Parts of a Dictionary Entry

③ pronunciation   ④ part-of-speech labels   ⑤ inflected forms

① entry word —— **blue** (blü) *n., adj.* **blu·er, blu·est;** *v.* **blued, blu·ing** or **blue·ing.** —*n.*

⑦ definition —— **1** the color of the clear sky in daylight or the color of the part of the spectrum between green and violet. **2** blue dye or pigment. **3 the blue, a** the sky: *up in the blue.* **b** the far distance. **c** the sea. **4 blues,** —— ⑧ hidden entry
pl. Informal. low spirits: *He's got the blues.* **5 blues,** *Music.* **a** a

⑥ restrictive label —— style of jazz characterized by a tendency to flatten the thirds by a semitone, producing minor sequences and harmonies that give the music a melancholy sound. The blues developed from black work songs and spirituals. **b** a song in this style (*used with a singular verb*).

⑨ idiom —— **out of the blue,** completely unexpected; from an unknown source or for an unknown reason: *Suddenly, out of the blue, she announced that she was quitting.*
—*adj.* **1** of or having the color of the clear sky in daylight or any tone of this color. **2** of animals or plants, bluish, or having parts that are blue or bluish (*used in compounds*): *blue spruce, blue flag, bluefish.* **3** of the skin, livid; ashen: *blue with cold.* **4** having or showing low spirits; sad, gloomy, or discouraged: *a blue mood. I was feeling very blue.* **5** dismal; dispiriting: *a blue day.* **6** *Informal.* indecent or off-color: *blue language, a blue joke.* **7** of or having to do with Conservatives.

⑨ —— **once in a blue moon,** hardly ever; rarely: *Once in a blue moon we get a letter from him.*
—*v.* **1** make blue. **2** using bluing on. [ME < OF *bleu* < Gmc.] —— ⑩ etymology
—**blue′ness,** *n.*

⑫ fistnote (homonym) —— ☛ *Hom.* **blew.**   ⑪ run-on entry

② homograph number

③ ⑤ ④

① —— **crab**¹ (krab) *n., v.* **crabbed, crab·bing.** —*n.* **1** any decapod crustacean having a short abdomen, or "tail", that is carried tucked up under a short, broad shell and having the first pair of legs modified into pincers. Most of the approximately 4500 species are marine, but some are found in fresh water and even on land. **2** any
⑥ —— of several other crustaceans resembling the true crab, such as the hermit crab. **3** a machine or apparatus for raising or moving heavy weights. **4 Crab,** *Astronomy or astrology.* Cancer. —— ⑪
⑧ —— **catch a crab,** make a faulty stroke in rowing.
—*v.* catch crabs for eating. [OE *crabba*] —**crab′ber,** *n.* ⑦
② —— **crab**² (krab) *n., v.* **crabbed, crab·bing.** —*n.* **1** crab apple. **2** a cross, sour, ill-natured person; one who is always complaining or finding fault. —*v.* **1** find fault; complain; criticize: *It doesn't do any good to crab about the weather.* **2** *Informal.* interfere with; spoil: *His lack of enthusiasm crabbed the deal.* [origin uncertain] —— ⑩

Gage
Canadian
Dictionary

A book in the

DICTIONARY OF

CANADIAN ENGLISH

series

Gage
Canadian
Dictionary

Walter S. Avis
Patrick D. Drysdale
Robert J. Gregg
Victoria E. Neufeldt
Matthew H. Scargill

 **gage** PUBLISHING LIMITED
TORONTO ONTARIO CANADA

Illustrations: *Lewis Parker, Lyle Glover,*
            and *Lazare and Parker*

Cover: *Brant Cowie/Artplus*

Data base design and creation: *Trigraph Inc., Toronto*
Phototypesetting on APS-Micro 5: *Trigraph Inc., Toronto*

Canadian Cataloguing in Publication Data

Main entry under title:
Gage Canadian dictionary

(Dictionary of Canadian English)
Revision of: Canadian senior dictionary, and, The Senior dictionary.
ISBN 0-7715-1980-X

1. English language in Canada—Dictionaries.
2. Canadianisms (English)—Dictionaries.*
3. English language—Dictionaries. I. Avis, Walter S., 1919–1979. II. Series.

PE3235.G34 1982   423   C82-095155-2

ISBN 0-7715-1980-X

1 2 3 4 5 6 7 8 9   RBW   89 88 87 86 85 84 83

Printed and bound in Canada

To the memory of
Walter S. Avis
1919–1979
scholar and teacher
of Canadian English

GAGE CANADIAN DICTIONARY

Editorial and Research

Co-ordinating Editor: *Patrick D. Drysdale*
Editor: *Victoria E. Neufeldt*

Editorial and Research Assistants: *Gordon Cluett, Sue Dickin, Cecil Lancefield, Casimire Pindel, Anne Rutledge, Dorothy Schweder, Mary Vasey, Nancy Visée, Pam Young*

Acknowledgments

The editors wish to acknowledge all the people in various specialized fields who provided information on concepts, terms, and usage, or checked definitions. It is not possible to name them all here, but included among them are *Dahn Batchelor, Mary Agnes Challoner, Gordon Cluett, John Freeman, Anita Janzen, Leonard Lee, Mick Lymburner, Aldred Neufeldt, Russell Roberts.*

Contents

Introduction

The *Gage Canadian Dictionary* is a major revision of the *Canadian Senior Dictionary* (1979) and the *Dictionary of Canadian English: The Senior Dictionary* (1973, 1967). With the addition of almost 3000 new entries plus additional meanings for many existing entries to expand its range and bring it up-to-date, as well as the thorough revision of much of the content of the previous edition, the new *Gage Canadian Dictionary* is an authoritative, contemporary dictionary of Canadian English that is comprehensive enough for general use by Canadians in schools, universities, homes, and offices.

During the course of this revision, over a period of more than three years, the great majority of existing entries were checked for accuracy, clarity, and up-to-dateness and a large proportion of these were revised or rewritten to improve them. In addition, certain new stylistic features, such as italic labels identifying definitions restricted to specific fields of knowledge or activity, have been introduced to make the dictionary easier to use, more informative, and more readable.

Among the important features of this new dictionary are the following:

—the revision of all entries for plants and animals to include identifying characteristics and the appropriate Latin names used in current biological classification;

—homonym notes to assist the user in locating entries;

—the use of metric units for all measurements given in the dictionary (e.g. the definition of a light-year or the size of an animal), as well as the inclusion of SI units and prefixes with clear definitions;

—additional charts and tables, including a comparative table for units of measurement (metric and non-metric);

—approximately 400 large, clear line-drawings—about 95 percent of these are new for this dictionary, having been specially drawn by first-rate Canadian artists, either for this particular edition or for the current editions of the *Canadian Intermediate Dictionary* or *Canadian Junior Dictionary* in the *Dictionary of Canadian English* series published by Gage.

While making revisions and additions, however, the editors have conscientiously endeavored to maintain the existing strengths of the dictionary and build on them wherever possible. The principle of clarity and simplicity of definition has been followed for all new and revised definitions. Moreover, the liberal use of illustrative phrases and sentences, far more extensive than in comparable desk dictionaries, has been continued. Such phrases and sentences are extremely useful to distinguish, clarify, and reinforce the definitions by showing how the entry words are (or were, in the case of archaic terms) actually used in the language. This feature, along with the inclusion of a great many idioms (another feature continued and expanded from the previous edition), also makes the *Gage Canadian Dictionary* extremely valuable for those learning English as a second language. Also continued from the previous edition are the etymologies (given throughout), usage notes (revised for this edition), and synonym studies.

The *Gage Canadian Dictionary* is the "senior" volume in the *Dictionary of Canadian English* series of graded dictionaries. The first, the *Canadian Junior Dictionary*, is designed for children in Grades 4, 5, and 6, who are beginning to acquire skill in the conscious use of language; the second, the *Canadian Intermediate Dictionary*, is a much larger volume and is tailored to the needs of students in senior elementary and junior high schools; The *Gage Canadian Dictionary* is intended for use in high schools and universities and for general adult use. Each book in the series is based on the needs and understanding of a particular range of users, who are thus able to find the information they want in a form they can understand. Moreover, all of these books adhere to the principles explained above (clarity of definition, use of illustrative sentences, etc.), adapted in each book to the audience for which it is intended.

Above all, these are Canadian dictionaries, and the present volume is the only adult-level dictionary currently available that can be said truly to reflect standard Canadian usage throughout.

The authors are all established scholars in the field of Canadian English, and their special

knowledge in this field is reflected in the text of this dictionary. Many entries are based on material collected for a *Dictionary of Canadianisms on Historical Principles* (Gage, 1967), which shows even more vividly the richness and variety of the particularly Canadian element of our vocabulary. In addition, every effort has been made to ensure that all entries in the *Gage Canadian Dictionary*, whether of terms peculiar to Canada or of terms which Canadian English shares with English speakers in other countries, reflect the usage generally accepted among Canadians throughout the country, with respect to style, vocabulary, spelling, and pronunciation. The numerous regionalisms included—e.g. *chuck*, *bluff*, *fire-reels*, *aboideau*—are identified as such. Because standard Canadian usage, especially in spelling and pronunciation, is more diverse than that of either Britain or the United States, the *Gage Canadian Dictionary* gives a much greater range of alternatives than is available in comparable British and U.S. dictionaries. For instance, Canadian usage is almost equally divided between *-our* and *-or* spellings in words such as *color/colour* and *honor/honour*, so both spellings must be accepted by a Canadian dictionary as "standard". (However, one spelling or the other must be placed first, and, based on their research, the editors of this dictionary have chosen to give this first place to the *-or* spelling.)

This is not the case for British and American dictionaries, however. The British standard spelling is *-our*, and British dictionaries reflect this by labelling *-or* spellings "U.S." The standard spelling in the United States, on the other hand, is *-or*, and American dictionaries label the *-our* spelling "Brit." (Neither British nor American dictionaries mention Canadian usage in such cases.)

In most other cases in which there are two or more acceptable spellings for a given word, however, surveys indicate that Canadian usage shows a definite preference for one (e.g. *centre*, *fibre*, *axe*, and *cheque* are much more common than *center*, *fiber*, *ax*, and *check*).

For further information on these matters, the reader is directed to the relevant portions of the *Guide to the dictionary*, which begins on page xiv. It is a great pity that such introductory matter in a dictionary is usually ignored. One cannot get the most out of a dictionary unless one knows the kind of information it contains and the ways in which this is arranged; moreover, a dictionary, like any other work, can be properly evaluated only if one knows what it aims to achieve. Particular care has been taken to make this *Guide* to the *Gage Canadian Dictionary* explicit and easy to read; it consists, for the most part, of simple, straightforward statements followed by extensive examples from the text of the dictionary.

Attention is drawn also to the sample entries on the front endpaper, in which the parts of a dictionary entry are identified by means of reference numbers, which are keyed to the relevant section numbers in the *Guide*. Thus the number 10, identifying the etymology, refers also to Section 10 of the second part of the *Guide*, on page xxvii. See also the table of contents (p. vii) for a list of the sections of the *Guide*.

The *Guide*, then, is the key to the dictionary and its wealth of information about words—their spelling, pronunciation, meaning, and origin. But, however interesting such information may be in itself, a dictionary contains much more than this. For one thing, it bears testimony to the customs and interests of the people whose language it describes; it is an inventory of the things which the people live with and talk about. *Muskeg*, for example, is not just a Canadian word; it is also a fact of Canadian life. The *Gage Canadian Dictionary* is thus a catalogue of the things relevant to the lives of Canadians at a certain point in history. It contains, therefore, some clues to the true nature of our Canadian identity.

Canadian English

by Walter S. Avis

The following essay was written by Walter S. Avis (1919–1979) for the first edition of the Dictionary of Canadian English: The Senior Dictionary, *published in 1967. Since this paper was written, the public awareness of a distinctively Canadian variety of English has increased considerably, some preferences of vocabulary, spelling, etc. have been changed, and certain trends that seemed apparent fifteen years ago have not, in fact, developed.*

However, the essay is still valuable for its historical information on the development of Canadian English and for its perspective on the general position of Canadian English in relation to its British and American counterparts. This essay is also significant for its early recognition of the importance for Canadians of a dictionary that truly reflects the English language as we ourselves use it.

V.N.
October 1982

Language in Canada, as in most countries, is taken for granted. Unfortunately, however, a great deal of nonsense is taken for granted by many Canadians. Some people, especially recent arrivals from the United Kingdom, refuse to accept the fact that the English spoken in Canada has any claim to recognition. Others, who themselves speak Canadian English, are satisfied with the view that British English is the only acceptable standard. To these people the argument that educated Canadians set their own standard of speech is either treasonable or ridiculous.

One Canadian I know had his eyes opened in a rather curious way. While shopping in a large Chicago department store, he asked where he might find chesterfields. Following directions to the letter, he was somewhat dismayed when he ended up at the cigar counter. He soon made other discoveries as well. Blinds were "shades" to his American neighbors; taps were "faucets," braces "suspenders," and serviettes "napkins."

Before long his American friends were pointing out differences between his speech and theirs. He said *been* to rhyme with "bean," whereas for them it rhymed with "bin"; and he said *shone* to rhyme with "gone," whereas for them it rhymed with "bone." In fact, their Canadian friend had quite a few curious ways of saying things: *ration* rhymed with "fashion" rather than with "nation"; *lever* with "beaver" rather than "sever"; *z* with "bed" rather than "bee." Moreover, he said certain vowels in a peculiar way, for *lout* seemed to have a different vowel sound from *loud*, and *rice* a different vowel from *rise*.

The Englishman is also quick to observe that Canadians talk differently from himself. For example, he doesn't say *dance, half, clerk, tomato, garage,* or *war* as Canadians do; and he always distinguishes *cot* from *caught*, a distinction that few Canadians make. He also finds that many of the words he used in England are not understood by people in Canada. Suppose he gets into a conversation about cars. Says he, "I think a car should have a roomy boot." No headway will be made till somebody rescues him by explaining that in Canada the boot is called a "trunk." Before the session is finished, he will probably learn that a bonnet is called a "hood" and the hood of a coupé is "the top of a convertible." Similarly, he must substitute *muffler* for *silencer, windshield* for *windscreen, truck* for *lorry,* and *gas* for *petrol.*

The examples I have mentioned suggest, quite correctly, that Canadian English, while different from both British and American English, is in large measure a blend of both varieties; and to this blend must be added many features which are typically Canadian. The explanation for this mixed character lies primarily in the settlement history of the country, for both Britain and the United States have exerted continuous influence on Canada during the past two hundred years.

As the several areas of Canada were opened to settlement, before, during and after the Revolutionary War in the 1770's, Americans were prominent among the settlers in many, if not in most, communities. American influence has been great ever since: Canadians often learn from American textbooks, read American novels and periodicals, listen to American radio programs, and watch American T.V. and movies. Moreover, Canadians

in large numbers are constantly moving back and forth across the border, as emigrants, as tourists, as students (especially on athletic scholarships), and as bargain hunters. Finally, Canada shares with the United States a large vocabulary denoting all manner of things indigenous to North America. One need only leaf through the full or concise *Dictionary of Canadianisms* or the *Dictionary of Americanisms* to appreciate this fact.

On the other hand, Britain has also made an enormous contribution to the settlement of English-speaking Canada. For more than a century and a half, Britishers in an almost continuous stream and speaking various dialects have immigrated to Canada. In most communities, especially those along the Canadian-American border (where most of Canada's population is still concentrated), these newcomers came into contact with already established Canadians; and, as might be expected, their children adopted the speech habits of the communities they moved into. Only in certain settlement areas where relatively homogeneous Old-Country groups established themselves did markedly British dialectal features survive through several generations. Such communities may be found in Newfoundland, the Ottawa Valley, the Red River Settlement in Manitoba, and on Vancouver Island. For the most part, however, the children of British immigrants, like those whose parents come from other European countries, adopt the kind of English spoken in Canada. Yet in the very process of being absorbed, linguistically speaking, they have made contributions to every department of the language.

That part of Canadian English which is neither British nor American is best illustrated by the vocabulary, for there are hundreds of words which are native to Canada or which have meanings peculiar to Canada. As might be expected, many of these words refer to topographical features, plants, trees, fish, animals, and birds; and many others to social, economic, and political institutions and activities. Few of these words, which may be called Canadianisms, find their way into British or American dictionaries, a fact which should occasion no surprise, for British and American dictionaries are based on British and American usage, being primarily intended for Britons and Americans, not for Canadians.

Prominent among Canadianisms are proper nouns, including names of regions: *Barren Grounds, French Shore, Lakehead*; names given to the natives of certain regions: *Bluenoses, Herringchokers*; names associated with political parties: *New Democratic Party, Union Nationale*. In addition, there are a host of terms identified with places or persons: *Digby chicken, McIntosh apple, Quebec heater, Winnipeg couch*.

Languages other than English have contributed many Canadianisms to the lexicon: (from Canadian French) *brulé, fameuse, lacrosse, Métis, portage*; (from Amerindian) *babiche, kokanee, pemmican, shaganappi*; (from Eskimo) *komatik, kuletuk, ooloo, oomiak*. Sometimes the origin of such loanwords is obscured in the process of adoption; thus *carry-all, mush, Siwash, snye*, and *shanty* derive from Canadian French *cariole, marche, sauvage, chenail*, and *chantier*.

Other Canadianisms are more or less limited to certain regions—to Newfoundland: *jinker, nunny bag, tickle, tilt*; to the Maritimes: *aboideau, gaspereau, longliner*; to Ontario: *concession road, dew-worm, fire-reels*; to the Prairie Provinces: *bluff* (clump of trees), *grid road, local improvement district*; to British Columbia: *rancherie, skookum, steelhead*; to the Northland: *bush pilot, cat-swing, cheechako*.

Hundreds of Canadian words fall into the category of animal and plant names: *caribou, fool hen, inconnu, kinnikinnick, malemute, oolichan, saskatoon, sockeye, whisky-jack* or *Canada jay*. Many more fall into the class of topographical terms: *butte, coulee, dalles, sault*. Yet another extensive class includes hundreds of terms of historical significance: *Family Compact, Klondiker, North canoe, Red River cart, wintering partner, York boat*.

For many terms there are special Canadian significations: *Confederation, Grit, height of land, reeve, riding, warden*. From the sports field come a number of contributions, especially from hockey and a game we used to call rugby, a term now almost displaced by the American term football: *boarding, blueline, convert, cushion, flying wing, puck, rouge, snap*. And in the same area there are a number of slang terms that merit mention: *chippy, homebrew, import, rink rat*.

In pronunciation, as in vocabulary, Canadians are neither American nor British, though they have much in common with both. Although most Canadians pronounce *docile* and *textile* to rhyme

with *mile*, as the British do, it is probable that most pronounce *fertile* and *missile* to rhyme with *hurtle* and *missal*, as the Americans do. And no doubt Canadians pronounce some words in a way that is typically Canadian. Most of us, for example, would describe the color of a soldier's uniform as *khaki*, pronounced (kär′kē). Yet no non-Canadian dictionary recognizes this Canadianism. Americans say (kak′ē), while the British say (kä′kē). In Canada, many people put flowers in a vase, pronounced (vāz); Americans use a (vās) and the British a (väz). To be sure, a number of Canadians say something like (väz), especially if the vase is Ming.

If we take imported dictionaries as our authority, such pronunciations as (kär′kē) and (vāz) are unacceptable. But surely the proper test of correctness for Canadians should be the usage of educated natives of Canada. Here are some other example of pronunciations widely heard among educated Canadians; few of them are recorded in our imported dictionaries: *absolve* (ab zolv′), *arctic* (är′tik), *armada* (är mad′ə), *chassis* (chas′ē), *culinary* (kul′ə ner′ē), *evil* (ē′vəl), *finale* (fə nal′ē), *fungi* (fung′gī), *jackal* (jak′əl), *longitude* (long′gə tüd′), *official* (ō fish′əl), *opinion* (ō pin′yən), *placate* (plak′āt), *plenary* (plen′ə rē), *prestige* (pres tēj′), *resources* (ri zôr′səz), *senile* (sen′īl), *species* (spē′sēz), *Trafalgar* (trə fol′gər).

Of course, not everyone uses all of these forms; yet all are used regularly by educated Canadians in large numbers. Who can deny that (ri zôr′səz) and (spē′sēz) are more often heard at all levels of Canadian society than (ri sôrs′əz) and (spē′shēz), the pronunciations indicated in nearly all available dictionaries? Surely, when the evidence of usage justifies it, forms such as these should be entered as variants in any dictionary intended to reflect Canadian speech.

Another of the functions of a dictionary is to record the spellings used by the educated people of the community. In spelling, as in vocabulary and pronunciation, Canadian usage is influenced by the practice of both the Americans and the British. In areas where American and British practices differ, Canadian usage is far from uniform. Until recent years, British forms have pre-dominated in most instances, for example, in *axe, catalogue, centre, colour, cheque, mediaeval, plough, skilful,* and *woollen* (and words of similar pattern), in spite of the obvious practical advantages of the American forms: *ax, catalog, center, check, color, medieval, plow, skillful,* and *woolen.* In some cases, however, American spellings have asserted themselves to the virtual exclusion of the corresponding British forms, as in *connection, curb, jail, net, recognize, tire,* and *wagon* for *connexion, kerb, gaol, nett, recognise, tyre,* and *waggon.*

In recent years there have been indications that American spellings are becoming more commonly used in Canada. Many have, for example, been adopted by Canadian newspapers, especially those in the larger centres, and by magazine and book publishers. Young people seem to use such spellings as *color, center, defense, medieval, program, skillful,* and *traveler* much more frequently than was formerly the case, the implication being that at least some American forms are accepted as proper in many Canadian schools. The fact is that usage is very much divided, varying from province to province and often from person to person. For the most part, however, Canadians respond to these variants with equal ease. Under such circumstances, a Canadian dictionary should include both forms, for here, as elsewhere, the lexicographer's obligation is to record usage, not to legislate it.

It has been argued in these pages that there is such a thing as a distinctive variety of Canadian English; yet it should be observed that this distinctive variety is referred to as "Canadian English" and not as "the Canadian language." The fact is that Canadians share one language with Britons, Americans, Australians, and a host of other people, both inside the Commonwealth and beyond it. To claim that there is a Canadian language, or, as many Americans do, an American language, is to distort the meaning of the word *language* for nationalistic purposes. On the other hand, it is a form of blindness to insist, as many do, that "English is English" and that only fools "dignify the slang and dialect" of Canada by giving it serious attention.

Guide to the dictionary

Locating an entry

All main entries—single words, compound nouns and noun phrases, contractions, affixes, combining forms, abbreviations—are to be found in the same alphabetical list. However, there is a system of priorities whereby, for example, prefixes come before abbreviations of the same spelling and abbreviations without periods come before the same forms with periods, as shown in the following sequence of entries from page 1:

ab–¹ *prefix.* from, away, away from, or off, as in *abnormal, abduct, abjure.* Also: **a-** before *m, p, v*; **abs-** before *c, t.* [< L *ab-* < *ab*, prep.]

ab–² *prefix.* to or toward; the form of **ad-** occurring before *b*, as in *abbreviate.*

AB¹ Alberta (*used esp. in computerized address systems*).

AB² the type of human blood containing both antigens A and B. It is one of the four blood types in the ABO system.

A.B. *U.S.* Bachelor of Arts; B.A. (for L *Artium Baccalaureus*).

A.B. or **a.b.** able-bodied (seaman); able seaman.

a·ba·ca (ab′ə kə *or* ab′ə kä′) *n.* **1** a plant (*Musa textilis*) of the Philippines related to the banana, from whose leafstalks Manila hemp is obtained. **2** Manila hemp. [< Malay]

For such entries it is advisable to be prepared to look a few lines above and below the place where one expects a particular item. Apart from such cases, there is only one place in the book to look for each entry.

Guide words

Guide words in a dictionary indicate the first and last entries commencing on each page. For example, on page 7 the guide words are *acceleration* and *accidental*, indicating that these two entries and all those that fall alphabetically between them are to be found on that page. Note that in this dictionary the guide words are placed above the outside column of each page so that they are easily seen when leafing through the book.

Homographs

Although homographs are spelled alike, they are different words because they have different meanings and origins. Homographs are entered separately and are distinguished from each other by means of small raised numerals called superscripts:

chuck¹ *v., n.* —*v.* **1** pat; tap, especially under the chin. **2** *Informal.* throw: *She chucked the apple core into the garbage.* **3** *Informal.* give up or finish with: *He's chucked his job.* —*n.* **1** a tap; slight blow under the chin. **2** a toss [probably imitative]

chuck² (chuk) *n.* **1** a device for holding a tool or piece of work in a machine. **2** a cut of beef between the neck and the shoulder. See **beef** for picture. [var. of *chock*]

chuck³ (chuk) *n. Cdn.* on the west coast, a large body of water, formerly especially a river, but now usually the ocean. [< Chinook jargon]

Note that homographs may be pronounced similarly, as above, or differently, as below:

slough¹ (slü *for 1 - 4*; *usually* slou *for 5*) *n.* **1** *Cdn. Western Canada.* a body of fresh water formed by rain or melted snow. **2** a soft, deep, muddy place; mud hole. **3** a backwater or side channel of a stream. **4** on the Pacific coast, a shallow or marshy inlet of the sea. **5** a state of hopeless discouragement or degradation. [OE *slōh*] ☛ *Hom.* **slew, slue** (slü).

slough² (sluf) *n., v.* —*n.* **1** the old skin shed, or cast off, by a snake. **2** a layer of dead skin or tissue that drops or falls off as a wound, sore, etc. heals. **3** anything that has been shed or cast off: *the slough of outmoded ideas, the slough of grief.* —*v.* **1** drop off; throw off; shed: *The snake sloughed its skin.* **2** be shed or cast; drop or fall: *A scab sloughs off when new skin takes its place.* **3** cast off as undesirable, tiresome, bothersome, etc. (*usually used with* **off**): *to slough off a heavy backpack. He sloughed off his depression and started anew.* **4** *Card games.* discard (a losing card). [ME *slugh(e), slouh* < Gmc.; cf. G *Schlauch* skin, bag]

Derivatives

Derivatives are words formed by adding prefixes or suffixes to other words or their roots. For example, the derivative *remake* is formed by adding the prefix *re-* to the verb *make*; the derivative *achievable* is formed by adding the suffix *-able* to the verb *achieve*, first dropping the final *e.*

Formed with suffixes

Derivatives formed with certain common suffixes are entered usually as "run-on" entries, that is they are printed in boldface type at the end of the entry for their root word. Thus *churlishly* and *churlishness* are shown at the end of the entry for churlish:

churl·ish (chèr′lish) *adj.* **1** rude; surly: *a churlish reply.*
2 niggardly; stingy; grudging; sordid. —**churl′ish·ly,** *adv.*
—**churl′ish·ness,** *n.*

For further information on such words, see Section 11, "Run-on entries," on p. xxviii. Derivatives formed with other suffixes are entered separately as main entries, as are all derivatives having meanings or pronunciations that cannot be inferred from those of their root words. Thus *absolutely* is an obvious derivative of *absolute*, but because it has a special meaning (and a special pronunciation) it has been entered separately:

ab·so·lute·ly (ab′sə lüt′lē *for 1, 2*; ab′sə lüt′lē *for 3*) *adv.* **1** in an absolute way; especially; completely: *The water is absolutely pure. This can opener is absolutely useless.* **2** positively or definitely: *He is absolutely the finest fellow I know. Can I try out your new car? Absolutely not!* **3** certainly; definitely yes: *"Are you going to the game?" "Absolutely!"*

Formed with prefixes

Derivatives formed with prefixes are listed in their alphabetical place in the dictionary, except for some words that are formed with *non-, over-, re-,* and *un-* and have meanings that can be inferred from those of the prefix and the root word. These words are listed (without meanings or other information besides syllabication and stress marks) in columns at the bottom of the pages on which they would appear if listed as main entries. For example, *non-absorbent* is found in the list at the bottom of page 772, but *non-conformist* has special meanings and therefore appears as a main entry in its proper place in the alphabetical list.

Sub entries

Hidden entries

Special uses of words, such as plural nouns, nouns or adjectives with articles, and capital-letter forms with special meanings, are treated as numbered definitions under the basic form of the word, with the special form shown in boldface type. Certain recognized phrases that do not merit separate entry are also printed in boldface type and explained within the entry for their main word (e.g. *red admiral*—a butterfly—is found under *admiral*). See section 8, "Hidden Entries," on p. xxvi, for more information and examples.

Idioms

Idiomatic expressions or phrases are defined under the entry for their most important word. For example, *have a care* will be found under *care*; *run for it, run in,* and *on the run* will be found under *run*. See Section 9, "Idioms," on p. xxvi, for more information and examples.

Noun phrases

Many noun phrases of two or more words function almost as if they were one-word compounds. They are found as main entries if they have a meaning that is not obvious from the meanings of their separate elements. Examples are:

affair of honor or **honour** a duel.

double agent a person who is ostensibly working as a secret agent for one side but is in fact working for the other. A double agent may even be deceiving both sides.

poor law *Historical.* a law providing for or regulating the relief or support of the poor through public funds.

See also section 8, "Hidden entries," p. xxvi for examples of noun phrases that are not entered separately, but are explained within the entry for their main word.

Proper names

Biographical and gazetteer entries are not given in this dictionary, the space thus saved being given to enlarging the coverage of the contemporary general vocabulary and to increasing the number of illustrative phrases and sentences. However, entries are given for a number of proper names that have passed into the general

xv

language and to others that are frequently met with in literature.

Place names

Many mythical and legendary places are entered:

As·gard (as′gärd, az′gärd, *or* ās′gärd) *n.* the home of the Norse gods and heroes.

Shan·gri–La or **Shan·gri·la** (shang′gri lä′) *n.* an idyllic earthly paradise. [an inaccessible land in *Lost Horizon*, a novel by James Hilton (1900-1954), an English author]

In addition, some historical places and geographical areas are listed:

A·ca·di·a (ə kā′dē ə) *n. Cdn.* **1** the areas of French settlement and culture in the Maritime Provinces. **2** the Maritime Provinces as a unit. **3** *Historical.* the French colony comprising the Maritime Provinces and adjacent parts of Quebec and New England. [probably after *Arcadia*]

Bab·y·lon (bab′ə lən *or* bab′ə lon′) *n.* **1** the capital of ancient Babylonia, on the Euphrates River and, later, of the ancient Chaldean empire. Babylon was noted for its wealth, power, magnificence, and wickedness. **2** any great, rich, or wicked city.

Entries are also provided for some "places" of the modern world that have acquired general or figurative significance:

Bay Street *Cdn.* **1** in Toronto, a street on which is situated the Toronto Stock Exchange and many financial houses. **2** the financial or moneyed interests of Toronto.

Broad·way (brod′wā′ *or* brôd′-) *n.* **1** in New York City, a street famous for its bright lights, theatres, night clubs, etc. **2** the New York commercial theatre.

Personal names

People entered are mainly: prominent figures of myth, legend, or literature, especially those whose names have acquired a general significance, representing some particular quality or ideal; central figures of great religions; people who have given their names to specific things or qualities:

Bal·der (bol′dər *or* bôl′dər) *n. Norse mythology.* the god of light, beauty, goodness, wisdom, and peace.

Bud·dha (bůd′ə, bü′də, *or* bud′ə) *n.* the title of Siddhartha Gautama (563?-483? B.C.), the Indian philosopher and teacher who founded Buddhism. Buddha means Enlightened One. [< Skt.]

Pro·me·the·us (prə mē′thē əs *or* prə mē′thyüs) *n. Greek mythology.* one of the Titans. He stole fire from heaven and taught men its use. Zeus punished him by chaining him to a rock.

Xan·thip·pe (zan tip′ē) *n.* a scolding woman; shrew. [< *Xanthippe*, the wife of Socrates, notorious as a scold]

In addition, information about many people is to be found in the etymologies of words derived from their names:

Bae·de·ker (bā′də kər) *n.* a guidebook for travellers. [< Karl *Baedeker* (1801-1859), German publisher of a series of guidebooks.]

Ba·co·ni·an (bā kō′nē ən) *adj., n.* —*adj.* **1** of or having to do with Francis Bacon (1561-1626), an English essayist, statesman and philosopher. **2** of or suggestive of his writings or philosophy. **3** of or having to do with the theory that Bacon wrote the plays of Shakespeare. —*n.* **1** a person who supports or follows the philosophy of Francis Bacon. **2** a person who supports the theory that Bacon wrote the plays of Shakespeare.

Parts of an entry

Note. Abbreviations used in the text of the dictionary are listed and explained on the inside back endpaper.

1. Entry word—spelling and syllabication

The first item in any dictionary entry is the entry word itself, which indicates the spelling of the basic form of the word. Main entries in this dictionary are set in large boldface type:

a·rise (ə rīz′) *v.* **a·rose, a·ris·en, a·ris·ing. 1** get up; . . .

ar·is·toc·ra·cy (ar′is tok′rə sē *or* er′is-) *n., pl.* **-cies. 1.** . . .

Note that syllabication, indicating where a word may be hyphenated, is shown by the placing of a midline dot between syllables. Syllabication is not shown in the case of entries made up of two or more words for each of which there is a main entry:

parliamentary secretary a member of the House of Commons appointed to assist a Cabinet Minister in his parliamentary work.

Variant spellings

Many words in Canadian English (and some words in all dialects of English) can be spelled in two or more ways. When both spellings are equally acceptable, they are shown as alternative entry words:

col·or *or* **col·our** (kul′ər) . . .

pro·gram *or* **pro·gramme** (prō′gram *or* prō′grəm) . . .

sul·phur *or* **sul·fur** (sul′fər) . . .

In such cases, the form given first is that which is considered to be somewhat more frequently used by educated writers across Canada. The form given first is also the one used for all occurrences of the word throughout this dictionary. It should be stressed, however, that though usage among individual writers and in particular regions may not be the same, any one writer will aim for consistency in his own work.
If one of two variants is considerably less common than the other, the less common variant is given toward the end of the main entry, before the etymology:

cen·tre (sen′tər) *n., v.* **-tred** *or* **-tered, -tring** *or* **-ter·ing.** —*n.* **1** a point within a circle or sphere equally distant from all parts of the
. . . .
centres on her childhood experiences. **4** mark or provide with a centre: *a smooth lawn centred by a pool.* Also, **center.** [ME < OF *centre* < L *centrum* < Gk. *kentron* sharp point]

axe (aks) *n., v.* —*n.* **1** a tool for chopping and splitting wood, etc., consisting of a heavy metal head attached to a long wooden handle,
. . . .
restrict, end, etc. *Several budget items were axed due to lack of funds.* Sometimes, **ax.** [OE *æx*] —**axe′like′,** *adj.*

For all words with two or more acceptable variants, each of the less common variants is entered in its proper alphabetical place as a cross-reference to the main entry:

cat·a·log (kat′ə log′) *n., v.* **-loged, -log·ing.** *Esp.U.S.* See **catalogue.** —**cat′a·log′er,** *n.*

cen·ter (sen′tər) See **centre.**
☛ *Spelling.* Compounds and derivatives beginning with **center-** are entered under their **centre-** forms.

col·our (kul′ər) See **color.**
☛ *Spelling.* Compounds and derivatives beginning with **colour-** are entered under their **color-** forms.

When there is also a slight difference in pronunciation, the less common variant is entered separately, with the more common form given as a one-word definition (a gloss), rather than as a cross-reference:

in·close (in klōz′) *v.* **-closed, -clos·ing.** enclose.

Spelling charts

It is often difficult to find the spelling of English words of which one knows only the pronunciation. The chart on the following two pages should help the reader to solve this difficulty. It gives the spellings for sounds occurring at the beginning, middle, and end of words.

Spellings of English Sounds

SOUND	BEGINNINGS OF WORDS	MIDDLES OF WORDS	ENDS OF WORDS
a	*a*nd, *au*nt	h*a*t, pl*ai*d, h*a*lf, l*au*gh	——
ā	*a*ge, *ai*d, *eigh*t, *eh*	f*a*ce, f*ai*l, str*aigh*t, p*a*yment, g*ao*l, g*au*ge, br*ea*k, v*ei*n, r*ei*gn n*ei*ghbor	s*ay*, w*eigh*, bouqu*et*, th*ey*, matin*ée*, *eh*
ä	*ah*, *a*lmond, *a*rt	c*a*lm, b*a*rn, baz*aa*r, s*e*rgeant, h*ea*rt	b*aa*, hurr*ah*
b	*b*ad	ta*b*le, ra*bb*it	ru*b*, e*bb*
ch	*c*ello, *ch*ild	ri*ch*ness, wat*ch*ing, righ*t*eous, ques*ti*on, na*t*ure	mu*ch*, ca*tch*
d	*d*o	do*d*o, do*dd*er	re*d*
e	*a*ny, *ae*rial, *ai*r, *e*nd	m*a*ny, s*ai*d, s*ay*s, l*e*t, br*ea*d, h*ei*fer, l*eo*pard, fri*e*nd, b*u*ry	——
ē	*ae*on, *e*qual, *ea*t, *ei*ther	C*ae*sar, m*e*tre, t*ea*m, n*ee*d, rec*ei*ve, p*eo*ple, k*ey*hole, mach*i*ne, bel*ie*ve, ph*oe*be	alg*ae*, qu*ay*, b*e*, fl*ea*, b*ee*, k*ey*, pit*y*
ėr	*er*mine, *ear*ly, *ir*k, *ur*ge	t*er*m, l*ear*n, f*ir*st, w*or*d, j*our*ney, t*ur*n, m*yr*tle	det*er*, voyag*eur*, f*ir*, c*ur*, b*urr*
f	*f*at, *ph*one	h*ei*fer, co*ff*ee, laug*h*ter, gop*h*er	roo*f*, bu*ff*, coug*h*, lym*ph*
g	*g*o, *gh*ost, *gu*ess	bo*g*us, bo*gg*le, ro*gu*ish, e*x*act	ba*g*, e*gg*, ro*gu*e
h	*h*e, *wh*o (hü), *wh*y (hwī)	block*h*ead	——
i	*e*namel, *i*n	mess*a*ge, b*ee*n, p*i*n, s*ie*ve, wom*e*n, b*u*sy, b*ui*ld, h*y*mn	——
ī	*ai*sle, *ay*e, *ei*ther, *eye*, *i*ce	h*eigh*t, l*i*ne, al*i*gn, m*igh*t, b*uy*ing, sk*y*lark	*ay*e, *eye*, l*ie*, h*igh*, b*uy*, sk*y*, r*ye*
j	*g*em, *j*am	ba*dg*er, sol*di*er, e*du*cate, tra*gi*c, exa*gg*erate, en*j*oy	bri*dge*, ra*ge*
k	*c*oat, *ch*emist, *k*ind, *qu*ick, *qu*ay	re*c*ord, a*cc*ount, e*ch*o, lu*ck*y, a*cqu*ire, ree*k*ing, li*qu*or, e*x*tra	ba*ck*, see*k*
l	*l*and, *ll*ama	on*l*y, fo*ll*ow	coa*l*, fi*ll*
m	*m*e	co*m*ing, cli*m*bing, su*mm*er	ru*m*, co*mb*, sole*mn*
n	*gn*aw, *kn*ife, *n*ut, *pn*eumonia	jack-*kn*ife, mi*n*er, ma*nn*er	ma*n*, i*nn*
ng	——	i*n*k, fi*n*ger, si*ng*er	ri*ng*, to*ngue*

SOUND	BEGINNINGS OF WORDS	MIDDLES OF WORDS	ENDS OF WORDS
o	*all*, *almond*, *auto*, *awful*, *encore*, *odd*, *aught*, *ought*	w*a*tch, app*a*l, w*a*lk, f*a*ll, t*au*t, t*au*ght, c*au*lk, c*a*wed, h*o*t, b*ou*ght, c*a*lm	p*aw*
ō	*open*, *oats*, *oh*, *own*	y*eo*man, s*e*wn, b*o*gus, b*oa*t, f*o*lk, br*oo*ch, s*ou*l, fl*ow*n	b*eau*, s*ew*, potat*o*, t*oe*, *oh*, th*ough*, bl*ow*
ô	*all*, *auto*, *awful*, *oar*, *order*	app*a*l, w*a*lk, t*a*ll, t*au*t, t*au*ght, c*au*lk, c*a*wed, b*oa*rd, b*o*rn, fl*oo*ring, b*ou*ght, m*ou*rn	p*aw*
oi	*oil*, *oyster*	b*oi*l, b*oy*hood	b*oy*
ou	*out*, *owl*	b*ou*nd, dr*ou*ght, h*ow*l	th*ou*, b*ough*, n*ow*
p	*pen*	ta*p*er, su*pp*er	u*p*
r	*run*, *rhythm*, *wrong*	pa*r*ent, hu*rr*y	bea*r*, bu*rr*
s	*cent*, *psalm*, *say*, *science*, *sword*	de*c*ent, ma*s*on, resu*sc*itate, ma*ss*ive, e*x*tra	ni*ce*, bogu*s*, mi*ss*, la*x*
sh	*chauffeur*, *schwa*, *she*, *sure*	o*ce*an, ma*ch*ine, spe*ci*al, in*s*urance, con*sci*ence, nau*se*a, ten*si*on, i*ss*ue, mi*ss*ion, na*ti*on	wi*sh*, ca*che*
t	*ptomaine*, *tell*, *Thomas*	la*t*er, la*tt*er, deb*t*or	bi*t*, mi*tt*, doub*t*
th	*thin*	too*th*paste	ba*th*
ŦH	*then*	fa*th*er	smoo*th*, ba*the*
u	*oven*, *up*	c*o*me, d*oe*s, fl*oo*d, tr*ou*ble, c*u*p	——
u̇	——	w*o*lf, g*oo*d, sh*ou*ld, f*u*ll	——
ü	*ooze*	n*eu*tral, m*o*ve, man*oeu*vre, f*oo*d, cr*ou*p, r*u*le, fr*ui*t	thr*ew*, sh*oe*, carib*ou*, thr*ough*, bl*ue*
yü	*euchre*, *ewe*, *use*, *you*, *Yule*	b*eau*ty, f*eu*d, d*u*ty	qu*eue*, f*ew*, *ewe*, adi*eu*, *you*, c*ue*
v	*very*	Step*h*en, o*v*er	o*f*, lo*ve*
w	*will*, *wheat*	ch*oi*r, q*u*ick, t*w*in	——
y	*young*	opin*i*on, hallelu*j*ah, can*y*on	——
z	*xylophone*, *zero*	rai*s*in, di*s*cern, *sc*issors, e*x*act, si*z*ing, da*zz*le	ha*s*, ma*ze*, bu*zz*
zh	——	ga*ge*d, divi*si*on, mea*s*ure, a*z*ure	rou*ge*
ə	*alone*, *essential*, *oblige*, *upon*	particul*a*r, fount*ai*n, mom*e*nt, penc*i*l, bott*le*, pris*m*, butt*o*n, caut*i*ous, circ*u*s, zeph*y*r	sof*a*

2. Homograph number

Words having identical spellings but different origins and meanings are called homographs. They are given as separate entries in this dictionary, with a superscript number following the entry word, to distinguish one homograph from another. The superscript also serves to indicate to the user that there is at least one other entry word with the same spelling. For example:

fair¹ (fer) *adj., adv., n.* —*adj.* **1** not favoring one more than the other or others; just; honest: *a fair judge.* **2** according to the rules: *fair play.* **3** pretty good; not bad; average: *She has a fair understanding of the subject. There is only a fair crop of wheat this year.* **4** favorable; likely; promising: *He is in a fair way to succeed.* **5** not dark; blond: *fair hair, a fair complexion.* **6** not cloudy or stormy; clear; sunny: *The weather will be fair today.* **7** pleasing to the eye or mind; beautiful: *a fair lady. He spoke fair words.* **8** of good size or amount; ample: *They own a fair piece of property.* **9** clean or pure; without blemishes: *fair water, a fair copy.* **10** easily read; plain: *fair handwriting.* **11** favorable; helpful, especially to a ship's course: *We had fair winds all the way.* **12** seeming good at first, but not really so: *His fair promises proved false.*
fair and square, *Informal.* just; honest.
fair to middling, moderately good; average.
—*adv.* **1** in an honest, straightforward manner; honestly: *fair-spoken, to play fair.* **2** directly; straight: *The stone hit him fair on the head.*
bid fair, seem likely; have a good chance.
—*n. Archaic.* a woman, especially a sweetheart. [OE *fæger*]
—**fair′ness,** *n.*
☛ Hom. **fare.**

fair² (fer) *n.* **1** a gathering of people for the purpose of showing goods, products, etc.; exhibition: *the Royal Winter Fair. At the county fair last year, prizes were given for the best farm products and livestock.* **2** a gathering of people to buy and sell, often held in a certain place at regular times during the year: *a trade fair.* **3** an entertainment and sale of articles; bazaar: *Our church held a fair to raise money.* [ME < OF *feire* < LL *feria* holiday]
☛ Hom. **fare.**

3. Pronunciation

Pronunciation respellings are given in parentheses immediately after the entry words. The symbols used are those shown in the key on the inside of the back cover; a short key is given below the guide words at the top of the outside column of each right-hand page:

but·tress (but′ris) *n., v.* —*n.* **1** a structure...

bu·ty·lene (byü′tə lēn′) *n.* a gaseous...

buzz (buz) *n., v.* —*n.* **1** a humming sound...

In the case of entries of two or more words, no respelling is given for words that are entered separately:

squadron leader **1** the leader of a squadron...

Whenever one word of a phrase is entered separately and the other is not, only the word that does not have its own main entry is respelled:

bu·tyr·ic acid (byü tir′ik) a colorless liquid...

delirium tre·mens (trē′mənz) delirium characterized...

Syllabication

Syllabication in the respellings is shown by small spaces between the syllables. This phonetic syllabication is not necessarily the same as the spelling divisions shown by midline dots in the entry words.

Stress

Three degrees of stress are indicated in this dictionary: primary stress (′), secondary stress (′), and weak stress (unmarked). Stress is not indicated for words of one syllable, but primary stress is shown in all respellings of more than one syllable:

boy (boi)...

boy·hood (boi′hůd)...

Secondary stress is given in the case of compounds, including those that are hyphenated:

black·ber·ry (blak′ber′ē *or* blak′bər ē)...

bird·bath (bėrd′bath′)...

bell·flow·er (bel′flou′ər)...

Fin·no–U·gric (fin′ō yü′grik or -ü′grik)...

tai·lor–made (tā′lər mād′)...

Except in compounds, secondary stress is not shown when the syllable carrying it comes next to the primary stress:

an·o·dyne (an′ə dīn′)...

cal·cite (kal′sīt)...

Certain adjectival compounds, such as *hard-hearted*, are pronounced with two strong stresses in most sentence positions, but with primary-secondary stress when occurring before a noun. Compare *She is very hardhearted* with *She's a hardhearted woman*. Such words are shown in the respellings as having two primary stresses (härd′härt′id), but it must be remembered that (härd′härt′id) also occurs.

Variant pronunciations

The respellings show pronunciation variants that are acceptable in at least some parts of Canada, for example:

call (kol *or* kôl)...

fu·tile (fyü′tīl *or* fyü′təl)...

le·ver (lē′vər *or* lev′ər)...

khak·i (kär′kē, kä′kē, *or* kak′ē)...

al·ti·tude (al′tə tyüd′ *or* al′tə tüd′, ol′tə tyüd′ *or* ol′tə tüd′, ôl′tə tyüd′ *or* ôl′tə tüd′)...

The first form given is the one considered to be most frequent in Canada as a whole, but, as with spelling, different forms are often preferred in different parts of the country or among different social groups. An individual's own usage is normally governed by that of the community to which he belongs, so that, unless otherwise indicated, all pronunciations given in this dictionary should be considered equally acceptable.

Variant pronunciations of compounds and some other long words are abbreviated in respelling, the part that is pronounced the same in each variant not being repeated but being replaced by a hyphen:

white·fish (wīt′fish′ *or* hwīt′-)...

dead·fall (ded′fol′ *or* -fôl′)...

Words containing combining forms may be treated in the same way as true compounds if the abbreviation is easily recognizable and pronounceable by itself:

au·to·crat (o′tə krat′ *or* ô′tə-)...

breadth·wise (bredth′wīz′ *or* bretth′-)...

Labelled pronunciations

Some words are pronounced differently when they occur as different parts of speech. In such cases the respellings are labelled in the following manner:

ac·cent (*n.* ak′sent; *v.* ak′sent *or* ak sent′)...

mod·er·ate (*adj., n.* mod′ər it; *v.* mod′ər āt′)...

Some words have unusual pronunciations when used by members of a profession or in other specialized contexts. In such cases the restricted pronunciation, preceded by an appropriate label, is given after the respelling for the general pronunciation:

an·gi·na (an jī′nə; *in medicine, often* an′jə nə) *n.* **1** any disease of the mouth or throat, such as quinsy, croup, mumps, or diphtheria, marked by painful attacks of suffocation. **2** angina pectoris. [< L *angina* quinsy < *angere* choke]

Pronunciation of foreign words

Where a foreign phrase is entered but has little currency in spoken English, the nearest possible approximation to the original pronunciation is given:

au jus (ō zhʏ′) *French.* in gravy or juice.

For words that have been anglicized but still sometimes have their original pronunciation when used in spoken English, the anglicized form is given first, followed by the labelled original form:

vo·ya·geur (voi′ə zhèr′; *French,* vwä yä zhœr′) *n., pl.* **-geurs** (-zhèrz; *French,* -zhœr′). *Cdn.* **1** *Historical.* a canoeman or boatman, especially a French Canadian, in the service of the early fur-trading companies. **2** a person who travels the northern wilderness, especially by canoe. [< F *voyageur,* ult. < *voyage* voyage]

4. Parts of speech

The part of speech is given for all one-word and hyphenated entries, the label following immediately after the pronunciation respelling:

ant (ant) *n.* any of a large family (Formicidae) of...

If a word is used as two or more parts of speech, these are listed, along with their inflected forms if required (see Section 5 below), and then the meanings are given for each part of speech in

turn. The most important part of speech and its meanings are normally given first:

an·te·pe·nul·ti·mate (an′tē pə nul′tə mit) *adj., n.* —*adj.* third from the end; last but two. —*n.* antepenult.

5. Inflected forms

Certain inflected forms—the plural of nouns, the past tense and past participle of verbs, and the comparative and superlative of adjectives and adverbs—are given whenever they are not regularly formed. They are set in boldface type and come immediately after the part-of-speech listing; syllabication is indicated by midline dots, as in the entry words:

lib·er·ate (lib′ər āt′) *v.* **-at·ed, -at·ing.**…

clar·i·fy (klar′ə fī′ *or* kler′ə fī) *v.* **-fied, -fy·ing.**…

da·tum (dā′təm *or* dat′əm) *n., pl.* **da·ta.**…

ox (oks) *n., pl.* **ox·en.**…

tes·ser·a (tes′ər ə) *n., pl.* **tes·ser·ae** (tes′ər ē′ *or* tes′ər ī′).…

safe (sāf) *adj.* **saf·er, saf·est;** *n.*…

good (gùd) *adj.* **bet·ter, best;** *n., interj.*…

wit·ty (wit′ē) *adj.* **-ti·er, -ti·est.**…

Note that the inflected forms are often abbreviated, the syllables shared with the entry word being omitted and replaced by a hyphen. Note also that the pronunciation of inflected forms is given wherever it is not obvious from that of the entry word (see *tessera* above), and when the inflected form is not itself an entry. Such respellings are abbreviated whenever this can be done

without giving rise to confusion or ambiguity:

hyp·no·sis (hip nō′sis) *n., pl.* **-ses** (-sēz).…

Inflected forms are given as main entries whenever they would not come immediately before or after their root word in alphabetical order. In such cases a form is cross-referred to the entry for its root word, where the full information is to be found:

came (kām) *v.* pt. of **come.**

nu·cle·i (nyü′klē ī′ *or* nü′klē ī′) *n.* pl. of **nucleus.**

ox·en (ok′sən) *n.* pl. of **ox.**

slid (slid) *v.* pt. and pp. of **slide.**

taught (tot *or* tôt) *v.* pt. and pp. of **teach.**

Variant inflected forms are given whenever appropriate:

ap·pen·dix (ə pen′diks) *n., pl.* **-dix·es or -di·ces.**…

car·i·bou (kar′ə bü′ *or* ker′ə bü′) *n., pl.* **-bou or -bous.**…

crow¹ (krō) *n., v.* **crowed** (or **crew** for 1), **crowed, crow·ing.**…

dive (dīv) *v.* **dived or dove, dived, div·ing;** *n.*…

kid·nap (kid′nap) *v.* **-napped or -naped, -nap·ping or -nap·ing.**…

trav·el (trav′əl) *v.* **-elled or -eled, -el·ling or -el·ing;** *n.*…

6. Restrictions of use

Words and meanings that are appropriate only under certain conditions are indicated in two ways: by italicized labels and by introductory phrases.

Restrictive labels

Labels are used mainly to indicate restrictions of usage in regard to level, style, currency, locality, etc. Those most commonly used are explained below, and further information may be had by looking up the entry word for each of these terms in the body of the dictionary.

Informal   The word or meaning is quite acceptable in everyday use but would be out of place in

formal speech or writing. Thus *Informal* simply means "not formal":

choos·y (chüz′ē) *adj.* **choos·i·er, choos·i·est.** *Informal.* particular or fussy in one's preferences; fastidious; selective. —**choos′i·ness,** *n.*

Slang   The word or meaning is not established in standard use but is used mainly in speech and only by certain groups, or by others in imitation or for special effects. When a word becomes generally known and acceptable, it ceases to be slang:

beef (bēf) *n., pl.* **beeves** (def. 2), **beefs** (def. 4); *v.* —*n.* **1** the meat from a steer, cow, or bull. **2** a steer, cow, or bull when full-grown and fattened for food. **3** *Informal.* strength or muscle; brawn. **4** *Slang.* complaint or grievance: *We answered all his beefs.* —*v.* **1** *Informal.* strengthen (*used with* **up**): *You could beef up your argument by adding more examples.* **2** *Slang.* complain: *She's*

always beefing about something. [ME < OF *boef* < L *bos, bovis* ox] —**beef′er,** *n.* —**beef′less,** *adj.*

rink rat *Cdn. Slang.* a young person who helps with the chores around a hockey rink, often in return for free skating, free admission to hockey games, etc.

Derogatory The word or meaning is not in polite use and is used as a term of insult:

rube (rüb) *n. Derogatory slang.* a rustic; an unsophisticated person. [< *Reuben,* a traditional rural name]

Offensive The word or meaning, though not necessarily intended to insult or denigrate, is considered offensive, either by the person(s) to whom it refers or by people in general:

Chi·na·man (chī′nə mən) *n., pl.* **-men.** *Offensive.* Chinese. ☛ *Usage.* See note at **Chinese.**

Dialect The word or meaning is used only in the folk-speech of certain people or geographical areas:

cadge (kaj) *v.* **cadged, cadg·ing. 1** *Dialect.* peddle. **2** *Informal.* beg. [origin uncertain] —**cadg′er,** *n.*

Poetic The word or meaning is used only in poetry or in prose written in a poetic style:

a·wea·ry (ə wēr′ē) *adj. Poetic.* weary; tired.

e·ven² (ē′vən) *n. Poetic.* evening.

Archaic The word or meaning is out of place except in writings of earlier times and in modern literature that is written in the style of an earlier period:

glis·ter (glis′tər) *v.* or *n. Archaic.* glisten; glitter; sparkle.

per·chance (pər chans′) *adv. Archaic or poetic.* perhaps.

Historical The word or meaning is used only with reference to things, institutions, etc. that existed in the past:

win·ter·er (win′tər ər) *n. Cdn. Historical.* **1** a seasoned fur trader or voyageur who spent his winters in the fur country. **2** a wintering partner.

Obsolete Neither the word nor meaning nor the thing it refers to remains in current use:

fee (fē) *n., v.* **feed, fee·ing.** —*n.* **1** a sum of money asked or paid for a service or privilege; charge: *Doctors and lawyers get fees for their services....* **5** *Obsolete.* gratuity; tip.
hold in fee, have absolute legal possession of.
—*v. Rare.* give a fee to. [ME < AF var. of OF *fieu* < Med.L *feudum* fief? < Gmc.; cf. OE *feoh* money, cattle]

Trademark The word or form is a proprietary name, owned by a particular company and valued by it as identifying its product. Trademarks have been labelled wherever possible, but the absence of such a label does not necessarily mean that a word is not a trademark:

Plex·i·glas (plek′sə glas′) *n. Trademark.* a light, transparent, acrylic plastic, often used in place of glass. [*pl*astic + fle*xi*ble + *glas*s]

Or·lon (ôr′lon) *n. Trademark.* any of several kinds of strong, elastic acrylic fibres that resist sun, water, and chemicals, and combine well with other fibres. Orlon is used for knitted clothing, rugs, draperies, etc.

Words that are trademarks are entered only when they are considered to be established as part of the general vocabulary. Some words that have passed into general use are shown as being derived from a trademark, even though the trademark is not entered separately:

ter·y·lene (ter′ə lēn′) *n.* **1 Terylene,** *Trademark.* a crease-resistant synthetic polyester fibre, much used for shirts, dresses, suits, etc. and often mixed with wool or other yarns. **2** any fibre of this kind.

vas·e·line (vas′ə lēn′) *n.* **1** petroleum jelly. **2 Vaseline,** *Trademark.* a brand of petroleum jelly. [coined from G *Wasser* water + Gk. *elaion* oil]

French, Latin, German, etc. Such language labels are used to distinguish words and phrases that, though used often in English writing and sometimes in speech, are still considered to be foreign. Such foreign words and phrases are usually italicized in print and underlined in writing or typing:

gar·çon (gär sôɴ′) *n., pl.* **-çons** (-sôɴ′). *French.* **1** a young man or boy. **2** a male servant. **3** waiter.

Füh·rer (fyü′rər; *German,* fy′rər) *n. German.* the title given to Adolf Hitler (1889-1945), the German dictator. Führer means leader.

per di·em (pər dē′əm *or* dī′əm) *Latin.* **1** per day; for each day. **2** an allowance of so much every day. [< L *per diem* per day]

Cdn. Indicates that a word or meaning originated in or is now peculiar to Canada:

reeve¹ (rēv) *n.* **1** *Cdn.* in Ontario and some western provinces, the elected head of a rural municipal council; in Ontario, also the elected head of a village or township council. **2** *Historical.* bailiff; steward; overseer. [OE (*ge*)*rēfa*]

snye or **sny** (snī) *n., pl.* **snyes** or **snies.** *Cdn.* a side channel of a stream. [< Cdn.F *chenail*; cf. F *chenal* channel]

Brit., Scottish, U.S., etc. Other national labels are used to distinguish words, meanings, or spellings that are used chiefly or solely in some particular part of the English-speaking world:

fen¹ (fen) *n. Brit.* a marsh; swamp; bog. [OE *fenn*]

boot¹ (büt) *n., v.* —*n.* **1** a covering for the foot and lower part of the leg, made of leather, rubber, or a synthetic material such as vinyl. **2** a kick. **3** the place for luggage in a horse-drawn coach. **4** *Brit.* the trunk of an automobile. **5** a bootlike protective covering or sheath for a mechanical device, etc. **6** an instrument of torture formerly used to crush a person's leg. **7** *U.S. Slang.* a new recruit in training in the United States Navy or Marines....

road agent *Esp.U.S. Historical.* a highwayman.

Architecture, Hockey, Law, Music, Sports, etc. Such field labels are used to show that a word or meaning is used with reference to a specialized field of knowledge or activity:

cross–check (kros′chek′) *v., n.* —*v.* **1** check again, or check against another source. **2** *Hockey or lacrosse.* give an illegal check by holding one's stick in both hands and thrusting it in front of an opponent's face or body. —*n.* **1** the act of cross-checking. **2** *Hockey or lacrosse.* an illegal check made by cross-checking.

celestial globe *Astronomy.* a globe indicating the position of the heavenly bodies, similar to a globe of the earth showing the geography of continents, oceans, etc.

Restrictive phrases

Phrases (such as "in ancient Rome," "especially in Ontario") are also sometimes used at the beginning of definitions to show limitations of meaning. They may indicate that a word is used with reference to one particular region or country:

bank barn *Cdn.* especially in Ontario, a two-storey barn built into a hill so as to permit entry to the bottom level from one side and to the top level from the other side.

Position

Note in the above examples that the position of both labels and phrases varies, depending on whether the restriction applies to a particular meaning (in which case it is placed after the numeral), to the meanings for one part of speech (placed after the part-of-speech label), or to the whole entry (placed before the part-of-speech label introducing the first group of meanings).

7. Definitions

Definitions are intended to be as simple and straightforward as possible. Where there is more than one meaning for an entry, each meaning is introduced by a boldface numeral; within a single meaning, different explanations or synonyms are separated by semicolons:

queer (kwēr) *adj., v., n.* —*adj.* **1** different from what is normal or usual; strange; odd; peculiar: *a queer remark, a queer noise, a queer reaction.* **2** *Informal.* eccentric or mildly crazy: *She's a little bit queer.* **3** *Informal.* not as it should be; causing doubt or suspicion: *There's something queer going on here....*

rum·pus (rum′pəs) *n. Informal.* a noisy disturbance or uproar; row. [origin uncertain]

Order of definitions

(*a*) Definitions are grouped by parts of speech, all the noun meanings for an entry being together, all the verb meanings being together, and so on.
(*b*) Within one part of speech, meanings are grouped in the order likely to be most useful to the reader. Normally, this is the order of frequency, the most commonly used meanings being given first. It is usual, therefore, for general meanings to be at the beginning of an entry and for specific, technical senses to come later. Sometimes, however, it is easier to understand the different meanings of a word if they are arranged in a historical or a logical order. For instance, it is usually desirable for closely related senses to be kept together, as in the entry for *bar¹*:

bar¹ (bär) *n., v.* **barred, bar·ring;** *prep.* —*n.* . . . **6** a counter over which drinks, especially alcoholic drinks, are served. **7** a room or establishment that has such a counter and in which alcoholic drinks are sold and consumed. **8** a counter, department, or other place, such as a self-serve area, where specific goods or services are sold: *a snack bar, a record bar, a gas bar.* **9 the bar, a** the profession of a lawyer. A person is called to the bar after passing the prescribed law examinations. **b** lawyers as a group: *Judges are chosen from the bar.* **10** the area or railing in a court of law that separates the bench and the lawyers' seats from the rest of the court. **11** *Esp.Brit.* the place where an accused person stands in a court of law. **12** a court of law. **13** anything like a court of law: *the bar of public opinion....*

Here definitions 6 to 8 cover one group of meanings, while definitions 9 to 13 cover another group. This is the most convenient order in which to place these entries, but it does not mean, for example, that sense 9 is necessarily less common than sense 7.

Parentheses in definitions

Parentheses are used to enclose words that are not strictly part of the meaning of the word being defined but are necessary in order to understand that meaning or its use. For instance, in defining a transitive verb, it is often necessary to indicate the type of word that occurs as its object:

ab·duct (ab dukt′) *v.* **1** carry off or take away (a person) by force or deceit. **2** of a muscle or group of muscles, serve to move (a limb, etc.) away from the median axis of the body or of one of its parts. Compare **adduct.** [< L *abductus,* pp. of *abducere* < *ab-* away + *ducere* lead] —**ab·duc′tion,** *n.*

The meaning of sense 1 of *abduct* is not complete unless one understands that the action is something that is done to persons; similarly, in

sense 2, the words in parentheses (the supplied object) are necessary to an understanding of the meaning. Other types of information are sometimes treated in the same way:

ac·cede (ak sēd′) v. -ced·ed, -ced·ing. 1 give in or agree (*to*): *to accede to a proposal, to accede to popular demand.* 2 come or attain (*to an office or dignity*): *When the king died, his oldest son acceded to the throne.* 3 become a party (*to*): *Our government acceded to the treaty.* [< L *accedere* < *ad-* to + *cedere* come]

In addition, as also seen in the above example, parentheses are used to enclose prepositions that follow verbs in specific meanings. Such required prepositions are printed in italics:

a·gree (ə grē′) v. -greed, -gree·ing. 1 have the same opinion or opinions: *I agree with you. The two partners usually agreed on important issues.* 2 be alike or be similar to; be in harmony; correspond (*with*): *Her story agrees with theirs.* 3 get along well together. 4 consent (*to*): *We agreed to their proposal. He agreed to accompany us.* 5 come to an understanding, especially in settling a dispute. 6 be suitable, healthful, etc. (*used with* **with**): *Bananas don't agree with him; they make him sick.* 7 *Grammar.* have the same number, case, gender, or person: *In English, the subject and verb of a sentence have to agree in number.* [ME < OF *agreer* < *a gre* to (one's) liking < L *ad* to, *gratum*, neut., pleasing]

In sense 1 of *agree, with* may be used but the verb may also occur without any preposition; in sense 2 the verb must be followed by *with*, and in sense 4, it must be followed by *to*. In such cases, the following preposition may be the only real clue as to which meaning of the verb is being used.

Expanded definitions

In many cases, especially with technical words, the normal style of gloss is not sufficient to explain a meaning, and a separate explanatory sentence is added, as in definition 4 of *aberration*:

ab·er·ra·tion (ab′ər ā′shən) n. 1 a wandering from the right path or usual course of action. 2 a deviation from a standard or ordinary type; abnormal structure or development. 3 a temporary mental disorder. 4 *Optics.* the failure of a lens or mirror to bring to a single focus the rays of light coming from one point. Aberration causes a blurred image or an image with a colored rim. 5 *Astronomy.* a slight change in the apparent position of a heavenly body, caused by the combined effect of the earth's motion and of light.

Examples

Illustrative phrases and sentences, printed in italics, are widely used to support the definitions. Such examples often show the type of context in which a word may be used in a particular meaning:

ac·tion (ak′shən) n. 1 the process of doing something or the state of being active or in operation: *to put a machine into action.* 2 habitual activity, especially when characterized by energy or initiative: *a man of action.* 3 something done; act. 4 **actions,** *pl.* conduct; behavior. 5 *Slang.* important or exciting activities or happenings: *to go where the action is.* 6 the effect or influence of a force or thing on something else: *the action of the wind on a ship's sails, the action of a drug....*

Examples are used also to highlight the contrast between related meanings of the same word:

a·bout (ə bout′) *prep., adv.* —*prep....* ...3 somewhere near; not far from: *The dog was about the house.* 4 approximately; near: *He is about my size....*

beat (bēt) v. **beat, beat·en** or **beat, beat·ing;** *n., adj....* —*n.* 1 a stroke or blow made again and again: *the beat of a drum, the beat of waves on a beach.* 2 pulsation; throb: *the beat of the heart.* 3 *Music.* **a** a unit of time or accent: *three beats to a measure.* **b** a stroke of the hand, baton, etc. showing a beat....

ob·scure (əb skyür′) *adj.* -scur·er, -scur·est; *v.* -scured, -scur·ing. —*adj.* 1 not clearly expressed: *an obscure passage in a book.* 2 not expressing meaning clearly: *an obscure style of writing.* 3 not well known; attracting no notice: *an obscure little village, an obscure poet, an obscure position in the government.* 4 not easily discovered; hidden: *an obscure path, an obscure meaning....*

Pictures and diagrams

The definitions are further supported and amplified by the various types of pictorial illustration that appear throughout the book. Some of these merely provide a picture or diagram of something hard to visualize from a verbal description:

A sickle

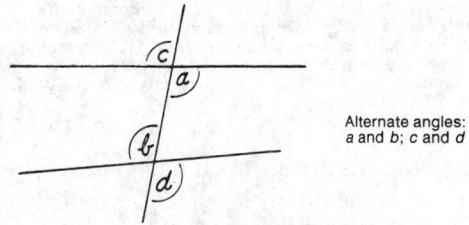

Alternate angles: *a* and *b*; *c* and *d*

Others give a considerable amount of more-or-less technical information, sometimes in diagram form, and these often label items that are entered elsewhere and are cross-referred to the same picture or diagram:

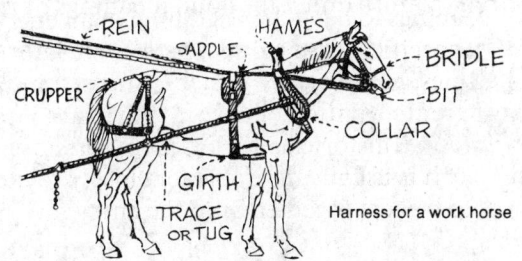

Harness for a work horse

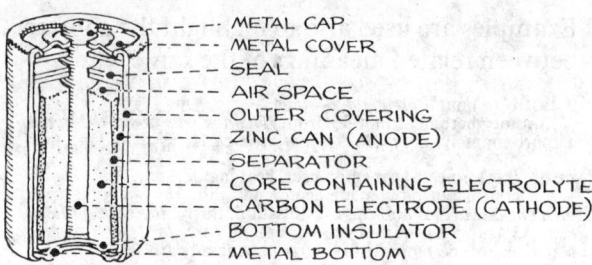

- METAL CAP
- METAL COVER
- SEAL
- AIR SPACE
- OUTER COVERING
- ZINC CAN (ANODE)
- SEPARATOR
- CORE CONTAINING ELECTROLYTE
- CARBON ELECTRODE (CATHODE)
- BOTTOM INSULATOR
- METAL BOTTOM

A carbon-zinc dry cell: a flashlight battery. The electrolyte, a paste of ammonium chloride, zinc chloride, manganese dioxide, and carbon, reacts with the zinc, causing it to become negatively charged. When the zinc anode and the carbon cathode are connected by a conducting wire, electrons flow from the anode to the cathode, producing an electric current.

Still others have captions which give information that, though not strictly part of a definition, is interesting and important for a full under-

standing of what the entry word represents:

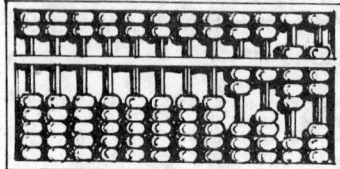

An abacus. The beads above the bar count 5 each when lowered to the bar. The beads below the bar count 1 each when raised. The beads of the abacus at left are set to show 7 in the units column, 8 in the 10's, 1 in the 100's, and 2 in the 1000's, for a total of 2187.

Charts and tables

The reader's attention is also drawn to the six full-page charts and tables, which give additional information to support the following entries: *alphabet, classification, element, geology, measure, money.*

8. Hidden entries

Certain special uses of words, such as plural nouns, nouns or adjectives with articles, or capital-letter forms with special meanings, are treated as numbered definitions, but the special form is shown in regular boldface type after the definition number:

a·crop·o·lis (ə krop′ə lis) *n.* **1** the fortified hill in the centre of an ancient Greek city, which served as its religious centre as well as its fortress. **2 the Acropolis,** the fortified hill of Athens, on which the Parthenon was built. [< Gk. *akropolis* < *akros* topmost, outermost + *polis* city]

af·fair (ə fer′) *n.* **1** something done or to be done; matter; concern: *That's my affair.* **2 affairs,** *pl.* matters of interest or concern, especially business, commercial, or public matters: *current affairs, affairs of state.* **3** an action, event, or procedure referred to in vague terms: *The party on Saturday night was a dull affair....*

Certain recognized noun phrases, etc. that do not merit separate entry are also printed in regular boldface type and explained within the entry for their basic, or main, word:

ad·mi·ral (ad′mə rəl) *n.* **1** the commander-in-chief of a fleet. **2** *Canadian Forces.* in Maritime Command... **6** any of various brightly colored butterflies (subfamily Nymphalinae), such as the **red admiral** or the **white admiral.** [earlier *amiral* < OF < Arabic *amir* chief. Related to AMIR.]

pol·y·he·dron (pol′i hē′drən) *n., pl.* **-drons, -dra** (-drə). a solid figure having four or more plane faces, all of which are polygons. The faces of a **regular polyhedron** are all identical polygons. A cube is a regular polyhedron with six square faces. [< NL < Gk. *polyedros* < *polys* many + *hedra* seat, side]

9. Idioms

An idiom is a phrase or expression which cannot be fully understood from the meanings of the words that form it. Idioms are defined under the entry for their most important word, and they are printed in boldface type. For example, the idioms *a run for* (one's) *money* and *in the long run* are explained under the noun meanings of *run:*

run (run) *v.* **ran, run, run·ning;** *n.* —*v.* **1** move the legs quickly; go

—*n.* **1** the act of running; *to set out at a run.* **2** a spell or period of

a run for (one's) **money,** **a** strong competition. **b** satisfaction for one's efforts.
in the long run, on the whole; in the end.

Verb phrases, such as *run down* and *run in,* and other idioms using *run* as a verb, such as *run for it,* are entered under the meanings of the verb:

run (run) *v.* **ran, run, run·ning;** *n.* —*v.* **1** move the legs quickly; go faster than walking: *A horse can run faster than a man.* **2** go

run down, a cease to go; stop working. **b** pursue till caught or killed; hunt down. **c** knock down by running against. **d** speak disparagingly against. **e** decline or reduce in vigor or health. **f** fall off, diminish, or decrease; deteriorate. **g** *Baseball.* put a base runner out after trapping him between bases.
run for it, run for safety.
run in, a *Informal.* arrest and put in jail. **b** pay a short visit.

10. Etymologies

The etymology, or origin, of a word is given at the end of all the definitions and is enclosed in square brackets:

a·dult (ə dult′ *or* ad′ult) *adj., n.* —*adj.* **1** fully developed and
. . . .
—*n.* **1** a grown-up person. **2** a person who has reached an age of legal responsibility: *In some provinces, one is an adult at 18.* **3** a full-grown animal or plant. [< L *adultus*, pp. of *adolescere*. See ADOLESCENT.] —**a·dult′ness**, *n.*

an·thrax (an′thraks) *n.* an infectious, often fatal, disease of cattle, sheep, etc. that may be transmitted to human beings. [< LL < Gk. *anthrax* carbuncle, live coal]

ax·le (ak′səl) *n.* **1** a bar or shaft on which or with which a wheel turns. **2** axletree. [OE *eaxl* shoulder, crossbar; influenced by ON *öxul* axle]

bar·ri·cade (bar′ə kād′ *or* ber′ə kād′, bar′ə kād′ *or* ber′ə kād′) *n., v.* **-cad·ed, -cad·ing.** —*n.* **1** a rough, hastily made barrier for defence. **2** any barrier or obstruction. **3** *Cdn.* large blocks of ice remaining frozen to a river or sea shore after the spring breakup. —*v.* block or obstruct with a barricade: *The road was barricaded with fallen trees.* [< F *barricade*, apparently < Provençal *barricada* < *barrica* cask; originally, made of casks. Related to BARREL.]

duc·at (duk′ət) *n.* **1** a gold or silver coin formerly used in some European countries. **2** *Slang.* a ticket. [ME < Ital. *ducato* < Med.L < L *dux, ducis* leader]

ki·osk (kē osk′ *or* kī′osk *for 1;* kē osk′ *for 2*) *n.* **1** a small building, usually with one or more sides open, used as a newsstand, bus shelter, telephone booth, etc. **2** in Turkey, Persia, etc., a light, open summerhouse. [< F < Turkish *kiushk* pavilion]

lem·on (lem′ən) *n., adj.* —*n.* **1** an acid-tasting, light-yellow citrus fruit growing in warm climates. **2** a thorny tree that bears this fruit. **3** a pale yellow. **4** *Slang.* a thing or person that is considered inferior or disagreeable: *The last car I bought was a lemon.* **5** a soft drink flavored with lemon juice. —*adj.* pale yellow. [ME < OF *limon* < Arabic *laimun* < Persian *limun*]

The arrow sign (<), used to connect the earlier forms of a word given as a chain in the square brackets, means "from," "derived from," or "taken from." Thus *adult* is from L *adultus*; *anthrax* is taken from the Late Latin word of the same form, which in its turn is taken from the Greek *anthrax* meaning "carbuncle" or "live coal." The arrow sign that stands at the opening of a square bracket is dropped if the word is found in Old English or Middle English, as in the case of *axle*, which is a native English word found in Old English as *eaxl* meaning "shoulder."

Usually, etymological forms and their meanings are given only where they are distinctive in regard to sense, spelling, or pronunciation. Otherwise only the language symbol is given and not the form. Thus *ducat* is found in Middle English; it is derived from the Italian *ducato*, which is from the Medieval Latin word of almost identical form (*ducatus*, not given), which is derived from the Latin *dux* meaning "leader."

For Latin and Greek forms, the genitive case is also given when it sheds light on the form of spelling of the derived word, as in the case of *dux, ducis* for *ducat*.

No etymology is given for the following entries:
(*a*) abbreviations;
(*b*) words, including compounds, made up of elements separately entered in the dictionary as English forms;
(*c*) phrases of two or more words that are separately entered. However, etymologies are given for such entries when the origin would not be evident from the etymologies of the separate words:

dog–train (dog′trān′) *n. Cdn.* a sled pulled by a team of dogs.

dog days in the northern hemisphere, a period of very hot, humid, and uncomfortable weather during July and August. [with reference to the rising of Sirius, the Dog Star]

Related words

It is often desirable to show relationships between different entries, as in the case of two words that come from an identical source but have acquired different forms as a result of different linguistic histories; such words are called doublets:

frail (frāl) *adj.* **1** not very strong; weak; physically delicate: *a frail child.* **2** easily broken, damaged, or destroyed; fragile: *Be careful, those branches are a very frail support.* **3** morally weak; liable to yield to temptation. [ME < OF *fraile* < L *fragilis* fragile. Doublet of FRAGILE.] —**frail′ly**, *adv.* —**frail′ness**, *n.*

frag·ile (fraj′īl *or* fraj′əl) *adj.* easily broken, damaged, or destroyed; delicate; frail. [< L *fragilis* (related to *frangere* break). Doublet of FRAIL.] —**frag′ile·ly**, *adv.* —**frag′ile·ness**, *n.*

In this case Latin *fragilis* became Old French *fraile*, resulting in the English form *frail*, while *fragile* was formed at a later date directly from the Latin.

Relationships that are slightly less close are shown by means of the phrase *related to*, or *akin to*:

ban·dit (ban′dit) *n., pl.* **ban·dits** *or* **ban·dit·ti** (-ē). a highwayman; robber. [< Ital. *bandito*, pp. of *bandire* banish, proscribe, ult. < Gmc. Akin to BAN.]

beck·on (bek′ən) *v.* signal by a motion of the head or hand: *He beckoned me to follow him.* [OE *bēcnan*, var. of *bīecnan*. Related to BEACON.]

Cross references are used to direct the reader to a related entry where the etymology he is studying is completed:

chap·el (chap′əl) *n.* **1** a building for worship, not so large as a church. . . . . [ME < OF *chapele* < LL *cappella*; originally a shrine in which was preserved the *cappa* or cape of St. Martin]

chap·lain (chap′lən) *n.* a clergyman officially authorized to perform religious functions for a family, court, society, public institution, or unit in the armed forces. [ME < OF *chapelain* < LL *capellanus* < *cappella*. See CHAPEL.]

Referring the reader from *chaplain* to *chapel* avoids the necessity of repeating information about the origin of Latin *capella*, at the same time establishing the relationship between the two words. Further examples of this device are:

ben·e·fice (ben′ə fis) *n.* a permanent office or position created by ecclesiastical authority. [ME< OF < L *beneficium* benefit < *beneficus* beneficent < *benefacere*. See BENEFACTOR.]

ben·e·fac·tor (ben′ə fak′tər *or* ben′ə fak′tər) *n.* a person who has helped others, either by gifts of money or by some kind act. [ME < LL *benefactor* < *benefacere* < *bene* well + *facere* do]

Occasionally no extra information is to be found at the etymology for a related word but it is worthwhile to compare the two and to note the relationship, or similarity, between the two. In such cases the direction *Cf.* is used:

as¹ (əz; *stressed,* az) *adv., conj., prep., pron.* —*adv.* **1** to the same

—*pron.* **1** a condition or fact that: *She is very careful, as her work shows.* **2** that: *Do the same thing as I do.* [OE (unstressed) *ealswā* quite so. Cf. ALSO.]

al·so (ol′sō *or* ôl′sō) *adv.* in addition; besides; too. [OE *ealswā* all so, quite so]

11. Run-on entries

Run-ons are derived forms listed after the etymology position in many entries. See the first two paragraphs of the discussion of derivatives on page xiv.
Further examples of run-on entries are:

ab·jure (ab jür′) *v.* **-jured, -juring. 1** renounce solemnly or on oath; swear to give up: *to abjure one's religion.* **2** abstain from; avoid: *to abjure alcohol.* [< L *abjurare* < *ab-* away + *jurare* swear] —**ab·jur′er,** *n.*

cool (kül) *adj., n., v.* —*adj.* **1** somewhat cold;...
cool (one's) **heels,** *Informal.* be kept waiting for a long time. [OE *cōl*] —**cool′ly,** *adv.* —**cool′ness,** *n.*

pat·ent (*n., adj. 1, v.* pat′ənt *or* pā′tənt;...
—*v.* get a patent for. [< L *patens, -entis,* ppr. of *patere* lie open] —**pat′ent·a·ble,** *adj.*

Note that the part of speech is given for run-on entries, and that syllabication and stress marks are indicated; the rest of the pronunciation and the meaning are to be inferred from those of the root word and the suffix.
Run-on entries may be given for words formed with the following suffixes:

Suffixes forming adjectives

-able	"able to be—"or "capable of being—"; added to verbs: *singable* = able to be sung; *adaptable* = capable of being adapted or capable of adapting.
-an **-ian** **-n**	"of or having to do with—"; added to nouns (names of places): *Albertan* = of or having to do with Alberta.

-less	"having no—"; added to nouns: *wingless* = having no wings; *conscienceless* = having no conscience.
-like	"like a—" or "like a—'s"; added to nouns: *flowerlike* = like a flower; *birdlike* = like a bird or like a bird's.

Suffixes forming nouns

-an **-ian** **-n**	"a native or inhabitant of—"; added to nouns (names of places): *Albertan* = a native or inhabitant of Alberta.
-er **-or**	"one that—s"; added to verbs: *deceiver* = one that deceives, *extractor* = one that extracts.
-ion **-ation** **-tion**	"a—ing or being—ed"; added to verbs: *decontamination* = a decontaminating or being decontaminated; *magnetization* = a magnetizing or being magnetized.
-ment	"a—ing or being—ed"; added to verbs: *encouragement* = an encouraging or being encouraged, or something that encourages; *impalement* = an impaling or being impaled.
-ness	"the fact or quality of being—"; added to adjectives: *exactness* = the fact or quality of being exact; *timeliness* = the fact or quality of being timely.

Suffixes forming adverbs

-ly	"in a—way or manner"; added to adjectives: *innocently* = in an innocent manner; *plainly* = in a plain way.
-ally	"in a—way or manner"; added to certain adjectives ending in *-ic*: *schematically* = in a schematic manner.

12. Fistnotes

Certain kinds of definition that do not fit into the above parts of an entry are given in fistnotes, so called because they are introduced by a printer's fist: ☛ Such notes are set in smaller type than the main text. There are five kinds of fistnote, distinguished from each other by an italic label following the fist: *Hom.* (Homonym), *Syn.* (Synonym), *Usage.*, *Spelling.*, and *Pronun.* (Pronunciation).

Homonyms

The listing of homonyms (words with identical pronunciations but different spellings) is a new feature of this edition. The inclusion of the homonym(s) of a given entry word can assist the user in finding a desired word when he is unsure of the spelling:

al·ter (ol′tər *or* ôl′tər) *v.* **1** make different; change; vary: *If this coat is too large, a tailor can alter it to fit you.* **2** become different; *Since her trip to Europe, her whole outlook has altered.* [ME < OF < LL *alterare* < L *alter* other] —**al′ter·a·ble**, *adj.* —**al′ter·a·bly**, *adv.*
☛ *Syn.* **1.** See note at **change.**
☛ *Hom.* **altar.**

ker·nel (kėr′nəl) *n.* **1** the softer part inside the hard shell of a nut or inside the stone of a fruit. **2** a grain or seed like wheat or corn. **3** the central or most important part: *the kernel of an argument.* [OE *cyrnel* < *corn* seed, grain]
☛ *Hom.* **colonel.**

Synonym studies

These notes bring out differences in meaning or usage between words that have very similar definitions. Usually, the basic meaning common to the synonyms being discussed is given first, followed by the particular shades of meaning that distinguish each individual word:

har·bor *or* **har·bour** (här′bər) *n., v.* —*n.* **1** a naturally or artificially sheltered area of deep water where ships may dock or anchor. A harbor may have loading and unloading facilities for passengers and cargo. **2** any place of shelter. —*v.* **1** give shelter to; give a place to hide: *The dog's shaggy hair harbors fleas.* **2** take shelter or refuge. **3** keep or nourish in the mind: *Don't harbor unkind thoughts.* [OE *hereborg* lodgings < *here* army + *beorg* shelter] —**har′bor·er** *or* **har′bour·er**, *n.* —**har′bor·less** *or* **har′bour·less**, *adj.*
☛ *Syn. n.* **1. Harbor, port** = place of shelter for ships. **Harbor** emphasizes shelter, and applies to a protected part of the sea, or other large body of water, where land or breakwaters shield against wind and heavy waves: *Many yachts are lying at anchor in the harbor.* **Port** emphasizes the idea of a place to put in to land or unload at the end of a voyage, and applies particularly to a harbor where commercial ships dock for loading and unloading: *The ship arrived in port. v.* **3.** See note at **cherish.**

A synonym study is given under the entry for the most common of the words discussed, cross-references to the study being given under the entries for the other words:

port¹ (pôrt) *n.* **1** a harbor; a place where ships and boats can take shelter from storms. **2** a city or town with a harbor where ships and boats may take on or unload cargo. **3** See **port of entry. 4** any place where one can find shelter. [OE < L *portus*]
☛ *Syn.* **1, 2.** See note at **harbor.**

Usage notes

A large number of fistnotes give information about usage, including contrasts of meaning (see *contemptuous* and *rugby*, below); shades of meaning, or connotations (see *ethnic*, below); levels of usage (see *hence*, below); and additional information about etymology (see *a⁴* and *Dutch*, below):

con·temp·tu·ous (kən temp′chü əs) *adj.* showing contempt; scornful: *a contemptuous look.* —**con·temp′tu·ous·ly**, *adv.* **con·temp′tu·ous·ness**, *n.*
☛ *Usage.* **Contemptuous** and **contemptible** are sometimes confused. The distinction will be clear if one observes that in **contemptible** the suffix **-ible** means deserving.

rug·by (rug′bē) *n.* **1** *Cdn.* a game played by teams of twelve men who carry, pass, or kick an oval ball towards the opposing team's goal; football. **2** rugger. [< *Rugby*, a famous school for boys in Rugby, England]
☛ *Usage.* **Rugby, rugger, soccer.** Though still heard in Canada, the term **rugby** (or **rugby football**) is being displaced by the American term **football.** As such, it is distinct from **rugger,** played with 15 players a side, and **soccer,** played with 11 players of whom only the goalie can play the ball with his hands.

eth·nic (eth′nik) *adj., n.* —*adj.* **1** of or having to do with various groups of people and their characteristics, customs, and languages. **2** *Cdn.* of or having to do with immigrants who are not native speakers of English or French: *ethnic dances, the ethnic vote.* **3** heathen or pagan.
—*n. Cdn. Informal.* an immigrant who is not a native speaker of English or French; a person of foreign birth or descent: *There are ethnics in Toronto from many parts of Europe.* [< L *ethnicus* < Gk. *ethnikos* < *ethnos* nation]
☛ *Usage.* **Ethnic,** *adj.* (def. 2) and *n.* This use of **ethnic** has become established in Canada and is spreading to the United States, though many people consider it unacceptable. While the word is useful in that it recognizes that different nationalities have individual qualities and customs, it becomes insulting if it is used to refer scornfully to people not of English or French descent.

hence (hens) *adv., interj.* —*adv.* **1** as a result of this; therefore: *The attempts to raise money have failed; hence the project will have to be abandoned.* **2** from now; from this time onward: *A year hence, the incident will have been forgotten.* **3** *Archaic.* from here; away: *She went hence many years ago.* **4** *Archaic.* from this world or life. **5** *Archaic.* from this source or origin: *Hence came several problems.*
—*interj. Archaic.* go away! begone!
hence with, *Archaic.* away with; take away.
[ME *hennes* < OE *heonan* + *-s,* adv. ending]
☛ *Usage.* **Hence** is a formal or archaic word for the less formal **consequently** or **therefore** and the general **so that:** *He has not answered our last letter; hence it would seem that he is not interested.* **Hence** is rare in current general writing.

a⁴ *prefix.* not or without; the form of **an⁻¹** occurring before consonants except *h,* as in *atypical, atonal.*
☛ *Usage.* **A-** meaning *not* is of Greek origin and is used in words taken directly, or through Latin, from Greek, as in *apathy.* It is also used as a naturalized English prefix in new formations, as in *achromatic.* **A-,** called alpha privative, corresponds to English **un-** and Latin **in-.**

Dutch (duch) *n., adj.* —*n.* **1 the Dutch,** *pl.* **a** the people of the Netherlands, a small country in W Europe. **b** *Esp.U.S.* the Pennsylvania Dutch. **c** *Obsolete.* the people of Germany, including the Netherlands. **2** the official language of the Netherlands. **3** *Obsolete.* the language of Germany and the Netherlands.
beat the Dutch, *Informal.* be very strange or surprising; outdo anything considered remarkable.
in Dutch, *Slang.* in trouble or disgrace: *He's in Dutch with his sister.*
—*adj.* **1** of or having to do with the Netherlands, its people, or their language. **2** *Esp.U.S.* Pennsylvania Dutch. **3** *Obsolete.* German.
go Dutch, *Informal.* have each person pay for himself.
[< MDu. *dutsch* Dutch, German]
☞ *Usage.* The numerous derogatory expressions compounded of **Dutch,** such as **Dutch courage** and **Dutch uncle,** are a legacy from the Dutch-English commercial rivalry of the 17th and 18th centuries.

Some usage notes give grammatical information:

a¹ (ə; *stressed,* ā *or* a) *adj. or indefinite article.* **1** a word used before singular nouns when the person or thing referred to is not specific: *There's a man at the door. I need a new coat.* **2** one: *I want a loaf of bread, a watermelon, and a dozen oranges. She took the stairs two at a time.* **3** any: *A thoughtful person would not have said that.* **4** a single: *not a one.* [var. of **an¹**]
☞ *Usage.* A is used before words pronounced with an initial consonant sound whether or not that sound is shown by the spelling, as in *a man, a year, a union, a hospital.* Most people now write *a hotel* or *a historian,* but some use *an* in these cases.
☞ *Usage.* A regularly comes before other modifiers but follows *many, such, what,* and any adjective preceded by *as, how, so,* or *too,* as in *many a person, such a bore, so fine a picture, too high a price.*

a⁻¹ *prefix.* **1** on or in: *We went aboard. They found him abed. He set the bells a-ringing. The room was abuzz with conversation.* **2** in the act of ——ing: *a-fishing = in the act of fishing.* [ME a < OE *an, on* in, on, at]
☞ *Usage.* a⁻¹. Adjectives originally formed with **a-** + noun (such as *alive, asleep*) are not used before a noun. We say *a man who is asleep* and *a man asleep,* but not *an asleep man.*

ad·her·ent (ad hēr′ənt) *n., adj.* —*n.* a faithful supporter; follower. —*adj.* sticking fast; attached. —**ad·her′ent·ly,** *adv.*
☞ *Syn. n.* See note at **follower.**
☞ *Usage.* Adherent. The preposition used with the noun adherent is of: *He was an adherent of the Liberal Party.*

Detailed grammatical information is given in the form of usage notes for such terms as *adverb* and *gerund:*

ad·verb (ad′vėrb) *n.* a word that extends or limits the meaning of verbs but is also used to qualify adjectives or other adverbs, especially in place, time, manner, or degree: *Soon, here, very, gladly,* and *not* are adverbs. *Abbrev.:* adv. [< L *adverbium < ad-* to + *verbum* verb]
☞ *Usage.* **Adverb. a. forms of adverbs.** Most adverbs are formed from adjectives or participles plus the ending *-ly: He rowed badly. She was deservedly popular. Surely you hear that.* There are a number of adverbs with the same forms as adjectives. Some of these are: *cheap, close, deep, even, first, high, loud, much, near, right, slow, smooth, tight, well, wrong.* Most of these adverbs have forms in *-ly* as well so that we can write: *He sang loud. He sang loudly.* The *-ly* forms are more common in formal English and the shorter forms in informal speech and writing. **b. comparison of adverbs.** Degrees of the condition or manner indicated by an adverb are shown by adding *-er, -est,* or by placing *more, most* before it: *hard, harder, hardest; slow, slower, slowest;* or *slowly, more slowly, most slowly. More* and *most* are used with most adverbs of more than one syllable.

ger·und (jer′ənd) *n. Grammar.* a verb form used as a noun. *Abbrev.:* ger. [< LL *gerundium,* ult. < L *gerere* bear]
☞ *Usage.* The English **gerund** ends in *-ing.* It has the same form as the present participle but differs in use. Gerund: *Running a hotel appealed to him.* Participle: *Running around the corner, he bumped into a cop.* A gerund may take an object (*running a hotel*) or a complement (*being a hero*), and it may serve in any of the functions of a noun: Subject: *Looking for an apartment always fascinated her.* Object: *He taught dancing.* Predicate noun: *Seeing is believing.* Adjectival use: *a fishing boat* (a boat for fishing, not a boat that fishes). Object of a preposition: *a great day for hiking.*

Spelling

A number of fistnotes deal with problems or variations of Canadian spelling:

ad·vis·er or **ad·vi·sor** (ad vīz′ər) *n.* **1** a person who gives advice. **2** a person whose work is giving advice, especially a teacher or professor appointed to advise students.
☞ *Usage.* **Adviser** has been the more common spelling, but the *-or* form, because of its similarity to *advisory,* is being increasingly used.

–or *suffix.* **1** a person or thing that ——s, as in *actor, accelerator, orator, survivor, sailor.* **2** an act, state, condition, quality, characteristic, etc., especially in words from Latin, as in *error, horror, labor, terror.* [< L]
☞ *Spelling.* **-or, -our.** In Canada usage varies in such words as **color/colour, honor/honour, labor/labour.** Both spellings are accepted, though **-or** is more common in printed materials. Exceptions are **glamour** (usually), **Honourable** (as a title), and **Saviour** (as a name for Jesus Christ). In British usage, which prefers **-our** spellings, derivatives ending in **-ation, -ary, -ific,** and **-ous** are spelled with **-or-.** Thus, *honorific,* **honorary, humorous, odoriferous** are so spelled on both sides of the Atlantic.

Hon·our·a·ble or **Hon·or·a·ble** (on′ər ə bəl) *adj.* **1** in Canada, a title given to members of the Privy Council (which includes the Federal Cabinet), to the Speakers of both the House of Commons and the provincial legislative assemblies, and to certain senior judges. **2** in Great Britain and elsewhere, a title of respect used under various conditions.
☞ *Usage.* **Honourable, Honorable.** The spelling *Honourable* is usually retained in Canada as an official title for Cabinet ministers, etc. *Abbrev.:* Hon.

Pronunciation

Variations in pronunciation are discussed in a similar way:

creek (krēk *or* krik) *n.* **1** a small freshwater stream. **2** a narrow bay, running inland for some distance. [ME *creke;* cf. MDu. *creke*]
☞ *Hom.* **creak** (krēk), **Creek.**
☞ *Pronun.* Most Canadians pronounce **creek** the same as **creak,** but in some regions, especially in parts of the West, the pronunciation (krik) is common.

been (bin *or* bēn) *v.* pp. of **be.**
☞ *Hom.* **bin** (bin), **bean** (bēn).
☞ *Pronun.* **Been.** The most common British pronunciation is (bēn), and the normal American pronunciation is (bin). In earlier English, (bēn) was the stressed form and (bin) the unstressed; many Canadian speakers still employ this distinction. Otherwise, Canadian usage varies between the two forms.

A a

a or **A** (ā) *n., pl.* **a's** or **A's. 1** the first letter of the English alphabet. **2** any speech sound represented by this letter, as in *cat, father, late,* etc. **3** a person or thing identified as *a,* especially the first in a series: *Company A in a battalion. A works twice as hard as B.* **4 A, a** a grade rating a person or thing as the best in a group: *grade A eggs.* **b** a person or thing receiving this rating: *All these exams are A's.* **5** *Music.* **a** the sixth tone in the scale of C major. **b** a symbol representing this tone. **c** a key, string, etc. that produces this tone. **d** a scale or key that has A as its keynote: *a symphony in A.* **6** *Algebra.* **a,** the first known quantity: *ax + by + c =* 0. **7 A, a** an antigen found in some human blood. **b** the type of human blood containing this antigen, one of the four main types in the ABO system. **8 A,** something shaped like the letter A. **9** (*adj.*) of or being an A or a.

a¹ (ə; *stressed,* ā *or* a) *adj. or indefinite article.* **1** a word used before singular nouns when the person or thing referred to is not specific: *There's a man at the door. I need a new coat.* **2** one: *I want a loaf of bread, a watermelon, and a dozen oranges. She took the stairs two at a time.* **3** any: *A thoughtful person would not have said that.* **4** a single: *not a one.* [var. of **an¹**]
☛ *Usage.* A is used before words pronounced with an initial consonant sound whether or not that sound is shown by the spelling, as in *a man, a year, a union, a hospital.* Most people now write *a hotel* or *a historian,* but some use *an* in these cases.
☛ *Usage.* A regularly comes before other modifiers but follows *many, such, what,* and any adjective preceded by *as, how, so,* or *too,* as in *many a person, such a bore, so fine a picture, too high a price.*

a² (ə; *stressed,* ā *or* a) *adj. or indefinite article.* **1** in each: *once a year.* **2** for each: *two dollars a dozen, forty dollars a day.* [OE *on on*]
☛ *Usage.* See first note at **a¹**.

a–¹ *prefix.* **1** on or in: *We went aboard. They found him abed. He set the bells a-ringing. The room was abuzz with conversation.* **2** in the act of ——ing: *a-fishing = in the act of fishing.* [ME *a <* OE *an, on in, on, at*]
☛ *Usage.* **a-¹.** Adjectives originally formed with a- + noun (such as *alive, asleep*) are not used before a noun. We say *a man who is asleep* and *a man asleep,* but not *an asleep man.*

a–² *prefix.* from, away, or off; the form of **ab-¹** occurring before *m, p,* and *v,* as in *avert.*
☛ *Usage.* See notes at **a¹**.

a–³ *prefix.* to or toward; the form of **ad-** occurring before *sc, sp,* and *st,* as in *ascribe, aspire, astringent.*

a–⁴ *prefix.* not or without; the form of **an-¹** occurring before consonants except *h,* as in *atypical, atonal.*
☛ *Usage.* A- meaning *not* is of Greek origin and is used in words taken directly, or through Latin, from Greek, as in *apathy.* It is also used as a naturalized English prefix in new formations, as in *achromatic.* A-, called alpha privative, corresponds to English **un-** and Latin **in-**.

a 1 anode. **2** alto. **3** are². **4** before (for L *ante*).
a. 1 about. **2** acre(s). **3** adjective. **4** alto. **5** in the year (for L *anno*). **6** anode. **7** anonymous. **8** answer. **9** before (for L *ante*). **10** *Heraldry.* argent. **11** *Sports.* assist; assists.
Å 1 ampere. **2** answer. **3** *A,* absolute temperature.
Å angstrom.
A1 or **A–1** *Informal.* A-one; first-class.
AA or **A.A. 1** *Psychology.* achievement age. **2** Alcoholics Anonymous. **3** anti-aircraft.
AAA or **A.A.A. 1** Amateur Athletic Association. **2** American Automobile Association.
aard·vark (ärd′värk′) *n.* an African burrowing mammal (*Orycteropus afer,* of the order Tubulidentata) having large, erect ears, a long movable snout, and a very long, flat, sticky tongue with which it catches ants and termites. An aardvark is about 1.5 m long. [< Afrikaans < Du. *aarde* earth + *vark* pig]

ab–¹ *prefix.* from, away, away from, or off, as in *abnormal, abduct, abuse.* Also: **a-** before *m, p, v;* **abs-** before *c, t.* [< L *ab- < ab,* prep.]

ab–² *prefix.* to or toward; the form of **ad-** occurring before *b,* as in *abbreviate.*

AB¹ Alberta (*used esp. in computerized address systems*).
AB² the type of human blood containing both antigens A and B. It is one of the four blood types in the ABO system.

A.B. *U.S.* Bachelor of Arts; B.A. (for L *Artium Baccalaureus*).
A.B. or **a.b.** able-bodied (seaman); able seaman.

a·ba·ca (ab′ə kə *or* ab′ə kä′) *n.* **1** a plant (*Musa textilis*) of the Philippines related to the banana, from whose leafstalks Manila hemp is obtained. **2** Manila hemp. [< Malay]

a·back (ə bak′) *adv. Archaic* (*except in* **taken aback**). toward the back; backward.
taken aback, taken by surprise; startled and confused: *She was taken aback by his angry outburst.* [OE *on bæc*]

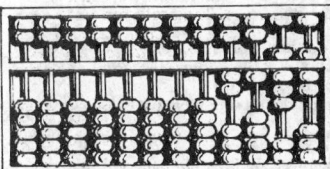
An abacus. The beads above the bar count 5 each when lowered to the bar. The beads below the bar count 1 each when raised. The beads of the abacus at left are set to show 7 in the units column, 8 in the 10's, 1 in the 100's, and 2 in the 1000's, for a total of 2187.

ab·a·cus (ab′ə kəs) *n., pl.* **-cus·es** or **-ci** (-sī′ *or* -sē′). **1** a calculating device consisting of a frame having rows of counters or beads that slide back and forth in grooves or on wires. **2** *Architecture.* a slab forming the top of the capital of a column. [< L < Gk. *abax, abacos*]

a·baft (ə baft′) *adv., prep.* —*adv.* of a ship or boat, at or toward the stern. —*prep.* behind; toward the stern from. [< *a-* on + ME *baft,* OE *beæftan < be* by + *æftan* behind]

ab·a·lo·ne (ab′ə lō′nē) *n.* any of several species of edible marine snail (genus *Haliotis*) found mainly along temperate Pacific coasts, having a single, flat, ear-shaped shell with a row of small holes along one side and a mother-of-pearl lining that is used for buttons and ornaments. [Am.Sp. *abulón*]

a·ban·don (ə ban′dən) *v., n.* —*v.* **1** give up entirely; relinquish: *to abandon a career, to abandon an idea.* **2** leave without intending to return; desert: *to abandon one's home.* **3** yield (oneself) completely (to a feeling, impulse, etc.): *to abandon oneself to grief.* —*n.* complete freedom from restraint; spontaneous exuberance or enthusiasm: *The crowd cheered with abandon.* [ME < OF *abandoner,* earlier *a ban doner* give over to another's jurisdiction < *a* to (< L *ad*) + *ban* power (< Gmc.) + *doner* give < L *donare* grant < *donum* gift] —**a·ban′don·er,** *n.*
☛ *Syn. v.* **2.** See note at **desert²**.

a·ban·doned (ə ban′dənd) *adj.* **1** deserted or forsaken: *an abandoned homestead.* **2** completely unrestrained; especially, disregarding accepted standards of sexual behavior.

a·ban·don·ment (ə ban′dən mənt) *n.* **1** abandoning or being abandoned. **2** freedom from restraint; abandon.

a·base (ə bās′) *v.* **a·based, a·bas·ing.** make lower in rank, esteem, or prestige; humiliate or degrade: *to abase oneself by accepting a bribe.* [ME < OF *abaissier* bring low < LL *bassus* low]

a·base·ment (ə bās′mənt) *n.* the act of abasing or the condition of being abased.

a·bash (ə bash′) *v.* embarrass and confuse; make uneasy or shy and slightly ashamed: *The boys were abashed when the teacher pointed out all their mistakes.* [ME < OF *esbaïss-,* a stem of *esbaïr* be astonished < VL *batare* gape] —**a·bash′ment,** *n.*

a·bate (ə bāt′) *v.* **a·bat·ed, a·bat·ing. 1** become less violent, intense, etc.: *The storm has abated.* **2** make less in amount, intensity, etc.: *The medicine abated his pain.* **3** *Law.* do away with; put an end to; annul: *to abate a nuisance, to abate a writ.* **4** deduct (part of a price, etc.). [ME < OF *abatre* beat down < *a-* to (< L *ad-*) + *batre* beat < VL *battere* < L *battuere*] —**a·bat′er,** *n.*

a·bate·ment (ə bāt′mənt) *n.* **1** the act or process of abating. **2** the amount abated; reduction.

ab·a·tis or **ab·at·tis** (ab′ə tis *or* ab′ə tē) *n., pl.* **ab·a·tis** or **ab·at·tis.** a barricade of trees cut down and placed with their sharpened branches directed toward the enemy. [< F *abatis* mass of things thrown down]

ab·at·toir (ab′ə twär′ *or* ab′ə twär′) *n.* slaughterhouse. [< F]

ab·ba·cy (ab′ə sē) *n., pl.* **-cies. 1** the position or power of an

abbot. **2** the term of office of an abbot. **3** a district ruled by an abbot. [< LL *abbatia* < *abbas* abbot. See ABBOT.]

Ab·bas·sid (ə bas'id *or* ab'ə sid) *n.* any of the caliphs of Baghdad belonging to the dynasty supposed to be descended from Abbas (A.D. 566-652), uncle and helper of Mohammed. This dynasty ruled the Moslem empire from A.D. 750 to 1258.

ab·bé (ab'ā *or* a bā') *n.* **1** a French abbot. **2** a title of respect given to a French priest or other cleric.

ab·bess (ab'is *or* ab'es) *n.* the woman in charge of an abbey of nuns. [ME < OF < LL *abbatissa* < *abbas, abbatis* abbot + *-issa* Gk. fem. suffix. See ABBOT.]

ab·bey (ab'ē) *n., pl.* **-beys. 1** the building or buildings where monks or nuns live a religious life governed by an abbot or abbess; a monastery or convent. **2** the monks or nuns living there. **3** a church or residence that was once an abbey or a part of an abbey: *Westminster Abbey.* [ME < OF < LL *abbatia* < *abbas, -atis* abbot. See ABBOT.]

ab·bot (ab'ət) *n.* the man in charge of an abbey of monks. [OE *abbad, abbod* < LL *abbas, -atis* < LGk. < Aramaic *abbā* father]

abbrev. or **abbr.** abbreviation; abbreviated.

ab·bre·vi·ate (ə brē'vē āt') *v.* **-at·ed, -at·ing. 1** make (a word or phrase) shorter so that a part stands for the whole: *We can abbreviate Alberta to Alta.* **2** make briefer; curtail. [< L *abbreviare* < *ad-* to + *brevis* short. Doublet of ABRIDGE.] —**ab·bre'vi·a'tor,** *n.*
☛ *Syn.* See note at **shorten.**

ab·bre·vi·a·tion (ə brē'vē ā'shən) *n.* **1** a shortened form of a word or phrase standing for the whole, such as *Ont.* for *Ontario* or *MP* for *Member of Parliament.* **2** the act of making shorter.
☛ *Usage.* **Period with abbreviations.** As a general rule, a period is used after an abbreviation. However, it is now usual to omit periods with the abbreviations of names of organizations commonly known by their initials: *CBC, NDP, RCMP.* On the other hand, initial abbreviations for provinces and countries usually have periods: *B.C., P.E.I., U.S.A.* There is a tendency not to use a period after an abbreviation that ends with the last letter of the word abbreviated, that is, a form which really is a contraction: *Dr, Mr, Mrs, vs, Wm.* This practice is more common in British than in Canadian and American usage.

ABC¹ (ā'bē'sē') *n.* Often, **ABC's: 1** the alphabet: *to learn one's ABC's.* **2** elementary principles: *This course is intended to teach you the ABC of flying.*

ABC² American Broadcasting Company.

A.B.C. book primer.

ab·di·cate (ab'də kāt') *v.* **-cat·ed, -cat·ing. 1** give up or renounce formally (a position of authority or responsibility): *When King Edward VIII abdicated his throne his brother became king.* **2** renounce a throne, office, etc.: *Why did the king abdicate?* [< L *abdicare* < *ab-* away + *dicare* proclaim] —**ab'di·ca'tion,** *n.* —**ab'di·ca'tor,** *n.*

ab·do·men (ab'də mən *or* ab dō'mən) *n.* **1** the part of the body containing the stomach, the intestines, and other digestive organs; belly. **2** the outer front surface of this. **3** the last of the three parts of the body of an insect or crustacean. [< L]

ab·dom·i·nal (ab dom'ə nəl) *adj.* of, in, or for the abdomen: *the abdominal muscles.* —**ab·dom'i·nal·ly,** *adv.*

ab·dom·i·nous (ab dom'ə nəs) *adj.* potbellied.

ab·duct (ab dukt') *v.* **1** carry off or take away (a person) by force or deceit. **2** of a muscle or group of muscles, serve to move (a limb, etc.) away from the median axis of the body or of one of its parts. Compare **adduct.** [< L *abductus,* pp. of *abducere* < *ab-* away + *ducere* lead] —**ab·duc'tion,** *n.*

ab·duc·tor (ab duk'tər) *n.* **1** a person who abducts another person. **2** any muscle whose function is to move a limb, etc. away from the median axis of the body or of one of its parts, as in raising an arm out to the side or spreading the fingers or toes. Compare **adductor.**

a·beam (ə bēm') *adv.* **1** directly opposite to the middle part of a ship's side. **2** straight across a ship.

a·bed (ə bed') *adv. Archaic.* in bed.

A·bel (ā'bəl) *n.* in the Bible, the second son of Adam and Eve, killed in jealousy by his older brother Cain (Gen. 4:1-15).

A·be·li·an group (ə bē'lē ən *or* ə bel'yən) *Mathematics.* a group of numbers or variables governed by the commutative law.

Ab·e·na·ki (ab'ə nak'ē) *n., pl.* **-ki** *or* **-kis;** *adj.* —*n.* **1** a member of an Amerindian people living mainly in southern Quebec and the State of Maine. **2** the Algonquian language spoken by the Abenaki. —*adj.* of or having to do with the Abenaki or their language. Also, **Abnaki.** [< Algonquin, literally, those living in the east, or easterners]

Ab·er·deen An·gus (ab'ər dēn' ang'gəs) a breed of entirely black, hornless beef cattle having a compact body and short legs.

Ab·er·do·ni·an (ab'ər dō'nē ən) *adj., n.* —*adj.* of or having to do with Aberdeen or its people. —*n.* a native or inhabitant of Aberdeen.

ab·er·rance (ab er'əns) *n.* the fact or condition of being aberrant.

ab·er·rant (ab er'ənt) *adj., n.* —*adj.* deviating from what is regular, normal, or right: *aberrant behavior.* —*n.* an aberrant person or thing. [< L *aberrans, -antis,* ppr. of *aberrare* < *ab-* away + *errare* wander]

ab·er·ra·tion (ab'ər ā'shən) *n.* **1** a wandering from the right path or usual course of action. **2** a deviation from a standard or ordinary type; abnormal structure or development. **3** a temporary mental disorder. **4** *Optics.* the failure of a lens or mirror to bring to a single focus the rays of light coming from one point. Aberration causes a blurred image or an image with a colored rim. **5** *Astronomy.* a slight change in the apparent position of a heavenly body, caused by the combined effect of the earth's motion and of light.

a·bet (ə bet') *v.* **a·bet·ted, a·bet·ting.** encourage or help, especially in doing something wrong: *One man did the actual stealing, but two others abetted him.* [ME < OF *abeter* arouse < *a-* to + *beter* to bait] —**a·bet'ment,** *n.* —**a·bet'tor, a·bet'ter,** *n.*

a·bey·ance (ə bā'əns) *n.* **1** temporary inactivity; a state of suspended action: *The whole question is being held in abeyance until a new committee is formed.* **2** *Law.* a lapse in succession of title until ownership or possession is established: *The inheritance was in abeyance until the rightful owner came forward.* [< AF *abeiance* expectation < L *ad-* at + VL *batare* gape]

ab·hor (ab hôr') *v.* **-horred, -hor·ring.** shrink from with horror; feel disgust or hate for; detest; loathe: *to abhor liquor, to abhor snakes.* [< L *abhorrere* < *ab-* from + *horrere* dread] —**ab·hor'rer,** *n.*
☛ *Syn.* See note at **hate.**

ab·hor·rence (ab hôr'əns) *n.* **1** a feeling of horror or disgust. **2** something that is abhorred.

ab·hor·rent (ab hôr'ənt) *adj.* causing horror or disgust; hateful. —**ab·hor'rent·ly,** *adv.*

a·bide (ə bīd') *v.* **a·bode** *or* **a·bid·ed, a·bid·ing. 1** put up with; endure; tolerate: *He cannot abide untidiness.* **2** stay; remain: *"Though much is taken, much abides."* **3** dwell; continue to live (in a place). **4** stand firm. **5** *Archaic.* wait for: *He shall abide my coming.*
abide by, a accept and act upon: *We must abide by their decision.* **b** remain faithful to; fulfil: *They abided by their promise.* [OE *ābīdan* stay on, and *onbīdan* wait for] —**a·bid'er,** *n.*

a·bid·ing (ə bīd'ing) *adj.* unending; enduring; lasting: *an abiding interest in conservation. We hope for an abiding peace.*

ab·i·gail (ab'ə gāl') *n.* a lady's maid. [< *Abigail,* a character in Beaumont and Fletcher's play *The Scornful Lady*]

a·bil·i·ty (ə bil'ə tē) *n., pl.* **-ties. 1** the power to perform or accomplish: *He has the ability to hold an audience spellbound.* **2** skill: *He has great ability as a hockey player.* **3** the power to do some special thing; mental gift; talent: *Musical ability often shows itself early in life.* [< F *habileté* < L *habilitas* < *habilis* apt, fit, easily handled]
☛ *Syn.* **3. Ability, talent** = power to do or for doing something. **Ability** applies to a demonstrated physical or mental power, which may be either natural or acquired, to do a certain thing well: *He has unusual ability in science.* **Talent** applies to a capacity for doing a special thing, which is inborn in a person, never acquired, and which is or can be developed through training and use: *His Scout activities revealed a talent for leadership, which he is developing at school this year.*
☛ *Usage.* A verb following **ability** is in the infinitive and is always preceded by *to: He has the ability to swim like a fish;* not: *He has the ability of swimming like a fish.*

ab in·i·tio (ab'in ish'ē ō) *Latin.* from the beginning.

ab·ject (ab'jekt) *adj.* **1** wretched; miserable: *abject poverty.* **2** deserving contempt; degraded: *an abject flatterer.* **3** showing humiliation or complete resignation: *abject submission, an abject apology.* [< L *abjectus,* pp. of *abjicere* < *ab-* down + *jacere* throw] —**ab·ject'ly,** *adv.*

ab·ju·ra·tion (ab'jə rā'shən) *n.* the act or an instance of abjuring.

ab·jure (ab jür') *v.* **-jured, -juring. 1** renounce solemnly or on oath; swear to give up: *to abjure one's religion.* **2** abstain from; avoid: *to abjure alcohol.* [< L *abjurare* < *ab-* away + *jurare* swear] —**ab·jur'er,** *n.*

abl. ablative.

ab·late (ab lāt') *v.* **-lat·ed, -lat·ing. 1** remove by burning off, wearing down, cutting away, etc.; remove by ablation. **2** become ablated. [< L *ablatus,* literally, having been carried away, pp. of *auferre* carry away]

ab·la·tion (ab lā'shən) *n.* **1** the removal of an organ or body part by surgery. **2** *Geology.* the erosion of glaciers or rocks, especially by melting or the action of water. **3** *Astronautics.* the vaporizing or

melting of the outer surface of the nose cone, etc. of a spacecraft, as on reentry into the earth's atmosphere.

ab·la·tive (ab′lə tiv) *adj., n.* —*adj.* of, having to do with, or being the grammatical case, found in Latin and some other languages, that shows that a noun or pronoun refers to a source, agent, cause, etc. of an action. —*n.* **1** the ablative case. **2** a word or construction in the ablative case. [< L *ablativus,* literally, of removal < *ablatus,* pp. of *auferre* < *ab-* away + *ferre* carry]
☛ *Usage.* **Ablative case.** The work done in Latin by ablative case endings is done in English by the prepositions *at, by, from, in,* and *with* placed before the noun: *at the store, by the thief.*

ab·laut (ab′lout; *German,* äp′lout) *n. Linguistics.* a change in the quality or length of a root vowel sound, indicating a grammatical distinction. Ablaut was a feature of the early Indo-European languages and is still found in modern English in such verbs as *ring.* (pt. *rang,* pp. *rung*) and *write* (pt. *wrote,* pp. *written*). [< G *Ablaut* < *ab-* off + *Laut* sound]

a·blaze (ə blāz′) *adv.* or *adj.* (*never precedes a noun*) **1** on fire; burning: *By the time we arrived, the whole building was ablaze.* **2** bright or glowing: *The great hall was ablaze with a hundred lights.* **3** in or into a state of great excitement or enthusiasm.

a·ble (ā′bəl) *adj.* **a·bler, a·blest. 1** having power, means, opportunity, time, etc. (*to*): *Little children are able to walk, but they are not able to earn a living.* **2** having the necessary qualifications; competent: *an able seaman.* **3** having more power or skill than most others have; clever: *She is an able teacher.* **4** competently done: *an able speech.* [ME < OF *hable, able* < L *habilis* fit, easily held or handled < *habere* hold]
☛ *Syn.* **1. Able, capable, competent** = having sufficient power to do or for doing something. **Able** (with *to*) emphasizes power to act or perform: *He is able to play the piano.* **Capable** emphasizes fitness for doing, capacity or ability to do something adequately, or, sometimes, general efficiency: *He has proved himself capable both as soldier and as administrator.* **Competent** emphasizes possession of sufficient skill or other requirements to do a certain kind of work satisfactorily: *A competent typist is not necessarily a competent secretary.*
☛ *Usage.* **Able** and **competent** may be followed by *to* plus an infinitive, but **capable** takes *of* plus a gerund: *able to think, competent to drive a car, capable of taking responsibility.*

–able *suffix.* **1** that can be —ed; able to be —ed: *obtainable = that can be obtained.* **2** likely to be or suitable for: *comfortable = suitable for comfort.* **3** inclined to: *peaceable = inclined to peace.* **4** deserving to be —ed: *lovable = deserving to be loved.* See also **-ible.** [< F < L *-abilis,* a suffix forming adjectives from verbs with infinitives in *-are,* being one form of the suffix *-bilis*]
☛ *Usage.* Instead of **-able,** a number of words have the spelling **-ible,** which originally belonged largely to words from Latin infinitives in *-ere* or *-ire* (as in *terrible*). The living suffix is **-able,** which should be used in coining occasional words like *jumpable.* If there is a related noun ending in *-ion,* the adjective suffix is usually **-ible.**

a·ble-bod·ied (ā′bəl bod′ēd) *adj.* physically fit; strong and healthy.

able-bodied seaman an experienced sailor, especially in a merchant navy, who is qualified to perform certain routine duties at sea. *Abbrev.:* A.B. or a.b.

able seaman 1 *Canadian Forces.* in Maritime Command, a person ranking next above an ordinary seaman and below a leading seaman. *Abbrev.:* A.B. or AB See chart at **rank**[1]. **2** able-bodied seaman.

a·bloom (ə blüm′) *adv.* or *adj.* (*never precedes a noun*) in bloom; blossoming.

ab·lu·tion (ab lü′shən) *n.* **1** the act of washing oneself: *to perform one's ablutions.* **2** the act of washing or cleansing as a religious ceremony of purification. **3** the water or other liquid used in washing. [< L *ablutio, -onis* < *abluere* < *ab-* away + *lavere* wash]

a·bly (ā′blē) *adv.* in an able manner; with skill.

ABM antiballistic missile.

Ab·na·ki (ab′nak′ē) *n., pl.* **-ki** or **-kis.** Abenaki.

ab·ne·gate (ab′nə gāt′) *v.* **-gat·ed, -gat·ing. 1** surrender; give up a right or privilege: *They abnegated their claim on the estate.* **2** deny; recant; renounce: *to abnegate one's God.* [< L *abnegare* < *ab-* off, away + *negare* deny] —**ab′ne·ga′tion,** *n.*

ab·nor·mal (ab nôr′məl) *adj.* **1** deviating from the normal, standard, or typical; markedly irregular: *The drug produces an abnormal dilation of the pupil of the eye.* **2** having to do with what is abnormal: *abnormal psychology.* —**ab·nor′mal·ly,** *adv.* —**ab·nor′mal·ness,** *n.*
☛ *Syn.* See note at **irregular.**

ab·nor·mal·i·ty (ab′nôr mal′ə tē) *n., pl.* **-ties. 1** an abnormal thing or happening. **2** an abnormal condition: *He suffers from an abnormality of the blood.*

a·board (ə bôrd′) *adv., prep.* —*adv.* **1** on board; on, in, or into a ship, train, bus, aircraft, etc.: *All passengers should now be aboard.* **all aboard,** everybody on (conductor's call directing passengers to enter a train, bus, etc. about to start).
—*prep.* on board of: *They went aboard the ship.*

hat, āge, fär; let, ēqual, tèrm; it, īce
hot, ōpen, ôrder; oil, out; cup, pùt, rüle,
əbove, takən, pencəl, lemən, circəs
ch, child; ng, long; sh, ship
th, thin; ᴛʜ, then; zh, measure

a·bode (ə bōd′) *n., v.* —*n.* a place to live in; dwelling; residence. —*v.* a pt. and a pp. of **abide.** [OE *ābād*]

a·boi·deau (ab′ə dō′; *French,* ä bwä dō′) *n., pl.* **-deaus** or **-deaux** (-dōz′; *French,* -dō′). *Cdn.* in Nova Scotia and New Brunswick: **1** a sluice-gate in the dikes along the Bay of Fundy. **2** one of these dikes. [< Cdn.F]

a·boi·teau (ab′ə tō′; *French,* ä bwä tō′) *n., pl.* **-teaus** or **-teaux** (-tōz′; *French,* tō′). *Cdn.* aboideau. [< Cdn.F]

a·bol·ish (ə bol′ish) *v.* do away with (a law, institution, or custom) completely; put an end to: *to abolish slavery.* [< F *aboliss-,* stem of *abolir;* fusion of two verbs, L *abolere* destroy, and L *abolescere* die out] —**a·bol′ish·ment,** *n.*
☛ *Syn.* **Abolish, annihilate, extinguish** = put an end to something. **Abolish** applies only to man-made things, usually long in existence, such as laws and customs: *Many countries have abolished hanging.* **Annihilate,** more general in application, suggests use of force and always retains its literal meaning of reducing to nothing, by wiping something out without a trace or by destroying its distinguishing qualities or form: *The enemy annihilated the regiment.* **Extinguish** applies to things or ideas which can be caused to die or be blotted out by overpowering force or circumstances: *You may extinguish a nation, but not the love of liberty.*

ab·o·li·tion (ab′ə lish′ən) *n.* **1** abolishing or being abolished. **2** the annulment of a specific law, especially: **a** *Historical.* the ending of slavery in the British Empire (1833) or the United States (1865). **b** the abolishing of capital punishment. [< L *abolitio, -onis*]

ab·o·li·tion·ist (ab′ə lish′ən ist) *n.* a person who wishes to abolish a particular law, custom, etc., especially one in favor of abolishing slavery.

ab·o·ma·sum (ab′ə mā′səm) *n.* the fourth stomach of cows, sheep, and other animals that chew the cud. The abomasum is the stomach that digests the food. [< NL < L *ab-* away from + *omasum* bullock's tripe]

A-bomb (ā′bom′) *n.* atomic bomb.

a·bom·i·na·ble (ə bom′ə nə bəl *or* ə bom′nə bəl) *adj.* **1** disgusting or detestable: *abominable treatment of prisoners.* **2** *Informal.* very unpleasant, distasteful, or inferior: *abominable roads, abominable taste.* [< F < L *abominabilis < abominari.* See ABOMINATE.] —**a·bom′i·na·ble·ness,** *n.* —**a·bom′i·na·bly,** *adv.*

abominable snowman a manlike monster supposed to inhabit the higher parts of the Himalaya mountains, where huge footprints have been found in the snow. It is called "yeti" by the Sherpa people, who inhabit this region.

a·bom·i·nate (ə bom′ə nāt′) *v.* **-nat·ed, -nat·ing. 1** feel disgust for; abhor; detest. **2** *Informal.* dislike. [< L *abominari* deplore as an ill omen < *ab-* off + *ominari* prophesy < *omen, ominis* omen] —**a·bom′i·na′tor,** *n.*

a·bom·i·na·tion (ə bom′ə nā′shən) *n.* **1** a revolting thing: *Anything that degrades man is an abomination.* **2** a shamefully wicked action or custom. **3** a feeling of disgust; hate; loathing.

ab·o·rig·i·nal (ab′ə rij′ə nəl) *adj., n.* —*adj.* **1** existing in a place from the beginning; being the first or the original one or ones: *aboriginal inhabitants.* **2** of or having to do with the original or earliest known inhabitants of a region or country: *aboriginal customs, aboriginal rights.* —*n.* aborigine. —**ab′o·rig′i·nal·ly,** *adv.*
☛ *Usage.* See note at **aborigine.**

ab·o·rig·i·ne (ab′ə rij′ə nē′) *n.* **1** one of the earliest known inhabitants of a country. **2** Usually, **Aborigine,** a member of a dark-skinned people who are the original inhabitants of Australia; a member of the Australoid race. [< L *aborigines < ab origine* from the beginning]
☛ *Usage.* In the singular both **aborigine** and **aboriginal** are used, but in the plural **aborigines** is more common than **aboriginals.**

a·born·ing (ə bôr′ning) *adv.* while just being born or produced (*used especially in* **die aborning**): *Their hopes died aborning.*

a·bort (ə bôrt′) *v.* **1** give birth before the fetus has developed enough to survive outside the womb; have a miscarriage. **2** cause to have an abortion. **3** *Biology.* fail to develop beyond the rudimentary stage. **4** bring to an end prematurely; cut short or cancel: *to abort a space flight.* **5** fail to develop. [< L *abortus,* pp. of *aboriri < ab-* amiss + *oriri* be born]

a·bor·tion (ə bôr′shən) *n.* **1** the intentional ending of a pregnancy and destruction of the fetus by causing the fetus to be expelled, especially before it is viable. **2** miscarriage (def. 2). **3** *Biology.* **a** failure to develop beyond the rudimentary stage. **b** a creature or an organ that is incompletely or imperfectly formed. **4** the failure of

anything to develop completely or properly. **5** anything incompletely or imperfectly developed: *Their revolutionary solar heating system turned out to be a sad abortion.*

a·bor·tion·ist (ə bôr′shən ist) *n.* a person who performs abortions, especially one who does so illegally.

a·bor·tive (ə bôr′tiv) *adj.* **1** unsuccessful; fruitless: *He made several abortive attempts to escape.* **2** *Biology.* not developed properly or completely; rudimentary. **3** causing abortion. **—a·bor′tive·ly,** *adv.* **—a·bor′tive·ness,** *n.*

ABO system a classification of human blood types based on the presence or absence of two antigens, called A and B, on the red cells. The four blood types in this system are A, B, AB, and O.

a·bound (ə bound′) *v.* **1** be plentiful: *Fish abound in the ocean.* **2** be rich (*in*): *Alberta abounds in oil.* **3** be well supplied or filled (*with*): *The ocean abounds with fish.* [ME < OF *abunder* < L *abundare* < *ab-* off + *undare* flow < *unda* a wave]

a·bout (ə bout′) *prep., adv.* **—prep. 1** of or having to do with: *a book about bridges.* **2** in connection with: *something peculiar about him.* **3** somewhere near; not far from: *The dog was about the house.* **4** approximately; near: *He is about my size.* **5** on every side of; all around; around: *a fence about the garden.* **6** on (one's person); with: *She has no money about her.* **7** in many parts of; everywhere in: *to scatter papers about the room.*
—adv. 1 nearly; almost: *The buckets and tubs are about full.* **2** somewhere near: *A tramp has been hanging about.* **3** all around; in every direction: *The boy looked about.* **4** in many places; here and there: *A rumor went about that he was ill.* **5** in the opposite direction: *Face about! After swimming a kilometre, we turned about and swam back to the shore.* **6** doing; working at: *An expert worker knows what he is about.* **7** one after another; by turns: *Turn about is fair play.* **8** stirring: *able to be up and about.*
about to, on the point of; going, intending, or ready to: *The plane is about to take off.*
[OE *onbūtan, abūtan* on the outside of]

a·bout-face (*n.* ə bout′fās′; *v.* ə bout′fās′) *n., v.* **-faced, -fac·ing. —n.** a complete change or reversal of direction, point of view, opinion, etc.: *She made an about-face and hurried back to the house. At the first hint of opposition, the policy committee did an about-face.* **—v.** turn or go in the opposite direction.

about turn *Military.* a command to face in the opposite direction.

a·bout-turn (ə bout′tèrn) *n. or v.* about-face.

a·bove (ə buv′) *adv., prep., adj., n.* **—adv. 1** overhead; in a higher place: *The sky is above.* **2** on the upper side or on top: *The leaves are dark above and light below.* **3** higher in rank or power: *the courts above.* **4** more than: *The cost of the repairs is not likely to be above $500.* **5** earlier, in a book or article: *as mentioned above.* **6** in heaven.
—prep. 1 in or to a higher place than: *Birds fly above the trees.* **2** higher than; over: *He kept his head above water. A captain is above a sergeant.* **3** too high in dignity or character for; superior to: *A great person should be above mean actions.* **4** more than: *The weight is above a tonne.* **5** beyond: *Turn at the first corner above the school.*
—adj. 1 made or mentioned above: *the above remark.* **2** above zero on the Fahrenheit scale of temperature: *It was 40 above that New Year's Day.*
—n. the above, something that is written above. [OE *abufan*]
☛ *Syn. prep.* **1, 2.** See note at **over.**

a·bove-board (ə buv′bôrd′) *adv. or adj.* in open sight; without tricks or concealment: *The official was always aboveboard in her conduct.*

a·bove-men·tioned (ə buv′men′shənd) *adj.* previously referred to; mentioned earlier.

ab o·vo (ab′ō′vō) *Latin.* from the beginning. [*literally,* from the egg]

Abp. Archbishop.

abr. abridged.

ab·ra·ca·dab·ra (ab′rə kə dab′ rə) *n.* **1** a word supposed to have magic power, used in incantations or as a charm to ward off disease. **2** meaningless talk; jargon. [< LL]

a·brade (ə brād′) *v.* **a·brad·ed, a·brad·ing.** wear away by rubbing; scrape off: *The rock had been abraded over the years by blowing sand.* [< L *abradere* < *ab-* off + *radere* scrape]

a·bra·sion (ə brā′zhən) *n.* **1** a place scraped or worn by rubbing: *Abrasions of the skin are painful.* **2** a scraping off; a wearing away by rubbing. [< L *abrasio, -onis* < *abradere. See* ABRADE.]

a·bra·sive (ə brā′siv or ə brā′ziv) *n., adj.* **—n.** a substance used for grinding, smoothing, or polishing. Sandpaper, pumice, and emery are abrasives. **—adj. 1** wearing away by rubbing; causing abrasion: *the abrasive action of water.* **2** causing or tending to cause

irritation or annoyance: *an abrasive personality.* **—a·bra′sive·ly,** *adv.* **—a·bra′sive·ness,** *n.*

a·breast (ə brest′) *adv. or adj.* (*never precedes a noun*) side by side: *The soldiers marched three abreast.*
abreast of or **abreast with,** up with; alongside of: *Keep abreast of what is going on.*

a·bri (ä brē′) *n., pl.* **a·bris** (ä brē′). *French.* a shelter.

a·bridge (ə brij′) *v.* **a·bridged, a·bridg·ing. 1** make shorter, especially written or printed matter; condense: *The novel was abridged for publication in the magazine.* **2** make less: *The rights of citizens must not be abridged without proper cause.* **3** *Archaic.* deprive (*of*): *to abridge citizens of their rights.* [ME < OF *abregier* < L *abbreviare* shorten. Doublet of ABBREVIATE.] **—a·bridg′a·ble or a·bridge′a·ble,** *adj.*

a·bridg·ment or **a·bridge·ment** (ə brij′mənt) *n.* **1** a shortened form, especially of a book or long article: *This book is an abridgment of a three-volume history.* **2** abridging or being abridged.

a·broad (ə brod′ or ə brôd′) *adv.* **1** outside one's country, especially overseas; to or in a foreign land or foreign lands: *We're going abroad this summer. He spent a year abroad, mostly in Norway.* **2** out of doors, especially away from one's home: *They travelled only by night because fewer enemy patrols were abroad then.* **3** going around; in circulation; current: *There is a rumor abroad that the mayor is resigning.* **4** far and wide; widely: *The news of his arrival spread abroad.*

ab·ro·gate (ab′rə gāt′) *v.* **-gat·ed, -gat·ing. 1** abolish or annul (a law or custom) by legislation; repeal. **2** do away with. [< L *abrogare* < *ab-* away + *rogare* demand] **—ab′ro·ga′tion,** *n.* **—ab′ro·ga′tor,** *n.*

a·brupt (ə brupt′) *adj.* **1** sudden; hasty; unexpected: *an abrupt turn.* **2** very steep. **3** short or sudden in speech or manner; blunt. **4** disconnected; *an abrupt rhythm, an abrupt style.* **5** *Botany.* truncate: *the abrupt top of a tulip-tree leaf.* [< L *abruptus,* pp. of *abrumpere* < *ab-* off + *rumpere* break] **—a·brupt′ly,** *adv.* **—a·brupt′ness,** *n.*
☛ *Syn.* **2.** See note at **steep.**

abs– *prefix.* from, away, or off; the form of **ab-**[1] occurring before *c* and *t* as in *abscond, abstain.*

abs. 1 absent. **2** absolute. **3** abstract.

Ab·sa·lom (ab′sə ləm) *n.* in the Bible, David's favorite son, who rebelled against his father (II Samuel 18).

ab·scess (ab′ses) *n.* a collection of pus in the tissues of some part of the body, caused by infection and often forming a red, swollen, painful lump on the skin. Pimples, boils, and carbuncles are abscesses. [< L *abscessus* < *abscedere* < *ab*(s)- away + *cedere* go]

ab·scessed (ab′sest) *adj.* having an abscess.

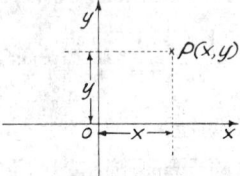

The abscissa of the point *p* is *x*; the ordinate is *y*.

ab·scis·sa (ab sis′ə) *n., pl.* **-scis·sas** or **-scis·sae** (-sis′ē *or* -sis′ī). *Mathematics.* the first number in an ordered pair; the horizontal co-ordinate, or *x*-value, in a system of cartesian co-ordinates. Compare **ordinate.** [< L (*linea*) *abscissa* (line) cut off < pp. stem (*ab*)*sciss-* of (*ab*)*scindere* cut]

ab·scond (ab skond′) *v.* go away suddenly and secretly; especially, flee from the law after stealing something: *She absconded with the association's funds.* [< L *abscondere* < *ab*(s)- away + *condere* store] **—ab·scond′er,** *n.*

ab·sence (ab′səns) *n.* **1** the state of being away: *absence from work.* **2** the time of being away: *an absence of two weeks.* **3** the fact of being without; lack: *darkness is the absence of light.* **4** absent-mindedness.

absence of mind absent-mindedness.

ab·sent (*adj.* ab′sənt; *v.* ab sent′) *adj., v.* **—adj. 1** not present; away: *John is absent from class today.* **2** lacking; not existing: *Trees are almost completely absent in some parts of the Prairies.* **3** absent-minded: *an absent reply.*
—v. take or keep (oneself) away: *to absent oneself from class.* [< L *absens, -entis,* ppr. of *abesse* < *ab-* away + *esse* to be]

ab·sen·tee (ab′sən tē′) *n., adj.* **—n.** a person who is absent or remains absent. **—adj.** of or for a voter or voters permitted to vote while absent from home.

ab·sen·tee·ism (ab′sən tē′iz əm) *n.* **1** the practice or habit of

being an absentee. **2** an economic system under which a landowner controls the use of land in a country or place where he does not live.

absentee landlord a landowner who draws an income from his land but lives in another part of the country, or in another place.

ab·sent·ly (ab′sənt lē) *adv.* without paying attention to what is going on around one; inattentively: *He had answered her absently and later on couldn't remember what he had said.*

ab·sent·mind·ed (ab′sənt mīn′did) *adj.* not aware of what is going on around one; having one's mind on other things. —**ab′sent-mind′ed·ly,** *adv.* —**ab′sent-mind′ed·ness,** *n.*

ab·sinthe (ab′sinth) *n.* a strong, green, somewhat bitter liqueur flavored with wormwood or a substitute and any of various other aromatics, such as aniseed or licorice. Also, **absinth.** [< F *absinthe* < L < Gk. *apsinthion* wormwood]

ab·sit o·men (ab′sit ō′mən) *Latin.* may the feared disaster, evil, etc. not take place. [literally, may this (evil) omen be absent]

ab·so·lute (ab′sə lüt′) *adj., n.* —*adj.* **1** complete; whole or entire; perfect: *absolute ignorance, absolute silence, absolute justice.* **2** not mixed with anything else; pure: *absolute alcohol.* **3** not limited or restricted by a constitution, parliament, etc.: *an absolute monarchy, an absolute ruler.* **4** not qualified or restricted in any way: *absolute freedom.* **5** certain; unquestionable; positive: *absolute proof, absolute certainty.* **6** not compared with or dependent on anything else; not relative: *absolute velocity, an absolute term in logic.* **7** real; actual: *an absolute truth.* **8** *Grammar.* of a word, phrase, etc.: **a** forming a part of a sentence, but not connected with it gramatically. In *The train being late, we missed the boat, the train being late* is an absolute phrase. **b** used without an expressed object. In *I will not ask again, ask* is an absolute verb. **c** having its noun understood, but not expressed. In *The older pupils may help the younger, younger* is an absolute adjective. In *Your house is larger than ours, ours* is an absolute pronoun. **9** *Physics.* of or having to do with the absolute-temperature scale. —*n.* **1** something that is absolute. **2 the absolute,** *Philosophy.* that which exists of itself and is conceivable without relation to other things. [< L *absolutus,* pp. of *absolvere.* See ABSOLVE.] —**ab′so·lute′ness,** *n.*

absolute alcohol ethyl alcohol that contains not more than one percent by weight of water.

absolute humidity the amount of water vapor present in a unit volume of air: *A cubic metre of air containing 10 grams of water vapor has an absolute humidity of 10.* Compare **relative humidity.**

ab·so·lute·ly (ab′sə lüt′lē *for 1, 2;* ab′sə lüt′lē *for 3*) *adv.* **1** in an absolute way; especially; completely: *The water is absolutely pure. This can opener is absolutely useless.* **2** positively or definitely: *He is absolutely the finest fellow I know. Can I try out your new car? Absolutely not!* **3** certainly; definitely yes: *"Are you going to go there?" "Absolutely!"*
☛ *Usage.* In speech **absolutely** has become generalized to mean "positively" or "quite": *He is absolutely the finest fellow I know.* As an answer to a question it usually means "yes." It is out of place in formal writing except in its original meaning of "completely."

absolute monarchy a monarchy in which the ruler has unlimited power.

absolute pitch 1 the pitch of a tone determined solely by the frequency of its vibrations. **2** the ability to identify a note by ear; perfect pitch.

absolute temperature thermodynamic temperature.

absolute value the value of a real number regardless of any accompanying sign: *The absolute value of +5, or −5, is 5.*

absolute zero the lowest temperature possible according to scientific theory, equal to −273.16°C, or zero kelvins. The temperature of zero thermal energy. Because the volume of a gas decreases as the temperature decreases, absolute zero is calculated as the theoretical temperature at which an ideal gas at a constant pressure would reach zero volume.

ab·so·lu·tion (ab′sə lü′shən) *n.* **1** *Christianity.* **a** release from the guilt or penalty of sins, pronounced by a priest in the name of God upon a person's confession of and sincere repentance for the sins. **b** the prescribed form of words by which such remission is granted. **2** the act of freeing or the state of being freed from guilt, blame, obligation, or promise.

ab·so·lut·ism (ab′sə lüt iz′əm) *n.* **1** a system or form of government in which the power of the ruler is not restricted; despotism. **2** the quality of being absolute; positiveness. **3** *Philosophy.* belief in absolute idealism, which holds that all things are manifestations of one universal spirit.

ab·so·lut·ist (ab′sə lüt′ist) *n., adj.* —*n.* a person in favor of despotism or absolutism. —*adj.* despotic.

ab·solve (ab zolv′ *or* ab solv′) *v.* **-solved, -solv·ing. 1** declare (a person) free from sin, guilt, or blame. **2** set free (from a promise or duty). [< L *absolvere* < *ab-* from + *solvere* loosen. Doublet of ASSOIL.]

hat, āge, fär; let, ēqual, tèrm; it, īce
hot, ōpen, ôrder; oil, out; cup, pút, rüle,
əbove, takən, pencəl, lemən, circəs
ch, child; ng, long; sh, ship
th, thin; ŦH, then; zh, measure

ab·sorb (ab zôrb′ *or* ab sôrb′) *v.* **1** take in or suck up (liquids): *A blotter absorbs ink.* **2** take in and make a part of itself; assimilate: *Canada has absorbed millions of immigrants.* **3** take up all the attention of; interest very much: *The puzzle has absorbed him for hours.* **4** take in and hold: *Anything black absorbs most of the light rays that fall on it; that is, few of the light rays are reflected from it.* **5** *Biology.* take (digested food, oxygen, etc.) into the blood stream by osmosis. **6** grasp with the mind; understand. **7** *Business.* **a** pay (a cost, tax, etc.) without adding it to the price of an article, etc.: *The manufacturer absorbed the new tax, and the prices remained the same.* **b** take up: *The market absorbed the whole production.* **8** take up the impact of (bumps, shocks, sound, etc.): *The ceiling insulation absorbed the noise of the children's party.* [< L *absorbere* < *ab-* from + *sorbere* suck in]
☛ *Syn.* **2. Absorb, assimilate** = take something in, both literally and as used figuratively with reference to ideas. **Absorb** = swallow up a thing so that it loses its individual character or disappears: *Large companies sometimes absorb smaller ones.* **Assimilate** adds to **absorb** the idea of converting what is absorbed into an essential part of what has taken it in: *A person who reads intelligently assimilates what he reads by making it a part of his own thinking.*

ab·sorbed (ab zôrbd′ *or* ab sôrbd′) *adj.* very much interested; completely occupied: *She was so absorbed in watching the chipmunk that she didn't hear her friend call.* —**ab·sorb′ed·ly,** *adv.*

ab·sorb·en·cy (ab zôr′bən sē *or* ab sôr′bən sē) *n.* **1** the quality of being absorbent. **2** the degree to which anything is absorbent. **3** the ability to be assimilated.

ab·sorb·ent (ab zôr′bənt *or* ab sôr′bənt) *adj., n.* —*adj.* able to take in moisture, light, or heat: *Towels are absorbent.* —*n.* any thing or substance that absorbs moisture, light, or heat.

ab·sorb·ing (ab zôr′bing *or* ab sôr′bing) *adj.* extremely interesting: *He has written an absorbing account of his adventure.* —**ab·sorb′ing·ly,** *adv.*

ab·sorp·tion (ab zôrp′shən *or* ab sôrp′shən) *n.* **1** the process of absorbing or of being absorbed: *the absorption of water by a sponge. In the absorption of light rays by black objects, the light rays are changed to heat.* **2** a great interest (*in* something). **3** *Biology.* the process of taking (digested food, oxygen, etc.) into the blood stream by osmosis. [< L *absorptio, -onis* < *absorbere.* See ABSORB.]

ab·sorp·tive (ab zôrp′tiv *or* ab sôrp′tiv) *adj.* able to absorb. —**ab·sorp′tive·ness,** *n.*

ab·stain (ab stān′) *v.* **1** do without something voluntarily; refrain (*from*): *Athletes usually abstain from smoking.* **2** decline to vote: *Several delegates abstained because they objected to the wording of the motion.* [< F *abstenir* < L *abstinere* < *ab(s)-* off + *tenere* hold]
☛ *Syn.* See note at **refrain**[1].

ab·stain·er (ab stān′ər) *n.* a person who abstains, especially from the use of alcoholic liquor.

ab·ste·mi·ous (ab stē′mē əs) *adj.* sparing in eating and drinking; moderate; temperate. [< L *abstemius* < *ab(s)-* off + *tem-,* root of *temetum* potent liquor] —**ab·ste′mi·ous·ly,** *adv.* —**ab·ste′mi·ous·ness,** *n.*

ab·sten·tion (ab sten′shən) *n.* the act or an instance of abstaining: *His abstention from voting was severely criticized.* [< F < L *abstentio, -onis* < *abstinere.* See ABSTAIN.]

ab·sti·nence (ab′stə nəns) *n.* **1** voluntary avoidance of indulgence in certain pleasures, foods, etc. **2** *Christianity.* the practice of avoiding certain foods, especially meat, as an act of penance. **3** the practice of refraining from drinking alcoholic liquor. [< L *abstinentia* < *abstinere.* See ABSTAIN.]

abs·ti·nent (ab′stə nənt) *adj.* abstemious.

ab·stract (*adj. n.* ab′strakt; *v.* ab strakt′ *for 1, 3, 4,* ab′strakt *for 2*) *adj., v., n.* —*adj.* **1** thought of apart from any particular object or real thing; not concrete: *A lump of sugar is real; the idea of sweetness is abstract.* **2** expressing a quality that is thought of apart from any particular object or real thing. In *Honesty is the best policy, honesty* is an abstract noun. **3** not practical; ideal; theoretical. **4** hard to understand; difficult: *abstract theories about the nature of the soul.* **5** *Art.* representing ideas or feelings by abstracting certain qualities or elements from real things so that the result has little or no direct resemblance to these things.
—*v.* **1** think of (a quality, such as redness, weight, or truth) apart from any object or real thing having that quality: *How can we abstract time from the hours, minutes, and seconds by which we*

measure it? **2** make an abstract of; summarize. **3** take away; remove: *We can abstract gold from ore. A thief abstracted my wallet from my pocket.* **4** withdraw (the attention). —*n.* a short statement giving the main ideas of an article, book, case in court, etc.; summary. **in the abstract,** in theory rather than in practice. [< L *abstractus,* pp. of *abstrahere* < *ab(s)-* away + *trahere* draw] —**ab·stract′er,** *n.* —**ab′stract·ly,** *adv.* —**ab′stract·ness,** *n.*

ab·stract·ed (ab strak′tid) *adj.* lost in thought; absent-minded. —**ab·stract′ed·ly,** *adv.*

abstract expressionism a movement in painting that flourished especially in the United States in the 1950's and that emphasized the spontaneous expression of the feelings of the artist through color and abstract forms.

ab·strac·tion (ab strak′shən) *n.* **1** the idea of a quality thought of apart from any particular object or real thing having that quality; abstract idea or term: *Whiteness, bravery, and length are abstractions. A line that has no width is only an abstraction.* **2** the formation of such an idea. **3** a taking away; removal: *After the abstraction of the juice from an orange, only the pulp and peel are left.* **4** the state of being lost in thought; absence of mind. **5** a work of abstract art.

ab·strac·tion·ism (ab strak′shən iz′əm) *n.* the processes or principles of abstract art.

ab·struse (ab strüs′) *adj.* hard to understand. [< L *abstrusus,* pp. of *abstrudere* < *ab(s)-* away + *trudere* thrust] —**ab·struse′ly,** *adv.* —**ab·struse′ness,** *n.*

ab·surd (ab zėrd′ *or* ab sėrd′) *adj.* plainly not true or sensible; so contrary to reason that it is laughable; foolish; ridiculous. [< L *absurdus* out of tune, senseless] —**ab·surd′ly,** *adv.* —**ab·surd′ness,** *n.*
➤ *Syn.* See note at **ridiculous.**

ab·surd·i·ty (ab zėr′də tē *or* ab sėr′də tē) *n., pl.* **-ties.** **1** something absurd. **2** an absurd quality or condition; folly.

a·bun·dance (ə bun′dəns) *n.* a quantity that is more than enough; great plenty; full supply. [ME < OF < L *abundantia* < *abundare.* See ABOUND.]

a·bun·dant (ə bun′dənt) *adj.* more than enough; very plentiful. —**a·bun′dant·ly,** *adv.*

a·buse (*v.* ə byüz′; *n.* ə byüs′) *v.* **a·bused, a·bus·ing;** *n.* —*v.* **1** use wrongly; make bad use of; misuse: *to abuse a privilege.* **2** treat badly; mistreat. **3** use harsh and insulting language to. —*n.* **1** a wrong or bad use. **2** a harsh or severe treatment of a person. **3** harsh and insulting language. **4** a bad practice or custom: *Abuses multiply when citizens are indifferent.* [ME < OF *abuser* < L *abusus,* pp. of *abuti* use up, misuse < *ab-* away + *uti* use] —**abus′er,** *n.*

a·bu·sive (ə byü′siv *or* ə byü′ziv) *adj.* **1** using harsh and insulting language; reviling. **2** containing abuse: *an abusive letter.* **3** abusing; treating badly. —**a·bu′sive·ly,** *adv.*

a·but (ə but′) *v.* **a·but·ted, a·but·ting. 1** touch at one end or edge; end (*on* or *against*): *The sidewalk abuts on the street. The street abuts against the railway.* **2** join at a boundary; border (*on* or *upon*): *Her land abuts on mine.* [< OF *abouter* join end to end (< *a-* to + *bout* end) and OF *abuter* touch with an end (< *a-* to + *but* end)]

a·but·ment (ə but′mənt) *n.* **1** *Architecture.* a support for an arch or bridge. **2** the point or place where a support joins the thing supported. **3** the fact or state of abutting.

a·but·ting (ə but′ing) *adj.* adjacent.

a·buzz (ə buz′) *adj.* (*never used before a noun*) **1** filled with buzzing sounds. **2** full of excited activity, conversation, etc.: *The town was abuzz with the story of his disappearance.*

a·bysm (ə biz′əm) *n.* abyss. [ME *abime* < OF *abisme* < L *abyssus.* See ABYSS.]

a·bys·mal (ə biz′məl) *adj.* **1** too deep to be measured; bottomless. **2** very great; profound; immeasurable: *abysmal ignorance, abysmal despair.* **3** *Informal.* immeasurably bad: *abysmal dialogue, abysmal taste.* —**a·bys′mal·ly,** *adv.*

a·byss (ə bis′) *n.* **1** a very deep crack in the earth; a seemingly bottomless hole; chasm. **2** the lowest depth; anything seemingly endless or measureless: *the abyss of despair.* **3** in the Bible, the chaos before Creation. [< L < Gk. *abyssos* < *a-* without + *byssos* bottom]

a·byss·al (ə bis′əl) *adj.* **1** of or having to do with the lowest depths of the ocean. **2** unfathomable.

Ab·ys·sin·i·an (ab′ə sin′ē ən) *adj., n.* —*adj.* Ethiopian. —*n.* **1** Ethiopian. **2** a breed of medium-sized cat having short, silky, brownish hair with darker markings.

ac– *prefix.* the form of **ad-** occurring before *c* and *q,* as in *accede, acquaint.*

Ac 1 actinium. **2** *Meteorology.* alto-cumulus.

AC, A.C., *or* **a.c.** alternating current.

A/C *or* **a/c** account.

A.C. 1 air commodore. **2** aircraftman.

a·ca·cia (ə kā′shə) *n.* **1** any of a large genus (*Acacia*) of flowering trees and shrubs of the pea family found in warm regions, having fluffy clusters or spikes of yellow or white flowers, and fernlike leaves or wide, flattened, leaflike stems. Some species yield tannin or gum arabic. **2** locust tree. [< L < Gk. *akakia,* a thorny Egyptian tree]

acad. academy.

ac·a·deme (ak′ə dēm′) *n.* **1** the academic environment; university life: *He has spent all his adult life in academe.* **2** higher learning as an institution: *The government has promised more money for academe.*

ac·a·de·mi·a (ak′ə dē′mē ə) *n.* academe.

ac·a·dem·ic (ak′ə dem′ik) *adj., n.* —*adj.* **1** of or having to do with schools, colleges, universities, and their studies. **2** concerned with education in the arts, history, philosophy, etc. rather than with commercial, technical, or professional training. **3** scholarly. **4** theoretical; not practical: *"Which came first, the chicken or the egg?" is an academic question.* **5** following established rules and traditions, especially in art, literature, etc.; formal or conventional. —*n.* **1** a person engaged in scholarly pursuits. **2 academics,** *pl.* academic courses or studies. —**ac′a·dem′i·cal·ly,** *adv.*

ac·a·dem·i·cal (ak′ə dem′ə kəl) *adj.* academic.

academic freedom 1 the freedom of a teacher to investigate and discuss controversial issues and problems without fear of losing his position or standing. **2** the freedom of an educational institution to decide the subjects it will teach and how it will teach them.

a·cad·e·mi·cian (ə kad′ə mish′ən *or* ak′ə də mish′ən) *n.* **1** a member of a society for encouraging literature, science, or art. **2** an artist, writer, or composer who follows traditional or conventional rules.

ac·a·dem·i·cism (ak′ə dem′ə siz′əm) *n.* the practice of following established rules and traditions, especially in art, literature, etc.; formalism or conventionalism.

academic year the part of the year during which a university or college is in regular session.

a·cad·e·mism (ə kad′ə miz′əm) *n.* academicism.

a·cad·e·my (ə kad′ə mē) *n., pl.* **-mies. 1** a place for instruction. **2** a private high school. **3** a school where some special subject can be studied: *a military academy, a naval academy.* **4** a society of authors, scholars, scientists, artists, etc. for encouraging literature, science, or art. **5 Academy,** near ancient Athens, a park where Plato taught. [< L *academia* < Gk. *Akadēmeia,* the grove where Plato taught]

A·ca·di·a (ə kā′dē ə) *n. Cdn.* **1** the areas of French settlement and culture in the Maritime Provinces. **2** the Maritime Provinces as a unit. **3** *Historical.* the French colony comprising the Maritime Provinces and adjacent parts of Quebec and New England. [probably after *Arcadia*]

A·ca·di·an (ə kā′dē ən) *n., adj.* —*n.* **1** a native or inhabitant of Acadia. **2** a person of Acadian descent. —*adj.* of or having to do with Acadia or, sometimes, Nova Scotia.

a·can·thus (ə kan′thəs) *n., pl.* **-thus·es, -thi** (-thī *or* -thē). **1** any of a genus (*Acanthus*) of herbs or shrubs native to the Mediterranean region, having large, usually spiny leaves. Some species are widely cultivated as ornamental plants. **2** *Architecture.* an ornamentation based on the leaves of *Acanthus spinosus,* used especially on classical Corinthian and Composite columns. See **order** for picture. [< L < Gk. *akanthos* < *akē* thorn]

a cap·pel·la (ä′kə pel′ə) *Music.* without instrumental accompaniment. [< Ital. *a cappella* in the manner of chapel (music)]

ac·a·rid (ak′ə rid′) *n.* any of an order (Acarina) of arachnids, including the mites and ticks.

acc. 1 accusative. **2** account.

ac·cede (ak sēd′) *v.* **-ced·ed, -ced·ing. 1** give in or agree (*to*): *to accede to a proposal, to accede to popular demand.* **2** come or attain (*to* an office or dignity): *When the king died, his oldest son acceded to the throne.* **3** become a party (*to*): *Our government acceded to the treaty.* [< L *accedere* < *ad-* to + *cedere* come]

accel. accelerando.

ac·cel·er·an·do (ak sel′ər an′dō) *adv. or adj. Music.* gradually increasing in speed. *Abbrev.:* accel. [< Ital.]

ac·cel·er·ate (ak sel′ər āt′) *v.* **-at·ed, -at·ing. 1** go or cause to go faster; increase in speed; speed up. **2** cause to happen sooner; hasten: *Sunshine, fresh air, and rest often accelerate a person's*

recovery from sickness. **3** *Physics.* change the velocity of (a moving object). [< L *accelerare* < *ad-* to + *celer* swift]

ac·cel·er·a·tion (ak sel′ər ā′shən) *n.* **1** accelerating or being accelerated. **2** a change in velocity. **Positive acceleration** is increase in velocity. **Negative acceleration** is decrease in velocity. **3** the rate of change in the velocity of a moving body.

ac·cel·er·a·tor (ak sel′ər ā′tər) *n.* **1** a device for increasing the speed of a machine, especially the pedal that controls the flow of gasoline to an automobile engine. **2** *Chemistry.* any substance that speeds up a chemical reaction; catalyst. **3** *Physics.* any of several kinds of apparatus used in nuclear research and in medicine and industry for accelerating electrically charged atomic particles to high velocities, thus building up extremely high amounts of energy in them.

ac·cent (*n.* ak′sent; *v.* ak′sent *or* ak sent′) *n., v.* —*n.* **1** a distinctive manner of pronunciation, intonation, etc. typical of a given region or group: *a Scottish accent, a Canadian accent. Hans still speaks English with a German accent.* **2** accents, *pl.* tone of voice or mode of speech: *speaking in tender accents.* **3** emphasis placed on a particular word or syllable; stress (def. 5). **4** a mark (such as ′ or ′) showing such emphasis; stress (def. 6). **5** a mark used in writing or printing to indicate a particular sound quality, length of vowel, contraction, etc., or to indicate that a normally silent vowel is to be pronounced. Accents are used as part of the spelling system of certain languages, such as French and Greek. The accent ` in Shakespeare's phrase *despised tears* indicates that the final vowel in *despised* is to be pronounced. **6** *Prosody.* rhythmical stress. **7** *Music.* **a** emphasis given to certain notes or chords in a piece of music, indicated by a symbol above the note or chord concerned. **b** the symbol itself. **c** the regularly recurring emphasis that determines the rhythm of a piece of music. **8** intensity or emphasis: *the accent is on style.* **9** a distinguishing mark or quality: *an accent of humor.* **10** a sharply contrasting detail or an object or substance used for such contrast: *a grey and beige color scheme with dark-green accents.*
—*v.* **1** pronounce or write with an accent. **2** emphasize; accentuate. [< L *accentus*, literally, song added to (speech) < *ad-* to + *cantus* singing < *canere* sing]
☛ *Syn. v.* **2. Accent, accentuate,** both mean "emphasize," although **accent** means only to mark or say something with emphasis. **Accentuate,** the more common word, means to give emphasis to something by intensifying it or making it conspicuous: *Throughout his speech he accented the gravity of the situation. Her white dress accentuated her sunburn.*
☛ *Usage.* **Accents.** French words in English sometimes keep their accent marks: *café, outré, attaché, crêpe, tête-à-tête, à la mode.* Words that are used frequently in English usually drop the accent marks after a time unless the marks are necessary to indicate pronunciation (as in *café, attaché*).

ac·cen·tu·al (ak sen′chü əl) *adj.* **1** of or formed by accent or stress. **2** having the same accent or stress as ordinary speech.

ac·cen·tu·ate (ak sen′chü āt′) *v.* -**at·ed,** -**at·ing. 1** emphasize: *Her black hair accentuated the whiteness of her skin.* **2** pronounce with an accent. **3** mark with an accent. **4** make worse; increase in severity: *The problems of the pioneers were accentuated by the harsh climate.* —**ac·cen′tu·a′tion,** *n.*
☛ *Syn.* **1.** See note at **accent.**

ac·cept (ak sept′) *v.* **1** take or receive (something offered or given); consent to take: *I accept the gift.* **2** agree to; consent to; say yes to: *to accept a proposal.* **3** take as true or satisfactory; believe in: *to accept a hypothesis. She refused to accept our story of what had happened.* **4** receive with liking and approval; approve: *He was soon accepted by his new classmates.* **5** regard as normal or inevitable: *to accept one's fate. The right to an education is generally accepted today.* **6** undertake as a responsibility: *to accept a position as cashier.* **7** *Business.* agree to pay, especially by signing: *to accept a note.* **8** say yes to an invitation, offer, etc.: *They invited me to go along and I accepted.* [< L *acceptare,* frequentative of *accipere* < *ad-* to + *capere* take] —**ac·cept′er,** *n.*
☛ *Syn.* **1.** See note at **receive.**
☛ *Usage.* **Accept, except** are often misspelled because of similarity in sound. **Accept,** always a verb, has as its basic meaning "take to (oneself)" and is a synonym of *receive: He accepted the gift.* **Except,** sometimes a verb, sometimes a preposition, has the basic sense of *taking out;* the verb is a synonym of *omit, exclude,* the preposition, a synonym of *but: We can call his career brilliant if we except that one serious blunder. Everyone except John went home.*

ac·cept·a·bil·i·ty (ak sep′ tə bil′ə tē) *n.* the quality of being acceptable or satisfactory.

ac·cept·a·ble (ak sep′tə bəl) *adj.* **1** worth accepting: *Flowers are an acceptable gift to a sick person.* **2** good enough but not outstanding; satisfactory: *an acceptable performance.*

ac·cept·a·bly (ak sep′tə blē) *adv.* in a way that pleases.

ac·cept·ance (ak sep′təns) *n.* **1** the taking of something offered or given. **2** a favorable reception; approval. **3** a belief; taking as true and satisfactory. **4** *Business.* **a** a promise or signed agreement to pay a draft or bill of exchange when it is due. **b** the draft or bill of exchange itself.

ac·cep·ta·tion (ak′sep tā′shən) *n.* **1** the usual meaning;

hat, āge, fär; let, ēqual, tèrm; it, īce
hot, ōpen, ôrder; oil, out; cup, pùt, rüle,
əbove, takən, pencəl, lemən, circəs

ch, child; ng, long; sh, ship
th, thin; ₮H, then; zh, measure

generally accepted meaning: *It is more important to know the acceptation of a word than its derivation.* **2** a favorable reception; approval. **3** a belief; taking as true and satisfactory.

ac·cept·ed (ak sep′tid) *adj.* generally approved; conventional: *the accepted behavior at formal dinners.*

ac·cep·tor (ak sep′tər) *n.* **1** a person who accepts. **2** a person who signs a draft or bill of exchange and agrees to pay it. **3** *Chemistry.* an atom sharing two electrons in bond with another atom but itself contributing neither electron. **4** *Electronics.* a circuit that allows reception of a certain frequency and no other.

ac·cess (ak′ses) *n., v.* —*n.* **1** the right to approach, enter, or use; admission: *All children have access to the library during the afternoon.* **2** the degree to which a place is reachable; approach: *Access to the mountain town was difficult because of the poor road.* **3** a way or means of approach: *A ladder was the only access to the attic. He has access to people who can help him get work.* **4** of a disease, the onset. **5** an outburst: *an access of pity and remorse.* —*v. Computer science.* get (information) out of a storage device: *The customer service department can access information on the company's product via the CRT's.* [ME < L *accessus* < *accedere.* See ACCEDE.]

ac·ces·sa·ry (ak ses′ə rē) See **accessory.**

ac·ces·si·bil·i·ty (ak ses′ə bil′ə tē) *n.* **1** the condition of being easy to reach or get at. **2** the condition of being open to influence.

ac·ces·si·ble (ak ses′ə bəl) *adj.* **1** capable of being entered or reached; approachable: *The camp is accessible only by boat or plane.* **2** easy to get at; easy to enter: *A telephone should be put where it will be accessible.* **3** capable of being influenced; susceptible (*to*); open (*to*): *accessible to pity, accessible to reason.* **4** obtainable. —**ac·ces′si·bly,** *adv.*

ac·ces·sion (ak sesh′ən) *n., v.* —*n.* **1** the act of attaining to a right, office, etc.: *the prince's accession to the throne.* **2** an increase; addition: *The accession of forty new members helped the club considerably.* **3** something added: *Each accession to the library means more expense.*
—*v.* enter (a book, painting, etc.) in a record of a collection. [< L *accessio, -onis* < *accedere.* See ACCEDE.]

ac·ces·so·rize (ak ses′ə rīz′) *v.* -**rized,** -**riz·ing.** provide or furnish with accessories: *to accessorize a basic dress.*

ac·ces·so·ry (ak ses′ə rē) *n., pl.* -**ries;** *adj.* —*n.* **1** something added that is useful in some way but not absolutely necessary: *He bought a mirror and some other accessories for his bicycle.* **2** something worn or carried, such as a hat, shoes, or scarf, that is chosen to set off or complement a dress, suit, etc.: *The appearance of a basic dress can be changed considerably by varying the style and color of the accessories.* **3** *Law.* a person who helps an offender against the law, without actually taking part in the commission of the offence. One who encourages, incites, or assists in the planning of a crime is called an **accessory before the fact.** One who hides the offender or fails to report the offence is called an **accessory after the fact.**
—*adj.* **1** additional; supplementary: *an accessory touch of color.* **2** helping as an accessory in an offence against the law.
☛ *Pronun.* This word is often mispronounced (a ses′ə rē). The first syllable is (ak-), as in **accident.**

access road *Cdn.* **1** a road built to permit entry to a place or an area that is otherwise sealed off, as by dense brush, muskeg, etc. **2** a road permitting entry to an expressway.

ac·ci·dence (ak′sə dəns) *n.* the part of grammar dealing with those changes in words that show case, number, tense, etc.

ac·ci·dent (ak′sə dənt) *n.* **1** something harmful or unlucky that happens unexpectedly and apparently by chance: *He was killed in an automobile accident. Many accidents happen in the home.* **2** something that happens without being planned, intended, or known in advance: *Their meeting was an accident.* **3** a nonessential quality or property. **4** an irregularity in surface or structure.
by accident, by chance; not on purpose: *I dropped it by accident.* [ME < OF < L *accidens, -entis,* ppr. of *accidere* < *ad-* to + *cadere* fall]

ac·ci·den·tal (ak′sə den′təl) *adj., n.* —*adj.* **1** happening unexpectedly or by chance: *They had searched for months, but the actual discovery of the treasure was accidental.* **2** of something harmful or unlucky; not intended or planned: *an accidental injury.* **3** nonessential; incidental: *Songs are essential to musical comedy,*

but accidental to Shakespeare's plays. **4** *Music.* of or designating an accidental.

—*n. Music.* a sign showing a change in a single note in a piece of music, that is not in the key indicated by the signature. Accidentals can indicate a sharp (♯), a flat (♭), or a natural (♮).

☛ *Syn. adj.* **2. Accidental, incidental** = not essential or of primary importance. **Accidental** emphasizes that what it describes is not an essential or necessary part, result, etc. of some larger thing or scheme of things: *Songs are essential to musical comedy, but accidental to Shakespeare's plays.* **Incidental** emphasizes that what it describes, although perhaps necessary, is subordinate to something else in importance: *My father pays my tuition, board, and room at college, but not incidental expenses such as laundry and haircuts.*

ac·ci·den·tal·ly (ak′sə den′təl ē *or* ak′sə dent′lē) *adv.* in an accidental manner; by chance.

ac·ci·dent–prone (ak′sə dənt prōn′) *adj.* tending to have accidents.

ac·cip·i·ter (ak sip′ə tər) *n.* any of a genus of small and medium-sized hawks having relatively short, rounded wings and a long tail.

ac·claim (ə klām′) *v., n.* —*v.* **1** show satisfaction and approval by words or sounds; shout welcome to; applaud: *The crowd acclaimed the fireman for rescuing two people from the burning house.* **2** announce with signs of approval; hail: *The newspapers acclaimed the fireman a hero.* **3** *Cdn.* elect to an office without opposition: *The voters acclaimed her mayor.*
—*n.* a shout or show of approval; applause; welcome. [< L *acclamare* < *ad-* to + *clamare* cry out]

ac·cla·ma·tion (ak′lə mā′shən) *n.* **1** a shout of welcome or show of approval by a crowd; applause. **2** an oral vote: *The club elected him president by acclamation.* **3** *Cdn.* the act or an instance of electing without opposition: *There were acclamations in five ridings.* **by acclamation,** *Cdn.* without opposition in an election: *Since no candidate opposed him, Mr. Kress was elected by acclamation.* [< L *acclamatio* a shouting. See ACCLAIM.]
☛ *Hom.* **acclimation.**

ac·cli·mate (ak′lə māt′ *or* ə klī′mit) *v.* **-mat·ed, -mat·ing.** acclimatize. [< F *acclimater* < à to (< L *ad-*) + *climat* climate]

ac·cli·ma·tion (ak′lə mā′shən) *n.* acclimatization.
☛ *Hom.* **acclamation.**

ac·cli·ma·ti·za·tion (ə klī′mə tə zā′shən *or* ə klī′mə tī zā′shən) *n.* acclimatizing or being acclimatized.

ac·cli·ma·tize (ə klī′mə tīz′) *v.* **-tized, -tiz·ing.** accustom or become accustomed to new climate or new surroundings or conditons: *It took him a long while to acclimatize himself to the high altitude. They soon became acclimatized to city life.*

ac·cliv·i·ty (ə kliv′ə tē) *n., pl.* **-ties.** an upward slope (of ground). [< L *acclivitas* < *acclivis, acclivus* ascending < *ad-* toward + *clivus* rising ground]

ac·co·lade (ak′ə lād′, ak′ə lād′ *or* ak′ə lād′) *n.* **1** a tap on the shoulder with the flat side of a sword, given to mark the bestowal of knighthood on a person. **2** praise; recognition; award. [< F < Ital. *accollata* an embrace about the neck < L *ad-* to + *collum* neck]

ac·com·mo·date (ə kom′ə dāt′) *v.* **-dat·ed, -dat·ing.** **1** have room for; hold comfortably: *This big bedroom will accommodate two beds.* **2** help out; oblige: *He wanted change for a quarter, but I could not accommodate him.* **3** furnish with lodging, sometimes with food as well. **4** supply; furnish. **5** provide (a person) with a loan of money. **6** make or become fit or suitable; adapt: *The eye can accommodate to objects at different distances.* **7** reconcile; adjust: *to accommodate differences.* [< L *accommodare* < *ad-* to + *commodare* make fit < *com-* with + *modus* measure]
—**ac·com′mo·dat′or,** *n.*
☛ *Syn.* **1.** See note at **contain. 7.** See note at **adjust.**

ac·com·mo·dat·ing (ə kom′ə dāt′ing) *adj.* obliging; willing to help. —**ac·com′mo·dat·ing·ly,** *adv.*

ac·com·mo·da·tion (ə kom′ə dā′shən) *n.* **1** lodging, sometimes with food as well: *The hotel has accommodations for one hundred people.* **2** a help; favor; convenience: *It will be an accommodation to me if you will meet me tomorrow instead of today.* **3** a loan. **4** a willingness to help out. **5** a fitting or being fitted to a purpose or situation; adjustment; adaptation: *The accommodation of our desires to a smaller income took some time.* **6** settlement of differences; reconciliation; compromise: *to arrange an accommodation with one's creditors.* **7** the adjustment of the lens of the eye for seeing objects at various distances.

ac·com·pa·ni·ment (ə kom′pə nē mənt *or* ə kump′nē mənt) *n.* **1** whatever goes along with something else: *Destruction and suffering are accompaniments of war.* **2** *Music.* a part added to help or enrich the main part.

ac·com·pa·nist (ə kum′pə nist) *n.* a person who plays a musical accompaniment.

ac·com·pa·ny (ə kum′pə nē) *v.* **-nied, -ny·ing. 1** go along with:

to accompany a friend on a walk. **2** be or happen in connection with: *Fire is accompanied by heat.* **3** cause to be attended by; supplement (*with*): *to accompany a speech with gestures.* **4** play or sing a musical accompaniment for or to. [ME < OF *acompagner* < à to + *compagne* companion. Related to COMPANION.]
—**ac·com′pa·ni·er,** *n.*
☛ *Syn.* **1. Accompany, attend, escort** = go with someone or something. **Accompany** = go along with as a companion or (of things) as a customary addition: *He accompanied the other boys to the game. Baked or fried potatoes often accompany steak.* **Attend** = go along with to serve or assist: *The student attended the professor on a field trip.* **Escort** = go along with as a protector: *He escorted a girl to the dance. Canadian destroyers escorted many Atlantic convoys during World War II.*

ac·com·plice (ə kom′plis) *n.* a person who aids another in committing a crime or other unlawful act or one who encourages another to commit such an act: *The thief could not have got into the house so easily without an accomplice.* [earlier *a complice* a confederate < F *complice* < L *complex* < *com-* together with + *plectere* twist]
☛ *Syn.* **Accomplice, confederate** in technical (legal) use mean "a partner in crime." **Accomplice** applies to a person who deliberately gives help of any kind to another in connection with an unlawful act or crime, either before, during, or after the act itself: *Without an accomplice the thief could not have got into the house and stolen the jewels.* **Confederate** applies to a person who joins with others, or another, for the purpose of committing an unlawful act: *The head of the smuggling ring has not been found, but his confederates are in jail.*

ac·com·plish (ə kom′plish) *v.* **1** succeed in completing; carry out (a promise, plan, etc.): *to accomplish a purpose.* **2** finish; complete: *to accomplish nothing.* [ME < OF *accompliss-*, a stem of *acomplir* < LL *accomplere* < *ad-* + *complere* fill up]
—**ac·com′plish·er,** *n.*
☛ *Syn.* **1, 2.** See note at **do.**

ac·com·plished (ə kom′plisht) *adj.* **1** successfully carried out; achieved: *an accomplished goal.* **2** expert; skilled: *an accomplished surgeon, an accomplished host, an accomplished liar.*

ac·com·plish·ment (ə kom′plish mənt) *n.* **1** the act of achieving or carrying out; successful completion: *the accomplishment of a purpose.* **2** something accomplished; achievement; completed undertaking: *the major accomplishments of modern technology.* **3** skill or talent especially in the social arts: *a man of accomplishment.*

ac·compt (ə kount′) *n. or v. Archaic.* account.

ac·cord (ə kôrd′) *v., n.* —*v.* **1** be in harmony (*with*); agree (*with*): *His account of the accident accords with yours.* **2** grant (a favor, request, etc.): *We should accord Tom praise for good work.* **3** make agree; harmonize; reconcile.
—*n.* **1** agreement; harmony: *Accord was finally reached. The various city groups are now in accord on the parks issue.* **2** an agreement between nations; treaty. **3** harmony of color, pitch, or tone.
of (one's) own accord, without being asked; without suggestion from another: *He is old enough now to go to bed of his own accord.*
with one accord, all agreeing; unanimously: *They cheered with one accord when she made the jump.*
[ME < OF *acorder* < VL *acchordare* bring into harmony < L *ad-* to + *chorda* string]

ac·cord·ance (ə kôr′dəns) *n.* agreement; harmony: *What he did was in accordance with what he said.*

ac·cord·ant (ə kôr′dənt) *adj.* agreeing; in harmony.

ac·cord·ing (ə kôr′ding) *adj.* **1 according as,** depending on how or whether: *His fortunes varied according as the market fluctuated.* **2 according to, a** on the authority of; as stated by: *According to this book, we are heading for a recession.* **b** on the basis of; in conformity with: *They try to spend according to their income. Bacteria are classified according to shape.*

ac·cord·ing·ly (ə kôr′ding lē) *adv.* **1** in agreement with something that has been stated. **2** for this reason; therefore.
☛ *Usage.* **Accordingly** is a conjunctive adverb most appropriately used in formal writing. A co-ordinate clause introduced by **accordingly** is preceded by a semicolon: *He was told to speak briefly; accordingly he cut short his remarks.*

ac·cor·di·on (ə kôr′dē ən) *n.* **1** a portable musical wind instrument with a bellows, metallic reeds, and keys, played by pressing the keys and the bellows to force air through the reeds: *In a piano accordion, one set of keys is like a piano keyboard and the other keys are buttons.* **2** (*adj.*) with folds like the bellows of an accordion: *a skirt with accordion pleats.* [< Ital. *accordare* harmonize]

ac·cost (ə kost′) *v.* come up and speak to; address: *A ragged beggar accosted him, asking for money.* [< F *accoster* < Ital. < LL *accostare* < L *ad-* to + *costa* side, rib]

ac·couche·ment (ə küsh′mənt; *French,* ä küsh mäN′) *n.* **1** a confinement for childbirth. **2** childbirth. [< F]

ac·count (ə kount′) *n., v.* —*n.* **1** a statement telling in detail about an event or thing; a report or story: *The newspaper published an account of the trial.* **2** an explanation or statement of reasons: *He could give no satisfactory account of his absence.* **3** sake: *Don't*

wait on my account. **4** worth or importance: *It was an error of no account. The extra expense is of little account in comparison with the total cost.* **5** profit; advantage: *She turned the incident to her own account.* **6** Usually, **accounts,** *pl.* a statement of money received and spent: *Businesses and factories keep accounts.* **7** an arrangement for purchasing goods or services on credit; charge account: *Her firm has an account with that new advertising agency.* **8** an arrangement for depositing one's money in a bank for safekeeping, or the money deposited; bank account.

call (or **bring**) **to account, a** demand an explanation of (someone). **b** scold; rebuke; reprimand.

on account, a on the instalment plan: *She bought the coat on account.* **b** as part payment: *If you accept five dollars on account, I can pay the rest next week.*

on account of, a because of: *The game was put off on account of rain.* **b** for the sake of.

take account of, take into account.

take into account, make allowance for; consider: *When planning a holiday, you have to take travelling time into account.*

—*v.* hold to be; think of as; consider: *Solomon was accounted wise. She accounted herself lucky to have escaped with her life.*

account for, a give a reason or explanation for: *He couldn't account for the strange message.* **b** be the main or only source or reason for: *Late frosts accounted for the poor fruit crop.* **c** give a reckoning of; tell what has happened to: *The treasurer of the club has to account for all the money received. Have all the passengers been accounted for?* **d** be responsible for the defeat, destruction, or death of: *His squadron accounted for twenty enemy aircraft in the battle.*

[ME < OF *acont,* n., *aconter,* v., < VL *accomptare* < L *ad-* up + *computare* count < *com-* together + *putare* reckon]

ac·count·a·bil·i·ty (ə koun′tə bil′ə tē) *n.* the state of being accountable; responsibility.

ac·count·a·ble (ə koun′tə bəl) *adj.* **1** responsible; liable to be called to account: *He was judged not accountable for his actions.* **2** explainable: *His bad temper is easily accountable; he has had a toothache all day.* —**ac·count′a·bly,** *adv.*

ac·count·an·cy (ə koun′tən sē) *n.* the profession or work of an accountant.

ac·count·ant (ə koun′tənt) *n.* a person trained in accounting, especially one whose work it is.

account executive *Advertising.* an executive in charge of the work for a particular client or clients.

ac·count·ing (ə koun′ting) *n.* **1** the system or procedures of recording, sorting, and analysing economic data related to business transactions and preparing statements of the results for individuals or businesses to use in making business decisions. **2** a statement of explanation or justification: *He was asked for an accounting of his time away from work.*

ac·cou·ter (ə kü′tər) See **accoutre.**

ac·cou·ter·ment (ə kü′tər mənt) See **accoutrement.**

ac·cou·tre (ə kü′tər) *v.* **-tred, -tring.** equip; array: *Knights were accoutred in armor.* Also, **accouter.** [< F *accoutrer*]

ac·cou·tre·ment (ə kü′tər mənt *or* ə kü′trə mənt) *n.* **1** the act of accoutring or the state of being accoutred. **2** Usually, **accoutrements,** *pl.* **a** clothing, equipment, accessories, etc. **b** *Military.* a soldier's outfit or equipment, other than clothing and weapons. Also, **accouterment.**

ac·cred·it (ə kred′it) *v.* **1** give (a person) credit for; regard (a person) as having: *to accredit her with kindness.* **2** consider (a thing) as belonging or due (to a person): *We accredit the invention of the telephone to Bell.* **3** accept as true; believe; trust. **4** give authority to. **5** send or provide with credentials or a recommendation: *An ambassador is accredited as the representative of his own country in a foreign land.* **6** recognize as coming up to an official standard. [< F *accréditer* < *à* to + *crédit* credit] —**ac·cred′i·ta′tion,** *n.*

☛ *Syn.* **1, 2.** See note at **credit.**

ac·cre·tion (ə krē′shən) *n.* **1** growth in size or amount: *the accretion of political power.* **2** a growing together of separate particles or parts. **3** an increase in size by gradual external addition: *the accretion of land by deposits of alluvial soil.* **4** something added to cause an increase in size. **5** a whole that results from such growths or additions. [< L *accretio, -onis* < *accrescere.* See ACCRUE.]

ac·cru·al (ə krü′əl) *n.* **1** the process of accruing; progressive growth: *Money left in a savings account increases by the accrual of interest.* **2** the amount accrued or accruing.

ac·crue (ə krü′) *v.* **-crued, -cru·ing.** come as a growth or result: *Interest on a term deposit accrues at a higher rate than on a regular savings account.* [< F < L *accrescere* < *ad-* to + *crescere* grow] —**ac·crue′ment,** *n.*

acct. **1** account. **2** accountant.

ac·cul·tu·ra·tion (ə kul′chə rā′shən) *n.* **1** the modification of the culture of one group through the influence of the culture of another

hat, āge, fär; let, ēqual, tėrm; it, īce
hot, ōpen, ôrder; oil, out; cup, pút, rüle,
əbove, takən, pencəl, lemən, circəs
ch, child; ng, long; sh, ship
th, thin; ŦH, then; zh, measure

group. **2** the conditioning of a child to the ways of a particular society.

ac·cu·mu·late (ə kyü′myə lāt′) *v.* **-lat·ed, -lat·ing.** **1** collect little by little: *He accumulated a fortune by hard work.* **2** grow in amount or number; mount up: *Dust had accumulated during the three weeks that we were gone.* [< L *ac-cumulare* < *ad-* up + *cumulus* heap]

☛ *Syn.* **1. Accumulate, amass** = collect a considerable or large amount. In figurative use, applied to resources, feelings, etc., **accumulate** emphasizes the idea, expressed in its literal meaning, of heaping up, little by little, pile on pile: *Through the years he accumulated sufficient money to buy a farm when he retired.* **Amass** emphasizes the idea of gathering to oneself as in a mass or in large amounts: *Before he was forty, he amassed a fortune.*

ac·cu·mu·la·tion (ə kyü′ myə lā′shən) *n.* **1** a mass of material collected: *His accumulation of old papers filled three trunks.* **2** a collecting together: *The accumulation of knowledge is one result of reading.*

ac·cu·mu·la·tor (ə kyü′myə lā′tər) *n.* **1** a person or thing that accumulates matter or objects. **2** *Brit.* storage battery. **3** a register or location in a calculator or computer where numerical data is stored and arithmetic operations performed.

ac·cu·ra·cy (ak′yə rə sē) *n.* the absence of errors or mistakes; correctness; exactness.

ac·cu·rate (ak′yə rit) *adj.* **1** making few or no errors: *an accurate observer.* **2** without errors or mistakes; exact; correct: *accurate measure.* [< L *accuratus* prepared with care, pp. of *accurare* take care of < *ad-* to + *cura* care] —**ac′cu·rate·ly,** *adv.* —**ac′cu·rate·ness,** *n.*

☛ *Syn.* **2.** See note at **correct.**

ac·curs·ed (ə kėr′sid *or* ə kėrst′) *adj.* **1** damnable; detestable; hateful. **2** under a curse.

ac·curst (ə kėrst′) *adj.* accursed.

accus. accusative.

ac·cu·sa·tion (ak′yə zā′shən) *n.* **1** a charge of having done something wrong, of being something bad, or of having broken the law. **2** the offence charged. **3** accusing or being accused.

ac·cu·sa·tive (ə kyü′zə tiv) *adj., n.* —*adj.* of, having to do with, or being the grammatical case found in some languages, that shows that a noun, pronoun, or adjective is not part of the subject of a sentence, but is a direct object of a verb or of any of certain prepositions. The English pronouns *me, her, him, us,* and *them* correspond roughly to the accusative case in languages such as German, Latin, and Greek. —*n.* **1** the accusative case. **2** a word or group of words in the accusative case.

ac·cu·sa·to·ry (ə kyü′zə tô′rē) *adj.* of a statement, manner, etc., containing or expressing an accusation; accusing: *an accusatory glance, an accusatory tone of voice.*

ac·cuse (ə kyüz′) *v.* **-cused, -cus·ing.** **1** charge with having done something wrong, with being something bad, or with having broken the law. **2** find fault with; blame. [ME < OF < L *accusare* < *ad-* to + *causa* cause] —**ac·cus′er,** *n.* —**ac·cus′ing·ly,** *adv.*

☛ *Syn.* **1.** See note at **charge.**

ac·cused (ə kyüzd′) *n.* **the accused,** *Law.* the person or persons appearing in court on a criminal charge. Compare **defendant.**

ac·cus·tom (ə kus′təm) *v.* make familiar with or used to, by habit or practice (*used with* **to**): *to accustom a hunting dog to the noise of a gun.* [ME < OF *acostumer* < *a-* to (< L *ad-*) + *costume* custom < L *consuescere* < *com-* + *suescere* accustom]

ac·cus·tomed (ə kus′təmd) *adj.* usual; customary: *By Monday he was back in his accustomed place.*

accustomed to, used to; in the habit of: *He was accustomed to hard work.*

ace (ās) *n., v.* —*n.* **1** a playing card, domino, or side of a die having one spot. **2** a single spot or point. **3** *Sports.* a point won by a single stroke. **4** a person expert at anything. **5** a combat pilot who has shot down a large number of enemy planes. **6** (*adj.*) of very high rank or quality; expert: *an ace football player.*

ace in the hole, a *Poker.* an ace dealt face downwards and not exposed until the end. **b** *Informal.* a decisive advantage that is kept hidden until needed.

ace up one's sleeve, *Informal.* a decisive advantage that is kept hidden until needed.

within an ace of, at the brink of; on the very point of: *I came within an ace of quitting.*

—*v.* **1** *Tennis.* serve an ace against (an opponent). **2** *Golf.* make an ace on (a hole). **3** *Slang.* achieve a high mark in (an examination, etc.). [ME < OF *as* < L *as, assis* smallest unit]

a·cer·bic (ə sėr′bik) *adj.* **1** sour in taste. **2** sharp, bitter, or harsh in tone, mood, or temper: *an acerbic remark, an acerbic columnist.* —**a·cer′bi·cal·ly,** *adv.*

a·cer·bi·ty (ə sėr′bə tē) *n., pl.* **-ties. 1** acidity combined with astringency; sharpness of taste; sourness. **2** harshness or bitterness of tone, mood, or temper. [< F *acerbité* < L *acerbitas* < *acerbus* bitter]

ac·e·tab·u·lum (as′ə tab′yə ləm) *n., pl.* **-la** (-lə). a socket in the hipbone into which the top part of the thighbone fits. See **pelvis** for picture. [< L *acetabulum* cup-shaped holder for vinegar < *acetum* vinegar]

ac·et·an·i·lid (as′ət an′ə lid) *n.* acetanilide.

ac·et·an·i·lide (as′ət an′ə līd′ *or* as′ət an′ə lid) *n.* a white crystalline compound, used in medicine to relieve pain and lessen fever. *Formula:* $C_6H_5NHCOCH_3$ [< *acetic* + *aniline*]

ac·e·tate (as′ə tāt′) *n.* a salt or ester of acetic acid. Cellulose acetate is used in making textile fibres, tool handles, industrial parts, cellophane, etc.

a·ce·tic (ə sē′tik *or* ə set′ik) *adj.* of or producing vinegar. [< L *acetum* vinegar]

acetic acid a very sour, colorless acid, present in vinegar. *Formula:* CH_3COOH

a·cet·i·fy (ə set′ə fī′) *v.* **-fied, -fy·ing.** turn into vinegar or acetic acid.

ac·e·tone (as′ə tōn′) *n.* a colorless, volatile, flammable liquid, used as a solvent for oils, fats, resins, cellulose, etc. and in making varnishes. *Formula:* C_3H_6O

a·cet·y·lene (ə set′ə lēn′ *or* ə set′ə lin) *n.* a colorless, gaseous hydrocarbon that burns with a bright light and a very hot flame. It is used mainly in preparing compounds to make synthetic fibres and vinyl plastics and, combined with oxygen, for welding and cutting metals. *Formula:* C_2H_2

ac·e·tyl·sal·i·cyl·ic acid (as′ə til sal′ə sil′ik *or* ə sē′təl sal′ə sil′ik) aspirin.

A·chae·an (ə kē′ən) *adj., n.* —*adj.* **1** of Achaea, an ancient province in southern Greece. **2** Greek. —*n.* a native or inhabitant of Achaea or Greece.

A·chai·an (ə kā′ən) *adj. or n.* Achaean.

A·cha·tes (ə kā′tēz) *n.* **1** the faithful companion of Aeneas in Virgil's *Aeneid.* **2** any faithful companion.

ache (āk) *v.* **ached, ach·ing;** *n.* —*v.* **1** be in continued pain. **2** *Informal.* be eager; wish very much. —*n.* a dull, steady pain. [OE *acan*] —**ach′ing·ly,** *adv.*
☛ *Syn. n.* See note at **pain.**

a·chene (ā kēn′) *n. Botany.* a small, dry, hard fruit that develops from a simple ovary, having a single seed and a thin outer covering that does not burst open when ripe. The achenes of some plants, such as the sunflower, are commonly called seeds. See **fruit** for picture. [< NL *achaenium* < Gk. *a-* not + *chainein* gape; because it ripens without bursting]

Ach·er·on (ak′ər on′) *n. Greek mythology.* **1** a river in Hades. **2** the lower world; Hades.

a·chieve (ə chēv′) *v.* **a·chieved, a·chiev·ing. 1** do; get done; carry out; accomplish: *to achieve one's purpose.* **2** get by effort: *He achieved distinction in mathematics.* [ME < OF *achever* < *venir*) *a chief* (come) to a head < LL *ad caput* (*venire*) —**a·chiev′a·ble,** *adj.* —**a·chiev′er,** *n.*

a·chieve·ment (ə chēv′mənt) *n.* **1** the act of achieving; completing successfully: *the achievement of one's purpose.* **2** something achieved, especially some plan or action accomplished with courage or unusual ability.
☛ *Syn.* **2.** See note at **exploit.**

achievement age a measure of a student's learning, determined from his score on a special test. It is the average age of all students having that particular score.

achievement quotient the ratio of a person's achievement age to his actual age, usually multiplied by 100.

A·chil·les (ə kil′ēz) *n. Greek mythology.* the hero of the *Iliad,* a Greek warrior who killed Hector at the siege of Troy, but was himself killed by Paris. Paris' arrow struck Achilles in the heel, his only vulnerable spot.

Achilles' heel a vulnerable area.

Achilles tendon the strong tendon joining the heel bone to the muscles of the calf: *The Achilles tendon helps to move the ankle joint.*

ach·ro·mat·ic (ak′rə mat′ik) *adj.* **1** capable of refracting white light without breaking it up into the colors of the spectrum. **2** having no hue: *Black, white, and neutral greys are achromatic colors.* **3** *Biology.* containing or consisting of material that resists ordinary stains: *achromatic cells.* **4** *Music.* having no accidentals or changes of key; diatonic: *an achromatic scale.* [< Gk. *achrōmatos* < *a-* without + *chrōma* color] —**ach′ro·mat′i·cal·ly,** *adv.*

ach·tung (äн′tùng) *interj. German.* **1** attention! **2** pay attention! look out!

ac·id (as′id) *n., adj.* —*n.* **1** *Chemistry.* any of various compounds that yield hydrogen ions when dissolved in water and usually reacts with a base to form a salt. The water solution of an acid turns blue litmus paper red. **2** a sour substance. **3** a harsh, biting, or bitter quality or character: *There was acid in his voice as he replied.* **4** *Slang.* LSD.
—*adj.* **1** of, having to do with, or containing an acid: *an acid solution.* **2** sharp or biting to the taste; sour. **3** harsh, biting, or bitter: *an acid comment, acid humor.* [< L *acidus* sour] —**ac′id·ly,** *adv.* —**ac′id·ness,** *n.*
☛ *Syn. adj.* See note at **sour.**

a·cid·ic (ə sid′ik) *adj.* **1** acid-forming. **2** acid: *Rainfall is growing more acidic in many parts of the world.*

a·cid·i·fi·ca·tion (ə sid′ə fə kā′shən) *n.* the action or process of acidifying or the state of being acidified.

a·cid·i·fy (ə sid′ə fī′) *v.* **-fied, -fy·ing. 1** make or become sour. **2** change into an acid. —**a·cid′i·fi′er,** *n.*

a·cid·i·ty (ə sid′ə tē) *n., pl.* **-ties.** an acid quality or condition; sourness: *the acidity of vinegar.*

ac·i·do·sis (as′ə dō′sis) *n.* a harmful condition in which the blood and tissues are less alkaline than is normal. [< *acid* + *-osis* process (< Gk.)]

acid precipitation acid rain.

acid rain rain or snow contaminated by acids formed when industrial pollutants, especially sulphur dioxide and nitrogen oxides, undergo chemical changes in the atmosphere.

acid salt a salt formed from an acid of which only part of the hydrogen has been replaced by a metal or radical.

acid test **1** a decisive test of the real worth of some person or thing. **2** a former test for gold, using nitric acid.

a·cid–tongued (as′id tungd′) *adj.* sarcastic; biting: *acid-tongued criticism.*

a·cid·u·late (ə sij′ə lāt′) *v.* **-lat·ed, -lat·ing.** make slightly acid or sour. —**a·cid′u·la′tion,** *n.*

a·cid·u·lous (ə sij′ə ləs) *adj.* slightly acid or sour. —**a·cid′u·lous·ly,** *adv.* —**a·cid′u·lous·ness,** *n.*

ack–ack (ak′ak′) *n. Informal.* Anti-aircraft fire. [British radio operator's code word for A.A. (anti-aircraft)]

ack·ee (ak′ē) *n.* **1** a tropical African tree (*Blighia sapida*) of the soapberry family, cultivated, especially in Jamaica, for its edible fruit. **2** the fruit of this tree, eaten as a cooked vegetable, usually with salt fish. Ackee resembles scrambled eggs in appearance and taste. [from an African name]

ac·knowl·edge (ak nol′ij) *v.* **-edged, -edg·ing. 1** admit to be true: *He acknowledges his own faults.* **2** recognize the merit, authority or claims of: *She was acknowledged to be the best player on the baseball team.* **3** express appreciation of (a gift, favor, etc.): *He acknowledged his help by inviting them to dinner.* **4** make known that one has received (a service, favor, gift, message, etc.). **5** *Law.* recognize or certify as genuine: *to acknowledge a contract before a notary public.* [blend of ME *aknowen* admit (< OE *oncnāwan*) and *knowleche* knowledge] —**ac·knowl′edg·er,** *n.*
☛ *Syn.* **1.** See note at **admit.**

ac·knowl·edg·ment or **ac·knowl·edge·ment** (ak nol′ij mənt) *n.* **1** a verbal, written, or other recognition of a gift, service, favor, etc.: *He waved in acknowledgment of the crowd's cheers. A receipt is an acknowledgment that a bill has been paid.* **2** the act of admitting the existence or truth of anything. **3** the recognition of authority or claims. **4** an expression of thanks. **5** an official certificate in legal form.

A.C.M. Air Chief Marshal.

ac·me (ak′mē) *n.* the highest point. [< Gk. *akmē* point]

ac·ne (ak′nē) *n.* a skin disease in which the oil glands in the skin become clogged and inflamed, often causing pimples. [? < Gk. *akmē* point]

ac·o·lyte (ak′ə līt′) *n.* **1** a person who helps a priest during certain religious services; server. **2** attendant or follower. [ME < Med.L *acolitus* < Gk. *akolouthos* follower]

ac·o·nite (ak′ə nīt′) *n.* **1** any of a genus (*Aconitum*) of plants of the buttercup family found in cool northern regions, having blue, purple, yellow, or white, hood-shaped flowers and, in some species, poisonous roots, seeds, and leaves. **2** a poisonous substance

obtained from the roots of some aconites, especially a drug obtained from *Aconitum napellus*, formerly used in medicine to deaden pain, slow down the pulse, etc. [< F *aconit* < L < Gk. *akoniton*]

a·corn (ā′kôrn) *n.* the nut, or fruit, of an oak tree. [OE *æcern*]

a·cous·tic (ə küs′tik) *adj.* **1** of or having to do with the sense of hearing: *acoustic nerves, an acoustic stimulus.* **2** having to do with the science of sound: *acoustic phonetics, acoustic energy.* **3** designed to carry sound or to aid in hearing: *An acoustic baffle has been installed in the concert hall.* **4** designed to deaden or absorb sound: *acoustic tile.* **5** operated by sound waves: *An acoustic mine is exploded by sound waves.* **6** of musical instruments, etc., not using electronic amplification: *an acoustic guitar.* [< F *acoustique* < Gk. *akoustikos* having to do with hearing < *akouein* hear]

a·cous·ti·cal (ə küs′ti kəl) *adj.* having to do with the science of sound: *an acoustical engineer.*

a·cous·ti·cal·ly (ə küs′tik lē) *adv.* with regard to acoustics.

a·cous·tics (ə küs′tiks) *n.* **1** the qualities of a room, hall, auditorium, etc. that determine how well sounds can be heard in it; acoustic qualities (*used with a plural verb*): *We enjoy singing in the auditorium because the acoustics are so good.* **2** the scientific study of sound (*used with a singular verb*): *Acoustics is taught in some universities.*

ac·quaint (ə kwānt′) *v.* **1** inform (a person) about a thing: *Acquaint him with your intention. He acquainted me of his plan.* **2** make familiar: *Let me acquaint you with the facts.*
be acquainted with, have personal knowledge of: *She is acquainted with my father.* [ME *acointe* < OF *acointer* < LL *adcognitare* < L *adcognitus, accognitus* < *ad-* to + *cognitus,* pp. of *cognoscere* know < *com-* with + *gnoscere* come to know]
☞ *Syn.* **1.** See note at **inform.**

ac·quaint·ance (ə kwān′təns) *n.* **1** a person known to one, but not a close friend. **2** a knowledge of persons or things gained from experience with them; personal knowledge.

ac·quaint·ance·ship (ə kwān′təns ship′) *n.* **1** personal knowledge; acquaintance. **2** the relation between acquaintances: *Their acquaintanceship dates from before the war.*

ac·qui·esce (ak′wē es′) *v.* **-esced, -esc·ing.** accept or agree to by keeping quiet or by not making objections: *We acquiesced in their plan because we could not suggest a better one.* [< F < L *acquiescere* < *ad-* to + *quiescere* to rest < *quies* rest]

ac·qui·es·cence (ak′wē es′əns) *n.* the act of acquiescing or the state of being acquiescent.

ac·qui·es·cent (ak′wē es′ənt) *adj.* acquiescing; consenting or accepting.

ac·quire (ə kwīr′) *v.* **-quired, -quir·ing. 1** receive or get as one's own: *to acquire land.* **2** get by one's own efforts or actions: *to acquire an education.* [ME *acquere* < OF *acquerre* < L *acquirere* < *ad-* to + *quaerere* seek] —**ac·quir′a·ble,** *adj.* —**ac·quir′er,** *n.*
☞ *Syn.* **1.** See note at **get.**

ac·quire·ment (ə kwīr′mənt) *n.* **1** the act of acquiring. **2** something acquired; attainment: *Her musical acquirements are remarkable for a girl of her age.*

ac·qui·si·tion (ak′wə zish′ən) *n.* **1** the act or process of acquiring: *He spent hundreds of hours in the acquisition of skill with a rifle.* **2** something acquired. [< L *acquisitio, -onis* < *acquirere.* See ACQUIRE.]

ac·quis·i·tive (ə kwiz′ə tiv) *adj.* fond of acquiring; likely to get and keep: *A miser is acquisitive of money. A great scholar is acquisitive of ideas.* —**ac·quis′i·tive·ly,** *adv.* —**ac·quis′i·tive·ness,** *n.*

ac·quit (ə kwit′) *v.* **-quit·ted, -quit·ting. 1** declare (a person) not guilty (of an offence): *The jury acquitted the innocent man of the crime.* **2** set free or release (from a duty, obligation, etc.). **3** pay off or settle (a debt, claim, etc.). **4** do (one's part); conduct (oneself): *The soldiers acquitted themselves well in battle.* [ME < OF *aquiter* < *a-* to (< L *ad-*) + *quitte* free < L *quietus* quiet] —**ac·quit′ter,** *n.*

ac·quit·tal (ə kwit′əl) *n.* **1** a setting free by declaring not guilty; release. **2** the performance of a duty, obligation, etc.).

ac·quit·tance (ə kwit′əns) *n.* **1** a release from a debt or obligation. **2** a payment of a debt; settlement of a claim. **3** a written statement showing that a debt has been paid; receipt for the full amount.

a·cre (ā′kər) *n.* **1** a unit for measuring land area, equal to about 4047 square metres. **2 acres,** *pl.* lands; property. **3** *Archaic.* field. **4** See *God's acre.* [OE *æcer* field]

a·cre·age (ā′kər ij) *n.* **1** the number of acres: *What is the acreage of the farm?* **2** area in acres; acres collectively: *We have most of our acreage in barley this year.* **3** a piece of land of several acres: *She bought a small acreage north of town.*

ac·rid (ak′rid) *adj.* **1** sharp, bitter, or stinging to the nose, mouth, or skin. **2** having or showing a sharp or irritating temper: *an acrid*

hat, āge, fär; let, ēqual, tèrm; it, īce
hot, ōpen, ôrder; oil, out; cup, pút, rüle,
əbove, takən, pencəl, lemən, circəs

ch, child; ng, long; sh, ship
th, thin; ᴛʜ, then; zh, measure

comment. [< L *acer, acris* sharp, after *acid*] —**ac′rid·ly,** *adv.* —**ac′rid·ness,** *n.*

a·crid·i·ty (ə krid′ə tē) *n.* bitterness or sharpness.

Ac·ri·lan (ak′rə lan′) *n. Trademark.* a synthetic acrylic fibre having a woolly texture, used for blankets, carpets, clothing, etc.

ac·ri·mo·ni·ous (ak′rə mō′nē əs) *adj.* sharp and bitter in temper, language, or manner. —**ac′ri·mo′ni·ous·ly,** *adv.* —**ac′ri·mo′ni·ous·ness,** *n.*

ac·ri·mo·ny (ak′rə mō′nē) *n., pl.* **-nies.** sharpness or bitterness in temper, language, or manner. [< L *acrimonia* < *acer* sharp]

ac·ro·bat (ak′rə bat′) *n.* a person who can perform on a trapeze, turn handsprings, walk on a tightrope, etc. [< F *acrobate* < Gk. *akrobatēs* < *akros* tip (of the toes) + *-batos* going]

ac·ro·bat·ic (ak′rə bat′ik) *adj.* **1** of an acrobat. **2** like an acrobat's. —**ac′ro·bat′i·cal·ly,** *adv.*

ac·ro·bat·ics (ak′rə bat′iks) *n.pl.* **1** the skills or performance of an acrobat. **2** feats like those of an acrobat.

ac·ro·gen (ak′rə jən) *n.* any flowerless plant in which growth occurs only from the tip of the main stem, such as a fern or moss. [< Gk. *akros* tip + E *-gen* growth < F < Gk. *-genēs* born]

a·cro·le·in (ə krō′lē in) *n.* a colorless, poisonous liquid that is used as a tear gas. *Formula:* C_3H_4O [< L *acer, acris* sharp + *olere* to smell + E *-in*]

ac·ro·me·gal·ic (ak′rō mə gal′ik) *adj.* **1** having to do with acromegaly. **2** affected with acromegaly.

ac·ro·meg·a·ly (ak′rō meg′ə lē) *n.* a disease caused by abnormal activity of the pituitary gland, in which the head, hands, and feet become permanently enlarged. [< F *acromégalie* < Gk. *akros* tip + *megas, -galou* big]

ac·ro·nym (ak′rə nim) *n.* a word formed from the first letters or syllables of other words, such as radar (RAdio Detecting And Ranging), snafu (Situation Normal—All Fouled Up), and Unesco (United Nations Educational, Scientific, and Cultural Organization). [< Gk. *akros* tip + dial. *onyma* name]

ac·ro·pho·bi·a (ak′rə fō′bē ə) *n. Psychiatry.* extreme, irrational fear of high places.

a·crop·o·lis (ə krop′ə lis) *n.* **1** the fortified hill in the centre of an ancient Greek city, which served as its religious centre as well as its fortress. **2 the Acropolis,** the fortified hill of Athens, on which the Parthenon was built. [< Gk. *akropolis* < *akros* topmost, outermost + *polis* city]

a·cross (ə kros′) *prep. adv.* —*prep.* **1** from one side to the other of; to the other side of; over: *a bridge laid across a river. She drew a line across the page.* **2** on the other side of; beyond: *across the sea.* **3** on top of and at an angle to: *She laid the board across the sawhorses. He put the coat across the back of a chair.* **4** into contact with: *We come across unusual words in some books.*
across country, by way of fields, woods, etc., ignoring the roads: *We followed the road for two kilometres and then struck out across country.*
—*adv.* **1** from one side to the other: *What is the distance across?* **2** on or to the other side: *He ran across without looking where he was going.*
come across See **come.**
get across See **get.**
put across See **put.**
[< *a-* on, in + *cross*]

a·cross-the-board (ə kros′ᴛʜə bôrd′) *adj.* affecting all members of a group; all-embracing: *The contract called for across-the-board raises in pay.*

Nᴏʀᴛʜ
Eᴀsᴛ
Wᴇsᴛ
Sᴏᴜᴛʜ   An acrostic of *news*

a·cros·tic (ə kros′tik) *n.* a composition in verse or an

arrangement of words in which the first, last, or certain other letters in each line, taken in order, spell a word or phrase. [< L < Gk. *akrostichis* < *akros* tip + *stichos* row]

ac·ryl·ate (ak′rəl āt′) *n.* a salt or ester of acrylic acid.

acrylate resin acrylic resin.

a·cryl·ic (ə kril′ik) *adj., n.* —*adj.* of or having to do with acrylic acid or its derivatives. —*n.* **1** an acrylic resin. **2** a paint made with an acrylic resin base. **3** a painting done with such paints: *We bought one of her latest acrylics.* **4** an acrylic textile fibre or fabric.

acrylic acid an unsaturated organic acid in the form of a colorless liquid, from which acrylic resins are derived by polymerization. *Formula:* CH_2:$COOH$

acrylic fibre any of various strong, lightweight, synthetic textile fibres made by polymerizing acrylonitrile, used especially for knitwear, pile fabrics, and carpets.

acrylic resin any of a group of transparent, colorless thermoplastics made by polymerizing acrylic acid or derivatives of it, used especially in sheet form for windows, etc. and in the manufacture of paints, rubber, and adhesives.

ac·ry·lo·ni·trile (ak′rə lō nī′trĭl) *n.* a colorless, volatile liquid used in the manufacture of acrylic textile fibres, synthetic rubber, and thermoplastics. *Formula:* CH_2:$CHCN$

act (akt) *n., v.* —*n.* **1** something done; a deed: *an act of kindness.* *Slapping his face was a childish act.* **2** the process of doing: *He was caught in the act of stealing.* **3** a main division of a play or opera. **4** one of several performances on a program: *the trained dog's act.* **5** a legislative decision; law. An Act of Parliament is a bill that has been passed by Parliament. **6** *Informal.* a display of affected or pretended behavior: *Her bad temper was just an act and failed to convince anyone.*
get into the act, *Informal.* to take part in or join: *Suddenly the new dance caught on and everyone was getting into the act.*
—*v.* **1** do something: *The firemen acted promptly and saved the house.* **2** behave: *to act like a fool, to act generously.* **3** behave like: *Most people act the fool now and then.* **4** have an effect or influence: *Yeast acts on dough and makes it rise.* **5** play a part; perform in a theatre. **6** serve or function (*as*): *He acted as interpreter at the conference. The foam acts as insulation.* **7** serve as representative or substitute (*for*): *She is acting for the board of directors in this matter.* **8** act in accordance with; follow or obey (*used with* **on**): *He said he would act on their advice.*
act out, **a** represent in actions, as in mime: *Charades is a game in which titles or sayings are acted out.* **b** *Psychiatry.* express subconscious feelings, attitudes, etc. in overt actions, without awareness of the cause: *Disturbed children sometimes act out the antisocial feelings of their elders.*
act up, *Informal.* **a** behave badly: *They left when their baby started acting up.* **b** be troublesome: *The knee I hurt last summer is acting up again.*
[ME < OF *acte*, n., < L *actus* a doing, *actum* (thing) done < *agere* do]
☛ *Usage.* In the sense 'behave,' **act** can be followed by an adverb or by certain adjectives: *He sometimes acts foolishly. He acts older than he is.*

ACTH a hormone obtained from the pituitary gland, used in treating arthritis, rheumatic fever, etc. [adreno- cortico- trophic hormone]

act·ing (ak′ting) *adj.* temporarily taking another's place and doing his duties: *While the principal was sick, one of the teachers was acting principal.*

ac·tin·ic (ak tin′ik) *adj.* **1** of actinism. **2** producing chemical changes by radiation. Actinic rays are important in photography. [< Gk. *aktis, -tinos* ray]

ac·tin·ide (ak′tin īd′) *n.* any chemical element belonging to the series having the atomic numbers 90 through 103. All actinides are naturally radio-active.

ac·tin·ism (ak′tən iz′əm) *n.* the property in light that causes chemical changes.

ac·tin·i·um (ak tin′ē əm) *n.* a radio-active, metallic chemical element resembling radium, found in pitchblende after uranium has been extracted. *Symbol:* Ac; *at.no.* 89; *at.wt.* (227); *half-life* 21.7 years.

ac·ti·nom·e·ter (ak′tə nom′ə tər) *n.* an instrument for measuring the intensity of radiation, especially from the sun.

ac·tin·on (ak′tə non′) *n.* a gaseous, radio-active element formed by the decay of actinium. *Symbol:* An; *at.no.* 86; *at.wt.* 219; *half-life* 3.9 seconds. [< *actinium*]

ac·ti·no·zo·an (ak′tə nə zō′ən) *n.* anthozoan. [< NL *Actinozoa* < Gk. *aktis, -tinos* ray + *zōia,* pl. of *zōion* animal]

ac·tion (ak′shən) *n.* **1** the process of doing something or the state of being active or in operation: *to put a machine into action.* **2** habitual activity, especially when characterized by energy or initiative: *a man of action.* **3** something done; act. **4 actions,** *pl.* conduct; behavior. **5** *Slang.* important or exciting activities or happenings: *to go where the action is.* **6** the effect or influence of a force or thing on something else: *the action of the wind on a ship's sails, the action of a drug.* **7** the way in which something moves or works. **8** the working parts of a machine, instrument, etc. The keys of a piano are part of its action. **9** a minor battle. **10** combat between military forces: *He was in the armed forces but was never in action.* **11** the events forming the story or plot of a play, novel, film, etc.: *Most of the action takes place in a small town in Manitoba.* **12** lawsuit: *to bring an action against someone.* **13** an appearance of movement or activity in a painting, drawing, or sculpture.
take action, begin to act, especially in order to stop or oppose something.
[ME < OF < L *actio, -onis* < *agere* do] —**ac′tion·less,** *adj.*
☛ *Syn.* **3.** See note at **act. 9.** See note at **battle.**

ac·tion·a·ble (ak′shən ə bəl) *adj.* giving cause for a lawsuit; justifying a lawsuit.

ac·ti·vate (ak′tə vāt′) *v.* **-vat·ed, -vat·ing. 1** make active. **2** *Physics.* make radio-active. **3** *Chemistry.* make capable of reacting or of speeding up a reaction. **4** purify (sewage) by treating it with air and bacteria. —**ac′ti·va′tion,** *n.*

ac·ti·va·tor (ak′tə vā′tər) *n.* **1** something that activates. **2** *Chemistry.* catalyst.

ac·tive (ak′tiv) *adj., n.* —*adj.* **1** capable of acting or reacting: *an active volcano.* **2** moving much or quickly; lively or brisk: *an active child.* **3** marked by much or constant activity: *an active stock market.* **4** taking an effective part in; participating: *She's an active member of the organization.* **5** real or effective: *an active interest in sports.* **6** in present use: *an active file.* **7** causing action or change: *an active ingredient.* **8** *Grammar.* of or designating a form (called the voice) of a verb that shows the grammatical subject of a clause as the logical subject, the agent of the action expressed in the verb. In *She broke the window, broke* is active; the subject *she* performs the action represented by the verb *broke.* Compare **passive** (def. 3). —*n. Grammar.* **1** the active voice. **2** a verb in the active voice. [ME < OF *actif* < L *activus* < *agere* act] —**ac′tive·ly,** *adv.* —**ac′tive·ness,** *n.*

active list a list of officers serving in the armed forces or available for service.

active service or **duty 1** military service with full pay and regular duties. **2** service in the armed forces in time of war.

ac·tiv·ism (ak′tə viz′əm) *n.* a doctrine or policy of direct, vigorous action or confrontation in supporting one's own point of view on a controversial social or political issue.

ac·tiv·ist (ak′tə vist) *n., adj.* —*n.* a person who practises activism. —*adj.* of or having to do with activism or activists.

ac·tiv·i·ty (ak tiv′ə tē) *n., pl.* **-ties. 1** the state of being active; movement; use of power: *physical activity, mental activity.* **2** action; doing: *the activities of enemy spies.* **3** vigorous action; liveliness: *no activity in the market.* **4** a thing to do: *A student who has too many outside activities may find it hard to keep up with his studies.* **5** anything active; active force.

act of God something that could not be foreseen or prevented by human beings; a happening beyond a person's control. Floods, storms, and earthquakes are called acts of God.

Act of Union an act of the British Parliament, passed in 1840, to unite the provinces of Upper and Lower Canada.

ac·tor (ak′tər) *n.* **1** a person who acts on the stage, in motion pictures, on radio, or on television. **2** any person who does something or takes part in something.
bad actor, *Informal.* a person, animal, or thing that is always misbehaving: *That horse is a bad actor.*

ACTRA Award (ak′trə) one of several awards presented annually by the Association of Canadian Television and Radio Artists for excellence in broadcasting.

ac·tress (ak′tris) *n.* a woman or girl who acts on the stage, in motion pictures, on radio, or on television.

ac·tu·al (ak′chü əl) *adj.* **1** existing as a fact; real: *What he told us was not a dream but an actual happening.* **2** now existing; present; current: *the actual state of affairs.* [ME < OF < LL *actualis* < L *actus* a doing. See ACT.] —**ac′tu·al·ness,** *n.*
☛ *Syn.* **1.** See note at **real¹.**

ac·tu·al·i·ty (ak′chü al′ə tē) *n., pl.* **-ties. 1** actual existence; reality. **2** an actual thing; fact.

ac·tu·al·ize (ak′chü əl īz′) *v.* **-ized, -iz·ing.** make actual; realize in action or as a fact. —**ac′tu·al·i·za′tion,** *n.*

ac·tu·al·ly (ak′chü əl ē) *adv.* really; in fact: *Are you actually going abroad this summer?*

ac·tu·ar·i·al (ak′chü er′ē əl) *adj.* **1** of actuaries or their work. **2** determined by actuaries.

ac·tu·ar·y (ak′chü er′ē) *n., pl.* **-ar·ies.** a person whose work is figuring risks, rates, premiums, etc. for insurance companies. [< L *actuarius* account keeper < *actus* a doing. See ACT.]

ac·tu·ate (ak′chü āt′) *v.* **-at·ed, -at·ing. 1** put into action: *This pump is actuated by a belt driven by an electric motor.* **2** influence to act: *She was actuated by love for her mother.* [< LL *actuare* < L *actus* a doing. See ACT.] **—ac′tu·a′tion,** *n.* **—ac′tu·a′tor,** *n.*
☛ *Syn.* See note at **move.**

a·cu·i·ty (ə kyü′ə tē) *n.* sharpness; acuteness. [< Med.L *acuitas,* ult. < L *acus* needle]

a·cu·men (ə kyü′mən *or* ak′yə mən) *n.* sharpness and quickness in seeing and understanding; keen insight. [< L *acumen* < *acuere* sharpen]

a·cu·mi·nate (ə kyü′mə nit *or* ə kyü′mə nāt′) *adj.* pointed: *a leaf with an acuminate tip.* [< L *acuminatus,* pp. of *acuminare* point < *acumen.* See ACUMEN.]

ac·u·punc·ture (ak′yə pungk′chər) *n.* a method of relieving pain and treating disease by inserting fine needles into the body at specific points. Acupuncture has been used in the Far East for thousands of years.

a·cute (ə kyüt′) *adj., n.* **—adj. 1** having a sharp point. **2** sharp and severe: *A toothache can cause acute pain.* **3** brief and severe: *An acute disease like pneumonia reaches a crisis within a short time.* **4** keen: *Dogs have an acute sense of smell. An acute thinker is clever and shrewd.* **5** high in pitch; shrill: *Some sounds are so acute that we cannot hear them.* **6** critical; crucial: *Their situation became acute when their food supplies were exhausted.* **7** of a vowel, having the mark (′) over it. **8** *Geometry.* less than a right angle. See **angle** for picture.
—n. an acute accent. [< L *acutus,* pp. of *acuere* sharpen]
—a·cute′ly, *adv.* **—a·cute′ness,** *n.*
☛ *Syn.* **4.** See note at **sharp.**

acute accent 1 a mark ′ written or printed to show the spoken quality of a particular letter in a word: *An acute accent placed over an e in French indicates that it is pronounced something like the beginning of the English* (ā) *sound.* **2** a mark ′ used to indicate emphasis or stress in pronunciation. A heavy acute accent is used in this dictionary to show which syllable of a word is stressed. A light accent is used to show a secondary stress in some longer words.

acute angle an angle less than a right angle. See **angle** for picture.

A.C.W. aircraftwoman.

ad (ad) *n. Informal.* advertisement.
☛ *Usage.* **Ad** is the clipped form of *advertisement,* has only one *d,* and should not be followed by a period.

ad– *prefix.* to or toward, as in *admit, administer, adverb, advert.* Also: **a-** before *sc, sp, st;* **ab-** before *b;* **ac-** before *c, q;* **af-** before *f;* **ag-** before *g;* **al** before *l;* **an-** before *n;* **ap-** before *p;* **ar-** before *r;* **as-** before *s;* **at-** before *t.* [< L *ad-* < *ad,* prep.]

A.D. in the year of the Lord; since Christ was born (for LL *anno Domini.*)

ad·age (ad′ij) *n.* a wise saying that has been much used; well-known proverb. [< F < L *adagium*]

a·da·gio (ə dazh′ē ō, ə daj′ē ō, *or* ə dä′jō) *adv., adj., n., pl.* **-gios.** *Music.* **—adv.** slowly. **—adj.** slow. **—n. 1** a slow part in a piece of music. **2** a composition to be played or sung at a slow tempo. **3** *Ballet.* a slow dance in which a man and woman do acrobatic feats. [< Ital. *ad agio* at ease]

Ad·am[1] (ad′əm) *n.* in the Bible, the first man. With his wife Eve, he was driven from the Garden of Eden for eating the forbidden fruit (Gen. 1:5).
the old Adam, human tendency to sin.
not to know (someone) from Adam, *Informal.* be unable to recognize; be completely unacquainted with someone.

Adam[2] (ad′əm) *adj., n.* **—adj.** of, like, or having to do with a graceful ornamented style of furniture and architecture. **—n. 1** this style of furniture or architecture. **2** a piece of furniture or architecture of this style. [after Robert and James *Adam,* 18th-century British designers]

ad·a·mant (ad′ə mənt) *n., adj.* **—n. 1** a legendary mineral so hard that it could not be cut or broken: *Adamant was identified at different times with the diamond and lodestone.* **2** any extremely hard substance. **—adj. 1** too hard to be cut or broken. **2** unyielding; firm; immovable. [< OF *adamaunt* the hardest stone (= diamond) < L < Gk. *adamas, -antos* < *a-* not + *damaein* conquer, tame]

ad·a·man·tine (ad′ə man′tīn, ad′ə man′tēn, *or* ad′ə man′tin) *adj.* **1** having a lustre like a diamond. **2** adamant.

Adam's ale water.

Adam's apple the lump in the front of the throat formed by the thyroid cartilage. [translation of Hebrew *tappūach hā′ādām,* lit. meaning either 'protrusion on (the neck of) a man' or 'fruit of Adam,' from the story of the forbidden fruit getting stuck in Adam's throat]

hat, āge, fär; let, ēqual, tėrm; it, īce
hot, ōpen, ôrder; oil, out; cup, pút, rüle,
ə·bove, tak·ən, penc·əl, lem·ən, circ·əs

ch, child; ng, long; sh, ship
th, thin; ᴛʜ, then; zh, measure

a·dapt (ə dapt′) *v.* **1** make or become fit or suitable; adjust: *Can you adapt yourself to a new job? He has adapted well to the new school.* **2** modify or alter for a different use: *The farmer can adapt the barn for use as a garage.* [< L *adaptare* < *ad-* to + *aptare* fit] **—a·dapt′er,** *n.*
☛ *Syn.* **1.** See note at **adjust.**
☛ *Usage.* **Adapt** meaning "make suitable" is followed by the preposition *to: His style is not adapted to adults.* **Adapt** meaning "revise" is followed by *for* or *from: The story was adapted for television. It was adapted from the novel.*

a·dapt·a·bil·i·ty (ə dap′tə bil′ə tē) *n.* the power to change easily to fit different conditions.

a·dapt·a·ble (ə dap′tə bəl) *adj.* **1** easily changed to fit different conditions: *an adaptable schedule.* **2** changing easily to fit different conditions: *an adaptable person.* **—a·dapt′a·ble·ness,** *n.*

ad·ap·ta·tion (ad′ap tā′shən) *n.* **1** adapting or being adapted. **2** something made by adapting: *A motion picture is often an adaptation of a novel.* **3** *Biology.* a change in structure, form, or habits to fit different conditions: *Wings are adaptations of the upper limbs for flight.*

a·dapt·er (ə dap′tər) *n.* **1** a person or thing that adapts. **2** a device for fitting together parts that do not match: *An adapter can be used to fit this nozzle onto a larger hose.* **3** a device for changing the function of a machine, apparatus, etc. Also, **adaptor.**

a·dap·tive (ə dap′tiv) *adj.* **1** able to adapt. **2** showing adaptation. **—a·dap′tive·ly,** *adv.* **—a·dap′tive·ness,** *n.*

a·dap·tor (ə dap′tər) See **adapter.**

A·dar (ə där′) *n.* in the Hebrew calendar, the twelfth month of the ecclesiastical year and the sixth month of the civil year.

ADC, A.D.C., or **a.d.c.** aide-de-camp.

add (ad) *v.* **1** join (one thing to another); put together; put with: *Add another stone to the pile. Add 8 and 2 and you have 10.* **2** make or form an addition; increase: *The fine weather added to our pleasure.* **3** say further; go on to say or write: *She said goodbye and added that she had had a pleasant visit.* **4** perform arithmetical addition: *The little boy is learning to add and subtract.*
add in, include.
add up, a find the sum of (a column, etc. of numbers). **b** *Informal.* make the correct total. **c** *Informal.* make sense; fit together: *There were many clues to the murder, but they just didn't add up.*
add up to, amount to.
[ME < L *addere* < *ad-* to + *dare* put]

ad·dax (ad′aks) *n.* a large, heavily built antelope (*Addax nasomaculatus*) of the deserts of N Africa, standing about 105 cm high at the shoulder and having very long, curving, ringed horns. [< L < an African word]

added line *Music.* ledger line.

ad·dend (ad′end *or* ə dend′) *n.* a number or quantity to be added to another number or quantity.

ad·den·da (ə den′də) *n.* pl. of **addendum.**

ad·den·dum (ə den′dəm) *n., pl.* **-da. 1** a thing to be added. **2** the thing added; appendix. [< L]

ad·der[1] (ad′ər) *n.* **1** the common viper (*Vipera berus*), a small poisonous snake of Europe and N Asia, from 45 to 75 cm long, usually having a black zigzag band along its back. It is the only poisonous snake native to Great Britain. **2** any of several vipers found in Africa, including the large, dangerous **puff adder** (*Bitis arietans*) and the small, less dangerous **night adders** (genus *Causus*). **3** Also, **death adder,** a very poisonous snake (*Acanthophis antarcticus*) of Australia, belonging to the same family as cobras and coral snakes, but resembling a viper. **4** Also, **blowing adder,** any of several species (genus *Heterodon*) of harmless snake found in the United States. **5** *Informal.* any snake thought to be poisonous. [OE *nædre*; in ME *a nadder* was taken as *an adder*]

ad·der[2] (ad′ər) *n.* a person or thing that adds, especially a device or machine that performs addition.

ad·der's–tongue (ad′ərz tung′) *n.* **1** any of various ferns (family Ophioglossaceae) of the northern hemisphere having a spore-bearing body resembling a spike or snake's tongue. **2** dogtooth violet.

add·i·ble (ad′ə bəl) *adj.* that can be added.

ad·dict (*n.* ad′ikt; *v.* ə dikt′) *n., v.* **—n. 1** a person who is dependant on a drug, especially a narcotic drug, such as morphine or heroin. **2** a person who has given himself up to a habit or

obsession: *a movie addict.* —*v.* cause (oneself or someone) to become dependant or obsessed (*usually used in the passive*): *addicted to heroin, addicted to detective novels.* [< L *addictus,* pp. of *addicere* adjudge, devote < *ad-* to + *dicere* say]

ad·dict·ed (ə dik′tid) *adj.* slavishly following (a habit or practice); strongly inclined: *He was addicted to cigars.*

ad·dic·tion (ə dik′shən) *n.* the condition of being addicted.

ad·dic·tive (ə dik′tiv) *adj.* that causes or tends to cause addiction.

ad·di·tion (ə dish′ən) *n.* 1 the act or process of adding. 2 the result of adding; something added. 3 a part added to a building. **in addition** or **in addition to,** besides; also. [ME < OF < L *additio, -onis* < *addere.* See ADD.]

ad·di·tion·al (ə dish′ən əl *or* ə dish′nəl) *adj.* added; extra; more. —**ad·di′tion·al·ly,** *adv.*

ad·di·tive (ad′ə tiv) *n., adj.* —*n.* any substance added in small amounts to a product to add or improve certain desirable qualities or to reduce the effects of undesirable ones: *Additives are put in processed foods to add a desirable color, act as a preservative, etc. There are additives in gasoline and fuel oil to increase the efficiency of combustion.* —*adj.* of, having to do with, or involving addition.

ad·dle (ad′əl) *v.* -**dled,** -**dling;** *adj.* —*v.* 1 make or become muddled: *The wine has quite addled her.* 2 of eggs, become rotten; spoil. —*adj.* 1 muddled; confused (*used only in compounds*): *They called him an addle-pated fool.* 2 of eggs, rotten. [OE *adela* liquid filth]

ad·dress (ə dres′; *also, for n. defs.* 2 *and* 3, ad′res) *n., v.* -**dressed** *or* -**drest, -dress·ing.** —*n.* 1 a speech, especially a formal one: *The prime minister gave a television address.* 2 the place at which a person, business, etc. may be found or reached: *Send the letter to her business address.* 3 the writing on an envelope, package, etc. that shows where it is to be sent: *The letter was returned because the address was incomplete.* 4 a location or place, especially with reference to its social desirability: *It's a very good address.* 5 manner in conversation: *She was a person of pleasant address.* 6 skill: *The new manager shows much address in getting people to help him.* 7 a formal request to those in authority to do a particular thing: *an address from the colonists to the king, listing grievances.* 8 **addresses,** *pl.* attentions paid in courtship. —*v.* 1 direct speech or writing to: *The Queen addressed Parliament.* 2 use titles or other forms in speaking or writing to: *How do you address a mayor?* 3 write on (a letter, package, etc.) the information that shows where it is to be sent. 4 apply (oneself) in speech (*to a person or group*): *He addressed himself to the chairman.* 5 apply or devote (oneself) (*to*): *She addressed herself to completing the report.* 6 deal with: *to address the problem at hand.* 7 direct to the attention: *to address a warning to a friend.* 8 *Golf.* prepare for a stroke by placing the head of a club behind (the ball). [ME < OF *adresser,* v. (noun partly < F *adresse*), earlier *adrecier* < VL *addirectaire* < L *ad-* to + *directus* straight] —**ad·dress′er** *or* **ad·dres′sor,** *n.*

☛ *Syn. n.* 1. See note at **speech.**
☛ *Usage.* **Addresses.** When the various parts of a person's address are written on the same line, they are separated by commas: *Send the money to Miss Louise Finney, 48 Pine St., Kingston, Ontario.*

ad·dress·ee (ə dres ē′ *or* ad′res ē′) *n.* the person to whom a letter, package, etc. is addressed.

ad·duce (ə dyüs′ *or* ə düs′) *v.* -**duced, -duc·ing.** give as a reason, proof, or example; cite: *The author has adduced some convincing data in support of his argument.* [< L *adducere* < *ad-* to + *ducere* lead]

ad·duct (ə dukt′) *v.* of a muscle or group of muscles, serve to draw (a limb, etc.) toward or beyond the median axis of the body or of one of its parts. Compare **abduct.** [< L *adductus,* pp. of *adducere.* See ADDUCE.]

ad·duc·tion (ə duk′shən) *n.* 1 the act of adducing; the bringing forward of proof, evidence, etc. 2 the act of adducting or the state of being adducted: *the adduction of the fingers of the hand.*

ad·duc·tor (ə duk′tər) *n.* any muscle whose function is to draw a limb, etc. toward the median axis of the body or one of its parts. Compare **abductor.**

ad·e·noid (ad′ə noid′) *adj.* 1 lymphoid. 2 like a gland; glandular.

ad·e·noi·dal (ad′ə noi′dəl) *adj.* 1 adenoid. 2 having adenoids (def. 2). 3 typical of a person affected with adenoids (def. 2): *adenoidal breathing.*

ad·e·noids (ad′ə noidz′) *n.pl.* 1 normal lymphoid tissue in the upper part of the throat, just behind the nose, that usually shrinks and disappears in childhood, but sometimes swells and gets in the way of natural breathing and speaking. 2 swollen adenoids: *He had adenoids as a child.* [< Gk. *adenoeidēs* < *adēn* gland, acorn]

ad·e·no·ma (ad′ə nō′mə) *n.* 1 a tumor originating in a gland. 2 a tumor resembling a gland. [< Gk. *adēn* gland + *-oma*]

ad·ept (*n.* ad′ept *or* ə dept′; *adj.* ə dept′) *n., adj.* —*n.* a thoroughly skilled or expert person. —*adj.* thoroughly skilled; expert. [< L *adeptus,* pp. of *adipisci* attain < *ad-* to + *apisci* get] —**a·dept′ly,** *adv.* —**a·dept′ness,** *n.*

ad·e·qua·cy (ad′ə kwə sē) *n.* the quality or state of being adequate; sufficiency.

ad·e·quate (ad′ə kwit) *adj.* 1 as much as is needed; fully sufficient: *His wages are adequate to support three people.* 2 suitable; competent: *an adequate person for the job.* [< L *adaequatus,* pp. of *adaequare* < *ad-* to + *aequus* equal] —**ad′e·quate·ly,** *adv.* —**ad′e·quate·ness,** *n.*
☛ *Syn.* 1. See note at **enough.**

ad·here (ad hēr′) *v.* -**hered, -her·ing.** 1 stick fast; remain attached (*to*): *Mud adheres to your shoes.* 2 hold closely or firmly (*to*): *to adhere to a plan.* 3 be devoted (*to*): *Most people adhere to the church of their parents.* [< L *adhaerere* < *ad-* to + *haerere* stick] —**ad·her′er,** *n.*
☛ *Syn.* 1. See note at **stick**[2].

ad·her·ence (ad hēr′əns) *n.* 1 an attachment or loyalty (to a person, group, belief, etc.); faithfulness. 2 a holding to and following closely: *rigid adherence to rules.*

ad·her·ent (ad hēr′ənt) *n., adj.* —*n.* a faithful supporter; follower. —*adj.* sticking fast; attached. —**ad·her′ent·ly,** *adv.*
☛ *Syn. n.* See note at **follower.**
☛ *Usage.* **Adherent.** The preposition used with the noun adherent is of: *He was an adherent of the Liberal Party.*

ad·he·sion (ad hē′zhən) *n.* 1 the action of sticking fast or joining or the state of being stuck or joined together. 2 a steady or devoted attachment; faithfulness. 3 an agreement; assent. 4 *Physics.* the attraction between the molecules of different substances. Capillary attraction, which causes the surface of water to rise against the inside of a glass tube, is the result of adhesion between the liquid and the solid. 5 *Medicine.* **a** the growing together of tissues that should be separate, usually as a result of inflammation. **b** tissues abnormally joined in this way. [< L *adhaesio, -onis* < *adhaerere.* See ADHERE.]

ad·he·sive (ad hē′siv *or* ad hē′ziv) *adj., n.* —*adj.* 1 holding fast; adhering easily; sticky. 2 smeared with a sticky substance for holding (something) fast: *adhesive tape.* —*n.* any substance, such as paste or gum, used to stick things together. —**ad·he′sive·ly,** *adv.* —**ad·he′sive·ness,** *n.*

ad hoc (ad′hok′) for or concerned with a particular purpose or case, without general application: *An ad hoc committee was appointed to discuss the problem. The decision was made ad hoc.* [< L *ad hoc* 'for this'.]

ad·hock·er·y (ad′hok′ə rē) *Slang.* the act or practice of making decisions, rules, etc. on an ad hoc basis, without considering wider applications or implications. Also, **ad hocery.**

ad ho·mi·nem (ad′ hom′ə nem) *Latin.* 1 appealing to personal prejudices, interests, etc. 2 attacking a person's character rather than replying to his arguments. [*literally,* to the man]

ad·i·a·bat·ic (ad′ē ə bat′ik) *adj. Physics.* of or involving expansion or contraction without gain or loss of heat: *the adiabatic expansion of air.* —**ad·i·a·bat·i·cal·ly,** *adv.*

a·dieu (ə dyü′ *or* ə dü′; *French,* ä dyœ′) *interj. or n.* **a·dieus** *or* **a·dieux** (ə dyüz′ *or* ə düz′). goodbye; farewell. [ME < OF *a dieu* to God]

ad in·fi·ni·tum (ad′ in′fə nī′təm) without limit; endlessly. [< L]

ad in·ter·im (ad′ in′tə rim) from or in the meantime; temporary. [< L]

a·di·os (ä′dē ōs′ *or* ad′ē ōs′) *interj., n.* —*interj.* goodbye. —*n.* a farewell. [< Sp. *a dios* to God]

ad·i·pose (ad′ə pōs′) *adj., n.* —*adj.* 1 of or having to do with animal fat; fatty: *adipose tissue.* 2 fat. —*n.* the fat found in fatty tissue. [< NL *adiposus* < L *adeps* fat] —**ad′i·pose·ness,** *n.*

ad·i·pos·i·ty (ad′ə pos′ə tē) *n.* 1 an adipose condition; fatness. 2 a tendency to become fat.

ad·it (ad′it) *n.* 1 an approach; entrance. 2 a nearly horizontal entrance to a mine. 3 admission; access. [< L *aditus* < *adire* approach < *ad-* to + *ire* go]

adj. 1 adjective; adjectival. 2 adjunct. 3 adjustment. 4 adjacent.

Adj. adjutant.

ad·ja·cen·cy (ə jā′sən sē) *n., pl.* -**cies.** nearness.

ad·ja·cent (ə jā′sənt) *adj.* lying near or close; adjoining: *The house adjacent to ours has been sold.* [ME < L *adjacens, -entis,* ppr. of *adjacere* < *ad-* near + *jacere* to lie. Doublet of EASE.] —**ad·ja′cent·ly,** *adv.*

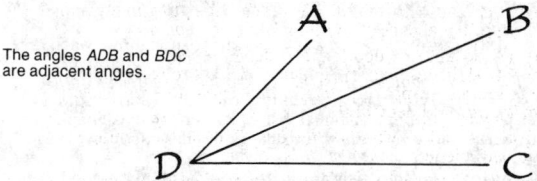

The angles *ADB* and *BDC*
are adjacent angles.

hat, āge, fär; let, ēqual, tèrm; it, īce
hot, ōpen, ôrder; oil, out; cup, pút, rüle,
əbove, takən, pencəl, lemən, circəs

ch, child; ng, long; sh, ship
th, thin; ŦH, then; zh, measure

adjacent angles *Mathematics.* two angles that have the same vertex and the same line for one of their sides.

ad·jec·ti·val (aj′ik tī′vəl *or* aj′ik tiv′əl) *adj., n.* —*adj.* **1** of or having to do with an adjective. The ending *-like* in *childlike* is an adjectival suffix. **2** used as an adjective. The form *toy* in *toy poodle* is an adjectival use of the noun *toy.* —*n.* a word or group of words used as an adjective. —**ad·jec·ti·val·ly,** *adv.*

ad·jec·tive (aj′ik tiv) *n., adj.* —*n.* a class of words that limit or add to the meaning of nouns. *Examples:* a *blue* shirt, a *powerful* car. —*adj.* **1** of an adjective. **2** used as an adjective. *Abbrev.:* adj. or a. [ME < LL *adjectivus* that which is added to < *adjicere,* *-jectum* put near < *ad-* to + *jacere* throw] —**ad′jec·tive·ly,** *adv.*

☛ *Usage.* **Adjectives. a. forms of adjectives.** Many English adjectives are made by the addition of a suffix to a noun or verb. Some of these suffixes such as *-some* (as in *winsome*) are no longer active. Among those still in use are: *-able* (*-ible*), as in *eatable, dirigible,* and *-ed* as in *sugared, four-footed, well-lighted; -escent,* as in *florescent; -ese,* as in *Burmese, journalese; -ful,* as in *playful, soulful; -ish,* as in *babyish, cattish, womanish; -less,* as in *harmless, fearless; -like,* as in *birdlike; -y,* as in *cranky, dreamy, corny.* **b. position of adjectives.** According to its use in a sentence, an adjective is attributive, appositive, or predicative. In English, **attributive adjectives** ordinarily stand immediately before the word they modify, as in *the tiny brook, horseless carriages;* but in certain phrases attributive adjectives may come after the noun: *the day following, his lady fair,* etc. **Appositive adjectives** follow the word they describe, and they are placed between commas: *The boy, weary and discouraged, went to sleep.* **Predicate adjectives** are used with some form of the verb *be* or some other linking verb (*taste, feel, turn,* etc.): *The day is warm. The train was crowded. That pie smells good. For a while I felt bad. How tall you have grown!* **c. comparison of adjectives.** Degrees of the quality named by an adjective are shown by adding *-er* or *est* to the adjective or by placing *more* or *most* before it: *warm, warmer, warmest; learned, more learned, most learned. More* and *most* are used with most adjectives of two syllables and all adjectives of three syllables or more.

adj. adjectival.

ad·join (ə join′) *v.* **1** be next to; be in contact with: *Canada adjoins the United States.* **2** be next to or close to each other; be in contact: *These two countries adjoin.* [ME < OF *ajoindre* < L *adjungere* < *ad-* to + *jungere* join]

ad·join·ing (ə joi′ning) *adj.* being next to or in contact with; bordering: *adjoining rooms.*

ad·journ (ə jèrn′) *v.* **1** suspend or break off for a time; especially, stop at the end of a session: *The judge adjourned the court for two hours. The meeting was adjourned at 10 o'clock.* **2** stop business or proceedings for a time: *The court adjourned for the weekend.* **3** *Informal.* go to another place: *After the meeting we adjourned to the cafeteria.* [ME < OF *ajorner* < *a-* for (< L *ad-*) + *jorn* day < LL *diurnum* < L *diurnum* (neut.) daily < *dies* day]

ad·journ·ment (ə jèrn′mənt) *n.* **1** an adjourning or being adjourned. **2** the time during which a court, legislature, etc. is adjourned.

Adjt. adjutant.

ad·judge (ə juj′) *v.* **-judged, -judg·ing. 1** decree or declare by law: *The accused woman was adjudged guilty.* **2** decide or settle by law; judge: *The boy's case was adjudged in the juvenile court.* **3** award or assign by law: *The property was adjudged to the rightful owner.* [ME < OF *ajugier* < L *adjudicare* < *ad-* to + *judicare* judge. Doublet of ADJUDICATE.] —**ad·judg′ment** or **ad·judge′ment,** *n.*

ad·ju·di·cate (ə jü′də kāt′) *v.* **-cat·ed, -cat·ing. 1** decide or settle by law. **2** act as judge; pass judgment. [< L *adjudicare.* Doublet of ADJUDGE.]

ad·ju·di·ca·tion (ə jü′də kā′shən) *n.* **1** the act or process of adjudicating. **2** a decision of a judge or court.

ad·ju·di·ca·tor (ə jü′də kā′tər) *n.* a judge.

ad·junct (aj′ungkt) *n.* **1** something added that is less important or not necessary, but helpful. **2** an assistant or associate of a more important person. **3** *Grammar.* a word or phrase that qualifies or modifies another word or phrase. Adjectives, adjectival phrases, adverbs, and adverbial phrases are adjuncts. [< L *adjunctus,* pp. of *adjungere* join to. See ADJOIN.]

ad·ju·ra·tion (aj′ə rā′shən) *n.* a solemn command; earnest appeal.

ad·jure (ə jür′) *v.* **-jured, -jur·ing. 1** command or charge (a person) on oath or under some penalty (to do something). **2** ask earnestly or solemnly: *I adjure you to speak the truth.* [ME < L *adjurare* < *ad-* to + *jurare* swear]

ad·just (ə just′) *v.* **1** fit or adapt (one thing to another): *to adjust a seat to the right height for a child.* **2** arrange or set (machinery or controls) to work as required: *to adjust a radio dial.* **3** arrange satisfactorily; set right; settle: *to adjust a difference of opinion.* **4** accommodate oneself; get used (to): *He soon adjusted to army life.* **5** decide the amount to be paid in settling (a bill, insurance claim, etc.). [< F *ajuster* < *a-* for (< L *ad-*) + *juste* right < L *justus*] —**ad·just′a·ble,** *adj.*

☛ *Syn.* **1. Adjust, adapt, accommodate** = suit one thing (or person) to another. **Adjust** emphasizes the idea of matching one thing to another: *I have to adjust my expenditure to my income.* **Adapt** emphasizes the idea of making minor changes in a thing (or person) to make it fit, suit, or fit into something: *I adapted the pattern to the material.* **Accommodate** emphasizes that the things to be fitted together are so different that one must be subordinated to the other: *We should not have to accommodate our beliefs to those of our employer.*

ad·just·er or **ad·jus·tor** (ə jus′tər) *n.* **1** a thing that adjusts something else. **2** a person who adjusts claims.

ad·just·ment (ə just′mənt) *n.* **1** the act or process of adjusting. **2** the state of being adjusted. **3** a means of adjusting, especially a mechanism or device to control machinery, etc.: *The radio has separate adjustments for volume and tone.* **4** a settlement of an insurance claim, etc.: *They accepted the adjustment.*

ad·ju·tan·cy (aj′ə tən sē) *n., pl.* **-cies.** the rank or position of an adjutant.

ad·ju·tant (aj′ə tənt) *n.* **1** *Military.* an officer who assists a commanding officer by sending out orders, writing letters, giving messages, etc. **2** helper; assistant. **3** adjutant stork. [< L *adjutans,* *-antis,* ppr. of *adjutare* assist, frequentative of *adjuvare* < *ad-* to + *juvare* help]

adjutant general *pl.* **adjutants general.** the adjutant of a division or a larger military unit.

adjutant stork either of two very large, carrion-eating storks (*Leptoptilos dubius* and *L. javanicus*) of India and SE Asia closely related to and resembling the African marabou, having grey and white plumage, a bare head and neck, and a large pouch of skin at the front of the neck. Also called **adjutant bird.** [named for their stiff-legged, military-style walk]

ad lib (ad′lib′) *v.* **-libbed, -lib·bing.** *Informal.* make up as one goes along; extemporize. [shortened form of *ad libitum*]

ad lib. ad libitum.

ad lib·i·tum (ad′lib′ə təm) **1** to any extent; without restriction. **2** *Music.* an instruction to change, omit, or expand a passage as the performer wishes. *Abbrev.:* ad lib. [< NL *ad libitum* at pleasure]

Adm. or **Adm** Admiral; Admiralty.

ad–man or **ad·man** (ad′man′) *n.* a person whose business is advertising.

ad·min·is·ter (ad min′is tər) *v.* **1** manage the affairs of (a business, a city, etc.); control on behalf of others; direct: *The Minister of Defence administers a department of the government. A housekeeper administers a household.* **2** give (*to*); apply; dispense: *A doctor administers medicine to sick people. Judges administer justice and punishment.* **3** offer or tender (an oath). **4** *Law.* settle or take charge of (an estate). **5** act as administrator or executor. **6** be helpful; add something; contribute: *to administer to a person's comfort or pleasure.* [ME < OF < L *administrare* < *ad-* to + *minister* servant]

ad·min·is·trate (ad min′ə strāt′) *v.* **-strat·ed, -strat·ing.** manage or direct the affairs of (a business, school, government, etc.)

ad·min·is·tra·tion (ad min′is trā′shən) *n.* **1** the managing of a business, office, etc.; management. **2** a group of persons in charge: *The university administration has improved the enrolment procedure.* **3 a** the management of public affairs by government officials. **b** the officials as a group; the government. **c** the period of office of these officials or of a government. **4** a giving out or dispensing (of medicine, justice, etc.): *The Red Cross handled the administration of aid to the refugees.* **5** *Law.* the management, settling, etc. (of an estate).

ad·min·is·tra·tive (ad min′is trə tiv *or* ad min′is trā′tiv) *adj.* having to do with administration; managing; executive. —**ad·min′is·tra·tive·ly,** *adv.*

ad·min·is·tra·tor (ad min′is trā′tər) *n.* **1** a person who administers. **2** *Law.* a person appointed by a court to take charge of or settle the estate of someone who has died without making a will

or appointing an executor, or at the executor's death. [< L]

ad·min·is·tra·trix (ad min′is trā′triks) *n.* a woman administrator.

ad·mi·ra·ble (ad′mə rə bəl) *adj.* 1 worth admiring. 2 excellent; very good. [< L *admirabilis*] —**ad′mi·ra·ble·ness,** *n.* —**ad′mi·ra·bly,** *adv.*

ad·mi·ral (ad′mə rəl) *n.* 1 the commander-in-chief of a fleet. 2 *Canadian Forces.* in Maritime Command the equivalent of a general. *Abbrev.:* Adm. or Adm See chart at **rank¹.** 3 a naval officer of similar rank in other countries. 4 any naval officer ranking above a commodore (or, in the U.S., above a captain). 5 *Cdn. Historical.* the leader of a fishing fleet in Newfoundland. 6 any of various brightly colored butterflies (subfamily Nymphalinae), such as the **red admiral** or the **white admiral.** [earlier *amiral* < OF < Arabic *amir* chief. Related to AMIR.]

admiral of the fleet the officer of the highest rank in the navies of certain countries, ranking above an admiral.

ad·mi·ral·ty (ad′mə rəl tē) *n., pl.* **-ties.** 1 a law or court dealing with affairs of the sea and ships. 2 **the Admiralty,** in the United Kingdom, a department of the Ministry of Defence responsible for naval affairs. 3 the office or authority of an admiral.

ad·mi·ra·tion (ad′mə rā′shən) *n.* 1 a feeling of wonder, pleasure, and approval. 2 the act of regarding with delight (something fine or beautiful): *They paused in admiration of the beautiful view.* 3 a person or thing that is admired: *The well-dressed woman was the admiration of everyone at the party.* 4 wonder.

ad·mire (ad mīr′) *v.* **-mired, -mir·ing.** 1 regard with wonder, approval, and delight: *to admire a brave deed. They stood for a while, admiring the view.* 2 think highly of; esteem: *I admire her very much.* 3 express admiration for: *He was so anxious to please that he enthusiastically admired every piece of furniture in the room.* [< L *admirari* < *ad-* at + *mirari* wonder < *mirus* wonderful]

ad·mir·er (ad mīr′ər) *n.* 1 a person who admires. 2 a person in love with or fond of another; suitor.

ad·mir·ing (ad mīr′ing) *adj.* showing or feeling admiration: *an admiring glance. He was surrounded by a group of admiring friends.* —**ad·mir′ing·ly,** *adv.*

ad·mis·si·bil·i·ty (ad mis′ə bil′ə tē) *n.* the quality or state of being admissible.

ad·mis·si·ble (ad mis′ə bəl) *adj.* 1 that can be permitted; allowable. 2 *Law.* that can be considered as evidence or proof. 3 having the right to enter or use (a position, occupation, group, place, etc.). —**ad·mis′si·ble·ness,** *n.* —**ad·mis′si·bly,** *adv.*

ad·mis·sion (ad mish′ən) *n.* 1 the act of allowing (a person, animal, etc.) to enter; entrance: *admission of aliens into a country.* 2 the power or right to enter or use an office, place, etc. 3 the price paid for the right to enter. 4 acceptance into an office or position. 5 an acknowledging: *His admission that he was to blame kept the others from being punished.* 6 an accepting as true or valid. 7 the fact or point acknowledged; something accepted as true or valid. [< L *admissio, -onis* < *admittere.* See ADMIT.]

ad·mit (ad mit′) *v.* **-mit·ted, -mit·ting.** 1 say that (an undesirable or damaging fact, etc.) is true or valid; acknowledge, often unwillingly or hesitantly: *He admitted that he had lied. She admitted her mistake.* 2 accept as true or valid: *to admit a hypothesis.* 3 allow to enter or use; let in: *The head waiter refused to admit him without a tie.* 4 give the right to enter to: *This ticket admits one person.* 5 allow; leave room for; permit (*usually used with* **of**): *His argument admits of no reply.* 6 give access or entry to: *The new window admits more light. The harbor admits three ships at one time.* 7 allow to attain (*to* a position, privilege, etc.): *She was admitted to the bar last year.* [ME < L *admittere* < *ad-* to + *mittere* let go]
☛ *Syn.* 1. **Admit, acknowledge, confess** = disclose or own that something is true. **Admit** = own or grant the existence or truth of something, usually after giving in to outside forces or the dictates of one's own conscience or judgment: *I admit that he is right.* **Acknowledge** = bring out into the open one's knowledge of the existence or truth of something, sometimes reluctantly: *They have now acknowledged defeat.* **Confess** =admit something unfavorable or criminal about oneself: *I confess I am a coward.*
☛ *Usage.* **Admit** is followed by *to* or *into* when it means "give the right to enter or allow to enter": *Fifty cents will admit you to the game. The butler would not admit him into the house.* **Admit** is followed by *of* when it means "leave room for": *His conduct admits of no complaint.*

ad·mit·tance (ad mit′əns) *n.* 1 a right to enter; permission to enter. 2 the act of admitting. 3 actual entrance.
☛ *Syn.* 1. See note at **admission.**

ad·mit·ted·ly (ad mit′id lē) *adv.* without denial; by general consent.

ad·mix (ad miks′) *v.* add in mixing; mix in.

ad·mix·ture (ad miks′chər) *n.* 1 mixture. 2 anything added in

mixing. [< L *admixtus,* pp. of *admiscere* < *ad-* in addition + *miscere* mix]

ad·mon·ish (ad mon′ish) *v.* 1 advise against something; warn: *The policeman admonished him for driving too fast.* 2 reprove gently: *The teacher admonished the student for his careless work.* 3 urge strongly; advise. 4 recall to a duty overlooked or forgotten; remind. [< *admonition*] —**ad·mon′ish·er,** *n.* —**ad·mon′ish·ment,** *n.*
☛ *Usage.* **Admonish.** *Of,* not *against,* is used after this rather formal synonym for *warn: John admonished them of the impending peril.*

ad·mo·ni·tion (ad′mə nish′ən) *n.* an act of admonishing; advice concerning the faults a person has shown or may show. [ME < OF < L *admonitio, -onis* < *ad-* to + *monere* warn]

ad·mon·i·to·ry (ad mon′ə tô′rē) *adj.* admonishing; warning.

ad nau·se·am (ad′nos′ē am *or* ad′nôs′ē am, ad′noz′ē am *or* ad′nôz′ē am) to a disgusting or sickening degree or extent. [< L *literally;* to (the point of) nausea]

a·do (ə dü′) *n.* bother, fuss, or trouble: *Without more ado, he started in on the cleaning.* [ME *at do* to do]
☛ *Syn.* See note at **stir.**

a·do·be (ə dō′bē) *n.* 1 sun-dried clay or mud. 2 a brick or bricklike piece of such material, used in building. 3 a building made of such bricks or material. 4 (*adj.*) built or made of such bricks or material: *Adobe houses are common in Mexico and the southwestern United States.* [< Sp. *adobe* < Arabic *at-tub* the brick]

ad·o·les·cence (ad′ə les′əns) *n.* 1 the period of physical and psychological growth between childhood and maturity. 2 the state of being adolescent.

ad·o·les·cent (ad′ə les′ənt) *n., adj.* —*n.* a person in the state of growth between childhood and maturity. —*adj.* 1 of, having to do with, or being in adolescence. 2 characteristic of an adolescent, especially with reference to immature behavior by an adult. [ME < OF < L *adolescens, -entis,* ppr. of *adolescere* < *ad-* to + *olescere* grow up. Related to ADULT.]

A·don·is (ə don′is *or* ə dō′nis) *n.* 1 *Roman and Greek mythology.* a handsome young man who was loved by Venus. 2 any very handsome young man.

a·dopt (ə dopt′) *v.* 1 take or use as one's own by choice: *to adopt a new technique. I liked your idea and adopted it.* 2 accept formally: *The club adopted the motion by a vote of 20 to 5.* 3 legally take (a child of other parents) and bring up as one's own. [< L *adoptare* < *ad-* to + *optare* choose] —**a·dopt′a·ble,** *adj.* —**a·dopt′er,** *n.*

a·dop·tion (ə dop′shən) *n.* the act of adopting or the state of being adopted: *the adoption of a new text for a course, the adoption of a child.*

a·dop·tive (ə dop′tiv) *adj.* 1 tending to adopt. 2 related by adoption: *adoptive parents.* —**a·dop′tive·ly,** *adv.*

a·dor·a·ble (ə dôr′ə bəl) *adj.* 1 worthy of adoration. 2 *Informal.* lovely; delightful. —**a·dor′a·bly,** *adv.*
☛ *Usage.* See note at **adore.**

ad·o·ra·tion (ad′ə rā′shən) *n.* 1 worship. 2 highest respect; devoted love.

a·dore (ə dôr′) *v.* **a·dored, a·dor·ing.** 1 respect very highly; love deeply. 2 *Informal.* like very much. 3 worship. [ME < OF < L *adorare* < *ad-* to + *orare* pray] —**a·dor′ing·ly,** *adv.*
☛ *Usage.* **Adore, adorable** are often used in informal speech to express general and undiscriminating approval: *I adore hamburgers. What an adorable hat she is wearing!*

a·dor·er (ə dôr′ər) *n.* 1 a devoted admirer; lover. 2 worshipper.

a·dorn (ə dôrn′) *v.* 1 add beauty to; make greater the splendor or honor of; add distinction to. 2 put ornaments on; decorate. [ME < OF < L *adornare* < *ad-* to + *ornare* fit out] —**a·dorn′er,** *n.*
☛ *Syn.* 2. See note at **decorate.**

a·dorn·ment (ə dôrn′mənt) *n.* 1 something that adds beauty; ornament; decoration. 2 the act of adorning or the state of being adorned.

a·down (ə doun′) *adv. or prep. Poetic.* down.

ad·re·nal (ə drē′nəl) *adj., n.* —*adj.* 1 near or on the kidney. 2 of or from the adrenal glands. —*n.* adrenal gland. [< L *ad-* near + *renes* kidneys]

adrenal gland either of the two ductless glands situated one on top of each kidney. The inner part of the gland, called the medulla, is controlled by the nervous system and produces adrenalin, the outer layer, called the cortex, is controlled by the pituitary gland and produces several hormones necessary to life. See **kidney** for picture.

ad·ren·al·in (ə dren′əl in) *n.* 1 a hormone secreted by the adrenal glands. 2 **Adrenalin,** *Trademark.* a white crystalline drug prepared from this hormone, used to stimulate the heart and stop bleeding. Adrenalin is obtained from the adrenal glands of animals.

ad·ren·al·ine (ə dren′əl in *or* ə dren′əl ēn′) *n.* adrenalin (def. 1).

a·drift (ə drift′) *adv. or adj.* (*never used before a noun*) 1 being

carried along by the current, without having control: *Having lost the paddle, we were adrift on the lake.* **2** without guidance, security, or purpose: *The team was adrift for three weeks while the coach was sick.*

a·droit (ə droit′) *adj.* **1** expert in the use of the hands; skilful. **2** clever with the mind; resourceful: *A good teacher is adroit in asking questions.* [< F *adroit* < *à droit* rightly < L *ad* to, *directus* straight] **—a·droit′ly,** *adv.* **—a·droit′ness,** *n.*
☛ *Syn.* See note at **dexterous.**

ad·sorb (ad zôrb′ *or* ad sôrb′) *v.* **1** cause (a gas, liquid, or dissolved substance) to adhere in a very thin layer of molecules to the surface of a solid. Water can be purified by passing through a charcoal filter because molecules of substance dissolved in the water are adsorbed on the charcoal particles. **2** become adsorbed. [< L *ad-* to + *sorbere* suck in]

ad·sorp·tion (ad zôrp′shən *or* ad sôrp′shən) *n.* the adhesion of a very thin layer of molecules of a liquid, gas, or dissolved substance to the surface of a solid with which it is in contact; adsorbing or being adsorbed.

ad·sorp·tive (ad zôrp′tiv *or* ad sôrp′tiv) *adj.* having to do with adsorption.

ADT *or* **A.D.T.** Atlantic Daylight Time.

ad·u·late (aj′ə lāt′) *v.* **-lat·ed, -lat·ing.** praise too much; flatter slavishly. [< L *adulari*] **—ad′u·la′tor,** *n.*

ad·u·la·tion (aj′ə lā′shən) *n.* too much praise; slavish flattery.

ad·u·la·to·ry (aj′ə lə tô′rē) *adj.* praising too much; slavishly flattering.

a·dult (ə dult′ *or* ad′ult) *adj., n.* **—adj. 1** fully developed and mature; full-grown; grown-up: *the adult population. An adult frog looks very different from a tadpole.* **2** of, intended for, or appealing to grown-up people: *adult education.* **3** appealing to sexual desires or interests: *adult movies, adult bookstores.* **4** Usually, **Adult,** of motion pictures, rated as recommended entertainment for adult people.
—n. 1 a grown-up person. **2** a person who has reached an age of legal responsibility: *In some provinces, one is an adult at 18.* **3** a full-grown animal or plant. [< L *adultus,* pp. of *adolescere.* See ADOLESCENT.] **—a·dult′ness,** *n.*
☛ *Pronun.* **Adult** is pronounced (ə dult′ *or* (ad′ult), the choice depending generally on which best fits the rhythm.

a·dul·ter·ant (ə dul′tər ənt) *n., adj.* **—n.** a substance used in adulterating. **—adj.** adulterating.

a·dul·ter·ate (ə dul′tər āt′) *v.* **-at·ed, -at·ing.** make lower in quality by adding inferior or impure materials: *to adulterate milk with water.* [< L *adulterare,* ult. < *ad-* to + *alter* other, different]

a·dul·ter·a·tion (ə dul′tər ā′shən) *n.* **1** the act of adulterating. **2** an adulterated substance; a product that has been adulterated.

a·dul·ter·er (ə dul′tər ər) *n.* a person, especially a man, guilty of adultery.

a·dul·ter·ess (ə dul′tər is *or* ə dul′tris) *n.* a woman guilty of adultery.

a·dul·ter·ous (ə dul′tər əs *or* ə dul′trəs) *adj.* having to do with, characterized by, or committing adultery: *an adulterous act.*
—a·dul′ter·ous·ly, *adv.*

a·dul·ter·y (ə dul′tər ē *or* ə dul′trē) *n., pl.* **-ter·ies.** sexual unfaithfulness of a husband or wife. [< L *adulterium*]

a·dult·hood (ə dult′hůd *or* ad′ult hůd′) *n.* the state or condition of being an adult.

ad·um·brate (ad um′brāt′ *or* ad′əm brāt′) *v.* **-brat·ed, -brat·ing. 1** indicate faintly; outline. **2** foreshadow. **3** overshadow; obscure. [< L *adumbrare* overshadow < *ad-* + *umbra* shade]
—ad′um·bra′tion, *n.*

adv. 1 adverb; adverbial. **2** advertisement. **3** advocate.

ad val. ad valorem.

ad va·lo·rem (ad′və lô′rəm) of merchandise, in proportion to the value: *an ad valorem tax.* *Abbrev.*: ad val. [< Med.L]

ad·vance (ad vans′) *v.* **-vanced, -vanc·ing;** *n.* **—v. 1** move forward; go forward: *The troops advanced.* **2** bring forward: *The troops were advanced.* **3** make progress; improve: *We advance in knowledge.* **4** help forward; further: *to advance the cause of peace.* **5** put forward; suggest: *He advanced a new idea to help solve the city's transportation problems.* **6** raise to a higher rank; promote: *to advance him from lieutenant to captain.* **7** rise in rank; be promoted: *to advance in one's profession.* **8** raise (prices or value): *to advance the price of milk.* **9** rise in price or value: *The stock advanced three points.* **10** make earlier; hasten: *to advance the time of the meeting.* **11** move the hands (of a clock or watch) forward: *In summer, the clocks are advanced one hour.* **12** in internal-combustion engines, cause the sparking action to take place earlier in the cycle. **13** supply beforehand: *to advance a salesman funds for expenses.* **14** lend (money), especially on security: *to advance a loan.* **15** put forward; offer or suggest: *to advance an opinion.*
—n. 1 a movement forward: *The army's advance was very slow.*

hat, āge, fär; let, ēqual, tèrm; it, īce
hot, ōpen, ôrder; oil, out; cup, pút, rüle,
ə̇bove, takən, pencəl, lemən, circəs
ch, child; ng, long; sh, ship
th, thin; ᴛʜ, then; zh, measure

2 the distance covered in such a movement. **3** (*adj.*) going before: *the advance guard.* **4** a command, signal, etc. to move forward. **5** a step forward; progress. **6** a rise in price or value. **7** the furnishing of money or goods before they are due or as a loan. **8** the money or goods furnished. **9** (*adj.*) made or provided ahead of time: *Customers were sent advance notice of the price increase.*
10 advances, *pl.* personal approaches toward another or others to settle a difference, to make an acquaintance, etc.
in advance, a in front; ahead. **b** ahead of time.
[ME < OF *avancier* < VL *abantiare* < LL *abante* < *ab* from + *ante* before]
☛ *Syn. v.* **1. Advance, proceed** = move forward. **Advance** means move forward toward a definite end or destination: *In two plays the team advanced to the one-yard line.* **Proceed** means move forward toward a goal, often after a break, interruption, or delay: *If we get the money to finish the hospital, we can proceed with construction.*

ad·vanced (ad vanst′) *adj.* **1** in front of others; forward. **2** ahead of most others in progress, ideas, etc.: *The advanced class has studied history for three years.* **3** far along in life; very old: *He lived to the advanced age of ninety years.* **4** increased: *advanced prices.* **5** ahead of the times; progressive; unconventional: *advanced ideas on social welfare.*

ad·vance·ment (ad vans′mənt) *n.* **1** a movement forward; advance. **2** progress; improvement. **3** promotion.

advance poll *Cdn.* in a general election: **1** an arrangement whereby persons expecting to be absent from their home riding on election day may cast their votes on an earlier date. **2** the number of votes cast in such a poll.

ad·van·tage (ad van′tij) *n., v.* **-taged, -tag·ing. —n. 1** a favorable condition, circumstance, or opportunity; benefit or profit: *Good health is always a great advantage. It would be to your advantage if you learned a second language.* **2** a better or superior position: *He had an advantage over his opponent in that he had more experience. She had the advantage of us because we had never been there before.* **3** *Tennis.* the first point scored after deuce.
have the advantage of (someone), know or recognize someone to whom one is not known: *You have the advantage of me; I'm afraid I don't know you.*
take advantage of, a make good use of for oneself: *She took advantage of the hubbub to slip out of the room.* **b** impose upon (a person or a person's good nature, innocence, ignorance, etc.); abuse.
to advantage, so as to produce a good effect or show the merits of: *a painting displayed to advantage.*
—v. give an advantage to; help; benefit. [ME < OF *avantage* < *avant* before < LL *abante*. See ADVANCE.]
☛ *Syn. n.* **4. Advantage, benefit, profit** = gain of some kind. **Advantage** applies to a gain resulting from a position of superiority, of any kind, over others: *The boy who can think for himself has an advantage when he begins work.* **Benefit** applies to gain in personal or social improvement: *His summer in Mexico was a benefit to him.* **Profit** applies especially to material gain, but also to gain in anything valuable, such as knowledge: *There is profit even in mistakes.*

ad·van·ta·geous (ad′vən tā′jəs) *adj.* giving advantage; favorable; helpful; profitable: *This advantageous position commands three roads.* **—ad′van·ta′geous·ly,** *adv.*
—ad′van·ta′geous·ness, *n.*

ad·vec·tion (ad vek′shən) *n.* the transference of heat, cold, or other property of air by the horizontal movement of a mass of air. [< L *advectio, -onis* a conveying < *advehere* carry to < *ad-* to + *vehere* carry] **—ad·vec′tion·al,** *adj.*

ad·vec·tive (ad vek′tiv) *adj.* of or having to do with advection.

ad·vent (ad′vent) *n.* **1** a coming; arrival: *the advent of spring.* **2 Advent, a** the birth of Christ. **b** the season of devotion including the four Sundays before Christmas. **3 Second Advent,** the coming of Christ at the Last Judgment. [< L *adventus* < *advenire* arrive < *ad-* to + *venire* come]

Ad·vent·ist (ad′ven tist *or* ad ven′tist) *n.* a member of a Christian denomination that believes that the second coming of Christ is near at hand.

ad·ven·ti·tious (ad′ven tish′əs) *adj.* **1** coming from outside; additional; accidental: *The romantic life of the author gives his book an adventitious interest.* **2** *Biology.* appearing in an unusual position or place: *Adventitious roots sometimes grow from leaves.* [< L *adventicius*] **—ad′ven·ti′tious·ly,** *adv.* **—ad′ven·ti′tious·ness,** *n.*

ad·ven·tive (ad ven′tiv) *adj. Biology.* introduced into a new environment; not native, though growing with cultivation.

Advent Sunday the first of the four Sundays in Advent.

ad·ven·ture (ad ven'chər) *n., v.* **-tured, -tur·ing.** —*n.* **1** a bold and difficult undertaking involving unknown risks and danger: *He had had many adventures in his career as a detective.* **2** the seeking or encountering of excitement and unknown risks or danger: *the spirit of adventure, yearning after adventure.* **3** an unusual or exciting experience: *It was an adventure to be entirely on his own in a strange city.* **4** *Archaic.* venture.
—*v.* **1** take part in daring or exciting undertakings: *a summer of adventuring in the wilderness.* **2** dare to do, go, etc.: venture: *to adventure upon an unknown shore.* [ME < OF *aventure* < L *adventura* (*res*) (thing) about to happen < *advenire* arrive. See ADVENT.]

ad·ven·tur·er (ad ven'chər ər) *n.* **1** a person who seeks or has adventures. **2** a soldier ready to serve in any army that will hire him; a mercenary. **3** a person who lives by his wits; a person who schemes to get money, social position, etc. **4** speculator.

ad·ven·ture·some (ad ven'chər səm) *adj.* bold and daring; adventurous.

ad·ven·tur·ess (ad ven'chər is) *n.* a woman who is an adventurer, especially one who schemes to get money, social position, etc.

ad·ven·tur·ism (ad ven'chər iz'əm) *n.* the attempting of projects without sufficient forethought or preparation; imprudence.

ad·ven·tur·ist (ad ven'chər ist') *n., adj.* —*n.* a person who attempts a project or undertakes a program without sufficient forethought. —*adj.* of or having to do with adventurists or adventurism.

ad·ven·tur·ous (ad ven'chər əs) *adj.* **1** fond of adventures; ready to take risks; daring: *a bold, adventurous explorer.* **2** full of risk; dangerous: *An expedition to the North Pole is an adventurous undertaking.* —**ad·ven'tur·ous·ly,** *adv.* —**ad·ven'tur·ous·ness,** *n.*

ad·verb (ad'vèrb) *n.* a word that extends or limits the meaning of verbs but is also used to qualify adjectives or other adverbs, especially in place, time, manner, or degree: *Soon, here, very, gladly,* and *not* are adverbs. *Abbrev.*: adv. [< L *adverbium* < *ad-* to + *verbum* verb]
☛ *Usage.* **Adverb. a. forms of adverbs.** Most adverbs are formed from adjectives or participles plus the ending -*ly*: *He rowed badly. She was deservedly popular. Surely you hear that.* There are a number of adverbs with the same forms as adjectives. Some of these are: *cheap, close, deep, even, first, high, loud, much, near, right, slow, smooth, tight, well, wrong.* Most of these adverbs have forms in -*ly* as well so that we can write: *He sang loud. He sang loudly.* The -*ly* forms are more common in formal English and the shorter forms in informal speech and writing. **b. comparison of adverbs.** Degrees of the condition or manner indicated by an adverb are shown by adding -*er*, -*est*, or by placing *more, most* before it: *hard, harder, hardest; slow, slower, slowest;* or *slowly, more slowly, most slowly. More* and *most* are used with most adverbs of more than one syllable.

ad·ver·bi·al (ad vèr'bē əl) *adj., n.* —*adj.* **1** of an adverb. **2** used as an adverb: *The form home in* I'm going home *is an adverbial use of the noun* home. —*n.* a word or group of words used as an adverb. —**ad·ver'bi·al·ly,** *adv.*

ad·ver·sar·y (ad'vər ser'ē) *n., pl.* **-sar·ies. 1** a person opposing or resisting another person; enemy. **2** a person or group on the other side in a contest. [< L *adversarius*]
☛ *Syn.* **2.** See note at **opponent.**

ad·ver·sa·tive (ad vèr'sə tiv) *adj., n. Grammar.* —*adj.* expressing contrast or opposition. *But* and *yet* are adversative conjunctions. —*n.* a word expressing contrast or opposition.

ad·verse (ad'vèrs *or* ad vèrs') *adj.* **1** unfavorable: *adverse criticism.* **2** harmful: *adverse influences. The climate had an adverse effect on his health.* **3** acting in a contrary direction; opposing: *Adverse winds hindered the ship.* [< L *adversus* over against, pp. of *advertere.* See ADVERT.] —**ad·verse'ly,** *adv.* —**ad·verse'ness,** *n.*
☛ *Pronun.* The stress is usually on the first syllable when the word precedes a noun (*ad'verse criticism*) and on the last syllable when it forms part of the predicate (*The winds were adverse*).

ad·ver·si·ty (ad vèr'sə tē) *n., pl.* **-ties. 1** a condition of unhappiness, misfortune, or distress. **2** a stroke of misfortune; an unfavorable or harmful thing or event.
☛ *Syn.* **1.** See note at **misfortune.**

ad·vert¹ (ad vèrt') *v.* direct attention (*to*); refer (*to*): *The speaker adverted to the need for more parks.* [ME *advert* < OF *avertir* < L *advertere* < *ad-* to + *vertere* turn]

ad·vert² (ad'vèrt) *n. Esp.Brit. Informal.* advertisement.

ad·ver·tise (ad'vər tīz') *v.* **-tised, -tis·ing. 1** give public notice of in a newspaper, over the radio, etc.: *The meeting was well advertised in the newspaper.* **2** ask by public notice (*for*): *to advertise for a job.* **3** make generally known. **4** praise the good qualities of (a product, etc.) in order to promote sales: *Manufacturers advertise things that they wish to sell.* **5** issue

advertising: *It pays to advertise.* **6** call attention to (oneself). [ME < OF *avertiss-*, a stem of *avertir* < *adverterre.* See ADVERT.]

ad·ver·tise·ment (ad'vər tīz'mənt, ad vèr'tis mənt, *or* ad vèr'tiz mənt) *n.* a public notice or announcement, as in a newspaper or magazine, over the radio, or on television.
☛ *Usage.* See note at **ad.**

ad·ver·tis·er (ad'vər tīz'ər) *n.* one who advertises.

ad·ver·tis·ing (ad'vər tīz'ing) *n.* **1** the business of preparing, publishing, or circulating advertisements. **2** advertisements.

ad·vice (ad vīs') *n.* **1** an opinion about what should be done: *Take the doctor's advice.* **2** Often, **advices,** *pl.* news or information, especially of a formal or official nature. [ME < MF *advis*, var. of OF *avis* < L *ad-* + *visum* thing seen]

ad·vis·a·bil·i·ty (ad vīz'ə bil'ə tē) *n.* the quality of being advisable; propriety; expediency.

ad·vis·a·ble (ad vīz'ə bəl) *adj.* to be recommended; wise; sensible. —**ad·vis'a·bly,** *adv.*

ad·vise (ad vīz') *v.* **-vised, -vis·ing. 1** give advice to: *Advise him to be cautious.* **2** give advice: *I shall act as you advise.* **3** give notice; inform (*often used with* **of**): *We were advised of the dangers before we began our trip.* [ME < OF *aviser* < *avis* opinion. See ADVICE.]

ad·vised (ad vīzd') *adj.* planned; considered; thought-out.

ad·vis·ed·ly (ad vīz'id lē) *adv.* after careful consideration; deliberately.

ad·vise·ment (ad vīz'mənt) *n.* careful consideration: *The lawyer took our case under advisement and said he would give us an answer in two weeks.*

ad·vis·er *or* **ad·vi·sor** (ad vīz'ər) *n.* **1** a person who gives advice. **2** a person whose work is giving advice, especially a teacher or professor appointed to advise students.
☛ *Usage.* **Adviser** has been the more common spelling, but the -*or* form, because of its similarity to *advisory,* is being increasingly used.

ad·vi·so·ry (ad vīz'ə rē) *adj., n.* —*adj.* **1** having power to advise: *an advisory committee.* **2** containing advice. —*n.* a bulletin or report containing advice or advance information: *a weather advisory.* —**ad·vi'so·ri·ly,** *adv.*

advl. adverbial.

ad·vo·ca·cy (ad'və kə sē) *n.* a statement in favor; a public recommendation; support: *The premier's advocacy got votes for the plan.*

ad·vo·cate (*v.* ad'və kāt'; *n.* ad'və kit *or* ad'və kāt') *v.* **-cat·ed, -cat·ing;** *n.* —*v.* speak in favor of; recommend publicly: *He advocates increased spending for public transportation.* —*n.* **1** a person who pleads or argues for: *an advocate of peace.* **2** a lawyer who pleads or argues in a law court; barrister. [ME *avocat* < OF < L *advocare* < *ad-* to + *vocare* call] —**ad'vo·ca'tion,** *n.* —**ad'vo·ca'tor,** *n.*

advt. advertisement.

Adzes.
A man using an adze to shape a log

adze (adz) *n.* a tool for shaping wood, resembling an axe, but having a curved blade with its cutting edge set across the end of the handle. Sometimes, **adz.** [OE *adesa*]

AEA *or* **A.E.A.** *Brit.* Atomic Energy Authority.

AEC *or* **A.E.C.** *U.S.* Atomic Energy Commission.

a·e·des (ā ē'dēz) *n., pl.* **-des.** any of a genus (*Aedes*) of chiefly tropical and subtropical mosquitoes, including vectors of disease, such as *A. aegypti,* which transmits yellow fever and dengue. Also, **aëdes.** [NL < Gk. *aēdēs* unpleasant < *a-* not + Gk. *hēdos* pleasant. 20c. Akin to HEDONISM.]

ae·dile (ē'dīl) *n.* in ancient Rome, an official in charge of public buildings, games, streets, and markets. Also, **edile.** [< L *aedilis* < *aedes* building]

ae·gis (ē'jis) *n.* **1** *Greek mythology.* a shield or breastplate originally used by Zeus and later by his daughter Athena. **2** protection: *under the aegis of the law. He sought the aegis of the ambassador.* **3** sponsorship; auspices: *under the aegis of the ministry of tourism.* [< L < Gk. *aigis*]

ae·gro·tat (ī'grō tat') *n.* **1** a certificate stating that a student is unable to write an examination because of illness. **2** a pass degree awarded on the basis of such a certificate. [< L *aegrotat* he is sick]

Ae·ne·as (i nē'əs) *n. Greek and Roman mythology.* a Trojan

hero, son of Anchises (a prince of Troy) and Venus. He escaped from burning Troy, carrying his father and leading his little son. After years of wandering he reached Italy, where, it is said, his descendants founded Rome.

Ae·ne·id (i nē′id) *n.* a Latin epic poem by Virgil, describing the wanderings of Aeneas.

Ae·o·li·an[1] (ē ō′lē ən) *adj.* **1** of Aeolus. **2 aeolian,** of, produced by, or carried by the winds. Also, **Eolian.**

Ae·o·li·an[2] (ē ō′lē ən) *n., adj.* —*n.* **1** a member of an ancient Greek people who lived in Boeotia, Thessaly, and NW Asia Minor. **2** Aeolic. —*adj.* of or having to do with the Aeolians or their dialect (Aeolic). Also, **Eolian.**

aeolian harp a box with six or more tuned strings fitted across openings in the top, usually placed in a window. Air currents vibrate the strings, causing them to produce musical sounds.

Ae·o·lic (ē ol′ik or e ō′lik) *n., adj.* —*n.* a dialect of ancient Greek, spoken mainly in Boeotia, Thessaly, and NW Asia Minor. —*adj.* Aeolian. Also, **Eolic.**

Ae·o·lus (ē′ə ləs) *n. Greek mythology.* the god of the winds.

ae·on (ē′ən or ē′on) See **eon.**

aer·ate (er′āt or ā′ər āt′) *v.* **-at·ed, -at·ing. 1** expose to air. **2** expose to and mix with air. Water in some reservoirs is aerated by being tossed high into the air in a fine spray. **3** charge with a gas. Soda water is water that has been aerated with carbon dioxide. **4** expose to chemical action with oxygen. Blood is aerated in the lungs. [< L < Gk. *aēr* air] —**aer·a′tion,** *n.* —**aer′a·tor,** *n.*

aer·i·al (*adj.* er′ē əl *or* ā ēr′ē əl; *n.* er′ē əl) *adj.* **1** of, having to do with, or existing in the air: *aerial spirits.* **2** done or performed up in the air instead of on the ground: *swallows performing an aerial ballet.* **3** like air; thin, light, and insubstantial as air. **4** ideal; imaginary. **5** of, having to do with, by, or involving an aircraft: *aerial navigation, aerial warfare, aerial bombardment.* **6** taken from or designed to be used in an aircraft: *an aerial photograph.* **7** *Botany.* growing in the air instead of in soil or water: *aerial ferns.* —*n.* a radio or television antenna. [< L < Gk. *aerios* < *aēr* air] —**aer′i·al·ly,** *adv.*
☛ *Pronun.* **Aerial.** For the highly literary uses of the adjective (defs. 3 and 4), it is better to retain the pronunciation with four syllables, and in verse the four syllables are often useful to the metre. For the more common uses of the adjective and for the noun, the pronunciation with three syllables is established and natural: *aerial warfare, a radio aerial.*

aer·i·al·ist (er′ē əl ist) *n.* an acrobat who performs feats on a trapeze, a high wire, etc.

aer·ie (er′ē *or* ēr′ē) *n., pl.* **-ies.** *Esp.U.S.* eyrie.

aer·o (er′ō) *adj.* of or having to do with aircraft or aviation.

aero– *combining form.* **1** air, as in *aerospace, aerodynamics.* **2** gas, as in *aerosol.* **3** aircraft or aviation, as in *aeronautics.* [< Gk. *aēr* air]

aer·o·bat·ic (er′ō bat′ik) *adj.* of or having to do with aerobatics.

aer·o·bat·ics (er′ō bat′iks) *n.* the performance of tricks, stunts, etc. with an aircraft in flight. [< *aero-* + (*acro*)*batics*]

aer·obe (er′ōb) *n.* a micro-organism, such as a bacterium, that can live only in air containing oxygen.

aer·o·bic (er ō′bik *or* ā′ər ō′bik) *adj.* **1** living and growing only where there is oxygen. Some bacteria are aerobic. **2** having to do with or caused by aerobic bacteria. [ult. < Gk. *aēr* air + *bios* life]

aer·o·bi·ol·o·gist (er′ō bī ol′ə jist) *n.* a person trained in aerobiology, especially one whose work it is.

aer·o·bi·ol·o·gy (er′ō bī ol′ə jē) *n.* the branch of biology that studies how bacteria, viruses, etc. are borne through the air.

aer·o·drome (er′ə drōm′) *n. Brit.* an airfield or small airport.

aer·o·dy·nam·ic (er′ō dī nam′ik) *adj.* of or having to do with aerodynamics: *Airplanes are supported in the air by aerodynamic forces.*

aer·o·dy·nam·ics (er′ō dī nam′iks) *n.* the branch of physics that deals with the motion of air and other gases, and with the forces that act on bodies moving through the air.

aer·o·em·bo·lism (er′ō em′bə liz′əm) *n.* **1** an embolism produced by bubbles of air or other gases. **2** decompression sickness, especially when caused by a too sudden ascent to high altitudes, as in an unpressurized aircraft.

aer·o·gram (er′ə gram) *n.* air letter. Also, **aerogramme.**

aer·o·lite (er′ə līt′) *n.* meteorite. [< *aero-* + *-lite* < F < Gk. *lithos* stone]

aer·o·log·ic (er′ō loj′ik) *adj.* of or having to do with aerology.

aer·ol·o·gist (er ol′ə jist′) *n.* a person trained in aerology, especially one whose work it is.

aer·ol·o·gy (er ol′ə jē) *n.* the branch of meteorology that deals with the study of the upper atmosphere.

aer·o·me·chan·ic (er′ō mə kan′ik) *adj., n.* —*adj.* of or having

hat, āge, fär; let, ēqual, tèrm; it, īce
hot, ōpen, ôrder; oil, out; cup, put, rüle,
əbove, takən, pencəl, lemən, circəs

ch, child; ng, long; sh, ship
th, thin; ŦH, then; zh, measure

to do with aeromechanics. —*n.* a mechanic who works on aircraft.

aer·o·me·chan·ic·al (er′ō mə kan′ik əl) *adj.* aeromechanic.

aer·o·me·chan·ics (er′ō mə kan′iks) *n.* (*used with a singular verb*) the branch of physics that deals with air and other gases, both in motion and at rest. It includes aerodynamics and aerostatics.

aer·o·naut (er′ə not′ *or* -nôt′) *n.* **1** a pilot of an airship or balloon; balloonist. **2** a person who travels in an airship or balloon. [< F *aéronaute* < Gk. *aēr* air + *nautēs* sailor]

aer·o·nau·tic (er′ə not′ik *or* -nô′tik) *adj.* of aeronautics or aeronauts.

aer·o·nau·ti·cal (er′ə not′ə kəl *or* -nô′tə kəl) *adj.* aeronautic. —**aer′o·nau′ti·cal·ly,** *adv.*

aer·o·nau·tics (er′ə not′iks *or* -nô′tiks) *n.* the science or art of the design, manufacture, and operation of aircraft.

aer·o·pause (er′ə poz′ *or* -pôz′) *n.* **1** level above the earth's surface beyond which the atmosphere has no effect on flight. **2** the upper limit of manned airborne flight.

aer·o·pho·bi·a (er′ō fō′bē ə) *n.* an abnormal fear of air or other gases, especially of drafts.

aer·o·plane (er′ə plān′) *n. Esp.Brit.* airplane.
☛ *Usage.* See note at **airplane.**

aer·o·quay (er′ə kē) *n.* an airport building comprising ticket offices, shops, restaurants, etc. as well as docklike bays at which aircraft take on and let off passengers.

aer·o·sol (er′ə sol′) *n.* **1** a suspension of fine solid or liquid particles in a gas. Smoke and fog are aerosols. **2** (*adj.*) of or designating an apparatus for dispensing a substance such as paint, insecticide, or shaving cream, under pressure as a mist or foam. The apparatus consists of a small metal can containing the paint, etc. mixed with a liquified gas that is under pressure and acts as a propellant, shooting the substance out when the valve is opened. **3** (*adj.*) contained in such an apparatus: *aerosol shaving cream.* **4** an aerosol container together with its contents. [< *aero-* + *sol*, short for *solution*]

aer·o·space (er′ə spās′) *n.* **1** the earth's atmosphere and space beyond it, considered as a continuous region or field. **2** the branch of science that deals with the earth's atmosphere and outer space, especially in relation to space travel. **3** the industry of designing, building and operating spacecraft, missiles, etc. **4** (*adj.*) of or having to do with aerospace, space travel, or the designing, building, and operating of spacecraft, etc.: *aerospace technology.*

aer·o·stat (er′ə stat′) *n.* any lighter-than-air aircraft, such as a balloon or dirigible. [< *aero-* + Gk. *statos* standing]

aer·o·stat·ic (er′ō stat′ik) *adj.* **1** of or having to do with aerostatics. **2** of or having to do with an aerostat.

aer·o·stat·ics (er′ō stat′iks) *n.* (*used with a singular verb*) the branch of physics that deals with the equilibrium of air and other gases, and with the equilibrium of solid objects floating in air and other gases.

Aes·cu·la·pi·us (es′kyə lā′pē əs *or* es′kyə lä′pē əs) *n. Roman mythology.* the god of medicine and healing.

Ae·sir (ā′sər *or* ē′sər) *n.pl.* the chief Scandinavian gods, especially Odin, Thor, Balder, Loki, and Freya.

Ae·so·pi·an (ē sō′pē ən) *adj.* **1** of or having to do with Aesop (620?-560? B.C.), a Greek writer of fables. **2** of or suggestive of his writings.

aes·thete (es′thēt *or* es′thēt) *n.* **1** a person who is sensitive to beauty; lover of beauty. **2** a person who pretends to care a great deal about beauty; a person who gives too much attention to beauty. Also, **esthete.** [< Gk. *aisthētēs* one who perceives]

aes·thet·ic (ēs thet′ik *or* es thet′ik) *adj., n.* —*adj.* **1** of or having to do with the beautiful, as distinguished from the useful, scientific, etc.: *aesthetic principles.* **2** characterized by good taste, beauty, etc.; artistic: *the aesthetic value of a work.* **3** sensitive to beauty: *an aesthetic mind.* —*n.* a set of principles for the appreciation of beauty in art and nature: *following an outdated aesthetic.* Also, **esthetic.**

aes·thet·i·cal·ly (ēs thet′ik lē *or* es thet′ik lē) *adv.* **1** in an aesthetic manner. **2** according to aesthetics: *an aesthetically pleasing color combination.* Also, **esthetically.**

aes·thet·i·cism (ēs thet′ə siz′əm *or* es thet′ə siz′əm) *n.* **1** the belief in beauty as the basic standard of value in human life,

underlying all moral and other considerations. 2 great love for and sensitivity to beauty and the arts. Also, **estheticism**.

aes·thet·ics (ēs thet′iks *or* es thet′iks) *n.* the study of beauty in art and nature; philosophy of beauty; theory of the fine arts. Also, **esthetics**.

aes·ti·val (es tī′vəl *or* es′tə vəl) See **estival**.

aes·ti·vate (es′tə vāt′) See **estivate**.

aet. or **aetat.** of or at the age of (for L *aetas, aetatis* age).

ae·ther (ē′thər) See **ether** (defs. 2 and 3).

ae·the·re·al (i thēr′ē əl) See **ethereal**.

ae·ti·ol·o·gy (ē′tē ol′ə jē) See **etiology**.

af– *prefix.* to or toward; the form of **ad–** occurring before *f*, as in *affix.*

AF, A.F., or **a.f.** audio frequency.

A.F. or **AF** Anglo-French.

a·far (ə fär′) *adv.* far; far away; far off.

a·feard or **a·feared** (ə fērd′) *adj. Archaic or dialect.* frightened; afraid.

af·fa·bil·i·ty (af′ə bil′ə tē) *n.* the state or quality of being affable; a courteous, pleasant, and friendly manner.

af·fa·ble (af′ə bəl) *adj.* easy to talk to; courteous, pleasant, and friendly. [< F < L *affabilis* able to be spoken to < *affari* < *ad–* to + *fari* speak] —**af′fa·ble·ness,** *n.* —**af′fa·bly,** *adv.*

af·fair (ə fer′) *n.* 1 something done or to be done; matter; concern: *That's my affair.* 2 **affairs,** *pl.* matters of interest or concern, especially business, commercial, or public matters: *current affairs, affairs of state.* 3 an action, event, or procedure referred to in vague terms: *The party on Saturday night was a dull affair.* 4 an object or group of objects referred to in vague terms: *This machine is a complicated affair.* 5 a sexual relationship between two people not married to each other, especially one that lasts only a short while. [ME < OF *afaire < a faire* to do < L *ad* to + *facere* do]

affair of honor or **honour** a duel.

af·fect¹ (ə fekt′) *v.* 1 make something happen to; have an effect on; influence: *The small amount of rain last year affected the growth of crops.* 2 act on in a harmful way: *The disease so affected his mind that he lost his memory.* 3 touch the heart of; stir the emotions of; move: *The story of their plight so affected him that he immediately offered to help.* [< L *affectus,* pp. of *afficere;* ult. < *ad–* to + *facere* do]

af·fect² (ə fekt′) *v.* 1 pretend to have or feel: *He affected ignorance of the fight, but we knew that he had seen it.* 2 be fond of; like: *She affects old furniture.* 3 assume falsely or ostentatiously: *He affects a taste for abstract painting though he knows little about art.* [< MF < L *affectare* strive for; ult. < *ad–* to + *facere* do]
☛ *Syn.* 1. See note at **pretend.**
☛ *Usage.* See note at **effect.**

af·fec·ta·tion (af′ek tā′shən) *n.* 1 an artificial or unnatural way of behaving or talking: *His British accent is an affectation, for he has never lived outside Alberta.* 2 outward appearance; pretence: *an affectation of ignorance.*

af·fect·ed¹ (ə fek′tid) *adj.* 1 acted on; influenced. 2 influenced injuriously. 3 touched in the heart; moved in feeling.

af·fect·ed² (ə fek′tid) *adj.* 1 put on for effect; unnatural; artificial: *His affected manner changed as soon as the guests had gone.* 2 behaving, speaking, writing, etc. unnaturally for effect: *She is very affected.* —**af·fect′ed·ly,** *adv.*

af·fect·ing (ə fek′ting) *adj.* causing emotion; touching the heart or moving the feelings. —**af·fect′ing·ly,** *adv.*

af·fec·tion (ə fek′shən) *n.* 1 friendly feeling; a warm liking; fondness. 2 a feeling; inclination. 3 a disease or unhealthy condition. 4 *Archaic.* a disposition; tendency.
☛ *Syn.* 1. See note at **love.**

af·fec·tion·ate (ə fek′shən it) *adj.* loving; fond; tender; having or showing affection. —**af·fec′tion·ate·ly,** *adv.*

af·fec·tive (ə fek′tiv) *adj.* of the feelings; emotional. —**af·fec′tive·ly,** *adv.*

af·fer·ent (af′ər ənt) *adj.* of nerves, blood vessels, etc., carrying inward to a central organ or point. Compare **efferent.** [< L *afferens, -entis,* ppr. of *afferre < ad–* to + *ferre* bring]

af·fi·ance (ə fī′əns) *v.* -anced, -anc·ing; *n.* —*v.* promise in marriage; betroth. [ME < OF *afiancer* to promise < *afiance,* n., trust] —*n.* 1 the pledging of faith; betrothal. 2 trust; confidence. [ME < OF *afiance < afier* to trust < VL *affidare < ad–* to + *fidare* trust < L *fidus* faithful]

af·fi·anced (ə fī′ənst *or* af′ē änst′) *adj.* promised in marriage; engaged or betrothed.

af·fi·da·vit (af′ə dā′vit) *n.* a statement written down and sworn to be true. An affidavit is usually made before a notary public or a commissioner of oaths. [< Med.L *affidavit* he has stated on oath]

af·fil·i·ate (*v.* ə fil′ē āt′; *n.* ə fil′ē it *or* ə fil′ē āt′) *v.* -at·ed, -at·ing; *n.* —*v.* 1 connect in close association: *The two clubs did not have the same members, but they were affiliated with each other.* 2 associate oneself (*with*): *to affiliate with a political party.* 3 bring into relationship; adopt.
—*n.* 1 an organization or group associated with other similar bodies. 2 a person or organization that is affiliated. [< LL *affiliare* adopt < L *ad–* to + *filius* son]

af·fil·i·a·tion (ə fil′ē ā′shən) *n.* association; relation.

af·fin·i·ty (ə fin′ə tē) *n., pl.* -ties. 1 a natural attraction to a person or liking for a thing: *an affinity for dancing. They have a strong affinity for each other.* 2 *Chemistry.* an attraction or force between certain particles or substances that causes them to combine chemically. 3 a close relationship or connection, as between biological groups, languages, etc. 4 a similarity or resemblance based on relationship or connection. 5 relationship by marriage or adoption. Compare **consanguinity.** 6 a person to whom one is especially attracted. [ME < OF *af(f)inite* < L *affinitas < ad–* on + *finis* boundary]

af·firm (ə fèrm′) *v.* 1 declare to be true; say firmly; assert. 2 confirm; ratify: *The higher court affirmed the lower court's decision.* 3 *Law.* declare solemnly, but without taking an oath. [ME < OF < L *affirmare < ad–* to + *firmus* strong]

af·fir·ma·tion (af′ər mā′shən) *n.* 1 *Law.* a solemn declaration made without taking an oath: *If a person's religion forbids him to take an oath, he can make an affirmation.* 2 an assertion; positive statement. 3 an affirming; confirmation; ratification.

af·firm·a·tive (ə fèr′mə tiv) *adj., n.* —*adj.* stating that a fact is so; saying yes. —*n.* 1 a word or statement that gives assent or indicates agreement. 2 **the affirmative,** the side arguing in favor of a question being debated.
in the affirmative, with an affirmative answer; with a word or statement meaning yes: *Asked whether she would stand for election, she replied in the affirmative.* —**af·firm′a·tive·ly,** *adv.*

af·fix (*v.* ə fiks′; *n.* af′iks) *v., n.* —*v.* 1 make firm or fix (one thing to or on another). 2 add at the end. 3 make an impression of (a seal, etc.). 4 connect with; attach: *to affix blame.*
—*n.* 1 something affixed. 2 a prefix or a suffix. *Un–* and *-ly* are affixes. [< Med.L *affixare,* ult. < L *ad–* to + *figere* fix] —**af·fixer,** *n.*
☛ *Syn. v.* 1. See note at **attach.**

af·fla·tus (ə flā′təs) *n.* a divine inspiration. [< L *afflatus < afflare < ad–* on + *flare* blow]

af·flict (ə flikt′) *v.* cause pain to; trouble greatly; distress: *to be afflicted with troubles.* [< L *afflictus,* pp. of *affligere < ad–* upon + *fligere* dash]

af·flic·tion (ə flik′shən) *n.* 1 a state of pain, trouble, or distress. 2 a cause of pain, trouble, or distress.

af·flic·tive (ə flik′tiv) *adj.* causing misery or pain; distressing.

af·flu·ence (af′lü əns) *n.* 1 wealth; riches. 2 abundant supply; great abundance. [< F L *affluentia < affluere.* See AFFLUENT.]

af·flu·ent (af′lü ənt) *adj., n.* —*adj.* 1 very wealthy. 2 abundant; plentiful. —*n.* a stream flowing into a larger stream, lake, etc. [< L *affluens, -entis,* ppr. of *affluere < ad–* to + *fluere* flow] —**af′flu·ent·ly,** *adv.*

af·flux (af′luks) *n.* a flow toward a place. [< Med.L *affluxus < affluere.* See AFFLUENT.]

af·ford (ə fôrd′) *v.* 1 have or spare the money for: *We can't afford a new car.* 2 manage to give, spare, have, etc.: *A busy person cannot afford delay. Can you afford the time?* 3 be able without difficulty; have the means: *I can't afford to take the chance.* 4 furnish from natural resources; yield: *Some trees afford resin.* 5 yield or give as an effect or a result; provide: *Reading affords pleasure.* [OE *geforthian* further, accomplish]

af·ford·a·ble (ə fôr′də bəl) *adj.* 1 of a price, low enough to be acceptable to the consumer: *an affordable price for oil.* 2 of goods or services, having such a price: *affordable merchandise.*

af·for·est (ə fôr′ist) *v.* plant an area with trees.

af·for·est·a·tion (ə fôr′is tā′shən) *n.* the act or practice of afforesting.

af·fran·chise (ə fran′chīz′) *v.* -chised, -chis·ing. enfranchise.

af·fray (ə frā′) *n.* a noisy quarrel; a fight in public; a brawl. [ME < OF *affrei,* ult. < L *ex–* out of + Gmc. **fridhu* peace]

af·fri·cate (af′rə kit) *n. Phonetics.* a sound that begins with a stop and ends with a fricative. The *ch* in *chin* is an affricate: it starts with *t* and ends with *sh.* [< L *affricatus,* pp. of *affricare < ad–* against + *fricare* rub]

af·fright (ə frīt′) *Archaic. v., n.* —*v.* frighten; terrify. —*n.* fright; terror.

af·front (ə frunt′) *n., v.* —*n.* **1** a word or act that openly expresses disrespect. **2** a slight or injury to one's dignity. —*v.* **1** insult openly; offend purposely: *The boy affronted the teacher by making a face at her.* **2** meet face to face; confront. [ME < OF *afronter* < *a front* against the forehead < L *ad frontem*]
☛ *Syn. n.* **1.** See note at **insult.**

Af·ghan (af′gan *or* af′gən) *n., adj.* —*n.* **1** a native or inhabitant of Afghanistan, a country in SW Asia. **2** Afghan hound. **3 afghan,** a knitted or crocheted blanket or large shawl, usually having a pattern of squares or zigzag stripes.
—*adj.* of or having to do with Afghanistan or its people.

Afghan hound a breed of tall, swift dog having a thick coat of long, silky hair, a long, narrow head, and a thin tail: *Afghan hounds came originally from the Middle East, where they were usually trained as hunting dogs.*

af·ghan·i (af gan′ē) *n.* **1** the basic unit of money in Afghanistan, divided into 100 puls. See table at **money. 2** a coin worth one afghani.

a·fi·cio·na·do (ə fē′syə nä′dō; *Spanish* ä fē′thyō nä′гнō) *n., pl.* -**dos. 1** a person who takes a very great interest in bullfighting, but who is not himself a bullfighter. **2** a person who is very enthusiastic about something.

a·field (ə fēld′) *adv. or adj.* (*never precedes a noun*) **1** away from home; away. **2** out of the way; astray.

a·fire (ə fīr′) *adv. or adj.* (*never precedes a noun*) **1** on fire; ablaze: *The whole house was afire.* **2** in or into a state of great excitement or enthusiasm: *afire with patriotism.*

a·flame (ə flām′) *adv. or adj.* (*never precedes a noun*) **1** in flames; ablaze. **2** in or into a state of great excitement or enthusiasm: *aflame with curiosity.* **3** bright or glowing: *a garden aflame with color.*

AFL–CIO *U.S.* a labor organization made up of the American Federation of Labor and the Congress of Industrial Organizations.

a·float (ə flōt′) *adv. or adj.* (*never precedes a noun*) **1** floating. **2** on shipboard; at sea. **3** adrift. **4** flooded. **5** in circulation; current: *Rumors of a revolt were afloat.*

a·flut·ter (ə flut′ər) *adv. or adj.* (*never precedes a noun*) **1** fluttering. **2** excited; confused.

A.F.M. Air Force Medal.

a·foot (ə fut′) *adv. or adj.* (*never precedes a noun*) **1** on foot; walking. **2** going on; in progress: *Preparations for dinner were afoot in the kitchen.*

a·fore (ə fôr′) *adv., prep., or conj.* Archaic *or* dialect. before. [OE *onforan* (< *on foran* in front) and *ætforan* (< *æt* at + *foran* in front)]

a·fore·men·tioned (ə fôr′men′shənd) *adj.* spoken of before; mentioned above.

a·fore·said (ə fôr′sed′) *adj.* spoken of before.

a·fore·thought (ə fôr′thot′ *or* -thôt′) *adj.* thought of beforehand; deliberately planned.

a·fore·time (ə fôr′tīm′) *adv.* in time past.

a for·ti·o·ri (ā′fôr′tē ôr′ī, ā′fôr′tē ôr′ē, *or* a′fôr′tē ôr′ē) *Latin.* for a still stronger reason; all the more.

a·foul (ə foul′) *adv. or adj.* (*never precedes a noun*) in a tangle; in a collision; entangled.
run afoul of, get into difficulties with.

Afr. Africa; African.

a·fraid (ə frād′) *adj.* **1** feeling fear; frightened: *afraid of the dark.* **2** sorry (*used to express polite regret or to soften an abrupt or possibly unwelcome statement*): *I'm afraid we won't be able to come after all. I'm afraid I'll have to ask you to leave.* [originally pp. of archaic v. *affray* frighten]
☛ *Syn.* **Afraid, frightened, terrified** = feeling fear. **Afraid,** which is never used before the noun, means being in a mental state ruled by fear which may have either a real or an imagined cause and may last a long or a short time: *I am afraid of snakes.* **Frightened,** commonly used instead of *afraid* before the noun, particularly means "made afraid suddenly, often only momentarily, by a real and present cause": *The frightened child ran home.* **Terrified** means "suddenly filled with a very great and paralysing fear": *The terrified mother watched the dog attack her child.*

A·frame (ā′frām′) *n.* a building having a two-sided roof that slopes steeply almost to the ground, forming triangular, or A-shaped, front and rear walls.

af·reet (af′rēt *or* ə frēt′) *n. Arabic mythology.* a powerful evil demon or giant. [< Arabic *ifrīt*]

a·fresh (ə fresh′) *adv.* once more; again.

Af·ric (af′rik) *adj.* African.

Af·ri·can (af′rə kən) *adj., n.* —*adj.* **1** of or having to do with Africa or its inhabitants. **2** of or designating a major race of mankind that includes most of the peoples traditionally inhabiting Africa south of the Sahara, distinguished by a combination of

hat, āge, fär; let, ēqual, tèrm; it, īce
hot, ōpen, ôrder; oil, out; cup, put, rüle,
əbove, takən, pencəl, lemən, circəs
ch, child; ng, long; sh, ship
th, thin; ℔, then; zh, measure

biological characteristics, including very dark skin, curly or woolly hair, and a genetic resistance to such diseases as malaria. The blacks of North and South America and the West Indies belong to the African race. —*n.* **1** a native or inhabitant of Africa. **2** a person whose recent ancestors come from Africa. **3** a member of the African race.

Af·ri·can·ist (af′rə kən ist) *n.* **1** an expert in African art, history, culture, etc. **2** a person who supports African nationalism and African interests.

Af·ri·can·ize (af′rə kən īz′) *v.* **1** make African. **2** turn over (the government, civil service, etc. of a former colony) to Africans.
—**af′ri·can·i·za′tion,** *n.*

African violet any of several small, tropical plants (genus *Saintpaulia*) of the gloxinia family having violet, pink, or white flowers, especially *S. ionantha,* cultivated in many varieties as a house plant in temperate climates.

Af·ri·kaans (af′rə käns′ *or* af′rə känz′) *n., adj.* —*n.* one of the official languages of the Republic of South Africa. Afrikaans developed from 17th-century Dutch. —*adj.* of or having to do with Afrikaans or Afrikaners. [< Afrikaans spelling of Du. *Afrikansch*]

Af·ri·kan·der (af′rə kän′der) *n.* **1** Afrikaner. **2** a breed of cattle found in southern Africa. [< Afrikaans *Afrikaander,* modelled after Du. *Hollander* Dutchman]

Af·ri·ka·ner (af′rə kä′nər) *n.* a native or inhabitant of the Republic of South Africa who is of European, especially Dutch, descent. [< Afrikaans *Afrikaander*]

Af·ro (af′rō) *n., pl.* **Af·ros;** *adj.* —*n.* a hairstyle that takes advantage of the character of very curly hair by leaving it bushy and clipping it into any of various rounded shapes. —*adj.* of, for, or designating such a hairstyle: *an Afro cut.* Also, **afro.**

Afro– combining form. **1** African: *An Afro-American is an American of African descent.* **2** African and—: *An Afro-Asian conference would involve both African and Asian nations.*

Af·ro-A·mer·i·can (af′rō ə mer′ə kən) *n., adj.* —*n.* an American of African descent or having some African ancestors. —*adj.* of or having to do with Afro-Americans or their history or culture.

Af·ro-A·sian (af′rō ä′zhən *or* af′rō ä′shen) *adj.* of, having to do with, or involving both Africa and Asia.

Af·ro-A·si·at·ic languages (af′ro ä′zhē at′ik *or* -shē at′ik) a family of languages spoken throughout N Africa and SW Asia, made up of the Berber, Chad, Cushitic, Egyptian, and Semitic language groups.

aft (aft) *adv., adj.* —*adv.* at, near, or toward the stern of a ship or boat or the tail of an aircraft; abaft. —*adj.* at or near the stern or tail: *the aft deck.* [OE *æftan* from behind]

af·ter (af′tər) *prep., adv., adj., conj.* —*prep.* **1** behind (in place): *in line one after another.* **2** next to; following: *day after day.* **3** in pursuit of; in search of: *Run after him. The spy was after a special set of documents.* **4** about; concerning: *Your aunt asked after you.* **5** later in time than: *after supper.* **6** considering; because of: *After the selfish way she acted, who could like her?* **7** in spite of: *After all her suffering, she is still cheerful.* **8** imitating; in imitation of: *He wrote a fable after the manner of Aesop.* **9** lower in rank or importance than: *A captain comes after a general.* **10** according to: *to act after one's own ideas.* **11** for: *named after his cousin.*

after all, a in spite of everything that has happened, been said, etc. to the contrary: *We decided to go after all.* **b** taking everything into consideration: *After all, what does it really matter?*
—*adv.* **1** behind: *to follow after.* **2** later: *three hours after.*
—*adj.* **1** later; subsequent: *In after years he regretted the mistakes of his boyhood.* **2** nearer or toward the stern: *after sails.*
—*conj.* later than the time that: *After he goes, we shall eat.* [OE *æfter* more to the rear, later]
➨ *Syn. prep.* See note at **behind.**

af·ter·beat (af′tər bēt′) *n. Music.* a note (or notes), especially in accompaniment, that follows the beat.

af·ter·birth (af′tər bėrth′) *n.* the placenta and membranes expelled from the uterus after childbirth.

af·ter·burn·er (af′tər bėr′nər) *n.* in a turbojet aircraft, an extra section between the turbojet engine and the tail pipe, in which additional fuel is sprayed into the burning exhaust gases, greatly increasing the thrust of the exhaust jet and thus permitting the aircraft to attain very high speeds.

af·ter·care (af′tər ker′) *n.* **1** the care or treatment of convalescent patients. **2** the assistance given to people who have been discharged from prisons, mental hospitals, etc.

af·ter·damp (af′tər damp′) *n.* a dangerous mixture of gases left in coal mines after an explosion of firedamp.

af·ter·deck (af′tər dek′) *n.* the deck toward or at the stern of a ship.

af·ter·din·ner (af′tər din′ər) *adj.* following dinner: *an after-dinner speech.*

af·ter·ef·fect (af′tər i fekt′) *n.* a result or effect that follows something.

af·ter·glow (af′tər glō′) *n.* **1** the glow in the sky after sunset. **2** the glow after something exciting has passed.

af·ter·grass (af′tər gras′) *n.* a second growth of grass in a field that has been cut.

af·ter·growth (af′tər grōth′) *n.* a second stage of growth and development; a second growth.

af·ter·im·age (af′tər im′ij) *n.* a sensation that persists or recurs after the stimulus is withdrawn.

af·ter·life (af′tər līf′) *n.* life or existence after death.

af·ter·mar·ket (af′tər mär′kət) *n.* the market for replacement parts and accessories for manufactured articles as distinct from the parts and accessories used in the original product: *There is a large aftermarket in the automotive industry.*

af·ter·math (af′tər math′) *n.* **1** a result; consequence: *The aftermath of war is hunger and disease.* **2** a crop gathered after the first crop. [< *after* + *math* a mowing < OE *mæth*]

af·ter·most (af′tər mōst′) *adj.* **1** nearest the stern of a ship. **2** hindmost; last.

af·ter·noon (*n.* af′tər nün′; *adj.* af′tər nün′) *n., adj.* —*n.* the part of the day between noon and evening. —*adj.* of, in, or suitable for the afternoon.

af·ter·shave (af′tər shāv′) *n.* **1** a usually scented, astringent lotion for applying to the face after shaving. **2** (*adj.*) of or designating a lotion, etc. for use after shaving.

af·ter·shock (af′tər shok′) *n.* a minor tremor, often one of a series, that closely follows an earthquake.

af·ter·taste (af′tər tāst′) *n.* a taste that remains after eating or drinking.

af·ter·thought (af′tər thot′ *or* -thôt′) *n.* **1** a thought that comes after the time when it could have been used. **2** a later thought or explanation.

af·ter·ward (af′tər wərd) *adv.* later. [OE *æfterweard*]

af·ter·wards (af′tər wərdz) *adv.* afterward.

ag– *prefix.* the form of **ad-** occurring before *g*, as in *agglutinate.*

Ag silver (for L *argentum*).

Ag. Agrégé.

A.G. **1** Attorney General. **2** Agent General. **3** air gunner. **4** Adjutant General.

a·ga (ä′gə) *n.* in Moslem countries, a commander or chief officer: *The Aga Khan is the leader of a Moslem sect.* Also, **agha.** [< Turkish]

a·gain (ə gen′ *or* ə gān′) *adv.* **1** once more; another time: *to try again.* **2** in return; in reply: *to answer again.* **3** to the same place or person; back: *Bring us word again.* **4** moreover; besides: *Again, I must say that you are wrong.* **5** on the other hand: *It might rain, and again it might not.*
again and again, often; frequently.

as much again, twice as much; twice as many. [OE *ongean*]

a·gainst (ə genst′ *or* ə gänst′) *prep.* **1** in an opposite direction to, so as to meet; upon; toward: *to sail against the wind.* **2** in opposition to: *against reason.* **3** directly opposite to; facing: *over against the wind.* **4** in contrast to or with: *The ship appeared against the sky.* **5** in contact with: *to lean against a wall.* **6** in preparation for: *Squirrels store up nuts against the winter.* **7** from: *A fire is a protection against cold.* [ME *agenes* (< OE *ongean*) + *-t* as in *amidst, amongst.* See AGAIN.]

a·gape¹ (ə gāp′) *adv. or adj.* (*never precedes a noun*) **1** gaping; with the mouth wide open in wonder or surprise. **2** wide open.

a·ga·pe² (ä′gä pā *or* ä′gə pē) *n. Christianity.* **1** unselfish, brotherly love; charity (def. 5). **2** love feast, especially of the early Christians. [< Gk. *agapē*]

a·gar (ä′gər *or* ag′ər) *n.* **1** agar-agar. **2** a preparation containing agar-agar.

a·gar-a·gar (ä′gər ä′gər *or* ag′ər ag′ər) *n.* an extract, resembling gelatin, obtained from certain seaweeds and used in making cultures for bacteria, fungi, etc. and as a glue. [< Malay]

ag·a·ric (ag′ə rik *or* ə gar′ik) *n.* any of a family (Agaricaceae) of fungi that includes most edible mushrooms and many poisonous mushrooms. [< L *agaricum* < Gk. *agarikon* < *Agaria*, place name]

ag·ate (ag′it) *n.* **1** a kind of quartz having different-colored stripes, clouded colors, or mosslike formations. **2** a gem made from this stone. **3** a playing marble that resembles an agate. **4** *Printing.* a 5½ point size of type. This sentence is set in agate. [< F *agathe* < L *achates* < Gk.] —**ag′ate-like′,** *adj.*

ag·ate·ware (ag′it wer′) *n.* steel or iron household ware covered with grey enamel.

a·ga·ve (ə gā′vē) *n.* **1** any of a genus (*Agave*) of tropical American plants having thick, fleshy leaves and tall flower stalks. Some species are commercially important as sources of soap, sisal, and alcoholic drinks. **2** (*adj.*) designating the family of tropical and temperate plants that includes the agaves, yuccas, and the tuberose. [< NL < Gk. *Agauē*, fem. proper name, noble]

Ag. de l'U. Agrégé de l'Université de Paris.

age (āj) *n., v.* **aged, age·ing** or **ag·ing.** —*n.* **1** time of life: *He died at the age of eighty.* **2** length of life; the time anything has existed: *Her actions belie her age. The age of these elms is greater than that of any other trees in the park.* **3** a period in life: *middle age.* **4** the latter part of life: *the wisdom of age.* **5** the full or average term of life: *The age of a horse is from 25 to 30 years.* **6** a period in history: *the golden age, the space age, the Ice Age.* **7** generation: *ages yet unborn.* **8** *Informal.* a long, or apparently long, time: *We haven's been to the movies in ages.* **9** *Psychology.* the level of a person's attainment, mentally, educationally, emotionally, etc., determined by tests.
of age, old enough to have full legal rights and responsibilities.
—*v.* **1** grow old: *He is aging rapidly.* **2** make old: *Fear and worry aged him.* **3** improve by keeping for a time; mature: *to age wine.* [ME < OF *aage* < VL *aetaticum* < L *aetas, -tatis* age]

–age *suffix.* **1** the act of: *breakage* = *the act of breaking.* **2** a collection of; group of: *baggage* = *a group of bags.* **3** the condition of; status of: *peerage* = *status of peers.* **4** the cost of: *postage* = *the cost of posting.* **5** a home of or for: *orphanage* = *a home for orphans.* [< OF < L *-aticum* < Gk.]

a·ged (ā′jid *for adj. 1, n. 3*; ājd *for adj. 2*) *adj., n.* —*adj.* **1** having lived a long time; old: *The aged woman was wrinkled and bent.* **2** of the age of: *a child aged six.* **3** characteristic of old age.
—*n.* **the aged,** *pl.* elderly people.

age·less (āj′lis) *adj.* never growing old.

age·long (āj′long′) *adj.* lasting a long time.

a·gen·cy (ā′jən sē) *n., pl.* **-cies.** **1** a means; action: *Snow is drifted by the agency of the wind.* **2** the business of a person or company that has the authority to act for another: *An agency rented my house for me.* **3** the office of such a person or company.

a·gen·da (ə jen′də) *n.* a list or plan of things to be done or accomplished: *The agenda of the next meeting is posted on the bulletin board. What's on our agenda for this afternoon?* [< L *agenda* things to be done, pl. of *agendum* < *agere* do]
➨ *Usage.* **Agenda** was originally a plural noun. It is now used as a singular noun and has the regular plural **agendas.**

a·gent (ā′jənt) *n.* **1** a person or company that has the authority to act for another. **2** a person who produces an effect: *The assassin was an agent of tragedy.* **3** an active power or cause that produces an effect: *Yeast is an important agent in the making of beer.* **4** a means; instrument. **5** secret agent. **6** a travelling sales representative. [< L *agens, -entis,* ppr. of *agere* do]

agent general *pl.* **agents general** or **agent generals.** a representative in the United Kingdom of certain Canadian provinces. *Abbrev.:* A.G.

a·gent pro·vo·ca·teur (ä zhän′ prô vô kä tœr′) *French.* a person who incites others to do something that will make them liable to punishment.

age of consent the age at which a person is legally able to agree to marriage, medical treatment, etc. without the consent of a parent or guardian.

age–old (āj′ōld′) *adj.* having existed for many ages; very old and still continuing: *the age-old question of astrology.*

ag·er·a·tum (aj′ər ā′təm *or* ə jer′ə təm) *n.* any of a genus (*Ageratum*) of tropical American annual plants of the composite family having compact heads of small blue, white, or pink flowers. [< NL < Gk. *agēraton* < *a-* without + *gēras* old age]

ag·glom·er·ate (*v.* ə glom′ər āt′; *n., adj.* ə glom′ər it′ *or* ə glom′ər āt′) *v.* **-at·ed, -at·ing;** *n., adj.* —*v.* gather together in a mass; cluster together. —*n.* **1** a mass; collection; cluster. **2** *Geology.* a rock composed of volcanic fragments fused by heat. —*adj.* packed together in a mass. [< L *agglomerare* < *ad-* to + *glomus, glomeris* ball]

ag·glom·er·a·tion (ə glom′ər ā′shən) *n.* **1** the act of agglomerating. **2** an agglomerated condition. **3** a mass of things gathered or clustered together.

ag·glu·ti·nate (*v.* ə glü′tə nāt′; *adj.* ə glüt′tə nit *or* ə glü′tə nāt′) *v.* **-nat·ed, -nat·ing;** *adj.* —*v.* **1** stick together; join together. **2** *Linguistics.* of a language, form words by joining words, or words and affixes, together. **3** *Bacteriology.* cause (cells, etc.) to mass together.
—*adj.* stuck or joined together: *"Never-to-be-forgotten" is an agglutinate word.* [< L *agglutinare* < *ad-* to + *gluten, glutinis* glue]

ag·glu·ti·na·tion (ə glü′tə nā′shən) *n.* **1** the process of agglutinating. **2** an agglutinated condition. **3** a mass of parts sticking together. **4** *Bacteriology.* the massing together of cells, etc. **5** *Linguistics.* the forming of words by joining separate words, or words and affixes, together.

ag·glu·ti·na·tive (ə glü′tə nə tiv *or* ə glü′tə nā′tiv) *adj.* **1** tending to stick together. **2** *Linguistics.* of a language, forming words by joining words, or words and affixes, together.

ag·gran·dize (ə gran′dīz′ *or* ag′rən dīz′) *v.* **-dized, -diz·ing.** increase in power, wealth, rank, etc.; make greater: *The dictator sought to aggrandize himself at the expense of his people.* [< F *agrandiss-,* a stem of *agrandir,* ult. < L *ad-* + *grandis* large] —**ag·gran′diz·er,** *n.*

ag·gran·dize·ment (ə gran′diz mənt) *n.* an increase in power, wealth, rank, etc.; making greater.

ag·gra·vate (ag′rə vāt′) *v.* **-vat·ed, -vat·ing. 1** make worse or more severe: *His bad temper was aggravated by his headache.* **2** *Informal.* annoy; irritate; exasperate. [< L *aggravare* < *ad-* on + *gravis* heavy. Doublet of AGGRIEVE.] —**ag′gra·vat′ing·ly,** *adv.* —**ag′gra·va′tor,** *n.*

ag·gra·va·tion (ag′rə vā′shən) *n.* **1** making or being made worse or more severe: *the aggravation of an illness.* **2** something that makes worse or more severe. **3** *Informal.* something that annoys or exasperates.

ag·gre·gate (*adj., n.* ag′rə git *or* ag′rə gāt′; *v.* ag′rə gāt′) *adj., n., v.* **-gat·ed, -gat·ing.** —*adj.* **1** formed by the collection of parts or units into one body, mass, or amount; collected; whole, or total: *The aggregate value of all the gifts was $1000.* **2** *Botany.* **a** of a flower, composed of many florets forming a head. **b** of a fruit, formed from the development together of several pistils of a single flower: *The raspberry and strawberry are aggregate fruits.* **3** *Geology.* composed of mineral crystals or rock fragments: *Granite is an aggregate rock.*
—*n.* **1** a mass of separate things joined together or associated; collection. *The report was an aggregate of the viewpoints of the committee members.* **2** the sum total; total amount. **3** *Geology.* an aggregate rock: *volcanic aggregates.* **4** material such as broken stone, sand, or gravel used to make concrete.
in the aggregate, together; as a whole.
—*v.* **1** collect together or unite. **2** amount to: *The money collected is expected to aggregate over $3000.* [< L *aggregare* < *ad-* to + *grex, gregis* flock] —**ag′gre·gate·ly,** *adv.*

ag·gre·ga·tion (ag′rə gā′shən) *n.* a collection of separate things into one mass or whole.

ag·gres·sion (ə gresh′ən) *n.* **1** the making by one nation of an unprovoked attack or assault on the rights or territories of another: *In 1914, Germany was guilty of aggression against Belgium.* **2** any unprovoked attack. **3** *Psychology.* an act or attitude of hostility, usually arising from feelings of inferiority or frustration. [< L *aggressio, -onis* < *aggredi* < *ad-* to + *gradi* to step]

ag·gres·sive (ə gres′iv) *adj.* **1** taking or tending to take the first step in an attack or quarrel: *aggressive behavior, an aggressive*

nation. **2** energetic and forceful: *an aggressive political campaign, an aggressive salesman.* —**ag·gres′sive·ly,** *adv.* —**ag·gres′sive·ness,** *n.*

ag·gres·sor (ə gres′ər) *n.* one that commits aggression; one that begins an attack or quarrel.

ag·grieve (ə grēv′) *v.* **-grieved, -griev·ing.** injure unjustly; cause grief or trouble to: *He was aggrieved at the insult from his friend.* [ME *agreve* < OF *agrever* < L *aggravare.* Doublet of AGGRAVATE.]

ag·grieved (ə grēvd′) *adj.* **1** injured or offended as to rights, position, etc.: *make amends to an aggrieved victim of injustice.* **2** feeling distressed or wronged, whether justly or not.

a·gha (ä′gə) *n.* aga.

a·ghast (ə gast′) *adj.* filled with extreme surprise or horror; shocked (*never used before a noun*): *They were aghast at the violence of the crime.* [ME pp. of obs. *agast* terrify < OE *on-* on + *gæstan* frighten. Related to GHOST.]

ag·ile (aj′īl *or* aj′əl) *adj.* **1** moving quickly and easily; nimble: *An acrobat has to be agile.* **2** able to think quickly; mentally nimble. [ME < OF < L *agilis* < *agere* move] —**ag′ile·ly,** *adv.* —**ag′ile·ness,** *n.*

a·gil·i·ty (ə jil′ə tē) *n.* the ability to move quickly and easily; activeness; liveliness; nimbleness.

ag·i·tate (aj′ə tāt′) *v.* **-tat·ed, -tat·ing. 1** move or shake violently. **2** disturb; excite (the feelings or the thoughts): *She was much agitated by the news of her brother's accident.* **3** argue about; discuss vigorously. **4** keep arguing about and discussing a matter to arouse public interest: *agitate for a shorter working week.* [< L *agitare* move to and fro < *agere* drive, move] —**ag′i·tat′ed·ly,** *adv.*

ag·i·ta·tion (aj′ə tā′shən) *n.* **1** a violent moving or shaking. **2** a disturbed, upset, or troubled state. **3** an argument or discussion to arouse public interest.

a·gi·ta·to (ä′jē tä′tō) *adj., adv.* —*adj. Music.* restless, agitated. —*adv.* in restless or agitated manner. [< Ital.]

ag·i·ta·tor (aj′ə tā′tər) *n.* **1** a person who tries to make people discontented with things as they are. **2** a device for shaking or stirring.

ag·it·prop (aj′it prop′) *n.* **1** political propaganda in the form of drama, music, or art, especially communist propaganda. **2** (*adj.*) of or having to do with such propaganda.

a·gleam (ə glēm′) *adj.* (*never precedes a noun*) gleaming.

a·gley (ə glā′ *or* ə glē′; *Scottish,* ə glī′) *adv. Scottish.* wrong; awry; askew; contrary to plan.

a·glit·ter (ə glit′ər) *adj.* (*never precedes a noun*) glittering.

a·glow (ə glō′) *adj.* (*never precedes a noun*) glowing; in a glow.

ag·lu *or* **ag·loo** (ag′lü) *n. Cdn.* a breathing-hole in ice, made by seals. [< Inuktitut (Eskimo)]

ag·nos·tic (ag nos′tik) *n., adj.* —*n.* a person who believes that nothing is known or can be known about the existence of God or about things outside human experience. —*adj.* of agnostics or their beliefs. [< Gk. *agnōstos* < *a-* not + *gnōstos* (to be) known] —**ag·nos′ti·cal·ly,** *adv.*

ag·nos·ti·cism (ag nos′tə siz′əm) *n.* the belief or intellectual attitude of agnostics.

Ag·nus De·i (ag′nəs dā′ē *or* dē′ī) **1** an image of a lamb as a symbol of Christ. **2** the part of the Mass beginning "Agnus Dei." **3** the music for it. **4** a blessed cake of wax bearing the image of a lamb. [< L *Agnus Dei* Lamb of God]

a·go (ə gō′) *adj., adv.* —*adj.* gone by; past (*always placed after the noun*): *a year ago.* —*adv.* in the past: *He went long ago.* [OE *āgān* gone by]

a·gog (ə gog′) *adj. or adv.* (*never precedes a noun*) in a state of great excitement, curiosity, etc. [? < F *en gogues* in happy mood]

ag·o·nize (ag′ə nīz′) *v.* **-nized, -niz·ing. 1** feel great anguish. **2** cause to suffer extreme pain; torture. **3** strive painfully; struggle. [< F *agoniser* < LL *agonizare* < Gk. *agōnizethai* struggle < *agōn* a contest] —**ag′o·niz′ing·ly,** *adv.*

ag·o·ny (ag′ə nē) *n., pl.* **-nies. 1** great pain or suffering. **2** the struggle often preceding death. [ME < OF < LL < Gk. *agōnia* struggle]

☞ *Usage.* **Agony.** Often used in informal English in a light vein in such expressions as: *My shoes hurt; I'm in agony. I have to do my Latin some time; I might as well get the agony over now.*

ag·o·ra¹ (ag′ə rə) *n., pl.* **-rae** (-rē *or* -rī). the marketplace in an ancient Greek city. **The Agora** in Athens was used for public assemblies. [< Gk.]

ag·o·ra² (äg′ə rä′) *n., pl.* **ag·o·rot. 1** a unit of money in Israel, worth 1/100 of a pound. **2** a coin worth one agora. [< Hebrew *agora* a small coin]

ag·o·ra·phobe (ag′ə rə fōb′ *or* ag′rə fōb′) *n.* a person suffering from agoraphobia.

ag·o·ra·pho·bi·a (ag′ə rə fō′bē ə *or* ag′rə fō′bē ə) *n.* a morbid fear of open spaces.

ag·o·rot (äg′ə rōt′) *n.* pl. of **agora²**.

a·gou·ti (ə gü′tē) *n., pl.* **-tis** *or* **-ties.** any of a genus (*Dasyprocta*) of tropical American rodents having long legs, small ears, a very short tail, and grizzled, reddish brown to blackish fur. [< F < Sp. *aguti* < native Indian name]

a·grar·i·an (ə grer′ē ən) *adj., n.* —*adj.* **1** having to do with land, its use, or its ownership. **2** for the support and advancement of the interests of farmers. **3** agricultural.
—*n.* a person who favors a new division of land. [< L *agrarius* < *ager* field]

a·grar·i·an·ism (ə grer′ē ən iz′əm) *n.* **1** the principles, methods, or practices of agrarians. **2** an agitation for a redistribution of landed property.

a·gree (ə grē′) *v.* **a·greed, a·gree·ing. 1** have the same opinion or opinions: *I agree with you. The two partners usually agreed on important issues.* **2** be alike or be similar to; be in harmony; correspond (*with*): *Her story agrees with theirs.* **3** get along well together. **4** consent (*to*): *We agreed to their proposal. He agreed to accompany us.* **5** come to an understanding, especially in settling a dispute. **6** be suitable, healthful, etc. (*used with* **with**): *Bananas don't agree with him; they make him sick.* **7** *Grammar.* have the same number, case, gender, or person: *In English, the subject and verb of a sentence have to agree in number.* [ME < OF *agreer* < *a gre* to (one's) liking < L *ad* to, *gratum*, neut., pleasing]
☞ *Syn.* **2. Agree, correspond, coincide** = be in harmony. **Agree** = not only to be consistent or harmonious in all essentials, but also to be without inconsistencies or contradictions: *The views of the two leaders agree.* **Correspond** = to agree or to equal in essentials or as a whole, in spite of differences: *Dominion Day corresponds to the American Independence Day.* **Coincide** = agree so closely as to be identical: *His tastes coincide with mine.*
☞ *Usage.* **Agree to, agree with.** One agrees *to* a plan and agrees *with* a person, but one thing agrees *with* another.

a·gree·a·bil·i·ty (ə grē′ə bil′ə tē) *n.* the quality of being agreeable.

a·gree·a·ble (ə grē′ə bəl) *adj.* **1** pleasant; pleasing: *agreeable manners.* **2** ready to agree; willing: *agreeable to a suggestion.* **3** in agreement; suitable (*to*): *music agreeable to the occasion.*
—**a·gree′a·ble·ness,** *n.* —**a·gree′a·bly,** *adv.*
☞ *Syn.* **1.** See note at **pleasant.**

a·greed (ə grēd′) *adj.* fixed by common consent.

a·gree·ment (ə grē′mənt) *n.* **1** an agreeing; an understanding reached by two or more nations, persons, or groups of persons among themselves. Nations make treaties and individuals make contracts; both are agreements. **2** sameness of opinion. **3** harmony; correspondence. **4** *Grammar.* correspondence of words with respect to number, case, gender, person.

a·gré·gé (ä′grā zhā′) *n. French.* a person who has passed a competitive examination conducted by the State for higher teaching appointments. *Abbrev.:* Ag.

ag. rep. *or* **ag–rep** (ag′rep′) *n. Cdn.* agricultural representative; an official appointed by a provincial government to act as adviser to farmers in a particular district.

ag·ri·busi·ness (ag′rə biz′nəs) *n.* the whole group of businesses and industries involved in the production, processing, and marketing of agricultural products, especially as distinct from small-scale farming.

agric. agriculture.

ag·ri·cul·tur·al (ag′rə kul′chər əl) *adj.* **1** having to do with farming; of agriculture. **2** promoting the interests or the study of agriculture. —**ag′ri·cul′tur·al·ly,** *adv.*

ag·ri·cul·tur·al·ist (ag′rə kul′chər əl ist) *n.* agriculturist.

ag·ri·cul·ture (ag′rə kul′chər) *n.* farming; the raising of crops and livestock; the science or art of cultivating the ground. [< L *agricultura* < *ager* field + *cultura* cultivation]

ag·ri·cul·tur·ist (ag′rə kul′chər ist) *n.* **1** a person trained in agriculture, especially one whose work it is. **2** farmer.

ag·ri·mo·ny (ag′rə mō′nē) *n., pl.* **-nies.** any of a genus (*Agrimonia*) of plants of the rose family, especially *A. eupatoria*, a tall European perennial having feathery leaves that yield a yellow dye, long spikes of small yellow flowers, and fruit like small burrs.

[< L *agrimonia,* var. of *argemonia* < Gk. *argemōnē*]

ag·ro·bi·ol·o·gist (ag′rō bī ə jist) *n.* a person trained in agrobiology, especially one whose work it is.

ag·ro·bi·ol·o·gy (ag′rō bī ol′ə jē) *n.* the study of plant nutrition and soil management.

a·grol·o·gist (ə grol′ə jist) *n.* a person trained in agrology, especially one whose work it is.

a·grol·o·gy (ə grol′ə jē) *n.* the branch of agriculture that deals with soils.

ag·ro·ma·ni·a (ag′rō mā′nē ə) *n.* an abnormal desire to live in the open country, away from people. [< Gk. *agros* field + *mania*]

ag·ro·nom·ic (ag′rə nom′ik) *adj.* of or having to do with agronomy.

a·gron·o·mist (ə gron′ə mist) *n.* a person skilled in agronomy.

a·gron·o·my (ə gron′ə mē) *n.* the science of managing farm land; the branch of agriculture dealing with crop production; husbandry. [< Gk. *agronomos* < *agros* land + *nemein* manage]

a·ground (ə ground′) *adv. or adj.* on or onto the shore or the bottom in shallow water: *The ship ran aground on a reef.*

agt. agent.

a·gue (ā′gyü) *n.* **1** a malarial fever with chills and sweating occurring at regular intervals. **2** a fit of shivering; chill. [ME < OF < L *acuta* (*febris*) severe (fever)]

a·gu·ish (ā′gyü ish) *adj.* **1** of or like ague. **2** causing ague. **3** liable to have ague.

ah (ä) *interj.* an exclamation of pain, sorrow, regret, pity, admiration, surprise, joy, dislike, contempt, etc. The meaning of *ah* varies according to the way it is said.

a·ha (ä hä′) *interj.* an exclamation of triumph, satisfaction, surprise, etc.

a·head (ə hed′) *adv.* **1** in front; before: *Walk ahead of me.* **2** forward; onward: *Go ahead with this work.* **3** in advance: *Columbus was ahead of his times in his belief that the world was round.*
get ahead, *Informal.* succeed.
get ahead of, surpass; excel.

a·hem (ə hem′) *interj.* a word used to represent the sound made by coughing or clearing the throat, sometimes done to attract attention, express doubt, or gain time.

a·hoy (ə hoi′) *interj.* a call used by sailors to attract the attention of persons at a distance: *When sailors call to a ship, they shout, "Ship ahoy!"*

aid (ād) *v., n.* —*v.* give support to; help: *The Red Cross aids flood victims.* —*n.* **1** help; support: *When my arm was broken, I could not dress without aid.* **2** a helper; assistant. [ME < OF *aidier* < L *adjutare,* frequentative of *adjuvare* < *ad-* to + *juvare* help]
☞ *Syn. v.* See note at **help.**

aide (ād) *n.* **1** an aide-de-camp. **2** an aid; helper. [< F]

aide–de–camp (ād′də kamp′; *French,* ed də kän′) *n., pl.* **aides-de-camp.** a military officer who acts as an assistant and secretary to a superior officer. *Abbrev.:* ADC, A.D.C., or a.d.c. [< F]

aide–mé–moire (ed me mwär′) *n. French.* **1** anything that reminds, such as a calendar note. **2** a written summary or outline of a communication or proposed agreement; memorandum.

ai·grette (ā′gret *or* ā gret′) *n.* **1** a tuft of feathers worn as an ornament on the head. **2** anything similar in shape or use. **3** egret. [< F *aigrette* egret]

ai·guille (ā gwēl′) *n.* **1** in mountainous regions, a thin sharp-pointed peak of rock. **2** an instrument for boring holes, used in masonry or blasting. [< F *aiguille* needle < LL *acicula, acucula,* dim. of L *acus* needle]

ail (āl) *v.* **1** be the matter with; trouble: *What ails the man?* **2** be ill; feel sick: *He is ailing.* [OE *eglan*]
☞ *Hom.* **ale.**

ai·lan·thus (ā lan′thəs) *n.* any of a small genus (*Ailanthus*) of trees and shrubs native to tropical Asia, having compound leaves with leaves growing along the side of the stalk. The tree of heaven is an ailanthus. [< NL < Amboinan (language of Amboina in the Dutch East Indies) *aylanto* tree of heaven; form influenced by Gk. *anthos* flower]

ai·ler·on (ā′lər on′) *n.* a small, movable section near the tip of the wing of an aircraft for controlling the side-to-side motion of the aircraft in flight. See **airplane** for picture. [< F *aileron,* dim. of *aile* < L *ala* wing]

ail·ment (āl′mənt) *n.* a disorder of the body or mind; illness; sickness.

aim (ām) *v.* **1** point or direct (a gun, blow, etc.) in order to hit a target: *aim a gun.* **2** direct (words or acts): *The Prime Minister's speech was aimed at men in his own party.* **3** *Informal.* intend: *I*

aim to go. **4** *Informal.* try; direct one's efforts: *He aims to be helpful.*
—*n.* **1** the act of aiming. **2** the direction aimed in; line of sighting. **3** purpose; intention. [ME < OF *esmer* < L *aestimare* appraise, and OF *aesmer* < VL *adaestimare*]

aim·less (ām′lis) *adj.* without aim or purpose. —**aim′less·ly**, *adv.* —**aim′less·ness**, *n.*

ain't (ānt) **1** am not, are not, or is not. **2** have not or has not.
☛ *Usage.* **Ain't** has long been used in English, though it is unacceptable to most educated speakers. It should not be used in formal English.

Ai·nu (ī′nü) *n., adj.* —*n.* **1** a member of a very primitive, light-skinned people in N Japan, now becoming extinct. **2** the language of this people. —*adj.* of this people or their language.

air (er) *n., v.* —*n.* **1** the mixture of gases that surrounds the earth; atmosphere. Air consists of nitrogen, oxygen, argon, carbon dioxide, hydrogen, and small quantities of neon, helium, and other inert gases. **2** the space overhead; sky: *Birds fly in the air.* **3** a light wind; breeze. **4** a melody; tune. **5** public mention: *He gave air to his opinions.* **6** the general character or appearance of anything: *an air of mystery.* **7** bearing; manner: *The famous man had an air of importance.* **8** airs, *pl.* unnatural or affected manners. **9** *Music.* **a** a composition to be played or sung as a solo: *Bach's Air on the G String.* **b** any tune or melody, especially a simple one. **c** the main melody in a harmonized composition, usually the soprano or treble part. **10** the medium through which radio waves travel. **11** (*adjl.*) conducting or supplying air: *an air duct.* **12** (*adjl.*) compressing or confining air: *an air valve.* **13** (*adjl.*) using or worked by compressed air: *an air drill.* **14** (*adjl.*) relating to aviation; done by means of aircraft: *air photography.*
get the air, *Slang.* be dismissed or rejected.
give the air, *Slang.* dismiss, especially scornfully.
in the air, a going around: *Wild rumors were in the air.* **b** uncertain.
into thin air, without leaving a trace; completely: *He just disappeared into thin air and hasn't been seen since.*
on the air, broadcasting.
off the air, a not broadcasting: *Our radio station is off the air from one till six a.m.* **b** not being broadcast: *That show is off the air now.*
out of thin air, by magic or as if by magic: *She suddenly appeared out of thin air. They seem to expect us to produce a workable plan out of thin air.*
take the air, a go outdoors; take a walk or ride. **b** start broadcasting.
up in the air, a *Informal.* uncertain; unsettled. **b** *Informal.* very angry or excited.
walk on air, *Informal.* be very happy or pleased.
—*v.* **1** put out in the air; let air through: *to air clothes.* **2** make known; mention publicly: *Do not air your troubles.* **3** take for a walk: *to air the dog.* **4** *Informal.* broadcast by radio or television: *The Olympic Games were aired to all of Canada.* [ME < OF < L *aer* < Gk. *aēr*]
☛ *Hom.* **e'er, ere, err, heir.**

air base headquarters and airport for military aircraft.

air bladder in most fish and in some animals and plants, a sac containing air. The air bladder in fish, usually called a swim bladder, acts as an aid in breathing and hearing or helps the fish to maintain buoyancy in the water.

air·borne (er′bôrn′) *adj.* **1** carried through the air: *airborne seeds, airborn bacteria.* **2** transported by aircraft: *airborne troops.* **3** of aircraft, in the air after taking off; flying: *After another delay, we were finally airborne.*

air brake a brake operated by a piston or pistons worked by compressed air.

air·brush (er′brush′) *n., v.* —*n.* a device, operated by compressed air, used to apply a fine spray of paint, liquid color, etc. onto a surface. —*v.* apply paint or color to (a photograph, etc.) with an airbrush, in order to remove blemishes or unwanted details or to improve finish: *to airbrush a photograph.*

air·bus (er′bus′) *n.* a passenger aircraft, operating on a regular route and as part of a frequent service, which one may board without an advance reservation, simply by paying cash as on a bus or streetcar.

air cadet a person under military age who is undertaking basic air-command training in an organization subsidized by the armed forces.

air chamber any compartment filled with air, especially one in a hydraulic engine.

air chief marshal an air-force officer ranking next above an air marshall. See chart at **rank¹**. *Abbrev.:* A.C.M.

air coach *Esp.U.S.* an aircraft with low passenger rates.

air cock a small opening or valve for letting air in or out.

Air Command *Cdn.* a major organizational element of the Canadian Forces, whose role is to provide combat-ready air defence forces over land and sea.

air commodore an air-force officer ranking next above a group

hat, āge, fär; let, ēqual, tèrm; it, īce
hot, ōpen, ôrder; oil, out; cup, pùt, rüle,
əbove, takən, pencəl, lemən, circəs
ch, child; ng, long; sh, ship
th, thin; ᴛH, then; zh, measure

captain and below an air vice-marshal. See chart at **rank¹**. *Abbrev.:* A.C.

air-con·di·tion (er′kən dish′ən) *v.* **1** supply with the equipment for air conditioning. **2** treat (air) by means of air conditioning.

air-con·di·tioned (er′kən dish′ənd) *adj.* having air conditioning.

air conditioner an apparatus used to air-condition a room, building, train, etc.

air conditioning a means of treating air in buildings, rooms, trains, etc. to regulate its temperature and humidity and to free it from dust.

air-cool (er′kül′) *v.* **1** remove heat produced in motor cylinders by combustion, friction, etc. by blowing air. **2** remove heat in (a room) by blowing cool air in. —**air′cool′er**, *n.*

air corridor an established route or passage along which aircraft are permitted to fly.

air·craft (er′kraft′) *n., pl.* **-craft.** a machine for navigation in the air, supported in the air either by aerodynamic forces acting on its surfaces (as an airplane, helicopter, or glider) or by buoyancy (as a dirigible).

aircraft carrier a warship designed as a base for aircraft.

air·craft·man (er′kraft mən) *n., pl.* **-men.** an air-force serviceman of the lowest rank. See chart at **rank¹**. *Abbrev.:* A.C.

air·craft·wom·an (er′kraft wùm′ən) *n., pl.* **-wom·en.** an air-force servicewoman of the lowest rank. See chart at **rank¹**. *Abbrev.:* A.W. or A.C.W.

air curtain a mass of heated or cooled air circulated around the entrance of a building, in front of and around storage areas, etc., to hold in or keep out warm air and to serve in place of a door.

air cushion 1 an inflatable rubber or rubberized casing for use as a cushion or pad. **2** the layer of air under pressure that supports a hovercraft.

air-cushion vehicle (er′kúsh′ən) hovercraft.

air cylinder a cylinder in which air is compressed by a piston, for checking the recoil of a gun.

air-drop (er′drop′) *n., v.* **-dropped, -drop·ping.** —*n.* a system of dropping food, supplies, etc. from aircraft, especially to allies who are caught behind enemy lines, living in occupied territory, etc.
—*v.* deliver (supplies, etc.) in this way.

Aire·dale (er′dāl′) *n.* a breed of large terrier having a wiry tan coat with a large, dark patch on the back and sides. [< *Airedale* in Yorkshire, England]

air express a quick or direct means of sending goods by aircraft.

air-ex·press (er′eks pres′) *v.* send by air express.

air·field (er′fēld′) *n.* the landing field of an airport.

air·flow (er′flō′) *n.* **1** the motion of air relative to the surface of a moving object, such as an aircraft or automobile. **2** a natural movement of air or wind. **3** (*adjl.*) resulting from air currents: *The airflow pattern changes when an aircraft crosses the sonic barrier.* **4** (*adjl.*) streamlined: *airflow design.*

air·foil (er′foil′) *n.* any surface, such as a wing, rudder, etc. designed to help lift or control an aircraft.

air force Often, **Air Force,** the branch of the armed forces of a nation responsible for military aircraft. In Canada, the function of an air force is served by Air Command of the Canadian Forces.

air·frame (er′frām′) *n.* the structure or framework, excluding engines, of an airplane, rocket, etc.

air freight 1 freight carried by aircraft. **2** the sending of freight carried by aircraft.

air-freight (er′frāt′) *v.* send by air freight.

air gun a gun worked by compressed air.

air hole 1 a hole that allows air to pass through. **2** a hole in the ice covering a body of water, often used as a breathing hole by seals, muskrats, etc. **3** air pocket.

air·i·ly (er′ə lē) *adv.* in an airy manner.

air·i·ness (er′ē nis) *n.* an airy quality.

air·ing (er′ing) *n.* **1** exposure to air for drying, warming, etc.; putting out in the air; letting air through. **2** a walk, ride, or drive in

the open air. **3** exposure to public discussion, criticism, etc.

air lane a regular route used by aircraft.

air·less (er′lis) *adj.* **1** without fresh air; stuffy. **2** without a breeze; still.

air letter a pre-stamped letter form used for international airmail, consisting of a single sheet of paper (for writing on) which is folded, sealed, and addressed on the outside, so that no envelope is required.

air·lift (er′lift′) *n., v.* —*n.* **1** a system of using aircraft for passenger transportation and freight conveyance to a place when land approaches are closed: *the Berlin airlift.* **2** something transported by such a system. —*v.* transport by such a system.

air·line (er′līn′) *n.* **1** a company operating a system of transportation by means of aircraft. **2** the system itself. **3** (*adj.*) of or having to do with an airline: *airline schedules.*

air·lin·er (er′lī′nər) *n.* a large aircraft operated by an airline for carrying passengers.

air lock an airtight compartment in which the air pressure can be adjusted, as between the outside air and the working compartment of a caisson.

air·mail or **air–mail** (er′māl′) *v., adj.* —*v.* send or transport by air mail. —*adj.* of, having to do with, or sent by air mail.

air mail 1 mail sent by aircraft. **2** the system of sending mail by aircraft.

air·man (er′mən) *n., pl.* **-men. 1** a man connected with flying, especially as a pilot, crew member, or ground technician. **2** aircraftman. See chart at **rank¹. 3** any man serving in an air force.

air marshal an air-force officer ranking next above an air vice-marshal and below an air chief marshal. See chart at **rank¹.** *Abbrev.*: A.M.

air mass a large area of the atmosphere that has nearly uniform temperature and humidity at any given level and moves horizontally over great distances without changing.

air mattress an inflatable rubber or rubberized casing designed for use as a mattress: *Air mattresses are often used by campers.*

air–mind·ed (er′mīn′did) *adj.* interested in aviation or aircraft. —**air′-mind′ed·ness,** *n.*

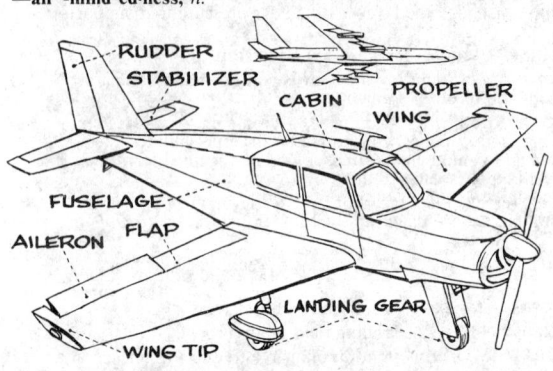

RUDDER
STABILIZER
CABIN
PROPELLER
WING
FUSELAGE
AILERON
FLAP
LANDING GEAR
WING TIP

Airplanes: a small, propeller-driven plane and, in the background, a jet airliner

air·plane (er′plān′) *n.* a mechanically driven, heavier-than-air aircraft supported in flight by the action of the air flowing past or thrusting upward on fixed wings.

☛ *Usage.* **Airplane, aeroplane. Airplane** is the usual form in North America. **Aeroplane** is more commonly used in England. In Canada the pronunciation (er′ə plān′) is used by some people who use the spelling **airplane.**

air plant a plant that grows on other plants and draws nourishment from the air and the rain. Many orchids are air plants.

air pocket a downward air current formed by the sudden sinking of cooled air causing a sudden, short drop in the altitude of an aircraft.

air·port (er′pôrt′) *n.* a place where aircraft regularly come to discharge or take on passengers or freight. It usually comprises several runways, buildings for passenger and staff facilities, and facilities for sheltering, repairing, and servicing aircraft.

air pressure 1 the force exerted by air confined in a restricted space. **2** atmospheric pressure: *Winds are caused by the flow of air from an area of high air pressure to an area of low air pressure.*

air pump a machine for forcing air into or out of something.

air raid an attack by aircraft.

air–raid shelter (er′rād′) a place for protection during an air raid.

air rifle a rifle that is worked by compressed air and shoots a single pellet or dart.

air rights the right to use the space above a building, road, railway, etc.: *A company has bought air rights over the freight yards in order to build a huge office block above the tracks.*

air sac an air-filled space in the body of a bird, connected with the lungs.

air shaft a passage for letting fresh air into a mine, tunnel, building, etc.

air·ship (er′ship′) *n.* a dirigible.

air·sick (er′sik′) *adj.* feeling nauseated and dizzy from the motion of an aircraft. —**air′sick′ness,** *n.*

air·space (er′spās′) *n.* **1** an enclosed area containing air. **2** space in the air, especially that belonging to a particular country: *a violation of our airspace.*

air speed the speed of an aircraft measured in relation to the movement of the air rather than to the ground.

air station a headquarters and airfield for air force operations and training.

air·stream (er′strēm′) *n.* the stream of air created around a moving object, such as an aircraft, train, or car; airflow.

air·strip (er′strip′) *n.* a paved or cleared strip on which planes can land and take off; a temporary airfield.

air·tight (er′tīt′) *adj.* **1** so tight that no air or gas can get in or out. **2** having no weak points open to attack: *an airtight explanation.*

air time 1 the time when a certain radio or television program begins to broadcast: *a few minutes to air time.* **2** an amount of broadcasting time: *The advertising program cost $75 000 in air time alone.*

air–to–air (er′tū er′) *adj.* between two flying aircraft: *air-to-air refuelling, air-to-air missiles.*

air valve a valve for controlling the flow of air into or out of something.

air vice–marshal an air-force officer ranking next above an air commodore and below an air marshal. See chart at **rank¹.** *Abbrev.*: A.V.M.

air·waves (er′wāvz′) *n.pl.* the medium by which radio and television signals are transmitted.

air·way (er′wā′) *n.* **1** a route for aircraft. **2** a passage for air. **3** a specified radio frequency for broadcasting. **4 airways,** *pl.* **a** airline. **b** channels for radio or television broadcasting.

air well air shaft.

air·wo·man (er′wùm′ən) *n., pl.* **-wo·men. 1** a woman who pilots an aircraft. **2** aircraftwoman. See chart at **rank¹.** *Abbrev.*: AW **3** any woman serving in an air force.

air·wor·thy (er′wèr′ᴛᴌē) *adj.* fit or safe for service in the air. —**air′wor′thi·ness,** *n.*

air·y (er′ē) *adj.* **air·i·er, air·i·est. 1** like air; not solid or substantial. **2** light as air; graceful; delicate. **3** light-hearted; gay. **4** open to currents of air; breezy. **5** reaching high into the air; lofty. **6** of air; in the air. **7** unnatural; affected: *His airy manner made him seem very haughty.* **8** flippant.

air·y–fair·y (er′ē fer′ē) *adj.* very fanciful or idealistic; unrealistic: *an airy-fairy scheme to make a million.*

aisle (īl) *n.* **1** a passage between rows of seats in a hall, theatre, school, church, etc. **2** the part of a church at the side of the nave, choir, or transept and set off by pillars. **3** any long or narrow passageway. See **basilica** for picture. [ME *ele* < OF < L *ala* wing; influenced in form by F *aile* and E *isle* and in meaning by *alley*]

aitch (āch) *n.* the letter *h* or the sound represented by it: *She drops her aitches when she speaks fast.*

a·jar¹ (ə jär′) *adv. or adj.* (*never precedes a noun*) of a door or gate, opened a little way. [ME *on char* on the turn; OE *cerr* turn] ☛ *Usage.* See note at **a¹.**

a·jar² (ə jär′) *adv.* not in harmony. [< *a-* in + *jar* discord]

a.k.a. also known as.

ak·ee (ak′ē) See ackee.

A·ke·la (ə kā′lə *or* ə kē′lə) *n.* cubmaster. [from *Akela,* the Lone Wolf, the leader of the wolf pack in Rudyard Kipling's *The Jungle Book*]

a·kim·bo (ə kim′bō) *adj. or adv.* (*never precedes a noun*) with the hands on the hips and the elbows bent outward. [ME *in kene bowe,* apparently, in keen bow, at a sharp angle]

a·kin (ə kin′) *adj.* (*never precedes a noun*) **1** related by blood: *Your cousins are akin to you.* **2** *Linguistics.* descended from the

same root: *Guest is akin to host.* **3** alike; similar: *The friends are akin in their love of sports.* [for *of kin*]

al– the form of **ad–** before *l*, as in *ally*.

–al¹ *suffix.* of; like; having the nature of: *natural = of nature or like nature; ornamental = having the nature of ornament.* [< L *-alis* pertaining to]

–al² *suffix.* the act of —ing: *refusal = the act of refusing.* [< L *-ale*, neut. of *-alis*]

Al aluminum.

AL Alabama.

à la or **a la** (aʹlə *or* äʹlə; *French,* ä lä) in the manner of; in the style of. [< F]
☛ *Usage.* à la, a la. Although originally French, **a la** is now regarded as an English preposition: *a la Hollywood, a la Winston Churchill.* In formal writing and some advertising (for cosmetics and fashionable clothes), the accent mark is usually kept. It is often dropped in informal writing.

Ala. Alabama.

al·a·bas·ter (alʹə basˌtər *or* alʹə basˌtər) *n., adj.* —*n.* **1** a smooth, white, translucent variety of gypsum. Alabaster is often carved into ornaments and vases. **2** a variety of calcite that is somewhat translucent and often banded like marble. —*adj.* smooth, white, and translucent like alabaster. [ME < OF < L < Gk. *alabast(r)os* alabaster]

à la carte (aʹlə kärtʹ *or* äʹlə kärtʹ; *French,* ä lä kärtʹ) according to the menu, on which each dish is priced separately. Compare **table d'hôte.** [< F *à la carte* according to the bill of fare]

a·lack (ə lakʹ) *interj. Archaic.* an exclamation of sorrow or regret; alas.

a·lack·a·day (ə lakʹə dāˌ) *interj. Archaic.* alas! alack!

a·lac·ri·ty (ə lakʹrə tē) *n.* **1** cheerful willingness: *The boy took to Latin with alacrity.* **2** liveliness. [< L *alacritas* < *alacer* brisk]

A·lad·din (ə ladʹən) *n.* in *The Arabian Nights,* a youth who found a magic lamp and a magic ring. By rubbing either one of them, he could call a powerful spirit, or genie, to do whatever he commanded.

Aladdin's lamp a means of making any dream come true.

à la king (aʹ lə kingʹ *or* äʹ lə kingʹ) creamed with mushrooms, pimento, and green pepper: *chicken à la king.*

à la mode, a la mode, or **a·la·mode** (aʹ lə mōdʹ *or* äʹ lə mōdʹ) *adv.* **1** according to the prevailing fashion; in style. **2** in a certain way. *Desserts à la mode are served with ice cream. Beef à la mode is cooked with vegetables.* [< F]

a·larm (ə lärmʹ) *n., v.* —*n.* **1** sudden fear; fright; excitement caused by fear of danger. **2** a warning of approaching danger. **3** something that gives such a warning. **4** a call to arms or action. **5** a device that makes a noise to warn or awaken people.
—*v.* **1** fill with sudden fear; frighten: *He was alarmed because his friends were late in returning.* **2** warn (anyone) of approaching danger. **3** call to arms. [ME < OF *alarme* < Ital. *allarme* < *all'arme!* to arms!]
☛ *Syn. n.* **1.** See note at **fear.** —*v.* **1.** See note at **frighten.**

alarm clock a clock that can be set to ring a bell, etc. at any desired time, especially to waken people from sleep.

a·larm·ing (ə lärʹming) *adj.* of a frightening nature.
—**a·larmʹing·ly,** *adv.*

a·larm·ist (ə lärʹmist) *n.* one who raises alarms without good reason.

a·lar·um (ə lärʹəm, ə lerʹəm, *or* ə lärʹəm) *n. Archaic.* alarm.

a·la·ry (āʹlə rē *or* alʹə rē) *adj. Zoology.* **1** of or having to do with wings. **2** wing-shaped. [< L *alarius* < *ala* wing]

a·las (ə lasʹ) *interj.* an exclamation of sorrow, grief, regret, pity, or dread. [ME < OF *a ah* + *las* miserable < L *lassus* weary]

Alas. Alaska.

A·las·ka cedar or **cypress** (ə lasʹkə) yellow cypress.

Alaska Highway a highway that extends from Dawson Creek, British Columbia, to Fairbanks, Alaska.

A·las·kan (ə lasʹkən) *adj., n.* —*adj.* of or having to do with Alaska, one of the United States. —*n.* a native or long-term resident of Alaska.

a·late (āʹlāt) *adj.* having wings or winglike parts. [< L *alatus* < *ala* wing]

alb (alb) *n.* a long, usually white robe with long sleeves, worn by Roman Catholic priests and by some Anglicans and Lutherans in certain church services. It is usually made or linen or linen-like fabric. [< L (*vestis*) *alba* white (robe)]

al·ba·core (alʹbə kôrˌ) *n., pl.* **-core** or **-cores.** a long-finned, edible fish related to the tuna, found in the Atlantic. [< Pg. *albacor* < Arabic *al-bakūra*]

Al·ba·ni·an (al bāʹnē ən) *n., adj.* —*n.* **1** a native or inhabitant of Albania, a country in SE Europe. **2** the language of the people of

hat, āge, fär; let, ēqual, tèrm; it, īce
hot, ōpen, ôrder; oil, out; cup, pu̇t, rüle,
əbove, takən, pencəl, lemən, circəs

ch, child; ng, long; sh, ship
th, thin; ᴛʜ, then; zh, measure

Albania. It is an Indo-European language. —*adj.* of or having to do with Albania, its people, or their language.

al·ba·tross (alʹbə trosˌ) *n.* **1** any of a family (Diomedeidae) of large ocean birds found especially from about the Tropic of Capricorn south to Antarctica, having very long, narrow wings, webbed feet, a stout, hooked bill, and black, brown, or mostly white plumage. The largest species is the wandering albatross (*Diomedea exulans*), whose wingspread may reach 3.5 metres, the greatest of any living bird species. **2** a burden that one is obliged to bear, especially as a consequence of one's own actions or mistakes (from Coleridge's "The Rime of the Ancient Mariner"; the Mariner shoots the albatross, which the other sailors thought a sign of good luck, and is then forced to wear the dead bird around his neck). **3** anything that continually presents problems or makes things difficult. [var. of obsolete *alcatras* frigate bird < Sp. < Pg. *alcatraz* < Arabic *al-qadus* the bucket < Gk. *kados* < Phoenician]

al·be·it (ol bēʹit *or* ôl bēʹit) *conj.* although; even though. [ME *al be it* although it be]

Al·ber·tan (al bèrʹtən) *n., adj.* —*n.* a native or long-term resident of Alberta. —*adj.* of or having to do with Alberta or Albertans.

al·bert·ite (alʹbər tītˌ) *n.* a bituminous mineral resembling asphalt. [< *Albert* County, New Brunswick. + *-ite*]

al·bi·nism (alʹbə nizˌəm) *n.* the absence of color; the condition of being an albino.

al·bi·no (al bīʹnō *or* al bēʹnō) *n., pl.* **-nos. 1** a person who from birth lacks normal pigment and therefore has a pale, milky skin, very light or white hair, and pink eyes. **2** a plant or animal lacking normal color, especially an animal having white hair or fur and red eyes. [< Pg. *albino* < *albo* < L *albus* white]

Al·bi·on (alʹbē ən) *n. Poetic.* England. [< L]

al·bum (alʹbəm) *n.* **1** a book with blank pages for holding pictures, stamps, autographs, etc. **2** a phonograph record or set of records, together with the cardboard slipcover or case in which it is sold and any additional material included in the package, such as lyrics of songs, posters, etc.: *He has just put out a new two-record album.* **3** the record or set itself. **4** the slipcover or case of a phonograph record or set of records. **5** a collection in the form of a book of pictures, musical compositions, souvenirs, etc.: *We made an album of our trip.* [< L *album,* neut. of *albus* white]

al·bu·men (al byüʹmən) *n.* **1** the white of an egg, consisting mostly of albumin dissolved in water. **2** *Chemistry.* albumin. **3** *Botany.* the food for a young plant stored in a seed; endosperm. [< L *albumen* < *albus* white]
☛ *Hom.* **albumin.**

al·bu·min (al byüʹmən) *n. Chemistry.* any of a class of proteins soluble in water and found in the white of egg and in many other animal and plant tissues and juices. [< F *albumine* < L *albumen, -inis.* See ALBUMEN.]
☛ *Hom.* **albumen.**

al·bu·mi·nose (al byüʹmə nōsˌ) *adj.* albuminous.

al·bu·mi·nous (al byüʹmə nəs) *adj.* **1** of albumin. **2** resembling albumin. **3** containing albumin.

al·bur·num (al bèrʹnəm) *n.* the lighter, softer part of wood between the inner bark and the harder centre of a tree; sapwood. [< L *alburnum* < *albus* white]

Al·can Highway (alʹkan) Alaska Highway. [< *Al*aska + *Can*ada]

al·ca·zar or **al·cá·zar** (alʹkə zärˌ *or* al kazʹər; *Spanish,* äl käʹthär) *n.* **1** a palace of the Spanish Moors. **2** **Alcázar,** the palace of the Moorish kings at Seville, Spain, later occupied by the Spanish royal family. [< Sp. < Arabic *al-qasr* the castle < L *castrum* fort]

al·che·mist (alʹkə mist) *n.* in the Middle Ages, a student of alchemy. Alchemists tried to turn base metals into gold and to find the elixir of life.

al·che·my (alʹkə mē) *n.* **1** medieval chemistry, especially the search for a process by which base metals could be turned into gold. **2** any magic power or process for changing one thing into another: *the lovely alchemy of spring.* [ME < OF *alkemie* < Med.L *alchimia* < Arabic *al-kīmiyā* < LGk. *chēmeia* the extracting of medical juices < Gk. *chymeia* infusion < *chymos* juice of a plant]

al·co·hol (alʹkə holˌ *or* alʹkə hôlˌ) *n.* **1** the colorless liquid in wine, beer, whisky, gin, etc. that makes them intoxicating; grain alcohol; ethyl alcohol. Alcohol is used in medicine, in

manufacturing, and as a fuel. *Formula*: C_2H_5OH **2** any intoxicating liquor containing this liquid. **3** *Chemistry.* any of a group of similar organic compounds. Alcohols contain a hydroxyl group and react with organic acids to form esters. Wood alcohol or methyl alcohol, CH_3OH, is very poisonous. [< Med.L *alcohol* (originally, "fine powder," then "essence") < Arabic *al-koh'l* powdered antimony]

al·co·hol·ic (al'kə hol'ik *or* al'kə hôl'ik) *adj., n.* —*adj.* **1** of or having to do with alcohol. **2** containing alcohol. **3** suffering from alcoholism.
—*n.* a person suffering from alcoholism.

al·co·hol·ism (al'kə hol iz'əm *or* al'kə hôl iz'əm) *n.* **1** continual excessive and compulsive consumption of alcoholic drinks. **2** a chronic disorder resulting from this.

Al·co·ran (al'kô rän' *or* al'kô ran') *n.* the Koran.

al·cove (al'kōv) *n.* **1** a recessed section of a room; nook: *Some bachelor apartments have an alcove for a bed.* **2** a hollow, usually arched space in a wall, etc.; niche. **3** summerhouse. [< F < Sp. *alcoba* < Arabic *al-qubba* the vaulted chamber]

Ald. alderman.

Al·deb·a·ran (al deb'ə rən) *n.* the brightest star in the constellation Taurus. [< Arabic *al-dabarān* the follower (i.e., of the Pleiades) < *dabar* follow]

al·de·hyde (al'də hīd') *n.* **1** a transparent, colorless liquid, with a suffocating smell, produced by the partial oxidation of ordinary alcohol. *Formula*: CH_3CHO **2** any similar organic compound. [short for NL *al(cohol) dehyd(rogenatum)*, alcohol deprived of its hydrogen]

al den·te (äl den'tā *or* al den'tē) *Italian.* of pasta, etc., cooked so as to be still firm when eaten; not cooked to the soft stage.

al·der (ol'dər *or* ôl'dər) *n.* any of a genus (*Alnus*) of shrubs or trees of the birch family found especially in cool, wet parts of the northern hemisphere, having toothed leaves and clusters of catkins that develop into woody cones. The bark of alders is used in tanning and dyeing. [OE *alor*]

al·der·man (ol'dər mən *or* ôl'dər mən) *n., pl.* **-men.** a member of the governing body of a city, elected by the people of a particular district or ward of the city. *Abbrev*: Ald. or Aldm. [OE *(e)aldorman < ealdor* elder, chief + *mann* man]

al·der·man·ic (ol'dər man'ik *or* ôl'dər man'ik) *adj.* of, having to do with, or characteristic of an alderman or aldermen.

Al·der·ney (ol'dər nē *or* ôl'dər nē) *n., pl.* **-neys.** any of various breeds of cattle, such as Jersey or Guernsey, that originally came from Alderney or any of the other Channel Islands.

Aldm. alderman.

ale (āl) *n.* an alcoholic drink brewed from malt with a type of yeast that rises to the top, and flavored with hops. [OE *alu*]
☛ *Hom.* ail.

a·lee (ə lē') *adv. or adj.* on or toward the side of a ship that is away from the wind. [< *a¹-* + *lee*]

ale·house (āl'hous') *n. Historical.* a place where ale or beer was sold and drunk.

a·lem·bic (ə lem'bik) *n.* **1** a glass or metal container formerly used in distilling. **2** something that transforms or refines: *Imagination is the alembic of the mind.* [ME < OF < Med.L *alembicus* < Arabic *al-anbiq* the still < Gk. *ambix* cup]

A·len·çon (ä län sôn'; *often,* ə len'sən) *n.* a kind of fine lace. [< *Alençon,* a city in NW France where this lace is made]

a·lert (ə lèrt') *adj., n., v.* —*adj.* **1** watchful; wide-awake: *A good hunting dog is alert to every sound and movement in the field.* **2** brisk; active; nimble: *A sparrow is very alert in its movements.* —*n.* **1** a signal warning of an air attack or other impending danger. **2** the period of time in which this warning is in effect: *We stayed at home throughout a hurricane alert.* **3** a signal to troops, etc. to be ready for action.
on the alert, on the lookout; watchful; wide-awake.
—*v.* call to arms; warn. [< F *alerte* < Ital. *all' erta* on the watch, ult. < L *erigere* raise up] —**a·lert'ly,** *adv.* —**a·lert'ness,** *n.*
☛ *Syn.* **adj. 1.** See note at **watchful.**

ALERT (ə lèrt') *n.* **1** *Trademark.* acronym for Alcohol Level Evaluation Roadside Test, a portable device for measuring the level of alcohol in a person's blood, used to test the driver of a motor vehicle for impairment. **2** Often, **Alert,** any similar portable device for measuring the level of alcohol in the blood.

A·le·ut (al'ē üt') *n.* **1** a native or inhabitant of the Aleutian Islands, southwest of Alaska. **2** The language of the Aleuts, which is distantly related to Eskimo. [< Russian]

al·e·vin (al'ə vin) *n.* a very young fish, especially a very young salmon. [< F < L *allevare* lift up, rear < *ad-* to + *levare* raise]

ale·wife¹ (āl'wīf') *n., pl.* **-wives.** a woman who keeps an alehouse.

ale·wife² (āl'wīf') *n., pl.* **-wives.** a food fish of the herring family found in sea and fresh waters of eastern North America; gaspereau. [origin uncertain]

Al·ex·an·dri·an (al'ig zan'drē ən) *adj.* **1** of or having to do with Alexander the Great. **2** of or having to do with Alexandria, a seaport in Egypt, or the culture that flourished there in ancient times.

al·ex·an·drine *or* **Al·ex·an·drine** (al'ig zan'drin) *n.* a line of poetry having six iambic feet, with a caesura (pause) after the third foot. *Example*:
He seeks | out might | y charms, | to trou | ble sleep | y minds.
[< F *alexandrin*; because this metre was used in OF poems on *Alexander* the Great]

al·fal·fa (al fal'fə) *n.* a European plant (*Medicago sativa*) of the pea family having clusters of small purplish flowers, compound leaves, and a deep taproot. It is widely cultivated for forage and hay. [< Sp. < Arabic *al-fishfisha* the best kind of fodder]

al fi·ne (äl fē'nā) *Italian. Music.* to the end.

al·fres·co *or* **al fres·co** (al fres'kō) *adv. or adj.* in the open air; outdoors. [< Ital.]

alg. algebra.

al·ga (al'gə) *n.* sing. of **algae.**

al·gae (al'jē *or* al'jī) *n.pl.* a large group of mainly aquatic, one-celled or multi-celled organisms traditionally classified as plants, having chlorophyll but lacking true stems, roots, and leaves. Seven phyla or divisions are generally recognized, but authorities differ on the placement of these phyla in a kingdom or kingdoms. [< L *algae,* pl. of *alga* seaweed]

al·gal (al'gəl) *adj.* of or having to do with algae.

al·ge·bra (al'jə brə) *n.* a generalization of arithmetic in which letters or other symbols are used to represent any one of a set of numbers. The symbols and numbers are combined by adding, subtracting, etc. to form expressions that are used in equations and inequations for representing problem situations. Algebra is also used to illustrate properties of numbers; for example, $x \times 0 = 0$ states that the product of x (*any* number) and zero is zero. *Abbrev*: alg [< Med.L < Arabic *al-jabr* the bone setting; hence, reduction (i.e., of parts to a whole)]

al·ge·bra·ic (al'jə brā'ik) *adj.* of or used in algebra: $(a + b)(a - b) = a^2 - b^2$ *is an algebraic statement.* —**al'ge·bra'i·cal·ly,** *adv.*

al·ge·bra·i·cal (al'jə brā'ə kəl) *adj.* algebraic.

al·ge·bra·ist (al'jə brā'ist) *n.* a person who is skilled in algebra.

Al·ge·ri·an (al jēr ē ən) *n., adj.* —*n.* a native or inhabitant of Algeria, a country in N Africa, or of Algiers, its capital. —*adj.* of or having to do with Algeria or its people.

al·gin (al'jən) *n.* **1** alginic acid. **2** alginate.

al·gi·nate (al'jə nāt') *n.* a soluble salt of alginic acid, used in the manufacture of textiles, as a thickening agent in foods and cosmetics, etc.

al·gin·ic acid (al jin'ik) an insoluble colloidal carbohydrate obtained from the cell walls of kelp, used in the manufacture of rubber tires, the preparation of emulsifiers, etc. *Formula*: $(C_6H_8O_6)_n$

Al·gol (al'gol) *n.* a bright binary star in the constellation Perseus that varies in brightness because its smaller, brighter component is periodically eclipsed by its larger, weaker one.

ALGOL *or* **Algol** (al'gol) *n.* a high-level computer programming language in which algorithms can be expressed in algebraic terms. It is designed for scientific and mathematical use. [an acronym for *algorithmic language.* 20c.]

al·go·log·i·cal (al'gə loj'ə kəl) *adj.* of or having to do with algology. —**al'go·log'i·cal·ly,** *adv.*

al·gol·o·gist (al gol'ə jist) *n.* a person trained in alogology, especially one whose work it is.

al·gol·o·gy (al gol'ə jē) *n.* the branch of botany that deals with the study of algae.

Al·gon·ki·an (al gong'kē ən) *n. or adj.* **1** See **Algonquian.** **2** *Obsolete.* Proterozoic.

Al·gon·kin (al gong'kin) *n.* Algonquin.

Al·gon·qui·an (al gong'kē ən *or* al gong'kwē ən) *n., adj.* —*n.* **1** a stock or family of languages spoken by a large number of confederacies, tribes, and bands of Amerindian peoples who traditionally occupied much of central and eastern North America, including large areas from Labrador south to Carolina and from the Atlantic west to the Rocky Mountains. Among the languages included in this family are Abenaki, Blackfoot, Cree, Malecite, Micmac, Ojibwa, and Ottawa. **2** a member of any of the Amerindian peoples speaking one of these languages. **3** Algonquin (def. 1).

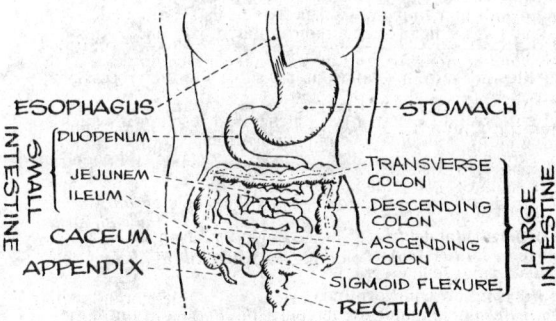

—*adj.* of, having to do with, or designating these peoples or their languages. [< *Algonquin*]

Al·gon·quin (al gong′kin *or* al gong′kwin) *n., adj.* —*n.* **1** a member of an Amerindian people living in eastern Ontario and Quebec. **2** a dialect of Ojibwa, spoken by these people. —*adj.* of, having to do with, or designating these people or their language.

al·go·rism (al′gə riz′əm) *n.* **1** the system of Arabic numerals, using nine digits and zero; decimal system of counting. **2** the skill of computing with any system of numbers. **3** algorithm. [ME < OF *algorisme* < Med.L *algorismus* < Arabic *al-khuwarizmi* < *al-Khowarizmi*, a famous Arab mathematician of the 9th century A.D.]

al·go·rithm (al′gə riŦH′əm) *n.* **1** *Mathematics.* a special procedure or set of rules for solving a certain type of problem, especially one involving repetition of an operation. **2** any set of rules or step-by-step procedure for accomplishing some end.

Al·ham·bra (al ham′brə) *n.* the palace of the Moorish kings near Granada, Spain. [< Sp. < Arabic *al-hamra′* the red (house)]

a·li·as (ā′lē əs) *n., pl.* **a·li·as·es;** *adv.* —*n.* an assumed name; other name: *The spy's real name was Harrison, but he sometimes went by the alias of Johnson.* —*adv.* otherwise called; with the assumed name of. [< L *alias* at another time]
☞ *Usage.* In law, **alias** is still often written in italics (Harrison *alias* Johnson), in which case it stands for the Latin *alias dictus,* meaning "otherwise called."

al·i·bi (al′ə bī′) *n., pl.* **-bis;** *v.* **-bied, -bi·ing.** —*n.* **1** *Law.* the plea that a person accused of a certain offence was somewhere else when the offence was committed. **2** *Informal.* an excuse. —*v. Informal.* make an excuse. [< L *alibi* elsewhere]

al·ien (ā′lē ən *or* āl′yən) *n., adj.* —*n.* **1** a person who is not a citizen of the country in which he lives. **2** a foreigner; stranger. —*adj.* **1** of or by another country; foreign: *an alien language, alien domination.* **2** unfamiliar; strange: *alien ideas.* **3** not characteristic or compatible; repugnant or opposed (*used with* **to**): *Unkindness is alien to her nature.* [ME < OF < L *alienus* < *alius* other]

al·ien·a·ble (ā′lē ən ə bəl *or* āl′yən ə bəl) *adj.* capable of being transferred to another person: *alienable property.*

al·ien·ate (ā′lē ən āt′ *or* āl′yən āt′) *v.* **-at·ed, -at·ing. 1** cause (a friend, etc.) to become indifferent or hostile; estrange: *Her moodiness is alienating many of her friends.* **2** turn away; divert: *to alienate someone's affections.* **3** cause to become withdrawn or isolated: *She is becoming more and more alienated. Many social pressures tend to alienate our youth.* **4** *Law.* transfer the ownership of (property) to another: *Enemy property was alienated during the war.*

al·ien·a·tion (ā′lē ən ā′shən *or* āl′yən ā′shən) *n.* **1** a turning away in indifference or hostility; estrangement. **2** withdrawal or detachment from one's society or environment; isolation: *Alienation can be a serious problem in an urbanized society.* **3** *Law.* a transfer of the ownership of property to another.

al·ien·ist (ā′lē ən ist *or* āl′yən ist) *n.* a psychiatrist, especially one who testifies in court. [< F *aliéniste* < L *alienus* insane]

al·i·form (al′i fôrm′) *adj.* of or having to do with wings; wing-shaped. [< L *ala* wing + E *-form*]

a·light[1] (ə līt′) *v.* **a·light·ed** *or* (*poetic*) **a·lit, a·light·ing. 1** get down; get off: *to alight from a horse.* **2** come down from the air and settle; come down from flight. **3** come by chance (*on* or *upon*). [OE *ālīhtan*, ult. < *līht* light (in weight); originally, with reference to taking one's weight off a horse or vehicle]

a·light[2] (ə līt′) *adv. or adj.* **1** lighted up; illuminated: *a face alight with joy.* **2** on fire: *The candles were still alight.* [OE *ālīht* illuminated]

a·lign (ə līn′) *v.* **1** bring into line or alignment: *to align the sights of a gun with the target, to align the wheels of a car.* **2** place in a line: *Lombardy poplars were aligned along the drive.* **3** form an alliance with or against a particular party, group, cause, etc.: *They aligned themselves against the supporters of capital punishment.* Also, **aline.** [< F *aligner* < *a-* to (< L *ad-*) + *ligner* < L *lineare* < *linea* line]

a·lign·ment (ə līn′mənt) *n.* **1** an arrangement in a straight line; formation in a line; bringing into line. **2** the line or lines so formed. **3** a joining together (of persons, nations, etc.) for a common purpose.

a·like (ə līk′) *adv., adj.* —*adv.* **1** in the same way: *Robert and his father walk alike.* **2** similarly; equally. —*adj.* like one another; similar: *These twins are very much alike.* [OE *gelīc, onlīc*]

al·i·ment (al′ə mənt) *n.* food; nourishment. [< L *alimentum* < *alere* nourish]

al·i·men·ta·ry (al′ə men′tə rē *or* al′ə men′trē) *adj.* **1** having to do with food and nutrition. **2** nourishing; nutritious. **3** providing support or sustenance.

The human alimentary canal

alimentary canal the parts of the body through which food passes. The mouth, esophagus, stomach, intestines, and anus are parts of the alimentary canal.

al·i·men·ta·tion (al′ə men tā′shən) *n.* **1** nourishment; nutrition. **2** maintenance; support.

al·i·mo·ny (al′ə mō′nē) *n.* **1** *Law.* money paid by a person for the support of his or her spouse under a separation agreement. Compare **maintenance.** **2** *Informal.* money paid for the support of a former spouse after divorce. [< L *alimonia* sustenance < *alere* nourish]

a·line (ə līn′) *v.* **a·lined, a·lin·ing.** See **align.**

a·line·ment (əl īn′mənt) See **alignment**

al·i·quant (al′ə kwənt) *adj.* not able to divide a number or quantity without leaving a remainder: *5 is an aliquant part of 14.* [< L *aliquantus* somewhat < *alius* some + *quantus* how much]

al·i·quot (al′ə kwət) *adj.* able to divide a number or quantity without leaving a remainder: *3 is an aliquot part of 12.* [< L *aliquot* some < *alius* some + *quot* how many]

a·lit (ə lit′) *v. Poetic.* a pt. and a pp. of **alight**[1].

a·live (ə līv′) *adj.* **1** living; not dead: *The man is alive.* **2** in continued activity or operation: *Keep the principles of liberty alive.* **3** of all living: *the happiest man alive.* **4** active; lively. **5** connected with a source of electricity; charged electrically. **6** of telephones, microphones, etc. not shut off; operating or functioning.
alive to, noticing; awake to; sensitive to.
alive with, full of; swarming with: *The streets were alive with people.*
look alive! hurry up! be quick! [OE *on life*]
☞ *Usage.* **Alive** is not normally used before a noun, where **live** (līv) and **living** may appear: *a live animal, living people.* **Alive** occurs after its noun or in the predicate: *the oldest man alive. He is still alive.*

a·liz·a·rin (ə liz′ə rin) *n.* a red dye prepared from coal tar, formerly obtained from madder. *Formula:* $C_{14}H_8O_4$ [< F *alizarine* < *alizari* < Sp. < Arabic *al-ʼuṣara(h)* the extract]

al·ka·li (al′kə lī′) *n., pl.* **-lis** or **-lies. 1** *Chemistry.* any base or hydroxide that is soluble in water, neutralizes acids and forms salts with them, and turns red litmus blue. Lye and ammonia are alkalis. **2** any salt or mixture of salts that neutralizes acids. Some desert soils contain much alkali. [< MF *alcali* < Arabic *al-qalī* the ashes of saltwort (a genus of plant)]

al·ka·line (al′kə līn′ *or* al′kə lin) *adj.* **1** of or like an alkali. **2** containing an alkali: *The soil around the slough was alkaline.*

alkaline–earth metals calcium, strontium, and barium. Some authorities include beryllium, magnesium, and radium.

alkaline earths the oxides of the alkaline-earth metals.

al·ka·lin·i·ty (al′kəl in′ə tē) *n.* an alkaline quality or condition.

al·ka·lize (al′kə līz′) *v.* **-lized, -liz·ing.** make alkaline. —**al′ka·li·za′tion,** *n.*

al·ka·loid (al′kə loid′) *n.* an organic substance containing nitrogen; a substance that resembles an alkali and contains nitrogen. Many alkaloids obtained from plants are drugs, such as cocaine, strychnine, morphine, and quinine. Alkaloids are often very poisonous.

Al·ko·ran (al′kô rän′ *or* al′kô ran′) *n.* Koran.

al·kyd (al′kid) *n.* **1** any of several synthetic resins made by heating certain organic acids with alcohols, used especially for paints and other finishes. **2** (*adj.*) of, containing, or designating any of these resins: *Alkyd paint is the common oil-base household paint that is thinned with turpentine or solvent.*

al·kyl (al′kəl) *n.* **1** any of a group of univalent hydrocarbon radicals having the general formula C_nH_{2n+1}. **2** (*adj.*) of, designating, or containing any of these radicals. **3** an organic compound consisting of such a radical bound with one or more metal atoms.

al·kyl·ate (al′kə lāt′) *v.* **-at·ed, at·ing.** subject to the process of alkylation.

al·kyl·a·tion (al′kə lā′shən) *n.* **1** a chemical reaction in which a hydrogen atom in an organic compound is replaced by an alkyl group. **2** the addition of an alkyl group to an organic compound in producing high-octane fuels.

all (ol *or* ôl) *adj., pron., n., adv.* —*adj.* **1** the whole of: *all Europe.* **2** every one of: *all men.* **3** the greatest possible: *He made all haste to reach home in time.* **4** any; any whatever: *The prisoner denied all connection with the crime.* **5** nothing but; only: *all words and no thought.*
all in, *Informal.* weary; worn out.
—*pron.* **1** the whole number; everyone: *All of us are going.* **2** the whole quantity; everything: *All that glitters is not gold.*
—*n.* everything one has: *He lost all in the fire.*
above all, before everything else.
after all, when everything has been considered; nevertheless.
all at once, suddenly.
all but, almost; nearly: *He was all but dead from fatigue, but he struggled on.*
all in all, on the whole; taking everything into consideration: *All in all it was an exciting election.*
at all, **a** under any conditions. **b** in any way.
for all (that), in spite of; notwithstanding.
in all, counting every person or thing; altogether: *There were 100 men in all.*
—*adv.* **1** wholly; entirely: *The cake is all gone.* **2** each; apiece: *The score was even at forty all.*
all of, as much as; no less than.
all that, *Informal.* to a particular extent or amount; very; so (*used with negatives*): *I wasn't all that keen on going.*
go all out, use all one's resources; go the whole way, without limiting oneself: *They decided to go all out and hire a band for the dance.*
[OE *eall*]
☛ Hom. **awl.**

al·la bre·ve (al′ə brā′vā) *Music.* **1** a measure having two or four beats in which a half note represents one beat. **2** the symbol indicating this. [< Ital.]

Al·lah (al′ə *or* ä′lə) *n.* the Moslem name of the one Supreme Being, or God.

all-A·mer·i·can (ol′ə mer′i kən *or* ôl′-) *adj.* **1** representing or typical of the United States or Americans. **2** composed entirely of Americans or American elements. **3** situated wholly within the borders of the United States. **4** of, having to do with, or involving all the nations of the western hemisphere.

al·lar·gan·do (ä′lär gän′dō) *adj. Music.* gradually becoming slower and louder. [< Ital.]

all-a·round (ol′ə round′ *or* ôl′-) *adj.* all-round.

al·lay (ə lā′) *v.* **-layed, -lay·ing. 1** put at rest; quiet: *His fears were allayed by the news of the safety of his family.* **2** relieve; check: *Her fever was allayed by the medicine.* **3** make less; weaken. [OE *ālecgan*]

all-Ca·na·di·an (ol′kə nā′dē ən *or* ôl′-) *adj.* **1** representing or typical of Canada or Canadians: *an all-Canadian menu.* **2** composed entirely of Canadians or Canadian elements: *an all-Canadian hockey team.* **3** situated wholly within Canada's borders: *an all-Canadian route.*

all clear a signal indicating the end of an air raid or other danger.

al·le·ga·tion (al′ə gā′shən) *n.* **1** an assertion without proof: *He makes so many wild allegations that no one will believe him.* **2** an assertion: *The lawyer's allegation was proved.* [ME < OF < L *allegatio, -onis* < *allegare* send a message, cite < *ad-* to + *legare* commission, ult. < *lex* law]

al·lege (ə lej′) *v.* **-leged, leg·ing. 1** assert without proof. **2** state positively; assert; declare: *This man alleges that his watch has been stolen.* **3** give or bring forward as a reason, argument, or excuse. [< AF *alegier* < L *ex-* out + *litigare* strive, sue; with sense of L *allegare* charge] —**al·leg′er,** *n.*

al·leged (ə lejd′) *adj.* **1** asserted without proof: *The alleged theft never really happened.* **2** asserted; declared. **3** brought forward as a reason.

al·leg·ed·ly (ə lej′id lē) *adv.* according to what is or has been alleged.

al·le·giance (ə lē′jəns) *n.* **1** the loyalty owed by a citizen to his country or by a subject to his ruler. **2** loyalty; faithfulness to a person, cause, etc. that is entitled to obedience or honor. [ME *alegeaunce* < OF *ligeance* < *lige* liege]

al·le·gor·i·cal (al′ə gôr′ə kəl) *adj.* explaining or teaching something by a story; using allegory. —**al′le·gor′i·cal·ly,** *adv.*

al·le·gor·ist (al′ə gôr′ist) *n.* a writer of allegories.

al·le·go·rize (al′ə gə rīz′) *v.* **-rized, -riz·ing. 1** make into an allegory. **2** treat or interpret as an allegory. **3** use allegory.

al·le·go·ry (al′ə gô′rē) *n., pl.* **-ries.** a long and complicated story with an underlying moral meaning different from the surface meaning. An allegory may be regarded as an extended metaphor. *Example: Pilgrim's Progress* by John Bunyan. [ME < L < Gk. *allēgoria* < *allos* other + *agoreuein* speak]
☛ *Syn.* An **allegory,** a **fable,** or a **parable** is a story made up to present ideas in a concrete, vivid way. The incidents of an **allegory** may stand for political, spiritual, or romantic situations; its characters may be types (*Mr. Worldly Wiseman*) or personifications (*Courtesy, Jealousy*). A **fable** has as its characters animals or inanimate objects that by acting and talking like human beings call attention to human weaknesses and teach a common-sense lesson that is usually stated at the end: *Aesop's fables.* A **parable** is a short story of everyday life used to teach a moral by comparison or by implication: *Jesus often used parables.*

al·le·gret·to (al′ə gret′ō) *adj., adv., n., pl.* **-tos.** *Music.* —*adj.* quick, but not as quick as allegro. —*adv.* in allegretto tempo. —*n.* such a part in a piece of music. [< Ital. *allegretto,* dim. of *allegro*]

al·le·gro (ə leg′rō *or* ə lā′grō) *adj., adv., n., pl.* **-gros.** *Music.* —*adj.* quick; lively. —*adv.* in allegro time. —*n.* such a part in a piece of music. [< Ital. < L *alicer,* unrecorded popular variant of *alacer* brisk]

al·le·lu·ia (al′ə lü′yə) *interj., n.* —*interj.* a liturgical form of hallelujah, meaning "praise ye the Lord." —*n.* a hymn of praise to the Lord. [< L < Gk. < Hebrew *hallēlūjāh* praise ye Jehovah]

al·le·mande (a′lə mand′; *French:* äl mänd′) *n.* **1** a German dance that became popular in France in the 1700's. **2** the music for such a dance. **3** *Music.* one of the movements of a classical suite. **4** in square dancing, a movement in which pairs of dancers interlace their right or left arms and turn in a circle.

al·ler·gen (al′ər jən) *n.* any substance that causes an allergic reaction. [< *aller(gy)* + *-gen*]

al·ler·gen·ic (al′ər jen′ik) *adj.* of or having to do with allergens.

al·ler·gic (ə lėr′jik) *adj.* **1** of or caused by allergy: *Hay fever is an allergic reaction.* **2** having an allergy: *Some people are allergic to milk.* **3** *Facetious.* having a strong dislike; averse (*to*): *She's allergic to work.*

al·ler·gist (al′ər jist′) *n.* a doctor who specializes in the diagnosis and treatment of allergies.

al·ler·gy (al′ər jē) *n., pl.* **-gies. 1** an unusual sensitiveness to a particular substance. Hay fever and asthma are often caused by allergies to certain pollens and dusts. **2** *Informal.* a strong dislike: *an allergy for work.* [< NL *allergia* < Gk. *allos* different, strange + *ergon* action]

al·le·vi·ate (ə lē′vē āt′) *v.* **-at·ed, -at·ing.** make easier to endure (suffering of the body or mind); relieve; lessen: *Heat often alleviates pain.* [< LL *alleviare* < L *ad-* up + *levis* light] —**al·le′vi·a′tor,** *n.*

al·le·vi·a·tion (ə lē′vē ā′shən) *n.* **1** alleviating or being alleviated. **2** something that alleviates.

al·le·vi·a·tive (ə lē′vē ə tiv *or* ə lē′vē ā′tiv) *adj., n.* —*adj.* alleviating. —*n.* anything that alleviates.

al·ley¹ (al′ē) *n., pl.* **-leys. 1** a narrow back street in a city or town; alleyway. **2** a path in a park or garden, bordered by trees. **3** a long, narrow enclosed place for bowling. **4** a building having a number of alleys for bowling. [ME < OF *alee* a going < *aler* go]

al·ley² (al′ē) *n., pl.* **-leys. 1** a large, white or colored glass marble used to shoot at the other marbles in a game. **2 alleys,** any game played with such marbles. [shortened form of *alabaster*]

al·ley·way (al′ē wā′) *n.* **1** an alley in a city or town. **2** a narrow passageway.

All Fools' Day April 1, April Fools' Day.

all fours 1 all four legs of an animal. **2** the arms and legs of a person; hands and knees.

all hail an exclamation of greeting or welcome.

All·hal·lows (ol′hal′ōz *or* ôl′-) *n.* November 1, All Saints' Day.

Allhallows Eve October 31, Halloween.

al·li·ance (ə lī′əns) *n.* **1** a union formed by agreement; joining of interests. An alliance may be a joining of family interests by

marriage, a joining of national interests by treaty, etc. 2 the nations, persons, etc. who belong to such a union. 3 an association; connection. 4 a similarity in structure or descent; relationship. [ME < OF *aliance* < *alier* unite < L *alligare* < *ad-* to + *ligare* bind]

al·lied (ə līd′ or al′īd) *adj.* 1 united by agreement or treaty; combined for some special purpose: *allied nations, allied armies.* 2 associated; connected: *allied industries. Reading and listening are allied activities.* 3 similar in structure or descent; related: *The dog and the wolf are allied animals.* 4 **Allied,** of, involving, or designating the Allies.

Al·lies (al′īz or ə līz′) *n.pl.* 1 the countries that fought against Germany and Austria in World War I. 2 the countries that fought against Germany, Italy, and Japan in World War II.

al·li·ga·tor (al′ə gā′tər) *n.* 1 either of two species of reptile (genus *Alligator* of the family Alligatoridae) having a long, thick body and tail, four short legs, powerful jaws with sharp teeth, and eyes and nostrils set on the top of the skull. The two species are the American alligator (*A. mississipiensis*) of the southern United States and the Chinese alligator (*A. sinensis*) of the Yangtze River Valley in China. 2 leather made from the hide of an alligator. 3 (*adj.*) made of this leather: *alligator shoes.* 4 *Cdn.* **a** formerly, a scow-like amphibious craft equipped with a winch and cable, used for towing log booms, breaking up logjams, etc.: *The first alligators, built about 1890, were steam driven, sidewheel vessels.* **b** a small gasoline or diesel-powered boat, usually equipped with a winch and cable, used for handling and hauling floating logs, breaking logjams, etc. [< Sp. *el lagarto* the lizard < L *lacertus* lizard]

alligator pear avocado.

all–im·por·tant (ol′im pôr′tənt or ôl′-) *adj.* essential; extremely important.

al·lit·er·ate (ə lit′ər āt′) *v.* -at·ed, at·ing. 1 a have the same first sound. **b** loosely, having the same first letter. 2 use alliteration. [back-formation from ALLITERATION.]

al·lit·er·a·tion (ə lit′ər ā′shən) *n.* 1 a repetition of the same first sound in a group of words or line of poetry. *Example:* "The sun sank slowly" shows alliteration of *s*. 2 less properly, repetition of the same first letter in a group of words or line of poetry. [< Med.L *alliteratio, -onis* < *ad-* to + L *litera* letter]

al·lit·er·a·tive (ə lit′ər ət iv or ə lit′ər ā′tiv) *adj.* 1 having words beginning with the same sound. 2 loosely, having words beginning with the same letter. —**al·lit′er·a′tive·ly,** *adv.* —**al·lit′er·a′tive·ness,** *n.*

al·lo·ca·ble (al′ə kə bəl) *adj.* capable of being allocated.

al·lo·cat·a·ble (al′ə kā′tə bəl) *adj.* allocable.

al·lo·cate (al′ə kāt′) *v.* -cat·ed, -cat·ing. 1 assign or set apart; designate; earmark: *funds allocated for capital expenditures.* 2 distribute; allot: *The money received has not yet been allocated.* 3 locate. [< Med.L *allocare* < L *ad-* to, at + *locus* place]

al·lo·ca·tion (al′ə kā′shən) *n.* an allotment, especially by government; distribution; assignment.

al·lo·morph (al′ə môrf′) *n.* 1 *Chemistry.* allotrope. 2 *Linguistics.* one of the variant forms of a morpheme: *com-* in *compress, col-* in *collect, con-* in *connect,* and *cor-* in *correct* are allomorphs of the morpheme *com-*. [< Gk. *allos* other + *morphē* form]

al·lo·path (al′ə path′) *n.* 1 a doctor who uses allopathy. 2 a person who favors allopathy.

al·lo·path·ic (al′ə path′ik) *adj.* of allopathy; using allopathy. —**al·lo·path′i·cal·ly,** *adv.*

al·lop·a·thist (ə lop′ə thist) *n.* allopath.

al·lop·a·thy (ə lop′ə thē) *n.* a method of treating a disease by using remedies to produce effects different from the symptoms produced by the disease. Compare **homeopathy.** [< G *Allopathie* < Gk. *allos* other + *patheia* suffering]

al·lo·phone (al′ə fōn′) *n.* any one of a family of similar speech sounds that are heard as the same sound by speakers of a given language or dialect. In English, the *t* in *top* and the *t* in *stop,* although different in quality, are allophones of the phoneme *t.* [< Gk. *allos* other + E *-phone* sound (< Gk. *phōnē*)]

al·lo·saur (al′ə sôr′) *n.* any of a genus (*Allosaurus*) of large, carnivorous dinosaurs whose fossilized remains have been found in Jurassic and Cretaceous rocks of North America. [< Gk. *allos* other + *sauros* lizard]

al·lot (ə lot′) *v.* -lot·ted, -lot·ting. 1 divide and distribute in parts or shares: *The profits have all been allotted.* 2 give as a share; assign: *The teacher allotted work to each student.* [< OF *aloter* < *a-* to (< L *ad-*) + *lot* lot < Gmc. Akin to LOT.]

☛ *Syn.* 1. **Allot, apportion** = to give out in shares. **Allot** emphasizes giving set amounts for a definite purpose or to particular persons, and does not suggest the way in which the shares are settled or distributed: *The Government is ready to allot homesteads in that area.* **Apportion** emphasizes division and distribution according to a fair plan, usually in proportions settled by some rule: *The reward money was apportioned among those who had helped in the rescue.* 2. See note at **assign.**

hat, āge, fär; let, ēqual, tèrm; it, īce
hot, ōpen, ôrder; oil, out; cup, pùt, rüle,
əbove, takən, pencəl, lemən, circəs

ch, child; ng, long; sh, ship
th, thin; ͪH, then; zh, measure

al·lot·ment (ə lot′mənt) *n.* 1 the act of alloting; a division or distribution in parts or shares. 2 something alloted; share or portion.

al·lo·trope (al′ə trōp′) *n.* an allotropic form.

al·lo·trop·ic (al′ə trop′ik) *adj. Chemistry.* occurring in two or more forms that differ in physical and chemical properties but not in the kind of atoms of which they are composed.

al·lot·ro·pism (ə lot′rə piz′əm) *n.* allotropy.

al·lot·ro·py (ə lot′rə pē) *n. Chemistry.* the property or fact of being allotropic. [< Gk. *allotropia* < *allos* other + *tropos* manner]

all–out (ol′out′ or ôl′-) *adj.* involving one's entire resources; total; complete: *an all-out effort to win, all-out war.*

all·o·ver (ol′ō′vər or ôl′-) *adj.* 1 covering the whole surface. 2 having a pattern that is repeated over the whole surface.

al·low (ə lou′) *v.* 1 let; permit: *The class was not allowed to leave until the bell rang.* 2 let have; give: *His father allows him $10 a week as spending money.* 3 admit; acknowledge; recognize: *The judge allowed the claim of the man whose property was damaged.* 4 add or subtract to make up for something: *to allow an extra hour for travelling time.* 5 permit to happen, especially through carelessness or neglect. 6 *Dialect.* say; think: *He allowed that he was going to the dance.*

allow for, take into consideration; provide for: *She purposely made the dress large to allow for shrinking.* [ME < OF *alouer* < L *allaudare* (< *ad-* to + *laus* praise) and Med.L *allocare* (< L *ad-* to, at + *locus* place)] —**al·low′er,** *n.*

☛ *Syn.* 1. See note at **permit.**

al·low·a·ble (ə lou′ə bəl) *adj.* allowed by law or by a person in authority; permitted by the rules of the game; not forbidden. —**al·low′a·ble·ness,** *n.* —**al·low′a·bly,** *adv.*

al·low·ance (ə lou′əns) *n.* 1 a limited share set apart; definite portion or amount given out: *Each child received a weekly allowance.* 2 an amount added or subtracted to make up for something: *a car trade-in allowance of $700.* 3 an allowing; conceding: *allowance of a claim.* 4 tolerance: *allowance of slavery.* 5 the variation in dimension allowed between machine parts that fit together. 6 in coinage, the variation from the standard permitted by the mint.

make allowance or **make allowance for,** take into consideration; allow for.

al·loy (*n.* al′oi; *v.* ə loi′) *n., v.* —*n.* 1 an inferior metal mixed with a more valuable one: *This gold is not pure; there is some alloy in it.* 2 a metal made by mixing and fusing two or more metals, or a metal and a non-metal: *Brass is an alloy of copper and zinc.* 3 any injurious addition.

—*v.* 1 make into an alloy. 2 make less valuable by mixing with a cheaper metal. 3 make worse; debase. [< F *aloi,* n., *aloyer,* v., OF *alei, aleier,* var. of *alier* unite, combine < L *alligare* < *ad-* to + *ligare* bind. Doublet of ALLY.]

all–pow·er·ful (ol′pou′ər fəl or ôl′-) *adj.* having power over all people, things, etc.; almighty; omnipotent.

all–pur·pose (ol′pèr′pəs or ôl′-) *adj.* suitable for all purposes for which a particular product, device, etc. is generally used: *All-purpose flour is as suitable for pastry and cakes as it is for bread.*

all right 1 all correct. 2 yes. 3 without doubt; certainly. 4 in good health. 5 satisfactory.

☛ *Usage.* See note at **alright.**

all–round (ol′round′ or ôl′-) *adj.* not limited or specialized; able to do many things; useful in many ways.

All Saints' Day November 1, a Christian church festival honoring all the saints; Allhallows.

All Souls' Day November 2, in the Roman Catholic Church, a day when services are held and prayers said for all the souls in purgatory.

all·spice (ol′spīs′ or ôl′-) *n.* 1 a spice made from the dried unripe berries of a West Indian tree (*Pimenta dioica*) of the myrtle family. Allspice has a flavor like a combination of cinnamon, nutmeg, and cloves. 2 the berry of this tree. 3 the tree itself.

all square *Informal.* 1 having paid what is due; having done what is needed. 2 having the same score; tied; even: *The teams were all square at the end of the second period.*

all–star (ol′stär′ or ôl′-) *adj.* made up of the best players or performers.

all–ter·rain vehicle (ôl′tə răn *or* ôl′-; ôl′ter′ān *or* ôl′-) a motor vehicle designed for travel off roads, on rough land, over snow, or through water, etc.

all–time (ôl′tīm′ *or* ôl′-) *adj. Informal.* **1** for all time up to the present. **2** that sets a record: *an all-time high in wheat prices.*

al·lude (ə lüd′) *v.* **-lud·ed, -lud·ing.** refer indirectly (*to*); mention in passing: *Do not ask him about his failure; do not even allude to it.* [< L *alludere* < *ad-* with + *ludere* play]
☛ *Syn.* See note at refer.
☛ *Usage.* Do not confuse **allude** with **elude.**

al·lure (ə lür′) *v.* **-lured, -lur·ing;** *n.* —*v.* tempt or attract very strongly; fascinate; charm. —*n.* fascination; charm. [ME < OF *alurer* < *a-* to (< L *ad-*) + *leurre* lure < Gmc. Related to LURE.] —**al·lur′er,** *n.*
☛ *Syn. v.* **2.** See note at **lure.**

al·lure·ment (ə lür′mənt) *n.* **1** charm; fascination. **2** temptation; attraction.

al·lur·ing (ə lür′ing) *adj.* **1** tempting; attracting. **2** charming; fascinating. —**al·lur′ing·ly,** *adv.* —**al·lur′ing·ness,** *n.*

al·lu·sion (ə lü′zhən) *n.* an indirect or passing reference. [< L *allusio, -onis* < *alludere.* See ALLUDE.]
☛ *Usage.* See note at **illusion.**

al·lu·sive (ə lü′siv) *adj.* containing an allusion; full of allusions. —**al·lu′sive·ly,** *adv.* —**al·lu′sive·ness,** *n.*

al·lu·vi·al (ə lü′vē əl) *adj., n.* —*adj.* consisting of or formed by sand or mud left by flowing water. A delta is an alluvial deposit at the mouth of a river. —*n.* alluvial soil.

al·lu·vi·um (ə lü′vē əm) *n., pl.* **-vi·ums** *or* **-vi·a** (-vē ə). the sand, mud, etc. left by flowing water. [< L *alluvium,* neut. of *alluvius* alluvial < *ad-* up + *luere* wash]

all–weath·er (ôl′weᴛʜ′ər *or* ôl′-) *adj.* **1** designed to be useable or practical in all kinds of weather: *an all-weather coat, an all-weather road.* **2** done or performed in all kinds of weather.

al·ly (*v.* ə lī′ *or* al′ī; *n.* al′ī *or* ə lī′) *v.* **-lied, -ly·ing;** *n., pl.* **-lies.** —*v.* **1** combine for some special purpose; unite by formal agreement (*to* or *with*). One nation allies itself with another to protect its people and interests. **2** associate; connect: *This newspaper is allied with three others.* **3** be similar in structure, descent, etc.; relate: *Dogs are allied to wolves.* —*n.* **1** a person or nation united with another for some special purpose. See also **Allies. 2** a related animal, plant, form, or thing. **3** a helper; supporter. [ME < OF *alier* < L *alligare* < *ad-* to + *ligare* bind. Doublet of ALLOY.]

al·ma ma·ter *or* **Al·ma Ma·ter** (al′mə mä′tər, äl′mə mä′tər *or* al′mä mä′tər) a person's school, college, or university. [< L *alma mater* bounteous mother]

al·ma·nac (ol′mə nak′ *or* ôl′mə nak′) *n.* a calendar or table showing the days, weeks and months. Many almanacs give information about the weather, sun, moon, stars, tides, church days, and other facts. [ME < Med.L, probably < LGk. < Arabic *al-manākh*]

al·ma·nack (ol′mə nak′ *or* ôl′mə nak′) See almanac.

Al·mey (al′mē) *n.* a Canadian variety of flowering crabapple having red wood, leaves, and flowers.

al·might·y (ol mīt′ē *or* ôl mīt′ē) *adj., adv., n.* —*adj.* **1** having supreme power; all-powerful. **2** *Informal.* great; very. —*adv. Informal.* exceedingly. —*n.* **the Almighty,** God. —**al·might′i·ly,** *adv.* —**al·might′i·ness,** *n.*

almighty dollar *Informal.* money thought of as all-powerful.

ALMOND

SEED   SHELL   FRUIT

al·mond (o′mənd *or* ä′mənd) *n.* **1** a small tree (*Prunus amygdalus*) of the rose family native to SW Asia but widely cultivated for its nutlike seeds. It is closely related to the peach. **2** the oval-shaped seed of this tree, eaten as a nut. **3** (*adj.*) shaped like an almond. **4** (*adj.*) made from almonds: *almond paste.* [ME < OF *almande* < L < Gk. *amygdalē*] —**al′mond-like,** *adj.*

al·mond–eyed (o′mənd īd′ *or* ä′mənd-) *adj.* having eyes that appear to be oval-shaped and to have pointed ends. The Chinese and Japanese are almond-eyed.

al·mon·er (al′mən ər *or* ol′mə nər) *n.* a person who distributes alms for a king, monastery, etc. [ME < OF *almosnier* < LL *elemosynarius* < L *eleemosyna* alms. See ALMS.]

al·mon·ry (al′mən rē *or* ol′mən rē) *n., pl.* **-ries.** a place where alms are distributed.

al·most (ol′mōst *or* ôl′mōst) *adv.* nearly: *Nine is almost ten.* [OE *eal māst* nearly]
☛ *Usage.* See note at **most.**

alms (omz *or* ämz) *n. sing. or pl.* money or gifts to help the poor. [OE *ælmysse* < VL *alimosina* < L *eleemosyna* < Gk. *eleēmosynē* compassion < *eleos* mercy]

alms·giv·er (omz′giv′ər *or* ämz′-) *n.* a person who helps the poor with money or other gifts.

alms·giv·ing (omz′giv′ing *or* ämz′-) *n. or adj.* giving help to the poor.

alms·house (omz′hous′ *or* ämz′-) *n.* a home for persons too poor to support themselves.

al·ni·co (al′ni kō′ *or* al nē′ kō) *n.* an alloy containing aluminum, nickel, and cobalt, much used in making magnets. [< *al*uminum + *ni*ckel + *co*balt]

al·oe (al′ō) *n., pl.* **-oes. 1** any of a large genus (*Aloe*) of mainly South African succulents belonging to the lily family, having a long spike of flowers and thick, fleshy narrow leaves. Some aloes are grown as house plants in temperate climates. **2 aloes,** a bitter drug made from the dried juice of the leaves of certain aloes (*used with a singular verb*). [OE *aluwe* < L < Gk.]

a·loft (ə loft′) *adv. or adj.* (*never precedes a noun*) **1** far above the earth; high up. **2** high above the deck of a ship; up among the sails, rigging, or masts of a ship. [ME < ON *á lopt* in the air]

a·lo·ha (ə lō′ə *or* ä lō′hä) *n. or interj.* **1** greetings; hello. **2** goodbye; farewell. [< Hawaiian]

a·lone (ə lōn′) *adj., adv.* —*adj.* **1** apart from other persons or things; solitary: *He was alone.* **2** without anyone else; only: *He alone remained.* **3** without anything more: *Meat alone is not the best diet for children.*
leave alone, not bother; not meddle with.
let alone, a not bother; not meddle with. **b** not to mention: *It would have been a hot day for summer, let alone early spring.*
—*adv.* only; merely; exclusively. [ME *al one* all (completely) one] —**a·lone′ness,** *n.*
☛ *Usage.* As an adjective, **alone** is most frequently used predicatively: *The little girl was alone.* Otherwise, it is usually used after the noun it modifies, rarely before the noun: *The dessert alone would have been enough for a whole meal.*

a·long (ə long′) *prep., adv.* —*prep.* from one end of something to the other: *Flowers are planted along the path. We walked along the street.* —*adv.* **1** further; onward: *Move along. Pass the word along.* **2** with one; at hand or accompanying one (*often used with* **with**): *He took his dog along. I'll go along with you.* **3** together (*with*); in association (*with*): *We had pop along with the food.* **4** *Informal.* there; present: *I'll be along in a minute.*
all along, from the very beginning: *He was here all along.*
get along, a *Informal.* manage with at least some success. **b** agree. **c** go away. **d** advance. **e** succeed; prosper. [OE *andlang*]

a·long·shore (ə long′shôr′) *adv.* near or along the shore.

a·long·side (*adv.* ə long′sīd′; *prep.* ə long′sīd′) *adv., prep.* —*adv.* at the side; close to the side; side by side.
alongside of, beside; next to.
—*prep.* by the side of; beside.

a·loof (ə lüf′) *adv., adj.* —*adv.* at a distance; withdrawn; apart: *One boy stood aloof from all the others.* —*adj.* unsympathetic; not interested; reserved. [< *a-* on + *loof* windward, probably < Du. *loef*] —**a·loof′ly,** *adv.* —**a·loof′ness,** *n.*

al·o·pe·cia (al′ə pē′shē ə) *n.* partial or complete loss of hair on the head; baldness.

a·loud (ə loud′) *adv.* **1** loud enough to be heard; not in a whisper. **2** in a loud voice; loudly.

alp (alp) *n.* a high mountain. [< L *Alpes* the Alps]

al·pac·a (al pak′ə) *n.* **1** a domesticated grazing animal (*Lama pacos*) raised in the mountains of Peru and Bolivia mainly for its long, soft, silky wool. It belongs to the same genus as the llama. **2** the wool of the alpaca. **3** a kind of warm, soft cloth made from this wool. **4** glossy, wiry cloth made of wool and cotton, usually black. [< Sp. < Arabic *al* the + Peruvian *paco* alpaca]

al·pen·horn (al′pən hôrn′) *n.* a long, powerful horn used in Switzerland for military signals and for calling cattle. [< G *Alpen* Alps + *Horn* horn]

al·pen·stock (al′pən stok′) *n.* a strong staff with an iron point, used in climbing mountains. [< G *Alpen* Alps + *Stock* stick]

al·pha (al′fə) *n.* **1** the first letter of the Greek alphabet (Α, α). **2** a beginning; first in a series. **3 Alpha,** *Astronomy.* the brightest star in a constellation: *Alpha Herculis is the brightest star in the constellation Hercules.*

COMPARATIVE TABLE OF ALPHABETS

The transliterations are those used in the etymologies of this dictionary.

GREEK Forms	Name	Sound	ARABIC Forms	Name	Sound	HEBREW Forms	Name	Sound	CYRILLIC Forms	Sound
A α	alpha	a	ا	alif		א	aleph	'	А а	a
B β	beta	b	ب	bā	b	ב	beth	b, bh	Б б	b
									В в	v
Γ γ	gamma	g, n	ت	tā	t	ג	gimel	g, gh	Г г	g
Δ δ	delta	d	ث	thā	th	ד	daleth	d, dh	Д д	d
E ε	epsilon	e	ج	jīm	j	ה	he	h	Е е	e
Z ζ	zeta	z	ح	ḥā	ḥ	ו	waw	w	Ж ж	zh
H η	eta	ē	خ	khā	kh	ז	zayin	z	З з	z
Θ θ	theta	th	د	dāl	d	ח	heth	ḥ	И и Й й	i, ī
I ι	iota	i	ذ	dhāl	dh	ט	teth	ṭ	К к	k
K κ	kappa	k	ر	rā	r	י	yod	y	Л л	l
Λ λ	lambda	l	ز	zāy	z	כ ך	kaph	k, kh	М м	m
M μ	mu	m	س	sīn	s	ל	lamed	l	Н н	n
N ν	nu	n	ش	shīn	sh	מ ם	mem	m	О о	o
Ξ ξ	xi	x	ص	ṣād	ṣ	נ ן	nun	n	П п	p
O o	omicron	o	ض	ḍād	ḍ	ס	samekh	s	Р р	r
Π π	pi	p	ط	ṭā	ṭ	ע	ayin	'	С с	s
P ρ	rho	r, rh	ظ	ẓā	ẓ	פ ף	pe	p, ph	Т т	t
Σ σ ς	sigma	s	ع	'ayn	'	צ ץ	sadhe	ṣ	У у	u
T τ	tau	t	غ	ghayn	gh	ק	qoph	q	Ф ф	f
Υ υ	upsilon	y, u	ف	fā	f	ר	resh	r	Х х	kh
Φ φ	phi	ph	ق	qāf	q	שׂ	sin	ś	Ц ц	ts
X χ	chi	ch	ك	kāf	k	שׁ	shin	sh	Ч ч	ch
Ψ ψ	psi	ps	ل	lām	l	ת	taw	t, th	Ш ш	sh
Ω ω	omega	ō	م	mīm	m				Щ щ	shch
			ن	nūn	n				Ъ ъ	''
			ه	hā	h				Ы ы	y
			و	wāw	w				Ь ь	'
			ي	yā	y				Э э	e
									Ю ю	yu
									Я я	ya

When *gamma* precedes *kappa*, *xi*, *khi*, or another *gamma*, it is transliterated *n*; the letter *upsilon* is transliterated *u* as the final element in diphthongs. The second lowercase form of *sigma* is used only in the final position.

The forms shown are those used when the letters are in isolation. These forms may change when used in conjunction with other letters. In the names of the Arabic letters, *ā* is pronounced like the *a* in *father*, *ī* like the *i* in *machine*, and *ū* like the *u* in *rule*. The letter *alif* represents no sound in itself.

Where two forms of a letter are shown, the second form is used at the end of a word. Where two transliterations are shown, the second is used when the letter falls at the end of a word. Hebrew letters are primarily consonants; vowels are shown by the addition of subscript and superscript dots.

The Cyrillic alphabet is used for writing Russian, Bulgarian, and various other Slavic languages.

alpha and omega the first and the last; the beginning and the end.

al·pha·bet (al′fə bet′) *n.* **1** a set of letters or characters representing sounds, used in writing a language. **2** the letters of a language, arranged in their conventional order. **3** the parts to be learned first; elementary principles. *Abbrev.*: ABC or ABC's. [< LL *alphabetum* < LGk. *alphabetos* < *alpha* + *beta*]

al·pha·bet·ic (al′fə bet′ik) *adj.* alphabetical.

al·pha·bet·i·cal (al′fə bet′ə kəl) *adj.* **1** arranged with the initial letters in the order of the alphabet. **2** of the alphabet.

al·pha·bet·ize (al′fə bə tīz′) *v.* **-ized, -iz·ing. 1** arrange in alphabetical order. **2** express by the letters of an alphabet.

al·pha·nu·mer·ic (al′fə nyü mer′ik *or* -nü mer′ik) *adj.* **1** consisting of both letters and numerals: *an alphanumeric postal code, alphanumeric information.* **2** producing or using both letters and numbers: *an alphanumeric typewriter keyboard.*

alpha particle *Physics.* a positively charged particle consisting of two protons and two neutrons, released in the disintegration of radium and similar radio-active substances.

alpha rays *Physics.* a stream of alpha particles.

Al·pine (al′pīn) *adj.* **1** of or like the Alps. **2 alpine, a** of, having to do with, or living or growing on mountains: *alpine meadows, alpine flowers.* **b** having to do with or designating downhill as opposed to cross-country skiing.

alpine fir 1 a fir (*Abies lasiocarpa*) found especially in the mountainous regions of western North America, having a narrow, tapering, spire-like crown and greyish-green or bluish-green curved needles. **2** the light, soft, relatively weak wood of this tree.

alpine larch a small larch tree (*Larix lyallii*) found on mountain slopes at or near the timberline, from southern British Columbia south into the United States, having a short, sturdy trunk and a ragged-looking crown with gnarled branches.

al·pin·ist (al′pə nist) *n.* mountain climber.

al·read·y (ol red′ē *or* ôl red′ē) *adv.* **1** before this time; by this time; even now: *The house is already full.* **2** so soon: *Must you go already?* [for *all ready*]

☞ *Usage.* **All ready,** as distinguished from the adverb **already,** is used as an adjective phrase meaning quite or completely ready: *He was all ready for his next job.*

al·right (ol rīt′ *or* ôl rīt′) *adv. Informal.* all right.

☞ *Usage.* **All right** is the correct spelling of both the adjective phrase (*He is all right*) and the sentence adverb meaning "yes, certainly" (*All right, I'll come*). The spelling **alright** is not used in formal nor in most informal writing. Occasionally it is found in advertising and in comic strips, but it is not as yet generally acceptable.

Al·sa·tian (al sā′shən) *n., adj.* —*n.* **1** a native or inhabitant of Alsace, a region in northeastern France. **2** *Brit.* German shepherd. —*adj.* of or having to do with Alsace or its people.

al·so (ol′sō *or* ôl′sō) *adv.* in addition; besides; too. [OE *ealswā* all so, quite so]

☞ *Usage.* **Also** is an adverb; it should not be used as a connective in place of *and: The principal was strict; she was also fair. He came with tents, cooking things, and* (not *also*) *about twenty kilograms of photographic equipment.*

al·so·ran (ol′sō ran′ *or* ôl′sō-) *n.* **1** a horse or dog that does not finish among the first three in a race. **2** a loser; a person who fails to win a contest, competition, etc., or to acquire distinction in any field.

alt. 1 alternate; alternating. **2** altitude. **3** alto.

Alta. Alberta.

Al·ta·ic (al tā′ik) *adj.* **1** of or having to do with a family of languages that includes Turkish, Mongolian, and Manchu. **2** of or having to do with the Altai Mountains in Central Asia.

Al·ta·ir (al tä′ir) *n.* a first magnitude star in the constellation Aquila. It is about ten times as bright as the sun. [< Arabic *al-ta'ir* bird, literally, flyer]

al·tar (ol′tər *or* ôl′tər) *n.* **1** a table or stand in the most sacred part of a church, synagogue, or temple. In Christian churches the Communion service or Mass is held at the altar. **2** a raised place built of earth or stone on which to make sacrifices or burn offerings to a god.

lead to the altar, marry. [OE < LL *altare* < L *altus* high]

☞ *Hom.* **alter.**

altar boy a boy who helps a priest during certain religious services, especially Mass; acolyte.

al·tar·piece (ol′tər pēs′ *or* ôl′tər-) *n.* a decorated panel or wall behind and above an altar in a church; reredos.

al·ta·zi·muth (al taz′i məth) *n.* an instrument equipped with a telescope for measuring angles vertically and horizontally, used in astronomy to determine the position of stars, planets, etc. and in surveying. A theodolite is a portable altazimuth. [< *altitude* + *azimuth*]

al·ter (ol′tər *or* ôl′tər) *v.* **1** make different; change; vary: *If this coat is too large, a tailor can alter it to fit you.* **2** become different: *Since her trip to Europe, her whole outlook has altered.* [ME < OF < LL *alterare* < L *alter* other] —**al′ter·a·ble,** *adj.* —**al′ter·a·bly,** *adv.*

☞ *Syn.* **1.** See note at **change.**

☞ *Hom.* **altar.**

al·ter·a·tion (ol′tər ā′shən *or* ôl′tər ā′shən) *n.* **1** a change in the appearance, form, or condition of anything: *to have alterations made in a dress.* **2** the act or process of making a change.

al·ter·a·tive (ol′tər ā′tiv *or* ôl′tər ā′tiv) *adj., n.* —*adj.* **1** causing change; having the power to cause change. **2** gradually restoring the healthy bodily functions. —*n.* a remedy that gradually restores health.

al·ter·cate (ol′tər kāt′ *or* ôl′tər kāt′) *v.* **-cat·ed, -cat·ing.** dispute angrily; quarrel. [< L *altercari* < *alter* other]

al·ter·ca·tion (ol′tər kā′shən *or* ôl′tər kā′shən) *n.* an angry dispute; quarrel: *The two teams had an altercation over the umpire's decision.*

al·ter e·go 1 another aspect of one's nature. **2** a very intimate friend. [< L *alter ego,* translation of Gk. *heteros egō*]

al·ter·nate (*v.* ol′tər nāt′ *or* ôl′tər nāt′; *adj.* ol tėr′nit *or* ôl tėr′nit, ol′tər nit *or* ôl′tər nit; *n.* ol′tər nit *or* ôl′tər nit) *v.* **-nat·ed, -nat·ing;** *adj., n.* —*v.* **1** occur by turns, first one and then the other; happen or be arranged by turns: *Squares and circles alternate in this row:* ☐ ○ ☐ ○ ☐ ○ ☐ ○. **2** take turns; do by turns: *We try to alternate work and pleasure.* **3** take turns: *Lucy and her brother will alternate in setting the table.* **4** interchange regularly. **5** *Electricity.* **a** reverse direction at regular intervals: *Some electric currents alternate 120 times a second.* **b** produce or be operated by such a current.
—*adj.* **1** placed or occurring by turns; first one and then the other: *The row has alternate squares and circles.* **2** every other: *The milkman comes on alternate days.* **3** reciprocal. **4** *Botany.* of leaves, flowers, etc., growing singly along either side of a stem, but not directly opposite each other. Compare **opposite.**
—*n.* **1** a person appointed to take the place of another if necessary; substitute. **2** a player who relieves another during a game. [< L *alternare* < *alternus* every second < *alter* other]

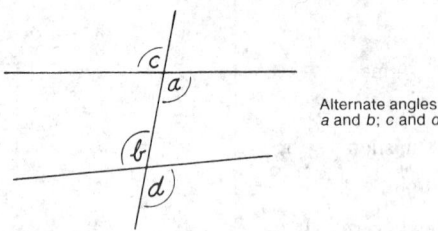

Alternate angles:
a and *b; c* and *d*

alternate angles two angles, both interior or both exterior but not adjacent, formed when two lines are crossed by a third and being on opposite sides of the third line. If the two lines are parallel, the alternate angles are equal.

al·ter·nate·ly (ol′tər nit lē *or* ôl′tər nit lē) *adv.* by turns, first one and then the other.

alternating current an electric current that reverses its direction at regular intervals. *Abbrev.:* A.C., a.c., or a-c.

al·ter·na·tion (ol′tər nā′shən *or* ôl′tər nā′shən) *n.* an alternating; occurring by turns, first one and then the other: *There is an alternation of red and white stripes on the sign outside a barber shop.*

alternation of generations the occurrence of different reproductive forms within the life cycle of an organism, usually a regular alternation of sexual and asexual generations. Alternation of generations occurs in many plants and some lower animals.

al·ter·na·tive (ol tėr′nə tiv *or* ôl tėr′nə tiv) *adj., n.* —*adj.* **1** giving or requiring a choice between only two things. **2** giving a choice from among more than two things: *There are several alternative routes from Ottawa to Toronto.* —*n.* **1** a choice between two things: *We have the alternative of going out or watching a TV movie.* **2** a choice from among more than two things: *We chose the second alternative.* **3** one of the things to be chosen: *John chose the former alternative and stayed in school.* —**al·ter′na·tive·ly,** *adv.*

☞ *Syn.* **n. 1, 2.** See note at **choice.**

☞ *Usage.* **Alternative** comes from Latin *alter,* meaning the second of two. Some writers, because of the word's origin, confine its meaning to one of two possibilities, but it is commonly used to mean one of several possibilities.

alternative conjunction a conjunction connecting terms that

are alternative. *Examples*: either...or, neither...nor, whether...or.

al·ter·na·tor (ol′tər nā′tər *or* ôl′tər nā′tər) *n.* a dynamo or generator for producing an alternating electric current.

al·the·a or **al·thae·a** (al thē′ə) *n.* **1** the rose of Sharon, a flowering garden shrub. **2** any of a genus (*Althaea*) of plants of the mallow family, such as the hollyhocks. [< L *althaea* < Gk. *althaia* wild mallow, ? < *althainein* heal]

alt·horn (alt′hôrn′) *n.* a brass musical instrument similar to the French horn. Also, **alto horn.** [< G]

al·though (ol ᴛʜō′ *or* ôl-) *conj.* even if; in spite of the fact that; though. [ME *al thogh* even though]
▸ *Usage.* **Although, though.** There is no difference in meaning between the subordinating conjunctions **although** and **though.** Either may be used to connect an adverbial clause with the main clause of a sentence. **Although** is more likely to introduce a clause that precedes a main clause, and **though** one that follows: *Although it rained all morning, they went on the hike. They went on the hike, though it rained all morning.*

al·tim·e·ter (al tim′ə tər *or* al′tə mē′tər) *n.* any instrument for measuring altitude. Altimeters are used in aircraft to indicate height above the earth's surface. [< L *altus* high + E *-meter*]

al·ti·tude (al′tə tyüd′ *or* al′tə tüd′, ol′tə tyüd′ *or* ol′tə tüd′, ôl′tə tyüd′ *or* ôl′tə tüd′) *n.* **1** the height above the earth's surface: *The airplane was flying at an altitude of 3000 metres.* **2** the height above sea level: *The altitude of Calgary, Alberta, is 1079 metres.* **3** a high place: *At these altitudes snow never melts.* **4** a position of high rank or great power. **5** *Geometry.* the vertical distance from the base of a figure to its highest point. **6** *Astronomy.* the angular distance of a star, planet, etc. above the horizon. *Abbrev.:* alt. [ME < L *altitudo* < *altus* high]

altitude sickness a condition resulting from deficiency of oxygen in the body because of the thinness of the air at high altitudes. It is characterized by sleepiness, headache, muscle weakness, etc., and, in extreme cases, by unconsciousness and failure of the respiratory and circulatory systems, resulting in death.

al·to (al′tō, ol′tō *or* ôl′tō) *n., pl.* **-tos;** *adj.* —*n.* **1** the lowest female singing voice. **2** the highest adult male singing voice, above tenor; counter tenor. Alto is now very rare; it has been replaced in music by the female voice that corresponds to it, originally called contralto but now usually called alto. **3** a singer whose range is alto. **4** the part sung by an alto. It is the second highest part in standard four-part harmony for men's and women's voices together. **5** an instrument having a range lower than that of the soprano, or treble, in a family of instruments. —*adj.* having to do with, having the range of, or designed for an alto. *Abbrev.:* a. *or* alt. [< Ital. < L *altus* high]

al·to·cu·mu·lus (al′tō kyü′myə ləs) *n., pl.* **-li** (-lī). a fleecy cloud formation having rounded heaps of white or greyish clouds, often partly shaded, at heights of between 2400 and 6000 metres. *Abbrev.:* Ac

al·to·geth·er (*adv.* ol′tə geᴛʜ′ər *or* ôl′tə geᴛʜ′ər; *n.* ol′tə geᴛʜ′ər *or* ôl′tə geᴛʜ′ər) *adv., n.* —*adv.* **1** completely; entirely: *altogether wicked.* **2** on the whole; considering everything: *Altogether, I'm sorry it happened.* **3** all included: *Altogether there were ten books.* —*n.* **the altogether,** *Informal.* the condition of being nude (*used in the phrase* **in the altogether**): *They went swimming in the altogether.* [ME *altogedere*]
▸ *Usage.* Do not confuse the adverb **altogether** with the adjective phrase **all together,** which means 'together in a group': *We found the boys all together in the kitchen.*

alto horn althorn.

al·to-re·lie·vo (al′tō ri lē′vō) *n., pl.* **-vos.** sculpture in high relief, in which the figures stand out at least half their thickness from the background. [< Ital.]

al·to-stra·tus (al′tō strā′təs *or* -strat′əs) *n., pl.* **-ti** (-tī *or* -tē). a bluish-grey, sheetlike cloud formation, ill-defined at the base, occurring at heights between 2400 and 6000 metres. *Abbrev.:* As [< L *altus* high + E *stratus*]

al·tru·ism (al′trü iz′əm) *n.* unselfishness; unselfish devotion to the interests and welfare of others. [< F *altruisme* < Ital. *altrui* of or for others < L *alter* other]

al·tru·ist (al′trü ist) *n.* an unselfish person; a person who works for the welfare of others.

al·tru·is·tic (al′trü is′tik) *adj.* thoughtful of the welfare of others; unselfish. —**al′tru·is′ti·cal·ly,** *adv.*

al·um (al′əm) *n.* **1** a white mineral salt used in medicine and in dyeing. Alum is sometimes used to stop the bleeding of a small cut. *Formula:* KAl(SO₄)₂·12H₂O **2** a colorless, crystalline salt containing ammonia, used in baking powder, in medicine, etc. *Formula:* NH₄Al(SO₄)₂·12H₂O [ME < OF < L *alumen*]

a·lu·mi·na (ə lü′mə nə) *n.* aluminum oxide, Al₂O₃. Clay is mostly alumina; emery, rubies, and sapphires are crystalline forms of alumina colored by various impurities. [< NL < L *alumen, -minis* alum]

hat, āge, fär; let, ēqual, tėrm; it, īce
hot, ōpen, ôrder; oil, out; cup, pút, rüle,
above, takən, pencəl, lemən, circəs

ch, child; ng, long; sh, ship
th, thin; ᴛʜ, then; zh, measure

a·lu·min·i·um (al′yü min′ē əm) *n. Esp.Brit.* aluminum.

a·lu·mi·nize (ə lü′mə nīz′) *v.,* —**nized,** —**niz·ing.** coat or treat with aluminum: *aluminized automobile mufflers.*

a·lu·mi·nous (ə lü′mə nəs) *adj.* **1** of or containing alum. **2** of or containing aluminum.

a·lu·mi·num (ə lü′mə nəm) *n.* a silver-white, very light, ductile, metallic chemical element that occurs in nature only in combination. It resists tarnish and is used for making utensils, instruments, etc. *Symbol:* Al; *at.no.* 13; *at.wt.* 26.9815. [< *alumina*]

aluminum hydroxide a white, tasteless, odorless powder used in medicine and for dyeing, waterproofing, and ceramic glazing. *Formula:* Al(OH)₃

aluminum oxide alumina.

aluminum phosphate a white powder, or colorless crystals, used in making dental cements and, in ceramics, as a flux. *Formula:* AlPO₄

aluminum sulphate a white crystalline salt, available in powder or crystals, used in medicine and in the paper and leather industries, also in dyeing and waterproofing. *Formula:* Al₂(SO₄)₃

a·lum·na (ə lum′nə) *n., pl.* **-nae.** a female graduate or former student of a school, college, or university. [< L]

a·lum·nae (ə lum′nē) *n.* pl. of **alumna.** See note at **alumni.**

a·lum·ni (ə lum′nī) *n.* pl. of **alumnus.**
▸ *Pronun.* Generally, two pronunciations are given in this dictionary for Latin-derived words ending in "-ae" and "-i". However, because of the distinction in meaning between **alumnae** and **alumni,** the two words should be kept separate, one pronunciation being given for each.

a·lum·nus (ə lum′nəs) *n., pl.* **-ni.** a graduate or former student of a school, college, or university. [< L *alumnus* foster child < *alere* nourish]

al·ve·o·lar (al vē′ə lər *or* al′vē ō′lər) *adj., n.* —*adj.* **1** *Anatomy.* **a** of the part of the jaws where the sockets of the teeth are. **b** of, like, or having to do with an alveolus or alveoli. **2** *Phonetics.* formed by touching the tip of the tongue to or bringing it near the upper alveoli. English *t* and *d* are alveolar sounds. —*n. Phonetics.* a speech sound formed in this manner.

al·ve·o·lus (al vē′ə ləs *or* al vē ō′ləs) *n., pl.* **-li** (-lī′ *or* lē′). **1** *Anatomy.* **a** a small vacuity, pit, or cell. The air cells of the lungs are alveoli. **b** the socket of a tooth. **2** Often *pl., Phonetics.* the ridge behind and above the upper teeth. [< L *alveolus,* dim. of *alveus* cavity]

al·way (ol′wā *or* ôl′wā) *adv. Archaic or poetic.* always.

al·ways (ol′wiz *or* ôl′wāz, ol′wiz *or* ôl′wāz) *adv.* **1** every time; at all times: *Water always has some air in it.* **2** all the time; continually: *Mother is always cheerful.* **3** forever; for all time to come: *I'll love you always.* [< all + way]

a·lys·sum (ə lis′əm) *n.* **1** any of a genus (*Alyssum*) of annual or perennial plants of the mustard family, having greyish leaves and fragrant yellow, white, pink, blue, or violet flowers. Alyssum is a popular garden flower. **2** sweet alyssum. [< NL < Gk. *alysson,* name of a plant thought to cure rabies]

am (am; *unstressed,* əm) *v.* the 1st pers. sing., present indicative of **be:** *I am a student. I am going home tomorrow.* [OE *eom*]

a.m. or **A.M.** before noon (*used especially to refer to a particular time after midnight and before midday*): *The appointment is for 10:00 a.m.* [for L *ante meridiem*]
▸ *Usage.* The abbreviations **a.m.** and **p.m.** are usually written in small letters except in headlines and tables. At the beginning of a sentence the first letter only is capitalized.

Am americium.

Am. **1** America. **2** American.

AM or **A.M.** amplitude modulation.

A.M. **1** air marshal. **2** Albert Medal. **3** *U.S.* Master of Arts; M.A. (for L *Artium Magister*).

AMA or **A.M.A.** American Medical Association.

a·ma·bi·lis fir (ə mä′bə lis) **1** a fir tree (*Abies amabilis*) of the western coast of North America, found especially on Vancouver Island and along the coast of the British Columbia mainland. **2** the light, soft wood of this tree, used for pulpwood and lumber.

a·mah (ä′mə *or* am′ə) *n.* in India, China, etc., a nurse or maid. [< Anglo-Indian < Pg. *ama*]

a·main (ə mān′) *adv. Archaic.* **1** at full speed. **2** in haste. **3** with full force; violently. [< *a-¹* in + *main* force]

a·mal·gam (ə mal′gəm) *n.* **1** an alloy of mercury with some other metal or metals. Tin amalgam is used in silvering mirrors. Silver amalgam is used as fillings for teeth. **2** a mixture; blend. [< Med.L. *amalgama* < Arabic < Gk. *malagma* emollient < *malassein* soften]

a·mal·gam·ate (ə mal′gə māt′) *v.* **-at·ed, -at·ing.** unite together; combine; mix; blend: *The two companies amalgamated to form one big company. Many different ethnic groups are being amalgamated in Canada.*

a·mal·gam·a·tion (ə mal′gə mā′shən) *n.* a union; combination; mixture; blend: *Our nation is an amalgamation of many races.*

a·man·u·en·sis (ə man′yə en′sis) *n., pl.* **-ses** (-sēz). a person who writes down what another says or copies what another has written. [< L *amanuensis* < (*servus*) *a manu* literally, hand servant + *-ensis* belonging to]

am·a·ranth (am′ə ranth′) *n.* **1** *Poetic.* an imaginary flower that never fades. **2** any of a genus (*Amaranthus*) of plants including some well-known garden plants, such as love-lies-bleeding, and many weeds, such as the pigweeds. **3** (*adj.*) designating a family (Amaranthaceae) of plants native to Africa and tropical America, made up chiefly of herbs but including a few shrubs and trees. The amaranth family includes the amaranths and the cockscomb. **4** dark reddish-purple. [< L < Gk. *amarantos* everlasting < *a-* not + *marainein* wither; influenced by Gk. *anthos* flower]

am·a·ran·thine (am′ə ran′thīn, am′ə ran′thēn, or am′ə ran′thin) *adj.* **1** never-fading; undying. **2** purple; purplish red.

am·a·ryl·lis (am′ə ril′is) *n.* **1** a widely cultivated, lily-like S African plant (*Amaryllis belladonna*) having clusters of very large, fragrant red, white, or rose flowers on a thick stalk and long narrow leaves that appear after the flowers have withered. **2** any of various other plants of the same family, having lilylike flowers. **3** (*adj.*) designating a family (Amaryllidaceae) of mostly tropical plants that grow from bulbs, corms, or rhizomes, having long narrow leaves and large fragrant flowers with six petals, including the daffodil, jonquil, century plant, and amaryllis. [< L < Gk. *Amaryllis*, typical name for a country girl]

a·mass (ə mas′) *v.* heap together; pile up; accumulate: *The miser amassed a fortune for himself.* [< F *amasser* < *a-* to (< L *ad-*) + *masse* mass < L *massa* kneaded dough. Related to MASS¹.]
☛ *Syn.* See note at **accumulate.**

am·a·teur (am′ə chər, am′ə chür′, am′ə tyūr′, or am′ə tèr′) *n., adj.* —*n.* **1** a person who undertakes some activity for pleasure, not for money or as a profession. **2** a person who does something without showing the proper skills. **3** an athlete who is not a professional. —*adj.* **1** of amateurs; made or done by amateurs. **2** being an amateur: *an amateur pianist.* [< F < L *amator* lover < *amare* love]

am·a·teur·ish (am′ə chür′ish, am′ə tyūr′ish, or am′ə tèr′ish) *adj.* done as an amateur might do it; not expert; not very skilful. —**am′a·teur′ish·ly,** *adv.*

am·a·teur·ism (am′ə chər iz′əm, am′ə chür iz′əm, am′ə tyūr iz′əm, or am′ə tèr′iz əm) *n.* **1** an amateurish way of doing things. **2** the position or rank of an amateur.

am·a·tol (am′ə tol′) *n.* an explosive substance composed of ammonium and trinitrotoluene. [< *ammonium* + *trinitrotoluene*]

am·a·to·ry (am′ə tô′rē) *adj.* of love; causing love; having to do with making love or with lovers. [< L *amatorius* < *amare* love]

a·maze (ə māz′) *v.* **a·mazed, a·maz·ing;** *n.* —*v.* surprise greatly; strike with sudden wonder. —*n. Poetic.* amazement. [OE *āmasian*]
☛ *Syn. v.* See note at **surprise.**

a·mazed (ə māzd′) *adj.* greatly surprised.

a·maz·ed·ly (ə māz′id lē) *adv.* lost in wonder or astonishment.

a·maze·ment (ə māz′mənt) *n.* great surprise; sudden wonder; astonishment.

a·maz·ing (ə māz′ing) *adj.* very surprising; wonderful; astonishing. —**a·maz′ing·ly,** *adv.*

Am·a·zon (am′ə zon′ or am′ə zən) *n.* **1** *Greek mythology.* a member of a race of female warriors supposed to live near the Black Sea. **2** Usually, **amazon,** a tall, strong, athletic woman. [ME < L < Gk.; origin uncertain]

Am·a·zo·ni·an (am′ə zō′nē ən) *adj.* **1** of or having to do with the Amazon River in South America or the region it drains. **2** of, having to do with, or characteristic of an Amazon. **3** Usually, **amazonian,** of a woman or girl, strong and athletic or warlike.

am·a·zon·ite (am′ə zə nit′) *n.* **1** a bright, bluish-green, semiprecious stone, a variety of feldspar. **2** a piece of this stone or a gem made from it. [< *Amazon* (River) + *-ite¹*]

am·bas·sa·dor (am bas′ə dər or am bas′ə dôr′) *n.* **1** the highest-ranking diplomatic representative sent by one government or ruler to another. **2** an official representative of a government or a ruler at the meetings of an international organization, on a special mission, etc.: *The Canadian ambassador to N.A.T.O.* **3** any representative of a group who reflects its typical qualities: *Visiting scouts can be ambassadors of good will for their country.* Also, **embassador.** [ME < MF *ambassadeur* < Ital. *ambasciatore*]

am·bas·sa·dor–at–large (am bas′ə dər ət lärj′) *n.* a minister or representative appointed for a special occasion, but not accredited to any government.

am·bas·sa·do·ri·al (am bas′ə dô′rē əl) *adj.* of an ambassador or ambassadors.

am·bas·sa·dor·ship (am bas′ə dər ship′) *n.* **1** the position or rank of an ambassador. **2** the term of office of an ambassador.

am·ber (am′bər) *n., adj.* —*n.* **1** a hard, translucent, fossilized resin, yellow or brownish yellow in color, used for jewellery. **2** the color of amber; brownish yellow. —*adj.* **1** made of amber. **2** brownish yellow. [ME < OF *ambre* < Arabic *'anbar* ambergris]

am·ber·gris (am′bər grēs′ or am′bər gris′) *n.* a waxlike, greyish substance secreted by sperm whales. Ambergris is used in making perfumes. [< F *ambre gris* grey amber]

ambi– *combining form.* on both sides or in both ways; both, as in *ambidextrous* (dextrous with both hands). [< L *ambi-* around or *ambo* both]

am·bi·ance (am′bē əns) See **ambience.**

am·bi·dex·ter·i·ty (am′bə deks ter′ə tē) *n.* **1** the ability to use both hands equally well. **2** unusual skilfulness. **3** deceitfulness.

am·bi·dex·trous (am′bə dek′strəs) *adj.* **1** able to use both hands equally well. **2** very skilful. **3** deceitful. [< LL *ambidexter* < L *ambi-* both + *dexter* right] —**am′bi·dex′trous·ly,** *adv.* —**am′bi·dex′trous·ness,** *n.*

am·bi·ence (am′bē əns) *n.* environment or atmosphere: *They felt uncomfortable in the formal ambience of the expensive restaurant.* Also, **ambiance.**

am·bi·ent (am′bē ənt) *adj.* surrounding: *the ambient temperature.* [< L *ambiens, -entis,* ppr. of *ambire* < *ambi-* around + *ire* go]

am·bi·gu·i·ty (am′bə gyü′ə tē) *n., pl.* **-ties. 1** a possibility of two or more meanings: *The ambiguity of the speaker's reply made it impossible to know which side he was on.* **2** a word or expression that can have more than one meaning. **3** lack of clarity; vagueness; uncertainty: *On his first day as a clerk in the office, the president's son was embarrassed by the ambiguity of his position.*

am·big·u·ous (am big′yü əs) *adj.* **1** having more than one possible meaning: *"After John hit Dick, he ran away," is ambiguous because one cannot tell which boy ran away.* **2** doubtful; not clear; uncertain: *He was left in an ambiguous position by his friend's failure to appear and help him.* [< L *ambiguus* < *ambigere* < *ambi-* in two ways + *agere* drive] —**am·big′u·ous·ly,** *adv.* —**am·big′u·ous·ness,** *n.*
☛ *Syn.* **1.** See note at **obscure.**

am·bit (am′bit) *n.* **1** the bounds or limits of a district, estate, etc. **2** sphere of influence; scope.

am·bi·tion (am bish′ən) *n.* **1** a strong desire for fame or honor; seeking after a high position or great power. **2** something strongly desired or sought after: *Her ambition was to be a great actress.* [ME < OF < L *ambition, -onis* a canvassing for votes < *ambire* < *ambi-* around + *ire* go] —**am·bi′tion·less,** *adj.*

am·bi·tious (am bish′əs) *adj.* **1** having ambition: *an ambitious person.* **2** strongly desiring a particular thing; eager: *ambitious to succeed, ambitious of power.* **3** requiring much skill or effort: *an ambitious undertaking.* —**am·bi′tious·ly,** *adv.* —**am·bi′tious·ness,** *n.*

am·biv·a·lence (am biv′ə lens′) *n.* the state or condition of having simultaneously conflicting feelings or attitudes, such as love and hate, towards persons, places, or things. [< *ambi-* + L *valentia* value < *valere* be worth]

am·biv·a·lent (am biv′ə lənt) *adj.* acting in opposite ways; having conflicting feelings or attitudes, such as love and hate, at the same time: *The politician was spurred on by the ambivalent mixture of a ruthless ambition and an earnest desire to serve his country.*

am·ble (am′bəl) *n., v.* **-bled, -bling.** —*n.* **1** the gait of a horse when it lifts first the two legs on one side and then the two on the other. **2** an easy, slow pace in walking. —*v.* **1** walk at an easy, slow pace. **2** (of a horse) move at an amble. [ME < OF *ambler* < L *ambulare* walk]

am·bler (am′blər) *n.* **1** a horse or mule that ambles. **2** a person who ambles.

am·bro·sia (am brō′zhə or am brō′zē ə) *n.* **1** *Greek and Roman mythology.* the food of the gods. **2** something especially pleasing to taste or smell. [< L < Gk. *ambrosia* < *ambrotos* < *a-* not + *brotos* mortal]

am·bro·sial (am brō′zhəl *or* am brō′zē əl) *adj.* **1** like ambrosia; especially pleasing to taste or smell. **2** divine; worthy of the gods.

Am·bro·sian chant (am brō′zhən) a style of plain song introduced by St. Ambrose in the cathedral of Milan about A.D. 384. The melody had more ornamentation than the later Gregorian chant.

am·bu·lance (am′byə ləns) *n.* a vehicle, boat, or aircraft equipped to carry sick or wounded persons. [< F *ambulance* < (*hôpital*) *ambulant* walking hospital) < L *ambulare* walk]

am·bu·lant (am′byə lənt) *adj.* walking.

am·bu·late (am′byə lāt′) *v.* **-lat·ed, -lat·ing.** walk; move about [< L *ambulare*] —**am′bu·la′tion,** *n.*

am·bu·la·to·ry (am′byə lə tô′rē) *adj., n., pl.* **-ries.** —*adj.* **1** having to do with walking; fitted for walking. **2** capable of walking, not bedridden. **3** moving from place to place. **4** not permanent; changeable. —*n.* a covered place for walking; cloister.

am·bus·cade (am′bəs kād′) *n. or v.* **-cad·ed, -cad·ing.** ambush. [< F *embuscade* < Ital. *imboscata* < *imboscare* ambush] —**am′bus·cad′er,** *n.*

am·bush (am′bŭsh) *n., v.* —*n.* **1** a surprise attack from some hiding place on an approaching enemy. **2** attackers so hidden. **3** the place where they are hidden. **4** the act of lying in wait: *They often trapped their enemies by ambush instead of meeting them in open battle.* —*v.* **1** attack from an ambush. **2** wait in hiding to make a surprise attack. **3** put (soldiers, etc.) in hiding for a surprise attack: *The general ambushed his troops in the woods on either side of the road.* [ME < OF *embusche,* n., *embuscher,* v. < *en* -in (< L *in-*) + *busche* wood, bush < VL *busca* < Gmc.]

a·me·ba (ə mē′bə) *n., pl.* **-bas** or **-bae** (-bē *or* -bī). See **amoeba.**

a·me·bic (ə mē′bik) See **amoebic.**

a·me·boid (ə mē′boid) See **amoeboid.**

a·meer (ə mēr′) *n.* See **emir.**

a·mel·io·ra·ble (ə mēl′yə rə bəl *or* ə mē′lē ə rə bəl) *adj.* that can be improved.

a·mel·io·rate (ə mēl′yə rāt′ *or* ə mē′lē ə rāt′) *v.* **-rat·ed, -rat·ing.** make better; become better; improve: *New housing ameliorated living conditions in the slums.* [< F *améliorer,* ult. < LL *meliorare* < L *melior* better]

a·mel·io·ra·tion (ə mēl′yə rā′shən *or* ə mē′lē ə rā′shən) *n.* improvement.

a·mel·io·ra·tive (ə mēl′yə rə tiv *or* ə mēl′yə rā′tiv, ə mē′lē ə rə tiv *or* ə mē′lē ə rā′tiv) *adj.* improving.

a·men (ā′men *or* ä′men′) *interj., n.* —*interj.* **1** be it so; may it become true. *Amen* is said after a prayer or wish. **2** *Informal.* an expression of approval. —*n.* the saying or writing of 'amen': *Several amens were heard from the crowd.* [< L < Gk. Hebrew *amen* truth, certainty < *aman* strengthen]

a·me·na·bil·i·ty (ə mē′nə bil′ə tē *or* ə men′ə bil′ə tē) *n.* the fact, quality, state, or condition of being amenable.

a·me·na·ble (ə mē′nə bəl *or* ə men′ə bəl) *adj.* **1** open to suggestion or advice; responsive; submissive: *A reasonable person is amenable to persuasion.* **2** accountable; answerable: *People living in a country are amenable to its laws.* [< AF *amener* < *a-* to (< L *ad-*) + *mener* lead < L *minare* drive (with shouts) < *minae* threats] —**a·me′na·ble·ness,** *n.* —**a·me′na·bly,** *adv.*

a·mend (ə mend′) *v.* **1** change the form of (a law, bill, motion, etc.) by addition, omission, etc. **2** change for the better; improve. **3** free from faults; make right; correct. [ME < OF *amender* < L *emendare* < *ex-* out of + *mendum, menda* fault. Doublet of EMEND.] —**a·mend′a·ble,** *adj.* —**a·mend′er,** *n.*

a·men·da·to·ry (ə men′də tôr′ē) *adj.* intended or tending to amend; corrective.

a·mende (ə mend′; *French,* ä mänd′) *n.* **1** recompense or satisfaction for an injury done. **2** a fine or penalty. [< F]

a·mend·ment (ə mend′mənt) *n.* **1** a change made in a law, bill, motion, etc. **2** a change for the better; improvement. **3** a change made to remove an error; correction.

a·mends (ə mendz′) *n.* (*used with singular or plural verb*) a payment for loss; satisfaction for an injury; compensation.

a·men·i·ty (ə men′ə tē *or* ə men′ə tē) *n., pl.* **-ties. 1** a pleasant way; polite act: *Saying "Thank you" and holding the door open for a person to pass through are amenities.* **2** a pleasant feature; something which makes life easier and more pleasant. **3** a pleasantness; agreeableness: *the amenity of a warm climate.* [ME < OF < L *amoenitas* < *amoenus* pleasant]

a·men·or·rhe·a (ā men′ə rē′ə) *n.* failure to menstruate; the absence of menstruation. [< NL *amenorrhea* < Gk. *a-* not + *men* month + *rhoia* flux, flow]

A·men-Ra (ä′men rä′) *n.* the principal god of ancient Egypt.

am·ent (am′ənt *or* ā′mənt) *n.* catkin. [< L *amentum* thong]

hat, āge, fär; let, ēqual, tèrm; it, īce
hot, ōpen, ôrder; oil, out; cup, pút, rüle,
əbove, takən, pencəl, lemən, circəs

ch, child; ng, long; sh, ship
th, thin; ŦH, then; zh, measure

Amer. 1 America. **2** American.

a·merce (ə mèrs′) *v.* **a·merced, a·merc·ing. 1** punish by a fine. **2** punish. [ME < AF *amercier* < *a merci* at the mercy (of)] —**a·merce′ment,** *n.* —**a·merc′er,** *n.*

A·mer·i·can (ə mer′ə kən) *n., adj.* —*n.* **1** an inhabitant or citizen of the United States, or of the earlier British colonies, not belonging to one of the aboriginal peoples. **2** a native or inhabitant of the western hemisphere. —*adj.* **1** of or having to do with the United States or its people: *an American citizen, American technology.* **2** of, having to do with, or found in the western hemisphere: *the Amazon and other American rivers. The American robin is a different bird from the European robin.*

A·mer·i·ca·na (ə mer′ə kä′nə, ə mer′ə kän′ə, *or* ə mer′ə kā′nə) *n. pl.* a collection of objects, documents, books, facts, etc. about America, especially its history.

American Beauty a variety of hybrid perennial rose with red blooms that was formerly very popular.

American eagle the bald eagle, especially as the emblem or a symbol of the United States.

American Indian Amerindian.

A·mer·i·can·ism (ə mer′ə kən iz′əm) *n.* **1** devotion or loyalty to the United States, its customs, traditions, etc. **2** a word, phrase, or meaning originating in the United States. **3** a custom or trait peculiar to the United States.

A·mer·i·can·i·za·tion (ə mer′ə kən ə zā′shən *or* ə mer′ə kən ī zā′shən) *n.* the act or process of making or becoming American in habits, customs, or character.

A·mer·i·can·ize (ə mer′ə kən īz′) *v.* **-ized, -iz·ing.** make or become American in habits, customs, or character.

American organ a kind of small reed organ; melodeon.

American plan a system used in hotels where one price covers room, board, and service. See also **European plan.**

am·er·i·ci·um (am′ər ish′ē əm) *n.* an artifical, radio-active metallic chemical element. *Symbol:* Am; *at.no.* 95; *at.wt.* (243). [< NL < *America*]

Am·er·ind (am′ər ind′) *n.* Amerindian.

Am·er·in·di·an (am′ər in′dē ən) *adj., n.* —*adj.* **1** of or designating a major race of mankind, the original inhabitants of the western hemisphere south of the Arctic coastal regions, distinguished by a combination of biological characteristics, including straight, dark hair and light to dark-brown skin. **2** designating the aboriginal languages of the western hemisphere south of the Arctic region, forming numerous distinct language families. **3** of or having to do with the Amerindian peoples, their cultures, or their languages. —*n.* a member of the Amerindian race.

am·e·thyst (am′ə thist) *n.* **1** a purple or violet variety of quartz, used for jewellery. **2** a piece of this stone, or a gem made from it. **3** a violet-colored corundum, used for jewellery. **4** purple; violet. [ME < OF < L < Gk. *amethystos* < *a-* not + *methy* wine; thought to prevent intoxication] —**am′e·thyst·like′,** *adj.*

Am·har·ic (am här′ik) *n., adj.* —*n.* the official and literary language of Ethiopia since the twelfth century, a Semitic language of the Ethiopic group. —*adj.* of or having to do with this language.

a·mi·a·bil·i·ty (ā′mē ə bil′ə tē) *n.* good nature; friendliness; pleasantness; agreeableness.

a·mi·a·ble (ā′mē ə bəl) *adj.* good-natured and friendly; agreeable: *an amiable smile.* [ME < OF *amiable* < LL *amicabilis* < L *amicus* friend. Doublet of AMICABLE.] —**a′mi·a·bly,** *adv.*

am·i·ca·bil·i·ty (am′ə kə bil′ə tē) *n.* friendliness.

am·i·ca·ble (am′ə kə bəl) *adj.* peaceable; friendly: *Instead of fighting, the two nations settled their quarrel in an amicable way.* [< LL *amicabilis* < L *amicus* friend. Doublet of AMIABLE.] —**am′i·ca·bly,** *adv.*

am·ice (am′is) *n.* an oblong piece of white linen worn by priests at Mass. It is placed around the neck and over the shoulders. [ME < OF *amis* < L *amictus* cloak]

a·mi·cus cu·ri·ae (ə mē′kəs kyür′ē ī *or* ə mī′kəs kyür′ē ē) *Law.* a person with no interest in a case who is called in to advise the judge. [< NL *amicus curiae* friend of the court]

a·mid (ə mid′) *prep.* in the middle of; among. [OE *amiddan* < *on middan* in the middle]

a·mid·ship (ə mid′ship) *adv.* amidships.

a·mid·ships (ə mid′ships) *adv.* in or toward the middle of a ship; halfway between the bow and stern.

a·midst (ə midst′) *prep.* amid.

a·mi·go (ə mē′gō) *n.* friend. [< Sp. < L *amicus*]

a·mine (ə mēn′ *or* am′in) *n. Chemistry.* any of a group of organic compounds formed from ammonia by replacement of one or more of its three hydrogen atoms by univalent hydrocarbon radicals. [< ammonia + *-ine²*]

a·mi·no acids (ə mē′nō *or* am′ə nō) *Chemistry.* certain complex organic compounds of nitrogen that combine in various ways to form proteins.

a·mir (ə mēr) *n.* in Moslem countries, a commander, ruler, or prince. Also, **ameer.** [< Arabic *amir* commander. Related to ADMIRAL.]

Am·ish (am′ish *or* ä′mish) *n., adj.* —*n.* **the Amish,** *pl.* the members of a strict Mennonite sect, founded in the 17th century in Switzerland. Today most Amish live in farming communities in southern Ontario and parts of the United States. They form part of the group often called Pennsylvania Dutch. —*adj.* of, having to do with, or designating this sect or its members. [after Jacob *Amen,* 17th cent. Mennonite preacher]

am·isk (am′isk) *n.* beaver. [< Cree]

a·miss (ə mis′) *adv., adj.* —*adv.* not the way it should be; out of order; at fault.
take amiss, be offended at because of a misunderstanding: *John had not meant to be rude to his mother but she took his answer amiss.* —*adj.* improper; wrong. [ME *a mis* by (way of) fault. Related to MISS¹.]

am·i·to·sis (am′ə tō′sis) *n. Biology.* a simple or direct method of cell division; reproduction without mitosis. In amitosis the cell separates into new cells without an exact division of the chromosomes. [< *a-⁴* not + *mitosis*]

am·i·ty (am′ə tē) *n., pl.* **-ties.** peace and friendship; friendly relations: *If there were amity between nations, there would be no wars.* [ME < OF *amitie,* ult. < L *amicus* friend]

am·me·ter (am′mē′tər *or* am′ē′tər) *n.* an instrument for measuring in amperes the strength of an electric current. [< *ampere* + *meter*]

am·mo (am′ō) *n. Informal.* ammunition.

am·mo·nia (ə mōn′yə *or* ə mō′nē ə) *n.* **1** a strong-smelling, colorless gas, consisting of nitrogen and hydrogen. *Formula:* NH₃ **2** this gas dissolved in water. Ammonia is very useful for cleaning. *Formula:* NH₃OH [< NL; so named because obtained from sal *ammoniac*]

am·mo·ni·ac (ə mō′nē ak′) *n., adj.* —*n.* a gum resin used for medicines and as a cement for porcelain; gum ammoniac. —*adj.* ammoniacal. [< L *ammoniacum* < Gk. *ammōniakon*; applied to a salt obtained near the shrine of Ammon in Libya]

am·mo·ni·a·cal (am′ə nī′ə kəl) *adj.* of or like ammonia.

ammonia water ammonia gas dissolved in water.

am·mon·i·fy (ə mon′ə fī′) *v.* combine or be combined with ammonia or an ammonium compound. —**am·mon′i·fi·ca′tion,** *n.*

am·mo·nite (am′ə nīt′) *n.* the fossil shell of a mollusc extinct in the Cretaceous period, coiled in a flat spiral and up to 2 m in diameter. [< NL *ammonites* < Med.L *cornu Ammonis* horn of Ammon]

am·mo·ni·um (ə mō′nē əm) *n.* a radical NH₄ or an ion NH₄+, a group of nitrogen and hydrogen atoms present in ammonia salts. Ammonium never appears in a free state by itself, but acts as a unit in chemical reactions.

ammonium chloride colorless crystals or a white powder used in medicine in printing on cloth, etc.; sal ammoniac. *Formula:* NH₄Cl

ammonium hydroxide an alkali formed when ammonia gas dissolves in water. *Formula:* NH₄OH

am·mu·ni·tion (am′yə nish′ən) *n.* **1** bullets, shells, gunpowder, etc. for guns or other weapons; military supplies that can be used against an enemy. **2** anything that can be shot, hurled, or thrown. **3** a means of attack or defence. [< obsolete F *amunition,* used for *munition*]

am·ne·sia (am nē′zhə *or* am nē′zē ə) *n.* loss of memory caused by injury to the brain, or by disease or shock. [< NL < Gk. *amnēsia* < *a-* not + *mnasthai* remember]

am·ne·si·ac (am nē′zē ak′) *adj., n.* —*adj.* of or resulting from amnesia. —*n.* a person suffering from amnesia.

am·ne·sic (am nē′zik *or* am nē′sik) *adj. or n.* amnesiac.

am·nes·ty (am′nis tē) *n., pl.* **-ties;** *v.* **-tied, -ty·ing.** —*n.* a general pardon for past offences against a government: *After order was restored, the king granted amnesty to those who had plotted against him.* —*v.* give amnesty to; pardon. [< L < Gk. *amnēstia* < *a-* not + *mnasthai* remember]

am·ni·on (am′nē ən) *n., pl.* **-ni·ons** *or* **-ni·a** (-nē ə). a membrane lining the sac that encloses the embryos of reptiles, birds, and mammals. [< Gk. *amnion,* dim. of *amnos* lamb]

am·ni·ote (am′nē ōt′) *n. Zoology.* any of the group of vertebrates, including reptiles, birds, and mammals that develop amnions in their embryonic stages.

am·ni·ot·ic (am′nē ot′ik) *adj.* **1** of or contained in the amnion. **2** having an amnion.

a·moe·ba (ə mē′bə) *n., pl.* **-bas** *or* **-bae** (-bē *or* -bī). any of a genus (*Amoeba*) of protozoans found in water or moist soil or living as parasites in man and animals. They move by forming temporary footlike projections which are constantly changing. Sometimes, **ameba.** [< Gk. *amoibē* change]

a·moe·bic *or* **a·me·bic** (ə mē′bik) *adj.* **1** of or like an amoeba or amoebas. **2** caused by amoebas.

a·moe·boid *or* **a·me·boid** (ə mē′boid) *adj.* of or like an amoeba; like that of an amoeba; related or having to do with amoebas.

a·mok (ə muk′ *or* ə mok′) *adv., adj., n.* —*adv. or adj.* amuck. —*n.* a violent nervous disorder, occurring chiefly among the Malays; a murderous frenzy. [< Malay]

A·mon (ä′mən) *n.* one of the chief gods of ancient Egypt, who became identified with the sun god Re and was then called **Amon-Re.**

a·mong (ə mung′) *prep.* **1** surrounded by: *a house among the trees.* **2** in with: *He fell among thieves.* **3** one of: *Canada is among the largest countries in the world.* **4** in the number or class of: *That book is the best among modern novels.* **5** in comparison with: *one among many.* **6** to each of; by or for distribution to: *He divided the chores among the three of them. They divided the money among themselves.* **7** by the combined action of: *Among them they saved the company. We decided among ourselves to call the whole thing off.* **8** by the reciprocal actions of: *They fought among themselves.* **9** by, with, or through the whole or aggregate of: *political unrest among the people.* [OE *amang* < *on gemang* in a crowd]
☛ *Usage.* See note at **between.**

a·mongst (ə mungst′) *prep.* among.

a·mon·til·la·do (ə mon′tə lä′dō; *Spanish,* ä mōn′tē lyä′ᴛнō), *n., pl.* **-dos** (-dōz; *Spanish,* -ᴛнōs). a pale, moderately dry sherry. [< Sp. *Montilla,* a district in Spain where this wine is made]

a·mor·al (ā môr′əl *or* a môr′əl) *adj.* not involving any question of morality; non-moral. [< *a-⁴* not + *moral*] —**a·mor′al·ly,** *adv.*

a·mo·ral·i·ty (ā′ mə ral′i tē *or* a′mə ral′i tē) *n.* the quality of being amoral: *the amorality of nature.*

a·morce (ə môrs′) *n.* **1** an explosive to set off the main charge; priming charge. **2** a percussion cap for a toy pistol. [< F < OF *amordre* bite]

am·o·ro·so (am′ə rō′sō) *adj., n.* —*adj. Music.* tender; loving. —*n.* lover. [< Ital. *amoroso* loving < LL *amorosus* < L *amor* love]

am·o·rous (am′ə rəs) *adj.* **1** inclined to love. **2** in love. **3** showing love; loving. **4** having to do with love or courtship. [ME < OF *amorous* < *amour* love < L *amor*] —**am′o·rous·ly,** *adv.* —**am′o·rous·ness,** *n.*

a·mor pa·tri·ae (ā′môr pa′trē ī′ *or* ā′môr pā′trē ē′) *Latin.* love of one's own country; patriotism.

a·mor·phous (ə môr′fəs) *adj.* **1** not consisting of crystals: *Glass is amorphous; sugar is crystalline.* **2** of no particular kind or type. **3** having no definite form; shapeless; formless; not organized. **4** *Geology.* lacking stratification or other division. **5** *Biology.* having no definite shape or structure. [< Gk. *amorphos* < *a-* without + *morphē* shape] —**a·mor′phous·ly,** *adv.*

am·or·tise (am′ər tīz′ *or* ə môr′tīz) *v.* **-tised, -tis·ing.** *Esp.Brit.* amortize.

am·or·ti·za·tion (am′ər tə zā′shən *or* ə môr′tə zā′shən) *n.* **1** amortizing or being amortized. **2** the money regularly set aside for this purpose.

am·or·tize (am′ər tīz′ *or* ə môr′tīz) *v.* **-tized, -tiz·ing. 1** set money aside regularly in a special fund for future wiping out of (a debt, etc.). **2** *Accounting.* write off (expenditures, debts, etc.) proportionately over a fixed period. [ME < OF *amortiss-,* a stem of *amortir* deaden < *a-* to (< L *ad-*) + *mort* death < L *mors, mortis*]

a·mor·tize·ment (ə môr′tiz mənt) *n.* amortization.

a·mount (ə mount′) *n., v.* —*n.* **1** a sum; total: *What is the amount of the day's sales?* **2** the full effect, value, or extent: *The amount of evidence against him is great.* **3** a quantity viewed as a whole: *a great amount of intelligence.* —*v.* **1** be equal (*to*); add up (*to*): *The loss from the flood amounts to*

ten million dollars. 2 be equivalent in quantity, value, force, effect, etc. (to): *Keeping what belongs to another amounts to stealing.* [ME < OF *amonter* < *a mont* up, literally, to the mountain < L *ad to, mons. montis* mountain]

☛ **Usage. Amount, number. Amount** is used of things viewed in the bulk, weight, or sum; **number** is used of persons or things that can be counted: *an amount of milk, a number of cans of milk.*

a·mour (ə mür′) *n.* 1 a love affair. 2 a secret or illicit love affair. [< F *amour,* probably < Provençal < L *amor* love]

a·mour–pro·pre (ä mür′prô′prə) *n. French.* conceit; self-esteem.

amp. ampere(s); amperage.

am·per·age (am′pər ij *or* am pēr′ij) *n.* the strength of an electric current measured in amperes. *Abbrev.:* a., a, or amp.

am·pere (am′pēr *or* am′per) *n.* an SI unit for measuring the rate of flow of an electric current, defined in terms of the magnetic force which a current produces. About one ampere of current is required to produce 100 watts of electric power. The ampere is one of the seven base units in the SI. *Symbol:* A [after André *Ampère* (1775-1836), a French physicist]

am·per·sand (am′pər sand′) *n.* the sign &, meaning "and." [alteration of *and per se* = and, & by itself = and]

☛ **Usage. The ampersand** is used chiefly in business correspondence and reference works.

am·phet·a·mine (am fet′ə mēn′ *or* am fet′ə min) *n.* a colorless, somewhat volatile, bitter-tasting liquid which has a strong stimulatory effect on the central nervous system, used in various preparations in medicine to treat nervous depression, overcome the effects of anesthetics, narcotics, etc., and lessen the appetite in dieting for weight reduction. The drug can have dangerous side effects and can also produce addiction. *Formula:* $C_9H_{13}N$ [*apha-methyl-beta-phenyl-ethyl- amine*]

amphi– *combining form.* 1 around; on both sides, as in *amphitheatre.* 2 in two ways; of two kinds, as in *amphibious.* [< GK. *amphi-* amphi, prep., adv.]

am·phib·i·an (am fib′ē ən) *n., adj.* —*n.* 1 any of a class (Amphibia) of cold-blooded vertebrates, most of which have completely scaleless skin, and which produce young that at first breathe by means of gills but usually undergo a complete physical change as they mature, becoming land-living animals with lungs and legs: *Frogs, toads, newts, and salamanders are amphibians.* 2 an animal or plant adapted to life in the water and on land: *Seals, beavers, and water snakes are sometimes called amphibians.* 3 an aircraft that can take off from and come down on either land or water. 4 a vehicle that can travel across land or water. —*adj.* 1 of or having to do with amphibians. 2 amphibious. [< NL *Amphibia,* neut. pl. of *amphibius* < Gk. *amphibios.* See AMPHIBIOUS.]

am·phib·i·ous (am fib′ē əs) *adj.* 1 able to live both on land and in water. 2 suited for use on land or water: *an amphibious tank.* 3 having two qualities, kinds, natures, or parts. 4 by the combined action of land, water, and air forces: *an amphibious attack.* [< Gk. *amphibios* living a double life < *amphi-* both + *bios* life] —**am·phib′i·ous·ly,** *adv.* —**am·phib′i·ous·ness,** *n.*

am·phi·bole (am′fə bōl′) *n.* any of a group of rock-forming silicate minerals, including hornblende and asbestos. [< F < L *amphibolus* < GK. *amphibolos* ambiguous < *amphi-* on both sides + *-bolos* struck]

am·phib·o·lite (am fib′ə līt′) *n.* a usually dark-green or black metamorphic rock composed mainly of amphiboles, especially hornblende.

am·phi·brach (am′fə brak′) *n. Prosody.* a measure or foot consisting of one strongly stressed syllable between two weakly stressed syllables, or one long syllable between two short syllables. *Example*:

Behind shut | the póstern, | the lights sank | to rest,
And into | the mídnight | we galloped | abreast.

[< L *amphibrachus* < Gk. *amphibrachys* short at both ends < *amphi-*both + *brachys* short]

am·phi·pod (am′fə pod′) *n.* any of an order (Amphipoda) of tiny crustaceans, such as the sand flea, having two sets of feet serving different purposes. Sand fleas have one set of feet used for jumping and another for swimming.

am·phi·the·a·tre (am′fə thē′ə tər) *n.* 1 a circular or oval building with tiers of seats around a central open space. 2 a theatre gallery, lecture hall, etc. with ascending rows of seats, especially when forming a semicircle. 3 a place for public contests and games. 4 a level place surrounded by a steeply rising slope. Sometimes, **amphitheater.** [< L < Gk. *amphitheatron* < *amphi-* on all sides + *theatron* theatre]

Am·phi·tri·te (am′fə trī′tē) *n. Greek mythology.* the goddess of the sea. Amphitrite was the wife of Poseidon.

am·pho·ra (am′fə rə) *n., pl.* **-rae** (-rē′ *or* -rī′). a tall two-handled

hat, āge, fär; let, ēqual, tèrm; it, īce
hot, ōpen, ôrder; oil, out; cup, pút, rüle,
əbove, takən, pencəl, lemən, circəs
ch, child; ng, long; sh, ship
th, thin; ᴛн, then; zh, measure

jar, used by the ancient Greeks and Romans. [< L < Gk. *amphoreus,* short for *amphiphoreus* < *amphi-* on both sides + *phoreus* bearer; with reference to the two handles]

am·ple (am′pəl) *adj.* **-pler, -plest.** 1 large or extensive: *an ample backyard, a figure of ample proportions.* 2 enough to easily meet all requirements; plentiful; abundant: *We had ample food for the trip.* [< F < L *amplus*] —**am′ple·ness,** *n.* —**am′ply,** *adv.*

am·pli·fi·ca·tion (am′plə fə kā′shən) *n.* 1 the act of amplifying; expansion. 2 a detail or example that amplifies a statement, narrative, etc. 3 an expanded statement, narrative, etc. 4 an increase in the strength of electric current.

am·pli·fi·er (am′plə fī′ər) *n.* 1 an electronic device in or attached to a radio, record player, etc. for strengthening electrical impulses. 2 loudspeaker. 3 any person or thing that amplifies.

am·pli·fy (am′plə fī′) *v.* **-fied, -fy·ing.** 1 make greater or stronger. 2 make fuller and more extensive; expand; enlarge: *to amplify a description, to amplify a point in argument.* 3 write or talk at length. 4 *Electronics.* increase the strength of (an electrical impulse) by means of an amplifier. [ME < OF *amplifier* < L *amplificare* < *amplus* ample + *facere* make]

am·pli·tude (am′plə tyüd′ *or* am′plə tüd′) *n.* 1 width; breadth; size. 2 abundance; fullness. 3 *Physics.* the maximum range of swing or vibration from the mean, or zero, position: *A pendulum swinging through 10° has an amplitude of 5°.* 4 *Electricity.* the maximum departure from the average cycle of an alternating current. [< L *amplitudo* < *amplus* ample]

amplitude modulation *Radio.* 1 a method of transmitting the sound signals of a broadcast by changing the strength, or amplitude, of the carrier waves to match the audio signals. 2 a broadcasting system that uses amplitude modulation. Compare **frequency modulation.** *Abbrev:* AM or A.M.

am·poule (am′pül *or* am pül′) *n.* a small, sealed glass container, usually holding one dose of a drug, medicine, etc. [< F < L. *ampulla* small bottle]

am·pul·la (am pül′ə) *n., pl.* **am·pul·lae** (-ē *or* -ī). 1 a two-handled, rounded glass or earthenware flask used in ancient Rome to hold oil, perfume, or wine. It was smaller than an amphora. 2 a vessel used in churches to hold consecrated oil. 3 *Biology.* a dilated part of a canal or duct. —**am·pul′lar,** *adj.* [< L]

am·pu·tate (am′pyə tāt′) *v.* **-tat·ed, -tat·ing.** cut off, especially in a surgical operation: *to amputate a leg.* [< L *amputare* < *ambi-* about + *putare* prune] —

am·pu·ta·tion (am′pyə tā′shən) *n.* the act of cutting off a leg, arm, finger, etc.; a cutting off.

am·pu·tee (am′pyə tē′) *n.* a person who has had an arm, leg, etc. amputated.

amt. amount.

a·muck (ə muk′) *adv. or adj.* in a murderous frenzy; with a crazy desire to attack. Also, **amok.**
run amuck, run about in a murderous frenzy. [< Malay *amok* engaging furiously in battle]

am·u·let (am′yə lit) *n.* some object worn as a magic charm against evil. [< L *amuletum*]

a·muse (ə myüz′) *v.* **a·mused, a·mus·ing.** 1 cause to laugh or smile. 2 keep pleasantly interested; cause to feel cheerful or happy; entertain: *The new toys amused the children.* [ME < OF *amuser* divert < *a-* + *muser* stare] —**a·mus′er,** *n.*

☛ **Syn. 2. Amuse, entertain** = keep pleasantly interested. **Amuse** emphasizes the idea of passing time by keeping one's attention occupied with something interesting and pleasing: *While waiting, she amused herself by counting the cars that passed.* **Entertain** emphasizes greater effort or more elaborate means to hold attention: *Some people entertain themselves by reading; others have to be entertained by the radio or television.*

a·mused (ə myüzd′) *adj.* pleasantly entertained. —**a·mus′ed·ly,** *adv.*

a·muse·ment (ə myüz′mənt) *n.* 1 the condition of being amused. 2 pleasant diversion: *They often window shop for amusement.* 3 something that amuses or entertains: *His favorite amusement at the Exhibition is the ferris wheel.*

a·mus·ing (ə myüz′ing) *adj.* 1 entertaining. 2 causing laughter, smiles, etc. —**a·mus′ing·ly,** *adv.*

am·yl (am′əl) *n.* a group of carbon and hydrogen atoms that acts as a unit in forming compounds. *Formula*: C_5H_{11} [< L *amylon*, starch, originally, unground < *a-* not + *mylē* mill]

am·yl·ase (am′ə lās′) *n.* an enzyme in saliva, the pancreatic juice, etc., or in parts of plants, that helps to change starch into sugar. [< *amyl*]

am·y·lop·sin (am′ə lop′sin) *n.* an enzyme in the pancreatic juice that changes starch into simpler compounds such as glucose. [< *amyl* + *trypsin*]

an¹ (ən; *stressed*, an) *adj. or indefinite article* (*used in place of* **a** *before an initial vowel sound*) **1** any: *Have you an answer to this accusation?* **2** one: *Take an orange.* **3** each; every: *twice an hour.* **4** for each: *He paid thirty cents an apple.* [OE *ān* one] ☛ *Usage.* See note at **a¹**.

an² (ən; *stressed*, an) *conj.* **1** *Dialect or informal.* and. **2** *Archaic.* if. [var. of *and*]

an–¹ *prefix.* not; without, as in *anhydrous.* Also, **a-**, before consonants except *h.* [< Gk.]

an–² the form of **ad-** before *n*, as in *annex.*

–an *suffix.* **1** of or having to do with —: *Mohammedan = of or having to do with Mohammed.* **2** of or having to do with — or its people: *Asian = of or having to do with Asia or its people.* **3** a native or inhabitant of —: *American = native or inhabitant of America.* [< L *-anus*]

ana– *prefix.* back; again; thoroughly; up, as in *anachronism, analysis.* [< Gk. *ana-* < *ana*, prep.]

–ana *suffix.* sayings, writings, or articles by, belonging to or associated with —: *Shakespeariana = things written by or associated with Shakespeare. Canadiana = things associated with Canada.* [< L *-ana*, neuter pl. of *-anus*, *-an*]

an·a·bap·tism (an′ə bap′tiz əm) *n.* **1** a second baptism. **2** the doctrines, principles, and practices of the Anabaptists.

An·a·bap·tist (an′ə bap′tist) *n.* a member of a Protestant sect opposing infant baptism and requiring adult baptism.

an·a·bi·o·sis (an′ə bī ō′sis) *n.* **1** a coming to life again from a deathlike condition; resuscitation. **2** a state of suspended animation, as produced in certain organisms by drying, etc. [NL < Gk. *anabiōsis* < *anabioein* to return to life < *ana-* back, again + *bios* life]

an·a·bi·ot·ic (an′ə bī ot′ik) *adj.* of, having to do with, or showing anabiosis.

an·a·bol·ic (an′ə bol′ik) *adj.* of or having to do with anabolism.

anabolic steroid any of various synthetic androgens used in medicine and by athletes to stimulate the growth of muscle and bone.

an·ab·o·lism (ə nab′ə liz′əm) *n.* the part of the process of metabolism concerned with the synthesis of complex molecules from simple ones, by which food is changed into living tissue. [< *ana-* + meta*bolism;* 19c.]

a·nach·ro·nism (ə nak′rə niz′əm) *n.* **1** the putting of a person, thing, or event in some time where he or it does not belong: *It would be an anachronism to speak of John Milton riding in an automobile.* **2** something placed or occurring out of its proper time. [< F < Gk. *anachronismos* < *ana-* backwards + *chronos* time]

a·nach·ro·nis·tic (ə nak′rə nis′tik) *adj.* having or involving an anachronism. —**a·nach′ro·nis′ti·cal·ly,** *adv.*

a·nach·ro·nous (ə nak′rə nəs) *adj.* placed or occurring out of the proper time. —**a·nach′ro·nous·ly,** *adv.*

an·a·co·lu·thon (an′ə kə lü′thon) *n., pl.* **-tha** (-thə) a change from one grammatical construction to another in the same sentence. [< LL < Gk. *anakolouthos* < *an-* not + *akolouthos* following]

an·a·con·da (an′ə kon′də) *n.* **1** a very large snake (*Eunectes murinus*), a tropical American boa, having olive-green skin, often with black rings or spots, and living in trees and in and around water. Although it is not so long as the largest python, averaging about 9 m, it has a much thicker body and is considered the largest snake in the world. **2** any large snake that kills its prey by coiling around it and squeezing until it suffocates. [? < Singhalese *henakandayā*, a kind of thin, green snake]

a·nad·ro·mous (ə nad′rə məs) *adj.* going up rivers from the sea to spawn. Salmon are anadromous. [< LGk. *anadromos* < *ana-* up + *dromos* a running]

a·nae·mi·a (ə nē′mē ə) See **anemia.**

a·nae·mic (ə nē′mik) See **anemic.**

an·aer·obe (an er′ōb *or* an ā′ər ōb′) *n.* **1** an organism that cannot live in the presence of free oxygen. **2** an organism that can live without free oxygen. [< NL *anaerobium* < Gk. *an-* without + *aēr* air + *bios* life]

an·aer·o·bic (an′er ō′bik *or* an ā′ər ō′bik) *adj.* living or growing where there is no free oxygen. Anaerobic bacteria get their oxygen by decomposing compounds containing oxygen.

an·aes·the·sia (an′is thē′zhə *or* an′is thē′zē ə) *n.* anesthesia.

an·aes·thet·ic (an′is thet′ik) *adj. or n.* anesthetic.

an·aes·the·tist (ə nēs′thə tist *or* ə nes′thə tist) *n.* anesthetist.

an·aes·the·tize (ə nēs′thə tīz′ *or* ə nes′thə tīz′) *v.* **-tized, -tiz·ing.** anesthetize. —**an·aes′the·ti·za′tion,** *n.*

an·a·gram (an′ə gram′) *n.* **1** a word or phrase formed from another by transposing the letters. *Example*: table—bleat. **2 anagrams,** *pl.* a game in which the players make words by changing and adding letters. [< NL *anagramma* < Gk. *anagrammatizein* transpose letters < *ana-* up or back + *gramma* letter]

a·nal (ā′nəl) *adj.* **1** of the anus. **2** near the anus.

an·a·lem·ma (an′ə lem′ə) *n.* a graduated scale in the shape of a figure eight, found on many globes, which shows the variation throughout the year between noon according to clock time and noon according to the position of the sun. The analemma also shows on which two days of the year the sun is directly overhead at mid-day in the low latitudes.

an·al·ge·si·a (an′əl jē′zē ə *or* an′əl jē′sē ə) *n.* the state of not being able to feel pain even while completely conscious. [< NL < Gk. *analgēsia* < *an-* not + *algein* feel pain]

an·al·ge·sic (an′əl jē′zik *or* an′əl jē′sik) *adj., n.* —*adj.* of, having to do with, or causing analgesia: *an analgesic drug.* —*n.* a drug or other agent that causes analgesia.

an·a·log (an′ə log′) See **analogue.**

an·a·log·i·cal (an′ə loj′ə kəl) *adj.* based on analogy; using analogy; having to do with analogy.

analogical change *Linguistics.* the alteration of a form to make it conform to a dominant pattern. *Examples*: the form *climbed* in place of earlier *clomb, crowed* in place of earlier *crew, horses* in place of earlier *hors.*

a·nal·o·gous (ə nal′ə gəs) *adj.* **1** alike in some way; similar; comparable. **2** *Biology.* corresponding in function, but not in structure and origin. —**a·nal′o·gous·ly,** *adv.*

an·a·logue (an′ə log′) *n.* something analogous.

analogue computer an electronic calculating machine or automatic control that deals directly with physical quantities (weights, voltages, etc.) rather than with a numerical code. See **digital computer.**

a·nal·o·gy (ə nal′ə jē) *n., pl.* **-gies. 1** a likeness in some ways between things that are otherwise unlike; similarity: *the analogy between words like "man" and "pan."* **2** a comparison of such things: *It is easy to draw analogies between the past and the present.* **3** *Biology.* correspondence in function but not in structure and origin. **4** *Logic.* the inference that things alike in some respects will be alike in others: *It is risky to argue by analogy.* [< L < Gk. *analogia* equality of ratios, proportion] ☛ *Usage.* One says **analogy** *between* things, and that one thing has **analogy** *to* or *with* another.

an·a·lyse *or* **an·a·lyze** (an′ə līz′) *v.* **-lysed** *or* **-lyzed, -lys·ing** *or* **-lyz·ing. 1** separate into its parts. **2** examine critically the parts or elements of; find out the essential features of: *analyse a sentence.* **3** examine carefully and in detail. **4** *Chemistry.* subject to analysis. **5** *Mathematics.* solve a problem by means of algebra especially by calculus. **6** examine minutely a mind or personality; psychoanalyse. —**an′a·lys′er** *or* **an′a·lyz′er,** *n.*

a·nal·y·sis (ə nal′ə sis) *n., pl.* **-ses** (-sēz′). **1** the separation of a whole into its parts. Compare **synthesis. 2** examination of the parts of a whole to discover their nature, relationship with each other and with the whole, etc. An analysis may be made of a book, a person's character, a medicine, soil, etc. **3** *Chemistry.* **a** the intentional separation of a substance into its ingredients or elements to determine their amount or nature. **b** the determination of the kind or amount of one or more of the constituents of a substance, whether actually obtained in separate form or not. **4** a statement giving the results of an analysis. **5** *Mathematics.* the branch of mathematics that deals with the methods and principles of algebra and calculus, as distinguished from synthetic geometry, group theory, and number theory. **6** psychoanalysis. [< Med.L < Gk. *analysis* a breaking up < *analyein* unloose < *ana-* up + *lyein* loose]

an·a·lyst (an′ə list) *n.* **1** a person who analyses, especially one who is skilled at analysis: *The analyst found traces of poison in the body.* **2** psychoanalyst. **3** systems analyst.

an·a·lyt·ic (an′ə lit′ik) *adj.* analytical.

an·a·lyt·i·cal (an′ə lit′ə kəl) *adj.* of analysis; using analysis. —**an′a·lyt′i·cal·ly,** *adv.*

analytic geometry *Mathematics.* the use of algebra and co-ordinates (or the calculus) to solve problems in geometry.

an·a·lyt·ics (an′ə lit′iks) *n.* mathematical or algebraic analysis.

an·a·lyze (an′ə līz′) See **analyse.**

An·a·ni·as (an′ə nī′əs) *n.* **1** in the Bible, a member of the church at Jerusalem. He and his wife were struck dead for lying (Acts 5: 1-10). **2** *Informal.* any liar.

an·a·paest or **an·a·pest** (an′ə pēst′ *or* an′ə pest′) *n.* *Prosody.* a measure or foot consisting of two weakly stressed syllables followed by a strongly stressed syllable, or two short syllables followed by one long syllable. *Example:*

From the cén | tre all round | to the sea

I am lord | of the fowl | and the brute.

[< L *anapaestus* < Gk. *anapaistos* < *ana-* back + *paiein* strike]

an·a·paes·tic or **an·a·pes·tic** (an′ə pēs′tik *or* an′ə pes′tik) *adj.* having to do with or consisting of anapests.

an·arch (an′ärk) *n.* an anarchic leader.

an·ar·chic (an är′kik) *adj.* lawless; favoring anarchy.

an·ar·chi·cal (an är′kə kəl) *adj.* anarchic.

an·ar·chism (an′ər kiz′əm) *n.* **1** the political theory that all systems of government and law are unnecessary and in fact harmful because they prevent individuals from reaching their greatest development. Anarchism advocates a society based on voluntary co-operation among individuals and groups. **2** the support or practice of anarchistic beliefs. **3** lawlessness or terrorism.

an·ar·chist (an′ər kist) *n.* **1** a person who favors and supports anarchism as a political idea. **2** a person who uses violent means to overthrow organized government. **3** a person who promotes disorder or rebels against established laws or customs.

an·ar·chis·tic (an′ər kis′tik) *adj.* of or having to do with anarchism or anarchists.

an·ar·chy (an′ər kē) *n.* **1** the absence of a system of government and law. **2** a state of political disorder and violence due to the absence of governmental authority. **3** disorder or confusion. [< Gk. *anarchia* < *an-* without + *archos* ruler]

an·a·tase (an′ə tās′) *n.* a variety of native titanium oxide; octahedrite. [< F *anatase* < Gk. *anatasis* extension < *ana-* up + *teinein* stretch, so named because of elongated crystals]

a·nath·e·ma (ə nath′ə mə) *n., pl.* **-mas.** **1** a solemn curse by church authorities excommunicating a person. **2** the act of denouncing and condemning a person or thing as evil; curse. **3** a person or thing accursed. **4** a person or thing that is detested and condemned. [< L < Gk. *anathema* thing devoted, esp. to evil < *ana-* up+ *tithenai* set]

a·nath·e·ma·tize (ə nath′ə mə tīz′) *v.* **-tized, -tiz·ing.** pronounce an anathema against; denounce; curse. —**a·nath′e·ma·ti·za′tion,** *n.* —**a·nath′e·ma·tiz′er,** *n.*

An·a·to·li·an (an′ə tō′lē ən) *adj., n.* —*adj.* of or having to do with Anatolia (Asia Minor) or its people. —*n.* a native or inhabitant of Anatolia.

an·a·tom·ic (an′ə tom′ik) *adj.* anatomical.

an·a·tom·i·cal (an′ə tom′ə kəl) *adj.* of anatomy; having to do with anatomy. —**an′a·tom′i·cal·ly,** *adv.*

a·nat·o·mist (ə nat′ə mist) *n.* **1** an expert in anatomy. **2** a person who dissects or analyses.

a·nat·o·mize (ə nat′ə mīz′) *v.* **-mized, -miz·ing.** **1** divide (a plant or a body) into parts to study the structure; dissect. **2** examine the parts of; analyse. —**a·nat′o·mi·za′tion.** *n.*

a·nat·o·my (ə nat′ə mē) *n., pl.* **-mies.** **1** the structure of an animal or plant: *The anatomy of an earthworm is much simpler than that of a man.* **2** the science of the structure of animals and plants. **3** a textbook or handbook dealing with this subject. **4** the dissecting of animals or plants to study their structure. **5** an examination of the parts or elements of a thing; analysis. **6** skeleton. [< LL *anatomia* < Gk. *anatomē* dissection < *ana-* up + *temnein* cut]

anc. ancient.

–ance *noun-forming suffix.* **1** the act or fact of ——ing: *avoidance = the act or fact of avoiding.* **2** the quality or state of being ——ed: *annoyance = the quality or state of being annoyed.* **3** the quality or state of being ——ant: *importance = the quality or state of being important.* **4** something that ——s: *conveyance = something that conveys.* **5** what is ——ed: *contrivance = what is contrived.* [< F < L *-antia, -entia*]

an·ces·tor (an′ses tər) *n.* **1** a person from whom one is descended, such as one's father, mother, grandfather, or grandmother. **2** an original model or type from which others are developed: *The horseless carriage is the ancestor of the modern automobile.* **3** *Biology.* an earlier species or type from which a later or existing species is descended: *The horse and the donkey have a common ancestor.* [ME < OF *ancestre* < L *antecessor* < *antecedere* < *ante* before + *cedere* go]

an·ces·tral (an ses′trəl) *adj.* **1** of or having to do with ancestors: *The ancestral home of the Acadians was France.* **2** inherited from ancestors: *Black hair is an ancestral trait in that family.* —**an·ces′tral·ly,** *adv.*

an·ces·tress (an′ses tris) *n.* a woman from whom one is descended.

an·ces·try (an′ses trē) *n., pl.* **-tries.** **1** one's parents, grandparents, and other ancestors: *Many of the early settlers in North America had English ancestry.* **2** a line of descent from ancestors; lineage. **3** honorable descent.

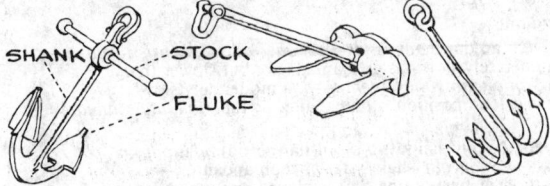

SHANK — STOCK

FLUKE

Anchors. The traditional ship's anchor on the left is still often used for boats, but ships now commonly use anchors of the type shown in the centre. The grapnel, on the right, is used for dories, etc.

an·chor (ang′kər) *n., v.* —*n.* **1** a heavy piece of shaped iron that is attached to a ship or boat by a cable and dropped to the bottom to keep the vessel from drifting. Anchors usually have hooks of some kind that dig into the bottom. **2** something used to hold something else in place. **3** something that makes a person feel safe and secure.

at anchor, held by an anchor.

cast anchor, drop the anchor.

ride at anchor, be kept at some place by being anchored.

weigh anchor, take up the anchor.

—*v.* **1** hold in place with an anchor: *to anchor a ship.* **2** drop anchor; stop or stay in place by using an anchor. **3** hold in place; fix firmly: *to anchor a tent to the ground.* [OE *ancor* < L *ancora, anchora* < Gk. *ankyra*]

an·chor·age (ang′kər ij) *n.* **1** a place to anchor. **2** money paid for the right to anchor. **3** anchoring or being anchored. **4** something to hold on to or depend on.

an·cho·ret (ang′kə rit *or* ang′kə ret′) *n.* anchorite.

anchor ice ground ice (def. 1).

an·cho·rite (ang′kə rīt′) *n.* **1** a person who lives alone in a solitary place for religious meditation. **2** hermit. [< Med.L *anachorita* < LL < Gk. *anachōrētēs* < *anachōreein* < *ana-* back + *chōreein* withdraw]

anchor man **1** *Sports.* **a** the last man to swim or run on a relay team. **b** the last player of a team to bowl in each frame. **c** the end man of a tug-of-war team. **2** *Radio and television.* the co-ordinator of a broadcast consisting of direct reports from several different cities or locations.

an·cho·vy (an′chō vē, an′chə vē, *or* an chō′vē) *n., pl.* **-vies.** any of a family (*Engraulidae*) of very small fishes distantly related to the herring, used for food and also for bait. Most species are found in warm seas. [< Sp., Pg. *anchova* < VL *apiuva,* probably < Gk. *aphyē*]

an·cienne no·blesse (äṅ syen nô bles′) *French.* **1** in France, the nobles before the Revolution in 1789. **2** the old nobility.

an·cien ré·gime (äṅ syaṅ rā zhēm′) *French.* **1** the social and political structure of France before the Revolution of 1789. **2** any former system; the old order of things.

an·cient (ān′shənt) *adj.* **1** of or belonging to times long past, especially the period before the fall of the Roman Empire in A.D. 476: *ancient history, ancient records. We saw the ruins of an ancient temple built six thousand years ago.* **2** of great age or early origin; very old: *the ancient hills, ancient freedoms.* **3** old-fashioned or antique: *He still wears that ancient coat.* **4** (*noml.*) a very old person. **5** (*noml.*) **the ancients,** **a** a people who lived in ancient times, especially the Greeks, Romans, and Hebrews. **b** the writers and artists of classical Greece and Rome. [ME < OF *ancien* < LL *antianus* former < L *ante* before] —**an′cient·ness,** *n.*

☛ *Syn. adj.* **2.** See note at **old.**

ancient history **1** history from the earliest times to the fall of the western part of the Roman Empire in A.D. 476. **2** *Informal.* a well-known fact or event of the recent past.

an·cient·ly (ān′shənt lē) *adv.* in ancient times.

an·cil·lar·y (an sil′ə rē *or* an′sə ler′ē) *adj.*, *n.* —*adj.*
1 subordinate; dependent: *He owns a factory and several ancillary
plants.* **2** assisting; auxiliary: *ancillary information.* —*n.*
something subordinate or auxiliary. [< L *ancillaris* < *ancilla*
handmaid]

an·con (ang′kon) *n.*, *pl.* **an·co·nes** (ang kō′nēz). *Architecture.* a
projection like a bracket, used to support a cornice. [< L < Gk.
ankōn bend]

-ancy *suffix.* a variant of *-ance*, as in *infancy*.

and (ənd *or* ən; *stressed*, and) *conj.* **1** as well as: *nice and cold.*
2 added to; with: *4 and 2 make 6. He likes ham and eggs.* **3** as a
result: *The sun came out and the grass dried.* **4** *Informal.* to: *try
and do better.* [OE]

and. andante.

an·dan·te (an dan′tē *or* än dän′tä) *adv.*, *adj.*, *n. Music.* —*adv.*
or adj. moderately slow; faster than adagio, but slower than
allegretto: *an andante movement.* —*n.* a moderately slow
movement or composition. *Abbrev.:* and. [< Ital. *andante* < *andare*
walk]

an·dan·ti·no (an′dan tē′nō *or* än′dän tē′nō) *adv.*, *adj.*, *n.*, *pl.*
-nos. *Music. adv. or adj.* slightly faster than andante. —*n.*
a composition or part of one that is played or sung andantino. [<
Ital. *andantino*, dim. of *andante*]

An·de·an (an dē′ən) *adj.* of or having to do with the Andes, a
mountain system in western South America.

and·i·ron (and′ī′ərn) *n.* one of a pair of metal supports for wood
burned in a fireplace; a firedog. [ME < OF *andier; -iron* by
association with *iron*]

and/or both or either.

☛ *Usage.* **And/or** is used primarily in business and legal writing. It is useful
when three choices exist (both items mentioned or either one of the two), but it
should not be overused. Writers can usually decide whether they mean *and* or
or.

an·dro·gen (an′drə jən) *n.* a male sex hormone, such as
testosterone, produced by the testes and the adrenal cortex or made
synthetically. Androgens promote the development of the male sex
organs and secondary masculine characteristics.

an·drog·e·nous (an droj′ə nəs) *adj.* **1** *Botany.* having flowers
with stamens and flowers with pistils in the same cluster. **2** having
both male and female characteristics. [< L < Gk. *androgynos* <
anēr, andros- man + *gynē* woman]

an·droid (an′droid) *n.* a robot, or automaton, having the form of
a human being.

An·drom·e·da (an drom′ə də) *n.* **1** *Greek mythology.* an
Ethiopian princess, who, to save her country, was to be sacrificed
to a sea monster. Perseus killed the monster and married
Andromeda. **2** *Astronomy.* a northern constellation.

an·ec·do·tal (an′ik dō′təl *or* an′ik dō′təl) *adj.* of anecdotes;
containing anecdotes.

an·ec·dote (an′ik dōt′) *n.* a short account of some interesting or
amusing incident or event: *Many anecdotes are told about Sir John
A. Macdonald.* [< Med.L *anecdota* < Gk. *anekdota* (things)
unpublished < *an-* not + *ek-* out + *didonai* give]
☛ *Syn.* See note at **story**[1].

a·ne·mi·a (ə nē′mē ə) *n.* an insufficiency of hemoglobin or of red
corpuscles in the blood. Also, **anaemia.** [< NL < Gk. *anaimia* lack
of blood < *an-* not + *haima* blood]

a·ne·mic (ə nē′mik) *adj.* of anemia; having anemia. Also,
anaemic.

an·e·mom·e·ter (an′ə mom′ə tər) *n.* an instrument for
measuring the speed or force of the wind. [< Gk. *anemos* wind + E
-meter]

a·nem·o·ne (ə nem′ə nē′) *n.* **1** any of a large genus (*Anemone*)
of small flowers of the buttercup family having lobed or divided
leaves and large, showy flowers. The prairie crocus is an anemone.
2 the sea anemone. [< L < Gk. *anemōnē* wind flower < *anemos*
wind]

a·nent (ə nent′) *prep. Archaic.* concerning; about. [OE *on emn,
on efn* on even (ground with)]

an·er·oid (an′ər oid′) *adj.*, *n.* —*adj.* using no liquid. —*n.*
an aneroid barometer. [< F *anéroïde* < Gk. *a-* without + LGk.
nēros wet]

aneroid barometer a barometer that records the changing
pressure of air on the flexible top of an air-tight metal box from
which some of the air has been pumped out. The barometers
commonly used in houses and offices are aneroid barometers.

an·es·the·sia (an′əs thē′zhə *or* an′əs thē′zē ə) *n.* an entire or
partial loss of the feeling of pain, touch, cold, etc., produced by
drugs, hypnotism, etc. or as the result of paralysis or disease.
General anesthesia is the loss of feeling in the whole body, causing
complete or partial unconsciousness. **Local anesthesia** is the loss of
feeling in only part of the body. Also, **anaesthesia.** [< NL < Gk.
anaisthēsia insensibility < *an-* without + *aisthēsis* sensation]

an·es·the·si·ol·o·gist (an′əs thē′zē ol′ə jist) *n.* a medical
doctor who specializes in anesthesiology; anesthetist (def. 2).

an·es·the·si·ol·o·gy (an′əs thē′zē ol′ə jē) *n.* a branch of
medicine dealing with anesthesia and the application of anesthetics.

an·es·thet·ic (an′əs thet′ik) *n.*, *adj.* —*n.* a substance that
produces anesthesia. Anesthetics used for surgical operations
include halothane, sodium pentothal, and nitrous oxide (to produce
general anesthesia) and procaine (for local anesthesia). —*adj.*
of, characterized by, or causing anesthesia. Also, **anaesthetic.**
—**an′es·thet′i·cal·ly,** *adv.*

an·es·the·tist (ə nēs′thə tist *or* ə nes′thə tist) *n.* **1** a person
whose work is giving anesthetics during surgical operations, etc. **2** a
medical doctor who specializes in the application of anesthetics.
Also, **anaesthetist.**

an·es·the·ti·za·tion (ə nēs′thə tə zā′shən *or* ə nes′-, ə nēs′thə
tī zā′shən *or* ə nes′-) *n.* **1** the act or process of anesthetizing. **2** the
state of being anesthetized. Also, **anaesthetization.**

an·es·the·tize (ə nēs′thə tīz′ *or* ə nes′thə tīz′) *v.* **-tized, -tiz·ing.**
1 make unable to feel pain, touch, cold, etc.; make insensible.
2 reduce (a person's) emotional or critical responses. Also,
anaesthetize. —**an·es′the·tiz′er,** *n.*

an·eu·rysm *or* **an·eu·rism** (an′yə riz′əm) *n.* a permanent
swelling of an artery, caused by pressure of the blood on a part
weakened by disease or injury. [< Gk. *aneurysma* dilation < *ana-*
up + *eurys* wide]

a·new (ə nyü′ *or* ə nü′) *adv.* **1** once more; again: *At each meeting
the question was raised anew.* **2** in a new form or way: *She crossed
out the whole paragraph and began anew.* [OE of *newe,* modelled
on OF *de neuf,* L *de novo*]

an·ga·koq *or* **an·ga·kok** (an′gə kok′) *n. Cdn.* an Inuit
shaman, the central religious figure in the traditional Inuit culture.
[< Eskimo]

an·gel (ān′jəl) *n.* **1** in certain religions, an immortal, spiritual
being who is an attendant and messenger of God. In medieval
Christian theology, angels were ranked in nine orders, and the word
angel was also specifically reserved for the lowest of these. **2** *Art.* a
representation of such a being, shown in human form but with
wings, white robes, and, often, a halo. **3** a person like an angel in
goodness, innocence, or loveliness. **4** any supernatural (but not
divine) spirit, either good or bad: *the angel of death.* **5** a person
who provides money for a business venture such as the production
of a play. **6** a shape like a traditional angel with wings, made as a
depression in soft snow by lying on one's back and moving the
outstretched arms up and down. **7** an old English gold coin in use
between 1465 and 1634. [OE *engel,* OF *angele* < L < Gk. *angelos*
messenger]

angel cake angel food cake.

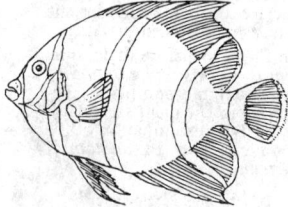

Angelfish (def. 2):
a young French angelfish
(*Pomacanthus arcuatus*),
native to the Caribbean

an·gel·fish (ān′jəl fish′) *n.*, *pl.* **-fish** *or* **fish·es.** **1** a small, tropical
freshwater fish (*Pterophyllum scalare*) native to South America,
usually silver and black in color and having a deep, narrow body
and long fins. Angel fish are popular for home aquariums. **2** any of
various brightly colored tropical marine fishes (family
Chaetodontidae) having a deep, narrow body. **3** a shark (*Squatina
squatina*) found in warm seas, having large winglike pectoral fins
and reaching a length of about 120 cm.

angel food cake a light, springy sponge cake containing whites
of eggs but no shortening or egg yolks.

an·gel·ic (an jel′ik) *adj.* **1** of angels; heavenly. **2** like an angel;
pure; innocent; good and lovely. —**an·gel′i·cal·ly,** *adv.*

an·gel·i·ca (an jel′ə kə) *n.* any of a genus (*Angelica*) of tall
perennial herbs of the carrot family found in the northern
hemisphere and New Zealand, having compound leaves and clusters
of white or greenish flowers. Some species of angelica yield an oil
used as a flavoring, in making perfume, etc. [< Med.L; named from
its use as an antidote]

an·gel·i·cal (an jel′ə kəl) *adj.* angelic.

An·ge·lus (an′jə ləs) *n. Roman Catholic Church.* **1** a prayer said in memory of Christ's assuming human form. **2** the bell, **Angelus bell**, rung at morning, noon, and night as a signal for the saying of this prayer. [from the first word in the prayer]

an·ger (ang′gər) *n., v.* —*n.* the feeling of wanting to retaliate that one has toward some person, animal, or thing that hurts, opposes, offends, or annoys; wrath; strong displeasure. —*v.* **1** make angry: *The boy's disobedience angered his father.* **2** become angry: *He angers easily.* [ME < ON *angr* trouble]
☛ *Syn. n.* **Anger, indignation, wrath** = the feeling of strong displeasure against anyone or anything that has hurt or wronged us or others. **Anger** is the general word for the emotion: *He never speaks in anger.* **Indignation** means anger mixed with scorn, caused by something mean, base, or unjust: *The atrocity caused widespread indignation.* **Wrath,** a formal word, means great anger or indignation: *His wrath was terrible to behold.*

An·ge·vin (an′jə vin) *adj., n.* —*adj.* **1** of or from Anjou. The Plantagenet family of the kings of England was Angevin. **2** of or belonging to the Plantagenet family. —*n.* **1** a member of the Plantagenet family. **2** a native or inhabitant of Anjou.

an·gi·na (an jī′nə; *in medicine, often* an′jə nə) *n.* **1** any disease of the mouth or throat, such as quinsy, croup, mumps, or diphtheria, marked by painful attacks of suffocation. **2** angina pectoris. [< L *angina* quinsy < *angere* choke]

angina pec·to·ris (pek′tə ris *or* pek tôr′is) a serious disease of the heart characterized by sharp chest pains and a feeling of suffocation, caused by a sudden decrease in the flow of blood of the heart muscles. [< NL *angina pectoris* angina of the chest]

an·gi·o·sperm (an′jē ō spėrm′) *n.* any plant belonging to the division Magnoliophyta (also called Angiospermae); any plant producing flowers and having its seeds enclosed in an ovary which becomes the fruit after fertilization. [< NL *angiospermus* < Gk. *angeion* vessel + *sperma* seed]

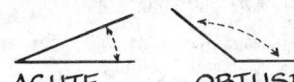

OBLIQUE ANGLES: RIGHT ANGLE:

ACUTE   OBTUSE

an·gle¹ (ang′gəl) *n., v.* **-gled, -gling.** —*n.* **1** the space between two lines extending in different directions from the same point or two surfaces extending from the same line. **2** the figure formed by two such lines or surfaces. **3** the difference in direction between two such lines or surfaces: *The roads lie at an angle of about 45 degrees.* **4** a corner. **5** *Informal.* point of view. **6** *Informal.* a means or method of obtaining an advantage, especially an unfair one: *She always has an angle for getting the better of you.* **7** one aspect of something; phase.
—*v.* **1** move at an angle. **2** present (something) with a particular point of view or a prejudice; slant. [ME < OF < L *angulus*]

an·gle² (ang′gəl) *v.* **-gled, -gling. 1** fish with a hook and line. **2** try to get something by using tricks or schemes (*used with* for): *to angle for an invitation.* [OE *angel* fish-hook]

An·gle (ang′gəl) *n.* a member of a Germanic tribe that migrated from what is now Denmark to England in the fifth century A.D.

angle iron a strip of iron or steel in the shape of an angle, used for joining two other pieces at an angle.

angle of attack the acute angle between the chord of an airplane wing or other airfoil and the direction of flight.

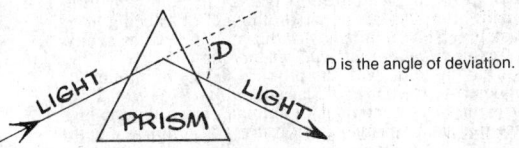

D is the angle of deviation.

angle of deviation the angle made between a ray of light as it enters a prism or other optical medium and the ray that emerges.

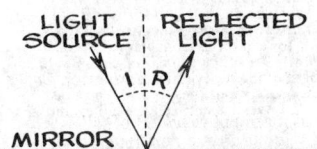

LIGHT SOURCE | REFLECTED LIGHT

MIRROR

I is the angle of incidence.
R is the angle of reflection.
The angle of incidence is always equal to the angle of reflection.

angle of incidence the angle made by a ray of light falling upon a surface with a line perpendicular to that surface.

hat, āge, fär; let, ēqual, tèrm; it, īce
hot, ōpen, ôrder; oil, out; cup, pút, rüle,
əbove, takən, pencəl, lemən, circəs
ch, child; ng, long; sh, ship
th, thin; ⟋H, then; zh, measure

angle of reflection the angle that a ray of light makes on reflection from a surface with a line perpendicular to that surface.

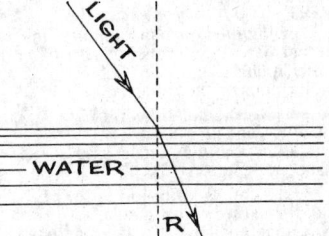

R is the angle of refraction.

angle of refraction the angle made between a ray of light refracted at a surface separating two media and a line perpendicular to the surface.

an·gler (ang′glər) *n.* **1** a person who fishes with a hook and line. **2** a person who tries to get something by using tricks and schemes. **3** any of an order (Pediculati, also called Lophiiformes) of bottom-living fishes that lure their prey within reach by means of a modified spine that projects from the head over the mouth, attracting other fish; especially, one species (*Lophius piscatorius*) found along the Atlantic coasts of North America and Europe.

an·gle·worm (ang′gəl wėrm′) *n.* earthworm.

An·gli·an (ang′glē ən) *adj., n.* —*adj.* of or having to do with the Angles, their dialect, or customs. —*n.* **1** an Angle. **2** the dialect of the Angles.

An·gli·can (ang′glə kən) *adj., n.* —*adj.* of or having to do with the Anglican Church of Canada, or the Church of England or other associated churches: *The first Anglican church in Canada was built in Halifax in 1750.* —*n.* a member of one of these churches.

Anglican Church of Canada a Christian church associated with the Church of England, until 1955 known as the Church of England in Canada.

An·gli·can·ism (ang′glə kən iz′əm) *n.* the principles and beliefs of the Church of England or of other churches associated with it.

An·gli·cism (ang′glə siz′əm) *n.* **1** a word, phrase, or meaning used in England, but not in widespread use in other English-speaking countries; a Briticism. **2** a custom or trait peculiar to the English.

An·gli·cize or **an·gli·cize** (ang′glə sīz′) *v.* **-cized, -ciz·ing.** make or become English in form, pronunciation, habits, customs, or character. *Cajole, lace,* and *cousin* are French words that have been Anglicized. —**An′gli·ci·za′tion** or **an′gli·ci·za′tion,** *n.*

Anglo– *combining form.* **1** English or English-speaking: *An Anglo-Canadian is an English-speaking Canadian.* **2** English and—: *Anglo-American means English (British) and American.* [< LL *Angli* the English]

An·glo–A·mer·i·can (ang′glō ə mer′ə kən) *adj., n.* —*adj.* **1** British and American. **2** of Americans, especially those of English descent. —*n.* an American, especially a United States citizen of English descent.

An·glo–Ca·na·di·an (ang′glō kə nā′dē ən) *adj., n.* —*adj.* **1** British and Canadian. **2** of or having to do with English-speaking Canadians. —*n.* an English-speaking Canadian; a Canadian whose native language is English.

An·glo–Cath·o·lic (ang′glō kath′ə lik *or* -kath′lik) *n., adj.* —*n.* a member of the Church of England who believes that it is and always has been a Catholic church. —*adj.* **1** of or having to do with Anglo-Catholics. **2** of or having to do with the Church of England as a Catholic church, as distinct from the Roman Catholic and Greek churches.

An·glo–Ca·thol·i·cism (ang′glō kə thol′ə siz′əm) *n.* the beliefs and practices of Anglo-Catholics.

An·glo–French (ang′glō french′) *n., adj.* —*n.* the French language as it developed in England after the Norman Conquest, especially after continental French began to have more influence in England than the dialect of the Normans. —*adj.* **1** of or referring to this language. **2** British and French: *an Anglo-French agreement.*

An·glo-In·di·an (ang′glō in′dē ən) *adj., n.* —*adj.* **1** English and Indian. **2** of or having to do with Anglo-Indians. —*n.* **1** a person of British birth living in India. **2** the dialect of English spoken by Anglo-Indians. **3** officially in India, an Indian citizen of mixed European, especially British, and Indian descent; Eurasian.

An·glo-I·rish (an′glō ī′rish) *n., adj.* —*n.* **1** the **Anglo-Irish**, *pl.* the inhabitants of Ireland who are of English birth or descent. **2** the kind of English spoken in Ireland. —*adj.* **1** of or having to do with the inhabitants of Ireland who are of English birth or descent. **2** of, having to do with, or involving Ireland and England. **3** of or having to do with the English spoken in Ireland.

An·glo-Nor·man (ang′glō nôr′mən) *n., adj.* —*n.* **1** any of the Normans who settled in England following the Norman Conquest in 1066. **2** a descendant of an English Norman. **3** the French dialect of the Normans as used in England after 1066.
—*adj.* of or referring to the Anglo-Normans or their dialect.

An·glo·phile (ang′glō fīl′) *n.* **1** a person who greatly admires England, its people, and its culture. **2** in Canada, a French Canadian who shows particular sympathy with the policies and culture of English-speaking Canada.

An·glo·phil·i·a (ang′glō fil′ēə) *n.* **1** a strong admiration for or devotion to England, its people, and its culture. **2** in Canada, a particular sympathy among French Canadians for the policies and culture of English-speaking Canada.

An·glo·phil·ic (ang′glə fil′ik) *adj.* **1** having to do with or characteristic of Anglophiles. **2** being an Anglophile.

An·glo·phobe (ang′glō fōb′) *n.* **1** a person who hates or fears England and its people. **2** in Canada, a French Canadian who hates or especially fears the policies and culture of English-speaking Canadians.

An·glo·pho·bi·a (ang′glō fō′bē ə) *n.* **1** a hatred or very great fear of England and anything English. **2** in Canada, a hatred or especial fear of the policies and culture of English-speaking Canadians.

An·glo·phone (ang′glō fōn′) *n. Cdn.* **1** a person in a bilingual or multilingual country whose native or principal language is English. **2** (*adj.*) of, having to do with, or made up of people whose native or principal language is English: *an Anglophone regiment.*

An·glo-Sax·on (ang′glō sak′sən) *n., adj.* —*n.* **1** a member of the nation that dominated England before the Norman conquest in 1066, descended from the Germanic tribes who conquered England in the fifth century A.D. **2** the language of the Anglo-Saxons; Old English. **3** a person who is English or of English descent. **4** plain, blunt English; that part of the English vocabulary descended from Old English, as opposed to the French and Latin elements, often with reference to its inclusion of words commonly considered offensive.
—*adj.* **1** of or having to do with the Anglo-Saxons or their language. **2** designating that part of the vocabulary of English that is derived from Old English, including words commonly considered offensive: *Food, horse, and hand are Anglo-Saxon words. She cursed him in Anglo-Saxon monosyllables.* *Abbrev.* AS or A.S.

An·go·ra (ang gô′rə) *n.* **1** Usually, **angora**, **a** the hair of the Angora rabbit. **b** yarn made from this hair, used especially for knitting. **c** (*adj.*) made from this yarn: *an angora sweater.* **d** mohair. **2** Angora cat. **3** Angora goat. **4** Angora rabbit. [< *Angora*, the former name of the Turkish province of Ankara, the original name of the Angora cat and Angora goat]

Angora cat a breed of cat having long, silky hair, a bushy tail, and a ruff of hair around the neck.

Angora goat a breed of goat having spiral horns and long, silky, curly hair that is used for making cloth. The hair of the Angora goat or cloth made from it is usually called mohair.

Angora rabbit a breed of rabbit having long, soft, usually white hair that is used for making yarns, especially for knitting. The Angora rabbit was developed from a species of European wild rabbit. [named after the Angora goat since it has similar hair]

an·gos·tu·ra (ang′gəs tyür′ə *or* ang′gəs tür′ə) *n.* **1** the bitter bark of a South American tree. **2 Angostura,** *Trademark.* Angostura Bitters. [after *Angostura*, a town in Venezuela]

Angostura Bitters *Trademark.* a bitter tonic derived from angostura bark and various other roots, barks, etc. It is sometimes used as a flavoring in food and cocktails.

an·gry (ang′grē) *adj.* **-gri·er, -gri·est. 1** feeling or showing anger: *an angry reply. He was angry with his brother.* **2** raging or stormy: *an angry sky.* **3** moved by anger: *angry words.* **4** inflamed and sore: *She had an angry cut on her arm.* [< *anger*] —**an′gri·ly,** *adv.* —**an′gri·ness,** *n.*
☛ *Usage.* **Angry.** In reference to a thing, **angry at** and **angry about** are used: *I was angry at his slipshod work. Do you ever get angry about the cheating you see?* In reference to a person, **angry with** is general: *He was angry with his son.*

Formal English uses **angry at** or **angry with,** making the following distinctions: when the angry feeling is being stressed, *at* is used; when the stress is on the directing of that anger upon a person, *with* is used: *We were angry at the boys for their tardiness. I was so angry with John that he drew back in fear.*

angst (ängst *or* angst) *n.* a continuous, vague feeling of anxiety or dread not consciously related to any specific thing in one's environment: *adolescent angst, the angst of the rootless and the lonely.*

ang·strom or **ång·ström** (ang′strəm) *n.* a unit for measuring length, equal to one ten-millionth of a millimetre, sometimes used to measure wavelengths of light. *Symbol:* A [after Anders John Angstrom (1814-1874), a Swedish physicist]

angstrom unit angstrom.

an·guish (ang′gwish) *n., v.* —*n.* very great pain or grief; great suffering or distress. —*v.* cause or feel anguish: *News of the flood anguished the nation. The boy anguished over the loss of his pet.* [ME < OF *anguisse* < L *angustia* tightness < *angustus* narrow]

an·guished (ang′gwisht) *adj.* **1** suffering anguish. **2** full of anguish; showing anguish.

an·gu·lar (ang′gyə lər) *adj.* **1** having angles; sharp-cornered: *an angular rock.* **2** measured by an angle: *angular distance.* **3** somewhat thin and bony; not plump: *He has a tall, angular body.* **4** stiff and awkward in manner or character: *angular compliments.* [< L *angularis* < *angulus* angle] —**an′gu·lar·ly,** *adv.*

an·gu·lar·i·ty (ang′gyə lar′ə tē *or* -ler′ə tē) *n., pl.* **-ties. 1** the quality or condition of being angular. **2 angularities,** *pl.* sharp corners.

an·hy·dride (an hī′drīd *or an* hī′drid) *n.* **1** any oxide that unites with water to form an acid or base. Sulphur trioxide, SO_3, is the anhydride of sulphuric acid. **2** any compound formed by the removal of water.

an·hy·drite (an hī′drīt) *n.* a white to bluish-grey mineral consisting of anhydrous sulphate of calcium. *Formula:* $CaSO_4$

an·hy·drous (an hī′drəs) *adj.* **1** without water: *an anhydrous region.* **2** *Chemistry.* containing no water of crystallization. [< Gk. *anydros* < *an-* without + *hydōr* water]

an·il (an′il) *n.* **1** a West Indian leguminous shrub from whose leaves and stalks indigo is made. **2** indigo. [< F < Pg. < Arabic *al-nil* < *al* the + *nil* indigo < Skt. *nīli* indigo < *nīla* dark blue]

an·ile (an′īl *or* ā′nīl) *adj.* old-womanish; suitable for a weak or doting old woman. [< L *anilis* < *anus* old woman]

an·i·line (an′ə lin, an′ə līn′, *or* an′ə lēn′) *n., adj.* —*n.* a poisonous, oily liquid, obtained from coal tar and especially from nitrobenzene, used in making dyes, plastics, etc. Aniline is a compound of carbon, nitrogen, and oxygen. *Formula:* $C_6H_5NH_2$ —*adj.* made from aniline. [< *anil*]

aniline dye 1 a dye made from aniline. **2** any artificial dye.

a·nil·i·ty (ə nil′ə tē) *n., pl.* **-ties. 1** an anile condition. **2** an anile act or notion.

an·i·ma (an′ə mə) *n. Latin.* life; soul.

an·i·mad·ver·sion (an′ə mad vėr′zhən) *n.* criticism; blame; unfavorable comment. [< L *animadversio, -onis* < *animadvertere.* See ANIMADVERT.]

an·i·mad·vert (an′ə mad vėrt′) *v.* make criticisms; express blame; comment unfavorably. [< L *animadvertere* < *animus* mind + *ad-* to + *vertere* turn]

an·i·mal (an′ə məl) *n., adj.* —*n.* **1** any living thing that is not a plant. Most animals can move about, whereas most plants cannot; most animals are unable to make their own food from carbon dioxide, water, nitrogen, etc., but most plants can. **2** any creature other than man; brute; beast. **3** a person thought of as being like a brute or beast; a person seemingly without human feelings. **4** any four-footed creature: *the animals and birds of the forest.*
—*adj.* **1** of or having to do with the physical nature of human beings, as opposed to the spiritual; carnal: *animal appetites.* **2** of, having to do with, or characteristic of animals, especially the higher animals other than man: *animal intelligence.* [< L *animal* < *anima* life, breath]
☛ *Syn. n.* **2. Animal, beast, brute** = a living creature of a lower order than man. **Animal,** the general word, suggests nothing more: *He likes animals.* **Beast** applies to four-legged animals, as distinct from birds, insects, etc.: *The horse is a noble beast.* **Brute,** used chiefly in formal or special styles, emphasizes lack of the power to reason which sets man above animals: *With the instinct of the brute, the deer found safety.* **4** Used figuratively, applied to man, **animal, beast,** and **brute** express attitudes of the speaker toward the persons named. **Animal,** objective, emphasizes the body: *Those boys are healthy young animals.* **Beast,** emotional, emphasizes giving up control over physical desires: *Living only for self-indulgence, he is a beast.* **Brute,** emotional, emphasizes lack of reason as shown by mental dullness or lack of control over violent feelings and inhuman treatment of others: *The brute of a guard beat him to a pulp.*

an·i·mal·cule (an′ə mal′kyül) *n.* a minute or microscopic animal, such as a protozoan or rotifer. [< NL *animalculum,* dim. of L *animal*]

an·i·mal·ism (an′ə məl iz′əm) *n.* **1** enjoyment of the natural

health and vitality typical of animals. 2 preoccupation with the satisfying of physical needs and desires. 3 the belief or doctrine that human beings are no more than animals and that they have no soul or spirit.

an·i·mal·ist (an′ə mə list′) *n.* 1 one who believes in animalism. 2 a sensualist. 3 an artist whose main subject is animal life.

an·i·mal·i·ty (an′ə mal′ə tē) *n.* 1 animal nature or character in man. 2 animal life.

an·i·mal·ize (an′ə mə līz′) *v.* -ized, -iz·ing. 1 change into animal matter: *Food assimilated into the body is animalized.* 2 make bestial; dehumanize. 3 make sensual.

animal kingdom one of the three basic groups into which all things found in nature are divided: *The animal kingdom includes all living and extinct animals, birds, fish, insects, etc.* Compare **mineral kingdom** and **plant kingdom.**

animal spirits natural liveliness; healthy cheerfulness.

an·i·mate (*v.* an′ə māt′; *adj.* an′ə mit) *v.* -mat·ed, -mat·ing; *adj.* —*v.* 1 give life to; make alive. 2 add liveliness or zest to: *Jim's funny stories animated the whole party.* 3 more to action; stir up; incite: *A fierce desire to succeed animated her efforts.* 4 inspire; encourage: *The soldiers were animated by their captain's brave speech.* 5 put into motion; cause to act or work: *Windmills are animated by the wind.* 6 produce as an animated cartoon: *to animate a children's story.* 7 make the drawings, etc. for an animated cartoon: *The television commercial was animated by a group of local artists.*
—*adj.* 1 living; having life: *Animate nature means all living plants and animals.* 2 lively; gay; vigorous. [< L *animare* < *anima* life, breath]

an·i·mat·ed (an′ə māt′id) *adj.* 1 lively; vigorous: *an animated discussion.* 2 joyful or vivacious: *an animated smile.* 3 simulating life: *animated dolls.* 4 made as an animated cartoon: *The movie has some animated sequences and some scenes with live actors.* 5 living, alive, animate. —**an′i·mat′ed·ly**, *adv.*

animated cartoon a series of drawings arranged to be photographed and shown in rapid succession as a motion picture. Each drawing shows a slight change from the one before it so that, when the film is projected, the figures in the drawings seem to move.

an·i·ma·tion (an′ə mā′shən) *n.* 1 an animating or being animated. 2 life. 3 liveliness; spirit. 4 the process or technique of making animated cartoons.

a·ni·ma·to (ä′ni mä′tō) *adj. Music.* lively; gay; vigorous. [< Ital.]

an·i·ma·tor (an′ə mā′tər) *n.* 1 a person or thing that animates. 2 a person who makes drawings for animated cartoons.

an·i·mism (an′ə miz′əm) *n.* 1 a belief in the existence of soul as distinct from matter; belief in spiritual beings, such as souls, angels, and devils. 2 a belief that there are living souls in trees, stones, stars, etc. [< L *anima* life, breath]

an·i·mist (an′ə mist) *n.* a person who believes in some form of animism.

an·i·mis·tic (an′ə mis′tik) *adj.* of or associated with animism.

an·i·mos·i·ty (an′ə mos′ə tē) *n., pl.* -ties. active or violent dislike; ill will: *He felt no animosity towards the winner.* [< L *animositas* < *animosus* spirited]

an·i·mus (an′ə məs) *n.* 1 active dislike or enmity; animosity. 2 an animating thought or spirit; intention: *Ambition was his animus.* [< L *animus* spirit, feeling]

an·i·on (an′ī ən) *n.* 1 a negatively charged ion that moves toward the positive pole in electrolysis. See **cathode** for picture. 2 an atom or group of atoms having a negative charge. [< Gk. *anion* (thing) going up, ppr. neut. of *anienai* < *ana-* up + *ienai* go]

an·ise (an′is) *n.* 1 an annual plant (*Pimpinella anisum*) of the parsley family native to the Mediterranean but widely cultivated in warm regions for its licorice-flavored seeds. 2 aniseed. [ME < OF *anis* < L < Gk. *anison*]

an·i·seed (an′ə sēd′ *or* an′is sēd′) *n.* the seed of anise, used as a flavoring or in medicine.

an·i·sette (an′ə set′ *or* an′ə zet′) *n.* a sweet, usually colorless liqueur flavored with aniseed.

ankh (angk) *n.* an ancient Egyptian symbol of life, in the form of a cross with a loop at the top instead of a vertical arm. See **cross** for picture.

an·kle (ang′kəl) *n.* 1 the part of the human leg between the foot and the calf: *slim ankles.* 2 the protruding part on the outside bottom end of each of the lower leg bones, just above the foot: *I bumped my ankle against the chair. He has a broken ankle.* 3 the joint formed by the lower leg bones and the talus, connecting the foot and the leg: *My ankle is still stiff from when I twisted it.* 4 the part of a stocking, sock, or boot that covers the ankle. 5 in a horse,

hat, āge, fär; let, ēqual, tèrm; it, īce
hot, ōpen, ôrder; oil, out; cup, put, rüle,
əbove, takən, pencəl, lemən, circəs

ch, child; ng, long; sh, ship
th, thin; ŦH, then; zh, measure

etc., the joint between the cannon bone and the pastern. [ME < Scand.; cf. Danish *ankel*]

an·kle·bone (ang′kəl bōn′) *n.* the protruding part ·on the outside of the bottom of each of the lower leg bones, just above the foot.

an·klet (ang′klit) *n.* 1 a short sock. 2 a chain or band worn around the ankle, especially as an ornament.

an·ky·lose (ang′kə lōs′) *v.* -losed, -los·ing. 1 make or become stiff, by or as if by ankylosis. 2 of bones, grow together; unite. [< Gk. *ankylosis* < *ankylos* crooked]

an·ky·lo·sis (ang′kə lō′sis) *n.* 1 a growing together of bones as a result of disease or injury. 2 stiffness of a joint caused by this. [< NL < Gk. *ankylosis* < *ankyloein* stiffen < *ankylos* crooked]

an·na (an′ə) *n.* 1 a unit of money formerly used in India, Pakistan, Burma, and British East Africa, equal to one sixteenth of a rupee. 2 a coin having this value. [< Hind. *ana*]

an·nal·ist (an′əl ist) *n.* a writer of annals.

an·nals (an′əlz) *n.pl.* 1 a written account of events year by year. 2 historical records; history. [< L *annales* (*libri* books) annual record < *annus* year]

An·na·mese (an′ə mēz′) *adj., n., pl.* -mese. —*adj.* of or associated with Annam or its people. —*n.* 1 a native or inhabitant of Annam. 2 the language spoken by the Annamese.

an·neal (ə nēl′) *v.* toughen (glass, metals, etc.) by heating and then cooling; temper. [OE *anǣlan* < *an-* on + *ǣlan* burn]

an·ne·lid (an′ə lid) *n.* any of more than 8000 species of segmented worms making up the phylum **Annelida.** Annelids are grouped into three classes: sea worms, earthworms, and leeches. [< F *annélide* < of *annel* ring < L *anellus*, double dim. of *anus* ring]

an·nex (*v.* ə neks′; *n.* an′eks) *v., n.* —*v.* 1 join or add to a larger thing: *Britain annexed Acadia in 1713.* 2 *Informal.* take as one's own; appropriate, especially without permission. —*n.* 1 something added or attached; an added part: *Our hotel has an annex.* 2 *Slang.* a backhouse; outhouse. [ME < Med.L *annexare* < L *annexus*, pp. of *annectere* < *ad-* to + *nectere* bind]
☞ *Syn. v.* 1. See note at **attach.**

an·nex·a·tion (an′ək sā′shən) *n.* 1 an annexing or being annexed: *the annexation of several suburbs to the metropolitan area.* 2 something annexed.

an·nex·a·tion·ist (an′ək sā′shən ist) *n.* 1 a person who favors or supports annexation, as between two cities, nations, etc. 2 Sometimes, **Annexationist,** *Cdn.* a person belonging to or supporting an Annexation Movement.

Annexation Movement the name given to groups in Canada that have advocated political union with the United States.

an·ni·hi·late (ə nī′ə lāt′) *v.* -lat·ed, -lat·ing. 1 destroy completely; wipe out of existence. 2 bring to ruin or confusion. [< LL *annihilare* < L *ad-* + *nihil* nothing] —**an·ni′hi·la′tor,** *n.*
☞ *Syn.* 1. See note at **abolish.**

an·ni·hi·la·tion (ə nī′ə lā′shən) *n.* 1 complete destruction. 2 *Nuclear physics.* **a** the destruction of a positron (positive electron) and an electron, the energy turning into one or more photons of radiation. **b** the uniting of an electron and a positron to produce a gamma ray.

an·ni·hi·la·tive (ə nī′ə lə tiv *or* ə nī′ə lā′tiv) *adj.* able or likely to annihilate.

an·ni·ver·sa·ry (an′ə vėr′sə rē *or* an′ə vèrs′rē) *n., pl.* -ries. 1 the yearly return of a date: *Tomorrow is the anniversary of her wedding.* 2 the celebration of the yearly return of a date. 3 (*adj.*) of or having to do with an anniversary: *an anniversary dinner.* [ME < L *anniversarius* returning annually < *annus* year + *vertere* turn]

an·no Dom·i·ni (an′ō dom′ə nē *or* -dom′ə nī) *Latin.* in the year of our Lord; any year since the birth of Christ. *Abbrev.:* A.D.

an·no·tate (an′ō tāt′) *v.* -tat·ed, -tat·ing. 1 provide with explanatory notes or comments: *Shakespeare's plays are often annotated to make them easier for modern readers to understand.* 2 make explanatory notes or comments. [< L *annotare* < *ad-* to + *nota* note] —**an′no·ta′tor,** *n.*

an·no·ta·tion (an′ō tā′shən) *n.* 1 the act of providing with notes; being provided with notes: *The book's annotation required hundreds of hours.* 2 a note added to explain or criticize: *The editor's annotations were printed in small type.*

an·nounce (ə nouns′) *v.* -nounced, -nounc·ing. 1 make known;

give formal or public notice of: *to announce a wedding in the papers. She announced that she was never going to school again.* 2 make known the presence or arrival of: *The butler announced each guest in a loud voice.* 3 give or be evidence of: *Black clouds announced the coming thunderstorm.* 4 *Radio and television.* act as an announcer; be an announcer for. [ME < OF *anoncier* < L *annuntiare* < *ad-* to + *nuntius* messenger. Doublet of ANNUNCIATE.]

➤ *Syn.* **1. Announce, proclaim, declare** = make known formally or publicly. **Announce** = give formal notice of something of interest to the public or a particular group: *They announced the birth of their first baby.* **Proclaim** = announce publicly and with authority something of importance to the general public: *The Prime Minister proclaimed an emergency.* **Declare** = make known clearly and plainly, often formally or officially: *An armistice was declared.*

an·nounce·ment (ə nouns′mənt) *n.* **1** the act of announcing. **2** a public or formal notice: *Announcements of marriages appear in the newspapers.*

an·nounc·er (ə noun′sər) *n.* a person who announces, especially a person in radio and television who introduces programs, reads news, etc.

an·noy (ə noi′) *v.* **1** disturb or trouble, often by repetition of an act; vex; irritate: *She annoys her little brother by teasing him. The speaker was annoyed at the interruption.* **2** harass by means of repeated attacks; harry or molest: *a series of raids designed to annoy the enemy.* [ME < OF *anuier* < LL *inodiare* < L *in odio* in hatred]

➤ *Syn.* **1.** See note at **worry.**

an·noy·ance (ə noi′əns) *n.* **1** the act of annoying. **2** a feeling of being bothered or irritated; vexation: *She replied with annoyance that she had heard that story before.* **3** anything that annoys: *The heavy traffic on our street is a great annoyance.*

an·noy·ing (ə noi′ing) *adj.* disturbing; irritating: *an annoying background hum.* —**an·noy′ing·ly,** *adv.* —**an·noy′ing·ness,** *n.*

an·nu·al (an′yü əl) *adj., n.* —*adj.* **1** coming once a year: *Your birthday is an annual event.* **2** in or for a year; covering the period of a year: *an annual salary of $16 000, annual rainfall, the earth's annual course around the sun.* **3** *Botany.* living only one year or season. —*n.* **1** a book, journal, etc. published once a year. **2** a plant that lives only one year or season. Compare **biennial, perennial.** [ME < OF *annuel* < LL *annualis* < L *annus* year.] —**an′nu·al·ly,** *adv.*

annual ring in a woody plant, one of the concentric circles that can be seen in a cross section of a stem; each ring is the layer of wood produced in one growing season.

an·nu·i·tant (ə nyü′ə tənt *or* ə nü′ə tənt) *n.* a person who receives an annuity.

an·nu·i·ty (ə nyü′ə tē *or* ə nü′ə tē) *n., pl.* **-ties.** **1** a sum of money paid every year. **2** the right to receive or duty to pay such a yearly sum. **3** an investment that provides a fixed yearly income during one's lifetime. [ME < OF *annuite* < Med.L *annuitas* < L *annus* year]

an·nul (ə nul′) *v.* **-nulled, -nul·ling.** do away with; destroy the force of; make void: *The judge annulled the contract because one of the signers was too young.* [ME < OF *anuller* < LL *annullare* < L *ad-* + *nullus* none]

an·nu·lar (an′yə lər) *adj.* ringlike; ring-shaped; ringed. [< *anularis* (sometimes misspelled *annularis* in late and poor MSS) < *anulus* ring. See ANNULUS.]

an·nu·let (an′yə lit) *n.* **1** a little ring. **2** *Architecture.* a narrow, ringlike moulding of wood, stone, etc. [< L *anulus* ring. See ANNULUS.]

an·nul·ment (ə nul′mənt) *n.* an annulling or being annulled; cancellation.

an·nu·lus (an′yə ləs) *n., pl.* **-li** (-lī′ *or* -lē′) *or* **-lus·es.** a ringlike part, band, or space. [< L *anulus* (sometimes misspelled *annulus* in late and poor MSS), dim. of *anus* ring]

an·num (an′əm) *n. Latin.* year (acc. of *annus*).

an·nun·ci·ate (ə nun′sē āt′ *or* ə nun′shē āt′) *v.* **-at·ed, -at·ing.** make known; announce. [< Med.L *annunciare* < L *annuntiare* < *ad-* to + *nuntius* messenger. Doublet of ANNOUNCE.]

an·nun·ci·a·tion (ə nun′sē ā′shən *or* ə nun′shē ā′shən) *n.* **1** an announcement. **2 the Annunciation, a** the angel Gabriel's announcement to the Virgin Mary that she was to be the mother of Christ (Luke 1: 26-33). **b** a painting, sculpture, etc. of this. **c** Lady Day.

an·nun·ci·a·tor (ə nun′sē ā′tər *or* ə nun′shē ā′tər) *n.* **1** an electrical device such as a buzzer or light, that indicates where a signal is coming from: *Annunciators are used in hotel switchboards, in manually operated elevators, etc.* **2** announcer.

an·ode (an′ōd) *n.* **1** the negatively charged electrode of a primary cell or storage battery, through which the electrons leave the cell

when the circuit is complete. See **dry cell** for picture. **2** the positive electrode in an electrolytic cell, that is connected to the positive terminal of a battery and carries electrons from the cell back to the battery. See **electrolysis** for picture. **3** the positively charged electrode in a vacuum tube, that attracts electrons from the cathode. See **cathode-ray tube** for picture. [< L < Gk. *anodos* < *ana-* up + *hodos* way]

an·o·dyne (an′ə dīn′) *n.* anything that lessens pain or provides comfort. [< L < Gk. *anodynos* < *an-* without + *odynē* pain]

a·noint (ə noint′) *v.* **1** put oil on; rub with ointment; smear: *Anoint sunburned skin with cold cream.* **2** put oil on in a ceremony as a sign of consecration to office; make sacred with oil: *The archbiship anointed the new king.* [< OF *enoint*, pp. of *enoindre* < L *inunguere* < *in-* on + *unguere* smear] —**a·noint′ment,** *n.*

a·nom·a·lous (ə nom′ə ləs) *adj.* departing from the common rule; irregular; abnormal: *A position as head of a department, but with no real authority, is anomalous.* [< LL < Gk. *anōmalos* < *an-* not + *homalos* even]

a·nom·a·ly (ə nom′ə lē) *n., pl.* **-lies.** **1** a departure from a general rule; irregularity. **2** something abnormal: *A dog that cannot bark would be an anomaly.*

a·nom·ic (ə nom′ik) *adj.* of, having to do with, or characterized by anomie.

an·o·mie (an′ə mē) *n.* a lack of standards for social or moral conduct in a person or society.

a·non (ə non′) *adv. Archaic.* **1** in a little while; soon. **2** at another time; again.
ever and anon, now and then. [OE *on ān* into one, *on āne* in one, at once]

anon. anonymous.

an·o·nym·i·ty (an′ə nim′ə tē) *n.* the quality or state of being anonymous: *He wrote under a pen name to preserve his anonymity.*

a·non·y·mous (ə non′ə məs) *adj.* **1** by or from a person whose name is not known or not given: *an anonymous letter, an anonymous poem.* **2** of unknown name; nameless: *The author of this poem is anonymous.* Abbrev.: a. or anon. [< Gk. *anōnymos* < *an-* without + (dialectal) *onyma* name] —**a·non′y·mous·ly,** *adv.*

a·noph·e·les (ə nof′ə lēz′) *n., pl.* **-les.** any of a genus (*Anopheles*) of mosquitoes that includes all the species known to transmit malaria to man. [< NL < Gk. *anōphelēs* harmful]

a·no·rak (an′ə rak′) *n.* **1** a waterproof, hooded outer coat of skins, often worn by Inuit when hunting in a kayak. The lower edge of the anorak can be fastened tightly around the opening in the kayak. **2** a parka, especially a waterproof one. [< Inuktitut (Eskimo), Greenland dial.]

an·o·rec·tic (an′ə rek′tik) *adj. or n.* anoretic.

an·o·ret·ic (an′ə ret′ik) *adj., n.* —*adj.* of, causing, or affected with anorexia. —*n.* **1** a person affected with anorexia. **2** something that causes anorexia.

an·o·rex·i·a (an′ə rek′sē ə) *n.* **1** chronic loss of appetite. **2** anorexia nervosa.

anorexia ner·vo·sa (nėr vō′sə) an emotional disorder characterized by a refusal to eat, resulting in excessive weight loss and malnutrition which, if not corrected, can end in death.

an·o·rex·ic (an′ə rek′sik) *n.* a person affected with anorexia.

an·os·mi·a (a noz′mē ə *or* a nos′mē ə) *n.* partial or complete loss of the sense of smell.

an·os·mic (a noz′mik *or* a nos′mik) *adj.* of or having to do with anosmia.

an·oth·er (ə nuᴛн′ər) *adj., pron.* —*adj.* **1** one more: *Have another glass of milk.* **2** different; not the same: *That is another matter entirely.* —*pron.* **1** one more: *Here is a piece of cake and then asked for another.* **2** a different one: *I don't like this book; give me another.* **3** one of the same kind: *His father is a scholar, and he is another.* [for *an other*]

ans. **1** answer. **2** answered.

An·schluss (än′shlùs) *n. German.* a union, especially that of Germany and Austria in 1938.

an·ser·ine (an′sər in′, an′sər ēn′, *or* an′sər in) *adj.* **1** of or belonging to the subfamily Anserine, which includes the geese. **2** of, like, or having to do with a goose or geese. **3** stupid; foolish. [< L *anserinus* < *anser* goose]

an·swer (an′sər) *n., v.* —*n.* **1** words spoken or written in return to a question: *The boy gave a quick answer.* **2** a gesture or act done in return: *A nod was her only answer.* **3** a solution to a problem: *What is the correct answer to this algebra problem?*
know all the answers, *Informal.* **a** be extremely well-informed. **b** make a boastful and annoying display of one's knowledge.
—*v.* **1** reply to: *He answered my question.* **2** make answer; reply: *I asked him a question, but he would not answer.* **3** reply or respond by act: *He knocked on the door, but no one answered.* **4** act or

move in response to: *She answered the doorbell.* **5** serve: *This will answer your purpose. Such a poor excuse will not answer.* **6** reply to (a charge): *to answer a summons.* **7** bear the consequences of; be responsible (*for*): *to answer for a crime, to answer for his safety.* **8** correspond (*to*): *This house answers to his description.*
answer back, *Informal.* reply in a rude, saucy way.
[OE *andswaru* < *and-* against + *swerian* swear] **—an'swer·less',** *adj.*

☛ *Syn. v.* **2. Answer, reply, respond** = say something in return to something said, asked, or demanded. **Answer** is the general word, meaning 'speak or write in return': *I called, but no one answered.* **Reply** is used in more formal style or to suggest more formal answering, as with thought and care: *I sent in my application, and the university replied immediately.* **Respond,** formal in this sense, suggests an action as an answer. *When we requested information and instructions, the chairman responded.*

an·swer·a·ble (an'sər ə bəl) *adj.* **1** responsible: *The club treasurer is held answerable to the club for the money that is given to him.* **2** that can be answered. **3** *Archaic.* corresponding.

answering service a business organization that takes the telephone calls of a subscriber in his absence and, when he returns, reports to him on the calls received.

ant (ant) *n.* any of a large family (Formicidae) of mainly wingless insects that live in the ground or in wood in highly organized groups called colonies, which are divided into smaller groups, each with a specialized function to perform. Ants belong to the same order as bees and wasps. [OE *æmete*] **—ant'like',** *adj.*

ant– the form of **anti-** before vowels and *h,* as in *antacid.*

–ant *suffix.* **1** —ing: *buoyant = buoying, compliant = complying, triumphant = triumphing.* **2** one that —s: *assistant = one that assists.* See also **-ent.** [< F < L *-ans, -antis; -ens, -entis*]

ant. **1** antonym. **2** antiquary.

ant·ac·id (ant as'id) *n., adj.* **—n.** a substance, such as baking soda or magnesia, that neutralizes acids. **—adj.** tending to neutralize acids; counteracting acidity.

an·tag·o·nism (an tag'ə niz'əm) *n.* active opposition; conflict; hostility.

an·tag·o·nist (an tag'ə nist) *n.* one who fights, struggles, or contends with another: *The knight defeated each antagonist.*
☛ *Syn.* See note at **opponent.**

an·tag·o·nis·tic (an tag'ə nis'tik) *adj.* having or showing conflict or hostility; opposing: *an antagonistic attitude. The two brothers have always been antagonistic.* **—an·tag'o·nis'ti·cal·ly,** *adv.*

an·tag·o·nize (an tag'ə nīz') *v.* **-nized, -niz·ing.** **1** arouse opposition, hostility, or enmity in: *Her unkind remarks antagonized people who had been her friends.* **2** oppose or counteract. [< Gk. *antagōnizesthai* < *anti-*against + *agōn* contest] **—an·tag'o·niz·er,** *n.*

ant·arc·tic (ant ärk'tik *or* ant är'tik) *adj., n.* **—adj.** Often, **Antarctic,** of, having to do with, referring to, or living or growing in the region south of the Antarctic Circle. **—n.**
the Antarctic, the south polar region; the region south of the Antarctic Circle. [ME < OF < L *antarcticus* < Gk. *antarktikos* opposite the north < *anti-* opposite + *arktikos* of the north. See ARCTIC.]

Antarctic Circle the parallel of latitude at 66°33′ south of the equator that marks the boundary of the south polar region.

An·tar·es (an ter'ēz) *n.* a first magnitude star in the constellation Scorpio.

ant·ar·thrit·ic (ant'är thrit'ik) *adj., n.* **—adj.** relieving or preventing arthritis. **—n.** a remedy for arthritis.

ant·asth·ma·tic (ant'az mat'ik *or* ant'as mat'ik) *adj., n.* **—adj.** relieving or preventing asthma. **—n.** a remedy for asthma.

ant bear the giant anteater of South America.

an·te (an'tē) *n., v.* **-ted** *or* **-teed, -te·ing.** **—n.** in the game of poker, a stake that every player must put up before receiving a hand or drawing new cards. **—v.** *Informal.* **1** in poker, put (one's stake) into the pool. **2** pay (one's share).
ante up, **a** in poker, put in one's stake. **b** pay one's share. [See ANTE-.]
☛ *Hom.* **anti-.**

ante– *prefix.* **1** before; earlier: *antenatal.* **2** in front of: *anteroom.* [< L *ante-* < *ante,* adv., prep.]
☛ *Hom.* **anti-.**

ant·eat·er (ant'ēt'ər) *n.* **1** any of a family (Myrmecophagidae) of toothless mammals found in the tropical forests of South America, having a long, tube-shaped head and muzzle with a small mouth opening and a long, slender, sticky, wormlike tongue with which it catches the ants and termites it eats. The giant, or great, anteater, the largest species, has a long, bushy tail and very strong front claws with which it rips open the nests of ants and termites. **2** any of several other mammals, such as the aardvark and the pangolin, that feed mainly on ants and termites but are not related to the true anteaters.

hat, āge, fär; let, ēqual, tėrm; it, īce
hot, ōpen, ôrder; oil, out; cup, pu̇t, rüle,
əbove, takən, pencəl, lemən, circəs

ch, child; ng, long; sh, ship
th, thin; ᴛʜ, then; zh, measure

an·te·bel·lum (an'tē bel'əm) *adj.* **1** before the war. **2** *U.S.* before the American Civil War. [< L *ante bellum* before the war]

an·te·ced·ence (an'tə sēd'əns) *n.* **1** a going before; precedence; priority. **2** *Astronomy.* the apparent motion of a planet from east to west.

an·te·ced·ent (an'tə sēd'ənt) *n., adj.* **—n.** **1** a previous thing or event; something happening before an event and leading up to another. **2** *Grammar.* a word, phrase, or clause that is referred to by a pronoun or relative adverb. In "This is the house that Jack built," *house* is the antecedent of *that.* In "I remember the house where I was born," *house* is the antecedent of *where.* **3** *Mathematics.* the first term of a ratio; the first or third term in a proportion. **4** *Logic.* a condition upon which a theoretical conclusion depends.
5 antecedents, *pl.* **a** past life or history: *No one knew the antecedents of the mysterious stranger.* **b** ancestors.
—adj. coming or happening before; preceding; previous. [< L *antecedens, -entis,* ppr. of *antecedere* < *ante-* before + *cedere* go]

an·te·cham·ber (an'tē chām'bər) *n.* anteroom.

an·te·date (an'tē dāt') *n., v.* **-dat·ed, -dat·ing.** **—n.** a date, set on a document or assigned to an event, earlier than the actual date. **—v.** **1** come before in time; occur earlier than. *Shakespeare's Hamlet antedates Macbeth by about six years.* **2** give too early a date to.

an·te·di·lu·vi·an (an'tē də lü've ən) *adj., n.* **—adj.** **1** of or having to do with the period before the Flood. **2** very old or old-fashioned. **—n.** **1** a person who lived before the Flood. **2** an old-fashioned or very old person. [< *ante-* + L *diluvium* deluge]

an·te·lope (an'tə lōp') *n., pl.* **-lope** *or* **-lopes.** **1** any of a large group of hoofed, cud-chewing, mainly African animals belonging to the same family as cattle, goats, etc., having hollow, non-branding horns that grow upward and backward and that are not shed. **2** a very swift, hoofed, cud-chewing animal (*Antilocapra americana*) of the North American plains that is the only member of the family Antilocapridae, having horns with a permanent bony core and a black, horny outer layer that is shed every year. Also called **pronghorn antelope, pronghorn.** [ME < OF *antelop* < Med.L < LGk. *antholops*]

an·te me·rid·i·em (an'tē mə rid'ē əm) *Latin.* before noon. *Abbrev.:* a.m. or A.M.

an·te·na·tal (an'tē nā'təl) *adj.* before birth.

an·ten·na (an ten'ə) *n., pl.* **-ten·nae** for 1; **-ten·nas** for 2. **1** one of two feelers on the head of an insect, lobster, etc. **2** *Radio and television.* a long wire or set of wires for sending out or receiving electromagnetic waves. [< L *antenna,* originally, sailyard]

an·ten·nae (an ten'ē *or* an ten'ī) *n. pl.* of **antenna** (def. 1).

an·te·nup·tial (an'tē nup'shəl) *adj.* before marriage.

an·te·pe·nult (an'tē pə nult' *or* -pē'nult) *n.* the third syllable from the end of a word. In *anthropology* the syllable *pol* is the antepenult.

an·te·pe·nul·ti·mate (an'tē pə nul'tə mit) *adj., n.* **—adj.** third from the end. **—n.** antepenult.

an·te·ri·or (an tēr'ē ər) *adj.* **1** toward the front; fore: *The anterior part of a fish's body contains the head and gills.* **2** going before; earlier; previous. [< L *anterior,* comparative of *ante* before]

an·te·room (an'tē rüm' *or* -ru̇m') *n.* a small room leading to a larger one; a waiting room.

an·them (an'thəm) *n.* **1** a song of praise, devotion, or patriotism. Most countries have a **national anthem.** **2** a piece of sacred music, usually with words from some passage in the Bible. [OE *antefne* < LL < Gk. *antiphōna* antiphon. Doublet of ANTIPHON.]

an·ther (an'thər) *n.* of a flower, the part of the stamen that bears the pollen. See **flower** for picture. [< NL < Gk. *anthēra,* fem. of *anthēros* flowery < *anthos* flower]

an·ther·id·i·um (an'thər id'ē əm) *n., pl.* **-id·i·a** (-id'ē ə). the part of a fern, moss, etc. that produces male reproductive cells. [< NL *antheridium.* dim. of Gk. *anthēra* anther. See ANTHER.]

ant·hill *or* **ant hill** (ant'hil') *n.* **1** a heap of dirt piled up by ants around the entrance to their underground nest. **2** a termite nest.

an·thol·o·gist (an thol'ə jist) *n.* a person who makes an anthology.

an·thol·o·gize (an thol'ə jīz') *v.* **-gized, -giz·ing.** compile an

anthology of or publish in an anthology: *His poems have never been anthologized.*

an·thol·o·gy (an thol′ə jē) *n., pl.* **-gies.** a collection of poems or prose selections from various authors. [< L < Gk. *anthologia* < *anthos* flower + *legein* gather]

an·tho·zo·an (an′thə zō′ən) *n.* any of a class (Anthozoa) of flowerlike marine animals having a body that is shaped somewhat like a cylinder, closed above and below by disks of tissue, the upper disk surrounded by a circle of hollow tentacles and having a mouth in the centre. Sea anemones and corals are anthozoans. [< Gk. *anthos* flower + *zōa* animals]

an·thra·cene (an′thrə sēn′) *n.* a colorless, crystalline, complex compound of hydrogen and carbon. It is obtained by distilling coal tar and is used in making alizarin dyes. *Formula*: $C_{14}H_{10}$ [< Gk. *anthrax* live coal]

an·thra·cite (an′thrə sīt′) *n.* a hard, shiny, black type of coal containing a high percentage of carbon and a low percentage of moisture, that burns with very little smoke. [< L < Gk. *anthrakitēs* coal-like < *anthrax* charcoal]

an·thrac·nose (an thrak′nōs) *n.* any of various fungus diseases of plants that form spores which break through the surface as blackish spots, often on fruit and leaves, sometimes destroying whole crops. [< Gk. *anthrax* carbuncle, charcoal + *nosos* disease]

an·thrax (an′thraks) *n.* an infectious, often fatal, disease of cattle, sheep, etc. that may be transmitted to human beings. [< LL < Gk. *anthrax* live coal]

anthropo– *combining form.* of human beings, as in *anthropology, anthropometry.* [< Gk. *anthrōpos* man]

an·thro·poid (an′thrə poid′) *adj., n.* —*adj.* manlike; used especially with reference to members of the ape family. —*n.* ape (def. 1). [< Gk. *anthrōpoeidēs* < *anthrōpos* man]

an·thro·poi·de·a (an′thrə poi′dē ə) *n. Zoology.* a suborder of mammals, including monkeys, baboons, apes, and man.

an·thro·po·log·i·cal (an′thrə pə loj′ə kəl) *adj.* of or having to do with anthropology. —**an′thro·po·log′i·cal·ly,** *adv.*

an·thro·pol·o·gist (an′thrə pol′ə jist) *n.* a person trained in anthropology, especially one whose work it is.

an·thro·pol·o·gy (an′thrə pol′ə jē) *n.* the science that deals with the origin, development, and customs of mankind. **Physical anthropology** deals with the physiological and anatomical evolution and the racial classifications of man; **cultural anthropology** deals with the social development, practices, and beliefs of man.

an·thro·po·met·ric (an′thrə pə met′rik) *adj.* of or having to do with anthropometry.

an·thro·po·met·ri·cal (an′thrə pə met′rə kəl) *adj.* anthropometric.

an·thro·pom·e·try (an′thrə pom′ə trē) *n.* the branch of anthropology that deals with measurement of the human body.

an·thro·po·mor·phic (an′thrə pə môr′fik) *adj.* attributing human form or qualities to gods, animals, etc. The religion of ancient Greece was anthropomorphic. [< Gk. *anthrōpomorphos* < *anthrōpos* man + *morphē* form]

an·thro·po·mor·phism (an′thrə pə môr′fiz əm) *n.* an attributing of human form or qualities to gods or things.

anti (an′tē) *n., pl.* **-tis;** *adj., prep. Informal.* —*n.* a person opposed to some plan, idea, political party, etc. —*adj.* opposed: *He is anti by nature.* —*prep.* against: *anti everything new.* [See ANTI-]
☛ *Hom.* ante.

anti– (an′tē) *prefix.* **1** against; opposed to ——: *anti-aircraft* = *against aircraft; anti-administration* = *opposed to the administration.* **2** not; the opposite of ——: *antisocial* = *the opposite of social; antiwarlike* = *not warlike.* **3** rival ——: *antipope* = *rival pope.* **4** preventing or counteracting ——: *antirust* = *preventing or counteracting rust.* **5** preventing, curing, or alleviating ——: *antiscorbutic* = *preventing, curing, or alleviating scurvy.* Also, **ant-** before vowels and h. [< Gk. *anti-* < *anti,* prep.]
☛ *Usage.* **Anti-,** in this dictionary, is hyphenated only before root words beginning with a vowel and before proper nouns and proper adjectives: *anti-intellectual, anti-Confederation, anti-American.*
☛ *Pronun.* The pronunciation given here (an′tē) is still the standard pronunciation in Canada. However, the variant pronunciation (an′tī), which is more typical of usage in the United States, is now making headway in Canada, especially in certain words, such as **antisocial** (an′tī sō′shəl). The same trend can be seen in certain words beginning with **semi-** and **multi-.**
☛ *Hom.* ante- (an′tē).

an·ti-air·craft (an′tē er′kraft′) *adj.* used in defence against enemy aircraft. *Abbrev.:* AA or A.A.

an·ti-at·om (an′tē at′əm) *n.* an atom of antimatter.

an·ti·bac·te·ri·al (an′tē bak tēr′ē əl) *adj.* counteracting or destroying viruses.

an·ti·bal·lis·tic missile (an′tē bə lis′tik) a ballistic missile designed to intercept and destroy other ballistic missiles in flight.

an·ti·bi·ot·ic (an′tē bī ot′ik) *n.* a product of an organism that destroys or weakens harmful micro-organisms. Penicillin is an antibiotic.

an·ti·bod·y (an′tē bod′ē) *n., pl.* **-bod·ies.** any of various proteins produced in the blood of animals or man in reaction to foreign substances called antigens, to provide immunity to diseases. Different antibodies are produced in reaction to different antigens.

an·tic (an′tik) *n.* **1** Often, **antics,** *pl.* a grotesque gesture or action; a silly trick: *The clown amused us by his antics.* **2** *Archaic.* a clown. [< Ital. *antico* old (with sense of *grottesco* grotesque) < *antiquus* ancient]

An·ti·christ (an′tē krīst) *n.* **1** the great enemy or opponent of Christ, expected by the early Christians to set himself against Christ just before the Second Coming of Christ (I John 2:18). **2** one who denies or opposes Christ. **3** one who sets himself up as Christ.

an·tic·i·pate (an tis′ə pāt′) *v.* **-pat·ed, -pat·ing.** **1** look forward to; expect: *He had anticipated a good vacation in the mountains; but when the time came, he was sick.* **2** do, make, or use in advance: *The Chinese anticipated some modern discoveries.* **3** take care of ahead of time: *The nurse anticipated all the patient's wishes.* **4** be before (another) in thinking, acting, etc. **5** consider or mention before the proper time. **6** cause to happen sooner; hasten. [< L *anticipare* < *ante-* before + *capere* take]

an·tic·i·pa·tion (an tis′ə pā′shən) *n.* **1** the act of looking forward; expectation: *The settler cut more wood than usual, in anticipation of a long winter.* **2** enjoyment in looking forward to something: *They were waiting for the holidays with great anticipation.* **3** action beforehand that provides for, takes into account, or prevents a later action or occurrence. **4** recognition, realization, or accomplishment beforehand.

an·tic·i·pa·tive (an tis′ə pā′tiv) *adj.* involving anticipation; having a tendency to anticipate.

an·tic·i·pa·to·ry (an tis′ə pə tô′rē) *adj.* anticipating.

an·ti·cler·i·cal (an′tē kler′ə kəl) *adj.* opposed to the influence of the church and clergy, especially in public affairs.

an·ti·cler·i·cal·ism (an′tē kler′ə kəl iz′əm) *n.* opposition to the influence of the church and clergy, especially in public affairs.

an·ti·cler·i·cal·ist (an′tē kler′ə kə list) *n.* a person who is opposed to the influence of the church or the clergy, especially in public affairs.

an·ti·cli·mac·tic (an′tē klī mak′tik) *adj.* of or like an anticlimax.

an·ti·cli·max (an′tē klī′maks) *n.* **1** an abrupt descent from the important to the trivial. *Example:* "Alas! Alas! what shall I do? I've lost my wife and best hat, too!" **2** a descent (in importance, interest, etc.) contrasting with a previous rise.

an·ti·cli·nal (an′tē klī′nəl) *adj.* of or like an anticline.

an·ti·cline (an′tē klīn′) *n. Geology.* an arch of stratified rock, in which the layers slope downward in opposite directions from the centre. Compare **syncline.** [< *anti-* + Gk. *klinein* lean; modelled on *incline*]

an·ti·co·ag·u·lant (an′tē kō ag′yə lənt) *n., adj.* —*n.* a substance or agent that prevents or slows up the clotting of blood, used in the treatment of certain heart diseases, etc. —*adj.* preventing or delaying coagulation.

an·ti·co·lo·ni·al·ism (an′tē kə lō′nē əl iz′əm) *n.* opposition to the system of one country ruling another as a colony.

an·ti·com·mun·ist or **an·ti-Com·mun·ist** (an′tē kom′yə nist) *n., adj.* —*n.* a person who is opposed to the principles and practices of communism. —*adj.* opposed to communism.

an·ti·con·vul·sant (an′tē kən vul′sənt) *n., adj.* —*n.* a substance or agent that prevents, or alleviates the effects of, convulsions. —*adj.* preventing, or alleviating the effects of, convulsions.

an·ti·cy·clone (an′tē sī′klōn) *n.* **1** an area in which winds rotate around and away from a centre of high pressure, which also moves. **2** an atmospheric disturbance at the fringes of such an area.

an·ti·cy·clon·ic (an′tē sī klon′ik) *adj.* of or having to do with an anticyclone.

an·ti·do·tal (an′tē dō′təl) *adj.* like an antidote; serving as an antidote.

an·ti·dote (an′tə dōt′ *or* an′tē dōt′) *n.* **1** a medicine or remedy that counteracts a poison: *Milk is an antidote for some poisons.* **2** anything that counteracts or relieves: *The plants and paintings served as an antidote to the impersonal atmosphere of the waiting room.* [< L < Gk. *antidoton* (thing) given against < *anti-* against + *didonai* give]

an·ti·freeze (an′tē frēz′) *n.* a substance added to a liquid to

lower its freezing point. Alcohol is much used as an antifreeze in automobile radiators.

an·ti·fric·tion (an′tē frik′shən) *n.* a substance that prevents or reduces friction.

an·ti·gen (an′tə jən) *n.* any substance that stimulates the production of antibodies or that reacts with antibodies that have already been formed. Bacteria, viruses, and other micro-organisms are sources of antigens. [< *anti*body + *gen* something that produces (< F < Gk. -*genēs* born, produced)]

An·tig·o·ne (an tig′ə nē′) *n. Greek mythology.* a daughter of Oedipus. She gave her dead brother a proper burial against the orders of her uncle; when he condemned her to be buried alive, she took her own life.

an·ti·he·ro (an′tē hē′rō) *n.* a person in a novel, play, etc. who, though the central character, has none of the qualities normally expected of a hero.

an·ti·he·ro·ic (an′tē hi rō′ik) *adj., n.* —*adj.* **1** opposed to the traditional or conventional idea of heroism; unlike a conventional hero. **2** opposed to the use of heroic couplets. —*n.* **1** an imitation, satire, burlesque, etc. composed to ridicule conventional or traditional heroism. **2** a mock-heroic poem, verse, etc. **3 antiheroics**, writings or actions that riducule the traditional or conventional idea of heroism.

an·ti·his·ta·mine (an′tē his′tə mēn′ *or* -his′tə min) *n.* a medicine used in the treatment of colds and allergies.

an·ti·knock (an′tē nok′) *n., adj.* —*n.* a substance added to the fuel of an internal-combustion engine to reduce noise caused by too rapid combustion. —*adj.* serving to reduce such noise.

an·ti·log·a·rithm (an′tē log′ə riтн′əm) *n.* a number corresponding to a given logarithm: *The antilogarithms of the logarithms* 1, 2, *and* 3 *are* 10, 100, *and* 1000.

an·ti·ma·cas·sar (an′tē mə kas′ər) *n.* a small covering to protect the back or arms of a chair, chesterfield, etc. [< *anti*-against + *macassar*, a hair oil from Macassar]

an·ti·mat·ter (an′tē mat′ər) *n.* a hypothetical form of matter composed of antiparticles.

an·ti·mis·sile (an′tē mis′īl *or* -mis′əl) *adj.* for use in defence against ballistic missiles, rockets, etc.

an·ti·mo·ny (an′tə mō′nē) *n.* a crystalline, metallic chemical element, having a bluish-white lustre that occurs chiefly in combination with other elements. It is used mainly in alloys to make them harder and in medicinal compounds. *Symbol:* Sb; *at.no.* 51; *at.wt.* 121.75 [< Med.L *antimonium*]

an·ti·neu·tron (an′tē nyü′tron *or* -nü′tron) *n.* the antiparticle of the neutron, having the same mass, etc. and an equal but opposite magnetic effect.

an·ti·nov·el (an′te nov′əl) *n.* a work of fiction that lacks most of the basic features of the traditional novel, such as character development or plot. [translation of F *anti-roman.* 20c.]

an·ti·nu·cle·ar (an′tē nyü′klē ər *or* -nü′klē ər) *adj.* opposing the use of nuclear energy, whether for military use or as a source of domestic power: *an antinuclear demonstration.*

an·ti·nu·cle·on (an′tē nyü′klē on′ *or* -nü′klē on′) *n.* an antiproton or antineutron.

an·ti–nuke (an′tē nyük′ *or* -nük′) *adj. Slang.* antinuclear. —**an′ti·nu′ker,** *n.*

an·ti·par·ti·cle (an′tē pär′tə kəl) *n.* an elementary particle having the same mass as a given particle but having an electric charge or magnetic effect, etc. of equal magnitude but opposite sign. If a particle collides with an antiparticle, both are annihilated. See **antineutron, antiproton, positron.**

an·ti·pas·to (an′tē pas′tō; *Italian,* än′tē päs′tō) *n., pl.* -**tos.** an Italian dish consisting of fish, meats, etc., served as an appetizer; hors d'oeuvres. [< Ital.]

an·tip·a·thet·ic (an tip′ə thet′ik *or* an′tē pə thet′ik) *adj.* having antipathy; contrary or opposed in nature or disposition: *Dogs and cats are antipathetic.*

an·tip·a·thet·i·cal (an tip′ə thet′ə kəl *or* an′tē pə thet′ə kəl) *adj.* antipathetic.

an·tip·a·thy (an tip′ə thē) *n., pl.* -**thies.** a strong or fixed dislike; a feeling against. [< L < Gk. *antipatheia* < *anti-* against + -*patheia* < *pathos* feeling]

an·ti·per·son·nel (an′tē pèr′sə nel′) *adj. Military.* directed against persons rather than against mechanized equipment, supplies, etc.

an·ti·phon (an′tə fon′) *n.* **1** a psalm, hymn, or prayer sung or chanted in alternate parts. **2** verses sung or chanted in response in a church service. [< LL < Gk. *antiphōna* sounding in response < *anti*- opposed to + *phōnē* sound. Doublet of ANTHEM.]

an·tiph·o·nal (an tif′ə nəl) *adj., n.* —*adj.* like an antiphon; sung or chanted alternately. —*n.* a book of antiphons.

hat, āge, fär; let, ēqual, tèrm; it, īce
hot, ōpen, ôrder; oil, out; cup, pùt, rüle,
əbove, takən, pencəl, lemən, circəs
ch, child; ng, long; sh, ship
th, thin; тн, then; zh, measure

an·tip·o·dal (an tip′ə dəl) *adj.* **1** on the opposite side of the earth. **2** directly opposite; exactly contrary.

an·ti·pode (an′tə pōd′) *n.* anything exactly opposite; direct opposite.

an·tip·o·de·an (an tip′ə dē′ən) *adj.* antipodal.

an·tip·o·des (an tip′ə dēz′) *n.pl.* **1** two places on directly opposite sides of the earth: *The North Pole and the South Pole are antipodes.* **2** a place on the opposite side of the earth. **3** two opposites or contraries: *Forgiveness and revenge are antipodes.* **4** the direct opposite. [< L < Gk. *antipodes*, pl. of *antipous* < *anti-* opposite to + *pous* foot]
☛ *Usage.* **Antipodes** is plural in form and plural or singular in use for defs. 2 and 4.

an·ti·pope (an′tē pōp′) *n.* a pope set up by a rival group in opposition to the true pope.

an·ti·pro·ton (an′tē prō′ton) *n.* the antiparticle of the proton, having the same mass, etc. as the proton and an equal but opposite electric charge.

an·ti·py·ret·ic (an′tē pī ret′ik) *adj., n.* —*adj.* checking or preventing fever. —*n.* any medicine or remedy for checking or preventing fever.

an·ti·quar·i·an (an′tə kwer′ē ən) *adj., n.* —*adj.* having to do with antiques or antiquaries: *The antiquarian section of the museum was full of old furniture and pottery.* —*n.* an antiquary. —**an′ti·quar′i·an·ism,** *n.*

an·ti·quar·y (an′tə kwer′ē) *n., pl.* -**quar·ies.** a student or collector of relics from ancient times. [< L *antiquarius*]

an·ti·quate (an′tə kwāt′) *v.* -**quat·ed,** -**quat·ing.** make old-fashioned; make out-of-date. [< L *antiquare* < *antiquus* ancient] —**an′ti·qua′tion,** *n.*

an·ti·quat·ed (an′tə kwāt′id) *adj.* **1** old-fashioned; out-of-date. **2** too old for work, service, etc.

an·tique (an tēk′) *adj., n., v.* —*adj.* **1** of a manufactured object, made in an earlier period, especially more than 100 years ago. **2** exhibiting or selling antique objects: *an antique auction.* **3** of, belonging to, or existing since times long ago; ancient. **4** in the style of former times: *antique manners. An antique gold finish is dull and slightly greenish.* **5** old-fashioned; out-of-date: *an antique hat.* —*n.* **1** a manufactured object made in an earlier period. To antique dealers an antique is more than 100 years old. Canada Customs defines an antique as being more than 50 years old. **2** any object or relic of ancient times. **3 the antique,** an antique style in art, especially that of ancient Greece or Rome: *the proportions of the antique.* **4** *Printing.* a style of type in which the lines are of equal thickness throughout. This sentence is in antique. —*v.* **1** make (furniture, etc.) look antique by finishing or refinishing in an antique style. **2** hunt for or collect antiques. [< L *antiquus* < *ante* before]

an·tiq·ui·ty (an tik′wə tē) *n., pl.* -**ties.** **1** oldness; great age. **2** times long ago; early ages of history. Antiquity usually refers to the period from 5000 B.C. to A.D. 476. **3** people of long ago. **4 antiquities,** *pl.* **a** things from times long ago. **b** the customs and life of olden times.

an·ti·ra·chit·ic (an′tē rə kit′ik) *adj.* preventing or curing rickets.

an·tir·rhi·num (an′tə rī′nəm) *n.* any of a large genus (*Antirrhinum*) of plants of the figwort family, such as the snapdragon.

an·ti·scor·bu·tic (an′tē skôr byü′tik) *adj., n.* —*adj.* preventing or curing scurvy. —*n.* a remedy for scurvy.

an·ti–Sem·ite (an′tē sem′īt) *n.* a person who is anti-Semitic.

an·ti–Se·mit·ic (an′tē sə mit′ik) *adj.* having or showing dislike or hatred for Jews; prejudiced against Jews.
☛ *Usage.* **Anti-Semitic.** This and the following word are based on a misunderstanding, since Jews form only one group of Semites. Other Semitic peoples include the Arabs, Syrians, etc.

an·ti–Sem·i·tism (an′tē sem′ə tiz′əm) *n.* a dislike or hatred for Jews; prejudice against Jews.
☛ *Usage.* See note at **anti-Semitic.**

an·ti·sep·sis (an′tə sep′sis) *n.* **1** the prevention of infection. **2** a method or medicine that prevents infection.

an·ti·sep·tic (an′tə sep′tik) *adj., n.* —*adj.* preventing infection. —*n.* a substance that prevents infection. Iodine, peroxide, mercurochrome, alcohol, and boric acid are antiseptics.

an·ti·sep·ti·cal·ly (an′tə sep′tik lē) *adv.* by the use of antiseptics.

an·ti·slav·er·y (an′tē slāv′ər ē *or* -slăv′rē) *adj.* opposed to slavery; against slavery.

an·ti·so·cial (an′tē sō′shəl) *adj.* 1 of, having to do with, or designating behavior that violates the generally accepted rules of social interaction, personal and property rights, etc.: *acting out one's antisocial feelings. Spreading disease, stealing, and murder are antisocial acts.* 2 unsociable: *He's rather antisocial and doesn't like parties.*

an·ti·spas·mod·ic (an′tē spaz mod′ik) *adj., n.* —*adj.* preventing or curing spasms. —*n.* a drug to prevent or cure spasms.

an·tis·tro·phe (an tis′trə fē) *n.* 1 a part of an ancient Greek ode sung by the chorus when moving from left to right. 2 a stanza following a strophe and usually in the same metre. [< LL < Gk. *antistrophē* a turning about < *anti-* against + *strephein* turn]

an·ti·tank (an′tē tangk′) *adj. Military.* designed for use against armored vehicles, especially tanks. *Abbrev.:* AT

an·tith·e·sis (an tith′ə sis) *n., pl.* **-ses** (-sēz′). 1 the direct opposite: *Hate is the antithesis of love.* 2 a contrast of ideas, expressed by parallel arrangements of words, clauses, etc. *Example:* "*To err is human; to forgive, divine.*" 3 opposition; contrast (*of* or *between*): *antithesis of theory and fact.* [< L < Gk. *antithesis* < *anti-* against + *tithenai* set]

an·ti·thet·ic (an′tə thet′ik) *adj.* 1 of or using antithesis. 2 contrasted; opposite.

an·ti·thet·i·cal (an′tə thet′ə kəl) *adj.* antithetic.

an·ti·tox·ic (an′tē tok′sik) *adj.* 1 counteracting diseases or poisonings caused by toxins. 2 having to do with or like an antitoxin.

an·ti·tox·in (an′tē tok′sin) *n.* 1 a substance formed in the body to counteract a disease or poison. 2 a serum containing antitoxin. Diphtheria antitoxin, obtained from the blood of horses infected with diphtheria, is injected into a person to make him immune to diphtheria, or to treat him if already infected.

an·ti·trades (an′tē trādz′) *n.* the winds that blow in the opposite direction to that of the trade winds, on a level above them in the tropic zone and at the earth's surface in the temperate zones.

an·ti·trust (an′tē trust′) *adj.* opposed to large corporations that control the trade practices of certain kinds of business.

an·ti·ven·in (an′tē ven′in) *n.* an antitoxin to counteract a particular venom, especially snake venom.

an·ti·vi·ral (an′tē vī′rəl) *adj.* counteracting or destroying viruses.

an·ti·vi·ta·min (an′tē vī′tə min) *n.* 1 any substance that prevents or inhibits the absorption of a vitamin. 2 an enzyme that destroys vitamins.

an·ti·viv·i·sec·tion (an′tē viv′ə sek′shən) *n.* opposition to the practice of cutting into or experimenting on living animals for scientific study.

an·ti·viv·i·sec·tion·ist (an′tē viv′ə sek′shən ist) *n.* a person opposed to the practice of vivisection.

ant·ler (ant′lər) *n.* 1 a branched horn of a deer or similar animal. 2 a branch of such a horn. [ME < OF *antoillier* < L *ante* before + *oculus* eye]

ant·lered (ant′lərd) *adj.* having antlers.

ant lion 1 any of several insects of the family Myrmeleontidae found in North America and Europe, resembling a dragonfly and having short antennae and four narrow wings usually marked with brown or black. The larva of the ant lion catches small insects for food by lying in wait in a pit it has dug and seizing any insect that falls or slides in. 2 the larva of the ant lion.

an·to·nym (an′tə nim′) *n.* a word that means the opposite of another word: *Right is the antonym of* wrong. *Abbrev.:* ant. [< Gk. *antonymia* < *anti-* opposite to + (dialectal) *onyma* word]

A number 1 *Informal.* A-one; first-class.

a·nus (ā′nəs) *n.* the opening at the lower end of the alimentary canal. [< L *anus*, originally, ring]

an·vil (an′vəl) *n.* 1 an iron or steel block on which metals are hammered and shaped. 2 the incus in the ear. [OE *anfilt*]

anvil chorus in opera, a stage device to create an atmosphere of tension and crisis by means of striking small steel bars, as in Verdi's *Il Trovatore.*

anx·i·e·ty (ang zī′ə tē) *n., pl.* **-ties.** 1 uneasy thoughts or fears about what may happen; a troubled, worried, or uneasy feeling: *We all felt anxiety when the airplane was caught in a hurricane.* 2 eager desire: *anxiety to succeed.* 3 *Psychiatry.* a state of abnormal fear or mental tension. [< L *anxietas* < *anxius* troubled. See ANXIOUS.]

anx·ious (angk′shəs *or* ang′shəs) *adj.* 1 uneasy because of thoughts or fears of what may happen; troubled; worried. 2 causing uneasy feelings or troubled thoughts. 3 eagerly desiring; wishing very much: *The boy was anxious for a new bicycle.* [< L *anxius* troubled < *angere* choke, cause distress] —**anx′ious·ly,** *adv.* —**anx′ious·ness,** *n.*

☛ *Syn.* 3. See note at eager.

☛ *Usage.* **Anxious.** The idiom is **anxious for** when eagerly desiring is meant: *He is anxious for news of her.* When worried is meant, the idioms are **anxious about,** referring to persons, and **anxious at,** referring to things: *Her mother was anxious about her. They became anxious at her delay.*

anxious seat *or* **bench** *U.S.* a seat near the pulpit at a revival meeting for those who are troubled about their religious life and want to strengthen their faith.

on the anxious seat, in an uneasy or troubled condition.

an·y (en′ē) *adj., pron., adv.* —*adj.* 1 one (no matter which) out of many: *Any book will do. You can come any day, but you really must come some day.* 2 some (*used in questions*): *Have you any fresh fruit?* 3 every: *any child knows that.* 4 no (*used with negatives and words like* **seldom** *and* **hardly**): *They seldom have any visitors. We don't have any fresh fruit.* 5 even one (*used with negatives and verbs like* **forbid** *or* **prohibit**): *He was forbidden to go to any movie.* —*pron.* 1 some (*used in questions*): *I need more paper, do you have any?* 2 none (*used with negatives and words such as* **seldom** *and* **hardly**): *I asked him for some paper, but he didn't have any.* —*adv.* 1 to some extent or degree; at all (*used in questions and with negatives*): *Has the sick child improved any?* 2 even a little (*used with negatives and in sentences expressing fear, a threat, etc.*): *If she leans over any farther, she'll fall.* [OE ǽnig]

an·y·bod·y (en′ē bud′ē *or* -bod′ē) *pron. or n., pl.* **-bod·ies.** 1 any person; anyone: *Has anybody been here?* 2 an important person: *Is he anybody?*

an·y·how (en′ē hou′) *adv.* 1 in any way whatever: *The answer is wrong anyhow you look at it.* 2 in any case; at least: *I can see as well as you, anyhow.* 3 carelessly; in ways that are not right and proper: *He does his work anyhow.*

any more *or* **anymore** (en′ē môr′) *adv.* these days or any longer (*used with negatives and in questions with a negative connotation*): *That book is not available any more. Who ever walks to work any more?*

☛ *Usage.* **Any more** is used only in negative constructions in most of Canada. In certain regions, however, it is also quite commonly used informally in positive constructions with the meaning "these days": *That's the trouble with the world any more.*

an·y·one (en′ē wun′ *or* en′ē wən) *pron.* any person; anybody.

an·y·place (en′ē plās′) *adv. Informal.* anywhere.

an·y·thing (en′ē thing′) *pron., n., adv.* —*pron.* any thing. —*n.* a thing of any kind whatever. —*adv.* at all.

an·y·time (en′ē tīm′) *adv.* at any time: *Feel free to drop in anytime.*

an·y·way (en′ē wā′) *adv.* 1 in any way whatever. 2 in any case; at least: *I am coming anyway, no matter what you say.* 3 carelessly; in ways not right and proper.

☛ *Usage.* The form *anyways* is usually regarded as non-standard and should be avoided.

an·y·where (en′ē wer′ *or* -hwer′) *adv.* in, at, or to any place.

an·y·wise (en′ē wīz′) *adv.* in any way; to any degree; at all.

An·zac (an′zak) *n.* 1 a soldier in the Australian and New Zealand Army Corps of World War I. 2 any Australian or New Zealand soldier. [an acronym for Austral¹ia and New Zealand Army Corps]

A-O.K. *or* **A-OK** (ā′ō kā′) *adj. or adv. Informal.* perfectly O.K.; working, functioning, etc. very well: *Everthing is A-O.K. now.* Also, A-okay.

A-one (ā′wun′) *adj. Informal.* first-rate; first-class; excellent. Also, A 1.

a·o·rist (ā′ə rist) *n.* 1 one of the past tenses of Greek verbs, showing that an action took place at some time in the past without indicating whether the act was completed, repeated, or continued. 2 a tense having a similar form or purpose in other languages. 3 a verb form in the aorist. [< Gk. *aoristos* < *a-* not + *horos* boundary]

a·or·ta (ā ôr′tə) *n., pl.* **-tas** *or* **-tae** (-tē *or* -tī). the main artery that carries the blood from the left side of the heart and, with its branches, distributes it to all parts of the body except the lungs. See **heart** for picture. [< NL or Med.L < Gk. *aortē* that which is hung]

a·or·tic (ā ôr′tik) *adj.* having to do with the aorta.

a·ou·dad (ä′ù dad′) *n.* a large wild sheep (*Ammotragus lervia*) of N Africa having characteristics of both sheep and goats; Barbary sheep. [< F < Berber *audad*]

ap-¹ the form of **ad-** before *p*, as in *apprehend.*

ap-² the form of **apo-** before vowels and *h*, as in *aphelion.*

Ap. April.

AP Associated Press.

a·pace (ə pās′) *adv.* swiftly; quickly; fast.

A·pach·e (ə pach′ē) *n., pl.* **Apache** or **Apaches**; *adj.* —*n.* **1** a member of a group of Amerindian peoples of the SW United States. **2** any of the Athapascan languages spoken by these peoples. —*adj.* of or having to do with the Apache or their languages. [apparently < Am.Sp. *ápachu* enemy]

a·pache (ə päsh′ *or* ə pash′) *n.* one of a band of gangsters of Paris, Brussels, etc. [F; special use of *Apache*]

ap·a·nage (ap′ə nij) See **appanage**.

a·part (ə pärt′) *adv.* **1** to pieces; in pieces; in separate parts: *Take the watch apart.* **2** away from each other: *Keep the dogs apart.* **3** to one side; aside: *He stood apart from the others.* **4** away from others; independently: *View each idea apart.* [ME < OF *à part* aside]

a·part·heid (ə pärt′hāt *or* ə pärt′hīt) *n.* in South Africa, the policy of economic and political segregation of the native people as a principle of society upheld by law; racial segregation. [< Afrikaans]

a·part·ment (ə pärt′mənt) *n.* a room or rooms to live in. [< F < Ital. *appartamento*, ult. < *a parte* apart]

apartment block a building containing a number of apartments.

apartment house apartment block.

ap·a·thet·ic (ap′ə thet′ik) *adj.* **1** with little interest in or desire for action; indifferent. **2** lacking in feeling. —**ap′a·thet′i·cal·ly,** *adv.*

ap·a·thy (ap′ə thē) *n., pl.* **-thies. 1** a lack of interest in or desire for activity; indifference: *The miser heard the old beggar's story with apathy.* **2** a lack of feeling. [< L < Gk. *apatheia* < *a-* without + *pathos* feeling]
☛ **Syn. 1.** See note at **indifference.**

ap·a·tite (ap′ə tīt′) *n.* a mineral consisting mainly of calcium phosphate, that occurs in the form of crystals or granular masses and is the main constituent of bones and teeth. *Formula:* $Ca_5(F,Cl,OH,\frac{1}{2}CO_3)(PO_4)_3$ [< Gk. *apatē* deceit + E *-ite,* so called because its various forms were often wrongly identified]
☛ *Hom.* **appetite.**

ape (āp) *n., v.* **aped, ap·ing.** —*n.* **1** any of the family of tail-less primates that most resemble man, having hairless hands, feet, and faces, long front limbs and short hind limbs, and showing a tendency to stand almost erect. Chimpanzees, gibbons, gorillas, and orangutans are apes. **2** any primate other than man. **3** a large, clumsy or boorish person. **4** a mimic.
go ape, *Slang.* become crazy or wildly enthusiastic: *to go ape over a new style of music. He went ape for a while, but has settled down now.*
—*v.* imitate; mimic. [OE *apa*] —**ape′like′,** *adj.*

APEC or **A.P.E.C.** Atlantic Provinces Economic Council.

a·pep·si·a (ə pep′sē ə) *n.* faulty digestion; dyspepsia. [< NL < Gk. *apepsia* < *a-* not + *peptein* to digest]

a·pe·ri·ent (ə pēr′ē ənt) *adj. or n.* laxative. [< L *aperiens, -entis,* ppr. of *aperire* open]

a·pe·ri·od·ic (ā′pēr ē od′ik) *adj.* **1** not periodic; irregular. **2** *Physics.* having irregular vibrations.

a·per·i·tif (ə per′ə tēf′; *French,* ä pä rē tēf′) *n.* an alcoholic drink taken before a meal to stimulate the appetite. [< F *apéritif*]

ap·er·ture (ap′ər chər *or* ap′ər chür′) *n.* **1** an opening; gap; hole. **2** in a camera, telescope, etc.: **a** the opening through which light passes. **b** the diameter of such an opening. [< L *aperture < aperire* open. Doublet of OVERTURE.]

a·pet·al·ous (ā pet′əl əs) *adj.* having no petals.

a·pex (ā′peks) *n., pl.* **a·pex·es** *or* **ap·i·ces. 1** the highest point; peak; tip: *the apex of a triangle.* **2** climax. [< L]

a·pha·sia (ə fā′zhə *or* ə fā′zē ə) *n.* a total or partial loss of the ability to use or understand words, usually caused by injury or disease that affects the brain. [< NL < Gk. *aphasia < a-* not + *phanai* speak]

a·pha·si·ac (ə fā′zē ak′) *adj.* aphasic.

a·pha·sic (ə fā′zik) *adj., n.* —*adj.* of, having to do with, or characterized by aphasia. —*n.* a person affected with aphasia.

a·phe·li·on (ə fē′lē ən) *n., pl.* **-lions** *or* **-li·a** (-lē ə) the point in the orbit of a planet or other heavenly body where it is farthest from the sun. Compare **perihelion.** [< NL *aphelium* < Gk. *apo-* away from + *hēlios* sun]

a·phid (ā′fid *or* af′id) *n.* any of a family (*Aphidae*) of tiny insects having a soft, pear-shaped body and a tube-shaped mouth adapted for piercing the stems, leaves, etc. of plants and sucking the juices. [< NL *aphis, aphidis*]

a·phis (ā′fis *or* af′is) *n., pl.* **aph·i·des** (ā′fə dēz′ *or* af′ə dēz′) **1** any of a genus (*Aphis*) of aphids. **2** any aphid.

aph·o·rism (af′ə riz′m) *n.* **1** a terse sentence expressing a general thought; maxim; proverb. *Example: "A living dog is better than a dead lion."* **2** a concise statement of a principle. [< LL <

Gk. *aphorismos* definition < *apo-* off + *horos* boundary]
☛ *Usage.* See note at **epigram.**

aph·o·rist (af′ər ist) *n.* a person who composes or uses aphorisms.

aph·o·ris·tic (af′ə ris′tik) *adj.* of, containing, or like an aphorism or aphorisms.

aph·o·rize (af′ər īz′) *v.* **-rized, -riz·ing.** compose aphorisms; write or speak in aphorisms.

aph·ro·dis·i·ac (af′rō diz′ē ak′) *adj., n.* —*adj.* arousing or increasing sexual desire. —*n.* any drug, food, etc. that arouses or increases sexual desire. [< Gk. *aphrodisiakos < aphrodisios* < Aphrodite, the goddess of love]

Aph·ro·di·te (af′rə dī′tē) *n. Greek mythology.* the goddess of love and beauty, corresponding to the Roman goddess Venus.

a·pi·an (ā′pē ən) *adj.* of or having to do with bees.

a·pi·a·rist (ā′pē ə rist) *n.* a person who keeps bees.

a·pi·a·ry (ā′pē er′ē) *n., pl.* **-ar·ies.** a place where bees are kept; group of beehives. [< L *apiarium < apis* bee]

a·pi·cal (ā′pə kəl *or* ap′ə kəl) *adj.* of the apex; at the apex; forming the apex.

ap·i·ces (ā′pə sēz′ *or* ap′ə sēz′) *n.* a pl. of **apex.**

a·pic·u·late (ə pik′yə lāt′) *adj.* of leaves, ending abruptly, in a short, distinct point. [< NL *apiculatus < apiculus* tip, dim. of L *apex, apicis* apex]

a·pi·cul·ture (ā′pə kul′chər) *n.* the raising and care of bees; beekeeping. [< L *apis* bee + E *culture*]

a·piece (ə pēs′) *adv.* for each one; each: *These apples are five cents apiece.*

à pied (ä pyä′) *French.* on foot.

A·pis (ā′pis) *n.* the sacred bull worshipped by the ancient Egyptians.

ap·ish (āp′ish) *adj.* **1** like an ape. **2** senselessly imitative. **3** rough; clumsy. **4** foolish; silly. —**ap′ish·ly,** *adv.*

A–plane (ā′plān′) *n.* an aircraft driven by atomic energy.

a·plen·ty (ə plen′tē) *adv. Informal.* in plenty.

a·plomb (ə plom′) *n.* complete self-confidence and assurance; poise. [< F *aplomb < à plomb* according to the plummet]

apo– *prefix.* from; away; quite, as in *apostasy.* Also, **ap-,** before vowels and *h.* [< Gk.]

Apoc. **1** Apocalypse. **2** Apocrypha. **3** Apocryphal.

a·poc·a·lypse (ə pok′ə lips′) *n.* **1** a revelation. **2 the Apocalypse,** the last book of the New Testament; book of Revelation. *Abbrev.:* Apoc. [< L *apocalypsis* < Gk. *apokalypsis < apo-* off, un- + *kalyptein* cover]

a·poc·a·lyp·tic (ə pok′ə lip′tik) *adj.* **1** of the Apocalypse. **2** like a revelation; giving a revelation.

a·poc·a·lyp·ti·cal (ə pok′ə lip′tə kəl) *adj.* apocalyptic.

a·poc·o·pe (ə pok′ə pē) *n.* the dropping out of the last sound, syllable, or letter in a word. *Th'* for *the* and *i'* for *in* are examples of apocope. [< L < Gk. *apokopē < apo-* off + *koptein* cut]

A·poc·ry·pha (ə pok′rə fə) *n.pl.* **1** fourteen books found in a Greek Bible of the 3rd century B.C. Eleven of them are included in the Roman Catholic Bible though none are included in the Jewish or, usually, the Protestant Bibles. **2 apocrypha,** any writings or statements of doubtful authorship or authority. [ME < LL *apocrypa,* neut. pl. of *apocryphus* < Gk. *apokryphos* hidden < *apo-* from + *kryptein* hide]

a·poc·ry·phal (ə pok′rə fəl) *adj.* **1** of doubtful authorship or authority. **2** false; counterfeit. **3 Apocryphal,** of the Apocrypha. *Abbrev.:* Apoc.

ap·o·cyn·thi·on (ap′ə sin′thē ən) *n.* the point in the lunar orbit of an earth-launched spacecraft where it is farthest from the moon. Compare **pericynthion, apolune.** [< *apo-* + *-cynthion* < Cynthia (goddess of) the moon]

ap·o·gee (ap′ə jē′) *n.* **1** the point in orbit of a satellite of the earth or an orbiting vehicle where it is farthest from the centre of the earth. Compare **perigee. 2** the farthest or highest point. [< F *apogée* < Gk. *apogaion < apo-* away from + *gē* or *gaia* earth]

à point (ä pwaN′) *French.* just right; just enough. A good chef cooks each dish *à point.*

a·po·lit·cal (ā′pə lit′ə kəl) *adj.* not concerned with politics or political issues: *an apolitical decision.*

A·pol·lo (ə pol′ō) *n., pl.* **-los.** 1 *Greek and Roman mythology.* the god of the sun, poetry, music, prophecy, and healing. The Greeks and Romans considered Apollo the highest type of youthful, manly beauty. He was the first Greek god accepted by the Romans. 2 any extremely handsome young man.

A·pol·li·on (ə pol′yən) *n.* the Devil (Rev. 9:11).

a·pol·o·get·ic (ə pol′ə jet′ik) *adj., n.* —*adj.* 1 making an apology; expressing regret or offering an excuse for a fault or failure: *an apologetic reply.* 2 suggesting uncertainty; unsure: *He answered the principal in an apologetic voice.* 3 defending by speech or writing.
—*n.* 1 a systematic defence of a doctrine, etc. 2 **apologetics,** the branch of theology that deals with the rational defence of a religious faith (*used with a singular verb*). —**a·pol′o·get′i·cal·ly,** *adv.*

ap·o·lo·gi·a (ap′ə lō′jē ə) *n.* a statement in defence or justification; apology. [< L < Gk.]

a·pol·o·gist (ə pol′ə jist) *n.* a person who defends an idea, belief, religion, etc. in speech or writing.

a·pol·o·gize (ə pol′ə jīz′) *v.* **-gized, -giz·ing.** 1 make an apology; express regret; acknowledge a fault; offer an excuse. 2 make a defence in speech or writing. —**a·pol′o·giz′er,** *n.*

ap·o·logue (ap′ə log′) *n.* a fable with a moral: *Aesop's fables are apologues.* [< F < L < Gk. *apologos* story, tale]

a·pol·o·gy (ə pol′ə jē) *n., pl.* **-gies.** 1 words of regret for an offence or accident; acknowledgment of a fault or failure; expressing regret and asking pardon: *to make an apology.* 2 a systematic defence of a doctrine, etc.; an explanation of the truth or justice of something: *He presented an effective apology for his course of action.* 3 a poor substitute: *It wasn't a dinner at all, but only an apology for one.* [< LL < Gk. *apologia* a speech in defence, ult. < *apo-* off + *legein* speak]
☛ *Syn.* 1. See note at **excuse.**

ap·o·lune (ap′ə lün′) *n.* the point in the lunar orbit of a moon-launched spacecraft where it is farthest from the moon. Compare **perilune, apocynthion.** [< *apo-* + *-lune* < L *luna* moon]

ap·o·phthegm (ap′ə them′) See **apothegm.**

ap·o·plec·tic (ap′ə plek′tik) *adj.* 1 of, having to do with, or causing apoplexy. 2 suffering from or showing symptoms of apoplexy. 3 of an emotional reaction, likely to bring on apoplexy; extreme: *an apoplectic rage.* —**ap′o·plec′ti·cal·ly,** *adv.*

ap·o·plex·y (ap′ə plek′sē) *n.* cerebrovascular accident; stroke. [< LL < Gk. *apoplēxia* < *apo-* off, from + *plēssein* strike]

a·port (ə pôrt′) *adv.* to the port side; to the left.

a·pos·ta·sy (ə pos′tə sē) *n., pl.* **-sies.** a complete forsaking of one's religion, faith, political party, or principles. [ME < LL < Gk. *apostasia* < *apo-* away from + *stenai* stand]

a·pos·tate (ə pos′tāt′ *or* ə pos′tit) *n., adj.* —*n.* a person who completely forsakes his religion, faith, political party, or principles. —*adj.* guilty of apostasy.

a·pos·ta·tize (ə pos′tə tīz′) *v.* **-tized, -tiz·ing.** forsake completely one's religion, faith, party, or principles.

a pos·te·ri·o·ri (ā′ pos tēr′ē ō′rī *or* ä′ pos tēr′ē ô′rē) from effect to cause; from particular cases to a general rule; based on actual observation or experience. [< Med.L *a posteriori* from what comes after]

a·pos·tle (ə pos′əl) *n.* 1 **Apostle,** one of the twelve disciples, **the Apostles,** chosen by Christ to go forth and preach the gospel to all the world. 2 any early Christian leader or missionary: *Paul was frequently called the "Apostle to the Gentiles."* 3 the first Christian missionary to any country or region. 4 a leader of any reform movement or belief. 5 in the Mormon Church, one of the council of twelve administrative officials. [OE < LL < Gk. *apostolos* messenger < *apo-* off + *stellein* send]

Apostles′ Creed the statement of belief that contains the fundamental doctrines of Christianity, beginning "I believe in God, the Father..." In its present form it dates back to about A.D. 600 and was formerly supposed to have been composed by the Apostles.

ap·os·tol·ic (ap′əs tol′ik) *adj.* 1 of the Apostles; having to do with the Apostles. 2 according to the beliefs and teachings of the Apostles. 3 of or having to do with the Pope; papal.

ap·os·tol·i·cal (ap′əs tol′ə kəl) *adj.* apostolic.

Apostolic Fathers 1 a group of early Christian authors who

lived very soon after the Apostles. 2 the writings attributed to these authors, written probably between A.D. 95 and 150.

Apostolic See the bishopric of the Pope.

apostolic succession especially in Roman Catholic, Greek Orthodox, and Anglican churches, the unbroken line of succession from the Apostles down to the present-day bishops and priests, by which it is held that religious authority has been transmitted.

a·pos·tro·phe¹ (ə pos′trə fē) *n.* a sign (′) used: **a** to show the omission of one or more letters in contractions, as in *o'er* for *over, thro'* for *through.* **b** to show the possessive forms of nouns or indefinite pronouns, as in *John's book, the lions' den, everybody's business.* **c** to form certain plurals, as in *2 o's, four 9's in 9999.* **d** to show that certain sounds represented in the usual spelling have not been spoken: *'lectric.* [< F < LL < Gk. *apostrophos* a turning away, omission (mark) < *apostrephein* avert, get rid of. See APOSTROPHE².]

a·pos·tro·phe² (ə pos′trə fē) *n.* the addressing of words to an absent person as if he were present or to a thing or idea as if it could understand and appreciate the words. *Example:* "*Western wind, when wilt thou blow".* [< LL < Gk. *apostrophē* < *apostrephein* < *apo-* away from + *strephein* turn]

a·pos·tro·phize (ə pos′trə fīz′) *v.* **-phized, -phiz·ing.** in a speech, poem, etc., address some thing or absent person, usually with emotion: *The poet apostrophizes judgment in these words:* "*Oh, judgment! thou art fled to brutish beasts.*"

apothecaries′ measure a system of units for measuring volume, traditionally used by pharmacists. One fluid ounce in apothecaries' measure is equal to about 28.4 cubic centimetres.

apothecaries′ weight a system of units for measuring mass, traditionally used by pharmacists. One ounce in apothecaries' weight is equal to about 31.1 grams.

a·poth·e·car·y (ə poth′ə ker′ē) *n., pl.* **-car·ies.** *Archaic.* pharmacist; druggist. [ME < LL *apothecarius* warehouseman < L *apotheca* storehouse < Gk. *apothēkē* < *apo-* away + *tithenai* put]

ap·o·thegm (ap′ə them′) *n.* a short, forceful saying; maxim. *Example:* "*Beauty is only skin-deep.*" Also, **apophthegm.** [< Gk. *apophthegma* < *apo-* forth + *phthengesthai* utter]

a·poth·e·o·sis (ə poth′ē ō′sis *or* ap′ə thē′ə sis) *n., pl.* **-ses** (-sēz). 1 the raising of a human being to the rank of a god; deification: *The apotheosis of the emperor became a Roman custom.* 2 glorification; exaltation. 3 a glorified ideal. [< L < Gk. *apotheosis,* ult. < *apo-* + *theos* god]

a·poth·e·o·size (ə poth′ē ə sīz′ *or* ap′ə thē′ə sīz′) *v.* **-sized, -siz·ing.** 1 raise to the rank of a god; deify. 2 glorify; exalt.

app. 1 apparent; apparently. 2 appendix; appended. 3 apprentice.

ap·pal *or* **ap·pall** (ə pol′ *or* ə pôl′) *v.* **-palled, -pall·ing.** fill with horror; dismay; terrify: *We were appalled at the thought of another war. She was appalled when she saw the river had risen to the doorstep.* [ME < OF *apallir* become or make pale < *a-* to (< L *ad-*) + *pale* < L *pallidus.* Related to PALE¹.]

ap·pall (ə pol′ *or* ə pôl′) See **appal.**

ap·pall·ing (ə pol′ing *or* ə pôl′ing) *adj.* dismaying; terrifying; horrifying. —**ap·pall′ing·ly,** *adv.*

ap·pa·loo·sa (ap′ə lü′sə) *n.* a breed of horse having mottled skin, spots or blotches of color on the rump, and a skimpy tail. [< *a Palouse* horse, named after the Palouse River country in Washington, where the breed is said to have been developed by the Nez Percé Indians]

ap·pa·nage (ap′ə nij) *n.* 1 land, property, or money set aside to support the younger children of kings, princes, etc. 2 a person's assigned portion; rightful property. 3 something that accompanies; an adjunct: *The millionaire had three houses, a yacht, and all the other appanages of wealth.* 4 a territory controlled by another country. Also, **apanage.** [< F *apanage* < *apaner* give bread to, ult. < L *ad-* to + *panis* bread]

ap·pa·ra·tus (ap′ə rā′təs *or* ap′ə rat′əs) *n., pl.* **-tus** *or* **-tus·es.** the things necessary to carry out a purpose or for a particular use: *apparatus for an experiment in chemistry, gardening apparatus, our digestive apparatus.* [< L *apparatus* preparation < *ad-* + *parare* make ready]

ap·par·el (ə par′əl *or* ə per′əl) *n., v.* **-elled** *or* **-eled, -el·ling** *or* **-el·ing.** —*n.* clothing; dress. —*v.* clothe; dress up. [ME < OF *apareil* < *apareiller* clothe, ult. < L *ad-* + *par* equal]
☛ *Syn.* See note at **dress.**

ap·par·ent (ə par′ənt *or* ə per′ənt) *adj.* 1 plain to see; so plain as not to be missed: *The flaw in the fabric was quite apparent.* 2 easily understood; obvious to the mind: *It was apparent that she was lying.* 3 according to appearances; seeming: *An apparent truth was really a lie.* [ME < OF *aparant,* ppr. of *apareir* < L *apparere.* See APPEAR.]
☛ *Syn.* 1. See note at **obvious.**

ap·par·ent·ly (ə par′ənt lē *or* ə per′ənt lē) *adv.* **1** seemingly; as far as one can judge by appearances: *Apparently the baby had chicken pox.* **2** clearly; plainly; obviously: *He had quite apparently hurt his leg.*

ap·pa·ri·tion (ap′ə rish′ən) *n.* **1** a ghost; phantom. **2** something strange, remarkable, or unexpected that comes into view. **3** the act of appearing; appearance. [< LL *apparitio, -onis* < L *apparere.* See APPEAR.]
☛ *Syn.* **1.** See note at **ghost.**

ap·peal (ə pēl′) *v., n.* —*v.* **1** make an earnest request (*to* or *for*); apply for help, sympathy, etc.: *The children appealed to their mother to know what to do on a rainy day.* **2** *Law.* **a** ask that a case be taken to a higher court to be reviewed or heard again. **b** apply for a retrial of (a case) before a higher court. **3** call on some person to decide some matter in one's favor. **4** be attractive, interesting, or enjoyable: *Blue and red appeal to me, but I don't like grey or yellow.*
—*n.* **1** an earnest request; call for help, sympathy, etc. **2** *Law.* **a** a request to have a case heard again before a higher court or judge. **b** the right to have a case heard again. **3** a call on some person for proof, decision, etc. **4** an attraction, interest. [ME < OF < L *appellare* accost, alteration of *appellere* < *ad-* up to + *pellere* drive] —**ap·peal′ing·ly,** *adv.*

ap·pear (ə pēr′) *v.* **1** be seen; come in sight: *One by one the stars appear.* **2** seem; look: *The apple appeared sound on the outside, but it was rotten inside.* **3** be published or otherwise presented to the public: *The book appeared in the autumn. The movie will appear soon.* **4** present oneself publicly or formally: *to appear on the stage.* **5** become known to the mind: *It appears that we must go.* **6** stand before an authority: *to appear in court.* [ME < OF *apareir* < L *apparere* < *ad-* + *parere* come in sight]
☛ *Syn.* **2.** See note at **seem.**

ap·pear·ance (ə pēr′əns) *n.* **1** the act of appearing: *John's appearance in the doorway, a singer's first appearance in a city.* **2** outward look; aspect: *The appearance of the house made us think that it was empty.* **3 appearances,** *pl.* outward show, especially when thought of in contrast to some underlying fault or misfortune: *After he lost his job, he found it hard to keep up appearances.* **4** a thing that appears in sight; object seen. **5** *Law.* **a** in criminal law, the accused's physical attendance in court to answer the charge or charges against him. **b** in civil law, a document advising the court of the defendant's or respondent's intention to participate in the proceedings personally or through a lawyer. **6** apparition.
☛ *Syn.* **2. Appearance, aspect** (def. 2) = the look or looks of a person or thing. **Appearance** is the general word applying to what one sees when looking at someone or something: *The appearance of the city is pleasing.* **Aspect** applies to the appearance at certain times or under certain conditions: *I love the bay in all its aspects, even its stormy, frightening aspect in winter.*

ap·pease (ə pēz′) *v.* **-peased, -peas·ing. 1** satisfy (an appetite or desire): *A good dinner will appease your hunger.* **2** make calm; quiet: *to appease a crying child.* **3** give in to the demands of (especially those of a potential enemy): *Hitler was appeased at Munich.* [ME < OF *apaisier* < *a-* to (< L *ad-*) + *pais* peace < L *pax*] —**ap·peas′er,** *n.* —**ap·peas′ing·ly,** *adv.*
☛ *Syn.* **2. Appease, pacify** = make calm. **Appease** = calm or quiet a person who is excited or upset by pleasing and contenting him or her: *When he left school to go to work, he had to appease his father.* **Pacify** = quiet people or things that are quarrelling or fighting among themselves or against some condition, by making peace though not necessarily by eliminating the cause of the disturbance: *He pacified the angry mob.*

ap·pease·ment (ə pēz′mənt) *n.* an appeasing or being appeased; pacification; satisfaction.

ap·pel·lant (ə pel′ənt) *n., adj.* —*n.* a person who appeals. —*adj.* **1** having to do with appeals. **2** in the process of appealing.

ap·pel·late (ə pel′it) *adj.* having to do with appeals. [< L *appellatus,* pp. of *appellare.* See APPEAL.]

appellate court a court having the power to re-examine and reverse the decisions of a lower court.

ap·pel·la·tion (ap′ə lā′shən) *n.* **1** a name or title. In *John the Baptist,* John's appellation is *the Baptist.* **2** the act of calling by a name.

ap·pel·la·tive (ə pel′ə tiv) *n., adj.* —*n.* **1** a descriptive name. **2** a common noun; one that can be applied to any member of a class. —*adj.* that names; naming.

ap·pend (ə pend′) *v.* add to a larger thing; attach as a supplement: *The amendments to the association's constitution are appended to it.* [< L *appendere* < *ad-* on + *pendere* hang]

ap·pend·age (ə pen′dij) *n.* **1** something attached; addition; adjunct. **2** *Biology.* any of various external or subordinate parts. Arms, tails, fins, legs, etc. are appendages.

ap·pend·ant (ə pen′dənt) *adj., n.* —*adj.* added; attached. —*n.* appendage.

ap·pen·dec·to·my (ap′ən dek′tə mē) *n., pl.* **-mies.** the surgical removal of the vermiform appendix. [< *appendix* + *ectomy* (< Gk. *ek* out of + *-tomia* a cutting < *temnein* cut)]

ap·pen·di·ces (ə pen′də sēz′) *n.* a pl. of **appendix.**

ap·pen·di·ci·tis (ə pen′də sī′tis) *n.* an inflammation of the vermiform appendix, the small saclike growth on the large intestine. [< L *appendix, -icis* + E *-itis*]

ap·pen·dix (ə pen′diks) *n., pl.* **-dix·es** or **-di·ces. 1** an addition at the end of a book or document, containing supplementary material. **2** an outgrowth of an organ, etc. The small saclike growth attached to the large intestine is the **vermiform appendix.** See **alimentary canal** for picture. [< L *appendix* < *appendere.* See APPEND.]
☛ *Syn.* **1.** See note at **supplement.**
☛ *Usage.* The English plural **appendixes** is rapidly overtaking the Latin **appendices** and occurs more frequently except in quite formal usage.

ap·per·cep·tion (ap′ər sep′shən) *n.* **1** the assimilation of a new perception by means of a mass of ideas already in the mind. **2** a clear perception; full understanding. [< F *aperception* < NL. Related to PERCEPTION.]

ap·per·cep·tive (ap′ər sep′tiv) *adj.* of or having to do with apperception.

ap·per·tain (ap′ər tān′) *v.* belong as a part; pertain; relate: *The control of traffic appertains to the police. Forestry appertains to geography, to botany, and to agriculture.* [ME < OF *apartenir* < LL *appertinere* < L *ad-* to + *pertinere* pertain]

ap·pe·tite (ap′ə tīt′) *n.* **1** a desire for food. **2** a desire: *an appetite for amusement.* [ME < OF < L *appetitus* < *ad-* + *petere* seek]
☛ *Hom.* **apatite.**

ap·pe·tiz·er (ap′ə tīz′ər) *n.* food or drink served, especially before a meal, to stimulate the appetite.

ap·pe·tiz·ing (ap′ə tīz′ing) *adj.* arousing or exciting the appetite: *appetizing food.* —**ap′pe·tiz′ing·ly,** *adv.*

ap·plaud (ə plod′ *or* ə plôd′) *v.* **1** express approval by clapping hands, shouting, etc.: *The crowd applauded lustily.* **2** express approval of (a person, speech, performance, etc.) in this way: *We applauded the speaker.* **3** approve; praise. [< L *applaudere* < *ad-* to + *plaudere* clap]

ap·plause (ə ploz′ *or* ə plôz′) *n.* **1** approval expressed by clapping the hands, shouting, etc. **2** approval; praise. [< L *applausus,* pp. of *applaudere.* See APPLAUD.]

ap·ple (ap′əl) *n.* **1** the firm, fleshy, roundish fruit of a tree widely grown in temperate regions. Apples belong to the same family as the quince, pear, and hawthorn. **2** the tree. **3** any of various other fruits or fruitlike products, such as the oak apple and love apple.
apple of (someone's) **eye,** a person or thing that one cherishes: *She is the apple of her father's eye.* [OE *æppel*]

apple butter a smooth, jamlike spread made by boiling tart apples and apple cider together to produce a purée, and then cooking this with sugar and spices such as cinnamon and cloves.

apple cart a cart for carrying apples.
upset the apple cart, *Informal.* spoil or disrupt a plan or program: *The delegates hoped that no one would upset the apple cart before the agreement was signed.*

ap·ple·jack (ap′əl jak′) *n.* an intoxicating liquor made from apple cider.

apple of discord 1 *Greek mythology.* a golden apple inscribed "For the fairest" and claimed by Aphrodite, Athena, and Hera. Paris awarded it to Aphrodite. **2** any cause of jealousy and trouble.

apple–pie order perfect order or condition.

ap·ple-pol·ish (ap′əl pol′ish) *v. Informal.* **1** curry favor with; flatter. **2** use flattery. —**ap′ple-pol′ish·er,** *n.*

ap·ple·sauce (ap′əl sos′ *or* -sôs′) *n.* **1** apples cut in pieces and cooked with sugar and water until soft. **2** *Slang.* nonsense.

apple slump brown betty.

ap·ple·wood (ap′əl wud′) *n.* the wood of the apple tree, used for cabinetmaking, firewood, etc.

ap·pli·ance (ə plī′əns) *n.* **1** a tool, small machine, or some other device used in doing something: *Can openers, vacuum cleaners, washing machines, refrigerators, etc. are household appliances.* **2** an applying; the act of putting into use.

ap·pli·ca·bil·i·ty (ap′lə kə bil′ə tē) *n.* the quality of being applicable.

ap·pli·ca·ble (ap′lə kə bəl *or* ə plik′ə bəl) *adj.* capable of being

put to practical use; appropriate; suitable; fitting: *The rule "Look before you leap" is almost always applicable.*

ap·pli·cant (ap′lə kənt) *n.* a person who applies (for money, position, help, office, etc.).

ap·pli·ca·tion (ap′lə kā′shən) *n.* 1 the act of using; the use: *The application of what you know will help you solve new problems.* 2 the act of applying; a putting on: *the application of paint to a house.* 3 ways of using: *Freedom is a word of wide application.* 4 something applied: *This application is made of cold cream and ointment.* 5 a request (for employment, an award, tickets, etc.): *He made an application for the position of clerk.* 6 continued effort; close attention: *By application to his work he won promotion.* [ME < MF < L *applicatio, -onis* a joining to < *applicare*. See APPLY.]
☞ *Syn.* 6. See note at **effort.**

ap·pli·ca·tor (ap′lə kā′tər) *n.* any device for applying medicine, polish, paints, cosmetics, etc.

ap·plied (ə plīd′) *adj.* put to practical use; used to solve actual problems: *Engineers study applied mathematics.*

applied science science that uses facts, laws, and theories to solve practical problems such as building a bridge, designing a radio, testing intelligence, etc.

ap·pli·qué (ap′lə kā′) *n., v.* **-quéd, -qué·ing.** —*n.* 1 the art or process of sewing or gluing pieces of fabric in various shapes and colors to a larger piece of fabric for decoration: *Appliqué is often used to decorate clothing, table linens, etc.* 2 a cutout piece of fabric attached to a larger piece as a decoration: *a skirt with butterfly appliqués.* 3 (*adj.*) trimmed with such pieces of fabric: *an appliqué skirt.*
—*v.* 1 trim or ornament with appliqué: *to appliqué a skirt.* 2 put on as appliqué: *to appliqué flowers on a table cloth.* 3 make by using appliqué: *an appliquéd wall hanging.* [< F *appliqué* < *appliquer* apply]

ap·ply (ə plī′) *v.* **-plied, -ply·ing.** 1 put: *to apply paint to a house.* 2 put to practical use; put into effect: *He knows the rule but does not know how to apply it.* 3 be useful or suitable; fit: *When does this rule apply?* 4 use for a special purpose: *to apply a sum of money to charity.* 5 make a formal request: *to apply for a job.* 6 use (a word or words) appropriately with reference to a person or thing: *to apply a nickname. Don't apply that adjective to me.* 7 set to work and stick to it: *He applied himself to learning French.* [ME < OF *aplier* < L *applicare* < *ad-* on + *plicare* fold, lay]

ap·pog·gia·tu·ra (ə poj′ə tyŭr′ə *or* ə poj′ə tŭr′ə) *n. Music.* a grace note. [< Ital. *appoggiatura* < *appoggiare* lean, ult. < L *ad-* on + *podium* podium]

ap·point (ə point′) *v.* 1 name to an office or position; choose: *This man was appointed postmaster.* 2 decide on; set: *to appoint a time for the meeting.* 3 fix; prescribe. 4 furnish; equip: *a well-appointed office.* [ME < OF *apointer* < *a-* to (< L *ad-* to) + *punctum* point. Related to POINT.] —**ap·point′er,** *n.*

ap·point·ee (ə poin′tē′) *n.* a person appointed.

ap·poin·tive (ə poin′tiv) *adj.* filled by appointment: *Positions in the Senate are appointive.*

ap·point·ment (ə point′mənt) *n.* 1 the act of naming to an office or position; choosing: *The appointment of Ann as secretary pleased her friends.* 2 an office or position. 3 an engagement to be somewhere or to meet someone. 4 **appointments,** *pl.* furniture; equipment.

ap·por·tion (ə pôr′shən) *v.* divide and give out in fair shares; distribute according to some rule: *The father's property was apportioned among his children after his death.* [< obsolete F *apportionner,* ult. < L *ad-* to + *portio, -onis* portion]
☞ *Syn.* See note at **allot.**

ap·por·tion·ment (ə pôr′shən mənt) *n.* the act of dividing and giving out in fair shares.

ap·pose (a pōz′) *v.* **-posed, -pos·ing.** 1 put next; place side by side. In the phrase *Louis Riel, the Métis leader,* the word *leader* is apposed to *Riel.* 2 put (one thing to another); apply: *An official seal was apposed to the document.* [< F *apposer* < *a-* to (< L *ad-*) + *poser* put (see POSE¹)]

ap·po·site (ap′ə zit) *adj.* appropriate; suitable; apt. [< L *appositus,* pp. of *apponere* < *ad-* near + *ponere* place]
—**ap′po·site·ly,** *adv.* —**ap′po·site·ness,** *n.*

ap·po·si·tion (ap′ə zish′ən) *n.* 1 the act of putting side by side. 2 a position side by side. 3 *Grammar.* **a** a placing together in the same relation. **b** the relation of two parts of a sentence when the one is added as an explanation to the other. In *Mr. Brown, our neighbor, has a new car, Mr. Brown* and *neighbor* are in apposition.

ap·pos·i·tive (ə poz′ə tiv) *n., adj. Grammar.* —*n.* a noun added to another noun as an explanation; word, phrase, or clause in apposition. —*adj.* placed beside another noun as an explanation.

ap·prais·al (ə prāz′əl) *n.* 1 an estimate of the value, amount, etc. 2 an appraising; valuation.

ap·praise (ə prāz′) *v.* **-praised, -prais·ing.** 1 estimate the value, amount, quality, etc. of: *An employer should be able to appraise ability and character.* 2 set a price on; fix the value of: *Property is appraised for taxation.* [< *praise,* ? after *prize³, apprize¹*]
—**ap·prais′ing·ly,** *adv.*
☞ *Syn.* 1. See note at **estimate.**

ap·praise·ment (ə prāz′mənt) *n.* appraisal.

ap·prais·er (ə prāz′ər) *n.* 1 a person authorized to fix the value of property, imported goods, etc. 2 a person who appraises.

ap·pre·ci·a·ble (ə prē′shə ə bəl *or* ə prē′shə bəl) *adj.* enough to be felt or estimated: *The difference between the two prices is appreciable.* —**ap·pre′ci·a·bly,** *adv.*

ap·pre·ci·ate (ə prē′shē āt′) *v.* **-at·ed, -at·ing.** 1 think highly of; recognize the worth or quality of; value; enjoy: *Almost everybody appreciates good food.* 2 have an opinion of the value, worth, or quality of; estimate: *to appreciate knowledge.* 3 be sensitive to; be aware of: *A musician can appreciate small differences in sounds.* 4 estimate correctly. 5 Raise in value: *New buildings appreciate the value of land.* 6 rise in value: *This land will appreciate as soon as good roads are built.* [< L *appretiare* appraise < *ad-* + *pretium* price. Doublet of APPRIZE¹.]
☞ *Syn.* 1. See note at **value.**

ap·pre·ci·a·tion (ə prē′shē ā′shən) *n.* 1 valuing highly; sympathetic understanding: *She has no appreciation of art and music.* 2 an appreciating; valuing. 3 favorable criticism. 4 a rise in value.

ap·pre·ci·a·tive (ə prē′shē ə tiv, ə prē′shē ā′tiv *or* ə prē′shə tiv) *adj.* having appreciation; showing appreciation; recognizing the value: *appreciative of the smallest kindness.* —**ap·pre′ci·a′tive·ly,** *adv.*

ap·pre·hend (ap′ri hend′) *v.* 1 understand; grasp with the mind: *They were able to apprehend his meaning from his gestures.* 2 anticipate with fear or dread: *No one had apprehended any violence.* 3 arrest: *The thief has been apprehended.* [< L *apprehendere* < *ad-* upon + *prehendere* seize]
☞ *Usage.* See note at **comprehend.**

ap·pre·hen·si·bil·i·ty (ap′ri hen′sə bil′ə tē) *n.* the quality or state of being apprehensible.

ap·pre·hen·si·ble (ap′ri hen′sə bəl) *adj.* capable of being apprehended; understandable. —**ap′pre·hen′si·bly,** *adv.*

ap·pre·hen·sion (ap′ri hen′shən) *n.* 1 expectation of evil; fear; dread. 2 understanding; grasping with the mind: *a clear apprehension of the facts.* 3 a seizing or being seized; arrest: *the apprehension of a suspect.* [< L *apprehensio, -onis* < *apprehendere.* See APPREHEND.]

ap·pre·hen·sive (ap′ri hen′siv) *adj.* 1 fearfully expecting danger or harm; afraid; anxious: *The captain was apprehensive for the safety of his passengers during the storm.* 2 quick to understand; able to learn. —**ap′pre·hen′sive·ly,** *adv.* —**ap′pre·hen′sive·ness,** *n.*

ap·pren·tice (ə pren′tis) *n., v.* **-ticed, -tic·ing.** —*n.* 1 a person learning a trade or craft by working at it under skilled supervision for a given length of time. 2 a beginner; learner. —*v.* bind or take as an apprentice. [ME < OF *aprentis* < *apprendre* learn < L *apprehendere.* See APPREHEND.]

ap·pren·tice·ship (ə pren′tis ship′) *n.* 1 the condition of being an apprentice. 2 the time during which one is an apprentice.

ap·prise (ə prīz′) *v.* **-prised, -pris·ing.** give notice to; inform (*often used with* **of**): *They were apprised by letter of a delay in the shipment.* [< F *appris,* pp. of *apprendre* learn < L *apprehendere.* See APPREHEND.]

ap·prize (ə prīz′) *v.* **-prized, -priz·ing.** 1 appraise. 2 esteem or appreciate. [ME < OF *apriser* < L *appretiare.* Doublet of APPRECIATE.]

ap·proach (ə prōch′) *v., n.* —*v.* 1 come near or nearer to: *We're approaching the town.* 2 come near or nearer to (in character, quality, amount): *The wind was approaching gale force.* 3 come near or nearer (in space, time, character, condition, or amount): *Winter approaches.* 4 bring near (to something): *Approach the magnet to this heap of filings.* 5 make advances or overtures to: *Will you approach your father with our plan for a party?*
—*n.* 1 the act of coming near or nearer: *the approach of night.* 2 a way by which a place or a person can be reached; access. 3 a nearness in quality, likeness, or character: *In mathematics there must be more than an approach to accuracy.* 4 Also, **approaches,** *pl.* an advance; overture: *Our approaches to the manager were met with disdain.* 5 a way of dealing with or accomplishing something: *a new approach to mathematics.* 6 *Golf.* a stroke by which a player tries to get his ball onto the putting green. [ME < OF *aprochier* < LL *appropiare* < L *ad-* to + *prope* near]

ap·proach·a·bil·i·ty (ə prōch′ə bil′ə tē) *n.* an approachable quality or condition.

ap·proach·a·ble (ə prōch′ə bəl) *adj.* **1** that can be approached: *The fishing camp was approachable from the south only.* **2** easy to approach: *He looks stern but is really quite approachable.*

ap·pro·ba·tion (ap′rə bā′shən) *n.* **1** approval; favorable opinion. **2** sanction. [ME < OF < L *approbatio, -onis* < *approbare* approve. See APPROVE.]

ap·pro·pri·a·ble (ə prō′prē ə bəl) *adj.* capable of being appropriated.

ap·pro·pri·ate (*adj.* ə prō′prē it; *v.* ə prō′prē āt′) *adj., v.* **-at·ed, -at·ing.** —*adj.* suitable; proper: *Blue jeans and a sweater are appropriate clothes for the hike.* —*v.* **1** set aside for some special use: *The government appropriated money for roads.* **2** take for oneself: *You should not appropriate other people's belongings without their permission.* [< LL *appropriatus,* pp. of *appropriare* < L *ad-* to + *proprius* one's own] —**ap·pro′pri·ate·ly,** *adv.* —**ap·pro′pri·ate·ness,** *n.* —**ap·pro′pri·a′tor,** *n.*
☛ *Syn. adj.* See note at fit¹.

ap·pro·pri·a·tion (ə prō′prē ā′shən) *n.* **1** a sum of money or other thing set aside for a special use. **2** the act or an instance of appropriating: *The appropriation of the land made it possible to have a park.*

ap·prov·al (ə prüv′əl) *n.* **1** an approving; favorable opinion: *This plan has the teacher's approval.* **2** consent: sanction: *The principal gave his approval to plans for the holiday.* **3 approvals,** *pl.* items sent to a customer on approval.
on approval, so that the customer can decide whether to buy or not; on trial: *We had the car for a day on approval.*

ap·prove (ə prüv′) *v.* **-proved, -prov·ing. 1** consent to; sanction: *Everyone approved the plan. Parliament has approved the bill.* **2** give approval; think well of; commend (*used with* **of**): *Her family did not approve of her plan to sell the farm.* **3** think or speak well of; be pleased with: *His boss approved his work.* **4** *Archaic.* prove to be (*often reflexive*). [ME < OF *aprover* < L *approbare* < *ad-* to + *probus* good] —**ap·prov′er,** *n.* —**ap·prov′ing·ly,** *adv.*
☛ *Syn.* **1.** See note at **praise. 3. Approve, sanction, ratify** mean to give formal consent or support. **Approve,** the general word, means to consent to something one thinks favorably of: *The school board approved the budget.* **Sanction,** more formal, means to give official consent or support: *Society does not sanction child labor.* **Ratify** is more formal still, expressing approval or confirmation: *The club council ratified the by-laws.*

approx. approximate; approximately.

ap·prox·i·mate (*adj.* ə prok′sə mit; *v.* ə prok′sə māt′) *adj., v.* **-mat·ed, -mat·ing.** —*adj.* **1** not accurate or precise, but nearly so; fairly close to the actual or the best: *an approximate fit. The approximate number of people expected is 500.* **2** set or located very close together. **3** very like: *The two samples are approximate in size.* —*v.* **1** come near to; approach: *Your account of what happened approximated the truth, but there were several small errors. The crowd approximated a thousand people.* **2** bring near. *Abbrev.:* approx. [< L *approximatus,* pp. of *approximare* < *ad-* to + *proximus* nearest < *prope* near] —**ap·prox′i·mate′ly,** *adv.*

ap·prox·i·ma·tion (ə prok′sə mā′shən) *n.* **1** an approximating; approach: *an approximation to the truth.* **2** a nearly correct amount; close estimate: *Forty thousand kilometres is an approximation of the circumference of the earth.*

ap·pur·te·nance (ə pėr′tə nəns) *n.* **1** an addition to something more important; added thing; accessory. **2** a right or privilege that is subordinate to another. [< AF *apurtenance.* Related to APPERTAIN.]

ap·pur·te·nant (ə pėr′tə nənt) *adj.* pertaining; belonging; appertaining (*to*).

Apr. April.

a·près–ski (ap′rā skē′) *n.* **1** a party or other social activity held in the evening after a day of skiing. **2** (*adj.*) of, for, or designating such an activity: *après-ski fashions.*

ap·ri·cot (ap′rə kot′ *or* ā′prə kot′) *n., adj.* —*n.* **1** a tree (*Prunus armeniaca*) of the rose family native to Africa and W Asia but cultivated throughout the warmer temperate regions of the world for its roundish, pale-orange or yellow, juicy fruit. **2** the fruit of this tree. **3** a pale orange yellow. —*adj.* pale orange-yellow. [earlier *apricock* (< Pg. *albricoque*), later influenced by F *abricot* < Pg. < Sp. < Arabic *al-burquq* < Gk., ult. < *praecox* or *praecoquis* early-ripe < *prae* before + *coquere* cook, ripen]

A·pril (ā′prəl) *n.* the fourth month of the year. It has 30 days. *Abbrev.:* Ap. or Apr. [< L *Aprilis*]

April fool any person who gets fooled on April Fools' Day.

April Fools' Day April 1, a day observed by fooling people with tricks and jokes.

a pri·o·ri (ā′prē ô′rī *or* ā′prī ô′rī) **1** from cause to effect; from a general rule to a particular case. **2** based on opinion or theory rather than on actual observation or experience. [< Med.L *a priori* from (something) previous]

a·pron (ā′prən) *n., v.* —*n.* **1** a garment worn over the front part of

hat, āge, fär; let, ēqual, tėrm; it, īce
hot, ōpen, ôrder; oil, out; cup, pùt, rüle,
əbove, takən, pencəl, lemən, circəs
ch, child; ng, long; sh, ship
th, thin; ᴛн, then; zh, measure

the body to protect one's clothes: *a kitchen apron, a carpenter's apron.* **2** a protective shield or structure to prevent the washing away of a surface, such as a sea wall, river bank, etc. **3** a platform at the bottom of a sluice to intercept the fall of water. **4** *Logging.* a platform at the bottom of a log chute used to break the fall of the logs as they enter the water. **5** a paved area adjacent to the hangars or terminal building of an airport, especially the area immediately in front of a hangar or terminal. **6** the part of a theatre stage that extends in front of the curtain. **7** *Geology.* a sheet of sand or gravel in front of a moraine.
—*v.* provide with an apron. [ME *a napron* taken as *an apron* < OF *naperon,* dim. of *nape* < L *mappa* napkin] —**a′pron·like′,** *adj.*

apron strings the ties used to fasten an apron.
tied to (one's) **mother's apron strings,** dependent on, or dominated by, one's mother.

ap·ro·pos (ap′rə pō′) *adv., adj.* —*adv.* fittingly; opportunely.
apropos of, with regard to.
—*adj.* fitting; suitable; to the point: *an apropos remark.* [< F *à propos* to the purpose]

apse (aps) *n.* a semicircular or many-sided recess in a church, usually at the east end, having an arched or vaulted roof. [< L *apsis* < Gk. *hapsis* loop, arch < *haptein* fasten]

apt (apt) *adj.* **1** fitted by nature; likely: *A careless person is apt to make mistakes.* **2** suitable; fitting: *an apt reply.* **3** quick to learn: *an apt pupil.* [ME < L *aptus* joined, fitted] —**apt′ly,** *adv.* —**apt′ness,** *n.*
☛ *Usage.* See note at **likely.**

apt. apartment.

ap·ter·ous (ap′tər əs) *adj. Biology.* wingless. Lice are apterous insects. [< Gk. *apteros* < *a-* without + *pteron* wing]

ap·ter·yx (ap′tər iks′) *n., pl.* **-yx·es** (-ik′siz). kiwi (def. 1). [< NL *apteryx* < *a-* without + Gk. *pteryx* wing]

ap·ti·tude (ap′tə tyüd′ *or* ap′tə tüd′) *n.* **1** a natural tendency; ability; capacity: *Edison had a great aptitude for inventing new things.* **2** readiness in learning; quickness to understand. **3** a special fitness. [< LL *aptitudo* < L *aptus* joined, fitted. Doublet of ATTITUDE.]

aptitude test a test given to a person to find out the sort of work, studies, etc. for which he is specially suited.

aq. aqua.

AQ achievement quotient.

aq·ua (ak′wə) *n., adj.* —*n.* **1** water. **2** *Chemistry.* a liquid solution: *aqua fortis.* **3** aquamarine. —*adj.* light bluish-green. *Abbrev.:* aq. [< L]

aq·ua·cade (ak′wə kād′) *n.* a water entertainment consisting of swimming, diving, water skiing, group formations, etc., usually performed to the accompaniment of music. [< *aqua* + (*caval*)*cade*]

aq·ua·cul·ture (ak′wə kul′chər) *n.* **1** the raising of water animals and plants, especially fish, for commercial purposes. **2** (*adj.*) of or designating aquaculture: *aquaculture technology.* Also, **aquiculture.**

aq·ua for·tis (ak′wə fôr′tis) nitric acid. [< L *aqua fortis* strong water]

aq·ua·lung (ak′wə lung′) *n.* **1** a diving apparatus consisting of cylinders of compressed air strapped to the diver's back and a watertight mask placed over the eyes and nose. The supply of air to the diver is regulated automatically by a valve. **2 Aqua-Lung,** *Trademark.* a brand of such an apparatus.

aq·ua·ma·rine (ak′wə mə rēn′) *n., adj.* —*n.* **1** a transparent, bluish-green precious stone; a variety of beryl. **2** a gem made from this stone. **3** a color ranging from pale to light bluish-green.
—*adj.* having the color aquamarine. [< L *aqua marina* sea water]

aq·ua·naut (ak′wə not′ *or* -nôt′) *n.* an underwater explorer. [< *aqua* + (*astro*)*naut*]

aq·ua·plane (ak′wə plān′) *n., v.* **-planed, -plan·ing.** —*n.* a wide board on which a person stands as it is towed by a speeding motorboat. —*v.* **1** ride on an aquaplane. **2** of a motor vehicle, ride on a film of water that is built up under the tires at high speed on wet roads, resulting in loss of control over braking and steering. [< L *aqua* water + E *plane*]

aq·ua re·gi·a (ak′wə rē′jē ə) a mixture of nitric acid and hydrochloric acid that will dissolve gold and platinum. [< NL *aqua regia* royal water, because it dissolves gold]

aq·ua·relle (ak′wə rel′) *n.* **1** a painting done with ink and transparent water colors. **2** the method of painting in this way.

a·quar·ist (ə qwer′ist) *n.* a person who keeps an aquarium.

a·quar·i·um (ə kwer′ē əm) *n., pl.* **a·quar·i·ums** or **a·quar·i·a** (ə kwer′ē ə). **1** a pond, tank, or glass bowl in which living fish, water animals, and water plants are kept. **2** a building used for showing collections of living fish, water animals, and water plants. [< L *aquarium*, neut. of *aquarius* of water < *aqua* water]

A·quar·i·us (ə kwer′ē əs) *n.* **1** *Astronomy.* a northern constellation thought of as representing a man standing with his left hand extended upward, and with his right pouring a stream of water out of a vase. **2** *Astrology.* **a** the 11th sign of the zodiac. The sun enters Aquarius about January 22. See **zodiac** for picture. **b** a person born under this sign.

a·quat·ic (ə kwat′ik *or* ə kwot′ik) *adj., n.* —*adj.* **1** growing or living in water: *Water lilies are aquatic plants.* **2** taking place in or on water: *Swimming and sailing are aquatic sports.* —*n.* **1** a plant or animal that lives in water. **2 aquatics,** *pl.* sports that take place in or on water.

aq·ua·tint (ak′wə tint′) *n.* **1** a process in which spaces, not lines, are etched by acid. **2** an etching made by this process. [< F *aquatinte* < Ital. *acqua tinta* < L *aqua* water, and *tincta* (fem.) dipped]

aq·ua·tone (ak′wə tōn′) *n.* **1** a process of photo-engraving in which the design is transferred to a sensitized aluminum plate coated with a mixture of gelatin and celluloid. **2** a print made by this process.

aq·ua vi·tae (ak′wə vī′tē *or* ak′wə vē′tī) **1** alcohol. **2** brandy; whisky, etc. [< NL *aqua vitae* water of life]

aq·ue·duct (ak′wə dukt′) *n.* **1** an artificial channel or large pipe for bringing water from a distance. **2** a structure that supports such a channel or pipe. **3** *Anatomy.* a canal or passage. [< L *aquaeductus* < *aqua* water + *ductus*, pp. of *ducere* lead, convey]

a·que·ous (ā′kwē əs *or* ak′wē əs) *adj.* **1** of water; like water; watery. **2** containing water; made with water. **3** produced by the action of water: *Aqueous rocks are formed of the sediment carried and deposited by water.*

aqueous humor or **humour** the watery liquid that fills the space in the eye between the cornea and the lens. See **eye** for picture.

aq·ui·cul·ture (ak′wə kul′chər) See **aquaculture.**

aq·ui·fer (ak′wə fər) *n.* a water-bearing, underground layer of porous rock, sand, etc. which can be used as a source of water for wells.

Aq·ui·la (ak′wə lə) *n.* a northern constellation thought of as resembling the outline of an eagle. It contains the star Altair. [< L *aquila* eagle]

aq·ui·line (ak′wə līn′ *or* ak′wə lin) *adj.* **1** of or like an eagle. **2** curved like an eagle's beak; hooked: *an aquiline nose.* [< L *aquilinus* < *aquila* eagle]

a·quiv·er (ə kwiv′ər) *adj.* trembling.

ar– *prefix.* to or toward; the form of **ad-** occurring before *r*, as in *arrive.*

Ar argon.

Ar. **1** Arabia; Arabic. **2** Aramaic.

AR Arkansas.

Ar·ab (ar′əb *or* er′əb) *n., adj.* —*n.* **1** a member of a Semitic people originally from the Arabian Peninsula between the Red Sea and the Persian Gulf, now widely scattered throughout the Near East and N Africa. **2** a member of any Arabic-speaking people. **3** a breed of horse originally from the Arabian Peninsula, noted for its swiftness, gracefulness, and spirit. **4** See **street Arab.** —*adj.* **1** of or having to do with the Arabs: *the Arab countries.* **2** of or having to do with the Arabian Peninsula; Arabian. ☛ *Usage.* **Arab, Arabian, Arabic** should not be used interchangeably. **Arab** applies most commonly to the people or their culture: *Arab customs, the Arab world.* **Arabian** usually applies more to the territory traditionally recognized as the home of these people, specifically to the Arabian peninsula: *Arabian sands.* **Arabic** applies to the language of the Arabs and to their literature, art, etc: *Arabic poetry.*

ar·a·besque (ar′ə besk′ *or* er′ə besk′) *n., adj., v.* —*n.* **1** an elaborate and fanciful design of flowers, leaves, geometrical figures, etc. **2** *Ballet.* a pose in which the dancer stands on one leg with the other leg extended horizontally behind him. Traditionally, one arm is extended in front and the other arm behind. **3** *Music.* **a** an ornamentation, often elaborate, of a melody. **b** a short, graceful composition, often highly ornamented, resembling a rondo: *Debussy's piano arabesques.* —*adj.* **1** carved or painted in arabesque. **2** like arabesque; elaborate; fanciful.

—*v.* **1** decorate with arabesques. **2** *Ballet.* execute an arabesque. [< F < Ital. *arabesco* < *Arabo* Arab]

A·ra·bi·an (ə rā′bē ən) *adj., n.* —*adj.* **1** of or having to do with the Arabian Peninsula: *the Arabian desert, Arabian flora.* **2** of or having to do with the Arabs. —*n.* Arab. ☛ *Usage.* See note at **Arab.**

Arabian camel a species of camel (*Camelus dromedarius*) found mainly in India, the Near East, and North Africa, used for riding and as a beast of burden, having long legs and one hump, and standing about 2 m high at the shoulder.

Arabian Nights *The Thousand and One Nights,* a collection of old tales from Arabia, Persia, and India, dating from the tenth century A.D.

Ar·a·bic (ar′ə bik *or* er′ə bik) *n., adj.* —*n.* a Semitic language that is the main language of Saudi Arabia, Yemen, South Yemen, Syria, Lebanon, Jordan, Iraq, Egypt, and parts of North Africa. —*adj.* of or having to do with the Arabs or their language. ☛ *Usage.* See note at **Arab.**

Arabic numerals or **figures** the figures 1, 2, 3, 4, 5, 6, 7, 8, 9, 0. The Arabic numerals are so called because they were introduced into western Europe by Arabian scholars, but most probably they were derived from India. A more accurate name for the Arabic figures is Hindu-Arabic.

ar·a·ble (ar′ə bəl *or* er′ə bəl) *adj.* fit for growing crops: *There is little arable land in the Canadian Shield.* [< L *arabilis* < *arare* plough]

Ar·a·by (ar′ə bē *or* er′ə bē) *n. Poetic.* Arabia.

A·rach·ne (ə rak′nē) *n. Greek mythology.* a maiden who dared to challenge Athena to a contest in weaving, and was changed by her into a spider.

a·rach·nid (ə rak′nid) *n.* any of a class (Arachnida) of small, air-breathing arthropods having four pairs of walking legs, no antennae or wings, and a body usually divided into only two segments. Spiders, scorpions, mites, etc. are arachnids. [< NL *Arachnida* < Gk. *arachnē* spider, web]

a·rach·ni·dan (ə rak′nə dən) *adj., n.* —*adj.* of or having to do with arachnids. —*n.* arachnid.

a·rach·noid (ə rak′noid) *adj., n.* —*adj.* **1** like a cobweb. **2** of or resembling an arachnid. **3** *Physiology.* of or having to do with the thin serous membrane that envelops the brain and spinal cord. **4** *Botany.* formed of, or covered with, fine hairs of fibres resembling cobwebs. —*n.* **1** arachnid. **2** the arachnoid membrane. [< NL < Gk. *arachnoeidēs* cobweblike < *arachnē* spider, web]

Ar·a·ma·ic (ar′ə mā′ik *or* er′ə mā′ik) *n., adj.* —*n.* a Semitic language or group of dialects, including Syriac and the language spoken in Palestine in the time of Christ. —*adj.* of or in Aramaic.

A·ra·wak (ä′rə wäk′) *n., pl.* **Arawak** or **-waks**; *adj.* —*n.* **1** a member of a group of Amerindian peoples of South America and, formerly, the West Indies. **2** a member of one of these peoples, now living mainly along the coast of Guyana. **b** their language. —*adj.* of or having to do with the Arawak or their language.

A·ra·wak·an (ä′rə wä′kən) *n., pl.* **Arawakan** or **-kans**; *adj.* —*n.* **1** a large family of Amerindian languages spoken by the Arawak (def. 1). **2** Arawak (def. 1). —*adj.* of, having to do with, or designating the Arawak peoples or their languages.

ar·ba·lest or **ar·ba·list** (är′bə list) *n.* a powerful crossbow having a steel bow. [< OF *arbaleste* < LL *arcu-ballista* < *arcus* bow + *ballista* military engine, ult. < Gk. *ballein* throw]

ar·bi·ter (är′bə tər) *n.* **1** a person chosen to decide a dispute. **2** a person with full power to decide. [< L *arbiter*]

ar·bi·tra·ble (är′bə trə bəl) *adj.* capable of being decided by arbitration.

ar·bi·trage (är′bə trij) *n. Business.* **1** the calculation of the prices of certain stocks, bonds, etc. in different places at the same time, allowing for exchange rates. **2** the buying and selling of stocks, bonds, etc. in several markets simultaneously, to take advantage of price differences between markets. [< F < *arbitrer* arbitrate < L *arbitrare* < *arbiter* arbiter]

ar·bi·tral (är′bə trəl) *adj.* of arbiters or arbitration.

ar·bit·ra·ment (är bit′rə mənt) *n.* **1** a decision by an arbitrator or arbiter. **2** the power to judge and decide.

ar·bi·trar·y (är′bə trer′ē) *adj.* **1** determined by caprice or whim: *Her sudden arbitrary decision to quit the team cost us the game.* **2** done or made at random without a reason: *An arbitrary selection of a single ticket decides the winner of a lottery.* **3** determined by the decision of a judge or tribunal rather than by a specific law. **4** despotic; absolute: *arbitrary rule.* —**ar′bi·trar′i·ly,** *adv.* —**ar′bi·trar′i·ness,** *n.*

ar·bi·trate (är′bə trāt′) *v.* **-trat·ed, -trat·ing.** **1** give a decision in a dispute; act as arbiter: *to arbitrate between two persons in a quarrel.* **2** settle by arbitration; submit to arbitration: *The two*

nations finally agreed to arbitrate their dispute. [< L arbitrari < arbiter. See ARBITER.]

ar·bi·tra·tion (är′bə trā′shən) *n.* the settlement of a dispute by the decision of a judge, umpire, or arbiter.

ar·bi·tra·tor (är′bə trā′tər) *n.* **1** a person chosen to decide a dispute. **2** a person with full power to judge and decide.

ar·bor¹ or **ar·bour** (är′bər) *n.* a shady place formed by trees or shrubs or often by vines growing on latticework. [ME < AF *erber* < LL *herbarium* < *herba* herb. Doublet of HERBARIUM.]

ar·bor² (är′bər) *n.* the main shaft or axle of a machine. [< F *arbre*]

Arbor Day or **Arbour Day** a day observed in certain Canadian provinces and in some other countries by planting trees. The date varies in different places.

ar·bo·re·al (är bô′rē əl) *adj.* **1** of trees; like trees. **2** living in or among trees: *A squirrel is an arboreal animal.*

ar·bo·re·tum (är′bə rē′təm) *n.* a place where trees and shrubs are grown for educational, scientific, and other purposes. [< L *arboretum* < *arbor* tree]

ar·bor·vi·tae (är′bər vī′tē *or* -vē′tī) *n., pl.* **-vi·tae** or **-vi·taes.** any of a genus (*Thuja*) of evergreen trees of the cypress family found in North America and E Asia, having small, fragrant, scalelike, overlapping leaves, small cones, and light, soft, fragrant wood that is highly resistant to decay. See also **eastern white cedar, western red cedar.** [< L *abor vitae* tree of life]

ar·bour (är′bər) See **arbor¹.**

ar·bu·tus (är byü′təs) *n.* **1** any of a genus (*Arbutus*) of shrubs and trees of the heath family, having broad, leathery, evergreen leaves, large clusters of flowers, and red, berrylike fruit. A common arbutus of warm temperate regions is the **strawberry tree,** native to southern Europe and Ireland. **2** See **trailing arbutus.** [< L]

arc (ärk) *n., v.* **arced** (ärkt), **arc·ing** (är′king). —*n.* **1** any continuous part of a circle or ellipse. **2** a curved line or path. **3** *Electricity.* a discharge of electricity seen as a curved stream of brilliant light or sparks, formed when a current jumps across a gap in a circuit or between electrodes. **4** *Astronomy.* the apparent path of a heavenly body above the horizon (**diurnal arc**) and below the horizon (**nocturnal arc**). —*v.* **1** *Electricity.* form an arc. **2** follow a curved path or course. [< L *arcus* bow]

ar·cade (är kād′) *n.* **1** a passageway with an arched roof. **2** any covered passageway: *Some buildings have arcades with small stores along either side.* **3** *Architecture.* a row of arches supported by columns. [< F < Provençal *arcado*, ult. < VL *arca.* See ARCH¹.]

Ar·ca·di·a (är kā′dē ə) *n.* **1** a mountain district in the southern part of ancient Greece, famous for the simple, contented life of its people. **2** any region of simple, quiet contentment. [< L < Gk.] —**Ar·ca′di·an,** *adj., n.*

Ar·ca·dy (är′kə dē) *n. Poetic.* Arcadia.

ar·cane (är kān′) *adj.* mysterious; esoteric: *an arcane science, arcane knowledge.* [< L See ARCANUM.]

ar·ca·num (är kā′nəm) *n., pl.* **-nums** or **-na** (-nə) a secret; mystery. [< L *arcanum* (thing) hidden < *arca* chest]

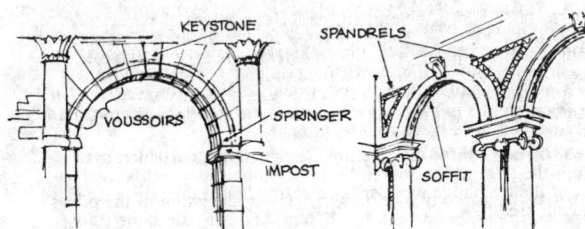

Arches: at the left, an ancient Roman arch; at the right, arches in a gallery at Osgoode Hall, Toronto

arch¹ (ärch) *n., v.* —*n.* **1** *Architecture.* a curved structure used in bridges, gateways, etc. as a support for the weight above it. **2** a structure containing an arch or arches, built as an ornament or gateway: *a triumphal arch.* **3** any curve in the shape of an arch. **4** *Anatomy.* the instep. Fallen arches cause flat feet. **5** something like an arch: *the great blue arch of the sky.* —*v.* **1** bend into an arch; curve. **2** furnish with an arch: *The rainbow arches the sky.* **3** form an arch over; span. [ME < OF < *arche* < VL *arca,* pl. < L *arcus* bow]

arch² (ärch) *adj.* **1** chief; principal: *the arch villain of a story. His arch rival for the position was a younger man.* **2** consciously playful or mischievous: *an arch look, an arch reply.* [< *arch-* (prefix)] —**arch′ly,** *adv.* —**arch′ness,** *n.*

hat, āge, fär; let, ēqual, tèrm; it, īce
hot, ōpen, ôrder; oil, out; cup, put, rüle,
əbove, takən, pencəl, lemən, circəs

ch, child; ng, long; sh, ship
th, thin; ᴛʜ, then; zh, measure

arch– *prefix.* chief; principal: *archbishop = principal bishop; archduke = principal duke.* Also, **archi-.** [ME *arche-* < OE *arce-* < L *archi-* < Gk. *arche-,* combining form of *archos* chief]

arch. **1** archaic; archaism. **2** architecture; architect. **3** archipelago.

Arch. **1** Archbishop. **2** Archdeacon. **3** Archduke.

archaeo– *combining form.* ancient; primitive, as in *archaeology.* [< Gk. *archaios* ancient < *archē* beginning]

ar·chae·o·log·i·cal (är′kē ə loj′ə kəl) *adj.* of or having to do with archaeology. Also, **archeological.**

ar·chae·ol·o·gist (är′kē ol′ə jist) *n.* a person trained in archaeology, especially one whose work it is. Also, **archeologist.**

ar·chae·ol·o·gy (är′kē ol′ə jē) *n.* the study of the people, customs, and life of ancient times. Students of archaeology excavate, classify, and study the remains of ancient cities, tools, monuments, etc. Also, **archeology.** [< Gk. < *archaios* ancient + *-logos* treating of]

ar·chae·op·ter·yx (är′kē op′tər iks) *n.* the oldest-known fossil bird of the European Upper Jurassic period, about the size of a crow, having teeth, a lizardlike tail, and well-developed wings. Also, **archeopteryx.** [< *archaeo-* + Gk. *pteryx* wing]

ar·cha·ic (är kā′ik) *adj.* **1** no longer in general use. **2** old-fashioned; out-of-date. **3** ancient. [< Gk. *archaikos,* ult. < *archē* beginning]

ar·cha·ism (är′kē iz′əm *or* är′kā iz′əm) *n.* **1** a word or expression no longer in general use. *In sooth* and *methinks* are archaisms meaning *in truth* and *it seems to me.* **2** the use of something out of date in language or art.

arch·an·gel (ärk′ān′jəl) *n.* an angel of a very high rank. [ME < LL < Gk. *archangelos* < *arch-* chief + *angelos* angel]

arch·bish·op (ärch′bish′əp) *n.* a bishop of the highest rank. He presides over a church district called an archbishopric or archdiocese.

arch·bish·op·ric (ärch′bish′əp rik) *n.* **1** a church district governed by an archbishop. **2** the position, rank, or dignity of an archbishop.

arch·dea·con (ärch′dē′kən) *n.* an assistant to a bishop. In the Anglican Church, he superintends the work of other members of the clergy.

arch·dea·con·ate (ärch′dē′kən it) *n.* the office of an archdeacon.

arch·dea·con·ry (ärch′dē′kən rē) *n., pl.* **-ries. 1** a district under the supervision of an archdeacon. **2** the position or rank of an archdeacon. **3** the residence of an archdeacon.

arch·di·oc·e·san (ärch′dī os′ə sən) *adj.* of or having to do with an archdiocese.

arch·di·o·cese (ärch′dī′ə sis *or* ärch′dī′ə sēs′) *n.* the church district governed by an archbishop.

arch·du·cal (ärch′dyü′kəl *or* ärch′dü′kəl) *adj.* of an archduke; of an archduchy.

arch·duch·ess (ärch′duch′is) *n.* **1** the wife or widow of an archduke. **2** a princess of the former ruling house of Austria-Hungary.

arch·duch·y (ärch′duch′ē) *n., pl.* **-duch·ies.** the territory under the rule of an archduke or archduchess.

arch·duke (ärch′dyük′ *or* ärch′dük′) *n.* a prince of the former ruling house of Austria-Hungary.

arched (ärcht) *adj.* having an arch or arches.

ar·che·go·ni·um (är′kə gō′nē əm) *n., pl.* **-ni·a** (-nē ə). *Botany.* the female reproductive organ in ferns, mosses, etc. [< NL *archegonium,* ult. < Gk. *archē* beginning + *genos* race]

arch·en·e·my (ärch′en′ə mē) *n., pl.* **-mies. 1** the chief enemy. **2** Satan.

ar·che·o·log·i·cal (är′kē ə loj′ə kəl) See **archaeological.**

ar·che·ol·o·gist (är′kē ol′ə jist) See **archaeologist.**

ar·che·ol·o·gy (är′kē ol′ə jē) See **archaeology.**

Ar·che·o·zo·ic (är′kē ə zō′ik) *n., adj. Geology.* —*n.* **1** the oldest era. During this era, commencing about 2 billion years ago, living things first appeared. See chart at **geology.** **2** the rocks formed during this era. —*adj.* of or having to do with this era or the rocks formed during it. [< *archeo-* (var. of *archaeo-*) + Gk. *zōē* life]

arch·er (är′chər) *n.* **1** a person who shoots with a bow and arrows. **2 Archer,** *Astronomy or astrology.* Sagittarius. [< AF < L *arcarius* < *arcus* bow]

arch·er·y (är′chər ē) *n.* **1** the practice or art of shooting with bows and arrows. **2** a troop of archers. **3** the weapons of an archer; bows, arrows, etc.

ar·che·typ·al (är′kə tī′pəl) *adj.* **1** serving as a model or pattern. **2** representative or typical: *the archetypal Hollywood heroine.*

ar·che·type (är′kə tīp′) *n.* **1** an original model or pattern from which copies are made, or out of which later forms develop: *That little engine is the archetype of huge modern locomotives.* **2** a perfect or typical example or specimen. [< L < Gk. *archetypon,* neut. of *archetypos* original]

ar·che·typ·i·cal (är′kə tip′ə kəl) *adj.* archetypal.

arch·fiend (ärch′fēnd′) *n.* **1** the chief fiend. **2** Satan.

archi– *prefix.* a variant of **arch-,** as in *archi-episcopal.*

ar·chi·e·pis·co·pal (är′kē i pis′kə pəl) *adj.* of or having to do with an archbishop.

Ar·chi·me·de·an (är′kə mē′dē ən) *adj.* of, having to do with, or invented by Archimedes.

Ar·chi·me·des principle (är′kə mē′dēz) *Physics.* the principle that the apparent loss of weight of a body when partly or totally immersed in a liquid is equal to the weight of the liquid displaced. [after *Archimedes* (287?-212 B.C.), a Greek mathematician, physicist, and inventor, who discovered this principle]

ar·chi·pe·lag·ic (är′kə pə laj′ik) *adj.* of, having to do with, or found in an archipelago.

ar·chi·pel·a·go (är′kə pel′ə gō′) *n., pl.* **-gos** or **-goes. 1** a sea having many islands in it. **2** a group of many islands: *The islands in the Arctic Ocean north of Canada are called the Canadian Archipelago.* Abbrev.: arch. [< Ital. *arcipelago* < *arci-* chief (ult. < Gk. *archi-*) + *pelago* sea (ult. < Gk. *pelagos*); originally, the Aegean]

ar·chi·tect (är′kə tekt′) *n.* **1** a person trained in architecture, especially one whose work is designing buildings and supervising their construction. **2** a designer, planner, or maker: *the architects of modern technology.* [< L *architectus* < Gk. *architekton* < *archi-* chief + *tekton* builder]

ar·chi·tec·ton·ic (är′kə tek ton′ik) *adj.* **1** having to do with architecture, construction, or design. **2** showing skill in construction or design. **3** directive; controlling.

ar·chi·tec·ton·ics (är′kə tek ton′iks) *n.* **1** the science of architecture. **2** skill in architecture. **3** any skill in the construction or design of a work of art. **4** the product of such skill; the design or structure of a work of art.

ar·chi·tec·tur·al (är′kə tek′chər əl) *adj.* of architecture; having to do with architecture. —**ar′chi·tec′tur·al·ly,** *adv.*

ar·chi·tec·ture (är′kə tek′chər) *n.* **1** the science or art of building; the planning and designing of buildings. **2** a style or special manner of building: *Greek architecture made much use of columns.* **3** construction: *the flimsy architecture of some buildings.* **4** a building; structure.

ar·chi·trave (är′kə trāv′) *n. Architecture.* **1** the beam resting directly on the top, or capital, of a column; the lowest part of an entablature, below the frieze. See **column** for picture. **2** the moulding around a door, window, or arch. [< Ital. *architrave* < *archi-* chief (ult. < Gk.) + *trave* beam < L *trabs, trabis*]

ar·chi·val (är kī′vəl) *adj.* of, having to do with, or kept in archives: *archival records.*

ar·chive (är′kīv) *n.* Usually, **archives,** *pl.* **1** a place where public records or historical documents are preserved: *The Dominion Archives are in Ottawa.* **2** the material kept in such a place. [< F < L *archivum* < Gk. *archeia* < *archē* government]

ar·chiv·ist (är′kiv ist) *n.* a person in charge of archives.

ar·chon (är′kon) *n.* **1** in ancient Athens, a chief magistrate. **2** ruler. [< Gk. *archōn,* ppr. of *archein* rule]

arch·way (ärch′wā′) *n.* **1** an entrance or passageway with an arch above it. **2** an arch covering a passageway.

arc lamp a lamp in which the light comes from an electric arc.

arc light 1 the brilliant light given by an arc lamp. **2** an arc lamp.

arc·tic (ärk′tik or är′tik) *adj., n.* —*adj.* **1** Often, **Arctic,** of, having to do with, referring to, or living or growing in the region north of the Arctic Circle: *the arctic fox.* **2** extremely cold; frigid: *a whole week of arctic temperatures.* —*n.* **1 the Arctic, a** the north polar region; the region north of the Arctic Circle. **b** the Arctic Ocean. **2 arctics,** *pl.* warm, waterproof overshoes. [ME < OF < L *arcticus* < Gk. *arktikos* of the Bear (constellation) < *arktos* bear]

arctic char or **Arctic char** a food fish of the salmon and trout family found throughout the Arctic, occurring in two varieties, one of which is landlocked, the other spending most of its life in the sea but moving into fresh water to spawn.

arctic circle or **Arctic Circle** the parallel of latitude at 66°33′ north of the equator that marks the boundary of the north polar region.

arctic cotton *Cdn.* any of several species of cotton grass, such as *Eriophorum scheuchzeri,* found in arctic regions.

arctic fox a fox of the arctic regions, valued for its fur. Its coat is bluish grey or brownish grey in summer and white in winter.

arctic hare *Cdn.* a large, thickset hare (*Lepus arcticus*) found in arctic Canada, from the tundra of the Northwest Territories up to the northern tip of Ellesmere Island, and also in Greenland. It is pure white in winter, except for its black-tipped ears, and varies in summer from bluish grey to almost white with a tinge of cinnamon or grey, depending on the latitude.

arctic tern an Arctic-breeding tern (*Sterna paradisaea*) noted for the length of its migrations, from its breeding grounds in the Arctic of the Old and New Worlds south to its winter range in the oceans of the southern hemisphere.

arctic willow a low-growing willow (*Salix arctica*) of arctic tundra and northern alpine regions having trailing, freely rooting branches and pale foliage.

Arc·tu·rus (ärk tyūr′əs or ärk tūr′əs) *n.* a first magnitude star in the constellation Boötes.

—ard or **—art** *noun-forming suffix.* designating a person characterized by a certain quality, behavior, actions, etc., especially excessively or conspicuously, as in *sluggard, drunkard, braggart, wizard.* [< OF < Gmc.; related to G *-hard, -hart* (literally, hardy or bold]

ARDA (är′də) *Cdn.* Agriculture and Rural Development Act.

Ar·den (är′dən) *n.* **1** a district or forest in the central and formerly also the eastern part of England. **2** a land of the imagination or of romance.

ar·den·cy (är′dən sē) *n.* the condition of being ardent.

ar·dent (är′dənt) *adj.* **1** full of zeal; very enthusiastic; eager. **2** burning; fiery; hot. **3** glowing. [ME < OF < L *ardens, -entis,* ppr. of *ardere* burn] —**ar′dent·ly,** *adv.*

ardent spirits strong alcoholic liquor.

ar·dor or **ar·dour** (är′dər) *n.* **1** eagerness; warmth of emotion; great enthusiasm: *patriotic ardor.* **2** burning heat. [ME < OF < L *ardor* < *ardere* burn]

ar·du·ous (är′jü əs) *adj.* **1** hard to do; requiring much effort; difficult: *an arduous lesson.* **2** using up much energy; strenuous: *an arduous effort to learn the lesson.* **3** hard to climb; steep: *an arduous hill.* [< L *arduus* steep] —**ar′du·ous·ly,** *adv.* —**ar′du·ous·ness,** *n.*

are[1] (är; *unstressed,* ər) *v.* the plural and the 2nd pers. sing., present indicative, of **be:** *we are, you are, they are.* [OE (Northumbrian) *aron*]

are[2] (er or är) *n.* a measure of area, equal to 100 square metres. *Symbol:* a [< F < L *area* area]

ar·e·a (er′ē ə) *n.* **1** the amount of surface; extent of surface: *The area of this floor is 60 square metres.* **2** region: *a mountainous area.* **3** range; scope: *The provincial governments often try to limit the area of federal responsibility.* **4** a field of study or activity: *He is working in the area of foreign policy.* **5** a level surface or space: *The playing area was marked off with white lines.* **6** a yard or court of a building. [< L *area* piece of level ground]

area code a three-digit number designating a particular area within the total region served by a telephone system. It is used as part of the telephone number for directly dialled long-distance calls between areas.

ar·e·al (er′ē əl) *adj.* of or having to do with area or an area. —**ar′e·al·ly,** *adv.*

ar·e·a·way (er′ē ə wā′) *n.* **1** a sunken area or court at the entrance to a cellar or basement. **2** an area serving as a passageway between buildings.

ar·e·ca (ar′i kə, er′i kə, or ə rē′kə) *n.* any of several tall, tropical Asian palms (genus *Areca*), especially the betel palm. [< Port. < Tamil *adaikay*]

a·re·na (ə rē′nə) *n.* **1** a building for indoor sports, having a central space for players or competitors that is surrounded by tiers of seats for spectators: *There is a hockey game at the arena tonight.* **2** any area where contests or shows take place. **3** the central area of an ancient Roman amphitheatre, where gladiators fought. **4** any sphere of public action, especially one involving conflict: *You have to have stamina to succeed in the political arena.* [< later var. of L *harena* sand; because the floors of Roman arenas were covered with sand]

ar·e·na·ceous (ar′ə nā′shəs *or* er′ə nā′ ... *adj.* sandy.
arena rat *Cdn. Slang* ...
aren't (ärnt) ... ns): *I'm too late,*
little area.
mething, as
. The spaces
(är′ē ōl′). [<
the hill of
Athens,
esponding
sually
rare
a single
dant lip,
ning
, a
ar·
2 *H* ... *dj.*
silve
Ar·g ... e or
inhab
Argen ... r its
people
Ar·ge
Argenti
ar·gen ... ns
in granit
importan
-*ite*¹]
ar·gil (är
< L < Gk.
ar·gil·la·c
containing
ar·gil·lite
intermediate
does not have
-*ite*¹]
Ar·give (är′j
1 a native or in
Ar·go (är′gō)
companions sail
ar·gon (är′gon,
odorless, inert ga
ordinary light bul
at.wt. 39.948. [< N
Ar·go·naut (är′g
of the men who sai
2 Often, **argonaut,** a
modern times, espec
British Columbia, in
Argō, the name of the
ar·go·sy (är′gə sē)
of such ships. [< Ital.
trading extensively wit
ar·got (är′gō *or* är′gə
particular class of perso
language, or jargon, of p
or way of life, especially
jargon. [< F]
ar·gu·a·ble (är′gyü ə b
disputed or questioned. —
ar·gue (är′gyü) *v.* **-gued,** -
disagrees. **2** give reasons for
question. He argued against
giving reasons: *He argued m*
reasoning; maintain: *Columb*
5 indicate; show; prove: *Her r*
objections; dispute. [ME < OF
of *arguere* make clear] —**ar′gu**
☛ *Syn.* **1.** See note at **discuss.**
ar·gu·ment (är′gyə mənt) *n.* ... discussion by persons who give reasons for and against different points of view; a debate: *He won the argument by producing figures to prove his point.* **2** an emotional disagreement; a dispute: *He had an argument with his*

Heart Attack Signals

- Vague chest tightness, discomfort, pain or a crushing radiating chest pain
- Heaviness, pressure, squeezing, fullness, burning or pain that may begin in the centre of chest and spread to the neck, jaws and shoulders
- Unusual pain that spreads down one or both arms
- Shortness of breath, paleness, sweating or weakness
- Nausea, vomiting and/or indigestion
- Feeling of extreme anxiety, fear and/or denial

Actions

If you experience these signals or notice them in others:

- Stop activity, sit or lie down
- If you have nitroglycerine, take as prescribed
- **CALL 911 TO GET HELP!**

For further information, contact the Heart and Stroke Foundation of Nova Scotia at 423-7530, or 1-800-423-4432.

Visit our website at <u>www.heartandstroke.ca</u>

hat, āge, fär; let, ēqual, tėrm; it, īce
hot, ōpen, ôrder; oil, out; cup, pu̇t, rüle,
əbove, takən, pencəl, lemən, circəs
ch, child; ng, long; sh, ship
th, thin; ᴛʜ, then; zh, measure

brother about who won the card game. **3** the reason or reasons given for or against something. **4** a short statement of what is in a book, poem, etc.
☛ *Syn.* **1. Argument, controversy, dispute** = a discussion by persons who disagree. **Argument** applies to a discussion in which each of two persons uses facts and reasons to try to win the other over: *He won the argument by producing figures.* **Controversy** applies chiefly to a formal argument between groups, often carried on in writing or speeches: *The Canadian school controversy still continues.* **Dispute** suggests contradicting rather than reasoning, and applies to an argument marked by feeling: *The dispute over the property was settled in court.*

ar·gu·men·ta·tion (är′gyə men tā′shən) *n.* **1** the process of arguing; reasoning. **2** discussion; debate.

ar·gu·men·ta·tive (är′gyə men′tə tiv) *adj.* **1** fond of arguing. **2** containing argument. —**ar′gu·men′ta·tive·ly,** *adv.*

Ar·gus (är′gəs) *n.* **1** *Greek mythology.* a giant with a hundred eyes. He was killed by Hermes, and his eyes were put in the peacock's tail. **2** any watchful guardian.

Ar·gus–eyed (är′gəs īd′) *adj.* watchful; observant.

ar·gyle or **Ar·gyle** (är gīl′) *adj.* of or having to do with a diamond-shaped pattern of various colors, often knitted into articles such as socks, neckties, etc. [< *Argyll,* a county in Scotland]

Ar·gy·rol (är′jə rōl′ *or* är′jə rol′) *n. Trademark.* a compound of silver and a protein, used in the treatment of inflamed mucous membranes. [< Gk. *argyros* silver]

a·ri·a (ä′rē ə *or* er′ē ə) *n.* an air or melody; a melody for a single voice with instrumental or vocal accompaniment. [< Ital. < L *aer* air < Gk.]

Ar·i·ad·ne (ar′ē ad′nē *or* er′ē ad′nē) *n. Greek mythology.* the daughter of Minos, king of Crete. She fell in love with Theseus and gave him a ball of thread to help him find his way out of the Labyrinth of the Minotaur.

Ar·i·an (er′ē ən) *adj., n.* —*adj.* of or having to do with the doctrine of Arius of Alexandria (4c.) who taught that Jesus Christ is not of the same substance as God the Father. —*n.* a believer in this doctrine.

ar·id (ar′id *or* er′id) *adj.* **1** dry; barren: *Desert lands are arid.* dull; uninteresting: *an arid, tiresome speech.* [< L *aridus* < *arere* dry] —**ar′id·ly,** *adv.* —**ar′id·ness,** *n.*
Syn. **1.** See note at **dry.**

rid·i·ty (ə rid′ə tē) *n.* **1** dryness; barrenness. **2** dullness; lack of erest, life, or spirit.

ies (er′ēz *or* er′ē ēz′) *n.* **1** *Astronomy.* a northern tellation thought of as having the shape of a ram. **2** *Astrology.* first sign of the zodiac. The sun enters Aries about March 21. **odiac** for picture. **b** a person born under this sign.
n. **Ares** (er′ēz).

t (ə rīt′) *adv.* correctly; rightly.

ar′il *or* er′il) *n. Botany.* an outside covering of certain he pulpy inner pod of the bittersweet is an aril. [< NL Med.L *arilli* raisins]

e (ar′ə lāt′ *or* er′ə lat′) *adj. Botany.* having an aril.

o (ä′rē ō′sō) *adj., adv., n., pl.* **-sos.** —*adj. or adv.* or like an aria or song. —*n.* a passage or piece of music as an aria or song. [< Ital. *arioso* songlike < *aria* aria]

rīz′) *v.* **a·rose, a·ris·en, a·ris·ing. 1** get up; rise: *The ose together.* **2** move upward; ascend: *Smoke arose mney.* **3** come into being or action; appear or begin: *A rose.* **4** be caused; result: *Many accidents arise through* [OE *ārīsan*]
ote at **rise.**

iz′ən) *v.* pp. of **arise.**

cy (ar′is tok′rə sē *or* er′is-) *n., pl.* **-cies. 1** people of e, or birth; a ruling body of nobles; nobility. **2** any sidered superior because of birth, intelligence, , or wealth; upper class. **3** a government in which a privileged upper class rules. **4** a country or state having such a government; oligarchy. **5** government by the best citizens. [< LL *aristocratia* < Gk. *aristokratia* < *aristos* best + *kratein* rule]

a·ris·to·crat (ə ris′tə krat′, ar′is- or, er′is-) *n.* **1** a person who belongs to the aristocracy; noble. **2** a person who has the tastes, opinions, manners, etc. of the upper classes. **3** a person who favors government by an aristocracy.

a·ris·to·crat·ic (ə ris′tə krat′ik, ar′is- or er′is-) *adj.* **1** having to do with, belonging to, or characteristic of aristocracy or aristocrats. **2** proud or distinguished: *an aristocratic bearing.*
—**a·ris′to·crat′i·cal·ly,** *adv.*

Ar·is·to·te·li·an (ar′is tə tēl′yən or er′is-) *adj., n.* —*adj.* having to do with the Greek philosopher Aristotle (384-322 B.C.) or his philosophy. —*n.* a follower of Aristotle.

arith. arithmetic; arithmetical.

a·rith·me·tic (*n.* ə rith′mə tik′, *adj.* ar′ith met′ik or er′ith met′ik) *n., adj.* —*n.* **1** the branches of mathematics dealing with computation using positive, real numbers, especially addition, subtraction, multiplication, and division. **2** a textbook or handbook on this subject. —*adj.* of, having to do with, or using arithmetic: *an arithmetic progression.* [ME < OF < L *arithmetica* < Gk. *arithmētikē* < *arithmos* number]

ar·ith·met·i·cal (ar′ith met′ə kəl or er′ith-) *adj.* of, having to do with, or using arithmetic. —**ar′ith·met′i·cal·ly,** *adv.*

a·rith·me·ti·cian (ə rith′mə tish′ən, ar′ith- or er′ith-) *n.* a person skilled in arithmetic.

arithmetic mean the average obtained by dividing the sum of several quantities by the number of quantities. To obtain the arithmetic mean of 3, 9, 18, and 42, add them up and divide the total by 4.

arithmetic progression a series in which there is always the same difference between a number and the one next after it. 2, 4, 6, 8, 10 are in arithmetical progression; so are 8, 5, 2, –1.

Ariz. Arizona.

Ar·i·zo·nan (ar′ə zō′nən) *adj., n.* —*adj.* of or having to do with Arizona. —*n.* a native or inhabitant of Arizona.

Ar·i·zo·ni·an (ar′ə zō′nē ən) *adj. or n.* Arizonan.

ark (ärk) *n.* **1** in the Bible, the large boat in which Noah saved himself, his family, and a pair of each kind of animal from the Flood. **2** *Informal.* any large, clumsy boat. **3** the Ark of the Covenant. [OE *arc* < L *arca* chest]

Ark. Arkansas.

Ark of the Covenant **1** the wooden chest or box in which the ancient Hebrews kept the two tablets of stone containing the Ten Commandments. **2** the wooden chest in a synagogue that symbolizes this.

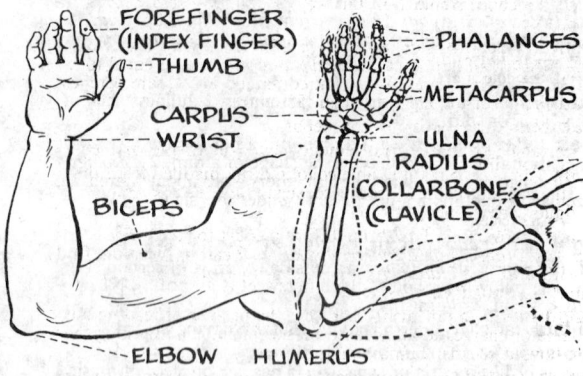

A human right arm, seen from the front

arm[1] (ärm) *n.* **1** the upper limb of the human body between the shoulder and the hand. **2** a forelimb of an animal. The front legs of a bear are sometimes called arms. **3** anything resembling an arm in shape or use: *the arm of a chair, an arm of the sea.* **4** the part of a garment covering the arm. **5** power; authority: *the strong arm of the law.*

arm in arm, with arms linked: *She walked arm in arm with her sister.*

at arm's length, a as far as the arm can reach: *He held the picture up at arm's length to look at it.* **b** far enough away to avoid familiarity: *She was never very friendly and kept everyone at arm's length.* **c** of business transactions or relationships, not involving direct influence by any of the parties over the other or others: *The new regulatory body will be at arm's length from both industry and government.*

with open arms, in a warm, friendly way; cordially. [OE *earm*]
—**arm′less,** *adj.*

arm[2] (ärm) *n., v.* —*n.* **1** any instrument used for fighting; weapon

(usually used in the plural): Arms may be used for defence or attack. **2 arms,** *pl.* fighting; war: *A soldier is a man of arms.* **3** a combatant branch of the armed forces.

arms, *pl.* the symbols and designs used in heraldry or, as emblems of official dignity, by governments, cities, corporations, etc.

bear arms, a serve as a soldier. **b** possess and display a coat of arms.

take up arms, arm for attack or defence: *The settler took up arms against the invaders.*

to arms! prepare for battle!

under arms, having weapons; equipped for fighting.

up in arms, a preparing for battle. **b** very angry; in rebellion.
—*v.* **1** supply with weapons; equip with armament. **2** take up weapons; prepare for war. **3** provide with a protective covering. **4** provide with a means of defence or attack: *Armed with additional statistics, he convinced the committee that more parks were necessary.* [sing. of arms, ME *armes* < OF < L *arma,* pl.]

Arm. Armenian.

ar·ma·da (är mad′ə or är mä′də) *n.* **1** a fleet of warships. **2** a fleet of military aircraft. **3 the Armada,** the Spanish fleet that was sent to attack England in 1588. [< Sp. < L *armata* armed force, originally pp. neut. pl. of *armare* to arm. Doublet of ARMY.]

ar·ma·dil·lo (är′mə dil′ō) *n., pl.* **-los.** any of a family (Dasypodidae) of burrowing mammals of South America and southern North America having an armor-like covering of small, jointed, bony plates, a long, narrow tongue adapted for catching insects, and strong claws. One species rolls up into a ball to protect itself when attacked. [< Sp. *armadillo* dim. of *armado* armed (one) < L *armatus,* pp. of *armare* arm]

Ar·ma·ged·don (är′mə ged′ən) *n.* **1** in the Bible, the scene of a great and final conflict between the forces of good and evil (Rev. 16:16). **2** any great and final conflict. [< LL < Gk., probably < Hebrew]

ar·ma·ment (är′mə mənt) *n.* **1** war equipment and supplies. **2** all the armed forces of a nation. **3** the act or process of preparing for war. **4** the weapons on a naval vessel, tank, aircraft, etc.

ar·ma·ture (är′mə chər) *n.* **1** armor. **2** a part of an animal or plant serving for offence (teeth, claws) or defence (shells, thorns): *A turtle's shell is an armature.* **3** wire wound round and round a cable. **4** a piece of soft iron placed in contact with the poles of a magnet. **5** a revolving part of an electric motor or generator. **6** a movable part of an electric relay or buzzer. **7** *Sculpture.* a framework which supports the clay or other substance used for modelling a figure. [< L *armatura* < *armare* arm. Doublet of ARMOR.]

arm·band (ärm′band′) *n.* a circlet of cloth, worn around the sleeve as a sign of rank, office, etc. Black armbands are usually a sign of mourning.

arm·chair (ärm′cher′) *n., adj.* —*n.* a chair with side pieces to support a person's arms or elbows. —*adj.* **1** of or having to do with an armchair. **2** of or having to do with actions, opinions, etc. based on theory rather than on practical experience or knowledge: *Armchair politicians have no idea of the real difficulties of government.* **3** sharing by reading, etc. in another's experiences: *an armchair explorer.* **4** of or having to do with work done by the intellect rather than by physical effort: *an armchair detective.*

armed[1] (ärmd) *adj.* **1** having an arm or arms. **2** having an arm or arms of a specified kind or number (*used in compounds*): *one-armed, long-armed.*

armed[2] (ärmd) *adj.* having, equipped with, or using weapons: *armed guards.*

armed forces the combined military strength of a nation, including sea, land, and air elements, or navy, army, and air force. Also called **armed services.**

Ar·me·ni·an (är mē′nē ən) *n., adj.* —*n.* **1** a native or inhabitant of Armenia, a former kingdom of SW Asia. **2** the Indo-European language of the Armenians. —*adj.* of or having to do with Armenia, its people, or their language.

arm·ful (ärm′ful′) *n., pl.* **-fuls.** as much as one arm or both arms can hold.

arm·hole (ärm′hōl′) *n.* a hole for the arm in a garment.

Ar·min·i·an (är min′ē ən) *adj., n.* —*adj.* of Arminius, an early Dutch theologian (1560-1609), or his doctrines. —*n.* a believer in Arminian doctrines.

ar·mi·stice (är′mə stis) *n.* a formal agreement between governments to cease hostilities on all fronts; especially, a permanent cessation of hostilities, as a preliminary to a peace treaty. [< NL *armistitium* < L *arma* arms + *sistere* stop, stand]

Armistice Day **1** November 11, the date of the cessation of fighting (1918) in World War I, now called **Remembrance Day.** **2** the anniversary of this date, celebrating also the cessation of fighting in World War II.

arm·let (ärm′lit) *n.* **1** an ornamental band for the upper arm. **2** a small inlet of the sea.

ar·moire (är′mwär′) *n.* a large, usually ornate, wardrobe, closet, or cupboard. [< F *armoire* < OF *armarie* < L *armarium* cabinet, ult. < *arma* weapons]

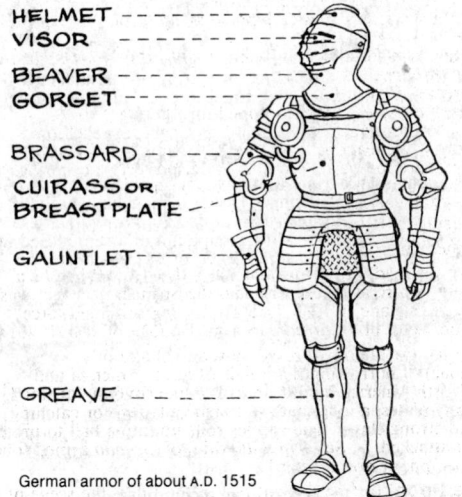

HELMET

VISOR

BEAVER

GORGET

BRASSARD

CUIRASS or
BREASTPLATE

GAUNTLET

GREAVE

German armor of about A.D. 1515

ar·mor or **ar·mour** (är′mər) *n., v.* —*n.* **1** a covering worn to protect the body in fighting. **2** any kind of protective covering. A diver's suit and the scales of a fish are armor. **3** the steel or iron plates or other protective covering of a warship, aircraft, or fortification. **4** the tanks and other armored vehicles of an army. **5** anything that protects or defends: *An informed public opinion is the best armor against propaganda.* —*v.* cover or protect with armor. [ME < OF *armeüre* < L *armatura* < *armare* arm. Doublet of ARMATURE.]

ar·mor·bear·er or **ar·mour·bear·er** (är′mər ber′ər) *n. Historical.* an attendant who carried the armor or weapons of a warrior.

ar·mored or **ar·moured** (är′mərd) *adj.* **1** covered or protected with armor: *an armored train, car, etc.* **2** using tanks, armored cars, etc.: *an armored regiment.*

ar·mor·er or **ar·mour·er** (är′mər ər) *n.* **1** a maker or repairer of armor. **2** a manufacturer of firearms. **3** a man in charge of firearms. The armorer of a warship takes care of the revolvers, pistols, and rifles on the ship.

ar·mo·ri·al (är mô′rē əl) *adj.* having to do with coats of arms or heraldry.

armorial bearings a coat of arms.

ar·mor·ies or **ar·mour·ies** (är′mər ēz′) *n.pl. Cdn.* a building where reserve units of the armed forces have their headquarters and training area.

armor plate or **armour plate** steel or iron plating to protect warships, forts, etc.

ar·mor·y or **ar·mour·y** (är′mər ē) *n., pl.* **-ies.** **1** a place where weapons are kept; arsenal. **2** *U.S.* a place where weapons are made; arsenal. **3** armories.

ar·mour (är′mər) See **armor.**

arm·pit (ärm′pit′) *n.* the hollow under the arm at the shoulder.

arm-twist·ing (ärm′twis′ting) *n.* strong pressure or influence used to get what one wants; forceful persuasion: *It took some arm-twisting, but we finally got him to agree to contribute.*

ar·my (är′mē) *n., pl.* **-mies.** **1** a large, organized group of personnel trained and armed for war, especially on land. **2** Often, **Army,** such a group serving as the land forces of a nation. In Canada, the function of an army is served by Mobile Command of the Canadian Forces. **3** a body organized on military lines: *the Salvation Army.* **4** a very large number; multitude: *an army of ants.* [ME < OF *armee* < L *armata.* Doublet of ARMADA.]

army ant any of various mainly tropical ants (subfamily Dorylinae) that migrate in large groups and devour other insects and small animals in their path.

army cadet a person under military age who is undertaking basic military training oriented in an organization subsidized by the armed forces.

army of occupation an army sent into a defeated country to enforce a treaty, keep order, etc.

army worm **1** the larva of a moth (*Pseudaletia unipuncta*). Army

hat, āge, fär; let, ēqual, tėrm; it, īce
hot, ōpen, ôrder; oil, out; cup, pùt, rüle,
əbove, takən, pencəl, lemən, circəs

ch, child; ng, long; sh, ship
th, thin; ₮ʜ, then; zh, measure

worms travel over the ground in multitudes, eating the vegetation they find in their path, thus often destroying or seriously damaging crops and grasses. **2** any of various other moth larvae that migrate in large numbers.

ar·ni·ca (är′nə kə) *n.* **1** a healing liquid used on bruises, sprains, etc., prepared from the dried flowers, leaves, or roots of a plant of the aster family. **2** the plant itself, which has showy yellow flowers. [< NL]

a·ro·ma (ə rō′mə) *n.* **1** a pleasant, sweet or savory, smell: *the aroma of a cake in the oven.* **2** a distinctive fragrance or flavor; subtle quality. [ME < OF < L < Gk. *arōma* spice]

ar·o·mat·ic (ar′ə mat′ik *or* er′ə-) *adj., n.* —*adj.* having a sweet or spicy smell; fragrant: *The cinnamon tree has an aromatic inner bark.* —*n.* a fragrant plant or substance.

a·rose (ə rōz′) *v.* pt. of **arise:** *She arose from her chair.*

a·round (ə round′) *prep., adv.* —*prep.* **1** in a circle about: *to travel around the world.* **2** closely surrounding: *She had a coat around her shoulders.* **3** on all sides of: *Woods lay around the house.* **4** *Informal.* here and there in: *He leaves his books around the house.* **5** *Informal.* somewhere near: *to play around the house.* **6** *Informal.* approximately; near in amount, number, etc. to: *That hat cost around five dollars.* **7** on the far side of: *just around the corner.* —*adv.* **1** in a circle. **2** in circumference: *The tree measures two metres around.* **3** on all sides: *A dense fog lay around.* **4** here and there: *We walked around to see the town.* **5** *Informal.* somewhere near: *Wait around awhile.* **6** in the opposite direction: *Turn around! You are going the wrong way.*
☞ *Usage.* See note at **round.**

a·rous·al (ə rou′zəl) *n.* the action of arousing or the state of being aroused.

a·rouse (ə rouz′) *v.* **a·roused, a·rous·ing.** **1** awaken. **2** stir to action; excite; stimulate. —**a·rous′er,** *n.*

ar·peg·gio (är pej′ē ō *or* är pej′ō) *n., pl.* **-gios.** *Music.* **1** the sounding of the notes of a chord in rapid succession instead of together. **2** a chord sounded in this way. [< Ital. *arpeggio* < *arpa* harp < Gmc.]

ar·pent (är′pənt; *French,* är pän′) *n. Cdn. Historical.* **1** an old French measure of land area, formerly used in Canada, equal to about 3400 square metres. An arpent contained 100 square perches. **2** a measure of length, equal to about 58 metres. [< F]

ar·que·bus (är′kwə bəs) *n.* harquebus.

arr. **1** arrange; arranged; arrangements. **2** arrival; arrive; arrived.

ar·rack (ar′ək *or* ə rak′) *n.* an alcoholic drink distilled from the sap of the coconut palm or from rice, sugar cane, etc. [< Arabic *'araq* liquor, sweet juice]

ar·raign (ə rān′) *v.* **1** *Law.* bring before a court for trial: *The tramp was arraigned on a charge of stealing.* **2** call in question; find fault with. [ME < AF *arainer* < VL < L *ad-* to + *ratio, -onis* account] —**ar·raign′er,** *n.*

ar·raign·ment (ə rān′mənt) *n.* **1** *Law.* the process of reading out the charge or charges to an accused person in court and asking the person how he pleads. **2** unfavorable criticism.

ar·range (ə rānj′) *v.* **-ranged, -rang·ing.** **1** put in the proper order: *The army is arranged for battle.* **2** settle (a dispute). **3** come to an agreement. **4** plan; prepare: *Can you arrange to meet me this evening?* **5** *Music.* adapt (a composition) to voices or instruments for which it was not written. [ME < OF *arangier* < *a-* to + *rang* rank¹ < Gmc.] —**ar·rang′er,** *n.*

ar·range·ment (ə rānj′mənt) *n.* **1** a putting or being in proper order. **2** a way or order in which things or persons are put: *You can make six arrangements of the letters A, B, and C.* **3** an adjustment; settlement. **4** Usually, **arrangements,** *pl.* a plan; preparation: *to make arrangements for a journey.* **5** something made by arranging separate parts or things in a particular way: *an unusual flower arrangement.* **6** *Music.* **a** an adaptation of a composition to voices or instruments for which it was not written. **b** a composition so adapted.

ar·rant (ar′ənt *or* er′ənt) *adj.* extreme; thoroughgoing; downright: *He was such an arrant liar that nobody ever believed him.* [var. of *errant*]

ar·ras (ar′əs *or* e′rəs) *n.* **1** a kind of tapestry. **2** a curtain or hangings of tapestry. [from *Arras,* a city in France]

ar·ray (ə rā′) *n., v.* —*n.* **1** order: *The troops were formed in battle array.* **2** a display of persons or things: *The array of good players on the other team made our side lose confidence.* **3** military force; soldiers. **4** clothes; dress: *bridal array.* **5** *Law.* the list of jurors summoned for a trial.
—*v.* **1** arrange in order: *The general arrayed his troops for the battle.* **2** dress in fine clothes; adorn. [ME < OF *a* to (< L *ad*) + *rei* order < Gmc.]

ar·rear·age (ə rēr′ij) *n.* debts; arrears.

ar·rears (ə rērz′) *n. pl.* **1** money due but not paid; debts. **2** unfinished work; things not done on time.
in arrears, behind in payments, work, etc. [ME < OF *arere* < LL *ad retro* to the rear]

ar·rest (ə rest′) *v., n.* —*v.* **1** seize a person or persons by legal authority; take to jail or court. **2** stop; check: *Filling a tooth arrests decay.* **3** catch and hold.
—*n.* **1** the seizing of a person or persons for the purpose of laying a criminal charge. **2** a stopping; checking.
under arrest, held by the police.
[ME < OF *arester* < VL *adrestare* < L *ad-* + *re-* back + *stare* stand] —**ar·rest′er,** *n.*
☛ *Syn. v.* **2.** See note at **stop.**

ar·rest·ing (ə rest′ing) *adj.* catching the attention; striking: *She is not beautiful, but she has arresting eyes.*

ar·ris (ar′is *or* er′is) *n. Architecture.* **1** a sharp edge formed by two straight or curved surfaces meeting at an angle. **2** a sharp ridge. A Doric column has arrises. [< OF *arest* < L *arista* ear of corn, fishbone]

ar·riv·al (ə rī′vəl) *n.* **1** the act of arriving; coming. **2** a person or thing that arrives.

ar·rive (ə rīv′) *v.* **-rived, -riv·ing. 1** reach the end of a journey; come to a place: *We arrived at noon.* **2** each (*used with* **at**): *You must arrive at a decision soon.* **3** come; occur: *The time has arrived for you to study.* **4** be successful. [ME < OF *ar(r)iver* < VL < L *ad ripam* to the shore]
☛ *Syn.* **2.** See note at **come.**
☛ *Usage.* Arrive is generally followed by *at,* especially when the place reached is only a temporary stopping point: *We arrived at the bridge. The train arrived at Winnipeg. He has not yet arrived at a decision.* But *arrive in* is used before the names of countries and, sometimes, cities or towns. *We arrived in Kingston a week ago.* In informal English, **arrive** is now often used without any preposition before the name of a city or town: *The flight arrived Saint John two hours late.*

ar·ro·gance (ar′ə gəns *or* er′ə gəns) *n.* too great pride; haughtiness.

ar·ro·gant (ar′ə gənt *or* er′ə gənt) *adj.* too proud; haughty. [ME < OF < L *arrogans, -antis,* ppr. of *arrogare* < *ad-* to + *rogare* ask] —**ar′ro·gant·ly,** *adv.*
☛ *Syn.* See note at **haughty.**

ar·ro·gate (ar′ə gāt′ *or* er′ə gāt′) *v.* **-gat·ed, -gat·ing. 1** claim or take without right: *The despotic king arrogated to himself the power that belonged to the nobles.* **2** claim for another without good reasons: *People are only too ready to arrogate dishonesty to a politician.* [< L *arrogare* < *ad-* to + *rogare* ask]

ar·ro·ga·tion (ar′ə gā′shən *or* er′ə gā′shən) *n.* the act of arrogating.

ar·ron·disse·ment (ä rôn dēs mäN′) *n., pl.* **-ments** (-mäN′). *French.* in France, the largest administrative subdivision of a department.

ar·row (ar′ō *or* er′ō) *n., v.* —*n.* **1** a slender shaft or stick designed to be shot from a bow, having a pointed tip, usually barbed, and feathers at the tail end. **2** anything resembling an arrow in shape or speed. **3** a sign (→) used to show direction or position in maps, on road signs, and in writing.
—*v.* **1** indicate with an arrow: *The main points are arrowed in the margin.* **2** move swiftly like an arrow: *Jet planes arrowed through the sky.* [OE *arwe*] —**ar′row·like′,** *adj.*

ar·row·head (ar′ō hed′ *or* er′ō-) *n.* **1** the head or tip of an arrow, especially a separately made piece of stone or metal. **2** any of a genus (*Sagittaria*) of water or marsh plants found mainly in temperate and tropical regions of the western hemisphere, typically having arrowhead-shaped leaves.

ar·row·root (ar′ō rüt′ *or* er′ō-) *n.* **1** a West Indian plant (*Maranta arundinacea*) having rhizomes that yield an easily digested starch. **2** the starch obtained from this plant. **3** any of various other plants having rhizomes or roots that yield starch.

ar·row·wood or **ar·row-wood** (ar′ō wůd′ *or* er′ō-) *n.* **1** a viburnum (*Viburnum dentatum*) of E North America having coarsely toothed, rounded or oval leaves and flat clusters of white flowers followed by bluish-black fruits. **2** any of various related or

similar shrubs having straight, tough, pliant branches formerly much used for making arrows.

ar·row·y (ar′ō ē *or* er′ō ē) *adj.* **1** of arrows. **2** like an arrow in shape or speed.

ar·roy·o (ə roi′ō) *n., pl.* **-roy·os. 1** the dry bed of a stream; gully. **2** a small river. [< Sp.]

arse (ärs) *n. Vulgar slang.* **1** buttocks. **2** anus. [OE *ears, ærs*]

ar·se·nal (är′sə nəl) *n.* a building for storing or manufacturing weapons and ammunition for the armed forces. [< Ital. *arsenale* < Arabic *dar accina′ah* house (of) the manufacturing]

ar·se·nate (är′sə nāt′ *or* är′sə nit) *n.* a salt of arsenic acid.
Arsenate of lead is a poison that is used to kill insects.

ar·se·nic (*n.* är′sə nik′; *adj.* är′sə nik′ *or* är sen′ik) *n., adj.* —*n.* **1** a greyish-white chemical element, having a metallic lustre and volatilizing when heated. *Symbol*: As; *at.no.* 33; *at.wt.* 74.9216. **2** a violently poisonous, tasteless, white compound of arsenic, used in industry and in medicine. *Formula*: As_2O_3 or As_3O_6 —*adj.* of or containing arsenic. [< L *arsenicum* < Gk. *arsenikon* < Hebrew < Old Persian **zarnika-* golden]

arsenic acid a colorless crystalline compound. *Formula*: H_3AsO_4

ar·sen·i·cal (är sen′ə kəl) *adj.* arsenious.

ar·se·ni·ous (är sē′nē əs) *adj.* **1** of arsenic. **2** containing arsenic.

ar·son (är′sən) *n.* the criminal offence of intentionally setting fire to a building or other property belonging to someone else, or to one's own insured property in order to collect insurance. [< OF < LL *arsio, -onis* a burning < L *ardere* burn]

ar·son·ist (är′sən ist′) *n.* a person who commits arson.

art¹ (ärt) *n.* **1** any form of human activity that is the product of imagination and skill and that appeals mainly to the imagination; especially, drawing, painting, and sculpture, and also architecture, poetry, music, dancing, etc. **2** works produced by such activity: *a museum of art.* **3** (*adj.*) of, for, or having to do with art or artists: *an art gallery.* **4** (*adj.*) having or showing the techniques or characteristics of art: *an art film.* **5** a branch or division of learning dealing mainly with human ideas and values and the development of the intellect, such as literature, philosophy, and history; one of the humanities. **6 arts,** *pl.* in universities, a group of studies that includes literature, languages, history, philosophy, etc. and that excludes the sciences and technical or professional studies. **7 the arts,** *pl.* fine arts: *The arts flourished in Elizabethan England.* **8** *Archaic.* learning or scholarship in general. **9** a craft or trade that requires skill and imagination: *the household arts of cooking and sewing, the weaver's art.* Writing compositions is an art. **10** a particular skill or set of working principles: *the art of making friends, the art of war. There is an art to organizing your work area.* **11** human skill or effort, as opposed to nature: *It was a well-kept, formal garden that owed more to art than to nature.* **12** artwork. **13** cunning; artfulness: *He swore he used no art to persuade them.* **14** Usually, **arts,** *pl.* cunning or skilful plans or tricks: *using arts and wiles to get one's way.* [ME < OF < L *ars, artis*]

art² (ärt) *v. Archaic or poetic.* 2nd pers. sing., present indicative, of **be.** *Thou art* means *you* (sing.) *are.* [OE *eart*]

art. **1** article. **2** artillery. **3** artist. **4** artificial.

-art *noun-forming suffix.* See **-ard.**

ARTC or **A.R.T.C.** Air Route Traffic Control.

ar·te·fact (är′tə fakt′) See **artifact.**

Ar·te·mis (är′tə mis) *n. Greek mythology.* the goddess of the hunt, and of the forests, wild animals, and the moon. She corresponds to the Roman goddess Diana.

ar·te·ri·al (är tēr′ē əl) *adj.* **1** *Anatomy.* having to do with or resembling the arteries. **2** *Physiology.* having to do with the bright-red blood of the arteries. **3** serving as a major route of transportation, supply, etc.: *an arterial highway.* **4** having a main channel with many branches.

ar·te·ri·o·scle·ro·sis (är tēr′ē ō sklə rō′sis) *n.* a hardening and thickening of the walls of the arteries. It makes circulation of the blood difficult.

ar·te·ri·o·scle·rot·ic (är tēr′ē ō sklə rot′ik) *adj., n.* —*adj.* of, having to do with, or afflicted with arteriosclerosis. —*n.* a person afflicted with arteriosclerosis.

ar·ter·y (är′tər ē) *n., pl.* **-ter·ies. 1** *Anatomy.* any of the blood vessels or tubes that carry blood from the heart to all parts of the body. **2** a main road; an important channel: *Yonge Street is one of the main arteries of Toronto.* [ME < L *arteria* < Gk.]

ar·te·sian well (är tē′zhən) a deep-drilled well, especially one from which water gushes up without pumping. [< F *artésien* of Artois, and old French province where such wells were first made]

art·ful (ärt′fəl) *adj.* **1** crafty; deceitful: *A swindler uses artful tricks to get money out of people.* **2** skilful; clever. **3** artificial.
—**art′ful·ly,** *adv.* —**art′ful·ness,** *n.*

ar·thrit·ic (är thrit′ik) *adj.* of, caused by, or affected with arthritis: *arthritic pain, arthritic joints.*

ar·thri·tis (är thrī′tis) *n. Medicine.* an inflammation of a joint or joints. [< L < Gk. *arthritis* < *arthron* joint]

ar·thro·plas·ty (är′thrə plas′tē) *n.* **1** the making of an artificial joint to replace a natural one. **2** surgery performed on a joint. [< Gk. *arthron* joint + *plastos* moulded]

ar·thro·pod (är′thrə pod′) *n.* any animal belonging to the phylum **Arthropoda**, a large group of invertebrate animals having a segmented body and legs, including insects, spiders, mites, scorpions, and crustaceans. Arthropods range in size from tiny mites only 0.1 mm long to a giant crab having a leg span of 3.4 m; they make up about three quarters of all the known species of animals on earth. [< *arthro-* joint (< Gk. *arthron*) + Gk. *pous, podos* foot]

Ar·thur (är′thər) *n. Medieval legend.* a king of ancient Britain who gathered about him a company of famous knights, who sat at a Round Table so that all would have equal rank. The real Arthur was a British chieftain or general of the 5th or 6th century A.D.

Ar·thu·ri·an (är thür′ē ən *or* är thyür′ē ən) *adj.* of or having to do with King Arthur and his knights.

ar·ti·choke (är′tə chōk′) *n.* **1** a plant (*Cynara scolymus*) of the composite family native to Europe and Asia, widely cultivated for its large flower heads having many fleshy bracts which are eaten as a vegetable. **2** the unopened flower head of this plant. **3** Jerusalem artichoke. [< Ital. *articiocco* < Provençal < Arabic *alkharshuf*]

ar·ti·cle (är′tə kəl) *n., v.* **-cled, -cling.** —*n.* **1** a literary composition, complete in itself, but forming part of a magazine, newspaper, or book: *an article on gardening in a newspaper.* **2** a clause in a contract, treaty, statute, etc.: *the third article of the club's constitution deals with fees.* **3** a particular thing; item: *Bread is a main article of food.* **4** one of the words *a, an* or *the* or the corresponding words in certain other languages. *A(n)* is the **indefinite article;** *the* is the **definite article.**
—*v.* **1** bind by a contract: *The apprentice was articled to serve the master craftsman for seven years.* **2** bring charges; accuse. [ME < OF < L *articulus,* dim. of *artus* joint]

Articles of Confederation *U.S.* the constitution adopted by the thirteen original states of the United States in 1781. It was replaced by the present Constitution in 1789.

ar·tic·u·lar (är tik′yə lər) *adj.* of the joints: *Arthritis is an articular disease.*

ar·tic·u·late (*adj.* är tik′yə lit; *v.* är tik′yə lāt′) *adj., v.* **-lat·ed, -lat·ing.** —*adj.* **1** uttered in distinct syllables of words: *A baby cries and gurgles, but does not use articulate speech.* **2** able to put one's thoughts into words: *Julia is the most articulate of the sisters.* **3** made up of distinct parts; distinct. **4** jointed; segmented.
—*v.* **1** speak distinctly: *Be careful to articulate your words so that everyone in the room can understand you.* **2** unite by joints. **3** fit together in a joint: *After his knee was injured, he was lame because the bones did not articulate well.* **4** form or join together in a system, sequence, etc.: *An articulated English program is being introduced in all schools.* [< L *articulatus,* pp. of *articulare* divide into single joints < *articulus.* See ARTICLE.] —**ar·tic′u·late·ly,** *adv.* —**ar·tic′u·la·tor,** *n.*

ar·tic·u·la·tion (är tik′yə lā′shən) *n.* **1** a way of speaking; enunciation. **2** a joint. **3** *Anatomy.* the act or manner of connecting by a joint or joints: *the articulation of the bones.* **4** the act or process of forming or joining together in a system, sequence, etc.: *the articulation of all manufacturing processes in the plant.*

ar·ti·fact *or* **ar·te·fact** (är′tə fakt′) *n.* anything made by human skill or work; an aritifical product. [< L *ars, artis* art + *factus* made]

ar·ti·fice (är′tə fis) *n.* **1** a clever device; trick: *She will use any artifice to get her way.* **2** trickery; craft: *His conduct is free from artifice.* **3** skill; cleverness. [< F < L *artificium* < *ars, artis* art + *facere* make]
☛ *Syn.* **1.** See note at **stratagem.**

ar·tif·i·cer (är tif′ə sər) *n.* **1** a skilled workman; craftsman. **2** a maker; inventor.

ar·ti·fi·cial (är′tə fish′əl) *adj.* **1** made by human skill or labor; not natural: *When you read at night, you read by artificial light.* **2** made as a substitute for or in imitation of; not real: *artificial flowers, artificial silk.* **3** assumed; false; affected: *an artificial tone of voice, an artificial manner.* **4** of plants, not native or growing naturally in a place; cultivated. [< L *artificialis*] —**ar′ti·fi′cial·ly,** *adv.* —**ar′ti·fi′cial·ness,** *n.*
☛ *Syn.* **1. Artificial, synthetic** = not natural. **Artificial** describes things which are made by human skill and labor, in contrast to those produced in nature, but which often correspond to natural things: *You can get burned by the artificial light of a sun lamp.* **Synthetic** describes things which are put together in a laboratory by chemical combination or treatment of natural substances, and which often serve as substitutes for natural products: *Nylon is a synthetic fabric.*

hat, āge, fär; let, ēqual, tèrm; it, īce
hot, ōpen, ôrder; oil, out; cup, put, rüle,
əbove, takən, pencəl, lemən, circəs
ch, child; ng, long; sh, ship
th, thin; ŦH, then; zh, measure

ar·ti·fi·ci·al·i·ty (är′tə fish′ē al′ə tē) *n., pl.* **-ties. 1** an artificial quality or condition. **2** something unnatural or unreal.

artificial respiration the process of restoring the breathing of a person by rhythmically forcing air into and out of his lungs, as by breathing directly into the mouth or alternately applying and releasing pressure on the diaphragm.

ar·ti·gi *or* **ar·tig·gi** (är′tə gē *or* är tē′gē) *n. Cdn.* atigi.

ar·til·ler·y (är til′ər ē) *n.* **1** mounted guns; cannon. **2** the part of an army that uses and manages big guns. **3** the science of firing, and co-ordinating the firing of, guns of larger calibre than machine guns. [ME < OF *artillerie* < *artiller* equip]

ar·til·ler·y·man (är til′ər ē mən) *n., pl.* **-men.** a soldier who belongs to the artillery; gunner.

ar·ti·san (är′tə zən *or* är′tə zan′) *n.* a workman skilled in some industry or trade; craftsman. [< F < Ital. *artigiano* < L *ars, artis* art]
☛ *Syn.* See note at **artist.**

art·ist (är′tist) *n.* **1** a person who draws or paints pictures, especially one who does so as a profession. **2** a person skilled in any of the fine arts, such as sculpture, music, or literature. **3** a person who does work with skill and good taste. **4** an actor, singer, musician, etc; artiste. [< F < Ital. *artista* < VL < L *ars, artis* art]
☛ *Syn.* **3. Artist, artisan** = a person who does work with skill. **Artist** emphasizes use of taste, imagination, and creative ability in addition to skill, and usually applies to a person working in the fine arts: *Her creative interpretation makes that dancer an artist.* **Artisan** emphasizes skill, and usually applies to a person working in the manual or industrial arts: *Factories want artisans in all departments.*

ar·tiste (är tēst′) *n.* a very skilful performer or worker. An artiste may be a singer, a dancer, or a cook. [< F]

ar·tis·tic (är tis′tik) *adj.* **1** of, having to do with, or characteristic of art or artists: *The artistic imagination.* **2** done or made with skill, imagination, and good taste: *an artistic design, an artistic presentation.* **3** having skill in art or an appreciation of art: *She is very artistic.*

ar·tis·ti·cal·ly (är tis′tik lē) *adv.* **1** with skill and good taste. **2** from an artistic point of view.

art·ist·ry (är′tis trē) *n., pl.* **-ries.** artistic work; workmanship of an artist.

art·less (ärt′lis) *adj.* **1** not artificial or studied; natural and uncontrived: *She walked with artless grace. Small children ask many artless questions.* **2** without guile or deceit; sincere; innocent: *artless flattery, an artless youth.* **3** lacking knowledge or skill; crude, uncultured, or clumsy. —**art′less·ly,** *adv.* —**art′less·ness,** *n.*

art·sy-craft·sy (ärt′sē kraft′sē) *adj.* of or having to do with an art or craft, especially when made, done, or working in a fussy, faddish, or superficial way.

art·work (ärt′wèrk′) *n.* pictures and other decorative or illustrative material in a magazine, book, etc.: *That magazine always has excellent artwork.*

art·y (är′tē) *adj.* **art·i·er, art·i·est.** *Informal.* making a pretence or show of being artistic. —**art′i·ness,** *n.*

Arty. artillery.

ar·um (er′əm) *n.* **1** of a genus (*Arum*) of Old World plants having small flowers densely clustered on an upright fleshy part called a spadix which is more or less enclosed by a leafy part called a spathe. **2** any of various other plants of the same family, such as the **water arum** or **wild calla** (*Calla palustris*), a common Canadian marsh plant having a greenish-white spathe surrounding a yellow spadix. **3** (*adj.*) designating the family (Araceae) of plants that includes the arums and other plants, such as the jack-in-the-pulpit, sweet flag, and skunk cabbage. [< L < Gk. *aron*]

-ary *suffix.* **1** a place for ——, as in *infirmary, library.* **2** a collection of ——, as in *dictionary, statuary.* **3** a person or thing that is, does, belongs to, etc. ——, as in *adversary, boundary, commentary.* **4** of or having to do with ——, as in *legendary, missionary.* **5** being; having the nature of ——, as in *secondary, supplementary.* **6** characterized by ——, as in *customary, honorary.* [< L *-arius* or (neut.) *-arium*]

Ar·y·an (ar′ē ən, er′ē ən, ar′yən *or* er′yən) *adj., n.* —*adj.* **1** of, having to do with, or designating the Indo-European family of languages or the hypothetical language from which they developed. **2** of or having to do with a hypothetical prehistoric people who

spoke this original language, or any of their supposed descendants.
3 of or having to do with the Indo-Iranian languages or the peoples
who speak them.
—*n.* **1** a member of the hypothetical prehistoric people who spoke
the Aryan language, or any of their supposed descendants. **2** a
member of any of the peoples speaking Indo-European languages.
3 in Nazi use, a non-Jewish person of European descent, especially
the so-called Nordic type. **4** the hypothetical parent language of the
Indo-European languages. [< Skt. *arya* noble]

as¹ (əz; *stressed*, az) *adv., conj., prep., pron.* —*adv.* **1** to the same
degree or extent; equally: *as black as coal.* **2** for example: *Some
animals, as dogs and cats, eat meat.*
—*conj.* **1** to the same degree or extent that: *She worked just so
much as she was told to.* **2** in the same way that: *Run as I do.*
3 during the time that; when; while: *She sang as she worked.*
4 because: *As he was a skilled worker, he received good wages.*
5 though: *Brave as they were, the danger made them afraid.* **6** that
the result was: *The child so marked the picture as to spoil it.*
as for, about; concerning; referring to: *We're leaving now; as for
Sonia, she'll have to come on her own.*
as from, as of.
as good as, practically; almost: *He looks as good as dead.*
as if, as it would be if: *The car looked as if it had been driven on
rough roads.*
as is, *Informal.* in the present condition: *If you buy the car as is,
you will have to put it in running order yourself.*
as it were, so to speak.
as of, beginning or on; dating from: *As of April 30, we will be on
daylight-saving time.*
as though, as it would be if.
as to, **a** about; concerning; referring to: *We have no information as
to the cause of the riot.* **b** according to: *The scarves were grouped
as to color.*
as well, also; besides.
as well as, in addition to.
as yet, up to this time; so far: *Nothing has been done as yet.*
—*prep.* in the character of; doing the work of: *Who will act as
teacher.*
—*pron.* **1** a condition or fact that: *She is very careful, as her work
shows.* **2** that: *Do the same thing as I do.* [OE (unstressed) *ealswā*
quite so. Cf. ALSO.]
☛ *Syn. conj.* **4.** See note at **because**.
☛ *Usage.* **As to** is often a clumsy substitute for a single preposition, usually
about or *of*. *Practice usually proves the best teacher as to* (in, for, of) *the use
of organ stops.*
☛ *Usage.* See note at **like¹**.

as² (as) *n., pl.* **as·ses** (as'iz). **1** an ancient Roman unit for
measuring mass, equal to about 328 grams. **2** the standard unit of
money in ancient Rome. **3** a bronze or copper coin worth one as. [<
L]

as— *prefix.* the form of **ad-** before *s*, as in *assist.*

As **1** arsenic. **2** altostratus.

AS or **A.S.** Anglo-Saxon.

as·a·fet·i·da or **as·a·foet·i·da** (as'ə fet'ə də *or* as'ə fĕ'tə də)
n. a gum resin with a garliclike odor, used in medicine and cooking.
Also, **assafetida, assafoetida.** [< Med.L *asafetida* < *asa* mastic (<
Persian *azā*) + L *fetidus* stinking]

as·bes·tos (as bes'təs *or* az bes'təs) *n.* **1** a mineral, a silicate of
calcium and magnesium, that does not burn or conduct heat, usually
occurring in fibres. **2** a fireproof fabric made of these fibres. [ME <
OF < L < Gk. *asbestos* unquenchable (originally, of quicklime) <
a- not + *sbennunai* quench]

as·bes·to·sis (as'bes tō'sis) *n.* a disease of the lungs caused by
the inhalation of asbestos dust and fibres over a period of time.

as·cend (ə send') *v.* **1** go up; rise; move upward: *He watched the
airplane ascend higher and higher.* **2** climb; go to or toward the top
of: *Another expedition is planning to ascend Mt. Everest.* **3** *Music.*
rise in pitch.
ascend the throne, become king, queen, etc. [ME < L *ascendere* <
ad- up + *scandere* climb]
☛ *Syn.* **2.** See note at **climb**.

as·cend·ance (ə sen'dəns) *n.* ascendancy. Also, **ascendence.**

as·cend·an·cy (ə sen'dən sē) *n.* a controlling influence;
domination; rule. Also, **ascendency.**

as·cend·ant (ə sen'dənt) *adj., n.* —*adj.* **1** ascending; rising.
2 superior; dominant; ruling; controlling. —*n.* **1** a position of power;
controlling influence. **2** *Astrology.* the sign of the zodiac rising
above the horizon at a certain time. **b** horoscope. Also, **ascendent.**
in the ascendant, **a** supreme; dominant. **b** increasing in influence.

as·cend·ency (ə sen'dən sē) See **ascendancy**.

as·cend·ent (ə sen'dənt) See **ascendant**.

as·cend·er (ə sen'dər) *n.* **1** a person or thing that ascends.
2 *Printing.* **a** the upper part of a lower-case letter, such as b, d, h,
or k. **b** any such letter.

ascend·ing (ə sen'ding) *adj.* **1** rising or sloping upwards;
mounting. **2** *Botany.* rising or gradually curving upwards to a
vertical position.

as·cen·sion (ə sen'shən) *n.* **1** the act of ascending; ascent.
2 Ascension, a the bodily passing of Christ from earth to heaven.
b Also, **Ascension Day.** a Christian church festival in honor of this on
the fortieth day after Easter. [< L *ascensio, -onis* < *ascendere*. See
ASCEND.]

as·cent (ə sent') *n.* **1** the act of going up; rising. **2** the act of
climbing. **3** a place or way that slopes up. [< *ascend*; modelled after
descent]

as·cer·tain (as'ər tān') *v.* find out; determine. [ME < OF
acertener < *a-* to + *certain* certain < L *certus* sure]
—**as'cer·tain'a·ble,** *adj.* —**as'cer·tain'a·bly,** *adv.*

as·cer·tain·ment (as'ər tān'mənt) *n.* ascertaining.

as·cet·ic (ə set'ik) *n., adj.* —*n.* **1** a person who practises unusual
self-denial and devotion, or severe discipline of self for religious
reasons. **2** a person who refrains from pleasures and comforts.
—*adj.* refraining from pleasures and comforts; self-denying. [< Gk.
askētikos < *askeein* exercise; hence, discipline] —**as·cet'i·cal·ly,**
adv.

as·cet·i·cism (ə set'ə siz'əm) *n.* **1** the life or habits of an
ascetic. **2** the doctrine that by abstinence and self-denial a person
can train himself to be in conformity with God's will.

as·cid·i·an (ə sid'ē ən) *n.* sea squirt.

as·cid·i·um (ə sid'ē əm) *n., pl.* **-cid·i·a** (-sid'ē ə). *Botany.* a
baglike or pitcherlike part of a plant. [< NL < Gk. *askidion*, dim of
askos bag]

as·co·my·cete (as'kō mī sēt') *n.* any of a class (Ascomycetes)
of fungi that includes yeasts, moulds, truffles, and mildews. [< Gk.
askos bag + *mykēs, mykētos* fungus]

a·scor·bic acid (ə skôr'bik *or a* skôr'bik) vitamin C. *Formula:*
$C_6H_8O_6$ [< *a-⁴* + *scorb*utic]

as·cot (as'kət *or* as'kot) *n.* a neck scarf with broad ends that is
worn turned over in a loose single knot at the throat, with the ends
laid one over the other. It is usually worn inside the collar. [from
Ascot, famous English race track]

as·cribe (əs krīb') *v.* **-cribed, -crib·ing.** **1** assign; attribute: *The
police ascribed the automobile accident to fast driving.* **2** consider
as belonging: *Men have ascribed their own characteristics to their
gods.* [ME < OF < L *ascribere* < *ad-* to + *scribere* write]
☛ *Syn.* **1.** See note at **attribute**.

as·crip·tion (əs krip'shən) *n.* **1** the act of ascribing: *the
ascription of selfishness to a miser.* **2** a statement or words
ascribing something. [< L *ascriptio, -onis* < *ascribere*. See ASCRIBE.]

a·sep·sis (ə sep'sis *or* ā sep'sis) *n.* **1** an aseptic condition.
2 aseptic methods or treatment.

a·sep·tic (ə sep'tik *or* ā sep'tik) *adj.* free from germs causing
infection. —**a·sep'ti·cal·ly,** *adv.*

a·sex·u·al (ā sek'shü əl) *adj. Biology.* **1** having no sex.
2 independent of sexual processes. In the liverworts and mosses,
and in some of the lower animals, sexual and asexual reproduction
alternate. —**a·sex'u·al·ly,** *adv.*

As·gard (as'gärd, az'gärd, *or* ās'gärd) *n.* the home of the Norse
gods and heroes.

ash¹ (ash) *n.* **1** what remains of a thing after it has been
thoroughly burned or oxidized by chemical means: *There was a
cigarette ash on the carpet. We cleaned the ashes out of the
fireplace.* **2 ashes,** *pl.* **a** ruins: *a whole city laid in ashes.* **b** the
remains of a dead person: *He was buried beside the ashes of his
forefathers.* **3** the light-grey color of ashes from wood. **4** fine
particles of lava from an erupting volcano. **5** (*adj.*) like ash in color,
etc. [OE *æsce*]

ash² (ash) *n.* **1** any of a genus (*Fraxinus*) of trees of the olive
family found in the northern hemisphere, having compound leaves
and greyish twigs. **2** the tough, straight-grained wood of an ash,
valued especially for making tool handles, etc. **3** see **mountain ash.**
[OE *æsc*]

a·shamed (ə shāmd') *adj.* **1** feeling shame; disturbed or
uncomfortable because one has done something wrong, improper,
or silly: *I was ashamed when I cried at the movies. He was
ashamed of his dishonesty.* **2** unwilling because of shame: *He was
ashamed to tell his parents that he had failed.*
☛ *Syn.* **1. Ashamed, humiliated, mortified** = feeling embarrassed and disgraced.
Ashamed emphasizes a feeling of having disgraced oneself by doing something
wrong, improper, or foolish: *I was ashamed when I cried at the movies.*
Humiliated emphasizes a painful feeling of being lowered and shamed in the
eyes of others: *Parents are humiliated if their children behave badly when
guests are present.* **Mortified** = feeling greatly embarrassed and humiliated,
sometimes ashamed: *He was mortified when he forgot his speech.*

A·shan·ti (ə shan′tē *or* ə shän′tē) *n., pl.* **-ti** *or* **-tis;** *adj.* —*n.* **1** the native people of the Ashanti region of Ghana. **2** a native of this region. **3** the language of its people.
—*adj.* of or having to do with the Ashanti region or its people.

ash·can (ash′kan′) *n.* any receptacle, such as a barrel, drum, or large can, for holding rubbish, garbage, ashes, etc.

ash·en[1] (ash′ən) *adj.* **1** like ashes; pale as ashes. **2** of ashes.

ash·en[2] (ash′ən) *adj.* **1** of the ash tree. **2** made from the wood of the ash tree.

Ash·ke·naz·ic (ash′kə naz′ik *or* äsh′kə nä′zik) *adj.* of, having to do with, or descended from the Ashkenazim.

Ash·ke·naz·im (ash′kə naz′im *or* äsh′kə nä′zim) *n.pl.* the Jews of central and eastern Europe, distinguished from the Spanish and Portuguese Jews, who are called the Sephardim. The Yiddish language developed among the Ashkenazim.

ash·lar *or* **ash·ler** (ash′lər) *n.* **1** a square stone used in building. **2** masonry composed of ashlars. [ME < OF *aisselier* < VL *axillarium* < *axis* plank]

a·shore (ə shôr′) *adv. or adj.* **1** to the shore; to land. **2** on the shore; on land.

Ash·to·reth (ash′tə reth′) *n.* Astarte. Also, **Ashtaroth.**

ash·tray (ash′trā′) *n.* a small receptacle to put tobacco ashes in.

Ash Wednesday the first day of Lent; the seventh Wednesday before Easter.

ash·y (ash′ē) *adj.* **ash·i·er, ash·i·est. 1** of or covered with ashes. **2** very pale; ashen.

A·sian (ā′zhən *or* ā′shən) *adj., n.* —*adj.* **1** of, having to do with, or characteristic of Asia or its people. **2** referring to the Asiatic race. —*n.* **1** a native or inhabitant of Asia. **2** a person whose recent ancestors come from Asia. **3** a member of the Asiatic.

Asian flu a kind of influenza, first identified in Hong Kong in 1957.

A·si·at·ic (ā′zhē at′ik *or* ā′shē at′ik) *adj., n.* —*adj.* **1** of or designating a major race of mankind that includes the traditional inhabitants of most of eastern Asia, Japan, Taiwan, the Philippines, and Indonesia, and usually, the Inuit of North America, Greenland, and Siberia. They are distinguished by a combination of biological characteristics, including straight, dark hair, light brown skin, and an inner fold in the upper eyelid. **2** Asian. —*n.* **1** a member of the Asiatic race. **2** Asian.

Asiatic cholera cholera.

a·side (ə sīd′) *adv., n.* —*adv.* **1** on or to one side: *Move the table aside. John spoke aside to Tom without our hearing him.* **2** out of one's thoughts, consideration, etc.: *Put your troubles aside.*
aside from, a apart from. **b** *Informal.* except for. —*n.* words meant not to be heard by someone; especially in the theatre, an actor's remark that is meant to be heard by the audience but not by the other characters in the play.

as·i·nine (as′ə nīn′) *adj.* **1** of asses. **2** like an ass. **3** stupid; silly. [< L *asininus* < *asinus* ass] —**as′i·nine·ly,** *adv.*

as·i·nin·i·ty (as′ə nin′ə tē) *n., pl.* **-ties.** silliness.

ask (ask) *v.* **1** try to find out by words; inquire: *Why don't you ask? She asked about our health. Ask the way.* **2** seek the answer to: *Ask any questions you wish.* **3** put a question to; inquire of: *Ask him how old he is.* **4** try to get by words; request: *Ask Kate to sing.* **5** claim; demand: *to ask too high a price for a house.* **6** invite: *She asked ten guests to the party.* **7** need; require: *This job asks hard work.*
ask for it, *Informal.* ask for trouble. [OE *āscian*]
☛ *Syn.* **1. ask, inquire** = try to find out by a question. **Ask** is the general word meaning to seek information from someone: *Joe asked about you.* **Ask** someone where that street is. **Inquire** is more formal, but suggests more strongly going into a subject, asking in an effort to get definite information: *He inquired about you, wanted to know when you were leaving. You had better inquire how to get there.*
☛ *Syn.* **4. Ask, request** (def. 1), **solicit** (def. 1). **Ask** is the general word: *I asked permission to do it.* **Request,** a more formal word, means to ask in a polite and more formal way: *We request contributions to the library.* **Solicit,** a formal word, means to request respectfully or earnestly: *They are soliciting funds for a new hospital.*

a·skance (ə skans′) *adv.* **1** with suspicion or disapproval: *The students looked askance at the suggestions of classes on Saturday.* **2** sideways; to one side. [origin uncertain]

a·skant (ə skant′) *adv.* askance.

a·skew (ə skyü′) *adv. or adj.* to one side; out of the proper position; turned or twisted the wrong way: *Her hat is on askew. The bottom line of printing is askew.*

a·slant (ə slant′) *adv., prep., adj.* —*adv.* in a slanting direction. —*prep.* slantingly across. —*adj.* slanting.

a·sleep (ə slēp′) *adj., adv.* —*adj.* (*never used before a noun or pronoun*) **1** in a condition of sleep; sleeping: *The cat is asleep.* **2** without feeling; numb: *My foot is asleep.* **3** sluggish; not alert; inactive: *asleep on the job.* **4** dead.

hat, āge, fär; let, ēqual, tèrm; it, īce
hot, ōpen, ôrder; oil, out; cup, pút, rüle,
ə above, takən, pencəl, lemən, circəs
ch, child; ng, long; sh, ship
th, thin; ᴛʜ, then; zh, measure

—*adv.* **1** into a condition of sleep: *The tired boy fell asleep.* **2** into a condition of numbness or inactivity.

a·slope (ə slōp′) *adv. or adj.* at a slant.

a·so·cial (ā sō′shəl) *adj.* **1** paying no attention to social customs or laws; not social. **2** avoiding association with others; not sociable.

asp[1] (asp) *n.* **1** the Egyptian cobra (*Naja haje*), a very poisonous snake, about 180 cm long. It was sacred to the Egyptians and became a symbol of royalty. **2** a small, poisonous snake (*Vipera aspis*) of Europe, a species of viper also called **asp viper.** [< L *aspis* < Gk.]

asp[2] (asp) *n. Archaic.* aspen. [OE *æspe*]

as·par·a·gus (əs par′ə gəs *or* əs par′-) *n.* **1** any of a genus (*Asparagus*) of perennial plants of the lily family having many-branched stems with tiny, scalelike leaves; especially, one species (*A. officinalis*) widely cultivated for its edible young shoots. Several other species (such as *A. plumosa*), usually called **asparagus ferns,** are grown as ornamental plants. **2** the young shoots of *A. officinalis,* which are cooked and eaten as a vegetable. [< L < Gk. *asparagos*]

a·spar·kle (ə spär′kəl) *adj.* sparkling.

as·pect (as′pekt) *n.* **1** one side, part, or view (of a subject): *various aspects of a plan.* **2** look; appearance: *aspect of the countryside.* **3** countenance; expression: *the solemn aspect of a judge.* **4** direction in which anything faces; exposure: *This house has a western aspect.* **5** a side fronting in a given direction: *the southern aspect of a house.* **6** *Astrology.* the relative position of planets as determining their supposed influence upon human affairs. **7** *Grammar.* **a** the nature of the action of a verb, regarded as beginning, continuing, ending, being repeated, etc. **b** a verb form that expresses action as beginning, continuing, ending, being repeated, etc.: *Aspects indicate a quality of the action; tenses indicate time.* **c** in English, a verb phrase performing a similar function. *He is walking* is, properly speaking, an aspect. **d** set of such forms or phrases for the various persons: *The Russian verb has many aspects.* **8** *Physics.* the position of a plane surface relative to a fluid or gas through which it moves. [< L *aspectus* < *aspicere* < *ad-* at + *specere* look]
☛ *Syn.* **2.** See note at **appearance.**

as·pec·tu·al (as pek′chü əl) *adj., n.* —*adj. Grammar.* of or having to do with aspect (def. 7). —*n. Grammar.* a verb form indicating aspect.

as·pen (as′pən) *n., adj.* —*n.* any of several trees (genus *Populus*) of the willow family having flattened leaf stalks that cause the leaves to flutter in the slightest breeze, such as the trembling aspen of North America and the common aspen (*P. tremula*) of Europe. See also **trembling aspen.** —*adj. Archaic.* trembling or quaking. [earlier meaning "of the asp"]

as·per·i·ty (as per′ə tē) *n., pl.* **-ties.** roughness; harshness; severity. [ME *asprete* < OF < L *asperitas* < *asper* rough]

as·perse (əs pèrs′) *v.* **-persed, -pers·ing. 1** spread damaging or false reports about; slander. **2** sprinkle. [< L *aspersus,* pp. of *aspergere* < *ad-* on + *spargere* sprinkle] —**as·per′er,** *n.*

as·per·sion (əs pèr′zhən *or* əs pèr′shən) *n.* **1** a damaging or false report; slander. **2** a sprinkling with water.

as·phalt (as′folt *or* as′fôlt) *n., v.* —*n.* **1** a dark-colored, almost solid, tarry substance found in natural deposits in many parts of the world and also obtained by evaporating petroleum; bitumen. **2** a mixture of this substance with crushed rock, used for pavements, roofs, etc. **3** (*adj.*) consisting of or covered with asphalt.
—*v.* surface or seal with asphalt. [< LL < Gk. *asphaltos*]

asphalt jungle *Informal.* a densely populated city area in which crime and violence are common.

as·phal·tum (as fal′təm) *n.* asphalt.

as·pho·del (as′fə del′) *n.* **1** any of various European plants (genera *Asphodelus* and *Asphodeline*) of the lily family, having spikes of white or yellow flowers. **2** an immortal flower of Greek legend, said to cover the fields of Elysium. [< L < Gk. *asphodelos*]

as·phyx·i·a (as fik′sē ə) *n.* suffocation or an unconscious condition caused by lack of oxygen and excess of carbon dioxide in the blood. [< NL < Gk. *asphyxia* < *a-* without + *sphyxis* pulse < *sphyzein* throb]

as·phyx·i·ant (as fik′sē ənt) *n., adj.* —*n.* a cause of asphyxiation. —*adj.* causing or producing asphyxiation.

as·phyx·i·ate (as fik′sē āt′) v. **-at·ed, -at·ing.** suffocate because of lack of oxygen and excess of carbon dioxide in the blood. —**as·phyx′·i·a′·tion,** n. —**as·phyx′i·a·tor,** n.

as·pic[1] (as′pik) n. a kind of jelly made of meat or fish stock, tomato juice, etc., often set in a mould with seafood, meat, etc. [< F]

as·pic[2] (as′pik) n. Poetic. asp[1]. [< F aspic, var. (by influence of piquer to sting) of L aspis. See ASP[1].]

as·pi·dis·tra (as′pə dis′trə) n. any of a genus (Aspidistra) of plants of the lily family native to E Asia, especially a cultivated species (A. lurida) commonly called the cast-iron plant, popular as a house plant. [< NL < Gk. aspis, aspidos shield + astra stars]

as·pir·ant (əs pīr′ənt or as′pə rənt) n., adj. —n. a person who aspires; a person who seeks a position of honor, advancement, etc. —adj. aspiring.

as·pi·rate (v. as′pə rāt′; adj., n. as′pə rit) v. **-rat·ed, -rat·ing;** adj., n. —v. Phonetics. **1** begin a word or syllable with an h-sound, as in hoot (hüt). **2** pronounce (a stop) with a following or accompanying puff of air. P is aspirated in pin but not in spin or nip. —adj. pronounced with a breathing or h-sound. The h in here is aspirate. —n. an aspirated sound. English p is an aspirate in pat, but not in tap. [< L aspirare. See ASPIRE.]

as·pi·ra·tion (as′pə rā′shən) n. **1** an earnest desire; longing. **2** an object of desire or ambition; goal. **3** the act of breathing, especially drawing air into the lungs. **4** Phonetics. **a** an aspirating (of sounds). **b** an aspirated sound.

as·pi·ra·tor (as′pə rā′tər) n. an apparatus or device employing suction: A vacuum cleaner is an aspirator.

as·pire (əs pīr′) v. **-pired, -pir·ing. 1** have an ambition for something; desire earnestly: Scholars aspire after knowledge. Tom aspired to be captain of the team. **2** rise high. [< L aspirare < ad- toward + spirare breathe] —**as·pir′ing·ly,** adv.

as·pi·rin (as′pə rin) n. **1** a white, crystalline powder, the acetate of salicylic acid, used in medicine to reduce fever, relieve pain, etc. Formula: $C_9H_8O_4$ **2** a tablet of aspirin. **3 Aspirin,** Trademark. a brand of such tablets. [< trademark]

a·squint (ə skwint′) adv. or adj. with a squint; sideways. [origin uncertain]

ass[1] (as) n. **1** donkey. **2** any of several wild animals (genus Equus) of Asia and Africa, smaller than the horse but very fast and having long, erect ears, a very short mane, and a long tail with a tuft of long hair at the end. The wild ass of Africa is the ancestor of the common domestic donkey. **3** a silly or stupid person; fool. [OE assa < Celtic < L asinus]

ass[2] (as) n. Vulgar slang. **1** buttocks. **2** anus. [variant of **arse**]

as·sa·fet·i·da or **as·sa·foet·i·da** (as′ə fet′ə də or as′ə fē′tə də) See **asafetida.**

as·sa·gai (as′ə gī′) n., pl. **-gais. 1** a slender spear or javelin of hard wood, often tipped with iron, used in S Africa. **2** a S African tree (Curtisea faginea) of the dogwood family whose wood is used for making such spears. [< Sp. azagaya < Arabic azzaghayah < Berber]

as·sail (ə sāl′) v. **1** set upon with violence; attack: to assail a fortress. **2** set upon vigorously with arguments, abuse, etc. **3** come over (a person); trouble: He was assailed with feelings of panic. [ME < OF asalir < VL adsalire < L ad- at + salire leap] —**as·sail′a·ble,** adj.
☛ Syn. 1. See note at **attack.**

as·sail·ant (ə sāl′ənt) n. a person who attacks: The injured man did not know his assailant.

as·sas·sin (ə sas′ən) n. **1** a murderer, especially of a politically important person. An assassin may be a hired murderer or a political fanatic. **2** any person who destroys or does serious damage: a character assassin. [< F < Ital. < Arabic hashshāshīn hashish eaters; with reference to murderers under the influence of hashish]

as·sas·si·nate (ə sas′ə nāt′) v. **-nat·ed, -nat·ing. 1** murder someone, especially a politically important person, by a sudden or secret attack. **2** destroy or do serious damage, especially by slander, treachery, etc. —**as·sas′si·na·tor,** n.

as·sas·si·na·tion (ə sas′ə nā′shən) n. the murder, especially of a politically important person, by a sudden or secret attack.

as·sault (ə solt′ or ə sôlt′) n., v. —n. **1** an attack, especially a sudden, vigorous attack. **2** the final phase of a military attack; closing with the enemy in hand-to-hand fighting. **3** Law. a threat or an attempt to do physical harm to another person. —v. make an assault on. [ME < OF asauter < VL < L ad- at + saltare leap] —**as·sault′er,** n.
☛ Syn. v. See note at **attack.**

assault and battery Law. the striking of a person; intentionally doing physical harm to a person.

as·say (ə sā′ or as′ā) v., n. —v. **1** analyse (an ore, alloy, etc.) to find out the quantity of gold, silver, or other metal in it. **2** try; test; examine. **3** (of ore) contain, as shown by analysis, a certain proportion of metal. **4** Archaic. attempt.
—n. **1** an analysis of an ore, alloy, etc. to find out the amount of metal in it. **2** a trial; test; examination. **3** the substance analysed or tested. **4** a list of the results of assaying an ore, drug, etc. [ME < OF a(s)sayer, ult. < LL < VL exagere weigh] —**as·say′er,** n.

as·se·gai (as′ə gī′) See **assagai.**

as·sem·blage (ə sem′blij) n. **1** a group of persons gathered together; assembly. **2** a collection; group. **3** a bringing together; coming together; meeting. **4** a putting together: the assemblage of the parts of a machine.

as·sem·ble (ə sem′bəl) v. **-bled, -bling. 1** gather or bring together: All the writer's papers have been assembled into one collection. They were finding it hard to assemble a crew for the yacht. **2** come together; meet: After lunch, the delegates assembled in the auditorium. **3** put together the parts of; fit together: The chair should be easy to assemble. [ME < OF as(s)embler < VL assimulare bring together < L assimulare compare, ult. < ad- to + similis like, or simul together] —**as·sem′bler,** n.
☛ Syn. 1. See note at **gather.**

as·sem·bly (ə sem′blē) n., pl. **-blies. 1** a group of people gathered together for some purpose; meeting. A reception or a ball may be called an assembly. **2** Often, **Assembly,** Cdn. in Quebec, the National Assembly. **3** any lawmaking body; especially, in some countries, the lower house or branch of a legislature. **4** the act of fitting together: the assembly of the parts of an automobile. **5** the set of parts fitted or required to be fitted together: the wing assembly of a model plane. **6** Military. a signal on a bugle or drum for troops to form in ranks. **7** the act of gathering or coming together: unlawful assembly.
☛ Syn. 1. See note at **meeting.**

assembly line a row of workers and machines along which work is passed until the final product is made: Automobiles are produced on an assembly line.

as·sem·bly·man (ə sem′blē mən) n., pl. **-men. 1** in Prince Edward Island, one of fifteen members of the Legislative Assembly elected by both property-holders and non-property-holders; a member of the Legislative Assembly who is not a councillor. **2** in the United States, a member of a lawmaking group.

as·sent (ə sent′) v., n. —v. express agreement; agree. —n. an acceptance of a proposal, statement, etc.; agreement. [ME < OF < L assentari < ad- along with + sentire feel, think] —**as·sent′er,** n. —**as·sent′ing·ly,** adv.
☛ Syn. v. See note at **consent.**

as·sert (ə sèrt′) v. **1** state positively; declare. **2** insist on (a right, a claim, etc.); defend: to assert one's independence.
assert oneself, put oneself forward; make oneself noticed, especially in insisting on one's rights: You'll never get waited on in that place if you don't assert yourself. [< L assertus, pp. of asserere < ad- to + serere join] —**as·sert′er** or **as·ser′tor,** n.
☛ Syn. 1. See note at **declare.**

as·ser·tion (ə sèr′shən) n. **1** a positive statement; declaration. **2** an insisting one's right, a claim, etc.

as·ser·tive (ə sèr′tiv) adj. **1** too confident and certain; positive: John is an assertive boy, always insisting on his rights and opinions. **2** declarative: an assertive sentence. —**as·ser′tive·ly,** adv. —**as·ser′tive·ness,** n.

as·sess (ə ses′) v. **1** estimate the value of (property or income) for taxation. **2** fix the amount of (a tax, fine, damages, etc.). **3** put a tax on or call for a contribution from (a person, property, etc.): Each member of the club will be assessed one dollar to pay for the trip. **4** portion out as a tax; apportion. **5** examine critically and estimate the merit, significance, value, etc. of: The committee met to assess the idea of establishing a new university. [ME < OF < VL assessare fix a tax < L assidere < ad- by + sedere sit] —**as·sess′a·ble,** adj.

as·sess·ment (ə ses′mənt) n. **1** the act of assessing. **2** the amount assessed. **3** an estimate; critical appraisal.

as·ses·sor (ə ses′ər) n. a person who estimates the value of property or income for taxation.

as·set (as′et) n. **1** something having value; resource or advantage: Her main asset as a politician is her ability to sway a crowd. **2** assets, pl. **a** the entire property of a person, company, etc. **b** property that can be used to pay debts. **c** Accounting. the entries on a balance sheet showing total resources. [< OF asez enough < L ad- + satis enough]

as·sev·er·ate (ə sev′ər āt′) v. **-at·ed, -at·ing.** declare solemnly; state positively. [< L asseverare < ad- + severus serious] —**as·sev′er·a·tive,** adj.

as·sev·er·a·tion (ə sev′ər ā′shən) *n.* a solemn declaration; emphatic assertion.

as·si·du·i·ty (as′ə dyü′ə tē *or* as′ə dü′ə tē) *n., pl.* **-ties.** careful and steady attention; diligence; perseverance.

as·sid·u·ous (ə sij′ü əs) *adj.* careful and attentive; diligent. [< L *assiduus* < *assidere* sit at. See ASSESS.] **—as·sid′u·ous·ly,** *adv.* **—as·sid′u·ous·ness,** *n.*

as·sign (ə sīn′) *v., n.* —*v.* **1** give as a share, task, duty, etc.: *The teacher has assigned ten problems for tonight's homework.* **2** appoint (to a post or duty): *The captain assigned two soldiers to guard the gate.* **3** name definitely; fix; set: *The judge assigned a day for the trial.* **4** ascribe; attribute: *His breakdown was assigned to overwork.* **5** *Law.* transfer or hand over (property, rights, etc.): *He was finally obliged to assign his farm to his creditors.* —*n. Law.* a person to whom property or a right is assigned; assignee. [ME < OF *assigner* < L *assignare* < *ad-* to, for + *signare* to mark < *signum* mark] **—as·sign′a·ble,** *adj.* **—as·sign′er,** *n.*

☛ *Syn. v.* **1. Assign, allot** = give something to a particular person or purpose as a share or responsibility. **Assign** emphasizes giving something that has been established as due by some plan or principle: *The teacher assigned me a seat near the window.* **Allot** suggests giving an amount or part that is set more or less by chance: *Each student was allotted two tickets.*

as·sig·nat (as′ig nat′; *French,* ä sē nyä′) *n.* a piece of paper money issued from 1789 to 1796 in France by a revolutionary government. Assignats were based on the value of confiscated lands. [< F < L *assignatum* < *assignare*. See ASSIGN.]

as·sig·na·tion (as′ig nā′shən) *n.* **1** an appointment for a meeting, especially a secret meeting between lovers; tryst. **2** the meeting or meeting place. **3** the act of assigning or alloting. **4** the assignment made.

as·sign·ee (ə sī nē′ *or* as′ə nē′) *n. Law.* a person to whom some property, right, etc. is transferred.

as·sign·ment (ə sīn′mənt) *n.* **1** something assigned, especially a piece of work to be done. **2** the act of assigning. **3** *Law.* a transfer of some property, right, etc.

as·sign·or (ə sī nôr′ *or* as′ə nôr′) *n. Law.* a person who transfers to another some property, right, etc.

as·sim·i·la·ble (ə sim′ə lə bəl) *adj.* that can be assimilated.

as·sim·i·late (ə sim′ə lāt′) *v.* **-lat·ed, -lat·ing. 1** absorb; digest: *Mary reads too fast to assimilate everything. The human body will not assimilate sawdust.* **2** make or become like (people of a nation, etc.) in customs and viewpoint: *Canada has assimilated people from many lands. Hungarians have assimilated readily in this country.* **3** *Phonetics.* make like. A consonant is frequently assimilated to the consonant it precedes; *ads-* becomes *ass-; comr-, corr-, disf-, diff-;* etc. **4** become like. [< L *assimilare* < *ad-* to + *similis* like] **—as·sim′i·la′tor,** *n.*

☛ *Syn.* **1.** See note at **absorb.**

as·sim·i·la·tion (ə sim′ə lā′shən) *n.* assimilating or being assimilated: *Nutrition depends on the assimilation of food.*

as·sim·i·la·tive (ə sim′ə lə tiv *or* ə sim′ə lā′tiv) *adj.* assimilating.

As·sin·i·boine (ə sin′ə boin′) *n., adj.* —*n.* **1** a member of an Amerindian people living mainly in Alberta, Saskatchewan and Montana: *The Assiniboines are a Siouan people.* **2** the Siouan language of the Assiniboines. —*adj.* of or having to do with the Assiniboines or their language.

as·sist (ə sist′) *v., n.* —*v.* **1** help; give aid to. **2** take part or have a hand (*in*): *He assisted in the scoring of the goal.* —*n.* **1** an instance of giving help: *With an assist from me, he soon climbed the fence.* **2** *Sports.* **a** the act of a player who helps a teammate score a goal, put an opposing player out, etc. **b** the credit given to a player for such an act. [< F < L *assistere* < *ad-* by + *sistere* take a stand]

☛ *Syn. v.* **1.** See note at **help.**

as·sist·ance (ə sis′təns) *n.* help; aid.

as·sist·ant (ə sis′tənt) *n., adj.* —*n.* **1** a helper; aid. **2** an assistant professor. —*adj.* helping; assisting.

assistant professor a college or university teacher ranking below an associate professor but above a lecturer.

as·size (ə sīz′) *n.* **1 assizes,** *pl.* **a** a periodical sessions of a court of law. **b** the time or the place of these sessions. **2** an inquest or the verdict of the inquest. [ME < OF *as(s)ise* < *aseeir* < VL *assedere* sit at < L *assidere*. See ASSESS.]

assn. or **Assn.** association.

assoc. or **Assoc.** associate; association.

as·so·ci·ate (*v.* ə sō′shē āt′; *n., adj.* ə sō′shē it *or* ə sō′shē āt′) *v.* **-at·ed, -at·ing.** *adj.* —*v.* **1** connect in thought: *We associate camping with summer.* **2** mix socially (*with*); keep company (*with*): *She associates only with people interested in sports.* **3** make (oneself or another person or persons) a partner or companion in some matter, organization, etc.: *He was associated with a law firm for several years. She has associated herself with the reform*

movement in the party. **4** join or combine (one with another) for a common purpose: *They have been associated in a number of business enterprises.* —*n.* **1** a partner or colleague. **2** a companion or friend. **3** something that is connected with or usually accompanies something else. **4** a member of an institution, association, etc., who does not have full rights and privileges. —*adj.* (*only before a noun*) **1** joined in companionship, interest, action, etc. **2** having partial rights and privileges in an institution, association, etc.: *an associate member.* [< L *associare* < *ad-* to + *socius* companion] **—as·so′ci·a·tor,** *n.*

associate professor a university or college teacher ranking below a professor but above an assistant professor.

as·so·ci·a·tion (ə sō′sē ā′shən *or* ə sō′shē ā′shən) *n.* **1** an associating or being associated. **2** a group of people joined together for some purpose; society. **3** companionship; partnership; friendship. **4** the connection of ideas in thought. *Abbrev.:* assn. or Assn., assoc. or Assoc.

association football soccer.

as·so·ci·a·tive (ə sō′shē ə tiv *or* ə sō′shē ā′tiv) *adj.* **1** of, having to do with, or dependent on association, as of ideas or images. **2** *Mathematics.* of or referring to a rule that any change in the grouping of elements in an operation will not affect the result: *Addition and multiplication are associative. Example:* $(7 + 3) + 8 = 7 + (3 + 8)$.

as·soil (ə soil′) *v. Archaic.* **1** absolve. **2** atone for. [ME < OF *assoil,* pres. indicative of *as(s)oldre* < L *absolvere.* Doublet of ABSOLVE.]

as·so·nance (as′ə nəns) *n.* **1** a partial rhyme in which the vowels are alike but the consonants are different. *Examples: brave—vain, lone—show.* **2** *Informal.* a resemblance in sound. *Example:* "So all day long the noise of battle rolled." [< F < L *assonans,* ppr. of *assonare* < *ad-* to + *sonare* sound]

as·sort (ə sôrt′) *v.* **1** sort out; classify; arrange in sorts. **2** furnish with an assortment of goods. **3** group (*with*). **4** agree in sort or kind; fall into a class. **5** associate (*with*). [< F *assortir* < *a-* to (< L *ad-*) + *sorte* sort < L *sors, sortis,* originally, lot] **—as·sort′er,** *n.*

as·sort·ed (ə sôr′tid) *adj.* **1** selected so as to be of different kinds; various: *assorted cakes.* **2** arranged by kinds; classified: *The socks are assorted by size.* **3** matched; suited to one another: *They are a poorly assorted couple, always quarrelling.*

as·sort·ment (ə sôrt′mənt) *n.* **1** a collection made up of various kinds of things, persons, etc.; miscellaneous collection: *an assortment of candy.* **2** the act of assorting; separation into classes.

ASSR or **A.S.S.R.** Autonomous Soviet Socialist Republic.

asst. or **Asst.** assistant.

as·suage (ə swāj′) *v.* **-suaged, -suag·ing. 1** make easier or milder: *to assuage pain.* **2** satisfy; appease; quench: *to assuage thirst.* [ME < OF *assuagier,* ult. < L *ad-* + *suavis* sweet] **—as·suag′er,** *n.*

as·suage·ment (ə swāj′mənt) *n.* **1** assuaging or being assuaged. **2** something that assuages.

as·sume (ə süm′ *or* ə syüm′) *v.* **-sumed, -sum·ing. 1** take for granted; suppose: *He assumed that the train would be on time.* **2** take upon oneself; undertake: *to assume the leadership of a group.* **3** take or put on oneself: *to assume an air of superiority.* **4** pretend: *to assume ignorance.* [ME < L *assumere* < *ad-* to + *sumere* take]

☛ *Syn.* **4.** See note at **pretend.**

as·sumed (ə sümd′ *or* ə syümd′) *adj.* **1** pretended; not real. **2** supposed.

as·sum·ing (ə süm′ing *or* ə syüm′ing) *adj.* taking too much on oneself; presumptuous.

as·sump·tion (ə sump′shən *or* ə sum′shən) *n.* **1** the act of assuming: *She bustled about with an assumption of authority.* **2** the thing assumed: *John's assumption that he would win the prize proved incorrect.* **3** presumption; arrogance; unpleasant boldness. **4 the Assumption,** *Christianity.* **a** the bodily taking of the Virgin Mary from earth to heaven after her death. **b** a Christian church festival in honor of this, held on August 15. [ME < L *assumptio, -onis* < *assumere.* See ASSUME.]

as·sur·ance (ə shür′əns) *n.* **1** making sure or certain. **2** a positive declaration inspiring confidence. **3** a security; certainty; confidence. **4** self-confidence. **5** impudence; too much boldness. **6** insurance.

☛ *Syn.* **4.** See note at **confidence.**

as·sure (ə shūr′) v. **-sured, -sur·ing. 1** make sure or certain: *The man assured himself that the bridge was safe before crossing it.* **2** tell confidently or postively: *The captain of the ship assured the passengers that there was no danger.* **3** make safe; secure. **4** make safe against loss; insure. **5** give or restore confidence to; reassure. [ME < OF *aseürer* < VL < L *ad-* + *securus* safe] **—as·sur′er**, *n.*

as·sured (ə shūrd′) *adj.*, *n.* —*adj.* **1** sure; certain. **2** confident; bold. **3** insured against loss. —*n.* **1** a person whose life or property is insured. **2** a person who is the beneficiary of an insurance policy. **—as·sur·ed·ly** (ə shūr′id lē), *adv.* **—as·sur′ed·ness**, (ə shūr′id nəs or ə shūrd′nəs), *n.*

As·syr·i·an (ə sir′ē ən) *n.*, *adj.* —*n.* **1** a native or inhabitant of Assyria, an ancient country and empire in SW Asia. **2** the Semitic language of the Assyrians. —*adj.* of or having to do with the Assyrians or their language.

AST or **A.S.T.** Atlantic Standard Time.

As·tar·te (as tär′tē) *n. Phoenician mythology.* the goddess of love and fertility, known to the Hebrews as Ashtoreth.

a·stat·ic (ā stat′ik) *adj.* **1** *Physics.* not tending to take a fixed or definite position: *A magnetic needle may be made astatic by neutralizing it.* **2** not stationary; unstable.

as·ta·tine (as′tə tēn′ or as′tə tin) *n.* a radio-active chemical element of the halogen group produced artificially by bombarding bismuth with alpha particles and also formed naturally by radio-active decay. *Symbol:* At; *at.no.* 85; *at.wt.* (210). [< Gk. *astatos* unstable + E *-ine²*]

as·ter (as′tər) *n.* **1** any of a genus (*Aster*) of perennial and annual plants of the composite family having daisylike, usually lavender, blue, pink, or white flowers. Many species are common North American wildflowers. **2** any of several other composite plants having similar flowers, such as the **China aster** (*Callistephus chinensis*), cultivated in several varieties as a garden flower, or the **golden asters** (genus *Chrysopsis*) of North America, having yellow flowers. [< L < Gk. *astēr* star]

as·ter·isk (as′tər isk′) *n.*, *v.* —*n.* a star-shaped mark (*) used in printed or written material to call attention to a footnote, indicate an omission, etc. —*v.* mark with an asterisk. [< LL < Gk. *asteriskos,* dim. of *astēr* star]

as·ter·ism (as′tər iz′əm) *n.* **1** *Astronomy.* **a** a group of stars. **b** a constellation. **2** *Geology.* a starlike figure produced in some crystallized minerals by reflected or transmitted light.

a·stern (ə stėrn′) *adv.* **1** at or toward the rear of a ship. **2** backward. **3** behind.

as·ter·oid (as′tər oid′) *n.*, *adj.* —*n.* **1** *Astronomy.* any of the many very small planets revolving about the sun between the orbit of Mars and the orbit of Jupiter. **2** any starfish. —*adj.* **1** starlike. **2** resembling a starfish. [< Gk. *asteroeidēs* starlike < *astēr* star]

as·the·ni·a (as thē′nē ə) *n.* lack or loss of strength; debility. [< NL *asthenia* < Gk. *astheneia* < *asthenēs* weak < *a-* without + *sthenos* strength]

as·then·ic (as then′ik) *adj.* **1** of or having to do with asthenia; weak. **2** characterized by a tall, lean physique.

asth·ma (az′mə or as′mə) *n.* a chronic disease that causes difficulty in breathing, a feeling of suffocation, and coughing. [ME *asma* < Med.L < Gk. *asthma* panting < *azein* breathe hard]

asth·mat·ic (az mat′ik or as mat′ik) *adj.*, *n.* —*adj.* **1** of or having to do with asthma. **2** suffering from asthma. —*n.* a person suffering from asthma.

as·tig·mat·ic (as′tig mat′ik) *adj.* **1** having astigmatism. **2** having to do with astigmatism. **3** corrected astigmatism.

a·stig·ma·tism (ə stig′mə tiz′əm) *n.* **1** a defect of an eye or of a lens that makes objects look indistinct or gives imperfect images. With perfect focus, all the rays of light from any one point of an object converge at one point on the retina of the eye or other receiving surface; with astigmatism they do not. **2** imperfect or distorting understanding or judgment. [< *a-¹* without + Gk. *stigma* point]

a·stir (ə stėr′) *adv.* or *adj.* (*never precedes a noun*) **1** out of bed; up and about: *It was only six o'clock, but already the house was astir.* **2** in motion.

as·ton·ish (əs ton′ish) *v.* surprise greatly; amaze: *The gift of ten dollars astonished the beggar.* [var. of *astoun* < OF *estoner* < VL *extonare*; cf. L *tonare* thunder]
➤ **Syn.** See note at **surprise.**

as·ton·ish·ing (əs ton′ish ing) *adj.* very surprising; amazing: *an astonishing sight.* **—as·ton′ish·ing·ly,** *adv.*

as·ton·ish·ment (əs ton′ish mənt) *n.* **1** great surprise; amazement; sudden wonder. **2** anything that causes great surprise.

as·tound (əs tound′) *v.* shock with alarm or surprise; surprise very greatly; amaze. [earlier *astoun.* See ASTONISH.] **—as·tound′ing·ly,** *adv.*

astr. astronomer; astronomy.

a·strad·dle (ə strad′əl) *adv.* or *adj.* astride.

as·tra·gal (as′trə gəl) *n. Architecture.* **1** a small, convex moulding cut into the form of a string of beads. **2** plain, convex moulding.

as·trag·a·lus (as trag′ə ləs) *n., pl.* **-li** (-lī or -lē′). the uppermost bone of the tarsus; anklebone; talus. [< L < Gk. *astragalos*]

as·tra·khan or **as·tra·chan** (as′trə kən) *n.* **1** the curly furlike wool of young lambs from Astrakhan, a district in the S Soviet Union. **2** a woollen cloth that looks like this. **3** a variety of apple having a reddish skin and crisp, white flesh.

as·tral (as′trəl) *adj.* **1** of or having to do with the stars. **2** consisting of stars; starry. [< LL *astralis* < L *astrum* star < Gk. *astron*]

astral body a spiritual counterpart, or double, of the human body, believed to be able to leave it at will.

astral lamp an oil lamp so made that it casts no shadow on the table below.

a·stray (ə strā′) *adj.* or *adv.* (*never precedes a noun*) off the right path or out of the right way.

a·stride (ə strīd′) *adj.*, *adv.*, *prep.* —*adj.* or *adv.* **1** with one leg on each side. **2** with legs far apart. —*prep.* with one leg on each side of (something).

as·trin·gen·cy (əs trin′jən sē) *n.* the property of being astringent.

as·trin·gent (əs trin′jənt) *adj.*, *n.* —*adj.* **1** causing the contraction of soft body tissues; styptic: *an astringent lotion.* **2** severe or austere: *astringent criticism.* —*n.* a substance or agent that has an astringent effect. Alum is an astringent. [< L *astringens, -entis,* ppr. of *astringere* < *ad-* to + *stringere* bind] **—as·trin′gent·ly,** *adv.*

astro- *combining form.* **1** a star, planet, or other heavenly body as in *astrophysics.* **2** space; outer space as in *astronaut.*

as·tro·bi·ol·o·gist (as′trō bī ol′ə jist) *n.* a person trained in astrobiology, especially one whose work it is.

as·tro·bi·ol·o·gy (as′trō bī ol′ə jē) *n.* the branch of biology that deals with the discovery and study of life on other planets, etc.

as·tro·bot·a·ny (as′trō bot′ə nē) *n.* the branch of botany that deals with the discovery and study of plant life on other planets, etc.

as·tro·chem·is·try (as′trō kem′is trē) *n.* the branch of chemistry that deals with the chemical properties of heavenly bodies.

astro compass an instrument used to determine direction by sighting on a heavenly body.

as·tro·dy·nam·ics (as′trō dī nam′iks) *n.* the branch of dynamics that deals with the motion of bodies in outer space and the forces acting upon them.

as·tro·labe (as′trə lāb′ or as′trə lab′) *n.* an astronomical instrument formerly used for measuring the altitude of the sun or stars. [ME < OF *astrelabe* < Med.L < Gk. *astrolabon,* orginally, star-taking < *astron* star + *lambanein* take]

as·trol·o·ger (əs trol′ə jər) *n.* a person who claims to interpret the influence of the stars and planets on persons, events, etc.

as·tro·log·i·cal (as′trə loj′ə kəl) *adj.* having to do with astrology.

as·trol·o·gy (əs trol′ə jē) *n.* **1** a pseudo-science that interprets the supposed influence of the stars and planets on persons, events, etc.; the study of the stars to foretell what will happen. **2** *Archaic.* practical astronomy. [ME < L < Gk. *astrologia* < *astron* star + *-logos* treating of]

astron. astronomer; astronomical; astronomy.

as·tro·naut (as′trə not′ or as′trə nôt′) *n.* a pilot or member of the crew of a spacecraft; a person who travels in outer space. [< *astro-* + (*Argo*)*naut*]

as·tro·nau·tics (as′trə no′tiks or as′trə nô′tiks) *n.* **1** the designing, manufacturing, and operating of space vehicles. **2** space travel.

as·tron·o·mer (əs tron′ə mər) *n.* a person trained in astronomy, especially one whose work it is.

as·tro·nom·ic (as′trə nom′ik) *adj.* astronomical.

as·tro·nom·i·cal (as′trə nom′ə kəl) *adj.* **1** of or having to do with astronomy. **2** enormous; like the numbers reported in astronomy. **—as′tro·nom′i·cal·ly,** *adv.*

astronomical unit a unit used in astronomy for measuring length or distance, equal to 149.600 gigametres, which is the mean distance of the earth from the sun. The astronomical unit is used with the SI.

astronomical year the period of the earth's revolution around the sun; solar year. It lasts 365 days, 5 hours, 48 minutes, and 45.51 seconds.

as·tron·o·my (əs tron′ə mē) *n.* **1** the science that treats of the sun, moon, and other heavenly bodies. It deals with their composition, motions, positions, distances, sizes, etc. **2** a textbook or handbook dealing with this science. *Abbrev.:* astr. [ME < L < Gk. *astronomia* < *astron* star + *nomos* distribution]

as·tro·phys·i·cal (as′trō fiz′ə kəl) *adj.* of or having to do with astrophysics.

as·tro·phys·ics (as′trō fiz′iks) *n.* the branch of astronomy that deals with the physical and chemical characteristics of heavenly bodies.

as·tute (əs tyüt′ *or* əs tüt′) *adj.* **1** having or showing a keen, discovering mind; clever; sagacious: *an astute remark.* **2** having or showing hard-headed shrewdness; crafty: *an astute business deal.* [< L *astutus* < *astus* sagacity] —**as·tute′ly,** *adv.* —**as·tute′ness,** *n.*
☛ *Syn.* See note at **shrewd.**

a·sun·der (ə sun′dər) *adv., adj.* —*adv.* in pieces; into separate parts. —*adj.* apart; separate. [OE *on sundran*]

a·swarm (ə swôrm′) *adv. or adj.* in a crowded, swarming state: *The bleachers were aswarm with baseball fans.*

a·sy·lum (ə sī′ləm) *n.* **1** *Historical.* an institution for the support and care of the mentally ill, the poor, the aged, etc. **2** a refuge; shelter: *The author who had been accused of a political crime was given asylum in another country.* [ME < L < Gk. *asylon* refuge < *a-* without + *sylē* right of seizure]

a·sym·met·ric (ā′sə met′rik *or* as′ə met′rik) *adj.* not symmetrical; lacking symmetry.

a·sym·met·ri·cal (ā′sə met′rə kəl *or* as′ə met′rə kəl) *adj.* asymmetric.

The outline of the tree on the left is asymmetric; the one on the right is symmetric.

a·sym·me·try (ā sim′ə trē *or* a sim′ə trē) *n.* lack of symmetry.

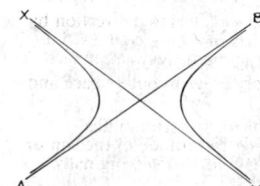

The lines AB and XY are asymptotes of an equilateral, or rectangular, hyperbola.

as·ymp·tote (as′im tōt′) *n. Mathematics.* a straight line that continually approaches a curve, but does not meet it within a finite distance. [< Gk. *asymptōtos* < *a-* not + *syn-* together + *ptōtos* apt to fall]

at¹ (ət; *stressed,* at) *prep.* **1** in; on; near: *at school, at the front door.* **2** toward; in the direction of: *to aim at the mark. Look at me.* **3** in a place or condition of: *at right angles, at war.* **4** on or near the time of: *at midnight.* **5** through; by way of: *Smoke came out at the chimney.* **6** engaged in; trying to do: *at work.* **7** because of; as a result of: *The shipwrecked sailors were happy at the arrival of the rescue ship.* **8** for: *two books at a dollar each.* **9** according to: *at will.* **10** from: *The sick man got good treatment at the hands of the doctor.* [OE *æt*]
☛ *Usage.* **At, in** are used to bring into a sentence a word stating a place or a time. **At** is used when the place or time is thought of as a point, as on a map or a clock. **In** is used when the place or time is thought of as having boundaries and the idea to be expressed is that of being *inside* or *within* the boundaries: *On our trip we stopped at Toronto and stayed two days in Montreal. We left Montreal at noon and in the afternoon drove to Quebec.*

at² (ät) *n.* **1** a unit of money in Laos, equal to ¹⁄₁₀₀ of a kip. **2** a coin worth one at. [< Thai]

at– *prefix.* to or toward; the form of **ad-** occurring before *t*, as in *attain.*

at. **1** atmosphere(s). **2** atomic.

At astatine.

AT antitank.

hat, āge, fär; let, ēqual, tèrm; it, īce
hot, ōpen, ôrder; oil, out; cup, put, rüle,
əbove, takən, pencəl, lemən, circəs
ch, child; ng, long; sh, ship
th, thin; ᴛʜ, then; zh, measure

At·a·lan·ta (at′ə lan′tə) *n. Greek mythology.* a maiden famous for her beauty and for her speed in running. She required each of her suitors to run a race with her; those who lost the race were killed.

at·a·vism (at′ə viz′əm) *n.* **1** in a plant or animal, the reappearance of a characteristic that has been absent for several generations. **2** an individual showing such a characteristic; throwback. [< L *atavus* ancestor]

at·a·vis·tic (at′ə vis′tik) *adj.* **1** having to do with atavism. **2** having a tendency to atavism.

a·tax·i·a (ə tak′sē ə) *n.* an inability to co-ordinate voluntary muscular movements, as in some nervous disorders. [< NL < Gk. *ataxia* < *a-* without + *taxis* order]

ATC or **A.T.C.** **1** air traffic control. **2** Air Transport Command.

ate (āt) *v.* pt. of **eat.**

A·te (ā′tē) *n. Greek mythology.* the goddess of recklessness and mischief, later regarded as the goddess of revenge.

–ate¹ *suffix.* **1** of or having to do with: *novitiate = having to do with novices.* **2** having; containing: *compassionate = having compassion.* **3** having the form of; like: *stellate = having the form of a star.* **4** become: *maturate = become mature.* **5** cause to be: *alienate = cause to be alien.* **6** produce: *ulcerate = produce ulcers.* **7** supply or treat with: *aerate = treat with air.* **8** combine with: *oxygenate = combine with oxygen.* [< L *-atus, atum,* pp. endings]

–ate² *suffix.* a salt made from —**-ic** acid: *nitrate = salt made from nitric acid.* [special use of *-ate¹*]

–ate³ *suffix.* the office, rule, or condition of: *caliphate = rule of a caliph.* [< L *-atus,* from 4th declension nouns]

at·el·ier (at′əl yā′) *n.* a workshop, especially an artist's studio. [< F *atelier* originally, pile of chips < OF *astele* chip < L *astula*]

a tem·po (ä tem′pō) *Music.* in time; returning to the former speed. [< Ital.]

Ath·a·na·sian Creed (ath′ə nā′zhən *or* ath′ə nā′shən) one of the three main Christian creeds or professions of faith, the other two being the Apostles' Creed and the Nicene Creed. Its authorship is unknown, but it was probably composed around A.D. 430. [< St. *Athanasius* (296 ?-373), bishop of Alexandria, formerly supposed to be the author of the creed]

Ath·a·pas·can (ath′ə pas′kən) *n., adj.* —*n.* **1** a major group of Amerindian languages spoken in northwestern Canada, Alaska, and the SW United States, including Chippewayan, Dogrib, Sarcee, Slave, and Navaho. **2** a member of a people speaking any of these languages. —*adj.* of, having to do with, or referring to this group of languages or any of the peoples speaking them.

a·the·ism (ā′thē iz′əm) *n.* the belief that there is no God. [< F *athéisme* < Gk. *atheos* denying the gods < *a-* without + *theos* a god]

a·the·ist (ā′thē ist) *n.* a person who believes that there is no God.

a·the·is·tic (ā′thē is′tik) *adj.* of atheism or atheists. —**a′the·is′ti·cal·ly,** *adv.*

a·the·is·ti·cal (ā′thē is′tə kəl) *adj.* atheistic.

ath·el·ing (ath′ə ling) *n.* an Anglo-Saxon prince or noble, especially a crown prince. [OE *ætheling* < *æthelu* noble family + *-ling* belonging to]

A·the·na (ə thē′nə) *n. Greek mythology.* the goddess of wisdom, arts, industries, and prudent warfare, corresponding to the Roman goddess Minerva. Also called **Pallas, Pallas Athena.**

ath·e·nae·um or **ath·e·ne·um** (ath′ə nē′əm) *n.* **1** a scientific or literary club. **2** a reading room; library. [< L < Gk. *Athēnaion* temple of Athena]

Ath·e·nae·um (ath′ə nē′əm) *n.* in Athens, the temple of Athena. Poets and learned men gathered there.

A·the·ne (ə thē′nē) *n.* Athena.

A·the·ni·an (ə thē′nē ən *or* ə thēn′yən) *adj., n.* —*adj.* of Athens, the capital of Greece, or its people. —*n.* **1** a person having the right of citizenship in ancient Athens. **2** a native or inhabitant of Athens.

ath·er·o·ma (ath′ə rō′mə) *n.* a fatty deposit on or in the inner lining of an artery. [< L < Gk. *athērē* mush + *-ōma* tumor]

ath·er·o·scle·ro·sis (ath′ə rō sklə rō′sis) *n.* a form of arteriosclerosis characterized by a narrowing and hardening of the arteries due to deposits of cholesterol and fatty acids along the artery walls.

a·thirst (ə thèrst′) *adj.* 1 thirsty. 2 eager.

ath·lete (ath′lēt) *n.* a person trained in exercises of physical strength, speed, and skill. Ballplayers, runners, boxers, and swimmers are athletes. [< L *athleta* < Gk. *athlētēs* < *athlēo* contend for a prize (*athlon*)]

athlete's foot a contagious skin disease of the feet, caused by a fungus; ringworm of the feet.

ath·let·ic (ath let′ik) *adj.* 1 active and strong; generally enjoying active games and sports and showing natural skill in them: *I'm not very athletic but I do enjoy swimming and horseback riding.* 2 of, like, or suited to an athlete. 3 having to do with active games and sports. —**ath·let′i·cal·ly,** *adv.*

ath·let·ics (ath let′iks) *n.* 1 (*usually pl. in use*) exercises of strength, speed and skill; active games and sports: *Athletics include baseball and basketball.* 2 (*usually sing. in use*) the practice and principles of athletic training: *Athletics is recommended for every student.*

athletic support an elasticized belt and pouch for supporting the genitals, worn by men for athletics and other physical activity.

at–home (ət hōm′) *n.* an informal reception, usually in the afternoon.

a·thwart (ə thwôrt′) *adv., prep.* —*adv.* crosswise; across from side to side. —*prep.* 1 across. 2 across the line or course of. 3 in opposition to; against. [< *a*- on + *thwart,* adv.]

at·i·gi (at′ə gē *or* ə tē′gē) *n.* Cdn. 1 a hooded, knee-length inner shirt made of summer skins with the hair inside against the body used in winter especially by Inuit, often for indoor wear. 2 a hooded outer garment of fur or other material; parka. Also, **artigi, artiggi.** [< Eskimo]

a·tilt (ə tilt′) *adj. or adv.* 1 at a tilt; tilted. 2 in a tilting encounter.

a·tin·gle (ə ting′gəl) *adj.* tingling; in a tingling or excited condition.

–ation *noun-forming suffix.* 1 the act or state of —ing: *admiration = act or state of admiring.* 2 the condition or state of being —ed: *cancellation = condition or state of being cancelled.* 3 the result of —ing: *civilization = result of civilizing.* [< L *-atio, -onis* < *-at-* of pp. stem (cf. *-ate¹*) + *-io* (cf. *-ion*)]

–ative *adjective-forming suffix.* 1 tending to —: *talkative = tending to talk.* 2 having to do with —: *qualitative = having to do with quality.* [< F *-ative* (fem. of *-atif* < L *-ativus*) or directly < L *-ativus* < *-at-* of pp. stem (cf. *-ate¹*) + *-ivus* (cf. *-ive*)]

At·lan·te·an (at′lan tē′ən) *adj.* 1 resembling Atlas; strong. 2 having to do with the legendary island of Atlantis. [< L *Atlanteus*]

At·lan·tic (at lan′tik) *n., adj.* —*n.* the Atlantic Ocean. —*adj.* 1 of the Atlantic Ocean: *Atlantic currents.* 2 on, in, over, or near the Atlantic Ocean: *Atlantic air routes.* 3 of or designating NATO: *the Atlantic alliance.* [< L < Gk. *Atlantikos* pertaining to Atlas]

Atlantic Charter the joint declaration of President Roosevelt and Prime Minister Churchill on August 14, 1941, asserting the need for guaranteed freedom of all nations.

Atlantic Provinces Newfoundland, Prince Edward Island, Nova Scotia, and New Brunswick.

Atlantic salmon a salmon (*Salmo salar*) found along the Atlantic coasts of North America and Europe, very highly valued as a game and food fish. The ouananiche, or landlocked salmon, is a variety of Atlantic salmon that spends all its life in fresh water.

At·lan·tis (at lan′tis) *n.* a legendary island in the Atlantic, said to have sunk beneath the sea. [< L < Gk.]

at·las (at′ləs) *n.* 1 **Atlas, a** *Greek mythology.* one of the Titans who rebelled against Zeus. He was punished by being made to support the heavens with his head and hands. **b** a person who bears a great burden. **c** a man who is exceptionally strong. 2 a book of maps. The first such books always had at the front a picture of Atlas supporting the world. 3 a book of plates, tables, or charts illustrating a particular subject. [< L < Gk.]

atm 1 standard atmosphere(s). 2 atmospheric.

at·mom·e·ter (at mom′ə tər) *n.* an instrument for measuring rate of evaporation. [< Gk. *atmos* vapor + E *-meter*]

at·mos·phere (at′məs fēr′) *n.* 1 air that surrounds the earth, consisting mainly of nitrogen and oxygen. More than 99 percent of the total mass of the earth's atmosphere lies in the region up to about 80 kilometres above the earth's surface. See also **troposphere, stratosphere, mesosphere, thermosphere, exosphere.** 2 the mass of gases that surrounds any heavenly body. 3 air in any given place: *a*

damp atmosphere. 4 standard atmosphere. 5 mental and moral environment; surrounding influence: *an atmosphere of poverty, the atmosphere of old Vienna.* 6 the coloring or feeling that pervades a work of art: *the sombre atmosphere of* The Scarlet Letter. [< NL *atmosphaera* < Gk. *atmos* vapor + *sphaira* sphere]

at·mos·pher·ic (at′məs fer′ik) *adj., n.* —*adj.* 1 of or having to do with the atmosphere: *Atmospheric conditions prevented observation of the stars.* 2 occurring in or produced by the atmosphere: *atmospheric moisture, atmospheric disturbances.* —*n.* **atmospherics,** *pl.* 1 interference in the form of crackling or hissing sounds in a radio receiver, caused by electrical disturbance in the atmosphere. 2 electrical disturbance in the atmosphere produced by a natural cause such as lightning.

at·mos·pher·i·cal (at′məs fer′ə kəl) *adj.* atmospheric. —**at′mo·spher′i·cal·ly,** *adv.*

atmospheric pressure the pressure exerted by the air on the surface of the earth and everything existing on it, caused by the force of gravity. The standard atmospheric pressure is about 101 kPa; the highest atmospheric pressure ever recorded was about 108 kPa, in Siberia.

at. no. atomic number.

at·oll (at′ol *or* ə tol′) *n.* a ring of coral that has built up on a sunken land bank or volcano top in the open sea, parts of the ring showing above water as solid coral islands that support vegetation. The pool in the centre of an atoll is called a lagoon. [< Maldive (lang. of the Maldive Islands in the Indian Ocean), ? < Malayalam *adal* uniting]

at·om (at′əm) *n.* 1 the smallest part of an element that has all the properties of the element and can take part in a chemical reaction without being permanently changed. The basic particles making up an atom are protons and neutrons making up its central portion, or nucleus, and electrons orbiting the nucleus. 2 the atom considered as a source of potential energy: *the power of the atom.* 3 a very small particle, thing, or quantity; bit: *not an atom of strength left. The plate was smashed to atoms.* [< L < Gk. *atomos* indivisible < *a-* not + *tomos* a cutting]

atom bomb atomic bomb.

a·tom·ic (ə tom′ik) *adj.* 1 of or having to do with atoms: *atomic research.* 2 of, having to do with, or using atomic energy or power: *an atomic submarine.* 3 of or using atomic weapons: *atomic warfare.* 4 extremely small; minute.

atomic age the era that began with the first use of atomic energy.

atomic bomb a bomb that uses the energy released by the very rapid splitting of atoms to cause an explosion of tremendous force.

atomic clock a highly accurate clock that is run by controlled radio waves.

atomic energy the energy that exists in atoms. Some atoms can be made to release this atomic energy, either slowly (in a reactor) or very suddenly (in a bomb); it is generated through alteration of an atomic nucleus, by fission or fusion.

at·o·mic·i·ty (at′ə mis′ə tē) *n.* 1 *Chemistry.* **a** the number of atoms in one molecule of an element. **b** valence. **c** the number of atoms or groups that can be replaced in the molecule of a compound. 2 the state or condition of being composed of atoms.

atomic number *Chemistry and physics.* a number used in describing a chemical element and giving its relation to other elements and determining its place in the periodic table. The atomic number of an element represents the number of protons (positive charges) in the nucleus of one of its atoms. *Abbrev.:* at. no.

atomic pile nuclear reactor.

atomic power nuclear power.

atomic theory *Chemistry and physics.* the theory that all matter is composed of atoms; especially, the modern theory that an atom is made of a positive nucleus around which electrons speed.

atomic weight the ratio of the average mass per atom of an element to one twelfth of the mass of an atom of carbon 12.

at·om·ize (at′əm īz′) *v.* **-ized, -iz·ing.** 1 reduce to atoms. 2 change (a liquid) into a fine spray. —**at′om·i·za′tion,** *n.*

at·om·iz·er (at′əm īz′ər) *n.* an apparatus used to blow a liquid in a spray of very small drops.

atom smasher cyclotron.

at·o·my¹ (at′ə mē) *n., pl.* **-mies.** 1 a very small thing; atom. 2 a tiny being; pygmy. [< L *atomi,* pl. of *atomus.* See ATOM.]

at·o·my² (at′ə mē) *n., pl.* **-mies.** *Archaic.* skeleton. [for *anatomy* taken as *an atomy*]

a·ton·al (ā tōn′əl) *adj.* *Music.* not having a central or dominant tone, or key; having all tones in equal relation to each other. Atonal music is often based on the chromatic scale of twelve tones. —**a·ton′al·ly,** *adv.* —**a′to·nal′i·ty,** *n.*

a·to·nal·i·ty (ā′tō nal′ə tē) *n. Music.* the state or condition of being atonal; absence of tonality.

a·tone (ə tōn′) *v.* **a·toned, a·ton·ing. 1** make amends or reparation (*for*): *to atone for a sin or crime. She tried to atone for her thoughtlessness by sending flowers to her hosts.* **2** expiate (a fault, etc.): *to atone guilt, to atone a loss.* [< *atonement*]

a·tone·ment (ə tōn′mənt) *n.* **1** a making up for something; giving satisfaction for a wrong, loss, or injury; amends. **2 the Atonement,** the reconciliation of God with sinners through the sufferings and death of Christ. **3** See **Day of Atonement.** [< *at onement* being at one, i.e., in accord; *onement* < ME *onen* unite, ult. < OE *ān* one]

a·top (ə top′) *adv., prep.* —*adv.* on or at the top. —*prep.* on the top of.

at·ra·bil·ious (at′rə bil′yəs) *adj.* **1** melancholy; hypochondriac. **2** bad-tempered. [< L *atra bilis* black bile]

a·tri·um (ā′trē əm *or* at′rē əm) *n., pl.* **a·tri·a** (ā′trē ə *or* at′rē ə). **1** the main room of an ancient Roman house. **2** a hall; court. **3** either of the upper chambers of the heart, that receive the blood from the veins. See **heart** for picture. **4** any of various other cavities in the body. [< L *atrium* (def. 1) < Etruscan]

a·tro·cious (ə trō′shəs) *adj.* **1** very wicked or cruel; very savage or brutal: *The crime was so atrocious that many details were never made public.* **2** *Informal.* very bad; abominable: *atrocious weather, an atrocious pun.* —**a·tro′cious·ly,** *adv.* —**a·tro′cious·ness,** *n.*

a·troc·i·ty (ə tros′ə tē) *n., pl.* **-ties. 1** very great wickedness or cruelty. **2** a very cruel or brutal act. **3** *Informal.* a very bad blunder. [< L *atrocitas* < *atrox, -ocis* fierce < *ater* dark]

at·ro·phy (at′rə fē) *n., v.* **-phied, -phy·ing.** —*n.* **1** the wasting away of tissue or an organ, etc. in the body: *muscular atrophy.* **2** the failure of a part or organ to develop properly. **3** any decline; degeneration: *the atrophy of a skill.* —*v.* waste away or cause to waste away. [< LL < Gk. *atrophia* < *a-* without + *trophē* nourishment]

at·ro·pin (at′rə pin) *n.* atropine.

at·ro·pine (at′rə pēn′ *or* at′rə pin) *n.* a poisonous drug obtained from belladonna and similar plants, used in medicine to relax muscles and dilate the pupil of the eye. *Formula:* $C_{17}H_{23}NO_3$ [< NL *Atropa* belladonna < Gk. *Atropos* one of the Fates]

At·ro·pos (at′rə pos′) *n. Greek mythology.* one of the three Fates. Atropos cuts the thread of life.

at·tach (ə tach′) *v.* **1** fasten (*to*): *He attached the boat to the pier by means of a rope.* **2** connect with for duty, etc: *He was attached as mate to the ship "Clio."* **3** add at the end; affix: *We attached our names to the petition.* **4** attribute: *The world at first attached little importance to the policies of Hitler.* **5** fasten itself; belong: *The blame attaches to you.* **6** bind by affection: *May is much attached to her cousin.* **7** *Law.* take (person or property) by legal authority: *Her property was attached by the court because she had not paid her debts.* [ME < OF *atachier* < L *ad-* to + Gmc. source of OF *tache* a fastening, a nail. Related to TACK.] —**at·tach′a·ble,** *adj.*

☞ *Syn.* **4. Attach, affix, annex** = to add one thing to another. **Attach,** the general word, used literally and figuratively, suggests only joining or fastening one thing to another by some means: *He attached a trailer to his car.* **Affix** suggests putting one thing, usually something smaller or less important, on another firmly and permanently: *He affixed his seal to the document.* **Annex** = add to and make a part of (usually something larger): *The Board annexed the suburb to the school district.*

at·ta·ché (ə tash′ā *or* at′ə shā′) *n.* a specialist on the official staff of an ambassador or minister to a foreign country: *a military attaché, a press attaché.* [< F]

attaché case a briefcase shaped like a small, thin suitcase with a rigid frame and sides.

at·tach·ment (ə tach′mənt) *n.* **1** attaching or being attached. **2** something that is or can be attached: *A vacuum cleaner has various attachments.* **3** a means of attaching; fastening. **4** affection. **5** *Law.* **a** the legal seizure of property. **b** the arrest of a person. **c** the writ authorizing an attachment.

at·tack (ə tak′) *v., n.* —*v.* **1** use force or weapons on to hurt; go against as an enemy; begin fighting against: *The dog attacked the cat.* **2** talk or write against. **3** begin to work vigorously on: *The hungry boy attacked his dinner as soon as it was served.* **4** act harmfully on: *Certain bacteria attack tooth enamel.* **5** make an attack: *The enemy attacked at dawn.* —*n.* **1** the act of attacking; especially, a hostile manoeuvre or onslaught; sharp criticism, etc.: *The attack of the enemy took the town by surprise. The chairman's speech consisted mainly of an attack on wasteful government spending.* **2** the sudden onset of illness, discomfort, etc.: *an attack of malaria, an attack of remorse.* [< F < Ital. *attaccare* (from the same source as OF *atachier*). See ATTACH.] —**at·tack′er,** *n.*

☞ *Syn.* v. **1. Attack, assail, assault** = set upon with force. **Attack,** the general word, emphasizes the idea of falling upon a person or enemy without warning, sometimes without cause, or of starting the fighting: *Germany attacked Belgium in 1914.* **Assail** = attack with violence and repeated blows: *The enemy assailed our defence positions.* **Assault** = attack suddenly with furious or brutal

hat, āge, fär; let, ēqual, tèrm; it, īce
hot, ōpen, ôrder; oil, out; cup, pùt, rüle,
əbove, takən, pencəl, lemən, circəs

ch, child; ng, long; sh, ship
th, thin; ŦH, then; zh, measure

force, and always suggests actual contact as in hand-to-hand fighting: *In a rage he assaulted his neighbor with a knife.*

at·tain (ə tān′) *v.* **1** arrive at; reach: *to attain years of discretion.* **2** gain; accomplish.

attain to, succeed in coming to or getting: *to attain to a position of great influence.* [ME < OF *ataindre* < VL *attangere* < L *ad-* to + *tangere* touch]

at·tain·a·bil·i·ty (ə tān′ə bil′ə tē) *n.* the quality of being attainable.

at·tain·a·ble (ə tān′ə bəl) *adj.* that can be attained: *The office of Prime Minister is one of the highest attainable in Canada.*

at·tain·der (ə tān′dər) *n. Historical.* the loss of property and civil rights as the result of being sentenced to death or being outlawed. [ME < OF *ataindre* attain; influenced by E *taindre* taint]

at·tain·ment (ə tān′mənt) *n.* **1** attaining. **2** something attained. **3** an accomplishment: *Leonardo da Vinci was a man of varied attainments; he was a painter, engineer, and inventor.*

at·taint (ə tānt′) *v., n.* —*v.* **1** *Historical.* punish or condemn by attainder. **2** *Archaic.* disgrace; sully. —*n. Archaic.* a disgrace. [< OF *ataint,* pp. of *ataindre.* See ATTAIN.] —**at·taint′ment,** *n.*

at·tar (at′ər) *n.* a perfume made from the petals of roses or other flowers. [< Persian *'aṭar* < Arabic *'uṭur* aroma]

attar of roses a fragrant oil made from rose petals.

at·tempt (ə tempt′) *v., n.* —*v.* **1** make an effort at; try. **2** try to take or destroy (life, etc.). —*n.* **1** a putting forth of effort to accomplish something, especially something difficult. **2** an attack: *The rebels made an unsuccessful attempt on the king's life.* [< OF < L *attemptare* < *ad-* to + *temptare* try]

☞ *Syn.* v. **1.** See note at **try.**

at·tend (ə tend′) *v.* **1** be present at: *Children must attend school.* **2** give care and thought; pay attention: *Attend to the laboratory instructions.* **3** apply oneself: *Attend to your music if you want to play well.* **4** go with; accompany: *Noble ladies attend the queen.* **5** go with as a result: *Danger attends delay. Success often attends hard work.* **6** wait on; care for; tend: *Nurses attend the sick.* **7** be ready; wait. [ME < OF < *atendre* < L *attendere* < *ad-* toward + *tendere* stretch]

☞ *Syn.* **4.** See note at **accompany.**

at·tend·ance (ə ten′dəns) *n.* **1** being present; attending: *Attendance at all classes is compulsory.* **2** the people present; number attending: *The attendance at church was over 200 last Sunday.*

dance attendance on, wait on with excessive attentions: *The ambitious courtier danced attendance on any noble he thought might help him.*

in attendance, waiting (*on*); on duty.

at·tend·ant (ə ten′dənt) *n., adj.* —*n.* **1** a person who waits on another, or provides a service: *An attendant will look after your coat. The prince had five attendants.* **2** an accompanying thing or event: *Hatred had developed as an attendant on fear.* **3** a person who is present; attendee.
—*adj.* **1** waiting on another to help or serve: *an attendant nurse.* **2** going with as a result; accompanying: *weakness attendant on illness, attendant circumstances.* **3** present: *attendant hearers.*

at·tend·ee (ə ten dē′) *n.* a person who is present at a meeting, function, etc.: *attendees at a conference.*

at·ten·tion (ə ten′shən) *n., interj.* —*n.* **1** the application of the mind to something; concentration: *He gave the speaker his undivided attention.* **2** notice or observation: *She called my attention to the cat stalking the squirrel.* **3** care and thought; consideration: *The matter requires our immediate attention.* **4** thoughtfulness and courtesy; attentiveness: *He showed his mother much attention.* **5 attentions,** *pl.* acts of courtesy or devotion, especially of a suitor. **6** *Military.* a standing position taken by a soldier, etc., in which the body is straight, with the heels together, arms straight down at the sides, and eyes looking forward. The position is taken to prepare for another command.
—*interj.* **1** an order to take notice. **2** *Military.* an order to assume the position of attention. [ME < L *attentio, -onis* < *attendere.* See ATTEND.]

at·ten·tive (ə ten′tiv) *adj.* **1** paying attention; observant. **2** considerate; thoughtful; solicitous: *an attentive host. The nurse*

was attentive to the patient's needs. —**at·ten′tive·ly,** *adv.*
—**at·ten′tive·ness,** *n.*

at·ten·u·ate (ə ten′yü āt′) *v.* **-at·ed, -at·ing. 1** make or become thin or slender. **2** weaken; reduce. **3** make less dense; dilute. **4** *Bacteriology.* make (micro-organisms, etc.) less harmful. [< L *attenuare* < *ad-* + *tenuis* thin]

at·ten·u·a·tion (ə ten′yü ā′shən) *n.* attenuating or being attenuated.

at·ten·u·a·tor (ə ten′yü ā′tər) *n.* a person or thing that attenuates, especially a device for reducing the amplitude of an electrical signal without distorting it.

at·test (ə test′) *v.* **1** give proof or evidence of: *The child's good health attests his parents' care.* **2** declare to be true or genuine; certify. **3** bear witness; testify: *The handwriting expert attested to the genuineness of the signature.* **4** put on oath. [< L *attestari* < *ad-* to + *testis* witness]

at·tes·ta·tion (at′es tā′shən) *n.* **1** the act of attesting. **2** proof; evidence. **3** testimony.

at·tic (at′ik) *n.* a room or space in a house just below the roof and above the other rooms. [< F *attique* < L *Atticus* Attic < Gk.]

At·tic (at′ik) *adj., n.* —*adj.* **1** of Attica or Athens; Athenian. **2** of a style of writing, etc., simple and elegant. —*n.* the speech of Attica, the dialect of ancient Greek used by Plato, Sophocles, Euripides, and Pericles. [< L *Atticus* < Gk. *Attikos*]

Attic salt or **wit** incisive wit.

at·tire (ə tīr′) *v.* **-tired, -tir·ing;** *n.* —*v.* clothe, especially in rich and formal clothes; array: *He was attired in full military uniform.* —*n.* clothes, especially rich or formal ones. [ME < OF *atirer* arrange < *a-* to (< L *ad-*) + *tire* row < Gmc.]
☞ *Syn.* See note at **dress.**

at·ti·tude (at′ə tyüd′ *or* at′ə tüd′) *n.* **1** a way of thinking, acting, or feeling: *His attitude toward school changed from dislike to great enthusiasm.* **2** a position of the body suggesting an action, purpose, emotion, etc: *She stood there in an attitude of defiance.* **3** the position of an aircraft, or spacecraft in relation to some line or plane, such as the horizon or the horizontal.
strike an attitude, pose for effect. [< F < Ital. *attitudine* < LL *aptitudo.* Doublet of APTITUDE.]

at·ti·tu·di·nal (at′ə tyü′də nəl *or* at′ə tü də nəl) of, having to do with, or expressing an attitude or attitudes.

attn. attention.

atto– (at′ə) SI *prefix.* one quintillionth; 10^{-18}. *Symbol:* a

at·tor·ney (ə tėr′nē) *n., pl.* **-neys. 1** a person who has legal power to act for another. **2** lawyer. *Abbrev.:* atty. [ME < OF *atourne,* pp. of *atourner* assign, appoint < *a-* to (< L *ad-*) + *tourner* turn < L *tornare* turn on a lathe < *tornus* lathe < Gk.]

attorney at law lawyer.

attorney general or **Attorney General** *pl.* **attorneys general** or **attorney generals. 1** a chief law officer. **2 Attorney General, a** the chief law officer of Canada: *The Attorney-General is the head of the Department of Justice and is a member of the Cabinet.* **b** the chief law officer of a province. Also, **attorney-general.**

at·tract (ə trakt′) *v.* **1** draw to oneself: *A magnet attracts iron.* **2** be pleasing to; win the attention and liking of: *Bright colors attract children.* [< L *attractus,* pp. of *attrahere* < *ad-* to + *trahere* draw]

at·trac·tant (ə trak′tənt) *n.* a substance that attracts, especially a pheromone or something imitating it.

at·trac·tion (ə trak′shən) *n.* **1** the act or power of attracting. **2** anything that delights or attracts people: *The elephants were the chief attraction at the circus.* **3** charm; fascination. **4** *Physics.* the force exerted by molecules on one another, tending to draw or hold them together.

at·trac·tive (ə trak′tiv) *adj.* **1** capable of winning attention and liking; pleasing or charming: *an attractive hat, an attractive personality. He is very attractive.* **2** having to do with or having the power to attract: *the attractive force of a magnet, an attractive job offer.* —**at·trac′tive·ly,** *adv.* —**at·trac′tive·ness,** *n.*

attrib. attribute; attributive.

at·trib·ut·a·ble (ə trib′yə tə bəl) *adj.* that can be attributed: *Some diseases are attributable to lack of cleanliness.*

at·trib·ute (*v.* ə trib′yüt; *n.* at′rə byüt′) *v.* **-ut·ed, -ut·ing;** *n.* —*v.* **1** consider as belonging to or appropriate to: *They attribute a great deal of intelligence to their dog.* **2** regard as an effect of; think of as caused by: *They attributed his success to intelligence and hard work.* —*n.* **1** a quality considered as belonging to a person or thing; a characteristic: *Prudence is an attribute of a judge.* **2** an object

considered appropriate to a person, rank, or office; symbol: *The eagle was the attribute of Jupiter.* **3** an adjective; a word or phrase used as an adjective. [ME < L *attributus,* pp. of *attribuere* < *ad-* to + *tribuere* assign, originally, divide among the tribes < *tribus* tribe]
☞ *Syn. v.* **Attribute, ascribe** = consider something as belonging or due to someone or something, and are often interchangeable. But **attribute** suggests believing something appropriate to a person or thing or belonging to it by nature or right: *We attribute importance to the words of great men.* **Ascribe** suggests guessing or basing a conclusion on evidence and reasoning: *I ascribe his failure to his careless habits.*

at·tri·bu·tion (at′rə byü′shən) *n.* **1** the act of attributing. **2** the thing attributed; attribute.

at·trib·u·tive (ə trib′yə tiv) *adj., n.* —*adj.* **1** *Grammar.* of an adjective or other modifier, expressing a quality or attribute, especially when coming before or immediately after the noun it modifies. An attributive adjective is in the same part of the sentence as the noun it modifies; a predicate adjective is separated from its noun by a linking verb. **2** that attributes. **3** of or like an attribute. —*n. Grammar.* an attributive noun or adjective. *General* is an attributive in *general store* and in *governor general.*
—**at·trib′u·tive·ly,** *adv.*
☞ *Usage.* **Attributive.** An adjective that stands before its noun is **attributive** (a *blue* shirt), as contrasted with a **predicate** adjective that is related to its noun by a linking verb (The shirt is *bluey*). An adjective that comes immediately after its noun is **postpositive** (the man *asleep*).

at·tri·tion (ə trish′ən) *n.* **1** a wearing away by rubbing: *Pebbles become smooth by attrition.* **2** any gradual process of wearing down: *a war of attrition.* **3** sorrow for one's sins, less perfect than contrition. [ME < LL *attritio, -onis* < *atterere* < *ad-* against + *terere* rub]

at·tune (ə tyün′ *or* ə tün′) *v.* **-tuned, -tun·ing. 1** bring into harmony; adjust: *He could not attune his ears to the sounds of the big city.* **2** make sensitive (*to*); make responsive (*to*): *His years in politics had attuned the minister to the shifts in public opinion.*
—**at·tune′ment,** *n.*

atty. attorney.

at.wt. atomic weight.

a·typ·i·cal (ā tip′ə kəl *or* a tip′ə kəl) *adj.* not typical; irregular; abnormal. —**a·typ′i·cal·ly,** *adv.*

Au gold (for L *aurum*).

au·berge (ō berzh′) *n.* inn. [< F]

au·burn (o′bərn *or* ô′bərn) *n. or adj.* reddish brown. [ME < OF *auborne* < L *alburnus* whitish < *albus* white; apparently confused with ME *brun* brown]

Au·bus·son (ō bY sôN′) *n.* French. **1** a rich tapestry of scenes or figures used for wall hangings, upholstery, etc. **2** a rug woven like an Aubusson tapestry. [< *Aubusson,* France, where these tapestries were first made in the 16th century]

A.U.C. from the founding of the city (of Rome) (for L *ab urbe condita*).

au cou·rant (ō kü räN′) *French.* in the current of events; well informed; up-to-date on the topics of the day.

auc·tion (ok′shən *or* ôk′shən) *n., v.* —*n.* **1** a public sale in which each thing is sold to the person who offers the most money for it. **2** auction bridge. —*v.* sell at an auction. [< L *auctio, -onis* < *augere* increase]

auction bridge a card game for four people playing in two opposing pairs. Tricks made by the highest-bidding team in excess of their bid may be counted toward a game. Compare **contract bridge.**

auc·tion·eer (ok′shən ēr′ *or* ôk′shən ēr′) *n., v.* —*n.* a man whose business is conducting auctions. —*v.* sell at an auction.

aud. auditor.

au·da·cious (o dā′shəs *or* ô dā′shəs) *adj.* **1** bold; daring. **2** too bold; impudent. —**au·da′cious·ly,** *adv.* —**au·da′cious·ness,** *n.*

au·dac·i·ty (o das′ə tē *or* ô das′ə tē) *n., pl.* **-ties. 1** boldness; reckless daring. **2** rudeness; impudence. [< L *audacia* < *audax* bold < *audere* dare]

au·di·bil·i·ty (o′də bil′ə tē *or* ô′də bil′ə tē) *n.* **1** being audible. **2** the relative loudness of a sound, usually measured in decibels.

au·di·ble (o′də bəl *or* ô′də bəl) *adj.* capable of being heard; loud enough to be heard. [< LL *audibilis* < L *audire* hear] —**au′di·bly,** *adv.*

au·di·ence (o′dē əns *or* ô′dē əns) *n.* **1** the people gathered to hear or see a performance or presentation: *The audience cheered the mayor's speech.* **2** the people reached by radio or television broadcasts, by books, etc.: *The book is intended for a juvenile audience.* **3** a chance to be heard; hearing: *The committee will give you an audience to hear you plan.* **4** a formal interview with a person of high rank: *The king granted an audience to the famous singer.* **5** the act or fact of hearing. [ME < OF < L *audientia* hearing < *audire* hear]

au·di·o (o′dē ō or ô′dē ō) *adj., n.* —*adj.* **1** of or having to do with sound. **2** *Television.* having to do with the broadcasting or receiving of sound: *An audio problem is a sound problem; a video problem involves the image that appears on the screen.* —*n.* sound reproduction.

audio frequency a frequency corresponding to audible sound vibrations, from about 20 Hz to about 20 000 Hz for the normal human ear. *Abbrev.*: AF, A.F., or a.f.

au·di·om·e·ter (o dē om′ə tər or ô dē om′ə tər) *n.* an instrument for measuring the power of hearing.

au·di·o·phile (o′dē ō fīl′ or ô′dē ō-) *n.* a person who is greatly interested in the high-fidelity reproduction of sound.

au·di·o·vid·e·o (o′dē ō vid′ē ō or ô′dē ō-) *adj.* of or having to do with the transmission or reception of both sounds and pictures.

au·di·o·vis·u·al (o′dē ō vizh′ü əl or ô′dē ō-) *adj.* **1** of or having to do with both hearing and sight. **2** of a teaching aid, involving the use of both hearing and sight: *Language courses often use audio-visual aids, such as motion pictures.*

au·dit (o′dit or ô′dit) *v., n.* —*v.* **1** examine and check (business accounts) officially. **2** at a college or university, attend a class as a listener without being allowed to take the examinations or get credit for the course. —*n.* **1** an official examination and check of business accounts. **2** a statement of an account that has been examined and checked authoritatively. [< L *auditus* a hearing < *audire* hear]

au·di·tion (o dish′ən or ô dish′ən) *n., v.* —*n.* **1** a trial performance in which an actor, singer, dancer, or other performer demonstrates his or her skills. **2** the act of hearing. **3** the power or sense of hearing. —*v.* **1** hold an audition: *The producer auditioned six singers for the lead in the musical.* **2** give an audition; perform at an audition: *She auditioned for the role of the maid.* [< L *auditio, -onis* a hearing < *audire* hear]

au·di·tor (o′də tər or ô′də tər) *n.* **1** a hearer; listener. **2** a person who audits business accounts. **3** at a college or university, a person permitted to attend a class as a listener without being allowed to take the examinations or get credit for the course.

auditor general or **Auditor General** *pl.* **auditors general** or **auditor generals.** in Canada, an officer, appointed by the Governor General, who is responsible for auditing the accounts of the federal government and making an annual report of his findings to Parliament.

au·di·to·ri·um (o′də tô′rē əm or ô′də tô′rē əm) *n.* **-to·ri·ums** or **-to·ri·a** (-tô′rē ə). **1** a large room for an audience in a church, theatre, school, etc.; a large hall. **2** a building especially designed for lectures, concerts, etc. [< L]

au·di·to·ry (o′də tô′rē or ô′də tô′rē) *adj., n., pl.* **-ries.** *-adj.* of or having to do with hearing, the sense of hearing, or the organs of hearing: *the auditory nerve.* *-n.* **1** *Archaic.* audience. **2** auditorium.

au fait (ō fā′) *French.* **1** well-informed; familiar (*with*). **2** expert; very skilled.

auf Wie·der·seh·en (ouf vē′dər zā′ən) *German.* goodbye; till we see each other again.

Aug. August.

Au·ge·an stables (o jē′ən or ô jē′ən) *Greek mythology.* the stables, sheltering 3000 oxen, that remained uncleaned for 30 years, until Hercules turned two rivers through them.

au·gend (o′jend or ô′jend) *n. Mathematics.* a number or quantity to which another, the addend, is to be added. [< L *augendum,* gerund of *augere* to increase]

au·ger (o′gər or ô′gər) *n.* **1** a tool for boring holes in wood. **2** a tool for boring holes in the earth: *a post-hole auger.* **3** a similar device having a continuous spiral channel inside a tube, used for moving bulk substances such as grain or snow: *An auger is used to move grain from an elevator to a boxcar.* [OE *nafugār,* originally, a nave borer < *nafu* nave of a wheel + *gār* spear; ME *a nauger* taken as *an auger*]
☛ *Hom.* **augur.**

aught¹ (ot or ôt) *n., adv.* —*n.* anything: *You may resign your job for aught I care.* —*adv.* in any degree; at all: *Help came too late to avail aught.* [OE *āwiht < ā* ever + *wiht* a thing]
☛ *Hom.* **ought.**

aught² (ot or ôt) *n.* zero; cipher; nothing. [< *naught; a naught* taken as *an aught; naught;* OE *nāwiht < nā* no + *wiht* a thing]
☛ *Hom.* **ought.**

au·gite (o′jīt or ô′jīt) *n.* a pure black, bluish, or greenish mineral, found mostly in volcanic rocks. [< L *augites* < Gk. *augitēs,* ult. < *augē* lustre]

aug·ment (og ment′ or ôg ment′) *v.* increase; enlarge: *He had to augment his income by working in the evenings.* —**aug·men′ta·ble,** *adj.* [ME < LL *augmentare* < *augmentum* < *augere* increase]
☛ *Syn.* See note at **increase.**

aug·men·ta·tion (og′men tā′shən or ôg′men tā′shən) *n.*

hat, āge, fär; let, ēqual, tèrm; it, īce
hot, ōpen, ôrder; oil, out; cup, pùt, rüle,
əbove, takən, pencəl, lemən, circəs

ch, child; ng, long; sh, ship
th, thin; ᴛʜ, then; zh, measure

1 enlargement; increase. **2** *Music.* the transformation of a melody by increasing the time values of the notes.

aug·ment·ed (og men′tid or ôg men′tid) *adj. Music.* of or having to do with an interval that is one half step higher than the corresponding normal interval.

au grat·in (ō grat′ən or ô grä′tən; *French,* ō grä taɴ′) *French.* with crumbs; cooked with crumbs and cheese; cooked with cheese. [lit., with grated (cheese)]

au·gur (o′gər or ô′gər) *n., v.* —*n.* **1** in ancient Rome, a priest who made predictions and gave advice. **2** a prophet; fortuneteller. —*v.* **1** predict; foretell. **2** be a sign or promise.
augur ill, be a bad sign.
augur well, be a good sign. [< L *augur,* apparently, Increase, Growth (of crops), personified in ritual service < *augere* increase]
☛ *Hom.* **auger.**

au·gu·ry (o′gyə rē or ô′gyə rē) *n., pl.* **-ries. 1** the art or practice of foretelling the future by the flight of birds, the appearance of the internal organs of sacrificed animals, thunder and lightning, etc. **2** a prediction; indication; sign; omen. **3** a rite or ceremony performed by an augur.

Au·gust (o′gəst or ô′gəst) *n.* the eighth month of the year. It has 31 days. *Abbrev.*: Aug. [after *Augustus* Cæsar (63 B.C.- A.D. 14), first emperor of Rome]

au·gust (o′gəst or ô′gəst, o gust′ or ô gust′) *adj.* inspiring reverence and admiration; majestic; venerable. [< L *augustus* < unrecorded *augus* increase, power < *augere* to increase] —**au·gust′ly,** *adv.* —**au·gust′ness,** *n.*

Au·gus·tan (o gus′tən or ô gus′tən) *adj., n.* —*adj.* of the Roman emperor Augustus or his reign. —*n.* any writer during the Augustan age of Latin or English literature.

Augustan age 1 the period of Latin literature covering the reign of Emperor Augustus, from 27 B.C. to A.D. 14. **2** the period of English literature from about 1700 to 1750, noted for classicism and elegance of style.

Au·gus·tin·i·an (o′gəs tin′ē ən or ô′gəs tin′ē ən) *adj., n.* —*adj.* of or having to do with Saint Augustine (A.D. 354-430), his teachings, or the religious orders named for him. —*n.* **1** a person who follows the teachings of Saint Augustine. **2** a member of any of the religious orders named for Saint Augustine.

au jus (ō zʜʏ′) *French.* in gravy or juice.

auk (ok or ôk) *n.* **1** any of various swimming and diving sea birds (family Alcidae) found along northern coasts. The **great auk,** (*Pinguinus impennis*), a flightless bird about the size of a goose, has been extinct for over a century. See also **auklet** and **razorbill. 2** (*adj.*) designating the family (Alcidae) of heavy-bodied, short-winged sea birds that includes the auks. Murres, guillemots, and puffins also belong to the auk family and are sometimes called auks. [< ON *álka*]

auk·let (ok′lit or ôk′lit) *n.* any of about six species of small sea birds (family Alcidae) of the N Pacific, having black-and-white plumage and, in breeding season, head plumes and brightly colored bill plates similar to those of the related puffins.

auld lang syne (old′ lang sīn′ or ôld′, old′ lang zīn′ or ôld′) *Scottish.* old times; long ago in one's life.

au na·tu·rel (ō nä tʏ rel′) *French.* **1** in the plainest or simplest manner. **2** natural; like life; nude.

aunt (ant) *n.* **1** a sister of one's father or mother. **2** one's uncle's wife. [ME < OF *ante* < L *amita* father's sister]
☛ *Pronun.* The pronunciation (ant) is usual in Canada, but (änt) is common in New Brunswick and parts of Nova Scotia.

au pair (ō per′) **1** a person, especially a girl or young woman, who works in another country as a housemaid, mother's helper, etc., usually temporarily in order to learn the language of the country. Au pairs usually receive a small wage in addition to board and room. **2** (*adj.*) of or designating such a person: *an au pair girl.* [< F *au pair* on equal terms; originally used to refer to an exchange student living with a family in a foreign country to learn the language, etc.]

au·ra (ô′rə) *n., pl.* **au·ras** or **au·rae** (ô′rē or ô′rī). something supposed to come from a person or thing and surround him or it as an atmosphere: *An aura of holiness surrounded the saint.* [< L < Gk.]

au·ral¹ (ô′rəl) *adj.* of or having to do with the ear or the sense of hearing. [< L *auris* ear]
☛ *Hom.* oral.

au·ral² (ô′rəl) *adj.* of or like an aura.
☛ *Hom.* oral.

au·rar (ou′rär *or* oe′rär) *n.* pl. of **eyrir**.

au·re·ate (ô′rē it *or* ô′rē āt′) *adj.* golden; gilded. [< L *aureatus* < *aurum* gold]

au·re·o·la (ô rē′ə lə) *n.* aureole.

au·re·ole (ô′rē ōl′) *n.* **1** an encircling radiance; halo. **2** *Astronomy.* a ring of light surrounding the sun. [< L *aureola* (*corona*) golden (crown) < *aurum* gold]

au·re·o·my·cin (ô′rē ō mī′sin) *n.* an antibiotic, similar to penicillin. [< L *aureus* golden + Gk. *mykēs* fungus]

au re·voir (ō rə vwär′) *French.* goodbye; till we see each other again.

au·ric (ôr′ik) *adj.* **1** of or having to do with gold. **2** containing gold, especially gold with a valence of 3.

au·ri·cle (ô′rə kəl) *n.* **1** atrium (def. 3). **2** the outer part of the ear. **3** an earlike part. [< L *auricula*, dim. of *auris* ear]

au·ric·u·lar (ô rik′yə lər) *adj.* **1** of, having to do with, or near the ear. **2** heard by or addressed to the ear. **3** shaped like an ear. **4** of or having to do with an auricle.

au·rif·er·ous (ô rif′ər əs) *adj.* yielding gold. [< L *aurifer* < *aurum* gold + *ferre* bear]

Au·ri·ga (ô rī′gə) *n.* a large northern constellation supposed to represent a charioteer kneeling in his chariot. [< L *Auriga* charioteer]

au·rist (ô′rist) *n.* a doctor who treats diseases of the ear. [< L *auris* ear]

au·rochs (ô′roks) *n., pl.* **-rochs. 1** a wild ox (*Bos primigenius*) extinct since the 17th century, thought to be one of the ancestors of the modern cattle breeds of Europe and America. It was a huge, black animal, about 185 cm high at the shoulder. **2** wisent. [< G *Auerochs* < OHG *ūr-ohso* < *ūr* wild bull + *ohso* ox]

au·ro·ra (ô rô′rə) *n.* **1** dawn. **2** streams or bands of light appearing in the sky at night. **3 Aurora,** *Roman mythology.* the goddess of the dawn, corresponding to the Greek goddess Eos. [< L]

aurora aus·tra·lis (os trā′lis *or* ôs trā′lis) streamers or bands of light appearing in the southern sky at night. [< NL]

aurora bo·re·al·is (bô′rē al′is *or* bō′rē ā′lis) streamers or bands of light appearing in the northern sky at night; northern lights. [< NL]

au·ro·ral (ô rô′rəl) *adj.* **1** of or like the dawn; first; rosy. **2** of the aurora borealis or the aurora australis. **3** shining; bright.

aurora trout a very rare, nonspotted subspecies of the brook trout found only in certain lakes of northern Ontario. It was originally described as a distinct species.

au·rous (ôr′əs) *adj.* **1** of or having to do with gold. **2** containing gold, especially gold with a valence of 1.

aus·cul·tate (os′kəl tāt′) *v.* **-tat·ed, -tat·ing.** *Medicine.* listen to; examine by auscultation.

aus·cul·ta·tion (os′kəl tā′shən *or* ôs′kəl tā′shən) *n.* **1** the act of listening. **2** *Medicine.* the act of listening, usually with a stethoscope, to sounds within the human body to determine the condition of the heart or lungs. [< L *auscultatio, -onis* < *auscultare* listen]

aus·pice (os′pis *or* ôs′pis) *n., pl.* **aus·pic·es** (os′pə siz *or* ôs′pə siz). **1** a favorable circumstance; indication of success. **2** an omen; sign. **3** a divination or prophecy, especially one made from the flight of birds.
under the auspices of, under the patronage of: *The school fair was held under the auspices of the Home and School Association.* [< F < L *auspicium* < *avis* bird + *specere* look at. See def. 3]

aus·pi·cious (os pish′əs *or* ôs pish′əs) *adj.* **1** with signs of success; favorable. **2** fortunate. **—aus·pi′cious·ly,** *adv.*
☛ *Syn.* 1. See note at **favorable**.

Aus·sie (os′ē *or* ôs′ē) *adj. or n. Slang.* Australian.

Aust. Austria; Austrian.

aus·tere (os tēr′ *or* ôs tēr′) *adj.* **1** harsh; stern: *Frank's father was a silent, austere man, very strict with his children.* **2** strict in moral discipline: *The Puritans were austere.* **3** severely simple: *The tall, plain columns stood against the sky in austere beauty.* **4** sour-tasting. [ME < OF < L < Gk. *austēros* < *auein* dry] **—aus·tere′ness,** *n.* **—aus·tere′ly,** *adv.*

aus·ter·i·ty (os ter′ə tē *or* ôs ter′ə tē) *n., pl.* **-ties. 1** sternness;

---

strictness; severity. **2** severe simplicity. **3** economic stringency or restriction. **4 austerities,** *pl.* severe practices, such as going without food or sitting up all night to pray.

Austl. **1** Australia. **2** Australasia.

aus·tral (os′trəl *or* ôs′trəl) *adj.* southern. [< L *australis* < *auster* the south wind]

Austral. **1** Australian; Australia. **2** Australasian.

Aus·tral·a·sian (os′trəl ā′zhən *or* ôs′trəl-, os′trəl ā′shən or ôs′trəl-) *adj., n.* **—***adj.* of or having to do with Australasia, the islands of the SW Pacific Ocean, or the people of these islands. **—***n.* a native or inhabitant of Australasia.

Aus·tral·ian (os trāl′yən *or* ôs trāl′yən) *n., adj.* **—***n.* a native or inhabitant of Australia, a country and island continent in the SW Pacific Ocean. **—***adj.* **1** of or having to do with the country of Australia or its people. **2** of, having to do with, or living or growing in the geographical region that includes the continent of Australia and nearby islands. **3** Australoid.

Australian ballot a ballot with the names of all candidates for election to public office on it. The ballot is marked by the voter in a private booth to guarantee secrecy.

Aus·tra·loid (os′trə loid′ *or* ôs′trə loid′) *adj., n.* **—***adj.* of or designating a major race of mankind that consists of the original inhabitants of the continent of Australia, distinguished by a combination of biological characteristics including medium brown to very dark skin and almost complete absence of blood type B. The Australoid race was separated from the rest of mankind for thousands of years before modern times. **—***n.* a member of the Australoid race.

Aus·tri·an (os′trē ən *or* ôs′trē ən) *n., adj.* **—***n.* **1** a native or inhabitant of Austria, a country in central Europe. **2** a person of Austrian descent. **—***adj.* of or having to do with Austria or its people.

Austrian pine a pine (*Pinus nigra*) native to N Europe but now commonly cultivated in Canada, having very long, stiff, dark-green needles.

Aus·tro·ne·sian (os′trə nē zhən *or* -shən) *adj., n.* **—***adj.* of or having to do with Austronesia, the islands of the central and S Pacific, or the peoples of these islands. **—***n.* Malayo-Polynesian.

aut– the form of **auto-** before vowels and *h*, as in *authentic.*

au·tar·chic (o tär′kik *or* ô tär′kik) *adj.* of, having to do with, or resembling autarchy.

au·tar·chy (o′tär kē *or* ô′tär kē) *n., pl.* **-chies.** absolute or autocratic rule; despotism. [< Gk. *autarchos* absolute ruler < *autos* self + *archein* rule]

au·tar·ky (o′tär kē *or* ô′tär kē) *n., pl.* **-kies.** the state of being self-sufficient, especially of being independent of imports from other nations. [< Gk. *autarkeia* < *auto-* self + *arkeein* suffice]

au·teur (ō tēr′) *n.* a film director, especially when considered as having the main creative role in a motion picture.

au·then·tic (o then′tik *or* ô then′tik) *adj.* **1** reliable: *an authentic account.* **2** genuine: *A comparison of signatures showed that the letter was authentic.* [ME < OF *autentique* < LL < Gk. *authentikos* < *auto-* by oneself + *hentēs* one who acts]
☛ *Syn.* 2. See note at **genuine**.

au·then·ti·cal·ly (o then′tik lē *or* ô then′tik lē) *adv.* **1** reliably. **2** genuinely.

au·then·ti·cate (o then′tə kāt′ *or* ô then′tə kāt′) *v.* **-cat·ed, -cat·ing. 1** establish the truth of; show to be valid or genuine. **2** establish the authorship of.
☛ *Syn.* 1. See note at **confirm**.

au·then·ti·ca·tion (o then′tə kā′shən *or* ô then′tə kā′shən) *n.* authenticating or being authenticated.

au·then·tic·i·ty (o′then tis′ə tē *or* ô′then tis′ə tē) *n.* **1** reliability. **2** genuineness: *to question the authenticity of a signature.*

au·thor (o′thər *or* ô′thər) *n., v.* **—***n.* **1** a person who writes books, stories, or articles. **2** an author's publications: *Do read this author.* **3** a person who creates or begins anything. **—***v.* be the author of; write: *She has authored a number of plays as well as two novels.* [ME < OF *autor* < L *auctor* < *augere* increase]

au·thor·ess (o′thər is *or* ô′thər is) *n. Rare.* a woman who writes books, stories, or articles.

au·thor·i·tar·i·an (ə thôr′ə ter′ē ən) *adj., n.* **—***adj.* favoring obedience to authority instead of individual freedom. **—***n.* a person who favors obedience to authority instead of individual freedom.

au·thor·i·tar·i·an·ism (ə thôr′ə ter′ē en iz′əm) *n.* the principle of obeying the authority of one person or of a small group of persons.

au·thor·i·ta·tive (ə thôr′ə tā′tiv) *adj.* **1** having authority;

officially ordered: *Authoritative orders came from the general.*
2 commanding: *In authoritative tones the policeman shouted,
"Keep back!"* **3** that ought to be believed or obeyed; having the
authority of expert knowledge. —**au·thor′i·ta′tive·ly,** *adv.*

au·thor·i·ty (ə thôr′ə tē) *n., pl.* **-ties. 1** the power to enforce
obedience; right to command or act: *Parents have authority over
their children.* **2** a person who has such power or right. **3 the
authorities,** **a** officials of the government. **b** persons in control. **4** a
government body that runs some activity or business on behalf of
the public: *the St. Lawrence Seaway Authority.* **5** an influence that
creates respect and confidence. **6** a source of correct information or
wise advice: *A good dictionary is an authority on the meanings of
words.* **7** an expert on some subject. [ME < OF *authorite* < L
auctoritas]

☛ **Syn. 1. Authority, control, influence** = power to direct or act on others.
Authority applies to legal power, given by a person's position or office, to give
commands and enforce obedience: *Teachers have authority over pupils.* **Control**
applies to power, given by a person's position, to direct people and things:
Parents have control over their children. **Influence** applies to personal power,
coming from a person's character, personality, or position, to shape the actions
of others: *Some teachers have great influence over young people.*

au·thor·i·za·tion (ô′thər ə zā′shən *or* ô′thər-, ô′thər ī zā′shən
or ô′thər-) *n.* **1** authorizing: *the general's authorization of the
attack.* **2** a legal right; sanction; warrant.

au·thor·ize (ô′thər īz′ *or* ô′thər īz′) *v.* **-ized, -iz·ing. 1** give
authority to; empower: *The Prime Minister authorized her to set up
a committee.* **2** give authoritative consent or approval to; sanction:
*The expenditure was never authorized by Parliament. This
dictionary authorizes the two spellings* honor *and* honour.

au·thor·ized (ô′thər īzd′ *or* ô′thər īzd′) *adj.* **1** having authority;
accepted as authoritative. **2** sanctioned by formal or legal authority.

Authorized Version the English translation of the Bible first
published in 1611; the King James Version. *Abbrev.:* A.V.

au·thor·ship (ô′thər ship′ *or* ô′thər ship′) *n.* **1** the occupation of
an author; writing. **2** the origin as to author: *What is the authorship
of that novel?* **3** the origin or source of anything.

au·tism (ô′tizm *or* ô′tism) *n.* a learning and behavior disorder
characterized by difficulty in understanding, or making sense of,
what one sees and hears, and in learning to talk and to understand
the meanings of words. Some children suffering from autism have
normal or even high intelligence, and many can be helped through
special educational programs to cope with their handicap.

au·tis·tic (ô tis′tik *or* ô tis′tik) *adj.* affected with autism.

au·to (ô′tō *or* ô′tō) *n., pl.* **au·tos.** automobile.

auto– *combining form.* **1** coming from or having to do with the
self: *An autobiography is the story of one's own life.* **2** independent:
An automobile is a self-propelled vehicle. [< Gk.]

Au·to·bahn (ou′tō bän′) *n., pl.* **Au·to·bah·nen** (ou′tō bä′nən).
in Germany, a four-lane express highway. [< G *Auto* motorcar +
Bahn road]

au·to·bi·og·ra·pher (ô′tə bī og′rə fər *or* ô′tə-) *n.* a person who
writes the story of his own life.

au·to·bi·o·graph·ic (ô′tə bī ə graf′ik *or* ô′tə-) *adj.* **1** having to
do with the story of one's own life. **2** telling or writing the story of
one's own life: *Her writings are all autobiographic.*

au·to·bi·o·graph·i·cal (ô′tə bī ə graf′ə kəl *or* ô′tə-) *adj.*
autobiographic. —**au′to·bi′o·graph′i·cal·ly,** *adv.*

au·to·bi·og·ra·phy (ô′tə bī og′rə fē *or* ô′tə-) *n., pl.* **-phies.**
the story of a person's life written by himself.

au·toch·tho·nous (ô tok′thə nəs *or* ô tok′thə nəs) *adj.*
originating where found; aboriginal; indigenous. [< Gk. *autochthon*
sprung from the land itself < *auto-* self + *chthōn* earth, soil]

au·to·clave (ô′tə klāv′ *or* ô′tə-) *n., v.* —*n.* **1** a strong, closed
vessel that develops superheated steam under pressure, used for
sterilizing, cooking, etc. **2** a strong vessel for effecting chemical
reactions under high pressure. —*v.* cook or sterilize in an
autoclave. [< F *autoclave* < *auto-* self + L *clavis* key]

au·toc·ra·cy (ô tok′rə sē *or* ô tok′rə sē) *n., pl.* **-cies. 1** a
government having absolute power over its citizens. **2** a country
having such a government. **3** absolute authority; unlimited power
over a group.

au·to·crat (ô′tə krat′ *or* ô′tə-) *n.* **1** a ruler having absolute power
over his subjects. **2** a person who uses power in a harsh way: *She
thinks her parents are autocrats.* [< Gk. *autokratēs* < *auto-* self +
kratos strength]

au·to·crat·ic (ô′tə krat′ik *or* ô′tə-) *adj.* of or like an autocrat;
absolute in authority; ruling without checks or limitations.
—**au′to·crat′i·cal·ly,** *adv.*

au·to·da·fé (ô′tō də fā′, ô′tō-, *or* ou′tō-) *n., pl.* **au·tos·da·fé.
1** a public ceremony accompanying the passing of sentence by the
Spanish Inquisition. **2** the carrying out of such a sentence. **3** the
burning of a heretic. [< Pg. *auto-da-fé* act of the faith < L *actus* act
and *fides* faith]

hat, āge, fär; let, ēqual, tèrm; it, īce
hot, ōpen, ôrder; oil, out; cup, pút, rüle,
əbove, takən, pencəl, lemən, circəs

ch, child; ng, long; sh, ship
th, thin; ŦH, then; zh, measure

au·to·gi·ro *or* **au·to·gy·ro** (ô′tə jī′rō *or* ô′tə-) *n., pl.* **-ros.
1** an aircraft powered by a single ordinary propeller but deriving its
lift mainly from a set of free-wheeling rotors that turn as the aircraft
moves forward. **2 Autogiro,** *Trademark.* a brand of such an aircraft.
[< Sp. *autogiro* < Gk. *auto-* self + *gyros* circle]

au·to·graph (ô′tə graf′ *or* ô′tə-) *n., v.* —*n.* **1** a persons's
signature. **2** something written in a person's own handwriting. —*v.*
1 write one's signature in or on. **2** write with one's own hand.

au·to·graph·ic (ô′tə graf′ik *or* ô′tə-) *adj.* **1** of or for an
autograph. **2** in one's own handwriting.

au·to·graph·i·cal (ô′tə graf′ə kəl *or* ô′tə-) *adj.* autographic.

au·to·in·tox·i·ca·tion (ô′tō in tok′sə kā′shən *or* ô′tō-) *n.*
poisoning by toxic substances produced within the body.

au·to·mat (ô′tə mat′ *or* ô′tə-) *n.* a restaurant in which food is
obtained from compartments that open when coins are inserted in
slots. [short for *automatic*]

au·to·mate (ô′tə mat′ *or* ô′tə-) *v.* **-mat·ed, mat·ing. 1** convert to
automatic operation or automation: *Fewer people are employed in a
plant when it is automated.* **2** make use of automation: *Many
industries now face the problem of whether to automate or not.*
[back formation from *automation*]

au·to·mat·ic (ô′tə mat′ik *or* ô′tə-) *adj., n.* —*adj.* **1** made without
thought or attention, as from force of habit, etc.; spontaneous or
mechanical: *His automatic reply to questions from reporters was,
"No comment."* **2** mainly or entirely involuntary; reflex: *Breathing
is automatic.* **3** of a mechanism, machine, etc., made or set to move
or act by itself; self-regulating or self-acting: *an automatic lock. Her
car has an automatic transmission.* **4** of a firearm, having a
mechanism for repeatedly firing, throwing out the used shell, and
reloading until the pressure on the trigger is released or the
ammunition is used up. **5** as a necessary consequence; without
exception, or restriction: *automatic promotion after a year of
service. Any violation of the rules means automatic disqualification.*
—*n.* **1** an automobile equipped with an automatic transmission: *Is
your car an automatic?* **2** an automatic firearm. [< Gk. *automatos*
self-acting]

au·to·mat·i·cal·ly (ô′tə mat′ik lē *or* ô′tə-) *adv.* in an automatic
manner.

automatic pilot a gyroscopic mechanism designed to keep an
aircraft, missile, etc. on a given course and at a given altitude
without human assistance.

au·to·ma·tion (ô′tə mā′shən *or* ô′tə-) *n.* a method of making a
manufacturing process, a production line, etc. operate more
efficiently by the use of built-in or supplementary controls in a
machine or number of machines. [< *automat*ic + *operation*]

au·tom·a·tism (ô tom′ə tiz′əm *or* ô tom′ə tiz′əm) *n.* **1** the
quality or state of being automatic. **2** an automatic action.
3 *Psychology.* **a** action not controlled by the conscious mind. **b** the
power of acting in such a way. **4** the suspension of conscious
control of the mind, as sought or practised by some artists and
writers, to permit free expression of the subconscious.

au·tom·a·ton (ô tom′ə ton′ *or* ô tom′ə ton′) *n., pl.* **-tons** *or* **-ta**
(-tə). **1** an apparatus that is made to resemble a human being or an
animal and operates by a concealed mechanism or by remote
control; robot. **2** a person or animal that acts or appears to act in an
automatic or mechanical way. [< Gk. *automaton,* neut., self-acting]

au·to·mo·bile (ô′tə mə bēl′ *or* ô′tə-) *n.* **1** a passenger vehicle
that carries its own engine and is driven on roads and streets; car.
2 (*adjl.*) of, having to do with, or for an automobile: *an automobile
engine.* [< F]

au·to·mo·bil·ist (ô′tə mə bēl′ist *or* ô′tə-) *n.* a person who uses
an automobile.

au·to·mo·tive (ô′tə mō′tiv *or* ô′tə-) *adj.* **1** of or having to do
with cars, trucks, and other self-propelled vehicles. Automotive
engineering deals with the design and construction of automobiles.
2 self-propelling.

au·to·nom·ic (ô′tə nom′ik *or* ô′tə-) *adj.* autonomous.

autonomic nervous system *Physiology.* the ganglia and
nerves of the nervous system of vertebrates, which control
digestive, reproductive, and other involuntary functions of the
body.

au·ton·o·mist (ô ton′ə mist′) *n.* a person who advocates
autonomy.

au·ton·o·mous (o ton′ə məs *or* ô ton′ə məs) *adj.* self-governing; independent. —**au·ton′o·mous·ly,** *adv.*

au·ton·o·my (o ton′ə mē *or* ô ton′ə mē) *n., pl.* -mies. 1 self-government; independence. 2 a self-governing community. [< Gk. *autonomia* < *auto-* of oneself + *nomos* law]

au·top·sy (o′top sē *or* ô′top sē, o′təp sē *or* ô′təp sē) *n., pl.* -sies. an examination and dissection of a dead body to find the cause of death or the nature or extent of the damage done to the body by disease, injury, etc. Compare **biopsy.** [< NL < Gk. *autopsia* < *auto-* for oneself + *opsis* a seeing]

au·to·route (o′tō rüt′ *or* ô′tō-) *n.* expressway. [< F]

au·to·sug·ges·tion (o′tō sə jes′chən *or* ô′tō-, o′tō səg jes′chən *or* ô′tō-) *n. Psychology.* the suggestion to oneself of ideas that produce subconscious changes in attitudes, behavior, or physical condition.

au·to·ther·a·py (o′tō ther′ə pē *or* ô′tō-) *n.* 1 self-treatment. 2 a spontaneous cure.

au·tumn (o′təm *or* ô′təm) *n.* 1 the season of the year between summer and winter; fall. 2 a time of maturity and the beginning of decay. 3 (*adjl.*) of, in, like, or characteristic of autumn: *autumn flowers, autumn rains.* [ME < OF < L *autumnus*]

au·tum·nal (o tum′nəl *or* ô tum′nəl) *adj.* of or coming in autumn.

autumnal equinox the equinox occurring about September 22.

aux·il·ia·ry (og zil′yə rē *or* ôg zil′yə rē, og zil′ə rē *or* ôg zil′ə rē) *adj., n., pl.* -ries. —*adj.* 1 supplementary or additional: *auxiliary troops. The building has an auxiliary power supply in case of a blackout.* 2 assisting or supporting: *Intellect and imagination should be auxiliary to each other.* 3 of a sailing vessel, equipped with an engine to supplement the power of the sails. —*n.* 1 a supplementary or supporting person, group, organization, or thing. 2 a sailing vessel equipped with an engine. 3 a naval vessel, such as a hospital ship, designed for duties other than fighting. 4 **auxiliaries,** *pl.* foreign or allied troops that help the army of a nation at war. 5 auxiliary verb. [< L *auxiliarius* < *auxilium* aid]

auxiliary verb a verb used to form the tenses, moods, aspects, or voices of other verbs, such as *be, can, do, have, may, must, shall,* and *will: I am going; he will go; they are lost; they were lost.*

Av (av) in the Hebrew calendar, the fifth month of the ecclesiastical year, and the eleventh month of the civil year.

av. 1 average. 2 avoirdupois.

av. *or* **Av.** Avenue.

AV audio-visual.

A.V. 1 Authorized Version. 2 audio-visual.

a·vail (ə vāl′) *v., n.* —*v.* 1 be of use or value to: *Money will not avail you after you are dead.* 2 help: *Talk will not avail without work.* **avail oneself of,** take advantage of; profit by; make use of: *While he was in Quebec he availed himself of the opportunity to improve his French.* —*n.* use; advantage or help for a purpose (*used especially with a negative meaning*): *Crying is of little avail now. He tried again and again, but to no avail.* [apparently < *a-* to (< L *ad-*) + *vail* < F < L *valere* be worth]

a·vail·a·bil·i·ty (ə vāl′ə bil′ə tē) *n.* the quality or state of being available: *The availability of water power helped make southern Ontario an industrial region.*

a·vail·a·ble (ə vāl′ə bəl) *adj.* 1 ready or handy to be used; that can be used: *The available water supply had dried up.* 2 that can be obtained: *All available tickets were sold.* 3 willing or free to do something: *He said he was available for the job now.* —**a·vail′a·bly,** *adv.*

av·a·lanche (av′ə lanch′) *n., v.* -lanched, -lanch·ing. —*n.* 1 a large mass of snow and ice, or of dirt and rocks, sliding or falling down a mountainside. 2 anything like an avalanche: *an avalanche of questions.* —*v.* move like an avalanche. [< F < Swiss F *lavenche* (< a pre-Latin Alpine language), influenced by F *avaler* go down < *à val* < L *ad vallem* to the valley]

avalanche lily any of several species (genus *Erythronium*) of wildflowers of the lily family found in the mountains of W North America, especially *E. grandiflorum,* the glacier lily.

Av·a·lon (av′ə lon′) *n. Celtic legend.* an earthly paradise in the western seas, to which King Arthur and other heroes were carried at death.

a·vant–garde (ä′vän gärd′) *n., adj.* —*n.* the people who develop new and experimental ideas, especially in the arts. —*adj.* of or having to do with such people or the movements started by

them: *an avant-garde artist, avant-garde ideas.* [< F *avant-garde* literally, advance guard]

a·vant–gard·ism (ä′vän gär′diz əm) *n.* 1 a movement or trend in the arts characterized by emphasis on what is new or startling. 2 the quality of being avant-garde.

a·vant–gard·ist (ä′vän gär′dist) *n.* a person who supports or belongs to the avant-garde in art, etc.

av·a·rice (av′ə ris) *n.* an extreme desire for money or property; greed: *It was avarice, not a desire for security, that made them scrimp and save all those years.* [ME < OF < L *avaritia* < *avarus* greedy]

av·a·ri·cious (av′ə rish′əs) *adj.* greedy for wealth. —**av′a·ri′cious·ly,** *adv.* —**av′a·ri′cious·ness,** *n.*

a·vast (ə vast′) *interj. Nautical.* a command to stop: *"Avast there!" shouted the sailor.* [probably < Du. *houd vast* hold fast]

a·va·tar (av′ə tär′) *n.* 1 *Hinduism.* the descent of a god to earth in bodily form; incarnation. 2 a manifestation in bodily form. [< Skt. *avatāra* descent < *ava* down + *tar-* pass over]

a·vaunt (a vont′, ə vônt′, *or* ə vänt′) *interj. Archaic.* a command to get out, go away, etc. [ME < OF *avant* < L *ab ante* forward, in front]

avdp. avoirdupois.

a·ve (ä′vā *or* ä′vē) *interj., n.* —*interj. Latin.* hail! farewell! —*n.* **Ave,** the prayer Ave Maria.

ave. *or* **Ave.** Avenue.

A·ve Ma·ri·a (ä′vä mə rē′ə *or* ä′vē mə rē′ə) *Roman Catholic Church.* 1 "Hail Mary!", the first words of the Latin form of a prayer. 2 the prayer.

A·ve Mar·y (ä′vē mer′ē) Ave Maria.

a·venge (ə venj′) *v.* a·venged, a·veng·ing. 1 inflict punishment in return for; take vengeance for: *to avenge an insult.* 2 take vengeance on behalf of (oneself or another): *The clan avenged their slain chief. He had the power to avenge himself on his betrayers.* 3 avenge oneself (*used in the passive*): *She swore to be avenged.* [ME < OF *avengier* < *a-* to (< L *ad-*) + *vengier* < L *vindicare* punish < *vindex* champion] —**a·veng′er,** *n.* ☛ **Syn. 1.** See note at **revenge.**

av·ens (av′inz) *n.* 1 any of several perennial plants (genus *Geum*) of the rose family found in temperate and arctic regions, including several common Canadian wildflowers, such as the three-flowered avens (*Geum triflorum*) of the Prairies. 2 See **mountain avens.** [ME < OF *avence*; origin unknown]

av·en·tu·rine (ə ven′chə rēn′ *or* ə ven′chə rin) *n.* a kind of quartz containing bright specks of mica or some other mineral. [< F < Ital. *avventurino* < *avventura* change < L *adventura*; because discovered accidentally. See ADVENTURE.]

av·e·nue (av′ə nyü′; *Esp.U.S.,* av′ə nü′) *n.* 1 a wide or main street. 2 a road or walk bordered by trees. 3 a way of approach or departure; passage: *avenues to fame.* 4 in some cities, a thoroughfare running at right angles to others usually called "streets." [< F *avenue,* fem. pp. of *avenir* < L *advenire* < *ad-* to + *venire* come]

a·ver (ə vėr′) *v.* a·verred, a·ver·ring. state to be true; assert. [ME < OF *averer,* ult < L *ad-* + *verus* true]

av·er·age (av′rij *or* av′ər ij) *n., adj., v.* -aged, -ag·ing. —*n.* 1 an arithmetical mean; the quantity found by dividing the sum of several quantities by the number of those quantities: *The average of 3, 5, and 10 is 6.* 2 a usual kind or quality; ordinary amount or rate: *His achievement at school was definitely above the average.* 3 *Business.* **a** a small charge payable by the master of a ship, covering the cost of pilotage, towing, etc. **b** a loss or expense arising as a result of damage at sea to ship or cargo. **c** the fair, proportionate distribution of such loss or expense among all the parties involved. —*adj.* 1 obtained by averaging; being an average: *an average price, the average temperature.* 2 usual; ordinary: *average intelligence.* —*v.* 1 find the average of. 2 amount on an average to; come close to: *The cost for lunch at the cafeteria averages about seven dollars a week.* 3 do, get, yield, etc. on an average: *He averages six hours work a day. We averaged eight litres per 100 kilometres.* 4 divide among several proportionately: *We averaged our gains according to what each had put in.* Abbrev.: av. [< F *avarie* damage to ship or cargo < Arabic *'awārīya* damage from sea water. In English, extended to "equal distribution" (at first, "of loss")]

a·ver·ment (ə vėr′mənt) *n.* a statement that something is true; assertion.

A·ver·nus (ə vėr′nəs) *n.* 1 *Roman mythology.* the lake on the shores of which lay the entrance to Hades. Avernus is the Latin name for Averno, a lake in the crater of an extinct volcano near Naples, Italy. 2 the lower world itself; Hades.

a·verse (ə vėrs′) *adj.* opposed; having an active distaste; reluctant (*used with* to): *He was averse to fighting.* [< L *aversus,* pp. of *avertere.* See AVERT.] —**a·verse′ness,** *n.*

a·ver·sion (ə vėr′zhən *or* ə vėr′shən) *n.* **1** a strong or fixed dislike; antipathy. **2** a thing or person disliked. **3** unwillingness.
☞ *Usage.* Either *to* or *for* follows **aversion:** *He has an aversion to moving fast and working hard. We'll eat alone; they have an aversion for fried shrimp.*

a·ver·sive (ə vėr′siv) *adj.* causing avoidance of an unpleasant stimulus; tending to repel: *Aversive conditioning is sometimes used by therapists to help a patient to overcome a serious bad habit, etc.*

a·vert (ə vėrt′) *v.* **1** prevent; avoid: *He averted the accident by a quick turn of his steering wheel.* **2** turn away; turn aside: *She averted her eyes from the wreck.* [ME < OF < L *avertere* < *ab-* from + *vertere* turn]

A·ves·ta (ə ves′tə) *n.* the sacred writings of the ancient Zoroastrian religion, still in use by the Parsees.

av·gas (av′gas′) *n.* aviation gasoline.

a·vi·an (ā′vē ən) *adj.* of or having to do with birds.

a·vi·ar·y (ā′vē er′ē) *n., pl.* **-ar·ies.** an enclosure or large cage in which to keep birds. [< L *aviarium* < *avis* bird]

a·vi·a·tion (ā′vē ā′shən *or* av′ē ā′shən) *n.* **1** designing, manufacturing, and operating of aircraft, especially airplanes. **2** airplanes, their personnel, and their equipment. [< F *aviation* < L *avis* bird]

a·vi·a·tor (ā′vē ā′tər *or* av′ē ā′tər) *n.* a person who flies an aircraft; pilot.

a·vi·a·trix (ā′vē ā′triks *or* av′ē ā′triks) *n.* a female aviator.

a·vi·cul·ture (ā′və kul′chər) *n.* the rearing or keeping of birds.

a·vi·cul·tur·ist (ā′və kul′chər ist) *n.* a bird expert or fancier.

av·id (av′id) *adj.* eager; greedy: *The miser was avid for gold.* [< L *avidus* < *avere* crave] —**av′id·ly,** *adv.*

a·vid·i·ty (ə vid′ə tē) *n.* **1** eagerness; greediness. **2** *Chemistry.* the relative strength of an acid or base.

a·vi·fau·na (ā və fon′ə) *n., pl.* the birds of a particular region, environment, or time.

A.V.M. Air Vice-Marshal.

av·o·ca·do (av′ə kä′dō) *n., pl.* **-dos. 1** the pear-shaped or egg-shaped fruit of a tropical American tree (*Persea americana*) of the laurel family, having a dark-green or blackish skin, soft, greenish-yellow, edible pulp, and a very large stone. **2** the tree producing this fruit. [< Sp. *avocado,* var. of *aguacate* < Mexican *ahuacatl*]

av·o·ca·tion (av′ə kā′shən) *n.* **1** something that a person does besides his regular business; a minor occupation; hobby: *Mrs. Gomez is a lawyer, but writing stories is her avocation.* **2** *Informal.* one's regular business; occupation. [< L *avocatio, -onis* < *avocare* < *ab-* away + *vocare* to call]
☞ *Usage.* See note at **vocation.**

av·o·cet (av′ə set′) *n.* any of several long-legged, web-footed wading birds (genus *Recurvirostra*) of temperate and tropical regions, having a long, slender bill that curves upward. [< F *avocette* < Ital. *avosetta*]

A·vo·gad·ro's law (ä′vō gäd′rōz) *Physics.* the law stating that equal volumes of different gases, under like conditions of pressure and temperature, contain the same number of molecules. [after Count Amedeo *Avogadro* (1776-1856), an Italian physicist, who stated it]

a·void (ə void′) *v.* **1** keep away from; keep out of the way of: *We avoided driving through large cities on our trip.* **2** *Law.* make void; annul. [< AF var. of OF *esvuidier* empty, quit < *es-* out (< L *ex-*) + *vuidier* < VL *vocitare* empty]

a·void·a·ble (ə voi′də bəl) *adj.* **1** that can be escaped or avoided. **2** *Law.* voidable.

a·void·ance (ə void′əns) *n.* **1** avoiding; a keeping away from. **2** the fact of being or becoming vacant: *the avoidance of the office of vice-president.* **3** *Law.* the act of making void; an invalidating; annulment.

av·oir·du·pois (av′ər də poiz′) *n.* **1** avoirdupois weight: *The package weighs three pounds avoirdupois.* **2** *Informal.* a person's mass, or weight. [ME < OF *aveir de peis* goods of weight < L *habere* have, *de* of, and *pensum* weight < *pendere* weight]

avoirdupois weight the ordinary system of weighing in Canada before the change to the **SI,** or metric system. One pound in avoirdupois weight is equal to about 0.454 kilograms. Compare **apothecaries' weight** and **troy weight.** See table at **weights and measures.**

av·o·set (av′ə set′) See **avocet.**

a·vouch (ə vouch′) *v.* **1** declare to be true. **2** guarantee. **3** acknowledge; affirm. [ME < OF *avochier* < *a-* to (< L *ad-*) + *vochier* call < L *vocare*]

a·vow (ə vou′) *v.* declare frankly or openly; confess; admit; acknowledge: *He avowed that he could not sing.* [ME < OF *avouer* < *a-* to (< L *ad-*) *vouer* vow < VL *votare*]

hat, āge, fär; let, ēqual, tėrm; it, īce
hot, ōpen, ôrder; oil, out; cup, pút, rüle,
əbove, takən, pencəl, lemən, circəs

ch, child; ng, long; sh, ship
th, thin; ŦH, then; zh, measure

a·vow·al (ə vou′əl) *n.* a frank or open declaration; confession; admission; acknowledgment.

a·vowed (ə voud′) *adj.* openly declared; admitted: *His avowed intention was to try for the party leadership.*

a·vow·ed·ly (ə vou′id lē) *adv.* admittedly; openly.

a·vun·cu·lar (ə vung′kyə lər) *adj.* **1** of an uncle. **2** like an uncle. [< L *avunculus* mother's brother, dim. of *avus* grandfather]

A.W. aircraftwoman.

a·wait (ə wāt′) *v.* **1** wait for; look forward to: *to await someone's arrival.* **2** be ready for; be in store for: *They had no idea what awaited them at the end of the trip.* [ME < OF *awaitier* < *a-* for (< L *ad-*) + *waitier* wait < Gmc.]
☞ *Usage.* See note at **wait.**

a·wake (ə wāk′) *v.* **a·woke** *or* **a·waked, a·wak·ing;** *adj.* —*v.* **1** cease or cause to cease sleeping; wake up: *We awoke from a sound sleep. The alarm clock awoke me.* **2** make or become active or alert: *The song awoke old memories.* —*adj.* (never used before a noun) **1** not asleep; roused from sleep: *Jerry is always awake early.* **2** on the alert; watchful: *awake to a danger.* [OE āwacian + OE onwǣcnan]

a·wak·en (ə wā′kən) *v.* awake.

a·wak·en·ing (ə wā′kən ing) *n., adj.* —*n.* a waking up or arousing: *an awakening to danger.* —*adj.* waking or reviving: *the awakening birds.*

a·ward (ə wôrd′) *v., n.* —*v.* **1** give after careful consideration; grant: *A medal was awarded to the woman who saved the child.* **2** decide or settle by law; adjudge: *The court awarded damages of $5000.* —*n.* **1** something given after careful consideration; a prize: *Frank's dog won the highest award.* **2** *Law.* a decision by a judge. [< AF var. of OF *esguarder* observe, decide < VL *ex-* from + *wardare* guard < Gmc.]

a·ware (ə wer′) *adj.* knowing; realizing; conscious: *I was too sleepy to be aware how cold it was.* [OE *gewær*] —**a·ware′ness,** *n.*
☞ *Syn.* See note at **conscious.**

a·wash (ə wosh′) *adv. or adj.* **1** level with the surface of the water; just covered with water. **2** carried about by water; floating.

a·way (ə wā′) *adv., adj.* —*adv.* **1** from a place; to a distance: *Get away from the fire.* **2** at a distance; far: *The sailor was far away from home.* **3** in another direction; aside: *turn away.* **4** out of one's possession, notice, or use: *He gave his boat away.* **5** out of existence: *The sounds died away.* **6** without stopping; continuously: *She worked away at her job.* **7** without waiting; at once.
away back, *Informal.* far back in space or time.
away with, (used in commands) take someone or something away: *Away with you* means go away.
do away with, **a** put an end to; get rid of. **b** kill.
—*adj.* **1** at a distance; far. **2** absent; gone. [OE *onweg*]

awe (o *or* ô) *n., v.* **awed, aw·ing.** —*n.* **1** wonder and reverence inspired by something sacred, mysterious, or magnificent: *They gazed in awe at the mountains towering above them.* **2** great respect and admiration mixed with fear, inspired by power and authority: *They stood in awe of the old woman's disapproval.* —*v.* **1** cause to feel awe; fill with awe: *The majesty of the mountains awed us.* **2** influence or restrain by awe. [ME *age* < ON *agi*]

a·wea·ry (ə wēr′ē) *adj. Poetic.* weary; tired.

a·weath·er (ə weŦH′ər) *adj. or adv.* on or toward the windward, or weather, side.

a·weigh (ə wā′) *adj.* raised off the bottom: *The ship sailed off as soon as its anchor was aweigh.*

awe·some (o′səm *or* ô′-) *adj.* **1** causing awe: *A great fire is an awesome sight.* **2** showing awe: *awesome admiration.*

awe–strick·en (o′strik′ən *or* ô′-) *adj.* filled with awe.

awe–struck (o′struk′ *or* ô′-) *adj.* filled with awe.

aw·ful (o′fəl *or* ô′-) *adj.* **1** dreadful; terrible: *an awful storm.* **2** *Informal.* very bad, great, ugly, etc.: *The room was in an awful mess.* **3** deserving great respect and reverence; sublime: *the awful power of God.* **4** filling with awe; impressive. **5** (advl.) *Informal.* very: *He was awful mad.* [< *awe* + *-ful*] —**aw′ful·ness,** *n.*
☞ *Usage.* In informal English **awful** = filling with awe. In familiar and informal English it is a general word of disapproval: *awful manners, an awful cold, an awful mistake.* As a result, the word is seldom used in careful writing; **awe-inspiring** has taken its place.

aw·ful·ly (o′flē *or* ô′flē, o′fə lē *or* ô′fəl ē) *adv.* **1** dreadfully; terribly. **2** *Informal.* very: *I'm awfully sorry that I hurt your feelings.*

a·while (ə hwīl′ *or* ə wīl′) *adv.* for a short time.

awk·ward (ok′wərd *or* ôk′wərd) *adj.* **1** clumsy; not graceful or skilful: *The seal is very awkward on land, but quite at home in the water.* **2** not well suited to use: *The handle of this pitcher has an awkward shape.* **3** not easily managed: *This is an awkward corner to turn.* **4** embarrassing: *He asked me an awkward question.* [< obs. *awk* perversely, in the wrong way (ME < ON *afug* turned the wrong way) + *-ward*] —**awk′ward·ly**, *adv.* —**awk′ward·ness**, *n.*
☛ *Syn.* **1. Awkward, clumsy, ungainly** = not graceful. **Awkward** = lacking grace, ease, quickness, and skill: *An awkward girl is no help in the kitchen.* **Clumsy** suggests moving heavily and stiffly: *The clumsy boy bumped into the furniture.* **Ungainly** = awkward in moving one's body: *He is as ungainly as a newborn calf.*

awl (ol *or* ôl) *n.* a pointed tool used for making small holes in leather or wood. [OE *al*]
☛ *Hom.* **all.**

A.W.L. *Military.* absent without leave. Also, **A.W.O.L.**

awn (on *or* ôn) *n.* one of the bristly hairs extending from the spikelets of some cereal grains and other grasses. [ME < ON *ögn* chaff]

awned (ond *or* ônd) *adj.* of cereal grains, etc., having awns; bearded.

awn·ing (on′ing *or* ôn′ing) *n.* a rooflike structure consisting of metal, canvas, wood, or plastic spread over a frame and attached over a door, window, etc. as a protection from the sun or rain. [origin uncertain]

a·woke (ə wōk′) *v.* pt. and pp. of **awake.**

A.W.O.L., a.w.o.l., or **AWOL** (ā′wol *when used as acronym*) A.W.L.

a·wry (ə rī′) *adv. or adj.* **1** with a twist or a turn to one side: *Her hat was blown awry by the wind.* **2** wrong: *Our plans have gone awry.* [< *a-* in + *wry*]

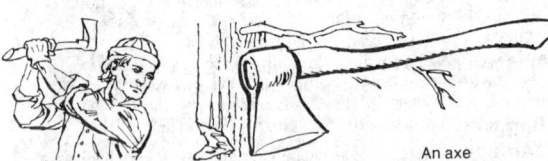

An axe

axe (aks) *n., v.* —*n.* **1** a tool for chopping and splitting wood, etc., consisting of a heavy metal head attached to a long wooden handle, the head having a blade, or cutting edge, parallel to the handle. **2** a tool or weapon similar to this.
get the axe, *Informal.* be dismissed from a job; get fired.
have an axe to grind, have a special, usually selfish, purpose or reason for being involved.
—*v.* **1** split, shape, or trim with an axe. **2** *Informal.* remove, restrict, end, etc.: *Several budget items were axed due to lack of funds.* Sometimes, **ax.** [OE *æx*] —**axe′like′**, *adj.*

ax·el (ak′səl) *n. Figure skating.* a jump in which the skater takes off from one foot, makes one and a half turns in the air, and lands on the other foot.

axe·man (aks′mən) *n., pl.* **-men.** a man who uses an axe in chopping or fighting.

ax·es¹ (ak′sēz) *n.* pl. of **axis.**

ax·es² (ak′səz) *n.* pl. of **axe.**

ax·i·al (ak′sē əl) *adj.* **1** of or forming an axis. **2** on or around an axis.

ax·il (ak′sil) *n. Botany.* the angle between the upper side of a leaf or stem and the supporting stem or branch. [< L *axilla* armpit]

ax·il·la (ak sil′ə) *n., pl.* **ax·il·lae** (-ē *or* -ī). **1** armpit. **2** axil. [< L]

ax·il·lar·y (ak′sə ler′ē) *adj.* **1** of or near the armpit. **2** in or growing from an axil.

ax·i·o·log·i·cal (ak′sē ə loj′ə kəl) *adj.* of or having to do with axiology. —**ax′i·o·log′i·cal·ly**, *adv.*

ax·i·ol·o·gist (ak′sē ol′ə jist) *n.* a person who studies or specializes in axiology.

ax·i·ol·o·gy (ak′sē ol′ə jē) *n.* the study of the nature and criteria of moral and aesthetic values and value judgments.

ax·i·om (ak′sē əm) *n.* **1** a statement seen to be true without

proof; a self-evident truth: *It is an axiom that if equals are added to equals the results will be equal.* **2** an established principle. [< L < Gk. *axiōma* < *axios* worthy]

ax·i·o·mat·ic (ak′sē ə mat′ik) *adj.* **1** self-evident: *That a whole is greater than any of its parts is axiomatic.* **2** full of axioms or maxims.

ax·is (ak′sis) *n., pl.* **ax·es** (-sēz). **1** an imaginary or real line that passes through an object and about which an object turns or seems to turn. The earth's axis is an imaginary line through the North and South Poles. **2** a central or principal line around which parts are arranged regularly. The axis of a cone is the straight line joining its apex and the centre of its base. **3** a central or principal structure extending lengthwise. The axis of a plant is the stem. The axis of the skeleton is the spinal column. **4** an important line of relation: *the Berlin-Rome axis.* **5 the Axis,** in World War II, Germany, Italy, Japan, and their allies. [< L]

ax·le (ak′səl) *n.* **1** a bar or shaft on which or with which a wheel turns. **2** axletree. [OE *eaxl* shoulder, crossbar; influenced by ON *öxul*]

ax·le·tree (ak′səl trē′) *n.* a crossbar that connects two opposite wheels.

ax·man (aks′mən) See **axeman.**

Ax·min·ster (aks′min stər) *n.* a kind of carpet with a finely tufted velvetlike pile. [< *Axminster,* a town in England where such carpets were first made]

ax·o·lotl (ak′sə lot′əl) *n.* any of several species (genus *Ambystoma*) of salamander found in certain lakes of Mexico and the W United States, that ordinarily never lose their gills and larval form but otherwise live and breed like other salamanders. [< Sp. < a Nahuatl word meaning "water doll"; literally, servant of water]

ax·on (ak′son) *n.* the part of a nerve cell that carries impulses away from the body of the cell. [< Gk. *axōn* axis]

ax·one (ak′sōn) *n.* axon.

ay¹ (ā) See **aye¹.**

ay² (ī) See **aye².**

a·yah (ä′yə) *n.* a native maid or nurse in India. [< Hind. *āya* < Pg. *aia* governess]

a·ya·tol·lah (ä′yə tō′lə) *n.* **1** a title of respect given to the most eminent scholars in Shiite Islamic theology and law. **2** *Informal.* a person having or aspiring to great authority: *the ayatollahs of the media.* [< Persian < *ayat* religious mark or sign + *ollah* Allah, God]

aye¹ or **ay** (ā) *adv.* always; ever. [ME < ON *ei*]
☛ *Hom.* **eye, I.**

aye² or **ay** (ī) *adv., n.* —*adv.* yes: *Aye, aye, sir.* —*n.* an affirmative answer, vote, or voter: *The ayes were in the majority when the vote was taken.* [origin uncertain]
☛ *Hom.* **eye, I.**

aye–aye (ī′ī′) *n.* a squirrel-like lemure of Malagasy. [< F < Malagasy *aiay*]

Ayr·shire (er′shər *or* er′shər) *n.* a breed of hardy dairy cattle that are red and white or brown and white. [< *Ayrshire,* a county in SW Scotland]

az. **1** azimuth. **2** azure.

AZ Arizona.

a·zal·ea (ə zāl′yə) *n.* **1** any of various species and cultivated varieties of rhododendron, especially those having funnel-shaped flowers and deciduous leaves. **2** the flower or cluster of flowers of any of these plants. [< NL < Gk. *azaleos* dry < *azein* parch]

a·zan (ä zän′ *or* ə zan′) *n.* the Moslem call to public prayer, proclaimed five times a day by the muezzin, or crier, from the minaret of a mosque. [< Arabic *adhān* invitation]

az·i·muth (az′ə məth) *n. Astronomy.* the angular distance east or west from the north point: *The azimuth of the North Star is 0 degrees. A star due northeast from the observer has an azimuth of 45 degrees E. Abbrev.:* az. [ME < OF *azimut* < Arabic *as-sumūt* the ways < *samt* way]

az·o (az′ō *or* ā′zō) *adj.* containing nitrogen. [< F *azote* nitrogen < Gk. *a-* not + *zōē* life, because nitrogen does not support life]

a·zo·ic (ə zō′ik) *adj.* **1** *Geology.* having no trace of life or organic remains. **2** of or having to do with geological time previous to the existence of living things. [< Gk. *azōos* without life + E *-ic*]

Az·tec (az′tek) *n., adj.* —*n.* **1** a member of an Amerindian people who ruled Mexico before its conquest by the Spaniards in 1519. **2** the language of the Aztecs. —*adj.* of or having to do with the Aztecs or their language.

az·ure (azh′ər *or* ā′zhər) *n., adj.* —*n.* **1** blue; sky blue. **2** *Poetic.* the clear sky. —*adj.* blue; sky blue. [ME < OF *l'azur* the azure < Arabic < Persian *lajward* lapis lazuli]

az·u·rite (azh′ú rīt′) *n.* a blue copper ore; a basic carbonate of copper. *Formula:* $2CuCO_3 \cdot Cu(OH)_2$

Bb

b or **B** (bē) *n., pl.* **b's** or **B's. 1** the second letter of the English alphabet. **2** any speech sound represented by this letter. **3** a person or thing identified as **b**, especially the second in a series: *Company B in a battalion.* **4 B, a** a grade rating a person or thing as good but not excellent, the second level from the top, or best: *grade B beef.* **b** a person or thing receiving this rating. **5** *Music.* **a** the seventh tone in the scale of C major. **b** a symbol standing for this tone. **c** a key or string that produces this tone. **d** a scale of key that has B as its keynote. **6** *Algebra.* Usually, **b**, the second known quantity: $ax + by + c = 0$. **7 B, a** an antigen found in some human blood. **b** the type of human blood containing this antigen, one of the four types in the ABO system. **8 B,** a symbol used on pencils to indicate the degree of softness of the lead: *A 2B pencil is quite soft; 6B is very soft.* Compare **H** and **HB. 9** something shaped like the letter B. **10** (*adj.*) of or being a B or b.

B boron.

B. 1 Bay. **2** Bible. **3** British. **4** bacillus.

B. or **b. 1** born. **2** book. **3** base. **4** baseman. **5** bat. **6** bass. **7** basso. **8** bachelor.

Ba barium.

BA or **B.A.** British Airways.

B.A. Bachelor of Arts (for L *Baccalaureus Artium*).

baa (bä *or* ba) *n., v.* **baaed, baa·ing.** bleat.

Ba·al (bā′əl *or* bāl) *n., pl.* **Ba·al·im** (bā′əl im). **1** any of a number of local deities among the ancient Semitic peoples. **2** the chief god of the Canaanites and Phoenicians. In some places he was the god of fertility; in others, he was the sun god. **3** a false god. [< Hebrew *bá'al* lord, master]

ba·ba (bä′bä; *French* bä bä′) *n.* a small, light cake, made with yeast and flavored with rum, kirsch, etc. [< F < Polish *baba*, originally, old woman]

bab·bitt (bab′it) *n., v.* —*n.* a whitish alloy of tin, antimony, and copper, or a similar alloy, used in bearings, etc. to lessen friction. —*v.* furnish (a bearing) with babbitt. [after Isaac *Babbitt* (1799-1862), an American inventor]

Bab·bitt (bab′it) *n.* a self-satisfied businessman who readily conforms to middle-class ideas of respectability and business success. [after the hero of the novel *Babbitt* by Sinclair Lewis]

Babbitt metal babbitt.

bab·bitt·ry or **Bab·bitt·ry** (bab′it rē) *n.* conformity to middle-class ideas of respectability and business success. [< *Babbitt*]

bab·ble (bab′əl) *v.* **-bled, -bling;** *n.* —*v.* **1** make indistinct sounds like a baby. **2** talk or speak foolishly. **3** talk too much; tell secrets. **4** reveal foolishly: *to babble a secret.* **5** murmur. —*n.* **1** talk that cannot be understood: *A confused babble filled the room.* **2** foolish talk. **3** a murmur: *the babble of the brook.* [ME *babel*; imitative] —**bab′bler,** *n.*

babe (bāb) *n.* **1** a baby. **2** an innocent or inexperienced person; a person who is like a child. **3** *Slang.* a girl or young woman, especially an attractive one. [ME]

babe in arms 1 a very young baby. **2** an innocent or gullible person.

babe in the wood or **woods** a naïve, gullible, or childlike person; one who is so innocent or inexperienced as to be a likely victim of an unscrupulous person or plan.

Ba·bel (bā′bəl *or* bab′əl) *n.* **1** Babylon. **2 Tower of Babel,** in the Bible, a high tower built to reach heaven. God punished the builders by changing their language into several new languages. When they could not understand one another, they had to leave the tower unfinished (Gen. 11:1-9). **3** Also, **babel. a** a confusion of many different sounds; noise. **b** a place of noise and confusion. [< Hebrew]

ba·biche (bä bēsh′ *or* bab′ish) *n. Cdn.* rawhide thongs or lacings: *Babiche is often used in making snowshoes.* [< Cdn.F < Algonquian]

bab·i·ru·sa, bab·i·rous·sa, or **bab·i·rus·sa** (bab′ə rü′sə *or* bä′bə rü′sə) *n.* a wild pig (*Babyrousa babyrussa*) of the East Indies. The boar has long, curved tusks. [< Malay *bābi* hog + *rūsa* deer]

ba·boo (bä′bü) See **babu.**

ba·boon (ba bün′) *n.* **1** any of various large, fierce monkeys of Africa and the Arabian peninsula having a doglike face and a short tail. **2** a clumsy, uncouth person; lout. [ME < OF *babouin* stupid person]

ba·bu (bä′bü) *n., pl.* **-bus.** in India: **1** a form of address more or less corresponding to *Mr.*, used before the full name or following the first name of a man. **2** *Historical.* **a** an Indian clerk who could write English. **b** *Derogatory.* an Indian person with some English education.

ba·bush·ka or **ba·boush·ka** (bə büsh′kə; *Russian,* bä′bùsh kə) *n.* a woman's scarf or kerchief worn on the head and knotted under the chin. [< Russian *babushka* grandmother, dim. of *baba* old woman]

ba·by (bā′bē) *n., pl.* **-bies;** *v.* **-bied, -by·ing.** —*n.* **1** a very young child. **2** the youngest of a family or group. **3** a person who acts like a baby; childish person. **4** a plan, idea, project, etc. that a person, group, etc. creates or is responsible for: *The society's baby for next year is the building of a new theatre.* **5** *Slang.* a girl or woman (*often used as a form of address*). **6** *Slang.* any person or thing: *That guy is a tough baby. This baby here is our best sedan.* **7** (*adj.*) **a** of or for a baby: *baby shoes.* **b** very young: *a baby bird.* **c** small of its kind: *my baby finger, a baby grand piano.* **d** like that of a baby or child: *a baby face.* —*v.* **1** treat as a baby; pamper or indulge. **2** operate or handle very carefully: *to baby a new car.* [ME *babe*] —**ba′by·like′,** *adj.*

baby beef 1 the prime beef of a calf that has been fattened for one to two years before slaughtering. **2** a calf thus fattened.

baby blue pale blue.

baby bonus *Cdn. Informal.* the Family Allowance.

baby boom the marked increase in the birth rate that characterized the period following the end of World War II: *The baby boom caused a shortage of schools in the Fifties and Sixties.*

baby buggy baby carriage.

baby carriage a light, four-wheeled carriage used for wheeling a baby about.

ba·by–faced (bā′bē fāst′) *adj.* **1** appearing to have extreme youth and innocence. **2** having a rather round, chubby, smooth face.

baby grand a small grand piano.

ba·by·hood (bā′bē hùd′) *n.* **1** the condition or time of being a baby. **2** babies as a group.

ba·by·ish (bā′bē ish) *adj.* like a baby; childish; silly. —**ba′by·ish·ly,** *adv.* —**ba′by·ish·ness,** *n.*

Bab·y·lon (bab′ə lən *or* bab′ə lon′) *n.* **1** the capital of ancient Babylonia, on the Euphrates River and, later, of the ancient Chaldean empire. Babylon was noted for its wealth, power, magnificence, and wickedness. **2** any great, rich, or wicked city.

Bab·y·lo·ni·an (bab′ə lō′nē ən) *adj., n.* —*adj.* of or having to do with Babylonia, an ancient empire in SW Asia or Babylon. —*n.* **1** a native or inhabitant of ancient Babylonia or Babylon. **2** the language of the ancient Babylonians.

baby's breath any of various plants (genus *Gypsophila*) of the pink family native to Europe, Asia, and Africa, having many tiny white or pink flowers on delicate branching stems: *Baby's breath is often used to add a dainty touch to bouquets and to flower arrangements.*

ba·by–sit (bā′bē sit′) *v.* **-sat, -sit·ting.** take care of a child or children during the temporary absence of the parents.

ba·by–sit·ter (bā′bē sit′ər) *n.* a person who baby-sits.

baby tooth one of the first set of teeth of a child or young animal; a temporary tooth; milk tooth.

bac·ca·lau·re·ate (bak′ə lô′rē it) *n.* **1** a degree of bachelor given by a university or college. **2** a speech delivered to a graduating class at commencement. [< Med.L. *baccalaureatus* < *baccalaureus* bachelor, var. of *baccalarius*, because of a supposed derivation from L *bacca* berry + *laurus* laurel]

bac·ca·rat or **bac·ca·ra** (bak′ə rä′ *or* bak′ə rä′) *n.* a kind of card game played for money. [< F]

Bac·chae (bak′ē or bak′ī) n. pl. **1** female companions or worshippers of Bacchus. **2** priestesses of Bacchus.

bac·cha·nal (bak′ə nal or bak′ə nal′) adj., n. —adj. having to do with Bacchus or his worship.
—n. **1** a worshipper of Bacchus. **2** a drunken reveller. **3** a wild, noisy party; bacchanalia. **4 Baccanals,** pl. Bacchanalia. [< L bacchanalis < Bacchus god of wine < Gk. Bakchos]

Bac·cha·na·li·a (bak′ə nāl′lē ə or bak′ə nāl′yə) n. pl. **1** in ancient Rome, a wild, noisy festival in honor of Bacchus. **2 bacchanalia,** a wild, noisy party; drunken revelry; orgy.

bac·cha·na·li·an (bak′ə nā′lē ən or bak′ə nāl′yən) adj., n. —adj. **1** having to do with the Bacchanalia. **2** drunken and riotous. —n. a drunken reveller.

bac·chant (bak′ənt) n., pl. **bac·chants** or **bac·chan·tes** (bə kan′tēz) **1** a priest or worshipper of Bacchus. **2** a drunken reveller. [< L bacchans, -antis, ppr. of bacchari celebrate the festival of Bacchus]

bac·chan·te (bə kan′tē, bə kant′, or bak′ənt) n. a priestess or female worshipper of Bacchus. [< F]

Bac·chic (bak′ik) adj. **1** of Bacchus or his worship. **2** Also, **bacchic,** drunken; riotous.

Bac·chus (bak′əs) n. Greek and Roman mythology. the god of wine. The Greeks also called him Dionysus.

bach (bach) v. Informal. live independently as a single person; keep house for oneself (often used with **it**): She's baching while her parents are away. He's been baching it for two years now. [< bachelor]

bach·e·lor (bach′ə lər or bach′lər) n. **1** an unmarried man. **2** (adj.) of, for, or designating a person who is not married or who lives alone: a bachelor apartment, a bachelor girl. **3** a bachelor apartment or flat: The apartments on this floor are all bachelors. **4** a person who holds the first degree offered by a university or college. **5** in the Middle Ages, a young knight serving under the banner of another. [ME < OF bacheler squire < Med.L baccalarius the holder of a small farm, a young man]

bach·e·lor-at-arms (bach′ə lər ət ärmz′ or bach′lər-) n., pl. **bachelors-at-arms.** bachelor (def. 5).

bach·e·lor·ette (bach′lə ret′) n. Cdn. a very small apartment consisting of one room with kitchen facilities and a bathroom; often, an illegal dwelling unit with less than the minimum floor space required by law.

bach·e·lor·hood (bach′ə lər hůd′ or bach′lər-) n. the condition of being a bachelor.

bachelor of arts a degree awarded by a university or college and involving at least three or four years' study beyond high school, the emphasis being generally on the liberal arts. Abbrev: B.A.

bach·e·lor's-but·ton (bach′ə lərz but′ən or bach′lərz-) n. **1** an annual plant (Centaurea cyanus) of the composite family, native to Europe but often grown in North America for its bright blue, mauve, pink, or white flowers; cornflower. **2** Often, **bachelor's buttons,** a perennial garden plant (Ranunculus acris) of the buttercup family native to Europe, having bright-yellow double flowers.

Bach·i·an (bäн′ē ən or bäk′ē ən) adj., n. —adj. **1** of or having to do with Johann Sebastian Bach (1685-1750), a German composer of music. **2** in the style of his music. —n. an interpreter or admirer of Bach's music.

ba·cil·lar (be sil′ər or bas′ə lər) adj. **1** of or like a bacillus. **2** characterized by bacilli. **3** rod-shaped.

ba·cil·li (bə sil′ī or bə sil′ē) n. pl. of **bacillus.**

ba·cil·li·form (ba sil′ə fôrm′) adj. rod-shaped. [< LL bacillus + E -form]

ba·cil·lus (bə sil′əs) n. **-cil·li. 1** any of a genus (Bacillus) of rod-shaped aerobic bacteria. **2** any rod-shaped bacterium. **3** any bacterium. [< LL bacillus, dim. of baculus rod]

back (bak) n., adj., v., adv. —n. **1** the part of a person's body opposite to his face and to the front part of his body: a broad back. She turned her back to the wind. **2** the upper part of an animal's body from the neck to the end of the backbone. **3** spinal column. **4** the side opposite or behind the front: the back of the head, the back of the room. **5** the upper, outer, or farther side or part: the back of the hand, the back of the garden. **6** the reverse or wrong side; the undecorated, unfinished, etc. side that is not meant to be displayed: the back of a rug. **7** the part of a chair, chesterfield, etc. that supports the back of a person sitting down. **8** support or help: Many of his friends backed his plan. **9** Sports. **a** a player whose position is behind the front line, as a halfback in football. **b** the position of such a player.

behind (someone's) **back,** secretly and with a mean or scheming purpose: He seemed to be a good friend but then I found out he was talking about me behind my back.

get (someone's) **back up,** Informal. make or become angry and stubbornly opposed: She didn't mean to be critical, so don't get your back up.

get off (someone's) **back,** Informal. stop nagging or criticizing someone: I finally told him if he didn't get off my back I wouldn't do it at all.

on (someone's) **back,** Informal. continually nagging or crticizing a person.

on (one's) **back,** helpless or incapacitated; especially, sick in bed: He's flat on his back with the flu.

put (someone's) **back up,** Informal. make angry and stubbornly opposed: It wasn't what she said, but the way she said it that put my back up.

turn (one's) **back on, a** reject or ignore in contempt, anger, or indifference: How can you turn your back on those people when they so obviously need help? **b** forsake; renounce: He turned his back on success and returned to his home town.

with (one's) **back to the wall,** in a desperate situation; no longer able to run away: Now, with their backs to the wall, they finally had to admit that they needed help.

—adj. **1** opposite or behind the front: the back seat of a car, the back fence. **2** belonging to the past; not current: the back numbers of a newspaper. **3** due but not yet paid; overdue: He still has some back debts to clear up. **4** Phonetics. pronounced at the back of the mouth. The o in go is a back vowel. **5** in distant or frontier regions: back country.

—v. **1** support or help (often used with **up**): Most of his friends backed his plan. If you make the request, we'll back you up. **2** take financial responsibility for: The show is backed by a group of local business people. **3** move backward: She backed away from the gun. He started the car and backed out into the street. **4** cause to move backward: to back a car. **5** countersign: to back a cheque. **6** bet on: to back a horse. **7** be a background for: A forest backed the little farm. **8** have the back facing towards (used with **on** or **onto**): Our house backs on a park. **9** provide with a back or backing: to back satin with crepe. The picture was backed with cardboard.

back and fill, a trim sails so as to keep a boat in a channel and floating with the current. **b** of cars and trucks, go forward and backward alternately in order to get out of mud or snow, or to make a difficult turn. **c** Informal. be undecided; keep changing one's mind.

back down, give up an attempt or claim; withdraw.

back into, Informal. gain (something) mainly by accident: He backed into a place on the hockey team when our star defenceman fell ill.

back off, move a short distance to the rear.

back out (of), Informal. **a** withdraw from an undertaking. **b** break a promise.

back up, move backward.

back water, a make a boat go backward. **b** reverse one's course; withdraw from a position, claim, etc.

—adv. **1** to or toward the rear; backward; behind: Please step back. **2** in or toward the past: some years back. **3** in return: Pay back what you borrow. **4** in the place from which something or somebody came: Put the books back. **5** in reserve: Keep back enough sugar to do the icing. **6** in check: Hold back your temper.

back and forth, first one way and then the other: He paced back and forth impatiently.

back of or **in back of,** behind: The garden is back of the house.

go back on, Informal. **a** fail to live up to: to go back on one's word. **b** not be faithful or loyal to: He went back on his friends. [OE bæc]

☛ Usage. **Back of, in back of.** The form **in back of,** still not accepted by some speakers, has become much more common throughout Canada. It is now widely accepted, along with the form **back of.**

back·ache (bak′āk′) n. a continuous pain in the back.

back bacon Cdn. bacon cut from the loin, having little fat and with a hamlike flavor.

back bench Usually **back benches,** pl. **1** the seats in a parliament or legislative assembly occupied by backbenchers. **2** the position or rank of a backbencher: He spent his entire political career on the back benches.

back-bench or **back·bench** (bak′bench′) adj. of or designating a backbencher or backbenchers: back-bench MPs, a back-bench revolt.

back·bench·er (bak′bench′ər) n. member of parliament or a legislative assembly who is not a member of the cabinet or one of the leading members of an opposition party.

back-bite (bak′bīt′) v. **-bit, -bit·ten** or **-bit, -bit·ing.** say spiteful or malicious things about (an absent person). —**back′bit′er,** n.

back·bone (bak′bōn′) n. **1** in human beings and other vertebrates, the series of small bones along the middle of the back; spinal column. See **spinal column** for picture. **2** anything like a backbone, such as the keel of a ship. **3** the most important part; the

chief strength or support: *She is the backbone of the organization.*
4 strength of character: *A coward lacks the backbone to stand up for his beliefs.*

back·break·ing (bak′brāk′ing) *adj.* physically very exhausting or tiring. —**back′break′ing·ly,** *adv.*

back·chat (bak′chat′) *n. Informal.* impudent or insolent retorts; talking back.

back–check¹ (bak′chek′) *n., v.* —*n.* the examination of completed work to verify its accuracy. —*v.* examine completed work to verify its accuracy.

back–check² (bak′chek′) *v. Hockey.* skate back toward one's own goal to cover an opponent's rush, used especially of forwards who have themselves been attacking.

back–comb (bak′kōm′) *v.* give (hair) a fuller appearance by lifting it in strands and combing the underlayers back toward the scalp.

back concessions *Cdn.* mainly in Ontario and Quebec, rural or bush districts, as opposed to urban centres: *He has a small farm on the back concessions.*

back country a region away from any centre of population; rural or undeveloped areas; backwoods.

back–country (bak′kun′trē) *adj.* of or having to do with the back country.

back·date (bak′dāt′) *v.* -dat·ed, -dat·ing. **1** put a date on (something) earlier than the actual date: **2** count as from a date earlier than the actual one.

back·door (bak′dôr′) *adj.* secret; underhand; sly.

back·drop (bak′drop′) *n.* **1** the curtain at the back of a stage. **2** a background.

back East *Cdn.* in or to eastern Canada: *Many people in western Canada speak of Ontario as being back East.*

back·er (bak′ər) *n.* a person who backs or supports another person, some plan or idea, a theatrical production, etc.

back·field (bak′fēld′) *n.* **1** *Football.* the players behind the front line: the quarterback, two halfbacks, flying wing, and fullback. In American football there is no flying wing. **2** *Baseball.* the outfield.

back·fill (bak′fil′) *v., n.* —*v.* refill (an excavation) with soil or other material. —*n.* the soil or other material used. —**back′fill′er,** *n.*

back·fire (bak′fīr′) *n., v.* -fired, -fir·ing. —*n.* **1** in an automobile engine, an explosion, either of fuel igniting too soon in a cylinder or of unburned exhaust gases in the muffler. **2** a fire set to check a forest fire or prairie fire by burning off the area in front of it. —*v.* **1** explode too soon. **2** use a backfire. **3** *Informal.* of a plan or scheme designed to gain something, have an unexpected result that is to the detriment or misfortune of the planner.

back formation a word formed from another word of which it appears to be the root. *Examples: burgle* from *burglar, edit* from *editor, pea* from *pease* taken as plural.

back·gam·mon (bak′gam′ən *or* bak′gam′ən) *n.* a game for two played on a special board with pieces moved according to the throw of dice. [< *back¹,* adj. + *gammon* game; because the men are sometimes set back]

back·ground (bak′ground′) *n.* **1** the part of a picture or scene farthest from the viewer: *In this photograph, the cottage stands in the foreground with the mountains in the background.* **2** a surface against which things are seen; a surface upon which things are made or placed: *a cotton print with pink flowers on a white background.* **3** earlier conditions or events that help to explain some later condition or event: *the background of the two-party system.* **4** one's past experience, knowledge, and training. **5** the accompanying music or sound effects in a play, motion picture, etc. **in the background,** out of sight; not in clear view.

back·hand (bak′hand′) *n., adj., v.* —*n.* **1** a stroke made with the back of the hand turned forward, especially in games like tennis or badminton. **2** handwriting in which the letters slope to the left. —*adj.* backhanded. —*v.* hit or catch backhanded.

back·hand·ed (bak′han′did) *adj.* **1** done or made with the arm across the body and the back of the hand turned forward. **2** slanting to the left. **3** awkward; clumsy. **4** ambiguous or sarcastic: *An example of a backhanded compliment is "I knew right away that you had made it yourself".* —**back′hand′ed·ly,** *adv.* —**back′hand′ed·ness,** *n.*

back·hoe (bak′hō′) *n., v.* -hoed, -hoe·ing. —*n.* a machine for digging trenches for water mains, etc. —*v.* use such a machine.

back·house (bak′hous′) *n.* **1** a small outside toilet; privy. **2** a small building at the back of a main one.

back·ing (bak′ing) *n.* **1** support; help. **2** financial support. **3** supporters; helpers. **4** something placed at the back of anything to support or strengthen it.

hat, āge, fär; let, ēqual, tèrm; it, īce
hot, ōpen, ôrder; oil, out; cup, pùt, rüle,
above, takən, pencəl, lemən, circəs

ch, child; ng, long; sh, ship
th, thin; ŦH, then; zh, measure

back·lash (bak′lash′) *n.* **1** a sudden hostile reaction to an earlier action or series of actions that were not originally seen as a serious threat: *a backlash of anger. The fear of rebellion resulted in a pro-government backlash.* **2** a jarring reaction between worn or badly fitting parts of a machine or mechanism. **3** the movement or play of such parts. **4** a tangle in the part of a fishing line still on the reel after a cast.

back·less (bak′lis) *adj.* **1** having no back. **2** of women's dresses, swim suits, etc., having the back of the bodice cut very low.

back·list (bak′list′) *n., v.* —*n.* **1** the books of a publisher that have been previously advertised and are still in print. **2** a list or catalogue of such books. —*v.* place on a backlist.

back·log (bak′log′) *n.* **1** an accumulation of orders, commitments, etc. that have not yet been filled: *The company hired extra staff to help clear the backlog of orders.* **2** a reserve supply; something saved or stored. **3** a large log at the back of a fire in a fireplace.

back number 1 an old issue of a magazine or newspaper. **2** *Informal.* a person or thing that is old-fashioned or out of date.

back order an order for goods not currently in stock, received and acknowledged for filling at a later date.

back–order (bak′ôr′dər) *v.* hold an order (for out-of-stock goods) for filling at a later date.

back·pack (bak′pak′) *n., v.* —*n.* **1** a lightweight bag of nylon, canvas, etc., usually attached to a tubular metal frame that is strapped onto a person's back, used for carrying food, clothing, equipment, etc. **2** (*adj.*) of or designating a way of travelling, especially on foot, while carrying all one's belongings in a backpack. —*v.* travel in this way: *They backpacked 200 kilometres last summer.*

back·pack·ing (bak′pak′ing) *n.* the action or sport of travelling, especially on foot, with all one's belongings carried in a backpack: *I had had no experience in wilderness backpacking.*

back·ped·al (bak′ped′əl) *v.* -alled, *or* aled, -al·ling *or* -al·ing. **1** move the pedals of a bicycle backward, especially to give a braking action. **2** *Boxing.* move backwards to keep away from an advancing opponent. **3** modify or retreat from (an opinion, promise, policy, etc.).

back·rest (bak′rest′) *n.* **1** anything that supports the back. **2** a support at the back, as on a lathe.

back road any little-used road, especially one in the country; side road.

back·room (bak′rüm′ *or* -rùm′) *adj.* **1** working behind the scenes or away from public view: *the backroom boys of politics.* **2** done, performed or decided without public knowledge: *She played a backroom role in the election.*

back·scratch·er (bak′skrach′ər) *n.* **1** any device for scratching the back. **2** *Informal.* a person who tries to gain advancement or maintain a position by flattering a superior; a toady.

back·scratch·ing (bak′skrach′ing) *n. Informal.* the giving and taking of favors for reciprocal advantage.

back seat 1 a seat at or in the back. **2** *Informal.* a place of inferiority or insignificance.

back–seat driver 1 a passenger in an automobile who criticizes and advises the driver. **2** a person who offers criticism and advice without himself assuming any responsibility.

back·set (bak′set′) *n.* a check to progress; setback.

back·sheesh *or* **back·shish** (bak′shēsh′) See **baksheesh.**

back·side (bak′sīd′) *n.* **1** the back. **2** the rump; buttocks.

back·slap·per (bak′slap′ər) *n. Informal.* **1** a person whose habit it is to slap others on the back. **2** any person whose friendly manner is so hearty and effusive as to seem insincere.

back·slide (bak′slīd′) *v.* -slid, -slid *or* -slid·den, -slid·ing. slide back into wrongdoing; lose one's enthusiasm, especially for religion. —**back′slid′er,** *n.*

back·space (bak′spās′) *v.* -spaced, -spac·ing. move the carriage or element carrier of a typewriter backward a space or a set number of spaces.

back–stab·ber (bak′stab′ər) *n. Informal.* a person who tries to harm another in secret, usually by slander or betrayal.

back·stage (bak′stāj′) *adv., adj.* —*adv.* 1 in the dressing rooms of a theatre. 2 toward the rear of a stage. —*adj.* 1 located backstage. 2 of or having to do with people and activities backstage. 3 not known to the general public; confidential: *backstage negotiations.*

back·stairs (bak′sterz′) *adj.* secret or underhand: *backstairs political bargaining.*

back stairs 1 stairs in the back part of a house, used mainly by servants. 2 a secret or underhand method or course: *Some people never do anything in the open but approach every deal by the back stairs.*

back·stay (bak′stā′) *n.* 1 a rope extending from the top of the mast to a ship's side and helping to support the mast. See **shroud** for picture. 2 a spring, rod, strap, etc. used for support at the back of something.

back·stitch (bak′stich′) *n., v.* —*n.* 1 a stitching method in which the thread doubles back each time on the preceding stitch. 2 a stitch made in this way. —*v.* sew with such stitches.

back·stop (bak′stop′) *n., v.* **-ped, -ping.** —*n. Sports.* 1 a fence or screen used to keep the ball from going too far away. 2 a player who stops balls that get past another player. —*v. Informal.* 1 serve as a backstop. 2 support; reinforce.

back·stroke (bak′strōk′) *n.* 1 a swimming stroke made with the swimmer lying on his back. 2 a backhanded stroke.

back talk *Informal.* a talking back; impudent answers.

back–to–back (bak′tə bak′) *adj.* 1 with the backs against each other or close together and the fronts or faces turned in opposite directions: *We placed the chairs back-to-back.* 2 *Informal.* consecutive: *They had four back-to-back wins.*

back·track (bak′trak′) *v.* 1 go back over a course of path. 2 withdraw from an undertaking, position, etc.: *Tom backtracked on the claim he made last week.*

back·up (bak′up′) *n.* 1 a person, group, or thing that serves as a support or reinforcement: *We need some sort of backup if we're going to convince them.* 2 (*adjl.*) serving as a support or reinforcement: *backup advice.* 3 an accumulation or buildup because of delay, obstruction, etc.: *a backup of traffic.*

back·ward (bak′wərd) *adv., adj.* —*adv.* 1 toward the back: *She glanced backward.* 2 with the back foremost: *The little girl was trying to walk backward. He tumbled backward.* 3 toward the starting point: *The rolling ball came to a stop and began to roll backward.* 4 opposite to the usual way; in the reverse way: *read backward.* 5 from better to worse: *Educational conditions in the town went backward.* 6 toward the past: *He looked backward forty years and talked about his childhood.* Also, **backwards.** —*adj.* 1 directed toward the back: *a backward look.* 2 with the back first. 3 directed to or toward the starting point; returning: *a backward movement.* 4 done in the reverse way or order: *a backward process.* 5 reaching back into the past. 6 slow in development: *Backward children need special help in school.* 7 shy; bashful. [ME *bakward* < *bak* back + *-ward*] —**back′ward·ness,** *n.*
☛ *Usage.* **Backward** and **backwards** are used interchangeably as adverbs: *Try doing the work backward. Try doing the work backwards.* Only *backward* is used as an adjective: *He hurried off without a backward glance.*

back·wards (bak′wərdz) *adv.* backward.
fall, lean, or **bend over backwards,** try extremely hard; be especially accommodating.
☛ *Usage.* See note at **backward.**

back·wash (bak′wosh′) *n.* 1 the water thrown back by oars, paddle wheels, the passing of a ship, etc. 2 a backward current.

back·wa·ter (bak′wo′tər *or* -wô′tər) *n.* 1 a stretch of still, often stagnant, water close to the bank of a river or stream. 2 a stretch of water that is held or pushed back, as by a dam. 3 a condition or place that is thought of as backward, stagnant, etc.: *The small, provincial town was often referred to as a cultural backwater.* 4 a backward current; backwash. 5 (*adjl.*) of or like a backwater: *backwater conditions.*

back·woods (bak′wùdz′) *n.pl., adj.* —*n.* uncleared forests or wild regions far away from towns. —*adj.* 1 of the backwoods. 2 crude; rough.

back·woods·man (bak′wùdz′mən) *n., pl.* **-men.** a person who lives or works in the backwoods.

back·yard (bak′yärd′) *n.* a yard behind a house: *They have a vegetable garden in their backyard.*
in (one's) **own backyard,** within one's own domain or area: *We have a lot of talented people right here in our own backyard.*

ba·con (bā′kən) *n.* salted and smoked meat from the back and sides of a pig. See **pork** for picture.
bring home the bacon, *Informal.* be successful; win the prize. [ME < OF < Gmc.]

Ba·co·ni·an (bā kō′nē ən) *adj., n.* —*adj.* 1 of or having to do with Francis Bacon (1561-1626), an English essayist, statesman and philosopher. 2 of or suggestive of his writings or philosophy. 3 of or having to do with the theory that Bacon wrote the plays of Shakespeare. —*n.* 1 a person who supports or follows the philosophy of Francis Bacon. 2 a person who supports the theory that Bacon wrote the plays of Shakespeare.

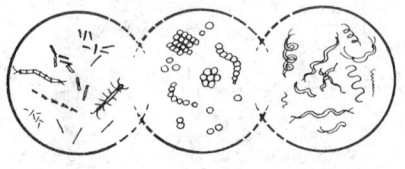

Three main tyes of bacteria, classified according to shape

BACILLI   COCCI   SPIRILLA

bac·te·ri·a (bak tēr′ē ə) *n.* a large, diverse group of one-celled micro-organisms found wherever there is life, in soil, water, and air, and within the bodies of other organisms. Many soil bacteria produce nitrogens that are useful for other organisms; some bacteria produce decay; some of the bacteria that live in other organisms cause disease. Bacteria have traditionally been classified as plants, but most authorities today place them in a separate kingdom.

bac·te·ri·al (bak tēr′ē əl) *adj.* of or caused by bacteria: *bacterial life, bacterial diseases.*

bac·te·ri·cid·al (bak tēr′ə sīd′əl) *adj.* destructive to bacteria.

bac·te·ri·cide (bak tēr′ə sīd′) *n.* a substance that destroys bacteria. [< *bacterium* + *-cide*²]

bac·te·ri·o·log·i·cal (bak tēr′ē ə loj′ə kəl) *adj.* having to do with bacteriology. —**bac·te′ri·o·log′i·cal·ly,** *adv.*

bac·te·ri·ol·o·gist (bak tēr′ē ol′ə jist) *n.* a person trained in bacteriology, especially one whose work it is.

bac·te·ri·ol·o·gy (bak tēr′ē ol′ ə jē) *n.* the science that deals with bacteria.

bac·te·ri·um (bak tēr′ē əm) *n. sing.* of **bacteria.** [< NL < Gk. *bactērion,* dim. of *baktron* stick, staff]

Bac·tri·an camel (bak′trē ən) a camel (*Camelus bactrianus*) of the highlands of central Asia, having two humps and somewhat shorter legs and a heavier build than the Arabian camel. It cannot travel as fast as the latter, but it can keep its pace longer in a caravan. [< *Bactria,* an ancient country in Asia]

bad (bad) *adj.* **worse, worst;** *adv.* —*adj.* 1 not good; not acceptable; poor or inferior in quality: *bad poetry, a bad shipment. The light was bad. That desk shows bad workmanship.* 2 unfavorable, unpleasant, or distressing: *bad news. He came at a bad time.* 3 severe: *a bad cold, a bad storm.* 4 evil; wicked: *a bad influence. They said he was bad through and through.* 5 naughty: *You're a bad boy!* 6 disagreeable or sullen: *a bad mood. She's in a bad temper.* 7 harmful: *It is bad for your eyes to read in dim light.* 8 sick; suffering: *He's feeling very bad with his cold.* 9 sorry; regretful: *I feel bad about losing your baseball.* 10 worthless; not valid: *a bad cheque, a bad debt.* 11 incorrect; faulty: *a bad guess, bad grammar.* 12 rotten; spoiled: *The fish is bad; we'll have to throw it out.* 13 run-down; partly ruined, especially because of neglect: *bad teeth. The car was in bad condition.* 14 (*noml.*) **the bad,** that which is bad; a bad condition, quality, etc.: *She realized she'd have to take the good with the bad.*
go bad, become spoiled or rotten: *We forgot about the leftovers and they went bad.*
in bad, *Informal.* in disfavor (with someone): *I'm in bad with my sister because I accidentally sat on her banjo.*
not bad, *Informal.* average; acceptable: *The movie's not bad, but I've seen better.*
not half bad, *Informal.* better than average; rather good: *I wasn't expecting much of the movie, but it's really not half bad.*
not so bad, *Informal.* better than expected: *I was dreading the test, but it wasn't so bad.*
to the bad, a toward a degenerative or ruined state: *a promising youth who went to the bad.* **b** in debt: *That last foolish deal put him several hundred dollars to the bad.*
—*adv. Slang.* badly: *It hurts bad.* [ME *badde,* ? < OE *bæddel* hermaphrodite] —**bad′ness,** *n.*
☛ *Hom.* **bade.**
☛ *Usage.* **Bad, badly.** Following a linking verb, formal English prefers the adjective **bad,** not the adverb **badly:** *He feels bad about the news.* Informal speech sometimes uses **badly:** *He feels badly about the news.* In both formal and informal writing, the adverb **badly** is used to modify verbs: *She sings badly.*

bad blood an unfriendly feeling; hate: *The bad blood between the two men grew to a full-scale feud.*

bad·die *or* **bad·dy** (bad′ē) *n., pl.* **-dies.** *Informal.* a bad person; an enemy or opponent, in public opinion, in a story or film, etc.: *The hero easily routs the baddies.*

bade (bad *or* bād) *v.* pt. of **bid** (defs. 1, 2, 5, 7).
☞ *Hom.* **bad** (bad).
☞ *Usage.* **Bade** is used chiefly in formal and literary English: *The king bade her remain.*

badge (baj) *n.* **1** something worn to show that a person belongs to a certain occupation, school, class, club, society, etc.: *The Red Cross badge is a red cross on a white background.* **2** a symbol; sign: *The traditional badge of office of a mayor is a chain.* [ME *bage*; origin unknown]

badg·er (baj'ər) *n., v.* —*n.* **1** any of various nocturnal burrowing animals of the weasel family having a wide, heavy body with long, grizzled fur, a long snout, and long, sharp claws on the forefeet. The American badger (*Taxidea taxus*), the only New World species, is found from the Canadian prairies south to Mexico. **2** the fur of a badger. —*v.* **1** keep after someone; try again and again to convince: *A car salesman has been badgering my father for weeks.* **2** harass by persistent questioning: *The judge objected to the way the lawyer was badgering the witness.* [? < *badge*; with reference to the white spot on its head]

bad·i·nage (bad'ə näzh' *or* bad'ə nij) *n.* good-natured joking; banter. [< F *badinage* < *badiner* banter < *badin* silly < VL *batare* gape]

bad·lands (bad'landz') *n.* a barren region marked by ridges, gullies, and weird rock formations caused by erosion, as found in parts of southern Saskatchewan and Alberta.

bad·ly (bad'lē) *adv.* **1** in a bad manner. **2** greatly; very much: *Rain is badly needed.*
☞ *Usage.* See note at **bad**.

bad·min·ton (bad'min tən) *n.* a game in which either two or four players use light rackets to volley a shuttlecock over a high net. [< *Badminton*, the Duke of Beaufort's estate in Gloucestershire, England]

bad–mouth (bad'mouth') *v. Slang.* speak badly of; disparage or criticize: *to bad-mouth a political opponent.*

bad–tem·pered (bad'tem'pərd) *adj.* **1** having a bad temper or disposition; angry or cross: *a bad-tempered horse.* **2** displaying irritation: *a bad-tempered remark.*

Bae·de·ker (bā'də kər) *n.* a guidebook for travellers. [< Karl *Baedeker* (1801-1859), German publisher of a series of guidebooks.]

baff (baf) *v., n.* —*v.* **1** *Golf.* strike the ground with the sole of the club in making a stroke. **2** *Scottish.* strike a blow. —*n.* **1** *Golf.* the act of baffing. **2** *Scottish.* a blow. [probably < OF *baffe* a blow]

baf·fle (baf'əl) *v.* **-fled, -fling;** *n.* —*v.* **1** be too hard for (a person) to understand or solve: *This puzzle baffles me.* **2** hinder or thwart. **3** struggle without success: *The ship baffled bravely with the storm.* —*n.* a wall, screen, or similar device controlling the flow of air, water, sound, etc. by hindering its movement or changing its course. [? < Scots *bauchle* ridicule] —**baf'fler,** *n.*
☞ *Syn. v.* **2.** See note at **frustrate**.

baf·fle·gab (baf'əl gab') *n. Slang.* meaningless or incomprehensible talk designed to impress or confuse a listener, avoid making a direct statement, etc.: *political bafflegab.*

baf·fle·ment (baf'əl mənt) *n.* the act of baffling or the state of being baffled.

baf·fling (baf'ling) *adj.* **1** puzzling. **2** hindering; thwarting.

bag (bag) *n., v.* **bagged, bag·ging.** —*n.* **1** a container made of paper, cloth, plastic, leather, etc. that can be pulled together or folded over to close at the top. **2** the amount that a bag can hold: *She ate a whole bag of cookies.* **3** a bag and its contents: *Could you buy a bag of milk?* **4** a baglike membrane or sac in an animal's body. **5** anything suggesting a bag by its use or shape. **6** the game killed or caught at one time by a hunter. **7** *Baseball.* a base. **8** *Slang.* an unattractive or disagreeable woman. **9** a person's particular interest, activity, skill, etc.: *Math was never his bag.*
bag and baggage, with all one's belongings; entirely.
in the bag, *Informal.* certain to succeed or be achieved; sure: *Don't worry; the contract's in the bag.*
leave (someone) **holding the bag,** *Informal.* leave (someone) to take all the responsibility or blame alone instead of sharing it: *We had agreed to do the dishes, but after dinner he suddenly remembered a phone call he had to make and left me holding the bag.*
—*v.* **1** put into a bag or bags: *to bag vegetables.* **2** swell or bulge: *His trousers bag at the knees.* **3** hang loosely. **4** *Hunting.* kill or catch. **5** *Slang.* catch; take; steal. [ME < ON *baggi* pack] —**bag'ger,** *n.*
☞ *Syn. n.* **1. Bag, sack** = a container made of paper, cloth, etc. that can be closed at the top. **Bag** is the general word, applying to any such container of suitable size and material: *Fresh vegetables are sometimes sold in cellophane bags.* **Sack,** in Canada and Great Britain, applies particularly to a large bag made of coarse cloth: *a sack of grain or potatoes.* In parts of the United States, **sack** is the general word.

ba·gasse (bə gas') *n.* the pulp of sugar cane after the juice has been extracted. [< F < Provençal *bagasso* husks]

bag·a·telle (bag'ə tel') *n.* **1** a mere trifle; thing of no importance.

hat, āge, fär; let, ēqual, tèrm; it, īce
hot, ōpen, ôrder; oil, out; cup, pút, rüle,
əbove, takən, pencəl, lemən, circəs

ch, child; ng, long; sh, ship
th, thin; ₮H, then; zh, measure

2 a game resembling billiards. **3** *Music.* a short, light composition. [< F < Ital. *bagatella*, dim. of *baga* berry]

ba·gel (bā'gəl) *n.* a doughnut-shaped roll of yeast dough that is simmered in water and then baked. [< Yiddish *beigel* < *beigen* twist; related to OE *bēag* ring]

bag·gage (bag'ij) *n.* **1** suitcases, bags, etc. packed with belongings, that a person takes with him on a trip; luggage. **2** the equipment that an army takes with it, such as tents, blankets, ammunition, etc. [ME < OF *bagage* < *bagues* bundles]
☞ *Syn.* **Baggage** (def. 1) and **luggage** are synonymous; however, the former term is usual in the United States, the latter in Great Britain. In Canada, both terms are used, but **luggage** often has special reference to suitcases, overnight bags, and other bags carried by hand; **baggage** is the usual term for heavier and more bulky items such as trunks, boxes, and crates, or for items that are checked or sent separately. Only **luggage** is used for suitcases, etc. when they are empty: *She bought a new set of luggage.*

baggage car a railway car used to carry passengers' baggage, mail bags, etc.

bag·gage·mas·ter (bag'ij mas'tər) *n.* a person in charge of receiving and dispatching baggage, especially at a railway station.

bag·gat·a·way (bə gat'ə wā') *n. Cdn. Historical.* a game of the Indians of eastern Canada, from which lacrosse developed. It was sometimes played between tribes, with as many as 200 men to a team. Also, **baggatiway.** [< Algonquian]

bag·ging (bag'ing) *n.* cloth for making bags.

bag·gy (bag'ē) *adj.* **-gi·er, -gi·est. 1** swelling; bulging. **2** hanging loosely: *baggy trousers.*

bag·man (bag'mən) *n.* **-men. 1** *Esp.Cdn. Informal.* a person who raises money for a political party. **2** *U.S. Slang.* a person who collects or pays out money for gamblers, racketeers, etc. **3** *Brit. Informal.* a travelling salesman.

bagn·io (ban'yō *or* bän'yō) *n., pl.* **bagn·ios. 1** brothel. **2** bathhouse. **3** prison. [< Ital. *bagno* bath or bathhouse < L < Gk. *balaneion* bath]

bag·pipe (bag'pīp') *n.* Usually, **bagpipes,** *pl.* a musical wind instrument in which the sound is produced by a reed melody pipe and several drone pipes supplied with air from a bag that is inflated by blowing through a mouthpiece or operating a bellows with the arm.

bag·pip·er (bag'pīp'ər) *n.* a person who plays the bagpipes.

ba·guette (ba get') *n.* **1** a gem cut in a narrow oblong shape. **2** such a shape. **3** *Architecture.* a small, half-round moulding.

bah (bä) *interj.* an exclamation of scorn or contempt.

Ba·ha·i (bə hä'ē) *n., adj.* —*n.* **1** a person who believes in Bahaism. **2** Bahaism. —*adj.* of or having to do with Bahaism. [< Persian]

Ba·ha·ism (bə hä'iz əm) *n.* a religious system founded in 1863 by Mussein Ali, a Persian religious leader who taught the basic unity of all religions.

Ba·ha·mi·an (bə hä'mē ən *or* bə hä'mē ən) *n., adj.* —*n.* a native or inhabitant of the Bahamas, a country consisting of a group of islands in the West Indies. —*adj.* of or having to do with the Bahamas.

Ba·ha·sa In·do·ne·sia (bä hä'sə in'dō nē'zhə) the official language of Indonesia, based on a form of Malay that was widely used in SE Asia as a lingua franca.

baht (bät) *n.* **1** the basic unit of money in Thailand, divided into 100 satang. See table at **money. 2** a coin worth one baht. [< Thai *bāt*]

bail¹ (bāl) *n., v.* —*n.* **1** a security necessary to set a person free from arrest until he is due to appear for trial. **2** the amount guaranteed.
go bail for, a supply bail for. **b** speak for; guarantee: *I'll go bail for his good behavior on the trip.*
—*v.* **1** obtain the freedom of (a person under arrest) by guaranteeing to pay bail. **2** deliver goods in trust without change of ownership.
bail out, supply bail for.
[ME < OF *bail* custody < *baillier* deliver < L *bajulare* carry]
☞ *Hom.* **bale.**

bail² (bāl) *n.* **1** the arched handle of a kettle or pail. **2** a hooplike support. The bails of a covered wagon hold up the canvas. [ME < ON *beygla* sword guard]
☞ *Hom.* **bale.**

bail³ (bāl) n., v. —n. a scoop or pail used to throw water out of a boat. —v. throw (water) out of a boat with a pail, a dipper, or any other container.
bail out, a make an emergency jump with a parachute from an aircraft. **b** throw accumulated water out of (something) with a pail, a dipper, or any other container.
[< F *baille* < L *bajulus* carrier]
☛ Hom. **bale.**

bail⁴ (bāl) n. **1** *Cricket.* either of two small bars that form the top of a wicket. **2** a partition separating horses in a stable. [ME < OF *bail* barrier]
☛ Hom. **bale.**

bail·a·ble (bāl′ə bəl) adj. **1** capable of being bailed. **2** permitting bail to be paid: *a bailable offence.*

bail·ee (bāl ē′) n. one to whom goods are committed in bailment.

bail·ey (bāl′ē) n., pl. **-eys.** the outer wall or court of a medieval castle. [var. of *bail⁴*]

Bail·ey bridge (bāl′ē) a portable bridge made from prefabricated steel sections in a lattice design. [after Sir Donald C. *Bailey*, a British engineer]

bail·ie (bāl′ē) n. in Scotland, an official of a town or city corresponding to an alderman. [ME < OF *baillis*, variant of *baillif.* See BAILIFF.]

bail·iff (bāl′if) n. **1** an official in charge of writs, processes, arrests, etc.; an assistant to a sheriff. **2** the officer of a court who has charge of prisoners while they are in the courtroom. **3** the overseer or steward of an estate. The bailiff collects rents, directs the work of employees, etc. for the owner. **4** in England, the chief magistrate in certain towns. [ME < OF *baillif* < *baillir* govern < *bail* guardian, manager < L *bajulus* carrier]

bail·i·wick (bāl′ə wik′) n. **1** the district over which a sheriff or bailiff has authority. **2** the place or locality that a person is identified with: *He is a big man in his own bailiwick.* **3** a person's field of knowledge, work, or authority. [< *bailie* + *wick* office < OE *wīce*]

bail·ment (bāl′mənt) n. **1** *Law.* the delivery of goods by one person to another in trust. **2** the act of bailing an accused person.

bails·man (bālz′mən) n., pl. **-men.** a person who gives bail.

Bai·ram (bī räm′) n. either of two Moslem festivals, the lesser Bairam, following immediately after Ramadan, or the greater Bairam, occurring 70 days later.

bairn (bern) n. *Scottish.* child. [OE *bearn* < pp. of *beran* to bear, influenced by ON *barn* child]

bait (bāt) n., v. —n. **1** anything, especially food, used to attract fish, birds, or animals to catch them. **2** anything used to tempt or attract.
—v. **1** put bait on (a hook) or in (a trap, etc.). **2** tempt or attract. **3** set dogs to attack (a chained animal, etc.): *Bears and bulls were formerly baited as sport.* **4** torment or worry by unkind or annoying remarks, etc. **5** *Archaic.* stop and feed: *The coachman baited his horses.* [ME < ON *beita* hunt with dogs, cause to bite and ON *beita* food, bait for fish, influenced also by ON *beit* pasture.] —**bait′er,** n.

bait·fish (bāt′fish′) n. fish caught for use as bait.

baize (bāz) n. a thick woollen or cotton cloth with a nap, used especially for table covers: *Baize is usually dyed green.* [< F *baies*, pl. of *bai* chestnut-colored < L *badius*]

bake (bāk) v. **baked, bak·ing;** n. —v. **1** cook (food) by dry heat without exposing it directly to the fire. Breads and cakes are cooked by baking. **2** dry or harden by heat: *to bake bricks or china.* **3** become baked: *Cookies bake quickly.* **4** make or become very warm: *I'm just going to lie in the sun and bake.*
—n. baking. [OE *bacan*]

bake·ap·ple (bāk′ap′əl) n. *Cdn., esp. Atlantic Provinces.* **1** a creeping plant (*Rubus chamaemorus*) of the rose family that grows in swampy areas, having single white flowers and amber-colored, edible berries like small raspberries; cloudberry. **2** the berry of this plant.

baked–apple (bākt′ap′əl) n. bakeapple.

Ba·ke·lite (bā′kə līt′) n. *Trademark.* a plastic used to make beads, stems of pipes, umbrella handles, fountain pens, electric insulators, etc. [after L. H. *Baekeland* (1863-1944), who invented it]

bak·er (bāk′ər) n. **1** a person who makes or sells bread, pies, cakes, etc. **2** a dish or utensil in which to bake something. **3** a small portable oven.

baker's dozen thirteen.

bak·er·y (bāk′ər ē or bāk′rē) n., pl. **-er·ies.** a baker's shop; a place where bread, pies, cakes, etc. are made or sold.

bake sale a sale of home-made baked goods, especially one held by a charitable organization, etc. to raise money.

bak·ing (bāk′ing) n. **1** the process of cooking in dry heat. **2** the process of drying or hardening by heat. **3** the amount baked at one time; a batch.

baking powder a mixture of bicarbonate of soda, starch, and an acid compound such as cream of tartar, used as a leavening agent in making biscuits, cakes, etc.

baking soda bicarbonate of soda.

bak·sheesh or **bak·shish** (bak′shēsh) n. in Egypt, Turkey, India, etc., money given as a tip. Also, **backsheesh, backshish.** [< Persian < *bakhshidan* give]

bal. balance.

bal·a·clav·a (bal′ə klav′ə or bal′ə klä′və) n. a type of knitted woollen headgear that covers all of the head and neck except the upper part of the face. [< *Balaklava*, site of a battle in the Crimean War]

bal·a·lai·ka (bal′ə lī′kə) n. a Russian musical instrument resembling a guitar, but having a triangular body. [< Russian]

bal·ance (bal′əns) n., v. **-anced, -anc·ing.** —n. **1** an instrument for weighing, especially a device consisting of a horizontal bar freely suspended from its centre and having a matched platform or shallow pan at either end; something to be weighed is placed on one platform and objects of known mass are added to the other until the bar is exactly horizontal. **2** equality in mass, amount, force, effect, etc. **3** a comparison of mass, value, importance, etc.; estimate. **4** good proportion in design, etc.; harmony: *a balance of colors.* **5** a steady condition or position; steadiness: *He lost his balance and fell off the ladder.* **6** mental steadiness; poise. **7** anything that counteracts the effect, mass, etc. of something else. **8** *Accounting.* **a** the difference between the credit and debit sides of an account. **b** equality of debit and credit in an account. **9** the part that is left over; remainder: *He was dismissed from school for the balance of the term.* **10** a wheel that regulates the rate of movement of a clock or watch. **11** the greatest mass, amount, or power. **12** *Dancing.* a balancing movement. **13 Balance,** *Astrology.* Libra.
in the balance, undecided.
—v. **1** weigh in a balance or in one's hands to see which of two things is heavier. **2** make or be equal to in mass, amount, force, effect, etc. **3** compare the value, importance, etc. of. **4** make or be proportionate to. **5** bring into or keep in a steady condition or position: *Can you balance a coin on its edge?* **6** counteract the effect, influence, etc. of; make up for. **7** *Accounting.* **a** make the credit and debit sides of (an account) equal: *to balance a budget.* **b** be equal in credit and debit: *The account doesn't balance.* **8** hesitate; waver. [ME < OF < LL *bilanx, bilancis* two-scaled < *bi-* two + *lanx* scale²] —**bal′anc·er,** n.

balance billing *Cdn.* a system by which a doctor charges more than the rates allowed under the provincial health program, billing the difference (or balance) to the patient.

balanced diet a diet having the correct amounts of all the kinds of food necessary for health.

balance of power 1 an even distribution of military and economic power among nations or groups of nations. **2** any even distribution of power. **3** the power of a small group to give control to a large group by joining forces with it.

balance of trade the difference between the value of all the imports and that of all the exports of a country.

balance sheet a written statement showing the profits and losses, the assets and liabilities, and the net worth of a business.

balance wheel a wheel for regulating motion. A clock or watch has a balance wheel that controls the movement of the hands.

bal·a·ta (bal′ə tə) n. **1** a hard, non-elastic, rubberlike substance made by drying the milky juice of a tropical American tree (*Manilkara bidentata*) of the sapodilla family, used in making golf balls, belting, etc. **2** the tree itself. [< Sp.]

bal·bo·a (bal bō′ə) n. **1** a unit of money in Panama. See table at **money. 2** a coin worth one balboa. [< Vasco de *Balboa* (1475-1517), a Spanish explorer]

bal·brig·gan (bal brig′ən) n. **1** a type of knitted cotton cloth, used for stockings, underwear, etc. **2** a similar type of knitted woollen cloth. **3** balbriggans, pl. knitted cotton stockings or pyjamas. [originally made at *Balbriggan*, Ireland]

bal·co·ny (bal′kə nē) n., pl. **-nies. 1** an outside projecting platform with an entrance from an upper floor of a building. **2** in a theatre or hall, a projecting upper floor with seats for an audience. [< Ital. *balcone* < *balco* scaffold < OHG *balcho* beam]

bald (bold or bôld) adj. **1** wholly or partly without hair on the head. **2** without its natural covering: *A mountain top with no trees or grass on it is bald.* **3** bare; plain; unadorned. **4** undisguised: *The bald truth is that he is a thief.* **5** of tires, having little or no tread remaining. **6** *Zoology.* having white on the head: *the bald eagle.*

[ME *balled*, apparently < obsolete *ball* white spot] —**bald′ly**, *adv.* —**bald′ness**, *n.*

bal·da·chin or **bal·da·quin** (bal′də kin *or* bôl′də kin) *n.* 1 a canopy of stone, metal, or other material over an altar, throne, etc. 2 a canopy of silk brocade or other fabric carried in solemn procession. 3 a similar canopy above a dais, etc. 4 a heavy brocade, formerly made of silk and gold. [< F *baldaquin* < Ital. *baldac(c)hino* < *Baldacco*, Italian name of Bagdad, where the silk was made]

bal·da·chi·no (bol′də kē′nō *or* bôl′də kē′nō) *n.* baldachin.

bald cypress a large coniferous tree (*Taxodium distichum*) of the same family as the redwood, native to swampy parts of the SE United States and Mexico, having feathery leaves, a thick trunk, and "knees", produced by the root system, that project above the surface of the water. It is named for the fact that, unlike most conifers, it loses its leaves each fall.

bald eagle a large North American eagle (*Haliaeetus leucocephalus*) having plumage that is mainly dark brown on the body and wings and pure white on the head, neck, and tail. Bald eagles feed mainly on fish.

Bal·der (bol′dər *or* bôl′dər) *n. Norse mythology.* the god of light, beauty, goodness, wisdom, and peace.

bal·der·dash (bol′dər dash′ *or* bôl′dər-) *n.* nonsense. [< 16th c. slang, meaning a senseless mixture of drinks such as milk and beer]

bald–faced (bold′fāst′ *or* bôld′-) *adj.* 1 of animals, having a white face or white markings on the face. 2 open and without shame or embarrassment: *a bald-faced lie.*

bald·head (bold′hed′ *or* bôld′-) *n.* 1 a person who has a bald head. 2 a breed of pigeon. 3 any of various birds with a whitish spot on the head.

bald·head·ed (bold′hed′id *or* bôld′-) *adj.* 1 designating a person having little or no hair on the head. 2 *Cdn.* devoid of trees or brush: *baldheaded prairie.*

bald·ing (bol′ding *or* bôl′ding) *adj.* going bald; becoming bald.

Bal·dor (bol′dər *or* bôl′dər) *n.* Balder.

bald·pate (bold′pāt′ *or* bôld′-) *n.* 1 a person who has a bald head. 2 a wild duck (*Anas americana*, also classified as *Mareca americana*) found throughout W North America, the male having a noticeable white patch on the forehead and crown; widgeon.

bald prairie that part of the western prairie which is almost without trees.

bal·dric (bol′drik *or* bôl′drik) *n.* a belt hung from one shoulder and across the chest to the opposite side of the body, used to support a sword, horn, etc. [ME *baudry* < OF *baudrei*, of obscure origin; akin to MHG *balderich* girdle]

Baldur (bol′dər *or* bôl′dər) See **Balder**.

bale¹ (bāl) *n., v.* **baled, bal·ing.** —*n.* a large bundle of merchandise or material securely wrapped or bound for shipping or storage: *a bale of paper.* —*v.* make into bales; tie in large bundles. [ME, probably < Flemish < OF < OHG *balla* ball¹]
☛ *Hom.* **bail.**

bale² (bāl) *n. Archaic or poetic.* 1 evil; harm. 2 sorrow; pain. [OE *bealu*]
☛ *Hom.* **bail.**

ba·leen (bə lēn′) *n.* 1 an elastic horny substance that grows in large, fringed, parallel plates or sheets from the roof of the mouth of baleen whales. It serves to trap the plankton taken into the whale's mouth with water. 2 baleen whale. [ME < OF *baleine* < L *ballena*, var. of *ballaena* < Gk. *phallaina* whale]

baleen whale any of a suborder (Mysticeti) of mostly large whales that includes the right whales, rorquals, and the blue whale, all lacking teeth but having baleen for trapping the plankton and small crustaceans on which they feed and having paired blowholes.

bale·ful (bāl′fəl) *adj.* evil; harmful. —**bale′ful·ly**, *adv.* —**bale′ful·ness**, *n.*

bal·er (bāl′ər) *n.* 1 a person who bales. 2 a machine that compresses and ties up into bundles such things as hay, straw, paper, and scrap metal.

Ba·li·nese (bä′lə nēz′) *n., pl.* **-nese;** *adj.* —*n.* 1 a native or inhabitant of Bali, an island in Indonesia. 2 the language of the Balinese. —*adj.* of or having to do with Bali, its people, or their language.

balk (bok *or* bôk) *v., n.* —*v.* 1 stop short and stubbornly; refuse to go on. 2 thwart; hinder; check: *The police balked the robber's plans.* 3 fail to use; let slip; miss. 4 *Sports.* make an incomplete or misleading move. —*n.* 1 a hindrance; check; defeat. 2 a blunder or mistake. 3 a ridge between furrows; a strip left unploughed. 4 a large beam or timber. 5 *Sports.* an incomplete or misleading motion, especially an illegal false move to throw the ball, made by a baseball pitcher when there are runners on base. Also, **baulk.** [OE *balca* ridge]

hat, āge, fär; let, ēqual, tėrm; it, īce
hot, ōpen, ôrder; oil, out; cup, pùt, rüle,
əbove, takən, pencəl, lemən, circəs
ch, child; ng, long; sh, ship
th, thin; ŧн, then; zh, measure

Bal·kan (bol′kən *or* bôl′kən) *adj., n.* —*adj.* 1 of or having to do with the Balkan peninsula. 2 of or having to with the countries of the Balkan peninsula or their inhabitants. 3 of or having to do with the Balkan Mountains.
—*n.* **the Balkans,** *pl.* the Balkan States.

bal·kan·ize (bol′kə nīz′ *or* bôl′kə nīz′) *v.* **-ized, -iz·ing.** break up into small ineffective or mutually hostile units: *The issue has turned province against province and threatens to balkanize the country.* —**bal′kan·i·za′tion,** *n.*

balk·y (bok′ē *or* bôk′ē) *adj.* **balk·i·er, balk·i·est.** balking or likely to balk: *a balky horse.* —**balk′i·ness,** *n.*

ball¹ (bol *or* bôl) *n., v.* —*n.* 1 a round or oval object that is thrown, kicked, knocked, bounced, or batted about in various games. 2 a game in which some kind of ball is thrown, hit, or kicked. 3 a ball in motion: *a fast ball.* 4 the game of baseball. 5 *Baseball.* pitched too high, too low, or not over the plate and not struck at by the batter. 6 bullet. 7 anything round or roundish; something that resembles a ball: *a ball of string, the ball of the thumb.* 8 a globe or sphere; the earth. 9 **balls,** *pl. Vulgar slang.* **a** testicles. **b** courage; nerve; spunk. **c** nonsense (*used also as an interjection*).
be on the ball, *Slang.* be mentally wide awake; be alert: *He's really on the ball today; he sold three cars before noon.*
have something on the ball, *Slang.* have quickness of mind and good judgment: *She must have something on the ball, because she's already figured out the answers. Anybody who would do a silly thing like that can't have much on the ball.*
keep the ball rolling, do one's part.
play ball, a begin a game or start in again after stopping. **b** get busy. **c** work together; co-operate: *If everyone will play ball, we can get the job done quickly.*
—*v.* make or form into a ball.
ball up, *Slang.* make or become messed up or confused: *He has balled it up so badly we will have to start over.*
[ME < ON *böllr*]
☛ *Hom.* **bawl.**

ball² (bol *or* bôl) *n.* 1 a large, formal party with dancing. 2 *Slang.* a very good time; a lot of fun: *We had a ball at the party.* [< F *bal* < *baler* to dance < LL *ballare*]
☛ *Hom.* **bawl.**

bal·lad (bal′əd) *n.* 1 a simple song. 2 a poem that tells a story in a simple verse form, especially one that tells a popular legend and is passed orally from one generation to another. 3 the music for such a poem. [ME < OF *balade* < Provençal *balada* dancing song]

bal·lade (bə läd′) *n.* 1 a poem having three stanzas of eight or ten lines each, followed by an envoy of four or five lines. The last line of each stanza and of the envoy are the same, and the same rhyme sounds recur throughout. 2 *Music.* an instrumental composition, usually rather simple and romantic: *Chopin's ballades.* [< F < OF *balade.* See BALLAD.]

bal·lad·eer (bal′ə dēr′) *n.* 1 a singer of ballads. 2 *Informal.* a singer of popular songs.

ball and chain 1 a heavy metal ball attached by a short chain to the leg of a prisoner to prevent his escaping. 2 *Informal.* anything that restricts one's freedom of action. 3 *Slang.* wife.

ball–and–socket joint a flexible joint formed by a ball or knob fitting in a socket, such as the shoulder or hip joint, and permitting some motion in every direction. See **socket** for picture.

bal·last (bal′əst) *n., v.* —*n.* 1 something heavy carried in a ship to steady it. 2 the weight carried in a balloon or dirigible to control it. 3 anything that steadies a person or thing. 4 the gravel or crushed rock used in making the bed for a road or railway track.
—*v.* 1 put ballast in (ships, balloons, etc.). 2 put gravel or crushed rock on. [apparently < Scand.; cf. ODanish *barlast* < *bar* bare + *last* load] —**bal′last·er,** *n.*

ballast tube in fluorescent lighting, etc., a device to keep the electric current constant, usually consisting of an iron wire in a vacuum tube filled with hydrogen. Its varying resistance counteracts changes of voltage.

ball bearing 1 a bearing in which the shaft turns upon a number of freely moving metal balls contained in a grooved ring around the shaft. Ball bearings are used to lessen friction. 2 any of the metal balls so used.

ball cock a valve for regulating the supply of water in a tank,

cistern, etc., opened or closed by the fall or rise of a hollow, floating ball.

bal·le·ri·na (bal′ə rē′nə) *n., pl.* **-nas.** a female ballet dancer. [< Ital.]

bal·let (bal′ā *or* ba lā′) *n.* **1** an artistic dance that usually tells a story or expresses a mood, performed by either a soloist or a group of dancers in a theatre, concert hall, etc. **2** the art of creating or performing ballets. **3** a performance of a ballet. **4** the music for a ballet. **5** a company of dancers that performs ballets. [< F *ballet*, dim. of *bal* dance. See BALL².]

bal·let·ic (ba let′ik) *adj.* of or having to do with ballet. —**bal·let′i·cal·ly,** *adv.*

bal·let·o·mane (ba let′ə mān′) *n.* a person who is enthusiastic about ballet. [< F *balletomane* < *ballet* + *-mane* < *manie* < Gk. *mania* enthusiasm]

ball hockey a hockey-like game played with hockey sticks and a tennis ball.

bal·lis·ta (bə lis′tə) *n., pl.* **-tae** (-tē *or* -tī). a machine used in wars in ancient times to throw stones and other heavy missiles. [< L *ballista*, ult. < Gk. *ballein* throw]

bal·lis·tic (bə lis′tik) *adj.* **1** having to do with the motion or throwing of projectiles. **2** having to do with the science of ballistics. —**bal·lis′ti·cal·ly,** *adv.*

ballistic missile a projectile powered by a rocket engine or engines but reaching its target as a result of aim at the time of launching, used especially as a long-range weapon of offence.

bal·lis·tics (bə lis′tiks) *n.* the science that deals with the motion of projectiles such as bullets, shells, and bombs.

bal·lo·net (bal′ə net′) *n.* a small bag inside a balloon or airship that holds air or gas to regulate ascent or descent. [< F *ballonnet*, dim. of *ballon* balloon]

bal·loon (bə lün′) *n., v.* —*n.* **1** an airtight bag filled with air or a gas lighter than air, so that it will rise and float. Small balloons are used as toys and decorations; larger balloons can be used as signals, advertisements, etc. **2** a large airtight bag from which is suspended either a gondola to carry two or more persons or a container to carry instruments. **Observation balloons** are used to observe and record data on weather, atmospheric radiation, etc. **3** (*adj.*) puffed out like a ballon: *balloon sleeves.* **4** in cartoons, a boxed space in which the words of a speaker are written. —*v.* **1** swell out like a balloon. **2** ride in a balloon. [< Ital. *ballone* < *balla* ball] —**bal·loon′like′,** *adj.*

balloon barrage an anti-aircraft screen of barrage balloons.

bal·loon·ist (bə lün′ist) *n.* **1** a person who goes up in balloons. **2** a pilot of a dirigible balloon.

balloon tire a large tire containing air under low pressure.

bal·lot (bal′ət) *n., v.* **-lot·ed, -lot·ing.** —*n.* **1** a piece of paper or other object used in voting. **2** the total number of votes cast. **3** vote; voting: *The ballot went in favor of the new party.* **4** a method of secret voting that uses paper slips, voting machines, etc. —*v.* vote or decide by using ballots. [< Ital. *ballotta*, dim. of *balla* ball]

ballot box the box into which voters put their ballots.

ball–peen hammer (bol′pēn′ *or* bôl′pēn′) a hammer having one end of the head rounded like a ball, for shaping metal, etc.

ball·play·er (bol′plā′ər *or* bôl′-) *n.* **1** a baseball player. **2** a person who plays ball.

ball·point *or* **ball–point** (bol′point′ *or* bôl′-) *n.* a pen having a small metal ball in place of a nib. The movement and pressure of writing make the ball turn against a cartridge of semisolid ink, transferring some of the ink to the paper.

ball·room (bol′rüm′ *or* bôl′-, bol′rùm′ *or* bôl′-) *n.* a large room for dancing.

bal·ly·hoo (*n.* bal′ē hü′; *v.* bal′ē hü′ *or* bal′ē hü′) *n., pl.* **-hoos;** *v.,* **-hooed, -hoo·ing.** *Slang.* —*n.* **1** noisy advertising; a sensational way of attracting attention. **2** an uproar or outcry. —*v.* advertise noisily; make exaggerated or false statements about. [origin uncertain] —**bal′ly·hoo′er,** *n.*

balm (bom *or* bäm) *n.* **1** any of various fragrant, oily, resinous substances obtained from certain tropical trees, used for relieving pain or healing. **2** any fragrant ointment or oil used for soothing or healing. **3** anything that soothes or comforts: *kind words that are a balm for wounded feelings.* **4** any of various plants of the mint family, especially a Eurasian herb (*Melissa officinalis*) cultivated for its fragrant leaves which are used as flavoring in foods and drinks and also for making perfume. [ME < OF *basme* < L < Gk. *balsamon* balsam. Doublet of BALSAM.]
☛ *Hom.* **bomb** (bom).

balm of Gilead **1** a fragrant ointment prepared from the resin

of a small evergreen tree (*Commiphora opobalsumum*) of Asia and Africa. **2** the tree itself. **3** a North American hybrid poplar (*Populus gileadensis*) closely resembling the balsam poplar but having a broader crown and leaves that are almost heart-shaped. **4** balsam fir.

bal·mor·al (bal môr′əl) *n.* a brimless Scottish cap having a round, soft, more or less flat crown that projects all around. See **cap** for picture.

Bal·mung (bäl′mùng) *n.* Siegfried's sword.

balm·y¹ (bom′ē *or* bäm′ē) *adj.* **balm·i·er, balm·i·est. 1** mild; gentle; soothing: *a balmy breeze.* **2** fragrant. [< *balm*] —**balm′i·ly,** *adv.* —**balm′i·ness,** *n.*

balm·y² (bom′ē *or* bäm′ē) *adj.* **balm·i·er, balm·i·est.** *Slang.* silly; crazy. [var. of *barmy*]

ba·lo·ney (bə lō′nē) *n.* **1** *Slang.* nonsense. **2** *Informal.* bologna. Also, **boloney.** [< *bologna*]

bal·sa (bol′sə *or* bôl′sə) *n.* **1** a tropical American tree (*Ochroma lagopus*) with very light, strong wood. **2** its wood. **3** a raft, especially one consisting of two or more floats fastened to a framework. [< Sp. *balsa* raft]

bal·sam (bol′səm *or* bôlsəm) *n.* **1** any of various fragrant, resinous substances containing benzoic acid, used in medicine and perfume. **2** any of various other fragrant and usually resinous substances used especially for healing or soothing. **3** any of various turpentines. **4** a tree that yields balsam, especially the balsam fir. **5** a garden plant (*Impatiens balsamina*) having large leaves and double, usually red or pink, flowers. **6** balm (def. 3). [< L < Gk. *balsamon.* Doublet of BALM.]

balsam fir **1** a fir (*Abies balsamea*) found throughout eastern Canada and parts of the Prairie Provinces and the N United States, having a narrow, symmetrical crown tapering to a spire-like top and shiny, dark-green needles. It is often used as a Christmas tree and its resin is used in making varnish. **2** the soft, light, weak wood of this tree, used especially for pulp.

balsam poplar **1** a poplar (*Populus balsamifera*) found throughout Canada and along the northern border of the United States, having oval leaves that are shiny dark green above and whitish green below and having resin-coated buds that give the tree a strong balsam odor; tacamahac. **2** the wood of this tree, used for lumber, veneer, etc.

Bal·tic (bol′tik *or* bôl′tik) *adj., n.* —*adj.* **1** having to do with the Baltic Sea. **2** having to do with the Baltic States. —*n.* a group of languages belonging to this region.

Baltimore oriole (bol′tə môr′ *or* bôl′tə môr′) North American oriole (*Icterus galbula*) common throughout central and eastern North America, having a loud, piping whistle. The adult male has a black head and back and mostly black wings, with a bright orange-yellow underside, rump, and upper tail feathers.

Ba·lu·chi (bə lü′chē) *n., pl.* **-chi. 1** a native or inhabitant of Baluchistan, a province of West Pakistan. **2** the language of Baluchistan.

bal·us·ter (bal′əs tər) *n.* one of a set of often ornamental posts supporting a railing or coping, as along the edge of a staircase, balcony, or terrace. [< F *balustre* < Ital. < L < Gk. *balaustion* pomegranate blossom; from the shape]

bal·us·trade (bal′əs trād′ *or* bal′əs träd′) *n.* an ornamental railing along a staircase, balcony, etc. together with its supporting balusters. [< F *balustrade* < *balustre.* See BALUSTER.]

bam·bi·no (bam bē′nō) *n., pl.* **-nos** *or* **-ni** (-nē). *Italian.* **1** a baby; little child. **2** an image or picture of the baby Jesus. [< Ital. *bambino*, dim. of *bambo* silly]

bam·boo (bam bü′) *n., pl.* **-boos. 1** any of a tribe (Bambuseae) of treelike tropical or semitropical grasses having hollow or solid, stiff, jointed stems and evergreen or deciduous leaves. **2** the stem of certain bamboos, used for building, furniture, poles, etc. **3** (*adj.*) made of bamboo: *a bamboo fishing pole, a bamboo chair.* [< Du. *bamboes*, probably < Malay]

Bamboo Curtain an imaginary wall or dividing line between China and non-communist nations.

bam·boo·zle (bam bü′zəl) *v.* **-zled, -zling.** *Informal.* **1** impose upon; cheat; trick. **2** puzzle; perplex. [origin uncertain] —**bam·boo′zler,** *n.*

ban¹ (ban) *v.* **banned, ban·ning;** *n.* —*v.* **1** prohibit; forbid by law or authority: *Swimming is banned in this lake.* **2** pronounce a curse on. —*n.* **1** the forbidding of an act or speech by authority of the law, the church, or public opinion; prohibition. **2** a solemn curse by the church; excommunication or condemnation. **3** a sentence of outlawry or banishment. [OE *bannan* summon]

ban² (ban) *n.* **1** a public proclamation or edict. **2** in medieval times: **a** the summoning of the king's vassals for war. **b** the whole body of these vassals. [fusion of OE *gebann* summons and Old North French *ban* proclamation, jurisdiction < Gmc.]

ban³ (bän) *n., pl.* **ba·ni** (bä′nē). a unit of money in Romania, equal to ¹⁄₁₀₀ of a leu. [< Romanian]

ba·nal (bā′nəl *or* bə nal′) *adj.* **1** commonplace; trite or trivial: *He made some banal remarks about the weather before coming to the point of his visit.* **2** *Historical.* available to the whole community: *banal mills.* [< F *banal* < *ban* proclamation < Gmc.; original sense "of feudal service"; later, "open to the community"] —**ba′nal·ly,** *adv.*

ba·nal·i·ty (bə nal′ə tē) *n., pl.* **-ties.** commonplaceness; triteness; triviality.

ba·nan·a (bə nan′ə) *n.* **1** the elongated, curved fruit of any of various tropical plants (genus *Musa*), having sweet, whitish pulp and a thick, yellow skin. **2** any of the treelike, herbaceous plants producing such fruit, especially *Musa sapientum*, widely cultivated in the tropics. **3** (*adj.*) designating a family (Musaceae) of plants that includes bananas, plantains, and the bird-of-paradise flower. **4 bananas,** *pl. Slang.* crazy or wildly enthusiastic, distressed, etc.: *The whole audience went bananas when he stepped onto the stage.* [< Pg. or Sp.]

banana belt *Cdn. Informal, often facetious.* a region having a relatively mild climate: *the banana belt of southwestern B.C.*

banana oil 1 a colorless liquid having a smell resembling that of bananas, used in flavorings and as a solvent. **2** *Slang.* pretentious but insincere talk; excessive flattery.

band¹ (band) *n., v.* —*n.* **1** a group of persons or animals moving or acting together: *a band of robbers, a band of wild dogs.* **2** a group of musicians organized to play together, especially on brass, woodwind, and percussion instruments: *We hired a five-piece band for our dance.* Compare **orchestra. 3** *Cdn.* a group of Canadian Indian people of a particular region or reserve, recognized by the Federal Government as an administrative unit. —*v.* unite or cause to unite in a group. [< MF *bande* < Med.L *banda*, prob. < Gmc. Related to BANNER.]

band² (band) *n., v.* —*n.* **1** a thin, flat strip of material for binding, trimming, etc.: *a narrow band of lace. The oak box was strengthened with bands of iron.* **2** a loop or ring of material used for holding something together: *I put a rubber band around the bundle of letters.* **3** a stripe: *a white cup with a gold band near the rim.* **4 bands,** *pl.* two strips hanging from the front of a collar in certain academic, clerical, or legal costume. **5** *Radio.* a particular range of wavelengths or frequencies. **6** any of a number of separate sections, or groups of grooves, on a phonograph record. **7** anything that binds or restrains. —*v.* **1** put a band on. **2** mark with stripes. [ME < MF *bande, bende* < Gmc. Related to BAND¹, BEND².]

band³ (band) *n.* anything that ties, binds, or unites. [ME < ON *band.* Related in Gmc. to BAND².]

band·age (ban′dij) *n., v.* **-aged, -ag·ing.** —*n.* **1** a strip of cloth or other material used in binding up and dressing a wound, injured leg or arm, etc. **2** something like this used to support or protect when there is no injury: *Race horses often have bandages on their legs.* —*v.* bind, tie up, or dress with a bandage. [< F *bandage* < *bande.* See BAND¹.] —**band′ag·er,** *n.*

Band–Aid (band′ād′) *n.* **1** *Trademark.* a small bandage for minor wounds, consisting of a thin gauze pad attached to the middle of a strip of adhesive tape. **2** any similar bandage. **3** Often, **band-aid, a** something quickly brought in or used as a temporary solution; stopgap: *The opposition leader dismissed the proposed tax cuts as nothing but economic band-aids.* **b** (*adj.*) serving as a stopgap; temporary or makeshift: *band-aid solutions.*

ban·dan·a *or* **ban·dan·na** (ban dan′ə) *n.* a large, colored handkerchief. [probably < Hind. *bandhnu* tying cloth to produce a design when dyed]

band–box (band′boks′) *n.* a light cardboard box for holding hats, collars, etc.

ban·deau (ban dō′ *or* ban′dō) *n., pl.* **-deaux** (-dōz′ *or* -dōz). **1** a band worn around the head. **2** a narrow band. **3** a narrow brassiere. [< F *bandeau,* dim. of *bande* band¹, ult. < Gmc.]

ban·de·role *or* **ban·de·rol** (ban′də rōl′) *n.* a small flag or steamer on a lance, mast, etc. [< F < Ital. *banderuola < bandiera* banner < LL *bandum* < Gmc.]

ban·di·coot (ban′də küt′) *n.* **1** any of about 20 species of small grey or tan marsupial (family Peramelidae) found in Australia and neighboring islands, resembling kangaroos but belonging to a different family. Bandicoots are active at night and sleep during the day. **2** bandicoot rat. [< Telegu *pandikokku* pig-rat]

bandicoot rat any of several large, burrowing ratlike rodents (genera *Bandicota* and *Nesokia*) found in India and Sri Lanka, having a body about 30 to 38 cm long and a very long tail, and having a short head and a broad muzzle. They live in forests, cultivated land, and towns, and destroy crops, stored grains, and poultry.

ban·dit (ban′dit) *n., pl.* **ban·dits** *or* **ban·dit·ti** (-ē). a highwayman;

hat, āge, fär; let, ēqual, tėrm; it, īce
hot, ōpen, ôrder; oil, out; cup, pút, rüle,
əbove, takən, pencəl, lemən, circəs
ch, child; ng, long; sh, ship
th, thin; ŦH, then; zh, measure

robber. [< Ital. *bandito,* pp. of *bandire* banish, proscribe, ult. < Gmc. Akin to BAN.]

ban·dit·ry (ban′dit rē) *n.* **1** the work of bandits. **2** bandits.

ban·dit·ti (ban dit′ē) *n.* a pl. of **bandit.**

band·mas·ter (band′mas′tər) *n.* the leader or conductor of a band (def. 2).

ban·do·lier *or* **ban·do·leer** (ban′də lēr′) *n.* **1** a broad belt worn over one shoulder and across the breast. Some bandoliers have loops for carrying cartridges; others have small cases for bullets, gunpowder, etc. **2** one of these cases. [< F *bandoulière* < Sp. *bandolera < banda* band¹, ult < Gmc.]

band saw a saw in the form of an endless steel belt.

band shell an outdoor platform for musical concerts that has a shell-shaped, rear wall extending up over the platform and serving as a sounding board.

bands·man (bandz′mən) *n., pl.* **-men.** a member of a band of musicians.

band·stand (band′stand′) *n.* an outdoor platform, usually roofed, for band concerts.

band·wag·on (band′wag′ən) *n.* a wagon that carries a musical band in a parade.

climb or **get on the bandwagon,** *Informal.* join what appears to be the winning side in a political campaign, contest, public issue, etc.

ban·dy (ban′dē) *v.* **-died, -dy·ing;** *adj.* —*v.* **1** throw back and forth; toss about. **2** give and take; exchange: *To bandy words with a foolish person is a waste of time.* —*adj.* bent or curved outward: *bandy legs.* [cf. F *bander* bandy, *se bander* band together < Gmc.]

ban·dy–leg·ged (ban′dē leg′id *or* -legd′) *adj.* having legs that curve outward; bowlegged.

bane (bān) *n.* **1** a cause of death, ruin, or harm: *Wild animals were the bane of the mountain village.* **2** destruction of any kind. [OE *bana* murderer]

bane·ber·ry (bān′ber′ē *or* bān′bər ē) *n., pl.* **-ries. 1** any of several plants (genus *Actaea*) of the buttercup family having spikes of small, white flowers and clusters of red or white, poisonous berries. **2** a berry of any of these plants.

bane·ful (bān′fəl) *adj.* deadly; harmful. —**bane′ful·ly,** *adv.*

bang¹ (bang) *n., v., interj.* —*n.* **1** sudden, loud noise: *the bang of a gun.* **2** a violent, noisy blow. **3** (*adv.*) violently and noisily: *The boy on the bicycle went bang into a tree.* **4** vigor; impetus: *They wanted to start the campaign off with a bang.* **5** *Slang.* thrill: *They really got a bang out of the incident.* —*v.* **1** make a sudden loud noise: *We heard the door bang.* **2** hit violently or sharply: *I banged my head when I fell. The snowball banged against the window.* **3** shut with a noise; slam: *She banged the door as she went out.* **4** handle roughly (usually used with **around**): *They really banged our suitcases around.* —*interj.* an imitation of gunfire: *"Bang! Bang!" shouted the children.* [? < ON *banga* to hammer]

bang² (bang) *n., v.* —*n.* **1** Usually, **bangs,** *pl.* a fringe of hair cut short and worn over the forehead: *She has long hair with bangs.* —*v.* cut hair in this way: *She wears her hair banged.* [< short for *bangtail* docked tail (of a horse)]

ban·gle (bang′gəl) *n.* **1** a ring worn around the wrist, arm, or ankle. **2** a small ornament suspended from a bracelet. [< Hind. *bangri, bangli* glass bracelet]

Bang's disease (bangz) an infectious disease in cattle that often results in abortion. [< Bernhard *Bang* (1848-1932), a Danish physician who described it]

ba·ni (bä′nē) *n.* pl. of **ban.³**

ban·ian (ban′yən *or* ban′yan) *n.* **1** a Hindu merchant of a caste that eats no meat. **2** See **banyan.** [< Pg. *banian,* probably < Arabic *banyan* < Gujarati (a lang. of western India), ult. < Skt.]

ban·ish (ban′ish) *v.* **1** condemn to leave a country; exile. **2** force to go away; send away; drive away. [ME < OF *baniss-,* a stem of *banir* < LL *bannire* ban · Gmc.] —**ban′ish·er,** *n.*

☛ **Syn. 1. Banish, exile, deport** = force to leave a country. **Banish** = to force a person, by order of authority, to leave his own or a foreign country, permanently or for a stated time: *Napoleon was banished to Elba.* **Exile** also means to compel a person to leave his own country or home, but the authority may be the force of circumstances or his own will: *The Kaiser was exiled from*

Germany after World War I. **Deport** = to banish a person from a country of which he is not a citizen: *We deport aliens who slip across our borders.*

ban·ish·ment (ban'ish mənt) *n.* **1** the act of banishing. **2** the state of being banished; exile.

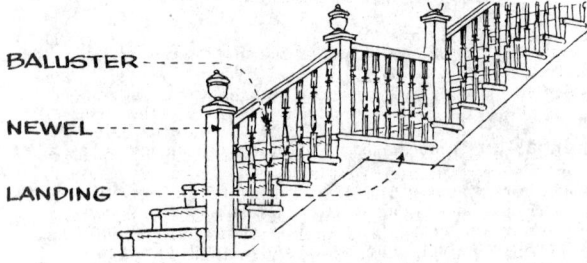

A staircase with banisters and a landing

ban·is·ter (ban'is tər) *n.* **1** Usually, **banisters,** *pl.* the railing of a staircase together with the supporting balusters. **2** the railing alone. **3** baluster. [var. of *baluster*]

ban·jo (ban'jō) *n., pl.* **-jos** or **-joes.** a stringed musical instrument played with the fingers or a plectrum. [< alteration of *bandore* < Sp. < LL < Gk. *pandoura,* a three-stringed instrument]

ban·jo·ist (ban'jō ist) *n.* a person who plays a banjo, especially a skilled player.

bank¹ (bangk) *n., v.* —*n.* **1** a long pile or heap: *a bank of snow.* **2** the ground bordering a river, lake, etc. **3** a shallow place in an ocean, sea, etc.; shoal: *the fishing banks of Newfoundland.* **4** a slope: *the bank of a corner on a race track.* **5** the tilting of an airplane to one side when making a turn. **6** *Mining.* **a** the top of a shaft. **b** the face being worked in a coal mine.
—*v.* **1** raise a ridge or mound about; border with a bank or ridge. **2** form into a bank; pile up; heap up: *The wind had banked snow against the wall.* **3** form banks: *Clouds are banking along the horizon.* **4** slope: *The pavement of a curve on an expressway should be well banked, upward and outward from the centre.* **5** make (an airplane) tilt when making a turn. **6** of an airplane, tilt when turning. **7** lessen the draft and cover (a fire) with ashes or fresh fuel so that it will burn slowly. [ME < ON; cf. Old Icelandic *bakki*]

bank² (bangk) *n., v.* —*n.* **1** an institution for keeping, lending, exchanging, and paying out money. **2** a container used for saving small sums at home: *a plastic piggy bank.* **3** *Gambling.* the funds kept by dealer or manager for use in a game. **4** *Games.* a stock of pieces from which players draw. **5** a place where something is stored for future use: *a blood bank, a data bank.*
—*v.* **1** operate or manage a bank. **2** keep money in a bank: *He banks at the branch near his office.* **3** put (money) in a bank: *She banked half her pay cheque.*
bank on, *Informal.* depend on; be sure of.
[< F *banque* < Ital. *banca,* originally, bench, later applied to the table used by money changers < Gmc.] —**bank'a·ble,** *adj.*

bank³ (bangk) *n., v.* —*n.* **1** a row or close arrangement of things: *a bank of switches, a bank of machines.* **2** a row of keys on an organ, typewriter, etc. **3** a tier or row of oars in a galley. **4** a bench for the rowers in a galley.
—*v.* arrange in rows. [ME < OF *banc* < LL *bancus* < Gmc. Akin to BENCH.]

bank account 1 an arrangement for depositing one's money in a bank for safekeeping until it is needed, involving a record of deposits and withdrawals: *to open a bank account.* **2** the sum of money kept by a bank for a person or company: *My bank account is very low right now.*

bank barn *Cdn.* especially in Ontario, a two-storey barn built into a hill so as to permit entry to the bottom level from one side and to the top level from the other side.

bank·book (bangk'bùk') *n.* a book in which a record of a person's account at a bank is kept.

bank discount an amount of money deducted from a loan by a bank at the time the loan is made, equal to the interest chargeable from the date the loan is made until the date when the final payment is due.

bank·er¹ (bangk'ər) *n.* **1** a person or company that manages a bank. **2** a dealer or manager in a gambling game. **3** *Informal.* any person who lends or advances money in order to make a profit: *a banker in a loan-shark operation.*

bank·er² (bangk'ər) *n.* **1** a fisherman who fishes off the Grand Banks. **2** a fishing vessel that operates off the Grand Banks.

bank holiday any day (from Monday to Friday inclusive) on which banks are legally closed; a legal holiday.

bank·ing (bangk'ing) *n.* the business of operating a bank.

bank note 1 a piece of paper currency. In Canada, all bank notes are issued by the Bank of Canada and serve as the currency of this country. **2** *Historical.* a note issued by a bank, that could be redeemed at any time for a specific amount of money, gold, etc.

Bank of Canada the agent of the Government of Canada that issues all Canadian bank notes and carries out monetary policy on behalf of the government.

bank rate the standard rate of discount for a specified type of note, security, etc., set by a central bank, such as the Bank of Canada, or by a chartered bank.

bank·roll (bangk'rōl') *n., v.* —*n. Informal.* the amount of money a person has in his possession or easily available. —*v. Slang.* provide or put up the money for: *A group of businessmen bankrolled the opera company's tour.*

bank·rupt (bangk'rupt) *n., adj., v.* —*n.* **1** a person declared by a law court to be unable to pay his debts and whose property is distributed among or administered on behalf of his creditors. **2** a person who is unable to pay his debts. **3** a person who is completely lacking in something: *a moral bankrupt.*
—*adj.* **1** unable to pay one's debts; declared legally unable to pay debts. **2** at the end of one's resources; destitute. **3** completely lacking in something: *The story was entirely bankrupt of any new ideas.*
—*v.* make bankrupt. [< F *banqueroute* < Ital. *bancarotta* < *banca* bank + *rotta,* fem. pp. of *rompere* break < L *rumpere*]

bank·rupt·cy (bangk'rəp sē or bangk'rupt sē) *n., pl.* **-cies.** the condition of being bankrupt.

ban·ner (ban'ər) *n.* **1** flag. **2** a piece of cloth with some design or words on it, attached by its upper edge to a pole or staff. **3** a newspaper headline in large type, usually extending across the entire width of the page. **4** (*adj.*) leading or outstanding; foremost: *a banner year in sports.* [ME < OF *baniere* < LL *bandum* < Gmc.]

ban·ner·et (ban'ər it) *n.* **1** *Historical.* a knight entitled to lead his vassals into battle under his own banner. **2** a rank of knighthood, senior to that of knight bachelor. [ME < OF *baneret* < *banere* banner + *-et* -ate¹]

ban·ner·ette or **ban·ner·et** (ban'ər et') *n.* a small banner.

ban·nock (ban'ək) *n.* **1** a flat cake, usually unleavened, made of oatmeal or barley flour. **2** *Cdn.* a flat, round cake, made of unleavened flour, salt, and water. Baking powder is sometimes added. [OE *bannuc* bit, piece]

banns (banz) *n. pl.* a public notice, given three times in church, that a man and a woman are to be married. [pl. of *bann,* var. of *ban* proclamation, OE *gebann*]

ban·quet (bang'kwit) *n., v.* **-quet·ed, -quet·ing.** —*n.* **1** a feast. **2** a formal dinner with speeches. —*v.* **1** entertain with a banquet: *The visiting celebrity was banqueted by the city.* **2** take part in a banquet. [< F < Ital. *banchetto,* dim. of *banco* bench < Gmc.]
☛ *Syn. n.* **1.** See note at **feast.**

ban·quette (bank ket') *n.* **1** a platform along the inside of a parapet or trench for soldiers to stand on when firing. **2** an upholstered bench, especially one along a wall in restaurants, etc. [< F]

ban·shee (ban'shē or ban shē') *n.* a spirit whose wails are supposed to mean that there will soon be a death in the family. [< Irish *bean sidhe* woman of the fairies]

ban·tam (ban'təm) *n.* **1** Often, **Bantam,** any of a number of breeds of dwarf ornamental fowl, raised mainly as a hobby because of the striking colors and arrangement of their feathers. Bantams usually weigh only about 680 g. **2** a very small person, especially one fond of fighting. **3** (*adj.*) small and light. **4** *Sports.* **a** a class for players under 15 years. **b** a player in such a class. **c** bantamweight. **5** (*adj.*) *Sports.* of or designating a class of players under 15 years: *a bantam hockey league.* [probably from *Bantam,* a city in Java]

ban·tam·weight (ban'təm wāt') *n.* a boxer who weighs at least 51 kg and not more than 54 kg.

ban·ter (ban'tər) *n., v.* **1** playful teasing; joking: *She didn't mind her friends' banter about her freckles.* —*v.* **1** tease or make fun of playfully. **2** talk in a joking way. [origin unknown] —**ban'ter·er,** *n.* —**ban'ter·ing·ly,** *adv.*

bant·ling (bant'ling) *n.* a young child; brat. [? alteration of G *Bänkling* bastard < *Bank* bench]

Ban·tu (ban'tü) *n., pl.* **-tu** or **-tus;** *adj.* —*n.* **1** a member of a large group of peoples who occupy central and southern Africa. The Bantu are not a uniform group, but include peoples of very different cultures. **2** a group of African languages widely spoken throughout central and southern Africa, including Swahili, Zulu, and Kikuyu. —*adj.* of or having to do with these peoples or their languages.

ban·yan (ban′yən *or* ban′yan) *n.* an east Indian tree (*Ficus bengalensis*) of the mulberry family, closely related to the fig but having inedible fruit. The branches of a banyan have hanging roots that grow down to the ground and start new trunks, so that one tree may cover several acres of ground. Also, **banian.** [var. of *banian*; originally a specific tree under which stood a banian pagoda]

ban·zai (bän′zī′) *interj.* 1 a Japanese greeting or patriotic cheer meaning: "May you live ten thousand years!" 2 the battle cry of Japanese soldiers in a banzai attack.

banzai attack a suicidal assault by Japanese soldiers, usually on an entrenched position.

ba·o·bab (bā′ō bab′ *or* bä′ō bab′) *n.* a tall, tropical African tree (*Adansonia digitata*) having a very thick trunk, sometimes up to 15 m in diameter. The fibres of baobab bark are used for making rope, cloth, etc. [? < native African]

Bap. or **Bapt.** Baptist.

bap·tism (bap′tiz əm) *n.* 1 a baptizing or being baptized. 2 the rite or sacrament of baptizing or being baptized. 3 an experience that cleanses a person or introduces him into a new kind of life.

bap·tis·mal (bap tiz′məl) *adj.* having to do with baptism; used in baptism: *baptismal vows.* —**bap·tis′mal·ly,** *adv.*

baptism of fire 1 the first time that a soldier is under fire. 2 a severe trial or test; ordeal.

Bap·tist (bap′tist) *n., adj.* —*n.* 1 a member of a Christian church that believes that baptism should be given to adults only, usually immersing the whole person under water. 2 **baptist,** a person who baptizes. —*adj.* of or having to do with the Baptists.

bap·tis·ter·y (bap′tis trē *or* bap′tis tər ē) *n., pl.* **-ter·ies.** a place where baptism is performed. A baptistery may be a section of a church or a separate building.

bap·tist·ry (bap′tis trē) *n., pl.* **-ries.** baptistery.

bap·tize (bap tīz′ *or* bap′tīz) *v.* **-tized, -tiz·ing.** 1 dip into water or wash with water as a sign of purification from sin and of admission into a Christian church. 2 purify; cleanse. 3 give a first name to (a person) at baptism; christen. 4 give a name to. [ME < OF *baptiser* < LL < Gk. *baptizein* < *baptein* dip] —**bap·tiz′er,** *n.*

BARS (DEF 5a)

BARS (DEF 5b)

bar¹ (bär) *n., v.* **barred, bar·ring;** *prep.* —*n.* 1 an evenly shaped piece of some solid, longer than it is wide or thick: *a bar of iron, a bar of soap, a bar of chocolate.* 2 a pole or rod put across a door, gate, window, etc. to fasten or shut off something. 3 anything that blocks the way or prevents progress: *A bar of sand kept boats out of the harbor. A bad temper is a bar to making friends.* 4 a band of color; stripe. 5 *Music.* **a** a unit of rhythm; measure. **b** the vertical line between two such units on a staff; bar line. 6 a counter over which drinks, especially alcoholic drinks, are served. 7 a room or establishment that has such a counter and in which alcoholic drinks are sold and consumed. 8 a counter, department, or other place, such as a self-serve area, where specific goods or services are sold: *a snack bar, a record bar, a gas bar.* 9 **the bar, a** the profession of a lawyer. A person is called to the bar after passing the prescribed law examinations. **b** lawyers as a group: *Judges are chosen from the bar.* 10 the area or railing in a court of law that separates the bench and the lawyers' seats from the rest of the court. 11 *Esp.Brit.* the place where an accused person stands in a court of law. 12 a court of law. 13 anything like a court of law: *the bar of public opinion.* —*v.* 1 put bars across; fasten or shut off with a bar: *He bars the doors every night.* 2 block; obstruct: *The exits were barred by chairs.* 3 exclude; forbid: *All talking is barred during a study period.* 4 mark with stripes or bands of color. —*prep.* except; excluding: *He is the best student, bar none.* [ME *barre* < OF < VL *barra* thick ends of bushes (collectively) < Celtic] ☛ *Hom.* **barre.**

bar² (bär) *n.* a unit for measuring pressure, equivalent to 100 kilopascals. *Symbol:* bar. [< Gk. *baros* weight] ☛ *Hom.* **barre.**

bar. 1 barometer; barometric. 2 barrel.

barb¹ (bärb) *n., v.* —*n.* 1 a point projecting backward from the main point. 2 *Zoology.* one of the hairlike branches on the shaft of a bird's feather. 3 a long, thin growth hanging from the mouth; barbel: *the barbs of a catfish.* 4 something sharp and wounding: *the stinging barbs of unfair criticism.*

hat, āge, fär; let, ēqual, tèrm; it, īce
hot, ōpen, ôrder; oil, out; cup, pủt, rüle,
əbove, takən, pencəl, lemən, circəs

ch, child; ng, long; sh, ship
th, thin; ᴛʜ, then; zh, measure

—*v.* equip with a barb; furnish with barbs. [ME < OF *barbe* < L *barba* beard]

barb² (bärb) *n.* 1 a kind of horse that has great speed, endurance, and gentleness. 2 a kind of domestic pigeon, related to the carrier pigeon, having a short, stout beak. [< F *barbe* < *Barbarie* Barbary]

Bar·ba·di·an (bär bā′dē ən) *n., adj.* —*n.* a native or inhabitant of Barbados, an island in the West Indies. —*adj.* of or having to do with Barbados or its people.

bar·bar·i·an (bär ber′ē ən) *n., adj.* —*n.* 1 a person belonging to a people or to a tribe thought to be uncivilized. 2 a foreigner differing from the speaker or writer in language and customs. In ancient times a barbarian was successively a person who was not a Greek, a person outside of the Roman Empire, or a person who was not a Christian. 3 a person without sympathy for literary culture or art; boor. —*adj.* 1 of or like a barbarian; not civilized; cruel and coarse. 2 differing from the speaker or writer in language and customs. [< F *barbarien* ult. < Gk. *barbaros* foreign. See BARBAROUS.] ☛ *Syn. adj.* 1. **Barbarian, barbaric, barbarous** = not considered civilized. **Barbarian** suggests nothing more: *The Roman Empire was conquered by barbarian peoples.* **Barbaric** emphasizes lack of refinement, taste, or moderation: *barbaric color schemes, a barbaric noise.* **Barbarous** emphasizes harshness and cruelty: *Torturing prisoners is a barbarous custom.*

bar·bar·i·an·ism (bär ber′ē ə niz′əm) *n.* the state or condition of being a barbarian.

bar·bar·ic (bär bar′ik *or* bär ber′ik) *adj.* 1 resembling barbarians; rough and rude. 2 crudely rich or splendid. [ME < L < Gk. *barbarikos* < *barbaros* foreign. See BARBAROUS.] —**bar·bar′i·cal·ly,** *adv.* ☛ *Syn.* 1. See note at **barbarian.**

bar·ba·rism (bär′bə riz′əm) *n.* 1 an act, custom, etc. that is brutal, harsh, or coarse. 2 the condition of being barbarous or a barbarian. 3 an act, expression, or object that offends against accepted standards of decency or good taste. 4 a word or construction that is considered substandard or wrong.

bar·bar·i·ty (bär bar′ə tē *or* bär ber′ə tē) *n., pl.* **-ties.** 1 brutal cruelty. 2 an act of cruelty. 3 a barbaric manner, taste, or style.

bar·ba·rize (bär′bə rīz′) *v.* **-rized, -riz·ing.** make or become barbarous. —**bar′ba·ri·za′tion,** *n.*

bar·ba·rous (bär′bə rəs) *adj.* 1 not civilized; primitive in culture and customs. 2 rough and rude; coarse; unrefined. 3 cruelly harsh; brutal: *the barbarous treatment of prisoners.* [< L *barbarus* < Gk. *barbaros* foreign, apparently originally, stammering < the reduplication of the syllable *bar* suggesting unintelligible speech] —**bar′ba·rous·ly,** *adv.* —**bar′ba·rous·ness,** *n.* ☛ *Syn.* 1. See note at **barbarian.**

Bar·ba·ry (bär′bə rē) *n.* the Moslem countries west of Egypt on the northern coast of Africa.

Barbary ape a tail-less monkey that lives in N Africa and on the Rock of Gibraltar.

Barbary sheep aoudad.

Barbary States a former name for Morocco, Algeria, Tunisia, and Tripoli, once noted as pirate strongholds.

bar·be·cue (bär′bə kyü′) *n., v.* **-cued, -cu·ing;** —*n.* 1 an outdoor grill or open fireplace for cooking meat, etc., usually over charcoal. 2 an outdoor meal prepared on a barbecue. 3 food prepared on a barbecue. 4 a feast at which animals are roasted whole. 5 an animal roasted whole. —*v.* 1 roast (meat, etc.) over an open fire. 2 cook (meat or fish) in a highly seasoned sauce. 3 roast (an animal) whole. [< Sp. *barbacoa* < Haitian *barboka* framework of sticks]

barbed (bärbd) *adj.* 1 having a barb or barbs. 2 sharp and wounding: *barbed sarcasm.*

barbed wire twisted wire with sharp points fixed to it at short intervals, used for fences, etc.

bar·bel (bär′bəl) *n.* 1 a long, thin growth hanging from the mouth of some fishes. 2 any of several large freshwater fishes (genus

FISH-HOOK BARB

ARROWHEAD BARB

Barbus) of Europe having such growths. [ME < OF < LL *barbellus*, dim. of *barbus* a kind of fish < L *barba* beard]

bar·bell (bär′bel′) *n.* a device for performing lifting exercises, similar to a dumbbell but having a longer bar and provision for weights at each end.

bar·ber (bär′bər) *n., v.* —*n.* a person whose business is cutting hair and shaving or trimming beards. —*v.* cut the hair or shave or trim the beard of. [ME < AF *barbour* < L *barba* beard]

bar·ber·ry (bär′ber′ē *or* bär′bər ē) *n., pl.* **-ries. 1** any of a genus (*Berberis*) of spiny shrubs having yellow flowers and sour, oblong, red berries. **2** the berry of a barberry. **3** (*adj.*) designating a family of mostly spiny shrubs or herbs found mainly in north temperate regions. The May apple and the barberries belong to the barberry family. [ME *barbere* < Med.L. *barbaris, berberis*]

bar·ber·shop (bär′bər shop′) *n., adj.* —*n.* a barber's place of business. —*adj.* of, having to do with, or suggesting a barbershop quartet: *barbershop harmony.*

barbershop quartet *or* **quartette** a male quartet that sings and improvises on popular sentimental ballads, usually in close harmony.

bar·bette (bär bet′) *n.* **1** a platform in a fort from which guns may be fired over the side. **2** an armored cylinder protecting a gun turret on a warship. [< F *barbette*, dim. of *barbe* beard < L *barba*]

bar·bi·can (bär′bə kan′ *or* bär′bə kən) *n.* a tower for defence built over a gate or bridge leading into a city or castle. [ME < OF *barbacane* < Med.L. *barbacana*]

bar·bi·tal (bär′bə tol′, bär′bə tôl′, *or* bär′bə tal′) *n.* a drug containing barbituric acid, used as a sedative or hypnotic.

bar·bi·tu·rate (bär bich′ə rāt′, bär bich′ə rit, bär′bə tyür′āt, *or* bär′bə tür′āt) *n.* **1** a salt or ester of barbituric acid. **2** any of several drugs derived from barbituric acid, used as sedatives or hypnotics.

bar·bi·tu·ric acid (bär′bə tyür′ik *or* bär′bə tür′ik) an acid much used as the basis of sedatives and hypnotics. *Formula:* $C_4H_4N_2O_3$ [*barbituric* < NL (*Usnea*) *barbata*, a kind of lichen (< L *barba* beard) + E *uric*]

barb·wire (bärb′wīr′) *n.* barbed wire.

bar·ca·role *or* **bar·ca·rolle** (bär′kə rōl′) *n.* **1** a traditional Venetian boat song. **2** any music in the style of a barcarole. [< F *barcarolle* < Ital. *barcarola* boatman's song < *barca* bark. See BARK³.]

B.Arch. Bachelor of Architecture.

bard (bärd) *n.* **1** a poet and singer of long ago. Bards sang their own poems to the music of their harps. **2** a poet. [< Irish and Scots Gaelic *bàrd* poet]

bar·dic (bär′dik) *adj.* of or having to do with bards or their poetry.

Bard of Avon Shakespeare.

bare¹ (ber) *adj.* **bar·er, bar·est;** *v.* **bared, bar·ing.** —*adj.* **1** without covering; not clothed; naked: *bare hands. Trees grew part way up the hill, but the top was bare.* **2** not concealed or not disguised; open: *the bare truth.* **3** not furnished; empty: *The room was bare.* **4** plain; unadorned: *He told us just the bare facts.* **5** much worn; threadbare. **6** only that and no more; mere: *She won by a bare five percent plurality. He earns a bare living by his work.* **7** *Archaic.* without a hat or other headdress.
lay bare, uncover; expose; reveal: *The plot was laid bare.*
—*v.* make bare; uncover; reveal: *to bare one's feelings. The dog bared its teeth.* [OE *bær*]
☛ *Hom.* **bear.**
☛ *Syn.* **1.** Bare, naked, nude = without covering. **Bare** emphasizes the idea of being without the usual covering and therefore lying open to view: *The sun burned her bare shoulders.* **Naked** emphasizes the idea of being stripped of all covering, especially customary protective covering, and laid open to view: *The little boy wandered naked through the streets.* **Nude** = unclothed, but expresses an objective attitude toward the body: *Many famous artists have painted nude models.*

bare² (ber) *v. Archaic.* a pt. of **bear¹.**
☛ *Hom.* **bear.**

bare·back (ber′bak′) *adv. or adj.* without a saddle; on the bare back of a horse, etc.: *to ride bareback, a bareback rider.*

bare·bones (ber′bōnz′) *n., adj.* —*n.* a very skinny person. —*adj.* meagre: *His barebones generosity will not make us rich.*

bare·faced (ber′fāst′) *adj.* **1** with the face bare. **2** not disguised. **3** shameless; impudent: *a barefaced lie.* —**bare′faced′ly,** *adv.*

bare·fist·ed (ber′fist′əd) *adj.* **1** without boxing gloves. **2** ruthless; unprincipled: *The industrialist was notorious for his barefisted treatment of competitors.*

bare·foot (ber′fut′) *adj. or adv.* without shoes and stockings on: *a barefoot child. If you go barefoot, watch out for broken glass.*

bare·foot·ed (ber′fut′id) *adj.* barefoot.

bare·hand·ed (ber′han′did) *adj. or adv.* **1** without any covering on the hands. **2** without weapons or tools in the hands: *He fought the dog barehanded.*

bare·head·ed (ber′hed′id) *adj. or adv.* wearing nothing on the head.

bare·knuck·le (ber′nuk′əl) *adj.* **1** without boxing gloves. **2** in which quarter is neither asked nor given: *a bare-knuckle argument.*

bare·leg·ged (ber′leg′id *or* ber′legd′) *adj. or adv.* without stockings.

bare·ly (ber′lē) *adv.* **1** only just; scarcely: *barely old enough to vote. He has barely enough money to live on.* **2** poorly or scantily: *a barely furnished room.* **3** *Archaic.* openly or plainly: *He put the question to them barely, and they were obliged to answer.*
☛ *Syn.* **1.** See note at **hardly.**

bare·ness (ber′nis) *n.* the state or condition of being bare; a lack of covering; lack of furnishings and contents.

barf (bärf) *v. Slang.* vomit. [imitative?]

bar·fly (bär′flī′) *n., pl.* **-flies.** a person who spends much time in bars or taverns.

bar·gain (bär′gən) *n., v.* —*n.* **1** an agreement to trade or exchange: *If you will take $5 for your book, it's a bargain.* **2** something offered for sale cheap, or bought cheap. **3** a good trade or exchange; price below the real value.
into the bargain, besides; also: *It's late and I'm tired into the bargain.*
strike a bargain, make a bargain; reach an agreement.
—*v.* **1** try to get good terms. **2** make a bargain; come to terms. **3** trade.
bargain for, be ready for; expect: *The rain wasn't so bad, but the hail was more than we bargained for.*
[ME < OF *bargaigne*] —**bar′gain·er,** *n.*

barge (bärj) *n., v.* **barged, barg·ing.** —*n.* **1** a large flat-bottomed boat for carrying freight. **2** a large boat furnished and decorated for use in excursions, pageants, and other special occasions. **3** a large motorboat or rowboat used by the commanding officer of a flagship. —*v.* **1** carry by barge. **2** move heavily or clumsily like a barge. **3** push oneself rudely or abruptly: *Everyone turned as she barged into the room.* **4** intrude (*used with* **in**): *He's forever barging in where he's not wanted.* [ME < OF < L < Gk. *baris* boat used on the Nile]

bar·gee (bär jē′) *n. Esp.Brit.* bargeman.

barge·man (bärj′mən) *n., pl.* **-men.** a man who works on a barge.

bar graph a chart or diagram showing different quantities by means of vertical or horizontal bars of proportional lengths.

bar·ite (ber′īt *or* bar′īt) *n.* a rock that consists mostly of barium sulphate.

bar·i·tone (bar′ə tōn′ *or* ber′ə tōn′) *n., adj.* —*n.* **1** a male voice between tenor and bass. **2** *Music.* **a** a singer with such a voice. **b** a part for such a voice or for a corresponding instrument. **c** an instrument playing such a part. —*adj.* **1** of or for a baritone. **2** that can sing or play a baritone part. [Gk. *barytonos* < *barys* deep + *tonos* pitch]

bar·i·um (bar′ē əm *or* ber′ē əm) *n.* a soft, silvery-white metallic element. *Symbol:* Ba; *at.no.* 56; *at.wt.* 137.34. [< NL < Gk. *barytēs* weight]

bark¹ (bärk) *n., v.* —*n.* **1** the tough outer covering of the stems and roots of woody plants, including an outside layer of dead cells, a cortex, which in twigs and small branches contains chlorophyll, and an inner layer, the phloem, containing the tubes which carry food along the stem or root. **2** any of several particular kinds of bark, such as tanbark, used in tanning, or circhona, used in medicine.
—*v.* **1** strip bark from; especially, cut out a ring of bark around a tree to kill it by interrupting the flow of food. **2** treat or tan with bark. **3** scrape the skin from (shins, knuckles, etc.): *I fell down the steps and barked my shins.* [ME < ON *börkr*]
☛ *Hom.* **barque.**

bark² (bärk) *n., v.* —*n.* **1** the short, sharp sound that a dog makes. **2** a sound like this: *the bark of a fox, a squirrel, a gun, or a cough.*
—*v.* **1** make this sound or one like it. **2** speak sharply or gruffly: *The officer barked out the order.* **3** *Informal.* cough. **4** *Informal.* call or shout to attract people into a circus tent, sideshow at a fair, store, etc.
bark at the moon, make a noise or fuss to no effect.
bark up the wrong tree, go after something by mistake or use wrong means to get at something.
[OE *beorcan*]
☛ *Hom.* **barque.**

bark³ (bärk) *n.* See **barque.**

bark beetle any of a family (Scolytidae) of small beetles that

bore through the bark and wood of trees. Bark beetles are carriers of the fungus that causes Dutch elm disease.

bar·keep (bär′kēp′) *n. Esp.U.S.* barkeeper.

bar·keep·er (bär′kēp′ər) *n.* a man who tends a bar where alcoholic drinks are sold.

bar·ken·tine (bär′kən tēn′) *n.* a three-masted ship with the foremast square-rigged and the other masts fore-and-aft-rigged. Also, **barquentine.** [< *bark*³; modelled on *brigantine*]

bark·er (bär′kər) *n.* **1** one that barks. **2** a person who stands in front of a circus tent, sideshow at a fair, store, etc. urging people to go in. [< *bark*²]

bar·ley (bär′lē) *n.* **1** any of various cereal grasses (genus *Horedum*) of temperate regions, especially *H. vulgare,* widely cultivated for forage and for its grain. **2** the grain or seed of barley, used in soups, etc. and also for making malt for beer and whisky. [OE *bærlic*]

Bar·ley·corn (bär′lē kôrn′) *n.* **John,** a name for intoxicating liquor, especially whisky.

barley sugar a clear, brittle candy, originally made by boiling sugar with an extract of barley.

barley water water in which barley has been boiled, formerly much used as a drink for invalids and babies.

bar line *Music.* the vertical line between two measures, or bars, on a staff.

barm (bärm) *n.* a foamy yeast that forms on malt liquors while they are fermenting. [OE *beorma*]

bar magnet a permanent magnet shaped like a bar or rod: *A bar magnet suspended from a string can serve as a compass.*

bar·maid (bär′mād′) *n.* a woman who works in a bar, serving alcoholic drinks to customers.

bar·man (bär′mən) *n., pl.* **-men.** barkeeper.

Bar·me·cide feast (bär′mə sīd′) **1** a pretended feast with empty dishes. **2** the empty pretence of hospitality, generosity, etc. [from *Barmecide,* a wealthy man in the *Arabian Nights* who gave a beggar a pretended feast on empty dishes]

bar mitz·vah (bär′mits′və) **1** a ceremony marking the formal admission of a boy into the Jewish religious community, usually held when the boy is thirteen years old. **2** a boy who has reached the age of thirteen, the age of religious responsibility. Also, **Bar Mitzvah.** [< Hebrew *bar mitzvāh* son of the commandment]

barm·y (bär′mē) *adj.* **barm·i·er, barm·i·est. 1** full of barm; fermenting. **2** *Informal.* silly; crazy; flighty.

barn (bärn) *n.* **1** a building for storing hay, grain, farm machinery, etc. and often for sheltering livestock. **2** any place that resembles a barn in use or appearance. [OE *bern < bere* barley + *ærn* storing place] **—barn′like′,** *adj.*

bar·na·cle (bär′nə kəl) *n.* any of a large group of marine crustaceans (subclass Cirripedia) that spend their entire adult life attached to some underwater object like a rock, ship bottom, or wharf pile, or a sea creature like a turtle or whale. In the first two or the three stages of a barnacle's life, it has no shell and can swim about freely. [ME *bernacle < OF* (cf. F *barnacle, bernicle*); earlier ME *bernake < OF bernaque*]

bar·na·cled (bär′nə kəld) *adj.* covered with barnacles.

barn dance 1 a dance held in a barn. **2** a lively dance resembling a polka.

barn raising a gathering of neighbors to build a barn. In pioneer days, such gatherings were usually social affairs, the day's work being followed by dancing, eating, and drinking.

barn·storm (bärn′stôrm′) *v. Informal.* **1** act plays, make speeches, etc. in small towns and country districts. **2** tour country districts giving short airplane rides, exhibitions of stunt flying, etc. **—barn′storm′er,** *n.*

barn swallow a swallow (*Hirundo rustica*) found throughout the world, having a dark steel-blue back and reddish-brown throat and breast, and a deeply forked tail. Barn swallows often nest in crevices of buildings.

barn·yard (bärn′yärd′) *n.* the yard around a barn for livestock, etc.

baro– *combining form.* weight; atmospheric pressure: *Barometer = something that measures (a meter of) atmospheric pressure.* [< Gk. *baros* weight]

bar·o·gram (bar′ə gram′ *or* ber′ə gram) *n.* a record made by a barograph or similar instrument.

bar·o·graph (bar′ə graf′ *or* ber′ə graf′) *n.* a barometer that automatically records pressure changes on a revolving drum.

ba·rom·e·ter (bə rom′ə tər) *n.* **1** an instrument for measuring atmospheric pressure. Barometers are used to indicate probable changes in the weather and for determining the height above sea level. **2** something that indicates changes: *Newspapers are often barometers of public opinion.*

hat, āge, fär; let, ēqual, tèrm; it, īce
hot, ōpen, ôrder; oil, out; cup, put, rüle,
əbove, takən, pencəl, lemən, circəs

ch, child; ng, long; sh, ship
th, thin; ᴛʜ, then; zh, measure

bar·o·met·ric (bar′ə met′rik *or* ber′ə met′rik) *adj.* **1** of a barometer. **2** indicated by a barometer.

bar·o·met·ri·cal (bar′ə met′rə kəl *or* ber′ə met′rə kəl) *adj.* barometric.

bar·on (bar′ən *or* ber′ən) *n.* **1** a nobleman of the lowest hereditary rank. **2** during the Middle Ages, an English nobleman who held his lands directly from the king. **3** a powerful merchant or financier: *a railway baron.* [ME < OF < OHG *baro* man, fighter] ☛ *Hom.* **barren.**
☛ *Usage.* In the United Kingdom, a **baron** is referred to as *Lord M—,* rather than as *Baron M—* as is the case in other European countries.

bar·on·age (bar′ən ij *or* ber′ən ij) *n.* **1** all the barons. **2** the nobility. **3** the rank or title of a baron.

bar·on·ess (bar′ən is *or* ber′ən is) *n.* **1** a noblewoman holding a rank equal to that of a baron. An English baroness has the title *Lady* before her name. **2** the wife or widow of a baron.

bar·on·et (bar′ən it *or* ber′ən it, bar′ən et′ *or* ber′ən et′) *n.* in the United kingdom, a man below a baron in rank and next above a knight. A baronet has *Sir* before his name and *Bart.* after it, as in *Sir John Brown, Bart. Abbrev.*: Bart. or Bt.

bar·on·et·cy (bar′ən it sē *or* ber′ən it sē) *n., pl.* **-cies. 1** the rank or position of a baronet. **2** a document that makes a person a baronet.

ba·ro·ni·al (bə rō′nē əl) *adj.* **1** of a baron; of barons. **2** suitable for a baron; splendid; stately; magnificent.

bar·o·ny (bar′ə nē *or* ber′ə nē) *n., pl.* **-nies. 1** the lands of a baron. **2** the rank or title of a baron. **3** a vast region or undertaking under private ownership or control.

ba·roque (bə rōk′ *or* bə rok′) *adj., n. —adj.* **1** of or having to do with a style of art, architecture, poetry, or music that flourished in Europe, especially in the seventeenth century, and was characterized by rich and elaborate ornamentation. **2** ornate or fantastic in style. **3** irregular in shape: *baroque pearls.* *—n.* the baroque style. [< F < Pg. *barroco* irregular]

bar·o·scope (bar′ə skōp′ *or* ber′ə skōp′) *n.* an instrument for showing changes in the pressure or density of the air. [< Gk. *baros* weight + E *-scope* instrument for viewing < Gk. *skopein* look at]

ba·rouche (bə rüsh′) *n.* a four-wheeled carriage with two seats facing each other, and a folding top. [< dial. G *Barutsche* < Ital. < L *birotus* two-wheeled < *bi-* two + *rota* wheel]

A barque of the late 19th century

barque (bärk) *n.* **1** *Poetic.* any boat or ship. **2** a sailing ship with three masts, square-rigged on the first two masts and fore-and-aft rigged on the other. Also, **bark.** [< F *barque* < Ital. *barca* < LL]

bar·quen·tine (bär′kən tēn′) See **barkentine.**

An aneroid barometer. A flexible box in this instrument expands or contracts with changes in air pressure and moves one of the pointers. The other pointer is set by hand and remains fixed, acting as a guide to how much the first pointer moves.

bar·rack[1] (bar′ək or ber′ək) n., v. —n. Usually, **barracks** (used with a sing. or pl. verb), **1** a building or group of buildings for members of the armed forces to live in. **2** Cdn. a building housing local detachments of the Royal Canadian Mounted Police. **3** Cdn. Informal. a training centre of the Royal Canadian Mounted Police: Her brother is training at the RCMP barracks in Regina. **4** a large, plain building housing many people. —v. house (soldiers, etc.) in barracks. [< F baraque < Ital. baracca]

bar·rack[2] (bar′ək or ber′ək) v. Brit. and Australian. Informal. express opinions noisily, especially to jeer (at a player, team, speaker, etc.). [< Australian slang barracking banter]

bar·ra·cu·da (bar′ə kü′də or bar′ə kü′də) n., pl. **-da** or **-das.** any of several pikelike fishes (genus Sphyraena) found in warm seas, having long, pointed jaws with razor-sharp teeth, and ranging in length from about 90 cm to about 120 cm. Because a barracuda will pursue anything that moves in the water, it is considered by some to be more dangerous than a shark. [< Sp. < West Indian name]

bar·rage (bə räzh′ for n. 1, 3 and v.; bär′ij for n. 2) n., v. **-raged,** **-rag·ing.** —n. **1** a barrier of artillery fire to check the enemy or to protect one's own soldiers in advancing or retreating. **2** an artificial barrier in a river; dam. **3** any heavy onslaught or attack: a barrage of words.
—v. fire with artillery at; subject to a barrage. [< F barrage < barrer to bar]

barrage balloon a large balloon intended to force enemy aircraft out of bombing range. It floats from a cable and is equipped with a self-sealing, bulletproof fabric.

bar·ra·try (bar′ə trē or ber′ə trē) n. **1** fraud or gross negligence of a ship's officer or seaman against owners, insurers, etc. **2** the act of stirring up lawsuits or quarrels. [ME < OF baraterie < barater to exchange, cheat. Related to BARTER.]

barre (bär) n. the supporting rail that ballet dancers use when practising. [< F]
☛ Hom. **bar.**

barred (bärd) adj. **1** having bars: a barred window. **2** marked with stripes: a chicken with barred feathers. **3** not permitted; forbidden: Smoking is barred in the library.

bar·rel (bar′əl or ber′əl) n., v. **-relled** or **-reled, -rel·ling** or **-rel·ing.** —n. **1** a large container shaped somewhat like a cylinder, having a flat, round top and bottom and slightly bulging sides, usually made of wide boards held together by hoops. **2** the amount that a barrel can hold. **3** a unit for measuring volume of oil, equal to about 0.159 m³ (159 L). **4** any container, case, or part shaped like a barrel: the barrel of a drum. **5** a metal tube of a firearm, through which the bullet travels. **6** Informal. a large quantity or number: a barrel of fun.
—v. **1** put in a barrel or barrels. **2** Informal. move in a rush: She was barrelling along the highway at 130 kilometres per hour. [ME < OF baril, probably < VL barra bar, stave]

barrel chair Esp.U.S. tub chair.

bar·rel·ful (bar′əl fül′ or ber′əl fül′) n. the amount that a barrel can hold.

barrel organ a hand organ.

bar·ren (bar′ən or ber′ən) adj., n. —adj. **1** not producing anything: A sandy desert is barren. **2** not able to bear offspring; sterile. **3** without interest; not attractive; dull. **4** fruitless; unprofitable.
—n. Cdn. **1** Usually, **barrens,** pl. a barren stretch of land; a wasteland. **2** the **Barrens,** pl. the Barren Ground. [ME < OF baraine] —**bar′ren·ness,** n.
☛ Hom. **baron.**

Barren Ground or **Grounds** Cdn. the treeless, thinly populated region in northern Canada, lying between Hudson Bay on the east and Great Slave Lake and Great Bear Lake on the west: Much of the Barren Ground is covered, in season, with short grass, moss, and small flowering plants.

Barren Lands Cdn. Barren Ground.

bar·rette (bə ret′) n. a pin with a clasp, used by women and girls for holding the hair in place. [< F barrette, dim. of barre bar]

bar·ri·cade (bar′ə kād′ or ber′ə kād′, bar′ə kād′ or ber′ə kād′) n., v. **-cad·ed, -cad·ing.** —n. **1** a rough, hastily made barrier for defence. **2** any barrier or obstruction. **3** Cdn. large blocks of ice remaining frozen to a river or sea shore after the spring breakup.
—v. block or obstruct with a barricade: The road was barricaded with fallen trees. [< F barricade, apparently < Provençal barricada < barrica cask; originally, made of casks. Related to BARREL.]

bar·ri·ca·do (bar′ə kä′dō or ber′ə kä′dō) n., pl. **-does.** barricade.

bar·ri·er (bar′ē ər or ber′ē ər) n. **1** something that stands in the way; something stopping progress or preventing approach. **2** something that separates or keeps apart. **3** Horse racing. a movable starting gate. [ME < AF barrere < LL barraria < barra bar < Celtic]

barrier reef a long line of rocks or coral reef not far from the mainland.

bar·ring (bär′ing) prep. except; not including: Barring accidents, we shall reach Vancouver at twelve o'clock.

bar·ris·ter (bar′is tər or ber′is tər) n. **1** a lawyer who pleads in court. **2** in the United Kingdom, a lawyer entitled to plead in any court, as opposed to a solicitor. [< bar + -ster]

bar·room (bär′rüm′ or -rùm′) n. a room with a bar for the sale of alcoholic drinks.

bar·row[1] (bar′ō or ber′ō) n. **1** a frame with two short handles at each end, used for carrying a load. **2** wheelbarrow. **3** handcart. [OE bearwe. Related to BEAR[1].]

bar·row[2] (bar′ō or ber′ō) n. a mound of earth or stones over an ancient or prehistoric grave. [OE beorg]

barrow pit especially in the West, a borrow pit.

bar sinister **1** bend sinister. **2** the fact or the stigma of being of illegitimate birth.

Bart. Baronet.

bar·tend·er (bär′tən′dər) n. a person who mixes or serves alcoholic drinks.

bar·ter (bär′tər) v., n. —v. **1** trade by exchanging one kind of goods or services for other goods or services without using money. **2** exchange (used with for): He bartered his boat for a car. **3** give or trade without an equal return (used with away): In his eagerness to make a fortune, he bartered away his freedom.
—n. **1** the act of bartering. **2** something bartered. —**bar′ter·er,** n.
[< OF barater to exchange. Related to BARRATRY.]

One of the bartizans on the walls of Glamis Castle in Scotland

bar·ti·zan (bär′tə zən or bär′tə zan′) n. Architecture. a small overhanging turret on a wall or tower. [alteration of bratticing < brattice parapet < OF bretesche, probably < OE brittisc British (type of fortification)]

Bart·lett pear (bärt′lit) a large, juicy kind of pear. [after E. Bartlett, who introduced it into America]

bar·y·on (bar′ē on′ or ber′ē on′) n. any of a class of elementary particles, including the proton and neutron and the hyperons, having a spin of ½ and generally having a mass greater than that of the mesons.

bar·y·sphere (bar′əs fēr′ or ber′əs fēr′) n. the heavy inside part of the earth within the outer crust. [< Gk. barys heavy + E sphere]

bas·al (bās′əl) adj. **1** of the base; at the base; forming the base. **2** fundamental; basic.

basal metabolism the amount of energy used by an animal or plant at rest, measured in terms of the rate at which oxygen is taken in. The basal metabolism for an average man 30 years old is between 1400 and 1500 calories per day.

ba·salt (bə solt′ or bə sôlt′, bä′solt or bä′sôlt, bas′olt or bas′ôlt) n. **1** a hard, dark-colored rock of volcanic origin. **2** basalt ware. [< LL basaltes, a manuscript corruption of L basanites < Gk. basanos touchstone]

ba·sal·tic (bə sol′tik or bə sôl′tik) adj. **1** of or having to do with basalt. **2** like basalt.

basalt ware a black, unglazed pottery having a dull gloss, developed by Josiah Wedgwood (1730-1795).

B.A.Sc. Bachelor of Applied Science.

bas·cule (bas′kyül) n. a device in which one end is counterbalanced by the other, as in a teeter-totter. [< F bascule seesaw, ult. < battre beat (influenced by bas low) + cul posterior]

bascule bridge a type of drawbridge that is raised and lowered by means of a bascule. See **bridge**[1] for picture.

base[1] (bās) n., v. **based, bas·ing.** —n. **1** an underlying support: The machine rests on a wide base of steel. **2** a fundamental

principle; basis; foundation. **3** the most important element of anything; essential part. **4** *Architecture.* **a** the part of a column on which the shaft rests. See **column** for picture. **b** the part at the bottom of a wall or monument. **5** *Biology.* **a** the part of an organ nearest its point of attachment. **b** the point of attachment. **6** *Chemistry.* a compound that reacts with an acid to form a salt. Calcium hydroxide is a base. **7** *Baseball.* any of the four corners of the diamond, which runners have to touch in order to score. **8** a starting place or goal in any of various sports and games. **9** the place from which a military force operates and from which supplies are obtained; headquarters. **10** a permanent camp or other place where units of the armed forces are stationed: *There is a large base at Gagetown, New Brunswick.* **11** the number that is a starting point for a system of numeration or logarithms. In arithmetic, 10 is the base of the decimal system. **12** *Geometry.* a line or surface forming that part of a geometrical figure on which it is supposed to stand: *Any side of a triangle can be its base.* **13** *Surveying.* a line used as the starting point. **14** *Linguistics.* the form of a word to which prefixes and suffixes are attached; root.

get to first base, make the first step successfully: *I worked on the problem for an hour, but couldn't even get to first base.*

off base, *Informal.* incorrect; absurdly mistaken: *I think your answer was off base.*

—*v.* **1** make or form a base or foundation for. **2** establish; found (*on* or *upon*): *Her large business was based on good service.* [ME < MF < L < Gk. *basis* base; literally, a step. Doublet of BASIS.]

☛ *Hom.* **bass¹.**

☛ *Syn.* **n. 1, 2. Base, basis, foundation** = the part of anything on which the rest stands for support. **Base,** chiefly used literally, applies to the bottom and supporting part of objects: *The Christmas tree must have a base.* **Basis,** chiefly used figuratively, applies to the part that supports beliefs, arguments, etc.: *The basis of his opinion is something he read in the paper.* **Foundation,** used literally and figuratively, emphasizes the firmness and solidness of the base or basis: *His honesty and willingness to work are the foundation of his success.*

☛ *Usage.* **Base.** The plural of this word is regular: **bases** (bā'siz). The plural of **basis** is spelled **bases** but pronounced (bā'sēz).

base² (bās) *adj.* **bas·er, bas·est;** *n.* —*adj.* **1** morally low; mean; selfish; cowardly: *To betray a friend is a base action.* **2** fit for an inferior person or thing; menial; unworthy: *No needful service is to be looked on as base.* **3** *Archaic.* of humble birth or origin. **4** having little comparative value; inferior: *Iron and lead are base metals; gold and silver are precious metals.* **5** debased; counterfeit: *base coin.* **6** deep or grave in sound. —*n.* the lowest male voice; bass. [ME < MF *bas* < LL *bassus* low. Doublet of BASSO.]

☛ *Hom.* **bass¹.**

☛ *Syn.* **adj. 1. Base, vile, low** = morally inferior and contemptible. **Base** = reduced to a low moral state, without honor or without moral standards, usually by selfishness or cowardliness: *To betray a friend for a reward is base.* **Vile** = without moral standards or sense of decency; evil; disgustingly dirty: *In the slums of some cities even small children learn vile language.* **Low** = without a sense of decency or of what is honorable: *To steal from the collection plate in church is low.*

base·ball (bās'bol' *or* -bôl') *n.* **1** a game played with bat and ball by two teams of nine players each, on a field with four bases. **2** the ball used in this game.

base·board (bās'bôrd') *n.* **1** a line of boards around the walls of a room, next to the floor. **2** a board forming the base of anything.

base·born (bās'bôrn') *adj.* **1** born of slaves, peasants, or other humble parents. **2** born of a mother who was not married; illegitimate.

base·burn·er (bās'bėr'nər) *n.* a stove or furnace fed automatically as the fuel below is burned.

base hit *Baseball.* a successful hitting of the ball by a batter so that he gets at least to first base without the help of an error.

base·less (bās'lis) *adj.* groundless; without foundation: *A rumor is baseless if it is not supported by facts.* —**base'less·ness,** *n.*

base line 1 a line used as a base for measuring or calculating, especially in land surveys, etc. **2** Often, **baseline,** a basic standard of value against which things are measured or compared: *the artistic baseline of the cinema.* **3** *Baseball.* a lane inside which a runner must keep when running between bases. **4** *Tennis.* the line marking the limit of play at either end of a court.

base·ly (bās'lē) *adv.* in a low, mean, or unworthy manner: *The prince acted basely towards the captives.*

base·man (bās'mən) *n., pl.* **-men.** *Baseball.* a player guarding one of the bases.

base·ment (bās'mənt) *n.* **1** the lowest storey of a building, partly or wholly below the ground; cellar. **2** (*adj.*) of, having to do with, or in a basement: *a basement rec room.*

base metal 1 any of the non-precious metals, such as lead, zinc, iron, etc. **2** the chief metallic element in an alloy.

base·ness (bās'nis) *n.* low, mean, or unworthy character or conduct.

ba·sen·ji (bə sen'jē) *n.* a breed of small dog originally from

hat, āge, fär; let, ēqual, tėrm; it, īce
hot, ōpen, ôrder; oil, out; cup, pùt, rüle,
əbove, takən, pencəl, lemən, circəs
ch, child; ng, long; sh, ship
th, thin; ᴛн, then; zh, measure

Africa, having a smooth, brown coat and a curled tail. Basenjis cannot bark. [< Afrikaans]

base runner *Baseball.* a member of the team at bat who is on a base or trying to reach a base.

ba·ses¹ (bā'sēz) *n.* pl. of **basis.**

bas·es² (bās'iz) *n.* pl. of **base¹.**

bash (bash) *v., n.* —*v. Informal.* strike violently: *He bashed the intruder on the head. They bashed down the door.* —*n.* **1** *Informal.* a smashing blow: *a bash on the head.* **2** *Slang.* an entertaining or exciting social event; a party or spree: *The mayor's fete was one of the most successful bashes of the year.* **3** *Slang.* an attempt: *Let me have a bash at it.* [? imitative]

ba·shaw (bə sho' *or* bə shô') *n.* **1** a pasha, a Turkish official. **2** an important person. [< Turkish *basha*]

bash·ful (bash'fəl) *adj.* uneasy and awkward in the presence of strangers; shy. [< *bash,* v. (var. of *abash*) + -*ful*] —**bash'ful·ly,** *adv.* —**bash'ful·ness,** *n.*

☛ *Syn.* See note at **shy¹.**

ba·sic (bā'sik) *adj., n.* —*adj.* **1** of, at, or forming the base; fundamental: *a basic principle. Addition, subtraction, multiplication, and division are the basic processes of arithmetic.* **2** being a basis or introduction; elementary: *a basic course in drawing.* **3** standard minimum, excluding extras: *a basic salary of $18 000.* **4** *Chemistry.* of, having the character of, or containing a base. —*n.* Usually, **basics,** *pl.* a fundamental fact, principle, etc.: *the basics of flying. Many parents felt that the schools were paying too little attention to basics.*

ba·si·cal·ly (bā'sik lē) *adv.* as a basic principle; fundamentally.

Basic English a simplified system of English, consisting of 850 essential words and a further 150 scientific words. It was invented by C. K. Ogden (1889-1957). [*Basic,* considered as an acronym for British, American, Scientific, International, Commercial]

ba·sic·i·ty (bā sis'ə tē) *n. Chemistry.* **1** the state or quality of being a base. **2** the ability of an acid to combine with bases, dependent on the number of replaceable hydrogen atoms contained in a molecule of the acid.

bas·il (baz'əl) *n.* **1** an annual herb (*Ocimum basilicum*) of the mint family having strongly aromatic leaves used as a seasoning in cookery; sweet basil: *Basil is especially good with tomatoes and tomato dishes.* **2** any of several other herbs (genus *Ocimum*) of the mint family, not used for cooking. [ME < OF *basile* < L < Gk. *basilikon* royal < *basileus* king]

bas·i·lar (bas'ə lər) *adj.* of the base; at the base.

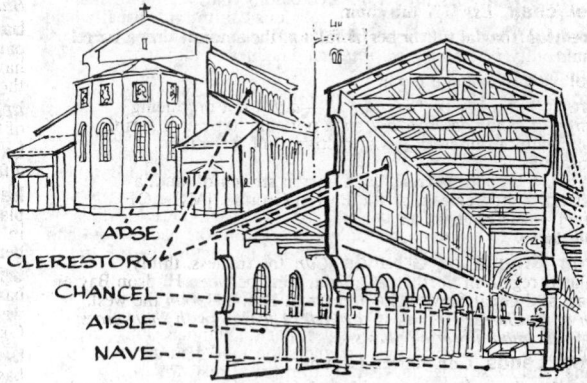

Basilica (def. 2). The 6th-century basilica of Sant' Apollinare in Classe, near Ravenna, Italy

ba·sil·i·ca (bə sil'ə kə) *n.* **1** an oblong hall with an aisle or gallery at each side, separated from the main area by a row of columns, and usually having an apse with a raised platform at one end. **2** an early Christian church built in this form. **3** a Roman Catholic church having certain rights and privileges. [< L < Gk. *basilikē* (*oikia*) royal (house) < *basileus* king]

bas·i·lisk (bas'ə lisk' *or* baz'ə lisk') *n.* **1** any of various tropical

American lizards (genus *Basiliscus*) of the same family as the iguanas, noted for their ability to run on their hind legs in an almost upright position. Male basilisks have a crest on the head. **2** a lizardlike reptile of classical legend whose breath and look were fatal. It had a black-and-yellow skin and fiery red eyes. [< L *basiliscus* < Gk. *basiliskos*, dim. of *basileus* king]

ba·sin (bā′sən) *n.* **1** a wide, shallow bowl, usually with sloping sides, used especially for holding liquids. **2** the amount that a basin can hold. **3** a relatively shallow depression in land, usually containing water. **4** a sheltered area where boats may be moored. **5** all the land drained by a river and the streams that flow into it: *the St. Lawrence basin.* [ME < OF *bacin* < LL *baccinum* < *bacca* water vessel < Celtic]

bas·i·net (bas′ə net′) *n.* a round steel helmet. [ME < OF *bacinet*, dim. of *bacin.* See BASIN.]

ba·sis (bā′sis) *n., pl.* **ba·ses** (-sēz). **1** the base or main part; foundation. **2** a fundamental principle or set of principles; criterion. **3** the principal ingredient: *The basis of this medicine is an oil.* [< L < Gk. *basis.* Doublet of BASE¹.]
☛ *Syn.* **1, 2.** See note at **base¹.**

bask (bask) *v.* **1** warm oneself pleasantly: *The cat was basking before the fire.* **2** take great pleasure: *He basked in the praise of his friends.* [ME < ON *bathask* bathe oneself]

bas·ket (bas′kit) *n.* **1** a container made of twigs, grasses, fibres, strips of wood, etc. woven together. **2** the amount that a basket holds: *She bought a basket of peaches.* **3** anything that looks like or is shaped like a basket. **4** the structure beneath a balloon for carrying passengers or ballast. **5** *Basketball.* **a** a net shaped like a basket but open at the bottom, used as a goal. **b** a score made by tossing the ball through the basket. [ME; origin unknown]
—**bas′ket·like′,** *adj.*

bas·ket·ball (bas′kit bol′ *or* bas′kit bôl′) *n.* **1** a game played with a large, round leather ball between two teams, usually of five players each. **2** the ball used in this game.

basket case *Informal.* a person who is completely incapacitated, especially as a result of mental or emotional breakdown. [originally applied, after World War I, to a person who had lost all four limbs]

bas·ket·ry (bas′kit rē) *n.* **1** basketwork; baskets. **2** the art or occupation of making baskets.

basket weave a weave in cloth that looks like the weave in a basket.

bas·ket·work (bas′kit wėrk′) *n.* **1** work woven as a basket is; wickerwork. **2** the art or occupation of making baskets.

basking shark a very large shark (*Cetorhinus maximus*) found chiefly in temperate seas, having two dorsal fins and very long gill clefts, and, unlike most sharks, not carnivorous, but feeding on plankton. It is named for its habit of floating at the surface of the water.

bas mitz·vah (bäs′mits′və) **1** a ceremony marking the formal admission of a girl into the Jewish religious community, usually held when the girl is thirteen years old. **2** a girl who is assuming religious responsibility. [< Hebrew *bat mitzvāh* daughter of the commandment]

Basque (bask) *n., adj.* —*n.* **1** a member of a people living in the Pyrenees in S France and in N Spain. **2** the language of the Basques, having no known relationship with any other language. **3** basque, a woman's garment consisting of a close-fitting bodice extending over the hips. —*adj.* of or having to do with the Basques or their language.

bas–re·lief (bä′ri lēf′ *or* bas′ri lēf′) *n.* relief sculpture in which the modelled forms stand out only slightly from the background and no part of the forms is undercut. See **relief** for picture. [< F < Ital. *basso-rilievo* low relief]

bass¹ (bās) *n., pl.* **bass·es**; *adj.* —*n.* **1** the lowest adult male singing voice: *He sings bass.* **2** a singer who has such a voice. **3** the part sung by a bass. Bass is the lowest part in standard four-part harmony for men's and women's voices together. **4** an instrument having the lowest range in a family of musical instruments, especially a double bass. **5** the lower half of the whole musical range for voice or instrument. Compare **treble.** **6** a deep, low-pitched voice or musical sound. —*adj.* **1** having to do with, having the range of, or designed for a bass. **2** having to do with or referring to the lower half of the musical range: *the bass clef.* [var. of *base²*; after Ital. *basso*]
☛ *Hom.* **base.**

bass² (bas) *n., pl.* **bass** *or* **bass·es.** **1** any of various perchlike, spiny-finned marine fishes (family *Serranidae*) found in temperate and warm seas throughout the world, highly valued as food and game fishes. **2** any of several large, important freshwater game

fishes (genus *Micropterus*) of the sunfish family native to eastern and central North America, especially the **largemouth bass** (*M. salmoides*) and **smallmouth bass** (*M. dolomieui*). [var. of *barse* perch, OE *bears*]

bass³ (bas) *n.* **1** basswood. **2** bast. [alteration of *bast*]

bass clef (bās′ klef′) *Music.* a symbol (𝄢) showing that the pitch of the notes on a staff is below middle C. In the bass clef, the F below middle C is on the fourth line from the bottom of the staff. See **clef** for picture.

bass drum (bās) a large double-headed drum that produces a deep sound of indefinite pitch. See **drum** for picture.

bas·set¹ (bas′it) *n.* a breed of hunting dog having short legs and a long body, similar to a dachshund, but bigger. [< F *basset*, dim. of *bas* low]

bas·set² (bas′it) *n., v.* —*n. Geology.* the edge of a rock stratum, etc. appearing at ground surface; outcropping. —*v.* appear or crop out at the surface.

basset hound a breed of heavily-built, short-haired hunting dog with a long body, short legs, and very long, drooping ears.

bass horn (bās) tuba.

bas·si·net (bas′ə net′ *or* bas′ə net′) *n.* **1** a baby's basketlike cradle. **2** a baby carriage of similar shape. [< F *bassinet*, dim. of *bassin* basin]

bass·ist (bā′sist) *n.* a person who plays a double bass, especially a skilled player.

bas·so (bas′ō; *Italian,* bäs′sō) *n., pl.* **bas·sos;** *Italian,* **bas·si** (bäs′sē). a singer with a bass voice. [< Ital. < LL *bassus* low. Doublet of BASE².]

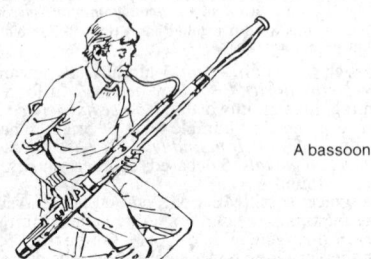

A bassoon

bas·soon (bə sün′ *or* bə zün′) *n.* a deep-toned wind instrument with a double reed, having a long wooden body with a second tube attached at the side, leading to a curved metal mouthpiece. [< F < Ital. *bassone* < *basso* bass]

basso pro·fon·do (prə fon′dō; *Italian,* prō fôn′dō) **1** the lowest bass voice. **2** a singer with such a voice. **3** a part for such a voice. [< Ital. *profondo* < L *profundus* deep]

basso pro·fun·do (prə fun′dō) basso profondo.

bass viol (bās′ vī′əl) **1** viola da gamba. **2** double bass.

bass·wood (bas′wüd′) *n.* **1** a tall North American shade tree (*Tilia americana*), a kind of linden, having heart-shaped leaves. **2** the light, fine-grained, white wood of this tree.

bast (bast) *n.* **1** tough fibres obtained from the phloem of plants such as flax and hemp, used in making rope, matting, etc. **2** phloem. [OE *bæst*]

bas·tard (bas′tərd) *n., adj.* —*n.* **1** a child born of parents not legally married. **2** anything inferior or not genuine. **3** *Slang.* a worthless, cruel, or unpleasant person.
—*adj.* **1** born of parents not legally married. **2** inferior; not genuine. **3** irregular or unusual in shape, size, style, etc. [ME < OF *bastard*, originally, mule < *bast* packsaddle + -*ard* (< Gmc.)]

bas·tard·ize (bas′tər dīz′) *v.* -ized, -iz·ing. **1** show or prove to be a bastard. **2** decrease the value or worth of; make inferior or corrupt; debase.

bas·tard·y (bas′tər dē) *n.* illegitimacy.

baste¹ (bāst) *v.* bast·ed, bast·ing. drip or pour melted fat or butter on (meat, etc.) while roasting: *Meat is basted to keep it from drying out and to improve its flavor.* —*bast′er,* *n.* [originally pp. of a verb < OF *basser* moisten. Related to BASIN.]

baste² (bāst) *v.* bast·ed, bast·ing. sew with long, loose stitches to hold the cloth until the final sewing. [ME < OF *bastir* < Gmc.; cf. OHG *bestan* tie up, sew with bast] —**bast′er,** *n.*

baste³ (bāst) *v.* bast·ed, bast·ing. beat; thrash. [< ON *beysta*]

Bas·tille (bas tēl′; *French,* bäs tēy′) *n.* **1** in Paris, an old fort used as a prison, especially for political offenders. It was captured and destroyed by a mob on July 14, 1789. **2** bastille *or* bastile, a prison, especially one considered oppressive. [< F < LL *bastilia* < *bastire* build]

bas·ti·na·do (bas'tə nä'dō or bas'tə nā'dō) n., pl. -does; v. -doed, -do·ing. —n. 1 a beating with a stick, especially on the soles of the feet. 2 a stick; cudgel. —v. beat or flog with a stick, especially on the soles of the feet. [< Sp. bastonada < baston cudgel, ult. < Gmc.]

bast·ings (bās'tingz) n.pl. long, loose stitches to hold cloth in place until the final sewing.

bas·tion (bas'chən or bas'tē ən) n. 1 a projecting part of a fortification made so that the defenders can fire at attackers from as many angles as possible. 2 any fortification or fortified area. 3 something that provides or acts as a stronghold: a bastion of freedom. [< F < Ital. bastione < bastire build < LL]

bas·tioned (bas'chənd or bas'tē ənd) adj. provided with or defended by bastions.

bat[1] (bat) n., v. bat·ted, bat·ting. —n. 1 Sports. a a specially shaped stick or club, used for hitting the ball as in baseball or cricket. b the act of hitting the ball with such a stick or club. c a turn at hitting the ball: It's her bat next. 2 Informal. a stroke or blow. 3 Slang. a drinking spree or binge. 4 batting (def. 1).
at bat, in position to bat; having a turn at batting.
go to bat for, Informal. support the cause of: I'm sure she'll go to bat for you if you explain exactly what happened.
right off the bat, Informal. immediately; without hesitation: He accepted the offer right off the bat.
—v. 1 hit with or as if with a bat. 2 use a bat: He's batting well this season.
bat around, a Baseball. go right through the batting order in one inning. b Slang. go here and there with no definite purpose: He is always batting around town in his new car. c Slang. discuss (a topic) freely and informally. [ME < OF batte club < battre strike] —bat'ter, n.

A little brown bat (Myotis lucifugus)—about 9 cm long; wingspread about 35 cm

bat[2] (bat) n. any of several hundred species making up an order (Chiroptera) of flying mammals, resembling other small mammals like mice and shrews in their general body form, but having membranes between the very long bones of the forelimbs, which enable them to fly, hind feet adapted for clinging, and a special radar-like sense organ that enables them to fly in the dark. Bats sleep during the day by clinging upside down to the ceilings in caves, dark corners of buildings, etc.
bats in the belfry, Informal. the state of being, or appearing, odd, peculiar, or insane.
blind as a bat, completely blind.
[alteration of ME bakkee < Scand.] —bat'like', adj.

bat[3] (bat) v. bat·ted, bat·ting. Informal. flutter; wink: He didn't bat an eye. [variant of obsolete bate flutter]

bat. 1 battalion. 2 battery.

batch[1] (bach) n. 1 a quantity of bread made at one baking. 2 a quantity of anything made as one lot or set: a batch of candy. 3 a number of persons or things taken together: a batch of essays. [ME bacche < OE bacan bake]

batch[2] (bach) n. or v. Informal. bach (shortened form of bachelor).

bate (bāt) v. bat·ed, bat·ing. abate; lessen; hold back.
with bated breath, holding the breath in great fear, awe, interest, etc.: The boys listened with bated breath to the sailor's stories of his adventures.
[var. of abate]

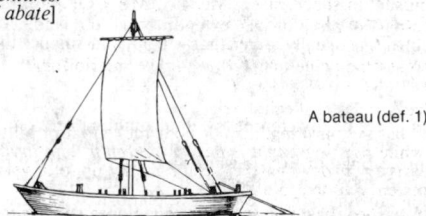

A bateau (def. 1)

ba·teau or **bat·teau** (ba tō') n., pl. -teaux (-tōz'). Cdn. 1 a light, flat-bottomed river boat about nine metres long, having a tapered bow and stern, and propelled by oars, poles, or sails. Bateaux were used especially in the late 18th and early 19th centuries to carry freight or passengers, especially on the upper St. Lawrence River. 2 any of several similar, usually smaller, light river boats. [< Cdn.F < F bâteau boat, ult. < OE bāt boat]

bath (bath) n., pl. baths (baᴛнz); v. —n. 1 a washing of the body.

hat, āge, fär; let, ēqual, tèrm; it, īce
hot, ōpen, ôrder; oil, out; cup, pùt, rüle, əbove, takən, pencəl, lemən, circəs
ch, child; ng, long; sh, ship
th, thin; ᴛн, then; zh, measure

2 the water, etc. for a bath: Your bath is ready. 3 a tub, room, or other place for bathing: In ancient Rome, baths were often elaborate public buildings which were used also as clubs. 4 a resort having baths for medical treatment. 5 a liquid for washing or dipping something, such as a solution for fixing photographic prints or film. 6 the container holding the liquid.
—v. 1 give a bath to. 2 take a bath. [OE bæth]

bathe (bāᴛн) v. bathed, bath·ing. 1 take a bath. 2 give a bath to. 3 apply water to; wash or moisten with any liquid: The doctor told her to bathe her eyes with the lotion. 4 go swimming; go into a pool, river, lake, etc. for pleasure. 5 cover; surround: The valley was bathed in sunlight. [OE bathian] —bath'er, n.

ba·thet·ic (bə thet'ik) adj. showing bathos; characterized by bathos.

bath·house (bath'hous') n. 1 a house or building fitted up for bathing. 2 a building containing one or more dressing rooms for swimmers.

bathing suit (bāᴛн'ing) a garment worn for swimming.

bath·o·lith (bath'ə lith') n. Geology. a great mass of intruded igneous rock, often forming the base of a mountain range and uncovered only by erosion. There is a batholith in British Columbia that is about 2400 by 160 kilometres. [< Gk. bathos depth + lithos stone]

ba·thos (bā'thos) n. 1 dullness or triteness in speech or writing, especially when immediately following more elevated expression. Example: The exile came back to his home, crippled, unfriended, and hatless. 2 strained or insincere pathos. [< Gk. bathos depth]

bath·robe (bath'rōb') n. a loose garment worn when going to and from a bath or when resting or lounging.

bath·room (bath'rüm' or -rùm') n. 1 a room fitted up for taking baths, usually equipped with a washbasin, a toilet, and a bathtub. 2 toilet.
go to the bathroom, Informal. urinate or defecate.

bath·tub (bath'tub') n. a tub to bath in.

bath·y·met·ric (bath'ə met'rik) adj. of or having to do with bathymetry. —bath'y·met'ri·cal·ly, adv.

ba·thym·e·try (bə thim'ə trē) n. the measurement of the depth of oceans, seas, and lakes.

bath·y·scaph (bath'ə skaf') n. a self-contained diving vessel for deep-sea observation, designed to reach great depths in the ocean, consisting of a heavy steel cabin for the observers attached to the underside of a large light hull called a float. The bathyscaph descends by allowing sea water into the float and ascends again by releasing iron ballast from the float. The record dive for a bathyscaph is 10 916 metres, made in 1960.

bath·y·scaphe (bath'ə skäf') n. bathyscaph.

bath·y·sphere (bath'ə sfèr') n. a ball-shaped, steel, watertight vessel having portholes, formerly used for observing plant and animal life in the ocean depths. The bathysphere was suspended from a boat by a cable and was able to descend to a depth of about 900 metres. [< Gk. bathys deep + E sphere]

ba·tik (bət ēk' or bat'ik) n., v. —n. 1 the art and method of making designs on cloth by dyeing only part at a time, the rest being protected by a removable coating of melted wax. 2 cloth dyed in this way. 3 a design formed in this way. 4 (adj.) of or like batik: a batik wall hanging.
—v. dye by batik. [< Malay]

ba·tiste (bə tēst') n. 1 a fine, thin cotton cloth in a plain weave. 2 any of various similar fabrics made of polyester, rayon, etc. [< F Baptiste, probably the name of the maker]

bat·man (bat'mən) n., pl. -men. a private soldier assigned to act as an officer's servant. [< OF bast packsaddle + man]

bat mitz·vah (bät'mits'və) bas mitzvah.

ba·ton (ba ton') n. 1 a staff or stick used as a symbol of office or authority. 2 a stick used by the leader of an orchestra, chorus, etc. to indicate the beat and direct the performance. 3 a stick passed from runner to runner in a relay race. 4 a light, hollow metal rod twirled by a drum major or majorette as a showy display. 5 Heraldry. a short, narrow, diagonal stripe on a shield, especially one running from upper left to lower right (from the bearer's point of view), indicating bastardy. [< F baton stick]

ba·tra·chi·an (bə trā'kē ən) n., adj. —n. an amphibian,

especially a frog or toad. —*adj.* of or having to do with amphibians, especially frogs and toads. [< Gk. *batrachos* frog]

bats·man (bats′mən) *n., pl.* **-men.** *Esp.Brit. Cricket.* a player who is batting.

batt. 1 battalion. 2 battery.

bat·tal·ion (bə tal′yən) *n.* 1 a formation of four companies within a regiment of infantry, usually commanded by a lieutenant-colonel. 2 any large number of soldiers organized to act together. 3 any large group organized to act together: *A battalion of volunteers helped to rescue the flood victims. Abbrev.:* Bn. [< F *bataillon* < Ital. *bataglione*, dim. of *battaglia* battle < LL *battalia.* See BATTLE.]

bat·teau (ba tō′) *n., pl.* **-teaux** (-tōz′). bateau.

bat·ten[1] (bat′ən) *v.* 1 grow fat. 2 fatten. 3 feed greedily. [< ON *batna* < *bati* improvement]

bat·ten[2] (bat′ən) *n., v.* —*n.* 1 a long, thick, board used for flooring. 2 a thin strip of wood used to reinforce or support lathing, etc., seal a joint, hold a tarpaulin in place over a ship's hatch, etc. 3 *Theatre.* **a** a wooden or metal bar from which to hang lights, scenery, etc. **b** the lights hung from such a bar. —*v.* fasten down or strengthen with strips of wood. [var. of *baton*]

bat·ter[1] (bat′ər) *v.* 1 beat with repeated blows; beat so as to bruise, break, or knock out of shape; pound: *Violent storms battered the coast for days.* 2 damage by hard use. [< *bat*[1]]

bat·ter[2] (bat′ər) *n.* a mixture of flour, milk, eggs, etc. that becomes solid when cooked. Cakes, pancakes, etc. are made from batter. [ME *batour*, probably < OF *bature* beating < *batre.* See BAT[3].]

bat·ter[3] (bat′ər) *n. Baseball and cricket.* a player who is batting. [< *bat*[1]]

battering ram 1 a heavy beam of wood with metal at the striking end, used in ancient and medieval warfare for battering down walls, gates, etc. 2 any heavy object used to break down a door, wall, etc.

bat·ter·y (bat′ər ē *or* bat′rē) *n., pl.* **-ter·ies.** 1 a container holding materials that produce electricity by chemical action; a single electric cell. See **dry cell** for picture. 2 a set of two or more electric cells that produce electric current: *a car battery.* 3 any set of similar or connected things: *a battery of loudspeakers, a battery of tests.* 4 a set of guns or other weapons such as mortars, machine guns, and artillery pieces for combined action in attack or defence. 5 a formation of several troops in an artillery regiment. 6 a platform or fortification equipped with big guns. 7 the armament, or one part of it, of a warship. 8 *Baseball.* the pitcher and catcher together. 9 *Law.* assault causing actual bodily harm. [< F *batterie* < *battre* beat < L *battuere.* Related to BAT[3], BATTLE.]

bat·ting (bat′ing) *n.* 1 sheets or layers of pressed cotton, wool, or a synthetic fibre, used for lining quilts, stuffing mattresses, packing, etc. 2 the act or manner of hitting a ball with a bat: *His batting has improved.*

batting average 1 *Baseball.* a player's ratio of base hits to the number of times at bat. 2 any record or indicator of performance or accomplishments: *Two promotions in two years is a pretty good batting average.*

bat·tle (bat′əl) *n., v.* **-tled, -tling.** —*n.* 1 a fight between opposing armed forces. 2 fighting or war: *wounds received in battle.* 3 any fight or contest: *a battle of words.* —*v.* 1 take part in a battle. 2 fight; struggle; contend. [ME *batayle* < OF *bataille* < LL *battalia* < L *battuere* beat. Related to BAT[3], BATTERY.] —**bat′tler,** *n.*

☛ *Syn.* 1. **Battle, action, engagement** = a fight between armed forces. **Battle** applies to a fight between large forces, such as armies, navies or air forces, lasting some time: *The battle for Caen lasted many weeks.* **Action** applies to a lively offensive or defensive part of a battle or campaign: *The Normandy landing during World War II was a decisive action.* **Engagement** emphasizes the meeting of forces, large or small, in combat: *The engagement at Dieppe cost the attacking Canadians many casualties.*

battle array 1 the order of troops, ships, etc. ready for battle. 2 armor and equipment for battle.

bat·tle–axe (bat′əl aks′) *n.* 1 a kind of axe used as a weapon of war. 2 *Slang.* an intolerant, overbearing woman. Sometimes, **battle-ax.**

battle cruiser a large, fast warship, not as heavily armored as a battleship.

battle cry 1 the shout of soldiers in battle. 2 a motto or slogan in any contest.

bat·tle·dore (bat′əl dôr′) *n.* 1 a small, light racket used in the game battledore and shuttlecock. 2 the game itself; battledore and shuttlecock. [ME *batyldore,* apparently < Pg. *batedor* beater < *bater* beat < L *battuere*]

battledore and shuttlecock an old-fashioned game resembling badminton, played by two persons.

battle dress a two-piece uniform consisting of trousers and a short, loose jacket, usually called a blouse, that ends in a fitted waistband. Battle dress is worn by the armed forces for field training and combat.

battle fatigue a neurosis caused by prolonged anxiety and emotional tension during combat.

bat·tle·field (bat′əl fēld′) *n.* the place where a battle is fought or has been fought.

bat·tle·front (bat′əl frunt′) *n.* the place where actual fighting between two armies is taking place.

bat·tle·ground (bat′əl ground′) *n.* battlefield.

bat·tle·ment (bat′əl mənt) *n.* 1 a wall for defence at the top of a tower or wall, with indentations through which soldiers could shoot. 2 a wall built like this for ornament. [ME *batelment* < OF *bateillier* fortify + E *-ment*]

bat·tle·ment·ed (bat′əl men′tid) *adj.* furnished with battlements.

battle royal 1 a fight in which several people take part; riot. 2 a long, hard fight.

bat·tle·scarred (bat′əl skärd′) *adj.* scarred from involvement in battles or fights: *a battle-scarred old coyote.*

bat·tle·ship (bat′əl ship′) *n.* the largest, most powerful, and most heavily armored type of warship. Battleships are seldom used now because they are very vulnerable to attacks from the air.

bat·tue (ba tyü′ *or* ba tü′) *n.* 1 the driving of game from cover toward the hunters. 2 a hunt where this is done. 3 a general slaughter. [< F *battue,* fem. pp. of *battre* beat < L *battuere*]

bat·ty (bat′ē) *adj.* **-ti·er, -ti·est.** *Slang.* crazy or odd. [< *bat*[2]]

bau·ble (bo′bəl *or* bô′bəl) *n.* 1 a showy trifle having no real value. Useless toys and trinkets are baubles. 2 a jester's staff. [ME *babel, babulle* < OF *babel, baubel* toy, of uncertain origin]

baulk (bok *or* bôk) See **balk.**

baux·ite (bok′sīt *or* bôk′sīt) *n.* a clay-like mineral from which aluminum is obtained. It is also used in making alum and fire bricks. *Formula:* $Al_2O_3.2H_2O$ [from Les *Baux,* France]

Ba·var·i·an (bə ver′ē ən) *n., adj.* —*n.* 1 a native or inhabitant of Bavaria, a state in SW Germany, formerly a duchy and a kingdom. 2 the German dialect spoken in Bavaria and in Austria. —*adj.* of or having to do with Bavaria, its people, or their dialect.

baw·bee (bo bē′ *or* bô bē′, bo′bē *or* bô′bē) *n. Scottish.* halfpenny.

bawd (bod *or* bôd) *n.* a woman who keeps a brothel. [ME < OF *bald* bold < Gmc.]

bawd·ry (bod′rē *or* bôd′rē) *n. Archaic.* lewd or obscene talk or writing.

bawd·y (bod′ē *or* bôd′ē) *adj.* **bawd·i·er, bawd·i·est;** *n.* —*adj.* humorously and exuberantly lewd or indecent: *bawdy songs.* —*n.* humorously lewd or obscene talk or writing. —**bawd′i·ly,** *adv.* —**bawd′i·ness,** *n.*
☛ *Hom.* body (bod′ē).

bawd·y–house (bo′dē hous′ *or* bô′dē-) *n.* brothel.

bawl (bol *or* bôl) *v., n.* —*v.* 1 shout or call out noisily: *The peddler bawled his wares in the street. The sergeant bawled out a command.* 2 weep loudly: *The small boy bawled whenever he hurt himself.*

bawl out, *Informal.* scold severely or loudly: *They got bawled out for leaving their bicycles in the driveway.*
—*n.* a loud shouting or weeping. [probably < Med.L *baulare* bark]
☛ *Hom.* ball.

bay[1] (bā) *n.* 1 a part of a sea or lake extending into the land; a wide indentation that is usually larger than a cove and smaller than a gulf. 2 **the Bay,** *Cdn. Informal.* **a** *Historical.* Hudson Bay. **b** the Hudson's Bay Company. [ME < OF *baie* < LL *baia*]
☛ *Hom.* bey.

bay[2] (bā) *n.* 1 a space or division of a wall or building between columns, pillars, buttresses, etc. 2 a space with a window or set of windows in it, projecting out from a wall. 3 a place in a barn for storing hay or grain; mow. 4 a compartment in an aircraft, especially one for carrying bombs. 5 a recess, platform, etc. for a specified purpose: *an unloading bay.* [ME < OF *baee* opening < VL *batare* gape.]
☛ *Hom.* bey.

bay[3] (bā) *n., v.* —*n.* 1 the long, deep howl or bark, especially as made by hounds, etc. when pursuing or closing in on prey. 2 the situation or position of a hunted animal when escape is impossible and it is forced to face its pursuers: *The quarry was brought to bay. The stag stood at bay on the edge of the cliff.* 3 the position or situation of a person forced to face an enemy, a serious difficulty,

persecution, etc. **4** the position of the pursuers or enemies who are being kept off: *The stag held the hounds at bay.*
bring to bay, put in a position from which escape is impossible.
—*v.* **1** utter a howl or prolonged barks: *The dogs sat and bayed at the moon.* **2** call out; shout. **3** bark at or pursue with barking. **4** bring to or hold at bay. [ME *bay, abay,* n. < OF *abai* a barking; ME *bayen,* v. (< OF *bayer* bark) and ME *abayen* (< OF *abayer* bark)]
☛ *Hom.* **bey.**

bay⁴ (bā) *n.* **1** laurel (def. 1), a shrub or tree of the Mediterranean region. Bay leaves are used for flavoring food. **2** any of several other trees resembling the laurel, such as a magnolia. **3 bays,** *pl.* **a** a laurel wreath worn by poets or victors. **b** honor; renown; fame. [< OF *baie* < L *baca* berry]
☛ *Hom.* **bey.**

bay⁵ (bā) *n., adj.* —*n.* **1** reddish brown. **2** a reddish-brown horse. —*adj.* reddish brown: *a bay mare.* [< OF *bai* < L *badius*]
☛ *Hom.* **bey.**

bay·ard (bā′ərd) *n., adj. Archaic.* —*n.* **1** a bay horse. **2** a mock-heroic name for any horse. —*adj.* bay-colored. [< OF *baiard* a red-brown horse < *bai* bay⁵]

Bay·ard (bā′ərd; French bä yär′) *n.* a man of heroic nature. [< Pierre du Terrail, Chevalier de *Bayard* (1473?-1524), a heroic French knight]

bay·ber·ry (bā′ber′ē *or* bā′bər ē) *n., pl.* **-ries. 1** a North American shrub (*Myrica pensylvanica*) of the wax-myrtle family, having clusters of round nuts covered with greyish-white wax. The leaves of the bayberry are aromatic, and candles made from the wax of the berries burn with a pleasant fragrance. **2** the fruit of this shrub. **3** a West Indian tree (*Pimenta racemosa*) of the myrtle family having leaves that yield an aromatic oil used in making bay rum.

Ba·yeux Tapestry (bā yü′; French, bä yœ′) a famous tapestry of the 11th century that pictures events leading to the Norman Conquest of England. [from *Bayeux,* a town in N France, where it is preserved]

bay laurel laurel (def. 1).

bay leaf the dried, aromatic leaf of the laurel (def. 1), used as a flavoring in making soups, stews, meat sauces, etc.

bay lynx bobcat.

bay·o·net (bā′ə nit *or* bā′ə net′) *n., v.* **-net·ed, -net·ing.** —*n.* a heavy, daggerlike blade for piercing or stabbing, made to be attached to the end of the barrel of a rifle. —*v.* pierce or stab with a bayonet. [< F *baïonnette*; from *Bayonne,* France]

bay·ou (bī′ü) *n., pl.* **-ous.** *Esp.U.S.* a marshy inlet or outlet of a lake, river, or gulf. [< Louisiana F < Choctaw *bayuk* small stream]

bay rum a fragrant liquid originally made from the leaves of the West Indian bayberry, used in medicine and cosmetics.

Bay Street *Cdn.* **1** in Toronto, a street on which is situated the Toronto Stock Exchange and many financial houses. **2** the financial or moneyed interests of Toronto.

A bay window

bay window 1 a window or set of windows projecting out from a wall, thereby providing extra space in a room. **2** a large abdomen: *He was a short, fat man, whose expensive watch chain called attention to his bay window.*

ba·zaar (bə zär′) *n.* **1** especially in Middle Eastern countries, a street or streets full of shops and stalls. **2** a place for the sale of many kinds of goods. **3** a sale of things donated by various people, held for some special purpose, often to raise money for charity. [< F < Arabic < Persian *bazar*]

ba·zoo·ka (bə zü′kə) *n.* a rocket gun used against tanks. [from its resemblance to a trombonelike instrument created and named by Bob Burns, an American humorist]

BB (bē′bē′) *n.* **1** a standard size of shot, approximately 0.45 cm in diameter. **2** a shot of this size, especially for use in an air rifle.

BBC or **B.B.C.** British Broadcasting Corporation.

BB gun air rifle. Also, **bee-bee gun.**

bbl. barrel(s).

bbls. barrels.

hat, āge, fär; let, ēqual, tèrm; it, īce
hot, ōpen, ôrder; oil, out; cup, pùt, rüle,
əbove, takən, pencəl, lemən, circəs

ch, child; ng, long; sh, ship
th, thin; ₮H, then; zh, measure

BC British Columbia (*used esp. in computerized address systems*).

B.C. 1 before Christ (*used to indicate years, numbering back from the birth of Christ*): *The year 350 B.C. is 100 years earlier than 250 B.C.* **2** British Columbia.

B.C.E. 1 Before the Common Era (*used to indicate years B.C.*). **2** Bachelor of Civil Engineering.

bch. bunch.

B.C.L. Bachelor of Civil Law.

B. Com. Bachelor of Commerce.

bd. 1 board. **2** bond. **3** bound.

B.D. Bachelor of Divinity.

bd. ft. board foot; board feet.

bdl. bundle.

Bdr or **Bdr.** Bombardier.

B.D.S. Bachelor of Dental Surgery.

be (bē) *v. pres. indic. sing.* **am, are, is,** *pl.* **are;** *pt. indic.* **was, were, was,** *pl.* **were;** *pp.* **been;** *ppr.* **be*ing. 1** have reality; live; exist: *The days of the pioneers are no more.* **2** take place; happen: *The circus was last month.* **3** have a particular place or position; remain; continue: *He will be here all year. The food is on the table.* **4** equal; represent: *Let "x" be the unknown quantity.* **5** belong to a particular group or class: *The new baby is a boy. My mother is a doctor. Elephants and mice are mammals.* **6** have or show a particular quality or condition: *I am sad. You are wrong. The book is red.* **7** Be is also used as an auxiliary verb with: **a** the present participle of another verb to form the progressive tense: *I am asking. She was asking. You will be asking.* **b** the past participle of another verb to form the passive voice: *I am asked. She was asked. You will be asked.* **8 Be** is also used to express future time, duty, intention, and possibility: *He is to arrive here at nine. No shelter was to be seen.* **9 Be** is also used as an auxiliary with the past participle of some intransitive verbs to form an archaic perfect tense: *The sun is risen.* [OE *bēon*]
☛ *Hom.* **bee.**

be- *prefix.* **1** thoroughly; all around, as in *bespatter.* **2** at; on; to; for; about; against, as in *bewail.* **3** make; cause to seem, as in *belittle.* **4** provide with, as in *bespangle.* [OE *be-,* unstressed form of *bī* by]

Be beryllium.

B.E. Bachelor of Engineering.

beach (bēch) *n., v.* —*n.* the almost flat shore of sand or small stones over which the water washes when high or at high tide. —*v.* run or drive up on shore: *We beached the boat in a little inlet. The newspaper reported that a whale was beached on the island.* [origin uncertain] —**beach′less,** *adj.*
☛ *Hom.* **beech.**

beach·comb (bēch′kōm′) *v.* live or work as a beachcomber.

beach·comb·er (bēch′kōm′ər) *n.* **1** a vagrant or loafer on beaches or in wharf areas, especially in islands of the south Pacific. **2** a long wave rolling in from the ocean. **3** *Cdn.* in British Columbia, a person who salvages logs broken loose from log booms and returns them to the logging companies for a fee.

beach·head (bēch′hed′) *n.* the first position established by an invading army on an enemy shore.

beach·wear (bēch′wer′) *n.* articles of clothing, such as bathing suits, shorts, or robes, for wearing at a beach.

bea·con (bē′kən) *n., v.* —*n.* **1** a fire or light used as a signal to guide or warn. **2** a marker, signal light, or radio station that guides aircraft through fogs, storms, etc. **3** a tall tower for a signal; lighthouse. **4** anything that guides or inspires. —*v.* **1** provide with a beacon or beacons. **2** serve as a beacon. [OE *bēacn*]

bead (bēd) *n., v.* —*n.* **1** a small ball or bit of glass, metal, etc. with a hole through it, so that it can be strung on a thread with others like it. **2 beads,** *pl.* **a** a string of beads. **b** a rosary; string of beads for keeping count in saying prayers. **3** any small, round object like a drop or bubble: *beads of sweat.* **4** a small metal knob or ball at the front of a rifle or pistol barrel, used for taking aim. **5** a narrow, semicircular moulding.
draw a bead on, aim at.
tell, count, or **say (one's) beads,** say prayers, using a rosary.
—*v.* **1** supply, trim, or cover with beads or beading: *beaded fabric,*

a beaded moulding. His forehead was beaded with sweat. 2 form into beads or drops: *Water will bead on an oily surface.* [OE *bedu* prayer. See def. 2b.] —**bead′like′**, *adj.*

bead·ed (bēd′id) *adj.* 1 trimmed with beads; having beads; covered with beads: *His brow was beaded with sweat.* 2 formed into beads; like beads.

bead·ing (bēd′ing) *n.* 1 a trimming made of beads threaded into patterns. 2 a narrow lace or openwork trimming through which ribbon may be run. 3 on woodwork, silver, etc., a pattern or edge made of small beads. 4 a narrow, rounded moulding.

bea·dle (bē′dəl) *n.* in the Church of England, a minor officer. Formerly, if a person slept in church, the beadle would wake him up. [OE *bydel*]

bea·dle·dom (bē′dəl dəm) *n.* stupid officiousness.

beads·man (bēdz′mən) *n., pl.* **-men.** a person who says prayers for others, especially one hired to do so.

beads·wom·an (bēdz′wŭm′ən) *n., pl.* **-wom·en.** a woman who says prayers for others, especially one hired to do so.

bead·work (bēd′wėrk′) *n.* beading.

bead·y (bēd′ē) *adj.* **bead·i·er, bead·i·est.** 1 small, round, and shiny. 2 trimmed with beads. 3 covered with drops or bubbles.

bea·gle (bē′gəl) *n.* a breed of small hunting dog having smooth hair, short legs, and drooping ears. [ME *begle* < ? OF *begueule* wide throat]

beak¹ (bēk) *n.* 1 a bird's bill, especially one that is strong and hooked and useful in striking or tearing. Eagles, hawks, and parrots have beaks. 2 a similar part in other animals, such as some turtles or fish. 3 the projecting bow of an ancient warship. 4 *Slang.* a person's nose, especially a large or hooked nose. 5 a spout. [ME < OF *bec* < L *beccus* < Celtic]

beak² (bēk) *n. Brit. Slang.* 1 magistrate. 2 a schoolmaster, especially a headmaster.

beaked (bēkt) *adj.* 1 having a beak. 2 shaped like a beak; hooked.

beak·er (bēk′ər) *n.* 1 a large cup or drinking glass. 2 the contents of a beaker. 3 a thin glass or metal cup with a small lip for pouring and no handle, used in laboratories. [ME < ON *bikarr* < LL *becarium,* var. of *bacarium.* Related to BASIN.]

beak·y (bēk′ē) *adj.* 1 having a beaklike nose; beaklike. 2 praying; meddlesome.

be–all and end–all 1 the main purpose or reason of anything. 2 *Informal.* the most important person or thing: *She thinks she is the be-all and end-all.*

beam (bēm) *n., v.* —*n.* 1 a large, long piece of timber, ready for use in building. 2 a similar piece of metal, stone, reinforced concrete, etc. 3 any of the main horizontal supports of a building or ship. 4 the part of a plough by which it is pulled. 5 the crossbar of a balance, from the ends of which the scales or pans are suspended. 6 the balance itself. 7 a ray or shaft of light: *the beam of a flashlight, a moonbeam.* 8 a bright look or smile. 9 a straight, narrow stream of electromagnetic radiation, nuclear particles, etc.: *a laser beam.* 10 a radio signal directed in a straight line, used to guide aircraft, ships, etc. 11 the side of a ship, or the direction at right angles to the keel, with reference to wind, sea, etc. 12 the greatest width of a ship.
off the beam, a of an aircraft, off the course indicated by directing signals. **b** *Informal.* on the wrong track; mistaken.
on the beam, a of a ship, at right angles to the keel. **b** of an aircraft, in the right path as indicated by directing signals.
c *Informal.* just right; on the right track.
—*v.* 1 send out rays of light; shine. 2 smile radiantly. 3 direct (a broadcast): *to beam programs at the Yukon.* [OE *bēam* tree, piece of wood, ray of light]
☞ *Syn.* 7. **Beam, ray** = a line of light. **Beam** applies to a shaft, long and with some width, coming from something that gives out light: *The beam from the flashlight showed a kneeling man.* **Ray** applies to a thin line of light, usually thought of as radiating, or coming out like the spokes of a wheel, from something bright: *There was not a ray of moonlight in the forest.*

beamed (bēmd) *adj.* furnished with beams: *a beamed ceiling.*

beam–ends (bēm′endz′) *n.pl.* the ends of a ship's beams.
on her beam-ends, of a ship, almost capsizing.
on (one's) beam-ends, seriously short of money; impoverished.

beam·er (bēm′ər) *n.* a bone implement for scraping hides, made from the cannon bone of a moose or caribou. It is used by holding it in both hands and pushing it along the skin away from the user.

beam·ing (bēm′ing) *adj.* 1 shining; bright. 2 smiling brightly; cheerful. —**beam′ing·ly**, *adv.*

beam–on (bēm′on′) *adv.* of a ship, with the beam ahead; against the beam.

bean (bēn) *n., v.* —*n.* 1 any of a number of climbing or bushy plants (genus *Phaseolus*) of the pea family, including many cultivated varieties, that produce edible, usually kidney-shaped seeds in long pods. The pods themselves of some of these plants are also edible when immature. 2 the dried mature seed of a bean plant: *Baked beans are often eaten as the main part of a meal.* 3 the immature green or yellow pod of a bean plant with its seeds, used as a vegetable, usually cooked. 4 any of various other seeds or fruits related to or resembling a bean: *Coffee beans are the seeds of the coffee plant.* 5 *Slang.* the head.
full of beans, *Slang.* lively; in high spirits: *She's really full of beans today.*
old bean, *Esp.Brit. Slang.* chap; friend (*used as a form of address*): *How are you, old bean?*
—*v. Slang.* hit (someone) on the head, especially with a baseball or other thrown object: *The pitcher beaned one batter twice.* [OE *bēan*] —**bean′like′**, *adj.*
☞ *Hom.* been (bēn).

bean·bag (bēn′bag′) *n.* a small cloth bag loosely filled with dry beans, used to toss in play: *Beanbags are often made in the shape of animals.*

beanie (bē′nē) *n.* a small cap, often having no peak, worn especially by schoolboys but often by students of both sexes.

bean·pole (bēn′pōl′) *n.* 1 a pole stuck in the ground for bean vines to climb on as they grow. 2 *Slang.* a tall, thin person.

bean sprout *n.* the sprout of any of various bean seeds used as a vegetable, either raw, as for salads, or cooked.

bean·stalk (bēn′stok′ *or* -stôk′) *n.* the stem of a bean plant.

bear¹ (ber) *v.* **bore, borne** or (for 6 when used in the passive voice) **born, bear·ing.** 1 carry; transport: *A voice was borne upon the wind.* 2 support: *The ice is too thin to bear your weight.* 3 put up with; abide; tolerate: *I can't bear that man.* 4 undergo or experience without giving way; endure: *He cannot bear any more pain.* 5 produce; yield: *This tree bears fine apples.* 6 give birth to; have (off-spring): *That woman has borne four boys. He was born on June 4.* 7 produce; create; cause to come into existence: *On the opening night of the play a star was born. The idea of the plot was born at a secret meeting.* 8 have a connection or effect; relate: *His answer did not bear on the question.* 9 behave; conduct: *He bore himself with great dignity.* 10 bring forward; give: *to bear company, to bear a hand. A person who has seen an accident can bear witness to what happened.* 11 hold in mind; harbor or cherish: *to bear a grudge, to bear affection for someone.* 12 have as an identification or characteristic: *He bears the name of John, the title of earl, and a reputation for learning.* 13 have as a duty, right, privilege, etc.: *The king bears sway over the empire.* 14 take on oneself as a duty: *to bear the cost, responsibility, etc. She couldn't bear to tell him.* 15 press; push: *Don't bear so hard on the lever.* 16 move; go: *The ship bore north.* 17 lie; be situated: *The land bore due north of the ship.* 18 allow; permit: *The accident bears two explanations.*
bear down (on), a put pressure on; press or push: *Don't bear down so hard on him.* **b** move toward; approach. **c** try hard; work seriously: *You'll have to bear down if you expect to pass the examination.*
bear out, support; prove.
bear up, keep one's courage; not lose hope or faith.
bear with, put up with; be patient with.
[OE *beran*]
☞ *Hom.* bare.
☞ *Syn.* 4. **Bear, endure, stand** = to undergo something hard to take. **Bear,** the general word, suggests only being able to hold up: *He is bearing his grief very well.* **Endure** = to bear hardship or misfortune for a long time without giving in: *The pioneers endured many hardships in settling the West.* **Stand** is the informal word used interchangeably with **bear,** but it suggests bearing stubbornly and bravely: *He can stand more pain than anyone else I know.* See note at **borne.**

bear² (ber) *n.* 1 any of a family (Ursidae) of large, heavily-built mammals found mainly in the temperate regions of the northern hemisphere, having thick, coarse, shaggy hair, a very short tail, short, rounded ears, and large, flat five-toed paws with powerful claws. Bears are carnivorous animals but they also feed on berries, young shoots and buds, etc. 2 a gruff, surly person. 3 a person who sells shares or stocks in anticipation of a price decline, in order to make a profit by buying later at the lower price. 4 (*adj.*) of, having to do with, or designating a stock market in which prices are declining. Compare **bull** (defs. 4 and 5). 5 **Bear.** See **Great Bear** and **Little Bear.** [OE *bera*]
☞ *Hom.* bare.

bear·a·ble (ber′ə bəl) *adj.* that can be borne; endurable: *The pain was severe but bearable.* —**bear′a·ble·ness,** *n.* —**bear′a·bly,** *adv.*

bear·bait·ing (ber′bāt′ing) *n.* a sport that was popular in England for several hundred years, in which dogs were set to torment a chained bear. Bearbaiting declined in popularity from the seventeenth century on and was finally outlawed by parliament in 1835.

bear·ber·ry (ber'ber'ē *or* ber'bər ē) *n., pl.* **-ries.** *Cdn.* **1** a trailing evergreen shrub (*Arctostaphylos uva-ursi*) of the heath family having small, pale-pink flowers, red berries, and astringent leaves. It is found especially in rocky or sandy regions of Canada and the United States and in the British Isles. **2** a closely related arctic and alpine shrub (*A. alpina*) having black berries.

TYPES
OF
BEARD

FULL · GOATEE · IMPERIAL
(EDWARD VII) (DISRAELI) (NAPOLEAN III)

beard (bērd) *n., v.* —*n.* **1** the hair that grows on the chin, cheeks, and upper throat of a man: *a three days' growth of beard.* **2** the growth formed by this hair, allowed to grow freely or cut or trimmed in any of various styles: *a full beard, an imperial beard.* **3** a tuft or growth of hair or bristles on the face or under the chin of any of certain animals or birds. **4** a tuft or crest of hairs or bristles on a plant, such as the awns of some grasses. —*v.* **1** face boldly; defy. **2** grasp by the beard. [OE] —**beard'like',** *adj.*

beard·ed (bēr'did) *adj.* having a beard.

bearded seal *Cdn.* a very large seal (*Erignathus barbatus*) found along the arctic coasts of the world, distinguished especially by its square foreflippers and long, whiskerlike bristles about the mouth.

beard·less (bērd'lis) *adj.* **1** having no beard. **2** too young to have a beard: *a beardless youth.*

bear·er (ber'ər) *n.* **1** a person or thing that carries. **2** a person who holds or presents a cheque, draft, or note for payment. **3** a tree or plant that produces fruit or flowers: *This apple tree is a good bearer.* **4** the holder of a rank or office. **5** pallbearer.

bear·ing (ber'ing) *n.* **1** a way of standing, sitting, walking, etc.; manner: *a military bearing.* **2** connection in thought or meaning; reference or relation: *His foolish question has no bearing on the problem.* **3** a part of a machine on which another part turns or slides. **4** a supporting part. **5** *Heraldry.* a device or figure on a shield; charge. **6** bearings, *pl.* **a** direction; position in relation to other things: *The pilot radioed his bearings.* **b** comprehension of one's position in relation to other things: *Without a guide in the bush, he would soon have lost his bearings.*
☞ *Syn.* **1.** Bearing, carriage = manner of carrying oneself. **Bearing** applies to a person's manner of managing his whole body, including his gestures, mannerisms, posture, the way he holds his head, and the way he walks and sits: *His manly bearing won the confidence of his employers.* **Carriage** applies only to a person's way of holding his head and body when he stands and walks: *Her awkward carriage prevented the pretty girl from becoming a model.*

bear·ish (ber'ish) *adj.* **1** like a bear; rough; surly. **2** marked by, tending toward, or expecting lower prices in the stock market. Compare **bullish.** —**bear'ish·ly,** *adv.* —**bear'ish·ness,** *n.*

bear·skin (ber'skin') *n.* **1** the skin of a bear with the fur attached. **2** a tall, black, fur cap worn by the members of certain regiments.

beast (bēst) *n.* **1** any animal except man. **2** any four-footed animal. **3** a coarse or brutal person. [ME < OF *beste* < LL *besta*] —**beast'like',** *adj.*
☞ *Syn.* See note at **animal.**

beast·ly (bēst'lē) *adj.* **-li·er, -li·est;** *adv.* —*adj.* **1** like a beast; brutal; coarse; vile. **2** *Informal.* very unpleasant; disagreeable: *a beastly headache.* —*adv. Informal.* very; unpleasantly: *It was beastly cold.* —**beast'li·ness,** *n.*

beast of burden an animal used for carrying loads.

beast of prey any animal that hunts and kills other animals for its food.

beat (bēt) *v.* **beat, beat·en** *or* **beat, beat·ing;** *n., adj.* —*v.* **1** strike again and again; strike; whip; thrash: *The cruel man beat his horse.* **2** throb: *Her heart beat fast with joy.* **3** drive by blows; force by blows: *He beat the savage dog away from him.* **4** defeat or overcome: *Their team beat ours by a huge score.* **5** *Informal.* baffle: *This problem beats me.* **6** *Informal.* cheat; swindle. **7** make flat; shape with a hammer: *to beat gold into thin strips.* **8** make flat by much walking; tread (a path). **9** mix by stirring; mix by striking with a fork, spoon, or other utensil: *to beat eggs.* **10** move up and down; flap: *The bird beat its wings.* **11** make a sound by being struck: *The drums beat loudly.* **12** mark (time) with drumsticks or by tapping with hands or feet: *to beat a tattoo.* **13** *Music.* show (a unit of time or accent) by a stroke of the hand, etc. **14** go through woods or

hat, āge, fär; let, ēqual, tèrm; it, īce
hot, ōpen, ôrder; oil, out; cup, put, rüle,
ə above, takən, pencəl, lemən, circəs

ch, child; ng, long; sh, ship
th, thin; ᴛʜ, then; zh, measure

underbrush in a hunt: *The men beat the woods in search of the lost child.* **15** move against the wind by a zigzag course: *The sailboat beat along the coast.* **16** outdo; surpass: *Nothing can beat yachting as a sport.*

beat about, search around; try to discover: *He beat about in vain for a fitting answer.*

beat a retreat, a a run away; retreat. **b** sound a retreat on a drum.

beat around (or **about**) **the bush,** approach matter indirectly; avoid coming to the point: *Stop beating around the bush and tell me what you want.*

beat back, force to retreat; push back: *The enemy advance was successfully beaten back.*

beat down, *Informal.* force to set a lower price.

beat it, *Slang.* go away; scram: *His sister got tired of his teasing and told him to beat it.*

beat off, a a drive off or away by blows: *He beat off the two men who attacked him.* **b** drive away; repel: *She beat off her fear by singing to herself.*

beat the rap, *Slang.* be freed from an accusation or charge without any penalty: *He was charged with dangerous driving, but managed to beat the rap.*

beat up, *Slang.* thrash severely.
—*n.* **1** a stroke or blow made again and again: *the beat of a drum, the beat of waves on a beach.* **2** pulsation; throb: *the beat of the heart.* **3** *Music.* **a** a unit of time or accent: *three beats to a measure.* **b** a stroke of the hand, baton, etc. showing a beat. **4** a regular round or route, especially one taken by a police officer or a sentry. **5** *Informal.* something that excels: *I've never seen the beat of that.* **6** *Slang.* beatnik. **7** a person's regular work or environment, sphere of knowledge, etc.: *That sort of thing is off my beat.*
—*adj.* **1** *Informal.* worn out; exhausted: *He was beat after a hard day at the factory.* **2** *Slang.* of or characteristic of beatniks: *the beat generation of the 50's.* [OE *bēatan*]
☞ *Hom.* **beet.**
☞ *Syn. v.* **1. Beat, hit, pound** = to strike. **Beat** = to strike again and again, but does not suggest how hard nor with what: *The cruel driver beat his horse.* **Hit** = to strike a single blow with force and aim: *The batter hit the ball.* **Pound** = to hit hard again and again with the fist or something heavy: *The child pounded the floor with a hammer.*

beat·en (bēt'ən) *v., adj.* —*v.* a pp. of **beat.**
—*adj.* **1** whipped; struck: *a beaten dog.* **2** shaped by blows of a hammer: *beaten silver.* **3** much walked on or travelled: *a beaten path.* **4** discouraged by defeat; overcome: *They were a beaten lot.* **5** exhausted.

beat·er (bēt'ər) *n.* **1** a person who beats, especially a man hired to rouse game during a hunt. **2** a device or utensil for beating eggs, cream, etc.: *an electric beater.* **3** *Cdn.* a young harp seal, about three or four weeks old, that is learning to swim and has developed its first spotted coat.

be·a·tif·ic (bē'ə tif'ik) *adj.* showing or producing blessedness; blissful: *The saint in the painting had a beatific smile.*

be·at·i·fi·ca·tion (bē at'ə fə kā'shən) *n.* **1** making blessed or being made blessed. **2** *Roman Catholic Church.* an official declaration by the Pope that a dead person is among the blessed in heaven.

be·at·i·fy (bē at'ə fī') *v.* **-fied, -fy·ing. 1** make supremely happy; bless. **2** *Roman Catholic Church.* declare (a dead person) by a papal decree to be among the blessed in heaven. [< L *beatificare* < *beatus* happy + *facere* make]

beat·ing (bēt'ing) *n.* **1** punishment by repeated blows; whipping. **2** defeat: *They took a beating in the game.* **3** throbbing; pulsation: *He could hear the beating of his own heart as he waited.*

be·at·i·tude (bē at'ə tyüd' *or* bē at'ə tüd') *n.* **1** supreme happiness; bliss. **2** a blessing. **3 the Beatitudes,** *pl.* the declarations of blessedness made by Jesus in the Sermon on the Mount (Matthew 5:3-12). [< L *beatitudo* < *beatus* blessed]

beat·nik (bēt'nik) *n.* a person who adopts a mode of life calculated to show indifference to or contempt for conventions and accepted standards in dress, speech, art expression, etc. [< *beat* + Yiddish *-nik*]

beat–up (bēt'up') *adj. Slang.* in very bad condition; worn out.

beau (bō) *n., pl.* **beaus** *or* **beaux** (bōz). **1** a young man courting a young woman; suitor; lover. **2** a man who pays much attention to the way he dresses and to the fashionableness or stylishness of his clothes. [< F *beau* handsome < L *bellus* fine]
☞ *Hom.* **bow².**

☛ *Usage.* Beaux is the more formal plural form; ordinarily, use **beaus.**

Beau Brum·mell (bō′brum′əl) **1** the nickname of George Bryan Brummell (1778-1840), an English leader in men's fashions. **2** any dandy.

Beau·fort scale (bō′fərt) an internationally used scale of wind velocities, using code numbers from 0 to 12.

beau geste (bō′zhest′) *pl.* **beaux gestes** (bō′zhest′). *French.* **1** a graceful or kindly act. **2** a pretence of kindness or unselfishness merely for effect.

beau i·de·al (bō′ī dē′əl; *French,* bō ē dā äl′) *pl.* **beau ideals or beaux ideals.** a perfect type of excellence or beauty; the highest ideal or model. [< F]

Beau·jo·lais (bō′zhə lā′ *or* bō′zhə lā′) *n.* a red or white table wine from the Beaujolais region in France.

beau monde (bō′ mond′) fashionable society. [< F]

beau·te·ous (byü′tē əs) *adj. Esp.Poetic.* beautiful.
—**beau′te·ous·ly,** *adv.* —**beau′te·ous·ness,** *n.*

beau·ti·cian (byü tish′ən) *n.* a specialist in the use of cosmetics, especially a person who works in a beauty salon.

beau·ti·ful (byü′tə fəl) *adj.* very pleasing to see or hear; delighting the mind or senses: *a beautiful picture, beautiful music.*
—**beau′ti·ful·ly,** *adv.* —**beau′ti·ful·ness,** *n.*

☛ *Syn.* **Beautiful, lovely, handsome** = pleasing the senses or mind. **Beautiful** suggests delighting the senses by excellence and harmony, and often also giving great pleasure to the mind by an inner goodness: *Looking at a beautiful painting always gives one satisfaction.* **Lovely** suggests appealing to the emotions and giving delight to the heart as well as to the senses and mind: *Her lovely smile shows a sweet disposition.* **Handsome** = pleasing to look at because well formed, well proportioned, etc.: *That is a handsome chest of drawers.*

beau·ti·fy (byü′tə fī) *v.* **-fied, -fy·ing. 1** make beautiful or more beautiful; embellish: *Flowers beautify a yard.* **2** become beautiful. [< *beauty* + *-fy*] —**beau′ti·fi′er,** *n.*

beau·ty (byü′tē) *n., pl.* **-ties. 1** a quality or combination of qualities that gives great pleasure to the senses or to the mind and spirit: *The richness and beauty of the great hall were almost beyond description. "A thing of beauty is a joy forever." There is great beauty in his poetry.* **2** a person or thing that has beauty, especially a beautiful woman: *She is a renowned beauty.* **3** a feature or trait that gives special pleasure to the mind or senses: *the beauties of the countryside in spring. The beauty of her writing style is its simplicity.* **4** *Informal.* a notable or exceptional example of its kind: *That catch was a beauty! You should see her black eye; it's a beauty!* [ME < OF *beaute* < *beau* beautiful < L *bellus* fine]

beauty parlor or **parlour** beauty salon.

beauty salon a place that provides women with such services as hairdressing, manicuring, and skin treatments.

beauty shop beauty salon.

beauty sleep *Informal.* **1** any short nap. **2** the hours of sleep taken before midnight, supposed to be those that are most beneficial.

beauty spot 1 a small, black patch worn on the face to show off by contrast the whiteness of the skin. **2** a mole or small spot or mark on the skin. **3** any place or natural feature of especial beauty.

beaux (bōz) *n.* a pl. of **beau.**

beaux–arts (bō zär′) *n.pl. French.* fine arts; painting, sculpture, music, etc.

A North American beaver—
about 75 cm long excluding
the tail; tail about 30 cm
long and 16 cm wide

bea·ver¹ (bē′vər) *n., pl.* **-vers** or (def. 1) **-ver;** *v.* —*n.* **1** either of two species comprising a family (Castoridae) of large rodents that live in and around water, having a thickset body, a broad, flat, scaly tail, which is used as a rudder in swimming, large webbed hind feet, and long, chisel-like front teeth. The North American beaver (*Castor canadensis*) has been an emblem of Canada for over two hundred years. Some authorities consider the North American beaver to be of the same species as the Old World beaver (*Castor fiber*). **2** the thick, soft, glossy, brown fur of a beaver, highly valued for coats, etc. **3** a man's high silk hat, formerly made of beaver fur. **4** a heavy woollen cloth. **5** *Informal.* an especially hard-working person; an eager beaver. **6 Beaver,** a member, aged five to seven, of the Boy Scouts.

—*v. Informal.* work hard or energetically (*often used with* **away**): *She has been beavering away all day.* [OE *beofor*]

bea·ver² (bē′vər) *n.* **1** a movable piece of armor that protects the chin and mouth. See **armor** for picture. **2** the movable front part of a helmet; a visor. [ME < OF *bavière,* originally, bib < *bave* saliva]

Beaver (bē′vər) *n., pl.* **-ver** or **-vers. 1** a group of Athapaskan Indians of the Peace River valley in Alberta. **2** a member of this group. **3** the language of this group. [translation of native name meaning "dwellers among beavers"]

bea·ver·board (bē′vər bôrd′) *n.* **1** a lightweight material resembling very thick, strong cardboard, used for making ceilings, partitions, etc. **2 Beaverboard,** a trademark for such material.

be·bop (bē′bop′) *n. Music.* a style of jazz that evolved in the 1940's, characterized by more complex harmony and more syncopation than in swing; bop. [imitative]

be·calm (bi kom′ *or* bi käm′) *v.* **1** keep (a ship, boat, etc.) from moving because of lack of wind (*usually used in the passive*): *We were becalmed for several hours.* **2** make calm; soothe.

be·came (bi kām′) *v.* pt. of **become.**

be·cause (bi koz′, bi kôz′, *or* bi kuz′) *conj.* for the reason that; since: *We play ball because we enjoy the game.*
because of, (*prep.*) by reason of; on account of: *We did not go because of the rain.*
[ME *bicause* by cause]

☛ *Syn.* **Because, as, since, for. Because** introduces a subordinate clause that gives the reason for the main clause: *Because we were late, we hurried.* **As** can be used in such clauses, but is less definite and more characteristic of informal speech than of writing. **Since** has a similar function but may be ambiguous since it can refer to time as well as cause: *Since she went away, he has taken to drink.* **For,** used only to introduce a clause following the main clause, is a more formal word.

be·chance (bi chans′) *v.* **-chanced, -chanc·ing.** *Archaic.* happen; happen to; befall.

beck (bek) *n.* a motion of the head or hand meant as a call or command.
at (one's) beck and call, ready to do whatever a person orders or wants: *She had three servants at her beck and call.*
[< *beck,* v., short for *beckon*]

beck·on (bek′ən) *v.* signal by a motion of the head or hand: *He beckoned me to follow him.* [OE *bēcnan,* var. of *bīecnan.* Related to BEACON.]

be·cloud (bi kloud′) *v.* **1** hide by a cloud or clouds. **2** make obscure: *Too many big words becloud the meaning.*

be·come (bi kum′) *v.* **be·came, be·come, be·com·ing. 1** come to be; grow to be: *He became wiser as he grew older.* **2** be suitable for; suit: *The rude comment did not become his position as chairman.* **3** look well on: *That dress becomes her.*
become of, happen to: *What will become of her? What has become of the box of candy?*
[OE *becuman*]

☛ *Usage.* **Become** is one of the common linking verbs: *At his words she became more angry.* **Become** differs from the linking verb *be* in that it adds a meaning of its own to its linking function, suggesting change or development rather than identity.

be·com·ing (bi kum′ing) *adj.* **1** suitable; appropriate: *becoming conduct for a formal occasion.* **2** that looks well on the person wearing it: *a becoming dress.* —**be·com′ing·ly,** *adv.*
☛ *Syn.* See note at **fitting.**

bec·que·rel (bek′ə rel′) an SI unit for measuring radio-activity, or the rate at which the atoms of radio-active elements disintegrate. One becquerel is equal to one disintegration per second. *Symbol:* Bq [after A.H. *Becquerel* (1852-1908), a French physicist]

B.Ed. Bachelor of Education.

bed (bed) *n., v.* **bed·ded, bed·ding.** —*n.* **1** anything to sleep or rest on. A bed usually consists of a mattress raised upon a support and covered with sheets and blankets. **2** any place where people or animals rest or sleep. **3** a flat base on which anything rests; foundation: *They set the lathe in a bed of concrete.* **4** the ground under a body of water: *the bed of a river.* **5** the piece of ground in a garden in which plants are grown. **6** *Geology.* a layer of stratum: *a bed of coal.*
bed and board, sleeping accommodation and meals.
get up on the wrong side of the bed, become irritable or bad-tempered.
go to bed with, *Informal.* have sexual intercourse with.
take to (one's) bed, stay in bed because of sickness or weakness.
—*v.* **1** provide with a bed or sleeping place; put to bed (*usually used with* **down**): *The man bedded his horse down with straw.* **2** go to bed; lie down to sleep (*used with* **down**): *He bedded down on a couch in the basement.* **3** fix or set in a permanent position; embed. **4** plant in a garden bed: *These roses should be bedded in rich soil.* **5** form a compact layer. **6** lay flat or in order. **7** *Informal.* have sexual intercourse with. [OE *bedd*]

be·daub (bi dob′ or -dôb′) v. **1** smear with something dirty or sticky. **2** ornament in a gaudy or showy way.

be·daz·zle (bi daz′əl) v. **-zled, -zling.** dazzle completely; confuse by dazzling: *He was bedazzled by the brilliant lights.*

bed·bug (bed′bug′) n. a small, reddish-brown bug (*Cimex lectularius*) about 5 mm long, having a broad, flat body covered with short hairs and bristles, small useless wings, and scent glands that give off a disagreeable odor. Bedbugs are bloodsucking parasites on human beings; they hide during the day in folds of mattresses, cracks in bedsteads, behind baseboards, etc. and come out at night to feed.

bed·cham·ber (bed′chām′bər) n. bedroom.

bed chesterfield a chesterfield that opens out into a bed.

bed·clothes (bed′klōz′ or bed′klōᴛʜz′) n.pl. sheets, blankets, quilts, etc.

bed·cov·er (bed′kuv′ər) n. a bedspread; coverlet.

bed·ding (bed′ing) n. **1** sheets, blankets, quilts, etc.; bedclothes. **2** material for beds: *Straw is used as bedding for cows and horses.* **3** a foundation; bottom layer.

be·deck (bi dek′) v. adorn; decorate.

be·dev·il (bi dev′əl) v. **-illed** or **-led, -il·ling** or **-il·ing. 1** trouble greatly; torment. **2** confuse completely; muddle. **3** put under spell; bewitch.

be·dev·il·ment (bi dev′əl mənt) n. **1** great trouble; torment. **2** complete confusion; muddle. **3** the state of being under a spell; being bewitched.

be·dew (bi dyü′ or bi dü′) v. make wet with dew or as if with dew: *Tears bedewed her cheeks.*

bed·fast (bed′fast′) adj. confined to bed; bedridden.

bed·fel·low (bed′fel′ō) n. **1** the person with whom one shares a bed. **2** a close associate: *The anti-war movement has produced some strange bedfellows.*

Bed·ford cord (bed′fərd) a heavy cloth ribbed like corduroy. [< *Bedford,* a town in S England]

be·dight (bi dīt′) v. **-dight, -dight** or **dight·ed, -dight·ing;** adj. *Archaic.* —v. adorn; array. —adj. adorned; arrayed. [< *be-* + *dight*]

be·dim (bi dim′) v. **-dimmed, -dim·ming.** make dim; darken; obscure.

be·di·zen (bi dī′zən or bi diz′ən) v. dress in gaudy clothes; ornament with showy finery. [< *be-* + *dizen*]

bed·lam (bed′ləm) n. **1** uproar; confusion: *When the home team won, there was bedlam in the arena. The whole house was bedlam for the first few days.* **2 Bedlam,** the traditional popular name for a hospital for the mentally ill in London, England, originally the Hospital of St. Mary of Bethlehem, but now officially named Bethlehem Royal Hospital. **3** *Archaic.* any insane asylum. [< ME *Bedlem,* a variant form of *Bethlehem*]

bed·lam·er (bed′ləm ər) n. *Cdn.* a young seal, especially a harp seal, about one to five years old, having a creamy brown coat with large, dark blotches on the flanks. [prob. a corruption of F *bête de la mer* sea beast]

bed·lam·ite (bed′ləm īt′) n. *Archaic.* an insane person; lunatic.

bed linen sheets and pillowcases for a bed.

Bed·ling·ton terrier (bed′ling tən) a breed of medium-sized terrier having rough, woolly fur, usually greyish brown, noted for its speed and pluck. It is usually clipped to resemble a lamb. [< *Bedlington,* a town in England]

Bed·ou·in (bed′ü in) n., adj. —n. **1** a nomad of the deserts and steppes of the Middle East and N Africa: *Most of the Bedouins of northern Africa are Berbers; those of the Middle East are Arabs.* **2** a wanderer; nomad. —adj. of or having to do with the Bedouins. [ME < OF < Arabic *badawin,* pl. of *badawiy* desert dweller]

bed·pan (bed′pan′) n. **1** a pan used as a toilet by sick people in bed. **2** a pan filled with hot coals for warming a bed.

bed·post (bed′pōst′) n. an upright support at a corner of a bed.

be·drag·gle (bi drag′əl) v. **-gled, -gling.** make wet or soiled with or as if with rain, mud, etc.

be·drag·gled (bi drag′əld) adj. **1** thoroughly wet and straggly or ragged-looking: *bedraggled hair. He arrived home two hours later, tired and bedraggled.* **2** soiled by or as if being dragged in dirt or mud: *a bedraggled hem.*

bed·rid (bed′rid′) adj. bedridden. [OE *bedreda, bedrida,* literally, bed rider]

bed·rid·den (bed′rid′ən) adj. confined to bed for a long time because of sickness or weakness. [var. (by confusion with *ridden*) of *bedrid*]

bed·rock (bed′rok′) n. **1** the solid rock beneath the soil and looser rocks. **2** a firm foundation. **3** the lowest level; bottom.

hat, āge, fär; let, ēqual, tèrm; it, īce
hot, ōpen, ôrder; oil, out; cup, pút, rüle,
əbove, takən, pencəl, lemən, circəs

ch, child; ng, long; sh, ship
th, thin; ᴛʜ, then; zh, measure

bed·room (bed′rüm′ or -rùm′) n. a room to sleep in.

bed·side (bed′sīd′) n. **1** the side of a bed. **2** (adj.) with or attending the sick: *Young doctors need bedside practice. She has a good bedside manner.*

bed·sore (bed′sôr′) n. a sore caused by lying too long in the same position.

bed·spread (bed′spred′) n. a cover that is spread over other bedclothes to keep them clean and neat.

bed·spring (bed′spring′) n. **1** a set of springs forming the part of the bed that supports the mattress. **2** one of these springs.

bed·stead (bed′sted′) n. the wooden or metal framework of a bed.

bed·straw (bed′stro′ or -strô′) n. any of a genus (*Galium*) of low-growing, perennial plants of the madder family having small, white, or yellow flowers. The plants were formerly dried and used as straw for beds.

bed·tick (bed′tik′) n. the cloth covering of a mattress or a box spring.

bed·tick·ing (bed′tik′ing) n. the strong cotton cloth from which bedticks are made.

bed·time (bed′tīm′) n. the usual time for going to bed.

bee¹ (bē) n. any of about 20 000 species making up a superfamily (Apoidea) of insects that feed their young with a mixture of pollen and honey stored in their nests. Some species of bees are social, living in large, highly organized colonies, but most species are solitary. The best-known social bees are the honeybees and the bumblebee.
have a bee in (one's) **bonnet,** *Informal.* **a** be preoccupied or overenthusiastic about one thing. **b** be slightly crazy.
[OE *bēo*]
☞ *Hom.* **be.**

bee² (bē) n. a gathering for work or amusement: *a husking bee, a spelling bee.* [? < E dialect *bean* or *been* help from neighbors < OE *bēn* prayer, related to ON *bón* petition. Compare ʙᴏᴏɴ.]

bee-bee gun air rifle; BB gun.

bee·bread (bē′bred′) n. a brownish, bitter substance consisting of pollen, or pollen mixed with honey, used by bees as food.

beech (bēch) n. **1** any of a genus (*Fagus*) of trees found in North America and Europe, having smooth, grey bark, dark-green, glossy leaves, and small, sweet, edible nuts. **2** the hard, heavy, strong wood of a beech. **3** (adj.) made of this wood: *a beech table.* **4** (adj.) designating a family (Fagaceae) of trees that includes some species highly valued for their timber. Beeches, oaks, and chestnuts belong to the beech family. [OE *bēce*]
☞ *Hom.* **beach.**

beech·nut (bēch′nut′) n. the small, triangular nut of the beech tree.

beech·wood (bēch′wùd′) n. the wood of a beech tree.

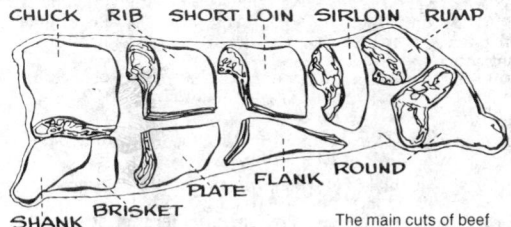

The main cuts of beef

beef (bēf) n., pl. **beeves** (def. 2), **beefs** (def. 4); v. —n. **1** the meat from a steer, cow, or bull. **2** a steer, cow, or bull when full-grown and fattened for food. **3** *Informal.* strength or muscle; brawn. **4** *Slang.* complaint or grievance: *We answered all his beefs.* —v. **1** *Informal.* strengthen (*used with* **up**): *You could beef up your argument by adding more examples.* **2** *Slang.* complain: *She's always beefing about something.* [ME < OF *boef* < L *bos, bovis* ox] —**beef′er,** n. —**beef′less,** adj.

beef·cake (bēf′kāk′) n. *Slang.* photographs or photography displaying men with muscular physiques. Compare **cheesecake.**

beef cattle cattle bred and raised primarily for meat.

beef·eat·er (bēf′ēt′ər) *n.* the common nickname for a yeoman of the guard who acts as a warder and official guide of the Tower of London.

beef extract an extract of beef or beef juices, for use in making broth, gravy, sauce, etc.

beef·steak (bēf′stāk′) *n.* a slice of beef for broiling or frying.

beef tea a strong beef broth.

beef·y (bēf′ē) *adj.* **beef·i·er, beef·i·est. 1** like beef: *a beefy taste.* **2** strong; muscular. **3** heavy; solid. —**beef′i·ness,** *n.*

bee·hive (bē′hīv′) *n.* **1** a hive or house for bees. See **hive** for picture. **2** a busy, swarming place.

bee·keep·er (bē′kēp′ər) *n.* a person who keeps bees for their honey and wax.

bee·keep·ing (bē′kēp′ing) *n.* the art of caring for and managing colonies of honeybees so that they will produce more honey than they need for themselves. The extra honey stored by the bees is collected for human use.

bee·line (bē′līn′) *n.* the straightest way or line between two places.
make a beeline for, *Informal.* go as quickly and directly as possible to: *The startled calf made a beeline for its mother.*

Be·el·ze·bub (bē el′zə bub′) *n.* **1** the Devil. **2** in Milton's poem *Paradise Lost,* the fallen angel next to Satan in power. [OE *Belzebub,* ultimately from Hebrew *ba'alzebūb,* the name of a Philistine god, lit., 'lord of the flies'. See BAAL.]

been (bin *or* bēn) *v.* pp. of **be.**
☛ *Hom.* **bin** (bin), **bean** (bēn).
☛ *Pronun.* Been. The most common British pronunciation is (bēn), and the normal American pronunciation is (bin). In earlier English, (bēn) was the stressed form and (bin) the unstressed; many Canadian speakers still employ this distinction. Otherwise, Canadian usage varies between the two forms.

beep (bēp) *n., v.* —*n.* **1** *Radio.* a short, sharp sound occurring as a signal. **2** any short, sharp sound: *the beep of a car horn.* —*v.* cause something to emit short, sharp sounds. —**beep′er,** *n.* [imitative]

beer (bēr) *n.* **1** any of various alcoholic, fermented beverages made from malt and, usually, hops, especially lager or Pilsener. **2** a bottle, can, or glass of beer: *She ordered two beers.* **3** a nonalcoholic or slightly alcoholic beverage made from roots or other parts of certain plants: *rootbeer, ginger beer.* **4** (*adj.*) of or for beer or the drinking of beer: *a beer glass, a beer parlor, a beer garden.* [OE *bēor*]
☛ *Hom.* **bier.**

beer and skittles *Informal.* enjoyment; material comforts: *Life is not all beer and skittles.*

beer parlor or **parlour** *Cdn.* a room in a hotel or tavern where beer is sold and drunk; beverage room.

Beer·she·ba (bēr shē′bə *or* bēr′shi bə) *n.* a city in central Israel, formerly near the southern boundary of Palestine.
from Dan to Beersheba, from one end of a place to the other.

beer·y (bēr′ē) *adj.* **beer·i·er, beer·i·est. 1** of beer. **2** like beer. **3** caused by beer. —**beer′i·ly,** *adv.*

beest·ings (bēs′tingz) *n.pl.* the first milk from a cow after it has given birth to a calf. [OE *bȳsting* < *bēost* beestings]

bees·wax (bēz′waks′) *n., v.* —*n.* a yellowish, pleasant-smelling wax given out by worker bees for constructing the cell walls of their honeycombs. Beeswax is processed for making candles, furniture polish, modelling wax, etc.
none of (someone's) beeswax, *Slang.* none of that person's concern: *What I do with my money is none of your beeswax.*
—*v.* rub, polish, or treat with beeswax.

bees·wing (bēz′wing′) *n.* **1** a thin film that forms in some old wines. **2** an old wine that has such a film.

beet (bēt) *n.* **1** a biennial plant (*Beta vulgaris*) of the goosefoot family widely cultivated in many varieties, especially in temperate regions, for its thick, fleshy, red, yellowish, or white root or its edible leaves. The red roots of some varieties are eaten as a vegetable; the white roots of other varieties yield sugar. See also **mangel** and **Swiss chard. 2** the root of a beet. [< L *beta*]
—**beet′like′,** *adj.*
☛ *Hom.* **beat.**

bee·tle¹ (bē′təl) *n., v.* —*n.* **1** any of an order (Coleoptera) of insects having four wings, the front pair of which are modified into horny coverings that are folded along the back when at rest, hiding the rear pair of wings. Beetles include some of the largest insects, such as an Asian beetle that is about 18 cm long, and others so small they are almost invisible to the naked eye. **2** any similar insect. —*v. Informal.* move quickly; scurry (*used with* **off, along,**

etc.): *beetling along the road. She grabbed his jacket and beetled off.* [OE *bitela* < *bītan* bite]
☛ *Hom.* **betel.**

bee·tle² (bē′təl) *n., v.* -**tled,** -**tling.** —*n.* **1** a heavy wooden mallet for ramming, crushing, or smoothing. **2** a wooden household utensil for beating or mashing. —*v.* pound with a beetle. [OE *bīetel* < *bēatan* beat]
☛ *Hom.* **betel.**

bee·tle³ (bē′təl) *v.* -**tled,** -**tling;** *adj.* —*v.* project; overhang: *Great cliffs beetled above the narrow path.* —*adj.* of eyebrows, shaggy and projecting: *His eyes were fierce beneath his beetle brows.* [< *beetle-browed*]
☛ *Hom.* **betel.**

bee·tle–browed (bē′təl broud′) *adj.* **1** having projecting or overhanging eyebrows. **2** scowling; sullen. [ME *bitel* biting + *brow.* Related to BEETLE¹.]

bee·tling (bēt′ling) *adj.* projecting; overhanging.

beet root the root of a beet plant.

beet sugar the sugar obtained from white beets.

beeves (bēvz) *n.* pl. of **beef¹** (def. 2).

be·fall (bi fol′ *or* bi fôl′) *v.* -**fell,** -**fall·en,** -**fall·ing. 1** happen to: *Be careful that no harm befalls you.* **2** happen. [OE *befeallan*]

be·fall·en (bi fol′ən *or* bi fôl′ən) *v.* pp. of **befall.**

be·fell (bi fel′) *v.* pt. of **befall.**

be·fit (bi fit′) *v.* -**fit·ted,** -**fit·ting.** be suitable or proper for: *clothes that befit the occasion.*

be·fit·ting (bi fit′ing) *adj.* suitable; proper. —**be·fit′ting·ly,** *adv.*

be·fog (bi fog′) *v.* -**fogged,** -**fog·ging. 1** surround with fog; make foggy. **2** obscure; confuse.

be·fool (bi fül′) *v. Archaic.* fool; deceive; dupe.

be·fore (bi fōr′) *prep., adv., conj.* —*prep.* **1** earlier than: *Come before five o'clock.* **2** rather than; sooner than: *We would choose death before dishonor.* **3** in the presence of or in sight of: *to stand before the king.* **4** in front or ahead of: *She walked before them.*
—*adv.* **1** earlier: *Come at five o'clock, not before.* **2** until now; in the past: *I didn't know that before.* **3** in front or ahead: *He went before to see if the road was safe.*
—*conj.* **1** previously to the time when: *Before she goes, I would like to talk to her.* **2** rather than; sooner than: *I'll give up the trip before I'll go with them.* [OE *beforan*]

be·fore·hand (bi fōr′hand′) *adv.* or *adj.* ahead of time; in advance: *I am going to get everything ready beforehand.*

be·fore·time (bi fōr′tīm′) *adv. Archaic.* formerly.

be·foul (bi foul′) *v.* **1** make dirty; cover with filth. **2** entangle: *The rope was befouled by weeds and sticks.* —**be·foul′ment,** *n.*

be·friend (be frend′) *v.* act as a friend to; help: *They were eager to befriend their new neighbors.*

be·fud·dle (bi fud′əl) *v.* -**dled,** -**dling. 1** stupefy; confuse. **2** make stupid with alcoholic drink. —**be·fud′dle·ment,** *n.*

beg (beg) *v.* **begged, beg·ging. 1** ask help or charity: *He was finally reduced to begging for a living.* **2** ask for (food, money, clothes, etc.) as a charity: *The tramp begged his meals.* **3** ask as a favor; ask earnestly or humbly: *He begged his mother to forgive him.* **4** ask formally and courteously: *I beg your pardon.*
beg off, ask to be excused or released from an engagement or obligation: *She asked me to go along, but I begged off.*
beg the question, take for granted the very thing argued about.
go begging, find no acceptance: *The architect's suggestion went begging.*
[ME *beggen* < AF *begger* < MF *begard,* of uncertain origin]
☛ *Syn.* **3. Beg, implore, beseech** = to ask earnestly. **Beg** = to ask earnestly or humbly: *He begged me to think about his offer.* **Implore,** more formal, adds to **beg** the idea of pleading with warm feeling or great humility: *We implored him not to ruin his life by doing anything so foolish.* **Beseech,** formal, suggests greater earnestness of humility than **beg:** *The mother besought the prince to pardon her son.*

be·gan (bi gan′) *v.* pt. of **begin.**

be·gat (bi gat′) *v. Archaic.* a pt. of **beget.**

be·get (bi get′) *v.* **be·got, be·got·ten** or **be·got, be·get·ting. 1** become the father of. **2** cause to be; produce: *Hate begets hate.* [ME *begete(n), begite(n),* alteration of earlier *beyiten* (OE *begitan*) under the influence of *gete(n)* get (< ON *geta*)]
—**be·get′ter,** *n.*

beg·gar (beg′ər) *n., v.* —*n.* **1** a person who makes his living by begging. **2** a very poor person. **3** a fellow: *That dog's a friendly little beggar.*
—*v.* **1** bring to poverty: *Your reckless spending will beggar your father.* **2** make to seem inadequate or useless: *The grandeur of Niagara Falls beggars description.*

beg·gar–lice (beg′ər līs′) *n., pl.* **beg·gar–lice.** beggar's-lice.

beg·gar·ly (beg′ər lē) *adj.* fit for a beggar; poor.
—**beg′gar·li·ness,** *n.*

beg·gar's-lice (beg′ərz līs′) *n., pl.* **beg·gar's-lice. 1** any of various plants of the borage family having prickly fruits that adhere to clothing, fur, etc. **2** beggarticks. **3** the prickly fruit of any of these plants.

beg·gar's-ticks (beg′ərz tiks′) *n., pl.* **beg·gar's-ticks.** beggarticks.

beg·gar·ticks (beg′ər tiks′) *n., pl.* **beg·gar·ticks. 1** any of a genus (*Bidens*) of weedy plants of the composite family having yellow flowers and small, pointed fruits with barbed awns that catch in clothing, fur, etc. **2** the fruit of any of these plants.

beg·gar·y (beg′ər ē) *n.* a condition of great poverty.

be·gin (bi gin′) *v.* **be·gan, begun, be·gin·ning. 1** do the first part; start: *Let's begin. She began to speak.* **2** do the first part of: *I began reading the book yesterday.* **3** come into being: *The club began two years ago.* **4** bring into being: *Two brothers began the club ten years ago.* **5** be near; come near: *That suit doesn't even begin to fit you.* [OE *beginnan*]

☛ *Syn.* **1. Begin, commence, start** = to get something going. **Begin** is the general word: *We will begin work soon.* **Commence** is formal and applies particularly to beginning a formal action or event: *The dedication ceremonies will commence at two o'clock.* **Start** emphasizes taking the first step in doing something, or setting about doing it: *At last they have started building that hotel.*

☛ *Usage.* **Begin** is followed by *at* when the meaning is "start from": *Let us begin at the third chapter.* It is followed by *on* or *upon* when the meaning is "set to work at": *We must begin on the government survey tomorrow.* When the meaning is "take first in an order of succession," the idiom is *begin with*: *We always begin with the hardest problems.*

be·gin·ner (bi gin′ər) *n.* **1** a person who is doing something for the first time; a person who lacks skill and experience. **2** a person who begins anything.

be·gin·ning (bi gin′iŋ) *n., adj.* —*n.* **1** a start: *make a good beginning.* **2** the time when anything begins: *"In the beginning God created the heaven and the earth."* **3** the first part: *The beginning of the book is good, but then it gets boring.* **4** a first cause; source; origin. —*adj.* **1** that begins; first in order: *a beginning course.* **2** for beginners: *a beginning dictionary.* **3** who is just starting: *a beginning student.*

be·gird (bi gèrd′) *v.* **-girt** or **-gird·ed, -gird·ed.** *Poetic.* encircle; gird around.

be·gone (bi gon′) *interj. or v.* be gone; go away; depart: *"Begone!" the old lady cried out to the tramp in her garden.*

be·go·ni·a (bi gō′nē ə *or* bi gōn′yə) *n.* **1** any of a large genus (*Begonia*) of flowering plants, including many varieties and hybrids grown for their showy, waxy flowers and often colored leaves. **2** (*adj.*) designating the family (Begoniaceae) of tropical and subtropical plants that includes the begonias and a few other species. Most of the plants belonging to the begonia family are herbs native to South America. [after Michel *Bégon* (1638-1710), a French colonial governor]

be·got (bi got′) *v.* a pt. and a pp. of **beget.**

be·got·ten (bi got′ən) *v.* a pp. of **beget.**

be·grimed (bi grīmd′) *adj.* made grimy; soiled and dirty.

be·grudge (bi gruj′) *v.* **-grudged, -grudg·ing. 1** be reluctant to give (something); grudge: *She is so stingy that she begrudges food to her dog.* **2** envy (someone) the possession of: *They begrudge us our new house.* —**be·grudg′ing·ly,** *adv.*

be·guile (bi gīl′) *v.* **-guiled, -guil·ing. 1** deceive; cheat: *His pleasant ways beguiled me into thinking that he was my friend.* **2** take away from deceitfully or cunningly. **3** entertain; amuse. **4** pass or while away (time) pleasantly. —**be·guil′er,** *n.*

☛ *Syn.* **4.** See note at **while.**

be·guil·ing (bi gīl′iŋ) *adj.* **1** deceiving. **2** entertaining; amusing. —**be·guil′ing·ly,** *adv.*

be·gum (bē′gəm) *n.* a Moslem title of honor for a woman, used especially in India and Pakistan. The title is equivalent to princess. [< Hind. *begam*]

be·gun (bi gun′) *v.* pp. of **begin.**

be·half (bi haf′) *n.* interest; favor; support: *His friends will act in his behalf.*
in behalf of, in the interest of; for: *He worked for weeks in behalf of the Community Chest.*
on behalf of, a as a representative of: *The lawyer spoke convincingly on behalf of his client.* **b** in behalf of.
[ME *behalve* beside, on the side of]

be·have (bi hāv′) *v.* **-haved, -hav·ing. 1** conduct (oneself): *The little boy behaves himself badly in school. The ship behaves well.* **2** act well; do what is right: *Did you behave today?* **3** act: *Water behaves in different ways when it is heated and when it is frozen.* [< *be-* + *have*]

☛ *Usage.* **Behave.** In speaking to or of children, **behave** (def. 2) = behave

hat, āge, fär; let, ēqual, tèrm; it, īce
hot, ōpen, ôrder; oil, out; cup, pút, rüle,
above, takən, pencəl, lemən, circəs

ch, child; ng, long; sh, ship
th, thin; ᴛʜ, then; zh, measure

properly or use good manners: *Did you behave at the party, Mary?* Otherwise, **behave,** meaning 'act or conduct oneself in a certain way', is ordinarily modified by a qualifying word: *He behaved well in spite of his boredom.*

be·hav·ior or **be·hav·iour** (bi hāv′yər) *n.* **1** a way of acting; actions; acts: *His sullen behavior showed that he was angry.* **2** manners; deportment.

☛ *Syn.* **1.** See note at **conduct.**

be·hav·ior·al or **be·hav·iour·al** (bē hāv′yər əl) *adj.* of or having to do with behavior: *Sociology and psychology are behavioral sciences.*

be·hav·ior·ism or **be·hav·iour·ism** (bi hāv′yər iz′əm) *n.* the theory that the objectively observable behavior of persons and animals are the chief or only subject matter of psychology.

be·hav·ior·ist or **be·hav·iour·ist** (bi hāv′yər ist) *n.* an adherent of behaviorism.

be·hav·ior·is·tic or **be·hav·iour·is·tic** (bi hāv′yər is′tik) *adj.* of or having to do with behaviorists or behaviorism.

be·hav·iour (bi hāv′yər) See **behavior.**

be·head (bi hed′) *v.* cut off the head of.

be·held (bi held′) *v.* pt. and pp. of **behold.**

be·he·moth (bi hē′məth *or* bē′ə məth) *n.* **1** in the Bible, a huge and powerful animal, possibly the hippopotamus (Job 40:15-24). **2** any large and powerful person or animal. **3** something that is especially large and powerful. [< Hebrew *b'hēmōth,* pl. of *b'hēmah* beast]

be·hest (bi hest′) *n.* a command or order. [OE *behæs* promise]

be·hind (bi hīnd′) *prep., adv., n.* —*prep.* **1** at the back of; in the rear of: *The child hid behind the door.* **2** at or on the far side of: *A beautiful valley lies behind the hill.* **3** concealed by: *Treachery lurked behind the spy's smooth manner.* **4** less advanced than: *He is behind the other children in his class.* **5** later than; after: *The milkman is behind his usual time today.* **6** remaining after: *The dead man left a family behind him.* **7** in support of; supporting: *His friends are behind him.*
—*adv.* **1** at or toward the back; in the rear: *The dog's tail hung down behind.* **2** farther back in place or time: *The rest of the hikers are still far behind.* **3** in reserve: *More supplies are behind.* **4** not on time; slow; late: *The train is behind today.*
—*n. Informal.* the fleshy part of the body where the legs join the back; buttocks; seat. [OE *behindan* < *be-* by + *hindan* from behind]

be·hind·hand (bi hīnd′hand′) *adj.* (*never used before a noun*) *or adv.* **1** behind time; late. **2** behind others in progress; backward; slow. **3** in debt; in arrears.

be·hold (bi hōld′) *v.* **be·held, be·hold·ing;** *interj.* —*v.* **1** see; perceive: *He beheld a strange figure approaching him.* **2** look at; observe: *He beheld the figure with apprehension.* —*interj.* look! see! [OE *behealdan*] —**be·hold′er,** *n.*

be·hold·en (bi hōl′dən) *adj.* under an obligation or in debt to somebody: *I am much beholden to you for your help.*

be·hoof (bi hüf′) *n. Archaic.* use; advantage; benefit: *The father toiled for his children's behoof.* [OE *behōf* need]

be·hoove (bi hüv′) *v.* **-hooved, -hoov·ing.** be necessary or proper for: *It behooves us to answer the challenge.* [OE *behōfian* to need]

be·hove (bi hōv′) *v.* **-hoved, -hov·ing.** behoove.

beige (bāzh) *n. or adj.* very light, greyish brown. [< F]

be·ing (bē′iŋ) *n., adj., v.* —*n.* **1** a person; living creature: *human beings.* **2** life; existence: *A new era came into being.* **3** nature; constitution: *Her whole being thrilled to the beauty of the music.* —*adj.*
for the time being, for the present time; for now: *Let's leave that problem for the time being and come back to it later.*
—*v.* ppr. of **be.**

be·jew·el (bi jü′əl) *v.* **-elled** or **-eled, -el·ling** or **-el·ing.** adorn with jewels, or as if with jewels: *The sky is bejewelled with stars.*

bel (bel) *n.* a unit for comparing levels of power, equal to ten decibels.

be·la·bor or **be·la·bour** (bi lāb′ər) *v.* **1** beat vigorously: *The man belabored his poor donkey.* **2** abuse or ridicule: *The politician was belabored by the press.* **3** work at or on longer than necessary; harp on: *to belabor a point in an argument.*

be·lat·ed (bi lāt′id) *adj.* delayed; happening or coming late or too

late: *a belated birthday card. Her belated attempt to make amends was rejected.* —be·**lat′ed·ly**, *adv.* —be·**lat′ed·ness**, *n.*

be·lay (bi lā′) *v.* be·**layed**, be·**lay·ing;** *n.* —*v.* **1** fasten (a line or rope) by winding it around a pin, cleat, piton, etc. **2** *Mountaineering.* secure (a climber) at the end of a rope. **3** *Nautical. Informal.* stop (*usually used in the imperative*): *Belay there!* —*n. Mountaineering.* **1** the action or method of obtaining a hold by securing a rope around an object. **2** an object, such as a projecting piece of rock, to which a rope is secured. [OE *belecgan*]

Belaying pins in a ship's rail

belaying pin a removable pin on the rail of a ship or boat, used for fastening rigging lines.

bel canto (bel kän′tō) *Music.* a style of singing marked by fullness and breadth of tone and the display of great technical skill. It originated in Italy in the 17th century. [< Ital. *bel canto*, literally, fine singing]

belch (belch) *v., n.* —*v.* **1** expel gas from the stomach through the mouth. **2** throw out with force: *The volcano belched fire and smoke.* —*n.* the act of belching. [cf. OE *bealcian*] —**belch′er,** *n.*

bel·dam or **bel·dame** (bel′dəm) *n.* **1** an old woman. **2** an ugly old woman; hag. [< *bel-* grand- (< OF *bel, belle* fair) + *dam* dame < OF *dame*]

be·lea·guer (bi lē′gər) *v.* **1** besiege: *The people of the beleaguered city refused to give in.* **2** torment; beset: *Beleaguered by debts, he was finally forced into bankruptcy.* [< Du. *belegeren* < *leger* camp]

bel·fry (bel′frē) *n., pl.* **-fries. 1** a tower or steeple containing a bell or bells. **2** a room in a tower, or a cupola or turret in which a bell or bells are hung. [ME *berfrey* < OF *berfrei* < Gmc.]

Belg. 1 Belgium. **2** Belgian.

Bel·gian (bel′jən) *n., adj.* —*n.* **1** a native or inhabitant of Belgium, a country in NW Europe. **2** a person of Belgian descent. **3** a breed of large, strong draft horse. —*adj.* of or having to do with Belgium or its people.

Belgian endive the whitish forced shoots of chicory, used raw in salads and also as a cooked vegetable.

Belgian hare a breed of large European rabbit having reddish-brown hair, raised in many countries for its fur and its meat: *The Belgian hare is the typical domestic rabbit.*

Be·li·al (bē′lē əl or bēl′yəl) *n.* **1** the Devil. **2** in Milton's poem *Paradise Lost*, a fallen angel.

be·lie (bi lī′) *v.* **-lied, -ly·ing. 1** give a false idea of; misrepresent: *Her frown belied her usual good nature.* **2** show to be false; contradict: *Her actions belie her words.* **3** fail to come up to; disappoint: *He stole again, and so belied our hopes.* [OE *belēogan*]

be·lief (bi lēf′) *n.* **1** the state or habit of having confidence in any person or thing; faith; trust: *a belief in God, belief in a person's honesty.* **2** mental acceptance as true or real; acceptance of a statement or fact: *a belief in the existence of ghosts. That statement is unworthy of belief.* **3** the thing believed; a statement or condition accepted as true: *His beliefs are different from mine.* **4** opinion: *It's my belief that we're in for a cold winter.* [ME *bileafe* < OE]

☛ *Syn.* **1. Belief, faith** (def. 1), **conviction** (def. 5) = what is held true. **Belief** is the general word: *His belief in superstition gets him into trouble.* **Faith** applies to a belief without proof, based on one's trust in a person or thing: *I have faith in his ability to succeed.* **Conviction** applies to a firm belief based on one's own certainty after one has been convinced by someone or something: *It is my conviction that he will succeed.*

be·liev·a·ble (bi lē′və bəl) *adj.* that can or is likely to be believed: *a believable story.* —be·**liev′a·bly,** *adv.* —be·**liev′a·bil′i·ty,** *n.*

be·lieve (bi lēv′) *v.* **-lieved, -liev·ing. 1** have faith; trust (*used with* **in**): *to believe in God. I believe in their sincerity.* **2** accept (a statement, fact, etc.) as true or real: *We believe that the earth revolves around the sun. I don't believe her story. Do you believe in ghosts?* **3** think that (another person) tells the truth: *I don't believe him.* **4** have religious faith: *All who believe are asked to pray for*

peace. **5** think or suppose: *I believe they're planning a big reception for the wedding.* [ME *bileve(n)* < OE]

be·liev·er (bi lēv′ər) *n.* a person who believes, especially a follower of some religion.

be·like (bi līk′) *adv. Archaic.* very likely; probably; perhaps.

be·lit·tle (bi lit′əl) *v.* **-tled, -tling.** cause to seem little, unimportant, or less important; speak slightingly of; disparage: *Jealous people belittled the explorer's great discoveries.* —be·**lit′tler,** *n.* —be·**lit′tling·ly,** *adv.*

bell¹ (bel) *n., v.* —*n.* **1** a hollow device of metal or sometimes glass, etc., usually shaped like a cup with a flared opening, that makes a musical sound when struck by a clapper or a hammer. **2** the sound of a bell. **3** on shipboard, the stroke of a bell to indicate a half hour of time. 1 bell = 12:30, 4:30, or 8:30; 2 bells =1:00, 5:00, or 9:00; and so on up to 8 bells = 4:00, 8:00, or 12:00. **4** Usually, **bells,** *pl.* a percussion instrument having metal tubes or bars that produce bell-like tones when struck. **5** anything shaped like a bell, such as the flared opening of a trumpet, etc., or the corolla of some flowers.
ring a bell, produce a response in one's mind; seem familiar: *I didn't recognize her at first, but the name rang a bell.* —*v.* **1** put a bell on. **2** swell out like a bell.
bell the cat, take on oneself a dangerous role for the common good. [OE *belle*] —**bell′-like′,** *adj.*
☛ *Hom.* **belle.**

bell² (bel) *v. or n.* bellow; roar; cry. [OE *bellan*]
☛ *Hom.* **belle.**

Bel·la Bel·la (bel′ə bel′ə) *n., pl.* **Bella Bella** or **Bella Bellas. 1** a member of an Amerindian people of the southern part of the British Columbia coast. **2** the Wakashan language of the Bella Bella.

Bel·la Coo·la (bel′ə kü′lə) *n., pl.* **Bella Coola** or **Bella Coolas. 1** a member of an Amerindian people living near Queen Charlotte Sound, B.C. **2** the Salishan language of the Bella Coola.

bel·la·don·na (bel′ə don′ə) *n.* **1** a very poisonous perennial plant (*Atropa belladonna*) of the nightshade family native to Europe, having reddish, bell-shaped flowers and small, shiny, black berries; deadly nightshade. **2** the dried leaves or roots of this plant, or any of the alkaloid drugs, such as atropine, prepared from them. [< Ital. *belladonna*, literally, fair lady]

belladonna lily an amaryllis (*Amaryllis belladonna*) of S Africa cultivated for its large, fragrant, white or pink flowers.

bell–bot·toms (bel′bot′əmz) *n.pl.* pants, or trousers, having legs that flare out downward from the knee into wide bottoms. —**bell′-bot′tom** or **bell′-bot′tomed,** *adj.*

bell–boy (bel′boi′) *n.* a man or boy whose work is carrying hand baggage and doing errands for the guests of a hotel or club.

bell buoy a buoy with a bell that is rung by the movement of the waves.

belle (bel) *n.* **1** a beautiful woman or girl. **2** the prettiest or most admired woman or girl: *the belle of the ball.* [< F *belle*, fem. of *beau.* See BEAU.]
☛ *Hom.* **bell.**

Bel·leek (bə lēk′) *n.* a kind of thin, delicate porcelain having a multicolored glaze. [< *Belleek*, a town in Northern Ireland, where this porcelain is made]

Bel·ler·o·phon (bə ler′ə fon′) *n. Greek mythology.* a hero who killed a dreadful monster, the chimera, with the help of the winged horse Pegasus.

belles–let·tres (bel′let′rə) *n.pl.* literature, such as poetry, drama, fiction and personal essays, considered for its artistic appeal rather than for any practical value such as giving information. [< F]

bell·flow·er (bel′flou′ər) *n.* **1** any of various plants (genus *Campanula*) found in temperate regions of the northern hemisphere having bell-shaped flowers, usually blue, purple, or white. Some bellflowers are grown as garden flowers. **2** (*adj.*) designating the family (Campanulaceae) of temperate and subtropical plants that includes the bluebell and the bellflowers.

bell glass a bell-shaped container or cover made of glass.

bell·hop (bel′hop′) *n. Informal.* bellboy.

bel·li·cose (bel′ə kōs′) *adj.* warlike; fond of fighting. [< L *bellicosus < bellum* war] —**bel′li·cose′ly,** *adv.*

bel·li·cos·i·ty (bel′ə kos′ə tē) *n.* a bellicose quality or attitude.

bel·lig·er·ence (bə lij′ər əns) *n.* **1** a warlike attitude; fondness for fighting. **2** fighting; war.

bel·lig·er·en·cy (bə lij′ər ən sē) *n.* **1** the state of being a belligerent. **2** belligerence.

bel·lig·er·ent (bə lij′ər ənt) *adj., n.* —*adj.* **1** having or showing an aggressive or quarrelsome attitude; warlike: *She gets very belligerent if you don't agree with her.* **2** at war; engaged in war; fighting. **3** having to do with nations or states at war. —*n.* **1** a person engaged in fighting with another person. **2** a nation

or state at war: *The belligerents agreed on a truce.* [< L
belligerans, -antis, ppr. of *belligerare* < *bellum* war + *gerere* wage]
—**bel·lig′er·ent·ly,** *adv.*

bell jar a bell-shaped container or cover made of glass, used
especially in scientific experiments requiring reduced air pressure.

bell·man (bel′mən) *n., pl.* **-men.** town crier.

Bel·lo·na (bə lō′nə) *n. Roman mythology.* the goddess of war;
the sister, wife, or, in some cases, daughter of Mars.

bel·low (bel′ō) *v., n.* —*v.* **1** roar as a bull does. **2** shout loudly:
The lifeguard bellowed at the boys to stay near the shore. **3** roar
with pain or anger: *The pain of the burn made him bellow.*
—*n.* **1** a roar like a bull's. **2** a deep, loud shout, roar of pain or
anger, etc. [ME *belwe,* akin to OE *bellan* roar and *bylgan* bellow]
—**bel′low·er,** *n.*

Bellows. Air is sucked into the bellows as the sides are
pulled apart. When the sides are pushed together, the
valve closes and air is forced out through the nozzle.

bel·lows (bel′ōz *or* bel′əs) *n.pl. or sing.* **1** an instrument for
producing a strong current of air, used for blowing a fire to make it
burn or for sounding an organ, accordion, etc. **2** in certain cameras,
the folding part behind the lens. [OE *belgas,* pl. of *belg* bag, belly]

bell·weth·er (bel′weŦH′ər) *n.* **1** a male sheep that wears a bell
and leads the flock. **2** any leader, especially of a group thought to
resemble sheep in lack of foresight, intelligence, etc.: *a bellwether
of the mob.* **3** *Cdn.* any person, group, or thing thought of as setting
a standard or pattern: *Our riding is considered the political
bellwether for the rest of the province.*

bel·ly (bel′ē) *n., pl.* **-lies;** *v.* **-lied, -ly·ing.** —*n.* **1** the lower part of
the human body that contains the stomach and intestines; abdomen.
2 the under part of an animal's body. **3** the stomach. **4** the bulging
part of anything. —*v.* swell out; bulge: *The ship's sails bellied in the
wind.* [ME *bely* < OE *belg, belig* bag]

bel·ly·ache (bel′ē āk′) *n., v.* **-ached, -ach·ing.** *Informal.* —*n.* **1** a
pain in the abdomen. **2** an excuse for complaining; grievance. —*v.*
complain or grumble, especially over trifles. —**bel′ly·ach′er,** *n.*

bel·ly·band (bel′ē band′) *n.* a strap around the middle of an
animal's body to keep a saddle, harness, etc. in place.

belly button *Informal.* navel.

bel·ly·flop (bel′ē flop′) *v.* **-flopped, -flop·ping;** *n. Slang.* —*v.*
1 ride prone on a sleigh, with the stomach downward. **2** *Diving.*
strike the water with the chest, or with the chest and abdomen. —*n.*
a dive or sleigh-ride executed in this manner.

bel·ly·ful (bel′ē fül′) *n. Informal.* an amount that is more than
one wants or can stand: *After listening to complaints for two hours,
the store clerk had had a bellyful.*

bel·ly–up (bel′ē up′) *adv.*
go belly-up, *Informal.* of an organization, business, etc., fail: *The
firm went belly-up after only a year.*

be·long (bi long′) *v.* have a proper place: *That book belongs on
this shelf.*
belong to, a be the property of. **b** be a part of; be connected with.
c be a member of. **d** be the duty or concern of: *This responsiblity
belongs to the club secretary.*
[ME *bilonge(n)* < *bi-* by + *longen* belong, ult. < OE *gelang*
belonging to]

be·long·ings (bi long′ingz) *n.pl.* the things that belong to a
person; possessions.

be·lov·ed (bi luv′id *ôr* bi luvd′) *adj., n.* —*adj.* dearly loved;
dear. —*n.* a person who is loved; darling.

be·low (bi lō′) *adv., prep.* —*adv.* **1** in or to a lower place: *She
stopped at the top of the hill and looked down on the road below.*
2 on or to a lower floor or deck; downstairs: *The sailor went below.*
3 on earth. **4** in hell. **5** at the bottom of the page or farther on in an
article, essay, book, etc.: *The problem is dealt with below.* **6** below
zero on the Fahrenheit scale of temperature: *It was four below last
night.*
—*prep.* **1** lower than; under: *below the third floor.* **2** lower in rank,
amount, or degree than: *an income below $10 000. The temperature
rarely goes below freezing.* **3** unworthy of; beneath: *He said it*

hat, āge, fär; let, ēqual, tèrm; it, īce
hot, ōpen, ôrder; oil, out; cup, pút, rüle,
əbove, takən, pencəl, lemən, circəs

ch, child; ng, long; sh, ship
th, thin; ŦH, then; zh, measure

would be below him to argue the point. [ME *biloghe* by low]
☛ *Syn. prep.* **1.** See note at **under.**

belt (belt) *n., v.* —*n.* **1** a strip of leather, cloth, etc. worn around
the body to hold in or support clothing, to hold tools or weapons, or
as a decoration. **2** any broad strip or band: *a belt of trees.* **3** a region
having distinctive characteristics; zone: *The wheat belt is the region
where wheat is grown.* **4** an endless band that transfers motion from
one wheel or pulley to another: *a fan belt.* **5** *Slang.* a sharp blow: *a
belt on the chin.* **6** *Slang.* a drink, as of liquor, especially when
gulped hurriedly or greedily: *He took a belt of whisky before
leaving.* **7** a jolt of excitement.
below the belt, unfair or unfairly: *He's hitting below the belt with his
personal remarks.*
tighten (one's) belt, become more thrifty; cut down on expenditures.
under (one's) belt, *Informal.* **a** in one's stomach: *With a good dinner
under his belt, he felt more relaxed.* **b** in one's possession or
experience; to one's credit: *With five years' training under her belt,
she could easily find another job.*
—*v.* **1** put a belt around. **2** fasten one with a belt. **3** beat with a belt.
4 hit suddenly and hard: *The boxer belted his opponent across the
ring.* **5** *Slang.* drink hurriedly or greedily (*usually used with* **down**):
They belted down a couple of drinks and took off. **6** *Slang.* sing
forcefully or raucously (*used with* **out**): *They stood around the
piano, belting out one song after another.* [OE *belt,* apparently ult.
< L *balteus* girdle]

Bel·tane (bel′tān) *n.* **1** in Scotland, May 1 (Old Style Calendar).
2 an ancient Celtic May-day celebration. [< Scots Gaelic *bealltainn*
May Day, the May festival]

belt·ed (bel′tid) *adj.* **1** having a belt: *a belted jacket.* **2** wearing a
special belt as a sign of honor: *a belted earl.* **3** marked by a belt or
band of color: *a belted kingfisher.*

belt·ing (bel′ting) *n.* **1** a material for making belts or lining
waistbands. **2** belts. **3** a beating.

belt line a railway, bus line, etc. that takes a more-or-less
circular route around a city or other special area.

be·lu·ga (bə lü′gə) *n.* **1** a white toothed whale (*Delphinapterus
leucas*) of the same family as the narwhal, found in the Arctic and
as far south as the Gulf of St. Lawrence, usually about four metres
long, having broad, rounded flippers and lacking a dorsal fin. It was
formerly called the "sea canary" by Arctic whalers because of its
musical trilling voice. Also called **white whale.** **2** a very large white
sturgeon (*Acipenser huso*) of the Black and Caspian seas and the
Sea of Azov. It is the largest inland fish, sometimes reaching a
length of seven metres, and is the source of most European caviar.
[def. 1 < Russian *beluga,* def. 2 < Russian *belukha*; both from
bielo- white]

bel·ve·dere (bel′və dēr′) *n.* a structure, sometimes set high on a
building, designed to be open on several sides to afford a wide
view. [< Ital. *belvedere* fine view]

B.E.M. British Empire Medal.

be·mire (bi mīr′) *v.* **-mired, -mir·ing. 1** make dirty with mud.
2 sink in mud.

be·moan (bi mōn′) *v.* **1** moan about; bewail. **2** mourn.

be·mock (bi mok′) *v. Archaic.* mock; mock at.

be·muse (bi myüz′) *v.* **-mused, -mus·ing.** bewilder; confuse;
stupefy. —**be·mused,** *adj.* —**be·mus′ed·ly,** *adv.* —**be·muse′ment,** *n.*

bench (bench) *n., v.* —*n.* **1** a long seat, usually of wood or stone.
2 the worktable of a carpenter, or of any worker with tools and
materials. **3** the seat where judges sit in a court of law. **4 the
bench, a** a judge or group of judges presiding in a court of law.
b the position or office of a judge: *The lawyer was appointed to the
bench.* **c** a court of law. **5** *Sports.* **a** the place where team members
sit while waiting their turn or opportunity to play. **b** these players
collectively. **6** a long, narrow, open plateau between a river or lake
bed and nearby hills: *Apples are grown on the benches of the
Okanagan Valley in British Columbia.* **7** a platform on which dogs
are placed for judging at a show. **8** a dog show.
on the bench, a sitting in a court of law as a judge. **b** sitting among
the substitute players.
—*v.* **1** furnish with benches. **2** assign a seat on a bench. **3** take (a
player) out of a game. [OE *benc*]

ben·cher (ben′chər) *n.* **1** a person who sits on a bench, especially
a judge, magistrate, etc. **2** in Canada, one of the elected officials of
a provincial law society, who, through committees, govern the

affairs of the society. **3** in England, one of the senior members governing a society of lawyers and law students called an Inn of Court.

bench·mark or **bench mark** (bench′märk′) *n.* **1** *Surveying.* a mark made on a rock or other permanent landmark of known position and elevation for use as a starting point or reference for topographical surveys. **2** a standard or point of reference for measuring or evaluating other things: *The court's ruling will serve as a benchmark for future cases.*

bench penalty or **bench minor** *Cdn. Hockey.* a minor (two-minute) penalty imposed against a team and served by a player designated by the team's coach or manager.

bench warrant a written order from a court of law or a judge for the arrest of an accused person or a witness who has not appeared in court as required.

bend¹ (bend) *v.* **bent, bend·ing;** *n.* —*v.* **1** make, be, or become curved or crooked: *The branch began to bend as I climbed along it.* **2** stoop; bow: *She bent to the ground and picked up a stone.* **3** force to submit: *"I will bend you or break you!" cried the villain.* **4** submit: *But the hero would not bend.* **5** move or turn in a certain direction; direct or apply (one's mind or effort): *He bent his mind to the task. She bent her steps toward home.* **6** fasten (a sail, rope, etc.).
—*n.* **1** a part that is not straight; curve or turn: *There is a sharp bend in the road here.* **2** the act of bending: *a bend of the knee.* **3** *Nautical.* a knot for tying two ropes together or tying a rope to something else.
the bends, *Informal.* decompression sickness.
around or **round the bend,** *Slang.* crazy: *That incessant noise is driving me around the bend.*
[OE *bendan* bind, band]

bend² (bend) *n.* *Heraldry.* a broad stripe extending across a shield from the upper right to the lower left, from the wearer's point of view. [OE *bend* strap, influenced by OF *bende* band]

bend·ed (ben′did) *v.* *Archaic.* pt. and a pp. of **bend.** *On bended knee, he asked her forgiveness.*

bend·er (ben′dər) *n.* **1** a person or thing that bends. **2** *Slang.* a drinking spree.

bend sinister *Heraldry.* a broad stripe drawn from the upper left to the lower right of a shield, (from the bearer's point of view), indicating bastardy.

be·neath (bi nēth′) *adv., prep.* —*adv.* below, underneath: *Whatever you drop will fall upon the spot beneath.* —*prep.* **1** below; under; lower than: *The dog sat beneath the tree.* **2** unworthy of; worthy not even of: *A traitor is so low that he is beneath contempt.* [OE *beneothan* < *be-* by + *neothan* below]
☞ *Syn. prep.* **1.** See note at **under.**

ben·e·dic·i·te (ben′ə dis′ə tē) *n., interj.* —*n.* **1** a blessing. **2 Benedicite, a** a hymn of praise to God. **b** a musical setting for such a hymn. —*interj.* bless (you, them, etc.). [< L *benedicite,* 2nd person pl. imperative of *benedicere* bless < *bene* well + *dicere* say]

ben·e·dict (ben′ə dikt′) *n.* **1** a recently married man, especially one who was a bachelor for a long time. **2** a married man. Also, **Benedick.** [< *Benedick,* character in Shakespeare's *Much Ado About Nothing*]

Ben·e·dic·tine (ben′ə dik′tēn or ben′ə dik′tin) *adj., n.* —*adj.* of Saint Benedict (480?-543?), the founder of the first order of monks, or of a religious order following his rule. —*n.* **1** *Roman Catholic Church.* a monk or nun following the rule of Saint Benedict or of the order founded by him. **2** a kind of liqueur. [< F *bénédictin*]

Benedictine rule the set of rules for a plan of life, used in monasteries and convents established by Saint Benedict.

ben·e·dic·tion (ben′ə dik′shən) *n.* **1** the asking of God's blessings at the end of a religious service. **2** a blessing. **3** mercy. [< L *benedictio, -onis* < *benedicere* bless. See BENEDICITE. Doublet of BENISON.]

Ben·e·dic·tus (ben′ə dik′təs) *n.* **1** a short hymn or canticle beginning in English "Blessed is He that cometh in the name of the Lord," taken from Psalm 118:26 and Matt. 21:9. **2** a canticle or hymn beginning in English "Blessed be the Lord God of Israel" (Luke 1:68). **3** a musical setting of either of these canticles. [< L *benedictus,* pp. of *benedicere.* See BENEDICITE.]

ben·e·fac·tion (ben′ə fak′shən) *n.* **1** a doing good; kind act. **2** a benefit conferred; gift for charity; help given for any good purpose.

ben·e·fac·tor (ben′ə fak′tər or ben′ə fak′tər) *n.* a person who has helped others, either by gifts of money or by some kind act. [ME < LL *benefactor* < *benefacere* < *bene* well + *facere* do]

ben·e·fac·tress (ben′ə fak′tris or ben′ə fak′tris) *n.* a woman

who has helped others, either by gifts of money or by some kind act.

ben·e·fice (ben′ə fis) *n.* a permanent office or position created by ecclesiastical authority. [ME< OF < L *beneficium* benefit < *beneficus* < *benefacere.* See BENEFACTOR.]

be·nef·i·cence (bə nef′ə səns) *n.* **1** the quality of being kind. **2** a charitable act or donation. [< L *beneficentia* < *beneficus.* See BENEFICE.]

be·nef·i·cent (bə nef′ə sənt) *adj.* **1** kindly; doing good. **2** having good results: *beneficent acts.*

ben·e·fi·cial (ben′ə fish′əl) *adj.* favorable; helpful; good for; productive of good: *Sunshine and moisture are beneficial to plants.* —**ben′e·fi′cial·ly,** *adv.*

ben·e·fi·ci·ar·y (ben′ə fish′ər ē or ben′ə fish′ē er′ē) *n., pl.* **-ar·ies. 1** a person who receives benefit: *All the children are beneficiaries of the new playground.* **2** a person who receives or is to receive money or property from an insurance policy, a will, etc.

ben·e·fit (ben′ə fit) *n., v.* **-fit·ed, -fit·ing.** —*n.* **1** anything for the good of a person or thing; an advantage: *Universal peace would be of great benefit to the world.* **2** *Archaic.* an act of kindness; a favor. **3** money paid to the sick, disabled, etc. **4** a performance at the theatre, a game, etc. to raise money that goes to a special person or persons or to a worthy cause.
—*v.* **1** give benefit to; be good for: *Rest will benefit a sick person.* **2** receive good; profit: *He benefited by the medicine. He will benefit from the new way of doing business.* [ME < AF *benfet* < L *benefactum* < *bene-* well + *factum,* pp. of *facere* do]
☞ *Syn. n.* **1.** See note at **advantage.**

benefit of clergy 1 *Historical.* the privilege of being tried in church courts instead of regular courts. **2** the services and rites or approval of the church.

Ben·e·lux (ben′ə luks′) *n.* the economic association of Belgium, the Netherlands, and Luxemburg, first organized in 1948 and now part of the European Common Market. [< *Bel*gium, *Ne*therlands, *Lux*emburg]

be·nev·o·lence (bə nev′ə ləns) *n.* **1** good will; kindly feeling. **2** an act of kindness; something good that is done; a generous gift. **3** *Historical.* a forced loan levied by certain medieval English kings. [ME < OF < L *benevolentia* < *bene* well + *velle* wish]

be·nev·o·lent (bə nev′ə lənt) *adj.* kindly; charitable. —**be·nev′o·lent·ly,** *adv.*

Ben·ga·lese (ben′gə lēz′ or beng′gə lēz′) *n., pl.* **-lese; adj.** —*n.* a native of Bengal. —*adj.* of Bengal, its people, or their language.

Ben·ga·li (ben go′lē or -gô′lē, beng gol′ or -gô′lē) *adj., n.* —*adj.* of Bengal, its people, or their language. —*n.* **1** a native of Bengal. **2** the language of Bengal.

ben·ga·line (beng′gə lēn′ or beng′gə lēn′) *n.* a corded silk or rayon cloth with wool or cotton in it. [< F]

be·night·ed (bi nīt′id) *adj.* **1** not knowing right from wrong; ignorant. **2** overtaken by night; being in darkness. [< obsolete verb *benight* < *be-* + *night*]

be·nign (bi nīn′) *adj.* **1** gentle; kindly: *a benign old lady.* **2** favorable; mild: *a benign climate.* **3** *Medicine.* **a** mild; doing no permanent harm: *benign leukemia.* **b** of tumors, not likely to recur after removal or to spread; not malignant. [ME *benigne* < OF < L *benignus* < *bene* well + *-gnus* born] —**be·nign′ly,** *adv.*

be·nig·nan·cy (bi nig′nən sē) *n.* a benignant quality.

be·nig·nant (bi nig′nənt) *adj.* **1** kindly; gracious: *a benignant rule.* **2** favorable; beneficial. —**be·nig′nant·ly,** *adv.*

be·nig·ni·ty (bi nig′nə tē) *n., pl.* **-ties. 1** the quality of kindliness or graciousness. **2** a kind act; favor.

ben·i·son (ben′ə zen or ben′ə sən) *n.* a blessing. [ME < OF *beneison* < L *benedictio, -onis.* Doublet of BENEDICTION.]

Ben·ja·min ·(ben′jə mən) *n.* **1** in the Bible, the youngest and favorite son of Jacob. **2** one of the twelve tribes of Israel.

Ben·nett buggy (ben′ət) *Cdn.* in the Depression of the 1930's, an automobile drawn by horses because the owner could not afford gas, oil, or a licence for it. Bennett buggies usually had the engine removed, and the horses were hitched to poles attached to the front bumper. [after R. B. *Bennett,* prime minister of Canada from 1930 to 1935, because his government had not succeeded in solving Canada's economic problems as promised.]

ben·ny (ben′ē) *n., pl.* **-nies.** *Slang.* an amphetamine tablet taken as a stimulant, especially Benzedrine. [shortened from *Benzedrine.* 20c.]

bent¹ (bent) *v., adj., n.* —*v.* pt. and pp. of **bend.** —*adj.* **1** not straight; curved; crooked. **2** strongly inclined; determined: *He was bent on going home.* —*n.* an inclination; a tendency: *a bent for drawing.*

bent² (bent) *n.* **1** any of a genus (*Agrostis*) of annual and perennial grasses found especially in temperate and cool parts of the world,

including several species, such as red top, valued for use as forage or in lawn mixtures. **2** any tiff or reedy grass. **3** *Archaic.* heath or moor. [OE *beonet-*]

bent grass bent[2] (def. 1).

ben·ton·ite (ben′tə nīt′) *n.* a highly absorbent clay formed from the decomposition of volcanic ash, used extensively in industry as a binding, filling, or filtering agent.

be·numb (bi num′) *v.* **1** make numb; deaden. **2** stupefy; make inactive: *A benumbing boredom had set in.* [OE *benumen,* pp. of *beniman* deprive < *be-* + *niman* take] —**be·numb′ing·ly,** *adv.*

Ben·ze·drine (ben′zə drēn′ or ben′zə drin) *n.* *Trademark.* amphetamine. *Formula:* $C_9H_{13}N$

ben·zene (ben′zēn or ben zēn′) *n.* a colorless, volatile, flammable liquid hydrocarbon that has a pleasant odor. It is obtained chiefly from coal tar and is used in the manufacture of many chemical products, including detergent, insecticides and motor fuels. *Formula:* C_6H_6 [< *benzoin*]

ben·zine (ben′zēn or ben zēn′) *n.* a clear, colorless, flammable liquid consisting of a mixture of hydrocarbons obtained by the fractional distillation of petroleum, used especially as a solvent and cleaning fluid. [< *benzoin*]

ben·zo·ate (ben′zō āt′ or ben′zō it) *n.* a salt or ester of benzoic acid. **Benzoate of soda** is used as a food preservative.

ben·zo·ic acid (ben zō′ik) an acid occurring in benzoin, cranberries, etc. that is used as an antiseptic or as a food preservative. *Formula:* C_6H_5COOH

ben·zo·in (ben′zō in) *n.* **1** a fragrant resin obtained from certain species of trees (genus *Styrax*) of Java, Sumatra, etc. and used in perfume and medicine. **2** a substance resembling camphor made from this resin. [< F *benjoin* < Sp. or Pg. < Arabic *luban jawi* incense of Java]

ben·zol (ben′zol or ben′zōl) *n.* **1** benzene. **2** a liquid containing about 70 percent of benzene and 20 to 30 percent of toluene. It is obtained from coal tar and is used in making dyes.

ben·zo·py·rene (ben′zō pī′rēn) *n.* a yellow, crystalline hydrocarbon found in coal tar and tobacco smoke. It is known to be carcinogenic. *Formula:* $C_{20}H_{12}$

benz·py·rene (benz pī′rēn) *n.* benzopyrene.

Be·o·thic (bē oth′ik or bē ot′ik) *n., pl.* **-thic** or **-thics.** Beothuk.

Be·o·thuk (bē oth′ək or bē ot′ək) *n., pl.* **-thuk** or **-thuks.** **1** an extinct tribe of North American Indians, the aboriginal inhabitants of Newfoundland. **2** a member of this tribe. The last Beothuk died in 1829. **3** the language of this tribe. Also, **Beothic.**

Be·o·wulf (bā′ə wûlf′) *n.* **1** an Old English epic poem in alliterative verse, composed in England probably about A.D. 700. **2** the hero of this poem.

be·praise (bi prāz′) *v.* **-praised, -prais·ing.** praise greatly; praise too much.

be·queath (bi kwēтн′ or bi kwēth′) *v.* **1** give or leave (property, etc.) by a will: *The father bequeathed the farm to his son.* **2** hand down to posterity: *One age bequeaths its civilization to the next.* [OE *becwethan* < *be-* to, for + *cwethan* say] —**be·queath′er,** *n.*

be·queath·al (bi kwēтн′əl) *n.* the act of bequeathing.

be·quest (bi kwest′) *n.* **1** something bequeathed; legacy: *Mr. Quail died and left a bequest of ten thousand dollars to the university.* **2** the act of bequeathing. [ME *biqueste*]

be·rate (bi rāt′) *v.* **-rat·ed, -rat·ing.** scold sharply; upbraid.

Ber·ber (bėr′bər) *n., adj.* —*n.* **1** a member of a group of peoples who are the original European, or Caucasoid inhabitants of N Africa. The Berbers, most of whom are now farmers, make up a considerable portion of the populations of Libya, Algeria, and Morocco. **2** a branch of the Afro-Asiatic language family, spoken by more than ten million people scattered through N Africa. **3** any one of these languages. —*adj.* of or having to do with the Berbers or their languages.

ber·ceuse (ber sœz′) *n.* French. **1** lullaby. **2** *Music.* a vocal or instrumental composition.

be·reave (bi rēv′) *v.* **be·reaved** or **be·reft, be·reav·ing. 1** deprive (*of*) ruthlessly; rob: *bereave of hope.* **2** leave desolate. [OE *bereafian* < *be-* away + *rēafian* rob]

be·reaved (bi rēvd′) *adj.* deprived (*of*) by death: *Bereaved of their mother at an early age, the children learned to take care of themselves.*

be·reave·ment (bi rēv′mənt) *n.* the fact or state of being bereaved, especially the loss of a relative or friend by death.

be·reft (bi reft′) *adj., v.* —*adj.* deprived; dispossessed: *Bereft of hope and friends, the old man led a wretched life.* —*v.* a pt. and a pp. of **bereave.**

be·ret (bə rā′ or ber′ā) *n.* a soft, round cap of wool, felt, etc. [< F *béret* < Provençal *birret* < LL *birretum.* See BIRETTA.]

hat, āge, fär; let, ēqual, tėrm; it, īce
hot, ōpen, ôrder; oil, out; cup, pùt, rüle,
əbove, takən, pencəl, lemən, circəs

ch, child; ng, long; sh, ship
th, thin; ŦH, then; zh, measure

berg (bėrg) *n.* iceberg.
☛ *Hom.* **burg.**

ber·ga·mot[1] (bėr′gə mot′) *n.* **1** a small citrus tree (*Citrus bergamia*) cultivated especially in S Italy for its pear-shaped fruit, whose rind yields a fragrant essential oil used in perfumes. **2** any of several plants of the mint family, such as a Mediterranean mint (*Mentha citrata*) that yields an oil with a similar fragrance. [from *Bergamo,* a town in Italy]

ber·ga·mot[2] (bėr′gə mot′) *n.* a kind of pear with a fine flavor. [< F *bergamote* < Ital. *bergamotta* < Turkish *beg-armudi* prince's pear < *beg* prince + *armudi* pear]

Berg·so·ni·an (berg sō′nē ən) *adj., n.* —*adj.* of or having to do with Henri Bergson (1859-1941), a French philosopher who thought of the universe as being in a continual process of creative evolution. —*n.* a person who supports or believes in the philosophy of Bergson.

be·rib·boned (bi rib′ənd) *adj.* **1** trimmed with many ribbons. **2** decorated with ribbons: *a beribboned general.*

ber·i·ber·i (ber′ē ber′ē) *n.* a disease caused by a lack of thiamine, affecting the heart or nervous system and in extreme cases resulting in heart failure or paralysis. [< Sinhala (language of Sri Lanka), a reduplication of *beri* weakness. 19c.]

ber·ke·li·um (bėr kē′lē əm) *n.* an artificial, radio-active, metallic element produced by bombarding americium with alpha particles. *Symbol:* Bk; *at.no.* 97; *at.wt.* (247). [< *Berkeley,* California (site of the University of California campus where berkelium was first produced in 1949)]

Berk·shire (bėrk′shər) *n.* a breed of black-and-white pig. [< *Berkshire,* a county in S England]

ber·lin (ber lin′ or bėr′lin) *n.* **1** a four-wheeled carriage with two hooded seats and a platform in the rear for footmen. **2** a soft woollen yarn. [from *Berlin,* Germany]

berm (bėrm) *n.* **1** a high embankment or ridge of earth, etc. functioning as a protective barrier or as a base or covering for a pipeline, etc.: *Berms are sometimes built along expressways to protect neighboring residential districts from traffic noise.* **2** a narrow strip of grass beside a street or road. **3** a narrow ledge, path, or shelf between a moat and a rampart in a fortification. [< F *berme* < Du. *berm,* prob. cognate with ON *barmr* brim. 18c.]

Ber·mu·da onion (ber myü′də) a large variety of onion with a mild flavor similar to that of the Spanish onion.

Bermuda shorts short pants that reach to just above the knee.

ber·ried (ber′ēd) *adj.* **1** of a lobster, crayfish, etc., bearing eggs. **2** having berries.

ber·ry (ber′ē) *n., pl.* **-ries;** *v.* **-ried, -ry·ing.** —*n.* **1** any small, juicy, edible fruit having many seeds instead of a single stone, or pit: *Strawberries and currants are berries.* **2** *Botany.* a simple fruit having two or more seeds in the pulp and having a skin or rind, such as grapes, tomatoes, currants, and bananas. **3** the dry seed or kernel of certain kinds of grain or other plants: *a wheat berry.* **4** the fruit of the coffee tree. Coffee is made from the beans found inside ripe coffee berries. **5** an egg of a lobster or fish.
—*v.* **1** gather or pick berries. **2** bear or produce berries: *a berrying shrub.* —**ber′ry·like′,** *adj.* [OE *berie*]
☛ *Hom.* **bury.**

ber·serk (bėr zėrk′ or bėr sėrk′) *adj.* or *adv.* in a frenzy. [< Icelandic *berserkr* (accus. sing. *berserk*) wild warrior < *ber-* bear + *serkr* shirt]

ber·serk·er (bėr′zėr kər or bėr′sėr kər) *n.* a fierce Norse warrior. [< Icelandic *berserkr*]

berth (bėrth) *n., v.* —*n.* **1** a place to sleep on a ship, train, or aircraft. **2** enough clear space around a ship for it to manoeuvre safely in the water; sea room. **3** the place where a ship stays when at anchor or at a wharf. **4** a place for a truck or other motor vehicle to load or unload, etc. **5** an appointment or position; job. **6** *Cdn.* stand of timber in which an individual or company has the right to fell trees; timber limited (def. 2).
give (a person or thing) **a wide berth,** keep well away from (a person or thing); pass well clear of: *He gave the dog a wide berth.*
—*v.* **1** put in a berth; provide with a berth. **2** have or occupy a berth. [? < *bear*[1]]
☛ *Hom.* **birth.**

ber·tha (bėr′thə) *n.* a woman's wide collar that often extends

over the shoulders. [after *Berthe*, mother of Charlemagne]

berth·ing (bėr′thing) *n.* a space to berth a ship, motorboat, etc. in a harbor or beside a pier.

Ber·til·lon system (bėr′tə lon′) a system, once widely used, for identifying persons, especially criminals, by their physical measurements, such as length of arms and legs and width and length of the skull. The Bertillon system has been replaced by fingerprinting. [after A. *Bertillon* (1853-1914), the French police officer who introduced the system]

ber·yl (ber′əl) *n.* 1 a very hard clear or cloudy mineral, usually green or greenish blue, a silicate of beryllium and aluminum. 2 a piece of this stone, or a gem made from it. Emeralds and aquamarines are beryls. [ME < OF < L < Gk. *bēryllos*, cognate with Skt. *vaidurya* cat's-eye]

be·ryl·li·um (bə ril′ē əm) *n.* a hard, strong, steel-grey metallic element, used mainly in alloys as a hardening agent. *Symbol*: Be; *at.no.* 4; *at.wt.* 9.0122. [< *beryl*]

B. ès A. Bachelier ès Arts; Bachelor of Arts.

be·seech (bi sēch′) *v.* **-sought** or **-seeched, -seech·ing.** ask earnestly; beg. [ME *bisechе*(n) < *be-* thoroughly + *sechе*(n) seek] **—be·seech′er,** *n.*
☛ *Syn.* See note at **beg.**

be·seech·ing (bi sēch′ing) *adj.* that beseeches. **—be·seech′ing·ly,** *adv.*

be·seem (bi sēm′) *v.* be proper for; be fitting to: *It does not beseem you to leave your friend without help.*

be·set (bi set′) *v.* **-set, -set·ting.** 1 attack on all sides; attack: *In the swamp we were beset by mosquitoes.* 2 continue to trouble; afflict: *a task beset with many difficulties.* 3 set; stud: *Her bracelet was beset with gems.* [OE *besettan* < *be-* around + *settan* set]

be·set·ting (bi set′ing) *adj.* habitually attacking or troubling: *Laziness is a loafer's besetting sin.*

be·shrew (bi shrü′) *v. Archaic.* call down evil upon; curse mildly. [ME *beshrewе*(n)]

be·side (bi sīd′) *prep., adv.* —*prep.* 1 by the side of; near; close to: *Grass grows tall beside the brook.* 2 compared with: *Lena seems dull beside her sister.* 3 in addition to; besides: *Other men beside ourselves were helping.* 4 away or aside from; not related to: *That question is beside the point.*
beside oneself, extremely excited or upset; wild or crazy: *beside oneself with fear. He was beside himself with joy.*
—*adv. Archaic.* in addition; besides. [OE *be sīdan* by side]
☛ *Usage.* Do not confuse the preposition **beside** with the adverb and preposition **besides.** Although both can mean 'in addition (to)', only **beside** can mean 'close to'.

be·sides (bi sīdz′) *adv., prep.* —*adv.* 1 also; moreover; further: *He didn't want to quarrel; besides, he wasn't completely sure he was right.* 2 in addition: *We tried two other ways besides.* 3 otherwise; else: *He is ignorant of politics, whatever he may know besides.*
—*prep.* 1 in addition to; over and above: *The picnic was attended by others besides our own club members.* 2 except; other than: *We spoke of no one besides you.*
☛ *Usage.* See note at **beside.**

be·siege (bi sēj′) *v.* **-sieged, -sieg·ing.** 1 make a long-continued attempt to get possession of (a place) by armed force; surround and try to capture: *For ten years the Greeks besieged the city of Troy.* 2 crowd around: *Hundreds of admirers besieged the astronaut.* 3 overwhelm with requests, questions, etc.: *During the flood the Red Cross was besieged with calls for help.* **—be·sieg′er,** *n.*

B. ès L. Bachelier ès Lettres; Bachelor of Letters.

B.E.S.L. British Empire Service League.

be·smear (bi-smēr′) *v.* 1 smear over. 2 sully; dishonor: *The lies and half-truths in the newspaper article besmeared the diplomat's reputation.*

be·smirch (bi smėrch′) *v.* 1 make dirty; soil. 2 sully; dishonor: *to besmirch a good reputation.* **—be·smirch′er,** *n.*

be·som (bē′zəm) *n.* a broom made of twigs. [OE *besma*]

be·sot (bi sot′) *v.* **-sot·ted, -sot·ting.** stupefy or make foolish, as with liquor, infatuation, etc.

be·sought (bi sot′ or bi sôt′) *v.* a pt. and a pp. of **beseech.**

be·spake (bi spāk′) *v. Archaic.* a pt. of **bespeak.**

be·span·gle (bi spang′gəl) *v.* **-gled, -gling.** adorn with spangles or anything like them.

be·spat·ter (bi spat′ər) *v.* 1 spatter all over; soil by spattering. 2 slander. **—be·spat′ter·er,** *n.*

be·speak (bi spēk′) *v.* **-spoke, -spo·ken** or **-spoke, -speak·ing.** 1 engage in advance; order; reserve: *to bespeak tickets to a play.*

2 show; indicate: *A neat appearance bespeaks care.* 3 *Archaic or poetic.* point to; foreshadow: *Her early successes bespeak a great future.*

be·spec·ta·cled (bi spek′tə kəld) *adj.* wearing glasses.

be·spoke (bi spōk′) *v.,* *adj.* —*v.* a pt. and a pp. of **bespeak.** —*adj. Esp.Brit.* made-to-order: *bespoke tailoring; a bespoke overcoat.*

be·spread (bi spred′) *v.* **-spread, -spread·ing.** spread over.

be·sprent (bi sprent′) *adj. Archaic or poetic.* sprinkled or strewn. [OE *besprenged,* pp. of *besprengan*]

be·sprin·kle (bi spring′kəl) *v.* **-kled, -kling.** sprinkle all over.

B. ès Sc. Bachelier ès Science; Bachelor of Science.

Bes·se·mer converter (bes′ə mər) a large container for making molten iron into steel by the Bessemer process.

Bessemer process a method of making steel by burning out carbon and impurities in molten iron with a blast of compressed air. [after Sir Henry *Bessemer* (1813-1898), the English engineer who invented the process]

Bessemer steel steel made by the Bessemer process.

best (best) *adj.* (superlative of **good**), *adv.* (superlative of **well**), *n., v.* —*adj.* 1 the most desirable, valuable, superior, etc.: *the best food, the best students, the best quality of crystal.* 2 of the greatest advantage, usefulness, etc.: *the best thing to do.* 3 largest; greatest: *We spent the best part of the day just getting organized.*
—*adv.* 1 in the most excellent way; most thoroughly: *Who reads best?* 2 in the highest degree: *I like this book best.*
had best, should; ought to; will be wise to: *We had best postpone the party.*
—*n.* 1 the person, thing, part, quality, or state that is best: *He is the best in the class. We want the best. The story represents journalism at its best.* 2 utmost: *I did my best to finish the work on time.*
(all) for the best, favorable in the end: *at first we were unhappy about the plan, but it turned out to be all for the best.*
at best, a even under the most favorable circumstances: *Summer is at best very short.* **b** even when interpreted most favorably: *It was a sad effort at best.*
get the best of, defeat.
make the best of, do as well as possible with: *We'll just have to make the best of a bad job.*
with the best, as well as anyone: *She can swim with the best.*
—*v. Informal.* outdo; defeat: *Our team was bested in the final game.* [OE *betst*]

be·stead (bi sted′) *v.* **-stead·ed, -stead·ed** or **-stead, -stead·ing;** *adj. Archaic.* —*v.* help; assist; serve. —*adj.* placed; situated. [< *be- + stead,* v., help]

bes·tial (bes′chəl or best′ē əl) *adj.* 1 beastly; brutal; vile. 2 of or having to do with beasts. [ME < OF < L *bestialis* < *bestia* beast] **—bes′tial·ly,** *adv.*

bes·ti·al·i·ty (bes′chē al′ə tē or bes′tē al′ə tē) *n.* 1 bestial character or conduct. 2 sexual activity between a person and an animal.

bes·ti·ar·y (bes′chē er′ē) *n.* a medieval collection of allegorical descriptions of real or mythical animals.

be·stir (bi stėr′) *v.* **-stirred, -stir·ring.** stir up; rouse; exert: *to bestir oneself to action.*

best man the chief attendant of the bridegroom at a wedding.

be·stow (bi stō′) *v.* 1 give (something) as a gift; give; confer (used with on or upon). 2 make use of; apply: *She bestowed a great deal of thought on the plan.* 3 *Archaic.* put safely; put; place. 4 *Archaic.* find quarters for; lodge. [ME *bistowе*(n)]

be·stow·al (bi stō′əl) *n.* the act of bestowing.

be·strad·dle (bi strad′əl) *v.* **-dled, -dling.** bestride; straddle.

be·strew (bi strü′) *v.* **-strewed, -strewn** or **-strewed, -strew·ing.** 1 strew; scatter; sprinkle: *The children bestrewed the path with flowers.* 2 strew (things) around; scatter about. 3 lie scattered over: *Flowers bestrewed the path.* [OE *bestrēowian*]

be·strid (bi strid′) *v.* a pt. and a pp of **bestride.**

be·strid·den (bi strid′ən) *v.* a pp. of **bestride.**

be·stride (bi strīd′) *v.* **-strode** or **-strid, -strid·den** or **-strid, -strid·ing.** 1 get on or sit on with one leg on either side: *One can bestride a horse, a chair, or a fence.* 2 stand over something with one leg on each side. 3 stride across; step over. [OE *bestrīdan*]

be·strode (bi strōd′) *v.* a pt. of **bestride.**

best·sell·er or **best seller** (best′ sel′ər) *n.* 1 anything, especially a book or phonograph record, that has a very large sale. 2 the author of a book with a very large sale.

bet (bet) *n., v.* **bet** or **bet·ted, bet·ting.** —*n.* 1 an agreement between two persons or groups that the one who is proved wrong about the outcome of an event will give a particular thing or sum of money to the one who is proved right: *I made a two-cent bet that I wouldn't pass.* 2 the thing or sum of money risked in a bet; the

stake: *I did pass; so I lost my bet* (that is my two cents.). **3** a thing to bet on: *That horse is a good bet.*
—*v.* **1** promise money or something else to a person if that person is proved right about the outcome of an event: *I bet you two cents I won't pass this test.* **2** make a bet: *Did you bet on the race?* **3** *Informal.* be very sure: *I bet you're wrong about that.*
you bet, *Informal.* certainly; of course: *You bet I'm going to object. "Are you going to the game?" "You bet!"*
[origin uncertain]

be·ta (bā′tə *or* bē′tə) *n.* **1** the second letter of the Greek alphabet (B, β). **2** the second of a series.

be·take (bi tāk′) *v.* **-took, -tak·en, -tak·ing.** (*used reflexively*) **1** go: *to betake oneself to the mountains.* **2** devote or apply (oneself) (*to*): *to betake oneself to hard work.*

be·tak·en (bi tāk′ən) *v.* pp. of **betake.**

beta particle an electron or positron emitted by a nucleus in the process of radio-active decay.

beta ray a stream of beta particles.

be·ta·tron (bā′tə tron′ *or* bē′tə-) *n.* an accelerator that uses magnetic induction produced by rapid changes in a magnetic field to increase the velocity of electrons. [< *beta ray* + *electron*]

be·tel (bē′təl) *n.* a climbing pepper plant (*Piper betle*) of tropical Asia, the dried leaves of which are commonly chewed, together with pieces of betel nut and lime, throughout S Asia. See also **betel nut, betel palm.** [< Port. < Malayalam *vettila*]
☛ *Hom.* **beetle.**

Be·tel·geuse (bē′təl jüz′) *n.* a very large reddish star in the constellation Orion. [< F ? < Arabic *bit-al-jāuza* house of the twins]

betel nut the seed of the betel palm, boiled and dried for chewing with betel leaves. See also **betel, betel palm.**

betel palm a palm (*Areca catechu*) of tropical Asia having pinnate leaves and producing large seeds called betel nuts.

bête noire (bet nwär′) a thing or person especially dreaded or detested. [< F *bête noire* black beast]

beth·el (beth′əl) *n.* **1** a holy place. **2** a church or chapel for seamen. [< Hebrew *beth-el* house of God]

be·think (bi thingk′) *v.* **-thought, -think·ing. 1** cause (oneself) to consider or reflect. **2** remind (oneself). **3** think about; call to mind. [OE *bethencan*]

be·thought (bi thot′ *or* bi thôt′) *v.* pt. and pp. of **bethink.**

be·tide (bi tīd′) *v.* **-tid·ed, -tid·ing.** happen or happen to; befall: *Woe betide anyone who touches Lisa's stamp collection.* [ME *betiden* < *be-* + *tiden* happen]

be·times (bi tīmz′) *adv. Archaic.* **1** early: *He rose betimes in the morning.* **2** soon; before it is too late. [ME *bitime* by time]

be·to·ken (bi tō′kən) *v.* be a sign or token of; indicate; show: *His smile betokens satisfaction.*

be·took (bi tuk′) *v.* pt. of **betake.**

be·tray (bi trā′) *v.* **1** deliver into the enemy's hands by treachery: *The traitor betrayed his country.* **2** be unfaithful to: *She betrayed her friends.* **3** mislead; deceive. **4** give away (a secret); disclose unintentionally. **5** reveal; show: *His mistakes betrayed his lack of education.* [ME *bitraie(n)* < *be-* (intensive) + *traie(n)* betray < OF < L *tradere* hand over] —**be·tray′er,** *n.*

be·tray·al (bi trā′əl) *n.* betraying or being betrayed.

be·troth (bi trōTH′ *or* bi troth′) *v.* promise in marriage; engage: *He betrothed his daughter to a rich man.* [ME *betrouthe(n),* var. of *betreuthien* < *be-* + *treuthe* < OE *trēowth* pledge]

be·troth·al (bi trōTH′əl *or* bi troth′əl) *n.* a promise of marriage; engagement.

be·trothed (bi trōTHd′ *or* bi trotht′) *n.* a person engaged to be married.

bet·ter¹ (bet′ər) *adj., adv., n., v.* —*adj.* **1** more desirable, valuable, etc.; of higher quality: *a better brand, better facilities.* **2** of greater advantage, usefulness, etc.: *a better thing to do.* **3** less sick: *The child is better today.* **4** larger or greater: *Four days is the better part of a week.*
—*adv.* **1** in a more excellent way; more thoroughly, desirably, etc.: *He'll do better next time.* **2** in a higher degree; more: *I know her better than I know her sister.*
better off, in a better condition: *The theatre was full, and we would have been better off if we had stayed at home watching television.*
had better, should; ought to; would be wise to: *You had better be there on time.*
think better of, think over and change one's mind.
—*n.* **1** a person, thing, part, quality, or state that is better: *That is the better of the two routes.* **2** Usually, **betters,** *pl.* one's superiors, especially in rank or merit: *They were told to listen to the advice of their betters.*
get or have the better of, be superior to; defeat.

hat, āge, fär; let, ēqual, tėrm; it, īce
hot, ōpen, ôrder; oil, out; cup, pút, rüle,
əbove, takən, pencəl, lemən, circəs

ch, child; ng, long; sh, ship
th, thin; ŦH, then; zh, measure

—*v.* **1** make or become better: *to better one's work, to better the lot of the poor.* **2** do better than; surpass: *They were unable to better the other school academically.* [OE *betera*]

bet·ter² or **bet·tor** (bet′ər) *n.* a person who bets.

better half *Informal.* wife.

bet·ter·ment (bet′ər mənt) *n.* **1** improvement: *Doctors work for betterment of their patients' health.* **2** Usually, **betterments,** *pl.* an improvement of real estate property.

bet·ty (bet′ē) *n.* a pudding made of diced bread or toast, fruit, and sweetening: *apple brown betty.*

be·tween (bi twēn′) *prep., adv.* —*prep.* **1** in or into the space, position, or time separating; in the middle in relation to two persons, things, etc.: *Many cities lie between Halifax and Toronto. There are no more holidays between now and the end of school. A sergeant ranks between a corporal and a warrant officer.* **2** in or into a position thought of as being in the middle in relation to two or more persons, things, or ideas: *Between dying in captivity and getting killed in escaping, he had little to choose from.* **3** within the range separating two or more quantities, qualities, or times: *a shade between pink and red. The temperature is probably between 20°C and 25°C. She made between $400 and $500 on the deal.* **4** connecting in space: *There is a paved highway between Flin Flon and The Pas.* **5** connecting in a state or condition; involving: *war between two nations. There was a strong bond of affection between them.* **6** in the joint ownership of: *They own the property between them.* **7** by the combined action or effort of: *The girls caught 12 fish between them. Settle the matter between you.* **8** in or into portions for: *The estate was divided between the grandchildren.* **9** restricted to: *We kept the matter between us.* **10** in or into a position separating: *They were fast friends and would let no quarrel come between them.* **11** through the range separating two or more conditions, qualities, or quantities: *all numbers between 1 and 50.*
between the devil and the deep blue sea See **devil.**
between you and me, as a secret; confidentially: *Between you and me, I don't think he has a chance of winning.*
no love lost between (persons), strong dislike involving two people; mutual enmity: *There's no love lost between them.*
—*adv.* in or into an intermediate space or time: *We could no longer see the moon, for a cloud had come between. The speeches seemed very long because there was no break between.*
in between, **a** in the middle: *We folded the blanket and put the mirror in between.* **b** in the middle of.
[OE *betwēonum* < *be-* by + *twā* two]
☛ *Usage.* **Between, among. Between** is used when the reference is to two persons or things only: *My sister and I had less than a dollar between us.* **Among** is usually preferred when the reference is to more than two persons or things: *The money was divided among the four of us.* However, **between** is used also when the reference is to a number of persons or things that are thought of in pairs: *Leave a line space between paragraphs.*
☛ *Usage.* **Between you and me.** Since prepositions are followed by the objective form of a pronoun, standard English requires *me* in this expression, not *I.* Similarly, standard English requires: *between you and him* (not *he*), *between you and us* (not *we*), etc.

be·tween·times (bi twēn′tīmz′) *adv.* at intervals.

be·twixt (bi twikst′) *prep. or adv.* between.
betwixt and between, in the middle; neither one nor the other. [OE *betweox*]

BeV *U.S.* gigaelectronvolt (GeV). [abbrev. of billion *e*lectron*v*olts]

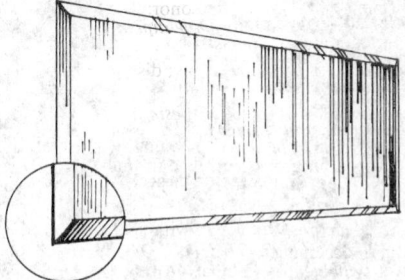

A mirror with
bevelled edges

bev·el (bev′əl) *n., v.* **-elled** or **-eled, -el·ling** or **-el·ing.** —*n.* **1** a sloping edge, as on plate glass, moulding, etc. **2** an instrument for

measuring or drawing angles or adjusting a surface or edge that is to be given a bevel. **3** (*adjl.*) slanting; oblique.
—*v.* cut at an angle other than a right angle; make slope: *This mirror has bevelled edges.* [? < OF]

bev·er·age (bev′ər ij *or* bev′rij) *n.* a liquid used or prepared for drinking. *Examples: milk, tea, coffee, beer, and wine.* [ME < OF *bevrage* < *bevre* drink < L *bibere*]

beverage room *Cdn.* beer parlor.

bev·y (bev′ē) *n., pl.* **bev·ies.** a small group: *a bevy of quail, a bevy of girls.* [ME *bevey* ? < AF *bevee* a drinking group]

be·wail (bi wāl′) *v.* mourn or lament: *to bewail one's fate.*

be·ware (bi wer′) *v. Formal.* be on one's guard; be cautious or wary (*used only in the imperative or infinitive*): *Beware of pickpockets.* [< *be* + *ware*]
☛ *Usage.* **Beware** is a formal word for "be careful." It is followed by *of* preceding a noun or pronoun or by *lest, how,* or *that*...not introducing a subordinate clause: *Beware of the sharpers at the fair. They were told to beware lest they wake him. We must beware how we approach him. Beware that you do not anger him.* Beware is sometimes followed directly by its object: *Beware the dog.*

be·wil·der (bi wil′dər) *v.* confuse completely; cause doubt and uncertainty: *The little girl was bewildered by the crowds. Difficult problems in arithmetic bewilder me.* [< *be-* + OE *wilder* lead astray] —**be·wil′der·ment,** *n.*
☛ *Syn.* See note at **puzzle.**

be·wil·der·ing (bi wil′dər ing) *adj.* perplexing; confusing: *a bewildering assortment of sizes and colors.* —**be·wil′der·ing·ly,** *adv.*

be·witch (bi wich′) *v.* **1** put under a spell; use magic on. **2** charm; delight; fascinate: *a smile that bewitches.* —**be·witch′er,** *n.*

be·witched (bi wicht′) *adj.* **1** under the influence of magic. **2** charmed; delighted; fascinated.

be·witch·ing (bi wich′ing) *adj.* fascinating; delightful; charming. —**be·witch′ing·ly,** *adv.*

be·wray (bi rā′) *v. Archaic.* reveal; make known. [ME *bewreie(n)* < *be-* + *wreie(n)* < OE *wrēgan* accuse]

bey (bā) *n., pl.* **beys. 1** in the Ottoman Empire, the governor of a province. **2** a Turkish title of respect for a person of rank. **3** formerly, a native ruler of Tunis or Tunisia. [< Turkish *beg*]
☛ *Hom.* **bay.**

be·yond (bi yond′) *prep., adv., n.* —*prep.* **1** on or to the farther side of: *He lives beyond the sea.* **2** farther on than: *The school is beyond the last house on this street.* **3** later than; past: *They stayed beyond the time set.* **4** out of the reach, range, or understanding of: *The dying man was beyond help.* **5** more than; exceeding: *The price of the suit was beyond what he could pay.* **6** in addition to; besides: *I will do nothing beyond the job given me.*
—*adv.* farther away: *Beyond were the hills.*
—*n.*
the beyond *or* **the great beyond,** life after death.
[OE *begeondan* < *be-* at, near + *geondan* beyond]

bez·el (bez′əl) *n.* **1** a slope, or bevel, especially on the edge of a cutting tool. **2** the sloping sides or faces of a cut jewel. **3** a grooved rim or ring holding a jewel, watch crystal, etc. in place. [< OF form of F *biseau*]

be·zique (bə zēk′) *n.* a card game resembling pinochle. [< F *bésigue,* origin uncertain]

bf. boldface (type).

B.F.A. Bachelor of Fine Arts.

bg. bag.

B.Gen *or* **BGen** brigadier-general.

Bha·ga·vad Gi·ta (bag′ə vəd gē′tə) a philosophical dialogue embodied in the *Mahabharata,* an ancient Sanskrit epic. [< Skt. *Song of the Blessed One*]

bhang (bang) *n.* **1** hemp. **2** cannabis (def. 2). [< Hind. < Skt. *bhanga* hemp]

bi- *prefix.* **1** twice, as in *biannual, bimonthly.* **2** doubly, as in *bipolar, biconcave.* **3** two as in *bicuspid, bilateral.* **4** having two, as in *bicarbonate, bichloride.* **5** appearance or occurrence in intervals of two; every two, as in *bimonthly, biennial.* [ME, < L]
☛ *Usage.* See note at **bimonthly.**

Bi bismuth.

bi·an·nu·al (bī an′yü əl) *adj.* occurring twice a year: *Our doctor recommends a biannual visit to the dentist.* —**bi·an′nu·al·ly,** *adv.*
☛ *Usage.* See note at **bimonthly.**

bi·as (bī′əs) *n., adv., v.* **bi·assed** or **bi·ased, bi·as·sing** or **bi·as·ing.**
—*n.* **1** a slanting or oblique line. Cloth is cut on the bias when it is cut diagonally across the weave. **2** (*adjl.*) slanting across the threads of cloth; oblique; diagonal: *a bias cut, cloth with a bias print.* **3** an inclination or preference that makes it difficult or impossible to judge fairly in a particular situation; a general opinion that has an unfair influence on a specific decision: *The newpaper account of the trial showed a bias in favor of the defendant.* **4** *Lawn bowling.* **a** the lopsided shape of a bowl that makes it swerve when rolled on the green. **b** the tendency of a bowl to swerve or the force that makes it do so. **5** *Statistics.* **a** the deviation of the true value of a statistic obtained in random sampling from its estimated value. **b** distortion of a statistic due to neglect of a factor or factors.
—*adv.* diagonally across the weave: *cloth cut bias.*
—*v.* cause to have an inclination or preference that interferes with fair judgment; prejudice: *Several bad experiences biassed him against teenage drivers.* [< F *biais* slant < VL *biaxius* having a double axis]

bi·assed *or* **bi·ased** (bī′əst) *adj.* having or showing bias (def. 3): *a biassed judge. He was biassed where his children were concerned.*

bi·ath·lon (bī ath′lən *or* bī ath′lon) *n.* an Olympic event or contest in which skiers with rifles race along a twenty-kilometre cross-country course, shooting at four targets spaced along the way. [< *bi-* + Gk. *athlon* contest, as in *pentathlon*]

bi·ax·i·al (bī ak′sē əl) *adj.* having two axes: *a biaxial crystal.* —**bi·ax′i·al·ly,** *adv.*

bib (bib) *n., v.* **bibbed, bib·bing.** —*n.* **1** a cloth worn under the chin, especially by babies and small children to protect their clothing. **2** the part of an apron or overalls extending above the waist in front. —*v. Archaic.* drink; tripple. [ME < *bib* drink, ? < L *bibere*]

Bib. 1 Bible. **2** Biblical.

bib and tucker *Informal.* clothes.

bib·cock (bib′kok′) *n.* a tap having a nozzle bent downward.

bi·be·lot (bib′lō; *French,* bē blō′) *n.* a small object valued for its beauty, rarity, or interest. [< F]

Bi·ble (bī′bəl) *n.* **1** the collection of sacred writings belonging to the Christian religion and comprising the Old and New Testaments. **2** the sacred writings of Judaism, identical with the Old Testament of the Christian Bible. **3** the sacred writings of any religion. **4** **bible,** any book accepted as an indisputable authority in a particular field: *The* Canada Year Book *is the Canadian geographer's bible.* [ME < OF < Med.L < Gk. *biblia,* pl. dim. of *biblos* book]
☛ *Usage.* **Bible,** referring to the Christian scriptures, is capitalized: *You will find it in the Bible.* Bible in the sense of an authoritative book is not capitalized: *"Smith's Manual," the botanist's bible, was most useful to the medical students.*

bib·li·cal *or* **Bib·li·cal** (bib′lə kəl) *adj.* **1** of or having to do with the Bible: *biblical literature.* **2** according to the Bible: *biblical history.* **3** in the Bible: *a biblical reference to Solomon.* —**bib′li·cal·ly** *or* **Bib′li·cal·ly,** *adv.*

biblio- *combining form.* book or books: *bibliophile = a lover of books.* [< Gk. *biblion* book]

bib·li·og·ra·pher (bib′lē og′rə fər) *n.* a person who investigates the authorship, edition, dates, etc. of books or other publications or manuscripts.

bib·li·o·graph·ic (bib′lē ə graf′ik) *adj.* bibliographical.

bib·li·o·graph·i·cal (bib′lē ə graf′ə kəl) *adj.* of bibliography. —**bib′li·o·graph′i·cal·ly,** *adv.*

bib·li·og·ra·phy (bib′lē og′rə fē) *n., pl.* **-phies. 1** a list of books, articles, etc. about a subject or person. **2** a list of books, articles, etc. by a certain author. **3** a study of the authorship, editions, dates, etc. of books, articles, etc.

bib·li·o·ma·ni·a (bib′lē ō mā′nē ə) *n.* an excessive preoccupation with collecting books.

bib·li·o·ma·ni·ac (bib′lē ō mā′nē ak′) *n.* a person who is excessively preoccupied with collecting books.

bib·li·o·phil (bib′lē ə fil′) *n.* bibliophile.

bib·li·o·phile (bib′lē ə fil′) *n.* a lover of books, especially one who likes to collect books.

bib·u·lous (bib′yə ləs) *adj.* **1** fond of drinking alcoholic liquor. **2** absorbent. —**bib′u·lous·ly,** *adv.* —**bib′u·lous·ness,** *n.* [< L *bibulus* < *bibere* drink]

bi·cam·er·al (bī kam′ər əl) *adj.* having or consisting of two legislative assemblies: *The Canadian Parliament is bicameral; it has both a Senate and a House of Commons.* [< *bi-* two + L *camera* chamber < Gk. *kamara*]

bi·car·bo·nate (bī kär′bə nit *or* bī kär′bə nāt′) *n.* sodium bicarbonate, especially when used in cooking as a leavening agent or in medicine as an antacid.

bicarbonate of soda sodium bicarbonate.

bice (bīs) *n.* **1** a kind of green paint. **2** a kind of blue paint. [< F *bis*]

bi·cen·ten·ar·y (bī′sen ten′ər ē *or* bī′sen tē′nə rē) *adj., n., pl.* **-nar·ies.** —*adj.* having to do with a period of 200 years. —*n.* **1** a period of 200 years. **2** a 200th anniversary. **3** its celebration.

bi·cen·ten·ni·al (bī′sen ten′ē əl *or* bī′sen tē′nē əl) *adj., n.* —*adj.* **1** having to do with a period of 200 years. **2** recurring every 200 years. —*n.* **1** a 200th anniversary. **2** its celebration.

bi·ceps (bī′seps) *n. sing. or pl.* **1** any muscle having two heads, or points of origin, especially the large muscle at the front of the upper arm or the large muscle at the back of the upper leg. **2** *Informal.* muscular strength, especially in the upper arm. [< L *biceps* two-headed < *bi-* two + *caput* head]

bi·chlo·ride (bī klô′rīd *or* bī klô′rid) *n.* **1** dichloride. **2** mercuric chloride; bichloride of mercury.

bichloride of mercury mercuric chloride.

bi·chro·mate (bī krō′māt) *n.* a salt containing two atoms of chromium combined with another element or radical.

bick·er (bik′ər) *v., n.* —*v.* **1** express annoyance to each other over trifles; squabble; engage in a petty quarrel: *The children bickered all afternoon.* **2** move quickly with a babbling or pattering noise: *a bickering stream.* **3** of light, a flame, etc., flash or flicker. —*n.* **1** a mild quarrel over a trifle or trifles: *After a short bicker, they decided on a movie they both wanted to see.* **2** a bickering sound. [ME *biker(en)*]

bi·col·ored *or* **bi·col·oured** (bī′kul′ərd) *adj.* having two colors: *bicolored roses.*

bi·con·cave (bī kon′kāv *or* bī′kon kāv′) *adj.* concave on both sides.

bi·con·cav·i·ty (bī′kon kav′ə tē) *n.* the quality or state of being biconcave.

bi·con·vex (bī kon′veks *or* bī′kon veks′) *adj.* convex on both sides.

bi·con·vex·i·ty (bī kon vek′sə tē) *n.* the quality or state of being biconvex.

bi·cul·tur·al (bī kul′chər əl) *adj.* **1** having two distinct cultures existing side by side in the same country, province, etc. **2** *Cdn.* having to do with the coexistence of English and French cultures.

bi·cul·tur·al·ism (bī kul′chər əl iz′əm) *n.* **1** the fact or condition of being bicultural. **2** a policy that favors a country, province, etc. being bicultural. **3** the practice or support of such a policy.

bi·cus·pid (bī kus′pid) *n., adj.* —*n.* a double-pointed tooth. A human adult has eight bicuspids. See **teeth** for picture. —*adj.* having two points. [< *bi-* two + L *cuspis, -pidis* point]

bi·cy·cle (bī′sə kəl) *n., v.* **-cled, -cling.** —*n.* a vehicle consisting of a metal frame with two wheels, set one behind the other, handles for steering, and a seat for the rider. An ordinary bicycle has pedals; a motor bicycle has an engine. —*v.* ride a bicycle. [< F *bicycle* < *bi-* two (< L *bis*) + Gk. *kyklos* circle, wheel] —**bi′cy·cler,** *n.*

bi·cy·clist (bī′sə klist) *n.* a bicycle rider; cyclist.

b.i.d. of medicine, (take) twice a day. [for L *bis in die*]

bid (bid) *v.* **bade** *or* **bid, bid·den** *or* **bid, bid·ding** (for defs. 1, 2, 5, 7), **bid, bid·ding** (for defs. 3, 4, 6); *n.* —*v.* **1** command: *Do as I bid you.* **2** say or tell: *His friends came to bid him goodbye.* **3** offer: *She bid $50 for the table.* **4** offer a price; state a price: *Several companies will bid for the contract.* **5** proclaim; declare: *He bade defiance to them all.* **6** *Card games.* state what one proposes to make or win. **7** *Archaic or dialect.* invite: *They bade him come again.*

bid fair, seem likely; have a good chance: *The plan bids fair to succeed.*

bid in, at an auction, overbid on behalf of the owner with the intention of keeping the article unsold.

bid up, at an auction, etc. raise the price of something by bidding more.

—*n.* **1** an offer of a specified amount, or price, as at an auction or for a contract: *Are you going to make a bid on that table?* **2** the amount of such an offer: *His bid was $140. The lowest bid for building the bridge was $800 000.* **3** an attempt to secure, achieve, etc.: *He made a bid for our sympathy.* **4** *Card games.* **a** the statement of what a player proposes to make or win. **b** the amount of the bid. **c** a player's turn to bid. **5** *Archaic.* an invitation. [OE *biddan* ask; meaning influenced by OE *bēodan* offer]

☛ *Usage.* In the sense "command," now somewhat archaic, **bid** in the active voice is usually followed by an infinitive without *to: You bade me forget what is unforgettable.* With the passive, *to* is used: *They were bidden to assemble.*

bid·da·ble (bid′ə bəl) *adj.* **1** obedient; docile. **2** that is suitable to bid on in card games.

bid·den (bid′ən) *v.* a pp. of **bid.**

hat, āge, fär; let, ēqual, tėrm; it, īce
hot, ōpen, ôrder; oil; out; cup, put, rüle, above, takən, pencəl, lemən, circəs
ch, child; ng, long; sh, ship
th, thin; ғн, then; zh, measure

bid·der (bid′ər) *n.* a person who bids, especially at an auction or in a card game.

bid·ding (bid′ing) *n.* **1** a request or command. **2** the offers, or bids, at an auction: *The bidding was slow at first but soon became lively.* **3** *Card games.* the bids collectively.

do (someone's) **bidding,** obey: *They did his bidding without question.*

bid·dy¹ (bid′ē) *n.* hen. [? imitative]

biddy² (bid′ē) *n.* a talkative old woman. [Anglo-Irish *Biddy,* dim. of *Bridget*]

bide (bīd) *v.* **bode** *or* **bid·ed, bid·ed, bid·ing.** *Archaic* (except in **bide one's time**). **1** dwell; abide. **2** stay or wait; tarry. **3** wait for. **4** bear; endure; suffer.

bide one's time, wait for a good chance: *If you bide your time, you will probably get a good bargain.* [OE *bīdan*]

bi·den·tate (bī den′tāt) *adj.* having two teeth.

bi·det (bē′dā *or* bē dā′) *n.* a bathroom fixture similar to a toilet but shallower and having taps and a drain like a sink, used for bathing the genital areas of the body.

bi·en·ni·al (bī en′ē əl) *adj., n.* —*adj.* **1** of plants, lasting two years. **2** occurring every two years. —*n.* **1** any plant that lives two years, usually producing flowers and seeds the second year. Carrots and onions are biennials. Compare **annual, perennial. 2** an event that occurs every two years. [< L *biennium* < *bi-* two + *annus* year] —**bi·en·ni·al·ly,** *adv.*

☛ *Usage.* See note at **bimonthly.**

bier (bēr) *n.* a movable stand on which a coffin or dead body is placed. [OE *bēr* < *beran* bear¹]

☛ *Hom.* **beer.**

biff (bif) *n. or v. Slang.* hit; slap. [probably imitative]

bif·fy (bif′ē) *n. Slang. Esp.Cdn.* **1** toilet. **2** bathroom. [origin uncertain]

bi·fid (bī′fid) *adj.* divided into two parts by a cleft. [< L *bifidus* < *bi-* two + *fid-* base of *findere* cleave]

bi·fo·cal (bī fō′kəl) *adj., n.* —*adj.* having two focuses: *Bifocal eye glasses have two parts: the upper part for far vision, the lower for near vision.* —*n.* **1 bifocals,** *pl.* eye glasses having bifocal lenses. **2** a bifocal lens.

Bif·rost (bēf′rost) *n. Norse mythology.* the rainbow bridge between heaven and earth.

bi·fur·cate (*v.* bī′fər kāt *or* bī fėr′kāt; *adj.* bī′fər kāt *or* bī fėr′kit) *v.* **-cat·ed, -cat·ing;** *adj.* —*v.* divide into two parts or branches. —*adj.* divided into two branches; forked. [< Med.L *bifurcatus* < L *bifurcus* < *bi-* two + *furca* fork]

bi·fur·ca·tion (bī′fər kā′shən) *n.* **1** a splitting into two parts. **2** the place where the split occurs.

big (big) *adj.* **big·ger, big·gest. 1** great in extent, amount, size, etc.; large: *a big room, a big book, big business.* **2** grown up: *He said he wants to be a firefighter when he's big.* **3** *Informal.* important; great: *This is big news.* **4** full or loud: *a big voice.* **5** generous: *She has a big heart and will always help you out.* **6** boastful: *big talk.* **7** (*adv.*) *Informal.* boastfully: *He talks big.* **8** *Informal.* popular: *CB radios are very big these days.*

big with child, pregnant. [ME] —**big′ness,** *n.*

☛ *Syn.* **1.** See note at **great.**

big·a·mist (big′ə mist) *n.* a person who commits bigamy.

big·a·mous (big′ə məs) *adj.* **1** guilty of bigamy. **2** involving bigamy. —**big′a·mous·ly,** *adv.*

big·a·my (big′ə mē) *n.* the criminal offence of marrying someone while still legally married to someone else. [ME < OF *bigamie* < *bigame* < Med.L *bigamus* < *bi-* twice + Gk. *gamos* married]

Big Ben (ben) in London, England, a huge bell in the clock tower of the Houses of Parliament.

Big Bertha *Informal.* **1** in World War I, a long-range gun used by the Germans to fire on Paris. **2** any powerful artillery gun. **3** anything large or of great range for its kind.

Big Brother a tyrannical dictator or government whose subjects are kept constantly under secret observation. [after the dictator,

who is frequently mentioned, but never appears, in George Orwell's novel *1984*, pub. 1949]

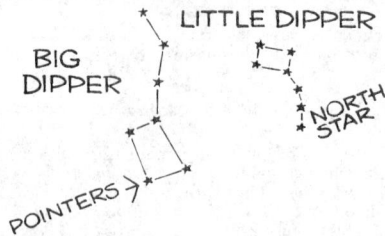

Big Dipper the seven principal stars in the constellation Ursa Major, arranged in a form that suggest a dipper. The two end stars of the Big Dipper are in a line with the North Star. Compare **Little Dipper.**

Big Four the United States, the United Kingdom, France, and the Soviet Union.

big game 1 large animals sought by hunters. Elephants, tigers, lions, moose, and elk are big game. 2 a very important thing that is sought.

big·gie (big'ē) *n. Slang.* a person or thing that is very important, influential, etc.: *Her next film promises to be a biggie.*

big gun *Slang.* an important or high-ranking person: *They brought in a couple of big guns from Toronto to negotiate the deal.*

big–head (big'hed') *n.* 1 any of several diseases of animals, especially sheep, characterized by swelling about the head. 2 infectious sinusitis in turkeys. 3 Also, **big head,** *Informal.* **a** a swelled head; conceit. **b** a conceited or arrogant person.

big–heart·ed (big'här'tid) *adj.* kindly; generous.

big–horn (big'hôrn') *n., pl.* **big·horn** or **big·horns.** a large, heavy-bodied wild mountain sheep (*Ovis canadensis*) found mainly in the Rocky Mountains, brown with a white muzzle and rump patch, having long, slender legs and huge brown horns that curl back and down from the forehead.

bight (bīt) *n.* 1 a long curve in a coastline, mountain range, etc. 2 bay. 3 a bend; angle; corner. 4 a loop of rope; the slack of rope between the fastened ends. 5 the width of sewing-machine stitch selected for making a buttonhole. [OE *byht*]
☛ *Hom.* bite.

big league 1 major league. 2 Often, **big leagues,** *pl.* the group, place, etc. that is recognized as the best and has the most power and influence within its sphere: *The star of the new musical is definitely from the big leagues.* —**big'-leagu'er,** *n.* —**big'-league',** *adj.*

big noise *Slang.* an important person; bigwig.

big·no·ni·a (big nō'nē ə) *n.* any of a genus (*Bignonia*) of mainly tropical American woody vines of the trumpet-creeper family, having compound leaves and trumpet- shaped flowers. [< NL, named after Abbé *Bignon,* librarian to Louis XIV]

big·ot (big'ət) *n.* a bigoted person; an intolerant, prejudiced person. [< F]

big·ot·ed (big'ət id) *adj.* sticking to an opinion, belief, party, etc. unreasonably and without tolerating other views; intolerant. —**big'ot·ed·ly,** *adv.*

big·ot·ry (big'ət rē) *n., pl.* **-ries.** bigoted conduct or attitude; intolerance.

big shot *Slang. n.* an important person; a big wheel. —**big'shot',** *adj.*

big time *Slang.* in public affairs, the arts, sports, etc., the top level of advancement or achievement. —**big'time',** *adj.*

big tree a giant coniferous tree (*Sequoiadendron giganteum*) found in California, not generally quite so tall as the redwood, but having a thicker trunk (the trunk of one specimen has a diameter of 10 m at the base).

big wheel *Informal.* an important and influential person, as in a particular organization, etc.: *He's a big wheel in publishing.*

big·wig (big'wig') *n. Informal.* an important person.

bi·jou (bē'zhü) *n., pl.* **-joux** (-zhüz). 1 a jewel. 2 something small and fine. [< F]

bi·ju·gate (bī'jə gāt' *or* bī jü'gāt) *adj. Botany.* having two pairs of leaflets. [< *bi-* two + L *jugatus* yoked]

bike (bīk) *n., v.* **biked, bik·ing.** —*v.* 1 bicycle. 2 motorcycle. —*v.* ride a bike. —**bik'er,** *n.* [< *bicycle*]

bi·ki·ni (bi kē'nē) *n.* a very brief, two-piece swimsuit for women

and girls. [< *Bikini,* an atoll in the Marshall Islands in the W Pacific Ocean, site of a series of U.S. atomic bomb tests]

bi·la·bi·al (bī lā'bē əl) *adj., n.* —*adj.* 1 having two lips. 2 *Phonetics.* produced by closing or nearly closing the lips: M, p, *and* b *are bilabial consonants.* —*n. Phonetics.* a bilabial speech sound.

bi·la·bi·ate (bī lā'bē āt' *or* bī lā'bē it) *adj. Botany.* having an upper and lower lip.

bi·lat·er·al (bī lat'ər əl) *adj.* 1 having two sides. 2 on two sides: *Symmetry on both sides of an axis is bilateral symmetry.* 3 affecting or influencing two sides equally: *a bilateral treaty.* —**bi·lat'er·al·ly,** *adv.*

bil·ber·ry (bil'ber'ē *or* bil'bər ē) *n., pl.* **-ries.** 1 any of several shrubs (genus *Vaccinium*) of the heath family, closely related to the blueberries, but having flowers that grow singly or in very small clusters. 2 the sweet, edible, bluish or blackish berry of any of these shrubs. [apparently Scand.; cf. Danish *böllebær*]

bil·bo (bil'bō) *n., pl.* **-boes.** *Archaic.* 1 Usually, **bilboes,** *pl.* a long iron bar with sliding shackles and a lock, formerly used to confine the feet of prisoners. 2 a sword. [apparently short for *Bilboa,* English name for Bilbao, a Spanish town, famous for its ironworks and steel]

bile (bil) *n.* 1 a bitter, yellow or greenish liquid secreted by the liver and stored in the gall bladder. It is discharged into the small intestine, where it aids digestion by neutralizing acids and emulsifying fats. 2 ill humor; anger. [< F < L *bilis*]

bilge (bilj) *n., v.* **bilged, bilg·ing.** —*n.* 1 the lowest part of a ship's hold; bottom of a ship's hull. 2 bilge water. 3 the bulging part of a barrel. 4 *Informal.* nonsense.
—*v.* 1 break in (the bottom of a ship). 2 spring a leak in the bilge. 3 come to rest or settle on the bilge. 4 bulge; swell out. [origin uncertain]

bilge water the dirty water that collects by seeping or leaking in the bottom of a ship or boat.

bil·har·zi·a (bil här'zē ə *or* -härt'sē ə) *n.* 1 a serious, debilitating disease of man in tropical and subtropical regions caused by a parasitic flatworm, a blood fluke, which is picked up in water as a tiny larva that burrows through the skin and enters the bloodstream; schistosomiasis. 2 any of a genus (*Schistosoma*) of flatworms causing this disease; schistosome.

bil·har·zi·a·sis (bil'här zī'ə sis *or* -härt sī'ə sis) *n.* bilharzia (def. l).

bil·i·ar·y (bil'ē er'ē) *adj.* 1 of bile. 2 carrying bile. 3 caused by trouble with the bile; bilious.

bi·lin·e·ar (bī lin'ē ər) *adj.* of, having to do with, or involving two lines.

bi·lin·gual (bī ling'gwəl *or* bī ling'gyə wəl) *adj., n.* —*adj.* 1 able to speak two languages, especially with the fluency of a native speaker. 2 of, containing, or written or expressed in two languages: *a bilingual dictionary, a bilingual meeting.* 3 *Cdn.* **a** able to speak both English and French. **b** having to do with or catering to speakers of both English and French: *bilingual courts, a bilingual hospital.*
—*n.* a bilingual person. [< L *bilinguis* speaking two languages < *bi-* two + *lingua* language] —**bi·lin'gual·ly,** *adv.*

bi·lin·gual·ism (bī ling'gwə liz'əm *or* bī ling'gyə wəl iz'əm) *n.* 1 the ability to speak two languages, especially with the fluency of a native speaker. 2 *Cdn.* the ability to speak both English and French. 3 the principle that two languages should enjoy equal status in a country, province, etc.

bi·lin·gual·ize (bī ling'gwə līz *or* bī ling'gyə wə līz') *v.* **-ized, -iz·ing.** *Cdn.* make bilingual: *to bilingualize the public service.* —**bi·lin'gual·i·za'tion,** *n.*

bil·ious (bil'yəs) *adj.* 1 having to do with bile. 2 suffering from or caused by some trouble with the bile or the liver: *a bilious person, a bilious attack.* 3 peevish; cross; bad-tempered. [< L *biliosus < bilis* bile] —**bil'ious·ly,** *adv.* —**bil'ious·ness,** *n.*

bilk (bilk) *v., n.* —*v.* 1 avoid payment of. 2 defraud; cheat; deceive. —*n.* 1 a fraud; deception. 2 a person who avoids paying his bills; petty swindler. [origin uncertain] —**bilk'er,** *n.*

bill¹ (bil) *n., v.* —*n.* 1 a list or statement showing an amount of money owed for work done or things supplied; an account: *We got the bill yesterday.* 2 the amount of money shown on such a statement: *Our phone bill was high last month.* 3 a piece of paper money: *a dollar bill.* 4 a written or printed public notice; advertisement; poster; handbill. 5 a written or printed statement; list of items: *a bill of fare.* 6 a theatre program. 7 the entertainment in a theatre. 8 a proposed law presented to a lawmaking body for its approval. In Canada, a bill becomes an act if it receives a majority vote in Parliament. 9 a bill of exchange. 10 a written request or complaint presented to a court.
fill the bill, *Informal.* satisfy requirements.
foot the bill, *Informal.* pay; settle the bill.

—v. **1** send a statement of charges to: *The store will bill us on the first of the month.* **2** enter or charge in a bill. **3** advertise or announce through public notices or posters: *It was billed as the greatest show on earth.* **4** list on a theatrical program, poster, etc.: *He was billed as the star.* [ME *bille,* Anglo-L *billa,* alteration of Med.L *bulla* document, seal, bull². See BULL².] —**bill′er,** *n.*

bill² (bil) *n., v.* —*n.* **1** the horny part of the jaws of a bird; beak. **2** a mouth part shaped like a bird's bill: *the bill of a turtle.* —*v.* **1** of doves, etc., touch or rub bills.

bill and coo, kiss, caress, and talk as lovers do. [OE *bile*]

bill³ (bil) *n.* **1** a spear with a hook-shaped blade. **2** a billhook; tool for pruning or cutting. [OE *bil*]

bil·la·bong (bil′ə bong′) *n. Australian.* **1** a branch of a river flowing away from the main stream. **2** a backwater; stagnant pool. [native Australian name < *billa* river + *bung* dual]

bill·board (bil′bôrd′) *n.* a large board, usually outdoors, on which advertisements or notices are displayed.

billed (bild) *adj.* having a bill or beak.

bil·let¹ (bil′it) *n., v.* **-let·ed, -let·ing.** —*n.* **1** a written order to provide board and lodging for troops, especially in a private home. **2** a place where a person is assigned to be lodged, especially as a guest in a private home: *We will require twenty billets for the visiting team.* **3** a job; position. —*v.* assign to lodging by billet or as a guest in a private home. [ME *billette,* dim. of *bille* bill¹]

bil·let² (bil′it) *n.* **1** a thick stick of wood, such as firewood. **2** a bar of iron or steel. [< F *billette,* dim. of *bille* log, tree trunk]

bil·let–doux (bil′ē dü′; *French,* bē ye dü′) *n., pl.* **bil·lets–doux** (bil′ē düz′; *French,* bē ye dü′). a love letter. [< F]

bill·fold (bil′fōld′) *n.* a folding case for carrying money, paper, etc.; wallet.

bill·head (bil′hed′) *n.* **1** a sheet of paper with the name and the address of a business firm printed at the top, used in making out bills. **2** the name and address of a business firm printed at the top of a sheet of paper.

bill·hook (bil′hůk′) *n.* a tool with a hooked blade, used for pruning or cutting.

bil·liard (bil′yərd) *adj., n.* —*adj.* of or for billiards. —*n. Billiards.* a score made by striking one ball so that it hits the other two; carom.

bil·liards (bil′yərdz) *n.* a game played with two white balls and a red one on a special table. A long stick called a cue is used to hit the balls. [< F *billard(s),* dim. of *bille* log, tree trunk]

bill·ing (bil′ing) *n.* **1** on a playbill or similar advertisement: **a** the order in which the names of the performers, acts, etc. are listed. **b** the position in such a listing: *She received star billing.* **2** a listing of the total amount of money owed by a client or customer: *They thought the company's billings were too high.*

bil·lings·gate (bil′ingz gāt′) *n,* vulgar, abusive language. [< *Billingsgate,* a fish market in London, England, once notorious for the abusive language used by the fish-sellers]

bil·lion (bil′yən) *n. or adj.* **1** in Canada, the United States, and France, a thousand million; 1 000 000 000. **2** in Britain and Germany, a million million; 1 000 000 000 000. [< F *billion* < *bi-* two (i.e., to the second power) + m*illion* million]

bil·lion·aire (bil′yən er′) *n.* a person whose wealth adds up to at least a billion dollars, pounds, marks, francs, etc.

bil·lionth (bil′yənth) *adj., n.* —*adj.* last in a series of a billion. —*n.* one of a billion equal parts.

bill of attainder *Historical.* an act of a lawmaking body that deprives a person of property and civil rights because of a sentence of death or outlawry.

bill of exchange a written instruction to pay a certain sum of money to a specified person.

bill of fare a list of the articles of food served at a meal or of those that can be ordered; menu.

bill of goods a shipment of merchandise.

sell a bill of goods, *Slang.* mislead or seek to mislead.

bill of health a certificate stating whether or not there are infectious diseases on a ship or in the port which the ship is leaving. A ship is not allowed to dock unless it has a clean bill of health from the port it left last.

clean bill of health, a a bill of health showing absence of infectious diseases. **b** *Informal.* a clean record; a favorable report.

bill of lading a receipt given by a shipping or express company, etc. showing a list of goods delivered to it for transportation.

bill of rights **1** a statement of the fundamental rights of the people of a nation. **2 Bill of Rights, a** in Canada, a statement of human rights and fundamental freedoms enacted by Parliament in 1960. **b** in the United Kingdom, a declaration of rights and liberties, which also established the succession to the throne, enacted under

hat, āge, fär; let, ēqual, tèrm; it, īce
hot, ōpen, ôrder; oil, out; cup, pût, rüle,
ǝbove, takǝn, pencǝl, lemǝn, circǝs

ch, child; ng, long; sh, ship
th, thin; ŦH, then; zh, measure

William III in 1689, **c** in the United States, the first ten amendments to the Constitution.

bill of sale a written statement transferring ownership of something from the seller to the buyer.

bil·low (bil′ō) *n., v.* —*n.* **1** a great wave or surge of the sea. **2** any great wave: *billows of smoke.* —*v.* **1** rise or roll, as big waves. **2** swell or bulge out, especially from the action of the wind: *skirts billowing in the wind.* [< ON *bylgja*]

bil·low·y (bil′ō ē) *adj.* **-low·i·er, -low·i·est. 1** rising or rolling in big waves. **2** swelling out; bulging.

bill·post·er (bil′pōs′tǝr) *n.* a person whose work is putting up advertisements or notices in public places.

bil·ly¹ (bil′ē) *n., pl.* **-lies.** a small club or stick, especially one carried by a police officer; truncheon. [< *billet²*]

bil·ly² (bil′ē) *n., pl.* **-lies.** billycan.

bil·ly·can (bil′ē kan′) *n.* a can or metal pot used for boiling water, especially over a camp fire, or for holding hot liquids, etc. [< native Australian *billa-* water + E *can*]

billy goat *Informal.* a male goat.

bil·tong (bil′tong) *n.* in South Africa, strips of dried lean meat of antelope, buffalo, etc. [< Afrikaans *biltong < bil* buttock + *tong* tongue]

bi·me·tal·lic (bī′mǝ tal′ik) *adj.* **1** using two metals. **2** of or based on bimetallism.

bi·met·al·lism (bī met′ǝl iz′ǝm) *n.* the use of gold and silver together, at a fixed ratio, as the standard of value for the currency of a country.

bi·mo·lec·u·lar (bī′mǝ lek′yǝ lǝr) *adj.* having to do with, or formed from, two molecules.

bi·month·ly (bī munth′lē) *adj., adv., n., pl.* **-lies.** —*adj.*
1 happening once every two months: *bimonthly meetings.*
2 happening twice a month.
—*adv.* **1** once every two months: *The magazine is published bimonthly.* **2** twice a month.
—*n.* a periodical published bimonthly.
☛ *Usage.* **Bimonthly, biweekly,** and **biyearly** originally meant 'every two months', etc. but are now often used to mean 'twice a month', etc. To avoid confusion, use *semi-monthly* or *twice a month* for one meaning and *every two months* for the other. However, **biannual** has only the one meaning: 'twice a year'. The word for 'every two years' is **biennial**.

bin (bin) *n., v.* —*n.* a box or enclosed place for holding grain, coal, etc. —*v.* put or store in a bin. [OE *binn*]
☛ *Hom.* **been.**

bi·na·ry (bī′nǝ rē) *adj., n., pl.* **-ries.** —*adj.* **1** having to do with, consisting of, or involving two; dual. **2** *Mathematics, Computer technology.* of, having to do with, using, or expressed in binary digits: *Binary notation is a number system used in computers.* —*n.* **1** something composed of two parts or things. **2** *Mathematics, Computer technology.* a number expressed in binary notation. [< L *binarius < bini* two at a time]

binary digit either of the digits 0 or 1, serving as the basic unit of information in a digital computing system. The two digits can be represented as the *off* and *on* states of an electric circuit. Also called **bit.**

binary scale a numerical system having a base of 2 rather than 10, so that 1 of the ordinary scale is expressed as 1, 2 as 10, 3 as 11, 4 as 100, and so on. It is used especially in digital computers.

binary star a pair of stars that revolve around a common centre of gravity, often appearing as a single object.

bi·nate (bī′nāt) *adj. Botany.* growing in pairs; double. [< NL *binatus < L bini* two at a time]

bin·aur·al (bin ôr′ǝl *or* bīn ôr′ǝl) *adj.* **1** of, for, or having to do with both ears: *a binaural stethoscope.* **2** of or having to do with two speakers, etc.; stereophonic: *binaural broadcasting.* **3** having two ears.

bind (bīnd) *v.* **bound, bind·ing;** *n.* —*v.* **1** tie together; hold together; fasten: *She bound the package with a bright ribbon.* **2** stick together. **3** hold by some force; restrain. **4** hold by a promise, love, duty, etc.; obligate: *in duty bound to help.* **5** put under legal obligation: *bound over to keep the peace.* **6** put under legal obligation to serve as an apprentice: *bound out to be a carpenter.* **7** put a bandage on: *bind up a wound.* **8** put a band or wreath around. **9** put a border or edge on to strengthen or

ornament. **10** tie up for the sake of appearance or convenience: *She bound her hair with red ribbons.* **11** fasten (sheets of paper) into a cover; put a cover on (a book): *The pages were bound into a small book.* **12** constipate.

bind hand and foot, a tie up thoroughly. **b** restrict or constrain without choice or freedom: *The strict contract bound us hand and foot.*

—*n.* **1** anything that binds or ties. **2** *Music.* a slur; tie. **3** *Informal.* something annoying; a nuisance. [OE *bindan*]

bind·er (bīn′dər) *n.* **1** a person who binds, especially a bookbinder. **2** anything that ties or holds together. **3** a cover for holding loose sheets of paper together. **4** a machine that cuts stalks of grain and ties them in bundles.

binder twine *Cdn.* a strong, coarse string used especially for binding up grain into sheaves.

bind·er·y (bīn′dər ē or bīn′drē) *n., pl.* **-er·ies.** a place where books are bound.

bind·ing (bīn′ding) *n., adj.* —*n.* **1** the covering of a book. **2** a strip protecting or ornamenting an edge: *Binding is sometimes used on the seams of dresses.* **3** the foot fastenings on a ski. —*adj.* **1** that binds, fastens, or connects. **2** having force or power to hold to some agreement, pledge, etc.; obligatory: *a binding contract.* —**bind′ing·ly,** *adv.*

binding energy *Physics.* the energy necessary to break a particular atomic nucleus into its smaller component particles.

bin·dle (bin′dəl) *n. Slang.* a bundle of clothing, toilet articles, etc., usually tied to a stick carried by a hobo over his shoulder. [? < *bundle*]

bin·dle·stiff (bin′dəl stif′) *n. Slang.* hobo.

bind·weed (bīnd′wēd′) *n.* any of various plants that twine around other plants or a support, especially any of several species (genus *Convolvulus*) in the morning-glory family, such as the **hedge bindweed** (*C. sepium*), or any of several species (genus *Polygonum*) of the buckwheat family, such as **black bindweed** (*P. convolvulus*).

binge (binj) *n. Slang.* **1** a heavy drinking session. **2** a bout or spree of indulgence in anything. [< dial. E *binge* to soak]

bin·go (bing′gō) *n., interj.* —*n.* **1** a game of chance in which each player has a card with randomly numbered squares, which he covers with markers as the numbers are drawn and called out by a caller. **2** an event at which people play bingo for prizes: *They held a bingo to raise money.* —*interj.* the word called out by the winner of a game of bingo. [origin uncertain]

bin·na·cle (bin′ə kəl) *n.* a box or stand that contains a ship's compass, placed near the man who is steering. [alteration of *bittacle* < Sp. *bitácula* or Pg. *bitácola* < L *habitaculum* dwelling place < *habitare* dwell]

bin·o·cle (bin′ə kəl) *n.* a telescope or field glass for both eyes.

bi·noc·u·lar (bə nok′yə lər or bī nok′yə lər) *adj., n.* —*adj.* of, having to do with, using, or for both eyes. —*n.* Usually, **binoculars,** *pl.* a double telescope joined as a unit for use with both eyes: *Field glasses and opera glasses are binoculars.* [< L *bini* two at a time + *oculi* eyes].

bi·no·mi·al (bī nō′mē əl) *adj., n.* —*adj.* consisting of two terms. —*n.* **1** *Mathematics.* an expression consisting of two terms connected by a plus or minus sign. **2** *Biology.* a two-part name by which a plant or animal is identified according to an international system of classification. The binomial of the North American beaver is *Castor canadensis.* [< LL *binomius* having two names + *bi-* two + *nomen* name] —**bi·no′mi·al·ly,** *adv.*

binomial theorem *Mathematics.* an algebraic system, invented by Sir Isaac Newton, for raising a binomial to any power. *Example:* $(a + b)^2 = a^2 + 2ab + b^2$

bi·nom·i·nal (bī nom′ə nəl) *adj.* having or using two names. Scientific classification by genus and species uses a binominal system.

bio– *combining form.* **1** life; living things: *biology = the science of life.* **2** biological: *biochemistry = biological chemistry.*

bi·o·chem·i·cal (bī′ō kem′ə kəl) *adj.* of or having to do with biochemistry. —**bi·o·chem′i·cal·ly,** *adv.*

bi·o·chem·ist (bī′ō kem′ist) *n.* a person trained in biochemistry, especially one whose work it is.

bi·o·chem·is·try (bī′ō kem′is trē) *n.* the chemistry of living animals and plants; biological chemistry.

bi·o·de·grad·a·ble (bī′ō di grā′də bəl) *adj.* capable of being broken down, or decomposed, by a natural process such as the action of bacteria: *Plastic containers are not biodegradable.*

bi·o·dyne (bī′ə dīn′) *n.* a substance, produced by an injured cell, that aids recovery by promoting growth, reproduction, etc. It is

similar in effect to a hormone. [< *bio-* + *-dyne* < Gk. *dynamis* power]

bi·o·feed·back (bī′ō fēd′bak′) *n.* the technique of controlling normally involuntary or unconscious body processes, such as heartbeat, body temperature, or blood pressure, by making them perceptible to the senses, often with the aid of electronic devices, and then using mental concentration to manipulate them.

biog. biographical; biography.

bi·o·gas (bī′ō gas′) *n.* a gas, such as methane, produced from the fermentation of animal dung and vegetable waste, especially for use as fuel.

bi·o·gen·e·sis (bī′ō jen′ə sis) *n.* **1** the theory that living things can be produced only by other living things. **2** the production of living things from other living things.

bi·o·ge·net·ic (bī′ō jə net′ik) *adj.* of or having to do with biogenesis.

bi·o·ge·og·ra·phy (bī′ō jē og′rə fē) *n.* the branch of biology that deals with the geographical distribution of plants and animals.

bi·og·ra·pher (bī og′rə fər) *n.* a person who writes a biography.

bi·o·graph·ic (bī′ə graf′ik) *adj.* biographical.

bi·o·graph·i·cal (bī′ə graf′ə kəl) *adj.* **1** of a person's life: *biographical information.* **2** having to do with biography. —**bi·o·graph′i·cal·ly,** *adv.*

bi·og·ra·phy (bī og′rə fē) *n., pl.* **-phies. 1** the written story of a person's life. **2** the part of literature that consists of biographies.

bi·o·log·ic (bī′ə loj′ik) *adj.* biological.

bi·o·log·i·cal (bī′ə loj′ə kəl) *adj., n.* —*adj.* **1** of plant and animal life. **2** having to do with biology. —*n.* a drug prepared from animal tissue or some other living source. —**bi·o·log′i·cal·ly,** *adv.*

biological clock a hypothetical mechanism inherent in living things that is responsible for various periodic physiological processes or responses, especially those synchronized to the cycle of day and night. It is the human biological clock that is responsible for the feeling known as jet lag.

biological warfare the waging of war by using disease-producing bacteria or other micro-organisms to destroy crops, livestock, or human life.

bi·ol·o·gist (bī ol′ə jist) *n.* a person trained in biology, especially one whose work it is.

bi·ol·o·gy (bī ol′ə jē) *n.* **1** the science of life or living matter in all its forms and phenomena; the study of the origin, reproduction, structure, etc. of plant and animal life. **2** the plant and animal life of a particular area or region. **3** the biological facts about a particular plant or animal. **4** a textbook or handbook dealing with biology.

bi·o·mass (bī′ō mas′) *n.* **1** the total amount or mass of living organisms in a given area: *the biomass of plankton.* **2** organic waste.

bi·ome (bī′ōm) *n.* an extensive ecological community, especially one having one dominant type of vegetation: *the tundra biome.*

bi·o·me·chan·ics (bī′ō mə kan′iks) *n.* the science that deals with the effects of forces on a living organism, especially the effects of gravity.

bi·o·met·rics (bī′ə met′riks) *n.* biometry (def. 2).

bi·om·e·try (bī om′ə trē) *n.* **1** the calculation of the probable duration of human life. **2** the branch of biology that deals with living things by measurements and statistics. [< Gk. *bios* life + E *-metry*]

bi·on·ic (bī on′ik) *adj.* **1** of or having to do with bionics. **2** in science fiction, designating a person, etc. having certain physiological parts or functions replaced or strengthened by electronic equipment.

bi·on·ics (bī on′iks) *n. (used with a singular verb).* the study of human and animal biological functions, especially functions of the brain, that might be applied to the development of electronic equipment, such as computers.

bi·o·phys·i·cal (bī′ō fiz′ə kəl) *adj.* of or having to do with biophysics.

bi·o·phys·i·cist (bī′ō fiz′ə sist) *n.* a person trained in biophysics, especially one whose work it is.

bi·o·phys·ics (bī′ō fiz′iks) *n. (used with a singular verb)* the science dealing with the application of the principles of physics to biology and biological problems.

bi·op·sy (bī′op sē) *n., pl.* **-sies.** the removal and examination of tissue taken from a living person or animal as an aid to medical diagnosis. A biopsy is often done to find out if cancer cells are present in a particular part of the body. Compare **autopsy.** [< *bio-* + Gk. *opsis* a viewing]

bi·o·sphere (bī′əs fēr′) *n.* the parts of the earth and its atmosphere in which living things are found.

bi·ot·ic (bī ot′ik) *adj.* of or having to do with life or living things. [< Gk. *biōtikos* < *bios* life]

bi·o·tin (bī′ə tin) *n.* a colourless crystalline vitamin of the B

complex that promotes growth and is found especially in yeast, liver, and egg yolk. *Formula*: $C_{10}H_{16}N_2O_3S$ [< Gk. *biotos* life + E -*in*]

bi·o·tite (bī'ə tīt') *n.* black or dark-colored mica. [after J. B. Biot, French mineralogist]

bip·a·rous (bip'ər əs) *adj.* **1** of animals, bringing forth two at a birth. **2** of flower clusters, having two axes or branches. [< *bi-* two + L *parere* to produce + E -*ous*]

bi·par·ti·san (bī pär'tə zən *or* bī pär'tə zan') *adj.* of or representing two political parties: *Bipartisan foreign policy has the support of the two main political parties of a nation.*

bi·par·tite (bī pär'tīt) *adj.* **1** having or consisting of two parts: *An oyster has a bipartite shell.* **2** *Botany.* divided into two parts nearly to the base: *a bipartite leaf.* [< L *bipartitus*, pp. of *bipartire* < *bi-* two + *partire* divide]

bi·par·ty (bī'pär'tē) *adj.* combining two different political groups, religious groups, etc.

bi·ped (bī'ped) *n., adj.* —*n.* an animal having two feet. Birds are bipeds. —*adj.* having two feet. [< L *bipes* < *bi-* two + *pes, pedis* foot]

bi·pet·al·ous (bī pet'əl əs) *adj. Botany.* having two petals.

bi·phen·yl (bī'fen'əl *or* -fē'nəl) *n.* a colorless, crystalline hydrocarbon used especially as a heat-transfer agent and fungicide and in the manufacture of dyes. *Formula*: $C_6H_5C_6H_5$

bi·pin·nate (bī pin'āt) *adj. Botany.* doubly pinnate. A leaf with leaflets on each side of a stalk is pinnate; a pinnate leaf with pinnate leaflets is bipinnate.

bi·plane (bī'plān') *n.* an airplane having two wings, one above the other.

bi·po·lar (bī pō'lər) *adj.* **1** of, having to do with, or occurring in both polar regions. **2** of or at both poles.

bi·ra·cial (bī rā'shəl) *adj.* of or having to do with two races: *a biracial community.*

birch (bėrch) *n., v.* —*n.* **1** any of a genus (*Betula*) of trees and shrubs found in the northern hemisphere, having light green oval or triangular leaves and usually light-colored, smooth outer bark that in many species peels off easily in thin layers. **2** the hard, close-grained wood of a birch, often used in making furniture. **3** (*adj.*) made of this wood: *a birch chair.* **4** a bundle of birch twigs or a birch stick, used for flogging. **5** (*adj.*) designating a family (Betulaceae) of deciduous trees and shrubs found mainly in the northern hemisphere, having simple, serrate leaves that grow alternately along the stems, and flowers in drooping catkins. Alders, hazelnuts, and birches belong to the birch family. —*v.* whip with a birch; flog. [OE *bierce*]

birch·bark (bėrch'bärk') *n.* **1** the bark of a birch, especially the white, or paper, birch. Birchbark was traditionally used by North American Indian peoples of the eastern woodlands to make canoes. **2** (*adj.*) made of or covered with birchbark: *a birchbark torch, a birchbark canoe.* **3** a canoe made of birchbark.

bird (bėrd) *n., v.* —*n.* **1** any of a class (Aves) of warm-blooded, egg-laying vertebrates having a body covered with feathers, and forelimbs modified into wings by means of which most species can fly. All birds have keen vision. **2** a bird hunted for sport; game bird. **3** *Informal.* a shuttlecock. **4** *Informal.* person: *He's a strange bird.* **5** *Brit. Slang.* a girl or young woman. **6** *Slang.* ballistic missile. **7** clay pigeon. **bird in the hand,** something certain because one already has it. **birds of a feather,** people with the same kind of ideas or interests. **for the birds,** not worth considering; ridiculous, boring, etc.: *The movie was for the birds. I think house cleaning is for the birds.* **give (someone) the bird,** jeer or ridicule someone. **kill two birds with one stone,** get two things done by one action. —*v.* engage in bird-watching. [OE *bridd*, bird] —**bird'like'**, *adj.* —**bird'er**, *n.*

bird·bath (bėrd'bath') *n.* a shallow basin raised off the ground and filled with water for birds to bathe in or drink from.

bird·brain (bėrd'brān') *n. Slang.* a stupid or scatterbrained person.

bird call 1 a sound that a bird makes. **2** an imitation of it. **3** an instrument for imitating the sound that a bird makes.

bird dog *n., v.* —*n.* **1** any of several breeds of dogs trained to locate game birds and to bring them back to the hunter after they have been shot. The various breeds of setter and retriever are usually trained as bird dogs. **2** *Informal.* a person whose work is seeking something for someone else, such as a talent scout or canvasser. —*v. Informal.* **1** pursue or follow closely. **2** look for new talent, prospective candidates, etc.

bird·house (bėrd'hous') *n.* a small roofed box with one or more openings, placed on a pole, in a tree, etc., for wild birds to nest in.

bird·ie (bėr'dē) *n.* **1** a little bird. **2** *Golf.* a score of one stroke less than par for any hole on a golf course.

bird·lime (bėrd'līm') *n., v.* -limed, -lim·ing. —*n.* **1** a sticky

hat, āge, fär; let, ēqual, tėrm; it, īce
hot, ōpen, ôrder; oil, out; cup, put, rüle,
əbove, takən, pencəl, lemən, circəs

ch, child; ng, long; sh, ship
th, thin; ͫH, then; zh, measure

substance smeared on trees to catch small birds. It is often made from the inner bark of holly or mistletoe. **2** anything that ensnares. —*v.* **1** smear with birdlime; lime. **2** catch (birds) with birdlime.

bird·man (bėrd'man') *n., pl.* -**men**. *Informal.* **1** an aviator. **2** a person who catches or sells birds; fowler. **3** one who studies birds; ornithologist.

bird of ill omen 1 a person who is always bringing bad luck. **2** an unlucky person.

bird of paradise any of about 40 species of songbird (family Paradiseidae) of New Guinea and nearby islands, the male of many species having vividly-colored plumes which it displays in elaborate rituals during the mating season. The largest of these birds is the cinnamon-colored great bird of paradise (*Paradisaea apoda*), having a yellow and emerald-green head and long, pale-yellow plumes rising over the back.

bird–of–paradise flower any of a genus (*Strelitzia*) of tropical African plants of the banana family, especially *S. reginae*, having large, showy, orange-and-purple blossoms resembling an exotic bird in flight.

bird of passage 1 a bird that flies from one region to another as the seasons change. **2** *Informal.* a person who roams from place to place.

bird of peace a dove.

bird of prey any of many species of bird that kill animals and other birds for food. Eagles, hawks, and owls are birds of prey.

bird·seed (bėrd'sēd') *n.* a mixture of small seeds used to feed birds.

bird's-eye (bėrdz'ī') *n.* **1** an allover woven pattern for cloth, consisting of small diamonds, each having a dot in the centre. **2** cloth of cotton, linen, or synthetic fibres woven with such a pattern. **3** any of various plants (especially of genera *Primula* and *Veronica*) having small, round, bright-colored flowers. **4** in wood, a small spot resembling birds' eye. **5** (*adj.*) having markings resembling birds' eyes.

bird's-eye view 1 a view from above or from a distance: *You get a bird's-eye view of the town from that hill.* **2** a general or overall view: *This summary will give you a bird's-eye view of the project.*

bird shot a small size of lead shot, used in shooting birds.

bird–watch (bėrd'woch') *v.* observe and study wild birds in their natural surroundings. [back formation < *bird watcher*]

bird–watch·er (bėrd'woch'ər) *n.* a person for whom bird watching is a pastime.

bird–watch·ing (bėrd'woch'ing) *n.* the observation and study of wild birds in their natural surroundings.

bi·reme (bī'rēm) *n.* in ancient times, a ship with two rows of oars on each side, one above the other. [< L *biremis* < *bi-* two + *remus* oar]

bi·ret·ta (bə ret'ə) *n.* a stiff, square cap having at the top three or four thin, upright pieces radiating out from the centre to the edge. Birettas are worn by Roman Catholic priests on certain occasions. [< Ital. *berretta* < LL *birretum* cap, dim. of L *birrus* cloak]

birl (bėrl) *v.* **1** rotate a log in the water by moving the feet while standing on it. **2** spin rapidly. —**birl·er**, *n.* [< *birr*, influenced by *whirl*]
☛ *Hom.* burl.

birr¹ (bėr) *n., v.* **birred, birr·ing.** —*n. Esp.Scottish.* **1** the force of the wind or of something moving; momentum. **2** vigor. **3** a whirring sound. —*v.* make or move with a whirring sound. [< ON *byrr* favoring wind]
☛ *Hom.* burr.

birr² (bėr) *n.* **1** the basic unit of money in Ethiopia, divided into 100 cents. See table at **money.** **2** a note worth one birr.

birth (bėrth) *n.* **1** a coming into life; a being born: *the birth of a child.* **2** a beginning or origin: *the birth of a nation.* **3** a bringing forth: *the birth of a plan.* **4** natural inheritance: *a musician by birth.* **5** descent; parentage: *She is of Spanish birth. He was a man of humble birth.* **6** noble family or descent: *He is a man of birth and breeding.* **7** *Archaic.* a person that is born or a thing that is produced.

give birth (to), a bear; bring forth. **b** be the origin or cause of.

[ME *birthe*, probably < ON *burthr*]
☛ *Hom.* **berth.**

birth control 1 the control of the birthrate by artificial means. **2** the use of contraceptive methods or devices.

birth·day (bėrth′dā′) *n.* **1** the day on which a person is born. **2** the day on which something began: *July 1, 1867, was the birthday of Canada.* **3** the anniversary of the day on which a person was born, or on which something began.

birthday honors or **honours** in the United Kingdom, the titles and decorations awarded annually by the sovereign on his or her official birthday.

birthday suit a state of nakedness; one's bare skin.

birth·mark (bėrth′märk′) *n.* a congenital spot or mark on the skin.

birth·place (bėrth′plās′) *n.* **1** the place where a person was born. **2** the place of origin.

birth rate the proportion of the number of births per year to the total population or to some other stated number.

birth·right (bėrth′rīt′) *n.* **1** the rights belonging to a boy or man because he is the eldest son. **2** a right enjoyed by a person because he was born in a certain country, or because of any other circumstance about his birth: *"Freedom is our birthright!" he shouted.*

birth·stone (bėrth′stōn′) *n.* a jewel associated with a certain month of the year. It is supposed to bring good luck when worn by a person born in that month.

bis (bis) *adv.* **1** twice; again; encore. **2** *Music.* a direction to repeat a passage. [< L *bis*]

bis·cuit (bis′kit) *n., pl.* **-cuits** or (rarely) **-cuit**; *adj.* —*n.* **1** a kind of bread baked in small, soft cakes, made with baking powder, soda, or yeast. **2** a cracker. **3** pottery or china that has been fired (baked) once but not yet glazed. **4** a pale brown. —*adj.* pale brown. [< OF *bescuit* < *bes* twice (< L *bis*) + *cuit*, pp. of *cuire* cook < L *coquere*]

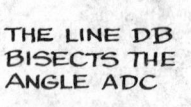
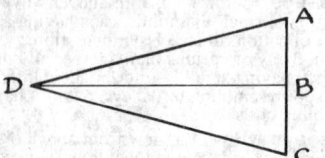

THE LINE DB BISECTS THE ANGLE ADC

bi·sect (bī sekt′) *v.* **1** divide into two parts; halves. **2** *Mathematics.* divide into two equal parts. [< *bi-* two + L *sectus,* pp. of *secare* cut]

bi·sec·tion (bī sek′shən) *n.* **1** the act of bisecting. **2** the place of bisecting. **3** one or two equal parts.

bi·sec·tor (bī sek′tər) *n. Mathematics.* a line that bisects something.

bi·sex·u·al (bī sek′shü əl) *adj., n.* —*adj.* **1** of, having to do with, or involving both sexes. **2** having male and female reproductive organs in one individual. Earthworms are bisexual. **3** sexually attracted to members of both sexes. —*n.* a plant or animal that is bisexual. —**bi·sex′u·al·ly,** *adv.*

bi·sex·u·al·ism (bī sek′shü ə liz′əm) *n.* a bisexual condition or quality.

bi·sex·u·al·i·ty (bī sek′shü al′ə tē) *n.* the quality or state of being bisexual.

bish·op (bish′əp) *n.* **1** in some Christian churches, a high ranking member of the clergy who has certain spiritual duties and who administers the religious affairs of a district called a diocese. **2** *Chess.* one of two pieces held by a player that may be moved diagonally across any number of unoccupied spaces of one color. [OE *bisc(e)op* < VL (*e*)*biscopus,* var. of L *episcopus* < Gk. *episkopos* overseer < *epi-* on, over + *skopos* watcher]

bish·op·ric (bish′əp rik) *n.* **1** the position, office, or rank of bishop. **2** a church district under the charge of a bishop; diocese. [OE *bisceoprīce < bisceop* bishop + *rīce* dominion. See BISHOP.]

bis·muth (biz′məth) *n.* a brittle, reddish-white, metallic chemical element. Some compounds are used in medicine and in alloys. Symbol: Bi; *at.no.* 83; *at.wt.* 208.980. [< G]

bi·son (bī′sən *or* bī′zən) *n., pl.* **-son.** either of two species making up a genus (*Bison*) of bovine animals found in Europe and North America. The North American bison (*Bison bison*) is commonly called a buffalo; the European bison (*Bison bonasus*) is the wisent. [< L < Gmc.]

bisque¹ (bisk) *n.* **1** a thick soup made from shellfish such as crayfish or lobsters, or from the meat of birds or rabbits. **2** a smooth, creamy soup made of strained tomatoes, asparagus, etc. **3** ice cream containing powdered macaroons or crushed nuts. [< F]

bisque² (bisk) *n.* biscuit (def. 3) that is purposely left unglazed, used especially in figurines, dolls, etc. [shortened from *biscuit.* 19c.]

bis·sex·tile (bī seks′til *or* bī seks′təl) *n., adj.* —*n.* leap year. —*adj.* containing the extra day of leap year. February is the bissextile month. [< L *bissextilis* (*annus*) leap (year) < *bis* twice + *sextus* sixth. The Julian calendar added an extra day after the *sixth* day before the calends of March.]

bis·tre (bis′tər) *n.* **1** a dark-brown coloring matter made from soot. **2** a dark brown. Also, **bister.** [< F *bistre*]

bis·tro (bē′strō) *n.* a small restaurant, wine bar, or café. [< F]

bi·sul·phate or **bi·sul·fate** (bī sul′fāt) *n.* a salt of sulphuric acid in which half of the hydrogen is replaced by a metal; acid sulphate.

bi·sul·phide or **bi·sul·fide** (bī sul′fīd *or* bī sul′fid) *n.* disulphide.

bit¹ (bit) *n., v.* **bit·ted, bit·ting.** —*n.* **1** the part of a bridle that goes in a horse's mouth. See **harness** for picture. **2** anything that curbs or restrains. **3** the biting or cutting part of a tool. **4** the part of a drill or similar tool that does the actual drilling or boring. A drill or brace and bit usually has several interchangeable bits. See **brace and bit** for picture. **5** the part of a key that goes into a lock and makes it turn.
take the bit in (one's) **teeth, a** of a horse, bite on the bit so that it cannot be pulled against the soft part of the mouth. **b** take control and act on one's own, especially in an irresponsible or wilful manner: *The young soldier took the bit in his teeth and charged the enemy, despite the order to wait for the lieutenant's signal.* —*v.* **1** put a bit in the mouth of; bridle. **2** curb; restrain. [OE *bite* a bite < *bītan* bite]
☛ *Hom.* **bitt.**

bit² (bit) *n.* **1** a small piece or amount. **2** a small degree or extent: *She wasn't a bit sorry. I'm a bit tired.* **3** bit part. **4** *Informal.* a short time: *Stay a bit longer.* **5** *Informal.* a group of actions, situations, or attitudes associated with a particular role, lifestyle, etc.: *the whole do-it-yourself bit.*
do (one's) **bit,** do one's share.
[OE *bita < bītan* bite]
☛ *Hom.* **bitt.**

bit³ (bit) *v.* pt. and pp. of **bite.**
☛ *Hom.* **bitt.**

bit⁴ (bit) *n.* the basic unit of information in an electronic computer; binary digit. [< *bi*nary dig*it*]
☛ *Hom.* **bitt.**

bitch (bich) *n., v.* —*n.* **1** a female dog, wolf, fox, etc. **2** *Slang.* a malicious, treacherous, or bad-tempered woman. **3** *Slang. Derogatory.* an immoral or lewd woman. **4** *Slang.* anything that is very unpleasant or difficult. —*v. Slang.* **1** complain; grumble: *He's always bitching about something.* **2** *Slang.* botch; bungle (*usually with* **up**). [OE *bicce*]

bitch·y (bich′ē) *adj. Slang.* ill-tempered or malicious. —**bitch′i·ness,** *n.*

bite (bīt) *v.* **bit, bit·ten** or **bit, bit·ing;** *n.* —*v.* **1** seize, cut into, or cut off with the teeth: *to bite into an apple, to bite one's fingernails.* **2** wound with teeth, fangs, or a sting: *That dog won't bite. A mosquito bit me.* **3** cut or pierce, as with a sword or other sharp weapon. **4** nip; snap: *a dog biting at fleas.* **5** cause a sharp, smarting pain to: *His fingers were bitten by frost.* **6** take a tight hold on; grip: *The wheels bite the rails.* **7** take a bait; be caught: *The fish are biting well today.* **8** eat into: *Acid bites metal.*
bite back, hold back (words, temper, etc.) by biting the lips.
bite off more than (one) **can chew,** attempt more than one is able to accomplish.
bite the bullet, brace oneself to confront or accept stoically (from a former practice, in battlefield surgery without anesthetic, of giving the patient a bullet to bite on).
bite the dust, *Informal.* **a** fall dead. **b** be defeated.
—*n.* **1** a piece bitten off; bit of food; mouthful: *Have the whole apple, not just a bite.* **2** a light meal; a snack: *We usually have a bite before going to bed.* **3** the act of biting: *The dog gave a bite or two at the bone.* **4** the result of a bite, wound, sting, etc.: *Mosquito bites itch.* **5** a sharp, smarting pain: *the bite of a cold wind.* **6** a cutting or wounding quality: *the bite of his sarcasm. There was a sharp bite to his humor.* **7** a tight hold or grip: *the bite of train wheels on the rails.* **8** action of acid in eating into a metal, etc. **9** an amount or part taken away: *Hotels took a big bite out of our travel budget.* **10** *Dentistry.* the way in which the upper and lower teeth meet when the mouth is closed naturally; occlusion. Braces are sometimes needed to correct a person's bite.
put the bite on, *Slang.* ask for or demand money from, as a loan or bribe.
[OE *bītan*] —**bit′er,** *n.*
☛ *Hom.* **bight.**

bit·ing (bīt′ing) *adj.* **1** sharp; cutting: *a biting wind.* **2** sarcastic; sneering: *a biting remark.* —**bit′ing·ly,** *adv.*

bit part a small role in a play or film, including some spoken lines.

bitt (bit) *n., v.* —*n.* a strong post on a ship's deck to which ropes, cables, etc. are fastened. —*v.* put (ropes, cables, etc.) around the bitts. [var. of BIT[1]]
☛ *Hom.* bit.

bit·ten (bit′ən) *v.* a pp. of **bite.**

bit·ter (bit′ər) *adj., n.* —*adj.* **1** having a sharp, harsh, unpleasant taste: *bitter medicine. Orange rind is bitter.* **2** unpleasant to the mind or feeling; hard to admit or bear: *a bitter defeat. Failure is bitter.* **3** (*noml.*) **the bitter,** that which is bitter: *You must take the bitter with the sweet.* **4** harsh or cutting: *bitter words.* **5** causing pain; sharp; severe: *a bitter wound, a bitter fight.* **6** of weather, very cold: *a bitter wind.* **7** expressing grief, pain, misery, etc.: *a bitter cry.*
to the bitter end, a until the very last. **b** to death.
—*n.* Brit. a somewhat bitter-tasting draft beer strongly flavored with hops. [OE *biter.* Related to BITE.] —**bit′ter·ly,** *adv.* —**bit′ter·ness,** *n.*

bitter end[1] *Informal.* the very end or last extremity, such as defeat or death.

bitter end[2] the inboard end of a ship's anchoring rope or cable.

bit·tern (bit′ərn) *n.* any of a small subfamily (Botaurinae) of wading birds of the same family as herons, resembling the herons, but having somewhat shorter legs and neck. Bitterns are solitary, secretive birds, seldom seen, but noted for their booming call. [ME < OF *butor*]

bit·ter·root (bit′ər rüt′) *n.* a low-growing herb (*Lewisia rediviva*) of the purslane family found in the Rocky Mountains, having small, fleshy leaves, large, showy pink flowers, and starchy, edible roots.

bit·ters (bit′ərz) *n.pl.* a liquid, usually alcoholic, flavored with some bitter plant. It is sometimes used as medicine.

bit·ter·sweet (bit′ər swēt′) *n., adj.* —*n.* **1** a woody climbing vine (*Solanum dulcamara*) of the nightshade family native to Europe but now common in North America, having clusters of purple flowers and poisonous leaves and poisonous scarlet berries: *The bittersweet is so named because its taste is at first bitter and then sweet.* **2** a North American climbing shrub (*Celastrus scandens*) having greenish-white flowers, short, pointed leaves, and orange berrylike fruits that open when ripe, showing red seeds. **3** sweetness and bitterness mixed.
—*adj.* being bitter and sweet at the same time; especially, being pleasant but including also suffering or regret: *bittersweet memories.*

bi·tu·men (bə tyü′mən, bə tü′mən, *or* bich′yü mən) *n.* **1** a heavy, almost solid form of petroleum occurring in natural deposits, as in the Athabasca tar sands. Bitumen is also often called pitch or asphalt. **2** any of various tarry substances obtained as a residue from the distillation of petroleum, coal tar, etc. [< L]

bi·tu·mi·nous (bə tyü′mə nəs *or* bə tü′mə nəs) *adj.* **1** containing or made with bitumen. **2** like bitumen.

bituminous coal a soft, black type of coal containing less carbon and more moisture than anthracite and burning with a smoky flame. It is the most important and most plentiful type of coal.

bi·va·lence (bī vā′ləns *or* biv′ə ləns) *n.* the quality or condition of being bivalent.

bi·va·lent (bī vā′lənt *or* biv′ə lənt) *adj. Chemistry.* **1** having a valence of two. **2** having two valences. [< *bi-* two + L *valens, -entis,* ppr. of *valere* be worth]

bi·valve (bī′valv′) *n., adj.* —*n.* any of a class (Bivalvia) of molluscs having gills for respiration and a shell consisting of two hinged sections, called valves. Clams, oysters, and mussels are bivalves. —*adj.* **1** having to do with, belonging to, or designating the class Bivalvia. **2** of a seed, etc., having or consisting of two similar parts: *a bivalve seed capsule.*

biv·ou·ac (biv′ü ak′) *n., v.* **-acked, -ack·ing.** —*n.* a temporary camp outdoors without tents or with very small tents as made by soldiers, etc. —*v.* camp outdoors in this way. [< F, probably < G *Beiwacht* additional night guards]

bi·week·ly (bī wēk′lē) *adj., n., pl.* **-lies;** *adv.* —*adj.* **1** happening once every two weeks. **2** happening twice a week; semiweekly. —*n.* a newspaper or magazine published biweekly. —*adv.* **1** once every two weeks. **2** twice a week; semiweekly.
☛ *Usage.* See note at **bimonthly.**

bi·year·ly (bī yēr′lē) *adj. or adv.* **1** once every two years. **2** *Informal.* twice a year; biannual.
☛ *Usage.* See note at **bimonthly.**

biz (biz) *n. Slang.* business: *The magazine biz.*

bi·zarre (bə zär′) *adj.* odd; queer; fantastic; grotesque. [< F <

hat, āge, fär; let, ēqual, tèrm; it, īce
hot, ōpen, ôrder; oil, out; cup, put, rüle,
əbove, takən, pencəl, lemən, circəs
ch, child; ng, long; sh, ship
th, thin; ŦH, then; zh, measure

Sp. *bizarro* brave < Basque *bezar* beard] —**bi·zarre′ly,** *adv.* —**bi·zarre′ness,** *n.*

B.J. Bachelor of Journalism.

bk. **1** bank. **2** book. **3** block.

Bk berkelium.

bkg. banking.

bks. **1** books. **2** barracks.

bkt. **1** basket. **2** bracket.

bl. **1** bale. **2** barrel. **3** blue.

b.l. or **B/L** bill of lading.

blab (blab) *v.* **blabbed, blab·bing;** *n.* —*v.* tell (secrets); talk too much. —*n.* **1** blabbing talk; chatter. **2** a person who blabs. [ME *blabbe*] —**blab′ber,** *n.*

blab·ber·mouth (blab′ər mouth′) *n. Informal.* a person who talks too much, especially one who reveals secrets.

black (blak) *adj., n., v.* —*adj.* **1** of the color of coal or soot; opposite to white: *This print is black.* **2** without any light; very dark: *The room was black as night.* **3** having a dark skin. **4** Often, **Black, a** of, having to do with, or being a black: *a black Trinidadian.* **b** by, for, or about blacks as a group: *black theatre, black studies.* **5** *Archaic.* having dark hair and eyes and, usually, dark skin. **6** covered with dirt, soot, grease, etc.: *The windows facing the highway were black.* **7** dismal; gloomy: *a black day.* **8** sullen; angry: *a black look.* **9** evil; wicked: *black magic.*
—*n.* **1** the color of coal or soot; the opposite of white: *Black is the darkest color; pure black reflects no light.* **2** black coloring matter. **3** black clothes; mourning. **4** Often, **Black,** a member of the African race or a person having some African ancestors. **5** *Archaic.* any person with dark hair, eyes, and skin. **6** *Chess, checkers, or backgammon.* **a** the black or dark-colored pieces. **b** the player holding these pieces. **c** the black or dark-colored squares or other shapes on the board.
in the black, showing a profit, or at least no loss.
—*v.* **1** make or become black. **2** put blacking on boots, shoes, etc. **black out, a** lose consciousness temporarily: *I don't know what happened after that, because I blacked out.* **b** darken completely. **c** hold back; suppress: *The government blacked out all news of the invasion.*
[OE *blæc*] —**black′er,** *n.*

black·a·moor (blak′ə mür′) *n.* a person with dark skin, especially a black African. [var. of *black Moor*]

black–and–blue (blak′ənd blü′) *adj.* severely bruised.

Black and Tan a member of the constabulary force sent to Ireland in 1919-1921 by the British government to put down the rebellion there, so called because members of the force wore a black and tan uniform.

black and white *n., adj.* —*n.* **1** print or writing: *I asked him to put his promise down in black and white.* **2** a drawing, photograph, motion picture, etc. in black, white, and shades of grey rather than in color. **3** (*adj.*) **black-and-white,** designating such a drawing, photograph, etc.: *a black-and-white studio portrait.*
—*adj.* having or showing a tendency to think, respond, etc. in terms of extremes, especially to view things as either all good or all evil: *His whole world is black and white. The book advocates a black-and-white morality.*

black art magic.

black·ball (blak′bol′ *or* -bôl′) *v., n.* —*v.* **1** vote against. **2** ostracize. —*n.* a vote against a person or thing. [from the practice of voting against a candidate by placing a black ball in the ballot box] —**black′ball′er,** *n.*

black bass bass[2] (def. 2).

black bear **1** a North American bear (*Ursus americanus;* formerly *Euarctos americanus*) found in forest regions and swamp areas from Mexico north to the edge of the tundra, about 170 cm long, able to swim and climb well, often climbing trees to eat young buds and fruit and to protect itself against attack. Most black bears are black except for a tan muzzle and a white V on the chest, but much lighter colors occur; cinnamon-colored black bears are common in western Canada. **2** a bear (*Selenarctos thibetanus*) found in the tropical forests of central and E Asia, having a black coat with a white V on the chest.

black belt **1** the highest major level of skill recognized in judo or

karate, symbolized by a black belt or sash. **2** a person who has achieved this level of skill.

black·ber·ry (blak′ber′ē or blak′bər ē) n., pl. **-ries;** v. **-ried, -ry·ing.** —n. **1** the small, black- or dark-purple, edible fruit of various bushes and vines (genus *Rubus*) of the rose family. **2** a bush or vine that produces blackberries. —v. gather blackberries.

black·bird (blak′bėrd′) n. **1** any of several mainly black species of songbird (family Icteridae) ranging in size from about 18 to 33 cm long. Among the species of blackbird found in Canada are the red-winged blackbird, the rusty blackbird, and the common grackle. **2** a European bird (*Turdus merula*) of the thrush family, the male having black feathers and an orange bill, and the female having dusky brown feathers and a dark bill. The blackbird is one of the commonest birds of the British Isles.

black blizzard *Cdn.* on the Prairies, a dust storm.

black·board (blak′bôrd′) n. a dark, smooth surface for writing or drawing on with chalk or crayon.

black book a book containing the names of people to be criticized or punished.

black box *Informal.* any self-contained electronic or automatic device for recording data, controlling a mechanical process, etc. One type is used to detect earthquakes and nuclear explosions.

black bread heavy, coarse, dark rye bread.

black·cap (blak′kap′) n. **1** a black raspberry. **2** a bird whose head has a black top, such as the chickadee.

black·cod (blak′kod′) n. *Cdn.* a large, dark-grey or black fish (*Anoplopoma fimbria*) of the N Pacific coasts, having a slender, streamlined body with two dorsal fins, one behind the other. The blackcod is an important commercial food fish. Also called **sablefish.**

Black Death a violent outbreak of bubonic plague that spread through Asia and Europe in the 14th century. It was at its worst in 1348.

black diamond 1 an opaque, dark type of diamond found chiefly in Brazil. **2 black diamonds,** *pl.* coal.

black·en (blak′ən) v. **-ened, -en·ing. 1** make or become black or very dark. **2** damage the reputation or good name of; defame. —**black′en·er,** n.

black eye 1 a bruise around an eye. **2** *Informal.* **a** a severe blow: *The insult gave his pride a black eye.* **b** a cause of disgrace or discredit. **c** disgrace or discredit: *The substandard housing in that section is a black eye to the whole community.*

black–eyed Su·san (blak′īd sü′zən) either of two North American wildflowers (*Rudbeckia hirta* and *R. serotina*) of the composite family having flower heads with bright golden-yellow ray flowers and a round-topped cluster of dark-brown or purplish disk flowers.

black·face (blak′fās′) n. **1** an actor made up as a caricature of a Negro, especially for a minstrel show. **2** the make-up for such a role. **3** *Printing.* a heavy style of type; boldface.

Black·feet (blak′fēt′) n.pl. Blackfoot confederacy.

black·fish (blak′fish′) n. **1** any of various dark-colored fishes, such as the sea bass, tautog, etc. **2** a small freshwater fish (*Dallia pectoralis*) of Alaska and Siberia having broad, fanlike pectoral fins and a slightly projecting lower jaw. **3** pilot whale.

black flag Jolly Roger.

black–fly (blak′flī′) n., pl. **-flies.** any of many species of small, mostly black or grey fly (family Simuliidae), found throughout the world and having mouth parts adapted for sucking blood. The bite of a black-fly can be very painful.

Black·foot (blak′fùt′) n., pl. **-foot. 1** a member of an Amerindian people of the Plains, one of the three Algonquian tribes forming the Blackfoot confederacy. **2** the Algonquian language spoken by the tribes of the Blackfoot confederacy. [a translation of the tribal name *Siksika*, believed to refer to their moccasins]

Blackfoot confederacy a confederacy of three Algonquian tribes of the Plains, the Blackfoot, Blood, and Piegan.

black–foot·ed ferret (blak′fùt′əd) a mink-sized mammal (*Mustela nigripes*) of the weasel family formerly found throughout the North American grasslands from Texas to the southern Canadian Prairies, having a creamy-white coat with black feet, tail, and face mask. This animal is now extinct in Canada and very rare in the remainder of its range.

Black Friar a Dominican friar.

Black Friday any Friday on which some calamity happens.

black grouse 1 a large N European grouse (*Lyrurus tetrix*), the [male] of which has bluish-black plumage and a lyre-shaped tail; the

female has mottled brown and black plumage. **2** a similar, related W Asian species (*Lyrurus mlokosiewiczi*).

black·guard (blag′ärd or blag′ərd) n., v. —n. scoundrel. —v. **1** abuse with vile language. **2** behave like a blackguard. [< *black* + *guard*] —**black′guard·ly,** adj., adv.

Black Hand any of various secret societies dedicated to violence and terrorism, such as a Sicilian organization, formed in the late 19th century, that operated in the United States in the early 20th century.

black·head (blak′hed′) n. **1** a small, black-tipped lump of dead cells and oil plugging a pore of the skin. **2** any of various birds that have a black head. **3** an infectious, often fatal disease that attacks turkeys.

black·heart (blak′härt′) n. **1** a variety of dark-skinned cherry. **2** a plant disease, especially of potatoes, in which the internal tissues turn black.

black hole¹ a hypothetical entity, a region in space, produced by the collapse of a star, resulting in such a strong gravitational field that anything caught in this field, including light, can never escape.

black hole² a cell or dungeon; a place of punishment. [< the *Black Hole of Calcutta*, a small cell in which many English prisoners were supposedly confined in 1756]

black·ing (blak′ing) n. a black polish used on shoes, stoves, etc.

black·ish (blak′ish) adj. somewhat black.

black·jack (blak′jak′) n., v. —n. **1** a club with a flexible handle, used as a weapon. **2** a large drinking cup or jug, formerly made of leather. **3** the black flag of a pirate. **4** a small oak tree (*Quercus marilandica*) of the S and SE United States having black bark. **5 a** a card game in which the players try to get a count of twenty-one. **b** a count of twenty-one with only two cards, namely an ace and a ten or any face card. —v. **1** hit (a person) with a blackjack. **2** coerce.

black lead graphite.

black·leg (blak′leg′) n. **1** *Informal.* swindler. **2** *Brit.* a worker who takes a striker's job. **3** an infectious, usually fatal disease of cattle and sheep.

black letter *Printing.* Gothic (a typeface).

black light invisible ultraviolet or infrared radiation.

black list a list of persons who are believed to deserve punishment, blame, suspicion, etc.

black–list (blak′list′) v. put on a black list.

black·ly (blak′lē) adv. **1** dismally; gloomily. **2** sullenly; angrily. **3** evilly; wickedly.

black magic evil magic

black·mail (blak′māl′) n., v. —n. **1** the extortion of money, etc. by threats, especially threats of disgracing a person by revealing his secrets. **2** the money or other advantage obtained in this way. —v. get or try to get blackmail from. [< *black* + *mail* rent, tribute, coin < OF *maille* < *mail, medaille* coin, medal] —**black′mail′er,** n.

Black Ma·ri·a (mə rī′ə) **1** a police patrol wagon or prison van. **2** hearse.

black mark a mark of criticism or punishment.

black market 1 the selling of goods at illegal prices or in illegal quantities. **2** a place where such trade is carried on.

black mar·ket·eer (mär′kə tēr′) one who deals on the black market.

Black Mass 1 a Mass for the dead at which black vestments are worn by the priest. **2** a ceremony in which the Mass of Christian worship is caricatured by so-called devil-worshippers.

black measles a severe form of measles.

black·ness (blak′nis) n. **1** the state of being black. **2** wickedness.

black nightshade a poisonous nightshade (*Solanum nigrum*) native to Europe, but now a common weed throughout eastern North America, having dark green leaves, white flowers, and black berries.

black oak an oak tree (*Quercus velutina*) of eastern North America having dark-grey or black bark rich in tannin.

black·out (blak′out′) n. **1** a turning out or concealing of all the lights of a city, district, etc. as a protection against an air raid. **2** a temporary loss of vision, memory, or consciousness due to lack of circulation of blood in the brain. It may occur as a result of extreme exertion, rapid changes of velocity or direction, as in an aircraft, etc. **3** a temporary failure of memory. **4** a turning off of all the lights on the stage of a theatre to suggest the passing of time, or to mark the end of a scene. **5** a failure in radio reception. **6** holding back news or other information by censorship: *News blackouts are common in wartime.*

black pepper a hot-tasting seasoning made from the ground dried berries of the pepper vine (*Piper nigrum*). Compare **white pepper.**

Black Power a movement among blacks, especially in the

United States, to obtain social equality by consolidating their political and economic resources, in order to bargain from a position of power, rather than by seeking integration into white society. Also, **black power.**

Black Rod 1 the chief usher in the British House of Lords, whose symbol of authority is a black rod. 2 in Canada, the chief usher of the Senate. 3 the chief usher in various other legislatures of the British Commonwealth.

black rot any of several diseases of cultivated plants caused by various bacteria or fungi and producing dark-brown discoloration and decay.

black sheep a person who has not lived up to the expectations of his family or group and is considered a disgrace to it.

Black·shirt (blak´shèrt´) 1 *Historical.* a member of the Italian Fascists, who wore a black shirt as part of their uniform. 2 a member of any similar fascist organization.

black·smith (blak´smith´) *n.* a person who makes and repairs things of iron, such as tools or horseshoes, using a forge. [with ref. to black metals, e.g., iron]

black·snake (blak´snāk´) *n.* 1 a harmless, swift-moving snake (*Coluber constrictor*) of southeastern Canada and the eastern United States, belonging to the same family as the garter snake, having a glossy black back and bluish-grey belly, and usually about 120 cm long. Blacksnakes eat insects, frogs, mice, and other snakes and will climb trees to get birds' eggs and young birds. 2 any of various other black or nearly black snakes, such as the poisonous Australian blacksnake (*Pseudechis porphyriacus*). 3 a heavy whip made of braided leather.

black spruce 1 a spruce (*Picea mariana*) found in moist climates throughout northern Canada up to the edge of the tundra, having small, egg-shaped cones and short, dark bluish-green needles. The black spruce is the commonest tree of the northern forest. 2 its soft, moderately light wood.

black tea tea made from leaves that have been allowed to wither and ferment in the air for some time, before being dried in ovens.

black·thorn (blak´thôrn´) *n.* 1 a thorny European shrub (*Prunus spinosa*), a species of plum having white flowers that appear before the leaves and bearing very small, bluish-black fruits usually called sloes. 2 a walking stick or club made from the stem of this shrub.

black tie 1 a black tie, especially a black bow tie, for wear with a dinner jacket or tuxedo. 2 a dinner jacket or tuxedo, as opposed to full evening dress, or tails: *The men will wear black tie for the dinner.*

black·top (blak´top´) *n., v.* **-topped, -top·ping.** —*n.* 1 asphalt mixed with crushed rock, used as a pavement for highways, roads, runways, etc. 2 any surface so paved, such as a highway, driveway, etc. —*v.* pave or surface a road with blacktop.

black walnut 1 a medium-sized North American walnut tree (*Juglans nigra*). 2 the heavy, hard, strong brown wood of this tree, highly valued for making furniture, interior panelling, etc. 3 the oily, round, edible nut of this tree.

black widow any of a genus (*Latrodectus*) of poisonous black spiders found in many warm regions of the world, especially *L. mactans*, which is found in the S United States, as well as many other regions, having a red hourglass-shaped spot on the underside of its abdomen. [named for its color and the fact that the female often eats the male after mating]

black·work (blak´wèrk´) *n.* iron wrought or forged by blacksmiths, not brightened by burnishing, filing, etc.

blad·der (blad´ər) *n.* 1 a soft, thin bag of membrane in the body of an animal, which holds urine received from the kidneys until it is discharged. 2 any similar bag that stores or holds liquid or air in an animal body: *the swim bladder of a fish.* 3 a strong bag, often made of rubber, that will hold liquids or air: *The rubber bag inside a football is a bladder.* 4 a hollow, air-filled bag in plants, as in certain seaweeds. [OE *blædre*]

blad·der·wort (blad´ər wèrt´) *n.* 1 any of a genus (*Utricularia*) of mainly small, rootless plants found throughout the world, but especially in tropical regions, having many small bladders or bags on their leaves in which they trap insect larvae, small crustaceans, etc. Most bladderworts are water or bog plants. 2 (*adj.*) designating a family (Lentibulariaceae) of carnivorous plants including the bladderworts, butterworts, etc.

blade (blād) *n.* 1 the cutting part of anything like a knife or sword. 2 sword. 3 swordsman. 4 a smart or dashing fellow. 5 a leaf of grass. 6 *Botany.* the flat, wide part of a leaf as distinguished from the stalk. 7 flat, wide part of anything: *the blade of an oar or paddle, the shoulder blade.* 8 *Phonetics.* the upper part of the tongue, just behind the tip. [OE *blæd*] —**blade´like´,** *adj.*

blad·ed (blād´id) *adj.* having a blade or blades.

blah (blä) *n., adj.* —*n. Slang.* 1 silly or boring talk or chatter. 2 **the blahs,** *pl.* a feeling of apathy, boredom, and vague dissatisfaction:

the February blahs. —*adj.* uninteresting and mediocre; insipid: *a blah speech.*

blain (blān) *n.* an inflamed swelling or sore; blister; pustule. [OE *blegen*]

blam·a·ble (blām´ə bəl) *adj.* deserving blame.

blame (blām) *v.* **blamed, blam·ing;** *n.* —*v.* 1 hold responsible (for something bad or wrong): *We blamed the fog for our accident.* 2 find fault with: *The teacher will not blame us if we do our best.*
be to blame, deserve blame: *Each person said somebody else was to blame.*
blame on, attribute to: *The accident was blamed on the icy road.*
—*n.* 1 the responsibility for something bad or wrong: *Lack of care deserves the blame for many mistakes.* 2 find fault; reproof. [ME < OF *blasmer* < L *blasphemare* < Gk. *blasphēmeein,* ult. < *blas-* false, slanderous + *phēmē* word. Doublet of BLASPHEME.] —**blam´er,** *n.*

☛ *Syn.* 2. Blame, censure, reproach = find fault with. **Blame,** the least formal word, means find fault with a person for doing something that is wrong or that the person passing judgment thinks is wrong: *We blame people for doing what they know is wrong.* **Censure** adds to *blame* the idea of expressing disapproval, often publicly: *People often censure the Government.* **Reproach** adds to *censure* the idea of expressing one's personal feelings of displeasure or resentment, sometimes unjustly: *She reproached him for being late.*

blame·less (blām´lis) *adj.* not deserving blame: *a blameworthy act.* —**blame´less·ly,** *adv.* —**blame´less·ness,** *n.*
☛ *Syn.* See note at **innocent.**

blame·wor·thy (blām´wèr´thē) *adj.* deserving blame.

blanch (blanch) *v.* 1 turn white; become pale: *to blanch with fear.* 2 loosen the skins of (raw vegetables, nuts, etc.) by plunging them first in boiling water and then in cold water. 3 keep (growing celery, etc.) from becoming green by covering with earth, etc. so as to exclude sunlight. 4 boil (vegetables, meat, etc.) briefly to prepare for freezing, remove a bitter taste, etc. 5 make white; bleach. [ME < OF *blanchir* < *blanc* white < Gmc.]

blanc·mange (blə mänzh´) *n.* a jellylike dessert made with milk, sugar, etc. thickened with cornstarch or gelatin. [ME < OF *blancmanger* white food]

bland (bland) *adj.* 1 smooth; mild; gentle; soothing: *a bland spring breeze, a bland diet.* 2 agreeable; polite, especially in an ingratiating manner. 3 lacking a distinctive character; uninteresting; dull: *a bland election campaign. His poems are very bland.* [< L *blandus* soft] —**bland´ly,** *adv.* —**bland´ness,** *n.*

blan·dish (blan´dish) *v.* coax by flattering. [ME < OF *blandiss-,* a stem of *blandir* < L *blandiri* flatter]

blan·dish·ment (blan´dish mənt) *n.* 1 the act of blandishing. 2 Usually, **blandishments,** *pl.* flattering remarks, etc. meant to persuade.

blank (blangk) *adj., n., v.* —*adj.* 1 not written or printed on: *blank paper.* 2 with spaces to be filled in: *a blank cheque.* 3 having or showing no idea or understanding: *His only answer was a blank stare. Her mind suddenly went blank in the middle of the exam.* 4 utter; absolute: *a blank refusal. He looked at her in blank dismay.* 5 incomplete or lacking some usual feature. A blank cartridge contains powder but no bullet.
—*n.* 1 a space left empty or to be filled in: *Leave a blank after each word.* 2 a paper with spaces to be filled in: *an application blank.* 3 an empty or vacant place or space: *His mind was a complete blank for several hours after the accident.* 4 a lottery ticket that does not win anything. 5 a partly formed piece ready to be stamped, filed, forged, etc. into a finished object: *a key blank.* 6 a mark, usually a long dash, indicating an omitted word, especially an oath or vulgarism. 7 blank cartridge. 8 the white spot in the centre of a target.
draw a blank, end an attempt without success; be unsuccessful: *He tried to get support for his nomination, but he drew a blank with us.*
—*v.* 1 become confused or distracted (used with **out**): *Just when I wanted to introduce them, I blanked out and couldn't remember their names.* 2 keep (an opponent) from scoring in a game. 3 hide; obscure. [F *blanc* white, shining < Gmc.] —**blank´ly,** *adv.* —**blank´ness,** *n.*

blank cartridge a cartridge with no bullet or shot.

blank cheque 1 a cheque form that has not been filled out. 2 a signed cheque that allows the bearer to fill in the amount. 3 *Informal.* freedom or permission to do as one pleases; carte blanche.

---

hat, āge, fär; let, ēqual, tèrm; it, īce
hot, ōpen, ôrder; oil, out; cup, pút, rüle,
əbove, takən, pencəl, lemən, circəs

ch, child; ng, long; sh, ship
th, thin; ᴛн, then; zh, measure

blan·ket (blang′kit) *n., v. —n.* **1** a soft, heavy covering woven from wool, cotton, or other material, used to keep people or animals warm. **2** anything like a blanket: *A blanket of snow covered the ground.* **3** (*adjl.*) covering all instances, members of a group or class, etc.: *a blanket insurance policy, a blanket wage increase.* —*v.* **1** cover with a blanket: *A blanket of snow covered the ground.* **2** cover; hinder; obscure: *Fog blanketed the city.* [ME < OF *blankete* < *blanc* white < Gmc. Related to BLANK.]

blank verse unrhymed poetry having a metre based on five iambic feet in each line: *Shakespeare's plays are written mainly in blank verse.*

blare (bler) *v.* **blared, blar·ing;** *n.* —*v.* **1** make a loud, harsh sound: *The trumpets blared, announcing the king's arrival.* **2** utter harshly or loudly. —*n.* **1** a loud, harsh sound: *The blare of the horn was startling.* **2** brilliance of color; glare. [ME < MDu. *blaren*]

blar·ney (blär′nē) *n., v.* **-neyed, -ney·ing.** —*n.* flattering, coaxing talk. —*v.* flatter; coax.
kiss the Blarney Stone, get skill in flattering and coaxing people. [< the *Blarney Stone,* a stone in a wall of Blarney Castle near Cork, Ireland, said to give skill in flattery to anyone who kisses it]

bla·sé (blä zā′ *or* blä′zā) *adj.* tired of pleasures; bored. [< F *blasé,* pp. of *blaser* exhaust with pleasure]

blas·pheme (blas fēm′) *v.* **-phemed, -phem·ing. 1** speak about God or sacred things with abuse or contempt; utter blasphemy. **2** utter profanities or curses. [ME *blasfemen* < OF *blasfemer* < L *blasphemare* < Gk. *blasphēmeein.* Doublet of BLAME.]
—blas·phem·er, *n.*

blas·phe·mous (blas′fə məs) *adj.* showing contempt for God or sacred things; profane: *a blasphemous utterance.*
—blas′phe·mous·ly, *adv.* **—blas′phe·mous·ness,** *n.*

blas·phe·my (blas′fə mē) *n., pl.* **-mies. 1** abuse of or contempt for God or sacred things. **2** irreverence or disrespect toward something considered immune from criticism.

blast (blast) *n., v.* —*n.* **1** a strong, sudden rush of wind or air: *the icy blasts of winter.* **2 a** the blowing of a trumpet, horn, etc. **b** the sound so made. **3** a current of air used in smelting, etc. A furnace is **in blast** when in operation; it is **out of blast** when stopped. **4** a charge of dynamite or some other explosive that blows up rocks, earth, etc. **5** a blasting; explosion. **6** a cause of withering, blight, or ruin. **7** *Slang.* an outburst of anger, severe criticism, etc. **8** *Slang.* a large, wild party.
in full blast, in full operation.
—*v.* **1** blow up (rocks, earth, etc.) with dynamite, or some other explosive. **2** wither; blight; ruin: *The intense heat blasted the vines. His conviction for fraud blasted his reputation.* **3** blow (a trumpet, horn, whistle, etc.). **4** criticize angrily and severely.
blast off, of rockets, missiles, etc., fire; take off: *Make ready to blast off.* [OE *blǣst*] **—blast′er,** *n.*

blast·ed (blas′tid) *adj.* **1** withered; blighted; ruined. **2** *Informal.* a word used as an intensive, to express impatience or anger: *This blasted pen won't write.*

blast furnace a furnace in which ores are smelted by blowing a strong current of air from the bottom to produce intense heat.

blas·to·derm (blas′tə dėrm′) *n. Biology.* a layer of cells formed by the growth of a fertilized egg. It later divides into three layers, from which all parts of the animal are formed. [< Gk. *blastos* germ + E *-derm* (< Gk. *derma* skin)]

blast·off *or* **blast–off** (blast′of′) *n.* the process or moment of launching a rocket, spacecraft, etc.

blas·tu·la (blas′chə lə) *n., pl.* **-lae** (-lē′ *or* -li′). *Zoology.* the embryo of an animal. It usually consists of a sac or hollow sphere formed by a single layer of cells. [< NL *blastula,* dim. of Gk. *blastos* sprout, germ]

blas·tu·lar (blas′chə lər) *adj.* having to do with, or resembling, a blastula.

blat (blat) *v.* **blat·ted, blat·ting. 1** cry like a calf or sheep; bleat. **2** *Informal.* say loudly and foolishly; blurt out. [imitative]

bla·tan·cy (blā′tən sē) *n.* a blatant quality.

bla·tant (blā′tənt) *adj.* **1** offensively obvious; forced on one's attention: *blatant lies, blatant stupidity.* **2** disagreeably noisy; clamorous. [coined by Spenser < L *blatire* babble] **—bla′tant·ly,** *adv.*

blath·er (blaᴛʜ′ər) *n., v.* —*n.* foolish talk. —*v.* talk foolishly. Also, **blether.** [ME < ON *blathr*]

blath·er·skite (blaᴛʜ′ər skīt′) *n. Informal.* a person who talks much and says little.

blaze[1] (blāz) *n., v.* **blazed, blaz·ing.** —*n.* **1** a bright flame or fire. **2** a glow of brightness; intense light; brilliance or glare: *the blaze of*

the noon sun. **3** a bright display. **4** a violent outburst: *a blaze of temper.*
—*v.* **1** burn with a bright flame; be on fire: *A fire was blazing in the fireplace.* **2** show bright colors or lights: *On Christmas Eve the big house blazed with lights.* **3** make a bright display. **4** burst out in anger or excitement: *He blazed at the insult.*
blaze away, fire a gun, etc.
[OE *blǣse*]
☛ *Syn. n.* **1.** See note at **flame.**

blaze[2] (blāz) *n., v.* **blazed, blaz·ing.** —*n.* **1** a mark made on a tree by chipping off a piece of bark. **2** a white mark on an animal's forehead. —*v.* **1** mark (a tree, trail, etc.) by chipping off a piece of the bark. **2** mark by blazing trees: *The hunters blazed a trail through the bush.* [< LG *blǣse*]

blaze[3] (blāz) *v.* **blazed, blaz·ing.** make known; proclaim. [< MDu. *blasen*]

blaz·er (blā′zər) *n.* **1** a jacket, often dark blue, cut like a suit coat, and usually worn by men as dressy but informal wear. **2** a similar loose or slightly fitted, unbelted jacket worn by women or men, usually having a notched collar and patch pockets.

bla·zon (blā′zən) *v., n.* —*v.* **1** make known; proclaim: *Big posters blazoned the wonders of the coming circus.* **2** decorate; adorn. **3** describe or paint (a coat of arms). **4** display; show.
—*n.* **1** coat of arms. **2** a description or painting of a coat of arms. **3** a display; a show. [ME < OF *blason* shield]

bla·zon·ry (blā′zən rē) *n.* **1** a bright decoration or display. **2** a coat of arms. **3** a description or painting of a coat of arms.

bldg. building.

bleach (blēch) *v., n.* —*v.* **1** whiten by exposing to sunlight: *Bleached bones lay on the deserts.* **2** whiten or lighten by using chemicals: *We bleached the stains out of the shirt.* **3** turn white or pale; lose color.
—*n.* **1** a chemical used in bleaching. **2** the act of bleaching. [OE *blǣcean* < *blāc, blǣce* pale. Related to BLEAK.]
☛ *Syn. v.* **1.** See note at **whiten.**

bleach·er (blēch′ər) *n.* **1** a person or thing that bleaches or an agent used in bleaching. **2 bleachers,** *pl.* the roofless rows or tiers of seats for spectators at outdoor games such as football or baseball.

bleaching powder 1 any powder used in bleaching. **2** chloride of lime.

bleak (blēk) *adj.* **1** swept by winds; bare: *bleak and rocky mountain peaks.* **2** chilly; cold: *a bleak wind.* **3** dreary; dismal: *All their savings were gone, and the future looked bleak.* [ME *bleke* pale < Scand., related to OE *blāc, blǣce.* See BLEACH.] **—bleak′ly,** *adv.* **—bleak′ness,** *n.*

blear (bler) *adj., v.* —*adj.* bleary. —*v.* make dim or blurred. [ME *blere(n)*]

blear–eyed (blēr′īd′) *adj.* having inflamed or watery eyes.

blear·y (blēr′ē) *adj.* **blear·i·er, blear·i·est.** of the eyes or vision, dim or blurred, especially from tiredness or tears. **—blear′i·ly,** *adv.* **—blear′i·ness,** *n.*

bleat (blēt) *n., v.* —*n.* **1** the cry made by a sheep, goat, or calf. **2** a sound like a bleat.
—*v.* **1** make the cry of a sheep, goat, or calf, or a sound like it. **2** complain, especially feebly or with a whine. **3** blather; babble. [OE *blǣtan*] **—bleat′er,** *n.*

bleb (bleb) *n.* **1** a blister. **2** a bubble. [probably imitative]

bled (bled) *v.* pt. and pp. of **bleed.**

bleed (blēd) *v.* **bled, bleed·ing.** *n.* —*v.* **1** lose blood: *This cut is bleeding.* **2** shed one's blood; suffer wounds or death: *He bled to death. He fought and bled for his country.* **3** take blood from: *Doctors used to bleed sick people.* **4** lose sap, juice, etc.: *The injured elm is bleeding.* **5** take sap, juice, etc. from. **6** feel pity, sorrow, or grief. **7** *Informal.* get money from by extortion. **8** *Printing.* **a** extend to the edge of a page, leaving no margin: *This photograph will look best on the page if it bleeds both sides.* **b** print (an illustration) or trim (a page) so that there is no margin.
bleed white, take all the power, strength, money, etc. of: *Blackmailers and gamblers have bled him white.*
—*n.* **1** *Printing.* **a** an illustration or page that bleeds. **b** the paper trimmed off such a page. **2** a valve or tap. [OE *blēdan* < *blōd* blood]

bleed·er (blēd′ər) *n.* a person suffering from a condition in which the blood fails to clot, so that bleeding is hard to stop; hemophiliac.

bleeding heart 1 a spring-flowering Japanese perennial herb (*Dicentra spectabilis* of the family Fumariaceae) widely cultivated for its drooping, heart-shaped, pink flowers. **2** any of several other cultivated plants of the same genus. **3** *Informal.* a person who is excessively sentimental and allows feelings of pity and sympathy to override his judgment.

bleep (blēp) *n., v.* —*n.* a short, high-pitched sound, especially a signal from electronic equipment, used as a warning, to indicate direction, etc.; beep. —*v. Radio and television.* Censor (a word,

etc.) in a broadcast by substituting a bleep (*often used with* **out**).

blem·ish (blem′ish) *n., v.* —*n.* **1** a stain; spot; scar: *A mole is a blemish on a person's skin.* **2** an imperfection; fault: *A quick temper was the only blemish in his character.* —*v.* **1** make stained or scarred. **2** injure; mar: *One bad deed can blemish a good reputation.* [ME < OF *blemiss-*, a stem of *ble(s)mir* make livid] —**blem′ish·er,** *n.*

blench¹ (blench) *v.* draw back; shrink away. [apparently OE *blencan* deceive]

blench² (blench) *v.* **1** turn pale. **2** make white. [var. of *blanch*]

blend (blend) *v.* **blend·ed** or **blent, blend·ing;** *n.* —*v.* **1** mix together; mix or become mixed so thoroughly that the things mixed cannot be distinguished or separated: *Oil and water will not blend. Blend the first three ingredients in a saucepan.* **2** make by mixing several kinds together: *blend tea.* **3** shade into each other, little by little; merge: *The colors of the rainbow blend into one another.* **4** go well together; harmonize: *The colors in that print do not blend.* —*n.* **1** the act of blending. **2** something produced by blending: *a blend of several coffees. This fabric is a blend.* **3** a word made by fusing two words, often with a syllable in common. *Blotch* is a blend of *blot* and *botch.* [ME < ON *blanda* mix] —**blend′er,** *n.*
☞ *Syn. v.* **1.** See note at **mix.**

blende (blend) *n.* **1** the chief ore of zinc; zinc sulphide. **2** any of certain other sulphides. [< G *Blende* < *blenden* blind, deceive; because the yield from the ore is disappointing]

blend·er (blen′dər) *n.* **1** a person or thing that blends. **2** a mechanical device for mixing things uniformly.

blen·ny (blen′ē) *n., pl.* **-ny** or **-nies. 1** any of a family (Blenniidae) of small, scaleless, bottom-living fishes found in the coastal waters of most oceans, having a large head and a tapering body. **2** any of numerous other, mostly small, fishes belonging to the same suborder (Blennioidei), typically having a slender, elongated body with a long dorsal fin. [< L *blennius,* var. of *blendius* < Gk. *blennos* < *blenna* slime]

blent (blent) *v. Poetic.* a pt. and a pp. of **blend.**

bless (bles) *v.* **blessed** or **blest, bless·ing. 1** make holy or sacred: *to bless a church.* **2** ask God's favor for: *Bless these little children.* **3** wish good to; feel grateful to: *They blessed him for his kindness.* **4** favor with prosperity, success, or happiness: *May this country always be blessed with prosperity.* **5** praise or glorify: *Bless the Lord, O my soul.* **6** guard; protect: *Heaven bless this house.* **7** make the sign of the cross over. [OE *blētsian* consecrate (i.e., with blood) < *blōd* blood]

bless·ed (bles′id *or* blest) *adj.* **1** holy; sacred. **2** in heaven; beatified. **3** fortunate; happy; successful. **4** bringing or accompanied by joy or happiness: *blessed ignorance.* **5** *Informal.* a word used as an intensive, to express annoyance or anger; darned; confounded: *Now where did I put the blessed thing?* —**bless′ed·ly,** *adv.* —**bless′ed·ness,** *n.*

Blessed Virgin the Virgin Mary.

bless·ing (bles′ing) *n.* **1** a prayer asking God to show His favor; benediction: *At the end of the church service, the bishop gave the blessing.* **2** a giving of God's favor. **3** a wish for happiness or success: *When she left home, she received her father's blessing.* **4** approval or consent: *The marriage had the blessing of all four parents.* **5** anything that makes one happy or contented; boon or benefit: *A good temper is a great blessing.*

blest (blest) *v., adj.* —*v.* a pt. and a pp. of **bless.** —*adj.* blessed.

bleth·er (bleᴛʜ′ər) *n. or v.* blather.

blew (blü) *v.* pt. of **blow²** and **blow³.**
☞ *Hom.* **blue.**

blight (blīt) *n., v.* —*n.* **1** any of several plant diseases that cause leaves, stems, or other parts to wither and die: *The apple crop was wiped out by a blight.* **2** a fungus, insect, etc. that causes such a disease: *Rust, smut, and mildew are blights.* **3** anything that destroys, impairs or prevents growth, etc.: *a region suffering from the blight of high unemployment.* **4** a person or thing that frustrates or disappoints hopes or ambitions. **5** the condition of being spoiled, ruined, etc.: *the causes of urban blight.* —*v.* **1** cause to wither and die: *Mildew blighted the June roses.* **2** destroy; ruin. **3** disappoint or frustrate: *All their hopes were blighted.* **4** suffer from blight. [origin uncertain]

blimp (blimp) *n. Informal.* **1** a small, non-rigid dirigible airship. **2** any dirigible. [apparently from Type *B limp,* the most common type of "limp dirigible" in World War I]

Blimp or **blimp** (blimp) *n.* an ultra-conservative, stupidly short-sighted person. [< *Colonel Blimp,* an English newspaper cartoon character created by David Low]

blind (blīnd) *adj., adv., v., n.* —*adj.* **1** not able to see; not having the sense of sight: *The man with the white cane is blind.* **2** of or for blind persons. **3** (*noml.*) **the blind,** *pl.* persons who are blind. **4** not based on evidence, judgment, or reason: *blind faith, a blind fury.* **5** unable or unwilling to understand or perceive (*used with* **to**): *blind*

hat, āge, fär; let, ēqual, tėrm; it, īce
hot, ōpen, ôrder; oil, out; cup, pút, rüle,
əbove, takən, pencəl, lemən, circəs

ch, child; ng, long; sh, ship
th, thin; ᴛʜ, then; zh, measure

to the beauty of one's environment. **6** hard to see; hidden: *a blind seam, blind curve on a highway.* **7** without an opening: *a blind wall.* **8** with only one opening: *a blind canyon.* **9** made or done without preparation, knowledge of certain facts, etc.: *a blind purchase.* **10** done without the help of sight, using only instruments: *The pilot made a blind landing.* **11** not producing buds, etc.: *a blind shoot.* **12** of a boil etc., not having come to a head.

turn a blind eye (to), refuse to see or take notice of.
—*adv.* **1** without being able to see properly: *driving blind in the fog.* **2** using only instruments: *to fly blind.* **3** without complete knowledge, etc.
—*v.* **1** make unable to see: *The bright lights blinded me for a moment. She was blinded in an accident in childhood.* **2** make hard to see; conceal: *Clouds blind the stars from view.* **3** rob of power to understand or judge: *His prejudices blinded him.*
—*n.* **1** a device on a spring roller that can be rolled down in front of a window in order to screen or shut out light or heat: *We have blinds on our bedroom windows.* **2** anything that conceals an action or purpose. **3** a hiding place for a hunter. [OE] —**blind′ly,** *adv.* —**blind′ness,** *n.*

blind alley 1 a passageway closed at one end. **2** anything that gives no chance for progress or improvement.

blind date 1 a social date arranged by a third person. **2** either of the two persons thus dated.

blind·er (blīn′dər) *n.* a leather flap designed to keep a horse from seeing to the side; blinker.

blind flying the act of piloting an airplane by instruments only.

blind·fold (blīnd′fōld′) *v., adj., n.* —*v.* cover the eyes to prevent seeing: *The robbers blindfolded, gagged, and bound their victim.* —*adj.* **1** with the eyes covered: *He said he could walk the line blindfold.* **2** reckless. —*n.* something covering the eyes to prevent seeing: *Putting a blindfold on the horse, the man led him from the burning barn.* [OE *blindfellian,* ult. < *blind* blind + *fell,* var. of *fiell* a fall; influenced by *fold*]

blind·man's buff (blīnd′manz buf′) a game in which a blindfolded person tries to catch and identify one of the other players.

blind pig *Slang.* a place where one can buy liquor illegally. Blind pigs usually operate outside the normal hours for taverns or bars.

blind spot 1 a round spot on the retina of the eye that is not sensitive to light: *The optic nerve enters the eye at the blind spot.* See **eye** for picture. **2** a matter on which a person does not know that he is prejudiced or poorly informed. **3** an area of poor radio reception. **4** an area of poor visibility: *There is a blind spot where the road dips on that steep curve.*

blind·stitch (blīnd′stich′) *v., n.* —*v.* sew with stitches not visible on the right side of the work. —*n.* Also, **blind stitch,** a stitch or stitching of this kind.

blind·worm (blīnd′wėrm′) *n.* a small, legless, burrowing lizard (*Anguis fragilis*) of Eurasia having a snakelike body and small eyes. Also called **slowworm.**

blink (blingk) *v., n.* —*v.* **1** look with the eyes opening and shutting: *Mary blinked at the sudden light.* **2** close the eyes and open them again quickly; wink: *We blink every few seconds.* **3** with an unsteady light: *A little lantern blinked in the night.* **4** with indifference at; ignore: *Don't blink the fact that there i[s a danger?] of war. She blinks at all his faults.*
—*n.* **1** a blinking. **2** a glimpse.

on the blink, *Informal.* not working properly; out of or[der: The TV] set is on the blink again.
[ME *blenken*]

blink·er (blingk′ər) *n., v.* —*n.* **1** blinder. **2** a warn[ing light with] flashing lights. —*v.* **1** put blinders on. **2** constrict [the vision of,] etc.: *blinkered by prejudice.*

blintz or **blintze** (blints) *n.* a thin, rolled [pancake with] cheese, fruit, jam, etc. [< Yiddish *blintz* < Uk[rainian]

blip (blip) *n.* **1** an image on a radar screen[, usually a bright] dot of light, showing that radar waves are [reflected from an] object. The blip shows the location of the [object and the speed at] which it is moving. **2** a short, light or cr[isp sound.]

bliss (blis) *n.* **1** great happiness; perfe[ct joy.] **2** blessedness. [OE *blīths < blīthe* blithe]
☞ *Syn.* **1.** See note at **happiness.**

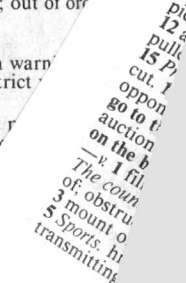

bliss·ful (blis′fəl) *adj.* very happy; joyful. —**bliss′ful·ly,** *adv.* —**bliss′ful·ness,** *n.*

blis·ter (blis′tər) *n., v.* —*n.* **1** a little baglike swelling in the skin filled with watery matter, often caused by a burn or by rubbing. **2** a swelling on the surface of a plant, on metal, or on painted wood, etc. **3** a bulge below the waterline in the hull of a ship, for protection against torpedoes. **4** a bulgelike, often transparent, projection on the fuselage of an aircraft, for an observer, navigator, or air gunner. **5** a bubblelike shell of transparent plastic used to protect and display merchandise. —*v.* **1** raise a blister on. **2** become covered with blisters; have blisters. **3** attack with sharp words. [ME < OF *blestre* tumor, lump < ON *blastr* swelling]

blister beetle any of various soft-bodied beetles (family Meloidae) having body fluids containing a substance that causes skin to blister.

blister rust a fungus disease of white pine trees.

blithe (blīTH *or* blīth) *adj.* **1** happy; cheerful; light-hearted: *She had a blithe and carefree spirit.* **2** airy; casual; unheeding: *blithe indifference.* [OE *blīthe*] —**blithe′ly,** *adv.* —**blithe′ness,** *n.*

blith·er·ing (blith′ər ing) *adj.* talking nonsense; jabbering; blathering: *a blithering idiot.* [var. of *blathering*]

blithe·some (blīTH′səm *or* blīth′səm) *adj.* cheerful and light-hearted. —**blithe′some·ly,** *adv.* —**blithe′some·ness,** *n.*

B.Litt. *or* **B.Lit.** Bachelor of Letters (or Literature) (for L *Baccalaureus Lit(t)erarum*).

blitz (blits) *n., v.* —*n.* **1** blitzkrieg. **2** a sudden, violent attack using many airplanes and tanks. **3** any concentrated effort: *The United Appeal launched a house-to-house blitz in a last attempt to meet their goal.* —*v.* to subject to a blitz. [< G *Blitz* lightning]

blitz·krieg (blits′krēg′) *n.* a type of offensive action designed by its speed and violence to crush the enemy quickly. [< G *Blitzkrieg* lightning war]

bliz·zard (bliz′ərd) *n.* **1** a violent, long-lasting, blinding snowstorm usually accompanied by temperatures of -10°C or colder: *Blizzards sometimes last for more than a day.* **2** any violent winter windstorm with much blowing snow. **3** *Informal.* an overwhelming number or amount: *a blizzard of angry letters.* [origin uncertain] —**bliz′zard·y,** *adj.*

blk. **1** black. **2** block. **3** bulk.

bloat (blōt) *v., n.* —*v.* **1** swell up; puff up: *His face was bruised and bloated after the fight.* **2** preserve (herring) by salting and smoking. —*n.* **1** a swelling of the stomach of cattle, sheep, etc. caused by an accumulation of gases brought on by eating moist feed that ferments. **2** *Informal.* needless or wasteful expansion of staff, budget, etc. [ME *blout* soft with moisture < ON *blautr* soft, pulpy]

bloat·ed (blō′tid) *adj.* **1** puffy and swollen. **2** pampered; glutted. **3** inflated. **4** cured as a bloater: *a bloated herring.*

bloat·er (blōt′ər) *n.* a herring preserved by salting and smoking.

blob (blob) *n., v.* **blobbed, blob·bing.** —*n.* **1** a small, soft drop or lump: *Blobs of wax covered the candlestick.* **2** a splash or daub of color. —*v.* mark or put on with blobs. [probably imitative]

bloc (blok) *n.* a group of persons, companies, or nations, etc. united for a purpose. [< F < OF *bloc.* See BLOCK.]

block (blok) *n., v.* —*n.* **1** a solid piece of wood, stone, metal, etc. **2** an obstruction; hindrance. **3** a space in a city or town bounded by four streets: *one city block.* **4** the length of one side of a block, in a city or town: *Walk one block east.* **5** a number of townships, usually surrounded by land that has not been surveyed: *the Peace River Block.* **6** a group of things of the same kind: *a block of seats in a theatre.* **7** a building containing a number of apartments: *an apartment block.* **8** a number of buildings close together. **9** a building containing offices, often an annex to another building. **10** a short section of railway track with signals for spacing trains. **11** a piece of wood placed under the neck of a person being beheaded. **12** a platform where things are put up for sale at an auction. **13** a pulley on a hook. **14** a mould on which things are shaped. **15** *Printing.* a piece of engraved metal, wood, or other substance; plate. **16** *Slang.* a person's head. **17** *Sports.* the hindering of an opponent's play.

on the block, a have one's head cut off. **b** be for sale at an auction.

put on the block, for sale, especially at an auction.

—*v.* **1** block so as to prevent passage or progress (*often used with* **up**): *The country roads were blocked with snow.* **2** put things in the way of; hinder: *Her sickness blocks my plans for the party.* **3** shape with a block. **4** shape with a mould: *Felt hats are blocked.* **5** *Sports.* hinder an opponent's play. **6** prevent (a nerve) from transmitting impulses. **7** plan roughly; outline (*usually used with* **in**

or **out**): *to block in a sketch.* **8** introduce an obstruction into, so as to make unfit for passage, etc. (*often used with* **off**): *to block off a street.* **9** support with or on a block. [ME < OF *bloc* < Gmc.]

block·ade (blok ād′) *n., v.* **-ad·ed, -ad·ing.** —*n.* **1** in war, the closing off of a harbor, city, etc. by enemy ships or other forces to keep people or supplies from getting through. **2** the forces used to set up a blockade. **3** anything that blocks up or obstructs.

run the blockade, try to get into or out of a port that is being blockaded.

—*v.* **1** put under blockade. **2** block up; obstruct. —**block·ad′er,** *n.*
☞ **Syn.** *n.* **1.** See note at **siege.**

blockade runner a ship that tries to get into or out of a port that is being blockaded.

block·age (blok′ij) *n.* **1** blocking or being blocked. **2** something that blocks: *We cleared the blockage from the pipe.*

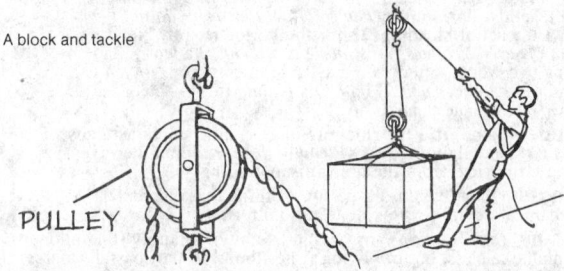

A block and tackle

PULLEY

block and tackle an arrangement of pulleys and ropes used in lifting heavy weights.

block·bust·er (blok′bus′tər) *n. Informal.* **1** an aerial bomb that weighs two or more tonnes, capable of destroying a large area. **2** any person or thing that has a very strong impact or effect: *The new musical is a blockbuster.* **3** a person, corporation, etc. that engages in blockbusting.

block·bust·ing (blok′bus′ting) *n.* the process or practice of developers buying up one or two houses in a city block or area and either razing them or letting them fall to ruin to induce other residents to sell their property quickly, often at a loss, for fear of depreciating property values.

block·head (blok′hed′) *n.* a stupid person; fool.

block heater an electrical device for keeping the engine block of a motor vehicle slightly warm, making it possible to start the engine even in extremely cold weather.

The three-storey concrete blockhouse of Fort Wellington at Prescott, Ontario

block·house (blok′hous′) *n.* **1** a military fortification built of heavy timbers or concrete, and having loopholes to shoot from. **2** a heavily reinforced building used as a control centre and place of observation for operations involving danger from intense heat, radiation, etc.: *The launching of space vehicles is controlled from a blockhouse.*

block·ish (blok′ish) *adj.* stupid. —**block′ish·ly,** *adv.* —**block′ish·ness,** *n.*

block plane a small plane used to smooth the ends of boards across the grain.

block printing printing from engraved blocks of wood, etc.

block signal a signal to show whether a short section of railway track ahead has a train on it or not.

block system the system of dividing a railway track into short sections with signals to warn a train when the section ahead is not clear.

block·y (blok′ē) *adj.* **block·i·er, block·i·est. 1** like a block; chunky. **2** having patches of light and shade. —**block′i·ness,** *n.*

bloke (blōk) *n. Esp.Brit. Informal.* fellow; chap.

blond (blond) *adj., n.* —*adj.* **1** light-colored: *blond hair, blond furniture.* **2** having yellow or light-brown hair, usually blue or grey eyes, and light skin; fair: *blond people.* —*n.* a blond man or boy. [< F < Gmc.]

☛ *Usage.* **Blond, blonde. As a noun, blond** is used for men and boys, while **blonde** is used for women and girls; in ambiguous or doubtful cases, **blond** is used: *Mary and her brother are both blonds.* The normal form of the adjective is **blond** for all cases, but some people prefer to use **blonde** as an adjective when referring to women or girls: *a blond young man, a blond actress* or *a blonde actress.* Those who make such distinctions are following a French grammatical pattern.

blonde (blond) *n., adj.* —*n.* a woman or girl having fair hair. —*adj.* blond. [< F *blonde*, feminine form of *blond*]
☛ *Usage.* See note at **blond.**

blood (blud) *n., pl.* (def. 9) **Bloods** or **Blood;** *v.* —*n.* **1** in vertebrates, the red liquid in the veins and arteries. Blood is circulated by the heart, carrying oxygen and digested food to all parts of the body and taking away waste materials. **2** the corresponding liquid in other animals. *The blood of most insects looks yellowish.* **3** bloodshed; slaughter. **4** family; birth; relationship; parentage; descent: *Love of the sea runs in his blood.* **5** high lineage, especially royal lineage: *a prince of the blood.* **6** temper; state of mind: *There was bad blood between them.* **7** a fashionable man; dandy. **8** of animals, pure breeding; thoroughbred stock. **9 Blood,** a member of an Amerindian people of the Plains, one of the three Algonquian tribes making up the Blackfoot confederacy.
blood is thicker than water, the ties that bind families are stronger than those that link friends.
draw first blood, hit or score first.
in cold blood, on purpose and without emotion: *He lay in wait for the spy and then shot him down in cold blood.*
make (one's) blood boil, make one very angry: *Unfair comments like that make my blood boil.*
make (one's) blood run cold, fill one with terror: *"The Arctic trails have their secret tales/That would make your blood run cold."*
—*v.* give the first taste or experience of blood to: *to blood a hunting dog, to blood raw troops in a battle.* [OE *blōd*]

blood–and–thun·der (blud´ ən thun´dər) *adj.* characterized by highly dramatic, sensational adventures: *a blood- and-thunder movie.*

blood bank 1 a place for storing blood to be used in transfusions. **2** the blood kept in storage.

blood bath savage or widespread killing; massacre.

blood brother 1 a brother by birth; real brother. **2** a person who goes through a ceremony of mixing some of his blood with another person's.

blood count a count of the number of red and white corpuscles in a sample of a person's blood.

blood·cur·dling (blud´kėr´dling) *adj.* terrifying; horrible: *a bloodcurdling story.*

blood donor a person who donates blood to a hospital or for storage in a blood bank.

blood·ed (blud´id) *adj.* **1** coming from good stock; of good breed: *blooded horses.* **2** having blood or a temperament of a certain kind (used only in compounds): *Snakes are called cold-blooded; lions are warm-blooded. She is very hot-blooded and gets angry quickly.*

blood fluke any of various parasitic flatworms (class Digenea) that live in the blood of man and other vertebrates.

blood group any of several groups into which human blood is classified.

blood·guilty (blud´gil´tē) *adj.* guilty of murder or bloodshed. —**blood´guilt´i·ness,** *n.*

blood heat the normal temperature of human blood, about 37°C.

blood·hound (blud´hound´) *n.* **1** a large breed of dog with a very keen sense of smell, long, drooping ears, and a wrinkled face. A trained bloodhound can follow a trail several hours old. **2** a keen and relentless pursuer. **3** *Slang.* detective.

blood·less (blud´lis) *adj.* **1** without blood; pale. **2** without bloodshed: *a bloodless revolution.* **3** without energy; spiritless. **4** cold-hearted or cruel. —**blood´less·ly,** *adv.* —**blood´less·ness,** *n.*

blood·let·ting (blud´let´ing) *n.* **1** taking blood from a vein as a treatment for disease. Bloodletting was formerly common, but few diseases are treated in this way today. **2** bloodshed.

blood·line (blud´līn´) *n.* a line of direct descent; family or pedigree.

blood money 1 money paid to have somebody murdered. **2** money paid as compensation to the next-of-kin of a person who has been murdered. In Anglo-Saxon England, blood money was paid to the family of a murdered man by the family of the murderer. **3** money gained at the cost of another person's life, freedom, welfare, etc.

blood poisoning a diseased condition that occurs when the bloodstream is invaded by poisonous substances or disease-causing bacteria from a local source of infection.

blood pressure the pressure of the blood against the inner walls of the blood vessels, varying with exertion, excitement, health, age, etc.

blood relation or **relative** a person related by birth.

hat, āge, fär; let, ēqual, tėrm; it, īce
hot, ōpen, ôrder; oil, out; cup, pùt, rüle,
əbove, takən, pencəl, lemən, circəs
ch, child; ng, long; sh, ship
th, thin; ᴛʜ, then; zh, measure

blood·root (blud´rüt´) *n.* a North American plant (*Sanguinaria canadensis*) of the poppy family having a red root, red sap, and a white flower that blooms in early spring.

blood royal the royal family.

blood·shed (blud´shed´) *n.* the shedding of blood; slaughter.

blood·shot (blud´shot´) *adj.* of the eyes, red and sore; tinged with blood: *Your eyes become bloodshot if you get dirt in them.*

blood sport any sport, such as fox hunting, that involves the killing of animals.

blood·stain (blud´stān´) *n.* a mark or stain left by blood.

blood·stained (blud´stānd´) *adj.* **1** stained with blood. **2** guilty of murder or bloodshed.

blood·stone (blud´stōn´) *n.* **1** a dark-green semiprecious stone having flecks of bright-red jasper or impure quartz through it. Bloodstone is a kind of translucent quartz. **2** a gem made from this stone.

blood·stream (blud´strēm´) *n.* the blood flowing in the circulatory system of a living body.

blood·suck·er (blud´suk´ər) *n.* **1** leech. **2** a person who gets all he can from others.

blood test an examination of a sample of a person's blood to determine the type of blood, to diagnose illness, etc.

blood·thirst·y (blud´thėrs´tē) *adj.* eager for bloodshed; cruel; murderous. —**blood´thirst´i·ly,** *adv.* —**blood´thirst´i·ness,** *n.*

blood transfusion an injection of blood from one person or animal into another.

blood type blood group.

blood vessel any tube in the body through which the blood circulates. Arteries, veins, and capillaries are blood vessels.

blood·y (blud´ē) *adj.* **blood·i·er, blood·i·est;** *adv., v.* **blood·ied, blood·y·ing.** —*adj.* **1** bleeding: *a bloody nose.* **2** covered or stained with blood: *a bloody bandage, a bloody sword.* **3** with much bloodshed: *a bloody battle.* **4** eager for bloodshed; cruel. **5** *Slang.* a word used as an intensive, especially to express irritation or anger; cursed; confounded: *He's a bloody fool.*
—*adv. Slang.* a word used as an intensive to express irritation or anger: *I worked bloody hard.*
—*v.* **1** cause to bleed: *His nose bloodied in the fight.* **2** stain with blood. —**blood´i·ly,** *adv.* —**blood´i·ness,** *n.*
☛ *Usage.* **Bloody,** in its slang use as an intensive, is sometimes considered vulgar.

bloom¹ (blüm) *n., v.* —*n.* **1** a flower; blossom. **2** the condition or time of flowering. **3** the condition or time of greatest health, vigor, or beauty: *in the bloom of youth.* **4** a glow of health and beauty. **5** the powdery or downy coating on some fruits and leaves. There is a bloom on grapes and plums and on the needles of some species of spruce.
—*v.* **1** have flowers; open into flowers; blossom: *Many plants bloom in the spring.* **2** be in the condition or time of greatest health, vigor, or beauty. **3** glow with health and beauty. [ME < ON *blóm*]

bloom¹ (blüm) *n.* **1** an unmelted, spongy mass of wrought iron. **2** a bar of iron or steel. [OE *blōma* lump]

bloom·er¹ (blüm´ər) *n.* something that blooms.

bloom·er² (blüm´ər) *n. Brit. Slang.* a blunder or mistake.

bloom·ers (blüm´ərz) *n.pl.* **1** loose trousers, gathered at the knee, formerly worn by women and girls for athletics. **2** underwear made like these. [first referred to in a magazine published by Amelia J. Bloomer in 1851]

bloom·ing (blüm´ing) *adj.* **1** having flowers; blossoming. **2** flourishing. **3** *Esp.Brit. Informal.* a word used as an intensive: *a blooming genius. It's a blooming shame.* —**bloom´ing·ly,** *adv.*
☛ *Usage.* **Blooming** (def. 3), in its informal usage, is a euphemism for **bloody** (def. 5).

bloop·er (blüp´ər) *n. Slang.* a silly or stupid, embarrassing mistake made in public; boner.

blos·som (blos´əm) *n., v.* —*n.* **1** a flower, especially of a tree or other plant that produces fruit: *apple blossoms.* **2** the condition or time of flowering: *a cherry tree in blossom.* —*v.* **1** have flowers; open into flowers. **2** open out; develop: *His talent blossomed under the teacher's expert guidance.* [OE *blōstma*]

blos·som·y (blos´əm ē) *adj.* full of blossoms.

blot (blot) v. **blot·ted, blot·ting;** n. —v. **1** make blots on; stain or spot. **2** dry ink, etc. with paper or other material that absorbs: *She blotted her signature before folding the letter.* **3** blemish; disgrace.
blot (one's) **copybook,** spoil one's record or reputation: *He failed to get his promotion after blotting his copybook at the staff party.*
blot out, a hide; cover up. **b** wipe out; destroy.
—n. **1** a spot or stain: *an ink blot.* **2** a blemish; disgrace. [ME; origin uncertain]

blotch (bloch) n., v. —n. **1** a large, irregular spot or stain. **2** a place where the skin is red or broken out. —v. cover or mark with blotches. [blend of *blot* and *botch*]

blotch·y (bloch′ē) adj. **blotch·i·er, blotch·i·est.** having blotches.

blot·ter (blot′ər) n. **1** a piece of blotting paper. **2** a book for writing down happenings or transactions: *A police station blotter is a record of arrests.* **3** anything that soaks up or absorbs: *He has a blotter of a mind; he remembers everything.* **4** *Slang.* drunkard.

blotting paper a soft paper used to dry writing by soaking up excess ink.

blouse (blouz *or* blous) n. **1** a loose or partly fitted, light garment for the upper part of the body, worn by women and girls. **2** any loosely fitted garment for the upper part of the body. Sailors wear blouses. **3** the upper part of a battle dress. **4** a kind of smock reaching to the knees, worn by European peasants and workmen to protect their clothes. [< F < Provençal (*lano*) *blouso* short (wool)] —**blouse′like′,** adj.

blow[1] (blō) n. **1** a hard hit; knock; stroke. **2** a sudden happening that causes misfortune or loss; severe shock; misfortune: *His mother's death was a great blow to him.* **3** a sudden attack or assault: *The army struck a swift blow at the enemy.*
at one blow, by one act or effort.
come to blows, start fighting.
without striking a blow, with no effort; without even trying. [ME *blaw*]
☞ *Syn.* **1.** Blow, stroke = a sudden, hard hit. **Blow,** both figuratively and literally, emphasizes the force, roughness, and heaviness of a hard knock against something or a hit with the fist or something heavy: *He got a blow on the head.* **Stroke** emphasizes the sharpness and precision of a hit with the hand or something long and narrow, but is most often used in specific senses, as in tennis or art, and figuratively: *His scar was made by a sword stroke across the face.*

blow[2] (blō) v. **blew, blown, blow·ing;** n. —v. **1** send forth a strong current of air. **2** move in a current, especially rapidly or with power: *The wind was blowing from the east.* **3** drive or carry by a current of air: *The wind blew the curtains.* **4** force a current of air into, through, or against: *She blew the embers into flame.* **5** clear or empty by forcing air through: *We blew the eggs before coloring them for Easter.* **6** produce or shape by means of blown or injected air: *to blow bubbles, to blow glass.* **7** cause a wind instrument to make a sound: *to blow a trumpet.* **8** make a sound by means of a current of air or steam: *The whistle blew at noon. The bugle blew taps.* **9** break by an explosion; blow up, open, etc.: *The thieves blew the safe.* **10** be out of breath: *The horse was blowing at the end of the race.* **11** make out of breath; cause to pant. **12** *Informal.* boast; brag. **13** of whales, spout water and air. **14** of insects, lay eggs in. Some flies blow fruit. **15** *Slang.* **a** spend recklessly: *She blew her whole allowance in the bookstore.* **b** treat; entertain. **16** melt: *A short circuit will blow a fuse.* **17** publish or spread (news). **18** *Slang.* handle badly; bungle: *The last time we asked him to help, he blew the job.* **19** *Slang.* leave; get out of: *He blew town.*
blow hot and cold, change from a favorable opinion to an unfavorable one; view with fluctuating enthusiasm.
blow in, a *Informal.* appear unexpectedly; drop in. **b** of an oil well, start production; come into production.
blow off, get rid of noisily.
blow (one's) **cool,** *Slang.* lose one's composure.
blow (one's) **top** (or **stack** or **cork,** etc.), *Slang.* become very angry.
blow out, a extinguish or be extinguished by a puff of breath or other current of air: *Please blow out the candle. The candle has blown out.* **b** have or cause to have a blowout.
blow over, a pass by or over: *The storm has blown over.* **b** be forgotten.
blow up, a explode. **b** fill with air. **c** *Informal.* become very angry. **d** *Informal.* scold; abuse. **e** arise; begin: *A storm suddenly blew up.* **f** enlarge (a photograph).
—n. **1** the act or fact of forcing air into, through, or against something: *One blow cleared the pipe.* **2** blowing: *a blow of the whistle.* **3** a gale of wind: *Last night's big blow brought down several trees.* [OE *blāwan*]

blow[3] (blō) v. **blew, blown, blow·ing;** n. —v. burst into flower; bloom (*now used mostly as a past participle*): *a full-blown rose.* —n. the state of blooming: *The garden was in full blow.* [OE *blōwan*]

blow–by–blow (blō′bī blō′) adj. of a report, account, etc., very detailed: *He gave us a blow-by-blow account of the game.*

blow–dry (blō′drī′) v. **blow-dried, blow-drying.** dry and style the hair using a blow dryer.

blow dry·er or **blow–dry·er** (blō′drī′ər) n. a hand-held electrical apparatus for drying the hair by means of a strong current of hot air. It has a nozzle for directing the air to a particular part of the hair so that the hair can be styled as it is being dried.

blow·er (blō′ər) n. **1** a person or thing that blows: *a glass blower.* **2** a fan or other machine for forcing air into a building, furnace, mine, etc. **3** whale. **4** *Informal.* telephone.

blow·fly (blō′flī′) n., pl. **-flies.** any of several species of large fly (family Calliphoridae), including bluebottles, having metallic blue, green, or bronze bodies and making a loud buzzing sound in flight. Blowflies are similar to the common housefly, except that they breed mainly in dead flesh, and their larvae will sometimes infest open wounds, causing serious disease.

blow·gun (blō′gun′) n. **1** a tube through which a person blows arrows or darts. **2** peashooter.

blow·hard (blō′härd′) n. *Slang.* braggart.

blow·hole (blō′hōl′) n. **1** a hole where air or gas can escape. **2** a hole for breathing, in the top of the head of whales and some other animals. **3** a hole in the ice where whales, seals, etc. come to breathe. **4** a defect in a piece of metal due to a bubble of air or gas. **5** a defect; flaw.

blown (blōn) adj., v. —adj. **1** out of breath; exhausted: *He was blown after climbing the steep hill.* **2** tainted by flies; flyblown; tainted. **3** shaped by blowing: *blown glass.* **4** of cattle, having the stomach distended by eating too much green food; bloated.
—v. pp. of **blow**[2] and **blow**[3].

blow·out (blō′out′) n. **1** the bursting of a container or casing, such as an automobile tire, by the pressure of the enclosed air, etc. on a weak spot. **2** the sudden, uncontrolled eruption of an oil or gas well. **3** the melting of an electric fuse caused by an overload in a circuit or line. **4** *Slang.* a big party or meal.

blow·pipe (blō′pīp′) n. **1** a tube for blowing air or gas into a flame to increase the heat. **2** blowgun. **3** a long metal tube used for blowing molten glass into the required shape. **4** *Medicine.* an instrument for blowing air into a body cavity for cleaning or examination.

blows·y or **blowz·y** (blouz′ē) adj. **blows·i·er, blows·i·est** or **blowz·i·er, blowz·i·est. 1** untidy; frowzy. **2** red-faced and coarse-looking. —**blows′i·ly** or **blowz′i·ly,** adv. —**blows′i·ness** or **blowz′i·ness,** n.

blow·torch (blō′tôrch′) n. a small torch that shoots out a hot flame. It is used to melt metal and burn off paint.

blow·up (blō′up′) n. **1** explosion. **2** *Informal.* **a** an outburst of anger. **b** a quarrel. **3** *Informal.* an enlargement (of a photograph).

blow·y (blō′ē) adj. **blow·i·er, blow·i·est.** windy.

B.L.S. Bachelor of Library Science.

bls. 1 barrels. **2** bales.

blub·ber (blub′ər) n., v. —n. **1** the fat of whales and some other sea animals. **2** a noisy weeping.
—v. **1** weep noisily. **2** utter while crying and sobbing: *The child blubbered an apology.* **3** disfigure or swell with crying: *a face all blubbered.* [probably imitative]

blu·cher (blü′chər *or* blü′kər) n. a shoe whose tongue and front part are made from one piece of leather. [after Field Marshal von Blücher (1742-1819), a Prussian general]

bludg·eon (bluj′ən) n., v. —n. a short, heavy club, used as a weapon. —v. **1** strike with a club. **2** bully; threaten. [origin unknown] —**bludg′eon·er,** n.

blue (blü) n., adj. **blu·er, blu·est;** v. **blued, blu·ing** or **blue·ing.** —n. **1** the color of the clear sky in daylight or the color of the part of the spectrum between green and violet. **2** blue dye or pigment. **3 the blue, a** the sky: *up in the blue.* **b** the far distance. **c** the sea. **4 blues,** pl. *Informal.* low spirits: *He's got the blues.* **5 blues,** *Music.* a style of jazz characterized by a tendency to flatten the thirds by a semitone, producing minor sequences and harmonies that give the music a melancholy sound. The blues developed from black work songs and spirituals. **b** a song in this style (*used with a singular verb*).
out of the blue, completely unexpected; from an unknown source or for an unknown reason: *Suddenly, out of the blue, she announced that she was quitting.*
—adj. **1** of or having the color of the clear sky in daylight or any tone of this color. **2** of animals or plants, bluish, or having parts that are blue or bluish (*used in compounds*): *blue spruce, blue flag, bluefish.* **3** of the skin, livid; ashen: *blue with cold.* **4** having or showing low spirits; sad, gloomy, or discouraged: *a blue mood. I was feeling very blue.* **5** dismal; dispiriting: *a blue day.* **6** *Informal.* indecent or off-color: *blue language, a blue joke.* **7** of or having to do with Conservatives.
once in a blue moon, hardly ever; rarely: *Once in a blue moon we get a letter from him.*

—*v.* **1** make blue. **2** using bluing on. [ME < OF *bleu* < Gmc.]
—**blue′ness**, *n.*
☛ *Hom.* **blew.**

Blue·beard (blü′bērd′) *n.* **1** *Legend.* a man who murdered six of his wives and hid their bodies in a room which he forbade anyone to enter. **2** any man who marries women with the intention of killing them.

Bluebeard's chamber any place where mysteries or terrible secrets are hidden.

blue·bell (blü′bel′) *n.* **1** a common wildflower (*Campanula rotundifolia*) of north temperate regions having long, slender stems and blue, bell-shaped flowers. Bluebells are found throughout most of Canada. **2** any of various other plants having bell-shaped blue flowers, such as a European woodland plant (*Endymion nonscriptus*, also classified as *Scilla nonscriptus*) of the lily family.

blue·ber·ry (blü′ber′ē or blü′bər ē) *n., pl.* **-ries.** **1** the small, sweet, blue berry of any of several shrubs (genus *Vaccinium*) of the heath family. **2** a shrub bearing these berries.

blue·bird (blü′bērd′) *n.* any of a small genus (*Sialia*) of North American songbirds, all three species about 18 cm long including the tail, and the males all having mainly bright-blue plumage. Bluebirds belong to the subfamily Turdinae, the thrushes.

blue·black (blü′blak′) *adj. or n.* bluish black; very dark blue.

blue blood **1** aristocratic descent. **2** aristocrat.

blue—blood·ed (blü′blud′id) *adj.* aristocratic.

blue·bon·net (blü′bon′it) *n.* **1** a round, brimless cap made of blue woollen cloth, formerly worn in Scotland. **2** a person wearing such a cap. **3** a Scot. **4** an annual lupin (*Lupinus subcarnosus*) of the SW United States, especially Texas, having clusters of small, bonnet-shaped, blue flowers.

blue book **1** a book that lists socially prominent people. **2** a booklet with a blue paper cover, used for writing answers to examinations. **3** an official statement of public accounts, published annually by the Government of Canada. **4** a parliamentary or other official publication.

blue·bot·tle (blü′bot′əl) *n.* **1** any of several species of blowfly having a bright, metallic-blue body. **2** any similar fly. **3** cornflower.

blue·coat (blü′kōt′) *n.* policeman.

blue—col·lar (blu′kol′ər) *adj.* of or having to do with industrial or manual workers as a group, or their jobs, attitudes, etc.: *He said he would prefer any blue-collar job to working in an office.* [referring to a common color for workshirts; coined in contrast to *white-collar*]

blue devils **1** the blues; low spirits. **2** delirium tremens; horrible things seen during delirium tremens.

blue·fin (blü′fin′) *n.* a type of tuna.

blue·fish (blü′fish′) *n., pl.* **-fish** or **-fish·es.** **1** a large, blue-and-silver game and food fish (*Pomatomus saltatrix*) of tropical and temperate parts of the Atlantic and Indian oceans, distantly related to the sea basses. **2** any of various other bluish fishes.

blue flag any of several blue-flowered wild irises, especially a common North American wildflower (*Iris versicolor*) found in marshy places.

blue goose *Cdn.* the snow goose in its "blue" color phase, with mainly bluish-grey upper parts and wings, greyish-brown or whitish under parts, and white head and neck.

blue·grass (blü′gras′) *n.* any of several grasses (genus *Poa*) having bluish-green stems, especially **Kentucky bluegrass** (*P. pratensis*), widely cultivated as a pasture, forage, and lawn grass.

blue gum any of several Australian eucalyptus trees, especially a tall species (*Eucalyptus globulus*) widely cultivated for its aromatic leaves, which yield a medicinal oil, and for its hard wood. The young leaves of the blue gum have a bluish tinge.

blue·ing (blü′ing) *n.* See **bluing.**

blue·jacket (blü′jak′it) *n.* a sailor in the navy.

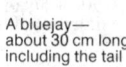
A bluejay— about 30 cm long including the tail

blue·jay (blü′jā′) *n.* a jay (*Cyanocitta cristata*) found in southern

hat, āge, fär; let, ēqual, tėrm; it, īce hot, ōpen, ôrder; oil, out; cup, pút, rüle, above, takən, pencəl, lemən, circəs ch, child; ng, long; sh, ship th, thin; ₮H, then; zh, measure

Canada and the United States, having a crest on the head, a very long tail, and a blue upper body and head, with a broad black band around the neck.

blue·jeans or **blue jeans** (blü′jenz′) *n.* men's or women's pants usually made of blue denim, having hip pockets and fell seams sewn in thread of a contrasting color.

blue laws any very strict and puritanical laws.

blue·line (blü′līn′) *n.* either of the two blue lines drawn midway between the centre of a hockey rink and each goal: *The blueline plays an important part in the rules of hockey.*

Blue·nose (blü′nōz′) *n. Informal.* **1** a Nova Scotian; less often, a New Brunswicker. **2** (*adj.*) of or associated with Nova Scotia. **3** a ship built in Nova Scotia and manned by Nova Scotians. **4 bluenose,** a prudish or puritanical person.

blue—pen·cil (blü′pen′səl) *v.* **-cilled** or **-ciled, -cil·ling** or **-cil·ing.** change or cross out, especially by using a pencil with a blue lead, such as editors usually use.

blue·point (blü′point′) *n.* a type of small, edible oyster harvested at Blue Point on Long Island, New York.

blue·print (blü′print′) *n., v.* —*n.* **1** an exact photographic copy of an original drawing of a building plan, map, etc., usually showing white lines on a blue background. **2** a detailed plan for any enterprise. —*v.* **1** make a blueprint of. **2** make or explain a plan in detail.

blue racer a dark-blue or greenish-blue subspecies of the blacksnake (*Coluber constrictor*) found in central and western North America.

blue ribbon first prize; highest honor.

blue spruce a spruce (*Picea pungens*) having bluish-green needles, native to the W United States but commonly used as an ornamental tree throughout North America.

blue·stock·ing (blü′stok′ing) *n. Informal.* a woman who displays great interest in intellectual or literary subjects. [< nickname *"Blue Stocking Society"* given to a group of English women who met (about 1750) to discuss literature]

blue·stone (blü′stōn′) *n.* **1** bluish sandstone. **2** blue vitriol.

blu·et (blü′it) *n.* a small plant of North America having pale bluish flowers. [< F *bluet,* dim of *bleu* blue < Gmc.]

blue vitriol hydrous copper sulphate. *Formula:* $CuSO_4.5H_2O$

blue whale a dark greyish-blue baleen whale (*Balaenoptera musculus*) found in all the oceans of the world. It is the largest animal that has ever existed on earth, reaching a maximum length of about 30 metres and weight of about 130 tonnes.

bluff¹ (bluf) *n., adj.* —*n.* **1** a high, steep bank or cliff. **2** *Cdn.* a clump of trees standing on the flat prairie; copse: *The farmhouse was screened from the wind and the sun by a poplar bluff.* —*adj.* **1** of a cliff, the bow of a ship, etc., rising steeply with a straight, broad front. **2** frank and rough in a good-natured way. [probably < Du. *blaf* broad flat face] —**bluff′ly,** *adv.* —**bluff′ness,** *n.*
☛ *Syn. adj.* **2.** See note at **blunt.**

bluff² (bluf) *n., v.* —*n.* **1** a show of pretended confidence, used to deceive or mislead. **2** a threat that cannot be carried out. **3** a person who bluffs.

call (someone's) **bluff,** challenge or expose a bluff: *He backed down when I called his bluff.*
—*v.* **1** deceive by a show of pretended confidence. **2** frighten with a threat that cannot be carried out.

bluff (one's) **way,** get something one wants by bluffing: *She bluffed her way through this test but she'll never make the final exam.* [? < Du. *bluffen,* baffle; mislead; brag] —**bluff′er,** *n.*

blu·ing or **blue·ing** (blü′ing) *n.* a blue liquid or powder put in water when rinsing white fabrics, in order to prevent them from turning yellow.

blu·ish (blü′ish) *adj.* somewhat blue.

blun·der (blun′dər) *n., v.* —*n.* a stupid mistake. —*v.* **1** make a stupid mistake. **2** do clumsily or wrongly; bungle. **3** move clumsily or blindly; stumble. **4** blurt out; say clumsily or foolishly. [ME *blondre(n)*; origin uncertain] —**blun′der·er,** *n.*

blun·der·buss (blun′dər bus′) *n.* **1** a short gun with a wide muzzle, formerly used to fire a quantity of shot a short distance. **2** a person who blunders. [alteration of Du. *donderbus* thunder box]

blunt (blunt) *adj., v.* —*adj.* **1** without a sharp edge or point.

2 plain-spoken; outspoken; frank. **3** slow in perceiving or understanding. —*v.* **1** make less sharp or keen: *to blunt a knife, to blunt someone's enthusiasm.* **2** become less sharp or keen. [ME; origin uncertain] —**blunt′ly,** *adv.* —**blunt′ness,** *n.*
☛ **Syn.** *adj.* **1.** See note at **dull. 2. Blunt, bluff, curt** = abrupt in speaking or manner. **Blunt** emphasizes speaking plainly and frankly in open disregard of the feelings of others and simple good manners: *He thinks that blunt speech proves he is honest.* **Bluff** suggests a frank and rough manner of speaking and acting combined with heartiness and genuineness: *Everyone likes the bluff policeman on the beat.* **Curt** = rudely abrupt and brief: *A curt nod was the only notice he gave that he knew she was there.*

blur (blėr) *v.* **blurred, blur·ring;** *n.* —*v.* **1** make confused in form or outline: *Mist blurred the hills.* **2** make dim: *Tears blurred my eyes.* **3** become dim or indistinct: *Her eyes blurred with tears.* **4** smear; blot; stain: *He blurred the writing by touching the ink before it was dry.* —*n.* **1** a blurred condition; dimness. **2** something seen dimly or indistinctly. **3** a smear; blot; stain. [? var. of *blear*]

blurb (blėrb) *n. Informal.* an advertisement or announcement, especially of a book, full of extremely high praise. [supposedly coined in 1907 by Gelett Burgess (1866-1951), an American humorist]

blur·ry (blėr′ē) *adj.* **1** dim; indistinct. **2** smeary; full of blots and stains. —**blur′ri·ness,** *n.*

blurt (blėrt) *v.* say suddenly or without thinking: *In his anger he blurted out the secret.* [imitative]

blush (blush) *n., v.* —*v.* **1** a reddening of the skin caused by shame, confusion, or excitement. **2** a rosy color.
at first blush, at first appearance or consideration.
—*v.* **1** make or become red because of shame, confusion, or excitement: *She was so shy that she blushed every time she was spoken to.* **2** be ashamed: *I blush to observe the errors in my manuscript.* **3** be or become rosy. [ME *blusche* < OE *blyscan* redden]

blus·ter (blus′tər) *v., n.* —*v.* **1** storm or blow noisily and violently: *The wind blustered around the house.* **2** talk noisily and boastfully or threateningly: *He blusters a lot but he's really a coward.* **3** do or say noisily and violently: *He blustered an oath and slammed the door.* **4** make or get by blustering. —*n.* **1** stormy noise and violence. **2** noisy and boastful or threatening talk. [apparently < LG *blüstern* blow violently]

blus·ter·y (blus′tər ē) *adj.* blustering.

blvd. boulevard.

BM *Informal.* bowel movement.

B. Mus. Bachelor of Music.

Bn. battalion.

BNA Act or **B.N.A. Act** British North America Act.

B'nai B'rith (bə nä′ brith′ *or* bə rēth′) a Jewish fraternal society.

BO or **B.O.** **1** body odor. **2** box office.

bo·a (bō′ə) *n., pl.* **bo·as. 1** any of various non-poisonous tropical snakes (family Boidae) that give birth to live young, unlike most snakes, and that kill their prey by coiling around it and squeezing until it suffocates. Boas range in length from about 45 cm to 9 m. One of the smallest boas, called the rubber boa, is found in the valleys in the extreme south of British Columbia. **2** a long scarf made of fur or feathers, worn around a woman's neck. [< L *boa,* a type of serpent]

boa constrictor 1 a large tropical American boa (*Constrictor constrictor*) having tan skin with brown markings and averaging about 340 cm in length. **2** any large snake that kills its prey by squeezing it until it suffocates.

boar (bôr) *n.* **1** an uncastrated male of the domestic pig. **2** wild boar. [OE *bār*]
☛ **Hom. bore.**

board (bôrd) *n., v.* —*n.* **1** a long, flat piece of sawed lumber for use in building, etc. **2** a flat piece of wood or other material used for some special purpose: *an ironing board.* **3 the boards,** *pl.* **a** the stage of a theatre. **b** *Cdn.* the wooden guard fence surrounding the ice of a hockey rink. **4** pasteboard: *a book with covers of board.* **5** a flat, specially marked piece of wood, cardboard, etc. on which to play a game: *a chessboard.* **6** a table to serve food on; table. **7** the food served on a table. **8** meals provided for pay. **9** a group of persons managing something; council: *a board of health.* **10** the side of a ship. **11** chalkboard; blackboard.
across the board, affecting everybody or everything of a group equally: *Prices have increased across the board again.*
go by the board, a of a ship mast, etc., fall over the side. **b** be given up, neglected, or ignored.
on board, on a ship, train, etc.
tread the boards, act in a play.

—*v.* **1** cover with boards (*usually used with* **up**): *to board up a broken window.* **2** provide with regular meals, or room and meals, for pay. **3** get meals, or room and meals, for pay: *Mr. Jones boards at our house.* **4** get on (a ship, train, etc.). **5** come alongside of or against (a ship). **6** *Cdn. Hockey.* bodycheck an opposing player into the boards. [OE *bord*]

board check *Hockey.* a check made by bodychecking an opposing player into the boards of a rink, the checker being subject to a penalty if the referee judges the act to have been violent; boarding.

board–check (bôrd′chek′) *v.* give a board check to (an opposing player).

board·er (bôr′dər) *n.* **1** a person who pays for regular meals, or for room and meals, at another's house. **2** a person assigned to go on board an enemy ship. **3** a resident pupil at a boarding school.
☛ **Hom. border.**

board foot a unit of measure equal to a board one foot square and one inch thick (about 30 cm^2 × 2.54 cm), used for measuring logs and lumber; 144 cubic inches (about 2250 cm^3). *Abbrev:* bd.ft.

board·ing (bôr′ding) *n.* **1** *Cdn. Hockey.* the act of checking an opposing player into the boards of the rink in a rough and illegal manner. **2** wood cut into boards: *We have to order the boarding for our new fence.* **3** a structure made of boards.

boarding house a house where meals, or room and meals, are provided for pay.

boarding school a school that provides lodging and food during the school term for some or all or its students or pupils.

board measure a system for measuring logs and lumber. The unit is the board foot.

board of control the executive branch of the governing council of certain large cities, consisting of the mayor and two or more controllers.

board of education a group of people, usually elected, who manage the schools in a certain area; school board.

board of health the department of a local government in charge of public health.

board of trade 1 an association of businessmen to protect and advance their interests. **2 Board of Trade,** in Great Britain, the governmental department in charge of commerce and industry.

board·room (bôrd′rüm′) *n.* a room that is regularly used to hold meetings of a board of directors, etc.

board·walk (bôrd′wok′ *or* -wôk′) *n.* a sidewalk or promenade made of boards.

boar·hound (bôr′hound′) *n.* any of several breeds of large dog, especially the Great Dane, formerly used in hunting wild boars.

boast (bōst) *v., n.* —*v.* **1** speak highly of oneself or one's accomplishments or possessions; brag. **2** brag about: *He boasts his skill at soccer. He boasted that he was the best player on the team.* **3** have and be proud of: *Our town boasts many fine parks.* —*n.* **1** a praising of oneself; bragging. **2** something to be proud of. [ME *boste(n);* origin uncertain] —**boast′er,** *n.* —**boast′ing·ly,** *adv.*
☛ **Syn.** *v.* **1. Boast, brag** = to praise oneself. **Boast** = talk too much about something one has done or about one's possessions, family, etc., even though there may be some reason to be proud: *He boasts about his new convertible.* **Brag** is informal, and always suggests showing off and exaggerating: *He is always bragging about what he can do with a car.*

boast·ful (bōst′fəl) *adj.* **1** boasting; speaking too well about oneself. **2** fond of boasting. —**boast′ful·ly,** *adv.* —**boast′ful·ness,** *n.*

boat (bōt) *n., v.* —*n.* **1** a small, open vessel for travelling on water. **2** ship. **3** a boat-shaped dish for gravy, sauce, etc.
burn (one's) boats, cut off all chances of retreat.
in the same boat, in the same position or condition; taking the same chances: *We're all in the same boat, so stop complaining.*
miss the boat, *Informal.* miss an opportunity; lose one's chances.
rock the boat, *Informal.* disturb the status quo.
—*v.* **1** use a boat; go in a boat. **2** put or carry in a boat. [OE *bāt*]

boat hook a pole having a metal hook at one end, used for pulling or pushing a boat, raft, etc.

boat·house (bōt′hous′) *n.* a house or shed for sheltering a boat or boats.

boat livery a boathouse where boats are hired out.

boat·load (bōt′lōd′) *n.* **1** as much or as many as a boat can hold or carry. **2** the load that a boat is carrying.

boat·man (bōt′mən) *n., pl.* **-men. 1** a man who rents out boats or takes care of them. **2** a man whose work is rowing or sailing small boats or who is skilled in their use.

boat·swain (bō′sən; *less often,* bōt′swān′) *n.* a ship's officer in charge of the deck crew, the anchors, ropes, rigging, etc. Also **bo's'n, bosun.**

bob[1] (bob) *v.* **bobbed, bob·bing;** *n.* —*v.* **1** move up and down, or to and fro, with short, quick motions: *bob a curtsy. The bird bobbed its head up and down.* **2** try to catch with the teeth

something floating or hanging: *One game at the party was to bob for apples in a bowl of water.*

bob up, appear suddenly or unexpectedly.

—*n.* a short, quick motion up and down, or to and fro. [ME; origin uncertain]

bob² (bob) *n., v.* **bobbed, bob·bing.** —*n.* **1** a short haircut. **2** a horse's docked tail. **3** a weight on the end of a pendulum or plumb line. **4** a float for a fishing line. **5** a bobsled.

—*v.* **1** cut (hair) short. **2** fish with a bob. [ME *bobbe* bunch; origin uncertain]

bob³ (bob) *n., v.* **bobbed, bob·bing.** —*n.* a light rap; tap. —*v.* rap lightly; tap. [ME; origin uncertain]

bob⁴ (bob) *n., pl.* **bob.** *Brit. Slang.* shilling. [origin uncertain]

bob·bin (bob′ən) *n.* a reel or spool for holding thread, yarn, etc. Bobbins are used in spinning, weaving, machine sewing, and lacemaking. Wire is also wound on bobbins. [< F *bobine*]

bob·bi·net (bob′ə net′) *n.* a cotton netting or lace made by machines. [< *bobbin* + *net¹*]

bob·by (bob′ē) *n., pl.* **-bies.** *Brit. Informal.* police constable. [after Sir *Robert* Peel (1788-1850), who improved the London police system]

bobby pin a flat wire clip for the hair, having prongs that press close together.

bob·by·socks (bob′ē soks′) *n.pl. Informal.* ankle-length socks, worn by young girls.

bob·by·sox·er (bob′ē sok′sər) *n. Informal.* an adolescent girl, especially one who enthusiastically follows every new fad.

bob·cat (bob′kat′) *n.* a lynx (*Lynx rufus*) found mostly in the United States, closely related to the Canada lynx but generally smaller and having much smaller ear tufts or none at all, and smaller paws. The bobcat has silky brownish fur with dark spots.

bob·o·link (bob′ə lingk′) *n.* a New World songbird (*Dolichonyx oryzivorus*) of the same family as the orioles and meadowlarks, that breeds in N North America and winters in central South America. The male in breeding season has a white back and rump and black under parts. [imitative]

bob·skate (bob′skāt′) *n.* a child's skate that consists of two sections of double runners and is adjustable to the size of the wearer's foot.

bob·sled (bob′sled′) *n., v.* **-sled·ded, -sled·ding.** —*n.* a long sled with two sets of runners, a continuous seat, a steering wheel, and brakes. —*v.* ride or coast on a bobsled.

bob·sleigh (bob′slā′) *n.* or *v.* **-sleighed, -sleigh·ing.** bobsled.

bob·stay (bob′stā′) *n.* on a ship, a rope or chain to hold a bowsprit down. See **bowsprit** for picture.

bob·tail (bob′tāl′) *n.* **1** a short tail; tail cut short. **2** a horse or dog having a bobtail. **3** (*adj.*) having a bobtail.

bob·white (bob′wīt′ *or* -hwīt′) *n.* a quail (*Colinus virginianus*) of southern Ontario and the eastern United States, a small, plump game bird having a reddish-brown back and striped sides. [imitative]

bob·wire (bob′wīr′) *n.* barbed wire.

Boche or **boche** (bosh *or* bōsh) *n. Derogatory.* a German. [<F *boche* < *tête de boche* blockhead, earlier *tête de caboche* < *caboche* skull, ult. < L *caput* head]

bock (bok) *n.* bock beer.

bock beer a strong, sweet dark beer brewed in the winter and stored until the spring. [< G *Bockbier* for *Eimbocker Bier* beer of *Eimbock*, variant of Einbeck, a city in Germany]

bode¹ (bōd) *v.* **bod·ed, bod·ing.** be a sign of; indicate beforehand: *Dark clouds boded rain.*

bode ill, be a bad sign.

bode well, be a good sign.

[OE *bodian* < *boda* messenger]

bode² (bōd) *v.* pt. of **bide.**

bod·ice (bod′is) *n.* **1** the part of a dress from the shoulders to the waist. **2** an outer garment for women and girls, worn over a blouse and laced up the front. The bodice is part of the traditional dress of peasant women in some European countries. [var. of pl. of *body,* part of a dress]

–bodied *combining form.* having a body of a certain kind: *a full-bodied wine, able-bodied helpers.*

bod·i·less (bod′ē lis) *adj.* **1** without a body; lacking the trunk. **2** having no material form: *bodiless spirits.*

bod·i·ly (bod′ə lē) *adj., adv.* —*adj.* of or in the body: *bodily pain, assault causing bodily harm.* —*adv.* **1** in person: *The man we thought dead walked bodily into the room.* **2** all together; as one unit; entirely: *The audience rose bodily. She carried the kicking child bodily from the room.*

bod·kin (bod′kin) *n.* **1** a large, blunt needle with a large eye, used for pulling tape or ribbon through a casing, etc. **2** a long ornamental

hat, āge, fär; let, ēqual, tėrm; it, īce
hot, ōpen, ôrder; oil, out; cup, put, rüle,
əbove, takən, pencəl, lemən, circəs
ch, child; ng, long; sh, ship
th, thin; ᴛʜ, then; zh, measure

hairpin. **3** a small, pointed tool for making holes in fabric or leather. **4** *Archaic.* dagger; stiletto. [ME *boydekyn* dagger; origin unknown]

bod·y (bod′ē) *n., pl.* **bod·ies;** *v.* **bod·ied, bod·y·ing.** —*n.* **1** the whole material part of a human being, animal, or plant: *This boy has a strong, healthy body.* **2** the main part, or trunk, of a human being or animal, excluding the head and limbs. **3** the main part of anything, such as the nave of a church, the hull of a ship. **4** the part of a vehicle that holds the passengers or the load. **5** the fuselage of an airplane. **6** the main part of a speech or document, excluding the introduction, etc. **7** a group of persons considered together; collection of persons or things: *A large body of children sang at the concert.* **8** *Informal.* a person: *He is a good-natured body.* **9** a dead person; corpse. **10** a mass; portion of matter: *A lake is a body of water.* **11** matter; substance; density; substantial quality: *Thick soup has more body than thin soup.* **12** that part of a garment that covers the trunk of the body.

keep body and soul together, keep alive.

—*v.* provide with a body; give substance to; embody.

body forth, be a sign of; represent.

[OE *bodig*]

☛ *Hom.* **bawdy.**

bod·y·check (bod′ē chek′) *n., v. Cdn.* —*n. Hockey, lacrosse, etc.* a defensive play by which a player impedes an opponent's progress by body contact. Also, **body check.** —*v.* employ a bodycheck. —**bod′y·check′er,** *n.*

bod·y·guard (bod′ē gärd′) *n.* **1** a man or men who guard a person. **2** a retinue; escort.

body politic the people forming a political group with an organized government.

body shirt or **bod·y·shirt** (bod′ē shėrt′) *n.* a shirt or blouse for women or girls that ends in a kind of brief pantie with a fastening at the crotch.

body snatcher a person who steals bodies from graves.

body stocking a lightweight, close-fitting, stretchable garment consisting of a top, briefs, and, often, stockings, in one piece. Body stockings may be worn for exercising, by dancers, or, when made of elastic fabric, as a light support for the body.

Boe·o·tian (bē ō′shən) *n., adj.* —*n.* **1** a native or inhabitant of Boeotia, a district in ancient Greece. The Boeotians were considered stupid. **2** a stupid person. —*adj.* **1** of or having to do with Boeotia or its people. **2** stupid.

Boer (bür *or* bôr) *n.* a Dutch colonist or a person of Dutch descent living in South Africa. [< Du. *boer* farmer]

Boer War the war between Great Britain and the Boers of South Africa, which lasted from 1899 to 1902.

bof·fo (bof′ō) *adj. Informal.* **1** outstandingly successful or popular: *a boffo moire.* **2** sensational; great.

bog (bog) *n., v.* **bogged, bog·ging.** —*n.* soft, wet, spongy ground; a marsh or swamp. —*v.* sink or get stuck in a bog.

bog down, get stuck as if in mud.

[< Irish or Scots Gaelic *bog* soft]

bo·gan (bō′gən) *n. Esp. Cdn.* in the Maritimes, a backwater or quiet tributary stream of a river. [< Algonquian *pokelogan.* Doublet of LOGAN.]

bo·gey¹ (bō′gē) *n., pl.* **-geys;** *v.* —*n. Golf.* **1** one stroke over par: *He shot a bogey on the seventh hole.* **2** the standard score that players try to equal; par. —*v.* play a hole in one stroke over par. [< Colonel *Bogey,* imaginary partner]

bo·gey² or **bo·gy** (bō′gē) *n., pl.* **-geys. 1** an evil spirit or goblin. **2** a person or thing that causes annoyance or fear; bugaboo: *His bogey was mathematics.* **3** *Slang.* an unidentified aircraft. Also, **bogie.** [< obsolete *bog* bugbear]

bog·gle (bog′əl) *v.* **-gled, -gling;** *n.* —*v.* **1** be or become overwhelmed, as by the unexpectedness, difficulty, etc. of something: *His mind boggled at the thought of so much responsibility.* **2** overwhelm: *The idea of him as a star boggles the mind.* **3** hesitate or shy away. **4** bungle; botch.

—*n.* the act or an instance of boggling. [? < *bogle*] —**bog′gler,** *n.* —**bog′gling·ly,** *adv.*

bog·gy (bog′ē) *adj.* **-gi·er, -gi·est.** soft and wet like a bog; marshy; swampy.

bo·gie (bō′gē) See **bogey²**.

bo·gle (bō′gəl) *n.* bogey[2]. [See BOGEY[2].]

bo·gus (bō′gəs) *adj.* not genuine; counterfeit; sham: *a bogus twenty-dollar bill.*

bo·gy (bō′gē) *n., pl.* **-gies.** See **bogey**[2].

Bo·he·mi·a (bō hē′mē ə *or* bō hēm′yə) *n.* **1** a former country in central Europe, now a region of Czechoslovakia. **2** a free and easy, unconventional sort of life; a place where artists, writers, etc. live such a life.

Bo·he·mi·an (bō hē′mē ən *or* bō hēm′yən) *n., adj.* —*n.* **1** a native or inhabitant of Bohemia. **2** the language of Bohemia; Czech. **3** Often, **bohemian**, an artist, writer, etc. who lives in a free and easy, unconventional way. **4** gypsy.
—*adj.* **1** of Bohemia, its people, or their language. **2** Often, **bohemian**, free and easy; unconventional.

Bo·he·mi·an·ism (bō hē′mē ən iz′əm *or* bō hēm′yən iz′əm) *n.* a free and easy way of living; unconventional habits.

bohemian waxwing a brownish-grey waxwing (*Bombycilla garrulus*) found throughout N Eurasia and NW North America.

Bo·hunk (bō′hungk) *n. Slang. Derogatory.* a central-European immigrant; hunky[2]. [< *Bohem*ian + *Hung*arian]

boil[1] (boil) *v., n.* —*v.* **1** of liquids, bubble up and give off steam or vapor: *Water boils when heated to about* 100°C. **2** cause to boil. **3** cook by boiling: *to boil eggs.* **4** of a container, have its contents boil: *The kettle is boiling.* **5** clean or sterilize by boiling. **6** be very excited; be stirred up, especially by anger: *He is still boiling over the incident.* **7** move violently.
boil down, a reduce the bulk of by boiling: *to boil a sauce down.* **b** reduce by getting rid of unimportant parts: *He boiled down his notes to a list of important facts.*
boil over, a come to the boiling point and overflow. **b** show excitement or anger.
—*n.* **1** boiling. **2** a boiling condition. [ME *boille* < OF *boillir* < L *bullire* form bubbles]
☛ **Syn.** *v.* **6. Boil, simmer, seethe,** figuratively used, mean "to be emotionally excited." **Boil** suggests being so stirred up by emotion, usually anger, that one's feelings and, often, blood are thought of as heated to boiling point: *My blood boils at the suggestion.* **Simmer** suggests less intense emotion or greater control, so that one's feelings are just below the boiling point: *I was simmering with laughter.* **Seethe** suggests being violently stirred up, so that a person's mind or feelings or a group of people are thought of as boiling and foaming: *The people seethed with discontent.*

boil[2] (boil) *n.* a hard, round abscess in the skin and the tissues just beneath it, consisting of pus around a hard core: *Most boils are caused by bacteria entering an oil or sweat gland, a hair follicle, or a small wound.*
blind boil, a boil that has no visible pus sac.
[OE *bȳl(e)*]

boil·er (boil′ər) *n.* **1** a container for heating liquids. **2** a tank for making steam to heat buildings or drive engines. **3** a tank for holding hot water.

boil·er·mak·er (boi′lər mā′kər) *n.* **1** a person who makes or repairs boilers. **2** *Informal.* a drink of whisky followed by beer.

boiling point the temperature at which a liquid boils. The boiling point of water at sea level is 100 degrees Celsius.

bois–brû·lé (bwä′brü lā′; *French*, bwä brv lā′) *Cdn. Historical.* Métis. [< Cdn. F. *bois brûlé* charred wood, referring to the dark complexion of most Métis]

bois·ter·ous (bois′tər əs *or* bois′trəs) *adj.* **1** noisily cheerful: *a boisterous game.* **2** violent; rough: *a boisterous wind, a boisterous child.* [ME *boistrous*, earlier *boistous*; origin unknown]
—**bois′ter·ous·ly,** *adv.* —**bois′ter·ous·ness,** *n.*

bo·la (bō′lə) *n.* a weapon consisting of stone or metal balls tied to cords. South American cowboys throw the bola so that it winds around the animal at which it is aimed. [< Sp. and Pg. *bola* ball < L *bulla* bubble]

bo·las (bō′ləs) *n.* bola.

bold (bōld) *adj.* **1** without fear; daring: *a bold knight, a bold explorer.* **2** showing or requiring courage: *a bold act.* **3** too free in manner; impudent: *The bold little boy made faces at us as we passed.* **4** striking; vigorous; free; clear: *The mountains stood in bold outline against the sky.* **5** steep; abrupt: *Bold cliffs overlooked the sea.*
make bold, take the liberty; dare.
[OE *bald*] —**bold′ly,** *adv.* —**bold′ness,** *n.*
☛ **Syn.** **3. Bold, brazen, forward** = too free in manner. **Bold** suggests lacking proper shame and modesty and pushing oneself forward too rudely: *He swaggered into school late with a bold look on his face.* **Brazen** = defiantly and insolently shameless: *He is brazen about being expelled.* **Forward** suggests being too sure of oneself, too disrespectful of others, too pert in pushing oneself forward: *With her forward ways, that girl will make no friends.*

bold·face (bōld′fās′) *n. Printing.* a heavy type that stands out clearly. **This sentence is in boldface.** *Abbrev.:* bf.

bole (bōl) *n.* the trunk of a tree. [ME < ON *bolr*]
☛ *Hom.* **boll, bowl.**

bo·le·ro (bə ler′ō) *n., pl.* **-ros. 1** a lively Spanish dance in 3/4 time. **2** the music for it. **3** a short, loose jacket worn open at the front. [< Sp.]

bol·i·var (bol′ə vər; *Spanish*, bō lē′vär) *n.* **1** a unit of money in Venezuela. See table at **money. 2** a coin worth one bolivar. [< Simon *Bolivar* (1783-1830), Venezuelan general and statesman]

bo·liv·i·a (bə liv′ē ə) *n.* a soft, woollen cloth resembling plush. [< *Bolivia*, a country in South America]

Bo·liv·i·an (bə liv′ē ən) *n., adj.* —*n.* a native or inhabitant of Bolivia, a country in central South America. —*adj.* of or having to do with Bolivia or its people.

boll (bōl) *n.* a rounded seed pod or capsule of a plant, especially that of cotton or flax. See **cotton** for picture. [var. of *bowl*]
☛ *Hom.* **bole, bowl.**

boll weevil a weevil (*Anthonomus grandis*) of the S United States, Mexico, and Central America, that is a serious pest of cotton plants, both as larva and adult, feeding on the buds and bolls.

boll·worm (bōl′wėrm′) *n.* any of various moth caterpillars, such as the **pink bollworm** (*Pectinophora gossypiella*), that feed on cotton bolls.

bo·lo (bō′lō) *n., pl.* **-los.** a long, heavy knife, used in the Philippine Islands. [< Sp. < Philippine dial.]

bo·lo·gna (bə lō′nē *or* bə lō′nə) *n.* a large sausage made of beef, veal, and pork. [< *Bologna*, a city in Italy]

bo·lom·e·ter (bō lom′ə tər) *n.* an instrument used to measure the intensity of radiant energy, especially in small amounts. [< Gk. *bolē* ray + E *-meter*]

bo·lo·ney (bə lō′nē) *n. Esp.Brit.* baloney.

Bol·she·vik (bol′shə vik′ *or* bōl′shə vik′) *n., pl.* **Bol·she·viks** or **Bol·she·vi·ki** (bol′shə vē′kē *or* bōl′shə vē′kē); *adj.* —*n.* **1** a member of the radical wing of the Russian Social Democratic Party, which seized power in November, 1917. The Bolsheviks formed the Communist party in 1918. **2** a Communist, especially in the Soviet Union. **3** Often, **bolshevik**, any extreme radical, especially a political revolutionary.
—*adj.* **1** of or having to do with the Bolsheviks or Bolshevism. **2** Often, **bolshevik**, extremely radical. [< Russian *bolshevik* < *bolshe* greater; because it was at one time the majority wing. Opposed to MENSHEVIK.]

Bol·she·vism or **bol·she·vism** (bol′shə viz′əm *or* bōl′shə viz′əm) *n.* **1** the doctrines and methods of the Bolsheviks. **2** extreme radicalism.

Bol·she·vist (bol′shə vist *or* bōl′shə vist) *n. or adj.* Bolshevik.

Bol·she·vis·tic (bol′shə vis′tik *or* bōl′shə vis′tik) *adj.* of, having to do with, or like the Bolsheviks.

Bol·she·vize or **bol·she·vize** (bol′shə vīz′ *or* bōl′shə vīz′) *v.* **-vized, -viz·ing.** make Bolshevistic. —**Bol′she·vi·za′tion** or **bol′she·vi·za′tion,** *n.*

bol·ster (bōl′stər) *n., v.* —*n.* **1** a long pillow for a bed. **2** a pad or cushion, often ornamental. —*v.* **1** support with or as if with a bolster (*often used with* **up**): *The baby was bolstered with pillows.* **2** give support or a boost to; prop (*often used with* **up**): *to bolster a theory with additional evidence.* [OE]

bolt[1] (bōlt) *n., v., adv.* —*n.* **1** a rod made to hold parts together, having a head at one end and a thread on the other. A bolt is placed through holes that have been drilled for it, and is held in place by a nut screwed onto the threaded end. **2** a sliding fastener for a door, gate, etc. **3** the part of a lock moved by a key. **4** a sliding bar that opens and closes the breech of a rifle, etc. The opening and closing of the bolt after firing ejects the used cartridge case and places a new one in position for firing. **5** a short arrow with a thick head. Bolts were shot from crossbows. **6** a discharge of lightning. **7** a sudden start; a running away. **8** a roll of cloth or wallpaper. **9** refusal to support one's political party or its candidates.
bolt from the blue, a sudden, unexpected happening; surprise.
shoot (one's) bolt, do as much or as well as one can; do all one can so that further effort is either useless or impossible: *He would like to have tried again for the championship, but he was over age and had shot his bolt.*
—*v.* **1** fasten with a bolt. **2** dash away; run away: *The horse bolted.* **3** break away from or refuse to support one's political party or its candidates. **4** move suddenly; rush. **5** swallow (food) without chewing. **6** of cultivated plants, go to seed too quickly. Some kinds of lettuce often bolt in hot weather.
—*adv.*
bolt upright, stiff and straight: *Awakened by a noise, he sat bolt upright in bed.*
[OE *bolt* arrow]

bolt[2] (bōlt) *v.* **1** sift through a cloth or sieve: *Flour is bolted to*

remove the bran. 2 examine carefully; separate. [ME *bulte* < OF *bulter*]

bolt·er¹ (bōl′tər) *n.* 1 a horse that runs away. 2 a person who breaks away from or refuses to support his political party or its candidates. [< *bolt¹*]

bolt·er² (bōl′tər) *n.* a cloth or sieve used for sifting flour, meal, etc. [< *bolt²*]

bo·lus (bō′ləs) *n.* 1 a small, rounded mass, especially of medicine. 2 a lump of masticated food, ready to swallow. 3 any small, rounded mass. [< L < Gk. *bōlos* lump]

bomb (bom) *n., v.* —*n.* 1 a container filled with an explosive charge or a chemical substance and exploded by a fuse or a timing mechanism, or by contact when something hits or touches it. 2 a container filled with liquid under pressure, such as paint, insect poison, etc.: *We used a bomb to rid the house of moths.* 3 a sudden, unexpected happening; disturbing surprise. 4 *Slang.* a miserable failure.
the bomb, nuclear weapons: *Many nations already have the bomb.*
—*v.* 1 attack, damage, or destroy with a bomb or bombs, especially by dropping bombs from aircraft. 2 *Slang.* fail completely and miserably: *All the jokes he made in his speech bombed because he was so nervous.* 3 *Slang.* move quickly: *bombing along the highway.* [< MF *bombe* < Ital. < L *bombus* < Gk. *bombos* boom¹]
☞ *Hom.* balm.

bom·bard (bom bärd′) *v.* 1 attack with heavy fire of shot and shell from big guns: *The artillery bombarded the enemy all day.* 2 drop bombs on: *Aircraft bombarded the hydro-electric plant and destroyed it.* 3 keep attacking vigorously: *The lawyer bombarded the witness with question after question.* 4 *Physics.* subject (atomic nuclei) to a stream of fast-moving particles, thus changing the structure of the nuclei. [< F *bombarder* < *bombarde* cannon < Med.L *bombarda* < L *bombus.* See BOMB.] —**bom·bard′ment**, *n.*

bom·bar·dier¹ (bom′bə dēr′ *or* bom′ə dēr′) *n.* 1 the member of the crew of a bomber who aims and releases the bombs. 2 a corporal in the artillery. *Abbrev.*: Bdr. [< MF *bombardier* < *bombarde* cannon. See BOMBARD.]

A bombardier

bom·bar·dier² (bom′bə dēr′) *n. Cdn.* 1 a large covered vehicle used for travelling over snow and ice, usually equipped with tracked wheels at the rear and a set of skis at the front. 2 **Bombardier,** *Trademark.* a brand of such machines. [after Armand *Bombardier* (1908-1964), inventor and manufacturer of the machine]

bom·ba·sine (bom′bə zēn′ *or* bom′bə zēn′) See **bombazine.**

bom·bast (bom′bast) *n.* high-sounding, pompous language. [earlier *bombace* < OF *bombace, bambace* < Med.L < Med.Gk. *bambax* cotton < Gk. *bombyx* silkworm, silk]

bom·bas·tic (bom bas′tik) *adj.* using bombast.
—**bom·bas′ti·cal·ly,** *adv.*

bom·ba·zine (bom′bə zēn′ *or* bom′bə zēn′) *n.* a twilled cloth made of silk and wool or cotton and wool. Also, **bombasine.** [< early modern F *bombasin* < Ital. *bambagino* made of cotton, ult. < Med.Gk. *bambax* cotton. See BOMBAST.]

bomb bay the space or compartment in the underside of a combat aircraft in which bombs are carried and from which they are dropped.

bombed (bomd) *adj. Slang.* completely under the influence of alcohol or drugs.

bomb·er (bom′ər) *n.* 1 a combat aircraft used to drop bombs on enemy troops, factories, cities, etc. 2 a person who throws or drops bombs.

bomb·proof (bom′prüf′) *adj., n.* —*adj.* strong or deep enough to be safe from bombs and shells. —*n.* a bombproof shelter.

bomb·shell (bom′shel′) *n.* 1 a bomb. 2 a sudden, unexpected happening; disturbing surprise.

bomb·sight (bom′sīt′) *n.* an instrument used to find that point in the flight of an airplane where dropping a bomb will cause the bomb to fall exactly on the target.

bomb·site (bom′sīt′) *n.* a district or area that has suffered damage from bombs.

bo·na fi·de (bō′nə fīd′, bō′nə fī′dē, *or* bō′nə fē′dā) in good faith; genuine; without make-believe or fraud. [< L]

bo·nan·za (bə nan′zə) *n.* 1 a rich mass of ore in a mine. 2 *Informal.* any rich source of profit. [< Sp. *bonanza* fair weather, prosperity < L *bonus* good]

hat, āge, fär; let, ēqual, tèrm; it, īce
hot, ōpen, ôrder; oil, out; cup, pùt, rüle,
əbove, takən, pencəl, lemən, circəs

ch, child; ng, long; sh, ship
th, thin; ŦH, then; zh, measure

Bo·na·part·ist (bō′nə pär′tist) *n.* a follower or supporter of Napoleon Bonaparte (1769-1821) and his family.

bon·bon (bon′bon′) *n.* a piece of candy. Bonbons often have fancy shapes. [< F]

bond¹ (bond) *n., v.* —*n.* 1 anything that ties, binds, or unites: *a bond of affection between sisters.* 2 a certificate of debt issued by a government or company that is borrowing money, promising to pay back, by a certain date, the money borrowed plus interest. 3 *Law.* a written agreement by which a person says he will pay a certain sum of money if he does not perform certain duties properly. 4 any agreement or binding engagement. 5 a person who acts as surety for another. 6 bond paper. 7 the condition of goods placed in a warehouse until taxes are paid: *Imported jewellery is held in bond until customs duty has been paid.* 8 a way of arranging bricks, stones, or boards to bind them together. 9 a substance that binds together the other ingredients of a mixture: *Cement is the bond in concrete.* 10 **bonds,** *pl.* **a** chains; shackles. **b** imprisonment.
—*v.* 1 issue bonds on; mortgage. 2 take out an insurance policy to pay for any losses caused by an employee: *The company bonds all its cashiers to protect itself in case any of them proves to be dishonest.* 3 put (goods) under bond. 4 bind or join firmly together. [var. of *band²*] —**bond′a·ble,** *adj.* —**bond′er,** *n.*
☞ *Syn. n.* 1. **Bond, tie,** used figuratively, mean something that joins people. **Bond** applies particularly to a connection that brings two people or a group so closely together that they may be considered as one: *The members of the club are joined by bonds of fellowship.* **Tie** may be used interchangeably with **bond,** but applies particularly to connections of a more involved and less voluntary nature: *When he went away, he severed all ties with his old life.*

bond² (bond) *adj.* in slavery; captive; not free. [ME < ON *bóndi* peasant, originally, dweller]

bond·age (bon′dij) *n.* 1 the lack of freedom; slavery. 2 the condition of being under some power or influence.

bond·ed (bon′did) *adj.* 1 guaranteed by a bond or bonds: *The company's drivers are bonded.* 2 put in a warehouse until taxes are paid.

bond·hold·er (bond′hōl′dər) *n.* a person who owns bonds issued by a government or company.

bond·maid (bond′mād′) *n.* a girl or woman slave.

bond·man (bond′mən) *n., pl.* **-men.** 1 a slave. 2 in the Middle Ages, a serf.

bond paper a good quality of strong paper, made at least partly from rag pulp: *Bond paper was originally used for documents.*

bond servant 1 a servant bound to work without pay, sometimes for a specified time only. 2 a slave.

bonds·man (bondz′mən) *n., pl.* **-men.** 1 a person who becomes responsible for another by giving a bond. 2 a slave. 3 in the Middle Ages, a serf.

bond·wom·an (bond′wùm′ən) *n., pl.* **-wom·en.** a female slave.

bone (bōn) *n., v.* **boned, bon·ing.** —*n.* 1 one of the parts of the skeleton of a vertebrate. 2 the hard substance of which bones are made. 3 anything like bone. Ivory is sometimes called bone. 4 **bones,** *pl.* **a** *Slang.* dice. **b** wooden clappers used in keeping time to music. **c** an end man in a minstrel show. **d** a skeleton. 5 a small thing given to soothe or make quiet, especially in order to avoid trouble: *throwing a bone to angry workers in the form of a small pay increase.*
feel in (one's) **bones,** be sure without knowing why.
have a bone to pick, having cause for argument or complaint.
make no bones, *Informal.* have no scruples; show no hesitation.
near the bone, a very exacting; mean: *A harsh employer comes near the bone.* **b** nearly indecent or obscene: *The speaker's jokes were very near the bone.*
—*v.* 1 take bones out of: *to bone fish.* 2 stiffen by putting whalebone or steel strips in. 3 *Informal.* study intensively, as for an examination (*usually used with* up): *You'd better bone up on your facts before you go for the interview.*
[OE *bān*] —**bone′less,** *adj.* —**bone′like′,** *adj.*

bone·black (bōn′blak′) *n.* a black powder made by roasting bones in closed containers, used to remove color from liquids and as a coloring matter.

bone china a particularly white and translucent type of china made by mixing bone ash or calcium phosphate with clay.

bone·dry (bōn′drī) *adj.* very dry.

bone meal crushed or ground bones, used as fertilizer and as food for animals.

bon·er (bōn′ər) *n. Slang.* a foolish mistake; stupid error; blunder.

bone·set (bōn′set′) *n.* a North American plant (*Eupatorium perfoliatum*) of the composite family having flat clusters of small white flowers formerly used in folk medicine.

bon·fire (bon′fīr′) *n.* a large fire built on the ground outdoors. [ME *bonefire* bone fire]

bon·go (bong′gō) *n., pl.* **—gos** or **goes.** one of a pair of small connected drums, one slightly larger than the other, that are played with the hands, usually while being held between the knees. [< Am. Sp.]

bon·ho·mie (bon′ə mē′) *n.* good nature; courteous and pleasant ways. [< F *bonhomie* < *bonhomme* good fellow]

Bon·homme (bo nom′; *French,* bôn ôm′) *n. Cdn.* a traditional character of the winter carnival in Quebec City. The Bonhomme is a giant snowman. [< Cdn. F *Bonhomme Carnaval* Carnival Fellow]

bo·ni·to (bə nē′tō) *n., pl.* **-tos** or **toes.** any of several food and game fishes (especially genus *Sarda*) of the mackerel family, steel blue and silvery in color, with dark, narrow stripes, found mainly in tropical seas. Bonitos are similar in form to tuna, but smaller. [< Sp. *bonito* pretty < L *bonus* good]

bon jour (bôN zhür′) *French.* good morning; good day.

bonk (bongk) *n.* or *v. Slang.* hit, especially on the head.

bon mot (bôN mō′) *pl.* **bons mots** (bôN mōz′; *French,* bôN mō′). *French.* a clever saying; witty remark.

bon·net (bon′it) *n., v.* —*n.* **1** a head covering usually tied under the chin with strings or ribbons, worn by babies and little girls. **2** a similar head covering formerly worn by girls and women. **3** a round, brimless cap worn by men and boys in Scotland. **4** war bonnet. **5** a metal covering or hood over a machine, chimney, etc. **6** *Esp.Brit.* the hood covering the engine of a car, truck, etc. —*v.* put a bonnet on. [ME < OF *bonet, bonnet,* originally, fabric for hats]

bon·nie or **bon·ny** (bon′ē) *adj.* **-ni·er, -ni·est. 1** pretty; handsome. **2** fine; excellent. **3** healthy-looking. [ME *bonie,* apparently < OF *bon, bonne* good < L *bonus*] —**bon′ni·ly,** *adv.* —**bon′ni·ness,** *n.*

bon·sai (bon′sī *or* bōn′sī) *n.* **1** a small potted tree or shrub that has been dwarfed by a special process that includes the pruning of branches and roots, placement in a shallow dish, etc. **2** the art of dwarfing trees and shrubs in this way.

bon soir (bôN swär′) *French.* good evening.

bon·spiel (bon′spēl′) *n. Curling.* a tournament among different clubs or among teams of the same club. [Scots < Du. *bond* contract, league + *spel* game]

bon ton (bôN tôN′) *French.* **1** good style; fashion. **2** fashionable society. **3** good breeding.

bo·nus (bō′nəs) *n., v.* —*n.* something extra; something given in addition to what is due: *The company gave all its employees a Christmas bonus.* —*v. Cdn.* offer a bonus for (work to be done, as for the construction of a railway line); subsidize. [< L *bonus* good]

bon vi·vant (bôN vē väN′) *pl.* **bons vi·vants** (bôN vē väN′). *French.* a person who is fond of good food and luxury.

bon vo·yage (bôN vwä yäzh′) *French.* goodbye; a farewell for someone going on a trip.

bon·y (bōn′ē) *adj.* **bon·i·er, bon·i·est. 1** of bone. **2** like bone. **3** full of bones. **4** having big bones that stick out. **5** thin. —**bon′i·ness,** *n.*

boo (bü) *n., pl.* **boos;** *interj., v.* **booed, boo·ing.** —*n. or interj.* a sound made to show dislike or contempt or to frighten. —*v.* **1** make such a sound. **2** cry "boo" at.

boob (büb) *n., v.* —*n. Slang.* **1** a stupid person; fool; dunce. **2** a silly mistake; booboo: *I made a real boob on the exam.* **3** *Vulgar slang.* a woman's breast. —*v. Slang.* make a silly mistake. [< *booby.* See BOOBY.]

boo-boo (bü′bü′) *n. Slang.* a silly mistake.

boob tube *Slang.* a television set.

boo·by (bü′bē) *n., pl.* **-bies. 1** a stupid person; fool; dunce. **2** a kind of large sea bird of the tropics. **3** the person who does worst in

a game or contest. [probably < Sp. *bobo* (defs. 1, 2) < L *balbus* stammering]

booby hatch 1 the covering over a hatchway on a boat. **2** *Slang.* an asylum for the insane.

booby prize a prize given to the person who does worst in a game or contest.

booby trap 1 a trick arranged to annoy some unsuspecting person. **2** a bomb arranged to explode when an object is grasped, pushed, etc. by an unsuspecting person.

boo·dle (bü′dəl) *n. Slang.* **1** graft; money from bribes. **2** caboodle. [Du. *boedel* goods]

boog·ie–woog·ie (bùg′ē wùg′ē) *n. Music.* a style of jazz characterized by a repeating rhythmic pattern of eighth notes in the bass, accompanying a melody that is often improvised. Boogie-woogie is usually played on the piano.

boo·hoo (bü′hü′) *v.* **-hooed, -hoo·ing;** *n., pl.* **-hoos.** —*v.* cry loudly. —*n.* loud crying.

book (bùk) *n., v.* —*n.* **1** a set of written or printed sheets of paper stitched or glued together along one edge and usually having attached covers at the front and back: *a book of poetry.* **2** a long work, or composition, that is written or printed: *She writes books about camping.* **3** a set of blank sheets bound together along one edge, used for taking notes, drawing, keeping records, etc. **4** a main division of a literary work: *the books of the Bible.* **5** something fastened together like a book: *a book of tickets, a book of matches.* **6** the words of an opera, operetta, etc.; libretto. **7** the **Book,** the bible. **8** something thought of as providing knowledge if it is studied or "read" like a book: *the book of nature, the book of life.* **9** a record of bets. **10** in certain card games, a trick or a specified number of tricks forming a set. **11** **books,** *pl.* the complete records of a business: *She keeps the books for their business.* **12** the **book,** the telephone directory of a particular town or city: *Are you in the book?*

bring to book, a demand an explanation from. **b** rebuke.

by the book, according to the proper or accepted way; strictly according to the rules: *When she was chairman, our meetings were always run by the book.*

close the books, stop entering items in an account book.

in (one's) **book,** *Informal.* in one's opinion or judgment: *In my book, swearing is always unnecessary.*

in (one's) **good** (or **bad**) **books,** in favor (or disfavor) with one: *He may be wild, but he is still in my good books.*

know like a book, understand very well; know everything about: *My mother knows me like a book, and can always tell when I have a problem.*

on the books, on the official list (of members of a club, university, etc.).

read like a book, guess accurately what a person is thinking, feeling, or planning: *He tried to hide it, but I can always read him like a book and I knew he was afraid.*

throw the book at, *Slang.* punish as severely as the law allows: *This is his third offence, so the judge will probably throw the book at him.*

—*v.* **1** enter in a book or list. **2** *Informal.* record a charge against a person at a police station: *She was booked on a charge of theft.* **3** engage a place, passage, etc.; make a reservation: *to book a room in a hotel, to book theatre tickets.* **4** hire; make engagements for: *The lecturer is booked for every night this week.* [OE *bōc*] —**book′er,** *n.* —**book′less,** *adj.*

book·bind·er (bùk′bīn′dər) *n.* a person whose work or business is binding books.

book·bind·er·y (bùk′bīn′dər ē *or* -bīn′drē) *n., pl.* **-er·ies.** an establishment for binding books.

book·binding (bùk′bīnd′ing) *n.* **1** the binding of a book. **2** the art or business of binding books.

book·case (bùk′kās′) *n.* a piece of furniture with shelves for holding books.

book club a business organization that regularly supplies selected books to subscribers.

book end a support placed at the end of a row of books to hold them upright.

book·ie (bùk′ē) *n. Informal.* bookmaker (def. 2).

book·ing (bùk′ing) *n.* **1** an engagement to perform, lecture, etc.: *The pianist has bookings for a six-week tour.* **2** a reservation: *He made a booking for his flight to Yellowknife. We have a booking at the hotel.*

book·ish (bùk′ish) *adj.* **1** fond of reading or studying. **2** knowing books better than real life. **3** having to do with books. **4** learned; pedantic. —**book′ish·ly,** *adv.* —**book′ish·ness,** *n.*

book·keep·er (bùk′kēp′ər) *n.* a person whose work is bookkeeping.

book·keep·ing (bùk′kēp′ing) *n.* the process or practice of recording, classifying, and summarizing data about the business transactions of a company, according to a particular system.

book learning knowledge learned from books, not from real life.

book·let (bùk′lit) *n.* a little book; a thin book or pamphlet. It usually has paper covers.

book·lore (bùk′lôr′) *n.* book learning.

book·mak·er (bùk′māk′ər) *n.* **1** a maker of books. **2** a person who makes a business of accepting bets on horse races.

book·mak·ing (bùk′māk′ing) *n.* **1** the business of taking bets on horse races, etc. at odds fixed by the takers. **2** the compiling and manufacture of books.

book·man (bùk′mən) *n.* **1** a scholar or literary man. **2** a publisher, editor, or other person engaged in the book business.

book·mark (bùk′märk′) *n.* **1** something put between the pages of a book to mark the place. **2** a bookplate.

book matches a strip of paper matches enclosed in a cardboard folder.

book·mo·bile (bùk′mə bēl′) *n.* a large van or trailer that serves as a travelling branch of a public library.

Book of Common Prayer the book containing the prayers and services of the Church of England or the Anglican Church of Canada.

Book of Mormon the sacred book of the Mormon Church.

Book of the Dead a collection of ancient Egyptian religious maxims that were intended to guide the soul on its way out of this world.

book·plate (bùk′plāt′) *n.* a label for pasting in books, having the owner's name or emblem printed on it.

book·rack (bùk′rak′) *n.* **1** a rack for holding an open book. **2** a rack for holding a row of books.

book review an article written about a book, discussing its merits, faults, etc.

book·sell·er (bùk′sel′ər) *n.* a person whose business is selling books.

book·shelf (bùk′shelf′) *n.* a shelf for holding books.

book·shop (bùk′shop′) *n.* bookstore.

book·stall (bùk′stol′ *or* -stôl′) *n.* a place where books, usually second-hand, are sold, often outdoors.

book·stand (bùk′stand′) *n.* **1** a stand for holding an open book. **2** a stand or counter for showing books for sale. **3** a place where books are sold.

book·store (bùk′stôr′) *n.* a store where books are sold.

book value the value of anything as it appears on the account books of the owner. It may be higher or lower than the real or present value.

book·work (bùk′wèrk′) *n.* **1** the keeping of records, ledgers, etc. for a business. **2** the study or use of books: *He always did far better in the laboratory than in his bookwork.*

book·worm (bùk′wèrm′) *n.* **1** any of various insects whose adult forms or larvae gnaw the bindings or pages of books. The silverfish is one of the most widely known kinds of bookworm. **2** a person who is excessively fond of reading and studying.

boom¹ (bùm) *n., v.* —*n.* **1** a deep, hollow sound like the roar of cannon or of big waves. **2** a sudden activity and increase in business, prices, or values of property; rapid growth: *Our town is having such a boom that it is likely to double its size in two years.* **3** (*adj.*) produced by a boom: *boom prices.*
—*v.* **1** make a deep, hollow sound: *The man's voice boomed out above the rest.* **2** utter with such a sound: *The big guns boomed their message.* **3** increase suddenly in activity; grow rapidly; *Business is booming.* [imitative] —**boom′er**, *n.*

boom² (bùm) *n.* **1** a long pole or beam, used to extend the bottom of a sail. See **sloop** for picture. **2** the lifting or guiding pole of a derrick. **3** *Lumbering.* **a** a chain, cable, or line of timbers used to keep logs from floating away. **b** the enclosure formed by such a chain, etc.: *The logs were held in booms upstream from the mill.* **c** a collection of logs held together by a chain, etc. for towing by water. [< Du. *boom* tree, pole]

boom·er·ang (bùm′ər ang′) *n., v.* —*n.* **1** a narrow, flat, curved or angular piece of wood used as a throwing weapon by native peoples of Australia. One type can be thrown so that it will return to the thrower if it misses its target. **2** anything that recoils or reacts to harm the doer or user. —*v.* act as a boomerang. [< native dial. of New South Wales]

booming ground *Cdn.* the part of a river, lake, or ocean where logs are dumped to be gathered into booms, or where booms of logs are held.

boom town a town that has grown up suddenly, usually as a result of an increase in economic activity. Boom towns are often found near newly discovered oil fields, gold strikes, etc.

hat, āge, fär; let, ēqual, tèrm; it, īce
hot, ōpen, ôrder; oil, out; cup, pùt, rüle,
əbove, takən, pencəl, lemən, circəs

ch, child; ng, long; sh, ship
th, thin; ᴛн, then; zh, measure

boon¹ (bün) *n.* **1** a blessing; great benefit. **2** *Archaic.* something asked or granted as a favor. [ME < ON *bón* petition]

boon² (bün) *adj.* **1** jolly; merry: *a boon companion.* **2** *Poetic.* kindly; pleasant. [ME < OF *bon* good < L *bonus*]

boon·docks (bün′doks) *n.pl. Slang.* rough backwoods; bush country. [< Tagalog *bundók* mountain]

boon·dog·gle (bün′dog′əl) *v.* **-gled, -gling;** *n.* —*v. Informal.* do trivial, unnecessary, or pointless work. —*n.* **1** *Informal.* trivial, unnecessary, or pointless work or its product. **2** *Cdn.* a device used to take up the slack in a chin strap, such as a large wooden bead. [origin uncertain] —**boon′dog′gler**, *n.*

boon·ies (bü′nēz) *n.pl. Slang.* boondocks.

boor (bùr) *n.* **1** a rude, bad-mannered, insensitive person. **2** a person who is clumsy and awkward in unfamiliar social situations; yokel. [< LG *bur* or Du. *boer* farmer]

boor·ish (bùr′ish) *adj.* rude; having bad manners; clumsy. —**boor′ish·ly**, *adv.* —**boor′ish·ness**, *n.*

boost (büst) *n., v. Informal.* —*n.* **1** a push or shove that helps a person in rising or advancing: *a boost over the fence.* **2** an increase: *a boost in salary.*
—*v.* **1** lift or push from below or behind. **2** raise; increase: *to boost prices, to boost sales.* **3** help by speaking well of or promoting activity: *to boost a new product.* [blend of *boom* and *hoist*]

boost·er (büst′ər) *n.* **1** a person or thing that boosts. **2** the first stage of a multistage rocket. **3** the device used to orbit an artificial satellite. **4** any auxiliary device for increasing force, power, etc. **5** *Informal.* booster shot.

booster cables a pair of heavy, insulated cables each fitted with a spring clip at each end for connecting the terminals of two batteries, used to start a motor vehicle with a weak or discharged battery by means of power from another battery. Also called **jumper cables.**

boost·er·ism (büs′tər iz′əm) *n.* the practice of promoting an event, region, city, etc. aggressively or extravagantly.

booster shot a supplementary injection of vaccine or serum, given to reinforce an earlier inoculation.

booster station a television or radio installation that picks up, amplifies, and relays signals from the main transmitting station.

boot¹ (büt) *n., v.* —*n.* **1** a covering for the foot and lower part of the leg, made of leather, rubber, or a synthetic material such as vinyl. **2** a kick. **3** the place for luggage in a horse-drawn coach. **4** *Brit.* the trunk of an automobile. **5** a bootlike protective covering or sheath for a mechanical device, etc. **6** an instrument of torture formerly used to crush a person's leg. **7** *U.S. Slang.* a new recruit in training in the United States Navy or Marines. **8 the boot,** *Slang.* rude or abrupt dismissal, as from a job.
bet your boots, depend on it; be sure: *You can bet your boots that our team will win.*
die with (one's) **boots on, a** die in battle; die fighting. **b** die working, especially for a cause.
have (one's) **heart in** (one's) **boots,** be dejected or discouraged.
lick (a person's) **boots,** flatter (a person); follow or obey slavishly.
the boot is on the other leg, the situation is reversed; the responsibility is on the other party.
too big for (one's) **boots,** *Informal.* having an excessively high opinion of oneself; conceited: *When he won the athlete-of-the-year award, he became much too big for his boots.*
wipe (one's) **boots on,** treat in an insulting way.

RETURNING BOOMERANG
NON-RETURNING BOOMERANG

Australian boomerangs

—v. **1** put boots on. **2** give a kick to; drive or move by kicking: *He booted the stone off the sidewalk.* **3** *Slang.* dismiss or get rid of rudely or abruptly (*usually used with* out). [ME < OF *bote* < Gmc.]

boot² (büt) *n., v.* —*n. Archaic.* profit; benefit.
to boot, in addition; besides: *He gave me his knife for my book and fifty cents to boot.*
—v. *Archaic.* benefit; avail. [OE *bōt* advantage]

boot·black (büt′blak′) *n.* a person whose work is shining shoes and boots.

boot·ed (bü′təd) *adj.* wearing boots: *He was booted and spurred.*

boot·ee (bü′tē) *n.* **1** a baby's soft shoe. **2** a woman's short boot.

Bo·ö·tes (bō ō′tēz) *n. Astronomy.* a northern constellation that includes the star Arcturus. [< L < Gk. *boōtēs* ox-driver < *bous* ox]

booth (büth) *n., pl.* **booths** (büᴛнz *or* büths). **1** a place where goods are displayed for sale at a fair, market, etc. **2** a small, closed place for a telephone, motion-picture projector, etc. **3** a small, closed place for voting at elections. **4** a partly enclosed space in a restaurant, café, etc., containing a table and seats for a few persons. [ME < Scand.; cf. ODanish *both*]

boot·jack (büt′jak′) *n.* a device to help in pulling off boots.

boot·leg (büt′leg′) *v.* **-legged, -leg·ging;** *adj., n.* —*v.* sell, transport, or make unlawfully.
—*adj.* made, transported, or sold unlawfully.
—*n. Informal.* alcoholic liquor made, sold or transported unlawfully. [modern use from the practice of smuggling liquor in boot legs]

boot·leg·ger (büt′leg′ər) *n. Informal.* a person who bootlegs.

boot·less¹ (büt′lis) *adj.* without shoes or boots.

boot·less² (büt′lis) *adj.* of no avail; useless. [< *boot²*]
—**boot′less·ly**, *adv.*

boot·lick (büt′lik′) *v. Informal.* fawn on a person to try to gain favor; toady: *He was determined to make it on his own, without bootlicking. They would bootlick anyone with influence.*

boot·lick·er (büt′lik′ər) *n. Informal.* a person who fawns on another in order to gain favor; flatterer; toady.

boots (büts) *n. Brit.* a servant who shines shoes and boots and does other menial tasks.

boots and saddles a bugle call to mount horses.

boot·strap (büt′strap′) *n.* **1** a strap or loop at the top of a boot, used for pulling it on. **2** (*adj.*) done or undertaken without outside help: *a bootstrap campaign.*
by (one's) **own bootstraps**, by one's own efforts; without help from others: *He raised himself to his present position by his own bootstraps.*

boot tree a wooden or metal device shaped like a foot and put into a boot to keep it in shape.

boo·ty (bü′tē) *n., pl.* **-ties. 1** things taken from the enemy in war. **2** things seized by violence and robbery; plunder: *The pirates fought over the booty from the raided town.* **3** any valuable thing or things obtained; prize. [Related to BOOT².]
☛ *Syn.* 1, 2. See note at **plunder.**

booze (büz) *n., v.* **boozed, booz·ing.** *Informal.* —*n.* **1** any intoxicating liquor. **2** a spree. —*v.* drink heavily. [probably < MDu. *busen* drink to excess] —**booz′er,** *n.*

booz·y (bü′zē) *adj.* **booz·i·er, booz·i·est. 1** rather drunk, especially as a habitual state. **2** involving the drinking of too much intoxicating liquor: *a long, boozy lunch.* —**booz′i·ly,** *adv.*
—**booz′i·ness,** *n.*

bop¹ (bop) *n., v.* **bopped, bop·ping.** *Slang.* —*n.* a blow with the hand, a club, etc. —*v.* hit; strike.

bop² (bop) *n.* bebop.

bor. borough.

bo·rac·ic (bə ras′ik) *adj.* boric.

bor·age (ber′ij *or* bôr′ij) *n.* **1** a plant (*Borago officinalis*) having hairy leaves and blue or purplish flowers, native to S Europe. It is used in salads, in flavoring beverages, and in medicine. **2** (*adj.*) designating the family (Boraginaceae) of flowering plants of temperate and tropical regions that includes borage, heliotrope, and forget-me-not. [< OF *bourrache* < Med.L *borrago* < *burra* rough hair]

bo·rate (bô′rāt *or* bô′rit) *n.* a salt or ester of boric acid.

bo·rat·ed (bô′rāt id) *adj.* mixed or treated with boric acid or borax.

bo·rax (bô′raks) *n.* white crystalline powder, used as an antiseptic, in washing clothes, in fusing metals, and in preserving foods; sodium borate. *Formula:* Na₂B₄O₇ [ME *boras* < Med.L < Arabic *buwraq* < Persian *bōrah*]

bor·a·zon (bôr′ə zon′) *n. Chemistry.* a crystalline compound of boron and nitrogen, harder than diamond and having a higher melting point. [< *bor*on + *azo* + *n*itrogen]

Bor·deaux (bôr dō′) *n.* a red or white wine made in the Bordeaux region of SW France.

Bordeaux mixture a liquid mixture of copper sulphate, lime, and water, used as a fungicide.

bor·del·lo (bôr del′ō) *n.* brothel. [< Ital. < Med.L *bordellus,* dim. of *borda* cottage]

bor·der (bôr′dər) *n., v.* —*n.* **1** an edge, rim, or outer part of something: *a plate with a fluted border.* **2** the line separating two countries, provinces, etc., or two geographical regions; boundary; frontier: *We reached Detroit by crossing the border at Windsor.* **3** a strip on or near the edge of anything for strength or ornament: *a handkerchief with a lace border. Our lawn has a border of flowers.*
—*v.* **1** form a boundary to; bound. **2** put a border on; edge. **3** touch at the border; be adjacent (*used with* on *or* upon). **4** approach in character; verge (*used with* on): *The accusations in the newspaper article border on libel.* [ME < OF *bordure* < *border* to border < *bord* side < Gmc.]
☛ *Hom.* **boarder.**

bor·der·er (bôr′dər ər) *n.* a person who lives on the border of a country or region.

bor·der·land (bôr′dər land′) *n.* **1** the land forming, or next to, a border. **2** an uncertain district, space, or condition: *the borderland between sleeping and waking.*

bor·der·line (bôr′dər līn′) *n., adj.* —*n.* a boundary; dividing line.
—*adj.* **1** on a border or boundary. **2** uncertain; in between.

bor·dure (bôr′jər) *n. Heraldry.* a border around a shield, covering one fifth of its surface. [earlier form of *border*]

bore¹ (bôr) *v.* **bored, bor·ing;** *n.* —*v.* **1** make a hole by means of a tool that keeps turning, or by penetrating as a worm does in fruit. **2** make (a hole, passage, entrance, etc.) by pushing through or digging out: *A mole has bored its way under the hedge.* **3** make a round hole in; hollow out evenly. **4** be capable of being bored by a tool: *Soft wood bores easily.*
—*n.* **1** a hole made by a revolving tool. **2** the hollow space inside a pipe, tube, or gun barrel: *He cleaned the bore of his gun.* **3** the distance across the inside of a hole or tube. [OE *borian*]
☛ *Hom.* **boar.**

bore² (bôr) *v.* **bored, bor·ing;** *n.* —*v.* make weary by dull or tiresome behavior or conversation. —*n.* a dull, tiresome person or thing. [origin unknown]
☛ *Hom.* **boar.**

bore³ (bôr) *v.* pt. of **bear¹.**
☛ *Hom.* **boar.**

bore⁴ (bôr) *n.* a sudden, high tidal wave that rushes up a channel with great force. [< ON *bára* wave]
☛ *Hom.* **boar.**

bo·re·al (bô′rē əl) *adj.* **1** northern. **2** of or having to do with Boreas.

Bo·re·as (bô′rē əs) *n.* the north wind. [< Gk.]

bore·dom (bôr′dəm) *n.* a bored condition; weariness caused by dull, tiresome people or events.

bor·er (bôr′ər) *n.* **1** a tool for boring holes. **2** an insect or worm that bores into wood, fruit, etc.

bore·some (bôr′səm) *adj.* boring; dull; tiresome.

bo·ric (bô′rik) *adj.* of or containing boron. Also, **boracic.**

boric acid a white crystalline substance used as a mild antiseptic, as a food preservative, etc. *Formula:* B(OH)₃

born (bôrn) *adj., v.* —*adj.* **1** brought into life; brought forth. **2** thought up; conceived. **3** by birth; by nature: *a born athlete.*
not born yesterday, not gullible or naïve: *You can't fool me with that trick—I wasn't born yesterday.*
—*v.* a pp. of **bear¹.** [pp. of *bear¹*]

borne (bôrn) *v.* a pp. of **bear¹.**

bo·ron (bô′ron) *n.* a non-metallic, chemical element found in borax. *Symbol:* B; *at.no.* 5; *at. wt.* 10.811. [blend of *borax* and *carbon*]

bor·ough (ber′ō) *n.* **1** a town or township having its own local government: *Etobicoke is a borough of Metropolitan Toronto.* **2** in England: **a** a town with a municipal corporation and a charter that guarantees the right of local self-government. **b** a town that sends representatives to Parliament. [OE *burg*]
☛ *Hom.* **burro, burrow.**

bor·row (bôr′ō) *v.* **1** get (something) from another person with the understanding that it is to be returned. **2** take and use as one's own: *Rome borrowed many ideas from Greece.* **3** take a word or expression from another language to use like a native word. The word *mukluk* was borrowed from Inuktitut. Many words we think of

as English were borrowed from French hundreds of years ago.
4 *Arithmetic.* in subtraction, decrease the digit in one column of the minuend by 1 in order to increase the value in the column on its right by 10; regroup.
borrow trouble, worry about something before there is reason to. [OE *borgian* < *borg* pledge, surety] —**bor′row·er,** *n.*

bor·row·ing (bôr′ō ing) *n.* **1** something borrowed. **2** a word taken direct from one language into another; loan word. The English word *voyageur* is a borrowing from Canadian French.

borrow pit *Cdn.* a pit or ditch from which earth has been dug for use as fill, especially in road or railway construction.

borsch (bôrsh) *n.* a Russian soup containing meat stock, beets, etc. [< Russian *borshch*]

borscht (bôrsht *or* bôrsh) *n.* borsch.

bor·zoi (bôr′zoi) *n.* a breed of tall, slender, swift dog having long, silky hair. The borzoi was developed in Russia and was originally used to hunt wolves. [< Russian *borzoy* swift]

bos·cage (bos′kij) *n.* a small woods; thicket. [ME < OF *boscage* < *bosc* < Gmc.; cf. Frankish *busk* woods. Related to BUSH.]

bosh[1] (bosh) *n. or interj. Informal.* nonsense; foolish talk or ideas. [< Turkish *boş* empty, worthless]

bosh[2] (bosh) *n.* **1** the lower, tapered part of a blast furnace. **2** a trough for cooling hot metal, such as ingots. [< G *Böschung* slope]

bosk (bosk) *n.* a grove; small woods; thicket. [var. of *busk*, dial. for *bush*]

bosk·y (bos′kē) *adj.* **1** wooded. **2** shady.

bo's'n (bō′sən) *n.* boatswain.

bos·om (bůz′əm *or* bü′zəm) *n., v.* —*n.* **1** the upper, front part of the human body, especially the female breasts. **2** the part of a garment covering the bosom. **3** the centre or inmost part: *He did not mention it even in the bosom of his family.* **4** the heart, thoughts, affections, desires, etc.: *He kept the secret in his bosom.* **5** the surface (of a sea, lake, river, the ground, etc.). **6** (*adj.*) close; trusted: *a bosom friend.* —*v.* cherish. [OE *bōsm*]

bos·om·y (bůz′əm ē *or* bü′zəm ē) *adj.* having large breasts.

bo·son (bō′son) *n.* any of a class of elementary particles that includes mesons and the photon, having a spin that is zero or an integral number.

boss[1] (bos) *Informal. n., v., adj.* —*n.* **1** a person who hires workers or watches over or directs them; foreman or manager. **2** a person who controls a political organization.
—*v.* **1** give orders to: *He likes to boss people. Don't boss me around!* **2** direct; control: *Who is bossing this job?*
—*adj.* **1** being in charge. **2** *Slang.* excellent: *a boss piece of writing.* [< Du. *baas*]

boss[2] (bos) *n., v.* —*n.* **1** an ornamentation of silver, ivory, or other material rising above a flat surface. **2** in machinery, the enlarged part of a shaft. **3** *Geology.* a domelike body of igneous rock protruding above the surface or into a stratum of other rock. —*v.* decorate with bosses. [ME *boce* < OF]

bos·sa no·va (bos′ə nō′və) **1** a dance originating in Brazil, resembling the samba. **2** the music for this dance. [< Pg., literally, new trend]

boss·y[1] (bos′ē) *adj.* **boss·i·er, boss·i·est.** *Informal.* fond of telling others what to do and how to do it; domineering. [< *boss*[1]]

boss·y[2] (bos′ē) *adj.* decorated with bosses. [< *boss*[2]]

bos·sy[3] *or* **bos·sie** (bos′ē′) *n.* a familiar name for a calf or cow. [< dial. E *borse, boss* young calf]

Boston bull (bos′tən) Boston terrier.

Boston fern a variety of sword fern having long, drooping fronds, popular as a house plant.

Boston ivy a woody Asian vine (*Parthenocissus tricuspidata*) of the grape family having broad, glossy, three-lobed leaves, widely cultivated as an ornamental covering for walls.

Boston Tea Party a raid on some British ships in Boston harbor in 1773. Disguised as Indians, colonists threw chests of tea overboard as a protest against taxation by the British Parliament.

Boston terrier a breed of small dog having smooth, short, dark hair with white feet, chest and face.

bo·sun (bō′sən) *n.* boatswain.

Bos·well (boz′wel *or* boz′wəl) *n.* an author of a biography of a close friend. [< James Boswell (1740-1795), the Scottish author of a famous biography of Samuel Johnson]

bot (bot) *n.* the larva of a botfly. It is a parasite of horses, cattle, and sheep. Also, **bott.** [ME; origin uncertain]

bo·tan·ic (bə tan′ik) *adj.* botanical. [< Med.L *botanicus* < Gk. *botanikos* < *botanē* plant]

bo·tan·i·cal (bə tan′i kəl) *adj.* **1** of or having to do with plants

hat, āge, fär; let, ēqual, tèrm; it, īce
hot, ōpen, ôrder; oil, out; cup, pút, rüle,
əbove, takən, pencəl, lemən, circəs
ch, child; ng, long; sh, ship
th, thin; ŦH, then; zh, measure

and plant life. **2** of or having to do with botany. —**bo·tan′i·cal·ly,** *adv.*

bot·a·nist (bot′ə nist) *n.* a person trained in botany, especially one whose work it is.

bot·a·nize (bot′ə nīz′) *v.* **-nized, -niz·ing. 1** study plants in their natural environment. **2** collect plants for study. **3** explore the plant life of. —**bot′a·niz′er,** *n.*

bot·a·ny (bot′ə nē) *n., pl.* **-nies. 1** the science of plants; the branch of biology that deals with the structure, growth, classification, diseases, etc. of plants. **2** the plant life of a particular area: *the botany of the Canadian Shield.* **3** the botanical facts and characteristics concerning a particular type or group of plants: *the botany of roses.* [< *botanic*]

Botany Bay (bot′ə nē) a bay on the southeastern coast of Australia, near Sydney. A penal colony was formerly located there.

Botany wool a fine merino wool used in high quality yarns and fabrics. [< *Botany Bay*, Australia, near which it was originally grown]

botch (boch) *v., n.* —*v.* **1** spoil by poor workmanship; bungle. **2** patch or mend clumsily. —*n.* **1** a poor piece of workmanship. **2** a clumsy patch. [ME *bocchen*; origin uncertain] —**botch′er,** *n.*

botch·y (boch′ē) *adj.* **botch·i·er, botch·i·est.** botched; poorly made or done.

bot·fly (bot′flī′) *n., pl.* **-flies.** any of various two-winged flies (families Gasterophilidae and Oestridae) whose larvae are parasites in mammals. Several species of botfly attack livestock.

both (bōth) *adj., pron., adv., conj.* —*adj.* two, when only two are considered; the one and the other: *Both houses are white.*
—*pron.* the two together: *Both belong to him.*
—*adv.* together; alike; equally: *He can both sing and dance.*
—*conj.* together; alike; equally: *He is both strong and healthy.* [ME, apparently < ON *báthar*]
☛ *Usage.* **Both** is used in informal English to emphasize the fact that two persons or places or things are involved in a situation: *The twins were both there.* Strictly speaking, the word *both* is redundant in this sentence, but it gives emphasis.

both·er (boŦH′ər) *v., n.* —*v.* **1** take trouble; concern oneself: *Don't bother about my breakfast; I'll eat what is here.* **2** make uneasy, worried, or annoyed; irritate: *Hot weather bothers me.* —*n.* **1** worry; fuss; trouble. **2** a person or thing that causes worry, fuss, or trouble. [apparently an Anglo-Irish modification of *pother*]

both·er·a·tion (boŦH′ər ā′shən) *n. or interj. Informal.* bother.

both·er·some (boŦH′ər səm) *adj.* causing worry or fuss; troublesome.

bots (bots) *n.* a disease of cattle caused by botfly larvae infesting the stomach and intestines. Also, **botts.**

bott (bot) *n.* See **bot.**

bot·tle (bot′əl) *n., v.* **-tled, -tling.** —*n.* **1** a container for holding liquids, made of glass, plastic, etc., usually without handles and with a narrow neck and mouth that can be closed with a cap or stopper. **2** the amount that a bottle can hold. **3** a bottle and its contents. **4 the bottle,** alcoholic liquor.
hit the bottle, *Slang.* drink alcoholic liquor to excess.
—*v.* **1** put into bottles: *to bottle milk.* **2** hold in; keep back; control: *to bottle one's feelings.*
bottle up, hold in; keep back; control: *to bottle up one's anger.* [ME *botel* < OF *bouteille* < VL *butticula*, dim. of LL *buttis* butt[4]] —**bot′tle-like′,** *adj.* —**bot′tler,** *n.*

bottle green a very dark green.

bot·tle·neck (bot′əl nek′) *n.* **1** the neck of a bottle. **2** a narrow passageway or street. **3** a person or thing that hinders progress. **4** a situation in which progress is hindered: *They have hit a bottleneck that could delay the decision for weeks.*

bot·tle·nose (bot′əl nōz′) *n.* bottlenosed dolphin.

bot·tle-nosed dolphin (bot′əl nōzd′) a dolphin (*Tursiops truncatus*) widely distributed in temperate and warm seas, having a short, somewhat upturned beak. Also called **bottlenose dolphin, bottlenose.**

bot·tom (bot′əm) *n., v., adj.* —*n.* **1** the lowest part: *The berries at the bottom of the basket were small.* **2** underside: *The bottom of the shelf was left unpainted. Don't set the glass on the table if the bottom is wet.* **3** the base on which something rests: *There is an inscription around the bottom of the statue.* **4** the ground under a

body of water: *the bottom of the sea.* **5** Often, **bottoms,** *pl.* the low land along a river. **6** the seat of a chair: *This chair needs a new bottom.* **7 bottoms,** *pl.* the trousers of pyjamas. **8** basis; source; origin: *He is at the bottom of this mischief.* **9** the buttocks. **10** the part of a ship's hull below the water line. **11** a ship, especially a cargo ship.

at bottom, basically; actually: *At bottom, he's a kind person.*

be at the bottom of, be the cause or source of.

bottom out, reach a low point and level off: *It seems the stock market has bottomed out.*

bottoms up! *Informal.* drain your glass! drink up!

get to the bottom of, discover the underlying source, cause, or meaning of.

—*v.* **1** put a seat on. **2** get to the bottom of; understand fully. **3** touch or rest on the bottom: *The submarine bottomed on the ocean floor.*

—*adj.* **1** lowest; last: *bottom prices. I bet my bottom dollar.* **2** underlying; fundamental. [OE *botm*]

bottom land the low land along a river.

bot·tom·less (bot′əm lis) *adj.* **1** without a bottom. **2** so deep that the bottom cannot be reached; extremely deep.

bot·tom·most (bot′əm mōst′) *adj.* deepest; lowest.

bot·tom·ry (bot′əm rē) *n., pl.* **-ries.** *Law.* a contract by which a shipowner mortgages his ship in order to get money to make a voyage. If the ship is lost, the lender loses the money. [< *bottom ship,* after Du. *bodemerij*]

botts (bots) See **bots.**

bot·u·lism (boch′ə liz′əm) *n.* acute food poisoning caused by a potent toxin produced in imperfectly preserved food, etc. by a bacterium (*Clostridium botulinum*). [< L *botulus* sausage; because originally thought to be produced especially by eating sausages]

bou·clé (bü klā′) *n.* **1** a crimped, looped yarn. **2** fabric made with this yarn, having a spongy feel and tiny loops and curls on its surface. [< F *bouclé* buckled]

bou·doir (bü′dwär *or* bü dwär′) *n.* a lady's private dressing room or sitting room. [< F *boudoir* < *bouder* sulk]

bouf·fant (bü fänt′; *French,* bü fäN′) *adj.* puffed out: *bouffant sleeves, a bouffant hairdo.* [< F]

bou·gain·vil·le·a (bü′gən vil′ē ə) *n.* any of several tropical climbing shrubs having large, brilliant, deep-red leaves surrounding tiny flowers. [after L. A. de *Bougainville* (1729-1811), a French navigator and explorer]

bough (bou) *n.* **1** one of the main branches of a tree. **2** a branch cut from a tree. [OE *bōg* bough, shoulder]

☛ *Hom.* **bow¹, bow³.**

☛ *Syn.* **1, 2.** See note at **branch.**

bought (bot *or* bôt) *v.* pt. and pp. of **buy.**

bought·en (bot′ən *or* bôt′ən) *adj.* Dialect. bought; not homemade.

☛ *Usage.* **Boughten** is a nonstandard expression used only in certain North American dialects: *Is that a boughten dress?*

bouil·la·baisse (bül′yə bās′; *French,* bü yä bes′) *n.* a fish chowder highly seasoned with wine, herbs, etc. [< F *bouillabaisse* < Provençal *bouiabaisso* < *boui* boil + *abaiso* go down (from its being brought quickly to boil and then simmered down)]

bouil·lon (bül′yon; *French,* bü yôn′) *n.* **1** a clear, thin soup or broth. **2** a liquid, nutritive medium used for growing cultures of bacteria. [< F *bouillon* < *bouillir* boil < L *bullire*]

boul·der (bōl′dər) *n.* a large rock rounded or worn by the action of water or weather. [for *boulderstone,* ME < Scand.; cf. Swedish *bullersten* < *bullra* roar + *sten* stone]

boul·e·vard (bül′ə värd′) *n.* **1** a broad street. **2** the strip of grass between a sidewalk and a curb. **3** the centre strip dividing any road into two lanes for traffic going in opposite directions. *Abbrev.:* blvd. [< F *boulevard,* originally, the passageway along a rampart < MLG < MDu. *bolwerc.* Akin to BULWARK.]

bounce (bouns) *v.* **bounced, bounc·ing;** *n.* —*v.* **1** spring, often repeatedly, into the air after striking something, as a rubber ball does: *The baby likes to bounce on the bed. The ball bounced off the porch railing.* **2** cause to bounce: *She bounced the basketball off the backboard.* **3** come or go energetically, noisily, angrily, etc.: *She bounced out of the room.* **4** *Slang.* throw out. **5** *Slang.* discharge from work or employment. **6** *Slang.* of a cheque, be returned by a bank as a result of the person who signed the cheque having insufficient funds in his account to meet it.

—*n.* **1** a bound; a spring; a bouncing. **2** impudence or bluster. **3** springiness; ability to bounce: *This ball has lots of bounce.* **4** *Informal.* energy; spirit: *He was in hospital for a week, but he is as full of bounce as ever.* **5 the bounce,** *Slang.* rude or abrupt dismissal or ejection: *The club owner gave him the bounce.* [ME *bunse(n);* cf. Du. *bonzen* thump] —**boun′cy,** *adj.* —**boun′ci·ness,** *n.*

bounc·er (boun′sər) *n.* **1** *Slang.* a man employed by a cabaret, restaurant, etc. to restrain or remove people who are drunk or disorderly. **2** any person or thing that bounces.

bounc·ing (boun′sing) *adj.* strong, healthy, and vigorous: *a bouncing baby boy.*

bouncing Bet soapwort.

boun·cy (boun′sē) *adj.* **boun·ci·er, boun·ci·est. 1** cheerful and spirited; exuberant: *A week after the accident, she was as bouncy as always.* **2** elastic: *a bouncy surface.* —**boun′ci·ly,** *adv.*

bound¹ (bound) *adj., v.* —*adj.* **1** under some obligation; obliged: *bound by law to keep the peace. He felt himself duty-bound to volunteer.* **2** certain; sure: *It's bound to rain before morning.* **3** confined (used especially in compounds): *housebound. We were snowbound for three days.* **4** *Informal.* determined; resolved: *She was bound to go, whether or not we were going.* **5** of a book, having covers; having a binding: *a newly bound book.*

bound up in or **with, a** closely connected with. **b** very devoted to.

—*v.* pt. and pp. of **bind.** [pp. of **bind**]

bound² (bound) *v., n.* —*v.* **1** spring lightly along; move by leaping: *The deer bounded into the woods and was gone.* **2** of a ball, etc., spring back after striking a surface; rebound; bounce: *The ball bounded from the wall and hit the car.* —*n.* **1** a leap or spring upward or onward. **2** the act of rebounding; bounce: *I caught the ball on the bound.* [< F *bondir* leap, originally, resound, ? < L *bombus.* See BOMB.]

bound³ (bound) *n., v.* —*n.* **1** Usually **bounds,** *pl.* a limit or limiting line: *the farthest bounds of the estate. Keep your hopes within bounds.* **2 bounds,** *pl.* land on or near a boundary.

out of bounds, outside the area allowed by rules, custom, or law: *He kicked the ball out of bounds. The town is out of bounds to the soldiers.*

—*v.* **1** be or form the boundary of: *A poplar bluff bounds the property to the north. The garden is bounded by a flagstone walk.* **2** be next to; adjoin (used with **on**): *Canada bounds on the United States.* [ME *bunne* < AF *bounde* < OF *bodne* < LL *butina*]

bound⁴ (bound) *adj.* going; on the way: *I am bound for home.* [ME *boun* < ON *búinn,* pp. of *búa* get ready]

bound·a·ry (boun′drē *or* boun′də rē) *n., pl.* **-ries. 1** a limiting line; something that functions as a dividing line, especially between properties, provinces, countries, etc.: *The Ottawa River forms part of the boundary between Ontario and Quebec.* **2** *Cricket.* **a** a limit of the field. **b** a hit to or beyond this limit.

bound·en (boun′dən) *adj.* **1** required; obligatory: *She considered it her bounden duty.* **2** Archaic. under obligation; obliged. [pp. of *bind*]

bound·er (boun′dər) *n. Esp.Brit. Informal.* a rude, vulgar person; upstart; cad.

bound·less (bound′lis) *adj.* **1** not limited; infinite; vast: *boundless space.* **2** seemingly without bounds; vast: *the boundless ocean.* —**bound′less·ly,** *adv.* —**bound′less·ness,** *n.*

boun·te·ous (boun′tē əs) *adj.* **1** generous; given freely. **2** plentiful; abundant. —**boun′te·ous·ly,** *adv.* —**boun′te·ous·ness,** *n.*

boun·ti·ful (boun′tə fəl) *adj.* **1** plentiful; abundant. **2** generous; giving freely. —**boun′ti·ful·ly,** *adv.* —**boun′ti·ful·ness,** *n.*

boun·ty (boun′tē) *n., pl.* **-ties. 1** something given with generosity. **2** generosity. **3** a reward or premium, especially one given by a government: *Governments have sometimes offered bounties for animals considered a nuisance.* [ME < OF *bonte* < L *bonitas* < *bonus* good]

bou·quet (bō kā′ *or* bü kā′ *for I;* bü kā′ *for 2) n.* **1** a bunch of flowers. **2** a fragrance; aroma. [< F *bouquet* little wood, dim. of OF *bosc* wood < Gmc. *busk.* See BOSCAGE.]

bour·bon (bèr′bən) *n.* a kind of whisky, distilled from a grain mash containing at least 51% corn. [< *Bourbon* County, Kentucky, where this whisky was originally made]

Bour·bon (bür′bən, *occasionally* bèr′bən) *n.* a person who clings to old ideas and opposes any change; an extreme conservative. [< *Bourbon,* the name of a former royal family of France, Spain, Naples, and Sicily]

Bour·bon·ism (bür′bən iz′ əm; *occasionally,* bèr′bən iz′ əm) *n.* **1** support of the Bourbons. **2** extreme conservatism in politics, etc.

bour·geois (bür zhwä′ *or* bür′zhwä) *n., pl.* **-geois;** *adj.* —*n.* **1** a person of the middle class. **2** a property owner or business person, as contrasted with a member of the working class. **3** *Cdn. Historical.* a partner in a fur-trading company, in charge of a trading post or expedition; wintering partner. **4** *Cdn. Historical.* employer; boss.

—*adj.* **1** of the middle class. **2** like the middle class; ordinary. **3** influenced chiefly by the interests of property ownership and business. [< F *bourgeois* < LL *burgensis* < *burgus* fort < Gmc. Doublet of BURGESS.]

bour·geoi·sie (bür′zhwä zē′) *n.* **1** the people of the middle class. **2** property owners and business people as a class, as contrasted with the proletariat. **3** the middle class. [< F]

bourn¹ or **bourne¹** (bôrn) *n.* a small stream; brook. [OE *burna*]

bourn² or **bourne²** (bôrn) *n.* **1** *Archaic.* a boundary; limit. **2** a goal. [< F *borne.* Akin to BOUND³.]

bourse (bürs) *n.* an exchange, especially the stock exchange in Paris or in any of certain other European cities. [< F *bourse*, originally, purse < LL *bursa* < Gk. *byrsa* hide, wineskin. Doublet of BURSA, PURSE.]

bout¹ (bout) *n.* **1** a trial of strength; contest. **2** a spell; a period, especially one involving illness, effort, or endurance: *I have just had a long bout of the flu. Are you ready for a bout of house-cleaning?* [var. of *bought* a bending, turn. Related to BOW¹.]

bout² (bü) *n. Cdn. Historical.* one of the paddlers or rowers at either end of a canoe, bateau, etc. [< Cdn.F < F *bout* end]

bou·tique (bü tēk′) *n.* a small shop or a department in a large store that specializes in fashionable clothes or accessories, or in gifts, etc. [< F]

bou·ton·niere or **bou·ton·nière** (bü′tə nyer′; *French,* bü tô nyer′) *n.* a flower or flowers worn in a buttonhole. [< F *boutonnière* buttonhole]

bou·vi·er (bü′vē ā′) *n.* bouvier des Flandres.

bouvier des Flan·dres (flan′dərz *or* flän′drə) a breed of large, heavily built dog having a rough, somewhat tousled coat, originally from Belgium where it was used especially for herding cattle.

bou·zou·ki (bü zü′kē) *n.* a Greek stringed musical instrument resembling a mandolin. [< Mod. Gk. *mpouzouki*, possibly < Turkish *büjük* large]

bo·vid (bō′vid) *adj., n.* —*adj.* belonging to or characteristic of the family Bovidae, a group of cud-chewing, hoofed mammals with permanent, non-branching, hollow horns. —*n.* an animal of the family Bovidae, including domestic cattle, true antelope, buffalo, bison, the yak, sheep, goats, and the musk-ox.

bo·vine (bō′vīn) *adj., n.* —*adj.* **1** belonging to or characteristic of a tribe (Bovini) of bovid mammals that includes buffalo, bison, the yak, and domestic cattle. **2** slow and somewhat stupid. **3** without emotion; stolid. —*n.* a bovine animal; ox (def. 2). [< LL *bovinus* < L *bos, bovis* ox, cow]

bow¹ (bou) *v., n.* —*v.* **1** bend the head or body in greeting, respect, worship, or submission. **2** show by bowing: *to bow one's thanks.* **3** cause to stoop: *The man was bowed by old age.* **4** submit; yield: *We must bow to necessity.*
bow and scrape, be too polite or slavish.
bow down, a weigh down: *bowed down with care.* **b** to worship.
bow out, a withdraw (from): *He sprained his wrist and had to bow out of the tennis tournament.* **b** usher out.
—*n.* a bending of the head or body in greeting, respect, worship, or submission.
make (one's) bow, a make an entrance. **b** make an initial appearance before the public as a performer. **c** retire from public notice.
take a bow, accept praise, applause, etc. for something done. [OE *būgan*]
☞ Hom. **bough, bow³.**

bow² (bō) *n., v.* —*n.* **1** a weapon for shooting arrows, usually consisting of a strip of springy wood with a string or cord stretched tight between the two ends. **2** a curve; bend. **3** a looped knot: *a bow of ribbon.* **4** a slender rod with horsehairs stretched on it, for playing a violin, etc. See **violin** for picture. **5** something curved; a curved part: *A rainbow is a bow.*
—*v.* **1** curve; bend. **2** play (a violin, etc.) with a bow. [OE *boga*]
—**bow′less,** *adj.* —**bow′-like′,** *adj.*
☞ Hom. **beau.**

bow³ (bou) *n.* **1** the forward part of a ship, boat, or airship. See **aft** for picture. **2** the person who rows with the oar nearest the bow of a boat. [probably < LG or Scand. origin. Akin to BOUGH.]
☞ Hom. **bough, bow¹.**

bowd·ler·ize (boud′lər īz′) *v.* **-ized, -iz·ing.** remove words and passages thought to be improper. [< Dr. T. *Bowdler* (1754-1825), who published an expurgated edition of Shakespeare in 1818]

bow·el (bou′əl) *n.* **1** a part of the bowels; intestine. **2** Usually, **bowels,** *pl.* a tube in the body into which digested food passes from the stomach; intestines. **3** bowels, *pl.* **a** the inner part; depths: *Miners dig for coal in the bowels of the earth.* **b** *Archaic.* pity; tender feelings. [ME < OF *boel* < L *botellus,* dim. of *botulus* sausage]

bowel movement **1** discharge of waste matter from the large intestine. **2** the waste matter discharged; feces.

bow·er¹ (bou′ər) *n.* **1** a shelter of leafy branches. **2** a

hat, āge, fär; let, ēqual, tèrm; it, īce
hot, ōpen, ôrder; oil, out; cup, pùt, rüle,
əbove, takən, pencəl, lemən, circəs
ch, child; ng, long; sh, ship
th, thin; ŦH, then; zh, measure

summerhouse or arbor. **3** *Archaic.* bedroom. [OE *būr* dwelling]
—**bow′er·like′,** *adj.*

bow·er² (bou′ər) *n.* an anchor carried at the bow of a ship. [< *bow³*]

bow·er³ (bou′ər) *n.* the high card in certain games. The **right bower** is a jack of the suit that is trump; the **left bower,** the jack of the suit of the same color as trump; the **best bower,** the joker. [< G *Bauer* jack (in cards), peasant]

bow·er⁴ (bou′ər) *n.* one who bows or stoops.

bow·er·y (bou′ər ē) *adj.* like a bower; leafy; shady.

bow·fin (bō′fin′) *n.* a voracious freshwater fish (*Amia calva*) found in shallow, weedy waters in E North America, having a dull-green, roundish body with a very long dorsal fin. The bowfin is the only living representative of the order Amiiformes. Also called **dogfish, mudfish.**

bow·head (bō′hed′) *n.* a right whale (*Balaena mysticetus*) having a very large head that is almost one third of its total length of about 18 m and a great mouth, with the lower lip curving upward in a high bow on each side.

bow·ie knife (bō′ē *or* bü′ē) a long, single-edged hunting knife carried in a sheath. [after Col. James *Bowie,* American pioneer]

bow·knot (bō′not′) *n.* a slipknot such as is made in tying shoelaces. It may be tied as a single bow or as a double bow.

bowl¹ (bōl) *n.* **1** a hollow, rounded dish. **2** the amount that a bowl can hold. **3** a bowl-shaped or concave part: *the bowl of a spoon or a pipe.* **4** a large drinking cup. **5** a drink. **6** a bowl-shaped structure such as an amphitheatre or a stadium. [ME *bolle* < OE *bolla*]
—**bowl′-like′,** *adj.*
☞ Hom. **bole, boll.**

bowl² (bōl) *n., v.* —*n.* **1** a fairly large, heavy ball used in certain games, especially the weighted or slightly flattened ball used in lawn bowling. **2** in lawn bowling or bowling, a throw. **3 bowls,** *pl.* (*usually used with a singular verb*) **a** lawn bowling. **b** skittles or tenpins.
—*v.* **1** *Bowling.* **a** take part in a game of bowling. **b** roll (a ball) in bowling. **2** roll or move along rapidly and smoothly: *Our car bowled along on the good road.* **3** *Cricket.* **a** a throw (the ball) to the batsman. **b** dismiss (a batsman), especially by knocking off the bails or knocking down a wicket.
bowl down, knock down.
bowl over, a knock over. **b** *Informal.* make helpless and confused; stun: *I was bowled over by the bad news.*
[ME *boule* < L *bulla* ball, bubble]
☞ Hom. **bole, boll.**

bowl·der (bōl′dər) See **boulder.**

bow·leg (bō′leg′) *n.* **1** a leg that curves outward at or below the knee. **2** an outward curve of the legs.

bow·leg·ged (bō′leg′id *or* -legd′) *adj.* having the legs curved outward at or below the knee.

bowl·er¹ (bōl′ər) *n.* **1** a person who bowls. **2** *Cricket.* the player who throws the ball at the wicket. [< *bowl²*, v.]

bowl·er² (bōl′ər) *n.* derby (def. 3). [< *bowl²*, n.]

bowl·ful (bōl′fùl) as much as a bowl can hold.

bow·line (bō′lən *or* bō′līn′) *n.* **1** a knot used in making a loop. **2** the rope tied to the edge of a square sail nearest the wind. It holds the sail steady when sailing into the wind. [ME; *bow³* + *line¹*]

bowline knot bowline (def. 1).

bowl·ing (bōl′ing) *n.* **1** a game played indoors, in which balls are rolled down an alley at bottle-shaped wooden pins. Fivepins, ninepins, and tenpins are forms of bowling. **2** lawn bowling.

bowling alley **1** *Bowling.* the lane or alley down which balls are rolled. **2** an establishment having a number of lanes for bowling: *There is a snack bar at the bowling alley.*

bowling green a smooth, flat stretch of grass for lawn bowling.

bow·man (bō′mən) *n., pl.* **-men.** a soldier armed with bow and arrows; archer.

bow net (bō) a wickerwork trap for catching lobsters and other shellfish. [< *bow²* + *net*]

bow·shot (bō′shot′) *n.* **1** a shot from a bow. **2** the distance that a bow will shoot an arrow.

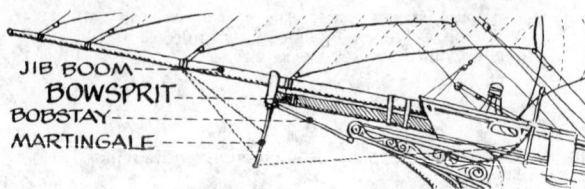

The bow of a French barkentine of the early 20th century

bow·sprit (bou′sprit′ *or* bō′sprit′) *n.* a pole or spar projecting forward from the bow of a ship. Ropes from the bowsprit help to steady sails and masts. [probably < LG or Du.]

bow·string (bō′string′) *n., v.* —*n.* 1 a strong cord stretched between the two ends of a bow and pulled back by the archer to send the arrow forward. 2 a cord like this. —*v.* strangle with a bowstring; garrote.

bow tie (bō) a necktie worn in a small bowknot.

bow window (bō) a curved bay window.

bow–wow (bou′wou′) *n., v.* —*n.* 1 the bark of a dog, or an imitation of this sound. 2 a child's word for a dog. —*v.* bark like a dog. [imitative]

box¹ (boks) *n., v.* —*n.* 1 a container, usually with a lid, made of wood, metal, cardboard, paper, etc. to pack or put things in. 2 the amount that a box can hold: *We ate a whole box of cereal.* 3 a separate, partly enclosed area in a theatre, etc. for a small group of people. 4 an enclosed space in a courtroom, as for a jury, witness, or prisoner. 5 a small shelter: *a sentry box.* 6 anything shaped or used like a box. 7 a hollow part that encloses or protects some piece of machinery. 8 the driver's seat on a coach, carriage, etc. 9 *Baseball.* a the place where a pitcher stands to throw the ball. b the place where the batter stands to hit the ball. 10 *Cdn.* an enclosed area for playing lacrosse. 11 a compartment for a horse in a stable or a vehicle. 12 in newspapers, magazines, etc., a space set off by enclosing lines. 13 a receptacle in a post office from which a subscriber collects mail.
—*v.* 1 pack in a box; put into a box. 2 confine as if in a box; surround or hem in (*usually used with* **in** *or* **up**): *We couldn't get out of our parking space because another car had boxed us in.*
box the compass, a a name the points of a compass in order. **b** go all the way around and end up where one started.
[specialization of meaning of *box³*] —**box′like′,** *adj.*

box² (boks) *n., v.* —*n.* a blow with the open hand or the fist, especially on the side of the head: *She gave him a box on the ear.* —*v.* 1 strike such a blow. 2 fight as a sport with the fists, which are usually covered with padded gloves: *He had not boxed since he left school.* [origin uncertain]

box³ (boks) *n.* 1 any of a genus (*Buxus*) of evergreen shrubs and small trees, especially the **common box** (*B. sempervirens*), often used for hedges, borders, etc. 2 the hard, durable wood of a box; boxwood. [< L *buxus* < Gk. *pyxos*]

box camera a simple camera in the form of a box which does not fold up and which has a fixed focus.

box·car (boks′kär′) *n.* a railway freight car enclosed on all sides.

box elder Manitoba maple.

box·er¹ (bok′sər) *n.* a person or machine whose work is to pack things in boxes. [< *box¹* + -*er*]

box·er² (bok′sər) *n.* 1 a person who fights with his fists, usually in padded gloves and according to special rules. 2 a breed of medium-sized dog having a stocky, strong body with a deep chest, short brownish hair, and a short, square muzzle. 3 **Boxer,** in China, a member of a society opposed to foreigners and Christianity. The Boxers rose in armed rebellion in 1900, but were defeated by foreign soldiers.

box·ing¹ (bok′sing) *n.* the sport of fighting with the fists. [< *box²*]

box·ing² (bok′sing) *n.* 1 the material used for boxes. 2 the sides of a window; casing. [< *box¹*]

Boxing Day December 26, a legal holiday in all provinces except Quebec. Formerly, "boxes" or presents were given on this day to employees, postmen, etc.

boxing gloves the padded gloves worn when boxing.

box kite a kite consisting of two rectangular boxes with open ends, joined together one above the other.

box lacrosse *Cdn.* a form of lacrosse played by teams of seven players on an enclosed playing area about the size of a hockey rink.

box office 1 the place where tickets are sold in a theatre, hall, etc. 2 the money taken in at the box office. 3 the power to attract ticket buyers, or a show or performer having this power: *Adventure movies are good box office.*

box pleat a double pleat with the cloth folded under at each side.

box score *Baseball.* a complete record of the plays of a game arranged in a table by the names of the players.

box seat a chair or seat in a box of a theatre, hall, auditorium, stadium, etc.

box set in a theatre, a stage set with back and side walls.

box spring a base for a bed, consisting of coil springs set in a cloth-covered frame: *A box spring is designed to be used under a mattress.*

box·wood (boks′wùd′) *n.* 1 the hard, fine-grained, durable wood of a box, especially the common box (*Buxus sempervirens*), used for making tool handles, musical instruments, inlays, etc. 2 a box tree or shrub.

boy (boi) *n., interj.* —*n.* 1 a male child. 2 son: *Is that your boy?* 3 a male servant. 4 a boy or man employed to run errands, carry things, etc. 5 *Informal.* any man; fellow: *the boys at the office. He's a local boy.*
—*interj. Informal.* an exclamation of surprise, admiration, pleasure, contempt, etc.: *Boy, is it hot! Boy, is he a liar!* [ME *boy, boi*; origin uncertain]
☛ *Hom.* **buoy.**

boy·cott (boi′kot) *v., n.* —*v.* 1 combine against and have nothing to do with (a person, business, nation, etc.). If people are boycotting someone, they do not associate with him, or buy from or sell to him, and they try to keep others from doing so. 2 refuse to buy or use (a product, etc.). —*n.* the act of boycotting. [after Captain *Boycott* (1832-1897), an English land agent in Ireland who was so treated] —**boy′cot·ter,** *n.*

boy·friend (boi′frend′) *n.* 1 a male companion of a girl or woman; escort, sweetheart, or lover: *She has a new boyfriend.* 2 a boy who is one's friend.

boy·hood (boi′hùd′) *n.* 1 the time or condition of being a boy. 2 boys as a group: *the boyhood of the nation.*

boy·ish (boi′ish) *adj.* 1 of a boy. 2 like a boy: *The warm spring weather made him feel almost boyish again.* 3 like a boy's: *a boyish grin.* 4 fit for a boy: *boyish games.* —**boy′ish·ly,** *adv.* —**boy′ish·ness,** *n.*

Boyle's law (boilz) *Physics.* the principle that at a constant temperature the volume of a gas varies inversely with the pressure to which it is subjected. [< Robert *Boyle* (1627-1691), an Irish scientist and philosopher who formulated this law]

Boy Scouts 1 a nonpolitical, nondenominational organization for boys and young men whose aim is to help them to learn co-operation, leadership, and self-reliance, to acquire knowledge and appreciation of the outdoors and to develop physically and spiritually. The Boy Scouts of Canada has five programs for different ages: *Beavers, Wolf Cubs, Scouts, Venturers,* and *Rovers.* 2 **Boy Scout,** a member, aged 11 to 14, of the Boy Scouts.

boy·sen·ber·ry (boi′zən ber′ē) *n., pl.* -**ries.** 1 a purple berry like a blackberry in size and shape, and like a raspberry in flavor, probably a cross of loganberry, raspberry, and blackberry. 2 the plant it grows on. [after R. *Boysen* of California, who developed it]

bp. birthplace.

Bp. Bishop.

B/P or **b/p** bills payable.

B.P.E. Bachelor of Physical Education.

B. Ped. Bachelor of Pedagogy (for L *Baccalaureus Paedagogiae*).

B.Péd. Bachelier de Pédagogie (Bachelor of Pedagogy).

B. Ph. Bachelor of Philosophy (for L *Baccalaureus Philosophiae*).

B.Pharm. Bachelor of Pharmacy (for L *Baccalaureus Pharmaciae*).

B.P.H.E. Bachelor of Physical and Health Education.

br. 1 branch. 2 brand. 3 brother. 4 bronze.

Br bromine.

Br. Britain; British.

bra (brä) *n.* brassiere.

brace (brās) *n., v.* **braced, brac·ing.** —*n.* 1 something that holds parts together or in place; a support: *An iron rod or a piece of timber used to support a roof or a wall is called a brace.* 2 a pair; couple: *a brace of ducks.* 3 a handle for a tool or drill used for

boring. See **drill**[1] for picture. **4** either of these signs { } used to
enclose words, figures, lines, or staves of music, indicating that
they are to be considered together. **5 braces,** *pl.* a pair of straps,
usually elasticized, for supporting trousers, worn over the shoulders
and fastened to the trousers at the back and front; suspenders.
6 Often, **braces,** *pl.* an arrangement of wires attached to crooked
teeth in order to correct their position. **7** a leather thong that slides
up and down the cord of a drum, used to regulate the tension of the
skins and thus the pitch.
—*v.* **1** give strength or firmness to; support. **2** enliven; invigorate:
The walk braced us for the next job.
brace (oneself) or **brace up,** *Informal.* summon one's strength or
courage.
[ME < OF *bracier* embrace < *brace* the two arms < L *bracchia,*
pl. of *bracchium* < Gk. *brachion* upper arm]

brace and bit a tool for boring, consisting of a bit fitted into a
crank-shaped handle.

brace·let (brās′lit) *n.* **1** a band or chain worn for ornament
around the wrist or arm. **2** the band of a wristwatch, especially a
metal band: *My watch has an expansion bracelet.* **3** *Informal.*
handcuff. [ME < OF *bracelet,* dim. of *bracel,* ult. < L *bracchium*
arm < Gk. *brachion*]

brac·er (brās′ər) *n.* **1** a person or thing that braces; a support.
2 *Slang.* a stimulating drink.

brachi·a (brak′ē ə *or* brā′kē ə) *n.* pl. of **brachium.**

bra·chi·al (brak′ē əl *or* brā′kē əl) *adj.* **1** of or having to do with
the arm or forelimb: *the brachial artery.* **2** armlike: *the brachial
appendages of a starfish.* [< L *bracchialis* of the arm < *bracchium*
arm < Gk. *brachion* upper arm]

brach·i·o·pod (brak′ē ə pod′ *or* brā′kē ə pod′) *n.* any of a
phylum (Brachiopoda) of small, invertebrate animals of the sea
bottom, all having a shell consisting of an upper and a lower valve,
and, inside the shell, two coiled arms called brachia on either side
of the mouth, used to draw in food-bearing water. Some
brachiopods look very much like clams, but the two groups are not
related. [< NL *brachiopoda,* pl. < Gk. *brachion* arm + *pous* foot]

bra·chi·um (brak′ē əm *or* brā′kē əm) *n.,* pl. **-chi·a. 1** the part of
the arm from the elbow to the shoulder; upper arm. **2** a
corresponding part in an animal. **3** *Zoology.* any armlike appendage.
[< L *bracchium* arm < Gk. *brachion* upper arm]

brach·y·ce·phal·ic (brak′ə sə fal′ik) *adj.* having a short, broad
skull; having a skull whose breadth is 80 percent or more of its
length; broad-headed. Compare **dolichocephalic.** [< Gk. *brachys*
short + *kephalē* head]

brac·ing (brās′ing) *adj., n.* —*adj.* giving strength and energy;
refreshing. —*n.* a brace or system of braces. —**brac′ing·ly,** *adv.*

brack·en (brak′ən) *n.* **1** a large, coarse fern (*Pteridium aquilinum*)
found almost throughout the world, having large, triangular fronds
and creeping underground stems. **2** any of various other large ferns,
especially of genus *Pteridium.* Also called **brake. 3** a growth or
clump of such ferns. [ME *braken,* apparently < Scand.]

brack·et (brak′it) *n., v.* —*n.* **1** a flat-topped piece of stone, wood,
etc., projecting from a wall or column to support a cornice, statue,
etc. **2** a usually L-shaped support fixed to a wall to hold a shelf,
light fixture, etc. **3** a small shelf supported by brackets. **4** a light
fixture projecting from a wall. **5** either of the signs [ ], used to
enclose words, symbols, or figures. **6** either of the signs ( );
parenthesis. **7** either of the signs ( ); brace. **8** the distance between
two shots, one fired beyond and one short of a target, in finding the
correct range for artillery. **9** a classification or grouping according to
age, income, etc.: *a middle-income bracket, the junior age bracket.*
—*v.* **1** support with brackets. **2** enclose within brackets. **3** consider
or think of together; group: *He is usually bracketed with the
avant-garde in music.* **4** fire beyond and short of (a target) in order
to find the correct range for artillery. [< F *braguette* < Sp.
bragueta, dim. of *braga* < L *bracae* breeches; by confusion with
brachia arms]

brack·ish (brak′ish) *adj.* **1** of water, slightly salty. **2** distasteful;
unpleasant. [< E dial. *brack* salty < MLG *brac;* cf. Du. *brak.* 16c.]
—**brack′ish·ness,** *n.*

bract (brakt) *n.* a small leaf at the base of a flower or flower stalk.
[< L *bractea* thin metal plate]

brad (brad) *n.* a small, thin nail with a small head. [var. of *brod* <
ON *broddr* spike]

brad·awl (brad′ol′ *or* brad′ôl′) *n.* an awl with a cutting edge for
making small holes for brads, etc.

brae (brā) *n. Scottish.* a slope; hillside. [ME *bra* < ON *brá-* (first
member of a compound) brow; intermediate sense being "brow of a
hill"]

hat, āge, fär; let, ēqual, tėrm; it, īce
hot, ōpen, ôrder; oil, out; cup, put, rüle,
əbove, takən, pencəl, lemən, circəs
ch, child; ng, long; sh, ship
th, thin; ŦH, then; zh, measure

brag (brag) *n., v.* **bragged, brag·ging.** —*n.* **1** a boast. **2** boastful
talk. **3** a person who boasts.
—*v.* boast. [ME; origin uncertain] —**brag′ger,** *n.*
☛ *Syn. v.* See note at **boast.**

brag·ga·do·ci·o (brag′ə dō′shē ō *or* brag′ə dō′chē ō) *n., pl.*
-ci·os. 1 a boasting or bragging. **2** a boaster; braggart. [coined by
Spenser as the name of a character in his *Faerie Queene*]

brag·gart (brag′ərt) *n.* **1** boaster. **2** (*adj.*) boastful. [< F *bragard*
< *braguer* brag]

brah·ma (brä′mə *or* brā′mə) *n.* a breed of large chicken with
feathered legs and small wings and tail. [< *Brahmaputra,* a river in
E India]

Brah·ma (brä′mə) *n.* **1** *Hinduism.* a divinity formerly widely
worshipped as the highest god, the creator of all things. **2** Brahman
(def. 3). [< Skt.]

Brah·man (brä′mən) *n., pl.* **-mans. 1** *Classical Hinduism.* the
eternal, supreme reality that is the basis of the universe. **2** a
member of the priestly caste, the highest caste in India. **3** any of
several breeds of humpbacked cattle developed in the S United
States by crossing breeds of Indian zebu cattle with American beef
breeds. Also, **Brahmin.**

Brah·man·ism (brä′mən iz′əm) *n.* **1** the religious beliefs and
practices of ancient India; the early form of Hinduism when the
priestly caste, the Brahmans, had great power and prestige and
when sacrificial rituals were very important. **2** the principles and
practices of the Brahmans themselves.

Brah·min (brä′mən) *n., pl.* **-min. 1** See **Brahman. 2** highbrow
intellectual, especially one belonging to an upper-class family.

braid (brād) *n., v.* —*n.* **1** a narrow length of hair, ribbon, straw,
etc. formed by weaving together three or more strands or bunches.
2 ribbon or cord, usually consisting of interwoven strands, used to
trim or bind clothing, etc. **3** a band, etc. for binding the hair.
—*v.* **1** weave together three or more strands or bunches of: *Her
mother always braids her hair.* **2** form or make in this way: *to braid
a rug.* **3** trim or bind with braid. **4** *Poetic.* bind or ornament (the
hair) with ribbons, flowers, etc. [OE *bregdan*] —**braid′er,** *n.*

braid·ed (brād′id) *adj.* **1** formed by weaving together three or
more strands of hair, ribbon, straw, etc. **2** trimmed or bound with
braid.

brail (brāl) *n., v.* —*n.* **1** a rope fastened to a sail, used in drawing
the sail up or in. **2** brailer. —*v.* **1** draw in, or furl, (a sail) using the
brails. **2** unload (fish) from a seine or trap onto a boat. [ME < OF
< VL *bracale* belt < *bracae* breeches. See BRACKET.]

brail·er (brā′lər) *n.* a scoop or basket used to brail fish.

braille or **Braille** (brāl) *n.* **1** a system of writing and printing for
blind people. The letters in braille are made of groups of raised dots
that are read by touch. **2** the letters themselves. [named after Louis
Braille (1809-1852), a French teacher of the blind]

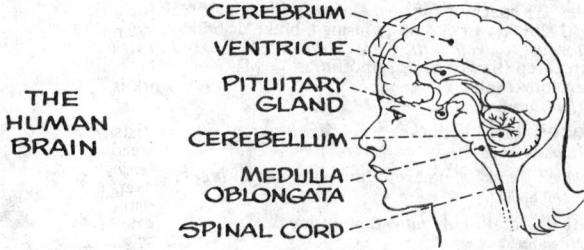

THE
HUMAN
BRAIN

CEREBRUM
VENTRICLE
PITUITARY
GLAND
CEREBELLUM
MEDULLA
OBLONGATA
SPINAL CORD

brain (brān) *n., v.* —*n.* **1** the mass of nerve tissue enclosed in the
skull of vertebrates. The brain interprets impulses received by the
senses of sight, touch, hearing, etc., controls and co-ordinates
bodily activities, and is the centre of thought and feeling. **2** in
invertebrates, the part of the nervous system corresponding to the
brain of vertebrates. **3** mind; intellect: *He has a good brain.*
4 *Slang.* a very intelligent person. **5** Usually, **brains,** *pl.*
a intelligence: *She has more brains than anyone else in the family.*
b the main planner of an organization or project: *She is the brains
of the firm.* **6** an electronic device thought of as comparable to a
brain.
beat (one's) **brains,** try hard to think of something.

have something on the brain, *Informal.* to be extremely interested in or eager about something: *She has ballet on the brain.*

pick (someone's) **brains,** to extract useful information or material from (someone).

—*v.* kill by smashing the skull of: *The trapper brained the injured wolf with a large stone.* [OE *brægen*]

brain cell a nerve cell in the brain.

brain·child (brān′chīld′) *n., pl.* **chil·dren.** an original product of a person's thought or imagination, such as an invention, idea, or plan, especially one that the person is particularly pleased with or proud of.

brain drain *Informal.* a departure of the most highly trained or educated people from a country or region because of better opportunities elsewhere.

brain·less (brān′lis) *adj.* 1 without a brain. 2 stupid; foolish. —**brain′less·ly,** *adv.* —**brain′less·ness,** *n.*

brain·pan (brān′pan′) *n.* the part of the skull enclosing the brain; cranium.

brain–pow·er (brān′pow′ər) *n.* 1 the power of the mind; brains. 2 intellect thought of as a force or as an instrument to be used.

brain·sick (brān′sik′) *adj.* crazy; insane.

brain·storm (brān′stôrm′) *n., v.* —*n.* 1 *Informal.* a sudden inspired idea. 2 a sudden and violent, but temporary, mental disturbance. —*v.* attempt to solve a problem in a group, committee, etc. by having the members suggest every possible solution they can think of. Discussion is postponed until suggestions are exhausted. —**brain′storm·er,** *n.*

brain trust or **brains trust** 1 a group of experts acting as advisers to an administrator, a political leader, or an executive. 2 a group of experts in various fields who discuss on the radio or television problems sent in for their attention.

brain·wash (brān′wosh′) *v.* change the ideas or beliefs of by brainwashing.

brain·wash·ing (brān′wosh′ing) *n.* 1 a process of systematic and intensive forced indoctrination designed to purge a person's mind of existing political, religious, or social beliefs and to replace them with a completely different set of beliefs. 2 *Informal.* persuasion through long or intensive exposure to advertising or propaganda.

brain wave 1 a rhythmic increase and decrease of voltage between parts of the brain that produces an electric current. Brain waves can be recorded by means of an electroencephalograph. 2 *Informal.* a sudden inspiration or bright idea.

brain·work (brān′wèrk′) *n.* work requiring the use of the mind, as distinguished from manual or mechanical work.

brain·y (brān′ē) *adj.* **brain·i·er, brain·i·est.** *Informal.* intelligent; clever. —**brain′i·ness,** *n.*

braise (brāz) *v.* **braised, brais·ing.** brown (meat) quickly and then cook it long and slowly in a covered pan with very little water. [< F *braiser* < *braise* hot charcoal < Gmc.]

brake[1] (brāk) *n., v.* **braked, brak·ing.** —*n.* 1 a device used to decrease or stop the motion of a wheel or vehicle by pressing or scraping. 2 a tool or machine for breaking up flax or hemp into fibres. 3 a machine for kneading or rolling. 4 a break (def. 7). —*v.* 1 slow down or stop by using a brake or brakes: *He had to brake fast to avoid hitting the car ahead. He braked the truck.* 2 break up (flax or hemp) into fibres. [< MLG or MDu. *braeke.* Akin to BREAK.]
☛ *Hom.* break.

brake[2] (brāk) *n.* thicket. [cf. MLG *brake*]
☛ *Hom.* break.

brake[3] (brāk) *n.* bracken. [probably var. of *bracken*]
☛ *Hom.* break.

brake[4] (brāk) *v. Archaic.* a pt. of **break.**
☛ *Hom.* break.

brake band on a winch, hoist, etc., a flexible band encircling the brake drum, that is tightened to slow down or stop a turning wheel or shaft.

brake drum on the wheel, axle, or transmission shaft of a vehicle, a metal cylinder against which a shoe or brake band is pressed in braking.

brake·man (brāk′mən) *n., pl.* **-men.** a person who works as assistant to the conductor or engineer of a railway train. Brakemen used to work the brakes on steam locomotives.

bram·ble (bram′bəl) *n.* 1 any of a genus (*Rubus*) of shrubs of the rose family, most of which have prickly stems. Blackberry and raspberry bushes are brambles. 2 any rough, prickly shrub. [OE *bræmbel,* var. of *brēmel* < *brōm* broom]

bram·bly (bram′blē) *adj.* **-bli·er, -bli·est.** 1 full of brambles. 2 like brambles; prickly.

bran (bran) *n.* the broken coat of the grains of wheat, rye, etc. separated from the flour or meal by bolting. Bran is used as fodder and in cereal, bread, and other foods. [ME < OF]

branch (branch) *n., v.* —*n.* 1 a subdivision of the stem of a large woody plant, especially a stem growing from the trunk or another stem of a tree or from the main or a secondary stem of a shrub. 2 any division or part of a main body or source, like a branch of a tree: *the branches of a deer's antlers, a branch of a river, a branch of a family.* 3 a division or part of a system, subject, etc. Botany is a branch of biology. 4 a local office: *The company's head office is in Moncton, but it has branches in several other cities.* —*v.* 1 put out branches; spread in branches (*often used with* **out**). 2 divide into branches: *The trunk branches near the ground. The road branches at the bottom of the hill.* 3 go in another direction; diverge from the main route, topic, etc. (*often used with* **off**). **branch out,** extend or expand business, activities, interests, etc.: *Her brokerage firm is considering branching out into investment counselling.* [ME < OF *branche* < LL *branca* paw] —**branch′less,** *adj.* —**branch′like′,** *adj.*
☛ *Syn.* 1. **Branch, bough, limb** = a part of a tree growing out from the trunk or from another similar part. **Branch** is the general word, and applies to any of the woody outgrowths, large or small, of a tree or shrub: *The branches waved in the breeze.* **Bough** applies particularly to a main branch, but often is used to suggest any branch covered with blossoms, fruit, etc., especially when it has been cut from the tree: *Those boughs of flowering plum are beautiful on the table.* **Limb** applies to a main or large branch: *The wind broke a whole limb from the tree.*

bran·chi·o·pod (brang′kē ə pod′) *n.* any of a subclass (Branchiopoda) of small, mainly freshwater crustaceans, including the water fleas, having many pairs of flattened appendages used for swimming, respiration, etc. [< NL < Gk. *branchia* gills + *pous, podos* foot]

branch·let (branch′lit) *n.* a small branch.

branch plant a business that is owned and controlled by a company having its headquarters elsewhere. A corporation may have branch plants in several countries, or in several parts of the same country.

branch–plant (branch′plant′) *adj.* characterized by or arising from the existence of branch plants and the resulting dependence on decisions made elsewhere: *a branch-plant economy.*

brand (brand) *n., v.* —*n.* 1 a certain kind, grade, or make: *a popular brand of shampoo, a good brand of coffee.* 2 brand name or trademark. 3 a mark made by burning the skin with a hot iron: *Cattle and horses on big ranches are marked with brands to show who owns them.* 4 branding iron. 5 a mark of disgrace. 6 a piece of wood that is burning or partly burned. 7 a disease of garden plants caused by a fungus (*Puccinia arenariae*), in which the leaves develop brown spots that look like burns. 8 *Archaic or poetic.* sword. —*v.* 1 mark by burning the skin with a hot iron: *In former times criminals were often branded.* 2 expose or mark as deserving disgrace: *He has been branded as a traitor.* [OE] —**brand′er,** *n.*

bran·died (bran′dēd) *adj.* prepared, mixed, or flavored with brandy.

branding iron an iron stamp for burning an identification mark on hide, wood, etc.

bran·dish (bran′dish) *v., n.* —*v.* wave or shake threateningly; flourish: *The knight drew his sword and brandished it at his enemy.* —*n.* a threatening shake; flourish. [< OF *brandiss-,* stem of *brandir* < *brand* sword < Gmc.]

brand name 1 a name given to a product or service by its manufacturer or seller to distinguish from similar ones produced or sold by someone else; trade name. A brand name may be registered and protected as a trademark. 2 a product with a well-known trade name. —**brand-name,** *adj.*

brand–new (brand′nyü′ *or* -nü′) *adj.* very new; as new as if just made.

bran·dy (bran′dē) *n., pl.* **-dies;** *v.* **-died, -dy·ing.** —*n.* 1 a strong alcoholic liquor distilled from wine. 2 an alcoholic liquor distilled from fermented fruit juice. —*v.* mix, flavor, or preserve with brandy. [< Du. *brandewijn* burnt (i.e., distilled) wine]

brant (brant) *n., pl.* **brants** or (esp. collectively) **brant.** a small wild goose (*Branta bernicla*) that breeds in the Arctic tundra and winters in the temperate regions of the Atlantic and Pacific oceans, having a black head, neck, and breast, dark grey upper parts, and a narrow white crescent on either side of the neck. [origin uncertain]

brash[1] (brash) *adj.* 1 hasty; rash. 2 impudent; saucy. [origin uncertain] —**brash′ly,** *adv.* —**brash′ness,** *n.*

brash² (brash) *n.* small fragments of ice broken off from an ice pack or floe. [? < MF *breche* breach]

bra·sier (brā′zhər *or* brā′zē ər) See **brazier.**

brass (bras) *n.* 1 a yellow metal, an alloy of copper and zinc. 2 something made of brass, such as door fittings or ornaments. 3 (*adj.*) made of brass. 4 a musical wind instrument, usually made of brass, such as the trumpet, trombone, and French horn. 5 often, **brasses,** *pl.* the section of an orchestra or band composed of brass instruments. 6 *Informal.* shamelessness; impudence. 7 high-ranking officials, especially military officers. 8 a memorial plate of brass marked with an effigy, coat of arms, inscription, etc. 9 *Esp.Brit. Dialect.* money. [OE *bræs*]

bras·sard (bras′ärd *or* brə särd′) *n.* 1 a band worn above the elbow as a badge. 2 armor for the upper part of the arm. See **armor** for picture. [< F *brassard* < *bras* arm]

bras·sart (bras′ərt) *n.* brassard (def. 2).

brass band a group of musicians playing brass wind instruments.

brass·bound (bras′bound′) *adj.* 1 *Informal.* keeping strictly to rule. 2 bound with brass: *a brassbound box.*

bras·se·rie (bras′ə rē) *n.* a bar or small restaurant serving food and alcoholic drinks, especially beer. [< F *brasser* brew, stir; 19c.]

brass hat *Slang.* a high-ranking military officer, such as a general or staff officer.

bras·siere *or* **bras·sière** (brə zēr′) *n.* a woman's undergarment worn to support the breasts. [< F *brassière* bodice < *bras* arm]

brass knuckles a metal bar that fits across the knuckles, used in fighting.

brass ring the highest prize, distinction, or position of honor, power, prominence, etc.: *As a politician he was not ambitious enough to reach for the brass ring.* [from a brass ring that used to hang above the riders on a merry-go-round; anyone catching hold of the ring got a free ride]

brass tacks *Informal.* the actual facts or details: *Let's get down to brass tacks.*

brass·ware (bras′ wer′) *n.* things made of brass.

brass·y (bras′ē) *adj.* **brass·i·er, brass·i·est.** 1 of brass. 2 like brass. 3 loud and harsh. 4 *Informal.* shameless; impudent. —**brass′i·ly,** *adv.* —**brass′i·ness,** *n.*

brat (brat) *n. Derogatory.* a child, especially an irritating one. [? special use of ME *brat* coarse garment, OE *bratt* cloak, covering, probably < Celtic; with reference to a bib] —**brat′ty** *or* **brat′tish,** *adj.* —**brat′ti·ness** *or* **brat′tish·ness,** *n.*

bra·va·do (brə vä′dō) *n.* a great show of boldness without much real courage; boastful defiance without much real desire to fight. [< Sp. *bravada* < *bravo.* See BRAVE.]

brave (brāv) *adj.* **brav·er, brav·est;** *n., v.* **braved, brav·ing.** —*adj.* 1 having the strength of mind to control fear and act firmly in the face of danger or difficulties; courageous: *He showed he was brave when he stood up to the bully.* 2 showing bravery: *a brave act.* 3 making a fine appearance; showy: *The fair had brave displays.* 4 *Archaic.* fine; excellent. —*n.* 1 a courageous person. 2 a North American Indian warrior. —*v.* 1 meet bravely: *Soldiers brave much danger.* 2 dare; defy: *She braved the king's anger.* [< F < Ital. *bravo* brave, bold < Sp. *bravo* vicious (as applied to bulls), ? < L *pravus*] —**brave′ly,** *adj.* —**brave′ness,** *n.*

brav·er·y (brā′vər ē *or* brāv′rē) *n., pl.* **-er·ies.** 1 strength of mind in the face of danger or difficulties; courage. 2 fine appearance; showy dress; finery.

bra·vo¹ (brä′vō) *interj., n., pl.* **-vos.** —*interj.* well done! fine! excellent! —*n.* the cry of "Bravo!" [< Ital. See BRAVE.]

bra·vo² (brä′vō) *n., pl.* **-voes** *or* **-vos.** a hired fighter or murderer. [< Ital. See BRAVE.]

bra·vu·ra (brə vyür′ə) *n.* 1 a piece of music requiring skill and spirit in the performer. 2 a display of daring; attempt at brilliant performance; dash; spirit. [< Ital. *bravura* bravery]

braw (bro *or* brô) *adj. Scottish.* 1 making a fine appearance. 2 excellent; fine. [var. of *brave*]

brawl¹ (brol *or* brôl) *n., v.* —*n.* 1 a noisy and disorderly quarrel: *The hockey game turned into a brawl.* 2 a babble. —*v.* 1 quarrel in a noisy and disorderly way. 2 babble. [ME *brallen*] —**brawl′er,** *n.*

brawl² (brol *or* brôl) *n.* 1 an old French folk dance similar to the cotillion. 2 the music for this dance. 3 *Slang.* a dance or party. [< *brawl¹* influenced by MF *branle* dance]

brawn (bron *or* brôn) *n.* 1 firm, strong muscles. 2 muscular strength: *Football requires brains as well as brawn.* 3 boiled and pickled meat from a boar or pig. [ME < OF *braon* < Gmc.]

hat, āge, fär; let, ēqual, tèrm; it, īce
hot, ōpen, ôrder; oil, out; cup, put, rüle,
above, takən, pencəl, lemən, circəs

ch, child; ng, long; sh, ship
th, thin; ʋH, then; zh, measure

brawn·y (bron′ē *or* brôn′ē) *adj.* **brawn·i·er, brawn·i·est.** strong; muscular. —**brawn′i·ness,** *n.*

bray¹ (brā) *n., v.* —*n.* 1 the loud, harsh sound made by a donkey. 2 any noise like it. —*v.* 1 make a loud, harsh sound: *The man brayed with laughter.* 2 utter in a loud, harsh voice. [ME < OF *braire*]

bray² (brā) *v.* pound or crush into fine bits; grind into a powder. [ME < OF *breier*]

Braz. Brazil; Brazilian.

braze¹ (brāz) *v.* **brazed, braz·ing.** 1 cover or decorate with brass. 2 make like brass. [OE *brasian* < *bræs* brass]

braze² (brāz) *v.* **brazed, braz·ing.** solder with any of various solders having a high melting point. [? < F *braser* < OF *braise* embers]

bra·zen (brā′zən) *adj., v.* —*adj.* 1 shameless; impudent. 2 made of brass. 3 like brass in color or strength. 4 loud and harsh. —*v.* make shameless or impudent.
brazen a thing out *or* **through,** act as if one did not feel ashamed of it.
[OE *bræsen* < *bræs* brass] —**bra′zen·ly,** *adv.* —**bra′zen·ness,** *n.*
➤ *Syn. adj.* 1. See note at **bold.**

bra·zier¹ (brā′zhər *or* brā′zē ər) *n.* a metal container to hold burning charcoal or coal: *Braziers are used in some countries for heating rooms.* Also, **brasier.** [< F *brasier* < *braise* hot coals]

bra·zier² (brā′zhər *or* brā′zē ər) *n.* a person who works with brass. Also, **brasier.** [< *braze¹*]

Bra·zil·ian (brə zil′yən) *n., adj.* —*n.* a native or inhabitant of Brazil, a country in South America. —*adj.* of or having to do with Brazil or its people.

Brazil nut 1 a large, triangular, edible nut of a tropical South American tree (*Bertholletia excelsa*). 2 the tree bearing these nuts.

bra·zil·wood (brə zil′wud′) *n.* the red wood of any of several tropical trees (genus *Caesalpina*) used in cabinetwork and, especially formerly, as a source of red or purple dye.

breach (brēch) *n., v.* —*n.* 1 an opening made by breaking down something solid; gap. 2 the breaking or neglect of a law, promise, duty, etc.: *For him to go away today would be a breach of duty.* 3 a breaking of friendly relations; quarrel. 4 a whale's leap clear of the sea. —*v.* 1 break through; make an opening in: *The enemy's fierce attack finally breached the wall.* 2 of whales, rise or leap clear of the sea. [ME *breche* < OF < Gmc.]
☛ *Hom.* **breech.**

breach of faith a breaking of a promise.

breach of promise a breaking of a promise to marry.

breach of the peace a public disturbance; riot.

bread (bred) *n., v.* —*n.* 1 a food made of flour or meal mixed with milk or water and, usually, yeast, that is kneaded, shaped into loaves, and baked. 2 food; livelihood. 3 *Slang.* money.
break bread, **a** share a meal. **b** administer or take Communion.
cast (one's) bread upon the waters, do good with little or no prospect of reward.
know which side (one's) bread is buttered on, know what is to one's advantage.
take the bread out of (someone's) mouth, **a** to take away a person's livelihood. **b** to take from a person what he is on the point of enjoying.
—*v.* cover with bread crumbs before cooking. [OE *brēad*]
—**bread′less,** *adj.*
☛ *Hom.* **bred.**

bread and butter 1 bread spread with butter. 2 *Informal.* necessities; a living.

bread–and–butter (bred′ən but′ər) *adj.* 1 *Informal.* prosaic; commonplace. 2 expressing thanks for hospitality: *a bread-and-butter letter.*

bread·bas·ket (bred′bas′kit) *n.* 1 a basket or tray for bread. 2 a region that is a chief source of grain: *The Prairies are the breadbasket of Canada.* 3 *Slang.* the stomach.

bread·board (bred′bôrd′) *n.* a board on which to slice bread, knead dough, roll pastry, etc.

bread·crumb *or* **bread–crumb** (bred′krum′) *n., v.* —*n.* 1 a

crumb of bread. **2** the soft part of bread as distinguished from the crust. —*v.* cover with breadcrumbs.

bread·fruit (bred′früt′) *n.* **1** a large, round, starchy, tropical fruit of the Pacific islands, much used for food. When baked, it tastes somewhat like bread. **2** the tree that it grows on.

bread line a line of people waiting to get food issued as charity or relief.

bread·stuff (bred′stuf′) *n.* **1** grain, flour, or meal for making bread. **2** bread.

breadth (bredth *or* bretth) *n.* **1** how broad a thing is; the distance across; width: *The breadth of his shoulders suggested great strength.* **2** a piece of a certain width: *a breadth of cloth.* **3** freedom from narrowness in views or taste: *She is known for her breadth of mind.* **4** great extent or scope: [ME *bredethe < brede* breadth, OE *brædu < brād* broad]

breadthways (bredth′wāz′ *or* bretth′-) *adv. or adj.* in the direction of the breadth.

breadth·wise (bredth′wīz′ *or* bretth′-) *adv. or adj.* breadthways.

bread·win·ner (bred′win′ər) *n.* the member of a family who earns the family's living.

break (brāk) *v.* broke, bro·ken, break·ing; *n.* —*v.* **1** cause to come to pieces by a blow or pull: *How did you break my glasses?* **2** come apart; crack; burst: *The plate broke into pieces when it fell on the floor.* **3** destroy evenness, wholeness, etc.: *to break a five-dollar bill.* **4** damage, ruin, or destroy: *She broke her watch by winding it too tightly.* **5** fracture the bone of: *to break one's arm.* **6** fail to keep; act against: *to break a law, to break a promise.* **7** escape or become free from: *to break jail. The boat broke its moorings in the storm.* **8** force open: *to break the enemy's ranks.* **9** force one's way: *to break loose from prison, to break into a house.* **10** come suddenly: *The storm broke within ten minutes.* **11** become less or stop suddenly: *The spell of rainy weather has broken.* **12** decrease the force of; lessen: *Because the bushes broke his fall, he was not hurt.* **13** be crushed; give way: *The dog's heart broke when his master died.* **14** dawn; appear: *The day is breaking.* **15** of plants: **a** to bud. **b** to flower too soon. **16** stop; put an end to: *to break one's fast.* **17** reduce in rank: *The captain was broken for neglect of duty.* **18** train to obey; tame: *to break a colt.* **19** ruin financially; make bankrupt. **20** go beyond; exceed: *The speed of the new train has broken all records.* **21** dig or plough (land), especially for the first time: *In the forests of Upper Canada the pioneers had to work hard to break the ground.* **22** of boxers, come out of a clinch. **23** make known; reveal: *to break the bad news gently.* **24** train away from a habit: *He's trying to break himself of nail biting.* **25** open an electric circuit.
break away, a leave or escape, especially suddenly: *He broke away from his captors. She finally broke away from her parents and got an apartment of her own.* **b** start before the signal: *The horse was disqualified for breaking away.*
break down, a go out of order; cease to work. **b** collapse; become weak: *His health broke down.* **c** begin to cry. **d** analyse; separate into components: *Water can be broken down into its component elements by passing an electric current through it. We broke our total holiday budget down into expenses for food, hotels, transportation and extras.*
break even, *Informal.* finish with the same amount one started with; not win or lose in: *He had hoped to sell his bicycle at a profit, but he could only break even.*
break in, a prepare for work or use; train. **b** enter illegally or by force: *The thieves broke in through the cellar.* **c** interrupt.
break into, a enter suddenly, by force, or illegally: *Our house was broken into while we were away. He broke into the room, yelling, "Who took my sweater?"* **b** begin suddenly: *I almost fell off when my horse broke into a gallop.* **c** interrupt: *He didn't want to break into the conversation, so he kept quiet.* **d** enter a profession or activity, especially with some difficulty: *She's been trying for months to break into the advertising business.*
break off, a stop suddenly. **b** stop being friends.
break out, a begin or arise suddenly or unexpectedly: *War broke out. Fire broke out in the basement.* **b** have an eruption of pimples, rashes, etc. on the skin: *The child broke out in measles.* **c** escape from prison: *Ten convicts have broken out in the last year.*
break trail, *Cdn.* move ahead of a dog team, vehicle, or person, making a way through deep snow: *The leader went ahead on snowshoes, breaking trail for the dogs.*
break up, a scatter: *The fog is breaking up.* **b** stop; put an end to: *We broke up our meeting early today.* **c** *Informal.* upset; disturb greatly. **d** break into pieces: *to break up lumps of earth.* **e** *Informal.* stop being friends: *They've broken up.*
break with, stop being friends with.
—*n.* **1** a broken place; gap; crack: *There's a break in the dam.* **2** a

breaking or shattering; fracture; rupture. **3** a forcing of one's way out. **4** an abrupt or marked change. **5** a short interruption in work, athletic practice, etc. **6** the act or fact of making an electric circuit incomplete. **7** a large, four-wheeled, horse-drawn carriage or wagon. **8** *Slang.* an awkward remark; mistake in manners. **9** *Slang.* a chance or opportunity.
get a break or **the breaks,** *Informal.* have things come easily; have lots of luck.
[OE *brecan*]
☛ *Hom.* brake.
☛ *Syn. v.* **1. Break, shatter, smash** = to make something come or go to pieces. **Break,** the general word = to divide something into two or more pieces by pulling, hitting, or striking it: *I broke the handle off a cup.* **Shatter** = to break suddenly into a number of pieces that fly in all directions. *I shattered the cup when I dropped it on the floor.* **Smash** = to break to pieces with sudden violence and noise: *He smashed the headlights when he hit the wall.*

break·a·ble (brāk′ə bəl) *adj.* that can be cracked or shattered, especially objects of glass, china, etc., or delicate mechanisms: *Is there anything breakable in this box?*

break·age (brāk′ij) *n.* **1** the act or fact of breaking; break. **2** damage or loss caused by breaking. **3** an allowance made for such damage or loss.

break and enter the act or an instance of breaking and entering. Also called **break and entry.**

break·a·way (brāk′ə wā′) *n.* **1** the act or fact of separating sharply from a group or pattern. **2** the separation of the shock wave from the fireball of an atomic explosion as it moves ahead. **3** *Slang.* in the theatre, a stage property made so that it breaks easily and harmlessly when struck by or against something. **4** a start: *Three of the horses in the race got well ahead of the others at the breakaway.* **5** *Hockey or lacrosse.* a situation in which a player of one team launches an attack on goal, the defensive players being caught out of position in their opponents' zone.

break·down (brāk′doun′) *n.* **1** a failure to work. **2** a loss of health; weakness; collapse: *a mental breakdown.* **3** a noisy, lively dance. **4** the division of a process into steps or stages; an analysis. **5** chemical decomposition or analysis.

break·er¹ (brāk′ər) *n.* **1** a wave that breaks into foam on the shore, rocks, etc. **2** a machine for breaking things into smaller pieces. **3** a person or thing that breaks. [< *break*]
☛ *Syn.* **1.** See note at wave.

break·er² (brāk′ər) *n.* a small water cask for use in a boat. [alteration of Sp. *barrica*]

break·fast (brek′fəst) *n., v.* —*n.* the first meal of the day. —*v.* eat breakfast. [< *break* + *fast²*]

breakfast food a cereal eaten at breakfast.

break–in (brāk′in′) *n.* burglary.

breaking and entering *Law.* the entry by force or guile into private or business premises with the object of committing a crime.

breaking point **1** the point at which a person's mental or physical endurance or resistance gives way under stress. **2** the point at which anything breaks under strain.

break·neck (brāk′nek′) *adj.* likely to cause a broken neck; very dangerous: *breakneck speed, a breakneck slope.*

break of day the dawn.

break·out (brāk′out′) *n.* **1** the act or condition of escaping from a prison, etc. **2** breakthrough (def. 2).

break·through (brāk′thrü′) *n.* **1** the solution of a problem, especially in science or technology, that has an important effect on all future research and development. The development of the transistor was a major breakthrough in electronics. **2** an offensive military operation that gets all the way through a defensive system into the unorganized area in the rear. **3** a solving of the major problem or problems hindering an undertaking, as in science.

break–up or **break up** (brāk′up′) *n.* **1** *Cdn.* the breaking of the ice on a river or lake in spring: *We stood on the bridge and watched the break-up.* **2** *Cdn.* especially in the North, the time when this happens; spring: *They planned to start work on the new road after break-up.* **3** a scattering; separation. **4** a stopping; end. **5** a collapse; decay.

break·wa·ter (brāk′wot′ər *or* -wô′tər) *n.* a wall or barrier built near the shore to break the force of waves and make an area of calm water for a harbor or beach.

bream¹ (brēm) *n., pl.* **bream** or **breams. 1** any of several European freshwater fishes (genus *Abramis*) of the minnow family, especially a common food and game fish (*A. brama*), having a deep, compressed body and silvery scales. **2** any of various other cyprinid fishes. **3** any of various freshwater sunfishes. **4** sea bream. [ME *breme < OF bre(s)me < Gmc.*]

bream² (brēm) *v. Archaic.* clean (a ship's bottom). [cf. MDu. *brem* broom]

breast (brest) *n., v.* —*n.* **1** either of the two milk-producing glands on the chest of the human female. **2** a similar gland in certain other

female mammals. **3** the upper, front part or the human body; chest. **4** the corresponding part in animals. **5** the upper, front part of a coat, dress, etc. **6** anything suggesting the human breast in shape or position. **7** the heart or feelings.
beat one's breast, express grief, guilt, remorse, etc. publicly and emotionally.
make a clean breast of, confess fully; tell everything.
—*v.* oppose; face; struggle with; advance against: *The experienced swimmer was able to breast the waves. He breasted every trouble as it came.* [OE *brēost*]

breast·beat·ing (brest′bēt′ing) *n.* the public, emotional expression of grief, guilt, remorse, etc.

breast·bone (brest′bōn′) *n.* the thin, flat bone in the front of the chest to which the ribs are attached; sternum. See **skeleton** for picture.

breast–feed (brest′fēd′) *v.* **-fed, -feed·ing.** feed a baby at the mother's breast rather than from a bottle; nurse; suckle.

breast·pin (brest′pin′) *n.* an ornamented pin worn on the breast, especially to close a garment.

breast·plate (brest′plāt′) *n.* **1** a piece of armor for the chest. See **armor** for picture. **2** in ancient times, a vestment set with jewels, worn by Jewish high priests.

breast stroke or **breast·stroke** (brest′strōk′) *n.* Swimming. a stroke performed while face down in the water, the swimmer bringing both arms forward from the breast and then sweeping them out to the sides and back down, while moving the legs in a frog kick.

breast·work (brest′wėrk′) *n.* a low, hastily built wall for defence.

breath (breth) *n.* **1** air drawn into and forced out of the lungs. **2** the act of breathing. **3** moisture from breathing: *You can see your breath on a very cold day.* **4** the ability to breathe easily: *Running makes a person lose his breath.* **5 a** a single drawing in and forcing out of air from the body. **b** the air drawn in. **c** the time required for one breath; a moment. **6** a slight movement of the air. **7** a whisper. **8** a short pause or rest; breather: *Let's take a breath here.* **9** life. **10** *Phonetics.* an expulsion of air without vibration of the vocal cords, as in pronouncing *s, f, p, t, k.* **11** the fragrance given off by flowers, etc. **12** a trace or suggestion: *a breath of suspicion.*
below (one's) **breath,** in a whisper.
catch (one's) **breath, a** a gasp; pant. **b** stop for breath; rest: *They sat down on a rock to catch their breath.*
hold (one's) **breath,** check exhalation.
in the same breath, at the same time or almost the same time.
out of breath, breathing very hard as a result of exertion: *She was so out of breath from the run that she could hardly speak.*
save (one's) **breath,** *Informal.* avoid useless effort in trying to convince: *I know he won't help, so you might as well save your breath.*
take (one's) **breath away,** leave one breathless because of awe, surprise, etc.
under or **below** (one's) **breath,** in a whisper: *She was talking under her breath so we couldn't hear her.*
[OE *brǣth* odor, steam]

breath·a·ble (brē′ŦHə bəl) *adj.* **1** suitable for being breathed: *The air in this place is hardly breathable.* **2** of a fabric, etc., allowing air to pass through. —**breath′a·bil′i·ty,** *n.*

breath·a·lyz·er (breth′ə līz′ər) *n.* a device for measuring the alcoholic content in a person's blood by a test of the breath. Also, **breathalyser.**

breathe (brēŦH) *v.* **breathed, breath·ing. 1** draw (air) into the lungs and force it out. **2** stop for breath; rest: *I need a moment to breathe.* **3** say softly; whisper; utter: *"Don't move until I give the signal," he breathed.* **4** be alive; live. **5** *Phonetics.* utter with breath and not with voice. **6** draw into the lungs; inhale. **7** send out from the lungs; exhale: *The dragon breathed fire and smoke.* **8** inspire; impart; give: *Her enthusiasm breathed new life into the team.* **9** blow lightly. **10** make apparent; show clearly: *His whole appearance breathes confidence.* **11** of a fabric, leather, etc., allow air to pass through: *Some synthetic fabrics are uncomfortable because they don't breathe.* **12** allow to rest after exertion: *to breathe a horse.*
breathe again or **breathe freely** or **easily,** feel relieved: *The guard passed and she could breathe again.*
breathe down (someone's) **neck,** pursue or watch a person closely: *His supervisor was always breathing down his neck.*
[ME *brethen* < *breth* breath]

breath·er (brē′ŦHər) *n.* **1** a short stop for breath; rest. **2** a small vent in an enclosure, container, etc. **3** a person or animal that breathes in a certain way: *a noisy breather.*

breath·ing (brē′ŦHing) *n.* **1** respiration. **2** a single breath. **3** the time needed for a single breath.

breathing space room or time enough to breathe easily; an opportunity to rest.

hat, āge, fär; let, ēqual, tėrm; it, īce
hot, ōpen, ôrder; oil, out; cup, put, rüle,
əbove, takən, pencəl, lemən, circəs

ch, child; ng, long; sh, ship
th, thin; ŦH, then; zh, measure

breathing spell a pause to catch one's breath.

breath·less (breth′lis) *adj.* **1** out of breath: *Running very fast makes you breathless.* **2** holding one's breath because of fear, interest, excitement, etc.: *The beauty of the scenery left Anne breathless.* **3** without breath; lifeless. **4** without a breeze. —**breath′less·ly,** *adv.* **-breath′less·ness,** *n.*

breath·tak·ing (breth′tāk′ing) *adj.* thrilling; exciting: *a breathtaking roller-coaster ride, a breathtaking view.* —**breath′tak′ing·ly,** *adv.*

breath·y (breth′ē) *adj.* characterized by audible sounds of breathing. —**breath′i·ly,** *adv.* —**breath′i·ness,** *n.*

brec·ci·a (brech′ē ə or bresh′ē ə) *n.* a kind of sedimentary rock consisting of angular fragments of older rocks naturally cemented together in a matrix. [< Ital. < Gmc. Akin to BREAK.]

Brecht·i·an (brek′tē ən or breн′tē ən) *adj.* of, having to do with, or characteristic of Bertolt Brecht (1898-1956), a German dramatist and director, or his works.

bred (bred) *v.* pt. and pp. of **breed.**
☛ *Hom.* **bread.**

breech (brēch) *n., v.* —*n.* **1** the lower part; back part. **2** in a firearm, the opening, directly behind the barrel, where the shells are inserted. **3** the rump or buttocks.
—*v.* **1** clothe with breeches. **2** provide (a gun) with a breech. [back formation from *breeches*]
☛ *Hom.* **breach.**

breech·cloth (brēch′kloth′) *n.* a covering for the loins consisting of a cloth or leather passed between the legs and fastened around the waist; loincloth. Breechcloths were formerly worn by some North American Indian peoples.

breech·clout (brēch′klout′) *n.* breechcloth.

breech·es (brich′iz or brē′chiz) *n.pl.* **1** short trousers covering the hips and thighs and fastened snugly at or just below the knees. **2** *Informal.* trousers; pants. [OE *brēc,* pl. of *brōc* breech]

breeches buoy a pair of short canvas trousers fastened to a belt or life preserver. A breeches buoy slides along a rope on a pulley and is used to move people from one ship to another or from ship to shore, especially in rescue operations.

breech·ing (brich′ing or brē′ching) *n.* the part of a harness that passes around a horse's rump.

breech·load·er (brēch′lōd′ər) *n.* a gun that is loaded from behind the barrel, instead of at the mouth.

breech·load·ing (brēch′lōd′ing) *adj.* of guns, loading from behind the barrel instead of at the mouth.

breed (brēd) *v.* **bred, breed·ing;** *n.* —*v.* **1** produce young; reproduce: *Rabbits breed rapidly.* **2** of animals, pair for reproduction; mate: *Polar bears breed only every other year.* **3** cause to mate. **4** develop (different or superior types of an animal or plant) by selective mating of outstanding individuals of one type or of two closely related types: *She breeds horses for harness racing.* **5** bring about; be the cause of: *Despair often breeds violence. Careless driving breeds accidents.* **6** be produced or caused; come into being. **7** bring up; nurture and train: *born and bred in the city.* **8** produce (fissionable material) by nuclear reaction.
—*n.* **1** a distinctive type of a particular species of animal or, sometimes, plant having recognizable inherited characteristics that are the result of a long period of selective mating. By mating only animals showing tendencies towards desired characteristics, mankind has produced many breeds of dog, horse, pigeon, etc. that suit specific purposes of usefulness or beauty. **2** kind; sort: *It takes a strong, tough breed of person to survive in the wilderness.* [OE *brēdan*]

breed·er (brēd′ər) *n.* **1** a person who breeds animals: *a cattle breeder, a dog breeder.* **2** an animal that produces offspring. **3** a source; cause: *Great inequalities are breeders of revolutions.* **4** breeder reactor.

breeder reactor a nuclear reactor that produces more fissionable material than it uses up in the chain reaction.

breed·ing (brēd′ing) *n.* **1** the producing of offspring. **2** the propagation of animals or plants, especially to produce different or superior varieties. **3** upbringing or training in social behavior: *Politeness is a sign of good breeding.* **4** good upbringing: *She is a woman of breeding.* **5** *Nuclear physics.* the process in a reactor by

which more fissionable material is produced than is consumed.

breeding ground 1 a place where animals, insects, etc. breed, or to which they return to breed. **2** a place where anything easily grows or flourishes: *Colonialism made Africa a breeding ground of nationalism.*

breeks (brēks) *n. Informal.* breeches.

breeze (brēz) *n., v.* **breezed, breez·ing.** —*n.* **1** a light wind. **2** *Informal.* a disturbance; quarrel. **3** *Informal.* an easy task: *That math problem was a breeze.*
shoot the breeze, *Slang.* engage in small talk; gossip.
—*v. Informal.* move or proceed easily or briskly: *She breezed through her homework.* [< OSp. and Pg. *briza* northeast wind]
☞ *Syn. n.* **1.** See note at **wind**[1].

breez·y (brē′zē) *adj.* **breez·i·er, breez·i·est. 1** that has a breeze; with light winds blowing. **2** brisk; lively; jolly: *We like his breezy joking manner.* —**breez′i·ly,** *adv.* —**breez′i·ness,** *n.*

Bren gun or **Bren** (bren) a fast, accurate, gas-operated machine gun used by the Allies in World War II. [<*Br*no, Czechoslovakia + *En*field, England, towns where these guns were manufactured]

br'er (brèr) *n. Southern U.S. Dialect.* brother (*used before a name*).

breth·ren (breTH′rən) *n.pl.* **1** *Archaic.* brothers. **2** the fellow members of a church, society, or religious order.
☞ *Usage.* See note at **brother.**

bret·on (bret′ən) *n.* a hat having a shallow crown and a slightly rolled brim. [< *Breton*]

Bret·on (bret′ən) *n., adj.* —*n.* **1** a native or inhabitant of Brittany, a region in NW France. **2** the Celtic language of the people of Brittany. —*adj.* of or having to do with Brittany, its people, or their language. [< F < L *Bretto, -onis*]

breve (brēv) *n.* **1** the curved mark (˘) put over a vowel or syllable to show that it is short. **2** *Music.* a note equal to two whole notes. [< Ital. < L *brevis* short]

bre·vet (brə vet′; *esp.Brit.,* brev′it) *n., adj., v.* **-vet·ted** or **-vet·ed, -vet·ting** or **-vet·ing.** —*n.* a commission promoting an army officer to a higher rank without an increase in pay.
—*adj.* having or giving rank by a brevet.
—*v.* give rank by a brevet. [ME < OF *brevet,* diminutive of *bref* letter < OF *bref* short. See **BRIEF.**]

bre·vi·ar·y (brē′vē er′ē *or* brev′ē er′ē) *n., pl.* **-ar·ies.** in the Roman Catholic Church, a book of prescribed prayers to be said daily by certain clergymen and religious. [< L *breviarium* summary < *brevis* short]

bre·vier (brə vēr′) *n.* a size of type; 8 point. This sentence is in brevier. [< G or OF < L *breviarium,* from its use in printing breviaries. See **BREVIARY.**]

brev·i·ty (brev′ə tē) *n., pl.* **-ties.** the quality of shortness or briefness. [< L *brevitas < brevis* short]

brew (brü) *v., n.* —*v.* **1** make beer, ale, etc. from malt, etc. by steeping, boiling, and fermenting. **2** make a drink by steeping, boiling, or mixing: *Tea is brewed in boiling water.* **3** bring about; plan; plot: *Those boys are brewing some mischief.* **4** begin to form; gather: *Dark clouds show that a storm is brewing.*
—*n.* **1** a drink made by brewing. **2** the quantity brewed at one time. **3** *Slang.* a glass or bottle of beer. [OE *brēowan*]

brew·er (brü′ər) *n.* a person who brews beer, ale, etc.

brew·er·y (brü′ər ē) *n., pl.* **-er·ies.** a place where beer, ale, etc. are brewed.

brew·ing (brü′ing) *n.* **1** the preparing of a brew. **2** the amount brewed at one time.

brew·is (brüz) *n.* in Newfoundland, a kind of stew prepared by boiling hardtack with codfish, pork fat, and vegetables.

bri·ar (brī′ər) See **brier.**

bri·ar-root (brī′ər rüt′) See **brier-root.**

bri·ar·wood (brī′ər wùd′) See **brierwood.**

bri·ar·y (brī′ər ē) See **briery.**

bribe (brīb) *n., v.* **bribed, brib·ing.** —*n.* **1** an inducement offered to a person to act dishonestly or against the law for the benefit of the giver. **2** a reward for doing something that one does not want to do: *He should not need a bribe to do well in school.* —*v.* influence by giving a bribe; give or offer a bribe to. [ME < OF *bribe* bit of bread given to a beggar] —**brib′a·ble,** *adj.* —**brib′er,** *n.*

brib·er·y (brīb′ər ē *or* brīb′rē) *n., pl.* **-er·ies. 1** the giving or offering of a bribe. **2** the taking of a bribe.

bric-a-brac or **bric-à-brac** (brik′ə brak′) *n.* a collection of interesting or curious knick-knacks used as decorations; small

ornaments, such as vases, old china, or small statues. [< F]
☞ *Usage.* **Bric-a-brac** is a collective noun; it never adds *s* to form the plural, nor is it ever modified by *a: The bric-a-brac showed evidence of her good taste.*

brick (brik) *n., pl.* **bricks** or (*esp. collectively*) **brick;** *v.* —*n.* **1** a block of clay baked by sun or fire, used in building and paving. **2** such blocks considered together as building material: *Our fireplace is built of brick.* **3** (*adj.*) made or built of bricks. **4** anything shaped like a brick: *a brick of ice cream.* **5** a light-colored, semisoft cheese made from whole milk, having numerous small holes and resembling mild Cheddar in flavor. A whole cheese is shaped like a brick. **6** *Informal.* a good fellow; a person who is generous and dependable.
—*v.* **1** build or pave with bricks. **2** cover or line with bricks: *Harry's father bricked the walk in front of his house.* **3** close or fill with bricks (*used with* **in** *or* **up**): *The old doorway was bricked up.* [< F *brique* < MDu. *bricke*] —**brick′like′,** *adj.*

brick·bat (brik′bat′) *n.* **1** a piece of broken brick, especially one used as a missile. **2** *Informal.* an insult.

brick·lay·er (brik′lā′ər) *n.* a person whose work is building with bricks.

brick·lay·ing (brik′lā′ing) *n.* the act or work of building with bricks.

brick-red (brik′red′) *adj.* yellowish red or brownish red.

brick·work (brik′wèrk′) *n.* **1** anything made of bricks. **2** the act or process of building with bricks; bricklaying.

brick·yard (brik′yärd′) *n.* a place where bricks are made or sold.

brid·al (brī′dəl) *adj., n.* —*adj.* of a bride or a wedding. —*n.* wedding. [OE *brȳdealo* bride ale]
☞ *Hom.* **bridle.**

bridal wreath a commonly cultivated shrub (*Spiraea prunifolia*) having long sprays of small, white flowers that bloom in the spring.

bride (brīd) *n.* a woman just married or about to be married. [OE *brȳd*]

bride·groom (brīd′grüm′) *n.* a man just married or about to be married. [OE *brȳdguma < brȳd* bride + *guma* man; influenced by *groom*]

brides·maid (brīdz′mād′) *n.* a young woman, usually unmarried, who attends the bride at a wedding.

bride·well (brīd′wel′) *n.* a house of correction for vagrants and disorderly persons; jail. [from a former prison at St. Bride's Well in London]

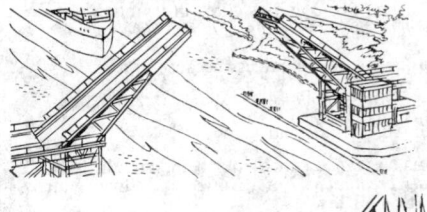

A bascule bridge on the Welland Canal in Ontario

The Quebec Bridge— the longest cantilever span in the world

The suspension bridge at Dunvegan, Alberta

bridge[1] (brij) *n., v.* **bridged, bridg·ing.** —*n.* **1** a structure built over a river, road, etc. to carry a road, walkway, or railway. **2** the platform above the deck of a ship for the officer in command. **3** the upper, bony part of the nose. **4** a mounting for a false tooth or teeth fastened to the real teeth nearby. **5** a movable piece of wood over which the strings of a violin, etc. are stretched. **6** *Music.* a passage in a composition connecting one theme, movement, etc. to another. **7** the curved central part of a pair of eyeglasses that rests on the nose. **8** *Electricity.* an apparatus for measuring the electrical

resistance of a conductor. **9** *Billiards.* a player's hand arched to steady the cue in long shots, or a notched wooden or metal piece at the end of a long rod used for the same purpose. **10** any other thing like a bridge in form or use.
burn (one's) **bridges,** cut off all chances of retreat.
—*v.* **1** build a bridge over: *The engineers bridged the river.* **2** form a bridge over; extend over; span: *A log bridged the brook.* **3** make a way over: *Politeness will bridge many difficulties.* [OE *brycg*]

bridge² (brij) *n.* a card game for two teams of two players each, played with 52 cards. Auction bridge and contract bridge are two varieties of this game. [origin uncertain]

bridge·a·ble (brij′ə bəl) *adj.* that can be bridged: *bridgeable differences.*

bridge·head (brij′hed′) *n.* **1** a position obtained and held by advance troops within enemy territory, used as a starting point for further attack. **2** any position taken as a foothold from which to make further advances: *She was able to make her first television job a bridgehead to a spectacular career in broadcasting.* **3** a fortification protecting the end of a bridge nearer to the enemy.

Bridge of Sighs 1 in Venice, the bridge through which prisoners were led for trial. **2** in New York City, the bridge leading to the Tombs prison.

bridge table a small, square or round table, about 75 centimetres square or 90 cm in diameter, having legs that fold under the table top, used for playing cards, etc.

bridge·work (brij′wèrk′) *n.* a number of false teeth in a mounting fastened to the adjacent natural teeth.

bridg·ing (brij′ing) *n.* the braces placed between two beams to strengthen them and to keep them apart.

bri·dle (brīd′əl) *n., v.* **-dled, -dling.** —*n.* **1** a harness fitted about a horse's head, consisting of a headstall, bit, and reins, used to guide or control the horse. See **harness** for picture. **2** anything that holds back or controls.
—*v.* **1** put a bridle on. **2** hold back; check; control: *Bridle your temper.* **3** hold the head up high with the chin drawn back to express pride, vanity, scorn or anger. **4** *Cdn.* the loop of a snowshoe in which the toe of the boot or moccasin is placed. [OE *brīdel, brigdels* < *bregdan* to braid] —**bri′dler,** *n.*
☛ *Hom.* bridal.

bridle path a path for people riding horses.

Brie (brē) *n.* a variety of soft, white cheese. [< F]

brief (brēf) *adj., n., v.* —*adj.* **1** lasting only a short time: *a brief meeting.* **2** using few words: *a brief announcement.*
—*n.* **1** a short statement or a summary. **2** a formal statement of opinion for submission to an authority: *She submitted a brief to the Royal Commission on Taxation.* **3** a statement of the facts and the points of law concerning a case to be pleaded in court. **4** *Informal.* a client; a case at law to plead. **5** a briefing. **6** *Roman Catholic Church.* a papal letter, less formal than a bull. **7 briefs,** *pl.* short, close-fitting underpants.
hold a brief for, argue for; support; defend.
hold no brief for, have no commitment or desire to argue for or support: *He is my friend, but I hold no brief for his political opinions.*
in brief, in a few words.
—*v.* **1** make a brief of; summarize. **2** furnish with a brief. **3** retain as a lawyer or counsel. **4** give a briefing to. [ME *bref* < OF < L *brevis* short] —**brief′ly,** *adv.* —**brief′ness,** *n.*
☛ *Syn. adj.* **1.** See note at **short.**

brief·case (brēf′kās′) *n.* a flat container for carrying loose papers, books, drawings, etc.

brief·ing (brēf′ing) *n.* **1** the act or an instance of giving necessary information or exact instructions for a specific job, assignment, etc.: *The briefing for the combat mission was given by the commanding officer.* **2** the information or instruction given.

bri·er¹ (brī′ər) *n.* **1** any of various kinds of thorny or prickly bush, especially the wild rose. **2** a thorn or thorny twig. **3** a tangled growth of briers. Also, **briar.** [OE *brēr*]

bri·er² (brī′ər) *n.* **1** an evergreen shrub (*Erica arborea*) of the heath family native to S Europe, having a hard, woody root used for making tobacco pipes. **2** a tobacco pipe made of brier-root. Also (especially def. 2), **briar.** [< F *bruyère* heath < Celtic]

Bri·er (brī′ər) *n. Cdn.* the competition or bonspiel that determines the curling champions of Canada. [< name of the trophy, formerly the Macdonald *Brier* Tankard, now the Labatt Tankard *Brier*]

bri·er–root (brī′ər rüt′) *n.* **1** the root of the brier (*Erica arborea*) used for tobacco pipes. **2** a pipe made of this root. Also, **briar-root.**

bri·er·wood (brī′ər wüd′) *n.* brier-root. Also, **briarwood.**

bri·er·y (brī′ər ē) *adj.* full of thorns or briers: *briery undergrowth.* Also, **briary.**

hat, āge, fär; let, ēqual, tèrm; it, īce
hot, ōpen, ôrder; oil, out; cup, pùt, rüle,
əbove, takən, pencəl, lemən, circəs
ch, child; ng, long; sh, ship
th, thin; ₮H, then; zh, measure

A mid-19th-century brig

FOREMAST — YARDS — MAINMAST — SPANKER

brig (brig) *n.* **1** a square-rigged ship with two masts. **2** the prison on a warship. [short for *brigantine*]

Brig. 1 Brigadier. **2** brigade.

bri·gade (bri gād′) *n., v.* —*n.* **1** a part of an army, usually made up of two or more regiments. **2** any group of people organized for a particular purpose: *A fire brigade puts out fires.* **3** *Cdn.* a fleet of canoes, bateaux, Red River carts, dog sleds, etc. carrying trade goods, supplies, etc. to and from inland posts.
—*v.* **1** form into a brigade. **2** form (people) as if into a brigade; combine; associate. [< F *brigade* < Ital. *brigata* < *brigare* strive, fight < *briga* strife < Celtic]

brig·a·dier (brig′ə dēr′) *n.* brigadier-general. [< F *brigadier* < *brigade.* See BRIGADE.]

brig·a·dier–gen·er·al (brig′ə dēr′ jen′ə rəl *or* brig′ə dēr′ jen′rəl) *n., pl.* **brig·a·dier–gen·er·als.** an officer in the armed forces, ranking next above a colonel and below a major-general. See **rank¹** for picture. *Abbrev.:* B.Gen. or BGen

brig·and (brig′ənd) *n.* a person who robs travellers on the road; a robber; bandit. [ME < OF < Ital. *brigante* fighter < *brigare* to brawl. See BRIGADE.]

brig·and·age (brig′ən dij) *n.* robbery; plundering.

brig·an·dine (brig′ən dēn′ *or* brig′ən dīn′) *n.* a coat of armor made of linen, leather, etc. strengthened with metal rings or thin metal pieces. [< MF *brigandine* armor for a brigand < *brigant* < Ital. *brigante* fighter. See BRIGAND.]

brig·an·tine (brig′ən tēn′) *n.* a two-masted ship having the foremast square-rigged and the mainmast fore-and-aft-rigged. [< F < Ital. *brigantino* < *brigare.* See BRIGAND, BRIGADE.]

bright (brīt) *adj.* **1** giving or reflecting much light; shining: *The sun is too bright to look at directly.* Chrome is very bright. **2** very light or clear: *a bright day.* **3** quick-witted; clever: *She's a bright girl and learns quickly.* **4** vivid; glowing: *bright colors.* **5** lively; cheerful: *a bright smile.* **6** likely to turn out well; favorable: *a bright outlook for the future.* **7** splendid; glorious: *The knight was a bright example of courage in battle.* **8** (*advl.*) in a bright manner: *The fire shines bright.* [OE *briht, beorht*] —**bright′ly,** *adv.* —**bright′ness,** *n.*
☛ *Syn. adj.* **1. Bright, radiant, brilliant** = shining. **Bright** is the general word, and applies to anything thought of as giving out or reflecting light: *Her silver earrings are bright.* **Radiant** suggests giving out light in rays as the sun does, shining with a light that comes from deep within the thing or person described: *Her radiant face told us of her happiness.* **Brilliant** = very bright or excessively bright and often suggests sparkling or flashing: *The surface of the water is brilliant in the sunlight.*

bright·en (brīt′ən) *v.* **1** become bright or brighter: *The sky brightened.* **2** make bright or brighter: *She brightened the room with flowers.* **3** make happy or cheerful. **4** become happy or cheerful: *Her face brightened.*

Bright's disease inflammation of the parts of the kidney that produce urine. A symptom of the disease is albumin in the urine. [after R. *Bright* (1789-1858), a British physician]

bright·work (brīt′wèrk′) *n.* polished metal-fittings or trim on ships, motor vehicles, etc.

brill (bril) *n., pl.* **brill** or **brills.** a European flatfish (*Scophthalmus rhombus*) closely related to the turbot, valued for food. [origin uncertain]

bril·liance (bril′yəns) *n.* **1** great brightness; radiance; sparkle. **2** splendor; magnificence. **3** great ability: *brilliance as a pianist.*

4 *Music.* clarity and vividness of sound: *the brilliance of modern high-frequency recordings.*

bril·lian·cy (bril′yən sē) *n.* brilliance.

bril·liant (bril′yənt) *adj., n.* —*adj.* **1** shining brightly; sparkling: *brilliant jewels, brilliant sunshine.* **2** splendid; magnificent; distinguished: *They say she has a brilliant future in politics.* **3** having or showing great ability: *a brilliant performance, a brilliant scholar.*
—*n.* **1** a diamond or other gem cut to sparkle brightly. **2** the smallest size of type; 3½ point: This sentence is set in brilliant. [< F *brilliant*, ppr. of *briller* shine, ? < L *beryllus* beryl] —**bril′liant·ly,** *adv.*
☛ *Syn. adj.* **1.** See note at **bright.**

bril·lian·tine (bril′yən tēn′) *n.* **1** an oily preparation used to make the hair glossy. **2** a glossy cloth of cotton and wool. [< F *brillantine*]

brim (brim) *n., v.* **brimmed, brim·ming.** —*n.* **1** the edge of a cup, bowl, etc.; rim. **2** the projecting edge of something: *The hat has a wide brim.* **3** *Archaic.* the edge of a body of water.
—*v.* fill or be full to the brim: *The pond is brimming with water as a result of the hard rains.* [ME *brimme*] —**brim′less,** *adj.*

brim·ful (brim′ful′) *adj.* full to the brim; full to the very top.

brim·mer (brim′ər) *n.* a cup, bowl, etc. full to the brim.

brim·stone (brim′stōn′) *n.* sulphur. [ME *brinston* < *brinnen* burn + *ston* stone]

brin·dle (brin′dəl) *adj., n.* —*adj.* brindled. —*n.* **1** a brindled color. **2** a brindled animal. [< *brindled*]

brin·dled (brin′dəld) *adj.* grey, tan, or tawny with darker streaks and spots. [earlier *brinded*, ME *brended.* Probably related to BRAND.]

brine (brīn) *n.* **1** very salty water: *Pickles are often kept in brine.* **2** a salt lake or sea; ocean. [OE *brȳne*]

bring (bring) *v.* **brought, bring·ing. 1** carry or take with oneself to a place; come to a place with: *I didn't bring enough money. He brought his cousin to the party. Bring me a clean plate, please. The bus brought us home from school.* **2** cause to come: *What brings you into town today?* **3** cause to do something; persuade; induce: *Our arguments finally brought him to agree. I can't bring myself to finish another page tonight.* **4** present before a law court: *He brought a charge against me.* **5** sell for: *Meat is bringing a high price this week.*
bring about, cause; cause to happen: *The flood was brought about by heavy rain.*
bring around or **bring round,** **a** restore to consciousness. **b** convince; persuade.
bring forth, **a** give birth to; bear. **b** reveal; show.
bring forward, **a** reveal; show. **b** *Accounting.* carry over from one page to another.
bring home to, **a** prove beyond doubt. **b** make realize.
bring in, **a** introduce or try out. **b** report or announce officially; return: *to bring in a verdict.* **c** cause to flow by drilling: *to bring in an oil well.*
bring off, cause to happen; carry to a successful conclusion.
bring on, cause; cause to happen: *I think my cold was brought on by lack of sleep.*
bring out, **a** reveal; show: *His paintings bring out the loneliness of the North.* **b** offer to the public: *She brought out a new book of poems.*
bring over, convince; persuade.
bring to, **a** restore to consciousness: *We tried to bring him to by loosening his clothing.* **b** stop; check. -
bring up, **a** care for in childhood. **b** educate or train, especially in social behavior: *His good manners showed that he had been well brought up.* **c** suggest for action or discussion. **d** stop suddenly: *The rider brought his horse up at the high fence.* **e** vomit.
[OE *bringan*] —**bring′er,** *n.*

bring·ing-up (bring′ing up′) *n.* **1** care in childhood. **2** education; training.

brink (bringk) *n.* **1** the edge at the top of a steep place. **2** any edge, such as the shore of a river, etc.
on the brink of, very near. [ME; probably < Scand.]

brink·man·ship (bringk′mən ship′) *n.* **1** the maintaining or urging of a foreign policy to the brink of war before giving ground. **2** the fact or process of manoeuvering any dangerous situation to the very limits of safety before giving ground.

brin·y (brīn′ē) *adj.* **brin′i·er, brin′i·est;** *n.* —*adj.* of or like brine; salty. —*n.* **the briny,** *Slang.* sea. —**brin′i·ness,** *n.*

bri·oche (brē ōsh′ or brē′ōsh) *n.* a roll or bun rich in butter and eggs. [< F]

bri·quette or **bri·quet** (bri ket′) *n.* **1** a block of compressed charcoal, coal dust, etc. used for fuel. **2** a small brick or similar block of anything else. [< F *briquette,* dim. of *brique* brick]

brisk (brisk) *adj.* **1** acting, moving, or happening quickly; energetic: *The storekeeper told us that business was brisk. He went for a brisk walk.* **2** keen; sharp: *brisk weather.* [? akin to *brusque*] —**brisk′ly,** *adv.* —**brisk′ness,** *n.*

bris·ket (bris′kit) *n.* **1** the meat from the breast of an animal. See **beef** for picture. **2** the breast of an animal. [ME < OF *bruschet* < Gmc.]

bris·tle (bris′əl) *n., v.* **-tled, -tling.** —*n.* **1** one of the short, stiff hairs of a hog or wild boar, used to make brushes. **2** any short, stiff hair of an animal or plant. **3** a synthetic substitute for a hog's bristles: *My toothbrush has nylon bristles.*
—*v.* **1** provide with bristles. **2** stand up straight: *The angry dog's hair bristled.* **3** cause (hair) to stand up straight. **4** have one's hair stand up straight: *The dog bristled.* **5** show that one is aroused and ready to fight: *The whole country bristled with indignation.* **6** be thick with; be thickly set: *Our path bristled with difficulties.* [ME *bristel* < OE *byrst* bristle]

bris·tle·tail (bris′əl tāl′) *n.* any of about 400 species making up two orders (Thysanura and Diplura) of mostly tiny, wingless insects found throughout the world, having compound eyes, long, segmented feelers, and two or two long, movable appendages at the end of the abdomen. Silverfish are bristletails.

bris·tly (bris′lē) *adj.* **-tli·er, -tli·est. 1** rough with bristles or hair that is like bristles. **2** resembling bristles; short and stiff; prickly.

Bris·tol board (bris′təl) a fine, smooth pasteboard.

Brit (brit) *n. Slang.* a Britisher; Englishman.

Brit. Britain; British; Briticism.

Bri·tan·ni·a (bri tan′yə) *n.* **1** *Poetic.* Great Britain. **2** *Poetic.* the British Empire. **3** a woman symbolizing Britain, shown (as on coins) with helmet, shield, and trident.

Britannia metal a white alloy of tin, copper, and antimony, used in making tableware.

Bri·tan·nic (bri tan′ik) *adj.* of Britain; British.

brit·ches (brich′iz) *n.pl. Informal.* breeches.

Brit·i·cism (brit′ə siz′əm) *n.* a word or phrase used especially by the British. *Wings* meaning *fenders* (of a car) is a Briticism.

Brit·ish (brit′ish) *adj., n.* —*adj.* of or having to do with Great Britain or the United Kingdom, or its people. —*n.* **the British,** the people of Great Britain or the United Kingdom. [OE *brittisc* < *Brittas* Britons < Celtic]

Brit·ish Co·lum·bi·an (kə lum′bē ən) *n., adj.* —*n.* a native or long-term resident of British Columbia. —*adj.* of or having to do with British Columbia or its people.

Brit·ish·er (brit′ish ər) *n.* a native or inhabitant of Great Britain.

British North America Act the Act of Parliament that in 1867 created the Government of Canada for the union of Ontario, Quebec, Nova Scotia, and New Brunswick. The other six provinces joined the federation as follows: Manitoba, 1870; British Columbia, 1871; Prince Edward Island, 1873; Alberta, 1905; Saskatchewan, 1905; and Newfoundland, 1949. *Abbrev.*: BNA Act or B.N.A. Act.

British subject a citizen of the United Kingdom or of any country that is a member of the Commonwealth of Nations.

British thermal unit a unit for measuring heat; the amount of heat necessary to raise the temperature of one pound of water one degree Fahrenheit (about 1.06 kJ). *Abbrev.*: B.T.U.

Brit·on (brit′ən) *n.* **1** a native or inhabitant of Great Britain. **2** a member of a Celtic people who lived in S Britain before the Roman conquest. [< Med.L *Brito, -onis* < Celtic]

brit·tle (brit′əl) *adj.* rigid but very easily broken; apt to break with a snap rather than bend: *Thin glass and dead twigs are brittle.* [ME *britel* < OE *brēotan* break] —**brit′tle·ness,** *n.*

bro. or **Bro.** brother.

broach (brōch) *n., v.* —*n.* **1** a pointed tool for making and shaping holes. **2** a sharp-pointed, slender rod on which meat is roasted. —*v.* **1** open by making a hole: *to broach a barrel of cider.* **2** begin to talk about: *to broach a subject.* [ME < OF < L *broccus* projecting] —**broach′er,** *n.*

broad (brod or brôd) *adj., n.* —*adj.* **1** large across; wide: *Many cars can go on that broad road.* **2** extensive: *a broad experience.* **3** not limited; liberal; tolerant: *broad ideas.* **4** not detailed; general: *Give a broad outline of the speech.* **5** clear; full: *broad daylight.* **6** plain; obvious; unmistakable: *a broad hint, a broad accent.* **7** coarse; not refined: *broad jokes.* **8** *Phonetics.* **a** pronounced with the vocal passage open wide. The *a* in *father* is broad. **b** indicating pronunciation in general terms: *a broad phonetic transcription.*
—*n. Slang.* a woman or girl. [OE *brād*] —**broad′ly,** *adv.*
☛ *Syn. adj.* **1.** See note at **wide.**

broad·axe (brod′aks′ or brôd′-) *n., pl.* **-ax·es.** an axe with a broad blade. Sometimes, **broadax.**

broad·brim (brod′brim′ or brôd′-) *n. Historical.* 1 a hat with a very wide brim, such as the kind once worn by the Quakers. 2 Quaker.

broad·cast (brod′kast′ or brôd′-) *v.* **-cast** (sometimes for def. 1) **-cast·ed, -cast·ing;** *n., adj., adv.* —*v.* 1 send out by radio or television: *Her speech will be broadcast tonight.* 2 scatter or spread widely: *to broadcast seed.*
—*n.* 1 a radio or television program. 2 the act of broadcasting.
—*adj.* 1 sent out by radio or television: *a broadcast message.* 2 scattered or spread widely: *broadcast sowing.*
—*adv.* over a wide surface: *He scattered the seed broadcast.*
—**broad′cast·er,** *n.*

broad·cloth (brod′kloth′ or brôd′-) *n.* 1 a fine, closely woven cloth with a smooth finish, made of cotton silk, rayon, synthetics, or blends of these fibres and used for shirts, dresses, pyjamas, etc. 2 a smooth, closely woven woollen cloth having a glossy surface and a short nap, used in making suits, coats, etc. [originally wider, or broader, than 29 inches (about 74 cm)]

broad·en (brod′ən or brôd′ən) *v.* make or become broad or broader: *to broaden one's outlook. The river broadens at its mouth.*

broad–gauge (brod′gāj′ or brôd′-) *adj.* of a railway, having a width of track greater than the standard gauge of 56½ inches (about 144 cm); especially of track of 66 inches (about 168 cm).

broad·gauged (brod′gājd′ or brôd′-) *adj.* broad-gauge.

broad jump long jump.
standing broad jump, a long jump from a standing start.

broad·loom (brod′lüm′ or brôd′-) *adj., n., v.* —*adj.* woven on a loom or machine at least 1.8 m wide: *a broadloom carpet.*
—*n.* carpeting made on a broad loom, sold by the metre or yard and cut to fit the exact dimensions of a room: *We have broadloom in the living room.*
—*v.* cover (a floor, walls, etc.) with such material: *We broadloomed the office.*

broad–mind·ed (brod′mīnd′id or brôd′-) *adj.* respecting opinions, customs, or beliefs, that are different from one's own; liberal; not prejudiced or bigoted. —**broad′-mind′ed·ly,** *adv.* —**broad′-mind′ed·ness,** *n.*

broad·sheet (brod′shēt′ or brôd′-) *n.* a large sheet of paper printed on one side as a newsletter, advertisement, etc.

broad·side (brod′sīd′ or brôd′-) *n.* 1 the whole side of a ship above the water line. 2 all the guns that can be fired from one side of a ship. 3 the firing of all these guns at the same time. 4 a violent attack in words; a storm of abuse: *He was met with a broadside from his sister the minute he got home.* 5 a broad surface or side, as of a house. 6 (*adv.*) with the side turned toward an object or point: *The ship drifted broadside to the pier.* 7 a large sheet of paper printed on one or both sides: *Boys were distributing broadsides announcing a big sale.*

broad·sword (brod′sôrd′ or brôd′-) *n.* a sword with a broad, flat blade.

broad·tail (brod′tāl′ or brôd′-) *n.* 1 Also, **broadtail sheep,** a kind of Asiatic sheep having a broad tail. 2 the skin of a prematurely born broadtail lamb, having dark, flat, wide curls. 3 a coat or other garment made from such skins.

Broad·way (brod′wā′ or brôd′-) *n.* 1 in New York City, a street famous for its bright lights, theatres, night clubs, etc. 2 the New York commercial theatre.

Brob·ding·nag (brob′ding nag′) *n.* the land of giants in Jonathan Swift's book *Gulliver's Travels.*

Brob·ding·nag·i·an (brob′ding nag′ē ən) *adj., n.* —*adj.* 1 of or like Brobdingnag. 2 gigantic; huge; enormous. —*n.* giant.

bro·cade (brō kād′) *n., v.* **-cad·ed, -cad·ing.** —*n.* a heavy cloth woven with a raised design on it: *silk brocade, velvet brocade.* —*v.* weave or decorate with raised designs. [< Sp., Pg. *brocado,* pp. of *brocar* embroider]

bro·cad·ed (brō kād′id) *adj.* woven or wrought into a brocade.

broc·co·li (brok′ə lē) *n.* 1 a variety of cabbage (*Brassica oleracea italica*) having dense clusters of green flower heads at the ends of the branches. 2 the flower heads and upper stems of this plant, cut for use as a cooked vegetable when the flower buds are still closed. [< Ital. *broccoli,* pl., sprouts < L *broccus* projecting]

bro·chure (brō shür′) *n.* a printed booklet or folder, usually having colorful pictures, that advertises or gives information about a place, a product, etc.: *The provincial government puts out a brochure on its parks.* [< F *brochure* < *brocher* stitch]

bro·gan (brō′gən) *n.* a heavy, strong work shoe reaching to the ankle. [< Irish, Scots Gaelic *brógan,* dim. of *bróg* shoe]

brogue¹ (brōg) *n.* 1 any heavy, strong shoe. 2 an oxford shoe made for comfort and long wear. [< Irish, Scots Gaelic *bróg* shoe]

brogue² (brōg) *n.* 1 an Irish accent in the speaking of English. 2 the accent or pronunciation peculiar to any dialect. [probably <

---

hat, āge, fär; let, ēqual, tèrm; it, īce
hot, ōpen, ôrder; oil, out; cup, pút, rüle,
əbove, takən, pencəl, lemən, circəs
ch, child; ng, long; sh, ship
th, thin; ᴛʜ, then; zh, measure

Irish *barróg* defect of speech]

broi·der (broi′dər) *v.* [ME < OF *broder;* influenced by archaic E *broid* braid] —**broi′der·y,** *n.*

broil¹ (broil) *v., n.* —*v.* 1 cook by placing on a rack directly over a fire or in a pan directly under an electric coil or gas flame; grill. 2 make or be very hot: *You will broil in this hot sun.* —*n.* broiled meat, etc. [ME *brule, bruyle* < OF *bruler, bruillir* burn]

broil² (broil) *n., v.* —*n.* an angry quarrel or struggle; brawl. —*v.* quarrel; fight. [< OF *brouiller* to disorder]

broil·er (broil′ər) *n.* 1 a person or thing that broils. 2 a pan or rack for broiling food. 3 a young chicken suitable for broiling.

broke (brōk) *v., adj.* —*v.* 1 a pt. of **break.** 2 *Archaic.* a pp. of **break.** broken. —*adj. Informal.* without money.

bro·ken (brō′kən) *v., adj.* —*v.* a pp. of **break.**
—*adj.* 1 crushed; in pieces: *a broken cup.* 2 weakened in strength, spirit, etc.; tamed; crushed: *He looked a broken man after his loss.* 3 rough; uneven: *broken ground, a broken voice.* 4 acted against; not kept: *a broken promise.* 5 imperfectly spoken: *He speaks broken French.* 6 interrupted: *broken sleep.* 7 bankrupt; ruined. —**bro′ken·ly,** *adv.* —**bro′ken·ness,** *n.*

bro·ken–down (brō′kən doun′) *adj.* 1 shattered; ruined: *broken-down health.* 2 unfit for use.

bro·ken–heart·ed (brō′kən här′tid) *adj.* crushed by sorrow or grief; heartbroken.

bro·ken–wind·ed (brō′kən win′did) *adj.* of a horse, breathing with sudden, short efforts; suffering from heaves.

bro·ker (brō′kər) *n.* a person who acts as an agent for other people in arranging contracts, purchases, or sales in return for a fee or commission. [ME < AF *brocour* tapster, retailer of wine. Akin to BROACH.]

bro·ker·age (brō′kər ij) *n.* 1 the business of a broker. 2 the money charged by a broker for his services.

brol·ly (brol′ē) *n. Brit. Informal.* umbrella.

brome (brōm) *n.* any of a genus (*Bromus*) of grasses of temperate regions, typically having loose, drooping clusters of flowers, especially any of several species, such as *B. inermis,* that are important for hay and as pasture grasses. Also called **brome grass.**

bro·mide (brō′mīd or brō′mid) *n.* 1 a compound of bromine with another element or radical. 2 potassium bromide, a drug used to induce sleep, as a tranquillizer, sedative, etc. Formula: KBr 3 a commonplace idea; trite remark.

bro·mid·ic (brō mid′ik) *adj. Informal.* like a bromide; commonplace; trite.

bro·mine (brō′mēn) *n.* a heavy, non-metallic element that evaporates quickly, resembling chlorine and iodine. Bromine is a dark-brown liquid that gives off an irritating vapor. It is used in drugs and dyes and in developing photographs. Symbol: Br; at.no. 35; at.wt. 79.909. [< Gk. *bromos* stench]

bronc (brongk) *n. Informal.* bronco.

bron·chi (brong′kī or brong′kē) *n. pl.* of **bronchus.** 1 the two main branches of the windpipe one going to each lung. 2 the smaller, branching tubes in the lungs.

bron·chi·a (brong′kē ə) *n.pl.* the bronchial tubes, especially the smaller tubes.

bron·chi·al (brong′kē əl) *adj.* of the bronchi or their branches.

bronchial tube either of the bronchi or any of their branching tubes. See **lung** for picture.

bron·chit·ic (brong kit′ik) *adj.* 1 of or having to do with bronchitis. 2 having bronchitis.

bron·chi·tis (brong kī′tis) *n.* inflammation of the lining of the bronchial tubes. [< NL < *bronchus* + *-itis*]

bron·cho (brong′kō) See **bronco.**

bron·cho·scope (brong′kə skōp′) *n. Medicine.* an instrument for examining and treating the bronchi.

bron·chus (brong′kəs) *n., pl.* **-chi** (-kī or -kē). one of the bronchi. [< NL < Gk. *bronchos*]

bron·co (brong′kō) *n., pl.* **-cos.** a western pony, often wild or

only half tamed. Also, **broncho**. [< Sp. *bronco* rough, rude; 19c.]

bron·co·bust·er (brong′kō bus′tər) *n. Slang.* in the West, one who breaks wild horses to the saddle.

bron·to·sau·rus (bron′tə sô′rəs) *n.* any of a genus (*Apatosaurus*, also called *Brontosaurus*) of giant, plant-eating dinosaurs having a long neck, small head, and long tail, and walking on four legs. [< NL < Gk. *brontē* thunder + *sauros* lizard]

Bronx cheer (brongks) *Slang.* a scornful noise made with the tongue and lips; raspberry (def. 4). [< *the Bronx*, a borough of New York City]

bronze (bronz) *n., adj., v.* **bronzed, bronz·ing. —n. 1** a brown metal, an alloy of copper and tin. **2** a similar alloy of copper with zinc or other metals. **3** a statue, medal, etc. made of bronze: *She won a bronze in the swimming competition.* **4** a moderate yellowish brown color.
—adj. 1 made of bronze. **2** having the color bronze. **—v.** tan: *The sailor was bronzed from the sun.* [< F < Ital. *bronzo* bell metal]

Bronze Age the period in human culture following the Stone Age, characterized by the use of bronze tools, weapons, etc. The European Bronze Age began about 3000 B.C.; that of the Middle East somewhat earlier.

bronze·smith (bronz′smith′) *n.* a man who works with bronze.

brooch (brōch) *n.* an ornamental pin having the point secured by a clasp or catch. [var. of *broach*, n.]

brood (brüd) *n., v. —n. 1** the young birds hatched at one time in the nest or cared for together. **2** young animals or humans who are cared for by the same mother. **3** a breed; kind. **4** (*adjl.*) kept for breeding: *a brood mare.*
—v. 1 sit on eggs in order to hatch them. **2** think or worry a long time about some one thing: *She broods a lot these days.* **3** dwell on it in thought: *For years he brooded vengeance.*
brood on or **over, a** keep thinking about. **b** hover over; hang close over.
[OE *brōd*]

brood·er (brüd′ər) *n.* **1** a closed place that can be heated, used in raising chicks, etc. **2** somebody or something that broods. **3** a hen brooding or ready to brood eggs.

brood·mare (brüd′mer′) *n.* a mare kept for breeding.

brood·y (brü′dē) *adj.* **1** inclined to ponder or think moodily on a subject. **2** of hens, ready to brood eggs. When hens become broody, they stop laying.

brook[1] (brük) *n.* a small, natural freshwater stream; creek. [OE *brōc*]

brook[2] (brük) *v.* put up with; endure; tolerate: *Her pride would not brook such insults.* [OE *brūcan* use]

brook trout a freshwater food and game fish (*Salvelinus fontinalis*) of North America having a long, quite narrow, deep body, a large head, and a square tail; speckled char, mud trout. The coloring of brook trout varies from olive green to dark brown.

broom (brüm *or* brům) *n.* **1** a long-handled brush for sweeping. **2** a shrub of the same family as the pea, having slender branches, small leaves, and yellow flowers.
a new broom, a new person or management that starts actively and tries to put everything right at once, from the saying "A new broom sweeps clean."
[OE *brōm*]

broom·ball (brüm′bol′ *or* -bôl′, brům′bol′ *or* -bôl′) *n. Cdn.* a game similar to hockey but using cornbrooms and a volleyball, usually played on a hockey rink.

broom·corn (brüm′kôrn′ *or* brům′-) *n.* a tall plant resembling corn, having flower clusters with long, stiff stems used for making brooms.

broom·stick (brüm′stik′ *or* brům′-) *n.* the long handle of a broom.

bros. or **Bros.** brothers.

broth (broth) *n.* **1** a thin soup made from water in which meat or fish and, often, vegetables have been boiled. **2** a thick soup, such as Scotch broth. **3** a medium in which cultures of bacteria are grown. [OE]

broth·el (broth′əl) *n.* an establishment where prostitutes are available to be hired for sexual acts. [ME < OE *brēothan* go to ruin]

broth·er (bruTH′ər) *n., pl.* **broth·ers** or (*archaic*) **breth·ren. 1** a son of the same parents; sometimes, a son only of the same mother or father (a half brother). **2** a male who is a very close friend or companion; one who fills the role of a brother: *My cousin is a brother to me.* **3** a male who shares a duty, purpose, ideal, or allegiance: *The two soldiers were brothers in arms. All men are brothers.* **4** a male fellow member of a church who is not a priest. **5** (*adjl.*) being in or of the same profession or calling: *brother officers.* [OE *brōther*] **—broth′er·less,** *adj.* **—broth′er·like,** *adj.*
☛ *Usage.* **Brothers** is the normal plural. **Brethren** is now used only of fellow members of a church or society, the names of certain religious groups, such as the *Plymouth Brethren.*

broth·er·hood (bruTH′ər hůd′) *n.* **1** the biological relationship between brothers: *He claimed brotherhood with the heir.* **2** a spiritual bond between brothers or as if between brothers: *The two inventors had worked closely together for so long that they had a strong feeling of brotherhood.* **3** an association of men with some common aim, characteristic, belief, profession, etc.: *the brotherhood of locomotive engineers.*

broth·er·in-law (bruTH′ər in lo′ *or* -lô′) *n., pl.* **broth·ers-in-law. 1** the brother of one's husband or wife. **2** the husband of one's sister. **3** the husband of the sister of one's wife or husband.

Brother Jonathan *Archaic.* **1** The United States or its people. **2** an inhabitant of the United States.

broth·er·ly (bruTH′ər lē) *adj.* **1** of or having to do with a brother, or brothers. **2** showing the affection of a brother; friendly; kindly: *He gave her a brotherly hug and wished her luck in the exam.* **—broth′er·li·ness,** *n.*

brougham (brō′əm *or* brü′əm) *n.* a closed four-wheeled carriage or automobile having an outside seat for the driver. [after Lord *Brougham* (1778-1868), a British statesman]

brought (brot *or* brôt) *v.* pt. and pp. of **bring.**

brou·ha·ha (brü hä′hä *or* brü′hä hä′) *n.* an uproar or commotion: *The proposed government spending cuts caused a nationwide brouhaha.* [< F, of imitative origin]

brow (brou) *n.* **1** the forehead. **2** the arch of hair over the eye; eyebrow. **3** the ridge or prominence above the eye, on which the eyebrow grows. **4** the edge of a steep place; top of a slope: *the brow of a hill.* [OE *brū*]

brow·beat (brou′bēt′) *v.* **-beat, -beat·en, -beat·ing.** frighten into doing something by overbearing looks or words; bully; intimidate. **—brow′beat·er,** *n.*

-browed (broud) *combining form.* having brows of a particular kind: *beetle-browed.*

brown (broun) *n., adj., v. —n.* **1** a color like that of toast, potato skins, and coffee. **2** a paint or dye having this color. **3** clothing having this color: *He was dressed in brown.*
—adj. 1 of or having a color like that of toast, potato skins, or coffee. **2** dark-skinned; tanned: *She was very brown from a summer in the sun.*
—v. make or become brown: *Brown the onions in butter.*
browned off, *Slang.* fed up; exasperated.
[OE *brūn*] **—brown′ness,** *n.*

brown bear the largest and most widespread species of bear (*Ursus arctos*), found throughout the northern parts of the world, having a short neck and large, doglike head and a thick coat of fur varying in color from cream to blueblack. The grizzly is a subspecies of the brown bear.

brown betty a baked pudding made of apples, bread crumbs, sugar, and spices.

brown bread bread made at least partly from whole wheat flour, sometimes containing extra bran and often flavored and colored with molasses or caramel.

brown coal lignite.

Brown·i·an motion (broun′ē ən) *Physics.* Brownian movement.

Brownian movement *Physics.* a rapid oscillatory motion often observed in very minute particles suspended in water or other liquids. [after Dr. Robert *Brown* (1773-1858), a Scottish botanist]

brown·ie (broun′ē) *n.* **1** a good-natured, helpful elf or fairy. **2 Brownie,** a member, aged six to nine, of the Girl Guides. **3** a small square or bar of a kind of rich chocolate cake usually containing nuts.

brown·ish (broun′ish) *adj.* rather brown.

brown race the Malay people living mainly in Malaya and Polynesia.

brown rice rice grains that have not had the outer layer containing the bran removed; unpolished rice.

brown shirt a member of the group of German storm troopers that was organized by Adolf Hitler in 1923 and discontinued in 1934.

brown·stone (broun′stōn′) *n.* **1** a reddish-brown sandstone, used as a building material. **2** a building, especially a house, built of this sandstone.

brown study the condition of being absorbed in thought; a serious reverie.

brown sugar refined sugar in which the crystals are coated with dark molasses-flavored syrup.

brown thrasher a thrasher (*Toxostoma rufum*) found in North America east of the Rockies, having bright reddish-brown upper parts and whitish under parts streaked with brown.

browse (brouz) *v.* **browsed, brows·ing;** *n.* —*v.* **1** feed on growing plants, especially the tender parts of trees and bushes: *The deer moved through the woods, browsing on young shoots and leaves.* **2** read here and there in a book or in books; especially, pass the time looking at books in a library or bookstore. **3** look casually at articles for sale in a store.
—*n.* **1** tender shoots, leaves, and twigs of trees and shrubs considered as food for animals. **2** the act of browsing. [apparently < early Mod.F *broust* a bud, shoot, *brouster* feed on buds and shoots < Gmc. 16c] —**brows′er,** *n.*

bru·in (brü′ən) *n.* a bear, especially a brown bear as featured in fables and children's stories. [< MDu. *bruin* brown]

bruise (brüz) *n., v.* **bruised, bruis·ing.** —*n.* **1** an injury to the body, caused by a fall or a blow, that breaks blood vessels without breaking the skin: *The bruise on my arm turned black and blue.* **2** an injury to the outside of a fruit, vegetable, plant, etc. **3** a hurt or injury: *His insult was a bruise to her pride.*
—*v.* **1** make or cause a bruise on: *I bruised my leg. Handle the tomatoes carefully so you don't bruise them.* **2** cause to be hurt: *The harsh words bruised her feelings.* **3** become bruised: *I bruise easily.* **4** pound or crush (drugs or food). [fusion of ME *bruse* < OE *brȳsan* crush and AF *bruser*, OF *bruisier* break, shatter]

bruis·er (brüz′ər) *n. Informal.* **1** a prize fighter. **2** a bully. **3** a very muscular person.

bruit (brüt) *v., n.* —*v.* spread (a report or rumor): *Rumors of the princess's engagement were bruited about.* —*n. Archaic.* a report or rumor. [< OF *bruit* noise, rumor < *bruire* roar]

bru·lé or **bru·le** (brü lā′ or brü′lē) *n. Cdn.* **1** a forest area that has been destroyed by fire. **2** rocky, untillable land. **3 Brulé,** a half-breed; a Métis. [< F *brûlé* burnt]

brum·ma·gem (brum′ə jəm) *adj., n. Informal.* —*adj.* cheap and showy. —*n.* anything cheap and showy. [alteration of *Birmingham,* England]

brunch (brunch) *n.* a meal, taken in the late morning, that combines breakfast and lunch. [< *br*eakfast + l*unch*]

bru·net (brü net′) *adj., n.* —*adj.* **1** dark-colored; having an olive color. **2** having dark-brown or black hair, usually brown or black eyes, and a dark skin. —*n.* a man or boy having dark hair. [< F *brunette,* fem., dim. of *brun* brown < Gmc.]

bru·nette (brü net′) *n.* a woman or girl having dark hair. [< F]

Brun·hild (brün′hild) *n.* in Germanic legend (especially in the *Nibelungenlied*), a queen of Iceland who, won by Siegfried's magic, becomes the wife of the King of Burgundy. In Norse legend, she is a Valkyrie and the daughter of Odin. Also, **Brynhild.**

Brünn·hil·de (brvn hil′də) *n.* in Wagner's opera *Die Walküre,* a Valkyrie cast into a magic sleep, from which Siegfried wakens her.

brunt (brunt) *n.* the main force or violence; hardest part: *to bear the brunt.* [ME *brunt* a blow; origin uncertain]

brush¹ (brush) *n., v.* —*n.* **1** a tool for cleaning, sweeping, scrubbing, painting, etc. A brush is made of bristles, hair or wires set in a stiff back or fastened to a handle. **2** a brushing; a rub with a brush. **3** a light touch in passing. **4** a short, brisk fight or quarrel. **5** the bushy tail of an animal, especially of a fox. **6** a piece of carbon, copper, etc. used to conduct the electricity from the revolving part of a motor or generator to the outside circuit. **7** the style of an artist: *He paints with a bold brush.*
—*v.* **1** clean, sweep, paint, etc. with a brush; use a brush on. **2** wipe away; remove: *The child brushed the tears from his eyes.* **3** touch lightly in passing. **4** move quickly.
brush aside or **away,** put aside; refuse to consider.
brush off, *Informal.* refuse or dismiss a request, person, etc. in a curt or disdainful way: *He brushed us off when we asked for his autograph.*
brush up or **brush up on,** refresh the memory by study; review: *I have to brush up on some theorems for the geometry test tomorrow.* [ME *brusshe* < OF *broisse* < Gmc.] —**brush′er,** *n.* —**brush′like′,** *adj.*

brush² (brush) *n.* **1** branches broken or cut off. **2** shrubs, bushes, and small trees growing thickly together. **3** a thinly settled country; backwoods. [ME *brusche* < OF *broche*]

brush·cut (brush′kut′) *n.* a very short haircut in which the hair on top of the head stands straight out from the scalp.

brush·off (brush′of′) *n. Informal.* a curt or offhand dismissal of a request, person, etc.: *When I asked for a date, I got a brushoff.*

brush·up (brush′up′) *n.* **1** a refreshing of memory or a reviewing of knowledge, skill, etc. **2** a smartening or freshening of one's appearance.

brush wolf *Cdn.* coyote.

brush·wood (brush′wůd′) *n.* brush² (defs. 1 and 2).

brush·work (brush′wėrk′) *n.* an artist's characteristic technique

in applying paint with a brush.

brush·y¹ (brush′ē) *adj.* **brush·i·er, brush·i·est.** like a brush; rough and shaggy. [< *brush¹*]

brush·y² (brush′ē) *adj.* **brush·i·er, brush·i·est.** covered with bushes, shrubs, etc. [< *brush²*]

brusque (brusk) *adj.* abrupt in manner or speech; blunt. [< F < Ital. *brusco* coarse < LL *bruscus,* blend of *ruscum* broom and Gaulish *brucus* broom] —**brusque′ly,** *adv.* —**brusque′ness,** *n.*

Brus·sels carpet (brus′əlz) a carpet with a pattern made of small loops of yarn having various colors.

Brussels lace a type of heavy lace with a very elaborate design.

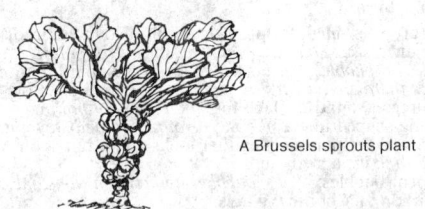

A Brussels sprouts plant

Brussels sprouts **1** a variety of cabbage (*Brassica oleracea gemmifera*) that bears many small green heads, like tiny cabbages, along its tall, thick stem. **2** the heads of this plant, eaten as a vegetable.

bru·tal (brü′təl) *adj.* coarse and savage. —**brut′al·ly,** *adv.*
☛ *Syn.* See note at **cruel.**

bru·tal·i·ty (brü tal′ə tē) *n., pl.* **-ties. 1** brutal conduct; cruelty; savageness. **2** a cruel or savage act.

bru·tal·ize (brü′təl īz′) *v.* **-ized, -iz·ing. 1** make brutal: *War brutalizes many people.* **2** treat brutally: *The judge had harsh criticism for police officers who brutalized people they were questioning.* —**bru′tal·i·za′tion,** *n.*

brute (brüt) *n.* **1** an animal without power to reason. **2** a cruel, coarse, or sensual person. **3** mankind's animal nature.
—*adj.* **1** not having power to reason: *brute creatures.* **2** cruel; coarse; sensual. **3** without feeling: *Man has struggled long against the brute forces of nature.* [< F *brut* < L *brutus* heavy, dull]
☛ *Syn. n.* **1, 2.** See note at **animal.**

brut·ish (brüt′ish) *adj.* coarse; savage. —**brut′ish·ly,** *adv.* —**brut′ish·ness,** *n.*

Bryn·hild (brin′hild or brvn′hild) *n.* Brunhild.

bry·ol·o·gy (brī ol′ə jē) *n.* a branch of botany that deals with mosses and liverworts. [< Gk. *bryon* moss + E -*logy*]

bry·o·ny (brī′ə nē) *n., pl.* **-nies.** any of a genus (*Bryonia*) of herbaceous climbing plants of the gourd family native to Europe and N Africa, having greenish flowers and red or black berries. [< L < Gk. *bryonia* < *bryein* swell]

bry·o·phyte (brī′ə fīt′) *n.* any of a division (Bryophyta) of plants having stems and leaves but no true roots, and reproducing by spores. The division includes the mosses and liverworts. [< NL *bryophia* < Gk. *bryon* tree moss + *phyton* plant < *phyein* grow]

Bryth·on (brith′ən) *n.* **1** any member of a large Celtic group once living in South Britain but later driven into Wales, Cornwall, and ancient Cumbria. **2** a Briton of Wales, Cornwall, or ancient Cumbria. [< Welsh *Brython* < Old Celtic *Britton* a Briton]

Bry·thon·ic (brithon′ik) *adj., n.* —*adj.* **1** of or having to do with the Brythons. **2** of, having to do with, or denoting the Celtic language group to which Breton, Cornish, and Welsh belong. —*n.* one of the two main divisions of the Celtic language (the other being Goidelic), including Breton, Cornish, and Welsh; Cymric.

b.s. **1** bill of sale. **2** balance sheet.

B.S. or **B.Sc.** Bachelor of Science (for L *Baccalaureus Scientiae*).

B.S.A. Bachelor of Science in Agriculture.

hat, āge, fär; let, ēqual, tėrm; it, īce
hot, ōpen, ôrder; oil, out; cup, půt, rüle,
above, takan, pencal, leman, circas

ch, child; ng, long; sh, ship
th, thin; ᴛʜ, then; zh, measure

B.Sc.A. Baccalauréat ès sciences appliquées.

B.Sc.Eng. Bachelor of Science in Engineering.

B.Sc.F. Bachelor of Science in Forestry.

B.Sc.M. Bachelor of Science in Medicine.

B.Sc.N. Bachelor of Science in Nursing.

B.Sc.Pharm. or **B.Sc.Phm.** Bachelor of Science in Pharmacy.

B.Sc.S.S. Bachelor of Science in Social Science.

B.S.F. Bachelor of Science in Forestry.

B.S.H.Ec. Bachelor of Science in Home Economics.

B.S.M. battery sergeant-major.

B.S.N. Bachelor of Science in Nursing.

B.S.P. Bachelor of Science in Pharmacy.

B.S.W. Bachelor of Social Work.

Bt. baronet.

B.Th. Bachelor of Theology (for L *Baccalaureus Theologiae*).

Btn. or **btn.** battalion.

Btu, BTU, or **B.T.U.** British thermal unit or units.

bu. 1 bushel(s). 2 bureau.

bub·ble (bub′əl) *n., v.* **-bled, -bling.** —*n.* 1 a thin round film of liquid enclosing air or gas: *soap bubbles. The surface of boiling water is covered with bubbles.* 2 a pocket of air or gas in a liquid or solid: *Sometimes there are bubbles in ice or in glass.* 3 the act or process of bubbling; a sound of bubbling: *the bubble of boiling water.* 4 something shaped like a bubble: *A round, domed skylight is often called a bubble.* 5 a plan or idea that looks good, but soon goes to pieces. 6 *Archaic.* a swindle.
—*v.* 1 have or form bubbles: *Water bubbled up between the stones.* 2 make sounds like water boiling; gurgle.
bubble over, a be very full; overflow. **b** be very enthusiastic: *The boys were bubbling over with ideas for the canoe trip.*
[ME *bobel*] —**bub′bling·ly,** *adv.*

bubble chamber a small vessel filled with a superheated liquid, especially pentane or hydrogen under pressure, through which sub-atomic particles make a bubbly track by means of which they may be isolated and identified.

bubble gum chewing gum that is very elastic and can be blown up into bubbles from the mouth.

bub·bly (bub′lē) *adj., n.* —*adj.* 1 full of bubbles. 2 showing enthusiasm or high spirits: *She has a bubbly personality.* —*n. Informal.* champagne.

bu·bo (byü′bō) *n., pl.* **bu·boes.** an inflammatory swelling of a lymphatic gland, especially in the groin or armpits. [< LL *bubo* < Gk. *boubon* groin]

bu·bon·ic (byü bon′ik) *adj.* of or having to do with inflamed swelling of the lymphatic glands, especially in the armpit and groin.

bubonic plague a dangerous disease, accompanied by fever, chills, and swelling of the lymphatic glands, carried to human beings by fleas from rats or squirrels.

buc·cal (buk′əl) *adj. Anatomy.* 1 of the cheek. 2 of the mouth or of the sides of the mouth. [< L *bucca* cheek, mouth]

buc·ca·neer (buk′ə nēr′) *n.* a pirate or freebooter. [< F *boucanier* < Tupi *boucan* frame for curing meat, as done by the French in Haiti]

Bu·ceph·a·lus (byü sef′ə ləs) *n.* the war horse of Alexander the Great.

Buch·man·ism (buk′mə niz′əm) *n.* a twentieth-century religious movement; Moral Rearmament. [< Frank *Buchman* (1878-1961), U.S. evangelist and founder of the movement]

buck¹ (buk) *n.* 1 an adult male deer, goat, hare, rabbit, antelope, or sheep. 2 *Informal.* a man, especially a young man who is lively, bold and dashing. 3 *Cdn. Informal.* a North American Indian man. [a fusion of OE *buc* male deer, and OE *bucca* male goat]
☛ *Usage.* **Buck** (def. 3) and the phrase **buck Indian** are now considered offensive.

buck² (buk) *v., n.* —*v.* 1 fight against; resist stubbornly: *The swimmer bucked the current with strong strokes. You can't buck progress.* 2 *Informal.* push or hit with the head; butt. 3 *Football.* charge into (the opposing line) with the ball. 4 of horses, jump into the air with back curved and come down with the front legs stiff. 5 throw or attempt to throw (a rider) in this way. 6 *Informal.* of an automobile, motor, etc., run unevenly; jerk, as when the fuel supply is low or the motor cold.
buck up, cheer up; be brave or energetic: *Buck up; everything will be all right.*
—*n.* a throw or an attempt to throw by bucking. [special use of *buck¹*] —**buck′er,** *n.*

buck³ (buk) *n., v.* —*n.* 1 a sawhorse; sawbuck. 2 *Gymnastics.* a padded, adjustable frame used for vaulting, etc. —*v.* cut wood, especially felled trees, into lengths, as with a bucksaw. —**buck′er,** *n.* [short for *sawbuck*]

buck⁴ (buk) *n.*
pass the buck, *Informal.* shift the responsibility, or blame to someone else: *Whenever his plans don't work out, he passes the buck and someone else gets blamed.*
[origin uncertain]

buck⁵ (buk) *n. Slang.* dollar.

buck·a·roo (buk′ə rü′ *or* buk′ə rü′) *n., pl.* **-roos.** cowboy. [< alteration of Sp. *vaquero* < *vaca* cow < L *vacca*]

buck·board (buk′bôrd′) *n.* an open four-wheeled carriage having a seat fastened to a platform of long, springy boards instead of having a body and springs.

buck·et (buk′it) *n., v.* **-et·ed, -et·ing.** —*n.* 1 a pail, especially a wooden one used for carrying water, milk, etc. 2 the amount that a bucket can hold. 3 the scoop of a dredging machine. 4 *Slang.* a ship, car, etc., especially one that is old and slow.
kick the bucket, *Slang.* die.
—*v.* 1 lift or carry in a bucket or buckets. 2 ride (a horse) hard. 3 *Informal.* **a** move fast. **b** move jerkily and irregularly. 4 swing forward too hurriedly before taking the stroke in rowing. 5 conduct a bucket shop. [ME < AF *buket* washtub, milk pail, perhaps < OE *būc* vessel, pitcher]

buck·et·ful (buk′it fùl′) *n., pl.* **-fuls.** the amount that a bucket can hold.

bucket seat a single, low-slung seat with a curved back, used especially in sports cars, small airplanes, etc.

bucket shop a fraudulent establishment conducted ostensibly for buying and selling stocks or commodities, but really for making bets on the rise and fall of their prices, with no actual buying and selling.

buck·eye (buk′ī′) *n. Esp.U.S.* any of various North American trees (genus *Aesculus*) of the horse chestnut family. The **Ohio buckeye** (*A. glabra*) gave Ohio the nickname "Buckeye State." [< *buck¹* + *eye*; with reference to mark on the seed]

Buckingham Palace the official London residence of all British sovereigns since 1837.

buck·le¹ (buk′əl) *n., v.* **-led, -ling.** —*n.* 1 a device used to fasten the loose end or both ends of a belt or strap, usually consisting of a metal or plastic frame through which the end of the belt or strap is pulled. 2 a metal ornament, especially one for a shoe. —*v.* fasten together with a buckle.
buckle down to, begin to work hard: *She promised to buckle down to her homework right after supper.*
[ME *bocle* < OF *boucle* < L *buccula* cheek strap on helmet, dim. of *bucca* cheek]

buck·le² (buk′əl) *v.* **-led, -ling;** *n.* —*v.* bend; bulge; give way under a heavy weight or strain: *The heavy snowfall caused the roof of the arena to buckle.* —*n.* a bend; bulge; kink or wrinkle. [< F *boucler* bulge]

buck·ler (buk′lər) *n.* 1 a small, round shield. 2 a protection; defence. [ME < OF *boucler* shield, originally, one with a boss < *boucle* boss < L *buccula*. See BUCKLE.]

buck private *U.S. Slang.* a common soldier below the rank of lance corporal.

buck·ram (buk′rəm) *n., v.* —*n.* 1 a coarse cotton or linen cloth made stiff with glue, used in bookbinding and to stiffen hats and other clothing. 2 (*adj.*) made of or resembling buckram. —*v.* pad or stiffen with buckram. [ME < AF ? ult. < *Bukhara*, var. of *Bokhara*]

A bucksaw

buck·saw (buk′so′ *or* -sô′) *n.* a saw set in a light H-shaped frame and held with both hands. Bucksaws are used for sawing wood.

buck·shee (buk′shē) *adj. Slang.* free: *We were given two buckshee tickets for the dance.* [< *baksheesh*]

buck·shot (buk′shot′) *n.* a coarse lead shot for shotgun shells, used for hunting large game such as deer.

buck·skin (buk′skin′) *n.* **1** the skin of a male deer. **2** a soft, strong, yellowish or greyish leather made from this skin, usually having a suede finish. Buckskin is tougher and coarser than deerskin. **3** a similar leather made from sheepskin. **4 buckskins,** *pl.* clothing, especially breeches, made from buckskins. (def. 2).

buck·thorn (buk′thôrn′) *n.* **1** any of several thorny trees or shrubs (genus *Rhamnus*) having small green flowers followed by bluish-black berries. **2** (*adj.*) designating the family (Rhamnaceae) of trees, shrubs, and climbing vines that includes the buckthorns.

buck·tooth (buk′tüth′) *n., pl.* **-teeth.** a tooth that sticks out.

buck·toothed (buk′tütht′ *or* -tüᴛʜd′) *adj.* having protruding upper-front teeth.

buck·wheat (buk′wēt′ *or* -hwēt′) *n.* **1** any of a genus (*Fagopyrum*) of annual plants native to Europe and Asia. Two species of buckwheat have been extensively grown in North America for their edible seeds, which are used as cereal grains; the plants have escaped from cultivation, becoming common weeds in many parts of Canada. **2** the seed of a buckwheat, used as food. **3 wild buckwheat,** a twining annual plant (*Polygonum convolvulus*) native to Europe, but now growing as a weed throughout Canada. Also called **black bindweed. 4** (*adj.*) designating a family (Polygonaceae) of annual or perennial herbs or shrubs found mainly in the northern hemisphere. Rhubarb, sorrel, dock and smartweed belong to the buckwheat family. [< *buck* (< OE *bōc* beech) + *wheat;* from its beechnut-shaped seeds]

buckwheat cake a pancake made of buckwheat flour.

bu·col·ic (byü kol′ik) *adj., n.* —*adj.* **1** of shepherds; pastoral: *Bucolic poetry is seldom written by shepherds themselves.* **2** rustic; rural. —*n.* a poem about shepherds. [< L *bucolicus* < Gk. *boukolikos* rustic < *boukolos* shepherd] —**bu·col′i·cal·ly,** *adv.*

bud (bud) *n., v.* **bud·ded, bud·ding.** —*n.* **1** on a plant, a small swelling that will develop into a flower, leaf, or branch. **2** a partly opened flower or leaf. **3** a person or thing not yet developed or mature. **4** anything in its beginning stage. **5** a minute, bud-shaped part or organ: *a taste bud.*
in bud, budding: *The pear tree is in bud.*
nip in the bud, stop at the very beginning.
—*v.* **1** put forth buds: *The rosebush has budded.* **2** graft (a bud) from one kind of plant into the stem of a different kind. See **graft** for picture. **3** begin to grow or develop. [ME *budde*] —**bud′der,** *n.*

Bud·dha (bùd′ə, bü′də, *or* bud′ə) *n.* the title of Siddhartha Gautama (563?-483? B.C.), the Indian philosopher and teacher who founded Buddhism. Buddha means Enlightened One. [< Skt.]

Bud·dhism (bùd′iz əm, bü′diz əm, *or* bud′iz əm) *n.* a religion based on the doctrine of Buddha that pain and suffering cannot be avoided so long as one is subject to worldly desires, but that through meditating and leading a strictly moral life one can eventually reach nirvana, a state of liberation and spiritual illumination that is beyond pleasure or pain. Buddhism is widely practised today in many parts of eastern and central Asia, especially in Burma, Thailand, Sri Lanka, Japan, Cambodia, Laos, and Tibet.

Bud·dhist (bùd′ist, bü′dist, *or* bud′ist) *n., adj.* —*n.* a believer in Buddhism. —*adj.* of or having to do with Buddha or Buddhism.

bud·dy (bud′ē) *n., pl.* **-dies. 1** a good friend; pal. **2** fellow (*used as a form of address*): *Say, buddy, can you change a quarter?*

buddy system an arrangement in dangerous kinds of work or sport, by which two people operate together as a safety precaution in case of accident.

budge (buj) *v.* **budged, budg·ing.** move or cause to move: *He wouldn't budge from his chair.* [< F *bouger* stir < VL *bullicare* boil furiously < *bullire* boil]

budg·er·i·gar (buj′ər i gär′) *n.* a small, long-tailed parrot (*Melopsittacus undulatus*) native to Australia, but very popular in many countries as a cage bird. The plumage of wild budgerigars is green below and yellow above, with blue and black stripes, but the cage birds have been bred to produce individuals of many different colors. [< native Australian *budgereegah* < *budgeri* good + *gar* cockatoo]

budg·et (buj′it) *n., v.* **-et·ed, -et·ing.** —*n.* **1** an estimate of the amount of money that will be spent for various purposes in a given time by a government, school, business, family, etc.: *We made a budget for our holiday trip so that we wouldn't run out of money before the end.* **2** the amount of money allotted for a particular use or period of time: *My budget won't allow any more movies this month.* **3** a stock or collection: *a budget of news.*
—*v.* **1** make a plan for spending or using: *to budget one's time. She budgets her earnings carefully.* **2** allot money for a particular purpose: *I forgot to budget for extras so I couldn't buy the record.* [ME < OF *bougette,* dim. of *bouge* bag < L *bulga* < Celtic]

budg·et·ar·y (buj′ə ter′ē) *adj.* of a budget.

budg·ie (buj′ē) *n. Informal.* budgerigar.

hat, āge, fär; let, ēqual, tèrm; it, īce
hot, ōpen, ôrder; oil, out; cup, pùt, rüle,
əbove, takən, pencəl, lemən, circəs

ch, child; ng, long; sh, ship
th, thin; ᴛʜ, then; zh, measure

bud·worm (bud′wèrm′) *n.* spruce budworm.

buff¹ (buf) *n., adj., v.* —*n.* **1** a strong, soft, dull-yellow leather having a fuzzy surface, made from buffalo skin or oxhide. **2** a soldier's coat made of this leather. **3** a dull yellow. **4** a polishing wheel or stick covered with leather. **5** *Informal.* bare skin: *swimming in the buff.*
—*adj.* **1** made of buff leather. **2** having the color buff.
—*v.* **1** polish with a buff. **2** stain or dye a dull yellow. [earlier *buffle* < F *buffle* < Ital. *bufalo.* See BUFFALO.]

buff² (buf) *n. Informal.* fan; enthusiast: *a hockey buff, a theatre buff.* [origin uncertain]

buff³ (buf) *n. Cdn. Informal.* buffalo.

The buffalo of North America—about 175 cm high at the shoulder

A water buffalo of India—about 155 cm high at the shoulder

buf·fa·lo (buf′ə lō′) *n., pl.* **-loes, -los,** *or* (*esp. collectively*) **-lo;** *v.* **-loed, -lo·ing.** —*n.* **1** a large mammal (*Bison bison*) of the North American plains having a prominent shoulder hump and a large head that is carried below the level of the shoulders, short, curved horns, and coarse, dark-brown hair that is long and shaggy on the forequarters. The buffalo is Canada's largest land mammal; a large bull may weigh up to one tonne. **2** any of several large hoofed mammals (family Bovidae) of Africa and India generally having long horns that curve upward and backward. Some species, such as the water buffalo of India, have been domesticated. **3** buffalo fish.
—*v. Slang.* make unable to answer, proceed, etc.; baffle: *We were all buffaloed by the last question on the exam.* [< Ital. *bufalo* < L *bubalus* < Gk. *boubalos* wild ox]

buffalo berry **1** a shrub (*Shepherdia argentea*) of the oleaster family native to W North America, having silvery foliage and edible red berries. **2** the berry of this shrub. **3** soapberry (def. 4).

buffalo fish any of several North American suckers (genus *Ictiobus*) having a deep body with a humped back.

buffalo grass a short grass (*Buchloe dactyloides*) of the plains east of the Rocky Mountains, valued especially for winter pasture.

buffalo jump a place where the Plains Indians slaughtered buffalo by stampeding them over a precipice.

buff·er¹ (buf′ər) *n.* **1** an apparatus that softens the shock of a blow. **2** anything helping to soften or sustain a shock or to neutralize opposing forces: *Mother was a buffer between my father's anger and me.* [< *buff* deaden force, (earlier meaning) strike; cf. OF *buffe* a blow]

buff·er² (buf′ər) *n.* a person or thing that polishes, especially a leather or cloth-covered device for polishing or buffing. [< *buff*]

buf·fer³ (buf′ər) *n. Slang.* a fellow, often used humorously or contemptuously of an older person. [origin uncertain]

buffer state a small country between two larger countries that are enemies or competitors, thought of as lessening the danger of open conflict between them.

buf·fet¹ (buf′it) *n., v.* **-fet·ed, -fet·ing.** —*n.* **1** a blow of the hand or fist. **2** a knock; stroke; hurt.
—*v.* **1** strike with the hand or fist. **2** knock about; strike; hurt: *The waves buffeted him.* **3** fight or struggle against: *He was exhausted from buffeting the storm.* [ME < OF *buffet,* dim. of *buffe* blow]

buf·fet² (bù fā′ *or* bu fā′) *n.* **1** a low cabinet with a flat top, for holding dishes, silver, and table linen. **2** a counter where food and drinks are served. **3** a restaurant with such a counter. **4** a meal at which guests serve themselves from food laid out on a table. [< F]

buffet car a railway car having a small area where light meals may be obtained.

buffet lunch a buffet (def. 4).

buffet supper a buffet (def. 4), served at night.

buf·fle·head (buf′əl hed′) *n.* a small, black-and-white, North

American diving duck (*Bucephala albeola*), the male of which has long, fluffy feathers forming puffs on the sides of the head. [< obs. *buffle* buffalo + *head*]

buf·fo (bü′fō; *Ital.*, büf′fō) *n., adj.*—*n.* a male singer of comic operatic roles, usually a basso.—*adj.* comic. [< Ital. *buffo*]

buf·foon (bu fün′) *n., v.*—*n.* 1 a person who amuses people with tricks, pranks, and jokes; clown. 2 a person given to coarse or undignified jesting.—*v.* behave like a buffoon. [< F *bouffon* < Ital. *buffone* < *buffa* jest]

buf·foon·er·y (bu fün′ər ē) *n., pl.* -er·ies. 1 the tricks, pranks, and jokes of a clown. 2 undignified or rude joking.

bug (bug) *n., v.* bugged, bug·ging.—*n.* 1 any of an order (Heteroptera) of sucking insects made up of about 20 000 species, including the bedbug, having generally horizontal wings that overlap on the body when at rest. Most families of bugs have scent glands that produce a characteristic odor. 2 any insect or insect-like animal. The ladybug and June bug are really beetles. Ants, spiders, cockroaches, etc. are sometimes called bugs, especially when thought of as pests. 3 *Informal.* a disease bacterium or virus: *the flu bug.* 4 *Informal.* a mechanical defect; any structural fault or difficulty: *a bug in the fire alarm system.* 5 *Informal.* a person who is very enthusiastic about something: *a camera bug.* 6 *Informal.* a very small hidden microphone, installed for the purpose of secretly listening in on or recording conversation.—*v.* 1 *Slang.* annoy; irritate: *His constant grumbling bugs me.* 2 *Informal.* fit (a room, telephone, etc.) with a very small concealed microphone. 3 *Informal.* secretly listening in on or record by means of a hidden microphone: *to bug a meeting.* [? < obsolete Welsh *bwg* ghost]

bug·a·boo (bug′ə bü′) *n., pl.* -boos. a cause of fear; something, usually imaginary, that frightens: *The child was frightened by tales of witches, ghosts, and other bugaboos.* [< *bug* bogy + *boo*, interjection]

bug·bear (bug′ber′) *n.* 1 bugaboo. 2 something that causes difficulties; a snag. [< *bug* bogy + *bear*²]

bug–eyed (bug′īd′) *adj. Slang.* having eyes wide open and bulging, especially from wonder or excitement.

bug·ger (bug′ər) *n., v.*—*n.* a person who commits buggery. —*v.* commit buggery (with). [< MDu. *bugger* < OF *bougre* < Med.L *Bulgarus* Bulgarian, the Orthodox Bulgarians being considered heretics. 16c.]

bug·ger·y (bug′ər ē) *n.* abnormal sexual relations involving anal intercourse between a man and another person or an animal.

A buggy

bug·gy¹ (bug′ē) *n., pl.* -gies. 1 a light, four-wheeled carriage drawn by one horse and having a single large seat. 2 a wheeled cart used for shopping in a grocery store, etc. 3 baby carriage. [origin uncertain]

bug·gy² (bug′ē) *adj.* -gi·er, -gi·est. swarming with bugs.

bu·gle¹ (byü′gəl) *n., v.* -gled, -gling.—*n.* a wind instrument like a small trumpet, made of brass or copper, and sometimes having keys, or valves. Bugles are sometimes used in the armed services for sounding calls and orders.—*v.* 1 blow a bugle. 2 direct or summon by blowing on a bugle. [ME < OF < L *buculus*, dim. of *bos* ox; with reference to early hunting horns]

bu·gle² (byü′gəl) *n.* a small, tubular glass or plastic bead used for trimming on dresses, blouses, etc. Also called **bugle bead**. [origin uncertain]

bu·gler (byü′glər) *n.* a person who blows a bugle.

bu·gloss (byü′glos) *n.* any of various weedy Eurasian plants of the borage family having bristly leaves and stems and small, bright-blue flowers. Some species, such as *Lycopsis arvensis*, have become naturalized in North America. [< F < L *buglossa* < Gk. *bouglōssos* ox-tongue < *bous* ox + *glōssa* tongue]

buhl (bül) *n.* wood inlaid in elaborate patterns with metal, tortoise shell, ivory, etc. and used for furniture. [< G spelling of F *boule* or *boulle*, after A.C. *Boule* or *Boulle* (1642-1732), a French cabinetmaker]

build (bild) *v.* **built** or (*archaic*) **build·ed, build·ing;** *n.*—*v.* 1 make by putting materials together; construct: *People build houses, dams, bridges, and roads.* 2 form gradually; develop: *to build a business, to build an empire.* 3 establish; base: *to build a case on facts.*

4 rely; depend: *We can build on that man's honesty.* 5 make a structure: *We've bought the land, but we won't start to build until next year.*

build up, a form gradually; develop: *to build up one's self-confidence. The firm has built up a wide reputation for fair dealing.* **b** gather; come together: *Clouds were building up on the horizon.* **c** fill with houses, etc. **d** accumulate, causing congestion: *The traffic always builds up at the toll bridge at rush hours.* **e** promote: *They're using TV ads to build up their new product.* —*n.* a form, style, or manner of construction; structure or physique: *An elephant has a heavy build.* [OE *byldan* < *bold* dwelling]

build·ed (bil′did) *v. Archaic.* a pt. and a pp. of **build.**

build·er (bil′dər) *n.* 1 a person or animal that builds. 2 a person in the construction business.

build·ing (bil′ding) *n.* 1 something built, such as a house, factory, barn, store, etc. 2 the business, art, or process of making houses, stores, bridges, ships, etc.

☛ *Syn.* 1. **Building, edifice, structure** = something constructed. **Building** is the general word and has a wide range of uses because it does not suggest purpose, size, materials, etc.: *From the hill we could see the buildings in the city.* **Edifice** is a formal word, applying to a large and imposing building: *The cathedral is a handsome edifice.* **Structure** emphasizes the type of construction: *The new library is a fireproof structure.*

build-up or **build–up** (bild′up′) *n.* 1 the act or process of building up: *a buildup of military strength.* 2 favorable publicity in advance; promotion: *The actor received a tremendous buildup in the local papers before the play opened.* 3 congestion: *a traffic buildup.*

built (bilt) *v.* a pt. and a pp. of **build.**

built–in (bilt′in′) *adj.* 1 built as part of a larger structure, especially a building; not detachable: *a built-in closet. We can't move the bookcase, because it's built-in.* 2 having as a part of one's nature, or as an integral part: *a built-in sense of humor.*

Bulb (def. 1): onions

bulb (bulb) *n.* 1 a kind of bud produced underground by certain plants, such as onions, lilies, and tulips, that permits the plants to survive cold or dry periods. It is in effect a compressed plant in a dormant state, consisting of a stem base, one or more growing buds, and root cells, surrounded by layers of fleshy leaves serving as a source of food. 2 any plant that produces bulbs. 3 a thick underground stem resembling a bulb, such as a corm or tuber. 4 an electric light bulb. 5 any object with a rounded end or swelling part: *the bulb of a thermometer.* [< L *bulbus* < Gk. *bolbos* onion] —**bulb′less,** *adj.*—**bulb′like′,** *adj.*

bulb·ar (bul′bər) *adj.* of or having to do with a bulb-shaped organ, especially the medulla oblongata, which is the lowest part of the brain.

bulb·let (bulb′lit′) *n.* a small flower or vegetable bulb.

bulb·ous (bul′bəs) *adj.* 1 shaped like a bulb; rounded and swollen: *a bulbous nose.* 2 producing or growing from bulbs: *Daffodils are bulbous plants.*

bul·bul (bùl′bùl) *n.* 1 any of a family (Pycnonotidae) of mainly brownish songbirds of tropical Asia and Africa. 2 a songbird often mentioned in Persian poetry, thought to be a nightingale. [< Arabic or Persian]

Bul·gar (bul′gär or bùl′gär) *adj. or n.* Bulgarian.

Bul·gar·i·an (bul ger′ē ən) *n., adj.*—*n.* 1 a native or inhabitant of Bulgaria, a country in SE Europe. 2 the Slavic language of the Bulgarians.—*adj.* of or having to do with Bulgaria, its people, or their language.

bulge (bulj) *v.* **bulged, bulg·ing;** *n.*—*v.* 1 swell outward: *His pockets bulged with apples and candy.* 2 cause to swell outward: *The apples bulged his pockets.* —*n.* 1 an outward swelling. 2 of a ship: **a** the bottom of the hull; bilge. **b** a structure attached outside the hull to protect it from mines, torpedoes, etc.; a blister. 3 a temporary increase: *The graph shows a bulge in the birth rate.* [ME < OF *boulge* < L *bulga* bag]

bulg·y (bul′jē) *adj.* bulging or bulges.—**bul′gi·ness,** *n.*

bulk (bulk) *n., v.*—*n.* 1 size, especially large size: *an elephant of great bulk.* 2 the largest part; main mass: *The ocean forms the bulk of the earth's surface.* 3 a ship's cargo or hold.

in bulk, a loose, not in packages. **b** in large quantities.

—v. **1** have size; be of importance. **2** grow large; swell. [< Scand.; cf. O Icelandic *bulki* heap]
☛ *Syn. n.* **1.** See note at **size**[1].

bulk carrier a lake freighter designed to carry bulk commodities such as ore and grain.

bulk·er (bul′kər) *n.* bulk carrier.

bulk·head (bulk′hed′) *n.* **1** one of the upright partitions dividing a ship into watertight compartments. **2** a similar partition in an aircraft, etc. **3** a wall or partition built to hold back water, earth, rocks, air, etc. **4** a boxlike structure covering the top of a staircase or other opening.

bulk·y (bul′kē) *adj.* **bulk·i·er, bulk·i·est. 1** taking up much space; large: *Bulky shipments are often sent by freight.* **2** hard to handle; clumsy: *She dropped the bulky package of curtain rods twice.* —**bulk′i·ly,** *adv.*—**bulk′i·ness,** *n.*

bull[1] (bul) *n., v.*—*n.* **1** the adult male of cattle, buffalo, etc. **2** the adult male of the moose, whale, elephant, seal, and other large animals. **3** (*adj.*) like a bull; large and strong. **4** a person whose size or loudness resembles that of a bull. **5** a person who tries to raise prices in the stock market, etc. **6** (*adj.*) marked by or having to do with rising prices in the stock market, etc. **7** *Slang.* foolish boastful talk. **8** bulldog. **9** *Esp.Brit.* bull's eye. **10** Bull, *Astronomy or astrology.* Taurus.
shoot the bull, *Slang.* talk idly; speculate or boast.
take the bull by the horns, deal bravely and directly with a dangerous or difficult situation.
—v. push or force one's way. [ME *bole* < ON *boli.* Related to BULLOCK.]

bull[2] (bul) *n. Roman Catholic Church.* a formal announcement or official order from the Pope. [< Med.L *bulla* document, seal < L *bulla* amulet, bubble]

bull[3] (bul) *n.* an absurd and amusing mistake in language, especially one that is self-contradictory. *Example: If you don't receive this letter, write and let me know.* [origin uncertain]

bull. bulletin.

bull·bait·ing (bul′bā′ting) *n. Historical.* a sport like bearbaiting, with the dogs tormenting a chained bull. See also **bearbaiting.**

bull·cook (bul′kuk′) *n.* a janitor or handyman in a lumber camp. In some camps it used to be his duty to prepare mash for the oxen used in hauling logs.

bull·dog[1] (bul′dog′) *n., v.* **-dogged, -dog·ging.**—*n.* **1** a breed of heavily built dog with a large head and short hair. Bulldogs are not large, but they are very muscular and courageous. **2** (*adj.*) like that of a bulldog: *bulldog courage.*—*v.* in the western parts of Canada and the United States, throw (a steer, etc.) to the ground by grasping its horns and twisting its neck.

bull·dog[2] (bul′dog′) *n. Cdn.* a kind of horsefly about the size of a bumblebee, having a vicious bite and a great appetite for blood. Also, **bulldog fly** or **bull fly.**

bull·doze (bul′dōz′) *v.* **-dozed, -doz·ing. 1** *Informal.* frighten by violence or threats; bully. **2** move, clear, dig, or level with a bulldozer. [back formation < *bulldozer*]

bull·doz·er (bul′dōz′ər) *n.* **1** a powerful tractor that moves dirt, etc. for grading, road building, etc. by means of a wide steel blade attached to the front. **2** *Informal.* one who bulldozes.

bul·let (bul′it) *n.* a round or pointed piece of lead, steel, or other metal designed to be shot from a rifle, pistol, or other relatively small firearm. [< F *boulette*, dim. of *boule* ball]

bul·let·head (bul′it hed′) *n.* **1** a short, round head. **2** a person with such a head. **3** *Informal.* a stubborn pig-headed person.

bul·let–head·ed (bul′it hed′id) *adj.* having a round head.

bul·le·tin (bul′ə tən) *n., v.*—*n.* **1** a short statement of news: *In times of crisis newspapers publish bulletins about the latest happenings. Doctors issue bulletins about the condition of a sick person.* **2** a magazine or newspaper appearing regularly, especially one published by a club or society for its members.—*v.* make known by a bulletin. [< F < Ital. *bullettino*, double dim. of *bulla* bull[2]]

bulletin board a board or a sheet of cork, etc. used for posting notices.

bul·let·proof (bul′it prüf′) *adj.* made so that a bullet cannot pass through: *a bulletproof jacket.*

bull·fight (bul′fīt′) *n.* a traditional public performance or ritual in which a man, called a matador, confronts a fierce bull in an arena and performs a series of skilful manoeuvres in avoiding the horns of the charging bull, usually killing the bull with a sword. Bullfights are common in Spain, Mexico, Columbia, Peru, and Venezuela.

bull·fight·er (bul′fīt′ər) *n.* matador.

bull·fight·ing (bul′fīt′ing) *n.* the act or ritual of fighting a bull in a public arena.

hat, āge, fär; let, ēqual, tėrm; it, īce
hot, ōpen, ôrder; oil, out; cup, put, rüle,
above, takən, pencəl, lemən, circəs

ch, child; ng, long; sh, ship
th, thin; ŦH, then; zh, measure

bull·finch (bul′finch′) *n.* **1** a small, plump-bodied finch (*Pyrrhula pyrrhula*) found in the forests of the British Isles, Europe, and Asia, having a short bill and black head, wings, and tail. The male bullfinch has a pinkish breast and a bluish back, the female a brownish-grey breast and back. **2** any of various other finches.

bull fly (bul′flī′) *n.* bulldog[2].

bull·frog (bul′frog′) *n.* any of a genus (*Rana*) of very large frogs found in North America, Africa, and India, the male having a loud call that has been compared to the bellow of a bull. The American bullfrog is olive green or reddish brown.

bull·head (bul′hed′) *n.* **1** any of several North American freshwater catfishes (genus *Ictalurus*, also called *Ameiurus*), such as the **brown bullhead** (*I. nebulosus*) of E and central North America. **2** any of various other large-headed fishes, such as a sculpin. **3** a stupid fellow; a blockhead.

bull·head·ed (bul′hed′id) *adj.* stupidly stubborn; obstinate. —**bull′head′ed·ness,** *n.*

bull·horn (bul′horn′) *n.* a megaphone with an electric amplifier.

bul·lion (bul′yən) *n.* bricks or bars of gold or silver. [< AF *bullion* < *bouillir* boil; influenced by OF *billon* debased metal]

bull·ish (bul′ish) *adj.* **1** like a bull. **2** marked by, tending toward, or expecting higher prices in the stock market. Compare **bearish.** —**bull′ish·ly,** *adv.*—**bull′ish·ness,** *n.*

bull–mar·ket (bul′mär′kit) *n.* a rising investment market.

bull mastiff a breed of large, powerful, thickset dog with a short brown or brindled coat, developed in the late 19th century in England from a cross between a bulldog and a mastiff.

bull·necked (bul′nekt′) *adj.* having a thick neck.

bull·ock (bul′ək) *n.* **1** a castrated ox or steer. **2** *Archaic.* a young bull. [OE *bulluc* bull calf]

bull pen *Esp.U.S.* **1** *Slang.* **a** a temporary prison. **b** a jail of any kind. **2** *Baseball.* a place outside the playing limits in which pitchers warm up during a game.

bull ring an enclosed arena for bullfights.

bull·roar·er (bul′rôr′ər) *n.* **1** a flat piece of wood tied to a string so as to produce a roaring sound when whirled in the air, used in religious rites by certain North American Indian tribes, Australian aborigines, etc. **2** a similar device used as a toy.

bull session an informal, rambling discussion, especially a freewheeling discussion among a small group of men.

bull's–eye (bulz′ī) *n.* **1** the centre of a target. **2** a shot that hits the centre. **3** a thick disk of glass set in a roof, pavement, the deck or side of a ship, etc. to let in light. **4** a convex lens with a short focal distance, used to concentrate light. **5** a lantern with such a lens. **6** any small, round opening or window.

bull terrier a breed of strong, active dog, having a long head and stiff, usually white, hair, originally bred as a cross between a bulldog and a terrier.

bull trout **1** salmon trout. **2** Dolly Varden trout.

bull·whip (bul′wip′ *or* -hwip′) *n., v.* **-whipped, -whip·ping.**—*n.* a long, heavy leather whip.—*v.* strike with a bullwhip.

bull work rough chores; manual labor: *He did the bull work around the camp.*

bul·ly (bul′ē) *n., pl.* **-lies;** *v.* **-lied, -ly·ing;** *adj., interj.*—*n.* a person who teases, frightens, or hurts smaller or weaker people. —*v.* **1** be a bully. **2** frighten into doing something by noisy talk or threats.
—*adj.* **1** *Informal.* first-rate; excellent. **2** jovial; gallant; spirited. —*interj. Informal.* bravo! well done! [origin uncertain]

bully beef canned or pickled beef. [? < F *bouilli* boiled beef < *bouillir* boil]

bul·ly·rag (bul′ē rag′) *v.* **-ragged, -rag·ging.** *Informal.* bully; tease; abuse.

bul·rush (bul′rush′) *n.* **1** any of a genus (*Typha*) of tall marsh plants found in North America, Europe, and Asia, having very long, stiff, flat leaves and long, thick, fuzzy, brown flower spikes; cat-tail: *Bulrushes are often used as decoration and also, sometimes, as torches outdoors.* **2** any of a genus (*Scirpus*) of

grasslike marsh plants of the sedge family found in North America, Europe, and Asia, having long, spongy, usually leafless stems and small flowers growing in a cluster of spikelets: *The stems of the common bulrush of Europe and Asia are used for making mats, baskets, chair seats, thatch, etc.* **3** the papyrus of Egypt, also belonging to the sedge family. [ME *bulrysche* < *bule* (see BULL[1], n. def. 2) + *rysche*, OE *rysc* rush]

bul·wark (bŭl′wərk) n., v.—n. **1** a support or safeguard; anything, person, or idea that serves as a defence: *They believe that free speech is a bulwark of democracy. Her common sense was our bulwark during the crisis.* **2** an earthwork or other wall for defence against an enemy. **3** a breakwater for protection against the force of the waves. **4** Usually, **bulwarks,** *pl.* the part of a ship's side that extends above the deck level. See **ship** for picture. —v. **1** defend; protect. **2** provide with a bulwark or bulwarks. [ME *bulwerk*, apparently < *bole* + *work*, a work made of tree trunks. Akin to BOULEVARD.]

bum[1] (bum) n., v. **bummed, bum·ming;** *adj.* **bum·mer, bum·mest.** *Informal.*—n. **1** an idle or good-for-nothing person; loafer. **2** a tramp or vagrant. **3** a person who devotes himself to a sport or recreation, to the exclusion of other activities or responsibilities: *a ski bum.*
on the bum, a living as a bum: *He spent two years on the bum.* **b** not functioning; in disrepair: *Our toaster is on the bum.*
the bum's rush, a forcible ejection (of a person from a place). —v. **1** loaf around; idle about. **2** live by taking advantage of the kindness of other people. **3** get something by taking advantage of the kindness of other people: *She tried to bum a ride.* —*adj.* **1** of poor quality. **2** injured or lame: *a bum knee.* [partly Scottish dial. *bum* a lazy, dirty person (a special use of *bum*[2]); partly a shortening of earlier American *bummer* loafter < G *Bummler*]—**bum′mer,** n.

bum[2] (bum) n. the fleshy part of a person's body, where the legs join the back; seat; buttocks. [ME, probably < *botem* bottom]

bum·bail·iff (bum bā′lif) n. *Brit.* a bailiff or sheriff's officer, especially one employed in serving attachments and making arrests. [< *bum*[2] + *bailiff*]

bum·ble (bum′bəl) n., v. **-bled, -bling.**—n. an awkward mistake. —v. act in a bungling or awkward way; blunder; botch. [origin uncertain]

bum·ble·bee (bum′bəl bē′) n. any of a tribe (*Bombini*) of large bees, especially any of a genus (*Bombus*) of social bees having a thick, hairy body usually banded with yellow. [< *bumble* buzz + *bee*]

bum·ble·dom (bum′bəl dəm) n. an incompetent, officious group of people. [< *Bumble*, the pompous beadle in Dickens' *Oliver Twist*, + *-dom*]

bum·boat (bum′bōt′) n. a boat used for peddling small wares and provisions to ships in port or off-shore. [? < LG *Bumboot*, a broad-beamed boat]

bum·mer (bum′ər) n. *Slang.* a bad or depressing experience or time: *The whole day was a bummer.*

bump (bump) v., n.—v. **1** push, throw, or strike (against something fairly large or solid). **2** move or proceed with bumps: *Our car bumped along the rough road.* **3** hit or come against with heavy blows: *That truck bumped our car.*
bump off, *Slang.* kill.
—n. **1** a blow, knock, or jolt. **2** a swelling caused by a blow or knock. **3** a projection or bulge: *a bump on a road.* **4** a rising air current that gives an aircraft a jolt. **5** an earthquake-like shock or concussion caused by rock subsidence in and around mines. [imitative]

bump·er (bump′ər) n. **1** the bar or bars of metal or hard rubber across the front and back of a car, bus, or truck that protect it from being damaged if bumped. **2** a person or thing that bumps. **3** a cup or glass filled to the brim. **4** *Informal.* something unusually large of its kind. **5** (*adj.*) unusually large: *We had a bumper crop of wheat last year.*

bumper sticker a piece of gummed paper having a slogan, catchword, or witty saying printed on it, for sticking on the bumper of a motor vehicle.

bump·kin (bump′kin) n. a person from the country who is socially awkward in unfamiliar surroundings, especially in cities. [< MDu. *bommekyn* little barrel]

bump·tious (bump′shəs) adj. unpleasantly assertive or conceited. [< *bump*]—**bump′tious·ly,** adv.—**bump′tious·ness,** n.

bump·y (bump′ē) adj. **bump·i·er, bump·i·est. 1** having bumps on the surface; uneven: *a bumpy road.* **2** causing bumps or jolts; rough: *a bumpy ride.*—**bump′i·ly,** adv.—**bump′i·ness,** n.

bun (bun) n. **1** a small piece of yeast dough that has been separately baked: *Buns are often slightly sweetened and may contain spice, raisins, or fruit.* **2** hair coiled at the back of the head in a knot suggesting a bun. [ME *bunne*; origin uncertain]

bu·na (byü′nə *or* bü′nə) n. an artificial rubber made from butadiene. [< *bu*tadiene + *Na*, symbol for sodium]

bunch (bunch) n., v.—n. **1** a group of things of the same kind growing, fastened, placed, or thought of together: *a bunch of grapes, a bunch of flowers.* **2** *Informal.* a group of people, animals, etc.: *They're a friendly bunch.* **3** *Informal.* a large quantity: *There is a whole bunch of paint in the basement.* —v. **1** come together in one place: *The sheep bunched in the shed to keep warm.* **2** bring together and make into a bunch: *We have bunched the flowers for you to carry home.*—**bunch′er,** n. [ME *bunche*; origin uncertain]
☛ *Syn.* n. **1.** See note at **bundle.**
☛ *Usage.* **Bunch.** Formal English limits the use of **bunch** to objects that grow together or can be fastened together: *a bunch of radishes, a bunch of flowers, a bunch of keys.* Informal English, however, clings to the older usage of **bunch,** applying it to a collection or group of any kind—including people: *A bunch of us meet at the Grill every night.*

bunch·ber·ry (bunch′ber′ē) n., *pl.* **-ries.** a small dogwood (*Cornus canadensis*) growing about 15-20 cm high, having showy blossoms consisting of four petal-like bracts surrounding a cluster of tiny flowers which mature into clusters of bright red berry-like fruits. The bunchberry is common throughout Canada.

bunch grass any of various grasses that grow in clumps or tufts, such as brome.

bunch·y (bun′chē) adj. **bunch·i·er, bunch·i·est. 1** having bunches. **2** growing in bunches.—**bunch′i·ness,** n.

bun·co (bung′kō) n., *pl.* **-cos;** v. **-coed, -co·ing.** *Informal.*—n. a scheme in which swindlers join to cheat an unsuspecting person. —v. swindle in this way. Also, **bunko.** [short for *buncombe*]

bun·combe (bung′kəm) n. *Informal.* bunkum.

Bund (bùnd; *German,* bùnt) n., *pl.* **Bün·de** (byn′də). *German.* an association; society; league.

Bun·des·rat (bùn′dəs rät′) n. **1** in West Germany, the upper house of the federal legislature. **2** in Switzerland or the former German Empire, the federal council or chief executive authority. [< G *Bund* league, federation + *Rat* council]

bun·dle (bun′dəl) n., v. **-dled, -dling.**—n. **1** a number of things tied or wrapped together. **2** a parcel or package. **3** *Informal.* a large number or amount; a bunch; a lot: *a bundle of money. The book gave us a bundle of new ideas.*
—v. **1** wrap or tie together; make into a bundle. **2** send away in a hurry; hustle (*usually used with* **off**): *They bundled him off to the hospital in spite of his protests.* **3** collect; gather together in a mass. **4** share a bed with one's sweetheart, while fully dressed (a courting custom formerly practised especially in New England.)
bundle up, dress warmly: *Make sure you bundle up when you go out.*
[cf. MDu. *bondel.* Akin to BIND.]—**bun′dler,** n.
☛ *Syn.* n. **1, 2. Bundle, bunch, parcel** = something fastened or wrapped together. **Bundle** suggests a number of things of the same or different sizes and shapes bound or wrapped together, often clumsily: *We gave away several bundles of old newspapers and magazines.* **Bunch** suggests a number of things of the same kind bound or fastened together, usually closely and neatly: *I bought a bunch of flowers.* **Parcel** suggests one or more things wrapped and tied neatly for mailing or carrying: *I had too many parcels to carry on the bus.*

bundle of nerves a person in a state of extreme nervousness and tension: *By the time we got there, she was a bundle of nerves.*

bung (bung) n., v.—n. **1** a stopper for closing the hole in the side or end of a barrel, keg, or cask. **2** bunghole.—v. *Brit. Slang.* hurl; throw.
bung up, a close (a bunghole) with a stopper. **b** stop up; choke up. **c** *Slang.* bruise.
[probably < MDu. *bonghe*]

bun·ga·low (bung′gə lō′) n. a one-storey house, often small; a house having no living space above the main floor. [< Hind. *bangla* of Bengal]

bung·hole (bung′hōl′) n. a hole in the side or end of a barrel, keg, or cask through which it is filled and emptied.

bun·gle (bung′gəl) v. **-gled, -gling;** n.—v. spoil by doing or making in a clumsy, unskilful way.—n. a clumsy, unskilful performance or piece of work. [origin uncertain]—**bun′gler,** n. —**bun′gling·ly,** adv.

bun·ion (bun′yən) n. an enlargement of the first joint of the big toe, causing the toe to be permanently bent inwards. [origin uncertain]

bunk[1] (bungk) n., v.—n. **1** a narrow bed attached to a wall like a shelf. **2** a narrow bed, usually one of two built one above the other. **3** *Informal.* any place to sleep.
—v. **1** *Informal.* spend the night (*at*): *It was too late to go home so Brigitta bunked at our house.* **2** sleep in or occupy a makeshift bed:

We bunked in an old barn. **3** provide with a bunk or bed: *This cabin bunks three people.* [? < *bunker*]

bunk² (bungk) *n. Slang.* insincere talk; humbug; bunkum. [short for *buncombe*]

bunk bed one of two single beds, usually built one above the other.

bunk·er (bungk′ər) *n., v.—n.* **1** a bin or other place for storing fuel on a ship. **2** a sandy hollow or mound of earth on a golf course, used as an obstacle. **3** a steel-and-concrete fortification, usually part of a defence system and built partly or entirely below ground.
—*v.* **1** hit (a golf ball) into a bunker. **2** supply (a ship) with coal or other fuel. [origin uncertain]

bunker fuel or **oil** a thick, heavy oil transported in bulk for use as fuel, especially for ships.

bunk·house (bungk′hous′) *n.* a building equipped with bunks for sleeping.

bun·ko (bung′kō) See **bunco.**

bun·kum (bung′kəm) *n. Informal.* insincere talk; humbug. Also, **buncum.** [after *Buncombe* Co., N.C., whose congressman kept making pointless speeches "for Buncombe"]

bun·ny (bun′ē) *n., pl.* **-nies.** a pet name for a rabbit. [origin uncertain]

Bun·sen burner (bun′sən) a gas burner with a very hot, blue flame, used in laboratories. Air is let in at the base of the burner and mixed with gas. [after Robert *Bunsen* (1811-1899), a German chemist who invented it]

bunt¹ (bunt) *v., n.—v.* **1** strike with the head or horns, as a goat does. **2** push; shove. **3** *Baseball.* hit a ball lightly so that it goes to the ground and rolls only a short distance.
—*n.* **1** push; shove. **2** *Baseball.* **a** a hit made by hitting the ball lightly so that it goes to the ground and rolls only a short distance. **b** a baseball that is bunted. [cf. *butt³*]—**bunt′er,** *n.*

bunt² (bunt) *n., v.—n.* **1** the central, bellying part of a square sail. **2** the bagging part of a fishing net.—*v.* swell out; belly: *sails bunting before the wind.*
bunt up, haul (a sail) up to a yard.
[origin uncertain]

bunt³ (bunt) *n.* **1** a disease of wheat in which a parasitic fungus turns the centre kernels into a foul-smelling black powder. **2** the fungus itself. [origin uncertain]

bun·ting¹ (bun′ting) *n.* **1** a thin cloth used for flags. **2** long pieces of cloth having the colors and designs of a flag, used to decorate buildings and streets on holidays and special occasions; flags. [? < ME *bonten* sift, since the cloth was used for sifting]

bun·ting² (bun′ting) *n.* any of numerous finches, especially of the New World genus *Passerina* and the Old World genus *Emberiza.* See also **indigo bunting, lark bunting, snow bunting.** [origin uncertain]

bunt·line (bunt′lin or bunt′līn′) *n.* a rope fastened to a sail, used to haul it up to the yard for furling. [< *bunt,* middle part of a sail (origin uncertain), + *line¹*]

Bun·yan (bun′yən) See **Paul Bunyan.**

buoy (boi or bü′ē) *n., v.—n.* **1** a floating object anchored on the water to warn or guide. Buoys mark hidden rocks or shallows, show the safe part of the channel, etc. **2** a cork or plastic belt, ring, or jacket used to keep a person from sinking; a life buoy or life preserver.
—*v.* **1** furnish or mark with a buoy or buoys. **2** keep from sinking (*often used with* **up**). **3** support or encourage (*often used with* **up**): *Hope buoyed him up when things began to go wrong.* [< OF *boie* (< Gmc.; akin to E *beacon*) and MDu. *boeie* (< OF *boie*)]
☛ *Hom.* **boy** (boi).

buoy·an·cy (boi′ən sē) *n.* **1** the power to float: *Wood has more buoyancy than iron.* **2** the power to keep things afloat: *Salt water has greater buoyancy than fresh water.* **3** a tendency to rise. **4** the ability to rise above or recover quickly from low spirits; light-heartedness; cheerfulness; hopefulness. **5** a body's loss in weight when immersed in a liquid.

buoy·ant (boi′ənt) *adj.* **1** able to float: *Wood and cork are buoyant in water; iron and lead are not.* **2** able to keep things afloat: *Air is buoyant; balloons float in it.* **3** tending to rise. **4** light-hearted; cheerful; hopeful: *Even in the hospital, his spirits were buoyant.*
—**buoy′ant·ly,** *adv.*

BUP British United Press.

bur (bėr) See **burr.**

Bur·ber·ry (bėr′bər ē) *n. Trademark.* **1** a kind of waterproof material for clothing. **2** a coat made of this material.

bur·ble (bėr′bəl) *v.* **-bled, -bling. 1** make a bubbling noise. **2** speak in a confused, excited manner. [probably imitative]

hat, āge, fär; let, ēqual, tėrm; it, īce
hot, ōpen, ôrder; oil, out; cup, pút, rüle,
əbove, takən, pencəl, lemən, circəs

ch, child; ng, long; sh, ship
th, thin; ŦH, then; zh, measure

bur·bot (bėr′bət) *n., pl.* **-bot** or **-bots.** a freshwater fish having a slender body, related to the cod. [< F *bourbotte* < L *barba* beard; influenced by F *bourbe* mud]

bur·den¹ (bėr′dən) *n., v.—n.* **1** something carried; a load of things, duty, work, etc. **2** anything difficult to carry or bear; a heavy load. **3** the quantity of freight that a ship can carry; the mass of a ship's cargo.
—*v.* **1** put a burden on; load. **2** load too heavily; oppress. [OE *byrthen.* Related to BEAR¹.]
☛ *Syn. n.* **1.** See note at **load.**

bur·den² (bėr′dən) *n.* **1** the main idea or message: *The burden of his speech was the conservation of our natural resources.* **2** a repeated verse in a song; chorus; refrain. [< MF *bourdon* humming, drone of bagpipe < LL *burda* pipe]

burden of proof the obligation of proving a statement or accusation that has been made. In any court case, the burden of proof lies with the accuser.

bur·den·some (bėr′dən səm) *adj.* hard to bear; very heavy or oppressive: *a burdensome tax, burdensome duties.*
—**bur′den·some·ly,** *adv.*—**bur′den·some·ness,** *n.*
☛ *Syn.* See note at **heavy.**

bur·dock (bėr′dok′) *n.* any of a genus (*Arctium*) of weedy herbs of the composite family, having broad, heart-shaped leaves and prickly fruits. [< *bur* + *dock⁴*]

bu·reau (byúr′ō) *n., pl.* **bu·reaus** or **bu·reaux** (byúr′ōz). **1** dresser. **2** a desk or writing table with drawers. **3** a certain kind of office or business: *a travel bureau.* **4** *Esp.U.S.* a branch of a government department. [< F *bureau* desk (originally cloth-covered) < OF *burel,* dim. of *bure* coarse woollen cloth < LL *burra*]

bu·reauc·ra·cy (byü rok′rə sē) *n., pl.* **-cies. 1** government by groups of officials. **2** the officials administering the government. **3** an excessive concentration of power in administrative offices. **4** excessive insistence on rigid routine; red tape.

bu·reau·crat (byúr′ə krat′) *n.* **1** an official in a bureaucracy. **2** a formal, pretentious government official. [blend of *bureau* + auto*crat*]

bu·reau·crat·ic (byúr′ə krat′ik) *adj.* **1** having to do with a bureaucracy or a bureaucrat. **2** arbitrary.—**bu′reau·crat′i·cal·ly,** *adv.*

bu·rette or **bu·ret** (byü ret′) *n.* a graduated glass tube with a valve at the bottom, used for accurately measuring out small amounts of a liquid or gas. [< F *burette,* dim. *buire* vase]

burg or **burgh** (bėrg) *n. Informal.* a town or city. [var. of *borough*]
☛ *Hom.* **berg.**

bur·geon (bėr′jən) *v., n.—v.* **1** bud; sprout: *burgeoning leaves.* **2** grow; flourish: *the burgeoning talent of the young painter.*—*n.* a bud or sprout. [ME < OF *burjon,* apparently < Gmc.]

bur·ger (bėr′gər) *n.* a citizen of a burgh or town; citizen.
☛ *Hom.* **burgher.**

–burger *combining form.* **1** a fried or grilled patty of —— in a split bun: *fishburger.* **2** a hamburger (def. 2) with ——: *cheeseburger.*

bur·gess (bėr′jis) *n.* **1** the citizen of a borough. **2** *Cdn.* in Saskatchewan, a property owner who has the right to vote on money by-laws in a municipality. [ME < OF *burgeis* < LL *burgensis* citizen. Doublet of BOURGEOIS¹.]

burgh (bėrg) *n.* **1** burg. **2** in some countries, a chartered town. [var. of *borough*]

burgh·er (bėr′gər) *n.* a citizen of a burgh or town; citizen.
☛ *Hom.* **burger.**

bur·glar (bėr′glər) *n.* a person who breaks into a dwelling to steal or commit some other crime. [< Anglo-L *burglator,* ? partly < OE *burgbryce*]

bur·glar·i·ous (bėr gler′ē əs) *adj.* having to do with burglary.
—**bur·glar′i·ous·ly,** *adv.*

bur·glar·ize (bėr′glər īz′) *v.* **-ized, -iz·ing.** *Informal.* break into (a dwelling) to steal.

bur·glar·proof (bėr′glər prüf′) *adj.* so strong or safe that burglars cannot break in.

bur·glar·y (bèr′glər ē) *n., pl.* **-glar·ies.** the act or criminal offence of breaking into a dwelling to steal or commit some other crime.

bur·gle (bèr′gəl) *v.* **-gled, -gling.** *Informal.* burglarize. [< *burglar*]

bur·go·mas·ter (bèr′gə mas′tər) *n.* in the Netherlands, Flanders, and Germany, the mayor of a town. [< Du. *burgemeester* < *burg* borough + *meester* master]

Bur·gun·di·an (bèr gun′dē ən) *n., adj.,—n.* a native or inhabitant of Burgundy, a region in E France.—*adj.* of or having to do with Burgundy or its people.

Bur·gun·dy (bèr′gən dē) *n., pl.* **-dies. 1** a red or white wine made in Burgundy, a region in E France. **2** a similar wine made elsewhere.

bur·i·al (ber′ē əl) *n.* **1** the act or process of putting a dead body in a grave, in a tomb, or in the sea; burying. **2** (*adjl.*) of or having to do with burying: *a burial service.*

burial ground a graveyard or cemetery.

burke (bèrk) *v.* **burked, burk·ing. 1** murder by suffocation so as to leave no marks on the body. **2** suppress; hush up. [< William Burke (1792-1829), hanged for murder; he suffocated his victims so that he could sell their unmarked bodies for dissection]

burl (bèrl) *n., v.—n.* a knot in wool, cloth, or wood.—*v.* remove knots from. [< MF *bourle* < LL *burra* flock of wool] ☛ **Hom. birl.**

bur·lap (bèr′lap) *n.* coarse and heavy plain-weave fabric made of jute, hemp, or cotton, used mainly for making sacks, wall coverings, and draperies, and sometimes clothing. [origin uncertain]

bur·lesque (bèr lesk′) *n., adj., v.* **-lesqued, -les·quing;—n. 1** a literary or dramatic composition in which a serious subject is treated ridiculously, or with mock seriousness: *The movie is a burlesque of the classical detective story.* **2** a cheap or debasing imitation or representation; mockery: *making a burlesque of parliamentary democracy.* **3** theatre entertainment featuring broadly humorous or bawdy skits or jokes, striptease, etc. —*adj.* of, having to do with, or characteristic of burlesque. —*v.* imitate or represent in a humorous or mocking way. [< F < Ital. *burlesco* < *burla* jest]—**bur·les′quer,** *n.*

bur·ley or **Bur·ley** (bèr′lē) *n., pl.* **-leys.** a kind of thin-leaved tobacco.

bur·ly (bèr′lē) *adj.* **-li·er, -li·est. 1** big, strong, and sturdy; husky. **2** bluff; rough. [OE *borlīce* excellently]—**bur′li·ly,** *adv.* —**bur′li·ness,** *n.*

Bur·man (bèr′mən) *n.* or *adj.* Burmese.

Bur·mese (bèr mēz′) *n., pl.* **-mese;** *adj.—n.* **1** a native or inhabitant of Burma, a country in SE Asia. **2** the Sino-Tibetan language of the Burmese. **3** Burmese cat. —*adj.* of or having to do with Burma, its people, or their language.

Burmese cat a breed of cat resembling the Siamese but having a dark-brown or grey coat.

burn[1] (bèrn) *v.* **burned** or **burnt, burn·ing;** *n.—v.* **1** be on fire; use up fuel while giving off heat and light and gases; blaze: *The campfire burned all night.* **2** set on fire; cause to burn, especially in order to destroy: *They raked up all the leaves and burned them.* **3** be destroyed or ruined by fire or heat: *Many important documents were burned in the fire. I forgot the roast and it burned to a crisp.* **4** ruin, damage, or injure by fire, heat, acid, electricity, or radiation: *I burned the roast. He burned his finger when he touched the hot pan.* **5** make or produce by burning: *The cigar ashes burned a hole in the tablecloth.* **6** become sunburned: *Do you burn easily?* **7** use as fuel: *The stove burns wood or coal. Our car burns too much gas.* **8** fire (a rocket engine): *The commander gave the order to burn the engines.* **9** give light; shine, as if from fire: *Lamps were burning in every room.* **10** feel hot: *the burning sands of the desert. His forehead burned with fever.* **11** produce or feel pain as if from fire or heat: *My hands were burning from the cold. That ointment burns.* **12** be or become very excited, eager, angry, etc.: *burning with enthusiasm, burning with resentment. It made me burn to see the way he got the better of them.* **13** *Informal.* make angry or annoyed (*usually used with* **up**): *Her smug attitude really burns me up.* **14** harden glaze, etc. by fire or heat: *to burn bricks.* **15** transform into energy by metabolism (*usually used with* **off** *or* **up**): *He's trying to burn off some weight by jogging.* **16** cauterize.

burn down, a burn to the ground: *Their house burned down but most of their possessions were saved.* **b** burn less strongly as fuel gets low: *We had to get more wood because the fire was beginning to burn down.*

burn (one's) boats or **bridges,** cut off all means of retreat for oneself; commit oneself to a particular course: *She burned her boats when she resigned from her old job before she had found a new one.*

burn out, a destroy the inside or contents of by burning: *The store*
was completely burned out, leaving just a shell. **b** cease to burn; become extinguished: *The campfire had burned out and we were in darkness.* **c** make or become unserviceable; make or become worn out, especially through long or improper use: *to burn out a motor. One of the light bulbs is burned out.* **d** deprive of a home through fire: *The family was burned out last year and had to live with relatives for two months. The marauders burned the villagers out of their homes.* **e** bring to a state of physical, mental, or emotional exhaustion: *He burned himself out with worry and overwork.*

burn up, burn completely: *By the time the police got there, the papers were burned up.*

—*n.* **1** an injury caused by fire, heat, acid, electricity, or radiation: *How do you treat a burn?* **2** a burned place or spot: *Those are cigarette burns on the floor.* **3** a sunburn. **4** the firing of a rocket engine, especially to change the course of a spacecraft in flight: *The burn lasted 43 seconds.* [coalescence of OE *beornan* be on fire and OE *bærnan* consume with fire]—**burn′a·ble,** *adj.*

☛ *Syn. v.* **4. Burn, scorch, sear** = to injure or be injured by fire, heat, or acid. **Burn,** the general word, suggests any degree of damage from slight injury to destruction by fire, heat, or acid: *The toast burned.* **Scorch** = to burn the surface enough to discolor it, sometimes to damage the texture, by heat or fire: *The cigarette scorched the paper.* **Sear** = to burn or scorch the surface enough to dry or harden it, by heat, fire, or acid, and applies particularly to burning the tissues of people or animals: *Wounds are cauterized by searing.*

☛ *Usage.* **Burn.** The past tense and past participle of **burn** are either **burned** or **burnt.** Many people keep **burned** for the verb and use **burnt** when the participle is adjectival: *They hastily burned all the old letters before they left. The partially burnt papers gave us little help in solving the mystery.*

burn[2] (bèrn) *n.* Scottish. a small stream; creek; brook. [OE *burna*]

burn·er (bèr′nər) *n.* **1** the part of a stove, furnace, etc. where the flame or heat is produced. **2** an apparatus or part that works by burning: *an oil burner. A combustion chamber in a jet engine is sometimes called a burner.* **3** any person or thing that burns. **on the back burner,** *Informal.* in or into a state of temporary inactivity; in or into abeyance: *The issue was put on the back burner until after the election.*

burn·ing (bèr′ning) *adj.* **1** glowing hot; hot. **2** vital; urgent. —**burn′ing·ly,** *adv.*

burning glass a convex lens used to produce heat or set fire to a substance by focussing the sun's rays on it.

bur·nish (bèr′nish) *v.* or *n.* polish; shine. [ME < OF *burniss-*, a stem of *burnir* make brown, polish < *burn* brown < Gmc.] —**bur′nish·er,** *n.*

bur·noose or **bur·nous** (bèr nüs′ *or* bèr′nüs) *n.* **1** a long, loose cloak with a hood, traditionally worn by Arabs and Moors. **2** a similar garment worn by women or men for casual wear. [< F *burnous* < Arabic *burnus*]

burn·out (bèrn′out′) *n.* **1** a failure due to burning or extreme heat. **2** the termination of operation of a jet or rocket engine, either the fuel has been used up or shut off. **3** the point at which burnout occurs.

burn·sides or **Burn·sides** (bèrn′sīdz) *n.pl.* a growth of hair on the cheeks but not on the chin. Also, **sideburns.** [after Gen. A. E. *Burnside*]

burnt (bèrnt) *v.* a pt. and a pp. of **burn**[1].
☛ *Usage.* See note at **burn**[1].

burnt offering 1 the burning of an animal, harvest, fruits, etc. on an altar as a religious sacrifice. **2** anything offered as a sacrifice.

burnt sienna 1 a dark-brown color. **2** a pigment of this color, especially when made by burning raw sienna to powder.

burnt umber 1 a reddish-brown color. **2** a pigment of this color.

bur oak a white oak (*Quercus macrocarpa*) of central and E North America having acorns partly enclosed in a deep cup covered with large, knobby scales.

burp (bèrp) *Informal. n., v.—n.* a belch.—*v.* **1** belch. **2** cause to belch: *to burp a baby.* [imitative]

burr[1] or **bur** (bèr) *n., v.—n.* **1** the prickly, clinging seedcase, fruit husk, or flowers of various plants. **2** a plant bearing burrs. **3** a person or thing that clings like a burr. **4** a rough ridge or edge left by a tool on metal, wood, etc. after cutting or drilling it. **5** any of several small cutting tools with a rough head, such as a dentist's drill. —*v.* remove burrs from. [ME, probably < Scand.; cf. Danish *borre* burdock]—**bur′ry,** *adj.* ☛ *Hom.* **birr.**

burr[2] (bèr) *n., v.—n.* **1** a prominent trilling of *r*, as in Scottish pronunciation. **2** a pronunciation in which *r* sounds are trilled: *a Scottish burr.* **3** a whirring sound. —*v.* **1** pronounce *r* with a trill: *He burrs his r's.* **2** speak with a burr. **3** make a whirring sound. [probably imitative]—**bur′ry,** *adj.* ☛ *Hom.* **birr.**

burr[3] (bèr) *n.* **1** a washer placed on the end of a rivet before swaging it. **2** a disk or blank punched out of a sheet of metal. [ME

burwe circle < Scand.; cf. Icelandic *borg* wall]
☞ *Hom.* **birr.**

bur·ro (bĕr′ō) *n., pl.* **-ros.** a small donkey, especially one used as a beast of burden in Latin America and the SW United States. [< Sp. *burro* < *burrico* small horse < LL *burricus*]
☞ *Hom.* **borough, burrow.**

bur·row (bĕr′ō) *n., v.—n.* **1** a hole dug in the ground by an animal for refuge or shelter: *Rabbits live in burrows.* **2** a similar passage for dwelling, shelter, or refuge.
—v. **1** dig a hole in the ground: *The mole soon burrowed out of sight.* **2** live in burrows. **3** hide. **4** dig; make burrows in: *Rabbits have burrowed the ground near the river.* **5** search. [cf. OE *beorg* burial place, *byrgen* grave]
☞ *Hom.* **borough, burro.**

bur·row·er (bĕr′ō ər) *n.* one who burrows.

bur·sa (bĕr′sə) *n., pl.* **-sae** (-sē *or* -sī) *or* **-sas.** a sac or pouch in the body, especially one located between joints and containing a lubricating fluid. [< LL *bursa* < Gk. *byrsa* hide, wineskin. Doublet of BOURSE, PURSE.]

bur·sar (bĕr′sər *or* bĕr′sär) *n.* a treasurer, especially of a university or college. [< Med.L *bursarius* < LL *bursa* purse]

bur·sa·ry (bĕr′sə rē) *n., pl.* **-ries.** **1** a grant of money to a student at a college or university. **2** a treasury, especially of a college or university.

bur·si·tis (bər sī′tis) *n.* inflammation of a bursa, usually in the shoulder or the hip. [*bursa* + *-itis*]

burst (bĕrst) *v.* **burst, burst·ing;** *n.—v.* **1** fly apart suddenly and with force; explode; break open: *The balloon burst when it touched the light bulb.* **2** be full to the breaking point: *The granaries were bursting with grain. He is bursting with enthusiasm.* **3** go, come, do, etc. by force or suddenly: *He burst into the room.* **4** open suddenly or violently: *The trees burst into bloom after the rain. The door burst open. She burst the lock with a screwdriver.* **5** act or change suddenly in a way suggesting a break or explosion: *She burst into loud laughter.* **6** cause to break open or into pieces; shatter: *to burst a blood vessel. The prisoner burst his chains.*
—n. **1** a sudden and violent issuing forth; sudden opening to view or sight. **2** a bursting; split; explosion. **3** an outbreak: *a burst of laughter.* **4** a sudden display of activity or energy: *a burst of speed.* **5** a series of shots fired by one pressure of the trigger of an automatic weapon. [OE *berstan*]

bur·then (bĕr′THən) *n. or v. Archaic.* burden[1].

bur·weed (bĕr′wēd′) *n.* any of various plants having burrs, such as a cocklebur or burdock.

bur·y (bĕr′ē) *v.* **bur·ied, bur·y·ing.** **1** put a dead body in the earth, a tomb, etc., usually with a ceremony of some kind. **2** cover up with earth or some other material: *The treasure was buried under the old oak tree. We found the essay buried under a lot of papers.* **3** hide from view: *He buried his face in his hands. The story of her exploits was buried in the back pages of the newspaper.* **4** occupy oneself with great concentration: *She buried herself in her work.* **5** put out of mind; put an end to: *They buried their differences and became friends again.* [OE *byrgan*]**—bur′i·er,** *n.*
☞ *Hom.* **berry.**

bus (bus) *n., pl.* **bus·es** *or* **bus·ses;** *v.* **bused** *or* **bussed, bus·ing** *or* **bus·sing.—n.** **1** a large motor vehicle with seats inside and sometimes also on the roof, used to carry passengers along a certain route. **2** *Informal.* an automobile or airplane. **3** (*adj.*) of, having to do with, or for buses: *a bus driver, a bus depot.*
miss the bus, *Slang.* lose an opportunity.
—v. transport or travel by bus: *He buses to work. We were bused to another airport.* [short for *omnibus*]

bus. business.

bus boy a waiter's assistant. He brings bread and butter, fills glasses, carries off dishes, etc.

bus·by (buz′bē) *n., pl.* **-bies.** **1** a tall fur hat with a cloth bag hanging from the top over the right side, worn by hussar regiments. **2** bearskin (def. 2).

bush (bŭsh) *n., v., adj.—n.* **1** any woody plant having many separate branches starting from or near the ground; shrub: *A bush is usually smaller than a tree.* **2** forested wilderness, especially the vast forests beyond settled areas. **3** *Cdn.* a tree-covered area on a farm; a bush lot or woodlot: *The bush was right behind the houses.* **4** *Cdn.* on the Prairies, wooded land on the edge of the plains: *There's more bush west of here.*
beat around (or **about**) **the bush,** approach a matter in a roundabout way; not come straight to the point: *Tell me the truth right away and don't beat around the bush.*
—v. **1** spread out like a bush; grow thickly (*often used with* **out**). **2** set (ground) with bushes; cover with bushes. **3** *Informal.* exhaust completely. **4** *Cdn.* set out bushes or small trees to mark (a route) across a frozen river, lake, etc. (*often used with* **out**).

hat, āge, fär; let, ēqual, tėrm; it, īce
hot, ōpen, ôrder; oil, out; cup, pŭt, rüle,
əbove, takən, pencəl, lemən, circəs
ch, child; ng, long; sh, ship
th, thin; ŦH, then; zh, measure

—adj. Slang. unpolished; rough-and-ready; suited to a bush league: *The course, the play, and the golfers were all bush.* [ME *busch*, var. of *busk* < ON *buskr* < Gmc. **busk-*]

bush·craft (bŭsh′kraft′) *n.* knowledge of how to keep alive and find one's way in the bush.

bushed (bŭsht) *adj.* **1** lost in the bush. **2** *Informal. Cdn.* acting strangely as a result of having been isolated from people. **3** *Informal.* exhausted.

bush·el[1] (bŭsh′əl) *n.* **1** a unit for measuring the volume of grain, fruit, vegetables, and other dry things, equal to about 0.036 m³. One bushel is equal to 4 pecks or 32 quarts. **2** a container holding a bushel. [ME < OF *boissiel*, dim. of *boisse* a measure]

bush·el[2] (bŭsh′əl) *v.* **-elled** *or* **-eled, -el·ling** *or* **-el·ing.** repair or alter (clothing). [origin uncertain]**—bush′el·ler** *or* **bush′el·er,** *n.*

Bu·shi·do *or* **bu·shi·do** (bü′shē dō′) *n.* in Japan, the moral code of the feudal knights and warriors; chivalry. In its fully developed form, Bushido lasted from the 12th to the 19th centuries. [< Japanese *bushi* warrior + *do* way]

bush·ing (bŭsh′ing) *n.* **1** a removable metal lining used to protect parts of machinery from wear. **2** a metal lining inserted in a hole, pipe, etc. to reduce its size. **3** a lining for a hole, to insulate one or more wires or other electrical conductors passing through. [< *bush* bushing < MDu. *busse* box]

bush league *Slang.* **1** *Baseball.* a minor league. **2** any second-rate or unimportant group or organization: *Her brilliant performance in court shows that this lawyer is no longer in the bush league.*—**bush′-league′,** *adj.*—**bush leaguer,** *n.*

bush line *Cdn.* an airline that transports freight and passengers over the northern bush country.

bush lot *Cdn.* that part of a farm where the trees have been left standing to provide firewood, fence posts, etc.; woodlot.

bush·man (bŭsh′mən) *n., pl.* **-men.** **1** *Australian.* a settler in the bush. **2** a person who knows much about living in the woods; woodsman. **3 Bushman, a** a member of a nomadic people of SW Africa: *The Bushmen were traditionally hunters.* **b** any of the Khoisan languages spoken by the Bushmen.

bush partridge *Cdn.* a bird found in Canada and the N United States; spruce grouse.

bush pilot *Cdn.* an aviator who does most of his flying in the bush country of the far north.

bush·rang·er (bŭsh′rān′jər) *n.* **1** a person who lives in the bush. **2** *Australian.* a criminal who hides in the bush and lives by robbery.

bush telegraph 1 any of various means of communication between natives in wild country: *The call to arms seemed to have spread instantly over the whole area by the amazing bush telegraph.* **2** grapevine (def. 2): *I heard on the bush telegraph that you were being nominated for president of our club.*

bush·whack (bŭsh′wak′ *or* -hwak′) *v.* **1** live or work in the bush or backwoods. **2** beat, cut, or make one's way through the bush. **3** ambush or raid, as in guerrilla warfare.

bush·whack·er (bŭsh′wak′ər *or* -hwak′ər) *n.* **1** a person who lives or works in the bush or backwoods. **2** a scythe for cutting bushes. **3** a guerilla fighter.

bush·work·er (bŭsh′wėrk′ər) *n. Cdn.* a person who works in the bush, especially a lumberjack.

bush·y (bŭsh′ē) *adj.* **bush·i·er, bush·i·est. 1** spreading out like a bush; growing thickly: *a bushy beard.* **2** overgrown with bushes: *a bushy hill.*—**bush′i·ness,** *n.*

bus·ied (biz′ēd′) *v.* pt. and pp. of **busy.**

bus·i·ly (biz′ə lē) *adv.* in a busy manner; actively.

busi·ness (biz′nis) *n.* **1** activities of buying and selling; trade; commercial dealings: *This store does a big business.* **2** a commercial enterprise; an industrial establishment: *a bakery business. They sold their business for ten million dollars.* **3** whatever one is busy at; one's work or occupation: *Business comes before pleasure.* **4** a matter or affair: *His dismissal was a sad business.* **5** the right to act; responsibility: *It's not your business to decide what he should do.* **6** *Theatre.* a movement or action in a play to add realism, reveal character, etc.
mean business, *Informal.* be in earnest; be serious.

mind (one's) **own business,** avoid interfering in the affairs of others. [< *busy* + *-ness*]
☞ *Syn.* 1. See note at **occupation.**

business card a calling card for use in business, printed with the owner's name, position, business address and telephone number, etc.

business college an institution that gives training in business-related subjects, especially secretarial skills such as shorthand, typewriting, and office procedures.

business end *Informal.* the area or part of something that does the important or essential work: *The nib is the business end of a pen.*

busi·ness·like (biz′nis lik′) *adj.* having system and method; well-managed; practical: *He ran his store in a businesslike manner.*

busi·ness·man (biz′nis man′ *or* biz′nis mən) *n., pl.* **-men. 1** a man in business. **2** a man who is good at business: *He's no businessman.*

business school business college.

busi·ness·wom·an (biz′nis wŭm′ən) *n., pl.* **-wom·en. 1** a woman in business. **2** a woman who is good at business: *She's more of a businesswoman than her mother.*

busk·er (bus′kər) *n. Brit.* a strolling entertainer of passers-by, theatre queues, etc. [< dial. *busk* peddle, provide entertainment, etc.]

bus·kin (bus′kin) *n.* **1** a boot reaching to the calf or knee, especially an open laced boot worn in ancient times. **2** a similar boot having a very thick sole, worn by actors in Greek and Roman tragedies. **3** tragedy; tragic drama. [probably < OF *brousequin* < MDu. *brosekin*]

bus·man (bus′mən) *n.* a conductor or driver of a bus.

busman's holiday a holiday spent in doing something similar to what one does at one's daily work: *A letter carrier who goes for a walk on his day off is taking a busman's holiday.*

buss (bus) *v. or n. Archaic or dialect.* kiss.

bus·ses (bus′iz) *n.* a pl. of **bus.**

bust¹ (bust) *n.* **1** a piece of sculpture representing a person's head, shoulders, and chest. **2** the breasts of a woman. **3** the measurement around a woman's body at the level of the breasts: *a 92-centimetre bust.* [< F < Ital. < L *bustum* funeral monument]

bust² (bust) *v.* **1** *Slang or dialect.* burst. **2** *Slang.* make or become bankrupt. **3** *Informal.* punch; hit: *He busted me on the nose.* **4** *Slang.* arrest: *She was busted for possessing stolen goods.* **5** *Slang.* reduce to a lower rank; demote: *He was busted to private.* **6** *Slang.* break or break down: *Don't bust my watch.* **7** tame: *bronco busting.* **8** break up (a monopoly, etc.).
—*n.* **1** *Slang.* a failure; flop. **2** *Informal.* a punch: *I gave him a bust on the head.* **3** *Informal.* spree. **4** *Slang.* a raid or arrest. [var. of *burst*]

bus·tard (bus′tərd) *n.* any of a family (Otididae) of large game birds having long legs and heavy bodies, found on the deserts and plains of Africa, Europe, and Asia. [blend of OF *bistarde* and *oustarde,* both < L *avis tarda* slow bird]

–busted *combining form.* having a certain kind of bust: *small-busted* = having a small bust.

bust·er (bus′tər) *n. Slang.* **1** boy, fellow, etc. (*used as a form of address*): *Look, buster, don't talk to me like that.* **2** something remarkable or outstanding. **3** a dashing fellow. **4** a wild frolic; spree. **5** *Australian.* a terrific gale.

bus·tle¹ (bus′əl) *v.* **-tled, -tling;** *n.*—*v.* **1** be noisily busy and in a hurry. **2** make (others) hurry or work hard.—*n.* noisy or excited activity: *There was a great bustle as the party broke up.* [? imitative]—**bus′tler,** *n.*
☞ *Syn. n.* See note at **stir¹.**

bus·tle² (bus′əl) *n.* a pad or framework used in the late 19th century to puff out the upper back part of a woman's skirts. [? special use of *bustle¹*]

bust–up (bust′up′) *n. Slang.* **1** a quarrel. **2** a fight.

bus·y (biz′ē) *adj.* **bus·i·er, bus·i·est;** *v.* **bus·ied, bus·y·ing.**—*adj.* **1** working; active: *a busy person.* **2** in use: *I tried to phone her but her line was busy.* **3** full of work or activity: *a busy day, a busy street.* **4** *Informal.* having too much design, ornament, etc.: *a busy drawing, busy decoration.* **5** meddlesome.
—*v.* make or keep busy: *The stage hands busied themselves in setting up the stage.* [OE *bisig*]—**bus′y·ness,** *n.*
☞ *Syn. adj.* 1. Busy, industrious, diligent = actively or attentively occupied. **Busy** = habitually active or working steadily or at the moment: *She is a busy woman, and it is hard to get an appointment with her.* **Industrious** =

hard-working by nature or habit: *He is an industrious worker.* **Diligent** = hard-working at a particular thing, usually something one likes or especially wants to do: *She is a diligent mother, and a poor housekeeper.*

bus·y·bod·y (biz′ē bod′ē) *n., pl.* **-bod·ies.** a person who pries into other people's affairs; meddler.

but (but; *unstressed,* bət) *conj., prep., adv., n.*—*conj.* **1** on the other hand; yet: *It rained, but I went anyway.* **2** without the result that; unless: *It never rains but it pours.* **3** other than: *We can do nothing but accept their conditions.* **4** that: *I don't doubt but he will come.* **5** that not: *He is not so sick but he can eat.*
—*prep.* **1** except; save: *He works every day but Sunday.* **2** other than: *No one replied but me.*
—*adv.* no more than; only; merely: *He is but a boy.*
all but, nearly; almost: *The book was all but finished when the author died.*
but for, were it not for; excepting; save: *He was right but for one thing.*
but that, were it not that: *I would have come but that I felt too ill.*
—*n.* objection: *Not so many buts, please.* [OE *būtan* without, unless < *be-* + *ūtan* outside < *ūt* out]
☞ *Hom.* **butt.**
☞ *Syn. conj.* 1. But, however express a relationship in which two things or ideas are thought of as standing in opposition or contrast to each other. **But** expresses the contrast or contradiction clearly and sharply by placing the two things or ideas side by side in perfect balance: *He is sick, but he can eat.* **However** is more formal, and suggests that the second idea should be compared and contrasted with the first: *We have not yet reached a decision; however, our opinion of your plan is favorable.*—*prep.* 1 See note at **except.**

bu·ta·di·ene (byü′tə di′ēn) *n.* a colorless, flammable gas obtained from petroleum, used especially in making synthetic rubber. *Formula:* C_4H_6 [< *butane* + *di-* + *-ene,* chemical suffix (< L *-enus*)]

bu·tane (byü′tān *or* byü tān′) *n.* a colorless, flammable gas obtained from natural gas or petroleum, used as a fuel. *Formula:* C_4H_{10} [< L *butyrum* butter < Gk. *boutyron*]

butch (büch) *n., adj. Slang.*—*n.* **1** a lesbian who is aggressively masculine in dress, manner, etc. **2** a tough or rugged man.—*adj.* aggressively masculine in appearance, manner, etc.

butch·er (büch′ər) *n., v.*—*n.* **1** a person whose work is killing animals to be sold for food. **2** a person who cuts up and sells meat. **3** a brutal killer or murderer. **4** *Informal.* a person who botches or bungles.
—*v.* **1** kill (animals) for food. **2** kill cruelly or needlessly: *Many village inhabitants were butchered in the invasion.* **3** spoil by poor work; botch: *He butchered the song by singing it much too loudly.* [ME < OF *bocher* < *boc* he-goat, buck1 < Gmc.]—**butch′er·er,** *n.*

butcher bird 1 any of various shrikes that impale their prey on thorns or wedge it into cracks in order to feed upon it or store it. **2** any of a genus (*Cracticus*) of Australian songbirds that treat their prey in a similar way.

butch·er·y (büch′ər ē) *n., pl.* **-er·ies. 1** brutal or wholesale killing or murder. **2** a slaughter house; butcher shop. **3** a butcher's work; the act or business of killing animals for food.

bu·te·o (byü′tē ō) *n.* any of a genus (*Buteo*) of hawks found in many parts of the world, having a thick-set body, broad wings, and a short, broad tail. Buteos will soar high in the air for hours while hunting.

but·ler (but′lər) *n.* **1** the chief male servant of a household, whose duties include supervising other servants, directing the serving of meals and personal services for his employers. **2** a male servant in charge of wines and liquors; wine steward. [ME < AF var. of OF *bouteillier* < *bouteille* bottle. See BOTTLE.]

butler's pantry a small room between the kitchen and dining room, for use by a butler, serving maid, etc.

butt¹ (but) *n., v.*—*n.* **1** the thicker end of anything: *The butt of a gun.* **2** the end that is left; a stub or stump: *a cigar butt.* **3** *Slang.* buttocks; rump.
—*v.* extinguish (a cigarette or cigar) by pressing and rubbing the lit end against something (*often used with* **out**). [fusion of ME *but, bott* (related to *buttocks*) and OF *bout* end < Gmc.]
☞ *Hom.* **but.**

butt² (but) *n., v.*—*n.* **1** target. **2** an object of ridicule or scorn: *He was the butt of their jokes.* **3 a** on a rifle, archery, or artillery range, a mound of earth or sawdust behind the target to stop shots. **b** a mound on which an archery target is set. **4** a joint where two boards or timbers meet end to end. **5** a hinge that fits behind two surfaces, as between the door and the jamb. **6** a small, open shelter for grouse shooting. **7 the butts,** a place to practise shooting in.
—*v.* **1** join end to end. **2** attach with a butt hinge. [< F *bout* end < Gmc.]
☞ *Hom.* **but.**

butt³ (but) *v., n.*—*v.* **1** strike or push by knocking hard with the head. **2** place (a timber, etc.) with its end against something; put

(planks, etc.) end to end. **3** cut off the rough ends of (boards, logs, etc.). **4** project; run out; jut (out or into): *One wing of the house butted out as far as the roadway.*
butt in, *Slang.* meddle; interfere.
—*n.* a push or blow with the head. [ME < OF *bouter* thrust < Gmc.]
☞ *Hom.* **but.**

butt⁴ (but) *n.* **1** a large barrel for wine or beer. **2** a former unit for measuring liquids, equal to two hogsheads, about 476 L. [ME < OF *botte* < LL *butta*]
☞ *Hom.* **but.**

butte (byüt) *n. Cdn.* a steep, often flat-topped hill standing alone. Buttes are common in southern Alberta. [< F]

butt–end·ing (but′end′ing) *n. Hockey.* the jabbing or thrusting of the handle end of the stick into an opponent's body.

but·ter (but′ər) *n., v.* —*n.* **1** the solid, yellowish fat obtained by churning cream or whole milk. **2** something like butter in consistency or use: *peanut butter, apple butter, cocoa butter.* **3** *Informal.* flattery.
—*v.* **1** put butter on. **2** *Informal.* flatter in order to get something (*used with* **up**): *We tried buttering him up, but he still wouldn't give us a ride.* [OE *butere* < L *butyrum* < Gk. *boutyron*] —**but′ter·less,** *adj.*

but·ter·ball (but′ər bol′ *or* -bôl′) *n.* **1** bufflehead. **2** *Informal.* a plump person.

but·ter·cup (but′ər kup′) *n.* **1** any of a number of wildflowers (genus *Ranunculus*) found especially in meadows and damp places, having yellow flowers and leaves that are usually deeply lobed. **2** (*adj.*) designating a large family (Ranunculaceae) of annual or perennial plants found in temperate and cold regions, especially in the northern hemisphere, including many herbs, such as the buttercups, columbines, and anemones, and a few woody vines, such as the clematis. The buttercup family is also called the crowfoot family.

but·ter·fat (but′ər fat′) *n.* the fatty content of milk from which butter is made. Whole milk from cows usually contains about 3.8 percent butterfat.

but·ter·fin·gered (but′ər fing′gərd) *adj.* always letting things drop or slip through one's fingers.

but·ter·fin·gers (but′ər fing′gərz) *n. Informal.* a clumsy or awkward person who drops things: *Don't let her handle the china; she's a real butterfingers.*

but·ter·fish (but′ər fish′) *n., pl.* **-fish** *or* **-fish·es.** a gunnel (*Pholis gunnellus*) of coastal regions of the North Atlantic, having a slippery body covered with fine scales.

but·ter·fly (but′ər flī′) *n., pl.* **-flies. 1** any of a large group of about six families of diurnal insects (order Lepidoptera) having a slender body, long, slender antennae with thick, knoblike tips, and four large, often brightly colored wings. Compare **moth. 2** a person who suggests a butterfly by delicate beauty, bright clothes, fickleness, etc. **3** a swimming stroke performed face down, in which the outstretched arms move in a circular motion together while the legs are kicking up and down together. **4 butterflies,** *pl.* an uneasy or queasy feeling caused by nervous anxiety about something that is to happen: *I get butterflies in my stomach just thinking about being in front of all those people.* [OE *buterflēoge*]

butterfly valve a valve consisting of a disk turning on an axis. A damper on a furnace and a throttle valve in a carburetor are examples.

butterfly weed a milkweed (*Asclepias tuberosa*) with orange-colored flowers.

but·ter·milk (but′ər milk′) *n.* **1** the sour, fat-free liquid left after butter has been churned from cream. **2** milk that has been soured by adding certain bacteria.

but·ter·nut (but′ər nut′) *n.* **1** a North American tree (*Juglans cinerea*) of the walnut family. **2** the oily, edible nut of this tree. **3** a brown dye made from butternut bark.

but·ter·scotch (but′ər skoch′) *n., adj.* —*n.* a candy made from brown sugar and butter. —*adj.* flavored with brown sugar and butter.

butter tart *Cdn.* a rich, sweet tart having a filling made from butter, brown sugar, corn syrup, raisins, spices, etc. Recipes for butter tarts vary somewhat and the filling may be runny or firm.

but·ter·wort (but′ər wèrt′) *n.* any of a genus (*Pinguicula*) of herbs of the bladderwort family having fleshy leaves that secrete a sticky substance that traps insect prey and digests it.

but·ter·y,¹ (but′ər ē) *adj.* **1** like butter. **2** containing butter; spread with butter. [< *butter*]

but·ter·y² (but′ər ē *or* but′rē) *n., pl.* **-ter·ies.** pantry. [ME < OF *boterie* < *botte* butt⁴ < LL *butta*]

but·tocks (but′əks) *n.pl.* the fleshy hind part of the body where the legs join the back; rump. [OE *buttuc* end, small piece of land]

hat, āge, fär; let, ēqual, tèrm; it, īce
hot, ōpen, ôrder; oil, out; cup, pùt, rüle;
əbove, takən, pencəl, lemən, circəs

ch, child; ng, long; sh, ship
th, thin; ᴛʜ, then; zh, measure

but·ton (but′ən) *n., v.* —*n.* **1** a knob or disk of plastic, metal, wood, etc. fixed on clothing or other things, serving to hold parts together when passed through a buttonhole or loop, or used simply to decorate. **2** a knob or small disk or plate that is pushed or turned to open or close an electric circuit: *an elevator button. You push that button to start the machine.* **3** a usually round badge of metal or plastic having a catchword, slogan, logo, etc. printed on it, and a pin at the back, for attaching to clothing: *The publisher was giving away buttons to promote the new book.* **4** anything that resembles or suggests a button. **5** a young or undeveloped mushroom. **6** a small knob on the end of a fencing foil. **7** *Slang.* the centre of the chin, especially as a target for a blow. **8 buttons,** *pl., Brit. Informal.* a bellboy or page in a hotel, etc.
on the button, *Informal.* exactly; precisely: *He was there at five o'clock on the button.*
—*v.* **1** close or fasten with buttons. **2** have buttons for fastening: *The dress buttons down the front.*
button up, *Informal.* complete satisfactorily: *button up the details of a contract.*
[ME < OF *boton* < *bouter* thrust. See BUTT³.] —**but′ton·less,** *adj.* —**but′ton·like′,** *adj.*

but·ton·ball (but′ən bol′ *or* but′ən bôl′) *n.* the common North American sycamore tree (*Platanus occidentalis*).

but·ton·hole (but′ən hōl′) *n., v.* **-holed, -hol·ing.** —*n.* **1** the slit through which a button is passed. **2** a flower or flowers worn in a buttonhole.
—*v.* **1** make buttonholes in. **2** sew with the stitch used in making buttonholes. **3** force someone to listen, as if by holding him by the buttonhole of his coat: *He buttonholed me as I tried to sneak out of the room.*

but·ton·hook (but′ən hùk′) *n.* a hook for pulling the buttons of shoes, gloves, etc. through the buttonholes.

but·ton·wood (but′ən wùd′) *n.* buttonball; sycamore.

Buttresses.
The one on the left
is a flying buttress.

but·tress (but′ris) *n., v.* —*n.* **1** a structure built against a wall or building to strengthen or support it. **2** something resembling a buttress, such as a projecting rock. **3** any support; prop: *The experience was a buttress to his faith.*
—*v.* **1** strengthen with a buttress. **2** support and strengthen; bolster: *The pilot's report of the flight was buttressed with photographs.* [ME < OF *bouterez* (pl.) < *bouter* thrust against. See BUTT³.]

bu·tyl (byü′təl) *n.* one of the three univalent radicals obtained from butane. Butyl is used in making inner tubes, insulation for electrical appliances, etc. *Formula:* C_4H_9

bu·ty·lene (byü′tə lēn′) *n.* a gaseous hydrocarbon of the ethylene series, often used in making synthetic rubber. *Formula:* C_4H_8

bu·ty·rate (byü′ti rāt′) *n.* any salt or ester of butyric acid.

bu·tyr·ic acid (byü tir′ik) a colorless liquid that has an unpleasant odor and is formed by fermentation in rancid butter, cheese, etc. *Formula:* $C_4H_8O_2$ [*butyric* < L *butyrum* butter < Gk. *boutyron*]

bux·om (buk′səm) *adj.* vigorously healthy and plump, used especially of a full-bosomed woman. [ME *buhsum* < OE *būgan* bend]

buy (bī) *v.* **bought, buy·ing;** *n.* —*v.* **1** get by paying a price: *You can buy a pencil for 20 cents.* **2** buy things. **3** bribe: *It was charged that two members of the jury had been bought.* **4** *Informal.* accept as valid, feasible, etc.: *If you say it's true, I'll buy it.*

buy into, obtain an interest or footing in by purchase: *He bought into the new aluminum company, obtaining 500 shares.*
buy off, get rid of by paying money to.
buy out, buy all the shares, rights, etc. of.
buy up, buy all that one can of; buy.
—*n.* **1** *Informal.* something bought; a purchase. **2** *Informal.* a bargain. [OE *bycgan*]
☛ *Hom.* **by, bye.**
☛ *Syn. v.* **1. Buy, purchase** = to get something by paying a price. **Buy** is the general word: *A person can buy anything in that store if he has the money.* **Purchase** is used in more formal style and suggests buying after careful planning or business dealings or on a large scale: *The bank has purchased some property on which to construct a new building.*
☛ *Usage.* **Buy** is used with *from* but, informally, also with *off*. *He bought it from a stranger he met on the street.* (Informal.) *He bought it off a kid at work.*
buy·er (bī′ər) *n.* **1** a person who buys. **2** a person whose work is buying goods, especially for a retail store.
buyer's market an economic situation in which the buyer has the advantage because goods are plentiful and prices tend to be low.
buzz (buz) *n., v.* —*n.* **1** a humming sound made by flies, mosquitoes, or bees. **2** a low, indistinct, murmuring sound of many people talking quietly: *The buzz of conversation stopped when the teacher entered the room.* **3** *Informal.* a telephone call: *Give me a buzz tonight.* **4** a busy movement; stir; state of activity or excitement. **b** the sound of such activity.
—*v.* **1** make a loud, steady humming sound on one pitch: *The radio needs to be fixed; it buzzes when you turn it on.* **2** make a low, indistinct murmuring sound: *The whole room buzzed with the news of the class excursion.* **3** murmur; whisper: *"Here they come," he buzzed in my ear.* **4** approach quickly and closely with an aircraft or a small boat: *A pilot buzzed our school yesterday.* **5** signal by pressing a buzzer: *She buzzed her secretary.* **6** *Informal.* to telephone: *I'll buzz you when I find out.*
buzz about, move about busily.
buzz off, *Slang.* go away.
[imitative]
buz·zard (buz′ərd) *n.* **1** any of several species of vulture of the western hemisphere, especially the turkey vulture, or turkey buzzard. **2** *Esp.Brit.* buteo. [ME < OF *busart*, ult. < L *buteo* hawk]
buzz bomb a type of unguided missile heavily loaded with explosives and propelled by a pulsejet, that was invented in Germany and used against England in World War II, especially in the bomb attacks on London. [with reference to the buzzing sound it made]
buzz·er (buz′ər) *n.* **1** something that buzzes, especially an electric device that makes a buzzing sound as a signal. **2** the sound of a buzzer: *At the buzzer, they all rushed from the room.*
buzz saw a circular saw.
B.V.M. Blessed Virgin Mary (for L *Beata Virgo Maria*).
B.W.I. British West Indies.
bx. box.
by (bī) *prep., adv., adj., n.* —*prep.* **1** near; beside: *The garden is by the house.* **2** along; over; through: *to go by the bridge.* **3** through the action of: *the thief was captured by a policeman. The house was destroyed by fire.* **4** through the means or use of: *They keep in touch by letter. He never travels by plane.* **5** combined with in multiplication or relative dimensions: *a room five by ten metres.* **6** in the measure of: *Eggs are sold by the dozen.* **7** to the extent of: *larger by half.* **8** according to: *They all work by the rules.* **9** in relation to: *She did well by her children.* **10** taken separately as units or groups in a series: *two by two. Algebra must be mastered step by step.* **11** during: *by day.* **12** not later than: *by six o'clock.* **13** toward: *The island lies south by east from here.*
by (oneself), **a** having no company; alone. **b** single-handed; unaided.
by the way, aside from the main point; incidentally: *By the way, what time is it?*
—*adv.* **1** at hand: *near by.* **2** past: *days gone by. A car dashed by.* **3** aside or away: *to put something by.* **4** *Informal.* at, in, or into another's house when passing: *Please come by and see me when you can.*
by and by, after a while; soon: *You will feel stronger by and by.*
by and large, on the whole; in general: *It has some faults, but by and large it is a good book.*
—*adj.* **1** situated at the side; out of the way. **2** away from the main purpose; secondary; private.
—*n.* See **bye.**
by the by, incidentally.
[OE *bī*]
☛ *Hom.* **buy, bye.**
☛ *Syn. prep.* **3. By, through** (def. 4), **with** (def. 4) = by means of. **By** in this sense is used before words for things: *She travelled by snowmobile.* **Through** is used before words for feelings or conditions or for people considered as intermediaries: *They lost the match through sheer carelessness. We found out through a friend in Vancouver.* **With** is used before things named as instruments: *We cut the meat with a knife.*

by– *combining form.* **1** secondary; minor; less important: *by-product* = *less important product.* **2** near by: *bystander* = *person standing near by.*
by-and-by (bī′ən bī′) *n.* the future.
bye[1] (bī) *n.* **1** *Sports.* **a** the condition of being the odd player or team not required to play one round of a contest in which players or teams are grouped in pairs: *Our team had a bye to the semifinal.* **b** the player or team not required to play a round. **2** *Cricket.* a run made on a missed ball. **3** *Golf.* the holes not played after one player has won.
by the bye, incidentally.
[var. of *by,* prep.]
☛ *Hom.* **buy, by.**
bye[2] or **'bye** (bī) *interj. Informal.* goodbye.
☛ *Hom.* **buy, by.**
bye-bye (bī′bī′) *interj. Informal.* good-bye.
by-e·lec·tion (bī′i lek′shən) *n.* an election held in one riding because of the death or resignation of its Member of Parliament or Legislative Assembly.
by·gone (bī′gon′) *adj., n.* —*adj.* gone by; past; former: *The Romans lived in bygone days.* —*n.* **1** something in the past. **2** the past.
let bygones be bygones, let the past be forgotten.
by-law (bī′lo′ or bī′lô′) *n.* **1** a local law; a law made by a city, company, club, etc. for the control of its own affairs: *Our city has by-laws to control parking, traffic, and building practices.* **2** a secondary law or rule; not one of the main rules. [ME, probably < earlier *byrlaw* < ON *býr* town + *lög* law; meaning influenced by *by-*]
by-line (bī′līn′) *n.* a line at the beginning of a newspaper or magazine article giving the name of the writer.
by·name (bī′nām′) *n.* a secondary name or nickname.
by-pass (bī′pas′) *n., v.* —*n.* **1** a road or passage around or to one side, especially a highway around a city or town. **2** a channel, pipe, etc. for a liquid or gas providing a secondary or alternative passage for a distance and connecting again with the main channel. **3** *Electricity.* a shunt.
—*v.* **1** provide a secondary passage for. **2** make a detour around: *by-pass a city.* **3** ignore an intermediate person or level in order to deal directly with a higher authority. **4** set aside or ignore (regulations, etc.) in order to reach a desired objective. **5** get away from; avoid; escape: *by-pass a question.* **6** *Military.* flank.
by-path (bī′path′) *n.* a side path; byway.
by-play (bī′plā′) *n.* especially in a dramatic production, a secondary action that is carried on on the side while the main action proceeds.
by-prod·uct (bī′prod′əkt) *n.* **1** something of value produced in making or doing something else: *Kerosene is a by-product of petroleum refining.* **2** a side effect; a secondary and sometimes unexpected result: *His new self-confidence is a by-product of his experience as club president.*
byre (bīr) *n.* a cowhouse or cow shed. [OE *byre*]
by-road (bī′rōd′) *n.* a side road.
By·ron·ic (bī ron′ik) *adj.* **1** of or having to do with the English poet George Gordon, Lord Byron (1788-1824), or his poetry. **2** having or showing qualities generally associated with Byron or his poetry; arrogant, cynical, unconventional, romantic, etc.
by·stand·er (bī′stan′dər) *n.* a person who stands near or looks on but does not take part.
by-street (bī′strēt′) *n.* a side street.
byte (bīt) *n. Computer technology.* a sequence of usually six or eight binary digits (bits) processed as a single unit of information by a computer. [probably a blend of *bite* and *bit*[4]. 20c.]
by-way or **by-way** (bī′wā′) *n.* a side path or road; a way that is little used.
by·word (bī′wèrd′) *n.* **1** a common saying; proverb. **2** a person or thing commonly or proverbially taken as typifying a certain characteristic, especially an unfavorable one: *He had become a byword throughout the region.* **3** an object of contempt; something scorned: *His cowardice made him a byword to all who knew him.* [OE *bīword*]
Byz·an·tine (biz′ən tēn′, bi zan′tin, or biz′ən tīn′) *adj., n.* —*adj.* **1** of or having to do with Byzantium, an ancient city on the Bosporus. **2** of or having to do with Byzantine art or architecture. **3** Sometimes, **byzantine,** complex; intricate and devious: *byzantine plots.*
—*n.* **1** a native or inhabitant of Byzantium. **2** *Architecture.* a style developed in Byzantium in the 5th and 6th centuries, characterized by rounded arches, domes, and a lavish use of mosaics and murals. **3** *Art.* a style developed in Byzantium in the 6th century, characterized by brilliant colors, formal designs, and distorted proportions. [< L *Byzantinus*]
Byzantine Empire the eastern part of the Roman Empire after the division in A.D. 395. It ceased to exist after the fall of its capital Constantinople in 1453.
Bz. benzene.

Cc

c or **C** (sē) *n.*, *pl.* **c's** or **C's. 1** the third letter of the English alphabet. **2** any speech sound represented by this letter. **3** a person or thing identified as *c*, especially the third in a series. **4** a person or thing considered as belonging to the third best group: *grade C eggs, C grade in Latin.* **5** *Music.* **a** the first tone in the scale of C major; the third tone of A minor. **b** a symbol representing this tone. **c** a key, string, etc. that produces this tone. **d** the scale or key that has C as its keynote. **6** the Roman numeral for 100. **7** *Algebra.* Usually *c*, the third known quantity: $ax + by + c = 0$. **8** something shaped like the letter C. **9** (*adj.*) of or being a C or c.

c centi- (an SI prefix).

c. 1 cent(s). **2** approximately (for L *circa*). **3** *Sports.* catcher. **4** century. **5** centre. **6** copyright. **7** cubic. **8** *Physics.* capacity. **9** cathode. **10** chapter. **11** current. **12** hundredweight. **13** city.

C 1 Celsius. **2** carbon. **3** central. **4** *Mathematics.* constant.

C. 1 Cape. **2** Catholic. **3** Conservative. **4** Celtic. **5** Church.

C1 chief petty officer 1st class.

C2 chief petty officer 2nd class.

C14 carbon 14.

ca about; approximately (for L *circa*). Also, **c.**

Ca calcium.

CA 1 California. **2** *Psychology.* chronological age.

C.A. 1 Chartered Accountant. **2** Central America. **3** Consular Agent. **4** Court of Appeal.

C/A or **c/a 1** capital account. **2** credit account. **3** current account.

CAA or **C.A.A.** Canadian Automobile Association.

Caa·ba (kä′bə) See **Kaaba.**

C.A.A.P. Certified Advertising Agency Practitioner.

CAAT or **C.A.A.T.** College of Applied Arts and Technology.

cab (kab) *n.* **1** an automobile that can be hired with a driver; taxi. **2** a horse-drawn carriage that can be hired with a driver. **3** the enclosed part of a locomotive, truck, etc. where the operator or driver stands or sits. [a shortened form of *cabriolet*]

CAB or **C.A.B. 1** Canadian Association of Broadcasters. **2** *U.S.* Civil Aeronautics Board.

ca·bal (kə bal′) *n.*, *v.* **-balled, -bal·ling. —n. 1** a small group of people working or plotting in secret. **2** a secret scheme of such a group; plot. —*v.* form such a group; conspire. [< F < Med.L *cabbala.* See **CABALA.**]

cab·a·la (kab′ə lə *or* kə bä′lə) *n.* **1** a secret religious philosophy of the Jewish rabbis, based on a mystical interpretation of the Scriptures. **2** a mystical belief; secret doctrine. [< Med.L *cabbala* < Hebrew *qabbalah* tradition]

cab·a·lis·tic (kab′ə lis′tik) *adj.* **1** of or suitable for the Jewish cabala. **2** having a mystical meaning; secret.

cab·al·le·ro (kab′ə ler′ō *or* kab′əl yer′ō; *Spanish,* kä′bä lyä′rō) *n., pl.* **-ros.** *Spanish.* **1** gentleman. **2** knight. [< Sp. < LL *caballarius* horseman < L *caballus* horse]

ca·ba·ña (kə ban′ə, kə bän′yə *or* kə bä′nə) *n.* **1** cabin (def. 1). **2** bathhouse. [< Sp. < LL *capanna.* Doublet of **CABIN.**]

cab·a·ret (kab′ə rā′ *or* kab′ə rā′) *n.* **1** a restaurant where singing and dancing are provided as entertainment. **2** the entertainment provided there. [< F *cabaret* tavern]

cab·bage (kab′ij) *n.* **1** a cultivated plant (*Brassica oleracea capitata*) having large, round leaves that are closely folded into a compact head growing from a short stem. **2** the head of a cabbage, used as a vegetable. **3** the Mediterranean plant (*Brassica oleracea*) of the mustard family from which the garden cabbage, cauliflower, Brussels sprouts, and broccoli have been developed. [< F *caboche* < Provençal, ult. < L *caput* head]

cabbage rose a Caucasian rose (*Rosa centifolia*) having large, double, very fragrant, pink flowers. It has been a popular garden rose for centuries.

cab·bage·town (kab′ij toun′) *n. Cdn.* a run-down urban area; slum. [< *Cabbagetown*, a depressed area on the east side of the older part of downtown Toronto, so-called from the supposed diet of the area's English population]

cab·by (kab′ē) *n., pl.* **-bies.** *Informal.* cabman.

ca·ber (kä′bər) *n.* a long, heavy pole or beam tossed as a trial of strength in Scottish Highland games. [< Scots Gaelic *cabar*]

cab·in (kab′ən) *n., v.* —*n.* **1** a small, often roughly built house; hut: *a hunting cabin in the woods.* **2** cottage (def. 1). **3** a room for passengers or crew in a ship or boat. **4** a place for passengers in an aircraft. —*v.* **1** live in a cabin. **2** *Archaic.* confine; cramp. [< F *cabane* < LL *capanna.* Doublet of **CABAÑA.**]

cabin boy a boy whose work is to wait on the officers and passengers on a ship.

cabin class a class of accommodation on a passenger ship, above tourist and below first class.

cabin cruiser a motorboat having a cabin and equipped with facilities for living on board.

cab·i·net (kab′ə nit *or* kab′nit) *n.* **1** an upright piece of furniture having shelves or drawers to store or display things: *a china cabinet, a medicine cabinet.* **2** (*adj.*) suitable in value, beauty, etc. for display in a cabinet. **3** an upright case holding a radio or television receiver, record turntable, etc. **4** a body of advisers to a head of state, a prime minister, etc. **5** Usually, **Cabinet**, in Canada: an executive committee of the federal government chosen by the prime minister, from members of the majority party in the House of Commons. Members of the Cabinet have the title of Minister of the Crown. **b** a similar committee of a provincial government. **6** (*adj.*) of or having to do with a political cabinet. **7** *Archaic.* a small private room. **8** (*adj.*) of a size suitable for a small room. [dim. of *cabin*]

cab·i·net·mak·er (kab′ə nit māk′ər *or* kab′nit-) *n.* a person skilled in constructing and finishing fine wooden furniture, especially one who makes it his or her work.

cab·i·net·mak·ing (kab′ə nit māk′ing *or* kab′nit-) *n.* the business, work, or art of a cabinetmaker.

cabinet minister the head of a department of the government of certain countries, including Canada, or of a province; a member of the cabinet.

cab·i·net·work (kab′ə nit wèrk′ *or* kab′nit-) *n.* **1** any beautifully made furniture or woodwork. **2** the making of such furniture and woodwork.

cabin fever *Cdn.* a state of mental depression or hysteria resulting from a long period of isolation and confinement, especially as occurs in isolated parts of the North toward the end of the long, dark winter.

cabin ship a ship carrying only one class of passengers.

ca·ble (kä′bəl) *n., v.* **-bled, -bling.** —*n.* **1** a strong, thick rope, usually made of wires twisted together. **2** the rope or chain by which an anchor is raised and lowered. **3** a cable's length. **4** an insulated bundle of wires made to carry an electric current. Telegraph messages are sent under the ground or under the ocean by cable. **5** a message sent by cable; cablegram. **6** an ornament with a design like that of a cable. **7** cable television. **8** (*adj.*) of or having to do with cable television. —*v.* **1** tie or fasten with a cable. **2** send (a message) by cable. [ME < OF < Provençal < L *capulum* halter]

cable car a car pulled by a moving cable that is operated by an engine.

ca·ble·gram (kä′bəl gram′) *n.* a message sent across the ocean by underwater cable.

cable's length a unit of length traditionally used at sea, defined as 607.56 feet (approx. 184 m) by the Canadian and British navies and 720 feet (approx. 220 m) by the United States navy.

cable stitch *Knitting.* a combination of stitches that produces a pattern resembling a twisted cable.

cable television a system by which signals from various television stations are picked up by a very tall or elevated central antenna and sent by cable to the sets of individual subscribers. A television set that is hooked up to cable television does not need any antenna.

cable TV cable television.

ca·ble·vi·sion (kä′bəl vi′zhən) *n.* cable television.

cab·man (kab′mən) *n., pl.* **-men.** a man who drives a cab.

cab·o·chon (kab′ə shon′) *n.* a rounded, unfaceted, highly polished gem. [<MF *cabochon* < *caboche* head. See CABBAGE.]

ca·boo·dle (kə bü′dəl) *n. Informal.* lot, pack, crowd (*used especially in the phrases* **the whole caboodle, the whole kit and caboodle**): *We put the whole caboodle into one box.*

ca·boose (kə büs′) *n.* **1** a small car on a freight train in which the train crew can work, eat, and sleep. It is usually the last car. **2** a kitchen on the deck of a ship. **3** *Cdn.* a mobile bunkhouse used by loggers, threshing crews, etc. **4** *Cdn.* a horse-drawn vehicle consisting of a small cabin mounted on runners and equipped with benches and a stove: *My aunt remembers driving to school in a caboose in winter.* **5** *Cdn.* in the North, a bunkhouse or cookhouse on runners for the crew of a cat train, etc. **6** *Cdn.* in the North, a portable house. [< Du. *kabuis* wretched hut, cabin < MLG *kabūse*; cf. CAMBOOSE]

cab·o·tage (kab′ə täzh′ *or* kab′ə tij; *French*, kä bô täzh′) *n.* **1** navigation or trade between ports along a coast. **2** transportation or trade between points within one country. [< F *cabotage* coastal trade < *caboter* sail along a coast]

cab·o·teur (kab′ə tèr′; *French*, kä bô tær′) *n. Cdn.* **1** a ship engaged in coastal trade, especially along the St. Lawrence River and in the Gulf of St. Lawrence. **2** a captain or a member of the crew of such a ship. [< Cdn.F < F. See CABOTAGE.]

cab·ri·ole (kab′rē ōl′) *n., adj.* —*n.* a curved, tapering furniture leg with a decorated foot, characteristic of Queen Anne and Chippendale furniture. The foot was usually carved as a claw grasping a ball. —*adj.* **1** in this style. **2** having such legs. [< F *cabriole*, var. of *capriole* a leap, because it resembled the foreleg of an animal making a capriole]

cab·ri·o·let (kab′rē ə lā′) *n.* **1** an automobile resembling a coupé but having a folding top. **2** a light one-horse carriage with one or two seats, two wheels, and, often, a folding top. [< F *cabriolet* < *cabrioler* caper < Ital. < L *caper* goat; from bouncing motion]

ca·ca·o (kə kā′ō *or* kə kä′ō) *n., pl.* **-ca·os.** **1** a tropical American evergreen tree (*Theobroma cacao*) that produces seeds from which chocolate, cocoa, and cocoa butter are obtained. **2** the seed of this tree, also called **cacao bean.** [< Sp. < Mexican *caca-uatl*]

cach·a·lot (kash′ə lot′ *or* kash′ə lō′) *n.* sperm whale. [< F < Pg. *cachalote*]

cache (kash) *n., v.* **cached, cach·ing.** —*n.* **1** a hiding place. **2** *Cdn.* a place for storing supplies, furs, equipment, etc. away from foraging animals and the weather. **3** the things hidden or stored in a cache. **4** *Cdn.* a supply of goods stockpiled for future use. **5** *Cdn.* a hut, tent, lean-to, or other structure used as a storehouse. **6** a blind used in hunting game. —*v.* **1** hide or conceal. **2** *Cdn.* deposit in a cache. [< F *cache* < *cacher* conceal]

ca·chet (ka shā′ *or* kash′ā) *n.* **1** a private seal or stamp: *The letter was sealed with the king's cachet.* **2** a distinguishing mark of quality or genuineness. **3** stylish distinction; prestige. **4** a capsule for enclosing a medicine with an unpleasant taste. **5** a slogan, design, etc. stamped or printed on mail. [< F *cachet* < *cacher* hide]

cach·in·nate (kak′ə nāt′) *v.* **-nat·ed, -nat·ing.** laugh loudly. [< L *cachinnare*]

cach·in·na·tion (kak′ə nā′shən) *n.* loud laughter.

ca·chou (kə shü′ *or* ka shü′) *n.* **1** a pill or lozenge, usually silvered, composed of cashew nut and other ingredients and used to perfume the breath, thus cloaking the odor of tobacco smoke, alcohol, etc. **2** catechu. [< F *cachou*]

☛ *Hom.* **cashew** (kə shü′).

ca·cique (kə sēk′) *n.* **1** *Historical.* a native Indian chief in Spanish America. **2** a local political boss in Latin America or Spain. **3** any of various tropical American orioles (especially of genus *Cacicus*). [< Sp. < Haitian]

cack·le (kak′əl) *v.* **-led, -ling;** *n.* —*v.* **1** of a hen, make a shrill, intermittent cry, especially after laying an egg. **2** laugh with shrill, harsh, or intermittent sounds: *The old man cackled after each joke.* **3** chatter. —*n.* **1** the shrill, intermittent cry that a hen makes, especially after laying an egg. **2** a burst of shrill, harsh, or intermittent laughter. **3** noisy chatter; silly talk. [ME *cakelen*; imitative]

ca·coph·o·nous (kə kof′ə nəs) *adj.* harsh and clashing; dissonant; discordant. —**ca·coph′o·nous·ly,** *adv.*

ca·coph·o·ny (kə kof′ə nē) *n., pl.* **-nies.** a harsh, clashing sound; dissonance; discord. [< NL *cacophonia* < Gk. *kakophōnia* < *kakos* bad + *phōnē* sound]

cac·tus (kak′təs) *n., pl.* **-tus·es** *or* **-ti** (-tī *or* -tē). any of a family (Cactaceae) of plants found especially in deserts, having thick, fleshy stems with spines or scales instead of leaves and often having large, showy flowers. [< L < Gk. *kaktos*]

cad (kad) *n.* a man who does not act like a gentleman; an ill-bred man. [< *caddie*]

ca·das·tral (kə das′trəl) *adj.* of, having to do with, or according to a cadastre: *cadastral survey.*

ca·das·tre (kə das′tər) *n.* a public register of the ownership, value, and extent of land as a basis of taxation. Also, **cadaster.** [< LL *capitastrum* register of poll tax < L *caput, -itis* head]

ca·dav·er (kə dav′ər) *n.* a dead body, especially a human body intended for dissection; corpse. [< L]

ca·dav·er·ous (kə dav′ər əs) *adj.* **1** of or like a cadaver. **2** pale and ghastly. **3** thin and worn. —**ca·dav′er·ous·ly,** *adv.* —**ca·dav′er·ous·ness,** *n.*

cad·die *or* **cad·dy** (kad′ē) *n., v.* **-died, -dy·ing.** —*n. Golf.* a person who helps a golf player by carrying his clubs, finding the ball, etc. —*v.* help a golf player in this way. [< F *cadet* younger brother. See CADET.]

cad·dis fly (kad′is) any of an order (Trichoptera) of aquatic insects found throughout the world, having two pairs of membranous wings and slender, jointed antennae. Many caddis flies resemble moths. See also **caddis worm.** [origin uncertain]

cad·dish (kad′ish) *adj.* like a cad; ungentlemanly. —**cad′dish·ly,** *adv.* —**cad′dish·ness,** *n.*

caddis worm the omnivorous larva of the caddis fly. It is found in fresh water, carrying around its own protective case that it has constructed of silk and bits of sand and debris.

cad·dy¹ (kad′ē) *n., pl.* **-dies.** a small box, can, or chest, often used to hold tea. [< Malay *kati* a small weight]

cad·dy² (kad′ē) *n., pl.* **-dies;** *v.* **-died, -dy·ing.** See **caddie.**

ca·dence (kā′dəns) *n.* **1** rhythm; the measure or beat of any rhythmical movement: *the steady cadence of a march.* **2** a fall of the voice, as at the end of a sentence. **3** a rising and falling sound; modulation: *She speaks with a pleasant cadence.* **4** *Music.* a series of chords, a trill, etc. that brings part of a composition to an end. [< F < Ital. *cadenza* < L *cadentia.* Doublet of CADENZA and CHANCE.]

ca·den·za (kə den′zə) *n. Music.* an elaborate flourish or showy passage for a solo voice or instrument in an aria, concerto, etc. [< Ital. < L *cadentia* < *cadere* fall. Doublet of CADENCE and CHANCE.]

ca·det (kə det′) *n.* **1** a young man or woman in training to be an officer in the armed forces. **2** a young man or woman undergoing training for a police force. **3** a person under military age who is undertaking basic military training in an organization subsidized by the armed forces. **4 Cadet,** a member of the Girl Guides, aged 15 to 17, who is training for leadership. **5** *Archaic.* a younger son or brother. [< F < Gascon *capdel* < L *capitellum,* dim. of *caput* head]

ca·det·ship (kə det′ship) *n.* the rank or position of a cadet.

cadge (kaj) *v.* **cadged, cadg·ing.** **1** *Dialect.* peddle. **2** *Informal.* beg. [origin uncertain] —**cadg′er,** *n.*

ca·di (kä′dē *or* kā′dē) *n., pl.* **-dis.** a Moslem judge responsible for making judgments in religious cases, such as those involving inheritance, marriage, or divorce. [< Arabic *qadi* judge]

Cad·me·an (kad′mē ən *or* kad mē′ən) *adj.* having to do with Cadmus. The Cadmean alphabet was the earliest form of writing used by the ancient Greeks.

cad·mi·um (kad′mē əm) *n.* a soft, bluish-white, ductile metallic chemical element, resembling tin, used in plating to prevent rust and in making certain alloys. *Symbol*: Cd; *at.no.* 48; *at.wt.* 112.40. [< NL < L *cadmia* zinc ore < Gk. *kadmeia*]

Cad·mus (kad′məs) *n. Greek mythology.* a Phoenician prince who killed a dragon and sowed its teeth. Armed men sprang up from the teeth and fought each other until only five survived. With these five men, Cadmus founded the Greek city of Thebes.

ca·dre (kä′dər; *in military use,* kad′rē) *n.* **1** framework. **2** the staff of trained military personnel necessary to establish and train a new military unit. **3** a similar group of people working closely together or as the nucleus of an organization. [< F < Ital. < L *quadrum* square]

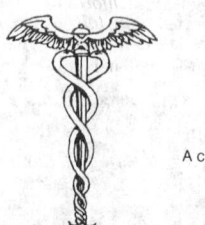

A caduceus

ca·du·ce·us (kə dyü′sē əs *or* kə dü′sē əs) *n., pl.* **-ce·i** (-sē ī′ *or* -sē ē′). a staff with two snakes twined around it and a pair of wings

on top. Mercury, or Hermes, the messenger of the gods, is usually shown carrying a caduceus. The caduceus is often used as an emblem of the medical profession. [< L < dial. Gk. *karykeion* herald's staff]

cae·cum (sē′kəm) *n., pl.* **-ca** (-kə). the large pouch, closed at one end, that forms the beginning of the large intestine. See **alimentary canal** for picture. [< L *caecum* blind (thing)]

Cae·sar (sē′zər) *n.* **1** a title of the Roman emperors from Augustus to Hadrian, and later of the heir to the throne. **2** emperor. **3** dictator; tyrant. [< Gaius Julius *Caesar* (100?-44 B.C.), a Roman general, statesman, and historian, conqueror of Gaul]

Cae·sar·e·an (si zer′ē ən *or* si zar′ē ən) *adj., n.* —*adj.* **1** of Julius Caesar or the Caesars. **2** by Caesarean section: *a Caesarean birth.* —*n.* Caesarean section. Also, **Caesarian** or (sometimes for *n.* and *adj.*, def. 2) **Cesarean** or **Cesarian.**

Caesarean section a method of delivering a child by cutting through the wall of the abdomen and uterus of the mother. [from the belief that Julius Caesar was born in this way]

Cae·sar·i·an (si zer′ē ən *or* si zar′ē ən) See **Caesarean.**

cae·sar·ism (sē′zər iz′ əm) *n.* dictatorship; autocracy.

cae·si·um (sē′zē əm) See **cesium.**

cae·su·ra (si zyūr′ə *or* si zhūr′ə) *n., pl.* **-sur·as.** a pause in a line of verse, generally agreeing with a pause required by the sense. The caesura is the chief pause if there is more than one. In Greek and Latin poetry the caesura falls within a foot, not far from the middle of a line. Whenever it occurs in English poetry, it usually comes near the middle of a line, either within or after a metrical foot. *Example: "To err is human,│to forgive, divine."* Also, **cesura.** [< L *caesura* cutting < *caedere* cut]

CAF or **C.A.F.** Canadian Armed Forces.

C.A.F. or **c.a.f.** **1** cost and freight. **2** cost, assurance, and freight.

ca·fé (ka fā′ *or* kə fā′) *n.* **1** a small, informal restaurant, especially one that serves light meals, often specializing in different coffees and teas, pastries, etc. **2** *French.* coffee. [< F]

☛ *Usage.* **Café** usually refers only to a small, informal place to eat. **Restaurant** may refer to any public eating place, from a very formal dining room to a small place with a counter and perhaps two or three tables.

ca·fé au lait (kä fā′ ō lā′ *or* kaf′ē-; *French,* kä fä ō le′) *French.* **1** coffee with milk or cream. **2** brownish yellow.

ca·fé noir (kä fä nwär′) *French.* coffee without milk or cream; black coffee.

caf·e·te·ri·a (kaf′ə tēr′ē ə) *n.* an informal restaurant, especially in an institution, such as a hospital or school or in an office building, where customers select their food at a counter and take it to the tables provided. [< Mexican Sp. *cafeteria* coffee shop]

caf·fè es·pres·so (kaf fā′ es pres′sō) *Italian.* espresso coffee.

caf·feine or **caf·fein** (kaf′ēn *or* kaf′ē in) *n.* a stimulating drug found in coffee and tea. *Formula:* $C_8H_{10}N_4O_2$ [< F *caféine* < *café* coffee]

caf·tan (kaf′tan *or* käf tän′) *n.* **1** a loose ankle-length, long-sleeved garment worn with a kind of sash. Caftans are traditionally worn in eastern Mediterranean countries. **2** a similar garment worn in western countries for lounging or recreation. Also, **kaftan.** [< Turkish *qaftan*]

cage (kāj) *n., v.* **caged, cag·ing.** —*n.* **1** a frame or box closed in with wires, bars, etc. Birds and wild animals are kept in cages. **2** anything shaped or used like a cage: *The car or closed platform of a mine elevator is a cage.* **3** a prison or anything that confines like a prison. **4** *Hockey.* the network structure forming the goal. **5** *Baseball.* a screen used to stop balls during batting practice. **6** *Basketball.* the basket. —*v.* put or keep in a cage. [ME < OF < L *cavea* cell < *cavus* hollow]

cage·ling (kāj′ling) *n.* a bird kept in a cage.

cag·er (kā′jər) *n. Slang.* a basketball player.

cag·ey (kā′jē) *adj.* **cag·i·er, cag·i·est. 1** *Informal.* shrewd: *a cagey lawyer.* **2** cautious; wary: *He was too cagey to commit himself completely.* —**cag′i·ly,** *adv.* —**cag′i·ness,** *n.*

CAHA or **C.A.H.A.** Canadian Amateur Hockey Association.

ca·hoots (kə hüts′) *n. Slang.*
in cahoots, in partnership, especially for a wrongful purpose; in league: *She was found to be in cahoots with the thief. The two of them are probably in cahoots.* [origin uncertain]

ca·hot (kə hō′) *n. Cdn.* **1** a ridge of snow on a road: *The cahots made the ride a very bumpy one.* **2** a ridge or bump in an unpaved road. [< F]

cai·man (kā′mən) *n., pl.* **-mans.** cayman.

Cain (kān) *n.* **1** in the Bible, the oldest son of Adam and Eve and

the murderer of his brother Abel (Genesis 4:1-17). **2** any murderer.
raise Cain, *Slang.* make a great disturbance.

caecum 161 calabash

hat, āge, fär; let, ēqual, tėrm; it, īce
hot, ōpen, ôrder; oil, out; cup, pút, rüle,
əbove, takən, pencəl, lemən, circəs

ch, child; ng, long; sh, ship
th, thin; ŦH, then; zh, measure

ca·ïque (kä ēk′) *n.* **1** a long, narrow Turkish rowboat, much used on the Bosporus. **2** a Mediterranean sailing ship. [< F < Ital. *caicco* < Turkish *qāyik*]

cairn (kern) *n.* **1** a pile of stones heaped up as a memorial, tomb, or landmark. **2** cairn terrier. [< Scots Gaelic *carn* heap of stones]

cairn·gorm (kern′gôrm′) *n.* **1** a yellow or smoky-brown variety of quartz. **2** a gem made of this stone. Cairngorms are often used for brooches and other ornaments, especially by the Scots. [< *Cairngorm,* a peak in the Grampians, Scotland]

cairn terrier a breed of small, long-haired, working terrier originally bred in Scotland, having a soft undercoat and a hard, wiry topcoat.

caisse pop·u·laire (kes′pop yə ler′; *French,* kes pop ʏ ler′) *Cdn.* especially in Quebec, credit union. [< Cdn. F]

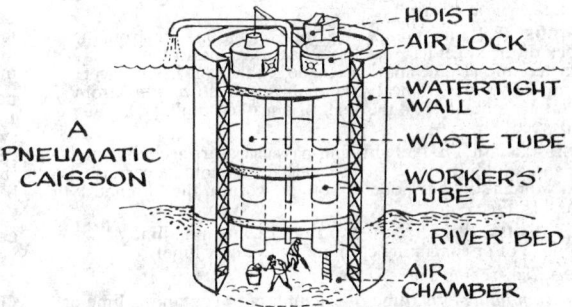

A PNEUMATIC CAISSON

HOIST
AIR LOCK
WATERTIGHT WALL
WASTE TUBE
WORKERS' TUBE
RIVER BED
AIR CHAMBER

cais·son (kā′son *or* kā′sən) *n.* **1** a watertight box or chamber within which work can be carried on under water. Caissons are used in the construction of bridge piers. **2** a watertight float used in raising sunken ships. **3** a box for ammunition. **4** a wagon to carry ammunition. [< F *caisson* < *caisse* chest < L *capsa* box]

caisson disease decompression sickness.

cai·tiff (kā′tif) *n., adj.* —*n. Archaic.* a mean, contemptible person; coward. —*adj.* vile; cowardly; contemptible. [ME < OF *catif* < L *captivus* captive. Doublet of CAPTIVE.]

ca·jole (kə jōl′) *v.* **-joled, -jol·ing.** persuade by flattery or false promises, especially to overcome reluctance; coax: *His older brother cajoled him into cutting the lawn.* [< F *cajoler*] —**ca·jol′er,** *n.* —**ca·jol′ing·ly,** *adv.*

ca·jol·er·y (kə jōl′ər ē *or* kə jōl′rē) *n., pl.* **-er·ies.** persuasion by flattering or deceitful words; flattery; coaxing.

cake (kāk) *n., v.* **caked, cak·ing.** —*n.* **1** a baked mixture of flour, sugar, eggs, flavoring, and other things: *a sponge cake, a fruit cake.* **2** batter that has been fried or baked in a small, flat, usually round shape: *buckwheat cakes.* **3** any small, flat mass of food fried on both sides: *a fish cake.* **4** a hard, shaped mass: *a cake of soap, a cake of maple sugar.*
take the cake, *Slang.* **a** win first prize. **b** excel. **c** used ironically: be the last or worst in a series of disappointments, troubles, etc. —*v.* form into a solid mass; harden: *Mud cakes as it dries.* [ME, probably < ON *kaka*]

cake flour a fine wheat flour having a low gluten content, used for baking cakes, cookies, etc.

cakes and ale good things; the pleasures of life.

cake·walk (kāk′wok′ *or* -wôk′) *n., v.* **1** *Historical.* among blacks of the United States, an entertainment in which people performed a kind of promenade or walk to music, with a prize of a cake for the best or most original steps. **2** a popular high-stepping dance based on this walk. **3** music for this dance. —*v.* do a cakewalk. —**cake′walk′er,** *n.*

cal. **1** calendar. **2** calibre. **3** calorie(s).

Cal. California.

cal·a·bash (kal′ə bash′) *n.* **1** a tropical American tree (*Crescentia cujete*) of the trumpet-creeper family, having funnel-shaped flowers and very large, hard-shelled fruits. **2** the fruit of this

tree. **3** a utensil, such as a bowl or dipper, made from the shell of this fruit. **4** gourd (def. 1). [< F *calebasse* < Sp. *calabaza*, probably < Persian *kharbuz* melon]

cal·a·boose (kal′ə büs′ *or* kal′ə büs′) *n. Informal.* a jail or prison. [< Sp. *calabozo* dungeon]

ca·la·di·um (kə lā′dē əm) *n.* any of several tropical American plants (genus *Caladium*) of the arum family grown in many varieties for their colorful foliage. Caladiums are popular as house plants in cooler regions. [< Malay *kelady*]

cal·a·man·co (kal′ə mang′kō) *n.* a glossy woollen cloth, checked or brocaded in the warp so that the pattern shows on one side only. [origin uncertain]

cal·a·mine (kal′ə mīn′ *or* kal′ə min) *n.* **1** a pink, odorless, tasteless powder consisting of zinc oxide and a small amount of ferric oxide, used in skin lotions and ointments. **2** *Obsolete.* hemimorphite. **3** *Obsolete.* smithsonite. [< F < Med.L *calamina* < L *cadmia.* See CADMIUM.]

ca·lam·i·tous (kə lam′ə təs) *adj.* causing a calamity; accompanied by a calamity; disastrous. **—ca·lam′i·tous·ly,** *adv.* **—ca·lam′i·tous·ness,** *n.*

ca·lam·i·ty (kə lam′ə tē) *n., pl.* **-ties. 1** an event causing great misery or destruction: *The fire was the worst calamity of the decade for the town.* **2** serious trouble; misery: *Calamity may come to anyone.* [< F *calamité* < L *calamitas*]
☛ *Syn.* **1.** See note at **disaster.**

cal·a·mus (kal′ə məs) *n., pl.* **-mi** (-mī′ *or* -mē′). **1** the aromatic rootstock of the sweet flag, used as a flavoring and in the manufacture of perfume and insecticide. **2** the plant itself; sweet flag. **3** any of various tropical Asian palms (genus *Calamus*) from which rattan is obtained. **4** the shaft of a feather; quill. [< L < Gk. *kalamos* reed]

ca·lash (kə lash′) *n.* **1** a light, four-passenger carriage with small wheels and a folding top. **2** *Archaic.* calèche. **3** a folding carriage top. **4** a woman's folding hood or bonnet, worn in the 18th and 19th centuries. [< F *calèche*]

cal·car·e·ous (kal ker′ē əs) *adj.* **1** of or containing lime or limestone. **2** of or containing calcium. [< L *calx* lime]

cal·ces (kal′sēz) *n.* a pl. of **calx.**

calci– *combining form.* lime or calcium; of or containing lime or calcium. Also (before vowels) **calc-.**

cal·cif·er·ous (kal sif′ər əs) *adj.* containing calcite. [calci- + -ferous containing (< L *ferre* bear)]

cal·ci·fi·ca·tion (kal′sə fə kā′shən) *n.* **1** the process of calcifying. **2** a calcified part. **3** the accumulation of calcium in certain soils.

cal·ci·fy (kal′sə fī′) *v.* **-fied, -fy·ing.** become hard by the deposit of lime. An injured cartilage sometimes calcifies.

cal·ci·mine (kal′sə mīn′ *or* kal′sə min) *n., v.* **-mined, -min·ing.** **—n.** a white or colored liquid consisting of a mixture of water, coloring matter, glue, etc., used especially on plastered ceilings and walls. **—v.** cover with calcimine.

cal·ci·na·tion (kal′sə nā′shən) *n.* **1** the act or operation of calcining. **2** anything formed by calcining.

cal·ci·na·tor (kal′sə nā′tər) *n.* a furnace or incinerator that reduces radio-active waste to ashes, so that it can be transported and dumped with greater care and safety.

cal·cine (kal′sīn *or* kal′sin) *v.* **-cined, -cin·ing. 1** heat (an inorganic substance) to a high temperature, but not high enough to melt or fuse it, in order to bring about evaporation of certain matter in it or cause chemical changes such as oxidation: *Limestone is calcined to produce lime.* **2** undergo this process. [ME < OF *calciner* < L *calx* lime]

cal·cite (kal′sīt) *n.* a mineral composed of calcium carbonate. It occurs as limestone, chalk, marble, etc. *Formula:* $CaCO_3$

cal·ci·um (kal′sē əm) *n.* a soft, silvery-white metallic element that is a part of limestone, chalk, milk, bone, etc. Calcium is used in alloys and its compounds are used in making plaster, in cooking, and as bleaching agents. *Symbol:* Ca; *at.no.* 20; *at.wt.* 40.08. [< L *calx, calcis* lime]

calcium carbide a heavy, grey crystalline compound that reacts with water to form acetylene gas. *Formula:* CaC_2

calcium carbonate a mineral occurring in rocks as marble and limestone, in animals as bones, shells, teeth, etc. and to some extent in plants; calcite. *Formula:* $CaCO_3$

calcium chloride a very absorbent compound of calcium and chlorine, used mainly as a drying agent, preservative, and refrigerant. *Formula:* $CaCl_2$

calcium hydroxide slaked lime. *Formula:* $Ca(OH)_2$

calcium light a strong, white light produced by making lime incandescent with a very hot flame; limelight.

calcium oxide quicklime. *Formula:* CaO.

calcium phosphate a compound of calcium and phosphoric acid, used in medicine, in making enamels, etc. It is found in bones and as rock. *Formula:* $Ca_3(PO_4)_2$

cal·cu·la·ble (kal′kyə lə bəl) *adj.* **1** that can be calculated. **2** reliable; dependable. **—cal′cu·la·bly,** *adv.*

cal·cu·late (kal′kyə lāt′) *v.* **-lat·ed, -lat·ing. 1** find out by adding, subtracting, multiplying, or dividing; figure: *to calculate the cost of furnishing a house.* **2** find out beforehand by any process of reasoning; estimate: *Calculate the day of the week on which Christmas will fall.* **3** rely; depend; count: *A waitress working evenings here can calculate on making $60 a week in tips.* **4** *Informal.* plan; intend: *That remark was calculated to hurt my feelings.* **5** *Informal.* think; believe; suppose. [< L *calculare* < *calculus* pebble used in counting, dim. of *calx* stone]

cal·cu·lat·ing (kal′kyə lāt′ing) *adj.* **1** that calculates: *calculating machines.* **2** shrewd; careful. **3** scheming; selfish. **—cal′cu·lat′ing·ly,** *adv.*

cal·cu·la·tion (kal′kyə lā′shən) *n.* **1** the act of calculating: *The calculation of the total cost will take some time.* **2** a result found by calculating: *All my calculations are correct.* **3** careful thinking; deliberate planning.

cal·cu·la·tive (kal′kyə lə tiv *or* kal′kyə lā′tiv) *adj.* **1** having to do with calculation. **2** tending to be calculating.

cal·cu·la·tor (kal′kyə lā′tər) *n.* **1** a machine that performs mathematical calculations mechanically, especially one that solves difficult mathematical problems. **2** a person who operates such a machine.

cal·cu·lus (kal′kyə ləs) *n., pl.* **-lus·es** *or* **-li** (-lī′ *or* -lē′). **1** *Mathematics.* a method of reasoning, using a highly specialized system of notation. See also, **differential calculus** and **integral calculus.** **2** a stone or hard mass formed in the body. **3** a hard substance that has collected on the teeth, formed by the action of bacteria on saliva and food particles; tartar. [< L *calculus.* See CALCULATE.]

cal·de·ra (kol′də rə *or* kal der′ə) *n.* a depression at the top of a volcano, larger than a crater, formed by an explosion or the collapse of part of the cone.

cal·dron (kol′drən *or* kôl′drən) *n.* cauldron.

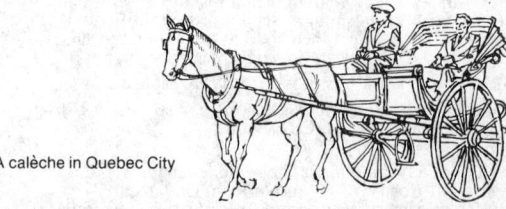

A calèche in Quebec City

ca·lèche (kə lesh′) *n. Cdn.* a light, two-wheeled, one-horse carriage for two passengers, having a seat in front for the driver and, usually, a folding top. Also, **calash.** [< F]
☛ *Usage.* The alternative form **calash** was once more common than it is today. Since the vehicle is now little used except as a conveyance for sightseers in Quebec City and Montreal, **calèche,** the French form of the word, is generally used.

Cal·e·do·ni·a (kal′ə dō′nē ə) *n. Poetic.* Scotland. **—Cal′e·do′ni·an,** *adj., n.*

cal·en·dar (kal′ən dər) *n., v.* **—n. 1** a table showing the months and weeks of the year and the day of the week on which each day of the month comes. **2** a system by which the beginning, length, and divisions of the year are fixed. **3** a list or schedule; record; register: *We have three winter carnivals on our calendar. The trial had to be delayed because the court calendar was filled.* **4** a volume or booklet issued by a university or college listing regulations, courses to be given, etc. **—v.** enter in a calendar or list; register. [ME < AF *calender* < L *calendarium* account book < *calendae* calends (day bills were due)]
☛ *Hom.* **calender.**

calendar day the 24 hours from one midnight to the next midnight.

calendar month one of the 12 parts into which a year is divided; month.

calendar year a period of 365 days (or in leap year, 366 days) that begins on January 1 and ends on December 31.

cal·en·der (kal′ən dər) *n., v.* **—n.** a machine in which cloth, paper, etc. is smoothed and glazed by pressing between rollers. **—v.**

make smooth and glossy by pressing in a calender. [< F *calandre* < L < Gk. *kylindros* cylinder]

☛ *Hom.* **calendar.**

cal·ends (kal′endz *or* kal′əndz) *n.pl.* in the ancient Roman calendar, the first day of the month. Also, **kalends.** [ME < L *calendae*]

ca·len·du·la (kə len′jə lə *or* kə len′dyə lə) *n.* any of a small genus (*Calendula*) of small, closely related herbs of the composite family having yellow or orange flowers. The best-known calendula is the pot marigold. [< NL *calendula*, dim. of *calendae* the calends]

cal·en·ture (kal′ən chər) *n.* a tropical fever accompanied by delirium. [< F < Sp. *calentura* < L *calere* be hot]

calf[1] (kaf) *n.*, *pl.* **calves.** 1 the young of the domestic cow or of a related animal such as the buffalo. 2 a young elephant, whale, seal, etc. 3 leather made from the skin of a calf. 4 *Informal.* a clumsy, silly boy or young man. 5 a small mass of ice that has become detached from a glacier, iceberg, etc.
kill the fatted calf, prepare a feast to celebrate something or to welcome someone. [OE]

calf[2] (kaf) *n.*, *pl.* **calves.** the thick, fleshy part of the back of the human leg below the knee. [< ON *kálfi*]

calf love puppy love.

calf·skin (kaf′skin′) *n.* 1 the skin of a calf. 2 leather made from it.

Cal·i·ban (kal′ə ban′) *n.* 1 in Shakespeare's play *The Tempest*, a beastlike slave. 2 any bestial or degraded man.

cal·i·ber (kal′ə bər) See **calibre.**

cal·i·brate (kal′ə brāt′) *v.* **-brat·ed, -brat·ing.** 1 determine, check, or adjust the scale of (a thermometer, gauge, or other measuring instrument). This is usually done by comparison with a standard instrument. 2 find the calibre of. —**cal′i·bra′tor,** *n.*

cal·i·bra·tion (kal′ə brā′shən) *n.* calibrating or being calibrated.

cal·i·bre (kal′ə bər) *n.* 1 diameter, especially inside diameter: *A .45 calibre revolver has a barrel with an inside diameter of 45/100 of an inch* (*about* 114 *mm*). 2 degree of quality or worth: *a person of high calibre. How can we improve the calibre of our schools?* Also, **caliber.** [< F *calibre* < Arabic *qalib* mould]

cal·i·co (kal′ə kō′) *n.*, *pl.* **-coes** *or* **-cos**; *adj.* —*n.* a cotton cloth that usually has colored patterns printed on one side. —*adj.* 1 made of calico. 2 spotted in colors. [< *Calicut*, India]

calico salmon *Cdn.* chum[3].

ca·lif (kā′lif *or* kal′if) See **caliph.**

Calif. California.

cal·if·ate (kal′ə fāt′ *or* kā′lə fāt′) See **caliphate.**

Cal·i·for·nia poppy (kal′ə fôrn′yə *or* kal′ə fôr′nē ə) a plant (*Eschscholtzia californica*) of the poppy family having finely divided bluish-green leaves and yellow, orange, or red flowers. It is native to the Pacific coast of North America.

cal·i·for·ni·um (kal′ə fôr′nē əm) *n.* a highly radio-active artificial element, produced by bombarding curium with helium isotopes. *Symbol:* Cf; *at.no.* 98; *at.wt.* (251). [after the University of California, where it was first produced in 1950]

cal·i·per (kal′ə pər) See **calliper.**

ca·liph (kā′lif *or* kal′if) *n.* a traditional title, since the time of Mohammed, of the religious and political leader of the Moslem community. The office of the caliph was suspended in 1926 until such time as the Moslem peoples can again form one community. Also, **calif, khalif.** [< OF *calife* < Med.L < Arabic *khalifah* successor, vicar]

cal·iph·ate (kal′ə fāt′ *or* kā′lə fāt′) *n.* the rank, reign, government, or territory of a caliph. Also, **califate.**

cal·is·then·ic (kal′is then′ik) See **callisthenic.**

cal·is·then·ics (kal′is then′iks) See **callisthenics.**

calk[1] (kok *or* kôk) See **caulk.**[1]

calk[2] (kok *or* kôk) See **caulk.**[2]

calk·er (kok′ər *or* kôk′ər) See **caulker.**

call (kol *or* kôl) *v.*, *n.* —*v.* 1 speak loudly; cry; shout (*often used with* **out**): *He called from downstairs. I called out all the names.* 2 of a bird or animal, utter its characteristic sound. 3 give a signal (*to*): *The bugle called the men to assemble.* 4 rouse; waken: *Call me at seven o'clock.* 5 summon or command: *Obey when duty calls.* 6 convene; assemble: *They have called a meeting for Thursday.* 7 bring to action; begin to consider: *Her case will be called in court tomorrow.* 8 give a name or label to: *They called the baby John. I hit him because he called me a coward.* 9 consider; think of as being: *Everyone called the party a success. I call that a rude remark.* 10 make a short visit or stop: *They called on us last night. We must call on our new neighbor.* 11 read over aloud: *The teacher called the roll of the class.* 12 end; stop: *The ball game was called*

hat, āge, fär; let, ēqual, tèrm; it, īce
hot, ōpen, ôrder; oil, out; cup, put, rüle,
əbove, takən, pencəl, lemən, circəs
ch, child; ng, long; sh, ship
th, thin; ŦH, then; zh, measure

on account of rain. 13 ring up on the telephone; telephone: *Call me tomorrow morning.* 14 demand payment of: *The bank called my loan.* 15 demand for payment: *The company will call its bonds on April first.* 16 *Poker.* demand a show of hands.
call back, a ask a person to return; recall: *Call the mailman back.* **b** take back; retract. **c** telephone to someone who has called earlier.
call down, *Informal.* scold.
call for, a go and get; stop and get: *You can call for the pictures any time after three o'clock.* **b** need; require: *This recipe calls for two eggs.*
call forth, bring into action or being; get: *a play that calls forth strong emotions.*
call in, a summon for advice or consultation: *to call in a lawyer, doctor, etc.* **b** withdraw from free action, circulation, or publicity: *to call in a book.* **c** collect as debts: *to call in a mortgage.*
call off, a order back; order away: *Call off your dog.* **b** cancel: *We called off our trip.* **c** read aloud from a list: *The names were called off alphabetically.*
call on *or* **upon, a** visit. **b** appeal to.
call out, a summon into service or action: *to call out troops.* **b** order (workers) to strike. **c** elicit; bring into play.
call up, a bring to mind; bring back. **b** telephone. **c** summon to the service of the country.
—*n.* 1 a shout; a cry. 2 the characteristic sound of a bird or other animal. 3 a signal given by sound: *Army calls are played on the bugle.* 4 an invitation; request; command; summons. 5 a claim or demand: *A busy person has many calls on his time.* 6 a need, occasion: *You have no call to meddle in other people's business.* 7 a short visit or stop. 8 a demand for payment. 9 a notice requiring actors and stagehands to attend a rehearsal. 10 the act of calling. 11 a calling by telephone: *I want to make a call to Montreal.* 12 *Poker.* the demand that all hands still active be shown after their players have matched the current bet. 13 *Square dancing.* an instruction that is chanted or shouted. 14 a calling, vocation.
on call, a subject to payment on demand. **b** available at any time: *There are three doctors on call tonight.*
within call, near enough to hear a call. [OE *callian*, dial. var. of *ceallian*]

☛ *Hom.* **caul.**

☛ *Syn. v.* 5. **Call, summon, invite** = ask or order someone to come. **Call** is the general and informal word: *The principal called the student leaders together for a talk.* **Summon** = call with authority, and is used especially of a formal calling to duty or to some formal meeting: *The principal summoned the student leaders to his office.* **Invite** = ask politely, and suggests giving a person a chance to do something he would like to do: *The principal invited the student leaders to come in and talk things over.*

cal·la (kal′ə) *n.* 1 a bog plant (*Calla palustris*) comprising a separate genus of the arum family found in northern temperate and subarctic regions, having heart-shaped leaves and a white spathe surrounding a yellow spadix whose flowers develop into brilliant red berries. Also called **wild calla, water arum,** *or* **water calla.** 2 calla lily. [< NL]

calla lily any of several plants (genus *Zantedeschia*) of the arum family cultivated as house or greenhouse plants, especially *Z. aethiopica*, native to southern Africa, having a large, white, flaring spathe surrounding a yellow spadix.

call·back (kol′bak′ *or* kôl′-) *n. Informal.* 1 a recalling of workers who were previously laid off. 2 an additional visit to a client or customer: *The salesman made no new calls, but spent the whole day on callbacks.*

call·boy (kol′boi′ *or* kôl′-) *n.* 1 a bellboy in a hotel, ship, etc. 2 a boy who calls actors from their dressing rooms when they are due to appear on the stage.

call·er (kol′ər *or* kôl′ər) *n.* 1 a person who makes a short visit. 2 a person who calls, especially a person who calls out the dance steps at a square dance.

☛ *Hom.* **collar** (kol′ər), **choler** (kol′ər).

call girl a prostitute with whom appointments may be made by telephone.

cal·lig·ra·pher (kə lig′rə fər) *n.* 1 a person having good handwriting, especially one practising the art of elegant penmanship. 2 a professional transcriber of manuscripts; penman.

cal·li·graph·ic (kal′ə graf′ik) *adj.* having to do with calligraphy.

cal·lig·ra·phy (kə lig′rə fē) *n.* 1 handwriting. 2 the art of beautiful handwriting. [< Gk. *kalligraphia* < *kallos* beauty + *graphein* write]

call·ing (kol′ing *or* kôl′ing) *n.* **1** a business; occupation; profession; trade. **2** an invitation; command; summons. **3** a spiritual or divine summons to a special service or office; call.

calling card a small card with a person's name on it. It is used when visiting someone, in acknowledging gifts, etc.

cal·li·o·pe (kə lī′ə pē′) *n.* **1** a musical instrument having a series of steam whistles played by a keyboard similar to that of an organ. **2 Calliope,** *Greek mythology.* the Muse of eloquence and heroic poetry. [< L < Gk. *Kalliopē* beautiful-voiced < *kallos* beauty + *ops* voice]

cal·li·op·sis (kal′ē op′sis) *n.* coreopsis.

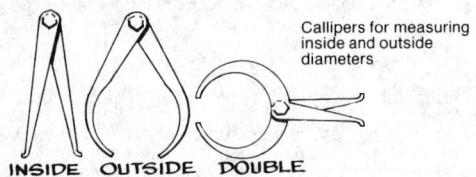

Callipers for measuring inside and outside diameters

INSIDE   OUTSIDE   DOUBLE

cal·li·per *or* **cal·i·per** (kal′ə pər) *n.* Usually, **callipers,** *pl.* an instrument used to measure the diameter or thickness of something.

cal·lis·then·ic *or* **cal·is·then·ic** (kal′is then′ik) *adj.* of callisthenics; developing a strong and graceful body.

cal·lis·then·ics *or* **cal·is·then·ics** (kal′is then′iks) *n.* **1** exercises without the use of special equipment, designed to develop a strong and graceful body. **2** the practice or art of callisthenics. [< Gk. *kallos* beauty + *sthenos* strength]

call loan a loan that must be paid back on demand.

call money a sum of money borrowed that must be paid back on demand.

call number a combination of letters and numbers that is part of a system by which a book is classified and assigned to a place on a library shelf.

cal·los·i·ty (kə los′ə tē) *n., pl.* **-ties. 1** callus (def. 1). **2** lack of feeling; hardness of heart.

cal·lous (kal′əs) *adj.* **1** hard; hardened. Parts of the skin that are subjected to friction often become callous. **2** unfeeling; insensitive: *Only a callous person can see suffering without trying to relieve it.* [< L *callosus* < *callus* hard skin] —**cal′lous·ly,** *adv.* —**cal′lous·ness,** *n.*
☛ *Hom.* **callus.**

call-out (kol′out′ *or* kôl′-) *n. Military.* an officer temporarily commissioned for a special assignment or duty.

cal·low (kal′ō) *adj.* **1** young and inexperienced. **2** not fully developed. **3** of birds, without feathers sufficiently developed for flight. [OE *calu* bald] —**cal′low·ness,** *n.*

call sign the combination of letters or letters and numbers used to identify a radio station, operator, office, etc.

call-up (kol′up′ *or* kôl′-) *n.* a summoning to training or duty, especially military training or duty.

cal·lus (kal′əs) *n., pl.* **-lus·es. 1** a hard, thickened place on the skin. **2** a new growth that unites the ends of a broken bone. **3** a substance that grows over the wounds of plants. [< L. Related to CALLOUS.]
☛ *Hom.* **callous.**

calm (kom *or* käm) *adj., n., v.* —*adj.* **1** not stormy or windy; quiet; still; not moving: *a calm sea.* **2** peaceful; not excited: *Although she was frightened, she answered with a calm voice.* **3** *Meteorology.* a condition in which the wind has a velocity of less than two kilometres per hour (on the Beaufort scale, force 0). —*n.* **1** the absence of motion or wind; quietness; stillness. **2** the absence of excitement; peacefulness. —*v.* **1** become calm: *The crying baby soon calmed down.* **2** make calm: *She soon calmed the baby.* [ME < OF *calme* < Ital. < VL < Gk. *kauma* heat of the day; hence, time for rest, stillness] —**calm′ly,** *adv.* —**calm′ness,** *n.*
☛ *Syn. adj.* **2. Calm, composed, collected** = not disturbed or excited. **Calm** = being or seeming to be completely undisturbed, showing no sign of being confused or excited: *Mother's calm behavior quieted the frightened boy.* **Composed** = calm as the result of having or having got command over one's thoughts and feelings and, sometimes, an inner peace: *She looked composed at the funeral.* **Collected** emphasizes having control over one's actions, thoughts, and feelings, especially at times of danger or disturbance: *He looked collected as he led the rescuers.*

cal·o·mel (kal′ə mel′) *n.* mercurous chloride, a white, tasteless, crystalline powder, used in medicine as a cathartic. *Formula:* Hg₂Cl₂ [< Gk. *kalos* beautiful + *melas* black]

ca·lor·ic (kə lôr′ik) *n., adj.* —*n.* heat. —*adj.* **1** having to do with heat. **2** of or having to do with calories.

cal·o·rie *or* **cal·o·ry** (kal′ə rē) *n., pl.* **-ries. 1** either of two units for measuring heat. A **calorie,** or **small calorie** represents the quantity of heat necessary to raise the temperature of a gram of water one degree Celsius. A **Calorie,** or **large calorie** represents the amount of heat necessary to raise the temperature of one kilogram of water one degree Celsius. A calorie is equal to about 4.18 joules; a Calorie is equal to about 4.18 kilojoules. **2** a unit corresponding to a Calorie, used to measure the heat or energy produced by food as it is burned in the body: *Thirty grams of brown sugar produce about 100 calories.* **3** an amount of food capable of producing energy equal to one Calorie. [< F < L *calor* heat]

cal·o·rif·ic (kal′ə rif′ik) *adj.* producing heat.

cal·o·rim·e·ter (kal′ə rim′ə tər) *n.* an apparatus for measuring the quantity of heat, the specific heat of different substances, the heat of chemical combination, etc.

cal·u·met (kal′yə met′) *n. Cdn.* a long, ornamented tobacco pipe formerly used by Amerindian peoples of the plains and eastern woodlands, especially in formal peacemaking ceremonies. [< F < L *calamus* < Gk. *kalamos* reed]

ca·lum·ni·ate (kə lum′nē āt′) *v.* **-at·ed, -at·ing.** say false and injurious things about; slander. [< L *calumniari* < *calumnia* false accusation. Doublet of CHALLENGE, v.]

ca·lum·ni·a·tion (kə lum′nē ā′shən) *n.* a slander; calumny.

ca·lum·ni·a·tor (kə lum′nē ā′tər) *n.* slanderer.

ca·lum·ni·ous (kə lum′nē əs) *adj.* slanderous.
—**ca·lum′ni·ous·ly,** *adv.*

cal·um·ny (kal′əm nē) *n., pl.* **-nies.** a false statement made to injure someone's reputation; slander. [< L *calumnia.* Doublet of CHALLENGE, n.]

Cal·va·dos *or* **cal·va·dos** (kal′və dōs′) *n.* a kind of brandy distilled from hard cider and originating in Normandy, France. [< *Calvados,* a department of NW France]

calve (kav) *v.* **calved, calv·ing. 1** give birth to a calf. **2** of a glacier, produce or set loose an iceberg or icebergs. When an advancing arctic glacier reaches the sea, the heavy weight of the ice in the water causes the glacier to calve huge chunks of ice that float away as icebergs. [OE *calfian* < *calf* calf¹]

calves (kavz) *n.* pl. of calf¹ and calf².

Cal·vin·ism (kal′vən iz′əm) *n.* the religious teachings of John Calvin (1509-1564), a French leader of the Protestant Reformation at Geneva, and his followers. Calvinism taught that only certain persons, the elect, were chosen by God to be saved and these could be saved only by God's grace.

Cal·vin·ist (kal′vən ist) *n.* a follower of the teachings of Calvin.

Cal·vin·is·tic (kal′vən is′tik) *adj.* of Calvinism.

calx (kalks) *n., pl.* **calx·es** *or* **cal·ces** (kal′sēz). **1** an ashy substance left after a metal or a mineral has been calcined or burned. **2** lime or chalk. [< L *calx* lime]

cal·y·ces (kal′ə sēz′ *or* kā′lə sēz′) *n.* a pl. of calyx.

Cal·y·do·ni·an (kal′ə dō′nē ən) *adj.* of Calydon, a city in ancient Greece. The **Calydonian boar** was a wild boar sent by Artemis to attack Calydon. Meleager finally killed it.

ca·lyp·so (kə lip′sō) *n.* **1** a kind of ballad that originated in Trinidad, characterized by syncopated rhythms and improvisation and usually having satirical or humorous lyrics. **2** the music characteristic of such ballads. **3** (*adj.*) of or designating these ballads or this music. **4 Calypso,** in Homer's *Odyssey,* a sea nymph who kept Ulysses on her island for seven years. [? < Calypso]

ca·lyx (kā′liks *or* kal′iks) *n., pl.* **ca·lyx·es** *or* **cal·y·ces. 1** *Botany.* the outer leaves that surround the unopened bud of a flower. The calyx is made up of sepals. See **flower** for picture. **2** *Zoology.* any cuplike structure or organ. [< L < Gk. *kalyx* covering]

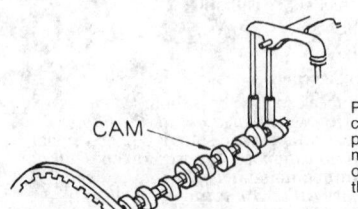

CAM

Part of an automobile camshaft. The cams produce the up-and-down motion of the push rods, opening and closing the piston valves.

cam (kam) *n.* a projection on a wheel or shaft that changes a regular circular motion into an irregular circular motion or into a back-and-forth motion. [< Du. *kam* cog, comb]

ca·ma·ra·de·rie (kä′mə rä′də rē) *n.* comradeship; friendliness and loyalty among comrades. [< F]

cam·a·ril·la (kam'ə ril'ə; *Spanish,* kä'mä rē'lyä) *n.* a group of private advisers, cabal; clique. [< Sp. *camarilla,* dim. of *cámara* chamber]

cam·as or **cam·ass** (kam'əs) *n.* any of a genus (*Camassia*) of plants of the lily family native to W North America, especially *C. quamash,* which has clusters of blue or white flowers and an edible bulb. The bulb was formerly a staple food of northwestern Indian peoples. [< Chinook *quamash* bulb]

cam·ber (kam'bər) *v., n.* —*v.* arch slightly; bend or curve upward in the middle. —*n.* a slight arch; an upward bend or curve in the middle, such as the curve of an airfoil, a ship's deck, or a piece of timber. [< F *cambre* bent < L *camur* crooked]

cam·bi·um (kam'bē əm) *n.* the layer of soft, growing tissue between the phloem (inner bark) and xylem (wood) of trees and shrubs, from which new bark and new wood grow. [< LL *cambium* exchange]

cam·boose (kam'büs') *n. Cdn. Historical.* 1 the living quarters of a gang of loggers or shantymen; shanty (def. 2). 2 an open fireplace in such a building. [< Cdn.F < F *cambuse* store, hut < Du. *kambuis* < MLG; cf. CABOOSE]

Cam·bri·a (kam'brē ə) *n.* an old name for Wales. [Variant of *Cumbria,* Med.L name for Wales < Welsh *Cymru* (*pronun.* kim'ri) Wales or *Cymry* Welshman]

Cam·bri·an (kam'brē ən) *adj., n.* —*adj.* 1 *Geology.* of, having to do with, or designating the first period of the Paleozoic era of geological time, or the rock formed during this time. The Cambrian period began about 600 million years ago. See chart at **geology.** 2 Welsh. —*n.* 1 **the Cambrian,** the Cambrian period or its rock system. 2 Welshman.

cam·bric (kām'brik) *n.* a fine, thin linen or cotton cloth. [< *Cambrai,* France]

cambric tea a drink made of hot water, milk, and sugar, often flavored with a little tea.

came (kām) *v.* pt. of **come.**

cam·el (kam'əl) *n.* 1 either of two species comprising a genus (*Camelus*) of large, cud-chewing desert mammals of Africa and Asia having one or two humps on the back in which fat is stored for use as food and as a source of water. See also **Arabian camel** and **Bactrian camel.** 2 a light yellowish-brown color. 3 (*adj.*) camel-hair: *a camel coat.* [< L *camelus* < Gk. *kamēlos;* of Semitic origin]

ca·mel·ia (kə mēl'yə or kə mē'lē ə) *n.* any of several E Asian evergreen shrubs and trees (genus *Camellia*), especially *C. japonica,* cultivated in several varieties as a greenhouse plant, having large, waxy, roselike flowers that may be white, pink, or red. [after G. J. *Kamel* or *Camellus* (1661-1706), missionary in Luzon]

ca·mel·o·pard (kə mel'ə pärd') *n. Archaic.* giraffe. [< LL < L < Gk. *kamēlopardalis* < *kamēlos* camel + *pardalis* leopard; so called from its camel-like neck and leopard-like spots]

Cam·e·lot (kam'ə lot') *n.* a legendary place in England where King Arthur had his palace and court.

camel hair or **camel's hair** 1 the hair of the camel, used especially for weaving into cloth. 2 a soft cloth, usually a light, yellowish brown in color, made from this hair or a blend of this hair and wool, etc. 3 (*adj.*) **camelhair** or **camel's-hair,** made of this cloth: *a camel-hair coat.*

Cam·em·bert (kam'əm bər') *n.* a rich, soft cheese. [after *Camembert,* France]

cam·e·o (kam'ē ō') *n., pl.* **-e·os.** 1 a precious or semiprecious stone, especially one made up of layers of different colors, carved so that there is a raised part of one color on a background of another color. Agates are commonly used for cameos. 2 the technique of carving cameos. 3 a short literary sketch of a certain character or event. 4 an appearance by a famous actor or actress in a minor film role, usually in a single brief scene, that presents a distinctive character or is especially suited to the star's talents: *In this movie, he has a cameo as an eccentric landlord.* [< Ital.]

cam·er·a (kam'ər ə or kam'rə) *n., pl.* **-er·as** for 1 and 2, **-er·ae** (-ər ē' or -ər ī') for 3. 1 a lightproof box or chamber for taking photographs or motion pictures, in which film or plates are exposed and the image is formed by means of a lens. 2 *Television.* the part of the transmitter that converts images into electronic impulses for transmitting. 3 a judge's private office.
in camera, a in a judge's private office. **b** of a trial, parliamentary session, or other meeting, with the press and public excluded. **c** privately.
[< L *camera* arched chamber, arch < Gk. *kamara.* Doublet of CHAMBER.]

camera lu·ci·da (lü'sə də) an instrument by which the image of an object is made to appear on a sheet of paper, etc. upon which it may be traced.

cam·er·a·man (kam'ər ə man' or kam'rə-) *n., pl.* **-men.** a man

hat, āge, fär; let, ēqual, tėrm; it, īce
hot, ōpen, ôrder; oil, out; cup, pût, rüle,
əbove, takən, pencəl, lemən, circəs

ch, child; ng, long; sh, ship
th, thin; ᴛн, then; zh, measure

who operates a camera, especially a motion-picture or television camera.

camera ob·scu·ra (ob skyür'ə) a camera in which images of external objects, received through an aperture, are exhibited in their natural colors on a surface arranged to receive them. The camera obscura is used for sketching, exhibition purposes, etc. [< NL]

cam·i·on (kam'ē ən) *n.* 1 a low, heavy cart; dray. 2 a truck for carrying cannon. [< F]

cam·i·sole (kam'ə sōl') *n.* a waist-length, sleeveless undergarment worn by women and girls, especially one trimmed with lace or embroidery and worn under a sheer blouse or shirt. [< F < Sp. *camisola,* dim. of *camisa* shirt. Akin to CHEMISE.]

cam·let (kam'lit) *n.* 1 a cloth of silk and wool made in the Orient. 2 a strong, waterproof cloth. [< F *camelot* < Arabic *khamlat* wool plush < *khaml* nap]

cam·o·mile (kam'ə mīl') *n.* 1 any of a genus (*Anthemis*) of aromatic herbs of the composite family, especially *A. nobilis,* a European plant having finely divided leaves and daisy-like flowers often used as medicine. 2 any plant of the related genus *Matricaria.* Also **chamomile.** [ME < OF < LL *camomilla,* var. of L *chamaemelon* < Gk. *chamaimēlon* earth apple]

Ca·mor·ra (kə môr'ə) *n.* 1 a secret society formed in Naples, Italy, about 1820, which developed into a powerful political organization. Later it was associated with blackmail, robbery, etc. 2 **camorra,** a secret society like the Camorra.

cam·ou·flage (kam'ə fläzh') *n., v.* **-flaged, -flag·ing.** —*n.* 1 an outward appearance that makes a person, animal, or thing seem to be part of its natural surroundings. The white fur of a polar bear is a natural camouflage, for it prevents the bear from being easily seen against the snow. 2 the practice of giving soldiers, weapons, etc. a false appearance to conceal them from the enemy. 3 materials or other means by which something or someone is disguised or concealed: *A camouflage of earth and branches effectively hid the guns.*
—*v.* give a false appearance to in order to conceal; disguise: *The hunters were camouflaged with shrubbery so that they blended with the green landscape. The boy camouflaged his embarrassment by laughing.* [< F *camouflage* < *camoufler* disguise] —**cam'ou·flag'er,** *n.*

camp (kamp) *n., v.* —*n.* 1 a temporary shelter such as a tent, trailer, or cabin, or the ground on which it is set up: *His camp was right in the bush. It took us three hours to get back to camp.* 2 a temporary community of people living in tents, trailers, cabins, etc. in the country, especially for holidays or outings: *a wilderness camp. They always go to camp for two weeks in summer.* 3 the people in a camp: *The camp was up by seven o'clock.* 4 a group of people who promote a particular theory, political doctrine, etc.: *the liberal camp.* 5 a way of thinking; an ideological outlook or position: *They're in the same camp, politically.* 6 military life. 7 a place where athletes train together. 8 *Slang.* a fashionably sophisticated kind of humor, based on the affectation of styles, decoration, etc. normally considered trite, corny, or vulgar.
break camp, pack up tents and equipment and leave.
make camp, set up a camp; set up tents, etc.: *We hiked until sunset and then made camp beside a creek.*
—*v.* 1 make a camp; put up tents, huts, etc.: *We decided to camp by the river the first night.* 2 live in a camp (*often used with* **out**): *We camped out all summer.* 3 live simply without comforts for a time: *We had to camp in the house until our furniture arrived.* [< F < Ital. < L *campus* field. Doublet of CAMPUS.] —**camp'er,** *n.*

cam·paign (kam pān') *n., v.* —*n.* 1 a series of related military operations that have some special purpose in view: *The general's staff planned a campaign to capture the enemy's most important city.* 2 a series of connected activities planned to achieve some goal or to acquire something; a planned course of action for some special purpose: *a campaign to raise money for a college, a campaign to advertise some article, a campaign to elect someone to political office.* —*v.* take part in or serve in a campaign; go on a campaign. [< F *campagne* open country < Ital. *campagna* < LL *campanea, campania* level country < L *campus* field. Doublet of CHAMPAIGN.] —**cam·paign'er,** *n.*

cam·pa·ni·le (kam'pə nē'lē) *n., pl.* **-ni·les** or **-ni·li** (-nē'lē). a bell tower, especially one that is near, but not attached to, a church. [< Ital. < LL *campana* bell]

cam·pan·u·la (kam pan'yə lə) *n.* any of a genus (*Campanula*) of

plants having bell-shaped flowers, including the bluebell and the bellflowers. [< LL *campanula*, dim. of *campana* bell]

camp bed a light folding cot or bed.

camp chair a lightweight folding chair.

cam·per (kamp′ər) *n.* **1** a person who camps. **2** a member of a summer camp for children or adolescents. **3** a vehicle equipped for camping, such as a small covered trailer or a pickup truck with a room-like unit fitted onto the back. Campers often have built-in beds, cupboards, etc.

camp·fire (kamp′fīr′) *n.* **1** a fire in a camp, for warmth or cooking. **2** a social gathering for soldiers, scouts, etc.

Camp Fire Girls *U.S.* an organization for promoting the health and welfare of young girls by training them in co-operation, outdoor activities, etc.

camp follower **1** a civilian hanger-on in an army camp, especially a prostitute or a seller of small wares. **2** *Informal.* any person who attaches himself for his own profit to a more important person, a group, a cause, etc.

camp·ground (kamp′ground′) *n.* **1** a place where a camp is. **2** the place where a camp meeting is held.

cam·phor (kam′fər) *n.* a white, crystalline compound with a strong odor and a bitter taste. Camphor is used in the manufacture of film, lacquers, etc., in medicine, and to protect clothes from moths. *Formula:* $C_{10}H_{16}O$ [< Med.L *camphora* < Arabic, ult. < Malay *kāpūr*]

cam·phor·at·ed (kam′fər āt′id) *adj.* containing camphor: *camphorated oil.*

camphor ball a small ball made of camphor, naphthalene, etc. used to keep moths out of clothes, furniture, etc.

cam·pi·on (kam′pē ən) *n.* any of various plants (genera *Lychnis* and *Silene*) of the pink family having pink, red, or white flowers. [< L *campus* field]

camp meeting a religious gathering held outdoors or in a tent, usually lasting several days.

cam·po·ree (kam′pə rē′) *n.* **1** a gathering of scouts or guides for competitions in campcraft, etc. **2** a kind of bivouac outing for a troop. [*camp* + *jamboree*]

camp robber *Cdn.* Canada jay.

camp·site (kamp′sīt′) *n.* **1** a place where people may camp: *Many provincial parks contain well-managed campsites.* **2** any place where someone camps or has camped: *We made our campsite in the bush.* **3** the site of an ancient or prehistoric camp: *The archaeologists found a Stone-Age campsite.*

camp·stool (kamp′stül′) *n.* a lightweight folding seat.

cam·pus (kam′pəs) *n.* the grounds and buildings of a university, college, or school. [< L *campus* field, plain. Doublet of CAMP.]

cam·py (kam′pē) *adj. Slang.* of, having to do with, or characterized by camp (def. 9).

cam·shaft (kam′shaft′) *n.* a rod or shaft on which a cam is fastened, or of which a cam forms an essential part. See **cam** for picture.

can[1] (kan; *unstressed*, kən) *v. pres. sing. and pl. (all persons)* **can**, *pt.* **could.** (*used as an auxiliary followed by an infinitive without* **to**) **1** have the knowledge or power to; be able to: *Can you come tomorrow? I can swim quite well. I can't see because you're standing in my way.* **2** have the right to, by permission, agreement, custom, or law: *You can cross the street here. You can go at 4 o'clock.* **3** be about to: *This calculator can do much more than the other one.* **4** be possible or probable: *It can't be that bad. Can he be serious?* [OE *can(n)* know, know how, can (infinitive, *cunnan*)]

☛ *Usage.* **Can, may.** In formal English we usually distinguish between **may**, meaning "be allowed to" or "have permission to", and **can**, meaning "know how to" or "be able to": *You may go now. You may if you can. He can walk with crutches.* In informal English **can** is widely used to mean both "be allowed to" and "be able to": *Can I go now? You can if you want to. I can run faster than any of my friends.* In both formal and informal English, **may** is used also to indicate that something is possible: *It may be all right for her, but it is not good for me.*

can[2] (kan) *n., v.* **canned, can·ning.** —*n.* **1** a metal container, usually having a separate lid: *a garbage can, an oil can, a milk can.* **2** a small metal container in which foods are sealed to preserve them for later use; tin can. **3** the contents of a can. **4** a can and its contents. **5** *Slang.* jail. **6** *Slang.* toilet. **7** *Slang.* **a** a depth charge. **b** destroyer.
in the can, *Slang.* of motion picture film, ready to show; completed.
—*v.* **1** preserve by putting in airtight cans or jars: *to can fruit.* **2** *Slang.* dismiss from a job: *He says he's been canned.* **3** *Slang.* put an end to; stop: *Can that racket!* **4** *Slang.* make a recording of: *to can applause for a later broadcast.* [OE *canne*] —**can′ner,** *n.*

can. **1** canon. **2** canto.

Can. **1** Canada. **2** Canadian.

Ca·naan (kā′nən) *n.* **1** a region in Palestine between the Jordan River and the Mediterranean. God promised Canaan to Abraham and his descendants. **2** a land of promise.

Ca·naan·ite (kā′nən īt′) *n.* an inhabitant of Canaan before its conquest by the Hebrews.

Can·a·da Act (kan′ə də) the Act of 1791 that divided the province of Quebec into Upper and Lower Canada.

Canada anemone a white-flowered anemone (*Anemone canadensis*) found in moist places across Canada.

Canada balsam a sticky, transparent, yellow resin obtained from the balsam fir. Because it is transparent when it solidifies, it is used as a cement and mounting medium for preparing specimens for examination through a microscope.

Canada Council a body founded by Parliament in 1957 to administer funds for the encouragement of writing, music, painting, and other cultural and scholarly activities. *Abbrev.:* C.C.

Canada Day Dominion Day.

Canada goose a large wild goose (*Branta canadensis*) of North America having a black head and neck, a white throat, and a brownish-grey body.

A Canada jay— about 28 cm long including the tail

Canada jay a jay (*Perisoreus canadensis*) that is common throughout Canada and the N United States, having loose, fluffy, grey feathers on the body and a white-and-black head without a crest; grey jay. The Canada jay has a number of nicknames, including lumberjack, moosebird, and whisky-jack.

Canada lynx a North American subspecies of the lynx (def. 1) sometimes classified as a separate species (*Felis canadensis*), found mainly in northern Canada and Alaska, having very large paws, pointed ears with long tufts, and a thick coat of long, silky, greyish fur mixed with black and dark brown. Its large, well-furred paws enable it to run fast over snow in winter.

Ca·na·di·an (kə nā′dē ən) *n., adj.* —*n.* a native, inhabitant, or citizen of Canada. —*adj.* of or having to do with Canada or its people. [< *Canada* < Cdn F < Iroquoian *kanata* village, community]

Ca·na·di·a·na (kə nā′dē an′ə *or* kə nā′dē ä′nə) *n.* things relating to Canada and its history, especially early Canadian furniture, textiles, books, etc.

Canadian Armed Forces Canadian Forces.

Canadian bacon *Esp.U.S.* back bacon.

Canadian English the kind of English spoken by English-speaking Canadians.

Canadian Forces the armed forces of Canada, made up of the sea, land, and air elements. *Abbrev.:* CF or C.F.

Canadian French the kind of French spoken by French-speaking Canadians.

Ca·na·di·an·ism (kə nā′dē ən iz′əm) *n.* **1** a word or expression originating in or peculiar to Canada. The words *muskeg* and *caribou* are Canadianisms. **2** a custom peculiar to Canada. **3** loyalty to Canada as an independent nation and devotion to her customs, traditions, and laws. **4** the state of being Canadian; the fact of Canada's existence as a separate entity.

Ca·na·di·an·ize (kə nā′dē ə nīz′) *v.* **-ized, -iz·ing.** **1** make Canadian in character or custom: *Our new neighbors have become so Canadianized they've already taken up curling.* **2** change the content or subject matter of a book, television program, scientific report, etc. to reflect Canadian situations or points of view. **3** bring under Canadian ownership or control: *to Canadianize a foreign-owned industry.*

Canadian Legion Royal Canadian Legion.

Canadian Radio–television and Telecommunications Commission a Federal Government body established in 1968 to regulate radio and television broadcasting in Canada. It has the power to enforce broadcasting policy and regulate public and private radio and television and cable systems. *Abbrev.:* CRTC

Canadian Shield a region of ancient rock, chiefly Precambrian granite, encircling Hudson Bay and covering nearly half the

mainland of Canada. The Canadian Shield is rich in minerals, especially gold, copper, nickel, and iron ore.

Canadian whisky a blended whisky containing a high proportion of rye whisky; rye (def. 6).

Ca·na·di·en (kə nä′dē en′; *French*, kä nä dyeN′) *n.* a French Canadian.

Ca·na·di·enne (kə nä′dē en′; *French*, kä nä dyen′) *n.* a French-Canadian girl or woman.

ca·naille (kə näl′; *French*, kä nī′) *n. French.* the lowest class of people; rabble; riffraff. [< F < Ital. *canaglia* < *cane* dog < L *canis*]

ca·nal (kə nal′) *n., v.* **-nalled** or **-naled, -nal·ling** or **nal·ing.** —*n.* 1 a waterway dug across land. Some canals are for boats and ships; others are for carrying water to places that need it. 2 a tube in the body or in a plant for carrying food, liquid, or air: *the alimentary canal.* 3 a long arm of a large body of water. 4 any of the long, narrow markings sometimes visible on the surface of the planet Mars. —*v.* 1 dig or cut a canal through or across. 2 furnish with canals. [< L *canalis* trench, pipe. Doublet of CHANNEL.]

canal boat a long, narrow boat used on canals. Canal boats are sometimes pulled along by horses.

ca·nal·i·za·tion (kə nal′ə zā′shən, kan′ə lə zā′shən *or* kan′ə lī zā′shən) *n.* 1 the act of canalizing. 2 a system of canals. 3 the draining of wounds by surgical means rather than by the use of tubes.

ca·nal·ize (kə nal′īz *or* kan′ə līz′) *v.* **-ized, -iz·ing.** 1 make a canal or canals through. 2 make into or like a canal. 3 lead in a desired direction so as to control or regulate; channel: *an attempt to canalize the energies of children into worth-while activities.*

can·a·pé (kan′ə pā′ *or* kan′ə pē) *n.* a cracker, a thin piece of toasted or fried bread, etc. spread with a seasoned mixture of fish, cheese, etc. [< F *canapé*, originally, a couch with curtains of mosquito netting. See CANOPY.]

ca·nard (kə närd′) *n.* a false rumor; an exaggerated report; hoax. [< F *canard*, literally, duck]

ca·nar·y (kə ner′ē) *n., pl.* **-nar·ies;** *adj.* —*n.* 1 a small yellow or greenish-yellow finch (*Serinus canaria*) native to the Canary Islands. Canaries are often kept as cage birds for their bright plumage and also for their singing. 2 canary yellow. 3 a usually sweet wine from the Canary Islands. —*adj.* canary yellow. [after the *Canary Islands*]

canary yellow light yellow.

ca·nas·ta (kə nas′tə) *n.* a card game similar to rummy, played by two to six players using two decks of cards. In canasta the players try to earn as many points as possible by getting sets of seven or more cards.

can·can (kan′kan′) *n.* a kind of dance marked by extravagant high kicking, performed by women (often in a chorus line) and originating in nineteenth-century Paris.

can·cel (kan′səl) *v.* **-celled** or **-celed, -cel·ling** or **-cel·ing;** *n.* —*v.* 1 cross out; mark, stamp, or punch something so that it cannot be used or used again: *to cancel a stamp.* 2 annul; make without value: *The debt was cancelled.* 3 *Mathematics.* **a** reduce a fraction by dividing both the numerator and the denominator by the same quantity. **b** reduce an equation by dividing both members by a common factor. 4 put an end to or withdraw; call off; stop: *He cancelled his order for the books. The meeting has been cancelled.* 5 balance or match; neutralize (*often used with* **out**): *crossness cancelled out by a smile.* 6 *Music.* nullify the power of a sharp or a flat by inserting the sign ♮. —*n.* cancellation. [< L *cancellare* cross out with latticed lines < *cancelli* crossbars, dim. of *cancri*, altered from *carcer*, originally, network, grating] —**can′cel·ler** or **can′cel·er,** *n.*

can·cel·la·tion (kan′sə lā′shən) *n.* 1 a cancelling or being cancelled. 2 the marks made when something is cancelled or crossed out: *You can hardly see the cancellation on this stamp.* 3 something cancelled.

can·cer (kan′sər) *n.* 1 **Cancer, a** *Astronomy.* a northern constellation thought of as having the shape of a crab. **b** *Astrology.* the fourth sign of the zodiac. The sun enters Cancer about June 21. See **zodiac** for picture. **c** a person born under this sign. **d** See **Tropic of Cancer.** 2 a harmful, uncontrolled growth of new tissue or cells in the body that tends to spread and destroy healthy tissue; a malignant tumor. 3 a condition marked by such harmful growths. 4 any evil or harmful thing that tends to spread: *the cancer of jealousy.* [< L *cancer* crab, tumor. Doublet of CANKER, CHANCRE.]

can·cer·o·gen·ic (kan′sər ə jen′ik) *adj.* carcinogenic.

can·cer·ous (kan′sər əs) *adj.* 1 of cancer: *a cancerous growth.* 2 having cancer: *a cancerous rat.*

can·de·la (kan dē′lə) *n.* an SI unit for measuring luminous

hat, āge, fär; let, ēqual, tèrm; it, īce
hot, ōpen, ôrder; oil, out; cup, pút, rüle,
əbove, takən, pencəl, lemən, circəs
ch, child; ng, long; sh, ship
th, thin; ℞H, then; zh, measure

intensity, or candlepower, which is the amount of light shining in one direction from a glowing object. One candela is the amount of light produced by the inside of a ceramic box that has been heated until it glows; the light is measured as it shines out through a hole in the box. The candela is one of the seven base units in the SI. *Symbol:* cd [< L *candela* candle]

can·de·la·bra (kan′də lä′brə) *n., pl.* **-bras** (-brəz). candelabrum.
☛ *Usage.* Though **candelabrum** is the original form, its plural **candelabra** is now often treated as singular, with its own plural **candelabras.**

can·de·la·brum (kan′də lä′brəm) *n., pl.* **-bra** (-brə) *or* **-brums.** an ornamental candlestick with several branches for holding candles. [< L *candelabrum* < *candela* candle]

can·des·cent (kan des′ənt) *adj.* glowing with heat; incandescent. [< L *candescens, -entis,* ppr. of *candescere* begin to glow] —**can·des′cent·ly,** *adv.*

can·did (kan′did) *adj.* 1 frank; sincere: *a candid reply.* 2 fair; impartial: *a candid decision.* 3 of a photograph, not posed: *The magazine story included several candid shots of the premier's family.* [< L *candidus* white] —**can′did·ly,** *adv.*
☛ *Syn.* 1. See note at **frank.**

can·di·da·cy (kan′də də sē) *n.* the state of being a candidate: *Please support my candidacy for treasurer.*

can·di·date (kan′də dāt′ *or* kan′də dit) *n.* 1 a person who seeks or is proposed for an honor, prize, position, office, etc.: *There were three possible candidates for the award. All the job candidates have been interviewed.* 2 a person who seems to have a particular fate in store: *a candidate for fame and fortune, a likely candidate for prison.* [< L *candidatus* clothed in a white toga]

can·di·da·ture (kan′də də chür′ *or* kan′də dā′chər) *n.* candidacy.

candid camera 1 a small camera with a fast lens for photographing persons unposed, and often unaware that their picture is being taken. 2 any very small camera.

can·died (kan′dēd) *adj.* 1 glazed, soaked, or cooked with sugar: *candied cherries, a candied apple.* 2 of honey, etc., crystallized. 3 made sweet or agreeable: *His candied words of congratulations hid a great bitterness.*

can·dle (kan′dəl) *n., v.* **-dled, -dling.** —*n.* 1 a stick of wax or tallow with a wick in it, burned to give light. 2 anything shaped or used like a candle: *Sulphur candles are burned to disinfect rooms.* 3 candela.
burn the candle at both ends, try to do more than one's energy or resources allow; make unreasonable demands on one's physical and mental resources.
not hold a candle to, not compare with: *The cake from the bakery could not hold a candle to the one John made.*
—*v.* 1 test eggs for freshness and quality by holding them in front of a light in order to see the size of the air pocket and the position and size of the yolk. 2 of ice, form into candle ice. [OE *candel* < L *candela* < *candere* shine]

can·dle·fish (kan′dəl fish′) *n.* oolichan.

can·dle·hold·er (kan′dəl hōl′dər) *n.* candlestick.

candle hour a unit of light equivalent to the energy derived in one hour from a source of light equal to one candle power.

candle ice *or* **candled ice** *Cdn.* ice on a river, lake, etc. that has deteriorated into candle-like shapes, usually occurring shortly before break-up.

can·dle·light (kan′dəl līt′) *n.* 1 the light from a candle or candles. 2 the time when candles are lighted; dusk; twilight; nightfall.

Can·dle·mas (kan′dəl məs) *n.* February 2, a Christian church festival in honor of the purification of the Virgin Mary and the presentation of the infant Jesus in the Temple. It is celebrated with lighted candles. [OE *candelmæsse*]

candle power the intensity of light given by a standard candle, used as a unit for measuring light. A light having 30 candle power gives 30 times as much light as one standard candle does.

can·dle·stick (kan′dəl stik′) *n.* a holder for a candle, to make it stand upright.

can·dle·wick (kan′dəl wik′) *n., adj.* —*n.* 1 the wick of a candle. 2 a soft, loosely twisted cotton thread similar to that used for

candlewicks. —*adj.* having a pattern made with tufts of such threads: *a candlewick bedspread.*

can·dor or **can·dour** (kan′dər) *n.* **1** frankness; open-heartedness in giving one's view or opinion. **2** fairness; impartiality. [< L *candor* whiteness, purity < *candere* shine]

can·dy (kan′dē) *n., pl.* **-dies;** *v.* **-died, -dy·ing.** —*n.* **1** a confection made with sugar or syrup and flavoring: *He doesn't eat much candy.* **2** a piece of this: *She took a candy from the box.* —*v.* **1** cook or soak in sugar, or glaze with sugar. **2** of honey, etc., become crystallized into sugar. **3** make sweet or agreeable. [< F (*sucre*) *candi* (sugar) candy < Persian *quand* sugar]

candy cane a stick of brittle, white peppermint candy having a spiralling red stripe and shaped like a walking stick with a curved handle.

candy floss spun sugar candy; cotton candy.

can·dy–pull (kan′dē pul′) *n.* **1** a social gathering where candy, while it is still soft enough to handle, is pulled and twisted to the color and consistency of taffy. **2** a turn at doing this.

candy stripe a narrow stripe of two alternating colors, generally red and white. —**can′dy·striped′,** *adj.*

can·dy–strip·er (kan′dē strīp′ər) *n.* a teenage girl who does volunteer work in a hospital. [from the uniform of a jumper with vertical red and white stripes, worn over a white blouse]

can·dy·tuft (kan′dē tuft′) *n.* any of various plants (genus *Iberis*) of the mustard family, widely cultivated for their clusters of white, pink, purple, or red flowers. [< *Candia*, former name of Crete + *tuft*]

cane (kān) *n., v.* **caned, can·ing.** —*n.* **1** a rod or stick, usually of wood and having a curved end, or head, for holding with the hand, used to help a person in walking. **2** a long, hollow or pithy, jointed stem, such as that of various woody grasses or reeds. **3** a plant having such stems, as sugar cane, bamboo, or rattan. **4** strips of such stems used for wickerwork, chair backs and seats, etc. **5** (*adjl.*) made of cane: *A cane chair bottom.* **6** a long, slender stem of woody plants such as roses and raspberries, usually growing directly from the ground. **7** any of a genus (*Arundinaria*) of coarse grasses of the S United States having long, stiff stems. **8** a flexible stick used for inflicting punishment. —*v.* **1** make or repair with strips of rattan, bamboo, etc.: *to cane a chair seat.* **2** beat with or as if with a flexible stick or rod. [< F < L *canna* < Gk. *kanna* reed. Doublet of CANNA.] —**can′er,** *n.*

cane·brake (kān′brāk′) *n.* a thicket of cane plants.

cane sugar sugar made from sugar cane.

ca·nine (kā′nīn) *adj., n.* —*adj.* **1** of or having to do with dogs. **2** like that of a dog: *His little brother followed him around with canine devotion.* **3** of or having to do with the dog family (Canidae), a group of meat-eating, four-footed animals that includes the domestic dog, wolf, coyote, Australian dingo, and jackal. —*n.* **1** dog. **2** any member of the dog family. **3** a canine tooth. [< L *caninus* < *canis* dog]

canine tooth one of the four pointed teeth next to the incisors; cuspid. See **tooth** for picture.

Ca·nis Ma·jor (kā′nis mā′jər) *Astronomy.* a group of stars southeast of Orion that contains Sirius, the brightest of the stars. [< L *canis major* greater dog]

Ca·nis Mi·nor (kā′nis mī′nər) *Astronomy.* a group of stars east of Orion, separated from Canis Major by the Milky Way. [< L *canis minor* lesser dog]

can·is·ter (kan′is tər) *n.* **1** a small covered box or can, especially one used for keeping tea, flour, sugar, coffee, and other dry products. **2** a bullet-filled case that is shot from a cannon. [< L *canistrum* < Gk. *kanastron* basket]

can·ker (kang′kər) *n., v.* —*n.* **1** a spreading sore, especially one in the mouth. **2** a disease of plants that causes slow decay. **3** anything that causes rot or decay or that destroys by a gradual eating away. —*v.* infect or be infected with canker; decay; rot. [OE *cancer* < L *cancer* crab, tumor, gangrene. Doublet of CANCER, CHANCRE.]

can·ker·ous (kang′kər əs) *adj.* affected with, caused by, or like canker.

can·ker·worm (kang′kər wėrm′) *n.* the larva of any of various geometrid moths, which injures or destroys fruit or shade trees by feeding on the buds and foliage; especially either of two North American tree pests, *Paleacrita vernata* or *Alsophila pometaria.*

Can·Lit (kan′lit′) *n.* *Cdn. Informal.* Canadian Literature.

can·na (kan′ə) *n.* any of a genus (*Canna,* constituting the family Cannaceae) of tropical herbs widely cultivated for their showy clusters of red or yellow flowers. [< L *canna* reed. Doublet of CANE.]

can·na·bis (kan′ə bis) *n.* **1** the dried flowering tops of the female hemp plant. Compare **marijuana, hashish. 2** hemp. [< L *cannabis* hemp < Gk. *kánnabis*]

canned (kand) *adj.* **1** preserved by being put in an airtight can or jar. **2** *Slang.* preserved on a phonograph record or tape; recorded: *canned music.* **3** *Informal.* drunk; intoxicated.

can·nel (kan′əl) *n.* cannel coal.

cannel coal a kind of bituminous coal in large lumps that burns with a bright flame and a lot of smoke. [apparently var. of *candle*]

can·ner·y (kan′ər ē) *n., pl.* **-ner·ies.** a factory where food is canned.

can·ni·bal (kan′ə bəl) *n.* **1** any person who eats human flesh. **2** an animal or fish that eats others of its own kind. **3** (*adjl.*) of or like cannibals. [< Sp. *Canibal* < *Caribe* Carib]

can·ni·bal·ism (kan′ə bəl iz′əm) *n.* **1** the practice of eating the flesh of one's own kind. **2** barbarity; extreme cruelty.

can·ni·bal·is·tic (kan′ə bəl is′tik) *adj.* of cannibals; characteristic of cannibals.

can·ni·bal·ize (kan′ə bəl īz′) *v.* **-ized, -iz·ing.** assemble or repair (a vehicle, piece of machinery, etc.) by using parts from others that are useless as a whole: *My brother cannibalized a radio set from two old ones that would not work.*

can·ni·kin (kan′ə kin) *n.* a small can; cup. [< *can²* + *-kin*]

can·ning (kan′ing) *n.* the process or business of preserving food by putting it in airtight cans or jars.

can·non (kan′ən) *n., pl.* **-non** or **-nons;** *v.* —*n.* **1** a big gun that is fixed to the ground or mounted on a carriage, especially the old-fashioned type of gun that fired cannon balls. **2** the cannon bone. **3** *Mechanics.* a hollow, cylindrical piece that revolves or is capable of revolving on and independently of a shaft. **4** the metal loop by which a bell is suspended; ear. **5** *Billiards.* a carom. —*v.* **1** fire a cannon. **2** attack with cannon. **3** *Billiards.* carom. **4** come into collision: *to cannon against a tree.* [< F *canon* < Ital. < L *canna* reed, tube < Gk. *kanna*]
☛ *Hom.* **canon.**

can·non·ade (kan′ən ād′) *n., v.* **-ad·ed, -ad·ing.** —*n.* **1** a continued firing of cannon. **2** *Informal.* a verbal assault: *a furious political cannonade.* —*v.* attack with cannon. [< F *canonnade*]

cannon ball a large iron or steel ball, formerly fired from cannons.

cannon bone in hoofed animals, the long bone between the hock and the fetlock. See **horse** for picture.

cannon cracker a large firecracker.

can·non·eer (kan′ən ēr′) *n.* an artilleryman; gunner.

can·non·ry (kan′ən rē) *n., pl.* **-ries. 1** a continuous firing of cannons. **2** artillery.

cannon shot 1 cannon balls or other shot for a cannon. **2** the range of a cannon.

can·not (kan′ot, ka not′, *or* kə not′) *v.* can not.

can·ny (kan′ē) *adj.* **-ni·er, -ni·est. 1** shrewd and cautious, especially in business. **2** thrifty. **3** *Esp.Scottish.* fortunate or lucky. **4** *Esp.Scottish.* nice, good, pleasant, etc. [< *can¹*] —**can′ni·ly,** *adv.* —**can′ni·ness,** *n.*

A modern canoe

ca·noe (kə nü′) *n., v.* **ca·noed, ca·noe·ing.** —*n.* a light, narrow boat having low, curving sides that come together in a point at each end, and that is moved by one or more paddles. —*v.* paddle a canoe; go in a canoe. [< Sp. < Haitian *canoa* < Arawakan]

ca·noe·ist (kə nü′ist) *n.* a person who paddles a canoe, especially one who is skilled at doing this.

ca·noe·man (kə nü′mən) *n., pl.* **-men.** *Cdn.* **1** voyageur. **2** a person skilled in handling a canoe.

Ca·no·la (kə nō′lə) *n.* *Cdn.Trademark.* **1** any of several varieties of the rape plant having seeds that contain no more than 5% erucic acid and no more than 3 mg per gram of glucosinolate (an anti-nutritional substance containing sulphur). **2** the seed or an edible oil or livestock meal prepared from the seed. [< *Can*ada + *col*za. 20c.]

can·on[1] (kan′ən) *n.* **1** a law of a church; a body of church law. **2** a rule by which a thing is judged; standard: *the canons of good taste.* **3** the official list of the books contained in the Bible; the books of the Bible accepted by the Christian church as being inspired by God. **4** the list of saints. **5** an official list. **6** the part of the Mass coming after the offertory. **7** *Music.* a kind of composition in the style of a fugue, the different voice parts repeating the same subject one after another either at the same or at a different pitch. **8** a large size of type; 48 point. [OE < L < Gk. *kanōn*]
☛ *Hom.* **cannon.**

can·on[2] (kan′ən) *n.* **1** a member of a group of clergymen belonging to a cathedral or to certain churches. **2** *Roman Catholic Church.* a member of a group of clergymen living according to a certain rule. [ME < OF < L *canonicus* canonical < *canon* canon[1]]
☛ *Hom.* **cannon.**

ca·ñon (kan′yən) See **canyon.**

ca·non·i·cal (kə non′ə kəl) *adj., n.* —*adj.* **1** according to or prescribed by the laws of a church. **2** in the canon of the Bible. **3** authorized; accepted. **4** *Music.* having to do with or in the form of a canon.
—*n.* **canonicals,** *pl.* the vestments worn by clergy for a church service. —**ca·non′i·cal·ly,** *adv.*

canonical hours in certain churches, the periods of the day fixed by canon law for prayer and worship.

can·on·i·za·tion (kan′ən ə zā′shən *or* kan′ən ī zā′shən) *n.* a canonizing or being canonized.

can·on·ize (kan′ən īz′) *v.* **-ized, -iz·ing. 1** declare (a dead person) to be a saint; place in the official list of saints: *Joan of Arc was canonized by the Roman Catholic Church in 1920.* **2** treat as a saint; glorify. **3** make or recognize as canonical. **4** authorize.

canon law the laws of a church that govern ecclesiastical affairs.

Can·o·pus (kə nō′pəs) *n.* a first magnitude star in the southern constellation Argo. It is the second brightest star in the sky; only Sirius is brighter.

can·o·py (kan′ə pē) *n., pl.* **-pies;** *v.* **-pied, -py·ing.** —*n.* **1** a covering fixed over a bed, throne, entrance, etc. or carried on poles over a person: *There is a striped canopy over the entrance to the hotel.* **2** a rooflike covering; a shelter or shade: *The trees formed a canopy over the old road.* **3** the sky. **4** the umbrella-like supporting surface of a parachute.
—*v.* cover with a canopy. [< F *canapé* < Med.L < L *conopeum* < Gk. *kōnōpeion* a couch with curtains of mosquito netting < *kōnōps* gnat]

ca·not du maître (kä nō dy me′trə) *Cdn. French.* Montreal canoe. [literally, master's canoe]

ca·not du nord (kä nō dy nôr′) *Cdn. French.* North canoe.

canst (kanst) *v. Archaic.* 2nd pers. sing., present tense, of **can**[1]. *Thou canst* means *You* (sing.) *can.*

cant[1] (kant) *n., v.* —*n.* **1** insincere talk; moral and religious statements that many people make, but few really believe or follow. **2** the peculiar language of a special group, inluding many words incomprehensible to outsiders: *thieves' cant.* **3** a whining manner of speaking, especially as adopted by beggars. **4** (*adj.*) of, marked by, or being cant: *the cant language of thieves.*
—*v.* use cant; talk in cant. [< L *cantus* song] —**cant′er,** *n.*
—**cant′ing·ly,** adv.

cant[2] (kant) *n., v.* —*n.* **1** a slope or bevel. **2** a sloping surface or edge. **3** an outside corner or angle, especially of a building. **4** a sudden movement producing a tilt. **5** the tilt or angle produced in this way.
—*v.* **1** give a cant, or slope, to; bevel. **2** tip or tilt. **3** overturn, especially with a sudden movement. [probably < MDu., MLG < OF < *cant* < L *cant(h)us* corner, side < Celtic]

can't (kant) cannot or can not.

Cantab. of Cambridge (for L *Cantabrigiensis*).

can·ta·bi·le (kän tä′bē lā′) *adj. or adv. Music.* in a smooth and flowing style; songlike. [< Ital. < L *cantare* < *canere* sing]

Can·ta·brig·i·an (kan′tə brij′ē ən) *adj.* —*adj.* of Cambridge, England, or Cambridge University. —*n.* **1** a native or inhabitant of Cambridge, England. **2** a student or graduate of Cambridge University. [< *Cantabrigia,* Latin form of *Cambridge*]

can·ta·loupe or **can·ta·loup** (kan′tə lōp′) *n.* **1** a cultivated variety of muskmelon (*Cucumis melo cantalupensis*) with a hard, rough rind and sweet, juicy orange flesh. **2** muskmelon. [< F *cantaloup* < Ital. *Cantalupo,* place where first cultivated]

can·tan·ker·ous (kan tang′kər əs) *adj.* showing a disagreeable and ill-natured disposition; quarrelsome and perverse: *a cantankerous way of speaking. She's very cantankerous these days.* [alteration, influenced by *rancorous,* of earlier *conteckerous* < ME *contecker* contentious person < *conteck* strife, quarrelling]
—**can·tan′ker·ous·ly,** *adv.* —**can·tan′ker·ous·ness,** *n.*

hat, āge, fär; let, ēqual, tèrm; it, īce
hot, ōpen, ôrder; oil, out; cup, put, rüle,
əbove, takən, pencəl, lemən, circəs
ch, child; ng, long; sh, ship
th, thin; ŦH, then; zh, measure

can·ta·ta (kən tä′tə *or* kən tat′ə) *n.* a musical composition consisting of a story or play to be sung, but not acted, by a chorus and soloists, usually with orchestral accompaniment. [< Ital. < L *cantare* < *canere* sing]

can·teen (kan tēn′) *n.* **1** a small container for carrying water or other drinks. **2** a place in a school, camp, factory, etc. where food and drink and, sometimes, other articles are sold or given out. **3** a store, recreation hall, or club for members of the armed forces. **4** a box of cooking utensils for use in camp. **5** a set of cutlery in a box or case. [< F < Ital. *cantina* cellar < LL *cant(h)us* side]

can·ter (kan′tər) *n., v.* —*n.* a horse's gait faster than a trot but slower than a gallop. —*v.* move with this gait. [for *Canterbury gallop,* the supposed easy pace of pilgrims riding to Canterbury]
☛ *Hom.* **cantor.**

Can·ter·bur·y bell (kan′tər ber′ē) a bellflower (*Campanula medium*) with tall stalks of bell-shaped flowers, usually purplish blue, pink, or white.

A cant-hook

cant–hook (kant′huk′) *n. Cdn.* a lever used for handling logs, consisting of a wooden handle with a blunt steel tip and a movable steel hook at its lower end. Compare **peavey.** [< *cant* a slabbed log < *cant*[2] + *hook*]

can·ti·cle (kan′tə kəl) *n.* **1** a song, hymn, or chant, especially a hymn with words taken from the Bible, used in certain church services. **2 Canticles,** Song of Solomon (*used with a singular verb*). Also called (in the Douay Bible) **Canticle of Canticles.** [< L *canticulum* little song < *cantus* song]

can·ti·lev·er (kan′tə lē′vər *or* -lev′ər) *n., v.* —*n.* a large, projecting bracket or beam that is fastened at one end only. —*v.* **1** build with cantilevers or a cantilever: *Our balcony is cantilevered; theirs is supported by pillars.* **2** extend outward on or as a cantilever: *The artist's studio cantilevers out over a sheer cliff.* [origin uncertain]

cantilever bridge a bridge made of two cantilevers whose projecting ends meet but do not support each other. See **bridge**[1] for picture.

can·tle (kan′təl) *n.* the part of a saddle that sticks up at the back. See **saddle** for picture. [< OF < Med.L *cantellus* little corner]

can·to (kan′tō) *n., pl.* **-tos.** **1** one of the main divisions of a long poem. A canto of a poem corresponds to a chapter of a novel. **2** *Music.* the soprano part; melody. [< Ital. < L *cantus* song]

can·ton (kan′ton *or* kan ton′; *French,* kän tôn′) *n., v.* —*n.* **1** a small part or political division of a country: *Switzerland is made up of 22 cantons.* **2** township. **3** in Quebec, a municipal unit roughly equal to a township.
—*v.* **1** divide into parts; subdivide. **2** allot quarters to or provide quarters for (soldiers, etc.). [< F *canton* corner, portion < OF *cant.* See CANT[2].]

can·ton·al (kan′tən əl) *adj.* of a canton.

Can·ton crepe (kan′tən) a soft silk cloth with a crinkled surface.

Can·ton·ese (kan′tən ēz′) *n., pl.* **-ese;** *adj.* —*n.* **1** a native or inhabitant of Canton, a city in S China. **2** the Chinese language spoken in Canton and the surrounding area, in Hongkong, etc.
—*adj.* of or having to do with Canton, its people or their language.

Can·ton flannel (kan′tən) a strong cotton cloth that is soft and fleecy on one side.

can·ton·ment (kan ton′mənt *or* kan tōn′mənt) *n.* a place where soldiers live; quarters. [< F]

can·tor (kan′tər *or* kan′tôr) *n.* **1** a man who leads the singing of a choir or congregation. **2** a soloist in a synagogue. [< L *cantor* singer < *canere* sing]
☛ *Hom.* **canter** (kan′tər).

Ca·nuck (kə nuk′) *n. or adj. Cdn. Informal.* **1** Canadian. **2** French Canadian. [origin uncertain]

can·vas (kan′vəs) *n., v.* —*n.* **1** a strong cloth made of cotton, flax, or hemp, used to make tents and sails, certain articles of clothing, etc. **2** (*adjl.*) made of canvas. **3** something made of canvas. **4** a sail or sails. **5** a piece of canvas on which to paint a picture, especially in oils. **6** a picture painted on canvas: *She's got seven canvases ready for the show.* **7** any coarse, stiffened fabric of wide weave used for working tapestry, as a basis for embroidery, etc. **8** *Rowing.* **a** either of the tapering covered ends of a racing boat. **b** the length of this: *They won the race by a canvas.*
under canvas, a in tents. **b** with sails spread: *The boat left the harbor under canvas.*
—*v.* cover, line, or furnish with canvas. [ME < OF *canevas* < L *cannabis* hemp]
☞ *Hom.* **canvass.**

can·vas·back (kan′vəs bak′) *n.* a North American diving duck (*Aythya valisineria*) having a long blackish bill and distinctive sloping forehead, the male having a rusty-brown head, black upper back, breast, and tail, and whitish back, wings and abdomen.

can·vass (kan′vəs) *v., n.* —*v.* **1** go about asking for subscriptions, votes, orders, etc.: *Each student canvassed his own block for contributions to the the Red Cross.* **2** ask for votes, orders, donations, etc.: *She's out canvassing.* **3** examine carefully; examine: *John canvassed the papers, hunting for notices of jobs.* **4** discuss: *The city council canvassed the mayor's plan thoroughly.* **5** examine and count the votes cast in an election.
—*n.* the act or process of canvassing, especially a personal visiting of homes or stores in a district to sell something, ask for votes, etc. [< *canvas*, originally, toss (someone) in a sheet, later, shake out, discuss] —**can′vass·er,** *n.*
☞ *Hom.* **canvas.**

can·yon (kan′yən) *n.* a narrow valley with high, steep sides, usually with a stream at the bottom. Also, **cañon.** [< Sp. *cañón* tube < L *canna* cane]

can·zo·net (kan′zə net′) *n.* a short, light song. [< Ital. *canzonetta*, ult. < L *cantare* sing]
☞ *Hom.* **canter** (kan′tər).

caou·tchouc (kou chük′ *or* kü′chŭk) *n.* the gummy, coagulated juice of various tropical plants; rubber. [< F < Sp. < South Am.Ind.]

Caps: several different types

cap (kap) *n., v.* **capped, cap·ping.** —*n.* **1** a close-fitting covering for the head usually having little or no brim. **2** a special head covering worn to show rank, occupation, etc.: *a nurse's cap.* **3** something that serves as a cover, especially to protect an end, tip, etc. or to close off the end of a pipe, tube, bottleneck, etc.: *a lens cap, a bottle cap.* **4** a top part like a cap: *The top of a mushroom is called a cap.* **5** the highest part; top. **6** a small quantity of explosive in a wrapper or covering. **7** capital letter: *a word written in caps.*
cap in hand, in humble fashion.
set (one's) **cap for,** *Informal.* try to get as one's husband or lover.
—*v.* **1** put a cap on. **2** put a top on; cover the top of: *pudding capped with whipped cream.* **3** match one thing with something good or better: *The two clowns kept on capping each other's jokes.* **4** form or serve as a cap, covering or crown to; lie on top of. **5** take off the cap as a mark of respect to another. **6** *Scottish.* confer an academic degree on. **7** place the white cap of a nurse upon (a nursing school graduate). **8** *Brit.* award a place on a team to.

cap the climax, go to the extreme limit; go beyond expectation or belief.
[OE *cæppe* < LL *cappa.* Doublet of CAPE¹. Cf. L *caput* head.]
—**cap′per,** *n.* —**cap′less,** *adj.* —**cap′like′,** *adj.*

cap. **1** capital letter. **2** capitalize. **3** capacity. **4** capital. **5** chapter (for L *caput*).

ca·pa·bil·i·ty (kā′pə bil′ə tē) *n., pl.* **-ties. 1** ability to learn or do; power or fitness; capacity. **2** legal or moral qualifications: *A contract has the capability of binding people to a common purpose.*

ca·pa·ble (kā′pə bəl) *adj.* having fitness, power, or ability; able; efficient; competent: *a capable teacher.*
capable of, a having ability, power, or fitness for: *Some airplanes are capable of going 1500 kilometres per hour.* **b** open to; ready for: *a statement capable of many interpretations.*
[< LL *capabilis* < L *capere* take] —**ca′pa·ble·ness,** *n.* —**ca′pa·bly,** *adv.*
☞ *Usage.* See note at **able.**

ca·pa·cious (kə pā′shəs) *adj.* able to hold much; roomy; large: *a capacious closet.* —**ca·pa′cious·ly,** *adv.* —**ca·pa′cious·ness,** *n.*

ca·pac·i·tor (kə pas′ə tər) *n.* condenser (def. 2).

ca·pac·i·ty (kə pas′ə tē) *n., pl.* **-ties. 1** the amount of room or space inside; the largest amount that can be held by a container: *This can has a capacity of four litres.* **2** the maximum number or amount that can be accommodated: *The theatre has a capacity of 500. The arena was filled to capacity.* **3** (*adjl.*) being a maximum number or amount: *a capacity crowd.* **4** the power or ability to receive and hold: *the capacity of a metal to retain heat.* **5** ability to learn or do; power or aptitude: *a great capacity for learning.* **6** a position or relation: *A person may act in the capacity of guardian, trustee, voter, friend, etc.* **7** *Archaic.* capacitance. [< L *capacitas* < *capere* take]

cap and bells a cap trimmed with bells, worn by a jester.

cap and gown a flat cap, or mortarboard, and loose gown, worn by university professors and students on certain occasions.

cap·a·pie *or* **cap·à·pie** (kap′ə pē′) *adv.* from head to foot; completely. [< F]

ca·par·i·son (kə par′ə sən *or* kə per′ə sən) *n., v.* —*n.* **1** an ornamental covering for a horse. **2** any rich clothing or equipment.
—*v.* dress richly; fit out. [< F *caparasson* < Provençal *capa* cape]

cape¹ (kāp) *n.* an outer garment, or part of one, without sleeves, that falls loosely from the shoulders. [< F < *cape* < Sp. < LL *cappa.* Doublet of CAP.]

cape² (kāp) *n.* **1** a point of land extending into the water. **2 the Cape,** the Cape of Good Hope. [< F *cap* < Provençal < L *caput* head]

Cape buffalo a large, wild buffalo (*Syncerus caffer*) of southern Africa having large horns that curve downward and then upward.

cap·e·lin (kāp′lin *or* kap′lin) See **caplin.** [< F < Provençal *capelan* chaplain]

Ca·pel·la (kə pel′ə) *n.* the brightest star in the constellation Auriga, one of the six brightest stars in the sky. [< L *capella,* dim. of *caper* goat]

ca·per¹ (kā′pər) *v., n.* —*v.* leap or jump about playfully.
—*n.* **1** a playful leap or jump. **2** a playful trick, scheme, or pursuit: *Her newest caper is to tell everyone she's an orphan.* **3** a dishonest scheme or enterprise; racket: *He got five years in jail for that caper.*
cut a caper *or* **cut capers,** behave in a frolicsome, playful way: *We really cut a caper at the party last night.*
[A shortened form of E *capriole,* first used in 16c. See CAPRIOLE.]

ca·per² (kā′pər) *n.* **1** a low, prickly Mediterranean shrub (*Capparis spinosa*) cultivated for its edible flower buds. **2** one of the flower buds of this plant, pickled for use as a condiment. [ME *capres,* meaning the flower buds of this shrub < F < L *capparis* < Gk. *kapparis*]

cap·er·cail·lie (kap′ər kāl′yē) *n.* a large, black grouse (*Tetrao urogallus*) of the woodlands of N Europe. [< Scots Gaelic *capullcoille*]

cape·skin (kāp′skin′) *n.* a soft, durable leather made of lambskin or sheepskin, used for gloves, jackets, etc. [< *Cape* of Good Hope, where the strong leather from its goats was first made]

Ca·pe·tian (kə pē′shən) *adj., n.* —*adj.* of or having to do with Hugh Capet (A.D. 938?-996), King of France from 987 to 996, or the kings named Capet who reigned over France till 1328. —*n.* one of these rulers.

cap gun a toy gun having a hammer action for setting off a small explosive charge, or cap; cap pistol.

ca·pi·as (kā′pē əs *or* kap′ē əs) *n. Law.* a writ ordering an officer to arrest a certain person. [< L *capias* you may take]

cap·il·lar·i·ty (kap′ə lar′ə tē *or* kap′ə ler′ə tē) *n.* **1** capillary

attraction or repulsion. 2 the quality of having or causing capillary attraction or repulsion.

cap·il·lar·y (kap′ə ler′ē *or* ka pil′ə rē) *n., pl.* **-lar·ies.** —*n.* **1** one of the very tiny blood vessels connecting the smallest arteries with the smallest veins. **2** any tube having a very slender opening, or bore. **3** (*adj.*) of, in, or having to do with capillaries. **4** (*adj.*) hairlike; very slender. [< L *capillaris* of hair, hairlike < *capillus* hair]

capillary attraction *Physics.* the force that causes a liquid to rise against a vertical surface, resulting when the attraction between the molecules of the liquid is less than the attraction between them and a solid surface. Capillary attraction causes the surface of water in a glass tube to be slightly higher at the sides where it touches the glass than in the middle. See **meniscus** for picture.

capillary repulsion *Physics.* the force that causes a liquid to move away from a vertical surface, resulting when the attraction between the molecules of the liquid is greater than the attraction between them and a solid surface. Capillary repulsion causes the surface of mercury in a glass tube to be slightly higher in the middle than at the sides where it touches the glass. See **meniscus** for picture.

capillary tube a tube with a very slender, hairlike opening or bore.

cap·i·tal¹ (kap′ə təl) *n., adj.* —*n.* **1** the city where the government of a country, province, or state is located. **2** a capital letter, as distinct from a, b, c, etc. **3** the amount of money or property that a company or a person uses in carrying on a business: *The Smith Company has a capital of $30 000.* **4** a source of power or advantage; resources. **5** national or individual wealth as produced by industry and available for reinvestment in the production of goods. **6** *Accounting.* **a** the net worth of a business after the deduction of taxes and other liabilities. **b** the total investment of owners in a business often expressed as capital stock. **7** capitalists as a group.

make capital of, take advantage of; use to one's own advantage: *He made capital of his mother's fame to get the job.*
—*adj.* **1** having to do with capital. **2** important; leading: *The invention of the telephone was a capital advance in communications.* **3** main; chief. **4** of the best kind; excellent: *A maple tree gives capital shade.* **5** involving death; punishable by death: *Murder is a capital crime in many countries.* [ME < OF < L *capitalis* chief, pertaining to the head < *caput* head. Doublet of CATTLE and CHATTEL.]
☞ *Hom.* **Capitol.**

cap·i·tal² (kap′ə təl) *n.* the top part of a column or pillar. See **column** for picture. [ME < OF *capitel* < L *capitellum,* dim. of *caput* head]
☞ *Hom.* **Capitol.**

capital goods *Economics.* goods such as machinery or equipment that can be used to produce other goods. Compare **consumer goods.**

cap·i·tal·ism (kap′ə təl iz′əm) *n.* an economic system in which the means of production, such as land or factories, are for the most part privately owned by individuals or corporations which compete with one another to produce goods and services that are offered on a free market for whatever profit may be made. Compare **communism** and **socialism.**

cap·i·tal·ist (kap′ə təl ist) *n.* **1** a person whose money and property are used in carrying on business. **2** *Informal.* a wealthy person. **3** a person who supports capitalism. **4** (*adj.*) capitalistic.

cap·i·tal·is·tic (kap′ə təl is′tik) *adj.* **1** of or having to do with capitalism. **2** favoring or supporting capitalism.
—**cap′i·tal·is′ti·cal·ly,** *adv.*

cap·i·tal·i·za·tion (kap′ə təl ə zā′shən *or* kap′ə təl ī zā′shən) *n.* **1** capitalizing or being capitalized. **2** the amount at which a company is capitalized; the capital stock of a business.

cap·i·tal·ize (kap′ə təl īz′) *v.* **-ized, -iz·ing. 1** write or print with a capital letter. **2** set the capital of (a company) at a certain amount. **3** turn into capital; use as capital. **4** take advantage; use to one's own advantage (*used with* **on**): *The children capitalized on the hot weather by setting up lemonade stands at the bus stops.*

capital letter the large form of a letter; A, B, C, D, etc., as distinguished from a, b, c, d, etc.

cap·i·tal·ly (kap′ə təl ē) *adv.* very well; excellently.

capital murder murder punishable by death.

capital punishment the death penalty for a crime.

capital ship a large warship; battleship.

capital stock capital used in carrying on a business. It is divided into shares.

cap·i·ta·tion (kap′ə tā′shən) *n.* **1** a tax or fee of a fixed amount per person. **2** the act or process of assessing by counting individuals. [< LL *capitatio, -onis* < L *caput* head]

hat, āge, fär; let, ēqual, tèrm; it, īce
hot, ōpen, ôrder; oil, out; cup, pùt, rüle,
əbove, takən, pencəl, lemən, circəs

ch, child; ng, long; sh, ship
th, thin; ᴛʜ, then; zh, measure

Cap·i·tol (kap′ə təl) *n.* **1** in Washington, D.C., the building in which the United States Congress meets. **2** *U.S.* Often, **capitol,** the building in which a state legislature meets. **3** in Rome: **a** the ancient temple of Jupiter on the Capitoline hill. **b** the Capitoline hill. [ME < ONF *capitolie* < L *Capitolium* chief temple (of Jupiter) < *caput* head]
☞ *Hom.* **capital.**

Cap·i·to·line (kap′ə tə līn′ *or* kə pit′ə līn′) *n., adj.* —*n.* in Rome, one of the seven hills on which ancient Rome was built. —*adj.* having to do with the hill or the Capitol.

ca·pit·u·late (kə pich′ə lāt′) *v.* **-lat·ed, -lat·ing. 1** surrender under certain terms or conditions: *The men in the fort capitulated on the condition that they be allowed to go free.* **2** give up completely; stop resisting: *He capitulated when he realized that arguing was useless.* [< Med.L *capitulare* draw up under separate heads, arrange in chapters < L *caput* head] —**ca·pit′u·la′tor,** *n.*

ca·pit·u·la·tion (kə pich′ə lā′shən) *n.* **1** the act of capitulating. **2** the terms or conditions of surrender. **3** statement of the main facts of a subject; summary.

cap·lin *or* **cape·lin** (kăp′lin *or* kap′lin) *n.* a small fish (*Mallotus villosus*) of the smelt family found in N Atlantic and Pacific coastal waters, used for food and as bait for cod.

Cap'n Captain.

ca·pon (kā′pon *or* kā′pən) *n.* a rooster that has been castrated to improve the flesh for eating. [OE *capūn* < OF < L *capo, caponis*]

ca·pon·ize (kā′pə nīz′) *v.* **-ized, -iz·ing.** make (a young male chicken) into a capon.

ca·pote (kə pōt′) *n.* **1** a long, cloaklike outer garment, usually having a hood. **2** a bonnet formerly worn by women and girls. [< F]

ca·pric·ci·o (kə prē′chē ō) *n., pl.* **-ci·os. 1** a caper; prank; caprice. **2** *Music.* a lively composition in a free, irregular style. [< Ital. *capriccio* < *capro* he-goat < L *caper.* Doublet of CAPRICE.]

ca·pric·ci·o·so (kə prē′chē ō′sō; *Ital.* kä′prēt chō′sō) *adj. Music.* to be played in a light, fanciful style.

ca·price (kə prēs′) *n.* **1** a sudden change of mind without any reason; unreasonable notion or desire: *Her decision to wear only blue clothes was pure caprice.* **2** a tendency to change suddenly and without reason. **3** capriccio (def. 2). [< F < Ital. *capriccio.* Doublet of CAPRICCIO.]

ca·pri·cious (kə prish′əs *or* kə prē′shəs) *adj.* likely to change suddenly and without reason; changeable; fickle: *a spoiled and capricious child, capricious weather.* —**ca·pri′cious·ly,** *adv.*
—**ca·pri′cious·ness,** *n.*

Cap·ri·corn (kap′rə kôrn′) *n.* **1** *Astronomy.* a southern constellation thought of as having the shape of a goat. **2** *Astrology.* **a** the tenth sign of the zodiac. The sun enters Capricorn about December 22. See **zodiac** for picture. **b** a person born under this sign. **3** See **Tropic of Capricorn.** [< L *capricornus* < *caper* goat + *cornu* horn]

cap·ri·ole (kap′rē ōl′) *n., v.* **-oled, -ol·ing.** —*n.* **1** a high leap made by a horse without moving forward. **2** a leap; caper. —*v.* **1** of a horse, make a high leap without moving forward. **2** leap; caper. [< F < Ital. *capriola* leap < *capriolo* roebuck, dim. of *caper* goat. See CAPRICCIO.]

caps *or* **caps. 1** capital letters. **2** capsule.

cap screw a bolt that screws into an opening, used to secure a cover, etc.

cap·si·cum (kap′sə kəm) *n.* **1** any of a genus (*Capsicum*) of small tropical shrubs of the nightshade family, some of which are widely grown for their edible fruit. Green peppers, chilies, and pimentos are the fruits of cultivated varieties of capsicum. **2** the fruit of any of these shrubs. [< NL < L *capsa* box]

cap·size (kap sīz′ *or* kap′sīz) *v.* **-sized, -siz·ing.** of a ship, boat, etc., turn bottom side up; upset; overturn. [origin unknown]

cap·stan (kap′stən) *n.* a machine for lifting or pulling that revolves on an upright shaft or spindle. Sailors on early sailing ships hoisted the anchor by turning the capstan by means of spokes inserted into the shaft; on later ships the capstan was operated by an engine. See **ship** for picture. [< Provençal *cabestan* < L *capistrum* halter < *capere* take]

capstan bar a pole used to turn a capstan.

cap·stone (kap′stōn′) *n.* the top stone of a wall or other structure.

cap·su·lar (kap′sə lər *or* kap′syə lər) *adj.* **1** of or having to do with a capsule. **2** in a capsule. **3** shaped like a capsule.

cap·sule (kap′səl *or* kap′syül) *n., v.* —*n.* **1** a small container of gelatin or other soluble substance for enclosing a dose of medicine. **2** the enclosed front section of a rocket, made to carry instruments, astronauts, etc. into space. In flight, the capsule can separate from the rest of the rocket and go into orbit or be directed back to earth. **3** any of various compact containers or coverings. **4** *Botany.* a dry seedcase that opens when ripe. **5** *Anatomy.* a membrane enclosing an organ; a membranous bag or sac. **6** a concise summary. **7** (*adj.*) condensed; concise: *She gave a capsule description of the entire plan.* —*v.* furnish with or enclose within a capsule: *It will be capsuled in a cylinder.* [< L *capsula,* dim. of *capsa* box]

cap·sul·ize (kap′sə līz′ *or* kap′syə līz′) *v.* **-ized, -iz·ing.** **1** condense into or express in a compact form. **2** enclose in a capsule.

Capt. *or* **Capt** captain.

cap·tain (kap′tən) *n.* **1** a leader; chief. **2** *Canadian Forces.* **a** an officer ranking next above a lieutenant and below a major. *Abbrev.*: Capt. *or* Capt **b** in Maritime Command, the equivalent of a colonel. *Abbrev.*: Capt.(N) *or* Capt(N) See chart at **rank**[1]. **3** an officer of similar rank in the armed forces of other countries. **4** the commander of a ship. **5** *Sports.* the leader of a team. *Abbrev.*: Capt. —*v.* lead or command as captain: *Tom will captain the team.* [ME < OF *capitain(e)* < LL *capitaneus* chief < L *caput* head. Doublet of CHIEFTAIN.]

cap·tain·cy (kap′tən sē) *n., pl.* **-cies.** the rank, commission, or authority of a captain.

cap·tain·ship (kap′tən ship′) *n.* **1** the rank, position, or authority of a captain. **2** ability as a captain; leadership.

cap·tion (kap′shən) *n., v.* —*n.* **1** a title or heading at the beginning of a page, article, chapter, etc. **2** an explanation or title accompanying a picture. **3** in motion pictures, subtitle. **4** of a legal document, the part that gives the time, place, or authority for the document. —*v.* put a caption on. [< L *captio, -onis* a taking < *capere* take]

cap·tious (kap′shəs) *adj.* **1** hard to please; faultfinding. **2** apt or designed to entrap or entangle by subtlety: *captious arguments.* [< L *captiosus* < *capere* take] —**cap′tious·ly,** *adv.* —**cap′tious·ness,** *n.*

cap·ti·vate (kap′tə vāt′) *v.* **-vat·ed, -vat·ing.** **1** hold captive by beauty or interest; charm; fascinate: *The children were captivated by the animal story.* **2** *Archaic.* capture. —**cap′ti·vat′ing·ly,** *adv.* —**cap′ti·va′tion,** *n.* —**cap′ti·va′tor,** *n.*

cap·tive (kap′tiv) *n., adj.* —*n.* a person or animal taken and held by force, skill, or trickery: *The army brought back a thousand captives.* —*adj.* **1** taken and held; captured or kept under control: *a captive balloon. The captive soldiers were kept in a special prison.* **2** obliged to participate; having no choice: *a captive audience, a captive market.* [ME < OF *captif* < L *captivus* < *capere* take. Doublet of CAITIFF.]

cap·tiv·i·ty (kap tiv′ə tē) *n., pl.* **-ties.** the state of being held captive: *Some animals cannot bear captivity and die after a few weeks in a cage.*

cap·tor (kap′tər) *n.* a person who takes or holds a prisoner.

cap·ture (kap′chər) *v.* **-tured, -tur·ing;** *n.* —*v.* **1** take by force, skill, or trickery; seize: *They were captured during the raid.* **2** attract: *The brightly-colored toy immediately captured the baby's attention.* **3** succeed in preserving: *The artist was able to capture the mood of a rainy fall day.* —*n.* **1** taking or being taken by force, skill, or trickery. **2** a person or thing taken in this way. [< F < L *captura* taking < *capere* take] —**cap′tur·er,** *n.*

cap·u·chin (kap′yü chin′ *or* kap′yü shin′) *n.* **1** any of a genus (*Cebus*) of South American monkeys typically having a thick, cowl-like crown of hair. **2** a woman's cloak with a hood. **3 Capuchin,** a friar belonging to a branch of the Franciscan order. Capuchins are distinguished by their long, pointed hood or cowl. [< F < Ital. *cappuccio* hood]

ca·put (kap′ət *or* kä′pət) *n., pl.* **cap·i·ta** (kap′ə tə). *Latin.* head.

cap·y·ba·ra (kap′ə bär′ə) *n.* either of two species of semiaquatic rodent constituting the genus *Hydrochoerus,* found in Central and South America. The best-known is *H. hydrochaeris* of South America, the largest living rodent, reaching a length of 1.2 metres. [< Pg. *capybara* < the Brazilian native name]

car (kär) *n.* **1** a passenger vehicle that carries its own engine and is used on roads and streets. **2** any vehicle that moves on wheels. **3** a vehicle that runs on rails and is used to carry passengers or freight, such as a railway car or a streetcar. **4** the closed platform of an elevator, balloon, etc. for carrying passengers or cargo. **5** *Poetic or archaic.* chariot. [ME < ONF *carre* < Med.L *carra* < L *carrus* two-wheeled cart]
☛ *Usage.* **Car** now commonly replaces *automobile, auto, motorcar,* and other terms for four-wheeled vehicles powered by a gasoline engine. But it is not used in referring to trucks, buses, and other specifically commercial vehicles.

ca·ra·ba·o (kä′rə bä′ō) *n., pl.* **-ba·os.** water buffalo. [< Sp. < Malay *karbau*]

car·a·bi·neer *or* **car·a·bi·nier** (kar′ə bə nēr′ *or* ker′ə bə nēr′) *n.* *Historical.* a cavalry soldier armed with a carbine. [< F]

car·a·cal (kar′ə kal′ *or* ker′ə kal′) *n.* a small, slender, long-legged wildcat (*Lynx caracal,* also classified as *Felis caracal*) of African and Asian desert regions, having reddish-brown fur with black-tipped ears. Also called **Persian lynx, desert lynx.**

car·a·cole (kar′ə kōl′ *or* ker′ə kōl′) *n., v.* **-coled, col·ing.** —*n.* a half turn to the right or left, made by a horse and rider. —*v.* make such half turns; prance from side to side. [< F < Ital. < Sp. *caracol* spiral shell]

car·a·cul (kar′ə kəl *or* ker′ə kəl) *n.* a type of flat, loose, curly fur made from the skin of newborn karakul lambs. Also, **karakul.** [< *Kara Kul,* a lake in Turkestan]

ca·rafe (kə raf′) *n.* a glass bottle for holding water, wine, etc. [< F < Ital. *caraffa* < Sp. < Arabic *gharrâf* drinking vessel]

car·a·ga·na (kar′ə gan′ə *or* ker′ə gan′ə) *n.* any of a genus (*Caragana*) of shrubs or small trees of the legume family, having feathery, pale-green foliage and yellow flowers that appear in early spring. Caraganas are widely grown on the Prairies as hedges and windbreaks because they can survive in a dry climate. [< NL < Tartar]

caragana break a hedge of caragana serving as a windbreak.

car·a·mel (kar′ə məl, ker′ə məl, *or* kär′məl) *n.* **1** sugar browned or burned over heat, used for coloring and flavoring food. **2** a small block of chewy candy flavored with this sugar. [< F < Sp. *caramelo*]

car·a·pace (kar′ə pās′ *or* ker′ə pās′) *n.* the shell on the back of a turtle, lobster, etc. [< F < Sp. *carapacho*]

car·at (kar′ət *or* ker′ət) *n.* a unit of mass for precious stones, equal to 200 mg. [< F < Ital. < Arabic < Gk. *keration,* a small horn-shaped bean used as a weight, dim. of *keras* horn]
☛ *Hom.* **caret, carrot, karat.**

car·a·van (kar′ə van′ *or* ker′ə van′) *n., v.* —*n.* **1** a group of people travelling together, especially for safety. **2** the vehicles or beasts of burden used by such a group. **3** *Esp.Brit.* a mobile home, especially one pulled by a car; trailer. **4** a covered vehicle, such as a camper or van. **5** *Military.* a mobile headquarters for a senior officer. —*v.* travel in a caravan. [< F *caravane* < Persian *karwan*]

car·a·van·sa·ry (kar′ə van′sə rē *or* ker′ə van′sə rē) *n., pl.* **-ries.** **1** an inn or hotel where caravans stop to rest in the Orient: *There used to be many caravansaries on the trade routes from China to Arabia.* **2** any large inn or hotel. [< Persian *karwansarai* < *karwan* caravan + *sarai* inn]

car·a·van·se·rai (kar′ə van′sə rī′ *or* -sə rä′, ker′ə van′sə rī′ *or* -sə rä′) *n.* caravansary.

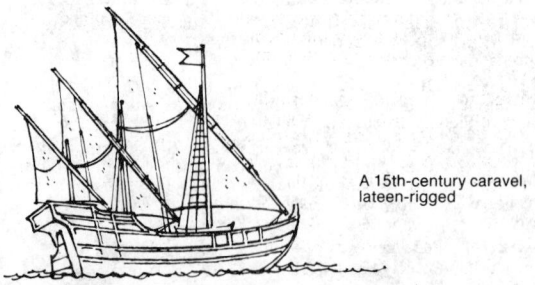

A 15th-century caravel, lateen-rigged

car·a·vel (kar′ə vel′ *or* ker′ə vel′) *n.* any of various small sailing ships of former times. One type was used by Columbus and other navigators of the same period. [< OF *caravelle* < Ital. < LL *carabus* < Gk. *karabos* kind of light ship < ancient Macedonian]

car·a·way (kar′ə wā′ *or* ker′ə wā′) *n.* **1** a biennial herb (*Carum carvi*) of the parsley family having finely divided leaves and a fragrant fruit used in cooking and medicine. **2** the dried fruit, usually called **caraway seed,** of this plant, used especially in flavoring cheeses and breads. [< Med.L *carui* < Arabic *karawya*]

car·bide (kär′bīd) *n.* a compound of carbon with a metal, especially calcium carbide.

car·bine (kär′bīn) *n.* a short, light rifle, originally designed for cavalry use. [< F *carabine*]

car·bi·neer (kär′bə nēr′) *n.* carabineer.

car·bo·hy·drate (kär′bō hī′drāt′) *n.* any of a group of compounds composed of carbon, hydrogen, and oxygen, that take part in the chemical processes in living plants and animals. Sugar and starch are carbohydrates. In sunlight, green plants make carbohydrates from carbon dioxide and water. [< *carbo(n)* + *hydrate*]

car·bo·lat·ed (kär′bə lāt′id) *adj.* containing carbolic acid.

car·bol·ic (kär bol′ik) *adj.* made from carbon or coal tar. [< L *carbo* coal + *oleum* oil]

carbolic acid a poisonous, corrosive, white crystalline compound present in coal tar and wood tar, used in solution as a disinfectant and antiseptic; phenol. *Formula:* C_6H_5OH

car·bo·lize (kär′bə līz′) *v.* **-lized, -liz·ing.** add carbolic acid to; treat with carbolic acid.

car·bon (kär′bən) *n.* **1** a very common non-metallic element found in combination with other elements in all plants and animals. Carbon forms organic compounds in combination with hydrogen, oxygen, etc. Diamonds and graphite are pure carbon; coal and charcoal are impure carbon. *Symbol:* C; *at.no.* 6; *at.wt.* 12.01115. **2** a piece of carbon used in batteries, arc lamps, etc. **3** a piece of carbon paper. **4** a copy made with carbon paper. [< F *carbone* < L *carbo, -onis* coal]

carbon 13 a heavy, stable isotope of carbon having a mass number of 13, used as a tracer in physiological studies, especially in cancer research.

carbon 14 a heavy radio-active isotope of carbon, produced by the bombardment of nitrogen atoms. It is used as a tracer in biological research and in carbon dating.

car·bo·na·ceous (kär′bə nā′shəs) *adj.* **1** of or containing carbon. **2** like or containing coal.

car·bo·na·do¹ (kär′bə nā′dō) *n.* —*n.* a piece of meat, fish, etc. scored and then broiled. —*v.* **1** score and broil. **2** *Archaic.* slash; hack. [< Sp. *carbonada* something cooked in coals < *carbon* charcoal < L *carbo, -onis*]

car·bo·na·do² (kär′bə nā′dō) *n.* a bulky dark-colored type of diamond, used for drills and found mostly in Brazil; black diamond. [< Pg. *carbonado* carbonized (from its color)]

carbon arc 1 a curved stream of light or sparks formed when a strong electric current jumps from one carbon electrode or conductor to another. **2** an arc lamp having carbon electrodes emitting such a stream of light or sparks.

car·bon·ate (*n.* kär′bən āt′ *or* kär′bən it; *v.* kär′bən āt′) *n., v.* **-at·ed, -at·ing.** —*n.* a salt or ester of carbonic acid. —*v.* **1** change into a carbonate. **2** charge with carbon dioxide. Soda water is carbonated to make it bubble and fizz. **3** burn to carbon; char; carbonize. —**car′bon·a′tion,** *n.*

carbon black a smooth, black pigment of pure carbon formed by deposits from burning gas, oil, etc.; a black soot, finer than lampblack.

carbon copy 1 a copy made by using carbon paper. **2** anything that appears to be a duplicate of something else: *His ideas are a carbon copy of his father's.*

carbon cycle 1 *Physics.* the process whereby nuclear changes in the interior of stars bring about the liberation of atomic energy that gradually transforms hydrogen to helium. **2** *Biology.* the circulation of carbon in nature.

carbon dating a method of determining the age of a once-organic archaeological or geological specimen by examining the extent to which the carbon 14 in it has disintegrated.

carbon dioxide a heavy, colorless, odorless gas, present in the atmosphere. Plants absorb it from the air to make plant tissue. The air that comes from an animal's lungs contains carbon dioxide. *Formula:* CO_2

car·bon·ic (kär bon′ik) *adj.* of or containing carbon.

carbonic acid the acid made when carbon dioxide is dissolved in water. *Formula:* H_2CO_3

Car·bon·if·er·ous (kär′bən if′ər əs) *n., adj.* —*n.* **1** *Geology.* the period, beginning approximately 315 million years ago, when the warm, moist climate produced a rank growth of tree ferns, horsetail rushes, and conifers, whose remains form the great coal beds. See the chart at **geology.** **2** the rocks and coal beds formed during this period. —*adj.* **carboniferous,** containing coal. [< *carbon* + *-ferous* containing (< L *ferre* to bear)]

car·bon·i·za·tion (kär′bən ə zā′shən *or* kär′bən ī zā′shən) *n.* carbonizing or being carbonized.

hat, āge, fär; let, ēqual, tėrm; it, īce
hot, ōpen, ôrder; oil, out; cup, pút, rüle,
above, takən, pencəl, lemən, circəs
ch, child; ng, long; sh, ship
th, thin; ᴛʜ, then; zh, measure

car·bon·ize (kär′bən īz′) *v.* **-ized, -iz·ing. 1** change into carbon by burning. **2** cover or combine with carbon.

carbon monoxide a colorless, odorless, poisonous gas, formed when carbon burns with an insufficient supply of air. It is part of the exhaust gases of automobile engines. *Formula:* CO

carbon paper a thin paper having a preparation of carbon or other inky substance on one surface, used for making copies of written or typed material. Carbon paper is placed between sheets of ordinary paper to make a copy of whatever is written or typed on the top sheet.

carbon tet·ra·chlo·ride (tet′rə klô′rīd *or* -klô′rid) a poisonous, colorless, nonflammable liquid, often used in fire extinguishers and in cleaning fluids. *Formula:* CCl_4

car·bo·run·dum (kär′bə run′dəm) *n.* **1** an extremely hard compound of carbon and silicon, used for grinding, polishing, etc. *Formula:* SiC **2 Carborundum,** the trademark for this compound. [< *carbo*n + *corundum*]

car·boy (kär′boi) *n.* a very large bottle of glass or plastic, usually enclosed in a protective box or crate, used for keeping liquids safely. [< Persian *qarabah* large flagon]

car·bun·cle (kär′bung kəl) *n.* **1** a severe abscess of the skin and tissues just beneath the skin, forming a hard, painful, dark red swelling that looks like a group of boils. A carbuncle discharges pus through several openings. **2** *Archaic.* a round garnet or other deep-red jewel not cut in facets. [ME < OF < L *carbunculus* < *carbo* coal]

car·bu·ret (kär′bə rāt′ *or* kär′byü ret′) *v.* **-ret·ted** *or* **-ret·ed, -ret·ting** *or* **-ret·ing. 1** mix (air or gas) with carbon compounds, such as gasoline, benzine, etc. **2** combine with carbon. [< *carbon*]

car·bu·re·tion (kär′bə rā′shən *or* kär′byü resh′ən) *n.* carburetting or being carburetted.

car·bu·re·tor (kär′bə rā′tər *or* kär′bə ret′ər) *n.* a device for sending air through or over a liquid fuel, so as to produce an explosive mixture. Also, **carburettor.**

car·ca·jou (kär′kə zhü′) *n. Cdn.* wolverine. [< Cdn.F < Algonquian]

car·ca·net (kär′kə net′) *n. Archaic.* an ornamental, usually jewelled necklace, collar, or headband. [< F *carcan* + E *-et*]

car·case (kär′kəs) *Brit.* See **carcass.**

car·cass (kär′kəs) *n.* **1** the body of a dead animal. A human body or corpse is sometimes contemptuously called a carcass. **2** the whole trunk of a butchered animal, after removal of the head, limbs, and offal. **3** the lifeless shell or husk of anything: *the carcass of his disappointed hopes.* **4** the shell or framework of a structure, as of a building, ship, or piece of furniture. **5** the foundation structure of a tire, consisting of layers of corded fabric. [< F < Ital. *carcassa*]

car·cin·o·gen (kär sin′ə jən) *n.* any substance or agent that causes cancer.

car·cin·o·gen·ic (kär′sin′ə jən′ik) *adj.* tending to cause cancer: *The drug was taken off the market because it was found to be carcinogenic.*

car·ci·no·ma (kär′sə nō′mə) *n., pl.* **-mas, -ma·ta** (-mə tə). a cancerous growth, especially in the skin or the lining of a tube or cavity in the body. [< L < Gk. *karkinōma* ulcer]

car coat a short topcoat for casual wear, cut for ease and comfort when driving.

card¹ (kärd) *n., v.* —*n.* **1** a piece of stiff paper, thin cardboard, or plastic, usually small and oblong: *a business card, a credit card.* **2** playing card. **3 cards,** *pl.* **a** any of various games played with a set of playing cards: *She enjoys cards.* **b** the playing of such a game: *Many of the guests were busy at cards.* **4** a piece of paper, usually folded, printed with a message or greeting and an illustration and sent in an envelope to mark a special occasion such as Christmas, a birthday, etc.: *Did you send him a card?* **5** compass card. **6** *Informal.* an amusing person. **7** *Brit.* cardboard.
a card up (one's) **sleeve,** a plan in reserve; extra help kept back until needed.
hold all the cards, have complete control (over).
in or **on the cards,** sure to happen: *It was in the cards that it would rain; nothing has gone right all day.*
play (one's) **cards well** (or **right,** etc.), deal or act cleverly.
put (one's) **cards on the table,** be perfectly frank about one's plans, resources, etc.

show (one's) cards, reveal one's plans. —*v.* **1** provide with a card. **2** put on a card. [< F *carte* < L *charta* < Gk. *chartēs* a leaf of papyrus. Doublet of CHART.]

card² (kärd) *n., v.* —*n.* a toothed tool or wire brush. —*v.* clean or comb with such a tool. [ME < OF *carde* < Provençal < L *carere* to card; influenced by L *carduus* thistle]

Card. Cardinal.

car·da·mom or **car·da·mum** (kär′də məm) *n.* **1** a spice consisting of the dried fruit, whole or ground, of a perennial East Indian herb (*Elettaria cardamomum*) of the ginger family. Cardamom is used in curry dishes and in Scandinavian pastries. **2** the plant producing this fruit, cultivated especially in S Asia and Central America. [< L < Gk. *kardamōmon*]

car·da·mon (kär′də mən) *n.* cardamom.

card·board (kärd′bôrd′) *n.* a fairly thick kind of stiff paper, used to make cards, boxes, cartons, etc.

card catalogue a reference catalogue of cards individually listing books and other items in a library or collection; card index.

card·er (kär′dər) *n.* a person or machine that cards wool, cotton, flax, etc.

card file a set of cards arranged systematically and containing data or information.

card game a game played with playing cards: *Would you like to learn a new card game?*

car·di·ac (kär′dē ak′) *adj., n.* —*adj.* **1** of or having to do with the heart: *cardiac symptoms.* **2** having to do with the upper part of the stomach. —*n.* a medicine that stimulates the heart. [< L *cardiacus* < Gk. *kardiakos* < *kardia* heart]

car·di·gan (kär′də gən) *n.* a sweater or knitted jacket that opens down the front and is usually collarless. [after the Earl of *Cardigan* (1797-1868)]

car·di·nal (kär′də nəl) *adj., n.* —*adj.* **1** of first importance; main; chief; principal: *His idea was of cardinal importance to the plan.* **2** bright red.
—*n.* **1** a bright red. **2** *Roman Catholic Church.* one of the high officials appointed by the Pope to the College of Cardinals, and second to him in rank. **3** Usually, **cardinals,** *pl.* cardinal numbers. **4** a North American songbird (*Richmondena cardinalis*) related to the finches, having a pointed crest on the head and a heavy, reddish bill, the male having bright-red plumage marked with grey and black, and the female being mainly brownish, with reddish wings, tail, and crest. [ME < OF < L *cardinalis* chief, having to do with a hinge < *cardo* hinge]

car·di·nal·ate (kär′də nəl āt′) *n.* the position or rank of cardinal.

cardinal flower a perennial plant (*Lobelia cardinalis*) that is a common wildflower of E North America and Central America and is also cultivated for its spikes of brilliant red flowers.

cardinal grosbeak a cardinal.

cardinal number any of the numbers one, two, three, fifteen, eight hundred, etc. that show quantity and are used in simple counting. Compare **ordinal number.**

cardinal points the four main directions of the compass: north, south, east, and west.

cardinal virtues prudence, fortitude, temperance, and justice. They were considered by the ancient philosophers to be the basic qualities of a good character.

card index a file of cards each referring to a separate item in a collection, list, research study, etc., so arranged as to aid in finding items desired; card catalogue.

card·ing (kär′ding) *n.* the preparation of the fibres of wool, cotton, flax, etc. for spinning by combing them.

cardio– *combining form.* **1** the heart: *Cardiology = the science of the heart.* **2** the heart and——: *Cardiovascular = relating to the heart and blood vessels.*

car·di·o·gram (kär′dē ə gram′) *n.* a graphic record of the action of the heart, made by a cardiograph.

car·di·o·graph (kär′dē ə graf′) *n.* an instrument that records the strength and nature of movements of the heart. [< Gk. *kardia* heart + *-graph*]

car·di·og·ra·phy (kär′dē og′rə fē) *n., pl.* **-phies.** an examination of the action of the heart by means of a cardiograph.

car·di·ol·o·gist (kär′dē ol′ə jist) *n.* one who studies the heart and its functions, or who specializes in the treatment of heart diseases.

car·di·ol·o·gy (kär′dē ol′ə jē) *n.* the study of the heart and its functions, and the diagnosis and treatment of heart diseases.

car·di·o·vas·cu·lar (kär′dē ō vas′kyə lər) *adj.* of or having to do with both the heart and the blood vessels: *Hardening of the arteries is a cardiovascular disease.*

car·di·tis (kär dī′tis) *n.* inflammation of the heart. [< NL < Gk. *kardia* heart + *-tis*]

card·sharp (kärd′shärp′) *n.* a person who cheats at cards, especially one who does so for a livelihood.

card·sharp·er (kärd′shärp′ər) *n.* cardsharp.

care (ker) *n., v.* **cared, car·ing.** —*n.* **1** a troubled state of mind because of fear of what may happen; worry: *Few people are completely free from care.* **2** serious attention; caution: *A good cook works with care.* **3** an object of worry, concern, or attention: *Keeping records is the care of the secretary of the club.* **4** watchful keeping; charge: *The child was left in her sister's care.* **5** food, shelter, and protection: *Your child will have the best of care.*
care of or **in care of,** at the address or in the charge of: *Send it care of his father. Symbol:* c/o
have a care, be careful.
take care, be careful.
take care of, **a** attend to; take charge of: *The waiter will take care of your order.* **b** look after; provide for: *She has a pension to take care of her basic needs. His brother took care of him while he was sick.* **c** be careful with; watch over: *Take care of your money.*
—*v.* **1** be concerned; feel an interest: *He cares about conservation. I don't care what they said.* **2** want; wish: *They said they didn't care to come.* **3** to object; mind (*usually used with negatives or in questions*): *Will he care if I borrow his sweater? They don't care if we come home late once in a while.*
care for, **a** have a liking or fondness for: *She doesn't care for him.* **b** want; wish: *I don't care for any dessert tonight.* **c** look after: *The nurse will care for him during the night.*
[OE *caru*] —**car′er,** *n.*
☛ *Syn. n.* **1.** Care, concern, solicitude = a troubled, worried, or anxious state of mind. **Care** emphasizes the idea of a burden which weighs a person down with responsibilities of worries and fears: *It is care that has made her sick.* **Concern** suggests uneasiness over someone or something one likes or is interested in: *He expressed concern over her health.* **Solicitude** suggests great concern, often together with loving care: *Her friends wait on her with solicitude.*

CARE (ker) Co-operative for American Remittances to Everywhere, Inc.

ca·reen (kə rēn′) *v.* **1** lean to one side; tilt; tip: *The ship careened in the strong wind.* **2** cause to lean to one side: *The strong wind careened the ship.* **3** lay (a ship) over on one side for cleaning, painting, repairing, etc. **4** rush along with a bobbing, leaning movement: *The waitress careened among the tables, balancing a heavy tray on one hand.* [< F < L *carina* keel]

ca·reer (kə rēr′) *n., v., adj.* —*n.* **1** a way of living; occupation; profession: *The boy planned to make law his career.* **2** a general course of action or progress through life: *It is interesting to read of the careers of great men and women.* **3** speed; full speed: *We were in full career when we struck the post.*
—*v.* rush along wildly; dash: *The runaway horse careered through the streets.*
—*adj.* having to do with someone who has seriously followed a profession: *a career diplomat.* [< F *carrière* race course < L *carrus* wagon]

ca·reer·ist (kə rēr′ist) *n.* a person interested only in advancing in his profession, often at the expense of other people.

care·free (ker′frē′) *adj.* without worry; light-hearted; happy.

care·ful (ker′fəl) *adj.* **1** thinking what one says; watching what one does; taking pains; watchful; cautious. **2** done with thought or effort; exact; thorough: *a careful investigation, a careful reading of a text.* **3** full of care or concern; attentive or protective: *She was always careful of the feelings of others.* **4** *Archaic.* anxious; worried. —**care′ful·ly,** *adv.* —**care′ful·ness,** *n.*
☛ *Syn.* **1.** Careful, cautious, wary = watchful in speaking and acting. **Careful** = being observant and giving serious attention and thought to what one is doing, especially to details: *He is careful to tell the truth at all times.* **Cautious** = very careful, looking ahead for possible risks or dangers, and guarding against them by taking no chances: *He is cautious about making promises.* **Wary** emphasizes the idea of being suspicious and on the alert for danger or trouble: *He is wary of people who suddenly become very friendly.*

care·less (ker′lis) *adj.* **1** not thinking what one says; not watching what one does; not taking enough pains; not watchful or cautious: *One careless step here could cost a life.* **2** done without enough thought or effort; not exact or thorough: *careless work, a careless worker.* **3** not troubling oneself; indifferent; unconcerned: *Careless of danger, he walked boldly into the enemy camp.* **4** carefree; untroubled. —**care′less·ly,** *adv.* —**care′less·ness,** *n.*

ca·ress (kə res′) *n., v.* —*n.* **1** a gentle, loving touch, stroke, or kiss. **2** any light or gentle touch: *the caress of a summer breeze.*
—*v.* touch or stroke gently, lightly, or lovingly: *He talked to the kitten softly as he caressed it. The wind caressed the treetops.* [< F *caresse* < Ital. *carezza* < L *carus* dear]

car·et (kar′ət *or* ker′ət) *n.* a mark (∧) to show where something

should be put in, used in writing and in proofreading. [< L *caret* is lacking, from *carere* be without; 17c.]
☛ *Hom.* **carat, carrot, karat.**

care·tak·er (ker′tāk′ər) *n.* **1** a person, especially a janitor, who takes care of a building, estate, etc. **2** (*adjl.*) of a government or management, carrying on the functions of an office on a temporary basis pending an election or the accession of a new administration.

care·worn (ker′wôrn′) *adj.* showing the effects of continuous worry and care.

car·fare (kär′fer′) *n.* the money that has to be paid for riding on a streetcar, bus, etc.: *He had just enough money for the carfare home.*

car·ful (kär′fŭl) *n., pl.* **-fuls.** as much as a car will hold; enough to fill a car: *a carful of children.*

car·go (kär′gō) *n., pl.* **-goes** or **-gos.** the load of goods carried on a ship or aircraft; freight: *a cargo of wheat.* [< Sp. *cargo* < *cargar* load, ult. < L *carrus* wagon]

car·hop (kär′hop′) *n. Informal.* a person who serves customers at a drive-in restaurant.

Car·ib (kar′ib or ker′ib) *n.* **1** a member of an Amerindian people who formerly inhabited NE South America and some islands in the Caribbean. **2** the language of the Caribs.

Car·ib·be·an (kar′ə bē′ən, ker′ə bē′ən, or kə rib′ē ən) *adj.* **1** of or having to do with the Caribbean Sea or the islands in it. **2** of or having to do with the Caribs or their language.

Car·i·boo (kar′ə bü′ or ker′ə bü′) *n.* **1 the Cariboo,** a region in the western foothills of the Cariboo Mountains in east central British Columbia, the site of a famous gold rush that began in 1860. **2** see **caribou.**

car·i·bou (kar′ə bü′ or ker′ə bü′) *n., pl.* **-bou** or **-bous.** **1** any of several subspecies of reindeer found in northern North America, of which the most widely spread are the **barren-ground caribou** (*Rangifer tarandus groenlandicus*) and the **woodland caribou** (*Rangifer tarandus caribou*). **2** the hide of a caribou: *a parka of caribou.* **3** (*adjl.*) made of this hide: *caribou mocassins.* [< Cdn.F < Algonquian *xalibu* pawer, from its habit of pawing snow in search of grass]

Caribou Eskimo a member of a group of Inuit living in the Barren Ground west of Hudson Bay. [with reference to their living on caribou]

car·i·ca·ture (kar′ə kə chür′ or ker′-, kar′ə kə chər or ker′-) *n., v.* **-tured, -tur·ing.** —*n.* **1** a picture, cartoon, description, etc. that deliberately exaggerates the peculiarities or defects of a subject. **2** the art of making such pictures or descriptions. **3** a very poor imitation. —*v.* make a caricature of. [< F < Ital. *caricatura* < *caricare* overload, exaggerate]

car·i·ca·tur·ist (kar′ə kə chür′ist or ker′-, kar′ə kə chər ist or ker′-) *n.* a person skilled in drawing caricatures, especially one whose work it is.

car·ies (ker′ēz or ker′ē ēz′) *n.* the decay of teeth, bones, or tissues: *Caries of the teeth is caused by bacteria.* [< L]

car·il·lon (kar′ə lon′, ker′ə lon′, or kə ril′yən) *n.* **1** a set of bells arranged for playing melodies: *There is a carillon in the Peace Tower in Ottawa.* **2** melody played on such bells. **3** a part of an organ that imitates the sound of bells. [< F, ult. < L *quattuor* four; originally consisted of four bells]

car·il·lon·neur (kar′ə lə nèr′ or ker′-) *n.* a person who plays a carillon.

car·i·o·ca (kar′ē ō′kə or ker′-) *n.* **1** a dance of South America. **2 Carioca,** a native or inhabitant of Rio de Janeiro. [< Brazilian Portuguese *carioca*]

car·i·ole[1] or **car·ri·ole**[1] (kar′ē ōl′ or ker′-) *n.* **1** a small, one-horse carriage. **2** a covered cart. [< F < Ital. *carriuola* < L *carrus* wagon]

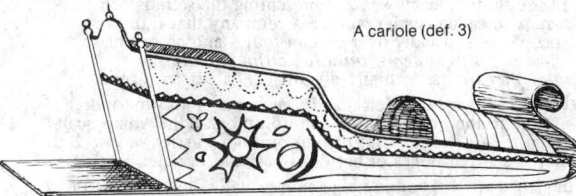
A cariole (def. 3)

car·i·ole[2] or **car·ri·ole**[2] (kar′ē ōl′ or ker′-) *n., v.* **-oled, -ol·ing. Cdn.** —*n.* **1** a light, open sleigh having a single seat for the driver, drawn by one or two horses or, sometimes, by dogs. **2** a light sleigh usually drawn by two horses and having seats for a driver and two passengers. **3** a dogsled, often ornately decorated,

hat, āge, fär; let, ēqual, tèrm; it, īce
hot, ōpen, ôrder; oil, out; cup, pút, rüle,
əbove, takən, pencəl, lemən, circəs

ch, child; ng, long; sh, ship
th, thin; ŦH, then; zh, measure

for carrying freight or equipped to carry one person lying down: *The sick trapper was brought to the post on a cariole.* —*v.* ride in a cariole. [< Cdn.F]

car·i·ous (ker′ē əs) *adj.* having caries; decayed. [< L *cariosus* < *caries* decay]

car jockey *Informal.* **1** a person employed by a hotel, restaurant, etc. to park customers' cars and return them to the customer when needed. **2** a person employed by a car rental agency to deliver cars to customers and to collect cars returned by customers.

cark·ing (kär′king) *adj.* troublesome; worrying. [< obs. *cark* burden, worry < AF *karke*, ult. < LL *carricare* load]

carl or **carle** (kärl) *n.* **1** *Archaic.* a peasant; rustic. **2** *Scottish.* a boor; churl. [< ON *karl* man]

car·lin or **car·line** (kär′lin or ker′lin) *n. Scottish.* **1** *Often derogatory.* a woman, especially an old woman. **2** a witch, or a woman charged with being a witch. [ME < Scand.; cf. ON *kerling* < *karl* man + *-ing*, a feminine suffix]

car·load (kär′lōd′) *n.* **1** the number or amount that an automobile can carry: *We passed a carload of people bound for the party.* **2** the amount that a freight car can hold or carry: *a carload of grain.*

Car·lo·vin·gi·an (kär′lə vin′jē ən) *adj.* or *n.* Carolingian.

Car·ma·gnole (kär′mən yōl′) *n.* a dance and song popular during the French Revolution. [< F < *Carmagnola,* a town in Piedmont taken by the revolutionaries]

car·man (kär′mən) *n., pl.* **-men.** *Rare.* **1** carter. **2** motorman.

Car·mel·ite (kär′məl īt′) *n.* a mendicant friar or nun of a religious order founded in the 12th century or earlier.

car·min·a·tive (kär min′ə tiv, kär′mə nə tiv, or kär′mə nā′tiv) *adj., n.* —*adj.* expelling gas from the stomach and intestines. —*n.* a medicine that does this. [< L *carminatus* carded; cleansed]

car·mine (kär′mən or kär′mīn) *n., adj.* —*n.* **1** a deep red with a tinge of purple. **2** a light crimson. **3** a crimson coloring matter found in cochineal, used to stain microscopic slides and formerly as a dye. —*adj.* **1** deep red with a tinge of purple. **2** light crimson. [< Med.L *carminium* < Arabic *qirmiz* the kermes insect, and L *minium* red lead. See CRIMSON.]

car·nage (kär′nij) *n.* the slaughter of a great number of people, as in war. [< F < Ital. *carnaggio* < L *caro, carnis* flesh]

car·nal (kär′nəl) *adj.* **1** having to do with the desires and pleasures of the body; sensual: *Gluttony and drunkenness have been called carnal vices.* **2** worldly; not spiritual. [< L *carnalis* < *caro, carnis* flesh. Doublet of CHARNEL.] —**car′nal·ly,** *adv.*

car·nal·i·ty (kär nal′ə tē) *n., pl.* **-ties. 1** worldliness. **2** sensuality.

car·na·tion (kär nā′shən) *n., adj.* —*n.* **1** any of numerous cultivated varieties of pink derived from the clove pink, widely grown in gardens and greenhouses for their large, many-petalled flowers which usually have a spicy fragrance. **2** the flower of a carnation: *He wore a carnation in his lapel.* **3** having the color carnation. **4** *Obsolete.* the pinkish color of fair skin. —*adj.* **1** having the color carnation. **2** *Obsolete.* of or having the color of fair skin. [< F < Ital. *carnagione* flesh color < *carnaggio.* See CARNAGE.]

car·nel·ian (kär nēl′yən or kär nēl′ē ən) *n.* **1** a red or reddish-brown variety of chalcedony used in jewellery. The color is caused by traces of iron oxide. **2** a gem made from this stone. Also called **cornelian.** [alteration of *cornelian;* influenced by L *caro* flesh]

car·nie (kär′nē) *n., pl.* **-nies.** *Slang.* **1** carnival. **2** a person who works or performs in a carnival. Also, **carny.**

car·ni·val (kär′nə vəl) *n.* **1** a place of amusement, especially a travelling show having merry-go-rounds, side shows, etc. **2** feasting and merrymaking; celebration. **3** an organized program of events involving a particular sport, institution, etc.: *a water carnival.* **4** a time of feasting and merrymaking just before Lent. [< Ital. *carnevale* < Med.L < L *carnem levare* the putting away of meat (before Lent)]

car·ni·vore (kär′nə vôr′) *n.* **1** any of an order (Carnivora) of mammals that feed chiefly on flesh or other animal matter rather than plants. Cats, dogs, weasels, raccoons, bears, seals, etc. are carnivores. **2** an insect-eating plant. [< F]

car·niv·o·rous (kär niv′ə rəs) *adj.* **1** feeding or subsisting on flesh or other animal matter. **2** of a plant, able to use animal substance as food. Carnivorous plants such as the pitcher plant trap

and digest insects and other small animals. **3** of or having to do with carnivores or the order Carnivora. [< L *carnivorus* < *caro, carnis* flesh + *vorare* devour]

car·no·tite (kär′nə tīt′) *n.* a yellowish, radio-active mineral found in the W and SW United States. It is a source of radium and uranium. [after Adolphe *Carnot* (1839-1920), a French inspector-general of mines]

car·ny (kär′nē) See **carnie.**

car·ob (kar′əb *or* ker′əb) *n.* **1** a Mediterranean evergreen tree (*Ceratonia siliqua*) of the pea family having compound leaves, red flowers, and long, blackish pods. **2** the edible pod of this tree, having a sweet pulp.

car·ol (kar′əl *or* ker′əl) *n., v.* **-olled** or **oled, -ol·ling** or **-ol·ing.** —*n.* **1** a song of joy. **2** a hymn of joy: *Christmas carols.* —*v.* **1** sing; sing joyously: *The birds were carolling in the trees.* **2** praise with carols. [ME < OF *carole*, probably < L < Gk. *choraulēs* flute player accompanying a choral dance < *choros* dance + *aulos* flute] —**car′ol·ler** or —**car′ol·er,** *n.*

Car·o·line (kar′ə līn′ *or* ker′-, kar′ə lin *or* ker′-) *adj.* of or having to do with Charles, especially Charles I or Charles II of England.

Car·o·lin·gi·an (kar′ə lin′jē ən *or* ker′-) *adj., n.* —*adj.* of or having to do with the second Frankish dynasty. It ruled in France from A.D. 751 to 987, in Germany from A.D. 751 to 911, and in Italy from A.D. 751 to 887. —*n.* a ruler during the Carolingian dynasty: *Charlemagne was a Carolingian.* Also, **Carlovingian.**

Car·o·lin·i·an (kar′ə lin′ē ən *or* ker′-) *adj., n.* —*adj.* of North Carolina and South Carolina, or of either of them. —*n.* a native or inhabitant of North Carolina or South Carolina.

car·om (kar′əm *or* ker′əm) *n., v.* —*n.* **1** *Billiards.* a kind of shot in which the ball struck with the cue hits two balls, one after the other. **2** a similar shot in other games. **3** a hitting and bouncing off. —*v.* **1** make a carom. **2** hit and bounce off. [< F < Sp. *carambola*, ? < Malay *carambil*, name of fruit]

ca·rot·id (kə rot′id) *n., adj.* —*n.* either of two large arteries, one on each side of the neck, that carry blood to the head. —*adj.* having to do with these arteries. [< F < Gk. *karōtides* < *karos* stupor (state produced by compression of carotids); 17c.]

ca·rous·al (kə rouz′əl) *n.* a noisy revel; drinking party.

ca·rouse (kə rouz′) *n., v.* **-roused, -rous·ing.** —*n.* a noisy feast; drinking party. —*v.* drink heavily; take part in noisy feasts or revels. [< obs. adv. < G *gar aus(trinken)* (drink) all up] —**ca·rous′er,** *n.*

car·ou·sel or **car·rou·sel** (kar′ə sel′ *or* ker′-, kar′ə zel′ *or* ker′-) **1** a merry-go-round. **2** at an airport, a revolving circular platform onto which the baggage of arriving passengers is delivered from a central chute. [< F < Ital. *carosello* < L *carrus* cart]

carp[1] (kärp) *v.* find fault; complain. [< ON *karpa* wrangle] —**carp′er,** *n.* —**carp′ing·ly,** *adv.*

carp[2] (kärp) *n., pl.* **carp** or **carps.** **1** a freshwater food fish (*Cyprinus carpio*) of the minnow family having large scales, a long dorsal fin, and two barbels on each side of the upper jaw. It is native to Asia, but has been introduced into Europe and North America. **2** any of various other comparatively large fishes of the same family. **3** any of various suckers. [ME < OF *carpe* < Provençal < LL *carpa* < Gmc.]

car·pal (kär′pəl) *adj., n.* —*adj.* of or having to do with the carpus. —*n.* a bone of the carpus. [< NL *carpalis* < Gk. *karpos* wrist]

☛ *Hom.* **carpel.**

car·pe di·em (kär′pē dē′em *or* dī′em) *Latin.* enjoy today; make the most of the present.

car·pel (kär′pəl) *n.* the central part of a flower containing the ovules, which develop into seeds. Some flowers, such as the pea and bean, have a simple pistil composed of only one carpel; other flowers, such as the iris and mock orange, have a compound pistil composed of several carpels fused together. See **flower** for picture. [< Gk. *karpos* fruit]

☛ *Hom.* **carpal.**

car·pen·ter (kär′pən tər) *n., v.* —*n.* a person skilled in carpentry, especially one whose work it is. —*v.* do carpentry. [ME < ONF *carpentier* < L *carpentarius* < *carpentum* wagon]

car·pen·try (kär′pən trē) *n.* the trade or art of building, finishing, and repairing wooden objects or structures.

car·pet (kär′pit) *n., v.* —*n.* **1** a thick, heavy, woven covering for floors and stairs. **2** the fabric used for such a covering; carpeting. **3** anything like a carpet: *A carpet of grass.*

on the carpet, a in the condition of being considered or discussed. **b** *Informal.* in the state of being scolded or rebuked. —*v.* cover with a carpet: *In the spring, the ground was carpeted with violets.* [ME < OF < Med.L *carpeta* thick cloth < L *carpere* card (wool)]

car·pet·bag (kär′pit bag′) *n.* a travelling bag made of carpeting: *Carpetbags were common in the nineteenth century.*

car·pet·bag·ger (kär′pit bag′ər) *n. Derogatory.* **1** *U.S. Historical.* a Northerner who went to the South to get political or other advantages during the time of disorganization that followed the Civil War. **2** *Esp.U.S.* a politician who stands for office or seeks influence for his own advantage in a region other than his own.

carpet beetle any of various small beetles (family Dermestidae, especially genus *Anthrenus*) whose larvae destroy carpets and other fabrics and furs. Also, **carpet bug.**

car·pet·ing (kär′pit ing) *n.* **1** a fabric for carpets. **2** carpets.

carpet sweeper a device for cleaning carpets and rugs.

carp·ing (kär′ping) faultfinding; naggingly critical: *a carping tongue, carping critics.*

car pool an arrangement by which members of a group take turns at providing transportation in their own cars, especially to and from work.

car·port (kär′pôrt′) *n.* a roofed shelter for one or more automobiles. It is usually attached to a house and open on at least one side.

carp·suck·er (kärp′suk′ər) *n.* quillback.

car·pus (kär′pəs) *n., pl.* **-pi** (-pī *or* -pē). *Anatomy.* **1** the group of short bones forming the joint between the forearm and the hand; the bones of the wrist. See **arm**[1] for picture. **2** the corresponding part of the foreleg of an animal; the knee joint. [< NL < Gk. *karpos* wrist]

car·rack (kar′ək *or* ker′ək) *n.* a large, regularly heavily armed, European merchant ship used from the 14th to the 17th centuries, similar to a caravel but larger and broader. The carrack was the forerunner of the three-masted ships. [ME < OF *carraque* < Sp. < Arabic *qaraqir*, pl.]

car·ra·geen or **car·ra·gheen** (kar′ə gēn′ *or* ker′ə gēn′) *n.* a small, purplish, edible seaweed (*Chondrus crispus*) found along rocky coasts of the North Atlantic, used especially as an emulsifying agent in medicines, certain foods, cosmetics, etc. [< *Carragheen*, near Waterford, Ireland, where it is abundant]

car·rel (kar′əl *or* ker′əl) *n.* an enclosed space for individual study in a library, usually containing a desk and bookshelves. [alteration of ME *carole* ring. See CAROL.]

car·riage (kar′ij *or* ker′ij; *for* 6, *also* kar′ē ij *or* ker′ē ij) *n.* **1** a vehicle that moves on wheels. Carriages are usually pulled by horses and are used to carry people. **2** a wheeled frame which supports a gun and by which it is moved from place to place. **3** a moving part of a machine that supports some other part: *the carriage of a typewriter.* **4** the manner of holding the head and body; bearing: *She has a queenly carriage.* **5** the act of taking persons or goods from one place to another; carrying; transporting: *carriage charges.* **6** the cost or price of carrying. **7** *Archaic.* management. [ME < ONF *cariage* < *carier.* See CARRY.]

☛ *Syn.* **4.** See note at **bearing.**

carriage bolt a bolt having a round shaft but for a square part just under the head, formerly used chiefly to fasten together parts of a carriage.

carriage trade the wealthy patrons, or customers, of a theatre, restaurant, store, etc. so called because such persons formerly drove in private carriages.

car·ri·er (kar′ē ər *or* ker′ē ər) *n.* **1** a person or thing that carries something: *Letter carriers deliver mail. Trains, buses, and ships are carriers.* **2** anything designed to carry something in or on. **3** a person or thing that carries or transmits a disease. Healthy persons who are immune to a particular disease may be carriers. **4** *Telecommunications.* a radio-frequency wave used to transmit, or carry, the audio-frequency waves representing the sounds being broadcast. Also called **carrier wave. 5** a company that transports goods, people, etc., usually over certain routes and according to fixed schedules: *Bus systems, railways, airlines, and truck companies are carriers.* **6** an aircraft carrier. **7** a carrier pigeon.

Car·ri·er (kar′ē ər *or* ker′ē ər) *n.* **1** a member of an Amerindian people living in the interior of British Columbia. **2** the Athapascan language of the Carriers. [from the custom of a Carrier widow carrying the charred bones of her dead husband in a net bag]

carrier pigeon **1** a homing pigeon, especially one trained to fly home from great distances carrying written messages. **2** a breed of large show pigeon.

carrier wave a radio wave whose intensity and frequency are varied in order to transmit a signal.

car·ri·ole (kar′ē ōl′ *or* ker′ē ōl′) See **cariole.**

car·ri·on (kar′ē ən *or* ker′ē ən) *n., adj.* —*n.* **1** dead and decaying flesh. **2** rottenness; filth.
—*adj.* **1** dead and decaying. **2** feeding on dead and decaying flesh. **3** rotten; filthy. [ME < OF *carogne*, ult. < L *caro* flesh. Doublet of CRONE.]

carrion crow a common European crow (*Corvus corone*).

car·ro·nade (kar′ə nād′ *or* ker′ə nād′) *n. Historical.* a short cannon with a large bore. [< *Carron*, Scotland]

car·rot (kar′ət *or* ker′ət) *n.* **1** a cultivated biennial herb (*Daucus carota sativa*) of the parsley family having feathery, finely divided leaves, flat clusters of tiny white flowers, and a long, thick, tapering orange root. See also **wild carrot.** **2** the root of this plant, eaten raw or cooked as a vegetable. **3** a promise of reward, used as an incentive or lure. [< F *carotte* < L < Gk. *karōton*]
☛ *Hom.* **carat, caret, karat.**

car·rot·y (kar′ət ē *or* ker′ət ē) *adj.* **1** like a carrot in color; orange red. **2** red-haired.

car·rou·sel (kar′ə sel′ *or* ker′-, kar′ə zel′ *or* ker′-) See **carousel.**

car·ry (kar′ē *or* ker′ē) *v.* **-ried, -ry·ing;** *n., pl.* **-ries.** —*v.* **1** take from one place to another: *Buses carry passengers. He carried the sleepy child up to bed.* **2** bear the weight of; hold up; support; sustain: *Those columns carry the roof.* **3** hold (one's body and head) in a certain way; have a certain kind of posture: *This boy carries himself well.* **4** capture; win: *Our troops carried the enemy's fort.* **5** get (a motion or bill) passed or adopted: *The motion to adjourn the meeting was carried.* **6** continue; extend: *to carry a road into the mountains.* **7** cover the distance; have the power of throwing or driving: *His voice carried easily to the back of the room. This gun will carry one kilometre.* **8** keep in stock: *This store carries men's clothing.* **9** of a newspaper, magazine, etc., print an article in its pages: *The evening newspapers carried a review of the new play.* **10** sing with correct or nearly correct pitch: *He can carry a tune.* **11** sing or play (a melody, part, etc.): *She will carry the soprano solos. The first violins carry the melody.* **12** influence greatly; lead: *His acting carried the audience.* **13** have as a result; have as an attribute, property, etc.; involve: *His judgment carries great weight.* **14** keep on the account books of a business. **15** *Mathematics.* transfer a number from one place or column in the sum to the next: *A 10 in the 1's column must be carried to the 10's column.*
carry away, arouse strong feeling in; influence beyond reason.
carry everything before (one), meet with uninterrupted success; be very successful in spite of opposition.
carry forward, **a** go ahead with; make progress with. **b** in bookkeeping, re-enter (an item or items already entered) on the next or a later page or column of an accounting record.
carry off, **a** win (a prize, honor, etc.). **b** succeed with: *It was her first speech, but she carried it off all right.*
carry on, **a** do; manage or conduct: *He carried on a successful business for many years.* **b** go ahead with; go on with after being stopped. **c** keep going; continue: *We must carry on in our effort to establish world peace.* **d** *Informal.* behave wildly or foolishly: *The small boys really carried on at the party.*
carry out, do; get done; accomplish; complete.
carry over, **a** have left over; be left over. **b** keep until later; continue; extend.
carry the ball, *Informal.* take the chief part in promoting or carrying through a plan or activity.
carry the day, **a** be victorious in battle. **b** be successful against opposition.
carry through, **a** do; get done; accomplish; complete. **b** bring through trouble; keep from being discouraged.
—*n.* **1** the distance covered or the distance that something goes. **2** the act of carrying boats and supplies from one body of water to another; portage. **3** a place where this is done. **4** *Golf.* the distance a ball travels in the air before hitting the ground. [< ONF *carier* < LL *carricare* < L *carrus* wagon, cart. Doublet of CHARGE.]
☛ *Syn. v.* **1. Carry, convey, transport** = to take or bring from one place to another. **Carry,** the general word, emphasizes the idea of holding and moving a person or thing in or with something, such as a vehicle, container, hands, or paws: *John was carrying a heavy box.* **Convey** emphasizes getting a person or thing to a place by some means or through some channel, and therefore is used figuratively in the sense of communicate: *Language conveys ideas.* **Transport** = to carry or convey people and goods in a ship, plane, or vehicle: *Trucks transport freight.*

car·ry·all¹ (kar′ē ol′ *or* ker′ē-, kar′ē ôl′ *or* ker′ē-) *n.* **1** *Cdn.* a covered one-horse carriage. **2** cariole. [alteration of *cariole*]

car·ry·all² (kar′ē ol′ *or* ker′ē-, kar′ē ôl′ *or* ker′ē-) *n.* **1** any of several vehicles so named because of their large capacity. **2** a large bag or basket.

carry cot a collapsible, boxlike cradle equipped with handles and used for carrying a baby: *Mother always uses the carry cot when she takes the baby out in the car.*

carry change the interest charged on money owing for goods or services bought on credit.

car·ry·ing-on (kar′ē ing on′ *or* ker′ē-) *n., pl.* **carry·ings-on.**

hat, āge, fär; let, ēqual, tèrm; it, īce
hot, ōpen, ôrder; oil, out; cup, pùt, rüle,
әbove, takәn, pencәl, lemәn, circәs
ch, child; ng, long; sh, ship
th, thin; ᴛʜ, then; zh, measure

Informal. **1** a loud disturbance; fuss. **2** conspicuous, uninhibited, or indiscreet behavior.

carrying place *Cdn.* a portage.

car·ry·o·ver (kar′ē ō′vәr *or* ker′ē-) *n.* the part left over.

car seat **1** the seat of an automobile. **2** a small, light seat for a child, designed to hook over a standard automobile seat.

car·sick (kär′sik′) *adj.* nauseated as a result of the motion of a car, train, etc. —**car′sick′ness,** *n.*

cart (kärt) *n., v.* —*n.* **1** a vehicle with two wheels, used to carry heavy loads: *Horses, donkeys, and oxen are often used to pull carts.* **2** a light wagon, used to deliver goods, etc. **3** a small, wheeled vehicle that is moved by hand.
put the cart before the horse, reverse the proper or natural order of things.
—*v.* carry in a cart. [ME < ON *kartr*]
☛ *Hom.* **carte.**

cart·age (kär′tij) *n.* **1** the act of carting. **2** the cost of carting.

carte¹ (kärt) *n.* **1** card. **2** bill of fare. **3** map; chart. [< F. See CARD¹.]
☛ *Hom.* **cart.**

carte² (kärt) *n. Fencing.* a thrust or parry. [< F *quarte* < Ital. *quarta* fourth]
☛ *Hom.* **cart.**

carte blanche (kärt blänsh′) *French.* **1** full authority; freedom to use one's discretion. **2** freedom to do whatever one pleases.

car·tel (kär tel′ *or* kär′tәl) *n.* **1** a combination of independent businesses formed to regulate prices, production, and marketing of goods. **2** a written agreement between countries at war for the exchange of prisoners or for some other purpose. **3** an alliance of political groups for a common cause. [< F < Ital. *cartello* little card¹, specifically one used for a written challenge to a duel]

car·tel·ize (kär tel′īz *or* kär′tәl īz′) *v.* **-ized, -iz·ing.** **1** combine in a cartel. **2** join with other businesses to form a cartel.

cart·er (kär′tәr) *n.* **1** a person whose work is driving a cart or truck. **2** a person who runs a trucking business.

Car·te·sian (kär tē′zhәn) *adj.* **1** of or having to do with René Descartes (1596-1650), a French philosopher and mathematician. **2** of or suggestive of his doctrines or methods. [< NL *Cartesianus* < *Cartesius,* Latinized form of *Descartes*]

Cartesian set *Mathematics and logic.* the set of all ordered pairs that can be formed by matching each member of one set in turn with each member of a second set.

Car·tha·gin·i·an (kär′thә jin′ē әn) *n., adj.* —*n.* a native or inhabitant of Carthage, an ancient city and seaport in N Africa. —*adj.* of or having to do with Carthage.

cart horse draft horse.

Car·thu·sian (kär thü′zhәn) *n., adj.* —*n. Roman Catholic Church.* a monk or nun of an order founded by St. Bruno in 1086. —*adj.* of this order. [< *Cartusia,* now *Chartreuse,* the village in the French Alps where the first monastery of the order was founded]

car·ti·lage (kär′tә lij) *n.* **1** a tough, elastic tissue that forms most of the skeleton of very young vertebrates and, in higher vertebrates, is for the most part changed into bone as the animal matures; gristle. Cartilage is found in adults at the ends of the long bones, between the bones of the spine, in the nose, etc. **2** a part formed of cartilage. [< F < L *cartilago*]

car·ti·lag·i·nous (kär′tә laj′ә nәs) *adj.* **1** of or like cartilage; gristly. **2** having the skeleton formed mostly of cartilage: *Sharks are cartilaginous fish.*

cart·load (kärt′lōd′) *n.* as much as a cart can hold or carry.

car·to·gram (kär′tә gram′) *n.* a map that gives information by means of dots, lines, etc.

car·tog·ra·pher (kär tog′rә fәr) *n.* a person skilled in making maps or charts, especially one whose work it is.

car·to·graph·ic (kär′tә graf′ik) *adj.* having to do with cartography or cartographers.

car·tog·ra·phy (kär tog′rә fē) *n.* the making of maps or charts. [< Med.L *carta* chart, map + E *-graphy*]

car·ton (kär′tәn) *n.* **1** a box or other container made of cardboard: *The books were packed in cartons. Milk can be bought in cartons.* **2** the amount that a carton can hold. **3** a carton and its

contents. [< F *carton* cardboard < Ital. *cartone* < *carta* < L *charta*. Related to CARD[1].]

car·toon (kär tün′) *n., v.* —*n.* **1** a humorous drawing, often having a caption, that shows ridiculous or exaggerated situations; a pictorial joke: *Many magazines and newspapers have cartoons.* **2** an exaggerated drawing or caricature, often accompanied by words, meant to make fun of a political figure or current happenings: *The editorial page of our paper has a cartoon every day.* **3** a comic strip. **4** a movie made up of a series of drawings; animated cartoon: *Cartoons often show animals engaging in human activities.* **5** a full-size sketch to be traced or copied as the design for a fresco, mosaic, tapestry, etc.
—*v.* **1** make a cartoon of. **2** make cartoons. [var. of *carton*; because drawn on paper]

car·toon·ist (kär tün′ist) *n.* a person skilled in drawing cartoons, especially one whose work it is.

car·tridge (kär′trij) *n.* **1** a cylindrical metal tube containing a charge of explosive and, usually, a bullet, for use in a rifle or pistol. **2** a shell for a shotgun. **3** a usually long, round case containing a refill of material, such as ink for a fountain pen. **4** a sealed plastic case containing a spool of film together with a take-up spool, designed for use with certain types of camera: *The cartridge is simply dropped into the back of the camera.* **5** a sealed plastic case containing film or magnetic tape in an endless loop wound on a single reel. The film or tape unwinds from the centre of the reel and rewinds around the outside. **6** (*adj.*) of a film projector or tape recorder, designed for use with cartridges. **7** a removable unit in the tone arm of a record player, containing the needle, or stylus, and a crystal or magnet that changes the movements of the needle into electric waves. [alteration of F *cartouche* roll or paper]

cartridge paper a heavy, uncoated type of paper used for drawing and also, especially formerly, for making cartridges or shells.

cart·wheel (kärt′wēl′ or -hwēl′) *n., v.* —*n.* **1** the wheel of a cart. **2** a sideways handspring or somersault, made with the arms and legs stretched out stiffly like the spokes of a wheel. **3** *Archaic. Slang.* a large coin, such as a large British penny or a silver dollar.
—*v.* **1** make a sideways handspring or somersault. **2** move like a rotating wheel.

carve (kärve) *v.* **carved, carv·ing. 1** cut into slices or pieces: *to carve the meat at the table.* **2** cut; make by cutting: *Statues are often carved from marble, stone, or wood.* **3** decorate with figures or designs cut on the surface: *to carve a wooden tray.* **4** cut (a design, etc.) on or into a surface: *They carved their initials on the tree.* **5** make as if by cutting: *He ruthlessly carved himself a financial empire.* [OE *ceorfan*]

car·vel (kär′vəl) *n.* caravel.

carv·en (kär′vən) *adj.* carved; decorated by carving.

carv·er (kär′vər) *n.* **1** a person who carves. **2** a large knife for carving meat.

carv·ing (kär′ving) *n.* **1** the act or art of a person who carves. **2** a piece of carved work; a carved decoration: *a wood carving.*

car·y·at·id (kar′ē at′id or ker′ē at′id) *n., pl.* **-ids, -i·des** (-ə dēz′). *Architecture.* a supporting column carved in the form of a woman. Compare **telamon.** [< L *Caryatides* < Gk. *Karyatides* women of Caryae]

ca·sa·ba (kə sä′bə) or **cas·sa·ba** (kə sä′bə) *n.* a variety of winter muskmelon with a yellow rind and sweet, green or white flesh. [< *Kasaba*, a town near Izmir (formerly Smyrna), Turkey]

Cas·a·no·va (kas′ə nō′və or kaz′ə nō′və) *n.* a man who has many affairs with women, especially an immoral adventurer with women. [< Giovanni Giacomo *Casanova* (1725-1798), an Italian adventurer, known for his *Memoirs*]

Cas·bah (käz′bä) *n.* **1** the native section of Algiers. **2** casbah, the Arab section of any city with a large Arab population. [< Arabic *qasaba* fortress, citadel]

cas·cade (kas kād′) *n., v.* **-cad·ed, -cad·ing.** —*n.* **1** a small waterfall. **2** anything like a waterfall: *a cascade of ruffles.* —*v.* fall, or cause to fall, in a cascade. [< F < Ital. *cascata* < L *cadere* fall]

cas·car·a (kas ker′ə) *n.* **1** a buckthorn (*Rhamnus purshiana*) found along the Pacific coast of North America, yielding cascara sagrada. **2** cascara sagrada. [< Sp. *cáscara* bark]

cas·car·a sa·gra·da (sə grä′də or sə grä′də) the dried bark of cascara, used as a laxative. [< Sp. *cáscara sagrada* sacred bark]

cas·ca·ril·la (kas′kə ril′ə) *n.* **1** Also, **cascarilla bark,** the bitter, aromatic bark of a West Indian shrub (*Croton eluteria*) of the spurge family used as flavoring for tobacco or as a tonic. **2** the shrub itself. [< Sp. *cascarilla,* dim. of *cáscara.* See CASCARA.]

case¹ (kās) *n.* **1** an instance; example: *a case of poor work.* **2** a set

of circumstances; situation; state: *You are in a worse case than I.* **3** the actual condition; real situation; true state: *He said he had done the work, but that was not the case.* **4** an instance of a disease or injury: *a case of measles.* **5** a person who has a disease or injury; patient. **6** a matter for a court of law to decide. **7** a statement of facts raising a point of view for a court to consider. **8** the set of arguments or supporting facts to justify an action, situation, etc.: *the case for a guaranteed annual income.* **9** *Informal.* a peculiar or unusual person. **10** *Grammar.* **a** a distinct form of a noun, pronoun, or adjective that shows its relation to other words in a sentence. **b** the relation shown by such a distinct form. English does not have a case system like German or Latin. English nouns and most pronouns have only two forms indicating grammatical relation: a common, or simple, form (e.g. *boy, woman,* somebody) and a possessive form (*boy's, woman's, somebody's*). Six English pronouns have three case forms: the subjective form (*I, we, he, she, they, who*), objective form (*me, us, him, her, them, whom*), and possessive form (*mine, ours, his, hers, theirs, whose*). English adjectives do not indicate grammatical relation at all.
in any case, under any circumstances; no matter what happens; in any event; anyhow: *In any case, you should prepare for the worst.*
in case, if it should happen that; if; supposing.
in case of, if there should be; in the event of: *In case of fire, walk to the nearest door.*
in no case, under no circumstances.
[ME < OF *cas* < L *casus* a falling, chance < *cadere* fall]

➤ **Syn. 1. Case, instance** = example. **Case** applies to a fact, actual happening, situation, etc. that is typical of a general kind or class: *His accident is a case of reckless driving.* **Instance** applies to an individual case used to illustrate a general idea or conclusion: *Going through a stop signal is an instance of his recklessness.*

➤ *Usage.* **Case.** Writers often make unnecessary and ineffective use of expressions containing the word *case: Although I read many stories, in not one case was I satisfied with the ending. She used the same plot before in the case of a short story about pioneer days.* In the first sentence, *case* is entirely unnecessary. The second can be improved by dropping *the case of.*

case² (kās) *n., v.* **cased, cas·ing.** —*n.* **1** a strong, heavy box: *a packing case. There is a big case full of books in the hall.* **2** the quantity in a box, etc.: *a case of ginger ale.* **3** a covering; sheath: *Put the knife back in the case.* **4** an outer protective part: *My watch has a steel case.* **5** a frame; casing. **6** *Printing.* a tray for type, with a space for each letter. **7** the covers and spine for a hard-bound book, especially before being attached to the book.
lower case, small letters.
upper case, capital letters.
—*v.* **1** put in a case; cover with a case. **2** *Slang.* look over carefully; inspect; examine: *The thieves cased the bank.* [ME < ONF *casse* < L *capsa* box < *capere* hold. Doublet of CASH¹, CHASE³.]

case–bound (kās′bound′) *adj.* hard-bound.

ca·se·fy (kā′sə fī′) *v.* **-fied, -fy·ing.** make or become like cheese. [< L *caseus* cheese + E *-fy*]

case·hard·en (kās′här′dən) *v.* **1** harden (iron or steel) on the surface. **2** render callous; make unfeeling.

case history all the facts about a person or group that may be useful in deciding what medical or psychiatric treatment, social services, etc. are needed.

ca·sein (kā′sēn or kā′sē in) *n.* the protein found especially in milk and which is the main ingredient of cheese. Casein is used in making plastics, paints, and adhesives. [< L *caseus* cheese]

case knife **1** a knife carried in a case. **2** a table knife.

case law law based on previous judicial decisions rather than on statutes.

case·mate (kās′māt) *n.* **1** a bombproof chamber in a fort or rampart, with openings through which cannon may be fired. **2** an armored enclosure protecting guns on a warship. [< F < Ital. *casamatta* (influenced by *casa* house), earlier *camata,* apparently < Gk. *chasmata* openings]

case·ment (kās′mənt) *n.* **1** a window opening on vertical hinges. **2** *Poetic.* any window. **3** a casing; covering; frame.

ca·se·ous (kā′sē əs) *adj.* of or like cheese. [< L *caseus* cheese]

ca·sern or **ca·serne** (kə zėrn′) *n.pl. Historical.* barracks or a billet for soldiers in a fortified town. [< F < Sp. *caserna* < L *casa* house]

case·work (kās′wėrk′) *n.* a thorough study of the character and present and past circumstances of a maladjusted person, family, or group, carried out by a social worker to serve as a basis for guidance or treatment. **—case′work′er,** *n.*

cash¹ (kash) *n., v.* —*n.* **1** money in the form of coins and bills; ready money. **2** money, or something recognized as the equivalent of money, such as a cheque, paid at the time of buying something: *I don't like charge accounts; I prefer to pay cash.* **3** *Informal.* the place in a store, restaurant, etc. where purchases are paid for: *You pay at the cash.*
—*v.* **1** get ready money for: *I'll have to cash a cheque to pay for it.* **2** give ready money for: *That teller will cash your cheque.*

cash in, a *Informal.* change (poker chips, etc.) into cash. **b** *Slang.* die.

cash in on, *Informal.* **a** make a profit from. **b** take advantage of; use to advantage.
[< F *caisse* < Provençal < L *capsa* box, coffer. Doublet of CASE², CHASE³.] **—cash′a·ble,** *adj.*

cash² (kash) *n., pl.* **cash. 1** in China, India, etc., a coin of small value. **2** in China, a copper coin with a square hole in it. [< Tamil *kasu*]

cash–and–car·ry (kash′ən kar′ē) *adj.* **1** with immediate payment for goods and without delivery service. **2** operated on this basis: *a cash-and-carry store.*

cash·book (kash′bùk′) *n.* a book in which a record is kept of money received and paid out.

cash crop a crop grown for sale, rather than for consumption on the farm.

cash·ew (kash′ū or kə shü′) *n.* **1** an evergreen tree (*Anacardium occidentale*) native to tropical and subtropical America cultivated for its kidney-shaped nuts. **2** the nut of this tree, edible when roasted. **3** (*adj.*) designating the family (Anacardiaceae) of trees and shrubs that includes the cashew as well as pistachio, mango, and the sumacs. [< F *acajou* < Brazilian Pg. *acajú* < Tupi-Guarani]
☛ *Hom.* cachou (kə shü′).

cash·ier¹ (kash ēr′) *n.* a person who has charge of money in a bank or business. [< F *caissier* treasurer < *caisse*. See CASH¹.]

cash·ier² (kash ēr′) *v.* dismiss from the armed forces for some dishonorable act; discharge in disgrace. [< Du. *casseren* < F < L *quassare* shatter and LL *cassare* annul]

cashier's cheque a cheque drawn by a bank on its own funds and signed by its cashier.

cash·mere (kash′mēr) *n.* **1** the soft, downy fibre forming the undercoat of a breed of goats raised especially in Kashmir and Tibet. **2** a fine, soft cloth made from this fibre. **3** any fine, soft woollen cloth. [< *Kashmir,* north of India]

cash on delivery payment when goods are delivered. *Abbrev.:* C.O.D. or c.o.d.

cash register a machine that records and shows the amount of a sale. It usually has a drawer to hold money.

cas·ing (kās′ing) *n.* **1** something to put around something else to cover or contain it; case: *The air in a rubber tire is contained inside a casing made of layers of rubberized cord fabric.* **2** a lining or liner, especially metal tube or pipe used to line a water, oil, or gas well. **3** a frame: *A window fits in a casing.* **4** a long, narrow space between two layers of fabric, formed by two parallel lines of stitching, used to insert a rod, as for curtains, or a drawstring or elastic, as for clothing. **5** a membrane used to encase sausage meat. It may be the cleaned intestine of cattle, pigs, etc. or a synthetic substitute.

ca·si·no (kə sē′nō) *n., pl.* **-nos. 1** a building or room for public shows, dancing, gambling, etc. **2** cassino. [< Ital. *casino,* dim. of *casa* house < L *casa*]

cask (kask) *n.* **1** a cylindrical container with outward-curving sides usually made of wooden staves bound by iron hoops, and having a flat top and bottom. Casks are used especially for holding beer, wine, etc. **2** the amount that a cask holds. **3** a cask and its contents. [< Sp. *casco* skull, cask of wine, ult. < L *quassare* break]

cas·ket (kas′kit) *n.* **1** a small box or chest used to hold jewels, letters, etc. **2** coffin. [origin uncertain]

casque (kask) *n.* armor for the head; helmet. [< F < Sp. *casco.* See CASK.]

cas·sa·ba (kə sä′bə) See casaba.

Cas·san·dra (kə san′drə) *n.* **1** *Greek mythology.* a daughter of King Priam of Troy. Apollo gave her the gift of prophecy, but later in anger decreed that no one should believe her. **2** any person who prophesies misfortune but is not believed.

cas·sa·tion (ka sā′shən) *n.* an annulment; reversal. [< LL *cassatio, -onis* < *cassare* annul]

cas·sa·va (kə sä′və) *n.* **1** any of several tropical American plants (genus *Manihot*) of the spurge family grown for their large, starchy rootstocks. **2** a starch from its roots, used as a staple food in the tropics. Tapioca is made from cassava. [< F *cassave* < Sp. < Haitian *cacábi* < Arawakan]

cas·se·role (kas′ə rōl′) *n.* **1** a baking dish in which food can be both cooked and served. **2** the food cooked and served in a casserole: *a chicken-and-rice casserole.* **3** a small, deep dish with a handle, used in chemical laboratories. [< F *casserole* < *casse* pan < VL *cattia* < Gk. *kyathion,* dim. of *kyathos* cup]

cas·sette (ka set′) *n.* **1** a sealed plastic case containing magnetic tape on a reel together with a take-up reel, designed for use with certain types of tape recorder. **2** (*adj.*) of a tape recorder, designed for use with cassettes. Cassette recorders are very simple to operate. **3** a lightproof plastic case, or magazine, for holding film, as

hat, āge, fär; let, ēqual, tèrm; it, īce
hot, ōpen, ôrder; oil, out; cup, pùt, rüle,
əbove, takən, pencəl, lemən, circəs

ch, child; ng, long; sh, ship
th, thin; ŦH, then; zh, measure

for a 35 mm camera. **4** a sealed plastic case containing a spool of film together with a take-up spool; cartridge (def. 3). **5** *Cdn. Historical.* a specially made box or trunk used by the fur traders for transporting personal effects on journeys inland. [< F *cassette* small case < OF *casse* case²]

cas·sia (kas′ē ə or kash′ə) *n.* **1** a spice similar to cinnamon, but coarser, obtained from the bark of a tropical Asian tree (*cinnamomum cassia*). **2** the tree itself. **3** any of a genus (*Cassia*) of mainly tropical herbs, shrubs, and trees of the pea family, especially any of several species whose leaves or pods yield a mild laxative. The laxative prepared from dried cassia leaves is called senna. **4** the pods or pulp of a cassia. [OE < L < Gk. < Hebrew *q'tsi'ah*]

cas·si·no or **ca·si·no** (kə sē′nō) *n.* a card game in which the ten of diamonds and the two of spades have special counting value. [var. of *casino*]

Cas·si·o·pe·ia (kas′ē ə pē′ə) *n.* **1** *Greek mythology.* the wife of an Ethiopian king and mother of Andromeda. **2** *Astronomy.* a northern constellation thought to resemble Cassiopeia sitting in a chair.

cas·sock (kas′ək) *n.* a long outer garment, usually black, worn by a clergyman. See picture in the next column. [< F *casaque* < Ital. *casacca*]

cas·socked (kas′əkt) *adj.* wearing a cassock.

cas·so·war·y (kas′ə wer′ē) *n., pl.* **-war·ies.** any of three species making up a genus (*Casuarius*) of large, flightless birds found in the forests of New Guinea, northern Australia, and nearby islands, having glossy black, hairlike plumage and a blue, featherless head and neck with a high, bony, helmetlike growth on the head. The cassowaries are the sole members of the family Casuariidae. [< Malay *kasuari*]

cast (kast) *v.* **cast, cast·ing;** *n., adj.* **—v. 1** throw, fling, or hurl. **2** throw one end of a fishing line out into the water. **3** throw off; discard; let fall: *The snake cast its skin.* **4** direct or turn: *He cast a glance of surprise at me.* **5** shape by pouring or squeezing into a mould to harden. Metal is first melted and then cast. **6** arrange: *He cast his plans into final form.* **7** *Theatre.* **a** assign the various parts of (a play). **b** appoint (actors) for the parts. **c** fill (a part) by assigning an actor to it. **8** add; calculate.
cast a ballot, vote.
cast about, search or seek; look around.
cast away, **a** abandon. **b** shipwreck.
cast down, **a** turn downward; lower. **b** make sad or discouraged: *He was cast down by the bad news.*
cast lots, use lots to decide something: *We cast lots for first chance to try out the raft.*
cast off, **a** let loose; set free: *to cast off a boat from its moorings.* **b** *Knitting.* make the last row of stitches.
cast on, *Knitting.* make the first row of stitches.
cast out, drive away; banish or expel.
cast up, **a** turn upward; raise: *He cast up his eyes and groaned in exasperation.* **b** add up; find the sum of.
—n. 1 the distance a thing is thrown: *She made a long cast with her line.* **2** the act of throwing a fishing line: *He made a skilful cast from the river bank.* **3** something made by casting; something that is moulded. **4** a mould used in casting. **5** a plaster support used to keep a broken bone in place while it is mending: *He had his arm in a cast for more than a month.* **6** the actors in a play. **7** the outward form or appearance: *His face had a gloomy cast.* **8** a kind or sort. **9** a slight amount of color; tinge: *a white dress with a pink cast.* **10** a slight squint.
—adj. made by casting. [ME < ON *kasta* throw]
☛ *Hom.* caste.
☛ *Syn. v.* **1.** See note at **throw.**

Castanets

cas·ta·net (kas′tə net′) *n.* a small rhythm instrument made of

ivory, hardwood, or plastic, consisting of two parts which are held in the hand and clicked together rhythmically, especially to accompany dancing. [< Sp. *castaneta* < L *castanea*. See CHESTNUT.]

cast·a·way (kast′ə wā′) *adj., n.* —*adj.* **1** thrown away; cast adrift. **2** outcast. —*n.* **1** a shipwrecked person. **2** an outcast.

caste (kast) *n.* **1** one of the four main social classes of India, formerly officially supported by the state and the Hindu religion. Castes have traditionally been hereditary; a person could never change his caste or marry somebody from another caste. **2** the system or basis of this division. **3** an exclusive social group; distinct class. **4** a social system having distinct classes separated by differences of birth, rank, wealth, or position.
lose caste, lose social rank or position.
[< Sp., Pg. *casta* race < L *castus* pure. Doublet of CHASTE.]
☛ *Hom.* cast.

cas·tel·lan (kas′tə lən) *n.* the governor of a castle. [< L *castellanus* occupant of a stronghold < *castellum*. See CASTLE.]

cas·tel·lat·ed (kas′tə lāt′id) *adj.* **1** like a castle; having turrets and battlements. **2** having many castles.

cast·er[1] (kas′tər) *n.* a person or thing that casts.

cast·er[2] or **cast·or** (kas′tər) *n.* **1** a small wheel on a swivel, set into the base of a piece of furniture or other heavy object to make it easier to move. **2** a bottle containing salt, mustard, vinegar, or other seasoning for table use. **3** a stand or rack for such bottles.

cas·ti·gate (kas′tə gāt′) *v.* -gat·ed, -gat·ing. criticize, rebuke, or punish severely. [< L *castigare*, ult. < *castus* pure]
—**cas′ti·ga′tion**, *n.* —**cas′ti·ga′tor**, *n.*

Cas·tile soap or **cas·tile soap** (kas′tēl *or* kas tēl′) **1** a pure, hard soap made from olive oil and sodium hydroxide. **2** any fine, mild soap made from another oil, such as coconut oil. [< *Castile*, a region in north and central Spain.]

Cas·til·ian (kas til′yən *or* kas til′ē ən) *n., adj.* —*n.* **1** a native or inhabitant of Castile, a region and former kingdom of Spain. **2** the standard form of Spanish used in Spain, originally the dialect of Castile. —*adj.* of or having to do with Castile, its people, or their dialect, or modern standard Spanish.

cast·ing (kas′ting) *n.* **1** something shaped by being poured into a mould to harden. **2** the process of making casts in a mould. **3** the assignment of the parts in a play, film, etc.

casting vote a vote by the presiding officer to decide a question when the votes of an assembly, council, board, or committee are evenly divided.

cast iron a hard, brittle form of iron containing carbon and silicon, made by re-melting pig iron and pouring it into moulds to harden.

cast-i·ron (kast′ī′ərn) *adj.* **1** made of cast iron. **2** hard; not yielding: *He has a cast-iron will.* **3** hardy; strong or impregnable: *a cast-iron stomach, a cast-iron alibi.*

cast-iron plant an aspidistra (*Aspidistra lurida*) often grown as a house plant, having long, tough, glossy leaves which grow from the base of the plant.

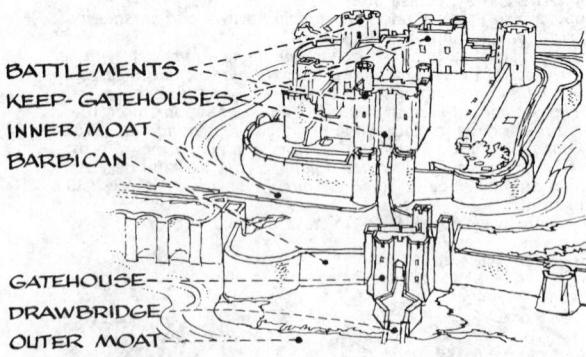

BATTLEMENTS
KEEP-GATEHOUSES
INNER MOAT
BARBICAN

GATEHOUSE
DRAWBRIDGE
OUTER MOAT

Caerphilly Castle in Glamorgan, Wales, built in the 13th century

cas·tle (kas′əl) *n., v.* -tled, -tling. —*n.* **1** a building or group of buildings with thick walls, towers, and other defences against attack. **2** a palace that once had defences against attack. **3** a large and imposing residence. **4** *Chess.* rook.
—*v.* **1** place in or as if in a castle. **2** *Chess.* **a** move the castle, or rook, and the king at the same time. **b** (of the king) be moved in this way. [< L *castellum*, dim. of *castrum* fort. Doublet of CHÂTEAU.]

castle in Spain a daydream; castle in the air.

castle in the air something imagined but not likely to come true; a daydream.

cast-off (kast′of′) *adj., n.* —*adj.* thrown away; abandoned. —*n.* **1** something that has been thrown away or put aside as no longer useful. **2** a person who has been abandoned or cast aside.

cas·tor[1] (kas′tər) See **caster**[2].

cas·tor[2] (kas′tər) *n.* **1** a hat made of beaver fur. **2** an oily substance with a strong odor, secreted by beavers. It is used in making perfume and in medicines. **3** beaver. [< L < Gk. *kastōr* beaver]

Cas·tor (kas′tər) *n.* **1** *Greek and Roman mythology.* the mortal twin brother of Pollux. **2** *Astronomy.* the second brightest star in the constellation Gemini. Pollux, the brightest star in the constellation, lies near it.

castor bean 1 the poisonous seed of the castor-oil plant.
2 castor-oil plant.

castor oil a yellow oil obtained from castor beans, used as a cathartic, a lubricant, etc.

cas·tor-oil plant (kas′tər oil′) a tall, tropical herb (*Ricinus communis*) of the spurge family, native to India, having very large, fanlike leaves. It is cultivated as an ornamental plant and also for its seeds, which yield an oil used as an industrial lubricant and also as a laxative.

cas·trate (kas′trāt) *v.* -trat·ed, -trat·ing. **1** remove the testicles of; geld. **2** take away the basic strength or vitality of. [< L *castrare*]

cas·tra·tion (kas trā′shən) *n.* the act of castrating.

cast steel steel that has undergone fusion.

cas·u·al (kazh′ü əl) *adj., n.* —*adj.* **1** happening by chance; not planned or expected; accidental: *a casual meeting.* **2** having or showing lack of concern or interest; careless, nonchalant, or indifferent: *He gave the painting only a casual glance. She takes a very casual approach to her work.* **3** informal; relaxed; easy-going: *casual manners, casual living.* **4** designed for informal use: *casual clothes, casual furniture.* **5** not given or done with any serious purpose or commitment; superficial: *a casual interest in the arts. He's just a casual acquaintance.* **6** happening, active, or employed on an irregular basis; occasional: *casual employment, a casual laborer.*
—*n.* **1** a casual laborer or worker. **2** a member of the armed forces temporarily attached to a post or station while awaiting transportation to his unit, to a permanent assignment, etc. [< L *casualis* < *casus* change] —**cas′u·al·ly**, *adv.* —**cas′u·al·ness**, *n.*

cas·u·al·ty (kazh′ü əl tē *or* kazh′əl tē) *n., pl.* -ties. **1** an accident. **2** an unfortunate accident; mishap. **3** a member of the armed forces who has been wounded, killed, or captured as a result of enemy action. **4** a person injured or killed in an accident or disaster, or as a result of enemy action: *The earthquake caused many casualties.*

cas·u·ist (kazh′ü ist) *n.* **1** a person who decides questions of right and wrong in conduct, duty, etc. **2** a person who reasons cleverly but falsely, especially in regard to right and wrong. [< F *casuiste* < L *casus* case]

cas·u·is·tic (kazh′ü is′tik) *adj.* **1** of or like casuistry. **2** too subtle; sophistical. —**cas′u·is′ti·cal·ly**, *adv.*

cas·u·is·ti·cal (kazh′ü is′tə kəl) *adj.* casuistic.

cas·u·ist·ry (kazh′ü is trē) *n., pl.* -ries. **1** the act or process of deciding questions of right and wrong in regard to conduct, duty, etc. **2** clever but false reasoning.

ca·sus bel·li (kā′səs bel′ī *or* kä′sùs bel′ē) *Latin.* a cause for war.

cat[1] (kat) *n., v.* cat·ted, cat·ting. —*n.* **1** a small domestic mammal (*Felis catus*) of the cat family having furry paws with soft pads and retractable claws, a rounded face with a short muzzle, short, pointed ears, and soft fur. Cats are kept as pets and for catching mice. **2** any of a family (Felidae) of mostly wild, flesh-eating, tree-climbing mammals characterized by lithe, muscular bodies, spiny tongues, teeth adapted for stabbing, holding, and cutting, but not for chewing, and claws that are retractable in all species but the cheetah. The cat family is divided into two main groups: the big roaring cats, including the lion, tiger, leopard, snow leopard, and jaguar; and the purring cats, including the lynx, wildcat, cougar, and domestic cat. **3** an animal resembling a cat. **4** a mean, spiteful woman. **5** catfish. **6** cat-o'-nine-tails. **7** the tackle for hoisting an anchor. **8** *Slang.* fellow; guy.
let the cat out of the bag, tell a secret: *It was supposed to be a surprise party, but he let the cat out of the bag.*
rain cats and dogs, rain very hard. —*v.* hoist (an anchor) and fasten it to a beam on the ship's side. [OE *catt(e)*, probably < LL *catta*]

cat[2] (kat) *n.* caterpillar tractor.

cat. 1 catalogue. 2 catechism.

cata– *prefix.* down; against; entirely, as in *cataract*. Also, **cat-** before vowels and *h*, as in *category, cathode.* [< Gk. *kata- < kata,* prep.]

ca·tab·o·lism (kə tab′ə liz′əm) *n. Biology.* the process of breaking down living tissues into simpler substances or waste matter, thereby producing energy. Also, **katabolism.** [probably < *metabolism*, by substitution of *cata-* down]

cat·a·chre·sis (kat′ə krē′sis) *n., pl.* **-ses** (-sēz). the misuse of words, especially the use of a word in an inappropriate or meaningless context. [< L < Gk. *katachrēsis* misuse < *kata-* amiss + *chrēsthai* use]

cat·a·clysm (kat′ə kliz′əm) *n.* 1 a flood, earthquake, or any sudden, violent change in the earth. 2 any violent change: *World War II was a cataclysm for all of Europe.* [< L *cataclysmos* < Gk. *kataklysmos* flood < *kata-* down + *klyzein* wash]

cat·a·clys·mal (kat′ə kliz′məl) *adj.* cataclysmic.

cat·a·clys·mic (kat′ə kliz′mik) *adj.* of or like a cataclysm; extremely sudden and violent.

cat·a·comb (kat′ə kōm′) *n.* Usually, **catacombs,** *pl.* an underground gallery forming a burial place. [< LL *catacumbae,* pl. < *cata* (< Gk. *kata*) *tumbas* (< Gk. *tymbos*) among the tombs]

cat·a·falque (kat′ə falk′) *n.* a stand or frame to support the coffin in which a dead person lies. [< F < Ital. *catafalco,* of uncertain origin]

Cat·a·lan (kat′ə lan′ *or* kat′ə lən) *n., adj.* —*n.* 1 a native or inhabitant of Catalonia, a region in NE Spain. 2 the Romance language of the Catalans, also spoken especially in Valencia, Andorra, and the Balearic Islands. —*adj.* of or having to do with Catalonia, its people, or their language.

cat·a·lep·sis (kat′ə lep′sis) *n.* catalepsy.

cat·a·lep·sy (kat′ə lep′sē) *n.* a kind of fit during which a person loses consciousness and the power to feel, and his muscles become rigid. [< LL *catalepsis* < Gk. *katalēpsis* seizure < *kata-* down + *lambanein* seize]

cat·a·lep·tic (kat′ə lep′tik) *adj., n.* —*adj.* 1 of catalepsy. 2 having catalepsy. —*n.* a person who has catalepsy.

cat·a·log (kat′ə log′) *n., v.* **-loged, -log·ing.** *Esp. U.S.* See **catalogue.** —**cat′a·log′er,** *n.*

cat·a·logue (kat′ə log′) *n., v.* **-logued, -logu·ing.** —*n.* 1 a list of items in a collection, identifying each item very briefly and sometimes describing it. A library has a catalogue of its books, arranged in alphabetical order. A company sometimes prints a catalogue with pictures and prices of the things that it sells. 2 a volume or booklet issued by a university or college listing rules, courses to be given, etc.; calendar. 3 a list; series: *a catalogue of lies, tricks, and deceits.* —*v.* make a catalogue of; put in a catalogue: *He catalogued all the insects in his collection.* [< F < LL < Gk. *katalogos* list < *kata-* down + *legein* count] —**cat′a·logu′er,** *n.*
☛ *Syn.* 1. See note at **list.**

ca·tal·pa (kə tal′pə) *n.* any of a small genus (*Catalpa*) of North American and Asian trees having large, heart-shaped leaves, clusters of bell-shaped flowers, and long pods. [< NL < Creek Indian *kutuhlpa*]

ca·tal·y·sis (kə tal′ə sis) *n., pl.* **-ses** (-sēz). *Chemistry.* the changing, especially the speeding up, of a chemical reaction by the presence of a substance that is not itself permanently changed. [< NL < Gk. *katalysis* dissolution < *kata-* down + *lyein* to loose]

cat·a·lyst (kat′ə list) *n.* 1 *Chemistry.* a substance that causes catalysis. 2 an agent that causes or speeds up the occurrence of an event, especially one that is not directly involved or affected by the results.

cat·a·lyt·ic (kat′ə lit′ik) *adj.* 1 of catalysis. 2 causing catalysis.

cat·a·lyz·er (kat′ə līz′ər) *n.* catalyst.

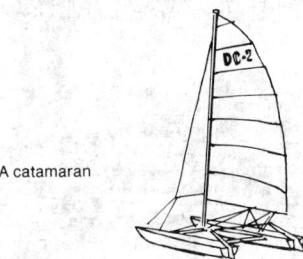
A catamaran

cat·a·ma·ran (kat′ə mə ran′) *n.* 1 a boat having two hulls or floats joined side by side by a frame. 2 *Cdn.* a type of platform on

hat, āge, fär; let, ēqual, tèrm; it, īce
hot, ōpen, ôrder; oil, out; cup, pút, rüle,
əbove, takən, pencəl, lemən, circəs

ch, child; ng, long; sh, ship
th, thin; ŦH, then; zh, measure

two runners, used for hauling lumber, etc. 3 a raft made of two or more logs fastened beside each other but some distance apart, used in parts of India, South America, etc. [< Tamil *kattamaram* tied tree]

cat·a·mount (kat′ə mount′) *n.* any of various wildcats, such as the cougar or lynx. [short for *catamountain* cat of (the) mountain]

cat·a·plex·y (kat′ə plek′sē) *n.* a momentary loss of muscular power and control, without loss of consciousness.

cat·a·pult (kat′ə pult′) *n., v.* —*n.* 1 an ancient military machine for shooting stones, arrows, etc. 2 slingshot. 3 a device for launching an aircraft from the deck of a ship. —*v.* shoot or launch by or as if by a catapult. [< L *catapulta* < Gk. *katapeltēs,* probably < *kata-* down + *pallein* hurl]

cat·a·ract (kat′ə rakt′) *n.* 1 a large, steep waterfall. 2 a violent rush or downpour of water; flood. 3 an opaque condition that develops in the lens of the eye, sometimes covering all of the lens and causing total blindness. A cataract is treated by removing the lens of the eye, after which most patients can see very well with the aid of glasses. [< L *cataracta* < Gk. *katarrhaktēs* < *kata-* down + *arassein* dash]

ca·tarrh (kə tär′) *n.* an inflamed condition of a mucous membrane, usually that of the nose or throat, causing a discharge of mucus or phlegm. [< F *catarrhe* < L < Gk. *katarrhous* < *kata-* down + *rheein* flow]

ca·tarrh·al (kə tär′əl) *adj.* 1 like catarrh. 2 caused by catarrh.

ca·tas·tro·phe (kə tas′trə fē) *n.* 1 a sudden, widespread, or extraordinary disaster; great calamity or misfortune. A big earthquake or flood is a catastrophe. 2 the outcome; unhappy ending: *The catastrophe of a tragedy usually brings death or ruin to the leading character.* 3 a disastrous end; ruin. [< Gk. *katastrophē* overturning < *kata-* down + *strephein* turn]
☛ *Syn.* 1. See note at **disaster.**

cat·a·stroph·ic (kat′ə strof′ik) *adj.* of or caused by disaster; calamitous.

Ca·taw·ba (kə tob′ə *or* kə tô′bə) *n., pl.* **-bas.** 1 a light-red grape of North America. 2 a light wine made from it. [< river in South Carolina along which the vine was first raised]

cat·bird (kat′bèrd) *n.* 1 a mainly slate-grey North American songbird (*Dumetella carolinensis*) belonging to the same family as the mockingbird and the thrashers. The catbird has a call like the mewing of a cat. 2 any of several Australian songbirds (family Ptilonorhynchidae) having a mewing call.

catbird seat a position of advantage or power; an enviable position: *He wasn't at all worried, since he was sitting in the catbird seat.*

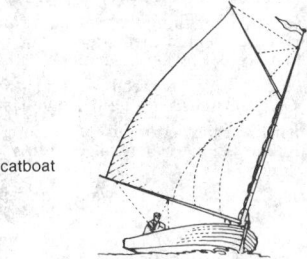
A catboat

cat·boat (kat′bōt′) *n.* a sailboat having a broad beam and one mast set far forward. It has no bowsprit or jib.

cat·call (kat′kol′ *or* -kôl′) *n., v.* —*n.* a shrill cry or whistle to express disapproval: *Poor actors are sometimes greeted by catcalls from the audience.* —*v.* 1 make catcalls. 2 attack with catcalls: *The audience catcalled the actor.*

catch (kach) *v.* **caught, catch·ing;** *n.* —*v.* 1 seize and hold, especially after chasing or going after: *She caught the child just as he reached the street. The thief was caught five days after the robbery.* 2 stop the motion of and hold on to: *I caught the ball with one hand. He caught the glass just before it fell.* 3 become affected by; take or get: *to catch the spirit of the celebration. Paper catches fire easily. I think I've caught a cold.* 4 become or cause to become accidentally hooked, pinched, or entangled: *My dress caught in the*

door. **5** start burning; take fire: *Tinder catches easily.* **6** come on suddenly; surprise in the act of doing something: *He was caught stealing. My mother caught me hiding her present.* **7** take or get suddenly or for a short while: *to catch a quick nap. They caught a glimpse of him before he disappeared into the crowd.* **8** attract: *Bright colors catch the eye. I tried to catch his attention but he didn't look my way.* **9** reach or get to in time: *If we hurry, we can just catch the next bus.* **10** take notice of; discover: *He thought I wouldn't catch his error.* **11** apprehend by the senses or intellect; hear, see, understand, catch, as by an effort: *I couldn't catch what he was saying.* **12** *Baseball.* act as catcher: *Who's catching?*
catch as catch can, grab or wrestle in any way.
catch at, try to take hold of; grab at: *He caught at the rope as it swung by him.*
catch it, *Informal.* be scolded or punished: *We'll catch it if we're late again.*
catch on, *Informal.* **a** understand; get the idea: *to catch on to a joke. They were kidding me but I didn't catch on.* **b** become popular; become widely used or accepted: *The song never caught on.*
catch up, a come up even with or overtake a person or thing going the same way: *He ran hard, trying to catch up with his sister.* **b** pick up suddenly; seize; grab: *He caught the laughing child up in his arms.* **c** become too much for: *His late nights were beginning to catch up with him.* **d** bring or become up-to-date; make up for lost time: *to catch up on the news. She's missed a lot of school, but it shouldn't take her too long to catch up.* **e** involve, especially unwillingly; ensnare (*used in the passive*): *They were both caught up in the scandal.* **f** absorb completely; engross (*used in the passive*): *He is all caught up in his new boat.* **g** take or hold up in loops or folds.
—*n.* **1** the act of catching: *Mario made a fine catch with one hand.* **2** a game of throwing and catching a ball: *They're outside playing catch.* **3** something caught, especially the total quantity caught: *They made a good catch today. Her catch was six trout.* **4** something that holds in place: *We can't fasten the windows because the catch is broken.* **5** *Informal.* a person worth catching as a spouse, especially because of wealth, position, etc. **6** a hidden or tricky condition or meaning; some difficulty that does not appear on the surface: *There's a catch to that question, so think carefully before you answer.* **7** (*adj.*) tricky or deceptive: *a catch question.* **8** a short stopping or blocking of the voice or breath: *There was a catch in his voice as he described the accident.* **9** *Music.* a round (def. 12). **10** a scrap or fragment of anything: *He sang catches of songs.* [ME < OF *cachier* < LL *captiare* < L *capere* take. Doublet of CHASE¹.]

catch–all (kach′ôl′ *or* -ôl′) *n.* **1** a container for odds and ends. **2** a term, question, etc. used to cover a number of possible examples: *The word etc. in this definition is a catch-all.*

catch–as–catch–can (kach′əz kach′kan′) *n., adj.* —*n.* a style of wrestling in which one may use the legs and feet, or hold one's opponent's legs and feet, to gain advantage. —*adj.* **1** unrestrained; free-for-all. **2** haphazard; random.

catch basin **1** a sievelike receptacle at the entrance of a sewer to retain matter that might block the flow of sewage. **2** a reservoir for catching and holding surface drainage over large areas.

catch·er (kach′ər) *n.* a person or thing that catches; especially, in baseball, the player who stands behind the batter to catch balls thrown by the pitcher that are not hit by the batter.

catch·ing (kach′ing) *adj.* **1** liable to spread from one to another; contagious; infectious: *Colds are catching.* **2** attractive; fascinating.

catch·ment (kach′mənt) *n.* **1** the act or fact of catching. **2** a reservoir for catching drainage. **3** the water collected in such a reservoir.

catchment basin *or* **area** a land area where the rainfall is drained by one river system.

catch·pen·ny (kach′pen′ē) *adj., n., pl.* **-nies.** —*adj.* showy but worthless or useless; made to sell quickly. —*n.* a showy but worthless article.

catch phrase a phrase designed to attract attention and be memorable; slogan: *Sheila is trying to think of a good catch phrase to advertise the contest.*

catch·pole *or* **catch·poll** (kach′pōl′) *n. Historical.* a deputy sheriff or bailiff whose duties included arresting debtors for nonpayment.

catch stitch a stitch that makes parallel rows of lines as in a herringbone design.

catch·up (kach′əp) *n.* ketchup.

catch·word (kach′wėrd′) *n.* **1** a word or phrase used again and again until it becomes accepted as representative of a party, point of view, etc.; slogan: *"Canada first" was a catchword of a late*

19th-century movement for cultural independence. **2** a word placed so as to catch attention, such as a guide word in a dictionary.

catch·y (kach′ē) *adj.* **catch·i·er, catch·i·est.** **1** easy to remember; attractive: *The new musical play has several catchy tunes.* **2** tricky; misleading; deceptive: *The third question on the test was catchy; nearly everyone in the class gave the wrong answer.* —**catch′i·ly,** *adv.* —**catch′i·ness,** *n.*

cate (kāt) *n. Archaic.* Usually, **cates,** *pl.* a delicacy; choice food. [var. of ME *acate* < ONF *acat* a purchase < *acater* buy < VL *acceptare* acquire < L *ad-* to + *capere* take]

cat·e·chet·i·cal (kat′ə ket′ə kəl) *adj.* **1** teaching by questions and answers. **2** like or according to a catechism.

cat·e·chise (kat′ə kīz′) *v.* **-chised, -chis·ing.** catechize. —**cat′e·chis′er,** *n.*

cat·e·chism (kat′ə kiz′əm) *n.* **1** a book of questions and answers, especially one used for teaching religious doctrine. **2** any set of questions.

cat·e·chist (kat′ə kist) *n.* a person who catechizes.

cat·e·chize (kat′ə kīz′) *v.* **-chized, -chiz·ing.** **1** teach by questions and answers. **2** question closely. [< L *catechizare* < Gk. *katēchizein* teach orally < *katēcheein* < *kata-* thoroughly + *ēcheein* sound] —**cat′e·chiz′er,** *n.* —**cat′e·chi·za′tion,** *n.*

cat·e·chu (kat′ə chü *or* kat′ə kyü′) *n.* any of several hard, brittle, astringent substances used in dyeing and tanning and in medicine, obtained from tropical plants, especially an acacia tree (*Acacia catechu*) of S Asia. [< NL < Malay *kachu*]

cat·e·chu·men (kat′ə kyü′mən) *n.* **1** a person who is being taught the elementary facts of Christianity. **2** a person who is being taught the fundamentals of any field of study. [< LL *catechumenus* < Gk. *katēchoumenos* one being instructed, ppr. passive of *katēcheein.* See CATECHIZE.]

cat·e·gor·i·cal (kat′ə gôr′ə kəl) *adj.* **1** without conditions or qualifications; positive. **2** of or in a category. —**cat′e·gor′i·cal·ly,** *adv.*

cat·e·gor·i·za·tion (kat′ə gər ə zā′shən *or* kat′ə gər ī zā′shən) *n.* the act or fact or process of categorizing.

cat·e·gor·ize (kat′ə gə rīz′) *v.* **-ized, -iz·ing.** place in a category; classify.

cat·e·gor·iz·er (kat′ə gə rī′zər) *n.* a person who categorizes.

cat·e·go·ry (kat′ə gô′rē) *n., pl.* **-ries.** a group or division in a general system of classification; class: *She groups all people into two categories: those she likes and those she dislikes.* [< L *categoria* < Gk. *katēgoria* assertion < *kata-* down + *agoreuein* speak]

cat·e·nar·y (kat′ə ner′ē *or* kə tē′nər ē) *n., pl.* **-nar·ies.** *adj. Mathematics.* —*n.* the curve formed by a heavy flexible cord hanging freely from two points not in a vertical line. —*adj.* of or having to do with a catenary. [< L *catenarius* relating to a chain < *catena* chain]

cat·e·nate (kat′ə nāt′) *v.* **-nat·ed, -nat·ing.** link together like a chain; connect in a series. [< L *catenare* < *catena* chain] —**cat′e·na′tion,** *n.*

ca·ter (kā′tər) *v.* **1** provide food or supplies: *He has a small hotel and also caters for weddings and parties.* **2** provide what is needed or wanted (*used with* **to**): *There is a new magazine catering to people interested in crafts.* [verbal use of *cater, n.,* ME *acatour* buyer of provisions < OF *acateor* < *acater* buy. See CATE.]

cat·er–cor·nered (kat′ər kôr′nərd) *adj. or adv.* kitty-corner. Also, **cater-corner.** [< E dial. *cater* diagonally (< F *quatre* four) + *cornered*]

ca·ter·er (kā′tər ər) *n.* a person who provides food or supplies for entertainments, parties, etc.

cat·er·pil·lar (kat′ər pil′ər) *n.* **1** the wormlike larva of certain insects, especially butterflies and moths, often brightly colored and covered with long hairs or spines. **2** caterpillar tractor. **3 Caterpillar,** *Trademark.* a brand of caterpillar tractor. [cf. OF *chatepelose* hairy cat]

A caterpillar tractor

caterpillar tractor a tractor that can travel over rough land on wheels that run inside two endless belts of linked, steel plates.

cat·er·waul (kat′ər wol′ *or* kat′ər wôl′) *v., n.* —*v.* **1** howl like a

cat; screech. **2** quarrel noisily. —*n.* such a howl or screech. [ME *caterwrawe* < *cater*, apparently, cat + *wrawe* wail, howl]

cat·fish (kat′fish′) *n., pl.* **-fish** or **-fish·es.** any of an order (Siluriformes) of mostly freshwater fishes of almost worldwide distribution, having long, whiskerlike barbels about the mouth.

cat·gut (kat′gut′) *n.* a very tough cord made from the dried and twisted intestines of sheep or other animals, used for stringing musical instruments and tennis rackets, and for surgical stitches. [origin uncertain]

Cath. Catholic.

ca·thar·sis (kə thär′sis) *n.* **1** a purging, especially of the digestive system. **2** an emotional purification or relief. [< NL < Gk. *katharsis*, ult. < *katharos* clean]

ca·thar·tic (kə thär′tik) *n.* a strong laxative. Epsom salts and castor oil are cathartics. —*adj.* of or bringing about catharsis; purifying.

Ca·thay (ka thā′) *n. Poetic or archaic.* China.

cat·head (kat′hed′) *n.* a projecting beam on a ship's side near the bow to which the hoisted anchor is fastened. See **capstan** for picture.

ca·the·dra (kə thē′drə *or* kath′ə drə) *n.* **1** a bishop's throne in a cathedral. **2** a seat of authority. See also **ex cathedra.** [< L < Gk. *kathedra* seat < *kata*- down + *hedra* seat. Doublet of CHAIR.]

ca·the·dral (kə thē′drəl) *n., adj.* —*n.* **1** the official church of a bishop. **2** a large or important church. —*adj.* **1** having a bishop's throne. **2** of, like, or having to do with a cathedral. [< Med.L *cathedralis* of the (bishop's) seat < L < Gk. *kathedra* seat. See CATHEDRA.]

Cath·e·rine wheel (kath′ə rin *or* kath′rin) **1** *Heraldry.* a figure of a wheel with projecting spikes. **2** a firework that revolves while burning; pinwheel. [< St. *Catherine* of Alexandria, condemned to torture on the wheel]

cath·e·ter (kath′ə tər) *n.* a slender tube to be inserted into a passage or cavity of the body. A catheter is used to distend a passage, remove urine from the bladder, etc. [< LL < Gk. *kathetēr* < *kata*- down + *hienai* send]

cath·ode (kath′ōd) *n.* **1** the positively charged electrode of a primary cell or storage battery. The cathode of a carbon-zinc dry cell is a mixture of manganese dioxide and carbon powder packed around a central carbon rod. See **dry cell** for picture. **2** the negative electrode of an electrolytic cell, through which electrons enter the cell. See **electrolysis** for picture. **3** *Electronics.* the electrode that is the main source of electrons in a vacuum tube. See **cathode-ray tube** for picture. [< Gk. *kathodos* a way down < *kata*- down + *hodos* way]

cathode ray a high-speed, invisible stream of electrons from the heated cathode of a vacuum tube.

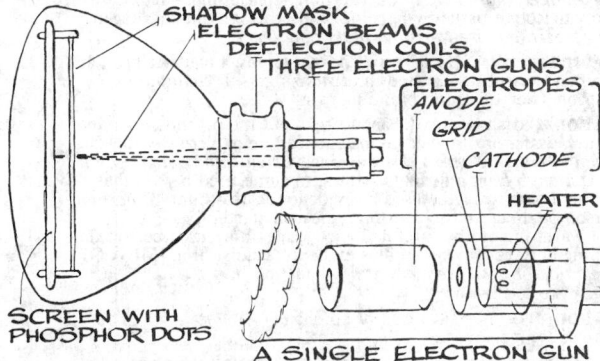

Cathode-ray tube: a color television picture tube

cathode–ray tube a kind of tapered vacuum tube used in electronic equipment to display information. A cathode at the narrow end is heated to give off electrons, which are accelerated as a beam through a collector and strike a fluorescent screen at the other end, causing it to glow.

cath·o·lic (kath′ə lik′ *or* kath′lik) *adj.* **1** very broad; general; all-inclusive; universal: *Music has a catholic appeal.* **2** having sympathies with all; broad-minded; liberal. **3** of the whole Christian church. [< L *catholicus* < Gk. *katholikos* < *kata*- in respect to + *holos* whole]

Cath·o·lic (kath′ə lik′ *or* kath′lik) *n., adj.* —*n.* **1** a member of the Christian church that recognizes the Pope as its supreme temporal leader and whose tenets include belief in the factual truth of the gospel of Christ as recorded in the Bible and interpreted by

hat, āge, fär; let, ēqual, tėrm; it, īce
hot, ōpen, ôrder; oil, out; cup, pút, rüle,
əbove, takən, pencəl, lemən, circəs
ch, child; ng, long; sh, ship
th, thin; ᴛн, then; zh, measure

the council of bishops together with the Pope, acceptance of seven sacraments (baptism, penance, Eucharist, confirmation, holy orders, matrimony, and extreme unction), and the doctrine of apostolic succession. The Catholic Church is the largest Christian denomination. **2** a member of any church that has its origins in or claims continuity with the ancient undivided Christian church. **3** a member of the ancient undivided Christian church. —*adj.* of or having to do with the Catholic Church or Catholicism.

Ca·thol·i·cism (kə thol′ə siz′əm) *n.* **1** the faith, doctrine, organization, and practice of the Catholic Church. **2 catholicism,** catholicity.

cath·o·lic·i·ty (kath′ə lis′ə tē) *n.* **1** universality; wide prevalence. **2** broad-mindedness; liberalness. **3 Catholicity,** Catholicism.

ca·thol·i·cize (kə thol′ə sīz′) *v.* **-cized, -ciz·ing.** make or become catholic or universal.

cat·house (kat′hous′) *n. Slang.* brothel.

cat·i·on (kat′ī′ən) *n.* an ion having a positive charge. During electrolysis, cations move toward the cathode. See **electrolysis** for picture. [< Gk. *kation* going down < *kata*- down + *ienai* go]

cat·kin (kat′kin) *n.* the downy or scaly spike of the flowers of willows, poplars, birches, etc.; ament. [< Du. *katteken* little cat]

cat·like (kat′līk′) *adj.* **1** like a cat. **2** noiseless; stealthy. **3** active; nimble.

cat·lin·ite (kat′lə nīt′) *n.* a smooth, hard, bright-red clay, used by Prairie Indians for tobacco pipes. [< George *Catlin* (1796-1872), an American artist + *ite*]

cat·mint (kat′mint′) *n. Esp.Brit.* catnip.

cat nap a short nap or doze.

cat·nip (kat′nip) *n.* a plant (*Nepeta cataria*) of the mint family having scented leaves that cats like. [< cat + nip, var. of *nep* catnip < L *nepeta*]

cat-o′-nine-tails (kat′ə nīn′tālz′) *n., pl.* **-tails.** a whip consisting of usually nine pieces of knotted cord fastened to a handle.

cat power *Cdn. Slang.* tracked work-vehicles, such as bulldozers, caterpillar tractors, etc.

cat-rigged (kat′rigd′) *adj.* rigged like a catboat.

cat's cradle a game in which a loop of string, stretched over the fingers in an intricate pattern, is passed from one player to another with the object of forming a new pattern each time.

cat's-eye (kats′ī′) *n.* **1** a gem showing beautiful changes of color suggesting a cat's eye. **2** one of a row of small reflectors set on a road or curb to act as guides by catching the headlights of approaching vehicles.

cat·skin·ner (kat′skin′ər) *n. Cdn.* a person who operates a caterpillar tractor. [< cat² + skinner, after *mule-skinner*]

cat's-paw or **cats·paw** (kats′po′ *or* -pô′) *n.* **1** a person used by another to do something unpleasant or dangerous. **2** a light breeze that ruffles a small stretch of water. **3** a type of hitch or knot, used for attaching a tackle to a hook.

cat·sup (kat′səp *or* kech′əp) *n.* ketchup.

cat-swing (kat′swing′) *n. Cdn.* cat-train. [< cat² + swing]

cat·tail or **cat-tail** (kat′tāl′) *n.* any of a genus (*Typha*) of tall marsh plants having long, flat leaves, and flowers that form long, thick brown spikes; bulrush (def. 1): *Cat-tails are often used as decoration.*

cat·tal·lo (kat′ə lō) *n. Cdn.* an experimental cross between beef cattle and North American buffalo. Cattalo are usually sterile.

cat·tish (kat′ish) *adj.* **1** catlike. **2** catty.

cat·tle (kat′əl) *n.* **1** domesticated bovine animals; cows, bulls, steers, or oxen. **2** *Archaic.* any farm animals; livestock. **3** *Derogatory.* human beings. [ME < OF *catel* < L *capitale* property, neut. of *capitalis.* Doublet of CAPITAL¹ and CHATTEL.]

cat·tle·man (kat′əl mən) *n., pl.* **-men.** a man who raises or takes care of cattle.

cat-train (kat′trān′) *n. Cdn.* a series of large sleds pulled by a caterpillar tractor. Cat-trains are used in the North for hauling goods over the frozen muskeg in wintertime.

cat·ty (kat′ē) *adj.* **-ti·er, -ti·est. 1** mean; spiteful. **2** catlike. **3** of or like cats. **—cat′ti·ly,** *adv.* **—cat′ti·ness,** *n.*

cat·ty-cor·nered (kat′ē kôr′nərd) *adj. or adv.* kitty-corner.

cat·walk (kat′wok′ *or* -wôk′) *n.* a high, narrow place to walk, as on a bridge.

Cau·ca·sian (ko kā′zhən *or* ko kā′shən, kô kā′zhən *or* kô kā′shən) *n., adj.* **—n. 1** a native or inhabitant of the Caucasus, a mountainous region in the S Soviet Union. **2** Caucasoid. **—adj. 1** of or having to do with the Caucasus or its inhabitants. **2** Caucasoid.

Cau·ca·soid (kôk′ə soid′) *adj., n.* **—adj. 1** European (def. 2). **2** *Obsolete.* of or having to do with the racial group including the European and Indian races. The human species was formerly classified into the Caucasoid, Mongoloid, and Negroid racial groups. **—n. 1** European (def. 3). **2** a member of the European or Indian race.

cau·cus (ko′kəs *or* kô′kəs) *n., v.* **—n. 1** in Canada and the United Kingdom, a meeting of the members of Parliament of one party to discuss policy, plan strategy, etc. **2** in the United States, a meeting of members or leaders of a political party to make plans, choose candidates, decide how to vote, etc. **3** a committee within a political party, whose function is to determine party policy. **—v.** hold a caucus. [prob. from Algonquian; cf. Virginian *caucauasu* counsellor. Formerly thought to be from Med.L *caucus,* *caucum* drinking vessel < Med.Gk. *kaukos.* 18c.]

cau·dal (ko′dəl *or* kô′dəl) *adj.* **1** of, at, or near the tail. **2** tail-like. [< NL *caudalis* < L *cauda* tail] **—cau′dal·ly,** *adv.*

cau·date (ko′dāt *or* kô′dāt) *adj.* having a tail.

cau·dil·lo (ko dēl′yō *or* kô dēl′yō *Spanish,* kou ᴛʜᴇ′lyō) *n.* a leader or head of state, especially a military one. [< Sp. < L *capitellum* little head]

cau·dle (ko′dəl *or* kô′dəl) *n.* a warm drink for sick people; gruel sweetened and flavored with wine, ale, spices, etc. [< ONF *caudel* < L *calidus* warm]

Caugh·na·waugh·a (kok′nə wo′gə) *n., pl.* **-waugh·a or -waugh·as.** a member of a band of Mohawks living on the Caughnawaugha Reserve on the south shore of the St. Lawrence opposite Montreal.

caught (kot *or* kôt) *v.* pt. and pp. of **catch.**
☛ *Hom.* **cot** (kot).

caul (kol *or* kôl) *n.* a portion of the membrane enclosing a child in the womb that is sometimes found clinging to the head at birth. It was supposed to be a good omen, especially against drowning. [ME *calle,* perhaps < OF *cale* a little cap]
☛ *Hom.* **call.**

caul·dron or **cal·dron** (kol′drən *or* kôl′drən) *n.* **1** a large kettle or boiler. **2** anything thought to resemble a boiling cauldron or its bubbling contents: *a cauldron of political intrigue and unrest.* [ME *caudron* < ONF < LL *caldaria* pot for boiling (L *calidus* warm)]

cau·li·flow·er (kol′ē flou′ər *or* kôl′ē flou′ər) *n.* **1** a garden plant (*Brassica oleracea botrytis*) that is a variety of cabbage, having a tightly set flower cluster that forms a solid, white head with a few leaves around it. **2** the head itself, eaten raw as in salads, or cooked as a vegetable. [half-translation of NL *cauliflora* < *caulis* cabbage + *flos, floris* flower]

cauliflower ear an ear that has been misshapen by injuries received in boxing, etc.

caulk¹ (kok *or* kôk) *v.* **1** fill up (a seam, crack, or joint) to make it watertight or airtight: *to caulk the seams of a boat, to caulk the cracks in a window frame.* **2** fill up the seams, cracks, or joints of something to make leakproof: *to caulk a boat, to caulk a window.* Sometimes, **calk. —caulk′er,** *n.* [< OF *cauquer* < L *calcare* tread, press in]
☛ *Hom.* **cock** (kok).

caulk² (kok *or* kôk) *n., v.* **—n. 1** a projecting piece on a horseshoe that catches in the ground or ice and prevents slipping. **2** one of a number of sharp spikes set into the sole of a boot or shoe or into a metal plate fitted over the sole to prevent slipping. **3** a metal plate studded with caulks and fastened to a boot or shoe. **4** a boot or shoe with caulks, worn especially by loggers, etc.
—v. 1 provide or fit with caulks: *caulked boots.* **2** wound with a caulk. Also, **calk.** [< L *calx* heel *or calcar* spur]

caus·a·ble (koz′ə bəl *or* kôz′ə bəl) *adj.* capable of being caused.

caus·al (koz′əl *or* kôz′əl) *adj.* **1** of, having to do with, or being a cause. **2** involving or having to do with cause and effect. **3** showing a cause or reason. Because is a casual conjunction. **—caus′al·ly,** *adv.*

cau·sal·i·ty (ko zal′ə tē *or* kô zal′ə tē) *n., pl.* **-ties. 1** the relation

between cause and effect; the principle that nothing can happen or exist without a cause. **2** a causal quality or agency.

cau·sa·tion (ko zā′shən *or* kô zā′shən) *n.* **1** causing or being caused. **2** whatever produces an effect; cause or causes. **3** the relation of cause and effect; the principle that nothing can happen or exist without a cause.

caus·a·tive (koz′ə tiv *or* kôz′ə tiv) *adj.* **1** being a cause; productive. **2** expressing causation. In *enrich, en-* is a causative prefix. **—caus′a·tive·ly,** *adv.* **—caus′a·tive·ness,** *n.*

cause (koz *or* kôz) *n., v.* **caused, caus·ing. —n. 1** whatever produces an effect; a person or thing that makes something happen: *The flood was the cause of much damage.* **2** an occasion for action; reason; ground; motive: *cause for celebration.* **3** a good reason; reason enough: *He was angry without cause.* **4** a subject or movement in which many people are interested and to which they give their support: *World peace is the cause she works for.* **5** *Law.* a matter for a court to decide; lawsuit.
make a common cause with, join efforts with; side with; help and support.
—v. produce an effect; make happen; make do; bring about: *What caused the fire?* [< L *causa*] **—caus′er,** *n.*
☛ *Syn. n.* **2.** See note at **reason.**

cause cé·lè·bre (kōz sā leb′rə) *French.* **1** *Law.* a famous case. **2** a notorious case or incident.

cause·less (koz′lis *or* kôz′lis) *adj.* **1** without any known cause; happening by chance. **2** without good reason; not having reason enough. **—cause′less·ly,** *adv.*

cau·se·rie (kō′zə rē′) *n.* **1** an informal talk or discussion; chat. **2** a short written article. [< F *causerie* < *causer* chat]

cause·way (koz′wā′ *or* kôz′-) *n., v.* **—n. 1** a raised road or path, usually built across wet ground or shallow water. **2** a paved road; highway. **—v. 1** provide with a causeway. **2** pave with cobbles or pebbles. [var. of *causey* (influenced by *way*) < ME *cauci* < ONF *caucie* < LL *calciata* paved way < L *calx* limestone]

caus·tic (kos′tik *or* kôs′tik) *n., adj.* **—n.** a substance that burns or eats away the chemical action; corrosive substance. **—adj. 1** able to burn or eat away by chemical action; corrosive. Lye is caustic soda or caustic potash. **2** sarcastic; stinging; biting: *The director's caustic remarks made the actors very angry.* [< L *causticus* < Gk. *kaustikos*]

caus·ti·cal·ly (kos′tik lē *or* kôs′tik lē) *adv.* sarcastically; stingingly; bitingly.

caustic soda a brittle, white alkaline compound used in bleaching and in making soap, rayon, paper, etc.; sodium hydroxide. *Formula:* $NaOH$

cau·ter·i·za·tion (ko′tər ə zā′shən *or* kô′-, ko′tər ī zā′shən *or* kô′-) *n.* the act of cauterizing or the state of being cauterized.

cau·ter·ize (ko′tər īz′ *or* kô′tər īz′) *v.* **-ized, iz·ing.** destroy defective tissue by burning with heat or a chemical agent: *Doctors often remove warts by cauterizing them.*

cau·ter·y (ko′tər ē *or* kô′tər ē) *n., pl.* **-ter·ies. 1** cauterizing. **2** an instrument or substance used in cauterizing. [< L *cauterium* < Gk. *kautērion,* dim. of *kautēr* branding iron]

cau·tion (ko′shən *or* kô′shən) *n., v.* **—n. 1** the practice of taking care to be safe, or of never taking chances; being very careful: *Use caution in crossing streets.* **2** a warning: *A sign with "Danger" on it is a caution.* **3** *Law.* a formal warning to an accused person that anything he says may be used as evidence against him. **4** *Informal.* a person or thing that is amusing, unusual, startling, etc.
—v. 1 warn; urge to be careful. **2** *Law.* warn an accused person that anything he says may be used as evidence against him. [ME < OF < L *cautio, -onis* < *cavere* beware] **—cau′tion·er,** *n.*
☛ *Syn. v.* See note at **warn.**

cau·tion·ar·y (ko′shən er′ē *or* kô′shən er′ē) *adj.* warning; urging care.

cau·tious (ko′shəs *or* kô′shəs) *adj.* very careful; taking care to be safe; never taking chances: *a cautious driver.* **—cau′tious·ly,** *adv.* **—cau′tious·ness,** *n.*
☛ *Syn.* See note at **careful.**

cav·al·cade (kav′əl kād′ *or* kav′əl kād′) *n.* **1** a procession of persons riding on horses, in carriages, or in automobiles. **2** a series of scenes or events: *a cavalcade of sports.* [< F < Ital. *cavalcata* < *cavalcare* ride horseback < LL *caballicare* < L *caballus* horse]

cav·a·lier (kav′ə lēr′) *n., adj.* **—n. 1** a courteous gentleman, especially as a lady's escort. **2** *Archaic.* a horseman, especially a mounted soldier or knight. **3 Cavalier,** a supporter of Charles I in his struggle with Parliament (1641-1649).
—adj. 1 free and easy; careless in manner; offhand: *a cavalier disregard for danger.* **2** haughty and arrogant; supercilious. **3 Cavalier, a** of or having to do with the supporters of Charles I in his struggle with Parliament. **b** of, having to do with, or designating a group of English lyric poets of the 17th century, most of whom

were associated with the court of Charles I. [< F < Ital. *cavalliere* < *cavallo* horse < L *caballus* horse] —**cav′a·lier′ly,** *adv.*

cav·al·ry (kav′əl rē) *n., pl.* **-ries. 1** army troops trained to fight on horseback or, in recent times, in armored vehicles. **2** a branch of an army made up of such troops. **3** (*adj.*) of, having to do with, or belonging to the cavalry. [< F *cavalerie* < Ital. *cavalleria* knighthood < *cavalliere.* See CAVALIER.]

cav·al·ry·man (kav′əl rē mən) *n., pl.* **-men.** a cavalry soldier.

cav·a·ti·na (kav′ə tē′nə) *n. Music.* a short, simple song; melody; air. [< Ital.]

cave (kāv) *n., v.* **caved, cav·ing.** —*n.* a hollow space underground, often having an opening in the side of a hill or cliff. —*v.* **1** form a cave in or under; hollow out. **2** take part in the sport or pastime of exploring caves.
cave in, a fall in or down; collapse: *The weight of the snow caused the roof of the arena to cave in.* **b** cause to fall in or down; smash. **c** *Informal.* yield completely; give in to an argument, strain, or hardship.
[ME < OF < L *cava* hollow (places)] —**cave′like′,** *adj.* **-cav′er,** *n.*

ca·ve·at (kā′vē at′) *n.* **1** a warning. **2** *Law.* a notice given to a law officer or some legal authority not to do something until the person giving notice can be heard. [< L *caveat* let him beware]

caveat emp·tor (emp′tôr) *Latin.* let the buyer beware; you buy at your own risk.

cave dweller 1 a person who lived in a cave in prehistoric times. **2** any person who lives in a cave.

cave·in (kāv′in′) *n.* **1** a falling-in, or collapse, of a mine, tunnel, etc. **2** the site of such a collapse.

cave man 1 a man who lived in a cave in prehistoric times. **2** *Informal.* a rough, crude man.

cav·ern (kav′ərn) *n.* a large cave. [ME < MF *caverne* < L *caverna* < *cavus* hollow]

cav·ern·ous (kav′ər nəs) *adj.* **1** like or characteristic of a cavern; large, dark, hollow, etc.: *a cavernous doorway, cavernous eyes.* **2** full of caverns: *cavernous mountains.* **3** full of small holes; porous. —**cav′ern·ous·ly,** *adv.*

cav·i·ar or **cav·i·are** (kav′ē är′ or kä′vē är′) *n.* a salty relish made from the eggs of sturgeon or other large fish.
caviar to the general, too good a thing to be appreciated by ordinary people.
[< F < Ital. < Turkish *khaviar*]

cav·il (kav′əl) *v.* **-illed** or **iled, -il·ling** or **-il·ing;** *n.* —*v.* find fault unnecessarily; raise trivial objections. —*n.* a petty objection; trivial criticism. [< F < L *cavillari* jeer] —**cav′il·ler** or **cav·il·er,** *n.*

cav·ing (kā′ving) *n.* the sport or pastime of exploring caves; spelunking.

cav·i·ty (kav′ə tē) *n., pl.* **-ties. 1** a hole; hollow place: *a cavity in a tooth.* **2** an enclosed space inside the body: *the abdominal cavity, the four cavities of the heart.* [< F *cavité* < LL *cavitas* < L *cavus* hollow]
☞ *Syn.* 1. See note at **hole.**

ca·vort (kə vôrt′) *v. Informal.* prance about; jump around in a frisky way: *The colt cavorted in the pasture.* [origin uncertain]

ca·vy (kā′vē) *n., pl.* **-vies.** any of a small family (Caviidae) of mostly rat-sized South American rodents having a very short tail and rough grey or brown hair; especially, any of the genus *Cavia,* which includes the guinea pig. [< NL *Cavia*]

caw (ko *or* kô) *n., v.* —*n.* the harsh cry made by a crow or raven. —*v.* make this cry. [imitative]

cay (kā *or* kē) *n.* a low island; reef; key. [< Sp. *cayo* shoal, rock]
☞ *Hom.* **key** (kē), **quay** (kē).

cay·enne (kī en′ *or* kā en′) *n.* red pepper. [< *Cayenne,* French Guiana]

cay·man (kā′mən) *n., pl.* **-mans.** a large alligator of tropical America. Also, **caiman.** [< Sp. *caiman* < Carib]

Ca·yu·ga (kā yü′gə *or* kī yü′gə) *n., adj.* —*n.* **1** a member of an Amerindian people living mainly in New York state and, later, in Ontario. The Cayuga belonged to the Iroquois Confederacy. **2** the Iroquoian language of the Cayuga. —*adj.* of or having to do with the Cayuga or their language.

cay·use (kī yüs′) *n.* in western Canada and the United States, an Indian pony. [after the *Cayuse* Indians]

Cb columbium.

CB Citizens' Band. See also **General Radio Service.**

C.B. 1 Cape Breton. **2** Companion of (the Order of) the Bath. **3** Confined to Barracks.

CBC the Canadian Broadcasting Corporation.

C.B.E. Commander of (the Order of) the British Empire.

CBS Columbia Broadcasting System, a United States network.

cc or **c.c.** cubic centimetre(s). Now written cm³.

hat, āge, fär; let, ēqual, tėrm; it, īce
hot, ōpen, ôrder; oil, out; cup, pùt, rüle,
əbove, takən, pencəl, lemən, circəs

ch, child; ng, long; sh, ship
th, thin; ᴛн, then; zh, measure

CC *Cdn.* Companion of the Order of Canada.

C.C. or **CC** Canada Council.

CCF or **C.C.F.** a Canadian political party established in 1932. It joined with the Canadian Labour Congress to form the New Democratic Party in 1961. The name CCF is an abbreviation for Co-operative Commonwealth Federation.

CCG Canadian Coast Guard.

C clef *Music.* a symbol that means that the line on which it is placed represents middle C.

cd. cord(s).

Cd cadmium.

C.D. or **CD 1** Civil Defence. **2** Canadian (Forces) Decoration.

CDC Canada Development Corporation.

cd.ft. cord foot; cord feet.

Cdn. Canadian.

Cdn. Fr. Canadian French.

Cdr. or **Cdr** commander.

CDS *Cdn.* Chief of the Defence Staff.

CDT or **C.D.T.** Central Daylight Time.

Ce cerium.

C.E. 1 civil engineer. **2** Church of England. **3** chief engineer. **4** chemical engineer. **5** Common Era (*used to indicate years* A.D.).

cease (sēs) *v., n.* —*v.* **ceased, ceas·ing. 1** come to an end: *The music ceased suddenly.* **2** *Poetic.* put an end to: *They have ceased their endeavors. Cease your complaining.* —*n. Archaic.* ceasing; cessation.
without cease, without ceasing; continuously: *It rained for hours without cease.*
[ME < OF < L *cessare*]
☞ *Syn.* 1. See note at **stop.**

cease–fire (sēs′fīr′) *n.* the formal cessation of combat between opposing armed forces, especially for a specified period of time in order to remove the dead and wounded, discuss peace, etc.

cease·less (sēs′lis) *adj.* never stopping; going on all the time; continual: *the ceaseless noise of distant traffic.* —**cease′less·ly,** *adv.* —**cease′less·ness,** *n.*

Ce·cro·pi·a moth (sə krō′pē ə) a large, colorful silkworm moth (*Samia cecropia*) of E North America having a wingspan of over 15 cm. [< NL *Cecropia,* a type of mulberry]

ce·cum (sē′kəm) See **caecum.**

ce·dar (sē′dər) *n.* **1** any of a genus (*Cedrus*) of North African and Asian evergreen trees of the pine family having long cones and short, sharp needles growing in spirals. The best known of these trees is the **cedar of Lebanon,** which often appears in art and literature as a symbol of power and long life. **2** any of various other trees, especially of the cypress family, such as arborvitae and junipers. **3** the durable, fragrant, usually reddish wood of any of these trees. Most kinds of cedar are insect repellant and resistant to decay. **4** (*adj.*) made of cedar: *a cedar chest.* [ME < OF *cedre* < L < Gk. *kedros*]

cedar waxwing a North American waxwing (*Bombycilla cedrorum*) found throughout most of the continent, smaller than the bohemian waxwing and having mainly cinnamon-brown upper parts and yellowish under parts.

cede (sēd) *v.* **ced·ed, ced·ing. 1** surrender; hand over to another: *In 1763, France ceded Canada to Britain.* **2** give up; yield: *His argument was so convincing that I ceded my point.* [< L *cedere* yield]
☞ *Hom.* **seed.**

ce·di (sā dē′) *n.* **1** the basic unit of money in Ghana, divided into 100 pesewas. See table at **money.** **2** a note worth one cedi.

ce·dil·la (sə dil′ə) *n.* a mark resembling a comma put under *c* (ç) before *a, o,* or *u* in certain words to show that it has the sound of *s. Example:* façade. [< Sp. *cedilla,* dim. of *ceda* < L *zeta,* the letter *z* < Gk.]

C.E.F. Canadian Expeditionary Force (World War I).

CEGEP Collège d'Enseignement Général et Professionel (General and Vocational College).

ceil (sēl) v. **1** put a ceiling in. **2** cover the ceiling of. [? < F *ciel* canopy, sky < L *caelum* heaven]
☛ *Hom.* **seal.**

cei·lidh (kā′lē) n. an informal social gathering featuring traditional Scottish or Irish songs and dances. [< Gaelic]

ceil·ing (sēl′ing) n. **1** the inside, top covering of a room; the surface opposite to the floor. **2** the greatest height to which an aircraft can go under certain conditions. **3** the distance between the earth and the lowest clouds. **4** an upper limit: *A ceiling was placed on the amount of rent landlords could charge.*
hit the ceiling, *Slang.* react with a strong burst of anger: *When she saw the repair bill she hit the ceiling.*
[< *ceil*]
☛ *Hom.* **sealing**

cel·an·dine (sel′ən dīn′) n. **1** a biennial herb (*Chelidonium majus*) of the poppy family having yellow flowers. **2** the **lesser celandine,** a perennial herb (*Ranunculus ficaria*) of the buttercup family native to Europe but now naturalized in North America. [ME < OF *celidoine* < L < Gk. *chelidonion* < *chelidōn* swallow[2]]

Cel·a·nese (sel′ə nēz′ *or* sel′ə nēz′) n. *Trademark.* an acetate rayon material.

cel·e·brant (sel′ə brənt) n. **1** a person who performs a ceremony or rite. **2** a priest who performs Mass. **3** anyone who celebrates; celebrator.

cel·e·brate (sel′ə brāt′) v. **-brat·ed, -brat·ing. 1** observe a special time or day with the proper ceremonies or festivities: *to celebrate Christmas, to celebrate a birthday.* **2** perform publicly with the proper ceremonies and rites: *The priest celebrates Mass in church.* **3** make known publicly; proclaim. **4** praise; honor: *to celebrate the glory of nature.* **5** observe a festival or event with ceremonies or festivities: *On her birthday she was too sick to celebrate.* **6** have a joyful time; make merry: *The people celebrated when the war ended.* [< L *celebrare*]

cel·e·brat·ed (sel′ə brāt′id) adj. famous; well-known; much talked about: *a celebrated author.*

cel·e·bra·tion (sel′ə brā′shən) n. **1** the act of celebrating. **2** whatever is done to celebrate something: *A Dominion Day celebration often includes a display of fireworks.*

cel·e·bra·tor (sel′ə brā′tər) n. a person who celebrates.

ce·leb·ri·ty (sə leb′rə tē) n., pl. **-ties. 1** a famous person; a person who is well known or much talked about. **2** fame; being well known or much talked about.

ce·ler·i·ac (sə ler′ē ak′) n. **1** a variety of celery (*Apium graveolens rapaceum*) cultivated for its edible, bulblike root. **2** the root itself, eaten raw or cooked as a vegetable.

ce·ler·i·ty (sə ler′ə tē) n. swiftness; speed. [ME < OF < L *celeritas < celer* swift]

cel·er·y (sel′ər ē *or* sel′rē) n. **1** a biennial herb (*Apium graveolens*) of the carrot family having long, crisp, pale-green stalks with leaves at the top; especially, a cultivated variety (*A. graveolens dulce*). **2** the stalks of this plant, eaten raw or cooked as a vegetable. [< F *céleri* < dial. Ital. < L < Gk. *selinon* parsley]

ce·les·ta (sə les′tə) n. a musical instrument with a keyboard, the tones being made by hammers hitting steel plates. [< F < L *caelestis* heavenly < *caelum* heaven]

ce·leste (sə lest′) n. celesta.

ce·les·tial (sə les′chəl) adj., n. —adj. **1** of or having to do with the sky or the heavens. The sun, moon, planets, and stars are celestial bodies. **2** heavenly; divine; very good or beautiful: *celestial music.* **3 Celestial,** of the Chinese people or the former Chinese Empire. **Celestial Empire** is a translation of a Chinese name for the empire.
—n. a heavenly being. [ME < OF *celestiel* < L *caelestis* heavenly < *caelum* heaven] —**ce·les′tial·ly,** adv.

celestial equator *Astronomy.* the imaginary great circle that represents the intersection of the plane of the earth's equator with the celestial sphere.

celestial globe *Astronomy.* a globe indicating the position of the heavenly bodies, similar to a globe of the earth showing the geography of continents, oceans, etc.

celestial navigation *Astronomy.* a method of navigation in which the position of a ship or an aircraft is calculated from the position of heavenly bodies.

celestial sphere *Astronomy.* the imaginary sphere that apparently encloses the universe, of a size approaching infinity.

ce·li·ac (sē′lē ak′) adj. **1** of or having to do with the abdominal cavity. **2** of or suffering from celiac disease. [< L *coeliacus* < Gk. *koiliakos* < *koilia* bowels, belly < *koilos* hollow]

celiac disease a chronic intestinal disorder of childhood, resulting in diarrhea, swelling of the abdomen, etc.

cel·i·ba·cy (sel′ə bə sē) n., pl. **-cies. 1** the state of being unmarried, especially because of religious vows. **2** habitual abstention from sexual intercourse.

cel·i·bate (sel′ə bit *or* sel′ə bāt′) n. **1** an unmarried person, especially one who takes a vow to remain single. **2** one who habitually abstains from sexual intercourse. —adj. being a celibate. [< L *caelibatus* < *caelebs* unmarried]

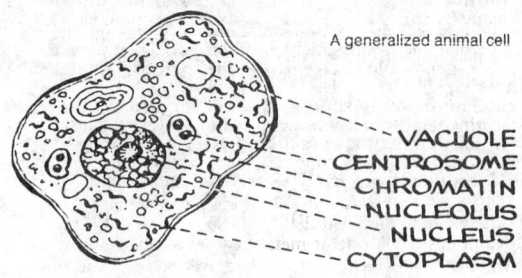

A generalized animal cell

VACUOLE
CENTROSOME
CHROMATIN
NUCLEOLUS
NUCLEUS
CYTOPLASM

cell (sel) n. **1** a small room in a prison, convent, or monastery. **2** a small, hollow place: *Bees store honey in the cells of a honeycomb.* **3** *Biology.* the smallest structural unit of living matter that can function independently. Most cells consist of protoplasm, have a nucleus near the centre, and are enclosed by a cell wall or membrane. Plants and animals are made of cells. **4** a device for producing electricity by chemical means, consisting of one positive and one negative electrode immersed in an electrolyte. **5** a small group that acts as the basic unit of an organization, especially a revolutionary political movement. **6** a small enclosed receptacle or cavity in an organism or tissue. [< L *cella* small room]
☛ *Hom.* **sell.**

cel·lar (sel′ər) n., v. —n. **1** an underground room or space, usually under a building used for storing food, fuel, etc. **2** such a room for wines. **3** a supply of wines.
—v. put into a cellar; store as if in a cellar. [ME *celer* < OF *celier* < L *cellarium < cella* small room]
☛ *Hom.* **seller.**

cel·lar·age (sel′ər ij) n. **1** the space in a cellar. **2** cellars. **3** a charge for storage in a cellar.

cel·lar·er (sel′ər ər) n. a person who takes care of a cellar and the food or wines in it.

cel·lar·et (sel′ə ret′) n. a cabinet to hold wine bottles, glasses, etc.

cel·lar·man (sel′ər mən) n., pl. **-men. 1** a man in charge of or employed in a cellar, especially a wine cellar. **2** a wine merchant.

cell block an individual building of cells in a prison.

cel·list or **'cel·list** (chel′ist) n. a person who plays the cello, especially a skilled player.

A cello

cel·lo or **'cel·lo** (chel′ō) n., pl. **-los.** the second largest instrument of the modern violin family, much larger than the violin and having a lower, mellow tone. When a cello is played it rests upright on the floor and is held between the knees of the player, who is seated. [shortened form of *violoncello*]

cel·lo·phane (sel′ə fān′) n. a shiny, transparent substance made from cellulose in the form of sheets somewhat like paper. It is used especially for packaging foods, candy, tobacco, etc. [< *cell(ul)o(se)* + Gk. *phanein* appear; orig. a trademark]

cel·lu·lar (sel′yə lər) adj. **1** having to do with cells. **2** consisting of cells: *All animal and plant tissue is cellular.*

cel·lule (sel′yül) n. a tiny cell. [< L *cellula,* dim. of *cella* small room]

cel·lu·loid (sel′yə loid′) n. **1** a hard, transparent, combustible substance made from cellulose nitrate and camphor, used now for

eyeglass frames, photographic film etc. Celluloid was the first plastic to be widely used commercially; it has now been largely replaced by less flammable plastics. **2 Celluloid,** *Trademark.* a brand of this substance. **3** (*adj.*) made of celluloid. **4** (*adj.*) of or having to do with motion pictures. [< *cellul(ose)* + *-oid*]

cel·lu·lose (sel′yə lōs′) *n.* a carbohydrate that is the chief constituent of the walls of plant cells and of plant fibres. It is used extensively in the manufacture of paper, plastics, textiles, explosives, etc. *General formula:* ($C_6H_{10}O_5$) [< L *cellula* small cell]

cellulose nitrate a nitric acid ester of cellulose; a group of compounds made by treating cellulose (wood, linen, cotton, etc.) with a mixture of nitric acid and sulphuric acid. It is used for manufacturing plastics, lacquers or varnishes, explosives, etc.

cel·lu·lous (sel′yə ləs) *adj.* **1** full of cells. **2** made of cells.

Celsius (sel′sē əs *or* sel′shəs) *adj.* of, based on, or according to a scale for measuring temperature, in which 0 degrees is the temperature at which water freezes and 100 degrees is the temperature at which water boils under normal atmospheric pressure. A **Celsius thermometer** is a thermometer marked off according to this scale. *Symbol:* C [< Anders *Celsius* (1701-1744), a Swedish astronomer, who invented it]

celt (selt) *n.* a prehistoric stone or metal tool shaped like an axe head with a bevelled edge.

Celt (kelt *or* selt) *n.* **1** a member of an ancient people of W Europe and the British Isles, including the Britons and Gauls. **2** a descendant of one of these peoples. The Irish, most Highland Scots, Welsh, and Bretons are Celts. Also, **Kelt.** [< L *Celtae,* pl. < Gk. *Keltoi*]

Celt·ic (kel′tik *or* sel′tik) *adj., n.* —*adj.* of the Celts or their language. —*n.* a group of Indo-European languages, including Irish and Scots Gaelic, Manx, Welsh, Breton, and Cornish. Also, **Keltic.**

Celtic cross a cross having a circle or circles intersecting the four arms. The design is of Celtic origin.

ce·ment (sə ment′) *n., v.* —*n.* **1** a fine, grey powder made by burning clay and limestone. **2** this substance mixed with water and sand, gravel, or crushed stone to form concrete, used to make sidewalks, basement walls and floors, etc.: *Cement becomes hard like stone.* **3** any soft substance that hardens to make things stick together: *rubber cement.* **4** a substance used to fill cavities in teeth or to fasten fillings into them. **5** anything that joins together or unites. —*v.* **1** fasten together with cement. **2** pour or spread concrete for: *The workmen were cementing the sidewalk.* **3** join firmly; make firm: *The shared dangers cemented their friendship.* [ME < OF *ciment* < L *caementum* chippings of stone < *caedere* cut] —**ce·ment′er,** *n.*

cem·e·ter·y (sem′ə ter′ē) *n., pl.* **-ter·ies.** a place for burying the dead; graveyard. [< LL *coemeterium* < Gk. *koimētērion* < *koimaein* lull to sleep]

cen. central.

ce·no·bite (sē′nə bīt′ *or* sen′ə bīt′) *n.* a member of a religious group living in a monastery or convent. Also, **coenobite.** [< LL *coenobita* < *coenobium* < Gk. *koinobion* convent < *koinos* common + *bios* life]

ce·no·bit·ic (sē′nə bit′ik *or* sen′ə bit′ik) *adj.* **1** of or having to do with a cenobite. **2** living in community: *Monks in a monastery are cenobitic.*

cen·o·taph (sen′ə taf′) *n.* **1** a monument in memory of a dead person whose body is elsewhere. **2** a monument in memory of many dead persons, such as all those from one country, city, etc. killed in a war. [< L *cenotaphium* < Gk. *kenotaphion* < *kenos* empty + *taphos* tomb]

Ce·no·zo·ic (sē′nə zō′ik *or* sen′ə zō′ik) *adj., n.* —*adj.* *Geology.* **1** of, having to do with, or designating the era extending from the end of the Mesozoic, about 70 million years ago, to the present time. The Cenozoic era is the age of mammals. See chart at **geology. 2** of, having to do with, or designating the rock formed during this era. —*n.* **the Cenozoic,** the Cenozoic era or its rock system. [< Gk. *kainos* recent + *zoē* life]

cen·ser (sen′sər) *n.* a container in which incense is burned. [ME < OF *(en)censier,* ult. < L *incensum* incense]
☛ *Hom.* censor, sensor.

cens et rentes (sän zä ränt′) *Cdn. French. Historical.* in New France and Lower Canada, a payment in cash and kind to a seigneur in recognition of his rights.

cens·i·taire (sän zi ter′) *n. Cdn. French. Historical.* in French Canada, a habitant qualified to vote.

cen·sor (sen′sər) *n., v.* —*n.* **1** a person authorized by a government or other organization to examine and, if necessary, change books, letters, motion pictures, etc. to ensure they contain nothing obscene, libellous, politically dangerous, etc. **2** in ancient Rome, a magistrate who took the census and supervised the

hat, āge, fär; let, ēqual, tèrm; it, īce
hot, ŏpen, ôrder; oil, out; cup, pŭt, rüle,
əbove, takən, pencəl, lemən, circəs
ch, child; ng, long; sh, ship
th, thin; ᴛʜ, then; zh, measure

conduct of citizens. **3** a person who exercises supervision over the morals or behavior of others. **4** a person who likes to find fault. —*v.* **1** examine as a censor, often making changes or cutting out parts: *All letters from the battlefront were censored.* **2** take out a part or parts of news reports, letters, books, motion pictures, etc.: *Two scenes in the movie had been censored.* [< L *censor* < *censere* appraise]
☛ *Hom.* censer, sensor.

cen·so·ri·al (sen sô′rē əl) *adj.* of or suitable for a censor.

cen·so·ri·ous (sen sô′rē əs) *adj.* too ready to find fault; severely critical. —**cen·so′ri·ous·ly,** *adv.* —**cen·so′ri·ous·ness,** *n.*

cen·sor·ship (sen′sər ship′) *n.* **1** the act, practice, or system of censoring: *Censorship of news is common in time of war.* **2** the position or work of a censor.

cen·sur·a·ble (sen′shər ə bəl) *adj.* worthy of censure. —**cen′sur·a·bil′i·ty,** *n.* —**cen′sur·a·bly,** *adv.*

cen·sure (sen′shər) *n., v.* **-sured, -sur·ing.** —*n.* **1** strong disapproval, especially official criticism or condemnation: *a vote of censure.* **2** an expression of such disapproval: *The minister's speech included a censure of the press for biased reporting.* —*v.* express disapproval of; criticize officially or publicly. [ME < OF < L *censura* < *censere* appraise] —**cen′sur·er,** *n.*
☛ *Syn. v.* See note at **blame.**

cen·sus (sen′səs) *n.* an official count of the people of a country or district. A census is taken to find out the number of people living there and the numbers in different age groups, occupations, etc. [< L < *censere* appraise]

cent (sent) *n.* **1** a unit of money in Australia, Bahamas, Barbados, Bermuda, Canada, Guyana, Hong Kong, Jamaica, Liberia, New Zealand, Singapore, Trinidad and Tobago, United States, West Indies (Leeward Islands, Windward Islands), and Zimbabwe, equal to $\frac{1}{100}$ of a dollar; in Ethiopia, $\frac{1}{100}$ of a birr; in Surinam, $\frac{1}{100}$ of a guilder; in the Netherlands $\frac{1}{100}$ of a gulden; in Sierra Leone, $\frac{1}{100}$ of a leone; in Malta, $\frac{1}{100}$ of a pound; in South Africa, $\frac{1}{100}$ of a rand; in Mauritius and Sri Lanka, $\frac{1}{100}$ of a rupee; in Kenya, Somalia, Tanzania, and Uganda, $\frac{1}{100}$ of a shilling. *Symbol:* ¢ **2** a coin worth one cent. [< F < L *centum* hundred]
☛ *Hom.* scent, sent.

cent. **1** central. **2** century. **3** centigrade.

cen·taur (sen′tôr) *n. Greek mythology.* one of a race of monsters that had the head, arms, and chest of a man, and the body and hind legs of a horse. [< L *centaurus* < Gk. *kentauros*]

cen·ta·vo (sen tä′vō) *n.* **1** a unit of money equal to $\frac{1}{100}$ of the basic unit of money in certain countries: $\frac{1}{100}$ of a peso in Argentina, Bolivia, Colombia, Cuba, the Dominican Republic, Mexico, and the Philippines; $\frac{1}{100}$ of an escudo in Mozambique and Portugal; $\frac{1}{100}$ of a colon in El Salvador; $\frac{1}{100}$ of a cordoba in Nicaragua; $\frac{1}{100}$ of a cruzeiro in Brazil; $\frac{1}{100}$ of a lempira in Honduras; $\frac{1}{100}$ of a quetzal in Guatemala; $\frac{1}{100}$ of a sol in Peru; $\frac{1}{100}$ of a sucre in Ecuador. **2** a coin worth one centavo. [< Sp. < L *centum* hundred]

cen·te·nar·i·an (sen′tə ner′ē ən) *n., adj.* —*n.* a person who is 100 years old or more. —*adj.* **1** 100 years old or more. **2** of 100 years.

cen·ten·ar·y (sen ten′ə rē, sen tē′nə rē, *or* sen′tə ner′ē) *n., pl.* **-ar·ies;** *adj.* —*n.* **1** a period of 100 years. **2** a 100th anniversary. **3** the celebration of the 100th anniversary. —*adj.* having to do with a period of 100 years. [< L *centenarius* relating to a hundred < *centum* hundred]

cen·ten·ni·al (sen ten′ē əl, sen ten′yəl, *or* sen tēn′yəl) *adj., n.* —*adj.* **1** of or having to do with 100 years or a 100th anniversary: *a centennial exhibition.* **2** 100 years old. —*n.* **1** a 100th anniversary. Canada celebrated its centennial in 1967. **2** the celebration of the 100th anniversary. [< L *cent(um)* hundred + E *(bi)ennial*] —**cen·ten′ni·al·ly,** *adv.*

cen·ter (sen′tər) See **centre.**
☛ *Spelling.* Compounds and derivatives beginning with **center-** are entered under their **centre-** forms.

cen·tes·i·mal (sen tes′ə məl) *adj.* **1** 100th. **2** divided into 100ths. [< L *centesimus* hundredth]

cen·tes·i·mo (sen tes′ə mō′) *n.* a unit of money in Uruguay, equal to $\frac{1}{100}$ of a peso. [< Sp. < L *centesimus* hundredth]

centi- *combining form.* **1** an SI prefix meaning one-hundredth. A

centimetre is one one-hundredth of a metre. *Symbol*: c **2** one hundred, as in *centigrade, centipede*. [< L *centum* hundred]

cen·ti·are (sen'tē er') *n.* 1/100 of an are; one square metre. [< F]

cen·ti·grade (sen'tə grād') *adj.* **1** divided into or consisting of 100 degrees. **2** Celsius. [< F < L *centum* hundred + *gradus* degree]

cen·time (sän tēm') *n.* **1** a unit of money equal to 1/100 of the basic unit in certain countries: 1/100 of a franc in Belgium, Benin, Burundi, Cameroon, Central African Republic, Chad, Congo Republic, France, Gabon, Ivory Coast, Luxembourg, Madagascar, Mali, Niger, Rwanda, Senegal, Switzerland, Togo, and Upper Volta; 1/100 of a dinar in Algeria; 1/100 of a gourde in Haiti; 1/100 of a dirham in Morocco. **2** a coin worth one centime. [< F < L *centum* hundred]

cen·ti·me·ter (sen'tə mē'tər) See **centimetre**.

cen·ti·me·tre (sen'tə mē'tər) *n.* an SI unit for measuring length, equal to one one-hundredth of a metre, or ten millimetres: *A nickel has a diameter of just over two centimetres. Symbol*: cm [< F]

cen·ti·mo (sen'tə mō') *n.* a unit of money equal to 1/100 of the basic unit in certain countries: 1/100 of a colon in Costa Rica; 1/100 of a guarani in Paraguay; 1/100 of a peseta in Spain; 1/100 of a bolivar in Venezuela. [< Sp. < F *centime*]

cen·ti·pede (sen'tə pēd') *n.* any of a class (Chilopoda) of small, wormlike arthropods having a long, flat body with a great many segments and one pair of legs to each segment. The front pair of legs is modified into poison fangs. [< L *centipeda* < *centum* hundred + *pes, pedis* foot]

cen·tral (sen'trəl) *adj., n.* —*adj.* **1** of the centre; being or forming the centre. **2** at, in, or near the centre: *the central part of the city.* **3** from the centre. **4** equally distant from all points; easy to get to or from: *They are looking for a good central location to set up their shop.* **5** main; chief: *What is the central idea in the story?* **6** *Anatomy.* **a** of or designating the brain and spinal cord as a major division of the nervous system of vertebrates. **b** arising from or affecting these parts of the nervous system: *central anesthesia.* —*n.* **1** a telephone exchange. **2** a telephone operator. [< L *centralis* < *centrum*. See CENTRE.] —**cen'tral·ly**, *adv.* —**cen'tral·ness**, *n.*

Central American *n., adj.* —*adj.* of or having to do with Central America or its people. —*n.* a native or inhabitant of Central America, the isthmus joining North and South America.

cen·tral·ism (sen'trə liz'əm) *n.* a theory or system of concentrating control in a central agency, especially a government.

cen·tral·ist (sen'trəl ist) *n.* a person who promotes or favors centralism.

cen·tral·i·za·tion (sen'trəl ə zā'shən *or* sen'trəl ī zā'shən) *n.* **1** the coming or bringing to a centre. **2** concentration at a centre: *Centralization of relief agencies may prevent waste of effort.* **3** the concentration of administrative power in a central government.

cen·tral·ize (sen'trəl īz') *v.* **-ized, -iz·ing. 1** collect at a centre; gather together. **2** bring or come under one control. —**cen'tra·liz'er**, *n.*

Central Powers during World War I, Germany and Austria-Hungary, sometimes also their allies Turkey and Bulgaria.

cen·tre (sen'tər) *n., v.* **-tred** *or* **-tered, -tring** *or* **-ter·ing.** —*n.* **1** a point within a circle or sphere equally distant from all parts of the circumference or surface. **2** the middle part or place: *the centre of a room, the centre of the forehead, the centre of the stage.* **3** a person or thing that is most important; the chief object of attention, interest, etc.: *He was the centre of attention. The new city hall was the centre of a huge controversy.* **4** a place of influence or activity; a main area or point: *a shopping centre, a community centre. Toronto is a centre for trade.* **5** *Sports.* the player who has the centre position of a forward line. **6** a political attitude or policy characterized by moderate views that are neither right (conservative) nor left (reformist or radical). **7** all the people and parties having moderate views. **8** a mass of nerve cells closely connected and acting together; nerve centre: *the respiratory centre, the centre of balance.* —*v.* **1** place in or at the centre. **2** gather together; concentrate: *She centred her hopes on obtaining the premiership. The troops were centred at a temporary camp.* **3** be concentrated; focus: *The story centres on her childhood experiences.* **4** mark or provide with a centre: *a smooth lawn centred by a pool.* Also, **center.** [ME < OF *centre* < L *centrum* < Gk. *kentron* sharp point]
  ☛ *Syn. n.* **1, 2.** See note at **middle.**
  ☛ *Usage.* **Centre around** (or **about**) is an informal idiom: *The story centres around a robbery.* The formal idiom is *centre on* or *upon.*

cen·tre·board (sen'tər bôrd') *n.* a movable keel of a sailboat. It is lowered through a slot in the bottom of a boat to prevent drifting to leeward. Also, **centerboard.**

centre field *Baseball.* the section of the outfield behind second base.

cen·tre·fold (sen'tər fōld') *n.* a large illustration that extends across the two facing pages forming the centre of a magazine.

centre ice *Hockey.* **1** the centre of the ice surface from which play begins at the start of each period. **2** the area of ice surface between the blue lines.

centre line *Hockey.* a red line passing through centre ice at an equal distance from each of the blue lines.

centre of gravity the point in something around which its mass is evenly balanced.

cen·tre·piece (sen'tər pēs') *n.* an ornamental piece of glass, lace, etc. for the centre of a dining table. Also, **centerpiece.**

cen·tric (sen'trik) *adj.* central. —**cen'tri·cal·ly**, *adv.*

–centric *combining form.* **1** having (something) as a centre: *heliocentric.* **2** having a centre or centres of a particular kind or number.

cen·trif·u·gal (sen trif'ə gəl *or* sen trif'yə gəl) *adj.* **1** moving away from the centre. **2** making use of or acted upon by centrifugal force. [< NL *centrifugus* < L *centrum* centre + *fugere* flee] —**cen·trif'u·gal·ly**, *adv.*

centrifugal force the inertia of a body that tends to move it away from the centre around which it revolves.

cen·tri·fuge (sen'trə fyüj') *n.* a machine for separating cream from milk, bacteria from a fluid, etc. by means of centrifugal force. [< F]

cen·tri·ole (sen'trē ōl') *n.* either of two bundles of rodlike bodies, within the centrosome of most animal cells, that form the spindle fibres along which chromatids move in the process of cell division.

cen·trip·e·tal (sen trip'ə təl) *adj.* **1** moving toward the centre. **2** making use of or acted upon by centripetal force. [< NL *centripetus* < L *centrum* centre + *petere* seek] —**cen·trip'e·tal·ly**, *adv.*

centripetal force a force that tends to move things toward the centre around which they are turning. Gravitation is a centripetal force.

cen·trist (sen'trist) *n.* a person who holds moderate views, especially in politics.

cen·tro·mere (sen'trə mēr') *n.* a structure or point by which two sister chromatids are joined to each other and to a spindle during cell division.

cen·tro·some (sen'trə sōm') *n.* a tiny spherical region in the cytoplasm of many animal cells, close to the nucleus, which contains the centrioles. [< centro- (< L *centrum* and Gk. *kentron*) + -some body (< Gk. *sōma*)]

cen·tro·sphere (sen'trə sfēr') *n.* **1** centrosome. **2** *Geology.* the extremely dense central part of the earth. [< centro- centre (< L *centrum* and Gk. *kentron*) + *sphere*]

cen·tu·ple (sen tü'pəl *or* sen'tə pəl) *adj., v.* **-pled, -pling.** —*adj.* 100 times as much or as many; a hundredfold. —*v.* make 100 times as much or as many; increase a hundredfold. [< F < LL *centuplus* hundredfold]

cen·tu·ri·on (sen tyür'ē ən *or* sen tür'ē ən) *n.* in the ancient Roman army, a commander of a group of about 100 soldiers. [< L *centurio, -onis* < *centuria*. See CENTURY.]

cen·tu·ry (sen'chə rē) *n., pl.* **-ries. 1** each 100 years, counting from some special time, such as the birth of Christ. **2** period of 100 years: *From 1824 to 1924 is a century.* **3** a group of 100 people or things. **4** in the ancient Roman army, a body of soldiers, originally probably consisting of 100 soldiers. **5** in ancient Rome, a division of the people for voting. Each century had one vote. **6** *Cricket.* a score of 100 runs. [< L *centuria* a division of a hundred units < *centum* hundred]
  ☛ *Usage.* **Centuries.** The fifth century A.D. runs from the beginning of the year 401 to the end of the year 500, the nineteenth century from January 1, 1801, through December 31, 1900. That is, to name the century correctly, add one to the number of its hundred. Similarly, the first century B.C. runs back from the birth of Christ through 100, the second century from 101 through 200, the fifth century from 401 through 500, and so on.

century plant a large, tropical American agave (*Agave americana*) that flowers only once, usually when it is more than 10 years old, and then dies.

ce·phal·ic (sə fal'ik) *adj.* **1** of or having to do with the head. **2** near, on, or in the head. **3** toward the head. [< L *cephalicus* < Gk. *kephalikos* < *kephalē* head]

cephalic index the ratio of the breadth of the human skull to its length, multiplied by 100. Also, **cranial index.**

ceph·a·lo·pod (sef'ə lə pod') *n.* any of a class (Cephalopoda) of molluscs including squids, octopuses, and cuttlefishes, having long, armlike tentacles around the mouth, a pair of large, highly

developed eyes, and a sharp, birdlike beak. [< NL *cephalopoda*, pl. < Gk. *kephalē* head + *pous, podos* foot]

ceph·a·lo·tho·rax (sef′ə lō thô′raks) *n.* the combined head and thorax of some animals, such as crabs, spiders, etc. [< *cephalo-* the head (< Gk. *kephalē*) + *thorax*]

Ce·phe·us (sē′fē əs *or* sē′fyüs) *n.* **1** *Greek mythology.* the father of Andromeda. **2** *Astronomy.* a northern constellation near Cassiopeia.

ce·ram·ic (sə ram′ik) *adj., n.* —*adj.* of or having to do with earthenware, porcelain, brick, etc. or with their manufacture. —*n.* **1 ceramics,** the art or process of making articles from baked clay (*used with a singular verb*): *Ceramics is taught in art class.* **2** an article of earthenware, porcelain, etc.: *They had some beautiful ceramics at the craft show.* [< Gk. *keramikos* < *keramos* potter's clay]

cer·a·mist (ser′ə mist) *n.* **1** an expert in ceramics. **2** a manufacturer of ceramics.

ce·rate (sēr′āt) *n.* a firm ointment made of lard or oil mixed with wax, resin, etc. [< L *ceratum,* pp. neut. of *cerare* to wax < *cera* wax]
☛ *Hom.* **serrate.**

Cer·ber·us (sèr′bər əs) *n.* **1** *Greek and Roman mythology.* a three-headed dog that guarded the entrance to Hades. **2** a surly, watchful guard.

cere (sēr) *n.* a waxy-looking membrane near the beak of certain birds, especially birds of prey and parrots, in which the nostrils open. [< L *cera* wax < Gk. *kēros*]
☛ *Hom.* **sear, sere.**

ce·re·al (sēr′ē əl) *n., adj.* —*n.* **1** any grass that produces a grain used as food. Wheat, rice, corn, oats, and barley are cereals. **2** the grain. **3** food, especially breakfast food, made from the grain. Oatmeal and corn flakes are cereals.
—*adj.* of or having to do with grain or the grasses producing it. [< L *Cerealis* of or having to do with Ceres]
☛ *Hom.* **serial.**

cer·e·bel·lar (ser′ə bel′ər) *adj.* of or having to do with the cerebellum.

cer·e·bel·lum (ser′ə bel′əm) *n.* **-bel·lums, -bel·la** (-bel′ə). a major division of the brain situated below the cerebrum. It controls the co-ordination of the muscles and the maintenance of bodily equilibrium. See **brain** for picture. [< L *cerebrum* dim. of *cerebrum* brain]

ce·re·bral (sə rē′brəl *or* ser′ə brəl) *adj.* **1** of the brain: *Paralysis may be caused by a cerebral hemorrhage.* **2** of the cerebrum: *The cerebral cortex is the outer layer of the cerebrum.* **3** involving or appealing to thought and reason; intellectual: *She enjoys cerebral games like chess.* [< L *cerebrum* brain]

cerebral palsy a disorder resulting from brain damage, especially before or during birth, and characterized by impaired muscular function, lack of co-ordination, spastic movement, etc.

cer·e·brate (ser′ə brāt′) *v.* **-brat·ed, -brat·ing.** use the brain; think.

cer·e·bra·tion (ser′ə brā′shən) *n.* **1** the action of the brain. **2** the act of thinking.

ce·re·bro·spi·nal (sə rē′brō spī′nəl *or* ser′ə brō spī′nəl) *adj.* of or affecting both the brain and spinal cord.

ce·re·bro·vas·cu·lar (sə rē′brō vas′kyə lər *or* ser′ə brō vas′kyə ler) *adj.* of or having to do with the blood vessels of the brain.

cerebrovascular accident sudden partial or complete loss of consciousness with paralysis and loss of sensation, caused by the rupture or the obstruction by a clot, etc. of an artery in the brain; stroke.

cer·e·brum (sə rē′brəm *or* ser′ə brəm) *n., pl.* **-brums, -bra** (-brə). **1** the part of the human brain that is responsible for mental activities such as memory, understanding, and the ability to reason, and also controls fine movements of the smaller muscles of the face, hands, and toes, and the senses of sight, hearing, etc. See **brain** for picture. **2** the part of the brain in all other vertebrates that corresponds structurally to the human cerebrum but has fewer functions. [< L]

cere·cloth (sēr′kloth′) *n.* **1** waxed cloth. **2** the waxed cloth in which a dead person is wrapped for burial. [originally *cered cloth; cere* wax < L *cerare* < *cera* wax. See CERE.]

cere·ment (sēr′mənt) *n.* Usually, **cerements,** *pl.* the cloth or garment in which a dead person is wrapped for burial; shroud. [< obs. *cere* wrap for burial, wax < L *cerare.* See CERECLOTH.]

cer·e·mo·ni·al (ser′ə mō′nē əl) *adj., n.* —*adj.* **1** of or having to do with ceremony: *a ceremonial occasion. The ceremonial costumes were beautiful.* **2** very formal; ceremonious.
—*n.* **1** formal actions suitable for an occasion. Kneeling is a ceremonial of religion. **2** a rite or ceremony. **3** a formality of

courtesy or manners. **4** the observance of these in social life.
—**cer′e·mo′ni·al·ly,** *adv.*
☛ *Usage.* **Ceremonial, ceremonious** differ in meaning and use. **Ceremonial** = having to do with ceremony, and applies to things involving or belonging to the ceremonies and formalities of the church, law, polite conduct, fraternities, etc.: *Shriners wear ceremonial costumes.* **Ceremonious** = full of ceremony, and applies to things done with ceremony or showy formality or to people who pay very strict attention to the details of polite conduct: *The banquet was a ceremonious affair.*

cer·e·mo·ni·ous (ser′ə mō′nē əs) *adj.* **1** full of ceremony. **2** very formal; extremely polite. —**cer′e·mo′ni·ous·ly,** *adv.* —**cer′e·mo′ni·ous·ness,** *n.*
☛ *Usage.* See note at **ceremonial.**

cer·e·mo·ny (ser′ə mō′nē) *n., pl.* **-nies. 1** a special form or set of acts to be done on special occasions such as weddings, funerals, graduations, Christmas, or Hanukkah. **2** very polite conduct; a way of conducting oneself that follows all the rules of polite social behavior: *The old gentleman showed us to the door with a great deal of ceremony.* **3** an empty form; meaningless formality. **4** formality; formalities: *The democratic prince disliked the traditional ceremony of court life.*
stand on ceremony, be very formal; insist on formal behavior: *The premier does not stand on ceremony but always makes the people he meets feel comfortable and relaxed.*
[< L *caerimonia* rite]
☛ *Syn.* **1. Ceremony, rite** = a form followed on special occasions. **Ceremony** applies to a special form or procedure used on religious, public, or other solemn occasions: *The graduation ceremony was inspiring.* **Rite** applies to a ceremonial procedure that is laid down to be followed in a religious service or other solemn ceremony and in which both the acts to be done and the words to be said are prescribed: *A priest went to administer the last rites to the dying victims of the explosion.*

Ce·res (sēr′ēz) *n. Roman mythology.* the goddess of agriculture, corresponding to the Greek goddess Demeter.

ce·re·us (sēr′ē əs) *n.* **1** any of a genus (*Cereus*) of tropical American cactuses. **2** the **night-blooming cereus,** any of several cactuses with fragrant flowers that open at night, such as *Selenicereus grandiflorus.* [< L *cereus* wax candle < *cera* wax]
☛ *Hom.* **serious.**

ce·rise (sə rēz′ *or* sə rēs′) *n. or adj.* bright pinkish red. [< F *cerise* cherry < VL < LGk. *kerasia* cherry tree < Gk. *kerasos* cherry. Doublet of CHERRY.]

ce·ri·um (sēr′ē əm) *n.* a greyish, metallic chemical element. *Symbol:* Ce; *at. no.* 58; *at.wt.* 140.12. [< NL *cerium,* from the asteroid *Ceres*]

cer·tain (sèr′tən) *adj., pron.* —*adj.* **1** settled; fixed; definite: *a certain hour. Each investor will receive a certain percentage of the profit.* **2** that cannot be disputed; established beyond any doubt: *It is certain that 2 and 3 do not make 6.* **3** sure to happen; inevitable: *Death is certain.* **4** bound to; sure to: *She is certain to do well in her profession.* **5** reliable; dependable: *The police have certain evidence of his guilt.* **6** definite but not named: *A certain person donated $2000 to the project.* **7** having or showing no doubt; confident; positive: *She was certain of her facts. His reply was quick and certain.* **8** of a particular but unspecified character, amount, or degree: *There was a certain reluctance in his voice, but he agreed to go. She had a certain charm that made it very inviting. To a certain extent we are all at fault.*
—*pron.* a definite but unspecified number; some particular ones: *Certain of the students will be asked to give a detailed report.*
for certain, surely, without a doubt: *It will rain for certain.*
[ME < OF < L *certus* sure] —**cer′tain·ness,** *n.*
☛ *Syn. adj.* **1.** See note at **sure.**

cer·tain·ly (sèr′tən lē) *adv.* **1** surely; without doubt. **2** *Informal.* yes; of course: *May I borrow your music? Certainly, you may.*
☛ *Usage.* **Certainly.** In informal speech **certainly** is often used as an intensifier or as an affirmative answer to questions: *I'm certainly pleased that you came. Are you going to the football game Friday? Certainly.*

cer·tain·ty (sèr′tən tē) *n., pl.* **-ties. 1** being certain; freedom from doubt: *The man's certainty was amusing, for we could all see that he was wrong.* **2** something certain; a fact: *The annual recurrence of the seasons is a certainty.*

cer·tes (sèr′tēz) *adv. Archaic.* certainly; in truth. [ME < OF < VL *certas* surely]

cer·ti·fi·a·ble (sèr′tə fī′ə bəl) *adj.* **1** that can be certified. **2** sick enough in the mind to be legally committed to a mental institution. —**cer′ti·fi′a·bly,** *adv.*

☛ hat, āge, fär; let, ēqual, tèrm; it, īce
hot, ōpen, ôrder; oil, out; cup, pùt, rüle,
ə above, takən, pencəl, lemən, circəs
ch, child; ng, long; sh, ship
th, thin; ŦH, then; zh, measure

cer·tif·i·cate (*n.* sər tif′ə kit; *v.* sər tif′ə kāt′) *n., v.* **-cat·ed,
-cat·ing.** —*n.* a written or printed statement that declares something
to be a fact: *Your birth certificate gives your full name and the date
and place of your birth.* —*v.* **1** give a certificate to. **2** authorize by a
certificate. [< Med.L *certificatum,* neut. pp. of *certificare.* See
CERTIFY.]

cer·ti·fi·ca·tion (sèr′tə fə kā′shən) *n.* **1** certifying or being
certified. **2** a certified statement.

cer·ti·fied (sèr′tə fīd′) *adj.* **1** guaranteed: *The water is certified to
be pure.* **2** having a certificate.

certified cheque a cheque that has been guaranteed as good by
the bank on which it is drawn. When a bank certifies a cheque,
money to cover it is immediately withdrawn from the account on
which the cheque is written.

certified mail a postal service that provides proof of delivery of
a letter or parcel by means of a card that is signed by the receiver
of the mail and is then returned to the sender. Certified mail is
similar to registered mail, but cheaper.

certified milk raw or pasteurized milk guaranteed to meet
certain official standards.

cer·ti·fi·er (sèr′tə fī′ər) *n.* one that certifies.

cer·ti·fy (sèr′tə fī′) *v.* **-fied, -fy·ing. 1** declare something as true
or correct by spoken, written, or printed statement: *The doctor
certified the cause of death as a heart attack.* **2** legally commit (a
person) to a mental institution. **3** guarantee the quality or value of.
4 assure; make certain. **5** *Banking.* guarantee in writing on the face
of (a cheque) that sufficient funds have been set aside from the
drawer's account to cover the cheque. **6** declare (a person) legally
insane. [ME < OF < Med.L *certificare* < *certus* sure + *facere*
make]

cer·ti·o·rar·i (sèr′shē ə rer′ē *or* -rer′ī) *n. Law.* an order from a
higher court to a lower one, calling for the record of a case for
review. [< LL *certiorari* be informed]

cer·ti·tude (sèr′tə tyüd′ *or* sèr′tə tüd′) *n.* certainty; sureness. [<
LL *certitudo* < *certus* sure]

ce·ru·le·an (sə rü′lē ən) *adj. or n.* sky blue. [< L *caeruleus* dark
blue]

ce·ru·men (sə rü′mən) *n.* a waxlike substance in the ears;
earwax. [< NL < L *cera* wax]

cer·vi·cal (sèr′və kəl *or* sèr vī′kəl) *adj.* of or having to do with a
cervix.

cer·vi·ces (sər vī′sēz) *n.* a pl. of **cervix.**

cer·vine (sèr′vīn *or* sèr′vin) *adj.* of or like a deer. [< L *cervinus*
< *cervus* deer]

cer·vix (sèr′viks) *n., pl.* **cer·vix·es** *or* **cer·vi·ces. 1** the neck,
especially the back of the neck. **2** a necklike part, especially the
narrow opening of the uterus. [< L]

Ce·sar·e·an *or* **Ce·sar·i·an** (si zer′ē ən *or* si zar′ē ən)
See **Caesarean.**

ce·si·um *or* **cae·si·um** (sē′zē əm) *n.* a silvery metallic
chemical element. *Symbol:* Cs; *at.no.* 55; *at.wt.* 132.905. [< NL
caesium < L *caesius* bluish-grey]

ces·sa·tion (se sā′shən) *n.* a ceasing; pause; stop: *There is still
hope for a cessation of fighting.* [< L *cessatio, -onis* < *cessare*
cease]

ces·sion (sesh′ən) *n.* a handing over to another; ceding; giving
up; surrendering. [< L *cessio, -onis* < *cedere* yield]
☛ *Hom.* **session.**

cess·pool (ses′pül′) *n.* **1** a pool or pit for house drains to empty
into. **2** any filthy place. [origin uncertain]

ces·tode (ses′tōd) *n.* any of a class (Cestoda) of flatworms that
live as parasites in the intestines of various animals. Tapeworms are
cestodes. [< Gk. *kestos* girdle]

ces·tus (ses′təs) *n.* a boxer's hand covering made of strips of
leather, often loaded with metal, used in ancient Rome. [< L
caestus, ? var. of *cestus* girdle < Gk. *kestos*]

ce·su·ra (sə zhür′ə *or* si zyür′ə) *n., pl.* **-su·ras, -su·rae** (-zhür′ē,
-zhür′ī, -zyür′ē *or* -zyür′ī). See **caesura.**

ce·ta·cean (sə tā′shən) *n., adj.* —*n.* any of an order (Cetacea) of
fishlike mammals that live in the water, especially in the ocean.
Whales, dolphins, and porpoises are cetaceans. —*adj.* of, having to
do with, or designating an animal of this order. [< NL < L *cetus*
whale < Gk. *kētos*]

ce·ta·ceous (sə tā′shəs) *adj.* cetacean.

ce·to·log·i·cal (sē′tə loj′i kəl) *adj.* of or having to do with
cetology.

ce·tol·o·gist (sē tol′ə jist′) *n.* a person trained in cetology,
especially one whose work it is.

ce·tol·o·gy (sē tol′ə jē) *n.* the branch of zoology that deals with
whales.

Ce·tus (sē′təs) *n.* a constellation near the celestial equator. [< L
Cetus < Gk. *Kētos* the Whale]

Cey·lo·nese (sē′lə nēz′) *n., pl.* **-nese;** *adj.* —*n.* a native or
inhabitant of Sri Lanka, an island country in the Indian Ocean.
—*adj.* of or having to do with Sri Lanka or its people.

cf. compare (for L *confer*).

c/f *Bookkeeping.* carried forward.

Cf californium.

CF Canadian Forces.

CFB Canadian Forces Base.

CFDC Canadian Film Development Corporation.

C.F.I. or **c.f.i.** cost, freight, and insurance.

CFL or **C.F.L.** Canadian Football League.

C.G.I.T. or **CGIT** Canadian Girls in Training.

C.G.M. Conspicuous Gallantry Medal.

ch. or **Ch. 1** chapter. **2** church. **3** chaplain. **4** child; children.
5 chain.

C.H. Companion of Honor.

Chab·lis (sha′blē *or* sha blē′) *n.* a dry white Burgundy wine from
the area around Chablis, France.

cha·bouk or **cha·buk** (chä′bük) *n.* in the Orient, a long whip
used to punish people. [< Persian or Hind. *chabuk*]

cha–cha (chä′chä′) *n.* cha-cha-cha.

cha–cha–cha (chä′ chä′ chä′) *n., v.* —*n.* **1** a ballroom dance
with a fast, strongly-marked rhythm, originally Latin American.
2 the music for such a dance. —*v.* dance the cha-cha-cha. Also,
cha–cha. [imitative]

cha·dor (chə dôr′) *n.* a large piece of cloth used as a long cloak
and veil by some Moslem women, especially in Iran.

chafe (chāf) *v.* **chafed, chaf·ing;** *n.* —*v.* **1** rub to make warm: *She
chafed her cold hands.* **2** wear or be worn away by rubbing. **3** make
or become sore by rubbing: *The rough collar chafed my neck.*
4 annoy or make angry: *Their teasing chafed him.* **5** become
annoyed or angry: *He chafed under their teasing.*
—*n.* **1** a sore or injury caused by chafing. **2** a state of irritation or
anger. [ME < OF *chaufer* < L *calefacere* < *calere* be warm +
facere make]

chaf·er (chāf′ər) *n.* any of various large beetles (subfamily
Melolonthinae of the family (Scarabaeidae), such as the cockchafer.
[OE *ceafor*]

chaff[1] (chaf) *n.* **1** husks of wheat, oats, rye, etc., especially when
separated from grain by threshing. **2** hay or straw cut fine for
feeding cattle. **3** worthless stuff. **4** strips of aluminum foil dropped
by aircraft to confuse enemy radar systems. [OE *ceaf*]

chaff[2] (chaf) *v., n.* —*v.* make fun of (someone) in a good-natured
way: *The girls chaffed the French boy about his English.* —*n.*
good-natured joking about a person to his face. [origin uncertain]

chaf·fer[1] (chaf′ər) *v., n.* —*v.* dispute about a price; bargain. —*n.*
a disputing about price; bargaining. [ME *chaffare* < OE *cēap*
bargain + *faru* journey]

chaf·finch (chaf′inch) *n.* a European Finch (*Fringilla coelebs*)
having black-and-white wings, the male having a reddish breast and
blue-grey head. The chaffinch has a pleasant, short song, and is
often kept as a cage bird. [OE *ceaffinc* < *ceaf* chaff[1] + *finc* finch]

chaff·y (chaf′ē) *adj.* **1** full of chaff. **2** worthless.

chafing dish a dish with a heating apparatus under it, used to
cook food at the table or to keep it warm.

cha·grin (shə grin′) *n., v.* —*n.* a feeling of embarrassment or
vexation caused by disappointment, failure, or humiliation. —*v.*
cause to feel chagrin. [< F < MF *chagrin* sad, gloomy]

chain (chān) *n., v.* —*n.* **1** a flexible, connected series of links or
rings used to bind, connect, or hold, or to decorate: *a gold chain, a
steel chain, a paper chain.* **2** a series of things joined or linked
together: *a mountain chain, a chain of happenings, a chain of
thoughts.* **3** anything that binds or restrains. **4** a measuring
instrument consisting of 100 links of iron or steel: *A surveyors'
chain is 66 feet long (about 20 m) an engineers' chain is 100 feet
long (about 30 m).* **5** a number of restaurants, stores, theatres, etc.
owned and operated by one person or company. **6 chains,** *pl.*
a bonds; fetters. **b** imprisonment; bondage. **7** *Chemistry.* a number
of atoms of the same element bonded together like a chain.
8 *Biology.* a group of organisms, as bacteria, connected end to end.
—*v.* **1** join together or fasten with a chain. **2** bind; restrain.
3 restrain with chains; fetter. [ME < OF *chaeine* < L *catena*]

chain gang in S United States, a gang of convicts, etc. chained
together while at work outdoors or on their way to work.

chain letter a letter that each receiver is asked to copy and send to several other people in order to get some supposed benefit.

chain mail a kind of flexible armor made of metal rings linked together.

chain·man (chān′mən) *n., pl.* **-men.** *Surveying.* a man who carries the measuring chain.

chain measure a system of measurement used in surveying:

> 100 links = 1 chain (about 20 m)
> 10 chains = 1 furlong
> 8 furlongs = 1 mile

chain reaction 1 *Chemistry or physics.* a process that goes on automatically when it has once been started because it yields energy or products that cause further reactions of the same kind. A reactor is designed to produce a controlled chain reaction; the explosion of an atomic bomb is an uncontrolled chain reaction. 2 any series of events or happenings, each caused by the one that precedes it.

chain saw a portable power saw having teeth linked together in an endless chain.

chain–smoke (chān′smōk′) *v.* **-smoked, -smok·ing.** smoke cigarettes one after another.

chain stitch a kind of stitch in which each stitch makes a loop through which the next stitch is taken.

chain–stitch (chān′stich′) *v.* sew or crochet using a chain stitch.

chain store one of a group of retail stores owned and operated by a single company.

chair (cher) *n., v.* —*n.* 1 a separate seat for one person, having legs and a back and, often, arms. 2 a seat of rank, dignity, or authority. 3 the position or authority of a person who has such a seat: *Professor Eagle occupies the chair of Philosophy at this university.* 4 the chairman of a meeting. 5 a covered chair carried on poles by two men; a sedan chair. 6 the electric chair. **take the chair, a** begin a meeting. **b** be in charge of or preside at a meeting: *Ms James will take the chair.* **c** begin a meeting: *The president took the chair at 2:00 p.m.* **get the chair,** *Informal.* die or be sentenced to die in the electric chair. —*v.* 1 put or carry in a chair. 2 carry high up, as if in a chair: *The winning team chaired their captain.* 3 put in a position of authority. 4 act as chairman of: *My brother chaired the meeting.* [ME < OF *chaiere* < L < Gk. *kathedra* seat. Doublet of CATHEDRA.]

chair lift an apparatus for conveying people, especially skiers, up a slope or between two points, consisting of a number of chairs suspended from an endless cable.

chair·man (cher′mən) *n., pl.* **-men.** 1 a person who presides at or is in charge of a meeting. 2 the head of a committee. 3 in New Brunswick, the elected head of a village council. 4 a man whose work is carrying or wheeling people in a chair.
☛ *Usage.* **Chairman, chairperson, chairwoman.** The word **chairman** may be used for either a man or a woman in charge of a meeting or committee. The word **chairperson** is now widely used, so that the term **chairwoman** is less frequently needed. Of the three terms, only **chairman** is used as a form of address: *Mr. Chairman, Madam Chairman.*

chair·man·ship (cher′mən ship′) *n.* 1 the position of chairman. 2 the length of time one is a chairman.

chair·per·son (cher′pèr′sən) *n.* 1 a person who presides at or is in charge of a meeting. 2 the head of a committee.
☛ *Usage.* See note at **chairman.**

chair·wom·an (cher′wùm′ən) *n., pl.* **-wom·en.** 1 a woman who presides at or is in charge of a meeting. 2 a woman at the head of a committee.
☛ *Usage.* See note at **chairman.**

chaise (shāz) *n.* 1 any of several kinds of light carriage, often with a folding top, having two or four wheels and drawn by one or two horses. 2 chaise longue. [< F *chaise* chair, var. of *chaire*, OF *chaiere.* See CHAIR.]

chaise longue (shāz′long′) a couchlike chair with a long seat, in which a person can sit with outstretched legs. [< F *chaise longue* long chair]

chaise lounge (shāz′lounj′) chaise longue.

chal·ced·o·ny (kal sed′ə nē *or* kal′sə dō′nē) *n., pl.* **-nies.** 1 a variety of quartz having a waxy lustre that occurs in various colors and forms. Agate, onyx, carnelian, jasper, etc. are chalcedony. 2 a gem made from this stone. [< L *chalcedonius* < Gk. *chalkēdōn*]

chal·cid (kal′sid) *n.* any of a large superfamily (Chalcidoidea) of mostly very small insects whose larvae live as parasites on other insects. [< Gk. *chalkos* copper; in reference to their color]

chal·co·py·rite (kal′kə pī′rīt *or* -pir′īt) *n.* a rich copper ore consisting of a sulphide of copper and iron; copper pyrites. *Formula*: CuFeS₂ [< Gk. *chalkos* copper + E *pyrite*]

Chal·da·ic (kal dā′ik) *adj. or n.* Chaldean.

Chal·de·a (kal dē′ə) *n.* a region of ancient Babylonia lying on

hat, āge, fär; let, ēqual, tèrm; it, īce
hot, ōpen, ôrder; oil, out; cup, pùt, rüle,
əbove, takən, pencəl, lemən, circəs

ch, child; ng, long; sh, ship
th, thin; ʈʜ, then; zh, measure

either side of the lower part of the Euphrates River, near the Persian Gulf.

Chal·de·an (kal dē′ən) *n., adj.* —*n.* 1 a member of an ancient Semitic people who dominated Babylonia from the late 700's to the late 600's B.C. 2 the Semitic language of the Chaldeans. 3 an astrologer or magician.
—*adj.* of or having to do with ancient Chaldea, its people, or their language. [< L *Chaldaeus* < Gk. *Chaldaios*]

Chal·dee (kal dē′ *or* kal′dē) *adj. or n.* Chaldean.

cha·let (shal′ā *or* sha lā′) *n.* 1 a herdsman's hut or cabin in the Alps. 2 a Swiss house with wide, overhanging eaves. 3 any house of similar design. [< Swiss F]

chal·ice (chal′is) *n.* 1 a cup; goblet, especially one used in the Communion service. 2 a flower shaped like a cup. [ME < OF < L *calix* cup]

chal·iced (chal′ist) *adj.* 1 having a flower shaped like a cup. 2 contained in a chalice.

chalk (chok *or* chôk) *n., v.* —*n.* 1 a soft, white or grey limestone, made up mostly of tiny fossil sea shells. Chalk is used for making lime. 2 a substance like chalk, especially in the form of a crayon used for writing or drawing on a hard, smooth surface such as a chalkboard. 3 a crayon of chalk. 4 a record of credit given; tally. **by a long chalk,** *Informal.* by far. **not by a long chalk,** *Informal.* not at all; by no means. —*v.* 1 mark, write, or draw with chalk. 2 mix or rub with chalk; whiten with chalk. 3 score; record. 4 of paint, become chalky or powdery when dry. **chalk up, a** write down; record. **b** score. [OE *cealc* < L *calx, calcis* lime] —**chalk′like′,** *adj.*
☛ *Hom.* **chock** (chok).

chalk·board (chok′bôrd′ *or* chôk′-) *n.* a board having a smooth, hard surface for writing or drawing on with chalk.

chalk talk a lecture illustrated by drawings and diagrams in chalk on a blackboard.

chalk·y (chok′ē *or* chôk′ē) *adj.* **chalk·i·er, chalk·i·est.** 1 of chalk; containing chalk. 2 like chalk; white as chalk: *The clown's face was chalky.* —**chalk′i·ness,** *n.*

chal·lenge (chal′ənj) *v.* **-lenged, -leng·ing;** *n.* —*v.* 1 call to engage in a fight or contest: *to challenge someone to a duel. The new school has challenged us to a basketball tournament.* 2 stop a person and question one's right to do what he is doing or to be where he is: *When she tried to enter the building, the guard challenged her.* 3 demand proof; question or dispute something: *My friends challenged my statement that Fredericton was the oldest city in Canada.* 4 *Law.* object formally, especially to a juror or jury. 5 demand action or effort from; stimulate: *The possibility of space travel has challenged the human imagination for centuries.*
—*n.* 1 a call to a fight or contest: *We have accepted the challenge.* 2 a call to justify or account for oneself or one's actions: *The sentry called out a challenge as they approached.* 3 a demand for proof; a questioning of the truth of something: *Their challenge led me to read up on the history of our country.* 4 *Law.* a formal objection especially to a juror or jury. [ME < OF *chalenge,* n., earlier *chalonge* (also OF *chalenger* < L *calumniari* to slander) < L *calumnia* false accusation. Doublet of CALUMNIATE, CALUMNY.]
—**chal′lenge·a·ble,** *adj.* —**chal′leng·er,** *n.*

chal·lis (shal′ē) *n.* a lightweight, usually printed, fabric of wool, wool and cotton, or a synthetic fibre, used for dresses, blouses, etc. [origin uncertain]

cha·lyb·e·ate (kə lib′ē it *or* kə lib′ē āt′) *adj., n.* —*adj.* containing salts of iron. —*n.* water, medicine, etc. containig salts of iron. [< NL *chalybeatus* < L < Gk. *chalyps* steel]

cham (kam) *n. Archaic.* khan¹.

cham·ber (chām′bər) *n., v.* —*n.* 1 *Archaic or poetic.* a room in a house, especially a bedroom. 2 a hall where a legislature or a governing body meets. 3 a group of lawmakers; a legislative or judicial body: *The Canadian Parliament has two chambers, the Senate and the House of Commons.* 4 a group of people organized for some business purpose: *Chamber of Commerce.* 5 **chambers,** *pl.* **a** a set of rooms in a building to live in or use as offices. **b** the office of a lawyer or judge. 6 an enclosed space, or cavity, in the body of an animal or plant: *The human heart has four chambers.* 7 an enclosed space in machinery, especially the part of the bore of a gun that holds the charge or any of the spaces for cartridges in a

revolver. **8** (*adj.*) of, having to do with, or performing chamber music: *a chamber group.* **9** chamber pot.
—*v.* provide with or put into a chamber. [ME < OF *chambre* < L *camera* < Gk. *kamaru* vaulted place. Doublet of CAMERA.]

cham·bered (chām′bərd) *adj.* having a chamber or chambers; divided into compartments.

cham·ber·lain (chām′bər lin) *n.* **1** the person who manages the household of a sovereign or a lord; steward. **2** a high official of a royal court. [ME < OF *chamberlenc* < L *camera* vault + Gmc. -*ling*]

cham·ber·maid (chām′bər mād′) *n.* a maid who makes the beds, cleans the bedrooms, etc., now especially in hotels.

chamber music music suited to a room or small hall; music for a trio, quartet, etc.

Chamber of Commerce an organization of business people whose aim is to increase business opportunities by improving the community in which they live.

chamber pot a receptacle for urine, etc., used in the bedroom.

cham·bray (sham′brā) *n.* a fine cloth, especially of cotton, in a plain weave, combining colored warp threads with white filling threads in various designs. [var. of *cambric*]

cha·me·le·on (kə mē′lē ən *or* kə mēl′yən) *n.* **1** any of a family (Chamaeleontidae) of mainly tree-dwelling Old World lizards having a prehensile tail, a very long, slender tongue, and the ability to change the color of their skin according to changes in their environment. **2** any of various New World lizards (family Iguanidae, especially of genus *Anolis*). **3** a changeable or fickle person. [< L *chamaeleon* < Gk. *chamaileōn*, literally, ground lion < *chamai* on the ground, dwarf + *leōn* lion]

cham·fer (cham′fər) *n., v.* —*n.* **1** a flat slanting surface made by cutting off an edge or corner; bevel. **2** a groove or furrow. —*v.* **1** cut off an edge or corner to make a slanting surface. **2** make a groove or furrow in; flute. [< F *chamfrai*⁻, apparently < *chant fraindre* (< L *cantum frangere*) break the side]

cham·ois (sham′ē *or, for def. 1,* sham wä′) *n., pl.* **-ois. 1** an animal (*Rupicapra rupicapra*) native to the mountains of Europe and SW Asia, belonging to the same family (Bovidae) as goats and antelope and having characteristics of both. **2** a very soft suede leather originally made from the hide of this animal, now made from the hide of sheep or goats. [< F < LL *camox*]

cham·o·mile (kam′ə mīl′) See **camomile.**

champ¹ (champ) *v.* **1** bite and chew noisily. **2** bite on impatiently: *The race horse champed its bit.*
champ (at) the bit, be restless or impatient: *After months with his leg in plaster, the boy was champing at the bit to go skiing again.* [? related to CHAP³]

champ² (champ) *n. Informal.* champion.

cham·pagne (sham pān′) *n., adj.* —*n.* **1** a sparkling, bubbling wine, first made in Champagne, France. **2** a very pale, yellowish brown or orange yellow. —*adj.* having the color champagne.

cham·paign (sham pān′) *n., adj.* —*n.* a wide plain; level, open country. —*adj.* level and open. [ME < OF *champaigne* < LL *campania* < L *campus* field. Doublet of CAMPAIGN.]

cham·pi·gnon (sham pin′yən *or* cham pin′yən; *French,* shäN pē nyôN′) *n.* an edible mushroom, especially the common meadow mushroom (*Agaricus campestris*) having a white cap with brown or pinkish gills underneath. [< MF]

cham·pi·on (cham′pē ən) *n., v.* —*n.* **1** a person, animal, or thing that wins first place in a game or contest: *the swimming champion of the world.* **2** (*adj.*) having won first place; ahead of all others: *a champion boxer, a champion rose.* **3** a person who fights or speaks for another; defender; supporter: *a great champion of peace.*
—*v.* fight or speak in behalf of; defend; support: *John championed his friends.* [ME < OF < LL *campio, -onis* < L *campus* field (i.e., of battle)] —**cham′pi·on·less,** *adj.*

cham·pi·on·ship (cham′pē ən ship′) *n.* **1** the position of a champion; first place. **2** defence; support. **3** a competition or series of competitions to decide a winner.

chance (chans) *n., v.* **chanced, chanc·ing.** —*n.* **1** an opportunity: *a chance to make some money.* **2** the likelihood of something happening; probability: *There's a good chance that he'll show up in time for dinner.* **3** fate; luck. **4** a happening: *Chance led to the finding of the diamond mine.* **5** a risk: *He took a chance when he swam the channel.* **6** (*adj.*) not expected or planned; happening by chance: *a chance meeting.* **7** *Baseball.* any handling of the ball which results in a put-out, an assist, or an error by a defensive player. **8** *Cricket.* a possible catch. **9** a ticket in a lottery or raffle.
by chance, a accidentally: *The meeting came about by chance.*

b by some turn of events: *If by chance the weather clears, we can go for a swim.*
on the chance, depending on the possibility.
on the off chance, depending on luck: *He went to the theatre on the off chance of getting a returned ticket.*
stand a chance, have favorable prospects: *Our team still stands a chance of winning the cup.*
—*v.* **1** happen. **2** accept the danger of; risk: *I wouldn't chance it without a life jacket.*
chance upon or **on,** happen to find or meet: *There they chanced on a real treasure—a first edition.*
[ME < OF *cheance* < L *cadentia* a falling < *cadere* fall. Doublet of CADENCE, CADENZA.]

chan·cel (chan′səl) *n.* the space around the altar of a church, used by the clergy and the choir. It is often separated from the rest of the church by a railing, lattice, or screen. See **apse** for picture. [ME < OF < L *cancelli* a grating]

chan·cel·ler·y (chan′sə lər ē *or* chan′slər ē) *n., pl.* **-ler·ies. 1** the position of a chancellor. **2** the office of a chancellor. **3** the office of an ambassador in a foreign country.

chan·cel·lor (chan′sə lər *or* chan′slər) *n.* **1** a high official who is the secretary of a monarch or noble, or the chief secretary of an embassy. **2** the prime minister or other very high official of some European countries. **3** any of various high British government officials, especially: **a** the Chancellor of the Exchequer. **b** the Lord Chancellor. **4** the honorary head of a university. The chancellor presides over convocation and is usually a member of the university senate and the board of governors. [ME < AF *canceler, chanceler* < LL *cancellarius* officer stationed at a tribunal < *cancelli* a grating, bars (which enclosed the chancel)]

Chancellor of the Exchequer in Great Britain, the highest official of the treasury.

chan·cel·lor·ship (chan′sə lər ship′ *or* chan′slər-) *n.* **1** the position of a chancellor. **2** the term of office of a chancellor.

chan·cer·y (chan′sər ē) *n., pl.* **-cer·ies. 1** a court that deals with cases involving fairness and justice outside the scope of common law or statute law. **2** an office where public records are kept. **3** the office of a chancellor. **4** the principle of equity; the spirit rather than the letter of the law. **5** *Wrestling.* a grip on the head.
in chancery, a in a court of equity. **b** in a helpless position. [var. of CHANCELLERY]

chan·cre (shang′kər) *n.* a hard, reddish ulcer or sore that is the first symptom of syphilis. [< F < L *cancer.* Doublet of CANCER, CANKER.]

chanc·y (chan′sē) *adj. Informal.* **1** subject to chance; risky; uncertain. **2** *Scottish.* lucky; favorable.

chan·de·lier (shan′də lēr′) *n.* a fixture with branches for lights, usually hanging from the ceiling. [ME < OF < VL *candelarius* < L *candela* candle < *candere* shine. Doublet of CHANDLER.]

chan·dler (chan′dlər) *n.* **1** a maker or seller of candles. **2** a dealer in groceries and supplies: *a ship chandler.* [ME < AF *chandeler* < VL *candelarius.* Doublet of CHANDELIER.]

chan·dler·y (chan′dlər ē) *n., pl.* **-dler·ies. 1** a storeroom for candles. **2** the warehouse, goods, or business of a chandler.

change (chānj) *v.* **changed, chang·ing;** *n.* —*v.* **1** become different: *He had changed since they had seen him last. The bus schedule has changed again.* **2** make different: *She changed the room by painting the walls green.* **3** put (one thing) in place of another; substitute: *to change dirty clothes for clean ones.* **4** pass from one position or state to another: *The wind changed from east to west.* **5** give and receive; exchange: *I changed seats with my brother.* **6** get or give small units of money that equal a larger unit: *to change a dollar bill for ten dimes.* **7** put fresh clothes or coverings on: *to change the baby, to change the bed.* **8** put on other clothing: *I want to change first.* **9** transfer from one bus, plane, etc. to another: *It's not a direct flight; you have to change at Winnipeg.*
change off, alternate with another person in doing something; take turns: *We changed off hoeing and raking to make the job easier.*
—*n.* **1** changing; passing from one position or state to another. **2** a changed condition. **3** the lack of sameness; variety: *Let me drive for a change.* **4** a thing to be used in place of another of the same kind: *a change of clothes.* **5** the money returned to a person when he has given an amount larger than the price of what he buys. **6** smaller units of money given in place of a large unit of money: *Please give me change for this dollar bill.* **7** coins: *I have a dollar and some change.* **8 changes,** *pl.* the different ways in which a set of bells can be rung.
ring the changes, a ring a set of bells in all its different ways. **b** do or express something in many different ways.
[ME < OF *changer* < LL *cambiare*] —**chang′er,** *n.*

☛ *Syn. v.* **1, 2. Change, alter** = make or become different. **Change** is the general word, but emphasizes the idea of a fundamental difference in the make-up of the person or thing, of making or becoming completely different: *She used to be shy, but has changed since she went to college.* **Alter** = change in one particular way, without changing the person or thing as a whole: *We can alter the kitchen enough to put in a freezer if we rehang the door.*

'change (chānj) *n.* an exchange; a place where people trade.

change·a·bil·i·ty (chān′jə bil′ə tē) *n.* a changeable quality or condition.

change·a·ble (chān′jə bəl) *adj.* **1** that can change; likely to change. **2** that can be changed; likely to be changed. **3** having a color or appearance that changes: *Silk is called changeable when it looks different in different lights.* —**change′a·ble·ness,** *n.* —**change′a·bly,** *adv.*

change·ful (chānj′fəl) *adj.* full of changes; likely to change; changing. —**change′ful·ly,** *adv.* —**change′ful·ness,** *n.*

change·less (chānj′lis) *adj.* not changing; not likely to change; constant; steadfast. —**change′less·ly,** *adv.* —**change′less·ness,** *n.*

change·ling (chānj′ling) *n.* **1** a child secretly substituted for another. **2** a strange, stupid, or ugly child, supposed to have been left by fairies in place of a child carried off by them.

change of heart a change of feeling; conversion.

change of life menopause.

change of venue **1** a change of the place of a trial. **2** a change in place for any activity.

change–o·ver (chānj′ō′vər) *n.* **1** conversion from one method, model, system, etc. to a completely different one. **2** a transfer of ownership or control.

chan·nel (chan′əl) *n., v.* -**nelled** or -**neled** -**nel·ling** or -**nel·ing.** —*n.* **1** the bed of a stream, river, etc. **2** a body of water joining two larger bodies of water: *the English Channel.* **3** the deeper part of a waterway: *There is shallow water on both sides of the channel in this river.* **4** a passage for liquids; groove. **5** means of communication or expression: *The information came through secret channels.* **6** a course of action; field of activity: *He sought to find a suitable channel for his enthusiasm.* **7** a narrow band of radio or television frequencies, sufficient for one-way transmission. —*v.* **1** to direct into a particular course; concentrate. **2** form a channel in; cut out as a channel: *The river had channelled its way through the rocks.* **3** convey through or as if through a channel. [ME < OF *chanel* < L *canalis.* Doublet of CANAL.]

chan·son (shän sôn′) *n. French.* song.

chan·son·nier (shän sô nyä′) *n. French.* a songwriter or singer, especially one who sings his own compositions in cabarets, etc.

chant (chant) *n., v.* —*n.* **1** song. **2** a song in which several syllables or words are sung on one tone. Chants are used in some church services. **3** a psalm, prayer, or other song for chanting. **4** a monotonous way of talking. —*v.* **1** sing. **2** sing to a chant, or in the manner of a chant. A choir chants psalms or prayers. **3** keep talking about; say over and over again: *We chanted, "Go, team, go!"* [ME < OF *chanter* < L *cantare* < *canere* sing]

chan·ter (chan′tər) *n.* **1** a person who sings or chants. **2 a** one who sings in a choir; chorister. **b** the chief singer in a choir; cantor. **3** a priest who sings Mass in a chantry. **4** in a bagpipe, the pipe on which the melody, or chant, is played.

chan·te·relle (shan′tə rel′ or chan′tə rel′) *n.* any of a genus (*Cantharellus*) of orange or yellow mushrooms with a funnel-shaped cap, especially *C. cibarius,* an edible species, yellow in color and having an apricotlike odor when fresh.

chan·teuse (shän tœz′) *n. French.* a female singer.

chant·ey (shan′tē or chan′tē) *n., pl.* **chant·eys.** See **shanty².**

chan·ti·cleer (chant′tə klēr′) *n.* rooster. [ME < OF *chantecler* < *chanter* sing + *cler* clear; from the name of the cock in the medieval tale of *Reynard the Fox*]

Chan·til·ly (shan til′ē; *French,* shän tē yē′) *n.* a type of fine lace, having a netlike pattern of six-pointed stars. [< *Chantilly,* a town in N France, formerly famous for lace manufacturing]

chan·try (chan′trē) *n., pl.* -**tries.** **1** a chapel attached to a church, used for the less important services. **2** an endowment to pay for the singing or saying of Masses for a person's soul. **3** a chapel, altar, or part of a church similarly endowed. **4** the priests thus endowed. [ME < OF *chanterie* < *chanter* sing]

chant·y (shan′tē or chan′tē) *n., pl.* **chant·ies.** See **shanty².**

Cha·nu·kah or **Cha·nuk·kah** (hä′nù kä′; *Hebrew,* Hä′nù kä′) See **Hanukkah.**

cha·os (kā′os) *n.* **1** great confusion; complete disorder: *The whirlwind left chaos behind it.* **2** the infinite space or formless matter thought to have existed before the universe came into being. [< L < Gk.]

cha·ot·ic (kā ot′ik) *adj.* in great confusion; very confused; completely disordered.

cha·ot·i·cal·ly (kā ot′ik lē) *adv.* in a chaotic manner; in great confusion or disorder.

chap¹ (chap) *v.* **chapped, chap·ping;** *n.* —*v.* of skin, crack open; make or become rough: *A person's lips often chap in cold weather.*

hat, āge, fär; let, ēqual, tėrm; it, īce
hot, ōpen, ôrder; oil, out; cup, pùt, rüle,
əbove, takən, pencəl, lemən, circəs

ch, child; ng, long; sh, ship
th, thin; ŦH, then; zh, measure

Cold weather chapped his hands. —*n.* a place where the skin is chapped. [ME *chappe*(n) cut]

chap² (chap) *n. Informal.* a fellow; man; boy. [a shortened form of *chapman*]

chap³ (chap) *n.* chop². [? < *chap¹*]

chap. **1** chapter. **2** chaplain. **3** chapel.

cha·pa·ra·jos (chä′pə rä′hōs) *n.pl.* in the SW United States, strong leather trousers worn by cowboys; chaps. [< Mexican Sp.]

chap·ar·ral (chap′ə ral′) *n.* in the SW United States, a thicket of low shrubs, etc., especially dwarf evergreen oaks. [< Sp. *chaparral* < *chaparro* evergreen oak]

chap·book (chap′bùk′) *n.* a small book or pamphlet of popular tales, ballads, etc., formerly sold on the streets. [because sold by *chapmen*]

cha·peau (sha pō′; *French,* shä pō′) *n., pl.* -**peaux** (-pō′) or -**peaus** (-pōz′). hat. [< F < OF *chapel* hat < VL *cappellum* < LL *cappa* cape. Related to CAP, CAPE.]

chap·el (chap′əl) *n.* **1** a building for worship, not so large as a church. **2** a small place for worship within a larger building. **3** a room or building for worship in a palace, school, etc. **4** a religious service in a chapel: *We were late for chapel.* **5** *Brit.* **a** a place of worship of Nonconformist groups. **b** Nonconformist doctrine or practices. **6** an association of journeymen printers for regulating conditions of work among themselves. [ME < OF *chapele* < LL *cappella;* originally a shrine in which was preserved the *cappa* or cape of St. Martin]

chap·er·on·age (shap′ər ōn′ij) *n.* the activities of a chaperone; protection of a chaperone.

chap·er·one or **chap·er·on** (shap′ər ōn′) *n., v.* -**oned,** -**on·ing.** —*n.* **1** a married woman or an older woman who accompanies a young unmarried woman in public for the sake of convention and protection. **2** an older person who attends young people's parties, student dances, etc. to ensure proper behavior. —*v.* act as a chaperone to. [< F *chaperon* hood, protector < *chape* cape < LL *cappa.* Related to CAP, CAPE.]

chap·fall·en (chap′fol′ən or -fôl′ən) *adj.* dejected; discouraged; humiliated. Also **chopfallen.**

chap·lain (chap′lən) *n.* a clergyman officially authorized to perform religious functions for a family, court, society, public institution, or unit in the armed forces. [ME < OF *chapelain* < LL *capellanus* < *cappella.* See CHAPEL.]

chap·lain·cy (chap′lən sē) *n.* the position of a chaplain.

chap·lain·ship (chap′lən ship′) *n.* chaplaincy.

chap·let (chap′lit) *n.* **1** a wreath worn on the head. **2** a string of beads. **3** *Roman Catholic Church.* **a** a string of beads, one third as long as a rosary, used for keeping count in saying prayers. **b** the prayers said with such beads. [ME *chapelet* < OF, dim. of *chapel* headdress. See CHAPEAU.]

chap·let·ed (chap′lit id) *adj.* wearing a wreath on the head.

chap·man (chap′mən) *n., pl.* -**men.** *Archaic.* **1** peddler. **2** a man whose business is buying and selling; merchant, trader; dealer. [OE *cēapman* < *cēap* trade + *man* man]

chaps (shaps or chaps) *n.pl.* backless leggings of tough leather, worn by cowboys to protect their legs when riding. [short for *chaparajos*]

chap·ter (chap′tər) *n., v.* —*n.* **1** a main division of a book or other writing, dealing with a certain part of the story or subject. **2** anything like a chapter; part; section: *The development of television is an interesting chapter in modern science.* **3** a local division of an organization; branch of a club, society, etc. **4** a group of clergymen, usually attached to a cathedral. **5** a meeting of such a group. —*v.* divide into chapters; arrange in chapters. [ME < OF *chapitre* < L *capitulum,* dim. of *caput* head]

chapter and verse **1** the exact reference for a passage of Scripture. **2** precise authority (*for*): *He cited chapter and verse for his opinions.* **3** exact information and complete detail.

chapter house **1** the building where the chapter of a cathedral holds its meetings. **2** the house of a college fraternity or sorority.

char¹ (chär) *v.* **charred, char·ring.** **1** burn to charcoal. **2** burn slightly; scorch. [? < *charcoal*]

char² (chär) *n., v.* **charred, char·ring.** *Esp.Brit.* —*n.* **1** charwoman. **2** an odd job; chore. —*v.* **1** do housework by the day or hour. **2** do odd jobs. [OE *cerr* turn, occasion]

char³ (chär) *n., pl.* **char.** any of a genus (*Salvelinus*) of mostly freshwater fish belonging to the salmon and trout family. The arctic char, brook trout, and lake trout are common Canadian char.

char-à–banc (shar′ə bang′ *or* sher′ə-, shar′ə bangk′ *or* sher′ə-; *French*, shä rä bän′) *n., pl.* **char-à-bancs** (-bangz′ *or* -bangks′; *French*, shä rä bän′). a large motorbus, used for excursions. [< F *char à bancs* car with benches]

char·ac·ter (kar′ik tər *or* ker′ik tər) *n.* **1** the combination of qualities or features that distinguishes one person, group, or thing from another; kind; sort; nature: *The sisters look alike but differ greatly in character. The character of the soil in the southern part of the province is different from that in the central part.* **2** the combined moral, emotional, and mental qualities that a person or group has: *a person of shallow, changeable character.* **3** moral firmness; integrity: *It takes character to endure hardship for very long.* **4** the estimate formed of a person's qualities; reputation: *His meanness was a stain on his character.* **5** position; status; role: *In his character as club secretary, he is responsible for all correspondence.* **6** a person or animal portrayed in a play, novel, or story: *The main character is a miner.* **7** (*adj.*) Theatre *or* film. of, for, or acting in roles that emphasize strong characteristics of personality that may be very different from those of the actor himself: *a character actress, a character part.* **8** *Informal.* a person who attracts attention for being different or eccentric: *I'd like to meet him; I hear he's really a character.* **9** *Biology.* a distinctive structure, function, or quality that is determined by heredity: *Marquis wheat is valued for its character of rust resistance.* **10** in writing or printing, a letter, symbol, or other mark: A, a, %, +, −, 1, 2, *and* 3 are characters. **11** a description of a person's qualities. **12** a written testimonial, especially from a former employer, describing the qualities and capacities of an employee.
in character, a *Theatre.* true to character: *The actor remained in character throughout the play.* **b** consistent with a person's known character; as expected: *Her stinging letter to the editor was entirely in character.*
out of character, a *Theatre.* not true to character. **b** not consistent with a person's known character; not as expected: *It was out of character for him to go off without letting anyone know.* [ME < OF *caractere* < L < Gk. *charaktēr* stamped mark < *charassein* engrave]
☛ *Syn. n.* **2. Character, personality, individuality** = the qualities that make a person what he is. **Character** applies to the moral qualities that determine the way a person thinks, feels, and acts in the important matters of life, especially in relation to the principles of right and wrong. **Personality** applies to the personal qualities that make one person different from another and determine the way he acts in his social and personal relations. **Individuality** applies to the particular qualities that make a person himself, an individual: *He has a weak character, but a winning personality and great individuality.*

char·ac·ter·is·tic (kar′ik tər is′tik *or* ker′ik tər is′tik) *adj., n.* —*adj.* distinguishing (a person or thing) from others; special: *Bananas have a characteristic smell.* —*n.* **1** a special quality or feature; whatever distinguishes one person or thing from others: *Cheerfulness is a characteristic that we admire in people. An elephant's trunk is its most noticeable characteristic.* **2** *Mathematics.* the integral part of a logarithm. In the logarithm 2.95424, the characteristic is 2 and the mantissa is .95424.
☛ *Syn. n.* **1.** See note at **feature.**

char·ac·ter·is·ti·cal·ly (kar′ik tər is′tik lē *or* ker′ik tər is′tik lē) *adv.* in a way that shows characteristics; specially; typically.

char·ac·ter·i·za·tion (kar′ik tər ə zā′shən *or* ker′-; kar′ik tər ī zā′shən *or* ker′-) *n.* **1** the act of characterizing; description of characteristics. **2** the creation of characters in a play, book, etc.

char·ac·ter·ize (kar′ik tər īz′ *or* ker′ik tər īz′) *v.* **-ized, -iz·ing.** **1** describe the special qualities or features of a person or thing; describe. **2** be a characteristic of; distinguish: *A camel is characterized by the humps on its back and the ability to do without water for several days.* **3** give character to: *The author characterized his heroine in a few short paragraphs.*

char·ac·ter·less (kar′ik tər lis *or* ker′ik tər lis) *adj.* **1** without character. **2** without distinction; uninteresting.

char·ac·ter·y (kar′ik tər ē *or* ker′ik tər ē) *n.* the signs or symbols used to express ideas.

cha·rade (shə räd′ *or* shə räd′) *n.* **1** a word represented by a pantomime, picture, or tableau. **2** **charades,** *pl.* a parlor game in which a word, title, proverb, etc. is acted out by a group of people while others try to guess what it is. **3** a very obvious pretence. [< F < Provençal *charrada* < *charra* chatter]

char·coal (chär′kōl′) *n., v.* —*n.* **1** the black substance, a form of carbon, made by partly burning wood or bones in a place from which the air is shut out. Charcoal is used as a fuel, filter, and absorbent. **2** a stick, pencil, or crayon of charcoal for drawing. **3** a drawing made with such a stick, pencil, or crayon.
—*v.* mark, write, or blacken with charcoal. [ME *charcole*]

charcoal burner 1 anything in which charcoal is burned, such as a stove. **2** a person whose work is making charcoal.

chard (chärd) *n.* a variety of white beet; Swiss chard. [< F *charde* < L *carduus* thistle, artichoke]

charge (chärj) *v.* **charged, charg·ing;** *n.* —*v.* **1** ask as a price; put on a price of: *He charged us $5 for repairing the radio.* **2** put down as an obligation or debt: *This store will charge things that you buy. Library books are charged at the exit.* **3** put down against: *Please charge my account.* **4** load; fill. A gun is charged with powder and shot. A battery is charged with electricity. **5** restore the active materials of a storage battery: *The battery of a car charges automatically when the motor is running.* **6** give a task, duty, or responsibility to: *The law charges the police with keeping order.* **7** give an order or command to; direct: *He charged us to keep the plan secret. The judge charged the jury.* **8** accuse, especially in a court of law: *The driver was charged with speeding.* **9** attack; rush with force: *The soldiers charged the enemy.* **10** attribute (a fault, etc.) to a person. **11** *Heraldry.* **a** place (a bearing or charge) on an escutcheon, shield, etc.: *to charge crosses on a field.* **b** bear upon (an escutcheon, shield, etc.) with a bearing or charge: *to charge a field with crosses.*
charge off, a subtract as a loss. **b** charge up.
charge up, put down as belonging: *A bad mistake must be charged up to experience.*
—*n.* **1** a price asked for or put on something. **2** a debt to be paid: *Taxes are a charge on property.* **3** the quantity needed to load or fill something. A gun is fired by exploding the charge of powder and shot. **4** an amount of electricity. **5** a task; duty; responsibility: *Arresting criminals is the charge of the police.* **6** care; management: *Doctors and nurses have charge of sick people.* **7** a person, persons, or thing under the care or management of someone: *Sick people are the charges of doctors and nurses.* **8** an order; command; direction: *a judge's charge to the jury.* **9** an accusation, especially in a court of law: *He admitted the charge and paid the fine.* **10** an attack; forceful rush: *The charge drove the enemy back.* **11** *Heraldry.* a device borne on an escutcheon; bearing.
in charge, in command; having control or management: *Who's in charge here?*
in charge of, having control, management, or supervision of: *Dr. Hsing is in charge of the case.*
in the charge of or in charge of, under the control or management of; in the custody of: *The suspect was placed in the charge of a police constable.* [ME < OF *charger* < LL *carricare* load < L *carrus* wagon. Doublet of CARRY.]
☛ *Syn. v.* **4. Charge, accuse** = put the blame on a person. *Charge* (followed by **with**) may suggest the blame for some minor wrongdoing, such as breaking a rule, but it commonly suggests a serious offence, such as breaking a law, and making a formal statement before the proper authority: *He was charged with leaving the grounds without permission.* **Accuse** (followed by **of**) suggests making the charge directly to the person blamed and expressing disapproval, but not necessarily taking him before authority: *He accused me of lying.*
—*n.* **7.** See note at **price.**

charge·a·ble (chär′jə bəl) *adj.* **1** that can be charged; likely to be charged: *If you take anything that belongs to someone else, you are chargeable with theft. Taxes are chargeable against the owners of property.* **2** liable to become a public charge.

charge account an arrangement with a business firm for purchasing goods or services on credit: *We have charge accounts at two department stores.*

charge card credit card.

charged (chärjd) *adj.* that has been loaded; filled.

char·gé d'af·faires (shär zhä′də fer′; *French*, shär zhä dä fer′) *pl.* **char·gés d'af·faires** (shär zhäz′də fer′; *French*, shär zhä dä fer′). an official who takes the place of an ambassador, minister, or other diplomat. [< F]

charge plate a credit card embossed with the holder's name and account number so that these may be printed on a bill, receipt, etc.

charg·er¹ (chär′jər) *n.* **1** a horse ridden in war. **2** a person or thing that charges. [< *charge*]

charg·er² (chär′jər) *n.* *Archaic.* a large, flat dish; platter. [< OF *chargeour* or *chargeoir* < *charger* load. See CHARGE.]

charg·ing (chär′jing) *n.* *Hockey.* an illegal action involving a direct forward attack of more than two steps against an opponent in an attempt to take him out of the play.

char·i·ot (char′ē ət *or* cher′ē ət) *n.* **1** a two-wheeled vehicle pulled by horses, used in ancient times for fighting, for racing, and in processions. **2** a four-wheeled carriage or coach. [ME < OF *chariot* < *char* < L *carrus* four-wheeled cart]

char·i·ot·eer (char′ē ə tēr′ *or* cher′ē ə tēr′) *n.* a person who drives a chariot.

char·ism (kar′əm or ker′iz əm) *n.* charisma.

charisma (kə riz′mə) *n.* **-ma·ta** (-mə tə). **1** *Theology.* a spiritual gift or grace giving a person the gift of prophesying, healing, etc. **2** magnetic and compelling personal power, especially as attributed to leaders who gain the enthusiastic support of large numbers of people. [< Gk. *charisma, -atos*]

char·is·mat·ic (kar′iz mat′ik or ker′iz mat′ik) *adj.* **1** of or having to do with a charisma. **2** having charisma; capable of inspiring popular allegiance.

char·i·ta·ble (char′ə tə bəl or cher′ə tə bəl) *adj.* **1** of or for charity. **2** generous in giving help to poor or suffering people. **3** kindly in judging people and their actions. **—char′i·ta·ble·ness,** *n.* **—char′i·ta·bly,** *adv.*

char·i·ty (char′ə tē or cher′ə tē) *n., pl.* **-ties. 1** the giving of help to the poor or suffering. **2** the help, money, etc. given. **3** a fund, institution, or organization for helping the poor or suffering. **4** kindness in judging the faults of other people. **5** love for one's fellow man. [ME < OF *charite* < L *caritas* dearness < *carus* dear]

cha·riv·a·ri (shiv′ə rē′ or shə riv′ə rē′) *n., pl.* **-ris.** shivaree. [< F]

char·la·tan (shär′lə tən) *n.* a person who pretends to have more knowledge or skill than he really has; quack. [< F < Ital. *ciarlatano*, ult. < Mongolian *dzar* proclaim, tell lies]

char·la·tan·ism (shär′lə tən iz′əm) *n.* the practices or methods of a charlatan; quackery.

char·la·tan·ry (shär′lə tən rē) *n.* charlatanism.

Charles's Wain (chärl′ziz wān′) Big Dipper. [OE *Carles Wægn* Carl's (Charlemagne's) wagon]

Charles·ton (chärl′stən) *n., v.* **—n.** a lively dance especially popular in the 1920's, in which the heels are kicked out to the side at each step. **—v.** dance the Charleston. [< *Charleston*, the early capital of South Carolina]

char·ley horse (chär′lē) *Informal.* a very painful cramp or stiffness in a muscle, especially of the leg or arm, caused by strain.

char·lock (chär′lək) *n.* wild mustard. [OE *cerlic*]

char·lotte russe (shär′lət rüs′) a dessert made of a mould of sponge cake filled with whipped cream or custard. [< F *charlotte russe* Russian charlotte (a type of charlotte)]

charm (chärm) *n., v.* **—n. 1** the power of delighting or fascinating; attractiveness: *We were much impressed with the grace and charm of our hostess.* **2** a very pleasing or fascinating quality or feature: *the charm of old ruins, the charm of novelty.* **3** a small ornament or trinket worn on a watch chain, bracelet, etc. **4** a word, verse, act, or thing supposed to have magic power to help or harm people. **—v. 1** please greatly; delight; fascinate; attract: *The old sailor's stories of his adventures charmed the boys.* **2** act on as if by magic: *Laughter charmed away his troubles.* **3** give magic power to; protect as by a charm: *Sir Galahad seemed to bear a charmed life.* [ME < OF *charme* < L *carmen* song, enchantment (? earlier *canmen*) < *canere* sing] **—charm′less,** *adj.*

☛ *Syn.* **v. 1. Charm, attract, allure** = win a person by pleasing. **Charm** emphasizes winning and holding a person's attention and admiration by giving delight: *Her beautiful voice charms everyone.* **Attract** emphasizes drawing attention and good will by being pleasing: *She attracts everyone she meets.* **Allure** emphasizes attracting a person by appealing to the senses and feelings: *Mountain scenery allures many tourists to the Rockies.*

charmed (chärmd) *adj.* **1** delighted; fascinated. **2** enchanted. **3** protected as by a charm: *He bears a charmed life.*

charm·er (chär′mər) *n.* one who charms, delights, or fascinates.

char·meuse (shär mœz′) *n.* a soft, lightweight fabric with a satiny finish. [< F, fem. of *charmeur*, literally, charmer.]

charm·ing (chär′ming) *adj.* very pleasing; delightful; fascinating; attractive. **—charm′ing·ly,** *adv.*

char·nel (chär′nəl) *n., adj.* **—n.** a charnel house. **—adj. 1** of or used for a charnel. **2** like a charnel; deathlike; ghastly. [ME < OF < LL *carnale*, originally neut. of L *carnalis*. Doublet of CARNAL.]

charnel house *Archaic.* a place where dead bodies or bones are laid.

Char·o·lais (shär′ə lā′) *n.* a breed of large, white beef cattle. [< F < *Charolles*, a province in France where the breed originated]

Char·on (ker′ən) *n.* Greek mythology. the boatman who ferried the spirits of the dead across the river Styx to Hades.

chart (chärt) *n., v.* **—n. 1** a map, especially one for the use of navigators. A sailor's chart shows the coasts, rocks, and shallow places of a sea. The course of a ship is marked on a chart. **2** an outline map for showing special conditions or facts other than just geographical information: *a weather chart.* **3** a sheet giving information in lists, pictures, tables, or diagrams. **4** such a list, table, picture, or diagram. **—v. 1** make a chart of; show on a chart: *chart a course.* **2** plan in

hat, āge, fär; let, ēqual, tėrm; it, īce
hot, ōpen, ôrder; oil, out; cup, put, rüle,
əbove, takən, pencəl, lemən, circəs
ch, child; ng, long; sh, ship
th, thin; ₮H, then; zh, measure

detail. [< F *charte* < L *charta* < Gk. *chartēs* leaf of paper. Doublet of CARD¹.] **—chart′less,** *adj.*
☛ *Syn.* **1.** See note at **map.**

char·ter (chär′tər) *n., v.* **—n. 1** a written grant by a government to a colony, a group of citizens, a commercial company, etc., bestowing the right of organization, with other privileges, and specifying the form of organization. All Canadian banks must have charters from the federal government. **2** a written order from the authorities of a society, giving to a group of persons the right to organize a new chapter, branch, or lodge. **3** a document setting forth aims and purposes of a group of nations, organizations, or individuals in a common undertaking: *the Charter of the United Nations.* **4** the hiring or leasing of a bus, ship, aircraft, etc. together with a driver or pilot, for temporary private use. **5** the contract or arrangement covering this. **6** (*adj.*) arranged by charter: *a charter flight.* **7** a special right, privilege, or immunity.
—v. 1 give a charter to. **2** hire or lease (a bus, ship, aircraft, etc.) for temporary private use: *We chartered a bus for the trip to the film festival.* [ME < OF *chartre* < L *chartula*, dim. of *charta.* See CHART.] **—char′ter·er,** *n.* **—char′ter·less,** *adj.*

chartered accountant a member of an accountants' institute that is chartered by the Crown. *Abbrev.:* C.A.

chartered bank in Canada, any of the privately owned banks chartered by Parliament and working under the provisions of the Bank Act with an extensive network of branches.

charter member one of the original members of a club, society, or company.

Chart·ism (chär′tiz əm) *n.* **1** in England, a reform movement organized by workingmen who drew up the People's Charter. The movement was active between 1838 and 1848. **2** the principles of this movement.

Chart·ist (chär′tist) *n., adj.* **—n.** an adherent of Chartism. **—adj.** of or having to do with Chartism.

chart·ist (chär′tist) *n.* a stock market specialist who predicts market trends on the basis of the analysis of charts recording the price and volume of shares traded on the world's stock exchanges.

char·treuse (shär trœz′; *also, for n. 2 and adj.,* shär trüz′) *n., adj.* **—n. 1** a green, yellow, or white liqueur first made by Carthusian monks. **2** a light, yellowish green. **—adj.** having the color chartreuse. [< F *chartreuse* Carthusian]

char·wom·an (chär′wum′ən) *n., pl.* **-wom·en.** a woman whose work is cleaning homes, offices, or public buildings; cleaning woman. [< OE *cerr* turn, occasion + *woman*]

char·y (cher′ē) *adj.* **char·i·er, char·i·est. 1** careful: *A cat is chary of wetting its paws.* **2** shy: *A bashful person is chary of strangers.* **3** sparing; stingy: *A jealous person is chary of praising others.* [OE *cearig* < *caru* care] a **—char′i·ly,** *adv.* **—char′i·ness,** *n.*
☛ *Hom.* **cherry.**

Cha·ryb·dis (kə rib′dis) *n.* a dangerous whirlpool off the northeastern coast of Sicily. See **Scylla.**
between Scylla and Charybdis, between two dangers, one of which must be met.

chase¹ (chās) *v.* **chased, chas·ing;** *n.* **—v. 1** run or follow after to catch or kill. **2** drive; drive away. **3** hunt. **4** follow; pursue: *The catcher chased the ball.* **5** *Informal.* rush; hurry: *He is always chasing about.*
—n. 1 going after to catch or kill: *The thieves were caught after a short chase.* **2** hunting as a sport: *He was very fond of the chase.* **3** a hunted animal: *The chase escaped the hunter.* **4** *Brit.* an open piece of privately owned ground or other place reserved for hunting animals.
give chase, run after; chase.
[ME < OF *chacier* < LL *captiare.* Doublet of CATCH.]

chase² (chās) *v.* **chased, chas·ing.** engrave. [var. of *enchase*]

chase³ (chās) *n.* **1** a groove; furrow; trench. **2** *Printing.* an iron frame to hold type that is ready to print or make plates from. [< F *châsse* < L *capsa* box. Doublet of CASE², CASH¹.]

chas·er¹ (chās′ər) *n.* **1** a person or thing that chases or pursues, such as a hunter or small, speedy aircraft or ship for pursuing the enemy. **2** a gun on the bow or stern of a ship, used when chasing, or being chased by, another ship. **3** *Informal.* a drink of water or something mild after a drink of strong liquor. [< *chase¹*]

chas·er² (chās′ər) n. 1 engraver. 2 a tool for engraving. [< chase²]

chasm (kaz′əm) n. 1 a deep opening or crack in the earth; a narrow gorge or abyss. 2 a wide difference of feelings or interests between people or groups: *The chasm between England and the American colonies grew wider and wider until it finally resulted in the American Revolution.* 3 a break in continuity. [< L *chasma* < Gk.]

chas·seur (sha sœr′) n. 1 a soldier of a group of cavalry or infantry equipped and trained to move rapidly. 2 hunter. 3 an attendant or servant in uniform. [< F]

chas·sis (shas′ē or chas′ē) n., pl. **chas·sis** (shas′ēz or chas′ēz). 1 the frame that supports the body of an automobile, aircraft, etc. 2 the frame that encloses and supports the working parts of a radio, television set, etc. 3 the frame on which a gun carriage moves backward and forward. 4 *Slang.* a person's body, especially a woman's. [< F < OF *châsse* frame or sash]

chaste (chāst) adj. 1 virginal. 2 abstaining from sexual activity outside of marriage. 3 decent or modest in speech or behavior. 4 simple in taste or style; not ornamented. [ME < OF < L *castus* pure. Doublet of CASTE.] —**chaste′ly**, adv. —**chaste′ness**, n.
☛ Hom. chased.

chas·ten (chās′ən) v. 1 punish with the intention of improving: *God chastened Job.* 2 make more restrained, humble, etc.; subdue: *The experience chastened them.* [obs. v. *chaste* < F < L *castigare* make pure < *castus* pure] —**chas′ten·er**, n.

chas·tise (chas tīz′) v. **-tised, -tis·ing.** 1 inflict punishment on, especially by beating or whipping. 2 rebuke or scold severely; castigate: *The coach chastised the players for being late.* [< obs. *chaste*. See CHASTEN.] —**chas·tise′ment**, n. —**chas·tis′er**, n.
☛ Syn. See note at punish.

chas·ti·ty (chas′tə tē) n. 1 purity; virtue. 2 decency; modesty. 3 simplicity of style or taste; absence of excessive decoration.

chas·u·ble (chaz′yə bəl or chaz′ə bəl) n. a sleeveless, capelike outer vestment worn over other vestments by a priest when celebrating Mass, or Eucharist. [ME *chesible* < OF < LL *casubula* < L *casa* cottage. Akin to CASSOCK.]

chat (chat) n., v. **chat·ted, chat·ting.** —n. 1 easy, familiar talk. 2 any of several birds having a chattering cry. —v. talk in an easy, familiar way. [short for *chatter*]

châ·teau or **cha·teau** (sha tō′ or shə tō′; *French*, shä tō′) n., pl. **-teaux** (-tōz′; *French*, -tō′). 1 in France, a castle. 2 a large country house in France. 3 a building resembling such a house. 4 *Historical.* in French Canada: **a** the residence of a governor or a seigneur. **b Château,** the Château St. Louis in Quebec City, the residence of the Governor of Quebec. [< F *château* < L *castellum* castle. Doublet of CASTLE.]

cha·teau·bri·and (sha tō brē än′) n. a thick tenderloin steak, usually grilled or broiled and served with a sauce. [after François René *Chateaubriand* (1768-1848), French statesman and writer]

chat·e·laine (shat′ə lān′) n. 1 the mistress, or lady, of a castle, château, or any large, fashionable household. 2 a chain or clasp formerly worn at a woman's waist for carrying keys, a watch, purse, etc. [< F *châtelaine*, fem. of *châtelain* keeper of a castle < L *castellanus*. See CASTELLAN.]

chat·tel (chat′əl) n. a movable possession; a piece of property that is not real estate. Furniture, automobiles, and domestic animals are chattels. [ME < OF *chatel* < L *capitale*, neut. of *capitalis*. Doublet of CAPITAL¹ and CATTLE.]

chat·ter (chat′ər) v., n. —v. 1 talk constantly, rapidly, and foolishly. 2 make rapid, indistinct sounds: *Monkeys chatter.* 3 rattle together: *Fear or cold sometimes make a person's teeth chatter.* —n. 1 rapid, foolish talk. 2 rapid, indistinct sounds: *The chatter of sparrows annoyed her.* [imitative] —**chat′ter·er**, n.

chat·ter·box (chat′ər boks′) n. a person who is given to chattering.

chat·ty (chat′ē) adj. **-ti·er, -ti·est.** 1 fond of friendly, familiar talk. 2 having the style and manner of friendly, familiar talk: *He wrote us a nice, chatty letter about his trip.* —**chat′ti·ly**, adv. —**chat′ti·ness**, n.

Chau·ce·ri·an (cho sēr′ē ən or chô sēr′ē ən) adj., n. —adj. 1 of or having to do with Geoffrey Chaucer (1340?-1400), an English poet and author of *The Canterbury Tales.* 2 of or suggestive of his writings. —n. a student of Chaucer or a specialist in his writings.

chauf·feur (shō′fər or shō fér′) n., v. —n. a man whose work is driving an automobile, usually as the employee of a private person or company: *The president of our bank has a chauffeur.* —v. act as a chauffeur to; drive around. [< F *chauffeur* stoker < *chauffer* heat; from the days of steam automobiles]

chaunt (chont or chônt) n. or v. *Archaic.* chant.

chau·tau·qua or **Chau·tau·qua** (shə tô′kwə or shə tô′kwə) n. an assembly for education and entertainment of adults by lectures, concerts, etc. held for several days. [with reference to meetings of a religious and educational nature, the first of which were held at *Chautauqua,* New York]

chau·vin·ism (shō′vən iz′əm) n. 1 unreasoning enthusiasm for the military glory of one's country; boastful, warlike patriotism. 2 a strong, unreasoning conviction of the natural superiority of one's own group, beliefs, etc. [< F *chauvinisme*, from Nicolas *Chauvin,* an over-enthusiastic French patriot and supporter of Napoleon I]

chau·vin·ist (shō′vən ist) n., adj. —n. a person given to chauvinism. —adj. chauvinistic.

chau·vin·is·tic (shō′vən is′tik) adj. 1 of or having to do with chauvinism or chauvinists. 2 showing chauvinism: *a chauvinistic remark.* —**chau′vin·is′ti·cal·ly**, adv.

Ch.B. Bachelor of Surgery (for L *Chirurgiae Baccalaureus*).

Ch.E. or **Che.E.** Chemical Engineer.

cheap (chēp) adj. 1 low in price or cost; not expensive: *Eggs are cheap now.* 2 costing less than it is worth. 3 charging low prices: *a cheap market.* 4 easily obtained; costing little effort: *a cheap victory.* 5 of little merit or value; common: *cheap entertainment, cheap jewellery.* 6 of little account; not esteemed: *Life was cheap in those days.* 7 of money, obtainable at a low rate of interest. 8 reduced in value or purchasing power, as money depreciated by inflation: *cheap silver.* 9 reduced in price for a special occasion or in prescribed circumstances: *cheap rates.* 10 (*advl.*) cheaply: *After the accident he sold his car cheap.* 11 stingy; mean: *Don't be so cheap!* **feel cheap,** feel inferior and ashamed. **on the cheap,** with little expense; at low cost: *travelling on the cheap, with a backpack.* [short for *good cheap* a good bargain; OE *cēap* price, bargain < Gmc. (cf. OHG *kouf*) < L *caupō* small tradesman] —**cheap′ness**, n.
☛ Hom. cheep.
☛ Syn. adj. 1. Cheap, inexpensive = costing little. Cheap = low in price, but often is used to express an attitude toward the thing, suggesting low quality that is worth no more or even less than the price: *Eggs are cheap now. I won't wear cheap shoes.* Inexpensive = not expensive, worth the price or even more, and usually expresses a more impersonal attitude: *An inexpensive car gives good mileage.*

cheap·en (chēp′ən) v. 1 make or become cheap; lower the price of. 2 lower the reputation of; reduce the dignity of: *He cheapened himself by his slovenly appearance.* —**cheap′en·er**, n.

cheap·ly (chēp′lē) adv. 1 at a low price; at small cost. 2 with little cost or effort.

Cheap·side (chēp′sīd′) n. in London, a famous street that was a busy market place in medieval times.

cheap·skate (chēp′skāt′) n. *Slang.* a stingy, miserly person.

cheat (chēt) v., n. —v. 1 deceive or trick; play or do business in a way that is not honest: *The peddler cheated the woman of ten cents in change.* 2 act in a dishonest way, by practising fraud or violating rules secretly: *to cheat at cards, to cheat in an exam.* 3 escape; foil: *to cheat death.*
—n. 1 a person who is not honest and does things to deceive and trick others. 2 a fraud or trick. [var. of *escheat*] —**cheat′a·ble**, adj. —**cheat′er**, n.
☛ Syn. v. Cheat, deceive, trick = use underhand means for a purpose. Cheat = do something dishonest in an underhand way to get something one wants: *He cheated to pass the test.* Deceive means to lead others to believe what is not true in order to hide the truth or to get what one wants: *He deceived the teacher by lying.* Trick emphasizes using a sly scheme or device to deceive and indirectly to get what one wants: *Mission Centre used fake plans to trick the spy.*

check (chek) v., n., interj. —v. 1 stop suddenly: *They checked their steps.* 2 hold back; control; restrain: *to check one's anger.* 3 rebuff; repulse; reverse: *to check an enemy attack.* 4 *Hockey.* impede the progress of (the puck-carrier), using either the stick or the body: *to check a person into the boards.* 5 correspond accurately when compared, usually with a duplicate or the original: *The two copies check.* 6 examine or compare to prove true or right: *Check your answers with mine.* 7 find out; investigate: *When he checked, he found the money was gone.* 8 mark something examined or compared with a check (✓): *How many answers did the teacher check as wrong?* 9 leave or take for safekeeping: *to check one's coat. The hotel checked our baggage.* 10 mark in a pattern of squares. 11 of wood, steel, paintwork, etc. crack or split. 12 cause to crack. 13 send (baggage) to a particular place: *I shall check my bag through to Halifax.* 14 *Chess.* have (an opponent's king) in a position of danger so that it must be moved or the danger avoided in some other way.
check in, a arrive and register at a hotel, etc. **b** *Slang.* die.
check off, mark as checked and found true or right.
check on or **check up on,** find out about; seek more information on: *The police were checking up on her.*
check out, a leave and pay for a hotel or motel room, or leave a hospital: *We checked out of the hotel at noon.* **b** in a supermarket or

other self-service store, check through and pay for one's purchases: *It took a long time to check out.* **c** *Slang.* die.
check up, examine or compare to prove true or correct.
—*n.* **1** a sudden stop: *The message gave a check to our plans.* **2** holding back; control; restraint. **3** any person, thing, or event that controls or holds back action. A rein used to prevent a horse from lowering his head is a check. **4** *Hockey.* **a** an impeding of the progress of the puck-carrier, by means of either the body or the stick. **b** a forward who is covered by an opposing forward: *The coach told him to keep better watch on his check.* **5** a rebuff; repulse; reverse. **6** a test for correctness made by comparing: *My work will be a check on yours.* **7** a mark (✓) to show that something has been counted, examined, verified, etc.: *He put a check beside the right answers.* **8** (*adj.*) used in checking. **9** a ticket or metal piece given in return for a coat, hat, baggage, package, etc. to show ownership. **10** a bill for a meal, etc. **11** *Esp.U.S.* See **cheque. 12** a pattern of squares: *Do you want a check or a stripe for your new dress?* **13** one of these squares: *The checks are small in this pattern.* **14** (*adj.*) marked in a pattern of squares. **15** a crack; split. **16** *Chess.* **a** a call warning that an opponent's king is in danger. **b** the position of an opponent's king when it is in danger and must be moved or the threatening piece blocked off or removed.
in check, held back; controlled.
—*interj. Chess.* a call warning that an opponent's king is in danger and must be moved. [ME < OF *eschec* a check at chess (v., *eschequier*), ult. < Persian *shāh* king, king at chess] —**check′a·ble,** *adj.*

☛ *Syn. v.* **1.** See note at **stop. 2. Check, restrain, curb** = hold someone or something back. **Check** suggests use of some means that slows up or stands in the way of action or progress: *The awning checked his fall.* **Restrain** suggests use of some force to keep down or within limits or to prevent completely: *A bystander restrained him from jumping off the bridge.* **Curb** suggests use of a control that pulls back suddenly or keeps from acting freely: *His good sense curbed his impulse to hit the man.*

check·book (chek′bùk′) *Esp.U.S.* See **chequebook.**

checked (chekt) *adj.* marked in a pattern of squares.

check·er[1] (chek′ər) *v., n.* —*v.* **1** mark in a pattern of squares of different colors. **2** mark off with patches different from one another: *The ground under the trees was checkered with sunlight and shade.* **3** have ups and downs; change.
—*n.* **1** a pattern of squares of different colors. **2** one of these squares. **3** one of the flat, round pieces used in the game of checkers. **4** *Obsolete.* checkerboard. Also, **chequer.** [ME < AF *escheker* < Med.L *scaccarium* chessboard]

check·er[2] (chek′ər) *n.* a person or thing that checks, especially a cashier in a self-service store or supermarket.

check·er·ber·ry (chek′ər ber′ē) *n., pl.* **-ries. 1** the red berry of any of various plants, especially the spicy, edible fruit of a North American wintergreen (*Gaultheria procumbens*). **2** a plant bearing such fruit.

check·er·board (chek′ər bôrd′) *n.* a square board marked in a pattern of 64 squares of two alternating colors and used in playing checkers or chess. Also, **chequerboard.**

check·ered (chek′ərd) *adj.* **1** marked in a pattern of squares of different colors. **2** marked in patches. **3** often changing; varied; irregular: *a checkered career.* Also, **chequered.**

check·ers (chek′ərz) *n.* a game played by two people, each having 12 round, flat pieces to move on a checkerboard (*used with a singular verb*). Also, **chequers.** British name: **draughts.**

check·list (chek′list′) *n.* a complete list of things, such as names, articles on inventory, steps in a procedure, etc., used for checking or comparing.

check mark a mark (✓) to show that something has been counted, examined, verified, etc.; a check (def. 7).

check·mate (chek′māt′) *v.* **-mat·ed, -mat·ing;** *n., interj.* —*v.* **1** *Chess.* put (an opponent's king) in check and so win the game. **2** defeat completely. **3** counteract a scheme or action of (an opponent), making it useless or ineffective: *The spy checkmated his pursuers at every turn.*
—*n.* **1** *Chess.* a move that ends the game by putting the opponent's king in check. **2** a complete defeat.
—*interj. Chess.* a declaration that the opposing king is in check. [ME < OF *eschec et mat* < Persian *shāh māt* king is dead]

check·off (chek′ôf′) *n.* **1** a system of collecting union dues through wage deductions made by the employer on the union's behalf. **2** the amount deducted under such a system.

check·out (chek′out′) *n.* **1** in a supermarket or other self-service store: **a** the process by which purchases are checked and paid for: *The check-out took only about a minute.* **b** the counter where this is done: *I went to the express check-out.* **2** in a hotel or motel, the time by which one must leave and pay for a room: *We missed the check-out and had to pay for an extra day.*

check·point (chek′point′) *n.* a point or place where a check is made, especially a place on a road or highway where vehicles or persons are inspected by authorities.

hat, āge, fär; let, ēqual, tèrm; it, īce
hot, ōpen, ôrder; oil, out; cup, pùt, rüle,
əbove, takən, pencəl, lemən, circəs

ch, child; ng, long; sh, ship
th, thin; ᴛʜ, then; zh, measure

check·rein (chek′rān′) *n.* **1** a short rein to keep a horse from lowering its head. **2** a short rein connecting the bit of one of a team of horses to the driving rein of the other.

check·room (chek′rüm′ *or* -rùm′) *n.* a place where coats, hats, baggage, packages, etc. can be left until required again.

check·up (chek′up′) *n.* **1** a careful examination. **2** a thorough physical examination.

Ched·dar (ched′ər) *n.* a hard, smooth, white or yellow cheese made in three main degrees of sharpness. Also, **cheddar.** [< *Cheddar,* in Somerset, England]

chee·cha·ko (chē cho′kō) *n. Cdn.* a newcomer; tenderfoot; greenhorn: *It took the cheechako many months to learn the ways of the Yukon.* [< Chinook jargon < Chinook *t'shi* new + *chakho* come]

cheek (chēk) *n.* **1** the side of the face below either eye. **2** something suggesting the human cheek in form or position. **3** *Informal.* saucy talk or behavior; impudence: *The boy's cheek annoyed the neighbors.*
cheek by jowl, a side by side; close together. **b** close; intimate; familiar.
[OE *cēce*]

cheek·bone (chēk′bōn′) *n.* a bone just below either eye.

–cheeked *combining form.* having cheeks of a particular kind: *rosy-cheeked.*

cheek pouch a pouch in the cheek. Squirrels have cheek pouches.

cheek strap one of the two side straps of a bridle. They connect the band around the head with the bit.

cheek·y (chēk′ē) *adj.* **cheek·i·er, cheek·i·est.** *Informal.* saucy; impudent. —**cheek′i·ly,** *adv.* —**cheek′i·ness,** *n.*

cheep (chēp) *v., n.* —*v.* make a short, sharp sound like a young bird; chirp; peep. —*n.* a short, sharp sound like that of a young bird; chirp; peep. [imitative] —**cheep′er,** *n.*
☛ *Hom.* **cheap.**

cheer (chēr) *n., v.* —*n.* **1** joy; gladness; comfort; encouragement: *The warmth of the fire and a good meal brought cheer to our hearts again.* **2** a shout of encouragement, approval, praise, etc. **3** food: *We were invited for Christmas cheer.* **4** a state of mind; condition of feeling: *My friends encouraged me to be of good cheer.*
what cheer? how are you?
—*v.* **1** fill with cheer; give joy to; gladden; comfort; encourage: *Our visit cheered the old lady.* **2** shout encouragement, approval, praise, etc. **3** urge on with cheers: *Everyone cheered our team.* **4** greet or welcome with cheers.
cheer up, make or become happier; be glad.
[ME *chere* < OF < LL *cara* face < Gk. *kara* head, face]
—**cheer′er,** *n.*

☛ *Syn. v.* **1. Cheer, gladden** = raise a person's spirits. **Cheer** suggests either making a person feel less downhearted by giving comfort and encouragement (often *cheer up*) or putting him in high spirits by giving pleasure or joy: *The news cheered everyone.* **Gladden** suggests putting a person in good spirits by giving delight and making him feel happy: *The sight of the countryside gladdened the crippled children.*

cheer·ful (chēr′fəl) *adj.* **1** full of cheer; joyful; glad: *a smiling, cheerful person.* **2** filling with cheer; pleasant; bright: *a cheerful sunny room.* **3** willing: *a cheerful giver.* —**cheer′ful·ly,** *adv.* —**cheer′ful·ness,** *n.*

cheer·i·o (chēr′ē ō′) *interj. n., pl.* **-i·os.** *Informal.* **1** goodbye! **2** hello! **3** hurrah!

cheer·lead·er (chēr′lē′dər) *n.* a person who leads the organized cheering of a crowd, especially at high-school or university sports events.

cheer·lead·ing (chēr′lē′ding) *n.* the act or practice of leading a crowd in cheers; being a cheerleader.

cheer·less (chēr′lis) *adj.* without joy or comfort; gloomy; dreary. —**cheer′less·ness,** *n.*

cheer·y (chēr′ē) *adj.* **cheer·i·er, cheer·i·est.** cheerful; pleasant; bright. —**cheer′i·ly,** *adv.* —**cheer′i·ness,** *n.*

cheese (chēz) *n., v.* —*n.* **1** a solid food made from the curds of milk. **2** a mass of this substance pressed into a shape. —*v. Slang.* upset or annoy (*used with* **off**): *His attitude cheeses me off. She's cheesed off about something.* [OE *cēse* < L *caseus*] —**cheese′like′,** *adj.*

cheese·burg·er (chēz′bėrg′ər) *n.* a hamburger with a slice of cheese melted on top of the meat.

cheese·cake (chēz′kāk′) *n.* **1** a dessert made of cream cheese or cottage cheese, eggs, sugar, etc. baked together. **2** *Slang.* photographs or photography emphasizing the figure and legs of an attractive young woman. Compare **beefcake.**

cheese·cloth (chēz′klôth′) *n.* a thin, loosely woven cotton cloth, originally used for wrapping cheese.

cheese·par·ing (chez′per′ing) *n., adj.* —*n.* **1** something as insignificant or worthless as the parings of rind from cheese. **2** stinginess; miserly. —*adj.* stingy; miserly.

chees·y (chēz′ē) *adj.* **chees·i·er, chees·i·est. 1** of or like cheese. **2** *Slang.* not well made; inferior.

chee·tah (chē′tə) *n.* a tall, rangy, long-legged African and Asian animal (*Acinonyx jubatus*) of the cat family, thought to be the fastest mammal on earth, having doglike feet with hard pads and claws that cannot be retracted, a small head, and a reddish-yellow coat with black spots. Cheetahs that have been captured and trained to hunt are often called hunting leopards. [< Hind. *chita*]

chef (shef) *n.* **1** a head cook. **2** a cook. [< F *chef* (*de cuisine*) < L *caput* head. Doublet of CHIEF.]

chef–d'oeu·vre (she dœ′vrə) *n., pl.* **chefs–d'oeuvre** (she dœ′vrə). masterpiece. [< F]

Che·khov·i·an (che kō′vē ən) *adj.* **1** of or having to do with Anton Chekhov (1860-1904), a Russian dramatist and writer of short stories. **2** of or suggestive of his writings.

che·la (kē′lə) *n., pl.* **-lae** (-lē *or* -lī). a pincer-like claw, such as that of a lobster, crab, or scorpion. [< L < Gk. *chēlē* claw]

che·lo·ni·an (ki lō′nē ən) *n., adj.* —*n.* any of an order (Chelonia) of reptiles, including tortoises and turtles, having the body enclosed in a protective bony shell. —*adj.* of, having to do with, or belonging to the order Chelonia. [< NL *Chelonia* < Gk. *chelōnē* tortoise]

chem. chemistry; chemical; chemist.

chem·ic (kem′ik) *adj. Archaic.* **1** chemical. **2** of alchemy.

chem·i·cal (kem′ə kəl) *adj., n.* —*adj.* **1** of, having to do with, used in, or produced by chemistry: *chemical knowledge, a chemical process, a chemical compound.* **2** producing or using chemicals: *the chemical industry.* **3** made of or working by chemicals: *a chemical fertilizer, a chemical toilet.*
—*n.* a substance that has been produced by chemical processes in a laboratory, using raw materials such as crude petroleum, rocks, or plant parts, or using basic substances already made in this way to produce more complex substances and finished products. Phosphates, coal, tar, plastics, drugs, paints, and insecticides are chemicals.

chemical engineering the science or profession of using chemistry for industrial purposes.

chem·i·cal·ly (kem′ik lē) *adv.* **1** according to chemistry. **2** by chemical processes.

chemical warfare the technique or use of gases, flames, smoke, or any chemicals other than explosives as weapons.

che·mise (shə mēz′) *n.* **1** a loose, shirtlike undergarment worn by women or girls. **2** a loose, straight-cut dress. [< F < LL *camisia* shirt < Celtic]

chem·ist (kem′ist) *n.* **1** a person trained in chemistry, especially one whose work it is. **2** *Esp.Brit.* druggist. [var. of *alchemist*]

chem·is·try (kem′is trē) *n., pl.* **-tries. 1** the science that deals with elements or simple substances, the changes that take place when they combine to form compounds, and the laws of their combination and behavior under various conditions. **2** the application of this to a certain subject: *the chemistry of foods.* **3** chemical processes, properties, phenomena, etc.: *Some teenagers have acne because of their body chemistry.*

chemo– *combining form.* of or involving chemical reactions: *chemotherapy.*

chem·o·sphere (kem′ə sfēr′) *n. Meteorology.* a region of the atmosphere beginning about 35 kilometres above the earth, where the sun's radiation produces predominant photochemical activity.

chem·o·ther·a·py (kem′ō ther′ə pē *or* kē′mō ther′ə pē) *n.* the treatment or control of disease by means of chemical agents.

chem·ur·gist (kem′ėr jist) *n.* a person trained in chemurgy, especially one whose work it is.

chem·ur·gy (kem′ėr jē) *n.* the branch of chemistry that deals with the use of farm products, such as casein and cornstalks, for purposes other than food and clothing. [< *chem*istry + *-urgy* < Gk. *ergon* work + *ia*]

che·nille (shə nēl′) *n.* **1** a fabric, usually cotton, made with a filling of rows of tufted cord arranged in various designs and forming a soft, piled surface: *Chenille is used for bedspreads, robes, rugs, etc.* **2** a tufted cord of silk, cotton, or worsted, used in embroidery, fringe, etc. [< F *chenille* caterpillar < L *canicula* little dog; from its furry look]

cheque (chek) *n.* **1** a written order directing a bank to take money from the account of the signer and pay it to the person or company named on it: *He pays his bills by cheque.* **2** a blank form on which to write such an order. Sometimes, *esp. U.S.,* **check.**

cheque·book (chek′buk′) *n.* a book of blank cheques. Sometimes, *esp. U.S.,* **checkbook.**

cheq·uer (chek′ər) See **checker.**

cheq·uer·board (chek′ər bôrd′) See **checkerboard.**

cheq·uered (chek′ərd) See **checkered.**

cheq·uers (chek′ərz) See **checkers.**

Cheq·uers (chek′ərz) *n.* the official country residence of the British prime minister, in Buckinghamshire, northwest of London.

chequing account a bank account against which cheques may be drawn.

cher·ish (cher′ish) *v.* **1** hold dear; treat with affection; care for tenderly: *He cherished his little daughter.* **2** keep in mind; cling to: *For many years the old woman cherished the hope that her wandering son would come home.* [ME < OF *cheriss*-, a stem of *cherir* < *cher* dear < L *carus*]
➤ *Syn.* 2. **Cherish, foster, harbor,** used figuratively, mean "keep and care for in the mind." **Cherish,** literally, means "hold dear," emphasizes treasuring an idea or feeling and watching over it with loving care: *He cherishes friendship.* **Foster** suggests nourishing an idea or feeling, and helping it to grow: *He tries to foster tolerance.* **Harbor,** literally, means "give shelter to," suggests letting in a bad idea or feeling and brooding over it: *He harbors a grudge.*

cher·no·zem (cher′nə zem′) *n.* a fertile soil typical of wet grasslands, consisting of a rich, black layer with a high organic content, overlying a layer of accumulated lime. [< Russian *chernozem* < *chernyi* black + *zemlja* land, soil]

Cher·o·kee (cher′ə kē *or* cher′ə kē′) *n., pl.* **-kee** *or* **-kees. 1** a member of an Amerindian people now living mostly in Oklahoma. **2** the Iroquoian language of the Cherokee. [alteration of native *Tsalagi* or *Tsaragi*]

che·root (shə rüt′) *n.* a cigar cut off square at both ends. [< F *chéroute* < Tamil *shuruttu* roll]

cher·ry (cher′ē) *n., pl.* **-ries;** *adj.* —*n.* **1** a small, round, edible, juicy fruit having a pit, or stone, in the centre, produced by any of various trees and shrubs (genus *Prunus*) of the rose family. **2** a tree or shrub that produces this fruit. **3** the wood of any of these trees or shrubs. **4** (*adjl.*) made of this wood. **5** a bright red.
—*adj.* bright red. [ME *chery*, back formation from *cherys* < ONF *cherise* < VL < LGk. *kerasia* cherry tree < Gk. *kerasos* cherry. Doublet of CERISE.]
➤ *Hom.* **chary.**

cherry picker a type of crane consisting of a jointed or telescoping arm with a large bucket at the end, in which a person can stand to carry out operations high above the ground, such as repairs to power lines.

cher·ry·stone (cher′ē stōn′) *n.* the *quahog,* a clam with a round, hard shell. Also called **cherrystone clam.**

chert (chėrt) *n.* a dark, impure mineral resembling flint and containing quartz and hydrated silica.

cher·ub (cher′əb) *n., pl.* **cher·u·bim** for 1 and 2, **cher·ubs** for 3 and 4. **1** one of the second highest order of angels. **2** a picture or statue of a child with wings, or of a child's head with wings but no body. **3** a beautiful or good child. **4** a person with a chubby, innocent face. [< Hebrew *kerūb*]

che·ru·bic (chə rü′bik) *adj.* **1** of or like a cherub; angelic. **2** innocent; good. **3** chubby. —**che·ru′bi·cal·ly,** *adv.*

cher·u·bim (cher′ə bim′ *or* cher′yə bim′) *n.* **1** pl. of **cherub. 2** (*pl., formerly used as sing.*) cherub.

cher·vil (chėr′vəl) *n.* an aromatic Eurasian herb (*Anthriscus cerefolium*) of the parsley family having finely divided leaves that are used to flavor soups, salads, fish, etc. [OE *cerfille* < L < Gk. *chairephyllon* < *chairein* rejoice + *phyllon* leaf]

cher·vo·nets (cher vô′nets) *n., pl.* **-von·tsi** (-vôn′tsē). **1** a former monetary unit of the Soviet Union. **2** a gold coin worth one chervonets. [< Russian]

Chesh·ire (chesh′ər) *n.* a crumbly cheese, similar to Cheddar, either white or colored red. Some red Cheshire develops a blue veining as it ripens. [< *Cheshire,* a county in W England]

Cheshire cat 1 anybody with a fixed grin. **2** the grinning cat in *Alice in Wonderland* by Lewis Carroll.

chess (ches) *n.* a game played on a chessboard by two people. Each has 16 pieces that have to be moved in various ways. [ME < OF *esches,* pl. of *eschec.* See CHECK.]

chess·board (ches'bôrd') *n.* a board marked in a pattern of 64 squares of two alternating colors, used in playing chess.

chess·man (ches'man' *or* -mən) *n., pl.* **-men.** one of the pieces used in playing chess.

chest (chest) *n.* **1** the part of the body of a person or animal enclosed by the ribs. **2** the front outside part of this. **3** the measurement around a person's body at the widest part of the chest: *He has a 100-centimetre chest.* **4** (*adj.*) of or involving the chest: *a chest cold.* **5** a large, sturdy box with a lid, used for storing or shipping things: *a linen chest, a tool chest.* **6** a piece of furniture with drawers. **7** a sealed container for gas, steam, etc. **8** *Rare* **a** a place where money of a public or charitable institution is kept; treasury. **b** the money itself. [OE *cest, cist* < L *cista* < Gk. *kistē* box]

–chested *combining form.* having a —chest: *broadchested = having a broad chest.*

ches·ter·bed (ches'tər bed') *n.* a chesterfield that can be opened out to form a bed.

ches·ter·field (ches'tər fēld') *n.* **1** a long, upholstered seat for several people, having a back and, usually, arms; sofa; couch. **2** a single-breasted, knee-length, man's overcoat usually having the buttons concealed by an overlapping flap. [after a 19th-century Earl of *Chesterfield*]

Chester White a breed of large, white pig.

chest·nut (ches'nut *or* -nət) *n., adj.* —*n.* **1** any of a genus (*Castanea*) of trees of the beech family native to north temperate regions having flowers in long catkins and producing burrlike fruits containing two or three edible nuts. **2** the nut of any of these trees. **3** the wood of any of these trees. **4** a reddish brown. **5** a brown or reddish-brown horse. **6** *Informal.* a stale joke or story. **7** See **horse chestnut, water chestnut.** —*adj.* having the color chestnut. [< obs. *chesten* chestnut (< OF *chastaigne* < L *castanea* < Gk. *kastanea* or *kastaneia* < *kastanon*) + *nut*]

che·tah (chē'tə) *n. Archaic.* See **cheetah.**

chet·nik (chet'nik) *n., pl.* **chet·ni·ci** (chet nē'tsē) *or* **-niks.** in Yugoslavia, one of a guerrilla force that was active against the Nazis during World War II. [< Serbian *chetnik < cheta* band]

che·val glass (shə val') a tall mirror mounted in a frame so that it swings between its supports. [*cheval* < F *cheval* horse, support < L *caballus* horse]

chev·a·lier (shev'ə lēr'; *French,* shə vä lyā') *n.* **1** *Archaic.* a knight. **2** in France, a member of the lowest rank in the Legion of Honor. [< F *chevalier < cheval* horse < L *caballus*]

Chev·i·ot (chev'ē ət *or* chē'vē ət *for 1 and 2*; shev'ē ət *for 3*) *n.* **1** a breed of sheep that originated in the Cheviot Hills on the boundary between England and Scotland. **2 cheviot, a** a rough woollen cloth with a nap, used for coats and suits. **b** a heavy, coarse cotton cloth used for shirts.

chev·ron (shev'rən) *n.* **1** a V-shaped bar, usually of cloth, often worn on the sleeve of a uniform by members of the armed forces, a police force, etc., to show rank or years of service: *A sergeant wears three chevrons.* **2** any V-shaped design. [ME < OF *chevron* rafter < *chevre* goat < L *caper*]

chev·y (chev'ē) *n., pl.* **chev·ies;** *v.* **chev·ied, chev·y·ing.** *Brit.* —*n.* **1** a hunting cry. **2** a hunt; chase. —*v.* **1** hunt; chase. **2** scamper; race. **3** worry. [shortened form of *Chevy Chase,* from the ballad of that name]

chew (chü) *v., n.* —*v.* **1** crush, grind, or gnaw with the teeth. **2** mark, crush, etc., as if by chewing (*usually used with* up): *The wheels of the truck had chewed up the lawn.* **3** *Informal.* consider or discuss at length (*used with* over): *She chewed it over for several days before making her decision.* **4** chew tobacco: *Does he chew?* **chew out,** *Informal.* reprimand. **chew the fat,** *Slang.* converse casually or idly: *We sat around for an hour or so, chewing the fat.* —*n.* **1** the act of chewing. **2** something chewed or to be chewed: *a chew of tobacco.* [OE *cēowan*] —**chew'a·ble,** *adj.* —**chew'er,** *n.*

chewing gum a gummy preparation for chewing, usually made of chicle that has been sweetened and flavored.

che·wink (chi wingk') *n.* towhee (def. 1). [imitative]

chew·y (chü'ē) *adj.* requiring chewing; becoming sticky and pliable when chewed.

Chey·enne (shī en') *n., pl.* **-enne** *or* **-ennes. 1** a member of an Amerindian people now living in Montana and Oklahoma. **2** the Algonquian language of the Cheyenne. [< the Sioux name *Shahi'yena, Shai-ena* people of alien speech]

chg. charge(s).

chgd. charged.

chi (kī) *n.* the 22nd letter of the Greek alphabet (Χ, χ), appearing as *ch,* but usually sounded as *k,* in English words of Greek origin.

Chi·an·ti (kē än'tē *or* kē an'tē) *n.* **1** a dry, red Italian wine. **2** any similar wine. [< the *Chianti* Mountains in Italy]

hat, āge, fär; let, ēqual, tèrm; it, īce
hot, ōpen, ôrder; oil, out; cup, put, rüle,
above, takən, pencəl, lemən, circəs

ch, child; ng, long; sh, ship
th, thin; ᴛʜ, then; zh, measure

chi·a·o (tyä'ü) *n., pl.* **chiao. 1** a unit of money in the People's Republic of China, equal to ¹⁄₁₀ of a yuan or 10 fen. **2** a coin worth one chiao. [< Chinese]

chi·a·ro·scu·ro (kē ä'rə skyür'ō; *Italian,* kyä'rō skü'rō) *n., pl.* **-ros. 1** the treatment of light and shade in a picture. **2** the effect of light and shade in a picture. **3** a style of painting, drawing, etc. that uses only light and shade. **4** a picture, especially a painting, in which chiaroscuro is used. **5** stylistic effects of variation, relief, contrast, etc. used in any of the arts. [< Ital. < *chiaro* clear (< L *clarus*) + *oscuro* dim (< L *obscurus*)]

chic (shēk *or* shik) *n., adj.* —*n.* style. —*adj.* stylish. [< F]
☛ **Hom. sheik** (shēk).

chi·cane (shi kān') *n., v.* **-caned, -can·ing.** —*n.* chicanery. —*v.* **1** use chicanery. **2** get by chicanery. [< F *chicane < chicaner* quibble]

chi·can·er·y (shi kān'ər ē) *n., pl.* **-er·ies.** low trickery; unfair practice; quibbling: *Only a dishonest lawyer would use chicanery to win a lawsuit.*

Chi·ca·no (chi kä'nō) *n., pl.* **-nos;** *adj.* —*n.* a citizen or inhabitant of the United States who is a native of Mexico or is of Mexican descent. —*adj.* of or having to do with Chicanos.

chi·chi (shē'shē') *adj. Informal.* very smart and stylish, especially in an affected, arty way: *a chi-chi little boutique.*

chick (chik) *n.* **1** a young chicken. **2** a young bird. **3** child. **4** *Slang.* an attractive girl. [ME *chicke,* var. of *chicken*]

chick·a·dee (chik'ə dē') *n.* any of several North American songbirds (genus *Parus*) of the titmouse family, having a plump body, long tail, short bill, and a large, black or brown, caplike patch on the top of the head. The **black-capped chickadee** (*P. atricapillus*) is the commonest species, found across North America. [imitative of its cry]

chick·a·ree (chik'ə rē') *n.* a North American red squirrel. See **red squirrel.** [imitative of its cry]

chick·en (chik'ən) *n., v.* —*n.* **1** the common domestic fowl, bred in many varieties for its flesh or eggs. All breeds of chicken are descended from a wild fowl (*Gallus gallus*) of the jungles of SE Asia. **2** a young hen or rooster. **3** the flesh of a chicken used for food. **4** any of various other birds when young. **5** *Cdn. Informal.* prairie chicken. **6** *Slang.* a young person, especially a girl. **7** (*adj.*) young or small: *a chicken lobster.* **8** *Slang.* coward: *Don't be such a chicken.* **9** (*adj.*) *Slang.* cowardly. **play chicken,** take part in any of various games in which each person risks his own safety on the assumption that the other person will give up or back down first. —*v. Slang.* back out, or withdraw, because of a loss of courage (*used with* out): *She chickened out at the last minute and refused to go on stage.* [OE *cicen*]

chick·en·burg·er (chik'ən bėrg'ər) *n.* a hamburger made with cooked chicken instead of ground beef.

chicken feed *Slang.* a small or insignificant amount of money: *He said he left the job because the pay was chicken feed.*

chick·en·heart·ed (chik'ən härt'id) *adj.* cowardly; timid.

chick·en·liv·ered (chik'ən liv'ərd) *adj. Informal.* cowardly.

chicken pox a contagious disease marked by pus-filled skin eruptions similar to those of smallpox but milder, and usually accompanied by a fever.

chicken wire a light wire netting of six-sided mesh, used for fencing, on cages for pets, to protect young trees, etc.

chick–pea (chik'pē') *n.* **1** an annual plant (*Cicer arietinum*) of the pea family, native to Asia but now widely grown in the western hemisphere for its edible seeds, which grow in short pods. **2** the seed of this plant, resembling the garden pea in shape and flavor.

chick·weed (chik'wēd') *n.* any of several plants (especially of genera *Stellaria* and *Cerastium*) of the pink family, some of which have leaves and seeds that are attractive to birds. The common chickweed (*Stellaria media*) is well-known as a weed in gardens.

chic·le (chik'əl) *n.* a tasteless, gumlike substance, the main ingredient of chewing gum, that is prepared from the milky juice of the sapodilla tree. [< Am.Sp. < Mexican *jiktli*]

chic·o·ry (chik'ə rē) *n., pl.* **-ries.** a European perennial herb (*Cichorium intybus*) of the composite family having small blue flowers. It is widely cultivated for its leaves, which are used in

salads and also for its roots, which are dried and ground for use as a coffee substitute. [< F *chicorée* < L < Gk. *kichōrion*]

chid (chid) v. a pt. and a pp. of **chide**.

chid·den (chid′ən) v. a pp. of **chide**.

chide (chīd) v. **chid·ed** or **chid, chid·ed, chid,** or **chid·den, chid·ing.** reproach; blame; scold: *She chided her son for getting his sweater dirty.* [OE *cīdan*] —**chid′er,** n. —**chid′ing·ly,** adv.
☛ *Syn.* See note at **scold.**

chief (chēf) n., adj. —n. 1 the head of a group; leader; the person highest in rank or authority. 2 the head of a tribe or clan. 3 *Heraldry.* the upper third of a shield.
in chief, at the head or in the highest position.
—adj. 1 leading; at the head; in authority: *the chief engineer of a building project.* 2 main; most important: *The chief attraction of the midway was the ferris wheel.* [ME < OF < L *caput* head. Doublet of CHEF.] —**chief′less,** adj.

chief·dom (chēf′dəm) n. the position or authority of a chief, or the territory ruled by him.

chief justice 1 in Canada and some other Commonwealth countries, a judge who is appointed as the senior judge of a supreme court. The Supreme Court of Canada is made up of the chief justice of Canada and eight puisne judges. 2 in the United States, a judge who presides over a court made up of a group of judges.

chief·ly (chēf′lē) adv. 1 mainly; mostly: *This juice is made up chiefly of tomatoes.* 2 first of all; above all.

chief of staff the senior staff officer serving as principal adviser to the commander of a military organization or formation.

chief petty officer 1 *Canadian Forces.* in Maritime Command, either of two ranks: chief petty officer 2nd class (*abbrev.*: C2), equivalent to a master warrant officer 1st class (*abbrev.*: C1), equivalent to a chief warrant officer. See chart at **rank¹.** 2 a naval non-commissioned officer of similar rank in other countries. *Abbrev.*: C.P.O. or CPO

chief·tain (chēf′tən) n. 1 the chief of a tribe or clan. 2 a leader; the head of a group. [ME *chevetaine* < OF < LL *capitaneus.* Doublet of CAPTAIN.]

chief·tain·cy (chēf′tən sē) n. the position or rank of a chieftain.

chief·tain·ship (chēf′tən ship′) n. chieftaincy.

chief warrant officer the highest ranking non-commissioned officer in the armed forces. *Abbrev.*: C.W.O. or CWO See chart at **rank¹.**

chif·fon (shi fon′ or shif′on) n. 1 a delicate, very thin, usually soft fabric, made of silk, rayon, etc. and used for dresses, scarves, veils, etc. 2 **chiffons,** pl. *Rare.* ribbons, laces, etc. used to ornament a woman's dress. 3 (*adjl.*) made of chiffon. 4 (*adjl.*) of fabric, soft and lightweight: *chiffon velvet.* 5 (*adjl.*) of cakes, etc., having a light texture, as from the addition of beaten egg whites. [< F *chiffon* < *chiffe* rag]

chif·fo·nier (shif′ə nēr′) n. a high chest of drawers, often having a mirror. [< F *chiffonnier* < *chiffon.* See CHIFFON.]

chig·ger (chig′ər) n. 1 the larva of any of various mites (family Trombiculidae) that sucks the blood of people and animals, causing intense irritation of the skin. 2 chigoe. [alteration of *chigoe*]

chi·gnon (shēn′yon; *French,* shē nyôn′) n. a knot or roll of hair worn at the back of the head by women. [< F *chignon* nape of the neck < VL *catenio* < L *catena* chain; referring to the vertebrae]

chig·oe (chig′ō) n. 1 a tropical flea (*Tunga penetrans*), the female of which burrows under the skin of people and animals, causing intense irritation; sand flea. 2 chigger. [< W Indian]

chi·hua·hua (chē wä′wä) n. an ancient breed of tiny dog originally developed in Mexico, having large, protruding eyes and large, erect ears. [< *Chihuahua,* a state and city in N Mexico]

chil·blain (chil′blān′) n. Usually, **chilblains,** pl. an itching sore or redness on the hands or feet, caused by cold. [< *chill* + *blain*]

Chil·cot·in (chil′kō′tin) n. 1 a tribe of Athapascan Indians living in the valley of the Chilcotin River, British Columbia. 2 a member of this tribe. 3 the Athapascan language of the tribe.

child (chīld) n., pl. **chil·dren.** 1 baby. 2 a boy or girl, especially one up to the early or mid teens. 3 a son or daughter: *All their children are already married.* 4 descendant. 5 an adult who behaves in a childish way, as if he has not grown up: *My father is such a child when he is sick.* 6 an adult who is more innocent, frank, and trusting than most other adults: *When it comes to politics or business dealings, Uncle Joe is a child.* 7 a product or result: *The new system is entirely the child of her brain.* 8 a person regarded as belonging to or produced by a particular time, place, or

environment: *a child of the sea, a child of the nuclear age.*
with child, pregnant.
[OE *cild*]

child·bear·ing (chīld′ber′ing) n., adj. —n. the act or process of giving birth to children. —adj. of or having to do with this act or process.

child·bed (chīld′bed′) n. the condition of a woman giving birth to a child.

child·birth (chīld′bėrth′) n. the act or process of giving birth to a child.

child·hood (chīld′hud′) n. 1 the condition of being a child: *the carefree days of childhood.* 2 the time during which one is a child: *His childhood was very happy.*

child·ish (chīl′dish) adj. 1 of a child. 2 like a child: *a childish person.* 3 not suitable for a grown person; weak; silly; foolish: *It was childish of her to make such a fuss.* —**child′ish·ly,** adv.
☛ *Usage.* **Childish, childlike** differ widely. **Childish** emphasizes the physical helplessness, lack of control over feelings, and undeveloped mind of a child, and therefore expresses an unfavorable opinion when used of an adult: *Such stupid behavior is childish.* **Childlike** emphasizes the innocence, simplicity, and frankness of children, and suggests a favorable opinion: *She has a childlike belief in her son's innocence.*

child·ish·ness (chīl′dish nis) n. 1 the fact or condition of being like a child. 2 weakness, silliness.

child labor or **labour** work done by children in factories, business, etc.

child·less (chīld′lis) adj. having no child. —**child′less·ness,** n.

child·like (chīld′līk′) adj. 1 like a child; innocent; frank; simple: *The charming old woman had an open, childlike manner.* 2 suitable for a child. —**child′like′ness,** n.
☛ *Usage.* See note at **childish.**

chil·dren (chil′drən) n. pl. of **child.**

children of Israel Israelites; Hebrews; Jews.

Children's Crusade an unsuccessful expedition to recover the Holy Sepulchre, undertaken by thousands of French and German children in 1212.

child's play something very easy to do.

chil·e (chil′ē) n. See **chili.**

Chil·e·an (chil′ē ən) n., adj. —n. a native or inhabitant of Chile, a country in SW South America. —adj. of or having to do with Chile or its people.

Chile saltpetre sodium nitrate.

chil·i (chil′ē) n., pl. **chil·ies.** 1 the small, hot-tasting pod, or fruit, of any of several varieties of pepper (def. 5), used for seasoning. Chilies are also dried and ground up to make red pepper. 2 chili con carne: *We had chili for supper last night.* Also, **chilli.** [< Sp. *chile* < Mexican *chilli*]
☛ *Hom.* **chilly.**

chil·i con car·ne (chil′ē kon kär′nē) ground or cubed beef cooked with chilies or chili powder and, usually, with red or kidney beans and tomatoes.

chili sauce a sauce made of red peppers, tomatoes, and spices. Also, **chilli sauce.**

Chil·kat (chil′kat) n. 1 a Tlingit Indian people formerly living mainly in SE Alaska, noted for their making of brightly-colored blankets of mountain-goat wool and cedar bark. 2 a member of this people.

chill (chil) n., adj., v. —n. 1 a moderate but unpleasant coldness: *a chill in the air.* 2 a sudden coldness of the body accompanied by shivering. 3 the state or condition of feeling cold; shivering. 4 unfriendliness; lack of warmth of feeling: *I felt the chill of his greeting.* 5 a check on enthusiasm; depressing influence: *The announcement of renewed fighting cast a chill over the assembled group.* 6 a sudden feeling of fear or dread: *A chill went through him at the thought of the coming night.* 7 *Metallurgy.* a metal mould, or a piece of iron in a sand mould for making chilled castings.
—adj. 1 unpleasantly cold. 2 cold in manner; unfriendly. 3 depressing; discouraging.
—v. 1 make cold: *We chilled the pop in the refrigerator.* 2 become cold; feel cold. 3 depress; dispirit. 4 *Metallurgy.* **a** harden (cast iron, etc.) on the surface by cooling it suddenly. **b** of cast iron, etc., become hard on the surface through sudden cooling. [OE *ciele*] —**chill′ness,** n.

chilled (child) adj. made cold.

chill·er (chil′ər) n. 1 a person or thing that chills. 2 *Informal.* a horror story or film.

chill factor wind chill.

chil·li (chil′ē) See **chili.**

chill·i·ness (chil′ē nis) n. the quality or state of being chilly.

chill·ing (chil′ing) adj. that chills: *a chilling wind, a chilling glance.* —**chill′ing·ly,** adv.

chilli sauce See **chili sauce.**

chill·y (chil′ē) *adj.* **chill·i·er, chill·i·est. 1** unpleasantly cool; rather cold: *a chilly day.* **2** cold in manner; unfriendly: *a chilly greeting.*
☛ *Hom.* **chili.**
☛ *Syn.* **1.** See note at **cold.**

Chil·tern Hundreds (chil′tərn) *Brit.* an office under the Crown that members of the House of Commons are said to apply for when they wish to resign.

chime (chīm) *n., v.* **chimed, chim·ing.** —*n.* **1** a set of bells tuned to the musical scale, usually played by hammers or simple machinery. **2** the musical sound made by a set of tuned bells. **3** a pleasantly harmonious sound, suggesting bells: *the chime of children's laughter.* **4** agreement; harmony. **5** carillon. **6** a set of metal tubes hung vertically from a frame, played by striking with a hammer held in the hand, used in orchestras. **7** an apparatus or arrangement for striking a bell or set of bells so as to produce a musical sound. —*v.* **1** make musical sounds on (a set of tuned bells). **2** ring out musically: *The bells chimed at midnight.* **3** speak or sing in cadence or singsong. **4** produce a musical sound from a bell (or the like) by striking it or using means other than ringing. **5** agree; be in harmony. **6** say or utter in cadence or singsong.
chime in, **a** be in harmony; agree: *His ideas chimed in with mine.* **b** *Informal.* break into or join in a conversation.
[ME *chymbe,* ult. < L < Gk. *kymbalon.* See CYMBAL.] —**chim′er,** *n.*

chi·me·ra or **chi·mae·ra** (kə mēr′ə or kī mēr′ə) *n., pl.* **-ras. 1** Chimera. *Greek mythology.* a female monster with a lion's head, a goat's body, and a serpent's tail, supposed to breathe out fire. **2** a horrible creature of the imagination. **3** an absurd or impossible idea; wild fancy: *The idea of changing lead to gold was a chimera.* [ME < OF < L < Gk. *chimaira* she-goat]

chi·mer·ic (kə mer′ik or kī mer′ik) *adj.* chimerical.

chi·mer·i·cal (kə mer′ə kəl or kī mer′ə kəl) *adj.* **1** unreal; imaginary. **2** absurd; impossible: *chimerical schemes for getting rich.* **3** wildly fanciful; visionary. —**chi·mer′i·cal·ly,** *adv.*

chim·ney (chim′nē) *n., pl.* **-neys. 1** an upright structure used to make a draft for a fire and carry away smoke. **2** the part of this structure that rises above a roof. **3** a glass tube put around the flame of a lamp. **4** a crack or opening in a rock, mountain, volcano, etc. [ME *chimenee* < OF *chemin
 < LL *caminata* < L *caminus* oven < Gk. *kaminos*] —**chim′ney·less,** *adj.*

chimney corner the corner or side of a fireplace; a place near the fire.

chimney piece mantlepiece.

chimney pot a pipe of earthenware or metal fitted on top of a chimney to increase the draft.

chimney swallow **1** the chimney swift of North America. **2** the European barn swallow.

chimney sweep a person whose work is cleaning out chimneys.

chimney swift a short-tailed, dark-grey swift (*Chaetura pelagica*) that often nests inside chimneys. The chimney swift ranges from southern Saskatchewan east to Nova Scotia and south to the upper Amazon region of South America.

chim·o (chē′mō or chī′mō) *interj. Cdn.* especially in the North, a call or exclamation of greeting. [< Eskimo]

chimp (chimp) *n. Informal.* chimpanzee.

chim·pan·zee (chim′pan zē′ or chim pan′zē) *n.* an anthropoid ape (*Pan troglodytes*) of Africa, smaller than a gorilla. The chimpanzee is probably the most intelligent ape. [< a native West African (Bantu) name]

chin (chin) *n., v.* **chinned, chin·ning.** —*n.* **1** the front of the lower jaw below the mouth. **2** the whole lower surface of the face, below the mouth. **3** *Informal.* a chat; gossip.
keep (one's) chin up, bear adversity without flinching or complaining.
—*v.* **1** (oneself) hang by the hands from an overhead bar and pull oneself up until one's chin is even with or above the bar. **2** *Informal.* chat; gossip. **3** *Informal.* place (a violin) under the chin in order to play it. [OE *cinn*] —**chin′less,** *adj.*

chi·na (chī′nə) *n.* **1** a fine, white, translucent ceramic ware made of pure clay that has been baked at high temperatures; porcelain. Colored designs can be baked into china. **2** dishes, vases, ornaments, etc. made of china. **3** ceramic dishes of any kind. [short for earlier *china-ware* ware from China]

Chi·na·man (chī′nə mən) *n., pl.* **-men.** *Offensive.* Chinese.
☛ *Usage.* See note at **Chinese.**

Chi·na·town (chī′nə toun′) *n.* a section of a city inhabited mainly by Chinese people and having a large number of Chinese stores, restaurants, etc.

chi·na·ware (chī′nə wer′) *n.* **1** dishes, vases, ornaments, etc. made of china. **2** earthen dishes of any kind.

chinch (chinch) *n. U.S.* **1** bedbug. **2** chinch bug. [< Sp. *chinche* < L *cimex, -micis* bedbug]

hat, āge, fär; let, ēqual, tėrm; it, īce
hot, ōpen, ôrder; oil, out; cup, put, rüle,
əbove, takən, pencəl, lemən, circəs

ch, child; ng, long; sh, ship
th, thin; ᵺ, then; zh, measure

chinch bug a small black-and-white bug (*Blissus leucopterus*) native to tropical America, which has extended its range northward to become a serious pest in grainfields in the United States.

chin·chil·la (chin chil′ə) *n.* **1** a small, stocky rodent (*Chinchilla laniger*) native to the mountains of South America, widely bred in captivity for its soft, fine silvery-grey fur. **2** the highly valued fur of a chinchilla. **3** (*adj.*) made of this fur: *a chinchilla coat.* **4** a thick woollen fabric woven in small, closely set tufts, used for overcoats. [< Sp. *chinchilla,* dim. of *chinche.* See CHINCH.]

chine (chīn) *n.* **1** the backbone; spine. **2** a piece of an animal's backbone with the meat on it, suitable for cooking. **3** a ridge; crest. [ME < OF *eschine* < Gmc.]

Chi·nee (chī′nē) *n. Derogatory slang.* a Chinese. [back formation < Chinese]

Chi·nese (chī nēz′) *n., pl.* **-nese;** *adj.* —*n.* **1** a native or inhabitant of China, a large country in E Asia. **2** a person of Chinese descent. **3** any of the Sino-Tibetan languages of China.
—*adj.* of or having to do with China, its people, or their languages.
☛ *Usage.* **Chinese** is preferred by natives of China (and others) to *Chinaman, Chinamen,* which are considered derogatory.

Chinese calendar the ancient lunar calendar formerly used in China, having cycles of 60 years, 12 months in a year, 29 or 30 days in a month, with an extra month added after each half cycle. The Chinese adopted the Georgian calendar in 1912, the first year of the Republic, and years are now counted from that date.

Chinese checkers a game played by two to six persons using small marbles on a board patterned as a six-pointed star. The object of the game is to be the first player to move all one's marbles into the corresponding positions on the opposite side of the board. Also, **Chinese chequers.**

Chinese Empire China before it became a republic in 1912, including Manchuria, Mongolia, Tibet, and Sinkiang.

Chinese lantern a lantern of thin, colored paper that can be folded up.

Chinese puzzle something that is very complicated and hard to solve. [from the wood and metal puzzles invented by the Chinese]

chink¹ (chingk) *n., v.* —*n.* a narrow opening; crack; slit: *The chinks between the logs of the cabin let in the wind and snow.* —*v.* **1** fill up the chinks in: *The cracks in the walls of the cabin were chinked with mud.* **2** make chinks in. [? < ME *chine* fissure < OE *cinu*]

chink² (chingk) *n., v.* —*n.* a short, sharp, ringing sound like coins or glasses hitting together. —*v.* **1** make a short, sharp, ringing sound. **2** cause to make such a sound: *He chinked the coins in his pocket.* [imitative]

Chink (chingk) *n. Derogatory slang.* a Chinese.

chi·no (chē′nō or shē′nō) *n.* **1** a twilled cotton or cotton-blend fabric of medium weight with a smooth, lustrous finish, used especially for sportswear. **2** chinos, *pl.* pants made of chino. **3** (*adj.*) made of chino: *chino pants.*

chi·noi·se·rie (shēn′wä zə rē′) *n.* **1** a style of design and decoration for furniture, ceramics, etc. based on traditional Chinese designs and motifs. **2** an article or articles made in this style: *She collects chinoiserie.*

chi·nook (shi nuk′) *n., v. Cdn.* —*n.* a warm, usually dry, winter wind that blows from the west or southwest across the Rocky Mountains from the Peace River to Colorado, sometimes extending across Alberta and into Saskatchewan. A chinook usually causes a dramatic rise in temperature. —*v.* blow a chinook: *It didn't chinook again until March.*

Chi·nook (chə nůk′ or shi nůk′) *n., pl.* **-nook** or **-nooks. 1** a member of an Amerindian people who lived along the Columbia River in the NE United States. **2** the Chinookan language of the Chinook and other peoples of the region. **3** Chinook jargon. **4** (*adj.*) of or having to do with the Chinook, their language, or Chinook jargon.

Chi·nook·an (shə nůk′ən) *n.* a family of languages spoken by Amerindian peoples of the N Pacific coast of North America.

chinook arch *Cdn.* an arch of blue sky above the western horizon, often seen just before or during a chinook.

Chinook jargon *Cdn.* a simple trade language of the Pacific coast of North America based on Chinook, with words from

Nootka, English, and French. Chinook jargon was formerly used by the Indian peoples and Europeans in their dealings with each other.

chinook salmon a spring salmon, especially a large one.

chintz (chints) *n.* a firm, plain-woven cotton fabric, usually printed with colorful designs and having a glazed surface. Chintz is used mostly for draperies and slipcovers. [originally pl., < Hind. *chint* < Skt. *citra* variegated]

chintz·y (chint′sē) *adj.* **1** like chintz. **2** *Informal.* showy or gaudy but cheap, trivial, or petty: *a chintzy motel room, a chintzy thing to do.*

chip (chip) *n., v.* **chipped, chip·ping.** —*n.* **1** a small, thin piece cut or broken off. **2** a place in china or stone from which a small piece has been broken: *One of the new plates has a chip.* **3** a small, thin piece of food or candy: *chocolate chips.* **4** potato chip (def. 1): *We ate a whole bag of chips.* **5** french fry: *fish and chips.* **6** *Games.* a round, flat piece of plastic, etc. used as a counter, to represent money, etc. **7** *Electronics.* **a** a tiny wafer of semiconductor material such as silicon used as the basis for an integrated circuit or an electronic component or device such as a transistor. **b** integrated circuit. **8** a strip of wood, palm leaf, or straw used in making baskets or hats. **9** a piece of dried dung, used for fuel in some regions: *buffalo chips.* **10** *Golf.* chip shot.

chip off the old block, *Informal.* a person who is like his parent.

chip on (one's) shoulder, *Informal.* **a** a readiness to quarrel or fight. **b** a permanent sense of grievance.

in the chips, *Slang.* wealthy; affluent.

when the chips are down, when the moment of decision or definite action arrives; in a crisis.

—*v.* **1** cut or break small pieces from wood, stones, dishes, etc.: *He chipped off the old paint.* **2** become chipped: *This china chips easily.* **3** shape by cutting at the surface or edge with an axe or chisel.

chip in, *Informal.* **a** join with others in giving (money or help). **b** put in (a remark) when others are talking.

cash in (one's) chips, **a** change (poker chips) into cash. **b** *Slang.* close or sell a business; retire; **c** *Slang.* die.

[OE *(for)cippian*]

chip·board (chip′bôrd′) *n.* a building material made in large rigid sheets, consisting of wood chips and fibres pressed together, using a synthetic resin as a binding agent.

Chip·e·wy·an (chip′ə wī′ən) *n., pl.* **-an** or **-ans. 1** a member of an Amerindian people living in northern Manitoba and Saskatchewan and the Northwest Territories. The Chipewyans were traditionally a nomadic people who hunted the caribou. **2** the Athapascan language of the Chipewyan. **3** (*adjl.*) of or having to do with the Chipewyans or their language.

chip·munk (chip′mungk) *n.* any of several small North American animals (genera *Eutamias* and *Tamias*) of the squirrel family that live mainly on the ground, having mostly brown fur with black stripes along the back that are separated by pale grey or creamy stripes. Chipmunks are smaller than squirrels and have a less bushy tail. [< obs. Cdn. dial. *chitmunk* < Algonquian; cf. Ojibwa *atchitamon* one who descends trees head first]

chipped beef *Esp.U.S.* dried, smoked beef sliced very thin and usually served hot, with a cream sauce.

Chip·pen·dale (chip′ən dāl′) *adj., n.* —*adj.* of, like, or having to do with a graceful, often richly ornamented style of furniture. —*n.* **1** this style of furniture. **Chinese Chippendale** reflects an Oriental influence. **2** a piece of furniture in this style. [after Thomas *Chippendale* (1718-1779), an English cabinetmaker]

chip·per (chip′ər) *adj. Informal.* lively; cheerful. [origin uncertain; cf. Northern E dial. *kipper* frisky]

Chip·pe·wa (chip′ə wä′ or chip′ə wâ′) *n., pl.* **-wa** or **-was.** Ojibwa.

chipping sparrow a small sparrow (*Spizella passerina*) found throughout North America except for the far North, having a reddish cap and black and white streaks on the side of the head. [< *chip,* imitative of its cry]

chip·py (chip′ē) *n., pl.* **-pies;** *adj.* —*n.* **1** chipping sparrow. **2** chipmunk. **3** *Slang.* **a** a frivolous young girl. **b** a woman of loose morals.

—*adj. Cdn. Slang.* **1** short-tempered; quarrelsome; aggressive: *He was known as a chippy player.* **2** having much rough and short-tempered play: *a chippy hockey game.*

chip shot *Golf.* a short, lofted shot used to get the ball onto the green.

chi·rog·ra·pher (kī rog′rə fər) *n.* a person who writes by hand.

chi·ro·graph·ic (kī′rə graf′ik) *adj.* of chirography.

chi·rog·ra·phy (kī rog′rə fē) *n.* handwriting. [< Gk. *cheir* hand + E *-graphy* writing < Gk. *graphein* write]

Chi·ron (kī′ron) *n. Greek mythology.* a wise and kindly centaur, teacher of many Greek heroes. Chiron was famous for his medical skill.

chi·rop·o·dist (kə rop′ə dist) *n.* a person trained and licensed to practise chiropody.

chi·rop·o·dy (kə rop′ə dē) *n.* the health specialty concerned with the diagnosis and treatment of disorders, injuries, and diseases of the human foot. Increasingly called **podiatry.** [< Gk. *cheir* hand + *pous, podos,* foot; originally, treatment of hands and feet]

chi·ro·prac·tic (kī′rə prak′tik) *n., adj.* —*n.* the treatment of disorders of the bones, muscles, and nerves by manipulation of the bony segments of the body, especially the spine. —*adj.* having to do with the treatment of diseases by manipulating the spine. [< Gk. *cheir* hand + *praktikos* referring to practice (< *prassein* do)]

chi·ro·prac·tor (kī′rə prak′tər) *n.* a person who is qualified to practise chiropractic and whose work it is.

chi·rop·ter (kī rop′tər) *n.* chiropteran.

chi·rop·te·ran (kī rop′tə rən) *n., adj.* —*n.* any mammal of the order Chiroptera, the bats. —*adj.* of, having to do with, or designating the order Chiroptera. [< NL < Gk. *cheir* hand + *pteron* wing]

chi·rop·ter·ous (kī rop′tə rəs) *adj.* chiropteran.

chirp (chėrp) *v., n.* —*v.* **1** make a short, sharp sound such as certain small birds and insects make: *The sparrows and crickets chirped outside the house.* **2** utter with a chirp. **3** greet or urge on by chirping: *He chirped his horses on.* **4** make any similar sound. —*n.* a short, sharp sound such as certain small birds and insects make. [? var. of *chirk* be cheerful, OE *circian* roar] —**chirp′er,** *n.*

chirp·y (chėr′pē) *adj.* **-i·er, -i·est.** *Informal.* **1** disposed to chirp. **2** lively and cheerful; enthusiastic. **chirp′i·ly,** *adv.* —**chirp′i·ness,** *n.*

chirr (chėr) *v., n.* —*v.* make a shrill, trilling sound: *The grasshoppers chirred in the fields.* —*n.* a shrill, trilling sound. Also, **churr.** [imitative]

chir·rup (chėr′əp or chir′əp) *v.* **-rupped** or **-ruped, -rup·ping or -rup·ing;** *n.* —*v.* **1** chirp again and again: *He chirruped to his horse to make it go faster.* **2** utter with chirps or sounds like this. —*n.* the sound of chirruping. [< *chirp*]

chi·rur·geon (kī rėr′jən) *n. Archaic.* surgeon. [ME < OF *cirurgien* < *cirurgie* surgery. See SURGERY.]

chi·rur·ger·y (kī rėr′jər ē) *n. Archaic.* surgery.

A chisel

chis·el (chiz′əl) *n., v.* **-elled** or **-eled, -el·ling** or **-el·ing.** —*n.* a cutting tool with a sharp edge at the end of a strong blade, used to cut or shape wood, stone, or metal. —*v.* **1** cut or shape with a chisel. **2** *Slang.* use unfair practices; cheat; swindle. [ME < OF < VL *cisellum,* var. of *caesellum* < L *caedere* cut]

chis·el·ler or **chis·el·er** (chiz′əl ər or chiz′lər) *n. Slang.* a cheat; swindler.

chi–square test or **chi–square** (kī′skwer′) *n. Statistics.* a test of the validity of a specific frequency distribution, made by matching the results obtained from the actual data with the results expected in theory.

chit¹ (chit) *n.* **1** child. **2** a saucy, forward girl. [related to KITTEN. Cf. dial. *chit* kitten.]

chit² (chit) *n.* **1** a note; memorandum. **2** a signed note or something like it, given for a purchase, a meal, etc. that is to be paid for later. [short for *chitty* < Hind. *chitthi* < Sanskrit *chitra* a spot, mark]

chit–chat (chit′chat′) *n.* **1** friendly, informal talk; chat. **2** gossip. [< *chat*]

chi·tin (kī′tin) *n.* a semi-transparent, horny substance forming the hard outer covering of beetles, lobsters, crabs, etc. [< F *chitine* < Gk. *chiton* tunic]

chi·tin·ous (kī′tə nəs) *adj.* of or like chitin.

chi·ton (kī′tən or kī′ton) *n.* in ancient Greece, a long, loose garment worn next to the skin by both men and women. [< Gk.]

chit·ter·lings (chit′ər lingz) *n.pl.* the small intestines of pigs, cooked as food. [ME; origin uncertain]

chiv·al·ric (shiv′əl rik *or* shə val′rik) *adj.* **1** having to do with chivalry. **2** chivalrous.

chiv·al·rous (shiv′əl rəs) *adj.* **1** having or showing the qualities of an ideal knight; brave, courteous, helpful, generous, and honorable: *a chivalrous action. He was a chivalrous escort.* **2** of or having to do with chivalry in the Middle Ages. —**chiv′al·rous·ly,** *adv.* —**chiv′al·rous·ness,** *n.*

chiv·al·ry (shiv′əl rē) *n.* **1** the qualities of an ideal knight. Chivalry includes bravery, honor, courtesy, respect for women, protection of the weak, generosity, and fairness to enemies. **2** in the Middle Ages, the rules and customs of knights; system of knighthood. **3** knights as a group. **4** gallant warriors or gentlemen. [ME *chivalrie* < OF *chevalerie* horsemanship, knighthood < Med.L *caballerius* horseman < L *caballus* horse]

chiv·a·ree (shiv′ə rē′) See **shivaree.**

chive (chīv) *n.* Usually, **chives,** *pl.* a plant (*Allium schoenoprasum*) closely related to and resembling the onion, but milder in flavor and having a very small bulb. The long, slender, hollow leaves of chives are used to flavor soups, stews, salads, etc. [ME < OF < L *caepa* onion]

chiv·vy *or* **chiv·y** (chiv′ē) *v.* pursue or nag; harass: *He was chivvied into taking up the challenge.*

Ch.J. Chief Justice.

chla·mys (klā′mis *or* klam′is) *n.* a short cloak worn by men in ancient Greece. [< L < Gk.]

chlo·ral (klôr′əl) *n.* a colorless, oily, liquid compound that is very irritating to the lungs, used in making DDT and chloral hydrate. *Formula:* CCl_3CHO **2** chloral hydrate. [< *chlor*ine + *alcohol*]

chloral hydrate a white, crystalline drug used to quiet nervousness and induce sleep. *Formula:* $CCl_3CH(OH)_2$

chlo·rate (klôr′āt *or* klôr′it) *n.* a salt of chloric acid.

chlo·ric (klôr′ik) *adj.* of or containing chlorine. **Chloric acid,** $HClO_3$, occurs as a colorless solution or in the form of chlorates.

chlo·ride (klôr′īd-) *n.* any of a group of chemical compounds consisting of chlorine and another element or radical, especially a salt of hydrochloric acid.

chloride of lime a white powder used for bleaching and disinfecting, made by treating slaked lime with chlorine. *Formula:* $CaOCl_2$

chlo·rin·ate (klôr′ə nāt′) *v.* **-at·ed, -at·ing. 1** combine or treat with chlorine: *Paper pulp is chlorinated to bleach it.* **2** disinfect with chlorine. The water in the city reservoirs is chlorinated.

chlo·rin·a·tion (klôr′ə nā′shən) *n.* chlorinating or being chlorinated.

chlo·rine (klôr′ēn *or* klôr ēn′) *n.* a poisonous, greenish-yellow, chemical element that is a gas at normal temperatures, used in making drugs, dyes, explosives, and plastics, and in bleaching and disinfecting. Chlorine has a sharp, unpleasant smell and is very irritating to the nose, throat, and lungs. *Symbol:* Cl; *at.no.* 17; *at.wt.* 35.453. [< Gk. *chlōros* green]

chlo·rite (klôr′īt) *n.* a salt of chlorous acid.

chlo·ro·form (klôr′ə fôrm′) *n., v.* —*n.* a colorless liquid with a sweetish smell, used as an anesthetic and to dissolve rubber, resin, wax, and many other substances. *Formula:* $CHCl_3$ —*v.* **1** make (a person or animal) unable to feel pain by giving chloroform. **2** kill with chloroform. [< *chloro-* (< *chlorine*) + *form*yl]

chlo·ro·my·ce·tin (klôr′ə mī′sə tin) *n. Trademark.* an antibiotic drug, used in treating bacterial and viral diseases, including typhoid fever and certain types of pneumonia. [< *chloro-* green (< Gk. *chlōros*) + Gk. *mykēs, -ētos* fungus]

chlo·ro·phyl *or* **chlo·ro·phyll** (klôr′ə fil′) *n.* **1** *Botany.* the green coloring matter of plants produced only in the presence of sunlight and where iron is available in the plant cell. It converts carbon dioxide and water into carbohydrates, such as starch and sugar. **2** a dark-green, waxy plant extract, containing chlorophyl, that is used as a dye and for its supposed deodorizing qualities. [< F *chlorophylle* < Gk. *chlōros* pale green + *phyllon* leaf]

chlo·ro·plast (klôr′ə plast′) *n. Botany.* the part of a plant cell that contains chlorophyl. [< Gk. *chlōros* pale green + *plastos* formed]

chlo·ro·prene (klôr′ə prēn′) *n.* a colorless liquid used in making synthetic rubber. *Formula:* C_4H_5Cl [< Gk. *chlōros* green + *iso*prene]

chlo·ro·quine (klôr′ə kwīn′) *n.* a medicine used against malaria.

chlo·ro·sis (klə rō′sis) *n.* **1** *Botany.* a blanching or yellowing of plants, usually resulting from a lack of iron and other minerals in the soil. **2** an iron-deficiency anemia affecting young girls and characterized by a greenish pallor, hysteria, etc. [< NL *chlorosis* < Gk. *chlōros* pale green + *-osis*]

chlo·rous (klôr′əs) *adj.* of or containing trivalent chlorine.

hat, āge, fär; let, ēqual, tėrm; it, īce
hot, ōpen, ôrder; oil, out; cup, pút, rüle,
above, takən, pencəl, lemən, circəs

ch, child; ng, long; sh, ship
th, thin; ᴛʜ, then; zh, measure

chm. *or* **chmn.** chairman.

Ch.M. Master of Surgery (for L *Chirurgiae Magister*).

chock (chok) *n., v., adv.* —*n.* **1** a block; wedge. A chock can be put under a barrel or wheel to keep it from rolling. A boat on a ship's deck is put on chocks. **2** on a ship or boat, a heavy piece of metal or wood with two arms curving inward for a rope to pass through. See **rowboat** for picture. —*v.* **1** provide or fasten with chocks. **2** put (a boat) on chocks. —*adv.* as close or as tight as can be: *chock up against the wall.* [apparently < ONF *choque* log]
☛ *Hom.* **chalk.**

chock-a-block (chok′ə blok′) *adj.* **1** with the blocks drawn close together. **2** jammed together; crowded; packed.

chock-full (chok′fùl′) *adj.* as full as can be; completely full. Also, **chuck-full.**

choc·o·late (chok′lit *or* chok′ə lit) *n., adj.* —*n.* **1** a dark-brown, bitter-tasting substance, the finely-ground roasted seeds of the cacao tree, used as a food or flavoring. The basic form of chocolate is a liquid, called **chocolate liquor,** that is produced when the seeds are ground. **2** a hot or cold drink made of chocolate or cocoa, milk or water, and sugar. **3** candy made of chocolate and sugar. **4** dark brown.
—*adj.* **1** made of or flavored with chocolate: *chocolate cake.* **2** dark brown. [< Sp. < Aztec *chocolatl*]

chocolate bar a confection consisting of an oblong piece or bar of chocolate or a mixture of things such as nuts, sugar, syrup, marshmallow, flavoring, etc. coated with chocolate.

choice (chois) *n., adj.* **choic·er, choic·est.** —*n.* **1** choosing; selection: *Leave the choice of background music to him.* **2** the power or chance to choose: *Her parents have given her a choice between tennis and golf lessons. He had no choice but to accept their statement.* **3** the person or thing chosen: *My choice was cabbage rolls.* **4** an alternative. **5** a quantity and variety to choose from: *There is a wide choice of vegetables in the market.* **6** best; cream: *a team made up of the choice of the league.*
—*adj.* **1** of fine quality; excellent; superior: *a choice steak.* **2** carefully chosen: *choice arguments.* [ME *chois* < OF *choisir* < Gmc.] —**choice′ly,** *adv.* —**choice·ness,** *n.*
☛ *Syn. n.* **2. Choice, alternative, preference** = the opportunity to choose or the thing to be chosen. **Choice,** the general and most informal word, emphasizes freedom in choosing, both in the way one chooses and in the number of possibilities from which to choose: *Take your choice of the puppies.* **Alternative** emphasizes limitation of the possibilities, usually to two but sometimes several, between which one must choose: *You have the alternative of sheltering from the rain or getting drenched.* **Preference** emphasizes choosing according to one's own liking: *Which is your preference?* —*adj.* **1.** See note at **fine.**

choir (kwīr) *n., v.* —*n.* **1** an organized group of singers who sing in church services. **2** the part of a church set aside for such a group. **3** any organized group of singers: *the university choir.* **4** instruments of the same class in an orchestra: *the string choir, a brass choir.* **5** in medieval Christian theology, any of the nine orders of angels. —*v. Poetic.* sing together. [ME *quer* < OF *cuer* < L *chorus.* Doublet of CHORUS.]

choir·boy (kwīr′boi′) a boy who sings in a church choir.

choir·mas·ter (kwīr′mas′tər) *n.* the director or conductor of a choir.

choke (chōk) *v.* **choked, chok·ing;** *n.* —*v.* **1** keep from breathing by squeezing or blocking up the windpipe: *The smoke almost choked the firemen.* **2** be unable to breathe: *He choked when some food stuck in his throat.* **3** check or extinguish by cutting off the supply of air: *to choke a fire.* **4** control; hold back; suppress (*used with* **down** *or* **back**): *He choked back his anger and said nothing.* **5** fill up or block; clog (*often used with* **up**): *a street choked with traffic. Sand is choking the river.* **6** in an internal-combustion engine, reduce or close the air intake in order to make a richer fuel mixture, especially in starting. **7** retard or stop the development or growth of: *The flowers had become choked by weeds.* **8** put an end to; stop (*used with* **off**): *to choke off rebellion. The rock slide choked off our water supply.*
choke up, fill with emotion; be or cause to be on the verge of tears: *He choked up from stage fright. We were all choked up when the hero in the movie died.*
—*n.* **1** the act of choking: *He gave a slight choke but then got his breath.* **2** the sound of choking: *We heard a choke behind us.* **3** something that chokes, such as a valve that cuts off the supply of air to an internal-combustion engine. **4** a narrow or constricted part

of a tube, etc. as in a chokebore. [OE *cēocian, var. of ācēocian]

choke·bore (chōk′bôr′) n. **1** a shotgun bore that narrows toward the muzzle in order to keep the shot from scattering too widely. **2** a shotgun with such a bore.

choke·cher·ry (chōk′cher′ē) n., pl. **-ries. 1** a North American shrub or small tree (Prunus virginiana) of the rose family having small, black or dark-red, edible, astringent fruit. **2** the fruit of this tree.

choke coil Electricity. a coil of wire around a core of iron or air, used to control alternating currents in an electric circuit.

choke·damp (chōk′damp′) n. a heavy, suffocating gas, mainly carbon dioxide and nitrogen, that gathers in mines, old wells, etc.

chok·er (chōk′ər) n. **1** a necklace that fits closely around the neck: a pearl choker. **2** a high, stiff, close-fitting collar, neckband, etc. **3** Cdn. Logging. a cable and hook used in hauling and loading logs. **4** any person or thing that chokes.

chol·er (kol′ər) n. **1** an irritable disposition; anger. **2** yellow bile, the one of the four humors of ancient physiology believed to cause irritability. **3** bilious disorder. [ME colre < OF < L < Gk. cholera cholera, apparently < cholē bile]
☛ Hom. **collar.**

chol·er·a (kol′ər ə) n. an acute, infectious disease of the stomach and intestines caused by a bacterium (Vibrio comma), characterized by vomiting, cramps, and diarrhea. Cholera is often fatal if untreated. [< L < Gk. See CHOLER.]

cholera mor·bus (môr′bəs) an old term applied to any inflammation of the intestines accompanied by diarrhea, fever, and pain. [< L cholera morbus cholera disease]

chol·er·ic (kol′ər ik) adj. easily made angry; irritable.

cho·les·ter·ol (kə les′tər ol′ or kə les′tər ōl′) n. a crystalline fatty alcohol produced by all vertebrate animals and found in the highest concentration in the brain, nerves and spinal cord. Cholesterol is used by the body to make acids which aid digestion and also to make some hormones. The human body produces most of its own cholesterol, but some enters the body in food and is not always properly absorbed. Formula: $C_{27}H_{45}OH$ [< Gk. cholē bile + stereos solid]

chomp (chomp) v. champ¹.

choose (chüz) v. **chose, cho·sen, choos·ing. 1** pick out; select from a number: He chose a book from the library. **2** prefer and decide on: I would never choose blue. **3** think fit; want and decide on: She did not choose to go. He chose to run for election. **4** make a choice; decide: You must choose.
cannot choose but, cannot take an alternative; must: Since he had received both first prizes, he could not choose but be satisfied. [OE cēosan] —**choos′er,** n.

choos·y (chüz′ē) adj. **choos·i·er, choos·i·est.** Informal. particular or fussy in one's preferences; fastidious; selective. —**choos′i·ness,** n.

chop¹ (chop) v. **chopped, chop·ping;** n. —v. **1** cut by hitting with something sharp: to chop wood with an axe. **2** cut into small pieces: to chop up cabbage. **3** make quick, sharp movements; jerk. **4** make by cutting: The explorer chopped his way through the bushes. **5** Tennis, cricket, etc. slice or cut at (a ball); hit with a chop stroke. —n. **1** a cutting stroke or blow. **2** a slice of lamb, pork, veal, etc. on a piece of rib, loin, or shoulder. **3** a short, irregular, broken motion of waves. **4** an area of rough or choppy water. [ME choppe(n)]
☛ Syn. v. **1.** See note at **cut.**

chop² (chop) n. **1** the jaw. **2** chops, pl. the cheeks or jaws, especially the fleshy covering of an animal's jaws: The cat is licking the milk off her chops.
lick (one's) chops, Slang. relish the prospect of something good to come: licking their chops over the prospect of a fat fee. [< chop¹]

chop³ (chop) v. **chopped, chop·ping.** change suddenly; shift quickly: The wind chopped around from west to north.
chop and change, change one's tactics or ways; make frequent changes; change about. [var. of obs. chap buy and sell, exchange. Related to CHEAP.]

chop·fall·en (chop′fol′ən or -fôl′ən) adj. chapfallen.

chop·house (chop′hous′) n. a restaurant that makes a specialty of serving chops, steaks, etc.

cho·pine (chō pēn′ or chop′in) n. a woman's shoe with a very thick sole, worn especially in the 17th century. [< Sp. chapin < chapa piece of leather]

chop·per (chop′ər) n., v. —n. **1** a person who chops. **2** a tool or machine for chopping, such as a short-handled axe or a heavy knife. **3** Informal. helicopter. **4** choppers, pl. Slang. teeth.

—v. Informal. fly or transport by helicopter: Workmen were choppered out to the rig.

chop·py¹ (chop′ē) adj. **-pi·er, -pi·est. 1** making quick, sharp movements; jerky: a choppy ride. **2** moving in short, irregular, broken waves: The lake is choppy today. [< chop¹] —**chop′pi·ness,** n.

chop·py² (chop′ē) adj. **-pi·er, -pi·est.** changing suddenly; shifting quickly. [< chop³]

Chopsticks

chop·stick (chop′stik′) n. one of a pair of small, shaped sticks used especially by the Chinese, Japanese, and Koreans to raise food to the mouth. [< Chinese Pidgin English chop quick + E stick¹]

chop su·ey (chop′sü′ē) a Chinese-American dish consisting of small pieces of meat with vegetables such as bean sprouts, mushrooms, and greens all cooked together in their own juices. Chop suey is usually served with rice. [alteration of Chinese tsa-sui odds and ends]

cho·ral (adj. kô′rəl; n. ko ral′ or ko räl′) adj., n. —adj. **1** of or having to do with a choir or chorus: She belongs to a choral group. **2** sung or designed to be sung by a choir or chorus: a choral arrangement of a song. —n. See **chorale.**
☛ Hom. **coral.**

cho·rale (ko ral′ or ko räl′) n. a slow, stately hymn tune, originally sung in unison, especially in the Lutheran church. [< G Choralgesang]

choral speaking the recitation of poetry, etc. by a group of people together.

chord¹ (kôrd) n. Music. a combination of three or more notes sounded together in harmony. [var. of cord, var. of accord, n.]
☛ Hom. **cord.**

chord² (kôrd) n. **1** Geometry. a straight line or segment between two points on a curve. **2** Anatomy. Archaic. See cord (def. 4). **3** Archaic or poetic. a string of a harp, etc. **4** a feeling, especially an emotional response: to touch a sympathetic chord. **5** Engineering. a main horizontal part of a truss. **6** Aeronautics. an imaginary straight line between the leading and trailing edges of an airfoil. [< L < Gk. chordē string made of gut; string of a lyre. Doublet of CORD.]
☛ Hom. **cord.**

chord·al (kôr′dəl) adj. Music. **1** of or having to do with the strings of an instrument. **2** of or having to do with chords.

chor·date (kôr′dāt) n., adj. —n. any of a phylum (Chordata) of animals that includes vertebrate and all other animals that have an internal skeleton (a notochord in primitive forms) and a central nervous system located along the back. —adj. of or having to do with this group. [< NL chordata < L chorda chord. See CHORD².]

chore (chôr) n. **1** an odd job; minor task, especially one that must be done daily: Feeding the chickens was John's chore on the farm. **2** a task that is disagreeable or irritating: He found the work quite a chore. [OE cyrr, var. of cierr, cerr turn, business. Cf. CHAR².]

cho·re·a (kô rē′ə) n. a nervous disorder characterized by involuntary twitching of the muscles; St. Vitus's dance. [< NL < Gk. choreia dance]

chore-boy (chôr′boi′) n. a person who does odd jobs or routine tasks around a farm, ranch, tourist resort, lumber camp, etc.

cho·re·o·graph (kôr′ē ə graf′) v. arrange or compose choreography for (a ballet, etc.).

cho·re·og·ra·pher (kôr′ē og′rə fər) n. a creator or designer of ballets and other stage dances.

cho·re·o·graph·ic (kôr′ē ə graf′ik) adj. **1** of or having to do with the art of dancing. **2** of or having to do with choreography.

cho·re·o·graph·i·cal·ly (kôr′ē ə graf′ə klē) adv. **1** in a choreographic manner. **2** in terms of choreography.

cho·re·og·ra·phy (kôr′ē og′rə fē) n. **1** the art of creating, designing, and arranging dances, such as ballet, for performance on stage. **2** the steps and sequences of such a dance. **3** notation used for representing dance movements. **4** the art of stage dancing. [< Gk. choreia dance + E -graphy writing < Gk. graphein write]

cho·ric (kô′rik) adj. of, having to do with, or for a chorus, especially one in an ancient Greek play.

chor·is·ter (kôr′əs tər) n. **1** a singer in a choir, especially a choirboy. **2** the leader of a choir. [< Med.L chorista chorister < L chorus. See CHORUS.]

cho·roid (kô′roid) n., adj. —n. the vascular membrane of the

eyeball between the retina and the sclera. See **eye** for picture. —*adj.* of or designating this membrane. [< Gk. *choroeidēs* < *chorion* membrane + *eidos* resemblance]

chor·tle (chôr′təl) *v.* **-tled, -tling;** *n.* chuckle and snort at the same time: *"He chortled in his joy."* —*n.* a combined chuckle and snort. [blend of *chuckle* and *snort;* coined by Lewis Carroll] —**chor′tler,** *n.*

cho·rus (kô′rəs) *n., pl.* **-rus·es;** *v.* **-rused, -rus·ing.** —*n.* **1** a group of singers who sing together, such as a choir. **2** a musical composition to be sung by a large number of singers in several harmonizing voice parts: *The opera ends in a splendid chorus.* **3** the part of a song that is repeated after each stanza; refrain. **4** a similar or identical utterance by many at the same time: *My question was answered by a chorus of No's.* **5** a group of singers and dancers: *He was in the chorus of our school musical.* **6** *Drama.* **a** an actor or group of actors who comment on the action of a play. **b** the part of a play performed by the chorus.
in chorus, all together at the same time.
—*v.* sing or speak all at the same time: *The birds were chorusing around me.* [< L < Gk. *choros* dance, band of dancers. Doublet of CHOIR.]

chose (chōz) *v.* pt. and an archaic pp. of **choose:** *Selma chose a red dress for the Christmas party.*

cho·sen (chō′zən) *v., adj.* —*v.* a pp. of **choose.** —*adj.* picked out; selected from a group: *the chosen book.*

Chosen People, The in the Bible, the Israelites.

chough (chuf) *n.* **1** either of two Old World birds (genus *Pyrrhocorax*) related to and resembling the crows, having glossy, blue-black plumage, a down-curved bill, and red legs. The common chough (*P. pyrrhocorax*) has a red bill; the alpine chough (*P. graculus*) has a yellow bill. **2** a similar but unrelated bird (*Corcorax melanorhamphus*) of Australia, having white wing patches and a black bill. [ME *choughe*]

chow (chou) *n.* **1** chow chow. **2** *Slang.* **a** food. **b** the time when food is served. [short for *chow-chow*]

chow chow or **Chow Chow** a breed of medium-sized dog having a curled tail, large head, compact body, and a thick, usually brown or black coat. [< Chinese dial.]

chow-chow (chou′chou′) *n.* **1** a Chinese mixed preserve. **2** any mixed pickles chopped up. [< Chinese Pidgin English]

chow·der (chou′dər) *n.* a thick soup or stew, often made of clams or fish with potatoes, onions, etc. in a milk base. [apparently < F *chaudière* pot, ult. < L *calidus* hot]

chow mein (chou′mān′) a Chinese-American dish consisting of a thickened stew of onions, celery, meat, etc. served over fried noodles. [< Chinese *ch'ao mien* fried flour]

Chr. Christ; Christian.

chres·tom·a·thy (kres tom′ə thē) *n., pl.* **-thies. 1** a collection of literary passages chosen to help in the learning of a language. **2** a selection of passages from the works of one author. [< Gk. *chrēstomatheia* < *chrēstos* useful + *matheia* learning]

chrism (kriz′əm) *n.* **1** the consecrated oil, used by some churches in baptism and other sacred rites. **2** a sacramental anointing; the ceremony of confirmation, especially as practised in the Greek church. [OE *crisma* < L *chrisma* < Gk. *chrisma* < *chriein* anoint]

chris·mal (kriz′məl) *adj.* having to do with chrism.

Christ (krīst) *n.* **1** the Messiah; the deliverer foretold by the ancient Jewish prophets. **2** Jesus of Nazareth, regarded by Christians as the incarnate Son of God and the true Messiah. [OE *Crīst* < L *Christus* < Gk. *Christos* one who is anointed, a translation of Hebrew *māshīax*]

Chris·ta·del·phi·an (kris′tə del′fē ən) *n.* a member of a religious sect founded in the United States about 1850 by Dr. John Thomas. This sect rejects the doctrine of the Trinity and holds that only the righteous attain immortality. [< L < Gk. *Christadelphos* brother of Christ < Gk. *Christos* Christ + *adelphos* brother + E *-ian*]

chris·ten (kris′ən) *v.* **1** admit to a Christian church by baptism; baptize. **2** give a name to (someone) at baptism. **3** give a name to: *The new ship was christened before it was launched.* **4** *Informal.* make the first use of. [OE *cristnian* make Christian < *cristen* Christian < LL < LGk. *christianos* Christian; belonging to Christ]

Chris·ten·dom (kris′ən dəm) *n.* **1** Christian countries; the Christian part of the world. **2** all Christians. [OE *cristendōm* < *cristen* Christian + *-dōm* state < *dōm* statute]

chris·ten·ing (kris′ən ing *or* kris′ning) *n.* the act or ceremony of baptizing and naming; baptism.

Chris·tian (kris′chən) *n., adj.* —*n.* **1** one who believes in Jesus as the Christ and follows his teachings; a believer in Christianity. **2** *Informal.* a decent person.
—*adj.* **1** of or having to do with Jesus Christ, his teachings, or Christianity: *the Christian religion, Christian ethics.* **2** being a

hat, āge, fär; let, ēqual, tèrm; it, īce
hot, ōpen, ôrder; oil, out; cup, pút, rüle,
əbove, takən, pencəl, lemən, circəs

ch, child; ng, long; sh, ship
th, thin; ᴛʜ, then; zh, measure

Christian or made up of Christians: *Christian countries, a Christian businessman.* **3** showing kindness, goodness, or humility: *a Christian act.* —**Chris′tian·like′,** *adj.* —**Chris′tian·ly,** *adj., adv.*

Christian Era the time since the birth of Christ. The label A.D. is used for dates in this era; B.C. for dates before it.

Chris·ti·an·i·ty (kris′chē an′ə tē) *n., pl.* **-ties. 1** a religion that grew out of Judaism and that separated itself from Judaism through its acceptance of Jesus of Nazareth as the Son of God and as the Messiah of Hebrew prophecy. The sacred Scriptures of Christianity, the Bible, comprise the Hebrew Bible (Old Testament) and the New Testament. **2** the Christian beliefs, spirit, or character. **3** all Christians; Christendom.

Chris·tian·ize (kris′chən īz′) *v.* **-ized, -iz·ing.** make Christian; convert to Christianity. —**Chris′tian·i·za′tion,** *n.* —**Chris′tian·iz′er.** *n.*

Christian name given name. It is so called from the traditional practice, in most Christian churches, of formally giving the name to an infant at christening.

Christian Science a Christian religion based on the belief that physical healing is possible through spiritual healing. Evil, pain, and disease are believed to be caused by a sinful mind, and they can be overcome through prayer and by following the teachings of Jesus. Christian Science was founded in the United States in the nineteenth century.

Christian Scientist a believer in Christian Science.

Christ·like (krīst′līk′) *adj.* like Jesus Christ; showing the spirit of Jesus Christ. —**Christ′like′ness,** *n.*

Christ·ly (krīst′lē) *adj.* of Christ; Christlike. —**Christ′li·ness,** *n.*

Christ·mas (kris′məs) *n.* **1** the yearly Christian celebration commemorating the birth of Christ; in most Christian churches, December 25. **2** the season of Christmas. [OE *Cristes mæsse* Christ's Mass]

Christmas Day December 25.

Christmas Eve December 24.

Christ·mas·tide (kris′məs tīd′) *n.* Christmastime. [< *Christmas* + *tide* time]

Christ·mas·time (kris′məs tīm′) *n.* the Christmas season, especially from Christmas Eve to New Year's Day, or, more traditionally, to Epiphany (January 6).

Christmas tree 1 an evergreen tree, such as a spruce or pine, or an imitation of one, hung with decorations at Christmastime. **2** *Cdn.* a party held at Christmastime for entertaining children and presenting gifts to them, usually sponsored by a church, school, or other organization.

chro·mate (krō′māt) *n.* a salt of chromic acid.

chro·mat·ic (krō mat′ik) *adj.* **1** of or having to do with color or colors. **2** *Music.* **a** of or involving the use of sharpened or flattened notes that are foreign to the diatonic key in which they occur: *chromatic chords, chromatic harmony.* **b** of, having to do with, or based on the chromatic scale. **c** designating an instrument capable of producing all the tones of the chromatic scale. [< L *chromaticus* < Gk. *chrōmatikos* < *chrōma, -atos* color] —**chro·mat′i·cal·ly,** *adv.*

chromatics *n.* (*used with a singular verb*). the scientific study of colors with reference to hue and intensity or brightness.

chromatic scale *Music.* a scale in which the octave is divided into 12 semitones.

chro·ma·tid (krō′mə tid) *n.* either of the two portions of a chromosome that has doubled in preparation for cell division, held together at the middle by a centromere. During cell division, the centromere of each doubled chromosome divides and the chromatids separate to become two complete chromosomes that are exactly the same as the parent chromosome.

chro·ma·tin (krō′mə tin) *n.* the substance in the nucleus of a plant or animal cell in a resting stage, made up of a spongy network of chromosomes. See **cell** for picture. [< Gk. *chrōma, chrōmatos* color]

chro·mat·o·gram (krō mat′ə gram′) *n.* the pattern formed on an adsorbent by the components of a mixture separated by chromatography.

chro·mat·o·graph (krō mat′ə graf′) *v., n.* —*v.* separate (the

component compounds of a mixture by chromatography. —*n.* a system for separating the component compounds of a mixture by chromatography.

chro·mat·o·graph·ic (krō mat′ə graf′ik) *adj.* of or having to do with chromatography. —**chro·mat′o·graph′i·cal·ly,** *adv.*

chro·ma·tog·ra·phy (krō′mə tog′rə fē) *n.* the separation of a mixture of liquids or gases for the purpose of analysis by passing it through an adsorbent, such as a column of clay. The different components of the mixture are adsorbed at different rates into different sections of the adsorbent.

chrome (krōm) *n., v.* —*n.* **1** chromium. **2** any of various pigments or dyes containing chromium. **3** chrome steel. —*v.* cover or plate with chrome. [< F < Gk. *chrōma* color]

chrome steel an extremely hard, strong steel containing chromium.

chrome yellow a yellow coloring matter made from lead chromate.

chro·mic (krō′mik) *adj.* of or containing chromium.

chro·mite (krō′mīt) *n.* **1** a mineral containing iron and chromium. *Formula*: FeCr$_2$O$_4$ **2** a salt of chromium.

chro·mi·um (krō′mē əm) *n.* a shiny, hard, brittle metallic element that does not rust or become dull easily; chrome. Chromium is used in alloys and in plating. *Symbol*: Cr; *at.no.* 24; *at.wt.* 51.996. [< Gk. *chrōma* color]

chromium steel chrome steel.

chro·mo (krō′mō) *n., pl.* **-mos.** a colored picture printed from a series of stones or plates. [< *chromo*lithograph < Gk. *chrōma* color + E *lithograph*]

chro·mo·some (krō′mə sōm′) *n.* any of the long, thin strands, or fibres, found in the nucleus of every plant and animal cell, composed of protein and DNA, which carry the coded information for heredity in units called genes. During cell division, the chromosomes form into pairs of short, fat rods, a characteristic number for each species. [< G *Chromosom* < Gk. *chrōma* color + *sōma* body]

chro·mo·sphere (krō′mə sfēr′) *n.* **1** a scarlet layer of gas around the sun, forming the lower part of the sun's atmosphere, below the corona. The chromosphere consists mainly of hydrogen. **2** a similar layer around a star. [< Gk. *chrōma* color + E *sphere*]

chron– *combining form.* the form of *chrono–* before vowels, as in *chronic.*

chron. **1** chronological. **2** chronology.

chron·ic (kron′ik) *adj.* **1** of a disease, lasting a long time: *The doctor told him rheumatism was a chronic disease.* **2** constant; habitual: *a chronic liar, a chronic smoker.* [< L *chronicus* < Gk. *chronikos* < *chronos* time]

chron·i·cal·ly (kron′ik lē) *adv.* in a chronic manner; always.

chron·i·cle (kron′ə kəl) *n., v.* **-cled, -cling.** —*n.* **1** a record of happenings in the order in which they happened. **2** a narrative; account. —*v.* record in a chronicle; write the history of; tell the story of. [ME < AF var. of OF *cronique* < L < Gk. *chronika* annals, neut. pl. of *chronikos*. See CHRONIC.]

chron·i·cler (kron′ə klər) *n.* the writer of a chronicle; a recorder of events; historian.

chrono– *combining form.* time: *chronometer = an instrument that measures time.* Also, before vowels, *chron-.* [< Gk. *chronos* time]

chron·o·graph (kron′ə graf) *n.* an instrument that measures very short intervals of time accurately; stop watch. [< Gk. *chronos* time + E *-graph*]

chro·nol·o·ger (krə nol′ə jər) *n.* chronologist.

chron·o·log·ic (kron′ə loj′ik) *adj.* chronological.

chron·o·log·i·cal (kron′ə loj′ə kəl) *adj.* arranged in the order in which the events happened: *In telling a story, a person usually arranges the events in chronological order.* —**chron′o·log′i·cal·ly,** *adv.*

chro·nol·o·gist (krə nol′ə jist) *n.* a person who investigates the exact dates of events and the order in which they happened.

chro·nol·o·gy (krə nol′ə jē) *n., pl.* **-gies. 1** an arrangement of time in periods; giving the exact dates of events arranged in the order in which they happened. **2** a table or list giving the exact dates of events arranged in the order in which they happened. [< Gk. *chronos* time + E *-logy*]

chro·nom·e·ter (krə nom′ə tər) *n.* a clock or watch that measures time very accurately, especially a *marine chronometer*, used to provide the exact time for observation of celestial bodies to determine the position of a ship at sea. [< Gk. *chronos* time + E *-meter*]

chron·o·scope (kron′ə skōp′) *n.* an instrument for measuring very small intervals of time, especially by visual means such as a pendulum or a falling rod. [< Gk. *chronos* time + E *-scope* instrument of viewing (< Gk. *skopein* look at)]

chrys·a·lid (kris′ə lid) *n., adj.* —*n.* chrysalis. —*adj.* of a chrysalis.

chrys·a·lis (kris′ə lis) *n.* **chrys·a·lis·es, chry·sal·i·des** (krə sal′ə dēz′). **1** the resting stage, or pupa, of a butterfly, during which it develops into a winged adult. **2** the hard outer covering of the butterfly during this stage. When the transformation has been completed, the chrysalis splits and the adult butterfly emerges. **3** a stage of development or change. [< L < Gk. *chrysallis* golden sheath < *chrysos* gold]

chry·san·the·mum (krə san′thə məm) *n.* **1** any of various plants (genus *Chrysanthemum*) of the composite family, some of which are widely cultivated for their large, showy, usually double flowers that bloom in late summer or autumn. **2** the flower of any of these plants: *Chrysanthemums are usually yellow, white, bronze, red, or rose.* [< L < Gk. *chrysanthemon* < *chrysos* gold + *anthemon* flower]

chrys·o·ber·yl (kris′ə ber′əl) *n.* **1** a yellow or pale-green semiprecious stone. **2** a piece of this stone, or a gem made from it. [< L < Gk. *chrysoberyllos* < *chrysos* gold + *beryllos* beryl]

chrys·o·lite (kris′ə līt′) *n.* **1** a green or yellow silicate of magnesium and iron, a semiprecious stone. **2** a piece of this stone, or a gem made from it. [< L < Gk. *chrysolithos* < *chrysos* gold + *lithos* stone]

chrys·o·prase (kris′ə prāz′) *n.* **1** a light-green kind of chalcedony, a semiprecious stone. **2** a piece of this stone, or a gem made from it. [< L < Gk. *chrysoprasos* < *chrysos* gold + *prason* leek]

chrys·o·tile (kris′ə tīl′) *n.* a green, grey, or white mineral occurring in the form of silky fibres; a variety of serpentine that constitutes commercial asbestos.

chub (chub) *n., pl.* **chub** or **chubs. 1** any of various freshwater game fishes of the cyprinid, or minnow, family. The lake chub (*Couesius plumbeus*) is found throughout Canada and in parts of the N United States. *Leuciscus cephalus* is a common European chub. **2** any of several North American whitefishes. [ME *chubbe*; origin unknown]

chub·by (chub′ē) *adj.* **-bi·er, -bi·est.** round and plump: *chubby cheeks.* —**chub′bi·ness,** *n.*

chuck[1] *v., n.* —*v.* **1** pat; tap; tap, especially under the chin. **2** *Informal.* throw: *She chucked the apple core into the garbage.* **3** *Informal.* give up or finish with: *He's chucked his job.* —*n.* **1** a tap; slight blow under the chin. **2** a toss [probably imitative]

chuck[2] (chuk) *n.* **1** a device for holding a tool or piece of work in a machine. **2** a cut of beef between the neck and the shoulder. See **beef** for picture. [var. of *chock*]

chuck[3] (chuk) *n. Cdn.* on the west coast, a large body of water, formerly especially a river, but now usually the ocean. [< Chinook jargon]

chuck–full (chuk′fūl′) *adj.* chock-full.

chuck·le (chuk′əl) *v.* **chuck·led, chuck·ling;** *n.* —*v.* laugh quietly, as when mildly amused: *He chuckled as he watched the antics of the puppy.* —*n.* a soft, quiet laugh. [< *chuck* cluck, laugh; imitative] —**chuck′ler,** *n.*

chuck·le·head (chuk′əl hed′) *n. Informal.* **1** a thick or large head. **2** a stupid person. —**chuck′le·head′ed,** *adj.* —**chuck′le·head′ed·ness,** *n.*

chuck race a chuckwagon race.

chuck·wag·on (chuk′wag′ən) *n.* in the western parts of Canada and the United States, a wagon that carries food and cooking equipment for cowboys, harvest hands, etc.

chuckwagon race *Cdn.* a race between chuckwagons drawn by horses, a thrilling and highly popular event at rodeos and stampedes in western Canada.

chuff (chuf) *n. or v.* chug. [imitative]

chug (chug) *n., v.* **chugged, chug·ging.** —*n.* a short, loud, explosive sound: *the chug of an engine.* —*v.* **1** make short, loud, explosive sounds. **2** *Informal.* go or move with short, loud, explosive sounds: *The engine chugged along.* [imitative]

chu·kar (chə kär′) *n.* a partridge (*Alectoris graeca*) native to SE Europe and Asia but introduced to many other countries as a game bird, having red legs and bill and mainly brown plumage barred with black. [< Hind. *chakor* < Skt. *chakora*]

chuk·ker or **chuk·kar** (chuk′ər) *n.* in polo, one of the periods of play, lasting about eight minutes. [< Hind. *chakar*]

chum[1] (chum) *n., v.* **chummed, chum·ming.** *Informal.* —*n.* a close friend. —*v.* be close friends: *Tom and Bill have chummed for years.* [? shortened form of *chamber mate, chamber fellow*]

chum² (chum) *n., v.* —*n.* bait for fish, especially chopped fish scattered on the water to attract fish. —*v.* scatter chum to attract fish. [origin unknown]

chum³ (chum) *n. Cdn.* a Pacific salmon (*Oncorhynchus keta*) found especially along the coasts of British Columbia and Alaska, metallic blue and silver in color and having pale pink flesh. [< Chinook jargon *tzum* spotted]

chum·my (chum'ē) *adj.* **-mi·er, -mi·est.** *Informal.* like a chum; very friendly; intimate. —**chum'mi·ly,** *adv.* —**chum'mi·ness,** *n.*

chump (chump) *n.* **1** *Informal.* a foolish or stupid person; blockhead. **2** a short, thick block of wood. **3** a thick, blunt end. **4** *Slang.* the head.
off one's chump, *Slang.* off one's head; out of one's senses. [origin uncertain]

chunk (chungk) *n. Informal.* **1** a thick piece or lump: *a chunk of earth.* **2** a considerable amount or part: *The preparation took quite a chunk out of the day.* [var. of *chuck²*]

chunk·y (chungk'ē) *adj.* **chunk·i·er, chunk·i·est.** *Informal.* **1** like a chunk; short and thick. **2** stocky. **3** containing chunks, as of meat or potatoes: *chunky soup.* —**chunk'i·ly,** *adv.* —**chunk'i·ness,** *n.*

church (chèrch) *n., v.* —*n.* **1** a building for public, especially Christian, worship or religious services: *There is a big church at the end of our street.* **2** public worship or religious service in a church: *They go to church regularly.* **3 the Church,** all Christians. **4** Usually, **Church,** a body or organization of persons having the same religious beliefs and usually under one authority; denomination: *the Presbyterian Church, the Roman Catholic Church.* **5** a group of people who worship together; congregation: *The whole church spent the weekend at the lake.* **6** the organization of a church; ecclesiastical authority or power: *The church forced Galileo to deny his discoveries.* **7** the profession of the clergy: *He has a brother in the church.* **8** (*adj.*) of or having to do with church or a church. —*v.* **1** bring to church. **2** conduct a special church ceremony for (especially a woman after childbirth). [OE *circe* < Gk. *kyriakon* (*doma*) (house) of the Lord < *kyrios* lord] —**church'less,** *adj.* —**church'like',** *adj.*

church day a day on which a festival of the Christian church is celebrated: *Ascension Day is a church day.*

churched (chèrcht) *adj.* associated with or belonging to a church.

church·go·er (chèrch'gō'ər) *n.* a person who goes to church, especially one who goes regularly.

Church·il·li·an (chèr chil'ē ən) *adj.* **1** of, having to do with, or resembling Sir Winston Churchill (1874-1965). **2** of or suggestive of his writings, speeches, etc: *Churchillian rhetoric.*

church·ly (chèrch'lē) *adj.* **1** of a church. **2** suitable for a church. —**church'li·ness,** *n.*

church·man (chèrch'mən) *n., pl.* **-men. 1** a member of the clergy. **2** a member of a church.

Church of Christ, Scientist the official name of the Christian Science Church.

Church of England the Christian church that is recognized as the national church of England. The Anglican Church of Canada is affiliated with the Church of England.

Church of Jesus Christ of Latter–day Saints the official name of the Mormon Church.

Church of the Brethren a Protestant sect practising adult baptism by immersion and opposed to oaths and military service. Its members are known as Dunkards.

church·ward·en (chèrch'wôr'dən) *n.* **1** in Anglican churches, a lay official who manages the business matters of a church. **2** a clay tobacco pipe with a very long stem.

church·wom·an (chèrch'wùm'ən) *n., pl.* **-wom·en.** a woman who is a member of a church.

church·yard (chèrch'yärd') *n.* the ground immediately surrounding and belonging to a church, especially a part used as a burial ground.

churl (chèrl) *n.* **1** a rude, surly person. **2** a person of low birth; peasant. **3** a person who is stingy in money matters; niggard; miser. [OE *ceorl* freeman (of low rank)]

churl·ish (chèr'lish) *adj.* **1** rude; surly: *a churlish reply.* **2** niggardly; stingy; grudging; sordid. —**churl'ish·ly,** *adv.* —**churl'ish·ness,** *n.*

churn (chèrn) *n., v.* —*n.* **1** a container or machine in which butter is made from cream or milk by beating and shaking. **2** a violent stirring.
—*v.* **1** stir or shake (cream or milk) in a churn. **2** make (butter) by using a churn. **3** stir violently; make or become foamy: *The propeller of the steamboat churned the waves.* **4** move as if beaten and shaken: *The excited crowd churned about the speaker's platform.* [OE *cyrn*] —**churn'er,** *n.*

churr (chèr) *v. or n.* chirr.

hat, āge, fär; let, ēqual, tèrm; it, īce
hot, ōpen, ôrder; oil, out; cup, pùt, rüle,
əbove, takən, pencəl, lemən, circəs

ch, child; ng, long; sh, ship
th, thin; ŦH, then; zh, measure

chute¹ (shüt) *n., v.* —*n.* **1** an inclined trough, tube, etc. used for dropping or sliding things such as mail, laundry, or coal to a lower level. **2** a narrow waterfall or rapids in a river. **3** a steep slope. **4** a narrow passageway or stall for controlling an animal while branding or disinfecting it. **5** a similar stall in which a rodeo animal is held before being released into the ring.
—*v.* send or go down a chute. [apparently blend of F *chute* fall (of water) and E *shoot*]
➡ Hom. **shoot.**

chute² (shüt) *n. or v.* **chut·ed, chut·ing.** *Informal.* parachute.
➡ Hom. **shoot.**

chut·ney (chut'nē) *n., pl.* **-neys.** a spicy sauce or relish made of fruits, herbs, pepper, etc. [< Hind. *chatni*]

chutz·pah (hùts'pä) *n. Slang.* excessive self-confidence; nerve; gall. [< Yiddish *khutspe*]

chyle (kīl) *n.* the milky fluid in the lymphatic vessels of the body, consisting of lymph and the digested fats that have been absorbed from the intestines. Chyle is carried by the lymphatic vessels, called lacteals, into the bloodstream. [< Med.L < Gk. *chylos* < *cheein* pour]

chyme (kīm) *n.* the thick semiliquid mass that is the product of the first stage of digestion in the stomach. The chyme passes from the stomach into the duodenum and small intestine, where digestion is completed. [< Med.L < Gk. *chymos* < *cheein* pour]

CIA or **C.I.A.** Central Intelligence Agency.

ciao (chou) *interj. Informal.* hello or goodbye. [< Ital.]

ci·bo·ri·um (sə bô'rē əm) *n., pl.* **-ri·a** (-rē ə). **1** a covered container used to hold the sacred bread of the Eucharist. **2** a dome-shaped canopy over an altar. [< Med.L *ciborium* canopy over an altar < L *ciborium* drinking cup < Gk. *kiborion* cuplike seed vessel]

ci·ca·da (sə kā'də *or* sə kä'də) *n., pl.* **-das, -dae** (-dē *or* -dī). any of a family (Cicadidae) of medium to large-sized insects, found mostly in tropical and subtropical regions, having two pairs of transparent wings and noted especially for the loud buzzing sound that the male makes by vibrating membranes on its abdomen. Several species of cicada have very long cycles of development; one species found in eastern North America lives underground as a larva for 17 years before becoming an adult. [< L]

cic·a·trice (sik'ə tris) *n.* cicatrix.

cic·a·trix (sik'ə triks') *n., pl.* **cic·a·tri·ces** (sik'ə trī'sēz). **1** *Medicine.* the scar left by a healed wound. **2** *Botany.* **a** the scar left on a tree or plant by a fallen leaf, branch, etc. **b** the scar on a seed where it was attached to the pod or seed container. [< L]

cic·a·trize (sik'ə trīz') *v.* **-trized, -triz·ing.** heal by forming a scar.

cic·e·ro·ne (sis'ə rō'nē) *n., pl.* **-nes.** a guide for sightseers who explains curiosities, antiquities, etc. [< Ital. < L *Cicero,-onis* Cicero]

Cic·e·ro·ni·an (sis'ə rō'nē ən) *adj.* **1** resembling the literary style of M. T. Cicero (106-43 B.C.), a Roman orator, writer, and statesman. **2** eloquent.

C.I.D. Criminal Investigation Department.

CIDA Canadian International Development Agency.

–cide¹ *combining form.* killing of: *regicide* (def. 1) = *killing of a king.* [< L *-cidium* the act of killing < *caedere* kill]

–cide² *combining form.* killer of: *regicide* (def. 2) = *killer of a king.* [< L *-cida* killer < *caedere* kill]

ci·der (sī'dər) *n.* **1** the juice pressed out of apples, for use as a drink and in making vinegar. **Sweet cider** is the unfermented juice; **hard cider,** the fermented juice. **2** the juice pressed from other fruits. [ME *sidre* < OF < LL *sicera* < Gk. < Hebrew *shēkār* liquor]

cider press a machine for pressing the juice out of apples.

ci·de·vant (sē də vän') *adj. French.* former; late: *The ci-devant general led the revolt against his government.*

CIE. or **cie.** company (for F *compagnie*).

C.I.F. or **c.i.f.** cost, insurance, and freight.

ci·gar (sə gär') *n.* a tight roll of dried tobacco leaves for smoking. [< Sp. *cigarro*]

cig·a·rette (sig'ə ret' *or* sig'ə ret') *n.* a small roll of finely cut

tobacco enclosed in a thin sheet of paper for smoking. Also, **cigaret.** [< F *cigarette,* dim. of *cigare* cigar]

cig·a·ril·lo (sig′ə ril′ō *or* sig′ə rē′yō) *n., pl.* **—los.** a small, thin cigar. [< Sp. *cigarillo* cigarette, dim. of *cigarro* cigar]

cil·i·a (sil′ē ə) *n. pl.* of **cil·i·um** (sil′ē əm). **1** eyelashes. **2** *Biology.* tiny hairlike projections found on the surface of many different types of cell, including those lining the human windpipe. In some one-celled animals cilia cover the entire surface of the organism and function like oars, allowing the animal to move through its liquid surrounding. [< L]

cil·i·ar·y (sil′ē er′ē) *adj.* **1** of or having to do with cilia. **2** of or having to do with the ciliary body in the eye.

ciliary body the part of the choroid layer of tissue in the front of the eyeball that contains the muscles used to focus the eye by changing the shape of the lens.

cil·i·ate (sil′ē āt′ *or* sil′ē it) *adj., n.* —*adj.* having cilia. —*n.* any of a large class (Cileatea) constituting a subphylum of protozoans having cilia on all or part of the body.

Ci·li·cian (sə lish′ən) *adj., n.* —*adj.* of or having to do with Cilicia, an ancient country in SE Asia Minor. —*n.* a native or inhabitant of Cilicia.

Cim·me·ri·an (sə mēr′ē ən) *n., adj.* —*n.* one of a mythical people said to live in perpetual mists and darkness. —*adj.* very dark and gloomy.

C. in C. Commander-in-Chief.

cinch (sinch) *n., v.* —*n.* **1** a strong band or belt, usually of leather, for fastening a saddle or pack on a horse. **2** *Informal.* a firm hold or grip. **3** *Informal.* something sure and easy: *We were a cinch to win the game.* —*v.* **1** fasten on with a cinch; bind firmly. **2** *Informal.* get a firm hold on. [< Sp. *cincha* < L *cincta* girdle < *cingere* bind]

cin·cho·na (sin kō′nə) *n.* **1** any of a genus (*Cinchona*) of tropical evergreen trees and shrubs of the madder family, native to South America. A few species of cinchona are cultivated in other parts of the world, especially Indonesia, because their bark is a source of quinine, quinidine, and other similar drugs. **2** the bitter bark of any species of cinchona tree from which these drugs are obtained. [< NL; after Francesca de Ribera, Countess *Chinchón* (?-1641 ?), the wife of a Spanish viceroy of Peru]

cinc·ture (singk′chər) *n., v.* **-tured, -tur·ing.** —*n.* **1** a belt; girdle. **2** a border; enclosure. —*v.* encircle; surround. [< L *cinctura* < *cingere* bind, gird]

cin·der (sin′dər) *n.* **1** a piece of burned-up wood or coal. **2 cinders,** *pl.* **a** wood or coal partly burned but no longer flaming. **b** ashes. [OE *sinder*]

Cin·der·el·la (sin′dər el′ə) *n.* **1** a girl who suddenly achieves success or fame after being neglected or ridiculed, etc. **2** any person whose real worth or beauty is not recognized. **3** (*adj.*) of or having to do with sudden or dramatic success: *a Cinderella story.* [< *Cinderella,* the beautiful young heroine of a fairy tale, who is cruelly treated by her stepmother and stepsisters but is then helped by her fairy godmother]

cin·e·aste *or* **cin·é·aste** (sin′ē ast′) *n.* a motion picture enthusiast. [<F < *ciné* cinema + *-aste* as in *enthusiaste* enthusiast. 20c.]

cin·e·ma (sin′ə mə) *n.* **1** a motion picture. **2** a motion-picture theatre. **3 the cinema,** motion pictures as an art form: *He is more interested in the cinema than in live theatre.* [short for *cinematograph*]

Cin·e·ma·scope (sin′ə mə skōp′) *n. Trademark.* a motion-picture process developed in the 1950's, in which the image is projected on a wide, curved screen to give some illusion of depth and of natural field of vision. The process involves the use of a special camera lens that photographs an area twice as large as an ordinary lens, but compresses it so that it can be recorded on regular film. This distorted film image is corrected before it reaches the screen by a special lens in the projector, which expands it to its normal width. [< *cinema + -scope*]

cin·e·mat·ic (sin′ə mat′ik) *adj.* of or having to do with motion pictures: *cinematic style, a cinematic presentation.*

cin·e·mat·o·graph (sin′ə mat′ə graf′) *n.* **1** *Brit.* a machine for projecting motion pictures on a screen. **2** a camera for taking motion pictures. Also, **kinematograph.** [< Gk. *kinema, -atos* motion + E *-graph*]

cin·e·ma·tog·ra·phy (sin′ə mə tog′rə fē) *n.* the art and science of making motion pictures. Also, **kinematography.**

ci·né·ma vé·ri·té (si nā mä′ vā ri tā′) *French.* a motion-picture style that aims to reflect reality by filming spontaneous action.

Cin·er·am·a (sin′ər am′ə *or* sin′ər äm′ə) *n. Trademark.* a wide-screen presentation of film using 70 mm film and a special lens to produce an image on a large, deeply curved screen, giving the illusion of three dimensions. [< *cine*ma + pano*rama*]

cin·e·rar·i·a (sin′ə rer′ē ə) *n.* any of several varieties of house and greenhouse plant derived from a perennial herb (*Senecio cruentus*) of the composite family, native to the Canary Islands. Cinerarias have heart-shaped leaves and clusters of daisylike flowers in several colors. [< NL < L *cinerarius* of ashes; with reference to down on leaves]

cin·e·rar·i·um (sin′ə rer′ē əm) *n.* **-rar·i·a.** a place for keeping the ashes of cremated bodies. [< L]

cin·e·rar·y (sin′ə rer′ē) *adj.* **1** used to hold the ashes of a cremated body. **2** of or for ashes.

cin·na·bar (sin′ə bär′) *n.* **1** a reddish or brownish mineral that is the chief source of mercury; native mercuric sulphide. *Formula:* HgS **2** artificial mercuric sulphide, used as a red pigment in making paints, dyes, etc. **3** a bright red; vermilion. [< L < Gk. *kinnabari;* ult. < Persian *šängärf*]

cin·na·mon (sin′ə mən) *n., adj.* —*n.* **1** a fragrant spice, used especially as a flavoring in baked goods, desserts, and candy, that is the dried inner bark of a tropical evergreen tree (*Cinnamomum zeylanicum*) of the laurel family. Most cinnamon comes from Sri Lanka and India. **2** this bark. **3** the tree or shrub yielding this bark. **4** the color of cinnamon, a light reddish brown. —*adj.* **1** flavored with cinnamon: *cinnamon rolls.* **2** having the color cinnamon. [ME < OF *cinnamome* < LL < Gk. *kinnamon;* of Semitic origin]

cinnamon bear a reddish-brown variety of the black bear of North America.

cin·quain (sing′kān) *n.* **1** a stanza of five lines. **2** a five-line poem, usually unrhymed, the lines having 2, 4, 6, 8, 2 syllables or 1, 2, 3, 4, 1 words, respectively. **3** any group of five.

cin·que·cen·to (ching′kwə chen′tō) *n., adj.* —*n.* the 16th century, especially with regard to the art and architecture of Italy at that time. —*adj.* of or having to do with the 16th century. [< Ital. *cinquecento* short for *mil cinque cento* one thousand five hundred]

☞ *Usage.* Note that *cinquecento* refers to the 1500's, and so to the sixteenth rather than the fifteenth century.

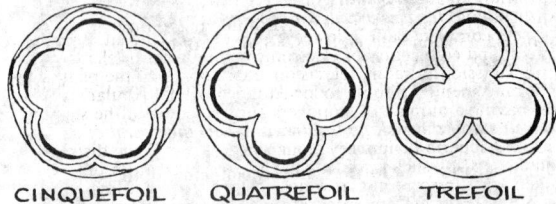

CINQUEFOIL　　QUATREFOIL　　TREFOIL

Circular architectural ornaments formed from five, four, and three arcs (or foils), respectively

cinque·foil (singk′foil′) *n.* **1** any of a genus (*Potentilla*) of plants of the rose family found mainly in the northern hemisphere, having compound leaves with three to seven leaflets and usually yellow or white flowers with five roundish petals. Several species of cinquefoil are common Canadian weeds. **2** *Architecture.* an ornament made up of five arcs or part circles joined in a circle. [ME *synkefoile* < OF (unrecorded) < L *quinquefolium* < *quinque* five + *folium* leaf]

ci·on (sī′ən) *n.* See **scion** (def. 1).

ci·pher (sī′fər) *n., v.* —*n.* **1** a method of secret writing based on a key or set pattern; code: *He sent me a telegram in cipher.* **2** something in secret writing or code. **3** the key to a method of secret writing or code. **4** a zero; 0. **5** a person or thing of no importance. **6** any Arabic numeral. **7** a pattern of interlaced initials; monogram. —*v.* **1** express (a message or information) in cipher. **2** *Rare.* do arithmetic or work out (a problem) by arithmetic. Also, **cypher.** [ME < Med.L *ciphra* < Arabic *sifr* empty. Doublet of ZERO.]

cir·ca (sèr′kə) *prep. or adv.* about: *Mohammed was born circa A.D. 570. Abbrev.:* c. *or* ca. [< L *circa* about]

cir·ca·di·an (sèr kā′ dē ən) *adj.* of, having to do with, or designating biological processes that have a cycle or periodicity of approximately 24 hours. [< L *circa* about + *dies* day + E *-AN;* 20c.]

Cir·cas·sian (sər kash′ən *or* sər kash′ē ən) *n., adj.* —*n.* **1** a native or inhabitant of Circassia, a region in southern Russia on the Black Sea. **2** a language of the northern Caucasus. —*adj.* of or having to do with Circassia, its people, or their language.

Circe (sèr′sē) *n.* **1** *Greek mythology.* an enchantress who changed men to beasts. **2** any enchantress.

cir·ci·nate (sėr′sə nāt′) *adj.* **1** rolled up into a coil. **2** *Botany.* coiled from tip toward the base: *The new leaves of a fern are circinate.* [< L *circinatus* made round, pp. of *circinare* < *circinus* pair of compasses < Gk. *kirkinos*]

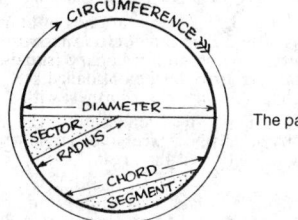

The parts of a circle

cir·cle (sėr′kəl) *n., v.* **-cled, -cling.** —*n.* **1** a continuously curving line, every point of which is equally distant from a fixed point called the centre. **2** a plane figure bounded by such a line. **3** a halo, crown, or anything shaped like a circle or part of one. **4** a ring: *The girls danced in a circle.* **5** a set of seats in the balcony of a theatre. **6** a complete series or course of something that is repeated; cycle: *A year is a circle of 12 months.* **7** *Astronomy.* **a** the orbit of a heavenly body. **b** the period of revolution of a heavenly body. **8** a group of people held together by the same interests: *the family circle; a circle of friends.* **9** a sphere of influence, action, etc. **10** a set of parts that form a connected whole: *the circle of the sciences.*
—*v.* **1** go around in a circle; revolve around: *The moon circles the earth. The airplane circled before it landed.* **2** identify by drawing a circle around: *Circle the number of the answer you think is correct.* [ME < OF *cercle* < L *circulus*, dim. of *circus* ring] —**cir′cler,** *n.*
☛ *Syn.* n. **8. Circle, clique** = a group of people held together by a common tie. **Circle** applies to a group held together around a person or a common interest, cause, occupation, etc.: *The book is praised in literary circles.* **Clique** applies to a small, exclusive, sometimes snobbish, group, and often expresses an attitude of disapproval on the part of the speaker: *Every school has its cliques.*

cir·clet (sėr′klit) *n.* **1** a small circle. **2** a round ornament worn on the head, neck, arm, or finger.

circs (sėrks) *n.pl. Informal.* circumstances: *We can't very well ask him again, under the circs.*

cir·cuit (sėr′kit) *n., v.* —*n.* **1** a complete course, journey, or route, especially one that is more or less circular or that goes around something: *It takes a year for the earth to make its circuit of the sun.* **2** the complete path followed by an electric current. **3** an arrangement and connection of electronic components or elements for the transmission of radio, television, etc.; hookup. **4** the plan of such an arrangement. **5** a route followed repeatedly at regular intervals, having a number of stopovers and returning to the starting point: *the circuit of a travelling theatre company, the circuit of a circuit court.* **6** a periodic journey along such a route. **7** the district or region covered by such a route. **8** a group or association of theatres, cinemas, resorts, etc. at which the same plays, films, or other entertainments are presented in turn. **9** an association of athletic teams or clubs or a series of sporting events involving the same players. **10** the distance around any space. **11** a line enclosing any space; boundary line. **12** the space enclosed.
—*v.* go round in or make a circuit. [ME < L *circuitus* a going around < *circum* around + *ire* go]

circuit breaker a switch that automatically opens or interrupts an electric circuit when the current gets too strong.

circuit court *Esp.U.S.* a law court that holds regular sessions in several districts or counties within its jurisdiction.

cir·cu·i·tous (sėr kyü′ə təs) *adj.* roundabout; not direct: *To avoid unpaved roads, we took a circuitous route home.* —**cir·cu′i·tous·ly,** *adv.* —**cir·cu′i·tous·ness,** *n.*

circuit rider *Historical.* a Methodist minister who rode from place to place over a circuit to preach.

cir·cuit·ry (sėr′kə trē) *n., pl.* **-ries. 1** the science of electrical or electronic circuits. **2** the component parts of a circuit.

cir·cu·lar (sėr′kyə lər) *adj., n.* —*adj.* **1** round: *The full moon is circular.* **2** moving in a circle; going around a circle: *a circular movement of the arms.* **3** having to do with a circle: *circular measure.* **4** sent to each of a number of people: *a circular letter.* **5** roundabout; indirect: *a circular explanation.* **6** in an argument, etc., using as one's proof an assertion that assumes what one is trying to prove: *Circular reasoning is futile because it inevitably comes back to the starting point.* **7** moving or occurring in a round or cycle of repetition: *a circular sequence of events.*
—*n.* a letter, notice or advertisement sent to each of a number of people. [ME < AF < LL *circularis* < *circulus*. See CIRCLE.] —**cir′cu·lar·ly,** *adv.*

cir·cu·lar·i·ty (sėr′kyə lar′ə tē or sėr′kyə ler′ə tē) *n., pl.* **-ties.** circular quality or form.

hat, āge, fär; let, ēqual, tėrm; it, īce
hot, ōpen, ôrder; oil, out; cup, put, rüle,
əbove, takən, pencəl, lemən, circəs
ch, child; ng, long; sh, ship
th, thin; ŦH, then; zh, measure

cir·cu·lar·ize (sėr′kyə lər īz′) *v.* **-ized, -iz·ing. 1** send circulars to. **2** make circular. —**cir′cu·lar·i·za′tion,** *n.* —**cir′cu·lar·iz′er,** *n.*

circular measure 1 a system for measuring angles. There are two main circular measures: **degree measure,** based on the division of a circle into 360 degrees, and **radian measure,** based on a standard angle in which the length of the arc subtending the angle is equal to the radius of the circle. See table at **measurement. 2** the measurement of the radius, circumference, area, etc. of a circle.

circular saw a thin steel disk with saw-teeth round its edge, turned at high speed by machinery.

cir·cu·late (sėr′kyə lāt′) *v.* **-lat·ed, -lat·ing. 1** move around in a circuit; follow a course, especially one that returns to the starting point: *The blood circulates through the body. The house is heated by hot water circulating through a system of pipes.* **2** pass from place to place or person to person freely and continuously: *The gossip circulated rapidly. Money circulates as it goes from person to person.* **3** send around from person to person or place to place: *He circulated the news of the holiday. The book has been widely circulated among our friends.* **4** move about in a social circle, especially move around at a party, etc., talking to different people. [< L *circulare* < *circulus.* See CIRCLE.]

circulating library lending library.

circulating medium the coins, notes, bills, etc. that are in use as money; currency.

cir·cu·la·tion (sėr′kyə lā′shən) *n.* **1** the movement of anything in a circuit, especially a closed circuit: *Open windows increase the circulation of air in a room. We are learning about the circulation of the blood.* **2** the passage of anything from person to person or place to place: *the circulation of money, the circulation of information or news, the circulation of magazines.* **3** the number of copies of a book, newspaper, magazine, etc. that are sent out during a certain time: *The magazine has a circulation of 50 000.*

cir·cu·la·tor (sėr′kyə lā′tər) *n.* a person or thing that circulates news, money, gossip, etc.

cir·cu·la·to·ry (sėr′kyə lə tô′rē) *adj.* having to do with circulation: *Arteries and veins are parts of the human body's circulatory system.*

circum– *prefix.* in a circle; around: *circumnavigate = navigate around; circumpolar = around the North or South Pole.* [< L]

cir·cum·am·bi·ent (sėr′kəm am′bē ənt) *adj.* surrounding; encircling.

cir·cum·cise (sėr′kəm sīz′) *v.* **-cised, -cis·ing.** cut off the foreskin of. [ME < L *circumcisus,* pp. of *circumcidere* < *circum* around + *caedere* cut] —**cir′cum·cis′er,** *n.*

cir·cum·ci·sion (sėr′kəm sizh′ən) *n.* the act or practice of circumcising, either for reasons of hygiene or as a religious rite.

cir·cum·fer·ence (sər kum′fər əns) *n.* **1** the boundary line of a circle. Every point on the circumference of a circle is at the same distance from the centre. See **circle** for picture. **2** the boundary line of any figure enclosed by a curve. **3** the distance around a circle or an object bounded by a curved surface: *The big tree had a circumference of three metres.* [< L *circumferentia* < *circum* around + *ferre* bear]

cir·cum·fer·en·tial (sər kum′fər en′shəl) *adj.* of a circumference; located at or near the circumference. —**cir·cum′fer·en′tial·ly,** *adv.*

cir·cum·flex (sėr′kəm fleks′) *n., adj.* —*n.* a mark (ˆ, ⌒, or ˜) used especially over a vowel in certain languages and phonetic spelling systems to show length, contraction, or quality. The circumflex was used originally in ancient Greek over long vowels to show a rising-falling tone. The circumflex in the French word *fête* (Old French *feste*) indicates that the *e* is long and at the same time marks the loss of the letter *s.* —*adj.* **1** of or characterized by the quality, length, etc. shown by a circumflex. **2** *Anatomy.* bending or curving around: *a circumflex nerve.* [< L *circumflexus* bent around < *circum* around + *flectere* bend]

circumflex accent a circumflex.

cir·cum·flu·ent (sər kum′flü ənt) *adj.* flowing around; surrounding. [< L *circumfluens, -entis,* ppr. of *circumfluere* < *circum* around + *fluere* flow]

cir·cum·fuse (sėr′kəm fyüz′) *v.* **-fused, -fusing. 1** pour or spread around. **2** surround; suffuse. [< L *circumfusus,* pp. of

circumfundere < circum around + *fundere* pour] —**cir′cum·fu′sion,** *n.*

cir·cum·lo·cu·tion (sèr′kəm lō kyü′shən *or* -lə kyü′shən) *n.* a roundabout way of speaking. *The wife of your father's brother* is a circumlocution for *Your aunt.* [< L *circumlocutio, -onis < circum* around + *loqui* speak]

cir·cum·nav·i·gate (sèr′kəm nav′ə gāt) *v.* **-gat·ed, -gat·ing.** sail completely around: *Magellan's ship circumnavigated the earth.* —**cir′cum·nav′i·ga′tor,** *n.*

cir·cum·nav·i·ga·tion (sèr′kəm nav′ə gā′shən) *n.* the act of sailing completely around.

cir·cum·po·lar (sèr′kəm pōlər) *adj.* **1** around the North or South Pole. **2** around either pole of the heavens.

cir·cum·scribe (sèr′kəm skrīb′ *or* sèr′kəm skrīb′) *v.* **-scribed, -scrib·ing.** **1** draw a line around; mark the boundaries of. **2** surround. **3** limit; restrict: *A prisoner's activities are circumscribed.* **4** *Geometry.* **a** draw (a figure) around another figure so as to touch as many points as possible: *A circle that is circumscribed around a square touches it at four points.* **b** be so drawn around: *A circle can circumscribe a hexagon.* [< L *circumscribere < circum* around + *scribere* write, draw] —**cir′cum·scrib′er,** *n.*

cir·cum·scrip·tion (sèr′kəm skrip′shən) *n.* **1** circumscribing or being circumscribed. **2** the thing that circumscribes, such as an outline or boundary or a restriction. **3** an inscription around a coin, medal, etc. **4** a space circumscribed. [< L *circumscriptio, -onis < circumscribere.* See CIRCUMSCRIBE.]

cir·cum·spect (sèr′kəm spekt′) *adj.* careful; cautious; prudent. [< L *circumspectus,* pp. of *circumspicere < circum* around + *specere* look] —**cir′cum·spect′ly,** *adv.* —**cir′cum·spect′ness,** *n.*

cir·cum·spec·tion (sèr′kəm spek′shən) *n.* care; caution; prudence.

cir·cum·stance (sèr′kəm stans′) *n.* **1** a condition that contributes to or modifies an act or event: *You ought to consider all the circumstances before you judge his action.* **2** a happening; occurrence: *Her arrival on the scene was a fortunate circumstance.* **3** circumstances, *pl.* financial condition: *A rich person is said to be in good or easy circumstances. A poor person is in bad or reduced circumstances.* **4** something that is not essential; additional information; detail: *It was his success, not the circumstances of the achievement, that interested his family.* **5** all the unavoidable factors contributing to an event or situation; the sum of the direct and indirect controlling influences (*used only as a singular noun and without* **the** *or* **a**): *a victim of circumstance.* **6** ceremony; display (*used only as a singular noun and without* **a**): *The royal procession advanced with pomp and circumstance.*

under no circumstances, never; no matter what the conditions are.
under the circumstances, because of conditions; things being as they are or were.

[< L *circumstantia* surrounding condition < *circumstans, -antis,* ppr. of *circumstare < circum* around + *stare* stand]

cir·cum·stan·tial (sèr′kəm stan′shəl) *adj.* **1** depending on or based on circumstances: *circumstantial evidence.* **2** incidental; not essential; not important: *Minor details are circumstantial compared with the main facts.* **3** giving full and exact details; complete: *a circumstantial report of an accident.* —**cir′cum·stan′tial·ly,** *adv.*

circumstantial evidence events or facts that make certain conclusions apparent. If stolen jewels are found in a man's possession, it is circumstantial evidence that he stole them; if somebody saw him steal them, that would be direct evidence.

cir·cum·stan·ti·ate (sèr′kəm stan′shē āt′) *v.* **-at·ed, -at·ing.** give the circumstances of; support or prove with details. —**cir′cum·stan′ti·a′tion,** *n.*

cir·cum·vent (sèr′kəm vent′ *or* sèr′kəm vent′) *v.* **1** defeat or get the better of by skilful planning; outwit; frustrate: *to circumvent the law. The rebels' plans to take over the radio station were circumvented by the police.* **2** avoid by going around: *We can circumvent the heavy traffic by taking this route.* **3** *Archaic.* surround, especially with evil, hatred, malice, etc., so as to trap or ensnare. [< L *circumventus,* pp. of *circumvenire < circum* around + *venire* come] —**cir′cum·ven′tor,** *n.*

cir·cum·ven·tion (sèr′kəm ven′shən) *n.* the act of circumventing.

cir·cus (sèr′kəs) *n.* **1** a travelling show of acrobats, clowns, horses, riders, and wild animals. **2** the performers who give the show or the performances they give. **3** *Informal.* an amusing person or thing. **4** *Informal.* a lively but disorderly time or place: *Our place was a circus that last night, as we were trying to get organized for the trip.* **5** in ancient rome, a round or oval, open-air stadium with

tiers of seats around it, used for chariot races, etc. **6** *Brit.* a more or less circular open area at an intersection of several streets (*used especially in place names*): *Picadilly Circus.* [< L *circus* ring. Doublet of CIRQUE.]

Circus Max·i·mus (mak′sə məs) in ancient Rome, a huge amphitheatre.

cirque (sèrk) *n.* **1** a circular space. **2** *Poetic.* a circlet; ring. **3** *Geology.* a steep-sided mountain rock basin, or hollow, formed by glacial erosion and often containing a small lake or glacier. [< F *cirque* < L *circus.* Doublet of CIRCUS.]

cir·rho·sis (sə rō′sis) *n.* a chronic progressive disease of the liver characterized by the death of liver cells and excessive formation of connective tisue followed by contraction of the organ. [< NL < Gk. *kirrhos* orange yellow]

cir·ri·ped (sir′ə ped′) *n.* any of a subclass (Cirripedia) of marine crustaceans, such as barnacles, that have threadlike appendages instead of legs. As adults cirripeds are parasitic or permanently attached to a surface. [< NL *Cirripeda* < L *cirrus* curl + *pes, pedis* foot]

cir·ro·cu·mu·lus (sir′ō kyü′myə ləs) *n.* a cloud made up of rows or groups of small, fleecy clouds. [< *cirrus* + *cumulus*]

cir·ro·stra·tus (sir′ō strā′təs *or* -strat′əs) *n.* a thin, veil-like cloud high in the air. [< *cirrus* + *stratus*]

cir·rus (sir′əs) *n., pl.* **cir·ri** (sir′ī *or* sir′ē). a thin, curling, wispy cloud very high in the air. [< L *cirrus* curl]

cis·al·pine (sis al′pīn *or* sis al′pin) *adj.* on the southern side of the Alps. [< L *cisalpinus < cis* on this (i.e., the Roman) side of + *alpinus < Alpes* the Alps]

cis·co (sis′kō) *n., pl.* **-coes** *or* **-cos.** any of various whitefishes (genus *Coregonus*) found throughout the lakes of Canada and the NE United States. Some ciscoes are valuable food fish. [< Cdn.F *ciscoette* < ? Algonquian]

Cis·ter·cian (sis tèr′shən) *n., adj.* —*n. Roman Catholic Church.* a monk or nun of a very strict order founded in France in 1098 as an offshoot of the Benedictines. —*adj.* of or having to do with this order. [< Med.L *Cistercium* Citeaux, where the order was founded]

cis·tern (sis′tərn) *n.* a large artificial reservoir, especially a tank, usually underground, for storing rainwater. [< L *cisterna* < *cista* box]

cit. **1** citation; cited. **2** citizen.

cit·a·del (sit′ə dəl *or* sit′ə del′) *n.* **1** a fortress commanding a city. **2** a strongly fortified place; stronghold. **3** a strong, safe place; refuge. [< F *citadelle* < Ital. *cittadella,* dim. of *città* city]

ci·ta·tion (sī tā′shən) *n.* **1** a quotation or reference given as an authority for facts, opinions, etc. **2** a specific mention in an official dispatch. **3** an honorable mention for bravery in war. **4** the commendation of a civilian for public service by some official or institution. **5** a summons to appear before a court of law.

cite (sīt) *v.* **cit·ed, cit·ing.** **1** quote (a passage, book or author), especially as an authority: *He cited the Bible and Shakespeare to prove his statement.* **2** refer to; mention as an example: *The lawyer cited another case similar to the one being tried.* **3** mention for bravery in war. **4** mention publicly in recognition of and praise for outstanding service to humanity, one's country, etc. **5** summon to appear before a court of law. **6** arouse to action; summon. [< F *citer* < L *citare* summon < *ciere* set in motion] —**cite′a·ble,** *adj.*
☞ *Hom.* **sight, site.**
☞ *Syn.* **1.** See note at **quote.**

cith·a·ra (sith′ə rə) *n.* an ancient musical instrument resembling a lyre. [< L < Gk. *kithara.* Doublet of GUITAR and ZITHER.]

cith·er (sith′ər) *n.* **1** cithern. **2** cithara.

cith·ern (sith′ərn) *n.* cittern.

cit·i·fied (sit′i fīd′) *adj. Informal.* having city ways or fashions.

cit·i·fy (sit′ə fī′) *v.* **-fied, -fy·ing.** cause to conform to an urban way of life.

cit·i·zen (sit′ə zən) *n.* **1** a person who by birth or by choice (i.e., naturalization) is a member of a nation or state, thereby owing allegiance to it and in turn being entitled to protection and the enjoyment of certain rights. **2** a civilian, as distinguished from a member of the armed forces, police, etc. **3** an inhabitant of a city or town; resident. [ME < AF *citisein* < OF *cite.* See CITY.]

cit·i·zen·ess (sit′ə zən is) *n.* a woman citizen.

citizen of the world a person who is interested in the affairs of the whole world; cosmopolitan.

cit·i·zen·ry (sit′ə zən rē) *n., pl.* **-ries.** citizens as a group.

citizens' band a range of radio frequencies reserved for use by the public. See also **General Radio Service.**

cit·i·zen·ship (sit′ə zən ship′) *n.* **1** the condition of being a citizen: *She has Canadian citizenship but her husband doesn't.* **2** the duties, rights, and privileges of a citizen.

cit·rate (sit′rāt) *n.* a salt or ester of citric acid.

cit·ric (sit′rik) *adj.* of or from fruits such as lemons, limes, oranges, etc.

citric acid a white, odorless, sour-tasting acid that occurs in such fruits as lemons, limes, etc. It is used as a flavoring, as a medicine, and in making dyes. *Formula:* $C_6H_8O_7$

cit·rine (sit′rin) *n. or adj.* pale yellow. [< F *citrin* < L *citrus* citrus tree]

cit·ron (sit′rən) *n.* 1 a pale-yellow citrus fruit resembling a lemon but larger, less acid, and with a thicker rind. 2 the tree (*Citrus medica*) that this fruit grows on. 3 a small, round variety of watermelon (*Citrullus vulgaris citroides*) generally considered inedible except for its rind, which is used in preserves. 4 the preserved or candied rind of either of these fruits. [< F < Ital. *citrone* < L *citrus* citrus tree]

cit·ron·el·la (sit′rən el′ə) *n.* 1 an oil used in making perfume, soap, liniment, etc. and for keeping mosquitoes away. 2 the fragrant tropical grass (*Cymbopogon nardus*) that yields this oil. [< NL; from its citronlike smell]

citron melon citron (def. 3).

cit·rous (sit′rəs) *adj.* having to do with fruits such as lemons, limes, oranges, etc.

cit·rus (sit′rəs) *n.* 1 any of a genus (*Citrus*) of trees or shrubs of the rue family grown in warm regions, bearing sweet or tart, edible fruit. 2 (*adj.*) of or designating this genus or the fruits borne by these trees or shrubs: *Oranges, lemons, limes, grapefruit, and citrons are citrus fruits.* [< L]

citrus fruit the fruit of a citrus tree.

cit·tern (sit′ərn) *n.* a musical instrument resembling a guitar, popular in the 16th and 17th centuries. [blend of L *cithara* cithara and E *gittern*]

cit·y (sit′ē) *n., pl.* **cit·ies.** 1 a large and important town. 2 in Canada, an incorporated community with fixed boundaries that has been granted status as a city by its provincial government, usually having more financial and social responsibilities and more sources of revenue than a town. A city is the largest urban municipal unit and in most provinces must have a minimum population of several thousand. 3 in Britain, a town or district that has a royal charter for the title of city and is usually a cathedral town. 4 in the United States, a municipality, usually with a large population, having a charter granted by the state. 5 the people living in a city. 6 the government of a city: *The city has decided to make more land available for parks.* 7 a city-state. 8 **the City,** in London, the business and financial district. 9 (*adj.*) of, having to do with, or in a city: *city politics. I hate city driving.* [ME < OF < L *civitas* citizenship, state, city < *civis* citizen]

city editor 1 the newspaper editor in charge of collecting and editing local news. 2 *Brit.* financial editor.

city fathers the councilmen, aldermen, magistrates, or other leading men of a city.

city hall 1 the headquarters of the local government in a city: *The mayor's office is in the city hall.* 2 a building housing a local government. 3 the officials of a municipal government, considered collectively.

city manager a person appointed by a city council or commission to manage the government of a city.

city of David 1 Jerusalem. 2 Bethlehem.

City of God heaven.

City of Seven Hills Rome.

cit·y·scape (sit′ē skāp′) *n.* 1 the visual aspects of a city; the buildings, streets, parks, etc. of a city viewed as scenery. 2 a photograph, painting, etc. of a city or part of a city.

city slicker *Slang.* a city dweller who is looked on with scorn or suspicion by rural people because of the way he dresses and behaves.

cit·y–state (sit′ē stāt′) *n.* an independent state consisting of a city and the territories depending on it, as in ancient Greece and Renaissance Italy.

civ·et (siv′it) *n.* 1 a fatty, yellowish, musky-smelling fluid secreted by civet cats, used as a fixative in perfumes. It can be removed from captive animals every two or three weeks. 2 civet cat. 3 the fur of a civet cat. [< F *civette* < Ital. < Arabic *zabad*]

civet cat any of various catlike carnivorous mammals (family Viverridae) of the Old World having anal glands that secrete civet, a fatty fluid with a powerful, musky smell.

civ·ic (siv′ik) *adj.* 1 of a city. 2 of or having to do with citizenship: *Every person has some civic duties, such as obeying the law, voting, or paying taxes.* 3 of citizens. [< L *civicus* < *civis* citizen]

civic centre 1 the headquarters of the government of a city. 2 a

hat, āge, fär; let, ēqual, tėrm; it, īce
hot, ōpen, ôrder; oil, out; cup, put, rüle,
əbove, takən, pencəl, lemən, circəs

ch, child; ng, long; sh, ship
th, thin; ᴛʜ, then; zh, measure

building serving as a centre for community activities, concerts, games, etc.

civ·ics (siv′iks) *n.* the study of the duties, rights, and privileges of citizens.

civ·ies (siv′ēz) See **civvies.**

civ·il (siv′əl) *adj.* 1 of a citizen or citizens; having to do with citizens. 2 of or having to do with the government, state, or nation: *civil servants.* 3 not connected with the armed forces or the church: *a civil court, a civil marriage.* 4 polite; courteous: *The boy answered our questions in a very civil way.* 5 having to do with the private rights of individuals or with legal proceedings connected with these rights: *a civil lawsuit.* 6 such as occurs among citizens of one community, state, or nation: *civil war, civil strife.* 7 of, belonging to, or in accordance with Roman civil law, or civil law derived from it. [< L *civilis* < *civis* citizen]
☛ *Syn.* 4. See note at **polite.**

civil defence or **defense** a program of procedures and planned action for civilian volunteers to cope with a general emergency, such as enemy attack or a major natural disaster.

civil disobedience refusal because of one's principles to obey the laws, especially by not paying taxes.

civil engineer a person trained in civil engineering, especially one whose work it is.

civil engineering the planning and directing of the construction of bridges, roads, harbors, etc.

ci·vil·ian (sə vil′yən) *n., adj.* —*n.* a person who is not in the armed forces. —*adj.* of civilians; not of the armed forces: *Soldiers often wear civilian clothes when on leave.*

ci·vil·i·ty (sə vil′ə tē) *n., pl.* **-ties.** 1 politeness; courtesy. 2 an act of politeness or courtesy.

civ·i·li·za·tion (siv′ə lə zā′shən *or* siv′ə lī zā′shən) *n.* 1 a civilized condition; an advanced stage of social and political organization. 2 the nations and peoples thought of as having reached an advanced stage of social and political organization. 3 civilizing or being civilized. 4 the total culture of a nation or people at a given time: *Inuit civilization, nineteenth-century Canadian civilization.*

civ·i·lize (siv′ə līz′) *v.* **-lized, -liz·ing.** 1 change a primitive social and political system to a much more complex one that includes knowledge of the arts and sciences: *The Romans civilized a great part of their world.* 2 improve in culture and good manners; refine: *They were given the job of trying to civilize their niece.* [< Med.L *civilizare* < L *civilis.* See CIVIL.] —**civ′i·liz′er,** *n.*

civ·i·lized (siv′ə līzd′) *adj.* 1 having a complex social and political system. 2 of nations or persons so advanced: *civilized entertainments.* 3 showing culture and good manners; refined.

civ·i·liz·ing (siv′ə līz′ing) *adj.* that civilizes; promoting civilization.

civil law 1 the body of law that regulates and protects private rights and is controlled and used by civil (not military) courts, opposed to *criminal law* and *military law.* 2 Roman law or a system of law based on Roman law.

civil liberty the right of a person to do, think, and say what he pleases as long as he does not harm anyone else or break established laws.

civil list 1 a list of sums appropriated to pay the members of the civil government and civil servants (obsolete in Canada). 2 in the United Kingdom, a list of sums appropriated by Parliament as allowances for the sovereign and members of the royal family.

civ·il·ly (siv′ə lē) *adv.* 1 politely; courteously. 2 according to the civil law.

civil marriage a marriage performed by a government official, rather than by a clergyman.

civil rights the rights of a citizen.

civil servant a member of the civil service. A cabinet minister has a staff of civil servants. A deputy minister is a civil servant.

civil service 1 the service responsible for the day-to-day administrative work of the various departments of the government of a country, province, etc., such as the collection of taxes and issuing of pensions. 2 the body of officials, clerks, etc. who do this work. The civil service is not usually affected by changes of government.

civil war 1 a war between two groups of citizens of one nation. 2 **Civil War, a** in England, the war between the king and Parliament, 1642-1646 and 1648-1652. **b** in the United States, the war between the northern and southern states, 1861-1865.

civil year the calendar year.

civ·vies (siv′ēz) *n.pl. Informal.* civilian clothes, as distinguished from military uniform. Also, **civies.**

ck. cask.

cl. 1 class. 2 clause. 3 clerk. 4 clergyman.

Cl chlorine.

clab·ber (klab′ər) *n., v.* —*n.* thick sour milk. —*v.* become thick in souring; curdle. [< Irish *clabar* curds, short for *bainne clabair* bonnyclabber (curdled milk)]

clack (klak) *v., n.* —*v.* 1 make or cause to make a short, sharp sound: *Her needles clacked as she knitted.* 2 chatter. —*n.* 1 a short, sharp sound: *We heard the clack of her heels on the sidewalk.* 2 chatter. [imitative] —**clack′er,** *n.*

clad[1] (klad) *v.* a pt. and a pp. of **clothe.**

clad[2] (klad) *v.* **clad, clad·ding.** sheathe or face (a surface, metal, etc.) with a protective coating, etc.: *Aluminum pots are sometimes clad with copper for better heat distribution.* [< OE *clæthan* clothe, now obsolete in that sense]

clad·ding (klad′ing) *n.* 1 material used for facing the outside walls of a building, etc.: *aluminum cladding for a house.* 2 a layer or coating of metal bonded to another metal, as for protection of the metal underneath. [See CLAD[2]]

claim (klām) *v., n.* —*v.* 1 say that one has and demand that others recognize (a right, title, possession, etc.); assert one's right to: *to claim a tract of land.* 2 demand as one's own or one's right: *Does anyone claim this pencil?* 3 declare as a fact; say strongly; maintain: *She claimed that her answer was correct.* 4 require; call for; deserve: *Business claims his attention.* —*n.* 1 a demand for something due; assertion of a right. 2 a right or title to something. 3 something that is claimed. 4 a piece of public land that a settler or prospector marks out for himself. When the government offers the land for sale, the settler must buy his claim or forfeit it. 5 the assertion of something as a fact.
jump a claim, illegally seize a piece of land that has been staked for mining by another but not yet formally recorded.
lay claim to, declare (one's) right to; assert (one's) ownership of; claim: *Since nobody laid claim to the record, we took it home.*
put in a claim or (someone's) **claim,** ask for as a right; claim: *I'm putting in my claim right now for my share of the saskatoons we picked.*
stake (out) a claim, claim an area of land for mining rights by setting out stakes to mark its boundaries: *After staking out a claim, a person must record his claim at the proper government office within a certain length of time to make it permanent.*
[ME < OF *claim*(e) < *clamer, v.* < L *clamare* call, proclaim] —**claim′a·ble,** *adj.* —**claim′er,** *n.*
☞ *Syn. v.* 2. See note at **demand.**

claim·ant (klām′ənt) *n.* one who makes a claim.

clair·voy·ance (kler voi′əns) *n.* 1 the power of knowing about things that are out of sight. 2 exceptional insight. [< F]

clair·voy·ant (kler voi′ənt) *adj., v.* —*adj.* 1 having the power of seeing things that are out of sight. 2 exceptionally keen. —*n.* a person who has, or claims to have, the power of seeing things that are out of sight: *The clairvoyant claimed to be able to locate lost articles, and to give news of faraway people.* [< F *clairvoyant* clear-sighted < *clair* clear + *voyant,* ppr. of *voir* see]

clam (klam) *n., v.* **clammed, clam·ming.** —*n.* 1 any of various bivalve molluscs having a shell closed by two muscles at opposite ends, and a powerful, muscular foot with which they burrow into sand or mud. Some clams, such as the quahog and soft-shell clam, are edible. 2 *Informal.* a person who speaks very little. —*v.* go out after clams; dig for clams.
clam up, *Slang.* refuse to speak or give information.
[apparently special use of *clam* pair of pincers; OE *clamm* fetter] —**clam′like,** *adj.*

clam·bake (klam′bāk′) *n.* 1 a picnic where clams are baked or steamed. A clambake may be an elaborate meal, with much to eat besides clams. 2 *Informal.* a large, noisy entertainment or social gathering.

clam·ber (klam′bər) *v., n.* —*v.* 1 climb, using both hands and feet; climb awkwardly or with difficulty; scramble. 2 of plants, climb by means of tendrils, etc. 3 climb or struggle into a position of eminence; attain with effort. —*n.* an awkward or difficult climb. [ME *clambre*(n). Related to CLIMB.] —**clam′ber·er,** *n.*

clam·my (klam′ē) *adj.* **-mi·er, -mi·est.** unpleasantly cold and damp. [ME; probably < *clammen* smear < OE *clæman*; cf. OE *clām* clay] —**clam′mi·ness,** *n.*

clam·or or **clam·our** (klam′ər) *n., v.* —*n.* 1 a loud, continual noise or uproar; shouting. 2 a noisy demand or complaint. 3 any loud, sustained noise. —*v.* 1 make a loud noise or continual uproar; shout. 2 demand or complain noisily. [ME < OF < L *clamor* < *clamare* cry out] —**clam′or·er** or **clam′our·er,** *n.*

clam·or·ous (klam′ər əs) *adj.* 1 noisy; shouting. 2 making noisy demands or complaints. —**clam′or·ous·ly,** *adv.* —**clam′or·ous·ness,** *n.*

clam·our (klam′ər) See **clamor.**

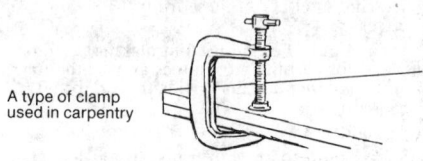

A type of clamp used in carpentry

clamp (klamp) *n., v.* —*n.* a mechanical device for binding or pressing two or more things firmly together. —*v.* put in a clamp or fasten together or strengthen with a clamp.
clamp down on, *Informal.* put pressure on; take strict measures against: *The police clamped down on careless driving.* [< MDu. *klampe*]

clan (klan) *n.* 1 especially in Scotland, a group of related families that claim to be descended from a common ancestor. 2 a group of people closely joined together by some common interest. [< Scots Gaelic *clann* family] —**clan′like,** *adj.*

clan·des·tine (klan des′tən) *adj.* secret; concealed; underhand: *a clandestine plan.* [< L *clandestinus* < *clam* secretly] —**clan·des′tine·ly,** *adv.*
☞ *Syn.* See note at **secret.**

clang (klang) *n., v.* —*n.* a loud, harsh sound such as that caused by metal striking metal: *The clang of the fire bell aroused the town.* —*v.* 1 make or cause to make such a sound. 2 strike together with a clang. [imitative]

clang·er (klang′ər) *n. Informal.* a bad or blatant mistake.

clan·gor or **clang·our** (klang′ər *or* klang′gər) *n.* a loud clang or continued clanging: *the clangor of many bells.* [< L *clangor* < *clangere* clang]

clan·gor·ous (klang′ər əs *or* klang′gər əs) *adj.* clanging.

clan·gour (klang′ər *or* klang′gər) *n.* See **clangor.**

clank (klangk) *n., v.* —*n.* a sharp, harsh sound like the rattle of a heavy chain. —*v.* 1 make a sharp, harsh sound: *The swords clashed and clanked as the men fought one another.* 2 cause to clank. [imitative; probably < Du. *klank*]

clan·nish (klan′ish) *adj.* 1 of or having to do with a clan. 2 closely united; not liking outsiders. —**clan′nish·ly,** *adv.* —**clan′nish·ness,** *n.*

clans·man (klanz′mən) *n., pl.* **-men.** a member of a clan.

clans·wom·an (klanz′wùm′ən) *n., pl.* **-wom·en.** a female member of a clan.

clap[1] (klap) *n., v.* **clapped, clap·ping.** —*n.* 1 a sudden noise, such as a single burst of thunder, the sound of the hands struck together, or the sound of a loud slap. 2 the act of clapping: *They gave the speaker a polite clap.* 3 a hit or blow; slap: *a clap on the shoulder.* —*v.* 1 strike together loudly: *to clap one's hands.* 2 applaud by striking the hands together. 3 strike lightly with a quick blow: *He clapped his friend on the back.* 4 put or place quickly and effectively: *The police clapped the thief into jail.* 5 of a bird, flap (the wings).
clap eyes on, *Informal.* look at; see: *I liked him from the first time I clapped eyes on him.*
[OE *clæppan*]

clap[2] (klap) *n.*
the clap, *Slang.* gonorrhea.
[< OF *clapoir* venereal sore; 16c.]

clap·board (klap′bôrd *or* klab′ərd) *n., v.* —*n.* a thin board, thicker along one edge than along the other, used to cover the outer walls of wooden buildings. —*v.* cover with clapboards.

clap·per (klap′ər) *n.* 1 a person or thing that claps, especially the movable part inside a bell that strikes the outside part, causing it to ring. 2 the movable part inside a bell that strikes the outer part. 3 a device for making noise: *We had horns and clappers at the party.*

clap·trap (klap′trap′) *n., adj.* —*n.* empty talk aimed at merely getting attention or applause. —*adj.* cheap and showy.

claque (klak) *n.* **1** a group of persons hired to applaud in a theatre. **2** a group that applauds or follows another person for selfish reasons. [< F *claque* < *claquer* clap]

clar·et (klar′ət *or* kler′ət) *n., adj.* —*n.* **1** a kind of dry red table wine, originally one made in Bordeaux, France. **2** a dark, purplish red. —*adj.* dark purplish red. [ME < OF *claret* light-colored, dim. of *cler.* See CLEAR.]

clar·i·fi·ca·tion (klar′ə fə kā′shən *or* kler′ə fə kā′shən) *n.* **1** the act or process of clarifying. **2** the state of being clarified.

clar·i·fi·er (klar′ə fī′ər *or* kler′ə fī′ər) *n.* **1** a substance used to clarify liquids. **2** a large metal pan used in clarifying sugar.

clar·i·fy (klar′ə fī′ *or* kler′ə fī) *v.* **-fied, -fy·ing. 1** make or become free of impurities; purify: *We clarified the cloudy liquid by using a filter.* **2** make clear to the understanding; explain: *The news reporter asked her to clarify her statement for the public.* [ME < OF *clarifier* < LL *clarificare* < L *clarus* clear + *facere* make]

A clarinet

clar·i·net (klar′ə net′ *or* kler′ə net′) *n.* a wind instrument consisting of a straight metal or wooden tube ending in a slightly flared bell, having a single reed and played by means of holes and keys. [< F *clarinette* < Ital. *clarinetto* < *clarino* trumpet, ult. < L *clarus* clear]

clar·i·net·tist *or* **clar·i·net·ist** (klar′ə net′ist *or* kler′ə net′ist) *n.* a person who plays a clarinet, especially a skilled player.

clar·i·on (klar′ē ən *or* kler′ē ən) *adj., n.* —*adj.* clear and shrill. —*n.* **1** a trumpet with clear, shrill tones. **2** *Poetic.* the sound made by this trumpet. **3** *Poetic.* a clear, shrill sound like it. [< Med.L *clario, -onis* < L *clarus* clear]

clar·i·ty (klar′ə tē *or* kler′ə tē) *n.* clearness. [< L *claritas*]

clar·sach (klär′saн) *n., pl.* **clar·saich** (klär′siн). the ancient festival harp of Ireland and Scotland, having from 29 to 58 strings. [< Gaelic]

clash (klash) *v., n.* —*v.* **1** make or cause to make a loud, harsh, discordant sound like that of two hard things running into each other, or of metal striking metal, or of bells rung together but not in harmony. **2** throw, shut, etc. with such a sound. **3** come into or be in conflict: *The two armies clashed. Your feeling and your judgment sometimes clash.* **4** of colors, look inharmonious together. —*n.* **1** a loud, harsh, discordant sound. **2** strong disagreement or conflict: *a clash of opinions.* [imitative] —**clash′er,** *n.* —**clash′ing·ly,** *adv.*

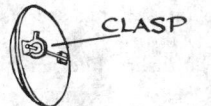

CLASP

A clasp on a brooch

clasp (klasp) *n., v.* —*n.* **1** a device, usually having a hook of some kind, to fasten two parts or pieces together: *This suede belt has a gold clasp.* **2** a close hold with the arms or hands. **3** a firm grip with the hand: *He gave my hand a warm clasp.* **4** a small bar of metal placed across the ribbon of a medal, indicating the battle area, etc. in which the medal was won. —*v.* **1** fasten together with a clasp. **2** hold closely with the arms or hands: *The mother clasped her baby to her breast.* **3** grip firmly with the hand. [ME *claspe(n)*] —**clasp′er,** *n.*

clasp knife a knife with a blade or blades folding into the handle; especially, one with a clasp to hold each blade open.

class (klas) *n., v.* —*n.* **1** a group of persons or things alike in some way; kind; sort. **2** a group of students taught together. **3** the meeting time for such a group: *The class was at nine o'clock.* **4** a group of students entering a school together and graduating in the same year: *The class of 1976 graduated in 1976.* **5** a rank or division of society: *the middle class.* **6** a system of ranks or divisions in society. **7** *U.S.* a group of military draftees of the same age. **8** high rank in society. **9** grade; quality: *First class is the best and most costly way to travel.* **10** *Informal.* elegance or style. **11** *Biology.* a major category in the classification of plants and animals, more specific than the phylum (or division) and more general than the order. See **classification** for chart.

—*v.* put or be in a class or group. [< L *classis* class, fleet < dial. Gk. *klasis* a calling, summoning]

class. **1** classical. **2** classified.

class·book (klas′bùk′) *n.* **1** a book in which a teacher records the absences and keeps the grades of students. **2** an annual book usually published by the graduating class of a high school or college. It contains pictures of the students, teachers, school buildings, etc.

class–cons·cious (klas′kon′shəs) *adj.* very aware of one's status as a member of a particular social or economic class.

class day *Esp.U.S.* the day on which the members of a class celebrate their graduation with special ceremonies.

clas·sic (klas′ik) *adj., n.* —*adj.* **1** of the highest rank or quality; serving as an example of excellence for its kind: *a classic example of clear, attractive handwriting; the classic 1937 Ford. The golf champion has a classic swing.* **2** having to do with the literature and art of ancient Greece and Rome; classical. **3** of or according to established principles of quality in the arts and sciences; simple, regular, and restrained: *the classic style of Bach's music. We admired the classic lines of the new bridge.* **4** established in literature, art, or history as a model or outstanding example: *the classic smile of the Mona Lisa.* **5** being an excellent model of its type: *the classic cowboy hero, a classic case of hysteria.* —*n.* **1** a work of literature or art long considered to be of the highest quality: The Tin Flute *is a classic.* **2** an author or artist of acknowledged excellence whose works serve as a standard, model, or guide: *Shakespeare is a classic.* **3** a famous traditional event: *The Kentucky Derby is a classic.* **4** something considered as a typical or outstanding example of its type. **5 the classics,** the literature of ancient Greece and Rome. [< L *classicus* < *classis.* See CLASS.]

clas·si·cal (klas′ə kəl) *adj.* **1** of, having to do with, or designating ancient Greece and Rome, especially with respect to their art and literature: *classical studies.* **2** knowledgeable about ancient Greece and Rome, especially their art and literature: *a classical scholar.* **3** modelled on or resembling this literature and art: Ulysses *is a classical poem by Tennyson.* **4** orthodox and sound, but not new or up to date: *classical physics.* **5** of or designating any music composed in the European tradition of written music as developed from early Christian church music, especially works composed during the last 300 years or so: *He prefers classical music to popular or folk music.* **6 Classical,** *Music.* of, having to do with, or designating the music of 18th century European composers such as Mozart and Haydn, as distinct from the Romantic music of composers like Beethoven and Tchaikovsky.

classical college *Cdn.* in French Canada, an educational establishment at the secondary-school and college levels that offers an eight-year course, mainly in the classics and liberal arts, leading to the B.A. degree which is conferred by the university to which the college is affiliated.

clas·si·cal·ly (klas′ik lē) *adv.* in a classical style; according to the manner of classic authors.

clas·si·cism (klas′ə siz′əm) *n.* **1** the principles of the literature and art of ancient Greece and Rome. They include simplicity, regularity, and restraint. **2** the following of these principles. **3** knowledge of the literature of ancient Greece and Rome; classical scholarship. **4** an idiom or form from Greek or Latin introduced into another language. **5** *Music.* a style developed in Europe during the latter half of the 18th century, characterized by simplicity, dignity, proportion, and elegance.

clas·si·cist (klas′ə sist) *n.* **1** a follower of the principles of classicism in literature and art. **2** an expert in the literature of ancient Greece and Rome. **3** a person who urges the study of Greek and Latin.

clas·si·fi·ca·tion (klas′ə fə kā′shən) *n.* **1** an arranging in classes or groups on the basis of similar qualities or features; grouping according to some system. **2** the arrangement or grouping so made: *This library has worked out a simple classification for its books.* **3** *Biology.* the arranging of plants and animals in groups according to shared characteristics such as body structure. See biological classification chart on the following page.

clas·si·fied (klas′ə fīd′) *adj.* **1** of government documents, having a classification as secret, confidential, or restricted. **2** *Informal.* secret.

The Biological Classification of Animals and Plants

ANIMALS		PLANTS	
Category	**Example**	**Category**	**Example**
SPECIES	*Canis latrans* The coyote.	SPECIES	*Rosa acicularis* The prickly rose, a wild rose.
GENUS	*Canis* Dogs and their close relatives; 8 species. (The coyote, domestic dog, dingo, wolves, and jackals.)	GENUS	*Rosa* Wild roses and garden roses.
FAMILY	*Canidae* Dog family, made up of 14 genera. (Dogs and their close relatives; also foxes, the African hunting dog, etc.)	FAMILY	*Rosaceae* Rose family, made up of about 100 genera. (Roses; also spireas, apples, pears, plums, strawberries, etc.)
ORDER	*Carnivora* Carnivorous, or meat-eating, animals, made up of 7 families. (Dog family; also cats, bears, weasels, skunks, etc.)	ORDER	*Rosales* Rose order, made up of about 3 families and 3200 species. (Rose family; also sycamore, mock orange, hydrangeas, clovers, etc.)
CLASS	*Mammalia* Mammals, made up of 18 orders. (Carnivorous animals; also man, apes, whales, camels, rodents, bats, etc.)	CLASS	*Magnoliopsida* (or *Dicotyledones*) Dicotyledons, made up of 74 orders. (All members of order Rosales; also willows, maples, cactuses, peppers, violets, daisies, etc.)
PHYLUM	*Chordata* Chordates, animals with some form of spinal cord, made up of 9 classes. (Mammals; also birds, reptiles, amphibians, fishes, etc.)	DIVISION	*Magnoliophyta* (or *Anthophyta*) The flowering plants, or angiosperms, made up of 2 classes. (All dicotyledons; also grasses, palms, bulrushes, lilies, orchids, etc.)
KINGDOM	*Animalia* All animals.	KINGDOM	*Plantae* All plants.

The chart above gives the main categories, or groupings, used in the classification of animals and plants. The examples (the *coyote* and the *rose*) are given to show how particular animals and plants fit into the system. As one goes up the hierarchy from the most specific to the most general, more and more animals or plants are included, and the relationships between the more general groups become more distant. For instance, coyotes are more closely related to dogs and wolves than to foxes; and coyotes, dogs, wolves, and foxes are more closely related to each other than they are to cats or bears.

classified advertisement an advertisement inserted in a special part of a newspaper, magazine, etc. under one of a set of special headings.

clas·si·fy (klas′ə fī′) v. **-fied, -fy·ing.** arrange in classes or groups; group according to some system: *In the post office, mail is classified according to the places where it is to go.* [< L *classis* class + E *-fy*] —**clas′si·fi′a·ble,** adj. —**clas′si·fi′er,** n.

class·less (klas′lis) adj. not divided into classes, especially social and economic classes: *a classless society.* —**class′less·ness,** n.

classmate (klas′māt′) n. a member of the same class in school.

class·room (klas′rüm′ *or* -rùm′) n. a room where classes meet in school; schoolroom.

class struggle any conflict between divisions of society, especially between capital and labor.

class·y (klas′ē) adj. **-i·er, -i·est.** *Informal.* of, or appearing to be of, high social or economic standing; stylish; elegant. —**class′i·ness,** n.

clat·ter (klat′ər) n., v. —n. **1** a rattling noise: *the clatter of dishes.* **2** noisy talk.
—v. **1** move or fall with a rattling noise; make a commotion: *The horses clattered over the stones.* **2** talk fast and noisily. **3** cause to clatter. [OE *clatrian*] —**clat′ter·er,** n.

clause (kloz *or* klôz) n. **1** that part of a sentence having a subject and predicate. In *He came before we left, He came* is a **main clause,** and *before we left* is a **subordinate clause.** A subordinate clause functions as a noun, adjective, or adverb. **2** a single provision of a law, treaty, or any other written agreement: *There is a clause in our contract that says we may not keep a dog in this building.* [< Med.L *clausa* for L *clausula* close of a period < *claudere* close]

claus·tro·pho·bi·a (klos′trə fō′bē ə *or* klôs′trə fō′bē ə) n. a morbid fear of enclosed spaces. [< NL < L *claustrum* closed place + E *-phobia* fear]

claus·tro·pho·bic (klos′trə fō′bik *or* klôs′trə fō′bik) adj. of or having to do with claustrophobia.

claus·tro·pho·bi·cal·ly (klos′trə fō′bə klē *or* klôs′trə fō′bə klē) adv. in a claustrophobic manner; in a way that is or feels confined or stifled.

cla·vate (klā′vāt) adj. club-shaped. [< L *clavatus* < *clava* club]

clave (klāv) v. *Archaic.* a pt. of **cleave².**

clav·i·chord (klav′ə kôrd′) n. an early stringed musical instrument with a keyboard. The piano evolved from it. [< Med.L *clavichordium* < L *clavis* key + *chorda* string]

clav·i·cle (klav′ə kəl) n. the collarbone. [< L *clavicula* bolt, dim. of *clavis* key]

clav·i·er¹ (klav′ē ər *or* klə vēr′) n. **1** the keyboard of a piano, organ, etc. **2** a soundless keyboard used for practice. [< F *clavier,* orig. key bearer < *clef* key < L *clavis*]

clav·i·er² (klə vēr′) n. any musical instrument having a keyboard, such as the harpsichord and the clavichord. [< G *Klavier* < F *clavier* keyboard, clavier¹]

claw (klo *or* klô) n., v. —n. **1** a sharp, hooked nail on each toe of a bird. **2** a similar nail on each toe of certain animals: *The cat's claws were dangerous.* **3** a foot with such sharp, hooked nails: *The gopher was held tightly in the hawk's claws.* **4** one of the pincers of a lobster, crab, etc. **5** anything like a claw. The part of a hammer used for pulling nails is the claw.
—v. scratch, tear, seize, or pull with claws or fingernails. [OE *clawu*] —**claw′-like′,** adj.

claw hammer 1 a hammer with one end of the head curved like a claw and forked for pulling nails. **2** *Informal.* a dress coat; swallowtail coat.

clay (klā) n. a stiff, sticky kind of earth with little or no animal or vegetable matter in it, that can be easily shaped when wet and hardens after drying or baking. Bricks and dishes may be made from clay. **2** earth. **3** in the Bible, the human body. [OE *clæg*]

clay·ey (klā′ē) adj. **clay·i·er, clay·i·est. 1** of, like, or containing clay. **2** covered or smeared with clay.

clay·more (klā′môr′) n. a heavy, two-edged sword, formerly used by Scottish Highlanders. [< Scots Gaelic *claidheamh mor* great sword]

clay pigeon a saucerlike clay disk thrown in the air as a flying target for skeet shooting.

CLC Canadian Labour Congress.

-cle suffix. **1** little, as in *corpuscle, particle.* **2** other meanings, as in *receptacle, vehicle.* [< L *-culus, -cula, -culum* (dim.) *or* < F *-cle* (< L)]

clean (klēn) adj., adv., v. —adj. **1** free from dirt or filth; not soiled or stained: *clean clothes.* **2** pure; innocent: *a clean heart.* **3** having the habit of keeping oneself clean: *Cats are clean animals.* **4** of atomic weapons, causing little or no radio-active fall-out. **5** fit for

food: *Moslems and Jews do not consider pork a clean meat.* **6** clear; even; regular: *a clean cut.* **7** clever; skilful; free from any clumsiness: *a clean jump.* **8** complete; entire; total: *a clean escape.* **9** honest; fair, as in sports: *a clean player, a clean fighter.* **10** having a few or no corrections or alterations: *I have to make a clean copy to hand in.* **11** blank; new: *I need a clean page.* **12** of printer's proofs, relatively free from corrections or alterations.
—adv. **1** completely; entirely; totally: *The horse jumped clean over the brook.* **2** in a clean manner.
—v. **1** make clean: *to clean a room.* **2** prepare fish, game, chicken, etc. for cooking by removing entrails, scales or feathers, etc. **3** undergo cleaning: *This room cleans easily because it doesn't have much furniture in it.* **4** do cleaning: *I'm going to clean this morning.*
clean out, a make clean by emptying: *Clean out your desk.* **b** empty; use up: *The girls cleaned out a whole box of cookies.* **c** *Slang.* leave without money; take all a person's money.
clean up, a make clean by removing dirt, rubbish, etc. **b** put in order. **c** *Informal.* finish; complete. **d** *Slang.* make money; profit. [OE *clæne*]
☞ *Syn.* v. **1. Clean, cleanse** = make free from dirt or filth. **Clean** is the general word meaning "to remove dirt, impurities, or stains," especially from objects: *The men cleaned the streets.* **Cleanse,** formal or archaic in the sense of "make clean," is used commonly in the sense of "make pure," applying particularly to removing impurities by chemical or other technical processes: *Health experts are trying to cleanse the air in cities. We cleanse wounds.*

clean-cut (klēn′kut′) adj. **1** having clear, sharp outlines. **2** well-shaped. **3** clear; definite; distinct. **4** having a neat and wholesome appearance: *a clean-cut young man.*

clean·er (klēn′ər) n. **1** a person whose work is keeping buildings, windows, etc., clean. **2** a tool or machine for cleaning. **3** anything that removes dirt, grease, or stains; cleanser.
take (someone) to the cleaners, *Slang.* take all a person's money, as in gambling.

cleaning lady cleaning woman.

cleaning woman a woman whose work is cleaning homes, offices, or public buildings.

clean-limbed (klēn′limd′) adj. having well-shaped limbs.

clean·li·ness (klen′lē nis) n. cleanness; habitual cleanness.

clean·ly (adv. klēn′lē; adj. klen′lē) adv., adj. —adv. in a clean manner: *The butcher's knife cut cleanly through the meat.* —adj. always keeping oneself or one's surroundings clean: *The cat is a cleanly animal.* [OE *clænlīce*]

clean·ness (klēn′nis) n. the quality or condition of being clean.

cleanse (klenz) v. **cleansed, cleans·ing. 1** make clean. **2** make pure. [OE *clænsian* < *clæne* clean] —**cleans′a·ble,** adj. —**cleans′er,** n.
☞ *Syn.* **1.** See note at **clean.**

cleans·er (klenz′ər) n. a substance that cleans, especially a soap, detergent, disinfectant, or bleaching agent used in household cleaning.

clean-shav·en (klēn′shāv′ən) adj. with the face shaved.

cleans·ing (klenz′ing) n., adj. —n. the act or process of making clean. —adj. that cleanses.

clean-up (klēn′up′) n. **1** a cleaning up. **2** *Slang.* an exceptional amount of money made on a transaction; profit.

clear (klēr) adj., v., adv., n. —adj. **1** not cloudy, misty, or hazy; bright; light: *a clear day.* **2** easy to see through; transparent: *clear glass.* **3** having a pure, even color: *a clear blue.* **4** easily seen, heard, or understood; plain; distinct: *a clear idea, a clear voice.* **5** sure; certain: *It is clear that it is going to rain.* **6** not blocked or obstructed; open: *a clear view.* **7** without touching; without being caught: *The ship was clear of the iceberg.* **8** free from blame or guilt; innocent: *A careful investigation showed that the suspect was clear.* **9** free from debts or charges: *clear profit.* **10** without limitation; complete: *the clear contrary.* **11** of lumber, free from knots or other imperfections.
—v. **1** make clear or free of obstruction: *He cleared the land of trees. He cleared his throat before he began to speak. She cleared her desk.* **2** become clear. *It rained and then it cleared.* **3** remove to leave a space clear: *She cleared the dishes from the table.* **4** get by or over without touching or being caught: *The horse cleared the fence.* **5** make free from blame or guilt; prove to be innocent: *The jury's verdict cleared the accused man.* **6** make as profit free from

debts or charges. **7** get (a ship or cargo) free by meeting requirements on entering or leaving a port. **8** leave a port after doing this. **9** get permission from an authority to proceed after inspection of goods, etc.: *It took us half an hour to clear customs.* **10** exchange (cheques and bills) and settle accounts between different banks. **11** settle a business account or certify a cheque as valid.

clear away or **off, a** remove to leave a space clear: *to clear away underbrush.* **b** clear dishes and so on from a table: *It's your turn to clear away.*

clear out, a make clear by throwing out or emptying. **b** *Informal.* go away; leave.

clear out or **off,** *Informal.* go away; leave: *You'll have to clear out of the gym by four o'clock because they need it for basketball practice. She cleared off as soon as she heard there was work involved.*

clear up, a make or become clear. **b** put in order by clearing. **c** explain: *John cleared up the question of why he had not been there by saying that he had been ill.* **d** become clear after a storm. —*adv.* **1** in a clear manner. **2** completely; entirely: *The bullet went clear through the door.*
—*n.*

in the clear, a between the outside parts; in interior measurement: *The house was 15 metres wide, in the clear.* **b** *Informal.* free of guilt or blame; innocent: *His report shows that the suspect is in the clear.* **c** free from limitations or encumbrances: *Having paid all his debts, he was finally in the clear again.* **d** in plain text; not in cipher or code. [ME *cler* < OF < L *clarus*] —**clear′ly,** *adv.* —**clear′ness,** *n.*

clear·ance (klēr′əns) *n.* **1** the act of clearing. **2** a clear space, especially the distance between objects or parts that allows free movement: *We had to wait for the other car to move, because there wasn't enough clearance to get our car out. The underpass has a clearance of four metres.* **3** the meeting of requirements to get a ship or cargo free on entering or leaving a port. **4** a certificate showing this. **5** official permission to go ahead; authorization to do a certain thing or have access to a certain place: *The pilot had to wait for clearance from the control tower.* **6** the exchanging of cheques and bills and settling of accounts between different banks.

clearance sale a sale held by a store, etc., to clear out old stock in order to make room for new.

clear–cut (klēr′kut′) *adj.* **1** having clear, sharp outlines. **2** clear; definite; distinct: *He had clear-cut ideas about his work.*

clear–eyed (klēr′īd′) *adj.* **1** having bright, clear eyes. **2** having acute and undistorted perception.

clear–head·ed (klēr′hed′id) *adj.* having or showing a clear understanding. —**clear′–head′ed·ly,** *adv.* —**clear′–head′ed·ness,** *n.*

clear·ing (klēr′ing) *n.* **1** an open space of cleared land in a forest. **2** exchanging of cheques and bills and settling of accounts between different banks.

clearing house a place where banks exchange cheques and bills and settle their accounts.

clear–sight·ed (klēr′sīt′id) *adj.* **1** able to see clearly. **2** able to understand or think clearly. —**clear′–sight′ed·ly,** *adv.* —**clear′–sight′ed·ness,** *n.*

clear·sto·ry (klēr′stô′rē) *n., pl.* **-ries.** See clerestory.

cleat (klēt) *n., v.* —*n.* **1** one of several studs or bars of leather, plastic, etc., attached to the sole of a football boot, soccer boot, etc., to prevent slipping. **2** a strip of wood, metal, leather, etc., fastened across anything for support or for sure footing. A gangway has cleats to keep people from slipping. **3** one of the raised bars placed at intervals across the track of a vehicle that travels over snow. The cleats on a snowmobile track make possible a firmer grip on snow. **4** a small, wedge-shaped block fastened to a mast, spar, etc. as a support, check, etc. **5** a piece of wood, metal, or plastic having projecting arms or ends, fixed to a boat, wharf, flagpole, etc. and used for securing ropes or lines. See rowboat for picture.
—*v.* fasten to or with a cleat. [ME *cleete*]

cleav·age (klēv′ij) *n.* **1** a split; division. **2** the action of cleaving, or splitting. **3** *Biology.* cell division, especially any of the series of divisions by which a fertilized egg develops into an embryo. **4** *Chemistry.* the breaking up of a molecule into simpler molecules. **5** *Mineralogy.* the tendency of a crystallized substance or rock to split along definite planes. **6** *Informal.* the division between a woman's breasts, especially as revealed by a low neckline.

cleave[1] (klēv) *v.* **cleft** or **cleaved** or **clove, cleft** or **cleaved** or **clo·ven, cleav·ing. 1** cut, divide, or split open: *With one blow of the axe he cleft the log in two.* **2** pass through; pierce; penetrate: *The airplane cleaved the clouds.* **3** make by cutting: *to cleave a path through the wilderness.* [OE *clēofan*] —**cleav′a·ble,** *adj.*

cleave[2] (klēv) *v.* **cleaved, cleaved, cleav·ing.** hold fast (*to*); cling; be faithful (*to*): *cleave to an idea.* [OE *cleofian*]

A cleaver

cleav·er (klēv′ər) *n.* **1** one that cleaves. **2** a cutting tool with a heavy blade and a short handle. A butcher uses a cleaver to chop through meat or bone.

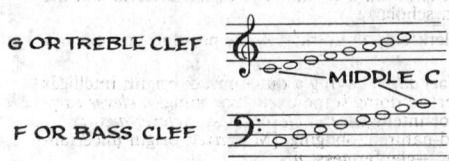

G OR TREBLE CLEF
MIDDLE C
F OR BASS CLEF

clef (klef) *n. Music.* a symbol indicating the pitch of the notes on a staff. [< F < L *clavis* key]

cleft (kleft) *v., adj., n.* —*v.* a pt. and a pp. of cleave[1].
—*adj.* split; divided.
—*n.* a space or opening made by splitting; crack. [OE *(ge)clyft*]

cleft palate a narrow opening running lengthwise in the roof of the mouth, caused by failure of the two parts of the palate to join.

clem·a·tis (klem′ə tis *or* klə mā′tis) *n.* any of a genus (*Clematis*) of mainly climbing shrubs of the buttercup family, some having evergreen leaves, cultivated in many species and varieties for their showy flowers. [< L < Gk. *klēmatis* < *klēma* vine branch]

clem·en·cy (klem′ən sē) *n., pl.* **-cies. 1** mercy; mildness in exercising authority or power: *The Crown recommended clemency for the defendant.* **2** mildness of climate or weather.
☛ *Syn.* **1.** See note at mercy.

clem·ent (klem′ənt) *adj.* **1** merciful. **2** mild. [< L *clemens, -entis*] —**clem′ent·ly,** *adv.*

clench (klench) *v., n.* —*v.* **1** close tightly together: *to clench one's fists, to clench one's teeth.* **2** grasp firmly; grip tightly: *The policeman clenched his prisoner's arm.* **3** clinch (a nail, etc.).
—*n.* a firm grasp; tight grip: *I felt the clench of his hand on my arm.* [OE *(be)clencan* hold fast] —**clench′er,** *n.*
☛ *Syn. v.* **1, 2. Clench, clinch** agree in their basic meaning of holding fast or making hold fast, but differ in emphasis and application. **Clench** emphasizes the idea of holding fast by clamping together and is used in the senses of close tightly (fist, teeth, lips, etc.) and grasp firmly (a hammer, etc.). **Clinch** emphasizes the idea of fastening firmly and securely, and applies chiefly to fastening nails and bolts, etc., or fastening things together.

clep·sy·dra (klep′sə drə) *n., pl.* **-dras, -drae** (-drē′ *or* -drī′). a device used in ancient times for measuring time by the flow of water, mercury, etc. through a small opening. [< L < Gk. *klepsydra* < *kleptein* steal + *hydōr* water]

clere·sto·ry (klēr′stô′rē) *n., pl.* **-ries. 1** *Architecture.* the upper part of the wall of a church, having windows in it above the roofs of the aisles. **2** any similar structure. Also, **clearstory.** [apparently < *clere* clear + *story*[2]]

cler·gy (klėr′jē) *n., pl.* **-gies. 1** a body or order of persons specially trained and ordained to perform religious services. Ministers, pastors, priests, and rabbis are members of the clergy. Compare laity. **2** all the persons commissioned or otherwise designated for religious duties, including deacons, religious, lay ministers, etc. [ME < OF *clergie,* ult. < L *clericus.* See CLERIC.]

cler·gy·man (klėr′jē mən) *n., pl.* **-men.** a man who is a member of the clergy.

Clergy Reserves *Cdn.* the lands set aside in Lower and Upper Canada in 1791 for the support of a Protestant clergy. In practice, this was interpreted to mean the Church of England clergy.

cler·ic (kler′ik) *n.* a member of the clergy. [< L *clericus* < Gk. *klērikos* < *klēros* clergy; originally, lot, allotment; first applied (in the Septuagint) to the Levites, the service of God being the priest's lot. Doublet of CLERK.]

cler·i·cal (kler′ə kəl) *adj., n.* —*adj.* **1** of or for a clerk or clerks: *Keeping records or accounts and copying letters are clerical jobs in an office.* **2** of, having to do with, or characteristic of the clergy or a member of the clergy: *clerical robes.* **3** supporting the power or influence of the clergy in politics.
—*n.* **1** a member of the clergy. **2** a supporter of the power or influence of the clergy in politics. **3** **clericals,** *pl.* the clothes worn by members of the clergy. [< LL *clericalis* < L *clericus.* See CLERIC.]
—**cler′i·cal·ly,** *adv.*

cler·i·cal·ism (kler′ə kəl iz′əm) *n.* **1** the power or influence of the clergy in politics. **2** the support of such power or influence.

cler·i·cal·ist (kler′ə kəl ist) *n.* a person who favors clericalism.

clerk (klėrk; *esp.Brit.*, klärk) *n., v.* —*n.* **1** a person whose work is waiting on customers and selling goods in a store; a salesman or saleswoman in a store. **2** a person whose work is keeping records or accounts, copying letters, etc. in an office. **3** an official who keeps records and takes care of regular business in a court of law, legislature, etc. **4** a layman who has minor church duties. **5** *Archaic.* clergyman. **6** *Archaic.* a person who can read and write; scholar. —*v.* work as a clerk in a store: *He clerks in a drugstore.* [party OE *clerc, cleric,* partly < OF *clerc* < L *clericus.* Doublet of CLERIC.]

clerk·ly (klėrk′lē *or* klärk′lē) *adj.* **1** of or like a clerk. **2** of the clergy. **3** *Archaic.* scholarly.

clerk·ship (klėrk′ship *or* klärk′-) *n.* the position or work of a clerk.

clev·er (klev′ər) *adj.* **1** having a quick mind; bright; intelligent. **2** skilful or expert in doing some particular thing: *a clever carpenter.* **3** showing skill or intelligence: *a clever trick, a clever answer.* **4** *Informal.* good-natured; obliging. [ME *cliver,* origin uncertain] —**clev′er·ly,** *adv.* —**clev′er·ness,** *n.*
☞ *Syn.* **1. Clever, ingenious** = having a quick mind. **Clever** is the general word, and suggests a natural quickness in learning things and skill in using the mind: *He had no training, but was clever enough to become a good salesman.* **Ingenious** = quick to see new ways of doing things, skilful in inventing and clever at making things: *Some ingenious person designed the first electric can opener.*

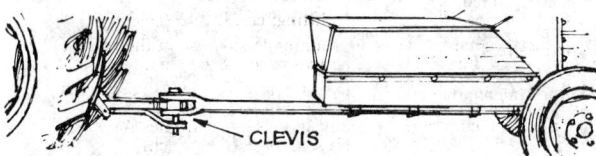

CLEVIS

clev·is (klev′is) *n.* a U-shaped piece of metal with a bolt or pin through the ends. A clevis may be used to fasten a wagon, plough, etc., to a tractor. [related to CLEAVE¹]

clew (klü) *n., v.* —*n.* **1** a ball of thread or yarn. **2** a lower corner of a sail. **3** a metal ring fastened there. —*v.* raise or lower a sail by the clews. [OE *cleowen*]
☞ *Hom.* **clue.**

cli·ché (klē shā′) *n.* a timeworn expression or idea. [< F *cliché,* pp. of *clicher* stereotype]

click (klik) *n., v.* —*n.* **1** a light, sharp sound: *We heard the click as he turned his key in the lock.* **2** a locking device in a ratchet mechanism, such as a pawl, that operates with a clicking sound. **3** *Phonetics.* any of a group of voiceless speech sounds characteristic especially of some African languages, made by sucking air into the mouth and rapidly drawing the tongue down from the teeth or the roof of the mouth. —*v.* **1** make a light, sharp sound. **2** cause to make such a sound: *The soldier clicked his heels together and saluted.* **3** *Slang.* get along well together; be congenial; hit it off: *We clicked from the start.* **4** *Informal.* succeed; go or do well: *This movie should click; it has well-known actors and a popular theme.* **5** *Informal.* suddenly make sense or become clear: *Then something clicked and he realized that he had seen the man before.* [imitative]

click beetle any of a family (Elateridae) of beetles that are able to right themselves with a clicking or snapping sound when put on their backs.

cli·ent (klī′ənt) *n.* **1** a person for whom a lawyer or other professional person acts. **2** customer. **3** in ancient Rome, a poor or humble person depending on a noble or wealthy man for assistance. **4** a personal follower; dependant. [< L *cliens, -entis* (related to *clinare* lean)] —**cli′ent·less,** *adj.*

cli·en·tele (klī ən tel′) *n.* **1** clients; customers. **2** personal followers. **3** a number of clients. [< F < L *clientela*]

cliff (klif) *n.* a steep, high face of rock or earth precipice: *Great cliffs overhung the canyon.* [OE *clif*] —**cliff′like′,** *adj.*

cliff dweller 1 a person living in a cave or house built in a cliff. **2** *Slang.* a person living in a high-rise apartment building.

cliff dwelling a cave or house built in a cliff.

cliff–hang·er (klif′hang′ər) *n. Slang.* **1** a story, motion picture, etc. that is full of suspense, especially a serial in which each episode ends with the hero or heroine in an extremely dangerous situation. **2** a race, election, or other contest in which the result is in doubt until the very end.

cliff swallow a swallow (*Petrochelidon pyrrhonota*) of North and South America having a relatively short, squarish tail. It builds a bottle-shaped nest of mud, straw, and feathers, usually attached to a cliff or wall.

hat, āge, fär; let, ēqual, tėrm; it, īce
hot, ōpen, ôrder; oil, out; cup, pút, rüle,
above, takən, pencəl, lemən, circəs

ch, child; ng, long; sh, ship
th, thin; ₮H, then; zh, measure

cli·mac·ter·ic (klī mak′tər ik *or* klī′mak ter′ik) *n., adj.* —*n.* **1** the time when some important event occurs, changing the course of things; crucial period. **2** the period of life around middle age when important physical and emotional changes usually take place. The climacteric in women is usually called the menopause. —*adj.* of, having to do with, or designating a climacteric. [< L < Gk. *klimaktērikos* of a critical period < *klimaktēr* rung of a ladder < *klimax* ladder]

cli·mac·tic (klī mak′tik) *adj.* of or forming a climax. —**cli·mac′ti·cal·ly,** *adv.*

cli·ma·graph (klī′mə graf′) *n.* a graph showing the typical climate of a selected location in terms of its average monthly temperature and precipitation. Also, **climograph.**

cli·mate (klī′mit) *n.* **1** the kind of weather patterns a place has over a period of years. Climate includes conditions of heat and cold, moisture and dryness, clearness and cloudiness, wind and calm. **2** any geographical region, with reference to its usual conditions of heat and cold, rainfall, wind, sunlight, etc: *The doctor ordered him to go to a drier climate.* **3** the prevailing state or trend: *the climate of public opinion.* [< L *clima, -atis* < Gk. *klima* slope (of the earth) < *klinein* incline]

cli·mat·ic (klī mat′ik) *adj.* of or having to do with climate.

cli·ma·tol·o·gist (klī′mə tol′ə jist) *n.* a person trained in climatology, especially one whose work it is.

cli·ma·tol·o·gy (klī′mə tol′ə jē) *n.* the science that deals with climate.

cli·max (klī′maks) *n., v.* —*n.* **1** the highest point; point of greatest interest; most exciting part. **2** the arrangement of ideas in a rising scale of force and interest. —*v.* bring or come to a climax. [< LL < Gk. *climax* ladder]

climb (klīm) *v., n.* —*n.* **1** go up, especially by using the hands or feet, or both; ascend: *The painter climbed the ladder. We had been climbing for hours but we had not reached the top of the mountain.* **2** rise slowly or with steady effort in rank or fortune: *It took her twelve years to climb to the position of executive director.* **3** grow upward by holding on or twining around: *Some vines climb.* **4** slope upward: *The road climbed for more than a kilometre before it began its descent toward the coast.* **5** increase: *The price of coffee has climbed during the past year.*
climb down, a go down by using the hands and feet. **b** *Informal.* give in; back down; withdraw from an impossible position or unreasonable attitude.
—*n.* **1** a climbing; ascent: *Our climb took two hours.* **2** a place to be climbed. **3** increase: *a climb in price.* [OE *climban*]
☞ *Hom.* **clime.**
☞ *Syn. v.* **1. Climb, ascend, mount** = go to or toward the top. **Climb** is the general word but suggests greater effort than do *ascend* and *mount: This car will never climb that hill.* **Ascend** is more formal, but suggests going straight up, or (in contrast to *climb*) up with ease: *She ascended the steps like a princess.* **Mount** is close to **ascend,** but in contrast to it can also mean to get on top of: *He mounted the stepladder. She mounted the stage.*

climb·er (klīm′ər) *n.* **1** a person or thing that climbs. **2** *Informal.* a person who is always trying to get ahead socially. **3** a spike attached to a shoe to help in climbing. **4** any climbing plant.

climbing iron one of a pair of frames having metal spikes, attached to boots to help in climbing.

clime (klīm) *n. Poetic.* **1** a country; region. **2** the climate. [< L *clima.* See CLIMATE.]
☞ *Hom.* **climb.**

clinch (klinch) *v., n.* —*v.* **1** fasten a driven nail, a bolt, etc. firmly by bending over or flattening the end that has been driven through something and projects from the other side. **2** fasten (things) together in this way. **3** fix firmly; settle decisively: *A deposit of five dollars clinched the bargain.* **4** *Boxing and wrestling.* grasp one another tightly; grapple: *When the boxers clinched, the crowd hissed.* **5** *Slang.* embrace. **6** clench.
—*n.* **1** *Boxing and wrestling.* a tight grasp; close grip: *The referee broke the boxers' clinch.* **2** *Slang.* embrace. **3** a kind of sailor's knot in which the end of the rope is lashed back. [var. of *clench*]
☞ *Syn. v.* **1.** See note at **clench.**

clinch·er (klin′chər) *n.* **1** a tool for clinching nails, bolts, etc. **2** *Informal.* an argument, statement, etc. that is decisive.

cling (kling) *v.* **clung, cling·ing. 1** attach oneself firmly; grasp; hold

tightly: *The child clung to his mother.* **2** stick; be attached: *A vine clings to its support.* **3** remain attached to a belief, idea, etc.: *They clung to the beliefs of their parents.* **4** keep or remain near: *clouds clinging to the mountains.* [OE *clingan*]

cling·ing (kling′ing) *adj.* that clings or holds fast.

cling·stone (kling′stōn′) *n., adj.* —*n.* a peach whose flesh clings to the stone. —*adj.* having such a stone.

clin·ic (klin′ik) *n.* **1** a part of a hospital where people are treated for certain kinds of illness without having to stay overnight: *They have the latest equipment in the eye clinic.* **2** a place, separate from a hospital, where a group of doctors work together: *My uncle is a heart specialist in the new clinic.* **3** a session held to treat or prevent certain illnesses or injuries, or to provide a special service: *a blood donor clinic, a rabies clinic for pets.* **4** the practical instruction of medical students by examining or treating patients in the presence of the students. **5** a class of students receiving such instruction. **6** a brief course of practical instruction in some non-medical field: *a football clinic, a writing clinic.* [< L < Gk. *klinikos* of a bed < *klinē* bed]

clin·i·cal (klin′ə kəl) *adj.* **1** of or having to do with a clinic. **2** having to do with the diagnosis and treatment of disease by observation of the patient, as opposed to dependence on laboratory tests: *clinical medicine.* **3** detached, unemotional, and thorough, suggesting a medical examination or report: *The interviewer looked the applicant over with a clinical eye and then said, "You'll do."* **4** bare, neat, and functional, suggesting a hospital: *The kitchen looked clinical, very different from the large, friendly kitchen in the old house.*

clin·i·cal·ly (klin′ik lē) *adv.* by clinical methods.

clinical thermometer a thermometer for measuring the temperature of the body.

cli·ni·cian (kli nish′ən) *n.* a person, such as a physician or psychiatrist, trained and specializing in the treatment of patients, as distinct from one specializing in medical research or laboratory work.

clink¹ (klingk) *n., v.* —*n.* a light, sharp, ringing sound like that of glasses hitting together. —*v.* **1** make a clink. **2** cause to clink. [ME, ? < Du. *klinken*]

clink² (klingk) *n. Informal.* a prison. [origin uncertain; possibly from the sound of fetters]

clink·er (klingk′ər) *n.* **1** a piece of the rough, hard mass left in a furnace or stove after coal has been burned; large, rough cinder. **2** a very hard brick. **3** a mass of bricks fused together. **4** slag. **5** *Informal.* a bad or stupid mistake, or its result. [< Du. *klinker* brick < *klinken* ring]

clink·er–built (klingk′ər bilt′) *adj.* made of boards or metal plates that overlap one another: *The lifeboat was clinker-built.* [*clinker*, dial. var. of *clincher*]

cli·nom·e·ter (klī nom′ə tər *or* klə nom′ə tər) *n.* an instrument for measuring deviation from the horizontal. [< L *clinare* incline + E *-meter*]

Clio (klī′ō) *n. Greek mythology.* the Muse of history.

clip¹ (klip) *v.* **clipped, clip·ping;** *n.* —*v.* **1** cut; cut out or cut short; trim with shears, scissors, or clippers: *to clip the hair. I often clip interesting newspaper articles to send to friends.* **2** cut or trim the hair of a person or animal: *Our dog is clipped every summer.* **3** shear off the fleece of a sheep. **4** damage (a coin) by cutting off the edge. **5** omit sounds in pronouncing. **6** *Informal.* move fast. **7** *Informal.* hit or punch sharply. **8** *Slang.* cheat, especially by overcharging: *We got clipped in that restaurant.* —*n.* **1** the act of clipping. **2** the amount of wool clipped from sheep at one shearing or during one season. **3** anything that has been clipped off, such as a section of filmed material. **4** *Informal.* a fast pace: *Our bus passed through the village at quite a clip.* **5** *Informal.* a sharp blow or punch. **6** *Informal.* one time; single occasion: *at one clip.* [ME *clippe(n)* < ON *klippa*]

clip² (klip) *v.* **clipped, clip·ping;** *n.* —*v.* hold tight; fasten: *to clip papers together.* —*n.* **1** something used for clipping (things) together: *a paper clip.* **2** of certain firearms: **a** a metal holder for cartridges. **b** the rounds it holds. [OE *clyppan* embrace]

clip·board (klip′bôrd′) *n.* a small board with a heavy spring clip at one end for holding papers while writing.

clip joint a business establishment, especially a restaurant, nightclub, etc., that regularly overcharges its customers.

clip–on (klip′on′) *adj.* designed to be attached by means of a clip: *clip-on earrings.*

clip·per (klip′ər) *n.* **1** a person who clips or cuts. **2** Often, **clippers,** *pl.* a tool for cutting. **3** a sailing ship of the mid-nineteenth century, built and rigged for great speed. **4** a large, fast aircraft.

clip·ping (klip′ing) *n.* a piece cut from or out of something, especially a piece cut out of a newspaper or magazine.

clique (klēk *or* klik) *n., v.* —*n.* a small, exclusive group of people within a larger group: *Members complained that the club was being run by a clique.* —*v. Informal.* form or associate in a clique. [< F *clique* < *cliquer* click]
  ☛ *Syn.* See note at **circle.**

cliqu·ey *or* **cliqu·y** (klē′kē *or* klik′ē) *adj.* cliquish.

cliqu·ish (klē′kish *or* klik′ish) *adj.* **1** like a clique. **2** tending to form a clique. —**cliqu′ish·ly,** *adv.* —**cliqu′ish·ness,** *n.*

clit·o·ral (klit′ə rəl *or* klī′tə rəl) *adj.* of or having to do with the clitoris.

clit·o·ris (klit′ə ris *or* klītə ris) *n.* a small, erectile organ that is part of the female genitals, situated at the front of the vulva. It is homologous to the male penis.

clo·a·ca (klō ā′kə) *n., pl.* **-cae** (-sē *or* -sī). **1** sewer. **2** privy. **3** a cavity in the body of birds, reptiles, amphibians, etc. into which the intestinal, urinary, and generative canals open. [< L *cloaca*, probably < *cluere* purge]

cloak (klōk) *n., v.* —*n.* **1** an outer garment, usually loose, with or without sleeves. **2** anything that hides or conceals. —*v.* **1** cover with a cloak. **2** hide; conceal: *to cloak evil purposes under friendly words.* [ME < OF *cloque* < LL *clocca*, originally, bell < OIrish *cloc.* Doublet of CLOCHE, CLOCK¹.]

cloak–and–dag·ger (klōk′ən dag′ər) *adj., adv.* —*adj.* of or having to do with spies and espionage, secret intrigue and adventure. —*adv.* in a manner suggestive of spies, secrecy, intrigue and adventure.

cloak·room (klōk′rüm′ *or* -rùm′) *n.* a room, especially in a school or other public building, where coats, hats, etc. can be left for a time.

clob·ber (klob′ər) *v. Slang.* **1** attack violently. **2** defeat severely.

cloche (klōsh) *n.* **1** a bell-shaped glass cover to protect tender plants. **2** a woman's close-fitting hat. [< F *cloche* bell, ult. < LL *clocca.* Doublet of CLOAK, CLOCK¹.]

clock¹ (klok) *n., v.* —*n.* an instrument for measuring and showing time, specifically one that is not carried around like a watch.
against the clock, under strong pressure from a deadline: *working against the clock to get the newsletter out on time.*
around the clock, all day and all night.
put or **turn the clock back,** return to an earlier time or to an out-of-date fashion or way of doing things.
—*v.* **1** measure or record the time of; time: *The coach clocked the three boys to see who was the fastest runner.* **2** record (time, distance, number, etc.) mechanically: *The racing car clocked 240 kilometres per hour.*
clock in or **out,** register on a time card the beginning or end of a day's work.
[ME < MDu. *clocke* < OF *cloque* or LL *clocca.* Doublet of CLOAK, CLOCHE.] —**clock′er,** *n.* —**clock′like′,** *adj.*

clock² (klok) *n.* an ornamental pattern sewn or woven on the side of a stocking, extending up from the ankle. [origin uncertain]

clock·mak·er (klok′māk′ər) *n.* a man whose business is making or repairing clocks.

clock radio a radio with a built-in clock that can be set to turn the radio on or off at any desired time, used as or instead of an alarm clock.

clock·wise (klok′wīz′) *adv. or adj.* in the direction in which the hands of a clock rotate.

clock·work (klok′wèrk′) *n.* **1** machinery used to run a clock, consisting of gears, wheels, and springs. **2** any mechanism like this. Many mechanical toys are run by clockwork.
like clockwork, with great regularity and smoothness.

clod (klod) *n.* **1** a lump of earth; lump. **2** earth; soil. **3** a stupid person; blockhead. [OE *clod*]

clod·hop·per (klod′hop′ər) *n.* **1** a clumsy boor. **2** a large, heavy shoe.

clog (klog) *v.* **clogged, clog·ging;** *n.* —*v.* **1** block by filling up; stop up: *Greasy water clogged the drain.* **2** become blocked or filled up: *The drain has clogged with leaves.* **3** hinder the operation or movement of; interfere with; hold back: *Heavy clothes clogged the swimmer. Sand clogged the reel of the fishing rod.* **4** perform a clog dance.
—*n.* **1** something that hinders or interferes. **2** any weight, such as a block of wood, fastened to the leg of an animal to hinder motion. **3** a heavy shoe with a wooden sole. **4** a lighter shoe with a wooden sole, used in clog dancing. **5** a clog dance. [ME *clogge* block; origin uncertain]

clog dance a dance performed while wearing clogs (def. 4) which produce a rhythmic clattering sound on the floor.
—**clog dancer.** —**clog dancing.**

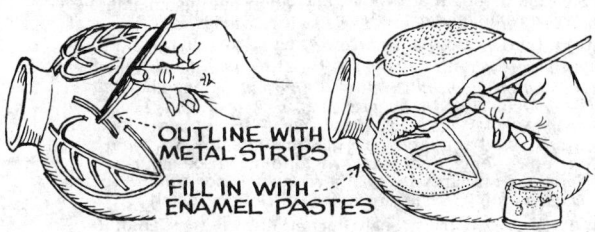

OUTLINE WITH METAL STRIPS

FILL IN WITH ENAMEL PASTES

The decoration of a cloisonné vase

cloi·son·né (kloi′zə nā′; *French*, klwä zô nā′) *n., adj.* —*n.*
1 enamelware in which the different colors of enamel are separated
by thin metal strips set on edge on the surface. **2** the method for
producing such enamelware. —*adj.* of, having to do with, or made
by cloisonné. [< F *cloisonné* partitioned < *cloison* partition, ult. <
L *clausus*, pp. of *claudere* close]

clois·ter (klois′tər) *n., v.* —*n.* **1** a covered walk along the wall of
a building, with a row of pillars on the open side. A cloister is often
built around the courtyard of a monastery, church, or university
building. **2** a place of religious retirement; convent or monastery.
3 a quiet place shut away from the world.
—*v.* shut away in a quiet place. [ME < OF < L *claustrum* closed
place, lock < *claudere* close]

clois·tral (klois′trəl) *adj.* **1** like a cloister. **2** of or suitable for a
convent, monastery, etc.

clomb (klōm) *v. Archaic.* a pt. and a pp. of **climb.**

clone (klōn) *n., v.* **cloned, clon·ing.** —*n.* **1** all the cells or
organisms derived from a single individual by means such as
cuttings or bulbs, by fission, or by the development of an
unfertilized ovum. **2** a single organism produced in this way. **3** a
person or thing that appears to be identical to another; carbon copy.
—*v.* produce a new, genetically identical individual by means of
cuttings or bulbs (for plants), fission, or the development of an
unfertilized ovum. [< Gk. *kton* a twig; 20c.]

clon·ing (klō′ning) **1** the technique of producing a duplicate of an
organism by replacing the nucleus of an unfertilized ovum, or egg,
with the nucleus of a body cell of the parent organism, causing the
ovum to develop into a new organism that is genetically identical to
the parent organism. **2** an individual produced by or as if by
cloning; a clone (defs. 2 and 3).

clo·nus (klō′nəs) *n.* a series of muscular spasms. [< NL < Gk.
klonus turmoil]

clop (klop) *n., v.* **clopped, clop·ping.** —*n.* a sharp, hard sound
such as is made by a horse's hoof on a paved road. —*v.* make such
a sound. [imitative]

close[1] (klōz) *v.* **closed, clos·ing;** *n.* —*v.* **1** shut: *Close the door.
The sleepy child's eyes are closing.* **2** stop up; fill; block: *to close a
gap.* **3** bring together; come together: *to close the ranks of troops.*
4 end; finish: *to close a debate. The meeting closed with a speech
by the president.* **5** come to terms; agree: *The labor union closed
with the company.* **6** grapple. **7** *Electricity.* unite the parts of (a
circuit) so as to make it complete.
close down, shut completely; stop.
close in, come near; approach from all sides: *The thief gave up when
the police closed in. Night closed in swiftly.*
close in on, come near and surround or shut in on all sides: *The
wolves closed in on the moose. I felt that the walls were closing in
on me.*
close out, a sell to get rid of: *to close out old stock.* **b** go out of
business: *They are closing out next month.*
close up, a shut completely; stop up; block. **b** bring or come
nearer together. **c** of a wound, heal.
—*n.* the end; finish [ME < OF *clos-*, stem of *clore* < L *claudere*
close] —**clos′a·ble,** *adj.* —**clos′er,** *n.*
☞ *Hom.* **clothes.**

close[2] (klōs) *adj.* **clos·er, clos·est;** *adv., n.* —*adj.* **1** with very little
in between; near together; near: *close teeth.* **2** fitting tightly; tight;
narrow: *close quarters.* **3** having its parts near together; compact: *a
close texture.* **4** intimate; dear: *a close friend.* **5** careful; exact: *a
close translation.* **6** thorough; strict: *close attention.* **7** stifling;
stuffy: *With the windows shut, the room soon became hot and
close.* **8** not fond of talking; keeping quiet about oneself. **9** secret;
hidden. **10** strictly guarded; confined: *to keep a man close at home.*
11 restricted; limited. **12** stingy. **13** hard to get; scarce. **14** nearly
equal; almost even: *a close contest.* **15** closed; shut; not open.
16 *Phonetics.* of a vowel, pronounced with some part of the tongue
raised to a point near the palate, as the vowels in *leap* and *loop.*
—*adv.* in a close manner.
close to the wind, a with the ship pointed as nearly as possible in

hat, āge, fär; let, ēqual, tėrm; it, īce
hot, ōpen, ôrder; oil, out; cup, pút, rüle,
above, takən, pencəl, lemən, circəs

ch, child; ng, long; sh, ship
th, thin; ŦH, then; zh, measure

the direction from which the wind is blowing. **b** *Informal.* just
barely following rules or laws.
—*n.* **1** an enclosed place. **2** the grounds around a cathedral or
abbey. [ME < OF < L *clausum* closed place < *claudere* close]
—**close′ness,** *n.*

close call *Informal.* a narrow escape from disaster: *I had a close
call this morning when a car went through a red light and almost
hit me.*

closed–cir·cuit (klōzd′sėr′kit) *adj.* denoting or having to do
with television broadcasting that is limited to a certain audience, as
in a chain of theatres, a school, etc.

closed season any part of the year when hunting or fishing is
restricted.

closed shop a factory or business that employs only members
of labor unions.

closed syllable a syllable that ends in a consonant sound.
Example: can- in *candy.* Compare **open syllable.**

close–fist·ed (klōs′fis′tid) *adj.* stingy.

close–fit·ting (klōs′fit′ing) *adj.* fitting tightly; tight.

close–grained (klōs′grānd′) *adj.* having a fine, close grain.
Mahogany is a close-grained wood.

close–hauled (klōs′hold′ *or* -hôld′) *adj.* having sails set for
sailing as nearly as possible in the direction from which the wind is
blowing.

close–knit (knōs′nit′) *adj.* firmly united by affection or common
interests: *a close-knit family.*

close–lipped (klōs′lipt′) *adj.* close-mouthed.

close·ly (klōs′lē) *adv.* in a close manner; to a close degree or
extent.

close–mouthed (klōs′mouŦHd′ *or* -moutht′) *adj.* tending to be
silent; taciturn; secretive.

close quarters a place or position with little space: *They were
living in very close quarters.*
at close quarters, very close; at close range: *I had never seen a bear
at close quarters before.*

close shave *Informal.* a narrow escape; close call.

clos·et (kloz′it) *n., v.* —*n.* **1** a small room or cupboard used for
storing clothes or household supplies: *Most houses and apartments
these days have built-in closets.* **2** a small, private room for prayer
or study. **3** water closet; toilet. **4** (*adj.*) private or secret;
unadmitted: *a closet drinker.* **5** speculative; theoretical, as opposed
to actual: *closet strategies, a closet politician.*
out of the closet, into the open; to public knowledge or view: *More
separatists were coming out of the closet.*
—*v.* shut up in a private room for a secret talk: *The president was
closeted with his personal advisers for several hours.* [ME < OF,
dim. of *clos.* See CLOSE[2].]

close–up (klōs′up′) *n.* **1** a picture taken at close range. **2** a close
view.

close–wo·ven (klōs′wō′vən) *adj.* woven so that the threads are
close together.

clo·sure (klō′zhər) *n.* **1** the act of closing or the condition of
being closed. **2** a thing that closes. **3** the end; finish; conclusion.
4 in a legislative body, a means of ending a debate and getting an
immediate vote on the question being discussed. In Canada, a
closure may be moved after due notice by a cabinet minister. [ME
< OF < LL *clausura* < L *clausus*, pp. of *claudere* close]

clot (klot) *n., v.* **clot·ted, clot·ting.** —*n.* **1** a half-solid lump;
thickened mass: *A clot of blood formed in the cut and stopped the
bleeding.* **2** a clod. —*v.* form into clots: *Milk clots when it turns
sour.* [OE *clott*]

cloth (kloth) *n., pl.* **cloths** (kloŦHz *or* kloths). **1** material made from
wool, cotton, silk, linen, hair, synthetic fibres, etc. by weaving,
knitting, or rolling and pressing. **2** a piece of such material used for
a special purpose: *a cloth for the table.* **3** (*adj.*) made of cloth. **4 the
cloth, a** the customary clothing worn by the clergy. **b** the clergy.
5 *Anglophone Africa.* a garment made of cloth that is not tailored or
cut: *He was wearing a ceremonial cloth.* [OE *clāth*]

clothe (klōŦH) *v.* **clothed** *or* **clad, cloth·ing.** **1** put clothes on, cover
with clothes; dress. **2** provide with clothes. **3** cover or wrap as if
with clothes: *The sun clothes the earth with light.* **4** provide;

furnish; equip: *A judge is clothed with the authority of the state.*
5 express: *The moral of a fable is usually clothed in simple words.*
[OE *clāthian < clāth* cloth]

☛ *Syn.* **1. Clothe, dress** = put clothes on. **Clothe** always requires an object and usually needs a modifying word or phrase telling how or with what: *He clothed himself in an old tweed suit.* **Dress** can be followed by an object and/or modifier but does not have to be. Without them it emphasizes the idea of getting ready, putting on whatever clothes are needed or appropriate: *She dressed in a hurry. It's time to dress for the party.*

clothes (klōz or klōᴛнz) *n.pl.* **1** coverings for a person's body; garments; apparel; clothing: *summer clothes.* **2** the coverings for a bed.
☛ *Hom.* **close¹** (klōz).

clothes·horse (klōz′hôrs′ or klōᴛнz′hôrs′) *n.* **1** a frame to hang clothes on in order to dry or air them. **2** *Informal.* a person who places great value on being well and fashionably dressed.

clothes·line (klōz′līn′ or klōᴛнz′līn′) *n.* a rope, wire, etc. to hang clothes on in order to dry or air them.

clothes moth any of various moths (family Tineidae, especially of genera *Tineda* and *Tinea*) whose larvae feed on wool, fur, or feathers.

clothes·peg (klōz′peg′ or klōᴛнz′peg′) *n.* **1** a peg for hanging clothes on. **2** a clothes pin.

clothes·pin (klōz′pin′ or klōᴛнz′pin′) *n.* a clip, usually of plastic or wood, to hold clothes on a clothesline.

clothes·press (klōz′pres′ or klōᴛнz′pres′) *n.* a chest, cupboard, or closet in which to keep clothes.

clothes tree an upright pole with branches on which to hang coats and hats.

cloth·ier (klōᴛн′yər or klōᴛн′ē ər) *n.* **1** a seller or maker of clothing. **2** a seller of cloth.

cloth·ing (klōᴛн′ing) *n.* **1** clothes. **2** covering.

Clo·tho (klō′thō) *n. Greek mythology.* one of the three Fates. Clotho spins the thread of life.

cloth of gold cloth made of gold threads woven with silk or wool threads.

cloth yard *Historical.* a unit of length for measuring cloth, set by Edward VI at 37 inches (about 94 cm). It was also used as a length for arrows.

clo·ture (klō′chər) *n. Esp.U.S.* closure (def. 4).

cloud (kloud) *n., v.* —*n.* **1** a white, grey, or almost black mass in the sky, made up of tiny drops of water or ice particles. **2** a mass of smoke or dust. **3** a great number of things moving close together through the air: *a cloud of birds, a cloud of arrows.* **4** a blemish or spot on a polished stone or gem. **5** anything that darkens or dims. **6** a cause of gloom, trouble, suspicion, or disgrace.
in the clouds, a far above the earth. **b** unreal; imaginary; fanciful; theoretical; not practical. **c** daydreaming; absent-minded.
under a cloud, a under suspicion; in disgrace. **b** in gloom or trouble.
—*v.* **1** cover with a cloud or clouds. **2** become cloudy: *The sky clouded.* **3** streak; spot. **4** make or become gloomy or troubled; darken; dim: *His face clouded as he thought of the quarrel.* **5** make or become suspected or disgraced. [OE *clūd* a mass of rock, hence, a mass of vapor] —**cloud′like′,** *adj.*

cloud·ber·ry (kloud′ber′ē) *n., pl.* **-ries.** *Cdn.* **1** a creeping herbaceous plant (*Rubus chamaemorus*) of the rose family found in northern latitudes, having white flowers and edible, amber-colored berries. **2** a berry produced by this plant, resembling a raspberry.

cloud·burst (kloud′bėrst′) *n.* a short, sudden, very heavy rainfall.

cloud chamber a large vessel filled with a vapor, especially a vapor of hydrogen and methyl alcohol, through which subatomic particles may be caused to move, leaving a trail by which they may be identified.

cloud·less (kloud′lis) *adj.* without clouds; clear; bright; sunny: *a cloudless sky, a cloudless day.* —**cloud′less·ly,** *adv.*
—**cloud′less·ness,** *n.*

cloud·let (kloud′lit) *n.* a little cloud.

cloud rack a group of broken clouds.

cloud seeding a scattering, usually from aircraft, of particles of carbon dioxide or certain other chemicals in clouds to produce rain.

cloud·y (kloud′ē) *adj.* **cloud·i·er, cloud·i·est. 1** having clouds; covered with clouds: *a cloudy sky.* **2** characterized by a sky covered with clouds: *The morning was cloudy and cold.* **3** of or like clouds: *A cloudy veil hid the mountaintop.* **4** of a liquid, not clear; murky: *The pond water was cloudy.* **5** streaked; spotted: *cloudy marble.* **6** of ideas, etc., dim or unclear; hazy; clouded by ignorance, etc.: *He had some cloudy, half-formed notions, but no real plan of*

action. **7** full of gloom or trouble; made dark or dim by grief, anger, fear, etc.: *a cloudy future.* —**cloud′i·ly,** *adv.* —**cloud′i·ness,** *n.*

clough (kluf or klou) *n.* a narrow valley; glen. [OE *clōh*]

clout (klout) *n., v.* —*n.* **1** *Informal.* a hit, especially with the hand; cuff: *a clout on the head.* **2** *Baseball. Informal.* a long hit. **3** *Informal.* power and influence: *That newspaper doesn't carry any real clout. She has a lot of political clout.* **4** *Archery.* **a** a white cloth on a frame, used as a target. **b** a shot that hits this. **5** *Archaic or dialect.* a piece of cloth or leather used to mend something.
—*v. Informal.* hit hard: *She finally got exasperated with his teasing and clouted him.* [OE *clūt* small piece of cloth or metal]

clove¹ (klōv) *n.* **1** the strongly fragrant dried flower bud of a tropical tree (*Eugenia aromatica*) of the myrtle family, used as a spice. **2** the tree itself. [ME *cloue* (apparently misread as *clove*) < OF *clou* < L *clavus* nail]

clove² (klōv) *n.* a small, separable section of a bulb: *a clove of garlic.* [OE *clufu*]

clove³ (klōv) *v.* a pt. of **cleave¹.**

clove hitch a knot used in tying a rope around a pole, spar, etc.

clo·ven (klō′vən) *v., adj.* —*v.* a pp. of **cleave¹.** —*adj.* split; divided.

cloven foot cloven hoof.

clo·ven–foot·ed (klō′vən fut′id) *adj.* **1** having cloven feet. **2** devilish.

cloven hoof a hoof divided into two parts. Cows have cloven hoofs. The Devil is traditionally pictured with cloven hoofs.

clo·ven–hoofed (klō′vən huft′ or -hūft′) *adj.* **1** having cloven hoofs. **2** devilish.

clove pink an Old World pink (*Dianthus caryophyllus*) having single, flesh-colored, clove-scented flowers. The many cultivated varieties of carnation are all derived from the clove pink.

clo·ver (klō′vər) *n.* **1** any of a genus (*Trifolium*) of low herbs of the pea family, having leaves consisting of three leaflets and rounded heads of small red, white, or yellow flowers. Several species of clover are grown as food for horses and cattle. **2** any of various related plants, such as sweet clover.
in clover, *Informal.* enjoying a life of pleasure and luxury without work or worry.
[OE *clāfre*]

clo·ver·leaf (klō′vər lēf′) *n.* a series of roads at the intersection of two highways, so arranged that traffic may move from one highway to the other without having to cross in front of other traffic.

clown (kloun) *n., v.* —*n.* **1** a person whose work is to amuse and entertain by tricks, jokes, and antics: *Circuses always have clowns.* **2** a bad-mannered, awkward, or uneducated person. —*v.* act like a clown; play tricks and jokes; act silly: *We were clowning around on the lawn.* [origin uncertain; cf. Icelandic *klumni* clumsy person, boor]

clown·er·y (kloun′ər ē) *n., pl.* **-er·ies.** the tricks and jokes of a clown; clownish act.

clown·ish (kloun′ish) *adj.* like a clown; like a clown's.
—**clown′ish·ly,** *adv.* —**clown′ish·ness,** *n.*

cloy (kloi) *v.* **1** overload with something originally pleasurable, such as rich or sweet food, so as to cause dislike: *He was cloyed with sweets before the holidays ended.* **2** disgust or make weary with too much of anything originally pleasant: *Her constant helpfulness soon begins to cloy.* [ME *acloy,* ancloy drive a nail into, stop up, fill full < OF *enclover* < *en-* in (< L *in-*) + *clou* nail (< L *clavus*)] —**cloy′ing·ly,** *adv.* —**cloy′ing·ness,** *n.*

club (klub) *n., v.* **clubbed, club·bing.** —*n.* **1** a heavy stick of wood, thicker at one end, used as a weapon. **2** *Sports.* a stick or bat used in some games to hit a ball: *golf clubs.* **3** a group of people joined together for some special purpose: *a tennis club.* **4** a building or rooms used by a club. **5** a playing card with one or more black designs on it shaped like this: ♣ **6** **clubs,** *pl.* a suit of cards marked with this design.
—*v.* **1** beat or hit with a club. **2** gather, unite, or combine for a common purpose (*usually used with* **together**). [ME < ON *klubba*]

club car a railway passenger coach for day travel, more luxurious than ordinary coaches.

club·foot (klub′fut′) *n., pl.* **-feet. 1** a deformity of the foot present at birth, in which the foot is twisted and misshapen, often resembling a club. **2** a foot having this deformity.

club·foot·ed (klub′fut′id) *adj.* having a clubfoot.

club·house (klub′hous′) *n.* a building used by a club.

club·man (klub′mən) *n., pl.* **-men.** a man who is a member of a fashionable club or clubs, especially one who makes frequent use of them.

club moss any of an order (Lycopodiales) of mosslike plants

having creeping or erect stems covered with tiny overlapping leaves that resemble pine needles.

club·room (klub′rüm′ or -rùm′) n. a room used for club meetings and activities.

club sandwich a sandwich consisting of toast and at least two layers of meats (especially chicken), lettuce, tomato, etc.

club steak a small piece of beef cut from the loin.

club·wom·an (klub′wùm′ən) n., pl. **-wom·en.** a woman who belongs to a fashionable club or clubs, especially one who makes frequent use of them.

cluck (kluk) n., v. —n. 1 the sound made by a hen calling her chickens. 2 a sound like this. 3 Slang. a stupid person; blockhead; fool.
—v. 1 of a hen, make a cluck when calling the chickens. 2 make a sound like this: She clucked her disapproval. [imitative]

clue (klü) n., v. —n. a guide to the solving of a mystery or problem: The police could find no clues to help them in solving the crime. This crossword puzzle has some very hard clues. —v. 1 indicate something by or as if by means of a clue. 2 Informal. tell; give information to: So what's happening? Clue me! She promised to clue him in on their doings.
clue up, Informal. provide (someone) with the essential details or information: The new minister is not yet clued up about the working of his department.
[var. of clew]
☛ Hom. clew.

clue·less (klü′lis) adj. Informal. 1 not having any idea; not knowing; in the dark: I always feel clueless about politics. 2 generally ignorant or incompetent: Boy, is she clueless— she just asked me where the cow's nest was!

clum·ber (klum′bər) n. a breed of spaniel with short legs, a long, heavy body, and a silky, mainly white coat. [< Clumber, an estate of the Duke of Newcastle, England]

clump (klump) n., v. —n. 1 a cluster: a clump of trees. 2 a lump: a clump of earth. 3 the sound of heavy, clumsy walking.
—v. 1 form a clump; plant in clusters. 2 walk heavily and clumsily. [earlier clumper, OE clympre lump of metal]

clump·y (klump′ē) adj. 1 full of clumps. 2 like clumps. 3 heavy and clumsy.

clum·si·ness (klum′zē nis) n. the state or condition of being clumsy; awkwardness.

clumsy (klum′zē) adj. -si·er, -si·est. 1 not graceful or skilful; awkward. 2 awkwardly done; poorly contrived: a clumsy apology. 3 not well-shaped or well-made. [< clumse be numb with cold, probably < Scand.] —clum′si·ly, adv.
☛ Syn. 1. See note at awkward.

clung (klung) v. pt. and pp. of cling.

Cluny lace a kind of lace made of heavy linen or cotton thread. [< Cluny, town in E France]

clus·ter (klus′tər) n., v. —n. 1 a number of things of the same kind growing or fastened together; bunch: a cluster of grapes, a cluster of curls. 2 a group of persons or things. 3 Phonetics. a sequence of two or more vowels or, especially, consonant sounds. Str- in string is a consonant cluster. 4 Astronomy. a group of stars relatively close to each other and often found to have a common motion in space. 5 U.S. a small metal device placed on the ribbon standing for a military medal, to show that the same medal has been awarded again.
—v. form into a cluster; gather in clusters; group together closely: The girls clustered around their teacher. [OE]

clutch[1] (kluch) n., v. —n. 1 a tight grasp; a firm hold by claw, paw, or hand: The eagle loosened its clutch and the rabbit escaped. 2 a grasping claw, paw, hand, etc.: He just managed to stay out of reach of the bear's clutches. 3 Usually, **clutches,** pl. control; power: in the clutches of the police. 4 any of several devices for connecting and disconnecting two working parts of a machine: The clutch in a car connects the engine with the drive shaft, which turns the wheels. 5 the lever or pedal that operates such a device.
—v. grasp tightly: The girl clutched her puppy to her breast.
clutch at, grasp eagerly for; try to seize or take hold of: She clutched at the branch, but missed it and fell.
[OE clyccan bend, clench]
☛ Syn. v. 1. See note at seize.

clutch[2] (kluch) n. 1 a nest of eggs. 2 a brood of chickens. 3 a group of people or things: There was a clutch of journalists covering the story. [var. of cletch < cleck hatch < ON klekja]

clutch bag a woman's handbag that is carried under the arm; a purse without handles.

clut·ter (klut′ər) n., v. —n. 1 a litter; confusion; disorder. 2 confused noise; loud clatter. —v. 1 litter with things: Her desk was all cluttered with books and papers. 2 make a confused noise; clatter loudly. [< clot]

hat, āge, fär; let, ēqual, tèrm; it, īce
hot, ōpen, ôrder; oil, out; cup, pùt, rüle,
əbove, takən, pencəl, lemən, circəs
ch, child; ng, long; sh, ship
th, thin; ᴛʜ, then; zh, measure

Clydes·dale (klīdz′dāl′) n. a breed of large, strong draft horses. [< Clydesdale, Scotland, where they were raised originally]

cm centimetre(s). The symbol for cubic centimetre is cm³.

Cm curium.

CM Cdn. Member of the Order of Canada.

CMA Canadian Medical Association.

Cmdr. or **Cmdr** commander.

Cmdre. or **Cmdre** commodore.

C.M.G. Companion of (the Order of) St. Michael and St. George.

CMHC or **C.M.H.C.** Central Mortgage and Housing Corporation.

cml. commercial.

CMM Cdn. Commander of the Order of Military Merit.

CN Canadian National Railways. Formerly, **CNR.**

CNIB Canadian National Institute for the Blind.

co- prefix. 1 with; together: co-operate = act with or together. 2 joint; fellow: co-author = joint or fellow author. 3 equally: co-extensive = equally extensive. [< L co-, var. of com-]

c.o. or **c/o** 1 in care of. 2 carried over.

Co cobalt.

Co. or **co.** 1 company. 2 county.

CO Colorado.

C.O. 1 Commanding Officer. 2 Informal. conscientious objector.

coach (kōch) n., v. —n. 1 Historical. a large, closed carriage with seats inside and a high seat in front for the driver, especially a stagecoach. 2 a passenger car of a railway train, containing adjustable seats but no sleeping accommodation. 3 a closed automobile having two doors. 4 bus. 5 a person who teaches or trains athletic teams, etc.: a football coach. 6 Baseball. a person stationed near first or third base to direct base runners and the batter. 7 a private teacher who helps a student prepare for a special test. 8 an instructor who supervises the training of actors, singers, etc.: a drama coach, a music coach.
—v. 1 carry or ride in a coach. 2 teach; train; instruct: He coached a winning team that fall. He coaches baseball. She coaches the young singer. 3 act as a coach: He is coaching this winter. 4 help to prepare for a special test. [ME < MF coche prob. < Magyar kocsi, after Kocs, a Hungarian village where coaches were supposedly made first]
☛ Usage. Coach (defs. 5-8). The senses of instructor, teacher, trainer, and the related verb meanings appear to derive from the idea of a university tutor being a means for carrying, or driving, the student through his examinations.

coach-and-four (kōch′ənd fôr′) n. a coach pulled by four horses.

coach dog Dalmatian.

coach·man (kōch′mən) n., pl. **-men.** a person whose work is driving a coach or carriage.

co·ad·ju·tor (kō aj′ù tər or kō′ə jü′tər) n. 1 an assistant; helper. 2 a bishop appointed to assist another bishop. [ME < LL < L co-with + adjutor helper < adjuvare < ad- + juvare help]

co·ag·u·lant (kō ag′yə lənt) n. a substance that produces coagulation.

co·ag·u·late (kō ag′yə lāt′) v. -lat·ed, -lat·ing. change from liquid form into a thickened mass; thicken; clot: Cooking coagulates the white of egg. Blood coagulates in air. [< L coagulare < coagulum means of curdling < co- together + agere drive] —co·ag′u·la·tor, n.

co·ag·u·la·tion (kō ag′yə lā′shən) n. 1 the act of coagulating. 2 a coagulated mass.

co·ag·u·la·tive (kō ag′yə lə tiv or kō ag′yə lā′tiv) adj. tending to coagulate or cause coagulation.

coal (kōl) n., v. —n. 1 a black or brownish-black combustible substance containing varying amounts of carbon, used as a natural fuel and for the manufacture of coal gas, coal tar, etc. Coal is a kind of sedimentary rock formed over millions of years from the partial decomposition of vegetable matter away from air and under varying degrees of pressure. 2 a piece of coal. 3 a piece of burning or charred coal, wood, etc.; ember. 4 charcoal.
call or **haul over the coals,** scold; blame.

heap coals of fire on (one's) **head,** make a person sorry by returning good for evil.
—*v.* supply with or take in coal: *The ship stopped to coal.* [OE *col* (def. 3)]
☛ *Hom.* cole.

coal·er (kōl′ər) *n.* 1 a ship, railway, freight car, etc. used for carrying or supplying coal. 2 a worker or merchant who supplies coal.

co·a·lesce (kō′ə les′) *v.* **-lesced, -lesc·ing.** 1 grow together. 2 unite into one body, mass, party, etc.; combine: *Two political groups coalesced to form a new party.* [< L *coalescere* < *co-* together + *alescere* grow]

co·a·les·cence (kō′ə les′əns) *n.* 1 growing together. 2 union; combination.

co·a·les·cent (kō′ə les′ənt) *adj.* growing together.

coal field a region where beds of coal are found.

coal·fish (kōl′fish′) *n.* pollock (def. 1).

coal gas 1 a gas made by distilling bituminous coal, used for heating and lighting. 2 the gas given off by burning coal.

coal hod coal scuttle.

coaling station a place where ships, trains, etc. are supplied with coal.

co·a·li·tion (kō′ə lish′ən) *n.* 1 a union; combination. 2 a formal arrangement by which statesmen, political parties, etc. agree to work together for a certain period of time or for a special purpose. [< Med.L *coalitio, -onis* < L *coalescere*. See COALESCE.]

coal measures beds of coal; strata containing coal.

coal mine a mine or pit where coal is dug from the earth.

coal oil 1 kerosene: *coal-oil lamps.* 2 petroleum.

coal pit 1 a coal mine. 2 a place where charcoal is made.

coal scuttle a bucket for holding or carrying coal.

coal tar a dark brown or black, heavy, sticky liquid obtained as a residue after the distillation of bituminous coal, used especially in making dyes, perfumes, medicines, and explosives.

coam·ing (kōm′ing) *n.* 1 a raised edge around a hatch or opening in the deck of a ship to prevent water from running down below. 2 any similar raised edge around an opening. [origin uncertain]

coarse (kôrs) *adj.* **coars·er, coars·est.** 1 made up of fairly large parts; not fine: *coarse sand.* 2 heavy and rough in appearance or texture; not smooth and fine: *Burlap is coarse fabric.* 3 common; of ordinary or inferior quality: *coarse food. The peasants wore the same coarse clothing, summer and winter.* 4 rude; rough; vulgar: *coarse manners, a coarse laugh.* [adjectival use of *course,* n., meaning "ordinary"] —**coarse′ly,** *adv.* —**coarse′ness,** *n.*
☛ *Hom.* course, corse.
☛ *Syn.* 4. **Coarse, vulgar** = not refined in feelings, manners, language, taste. **Coarse** emphasizes roughness and crudeness: *The soldier's coarse language was fit only for the barracks.* **Vulgar** suggests being deliberately and grossly rude, indelicate, or unrefined: *He is so vulgar that no one at school likes him.*

coarse–grained (kôrs′grānd′) *adj.* 1 having a coarse texture; made up of large, coarse fibres. 2 not delicate or refined; crude.

coars·en (kôr′sən) *v.* make or become coarse.

coast (kōst) *n., v.* —*n.* 1 the land along the edge of the sea; seashore. 2 a region near a coast. 3 **the Coast,** in Canada and the United States, the region along the Pacific Ocean. 4 a ride or slide down a hill without the use of power. 5 a slope for sliding downhill on a sleigh, etc.
the coast is clear, no one is in the way; the danger or hindrance is gone.
—*v.* 1 go along or near the coast of. 2 sail from port to port of a coast. 3 ride or slide down a hill without using power. [ME < OF < L *costa* side]
☛ *Syn.* n. 1. See note at **shore.**

coast·al (kōs′təl) *adj.* of, near, or along a coast.

coastal plain a flat stretch of land along a coast.

coast·er (kōs′tər) *n.* 1 a person or thing that coasts. 2 a ship trading along a coast. 3 a sleigh to coast on. 4 an amusement railway whose track dips and curves abruptly; roller coaster. 5 a little tray or mat on which a glass or bottle may be placed to protect the surface underneath.

coaster brake a brake on the rear wheel of a bicycle, worked by pushing back on the pedals.

coast guard 1 in Canada, a government service responsible mainly for search-and-rescue operations at sea, establishing and maintaining lighthouses, buoys, and other navigation aids, and icebreaking and moving cargo in the North. 2 a coastal patrol and police whose work is preventing smuggling and protecting lives and property along the coast: *The coast guard is often part of the armed forces of a country.* 3 a member of such a patrol.

coasting trade 1 the trade carried on by ships between the ports of one country. 2 the trade carried on by ships along the coasts of several countries.

coast·land (kōst′land′) *n.* the land along a coast.

coast·line (kōst′līn′) *n.* the outline of a coast.

Coast Salish 1 a North American Indian people living in southern British Columbia, including the southeastern part of Vancouver Island, famous for their skill in basketry. 2 a member of this people.

coast·ward (kōst′wərd) *adv. or adj.* toward the coast.

coast·ways (kōst′wāz′) *adv.* coastwise.

coast·wise (kōst′wīz′) *adv. or adj.* along the coast.

coat (kōt) *n., v.* —*n.* 1 an outer garment of cloth, fur, etc. with sleeves. 2 an outer covering: *a dog's coat of hair, a coat of bark on a tree.* 3 a layer covering a surface: *a coat of paint.*
—*v.* 1 provide with a coat. 2 cover with a layer: *The old books were coated with dust.* [ME < OF *cote* < Gmc.] —**coat′er,** *n.*
—**coat′less,** *adj.*
☛ *Hom.* cote.

coated paper paper that has been coated with clay or sizing to give a glossy, smooth surface especially suitable for reproducing half-tone illustrations.

co·a·ti (kō ä′tē) *n., pl.* **-ties.** any of a genus (*Nasua*) of tropical American mammals related to and somewhat resembling raccoons, but larger and having a long, flexible snout and coarse grey, reddish, or brown fur. [< Tupi-Guarani, an Indian language family of central South America]

coat·ing (kōt′ing) *n.* 1 a layer covering a surface: *a coating of paint.* 2 cloth for making coats.

coat of arms 1 a group of symbols or designs which show the marks of distinction of a noble family, a government, a city, etc.: *In the Middle Ages, each knight or lord had his own coat of arms.* 2 a shield, or drawing of a shield, marked with such symbols or designs. [translation of F *cotte d'armes,* a light coat decorated with heraldic designs worn over armor by knights in the Middle Ages]

coat of mail a garment made of metal rings or plates, worn as armor.

coat·tail (kōt′tāl′) *n.* 1 the back part of a coat below the waist; one of a pair of tails or flaps on such a part of a coat. 2 **coattails,** *pl.* the skirts of a formal coat.
ride on (someone's) **coattails,** advance in career or popularity by associating with a more successful or more popular person.

co·au·thor (kō o′thər *or* -ô′thər) *n., v.* —*n.* a joint author. —*v. Informal.* write with the help of another.

coax (kōks) *v.* 1 persuade by soft words; influence by pleasant ways: *She coaxed her father to let her go to the dance.* 2 get by coaxing: *The nurse coaxed a smile from the baby.* [< obs. *cokes* a fool] —**coax′er,** *n.*

co·ax·i·al (kō ak′sē əl) *adj.* 1 having a common axis. 2 of or having to do with a coaxial cable.

coaxial cable 1 a cable enclosing two or more concentric insulated conductors capable of operating singly or in combination to carry radio, television, telegraph, and telephone signals. 2 a large cable containing a system of many coaxial cables to carry several video circuits and a large number of telephone circuits.

cob (kob) *n.* 1 the centre part of an ear of corn, on which the kernels grow. 2 a strong horse with short legs, often used for riding. 3 a male swan. [ME *cob, cobbe* < Scand. and LG, a word suggesting something round or plump]

co·balt (kō′bolt *or* kō′bôlt) *n.* 1 a silver-white metallic element with a pinkish tint that occurs with and is similar to nickel and iron, used especially in alloys and for making pigments. *Symbol:* Co; *at.no.* 27; *at.wt.* 58.9332. 2 cobalt blue. [< G *kobalt,* var. of *kobold* goblin]

cobalt blue 1 a bright-blue pigment made from a mixture of cobalt and aluminum oxides. 2 bright medium blue.

cobalt bomb *Cdn.* a device for the use of cobalt 60 in the treatment of cancer.

cobalt 60 a heavy radio-active form of cobalt used as a source of gamma rays for radiotherapy, in industry for detecting flaws in the internal structure of materials, etc.

cob·ble¹ (kob′əl) *v.* **-bled, -bling.** 1 mend (shoes, etc.); repair; patch. 2 put together clumsily. [probably akin to COB]

cob·ble² (kob′əl) *n., v.* **-bled, -bling.** 1 cobblestone. 2 a round lump of coal about the size of a cobblestone. —*v.* pave with cobblestones. [apparently dim. of ME *cob, cobbe.* See COB.]

cob·bler (kob′lər) *n.* 1 a person whose work is mending or making shoes; shoemaker. 2 a clumsy workman. 3 a fruit pie baked

in a deep dish, usually with a crust only on top. **4** an iced drink made of wine, fruit juice, etc.

cob·ble·stone (kob′əl stōn′) *n.* a rounded stone formerly much used in paving streets, sidewalks, etc.

co–bel·lig·er·ent (kō′bə lij′ər ənt) *n.* a nation that helps another nation carry on a war.

co·bra (kō′brə) *n.* **1** any of several very poisonous snakes (genus *Naja*) of Asia and Africa that when excited will spread out their upper ribs, causing the skin just below the head to expand into a hoodlike shape. **2** any of various related snakes. [short for Pg. *cobra de capello* snake with a hood]

cob·web (kob′web′) *n.* **1** a spider's web or the stuff it is made of. **2** anything fine-spun or entangling like a spider's web. [OE (*ātor*)*coppe* spider + *web*]

cob·web·by (kob′web′ē) *adj.* **1** of or like a cobweb. **2** covered with cobwebs.

co·ca (kō′kə) *n.* **1** any of several South American shrubs (genus *Erythroxylon*), especially *E. coca* from whose leaves cocaine and other alkaloids are obtained. **2** the dried leaves of a coca. [< Peruvian *cuca*]

co·caine (kō kān′ *or* kō′kān) *n.* a white, bitter, crystalline drug obtained from coca leaves, used to deaden pain and as a stimulant. *Formula:* $C_{17}H_{21}NO_4$ Also, **cocain.** [< *coca*]

coc·cus (kok′əs) *n., pl.* **coc·ci** (kok′ī *or* kok′sī). **1** a bacterium shaped like a sphere. See **bacteria** for picture. **2** *Botany.* one of the carpels making up the compound pistil of such plants as the carrot and celery. Each coccus contains one seed and breaks away when the fruit is mature. [< NL < Gk. *kokkos* seed]

coc·cyx (kok′siks) *n., pl.* **coc·cy·ges** (kok sī′jēz). in man and tailless apes, a small triangular bone at the base of the spinal column. It consists of several fused vertebrae. See **spinal column** and **pelvis** for pictures. [< L < Gk. *kokkyx*, originally, cuckoo; because shaped like cuckoo's bill]

Co·chin *or* **co·chin** (kō′chin *or* koch′in) *n.* a breed of large domestic fowl developed in Asia, having thickly feathered legs. [after *Cochin China*, a former French colony in S Indo-China, now part of South Vietnam]

coch·i·neal (koch′ə nēl′ *or* koch′ə nēl′) *n.* a bright-red dye made from the dried bodies of the females of a scale insect that lives on cactus plants of tropical America. [< F < Sp. *cocinilla*, ult. < L *coccinus* scarlet < Gk. *kokkos* berry (gall) of a kind of oak]

coch·le·a (kok′lē ə) *n., pl.* **-le·ae** (-lē ē′ *or* -lē ī′). *Anatomy.* a spiral-shaped cavity of the inner ear, containing the sensory ends of the auditory nerve. See **ear** for picture. [< L < Gk. *kochlias* snail]

coch·le·ar (kok′lē ər) *adj.* of the cochlea.

cock¹ (kok) *n., v.—n.* **1** an adult male chicken; rooster. **2** the adult male of other birds. **3** a tap used to turn the flow of a liquid or gas on or off. **4** the hammer of a gun. **5** the position of the hammer of a gun when it is pulled back ready to fire. **6** weathercock. **7** *Informal.* leader; head; main person. **8** *Curling.* the mark aimed at. **cock of the walk,** a person who has power over a group or situation: *It was the first time he had ever been in charge of anything and he really thought he was cock of the walk.*
—*v.* pull back the hammer of (a gun), ready to fire. [OE *cocc*]
☛ *Hom.* **caulk** (kok).

cock² (kok) *v., n.—v.* **1** turn or tilt upward to one side: *The little bird cocked his eye at me.* **2** set (one's hat) at a jaunty angle on the head. **3** turn up the brim of (one's hat).
—*n.* **1** an upward turn or tilt of the nose, eye, or ear. **2** the turn of a hat brim. [apparently < *cock¹*]
☛ *Hom.* **caulk** (kok).

cock³ (kok) *n., v.—n.* a small pile of hay, rounded on top.—*v.* make such piles. [ME]
☛ *Hom.* **caulk** (kok).

cock·ade (kok ād′) *n.* a knot of ribbon or a rosette worn on the hat as a badge. [alteration of *cockard* < F *cocarde* < *coq* cock]

cock–a–hoop (kok′ə hüp′) *adj. Esp.Brit.* elated; triumphant and boastful.

Cock·aigne (kok ān′) *n.* an imaginary land of luxury and idleness. [ME < OF *cokaigne* < MLG *kokenje* little sugar cake, ult. < L *coquere* cook]

cock·a·lo·rum (kok′ə lôr′əm) *n.* **1** a little man with an exaggerated sense of his own importance. **2** boastful talk. [< *cock¹* + fanciful ending *-alorum*, based on L gen. pl. *-orum*; 18c.]

cock–and–bull story an absurd, incredible story.

cock·a·too (kok′ə tü′ *or* kok′ə tü′) *n., pl.* **-toos.** any of various large parrots (especially genus *Kakatoe*) of Australia and the East Indies, having mainly white plumage and a crest on the head. [< Du. *kaketoe* < Malay *kakatua*]

cock·a·trice (kok′ə tris) *n.* a fabled serpent whose look was

hat, āge, fär; let, ēqual, tèrm; it, īce
hot, ōpen, ôrder; oil, out; cup, pút, rüle,
əbove, takən, pencəl, lemən, circəs
ch, child; ng, long; sh, ship
th, thin; ŦH, then; zh, measure

supposed to cause death. [ME < OF *cocatris* (influenced by *coq* cock), ult. < L *calcare* tread]

cock·boat (kok′bōt′) *n.* a small rowboat.

cock·chaf·er (kok′chāf′ər) *n.* a large European beetle (*Melolontha melolontha*) that destroys plants. The larva of the cockchafer feeds on roots and the adult feeds on the green parts of plants.

cock·crow (kok′krō′) *n.* **1** the crowing of a rooster. **2** the time when roosters begin to crow; dawn.

cocked hat 1 a hat with the brim turned up. **2** a hat pointed in front and at the back.
knock into a cocked hat, *Slang.* defeat; destroy completely; ruin.

cock·er (kok′ər) *n.* cocker spaniel.

cock·er·el (kok′ər əl *or* kok′rəl) *n.* a young rooster, not more than one year old.

cocker spaniel a breed of small spaniel having long, silky hair and drooping ears.

cock–eyed (kok′īd′) *adj.* **1** cross-eyed. **2** *Slang.* tilted or twisted to one side. **3** *Slang.* foolish; silly.

cock·fight (kok′fīt′) *n.* a fight between roosters or between gamecocks armed with steel spurs.

cock·fight·ing (kok′fīt′ing) *n.* fighting by roosters or gamecocks for the entertainment of spectators. Cockfighting is illegal in Canada.

cock·horse (kok′hôrs′) *n.* a child's hobbyhorse; rocking horse.

cock·le¹ (kok′əl) *n., v.* **-led, -ling.—n.** **1** any of various saltwater clams (family Cardiidae) having a shell consisting of two round, convex valves with ridges radiating out from the hinge; especially, a common edible European species (*Cardium edule*). **2** cockleshell. **3** a wrinkle or pucker, as in paper or cloth.
cockles of (one's) heart, the inmost part of one's heart or feelings: *a welcome that warms the cockles of one's heart.*
—*v.* wrinkle; pucker: *Paper sometimes cockles when you paste it.* [ME < MF *cokille* < VL < L *conchylia*, pl. of *conchylium* < Gk. *konchylion*, ult. < *konchē* conch]

cock·le² (kok′əl) *n.* any of several weeds often found in grainfields, especially several plants (such as *Saponaria vaccaria* and *Lychnis alba*) of the pink family. [OE *coccel*, ? < L < Gk. *kokkos* berry]

cock·le·boat (kok′əl bōt′) *n.* a small, light, shallow boat.

cock·le·bur (kok′əl bèr′) *n.* any of a genus (*Xanthium*) of plants of the composite family found especially along roadsides and in pastures and fields, having spiny burrs.

cock·le·shell (kok′əl shel′) *n.* **1** the shell of a cockle or one of the valves of the shell. **2** a small, light, shallow boat.

cock·loft (kok′loft′) *n.* a small attic; garret.

Cock·ney *or* **cock·ney** (kok′nē) *n., pl.* **-neys;** *adj.—n.* **1** a native or inhabitant of London, England, especially a native of its East End or the City of London proper who speaks a particular dialect. **2** this dialect.—*adj.* **1** of or like this dialect. **2** of or like Cockneys. [ME *cokeney* cock's egg, pampered child, city fellow < *cocken* of cocks (OE *cocc*) + *ey* egg (OE *æg*)]

cock·pit (kok′pit′) *n.* **1** a place where the pilot sits in an aircraft. **2** the open place in a boat where the pilot or passengers sit. **3** an enclosed place for cockfights. **4** a scene of many fights or battles: *Belgium is often called the cockpit of Europe.* **5** *Historical.* an apartment or rooms below deck in a warship, used as quarters for junior officers, or as a hospital during battle.

cock·roach (kok′rōch′) *n.* any of an order (Blattaria) of insects, most of which are active at night, having long feelers and a long, flat, shiny body. Some species of cockroach are household pests. [alteration of Sp. *cucaracha*]

cocks·comb (koks′kōm′) *n.* **1** the fleshy, red crest on the head of a rooster. **2** a pointed cap somewhat like this, worn by a jester or clown. **3** any of several garden plants (genus *Celosia*) of the amaranth family having large, feathery red, orange, or yellow flower heads. **4** *Obsolete.* coxcomb.
☛ *Hom.* **coxcomb.**

cocks·foot (koks′fút′) *n.* orchard grass.

cock·spur (kok′spèr′) *n.* **1** the spur on the leg of a rooster. **2** a

North American hawthorn (*Crataegus crusgalli*) having wide-spreading branches and long, slender thorns.

cock·sure (kok'shūr′) *adj.* **1** too sure; cocky: *Her cocksure attitude is very irritating.* **2** perfectly sure; absolutely certain: *He hesitated, not being cocksure of his position.* —**cock′sure′ness,** *n.*

cock·swain (kok'sən *or* -swān′) See **coxswain.**

cock·tail (kok'tāl′) *n.* **1** an iced drink, often composed of gin or whisky mixed with bitters, vermouth, fruit juices, etc. **2** an appetizer: *a tomato-juice cocktail.* **3** shellfish served in a small glass with a highly seasoned sauce: *a sea-food cocktail.* **4** mixed fruits, diced and usually served in a glass. **5** (*adj.*) of, for, or involving the serving and drinking of cocktails: *a cocktail party.* **6** (*adj.*) of clothing, semiformal: *a cocktail dress.*

cocktail table coffee table.

cock·y (kok'ē) *adj.* **cock·i·er, cock·i·est.** *Informal.* conceited; swaggering. —**cock′i·ly,** *adv.* —**cock′i·ness,** *n.*

co·co (kō'kō) *n., pl.* **co·cos. 1** coconut palm. **2** its fruit. **3** (*adj.*) made of the fibres of coconut husks: *coco mats.* [< Pg. *coco* grinning face]
☛ *Hom.* **cocoa.**

co·coa (kō'kō) *n.* **1** a reddish-brown powder made from chocolate liquor by pressing out most of the fat. **2** a hot drink made from cocoa, milk or water, and sugar. **3** medium reddish-brown. —*adj.* having the color cocoa. [var. of *cacao*]
☛ *Hom.* **coco.**

cocoa bean the seed of the cacao.

cocoa butter a yellowish-white fat obtained from chocolate liquor, used in making soap, cosmetics, candy, etc.

co·co·nut (kō'kə nut′ *or* kō'kə nət) *n.* **1** the large, roundish fruit of the coconut palm, having edible white meat in a hard brown shell. The shell of a coconut is enclosed in a thick, fibrous husk which is itself covered by a smooth rind. **2** the meat of the coconut, usually shredded, used as a food or flavoring.

coconut milk a sweet liquid found in the hollow centre of an unripe coconut: *Coconut milk is good to drink.*

coconut oil the oil obtained from the dried meat of coconuts, used for making soap, candles, etc.

coconut palm a tall, tropical palm (*Cocos nucifera*) which produces coconuts. It has a crown of giant leaves with many leaflets growing along the centre rib.

co·coon (kə kün′) *n., v.* —*n.* **1** a covering prepared by the larva of many kinds of insect, including the ant and the moth, to protect itself while it is changing into an adult. Cocoons are usually of silk fibres produced by the insect, but some kinds include bits of leaves, twigs, etc. **2** any similar protective covering. —*v.* wrap or enclose in or as if in a cocoon; encase. [< F *cocon* < *coque* shell]

coco palm coconut palm.

cod (kod) *n., pl.* **cod** *or* **cods. 1** a very important food fish (*Gadus morhua*) of the colder parts of the N Atlantic Ocean, having soft fins, a barbel on the chin, and a small, square tail. The cod is the source of cod-liver oil. **2** any of several related fishes, especially a closely related Pacific fish (*Gadus macrocephalus*). **3** (*adj.*) designating a family of fish found in cold and temperate waters, including the cods, haddock, hakes, and pollocks. Some of the world's most valuable food fishes are in the cod family. [ME; origin uncertain]

C.O.D. *or* **c.o.d.** cash on delivery; collect on delivery.

co·da (kō'də) *n.* **1** *Music.* a separate and distinct passage at the end of a movement of composition, designed to bring it to a satisfactory close. **2** *Ballet.* the concluding section of a *pas de deux.* [< Ital. < L *cauda* tail]

cod·der (kod'ər) *n. Cdn. Maritimes.* **1** a boat used for cod fishing. **2** a cod fisherman.

cod·dle (kod'əl) *v.* **-dled, -dling. 1** treat tenderly; pamper: *coddle sick children.* **2** cook in hot water without boiling: *coddle an egg.* [var. of n. *caudle* gruel < OF < L *calidus* hot] —**cod′dler,** *n.*

code (kōd) *n., v.* **cod·ed, cod·ing.** —*n.* **1** a collection of the laws of a country. **2** any set of rules: *A moral code is made up of the notions of right and wrong conduct held by a person, a group of persons, or a society.* **3** a system of signals for sending messages by telegraph, flags, etc. The Morse code is used in telegraphy. **4** a system of symbols for representing information in a computer. **5** a system of secret writing; arrangement of words, figures, etc. to keep a message short or secret.
—*v.* **1** change or translate into a code; encode. **2** mark, provide, or program with a code. [< F < L *codex* codex. Doublet of CODEX.]

co·de·in (kō'dēn *or* kō'dē in) See **codeine.**

co·deine (kō'dēn *or* kō'dē in) *n.* a white crystalline drug

obtained from opium, used to relieve pain and cause sleep. [< Gk. *kōdeia* poppy head]

co·dex (kō'deks) *n., pl.* **co·di·ces.** a manuscript; a volume of manuscripts. [< L *codex,* var. of *caudex* tree trunk, block, book. Doublet of CODE.]

cod·fish (kod'fish′) *n., pl.* **-fish** *or* **-fish·es.** cod.

codg·er (koj'ər) *n. Informal.* a peculiar person. [origin uncertain]

cod·haul·er (kod'hol'ər *or* -hôl'ər) *n. Cdn. Slang.* Newfoundlander.

co·di·ces (kō'də sēz′ *or* kod'ə sēz′) *n.* pl. of **codex.**

cod·i·cil (kod'ə səl) *n.* **1** *Law.* something added to a will to change it, add to it, or explain it. **2** something added. [< L *codicullus,* dim. of *codex.* See CODEX.]

cod·i·cil·la·ry (kod'ə sil'ə rē) *adj.* of the nature of a codicil.

cod·i·fi·ca·tion (kō'də fə kā'shən *or* kod'ə fə kā'shən) *n.* **1** the act or process of arranging according to a system. **2** the state or fact of being so arranged.

cod·i·fy (kō'də fī′ *or* kod'ə fī′) *v.* **-fied, -fy·ing.** arrange (laws, etc.) according to a system: *The laws of France were codified between 1804 and 1810 by order of Napoleon I.* [< *code* + *-fy*] —**cod′i·fi′er,** *n.*

cod·lin (kod'lin) *n.* codling[1].

cod·ling[1] (kod'ling) *n.* **1** a small, unripe apple. **2** a kind of long, tapering apple. [ME *querd(e)lyng(e)* apple with a hard core, apparently < AF *quer de lion* heart of lion]

cod·ling[2] (kod'ling) *n.* **1** a young or small cod. **2** hake.

codling moth a small moth (*Carpocapsa pomonella*) whose larvae destroy apples, pears, etc.

cod–liver oil (kod'liv'ər) the oil extracted from the liver of cod or of related species of fish, used in medicine as a source of vitamins A and D.

cod·piece (kod'pēs′) *n.* a pouch or flap attached to the front of men's breeches or pants to cover the genitals, worn especially in the 15th and 16th centuries in Europe and Britain.

co·ed *or* **co·ed** (kō'ed′) *n., adj.* —*n. Informal.* a female student at a co-educational school, college, or university. —*adj.* co-educational.

co·ed·u·ca·tion (kō'ej ù kā'shən) *n.* the education of boys and girls or men and women together in the same school or classes.

co·ed·u·ca·tion·al (kō'ej ù kā'shən əl) *adj.* **1** educating boys and girls or men and women together in the same school or classes. **2** having to do with co-education. —**co′-ed·u·ca′tion·al·ly,** *adv.*

co·ef·fi·cient (kō'ə fish'ənt) *n., adj.* —*n.* **1** *Mathematics.* a number or symbol put before and multiplying another. In $3x$, 3 is the coefficient of x; in axy, a is the coefficient of xy. **2** *Physics.* a ratio used as a multiplier to calculate the behavior of a substance under different conditions of heat, light, etc.: *coefficient of expansion.* —*adj.* co-operating.

coe·la·canth (sē'lə kanth′) *n.* any of an order (Crossopterygii) of fishes having rounded scales and lobed, limblike pectoral fins. They were thought to have been long extinct until a living specimen (*Latimeria chalumnae*) was found near the S coast of Africa in 1938. Other specimens have been found since then. [< NL *coelacanthus* < Gk. *koilos* hollow + *akantha* thorn, spine]

coe·len·ter·ate (si len'tər āt′ *or* si len'tər it) *n.* any of a phylum (Coelenterata) of mostly marine invertebrates having a saclike body with a single opening. The phylum includes the jellyfishes, corals, hydras, and sea anemones. [< NL *coelenterata,* pl. < Gk. *koilos* hollow + *enteron* intestine]

coe·li·ac (sē'lē ak′) *adj. Anatomy.* of or in the abdominal cavity. [< L < Gk. *koiliakos* < *koilia* belly, bowels < *koilos* hollow]

coe·no·bite (sē'nə bīt′ *or* sen'ə bīt′) See **cenobite.**

co·e·qual (kō ē'kwəl) *adj., n.* —*adj.* equal in rank, degree, etc. —*n.* one that is co-equal. —**co·e′qual·ly,** *adv.*

co·erce (kō ėrs′) *v.* **co·erced, co·erc·ing. 1** compel; force: *The prisoner was coerced into confessing to the crime.* **2** control or restrain by force. [< L *coercere* < *co-* together + *arcere* restrain] —**co·erc′er,** *n.*

co·er·cion (kō ėr'shən) *n.* **1** the use of force; compulsion; constraint. **2** government by force.

co·er·cive (kō ėr'siv) *adj.* **1** compelling; forcing. **2** restraining. —**co·er′cive·ly,** *adv.* —**co·er′cive·ness,** *n.*

co·e·val (kō ē'vəl) *adj., n.* —*adj.* **1** of the same age, date, or duration. **2** contemporary. —*n.* a contemporary. [< LL *coaevus* < *co-* equal + *aevum* age] —**co·e′val·ly,** *adv.*

co·ex·ec·u·tor (kō'eg zek'yə tər) *n.* a person who, along with another, is an executor of a will.

co·ex·ist (kō'eg zist′) *v.* exist together or at the same time: *Orange trees have co-existing fruit and flowers.*

co·ex·ist·ence (kō′eg zis′təns) *n.* **1** existence together or at the same time. **2** living together in peace in spite of recognized differences of opinion, political philosophy, etc.

co·ex·ist·ent (kō′eg zis′tənt) *adj.* co-existing.

co·ex·tend (kō′eks tend′) *v.* extend equally or to the same limits.

co·ex·ten·sion (kō′eks ten′shən) *n.* **1** extension over an equal amount of space. **2** extension over exactly the same time.

co·ex·ten·sive (kō′eks ten′siv) *adj.* extending equally; extending over the same space or time. —**co·ex·ten′sive·ly,** *adv.*

C. of E. Church of England.

cof·fee (kof′ē) *n.* **1** a dark-brown drink or flavoring made from the roasted and ground beans, or seeds, of the coffee tree. **2** coffee beans, especially when roasted and ground: *a kilogram of coffee.* **3** coffee tree. **4** a medium to dark-brown color. **5** a cup of coffee: *They ordered two coffees.* **6** a social gathering at which coffee is served. [< Turkish *qahveh* < Arabic *qahwa*]

coffee bean the seed of the coffee tree, roasted and ground to make coffee.

coffee house **1** a small, informal restaurant that serves coffee and other refreshments and usually has some live entertainment: *She got her start as a folk singer by singing in coffee houses.* **2** *Historical.* in 18th-century England, a place where coffee and refreshments were sold, that served as a gathering place for people with similar interests.

coffee klatsch or **klatch** (kläch) *n.* a get-together at which coffee is served. [*coffee* + G *Klatsch* chitchat]

coffee mill a machine for grinding coffee.

coffee pot a covered container for making or serving coffee.

coffee shop an informal restaurant, as in a hotel, where coffee and other refreshments and light meals are sold, usually one in which customers are served at a counter or in which they select their food at a counter and take it to tables to eat.

coffee table a low table, usually placed in front of a chesterfield and used for serving coffee and other refreshments, etc.

coffee–table book (kof′ē tā′bəl) a book, usually large, expensive, and lavishly illustrated, designed mainly for display, as on a coffee table, and for casual browsing.

coffee tree any of several tall tropical evergreen shrubs (genus *Coffea*) of the madder family, the seeds of which are used to make coffee; especially, *C. arabica,* probably native to Ethiopia, but cultivated in many tropical parts of the world and accounting for the bulk of commercial coffee production.

cof·fer (kof′ər) *n., v.* —*n.* **1** a box, chest, or trunk, especially one used to hold money or other valuable things. **2** an ornamental panel in a ceiling, etc. **3** cofferdam. **4** coffers, *pl.* treasury; funds. —*v.* **1** deposit or enclose in or as if in a coffer. **2** build or ornament with coffers: *a coffered ceiling.* [ME < OF *cofre* < L < Gk. *kophinos* basket. See COFFIN.]

cof·fer·dam (kof′ər dam′) *n.* a watertight enclosure built in a shallow river, lake, etc. It is pumped dry so that the foundations of a bridge, etc. may be built.

cof·fin (kof′ən) *n., v.* —*n.* a box into which a dead person is put to be buried; a casket. —*v.* **1** put into a coffin. **2** shut up tightly. [ME < OF *cofin* < L *cophinus* < Gk. *kophinos* basket]

cog[1] (kog) *n.* **1** one of a series of teeth on the edge of a wheel that transfer motion by locking into the teeth of a similar wheel. **2** a wheel with such a row of teeth on it. **3** a person who plays a small but necessary part in a large and complex organization.
slip a cog, *Informal.* make a mistake.
[ME *cogge* < Scand.; cf. Swedish *kugge*]

cog[2] (kog) *n.* a projection, or tenon, on a wooden beam, etc. that fits into a hole, or mortise, in another beam to form a joint.

co·gen·cy (kō′jən sē) *n.* a forcible quality; power of convincing.

co·gent (kō′jənt) *adj.* forcible; convincing: *The lawyer's cogent arguments convinced the jury.* [< L *cogens, -entis,* ppr. of *cogere* < *co-* together + *agere* drive] —**co′gent·ly,** *adv.*
☛ *Syn.* See note at **valid.**

cogged (kogd) *adj.* having cogs.

cog·i·tate (koj′ə tāt′) *v.* **-tat·ed, -tat·ing.** think over; consider with care; meditate; ponder. [< L *cogitare* < *co-* (intensive) + *agitare* consider < *agere* discuss] —**cog′i·ta·tor,** *n.*

cog·i·ta·tion (koj′ə tā′shən) *n.* deep thought; careful consideration; pondering; meditation.

cog·i·ta·tive (koj′ə tā′tiv) *adj.* thoughtful; meditative. —**cog′i·ta·tive·ly,** *adv.*

co·gnac (kōn′yak or kon′yak; *French,* kô nyäk′) *n.* a fine brandy, originally produced in W France. [< F < *Cognac,* a town and region in France]

hat, āge, fär; let, ēqual, tèrm; it, īce
hot, ōpen, ôrder; oil, out; cup, put, rüle,
above, takən, pencəl, lemən, circəs
ch, child; ng, long; sh, ship
th, thin; ᴛʜ, then; zh, measure

cog·nate (kog′nāt) *adj., n.* —*adj.* **1** related by family or origin. English, Dutch, and German are cognate languages. **2** having a similar nature or quality. —*n.* a person, word, or thing related to another by having a common source. German *Wasser* and English *water* are cognates. [< L *cognatus* < *co-* together + *gnatus* born]

cog·ni·tion (kog nish′ən) *n.* **1** the mental process by which knowledge is acquired; perception. **2** that which is known, perceived, or recognized. [< L *cognitio, -onis* < *cognoscere* < *co-* (intensive) + *gnoscere* known]

cog·ni·tive (kog′nə təv) *adj.* **1** of, having to do with, or involving cognition: *cognitive studies.* **2** having to do with factual knowledge and understanding, especially as opposed to feelings and emotion.

cog·ni·za·ble (kog′nə zə bəl) *adj.* **1** that can be known or perceived; recognizable. **2** within the jurisdiction of a court of law.

cog·ni·zance (kog′nə zəns or kon′ə zəns) *n.* **1** knowledge; perception; awareness: *The dictator had cognizance of plots against him.* **2** *Law.* **a** knowledge upon which a judge is bound to act without having it proved in evidence. **b** the right or power to deal with (something) judicially. **3** jurisdiction; responsibility; charge. [ME *conisance* < OF *conoissance* < *conoistre* know < L *cognoscere.* See COGNITION.]

cog·ni·zant (kog′nə zənt or kon′ə zənt) *adj.* aware: *The general was cognizant of the enemy's movements.*

cog·no·men (kog nō′mən) *n.* **1** a surname; family name; last name. **2** any name, especially a descriptive nickname. **3** in ancient Rome, the third or family name of a person, as *Cicero* in *Marcus Tullius Cicero.* [< L *cognomen* < *co-* with + *nomen* name; form influenced by *cognoscere* recognize]

co·gno·scen·ti (kon′yō shen′tē or kog′nə shen′tē) *n., pl.* of **cognoscente.** people having or claiming to have a keen appreciation of or expert knowledge in a particular field, as in art, literature, or politics. [< obsolete Ital.; ult. < L *cognoscere* to know]

cog·wheel (kog′wēl′ or -hwēl′) *n.* a wheel with teeth cut in the rim that fit with teeth or grooves in another wheel or in a rack or worm so that one can drive the other; gear. See **gear** for picture.

co·hab·it (kō hab′it) *v.* **1** live together as husband and wife, especially when not legally married. **2** *Archaic.* live in the same place or territory. [< LL *cohabitare* < L *co-* with + *habitare* dwell]

co·hab·i·ta·tion (kō hab′ə tā′shən) *n.* the act or state of living together as husband and wife, especially when not legally married.

co–heir (kō er′) *n.* an heir with another or others.

co–heir·ess (kō er′is) *n.* an heiress with another or others.

co·here (kō hēr′) *v.* **-hered, -her·ing.** **1** stick or hold together as parts of the same mass or substance: *the particles making up a brick cohere.* **2** be connected logically; be consistent. [< L *cohaerere* < *co-* together + *haerere* stick]

co·her·ence (kō hēr′əns) *n.* **1** a logical connection; consistency. **2** a sticking together; cohesion.

co·her·en·cy (kō hēr′ən sē) *n.* coherence.

co·her·ent (kō hēr′ənt) *adj.* **1** logically connected; consistent in structure and thought: *A sentence that is not coherent is hard to understand.* **2** sticking together; holding together. —**co·her′ent·ly,** *adv.*

co·he·sion (kō hē′zhən) *n.* **1 a** a sticking together. **b** tendency to hold together: *Wet sand has more cohesion than dry sand.* **2** *Physics.* an attraction between molecules of the same kind, by which the elements of a substance are held together. The tendency of water to form into drops is a result of cohesion. Compare **adhesion** (def.4). **3** *Botany.* the union of one part with another. [< stem of L *cohaesus* pressed together, pp. of *cohaerere.* See COHERE.]

co·he·sive (kō hē′siv) *adj.* sticking together; tending to hold together. —**co·he′sive·ly,** *adv.* —**co·he′sive·ness,** *n.*

co·ho (kō′hō) *n., pl.* **-hoes** or **-ho.** *Cdn.* a Pacific salmon (*Oncorhynchus kisutch*) found along the coast from S California to Alaska, metallic blue and silver in color and having red flesh that fades when cooked. The coho is very highly valued as a food and game fish. Also, **cohoe.** [origin uncertain]

co·hort (kō′hôrt) *n.* **1** in ancient Rome, a part of a legion. There were from 300 to 600 soldiers in each cohort, and ten cohorts in each legion. **2** a group or band, especially of soldiers. **3** *Informal.* a

companion or associate. [< L *cohors, -ortis* court, enclosure. Doublet of COURT.]

coif (koif *for n. 1 and v. 1,* kwäf *for n. 2 and v. 2*) *n., v.* —*n.* **1** a cap or hood that fits closely around the head. **2** coiffure. —*v.* **1** provide or cover with a coif or something like a coif. **2** arrange or dress the hair. [ME < OF *coife* < LL *cofia* < Gmc.]

coif·feur (kwä fèr′; *French,* kwä fœr′) *n.* hairdresser. [< F *coiffeur* < *coiffer* coif]

coif·fure (kwä fyür′; *French,* kwä fyr′) *n.* a style of arranging the hair. [< F *coiffure* < *coiffer* coif]

coign (koin) *n.* a projecting corner. [var. of *coin*]

coign of vantage a good location for watching or doing something.

coil¹ (koil) *v., n.* —*v.* **1** wind around and around in a series of circles to form a spiral or a tube: *The sailor coiled the rope so it would not take up much space.* **2** form or lie in a series of circles: *The snake coiled around a branch.* **3** move in a winding course. —*n.* **1** one of a series of circles forming a spiral: *One coil of the rope was smaller than the others.* **2** a series of such circles: *The coil of hose was hung on the wall.* **3** a series of connected pipes arranged in a coil or row, as in a radiator. **4** a spiral of wire for conducting electricity. **5** a twist of hair. **6** a small pile of hay rounded on top; cock. [< OF *coillir* < L *colligere.* See COLLECT.] —**coil′er,** *n.*

coil² (koil) *n. Archaic.* disturbance; trouble. [origin uncertain]

coin (koin) *n., v.* —*n.* **1** a piece of metal stamped by a government for use as money. Nickels, dimes, and quarters are coins. **2** metal money: *The Mint makes coins by stamping metal.*
pay (someone) **back in** (his) **own coin,** treat someone as he treated oneself or others.
the other side of the coin, the opposite view, aspect, or opinion. —*v.* **1** make (money) by stamping metal; mint. **2** make (metal) into money. **3** make up; invent a word or phrase: *The word chortle was coined by Lewis Carroll.*
coin money, *Informal.* become rich; have a prospering business: *He's coining money in the oil industry.*
[ME < OF *coin* corner < L *cuneus* wedge]

coin·age (koin′ij) *n.* **1** the making of coins. **2** coins; metal money. **3** a system of coins: *Canada has a decimal coinage.* **4** a word or phrase that has been made up, or invented.

co·in·cide (kō′in sīd′) *v.* **-cid·ed, -cid·ing. 1** occupy the same place in space: *If these triangles △ △ were placed one over the other, they would coincide.* **2** occupy the same time; occur at the same time: *The working hours of the two friends coincide.* **3** correspond exactly; agree: *Her opinion coincides with mine.* [< Med.L *coincidere* < L *co-* together + *in* upon + *cadere* fall]
☛ *Syn.* **3.** See note at **agree.**

co·in·ci·dence (kō in′sə dəns) *n.* **1** an exact correspondence; agreement; especially, the chance occurrence of two things together in such a way as to seem remarkable, fitting, etc. **2** the act or condition of coinciding.

co·in·ci·dent (kō in′sə dənt) *adj.* **1** coinciding; happening at the same time. **2** occupying the same place or position. **3** in exact agreement (*used with* **with**). —**co·in′ci·dent·ly,** *adv.*

co·in·ci·den·tal (kō in′sə den′təl) *adj.* involving or resulting from coincidence. —**co·in′ci·den′tal·ly,** *adv.*

coin·er (koin′ər) *n.* **1** a person who makes coins. **2** a maker of counterfeit coins. **3** a maker; inventor.

coin-op·er·at·ed (koin′op′ə rā′tid) *adj.* worked by the insertion of a coin or coins: *Machines that sell candy, cigarettes, etc. are coin-operated.*

co-in·sur·ance (kō′in shür′əns) *n.* insurance held jointly with another or others.

Coin·treau (kwän′trō; *French,* kwan trō′) *n.* a clear, orange-flavored liqueur, a French brand of curaçao.

coir (koir) *n.* a fibre obtained from the outer husks of coconuts, used to make rope, mats, etc. [< Malayalam *kayar* cord]

co·i·tus (kō′it əs) *n.* sexual intercourse.

coke¹ (kōk) *n., v.* **coked, cok·ing.** —*n.* a fuel made from coal by heating it in a closed oven until the gases have been removed. Coke burns with much heat and little smoke; it is used in furnaces, for melting metal, etc. —*v.* change into coke. [? var. of *colk* core]

coke² (kōk) *n. Slang.* cocaine.

Coke (kōk) *n. Trademark.* Coca-Cola, a carbonated soft drink made from a secret recipe.

col (kol) *n.* a gap or depression in a range of mountains or hills, usually providing a pass through the range.

col– *prefix.* together or altogether; the form of **com-** occurring before *l,* as in *collapse.*

col. 1 column. **2** colony.

Col. or **Col** colonel.

co·la (kō′lə) *n.* **1** any of various carbonated soft drinks flavored with kola nuts, coca, etc. **2** See **kola.**

COLA cost-of-living allowance.

col·an·der (kul′ən dər *or* kol′ən dər) *n.* a vessel or dish with many small holes for draining off liquids from foods. [< VL *colator* or Med.L *colatorium* < L *colare* strain]

Col·by (kōl′bē) *n.* a soft cheese, made by stirring curd as the whey drains off instead of allowing it to settle.

col·chi·cum (kol′chə kəm) *n.* **1** any of a genus (*Colchicum*) of Old World plants of the lily family having crocus-like flowers that bloom in autumn. Some colchicums are grown as garden plants. **2** the dried corms or seeds of a colchicum, from which an alkaloid is extracted that is used in the treatment of gout. [< L < Gk. *kolchikon* < *Colchis*]

Col·chis (kol′kis) *n.* an ancient country on the eastern shore of the Black Sea. In Greek legend it is the country where the Golden Fleece was found by Jason and the Argonauts.

cold (kōld) *adj., n.* —*adj.* **1** much less warm than the body: *Snow and ice are cold.* **2** having a relatively low temperature; less warm than desired: *This coffee is cold.* **3** not kind and sympathetic; indifferent or unfriendly: *a cold person, a cold greeting.* **4** not influenced by emotion; objective: *cold logic.* **5** faint; weak; not fresh: *a cold trail, a cold scent.* **6** suggesting coolness: *Blue and green are called cold colors.* **7** feeling not enough warmth; feeling uncomfortable because of lack of warmth: *He's always complaining that he's cold.*
—*n.* **1** the lack of heat or warmth; low temperature: *the cold winter.* **2** a common infection that produces a stuffy or running nose and, often, a cough or sore throat.
catch cold or **take cold,** become sick with a cold.
(out) in the cold, all alone; neglected; ignored.
throw or **pour cold water on,** actively discourage or belittle: *to throw cold water on someone's plans.*
[OE *cald*]
☛ *Syn. adj.* **1, 2. Cold, chilly, cool** = having a low temperature, especially in comparison with body heat. **Cold** = having a low temperature, judged by the standard of normal body heat: *A cold wind is blowing.* **Chilly** = cold enough to be comfortable and make a person shiver a little: *Without my coat I feel chilly.* **Cool** = neither hot nor cold, but closer to cold: *After the hot day the evening seems cool.*

cold–blood·ed (kōld′blud′id) *adj.* **1** having blood whose temperature varies with that of the surroundings. Snakes and turtles are called cold-blooded, but their blood temperature is actually very close to that of the air or water around them. **2** feeling the cold because of poor circulation. **3** characterized by a lack of normal feelings of consideration, pity, or kindness; emotionless and cruel: *deliberate, cold-blooded murder. The cold-blooded pirates sold all their captives into slavery.* —**cold′-blood′ed·ly,** *adv.* —**cold′-blood′ed·ness,** *n.*

cold chisel a strong, steel chisel for cutting cold metal.

cold comfort little or no comfort; something that might be expected to cheer or console but does not, because of particular circumstances or a particular point of view.

cold cream a creamy, soothing, oil-based salve for softening or cleansing the skin.

cold cuts cooked or prepared meats or fowl, such as beef, chicken, salami, ham, etc., sliced and served cold.

cold feet sudden fear or timidity; loss of courage: *He suddenly got cold feet and refused to go on stage.*

cold frame a low box with a clear glass or plastic top, built on the ground outdoors and used to protect young or delicate plants from cold while allowing them exposure to sunlight.

cold front *Meteorology.* the front edge of a cold air mass advancing into and replacing a warm one.

cold–heart·ed (kōld′här′tid) *adj.* lacking in feeling; unsympathetic; unkind. —**cold′-heart′ed·ly,** *adv.* —**cold′-heart′ed·ness,** *n.*

cold light light without heat. Phosphorescence and fluorescence are kinds of cold light.

cold·ly (kōld′lē) *adv.* in a cold manner; without friendliness, warmth, or sympathy.

cold·ness (kōld′nis) *n.* **1** the state or quality of being cold. **2** a lack of warmth of feeling or friendliness; indifference.

cold pack 1 something cold put on the body for medical purposes. **2** a method of canning fruits or vegetables.

cold–pack (kōld′pak′) *v.* **1** put a cold pack on. **2** can (food) by cold pack.

cold rubber a tough synthetic rubber formed at a low temperature.

cold shoulder *Informal.* deliberately unfriendly or indifferent treatment; conscious neglect.

cold–shoul·der (kōld′shōl′dər) *v. Informal.* treat in an unfriendly or indifferent way.

cold snap a sudden spell of cold weather.

cold sore a sore on or near the lips, often accompanying a cold or fever, consisting of a group of small blisters that break and form a crust before they begin to heal. It is a form of herpes simplex.

cold steel a steel weapon, such as a knife or sword.

cold storage storage in a very cold place. Perishable foods are put in cold storage to keep them from spoiling.

cold sweat perspiration caused by fear, nervousness, pain, or shock, often accompanied by a cold or clammy feeling: *She broke out in a cold sweat just thinking about her narrow escape.*

cold turkey *Slang.* **1** sudden, total withdrawal from a drug to which one has become addicted: *She said the only way she could quit smoking was cold turkey. He decided to quit cold turkey.* **2** without preparation beforehand; without preliminaries: *He approached the manager cold turkey and asked for a raise.* —**cold′-tur′key,** *adj.*

cold war a prolonged contest for national advantage, conducted by diplomatic, economic, and psychological rather than military means.

cold wave¹ a period of very cold weather.

cold wave² a process by which hair is pressed into permanent waves or curls by the application of chemicals rather than heat.

cole (kōl) *n. Rare.* any of various plants of the genus *Brassica,* especially rape or cabbage. [OE *cāl,* var. of *cāw(e)l* < L *caulis* cabbage]
☛ *Hom.* **coal.**

co·le·op·ter·an (kō′lē op′tər an *or* kol′ē op′tər ən) *n., adj.* —*n.* any insect of the order Coleoptera; beetle¹. —*adj.* of, having to do with, or belonging to the order Coleoptera.

co·le·op·ter·ous (kō′lē op′tər əs *or* kol′ē op′tər əs) *adj.* coleopteran. [< Gk. *koleopteros* < *koleos* sheath + *pteron* wing]

cole·slaw (kōl′slo′ *or* -slô′) *n.* a salad made of shredded raw cabbage. [< Du. *kool sla* cabbage salad]

co·le·us (kō′lē əs) *n.* any of a genus (*Coleus*) of tropical plants of the mint family, grown for their showy, colorful leaves. [< NL < Gk. *kileos* sheath; from the union of the filaments]

cole·wort (kōl′wèrt′) *n.* **1** cole. **2** any kind of cabbage having a loosely packed head of curly leaves, such as kale.

col·ic (kol′ik) *n.* severe pains in the abdomen resulting from muscular spasms. [< LL < Gk. *kolikos* of the colon]

col·ick·y (kol′ik ē) *adj.* **1** of colic. **2** having colic.

col·i·form (kō′li fôrm′ *or* kol′i fôrm′) *adj.* of, like, or designating any of various bacilli normally found in the colon of vertebrates and excreted in the feces. Coliform bacteria from human and animal feces may contaminate water and cause disease.

col·i·se·um (kol′ə sē′əm) *n.* **1** a large building or stadium for games, contests, etc. **2 Coliseum,** Colosseum. [< Med.L var. of LL *colosseum.* See COLOSSEUM.]

co·li·tis (kō lī′tis *or* kə lī′tis) *n.* inflammation of the colon, often causing severe pain in the abdomen. [< NL *colitis* < Gk. *kolon* colon + *-itis*]

coll. **1** college. **2** collection; collector. **3** colleague. **4** colloquial. **5** collegiate.

col·lab·o·rate (kə lab′ə rāt′) *v.* **-rat·ed, -rat·ing. 1** work together: *Two authors collaborated on that book.* **2** aid or co-operate with someone traitorously. [< L *collaborare* < *com-* with + *laborare* work]

col·lab·o·ra·tion (kə lab′ə rā′shən) *n.* the act of collaborating.

col·lab·o·ra·tive (kə lab′ə rə tiv *or* kə lab′ə rā′tiv) *adj.* of or resulting from collaboration.

col·lab·o·ra·tor (kə lab′ə rā′tər) *n.* **1** a person who works with another, usually in literary work. **2** a person who aids or co-operates with someone traitorously.

col·lage (kə läzh′) *n.* a picture made by pasting on a background an arrangement of items with different textures, colors and shapes, such as portions of photographs, newspapers, fabric, string, etc. [< MF *collage* a gluing < OF *colle* < VL *colla* < Gk. *kolla* glue]

col·la·gen (kol′ə jen) *n.* any of a group of fibrous proteins found in connective tissue, as skin, ligaments, tendons, bone, and cartilage. It forms gelatin when dissolved in boiling water.

col·lapse (kə laps′) *v.* **-lapsed, -laps·ing;** *n.* —*v.* **1** fall suddenly down or in as a result of outside pressure or loss of support; cave in: *They escaped from the burning building just before it collapsed.*

hat, āge, fär; let, ēqual, tèrm; it, īce
hot, ōpen, ôrder; oil, out; cup, pút, rüle,
əbove, takən, pencəl, lemən, circəs

ch, child; ng, long; sh, ship
th, thin; ʈH, then; zh, measure

A football will collapse if the air leaks out. **2** break down; fail suddenly: *Both his health and his business collapsed within a year.* **3** fold or push together: *to collapse a telescope.*
—*n.* **1** a falling in; sudden shrinking together: *A heavy flood caused the collapse of the bridge.* **2** a breakdown; failure: *She is suffering from a nervous collapse.* [< L *collapsus,* pp. of *collabi* < *com-* (intensive) + *labi* fall]

col·laps·i·ble (kə lap′sə bəl) *adj.* made so that it can be folded or pushed into a smaller space.

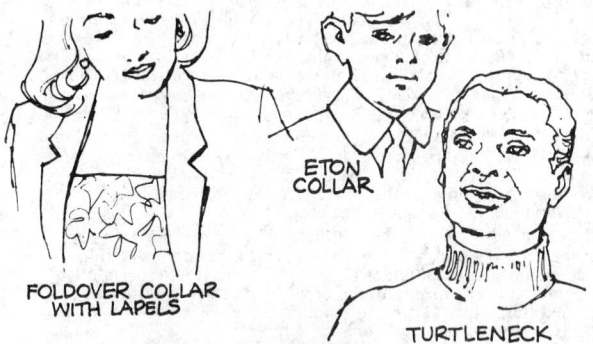

ETON COLLAR

FOLDOVER COLLAR WITH LAPELS

TURTLENECK

col·lar (kol′ər) *n., v.* —*n.* **1** a piece or band of cloth that finishes or is attached to the neckline of a garment, designed to stand up around the neck or lie folded over at the base of the neck, sometimes extending over the shoulders. See **lapel** for picture. **2** a piece of jewellery resembling a collar worn around the neck or over the chest and shoulders. **3** a band of leather, metal, etc. for the neck of a dog or other pet animal. **4** a thick, padded oval ring that forms part of the harness of a draft animal, fitting around the neck and resting against the shoulders and chest: *A horse's collar bears the weight of the load it is pulling.* See **harness** for picture. **5** a distinctive marking around the neck of an animal or bird, suggesting a collar: *The cliff swallow has a dark blue head and back and a grey collar around the back of the neck.* **6** a ring, disk, or flange on a rod, shaft, etc. that keeps a part from moving to the side. **7** a short pipe connecting two other pipes.
—*v.* **1** put a collar on. **2** seize by the collar; capture. **3** *Informal.* lay hold of; take. [ME < AF < L *collare* < *collum* neck] —**col′lar·less,** *adj.* —**col′lar·like′,** *adj.*
☛ *Hom.* **caller, choler.**

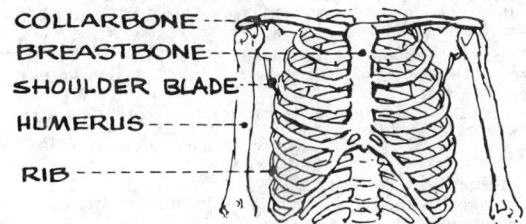

COLLARBONE
BREASTBONE
SHOULDER BLADE
HUMERUS
RIB

Part of the upper human skeleton, shown from the front

col·lar·bone (kol′ər bōn′) *n.* the bone connecting the breastbone and the shoulder blade; clavicle.

col·late (kə lāt′ *or* kol′āt) *v.* **-lat·ed, -lat·ing. 1** examine and compare carefully in order to note similarities and differences, check for accuracy, etc.: *to collate a copy of a document with the original, to collate the data from several experiments.* **2** arrange in proper order; put together in sequence: *to collate the pages of a report, to collate the sections of a book for binding.* [< L *collatus,* pp. to *conferre* < *com-* together + *ferre* bring]

col·lat·er·al (kə lat′ər əl) *adj., n.* —*adj.* **1** parallel; side by side. **2** related but less important; secondary; indirect. **3** in a parallel line of descent; descended from the same ancestors, but in a different

line: *Cousins are collateral relatives.* **4** additional. **5** secured by stocks, bonds, etc. —*n.* **1** a collateral relative. **2** stocks, bonds, etc. pledged as security for a loan. [< Med.L *collateralis* < *com-* together + L *lateralis* lateral] —**col·lat′er·al·ly,** *adv.*

col·la·tion (kə lā′shən) *n.* **1** the act or process of collating. **2** a light meal. Originally, in Benedictine monasteries, a light meal following readings of the Lives of the Fathers (*collationes patrum*). [ME < OF < L *collatio, -onis* a putting together]

col·la·tor (kə lā′tər *or* kol′āt ər) *n.* a person who collates.

col·league (kol′ēg) *n.* an associate; a fellow worker: *The doctor invited a colleague to examine the patient.* [< F *collègue* < L *collega* < *com-* together + *legare* send or choose as deputy]

col·lect¹ (kə lekt′) *v., adj., adv.* —*v.* **1** gather together; pick up: *The teacher collected the questionnaires.* **2** come together in one place; assemble: *A crowd soon collects at the scene of an accident.* **3** pile up; form into a mass; accumulate: *Drifting snow collects behind snow fences.* **4** gather together as a hobby: *to collect stamps.* **5** ask and receive payment for bills, debts, dues, taxes, etc. **6** regain control of: *After a shock a person must collect himself.* —*adj. or adv.* that is to be paid for by the receiver: *a collect telegram, telephone collect.* [< L *collectus,* pp. of *colligere* < *com-* together + *legere* gather]
☛ *Syn. v.* **1.** See note at **gather.**

col·lect² (kol′ekt) *n.* a short prayer used in certain church services. [ME < OF *collecte* < Med.L, short for *oratio ad collectam* prayer on assembly < L *collecta* a gathering in or gathering together < *colligere.* See COLLECT¹.]

col·lect·a·ble *or* **col·lect·i·ble** (kə lek′tə bəl) *adj., n.* —*adj.* that may be collected. —*n.* anything having a current attraction for collectors; an item that might be part of a collection, especially something other than an antique or work of art, or traditionally collected items such as coins or stamps: *a store window full of old picture frames, bottles, and other collectables.*

col·lect·ed (kə lek′tid) *adj.* **1** brought together; gathered together: *the author's collected works.* **2** not confused or disturbed; calm; in control of one's emotions. —**col·lect′ed·ly,** *adv.* —**col·lect′ed·ness,** *n.*
☛ *Syn.* **2.** See note at **calm.**

col·lect·i·ble (kə lek′tə bəl) *adj.* collectable.

col·lec·tion (kə lek′shən) *n.* **1** the act or practice of collecting. **2** a group of things gathered from many places and belonging together: *The library has a large collection of books.* **3** a collecting of money, especially for church expenses or charity. **4** the money collected: *The collection was larger than expected.* **5** something that has come together in one place; accumulation; heap: *There was a collection of debris on the porch.*

col·lec·tive (kə lek′tiv) *adj., n.* —*adj.* **1** of a group; as a group; taken all together: *a collective effort, a collective decision.* **2** formed by collecting. **3** functioning or operating on the principle of collectivism. —*n.* **1** collective noun. **2** a farm, factory, or other organization with collectivistic management. —**col·lec′tive·ly,** *adv.*

collective bargaining negotiation about wages, hours, and other working conditions between workers organized as a group and their employer or employers.

collective noun a noun that is singular in form but refers to a collection of things or persons. *Crowd, team, bunch,* and *orchestra* are collective nouns.
☛ *Usage.* A collective noun is used with a singular verb when it refers to a group as a whole (*The committee was silent*), but with a plural verb when it refers to a group in which the individuals are thought of as acting separately (*The committee were asked to prepare separate reports*).

col·lec·tiv·ism (kə lek′tiv iz′əm) *n.* the control of the production of goods and services and the distribution of wealth by people as a group or by a government.

col·lec·tiv·ist (kə lek′tiv ist) *n., adj.* —*n.* a person who favors or supports collectivism. —*adj.* collectivistic.

col·lec·tiv·is·tic (kə lek′tiv is′tik) *adj.* of collectivism or collectivists.

col·lec·ti·vize (kə lek′tə vīz′) *v.* **-vized, -viz·ing.** make (a state, economy, agricultural community, etc.) collective; transfer ownership of, from an individual or individuals to the state or all the people collectively. —**col·lec′ti·vi·za′tion,** *n.*

col·lec·tor (kə lek′tər) *n.* **1** a person who collects things as a hobby: *a coin collector.* **2** something that collects or appears to collect: *All these ornaments are just dust collectors.* **3** a person hired to collect money owed: *St. Matthew was a tax collector.* **4** in a vacuum tube, the positive electrode that attracts electrons from the emitter.

collector's item something worth adding to a collection.

col·lec·tor·ship (kə lek′tər ship′) *n.* **1** the office of a collector. **2** the district covered by a collector.

col·leen (kol′ēn *or* kə lēn′) *n. Irish.* girl. [< Ir. *cailín,* dim. of *caile* girl]

col·lege (kol′ij) *n.* **1** an institution that offers training or instruction in one or more particular occupations or professions and gives degrees or diplomas: *the Victoria College of Art. My cousin is taking a course in computer programming at a community college.* **2** *Informal.* university: *She's planning to go to college in the fall.* **3** one of the main academic divisions of a university, offering courses of study leading to a degree in a particular academic or professional field; faculty. All universities have a college of arts and most have several professional colleges such as engineering, agriculture, medicine, or education. **4** an institution within a university, either offering undergraduate courses in particular subject areas or organized as a social and residential unit with courses in a limited range of subjects: *Students at Erindale College get their degree from the University of Toronto.* **5** an organized association of persons having certain powers, rights, duties, and purposes: *the electoral college.* **6** a building or buildings used by a college. **7** (*adj.*) of or associated with college or university. [ME < OF *colege* < L *collegium* < *collega.* See COLLEAGUE.]

collège classique (kô lezh klä sēk′) *Cdn. French.* classical college.

College of Cardinals the cardinals of the Roman Catholic Church collectively. The College of Cardinals elects and advises the Pope.

col·le·gi·al (kə lē′jē əl) *adj.* characterized by equal sharing of power or authority among colleagues: *a collegial system of cabinet government.*

col·le·gi·al·i·ty (kə lē′jē al′ə tē) *n.* the sharing of authority and power among colleagues; especially, in the Roman Catholic Church, the sharing of authority by the Pope and bishops.

col·le·giate (kə lē′jit *or* kə lē′jē it) *adj., n.* —*adj.* **1** *Cdn.* of or like a high school or high-school students. **2** of or like a college. **3** of or like college students. —*n. Cdn.* **1** collegiate institute. **2** *Informal.* any large high school.

collegiate church **1** a church that has a chapter or college but no bishop's see. **2** *U.S.* an association of churches administered by several pastors jointly. **3** a church belonging to such an association. **4** in Scotland, a church served by two or more ministers of equal rank.

collegiate institute *Cdn.* in some provinces, a secondary school providing specified facilities, or having a set minimum number of specialist teachers, over and above those required in a high school.

col·lide (kə līd′) *v.* **-lid·ed, -lid·ing.** **1** come violently into contact; come together with force; crash: *Two large ships collided in the harbor.* **2** clash; conflict. [< L *collidere* < *com-* together + *laedere,* originally, strike]

col·lie (kol′ē *or* kō′lē) *n.* a breed of large, thick-haired dog having a long, pointed nose and a bushy tail. Collies came originally from Scotland where they were trained to tend sheep. [origin uncertain]

col·lier (kol′yer) *n.* **1** a ship for carrying coal. **2** a coal miner. [ME *colier* < *col* coal]

col·lier·y (kol′yer ē) *n., pl.* **-lier·ies.** a coal mine and its buildings and equipment.

col·li·mate (kol′ə māt′) *v.* **-mat·ed, -mat·ing.** **1** bring into line; make parallel. **2** adjust accurately the line of sight of (a surveying instrument, telescope, etc.) [< L *collimare,* misreading for *collineare,* ult. < *com-* together + *linea* line] —**col′li·ma′tion,** *n.*

col·li·ma·tor (kol′ə mā′tər) *n. Optics.* **1** a small fixed telescope used for adjusting the line of sight of other instruments. **2** in a spectroscope, a tube used to throw parallel rays of light on the prism. **3** the lens of this tube.

col·lin·e·ar (kə lin′ē ər) *adj. Geometry.* lying in the same straight line: *collinear points.* —**col·lin′e·ar·ly,** *adv.*

col·li·sion (kə lizh′ən) *n.* **1** a violent rushing against; hitting or striking violently together. **2** a clash; conflict. [< LL *collisio, -onis* < L *collidere.* See COLLIDE.]

col·lo·cate (kol′ō kāt′) *v.* **-cat·ed, -cat·ing.** **1** place together. **2** arrange. [< L *collocare* < *com-* together + *locare* place]

col·lo·ca·tion (kol′ō kā′shən) *n.* an arrangement: *the collocation of words in a sentence.*

col·lo·di·on (kə lō′dē ən) *n.* a glue-like solution of cellulose nitrate in ether and alcohol that dries very rapidly, leaving a tough, waterproof, transparent film. Collodion is used for covering burns and wounds. [< Gk *kollōdēs* gluey < *kolla* glue]

col·loid (kol′oid) *n.* **1** a solid, liquid, or gaseous substance made up of very small particles, such as single large molecules or groups

of smaller molecules, that will remain suspended without dissolving in a different medium. A colloid may be suspended in a solid, liquid, or gas. **2** a state of matter consisting of such a substance together with the medium in which it is suspended. Fog and the protoplasm of plant and animal cells are colloids. [< Gk. *kolla* glue]

col·loi·dal (kə loi′dəl) *adj.* **1** in the form of a colloid. **2** of, like, or containing a colloid.

col·lop (kol′əp) *n.* **1** a small slice of meat. **2** a small slice or piece of anything. **3** a fold of flesh or skin on the body. [ME *colope*; origin uncertain]

colloq. colloquial; colloquialism.

col·lo·qui·al (kə lō′kwē əl) *adj.* used in everyday informal talk, but not in formal speech or writing. *They've had it* and *It's a cinch* are colloquial expressions. —**col·lo′qui·al·ly,** *adv.*
☛ *Usage.* **Colloquial** = conversational, used in speaking. Since the speech of people varies with their education, work, and social status, there are obviously many different types of colloquial English. Since the bulk of conversation is informal, **colloquial** suggests informal rather than formal English. It need not, however, mean the speech of uneducated people. As used in many dictionaries, **colloquial** refers to informal cultivated English; the equivalent label in this dictionary is *Informal*. See note at **informal.**

col·lo·qui·al·ism (kə lō′kwē əl iz′əm) *n.* **1** a colloquial word or phrase. **2** colloquial style or usage.

col·lo·qui·um (kə lō′kwē əm) *n., pl.* **-qui·ums** or **-qui·a. 1** a meeting or conference, especially of scholars, scientists, etc. on a particular subject. **2** seminar. [< L *colloquium* conversation]

col·lo·quy (kol′ə kwē) *n., pl.* **-quies. 1** a talking together; conversation; conference. **2** a written dialogue: *Erasmus' Colloquies.* [< L *colloquium* < *colloqui* < *com-* with + *loqui* speak]

col·lude (kə lüd′) *v.* **-lud·ed, -lud·ing.** act together through a secret understanding; conspire in a fraud. [< L *colludere* < *com-* with + *ludere* play]

col·lu·sion (kə lü′zhən) *n.* a secret agreement for some wrong purpose. [< L *collusio, -onis* < *colludere.* See COLLUDE.]

col·lu·sive (kə lü′siv) *adj.* involving collusion; fraudulent. —**col·lu′sive·ly,** *adv.*

Colo. Colorado.

co·logne (kə lōn′) *n.* a fragrant liquid, not so strong as perfume. [< F *eau de Cologne,* meaning water of Cologne < *Cologne,* West Germany, where it was first made]

Co·lom·bi·an (kə lum′bē ən) *n., adj.* —*n.* a native or inhabitant of Colombia, a country in NW South America. —*adj.* of or having to do with Colombia or its people.

co·lon¹ (kō′lən) *n.* a mark (:) of punctuation used after an introductory sentence to show that a list, explanation, illustration, long quotation, etc. follows. [< L < Gk. *kōlon* limb, clause]

co·lon² (kō′lən) *n., pl.* **co·lons** or **co·la** (kō′lə). the main part of the large intestine, from the caecum to the rectum. See **alimentary canal** for picture. [ME < L < Gk. *kolon*]

co·lon³ (kō lōn′) *n., pl.* **co·lons** or **co·lo·nes** (kō lō′nās). **1** the basic unit of money in El Salvador, divided into 100 centavos. **2** the basic unit of money in Costa Rica, divided into 100 centimos. See table at **money. 3** a coin worth one colon. [< Sp. *colón* < Cristóbal *Colón* Christopher Columbus]

co·lon⁴ (lôn′) *n. French.* a French settler or the descendant of a French settler; a colonial.

colo·nel (kèr′nəl) *n.* an officer in the armed forces ranking next above a lieutenant-colonel and below a brigadier-general. *Abbrev.:* Col. or Col See chart at **rank¹.** [earlier also *coronel* < F *coronel* var. of *colonel* < Ital. *colonnello* commander of a regiment, ult. < *colonna* column < L *columna*]
☛ *Hom.* **kernel.**
☛ *Spelling.* **Colonel** is a spelling that has survived a change of pronunciation. The word, from the French, has two parallel forms **colonel, coronel,** each pronounced in three syllables. For 150 years the word has been pronounced (kèr′nəl), from the **coronel** form, but the spelling has survived as **colonel.**

Colonel Blimp See **Blimp.**

colo·nel·cy (kèr′nəl sē) *n., pl.* **-cies.** the rank, commission, or authority of a colonel.

co·lo·ni·al (kə lō′nē əl) *adj., n.* —*adj.* **1** of, or having to do with, or inhabiting a colony or colonies. **2** possessing or made up of colonies: *the British colonial empire.* **3** Often, **Colonial,** having to do with, prevailing in, or characteristic of the colonies of the British Empire, especially the 13 colonies that became the United States: *colonial furniture, colonial architecture.*
—*n.* a person living in a colony. —**co·lo′ni·al·ly,** *adv.*

co·lo·ni·al·ism (kə lō′nē ə liz′əm) *n.* **1** the practice or policy of a nation that rules or seeks to rule over other countries as colonies. **2** the state of being a colony.

co·lo·ni·al·ist (kə lō′nē ə list) *n., adj.* —*n.* a person who supports or practises colonialism. —*adj.* **1** of or having to do with colonialism or colonialists. **2** supporting or practising colonialism.

hat, āge, fär; let, ēqual, tèrm; it, īce
hot, ōpen, ôrder; oil, out; cup, put, rüle,
above, takən, pencəl, lemən, circəs
ch, child; ng, long; sh, ship
th, thin; ᴛʜ, then; zh, measure

col·o·nist (kol′ə nist) *n.* **1** a person who helps to found a colony. **2** a person who lives in a colony during the period of settlement; settler.

colonist car *Cdn. Historical.* a railway coach having wooden seats and rough berths for sleeping, sometimes also having cooking facilities.

col·o·ni·za·tion (kol′ə nə zā′shən *or* kol′ə nī zā′shən) *n.* the establishment of a colony or colonies: *the colonization of North America.*

col·o·nize (kol′ə nīz′) *v.* **-nized, -niz·ing.** establish a colony or colonies in: *French fishermen colonized this coast. France colonized parts of Canada before England did.* —**col′o·niz′er,** *n.*

col·on·nade (kol′ə nād′) *n. Architecture.* a series of columns set the same distance apart. [< F < Ital. *colonnata* < *colonna* column < L *columna*]

col·on·nad·ed (kol′ə nād′id) *adj.* having a colonnade.

col·o·ny (kol′ə nē) *n., pl.* **-nies. 1** a group of people who leave their own country and go to settle in another land, but who still remain citizens of their original country. **2** the settlement made by such a group of people. **3** a territory distant from the country that governs it. **4** a group of people of one country, faith, or occupation living as a group: *There is a large Chinese colony in Vancouver. There are several Doukhobor colonies in British Columbia. There is an artists' colony in Paris.* **5** *Biology.* a group of animals or plants of the same kind, living or growing together: *a colony of ants. A coral island is a colony.* **6** *Bacteriology.* a mass of bacteria arising from a single cell, living on or in a solid or partially solid medium. **7 the Colonies, a** the thirteen British colonies that became the United States of America: New Hampshire, Massachusetts, Rhode Island, Connecticut, New York, New Jersey, Pennsylvania, Delaware, Maryland, Virginia, North Carolina, South Carolina, and Georgia. **b** the colonies, as opposed to self-governing dominions, within the British Empire. [< L *colonia* < *colonus* cultivator, settler < *colere* cultivate]

col·o·phon (kol′ə fon′ *or* kol′ə fən) *n.* **1** the words or inscription formerly placed at the end of a book, telling the name of the publisher, the date of publication, etc. Nowadays, much of this information is usually found on the title page. **2** a small design or device of a publisher placed on the last page or on the title page of a book. [< LL < Gk. *kolophōn* summit, final touch]

col·or or **col·our** (kul′ər) *n., v.* —*n.* **1** the sensation produced by the different effects of waves of light striking the retina of the eye. Different colors are produced by rays of light having different wave lengths. **2** any color other than black, white, or grey; chromatic color: *Most of the photographs are in color.* **3** a paint, dye, or pigment: *oil colors.* **4** the natural healthy color of a person's face: *The color drained from his face and we thought he would faint.* **5** a flush caused by blushing: *The color rushed to her face when her mistake was pointed out.* **6** the color of a person's skin due to pigment. **7** an outward appearance; show: *His lies had some color of truth.* **8** a distinguishing quality; vividness: *His gift for description adds color to his stories.* **9** character; tone: *a horse of a different color.* **10** *Music.* **a** a quality of tone by which any musical instrument or combination of instruments can be recognized, used especially in orchestration; tone color; timbre. **b** the quality of expression in a musical performance or style of musical interpretation which may produce an emotional reaction in the listener or audience: *His playing has color and vigor.* **11 colors** or **colours,** *pl.* a badge, ribbon, dress, etc. worn to show allegiance. **12 the colors** or **colours, a** the flag of a nation, regiment, etc.: *He carried the colors in the parade.* **b** the ceremony of raising the flag in the morning and lowering it in the evening. **c** the army, navy, or air force: *Soldiers, sailors, and airmen serve the colors.*
change color (or **colour**), react by becoming either pale or red in the face: *She took the news calmly and didn't even change color.*
give or **lend color** (or **colour**) **to,** cause to seem true or likely.
lose color (or **colour**), become pale: *He lost a lot of color during his illness.*
show (one's) **true colors** (or **colours**), **a** show oneself as one really is. **b** declare one's opinions or plans.
with flying colors (or **colours**), with great success; triumphantly: *He passed the examination with flying colors.*
—*v.* **1** give color to; change the color of. **2** become red in the face; blush. **3** present so as to give a wrong idea; put in a false light: *The general colored his report of the battle to make his own mistakes seem the fault of his officers.* **4** give a distinguishing

quality to; affect: *Her report was colored by her desire to impress the audience. Love of nature colored all of Sir Charles Roberts' writing.* [ME < OF < L] —**col′or·er** or **col′our·er**, *n.*

☛ *Syn. n.* **1. Color, hue, shade** = a sensation produced by the effect of waves of light striking the retina of the eye. **Color** is the general word: *Her dress is the color of grass.* **Hue** is poetic in the general meaning of color. Technically, **hue** = the quality of a color that gives the name: red, blue, etc. It is also used to suggest partial alteration of a color: *This pottery is blue with a greenish hue.* **Shade** applies to a degree of intensity of color: *I like a blue car, but of a lighter shade than navy.*

col·or·a·ble or **col·our·a·ble** (kul′ər ə bəl) *adj.* **1** capable of being colored. **2** apparently plausible but actually specious or deceptive.

Col·o·ra·do potato beetle (kol′ə rad′ō or kol′ə rä′dō) potato beetle.

col·or·ant (kul′ər ənt) *n.* a coloring agent, such as a pigment or dye. [< F *colorant,* ppr. of *colorer* to color < L *colorare*]

col·or·a·tion or **col·our·a·tion** (kul′ər ā′shən) *n.* a coloring; way in which something is colored: *The coloration of some animals is like that of their surroundings.*

col·o·ra·tu·ra (kul′ə rə tyür′ə or kul′ə rə tür′ə) *n.* **1** *Music.* ornamental passages such as trills, runs, etc. **2** (*adj.*) characterized by or suitable for such ornamental passages. **3** a vocal composition containing such passages. **4** a soprano who specializes in singing such music. [< Ital. < L *color* color]

color bar or **colour bar** **1** the denial, especially to blacks, of rights, privileges, and opportunities enjoyed by white people. **2** the denial of rights, privileges, and opportunities on the grounds of skin color.

col·or·bear·er or **col·our·bear·er** (kul′ər ber′ər) *n.* a person who carries the flag or colors; standard bearer.

col·or–blind or **col·our–blind** (kul′ər blīnd′) *adj.* unable to tell certain colors apart; unable to perceive certain colors or, in certain cases, any colors. —**col′or-blind′ness** or **col′our-blind′ness,** *n.*

col·or–code or **col·our–code** (kul′ər kōd′) *v.* **col·or-cod·ed** or **col·our-cod·ed, col·or-cod·ing** or **col·our-cod·ing.** use standard colors as a means of identification: *The wires in the electrical system are color-coded.*

col·ored or **col·oured** (kul′ərd) *adj., n.* —*adj.* **1** having color; not black, white, grey, or clear: *colored water. He prefers colored shirts to white ones.* **2** having a certain color (used in compounds): *red-colored leaves.* **3** belonging to a non-European race or having non-European ancestors. **4** tinged by emotion, prejudice, desire for effect, etc: *The newspaper published a colored account of the political convention.*
—*n.* **1** *Esp.U.S.* a person of African descent or having some African ancestors. **2** *South African.* a person of racially mixed descent.

col·or·fast or **col·our·fast** (kul′ər fast′) *adj.* resistant to loss or change of color by fading or washing.

color film or **colour film** **1** a film for making photographs in color. **2** a motion picture made with such film.

col·or·ful or **col·our·ful** (kul′ər fəl) *adj.* **1** abounding in color. **2** picturesque; vivid. —**col′or·ful·ly** or **col′our·ful·ly,** *adv.* —**col′or·ful·ness** or **col′our·ful·ness,** *n.*

col·or·ing or **col·our·ing** (kul′ər ing) *n.* **1** the pattern, kind, or degree of color or colors that a person or thing has: *His coloring is much better since his health improved.* **2** a substance used to color something; pigment. **3** a false appearance: *His lies have a coloring of truth.*

coloring matter or **colouring matter** a substance used to color; pigment.

col·or·ist or **col·our·ist** (kul′ər ist) *n.* **1** an artist who is skilful in painting with colors. **2** a user of color.

col·or·less or **col·our·less** (kul′ər lis) *adj.* **1** without color. **2** without excitement or variety; uninteresting: *a colorless personality.* —**col′or·less·ly** or **col′our·less·ly,** *adv.* —**col′or·less·ness** or **col′our·less·ness,** *n.*

color line or **colour line** a distinction in social, economic, or political privileges between members of different races.

color photography or **colour photography** photography using color film.

co·los·sal (kə los′əl) *adj.* **1** huge; gigantic; vast. **2** *Informal.* remarkable; outstanding: *a colossal blunder. Her new film is colossal.* [< *colossus*] —**co·los′sal·ly,** *adv.*

Col·os·se·um (kol′ə sē′əm) *n.* in Rome, a large, outdoor theatre, completed in A.D. 80. The Colosseum was used for games and contests. Also, **Coliseum.** [< LL *colosseum,* neut. of L *colosseus* gigantic < *colossus* < Gk. *kolossos* gigantic statue]

co·los·sus (kə los′əs) *n., pl.* **-los·sus·es** or **-los·si** (-los′ī or -los′ē). **1** a huge statue. **2** anything huge; gigantic person or thing. [< L < Gk. *kolossos*]

Colossus of Rhodes (rōdz) a huge statue of Apollo made on the island of Rhodes about 280 B.C. It was one of the seven wonders of the ancient world.

co·los·to·my (kə los′tə mē) *n., pl.* **-mies.** the making of an artificial opening in the colon. [< *colon²* + Gk. *stoma* opening]

co·lot·o·my (kə lot′ə mē) *n., pl.* **-mies.** a surgical incision into the colon. [< *colon²* + Gk. *-tomia* -cutting]

col·our (kul′ər) See **color.**

☛ *Spelling.* Compounds and derivatives beginning with **colour-** are entered under their **color-** forms.

col·por·teur (kol′pôr′tər) *n.* **1** a person who travels about and distributes Bibles, tracts, etc. **2** a hawker of books, broadsides, newspapers, etc. [< F *colporteur* < *colporter* hawk, carry for sale (on the neck) < *col* neck (< L *collum*) + *porter* carry (< L *portare*)]

colt (kōlt) *n.* **1** a young horse, donkey, etc., especially a male horse under four or five years old. **2** a young or inexperienced person. [OE]

Colt a famous type of revolver. [< Samuel *Colt* (1814-1862), the inventor]

col·ter (kōl′tər) See **coulter.**

colt·ish (kōl′tish) *adj.* like a colt; lively and frisky. —**colt′ish·ly,** *adv.*

colts·foot (kōlts′füt′) *n.* a common European perennial plant (*Tussilago farfara*) of the composite family having heart-shaped leaves and yellow daisylike flowers. [from the shape of the leaves, resembling the imprint of a colt's foot]

Co·lum·bi·a (kə lum′bē ə) *n.* a name for the United States of America. Columbia is often represented as a woman dressed in red, white, and blue. [after Christopher *Columbus*]

col·um·bine (kol′əm bīn′) *n.* **1** any of a genus (*Aquilegia*) of perennial plants of the buttercup family having showy drooping flowers with five petals each forming a wide-mouthed tube ending in a hooked spur pointing upward. Several species of columbine grow wild in Canada. **2 Columbine,** in traditional Italian comedy and in pantomime, a girl who is the sweetheart of Harlequin. [ME < OF < LL *columbina* < L *columbina,* fem., dovelike < *columba* dove]

co·lum·bi·um (kə lum′bē əm) *n.* a rare, steel-grey, metallic chemical element that resembles tantalum in its chemical properties; niobium. *Symbol:* Cb; *at.no.* 41; *at.wt.* 92.91. [< NL < *Columbia,* the United States]

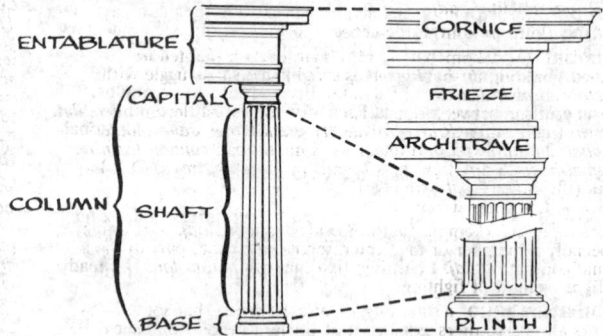

col·umn (kol′əm) *n.* **1** *Architecture.* a slender, upright structure; pillar. Columns are usually made of stone, wood, or metal, and are used mainly as supports or ornaments to a building. Sometimes a column stands alone as a monument. **2** anything that seems slender and upright like a column: *a column of smoke, a long column of figures, the spinal column.* **3** *Military.* a formation in which troops, units, armored vehicles, etc. follow one behind the other. **4** a line of ships or aircraft, one behind the other. **5** any similar line of persons, things, etc.: *A long column of cars followed the procession down the street.* **6** a narrow division of a page reading from top to bottom, kept separate by a line or a blank space. A newspaper often has eight columns on a page. **7** a part of a newspaper or periodical used for a special subject or written by a special writer. **8** a line or series of letters, figures, etc. arranged vertically. [< L *columna*]

☛ *Pronun.* **column.** In sense 6, **column** is occasionally pronounced (kol′yəm) although considered by most to be substandard. This pronunciation is also used humorously.

co·lum·nar (kə lum′nər) *adj.* **1** like a column. **2** made of columns. **3** written or printed in columns.

col·umned (kol′əmd) *adj.* **1** having columns. **2** formed into columns.

co·lum·ni·a·tion (kə lum′nē ā′shən) *n.* the use or arrangement of columns in a building.

col·um·nist (kol′əm ist *or* kol′əm nist) *n.* a person who writes or selects and edits the material for a special column in a newspaper.
☛ *Pronun.* **Columnist** is sometimes pronounced (kol′yəm ist). See note at **column.**

col·za (kol′zə) *n.* **1** cole seed. **2** an oil made from these seeds, used as a fuel in lamps, as a lubricant, etc. [< Du. *koolsaad,* literally, cabbage seed]

com– *prefix.* **1** with; together: *commingle = mingle with one another. Compress = press together.* **2** altogether; completely: *comprehend = grasp the meaning completely.* Used before *b, m, p,* and, occasionally, before *f* and vowels. Also: **co–** before vowels and *h*; **col–** before *l*; **cor–** before *r*; **con–** before all other consonants. [< L *com– < cum,* prep.]

com. 1 comedy. **2** commerce. **3** common; commonly. **4** communication.

Com. 1 Commander. **2** Commodore. **3** Commissioner. **4** committee. **5** Communist.

co·ma¹ (kō′mə) *n., pl.* **co·mas.** a prolonged unconsciousness caused by disease, injury, or poison; stupor. [< Gk. *kōma*]

co·ma² (kō′mə) *n., pl.* **co·mae** (-mē *or* -mī). **1** a cloudlike mass around the nucleus of a comet. **2** *Botany.* a tuft of hairs at the end of a seed. [< L < Gk. *komē* hair]

Co·man·che (kə man′chē) *n., pl.* **-che** *or* **-ches. 1** a member of an Amerindian people formerly inhabiting W North America from Wyoming to N Mexico, now living mainly in Oklahoma. **2** the Shoshonean language of the Comanche. [< Mexican Sp. *Comanche* < Shoshonean *Komanchi*]

co·mat·ik (kō′mə tik′) See **komatik.**

com·a·tose (kom′ə tōs′ *or* kō′mə tōs′) *adj.* **1** in a stupor or coma; unconscious. **2** drowsy; lethargic. [< F < Gk. *kōma, -atos* sleep]

comb¹ (kōm) *n., v.* —*n.* **1** a narrow, short, often somewhat flexible strip of metal, rubber, etc. with teeth, used to arrange or clean the hair or to hold it in place. **2** anything shaped or used like a comb. One kind of comb cleans and takes out the tangles in wool or flax. **3** a currycomb. **4** the thick, red, fleshy crest on the top of the head in some fowls. **5** honeycomb (def. 1). **6** the top of a wave rolling over or breaking. —*v.* **1** arrange, clean, or take out tangles in, with a comb. **2** search through; look everywhere in: *We had to comb the whole city before we found our lost dog.* **3** of waves, roll over or break at the top. [OE] —**comb′like′,** *adj.*

comb² (küm *or* kōm) See **combe.**

com·bat (*v. n.* kom′bat; *v.,* also, kəm bat′) *v.* **-bat·ted** *or* **-bat·ed, -bat·ting** *or* **-bat·ing**; *n.* —*v.* fight against; struggle with: *Doctors combat disease.* —*n.* **1** fighting between opposing armed forces; battle: *Bombers flew over us as we entered the combat. My grandfather was wounded in combat.* **2** (adjl.) designed for or used in combat: *combat training, combat boots.* **3** any fight or struggle. [< F *combattre* < LD < L *com–* (intensive) + *battuere* beat]
☛ *Syn. n.* **1.** See note at **fight.**

com·bat·ant (kəm bat′ənt *or* kom′bə tənt) *n., adj.* —*n.* a fighter, especially a member of the armed forces who takes part in the actual combat. —*adj.* **1** battling; fighting: *combatant forces.* **2** ready to fight or fond of fighting.

combat fatigue a state of mental exhaustion that sometimes occurs among soldiers as a result of warfare in the front lines.

com·bat·ive (kəm bat′iv *or* kom′bə tiv) *adj.* ready to fight or oppose; fond of fighting. —**com·bat′ive·ly,** *adv.* —**com·bat′ive·ness,** *n.*

combat team two or more units of different military branches acting together in battle.

combe or **comb** (küm *or* kōm) *n.* a narrow valley; deep hollow surrounded on three sides by hills. [OE *cumb,* probably < Celtic]

comb·er (kōm′ər) *n.* **1** a person or thing that combs wool, flax, etc. **2** a wave that rolls over or breaks at the top; breaker.

com·bi·na·tion (kom′bə nā′shən) *n.* **1** combining or being combined; union: *The combination of flour and water makes paste.* **2** one whole made by combining two or more different things. **3** persons or groups joined together for some common purpose. **4** a series of numbers or letters used in opening a combination lock. **5** the mechanism of such a lock. **6** an undergarment consisting of an undershirt and underpants in one piece. **7** *Mathematics.* **a** the arrangement of individual items of a set into groups of a certain size, without regard to order. The possible combinations of *a, b,* and *c,* taken two at a time, are *ab, ac,* and *bc.* **b** a group formed in

hat, āge, fär; let, ēqual, tèrm; it, īce
hot, ōpen, ôrder; oil, out; cup, pút, rüle,
əbove, takən, pencəl, lemən, circəs
ch, child; ng, long; sh, ship
th, thin; ᴛʜ, then; zh, measure

this way. **8** *Chemistry.* the union of substances to form a compound.

combination lock a lock that is opened either by turning a dial through a pre-selected sequence of numbers or by setting a series of dials at pre-selected numbers. Turning the dial or dials to the correct position aligns the tumblers inside so that the locking mechanism can be released.

com·bine (*v. 1, 2* kəm bīn′; *v. 3* kom′bīn; *n.* kom′bīn) *v.* **-bined, -bin·ing**; *n.* —*v.* **1** join together; unite. **2** *Chemistry.* unite to form a compound. Two atoms of hydrogen combine with one of oxygen to form water. **3** use a combine: *We combined the wheat last week.* —*n.* **1** a group of people joined together for business or political purposes; combination: *The companies formed a combine to keep prices up.* **2** a machine that cuts and threshes grain in one operation. It separates the seeds from the stalks as it moves across a field. [< LL *combinare* < *com–* together + *bini* two by two] —**com·bin′a·ble,** *adj.*
☛ *Syn. v.* **1.** See note at **join.**

com·bined (kəm bīnd′) *adj.* **1** joined together; united. **2** done by groups, persons, etc. acting together: *a combined effort.*

combined operations 1 military operations carried on by two or more allies acting together. **2** military operations in which land, sea, and air forces co-operate; amphibious operations.

comb·ings (kōm′ingz) *n.pl.* the hairs removed by a comb.

combining form a form of a word used for combining with other words or word elements, or with suffixes or prefixes. *Examples*: multi-, as in *multilingual* and *multimillionaire*; -phone, as in *telephone* and *Anglophone.*

com·bo (kom′bō) *n., pl.* **-bos.** *Informal.* a small group of jazz musicians playing together regularly. [shortened form of *combination*]

com·bus·ti·bil·i·ty (kəm bus′tə bil′ə tē) *n.* a combustible quality or condition; inflammability.

com·bus·ti·ble (kəm bus′tə bəl) *adj., n.* —*adj.* **1** capable of taking fire and burning; easily burned: *Gasoline is highly combustible.* **2** easily excited; fiery. —*n.* a combustible substance.

com·bus·tion (kəm bus′chən) *n.* **1** the act or process of burning: *The explosion in the coal mine was caused by the combustion of gases.* **2** *Chemistry.* a rapid oxidation accompanied by high temperature and, usually, by light. **3** a slow oxidation not accompanied by high temperature and light. The cells of the body transform food into energy by combustion. **4** violent excitement; tumult. [< LL *combustio, -onis* < L *comburere* burn together < *co-urere* burn together or simultaneously and *amburere* burn on both sides]

Comdr. Commander.

Comdt. Commandant.

come (kum) *v.* **came, come, com·ing**; *interj.* —*v.* **1** move toward; approach: *Come this way.* **2** reach a particular place in space or time; arrive: *We come now to a different kind of poem. The time has come for us to decide. The girls come home today.* **3** appear: *Light comes and goes.* **4** reach; extend: *The dress comes to her knees.* **5** progress (often used with **along**): *She's coming along well now. How is your project coming?* **6** arrive, happen, or belong at a certain position in a series: *She came second in the high jump.* **7** happen; take place; occur: *Come what may.* **8** be caused; result: *You see what comes of meddling.* **9** be derived; originate: *He comes of a poor family. Milk comes from cows.* **10** turn out to be; become: *His dream came true.* **11** enter or be brought into a particular state or condition: *to come into use. My shoelace came undone. When will you come to your senses?* **12** occur to the mind: *The solution of the problem has just come to me.* **13** be available or obtainable: *This sweater comes in white and yellow.* **14** amount or add up (*to*): *The bill comes to $100.*
come about, a take place; happen: *Their meeting came about by accident.* **b** *Nautical.* turn around; change direction.
come across, a meet or find by chance: *We came across some of my old toys when we were cleaning out the basement yesterday.* **b** have the desired effect; succeed: *The actor's attempt to portray terror didn't come across.* **c** *Informal.* give an impression of; appear: *He comes across very tough, but he's nice when you get to know him.* **d** *Slang.* give in to a demand, a persistent request, etc.; hand over money, information, etc.: *She came across with a $100 donation.*
come around or **come round, a** return to consciousness or health;

recover. **b** give in; yield; agree. **c** turn around; change direction.

come at, a reach; get. **b** rush toward; attack.

come back, a return. **b** be remembered: *The forgotten name came back to him the next day.* **c** *Informal.* return to a former position or condition: *She's making an effort to come back by appearing as a guest artist on television shows.*

come between, cause separation or unfriendly feeling: *The two friends vowed that they wouldn't let anything come between them.*

come by, get; obtain; acquire: *How did you come by that black eye?*

come down, a lose position, money, rank, etc.: *He has certainly come down in the last year.* **b** be handed down or passed along: *Many fables have come down through the ages.* **c** *Informal.* become ill (*with*): *He came down with a bad cold.*

come down on, a *Informal.* scold; blame. **b** attack suddenly.

come forward, offer oneself for work or duty; volunteer.

come from, a be born in or to; be descended from; descend from: *She comes from a large family.* **b** be a native or former resident of: *They come from Manitoba.*

come in, a enter: *Please come in.* **b** begin to be used; be brought into use or fashion: *Steamboats came in soon after the invention of the steam engine.* **c** of trains, planes, etc., arrive: *We got there just as the train came in.* **d** of an oil well, begin producing: *This was the first oil well in the area to come in.*

come in for, get; receive: *He came in for a lot of criticism on his handling of the deal.*

come into, acquire, especially by inheriting: *She has come into a lot of money.*

come off, a happen; take place; occur: *When is the final game going to come off?* **b** reach the end; emerge, as from a contest: *She tried out for the team yesterday and came off with flying colors.* **c** become detached: *The label came off when I soaked the jar in water.* **d** *Informal.* turn out to be effective or successful: *His jokes didn't come off at all.*

come off it!, *Slang.* stop acting or talking like that.

come on, a develop; progress: *Our garden is coming on fine.* **b** meet by chance; find: *When I turned the corner, I came on a strange sight.* **c** *Theatre.* make an entrance onto the stage: *The murderer comes on in the second act.* **d** *Slang.* make an impression: *He comes on too strong.*

come on!, *Informal.* hurry: *Come on! We're going to be late!* **b** stop behaving that way: *Oh, come on! You know he didn't mean it that way.* **c** an expression of disbelief: *Eighty thousand dollars for that house? Come on!*

come out, a be revealed or made public: *The details of the scandal never came out.* **b** be offered to the public: *A new model came out last year.* **c** result; end: *How did your pictures come out?* **d** put in an appearance; offer to take part: *Quite a few students came out for drama this year.* **e** state publicly: *She came out strongly in favor of the expressway.* **f** be introduced to society; make a debut.

come out with, a *Informal.* say openly: *That child comes out with the strangest qustions.* **b** offer to the public: *The publisher has come out with a new edition.*

come over, a happen to; influence or possess: *A strange feeling came over me. I don't know what's come over her; she's so grumpy lately.* **b** *Informal.* visit: *When are you coming over?*

come through, a be successful; win. **b** last through successfully. **c** *Slang.* hand over; pay.

come to, a return to consciousness: *The boxer came to in the dressing room.* **b** turn a ship's bow toward the wind. **c** to anchor.

come up, arise; develop: *The question is sure to come up in class.*

come upon, meet or find by chance: *We came upon them at the plaza this morning.*

come up with, provide; produce, especially in working on a problem: *He couldn't come up with the right answer.*

—*interj.* here! look! stop! (used to express irritation or impatience). [OE *cuman*]

☛ *Usage.* **Come, arrive, reach.** In the sense of getting to a point or place, **come** is followed by **to**, **arrive** is followed by **at**, and **reach** requires no preposition: *We came to a conclusion. We arrived at a decision. We reached an agreement.*

come-all-ye (kum′ol yē′ *or* -ôl yē′) *n.* a folk song or ballad of England, Ireland, or Canada. [< *Come all ye*, a frequent first line in such ballads]

come·back (kum′bak′) *n. Informal.* **1** a return to a former condition or position. **2** a clever or sharp reply: *She's always ready with a good comeback.* **3** a cause for complaint: *When you buy an appliance "as is," you have no comeback if it doesn't work.*

co·me·di·an (kə mē′dē ən) *n.* **1** an actor in comedies; an actor of comic parts. **2** an entertainer who tells jokes or funny stories, sings funny songs, etc.; a comic. **3** *Archaic.* a writer of comedies. **4** a person who amuses others with his funny talk and actions. [< F *comédien*]

co·me·di·enne (kə mē′dē en′) *n.* **1** an actress in comedies; an actress of comic parts. **2** a female entertainer who tells jokes or

funny stories, sings funny songs, etc. [< F *comédienne*, fem. of *comédien*]

come·down (kum′doun′) *n. Informal.* a loss of position, rank, money, etc.

com·e·dy (kom′ə dē) *n., pl.* **-dies. 1** an amusing play or show having a happy ending. **2** such plays or shows as a class; the branch of drama concerned with such plays. **3** an amusing happening; funny incident. **4** the comic element of drama or literature, or of life in general: *the human comedy.* **5** any literary work having a theme suited to comedy or using the methods of comedy. [ME < OF < L *comoedia* < Gk. *kōmōidia* + *kōmōidos* comedian < *kōmos* merrymaking + *aoidos* singer]

come·li·ness (kum′lē nis) *n.* **1** pleasant appearance. **2** fitness; suitableness; propriety.

come·ly (kum′lē) *adj.* **-li·er, -li·est. 1** having a pleasant appearance; attractive. **2** fitting; suitable; proper. [OE *cymlic*]

come–on (kum′on′) *n. Slang.* something offered to attract, especially something extra promised in a sales promotion; gimmick: *The offer of a free sample is just a come-on.*

com·er (kum′ər) *n.* **1** a person who comes. **2** a person who has recently come. **3** *Informal.* a person who shows promise or seems likely to succeed.

co·mes·ti·ble (kə mes′tə bəl) *n., adj.* —*n.* something to eat; an article of food. —*adj.* eatable. [< LL *comestibilis* < L *comestus*, var. of *comesus*, pp. of *comedere* < *com-* with + *edere* eat]

com·et (kom′it) *n. Astronomy.* a starlike object that travels in an oval orbit around the sun, having a head consisting of an icy nucleus of frozen gases, ice, and dust surrounded by a hazy cloud, and, often, a long, shining tail. Some comets are visible to the naked eye when they are near the sun. [ME *comete* < OF < L *cometa* < Gk. *kométēs* wearing long hair < *komē* hair]

come·up·pance (kum′up′əns) *n. Informal.* whatever penalty, change of luck, etc. one deserves; one's just deserts.

com·fit (kum′fit *or* kom′fit) *n.* a piece of candy; sweetmeat. [ME < OF *confit* < L *confectus* prepared, pp. of *conficere* < *com-* together + *facere* make]

com·fort (kum′fərt) *v., n.* —*v.* **1** ease the grief or sorrow of (someone); cheer. **2** give ease to. **3** *Archaic or formal.* help; support.
—*n.* **1** anything that makes trouble or sorrow easier to bear. **2** freedom from pain or hardship; ease. **3** a person or thing that makes life easier or takes away hardship. **4** *Archaic or formal.* help or support: *giving aid and comfort to the enemy.* [ME < OF *confort* < LL *confortare* strengthen < *com-* together + *fortis* strong]
—**com′fort·ing·ly,** *adv.*

☛ *Syn. v.* **1. Comfort, console** = ease sorrow, trouble, or pain. **Comfort** = ease the grief or sorrow of a person by making him more cheerful and giving him hope or strength: *Neighbors comforted the mother of the burned child.* **Console** = make grief or trouble easier to bear by doing something to lighten it or make the person forget it temporarily: *Her music consoled the widow.* —*n.* **2.** See note at **ease.**

com·fort·a·ble (kum′fər tə bəl) *adj.* **1** giving a feeling of ease: *That's a very comfortable chair. A soft, warm bed is comfortable.* **2** in comfort; at ease; free from pain or hardship. **3** easy; tranquil; undisturbed: *a comfortable sleep.* **4** *Informal.* enough for one's needs; adequate: *He has a comfortable income.*
—**com′fort·a·ble·ness,** *n.* —**com′fort·a·bly,** *adv.*

com·fort·er (kum′fər tər) *n.* **1** a person or thing that gives comfort. **2** a padded or quilted covering for a bed. **3** *Brit.* a long woollen scarf. **4** the **Comforter,** *Christianity.* the Holy Spirit.

com·fort·less (kum′fərt lis) *adj.* **1** bringing no comfort or ease of mind: *comfortless words.* **2** without the comforts of life: *a bare and comfortless room.*

comfort station a public lavatory.

com·fy (kum′fē) *adj.* **-fi·er, -fi·est.** *Informal.* comfortable.

com·ic (kom′ik) *adj., n.* —*adj.* **1** of comedy or in comedies: *a comic actor.* **2** amusing, funny.
—*n.* **1** the amusing or funny side of literature, life, etc. **2** *Informal.* a comic book. **3** *Informal.* a comic strip. **4** comedian. **5 comics,** *pl.* the page or section of a newspaper containing comic strips. [< L *comicus* < Gk. *kōmikos* < *kōmos* merrymaking]

com·i·cal (kom′ə kəl) *adj.* **1** amusing; funny. **2** *Informal.* queer; strange; odd. —**com′i·cal·ly,** *adv.* —**com′i·cal·ness,** *n.*

comic book a book or magazine made up of one or more comic strips.

comic opera an amusing opera having a happy ending.

comic strip a series of drawings that tell a funny story, an adventure, or a series of incidents.

Com·in·form (kom′in fôrm′) *n.* an international Communist organization intended to co-ordinate the propoganda of Communist parties throughout the world, formed in 1947 by the signatories of the Warsaw Pact and dissolved in 1956. [< *Communist Inform*ation Bureau]

com·ing (kum'ing) *n., adj.* —*n.* the approach; arrival. —*adj.*
1 now approaching; next: *this coming spring.* **2** *Informal.* on the
way to importance or fame.

Com·in·tern (kom'in tėrn') *n.* the Third Communist
International, an organization to spread communism, founded at
Moscow in 1919 and dissolved in 1943. [< *Com*munist *Intern*ational]

co·mi·ti·a (kə mish'ē ə) *n.pl.* in ancient Rome, a meeting of
citizens to pass laws, elect officials, etc. [< L *comitia,* pl. of
comitium meeting place]

com·i·ty (kom'ə tē) *n., pl.* **-ties.** courtesy; civility. [< L *comitas*
< *comis* friendly]

com·ma (kom'ə) *n.* a mark (,) of punctuation, used to show a
slight separation of elements within a sentence. Commas are
generally used where a slight pause or rise in the voice could be
made in speaking, as after an introductory word or phrase, between
words in a list, or before and after non-essential phrases or clauses
inserted into the middle of a sentence. [< L < Gk. *komma* piece
cut off < *koptein* to cut]

comma bacillus a comma-shaped bacterium (*Vibrio comma*)
that causes cholera in human beings.

com·mand (kə mand') *v., n.* —*v.* **1** give an order to; direct: *The
captain commanded the men to fire.* **2** give orders. **3** have authority
or power over; be in control of: *The captain commands his ship.*
4 be commander. **5** have a position of control over; overlook: *A
hilltop commands the plain around it.* **6** have ready for use: *With
the political knowledge that she commands, she can answer almost
any question on current affairs.* **7** ask for and get; force to be given:
Food commands a higher price when it is scarce. —*n.* **1** an order;
direction: *They obeyed the captain's command.* **2** authority; power;
control: *The general is in command of the army.* **3** the position of a
person who has the right to command. **4** the soldiers, ships, district,
etc. under an officer who is appointed to command them: *The
captain knew every man in his command.* **5** one of the main tactical
formations of the Canadian Forces: *Maritime Command.* **6** mastery
or control by position: *The hill fort had commanded of the plain
below.* **7** outlook (over); range of vision. **8** the ability to use;
mastery: *An effective speaker or writer must have a good command
of the language.* **9** a royal invitation.
at (one's) **command,** at one's disposal; available: *He always seems
to have the right words at his command.*
[ME < OF *comander* < LL *commandare* < L *com*- with +
mandare commit, command]

com·man·dant (kom'ən dant') *n.* **1** the officer in command of a
military base, camp, etc. **2** the officer in charge of a military college
or training school. *Abbrev.:* Comdt. [< F, originally ppr. of
commander command]

com·man·deer (kom'ən dēr') *v.* **1** seize (private property) for
military or public use: *All the automobiles in the town were
commandeered by the army.* **2** force into military service.
3 *Informal.* take by force. [< Afrikaans *commandeeren* < F
commander]

com·mand·er (kə man'dər) *n.* **1** a person who commands.
2 *Canadian Forces.* in Maritime Command, the equivalent of a
lieutenant-colonel. *Abbrev.:* Cdr. or Cdr See chart at **rank**[1]. **3** a
naval officer of similar rank in other countries. **4** a member of a
high rank in an order of knighthood or a society.

com·mand·er-in-chief (kə man'dər in chēf') *n., pl.*
com·mand·ers-in-chief. a person who has complete command of the
armed forces of a country in a theatre of war, a garrison, etc.
Abbrev.: C. in C.

com·mand·ing (kə man'ding) *adj.* **1** in command: *a
commanding officer.* **2** controlling; powerful: *commanding
influences.* **3** authoritative; impressive: *a commanding voice.*
4 having a position of control. —**com·mand'ing·ly,** *adv.*

com·mand·ment (kə mand'mənt) *n.* **1** an order; law. **2** in the
Bible, one of the ten laws that God gave to Moses.

command module the main section of a spacecraft, designed
to carry the crew and equipment for communication, flight, and
re-entry. A smaller section may be detached from the command
module for short independent flights or landing on a planet or the
moon.

com·man·do (kə man'dō) *n., pl.* **-dos** or **-does. 1** a soldier who
makes brief, daring raids in enemy territory and does close-range
fighting. **2** a group of such soldiers. **3** (*adj.*) having to do with,
involving, or designating a commando: *a commando raid.* [<
Afrikaans < Pg.]

command performance a stage performance, etc. given
before royalty by request or order.

com·me·dia dell'ar·te (kôm mä'dyä del lär'tä) *Italian.* a form
of comedy originating in the sixteenth century in Italy, in which a
company of professional actors play stock characters in
conventional situations but improvise their speeches and comic
actions.

hat, āge, fär; let, ēqual, tėrm; it, īce
hot, ōpen, ôrder; oil, out; cup, pu̇t, rüle,
əbove, takən, pencəl, lemən, circəs

ch, child; ng, long; sh, ship
th, thin; ᴛʜ, then; zh, measure

comme il faut (kô mēl fō') *French.* as it should be; proper; in
accordance with etiquette.

com·mem·o·rate (kə mem'ə rāt') *v.* **-rat·ed, -rat·ing. 1** preserve
the memory of: *Roman emperors built arches to commemorate
their victories.* **2** honor the memory of by some ceremony:
Christmas commemorates Christ's birth. [< L *commemorare* <
com- together + *memorare* remind]

com·mem·o·ra·tion (kə mem'ə rā'shən) *n.* **1** the act of
commemorating. **2** a service, celebration, etc. in memory of some
person or event.
in commemoration of, in honor of the memory of.

com·mem·o·ra·tive (kə mem'ə rə tiv *or* kə mem'ə rā'tiv) *adj.,
n.* —*adj.* calling to remembrance; honoring the memory of. —*n.*
a postage stamp issued to commemorate some preson, event, etc.
—**com·mem'o·ra'tive·ly,** *adv.*

com·mence (kə mens') *v.* **-menced, -menc·ing.** begin; start. [ME
< OF *comencer* < VL < L *com*- together + *initiare* begin (ult. <
inire begin < *in*- in + *ire* go)] —**com·menc'er,** *n.*
☞ *Syn.* See note at **begin.**

com·mence·ment (kə mens'mənt) *n.* **1** a beginning; start. **2** the
day when a school or college gives diplomas, certificates, etc. to
students who have completed the required course of study;
graduation day. **3** the ceremonies held on this day.

com·mend (kə mend') *v.* **1** praise. **2** mention favorably;
recommend. **3** hand over for safekeeping: *She commended the child
to her aunt's care.* [ME < L *commendare* < *com*- (intensive) +
mandare commit, command, Cf. COMMAND.]
☞ *Syn.* **1.** See note at **praise.**

com·mend·a·ble (kə men'də bəl) *adj.* worthy of praise;
deserving approval. —**com·mend'a·bly,** *adv.*

com·men·da·tion (kom'ən dā'shən) *n.* the act of commending,
especially recommendation or praise.

com·mend·a·to·ry (kə men'də tô rē) *adj.* **1** praising; expressing
approval. **2** mentioning favorably; recommending.

com·men·su·ra·ble (kə men'sə rə bəl *or* kə men'shə rə bəl)
adj. **1** measurable by the same set of units: *Greenness and mass are
not commensurable.* **2** corresponding in size, amount, or degree;
proportionate: *He was a big man, very tall and of commensurable
mass.* —**com·men'su·ra·ble·ness,** *n.* —**com·men'su·ra·bly,** *adv.*

com·men·su·rate (kə men'sə rit *or* kə men'shə rit) *adj.* **1** in the
proper proportion; proportionate: *The pay should be commensurate
with the work.* **2** of the same size, extent, etc.; equal. **3** measurable
by the same set of units; commensurable. [< LL *commensuratus,*
pp. of *commensurare* < L *com*- together + *mensurare* measure <
mensura a measure] —**com·men'su·rate·ly,** *adv.*
—**com·men'su·rate·ness,** *n.*

com·ment (kom'ənt) *n., v.* —*n.* **1** a short statement, note, or
remark that explains, praises, or finds fault with something that has
been written, said, or done. **2** a remark. **3** talk; gossip.
—*v.* **1** make a comment or comments: *Everyone commented on his
strange behavior.* **2** talk; gossip. [ME < LL *commentum* <
commentus, pp. of L *comminisci* < *com*- with + *minisci* think]

com·men·tar·y (kom'ən ter'ē) *n., pl.* **-tar·ies. 1** a series of notes
for explaining the hard parts of a book; explanation or
interpretation: *Bibles are often provided with commentaries.*
2 anything that explains or illustrates; comment: *The way she
dresses is usually a commentary on her mood.* **3** an explanatory
essay or treatise. **4** a description of a sporting event, ceremony,
etc., especially one given on radio or television.

com·men·ta·tor (kom'ən tā'tər) *n.* **1** a person who describes
and discusses news events, etc. while they are in progress,
especially for radio or television: *a sports commentator, a
fashion-show commentator.* **2** a person who gives a commentary. [< L]

com·merce (kom'ėrs) *n.* buying and selling in large amounts
between different places; business. [< F < L *commercium,* ult. <
com- with + *merx, mercis* wares]
☞ *Syn.* See note at **trade.**

com·mer·cial (kə mėr'shəl) *adj., n.* —*adj.* **1** of, for, or having to
do with commerce: *commercial law; a piece of commercial
property.* **2** made, done, or operating mainly for profit, especially at
the expense of quality, artistic merit, etc.: *Her recent plays are very
commercial. Their restaurant is very small and not at all
commercial.* **3** supported or subsidized by an advertiser: *commercial*

television. **4** for business purposes, especially in advertising: *commercial art.* **5** of chemicals, etc., being of average or inferior quality for use in large quantities in industry.
—**com·mer′cial·ly,** *adv.*

com·mer·cial·ism (kə mėr′shəl iz′əm) *n.* the aims, methods, and spirit of commerce, especially as showing too great a concern for profit and success: *Commercialism has almost ruined him as an artist.*

com·mer·cial·ize (kə mėr′shəl īz′) *v.* **-ized, -iz·ing.** make a matter of business or trade; apply the methods of business to, often suggesting the loss of some quality or standard: *It's a pity his photography has become so commercialized.*
—**com·mer′cial·i·za′tion,** *n.*

commercial traveller or **traveler** sales representative.

com·mi·na·tion (kom′ə nā′shən) *n.* **1** in Anglican churches, a recital of divine threats against sinners. **2** a threat; denunciation. [< L *comminatio, -onis* < *comminari* < *com-* with + *minari* threaten]

com·min·gle (kə ming′gəl) *v.* **-gled, -gling.** mingle together; blend.

com·mi·nute (kom′ə nyüt′ *or* kom′ə nüt′) *v.* **-nut·ed, -nut·ing.** reduce to a powder or to small fragments; pulverize. In a **comminuted fracture** part of the bone is broken into small fragments. [< L *comminutus,* pp. of *comminuere* < *com-* intensive + *minuere* make smaller < *minus* less] —**com′mi·nu′tion,** *n.*

com·mis·er·ate (kə miz′ər āt′) *v.* **-at·ed, -at·ing.** feel or express sorrow for; sympathize with; pity. [< L *com-* with *miserari* < *com-* + *miser* wretched]

com·mis·er·a·tion (kə miz′ər ā′shən) *n.* pity; sympathy.

com·mis·sar (kom′ə sär′) *n. Historical.* the head of a government department in the Soviet Union. [< Russian *kommisar* < F *commissaire*]

com·mis·sar·i·at (kom′ə ser′ē ət) *n.* **1** a food supply. **2** *Historical.* a department of the Soviet government. [< F < Med.L *commissarius.* See COMMISSARY.]

com·mis·sar·y (kom′ə ser′ē) *n., pl.* **-sar·ies. 1** a store handling food and supplies in a mining camp, lumber camp, etc. **2** a deputy; representative. [< Med.L *commissarius* < L *commissus* entrusted, pp. of *committere.* See COMMIT.]

com·mis·sion (kə mish′ən) *n., v.* —*n.* **1** a written paper giving certain powers, privileges, and duties. **2** an official certificate giving rank and authority as an officer in the armed forces: *My brother has received his commission as a lieutenant in the infantry.* **3** the rank and authority given. **4** a giving of authority. **5** the authority, power, or right given. **6** the thing for which authority is given; task entrusted to a person. **7** a group of people appointed or elected with authority to do certain things. **8** doing or committing, as a crime: *People are punished for the commission of crimes.* **9** pay based on a percentage of the amount of business done: *She gets a commission of 10 percent on all the sales she makes.*
in commission, a in service or use. **b** ready for service or use; in working order.
out of commission, a not in service or use. **b** not ready for use; not in working order.
—*v.* **1** give a commission to. **2** give authority to; give (a person) the right or power (to do something): *Some businessmen commission others to buy or sell property for them.* **3** put in service or use; make ready for service or use. A new warship is commissioned when it has the officers, sailors, and supplies needed for a voyage. [ME < OF < L *commissio, -onis* < *committere.* See COMMIT.]

com·mis·sion·aire (kə mish′ən er′) *n.* **1** a person whose job is to open doors, carry bags, etc. at the entrance of a hotel or a club. **2** a member of the Corps of Commissionaires: *Some Canadian cities employ commissionaires to check parking meters and to issue parking tickets to persons whose cars are parked overtime.* [< F]

com·mis·sioned (kə mish′ənd) *adj.* having a commission: *a commissioned officer.*

com·mis·sion·er (kə mish′ən ər *or* kə mish′nər) *n.* **1** a member of a commission. **2** an official in charge of some department of a government: *a police commissioner.* **3** one of a group of persons elected or appointed to govern a city or a county. **4 Commissioner, Cdn. a** the highest ranking officer of the Royal Canadian Mounted Police. **b** the chief executive officer of the Yukon Territory or the Northwest Territories. **5** a person who directs the operation of a professional sport or sport league.

commission merchant a person who buys or sells goods for others who pay him a commission.

com·mit (kə mit′) *v.* **-mit·ted, -mit·ting. 1** hand over for safekeeping; deliver: *He committed himself to the doctor's care.* **2** put officially in the care of an institution, such as a mental hospital or prison: *The judge committed the accused for psychiatric assessment.* **3** refer to a committee for consideration. **4** do something that is an offence: *to commit a crime, to commit a sin.*

5 reveal one's opinion. **6** involve; pledge: *He would not commit himself in any way.*
commit to memory, learn by heart.
commit to paper or **writing,** write down.
[ME < L *committere* < *com-* with + *mittere* send, put]
—**com·mit′ta·ble,** *adj.*

☛ *Syn.* **1. Commit, consign, entrust** = hand over a person or thing. **Commit** = hand over to be kept safe or taken care of: *The court committed the financial affairs of the orphan to a guardian.* **Consign** suggests formally handing over control: *He consigned his share of the bonds to his sister.* **Entrust** = commit with trust and confidence in the receiver: *I entrusted my door key to my neighbor.*

com·mit·ment (kə mit′mənt) *n.* **1** committing or being committed. **2** a pledge; promise: *He made a commitment to look after his younger brother.* **3** an official order sending a person to prison or to a mental institution. **4** an agreement to assume a future financial obligation. **5** something pledged or committed.

com·mit·tal (kə mit′əl) *n.* the act of committing or the state of being committed.

com·mit·tee (kə mit′ē) *n.* a group of persons appointed or elected by a legislature, club, etc. to consider, investigate, or act on certain matters and report to the main body.
in committee, under consideration by a committee: *The bill is still in committee.* [< AF *committee* committed]

☛ *Usage.* **Committee** is a collective noun, to be used with a singular or plural verb depending on whether the group or the individuals are meant: *The committee meets today at four. The committee get together with difficulty. See note at* **collective noun.**

com·mit·tee·man (kə mit′ē mən) *n., pl.* **-men.** a member of a committee.

committee of the whole a committee made up of all the members present of a legislature, club, etc.

com·mix (kə miks′) *v.* mix together.

com·mix·ture (kə miks′chər) *n.* mixture.

com·mode (kə mōd′) *n.* **1** chest of drawers. **2** a stand in a bedroom, to hold a washbasin, pitcher of water, chamber pot, etc.; washstand. [< F < L *commodus* convenient < *com-* with + *modus* measure]

com·mo·di·ous (kə mō′dē əs) *adj.* **1** roomy. **2** convenient; handy. [< Med.L *commodiosus* < L *commodus.* See COMMODE.]
—**com·mo′di·ous·ly,** *adv.* —**com·mo′di·ous·ness,** *n.*

com·mod·i·ty (kə mod′ə tē) *n., pl.* **-ties. 1** anything that is bought and sold; an article of trade or commerce: *Groceries are commodities.* **2** a useful thing.

com·mo·dore (kom′ə dôr′) *n.* **1** *Canadian Forces.* in Maritime Command, the equivalent of a brigadier-general. See chart at **rank¹.** **2** a naval officer of similar rank in other countries. *Abbrev.:* Cmdre. *or* Cmdre **3** the chief officer of a merchant fleet, yacht club, power squadron, etc. [earlier *commandore,* ? < Du. *kommandeur* < F *commandeur* < *commander* to command]

com·mon (kom′ən) *adj., n.* —*adj.* **1** belonging equally to each or all of a group; shared by all; joint: *The two cousins soon discovered that they had a lot of common interests. The house was the common property of the three brothers.* **2** widespread; general: *common knowledge, a common nuisance.* **3** generally accepted; usual; popular as opposed to scientific or technical: *The common name for* Equus caballus *is* horse. **4** often met with; usual; familiar: *Snow is common in cold countries. The dandelion is a common weed.* **5** of the most familiar or abundant kind: *common salt.* **6** of or having to do with the community as a whole; public: *the common good.* **7** without special rank or title: *the common people. A common soldier is a private.* **8** no more or greater than ordinary or average: *common courtesy.* **9** below ordinary; of poor quality; inferior: *a common grade of cloth.* **10** coarse; vulgar: *That was a common thing to say.* **11** *Grammar.* **a** designating gender that may be either masculine or feminine. The word *parent* is of common gender; *mother* is of feminine gender. **b** See **common noun.**
12 *Mathematics.* belonging equally to two or more quantities: *a common factor, a common multiple.*
—*n.* **1 the Commons,** the House of Commons. **2** Also, **commons,** *pl.* land owned or used by all the people of a town, village, etc. **3** *Law.* the right to use and take profit from land belonging to another, such as the right to fish or pasture animals, which a person shares with the owner or others. **4** *Archaic.* **commons,** *pl.* the common people. **5 commons,** a dining hall, especially one attached to a college, etc. **6 commons,** *pl.* food or rations served to all members of a group (*sometimes used with a singular verb*).
in common, equally with another or others; owned, used, done, etc. by both or all.
short commons, means too little food: *The prisoners were kept on short commons.*
[ME < OF *comun* < L *communis*] —**com′mon·ness,** *n.*

☛ *Syn. adj.* **2.** See note at **general. 4 Common, ordinary** = usual. **Common** = often met with or usual because shared by many people or things: *Colds are common in winter.* **Ordinary** = usual because in agreement with the normal standards and order of things: *I use ordinary gasoline.*

☛ *Usage.* **Common, mutual.** Formal English distinguishes between **common** =

belonging equally to each or all, and **mutual** = each to the other: *The estate is the common property of the five brothers. Bud and Mary felt a mutual dislike.*

com·mon·age (kom′ən ij) *n.* **1** the right to pasture animals on land owned by the town, village, etc. **2** the ownership of land in common. **3** land owned in common. **4** the common people.

com·mon·al·i·ty (kom′ə nal′tē) *n., pl.* **-ties. 1** the quality of being shared; possession in common: *a commonality of purpose.* **2** commonalty (def. 1).

com·mon·al·ty (kom′ən əl tē) *n., pl.* **-ties. 1** the common people; persons without rank or title; the middle and lower classes of society. **2** people as a group. **3** the members of a corporation.

common carrier a person or company whose business is conveying goods or people for pay. A railway company is a common carrier.

common council the lawmaking group of a city, town, etc.

common denominator 1 *Mathematics.* a denominator that is a common multiple of the denominators of a group of fractions. A common denominator of $\frac{1}{2}$, $\frac{2}{3}$, and $\frac{3}{4}$ is 12, because these three fractions can also be expressed as $\frac{6}{12}$, $\frac{8}{12}$, and $\frac{9}{12}$. **2** a quality, attribute, opinion, etc. shared by all the persons or things in a group.

common divisor a number that will divide two or more other numbers without a remainder. A common divisor of 4, 6, 8 and 10 is 2.

com·mon·er (kom′ən ər) *n.* **1** one of the common people; a person who is not a nobleman. **2** a member of the House of Commons.

Common Era Christian Era.

common fraction a fraction in which both the numerator and the denominator are whole numbers; simple fraction. *Examples:* $\frac{5}{8}$, $\frac{213}{500}$, $\frac{8}{15}$. Compare **complex fraction.**

common gender *Grammar.* **1** a classification consisting of nouns that are considered to be either masculine or feminine, so that they may be replaced in different contexts by *he* or *she.* *Examples: friend, person, writer.* **2** a classification consisting of nouns that are considered to be masculine, feminine, or neuter, so that they may be replaced by *he, she* or *it. Examples: baby, dog.*

common law the body of law based on custom and usage dating from the ancient unwritten laws of England, and recognized and confirmed by the judgments of the courts. It is distinguished from civil law and canon law and law created by statute.

com·mon-law (kom′ən lô′ *or* -lô′) *adj.* **1** of, having to do with, or based on a common-law marriage: *a common-law husband.* **2** of, having to do with, or based on common law.

common-law marriage a marriage that has not been solemnized in the normal way, but is legally recognized for certain purposes, such as allowances for widow or dependants, inheritance rights, etc. For a relationship to be recognized as a common-law marriage, each of the two partners must agree to the arrangement, and both must be legally able to marry.

common logarithm *Mathematics.* a logarithm having a base of 10.

com·mon·ly (kom′ən lē) *adv.* usually; as a rule; generally: *Arithmetic is commonly taught in elementary schools.*

common market 1 an association of countries to promote mutual free trade. **2 Common Market,** the European Economic Community.

common multiple a number that can be divided by two or more other numbers without a remainder: *12 is a common multiple of 2, 3, 4, and 6.*

common noun any noun that is not a proper noun. A common noun refers to a condition, quality, idea, etc. or to a person, animal, or thing as a member of a class. In the sentence *"The dog's name is Sam,"* *dog* and *name* are common nouns; *Sam* is a proper noun.
☛ *Usage.* Common nouns are not usually capitalized unless they are used to begin a sentence. Compare **proper noun.**

com·mon-or-gar·den (kom′ən ər gär′dən) *adj. Informal.* ordinary; familiar; everyday: *common-or-garden pencils.*

com·mon·place (kom′ən plās′) *n., adj. —n.* **1** an ordinary or everyday thing: *Sixty years ago broadcasting was a novelty; today it is a commonplace.* **2** an ordinary or obvious remark. **3** one of a collection of notable passages written down for reference. *—adj.* not new or interesting; everyday; ordinary: *We thought the speech rather commonplace.* **—com′mon·place′ness,** *n.*

common pleas lawsuits between private individuals that do not involve criminal cases.

com·mons (kom′ənz) *n.pl.* **1** the common people; people who are not of the nobility. **2** a dining hall or building where food is served to a large group at common tables. **3** the food served. **4** food: *The poor orphans were kept on short commons.* **5 the Commons, a** House of Commons. **b** the members of the House of Commons.

hat, āge, fär; let, ēqual, tèrm; it, īce
hot, ōpen, ôrder; oil, out; cup, pùt, rüle,
əbove, takən, pencəl, lemən, circəs

ch, child; ng, long; sh, ship
th, thin; ᴛʜ, then; zh, measure

common school in the United States and formerly in Canada, an elementary public school.

common sense ordinary good judgment; practical intelligence: *It's just common sense to carry a spare tire in the car.* **—com′mon-sense′,** *adj.*

common stock ordinary stock in a company, without a definite dividend rate. A holder of common stock is entitled to dividends only if there is any profit left after all other claims have been paid. Compare **preferred stock.**

com·mon·weal (kom′ən wēl′) *n.* **1** the general welfare; public good. **2** *Archaic.* commonwealth.

com·mon·wealth (kom′ən welth′) *n.* **1 the Commonwealth,** Commonwealth of Nations. **2** the people who make up a nation; citizens of a state. **3** a democratic state; republic. **4** a group of persons, nations, etc. united by some common interest.

Commonwealth of Nations an association of a large number of countries, many of them now completely independent, that were once under British law and government. All the independent members of the Commonwealth of Nations, including Canada and the United Kingdom, have equal status.

com·mo·tion (kə mō′shən) *n.* **1** confusion; agitation; violent movement: *We saw a great commotion in the water and then a dolphin surfaced.* **2** public disturbance; insurrection. [< L *commotio, -onis < commovere < com-* with + *movere* move]

com·mu·nal (kom′yə nəl *or* kə myü′nəl) *adj.* **1** of a community; public. **2** owned jointly by all; used or participated in by all members of a group or community. **3** of a commune. **—com′mu·nal·ly,** *adv.*

com·mu·nal·ism (kom′yə nəl iz′əm *or* kə myü′nəl iz′əm) *n.* a theory or system of government according to which each commune is virtually an independent state and the nation is merely a federation of communes.

com·mune¹ (*v.* kə myün′; *n.* kom′yün) *v.* **-muned, -mun·ing;** *n.* *—v.* talk intimately. *—n.* intimate talk. [< OF *communer < comun.* See COMMON.]

com·mune² (kom′yün) *n.* **1** a community of people sharing living accommodation, possessions, and responsibilities. **2** the smallest division for local government in France, Belgium, Switzerland, and Italy. **3** the government or inhabitants of such a division. **4 Commune,** in France: **a** a revolutionary group that governed Paris 1792-1794. **b** a similar group that governed Paris from March 18 to May 28, 1871. [< F *commune,* alteration of OF *comugne < VL communia,* originally neut. pl. of L *communis.* See COMMON.]

com·mu·ni·ca·ble (kə myü′nə kə bəl) *adj.* that can be communicated: *Ideas are communicable by words. Scarlet fever is a communicable disease.* **—com·mu′ni·ca·bly,** *adv.*

com·mu·ni·cant (kə myü′nə kənt) *n., adj. —n.* **1** a person who receives Holy Communion. **2** a regular attender at a church. **3** a person who gives information by talking, writing, etc. *—adj.* communicating.

com·mu·ni·cate (kə myü′nə kāt′) *v.* **-cat·ed, -cat·ing. 1** exchange information or signals by talk, writing, gestures, etc.; send and receive messages: *The searchers communicated by two-way radio.* **2** pass along; transmit: *A stove communicates heat to a room. He didn't say anything, but he soon communicated his uneasiness to the rest of us.* **3** get in touch with; get through to: *It was impossible to communicate with my family during the storm. The teacher could not communicate with some of the pupils.* **4** be connected: *The dining room communicates with the kitchen.* **5** receive Holy Communion. [< L *communicare < communis.* See COMMON.] **—com·mu′ni·ca′tor,** *n.*
☛ *Syn.* **1. Communicate, impart** = pass knowledge, ideas, or information along. **Communicate,** the general word, emphasizes the idea of passing something along from one person or thing to another: *He has not communicated his wishes to me.* **Impart** emphasizes the idea of giving to another a share of what one has: *A teacher imparts knowledge to his students.*

com·mu·ni·ca·tion (kə myü′nə kā′shən) *n.* **1** the act or fact of passing along; transmitting. **2** a giving or exchanging of information by talking, writing, etc.: *The government leaders are in close communication on this issue.* **3** information given in this way; message: *A communication has been received from the embassy.* **4** a means of going from one place to the other; connection; passage: *There is no communication between these two rooms.* **5 communications,** *pl.* **a** a system for sending or receiving messages,

as by telephone, television, or radio. **b** (*used with a singular verb*) the art and technology of communicating, especially by mechanical or electronic means.

communications satellite an artificial satellite used for radio and television communication. A communication satellite reflects or relays radio and television signals.

com·mu·ni·ca·tive (kə myü′nə kə tiv *or* kə myü′nə kā′tiv) *adj.* **1** ready to give information; talkative. **2** of or having to do with communication. —**com·mu′ni·ca′tive·ly,** *adv.* —**com·mu′ni·ca′tive·ness,** *n.*

com·mun·ion (kə myün′yən) *n.* **1** the act of sharing; a having in common. **2** an exchange of thoughts and feelings; intimate talk; fellowship. **3** a close spiritual relationship. **4** a group of people having the same religious beliefs. **5 Communion,** *Christianity.* the commemoration of Christ's Last Supper, in which bread and wine are consecrated and taken as the body and blood of Christ or as symbols of them; the Eucharist; Holy Communion. [ME < L *communio, -onis* < *communis.* See COMMON.]

com·mu·ni·qué (kə myü′nə kā′ *or* kə myü′nə kā′) *n.* an official bulletin, statement, or other communication. [< F]

com·mu·nism (kom′yə niz′əm) *n.* **1** the political, social, and economic system of certain countries, such as the U.S.S.R. and the People's Republic of China, in which the state, governed by a single party without formal opposition, owns all property, controls the production and distribution of goods and services, and, to a great extent, controls the social and cultural life of the people. **2** Often, **Communism,** a philosophy or system derived from Marxism, advocating state ownership of land and property and seeking the overthrow of non-communist societies on behalf of the working people, or proletariat, of the world. **3** any economic system based on ownership of all property and the means of production and distribution by the community or state. Compare **capitalism** and **socialism.** [< F *communisme* < *commun,* OF *commun.* See COMMON.]

com·mu·nist (kom′yə nist) *n.* **1** a person who favors and supports communism. **2 Communist,** a member of the Communist Party. **3** (*adj.*) of, having to do with, or characteristic of communism or communists; communistic: *communist doctrine.*

com·mu·nis·tic (kom′yə nis′tik) *adj.* **1** of or having to do with communists or communism. **2** favoring communism. —**com′mu·nis′ti·cal·ly,** *adv.*

Communist Party a political party that is dedicated to the establishment of communism, especially as derived from the principles of Marxism.

com·mu·ni·ty (kə myü′nə tē) *n., pl.* **-ties. 1** a group of people having common ties or interests and living in the same locality or district and subject to the same laws: *a farming community. This lake provides water for six communities.* **2** a group of people living together: *a community of monks.* **3** the public: *the approval of the community.* **4** ownership together; sharing together: *community of food supplies, community of ideas.* **5** *Ecology.* a group of animals and plants living in a particular region under similar conditions and interacting with one another, especially in food relationships. **6** likeness, similarity; identity: *Community of interests causes people to work together.* [ME *com(m)unete* < OF < L *communitas* < *communis.* See COMMON.]

community centre 1 a hall used for recreation, entertainment, public meetings, etc. in a community. **2** *Cdn.* an arena run by the community as a centre for sporting events, skating, dancing, and other forms of entertainment.

Community Chest a fund of money contributed voluntarily by people, usually once a year, to support various charitable organizations, in their community. The United Way is a kind of Community Chest.

community college *Cdn.* an institution for post-secondary and adult education, especially for training in particular occupations and skills. Community colleges offer diploma courses in many trades and also have courses for the personal interest of people in the community, ranging from philosophy and art appreciation to orienteering.

com·mu·nize (kom′yə nīz′) *v.* **-nized, -nizing. 1** subject all property to state ownership. **2** enforce the practice or adoption of communism. —**com′mu·ni·za′tion.**

com·mu·tate (kom′yə tāt′) *v.* **-tat·ed, -tat·ing.** *Electricity.* reverse the direction of (current). [back formation from *commutation*]

com·mu·ta·tion (kom′yə tā′shən) *n.* **1** an exchange; substitution. **2** the reduction (of an obligation, penalty, etc.) to a less severe one: *The prisoner obtained a commutation of his* sentence from death to life imprisonment. **3** *Electricity.* a reversal of the direction of a current by a commutator. **4** regular, daily travel back and forth to work by train, bus, automobile, etc.

com·mu·ta·tive (kə myü′tə tiv *or* kom′yə tā′tiv) *adj.* **1** of or having to do with, or involving substitution or exchange. **2** *Mathematics.* designating an operation in which the ordering of the elements does not affect the result. Addition and multiplication are commutative because it does not matter which quantity is placed first; subtraction and division are not commutative because reversing the order of the quantities will produce a different answer.

com·mu·ta·tor (kom′yə tā′tər) *n.* **1** a device for reversing the direction of an electric current. **2** a revolving part in a dynamo or motor that carries the current to or from the brushes. See **generator** for picture.

com·mute (kə myüt′) *v.* **-mut·ed, -mut·ing. 1** change (an obligation, penalty, etc.) to an easier one: *The prisoner's sentence of death was commuted to one of life imprisonment.* **2** travel as a commuter. **3** *Electricity.* reverse the direction of (a current) by a commutator. **4** exchange; substitute; change: *to commute foreign currency into Canadian dollars.* [< L *commutare* < *com-* (intensive) + *mutare* change]

com·mut·er (kə myüt′ər) *n.* a person who regularly travels a long distance between his home in one community and his work in another, especially one who travels by train, bus, etc. from a small community or suburb into a city to work.

comp. 1 compound. **2** compare; comparative. **3** composition. **4** compositor. **5** composer.

com·pact¹ (*adj.* kəm pakt′ *or* kom′pakt; *n.* kom′pakt; *v.* kəm pakt′) *adj., n., v.* —*adj.* **1** firmly packed together; closely joined: *The leaves of the cabbage were folded into a compact head.* **2** using few words; brief, well organized, and to the point: *a compact style of writing.* **3** *Poetic.* composed or made (*of*): *It was a tale compact of moonstruck fancy.* —*n.* **1** the second smallest of the four basic sizes of automobile, generally larger than a subcompact and smaller than an intermediate. **2** a small case for carrying face powder or rouge, having a hinged lid with a mirror. —*v.* **1** pack firmly together; join closely. **2** make by putting together firmly. **3** condense. [< L *compactus,* pp. of *compingere* < *com-* together + *pangere* fasten] —**com·pact′ly,** *adv.* —**com·pact′ness,** *n.*

com·pact² (kom′pakt) *n.* agreement: *We made a compact not to tell anyone what we had heard.* [< L *compactum* < *compacisci* < *com-* (intensive) + *pacisci* contract]

com·pan·ion¹ (kəm pan′yən) *n., v.* —*n.* **1** a person who goes along with or accompanies another; a person who shares in what another is doing; comrade. **2** anything that matches or goes with another in kind, size, color, etc. **3** a person paid to live or travel with another as a friend and helper. **4 Companion,** **a** in certain orders of knighthood, a member of the lowest rank. **b** *Cdn.* a member of the highest rank of the Order of Canada. —*v.* be a companion to; go along with. [ME < OF *compaignon* < LL *companio, -onis* < L *com-* together + *panis* bread] —**com·pan′ion·less,** *adj.*

com·pan·ion² (kəm pan′yən) *n.* **1** a covering over the top of a companionway. **2** companionway. [< Du. *kompanje* quarterdeck < OF *compagne* steward's room in a galley < VL *compania* < L *com-* together + *panis* bread]

com·pan·ion·a·ble (kəm pan′yən ə bəl) *adj.* suited to companionship; agreeable; pleasant; sociable: *a companionable disposition, a companionable evening.* —**com·pan′ion·a·ble·ness,** *n.* —**com·pan′ion·a·bly,** *adv.*

com·pan·ion·ate (kəm pan′yən it) *adj.* of or like companions.

com·pan·ion·ship (kəm pan′yən ship′) *n.* an association as companions; fellowship.

com·pan·ion·way (kəm pan′yən wā′) *n.* a stairway leading from one deck to another on a ship.

com·pa·ny (kum′pə nē *or* kump′nē) *n., pl.* **-nies. 1** a group of people joined together for some purpose: *a business company, a company of actors.* **2** a gathering of persons for social purposes: *He's quite shy in company.* **3** a companion or companions: *You are known by the company you keep.* **4** companionship: *They enjoy each other's company. The dog gives him company.* **5** a guest or guests: *We had company last night.* **6** a group of people. **7** a part of an army commanded by a captain. **8** a troop of Girl Guides. **9** a ship's crew; the officers and sailors of a ship. **10** partners not named in the title of a firm.
bear (someone) **company,** accompany.
keep company, go with; carry on courtship: *They have been keeping company for several months.*
keep (someone) **company,** stay with for companionship; accompany: *My sister kept me company while I was sick.*
part company, a go separate ways. **b** end companionship.
[ME < OF *compagnie* < *compagne* companion < LL *companio.* See COMPANION¹.]

Company of New France a company founded in 1627 in Paris by Cardinal Richelieu to foster immigration to New France and to maintain loyalty to the French Crown and the Catholic Church. The company, which was granted the monopoly of all French commerce in North America and sovereignty over the territories of the New World, ceased to function in 1657.

company town a town built by a company for its workers, to whom it rents houses, provides services, etc.

company union 1 a union of workers in one factory, store, etc. that is not part of a larger union. 2 a union of workers dominated by the employers.

compar. comparative.

com·pa·ra·ble (kom′pə rə bel *or* kəm per′ə bəl) *adj.* 1 able to be compared; having qualities in common: *A fire is comparable with the sun; both give light and heat.* 2 fit to be compared: *A cave is not comparable to a house as a comfortable place to live in.* —**com′pa·ra·ble·ness,** *n.* —**com′pa·ra·bly,** *adv.*
☛ *Pronun.* Although many people avoid the pronunciation (kəm per′ə bəl), the form has wide currency among educated Canadians.

com·par·a·tive (kəm per′ə tiv *or* kəm par′ə tiv) *adj., n.* —*adj.* 1 that compares; of or having to do with comparison: *the comparative method of studying.* 2 measured by comparison with something else; relative; not absolute: *Screens give us comparative freedom from flies.* 3 *Grammar.* of or designating the second degree of comparison of an adjective or adverb. *Better* is the comparative form of *good.*
—*n.* 1 *Grammar.* the second degree of comparison of an adjective or adverb. 2 a form or combination of words that shows this degree. *Fairer, better,* and *more slowly* are the comparatives of *fair, good,* and *slowly.*

com·par·a·tive·ly (kəm per′ə tiv lē *or* kəm par′ə tiv lē) *adv.* 1 by comparison; relatively. 2 rather; somewhat. 3 in a comparative manner.

com·par·a·tor (kəm per′ə tər *or* kəm par′ə tər) *n.* a device for making direct comparisons, as of measurements in different systems. There are comparators for comparing quantities in the metric and imperial systems.

com·pare (kəm per′) *v.* **-pared, -par·ing;** *n.* —*v.* 1 find out or point out how persons or things are alike and how they differ: *He compared the two books to see which one had the better bibliography.* 2 think, speak, or write of as similar; liken (*to*): *to compare life to a river.* 3 examine two or more things to find similarities and differences: *We compared the fins of a fish with the wings of a bird.* 4 be considered like as equal: *Artificial light cannot compare with daylight.* 5 *Grammar.* change the form of (an adjective or adverb) to show the comparative and superlative degrees; name the positive, comparative, and superlative degrees of. **not to be compared with, a** very different from. **b** not nearly so good as.
—*n.* comparison: *beauty beyond compare.* [< F < L *comparare* < *com-* with + *par* equal]
☛ *Usage.* **Compare, contrast. Compare** is commonly used in two senses: **a** to point out likenesses (used with *to*): *She compared his poetry to a meandering stream.* **b** to examine two or more objects to find both likenesses and differences (used with *with*): *The teacher compared his poem with one of Robert Frost's.* **Contrast** means to point out differences: *I contrasted John's report card with Mary's to show him how poorly he was doing.*

com·par·i·son (kəm per′ə sən *or* kəm par′ə sən) *n.* 1 the act or process of comparing; finding the likenesses and differences: *The teacher's comparison of the heart to a pump helped the student to understand its action.* 2 likeness; similarity: *There is no comparison between these two cameras; one is much better than the other.* 3 *Grammar.* a change in an adjective or adverb to show differences of degree. The three degrees of comparison are positive, comparative, and superlative. Examples: *good, better, best; cold, colder, coldest; helpful, more helpful, most helpful.*
in comparison with, compared with: *Even a large lake is small in comparison with an ocean.*
[ME < OF *comparison* < L *comparatio* < *comparare.* See COMPARE.]

com·part·ment (kəm pärt′mənt) *n.* 1 a separate division or section of anything; part of an enclosed space set off by walls or partitions: *a storage compartment. The human heart has four compartments.* 2 a separate category or aspect: *the compartments of the mind.* [< F *compartiment* < Ital. *compartimento* < LL < L *com-* with + *partiri* share]

com·part·men·tal·iz·a·tion (kəm pärt′men′tə lə zā′shən *or* kəm pärt′men′tə lī zā′shən) *n.* division into isolated compartments or categories.

com·part·men·tal·ize (kom′pärt men′tə līz′) *v.* **-ized, -izing.** divide into isolated compartments or categories: *He has a tendency to compartmentalize.*

hat, āge, fär; let, ēqual, tėrm; it, īce
hot, ōpen, ôrder; oil, out; cup, pùt, rüle,
əbove, takən, pencəl, lemən, circəs

ch, child; ng, long; sh, ship
th, thin; ŦH, then; zh, measure

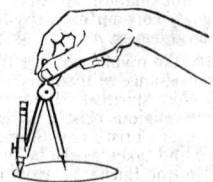

Compass (def. 1). A simple compass card. Turning it so that the needle points to the N (for 'north') enables the user to judge the other points of direction accurately.

Compass (def. 2). The pointed arm remains fixed so that the other arm moves in a circle.

com·pass (kum′pəs) *n., v.* —*n.* 1 an instrument for showing directions, consisting of a magnetized needle suspended by the middle so that it is free to point to the North Magnetic Pole, which is near the North Pole. 2 Sometimes, **compasses,** *pl.* an instrument for drawing circles and curved lines and for measuring distances, consisting of two arms, joined at one end so that they may be moved closer or farther apart, with one arm ending in a point, for use as a pivot, and the other holding a pencil, etc. 3 a boundary or circumference: *The castle had a large dungeon within the compass of its walls.* 4 the extent within limits; scope; range: *The old sailor had had many adventures within the compass of his lifetime.* 5 the range of a voice or musical instrument. 6 a circuit; going around.
—*v.* 1 make a circuit of; go around; move around: *The astronaut compassed the earth many times.* 2 form a circle around; hem in; surround: *a farm house compassed by trees.* 3 do; accomplish; get. 4 plot; scheme. 5 grasp with the mind; understand completely. [ME < OF *compas* < *compasser* divide equally < VL *compassare* measure off < *compassus* equal step < L *com-* with + *passus* step]
☛ *Syn.* 3. See note at **range.**

compass card a circular card set beneath the needle of a compass showing the 32 points of direction and the degrees of the circle.

com·pas·sion (kəm pash′ən) *n.* feeling for another's sorrow or hardship that leads one to help the sufferer; sympathy; pity. [ME < OF < L *compassio, -onis* < *compati* < *com-* with + *pati* suffer]
☛ *Syn.* See note at **pity.**

com·pas·sion·ate (kəm pash′ən it) *adj.* 1 desiring to relieve another's suffering; sympathetic; merciful. 2 of military leave, etc., granted to a person on the basis of unusual circumstances such as family illness or death. —**com·pas′sion·ate·ly,** *adv.*

compass saw a handsaw with a very narrow, straight blade for cutting curves.

com·pat·i·bil·i·ty (kəm pat′ə bil′ə tē) *n.* the ability to exist together; ability to get on well together; agreement; harmony.

com·pat·i·ble (kəm pat′ə bəl) *adj.* 1 able to exist together in harmony; that can get on well together: *My two sisters are always arguing; they don't seem to be compatible.* 2 *Television.* having to do with or designating the type of color broadcasting that permits reception in black and white on sets that are not built for color reception. [< Med.L *compatibilis* < L *compati* suffer with. See COMPASSION.] —**com·pat′i·bly,** *adv.*

com·pa·tri·ot (kəm pā′trē ət *or* kəm pat′rē ət) *n., adj.* —*n.* a fellow countryman. —*adj.* of the same country. [< LL *compatriota* < *com-* with + *patriota* fellow countryman < Gk. *patriōtēs* < *patria* clan < *patēr* father]

com·peer (kəm pēr′ *or* kom′pēr) *n.* 1 an equal; peer. 2 a comrade; companion. [ME < OF *comper* < L *compar* < *com-* with + *par* equal]

com·pel (kəm pel′) *v.* **-pelled, -pel·ling.** 1 force or oblige; urge irresistibly: *The cold finally compelled him to surrender. The holdup men compelled the employees to lie face down on the floor.* 2 cause or get by force: *His tone of voice compelled obedience. Such brave actions compel our respect.* 3 *Archaic.* drive or herd together. [< L *compellere* < *com-* (intensive) + *pellere* drive] —**com·pel′er,** *n.*
☛ *Syn.* 1. **Compel, impel** = force. **Compel** = force a person to do something against his or her will: *It is impossible to compel a person to love his fellow men.* **Impel** = force to move forward, but is most often used figuratively to mean "drive by strong inner desire": *Hunger impelled him to beg.*

com·pel·ling (kəm pel′ing) *adj.* **1** forcing attention or interest: *She has compelling beauty.* **2** strongly persuasive or convincing: *a compelling argument.* —**com·pel′ling·ly,** *adv.*

com·pen·di·ous (kəm pen′dē əs) *adj.* brief but comprehensive; concise. [ME < LL *compendiosus* < *compendium*. See COMPENDIUM.] —**com·pen′di·ous·ly,** *adv.*

com·pen·di·um (kəm pen′dē əm) *n., pl.* **-di·ums, -di·a** (-dē ə). a summary that gives much information in a little space; concise treatise. [< L *compendium* a saving, shortening < *compendere* < *com-* together + *pendere* weigh]

com·pen·sate (kom′pən sāt′) *v.* **-sat·ed, -sat·ing. 1** make an equivalent or satisfactory return to; reimburse or pay: *The hunter agreed to compensate the farmer for shooting his cow.* **2** balance by equal weight, power, etc.; make up; offset: *A hockey player who is not a very fast skater can sometimes compensate by good positional play.* **3** *Mechanics.* adjust so as to offset variations or produce equilibrium; counterbalance: *Watches and clocks are compensated in order to keep the wheels and springs properly balanced.* [< L *compensare* < *com-* with + *pensare* weigh < *pendere*] —**com′pen·sa′tor,** *n.*
☛ *Syn.* **1.** See note at **pay.**

com·pen·sa·tion (kom′pən sā′shən) *n.* **1** something given (or received) as an equivalent; a satisfactory return for a loss or injury, or for a service: *She received compensation from the government for the injury she suffered during the robbery.* **2** offsetting or counterbalancing by an equivalent power, weight, etc.; the act of compensating. **3** anything regarded as an equivalent reasonable substitute: *Age has its compensations.* **4** *Biology.* the counterbalancing of an organic defect or malfunction by increased development or activity of another organ or part. **5** *Psychology.* the attempt to counterbalance a real or imagined defect or failure by increasing achievement in some other field: *I think his aggressive behavior is just a compensation for shyness.*

com·pen·sa·tive (kom′pən sā′tiv *or* kəm pen′sə tiv) *adj.* compensating.

com·pen·sa·to·ry (kəm pen′sə tô′rē) *adj.* compensating.

com·pete (kəm pēt′) *v.* **-pet·ed, -pet·ing. 1** try hard to obtain something wanted by others; be rivals; contend. **2** take part (in a contest): *An injury kept him from competing in the final race.* [< L *competere* < *com-* together + *petere* seek]
☛ *Syn.* **1.** See note at **contend.**

com·pe·tence (kom′pə təns) *n.* **1** the quality or state of being competent: *No one doubted the guide's competence.* **2** enough money or property to provide a comfortable living.

com·pe·ten·cy (kom′pə tən sē) *n.* competence.

com·pe·tent (kom′pə tənt) *adj.* **1** able; fit: *a competent cook.* **2** *Law.* legally qualified: *The court ruled that the witness was not competent to judge the sanity of the accused.* **3** rightfully belonging; proper or permissible (*to*): *It is not competent to the jury to pronounce the sentence.* [< L *competens, -entis* being fit, ppr. of *competere* meet. See COMPETE.] —**com′pe·tent·ly,** *adv.*
☛ *Syn.* **1.** See note at **able.**
☛ *Usage.* See note at **able.**

com·pe·ti·tion (kom′pə tish′ən) *n.* **1** an effort to obtain something wanted by others; rivalry: *the spirit of competition. There is competition among business firms for trade.* **2** a contest, especially one in which there is a prize for the winner.
in competition with, competing against: *She was in competition with five other dancers.*

com·pet·i·tive (kəm pet′ə tiv) *adj.* **1** of, based on, or determined by competition: *a competitive examination for a job.* **2** characterized by a drive to excel; concerned with trying to do better than others: *A first-rate athlete must possess a competitive spirit.* —**com·pet′i·tive·ly,** *adv.* —**com·pet′i·tive·ness,** *n.*

com·pet·i·tor (kəm pet′ə tər) *n.* a person who competes.

com·pi·la·tion (kom′pə lā′shən) *n.* **1** the act of compiling. **2** a book, list, etc. that has been compiled.

com·pile (kəm pīl′) *v.* **-piled, -pil·ing. 1** collect and bring together in one list or account. **2** make (a book, report, etc.) out of various materials. [ME < OF *compiler* < L *compilare* steal, originally, pile up < *com-* together + *pilare* press] —**com·pil′er,** *n.*

com·pla·cence (kəm plā′səns) *n.* complacency.

com·pla·cen·cy (kəm plā′sən sē) *n., pl.* **-cies. 1** the state or condition of being pleased with oneself; self-satisfaction: *The defendant's complacency during the trial angered the jury.* **2** contentment.

com·pla·cent (kəm plā′sənt) *adj.* pleased with oneself; self-satisfied: *The winner's complacent smile annoyed some people.* [<

L *complacens, -entis,* ppr. of *complacere* < *com-* with + *placere* please] —**com·pla′cent·ly,** *adv.*

com·plain (kəm plān′) *v.* **1** say that something is unsatisfactory; find fault. **2** talk about one's pains, troubles, etc. **3** make an accusation or charge: *She complained to the police about her neighbor's dog.* [ME < OF *complaindre* < VL *complangere* < L *com-* (intensive) + *plangere* lament] —**com·plain′er,** *n.* —**com·plain′ing·ly,** *adv.*
☛ *Syn.* **1. Complain, grumble** = find fault, express discontent. **Complain** = say one is discontented with some situation: *He is always complaining about the weather.* **Grumble** = mutter complaint in a bad-tempered way: *He is grumbling about the food.*

com·plain·ant (kəm plān′ənt) *n.* a person who complains, especially one who brings a lawsuit or lays a criminal charge against another: *The complainant accused the defendant of cheating him.*

com·plaint (kəm plānt′) *n.* **1** a voicing of dissatisfaction; complaining; finding fault: *Her letter is filled with complaints about her new job.* **2** a cause for complaining. **3** a formal accusation. **4** a sickness or ailment: *Influenza is a common complaint.*

com·plai·sance (kəm plā′zəns *or* kəm plā′səns, kom′plə zəns *or* kom′plə sans) *n.* **1** willingness to please or oblige; agreeableness; courtesy. **2** an obliging or courteous act. [< F]

com·plai·sant (kəm plā′zənt *or* kəm plā′sənt, kom′plə zənt *or* kom′plə sant) *adj.* inclined to do what is asked; willing to please; obliging; courteous. [< F *complaisant,* ppr. of *complaire* acquiesce < L *complacere* < *com-* (intensive) + *placere* please] —**com·plai′sant·ly,** *adv.*

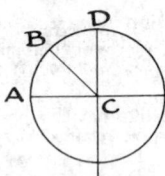

THE ARC BD IS THE COMPLEMENT OF THE ARC AB, AND THE ANGLE BCD IS THE COMPLEMENT OF THE ANGLE ACB

com·ple·ment (*n.* kom′plə mənt; *v.* kom′plə ment′) *n., v.* —*n.* **1** something that completes or makes perfect; something necessary to make a whole. **2** the full quantity or number; the required amount: *The ship now had its full complement of men.* **3** *Grammar.* a word or group of words used after a verb to describe or identify the subject or direct object of the sentence. In *The man is feeble, feeble* is a complement describing the subject *man.* In *She is chairman, chairman* is a complement identifying the subject *she.* In *They made him king, king* is a complement identifying the object *him.* **4** *Geometry.* either one of a pair of angles that together measure 90°. The complement of a 70° angle is a 20° angle. **5** either of a pair of complementary colors. The complement of red pigment is green. **6** *Music.* either of two intervals which together make up an octave. **7** either of two parts that complete each other. —*v.* supply a lack of any kind; complete: *My furniture just complemented my sister's, so that together we had what we needed.* [ME < L *complementum* < *complere.* See COMPLETE.]
☛ *Hom.* **compliment.**
☛ *Syn. v.* **Complement, supplement** = add to something to complete or enhance it. **Complement** = complete by supplying something that is missing but necessary to make a perfect whole: *The information from the encyclopedia complemented what he already had, and he was ready to write his essay.* **Supplement** = add something to make better or bigger or richer in some way: *School activities supplement one's education.*
☛ *Usage.* **Complement, compliment** (*n.*). **Complement** = something that completes or makes perfect: *She has her full complement of good looks.* **Compliment** means something said in praise: *He paid her a nice compliment.*

com·ple·men·tal (kom′plə men′təl) *adj.* complementary.

com·ple·men·ta·ry (kom′plə men′tə rē *or* kom′plə men′trē) *adj.* forming a complement; completing something; supplying what is lacking or needed.
☛ *Hom.* **complimentary.**

complementary angles two angles which together total 90°.

complementary colors *or* **colours 1** any two colors of the spectrum which, when combined in the right proportions, produce white light. Red and blue-green are complementary colors. **2** any two pigments which, when combined in the right proportions, produce dark grey or black. Red and green are complementary colors in paint.

com·plete (kəm plēt′) *adj., v.* **-plet·ed, -plet·ing.** —*adj.* **1** with all the parts; lacking nothing; whole; full: *a complete set of Dickens' novels.* **2** thorough; total; entire: *complete surprise, complete confidence.* **3** ended; finished; done: *My homework is complete.* —*v.* **1** make up all the parts of; make whole or entire: *She completed her set of dishes by buying a sugar bowl.* **2** make perfect or thorough: *The good news completed my happiness.* **3** get done; end; finish: *She completed her homework early in the evening.* [ME < OF *complet* < L *completus,* pp. of *complere* < *com-* (intensive) + *plere* fill] —**com·plete′ly,** *adv.* —**com·plete·ness,** *n.*

☛ *Syn. adj.* **1. Complete, entire** = with all the parts. **Complete** = with all the parts needed to make something whole or full: *I have the complete story now.* **Entire** = with no parts taken away: *He gave the entire day to his work, not even taking time for lunch.*

com·ple·tion (kəm plē′shən) *n.* **1** the act of completing; finishing. **2** the condition of being completed: *The work is near completion.*

com·plex (*adj.* kəm pleks′ *or* kom′pleks; *n.* kom′pleks) *adj., n.* —*adj.* **1** not simple; involved; complicated: *The instructions for building the radio were too complex for us to follow.* **2** made up of a number of connected or interwoven parts; composite: *A complex sentence has one or more clauses besides the main clause.* —*n.* **1** an interconnected or complicated whole: *The whole complex of charges and countercharges had to be sorted out before they could begin to work on a settlement of the dispute.* **2** a group of related or connected units such as buildings or roads: *The new civic complex includes a library, museum, and auditorium.* **3** *Psychology.* a system of related ideas, feelings, memories, etc. of which a person is usually not aware, which strongly influence his behavior in certain ways. **4** *Informal.* an exaggerated mental tendency; obsession: *He's got such a complex about fresh air that he can hardly stay in a room with the windows closed.* [< L *complexus,* pp. of *complecti* embrace < *com-* together + *plectere* twine] —**com·plex′ly,** *adv.* —**com·plex′ness,** *n.*

complex fraction a fraction having a fraction in the numerator, in the denominator, or in both; compound fraction. Compare **common fraction.** *Examples:* $\frac{1\frac{1}{3}}{3}$, $\frac{1}{3\frac{1}{4}}$, $\frac{\frac{4}{7}}{18}$

com·plex·ion (kəm plek′shən) *n.* **1** the color, quality, and general appearance of the skin, particularly of the face. **2** general appearance; nature; character. **3** in medieval physiology, the combination of the four humors (cold, heat, dryness, and moisture) in certain proportions, believed to determine the nature of an animal, plant, or human body. [ME < LL *complexio, -onis* constitution < L *complexio* combination < *complexus.* See COMPLEX.]

com·plex·ioned (kəm plek′shənd) *adj.* having a certain kind of complexion: *dark-complexioned.*

com·plex·i·ty (kəm plek′sə tē) *n., pl.* **-ties. 1** the state or quality of being complex: *The complexity of the road map puzzled Tom.* **2** something complex; a difficulty or complication.

complex sentence a sentence having one main clause and one or more subordinate clauses. *Example: When the engineer pulls the cord, the whistle blows.*

com·pli·ance (kəm plī′əns) *n.* **1** the act of complying or doing as another wishes; act of yielding to a request or command. **2** a tendency to yield to others. **in compliance with,** complying with; in accordance with.

com·pli·an·cy (kəm plī′ən sē) *n.* compliance.

com·pli·ant (kəm plī′ənt) *adj.* complying; yielding; obliging: *A compliant person gives in to other people.* —**com·pli′ant·ly,** *adv.* ☛ *Syn.* See note at **obedient.**

com·pli·cate (*v.* kom′plə kāt′; *adj.* kom′plə kit) *v.* **-cat·ed, -cat·ing;** *adj.* —*v.* **1** make hard to understand, settle, cure, etc.; mix up; confuse. **2** make worse or more mixed up: *a headache complicated by eye trouble.* —*adj. Biology.* folded lengthwise, as certain types of leaf or insect wing. [< L *complicare* < *com-* together + *plicare* fold]

com·pli·cat·ed (kom′plə kāt′id) *adj.* made up of many parts; involved; intricate.

com·pli·ca·tion (kom′plə kā′shən) *n.* **1** a complex or confused condition that is hard to understand, settle, cure, etc. **2** a difficulty or problem added to one or more already existing: *Pneumonia was the complication they most feared.* **3** the act or process of complicating. **4** an element in a story or play which complicates the plot.

com·plic·i·ty (kəm plis′ə tē) *n., pl.* **-ties.** a partnership in wrongdoing; the fact or state of being an accomplice: *Knowingly receiving stolen goods is complicity in theft.* [< F *complice* a confederate < LL *complex, -plicis* interwoven < L *complicare* < *com-* together + *plicare* fold]

com·pli·ment (*n.* kom′plə mənt; *v.* kom′plə ment′) *n., v.* —*n.* **1** something good said about a person; something said in praise or congratulation. **2 compliments,** *pl.* greetings: *In the box of flowers was a card reading "With the compliments of a friend."* —*v.* **1** praise or congratulate; pay a compliment to. **2** give something to (a person) as a polite attention. [< F < Ital. < Sp. *cumplimiento* fulfillment of courtesy < *cumplir* fulfil < L *complere* fill up] —**com′pli·ment·er,** *n.* ☛ *Hom.* **complement.** ☛ *Usage.* See note at **complement.**

com·pli·men·ta·ry (kom′plə men′tə rē *or* kom′plə men′trē) *adj.* **1** giving or containing a compliment; expressing courtesy;

admiration, or praise. **2** given free: *a complimentary ticket to a concert.* ☛ *Hom.* **complementary.**

com·plin (kom′plin) *n.* **1** the last of the seven canonical hours. **2** the service for it, now usually following vespers. [ME < OF *complie* < L *completa (hora)* completed hour]

com·pline (kom′plin *or* kom′plīn) *n.* complin.

com·ply (kəm plī′) *v.* **-plied, -ply·ing.** act in agreement (with a request or a command): *We should comply with the doctor's orders.* [< Ital. *complire* < Sp. *cumplir* < L *complere* complete; influenced by *ply¹*] —**com·pli′er,** *n.*

com·po·nent (kəm pō′nənt) *n., adj.* —*n.* **1** a part; a constituent element: *A chemist can separate a medicine into its components.* **2** one of the main units or parts of an electrical, electronic, or mechanical system. A printer is one of the components of a computer. —*adj.* **1** forming a part; constituent: *Blade and handle are the component parts of a knife.* **2** made up of separate units, or components: *In a component stereo system, the amplifier and loudspeakers are separate units.* [< L *componens, -entis,* ppr. of *componere* < *com-* together + *ponere* put] ☛ *Syn. n.* See note at **element.**

com·port¹ (kom′pôrt) *n.* compote.

com·port² (kəm pôrt′) *v.* **1** behave (*used with a reflexive pronoun*): *She comported herself with dignity throughout the trial.* **2** agree or suit (*used with* **with**): *His silliness at the meeting did not comport with what we had heard of him.* [< F *comporter* < L *comportare* < *com-* together + *portare* carry]

com·port·ment (kəm pôrt′mənt) *n.* behavior.

com·pose (kəm pōz′) *v.* **-posed, -pos·ing. 1** make up; form the substance or the parts of (*usually used in the passive*): *The ocean is composed of salt water. The Commonwealth is composed of a large number of countries.* **2** create, especially in music or in words: *to compose a symphony, to compose a poem.* **3** create works of music, literature, etc.: *She composes only early in the morning.* **4** get oneself ready; put into a proper state: *She composed herself for a long wait.* **5** make oneself or one's mind calm and quiet; put into a state of repose: *He tried to compose himself before entering the room.* **6** arrange the parts or elements of; put together in a pleasing or artistic way: *He composes his photographs very carefully.* **7** put into a proper or effective order or arrangement: *to compose pieces of evidence into a coherent argument.* **8** arrange or set up type for printing. [ME < OF *composer* < *com-* together + *poser* place (see POSE¹)]

com·posed (kəm pōzd′) *adj.* calm; quiet; self-controlled; tranquil. ☛ *Syn.* See note at **calm.**

com·pos·ed·ly (kəm pōz′id lē) *adv.* in a composed manner.

com·pos·er (kəm pōz′ər) *n.* a person who composes, especially a writer of music.

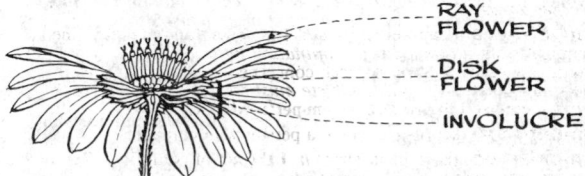

RAY FLOWER

DISK FLOWER

INVOLUCRE

Composite flower: a cross section of a daisy, seen from slightly below

com·pos·ite (kom′pə zit; *sometimes,* kəm poz′it) *adj., n.* —*adj.* **1** made up of various parts; compound: *The photographer made a composite picture by putting together parts of several others.* **2** designating a very large plant family (Compositae; also called Asteraceae), consisting mainly of herbs but including a few shrubs and trees, having flower heads made up of many tiny flowers called florets bunched together so that they appear to be single blooms. The composite family includes the dandelion, artichoke, sagebrush, thistles, and daisies. **3** belonging to the composite family. Goldenrod is a composite plant. **4** *Architecture.* of, having to do with, or

designating one of the five classical orders of architecture. The characteristic Composite column is 10 diameters high and has a capital showing acanthus leaves like the Corinthian, but topped by large volutes similar to those of the Ionic order. See **order** for picture.
—*n.* **1** a composite plant: *Many common weeds are composites.* **2** any composite thing; something made up of distinct parts. [< L *compositus*, pp. of *componere* < *com-* together + *ponere* put. Doublet of COMPOST.] —**com′pos·ite·ly,** *adv.*

composite number a number that can be exactly divided by some number other than itself or 1; a number that has more than 2 factors. Thus 8 is a composite number with four factors: 1, 2, 4, and 8; 5 is not a composite number; its only factors are 5 and 1.

composite school (kom′pə zit) *Cdn.* a secondary school in which a student may receive academic, commercial, or industrial training.

com·po·si·tion (kom′pə zish′ən) *n.* **1** the make-up of anything or the way it is put together; constitution: *We are studying the composition of light.* **2** a putting together of a whole: *Writing sentences, painting pictures, and setting type in printing are all forms of composition.* **3** the thing composed, such as a piece of music, writing, etc. **4** a short essay written as a school exercise. **5** a substance formed by a mixture of different ingredients, used especially in various industries and trades to refer to a particular mixed substance regularly used or manufactured: *The table top is of a composition resembling marble. Shoes can have leather soles or composition soles. Composition picture frames are usually a mixture of wood flakes or chips and a plastic binding agent shaped and hardened in a mould.* **6** an agreement; settlement.
—**com′po·si′tion·al,** *adj.*

com·pos·i·tor (kəm poz′ə tər) *n.* typesetter.

com·post (kom′pōst) *n., v.* —*n.* **1** a mixture of decayed vegetable or animal matter, such as leaves or manure, used to fertilize and condition soil. **2** mixture. —*v.* **1** fertilize with compost. **2** convert into compost. [ME < OF < L *compositus,* pp. of *componere.* See COMPOSITE.]

com·po·sure (kəm pō′zhər) *n.* calmness; quietness; self-control.

com·pote (kom′pōt) *n.* **1** a dish with a supporting stem, used for fruit, candy, etc. **2** stewed fruit. [< F < OF *compote* < L *compos(i)ta,* fem. of *compositus.* See COMPOSITE.]

com·pound¹ (*adj.* kom′pound *or* kom pound′; *n.* kom′pound; *v.* kom pound′) *n., adj., v.* —*n.* **1** a word made by joining together two or more separate words. The words *highway* and *landlocked* are compounds. **2** *Chemistry.* a substance formed by the chemical combination of two or more elements in fixed proportions. The elements lose their individual chemical properties and the compound has new properties. Water is a compound of hydrogen and oxygen. Compare **mixture** (def. 3). **3** something made by combining or mixing parts; combination or mixture: *Her success in business was due to a compound of common sense and long experience.*
—*adj.* having more than one part: *a compound sentence. A clover leaf is a compound leaf.*
—*v.* **1** increase or complicate by adding a new element: *The weekend visitors compounded the space problem at our cottage by bringing along their St. Bernard.* **2** calculate interest on a sum of money borrowed plus the accumulated unpaid interest: *The interest is compounded semi-annually.* **3** *Law.* accept or agree to accept payment not to prosecute: *It is unlawful to compound an indictable offence.* **4** mix or combine: *to compound ingredients.* **5** make by mixing or combining: *to compound a medicine.* **6** settle (a quarrel or a debt) by a compromise. [ME *compoune* < OF *compondre* < L *componere* < *com-* together + *ponere* put] —**com·pound′a·ble,** *adj.*
—**com·pound′er,** *n.*

com·pound² (kom′pound) *n.* an enclosed yard with buildings in it. [probably < Malay *kampong*]

compound eye *Biology.* an eye made up of many elements, each of which is sensitive to light and forms a part of the total image. Most insects and some crustaceans have compound eyes.

compound flower *Botany.* a flower head made up of many small flowers that appear to be a single bloom. The dandelion, aster, and dahlia are examples of plants that have compound flowers.

compound fraction a complex fraction.

compound fracture a fracture in which a broken bone cuts through the flesh and sticks out.

compound interest the interest paid on both the original sum of money borrowed and on the unpaid interest that has accumulated.

compound number a quantity expressed in two or more kinds of related units. *Examples:* 63° 30′; 12 h 30 min.

compound sentence a sentence made up of co-ordinate independent clauses. *Examples: He ran away from home, but he soon came back. The winds blew, the rains fell, and the water covered the earth.*
☛ *Usage.* See note at **clause.**

com·pre·hend (kom′pri hend′) *v.* **1** understand fully with the mind: *They did not at first comprehend the significance of the new government bill.* **2** include; contain: *His report comprehended all the facts.* [ME < L *comprehendere* < *com-* (intensive) + *prehendere* seize) —**com′pre·hend′er,** *n.* —**com′pre·hend′ing·ly,** *adv.*
☛ *Syn.* **2.** See note at **include.**
☛ *Usage.* **Comprehend, apprehend** = take hold of something with the mind; grasp. **Comprehend** = take complete hold of the meaning of something and understand it fully and perfectly: *He comprehends atomic energy.* **Apprehend** = take hold of a fact or idea but without necessarily seeing its relationships or implications: *He dimly apprehended what the foreign sailors were talking about.*

com·pre·hen·si·bil·i·ty (kom′pri hen′sə bil′ə tē) *n.* the quality of being understandable; intelligibility.

com·pre·hen·si·ble (kom′pri hen′sə bəl) *adj.* understandable.
—**com′pre·hen′si·bly,** *adv.*

com·pre·hen·sion (kom′pri hen′shən) *n.* **1** the act or power of understanding; ability to get the meaning: *Calculus is beyond his comprehension.* **2** the act or fact of including. **3** comprehensiveness. [< L *comprehensio, -onis* < *comprehendere.* See COMPREHEND.]

com·pre·hen·sive (kom′pri hen′siv) *adj.* **1** including much; covering everything or nearly everything: *The term's work ended with a comprehensive review.* **2** able to understand many things: *a comprehensive mind.* —**com′pre·hen′sive·ly,** *adv.*
—**com′pre·hen′sive·ness,** *n.*

comprehensive school *Cdn.* a composite school.

com·press (*v.* kəm pres′; *n.* kom′pres) *v., n.* —*v.* **1** make smaller and more compact by pressure or as if by pressure: *Paper is compressed into bales for recycling. He had to compress his speech because the meeting was running late.* **2** squeeze together: *We could see he was angry by the way he compressed his lips.* —*n.* **1** a pad of cloth applied to some part of the body to stop bleeding or to provide medication, etc. **2** a machine for compressing material for packing. [ME < F *compresse, compresser* < LL *compressare,* frequentative of L *comprimere* < *com-* together + *premere* press]

com·pressed (kəm prest′) *adj.* **1** squeezed together. **2** made smaller by pressure. **3** *Biology.* not thick or rounded; appearing flattened: *A puffin has a deep, compressed bill. A halibut has a compressed body.*

compressed air air put under extra pressure so that it has a great deal of force when released. Compressed air is used to inflate tires and to operate certain kinds of brakes and guns.

com·press·i·bil·i·ty (kəm pres′ə bil′ə tē) *n.* a compressible quality.

com·press·i·ble (kəm pres′ə bəl) *adj.* that can be compressed.

com·pres·sion (kəm presh′ən) *n.* **1** the act or process of compressing. **2** a compressed condition. **3** the reduction in volume of a gas by the application of pressure: *A car with worn piston rings will have poor compression.*

com·pres·sive (kəm pres′iv) *adj.* compressing; tending to compress.

com·pres·sor (kəm pres′ər) *n.* **1** one that compresses, especially a machine for compressing air, gas, etc. **2** *Anatomy.* a muscle that compresses a part of the body. [< L]

com·prise (kəm prīz′) *v.* **-prised, -pris·ing.** consist of; include: *Canada comprises ten provinces and two territories.* [ME < OF *compris,* pp. of *comprendre* < L *comprehendere.* See COMPREHEND.]
☛ *Syn.* See note at **include.**

com·pro·mise (kom′prə mīz′) *v.* **-mised, -mis·ing;** *n.* —*v.* **1** settle a dispute by agreeing that the person or group on each side will give up a part of what he demands. **2** put in danger or under suspicion, especially one's reputation or character: *You will compromise your good name if you go along with such a cheap trick.* —*n.* **1** a settlement of a dispute by a partial yielding on both sides. **2** the result of such a settlement. **3** anything halfway between two different things. **4** an exposing to danger, suspicion, etc.; an endangering: *Such a compromise of his reputation was most unwise.* [ME < OF *compromis* < L *compromissum* < *compromittere* < *com-* together + *promittere* promise]
—**com′pro·mis′er,** *n.*

Comp·tom·e·ter (komp tom′ə tər) *n. Trademark.* a machine that adds, subtracts, divides, and multiplies.

comp·trol·ler (kən trōl′ər) See **controller** (def. 1).

comp·trol·ler·ship (kən trōl′ər ship′) See **controllership.**

com·pul·sion (kəm pul′shən) *n.* **1** a compelling or being compelled, or forced: *He claimed that he had signed the confession under compulsion.* **2** *Psychology.* **a** an irresistible impulse to behave or act in a certain way, regardless of whether it is reasonable to do so. **b** an act resulting from such an impulse. [ME < LL *compulsio, -onis* < L *compellere.* See COMPEL.]

com·pul·sive (kəm pul′siv) *adj., n.* —*adj.* **1** of, having to do with, or caused by obsession or compulsion: *a compulsive liar. He was compulsive about cleanliness.* **2** using compulsion. —*n.* a person who has an obsession, or compulsion. —**com·pul′sive·ly,** *adv.*

com·pul·so·ry (kəm pul′sə rē) *adj.* **1** required; obligatory: *Attendance at school is compulsory for children.* **2** compelling; using force. —**com·pul′so·ri·ly,** *adv.*

com·punc·tion (kəm pungk′shən) *n.* **1** the pricking of conscience; remorse: *The murderer did his work cruelly and without compunction.* **2** a slight or passing regret: *He had no compunction about declining the offer.* [ME < LL *compunctio, -onis* pricking, remorse < L *compungere* < *com-* (intensive) + *pungere* prick]

com·pu·ta·tion (kom′pyə tā′shən) *n.* a reckoning; calculation. Addition and subtraction are forms of computation.

com·pute (kəm pyūt′) *v.* **-put·ed, -put·ing.** find out by mathematical work; reckon; calculate. [< L *computare* < *com-* up + *putare* reckon. Doublet of COUNT[1].] —**com·put′a·ble,** *adj.*

com·put·er (kəm pyūt′ər) *n.* **1** an electronic machine that can store large amounts of coded data and can be set, or programmed, to perform mathematical and logical operations at high speed, without the intervention of a human operator during the operation. See also **analog computer, digital computer. 2** a person skilled or trained in computing.

com·put·er·ize (kəm pyū′tə rīz′) *v.* **-ized, -iz·ing. 1** perform, regulate, or produce by means of an electronic computer: *computerized bookkeeping, computerized exam results.* **2** store in a computer: *to computerize data.* **3** furnish or equip with a computer or computers. —**com·put′er·iz′a·ble,** *adj.* —**com·put′er·i·za′tion,** *n.*

com·rade (kom′rad, kom′rid *or* kom′rād) *n.* **1** a companion and friend; partner. **2** a person who shares in what another is doing; partner; fellow worker. **3** a fellow member of a union, political party, etc., especially of the Communist Party. [< F < Sp. *camarada* room-mate < L *camera.* See CHAMBER.]

com·rade–in–arms (kom′rad in ärmz′) *n.* a fellow soldier.

com·rade·ly (kom′rad lē *or* kom′rid lē) *adj.* of, characteristic of, or like a comrade or comrades: *They sat around the fire in comradely silence.* —**com′rade·li·ness,** *n.*

com·rade·ship (kom′rad ship′ *or* kom′rid ship′) *n.* **1** the condition of being a comrade. **2** the relation of comrades; friendship; fellowship.

comte (kônt) *n. French.* a count or earl.

com·tesse (kôn tes′) *n. French.* countess.

con[1] (kon) *adv., n.* —*adv.* against: *The two debating teams argued the question pro and con.* —*n.* a reason against. The pros and cons of a question are the arguments for and against it. [short for L *contra* against]

con[2] (kon) *v.* **conned, con·ning. 1** learn well enough to remember; study. **2** examine carefully; pore over. [var. of *can[1]*]

con[3] (kon) *v.* **conned, con·ning;** *n.* —*v.* direct the steering of: *He conned the ship between the rocks.* —*n.* **1** the act or process of conning. **2** the post or station from which this is done. [var. of *cond* < OF *conduire* lead, guide < L *conducere* conduct]

con[4] (kon) *v.* **conned, con·ning;** *n. Slang.* —*v.* trick; swindle: *He was conned into buying a used car that was worthless.* —*n.* **1** a swindle: *The whole thing was just a con, but I fell for it.* **2** (adjl.) of or designating a swindle or a swindler: *a con game, a con artist.* [< *confidence game, man,* etc.]

con[5] (kon) *n. Slang.* a convict.

con– *prefix.* together or altogether; the form of **com-** occurring before all consonants except *b, m,* and *p* and, sometimes, *f,* as in *conclusion, confederation.*

con. 1 conclusion. **2** contra. **3** concession road. **4** *Music.* concerto. **5** continued.

Con. 1 Conservative. **2** Consul.

con a·mo·re (kôn ä mô′rā) *Italian.* **1** with love; with tenderness. **2** heartily; with enthusiasm. **3** *Music.* with sentiment.

con brio (kôn brē′ō) *Italian. Music.* to be played spiritedly.

con·cat·e·nate (kon kat′ə nāt′) *v.* **-nat·ed, -nat·ing;** *adj.* —*v.* link together. —*adj.* linked together. [< L *concatenare* < *com-* together + *catena* chain]

con·cat·e·na·tion (kon kat′ə nā′shən) *n.* **1** linking or being linked together. **2** a connected series of things or events.

hat, āge, fär; let, ēqual, tèrm; it, īce
hot, ōpen, ôrder; oil, out; cup, pùt, rüle,
əbove, takən, pencəl, lemən, circəs

ch, child; ng, long; sh, ship
th, thin; ᴛʜ, then; zh, measure

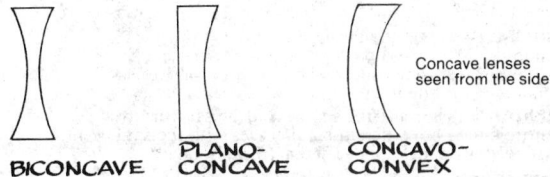

Concave lenses seen from the side

BICONCAVE   PLANO-CONCAVE   CONCAVO-CONVEX

con·cave (*adj.* kon kāv′, kon′kāv, *or* kong′kāv; *n.* kon′kāv *or* kong′kāv) *adj., n.* —*adj.* hollow and curved like the inside of a circle or sphere. —*n.* a concave surface or thing. [< L *concavus* < *com-* (intensive) + *cavus* hollow] —**con·cave′ly,** *adv.*

con·cav·i·ty (kon kav′ə tē) *n., pl.* **-ties. 1** a concave condition or quality. **2** a concave surface or thing.

con·ca·vo·con·vex (kon kā′vō kon veks′) *adj.* concave on one side and convex on the other. In a concavo-convex lens, the concave side has the greater curvature. See **concave** for picture.

con·ceal (kən sēl′) *v.* **1** hide. **2** keep secret. [ME < OF *conceler* < L *concelare* < *com-* (intensive) + *celare* hide] —**con·ceal′er,** *n.*
☛ *Syn.* **1.** See note at **hide[1].**

con·ceal·ment (kən sēl′mənt) *n.* **1** concealing or being concealed. **2** a means or place for hiding.

con·cede (kən sēd′) *v.* **-ced·ed, -ced·ing. 1** admit as true; admit: *We conceded that he was right.* **2** give (what is asked or claimed); grant; yield: *He conceded us the right to walk through his land.* [< L *concedere* < *com-* together + *cedere* yield]

con·ceit (kən sēt′) *n.* **1** too high an opinion of oneself or of one's ability, importance, etc: *In his conceit the track star thought no one could outrun him.* **2** a fanciful notion; witty thought or expression, often a far-fetched one. [< *conceive,* on analogy with *deceit*]
☛ *Syn.* See note at **pride.**

con·ceit·ed (kən sēt′id) *adj.* having too high an opinion of oneself or one's ability, importance, etc.; vain. —**con·ceit′ed·ly,** *adv.* —**con·ceit′ed·ness,** *n.*

con·ceiv·a·ble (kən sēv′ə bəl) *adj.* that can be conceived or thought of; imaginable: *We should take every conceivable precaution against fire.* —**con·ceiv′a·ble·ness,** *n.* —**con·ceiv′a·bly,** *adv.*

con·ceive (kən sēv′) *v.* **-ceived, -ceiv·ing. 1** form in the mind; think up, plan, or devise: *The plan was poorly conceived. She has conceived a better design for a house that uses solar heating.* **2** develop an idea, feeling, etc.; form in one's mind: *He conceived a strong dislike for his aunt.* **3** have as an idea or opinion; imagine or believe (*often used with* **of**): *It's hard to conceive of such things ever happening. They conceived themselves to be under the protection of the embassy.* **4** become pregnant. **5** become pregnant with: *She conceived a child.* **6** put in words; express: *The warning was conceived in the plainest language.* [ME < OF *conceveir* < L *concipere* take in < *com-* (intensive) + *capere* take] —**con·ceiv′er,** *n.*
☛ *Syn.* **1.** See note at **imagine.**

con·cen·trate (kon′sən trāt′) *v.* **-trat·ed, -trat·ing;** *n.* —*v.* **1** bring or come together to one place: *A convex lens is used to concentrate rays of light.* **2** pay close attention; focus the mind: *He concentrated upon the problem.* **3** increase the proportion of a substance in a solution or mixture: *We concentrated the solution by boiling off some of the water.* **4** *Mining.* remove rock, sand, etc. from (metal or ore). —*n.* something that has been concentrated: *lemon juice concentrate.* [< *con-* together + L *centrum* centre] —**con′cen·tra′tor,** *n.*

con·cen·trat·ed (kon′sən trāt′id) *adj.* **1** brought together in one place. **2** of liquids and solutions, made stronger. —**con′cen·trat′ed·ly,** *adv.*

con·cen·tra·tion (kon′sən trā′shən) *n.* **1** concentrating or being concentrated. **2** close attention: *He gave the problem his full concentration.* **3** the strength of a solution.

concentration camp a camp where political enemies, prisoners of war, and interned foreigners are held.

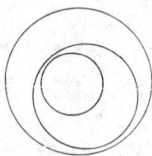

Eccentric circles

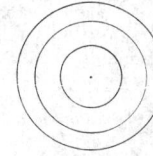

Concentric circles

con·cen·tric (kən sen′trik) *adj.* having the same centre. Concentric circles are different-sized circles with the same centre. Compare **eccentric** (def. 2). —**con·cen′tri·cal·ly,** *adv.*

con·cen·tri·cal (kən sen′trə kəl) *adj.* concentric.

con·cept (kon′sept) *n.* a general notion; an idea of a class of objects; idea: *the concept of equality, basic concepts of chivalry.* [< L *conceptus,* pp. of *concipere.* See CONCEIVE.]

con·cep·tion (kən sep′shən) *n.* **1** a thought; idea; impression: *His conception of the problem is different from mine.* **2** the act or power of conceiving. **3** the state of being conceived. **4** becoming pregnant. **5** a design; plan, or concept.

con·cep·tu·al (kən sep′chü əl) *adj.* having to do with concepts or general ideas. —**con·cep′tu·al·ly,** *adv.*

con·cep·tu·al·ize (kən sep′ chü ə līz′) *v.* **-ized, -iz·ing.** form an idea of; interpret or think about in terms of concepts. —**con·cep′tu·al·iz′er,** *n.*

con·cern (kən sèrn′) *v., n.* —*v.* **1** have to do with; relate to: *The letter concerns the proposal for a new bridge. Nine students from our class are concerned in the play.* **2** involve the interests of; be the proper business or affair of: *The message is private; it concerns nobody but me.* **3** trouble; make anxious: *He didn't want to concern his friends with the details of the accident.*
as concerns, about; with reference to.
concern (oneself), **a** take an interest; be busy: *She will concern herself in the water sports program.* **b** be troubled or worried; be anxious or uneasy: *Don't concern yourself; I have everything ready.* —*n.* **1** whatever has to do with a person or thing; matter; business; affair: *Keeping the books is his partner's concern.* **2** a troubled state of mind; worry; anxiety; uneasiness: *The mother's concern over her sick child kept her awake all night.* **3** a business company; firm: *He works for a big manufacturing concern in Toronto.* **4** relation; reference: *The special concern of her new book on Saskatchewan history is with the period just after the Depression.*
of concern, of importance; of interest: *a matter of concern to the ratepayers.*
[< Med.L *concernere* relate to < LL *concernere* mingle with, mix < L *concretus,* pp. of *concrescere* < *com-* together + *crescere* grow]
☞ *Syn.* **2.** See note at **care.**
☞ *Usage.* **Concern** (*v.*) used with *in* or *with* means "take part in or have to do with": *They could not prove he was concerned with the crime.* **Concern** used with *about* or *for* means "be worried": *Are you concerned about his escape? Naturally we were concerned for him when we heard of the accident.*

con·cerned (kən sèrnd′) *adj.* **1** interested; caring: *Concerned citizens will attend the meeting on pollution.* **2** involved; having a connection: *All the students concerned in the school play were given time off for the dress rehearsal.* **3** troubled; worried; anxious. —**con·cern′ed·ly,** *adv.*

con·cern·ing (kən sèr′ning) *prep.* having to do with; with regard to; regarding; relation to; about: *The policeman asked many questions concerning the accident.*

con·cern·ment (kən sèrn′mənt) *n.* **1** importance; interest. **2** worry; anxiety. **3** affair.

con·cert (*n. and adj.* kon′sərt; *v.* kən sèrt′) *n., adj., v.* —*n.* **1** a musical performance in which several musicians or singers take part. **2** agreement; harmony; union.
in concert, all together; in harmony or agreement.
—*adj.* **1** used in concerts; for concerts. **2** performing in a concert or concerts: *a concert pianist.*
—*v.* arrange by agreement; plan or make together. [< F < Ital. *concerto,* probably < *concertare* < L *com-* with + *certare* strive. Doublet of CONCERTO.]

con·cert·ed (kən sèr′tid) *adj.* **1** arranged by agreement; planned or made together; combined: *a concerted attack.* **2** *Music.* arranged in parts for several voices or instruments. —**con·cert′ed·ly,** *adv.*

concert grand a grand piano having the volume and brilliancy of tone required for use in a large hall or with an orchestra.

con·cer·ti·na (kon′sər tē′nə) *n.* a small musical instrument resembling an accordion. [< *concert*]

con·cert·mas·ter (kon′sərt mas′tər) *n.* the leader, usually the first violinist, of an orchestra, ranking next to the conductor.

con·cert·meis·ter (kon′ sərt mīs′tər) *n.* concertmaster. [< G]

con·cer·to (kən cher′tō) *n., pl.* **-tos** or (Italian) **-ti** (tē). a musical composition, usually in three movements and usually written for one or more solo instruments, such as a violin, piano, etc., accompanied by an orchestra. [< Ital. Doublet of CONCERT.]

concerto grosso (kən cher′tō grō′sō) a concerto for a group of solo instruments and a full orchestra. [< Ital.]

concert pitch 1 *Music.* a slightly heightened pitch, often used for tuning instruments for concert use. **2** the height of fitness, readiness, co-ordination, etc.: *Our Olympic runners were at concert pitch.*

con·ces·sion¹ (kən sesh′ən) *n.* **1** the act of conceding; granting; yielding: *Concession to popular demands was the monarch's weakness.* **2** anything yielded or conceded; admission; acknowledgment: *As a concession, Mother let me stay up an hour longer.* **3** something conceded or granted by a government or controlling authority; grant. Land, privileges, etc. given by a government to a business company are called concessions. A circus leases space for booths as concessions. **4** a privilege or space granted or leased for a particular use within specified premises: *There is a soft-drink concession at the ball park.* [< L *concessio, -onis* < *concedere.* See CONCEDE.]

con·ces·sion² (kən sesh′ən) *n. Cdn.* **1** mainly in Ontario and Quebec, a subdivision of land in township surveys, formerly one of the rows of thirty-two 200-acre lots into which each new township was divided. **2** concession road. **3 concessions,** *pl.* rural or bush districts: *He relies on the concessions for his political support.* [< Cdn.F]

con·ces·sion·aire (kən sesh′ən er′) *n.* a person, business company, etc. to whom a concession has been granted. [< F *concessionnaire*]

con·ces·sion·ar·y (kən sesh′ə ner′ē) *adj.* of, having to do with, or obtained by a concession.

concession road *Cdn.* especially in Ontario, a rural road following the road allowance between concessions, running as a rule east and west and connected to other concession roads by north-south side roads. Concession roads are usually 1¼ miles (2 km) apart.

con·ces·sive (kən ses′iv) *adj.* **1** yielding; making or implying concession. **2** *Grammar.* expressing concession. *Though* and *although* introduce concessive clauses.

conch (konch *or* kongk) *n., pl.* **conch·es** (kon′chiz) **or conchs** (kongks). **1** any of various large marine snails having a spiral shell with the outermost spiral roughly triangular in outline and with a wide lip often curled back, revealing a smooth, pearly lining; especially, any member of the plant-eating genera *Strombus* and *Cassis* found mainly in the Caribbean. **2** the shell of a conch, used as an ornament or for making cameos. **3** concha. [< L *concha* < Gk. *konchē*]

con·cha (kong′kə) *n.* **1** *Anatomy.* any of various shell-shaped structures, such as the external ear or a thin bone in the nose. **2** *Architecture.* the half dome of an apse. [< L *concha* conch]

con·chi·lite (kong′kə līt′) *n.* a bowl-shaped rock composed chiefly of limonite and goethite, having a smooth or irregularly scalloped outline resembling an oyster shell and varying in diameter from about 3 cm to 90 cm, discovered in 1943 on the bedrock floor of Finlayson Lake (Ont.).

con·cho·log·i·cal (kong′kə loj′ə kəl) *adj.* of or having to do with conchology.

con·chol·o·gist (kong kol′ə jist) *n.* a person trained in conchology, especially one whose work it is.

con·chol·o·gy (kong kol′ə jē) *n.* the branch of zoology that deals with shells and shellfish. [< Gk. *konchē* shell + E *-logy*]

con·ci·erge (kon′sē erzh′; *French,* kôn syerzh′) *n.* **1** doorkeeper. **2** janitor. [< F]

con·cil·i·ar (kən sil′ē ər) *adj.* of or having to do with a council or councils.

con·cil·i·ate (kən sil′ē āt′) *v.* **-at·ed, -at·ing. 1** win over; soothe: *She conciliated her angry little sister by promising to take her to the zoo.* **2** gain (good will, regard, favor, etc.) by friendly acts. **3** reconcile; bring into harmony. [< L *conciliare* < *concilium.* See COUNCIL.] —**con·cil′i·at′ing·ly,** *adv.*

con·cil·i·a·tion (kən sil′ē ā′shən) *n.* conciliating or being conciliated.

con·cil·i·a·tive (kən sil′ē ə tiv *or* kən sil′ē ā′tiv) *adj.* conciliatory.

con·cil·i·a·tor (kən sil′ē ā′tər) *n.* a person who conciliates; arbitrator; peacemaker.

con·cil·i·a·to·ry (kən sil′ē ə tô′rē) *adj.* tending or calculated to win over, soothe, or reconcile: *They hoped the apology would have a conciliatory effect on the angry tenants. He spoke to the crowd in a conciliatory tone of voice.*

con·cise (kən sīs′) *adj.* expressing much in a few words; brief but full of meaning. [< L *concisus*, pp. of *concidere* < *com*- (intensive) + *caedere* cut] —**con·cise′ly**, *adv.* —**con·cise′ness**, *n.*

con·ci·sion (kən sizh′ən) *n.* the quality or state of being concise; conciseness.

con·clave (kon′klāv *or* kong′klāv) *n.* **1** a private meeting. **2** *Roman Catholic Church.* **a** a meeting of the cardinals for the election of a pope. **b** the rooms where the cardinals meet in private for this purpose. [ME < OF < L *conclave* a room that can be locked < *com*- with + *clavis* key]

con·clude (kən klüd′) *v.* **-clud·ed, -clud·ing. 1** end; finish: *She concluded her speech with a funny story.* **2** arrange; settle: *The two countries concluded a trade agreement.* **3** find out by thinking; reach or arrive at a decision, judgment, or opinion by reasoning; infer: *From the clues we found, we concluded that the thief must have left in a hurry.* **4** decide; resolve: *I concluded not to go.* [< L *concludere* < *com*- (intensive) + *claudere* close] —**con·clud′er**, *n.*
☛ *Syn.* **1.** See note at **end.**
☛ *Usage.* **Conclude** is used: **a** with *by* before the -*ing* form of the verb: *He concluded his remarks by quoting a passage from Chaucer.* **b** (def. 1) with *with* before a noun: *I will conclude my remarks with a plea addressed to your president.* **c** (def. 3) with *from* when it means "infer": *I must conclude from what you say that you are dissatisfied.*

con·clu·sion (kən klü′zhən) *n.* **1** an end. **2** the last main division of a speech, essay, etc. **3** a final result; outcome. **4** an arrangement; settlement: *the conclusion of a peace treaty between enemies.* **5** a decision, judgment, or opinion reached by reasoning.
in conclusion, finally; lastly; to conclude.
try conclusions, *Archaic.* engage in a struggle (*with*).
[ME < L *conclusio, -onis* < *concludere.* See CONCLUDE.]

con·clu·sive (kən klü′siv) *adj.* decisive; convincing; definite: *conclusive evidence.* —**con·clu′sive·ly**, *adv.* —**con·clu′sive·ness**, *n.*

con·coct (kən kokt′ *or* kon kokt′) *v.* **1** prepare by putting together ingredients: *The chef has concocted a delicious new dessert.* **2** make up, especially something complicated; invent; devise: *What fantastic money-making scheme have you concocted this time? She concocts really clever mystery stories.* [< L *concoctus*, pp. of *concoquere* < *com*- together + *coquere* cook] —**con·coct′er**, *n.*

con·coc·tion (kən kok′shən *or* kon kok′shən) *n.* **1** the act of concocting. **2** the thing concocted.

con·com·i·tance (kən kom′ə təns *or* kon kom′ə təns) *n.* accompaniment.

con·com·i·tant (kən kom′ə tənt *or* kon kom′ə tənt) *adj., n.* —*adj.* accompanying; attending: *a concomitant result.* —*n.* an accompanying thing, quality, or circumstance; accompaniment. [< L *concomitans, -antis*, ppr. of *concomitari* < *com*- (intensive) + *comitari* accompany] —**con·com′i·tant·ly**, *adv.*

con·cord (kon′kôrd *or* kon′gkôrd) *n.* **1** agreement; harmony. **2** *Music.* a harmonious combination of tones sounded together. **3** treaty. [ME < OF < L *concordia*, ult. < *com*- together + *cor, cordis* heart]

Concord grape (kong′kərd *or* kon′kôrd) a large, sweet, bluish-black variety of grape used for making jelly, juice, or wine.

con·cord·ance (kən kôr′dəns *or* kon kôr′dəns) *n.* **1** an agreement; harmony. **2** an alphabetical list of the principal words or all the words occurring in a particular body of writing, with identification of the passages in which they occur: *a concordance of Shakespeare.*

con·cord·ant (kən kôr′dənt *or* kon kôr′dənt) *adj.* agreeing; harmonious. —**con·cord′ant·ly**, *adv.*

con·cor·dat (kon kôr′dat) *n.* **1** an agreement; compact. **2** a formal agreement between the Pope and a government about church affairs. **3** a similar agreement between any religious body and a government. [< F < LL *concordatum*, pp. neut. of *concordare* make harmonious]

con·course (kon′kôrs *or* kon′gkôrs) *n.* **1** a running, flowing, or coming together; confluence: *The fort was built at the concourse of two rivers.* **2** a crowd. **3** a place where crowds gather or wait: *the main concourse of a railway station.* [ME < OF *concours* < L *concursus* < *concurrere* < *com*- together + *currere* run]

con·cres·cence (kon kres′əns) *n.* **1** a growing together of parts. **2** an increase by the adding of particles. [< L *concrescentia* < *concrescere.* See CONCRETE.]

con·crete (*adj., n. and v.*1 kon′krēt *or* kon krēt′; *v.* 2 kon krēt′) *adj., n., v.* **-cret·ed, -cret·ing.** —*adj.* **1** existing of itself in the material world, not merely as an idea or as a quality; real: *All actual objects are concrete. A painting is concrete; its beauty is abstract.* **2** not abstract or general; specific; particular: *The lawyer gave concrete examples of the prisoner's cruelty.* **3** naming a thing, especially something perceived by the senses. *Sugar* and *people* are concrete nouns; *sweetness* and *humanity* are abstract nouns. **4** made of concrete: *a concrete sidewalk.* **5** formed into a mass; solid; hardened.
—*n.* **1** a mixture of crushed stone or gravel, sand, cement, and water that hardens as it dries. **2** the hard substance resulting from the hardening of this mixture: *He fell and hurt his head on the concrete.*
—*v.* **1** cover with concrete. **2** form or mix into a mass; harden into a mass. [< L *concretus*, pp. of *concrescere* < *com*- together + *crescere* grow] —**con·crete′ly**, *adv.* —**con·crete′ness**, *n.*

con·cre·tion (kon krē′shən) *n.* **1** forming into a mass; solidifying. **2** a solidified mass; hard formation. Gallstones are concretions.

con·cu·bi·nage (kon kyü′bə nij) *n.* **1** the condition of living together without legal marriage. **2** the condition of being a concubine.

con·cu·bine (kong′kyü·bīn *or* kon′kyə bīn′) *n.* **1** a woman who lives with or has a continuing sexual relationship with a man without being legally married to him; mistress. Concubine was the usual word for a mistress before about the 17th century. **2** in certain polygamous societies, such as that of the ancient Hebrews, a wife having an inferior social and legal status; a secondary wife. [< L *concubina* < *com*- with + *cubare* lie]

con·cu·pis·cence (kon kyü′pə səns) *n.* sensual desire; lust.

con·cu·pis·cent (kon kyü′pə sənt) *adj.* **1** eagerly desirous. **2** lustful; sensual. [< L *concupiscens, -entis*, ppr. of *concupiscere* < *com*- (intensive) + *cupere* desire]

con·cur (kən kėr′) *v.* **-curred, -cur·ring. 1** be of the same opinion; agree: *The judges all concurred in giving John the prize.* **2** work together: *The events of the week concurred to make it a great holiday.* **3** come together; happen at the same time. [< L *concurrere* < *com*- together + *currere* run] —**con·cur′rer**, *n.*
☛ *Syn.* **1.** See note at **consent.**

con·cur·rence (kən kėr′əns) *n.* **1** the holding of the same opinion; agreement. **2** a working together. **3** a happening at the same time. **4** *Geometry.* coming together; meeting at a point.

con·cur·rent (kən kėr′ənt) *adj., n.* —*adj.* **1** existing side by side; happening at the same time. **2** co-operating. **3** having equal authority or jurisdiction; co-ordinate. **4** agreeing; consistent; harmonious. **5** coming together; meeting in a point.
—*n.* a concurrent thing or event. —**con·cur′rent·ly**, *adv.*

con·cuss (kən kus′) *v.* **1** agitate or shake violently by or as if by a blow. **2** *Medicine.* injure (the brain) by concussion. [< L *concussus* < *concutere.* See CONCUSSION.]

con·cus·sion (kən kush′ən) *n.* **1** a sudden, violent shaking; shock: *The concussion caused by the explosion broke many windows.* **2** an injury to the brain, spine, etc. caused by a blow fall, or other shock. [< L *concussio, -onis* < *concutere* shake violently < *com*- (intensive) + *quatere* shake]

con·cus·sive (kən kus′iv) *adj.* **1** of or having to do with concussion. **2** tending to cause concussion.

con·demn (kən dem′) *v.* **1** express strong disapproval of: *We should condemn cruelty wherever we find it.* **2** show to be guilty of crime or wrong; convict: *The prisoner is sure to be condemned. Her letters are enough to condemn her.* **3** pass sentence on; doom: *He was condemned to death.* **4** assign to an unpleasant fate or condition: *Poverty condemned them to a life of frustration.* **5** declare not sound or suitable for use: *This bridge has been condemned because it is no longer safe for traffic.* **6** *U.S.* expropriate. [ME < OF *condem(p)ner* < L *condemnare* < *com*- (intensive) + *damnare* cause loss to, condemn < *damnum* loss] —**con·demn′er**, *n.*

con·dem·na·ble (kən dem′nə bəl) *adj.* that should be condemned; blamable.

con·dem·na·tion (kon′dem nā′shən) *n.* **1** strong disapproval: *He expressed his condemnation of the new plan.* **2** condemning or being condemned: *the condemnation of a prisoner by a judge, the condemnation of an unsafe bridge.* **3** a cause or reason for condemning: *Her refusal to help was her condemnation.*

hat, āge, fär; let, ēqual, tėrm; it, īce
hot, ōpen, ôrder; oil, out; cup, půt, rüle,
əbove, takən, pencəl, lemən, circəs

ch, child; ng, long; sh, ship
th, thin; ŦH, then; zh, measure

con·dem·na·to·ry (kən dem′nə tô′rē) *adj.* condemning; expressing condemnation.

con·den·sa·ble (kən den′sə bəl) *adj.* capable of being condensed.

con·den·sate (kon′den sāt′ *or* kən den′sāt) *n.* something formed or produced by condensation.

con·den·sa·tion (kon′dən sā′shən) *n.* **1** condensing or being condensed: *the condensation of a story, the condensation of steam into water.* **2** something condensed; a condensed mass: *A cloud is a condensation of water vapor in the atmosphere. There is a condensation of the book in that magazine.* **3** *Chemistry.* a reaction in which two or more molecules unite to form a larger, more dense, and more complex molecule, often with the separation of water or some other simple substance.

con·dense (kən dens′) *v.* **-densed, -dens·ing. 1** make or become denser or more compact; reduce the volume of: *Milk is condensed before it is canned.* **2** make stronger; concentrate: *Light is condensed by means of lenses.* **3** change from a gas or vapor to a liquid. If steam comes in contact with cold surfaces, it condenses or is condensed into water. **4** put into fewer words; express briefly: *He condensed the paragraph into one line.* [< L *condensare* < *com-* together + *densus* thick]

condensed milk sweetened evaporated milk.

con·dens·er (kən den′sər) *n.* **1** whatever condenses something. **2** a device for receiving and holding a charge of electricity. **3** an apparatus for changing gas or vapor into a liquid. **4** a strong lens or lenses for concentrating light upon a small area.

con·de·scend (kon′di send′) *v.* **1** come down willingly or graciously to the level of one's inferiors in rank: *The king condescended to eat with the beggars.* **2** grant a favor in a haughty or patronizing way. **3** stoop or lower oneself: *He would not condescend to taking a bribe.* [ME < OF *condescendre* < LL *condescendere* < L *com-* together + *descendere* descend]

con·de·scend·ing (kon′di sen′ding) *adj.* showing condescension; patronizing; acting in a way that shows scorn for others. **—con′de·scend′ing·ly,** *adv.*

con·de·scen·sion (kon′di sen′shən) *n.* **1** the act or an instance of condescending. **2** a patronizing attitude: *I could feel the condescension of the hotel clerk in the way he looked at my old luggage.* [< LL *condescensio, -onis* < *condescendere.* See CONDESCEND.]

con·dign (kən dīn′) *adj.* deserved; adequate; fitting: *a condign punishment.* [ME < OF *condigne* < L *condignus* very worthy < *com-* (intensive) + *dignus* worthy]

☛ *Usage.* Because **condign** is so often coupled with *punishment,* it is sometimes misunderstood and used incorrectly as a synonym for *severe.*

con·di·ment (kon′də mənt) *n.* something, such as pepper and spices, used to give flavor and relish to food. [< L *condimentum* spice < *condire* to spice, preserve]

con·di·tion (kən dish′ən) *n., v.* **—n. 1** the state in which a person or thing is: *The accident victim was in critical condition in the hospital. Her car is several years old, but still in very good condition.* **2** physical fitness; good health: *People who take part in sports must keep in condition.* **3** rank; social position: *The Premier's parents were people of humble condition.* **4** anything on which something else depends; that without which something else cannot occur or exist: *Available oxygen is a condition of human life. A condition of employment as a sales representative is a willingness to travel.* **5** something demanded as an essential part of an agreement. **6** *Grammar.* a clause that expresses or contains a condition. **7** an ailment or disease: *My uncle has a heart condition.* **8 conditions,** *pl.* circumstances that affect an activity or situation: *poor driving conditions. The working conditions here are excellent.* **on condition that,** if; provided that: *I'll go on condition that you will too.*
—v. 1 put in good condition: *Exercise conditions your muscles.* **2** be a condition of: *Ability and effort condition success.* **3** make depend on (a condition); subject to (a condition): *The gift to the boy was conditioned on his good behavior.* **4** *Archaic.* make conditions; make it a condition. **5** shape behavior of by repeated exposure to particular conditions, with which responses become associated: *This dog has been conditioned to expect food when he obeys a command.* **6** make accustomed to: *Many years of running the store had conditioned her to hard work.* [< L *condicio, -onis* agreement < *condicere* < *com-* together + *dicere* say] **—con·di′tion·er,** *n.*

☛ *Syn. n.* **1.** See note at **state.**

con·di·tion·al (kən dish′ən əl *or* kən dish′nəl) *adj., n.* **—adj. 1** depending on something else; not absolute; limited: *You may go if the sun shines* is a conditional promise. **2** expressing or containing a condition. "If the sun shines" is a conditional clause. **—n.**

Grammar. a word, phrase, clause, mood, or tense that expresses a condition. **—con·di′tion·al·ly,** *adv.*

con·di·tioned (kən dish′ənd) *adj.* **1** put under a condition; subject to certain conditions. **2** in a particular kind of condition. **3** *Psychology.* of or designating a response produced by repeated exposure to particular conditions; learned: *a conditioned reflex.* **4** accustomed (*to*): *conditioned to cold.*

conditioned response or **reflex** *Psychology.* a learned response which is predictable as a result of the subject having been repeatedly subjected to a certain stimulus or set of stimuli.

con·do (kon′dō) *n., pl.* **-dos** or **does.** *Informal.* condominium (defs. 1 and 2).

con·dole (kən dōl′) *v.* **-doled, -dol·ing.** express sympathy; sympathize (*used with* with): *The widow's friends condoled with her at the funeral.* [< L *condolere* < *com-* with + *dolere* grieve, suffer]

con·do·lence (kən dō′ləns) *n.* an expression of sympathy: *Her friends sent her their condolences.*

con·dom (kon′dəm *or* kun′dəm) *n.* a thin, usually rubber sheath worn over the penis during sexual intercourse to prevent venereal infection and as a contraceptive.

con·do·min·i·um (kon′də min′ē əm) *n.* **1** a residential structure in which apartments or townhouses are individually owned as pieces of real estate while the land and common facilities are jointly owned. **2** a unit in such a structure. **3** a joint control, especially of two or more countries over the government of another country. **4** a country whose government is controlled jointly by two or more others: *The Anglo-Egyptian Sudan was a condominium.* [< NL < L *com-* with + *dominium* lordship]

con·do·na·tion (kon′dō nā′shən) *n.* the forgiving of an offence, especially by ignoring or overlooking it.

con·done (kən dōn′) *v.* **-doned, -don·ing.** forgive or overlook an offence or fault: *His parents had always condoned his temper tantrums when he was small.* [< L *condonare* < *com-* (intensive) + *donare* give]

con·dor (kon′dər) *n.* either of two very large New World vultures, now in danger of extinction. The Andean condor (*Vultur gryphus*), found in the high Andes Mountains of South America, has black plumage with a white neck ruff and white wing patches. The California condor (*Gymnogyps californianus*) of the mountains of California, has black plumage with white wing bands. [< Sp. *cóndor* < Peruvian *cuntur*]

con·duce (kən dyüs′ *or* kən düs′) *v.* **-duced, -duc·ing.** lead; contribute; be favorable (*to*): *Darkness and quiet conduce to sleep.* [< L *conducere* < *com-* together + *ducere* lead]

con·du·cive (kən dyü′siv *or* kən dü′siv) *adj.* helpful; favorable: *Exercise is conducive to health.* **—con·du′cive·ly,** *adv.*

con·duct (*n.* kon′dukt; *v.* kən dukt′) *n., v.* **—n. 1** behavior; way of acting: *Her rude conduct was inexcusable. He won a medal for good conduct.* **2** direction; management: *the conduct of an office.* **3** a leading; guidance: *Give the messenger safe conduct to the king.* **—v. 1** act or behave in a certain way: *The way she conducted herself throughout the crisis showed that she had great courage.* **2** direct; manage. **3** direct an orchestra, choir, etc. as leader. **4** go along with and show the way to; guide: *The butler conducted him to the library.* **5** transmit (heat, electricity, etc.); be a channel to. [< L *conductus,* pp. of *conducere* < *com-* together + *ducere* lead]

☛ *Syn. n.* **1. Conduct, behavior** = way of acting. **Conduct** applies to a person's general manner of acting, especially in relation to others and to the principles of right and wrong set up by society: *His conduct is always admirable.* **Behavior,** used of people and animals, applies to the way of acting toward and in front of others, especially in certain situations: *His behavior shows his lack of consideration for others.* **—v.** See note at **manage. 4.** See note at **guide.**

con·duct·ance (kən duk′təns) *n.* **1** the power of conducting electricity as affected by the shape, length, etc. of the conductor. **2** the ease with which a substance or a solution of it permits the passage of an electrical current. Its unit of measurement is the mho, or reciprocal ohm.

con·duct·i·bil·i·ty (kən duk′tə bil′ə tē) *n.* the power of conducting heat, electricity, etc.

con·duct·i·ble (kən duk′tə bəl) *adj.* **1** capable of conducting heat, electricity, etc. **2** capable of being conducted.

con·duc·tion (kən duk′shən) *n.* **1** *Physics.* the transmission of heat, electricity, etc. by the transferring of energy from one particle to another. **2** conveying.

con·duc·tive (kən duk′tiv) *adj.* **1** having conductivity. **2** of conduction.

con·duc·tiv·i·ty (kon′duk tiv′ə tē) *n.* **1** the power of conducting heat; electricity; etc. **2** the ability of a given substance to conduct electricity between opposite faces of a one-centimetre cube of the material, measured in mhos, or reciprocal ohms, per centimetre cube. **3** the rate of transfer of heat by conduction between opposite faces of a one-centimetre cube of a substance, having unit temperature difference between opposite faces.

con·duc·tor (kən duk′tər) n. 1 a person who conducts; director; manager; leader; guide. 2 the director of an orchestra, chorus, etc. The conductor of an orchestra trains the musicians to work together, selects the music to be used, and directs the players during a performance. 3 the person in charge of a streetcar, bus, railway train, etc. The conductor usually collects the tickets or fares from the passengers. 4 anything that transmits heat, electricity, light, sound, etc. Copper is a good conductor of heat and electricity. —con′duc·tor′i·al, adj.

con·duit (kon′dyü it, kon′dü it, or kon′dit) n. 1 a channel or pipe for carrying liquids over long distances. 2 a tube or underground passage for electric wires. [ME < OF conduit < Med.L conductus a leading, a pipe < L conductus contraction < conducere < com- together + ducere draw]

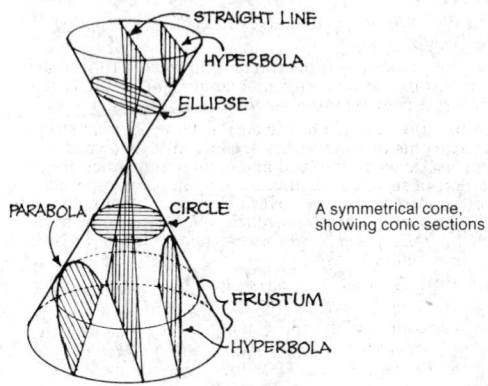

A symmetrical cone, showing conic sections

cone (kōn) n. 1 Geometry. a surface traced by a moving straight line, one point or end of which is fixed, the opposite end passing through all the points of a closed fixed curve. When the fixed curve is a circle and the line from the vertex to the centre of this circle forms a right angle with it, making a symmetrically tapered shape, the surface is called a **right circular cone**. 2 a solid figure bounded by such a surface. 3 anything shaped somewhat like a cone with evenly tapered sides: an ice-cream cone, the cone of a volcano. 4 Botany. a the reproductive structure of trees of the pine family, consisting of clusters of overlapping woody scales arranged along an axis, with the ovules contained between the scales. b a similar reproductive structure in various other plants, such as horsetails or club mosses. [ME < L conus < Gk. kōnos pine cone, cone] —cone′less, adj.

cone·flow·er (kōn′flou′ər) n. any of various North American plants of the composite family having flower heads with a raised or cone-shaped central disk surrounded by ray flowers, especially the **prairie coneflower** (Ratibida columnifera) or any of several plants of the genera Rudbeckia and Echinacea.

Con·el·rad (kon′əl rad′) n. U.S. a system for broadcasting instructions, etc. over radio stations while shifting frequencies, going on and off the air irregularly, etc. to keep enemy airplanes from utilizing the beams of the station for navigation. [short for Control of Electromagnetic Radiation]

con·es·to·ga wagon (kon′is tō′gə) a covered wagon with broad wheels, formerly used, especially by American pioneers, for travelling on soft ground or on the prairie. [< Conestoga, Pa., where such wagons were first built]

co·ney¹ (kō′nē) See cony.

co·ney² (kō′nē) n. inconnu. Also, cony.

con·fab (n. kon′fab′; v. kən fab′ or kon′fab) n., v. -fabbed, -fab·bing. Informal. —n. a conversation or conference. —v. have a conversation or conference.

con·fab·u·late (kən fab′yə lāt′) v. -lat·ed, -lat·ing. talk together informally and intimately; chat. [< L confabulari < com- together + fabula fable]

con·fab·u·la·tion (kən fab′yə lā′shən) n. an informal, intimate talking together; chat.

con·fec·tion (kən fek′shən) n. 1 a piece of candy, candied fruit, jam, etc. 2 an elaborate hat or dress. [< L confectio, -onis < conficere < com- with + facere make]

con·fec·tion·er (kən fek′shən ər) n. a person whose business is making or selling candies, ice cream, etc.

confectioners' sugar U.S. icing sugar.

con·fec·tion·er·y (kən fek′shən er′ē) n., pl. -er·ies. 1 candies, sweets, etc.; confections. 2 the business of making or selling

hat, āge, fär; let, ēqual, tèrm; it, īce
hot, ōpen, ôrder; oil, out; cup, put, rüle,
ə above, takən, pencəl, lemən, circəs

ch, child; ng, long; sh, ship
th, thin; ᵮн, then; zh, measure

confections. 3 a place where confections, ice cream, etc. are made or sold; candy shop.

con·fed·er·a·cy (kən fed′ər ə sē or kən fed′rə sē) n., pl. -cies. 1 a union of countries or states; group of people joined together for a special purpose. 2 a league; alliance. 3 conspiracy. 4 **Confederacy**, Confederate States of America.

con·fed·er·ate (adj. n. kən fed′ər it or kən fed′rit; v. kən fed′ər āt′) adj., n., v. -at·ed, -at·ing. —adj. 1 joined together for a special purpose; allied. 2 **Confederate**, of or belonging to the Confederate States of America: the Confederate uniform. —n. 1 a country, person, etc. joined with another for a special purpose; ally; companion. 2 an accomplice; partner in crime: The thief was arrested, but his confederate escaped. 3 **Confederate**, U.S. a person who lived in and supported the Confederate States of America. —v. 1 enter a union or alliance: Newfoundland confederated with Canada in 1949. Four provinces of Canada confederated in 1867. 2 join together for a special purpose; ally. [< L confoederatus, pp. of confoederare unite in a league < com- together + foedus, -deris league]
☛ Syn. n. 2. See note at accomplice.

Confederate States of America U.S. the group of eleven southern states that seceded from the United States in 1860 and 1861. Their secession lasted until 1865.

con·fed·er·a·tion (kən fed′ər ā′shən) n. 1 a federation; the act of joining together in a league; state of being united in a league or alliance: The conference devised a scheme for the confederation of the foreign colonies. 2 a group of countries, states, etc. joined together for a special purpose; league. 3 **Confederation**, Cdn. the name given to the federation of Ontario, Quebec, Nova Scotia, and New Brunswick in 1867. Six other provinces have joined Confederation since 1867. 4 **the Confederation**, a Cdn. the ten provinces of Canada. b the confederation of the American states from 1781 to 1789.

con·fer (kən fer′) v. -ferred, -fer·ring. 1 consult together; exchange ideas; talk things over: The Prime Minister often confers with his advisers. 2 give; award; bestow (on): The general conferred a medal on the brave soldier. [< L conferre < com- together + ferre bring]
☛ Syn. 1. See note at consult. 2. See note at give.

con·fer·ee (kon′fər ē′) n. 1 a person who takes part in a conference. 2 a person on whom something is conferred.

con·fer·ence (kon′fər əns or kon′frəns) n. 1 a meeting of interested persons to discuss a particular subject: A conference was called to discuss getting a playground for the school. 2 the act of taking counsel, the act of talking something over; consultation with a person or a group of persons: You cannot see Mr. Smith just now; he is in conference. 3 an association of schools, churches, etc. joined together for some special purpose. 4 Sports. a league or division of a league.

con·fer·ment (kən fer′mənt) n. a giving; bestowal.

con·fess (kən fes′) v. 1 acknowledge; admit; own up. 2 concede; grant: I confess you are right on one point. 3 admit one's guilt. 4 tell (one's sins) to a priest in order to obtain forgiveness. 5 of a priest, hear (a person) tell his sins in order to obtain forgiveness; act as a confessor. [ME < OF confesser < LL confessare < L confiteri < com- (intensive) + fateri confess]
☛ Syn. 1. See note at admit.

con·fessed (kən fest′) adj. acknowledged; admitted.

con·fess·ed·ly (kən fes′id lē) adv. by acknowledgment; admittedly.

con·fes·sion (kən fesh′ən) n. 1 acknowledgment; admission; owning up. 2 admission of guilt. 3 the telling of one's sins to a priest in order to obtain forgiveness. 4 the thing confessed. 5 an acknowledgment of belief; profession of faith. 6 the belief acknowledged; creed.

con·fes·sion·al (kən fesh′ən əl or kən fesh′nəl) n., adj. —n. 1 a small booth where a priest hears confessions. 2 the practice of confessing sins to a priest. —adj. of or having to do with confession.

confession of faith 1 an acknowledgment of belief. 2 the belief acknowledged; creed.

con·fes·sor (kən fes′ər) n. 1 a person who confesses. 2 a priest

who has the authority to hear confessions. **3** a person who acknowledges belief.

con·fet·ti (kən fet′ē) *n.* bits of colored paper thrown about at carnivals, weddings, etc. [< Ital. *confetti*, pl., sweetmeats]

con·fi·dant (kon′fə dant′ *or* kon′fə dant′) *n.* a person entrusted with one's secrets, private affairs, etc.; a close friend.

con·fi·dante (kon′fə dant′ *or* kon′fə dant′) *n.* a woman entrusted with one's secrets, etc.; a close woman friend.

con·fide (kən fīd′) *v.* **-fid·ed, -fid·ing. 1** tell as a secret: *He confided his troubles to his brother.* **2** hand over (a task, person, etc.) in trust; give to another for safekeeping: *The collection of dues is confided to the treasurer.*
confide in, a entrust a secret to: *She always confides in her sister.* **b** put trust in: *to confide in God.*
[< L *confidere* < *com-* (intensive) + *fidere* trust] —**con·fid′er,** *n.*

con·fi·dence (kon′fə dəns) *n.* **1** a firm belief; trust. **2** a firm belief in oneself and one's abilities. **3** boldness; too much boldness: *Although he could not swim, he dived into the water with confidence.* **4** a feeling of trust; assurance that a person will not tell others what is said: *The story was told to me in strict confidence.* **5** something told as a secret. **6** political support for the actions or policy of the cabinet, as expressed by the majority vote of a legislature: *A government that loses a vote of confidence must resign.*
☛ *Syn. n.* **2. Confidence, assurance** = a firm belief in oneself. **Confidence** emphasizes its basic meaning of faith or trust, and means "a strong belief in oneself and one's abilities": *He tackles his work with confidence.* **Assurance** emphasizes its basic meaning of certainty, and means "sureness of oneself and lack of fears or doubts about one's abilities": *He went into the contest with the assurance of a born fighter.*

confidence game a type of fraud in which a swindler works on his victim after gaining his confidence.

confidence man a swindler who uses the confidence game.

con·fi·dent (kon′fə dənt) *adj., n.* —*adj.* **1** firmly believing; certain; sure. **2** sure of oneself and one's abilities. **3** too bold; too sure. —*n.* a close, trusted friend; confidant. —**con′fi·dent·ly,** *adv.*
☛ *Syn. adj.* **1.** See note at **sure.**

con·fi·den·tial (kon′fə den′shəl) *adj.* **1** intended for or restricted to secret or private use: *The detective's report to her superior was confidential.* **2** showing trust or intimacy: *He spoke in a confidential tone of voice.* **3** trusted with secrets, private affairs, etc.: *a confidential secretary.* —**con′fi·den′tial·ly,** *adv.*
—**con′fi·den′tial·ness,** *n.*
☛ *Syn.* **3.** See note at **familiar.**

con·fi·den·ti·al·i·ty (kon′fə den′shē al′ə tē) *n.* the fact or quality of being confidential.

con·fid·ing (kən fīd′ing) *adj.* trustful; trusting. —**con·fid′ing·ly,** *adv.*

con·fig·u·ra·tion (kən fig′yə rā′shən *or* kən fig′ər ā′shən) *n.* **1** the relative position of parts; manner of arrangement; form; shape; outline: *Geographers study the configuration of the earth's surface.* **2** *Astronomy.* **a** the relative position of heavenly bodies, especially of the sun, moon, and planets. **b** any grouping of stars. **3** the relative spatial positions of atoms in a molecule. [< L *configuratio, -onis* < *configurare* form after some pattern < *com-* with + *figura* a form]

con·fig·u·ra·tive (kən fig′yər ə tiv *or* kən fig′ər ə tiv) *adj.* of or having to do with configuration.

con·fine (*v.* kən fīn′; *n.* kon′fīn) *v.* **-fined, -fin·ing;** *n.* —*v.* **1** keep within limits; restrict. **2** keep indoors; shut in. **3** imprison.
be confined, give birth to a child.
—*n.* Usually, **confines,** *pl.* a boundary; border; limit: *These people have never been beyond the confines of their own valley.* [< F *confiner* < *confins,* pl., bounds < L *confinium* < *com-* together + *finis* end, border] —**con·fin′er,** *n.*

con·fined (kən fīnd′) *adj.* **1** restricted. **2** imprisoned.

con·fine·ment (kən fīn′mənt) *n.* **1** confining or being confined. **2** imprisonment. **3** the period for which a mother is confined to bed during and after childbirth. [< F *confinement* < *confiner.* See CONFINE.]

con·firm (kən fèrm′) *v.* **1** make official by formal statement; approve; consent to: *Parliament confirmed the treaty.* **2** prove to be true or correct; make certain: *to confirm a rumor.* **3** support; strengthen in an opinion, etc.: *A sudden storm confirmed my decision not to leave.* **4** administer the religious rite of confirmation to. [ME < OF *confermer* < L *confirmare* < *com-* (intensive) + *firmus* firm] —**con·firm′a·ble,** *adj.* —**con·firm′er,** *n.*
☛ *Syn.* **1. Confirm, corroborate, authenticate** = prove to be true or genuine. **Confirm** = make certain that something is true or correct, by facts or a statement that cannot be doubted: *The mayor confirmed the report that he had resigned.* **Corroborate** = make more certain that something suspected is true,

by a statement or new evidence: *Finding the weapon corroborates the police theory.* **Authenticate** = prove something is genuine or reliable, by the evidence of someone who knows: *Handwriting experts authenticated the will.*

con·fir·ma·tion (kon′fər mā′shən) *n.* **1** the act or process of confirming. **2** something that confirms; proof: *The lab has sent confirmation of the diagnosis.* **3** an assurance that one's plans have not been changed: *The airline requires confirmation of your reservation.* **4** *Christianity.* a rite in many churches in which a baptized person is confirmed in his faith and admitted to full church membership. **5** *Judaism.* a ceremony in which a young person is confirmed in the Jewish faith.

con·firm·a·tive (kən fèr′mə tiv) *adj.* confirmatory.

con·firm·a·to·ry (kən fèr′mə tô′rē) *adj.* confirming.

con·firmed (kən fèrmd′) *adj.* **1** firmly established; proved: *confirmed results.* **2** habitual; constant; permanent: *a confirmed bachelor.*

con·fis·cate (kon′fis kāt′) *v.* **-cat·ed, -cat·ing. 1** seize for the public treasury: *The government confiscated the property of all traitors.* **2** seize by authority; take and keep: *The customs officer confiscated the smuggled cigarettes.* [< L *confiscare,* originally, lay away in a chest < *com-* (intensive) + *fiscus* chest, public treasury] —**con′fis·ca′tor,** *n.*

con·fis·ca·tion (kon′fis kā′shən) *n.* confiscating or being confiscated: *the confiscation of wealth.*

con·fis·ca·to·ry (kon fis′kə tô′rē) *adj.* of the nature of confiscation or tending to confiscate.

con·fla·gra·tion (kon′flə grā′shən) *n.* a great, destructive fire: *A conflagration destroyed most of the city.* [< L *conflagratio, -onis* < *conflagrare* < *com-* (intensive) + *flagrare* burn]

con·flict (*n.* kon′flikt; *v.* kən flikt′) *n., v.* —*n.* **1** a prolonged fight or struggle. **2** direct opposition; a disagreement; clash: *A conflict of opinions divided the members into two groups.* —*v.* **1** be directly opposed; disagree; clash: *The date conflicts with his vacation plans. Their stories of the accident conflict.* **2** *Archaic.* fight; battle. [< L *conflictus,* pp. of *confligere* < *com-* together + *fligere* strike]
☛ *Syn. n.* **1.** See note at **fight.**

con·flict·ing (kən flik′ting) *adj.* that conflicts; disagreeing; clashing.

conflict of interest a clash, or opposition, between the private interests and the public responsibilities of a person in a position of trust, such as a government official.

con·flu·ence (kon′flü əns) *n.* **1** a flowing together: *the confluence of two rivers.* **2** the place where two or more rivers, streams, etc. come together: *They pitched camp at the confluence of the two streams.* **3** a coming together of people or things; throng.

con·flu·ent (kon′flü ənt) *adj., n.* —*adj.* **1** flowing or running together; blending into one: *confluent rivers.* **2** *Medicine.* **a** tending to join or run together: *confluent eruptions of the skin.* **b** characterized by such eruptions. —*n.* **1** a stream which unites and flows with another of nearly equal size. **2** a smaller stream flowing into a larger one. [< L *confluens, -entis,* ppr. of *confluere* < *com-* together + *fluere* flow]

con·flux (kon′fluks) *n.* confluence.

con·form (kən fôrm′) *v.* **1** act according to law or rule; adapt oneself to or accept the normal standards of business, conduct, worship, etc. **2** be similar in form or character: *The path conforms to the shoreline of the lake.* **3** make similar in form or character: *to conform the path to the shoreline. The stranger never conformed his ways to theirs.* **4** *Brit.* comply with the usages of the Church of England. **5** in the British Isles, comply with the usages of the Church of England. [ME < OF *conformer* < L *conformare* < *com-* with + *forma* a shape] —**con·form′er,** *n.*

con·form·a·ble (kən fôr′mə bəl) *adj.* **1** similar. **2** in agreement; agreeable; harmonious: *The committee felt that the proposal was not conformable to their interests.* **3** obedient; submissive: *The boy was usually conformable to his father's wishes.* —**con·form′a·bly,** *adv.* —**con·form′a·ble·ness,** *n.*

con·form·ance (kən fôr′məns) *n.* the act of conforming; conformity.

con·for·ma·tion (kon′fôr mā′shən) *n.* **1** a structure; shape; the form of a thing resulting from the arrangement of its parts. **2** a symmetrical arrangement of the parts of a thing. **3** a conforming; adaptation.

con·form·ist (kən fôr′mist) *n., adj.* —*n.* **1** a person who tends to conform to generally accepted usage in behavior, dress, etc. **2** *Brit.* a person who complies with the usages of the Church of England. —*adj.* of or having to do with conformity or conformism.

con·form·i·ty (kən fôr′mə tē) *n., pl.* **-ties. 1** a similarity; correspondence; agreement. **2** behavior in agreement with generally accepted standards of business, law, conduct, or worship; fitting oneself and one's thoughts or actions to the ideas of others; compliance. **3** obedience; submission. **4** in the British Isles, compliance with the usages of the Church of England.

con·found (kən found′ *or* kon found′ *for 1-5;* kon′found′ *for 6*) *v.* **1** confuse; mix up; bewilder: *The shock confounded her.* **2** be unable to tell apart: *He confounds "deprecate" and "depreciate."* **3** surprise and puzzle. **4** *Archaic.* make uneasy and ashamed. **5** *Archaic.* defeat; overthrow. **6** damn. *Confound* is used as a mild oath. [ME < OF *confondre* < L *confundere* < *com-* together + *fundere* pour] **—con·found′er,** *n.*

con·found·ed (kən foun′did *or* kon foun′did) *adj.* **1** damned. *Confounded* is used as a mild oath. **2** hateful; detestable. **—con·found′ed·ly,** *adv.*

con·fra·ter·ni·ty (kon′frə tėr′nə tē) *n., pl.* **-ties. 1** brotherhood. **2** a group of men united for some purpose or in a profession. [ME *confraternite* < Med.L *confraternitas* < *confrater.* See CONFRERE.]

con·frere (kon′frer) *n.* a fellow member; colleague. [< F *confrère* < OF < Med.L *confrater* < L *com-* together + *frater* brother]

con·front (kən frunt′) *v.* **1** meet face to face, especially as opponents; stand facing. **2** face boldly; oppose. **3** bring face to face; place before: *The lawyer confronted the prisoner with the forged cheque.* **4** compare. [< F *confronter* < Med.L *confrontare* < L *com-* together + *frons, frontis* forehead]

con·fron·ta·tion (kon′frən tā′shən) *n.* **1** meeting or being met face to face. **2** an open clash between opposing groups, parties, or individuals: *He doesn't believe in confrontation, and would rather try to talk things out reasonably.* **3** (*adj.*) designating tactics or a strategy based on open clashes: *confrontation politics.*

con·fron·ta·tion·ist (kon′frun tā′shə nist′) *n.* a person who advocates or practises tactics or a strategy of confrontation.

Con·fu·cian (kən fyü′shən) *adj., n.* **—adj.** of or having to do with Confucius, his teachings, or his followers. **—n.** a follower of Confucius or his teachings.

Con·fu·cian·ism (kən fyü′shən iz′əm) *n.* a philosophical system based on the belief in the natural goodness of all human beings, that for more than 2000 years dominated the social and political order in China. Confucianism teaches that the greatest virtues are love, justice, reverence, wisdom, and sincerity, and emphasizes respect for parents and ancestors.

Con·fu·cian·ist (kən fyü′shə nist) *n., adj.* **—n.** a supporter or follower of Confucianism. **—adj.** of or having to do with Confucianism.

Con·fu·cius (kən fyü′shəs) *n.* 551 ?-478 B.C., a Chinese philosopher and teacher whose teachings form the basis of Confucianism. [latinized form of *Kung Fu-tse* Kung the master]

con·fuse (kən fyüz′) *v.* **-fused, -fus·ing. 1** mix up; throw into disorder. **2** bewilder: *So many people talking to me at once confused me.* **3** be unable to tell apart; mistake (one thing for another): *Even their own mother sometimes confused the twins.* **4** make uneasy and ashamed; embarrass: *Confused by her blunder, she could not say anything for a moment.* [< *confused* < F *confus* < L *confusus,* pp. of *confundere.* See CONFOUND.] **—con·fus′ing·ly,** *adv.*

▸ *Syn.* **4. Confuse, embarrass, disconcert** = disturb a person. **Confuse** = make a person so uneasy and bewildered that he cannot think clearly or act sensibly: *Honking at a driver who has stalled his car often confuses him.* **Embarrass** = make one so uneasy and self-conscious that he cannot talk or act naturally: *Meeting strangers embarrasses her.* **Disconcert** = disturb someone so suddenly or badly that for a moment he loses his poise and ability to handle the situation: *Forgetting the words disconcerted the singer.*

con·fused (kən fyüzd′) *adj.* **1** mixed up; disordered. **2** bewildered.

con·fus·ed·ly (kən fyüz′id lē *or* kən fyüzd′lē) *adv.* in a confused manner.

con·fu·sion (kən fyü′zhən) *n.* **1** the act or fact of confusing. **2** a confused condition; disorder: *There was confusion in the busy street after the accident.* **3** a failure to distinguish clearly: *confusion between red and orange.* **4** bewilderment; inability to think clearly: *In her confusion she quite forgot her appointment.* **5** uneasiness and shame.

con·fu·ta·tion (kon′fyə tā′shən) *n.* **1** the act of confuting. **2** the thing that confutes.

con·fute (kən fyüt′) *v.* **-fut·ed, -fut·ing. 1** prove (an argument, testimony, etc.) to be false or incorrect: *The lawyer confuted the testimony of the witness by showing actual photographs of the accident.* **2** prove (a person) to be wrong; overcome by argument: *The speaker confuted his opponents by facts and logic.* [< L *confutare*] **—con·fut′er,** *n.*

▸ *Usage.* **Confute, refute** = prove an adversary to be wrong. But **confute** is more intensive and has the force of "silencing or overcoming" a person by refutation.

con·ga (kong′gə) *n., v.* **-gaed** *or* **con·ga'd, con·ga·ing. —n. 1** a Cuban dance of African origin, usually performed by a group of people moving one behind the other in a single line. **2** music for this dance, having a strong, syncopated rhythm in 4/4 time. **3** a tall,

hat, āge, fär; let, ēqual, tėrm; it, īce
hot, ōpen, ôrder; oil, out; cup, put, rüle,
əbove, takən, pencəl, lemən, circəs
ch, child; ng, long; sh, ship
th, thin; ŦH, then; zh, measure

narrow, low-toned drum that is beaten with the hands. Also called **conga drum.** See **drum** for picture. **—v.** dance the conga. [< Sp.]

con·gé (kon′zhā; *French,* kôn zhā′) *n.* **1** dismissal; permission to leave. **2** formal leave-taking or departure. [< F < L *commeatus* going to and fro < *com-* (intensive) + *meare* wander]

con·geal (kən jēl′) *v.* **1** harden or make solid by cold; freeze. **2** thicken, clot: *The blood around the wound had congealed.* [ME < OF *congeler* < L *congelare* < *com-* (intensive) + *gelare* freeze] **—con·geal′er,** *n.* **—con·geal′ment,** *n.*

con·ge·ner (kon′jə nər) *n.* a person or thing of the same kind or class. [< L *congener* of the same kind < *com-* (intensive) + *genus, -neris* kind]

con·ge·ni·al (kən jē′nē əl *or* kən jēn′yəl) *adj.* **1** having similar tastes and interests; getting on well together: *congenial companions.* **2** agreeable; suitable: *congenial work.* [< NL *congenialis < L *com-* together + *genialis* < *genius* spirit] **—con·gen′ial·ly,** *adv.*

con·ge·ni·al·i·ty (kən jē′nē al′ə tē *or* kən jēn yal′ə tē) *n.* a congenial quality.

con·gen·i·tal (kən jen′ə təl) *adj.* existing before or at birth, but not inherited: *A clubfoot is a congenital deformity.* Compare **hereditary.** [< L *congenitus* born with < *com-* with + *genitus* born]

con·gen·i·tal·ly (kən jen′ə təl ē) *adv.* from the time of birth.

con·ger (kong′gər) *n.* conger eel.

con·ger eel (kong′gər) *n.* **1** a large, scaleless ocean eel (*Conger conger*) found along the coasts of Europe, Asia, and Africa, and the Atlantic coast of America. The conger eel is an important food fish of Europe. **2** any other eel of the same family (Congridae, the conger eel family). [ME < OF *congre* < L < Gk. *gongros*]

con·ge·ries (kon jēr′ēz *or* kon jēr′ē ēz′) *n.sing. and pl.* a collection; heap; mass. [< L *congeries* < *congerere.* See CONGEST.]

con·gest (kən jest′) *v.* **1** fill too full; overcrowd; clog: *The rush-hour traffic congested the streets.* **2** cause too much blood to gather in (a part of the body): *An infection of the mucous membrane in the nose will congest the nasal passages.* [< L *congestus,* pp. of *congerere* < *com-* together + *gerere* carry]

con·gest·ed (kən jes′təd) *adj.* **1** overcrowded; clogged: *congested hallways.* **2** of a body organ or tissue, containing too much blood: *congested mucous membranes, congested lungs.*

con·ges·tion (kən jes′chən) *n.* the quality or state of being congested: *traffic congestion. Congestion of the lungs may lead to pneumonia.*

con·ges·tive (kən jes′tiv) *adj.* accompanied by congestion; produced by congestion; causing congestion.

con·glom·er·ate (*adj. and n.* kən glom′ər it; *v.* kən glom′ər āt′) *adj., v.* **-at·ed, -at·ing. —adj. 1** gathered into a rounded mass; clustered. **2** made up of miscellaneous materials gathered from various sources. **3** *Geology.* of or forming a conglomerate. **—n. 1** a mass formed of fragments. **2** *Geology.* a kind of sedimentary rock consisting of waterworn boulders, pebbles, etc. held together by a natural cementing material. **3** a large, widely diversified corporation consisting of a number of companies dealing in different products or services. **—v.** collect together or accumulate into a mass or cluster. [< L *conglomerare* < *com-* together + *glomus, -meris* ball]

con·glom·er·a·tion (kən glom′ər ā′shən) *n.* **1** a mixed-up mass of various things or persons; mixture. **2** conglomerating or being conglomerated.

Con·go·lese (kong′gə lēz′) *n., adj.* **—n.** a native or inhabitant of the Congo region, the former French Congo, the former Belgian Congo, or either of the Congo republics. **—adj.** of or having to do with any of these regions.

congo snake *or* **eel** a snakelike amphibian (*Amphiuma means*) found in swampy regions of the SE United States, having gill slits and two pairs of very small, weak legs.

con·grat·u·late (kən grach′ü lāt′) *v.* **-lat·ed, -lat·ing.** express one's pleasure to someone at his happiness or good fortune. [< L *congratulari* < *com-* with + *gratulari* show joy] **—con·grat′u·la′tor,** *n.*

con·grat·u·la·tion (kən grach′ü lā′shən) *n.* **1** congratulating or wishing a person joy: *a letter of congratulation.* **2 congratulations,**

pl. an expression of pleasure at another's happiness or good fortune: *Congratulations on winning the tournament.*

con·grat·u·la·to·ry (kən grach′ŭ lə tô′rē) *adj.* expressing pleasure at another's happiness or good fortune.

con·gre·gate (kong′grə gāt′) *v.* **-gat·ed, -gat·ing.** come together into a crowd or mass; assemble. [< L *congregare* < *com-* together + *grex, gregis* flock]

con·gre·ga·tion (kong′grə gā′shən) *n.* **1** coming together into a crowd or mass; assembling. **2** a gathering of people or things; assembly. **3** a group of people gathered together for religious worship or instruction. **4** *Roman Catholic Church.* **a** a committee of cardinals or other clergymen. **b** a religious community or order having a common rule and with or without solemn vows.

con·gre·ga·tion·al (kong′grə gā′shən əl *or* kong′grə gāsh′nəl) *adj.* **1** of a congregation; done by a congregation. **2 Congregational,** of or belonging to Congregationalism or Congregationalists.

con·gre·ga·tion·al·ism (kong′grə gā′shən əl iz′əm *or* kong′grə gāsh′nəl iz′əm) *n.* **1** a system of church government in which each individual church governs itself. **2 Congregationalism,** the principles and system of organization of a Protestant denomination in which each individual church governs itself.

Con·gre·ga·tion·al·ist (kong′grə gā′shən əl ist *or* kong′grə gāsh′nəl ist) *n.* **1** a member of a Congregational church. **2** a believer in Congregationalism.

con·gress (kong′gris) *n.* **1** a formal meeting of representatives of interested groups to discuss some subject: *They attended an international congress on conservation.* **2** an organization of people for the purpose of promoting a common interest or concern: *the Canadian Labour Congress.* **3** the lawmaking body of a nation, especially of a republic. **4 Congress,** in the United States: **a** the national lawmaking body, consisting of the Senate and House of Representatives, with members from each state. **b** its session. **5** the act or action of meeting or coming together. [< L *congressus* < *congredi* < *com-* together + *gradi* go]

congress boot *U.S.* an ankle-high man's shoe having an elastic insert in each side; gaiter. Also called **congress gaiter** or **congress shoe.** [from its popularity, esp. in the late 19c., with U.S. congressmen]

con·gres·sion·al (kən gresh′ən əl *or* kən gresh′nəl) *adj.* **1** of or having to do with a congress. **2 Congressional,** of or having to do with Congress.

con·gress·man (kong′gris mən) *n., pl.* **-men.** Often, **Congressman,** in the United States: **1** a member of Congress. **2** a member of the House of Representatives.

con·gress·wom·an (kong′gris wŭm′ən) *n., pl.* **-wom·en.** in the United States, a female member of Congress or of the House of Representatives.

con·gru·ence (kong′grü əns) *n.* agreement; harmony.

con·gru·en·cy (kong′grü ən sē) *n.* congruence.

con·gru·ent (kong′grü ənt) *adj.* **1** agreeing; harmonious. **2** *Geometry.* exactly coinciding: *congruent triangles.* **3** *Mathematics.* producing the same remainder when divided by a given number. [< L *congruens, -entis,* ppr. of *congruere* agree] —**con′gru·ent·ly,** *adv.*

con·gru·i·ty (kən grü′ə tē) *n., pl.* **-ties. 1** agreement; harmony. **2** *Geometry.* the exact coincidence of lines, angles, figures, etc. **3** a point of agreement.

con·gru·ous (kong′grü əs) *adj.* **1** agreeing; harmonious. **2** fitting; appropriate. **3** *Geometry.* exactly coinciding. [< L *congruus* < *congruere* agree] —**con′gru·ous·ly,** *adv.* —**con′gru·ous·ness,** *n.*

con·i·bear trap (kō′nē ber′) *Cdn.* a heavy steel trap that kills large animals, such as beavers, instantly. [after F *Conibear,* a Canadian expert on trapping]

con·ic (kon′ik) *adj., n. —adj.* **1** of or having to do with a cone. **2** like a cone; conical. —*n. Geometry.* **1** a curve forming the edge of the plane surface produced when a piece is cut from a right circular cone. Depending on the angle at which the cut is made, the conic will be a circle, ellipse, parabola, or hyperbola. See **cone** for picture. **2 conics,** the branch of geometry dealing with circles, ellipses, parabolas, and hyperbolas (*used with a singular verb*).

con·i·cal (kon′ə kəl) *adj.* **1** like a cone; cone-shaped: *The wizard wore a conical hat.* **2** conic. —**con′i·cal·ly,** *adv.*

conic section *Geometry.* **1** a conic. **2 conic sections,** a branch of geometry; conics (*used with a singular verb*).

co·ni·fer (kō′nə fər *or* kon′ə fər) *n.* any tree or shrub of the order Coniferales, most species having small, needle-shaped, evergreen leaves and all bearing their seeds in cones. Pines, spruces, firs, hemlocks, junipers, and cypresses are conifers. [< L *conifer* cone-bearing < *conus* cone (< Gk. *kōnos*) + *ferre* to bear]

co·nif·er·ous (kō nif′ər əs) *adj.* **1** bearing cones. **2** belonging to or having to do with the conifers.

conj. 1 conjunction. **2** conjugation.

con·jec·tur·al (kən jek′chər əl) *adj.* **1** involving conjecture. **2** inclined to conjecture. —**con·jec′tur·al·ly,** *adv.*

con·jec·ture (kən jek′chər) *n., v.* **-tured, -tur·ing. —n. 1** the formation of an opinion admittedly without sufficient evidence for proof; guessing. **2** an opinion based on guesswork: *There were many conjectures about how he died, but no one knew for certain.* —*v.* form an opinion based on guesswork; guess. [ME < L *conjectura* < *conjicere* < *com-* together + *jacere* throw] —**con·jec′tur·a·ble,** *adj.* —**con·jec′tur·a·bly,** *adv.* —**con·jec′tur·er,** *n.* ☛ *Syn.* See note at **guess.**

con·join (kən join′) *v.* join together; unite; combine. [ME *conjoignen < OF conjoindre < L conjungere < com-* together + *jungere* join] —**con·join′er,** *n.*

con·joint (kən joint′ *or* kon′joint) *adj.* **1** joined together; united; combined. **2** formed by two or more in combination; joint. [< F *conjoint,* pp. of *conjoindre.* See CONJOIN.] —**con·joint′ly,** *adv.*

con·ju·gal (kon′jə gəl) *adj.* of or having to do with marriage or the relationship between husband and wife: *conjugal happiness.* [< L *conjugalis < com-* with + *jugum* yoke] —**con·ju·gal·ly,** *adv.*

con·ju·gate (*v.* kon′jə gāt′; *adj. n.* kon′jə git *or* kon′jə gāt′) *v.* **-gat·ed, -gat·ing;** *adj., n. —v.* **1** *Grammar.* give the forms of (a verb) according to a systematic arrangement. **2** join together; couple. —*adj.* **1** joined together; coupled. **2** *Grammar.* derived from the same root. —*n. Grammar.* a word derived from the same root as another. [< L *conjugare < com-* with + *jugum* yoke]

con·ju·ga·tion (kon′jə gā′shən) *n.* **1** *Grammar.* **a** a systematic arrangement of the forms of a verb. **b** a group of verbs having similar forms in such an arrangement. **c** the act of giving the forms of a verb according to such an arrangement. **2** a joining together; coupling.

con·junct (kən jungkt′ *or* kon′jungkt) *adj.* joined together; joint; associated; combined. [< L *conjunctus,* pp. of *conjungere.* See CONJOIN.]

con·junc·tion (kən jungk′shən) *n.* **1** joining or being joined together; union; combination: *A severe illness in conjunction with the hot weather has left the baby very weak.* **2** *Grammar.* a word that expresses a particular connection between words, phrases, clauses, or sentences. *And, but,* and *or* are **co-ordinating conjunctions;** *if, as, because,* etc. are **subordinating conjunctions;** *either. . .or, both. . .and* are **correlative conjunctions. 3** *Astronomy.* the apparent nearness of two or more heavenly bodies. ☛ *Usage.* **Conjunctions** are used to connect words, phrases, clauses, or sentences. Some conjunctions also serve the double purpose of introducing a clause and connecting it with the rest of the sentence. Conjunctions are classified as follows: **a Co-ordinating:** those that connect words, phrases, clauses, or sentences of equal rank: *and, but, for, nor, or so, yet.* **b Correlative:** co-ordinating conjunctions that are used in pairs: *both. . .and, either. . .or, neither. . .nor,* not only. . .but also, *whether. . .or.* **c Subordinating:** those that serve to introduce and to connect subordinate clauses with the main clauses of sentences: *after, although, as, because, before, if, since, when, whenever, where,* while, and so on. **d** See also **conjunctive adverbs,** under **conjunctive.**

con·junc·ti·va (kon′jungk tī′və *or* kən jungk′ti və) *n., pl.* **-vas, -vae** (-vē *or* -vī). *Anatomy.* the mucous membrane that covers the front of the eyeball and the inner surface of the eyelids. [< NL (*membrana*) *conjunctiva* connecting membrane]

con·junc·tive (kən jungk′tiv) *adj., n. —adj.* **1** joining together; connecting; uniting; combining. **2** joined together; joint; united; combined. **3** *Grammar.* **a** like a conjunction; like that of a conjunction. *Then* is a conjunctive adverb. **b** connecting words, phrases, or clauses in both meaning and construction. *And, also,* and *moreover* are conjunctive conjunctions. —*n.* a conjunctive word; conjunction. —**con·junc′tive·ly,** *adv.* ☛ *Usage.* **Conjunctive adverbs.** A number of words that are ordinarily used as adverbs are sometimes used also to connect independent clauses or sentences. They are called **conjunctive adverbs.** Even though they serve as connectives, their adverbial meaning remains important. The most common are: *accordingly, also, anyhow, anyway* (informal), *besides, consequently, furthermore, hence, however, indeed, likewise, moreover, namely, nevertheless, then, therefore.* In a compound sentence, it is normal to use a semicolon before a clause introduced by a conjunctive adverb: *He is extremely conceited; however, he is so charming that people overlook it.*

con·junc·ti·vi·tis (kən jungk′tə vī′tis) *n.* an inflammation of the conjunctiva. [< NL *conjunctivitis < conjunctiva + -itis* (< Gk.)]

con·junc·ture (kən jungk′chər) *n.* **1** a combination of events or circumstances. **2** a critical state of affairs; crisis.

con·ju·ra·tion (kon′jə rā′shən) *n.* **1** the act of invoking by a sacred name. **2** a magic form of words used in conjuring; magic spell. **3** the practice of magic: *In the fairy tale, the princess was changed into a toad by conjuration.* **4** *Archaic.* a solemn appeal.

con·jure (kun′jər *or* kon′jər *for* 1-5; kən jür′ *for* 6) *v.* **-jured, -jur·ing. 1** compel to appear by incantation (*often used with* **up**):

The wizard conjured a dragon. **2** summon a devil, spirit, etc. by incantation: *The wizard began to conjure.* **3** practise magic; be a conjurer. **4** cause to appear in the mind; evoke (*used with* **up**): *The song conjured up many memories.* **5** perform tricks by sleight of hand. **6** make a solemn appeal to; entreat: *I conjure you not to betray your country.*

(a person or thing) **to conjure with,** one that has great importance or influence: *Since her last novel, she has become a name to conjure with.* [ME < OF < L *conjurare* make a compact < *com-* together + *jurare* swear]

con·jur·er or **con·jur·or** (kun′jər ər *or* kon′jər ər) *n.* **1** a sorcerer or wizard. **2** a person who performs tricks by sleight of hand; magician or juggler. **3** shaman or medicine man.

conk (kongk) *n., v. Slang.* —*n.* **1** a punch or hit, especially on the head. **2** the head. —*v.* punch or hit (someone), especially on the head.
conk out, a of a car, machine, etc., break down suddenly: *The car conked out in the middle of an intersection.* **b** be overcome with fatigue or weakness; collapse: *I'm so tired, I'm about ready to conk out.* [prob. < E *conch*]

con mo·to (kôn mō′tō) *Italian. Music.* with spirited movement (used as a direction).

Conn. Connecticut.

con·nect (kə nekt′) *v.* **1** join, fasten, or link (one thing to another or two things together); unite: *to connect plumbing pipes.* **2** join in some business or interest; bring into some relation: *This store is connected with a major chain.* **3** think of one thing as being associated with or the cause of another: *We usually connect spring with sunshine and flowers.* **4** be or become connected. **5** establish a line of communication in a telephone system (*used with* **with**): *Could you please connect me with Mr. LeBlanc's office?* **6** of an airline flight, bus run, etc., be so arranged that passengers can change to another aircraft, bus, etc. without delay. **7** *Informal.* achieve one's aim; be successful, especially in hitting or throwing: *to connect for a home run. His first punch went wild, but the second one connected.* [< L *connectere* < *com-* together + *nectere* tie] —**con·nect′er** or **con·nec′tor,** *n.*
☛ *Usage.* **Connect** may be used with *to, with,* or *by: Now let's connect this wire to that. Be sure this piece connects with that. The two towns are connected by a railway.* **Up** is unnecessary after **connect:** *You should connect this wire* (up) *with that.*

con·nect·ed (kə nek′tid) *adj.* **1** joined together; fastened together. **2** joined in orderly sequence: *connected ideas.* **3** having ties and associates: *She is well connected socially.* —**con·nect′ed·ly,** *adv.*
☛ *Usage.* **Connected with** and **in connection with** are wordy expressions, usually for *in* or *with: The social life in connection with a college residence* (in a college residence) *will be something you have never experienced before.*

connecting rod a bar connecting two or more moving parts in a machine. See **dead centre** for picture.

con·nec·tion (kə nek′shən) *n.* **1** the act of connecting or state of being connected. **2** something that connects; a connecting part: *There is a loose connection in the wiring.* **3** any kind of practical relation with another thing or person: *He has no connection with his brother's firm.* **4** Usually, **connections,** *pl.* a group of people with whom one is associated in business dealings, etc.: *He'll probably be able to get tickets through his connections in the city.* **5** thinking of persons or things together; linking together of words or ideas in a logical order. **6** the scheduled meeting of trains, ships, airplanes, etc. so that passengers can change from one to the other without delay. **7** a line of communication between two points in a telephone system: *We had a bad connection and couldn't hear her very well.* **8** a related person; relative: *She is a connection of ours by marriage.* **9** a religious denomination.
in connection with, in regard or reference to.
☛ *Usage.* See note at **connected.**

con·nec·tive (kə nek′tiv) *adj., n.* —*adj.* that connects. —*n.* **1** something that connects. **2** *Grammar.* a word used to connect words, phrases, and clauses. Conjunctions and relative pronouns are connectives.

connective tissue tissue that connects, supports, or encloses other tissues and organs in the body.

con·nex·ion (kə nek′shən) *Esp.Brit.* See **connection.**

con·nie or **co·ny** (kon′ē) *n. Cdn.* inconnu.

con·ning tower (kon′ing) **1** on a submarine, a small tower on the deck, used as an entrance and as a place for observation. **2** an armored control station on the deck of a warship, occupied by the captain during battle. **3** any similar observation tower from which supervision can be carried out. [conning, ppr. of *con* direct the steering of (a ship), var. of earlier *cond,* shortened from ME *condue, condye* guide < OF *conduire* < L *conducere.* See CONDUCT.]

---

hat, āge, fär; let, ēqual, tèrm; it, īce
hot, ōpen, ôrder; oil, out; cup, pùt, rüle,
əbove, takən, pencəl, lemən, circəs
ch, child; ng, long; sh, ship
th, thin; ŦH, then; zh, measure

con·nip·tion (kə nip′shən) *n. Informal.* Often, **conniptions,** *pl.* a fit of rage, hysteria, etc.; tantrum.

con·niv·ance (kə nīv′əns) *n.* **1** the act of conniving; pretended ignorance or secret encouragement of wrongdoing. **2** *Law.* guilty assent to, or knowledge or encouragement of, wrongdoing, without participation in it.

con·nive (kə nīv′) *v.* **-nived, -niv·ing. 1** shut one's eyes to something wrong; give aid to wrongdoing by not telling of it (*used with* **at**): *The mayor was accused of conniving at the misuse of public funds.* **2** co-operate secretly; conspire (*with*): *The general connived with the enemies of his country.* [< L *connivere* shut the eyes, wink < *com-* together + *niv-* press (related to *nictere* wink)] —**con·niv′er,** *n.*

con·nois·seur (kon′ə sèr′) *n.* a person having thorough knowledge and able to make fine distinctions and critical judgments, especially in art and matters of taste: *a connoisseur of wine, a connoisseur of antique furniture.* [< F *connoisseur* (now *connaisseur*), ult. < L *cognoscere* < *co-* (intensive) + *gnoscere* recognize]

con·no·ta·tion (kon′ə tā′shən) *n.* **1** what is suggested by a word or expression in addition to its basic meaning. The connotations associated with words can determine the emotional effect of a statement, etc. and often indicate the attitude of the speaker or writer. The word *slender,* for instance, usually has a more favorable connotation than *thin.* Compare **denotation.** **2** the suggestion of a meaning in addition to the basic meaning; connoting.

con·no·ta·tive (kon′ə tā′tiv *or* kə nōt′ə tiv) *adj.* **1** connoting; having connotation. **2** having to do with connotation.

con·note (kə nōt′) *v.* **-not·ed, -not·ing.** suggest in addition to the literal meaning; imply. *Portly, corpulent,* and *obese* all mean fleshy; but *portly* connotes dignity; *corpulent,* bulk; and *obese,* an unpleasant excess of fat. [< Med.L *connotare* < L *com-* with + *notare* to note]

con·nu·bi·al (kə nyü′bē əl *or* kə nü′bē əl) *adj.* of or having to do with marriage. [< L *connubialis* < *connubium* marriage < *com-* (intensive) + *nubere* marry] —**con·nu′bi·al·ly,** *adv.*

co·noid (kō′noid) *adj., n.* —*adj.* shaped like a cone. —*n.* **1** *Geometry.* a surface formed by the revolution of a conic section about its axis. **2** something shaped like a cone, such as a bullet. [< Gk. *kōnoeidēs* < *kōnos* cone + *eidos* form]

co·noi·dal (kə noi′dəl) *adj.* conoid.

con·quer (kong′kər) *v.* **1** get by fighting; win in war: *to conquer a country.* **2** overcome by force; defeat; get the better of: *to conquer an enemy, to conquer a bad habit.* **3** be victorious; be the conqueror: *The general said he would conquer or die.* [ME < OF *conquerre* < L *conquaerere* < *com-* (intensive) + *quaerere* seek] —**con′quer·a·ble,** *adj.*
☛ *Syn.* See note at **defeat.**

con·quer·or (kong′kər ər) *n.* **1** a person who conquers, especially in war. **2 the Conqueror,** King William I of England. As Duke of Normandy, he conquered England in 1066, and reigned as king till his death in 1087.

con·quest (kon′kwest *or* kong′kwest) *n.* **1** the act of conquering. **2** the thing conquered; land, people, etc. conquered. **3** a person whose love or favor has been won. **4 the Conquest, a** the conquering of the English throne by William, Duke of Normandy, in 1066. **b** *Cdn.* the British takeover of French possessions in North America with the signing of the Treaty of Paris in 1763. [ME < OF *conqueste* < *conquest,* pp. of *conquerre.* See CONQUER.]
☛ *Syn.* **1.** See note at **victory.**

con·quis·ta·dor (kon kwis′tə dôr′ *or* kon kis′tə dôr′) *n., pl.* **-dors** *or* **-dores. 1** one of the Spanish conquerors who came to South America and the southern parts of North America in the 16th century to look for gold. The conquistadors conquered the Indian civilizations of Mexico and South America in their search for treasure. **2** any conqueror. [< Sp. *conquistador* < *conquistar* conquer]

con·san·guin·e·ous (kon′sang gwin′ē əs) *adj.* descended from the same parent or ancestor; related by blood. [< L *consanguineus* < *com-* together + *sanguis, -guinis* blood] —**con′san·guin′e·ous·ly,** *adv.*

con·san·guin·i·ty (kon′sang gwin′ə tē) *n.* **1** relationship by descent from the same parent or ancestor; relationship by blood:

Brothers and cousins are united by ties of consanguinity. **2** any close relationship or connection.

con·science (kon'shəns) *n.* **1** the sense or awareness of moral right and wrong with respect to one's own conduct or intentions, including the feeling that one ought to do what is right: *Her conscience prompted her to return the book she had stolen.* **2** obedience to the dictates of conscience: *A person of conscience would not have acted in that way.*
in all conscience, **a** reasonably; fairly. **b** surely; certainly.
on (one's) **conscience,** troubling one's conscience; making one feel guilty: *Her theft of the book had been on her conscience for a long time.* [ME < OF < L *conscientia* < *conscire* < *com-* with + *scire* know] —**con'science·less,** *adj.*

conscience money money paid voluntarily by a person whose conscience bothers him because of some dishonest act or a feeling of moral responsibility for an accident, etc.

con·science–strick·en (kon'shəns strik'ən) *adj.* suffering from a feeling of having done wrong.

con·sci·en·tious (kon'shē en'shəs) *adj.* **1** careful to do what one knows is right; controlled by conscience. **2** done carefully and properly: *Conscientious work is careful and exact.* —**con'sci·en'tious·ly,** *adv.* —**con'sci·en'tious·ness,** *n.*

conscientious objector a person whose beliefs do not let him act as a combatant in time of war.

con·scion·a·ble (kon'shən ə bəl) *adj.* according to conscience; just. —**con'scion·a·bly,** *adv.*

con·scious (kon'shəs) *adj.* **1** aware; knowing: *conscious of a sharp pain.* **2** capable of thought, will, or feeling; mentally awake: *Man is a conscious animal. After about five minutes he became conscious again.* **3** known to oneself; felt: *conscious guilt.* **4** meant; intended; deliberate: *a conscious lie. She's making a conscious effort to improve her writing.* **5** self-conscious. **6** aware of or concerned with (*used in compounds*): *clothes-conscious.* [< L *conscius* < *conscire* < *com-* (intensive) + *scire* know] —**con'scious·ly,** *adv.*
☛ *Syn.* **1. Conscious, aware** = knowing that something exists. **Conscious** emphasizes the idea of realizing or knowing in one's mind that one sees, feels, hears, etc. something either physically or emotionally: *He was conscious of a great uneasiness.* **Aware** emphasizes the idea of noticing something one sees, smells, hears, tastes, feels, or is told: *I was aware that someone was talking, but not conscious of what was being said.*

con·scious·ness (kon'shəs nis) *n.* **1** the state of being conscious; awareness. People and animals have consciousness; plants and stones do not. **2** all the thoughts and feelings of a person or group of people: *the moral consciousness of our generation.* **3** awareness of what is going on about one: *A severe shock often makes a person lose consciousness for a time.* **4** *Philosophy.* the power of the mind, whether rational or not, to be aware of acts, sensations, emotions, etc. **5** *Psychology.* the mental activity of which the individual is aware, in contrast to unconscious mental activity.

con·script (*v.* kən skript'; *adj. and n.* kon'skript) *v., adj., n.* —*v.* **1** compel by law to enlist in the armed forces; draft. **2** take for government use: *The dictator proposed to conscript both capital and labor.* —*adj.* conscripted; drafted. —*n.* a person who has been conscripted into the armed forces. [< L *conscriptus,* pp. of *conscribere* < *com-* (intensive) + *scribere* write]

conscript fathers (kon'skript) **1** in ancient Rome, the senators. **2** the senators or legislators of any nation.

con·scrip·tion (kən skrip'shən) *n.* **1** the compulsory enlistment of people in the armed forces; draft. **2** the act or system of forcing contributions of money, labor, or other service to the government or as the government directs.

con·se·crate (kon'sə krāt') *v.* **-crat·ed, -crat·ing;** *adj.* —*v.* **1** set apart as sacred; make holy: *A church is consecrated to God.* **2** make an object of veneration or cherished regard; hallow: *Time has consecrated these customs.* **3** devote to a purpose; dedicate: *He has consecrated his life to music.* —*adj.* Archaic. consecrated. [< L *consecrare* < *com-* (intensive) + *sacer* sacred] —**con'se·cra'tor,** *n.*
☛ *Syn. v.* **3.** See note at **devote.**

con·se·crat·ed (kon'sə krāt'id) *adj.* set apart as sacred; made holy.

con·se·cra·tion (kon'sə krā'shən) *n.* **1** the act of consecrating or the condition of being consecrated. **2** an ordination to a sacred office, especially to that of bishop.

con·sec·u·tive (kən sek'yə tiv) *adj.* **1** following without interruption; successive: *Monday, Tuesday, and Wednesday are consecutive days.* **2** characterized by logical order; proceeding from

one part to another in logical sequence: *consecutive reasoning.* **3** *Music.* of or designating intervals of the same kind: *consecutive thirds, fifths, octaves, etc.* [< F *consécutif* < L *consecutivus* < *consecutus* following closely, pp. of *consequi* < *com-* (intensive) + *sequi* follow] —**con·sec'u·tive·ly,** *adv.* —**con·sec'u·tive·ness,** *n.*
☛ *Syn.* **1.** See note at **successive.**

con·sen·sus (kən sen'səs) *n.* general agreement. The consensus of opinion means the opinion of all or most of the people consulted. [< L *consensus* < *consentire.* See CONSENT.]

con·sent (kən sent') *v.* —*v.* agree; give approval or permission: *My father would not consent to my leaving school.* —*n.* agreement; approval; permission. [ME < OF *consentir* < L *consentire* < *com-* together + *sentire* feel, think]
☛ *Syn. v.* **Consent, assent, concur** = agree. **Consent** = agree *to* something asked for, by giving approval willingly or by giving in to the wishes of others: *He consented to run for president.* **Assent** = agree *with,* think along with, something stated or put forward for consideration, by accepting it or expressing agreement: *He assented to the suggested change in plans.* **Concur** = agree *with* others, by having the same opinion: *The majority concurred in the decision to raise the dues.*

con·se·quence (kon'sə kwens *or* kon'sə kwəns) *n.* **1** a result of some previous action or occurrence; effect: *The consequence of breaking his leg was the loss of his job.* **2** a logical result; deduction; inference. **3** importance: *This matter is of little consequence.* **4** importance in rank or position: *She is a person of consequence in the community.*
in consequence (of), as a result (of).
take the consequences, accept any undesirable results of one's actions: *Do it your way if you like, but you'll have to take the consequences if it doesn't work out.*
☛ *Syn.* **1.** See note at **effect. 3.** See note at **importance.**

con·se·quent (kon'sə kwent *or* kon'sə kwənt) *adj., n.* —*adj.* **1** following as a natural result or effect; resulting: *His illness and consequent absence put him behind in his work.* **2** following logical sequence; logically consistent: *the consequent development of an idea.* **3** logically consistent. —*n.* **1** anything that follows something else; result; effect. **2** *Mathematics.* the second term of a ratio. In the ratio 1:4, 4 is the consequent, and 1 the antecedent. **3** *Logic.* the second term, or conclusion, of a conditional proposition. [< L *consequens, -entis,* ppr. of *consequi.* See CONSECUTIVE.]

con·se·quen·tial (kon'sə kwen'shəl) *adj.* **1** following as an effect; resulting. **2** self-important; pompous. —**con'se·quen'tial·ly,** *adv.* —**con'se·quen'tial·ness,** *n.*

con·se·quent·ly (kon'sə kwent'lē *or* kon'sə kwənt lē) *adv.* as a result; therefore.
☛ *Syn.* See note at **therefore.**

con·ser·va·tion (kon'sər vā'shən) *n.* **1** a preserving from harm or decay; protecting from loss or from being used up: *the conservation of natural resources.* **2** the official protection and care of forests, rivers, wildlife, etc. **3** a forest, etc. or a part of it, under official protection and care.

conservation energy *Physics.* the principle that the total amount of energy in the universe does not vary, although energy can be changed from one form into another.

con·ser·va·tion·ist (kon'sər vā'shən ist) *n.* a person who believes in and advocates conservation of the forests, rivers, wildlife, etc. of a country.

con·serv·a·tism (kən sėr'və tiz'əm) *n.* **1** an inclination to keep things as they are; opposition to change. **2** Often, **Conservatism,** the principles and practices of a conservative political party.

con·serv·a·tive (kən sėr'və tiv) *adj., n.* —*adj.* **1** inclined to keep things as they are or were in the past; opposed to change. **2** Often, **Conservative, a** of or belonging to a political party that opposes changes in national institutions. **b** of Conservatives or their party. **3** cautious; moderate: *conservative business methods.* **4** free from novelties and fads: *It is economical to choose suits of a conservative style.* **5** having the power to preserve from harm or decay; conserving; preserving. —*n.* **1** a conservative person. **2** Often, **Conservative, a** a member of a conservative political party. **b** in Canada, a member of the Progressive-Conservative Party, one of the principal political groups; a person who supports the views and principles of this party. **c** in Great Britain, a member of the Conservative Party. **3** a means of preserving. —**con·serv'a·tive·ly,** *adv.* —**con·serv'a·tive·ness,** *n.*

Conservative Party **1** in Great Britain, a political party that favors existing national institutions or a return to some of those recently existing. **2** in Canada, the Progressive-Conservative Party.

con·ser·va·toire (kən sėr'və twär') *n.* a school for instruction in music; conservatory. [< F]

con·ser·va·tor (kən sėr'və tər *or* kon'sər vā'tər) *n.* a preserver; guardian.

con·serv·a·to·ry (kən sėr'və tô'rē) *n., pl.* **-ries. 1** a greenhouse

or glass-enclosed room for growing and displaying plants. **2** a school for instruction in music.

con·serve (*v.* kən sėrv′; *n.* kon′sėrv *or* kən sėrv′) *v.* **-served, -serv·ing;** *n.* —*v.* **1** keep from harm or decay; protect from loss or from being used up. **2** preserve (fruit) with sugar. —*n.* Often, **conserves,** *pl.* preserves or jam, especially when made from a mixture of different fruits. [ME < OF *conserve, conserver* < L *conservare* < *com-* (intensive) + *servare* preserve] —**con·serv′a·ble,** *adj.* —**con·serv′er,** *n.*

con·sid·er (kən sid′ər) *v.* **1** think about in order to decide: *Take time to consider the problem.* **2** think to be; think of as: *We consider E.J. Pratt a great Canadian poet.* **3** allow for; take into account: *This watch runs very well, if you consider how old it is.* **4** be thoughtful of (others and their feelings). **5** think carefully; reflect: *He considered for a while before answering.* **6** *Archaic.* look at carefully. [< L *considerare,* originally, examine the stars < *com-* (intensive) + *sidus* star; with reference to augury]
☛ *Syn.* **1. Consider, study, weigh** = think about something in order to decide. **Consider** = think something over, to give it some careful thought before making a decision about it: *He considered going to college.* **Study** = think out, to consider with serious attention to details: *He studied ways to support himself.* **Weigh** = balance in the mind, to consider carefully both or all sides of an idea or action: *He weighed the idea of going to the local junior college.*

con·sid·er·a·ble (kən sid′ər ə bəl *or* kən sid′rə bəl) *adj., n.* —*adj.* **1** rather large in amount, extent, number, etc.: *a considerable sum of money. She has considerable influence in political circles.* **2** worthy of regard; important: *the most considerable poet of the age.* —*n. Dialect or informal.* a large quantity or amount.
☛ *Usage.* **Considerable, considerably.** In formal and informal writing, it is important to distinguish between the adverb **considerably** and the adjective **considerable:** *The teacher's explanation helped them considerably* (modifies verb *helped*). *The teacher's explanation was of considerable help to them* (modifies noun *help*).

con·sid·er·a·bly (kən sid′ər ə blē *or* kən sid′rə blē) *adv.* a good deal; much.
☛ *Usage.* See note at **considerable.**

con·sid·er·ate (kən sid′ər it *or* kən sid′rit) *adj.* thoughtful of others and their feelings. —**con·sid′er·ate·ly,** *adv.* —**con·sid′er·ate·ness,** *n.*
☛ *Syn.* See note at **thoughtful.**

con·sid·er·a·tion (kən sid′ər ā′shən) *n.* **1** careful thought about something before making a decision: *Please give careful consideration to this question.* **2** something thought of as a reason; something to be considered: *Price and quality are two important considerations in buying anything.* **3** money or other payment: *He said he would cut the grass for a small consideration.* **4** thoughtfulness for others and their feelings. **5** importance.
in consideration of, a because of: *In consideration of his wife's poor health, he moved to a milder climate.* **b** in return for: *She gave him a present in consideration of his helpfulness.*
on no consideration, not at all; never.
take into consideration, allow for; take into account; consider: *The judge took the boy's age into consideration.*

con·sid·ered (kən sid′ərd) *adj.* **1** carefully thought out: *in my considered opinion.* **2** honored; respected: *He is highly considered as a poet.*

con·sid·er·ing (kən sid′ər ing *or* kən sid′ring) *prep., adv.* —*prep.* taking into account; making allowance for: *Considering her age, she reads well.* —*adv.* taking everything into account: *He does very well, considering.*

con·sign (kən sīn′) *v.* **1** hand over; deliver: *The man was consigned to prison. The father consigned the child to his sister's care.* **2** transmit; send: *The order will be consigned to them by express.* **3** set apart; assign. [< F *consigner* < L *consignare* furnish with a seal < *com-* with + *signum* seal] —**con·sign′a·ble,** *adj.*
☛ *Syn.* **1.** See note at **commit.**

con·sign·ee (kon′sī nē′) *n.* the person or company to whom goods are consigned.

con·sign·er (kən sīn′ər) *n.* consignor.

con·sign·ment (kən sīn′mənt) *n.* **1** the act of consigning. **2** a shipment sent to a person or company for safekeeping or sale.
on consignment, of goods, sent to a retailer under an arrangement by which the retailer does not pay the distributor until the goods have been sold.

con·sign·or (kən sīn′ər *or* kon′sī nôr′) *n.* a person or company who consigns goods to another.

con·sist (kən sist′) *v.* **1** be made up; be formed: *A week consists of seven days.* **2** agree; be in harmony.
consist in, have a basis in or be made up of: *Happiness for him consists in being left alone.*
[< L *consistere* come to a stand, exist, consist < *com-* together + *sistere* stand]

con·sist·ence (kən sis′təns) *n.* consistency.

con·sist·en·cy (kən sis′tən sē) *n., pl.* **-cies. 1** holding together; firmness or density. **2** degree of firmness or density: *Icing for a*

hat, āge, fär; let, ēqual, tèrm; it, īce
hot, ōpen, ôrder; oil, out; cup, pút, rüle,
əbove, takən, pencəl, lemən, circəs
ch, child; ng, long; sh, ship
th, thin; ŦH, then; zh, measure

cake must be of the right consistency to spread easily without dripping. **3** keeping to a single set of principles, course of action, etc.: *He was much admired for his consistency of purpose.* **4** harmony; agreement; accordance: *It's not always easy to maintain consistency between principles and practice.*

con·sist·ent (kən sis′tənt) *adj.* **1** keeping or inclined to keep to the same principles, course of action, etc.: *What a consistent person says or does today agrees with what he said or did yesterday.* **2** in agreement; in accord; compatible: *Driving an automobile at very high speed is not consistent with safety. So much noise is not consistent with comfort.* —**con·sist′ent·ly,** *adv.*

con·sis·to·ry (kən sis′tə rē) *n., pl.* **-ries. 1** a church council or court, especially one composed of the Pope and cardinals; the College of Cardinals. **2** a meeting of such a council or court. **3** the place where it meets. [< ONF *consistorie* < L *consistorium* place of assembly < *consistere.* See CONSIST.]

con·so·la·tion (kon′sə lā′shən) *n.* **1** comfort. **2** a comforting person, thing, or event.

consolation prize a prize given to a person or team that has not won but has done well.

con·sol·a·to·ry (kən sol′ə tô′rē) *adj.* consoling; comforting.

con·sole[1] (kən sōl′) *v.* **-soled, -sol·ing.** comfort. [< L *consolari* < *com-* (intensive) + *solari* soothe] **con·sol′a·ble,** *adj.* —**con·sol′er,** *n.*
☛ *Syn.* See note at **comfort.**

con·sole[2] (kon′sōl) *n.* **1** the desklike part of an organ, containing the keyboard, stops, and pedals. **2** a cabinet for a television set, record player, or radio made to stand on the floor. **3** a panel of buttons, switches, dials, etc. used to control electrical or other apparatus; control panel. **4** *Architecture.* a heavy, ornamental bracket. [< F]

console table (kon′sōl) **1** a table supported against a wall by one or more consoles, or brackets. **2** any narrow table designed to be placed against a wall, often having curved or carved legs at the front, that resemble consoles.

con·sol·i·date (kən sol′ə dāt′) *v.* **-dat·ed, -dat·ing. 1** unite; combine; merge: *The two territories were consolidated by the government into one administrative district.* **2** make secure; strengthen: *to consolidate an empire. The army spent a day in consolidating its gains by digging trenches.* **3** make or become solid. [< L *consolidare* < *com-* (intensive) + *solidus* solid]

con·sol·i·dat·ed (kən sol′ə dāt′id) *adj.* united; combined.

Consolidated Revenue Fund *Cdn.* the pooled income of the Federal Government.

consolidated school a school for pupils from several school districts; a school built to replace two or more smaller ones, especially in country districts, so as to provide a greater range of facilities.

con·sol·i·da·tion (kən sol′ə dā′shən) *n.* consolidating or being consolidated.

con·sol·ing (kən sōl′ing) *adj.* that consoles. —**con·sol′ing·ly,** *adv.*

con·sols (kon′solz *or* kən solz′) *n.pl.* bonds of the government of Great Britain. [short for *consolidated annuities*]

con·som·mé (kon′sə mā′) *n.* a clear soup made by boiling meat with seasoning and, sometimes, vegetables in water. [< F *consommé,* pp. of *consommer* < L *consummare* finish. See CONSUMMATE.]

con·so·nance (kon′sə nəns) *n.* **1** harmony; agreement; accordance. **2** *Music.* harmony of sounds; a simultaneous combination of tones that is agreeable to the ear. Compare **dissonance. 3** a partial rhyme in which the consonant sounds are alike but the vowels are different. *Examples: lame/loam, seed/side.*

con·so·nan·cy (kon′sə nən sē) *n.* consonance.

con·so·nant (kon′sə nənt) *n., adj.* —*n.* **1** a speech sound formed by completely or partially blocking the breath. All languages have both consonants and vowels. The first and last sounds in *tab* are consonants. **2** any letter of the alphabet that is not a vowel. —*adj.* **1** harmonious; in agreement; in accord. **2** *Music.* characterized by consonance; agreeing in sound. **3** consonantal. [< L *consonans, -antis,* ppr. of *consonare* < *com-* together + *sonare* sound] —**con′so·nant·ly,** *adv.*

con·so·nan·tal (kon′sə nan′təl) *adj.* having to do with a consonant or its sound.

con·sort (*n.* kon′sôrt; *v.* kən sôrt′) *n.*, *v.* —*n.* **1** a husband or wife, especially of a monarch. **2** an associate. **3** a ship accompanying another; an escort vessel.
—*v.* **1** keep company; associate: *Do not consort with thieves.* **2** agree; accord. [< MF < L *consors, -ortis* sharer < *com-* with + *sors* lot]

con·sor·ti·um (kən sôr′shē əm *or* kən sôr′tē əm) *n.*, *pl.* **-ti·a** (-shē ə). **1** a partnership; association. **2** an agreement among bankers of several nations to give financial aid to another nation. **3** a group, association, etc. formed by such an agreement. [< L *consortium* partnership]

con·spec·tus (kən spek′təs) *n.* **1** a general or comprehensive view. **2** a short summary or outline of a subject; digest; résumé. [< L *conspectus* < *com-* + *specere* look at]

con·spic·u·ous (kən spik′yü əs) *adj.* **1** easily seen; obvious or showy: *A traffic sign should be conspicuous.* **2** attracting attention; striking or remarkable: *conspicuous gallantry, a conspicuous lack of tact.* [< L *conspicuus* visible < *conspicere* < *com-* (intensive) + *specere* look at] —**con·spic′u·ous·ly,** *adv.* —**con·spic′u·ous·ness,** *n.*
☛ *Syn.* **1.** See note at **prominent.**

con·spir·a·cy (kən spir′ə sē) *n.*, *pl.* **-cies. 1** a secret scheming or planning together to do something treacherous or evil. **2** the plot or scheme itself: *The conspiracy was revealed as a result of a neighbor's complaint.* **3** *Law.* an agreement between two or more persons to commit an illegal act: *The four contractors were charged with conspiracy to commit fraud.* **4** a happening or acting together as if by evil design: *It was a conspiracy of the elements to ruin our camping trip.*

con·spir·a·tor (kən spir′ə tər) *n.* a person who conspires; plotter: *A group of conspirators planned to kill the dictator.*

con·spir·a·to·ri·al (kən spir′ə tôr′ē əl) *adj.* having to do with conspiracy or conspirators.

con·spire (kən spīr′) *v.* **-spired, -spir·ing. 1** plan secretly with others to do something wrong; plot. **2** act together; as if by design: *The rain, the cold, and the mosquitoes conspired to ruin the concert in the park. All things conspired to make her birthday a happy one.* [ME < OF *conspirer* < L *conspirare* < *com-* together + *spirare* breathe] —**con·spir′er,** *n.*
☛ *Syn.* **1.** See note at **plot.**

const. *Mathematics.* constant.

Const. Constable.

con·sta·ble (kon′stə bəl) *n.* **1** a police officer, especially a police officer of the lowest rank. **2** especially in medieval England and France, the chief officer of a royal household. **3** the keeper of a royal fortress or castle. [ME < OF *conestable* < LL *comes stabuli* count of the stable; later, chief household officer]

con·stab·u·lar·y (kən stab′yə ler′ē) *n.*, *pl.* **-lar·ies;** *adj.* —*n.* **1** the constables of a district. **2** a police force organized like an army; provincial police. —*adj.* of the constables of a district; of police officers, or a police force.

con·stan·cy (kon′stən sē) *n.* **1** the condition of being always the same; absence of change. **2** firmness in belief or feeling; faithfulness; loyalty.

con·stant (kon′stənt) *adj.*, *n.* —*adj.* **1** always the same; not changing: *If you walk due north, your direction is constant.* **2** never stopping; incessant; continuous or continual: *three days of constant rain, a constant smoker. The clock makes a constant ticking sound.* **3** faithful; loyal; steadfast: *A constant friend helps you when you are in trouble.* **4** *Mathematics and physics.* retaining the same value; remaining the same in quantity, size, etc.: *a constant force.* —*n.* **1** something that is always the same; a number or quantity that does not change. **2** *Mathematics.* a quantity assumed to be invariable throughout a given calculation or discussion. **3** *Physics.* a numerical quantity expressing a relation or value, as of a physical property of a substance, that remains unchanged under certain conditions. [ME < OF < L *constans, -antis,* ppr. of *constare* stand firm < *com-* (intensive) + *stare* stand] —**con′stant·ly,** *adv.*
☛ *Syn. adj.* **5.** See note at **faithful.**

con·stel·la·tion (kon′stə lā′shən) *n.* **1** *Astronomy.* **a** any of the 88 recognized groups of stars traditionally thought of as forming outlines of animals, objects, or persons: *The Big Dipper is in the constellation Ursa Major.* **b** the part of the heavens occupied by such a group. **2** a brilliant gathering: *There was a constellation of ministers and ambassadors at the reception.* [< LL *constellatio, -onis* < L *com-* together + *stella* star]

con·ster·na·tion (kon′stər nā′shən) *n.* great dismay; paralysing terror: *To our consternation the train rushed on toward the burning bridge.* [< L *consternatio, -onis* < *consternare* terrify, var. of

consternere lay low < *com-* (intensive) + *sternere* strew]
☛ *Syn.* See note at **dismay.**

con·sti·pate (kon′stə pāt′) *v.* **-pat·ed, -pat·ing.** cause constipation in. [< L *constipare* < *com-* together + *stipare* press. Doublet of COSTIVE.]

con·sti·pat·ed (kon′stə pāt′id) *adj.* suffering from constipation.

con·sti·pa·tion (kon′stə pā′shən) *n.* a condition in which the bowels are sluggish or inactive, so that it is difficult or imposible to discharge waste matter from the body.

con·stit·u·en·cy (kən stich′ü ən sē) *n.*, *pl.* **-cies. 1** a district represented by a single member in a legislature. Each federal constituency, or riding, in Canada is represented by a member of parliament. **2** the body of voters in such a district. **3** the people who support or are served by a business, institution, etc.

con·stit·u·ent (kən stich′ü ənt) *adj.*, *n.* —*adj.* **1** forming a necessary part; necessary in the composition; composing: *Flour, liquid, salt, and yeast are constituent parts of bread.* **2** appointing; electing. **3** having the power to make or change a political constitution: *a constituent assembly.* —*n.* **1** a necessary part of a whole; ingredients; component. **2** a person who has the right to vote or appoint; a voter in a constituency: *Many of the MP's constituents protested his stand on the issue.* [< L *constituens, -entis,* ppr. of *constituere.* See CONSTITUTE.]

con·sti·tute (kon′stə tyüt′ *or* kon′stə tüt′) *v.* **-tut·ed, -tut·ing. 1** make up; form: *Seven days constitute a week. Hailstorms constitute a serious threat to standing crops.* **2** appoint; elect: *Mr. Chang was constituted president of the Home and School Association.* **3** set up; found; establish: *Our association has been constituted as a social and recreational organization.* **4** make by combining parts; frame: *The cabin is well constituted and will withstand the severest weather.* **5** give legal form to: *to constitute a lease.* [< L *constitutus,* pp. of *constituere* < *com-* (intensive) + *statuere* set up] —**con′sti·tu·tor,** *n.*

con·sti·tu·tion (kon′stə tyü′shən *or* kon′stə tü′shən) *n.* **1** a person's physical or mental nature or make-up: *A person with a good constitution is strong and healthy.* **2** the way in which anything is organized; structure: *The constitution of the world is the arrangement of all the things in it.* **3** the system of fundamental principles according to which a nation, state, or group is governed: *Our club has a written constitution.* **4** a document stating these principles. **5** an appointing; making. **6** a setting up; establishment. **7** a law; decree.

con·sti·tu·tion·al (kon′stə tyü′shən əl *or* kon′stə tü′shən əl) *adj.*, *n.* —*adj.* **1** of or in the constitution of a person or thing: *A constitutional weakness makes him subject to colds.* **2** of, in, or according to the constitution of a nation, state, or group: *Some lawyers are experts in constitutional law.* **3** for one's health. —*n. Informal.* a walk or other exercise taken for one's health. —**con·sti·tu′tion·al·ly,** *adv.*

con·sti·tu·tion·al·i·ty (kon′stə tyü′shən al′ə tē *or* kon′stə tü′shən al′ə tē) *n.* accordance with the constitution of a nation, state, or group: *The constitutionality of the new law was disputed.*

constitutional monarchy a monarchy in which the ruler has only the powers given to him by the constitution and laws of the nation.

con·sti·tu·tive (kon′stə tyü′tiv *or* kon′stə tü′tiv) *adj.* having power to establish or enact; making a thing what it is; formative; constituent; essential. —**con′sti·tu′tive·ly,** *adv.*

con·strain (kən strān′) *v.* **1** force or compel physically or by moral means: *He was constrained to accept his employer's decision or leave his job.* **2** confine; imprison. **3** repress; restrain. [ME < OF *constreindre* < L *constringere* < *com-* together + *stringere* pull tightly] —**con·strain′er,** *n.*

con·strained (kən strānd′) *adj.* **1** forced and stiff; unnatural: *a constrained smile.* **2** pt. and pp. of **constrain.**

con·straint (kən strānt′) *n.* **1** confinement. **2** restraint. **3** a holding back of natural feelings; forced or unnatural manner; embarrassed awkwardness. **4** force; compulsion. [ME < OF *constreinte,* fem. pp. of *constreindre.* See CONSTRAIN.]

con·strict (kən strikt′) *v.* draw together; contract; compress: *A tourniquet stops the flow of blood by constricting the blood vessels.* [< L *constrictus,* pp. of *constringere.* See CONSTRAIN.]

con·stric·tion (kən strik′shən) *n.* **1** the act of drawing together; contraction; compression. **2** a feeling of tightness: *He coughed and complained of a constriction in his chest.* **3** a constricted part. **4** something that constricts.

con·stric·tive (kən strik′tiv) *adj.* drawing together; contracting; compressing. —**con·stric′tive·ly,** *adv.*

con·stric·tor (kən strik′tər) *n.* **1** any snake, such as a boa or python, that kills its prey by squeezing it with its coils. **2** *Anatomy.* a muscle that constricts some part of the body.

con·struct (*v.* kən strukt′; *n.* kon′strukt) *v.*, *n.* —*v.* **1** put

together; build. 2 *Mathematics.* draw (a geometrical figure) so as to fulfil given conditions. —*n.* something systematically put together or constructed. [< L *constructus,* pp. of *construere* < *com-* together + *struere* pile]

☛ *Syn.* 1. See note at **make.**

con·struc·tion (kən struk′shən) *n.* 1 the act of constructing, building, or putting together. 2 the way in which a thing is constructed. 3 the thing constructed; building. 4 a meaning; explanation; interpretation: *He put an unfair construction on what she said.* 5 *Grammar.* **a** the arrangement, connection, or relation of words in a sentence, clause, phrase, etc. **b** any meaningful sequence or grouping.

con·struc·tion·al (kən struk′shən əl) *adj.* having to do with construction; structural.

con·struc·tion·ist (kən struk′shən ist) *n.* a person who gives a certain interpretation to laws, a constitution, etc.: *a strict constructionist.*

con·struc·tive (kən struk′tiv) *adj.* 1 building up so as to improve; helpful: *People appreciate constructive suggestions, not destructive criticisms.* 2 having to do with construction; structural. 3 *Law.* not done or expressed directly but inferred or construed as such: *constructive fraud.* —**con·struc′tive·ly,** *adv.* —**con·struc′tive·ness,** *n.*

con·struc·tiv·ism (kən struk′tə viz′əm) *n.* an art movement originating in the Soviet Union in the 1920's, characterized by the abstract arrangement of planes and masses, using materials such as glass and plastic.

con·struc·tiv·ist (kən struk′tə vist′) *n., adj.* —*n.* an artist who follows the principles of constructivism. —*adj.* of or having to do with constructivism or constructivists.

con·struc·tor (kən struk′tər) *n.* a person who constructs; builder.

con·strue (kən strü′) *v.* -strued, -stru·ing. 1 show the meaning of; explain; interpret: *Different lawyers may construe the same law differently.* 2 put a particular interpretation on: *His inability to hold a job can only be construed as indifference.* 3 translate. 4 *Grammar.* analyse the arrangement of words in (a sentence, clause, phrase, etc.). [< L *construere.* See CONSTRUCT.] —**con·stru′a·ble,** *adj.*

con·sue·tude (kon′swə tyüd′ *or* kon′swə tüd′) *n.* custom, especially one considered as having the force of law. [ME < L *consuetudo* for *consuescere* to accustom]

con·sul (kon′səl) *n.* 1 an official appointed by the government of a country to look after its business interests in a foreign city and also to assist citizens of his country living there. 2 in ancient Rome, either of the two chief magistrates of the republic. 3 any of the three chief magistrates of the First Republic of France (1799-1804). [< L *consul,* probably originally, one who consults the senate]

con·su·lar (kon′sə lər *or* kon′syə lər) *adj.* 1 of or belonging to a consul. 2 serving as a consul; having the duties of a consul.

con·su·late (kon′sə lit *or* kon′syə lit) *n.* 1 the official residence or offices of a consul. 2 the duties, authority, and position of a consul. 3 a consul's term of office. 4 government by consuls: *France was governed by a consulate from 1799 to 1804.*

consul general *pl.* **consuls general.** a consul of the highest rank. He is stationed at an important place or has authority over several other consuls.

con·sul·ship (kon′səl ship′) *n.* 1 the duties, authority, and position of a consul. 2 a consul's term of office.

con·sult (kən sult′) *v.* 1 seek information or advice from; refer to: *Consult a dictionary for the meaning of a word.* 2 exchange ideas; talk things over: *He is consulting with his lawyer.* 3 take into consideration; have regard for: *A good ruler consults the interests and feelings of his people.* [< L *consultare* < *consulere* take counsel, consult]

☛ *Syn.* 2. **Consult, confer** = talk something over with someone in order to make a decision. **Consult** = talk over something of importance with another or others who are in a position to give wise advice: *He decided to consult with his attorney before buying the property.* **Confer** = exchange ideas, opinions, or information with another, usually as equals: *The manager conferred with the committee of employees.*

con·sul·tan·cy (kən sul′tən sē) *n.* consultation, especially the work done by a professional consultant.

con·sult·ant (kən sul′tənt) *n.* 1 a person who consults another. 2 a person who gives professional or technical advice: *a medical consultant.*

con·sul·ta·tion (kon′səl tā′shən) *n.* 1 the act of consulting; act of seeking information or advice. 2 a meeting to exchange ideas or talk things over.

con·sult·a·tive (kən sul′tə tiv) *adj.* having to do with consultation; advisory.

con·sult·ing (kən sul′ting) *adj.* 1 that consults or asks advice. 2 employed in giving professional advice.

con·sum·a·ble (kən süm′ə bəl *or* kən syüm′ə bəl) *adj., n.* —*adj.*

hat, āge, fär; let, ēqual, tèrm; it, īce
hot, ōpen, ôrder; oil, out; cup, pùt, rüle,
əbove, takən, pencəl, lemən, circəs

ch, child; ng, long; sh, ship
th, thin; ᴛʜ, then; zh, measure

intended to be used up: *consumable supplies.* —*n.* an article that is intended to be used up: *Government offices have been told to cut expenditures on paper, pencils, and other consumables.*

con·sume (kən süm′ *or* kən syüm′) *v.* -sumed, -sum·ing. 1 eat or drink up. 2 destroy; burn up. 3 use up; spend: *A student consumes much of his time in studying.* 4 waste away; be destroyed. 5 waste (time, money, etc.).
consumed with, absorbed by: *consumed with envy.* [ME < L *consumere* < *com-* (intensive) + *sumere* take up] —**con·sum′a·ble,** *adj.*

con·sum·ed·ly (kən sü′mid lē *or* kən syü′mid lē) *adv.* very much; too much.

con·sum·er (kən sü′mər *or* kən syü′mər) *n.* 1 a person who buys and uses food, clothing, or anything grown or made by producers. 2 a person or thing that uses up, makes away with, or destroys.

consumer goods *Economics.* goods that people use or consume to satisfy their wants: *Food and clothing are two kinds of consumer goods.* Compare **capital goods.**

con·sum·er·ism (kən sü′mər iz′əm *or* kən syü′mər iz′əm) *n.* 1 support for the rights of the consumer. 2 the theory that a continued increase in the consumption of goods is economically desirable for a society.

con·sum·er·ist (kən sü′mər ist *or* kən syü′mər ist) *n.* a person who supports or practises consumerism.

consumer price index a measure of the change in the cost of living relative to a particular period in the past, represented as a percentage increase over or decrease from the cost of selected goods in the base period.

con·sum·mate (*v.* kon′sə māt′; *adj.* kən sum′it *or* kon′sù mit) *v.* -mat·ed, -mat·ing; *adj.* —*v.* 1 complete; fulfil: *His ambition was consummated when he won the first prize.* 2 complete (marriage) by sexual intercourse. —*adj.* 1 complete; perfect; in the highest degree: *The paintings of great artists show consummate skill.* 2 accomplished; supremely qualified: *a consummate artist.* [< L *consummare* bring to a peak < *com-* (intensive) + *summa* highest degree] —**con·sum′mate·ly,** *adv.*

con·sum·ma·tion (kon′sə mā′shən) *n.* a completion; fulfilment.

con·sump·tion (kən sump′shən) *n.* 1 the act of using or using up: *We took along some food for consumption on our trip.* The science of economics deals with the production, distribution, and consumption of wealth.* 2 the amount used up: *Our hydro consumption was up again last month.* 3 a wasting disease of the lungs or of some other part of the body; tuberculosis of the lungs. [< L *consumptio, -onis* < *consumere.* See CONSUME.]

con·sump·tive (kən sump′tiv) *adj.* —*adj.* 1 having or likely to have tuberculosis of the lungs. 2 of tuberculosis of the lungs. 3 tending to consume; destructive; wasteful. —*n.* a person who has tuberculosis of the lungs. —**con·sump′tive·ly,** *adv.* —**con·sump′tive·ness,** *n.*

cont. 1 continue; continued. 2 continent; continental. 3 contents; containing.

Cont. Continental.

con·tact (kon′takt) *n., adj., v.* —*n.* 1 the condition of touching; touching together: *This insecticide should not come in contact with the skin. When two balls are in contact, one can be moved by touching the other.* 2 the state of being in communication; connection; association: *He has kept in contact with his school friends. The control tower lost contact with the pilot.* 3 a person with whom one can get in touch, especially for business purposes: *She has a useful contact in an advertising agency.* 4 *Electricity.* **a** the connection between two conductors of electricity through which a current passes. **b** a device or component for producing such a connection: *The light went out when the wire broke off at the contact.* 5 *Medicine.* **a** exposure to a contagious disease. **b** a person who has been exposed to a contagious disease. 6 *Geology.* the surface of the boundary between adjacent rocks. 7 **contacts,** *pl. Informal.* contact lenses. —*adj. Aeronautics.* within sight of the ground: *a contact approach.* —*v.* get in touch with; communicate with: *There's been an accident! Contact the doctor immediately!* [< L *contactus* a touching < *contingere* < *com-* with + *tangere* touch]

contact flying flying an aircraft within sight of the ground. In

contact flying, the pilot directs the aircraft by referring to known points or objects on the ground. Compare **instrument flying.**

contact lens a small, thin plastic lens ground to an optical prescription and worn directly over the pupil of the eye to correct defective vision. A contact lens fits the curve of the cornea and floats on a thin layer of tears.

con·ta·gion (kən tā′jən) *n.* **1** the spreading of disease by contact. **2** a disease spread in this way; contagious disease. **3** a means by which disease is spread. **4** the tendency of any influence or emotional or mental state to spread from one person to another: *the contagion of a smile, the contagion of political graft.* **5** a spreading influence or emotional state, especially one that is unpleasant or destructive: *A contagion of fear swept through the crowd and caused a panic.* [< L *contagio, -onis* a touching < *contingere.* See CONTACT.]

con·ta·gious (kən tā′jəs) *adj.* **1** of a disease, communicable by direct contact with a person who has a disease, or with the person's clothing, etc. Compare **infectious. 2** carrying a disease-producing agent; liable to transmit an infectious disease: *He has not completely recovered, but he is no longer contagious.* **3** used for patients with contagious diseases: *the contagious ward in a hospital.* **4** tending to spread rapidly from one person to another; infectious: *Yawning is contagious.* —**con·ta′gious·ly,** *adv.* —**con·ta′gious·ness,** *n.*

con·tain (kən tān′) *v.* **1** have within itself; hold as contents; include: *This purse contains plenty of money.* **2** be capable of holding: *That pitcher contains a litre.* **3** be equal to: *A metre contains 100 centimetres.* **4** control; hold back; restrain: *He contained his anger.* **5** in warfare, control or restrain (enemy forces) by stopping, holding, or surrounding: *The British fleet under Admiral Nelson contained Napoleon's ships at Trafalgar.* **6** *Mathematics.* be exactly divisible by; be divisible by without a remainder: *12 contains 2, 3, 4, and 6.* [ME < OF *contenir* < L *continere* < *com-* together + *tenere* hold] —**con·tain′a·ble,** *adj.*

☛ *Syn.* **1, 2. Contain, hold, accommodate** = have within itself or be capable of having and keeping. **Contain** emphasizes the idea of actually having something within itself as contents or parts: *The house contains five rooms.* **Hold** emphasizes the idea of being capable of taking in and keeping or of having room, but is often used interchangeably with **contain:** *A paper bag won't hold water. My car holds six people.* **Accommodate** = hold comfortably: *Most hotel rooms accommodate two people.*

con·tain·er (kən tān′ər) *n.* **1** a person or thing that contains, especially a box, tin, jar, basket, etc. used to hold something for storage or transport. **2 a** a very large, boxlike, standard-sized receptacle for transporting an assortment of cargo. **b** (*adj.*) of or having to do with the use of such containers: *a container flatcar, a container service.*

con·tain·er·ize (kən tā′nə rīz′) *v.* **-ized, -iz·ing.** pack (cargo) in very large standardized containers. —**con·tain′er·iz·a′tion,** *n.*

con·tain·ment (kən tān′mənt) *n.* **1** the act or process of holding or confining. **2** the confinement of a hostile or potentially hostile force within its existing geographical boundaries. **3** (*adj.*) designating a policy, method, or place of holding or confining: *Containment labs are used in biological research to ensure that micro-organisms used in experiments cannot escape.*

con·tam·i·nant (kən tam′ə nənt) *n.* something that contaminates.

con·tam·i·nate (kən tam′ə nāt) *v.* **-nat·ed, -nat·ing.** make impure by contact; defile; pollute: *Flies can contaminate food.* [< L *contaminare* < *contamen* contamination < *com-* with + *tag-,* root of *tangere* touch] —**con·tam′i·na′tor,** *n.*

con·tam·i·na·tion (kən tam′ə nā′shən) *n.* **1** a contaminating or being contaminated; pollution: *Food should be kept covered to avoid contamination by flies.* **2** anything that contaminates; an impurity.

contd. continued.

con·temn (kən tem′) *v.* view with contempt; despise; scorn. [< L *contemnere* < *com-* (intensive) + *temnere* disdain, originally, cut]

con·tem·plate (kon′təm plāt′) *v.* **-plat·ed, -plat·ing. 1** look at for a long time; gaze at: *to contemplate the evening sky.* **2** think about for a long time; consider thoughtfully: *He contemplated his past life, with its successes and failures.* **3** meditate: *I sometimes like to sit and contemplate.* **4** have in mind; consider; intend: *She contemplated going to Europe after graduation. She is contemplating a change of work.* [< L *contemplari* survey < *com-* with + *templum* restricted area marked off for the taking of auguries]

con·tem·pla·tion (kon′təm plā′shən) *n.* **1** the act of looking at or thinking about something for a long time. **2** deep thought; meditation: *sunk in contemplation.* **3** expectation; intention.

con·tem·pla·tive (kən tem′plə tiv *or* kon′təm plā′tiv) *adj., n.*

—*adj.* **1** thoughtful; meditative. **2** devoted to religious meditation and prayer. —*n.* a person who leads a contemplative life, especially a monk or a nun. —**con′tem·pla′tive·ly,** *adv.*

con·tem·po·ra·ne·i·ty (kən tem′pə rə nē′ə tē) *n.* the quality or state of being contemporaneous.

con·tem·po·ra·ne·ous (kən tem′pə rā′nē əs) *adj.* belonging to the same period of time. [< L *contemporaneus* < *com-* with + *tempus, -poris* time] —**con·tem′po·ra′ne·ous·ly,** *adv.* —**con·tem′po·ra′ne·ous·ness,** *n.*

con·tem·po·rar·y (kən tem′pə rer′ē) *adj., n., pl.* **-rar·ies.** —*adj.* **1** belonging to or living in the same period of time. **2** of or having to do with the present time; current: *contemporary theatre, contemporary attitudes.* **3** of the same age or date. —*n.* **1** a person who belongs to the same period of time as another or others: *Shakespeare and Ben Jonson were contemporaries.* **2** a person, magazine, etc. of the same age or date: *We all tend to seek the society of our contemporaries.* [< *com-* together + L *temporarius* belonging to time < *tempus, -poris* time]

con·tempt (kən tempt′) *n.* **1** the feeling that a person, act, or thing is mean, low, or worthless; scorn; a despising: *We feel contempt for a liar.* **2** the condition of being scorned or despised; disgrace: *A traitor is held in contempt.* **3** *Law.* disobedience to or open disrespect for the rules or decisions of a court, lawmaking body, etc. A person can be put in jail for **contempt of court.** [< L *contemptus* < *contemnere.* See CONTEMN.]

☛ *Syn.* **1.** See note at **scorn.**

con·tempt·i·ble (kən temp′tə bəl) *adj.* deserving contempt or scorn; mean; low; worthless: *a contemptible act.* —**con·tempt′i·ble·ness,** *n.* —**con·tempt′i·bly,** *adv.*

☛ *Usage.* See note at **contemptuous.**

con·temp·tu·ous (kən temp′chü əs) *adj.* showing contempt; scornful: *a contemptuous look.* —**con·temp′tu·ous·ly,** *adv.* —**con·temp′tu·ous·ness,** *n.*

☛ *Usage.* **Contemptuous** and **contemptible** are sometimes confused. The distinction will be clear if one observes that in **contemptible** the suffix **-ible** means deserving.

con·tend (kən tend′) *v.* **1** fight; struggle: *The Arctic explorers had to contend with extreme cold, hunger, and loneliness.* **2** take part in a contest; compete: *Five runners were contending in the first race.* **3** argue; dispute. **4** declare to be a fact; maintain as true: *Columbus contended that the earth was round.* [< L *contendere* < *com-* (intensive) + *tendere* stretch] —**con·tend′er,** *n.*

☛ *Syn.* **2. Contend, compete** = take part in a contest for something. **Contend** emphasizes the idea of trying hard and struggling against opposition: *Our football team is contending with one from the next town for the championship.* **Compete** emphasizes the idea of rivalry and trying hard to win, as well as contending with another: *Only two boys are competing for the cup.*

con·tent¹ (kon′tent) *n.* **1** Usually, **contents,** *pl.* what is contained in anything; all things inside. **2** the facts or ideas stated; what is written in a book or said in a speech: *The content of his speech was good, but the form was not.* **3** the proportion of a certain substance contained in something else: *Cream has a higher fat content than milk.* **4** the power of containing; capacity: *What is the content of the gas tank of this car?* **5** the subject matter or range of any field of study: *the content of our mathematics course.* [< L *contentum,* pp. neut. of *continere.* See CONTAIN.]

con·tent² (kən tent′) *v., adj., n.* —*v.* **1** satisfy the requirement or desires of: *Nothing contents her; she is always complaining.* **2** limit (oneself) to a particular action, etc.: *He contented himself with writing a letter to the editor.* —*adj.* **1** not desiring anything more or anything different than what one has; satisfied: *We'll have to be content with whatever accommodations we get.* **2** willing; ready. —*n.* contentment; satisfaction; ease of mind. **to** (one's) **heart's content,** to one's full satisfaction; as much as one pleases: *When exams are over you'll be able to play tennis to your heart's content.* [< Med.L *contentare* < L *contentus* satisfied, pp. of *continere.* See CONTAIN.]

☛ *Syn. v.* **1.** See note at **satisfy.**

con·tent·ed (kən ten′tid) *adj.* satisfied; pleased; easy in mind: *A contented person is happy with what he has.* —**con·tent′ed·ly,** *adv.* —**con·tent′ed·ness,** *n.*

con·ten·tion (kən ten′shən) *n.* **1** a statement or point that one has argued; statement maintained as true: *Columbus's contention that the earth was round proved to be true.* **2** arguing; disputing; quarrelling: *The main subject of contention was the proposed change in the school curriculum.* **3** an argument or dispute. **4** a struggle; contest. [< L *contentio, -onis* < *contendere.* See CONTEND.]

con·ten·tious (kən ten′shəs) *adj.* **1** quarrelsome; fond of arguing; given to disputing: *A contentious person argues and disputes about trifles.* **2** characterized by contention: *a contentious election campaign.* —**con·ten′tious·ly,** *adv.* —**con·ten′tious·ness,** *n.*

con·tent·ment (kən tent′mənt) *n.* satisfaction; being pleased; ease of mind.

con·ter·mi·nous (kən tèr′mə nəs) *adj.* coterminous.

con·test (*n.* kon′test; *v.* kən test′) *n., v.* —*n.* **1** a game or competition, especially one in which the entries are rated by judges: *a ploughing contest, a baking contest, a contest to find a name for a new park.* **2** a fight or struggle. **3** an argument or dispute. —*v.* **1** try to win. **2** fight or struggle for: *The soldiers contested every spot of ground.* **3** argue against; dispute about: *The lawyer contested the claim and tried to prove that it was false.* **4** take part in a contest. [< F *contester* < L *contestari* call to witness < *com-* (intensive) + *testis* witness] —**con·test′a·ble,** *adj.*

con·test·ant (kən tes′tənt) *n.* a person who contests, especially a person who takes part in a game or competition: *The contestant whose name is selected will win a trip to Paris.*

con·text (kon′tekst) *n.* **1** the spoken or written text in which a particular word or group of words occurs: *It's unfair to judge his statement without knowing the context in which he made it.* **2** the immediate environment; attendant circumstances or conditions; background: *the political context of his speech.* [< L *contextus* < *contexere com-* together + *texere* weave]

con·tex·tu·al (kən teks′chü əl) *adj.* having to do with the context; depending on the context.

con·ti·gu·i·ty (kon′tə gyü′ə tē) *n., pl.* -**ties. 1** nearness: *The contiguity of the house and garage was a convenience in bad weather.* **2** contact. **3** a continuous mass; unbroken stretch.

con·tig·u·ous (kən tig′yü əs) *adj.* **1** in actual contact; touching: *A fence showed where the two farms were contiguous.* **2** adjoining; near. [< L *contiguus* < *com-* with + *tag-*, root of *tangere* touch. Related to CONTACT.] —**con·tig′u·ous·ly,** *adv.* —**con·tig′u·ous·ness,** *n.*

con·ti·nence (kon′tə nəns) *n.* **1** self-control; self-restraint; moderation. **2** chastity.

con·ti·nen·cy (kon′tə nən sē) *n., pl.* -**cies.** continence.

con·ti·nent[1] (kon′tə nənt) *n.* **1** one of the seven great masses of land on the earth. The continents are Asia, Africa, North America, South America, Europe, Australia, and Antarctica. **2** the mainland. **3 the Continent,** the mainland of Europe. It does not include the British Isles. [< L *continens,* short for *terra continens* land held together. See CONTINENT[2].]

con·ti·nent[2] (kon′tə nənt) *adj.* **1** showing restraint with regard to the desires or passions; using self-control; temperate. **2** chaste. [< L *continens, -entis,* ppr. of *continere.* See CONTAIN.]

con·ti·nen·tal (kon′tə nen′təl) *adj., n.* —*adj.* **1** of, having to do with, or characteristic of a continent: *continental rivers.* **2** Usually, **Continental,** of, having to do with, or characteristic of the mainland of Europe; of or like that of the Continent: *Continental customs differ from those of England.* **3 Continental,** in the United States, of or having to do with the thirteen colonies at the time of the American Revolution. —*n.* **1** Usually, **Continental,** a person living on the Continent. **2 Continental,** in the United States: **a** a soldier of the American army during the American Revolution. **b** a piece of paper money issued during the American Revolution. It was considered almost worthless by the time the war was over.

continental bed a bed that has no headboard or footboard, being made up of a spring mattress set on top of a box-spring base that has short legs.

continental drift *Geology.* the theory that the earth's land masses move gradually over the surface of the earth on a substratum of magma. See also **plate techtonics.**

con·ti·nen·tal·ism (kon′tə nen′təl iz′əm) *n. Cdn.* a policy advocating economic and political union of the countries of a continent, especially the union of Canada and the United States.

con·ti·nen·tal·ist (kon′tə nen′tə list) *n., adj. Cdn.* —*n.* an advocate or supporter of continentalism. —*adj.* having to do with, reflecting, or favoring continentalism: *a continentalist businessman, a continentalist bias.*

continental shelf the submerged shelf of land that borders most continents and ends in a steep slope (the **continental slope**) to deep water.

con·tin·gen·cy (kən tin′jən sē) *n., pl.* -**cies. 1** uncertainty of occurrence; dependence on change. **2** an accidental happening; unexpected event; chance. **3** a happening or event depending on something that is uncertain; possibility: *The explorer carried supplies for every contingency.*

con·tin·gent (kən tin′jənt) *adj., n.* —*adj.* **1** conditional; depending on something not certain: *Our plans for a picnic tomorrow are contingent upon pleasant weather.* **2** likely to happen or not to happen; possible; uncertain: *The traveller set aside five dollars a day for contingent expenses.* **3** happening by chance;

hat, āge, fär; let, ēqual, tėrm; it, īce
hot, ōpen, ôrder; oil, out; cup, pùt, rüle,
above, takən, pencəl, lemən, circəs

ch, child; ng, long; sh, ship
th, thin; ₮H, then; zh, measure

accidental; unexpected. **4** *Law.* dependent on events or circumstances that may or may not occur. —*n.* **1** a share of soldiers, workers, etc. furnished to a force from other sources: *Canada sent a large contingent of troops to France in World War I.* **2** a group that is part of a larger group: *The Kingston contingent had seats together at the convention.* **3** an accidental or unexpected event. [< L *contingens, -entis* touching, ppr. of *contingere.* See CONTACT.] —**con·tin′gent·ly,** *adv.*

con·tin·u·al (kən tin′yü əl) *adj.* **1** repeated many times; very frequent: *continual interference.* **2** never stopping: *the continual flow of the river.* —**con·tin′u·al·ly,** *adv.*

☛ *Usage.* **Continual, continuous. Continual** in most instances (def. 1) means repeated frequently or at close intervals: *Dancing requires continual practice.* It may also mean (def. 2) without a break in time: *a continual noise.* **Continuous** means ceaseless, without interruption in time or space: *a continuous procession of cars.*

con·tin·u·ance (kən tin′yü əns) *n.* **1** staying; remaining: *A public official is paid during his continuance in office.* **2** a continuing: *We admired his continuance of work in spite of illness.* **3** the time during which anything lasts; duration. **4** a continuation; sequel: *the continuance of a story.* **5** *Law.* an adjournment or postponement.

con·tin·u·a·tion (kən tin′yü ā′shən) *n.* **1** the going on with an activity or process: *He was looking forward to university as a continuation of his education.* **2** going on with a thing after stopping; beginning again: *They voted for a continuation of the discussion at the next meeting.* **3** anything by which a thing is continued; an added part: *The continuation of the story will appear in next month's magazine.* **4** the act or fact of not stopping.

continuation school *Cdn.* formerly in Ontario, a small secondary school administered by an elementary-school board.

con·tin·ue (kən tin′yü) *v.* -**tin·ued, -tin·u·ing. 1** keep up; keep on; go on; go on with: *The road continues for quite a distance. We continued our work at the hospital.* **2** go on, or go on with (something), after stopping; begin again: *He ate lunch and then continued his work.* **3** last; endure: *The king's reign continued for twenty years.* **4** cause to last. **5** extend in space: *The farmer continued his fence from the pasture to the highway.* **6** stay: *The children must continue in school till the end of June.* **7** allow to stay in a position; maintain; retain: *The club continued the president in office for another term.* **8** put off until a later time; postpone; adjourn: *The judge has continued the case until next month.* [ME < OF *continuer* < L *continuare* < *continere* hold together. See CONTAIN.] —**con·tin′u·a·ble,** *adj.*

☛ *Syn.* **3. Continue, last, endure** = go on for a long time. **Continue** emphasizes the idea of going on and on without an end, usually without a break: *The heavy snow continued all winter.* **Last** emphasizes the idea of holding out, either in good condition or full strength or for an unusually long time: *These flowers lasted for two weeks.* **Endure** emphasizes the idea of going on, or surviving, in spite of difficulties, dangers, or pressures of any kind: *These monuments will endure for centuries.*

con·ti·nu·i·ty (kon′tə nyü′ə tē *or* kon′tə nü′ə tē) *n., pl.* -**ties. 1** being a connected whole or an unbroken series: *The story lacked continuity because there were too many unconnected happenings.* **2** a detailed plan of the sequence of scenes in a motion picture. **3** *Radio or television.* **a** any connecting comments or announcements between the parts of a program. **b** a script for such comments or announcements.

con·tin·u·ous (kən tin′yü əs) *adj.* without a stop or break; connected; unbroken: *a continuous line, a continuous sound, continuous work, a continuous line of cars.* —**con·tin′u·ous·ly,** *adv.* —**con·tin′u·ous·ness,** *n.*

☛ *Usage.* See note at **continual.**

con·tin·u·um (kən tin′yü əm) *n., pl.* -**tin·u·a.** a continuous quantity; an unbroken series, etc. [< L]

con·tort (kən tôrt′) *v.* twist or bend out of shape; distort: *The clown distorted his face.* [< L *contortus,* pp. of *contorquere* < *com-* (intensive) + *torquere* twist]

con·tor·tion (kən tôr′shən) *n.* **1** a twisting or bending out of shape; a distorting. **2** a contorted condition; distorted form or shape.

con·tor·tion·ist (kən tôr′shən ist) *n.* a person who can twist or bend his body into odd and unnatural positions.

con·tour (kon′tür) *n., v.* —*n.* **1** the outline of a figure, land mass, body of water, etc.: *The contour of the Atlantic coast of Canada is very irregular.* **2** a line representing such outline or shape. **3** (*adj.*) showing the outlines of hills, valleys, etc. at regular

intervals above sea level: *a contour map.* **4** (*adjl.*) following the contours of uneven ground in such a way as to minimize erosion: *In contour ploughing, the furrows are made horizontally around the slopes of a hill instead of from top to bottom.* **5** (*adjl.*) shaped to fit the contour of a particular object: *a contour chair.*
—*v.* **1** build (a road, etc.) to follow natural contours. **2** shape to fit the contour of something: *bucket seats contoured to fit the body.* **3** mark with contour lines. **4** make an outline of. [< F < Ital. *contorno* < *contornare* encircle < L *com-* with + *tornus* turning lathe < Gk. *tornos*]
☞ *Syn. n.* See note at **outline.**

contour line a line on a map, showing the outline from above of a section of the earth's surface at a particular height above sea level. A 3000 metre contour line on a map of a mountain shows what its outline would look like from the top if a horizontal cross section were made at that height.

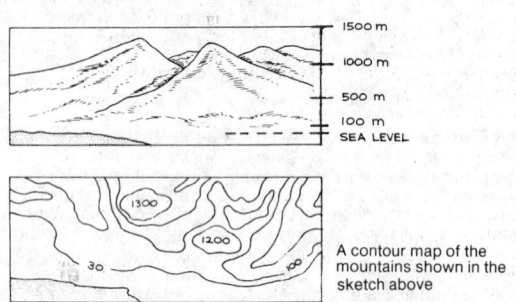

1500 m
1000 m
500 m
100 m
SEA LEVEL

A contour map of the mountains shown in the sketch above

contour map a map showing elevations and depressions of the earth's surface by means of a series of contour lines made at regular intervals above or below sea level.

contr. contract; contracted; contraction.

contra– *prefix.* in opposition; against: *contradistinction = distinction by opposition or contrast.* [< L *contra-* < *contra* against, adv., prep.]

con·tra·band (kon′trə band′) *n., adj.* —*n.* **1** goods that may not legally be imported or exported: *The plumage of endangered species of birds, such as the ostrich or egret is contraband in Canada. Some goods, such as firearms, are contraband except under certain circumstances.* **2** trading contrary to law; smuggling. **3** smuggled goods: *The customs official was looking for contraband.* **4** *U.S.* a black slave who escaped to or was brought within the Union lines during the Civil War.
—*adj.* against the law; prohibited: *contraband trade.* [< Sp. < Ital. *contrabando* < *contra-* against (< L) + *bando* < LL *bandum* ban < Gmc.]

contraband of war any materials supplied to warring nations by neutral countries and subject to seizure by the opposite side according to international law: *Ammunition is always contraband of war.*

con·tra·bass (kon′trə bās′) *n.* **1** the lowest bass instrument of a family of instruments, especially the double bass of the violin family. **2** (*adjl.*) having a pitch an octave lower than normal bass.

con·tra·cep·tion (kon′trə sep′shən) *n.* the intentional prevention of conception. [< *contra-* + *conception*]

con·tra·cep·tive (kon′trə sep′tiv) *n., adj.* —*n.* a substance or device for preventing pregnancy or conception. —*adj.* of or for contraception.

con·tract (*v.* kən trakt′ *for 1-4, 6,* kon′trakt *or* kən trakt′ *for 5;* *n.* kon′trakt) *v., n.* —*v.* **1** make or become narrower or shorter; make or become smaller; draw together; shrink: *Wrinkling the forehead contracts the brows. Rubber stretches and contracts.* **2** *Grammar.* shorten (a word, etc.) by omitting some of the letters or sounds: *In talking we contract* do not *to* don't. **3** form; enter upon; bring on oneself: *to contract a bad habit.* **4** get; catch a disease: *He contracted malaria in the tropics.* **5** make a contract; enter into a legal agreement: *The builder contracted to build the new library.* **6** *Anatomy.* draw together and thicken muscle fibre to move a part of the body.
—*n.* **1** an agreement, especially a written agreement that can be enforced by law: *All professional hockey players sign contracts each year, agreeing to play for a certain salary.* **2** a formal agreement of marriage. **3** contract bridge. **4** in contract bridge, the tricks that the declarer undertakes to win. [< L *contractus,* pp. of *contrahere* < *com-* together + *trahere* draw]

contract bridge a card game played by four people divided into two opposing pairs. The highest bidder can score toward a game only as many points as he promises to make in his bid.

con·tract·i·ble (kən trak′tə bəl) *adj.* capable of being contracted.

con·trac·tile (kən trak′tīl *or* kən trak′təl) *adj.* **1** capable of contracting: *Muscle is contractile tissue.* **2** producing contraction: *Cooling is a contractile force.*

con·trac·til·i·ty (kon′trak til′ə tē) *n.* the ability to contract.

con·trac·tion (kən trak′shən) *n.* **1** contracting or being contracted: *Cold causes the contraction of liquids, gases, and metals, whereas heat causes expansion.* **2** something contracted; shortened form: Can't *is a contraction of* cannot. **3** *Anatomy.* the drawing together and thickening of muscle fibre.

con·trac·tive (kən trak′tiv) *adj.* **1** capable of contracting. **2** producing contraction. **3** of contraction.

con·trac·tor (kon′trak tər *or* kən trak′tər *for 1;* kən trak′tər *for 2*) *n.* **1** a person who agrees to furnish materials or to do a piece of work for a certain price, especially for the construction of buildings. **2** *Anatomy.* a muscle that draws together some part or parts of the body.

con·trac·tu·al (kən trak′chü əl) *adj.* **1** of or having to do with a contract. **2** having the nature of a contract. —**con·trac′tu·al·ly,** *adv.*

con·tra·dict (kon′trə dikt′) *v.* **1** express the opposite of a statement; declare to be false or untrue: *She contradicted his version of the accident.* **2** deny the statement of another person: *to contradict a guest is rude.* **3** be contrary to; be inconsistent with: *His quick anger contradicted his previous statement that he never lost his temper.* [< L *contradictus,* pp. of *contradicere,* earlier *contra dicere* say in opposition]
☞ *Syn.* 1, 2. See note at **deny.**

con·tra·dic·tion (kon′trə dik′shən) *n.* **1** denying what has been said. **2** a statement or act that contradicts another; denial: *His statement was a clear contradiction of what his father had said.* **3** a contrary condition; disagreement; opposition: *a contradiction in terms.* **4** inconsistency.

con·tra·dic·to·ry (kon′trə dik′tə rē *or* kon′trə dik′trē) *adj.* **1** contradicting; contrary; in disagreement: *First reports of the election were so contradictory that we could not tell who had won.* **2** inclined to contradict.

con·tra·dis·tinc·tion (kon′trə dis tingk′shən) *n.* a distinction made by opposition or contrast: *The author emphasizes the importance of quality control in contradistinction to speed of production.*

con·trail (kon′trāl) *n.* the trail of vapor left by an aircraft flying at a high altitude; vapor trail. [< *condensation* + *trail*]

con·tral·to (kən tral′tō) *n.* -tos; *adj.* —*n.* **1** the lowest female singing voice; alto. **2** a singer who has such a voice. **3** the part sung by a contralto.
—*adj.* having to do with, having the range of, or designed for a contralto. [< Ital. *contralto* < *contra-* counter to (< L) + *alto* high < L *altus*]

con·tra·po·si·tion (kon′trə pə zish′ən) *n.* a placing over against; opposite position; contrast.

con·trap·tion (kən trap′shən) *n. Informal.* a contrivance; device; gadget. [? < *contrive*]

con·tra·pun·tal (kon′trə pun′təl) *adj. Music.* **1** of or having to do with counterpoint. **2** according to the rules of counterpoint. [< Ital. *contrapunto* (now *contrappunto*) counterpoint]
—**con′tra·pun′tal·ly,** *adv.*

con·tra·pun·tist (kon′trə pun′tist) *n.* a person skilled in the rules and practice of counterpoint.

con·tra·ri·e·ty (kon′trə rī′ə tē) *n., pl.* -ties. **1** the state or quality of being contrary. **2** something contrary; a contrary fact or statement.

con·tra·ri·wise (kon′trer ē wīz′ *for 1 and 2;* kon′trer ē wīz′ *or* kən trer′ē wīz′ *for 3*) *adv.* **1** in the opposite way or direction. **2** on the contrary. **3** perversely.

con·tra·ry (kon′trer ē *for adj. 1, 2, 3, n., and adv.;* kon′trer ē *or* kən trer′ē *for adj. 4*) *adj., n., pl.* -ries; *adv.* —*adj.* **1** opposed in purpose, character, etc.; opposite; completely different: *Contrary to all expectations, the party was a great success. The plan is contrary to government policy.* **2** opposite in direction, position, etc. **3** unfavorable: *a contrary wind.* **4** opposing others; stubborn; perverse.
—*n.* a fact or quality that is the opposite of something else; the opposite: *What he has just told us is the contrary of what we heard yesterday.*
on the contrary, exactly opposite to what has been said: *He didn't go straight home; on the contrary, he stopped at three different stores and even visited a friend.*
to the contrary, with the opposite effect.
—*adv.* in opposition. [ME < AF *contrarie* < L *contrarius* < *contra* against] —**con′tra·ri·ly,** *adv.* —**con′tra·ri·ness,** *n.*
☞ *Syn. adj.* 1. See note at **opposite.**

con·trast (*n.* kon′trast; *v.* kən trast′) *n., v.* —*n.* **1** a great difference; difference; striking difference: *the contrast between black and white.* **2** anything that shows differences when put side by side with something else: *Black hair is a sharp contrast to light skin.* **3** *Arts.* the usage of varied colors, shapes, sounds, etc. to heighten the effect of a composition.
—*v.* **1** compare two things so as to show their differences: *My project was to contrast the climate of the Mackenzie Valley and that of the District of Keewatin.* **2** show differences when compared or put side by side: *Blue and yellow contrast prettily in a design.* **3** form a contrast to; set off (*used with* **with**): *The strained language of his speeches contrasts oddly with the ease and naturalness of his letters.* **4** put close together to heighten an effect by emphasizing differences. [< F < Ital. *contrasto* < *contrastare* < VL *contrastare* < L *contra-* against + *stare* stand] —**con·trast′a·ble**, *adj.* —**con·trast′ing·ly**, *adv.*
☛ *Usage.* See note at **compare.**

con·trast·ive (kən tras′tiv) *adj.* having to do with or involving contrast: *A contrastive study of English and French grammar would show the ways in which the structures of the two languages are different.*

con·tra·vene (kon′trə vēn′) *v.* **-vened, -ven·ing. 1** conflict with; oppose: *A dictatorship contravenes the liberty of individuals.* **2** contradict. **3** violate; infringe. [< LL *contravenire* < L *contra-* against + *venire* come] —**con·tra·ven′er**, *n.*

con·tra·ven·tion (kon′trə ven′shən) *n.* **1** a conflict; opposition. **2** contradiction. **3** a violation; infringement.

con·tre·danse (kôn′trə däns′) *n.* French. **1** a dance in which the partners stand in two lines facing each other. **2** the music written for such a dance. [< E *country-dance*]

con·tre·temps (kôn′trə tän′) *n., pl.* **-temps** (-tänz′). *French.* an unfortunate accident; embarrassing or awkward happening. [< OF *contrestant,* ppr. of *contrester* oppose < VL *contrastare* (see CONTRAST); influenced by F *temps* time < L *tempus*]

con·trib·ut·a·ble (kən trib′yə tə bəl) *adj.* **1** capable of being contributed; payable as a contribution. **2** of persons, subject to contribution.

con·trib·ute (kən trib′yüt) *v.* **-ut·ed, -ut·ing. 1** give (money, help, etc.) along with others; furnish as a share: *We should also contribute to the Red Cross. Everyone was asked to contribute suggestions for the party.* **2** write (articles, stories, etc.) for a newspaper or magazine. **3** contribute to, help bring about: *Poor food contributed to the child's illness.* [< L *contributus,* pp. of *contribuere* bring together, collect < *com-* together + *tribuere* bestow, assign, originally, divide among the tribes < *tribus* tribe]

con·tri·bu·tion (kon′trə byü′shən) *n.* **1** the act of contributing; giving of money, help, etc. along with others. **2** the money, help, etc. given; gift. **3** an article, story, etc. written for a newspaper or magazine. **4** a tax; levy.

con·trib·u·tive (kən trib′yə tiv) *adj.* contributing; helping to bring about. —**con·trib′u·tive·ly**, *adv.* —**con·trib′u·tive·ness**, *n.*

con·trib·u·tor (kən trib′yə tər) *n.* **1** a person or thing that contributes. **2** a person who writes articles, stories, etc. for a newspaper or magazine.

con·trib·u·to·ry (kən trib′yə tô′rē) *adj., n.* —*adj.* contributing; helping to bring about: *The workman's carelessness was a contributory cause of the accident.* —*n.* a person or thing that contributes.

con·trite (kon′trīt *or* kən trīt′) *adj.* **1** sad and humbled by a sense of having done wrong; penitent. **2** showing deep regret and sorrow: *He wrote an apology in contrite words.* [< L *contritus* crushed, pp. of *conterere* < *com-* (intensive) + *terere* rub, grind] —**con·trite′ly**, *adv.* —**con·trite′ness**, *n.*

con·tri·tion (kən trish′ən) *n.* **1** sorrow for one's sins; being contrite; sincere penitence. **2** deep regret.

con·triv·ance (kən trīv′əns) *n.* **1** something invented; a mechanical device. **2** the act or manner of planning or designing: *By careful contrivance he managed to fit all his appointments into one afternoon.* **3** the power or ability of contriving. **4** a plan; scheme.

con·trive (kən trīv′) *v.* **-trived, -triv·ing. 1** invent; design: *to contrive a new kind of engine.* **2** scheme; plot: *to contrive a robbery.* **3** manage; arrange to have something happen: *I will contrive to be there by ten o'clock.* **4** bring about. [ME < OF *controver* < *con-* (< L *com-*) (intensive) + *trover* find < L *turbare* stir up < *turba* commotion] —**con·triv′er**, *n.*

con·trol (kən trōl′) *n., v.* **-trolled, -trol·ling.** —*n.* **1** power or authority; command: *He has no control over his temper. The rebels are in control of the capital.* **2** restraint: *She showed great control in not losing her temper.* **3** regulation: *birth control, gun control.* **4** a means of regulation or restraint; check: *They argued that the new law was not effective as a control against price increases.* **5** a device that regulates the working of a machine: *The control for our furnace is in the front hall.* **6 controls,** the instruments and devices by which a car, locomotive, etc. is operated: *After the crash, the*

hat, āge, fär; let, ēqual, tèrm; it, īce
hot, ōpen, ôrder; oil, out; cup, pút, rüle,
əbove, takən, pencəl, lemən, circəs

ch, child; ng, long; sh, ship
th, thin; ɟH, then; zh, measure

pilot was found dead at the controls. **7** a standard of comparison for testing the results of scientific experiments. **8** a spirit that directs a medium in a spiritualistic séance. **9** (*adj.*) serving as a control: *a control experience.* **10** (*adj.*) equipped with a control or controls: *a control room.*
—*v.* **1** exercise power or authority over; command or direct: *A ship's captain has control of the ship and its crew.* **2** hold back; keep down; restrain: *to control an impulse, to control a forest fire.* **3** regulate: *to control prices and wages.* **4** check or verify (an experiment, the effects of a drug, testimony, etc.) by some standard of comparison or by independent investigation. **5** *Accounting.* check, verify, or regulate (expenditures, accounts, etc.). [< F *contrôler* < OF *contreroller* < *controlle* register < *contre* against (< L *contra*) + *rolle* roll < L *rotulus,* dim. of *rota* wheel] —**con·trol′ling·ly**, *adv.*
☛ *Syn. n.* **1.** See note at **authority.**

con·trol·la·ble (kən trōl′ə bəl) *adj.* that can be controlled; capable of being checked or restrained.

con·trol·ler (kən trōl′ər) *n.* **1** a person employed to supervise expenditures or to manage financial affairs. **2** a person who controls, directs, or regulates: *an air traffic controller.* **3** a device that controls or regulates the speed of a machine. **4** in certain city councils, a member of the board of control. Also (def. 1), **comptroller.**

con·trol·ler·ship (kən trōl′ər ship′) *n.* the position or office of a controller.

control panel a panel containing all the instruments necessary for the control and operation of a complex mechanism such as an electronic computer or an aircraft.

control rod 1 in a nuclear reactor, a mechanism, containing fuel or other matter, used to control the rate of a chain reaction. **2** in an aircraft, a rod for transmitting movements from the controls in the cockpit to the rudder, ailerons, etc.

control room 1 in a radio or television studio, a sound-proof room from which the transmission of a broadcast can be controlled. **2** a room containing all the instruments necessary to control a complex operation, such as the launching of a rocket.

control stick the lever that controls the direction of an aircraft's movement.

control tower at an airfield, the building from which the taking off and landing of aircraft is controlled.

con·tro·ver·sial (kon′trə vèr′shəl) *adj.* **1** of, open to, or arousing controversy: *a controversial question. She is a controversial politician.* **2** fond of controversy. —**con′tro·ver′sial·ly**, *adv.*

con·tro·ver·sial·ist (kon′trə vèr′shəl ist) *n.* a person who takes part in or is skilled in controversy.

con·tro·ver·sy (kon′trə vèr′sē) *n., pl.* **-sies. 1** the act of arguing a question about which differences of opinion exist; debate; dispute: *The controversy between the company and the union ended in a strike.* **2** a quarrel; wrangle. [< L *controversia* < *controversus* < *contro-* against + *versus,* pp. of *vertere* turn]
☛ *Syn.* **1.** See note at **argument.**

con·tro·vert (kon′trə vèrt′ *or* kon′trə vèrt′) *v.* **1** dispute; deny; oppose: *The statement of the last witness controverts the evidence of the first two.* **2** dispute about; discuss; debate. [< L *contro-* against + *vertere* turn] —**con′tro·vert′er**, *n.*

con·tro·vert·i·ble (kon′trə vèr′tə bəl) *adj.* that can be controverted; debatable. —**con·tro·vert′i·bly**, *adv.*

con·tu·ma·cious (kon′tyü mā′shəs *or* kon′tù mā′shəs) *adj.* stubbornly rebellious; obstinately disobedient. —**con′tu·ma′cious·ly**, *adv.* —**con′tu·ma′cious·ness**, *n.*

con·tu·ma·cy (kon′tyü mə sē *or* kon′tù mə sē) *n., pl.* **-cies.** stubborn resistance to authority; obstinate disobedience. [< L *contumacia* < *contumax* insolent < *tumere* swell up]

con·tu·me·li·ous (kon′tyü mē′lē əs *or* kon′tù mē′lē əs) *adj.* contemptuously insolent; insulting. —**con′tu·me′li·ous·ly**, *adv.* —**con′tu·me′li·ous·ness**, *n.*

con·tu·me·ly (kon′tyü mə lē, kon′tù mə lē, kən tyü′mə lē *or* kən tü′mə lē) *n., pl.* **-lies. 1** insolent contempt; insulting words or actions; humiliating treatment. **2** a humiliating insult. [< L *contumelia,* originally, insolent action < *tumere* swell up]

con·tuse (kən tyüz′ *or* kən tüz′) *v.* **-tused, -tus·ing.**

injure without breaking the skin, bruise. [< L *contusus*, pp. of *contundere* < *com-* (intensive) + *tundere* pound]

con·tu·sion (kən tyü′zhən *or* kən tü′zhən) *n.* a bruise.

co·nun·drum (kə nun′drəm) *n.* **1** a riddle; a puzzling question whose answer involves a pun or play on words. *When is a door not a door?* is a conundrum. The answer to this conundrum is *When it's ajar.* **2** any puzzling problem. [origin unknown]

con·ur·ba·tion (kon′ėr bā′shən) *n.* a number of urban communities that have expanded and thus grown so close together that they can be considered as one large community.

con·va·lesce (kon′və lĕs′) *v.* **-lesced, -lesc·ing.** regain strength after illness; make progress toward health. [< L *convalescere* < *com-* (intensive) + *valescere* grow strong < *valere* be strong]

con·va·les·cence (kon′və les′əns) *n.* **1** a gradual recovery of health and strength after illness. **2** the time during which a person is convalescing.

con·va·les·cent (kon′və les′ənt) *adj., n.* —*adj.* **1** recovering health and strength after illness: *Such exercise is too strenuous for a convalescent.* **2** of or for persons who are convalescing: *the convalescent ward of a hospital, a convalescent diet.* —*n.* a person recovering after illness.

con·vec·tion (kən vek′shən) *n.* **1** *Physics.* the transfer of heat from one place to another by the circulation of heated particles of a gas or liquid: *A forced-air furnace system heats a room by convection.* **2** the act or process of conveying. [< L *convectio, -onis* < *convehere* < *com-* together + *vehere* carry]

con·vec·tion·al (kən vek′shə nəl) *adj.* of or characterized by convection.

con·vec·tive (kən vek′tiv) *adj.* **1** capable of conveying; transporting. **2** having to do with or resulting from convection.

con·vec·tive·ly (kən vek′tiv lē) *adv.* by means of convection.

con·vec·tor (kən vek′tər) *n.* a convective agent.

con·vene (kən vēn′) *v.* **-vened, -ven·ing.** **1** meet for some purpose; gather together; assemble: *Parliament convenes in Ottawa at least once a year.* **2** call together (members of an organization, etc.) [< L *convenire* < *com-* together + *venire* come]

con·ven·er (kən vē′nər) *n.* convenor.

con·ven·ience (kən vēn′yəns *or* kən vēn′ē əns) *n.* **1** the fact or quality of being convenient: *Many people appreciate the convenience of frozen foods.* **2** comfort; advantage: *Many provincial parks have camping places for the convenience of tourists.* **3** anything handy or easy to use; something that increases comfort and saves trouble or work: *A folding table is a convenience in a small room. Their house is filled with electrical appliances and other modern conveniences.* **4** Often, **conveniences,** *pl.* toilet or washroom. **5** (*adj.*) intended or prepared for people's convenience: *He lives on convenience foods.*
at (one's) **convenience,** so as to suit one as to time, place, or other conditions: *Write at your convenience.*

convenience store a small store, often a franchise or one of a chain of stores, that is open every day until late evening and specializes in selling basic food items, such as milk and bread, and a variety of small dry-goods items.

con·ven·ien·cy (kən vēn′yən sē *or* kən vēn′ē ən sē) *n., pl.* **-cies.** convenience.

con·ven·ient (kən vēn′yənt *or* kən vēn′ē ənt) *adj.* **1** saving trouble; well arranged; easy to use: *to use a convenient tool, to take a convenient bus, to live in a convenient house.* **2** within easy reach; handy: *To meet at a convenient place.* **3** easily done; not troublesome.
convenient to, *Informal.* near; easy to reach from: *The library is convenient to our apartment.* [< L *conveniens, -entis,* ppr. of *convenire* meet, agree, be suitable. See CONVENE.] —**con·ven′ient·ly,** *adv.*

con·ven·or *or* **con·ven·er** (kən vē′nər) *n.* a person who is responsible for calling together the members of a committee, club, etc. and who often acts as their chairman.

con·vent (kon′vənt *or* kon′vent) *n.* **1** a community of persons dedicated to a religious life; in modern usage, a community of nuns. **2** the building or buildings in which they live. [ME < AF *covent* < L *conventus* assembly < *convenire.* See CONVENE.]

con·ven·ti·cle (kən ven′tə kəl) *n.* **1** a secret or unauthorized meeting, especially for religious worship. **2** a secret religious meeting or assembly of certain Protestants who dissented from the doctrines and forms of the Church of England during the 16th and 17th centuries. **3** the place of such a meeting. [< L *conventiculum,* dim. of *conventus* assembly. See CONVENT.]

con·ven·tion (kən ven′shən) *n.* **1** a meeting for some purpose; gathering; assembly. A political party holds a convention to choose

candidates for public offices. **2** the delegates to a meeting or assembly. **3** an agreement. A convention signed by two or more countries is usually about less important matters than those in a treaty. **4** general agreement; common consent; custom. **5** a custom approved by general agreement; rule based on common consent: *Using the right hand to shake hands is a convention.* **6** *Arts.* a procedure or detail not taken literally, but accepted by the beholder, reader, etc. as fitting: *It is a convention of the theatre that asides spoken by a character are not heard by other persons on stage.* [< L *conventio, -onis* < *convenire.* See CONVENE.]

con·ven·tion·al (kən ven′shən əl) *adj.* **1** depending on conventions; customary: *"Good morning" is a conventional greeting.* **2** ordinary; not interesting; not original: *conventional furniture.* **3** *Art.* following custom rather than nature. Flowers and leaves are often drawn in a conventional design without any idea of making them look real. **4** of weapons, warfare, etc., not nuclear or biological. —**con·ven′tion·al·ly,** *adv.*
☛ *Syn.* **1.** See note at **formal.**

con·ven·tion·al·ism (kən ven′shən əl iz′əm) *n.* **1** a tendency to follow conventional usages; adherence to custom. **2** something conventional; formal usage, word, phrase, etc.

con·ven·tion·al·i·ty (kən ven′shən al′ə tē) *n., pl.* **-ties. 1** a conventional quality or character: *the conventionality of modern life.* **2** conventional behavior; adherence to custom. **3** a conventional custom or rule: *The girls at boarding school were required to observe the conventionalities very strictly.*

con·ven·tion·al·ize (kən ven′shən əl īz′) *v.* **-ized, -iz·ing. 1** make conventional. **2** draw or design according to a particular or conventional style, rather than according to nature; stylize or simplify. —**con·ven′tion·al·i·za′tion,** *n.*

con·ven·tu·al (kən ven′chü əl) *adj., n.* —*adj.* of or like a convent. —*n.* a member of a convent.

con·verge (kən vėrj′) *v.* **-verged, -verg·ing. 1** tend to meet in a point. **2** turn toward each other: *If you look at the end of your nose, your eyes converge.* **3** come together; centre: *The interest of all the students converged upon the celebration.* **4** cause to converge. [< LL *convergere* < L *com-* together + *vergere* incline]

con·ver·gence (kən vėr′jəns) *n.* **1** the act, process, or fact of converging; tendency to meet in a point. **2** the point of meeting. **3** *Biology.* the tendency in animals or plants not closely related to develop similar characteristics when living under the same conditions.

con·ver·gen·cy (kən vėr′jən sē) *n., pl.* **-cies.** convergence.

con·ver·gent (kən vėr′jənt) *adj.* tending to converge; inclining toward each other or toward a common point.

con·vers·a·ble (kən vėr′sə bəl) *adj.* **1** easy or pleasant to talk to. **2** fond of talking. **3** having to do with or proper for social intercourse. —**con·vers′a·bly,** *adv.*

con·ver·sant (kən vėr′sənt *or* kon′vər sənt) *adj.* familiar by use or study; acquainted: *He is not conversant with the history of philosophical thought.* —**con·ver′sant·ly,** *adv.*

con·ver·sa·tion (kon′vər sā′shən) *n.* **1** informal or friendly talk; the exchange of thoughts by talking informally: *There is much pleasure in good conversation.* **2** a talk; a meeting for the purpose of informal talk: *The professor invited his students to his home for a conversation.*

con·ver·sa·tion·al (kon′vər sā′shən əl *or* kon′vər sāsh′nəl) *adj.* **1** of or having to do with conversation. **2** fond of conversation; good at conversation. **3** characteristic of conversation.

con·ver·sa·tion·al·ist (kon′vər sā′shən əl ist *or* kon′vər sāsh′nəl ist) *n.* a person who is fond of or good at conversation; one who cultivates the art of conversation.

con·ver·sa·tion·al·ly (kon′vər sā′shən əl ē *or* kon′vər sāsh′nəl ē) *adv.* in a conversational, informal manner.

con·verse¹ (*v.* kən vėrs′; *n.* kon′vėrs) *v.* **-versed, -vers·ing;** *n.* —*v.* talk informally together: *The two old veterans liked conversing about their experiences during the war.* —*n.* conversation. [ME < OF *converser* < L *conversari* live with < *com-* with + *versari* live, be busy < *verti* turn] —**con·vers′er,** *n.*

con·verse² (*adj.* kən vėrs′ *or* kon′vėrs; *n.* kon′vėrs) *adj., n.* —*adj.* **1** opposite; contrary. **2** reversed in order; turned about. —*n.* **1** something that is opposite or contrary. **2** something that is turned around: *"Honest but poor" is the converse of "Poor but honest."* [< L *conversus* turned around, pp. of *convertere.* See CONVERT.]

con·verse·ly (kən vėrs′lē *or* kon′vėrs lē) *adv.* if or when turned the other way around: *Six is more than five; conversely, five is less than six.*

con·ver·sion (kən vėr′zhən *or* kən vėr′shən) *n.* **1** the act of converting or the process of being converted: *the conversion of inches into centimetres, the unlawful conversion of public money to one's own use.* **2** the act or experience of adopting a religion: *He told them about his conversion several years before.* **3** *Football.* the act or fact of kicking a point after a touchdown. **4** *Logic.* an

operation involving the transposition of the subject and predicate of a proposition.

con·vert (v. kən vėrt'; n. kon'vėrt) v., n. —v. **1** change; turn: *These machines convert pulp into paper. One last effort converted defeat into victory.* **2** change or cause to change from one religion, political party, etc. to another: *The missionaries converted many people to Christianity.* **3** cause to adopt a religion: *She was converted at a prayer meeting.* **4** take and use unlawfully: *The dishonest treasurer converted the club's money to his own use.* **5** turn the other way around; invert; transpose. **6** exchange for an equivalent: *He converted his Canadian dollars into French francs before he left.* **7** exchange (a bond or other security) for another type of security, as common stock. **8** *Football.* kick a goal after a touchdown.
—n. **1** a person who has been converted. **2** *Football.* **a** a goal kicked after a touchdown. **b** the point made by successfully kicking such a goal. [< L *convertere* < *com-* (intensive) + *vertere* turn]
☛ *Syn. v.* **1.** See note at **transform.**

con·vert·er (kən vėr'tər) n. **1** a device for changing alternating electrical current into direct current. **2** a device for adapting a television set to receive more channels than it was designed for. **3** a furnace in which pig iron is changed into steel by the Bessemer process. **4** any person or thing that converts.

con·vert·i·bil·i·ty (kən vėr'tə bil'ə tē) n. the quality of being convertible.

con·vert·i·ble (kən vėr'tə bəl) adj., n. —adj. **1** capable of being converted: *Wood is convertible into paper. A dollar bill is convertible into coins.* **2** of an automobile, having a top that may be folded down. **3** of securities, that can be exchanged for others of the same value.
—n. an automobile with a cloth roof that can be folded down behind the rear seat. —**con·vert'i·bly,** adv.

con·vert·i·plane (kən vėr'tə plän') n. an aircraft that operates like a conventional airplane in level flight, but that takes off and lands like a helicopter. [< *convert*ible + air*plane*]

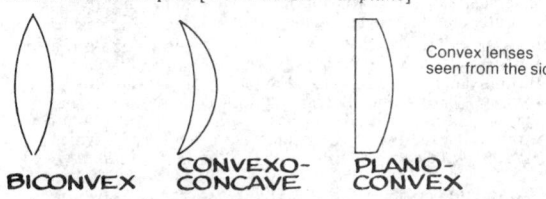

Convex lenses seen from the side

BICONVEX CONVEXO-CONCAVE PLANO-CONVEX

con·vex (kon veks' or kon'veks) adj., n. —adj. curved out, like the outside of a circle or sphere: *The crystal of a watch is slightly convex.* —n. a convex surface or thing. [< L *convexus* vaulted, probably < *com-* around + *vac-* bend (related to *vacillare* totter, sway)] —**con·vex'ly,** adv.

con·vex·i·ty (kon vek'sə tē) n., pl. **-ties.** **1** a convex condition or quality. **2** a convex surface or thing.

con·vex·o·con·cave (kon vek'sō kon kāv') adj. convex on one side and concave on the other. In a convexo-concave lens, the convex side has the greatest curvature. See **convex** for picture.

con·vey (kən vā') v. **1** carry; transport: *A bus conveys passengers.* **2** transmit; conduct: *A wire conveys an electric circuit.* **3** express; make known; communicate: *His words convey no meaning to me.* **4** *Law.* transfer the ownership of (property) from one person to another: *The old farmer conveyed his farm to his son.* [ME < OF *conveier* < VL < L *com-* with + *via* road. Doublet of CONVOY.] —**con·vey'a·ble,** adj.
☛ *Syn.* **1.** See note at **carry.**

con·vey·ance (kən vā'əns) n. **1** the act of carrying; transportation; transmission. **2** anything that carries people and goods; vehicle. **3** communication. **4** *Law.* **a** transfer of the ownership of property from one person to another. **b** a written statement that shows such a transfer; deed.

con·vey·anc·er (kən vā'ən sər) n. a lawyer who investigates the ownership of property and prepares contracts, deeds, etc., for its transfer from one person to another.

con·vey·anc·ing (kən vā'ən sing) n. the preparation of deeds, etc. for the transfer of the ownership of property from one person to another.

con·vey·or or **con·vey·er** (kən vā'ər) n. **1** a person or thing that conveys. **2** a mechanical device that carries things from one place to another by means of a moving endless belt or a series of rollers: *Grain is carried from one level of an elevator to another by means of a conveyor.*

conveyor belt conveyor (def. 1).

con·vict (v. kən vikt'; n. kon'vikt) v., n. —v. **1** prove guilty. **2** declare guilty: *The jury convicted the prisoner of murder.* **3** impress with a sense of guilt: *a person convicted of sin.*

hat, āge, fär; let, ēqual, tèrm; it, īce
hot, ōpen, ôrder; oil, out; cup, pút, rüle,
əbove, takən, pencəl, lemən, circəs
ch, child; ng, long; sh, ship
th, thin; ŦH, then; zh, measure

—n. **1** a person convicted by a court. **2** a person serving a prison sentence for some crime. [< L *convictus,* pp. of *convincere.* See CONVINCE.]

con·vic·tion (kən vik'shən) n. **1** convicting or being convicted: *a conviction for theft.* **2** the appearance or condition of being convinced: *She spoke with conviction on the benefits of regular exercise.* **3** a firm belief. **4** *Rare.* the act of convincing (a person).
☛ *Syn.* **3.** See note at **belief.**

con·vince (kən vins') v. **-vinced, -vinc·ing.** make a person feel sure; cause to believe; persuade by argument or proof: *The mistakes Nan made convinced the teacher that she had not studied her lesson.* [< L *convincere* < *com-* (intensive) + *vincere* overcome]
☛ *Syn.* See note at **persuade.**
☛ *Usage.* **Convince** is followed by *of* plus a noun or by a *that-*clause: *I can easily convince you of his innocence. You will soon be convinced that I am right.*

con·vin·ci·ble (kən vin'sə bəl) adj. capable of being convinced.

con·vinc·ing (kən vin'sing) adj. that convinces: *a convincing argument.* —**con·vinc'ing·ly,** adv. —**con·vinc'ing·ness,** n.

con·viv·i·al (kən viv'ē əl) adj. **1** fond of eating and drinking with friends; jovial; sociable. **2** of or suitable for a feast or banquet; festive. [< LL *convivialis* < L *convivium* feast < *com-* with + *vivere* live] —**con·viv'i·al·ly,** adv.

con·viv·i·al·i·ty (kən viv'ē al'ə tē) n., pl. **-ties.** **1** a fondness for eating and drinking with friends; good-fellowship. **2** eating and drinking with friends; festivity.

con·vo·ca·tion (kon'və kā'shən) n. **1** a calling together; an assembling by a summons. **2** an assembly; a number of persons gathered in answer to a summons: *The convocation of clergy passed a resolution condemning war.* **3** at certain universities: **a** the officials and graduates as a legislative, advisory, or electoral body. **b** a meeting of this body. **4** at other universities: **a** an assembly of the members of a university for a specific purpose. **b** a ceremony at which degrees are conferred.

con·voke (kən vōk') v. **-voked, -vok·ing.** call together; summon to assemble. [< L *convocare* < *com-* together + *vocare* call] —**con·vok'er,** n.

con·vo·lute (kon'və lüt') adj., v. **-lut·ed, -lut·ing.** —adj. coiled; rolled up into a spiral shape with one part over another. —v. coil. [< L *convolutus,* pp. of *convolvere* < *com-* together + *volvere* roll]

con·vo·lut·ed (kon'və lüt'id) adj. having convolutions; coiled; twisted.

con·vo·lu·tion (kon'və lü'shən) n. **1** a coiling, winding, or twisting together. **2** a coil; winding; twist. **3** *Anatomy.* an irregular fold or ridge on the surface of the brain.

con·vol·vu·lus (kən vol'vyə ləs) n., pl. **-lus·es, -li** (-lī' or -lē'). any of a genus (*Convolvulus*) of plants, usually vines, having flowers shaped like trumpets. The morning glory is a convolvulus. [< L *convolvulus* bindweed < *convolvere* roll around; with reference to its twining stems. See CONVOLUTE.]

con·voy (kon'voi) v., n. —v. accompany in order to protect; escort: *Warships convoy merchant ships in wartime.*
—n. **1** an escort; protection: *The gold was moved from the truck to the vault under convoy of armed guards.* **2** warships, soldiers, etc. that convoy; a protecting escort. **3** the ship, fleet, supplies, etc. accompanied by a protecting escort. **4** the act of escorting for protection: *The convoy of merchant ships was continued throughout the war.* [ME < OF *convoier, conveier.* Doublet of CONVEY.]

con·vul·sant (kən vul'sənt) adj., n. —adj. that causes convulsions. —n. a drug or other agent that causes convulsions.

con·vulse (kən vuls') v. **-vulsed, -vuls·ing.** **1** shake violently: *An earthquake convulsed the island.* **2** cause violent disturbance in; disturb violently: *Rage convulsed his face.* **3** throw into convulsions; affect with muscular spasms: *The sick child was convulsed before the doctor came.* **4** throw into a fit of laughter; cause to shake with laughter: *The clown convulsed the audience with his funny acts.* [< L *convulsus,* pp. of *convellere* tear away < *com-* (intensive) + *vellere* tear]

con·vul·sion (kən vul'shən) n. **1** Often, **convulsions,** pl. a violent, involuntary contracting and relaxing of the muscles; spasm. **2** a fit of laughter. **3** a violent disturbance: *The country was undergoing a political convulsion.*

con·vul·sive (kən vul′siv) *adj.* **1** sudden, violent, etc., like a convulsion: *The dog made convulsive efforts to free itself from the chain.* **2** having convulsions. **3** producing convulsions. —**con·vul′sive·ly**, *adv.*

co·ny or **co·ney** (kō′nē) *n., pl.* **-nies. 1** rabbit. **2** rabbit fur. **3** pika. **4** in the King James Version of the Bible, the hydrax (Deuteronomy 14:7).

coo (kü) *n., v.* **cooed, coo·ing.** —*n.* a soft, murmuring sound made by doves or pigeons. —*v.* **1** make a soft, murmuring sound. **2** murmur softly; speak in a soft, loving manner. [imitative] —**coo′er**, *n.*

coo·ee (kü′ē) *n., pl.* **-ees;** *interj., v.* —*n.* or *interj.* in Australia, a long, shrill signal call of the aborigines, adopted by the colonists. —*v.* make this call.

coo·ey (kü′ē) *n., pl.* **-eys,** or *interj.* See **cooee.**

cook (kük) *v., n.* —*v.* **1** prepare for eating by applying heat, as in boiling, baking, frying, or broiling: *We use coal, wood, gas, oil, and electricity for cooking.* **2** undergo cooking; be cooked. **3** act as cook; work as cook: *He cooked for the whole camp.* **4** apply heat or fire to. **5** *Informal.* subject to heat or fire. **6** *Informal.* tamper with (accounts, etc.); doctor; falsify: *She was caught cooking the company's books.*
cook up, *Informal.* **a** make up; prepare. **b** prepare falsely: *The young liar had cooked up a story to explain his absence.*
—*n.* a person who cooks. [OE *cōc* < LL *cocus* < L *coquus*]

cook·book (kük′bük′) *n.* a book containing directions for cooking various kinds of food; book of recipes.

cook·er (kük′ər) *n.* an apparatus or container to cook things in.

cook·er·y (kük′ər ē) *n., pl.* **-er·ies. 1** the art or occupation of cooking. **2** *Cdn.* a cookhouse at a lumber camp or mine. **3** a place for cooking.

cook·house (kük′hous′) *n.* a room or place for cooking, especially in a large camp.

cook·ie (kük′ē) *n.* **1** any of various kinds of small, sweet, more or less flat cake. Sometimes, **cooky. 2** *Slang.* person: *a shrewd cookie.* [Du. *koekje* little cake]

cook–out (kük′out′) *n.* the cooking and eating of a meal out-of-doors; a picnic, etc. where the food is cooked outdoors.

cook·shop (kük′shop′) *n.* a place where food is cooked and sold; small restaurant.

cook·stove (kük′stōv′) *n.* a stove for cooking.

cook·y (kük′ē) *n., pl.* **cook·ies.** See **cookie.**

cool (kül) *adj., n., v.* —*adj.* **1** somewhat cold; more cold than hot: *We sat in the shade where it was cool.* **2** allowing or giving a cool feeling: *cool clothes.* **3** not excited; calm and unemotional. **4** having or showing little enthusiasm or interest; not cordial: *a cool greeting.* **5** bold; impudent: *a cool customer.* **6** *Informal.* without exaggeration or qualification: *a cool million dollars.* **7** of colors suggesting coolness: *Blue and green are called cool colors. The chesterfield and chair were a cool grey.* **8** *Slang.* admirable; excellent. **9** *Slang.* relaxed and restrained in a sophisticated way: *cool jazz.*
—*n.* **1** a cool part, place, or time: *the cool of the evening.* **2** *Slang.* control of one's actions, feelings, etc.; self-control: *Maintain your cool.*
—*v.* **1** become cool: *Let the cake cool before you put on the icing.* **2** make cool.
cool it, *Slang.* calm down; regain one's self-control: *He told his excited little brother to cool it.*
cool (one's) heels, *Informal.* be kept waiting for a long time.
[OE *cōl*] —**cool′ly,** *adv.* —**cool′ness,** *n.*
☛ **Syn. adj. 1.** See note at **cold.**

cool·ant (kül′ənt) *n.* a cooling agent, used for machinery, etc.

cool·er (kül′ər) *n.* **1** an apparatus or container that cools foods or drinks, or keeps them cool. **2** anything that cools, such as a cool drink. **3** *Slang.* a jail: *He got drunk and landed in the cooler.*

cool–head·ed (kül′hed′id) *adj.* calm; not easily excited. —**cool′-head′ed·ly,** *adv.* —**cool′-head′ed·ness,** *n.*

coo·lie (kü′lē) *n.* **1** an unskilled laborer in parts of Asia. **2** any laborer who does hard work for very little pay. [probably < Tamil *kuli* hire, hired servant]
☛ **Hom. coulee.**

coo·ly (kü′lē) *n., pl.* **-lies.** See **coolie.**

coomb (küm *or* kōm) See **combe.**

coon (kün) *n.* **1** *Informal.* raccoon. **2** *Derogatory slang.* a Negro.

coon·skin (kün′skin′) *n., adj.* —*n.* the skin of a raccoon, used in making caps, coats, etc. —*adj.* made of coonskin.

coop (küp) *n., v.* —*n.* **1** a small cage or pen for chickens, rabbits, etc. **2** *Slang.* jail. —*v.* **1** keep or put in a coop. **2** confine, especially

in a very small space: *The children were cooped up indoors by the rain.* [ME *cupe* basket < L *cupa* cask]
☛ **Hom. coupe.**

co–op (kō′op *or* kō op′) *n. Informal.* co-operative.

coop·er (küp′ər) *n., v.* —*n.* a person who makes or repairs barrels, casks, etc. —*v.* make or repair (barrels, casks, etc.). [? < MDu., MLG *kuper* < L *cuparius* < *cupa* cask]

coop·er·age (küp′ər ij) *n.* **1** the work done by a cooper. **2** the price paid for such work. **3** the shop where such work is done.

co–op·er·ate or **co·op·er·ate** (kō op′ər āt′) *v.* **-at·ed, -at·ing.** work together; unite in producing a result. [< LL *cooperari* < *co-*together + *operari* to work < L *opera* effort, work] —**co·op′er·a′tor,** *n.*

co–op·er·a·tion or **co·op·er·a·tion** (kō op′ər ā′shən) *n.* **1** the act of working together; united effort or labor. **2** a co-operative combination of persons or groups. **3** *Ecology.* an interaction between individuals or organisms in a community, colony, etc. that is on the whole beneficial to all.

co–op·er·a·tive or **co·op·er·a·tive** (kō op′ər ə tiv *or* kō op′ər ā′tiv) *adj., n.* —*adj.* **1** wanting or willing to work together with others. **2** of, having to do with, or being a co-operative. —*n.* an enterprise owned jointly by a group of people and operated for their mutual benefit. Co-operatives may take the form of stores, farm marketing agencies, etc. —**co·op′er·a′tive·ly,** *adv.* —**co·op′er·a′tive·ness,** *n.*

Co–operative Commonwealth Federation a Canadian political party the CCF, established in 1932. The federal CCF ceased to exist on a national level after the New Democratic Party was formed in 1961. See also **New Democratic Party.**

co–operative store a store where merchandise is sold to members who share in the profits and losses according to the amount they buy.

co–opt (kō opt′) *v.* **1** of a committee, etc., add or elect a new member. **2** persuade or oblige to join one's own system, culture, side in a dispute, etc.; take over. —**co·op′tion,** *n.*

co–or·di·nate or **co·or·di·nate** (*adj. and n.* kō ôr′də nit *or* kō ôr′də nāt′; *v.* kō ôr′də nāt′) *adj., n., v.* **-nat·ed, -nat·ing.** —*adj.* **1** equal in importance; of equal rank. **2** made up of co-ordinate parts. **3** *Grammar.* grammatically equivalent. A compound sentence contains two or more co-ordinate clauses. **4** *Mathematics.* having to do with or involving the use of co-ordinates. **5** *Chemistry.* in which one atom shares two electrons with another atom: *a co-ordinate bond.*
—*n.* **1** a co-ordinate person or thing. **2** *Mathematics.* any of two or more magnitudes that define the position of a point, line, or plane by reference to a fixed figure, system of lines, etc.
—*v.* **1** make co-ordinate; make equal in importance. **2** arrange in proper order or relation; harmonize; adjust: *A swimmer should co-ordinate the movements of his arms and legs.* [< *co-* with + L *ordinatus,* pp. of *ordinare* regulate < *ordo, -inis* rank, order]
—**co·or′di·nate·ly,** *adv.* —**co·or′di·nate·ness,** *n.* —**co·or′di·na′tor,** *n.*

co–or·di·na·tion or **co·or·di·na·tion** (kō ôr′də nā′shən) *n.* **1** the condition of working together smoothly and easily, often used with reference to muscles: *She became a better swimmer as her co-ordination improved.* **2** arrangement in the proper order or proper relation: *She made an outline for her composition to help in the co-ordination of her ideas.* **3** putting or being put into the same order or rank.

co–or·di·na·tive or **co·or·di·na·tive** (kō ôr′də nə tiv *or* kō ôr′də nā′tiv) *adj.* co-ordinating.

coot (küt) *n.* **1** any of a genus (*Fulica*) of dark-grey inland marsh birds of the rail family, resembling ducks, but having a smaller bill and toes with scallop-like lobes of skin along the sides; mud hen. **2** a North American scoter. **3** *Informal.* a foolish or simple person: *The poor coot couldn't even remember where his hotel was.* [? < Du. *koet*]

coot·ie (küt′ē) *n. Slang.* louse.

cop¹ (kop) *n. Slang.* a police officer. [short for *copper* policeman < *cop²*]

cop² (kop) *v.* **copped, cop·ping. 1** *Slang.* steal. **2** capture; seize; nab.
cop a plea, plead guilty to one charge in order to avoid being tried for a more serious one.
cop out, *Slang.* avoid responsibility, commitment, challenge, etc. by withdrawing from the situation or by simply failing to act. [OE *coppian*]

cop. **1** copper. **2** copyright; copyrighted.

co·pa·cet·ic (kō′pə set′ik *or* kō′pə sē′tik) *adj. Slang.* completely satisfactory: *checking to see that everything was copacetic.* [origin unknown; 20c.]

co·pal (kō′pəl) *n.* a hard, lustrous resin from various tropical trees, used chiefly in making varnish. [< Sp. < Mexican *kopalli*]

co·part·ner (kō pärt′nər) *n.* a fellow partner; associate.

co·part·ner·ship (kō pärt′nər ship′) *n.* partnership.

cope[1] (kōp) *v.* **coped, cop·ing.** strive or fight with some degree of success; struggle on even terms; deal successfully: *He said he just couldn't cope any more. She was too weak to cope with the extra work.* [ME < OF *coper* strike < *coup.* See COUP.]

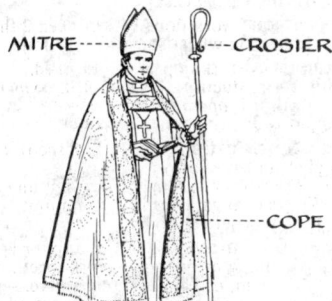

MITRE · · · · · · CROSIER

COPE

cope[2] (kōp) *n., v.* **coped, cop·ing.** —*n.* **1** a long cape worn by clergymen during certain religious rites. **2** anything like a cope; a cloaklike covering, such as a canopy, a high, arched roof, or the sky. **3** *Architecture.* a coping. —*v.* **1** cover with a cope or something like a cope. **2** provide with a coping or something like a coping. [OE *cāpe < Med.L *capa* cloak, var. of LL *cappa* hood, apparently < L *caput* head]

COPE *Cdn.* Committee for Original Peoples' Entitlement.

co·peck (kō′pek) See **kopeck.**

co·pe·pod (kō′pə pod′) *n.* any of a large subclass (Copepoda) of mostly very tiny crustaceans found as a constituent of plankton in fresh and salt water.

Co·per·ni·can (kə pėr′nə kən) *adj.* of or having to do with Nikolaus Copernicus (1473-1543), a Polish astronomer, or his system of astronomy. The Copernican system is the theory that the earth revolves on its axis and the planets move in orbits around the sun.

cope·stone (kōp′stōn′) *n.* **1** the top stone of a wall; a stone used for or in a coping. **2** a finishing touch; climax. [< *cop*[2] + *stone*]

cop·i·er (kop′ē ər) *n.* **1** a person who copies; imitator. **2** a person who makes written copies; copyist. **3** a machine that makes copies; duplicator.

co·pi·lot (kō′pī′lət) *n.* the assistant or second pilot in an aircraft.

cop·ing (kō′ping) *n.* the top layer of a brick or stone wall. It is usually built with a slope to shed water. [< *cope*[2]]

coping saw a saw with a narrow blade set in a U-shaped frame, used for cutting curves in wood. A coping saw has between three and five teeth per centimetre. Compare **fret saw.**

co·pi·ous (kō′pē əs) *adj.* **1** plentiful; abundant: *copious rainfall; a copious harvest.* **2** containing much matter. **3** containing many words; wordy: *a copious argument.* [< L *copiosus* < *copia* plenty < *copis* well supplied < *co-* with + *ops* resources] —**co′pi·ous·ly,** *adv.* —**co′pi·ous·ness,** *n.*

co·pla·nar (kō plā′nər) *adj.* *Mathematics.* (of points, lines, figures) lying in the same plane. A circle is a set of coplanar points.

co·pol·y·mer (kō pol′i mər) *n.* a chemical compound made up of large molecules, formed by the polymerization of two or more different compounds (monomers).

co·pol·y·mer·ize (kō pol′i mər īz′) *v.* **-ized, -iz·ing.** polymerize two different compounds to produce a copolymer.

cop-out (kop′out′) *n.* *Slang.* **1** the act or an instance of copping out; an avoidance of responsibility, commitment, etc. **2** an excuse for copping out: *What kind of a cop-out is that?* **3** a person who cops out.

cop·per[1] (kop′ər) *n., v., adj.* —*n.* **1** a tough, reddish-brown metallic chemical element that is easily shaped into thin sheets or fine wire and resists rust. Copper is an excellent conductor of heat and electricity. *Symbol:* Cu; *at.no.* 29; *at.wt.* 63.54. **2** a copper or bronze coin, especially a penny. **3** a large boiler or cauldron. **4** a reddish brown. —*v.* cover with copper. —*adj.* **1** made of copper. **2** having the color copper. [OE *coper* < L *cuprum,* for earlier *aes Cyprium* metal of Cyprus]

cop·per[2] (kop′ər) *n. Slang.* a police officer; cop.

cop·per·as (kop′ər əs) *n.* a green sulphate of iron, used in dyeing, photography, making ink, etc. *Formula:* $FeSO_4 \cdot 7H_2O$ [ME < OF *couperose* < Med.L (*aqua*) *cuprosa* (water) of copper < L *cuprum.* See COPPER.]

hat, āge, fär; let, ēqual, tèrm; it, īce
hot, ōpen, ôrder; oil, out; cup, pùt, rüle,
əbove, takən, pencəl, lemən, circəs

ch, child; ng, long; sh, ship
th, thin; ᴛʜ, then; zh, measure

Copper Eskimo a member of a group of Inuit living along the Arctic coast near the Coppermine River. [with reference to their use of copper tools]

cop·per·head (kop′ər hed′) *n.* a poisonous snake (*Agkistrodon contortrix*) of the eastern and central United States having a copper-colored head. It is closely related to the water moccasin.

cop·per·plate (kop′ər plāt′) *n.* **1** a thin, flat piece of copper on which a design, writing, etc. is engraved or etched. **2** an engraving, picture, or print made from a copperplate. **3** copperplate printing or engraving. **4** a type of elegant handwriting.

cop·per·smith (kop′ər smith′) *n.* a man who makes things out of copper.

copper sulphate a sulphate of copper that is white in its powdery anhydrous form and blue in its crystalline hydrous form. It is used chiefly in the dyeing of textiles, in electroplating, and as a fungicide. *Formula:* $CuSO_4$

cop·per·y (kop′ər ē) *adj.* **1** of or containing copper. **2** like copper. **3** copper-colored.

cop·pice (kop′is) *n.* copse.

cop·ra (kop′rə) *n.* the dried meat of ripe coconuts, which yields coconut oil, the basic cooking oil of the tropics, and coconut meal, a valuable high-protein food for livestock. [< Pg. < Malayalam *koppara*]

copse (kops) *n.* a thicket of small trees, bushes, shrubs, etc.; **bluff**[1] (def. 2). [< OF *copeiz* a cut-over forest < *couper* cut, ult. < L < Gk. *kolaphos* a blow]

Copt (kopt) *n.* **1** a native of Egypt descended from the ancient Egyptians. **2** a member of the Coptic Church. [< NL *Coptus* < Arabic *Quft, Qubt* the Copts]

cop·ter (kop′tər) *n. Informal.* helicopter.

Cop·tic (kop′tik) *adj., n.* —*adj.* of or having to do with the Copts. —*n.* the language formerly spoken by the Copts. Coptic is now used only in the rituals of the Coptic Church.

Coptic Church the national Christian church of Egypt and of Ethiopia.

cop·u·la (kop′yə lə) *n., pl.* **-las, lae** (-lē′; *or* -lī′). **1** linking verb. **2** something that serves to connect or link. [< L *copula* bond. Doublet of COUPLE.]

cop·u·late (kop′yə lāt′) *v.* **-lat·ed, -lat·ing.** of human beings or animals, come together in sexual union. [< L *copulare* < *copula.* See COPULA.]

cop·u·la·tion (kop′yə lā′shən) *n.* **1** sexual union between male and female human beings or animals. **2** *Grammar or logic.* a joining or being joined together; connection.

cop·u·la·tive (kop′yə lə tiv *or* kop′yə lā′tiv) *adj., n.* —*adj.* **1** serving to couple or connect. **2** *Grammar.* a serving to connect words or clauses of equal rank: And *is a copulative conjunction.* **b** being a copula: Be *is a copulative verb.* —*n.* a copulative word. In *He became captain, became* is a copulative. —**cop′u·la′tive·ly,** *adv.*

cop·y (kop′ē) *n., pl.* **cop·ies;** *v.* **cop·ied, cop·y·ing.** —*n.* **1** anything made to be just like another; anything made on the pattern or model of another; duplicate; reproduction: *One written page, picture, dress, or chair can be an exact copy of another.* **2** *Archaic.* something to be followed as a pattern or model, especially for penmanship. **3** one of a number of books, newspapers, magazines, pictures, etc. made at the same printing. **4** the material to be set up in type for a book, newspaper, or magazine. **5** *Journalism.* source material for an article, news report, etc.: *She's always good copy, with her unusual ideas and colorful way of talking.* —*v.* make a copy; make a copy of: *Copy this page. She copied her friend's hat.* **2** be like; follow as a pattern or model: *The little boy copied his father's way of walking.* [ME < OF *copier* < Med.L *copia* transcript < L *copia* plenty. See COPIOUS.]

☛ *Syn. v.* **1. Copy, imitate** = try to make a thing like something else by following a pattern or model. **Copy** = follow a model as closely and exactly as possible: *He copied all the pictures in his book.* **Imitate** = try to make or do something like a pattern or model: *Sometimes a teacher asks a class to imitate something written by a great author.*

cop·y·book (kop′ē bùk′) *n., adj.* —*n.* a book with models of handwriting to be copied in learning to write. —*adj.* commonplace; conventional; ordinary: *a copybook speech.*

co·py·cat (kop′ē kat′) *n. Scornful.* a person who slavishly

imitates another in dress, behavior, etc. (*a word used especially by children*).

copy desk the desk in a newspaper office where news stories and articles are edited before being set up for printing.

copy editor a person who edits written material and prepares it for publication.

cop·y·hold (kop′ē hōld′) *n. Brit. Historical.* 1 ownership of land proved by a copy of the roll of a manorial court. 2 the land held in this way.

cop·y·hold·er (kop′ē hōl′dər) *n.* 1 a person who reads manuscripts aloud to a proofreader. 2 *Law.* a person who owns land by copyhold.

cop·y·ist (kop′ē ist) *n.* 1 a person who makes written copies. 2 a person who copies; imitator.

cop·y·right (kop′ē rīt′) *n., v.* —*n.* a right to copy, granted by law to an author, composer, artist, etc., making him or her for a certain number of years the only person who can sell, print, publish, or copy a particular work, or who can authorize others to do so: *Because Shakespeare's plays are not in copyright, anyone can produce them on stage without paying a fee.* —*v.* protect by getting a copyright: *Books, pieces of music, plays, etc. are usually copyrighted.*

cop·y·writ·er (kop′ē rī′tər) *n.* a person whose work is writing advertisements and other publicity material to be used in newspapers, magazines, radio, or television.

co·quet (kō ket′) *v.* -**quet·ted**, -**quet·ting**. 1 flirt. 2 trifle. [< F *coqueter* < *coquet*, dim. of *coq* cock]

co·quet·ry (kō′kə trē *or* kō ket′rē) *n., pl.* -**ries.** 1 flirting. 2 trifling.

co·quette (kō ket′) *n.* a woman who tries to attract men merely to please her vanity; flirt. [< F *coquette*, fem. of *coquet.* See COQUET.]

co·quet·tish (kō ket′ish) *adj.* 1 of a coquette. 2 like a coquette; like a coquette's. —**co·quet′tish·ly,** *adv.*

co·qui·na (kō kē′nə) *n.* a soft, whitish rock composed of fragments of sea shells and corals. [< Sp. *coquina* shellfish. Akin to CONCH.]

cor- *prefix.* together or altogether; the form of **com-** occurring before *r*, as in correspond.

cor. 1 corner. 2 coroner. 3 correction; corrected. 4 corresponding.

Cor. Coroner.

cor·a·cle (kôr′ə kəl) *n.* a light, bowl-shaped boat used for many centuries in the British Isles for river fishing, originally made of woven reeds, grasses, or branches with a covering of hides. The coracles used today in Wales and Ireland have a covering of canvas and tar. [< Welsh *corwgl* < *corwg* round body or vessel, torso, carcass]

cor·a·coid (kôr′ə koid′) *n., adj.* —*n.* 1 in birds and reptiles, the bone between the shoulder blade and the breastbone. 2 in mammals, a bony process extending from the shoulder blade to or toward the breastbone. —*adj.* of this bone or process. [< NL < Gk. *korakoeidēs* < *korax, -akos* crow + *eidos* form]

cor·al (kôr′əl) *n., adj.* —*n.* 1 any of various marine polyps (class Anthozoa) having a stony, horny, or leathery external or internal skeleton. Most corals live in colonies, with their bodies joined together by membranes and their skeletons cemented together. 2 the stony or horny substance that forms the skeleton of certain of these animals, especially any of the order Madreporaria, colonies of which form coral reefs and islands. 3 a colony of certain of these animals which, together with the skeletons of dead individual animals, form a single mass. 4 a piece of the skeletal material of certain of these animals, especially any of several corals of the genus *Corallium*, whose pink or red internal skeleton is used for jewellery. 5 (*adj.*) made of coral: *a coral necklace.* 6 a deep, somewhat yellowish, pink. —*adj.* having the color coral. [ME < OF < L *corallum* < Gk. *koral(l)ion*]
🖝 Hom. **choral.**

coral reef a reef consisting mainly of coral produced by many colonies of coral polyps over a period of centuries, with new animals building on the skeletons left behind by animals that have died.

cor·al·root (kôr′əl rüt′) *n.* any of a genus (*Corallorhiza*) of orchids found in northern temperate regions, having leafless stems, pink, purple, or greenish flowers, and branched underground stems resembling coral.

coral snake 1 any of a genus (*Micrurus*) of poisonous snakes of tropical and subtropical America typically marked with red, black, and yellow or white bands around the body. Coral snakes are related to the cobras and mambas. 2 any of various brightly colored African and Asian snakes belonging to the same family (Elapidae).

cor·bel (kôr′bəl) *n., v.* -**belled** *or* -**beled**, -**bel·ling** *or* -**bel·ing.** —*n. Architecture.* a bracket of stone, wood, etc. on the side of a wall. It helps support a projecting ledge above. —*v.* furnish with corbels; support by corbels. [ME < OF *corbel*, dim. of *corp* raven < L *corvus*]

cor·bie (kôr′bē) *n. Scottish.* a raven or crow. [alteration of ME *corbin* < OF < L *corvinus* of a raven < *corvus* raven]

cord (kôrd) *n., v.* —*n.* 1 heavy, thick string of several strands or fibres twisted together; thin rope. 2 a thin, flexible, insulated cable having a plug at one end, used to connect an electrical appliance to a source of power. 3 a similar cable for connecting a desk telephone to the main telephone line. 4 *Anatomy.* a structure in an animal body that resembles a cord. The spinal cord is in the backbone. The vocal cords are in the throat. 5 any force or influence that ties or restrains: *a cord of affection.* 6 a ridge on cloth. 7 cloth made with such ridges. 8 **cords,** *pl.* trousers made of corduroy or other cloth with ridges. 9 a unit for measuring cut firewood, equal to 128 cubic feet (about 3.6 m³). A standard cord is a stack of 4-foot lengths of wood measuring 8 feet long by 4 feet high (about 1.2 m × 2.4 m × 1.2 m). Since fireplaces have become smaller, dealers usually sell wood in **face cords** for which the wood is cut in 2-foot (about 60 cm) lengths.
—*v.* 1 fasten or tie with heavy string or cord, or provide with cord. 2 pile (wood) in cords. [ME < OF *corde* < L < Gk. *chordē* gut. Doublet of CHORD².] —**cord·less,** *adj.*
🖝 Hom. **chord.**

cord·age (kôr′dij) *n.* 1 cords; ropes. The cordage of a ship is also called its rigging. 2 a quantity of wood measured in cords.

cor·date (kôr′dāt) *adj.* heart-shaped. [< NL *cordatus* < L *cor, cordis* heart]

cord·ed (kôr′did) *adj.* 1 having ridges on it; ribbed. 2 fastened with a cord; bound with cords. 3 made of cords; furnished with cords. 4 of wood, piled in cords.

cor·delle (kôr del′ *or* kôr′dəl) *n. v.* -**elled**, -**el·ling.** *Cdn.* —*n.* a towline. —*v.* tow a canoe, etc. with a cordelle. [< Cdn.F < F *cordelle*, dim. of OF *corde.* See CORD.]

cor·dial (kôr′jəl *or* kôr′dē əl) *adj., n.,* —*adj.* 1 warm; friendly: *His host gave him a cordial welcome.* 2 strengthening; stimulating: *a cordial drink.* —*n.* 1 a food, drink, or medicine that strengthens or stimulates. 2 liqueur. [ME < Med.L *cordialis* < L *cor, cordis* heart] —**cor′dial·ly,** *adv.* —**cor′dial·ness,** *n.*

cor·dial·i·ty (kôr jal′ə tē *or* kôr′dē al′ə tē) *n., pl.* -**ties.** a cordial quality or feeling; warmth: *The cordiality of his welcome made Tom feel at home.*

cor·di·er·ite (kôr′dē ə rīt′) *n.* a blue crystalline mineral, a silicate of magnesium and aluminum, containing some iron. *Formula:* $(MgFe_2)Al_4Si_5O_{18}$

cor·dil·le·ra (kôr′dəl yer′ə *or* kôr dil′ər ə) *n.* a long mountain range; chain of mountains. [< Sp., ult. < L *chorda* rope, cord. See CORD.]

Cor·dil·le·ran (kôr′dil yər′ən *or* kôr dil′ər ən) *adj.* 1 of the Cordilleras, a mountain system in W North America and South America. 2 in the Cordilleras.

cord·ite (kôr′dīt) *n.* a smokeless gunpowder composed chiefly of nitroglycerin and guncotton. [< *cord*, n.]

cor·do·ba (kôr′də bə) *n.* 1 the basic unit of money in Nicaragua, divided into 100 centavos. See table at **money.** 2 a coin or note worth one cordoba. [< Francisco de *Córdoba* (1475-1526), a Spanish explorer]

cor·don (kôr′dən) *n., v.* —*n.* 1 a line or circle of soldiers, police, ships, forts, etc. placed at intervals around an area to guard it. 2 a cord, braid, or ribbon worn as an ornament or badge of honor. —*v.* put a protective line or barrier around (*usually used with* **off**): *The area around the famous painting was cordoned off.* [< F *cordon* < *corde* cord]

cor·do·van (kôr′də vən *or, for n.* 1 *and adj.* 1, kôr dō′vən) *n., adj.* —*n.* 1 a kind of soft, fine-grained leather first made in Córdoba, Spain. Cordovan was originally made of goatskin, but now is usually made of split horsehide. 2 **Cordovan,** a native or inhabitant of Córdoba. —*adj.* 1 made of cordovan. 2 **Cordovan,** of or having to do with Córdoba. [< Sp. *cordobán* < *Córdoba,* a city in S Spain]

cor·du·roy (kôr′də roi′ *or* kôr′də roi′) *n., v.* —*n.* 1 cloth, usually of cotton, having a thin but twill weave, having a thick, velvetlike cut pile in wide or narrow ridges called wales. 2 (*adj.*) having ridges like corduroy. 3 *Cdn.* a corduroy road or bridge. 4 **corduroys,** *pl.* corduroy trousers. 5 (*adj.*) —*v.* surface or bridge with logs laid crosswise: *They corduroyed the muddy portage road.* [< *cord* + obs. *duroy,* a kind of woollen cloth produced formerly]

corduroy bridge *Cdn.* 1 a corduroy road. 2 a bridge built over a stream or river and having a surface of logs laid crosswise.

corduroy road *Cdn.* a road or stretch of road surfaced with logs laid crosswise, usually across low-lying, swampy or muddy land.

cord·wain (kôrd′wān′) *n. Archaic.* Cordovan leather. [ME < AF *cordewan*, OF *cordouan* < Sp. *cordobán*. See CORDOVAN.]

cord·wain·er (kôrd′wān′ər) *n. Obsolete.* shoemaker. [< AF *cordewaner* < *cordewan* Cordovan < Sp. *cordobán* < *Córdoba*]

cord·wood (kôrd′wŭd′) *n.* **1** wood sold or stacked in cords. **2** wood or standing timber suitable for use as firewood.

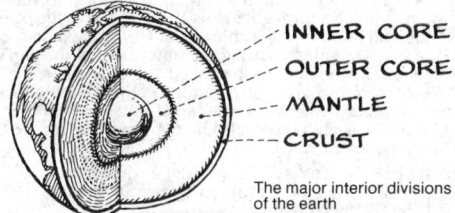

INNER CORE
OUTER CORE
MANTLE
CRUST

The major interior divisions of the earth

core (kôr) *n., v.* **cored, cor·ing.** —*n.* **1** the hard central part of some fruits, such as apples and pears, that contains seeds. **2** the central part of the earth, beginning at a depth of about 2880 km and having a radius of about 3400 km, believed by most geologists to consist of iron with a small amount of nickel. **3** a base layer of low-grade wood, platewood, etc. to which veneers or plastic laminates are glued: *The wall units are constructed of elm veneers on a platewood core.* **4** *Electricity.* **a** the conducting wire and its insulation in a subterranean or submarine cable. **b** a bar of soft iron, bundle of iron wires, etc. forming the centre of an electromagnet, induction coil, etc., and serving to increase and concentrate the induced magnetic field. **5** *Metallurgy.* an inner mould made of sand and other ingredients filling the space intended to be left hollow in a hollow casting. **6 a** the heartwood of a tree. **b** the lumber from this wood, usually soft and inexpensive, used as a base for veneers. **7** a central strand around which other strands are wound or woven in making certain kinds of rope, cord, or thread. **8** a cylindrical portion of rock or other material extracted from the centre of a mass by cutting or drilling. **9** the area in the centre of a nuclear reactor where the reaction takes place. **10** the central or most important part: *the core of a boil, the core of a hurricane, the core of an argument.* —*v.* take out the core of: *The cook cored the apples.* [ME; origin uncertain] —**cor′er,** *n.*
☛ *Hom.* **corps.**

CORE (kôr) *n. U.S.* Congress of Racial Equality.

co·re·op·sis (kō′rē op′sis) *n.* any of a genus (*Coreopsis*) of plants of the composite family having yellow, red-and-yellow, or reddish flowers shaped like daisies. [< NL < Gk. *koris* bedbug + *opsis* appearance; from the shape of the seed]

co·re·spond·ent (kō′rə spon′dənt *or* kôr′ə spon′dənt) *n. Law.* a person accused of adultery with one (husband or wife) who is being sued for divorce.

Cor·fam (kôr′fam) *n. Trademark.* a porous, leatherlike, synthetic plastic used especially for the manufacture of footwear. [arbitrary coinage]

cor·gi (kôr′gē) *n.* Welsh corgi.

co·ri·an·der (kō′rē an′dər) *n.* **1** an annual herb (*Coriandrum sativum*) of the parsley family native to the Mediterranean region, but widely cultivated for its tiny, seedlike, sweet-smelling fruits. **2** its fruit, used as a spice and as a flavoring in liqueurs and medicines. [< F *coriandre* < L < Gk. *koriandron*, var. of *koriannon*, the name of this plant]

Co·rin·thi·an (kə rin′thē ən) *n., adj.* —*n.* a native or inhabitant of Corinth, a seaport in S Greece. —*adj.* **1** of or having to do with Corinth or its people. **2** *Architecture.* of, having to do with, or designating the latest of the three orders of ancient Greek architecture. The characteristic Corinthian column is 10 diameters high and has a slender, deeply fluted shaft with a bell-shaped capital carved with an ornate design of acanthus leaves. See *order* for picture.

cork (kôrk) *n., v.* —*n.* **1** the light, thick, outer bark of the cork oak, used for bottle stoppers, floats for fishing lines, inner soles of shoes, floor and wall coverings, etc. **2** anything made of cork, especially a stopper for a bottle: *Bottles of wine are usually closed with a cork.* **3** any stopper made of other materials such as glass, rubber, etc. **4** (*adj.*) made of cork or with cork. **5** *Botany.* the outer bark of woody plants, consisting of layers of dead tissue produced by the cork cambium. —*v.* **1** stop up with a cork. **2** confine; restrain; check. **3** blacken with burnt cork. [< Sp. *alcorque* < Arabic < L *quercus* oak]

cork·age (kôr′kij) *n.* a charge made by a hotel or restaurant for uncorking and serving wine supplied by a client.

hat, āge, fär; let, ēqual, tèrm; it, īce
hot, ōpen, ôrder; oil, out; cup, pút, rüle,
above, takən, pencəl, lemən, circəs
ch, child; ng, long; sh, ship
th, thin; ŦH, then; zh, measure

cork oak an evergreen oak (*Quercus suber*) of the Mediterranean from whose inner bark cork is obtained. Cork oaks are also cultivated in India and the S United States.

cork·screw (kôrk′skrü′) *n., v.* —*n.* **1** a tool with a screw, or spiral, for pulling out the corks of bottles. **2** (*adj.*) shaped like a corkscrew; spiral: *The plane did a corkscrew dive.* —*v.* move or advance in a spiral or zigzag course.

cork·y (kôr′kē) *adj.* **cork·i·er, cork·i·est.** *Informal.* **1** of cork. **2** like a cork: *a corky flavor.* —**cork′i·ness,** *n.*

corm (kôrm) *n. Botany.* a fleshy, bulblike underground stem that has leaves and buds on the upper surface and roots usually on the lower. [< NL *cormus* < Gk. *kormos* stripped tree trunk < *keirein* shear]

cor·mo·rant (kôr′mə rənt) *n.* **1** any of a family (Phalacrocoracidae) of large, mainly black, web-footed sea birds having a long, hooked bill and an often bright-colored pouch of naked skin under the mouth. Cormorants are used in the Far East for catching fish. **2** a greedy person. [ME < OF *cormaran* < *corp* raven (< L *corvus*) + *marenc* of the sea < L *mare*]

corn¹ (kôrn) *n., v.* —*n.* **1** a tall cereal plant (*Zea mays*) having seeds, or kernels, that grow in rows along a thick, woody axis called a cob; maize; Indian corn. **2** the kernels, used for food or fodder. **3** any small, hard seed or grain, especially of cereal plants. **4** in England, grain in general, especially wheat. **5** in Scotland and Ireland, oats. **6** any small, hard particle, as of sand or salt. **7** corn snow. **8** *Slang.* anything trite, too sentimental, or unsophisticated. —*v.* **1** preserve (meat) with strong salt water or by dry salt. **2** form into grains, as gunpowder; granulate. [OE]

corn² (kôrn) *n.* a hardening and thickening of the skin, usually on a toe. Corns are caused by pressure or rubbing and are often very painful. [ME < OF *corn* horn < L *cornu*]

corn·ball (kôrn′bol′ *or* kôrn′bôl′) *n. Slang.* **1** corny: *cornball humor.* **2** an unsophisticated person.

corn boil corn roast.

corn borer the larva of any of various moths, such as *Pyrausta nubilalis*, that attacks corn plants.

corn bread a type of bread made of corn meal instead of flour.

corn·cob (kôrn′kob′) *n.* **1** the central, woody part of an ear of corn, on which the kernels grow. **2** a tobacco pipe with a bowl hollowed out of a piece of dried corncob.

corn cockle a European annual plant (*Agrostemma githago*) of the pink family having purplish red flowers and poisonous seeds. It is now naturalized in North America, where it has become a weed in grainfields.

corn crake a short-billed rail (*Crex crex*) native to Europe and Asia, commonly found in European grainfields.

corn·crib (kôrn′krib′) *n.* a bin or small, ventilated building for storing unshelled corn.

cor·ne·a (kôr′nē ə) *n.* the transparent part of the outer coat of the eyeball. The cornea covers the iris and the pupil. See *eye* for picture. [< Med.L *cornea* (*tela*) horny (web) < L *cornu* horn]

cor·ne·al (kôr′nē əl) *adj.* of or having to do with the cornea.

corned (kôrnd) *adj.* **1** preserved with strong salt water or dry salt: *corned beef.* **2** *Slang.* drunk.

cor·nel (kôr′nəl) *n.* dogwood. [< G < Med.L *cornolius*, ult. < L *cornus*]

cor·nel·ian (kôr nēl′yən) *n.* carnelian.

cor·ne·ous (kôr′ nē əs) *adj.* horny; of or like horn. [< L *corneus* < *cornu* horn]

cor·ner (kôr′nər) *n., v.* —*n.* **1** the point or place where lines or surfaces meet: *A diagonal joins two opposite corners of a rectangle.* **2** the space between two lines or surfaces near where they meet; angle: *There was a bookcase in the far corner of the room.* **3** the place where two streets meet. **4** (*adj.*) at a corner: *the corner drugstore.* **5** (*adj.*) for a corner: *a corner shelf.* **6** something that forms, protects, or decorates a corner: *The leather wallet has gold corners.* **7** a secret or secluded place. **8** a place that is far away; region; part: *People have searched in all corners of the earth for gold.* **9** an awkward or difficult position; a place from which escape is impossible: *a tight corner.* **10** *Business.* a buying up of the available supply of some stock or article to raise its price: *a corner in cotton.*

cut corners, **a** shorten the way by going across corners. **b** save money, effort, time, etc., by cutting down.

turn the corner, pass the worst or most dangerous point.

—*v.* **1** put in a corner; drive into a corner. **2** force into an awkward or difficult position; drive into a place from which escape is impossible. **3** *Business.* buy up all or nearly all that can be had of (something) to raise its price: *Some speculators have tried to corner wheat.* **4** drive a car around a sharp corner. **5** of an automobile, round sharp corners at relatively high speeds without sway. [ME < AF var. of OF *cornere* < L *cornu* horn, tip]

cor·ner·stone (kôr′nər stōn′) *n.* **1** a stone at the corner of two walls which it holds together. **2** such a stone built into the corner of a building as its formal beginning. The laying of a cornerstone is often accompanied with ceremonies. **3** a main part on which something else rests; foundation; basis: *Clear thinking is the cornerstone of good writing.*

cor·ner·ways (kôr′nər wāz′) *adv.* cornerwise.

cor·ner·wise (kôr′nər wīz′) *adv.* **1** with the corner in front; so as to form a corner. **2** from corner to corner; diagonally.

cor·net[1] (kôr net′ *for 1;* kôr′nit *or* kôr net′ *for 2*) *n.* **1** a valved brass wind instrument resembling a trumpet, now used mostly in brass bands. The cornet was very popular for all orchestral music in the late nineteenth century, before the valve trumpet was adopted. **2** a piece of paper rolled into a cone and twisted at one end, used to hold candy, nuts, etc. [ME < OF, ult. < L *cornu* horn]

cor·net[2] (kôr′nit *or* kôr net′) *n.* **1** a large, spreading, white cap worn by Sisters of Charity. **2** *Historical.* an officer in a British cavalry troop who carried the flag. [< F *cornette,* dim. of *corne,* ult. < L *cornua* horns]

cor·net·tist *or* **cor·net·ist** (kôr net′ist) *n.* a person who plays the cornet, especially a skilled player.

corn·field (kôrn′fēld′) *n.* a field of growing corn.

corn·flow·er (kôrn′flou′ər) *n.* bachelor's-button.

corn·husk (kôrn′husk′) *n.* the husk of an ear of corn.

cor·nice (kôr′nis) *n., v.* **-niced, -nic·ing.** —*n.* **1** *Architecture.* the moulded, projecting, topmost part of the upper section of a wall or storey supported on columns or pilasters; the top part of an entablature. See **column** for picture. **2** an ornamental moulding around the top of a wall. **3** any of various other ornamental mouldings, as for concealing a curtain rod or otherwise decorating the top of a window. —*v.* furnish or decorate with a cornice. [< F < Ital. < Med.Gk. *korōnis* copestone < Gk. *korōnis* something bent]

Cor·nish (kôr′nish) *adj., n.* —*adj.* of or having to do with Cornwall, a county in SW England, its people, or the language formerly spoken by them. —*n.* **1** the ancient Celtic language of Cornwall. **2** Rock Cornish; Cornish hen.

Cornish hen Rock Cornish.

Cor·nish·man (kôr′nish mən) *n., pl.* **-men.** a native or inhabitant of Cornwall.

corn·meal (kôrn′mēl′) *n.* meal made from ground-up corn.

corn pone in the S United States, a flat loaf of cornmeal shaped by hand; corn bread made without milk or eggs.

corn roast a picnic held usually in the fall, at which corn is roasted or boiled for eating off the cob.

corn silk the long, glossy styles that emerge in a silky tuft from the tip of an ear of corn.

corn snow snow consisting of granular particles suggesting cornmeal, formed by alternate periods of thawing and freezing.

corn·stalk (kôrn′stok′ *or* -stôk′) *n.* a stalk of a corn plant.

corn·starch (kôrn′stärch′) *n.* a starchy flour made from Indian corn, used to thicken puddings, etc.

corn stook a stack of cornstalks cut and set up on end together in a field.

corn sugar sugar made from cornstarch.

corn syrup syrup made from corn.

cor·nu·co·pi·a (kôr′nyə kō′pē ə) *n.* **1** a horn-shaped container or ornament. **2** a decorated curved horn overflowing with fruits and flowers, used as a symbol of a good harvest or any time of prosperity. **3** an overflowing supply; abundance. [< LL *cornucopia,* for L *cornu copiae* horn of plenty]

corn·y (kôr′nē) *adj.* **corn·i·er, corn·i·est.** *Informal.* too trite, sentimental, or unsophisticated: *corny jokes. That movie has some corny scenes.*

co·rol·la (kə rol′ə) *n.* the internal envelope or floral leaves of a flower, usually of some color other than green; the petals. The corolla can consist of separate petals, as in the rose, or fused petals,

as in the morning glory. [< L *corolla* garland, dim. of *corona* crown]

cor·ol·lar·y (kə rol′ə rē *or* kôr′ə ler′ē) *n., pl.* **-lar·ies.** **1** something proved incidentally in proving something else. **2** an inference; deduction. **3** a natural consequence or result: *She believes her good health is a corollary of her simple way of life.* **4** (*adj.*) like a corollary; resulting. [< LL *corollarium* < L *corollarium* gift < *corolla* garland. See COROLLA.]

co·ro·na (kə rō′nə) *n., pl.* **-nas, -nae** (-nē). **1** *Meteorology.* a ring of usually colored light visible around a shining body such as the sun or moon when it is seen through a thin cloud of water droplets or, sometimes, dust particles in the atmosphere. Compare **halo** (def. 1). **2** *Astronomy.* a layer of gases forming the outer part of the sun's atmosphere. The corona is visible to the naked eye only when the direct rays of the sun are blocked during a total eclipse. **3** an upper or crownlike part. **4** *Botany.* the trumpet-shaped inner part of the corolla of some flowers, such as the daffodil. **5** a kind of cigar. [< L *corona* crown. Doublet of CROWN.]

Corona Aus·tral·is (o strā′lis *or* ô strā′lis) a southern constellation near Sagittarius; the Southern Crown; Wreath. [< L *Corona australis* the Southern Crown]

Corona Bo·re·al·is (bôr′ē al′is *or* bôr′ē ā′lis) a northern constellation, the Northern Crown. [< L *Corona borealis* the Northern Crown]

cor·o·nach (kôr′ə nəh) *n. Scottish* and *Irish.* a dirge.

cor·o·nal (*n.* kôr′ə nəl; *adj.* kə rō′nəl *or* kôr′ə nəl) *n., adj.* —*n.* **1** a crown or coronet. **2** garland. —*adj.* of or having to do with a crown or a corona.

cor·o·nar·y (kôr′ə ner′ē) *adj., n.* —*adj.* **1** of or designating either or both of the two arteries branching from the aorta that supply blood to the muscular tissue of the heart. **2** having to do with or resembling a crown. —*n.* coronary thrombosis. [< L *coronarius* encircling < *corona* crown]

coronary thrombosis the stopping up, or occlusion, of a coronary artery by a blood clot (thrombus), usually as a result of atherosclerosis and usually leading to the destruction of muscle tissue in the heart. Compare **myocardial infarction.**

cor·o·na·tion (kôr′ə nā′shən) *n.* **1** the ceremony of crowning a monarch. **2** (*adj.*) of or having to do with a coronation: *coronation robes.*

cor·o·ner (kôr′ə nər) *n.* a person, usually a medical doctor, appointed by a provincial government for a particular community or area to investigate the cause of any sudden or unexpected death that may be the result of a crime or of a situation that could be dangerous to other people. [ME < AF *corouner* officer of the crown < *coroune.* See CROWN.]

coroner's inquest an inquiry by a coroner, usually with a jury, into the cause of a death that is not clearly due to natural causes.

coroner's jury a group of persons chosen to witness a coroner's investigation and to determine the cause of any death not clearly due to natural causes.

cor·o·net (kôr′ə net′) *n.* **1** a small crown worn as a mark of noble rank below that of a monarch. A monarch wears a crown; princes and nobles wear coronets. **2** a circle of gold, jewels, or flowers worn around the head as an ornament. [< MF *coronete,* dim. of OF *corone* crown < L *corona*]

Corp. **1** Corporation. **2** Corporal.

cor·po·ral[1] (kôr′pə rəl *or* kôr′prəl) *adj.* of or having to do with the body: *corporal punishment.* [< L *corporalis* < *corpus* body] —**cor′po·ral·ly,** *adv.*

cor·po·ral[2] (kôr′pə rəl *or* kôr′prəl) *n.* **1** *Canadian Forces.* a non-commissioned officer ranking next above a private and below a master corporal. See chart at **rank**[1]. **2** a non-commissioned officer of similar rank in the armed forces of other countries. **3** in the RCMP, a non-commissioned officer senior to a first constable and junior to a staff sergeant. *Abbrev.:* Cpl. or Cpl [< F *corporal,* former var. of *caporal* < Ital. *caporale* < *capo* head < L *caput*]

cor·po·ral·cy (kôr′pə rəl sē *or* kôr′prəl sē) *n.* the rank or position of a corporal.

corporal punishment physical punishment; punishment given by striking the body, as in spanking, strapping, beating, or whipping.

cor·po·rate (kôr′pə rit *or* kôr′prit) *adj.* **1** forming a corporation; incorporated. **2** belonging to a corporation; having to do with a corporation. **3** united; combined. [< L *corporatus,* pp. of *corporare* form into a body < *corpus* body]

cor·po·rate·ly (kôr′pə rit lē *or* kôr′prit lē) *adv.* **1** in a corporate capacity. **2** bodily; in the body.

cor·po·ra·tion (kôr′pə rā′shən) *n.* **1** a group of persons having a charter that gives them as a group certain legal rights and privileges distinct from those of the individual members of the group. A corporation can buy and sell, own property, etc., as if it were a

single person. 2 a group of persons with authority to act as a single person. The mayor and aldermen of a city are a corporation. 3 *Informal.* a prominent abdomen.

cor·po·re·al (kôr pô′rē əl) *adj.* 1 of or for the body; bodily: *Food and water are corporeal nourishment.* 2 of a material nature; tangible: *Land, trees, and buildings are corporeal things.* [< L *corporeus* < *corpus* body] —**cor·po′re·al·ly,** *adv.*

corps (kôr) *n., pl.* **corps** (kôrz). 1 a military formation made up of more than one division. 2 a branch of the armed forces that provides special services: *the Signal Corps.* 3 a group of people organized for working together: *a corps of volunteers.* 4 corps de ballet. [< F < OF *corps* < L *corpus* body. Doublet of CORPSE, CORPUS, CORSE.] ☛ *Hom.* **core.**

corps de bal·let (kôr′də ba lā′; *French,* kôr də bä lā′) all the dancers in a ballet company not classed as soloists. The members of the corps de ballet usually dance as a group. [< F]

corpse (kôrps) *n.* a dead body, especially of a human being. [ME < OF *cors* < L *corpus* body. Doublet of CORPS, CORPUS, CORSE.]

Corps of Commissionaires an organization of former members of the armed forces who can be hired as gatekeepers, guards, night watchmen, etc. Members of the Corps of Commissionaires, who wear dark-blue uniforms, are often employed to protect property.

cor·pu·lence (kôr′pyə ləns) *n.* fatness.

cor·pu·len·cy (kôr′pyə lən sē) *n.* corpulence.

cor·pu·lent (kôr′pyə lənt) *adj.* fat. [< L *corpulentus* < *corpus* body] —**cor′pu·lent·ly,** *adv.*

cor·pus (kôr′pəs) *n., pl.* **-po·ra** (-pə rə). 1 a complete collection of writings on some subject, or of some period, or of laws, etc. 2 any body of material, data, etc., especially as the object of study or research. 3 a body, especially the dead body of a person or animal. [< L *corpus* body. Doublet of CORPS, CORPSE, CORSE.]

Cor·pus Chris·ti (kôr′pəs kris′tē) *Christianity, esp. Roman Catholic Church.* the feast in honor of the Eucharist, celebrated on the Sunday following Trinity Sunday. [< L *corpus Christi* body of Christ]

cor·pus·cle (kôr′pəs əl *or* kôr′pus əl) *n.* 1 any of the cells that float in the blood, lymph, etc. Red corpuscles carry oxygen and carbon dioxide; some white corpuscles destroy disease germs. 2 a very small particle. [< L *corpusculum,* dim. of *corpus* body]

cor·pus·cu·lar (kôr pus′kyə lər) *adj.* of corpuscles; consisting of corpuscles; like that of corpuscles.

cor·pus de·lic·ti (kôr′pəs di lik′tī *or* di lik′tē) 1 *Latin.* the actual facts which prove a crime or offence against the law has been committed. 2 *Informal.* the body of a murdered person. [< L *corpus delicti* body of the crime]

cor·pus ju·ris (kôr′pəs jür′is) a complete collection of laws. [< L]

corr. 1 correspondent; corresponding; correspondence. 2 correct; corrected.

cor·ral (kə ral′) *n., v.* **-ralled, -ral·ling.** —*n.* 1 an enclosed space for keeping horses, cattle, etc., captured or kept. 2 a circular camp formed by wagons, carts, etc., for defence against attack. 3 a trap for game, fish, etc.
—*v.* 1 drive into or keep in a corral. 2 hem in; surround; capture. 3 form (wagons) into a circular camp. 4 *Slang.* catch; get; collect: *Our club has corralled several new members.* [< Sp. *corral* < *corro* ring. Doublet of CRAWL[2].]

cor·rect (kə rekt′) *adj., v.* —*adj.* 1 agreeing with fact or reason; free from mistakes or faults; right: *the correct answer.* 2 agreeing with a general standard of good taste; proper: *correct manners.*
—*v.* 1 change to what is right; remove mistakes or faults from: *Correct any wrong spellings that you find.* 2 alter or adjust to agree with some standard: *to correct the reading of a barometer.* 3 point out or mark the errors of: *The teacher corrects the test papers and returns them to the students.* 4 set right by punishing; find fault with in order to improve; punish: *The mother corrected the child.* 5 counteract something hurtful; cure; overcome: *to correct a bad habit. He was given medicine to correct his stomach trouble.* [< L *correctus,* pp. of *corrigere* make straight < *com-* + *regere* direct] —**cor·rect′a·ble,** *adj.* —**cor·rect′ly,** *adv.* —**cor·rect′ness,** *n.* —**cor·rec′tor,** *n.*
☛ *Syn. adj.* 1. **Correct, accurate, exact** = without error or mistake. **Correct,** the most general word, suggests only the absence of mistakes or errors: *He gave correct answers to the questions.* **Accurate** emphasizes the suggestion of careful effort to make something agree with facts or a model: *He gave an accurate account of the incident.* **Exact** emphasizes the suggestion of complete agreement in every detail with the facts or model: *His painting is an exact copy of the original.*

cor·rect·ed (kə rek′tid) *adj.* made free from mistakes or faults.

cor·rec·tion (kə rek′shən) *n.* 1 the act or process of correcting. 2 something put in place of an error or mistake. 3 a punishment; rebuke; scolding. 4 an amount added or subtracted to correct a

hat, āge, fär; let, ēqual, tèrm; it, īce
hot, ōpen, ôrder; oil, out; cup, pút, rüle,
əbove, takən, pencəl, lemən, circəs

ch, child; ng, long; sh, ship
th, thin; ᴛʜ, then; zh, measure

result. 5 the counteracting or neutralizing of harmful or unpleasant effects, as of a medicine.

cor·rec·tion·al (kə rek′shən əl) *adj.* of or having to do with correction; corrective.

cor·rec·tive (kə rek′tiv) *adj., n.* —*adj.* tending to correct; setting right; making better: *Corrective exercises will make weak muscles strong.* —*n.* something that tends to correct or set right anything that is wrong or hurtful. -**cor·rec′tive·ly,** *adv.*

cor·re·late (kôr′ə lāt′) *v.* **-lat·ed, -lat·ing;** *n.* —*v.* 1 be related one to the other; have a mutual relation: *The results of the study on television advertising correlate closely with earlier findings.* 2 place in or bring into proper relation with one another; show the connection or relation between: *Try to correlate your conclusions with the facts.* —*n.* either of two related things, especially when one implies the other. [< *cor-* together + *relate*]

cor·re·lat·ed (kôr′ə lāt′id) *adj.* related one to another.

cor·re·la·tion (kôr′ə lā′shən) *n.* 1 the mutual relation of two or more things: *There is a close correlation between climate and vegetation.* 2 correlating or being correlated.

cor·rel·a·tive (kə rel′ə tiv) *adj., n.* —*adj.* 1 mutually dependent; so related that each implies the other. 2 *Grammar.* having a mutual relation and commonly used together. Conjunctions used in pairs, such as *either. . . or* and *both. . . and,* are correlative words. —*n.* 1 either of two closely related things. 2 *Grammar.* a correlative word. —**cor·rel′a·tive·ly,** *adv.*

cor·re·spond (kôr′ə spond′) *v.* 1 be in harmony; agree: *His friendly manner corresponded with what they had been told of him.* 2 be similar; have the same function, value, effect, etc., in its own context: *The arms of a man correspond to the wings of a bird.* 3 agree in amount or position. 4 exchange letters; write letters to each other. [< Med.L *correspondere* < L *com-* together, with + *respondere* answer]
☛ *Syn.* 1. See note at **agree.**

cor·re·spond·ence (kôr′ə spon′dəns) *n.* 1 an agreement; harmony: *There was no correspondence between the two accounts of the events.* 2 a similarity; resemblance: *Historians have noted a correspondence between the careers of the two women.* 3 an exchange of letters; letter writing. 4 letters: *She found a pile of correspondence on her desk when she returned from her holidays.* 5 *Mathematics.* a matching of the members of one set of objects with the members of a second set of objects.

correspondence course a set of lessons on a certain subject given by a correspondence school.

correspondence school a school that gives lessons by mail. Instructions, explanations, and questions are sent to the student, and he returns his written answers for correction or approval.

cor·re·spond·ent (kôr′ə spon′dənt) *n., adj.* —*n.* 1 a person who exchanges letters with another. 2 a person employed by a newspaper, a radio or television network, etc., to send news from a distant place. A foreign correspondent is a reporter who gathers news in another country. 3 a person or company that has regular business with another in a distant place: *This important bank has correspondents in all the large cities of the world.* 4 anything that corresponds to something else.
—*adj.* corresponding; in agreement.

cor·re·spond·ing (kôr′ə spon′ding) *adj.* 1 agreeing; in harmony. 2 similar; matching. 3 handling or carrying on correspondence. —**cor′re·spond′ing·ly,** *adv.*

cor·ri·da (kə rē′də; *Spanish,* kô rē′ᴛʜə) *n.* bullfight.

cor·ri·dor (kôr′ə dər *or* kôr′ə dôr′) *n.* 1 a long hallway; passage in a large building from which doors lead into separate rooms. 2 a narrow strip of land connecting two parts of a country or an inland country with a seaport. [< F < Provençal *corredor* < *correr* run < L *currere*]

cor·rie (kôr′ē) *n. Scottish.* a circular hollow on a mountainside; cirque. [< Scots Gaelic *coire,* literally, cauldron]

cor·ri·gen·dum (kôr′ə jen′dəm) *n., pl.* **-da** (-də). 1 an error in a book, manuscript, etc., to be corrected. 2 **corrigenda,** *pl.* a list of errors with their corrections, in a book. [< L *corrigendum* (thing) to be corrected < *corrigere.* See CORRECT.]

cor·ri·gi·ble (kôr′ə jə bəl) *adj.* 1 that can be corrected. 2 yielding to correction; willing to be corrected. —**cor′ri·gi·bil′i·ty,** *n.* —**cor′ri·gi·bly,** *adv.* [Med.L *corrigibilis* < L *corrigere.* See CORRECT.]

cor·rob·o·rate (kə rob′ə rāt′) v. **-rat·ed, -rat·ing.** make more certain; confirm: *Witnesses corroborated the policeman's statement.* [< L *corroborare* strengthen < *com-* + *robur* oak] —**cor·rob′o·ra′tor,** n.
☛ *Syn.* See note at **confirm.**

cor·rob·o·ra·tion (kə rob′ə rā′shən) n. **1** confirmation by additional proof. **2** something that corroborates; additional proof.

cor·rob·o·ra·tive (kə rob′ər ə tiv *or* kə rob′ə rā′tiv) adj. corroborating; confirming. —**cor·rob′o·ra′tive·ly,** adv.

cor·rob·o·ra·to·ry (kə rob′ə rə tô′rē) adj. corroborative.

cor·rob·o·ree (kə rob′ər ē) n. **1** a tribal dance of Australian aborigines, held at night. **2** *Esp.Australian.* a noisy gathering or celebration. [< Australian native name]

cor·rode (kə rōd′) v. **-rod·ed, -rod·ing. 1** eat or wear away gradually, especially by chemical action: *Rust had corroded the steel rails. Iron corrodes quickly.* **3** destroy or cause to deteriorate gradually: *natural generosity corroded by ambition.* [< L *corrodere* < *com-* + *rodere* gnaw]

cor·rod·i·ble (kə rō′də bəl) adj. capable of being corroded. —**cor·rod′i·bil′i·ty,** n.

cor·ro·sion (kə rō′zhən) n. **1** the act or process of corroding. **2** a corroded condition. **3** a product of corroding, such as rust. [< LL *corrosio, -onis* < *corrodere.* See CORRODE.]

cor·ro·sive (kə rō′siv) adj., n. —adj. producing corrosion; corroding; eating away. —n. a substance that corrodes: *Most acids are corrosive.* —**cor·ro′sive·ly,** adv.

corrosive sublimate mercuric chloride.

cor·ru·gate (kôr′ə gāt′) v. **-gat·ed, -gat·ing.** bend or shape a surface or a thin sheet of material into wavelike folds; make wrinkles in; furrow. [< L *corrugare* < *com-* (intensive) + *ruga* wrinkle]

cor·ru·gat·ed (kôr′ə gāt′id) adj. bent or shaped into a row of wavelike ridges: *corrugated iron, corrugated paper.*

corrugated iron sheet iron or steel, usually galvanized, that is shaped into curved ridges. It is sometimes used for roofs, walls, etc.

corrugated paper paper or cardboard that is bent into a row of wavelike ridges, used in wrapping packages, etc.

cor·ru·ga·tion (kôr′ə gā′shən) n. **1** corrugating or being corrugated. **2** one of a series of wavelike ridges; a wrinkle; furrow.

cor·rupt (kə rupt′) adj., v. —adj. **1** dishonest; especially, influenced by or involving bribes: *a corrupt judge.* **2** depraved or wicked. **3** of a text or manuscript, debased or made meaningless by errors, alterations, insertions, etc. **4** of a dialect, etc., considered inferior to the standard form of the language because of changes that have taken place in structure, vocabulary, or pronunciation: *Dante's writings helped Italian to become accepted as a literary language rather than just a corrupt form of Latin.* **5** rotten; decayed.
—v. **1** make or become dishonest. **2** deprave. **3** alter (a text, word, etc.) from its original or correct form. **4** make or become tainted or rotten. [< L *corruptus,* pp. of *corrumpere* < *com-* + *rumpere* break] —**cor·rupt′er** or **cor·rupt′or,** n. —**cor·rupt′ly,** adv. —**cor·rupt′ness,** n.
☛ *Syn.* adj. **1. Corrupt, depraved** = made morally bad. **Corrupt** emphasizes the idea that the person or thing was good, pure, honorable and has been made bad by evil influences: *The Medical Association took away the licence of the doctor because of his corrupt practices.* **Depraved** emphasizes the idea that a person's morals have become worse and worse until his character, desires, pleasures, etc., are evil: *This murder was committed by a depraved criminal.*

cor·rupt·i·bil·i·ty (kə rup′tə bil′ə tē) n. the quality of being corruptible.

cor·rupt·i·ble (kə rup′tə bəl) adj. **1** that can be corrupted. **2** liable to be corrupted; perishable. —**cor·rupt′i·ble·ness,** n. —**cor·rupt′i·bly,** adv.

cor·rup·tion (kə rup′shən) n. **1** moral deterioration; depravity. **2** dishonesty or a dishonest practice, especially bribery. **3** alteration of a text or manuscript from its correct form. **4** an altered, or corrupt, form of a word. **5** rot; decay. **6** *Archaic.* a corrupting influence.

cor·rup·tive (kə rup′tiv) adj. tending to corrupt; causing corruption.

cor·sage (kôr säzh′) n. **1** a single flower or a small bouquet to be worn on a woman's dress. **2** the upper part of a dress; bodice. [< F < OF *cors* body < L *corpus*]

cor·sair (kôr′ser) n. **1** a privateer, especially a Saracen or Turkish privateer of the Barbary Coast. **2** pirate. **3** the ship of a pirate or a privateer. [< F *corsaire* < Ital. < VL *cursarius* runner < L *cursus* a run. Doublet of HUSSAR.]

corse (kôrs) n. *Archaic and poetic.* corpse. [ME < OF *cors* < L

corpus body. Doublet of CORPS, CORPSE, CORPUS.]
☛ *Hom.* coarse, course.

corse·let (kôrs′lit *for I;* kôr′sə let′ *for 2)* n. **1** a piece of armor for the body. Also, **corslet. 2** a light corset, with few or no stays. [< F *corselet,* double of dim. of OF *cors* body. See CORPSE.]

cor·set (kôr′sit) n., v. —n. **1** a firm, close-fitting undergarment stiffened and reinforced by stays, worn especially by women to support or shape the torso. **2** a similar garment worn by men or women because of injury, weakness, or deformity. **3** a medieval outer garment for the upper body.
—v. **1** dress in or fit with a corset. **2** control or restrict as if by a corset. [< F *corset,* dim. of OF *cors* body. See CORPSE.]

Cor·si·can (kôr′sə kən) n., adj. —n. **1** a native or inhabitant of Corsica, a French island in the Mediterranean Sea. **2 the Corsican,** Napoleon Bonaparte. —adj. of or having to do with Corsica or its people.

cors·let (kôrs′lit) See **corselet** (def. 1).

cor·tege or **cor·tège** (kôr tāzh′ *or* kôr tezh′) n. **1** a procession: *a funeral cortege.* **2** a group of followers, attendants, etc.; retinue. [< F < Ital. *corteggio* < *corte* court]

Cor·tes (kôr′tez *or* kôr′tes) n. in Spain, the national legislature.

cor·tex (kôr′teks) n., pl. **-ti·ces** (-tə sēz′). **1** *Botany.* a complex layer of tissue between the epidermis or corky layer and the vascular tissue of a stem or root, made up mainly of parenchyma cells. **2** the bark or rind of a plant used as medicine. **3** *Anatomy.* **a** the outer part of an internal organ such as the kidneys or the adrenal glands. **b** the thin layer of grey matter that covers the cerebrum of the brain: *the cerebral cortex.* [< L *cortex* bark]

cor·ti·cal (kôr′tə kəl) adj. **1** of or having to do with a cortex. **2** consisting of cortex. —**cor′ti·cal·ly,** adv.

cor·ti·cate (kôr′tə kāt′) adj. having a cortex; covered with bark. [< L *corticatus* < *cortex* bark]

cor·ti·cat·ed (kôr′tə kāt′id) adj. corticate.

cor·ti·sone (kôr′tə zōn′) n. one of the hormones produced by the cortex of the adrenal glands, necessary for the regulation of many functions of the body. Cortisone is used in the treatment of various diseases, including arthritis and leukemia. *Formula:* $C_{21}H_{28}O_5$

co·run·dum (kə run′dəm) n. an extremely hard mineral, aluminum oxide, sometimes containing iron, magnesia, or silica. Dark-colored corundum is used for polishing and grinding. Sapphires and rubies are transparent varieties of corundum. *Formula:* Al_2O_3 [< Tamil *kurundam;* cf. Skt. *kuruvinda* ruby]

cor·us·cate (kôr′əs kāt′) v. **-cat·ed, -cat·ing.** give off flashes of light; sparkle; glitter. [< L *coruscare* < *coruscus* darting, flashing]

cor·us·ca·tion (kôr′əs kā′shən) n. **1** a flash of light; sparkle. **2** a flashing; sparkling.

cor·vée (kôr vā′) n. **1** unpaid work done by a peasant for his feudal lord. **2** unpaid or partly unpaid labor imposed by authorities on the residents of a district. [< F < Med.L *corrogata (opera)* (work) requisitioned < L *corrogare* < *com-* together + *rogare* ask]

cor·vette or **cor·vet** (kôr vet′) n. **1** *Historical.* a warship equipped with sails and only one tier of guns. **2** a small, fast warship for use in antisubmarine and convoy work. [? < MDu. *korf,* a kind of ship < L *corbis* basket]

cor·vine (kôr′vīn *or* kôr′vin) adj. of or like a crow. [< L *corvinus* < *corvus* crow]

Cor·y·bant (kôr′ə bant′) n., pl. **Cor·y·ban·tes** (kôr′ə ban′tēz) or **Cor·y·bants. 1** one of the attendants of Cybele, an ancient nature goddess of Asia Minor. The Corybantes followed her over the mountains by torchlight with wild music and dancing. **2** a priest of Cybele.

Cor·y·ban·tic (kôr′ə ban′tik) adj. **1** of the Corybantes. **2** resembling the Corybantes or their rites.

cor·ymb (kôr′imb *or* kôr′im) n. *Botany.* a flat cluster of flowers in which the outer flowers blossom first. Small flowers on short stems grow from a longer, central stem to form a round, rather flat cluster. Cherry blossoms are corymbs. [< L *corymbus* < Gk. *korymbos* top, cluster]

co·rym·bose (kə rim′bōs) adj. **1** growing in corymbs. **2** of or like a corymb.

cor·y·phée (kôr′ə fā′) n. *Ballet.* a leading member of the corps de ballet. A coryphée dances in the front row of the corps de ballet or in a small group. [< F < L < Gk. *koryphaios* leader < *koryphē* head]

co·ry·za (kə rī′zə) n. a cold in the head. [< LL < Gk. *koryza* catarrh]

cos¹ or **cos lettuce** (kos) n. romaine. [< the island of *Cos* in the Aegean Sea]

cos² cosine.

cos. 1 companies. 2 countries.

Cosa Nostra a secret criminal society; the Mafia. [< Ital.; literally, "our affair"]

cosec cosecant.

co·se·cant (kō sē′kənt *or* -sē′kant) *n. Trigonometry.* the ratio of the length of the hypotenuse to the length of the opposite side; the secant of the complement of a given angle or arc. See **sine** for picture.

co·sig·na·to·ry (kō sig′nə tô′rē) *adj., n., pl.* **-ries.** —*adj.* signing along with another or others. —*n.* a person who signs something along with another or others.

co·sine (kō′sīn′) *n. Trigonometry.* the ratio of the length of the adjacent side to the length of the hypotenuse; the sine of the complement of a given angle or arc. See **sine** for picture.

co·si·ness (kō′zē nis) *n.* being cosy. Also, **coziness.**

cos·met·ic (koz met′ik) *n., adj.* —*n.* a preparation for beautifying the skin, hair, nails, etc. Powder, lipstick, and face creams are cosmetics. —*adj.* 1 beautifying to the skin, hair, nails, etc. 2 of or having to do with cosmetics. —**cos·met′i·cal·ly,** *adv.* [< Gk. *kosmētikos* of order, adornment < *kosmos* order]

cos·mic (koz′mik) *adj.* 1 of or belonging to the cosmos; having to do with the whole universe: *Cosmic forces produce stars and meteors.* 2 vast. [< Gk. *kosmikos* < *kosmos* order, world]

cos·mi·cal·ly (koz′mik lē) *adv.* according to cosmic laws; on a vast or cosmic scale.

cosmic dust fine particles of matter falling upon the earth from outer space.

cosmic noise radio-frequency radiation from the Milky Way that may be detected by radio receivers.

cosmic rays streams of mostly electrically charged particles that travel through space at speeds nearly equal to that of light; some of these enter the earth's atmosphere, where they collide with atoms in the air, producing secondary cosmic rays of enormous energy which are eventually converted into heat. The radiation from cosmic rays in outer space is a hazard for space travellers.

cos·mo·gon·ic (koz′mə gon′ik) *adj.* of or having to do with cosmogony.

cos·mog·o·nist (koz mog′ə nist) *n.* a person who studies cosmogony or who advocates a particular cosmogony.

cos·mog·o·ny (koz mog′ə nē) *n., pl.* **-nies.** 1 the creation or origin of the universe: *Cosmogony has puzzled philosophers throughout history.* 2 any theory of its creation or origin. [< Gk. *kosmogonia* < *kosmos* world + *gonos* birth]

cos·mog·ra·pher (koz mog′rə fər) *n.* a person trained in cosmography, especially one whose work it is.

cos·mo·graph·ic (koz′mə graf′ik) *adj.* of or about cosmography.

cos·mog·ra·phy (koz mog′rə fē) *n.* 1 the science that describes and maps the general appearance and structure of the universe. Cosmography includes astronomy, geography, and geology. 2 a general description of the universe or the earth. [< Gk. *kosmographia* < *kosmos* world + *graphein* write]

cos·mo·log·i·cal (koz′mə loj′ə kəl) *adj.* of or having to do with cosmology.

cos·mol·o·gist (koz mol′ə jist) *n.* a person trained in cosmology, especially one whose work it is.

cos·mol·o·gy (koz mol′ə jē) *n.* 1 the branch of learning that deals with the description of the universe as an ordered whole made up of parts and subject to laws by which it functions. Cosmology may be considered as a branch of philosophy or of natural science. 2 a particular theory or account of the structure and workings of the universe. [< Gk. *kosmos* world + E *-logy*]

cos·mo·naut (koz′mə not′ *or* koz′mə nôt′) *n.* astronaut.

cos·mop·o·lis (koz mop′ə ləs) *n.* a cosmopolitan city.

cos·mo·pol·i·tan (koz′mə pol′ə tən) *adj., n.* —*adj.* 1 made up of elements or people from many parts of the world: *a cosmopolitan art collection. Paris is a cosmopolitan city.* 2 familiar with and feeling at home in many parts of the world: *a cosmopolitan person.* 3 sophisticated and urbane. 4 of animals or plants, found in almost all parts of the world. —*n.* 1 a person who feels at home in many parts of the world. 2 an organism found in almost all parts of the world.

cos·mo·pol·i·tan·ism (koz′mə pol′ə tən iz′əm) *n.* the quality or condition of being cosmopolitan.

cos·mop·o·lite (koz mop′ə līt′) *n.* 1 a cosmopolitan person. 2 an animal or plant found in all or many parts of the world. [< Gk. *kosmopolitēs* < *kosmos* world + *politēs* citizen < *polis* city]

cos·mos (koz′məs *or* koz′mos) *n.* 1 the universe thought of as an orderly, harmonious system. 2 any complete system that is orderly and harmonious. 3 order; harmony. Cosmos is the opposite

hat, āge, fär; let, ēqual, tèrm; it, īce
hot, ōpen, ôrder; oil, out; cup, pût, rüle,
əbove, takən, pencəl, lemən, circəs

ch, child; ng, long; sh, ship
th, thin; ₮H, then; zh, measure

of chaos. 4 any of a genus (*Cosmos*) of garden plants of the composite family, especially a tall plant (*C. bipinnatus*) with much-divided leaves and white, pink, purple, or orange flowers that bloom from midsummer through fall. [< NL < Gk. *kosmos* order, world]

cos·mo·tron (koz′mə tron′) *n.* a nuclear accelerator designed to produce particles with energy of over two billion electron volts. [apparently < *cosmic* + *cyclotron*]

Cos·sack (kos′ak) *n., adj.* —*n.* a member of a people living in S Soviet Union, traditionally famous as horsemen. —*adj.* of, having to do with, or characteristic of the Cossacks. [< Russian *kozak, kazak*]

cos·set (kos′it) *n., v.* —*n.* a pet, especially a pet lamb. —*v.* make a pet of; treat as a pet; pamper. [OE *cossettan* kiss < *coss* a kiss]

cost (kost) *n., v.* **cost, cost·ing.** —*n.* 1 the price paid: *The cost of this hat was $18.* 2 a loss or sacrifice: *The fox escaped from the trap at the cost of a leg.* 3 outlay or expenditure of time, labor, trouble, effort, etc. 4 **costs,** *pl.* the expenses of a lawsuit or case in court.
at all costs *or* **at any cost,** regardless of expense; by all means; no matter what must be done: *They had to catch the next boat at all costs, or lose their chance to escape.*
—*v.* 1 have a price of: *This hat costs $18.* 2 require spending of money, effort, suffering, etc.: *The other hat costs a lot more. The school play cost much time and effort.* 3 estimate the expenditure required for the production or completion of: *The company is costing a new project.* 4 cause someone the loss or sacrifice of: *The accident almost cost him his life. Her many absences finally cost her her job.* [ME < OF *cost* < *coster* < L *constare* < *com-* with + *stare* stand]
☞ *Syn. n.* 1. See note at **price.**

cos·ta (kos′tə) *n.* a rib or riblike structure or marking of a plant or animal.

cost accountant an accountant who specializes in cost accounting.

cost accounting 1 a system of accounting that records all expenses, including overhead, incurred in making and distributing a product. 2 the keeping of such accounts.

cos·tal (kos′təl) *adj.* near, on, or having to do with a rib or the ribs. [< LL *costalis* < L *costa* rib]

co–star (*n.* kō′stär′; *v.* kō′stär′) *n., v.* **-starred, -star·ring.** —*n.* an actor or actress of equal prominence with another (or others) playing a leading role in a motion picture, play, etc. —*v.* be or cause to be a co-star.

cos·tard (kos′tərd) *n.* a variety of large English apple. [earlier meaning, "a ribbed apple"; probably < OF *coste* rib < L *costa*]

Cos·ta Ri·can (kos′tə rē′kən) *n., adj.* —*n.* a native or inhabitant of Costa Rica, a country in Central America. —*adj.* of or having to do with Costa Rica or its people.

cos·ter (kos′tər) *n.* costermonger.

cos·ter·mon·ger (kos′tər mung′gər *or* -mong′gər) *n. Brit.* a person who sells fruit, vegetables, fish, etc., from a handcart or stand in the street. [earlier *costardmonger* < *costard* + *monger* dealer, trader]

cos·tive (kos′tiv) *adj.* 1 constipated. 2 producing constipation. [ME < OF *costive* < L *constipatus,* pp. of *constipare.* Doublet of CONSTIPATE.] —**cos′tive·ly,** *adv.* —**cos′tive·ness,** *n.*

cost·li·ness (kost′lē nis) *n.* great cost; expensiveness.

cost·ly (kost′lē) *adj.* **-li·er, -li·est.** 1 of great value: *costly jewels.* 2 costing much: *costly mistakes.* 3 costing too much.
☞ *Syn.* 2. See note at **expensive.**

cost of living the average price paid by a person, family, etc., for food, rent, clothing, transportation, etc., within a given period.

cost of living index consumer price index.

cost plus an arrangement or contract under which the selling price is based on the cost of production plus an agreed profit.

cos·tume (*n.* kos′tyüm *or* kos′chüm; *v.* kos tyüm′ *or* kos chüm′) *n., v.* **-tumed, -tum·ing.** —*n.* 1 a style of dress of a particular time, place or social class, including garments, hairstyles, jewellery or other ornaments, etc. 2 dress belonging to another time or place, worn on the stage, at masquerades, etc.: *The actors wore*

Spanish costumes. **3** a complete set of outer garments: *a street costume, a hunting costume.*
—*v.* provide a costume or costumes for; dress. [< F < Ital. < VL *consuetumen* custom. Doublet of CUSTOM.]

cos·tum·er (kos tyüm′ər *or* kos′chüm ər) *n.* a person who makes, sells, or rents costumes or dresses.

cos·tum·i·er (kos tyüm′ē ər; *French,* kôs tỷ myā′) *n.* costumer.

co·sy (kō′zē) *adj.* **co·si·er, co·si·est;** *n., pl.* **co·sies.** —*adj.* warm and comfortable; snug: *She liked to read in a cosy corner by the fire.* —*n.* a cover, usually of padded or knitted cloth, used to keep a teapot warm. Also, **cozy.** [< Scand., origin uncertain] —**co′si·ly,** *adv.* —**co′si·ness,** *n.*
☞ *Syn. adj.* See note at **snug.**

cot¹ (kot) *n.* **1** a narrow bed, sometimes made of canvas stretched on a frame that folds together. **2** *Brit.* a child's crib. [< Anglo-Indian < Hind. *khāt*; cf. Skt. *khatvā*]
☞ *Hom.* **caught** (kot).

cot² (kot) *n.* **1** a cottage; small house. **2** something small built for shelter or protection. **3** a protective covering; sheath: *a cot for an injured finger.* [OE]
☞ *Hom.* **caught.** (kot).

cot³ cotangent.

co·tan·gent (kō tan′jənt) *n. Trigonometry.* the ratio of the length of the adjacent side (not the hypotenuse) to the length of the opposite side; the tangent of the complement of a given angle or arc. See **sine** for picture.

COTC or **C.O.T.C.** Canadian Officers Training Corps.

cote (kōt) *n.* a shelter or shed for small animals, birds, etc.: *a dovecote.* [OE. Related to COT².]
☞ *Hom.* **coat.**

co·teau (kə tō′; *French,* kō tō′) *n.* **1** a small hill; hillock. **2** a line of hills or ridges, often functioning as a watershed. [< Cdn.F]

co·ten·ant (kō ten′ənt) *n.* one of a group of tenants of the same place; joint tenant.

co·te·rie (kō′tə rē) *n.* a set or circle of acquaintances; group of people who often meet socially. [< F *coterie,* originally, an association for tenants of the same farm owner < OF *cotier* cotter < *cote* hut < MDu. *kote*]

co·ter·mi·nous (kō tèr′mə nəs) *adj.* **1** having a common boundary; bordering; meeting at their ends. **2** having the same boundaries or limits; co-extensive. Also, **conterminous.** [< L *conterminus* < *com-* with + *terminus* boundary]

co·til·lion (kə til′yən) *n.* **1** a dance with complicated steps and frequent changing of partners, led by one couple. **2** quadrille. **3** a piece of music for a cotillion. [< F *cotillon,* originally, petticoat, dim. of *cotte* coat]

co·to·ne·as·ter (kə tō′nē as′tər) *n.* any of a genus (*Cotoneaster*) of widely cultivated flowering shrubs of the rose family.

Cots·wold (kots′wōld *or* kots′wəld) *n.* a breed of large sheep having long wool. [< *Cotswolds,* hills in SW England]

cot·tage (kot′ij) *n.* **1** a small, usually simply built and uninsulated house for summer holiday use, as at a resort. **2** a small house, especially in a rural area. [< *cot²*]

cottage cheese a soft, white cheese made from the curds of sour skim milk.

cottage pudding cake covered with a sweet sauce.

cot·tag·er (kot′ij er) *n.* **1** a person who lives in a cottage. **2** a summer resident in a rural or resort area.

cot·ter¹ (kot′ər) *n.* **1** a wedge or other tapered piece used to hold parts of a structure together. **2** cotter pin. [origin uncertain]

cot·ter² or **cot·tar** (kot′ər) *n.* in Scotland, a man who works for a farmer and is allowed to use a small cottage and a plot of land. [< Med.L *cotarius* < *cota* < OE *cot* cot²]

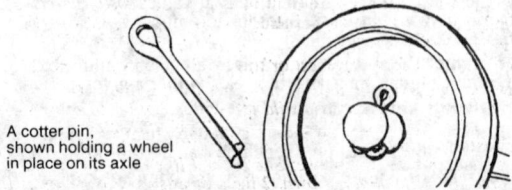

A cotter pin, shown holding a wheel in place on its axle

cotter pin a long metal strip, round on one side and flat on the other, that is bent double and used for inserting into a slot or hole to hold small parts of machinery together. The two ends of the

cotter pin are flared out after it is inserted, to keep it in place.

cot·to·lene (kot′ə lēn′) *n.* a preparation of cottonseed oil, used as a shortening in cooking.

A cotton plant, showing immature and mature bolls

cot·ton (kot′ən) *n., v.* —*n.* **1** soft, downy white or yellowish fibres obtained from the seed pods of any of several plants (genus *Gossypium*) of the mallow family, and used in making fabrics, threads, etc. The cotton is attached to the seeds in a fluffy mass. **2** any of the plants that produce these fibres: *Cotton grows in warm climates.* **3** the crop of such plants. **4** thread or cloth made from cotton fibres. **5** (*adj.*) made of cotton. **6** any downy substance resembling cotton fibres, growing on other plants.
—*v. Informal.* **1** agree; get along. **2** take a liking (*to*): *I cottoned to her at once.*
cotton on, *Informal.* understand: *He still hasn't cottoned on that it was only a joke.*
cotton up, *Informal.* flatter (*used with* **to**): *Did you see the way he was cottoning up to the coach?*
[ME < OF *coton* < Ital. *cotone* < Arabic *qutn*]

cotton batting soft, fluffy cotton pressed into thin layers, used as padding in quilting, for dressing wounds, etc.

cotton candy a light, fluffy candy made by spinning melted sugar.

cotton gin a machine for separating the fibres of cotton from the seeds.

cotton grass any of a genus (*Eriophorum*) of sedges found in north temperate and arctic regions having spikes of flowers that resemble tufts of cotton.

cotton sedge *Cdn.* cotton grass.

cot·ton·seed (kot′ən sēd′) *n., pl.* **-seed** *or* **-seeds.** the seed of cotton, used for making cottonseed oil, fertilizer, cattle food, etc.

cottonseed oil oil pressed from cottonseed, used for cooking, for making soap, etc.

cot·ton·tail (kot′ən tāl′) *n.* any of several species of rabbit (genus *Sylvilagus*), the common wild rabbit of North America, having brownish or greyish fur and a fluffy tail with a white or light grey underside.

cot·ton·wood (kot′ən wůd′) *n.* any of various North American poplars, such as the *eastern cottonwood* (*Populus deltoides*) and the *black cottonwood* (*P. trichocarpa*), both of which are native to Canada. They are named for the cottony tufts of hairs on the seeds, characteristic of poplars.

cotton wool 1 cotton batting. **2** raw cotton.

cot·ton·y (kot′ən ē) *adj.* **1** of cotton. **2** like cotton; soft; fluffy; downy.

cot·y·le·don (kot′ə lē′dən) *n.* an embryo leaf in the seed of a plant; the first leaf, or either of the first pair of leaves, growing from a seed. [< L < Gk. *kotylēdōn* cup-shaped hollow < *kotylē* small vessel]

cot·y·le·don·ous (kot′ə lē′dən əs) *adj.* having cotyledons.

couch (kouch) *n., v.* —*n.* **1** chesterfield; sofa. **2** any long piece of furniture for reclining or sitting on, especially one that is upholstered. **3** any place to sleep or rest: *The deer sprang up from its grassy couch.* **4** *Poetic.* bed. **5** *Archaic.* the burrow or den of a wild animal. **6** a frame on which barley is spread to be malted.
—*v.* **1** put on a couch. **2** lie down on a couch. **3** put in words; express: *Some poets couch their ideas in beautiful language.* **4** lower; bring down; put in a level position ready to attack: *The knights couched their lances and prepared to charge.* **5** lie hidden ready to attack. [ME < OF *couche* < *coucher* lay in place < L *collocare* < *com-* (intensive) + *locus* a place] —**couch′like**′, *adj.*

couch·ant (kouch′ənt) *adj. Heraldry.* lying down, but with the head raised. [< F *couchant,* ppr. of *coucher* lie]

couch grass a coarse, perennial grass (*Agropyron repens*) that is native to Europe but has become a common weed in North

America, having long, wiry, white or yellowish underground stems by which it spreads; quack grass.

cou·gar (kü′gər) *n.* a large, usually sand-colored wild animal (*Felis concolor*) of the cat family found in many parts of North and South America, having short, black ears and a very long, black-tipped tail; mountain lion. [< F *couguar* < NL < Tupi-Guarani *guaçu ara*]

cough (kof) *v., n.* —*v.* force air from the lungs suddenly with a short, harsh noise or series of noises.
cough up, a expel from the throat or lungs by coughing. **b** *Slang.* give; bring out; produce; pay what is due.
—*n.* **1** the act of coughing. **2** the sound of coughing. **3** repeated acts of coughing. **4** a condition marked by frequent coughing: *She has a bad cough.*
[ME *coghen*, related to OE *cohhetan*]

cough drop a small tablet containing medicine to relieve coughs, hoarseness, etc.

cough·ing (kof′ing) *n.* the forcing of air from the lungs with a harsh sound.

could (kud; *unstressed*, kəd) *v.* pt. of **can.** [OE *cūthe*; the *l* was inserted on analogy with *should*, *would*.]
☛ *Usage.* **Could, might. Could,** the past of **can,** and **might** are now used chiefly to convey a shade of doubt, or a slight degree of possibility: *It might be all right for her, but it isn't for me. Perhaps I could write a poem, but I doubt it.*

could·n't (kud′ənt) could not.

couldst (kudst) *v. Archaic or poetic.* 2nd pers. sing., past tense, of **can.** *Thou couldst* means *You* (sing.) *could.*

cou·lee (kü′lē) *n.* **1** *Cdn. esp.Prairies.* a deep, narrow ravine that is usually dry in summer. **2** a stream of lava. [< F *coulée*, fem. pp. of *couler* flow < L *colare* strain]
☛ *Hom.* **coolie.**

cou·loir (kü lwär′) *n.* a deep gorge or gully on the side of a mountain. [< F < OF *couloir* passage, literally, a slide, glide < *couler* flow. See COULEE.]

cou·lomb (kü lom′) *n.* an SI unit for measuring the quantity, or charge, of electricity flowing past a given section of an electric current within a given time. One coulomb is the electric charge furnished by a current of one ampere in one second. *Symbol:* C [after Charles A. de *Coulomb* (1736-1806), a French physicist]

coul·ter or **col·ter** (kōl′tər) *n.* a sharp blade or disk on a plough to cut the earth ahead of the ploughshare.

coun·cil (koun′səl) *n.* **1** a group of people called together to give advice, talk things over, or settle questions: *council of war.* **2** a small group of people elected by citizens to make laws for and govern a township, city, municipal district, etc. **3** a group of people appointed to advise a monarch, governor, etc.: *the Privy Council.* **4** the deliberation or consulation that takes place at the meeting of a council.
in council, a at a meeting of a council. **b** in consultation; deliberating together: *The family is in council planning a vacation.* [ME < OF *concile* < L *concilium* < *com-* together + *calare* call]
☛ *Hom.* **counsel.**
☛ *Usage.* **Council, counsel. Council** is a noun: *They called together a council* (group) *of the town's industrial leaders.* **Counsel** may be a noun or a verb: *Mrs. Smith could always be counted on for good counsel* (advice). *Each side tried to get Mr. Avery as its counsel* (adviser). *I do not like to counsel* (advise) *you on that point.*

coun·cil·lor or **coun·cil·or** (koun′sə lər or koun′slər) *n.* **1** an elected member of a council of a town, village, etc. **2** *Cdn.* in Prince Edward Island, a member of the Legislative Assembly elected by the property owners.

Council of the Northwest Territories the legislative body responsible for local government in the Northwest Territories, consisting of 15 elected members. It has powers similar to those of a provincial legislature, but all natural resources except game are under federal control.

Council of Trent the council of the Roman Catholic Church held at Trent, Italy, from time to time between 1545 and 1563. It formulated many of the present Catholic doctrines, corrected certain abuses within the church, and organized the Catholic opposition to the Protestant movement.

council of war 1 a conference of high officers of the armed forces to give advice and talk over matters of special importance. **2** an important conference to decide on a plan of action.

coun·ci·lor (koun′sə lər or koun′slər) See **councillor.**

coun·sel (koun′səl) *n., v.* **-selled** or **-seled, -sel·ling** or **-sel·ing.** —*n.* **1** the act of talking things over; consultation or deliberation: *There was little time for counsel.* **2** advice: *A wise person gives good counsel.* **3** a lawyer or group of lawyers: *He is acting as counsel for the defence.* **4** *Archaic.* wisdom; prudence.
hold or **take counsel,** talk things over; consult or deliberate: *The stranded travellers held counsel to decide what they should do next. He took counsel with his friends.*

---

hat, āge, fär; let, ēqual, tèrm; it, īce
hot, ōpen, ôrder; oil, out; cup, pùt, rüle,
ə above, təkən, pencəl, lemən, circəs

ch, child; ng, long; sh, ship
th, thin; ᴛʜ, then; zh, measure

keep (one's) own counsel, keep quiet about one's ideas and plans; not tell one's secrets.
—*v.* **1** give advice to; advise: *She counsels high school students.* **2** recommend: *He counselled immediate action.* **3** exchange ideas; consult together; deliberate. [ME < OF *conseil* < L *consilium* < *consulere* consult, originally, convoke < *com-* together + *sel-* take]
☛ *Hom.* **council.**
☛ *Syn. n.* **2.** See note at **advice.**
☛ *Usage.* See note at **council.**

coun·sel·lor or **coun·sel·or** (koun′sə lər or koun′slər) *n.* **1** a person who gives advice; adviser. **2** lawyer. **3** a person who supervises, especially at a summer camp.

count¹ (kount) *v., n.* —*v.* **1** name numbers in order: *Wait till I count ten.* **2** add; find how many: *He counted the books and found there were fifty.* **3** include in counting; take into account: *Let's not count that game.* **4** be included in counting; be taken into account: *Your first race is only for practice; it won't count.* **5** have value, significance, or influence: *She's one of the people who count in the company. His promise counts for little.* **6** depend; rely; trust (*used with* **on**): *Can I count on you to help?* **7** plan or expect (*used with* **on**): *You should count on spending at least $10 for dinner.*
count in, *Informal.* include: *Count me in for the party!*
count off, divide into equal groups by counting: *Count off in fours, from the left.*
count out, a not include in a plan: *If you go skiing, count me out.* **b** *Boxing.* declare (a fallen fighter) the loser when he cannot get up after ten seconds have been counted: *He was counted out in the third round of the fight.*
—*n.* **1** the act of counting or adding up. **2** the total number of individuals or units in a given sample: *a blood count.* **3** *Law.* a separate charge in an indictment: *three counts of theft.* **4** *Boxing.* the act of calling off up to ten seconds to give a fallen fighter time to get up before he is declared the loser. [ME < OF *conter* < L *computare* < *com-* up + *putare* reckon. Doublet of COMPUTE.]

count² (kount) *n.* a European nobleman having a rank about the same as that of a British earl. [< OF *conte* < L *comes, -itis* companion < *com-* with + *ire* go]

count·a·ble (koun′tə bəl) *adj.* capable of being counted.

count down or **count–down** (kount′doun) *n.* **1** the period of time immediately preceding the firing of a missile, rocket, etc. **2** the calling out of the minutes (and seconds, in the last stage) of this period as they pass.

coun·te·nance (koun′tə nəns) *n., v.* **-nanced, -nanc·ing.** —*n.* **1** an expression of the face: *His angry countenance frightened us all.* **2** face; features: *The king had a noble countenance.* **3** approval; encouragement: *He gave countenance to our plan, but no active help.* **4** calmness; composure.
keep (one's) countenance, a be calm; not show feeling. **b** keep from smiling or laughing.
lose countenance, get excited.
put out of countenance, embarrass and confuse; make uneasy and ashamed.
—*v.* tolerate; sanction: *A dictator will not countenance opposition.* [ME < OF *contenance* < Med.L *continentia* demeanor < L *continentia* self-control < *continere.* See CONTAIN.]
—**coun′te·nanc·er,** *n.*
☛ *Syn. n.* **1, 2.** See note at **face.**

count·er¹ (koun′tər) *n.* **1** something used for counting. **2** an imitation coin. **3** a fixture in a store, restaurant, etc., having a long, flat, relatively narrow top surface for displaying goods, serving food, etc., and closed sides, usually with shelves or drawers: *a lunch counter.* **4** a similar fixture built in against one wall in a kitchen or bathroom and usually including a sink or washbasin. [< AF *counteour* < *conter.* See COUNT¹.]

count·er² (koun′tər) *n.* a person or thing that counts. [< *count¹*]

coun·ter³ (koun′tər) *adv., adj., v., n.* —*adv.* in the opposite direction; opposed; contrary: *His wild idea runs counter to common sense.*
—*adj.* opposite; contrary.
—*v.* **1** go or act counter to; oppose: *She did not like our plan; so she countered it with one of her own.* **2** meet or answer a blow or move with another in return.
—*n.* **1** that which is opposite or contrary to something else. **2** a blow or move to answer or meet another. **3** a stiff piece inside the back of a shoe around the heel. **4** the part of a ship's stern from the

water line up to the end of the curved part. **5** the depressed part of the face of a type, coin, medal, etc. [< F < L *contra* against]

coun·ter– *combining form.* **1** against; in opposition to, as in *counteract.* **2** in return, as in *counterattack.* **3** corresponding or complementary, as in *counterpart.* [see COUNTER³]

☛ *Usage.* **Counter–.** As with many such combining forms, usage is divided as to whether or not **counter** should be followed by a hyphen when used in combinations. In this dictionary a hyphen is used before a following "r" and in most nouns, adjectives, and adverbs in which the primary stress falls on the second element of the compound: *counter-revolution, counter-offensive*; but *counterattack, counterpane,* etc.

coun·ter·act (koun′tər akt′) *v.* act against; neutralize the action or effect of; hinder.

coun·ter·ac·tion (koun′tər ak′shən) *n.* an action opposed to another action; hindrance.

coun·ter·ac·tive (koun′tər ak′tiv) *adj., n.* —*adj.* tending to counteract. —*n.* something that counteracts.

coun·ter·at·tack (koun′tər ə tak′) *n., v.* —*n.* an attack made to counteract an attack. —*v.* attack in return.

coun·ter·bal·ance (*n.* koun′tər bal′əns; *v.* koun′tər bal′əns) *n., v.* -anced, -anc·ing. —*n.* **1** a mass balancing another mass. **2** influence, power, etc. balancing or offsetting another. —*v.* act as a counterbalance to; offset; neutralize: *The two friends' different personalities seem to counterbalance each other.*

coun·ter·charge (*n.* koun′tər chärj′; *v.* koun′tər chärj′) *n., v.* -charged, -charg·ing. —*n.* a charge or accusation made to oppose one made by an accuser. —*v.* charge or accuse, (someone) after being oneself charged or accused.

coun·ter·check (koun′tər chek′) *n., v.* —*n.* **1** something that restrains or opposes; an obstacle. **2** a check made upon a check; double check for verification. —*v.* **1** restrain or oppose by some obstacle. **2** make a second check of; check again.

counter cheque a blank cheque obtainable for use in a bank or at a store.

coun·ter·claim (koun′tər klām′) *n., v.* —*n.* an opposing claim; claim made by a person to offset a claim made against him. —*v.* ask for or make a counterclaim.

coun·ter·clock·wise (koun′tər klok′wīz′) *adv. or adj.* in the direction opposite to that in which the hands of a clock move.

coun·ter·cul·ture (koun′tər kul′chər) *n.* a movement or group that rejects the values and mores of the prevailing culture in a particular society and pursues a quite different lifestyle: *the hippie counterculture of the Sixties.*

coun·ter·cur·rent (koun′tər kėr′ənt) *n., adv.* —*n.* a current running in the opposite direction; an opposing current. —*adv.* in an opposite manner or direction; contrary.

coun·ter·es·pi·o·nage (koun′tər es′pē ə näzh′ or koun′tər es′pē ə nij) *n.* the taking of measures to prevent or confuse enemy espionage.

coun·ter·feit (koun′tər fit) *v., n., adj.* —*v.* **1** copy (money, hand-writing, pictures, etc.) in order to deceive or defraud: *He was sent to prison for counterfeiting five-dollar bills.* **2** resemble closely. **3** pretend; dissemble: *She counterfeited a grief she did not feel.* —*n.* a copy made to deceive or defraud and passed as genuine: *The store manager refused to accept the fifty-dollar bill because he suspected it was a counterfeit.* —*adj.* **1** not genuine; sham. **2** pretended; dissembled. [ME < OF *contrefait* imitated, pp. of *contrefaire* < *contre-* against (< L *contra-*) + *faire* make < L *facere*] —**coun′ter·feit′er,** *n.*

☛ *Syn. adj.* **1.** See note at **false.**

coun·ter·foil (koun′tər foil′) *n.* the part of a cheque, receipt, etc. kept as a record. [< *counter-* + *foil* leaf]

coun·ter·in·tel·li·gence (koun′tər in tel′ə jəns) *n.* **1** a government or military department whose work is to track down and prevent espionage, sabotage, etc. **2** the system or methods used by such a department.

coun·ter·ir·ri·tant (koun′tər ir′ə tənt) *n.* an agent used to produce superficial irritation or inflammation on a part of the body in order to relieve a deep-seated congestion or inflammation by bringing blood to the surface.

coun·ter·mand (*v.* koun′tər mand′ or koun′tər mand′; *n.* koun′tə mand′) *v., n.* —*v.* **1** withdraw or cancel (an order, command, etc.). **2** recall or stop by a contrary order; order back. —*n.* an order that cancels or is contrary to a previous order. [ME < OF *contremander* < L *contra-* against + *mandare* order]

coun·ter·march (koun′tər märch′) *v. or n.* march in the opposite direction; march back.

coun·ter·meas·ure (koun′tər mezh′ər) *n.* a measure or move taken to offset another.

coun·ter·mine (koun′tər mīn′) *n., v.* -mined, -min·ing. —*n.* a submarine mine intended to set off enemy mines prematurely. —*v.* place countermines (against).

coun·ter·mis·sile (koun′tər mis′īl or -mis′əl) *n.* a missile designed to intercept and destroy another missile.

coun·ter–of·fen·sive (koun′tər ə fen′siv) *n.* an attack on a large scale undertaken by a defending force to take the initiative back from an attacking force.

coun·ter·pane (koun′tər pān′) *n.* an outer covering for a bed; bedspread. [alteration of *counterpoint* < OF *contrepoint* bed covering < Med.L *culcita puncta* quilt, stitched mattress. The latter part of the English word was altered to *pane* from association with ME *pane* piece of cloth < OF *pan.* See PANE.]

coun·ter·part (koun′tər pärt′) *n.* **1** a person or thing closely resembling another. **2** a person or thing that corresponds to another; equivalent: *The federal energy minister is holding talks with his provincial counterparts.* **3** a person or thing that complements another: *Night is the counterpart of day.* **4** a copy or duplicate, especially of a legal document.

coun·ter·plot (koun′tər plot′) *n., v.* -plot·ted, -plot·ting. —*n.* a plot to defeat another plot. —*v.* resist or oppose with a counterplot.

coun·ter·point (koun′tər point′) *n., v.* —*n.* **1** *Music.* **a** a melody added to another as an accompaniment. **b** the art of combining two or more melodies so that they form a harmonious unit but the individual melodies can still be distinguished. **c** the style of composition resulting from the way in which more or less individual melodies are combined according to fixed rules. **2** an element, theme, item, etc. that contrasts with or complements another; foil. —*v.* arrange in counterpoint. [< F *contrepoint*]

coun·ter·poise (koun′tər poiz′) *n., v.* -poised, -pois·ing. —*n.* **1** a mass balancing another mass. **2** an influence, power, etc. balancing or offsetting another. **3** balance; equilibrium. —*v.* act as a counterpoise to; offset. [ME < OF *countrepeis* < *contre-* against + *peis* weight, later, *pois* < L *pensum* < *pendere* weigh]

coun·ter·pro·duc·tive (koun′tər prē duk′tiv) *adj.* acting against or hindering the achievement of a goal; not productive or useful.

coun·ter–ref·or·ma·tion (koun′tər ref′ər mā′shən) *n.* **1** a reform movement opposed to a previous reform movement. **2 Counter-Reformation,** the movement in the Roman Catholic Church during the 16th and 17th centuries to correct certain abuses within the church, formulate many doctrines of the church, and organize Catholic opposition to Protestantism.

coun·ter–rev·o·lu·tion (koun′tər rev′ə lü′shən) *n.* a revolution against a government established by a previous revolution.

coun·ter·scarp (koun′tər skärp′) *n.* the outer slope or wall of a moat, ditch, etc. in a fortification. [< F *contrescarpe*]

coun·ter·shaft (koun′tər shaft′) *n.* a shaft that transmits motion from the main shaft to the working parts of a machine.

coun·ter·sign (koun′tər sīn′) *n., v.* —*n.* **1** a password given in answer to the challenge of a sentinel: *The soldier had to give the countersign before he could pass the sentry.* **2** a secret sign or signal given in answer to another. **3** a signature added to another signature to confirm it. —*v.* sign (something already signed by another) to confirm it. [< F *contresigne*]

coun·ter·sink (koun′tər singk′) *v.* -sunk, -sink·ing; *n.* —*v.* **1** enlarge the upper part of (a hole) to make room for the head of screw, bolt, etc. **2** sink the head of (a screw, bolt, etc.) into such a hole so that it is even with or below the surface. —*n.* **1** a countersunk hole. **2** a tool for countersinking holes.

coun·ter·ten·or (koun′tər ten′ər) *n.* **1** the highest adult male singing voice, above tenor. Countertenor usually involves falsetto in its upper range. **2** a singer who has such a voice. **3** the part sung by a countertenor. **4** (*adj.*) having to do with, having the range of, or designed for a countertenor.

coun·ter·vail (koun′tər vāl′ or koun′tər vāl′) *v.* **1** counteract; avail against. **2** compensate; offset; make up for. **3** *Obsolete.* be of equal force in opposition. [ME < AF *countrevaloir* < L *contra valere* be of worth against]

coun·ter·weight (koun′tər wāt′) *n.* a mass that balances another mass.

count·ess (koun′tis) *n.* **1** the wife or widow of an earl or count. **2** a woman whose rank is equal to that of an earl or count. [ME < OF *contesse* < Med.L *comitissa,* fem. of L *comes.* See COUNT².]

counting house a building or office used for keeping accounts and doing business.

counting room an office used for keeping accounts and doing business.

count·less (kount′lis) *adj.* too many to count; very many;

innumerable: *the countless grains of sand on the seashore, the countless stars.*

coun·tri·fy (kun′trə fī) *v.* **-fied, fy·ing.** cause to conform to a rural way of life.

coun·try (kun′trē) *n., pl.* **-tries. 1** an expanse of land characterized by a particular geography, population, etc.; a region or district: *Cossack country. They live in the hill country to the north.* **2** a nation; state: *He came from France, a country across the sea.* **3** the people of a nation. **4** the land where a person was born or is a citizen: *In my own country the customs are very different.* **5** land with few houses, away from cities or industrial areas; uncultivated land or farmland: *We drove out into the country.* **6** (*adj.*) of, in, or like the country as opposed to the city; rural: *He likes country food and country air.* **7** country music. **8** (*adj.*) of or having to do with country music.
across country See **across.**
[ME < OF *contree* < VL *contrata* region lying opposite < L *contra* against]

country and western country music.

country club a club in the country near a city, or in the suburbs, having a clubhouse and facilities for outdoor sports.

country cousin a person from the country who finds the city confusing or frightening.

coun·try–dance (kun′trē dans′) *n.* a dance in which partners face each other in two long lines. The Virginia reel is a country-dance.

coun·try·folk (kun′trē fōk′) *n.* the people who live in the country.

country gentleman a gentleman who lives on his estate in the country.

country house a home in the country.

coun·try·man (kun′trē mən) *n., pl.* **-men. 1** a man of one's own country; compatriot: *They met many of their countrymen in their travels through Europe.* **2** a man who lives in the country; a rustic.

country marriage *Cdn. Historical.* among fur traders and pioneers, a common-law marriage between a white man and an Indian or Métis woman.

country music a style of music that developed from the traditional folk music of white people in the S United States. Modern country music has spread throughout North America and other countries and contains many elements of blues, popular music, and rock.

coun·try·seat (kun′trē sēt′) *n.* a residence or estate in the country, especially a fine one.

coun·try·side (kun′trē sīd′) *n.* **1** land outside cities and towns, especially with reference to its features such as trees, flowers, hills and valleys, and its general appearance: *The countryside looked beautiful in the fall sun.* **2** a certain section of the country. **3** its people.

coun·try–wide (kun′trē wīd′) *adj.* nation-wide.

country wife *Cdn. Historical.* an Indian or Métis common-law wife of a white fur trader or pioneer.

coun·try·wom·an (kun′trē wum′ən) *n., pl.* **-wom·en. 1** a woman of one's own country; compatriot. **2** a woman living in the country; a rustic.

count·ship (kount′ship) *n.* **1** the title or rank of a count. **2** the territory owned by or under the control of a count.

coun·ty (koun′tē) *n., pl.* **-ties. 1** an administrative district of a country, province, state, etc. The county form of municipal government is used in Nova Scotia, New Brunswick, Quebec, Ontario, and Alberta. **2** in Great Britain and Ireland, one of the districts into which the country is divided for administrative, judicial, and political purposes. **3** the people of a county. [ME < AF *counte* < *counte*, var. of OF *conte*. See COUNT².]

county court a court having limited jurisdiction in the county or district where it is held.

county seat a town or city where the county government is located.

county town *Brit.* county seat.

coup (kü) *n., pl.* **coups** (küz). **1** a sudden, brilliant action; an unexpected, clever move; master stroke. **2** a stroke or blow. **3** a cleverly organized crime. **4** coup d'état. [< F < L < Gk. *kolaphos*]
☞ *Hom.* coo.

coup de grâce (kü′də gräs′) **1** an action that gives a merciful death to a suffering animal or person. **2** a finishing stroke: *The runner's final sprint gave the coup de grâce to his opponents.* [< F *ccup de grâce*, literally, stroke of grace]

coup d'é·tat (kü′dā tä′) *Politics.* a sudden and decisive use of force by a small group of people, especially in the violent overthrow of a government. [< F *coup d'état*, literally, stroke of state]

coup d'oeil (kü dœ′ē) *French.* a view taken in at a glance.

hat, āge, fär; let, ēqual, tėrm; it, īce
hot, ōpen, ôrder; oil, out; cup, pút, rüle,
əbove, takən, pencəl, lemən, circəs

ch, child; ng, long; sh, ship
th, thin; ŦH, then; zh, measure

coupe (küp) *n.* a closed, two-door automobile, usually seating two to five people.
☞ *Hom.* coop.

cou·pé (kü pā′ *for 1,* kü pā′ *or* küp *for 2*) *n.* **1** a closed carriage with a seat for two people inside and a seat for the driver outside. **2** coupe. [< F *coupé,* pp. of *couper* cut]

cou·ple (kup′əl) *n., v.* **-pled, -pling. —n. 1** two things of the same kind that go together; a pair. **2** a man and woman who are married, engaged, or paired together for a dance, party, game, etc. **3** *Informal.* a few; several (*used with of*): *It shouldn't take longer than a couple of days.*
—v. 1 join together; join together in pairs. **2** copulate. **3** *Electricity.* connect by a coupler. [ME < OF *cople* < L *copula* bond. Doublet of COPULA.]
☞ *Syn. n.* **1.** See note at **pair.**
☞ *Usage.* **Couple** = strictly two persons or things associated in some way: *a married couple.* In everyday speech **couple** is equivalent to the numeral two: *He borrowed a couple of pencils.*

cou·pler (kup′lər) *n.* **1** in an organ, a device for coupling keys or keyboards so they can be played together. **2** a device used to join together two railway cars. **3** a device used to connect electric circuits in order to transfer energy from one to the other. **4** any person or thing that couples.

cou·plet (kup′lit) *n.* **1** two successive lines of verse that rhyme and have the same number of metrical feet. *Example:*

Be not the first by whom the new are tried,

Nor yet the last to lay the old aside.

2 a couple; pair. [< F *couplet,* dim. of *couple* couple]

cou·pling (kup′ling) *n.* **1** the act or process of joining. **2** a device for joining parts of machinery. **3** a device used to join two railway cars. **4** a device or arrangement for transferring electrical energy from one circuit to another.

cou·pon (kü′pon *or* kyü′pon) *n.* **1** a part of a ticket, advertisement, package, etc. that entitles the person who holds it to get something in exchange: *She saved the coupons that came with each box of soap to get free cups and saucers.* **2** a printed statement of interest due on a bond, which can be cut from the bond and presented for payment. [< F *coupon* < *couper* cut]

cour·age (kėr′ij) *n.* bravery; the strength of mind to control fear and act firmly in the face of danger or difficulties.
have the courage of (one's) **convictions,** act as one believes one should.
[ME < OF *corage, curage* < *cuer* heart < L *cor*]
☞ *Syn.* **1. Courage, bravery** = fearlessness. **Courage** applies to moral strength that makes a person face any danger, trouble, or pain steadily and without fear: *Although blinded by the explosion, he faced the future with courage.* **Bravery** applies to a kind of courage that is shown by bold, fearless, daring action in the presence of danger: *The Commandos are famous for their bravery.*

cou·ra·geous (kə rā′jəs) *adj.* full of courage; brave.
—cou·ra′geous·ly, *adv.* **—cou·ra′geous·ness,** *n.*
☞ *Syn.* See note at **brave.**

cou·reur de bois (kü rėr′də bwo′; *French,* kü rœr də bwä′) *pl.* **coureurs de bois.** (kü rėr′ də bwo′; *French,* kü rœr də bwä′). *Cdn. Historical.* in the North and Northwest, a French or Métis fur trader or woodsman: *Radisson and Groseilliers were coureurs de bois.* [< Cdn. F]

cour·i·er (kėr′ē ər *or* kür′ē ər) *n.* **1** a person whose work is carrying messages, especially official government messages. **2** a secret agent who transfers information to and from other agents. **3** a person who goes with a group of travellers and takes care of hotel reservations, tickets, etc. [< F *courrier* < Ital. < L *curriere* run]

course (kôrs) *n., v.* **coursed, cours·ing. —n. 1** an onward movement: *the course of events. She gets little rest in the course of her daily work.* **2** a direction taken: *The ship's course was east.* **3** a line of action or conduct: *The only sensible course was to go home.* **4** a way; path or track; channel: *the course of a stream.* **5** a series of similar things arranged in some regular order: *a course of medical treatment, a course of lectures in history.* **6** the regular order; the ordinary way of proceeding: *the course of nature.* **7** in a university, college, or school: **a** a body of presented studies that make up a curriculum leading to a degree or diploma: *a hairdressing course, the course work for an M.A.* **b** a unit within such a body of studies; subject: *How many courses are you taking next year?* **8** a part of a meal served at one time: *Soup was the first course.* **9** an area marked out for a game or sport: *a race course, a golf course.*

10 a layer of bricks, stones, shingles, etc.; row. **11** the lowest square sail on any mast of a square-rigged ship.
in due course, at the proper or usual time; after a while.
in the course of, during; in the process of.
of course, a as might be expected; needless to say; naturally: *Of course it will rain on the weekend.* **b** certainly; without question: *Of course I'll do it.*
—*v.* **1** race; run: *The blood courses through the arteries.* **2** hunt with hounds. **3** cause (hounds) to hunt for game. [< F *cours* < L *cursus* a running, and < F *course* < Ital. *corsa* a running < L *currere* run]
☛ *Hom.* **coarse, corse.**

cours·er (kôr′sər) *n. Poetic.* a swift horse. [ME < OF *coursier* < *cours* a running < L *cursus*]

court (kôrt) *n., v.* —*n.* **1** a space partly or wholly enclosed by walls or buildings. **2** a short street, especially a wide lane opening off a street and having buildings on three sides. **3** a place marked or walled off for any of various games: *a tennis court, a squash court.* **4** the residence of a king, queen, or other sovereign; a royal palace. **5** the family, household, or followers of a sovereign. **6** a sovereign and his advisers as a ruling power. **7** a formal assembly held by a sovereign. **8** *Law.* **a** a place where justice is administered. **b** the persons who are chosen to administer justice; a judge or judges. **c** an assembly of such persons to administer justice. **d** a session of a judicial body. **9** attention paid to get favor; effort to please. **10** the act of wooing; seeking to marry.
hold court, a of a sovereign, hold a formal assembly. **b** receive or entertain (people) in a lordly way.
out of court, a without a trial or other legal proceedings; privately: *The case was settled out of court.* **b** not important enough to be considered.
pay court to, a pay attention to (a person) to get his favor; try to please. **b** woo.
—*v.* **1** pay attention to (a person) to get his favor; try to please. **2** try to gain the love of, especially with the intention of marrying; woo. **3** try to get; act so as to get; seek: *It is foolish to court danger.* **4** lay oneself open to, especially unthinkingly or foolishly: *Taking a shortcut through that yard when the dog is around is courting disaster.* [ME < OF *cort* < L *cohors* enclosure, retinue. Doublet of COHORT.]

court card the king, queen, or jack, of any suit of playing cards.

cour·te·ous (kėr′tē əs) *adj.* polite; thoughtful of others: *It is a courteous act to help an old lady cross the street.* [ME < OF *corteis* < *cort.* See COURT.] —**court′te·ous·ly,** *adv.*
—**cour′te·ous·ness,** *n.*
☛ *Syn.* See note at **polite.**

cour·te·san (kôr′tə zən *or* kôr′tə zan′) *n.* **1** a prostitute whose clients are men of high rank, especially men at court. **2** any prostitute. [< F *courtisane* < Ital. *cortigiana* woman of the court < *corte* < L *cohors.* Related to COURT.]

cour·te·sy (kėr′tə sē) *n., pl.* **-sies. 1** polite or gracious behavior; thoughtfulness for others. **2** Usually, **courtesies,** *pl.* a polite or thoughtful act or expression: *They exchanged courtesies and each went his way.*
by courtesy, as a favor, rather than as something rightfully owing.
by courtesy of or **through the courtesy of,** with the consent of; with the permission or approval of: *The poem is included in the book by courtesy of the author.*
[ME < OF *cortesie* < *corteis.* See COURTEOUS.]

cour·te·zan (kôr′tə zən *or* kôr′tə zan′) See **courtesan.**

court·house (kôrt′hous′) *n.* a building where law courts are held.

cour·ti·er (kôr′tē ər) *n.* **1** a person often present at the court of a king, prince, etc.; court attendant. **2** a person who tries to win the favor of another by flattering and pleasing him.

court·li·ness (kôrt′lē nis) *n.* politeness; elegance; polish.

court·ly (kôrt′lē) *adj.* **-li·er, -li·est. 1** suitable for a royal court; polite; elegant: *courtly manners, courtly hospitality.* **2** of or having to do with a royal court.

court–mar·tial (kôrt′mär′shəl) *n., pl.* **courts·mar·tial;** *v.* **-tialled** or **-tialed, -tial·ling** or **-tial·ing.** —*n.* **1** a court made up of commissioned officers in the armed forces for the purpose of trying armed forces personnel accused of breaking military law. **2** a trial by such a court: *The captain's court-martial will be held next week.*
—*v.* try by such a court.

Court of St. James's the official name for the British court, which gets its name from St. James's Palace in London, where royal receptions were formerly held.

court plaster cloth with a sticky substance on one side, used for covering and protecting slight cuts.

court·room (kôrt′rüm′ *or* -rùm′) *n.* a room where a law court is held.

court·ship (kôrt′ship) *n.* the condition or time of courting with the intention of marrying; wooing.

court tennis a game in which a ball is hit back and forth over a low net. It is played on an enclosed court, as distinguished from lawn tennis which is played outdoors.

court·yard (kôrt′yärd) *n.* a space enclosed by walls in or near a large building.

cous·in (kuz′ən) *n.* **1** the son or daughter of one's uncle or aunt. First cousins have the same grandparents; second cousins have the same great-grandparents; and so on for third and fourth cousins. Your father's or mother's first cousin is your first cousin once removed. **2** a distant relative. **3** a person who is related by culture, race, etc.: *our English cousins.* **4** any person or thing thought of as related to another: *A good swimmer is first cousin to a beaver.* **5** *Formal.* a title used by a sovereign in addressing another sovereign or a great nobleman. [ME < OF *cosin, cusin* < L *consobrinus* mother's sister's child < *com-* together + *soror* sister]
☛ *Hom.* **cozen.**

cous·in–ger·man (kuz′ən jėr′mən) *n., pl.* **cous·ins-ger·man.** a son or daughter of one's uncle or aunt; first cousin. [< F *cousin-germain; germain* < L *germanus*]

cous·in·ly (kuz′ən lē) *adj., adv.* —*adj.* of, like, or characteristic of a cousin. —*adv.* in a cousinly manner.

cous·in·ship (kuz′ən ship′) *n.* the relationship of a cousin or cousins.

couth (küth) *adj., n.* —*adj.* sophisticated; refined. —*n.* sophistication; refinement: *His writing style is colorful but lacks couth.* [back formation from *uncouth*]

cou·tu·ri·er (kü tür′ē ər; *French,* kü ty ryā′) *n.* a male dressmaker or dress designer. [< F *couturier* tailor < *couture* sewing < VL < L *consuere* < *com-* together + *suere* sew]

cou·tu·ri·ère (kü tür′ē er′; *French,* kü ty ryer′) *n.* a woman dressmaker or dress designer. [< F. See COUTURIER.]

co·va·lence (kō vā′ləns) *n. Chemistry.* **1** a bond in which two atoms share a pair of electrons. **2** the ability to form such a bond. **3** the total of the pairs of electrons which one atom can share with surrounding atoms. —**co·va′len·cy,** *n.*

co·va·lent (kō vā′lənt) *adj.* of or having to do with covalence.

cove (kōv) *n.* **1** a small, sheltered bay; an inlet on the shore; the mouth of a creek. **2** a sheltered nook. [OE *cofa* chamber]

cov·en (kuv′ən) *n.* **1** a gathering of witches. **2** a company or community of witches; especially, traditionally, a group of thirteen.

cov·e·nant (kuv′ə nənt) *n., v.* —*n.* **1** a solemn agreement between two or more persons or groups to do or not to do a certain thing; compact. **2 Covenant, a** the agreement signed by Scottish Presbyterians and members of the English Parliament in 1643. It set up the Presbyterian Church in England. **b** an earlier agreement signed by Scottish Presbyterians in 1638, for the defence of the Presbyterian faith. **c** the Covenant of the League of Nations. **3** in the Bible, the solemn promises of God to mankind; the compact between God and mankind. **4** a legal contract or agreement. —*v.* **1** solemnly agree (to do certain things). **2** enter into a covenant or formal agreement. [ME < OF *covenant* < *covenir* < L *convenire.* See CONVENE.]

cov·e·nant·er (kuv′ə nən tər; *also* kuv′ə nan′tər *for* 2) *n.* **1** a person who makes a solemn agreement. **2 Covenanter,** a person who signed and supported either of the Covenants of the Scottish Presbyterians in the 17th century.

Covenant of the League of Nations the constitution of the League of Nations. It comprises the first part of the Treaty of Versailles that was signed in 1919.

cov·e·nan·tor (kuv′ə nən tər) *n. Law.* a person who makes a covenant and assumes its obligations.

Cov·en·try (kuv′ən trē *or* kov′ən trē) *n.*
send to Coventry, refuse to associate with; ostracize.
[< *Coventry,* city in central England]

cov·er (kuv′ər) *v., n.* —*v.* **1** put something over or around so as to protect, keep warm, hide, etc.: *He covered the sleeping child with his coat. Pull the blind to cover the window.* **2** lie thickly on the surface of, be spread or scattered over: *Dust covered his shoes. Snow covered the ground.* **3** clothe; wrap up: *People in the Arctic cover themselves with furs.* **4** extend over; occupy: *Their farm covers 300 hectares.* **5** invest (oneself or one's reputation): *He covered himself with glory.* **6** hide; conceal: *to cover a mistake.* **7** protect, screen, or shelter: *to cover someone's retreat.* **8** go over; travel: *We covered more than 500 kilometres on the first day of our trip.* **9** include; take in: *The review covered everything we learned last term.* **10** be enough for; provide for: *I had just enough money to cover the cost of the meal plus a tip.* **11** aim straight at: *to cover a person with a pistol.* **12** have within range: *The guns of the fort on*

the hill covered the territory down to the sea. **13** put one's hat or cap on: *Cover your head when you are in the sun.* **14** protect by insurance; insure against a particular risk: *The house is covered but not the contents.* **15** *Journalism.* act as a reporter or photographer of an event or subject: *She covers the city police court.* **16** *Sports.* watch over and try to thwart an opposing player. **17** *Card games.* put a higher-ranking card on (a card played earlier). **18** stand behind; support: *The shortstop covered the second baseman in case the ball got by him.* **19** *Informal.* act as a substitute while someone is absent: *He is covering for the manager while she's away.* **20** deposit the equivalent of (money deposited in betting); accept the conditions of (a bet). **21** *Business.* buy (commodities, securities, etc.) for future delivery as a protection against loss. **22** (of a male animal) copulate with (the female). **23** brood or sit on (eggs or chicks).

cover up, a cover completely; hide; conceal: *He did his best to cover up his error.* **b** hide knowledge or an act in order to protect oneself or someone else: *He's obviously trying to cover up. She will always cover up for a colleague.* **c** seek to protect oneself: *The boxer covered up under the onslaught of blows.*
—*n.* **1** anything that covers: *She always puts covers on her school books.* **2** protection; shelter: *We took cover in an old barn during the storm. The soldiers attacked under cover of dark.* **3** *Hunting.* a covert (def. 2). **4** something that hides or disguises, such as a false identity: *Her job as newspaper reporter was just a cover for her activities as a spy.* **5** *Sports.* a player who watches over and tries to thwart an opposing player. **6** a place for one person at a table, set with a plate, knife, fork, spoon, napkin, etc. **7** funds adequate to cover or meet a liability or secure against possible loss. **8** *Philately.* **a** an envelope or wrapper with stamp and any postal markings affixed. **b** a letter addressed on the reverse side after folding to form an envelope.
blow (someone's) **cover** or **disguise,** expose someone's false identity: *The spy posed as a bookseller until an alert scholar blew his cover.*
break cover, come out of hiding, especially suddenly: *He broke cover and ran for the house.*
under cover, a hidden; secret; disguised. **b** secretly.
[ME < OF *covrir* < L *cooperire* < *co-* up + *operire* cover]
—**cov′er·er,** *n.* —**cov′er·less,** *adj.*

cov·er·age (kuv′ər ij) *n.* **1** the section of the potential buying public presumably reached by a given advertising campaign, medium, etc. **2** the scope and manner of presenting information by a reporter, newspaper, etc. **3** an amount held to meet liabilities: *a 60% gold coverage of paper money.* **4** in insurance, the risks covered by a policy.

cov·er·alls (kuv′ər olz′ or -ôlz′) *n.pl.* a strong outer garment that includes shirt and pants in a single unit, usually worn to protect other clothing. Mechanics usually wear coveralls.

cover charge a charge made in some nightclubs, discothèques, restaurants, etc. for service, entertainment, etc. in addition to the charge for food or drink.

cover crop a crop sown in a field or orchard to protect the soil, especially in winter.

cov·ered (kuv′ərd) *adj.* **1** having a cover or covering. **2** wearing one's hat or cap.

covered wagon a large wagon having a removable, arched canvas cover.

cover girl an attractive girl or woman whose picture is used on the cover of a magazine.

cov·er·ing (kuv′ər ing or kuv′ring) *n.* anything that covers.

cov·er·let (kuv′ər lit) *n.* **1** an outer covering for a bed; bedspread. **2** any covering. [ME *coverlite,* apparently < OF *covrir* (see COVER) + *lit* bed < L *lectus*]

cov·er·lid (kuv′ər lid) *n.* coverlet.

cov·ert (kuv′ərt) *adj., n.* —*adj.* secret; hidden; disguised: *covert glances.* —*n.* **1** a shelter; hiding place. **2** a thicket in which animals hide. [ME < OF *covert,* pp. of *covrir.* See COVER.] —**cov′ert·ly,** *adv.* —**cov′ert·ness,** *n.*
☛ *Syn. adj.* See note at **secret.**

co·vert cloth (kō′vərt or kuv′ərt) cloth of wool, silk and wool, or rayon, usually brownish, used for coats.

cov·er·ture (kuv′ər chür′ or kuv′ər chər) *n.* **1** a cover; a covering. **2** a shelter; hiding place.

cov·er-up (kuv′ər up′) *n.* a stratagem, action, or device designed to conceal something, especially a serious mistake or a crime.

cov·et (kuv′it) *v.* desire eagerly (something that belongs to another). [ME < OF *coveitier,* ult. < L *cupere* desire] —**cov′et·er,** *n.*
☛ *Usage.* See note at **envy.**

cov·et·ous (kuv′ə təs) *adj.* desiring things that belong to others. —**cov′et·ous·ly,** *adv.* —**cov′et·ous·ness,** *n.*

hat, āge, fär; let, ēqual, tėrm; it, īce
hot, ōpen, ôrder; oil, out; cup, put, rüle,
above, takən, pencəl, lemən, circəs
ch, child; ng, long; sh, ship
th, thin; ᴛʜ, then; zh, measure

cov·ey (kuv′ē) *n., pl.* **-eys. 1** a brood of partridges, quail; etc. **2** a small flock, especially of partridges, quail, etc.; group. [ME < OF *covee* < *cover* incubate < L *cubare* lie]

cow¹ (kou) *n., pl.* **cows** or (*archaic or dialect*). **kine. 1** the full-grown female of any bovine animal, especially of domestic cattle. **2** the female of various other large mammals: *an elephant cow, a buffalo cow, a cow moose.* [OE *cū*] —**cow′-like′,** *adj.*

cow² (kou) *v.* make afraid; frighten: *Don't let his threats cow you.* [? < ON *kúga*]

cow·ard (kou′ərd) *n.* **1** a person who lacks courage or gives in to fear; a person who runs from danger, trouble, etc. **2** (*adj.*) lacking courage; cowardly. [ME < OF *coart* < *coe* tail < L *coda,* dial. var. of *cauda;* with reference to an animal with its tail between its legs]

cow·ard·ice (kou′ər dis) *n.* lack of courage; the quality of being easily overcome by fear in the face of danger, pain, etc.

cow·ard·li·ness (kou′ərd lē nis) *n.* the state or quality of being cowardly.

cow·ard·ly (kou′ərd lē) *adj., adv.* —*adj.* **1** lacking courage. **2** of a coward; suitable for a coward. —*adv.* in a cowardly manner.
☛ *Syn.* **1.** See note at **timid.**

cow·bane (kou′bān′) *n.* any of several poisonous plants of the parsley family, especially a North American species (*Oxypolis rigidior*).

cow·bell (kou′bel′) *n.* a bell hung around a cow's neck to indicate where the cow is.

cow·bird (kou′bėrd′) *n.* a small North American blackbird (*Molothrus ater*), the adult male having mainly black plumage with a brown head and neck, the female having brownish grey plumage. Cowbirds are parasitic, laying their eggs in the nests of other small birds.

cow·boy (kou′boi′) *n.* especially in western Canada and the United States, a hired man who looks after cattle on a ranch and on the range. A cowboy performs many of his duties on horseback.

cow·catch·er (kou′kach′ər) *n.* a metal apron at the bottom of the front of a locomotive, designed to roll to one side any obstruction on the tracks.

cow·er (kou′ər) *v.* **1** crouch in fear or shame. **2** draw back tremblingly from another's threats, blows, etc. [ME *couren* < Scand.]

cow·fish (kou′fish′) *n., pl.* **-fish** or **-fish·es. 1** any of several small tropical fishes (family Ostraciidae) having hornlike projections above the eyes, such as *Lactophrys quadricornis.* **2** any of various sea mammals, such as a sea cow.

cow·girl (kou′gėrl′) *n.* a woman or girl who looks after cattle.

cow hand a cowboy or cowgirl.

cow·herd (kou′hėrd′) *n.* a person whose work is looking after cattle while they are at pasture.

cow·hide (kou′hīd′) *n.* **1** the hide of a cow. **2** leather made from it.

Cow·i·chan (kou′i chən) *n.* **1** a member of a Salishan people living mainly on Vancouver Island, noted for their knitting of distinctively patterned sweaters. **2** Cowichan sweater.

Cowichan sweater *Cdn.* a heavy sweater of unbleached wool, knitted by the Cowichans of Vancouver Island, distinguished by symbolic knitted designs, originally black and white, now sometimes multicolored. See also **siwash** (def. 1).

cowl (koul) *n., v.* —*n.* **1** a monk's cloak with a hood. **2** the hood itself. **3** anything shaped like a hood, such as a covering for the top of a chimney, designed to increase the draft. **4** the part of an automobile body that includes the windshield and the dashboard. **5** a cowling. **6** a covering for the top of a chimney, designed to increase the draft.
—*v* **1** put a monk's cowl on. **2** cover with a cowl or something resembling a cowl. [OE *cūle, cug(e)le* < LL *cuculla,* var. of L *cucullus* hood]

cow·lick (kou′lik′) *n. Informal.* a small tuft of hair that will not lie flat, usually just above the forehead.

cowl·ing (koul′ing) *n.* a metal covering over an aircraft engine.

cow·man (kou′mən) *n., pl.* **-men.** an owner of cattle; ranchman.

co-work·er (kō wėr′kər) *n.* one who works with a person; fellow worker: *She's one of his co-workers.*

cow·poke (kou′pōk′) *n. Informal.* cowboy.

cow·pox (kou′poks′) *n.* a disease of cows causing small pustules on their udders. The vaccine for smallpox is obtained from cows that have cowpox.

cow·punch·er (kou′pun′chər) *n. Informal.* cowboy.

cow·rie or **cow·ry** (kou′rē) *n.* 1 a glossy, yellow sea shell, used as money in some parts of Africa and Asia. 2 the mollusc that forms this shell. [< Hind. *kauri*]

cow·skin (kou′skin′) *n.* cowhide.

cow·slip (kou′slip) *n.* 1 a Eurasian primrose (*Primula veris*) having crinkled leaves and clusters of bright-yellow flowers that bloom in spring. 2 marsh marigold. [OE *cūslyppe* < *cū* cow + *slyppe* slime]

Cow·town (kou′toun′) *n.* in western Canada and the United States, a town that is largely dependent on the cattle business; a market or shipping centre for cattle.

cox (koks) *n., v.* —*n.* coxswain. —*v.* 1 act as a coxswain. 2 be a coxswain of.

cox·comb (koks′kōm′) *n.* 1 a vain, empty-headed man; a conceited dandy. 2 See **cockscomb** (def. 2). [var. of *cock's comb*] ☛ Hom. cockscomb.

cox·comb·ry (koks′kōm′rē) *n., pl.* **-ries.** 1 silly vanity; empty-headed conceit. 2 an example of this.

cox·swain (kok′sən or -swān′) *n.* a person who steers a boat, racing shell, etc. and is in charge of the crew. Also, **cockswain.** [< *cock* cockboat + *swain*]

coy (koi) *adj.* 1 shy; modest; bashful. 2 pretending to be shy: *The actress wore a coy smile.* [ME < OF *coi* < L *quietus* at rest. Doublet of QUIET and QUIT, adj.] —**coy′ly,** *adv.* —**coy′ness,** *n.*

coy·o·te (kī′ōt or kī′ūt′; *also, esp. U.S.* kī ō′tē) *n., pl.* **-tes** or (*esp. collectively*) **-te.** a North American wild animal (*Canis latrans*) of the dog family found throughout the continent, but especially on the plains, resembling a small wolf, having a buff coat and a bushy black-tipped tail, and noted for its nighttime calls that range from long mournful howls to short barks. Coyotes feed mainly on small wild animals such as gophers, rats, mice, and hares. [< Mexican Sp. < Nahuatl *koyotl*]

coy·pu (koi′pü) *n., pl.* **-pus** or (*esp. collectively*) **-pu.** a large beaverlike water rodent (*Myocastor coypus*) native to South America, having an undercoat of soft reddish-brown fur called nutria that is commercially valuable. [< S. *coipu* < Araucanian (S Am. Ind. linguistic stock) *koypu*]

coz (kuz) *n. Informal.* cousin.

coz·en (kuz′ən) *v.* 1 cheat; defraud (*usually used with* **out of** or **of**): *The child was cozened out of his inheritance.* 2 deceive; beguile: *They cozened her into signing the papers.* [origin unknown] —**coz′en·er,** *n.* ☛ Hom. cousin.

coz·en·age (kuz′ən ij) *n.* a cozening; fraud; deception.

co·zy (kō′zē) See **cosy.** —**co′zi·ly,** *adv.* —**co′zi·ness,** *n.*

cp. 1 compare. 2 coupon(s).

c.p. 1 candle power. 2 chemically pure.

CP 1 Canadian Pacific. 2 Canadian Press. 3 Command Post.

C.P. 1 Common Prayer. 2 Communist Party. 3 *Cdn. French.* a Conseil privé (Privy Council). b Conseiller privé (Privy Councillor).

C.P.A. Certified Public Accountant.

cpd. compound(s).

Cpl. or **Cpl** corporal.

CPI *Cdn.* Consumer Price Index.

cpm or **c.p.m.** cycles per minute.

C.P.O. or **CPO** chief petty officer.

CPR Canadian Pacific Railway.

cr. 1 credit; creditor. 2 crown.

Cr chromium.

Cr. 1 Crescent. 2 Creek.

C.R. *Cdn. French.* Conseiller de la reine (Queen's Counsel).

crab[1] (krab) *n., v.* **crabbed, crab·bing.** —*n.* 1 any decapod crustacean having a short abdomen, or "tail", that is carried tucked up under a short, broad shell and having the first pair of legs modified into pincers. Most of the approximately 4500 species are marine, but some are found in fresh water and even on land. 2 any of several other crustaceans resembling the true crab, such as the hermit crab. 3 a machine or apparatus for raising or moving heavy weights. 4 **Crab,** *Astronomy or astrology.* Cancer.
catch a crab, make a faulty stroke in rowing.
—*v.* catch crabs for eating. [OE *crabba*] —**crab′ber,** *n.*

crab[2] (krab) *n., v.* **crabbed, crab·bing.** —*n.* 1 crab apple. 2 a cross, sour, ill-natured person; one who is always complaining or finding fault. —*v.* 1 find fault; complain; criticize: *It doesn't do any good to crab about the weather.* 2 *Informal.* interfere with; spoil: *His lack of enthusiasm crabbed the deal.* [origin uncertain]

crab apple 1 any of several small trees (genus *Malus*) of the rose family having fragrant white, pink, or red flowers and small, very tart applelike fruit. 2 the fruit of any of these trees, used especially for jellies and preserves.

crab·bed (krab′id *or* krabd) *adj.* 1 crabby. 2 hard to understand; perplexing. 3 hard to read or decipher because irregular: *The teacher objected to crabbed handwriting.* [< *crab*[1]] —**crab′bed·ly,** *adv.* —**crab′bed·ness,** *n.*

crab·by (krab′ē) *adj. Informal.* cross, peevish, or ill-natured.

crab grass any of various coarse grasses (genus *Digitaria*) that spread rapidly. Crab grass is considered a lawn pest.

crab louse a parasitic louse (*Phthirus pubis*) that infests the pubic area of the human body.

crab·wise (krab′wīz′) *adv. or adj.* moving sideways like a crab: *The car went out of control and slid crabwise into the fence.*

crack (krak) *n., v.* —*n.* 1 a place, line, surface, or opening made by breaking without separating into parts: *a crack in a cup.* 2 a sudden, sharp noise: *the crack of a whip.* 3 *Informal.* a blow that makes a sudden, sharp noise. 4 a narrow opening: *There are cracks between the boards of the old floor.* 5 *Informal.* an instant; moment. 6 *Slang.* a try; effort; attempt: *Let me take a crack at opening the jar.* 7 *Slang.* a joke. 8 *Slang.* a nasty or sharp remark: *What do you mean by that crack?* 9 *Informal.* a superior person or thing: *She is a crack at skiing.* 10 (*adj.*) *Informal.* very good, excellent; first-rate: *a crack shot, a crack regiment.*
—*v.* 1 break without separating into parts: *to crack a window.* 2 break with a sudden, sharp noise: *The tree cracked and fell.* 3 make or cause to make a sudden, sharp noise: *The whip cracked. He cracked the whip.* 4 *Informal.* hit with a sudden, sharp noise. 5 of the voice, change or cause to change sharply in pitch or quality because of hoarseness or emotion. 6 *Slang.* give way; break down. 7 *Slang.* break into: *to crack a safe.* 8 *Chemistry.* separate (petroleum, coal tar, etc.) into various substances. 9 solve; decipher: *to crack a code.*
crack a bottle, *Informal.* open a bottle and drink what is in it.
crack a joke, tell a joke; say something funny.
crack down, *Informal.* take stern measures.
crack up, a crash or smash. b *Informal.* suffer a breakdown in mental or physical health. c *Informal.* respond or cause to respond with a fit of laughter: *I almost cracked up when he said that. This TV program always cracks her up.* d *Informal.* praise; tout: *That book is not what it's cracked up to be.*
get cracking, *Informal.* get started quickly: *We'd better get cracking if we want to catch that bus.*
[OE *cracian,* v., and ME *crak,* n., both < Gmc.]

crack–brained (krak′brānd′) *adj. Informal.* crazy; insane.

crack–down (krak′doun′) *n. Informal.* swift disciplinary action: *The police intensified their crackdown on drunken drivers.*

cracked (krakt) *adj.* 1 broken without separating into parts. 2 of the voice, lacking evenness; broken; having harsh notes. 3 *Informal.* crazy; insane.

crack·er (krak′ər) *n.* 1 a thin, crisp biscuit or wafer: *a soda cracker, a graham cracker.* 2 a small paper roll used as a party favor containing a motto, a paper cap, etc. A cracker explodes when it is pulled at both ends. 3 *U.S.* a poor white person living in the hills and backwoods regions of Georgia, Florida, etc. 4 a person or instrument that cracks.

cracker barrel an open barrel for salted crackers, formerly common in grocery and country stores.

crack·er–bar·rel (krak′ər bar′əl *or* -ber′əl) *adj.* of or having the informality and simplicity of country people; down-to-earth: *cracker-barrel humor.*

crack·er·jack (krak′ər jak′) *n., adj. Slang.* —*n.* an especially fine person or thing. —*adj.* of superior ability or quality.

Cracker Jack *Trademark.* a kind of candied popcorn.

crack·ing (krak′ing) *n.* the process of changing certain hydrocarbons in petroleum and other oils into lighter hydrocarbons by heat and pressure. Gasoline may be produced by cracking.

crack·le (krak′əl) *v.* **-led, -ling;** *n.* —*v.* 1 make slight, sharp sounds: *A fire crackled on the hearth.* 2 of china, glass, etc., become minutely cracked.
—*n.* 1 a slight, sharp sound, such as paper makes when it is crushed. 2 very small cracks on the surface of some kinds of china, glass, etc. 3 china, glass, etc. made with such a surface; crackleware. [< *crack*]

crack·le·ware (krak′əl wer′) *n.* ceramic ware made with a crackled glaze.

crack·ling (krak′ling) *n.* 1 Usually, **cracklings,** *pl.* the crisp

remains of rendered animal fat, especially from pork. 2 the crisp, browned skin of roasted pork.

crack·nel (krak′nəl) *n.* **1** a hard, brittle biscuit. **2 cracknels,** *pl.* **a** small pieces of fat pork fried crisp. **b** cracklings. [< F *craquelin* < MDu. *crakelinc*]

crack of doom **1** the signal for the Last Judgment. **2** a signal for the end of everything.

crack·pot (krak′pot′) *Slang. n., adj.* —*n.* a very eccentric or crack-brained person. —*adj.* eccentric; crack-brained; impractical.

cracks·man (kraks′mən) *n., pl.* **-men.** a burglar, especially a safe-cracker.

crack–up (krak′up′) *n.* **1** a smash-up; crash: *That pilot has been in more than one crack-up.* **2** *Informal.* a mental or physical collapse.

cra·dle (krā′dəl) *n., v.* **-dled, -dling.** —*n.* **1** a baby's little bed, usually on rockers or swinging on a frame. **2** the place where a thing begins its growth: *The authorities seem to disagree on where we should look for the cradle of civilization.* **3** a frame to support a ship, aircraft, or other large object while it is being built, repaired, lifted, etc. **4** the part of a telephone that supports the receiver. **5** a box on rockers designed to wash gold from the earth. **6** a frame attached to a scythe for laying grain evenly as it is cut. **7** cradle scythe.

rob the cradle, *Informal.* choose as a companion, or marry, a person much younger than oneself.
—*v.* **1** hold as in a cradle: *She cradled the child in her arms.* **2** put or rock in a cradle. **3** shelter or train in early life. **4** support (a ship, etc) in a cradle. **5** wash (gold from earth) in a cradle. **6** cut with a cradle scythe. [OE *cradol*] —**cra′dle-like′,** *adj.*

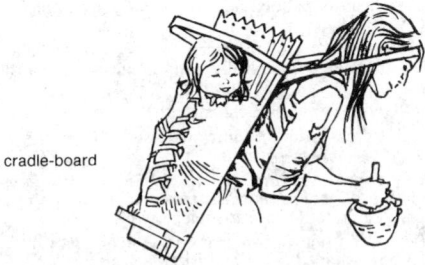

A cradle-board

cra·dle–board (krā′dəl bôrd′) *n. Cdn.* a North American Indian device for carrying a baby, consisting of a thin, rectangular board to which a kind of bag is fastened, formerly widely used throughout North America except in the Arctic.

cradle hill *Cdn. esp. Maritimes.* a small mound such as might have originally been formed at the base of an uprooted tree.

cradle scythe a scythe with a frame attached to it for laying grain evenly as it is cut.

cradle song or **cra·dle·song** (krā′dəl song′) *n.* lullaby.

craft (kraft) *n., pl.* **crafts** for 2, 4, **craft** for 6; *v.* —*n.* **1** skill or art, especially in handwork; craftsmanship: *The craft of the artist is evident in the fine detail of the carving.* **2** a trade or a kind of work requiring special skill: *Carpentry and weaving are crafts.* **3** the persons practising a skilled trade: *Carpenters compose a craft.* **4** an article made by hand. **5** skill in deceiving others; slyness; trickiness: *He used craft to get all their money from them.* **6** a boat, ship, aircraft, or spacecraft. **7** (*adjl.*) of or for a craft or crafts: *craft supplies, a craft sale.*
—*v.* construct or form (*usually used in the passive*): *The store is featuring oak furniture crafted in England. This quilt was crafted by hand.* [OE *cræft*]
☛ *Syn.* **4.** See note at **cunning.**

craft·i·ness (kraf′tē nis) *n.* skill in deceiving others; being crafty; cunning.

crafts·man (krafts′mən) *n.* **-men. 1** a person who practises a trade or handicraft. **2** a person who is highly skilled in the techniques of a craft or art: *a craftsman in wood. Her latest work shows she is a craftsman.*

crafts·man·like (krafts′mən līk′) *adj.* showing craftsmanship: *a craftsmanlike piece of work.*

crafts·man·ship (krafts′mən ship′) *n.* skill in artistic or exacting work; skilled workmanship.

crafts·peo·ple (krafts′pē′pəl) *n.pl.* people who are craftsmen; craftspersons.

crafts·per·son (krafts′pėr′sən) *n.* craftsman.

crafts·wom·an (krafts′wùm′ən) *n., pl.* **crafts·wom·en. 1** a woman who practises a trade or handicraft. **2** a woman who is highly skilled in the techniques of a craft or art.

hat, āge, fär; let, ēqual, tèrm; it, īce
hot, ōpen, ôrder; oil, out; cup, pùt, rüle,
əbove, takən, pencəl, lemən, circəs

ch, child; ng, long; sh, ship
th, thin; ŦH, then; zh, measure

craft union a labor union made up of persons in the same craft. Unions of carpenters, plumbers, or bricklayers are craft unions.

craft·y (kraf′tē) *adj.* **craft·i·er, craft·i·est.** skilful in deceiving others; sly; tricky: *The crafty thief escaped by disguising himself as a waiter.* —**craft′i·ly,** *adv.*

crag (krag) *n.* a steep, rugged rock or cliff; a projecting rock. [< Celtic (compare Welsh *craig*)]

crag·ged (krag′id) *adj.* craggy.

crag·gy (krag′ē) *adj.* **-gi·er, -gi·est. 1** with many crags; rocky: *a craggy hillside.* **2** suggesting the hardness and unevenness of a crag; rugged; rough: *a craggy face.* —**crag′gi·ly,** *adv.* —**crag′gi·ness,** *n.*

crake (krāk) *n.* any of various short-billed rails, especially of Europe. [ME < ON *kráka* crow]

cram (kram) *v., n.* —*v.* **crammed, cram·ming. 1** force; stuff: *He crammed all his clothes quickly into the bag.* **2** fill too full: *The hall was crammed with people.* **3** eat too fast or too much. **4** *Informal.* stuff with knowledge or information. **5** *Informal.* learn hurriedly: *He is cramming facts and dates for his history examination.*
—*n.* **1** a crammed or crowded condition; crush. **2** the act of cramming a subject especially in preparation for an examination. **3** information acquired by cramming. **4** a person who crams. [OE *crammian* < *crimman* insert] —**cram′mer,** *n.*

cram·bo (kram′bō) *n.* a game in which a player must think up a rhyme for a word or line given by another. [< earlier *crambe* < L *crambe* (*repetita*) cabbage (served up again)]

cramp¹ (kramp) *n., v.* —*n.* **1** a painful, involuntary contracting of muscles from a sudden chill, strain, etc.: *The swimmer was seized with a cramp.* **2** a temporary paralysis of particular muscles as a result of overexercising them: *Writer's cramp can be brought on by excessive writing.* **3 cramps,** *pl.* sharp, continuous pains in the abdomen.
—*v.* cause a painful numbness or stiffness: *I was cramped from sitting in one position so long.* [< F < Frankish *crampo* crampon (def. 1). Akin to CRAMP².]

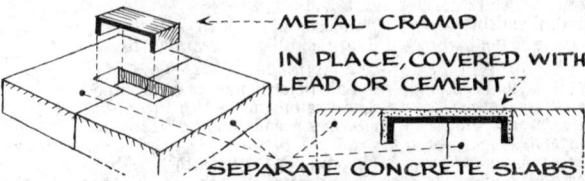

← METAL CRAMP
IN PLACE, COVERED WITH
LEAD OR CEMENT
SEPARATE CONCRETE SLABS

cramp² (kramp) *n., v., adj.* —*n.* **1** a small metal bar with both ends bent, used in building to hold timbers, stone or concrete blocks, etc. permanently in place. **2** a clamp. **3** something that confines or hinders; limitation; restriction.
—*v.* **1** fasten together with a cramp. **2** confine in a small space; limit; restrict: *If the flowerpot is too small, it will cramp the roots of the plant. The three girls were cramped up in one little tent. Cramped handwriting is small and hard to read.* **3** turn the wheels of an automobile, etc. sharply.

cramp (one's) style, *Slang.* restrict or interfere with one's natural or usual behavior.
—*adj.* cramped. [< MDu.; cf. MLG *krampe*]

A crampon harnessed to a boot

cram·pon (kram′pən) *n.* **1** a strong iron bar with hooks at one end, used to lift heavy things; grappling iron. **2** an iron plate set with spikes, that is fastened to the bottom of a shoe to prevent slipping when climbing, walking on ice, etc. [< F < Frankish *crampo* crampon (def. 1). Akin to CRAMP².]

cran·ber·ry (kran′ber′ē or kran′bər ē) *n., pl.* **-ries. 1** a firm,

sour, dark-red berry produced by any of several climbing or trailing plants (genus *Vaccinium*) of the heath family. Cranberries are used for jelly, sauces, etc. **2** a plant that produces these berries. **3** any of several species of viburnum often grown for ornament. The **highbush cranberry** (*Viburnum trilobum*) has edible fruit. [< LG *kraanbere*]

cranberry bog a marsh where cranberries grow.

crane (krān) *n., v.* **craned, cran·ing.** —*n.* **1** a machine with a long, swinging arm, for lifting and moving heavy weights. **2** any of several devices usually consisting of a horizontal arm swinging on a vertical axis, such as a metal arm in a fireplace used to hold a kettle over the fire, or a boom for holding a motion-picture or television camera. **3** any of a family (Gruidae) of tall, grey, brown, or white wading birds having long legs, a long neck and bill, and a partly naked head. Cranes resemble herons but they fly with the neck stretched out while herons fly with the neck curved back. **4** any of various herons, especially the great blue heron.
—*v.* **1** move by, or as if by, a crane. **2** stretch (the neck) as a crane does: *He craned his neck, trying to see over the crowd.* [OE *cran*] —**crane′like′** *adj.*

crane fly any of a family (Tipulidae) of flies having a long, slender body, two narrow wings, and very long legs. Crane flies look like large mosquitoes but do not bite.

cranes·bill (krānz′bil′) *n.* geranium (def. 2), especially any of several wild species, so called from the long, slender, beaklike projection of the fruit. Also, **crane's-bill.**

cran·i·al (krā′nē əl) *adj.* of, from, or having to do with the skull.

cranial index the cephalic index.

cranial nerve any of the nerves beginning in the lower part of the brain, which control certain bodily senses and movements. Mammals, birds, and reptiles have twelve pairs of cranial nerves.

cra·ni·ol·o·gist (krā′nē ol′ə jist) *n.* a person trained in craniology, especially one whose work it is.

cra·ni·ol·o·gy (krā′nē ol′ə jē) *n.* the science that deals with the size, shape, and other characteristics of skulls. [< Gk. *kranion* skull + E *-logy*]

cra·ni·om·e·try (krā′nē om′ə trē) *n.* the science of measuring skulls; measurement of skulls. [< Gk. *kranion* skull + E *-metry*]

cra·ni·ot·o·my (krā′nē ot′ə mē) *n.* a surgical operation that involves the opening of the skull. [< Gk. *kranion* skull + *-tomia* a cutting]

cra·ni·um (krā′nē əm) *n., pl.* **-ni·ums, -ni·a** (-nē ə). **1** the skull of a vertebrate. **2** the part of the skull enclosing the brain. [< LL < Gk. *kranion*]

crank (krangk) *n., v., adj.* —*n.* **1** a part or handle of a machine connected at right angles to a shaft to transmit motion. **2** *Informal.* a person with queer notions or habits, especially one possessed by some idea: *The police got a few calls from cranks when they asked for information about the missing boy.* **3** from or by a crank or a person thought to be a crank: *a crank call.* **4** *Informal.* a cross or ill-tempered person; grouch: *I wouldn't ask any favors of that old crank.* **5** a fanciful turn of speech: *quips and cranks.* **6** a fantastic or queer idea or action.
—*v.* **1** work or start by means of a crank: *to crank a window open.* **2** bend into the shape of a crank. **3** *Slang.* hit hard; slam: *He cranked a shot into the net.*
—*adj.* of machinery, loose and unsteady. [OE *cranc*]

crank·case (krangk′kās′) *n.* a heavy, metal case forming the bottom part of an internal-combustion engine. The crankcase of a gasoline engine encloses the crankshaft, connecting rods, etc.

crank·shaft (krangk′shaft′) *n.* a shaft turning or turned by a crank.

crank·y (krangk′ē) *adj.* **crank·i·er, crank·i·est. 1** cross; irritable; ill-natured. **2** odd; queer. **3** liable to capsize; loose; shaky. —**crank′i·ly,** *adv.* —**crank′i·ness,** *n.*

cran·nied (kran′ēd) *adj.* full of crannies.

cran·ny (kran′ē) *n., pl.* **-nies.** a small, narrow opening; crack; crevice. [< F *cran* fissure, ult. < Med.L *crena* notch]

crap (krap) *n., v.* **crapped, crap·ping.** —*n.* **1** *Slang.* nonsense. **2** *Slang.* dirt or garbage. **3** *Vulgar slang.* excrement; feces. —*v. Vulgar slang.* defecate. —**crap·py,** *adj.*

crape (krāp) *n.* **1** a piece of black crepe used as a sign of mourning. **2** See **crepe** (def. 1).
➤ **Hom. crepe.**

crap·pie (krap′ē) *n.* either of two small North American freshwater fishes (*Pomoxis annularis* or *P. nigromaculatus*) of the sunfish family that are edible. [< Cdn.F *crapet*]

craps (kraps) *n.* a gambling game played with two dice. [<

Louisiana F *craps* the game of hazard < F *craps, crabs* < E *crabs* the lowest throw in hazard]

crap·shoot·er (krap′shüt′ər) *n.* a person who plays craps.

crash¹ (krash) *n., v.* —*n.* **1** a sudden, very loud noise like many dishes falling and breaking, or like sudden, loud band music: *a crash of thunder. There was a crash as the platform collapsed. The huge tree fell with a crash.* **2** a hitting, colliding, or breaking with force and a loud noise; a violent impact or fall: *the crash of an airplane.* **3** an instance of this: *There was a serious car crash at this intersection last night.* **4** a sudden and severe decline or failure, as in business: *a stock market crash.* **5** (*adj.*) *Informal.* characterized by great hurry or speed and by concentrated effort: *a crash course in Italian, a crash campaign to raise money.*
—*v.* **1** make a sudden, loud noise: *The thunder crashed.* **2** fall, hit, or break with force and a loud noise: *The dishes crashed to the floor.* **3** go or move into or through with force and a loud noise: *A bullet crashed through the window. He crashed into the room.* **4** collide: *The two cars crashed right in front of our house.* **5** of a pilot or aircraft, make a crash landing. **6** fail or decline suddenly: *The stock market crashed.* **7** *Informal.* enter or attend without an invitation, ticket, etc.: *to crash a party.* [blend of *craze* shatter and *mash*] —**crash′er,** *n.*

crash² (krash) *n.* a coarse linen cloth, used for towels, curtains, upholstering, etc. [probably < Russian; cf. Russian *krashenina* colored linen]

crash dive **1** a fast descent made by a submarine in an emergency. **2** a downward plunge by an aircraft, ending in a crash.

crash–dive *v.* **-dived, -div·ing. 1** of a submarine, make a fast descent in an emergency. **2** of an aircraft, make a downward plunge that ends in a crash.

crash helmet a heavily padded helmet worn by automobile racers, etc.

crash–land (krash′land′) *v.* of an aircraft or its pilot, make a forced landing in an emergency, usually with damage to the aircraft.

crash landing a forced landing made by an aircraft in an emergency, usually with damage to the aircraft.

crass (kras) *adj.* **1** gross; stupid. **2** thick; coarse. [< L *crassus* thick] —**crass′ly,** *adv.* —**crass′ness,** *n.*

crate (krāt) *n., v.* **crat·ed, crat·ing.** —*n.* a large frame, box, basket, etc. used to pack furniture, glass, fruit, etc. for shipping or storage. —*v.* pack in a crate. [< L *cratis* wickerwork]

cra·ter¹ (krā′tər) *n.* **1** a depression around the opening at the top of a volcano. **2** a bowl-shaped hole: *The battlefield was full of craters made by exploding shells.* **3** a round, ringlike elevation on the surface of the moon, resembling the crater of a volcano. [< L < Gk. *kratēr* bowl < *kra-* mix]

crat·er² (krāt′ər) *n.* a person or thing that packs or stores goods in a crate.

cra·vat (krə vat′) *n.* **1** a scarf or cloth formerly worn around the neck. A cravat was wound around the neck several times outside the standing collar of the shirt. **2** ascot. [< F *cravate*, special use of *Cravate* Croat]

crave (krāv) *v.* **craved, crav·ing. 1** long for; yearn for; desire strongly: *The thirsty man craved water.* **2** ask earnestly; beg: *to crave a favor.* [OE *crafian* demand]

cra·ven (krā′vən) *adj., n.* —*adj.* cowardly: *a craven act.* —*n.* coward.
cry craven, surrender; admit defeat.
[ME *cravant*; origin uncertain] —**cra′ven·ly,** *adv.* —**cra′ven·ness,** *n.*

Crav·en·ette (krā′vən et′ *or* krav′ən et′) *n. Trademark.* a waterproofed cloth used for raincoats, topcoats, etc. [< *Craven Street,* in London, England]

crav·ing (krā′ving) *n.* a longing or yearning; strong desire.
➤ *Syn.* See note at **desire.**

craw (kro *or* krô) *n.* **1** the crop of a bird or insect. **2** the stomach of any animal. [ME *crawe* < OE **craga* neck]

craw·fish (kro′fish′ *or* krô′-) *n., pl.* **-fish** *or* **-fish·es**; *v.* —*n.* crayfish. —*v. Informal.* move backwards; back out of something; retreat. [var. of *crayfish*]

crawl¹ (krol *or* krôl) *v., n.* —*v.* **1** move slowly, with the body close to or dragging on the ground. Worms, snakes, and insects crawl. **2** move slowly on hands and knees; creep: *to crawl through a hole in a fence. Babies usually crawl before they learn to walk.* **3** move slowly: *The traffic crawled on the icy roads.* **4** swarm with crawling things: *The ground was crawling with ants.* **5** feel creepy: *My flesh crawled at the thought of the huge snakes.* **6** behave or move slavishly or abjectly; fawn. **7** swim with alternate overarm strokes and a continuous kicking motion.
—*n.* **1** a slow movement; crawling: *The traffic was moving at a crawl.* **2** a fast way of swimming, usually alternate overarm strokes and a continuous kicking motion. [ME ? < ON *krafla*] —**crawl′er,** *n.*

crawl² (krol *or* krôl) *n.* an enclosure made with stakes in shallow water, used to hold turtles, fish, etc. [< Du. *kraal* < Sp. *corral.* Doublet of CORRAL.]

crawl·y (krol′ē *or* krôl′ē) *adj.* **crawl·i·er, crawl·i·est.** feeling as if things are crawling over one's skin; creepy.

cray·fish (krā′fish′) *n., pl.* **-fish** *or* **-fish·es.** any of numerous freshwater decapod crustaceans, especially of the genera *Astacus* and *Cambarus,* resembling small lobsters, found almost throughout the world, having a segmented body with a long abdomen ending in a fanlike part, and having four pairs of legs, one pair of pincers, and two pairs of feelers. Crayfish often move backwards. [ME *crevise* < OF *crevice* crab < OHG *krebiz,* influenced by E *fish.* Akin to CRAB¹.]

cray·on (krā′on *or* krā′ən) *n., v.* **-oned, -on·ing.** —*n.* **1** a stick or pencil of chalk, charcoal, or a waxlike, colored substance, for drawing or writing. **2** a drawing made with crayons. —*v.* draw with a crayon or crayons. [< F *crayon* < *craie* chalk < L *creta*]

craze (krāz) *n., v.* **crazed, craz·ing.** —*n.* something everybody is very much interested in for a short time; a fad.
—*v.* **1** make crazy: *She was nearly crazed with the pain.* **2** make tiny cracks all over the surface of earthenware, pottery, etc. **3** of pottery, etc., develop a mesh of tiny cracks. [ME *crase(n)* break; ? < ON *krasa*]

cra·zy (krā′zē) *adj.* **-zi·er, -zi·est;** *n., pl.* **-zies.** —*adj.* **1** affected with madness; insane. **2** distracted or temporarily out of control as a result of some violent emotion: *crazy with fear, a thrill-crazy mob.* **3** *Informal.* very foolish or wild; not sensible: *a crazy driver. He has some crazy idea about walking from Dawson to White Horse.* **4** *Informal.* very enthusiastic; excessively preoccupied (used with **about**): *She's crazy about cars.* **5** *Informal.* extremely fond; infatuated (used with **about**): *He's crazy about her.* **6** *Informal.* unusual and conspicuous; odd: *She likes crazy jewellery.* **7** not strong or sound; shaky and frail: *a crazy old bridge.*
—*n. Slang.* an insane, wild, or very eccentric person.
like crazy, *Informal.* to an extreme degree; extremely hard, fast, etc.: *laughing like crazy. He took off on his bike, pedalling like crazy.*
[< *craze.* 16c.] —**cra′zi·ly,** *adv.* —**cra′zi·ness,** *n.*
➤ *Syn.* **1, 2.** See note at **mad.**

crazy bone the funny bone.

crazy quilt a quilt made of pieces of cloth of various shapes, colors, and sizes, sewed together with no definite pattern.

creak (krēk) *v., n.* —*v.* squeak loudly: *The hinges on our doors creak because they need oiling.* —*n.* a creaking noise. [ME *creke(n);* apparently imitative]
➤ *Hom.* **creek, Creek.**

creak·y (krēk′ē) *adj.* **creak·i·er, creak·i·est.** likely to creak; creaking. —**creak′i·ly,** *adv.* —**creak′i·ness,** *n.*

cream (krēm) *n., v., adj.* —*n.* **1** the yellowish part of milk that contains fat. Cream rises to the top when milk that is not homogenized is allowed to stand. Butter is made from cream. **2** *(adj.)* containing or made of cream or milk: *cream sauce, cream soup.* **3** food made of cream; food like cream: *ice cream, chocolate creams.* **4** an oily preparation put on the skin to make it smooth and soft. **5** a yellowish white. **6 the cream,** the best part of anything: *the cream of the crop. The cream of a class is made up of the best students.* **7** a thick, sweet liqueur; crème.
—*v.* **1** put cream in. **2** take or skim cream from. **3** form like cream on the top; froth. **4** allow (milk) to form cream. **5** cook with cream, milk, or a sauce of cream or milk with butter and flour. **6** make into a smooth mixture like cream: *to cream butter and sugar together in making a cake.* **7** *Slang.* **a** *Sports.* defeat soundly or decisively. **b** hurt or damage severely, especially as a result of hard blows or forceful impact.
—*adj.* having the color cream. [ME *creme* < OF *cresme* < LL *crama* cream < Gaulish, and < Ecclesiastical L *chrisma* ointment < Gk. *chrisma* < *chriein* anoint]

cream cheese a soft, white cheese made from cream or milk and cream.

cream·er (krēm′ər) *n.* **1** a small pitcher for holding cream. **2** a machine for separating cream from milk; separator. **3** a refrigerator in which milk is placed while the cream is rising. **4** a liquid or powder manufactured from any of various edible oils, used especially as a substitute for cream or milk in coffee or tea.

cream·er·y (krēm′ər ē) *n., pl.* **-er·ies.** **1** a place where butter and cheese are made. **2** a place where cream, milk, and butter are sold or bought. **3** a place where milk is set for cream to rise.

cream of tartar a very sour, white powder used in cooking and in medicine; potassium bitartrate. Cream of tartar is obtained from the deposit in wine casks. Formula: $KHC_4H_4O_6$

cream sauce a sauce made of cream or milk with flour and butter.

cream·y (krēm′ē) *adj.* **cream·i·er, cream·i·est.** **1** like cream;

hat, āge, fär; let, ēqual, tèrm; it, īce
hot, ōpen, ôrder; oil, out; cup, pùt, rüle,
əbove, takən, pencəl, lemən, circəs

ch, child; ng, long; sh, ship
th, thin; ŦH, then; zh, measure

smooth and soft. **2** having much cream in it. **3** having the color of cream; yellowish white. —**cream′i·ly,** *adv.* —**cream′i·ness,** *n.*

crease (krēs) *n., v.* **creased, creas·ing.** —*n.* **1** a ridge or groove in a pliable substance, made by or as if by folding and pressing; a fold or wrinkle. **2** *Cdn. Hockey and lacrosse.* a small area marked off in front of each goal. The crease is reserved for the goal tender and prohibited to attacking players except when the puck or ball is inside it. **3** *Cricket.* **a** either of two lines at each end of the pitch that define the positions of the bowler and the batsman. **b** the space enclosed by these two lines.
—*v.* **1** make a crease or creases in. **2** become creased or wrinkled: *This skirt creases badly.* **3** graze with a bullet. [origin unknown] —**creas′er,** *n.* —**crease′less,** *adj.*
➤ *Hom.* **creese.**

cre·ate (krē āt′) *v.* **-at·ed, -at·ing.** **1** make a thing that has not existed before: *The Bible says that God created all things.* **2** make something original by intelligence and skill: *She created this garden in the desert.* **3** give rise to; cause: *He was created a knight.* **4** produce or bring about: *to create a disturbance, to create new jobs.* **5** be the first to act (a particular part or role) in a play. [< L *creare*]

cre·a·tion (krē ā′shən) *n.* **1** creating or being created. **2** all things created; the world and everything in it; the universe. **3** a thing produced by intelligence and skill, usually something important or original: *That painting is a magnificent creation.* **4 the Creation,** the creating of the universe by God.

cre·a·tion·ism (krē ā′shən iz′əm) *n.* the theory that the universe and everything in it were specially created by God and are not the result of accident or evolution.

cre·a·tion·ist (krē ā′shən ist′) *n.* a person who believes in creationism. —**cre·a′tion·is′tic,** *adj.*

cre·a·tive (krē ā′tiv) *adj.* **1** having the power to create; inventive; productive: *Sculptors are creative artists.* **2** showing originality or imagination; artistic: *creative engineering, creative writing.* —**cre·a′tive·ly,** *adv.* —**cre·a′tive·ness,** *n.*

cre·a·tiv·i·ty (krē′ā tiv′ə tē) *n.* creative ability; the quality of being creative.

cre·a·tor (krē ā′tər) *n.* **1** a person who creates. **2 the Creator,** God.

crea·ture (krē′chər) *n.* **1** anything created. **2** a living being; an animal or person. **3** a person who is completely under the influence of another; a person who is ready to do anything that another asks. [< L *creatura* < *creare* create]

creature comforts the things that give bodily comfort. Food, clothing, and shelter are creature comforts.

crèche (kresh *or* krāsh) *n.* **1** a place where children are taken care of while their mothers are at work; day nursery. **2** a model showing the Christ child in the manger, with attendant figures, that is often displayed in homes, churches, etc. at Christmas. [< F < Gmc. Akin to CRIB.]

cre·dence (krē′dəns) *n.* **1** belief: *Never give credence to gossip.* **2** an introduction or recommendation in confidence; credential: *a letter of credence.* [< Med.L *credentia* < L *credere* believe]

cre·den·tial (kri den′shəl) *n.* **1** something that gives or recommends credit or confidence. **2 credentials,** letters of introduction, entitling the bearer to credit or confidence; references: *After showing his credentials, the new inspector was allowed to see the bank's records.*

cred·i·bil·i·ty (kred′ə bil′ə tē) *n.* the fact or quality of being credible.

cred·i·ble (kred′ə bəl) *adj.* believable; reliable; trustworthy: *It seems hardly credible that Bill has grown so tall in one year.* [ME < L *credibilis* < *credere* believe] —**cred′i·ble·ness,** *n.* —**cred′i·bly,** *adv.*
➤ *Usage.* **Credible, creditable,** and **credulous** are sometimes confused. **Credible** = believable: *His story is too full of coincidences to be credible.* **Creditable** = bringing honor or praise: *He turned in a creditable performance, though his heart was no longer in his acting.* **Credulous** = too ready to believe: *He was credulous enough to think he would really be given the job.*

cred·it (kred′it) *n., v.* —*n.* **1** belief in the truth of something; faith; trust: *They placed little credit in his story of having been robbed.* **2** confidence or trust in a person's ability and intention to pay later for something he wishes to buy now: *to get credit for a purchase.* **3** the time allowed for delayed payment: *They give only*

short-term credit. **4** the amount of money a person has in an account: *He had a credit of $5000 in his savings account.* **5** *Accounting.* **a** an entry of money paid on account. **b** the right-hand side of an account where such entries are made. **c** the amount entered or shown on this side. **6** reputation with respect to payment of debts: *If you pay your bills on time, your credit will be good.* **7** good reputation: *a man of credit.* **8** recognition; honor: *The person who does the work should get the credit.* **9** a source of honor or praise: *The author's latest novel is a credit to her.* **10** an acknowledgment of the authorship, source, etc. of material used in a publication, work done on a dramatic show, radio or television program, etc.: *He was promised a credit for his contribution to the documentary.* **11** Usually, **credits,** *pl.* a listing of the producers, directors, actors, technicians, and others who have contributed their skills to a motion picture, radio or television program, or a play.
do credit to, bring honor or recognition to: *Her quick action did credit to her courage.*
give (someone) **credit for,** believe or acknowledge that a person has: *Give him credit for some intelligence and let him try the job himself.*
give credit to, believe; have faith in; trust.
on credit, on a promise to pay later: *She bought her car on credit.*
—*v.* **1** believe in the truth of something; have faith in; trust: *It was difficult to credit the boy's strange explanation for his absence.* **2** add to (an account) as a deposit. **3** enter on the credit side of an account. **4** assign to as a credit. **5** put an entry on the record of (a student) showing that he has passed a course of study. **6** give recognition to; attribute to: *He credited her with the original idea.*
credit (someone) **with,** attribute to a person: *You will have to credit him with some sense for not panicking during the fire.*
[< F < Ital. < L *creditum* a loan < *credere* trust, entrust]
☛ *Syn.* **1. Credit, accredit** = believe someone or something responsible for saying, doing, feeling, or causing something. **Credit** emphasizes the idea of believing, not always with enough reason or evidence: *He credits me with doing things I never thought of.* **Accredit** emphasizes the idea of accepting because of some proof: *We accredit Peary with having discovered the North Pole.*
☛ *Usage.* See note at **credible.**
cred·it·a·ble (kred′ə tə bəl) *adj.* bringing credit or honor: *a creditable record of perfect attendance.* —**cred′it·a·ble·ness,** *n.* —**cred′it·a·bly,** *adv.*
☛ *Usage.* See note at **credible.**
credit bureau a business that collects information regarding the credit ratings of individuals or companies and offers this information as a service to subscribers.
credit card an identification card entitling its holder to charge the cost of goods or services.
Cred·i·tiste (kred′i tēst′) *adj., n. Cdn.* —*adj.* of or having to do with the Social Credit Rally. —*n.* a member of this party. [< Cdn.F *Créditiste*]
Creditiste Party Social Credit Rally.
cred·i·tor (kred′ə tər) *n.* a person to whom money or goods are due; one to whom a debt is owed.
credit rating the financial standing and reputation of a company or individual, used to set the amount of money or credit that one may borrow or obtain.
credit union a co-operative association that makes loans to its members at low rates of interest.
cre·do (krē′dō *or* krā′dō) *n., pl.* **-dos. 1** a creed: *His credo in art was purity of form.* **2** Also, **Credo,** **a** the Apostles' Creed or the Nicene Creed. **b** the music that accompanies either of these Creeds. [< L *credo* I believe. Doublet of CREED.]
cre·du·li·ty (krə dyü′lə tē *or* krə dü′lə tē) *n.* an excessive readiness to believe.
cred·u·lous (krej′ů ləs) *adj.* too ready to believe; easily deceived. [< L *credulus* < *credere* believe] —**cred′u·lous·ly,** *adv.* —**cred′u·lous·ness,** *n.*
☛ *Usage.* See note at **credible.**
Cree (krē) *n., pl.* **Cree** *or* **Crees;** *adj.* —*n.* **1** a member of an Amerindian people living mainly in the Prairie Provinces. **2** the Algonquian language of the Cree. —*adj.* of or having to do with the Cree or their language.
creed (krēd) *n.* **1** a formal statement of the essential points of religious belief as authorized by a church. **2** a set of beliefs, principles, or opinions: *It was his creed that work should come before play.* [OE *crēda* < L *credo* I believe. Doublet of CREDO.]
creek (krēk *or* krik) *n.* **1** a small freshwater stream. **2** a narrow bay, running inland for some distance. [ME *creke;* cf. MDu. *creke*]
☛ *Hom.* creak (krēk), Creek.
☛ *Pronun.* Most Canadians pronounce **creek** the same as **creak,** but in some regions, especially in parts of the West, the pronunciation (krik) is common.
Creek (krēk) *n., pl.* **Creek** *or* **Creeks. 1** a group of Indian tribes formerly living in Alabama, Georgia, and N Florida, now living in

Oklahoma. **2** a member of this group of tribes. **3** their language.
☛ *Hom.* creak (krēk), creek.
creel (krēl) *n.* **1** a basket for holding fish that have been caught. **2** a basketlike trap for fish, lobsters, etc. [ME *crele* ? < OF *creil,* ult. < L *cratis* wickerwork]
creep (krēp) *v.* **crept, creep·ing;** *n.* —*v.* **1** move with the body close to the ground or floor; crawl: *The cat crept toward the mouse. A baby creeps on its hands and knees.* **2** move slowly. **3** grow along the ground or over a wall by means of clinging stems: *a creeping plant. Ivy had crept up the wall of the old house.* **4** move or behave in a timid, stealthy, or servile manner: *The robbers crept toward their victims.* **5** develop gradually but persistently: *creeping materialism.* **6** slip slightly out of place: *The hall rug creeps so we always have to put it back in place.* **7** feel as if things were creeping over the skin; shiver; shudder: *I could feel my flesh creep, and my hair stood on end.*
—*n.* **1** creeping; slow movement. **2** *Geology.* slow movement of soil or disintegrated rock down a slope, due to gravity, frost, or ground water: *tangential creep, continental creep.* **3** *Physics.* the process of softening, flexing, or melting of material with accompanying changes in shape and dimension that result from increased stress or temperature. **4 the creeps,** *Informal.* a feeling as if things were creeping over one's skin. **5** *Slang.* a person who gives one the creeps; an undesirable or unlikable person. [OE *crēopan*]
creep·er (krēp′ər) *n.* **1** a person or thing that creeps. **2** any plant that grows along a surface, sending out rootlets from the stem, such as the Virginia creeper and ivy. **3** any of a family (Certhiidae) of small, mostly brownish birds that climb along the trunk and branches of trees looking for insects. The one North American species is the **brown creeper** (*Certhia familiaris*). **4** a piece of canvas or other material that is attached to the bottom of a ski for better gripping in climbing uphill. **5** climbing iron.
6 creepers, *pl.* a one-piece garment combining top and pants, worn by babies.
creep·y (krēp′ē) *adj.* **creep·i·er, creep·i·est. 1** having a feeling of horror, as if things were creeping over one's skin: *The ghost story made us feel creepy.* **2** causing such a feeling: *a creepy howl.* **3** creeping; moving slowly. —**creep′i·ly,** *adv.* —**creep′i·ness,** *n.*
creep·y–crawl·y (krēp′ē krol′ē *or* krēp′ē krôl′ē) *adj., n., pl.* **creep·y–crawl·ies.** —*adj.* making one feel shivery or afraid: *I had a nightmare in which there were creepy-crawly things all over me.*
—*n.* **1** a small insect or other creature, especially when thought of as frightening. **2 the creepy-crawlies,** *pl.* the feeling of fear such insects may give: *He looked dazed, as if he had the creepy-crawlies again.*
creese (krēs) *n. Rare.* See **kris.**
cre·mate (kri māt′ *or* krē′māt) *v.* **-mat·ed, -mat·ing.** burn to ashes; especially, burn a dead body to ashes. [< L *cremare* burn]
cre·ma·tion (kri mā′shən) *n.* the burning of a dead body to ashes instead of burying it.
cre·ma·tor (kri mā′tər *or* krē′mā tər) *n.* **1** a person who cremates. **2** a furnace for cremating. [< LL]
cre·ma·to·ri·um (krē′mə tô′rē əm *or* krem′ə tô′rē əm) *n., pl.* **-ums** *or* **-ria. 1** a furnace for cremating. **2** an establishment that has a furnace for cremating.
cre·ma·to·ry (krē′mə tô′rē *or* krem′ə tô′rē) *adj., n., pl.* **-ries.** —*adj.* of or having to do with cremation. —*n. Esp.U.S.* crematorium.
crème (krem) *n. French.* **1** cream. **2** a thick, sweet liqueur.
crème de ca·ca·o (krem′də kə kā′ō *or* -kə kā′ō) chocolate-flavored liqueur. [< F]
crème de la crème (krem′də lä krem′) *French.* the very best; most select. [literally, cream of the cream]
crème de menthe (krem də mäNt′) *French.* a liqueur flavored with mint.
Cre·mo·na (kri mō′nə) *n.* any of the fine violins made in Cremona, Italy, by the Amati, Guarneri, and Stradivari families during the 16th, 17th, and 18th centuries.
cre·nate (krē′nāt) *adj.* with a scalloped edge. [< NL *crenatus* < Med.L *crena* notch]
cre·na·tion (kri nā′shən) *n.* a crenate formation.
cren·el·ate (kren′əl āt′) See **crenellate.**
cren·el·late (kren′əl āt′) *v.* **-lat·ed, -lat·ing.** furnish with battlements. [< F *créneler* < *crenel* notch, ult. < Med.L *crena*] —**cren′el·la′tion,** *n.*
Cre·ole (krē′ōl) *n., adj.* —*n.* **1** a person who is a descendant of the original French settlers of Louisiana, and who has preserved their language and culture. **2** a person of French or Spanish ancestry born in Spanish America or the West Indies. **3** a black person or one of mixed black and European ancestry born in Spanish America or the West Indies. **4** the dialect of French spoken by many blacks in Louisiana. **5** Haitian Creole. **6 creole,** a language that is based on two or more languages and that is the mother tongue of a community of speakers. Creoles develop from extended

contact between peoples speaking different languages. —*adj.* **1** of or having to do with Creoles. **2** creole, of, having to do with, or characteristic of a creole. [< F *créole* < Sp. < Pg. *crioulo* < *criar* bring up < L *creare* create]

cre·o·lized (krē′ə līzd′) *adj.* designating a language that is a creole.

cre·o·sol (krē′ə sōl′ *or* krē′ə sol′) *n.* a colorless, oily liquid obtained from wood tar and a resin of the guaiacum tree, used as an antiseptic. *Formula:* $C_8H_{10}O_2$ [< *creosote*]

cre·o·sote (krē′ə sōt′) *n., v.* **-sot·ed, -sot·ing.** —*n.* **1** an oily liquid with a penetrating odor, obtained by distilling wood tar. It is used to preserve wood and in cough medicine. **2** a similar substance obtained from coal tar. —*v.* treat with creosote. [originally, a meat preservative; < Gk. *kreo-* (for *kreas* flesh) + *sōtēr* savior < *sōzein* save]

crepe *or* **crêpe** (krāp) *n.* **1** a kind of cloth woven with a crinkled surface. **2** crepe paper. **3** crepe rubber. **4** (*adj.*) made of crepe: *a crepe dress, crepe soles.* **5** Usually, **crêpe,** a large, very thin pancake usually served folded or rolled up with a filling. **6** See **crape** (def. 1). [< F *crêpe* < L *crispa* curled]
☛ *Hom.* **crape.**

crepe de Chine (krāp′də shēn′) a soft, thin, medium-weight, silk crepe. [< F *crêpe de Chine* China crepe]

crepe paper thin, crinkled, stretchy paper used for making party decorations, etc.

crepe rubber crude or synthetic rubber, made with a crinkled surface and used especially for the soles of shoes.

crep·i·tant (krep′ə tənt) *adj.* crackling; rattling.

crep·i·tate (krep′ə tāt′) *v.* **-tat·ed, -tat·ing.** crackle; rattle. [< L *crepitare* crackle < *crepare* crack]

crep·i·ta·tion (krep′ə tā′shən) *n.* a crepitating.

crept (krept) *v.* pt. and pp. of **creep.**

cre·pus·cu·lar (kri pus′kyə lər) *adj.* **1** of twilight; resembling twilight; dim; indistinct. **2** of certain birds, insects, etc., appearing or flying by twilight. [< L *crepusculum* twilight]

cres. *or* **cresc.** crescendo.

Cres. Crescent.

cre·scen·do (krə shen′dō) *n., pl.* **-dos;** *adj., adv., v.* —*n.* **1** *Music.* **a** a gradual increase in loudness. **b** a symbol (<) indicating this, placed over the affected passage of music. **c** a passage to be played or sung with a crescendo. **2** any gradual increase in force, loudness, etc.: *a crescendo of cheers.* **3** the peak of such an increase; climax: *Complaints reached a crescendo.* —*adj. or adv.* gradually increasing in volume, etc. —*v.* increase gradually in volume, etc. *Abbrev.:* cres. or cresc. [< Ital. *crescendo,* ppr. of *crescere* increase < L]

A crescent shape

The moon as a crescent

cres·cent (kres′ənt) *n., adj.* —*n.* **1** the shape of the moon as seen from the earth in its first or last quarter. **2** anything having this or a similar shape. A curved street or a curved row of houses is sometimes called a crescent. **3** a light roll, made of yeast dough, shaped like a crescent moon. **4** the emblem of the former Turkish Empire and of the present republic of Turkey. **5** the Turkish or Islamic power. —*adj.* **1** shaped like the moon in its first or last quarter. **2** growing; increasing. [< L *crescens, -entis,* ppr. of *crescere* grow] —**cres′cent·like′,** *adj.*

cre·sol (krē′sōl *or* krē′sol) *n.* an oily liquid obtained from tar, used as a disinfectant. *Formula:* C_7H_8O [var. of *creosol*]

cress (kres) *n.* any of various plants (family Cruciferae, the mustard family) having leaves with a peppery taste used in salads and as a garnish. [OE *cresse*]

cres·set (kres′it) *n.* a metal container for burning oil, wood, etc. to give light. Cressets are mounted on poles or hung from above. [ME < OF *cresset,* earlier *craisset* < *crois* cross < L *crux* (with reference to light from the Cross of Christ); influenced by *craisse* grease]

crest (krest) *n., v.* —*n.* **1** a tuft of hair or feathers, or a growth of skin on the head of a bird or animal. **2** a decoration, plumes, etc. on the top of a helmet. **3** a decoration at the top of a coat of arms. A family crest is sometimes put on silverware, dishes, stationery, etc. **4** an emblem, usually of felt cloth, worn by members of various

hat, āge, fär; let, ēqual, tèrm; it, īce
hot, ōpen, ôrder; oil, out; cup, pùt, rüle,
əbove, takən, pencəl, lemən, circəs

ch, child; ng, long; sh, ship
th, thin; ᴛʜ, then; zh, measure

organizations, athletic teams, etc.: *a hockey crest. The soldier wore his regimental crest on the breast pocket of his blue blazer.* **5** a similar emblem awarded as a sign of merit in studies, athletics, etc. **6** the top part; the top of a hill, wave, ridge, etc.; peak; summit. **7** among Indian peoples of the West Coast: **a** the symbol of a particular clan or similar social group. **b** the social group identified by this symbol. —*v.* **1** furnish with a crest. **2** of waves, form or rise into a crest. **3** serve as a crest to; top; crown. **4** reach the crest or summit of (a hill, wave, etc.). [ME < OF *creste* < L *crista* tuft] —**crest′like′,** *adj.*

crest·ed (kres′tid) *adj.* having a crest: *a crested bird, a crested shield.*

crest·fall·en (krest′fol′ən *or* -fôl′ən) *adj.* dejected; discouraged. —**crest′fall′en·ly,** *adv.*

cre·ta·ceous (kri tā′shəs) *adj., n.* —*adj.* **1** like chalk; containing chalk. **2 Cretaceous,** of or having to do with the geological period when most of the chalk deposits were made; of or having to do with rocks formed in this period. —*n.* **Cretaceous,** *Geology.* **a** the period, beginning approximately 130 million years ago, when most of the chalk deposits were made. **b** the group of rocks formed in this period. See chart at **geology.** [< L *cretaceus* < *creta* chalk < *Creta,* the island of Crete]

Cre·tan (krē′tən) *n., adj.* —*n.* a native or inhabitant of Crete, a Greek island in the Mediterranean Sea, SE of Greece. —*adj.* of or having to do with Crete or its people.
☛ *Hom.* **cretin** (krē′tən).

cre·tin (kret′ən *or* krē′tən) *n.* a person who is severely mentally retarded, especially one afflicted with cretinism. [< F *crétin* < Swiss dial. < OF *chrestien* < L *Christianus* Christian; came to mean "man," then "fellow," then "poor fellow"]
☛ *Hom.* **Cretan** (for second pronun. of **cretin**).

cre·tin·ism (kret′ən iz′əm *or* krē′tən iz′əm) *n.* an abnormal condition, usually present from birth, in which physical and mental growth is stunted because the thyroid gland cannot produce enough thyroid hormone.

cre·tonne (kri ton′ *or* krē ton′) *n.* a strong cotton cloth with designs printed in colors on one or both sides, used for curtains, furniture covers, etc. [< F *cretonne,* probably < *Creton,* a village in Normandy, France]

cre·vasse (krə vas′) *n., v.* —*n.* a deep crack or crevice in the ice of a glacier. —*v.* make crevasses in. [< F *crevasse* < OF *crevace.* Doublet of CREVICE.]

crev·ice (krev′is) *n.* a narrow split or crack. [ME *crevace* < OF < VL *crepacia* < L *crepare* crack. Doublet of CREVASSE.]

crew¹ (krü) *n., v.* —*n.* **1** a group of people who work together; gang: *A camera crew looks after the filming of a television program. A repair crew is working on the hydro lines.* **2** the people who operate a ship, sometimes including the officers and captain. **3** the people who operate an aircraft. **4** a team of people who man a boat. **5** *Informal.* a group or crowd: *The whole crew came to our place for dinner.* —*v.* **1** staff (a ship) with a crew. **2** act as a crew or as a member of a crew. [ME *crue* < MF *creüe* increase, reinforcement < *creistre* grow < L *crescere*]

crew² (krü) *v.* a pt. of **crow¹.**

crew cut a close-cropped haircut for men.

crew·el (krü′əl) *n.* a loosely twisted woollen yarn, used for embroidery. [origin uncertain]
☛ *Hom.* **cruel.**

crew neck a plain, round neckline on a pullover, sweatshirt, etc., fitting closely around the base of the neck.

crib (krib) *n., v.* **cribbed, crib·bing.** —*n.* **1** a small bed with high sides to keep a baby from falling out. **2** a rack or manger for horses and cows to eat from. **3** a building or box for storing grain, salt, etc.: *a corn crib.* **4** a framework of logs or timbers used in building. The wooden lining inside a mine shaft is a crib. **5** *Informal.* the use of another's ideas as one's own. **6** *Informal.* notes or helps that are used dishonestly or unfairly in doing schoolwork or in examinations. **7** a small room or house. **8** the cards discarded from each hand in cribbage and scored by the dealer after the deal has been played. **9** *Informal.* cribbage. **10** *Cdn.* a raft of logs lashed together for floating downstream. —*v.* **1** provide with a crib. **2** *Informal.* use (another's words or

ideas) as one's own. **3** *Informal.* use notes or helps unfairly in doing schoolwork or in examinations. **4** shut up in a small space. [OE *cribb*]

crib·bage (krib′ij) *n.* a card game for two, three, or four people. The players keep score with a narrow board having holes into which movable pegs fit.

crib·bing (krib′ing) *n. Mining.* **1** the lining of timber in a shaft; crib. **2** the pieces of timber used in a crib.

crick[1] (krik) *n.* a sudden muscular cramp; painful stiffness of muscles. [origin uncertain]

crick[2] (krik) *n. Dialect.* creek (def. 1).

crick·et[1] (krik′it) *n.* any of a large family (Gryllidae) of insects resembling grasshoppers, having long, threadlike antennae, long hind legs for jumping, and two pairs of wings. Male crickets produce the characteristic chirping noise by rubbing a kind of scraper on one of the leathery forewings against a row of teeth on the other. [ME < OF *criquet*; imitative]

crick·et[2] (krik′it) *n., adj., v.* —*n.* **1** an outdoor game played by two teams of eleven players each, with ball, bats, and wickets. **2** *Informal.* fair play; good sportsmanship. —*adj. Informal.* fair; according to good sportsmanship. —*v.* play the game of cricket. [< OF *criquet* goal post, stick, probably < MDu. *cricke* stick to lean on]

crick·et[3] (krik′it) *n.* a small, low, wooden stool. [origin uncertain]

crick·et·er (krik′ə tər) *n.* a person who plays cricket.

cried (krīd) *v.* pt. and pp. of **cry.**

cri·er (krī′ər) *n.* **1** an official who shouts out public announcements. **2** a person who shouts out announcements of goods for sale. **3** a person who cries.

cries (krīz) *n.* pl. of **cry.**

crime (krīm) *n.* **1** an act that is against the law. **2** the activity of criminals; violation of law. **3** a wrong act; sin (def. 2). [ME < OF < L *crimen* accusation, offence]
☛ *Syn.* **1. Crime, offence** = an act that breaks a law. **Crime** applies particularly to an act that breaks a law that has been made by men for the public good: *Murder and swindling are crimes.* **Offence** is more general, and applies to an act, not always serious, that breaks any moral, public, or social law: *Lying and cruelty are offences.*

Cri·me·an (krī mē′ən) *adj.* of or having to do with the Crimea, a peninsula in SW Russia, extending into the Black Sea.

crim·i·nal (krim′ə nəl or krim′nəl) *n., adj.* —*n.* a person guilty of a crime. —*adj.* **1** guilty of crime. **2** having to do with crime: *criminal court, criminal law.* **3** like crime; wrong; sinful. [< L *criminalis* < *crimen.* See CRIME.]

crim·i·nal·i·ty (krim′ə nal′ə tē) *n., pl.* **-ties. 1** the fact or quality of being a criminal; guilt. **2** a criminal act.

crim·i·nal·ly (krim′ə nəl ē or krim′nəl ē) *adv.* **1** in a criminal manner. **2** according to criminal law.

crim·i·nate (krim′ə nāt′) *v.* **-nat·ed, -nat·ing. 1** accuse of a crime. **2** furnish evidence as to the guilt of (someone). [< L *criminare < crimen.* See CRIME.]

crim·i·na·to·ry (krim′ə nə tô′rē) *adj.* criminating.

crim·i·no·log·i·cal (krim′ə nə loj′ə kəl) *adj.* of or having to do with criminology. —**crim′i·no·log′i·cal·ly,** *adv.*

crim·i·nol·o·gist (krim′ə nol′ə jist) *n.* a person trained in criminology, especially one whose work it is.

crim·i·nol·o·gy (krim′ə nol′ə jē) *n.* the scientific study of crime and criminals, and of the treatment of criminals. [< L *crimen, -minis* crime + E *-logy*]

crimp[1] (krimp) *v., n.* —*v.* **1** press into small, narrow folds; make wavy: *The girl crimped her hair before going to the party.* **2** pinch, fold, or bend into shape. —*n.* **1** a crimping. **2** something crimped; fold; wave. **3** a waved or curled lock of hair. **4** the natural curl or wave in wool fibre. **put a crimp in,** *Slang.* interfere with; hinder. [OE (ge)crympan] —**crimp′ler,** *n.*

crimp[2] (krimp) *n., v. Historical.* —*n.* a person who made a business of forcing or tricking men into becoming sailors, soldiers, etc. —*v.* force or trick (men) into becoming sailors, soldiers, etc. [origin uncertain]

crim·ple (krim′pəl) *v.* **-pled, -pling.** wrinkle; crumple; curl. [< *crimp*[1]]

crimp·y (krimp′ē) *adj.* **crimp·i·er, crimp·i·est.** having small, narrow folds; wavy.

crim·son (krim′zən) *n., adj., v.* —*n.* a deep red. —*adj.* having the color crimson: *a crimson rose.* —*v.* turn deep red: *His face crimsoned with shame.* [< Ital.

cremesion < cremisi, chermisi the color crimson < Arabic *qirmazi < qirmiz* the kermes insect (from which a red dye was derived) < Skt. *Krmis* worm, insect]

cringe (krinj) *v.* **cringed, cring·ing;** *n.* —*v.* **1** shrink from danger or pain; crouch in fear. **2** bow down timidly; try to get favor or attention by servile behavior: *The beggar cringed as he put out his hand for money.* —*n.* a cringing. [ME *crengen* < OE *cringan* give way] —**cring′er,** *n.* —**cring′ing·ly,** *adv.*

crin·gle (kring′gəl) *n.* a small loop or ring of rope on the edge of a sail. The sail can be fastened by putting a rope through the cringle. [apparently < LG *kringel,* dim. of *kring* ring]

crin·kle (kring′kəl) *v.* **-kled, -kling;** *n.* —*v.* **1** become or cause to be wrinkled: *His suit was crinkled from lying on the floor.* **2** rustle: *Paper crinkles when it is crushed.* —*n.* **1** a wrinkle; ripple. **2** a rustle. [ME *crenkle(n)* < OE *crincan* bend]

crin·kly (kring′klē) *adj.* **crin·kli·er, crin·kli·est.** full of crinkles.

cri·noid (krī′noid *or* krin′oid) *n., adj.* —*n.* any of a class (Crinoidea) of sea animals resembling flowers, with a more or less cup-shaped body and long, feathery arms. Some crinoids, such as the sea lilies, have long stalks by which they are attached to the sea bottom; others swim about freely. —*adj.* **1** of or designating the class Crinoidea. **2** shaped like a lily. [< Gk. *krinoeidēs < krinon* lily]

crin·o·line (krin′ə lin *or* krin′ə lēn′) *n.* **1** a stiff cloth used as a lining to hold a skirt out, make a coat collar stand up, etc. **2** a petticoat of crinoline to hold a skirt out. **3** hoop skirt. [< F < Ital. *crinolino < crino* horsehair (< L *crinis* hair) + *lino* thread < L *linum*]

crip·ple (krip′əl) *n., v.* **-pled, -pling.** —*n.* a person or animal that is partly disabled, especially one that is lame. —*v.* **1** make a cripple of. **2** damage; disable; weaken: *The ship was crippled by the storm.* [OE *crypel.* Related to CREEP.] —**crip′pler,** *n.*
☛ *Syn. v.* **1. Cripple, disable** = deprive of the ability or power to carry on normal activities. **Cripple** = deprive a person or animal of the use of a leg, foot, or arm: *He was crippled when he broke his hip.* **Disable** = deprive of the ability to work or act normally: *The man is disabled by a heart condition.*

cri·sis (krī′sis) *n., pl.* **-ses (-sēz). 1** the turning point in a serious illness, after which it is known whether the patient is expected to live or die. **2** an important or deciding event. **3** a time or state of danger or anxious waiting: *England faced a crisis during the Battle of Britain.* [< L < Gk. *krisis < krinein* decide]
☛ *Syn.* **3.** See note at **emergency.**

crisp (krisp) *adj., v., n.* —*adj.* **1** firm and stiff, but breaking or snapping easily and sharply: *Dry toast and fresh celery are crisp.* **2** fresh; sharp and clear; bracing: *The air was cool and crisp.* **3** clear-cut; decisive: *"Don't talk; fight" is a crisp sentence.* **4** curly and wiry: *crisp hair.* —*v.* make or become crisp. —*n.* **1** something crisp. **2** *Esp.Brit.* a potato chip. [< L *crispus* curled] —**crisp′ly,** *adv.* —**crisp′ness,** *n.*

crisp·er (kris′pər) *n.* a compartment in a refrigerator for storing fresh vegetables and fruit.

crisp·y (kris′pē) *adj.* **crisp·i·er, crisp·i·est.** crisp.

criss·cross (kris′kros′) *adj., adv., v., n.* —*adj.* marked or made with crossed lines; crossed; crossing: *Plaids have a crisscross pattern.* —*adv.* crosswise. —*v.* **1** mark or cover with crossed lines. **2** come and go across: *Buses and cars crisscross the city.* —*n.* a mark or pattern made of crossed lines. [alteration of *Christ's cross*]

cri·te·ri·a (krī tēr′ē ə) *n.* a pl. of **criterion.**

cri·te·ri·on (krī tēr′ē ən) *n.* **-te·ri·a** or **-te·ri·ons.** a rule or standard for making a judgment; test: *Wealth is only one criterion of success.* [< Gk. *kritērion < krinein* judge]
☛ *Syn.* See note at **standard.**

crit·ic (krit′ik) *n.* **1** a person who makes judgments of the merits and faults of books, music, pictures, plays, acting, etc. **2** a person whose profession is preparing such judgments for a newspaper, magazine, radio, television program, etc. **3** a person who disapproves or finds fault; faultfinder. [< L *criticus* < Gk. *kritikos* critical < *krinein* to judge]

crit·i·cal (krit′ə kəl) *adj.* **1** inclined to find fault or disapprove: *a critical disposition.* **2** skilled as a critic. **3** coming from one who is skilled as a critic: *a critical judgment.* **4** belonging to the work of a critic: *critical essays.* **5** of a crisis; important at a time of danger and difficulty: *the critical moment.* **6** full of danger or difficulty: *His delay was critical.* **7** of supplies, labor, or resources, necessary for some work or project but existing in inadequate supply. **8** *Physics and mathematics.* of or having to do with a point at which some action, property, or condition undergoes a change. **9** *Nuclear physics.* having to do with, or capable of producing, a chain reaction: *critical mass.* **10** of or involving the operation of an atomic

reactor: *a critical experiment.* —**crit′i·cal·ly,** *adv.* —**crit′i·cal·ness,** *n.*

critical angle 1 *Optics.* the smallest possible angle of incidence that gives total reflection. 2 *Aeronautics.* the angle of attack of a wing at which maximum lift is momentarily reached and above which turbulence occurs, drag is greatly increased, lift is destroyed, and the airfoil tends to stall.

critical mass *Nuclear physics.* the minimum quantity of fissionable material required in a reactor to produce or maintain a chain reaction.

crit·i·cise (krit′ə sīz′) *v.* **-cised, -cis·ing.** See **criticize.** —**crit′i·cis′er,** *n.*

crit·i·cism (krit′ə siz′əm) *n.* 1 disapproval; fault-finding. 2 the making of judgments; the act of approving or disapproving; an analysis of merits and faults. 3 the rules and principles used in making careful judgments of the merits and faults of books, music, pictures, plays, acting, etc. 4 a critical comment, essay, review, etc.
☛ *Syn.* 4. See note at **review.**
☛ *Usage.* Note that **criticism** (defs. 2-4) involves the making of judgments (favorable or unfavorable) after careful consideration; it does not necessarily involve fault-finding (def. 1).

crit·i·cize (krit′ə sīz′) *v.* **-cized, -ciz·ing.** 1 disapprove; find fault with: *Do not criticize him until you know all the facts.* 2 judge as a critic; discuss the merits and faults of. 3 act or speak as a critic. —**crit′i·ciz′er,** *n.*

cri·tique (kri tēk′) *n.* 1 a critical essay or review. Some newspapers regularly publish critiques of new books. 2 the art of criticism; criticism. [< F < Gk. *kritikē* (*technē*) the critical art, fem. of *kritikos.* See **CRITIC.**]

crit·ter (krit′ər) *n. Dialect.* 1 any living creature. 2 an animal, especially a cow, raised as livestock.

croak (krōk) *n., v.* —*n.* a deep, hoarse sound, made by a frog, crow, raven, etc.
—*v.* 1 make a deep, hoarse sound. 2 utter in a deep, hoarse voice. 3 be always prophesying misfortune; be dissatisfied; grumble. 4 *Slang.* die. [OE **cracian;* related to *cracettan* of the same meaning] —**croak′er,** *n.*

croak·y (krōk′ē) *adj.* **croak·i·er, croak·i·est.** 1 deep and hoarse; making a croaking sound. 2 having a tendency to croak. —**croak′i·ly,** *adv.* —**croak′i·ness,** *n.*

Croat (krō′at) *n.* a native or inhabitant of Croatia, a constituent republic of Yugoslavia.

Cro·a·tian (krō ā′shən) *n., adj.* —*n.* 1 Croat. 2 a Slavic language spoken by the Croats, closely related to Serbian. Croatian is written with the Latin alphabet while Serbian uses the Cyrillic alphabet. —*adj.* of or having to do with Croatia, the Croats, or their language.

cro·chet (krō shā′) *n., v.* **-cheted** (-shād′), **-chet·ing** (-shā′ing). —*n.* a kind of lacy needlework made by interlocking loops of a single thread, using a hooked needle. Crochet may be fine or heavy, and is used for making sweaters, shawls, doilies, tablecloths, etc. —*v.* 1 make of crochet: *to crochet a shawl.* 2 do crochet: *I like to crochet.* [< F *crochet,* dim. of *croc* hook < Gmc. Doublet of **CROCKET, CROTCHET.**] —**cro·chet′er** (-shā′ər), *n.*

crock (krok) *n.* 1 a pot or jar made of baked clay. 2 *Slang.* a bottle of liquor. 3 *Slang.* a worthless, old, or decrepit person, horse, car, etc. [OE *crocc(a)*]

crocked (krokt) *adj. Slang.* drunk.

crock·er·y (krok′ər ē *or* krok′rē) *n.* dishes, jars, etc. made of baked clay; earthenware.

crock·et (krok′it) *n. Architecture.* an ornament, usually made to resemble foliage, along the edges of a spire, pinnacle, gable, etc. [< AF *croket,* var. of OF *crochet,* dim. of *croc* hook < Gmc. Doublet of **CROCHET, CROQUET, CROTCHET.**]

croc·o·dile (krok′ə dīl′) *n.* any of a family (Crocodylidae) of large, tropical, aquatic reptiles having a thick, scaly skin, a long, round body, four short legs, and a powerful tail. Crocodiles closely resemble alligators, to which they are related, but they are faster moving and have a narrower snout. [ME < OF < LL *crocodilus* < Gk. *krokodilos,* earlier, lizard < *krokē* pebble + *drilos* worm]

crocodile tears pretended or insincere grief.

croc·o·dil·i·an (krok′ə dil′ē ən) *adj., n.* —*adj.* of or like a crocodile. —*n.* any of a group of reptiles that includes crocodiles, alligators, etc.

cro·cus (krō′kəs) *n., pl.* **cro·cus·es** *or* **cro·ci** (-sī *or* -sē). 1 any of a large genus (*Crocus*) of small plants of the iris family, growing from a fleshy underground stem and having long, slender leaves and a single large, cup-shaped flower that may be white, yellow or purple. Crocuses bloom early in spring and are popular garden plants. 2 *Cdn.* a small wildflower (*Anemone patens*) of central North America, a species of anemone having fine silky hairs on the stem and leaves and a single large, mauve, cup-shaped flower that blooms very early in spring; pasqueflower. The crocus is the floral

hat, āge, fär; let, ēqual, tèrm; it, īce
hot, ōpen, ôrder; oil, out; cup, pùt, rüle,
 əbove, takən, pencəl, lemən, circəs

ch, child; ng, long; sh, ship
th, thin; ŦH, then; zh, measure

emblem of Manitoba. 3 the flower of a crocus. 4 a deep-yellow color; saffron. 5 a polishing powder consisting of iron oxide: *jeweller's crocus.* [< L < Gk. *krokos* < Semitic]

Croe·sus (krē′səs) *n.* 1 King of Lydia from 560 to 546 B.C., famous for his great wealth. 2 any very rich person.

croft (kroft) *n. Brit.* 1 a small enclosed field. 2 a very small rented farm. [OE]

croft·er (krof′tər) *n. Brit.* a person who cultivates a small farm.

crois·sant (krwä′säN; *French,* krwä säN′) *n.* a small roll of bread shaped like a crescent. [< F *croissant* ppr. of *croître* grow < L *crēscere.* See **CRESCENT.**]

croix de guerre (krwä′də ger′) in France, a medal given to servicemen for bravery under fire. [< F *croix de guerre* war cross]

cro·ki·nole (krō′kə nōl′) *n.* a table game for two or four players in which each player tries to flick polished wooden or plastic disks into or near the centre of a round board, at the same time trying to knock out the disks of the opposing player or players. [< F *croquignole* a flick, fillip]

Cro-Mag·non (krō mag′non) *n.* an early type of man generally considered to be a race of modern man (*Homo sapiens*), known from skeletal remains found in S Europe, along with artifacts of bone and stone. [< *Cro-Magnon* cave, near Dordogne, SW France, where their remains have been found]

crom·lech (krom′lek) *n.* 1 a circle of upright stones erected in prehistoric times. 2 upright stones with a large, flat stone laid horizontally on them. [< Welsh *cromlech* < *crom* bent + *llech* flat stone]

crone (krōn) *n.* a shrivelled, wrinkled, old woman. [< MDu. *croonje* < OF *carogne* carcass, hag. Doublet of **CARRION.**]

Cro·nus (krō′nəs) *n. Greek mythology.* a Titan who was ruler of the universe until overthrown by his son Zeus. Cronus corresponds to the Roman god Saturn.

cro·ny (krō′nē) *n., pl.* **-nies.** a very close friend; chum. [origin uncertain]

crook (krùk) *n., v.* **crooked** (krùkt), **crook·ing;** *adj.* —*n.* 1 something having a hooked or bent form or part, such as a crosier or a shepherd's staff. 2 a hooked or bent part of something: *the crook of a hockey stick, the crook of an umbrella handle.* 3 a bend or curve: *a crook in a stream.* 4 *Informal.* a thief or swindler. —*v.* bend or curve: *She beckoned to the children by crooking her finger at them.*
—*adj. Austral. Slang.* 1 bad, unpleasant, or unsatisfactory. 2 bad-tempered. 3 sick. [ME *crōc* < ON *krókr*]

crook·ed (krùk′id) *adj.* 1 not straight; bent, curved, or twisted: *narrow, crooked streets, a crooked piece of lumber. Your skirt is crooked.* 2 not perpendicular or parallel; slanted: *The picture on the wall is crooked.* 3 dishonest: *a crooked politician, a crooked deal.* —**crook′ed·ly,** *adv.* —**crook′ed·ness,** *n.*

crooked knife *Cdn.* a wood-working knife having a blade that ends in a hook, used widely in the North, especially by the Indians, in making snowshoe frames, pelt stretchers, canoes, etc. [translation of Cdn.F *couteau croché*]

crook·neck (krùk′nek′) *n.* a variety of squash having a long, curved neck.

crook·necked (krùk′nekt′) *adj.* having a hooked or curved neck.

croon (krün) *v., n.* —*v.* 1 murmur; hum; sing in a low tone: *The mother was crooning to her baby.* 2 sing in a low voice with exaggerated emotion. —*n.* a low singing; humming or murmuring. [ME < MDu. *kronen* murmur] —**croon′er,** *n.*

crop (krop) *n., v.* **cropped, crop·ping.** —*n.* 1 a product grown or gathered for use, especially for use as food or fibre: *Wheat is the main crop of the Prairie Provinces.* 2 the total amount of a grain, vegetable, or fruit produced in one season: *The potato crop was very small this year.* 3 anything taken as a crop; group; collection: *a crop of new paperbacks in the bookstore.* 4 the act of clipping or cutting off short. 5 a short haircut. 6 a piece cut off or a notch cut in the ear of an animal. 7 a the baglike swelling in a bird's food passage where food is prepared for digestion. b a similar organ in other animals or in insects. 8 a short whip having a loop instead of a lash: *a riding crop.* 9 the handle of a whip. 10 *Mining.* an outcrop of a vein or seam.
—*v.* 1 plant and cultivate a crop. 2 cut or bite off the top of: *Sheep*

crop grass very short. **3** clip; cut short (the tail, ear, hair, edge of a book, etc.). **4** *Mining.* come to the surface of the ground, as a vein of ore.

crop out, appear or come to the surface: *Great ridges of rock cropped out all over the hillside.*

crop up, appear or occur unexpectedly: *All sorts of difficulties cropped up.*

[OE *cropp* sprout, craw]

➤ **Syn.** n. **1.** Crop, yield, harvest = a product of the land, grown or gathered for use. **Crop** is the general word, applying to the product while growing and when gathered: *The tomato crop was damaged by frost.* **Yield** applies to the quantity or amount of a crop produced: *The yield from those trees was poor this year.* **Harvest,** more formal, emphasizes the idea of gathering and applies to the process or time of gathering or to the amount gathered in one season: *The wheat is ready for harvest.*

crop·land (krop′land′) *n.* land under cultivation for crops. Also, **croplands.**

crop·per (krop′ər) *n.* **1** a person or thing that crops. **2** a person who raises a crop or crops, especially a sharecropper. **3** a plant that furnishes a crop: *The soybean is a hardy cropper.* **4** *Informal.* a heavy fall. **5** *Informal.* a failure; collapse.
come a cropper, *Informal.* **a** fall heavily. **b** fail; collapse.

crop rotation *Agriculture.* a way of conserving the fertility of soil by successively planting on the same ground different crops with varying food requirements.

cro·quet (krō kā′) *n., v.* **-quet·ted** or **-quet·ed** (-kād′), **-quet·ting** or **quet·ing** (-kā′ing). —*n.* **1** an outdoor game played by driving wooden balls through small wire arches by means of mallets. **2** a driving away of an opponent's ball by striking one's own when the two are in contact. —*v.* drive away (an opponent's ball) by striking one's own ball when the two are in contact. [< F *croquet*, dial. var. of *crochet*. See CROCHET.]

cro·quette (krō ket′) *n.* a small ball or cake of chopped or ground cooked meat, fish, vegetable, etc., coated with crumbs and fried. [< F *croquette* < *croquer* crunch]

cro·sier or **cro·zier** (krō′zhər) *n.* **1** an ornamental staff carried by or before bishops and also abbots and abbesses. **2** *Botany.* the curled top of a young fern. [ME < OF *crossier* crook bearer < VL *croccia* crook < Gmc.]

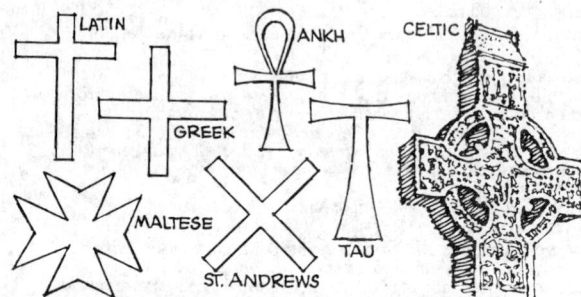

LATIN   ANKH   CELTIC
GREEK
MALTESE   TAU
ST. ANDREWS

Crosses (def. 3); at the far right, a 5th-century Irish stone cross

cross (kros) *n., v., adj.* —*n.* **1** an upright post with another across it near the top, upon which condemned persons were executed by the ancient Romans. **2 the Cross, a** the cross on which Jesus died. **b** the sufferings and death of Jesus; the Atonement. **3** any object, design, or mark shaped somewhat like a cross, consisting of at least two lines which cross. A cross is the main symbol of the Christian religion. A person who cannot write his name represents his signature with a cross. **4** a crossing; lying or going across. **5** a burden of duty; suffering or trouble that must be endured. **6** the act of crossing breeds, varieties, or species of animals or plants. **7** the result of such crossing: *Our dog is a cross between chihuahua and fox terrier.* **8** something that is like a combination of two different things or is intermediate between them: *Documentary drama is a cross between theatre and journalism.* **9** *Boxing.* a countering blow crossing over the opponent's lead.
take the cross, join a crusade.
—*v.* **1** draw a line across: *In writing you cross the letter* t. **2** cancel by drawing a line or lines through (*used with* **off** *or* **out**): *Cross my name off your list. He crossed out the wrong word.* **3** set or lay crosswise one over the other; put one thing across another: *He crossed his arms.* **4** go across; go to the other side of: *to cross a bridge.* **5** lie or extend across; form a cross: *Lansdowne Avenue crosses Main Street. The two streets cross.* **6** meet and pass: *Our letters crossed in the mail, and I got hers the same day she got mine.* **7** trace the form of a cross with the right hand as an act of

Christian devotion (*used with a reflexive*): *He knelt and crossed himself.* **8** oppose or hinder; thwart: *crossed in love. If anyone crosses him, he gets very angry.* **9** cause (two different breeds, varieties, or species of animals or plants) to mate in order to produce a new kind: *Canadian breeders have crossed domestic cattle with buffalo to produce the* **cattalo.**

cross (one's) **fingers,** put one finger over another in a superstitious gesture intended to keep trouble away, or when saying something but keeping back part of one's thoughts.

cross (one's) **heart,** make the sign of the cross over one's heart when swearing that something is true.

cross (one's) **mind,** occur to one; be thought of: *It never crossed my mind that he might forget.*

cross (someone's) **path,** meet a person.

cross swords, a fight with swords in single combat. **b** engage in controversy.

cross the floor, of a member of a legislature, leave one's party by moving from one's assigned seat with that party to a seat in another section of the chamber.

—*adj.* **1** in a bad temper; grumpy. **2** lying across: *a cross timber.* **3** moving or going across: *cross traffic.* **4** crossbred. [OE *cros* < OIrish *cros* < L *crux.* Doublet of CRUX.] —**cross′ly,** *adv.* —**cross′ness,** *n.*

cross– *combining form.* **1** cross-shaped: *cross-stitch = a stitch crossed over another.* **2** moving across: *crossfire = lines of fire crossing one another.* **3** counter: *cross-purpose = a purpose counter to another.* **4** across regular lines of affinity: *cross-fertilization = fertilization of one plant by pollen from another.*

cross·bar (kros′bär′) *n.* a bar, line, or stripe going crosswise.

cross·beam (kros′bēm′) *n.* a large beam that crosses another or extends from wall to wall.

cross·bill (kros′bil′) *n.* any of a small genus (*Loxia*) of finches having a strong bill with points that cross each other, with which the birds pry open conifer cones in order to feed on the seeds.

cross·bones (kros′bōnz′) *n.pl.* two large bones placed crosswise. A pirate flag has crossbones below a skull as a symbol of death. Poisonous products are marked with a skull and crossbones.

cross·bow (kros′bō′) *n.* a medieval weapon consisting of a bow fixed across a wooden stock with a groove along the middle to direct an arrow or a stone.

cross·bow·man (kros′bō′mən) *n., pl.* **-men.** *Historical.* a soldier who used a crossbow.

cross·bred (kros′bred′) *adj., n.* —*adj.* produced by crossbreeding. —*n.* an animal or plant produced by crossbreeding.

cross·breed (kros′brēd′) *v.* **-bred, -breed·ing;** *n.* —*v.* breed by mixing kinds, breeds, or races. —*n.* an individual or breed produced by crossbreeding. A mule is a crossbreed, developed by crossing a horse and a donkey.

cross bun a bun marked with a cross on the top. Hot cross buns are traditionally eaten on Good Friday.

cross·check (kros′chek′) *v., n.* —*v.* **1** check again, or check against another source. **2** *Hockey or lacrosse.* give an illegal check by holding one's stick in both hands and thrusting it in front of an opponent's face or body. —*n.* **1** the act of cross-checking. **2** *Hockey or lacrosse.* an illegal check made by cross-checking.

cross·coun·try (kros′kun′trē) *adj.* **1** across fields or open country instead of by road or over a track: *a cross-country race.* **2** going or reaching across a country: *to fly cross-country.* **3** of or designating the sport of skiing over relatively flat country, using long, narrow skis. Also called **Nordic.** Compare **downhill. 4** for use in cross-country skiing: *cross-country skis.*

cross·cur·rent (kros′ker′ənt) *n.* **1** a current of air blowing across another. **2** a contradictory tendency or trend: *the crosscurrents of political thought.*

cross·cut (kros′kut′) *adj., n., v.* **-cut, -cut·ting.** —*adj.* **1** of a cut, incision, etc., made across or obliquely. **2** made or used for cutting across: *crosscut teeth on a saw.*
—*n.* **1** a cut, course, or path across. **2** crosscut saw.
—*v.* cut or go across.

crosscut saw a saw used or made for cutting across the grain of wood.

crosse (kros) *n.* a lacrosse stick. [< Cdn.F < F *crosse* a hooked stick]

cross·ex·am·i·na·tion (kros′eg zam′ə nā′shən) *n.* **1** *Law.* examination to check a previous examination, especially the questioning of a witness by the lawyer for the opposing side to test the truth of the witness's evidence. **2** a close or severe questioning.

cross·ex·am·ine (kros′eg zam′ən) *v.* **-ined, -in·ing. 1** *Law.* question closely to test the truth of evidence given. **2** question closely or severely. —**cross′-ex·am′in·er,** *n.*

cross–eye (kros′ī′) *n.* a strabismus, especially the form in which both eyes are turned toward the nose.

cross-eyed (kros'īd') *adj.* having one eye or both eyes turned in toward the nose.

cross-fer-ti-li-za-tion (kros'fėr'tə lə zā'shən or kros'fėr tə lī zā'shən) *n. Botany.* the fertilization of one flower by pollen from another.

cross-fer-ti-lize (kros'fėr'tə līz') *v.* **-lized, -liz-ing. 1** cause the cross-fertilization of. **2** be subjected to cross-fertilization.

cross-fire (kros'fīr') *n.* **1** gun-fire coming from two or more opposite directions so as to cross. **2** a verbal attack from two or more sources or directions.

cross-grained (kros'grānd') *adj.* **1** of wood, having the grain running across the regular grain; having an irregular or gnarled grain. **2** hard to get along with; contrary.

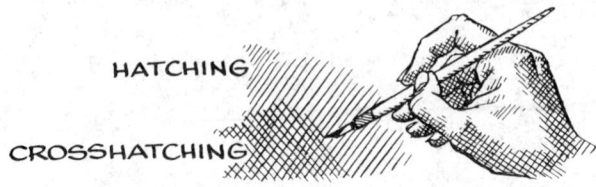

HATCHING

CROSSHATCHING

cross-hatch (kros'hach') *v.* mark or shade with two sets of parallel lines crossing each other.

cross-hatch-ing (kros'hach'ing) *n.* shading made with intersecting sets of parallel lines.

cross-ing (kros'ing) *n.* **1** a place where things cross each other. **2** a place at which a street, river, etc. may be crossed. **3** the act of crossing, especially a voyage across water.

crossing guard a member of a school patrol, or other individual, who escorts children across busy streets.

cross-jack (kros'jak') *n.* a square sail on the lower yard of a mizzenmast.

cross-leg-ged (kros'leg'id or kros'legd') *adj.* **1** with the ankles crossed and the knees bent and spread wide apart: *We all sat cross-legged on the floor.* **2** with one leg crossed in front of the other: *standing cross- legged.*

cross-let (kros'lit) *n.* a small cross.

Cross of Valour *Cdn.* Canada's highest award for bravery, given for extraordinary heroism in circumstances of extreme peril. It is the highest of a series of three bravery decorations, the other two being the Star of Courage and the Medal of Bravery. *Abbrev.:* CV Also, **Cross of Valor.**

cross-o-ver (kros'ō'vər) *n.* **1** a place at which a crossing is made. **2** anything that crosses over or connects, as a bridge over a highway.

cross-patch (kros'pach') *n. Informal.* a cross, bad-tempered person.

cross-piece (kros'pēs') *n.* a piece that is placed across something.

cross-pol-li-nate (kros'pol'ə nāt') *v.* **-nat-ed, -nat-ing. 1** cause cross-pollination in. **2** be subjected to cross-pollination.

cross-pol-li-na-tion (kros'pol'ə nā'shən) *n.* the transfer of pollen from the anther of one flower to the stigma of another. Insects and wind are agents of cross-pollination.

cross-pur-pose (kros'pėr'pəs) *n.* an opposing or contrary purpose.
at cross-purposes, a misunderstanding each other's purpose. **b** acting under such a misunderstanding.

cross-ques-tion (kros'kwes'chən) *v., n.* —*v.* question closely or severely; cross-examine. —*n.* a question asked in cross-examining.

cross-rail (kros'rāl') *n.* a piece of wood, metal, etc. that lies across something.

cross-re-fer (kros'ri fėr') *v.* **-ferred, -fer-ring. 1** refer from one part to another. **2** make a cross reference.

cross-ref-er-ence (kros'ref'ər əns) *n., v.* **-er-enced, -er-enc-ing.** —*n.* a reference or instruction in one part of a book, index, etc. to another part for more information. Under **crupper,** the instruction "See **harness** for picture" is a cross-reference. —*v.* cross-refer.

cross-road (kros'rōd') *n.* **1** a road that crosses another. **2** a road connecting main roads. **3 crossroads, a** a place where roads cross (*used with a singular or plural verb*): *He said he would wait for them at the crossroads.* **b** a critical point, especially where a decision has to be made (*used with a singular verb*): *The country is now at an economic crossroads.*

cross-ruff (kros'ruf') *n. Card games.* a play in which each of two partners leads a card that the other can trump.

hat, āge, fär; let, ēqual, tėrm; it, īce
hot, ōpen, ôrder; oil, out; cup, pút, rüle,
above, takən, pencəl, lemən, circəs
ch, child; ng, long; sh, ship
th, thin; ŦH, then; zh, measure

cross section 1 a cutting across; a cutting made at right angles to an axis: *Tomatoes are usually sliced by making a series of cross sections.* **2** a part cut off by making a cross section. **3** a drawing, etc. of the surface exposed by such a cutting. **4** a small selection of people, things, etc. thought to be typical of all the members of a larger, whole group to which they belong, and chosen to stand for the whole group; a representative sample: *The newspaper wanted to get the views of a cross section of the community.*

cross-staff (kros'staf') *n.* a surveying instrument for measuring distances at right angles to the main line.

cross-stitch (kros'stich') *n., v.* —*n.* **1** one stitch crossed over another, forming an X. **2** embroidery made with this stitch. —*v.* embroider or sew with one stitch crossed over another.

cross street 1 a street that crosses another. **2** a street connecting main streets.

cross-trees (kros'trēz') *n.pl.* two horizontal bars of wood near the top of a ship's mast.

cross-walk (kros'wok' or -wôk') *n.* a street crossing marked with white lines: *In some cities approaching vehicles must stop when pedestrians are using a crosswalk.*

cross-way (kros'wā') *n.* crossroad.

cross-ways (kros'wāz') *adv.* crosswise.

cross-wise (kros'wīz') *adv.* **1** so as to cross; across. **2** in the form of a cross. **3** opposite to what is required; wrongly.

cross-word puzzle (kros'wėrd') a puzzle with numbered clues to certain words and with sets of blank squares to be filled in, one letter to a square, with the answers. Some of the words read across and some downwards so that some letters belong to two words that cross each other.

cross-yard (kros'yärd') *n.* on a ship, a pole or spar fastened crosswise.

crotch (kroch) *n.* **1** a forked piece or part; place where a tree, bough, etc. divides into two limbs or branches. **2** the place where the human body divides into its two legs. [var. of *crutch*]

crotched (krocht) *adj.* having a crotch; forked.

crotch-et (kroch'it) *n.* **1** an odd notion; unreasonable whim. **2** a small hook or hooklike part. **3** *Music.* a quarter note. [ME < OF *crochet,* dim. of *croc* hook < Gmc. Doublet of CROCHET, CROCKET.]

crotch-et-y (kroch'ə tē) *adj.* full of odd notions or unreasonable whims. —**crotch'et-i-ness,** *n.*

crot-on (krō'tən) *n.* **1** any of a genus (*Codiaeum*) of shrubs of the spurge family, especially a tropical shrub (*C. variegatum*) native to Malaysia, widely cultivated for its showy, many-colored leaves that may be flat or crinkled and may have smooth or deeply lobed edges. **2** any of a genus (*Croton*) of mostly tropical shrubs, trees, and herbs also of the spurge family, especially one (*C. tiglium*) whose seeds yield croton oil. [< NL < Gk. *krotōn* tick[2]]

croton bug a small, winged cockroach (*Blatella germanica*).

croton oil a thick, bitter oil obtained from the seeds of the croton (def. 2), used as a counter-irritant and formerly also used internally as a strong cathartic.

crouch (krouch) *v., n.* —*v.* **1** stoop low with legs bent like an animal ready to spring, or in hiding, or shrinking in fear. **2** bow down in a timid or slavish manner; cower. **3** bend low. —*n.* **1** the act or state of crouching. **2** a crouching position. A baseball catcher's squatting stance is called a crouch. [ME < OF *crochir* < *croc* hook < Gmc.]

croup[1] (krüp) *n.* an inflammation or diseased condition of the throat and windpipe characterized by a hoarse cough and difficult breathing. [< *croup,* v., ? blend of *croak* and *whoop*]

croup[2] (krüp) *n.* the rump of a horse, etc. [ME < OF *croupe* < Gmc.]

crou-pi-er (krü'pē ər) *n.* the attendant at a gambling table who rakes in the money and pays the winners. [< F *croupier* < *croupe;* see CROUP[2]; originally, one who rides behind]

croup-y (krüp'ē) *adj.* **1** sick with croup. **2** hoarse and having difficulty in breathing. **3** of croup; resembling croup.

crou-ton (krü'ton) *n.* a small piece of toasted or fried bread, often served in soup. [< F *croûton* < *croûte* crust < L *crusta*]

crow[1] (krō) *n., v.* **crowed** (or **crew** for 1), **crowed, crow-ing.** —*n.* **1** a loud cry made by a rooster. **2** a happy sound made by a baby.

—*v.* **1** make the cry of a rooster. **2** make the happy sound of a baby. **3** show happiness and pride; boast: *The winning team crowed over its victory.* [OE *crāwan*; imitative]

crow² (krō) *n.* **1** any of various large, glossy-black birds (genus *Corvus*) that are somewhat smaller than most ravens, having a loud, harsh call. The common crow of North America is *Corvus brachyrhynchos.* **2** any of various other birds of the same family (Corvidae). **3** crowbar.
as the crow flies, in a straight line: *It's about five kilometres away as the crow flies, but nearly ten by road.*
eat crow, *Informal.* be forced to do something very disagreeable and humiliating.
[OE *crāwe*]

Crow (krō) *n., pl.* **Crow** or **Crows. 1** a tribe of Indians living in Montana and Wyoming. **2** a member of this tribe. **3** the Siouan language of this tribe.

crow·bar (krō′bär′) *n.* a strong iron or steel bar, used as a lever.

crow·ber·ry (krō′ber′ē) *n., pl.* **-ries. 1** a low-growing evergreen shrub (*Empetrum nigrum*) of the cool regions of the northern hemisphere having a small, black, berrylike fruit that is edible but insipid in taste. **2** any of various other plants of the same family (Empetraceae). **3** the fruit of any of these plants.

crow-boot (krō′būt′) *n.* Cdn. a mukluk, usually made of muskrat fur and having a thick moosehide sole.

crowd (kroud) *n., v.* —*n.* **1** a large number of people together: *A crowd gathered to hear the speaker.* **2** the common people; people in general; the masses: *Many newspapers appeal to the crowd.* **3** *Informal.* group; set: *The boy went out with his crowd to the dance.* **4** a large number of things together.
—*v.* **1** collect in large numbers. **2** fill; fill too full: *to crowd a bus.* **3** push; shove. **4** press forward; force one's way: *to crowd into a building.*
crowd on sail, raise more sails to make a ship go faster.
[OE *crūdan* press]
☛ *Syn. n.* **1. Crowd, throng, swarm** = a large number of people together. **Crowd** applies to a large number of people pressed closely together without much order: *A crowd was waiting in the lobby.* **Throng** suggests still larger numbers and more movement of pressing together and pushing forward: *At Christmas there are throngs in the streets.* **Swarm** emphasizes the idea of a large, confused, moving mass: *A swarm of students gathered.*

crowd·ed (kroud′id) *adj.* **1** filled with a crowd. **2** filled; filled too full; packed. **3** close together; too close together. —**crowd′ed·ly,** *adv.* —**crowd′ed·ness,** *n.*

crow·foot (krō′fůt′) *n., pl.* **-foots** for 1, **-feet** for 3, 4, 5. **1** any of several plants (genus *Ranunculus*) having yellow or white flowers and deeply lobed leaves that look somewhat like a bird's foot. See also **buttercup. 2** (*adj.*) designating the family (Ranunculaceae) that includes the crowfoots, buttercups, columbines, and anemones, more often called the buttercup family. **3** an arrangement of small ropes used to suspend awnings, etc. on a ship. **4** a piece of zinc used as one of the poles or electrodes in some kinds of batteries. **5** *Historical.* an iron ball having four spikes, thrown on the ground to hinder the advance of enemy cavalry.

crown (kroun) *n., v.* —*n.* **1** a head covering of precious metal and jewels, worn by a monarch. **2 the Crown, a** the power and authority of a monarch, or of the officials who exercise that authority; royal power. **b** a monarch acting in his official capacity. **3** a monarch; a king, queen, etc. **4** (*adj.*) of a crown; having to do with a crown: *the crown jewels.* **5** a design or thing shaped like a crown. **6** a wreath for the head: *The winner of the race received a crown.* **7** an honor; reward. **8** the head. **9** the top; highest part: *the crown of the head, the crown of a hat.* **10** the highest state or quality of anything. **11 a** the part of a tooth outside the gum. **b** the chewing surface of a tooth. **c** an artificial substitute for either of these. **12** a former British silver coin, worth 5 shillings. **13** the end of an anchor between the arms. **14** *Botany.* **a** the corona of a flower or seed. **b** the top of a root of a plant, from which the stem arises. **c** the leaves and branches of a tree or shrub. **15** the crest of a bird. **16** the tip of a deer's horn. **17** a size of printing paper, usually 38.1 × 50.8 cm.
—*v.* **1** put a crown on; make king, queen, etc. **2** honor; reward. **3** be on top of; cover the highest part of: *A fort crowns the hill.* **4** make perfect or complete; add the finishing touch to: *Success crowned his efforts.* **5** supply (a tooth) with a crown. **6** *Checkers.* make a king of (a piece that has been moved across the checkerboard). **7** *Informal.* hit on the head. **8** of forest fires, spread rapidly from treetop to treetop. [ME < AF *coroune* < L *corona* garland, wreath, crown. Doublet of CORONA.]
☛ *Syn. n.* **8, 10.** See note at **top.**

Crown attorney *Cdn.* a lawyer who represents the Crown (in essence, the people) in a trial.

crown colony a colony under the power and authority of the British government.

Crown corporation *Cdn.* a legal agency or company through which the Government of Canada or one of the provincial governments carries on certain activities. Air Canada, the CBC, and the St. Lawrence Seaway Authority are Crown corporations.

crown court *Brit.* a court of criminal jurisdiction holding periodic sessions in towns of England and Wales.

crown fire *Cdn.* a forest fire that spreads from treetop to treetop.

crown glass 1 a very clear glass used in optical instruments. **2** an old kind of window glass that is in round sheets with a thick part in the middle.

crown jewels jewels that are a traditional part of the regalia of a royal family: *The British crown jewels are kept in the Tower of London.*

crown land 1 public land; land belonging to a government. **2** land that is the personal property of a monarch.

crown prince the oldest living son of a king, queen, etc.; the heir apparent to a kingdom.

crown princess 1 the wife of a crown prince. **2** a girl or woman who is heir apparent to a kingdom.

Crown prosecutor *Cdn.* Crown attorney.

crow's-foot (krōz′fůt′) *n., pl.* **-feet. 1** Usually, **crow's-feet,** *pl.* a wrinkle at the outer corner of the eye. **2** a three-pointed embroidered design used to finish the ends of seams, openings, etc. **3** crowfoot (def. 4).

crow's-nest or **crows-nest** (krōz′nest′) *n.* **1** a small, enclosed platform near the top of a ship's mast, used by the lookout. **2** any similar platform ashore.

cro·zier (krō′zhər) See **crosier.**

CRT *n., pl.* **CRT's** or **CRTs** cathode-ray tube.

CRTC Canadian Radio-television and Telecommunications Commission.

cru·cial (krü′shəl) *adj.* **1** very important; critical; decisive. **2** very trying; severe. **3** having the form of a cross; cross-shaped. [< NL (medical) *crucialis* < L *crux, crucis* cross; with reference to the fork of a road] —**cru′cial·ly,** *adv.*

cru·ci·ble (krü′sə bəl) *n.* **1** a container in which metals, ores, etc. can be melted. **2** a severe test or trial. [< Med.L *crucibulum* originally, night lamp]

cru·ci·fix (krü′sə fiks′) *n.* **1** a cross with a figure of the crucified Christ on it. **2** a cross. [< LL *crucifixus,* alteration of L *cruci fixus* fixed to a cross < *crux* cross and *fixus,* pp. of *figere* fasten]

cru·ci·fix·ion (krü′sə fik′shən) *n.* **1** the act of crucifying. **2 the Crucifixion, a** the crucifying of Christ. **b** a picture, statue, etc. of Christ's death on the cross.

cru·ci·form (krü′sə fôrm′) *adj.* shaped like a cross. [< L *crux, crucis* cross + E *-form* shaped (< L *-formis*)]

cru·ci·fy (krü′sə fī′) *v.* **-fied, -fy·ing. 1** put to death by nailing or binding the hands and feet to a cross. **2** treat severely; persecute; torture. **3** blame and punish for the errors and crimes of someone else: *The newspapers crucified the mayor for a mistake made by his secretary.* [ME < OF *crucifier* < LL *crucifigere* (alteration of L *cruci figere;* see CRUCIFIX); influenced by OF verbs ending in *-fier* (< L *-ficare*)] —**cru′ci·fi′er,** *n.*

crud (krud) *n.* *Slang.* **1** a deposit or accumulation of unpleasantly dirty, slimy, or sticky material: *When we emptied the bottle, there was this crud at the bottom of it.* **2** anything contemptible or worthless: *Don't give me that crud.* **3** an unpleasant or despicable person.

crude (krüd) *adj., n.* —*adj.* **crud·er, crud·est. 1** in a natural or raw state; not yet prepared for use; unprocessed: *crude rubber.* **2** not skilfully or carefully made or done; rough, careless, or unfinished: *a crude shack, a crude attempt.* **3** lacking taste, grace, or tact; rude or vulgar: *a crude remark.* **4** bare and undisguised or unadorned: *the crude truth.* **5** *Archaic.* immature; unripe.
—*n. Informal.* crude oil; petroleum. [< L *crudus* raw] —**crude′ly,** *adv.* —**crude′ness,** *n.*
☛ *Syn.* **1.** See note at **raw.**

crude oil petroleum as it comes from the well, before it is refined.

cru·di·ty (krü′də tē) *n., pl.* **-ties. 1** a crude quality or condition; roughness; lack of finish. **2** a crude action, thing, etc.

cru·el (krü′əl) *adj.* **1** fond of causing pain to others and delighting in their suffering; not caring about the pain and suffering of others: *a cruel master.* **2** showing a cruel nature: *cruel acts.* **3** causing pain and suffering: *a cruel war.* [ME < OF < L *crudelis* rough. Related to CRUDE.] —**cru′el·ly,** *adv.* —**cru′el·ness,** *n.*
☛ *Hom.* **crewel.**
☛ *Syn.* **1. Cruel, brutal, pitiless** = unfeeling in treatment of people and animals.

Cruel emphasizes the idea of being completely untouched by the suffering of others and suggests taking pleasure in watching it or in causing pain: *Most people abhor cruel behavior.* **Brutal** suggests the cruelty of a wild animal, shown by unrestrained force and fury: *The brutal captors beat their prisoners.* **Pitiless** means completely without pity or willingness to show mercy to those who are suffering: *The pitiless woman refused to help the poor sick girl.*

cru·el·ty (krü′əl tē) *n., pl.* **-ties. 1** the state or condition of being cruel; readiness to give pain to others or to delight in their suffering. **2** a cruel act.

cru·et (krü′it) *n.* **1** a glass bottle to hold vinegar, oil, etc. for the table. **2** a set of such bottles on a stand. [ME < OF *cruet,* dim. of *cruie* pot < Gmc.]

cruise (krüz) *v.* **cruised, cruis·ing;** *n.* —*v.* **1** sail about from place to place on pleasure or business; sail over or about: *He bought a yacht so that he could cruise along the coast.* **2** journey or travel from place to place, with or without a special destination: *The taxi cruised about in search of passengers. Many police cars are cruising the streets.* **3** travel in an aircraft or automobile at the speed of maximum mechanical efficiency. **4** *Lumbering.* examine a tract of forest to estimate the value of the timber on it, especially for a logging company. —*n.* the act of sailing about from place to place on pleasure or business. [< Du. *kruisen* move, especially, sail crosswise < *kruis* cross < L *crux*]
☛ *Hom.* **cruse.**

cruis·er (krü′zər) *n.* **1** a warship with less armor and more speed than a battleship. **2** an aircraft, taxi, power boat, etc. that cruises. **3** a police car connected with headquarters by radio; a patrol car or squad car used for patrolling streets and highways. **4** a person employed by a logging company to estimate the volume of timber standing on a particular acreage. **5** a person who goes on a cruise. **6** cabin cruiser.

crul·ler (krul′ər) *n.* a kind of doughnut made by twisting together pieces of rich, sweet dough and frying them in fat. [apparently < Du. *kruller* < *krullen* curl]

crumb (krum) *n., v.* —*n.* **1** a very small piece of bread, cake, etc. broken from a larger piece. **2** the soft, inside part of bread. **3** a little bit: *a crumb of comfort.* **4** *Informal.* a worthless person; a person of no importance. —*v.* **1** break into crumbs. **2** cover with crumbs for frying or baking. **3** *Informal.* brush or wipe the crumbs from (a tablecloth, etc.). [OE *cruma*]

crum·ble (krum′bəl) *v.* **-bled, -bling. 1** break into very small pieces or crumbs. **2** fall to pieces; decay: *The old wall was crumbling away at the edges.* [earlier *crimble* < OE *(ge)crymman* < *cruma* crumb]

crum·bly (krum′blē) *adj.* **-bli·er, -bli·est.** tending to crumble; easily crumbled. —**crum′bli·ness,** *n.*

crumb·y (krum′ē) *adj.* **crumb·i·er, crumb·i·est. 1** full of crumbs. **2** soft like the inside part of bread. **3** *Slang.* crummy. —**crumb′i·ness,** *n.*

crum·my (krum′ē) *adj.* **-mi·er, -mi·est;** *n., pl.* **-mies.** *Slang.* —*adj.* cheap; shoddy; inferior. —*n.* *Logging.* an old truck or van used to take loggers to and from their work site. —**crum′mi·ness,** *n.*

crump (krump) *v.* or *n.* crunch.

crum·pet (krum′pit) *n.* a round, flat cake, thicker than a pancake, baked on a griddle. Crumpets are usually toasted and eaten while hot. [OE *crompeht* full of crumples]

crum·ple (krum′pəl) *v.* **-pled, -pling;** *n.* —*v.* **1** crush together; wrinkle: *He crumpled the letter into a ball.* **2** fall down; collapse: *The boxer crumpled to the floor.* —*n.* a wrinkle made by crushing something together. [OE *crump* bent]

crunch (krunch) *v., n.* —*v.* **1** crush noisily with the teeth. **2** produce a crunching noise: *The hard snow crunched under our feet.* **3** proceed with a crunching noise: *The children crunched through the snow.* —*n.* **1** the act or sound of crunching. **2** *Slang.* a crucial stage or turning point; crisis. [earlier *cra(u)nch;* apparently influenced by *crush, munch*]

crup·per (krup′ər) *n.* **1** a strap attached to the back of a harness and passing under a horse's tail. See **harness** for picture. **2** the rump of a horse. [ME < OF *cropier* < *crope* croup[2] < Gmc.]

cru·ral (krür′əl) *adj.* of the leg. [< L *cruralis* < *crus, cruris* leg]

cru·sade (krü sād′) *n., v.* **-sad·ed, -sad·ing.** —*n.* **1** Often, **Crusade,** any one of the Christian military expeditions between the years 1096 and 1272 whose aim was to recover the Holy Land from the Moslems. **2** a war having a religious purpose and approved by religious authorities. **3** an evangelistic campaign; a revival. **4** a vigorous campaign against a public evil or in favor of some new idea: *the crusade against tuberculosis.* —*v.* take part in a crusade. [anglicization of earlier *crusada* < Sp. *cruzada,* ult. < L *crux* cross]

cru·sad·er (krü sād′ər) *n.* a person who takes part in a crusade.

---

hat, āge, fär; let, ēqual, tėrm; it, īce
hot, ōpen, ôrder; oil, out; cup, pùt, rüle,
əbove, takən, pencəl, lemən, circəs

ch, child; ng, long; sh, ship
th, thin; ᴛʜ, then; zh, measure

cruse (krüz *or* krüs) *n. Archaic.* a jug, pot, or bottle made of earthenware. [< MDu. *croes*]
☛ *Hom.* **cruise** (krüz).

crush (krush) *v., n.* —*v.* **1** squeeze together so violently as to break or bruise. **2** wrinkle or crease by wear or rough handling: *His hat was crushed when the girl sat on it.* **3** break into fine pieces by grinding, pounding, or pressing. **4** flatten by heavy pressure. **5** subdue; conquer. —*n.* **1** a crushing or being crushed. **2** a violent pressure like grinding or pounding. **3** a mass of people crowded close together. **4** *Slang.* **a** a sudden, strong liking for a person. **b** the object of a sudden, strong liking. [ME *crusch(en),* apparently < OF *croissir* < Gmc.] —**crush′a·ble,** *adj.* —**crush′er,** *n.*

crust (krust) *n., v.* —*n.* **1** the hard, outside part of bread, rolls, etc. **2** a piece of this; any hard, dry piece of bread, etc. **3** the baked outside covering of a pie. **4** any hard outside covering: *The snow had a crust that was thick enough to walk on.* **5** *Geology.* the outer layer of the earth, about 30 to 50 kilometres thick, composed of rock. See **core** for picture. **6** *Slang.* nerve; impudence; gall: *She has a lot of crust to come barging in here like that.* —*v.* **1** cover or become covered with a crust. **2** form or collect into a crust. [< L *crusta* rind] —**crust′like′,** *adj.*

crus·ta·cean (krus tā′shən) *n., adj.* —*n.* any of a large class Crustacea of arthropods, most of them water animals having hard shells, jointed bodies with appendages, and two pairs of antennae. Barnacles, crabs, lobsters, shrimps, and wood lice are crustaceans. —*adj.* of or having to do with crustaceans. [< NL < L *crusta* shell, rind]

crus·ta·ceous (krus tā′shəs) *adj.* **1** crustacean. **2** having a shell or crust. **3** like a crust.

crust·y (krus′tē) *adj.* **crust·i·er, crust·i·est. 1** having a crust; crustlike: *crusty bread.* **2** bad-tempered or harsh in manner, speech, etc. —**crust′i·ly,** *adv.* —**crust′i·ness,** *n.*

crutch (kruch) *n.* **1** a support to help a lame or disabled person walk, usually consisting of a long, rubber-tipped staff with a padded crosspiece at the top that fits under the armpit and a handgrip lower down. **2** a support or brace with a forked top. **3** anything that serves as a prop or support: *She is such a poor manager that she has to use her assistant as a crutch.* [OE *crycc*]

crux (kruks) *n., pl.* **crux·es** *or* **cru·ces** (krü′sēz). **1** the essential or crucial part; the most important point. **2** a puzzling or perplexing question; difficult point to explain. **3 Crux,** *Astronomy.* Southern Cross. [< L *crux, crucis* cross. Doublet of CROSS.]

cru·zei·ro (krü zer′ō) *n.* **1** the basic unit of money in Brazil, divided into 100 centavos. See table at **money. 2** a coin worth one cruzeiro. [< Pg.]

cry (krī) *v.* **cried, cry·ing;** *n., pl.* **cries.** —*v.* **1** make a sound that shows pain, fear, sorrow, etc. **2** shed tears; weep. **3** of an animal, make its usual noise or call. **4** call loudly; shout. **5** announce in public: *Peddlers cried their wares in the street. The king ordered the news cried in the streets.*
cry down, make little of; speak of as unimportant or of little value; deprecate.
cry for, a ask earnestly for; beg for. **b** need very much.
cry off, break an agreement; refuse to do something.
cry (one's) eyes or **heart out,** shed many tears.
cry out, a call loudly; shout. **b** scream; yell. **c** complain.
cry up, praise; speak of as important or valuable.
—*n.* **1** a sound made by a person or animal that shows some strong feeling, such as pain, fear, anger, or sorrow; noise that shows grief, pain, etc. **2** a spell of shedding tears; fit of weeping. **3** the noise or call of an animal: *a gull's cry, the cry of the wolf.* **4** a loud call; shout: *a cry for help.* **5** a call to action; slogan: *"Forward" was the army's cry as it attacked.* **6** a public announcement; proclamation: *a peddler's cry.* **7** an opinion generally expressed; public voice. **8** an appeal; entreaty. **9 a** the yelping of hounds in the chase. **b** a pack of hounds.
a far cry, a a long way. **b** a great difference.
in full cry, in close pursuit.
[ME < OF *crier* < L *quiritare,* originally, implore the aid of the *Quirites* or Roman citizens]

cry·ba·by (krī′bā′bē) *n., pl.* **-bies.** a person who cries easily or pretends to be hurt.

cry·ing (krī′ing) *adj.* **1** that cries. **2** demanding attention; very bad: *a crying evil.*

cry·o·bi·ol·o·gist (krī′ō bī ol′ə jist′) *n.* a person trained in cryobiology, especially one whose work it is.

cry·o·bi·ol·o·gy (krī′ō bī ol′ə jē) *n.* the branch of biology dealing with the effects of very low temperatures on organisms, especially warm-blooded animals.

cry·o·gen (krī′ə jən) *n.* a substance for producing low temperatures. [< Gk. *kryos* frost + *-gen*]

cry·o·gen·ic (krī′ə jen′ik) *n., adj.* —*n.* **cryogenics,** the branch of physics dealing with the production of extremely low temperatures, approaching absolute zero, and the effect of such temperatures on matter (*used with a singular verb*). —*adj.* of or having to do with cryogenics.

cry·o·lite (krī′ə līt′) *n.* a fluoride of sodium and aluminum found in Greenland. It is used in making soda, aluminum, etc. *Formula:* Na_3AlF_6 [< Gk. *kryos* frost + E *-lite* (< F < Gk. *lithos* stone)]

crypt (kript) *n.* an underground room or vault. The crypt beneath the main floor of a church was formerly often used as a burial place. [< L *crypta* < Gk. *kryptē* vault < *kryptos* hidden. Doublet of GROTTO.]

cryp·tic (krip′tik) *adj.* having a hidden meaning; secret; mysterious: *a cryptic message, a cryptic reply.* [< LL *crypticus* < Gk. *kryptikos* < *kryptos* hidden] —**cryp′ti·cal·ly,** *adv.*

cryp·ti·cal (krip′tə kəl) *adj.* cryptic.

crypto– *combining form.* secret or hidden, as in *cryptogram.* [Gk. *kryptos* hidden]

cryp·to·gam (krip′tə gam′) *n.* any plant that does not produce flowers or seeds, but reproduces by means of spores, including algae, fungi, ferns, and mosses. [< NL *cryptogamia* < Gk. *kryptos* hidden + *gamos* marriage]

cryp·to·gram (krip′tə gram′) *n.* something written in secret code or cipher.

cryp·to·graph (krip′tə graf′) *n.* cryptogram.

TOURMALINE

AMETHYST
QUARTZ

Crystal (def. 5): mineral crystals

crys·tal (kris′təl) *n., adj.* —*n.* **1** a clear, transparent mineral, a kind of quartz, that looks like ice. **2** a piece of crystal cut to a special shape for use or ornament. Crystals are used as beads, and hung around lights. **3 a** a glass of great brilliance and transparency, used especially in making drinking glasses, serving dishes, etc.: *The wine glasses were made of crystal.* **b** glasses, dishes, etc. made of crystal: *Crystal glistened on the dinner table.* **4** the glass over the face of a watch. **5** a regularly shaped mass with angles and flat surfaces, into which a substance solidifies: *Crystals of sugar can be distinguished from crystals of snow by their difference in form.* **6** a piece of quartz used to control the frequency of a radio-frequency oscillator or filter.
—*adj.* **1** made of crystal: *crystal ornaments.* **2** clear and transparent like crystal. [ME < OF < L *crystallus* < Gk. *krystallos* clear ice, ult. < *kryos* frost]

crystal ball a ball of crystal or glass, used in crystal gazing.

crys·tal–clear (kris′təl klēr′) *adj.* **1** as clear as crystal; extremely clear and transparent. **2** very easy to understand; simple and lucid.

crystal detector *Electronics.* a device used in early radios for rectifying alternating currents, consisting of a crystal embedded in soft metal.

crystal gazing **1** the act or practice of staring into a crystal ball, supposedly to induce a vision of remote events, future happenings, etc. **2** *Informal.* speculation about the future.

crys·tal·line (kris′tə līn′ or kris′təl in) *adj.* **1** consisting of crystals; solidified in the form of crystals: *Sugar and salt are crystalline.* **2** of rocks, composed of crystals. **3** of or having to do with crystals and their formation. **4** made of crystal. **5** clear and transparent like crystal.

crystalline lens the lens of the eye.

crys·tal·li·za·tion (kris′təl ə zā′shən or kris′təl ī zā′shən) *n.* **1** crystallizing or being crystallized. **2** a crystallized substance or formation. **3** the taking on of a fixed, concrete, or permanent form: *The meeting resulted in the crystallization of our plans.*

crys·tal·lize (kris′təl īz′) *v.* **-lized, -liz·ing. 1** form into crystals; solidify into crystals: *Water crystallizes to form snow.* **2** form into

definite shape: *His vague ideas crystallized into a clear plan.* **3** coat with sugar. —**crys′tal·liz′er,** *n.*

crys·tal·lized (kris′təl īzd′) *adj.* formed into crystals.

crys·tal·log·ra·pher (kris′tə log′rə fər) *n.* a person trained in crystallography, especially one whose work it is.

crys·tal·log·ra·phy (kris′tə log′rə fē) *n.* the science that deals with the form, structure, and properties of crystals. [< Gk. *krystallos* crystal + E *-graphy*]

crys·tal·loid (kris′təl oid′) *adj., n.* —*adj.* like crystal. —*n. Chemistry.* a substance (usually capable of crystallization) that, when dissolved in a liquid, will diffuse readily through vegetable or animal membranes. [< Gk. *krystalloeidēs* < *krystallos* crystal + *eidos* form]

crystal set an early type of radio receiver in which radio signals were demodulated by means of a crystal detector. Earphones were needed for listening to it because it had no amplifier.

Cs 1 cesium. **2** cirro-stratus.

C.S. 1 Civil Service. **2** Christian Science.

CSC 1 Civil Service Commission. **2** Canadian Services College.

CST or **C.S.T.** Central Standard Time.

ct. 1 cent. **2** county. **3** court. **4** one hundred (for L *centum*).

CT Connecticut.

cten·o·phore (ten′ə fôr′ or tē′nə-) *n.* any of a phylum (Ctenophora) of marine invertebrates having a jellyfish- like body with eight bands of cilia by means of which they swim. [< NL *ctenophora* the class name < Gk. *kteis, ktenos* comb + *phorein* to bear]

ctn cotangent.

ctn. carton(s).

CTV Canadian Television (Canadian Television Network, Ltd.).

cu. cubic.

Cu 1 copper. **2** cumulus.

cub (kub) *n.* **1** a young bear, fox, lion, etc. **2 Cub,** a member of the Wolf Cubs, a program of the Boy Scouts. **3** an inexperienced or awkward boy. **4** a boy who behaves badly. [origin uncertain]

Cu·ban (kyü′bən) *n., adj.* —*n.* a native or inhabitant of Cuba, an island country in the West Indies. —*adj.* of or having to do with Cuba or its people.

cub·by·hole (kub′ē hōl′) *n.* a small, enclosed space. [< *cubby* (dim. of Brit. dial. word *cub* shed, coop) + *hole*]

cube (kyüb) *n., v.* **cubed, cub·ing.** —*n.* **1** a solid with six equal, square sides. **2** *Mathematics.* the product obtained when a number is cubed: *The cube of 4 is 64.* **3** an ice cube.
—*v.* **1** make or form into the shape of a cube: *The beets we had for supper were cubed three times as a factor: 5 cubed is 125, for $5 \times 5 \times 5 = 125$.* [< L *cubus* < Gk. *kybos* cube, die]

cu·beb (kyü′beb) *n.* **1** the dried, unripe berry of a tropical shrub (*Piper cubeba*) of the pepper family, used as a spice and in medicine. Cubebs were formerly crushed and smoked in pipes or cigarettes for the treatment of catarrh. **2** a cigarette made from these berries. [< F *cubèbe* < Arabic *kabāba*]

cube root *Mathematics.* a number used as the factor of a cube: *The cube root of 125 is 5.*

cu·bic (kyü′bik) *adj.* **1** shaped like a cube. **2** having length, breadth, and thickness. A cubic centimetre is the volume of a cube whose edges are one centimetre long. The cubic content of a room is the number of cubic metres it contains. **3** *Mathematics.* having to do with or involving the cubes of numbers. *Abbrev.:* cu.

cu·bi·cal (kyü′bə kəl) *adj.* shaped like a cube.
☛ *Hom.* cubicle.

cu·bi·cle (kyü′bə kəl) *n.* a small room or compartment, especially one of the divisions of a large dormitory. [< L *cubiculum* bedroom < *cubare* lie]
☛ *Hom.* cubical.

cubic measure a unit or series of units for measuring volume or capacity:

    1000 cubic millimetres = 1 cubic centimetre
    1000 cubic centimetres = 1 cubic decimetre
    1000 cubic decimetres = 1 cubic metre

cub·ism (kyü′biz əm) *n. Art.* a style (developed in the early part of the 20th century) in which people, objects, etc. are represented by means of geometric forms, including squares, triangles, etc. as well as cubes.

cub·ist (kyüb′ist) *n., adj.* —*n.* an artist or sculptor whose art is based on the theories of cubism. —*adj.* of or having to do with cubism or cubists. —**cu·bis′tic,** *adj.* —**cu·bis′ti·cal·ly,** *adv.*

cu·bit (kyü′bit) *n.* an ancient unit for measuring length, varying from about 45 to 50 cm. The cubit was based on the length of the

arm from the elbow to the tip of the middle finger. [< L *cubitum* elbow, cubit]

Cub·mas·ter (kub′mas′tər) *n.* Pack Scouter.

cu·boid (kyü′boid) *adj., n.* —*adj.* shaped like a cube. —*n.* something shaped like a cube.

cub reporter a young, inexperienced newspaper reporter.

cuck·old (kuk′əld) *n., v.* —*n.* the husband of an unfaithful wife. —*v.* make a cuckold of. [ME *cukeweld* < OF *cucuault* < *coucou* cuckoo; from the cuckoo's habit of laying its eggs in another bird's nest]

cuck·old·ry (kuk′əl drē) *n.* making a cuckold of a husband.

cuck·oo (*n., v.* kü′kü *or, sometimes,* kůk′kü; *adj.* kü′kü) *n., pl.* **-oos;** *adj., v.* —*n.* **1** any of a family (Cuculidae) of birds having a long, slender body, greyish-brown and white plumage, and pointed wings. Many species, including the well-known European cuckoo (*Cuculus canorus*) lay their eggs in the nests of other birds, which then hatch them and raise the baby cuckoos. **2** the two-note call of a cuckoo, that resembles its name. **3** *Slang.* an eccentric or mildly crazy person. —*adj. Slang.* foolish or crazy. —*v.* make the sound of a cuckoo or an imitation of it. [imitative]

cuckoo clock a clock with a toy bird that pops out of a little door at regular intervals and makes a sound like that of a European cuckoo to mark the hour, half-hour, etc.

cu·cul·late (kyü′kə lāt′ *or* kyə kul′āt) *adj.* **1** shaped like a hood: *a cucullate leaf.* **2** having a hoodlike part. [< LL *cucullatus* < L *cucullus* cap]

cu·cum·ber (kyü′kum bər) *n.* **1** the long, fleshy fruit of a vine (*Cucumis sativus*) of the gourd family, having a green skin and white flesh, commonly used as a vegetable. Cucumbers are eaten raw, often in salads, and are also pickled. **2** the vine it grows on. **cool as a cucumber, a** very cool. **b** calm and unruffled; not excited. [ME < OF *cocombre* < L *cucumis*]

cud (kud) *n.* **1** food that has been brought up into the mouth from the first and second stomachs of cattle, deer, camels, and other ruminants to be chewed before being swallowed again. **2** *Dialect.* a quid of tobacco. **chew the cud,** think or ponder something; ruminate. [OE *cudu;* var. of *cwidu*]

cud·dle (kud′əl) *v.* **-dled, -dling;** *n.* —*v.* **1** hold closely and lovingly in one's arms or lap: *The mother cuddled her baby.* **2** lie close and snug; curl up: *The two puppies cuddled together in front of the fire.* **3** hug. —*n.* a hug. [origin uncertain]

cud·dy (kud′ē) *n., pl.* **-dies. 1** a small cabin on a boat. **2** a small room or cupboard. [origin uncertain]

cudg·el (kuj′əl) *n., v.* **-elled** *or* **-eled, -el·ling** *or* **-el·ing.** —*n.* a short, thick stick used as a weapon; club. **take up the cudgels for,** defend strongly. —*v.* beat with a cudgel. **cudgel (one's) brains,** try very hard to think. [OE *cycgel*]

cue¹ (kyü) *n., v.* **cued, cu·ing** *or* **cue·ing.** —*n.* **1** a hint or suggestion as to what to do or when to act: *Being a stranger, he took his cue from the actions of the natives.* **2** an action or speech on or behind the stage, which gives the signal for an actor, singer, musician, etc. to enter or to begin. In a play the last word or words of one actor's speech is the cue for another to come on the stage, begin speaking, etc. **3** the part one is to play; course of action. **on cue,** at the right moment: *They started on cue.* —*v.* give a cue to; give a suggestion, hint or signal to: *Don't forget to cue him about when to start the song.* [probably < F *queue* tail, end < L *coda,* dial. var. of *cauda;* with reference to the end of a preceding actor's speech]
☛ Hom. **queue.**

cue² (kyü) *n.* **1** queue; pigtail. **2** *Billiards, etc.* a long, tapering stick used for striking the ball. [var. of *queue*]
☛ Hom. **queue.**

cues·ta (kwes′tə) *n.* a ridge or hill that has a steep face on one side and a gentle slope on the other. [< Sp. < L *costa* side, rib]

cuff¹ (kuf) *n.* **1** the part of a sleeve or glove that goes around the wrist. **2** a turned-up fold around the bottom of a trouser leg. **3** the part of a long glove or gauntlet that covers the wrist or part of the arm. **4** handcuff. **off the cuff,** without preparation; impromptu: *He had no notes but spoke off the cuff.* **on the cuff,** on credit. [ME *cuffe* glove; origin uncertain] —**cuff′less,** *adj.*

cuff² (kuf) *v. or n.* hit with the hand; slap. [origin uncertain]

cuff link a device for linking together the open ends of a shirt cuff.

cu. ft. cubic foot (feet).

---

hat, āge, fär; let, ēqual, tėrm; it, īce
hot, ōpen, ôrder; oil, out; cup, pút, rüle,
əbove, takən, pencəl, lemən, circəs
ch, child; ng, long; sh, ship
th, thin; ₮H, then; zh, measure

cui bo·no (kwē′bō′nō *or* kī′bō′nō) *Latin.* **1** for whose benefit? **2** of what good? for what use?

cu. in. cubic inch(es).

cui·rass (kwi ras′) *n.* **1** a piece of armor for the body, that is made of a breastplate and fastened to a plate protecting the back. **2** the breastplate alone. **3** the armor plate of a warship. [ME < OF *cuirasse* < Ital. *corazza* < VL < LL *coriacea* (*vestis*) (garment) of leather < L *corium* leather; form influenced by F *cuir* leather < L *corium*]

cui·ras·sier (kwē′rə sēr′) *n.* a cavalry soldier wearing a cuirass.

cui·sine (kwi zēn′) *n.* **1** a style of cooking or preparing food. **2** food. **3** a kitchen. [< F < L *cocina,* var. of *coquina* < *coquus* a cook]

cuisse (kwis) *n.* a piece of armor to protect the thigh. See **armor** for picture. [< F *cuisse* thigh < L *coxa* hip]

cuke (kyük) *n. Informal.* cucumber.

cul-de-sac (kul′də sak′ *or* kůl′də sak′; *French,* kyd säk′) *n.* a street or passage open at only one end; blind alley. [< F *cul-de-sac* bottom of the sack]

cu·lex (kyü′leks) *n., pl.* **-li·ces** (-lə sēz′). any of a genus (*Culex*) of mosquitoes found throughout the world, and including the common mosquito (*C. pipiens*) of North America and Europe. [< L *culex* gnat]

cu·li·nar·y (kul′ə ner′ē *or* kyü′lə ner′ē) *adj.* **1** having to do with cooking or the kitchen: *Mother is often praised for her culinary skill.* **2** used in cooking. [< L *culinarius* < *culina* kitchen]

cull (kul) *v., n.* —*v.* **1** pick out; select: *The lawyer culled a few important facts from the mass of evidence.* **2** pick over; make selections from. —*n.* something picked out as being inferior or worthless. Poor fruit, stale vegetables, and lumber and animals not up to standard are called culls. [ME < OF *cuillir* < L *colligere.* See COLLECT.] —**cull′er,** *n.*

cul·let (kul′it) *n.* broken or waste glass used to speed up the melting process in the manufacture of new glass.

culm¹ (kulm) *n.* **1** coal dust. **2** hard coal of poor quality. [? related to COAL]

culm² (kulm) *n. Botany.* the jointed stem characteristic of grasses, usually hollow. [< L *culmus* stalk]

cul·mi·nate (kul′mə nāt′) *v.* **-nat·ed, -nat·ing. 1** rise to or form a highest point: *The church tower had a long winding staircase that culminated in a lookout platform.* **2** reach the decisive point or climax: *The dramatic action of the play culminates in a murder.* [< LL *culminare* < L *culmen* top]

cul·mi·na·tion (kul′mə nā′shən) *n.* **1** the highest point; climax. **2** a reaching of the highest point.

cu·lottes (kyü lots′) *n.pl.* a divided skirt. [< F]

cul·pa·bil·i·ty (kul′pə bil′ə tē) *n.* the fact or condition of being culpable.

cul·pa·ble (kul′pə bəl) *adj.* deserving blame. [ME < OF < L *culpabilis* < *culpa* fault] —**cul′pa·ble·ness,** *n.* —**cul′pa·bly,** *adv.*

cul·prit (kul′prit) *n.* **1** a person guilty of a fault or a crime; offender. **2** a prisoner in court who has been accused of a crime. [apparently < AF *cul. prit.* earlier *cul. prist,* short for *culpable,* deserving punishment < L *culpabilis* and *prist,* var. of OF *prest* ready (for trial), ult. < L *praesto* on hand]

cult (kult) *n.* **1** a system of religious worship: *Buddhism includes many cults.* **2** great admiration for a person, thing, idea, etc.; worship: *In the Soviet Union, the cult of Stalin was discouraged after his death.* **3** a group showing such admiration; worshippers. [< L *cultus* worship < *colere* worship]

cult·ish (kult′ish) *adj.* of, having to do with, or characteristic of cults: *the cultish aspects of astrology.*

cult·ist (kult′ist) *n.* a person who tends to follow or practise cults.

cul·ti·va·ble (kul′tə və bəl) *adj.* that can be cultivated.

cul·ti·vat·a·ble (kul′tə vā′tə bəl) *adj.* cultivable.

cul·ti·vate (kul′tə vāt′) *v.* **-vat·ed, -vat·ing. 1** prepare and use (land) to raise crops by ploughing it, planting seeds, and taking care of the growing plants. **2** help (plants) grow by labor and care. **3** loosen the ground around (growing plants) to kill weeds, etc. **4** improve; develop by study or training: *It takes time, thought, and*

effort to cultivate your mind. **5** give time, thought, and effort to mastering; practise: *An artist cultivates his craft.* **6** promote the growth or development of (an art, science, etc.). **7** establish or strengthen: *Friendships cultivated in school often last a lifetime.* **8** seek better acquaintance with; try to win the friendship of. [< Med.L *cultivare* < *cultivus* under cultivation < L *cultus*, pp. of *colere* till]

cul·ti·vat·ed (kul′tə vā′tid) *adj.* **1** prepared and used to raise crops: *A field of wheat is cultivated land; a pasture is not.* **2** produced by cultivation; not wild: *All hybrid tea roses are cultivated flowers.* **3** improved; developed. **4** cultured; refined.

cul·ti·va·tion (kul′tə vā′shən) *n.* **1** the act or practice of cultivating. **2** the result of improvement or growth through education or experience; culture: *a man of cultivation.* **under cultivation,** of land, planted with crops or prepared for planting: *Most of their land is now under cultivation.*

cul·ti·va·tor (kul′tə vā′tər) *n.* **1** a tool or machine used to loosen the ground and destroy weeds. A cultivator is pulled or pushed between rows of growing plants. **2** a person or thing that cultivates.

cul·tur·al (kul′chər əl) *adj.* of or having to do with culture: *Music and art are cultural studies.* —**cul′tur·al·ly,** *adv.*

cultural lag or **culture lag** *Sociology.* delay in the adaptation of one aspect of a culture to accommodate changes in another aspect; especially delay in the adaptation of social institutions to technological advances.

cul·ture (kul′chər) *n., v.* **-tured, -tur·ing.** —*n.* **1** fineness of feelings, thoughts, tastes, manners, etc. **2** the arts, beliefs, habits, institutions, and other human endeavors considered together as being characteristic of a particular community, people, or nation. Modern Canadian culture is strongly influenced by television and other mass media. **3** the development of the mind or body by education, training, etc. **4** the preparation of land to raise crops by ploughing, planting, and the necessary care; cultivation. **5** proper care given to the raising of bees, fish, silkworms, etc. **6** *Biology.* **a** the growth of living micro-organisms such as bacteria in a special medium for scientific study or medicinal use. **b** a group or colony of micro-organisms produced in this way. —*v.* **1** cultivate. **2** *Biology.* grow bacteria, etc. in a special nutrient medium for scientific study or medicinal use. [< F < L *cultura* a tending < *colere* cultivate]
☛ *Syn. n.* **1.** See note at **education.**

cul·tured (kul′chərd) *adj.* **1** having or showing culture; refined. **2** produced or raised under artificial conditions, as in a laboratory, etc.: *cultured pearls.*

cultured pearl a natural pearl artificially cultivated by introducing a foreign body into an oyster, so causing the oyster to secrete a protective substance that hardens round the irritant.

culture lag cultural lag.

cul·tus[1] (kul′təs) *n.* a religious cult. [< L. See CULT.]

cul·tus[2] (kul′təs) *adj. Cdn. West Coast.* worthless; unimportant; bad. [< Chinook jargon < Chinook *cultus* worthless]

cul·ver·in (kul′vər in) *n.* **1** a musket used in the Middle Ages. **2** a long, heavy cannon, used in the 16th and 17th centuries. [ME < OF *coulevrine* < *couleuvre* < L *colubra* serpent]

cul·vert (kul′vərt) *n.* a small channel or drain that allows water to run under a road, railway, canal, etc. [origin uncertain]

cum (kum) *prep.* combined with or together with (used especially to form compounds): *an antique-cum-junk shop.*

cum·ber (kum′bər) *v., n.* —*v.* **1** burden; trouble: *Household cares cumber a busy mother.* **2** hinder; hamper: *The lumberman's heavy boots cumbered him in walking.* —*n.* hindrance. [ME, probably < OF *combrer* impede < *combre* barrier < Celtic] —**cum′ber·er,** *n.*

cum·ber·some (kum′bər səm) *adj.* clumsy; unwieldy; burdensome: *The armor worn by medieval knights seems cumbersome to us today. Long, badly constructed sentences are cumbersome.* —**cum′ber·some·ly** *adv.* —**cum′ber·some·ness,** *n.*

cum·brous (kum′brəs) *adj.* cumbersome. —**cum′brous·ly,** *adv.* —**cum′brous·ness,** *n.*

cum·in or **cum·min** (kum′ən) *n.* **1** a small, Mediterranean annual herb (*Cuminum cyminum*) of the parsley family widely cultivated for its aromatic seeds, which are used as a flavoring. **2** the seeds of this plant. [OE *cymen* < L *cuminum* < Gk. *kyminon*]

cum lau·de (kúm lou′dā *or* kum lô′dē) *Latin.* **1** with praise or honor. To graduate *cum laude* is to graduate with high rank. **2** a person who has graduated from a high school or university with high honors.

cum·mer·bund (kum′ər bund) *n.* a broad sash worn around the

waist. Also, **kummerbund.** [< Hind. *kamarband* < Persian *kamar* waist, loins (< Arabic) + *band* band, bandage]

cum·quat (kum′kwot) See **kumquat.**

cu·mu·late (kyū′myə lāt′) *v.* **-lat·ed, -lat·ing;** *adj.* —*v.* heap up; accumulate. —*adj.* heaped up. [< L *cumulare* < *cumulus* heap]

cu·mu·la·tion (kyū′myə lā′shən) *n.* **1** heaping up; accumulating. **2** a heap; accumulation.

cu·mu·la·tive (kyū′myə lə tiv *or* kyū′myə lā′tiv) *adj.* heaped up; accumulated; increasing or growing in amount, force, etc., by additions: *a cumulative argument.* A cumulative dividend is one that must be added to future dividends if not paid when due. —**cu′mu·la·tive·ly,** *adv.* —**cu′mu·la·tive·ness,** *n.*

cu·mu·lo–cir·rus (kyū′myə lō sir′əs) *n., pl.* **-cir·ri** (-sir′ī *or* -sir′ē). a cloud that is part cumulus, part cirrus.

cu·mu·lo–nim·bus (kyū′myə lō nim′bəs) *n., pl.* **-bus·es** or **-bi** (-bī *or* -bē). a massive cloud formation having peaks that resemble mountains.

cu·mu·lo–stra·tus (kyū′myə lō strā′təs *or* -strat′əs) *n.* a cumulus cloud with its base spread out horizontally like a stratus cloud.

cu·mu·lous (kyū′myə ləs) *adj.* of or like cumulus clouds.

cu·mu·lus (kyū′myə ləs) *n., pl.* **-li** (-lī′ *or* -lē′). **1** a cloud formation of rounded heaps having a flat base. **2** a heap. [< L *cumulus* heap]

cu·ne·ate (kyū′nē it *or* kyū′nē āt′) *adj.* tapering to a point at the base; wedge-shaped. [< L *cuneatus* < *cuneus* wedge]

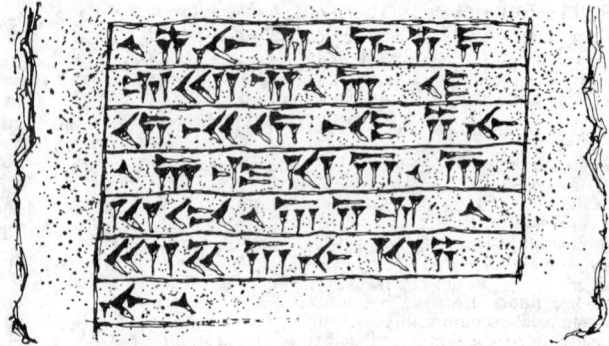

(WORD SEPARATOR)

i *ya* *m* *C* *i* *ça* *ta* *kh* *ma*

This *Ciçatakhma*

A section of a cuneiform inscription in Old Persian carved on the rock face of a mountain in Iran by order of the Persian king, Darius I, c. 500 B.C. The inscription describes the first year of his reign, during which he put down several rebellions against his rule. The part shown means "this is Ciçatakhma. He lied thus—he said, 'I am king'."

cu·ne·i·form (kyū′nē ə fôrm′ *or* kyū nē′ə-) *n., adj.* —*n.* **1** the wedge-shaped characters used in the writing of ancient Babylonia, Assyria, Persia, etc. **2** a wedge-shaped bone, especially one of the three bones of the human ankle. —*adj.* **1** wedge-shaped. **2** of or having to do with cuneiform characters. **3** of or denoting any wedge-shaped bone. [< L *cuneus* wedge + E -*form* shaped (< L -*formis*)]

cun·ner (kun′ər) *n.* a small fish (*Tautogolabrus adspersus*), a kind of wrasse, found off the Atlantic coast of North America, from Newfoundland south to New England. [origin unknown]

cun·ning (kun′ing) *adj., n.* —*adj.* **1** clever in getting what one wants or in deceiving one's enemies; crafty; wily: *a cunning rogue.* **2** showing craftiness or wiliness: *a cunning plot.* **3** *Archaic.* having or showing skill or cleverness: *cunning hands, cunning workmanship.* **4** *Informal.* attractively small, delicate, quaint, etc.; cute: *a cunning baby.* —*n.* **1** craftiness; wiliness: *A fox has a great deal of cunning.* **2** *Archaic.* skill or cleverness. [OE *cunnan < cunnan* know (how). Related to CAN[1].] —**cun′ning·ly,** *adv.* —**cun′ning·ness,** *n.*
☛ *Syn. adj.* **1.** See note at **sly.** —*n.* **1. Cunning, craft** = skill in getting what one wants. **Cunning** suggests slyness and the use of clever tricks or false appearances to hide one's real purpose and get the better of others: *He has the cunning of a cat chasing a mouse.* **Craft** suggests skill in deceiving others by clever and artful plans, devices, and underhand methods: *He has the craft of a successful swindler.*

cup (kup) *n., v.* **cupped, cup·ping.** —*n.* **1** a small but rather deep dish to drink from, usually having one curved handle. **2** as much as a cup holds; a cupful: *He ordered a cup of tea.* **3** a unit for measuring capacity or volume, used especially in cooking. One cup is equal to about 227 mL. **4** something resembling a cup in shape or function. **5** an ornamental cup, vase, etc. given to the winner of a contest; a trophy. **6** a mixed drink: *a claret cup.* **7** *Christianity.* **a** the chalice or other vessel used in Communion. **b** the consecrated wine, etc. contained in this vessel. **8** something to be experienced or endured; one's lot or fate: *It was a bitter cup for him.*
in (one's) **cups,** drunk.
—*v.* **1** curve or shape (one's hands, etc.) to resemble a cup: *She cupped her hands to catch the ball. The old man cupped a hand behind one ear.* **2** put into or take in a cup. **3** *Medicine. Historical.* bleed (a person) by means of a cupping glass. [OE *cuppe* < LL *cuppa*; cf. L *cupa* tub] —**cup′like′,** *adj.*

CUP 1 Canadian University Press. **2** Cambridge University Press.

cup·bear·er (kup′ber′ər) *n.* **1** a person who fills and passes around the cups in which drinks are served. **2** *Historical.* in royal households, a noble who tasted the wine before handing it to his master.

cup·board (kub′ərd) *n.* **1** a closet or cabinet with shelves for dishes, food, etc. **2** a closet for storing clothing, linens, etc.

cupboard love insincere expressions of love for selfish reasons; affection offered for the sake of something, such as food and care to be received in return.

cup·cake (kup′kāk′) *n.* a small cake baked in a cup-shaped container.

CUPE (kyü′pē) *n.* Canadian Union of Public Employees.

cup·ful (kup′fùl) *n., pl.* **-fuls.** as much as a cup can hold.

Cu·pid (kyü′pid) *n.* **1** *Roman mythology.* the god of love, the son of Venus, corresponding to the Greek god Eros. Cupid was usually represented as a winged boy with bow and arrows. **2 cupid,** a figure of a naked winged boy used as a symbol of love: *Valentine cards often have cupids on them.*

cu·pid·i·ty (kyü pid′ə tē) *n.* eager desire, especially to possess something; greed. [< L *cupiditas* < *cupidus* desirous < *cupere* long for, desire]

cu·po·la (kyü′pə lə) *n.* **1** a round dome forming the roof of a building or part of a building. **2** a small structure on top of a roof. **3** a domelike thing or part. [< Ital. < LL *cupula,* dim. of L *cupa* tub]

cupping glass *Medicine. Historical.* a kind of glass cup in which a partial vacuum could be created by suction or heat; it was applied to a person's skin to draw blood to the surface for slow bloodletting.

cu·pre·ous (kyü′prē əs) *adj.* **1** of or containing copper. **2** copper-colored. [< L *cupreus* < *cuprum* copper]

cu·pric (kyü′prik) *adj. Chemistry.* of or containing divalent copper.

cu·prous (kyü′prəs) *adj. Chemistry.* of or containing monovalent copper.

cu·prum (kyü′prəm) *n.* copper. [< L. See COPPER.]

CUPW Canadian Union of Postal Workers (*sometimes treated as a noun and pronounced* kup′dub′əl yü′).

cur (kėr) *n.* **1** a worthless dog; mongrel. **2** an ill-bred, despicable person. [ME *curre*]

cur·a·bil·i·ty (kyür′ə bil′ə tē) *n.* being curable.

cur·a·ble (kyür′ə bəl) *adj.* that can be cured. —**cur′a·ble·ness,** *n.* —**cur′a·bly,** *adv.*

cu·ra·çao (kyür′ə sō′) *n.* a liqueur or cordial flavored with orange peel. [< *Curaçao,* a Dutch island in the West Indies]

cu·ra·cy (kyür′ə sē) *n., pl.* **-cies.** the position, rank, or work of a curate.

cu·ra·re (kyü rä′rē) *n.* a poisonous, blackish, resinlike extract of certain tropical American plants, especially *Chondodendron* species of the family Menispermaceae and *Strychnos* species of the family Loganiaceae, which causes paralysis of the muscles. It is used medicinally as a muscle relaxant and has long been used by South American Indian peoples as an arrow poison in hunting game. Also, **curari.** [< Sp. *curaré* or Portuguese *curare* < Tupi]

cu·rate (kyür′it) *n.* a member of the clergy who is an assistant to a pastor, rector, or vicar. [< Med.L *curatus* < *cura* cure (def. 5) < L *cura.* Doublet of CURÉ.]

cur·a·tive (kyür′ə tiv) *adj.* —*adj.* having the power to cure; curing; tending to cure. —*n.* a means of curing. —**cur′a·tive·ly,** *adv.* —**cur′a·tive·ness,** *n.*

cu·ra·tor (kyü rā′tər) *n.* a person in charge of all or part of a museum, library, etc. [< L *curator* < *curare* care for < *cura* care]

curb (kėrb) *n., v.* —*n.* **1** a raised border of concrete or stone along the edge of a street, driveway, etc. **2** an enclosing framework or

hat, āge, fär; let, ēqual, tèrm; it, īce
hot, ōpen, ôrder; oil, out; cup, pùt, rüle,
əbove, takən, pencəl, lemən, circəs

ch, child; ng, long; sh, ship
th, thin; ŦH, then; zh, measure

border supporting the base or outer edge of a dome, shaft, etc. **3** a chain or strap fastened to a horse's bit and passing under its lower jaw. When the reins are pulled tight, the curb checks the horse. **4** anything that checks or restrains. **5** a market that deals in stocks and bonds not listed on the regular stock exchange. The name comes from the fact that such markets originally conducted their business on the streets.
—*v.* **1** hold in check; restrain. **2** provide with a curb. [ME < OF *courbe* < L *curvus* bent]
☛ *Syn. v.* **1.** See note at **check.**

curb bit a horse's bit having a curb.

curb·ing (kėr′bing) *n.* **1** material for making a curb. **2** a raised border of concrete, etc.; curb.

curb roof a roof having two slopes on each side.

curb·stone (kėrb′stōn′) *n.* a stone or stones forming a curb; a raised border of concrete, etc. along the sides of a street, driveway, etc.

cur·cu·li·o (kėr kyü′lē ō′) *n., pl.* **-li·os.** any of various American weevils, especially any that are pests of fruit trees, such as *Conotrachelus nenuphar.* [< L]

curd (kėrd) *n., v.* —*n.* Often, **curds,** *pl.* the thick part of milk that separates from the watery part when milk sours. —*v.* form into curds; curdle. [ME *curd, crud*]

cur·dle (kėr′dəl) *v.* **-dled, -dling. 1** form into curds. Milk curdles when it is kept too long. **2** thicken.
curdle the blood, horrify; terrify.
[< *curd*]

cur·dled (kėr′dəld) *adj.* formed into curds.

curd·y (kėr′dē) *adj.* **1** full of curds. **2** like curdled milk.

cure (kyür) *v.* **cured, cur·ing;** *n.* —*v.* **1** bring back to health or to a normal, sound, or proper condition: *The sick child was soon cured. The punishment was meant to cure her of lying.* **2** get rid of: *to cure a cold, to cure a bad habit.* **3** prepare for keeping; preserve: *They cured the meat by drying and salting it.* **4** treat (a substance) by chemical or physical means in order to prepare it for use: *Rubber is cured by vulcanizing it. Tobacco is cured by drying.* **5** become cured.
—*n.* **1** recovery from a disease; bringing or being brought back to health: *His cure took a long time.* **2** a period or course of treatment for a disease: *a rest cure.* **3** something that restores to health; a successful medical treatment, drug, etc.: *Researchers have not yet found a cure for cancer.* **4** anything that permanently relieves or corrects a problem or a harmful situation: *The cure for laziness. The tax cuts are not a cure for inflation, but merely a stopgap.* **5** spiritual charge; religious care. **6** a method of process of curing meat, fish, etc. [ME < OF *curer* < L *curare* care for < *cura* care] —**cure′less,** *adj.* —**cur′er,** *n.*
☛ *Syn. v.* **1. Cure, heal, remedy** = make well or right. **Cure** applies particularly to bringing back to health after sickness and disease: *The new treatment cured his skin disease.* **Heal** = make whole, and is used particularly of wounds, burns, etc.: *This medicine will heal that cut.* **Remedy** = put right, and applies to curing or relieving any unhealthy physical or mental condition: *The operation remedied his twisted foot.*

cu·ré (kyü rā′; French, kʏ rā′) *n.* a parish priest. [< F < Med.L *curatus.* Doublet of CURATE.]

cure-all (kyür′ol′ *or* -ôl′) *n.* a remedy supposed to cure all diseases or evils.

cur·few (kėr′fyü) *n.* **1** the giving of a signal, such as a bell ringing, at a fixed time every evening. In the Middle Ages, it announced the time to put out lights and cover fires. More recently it has been used as a direction for persons, usually children, to leave streets and public places. **2** the signal given: *"The curfew tolls the knell of parting day."* **3** the time when it is given: *Everyone was indoors before curfew.* **4** a formal regulation forbidding persons to be on the streets after a certain hour. [ME < AF *coeverfu* < *covrir* cover (< L *cooperire*) + *feu* fire < L *focus* hearth]

cu·ri·a (kyür′ē ə) *n., pl.* **cu·ri·ae** (kyür′ē ē′ *or* kyür′ē ī′). **1** in ancient Rome: **a** the meeting place of the tribes. **b** one of the ten divisions of each of the three tribes into which all Roman citizens were divided. **c** the meeting place of one of these divisions. **2** a medieval council or court of law. **3 Curia,** *Roman Catholic Church.* a group of high officials who assist the Pope in the government and administration of the Church; the papal court. [< L]

cu·rie (kyür′ē *or* kyü rē′) *n.* a unit for measuring radio-activity,

equal to 37 gigabecquerels. *Symbol:* Ci [after Mme. Marie *Curie* (1867-1934), a French physicist and chemist]

cu·ri·o (kyür′ē ō′) *n., pl.* **cu·ri·os.** an object valued as a curiosity: *The traveller brought back many curios from foreign lands.* [short for *curiosity*]

cu·ri·os·i·ty (kyür′ē os′i tē) *n., pl.* **-ties. 1** an eager desire to know: *Her curiosity made her open the forbidden door.* **2** the condition of being too eager to know: *Curiosity killed the cat.* **3** a strange, rare, or novel object. **4** an odd, unusual, or interesting quality: *He was intrigued with the curiosity of the place.*

cu·ri·ous (kyür′ē əs) *adj.* **1** eager to know: *a curious student.* **2** too eager to know; prying: *That old woman is curious about other people's business.* **3** strange; odd; unusual: *a curious old book.* **4** *Archaic.* very careful; exact: *a curious inquiry into the customs of the Blackfoot.* **5** *Informal.* very odd; eccentric: *curious notions.* [ME < *curios* < L *curiosus* inquisitive, full of care, ult. < *cura* care] —**cu′ri·ous·ly,** *adv.* —**cu′ri·ous·ness,** *n.*

☛ *Syn.* **1, 2. Curious, inquisitive, prying** = eager to find out about things. **Curious** = eager to learn things, but sometimes suggests being too eager to know about other people's business: *A normal child is curious about how things work.* **Inquisitive** suggests constantly asking questions to find out what one wants to know, especially about personal matters: *She is too inquisitive about my dates.* **Prying** adds to *inquisitive* the idea of peeping and of busying oneself about other people's business: *I had a prying landlady.*

cu·ri·um (kyür′ē əm) *n.* a radio-active chemical element produced by the bombardment of plutonium and uranium by helium ions. *Symbol:* Cm; *at.no.* 96; *at.wt.* (247); *half-life* 1.6 × 10⁷ years. [after Mme. Marie *Curie* (1867-1934), a French physicist and chemist]

curl (kėrl) *v., n.* —*v.* **1** twist or roll into a coil or coils (*sometimes used with* up): *to curl up a piece of paper. She uses a curling iron to curl her hair.* **2** take the form of ripples or twists (*often used with* up): *Paper curls when it burns.* **3** grow in coils or spirals: *My hair curls naturally.* **4** move or progress in curves or twists: *smoke curling from the chimney. A stream curled through the woods.* **5** form into a curve; twist: *Her lip curled in a sneer.* **6** *Curling.* **a** slide a curling stone down the ice. **b** engage in the game of curling.

curl up, a take a comfortable position sitting or lying down with one's legs drawn up: *The child curled up in the big chair and went to sleep.* **b** *Informal.* collapse; break down.

—*n.* **1** a curled lock of hair. **2** something shaped like this. **3** a curling or being curled.

in curl, curled: *keeping hair in curl.*
[ME *curle(n), crulle(n)* < *crul* curly]

curl·er (kėr′lər) *n.* **1** a person who takes part in the game of curling. **2** a device on which hair is twisted to make it curl.

cur·lew (kėr′lü) *n., pl.* **-lew** or **-lews.** any of a genus (*Numenius*) of medium-sized or large wading birds related to the sandpipers, having a long, thin, downward-curving bill. They breed in temperate and subarctic regions of the northern hemisphere and migrate to the southern hemisphere for winter. [ME < OF *courlieu;* imitative]

curl·i·cue (kėr′lə kyü′) *n.* a fancy twist, curl, flourish, etc.: *curlicues in handwriting.* [< *curly* + *cue²*]

curl·ing (kėr′ling) *n.* a game played on ice, in which large, heavy, round stones are slid towards a target at the end of the rink.

curling iron an instrument for curling hair by means of heat and, sometimes, steam, consisting of a usually metal rod that is heated and around which a strand of hair to be curled is wound.

A curling stone   A woman curling

curling stone or **rock** the object, usually made of granite, that is slid down the ice in the game of curling.

curling tongs curling iron.

curl·pa·per (kėrl′pā′pər) *n.* a piece of folded paper over which a lock of hair is rolled up tightly to curl it.

curl·y (kėr′lē) *adj.* **curl·i·er, curl·i·est. 1** curling; having a tendency to curl; wavy: *curly hair.* **2** having curls: *a curly head.* —**curl′i·ness,** *n.*

cur·mudg·eon (kər muj′ən) *n.* a rude, stingy, bad-tempered man. [origin unknown] —**cur·mudg′eon·ly,** *adj.*

cur·rach or **cur·ragh** (kur′əн *or* kur′ə) *n.* coracle. [< Irish and Scots Gaelic *currach;* 15c.]

cur·rant (kėr′ənt) *n.* **1** a small, seedless raisin, used in cakes, etc. **2** a small, sour, edible berry that is the fruit of any of several shrubs (genus *Ribus*) of the saxifrage family. Currants may be red, white, or black and are used for jelly, wine, preserves, etc. **3** a shrub that produces these berries. [ME (*raysons of*) *Coraunte* < AF (*raisins de*) *Corauntz* raisins of Corinth]

cur·ren·cy (kėr′ən sē) *n., pl.* **-cies. 1** the money in actual use in a country: *Canadian currency cannot be used in Mexico.* **2** a passing from person to person; circulation: *The town gossips gave the rumor currency.* **3** general use or acceptance; common occurrence: *The word* fire-reels, *which was the common term for a fire engine in Toronto and Montreal, is now passing out of currency.*

cur·rent (kėr′ənt) *n., adj.* —*n.* **1** a flow or stream of water or air in one direction, especially within a larger body of water or air: *Stay near the shore so you don't get caught in the current.* **2** a flow of electricity along a wire, etc. **3** the rate or amount of such a flow, usually expressed in amperes: *Heating requires much more current than lighting does.* **4** a course or tendency of events, ideas, etc.; a general direction or drift: *the current of public opinion.* —*adj.* **1** of or at the present time: *current fashions, the current month. Her current job involves a lot of travelling.* **2** most recent: *The current issue of a magazine is the one most recently published.* **3** generally used or accepted; common or prevalent: *Many slang expressions of the seventies are not longer current.* **4** going around; passing from person to person: *A rumor is current that prices will go up.* [ME < OF < L *current, -entis,* ppr. of *currere* run]

☛ *Syn. n.* **1.** See note at **stream.** —*adj.* **2. Current, present, prevailing** = generally used or occurring at a certain time. **Current** emphasizes the notion of continuity in circulation or use at a given time: *English usage current in the 17th century.* **Present** means here and now: *This apartment meets my present needs.* **Prevailing** emphasizes relative predominance or vogue: *This bathing suit agrees with the prevailing fashion.*

cur·rent·ly (kėr′ənt lē) *adv.* at the present time or in the present period: *The prime minister is currently vacationing in the Maritimes. Her songs are currently very popular.*

cur·ri·cle (kėr′i kəl) *n.* a two-wheeled carriage drawn by two horses. [< L *curriculum.* See CURRICULUM.]

cur·ric·u·lar (kə rik′yə lər) *adj.* having to do with a curriculum.

cur·ric·u·lum (kə rik′yə ləm) *n., pl.* **-lums** or **-la** (-lə). **1** the whole range of studies offered in a school, college, etc. or in a type of school: *the university curriculum. Our high-school curriculum includes English, mathematics, science, history, and foreign languages.* **2** a program of studies leading to a particular degree, certificate, etc.: *the curriculum of the Law School.* [< L *curriculum* race course, chariot, dim. of *currus* chariot < *currere* run]

curriculum vi·tae (vē′tī) *pl.* **curricula vitae.** a summary of one's life, listing schools, colleges, etc. attended, jobs held, prizes or other distinctions gained, etc., used especially to accompany job applications. [< L; literally, course of life]

☛ *Syn.* **Curriculum vitae, résumé** = summary of one's life, qualifications, etc. **Résumé** is the general term; **curriculum vitae** is used mainly in academic and professional situations.

cur·ri·er (kėr′ē ər) *n.* **1** a person who curries tanned leather. **2** a person who curries horses, etc. [ME < OF *corier* < L *coriarius* tanner < *corium* leather]

cur·rish (kėr′ish) *adj.* of or like a cur; snarling; ill-bred; worthless. —**cur′rish·ly,** *adv.* —**cur′rish·ness,** *n.*

cur·ry¹ (kėr′ē) *v.* **-ried, -ry·ing. 1** rub and clean (a horse, etc.) with a brush or currycomb. **2** prepare (tanned leather) for use by soaking, scraping, beating, coloring, etc.

curry favor, seek a person's favor by flattery, constant attentions, etc.
[ME < OF *correiier* put in order < *con-* (intensive) + *reiier* arrange < Gmc.]

cur·ry² (kėr′ē) *n., pl.* **-ries;** *v.* **-ried, -ry·ing.** —*n.* **1** a spicy dish consisting especially of meat, fish, or eggs prepared with a sauce seasoned with pungent spices such as cayenne, ginger, coriander, etc. Curries are common in S Asia, the West Indies, etc. **2** a sauce seasoned with such spices. **3** curry powder. —*v.* prepare with curry sauce or powder: *curried lamb.* [< Tamil *kari*]

cur·ry·comb (kėr′ē kōm′) *n., v.* —*n.* a brush with metal teeth for rubbing and cleaning a horse. —*v.* use a currycomb on; brush with a currycomb.

curry powder a finely ground mixture of spices, such as turmeric, cumin, coriander, cayenne, ginger, etc., used especially to make curries.

curse (kėrs) *v.* **cursed** or **curst, curs·ing;** *n.* —*v.* **1** call on a supernatural or divine being to bring evil or harm to: *to curse one's enemies.* **2** bring evil or harm to; torment or afflict: *cursed with poverty, cursed by the gods.* **3** rail at by using blasphemous words; revile: *to curse one's fate, to curse the gods.* **4** use blasphemous or obscene words to express anger, hatred, frustration, etc.; swear or

swear at: *He cursed when he hit his thumb with the hammer. She cursed her servant for his clumsiness.* **5** excommunicate. **be cursed with,** have and suffer from: *Job was cursed with boils.* —*n.* **1** the words that a person says when he curses someone or something. **2** a person or thing that is or ought to be cursed; a source of evil or harm: *The stolen money proved to be a curse to them. Malaria was the curse of the expedition.* **3** harm or evil that comes as if in answer to a curse or as a retribution: *They claimed that there was a curse on the diamond.* **4** blasphemous or obscene words used to express anger, hatred, frustration, etc.: *Their talk was full of curses.* **5 the curse,** *Informal.* **a** menstruation. **b** an occurrence of menstruation; period. **6** a sentence of excommunication. [OE *cūrs,* n., *cursian,* v.] —**curs′er,** *n.*
☛ *Syn.* v. **3. Curse, swear** = use profane or foul language. **Curse** emphasizes anger or hatred: *He cursed the poor waitress who had spilled soup on him.* **Swear** (def. 8) suggests using the names of holy persons or things or similar words to punctuate one's speech or express feelings: *He swore horrible oaths when he hurt himself.*

curs·ed (kėr′sid *or* kėrst) *adj.* **1** under a curse. **2** deserving a curse; evil; hateful. —**curs′ed·ly,** *adv.* —**cur′sed·ness,** *n.*

cur·sive (kėr′siv) *adj., n.* —*adj.* written with the letters joined together. Ordinary handwriting is cursive. —*n.* **1** a letter made to join other letters. **2** a style of printing type imitating handwriting. **3** cursive script. [< Med.L *cursivus* < *cursus,* pp. of L *currere* run] **cur′sive·ly,** *adv.*

cur·so·ri·al (kėr sô′rē əl) *adj.* **1** for running. **2** having legs fitted for running: *The ostrich is a cursorial bird.*

cur·so·ry (kėr′sə rē) *adj.* hasty; superficial; without attention to details: *Even a cursory reading of the letter showed many errors.* [< LL *cursorius* of a race < *currere* run] —**cur′so·ri·ly,** *adv.* —**cur′so·ri·ness,** *n.*

curst (kėrst) *adj., v.* —*adj.* cursed. —*v.* a pt. and a pp. of **curse.**

curt (kėrt) *adj.* short; rudely brief; abrupt: *Her curt answer made him angry.* [< L *curtus* cut short] —**curt′ly,** *adv.* —**curt′ness,** *n.*
☛ *Syn.* See note at **blunt.**

cur·tail (kėr tāl′) *v.* cut short; cut off part of; reduce; lessen. [< *curtal,* adj., cut short (especially of tails) < OF *cortald* < L *curtus;* influenced by *tail*]
☛ *Syn.* See note at **shorten.**

cur·tail·ment (kėr tāl′mənt) *n.* curtailing; diminution.

cur·tain (kėr′tən) *n., v.* —*n.* **1** a piece of cloth or other similar material hung at windows or in doorways to protect from sun, wind, or rain, to separate, conceal, or darken, or to decorate. **2** *Theatre.* **a** a movable hanging screen that separates the stage from the part where the audience sits. **b** the opening or raising of the curtain at the beginning of an act or scene, or the fall or closing of the curtain at the end of an act or scene. **3** anything that hides or acts as a barrier: *a curtain of fog. They had placed a curtain of secrecy over all their movements.* **4** the part of a wall between two bastions, towers, or the like. **bring down the curtain on,** terminate; end: *The merger brought down the curtain on the independent company.* **draw the curtain over** or **on,** conceal. **raise the curtain on,** disclose; reveal. —*v.* **1** provide with or as if with a curtain. **2** hide or cover with or as if with a curtain. **curtain off,** separate or divide by means of a curtain or curtains. [ME < OF *curtine* < LL *cortina*] —**cur′tain·less,** *adj.*

curtain call a call for an actor, musician, etc. to return to the stage and acknowledge the applause of the audience.

curtain lecture a scolding given by a wife to her husband. [originally with reference to the old-fashioned curtained bed]

curtain raiser 1 *Theatre.* a short play given before the main play. **2** a little thing used to introduce something bigger: *The walkout of a few workers was the curtain raiser to a major strike.*

curtain wall a wall between columns or piers of a frame or skeleton of a building which supports no load other than its own weight, and is not supported by girders or beams.

cur·te·sy (kėr′tə sē) *n., pl.* **-sies.** *Law.* the right a husband has, under certain conditions, in the land left by his dead wife. [var. of *courtesy*]

curt·sey (kėrt′sē) *n., pl.* **-seys;** *v.* **-seyed, -sey·ing.** See **curtsy.**

curt·sy (kėrt′sē) *n., pl.* **-sies;** *v.* **-sied, -sy·ing.** —*n.* a bow of respect or greeting by women, made by bending the knees and lowering the body slightly. —*v.* make a curtsy. [var. of *courtesy*]

cu·rule chair (kyūr′ül) a special seat used by the highest civil officials in ancient Rome. [< L *curulis* < *currus* chariot]

cur·va·ceous (kėr vā′shəs) *adj. Informal.* of a girl or woman, having a full figure, attractively well-developed.

cur·va·ture (kėr′və chər *or* kėr′və chūr′) *n.* **1** curving or bending. **2** a curved condition, especially an abnormal one: *a curvature of the spine.* **3** a curved piece or part; curve. **4** the degree of curving; curve: *the curvature of the earth's surface.*

hat, āge, fär; let, ēqual, tėrm; it, īce
hot, ōpen, ôrder; oil, out; cup, pùt, rüle,
əbove, takən, pencəl, lemən, circəs

ch, child; ng, long; sh, ship
th, thin; ŧH, then; zh, measure

curve (kėrv) *n., v.* **curved, curv·ing.** —*n.* **1** a line that has no straight part. **2** something having the shape of a curve; bend: *The automobile had to slow down for the curves in the road.* **3** *Baseball.* a ball pitched with a spin that causes it to swerve just before it reaches the batter: *A good curve is difficult to hit.* **4** the degree or manner to or in which something curves. **5** *Mathematics.* a line whose course can be defined by an equation, such as a parabola or a straight line. **6** a line on a graph, representing statistical data, such as economic trends: *the cost-of-living curve.* —*v.* **1** bend so as to form a curve. **2** move in the course of a curve. [< L *curvus* bending]

curved (kėrvd) *adj.* bent so as to form a curve.

cur·vet (*n.* kėr′vit; *v.* kėr vet′ *or* kėr′vit) *n., v.* **-vet·ted or -vet·ed, -vet·ting** *or* **-vet·ing.** —*n.* a leap in the air made by a horse. The forelegs are first raised and then the hind legs, so that all legs are off the ground for a second. —*v.* **1** of a horse, make a leap in the air. **2** make (a horse) leap in the air. [<Ital. *corvetta,* dim. of *corvo* curve < L *curvus* bending. Doublet of CAVORT.]

cur·vi·lin·e·al (kėr′və lin′ē əl) *adj.* curvilinear.

cur·vi·lin·e·ar (kėr′və lin′ē ər) *adj.* consisting of a curved line or lines; enclosed by curved lines.

cush·ion (kùsh′ən) *n., v.* —*n.* **1** a soft pillow or pad used to sit, lie, or kneel on. **2** anything used or shaped like a cushion. Air or steam forms a cushion in some machines to protect them from sudden shocks or jars. **3** anything that lessens the effects of distress or adversity, relieves a burden, or makes for greater comfort or ease: *a cushion of savings against sickness or retirement.* **4** *Cdn.* the enclosed ice surface, especially an outdoor one, on which hockey is played. **5** the elastic lining of the sides of a billiard table. **6** the layer of soft rubber in the casing of a pneumatic tire. —*v.* **1** put or seat on a cushion; support with cushions. **2** supply with a cushion. **3** protect from sudden shocks or jars with a cushion of steam. **4** ease the effects of; protect: *His family's wealth had always cushioned him against failure.* [ME < OF *coussin,* probably < VL *coxinum* < L *coxa* hip] **-cush′ion·like′,** *adj.*

cush·y (kùsh′ē) *adj.* **cush·i·er, cush·i·est.** *Slang.* luxuriously comfortable and easy: *a cushy job, a cushy life.*

cusk (kusk) *n., pl.* **cusk** or **cusks.** a large food fish (*Brosme brosme*) of the cod family found along the North American and European coasts of the Atlantic, having a barbel on the chin, a single, long dorsal fin, and a single, long anal fin. [origin unknown]

CUSO Canadian Universities Service Overseas.

cusp (kusp) *n.* **1** a pointed end; point: *A crescent has two cusps.* **2** a blunt or pointed protuberance of the crown of a tooth. [< L *cuspis, -pidis*]

cus·pid (kus′pid) *n.* a tooth having one cusp; a canine tooth. [< L *cuspid-, cuspis* point, cusp]

cus·pi·dal (kus′pə dəl) *adj.* **1** of or having to do with a cusp. **2** having a pointed end.

cus·pi·date (kus′pə dāt′) *adj.* having a sharp, pointed end.

cus·pi·dor (kus′pə dôr′) *n.* a container to spit into; spittoon. [< Pg. *cuspidor* spitter < *cuspir* spit < L *conspuere* spit on < *com-* + *spuere* spit]

cuss (kus) *n., v. Informal.* —*n.* **1** a curse. **2** an odd or troublesome person or animal: *Tell that cuss to get over here now.* —*v.* curse (often used with **out**): *He cussed me out for a whole half minute.* [var. of *curse*]

cuss·ed (kus′id) *adj. Informal.* **1** cursed. **2** stubborn. **-cuss·ed·ly,** *adv.* —**cuss′ed·ness,** *n.*

cus·tard (kus′tərd) *n.* a baked, boiled, or frozen food made of eggs and milk, usually sweetened. [var. of *crustade* < F < Provençal *croustado* pasty[2] < L *crustare* encrust < *crusta* crust]

custard apple 1 any of various shrubs or small trees (genus *Annona*) of tropical America, especially *A. reticulata* of the West Indies, having dark-brown fruit with a sweet, reddish-yellow, very soft pulp. **2** (*adj.*) **custard-apple,** designating a family (Annonaceae) of shrubs and trees that includes the custard apple, pawpaw, and soursop.

cus·to·di·al (kus tō′dē əl) *adj.* having to do with custody or custodians.

cus·to·di·an (kus tō′dē ən) *n.* **1** the person in charge; guardian

or keeper: *the custodian of a museum, the legal custodian of a child.* **2** caretaker; janitor.

cus·to·di·an·ship (kus tō′dē ən ship′) *n.* the position or duties of a custodian.

cus·to·dy (kus′tə dē) *n., pl.* **-dies. 1** the keeping; charge; care: *Parents have the custody of their young children.* **2** being confined or detained; imprisonment.
in custody, in the care of the police; in prison.
take into custody, arrest.
[< L *custodia* < *custos, -odis* guardian]

cus·tom (kus′təm) *n., adj.* —*n.* **1** a usual action; habit: *It was his custom to rise early.* **2** a habit maintained for so long that it has almost the force of law. **3** the regular business given by a customer: *He threatened to take his custom to another store.* **4 customs,** *pl.* **a** duty paid to the government on things brought in from a foreign country. **b** the office at a seaport, international airport, or border-crossing point where imported goods are checked. **c** the department of the government that collects duty. **5** in feudal times, a tax or service regularly due from tenants to their lord.
—*adj.* **1** made or done specially for an individual customer; made or done to order: *a car with custom fenders, custom threshing.* **2** making or doing things to order; not selling mass-produced goods or services: *a custom tailor.* [ME < OF *custume* < VL *consuetumen* < L *consuescere.* Doublet of COSTUME.]
☛ *Syn. n.* **1.** See note at **habit.**

cus·tom·ar·i·ly (kus′təm er′ə lē) *adv.* in a customary manner; usually.

cus·tom·ar·y (kus′təm er′ē) *adj.* according to custom; as a habit; usual.
☛ *Syn.* See note at **usual.**

cus·tom–built (kus′təm bilt′) *adj.* built according to the specifications of an individual customer: *a custom-built bedroom suite.*

cus·tom·er (kus′təm ər) *n.* **1** a person who buys, especially a regular patron of a particular store. **2** *Informal.* a person; fellow: *Don't get mixed up with him; he's a rough customer.*

cus·tom·ize (kus′tə mīz′) *v.* —**ized,** —**iz·ing.** make or alter according to individual requirements; make or alter to order: *to customize a van.*

cus·tom–made (kus′təm mād′) *adj.* made according to the specifications of an individual customer: *custom-made draperies.*

customs house a government building or office where taxes on things brought into a country are collected.

customs officer a government official who examines goods being brought into a country and charges any taxes that may be payable.

cut (kut) *v.* —**cut, cut·ting;** *adj., n.* —*v.* **1** open, remove, or separate with something sharp: *to cut meat, timber, grass, one's nails, etc.* **2** make or prepare by cutting: *He cut a hole through the wall with an axe.* **3** make a cut, opening channel, etc.: *This knife cuts well. The river has cut deep through the rock.* **4** be cut; admit of being cut: *Stale bread cuts better than fresh bread.* **5** pierce or wound with something sharp: *She cut her finger on the broken glass.* **6** reduce; decrease: *to cut expenses.* **7** prepare (a stencil) for mimeographing or the like: *to cut a stencil.* **8** go by a direct way; go: *He cut across the field to save time.* **9** cross; divide by crossing: *A brook cuts that field.* **10** make a recording on: *to cut a record, tape, etc.* **11** hit or strike sharply: *The cold wind cut me to the bone.* **12** *Sports.* hit with a slicing stroke: *He cut the ball so that it bounded almost backward.* **13** hurt the feelings of: *His mean remarks cut me.* **14** *Informal.* refuse to recognize socially: *Everyone in the class cut the boy who came first in the test by cheating.* **15** *Informal.* be absent from (a class, lecture, etc.): *He wanted to cut history when he heard there was going to be a test.* **16** makes less sticky or stiff; dissolve: *Gasoline cuts grease and tar.* **17** draw (a card) at random from a pack. **18** divide (a pack of cards) at random. **19** *Informal.* do; perform; make: *to cut a caper.* **20** shorten by omitting some part or parts: *Your speech will be more effective if you cut it in several places.* **21** come to an end; conclude; stop (especially as an order to stop cameras filming a motion picture or television scene).
cut across, go straight across or through.
cut back, a go back suddenly. **b** shorten (a plant) by cutting off the end. **c** reduce output, expenditure, etc.
cut both ways, have disadvantages or bad effects as well as advantages or good effects.
cut down, a cause to fall by cutting. **b** reduce; decrease.
cut in, a go in suddenly. **b** break in; interrupt. **c** interrupt a dancing couple to take the place of one of them. **d** move a vehicle suddenly into a line of moving traffic. **e** connect, join, etc., especially to a machine or working part.

cut off, a remove from the outside of something by cutting: *to cut off the bark of a tree.* **b** shut off: *Our power was cut off for an hour.* **c** stop suddenly. **d** break; interrupt. **e** disinherit.
cut out, a remove from inside of by cutting: *He cut the core out of the apple.* **b** take out; leave out. **c** take the place of; get the better of. **d** make by cutting; make; form: *Her cousin showed her how to cut out paper dolls.* **e** *Slang.* stop doing, using, making, etc.: *to cut out candy. He was told to cut out the teasing.* **f** move out of an assigned or expected position: *The reckless driver suddenly cut out from his own lane.*
cut short See **short.**
cut teeth See **teeth.**
cut up, a cut into small pieces. **b** *Informal.* hurt. **c** *Slang.* show off; play tricks.
cut up rough, a become physically violent. **b** make difficulties. **c** misbehave badly.
—*adj.* **1** that has been cut: *a cut pie.* **2** shaped or formed by cutting. **3** reduced: *at cut prices.*
—*n.* **1** a wound or opening made by cutting. **2** a passage, channel, etc. made by cutting or digging. **3** a piece cut off or cut out: *a cut of meat.* **4** the way in which a thing is cut; style; fashion. **5** a decrease, reduction. **6** a way straight across or through; short cut. **7** a sharp blow or stroke. **8** *Sports.* a slicing stroke. **9** an action or speech that hurts feelings. **10** *Informal.* refusal to recognize socially. **11** *Informal.* an absence from a class, lecture, etc. **12** *Logging.* the amount of wood cut: *Nearly half the cut is pulpwood.* **13** *Printing.* **a** a block or plate with a picture engraved on it. **b** a picture made from such a block or plate. **14** *Informal.* a share: *Each partner has a cut of the profits.* **15 a** a random division of a pack of playing cards. **b** the random selection of one card.
a cut above, *Informal.* somewhat superior to: *He's a cut above the average politician, but he's no statesman.*
[ME *cutte(n)*; origin uncertain]
☛ *Syn. v.* **1. Cut, chop, hack** = separate or remove with something sharp. **Cut** is the general word: *He cut some branches for kindling.* **Chop** = cut by hitting: *to chop wood.* **Hack** = cut or chop roughly and unevenly: *She hacked desperately at the rope to free herself.*

cut–and–dried (kut′ən drīd′) *adj.* **1** ready for use; prepared in advance: *a cut-and-dried scheme.* **2** dull; routine; lacking suspense or vitality: *a cut-and-dried lecture.*

cut and fill a system by which material excavated to make a road, canal, etc. is used to form an adjacent embankment.

cut and thrust 1 hand to hand fighting, especially with swords. **2** *Fencing.* the action of cutting and thrusting. **3** vigorous and lively interchange: *the cut and thrust of debate.*

cu·ta·ne·ous (kyü tā′nē əs *or* kyü tā′nyəs) *adj.* of, on, or having to do with the skin. [< Med.L *cutaneus* < L *cutis* skin]

cut·a·way (kut′ə wā′) *n., adj.* —*n.* a coat having the lower part cut back in a curve or slope from the waist in front to the tails in back. Cutaways are used by men for formal wear in the daytime.
—*adj.* of or designating a drawing or model of a building, machine, etc. having part of the outside wall or surface cut away to show its internal structure or workings.

cut·back (kut′bak′) *n.* a reduction in output, expenditure, etc.: *The company has had to make cutbacks in expenditures because of a slump in sales.*

cut·bank (kut′bangk′) *n.* the outer side of a stream or river where the force of the current has cut away the earth, leaving an overhanging bank.

cute (kyüt) *adj.* **cut·er, cut·est.** *Informal.* **1** pleasing or attractive, especially in a pretty, lovable, dainty, or delicate way: *a cute puppy, a cute dress, a cute girl.* **2** clever; shrewd; cunning: *a cute trick.* **3** consciously stylish or mannered: *cute dialogue.* [var. of *acute*] —**cute′ly,** *adv.* —**cute′ness,** *n.*

cut·ey (kyü′tē) See **cutie.**

cut glass glass shaped or decorated by grinding and polishing.

cu·ti·cle (kyü′tə kəl) *n.* **1** the outer layer of skin of vertebrates; epidermis. **2** the strip of hardened or dead skin at the base of a fingernail or toenail. **3** *Botany.* a very thin film covering the surface of a plant. [< L *cuticula,* dim. of *cutis* skin]

cut·ie (kyü′tē) *n. Informal.* a cute person. Also, **cutey.**

cu·tin (kyü′tən) *n. Botany.* a waxy substance that is the chief ingredient of the outer skin of many plants. [< L *cutis* skin]

cu·tis (kyü′tis) *n.* the skin beneath the epidermis; derma. [< L]

cut·lass (kut′ləs) *n.* a short, heavy, slightly curved sword with a single-edged blade. [< F *coutelas* < L *culter* knife]

cut·ler (kut′lər) *n.* a person who makes, sells, or repairs knives, scissors, and other cutting instruments. [ME < OF *coutelier* < *coutel* small knife < L *cultellus,* dim. of *culter* knife]

cut·ler·y (kut′lər ē) *n.* **1** knives, forks, and spoons for table use. **2** knives, scissors, and other cutting instruments. **3** the business of a cutler.

cut·let (kut′lit) *n.* **1** a slice of meat from the leg or ribs for broiling or frying: *a veal cutlet.* **2** a flat, fried cake of chopped meat or fish; croquette. [< F *côtelette,* dim. of *côte* < L *costa* rib]

cut·line (kut′līn′) *n.* **1** a caption to an illustration, cartoon, etc. **2** *Cdn.* a survey or other line cut through bush.

cut·off (kut′of′) *n.* **1** the act of cutting off, especially the limit set for an activity, process, etc. **2** a short way across or through; a road or passage shorter than the one normally used. **3 a** a new passage cut by a river across a bend. **b** the water in the old channel, thus cut off. **4** a stopping of the passage of steam or working fluid to the cylinder of an engine. **5** the mechanism or device that does this. **6** the point in an electrical circuit at which a mechanism prevents the flow of current of certain frequencies to or from the circuit. **7** *Baseball.* the interception of a ball thrown to a base from the outfield. **8 cutoffs,** *pl. Informal.* jeans or other pants that have been cut to serve as shorts.

cut·out (kut′out′) *n.* **1** a shape or design that has been cut out or is to be cut out: *Some books for children have cutouts.* **2** a device that allows the exhaust gases of an internal combustion engine to pass straight into the air instead of going through a muffler. **3** a device for breaking an electric current.

cut·o·ver (kut′ō′vər) *adj.* from which the tress have been cut: *cutover land.*

cut·price (kut′prīs′) *adj. Brit.* cut-rate.

cut·purse (kut′pèrs′) *n.* thief; pickpocket. [from the former practice of stealing purses by cutting them from belts, where they used to be hung]

cut·rate (kut′rāt′) *adj.* having or featuring a price or prices below what is usual: *cut-rate merchandise, a cut-rate store.*

cut·ter (kut′ər) *n.* **1** a person who cuts, especially one whose work is cutting cloth to be made up into clothes. **2** a tool or machine for cutting: *a meat cutter.* **3** a small, light sleigh, usually pulled by one horse. **4** a kind of sleigh pulled as a trailer by a snowmobile. **5** a small sailboat with one mast. **6** a boat belonging to a warship, used to carry people and supplies to and from the ship. **7** a small, armed ship used for patrolling coastal waters.

cut·throat (kut′thrōt′) *n., adj.* —*n.* **1** murderer. **2** cutthroat trout. —*adj.* **1** murderous. **2** relentless; merciless: *cutthroat competition.*

cutthroat trout a large trout (*Salmo clarki*) distinguished by bright-red streaks under the lower jaw, found mainly in the Rocky Mountain region and highly valued as a game fish.

cut·ting (kut′ing) *n., adj.* —*n.* **1** something cut off or out; especially: **a** a small shoot cut from a plant to grow a new plant. **b** a newspaper or magazine clipping. **2** a place or way cut through high ground for a road, track etc. **3** the act of that cuts. **4** (*adjl.*) designed to cut; sharp or keen: *the cutting edge of a knife.* **5** (*adjl.*) on which things can be cut: *a cutting table.* —*adj.* **1** that hurts the feelings; sarcastic: *a cutting remark.* **2** cold and piercing: *a cutting wind.* —**cut′ting·ly,** *adv.*

cutting horse a saddle horse trained to be used in separating an individual cow, etc. from a herd.

cut·tle (kut′əl) *n.* cuttlefish.

cut·tle·bone (kut′əl bōn′) *n.* the hard internal shell of cuttlefish, used as a food supplement for caged birds and, in powder form, as a polishing agent.

cut·tle·fish (kut′əl fish′) *n., pl.* **-fish** or **-fish·es.** any of various marine molluscs (order Sepioidea) characterized by a broad flattened body and a thick, calcified internal shell and having ten sucker-bearing arms, two of which are longer tentacles used in capturing prey. Cuttlefish belong to the same class (Cephalopoda) as octopuses and squids. [*cuttle,* OE *cudele* cuttlefish]

cut·up (kut′up′) *n. Slang.* a person who shows off or behaves like a clown.

cut·wa·ter (kut′wot′ər *or* -wô′tər) *n.* **1** the front part of a ship's prow. **2** the wedge-shaped edge of a bridge pier, designed to break the force of the current.

cut·work (kut′wèrk′) *n.* openwork embroidery in which part of the cloth is cut away.

cut·worm (kut′wèrm′) *n.* the larva of any of various moths (family Noctuidae) that feeds on young plant stems at night, cutting them off near ground level. Cutworms are pests in gardens.

cu. yd. cubic yard(s).

CV *Cdn.* Cross of Valor.

C.V.O. Commander (of the Royal) Victorian Order.

C.V.S.M. Canadian Volunteer Service Medal.

C.W.A.C. or **CWAC** Canadian Women's Army Corps.

C.W.O. or **CWO** chief warrant officer.

cwt. hundredweight.

–cy *noun-forming suffix.* **1** the office, position, or rank of, as in *captaincy.* **2** the quality, state, condition, or fact of being, as in *bankruptcy.* [(directly or < F *-cie*) < L *-cia,* Gk. *-keia;* (directly or

hat, āge, fär; let, ēqual, tèrm; it, īce
hot, ōpen, ôrder; oil, out; cup, put, rüle,
əbove, takən, pencəl, lemən, circəs
ch, child; ng, long; sh, ship
th, thin; ᴛʜ, then; zh, measure

< F *-cie* or *-tie*) < L *-tia,* Gk. *-tia, -teia*]

cy·an·a·mide (sī an′ə mīd′ *or* sī an′ə mid) *n.* **1** a white or colorless crystalline chemical compound. *Formula:* CH_2N_2 **2** a salt of this compound.

cy·a·nate (sī′ə nāt′) *n.* a salt of cyanic acid.

cy·an·ic (sī an′ik) *adj.* **1** of cyanogen; containing cyanogen. **2** blue. [< Gk. *kyanos* dark blue]

cyanic acid a colorless, poisonous liquid. *Formula:* HOCN

cy·a·nide (sī′ə nīd′ *or* sī′ə nid) *n.* a salt of hydrocyanic acid, especially potassium cyanide (a powerful poison).

cy·a·nite (sī′ə nīt′) *n.* a silicate of aluminum usually occurring in blue, blade-shaped crystals. *Formula:* Al_2SiO_5 Also, **kyanite.** [< Gk. *kyanos* blue substance + E- *ite*]

cy·an·o·gen (sī an′ə jən) *n.* **1** a colorless, poisonous, flammable gas having the odor of bitter almonds. *Formula:* C_2N_2 **2** a univalent radical (-CN) consisting of one atom of carbon and one of nitrogen. [< F *cyanogène* < Gk. *kyanos* dark-blue substance + *-genēs* born, produced]

cy·a·no·sis (sī′ə nō′sis) *n.* blueness or lividness of the skin, caused by lack of oxygen in the blood. [< NL < Gk. *kyanōsis* dark-blue color < *kyanos* dark blue]

cy·a·not·ic (sī′ə not′ik) *adj.* of, having to do with, or affected with cyanosis.

cy·ber·nate (sī′bər nāt′) *v.* **—nat·ed, —nat·ing.** operate or control (a process, industry, etc.) by cybernation: *a cybernated bakery, a cybernated world.*

cy·ber·na·tion (sī′bər nā′shən) *n.* automation in manufacturing, etc. by means of computers.

cy·ber·net·ic (sī′bər net′ik) *adj.* of or having to do with cybernetics.

cy·ber·net·ics (sī′bər net′iks) *n.* the comparative study of complex calculating machines and the human nervous system in order to understand better the functioning of the human brain. [< Gk. *kybernētikos* of a pilot < *kybernētēs* pilot < *kybernain* steer]

cy·cad (sī′kad) *n.* any of an order (Cycadales) of large, palmlike, tropical or subtropical plants having long, fernlike leaves at the top of a thick, unbranched stem that resembles a column. There is only one surviving family (Cycadaceae) of cycads, which includes the sago palm. [< NL *cycas, -adis* < Gk. *kykas,* scribal mistake for *koïkas,* pl. of *koïx* palm]

cy·cla·mate (sī′klə māt′) *n.* any of a group of salts of sodium or calcium formerly extensively used as substitutes for sugar. [< *cyclo*hexyl -sulph*amate.* 20c.]

cyc·la·men (sī klə mən *or* sik′lə mən) *n.* any of a genus (*Cyclamen*) of plants of the primrose family, having heart-shaped leaves and showy white, purple, pink, or crimson flowers, whose five petals bend backwards. [< NL < L < Gk. *kyklaminos*]

cy·cle (sī′kəl) *n., v.* **-cled, -cling.** —*n.* **1** a period of time or complete process of growth or action that repeats itself in the same order: *The seasons of the year—spring, summer, autumn, and winter—make a cycle.* **2** a complete set or series. **3** all the stories, poems, legends, etc. about a great hero or event: *There is a cycle of stories about the adventures of King Arthur and his knights.* **4** a very long period of time; age. **5** a bicycle, tricycle, or motorcycle. **6** *Electricity.* a complete or double alternation or reversal of an alternating current. The number of cycles per second is the measure of frequency. **7** *Biology.* a recurring series of changes. **8** *Botany.* a closed circle or whorl of leaves. **9** *Astronomy.* an orbit or circle in the heavens: *the cycle of a planet.* **10** *Physics.* a series of operations by which a substance or operation is finally brought back to the initial state. **11** the series of strokes of a piston in the cylinder of an engine. —*v.* **1** pass through a cycle; occur over and over again in the same order. **2** ride a cycle, especially a bicycle. [< LL *cyclus* < Gk. *kyklos* wheel]

cy·clic (sī′klik *or* sik′lik) *adj.* **1** of a cycle. **2** moving or occurring in cycles. **3** *Chemistry.* **a** containing a ring of atoms. **b** of or having to do with an arrangement of atoms in a ring or closed chain.

cy·cli·cal (sī′klə kəl *or* sik′lə kəl) *adj.* cyclic.

cy·clist (sī′klist) *n.* the rider of a cycle, especially a bicycle or motorcycle.

cyclo– *combining form.* **1** circle or circular, as in *cycloid.* **2** cyclic, as in *cyclopropane.* [< Gk. *kyklos* wheel]

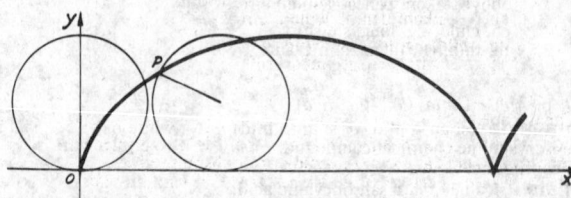

cy·cloid (sī'kloid) *adj., n.* —*adj.* like a circle. —*n. Geometry.* a curve traced by a point on the circumference, on a radius, or on a prolonged radius of a circle when the circle is rolled along a straight line and kept in the same plane.

cy·clom·e·ter (sī klom'ə tər) *n.* an instrument that records the number of revolutions that a wheel makes, used to measure the distance that a vehicle travels.

cy·clone (sī'klōn) *n.* **1** a severe windstorm resulting from a condition of low pressure, with moving in a spiral toward the centre, where the air pressure is lowest. Hurricanes and typhoons are cyclones. **2** a low-pressure condition or weather system that can produce such storms. Cyclones are sometimes thousands of kilometres across. **3** any violent windstorm with spiralling winds, such as a tornado. [< Gk. *kyklōn,* ppr. of *kykloein* move around in a circle]

cy·clon·ic (sī klon'ik) *adj.* **1** of a cyclone. **2** like a cyclone.

cy·clon·i·cal (sī klon'ə kəl) *adj.* cyclonic. —**cy·clon'i·cal·ly,** *adv.*

cy·clo·pae·di·a (sī'klə pē'dē ə) See **cyclopedia.**

cy·clo·pae·dic (sī klə pē'dik) See **cyclopedic.**

Cy·clo·pe·an (sī'klə pē'ən) *adj.* **1** of or having to do with the Cyclopes. **2** Usually, **cyclopean,** huge; gigantic.

cy·clo·pe·di·a or **cy·clo·pae·di·a** (sī'klə pē'dē ə) *n.* a book giving information on all branches of one subject. A cyclopedia is different from an encyclopedia in that it usually does not go beyond one field or classification of knowledge. [shortened form of *encyclopedia*]

cy·clo·pe·dic or **cy·clo·pae·dic** (sī'klə pē'dik) *adj.* **1** wide and varied. **2** having to do with a cyclopedia.

cy·clo·pro·pane (sī'klə prō'pān) *n.* a colorless, flammable gas used as an anaesthetic. *Formula:* C_3H_6

Cy·clops (sī'klops) *n., pl.* **Cy·clo·pes** (sī klō'pēz). *Greek mythology.* one of a group of one-eyed giants. [< L < Gk. *Kyklōps < kyklos* circle + *ōps* eye]

cy·clo·ram·a (sī'klə ram'ə) *n.* **1** a large picture of a landscape, battle, etc. on the wall of a circular room. **2** *Theatre.* a curved screen crossing the width of a stage and used as a background for the scenery. [< *cyclo-* + Gk. *horama* spectacle]

cy·clo·tron (sī'klə tron') *n.* a type of accelerator in which charged particles are accelerated in a spiral inside two hollow, D-shaped metal electrodes. [< *cyclo-* + *-tron* (as in *electron*)]

cyg·net (sig'nit) *n.* a young swan. [ME < OF *cygne* < L *cygnus,* earlier *cycnus* < Gk. *kyknos*]
☞ *Hom.* **signet.**

Cyg·nus (sig'nəs) *n. Astronomy.* a northern constellation in the Milky Way, thought of by the ancients as being arranged in the shape of a swan. [< L *cygnus* swan]

cyl. cylinder; cylindrical.

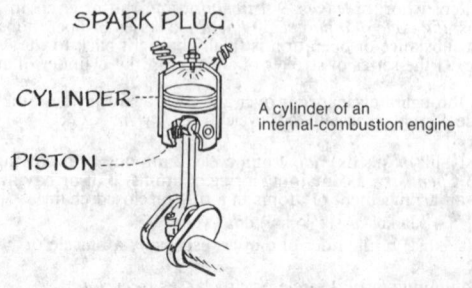

A cylinder of an internal-combustion engine

cyl·in·der (sil'ən dər) *n.* **1** a solid bounded by two equal, parallel

circles and a curved surface, formed by moving a straight line of fixed length so that its ends always lie on the two parallel circles. **2** the volume of such a solid. **3** any long, round object, solid or hollow, with flat ends: *Rollers and tin cans are cylinders.* **4** the part of a revolver that contains chambers for cartridges. **5** the piston chamber of an engine. **6 a** a vessel or container having the form of a cylinder. **b** its contents. [< L *cylindrus* < Gk. *kylindros < kylindein* to roll]

cy·lin·dric (sə lin'drik) *adj.* cylindrical.

cy·lin·dri·cal (sə lin'drə kəl) *adj.* shaped like a cylinder; having the form of a cylinder. —**cy·lin'dri·cal·ly,** *adv.*

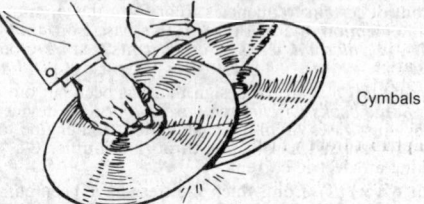

Cymbals

cym·bal (sim'bəl) *n.* one of a pair of metal plates, used as a musical instrument. Cymbals are struck together to make a ringing sound. A cymbal can also be struck with a drumstick, hammer, or wire brush. [OE < L *cymbalum* < Gk. *kymbalon < kymbē* hollow of a vessel]
☞ *Hom.* **symbol.**

cyme (sīm) *n. Botany.* a flower cluster in which there is a flower at the top of the main stem and of each branch of the cluster. The flower in the centre opens first. The sweet william has cymes. [< F < L *cyma* < Gk. *kyma* something swollen, sprout < *kyein* be pregnant]

cy·mose (sī'mōs *or* sī mōs') *adj. Botany.* **1** having a cyme or cymes. **2** like a cyme.

Cym·ric (kim'rik) *n., adj.* —*n.* **1** Welsh. **2** the group of Celtic languages that includes Briton, Cornish, and Welsh; the Brythonic languages. —*adj.* **1** of or having to do with the Brythons or their languages. **2** of or having to do with the Welsh people or Welsh.

Cym·ry (kim'rē) *n.* **1** the branch of the Celts that includes the Welsh, Cornish, and Bretons. **2** the Welsh people.

cyn·ic (sin'ik) *n., adj.* —*n.* **1** a person inclined to believe that the motives for people's actions are insincere and selfish. **2** a sneering, sarcastic person. **3 Cynic,** in ancient Greece, a member of a group of philosophers who taught that self-control is the essential part of virtue. They despised pleasure, money, and personal comfort. —*adj.* **1** cynical. **2 Cynic,** of or having to do with the Cynics or their doctrines. [< L *cynicus* < Gk. *kynikos* doglike < *kyōn* dog]

cyn·i·cal (sin'ə kəl) *adj.* **1** doubting the sincerity and goodness of others. **2** sneering; sarcastic. —**cyn'i·cal·ly,** *adv.* —**cyn'i·cal·ness,** *n.*
☞ *Syn.* **1. Cynical, pessimistic** = doubting and mistrustful. **Cynical** emphasizes the idea of doubting the honesty, sincerity, and disinterestedness of people and their motives for doing things: *People cannot make friends with a person who is cynical about friendship.* **Pessimistic** emphasizes the idea of always looking on the dark side of things and expecting the most unpleasant or worst things to happen: *He has a very pessimistic attitude toward the value of his work.*

cyn·i·cism (sin'ə siz'əm) *n.* **1** a cynical quality or disposition. **2** a cynical remark. **3 Cynicism,** the doctrines of the Cynics.

cy·no·sure (sī'nə shūr' *or* sin'ə shūr') *n.* **1** something that is the centre of attraction or interest: *He was the cynosure of all eyes.* **2 Cynosure,** *Astronomy.* **a** the constellation containing the North Star, now usually called Ursa Minor, or Little Bear. **b** the North Star. **3** something used for guidance or direction. [< L *Cynosura* (def. 3) < Gk. *kynosoura* dog's tail + *kyōn* dog + *oura* tail]

Cyn·thi·a (sin'thē ə) *n.* **1** Artemis, the goddess of the moon. **2** moon.

cy·pher (sī'fər) See **cipher.**

cy·press (sī'prəs) *n.* **1** any of a genus (*Cupressus*) of evergreen trees found in North America, S Europe, and Asia, having small, scalelike, overlapping leaves and round, upright cones. There are no cypresses native to Canada. **2** any of several related trees, such as the yellow cypress. **3** (*adj.*) designating the family (Cupressaceae) of coniferous trees that includes the true cypresses, junipers, and arborvitae. **4** any of various other coniferous trees, such as the bald cypress. [ME < OF < L *cupressus* < Gk. *kyparissos*]

Cyp·ri·an (sip'rē ən) *n., adj.* —*n.* a native or inhabitant of Cyprus, an island in the E Mediterranean Sea, south of Turkey. —*adj.* of or having to do with Cyprus or its people.

cyp·ri·nid (sip'rə nid) *n., adj.* —*n.* any of a family (Cyprinidae) of mainly soft-finned, freshwater fishes found in North America, Africa, Europe, and Asia, having toothless jaws, sometimes with

barbels. Carps, minnows, and goldfish are cyprinids. —*adj.* of, having to do with, or designating this family of fishes. The cyprinid family is also called the minnow family. [< L *cyprinus* carp (< Gk.) + E *-oid* resembling (< Gk. *eidos* form)]

cyp·ri·noid (sip′rə noid′) *n. or adj.* ciprinid.

Cyp·ri·ot (sip′rē ət) *n., adj.* —*n.* a native or inhabitant of Cyprus, an island country in the E Mediterranean sea, south of Turkey. —*adj.* of or having to do with Cyprus or its people.

cyp·ri·pe·di·um (sip′rə pē′dē əm) *n., pl.* **-di·a** (-dē ə). **1** any of a genus (*Cypripedium*) of orchids having large, drooping flowers with a pouchlike lip. See also **lady's-slipper. 2** any of a genus (*Paphiopedilum*) of tropical Old World orchids which have been much used by orchid breeders to produce cultivated varieties and hybrids. This genus is closely related to the genus *Cypripedium*, and is included in that genus by some authorities. [< NL *cypripedium*, apparently, alteration of *cypripodium* < Gk. *Kypris* Aphrodite + *podion*, dim. of *pous, podos* foot]

Cy·ril·lic (si ril′ik) *adj.* of, having to do with, or designating an ancient Slavic alphabet from which the Russian, Bulgarian, and Serbian alphabets have developed. [< St. *Cyril*, an apostle to the Slavs in the 9th century, who is traditionally supposed to have invented it]

cyst (sist) *n.* **1** an abnormal, saclike growth in animals or plants that usually contains fluid and has no outside opening. **2** a saclike structure in animals or plants. [< NL *cystis* < Gk. *kystis* pouch, bladder]

cyst·ic (sis′tik) *adj.* **1** of or like a cyst. **2** having a cyst or cysts.

–cyte *combining form.* cell: *leucocyte = a white* (*blood*) *cell.* [< Gk. *kytos* anything hollow]

Cyth·er·e·a (sith′ər ē′ə) *n. Greek mythology.* Aphrodite, the goddess of love and beauty.

cyto– *combining form.* cell; cells: *cytology = the study of cells.* Also, **cyt-** before vowels. [< Gk. *kytos* anything hollow]

cy·to·ge·net·ics (sī′tō jə net′iks) *n. Biology.* the study of the relation of cells to the phenomena of heredity and variation.

cy·tol·o·gist (sī tol′ə jist) *n.* a person trained in cytology, especially one whose work it is.

cy·tol·o·gy (sī tol′ə jē) *n.* the branch of biology that deals with the formation, structure, and function of the cells of animals and plants. [< Gk. *kytos* receptacle, cell + E *-logy*]

cy·to·plasm (sī′tə plaz′əm) *n. Biology.* the living substance or protoplasm of a cell, exclusive of the nucleus. [< Gk. *kytos* receptacle, cell + E *-plasm* something moulded (< Gk. *plasma*)]

cy·to·plas·mic (sī′tə plaz′mik) *adj.* having to do with cytoplasm.

hat, āge, fär; let, ēqual, tèrm; it, īce
hot, ōpen, ôrder; oil, out; cup, put, rüle,
əbove, takən, pencəl, lemən, circəs

ch, child; ng, long; sh, ship
th, thin; ŦH, then; zh, measure

CZ Canal Zone.

czar or **tsar** (zär) *n.* **1** emperor. It was the title of the former emperors of Russia. **2** autocrat; a person with absolute power: *Al Capone was a czar of crime.* [< Russian *tsar* < Old Church Slavic < Gothic < L *Caesar* Caesar]

czar·das (chär′däsh) *n.* **1** a complex Hungarian national dance having a slow first section followed by a fast one. **2** the music for such a dance. [< Hungarian *csárdás*]

czar·dom or **tsar·dom** (zär′dəm) *n.* **1** the position or power of a czar. **2** the territory ruled by a czar.

czar·e·vitch or **tsar·e·vitch** (zär′ə vich′) *n.* **1** the eldest son of a Russian czar. **2** the son of a Russian czar. [< Russian *tsarevich*]

cza·rev·na or **tsa·rev·na** (zä rev′nə) *n.* **1** the daughter of a Russian czar. **2** the wife of a czarevitch. [< Russian *tsarevna*]

cza·ri·na or **tsa·ri·na** (zä rē′nə) *n.* the wife of a czar; a Russian empress. [< G *Zarin* (earlier *Czarin*), fem. of *Zar* < Russian *tsar.* See CZAR.]

czar·ism or **tsar·ism** (zär′iz əm) *n.* **1** the Russian government under the czars. **2** autocratic government; despotism.

czar·ist or **tsar·ist** (zär′ist) *n., adj.* —*n.* a supporter of the government of the czars in Russia. —*adj.* **1** of or having to do with the czars or Russia under the czars. **2** characteristic of czarism.

Czech (chek) *n., adj.* —*n.* **1** a native or inhabitant of Czechoslovakia, a country in Central Europe, especially of Bohemia, Moravia, or Silesia, which are provinces of Czechoslovakia. **2** the Slavic language of the Czechs. —*adj.* of or having to do with Czechoslovakia, its people, or their language.

Czech·ish (chek′ish) *adj.* Czech.

Czech·o·slo·vak (chek′ə slō′vak) *n., adj.* —*n.* a native or inhabitant of Czechoslovakia. —*adj.* of or having to do with Czechoslovakia or its people.

Czech·o·slo·va·ki·an (chek′ə slō vak′ē ən) *adj. or n.* Czechoslovak.

Dd

d or **D** (dē) *n., pl.* **d's** or **D's. 1** the fourth letter of the English alphabet. **2** any speech sound represented by this letter. **3** a person or thing identified as *d*, especially the fourth in a series. **4 D, a** a grade rating a person's work or performance as being below average and barely acceptable. **b** a person receiving this rating. **5** *Music.* **a** the second tone in the scale of C major. **b** a symbol representing this tone. **c** a key, etc. of a musical instrument that produces this tone. **d** the scale or key that has D as its keynote. **6** the Roman numeral for 500. **7 D,** something shaped like the letter D. **8** (*adj.*) of or being a D or d.

d 1 day. **2** deci- (an SI prefix). **3** *d* diameter.

d. 1 died; dead. **2** *Historical.* in the United Kingdom and some other countries, penny or pence. **3** dime. **4** dollar. **5** day. **6** date. **7** delete. **8** daughter. **9** degree. **10** dyne.

D 1 deuterium. **2** *Physics.* density.

D. 1 Doctor (in academic degrees). **2** December. **3** *U.S. Politics.* Democrat; Democratic. **4** Dutch. **5** Duke. **6** Duchess. **7** Don (Spanish title). **8** God (L *deus*). **9** Lord (L *dominus*).

da deca- (an SI prefix).

D.A. *U.S.* District Attorney.

dab¹ (dab) *v.* **dabbed, dab·bing;** *n.* —*v.* **1** touch lightly; pat with something soft or moist; tap: *He dabbed at the spot with his napkin.* **2** put on with light strokes: *She dabbed some powder on her nose.* —*n.* **1** a quick, light touch or blow; pat; tap. **2** a small, soft or moist mass: *a dab of butter.* **3** a little bit. [ME] —**dab′ber,** *n.*

dab² (dab) *n.* any of various flounders, especially any of a genus (*Limanda*) of fishes found in the North Pacific and North Atlantic oceans. [origin uncertain]

dab³ (dab) *n. Informal.* expert. [origin uncertain]

dab·ble (dab′əl) *v.* **-bled, -bling. 1** dip (hands, feet, etc.) in and out of water; splash. **2** work at a little; do in a half-hearted or superficial way: *to dabble at painting, to dabble in stocks.* [< Flemish *dabbelen*] —**dab′bler,** *n.*

da capo (dä kä′pō) *Italian. Music.* **1** from the beginning (a direction to repeat a passage). **2** the passage to be repeated. *Abbrev.:* d.c. [literally, from the head]

dace (dās) *n., pl.* **dace** or **daces. 1** any of several small freshwater cyprinid fishes of North America, such as the **pearl dace** (*Semotilus margarita*), common in Canadian waters from the Maritimes to the Rocky Mountains. **2** a small, slender freshwater cyprinid fish (*Leuciscus leuciscus*) of Europe. [ME *darse* < OF *dars* dart < Med.L *darsus*]

da·cha (däch′ə) *n.* a Russian summer cottage.

dachs·hund (dash′hund′ *or* daks′hund′; *German,* däks′hunt′) *n.* a breed of small dog having a long body, long, drooping ears, a slender muzzle, and very short legs. The dachshund was originally developed in Germany for hunting badgers. [< G *Dachshund* < *Dachs* badger + *Hund* dog]

Da·cia (dā′shə) *n.* an ancient Roman province in S Europe.

da·coit (də koit′) *n.* in India or Burma, a member of a gang of robbers. [< Hind. *dakait* < *daka* gang-robbery]

Da·cron (dak′ron *or* dā′kron) *n.* **1** *Trademark.* a synthetic polyester fibre used for dress fabrics, carpets, etc. **2** Sometimes, **dacron,** any similar fibre or a fabric, etc. made from it; terylene.

dac·tyl (dak′təl) *n.* a foot consisting of one strongly stressed syllable followed by two weakly stressed syllables or one long syllable followed by two short syllables. *Example:* "Táke her up ténderly." [< L < Gk. *daktylos* finger. Doublet of DATE².]

dac·tyl·ic (dak til′ik) *adj.* **1** of dactyls. **2** consisting of dactyls. —**dac′tyl·i·cal·ly,** *adv.*

dac·ty·lol·o·gy (dak′tə lol′ə jē) *n.* the language of signs made with fingers, such as used by the deaf. [< Gk. *daktylos* finger + E *-logy*]

dad (dad) *n. Informal.* father.

Da·da or **da·da** (dä′də) *n.* Dadaism.

Da·da·ism or **da·da·ism** (dä′də iz′əm) *n.* a style in art and literature developed during World War I, characterized by the use of unconventional materials and techniques, by witty satire of all previous art forms and methods, and by an attitude of revolt against existing standards. [< F *dada* horse, hobbyhorse (a child's word) + E *-ism*]

Da·da·ist or **da·da·ist** (dä′də ist) *n., adj.* —*n.* a follower of Dadaism. —*adj.* of or having to do with Dadaism. —**Dadaistic or dadaistic,** *adj.*

dad·dy (dad′ē) *n., pl.* **-dies.** *Informal.* father.

dad·dy–long·legs (dad′ē long′legz′) *n.sing. or pl.* **1** any of an order (Opiliones) of arachnids resembling spiders but having a rounded body without a "waist" and four pairs of very long, thin, bent legs. **2** *Brit.* crane fly.

da·do (dā′dō) *n., pl.* **-does** or **-dos. 1** *Architecture.* the part of a pedestal between the base and the cap. **2** the lower part of an inside wall when covered with a special finish of wood, wallpaper, etc. [< Ital. *dado* die² < L *datus* given]

dae·dal (dē′dəl) *adj. Poetic.* **1** ingenious; skilful: *the sculptor's daedal hand.* **2** intricately made; with complex ornamentation. **3** like a maze; complex. [< L < Gk. *daidalos* skilful; skilfully wrought < *daidallein* work cunningly]

Dae·da·li·an or **Dae·da·le·an** (di dā′lē ən *or* di dal′yən) *adj.* **1** skilful; ingenious. **2** intricate; mazelike.

Daed·al·us (ded′ə ləs *or* dē′də ləs) *n. Greek mythology.* a skilful builder who built the Labyrinth in Crete and who invented wings by means of which he and his son Icarus escaped from imprisonment in the Labyrinth.

dae·mon (dē′mən) *n.* **1** an attendant or guardian spirit. **2** *Greek mythology.* a supernatural being halfway between a god and a human being. [< L < Gk. *daimon*]

daf·fo·dil (daf′ə dil′) *n., adj.* —*n.* **1** any of various plants (genus *Narcissus*) of the amaryllis family having long, slender leaves and yellow or yellow-and-white flowers with a trumpet-shaped corona growing out from the centre of its petals. **2** the flower of any of these plants. **3** a bright yellow. —*adj.* bright yellow. [var. of *affodill* < VL *affodillus* < L < Gk. *asphodelos*]

daff·y (daf′ē) *adj.* **daff·i·er, daff·i·est.** *Informal.* **1** foolish; silly. **2** crazy; insane.

daffy on, crazy about: *The girl was daffy on the young soldier.*

daft (daft) *adj.* **1** silly; foolish. **2** crazy; insane. [OE (*ge)d fte* gentle] —**daft′ly,** *adv.* —**daft′ness,** *n.*

dag (dag) *n. Cdn.* a heavy, flat, double-edged triangular blade, used by the Indians as a weapon and tool. [< Cdn.F < F *dague* dagger]

D.A.G. Deputy Adjutant General.

dag·ger (dag′ər) *n., v.* —*n.* **1** a small weapon with a short pointed blade, used for stabbing. **2** *Printing.* a sign (†) to refer the reader to a footnote, a note at the back of the book, etc.

look daggers at, look at (someone or something) with hatred or anger.

—*v.* **1** stab with a dagger. **2** mark with a dagger sign. [probably < obs. *dag* stab]

da·go or **Da·go** (dā′gō) *n., pl.* **-gos** or **-goes.** *Derogatory slang.* a person of Spanish, Portuguese, or, nowadays especially, Italian origin. [supposedly < *Diego* James, a common Spanish name]

da·guerre·o·type (də ger′ə tīp′ *or* də ger′ē ə tīp′) *n.* **1** an early photographic process. In daguerreotype, the pictures were made on light-sensitive silver-coated metal plates. **2** a picture made in this way. [after L. *Daguerre* (1789-1851), its inventor]

dahl·ia (dāl′yə *or* dal′yə) *n.* **1** any of a genus (*Dahlia*) of tall perennial plants of the composite family native to Mexico and Central America, including many cultivated varieties grown for their large, showy flower heads that appear in late summer and fall. **2** the flower head of a dahlia. [< NL; after A. *Dahl*, Swedish botanist]

Dail Eir·eann (dol′ âr′ən, dôl′, *or* doil′) the lower house of parliament of the Republic of Ireland. [< Irish *dáil* assembly, and *Éireann,* gen. of *Éire* Ireland]

dai·ly (dā′lē) *adj., n., pl.* **-lies;** *adv.* —*adj.* done, happening, or appearing every day, or every day but Sunday: *a daily paper, a daily visit.*

—*n.* a newspaper appearing every day, or every day but Sunday. —*adv.* every day; day by day.

daily double *Horse racing.* a bet or a form of betting in which a person bets on two horses at once in two separate races, usually the first two races of the day. To win the daily double, the bettor must have picked the winning horse in each of the two races.

dai·mio (dī′myō) *n., pl.* **-mio** or **-mios.** in Japan, one of the great feudal nobles who, from the 14th to the 19th century, were vassals of the emperor. [< Japanese < Chinese *dai* great + *mio* name]

dain·ti·ness (dān′tē nis) *n.* the quality of being dainty.

dain·ty (dān′tē) *adj.* **-ti·er, -ti·est;** *n., pl.* **-ties.** —*adj.* **1** having delicate beauty; pretty and graceful: *a dainty flower.* **2** having or showing delicate and refined tastes and feelings; particular: *She is dainty about her eating.* **3** overly refined and delicate; too particular. **4** good to eat; delicious: *a dainty morsel.* —*n.* something very good to eat; a delicious bit of food. [< OF *deinte* < L *dignitas* worthiness. Doublet of DIGNITY.] —**dain′ti·ly,** *adv.*
☛ *Syn. adj.* **1.** See note at **delicate.**

dai·qui·ri (dak′ər ē *or* dī′kər ē) *n.* a cocktail made from rum, lime juice, and sugar. [< *Daiquiri* Cuba]

dair·y (der′ē) *n., pl.* **dair·ies. 1** a room or building where milk and cream are kept and made into butter and cheese. **2** a business that processes and sells or distributes milk and milk products. **3** dairy farm. [ME *deierie* < *deie* maid (OE *dæge* breadmaker)]

dairy cattle cows kept to give milk for human consumption.

dairy farm a farm where milk and milk products are produced.

dair·y·ing (der′ē ing) *n.* the business of raising cows to produce milk and cream, or of making butter and cheese.

dair·y·maid (der′ē mād′) *n.* a girl or woman who works in a dairy.

dair·y·man (der′ē mən) *n., pl.* **-men. 1** a person who owns or manages a dairy farm. **2** a person who works in a dairy.

da·is (dā′is) *n.* a raised platform at one end of a hall or a large room. A throne, seats of honor, a lecture desk, etc. are set on a dais. [ME < OF *deis* < L *discus* quoit, dish < Gk. *diskos*. Doublet of DESK, DISCUS, DISH, and DISK.]

dai·sy (dā′zē) *n., pl.* **-sies. 1** any of several plants (genus *Chrysanthemum*) of the composite family, especially the ox-eye daisy or the Shasta daisy. Daisies have tall, leafy stems and showy flower heads consisting of a yellow central disk surrounded by usually white, petal-like ray flowers. **2** any of various other plants of the composite family having similar flowers, such as the **English daisy** (*Bellis perennis*) or the **Michaelmas daisies** (genus *Aster*). **3** the flower of any of these plants. **4** *Slang.* a first-rate person or thing. [OE *dæges ēage* day's eye]

Da·ko·ta (də kō′tə) *n., pl.* **-tas** or **-ta;** *adj.* —*n.* **1** a member of an Amerindian people living on the plains of southern Canada and the N United States. **2** the Siouan language of the Dakotas. —*adj.* of or having to do with the Dakotas or their language.

Da·lai La·ma (dä lī′ lä′mə) the chief priest of the religion of Lamaism in Tibet and Mongolia.

da·la·si (də lä′sē) *n., pl.* **dalasi.** the basic unit of money in The Gambia, divided into 100 butut. See table at **money.**

dale (dāl) *n.* valley. [OE *dæl*]

dalle (dal) *n.* dalles.

dalles (dal′əs *or* dalz) *n.pl. Cdn.* a narrow stretch of river between high rock walls, characterized by whirlpools, rapids, and treacherous currents. [< Cdn.F < F *dalle* gutter]

dal·li·ance (dal′ē əns) *n.* **1** flirtation; dallying. **2** playing; trifling.

Dall sheep (dol) *Cdn.* a white North American sheep (*Ovis dalli*) of the western mountains found from northern British Columbia to the Arctic Ocean. [after W.H. *Dall* (1845-1927), American naturalist]

Dall's sheep Dall sheep.

dal·ly (dal′ē) *v.* **-lied, -ly·ing. 1** loiter; linger idly; waste time: *He was late because he dallied along the way. She dallied away the whole afternoon.* **2** play or toy (*with*). **3** behave in a playful manner, especially flirt with a person. [< OF *dalier* chat] —**dal′ly·ing·ly,** *adv.*
☛ *Syn.* **2.** See note at **trifle.**

Dal·ma·tian (dal mā′shən) *n., adj.* —*n.* **1** a breed of medium-sized, short-haired dog, usually white with black spots; coach dog. **2** a native or inhabitant of Dalmatia, a region in Yugoslavia. —*adj.* of or having to do with Dalmatia or its people.

Dal·to·ni·an (dol tō′nē ən *or* dôl tō′nē ən) *adj., n.* —*adj.* **1** of or having to do with John Dalton (1766-1844), an English chemist and physicist who described color-blindness and was himself color-blind. **2** of or suggestive of his writings and theories. **3** of or having to do with color-blindness. —*n.* a person who is color-blind.

Dal·ton·ism or **dal·ton·ism** (dol′tə niz′əm *or* dôl′tə niz′əm) *n.* color-blindness, especially the inability to distinguish red from green. [< F *daltonisme* < John *Dalton* + *-isme* ism. See DALTONIAN.]

dam¹ (dam) *n., v.* **dammed, dam·ming.** —*n.* **1** a wall built to hold back flowing water. **2** the water held back by a dam. **3** anything resembling a dam. **4** on the Prairies, a reservoir of water collected from the spring thaw and from rainfall, used for watering cattle, etc.; dugout; pothole. —*v.* **1** provide with a dam; hold back by means of a dam: *Beavers had dammed the stream.* **2** hold back; block: *He tried to dam back his tears.* [ME < MLG or MDu. *dam*; akin to OE *fordemman* dam up] —**dam′like′,** *adj.*
☛ *Hom.* **damn.**

dam² (dam) *n.* **1** the female parent of four-footed animals. **2** *Archaic.* mother. [var. of *dame*]
☛ *Hom.* **damn.**

dam·age (dam′ij) *n., v.* **-aged, -ag·ing.** —*n.* **1** injury or harm that lessens value or usefulness. **2** *Slang.* cost; price: *What's the damage?* **3 damages,** *pl.* money claimed by law or paid to make up for some harm done to a person or his property. —*v.* injure or harm so as to lessen value or usefulness; harm; hurt: *I damaged my sweater in football practice.* [ME < OF < *dam* < L *damnum* loss, hurt] —**dam′age·a·ble,** *adj.* —**dam′ag·ing·ly,** *adv.*
☛ *Syn. v.* See note at **harm.**

dam·a·scene (dam′ə sēn′ *or* dam′ə sēn′) *v.* **-scened, -scen·ing;** *n., adj.* —*v.* ornament (metal) with inlaid gold or silver or with a wavy design. —*n.* ornamentation of this kind. —*adj.* of, having, or resembling such ornament. [< L *Damascenus* < Gk. *Damaskēnos* of Damascus]

Dam·a·scene (dam′ə sēn′ *or* dam′ə sēn′) *adj., n.* —*adj.* of or having to do with the city of Damascus. —*n.* a native or inhabitant of Damascus.

Damascus steel a kind of ornamented steel, used in making swords, etc.

dam·ask (dam′əsk) *n., adj., v.* —*n.* **1** reversible linen, silk, or cotton fabric with woven designs. **2** a linen material of this type, used especially for tablecloths and serviettes. **3** damascened metal. **4** a rose color; pink. —*adj.* **1** made of damask. **2** pink; rose-colored: *damask cheeks.* **3** of or named after the city of Damascus. —*v.* **1** damascene. **2** weave with the design of damask fabric. [< L *Damascus* < Gk. *Damaskos* Damascus]

dame (dām) *n.* **1 Dame, a** in the United Kingdom, the title of a woman who belongs to an order of knighthood. It is used before the given name. **b** the legal title of the wife or widow of a knight or baronet. **2** *Archaic.* the woman in authority in a household. **3** *Archaic.* lady. **4** an elderly woman. **5** *Slang.* any woman or girl. [ME < OF < L *domina* mistress]

damn (dam) *v., n., adj., adv., interj.* —*v.* **1** declare to be bad or inferior; condemn: *The throne speech was damned by the press.* **2** cause to fail; ruin. **3** swear at; curse. **4** doom to eternal punishment; condemn to hell. **5** prove the guilt of (a person): *damning evidence.*
damn with faint praise, praise with so little enthusiasm as to condemn.
—*n.* **1** an utterance of *damn* as a curse. **2** *Slang.* the smallest amount or degree: *not worth a damn. He didn't care a damn.* —*adj. or adv. Slang.* damned (*used as an intensifier*): *It's a damn shame. She's a damn good writer.* —*interj.* an exclamation of anger, frustration, etc. [ME < OF *damner* < L *damnare* condemn < *damnum* loss]
☛ *Hom.* **dam.**

dam·na·ble (dam′nə bəl) *adj.* **1** abominable; outrageous; detestable. **2** deserving damnation. —**dam′na·ble·ness,** *n.* —**dam′na·bly,** *adv.*

dam·na·tion (dam nā′shən) *n.* **1** damning or being damned; condemnation. **2** a condemnation to eternal punishment. **3** a curse.

dam·na·to·ry (dam′nə tô′rē) *adj.* damning; assigning to damnation; condemnatory.

damned (damd) *adj., adv.* —*adj.* **1** condemned to eternal punishment. **2** (*noml.*) **the damned,** *pl.* all the souls condemned to eternal punishment. **3** *Slang.* detestable or abominable (*used as an intensifier*): *That's a damned lie! When we got there the damned place was closed.* **4** *Slang.* extraordinary (*used in the superlative*): *It was the damnedest thing I ever saw.*

do (one's) **damnedest,** *Informal.* do one's best or utmost: *She'll do her damnedest to get the job done on time.* —*adv. Slang.* very: *He should be damned glad to get the work.*

Dam·o·cles (dam′ə klēz′) *n.* a flatterer and courtier of

Dionysius, King of Syracuse. Damocles thought Dionysius must be the happiest of men, but Dionysius asked him to share the happiness of a king. He gave a banquet for Damocles, seating his guest beneath a naked sword that hung above his head by a single hair. By this means Damocles was made aware of the dangers surrounding kings.

sword of Damocles, any imminent danger.

dam·oi·selle (dam′ə zel′) *n. Archaic.* damsel.

Da·mon (dā′mən) *n. Legend.* a man who pledged his life for his friend Pythias (or Phintias), who had been sentenced to death.
Damon and Pythias, any loyal and devoted friends.

dam·o·sel or **dam·o·zel** (dam′ə zel′ *or* dam′ə zel′) *n. Archaic.* damsel.

damp (damp) *adj., n., v.* —*adj.* slightly wet; moist. —*n.*
1 moisture: *One could feel the damp in the morning air.*
2 something that checks or deadens: *His ill-humored objections put a damp on our spirits.* **3** any foul or explosive gas that collects in mines, such as chokedamp or firedamp: *The mine disaster was caused by exploding damp.*
—*v.* **1** moisten; dampen. **2** slow down the combustion of a fire by cutting off most of the air supply: *She damped down the fire for the night.* **3** discourage; check. **4** *Music.* stop the vibrations of (a string, etc.). [< MDu. or MLG *damp* vapor] —**damp′ly,** *adv.*
—**damp′ness,** *n.*
☛ *Syn. adj.* **Damp, moist, humid** = rather wet. **Damp** means more wet than dry, although not completely covered or soaked with liquid, and often suggests the idea that the wetness is unpleasant or unwanted: *This house is damp in rainy weather.* **Moist** suggests less wetness than **damp,** and often implies a pleasant or desirable degree of wetness: *Keep the soil moist.* **Humid** is literary or scientific, but is used commonly to describe a high degree of moisture in the air: *In the East the air is humid in summer.*

damp·en (dam′pən) *v.* **1** make moist or slightly wet: *We dampen clothes before ironing them.* **2** deaden; depress; discourage.
—**damp′en·er,** *n.*

damp·er (dam′pər) *n.* **1** a person or thing that discourages or depresses. **2** a movable plate to control the draft in a stove or furnace. **3** *Music.* **a** a device for checking vibration and reducing the volume of sound, especially of piano strings. **b** a mute for muffling the sound of a horn, etc. **4** *Electricity.* **a** a device for checking the vibration of a magnetic needle. **b** a piece of copper in or near the poles of a synchronous machine to decrease hunting.
put a damper on, suppress; curb; curtail; squelch: *The chairman put a damper on every suggestion the committee made.*

damp·ing–off (damp′ing of′) *n.* the decaying of newly planted seedlings, cuttings, etc. at the surface of the ground.

dam·sel (dam′zəl) *n.* a maiden or a young girl. [ME *dameisele* < OF, ult. < L *domina* lady, mistress. Doublet of DEMOISELLE.]

damsel fly of a suborder (Zygoptera) of insect resembling dragonflies but smaller and having the wings closed together vertically over the back when at rest.

dam·son (dam′zən) *n.* **1** a small Asiatic tree (*Prunus institia*) of the rose family cultivated for its small, dark-purple, edible plums. **2** the fruit of this tree, having an acid taste and used especially in jams and preserves. [< L (*prunum*) *damascenum* (plum) of Damascus]

dan (dan) *n. Cdn.* in the North: **1** a sealskin used as a container for oil. **2** a buoy made of inflated sealskin or sheepskin sewn airtight, used as a mark in deep-sea fishing. [origin uncertain]

Dan (dan) *n.*
from Dan to Beersheba, from one end of the country to the other. [< the names of two towns in ancient Palestine, *Dan,* at the northern boundary, and *Beersheba,* at the southern boundary]

Dan. 1 Daniel. **2** Danish.

Da·na·id or **Da·na·ïd** (dan′ē id) *n.* one of the Danaides.

Da·na·i·des or **Da·na·ï·des** (də nā′ə dēz′) *n.pl.*
Greek mythology. the fifty daughters of Danaus, King of Argus. All but one killed their husbands on their wedding night, and were condemned to draw water with a sieve forever in Hades.

dance (dans) *v.* **danced, danc·ing;** *n.* —*v.* **1** move in rhythm, usually in time with music. **2** do or take part in (a dance). **3** jump up and down; move in a lively way. **4** bob up and down. **5** cause to dance; lead or conduct by dancing: *He danced his partner across the ballroom floor.*
dance attendance on, wait on often and attentively; be excessively polite and obedient to.
—*n.* **1** a movement in rhythm, usually in time with music. **2** some special groups of steps, etc: *The waltz and fox trot were the dances she knew best.* **3** the art of dancing. **4** one round of dancing. **5** a piece of music for dancing or in a dance rhythm. **6** a party where people dance. **7** a movement up and down; lively movement. **8** the dance, the art of dancing; ballet. **9** (*adjl.*) of or for dancing.
lead someone a dance, cause a person trouble, especially by luring him into a vain pursuit.
[ME < OF *danser,* probably < Gmc.] —**danc′ing·ly,** *adv.*

hat, āge, fär; let, ēqual, tèrm; it, īce
hot, ōpen, ôrder; oil, out; cup, pùt, rüle,
əbove, takən, pencəl, lemən, circəs
ch, child; ng, long; sh, ship
th, thin; ᴛʜ, then; zh, measure

dance hall a public hall or room for dancing.

dance of death a representation of a medieval dance in which a skeleton, symbolizing Death, dances with people to remind them of human mortality.

danc·er (dan′sər) *n.* **1** a person who dances. **2** a person whose occupation is dancing.

dan·de·li·on (dan′də lī′ən) *n.* any of a genus (*Taraxacum*) of plants of the composite family, native to Europe and Asia but now found throughout the temperate regions of North America, having long, often toothed leaves radiating from the base of the plant and a single, bright-yellow head made up of many ray flowers. The common dandelion (*T. officinale*) occurs as a weed throughout Canada and is also grown for its edible leaves and flowers. [< F *dent de lion* lion's tooth; from its toothed leaves]

dan·der (dan′dər) *n. Informal.* temper; anger.
get (one's) dander up, get angry; lose one's temper. [origin uncertain]

Dan·die Din·mont (dan′dē din′mont) a breed of small terrior originally developed in the border country of England and Scotland, having a long body, long ears, short legs, and a rough coat. [< *Dandie Dinmont* (a character in Sir W. Scott's *Guy Mannering*), who owned such terriers]

dan·dle (dan′dəl) *v.* **-dled, -dling. 1** move (a child, etc.) up and down on one's knee or in one's arms. **2** pet; pamper. [? < earlier Ital. *dandolare,* var. of *dondolare* swing] —**dan′dler,** *n.*

dan·druff (dan′drəf) *n.* small, whitish scales that flake off the scalp. [origin uncertain]

dan·dy (dan′dē) *n., pl.* **-dies;** *adj.* **-di·er, di·est.** —*n.* **1** a man who is too careful of his dress and appearance. **2** *Slang.* anything that is excellent or pleasing. —*adj.* **1** of a dandy; too carefully dressed. **2** excellent; first-rate: *Everything is just dandy.* [originally Scottish, ? < *Dandy,* a Scottish var. of *Andrew*]

Dane (dān) *n.* **1** a native or inhabitant of Denmark, a country in N Europe. **2** a person of Danish descent. **3** *Historical.* a person from any part of what is now Scandinavia: *King Alfred fought many battles against the Danes.*
☛ *Hom.* deign.

Dane·geld or **dane·geld** (dān′geld′) *n.* from the 10th to 12th centuries, an annual tax levied in Britain to buy off the Danish invaders, later continued as a land tax. [ME *Dane* Dane (< ON) + ON *gield* payment]

Dane·law (dān′lo′ *or* -lô′) *n.* **1** a set of laws enforced by the Danes when they held NE England in the ninth and tenth centuries A.D. **2** the part of England under these laws.

dan·ger (dān′jər) *n.* **1** a chance of harm; nearness to harm; risk or peril: *A mountain climber's life is full of danger.* **2** anything that may cause harm: *Hidden rocks are a danger to ships.*
in danger of, liable to (with the accompanying threat of injury, harm, or death): *The old bridge is in danger of collapsing. The sick man is in danger of dying.*
[ME < OF *dangier* < L *dominium* sovereignty < *dominus* master]
☛ *Syn.* **1. Danger, peril** = threat of harm. **Danger** is the general word, always suggesting there is a definite chance of harm, but the harm is not always near or certain: *Miners at work are always in danger.* **Peril** suggests great harm is very near at hand and probable: *When a mine caves in, the miners are in peril.*

dan·ger·ous (dān′jər əs) *adj.* likely to cause harm; not safe; risky. —**dan′ger·ous·ly,** *adv.* —**dan′ger·ous·ness,** *n.*

dan·gle (dang′gəl) *v.* **-gled, -gling. 1** hang and swing loosely: *The curtain cord dangles.* **2** hold or carry (something) so that it swings loosely: *The nurse dangled the toys in front of the baby.* **3** be a hanger-on or follower: *He was always dangling after the older boys.* **4** hold before a person as a temptation: *to dangle false hopes before a person.* [< Scand.; cf. Danish *dangle*] —**dan′gler,** *n.*

dangling participle a participle, past or present, that is not logically or grammatically attached to the noun or pronoun it is intended to modify. Also called **unattached participle.**
☛ *Usage.* The **dangling participle** can have ambiguous and often ludicrous effects. Thus, in *Swimming in the pond, the car was out of sight,* the participle *swimming* seems to refer to the car, which is logically ludicrous. Such a faulty sentence can be improved in several ways. The **dangling participle** can be attached to a noun or pronoun capable of modification: *Swimming in the pond, I could not see the car.* The **participial phrase** can be replaced by a clause: *when I was swimming in the pond, I could not see the car.* Do not confuse a phrase containing a dangling or unattached participle with an **absolute phrase** (see **absolute,** def. 8).

Dan·iel (dan′yəl) *n.* **1** in the Bible, a Hebrew prophet whose great faith in God kept him unharmed in the lions' den (Dan. 6:16-27). **2** an upright judge or other person of great wisdom.

Dan·ish (dā′nish) *adj., n.* —*adj.* of or having to do with Denmark, the Danes, or their language.
—*n.* **1** the Germanic language of the Danes. **2 the Danish,** *pl.* the people of Denmark. **3** *Informal.* Danish pastry: *Let's have a Danish for dessert.* [OE *Denisc*]

Danish pastry 1 a rich, flaky pastry made with yeast. **2** a piece of such pastry.

dank (dangk) *adj.* unpleasantly damp; moist; wet: *The cave was dark, dank, and chilly.* [ME; cf. Swedish *dank* marshy spot]
—**dank′ly,** *adv.* —**dank′ness,** *n.*

danse ma·ca·bre (däns mä kä′brə) *French.* dance of death.

dan·seur (dän sœr′) *French.* a male dancer, especially one in a ballet company. [< OF *danser.* See DANCE.]

dan·seuse (dän sœz′) *n., pl.* **-seuses** (-sœz′). a female dancer, especially in a ballet. [< F]

Dan·u·bi·an (dan yü′bē ən) *adj.* of or having to do with the Danube River or the people living near it.

Daph·ne (daf′nē) *n. Greek mythology.* a nymph who was pursued by Apollo and was saved by being changed into a laurel tree.

dap·per (dap′ər) *adj.* **1** neat; trim; spruce. **2** small and active. [ME < MDu. *dapper* agile, strong] —**dap′perly,** *adv.*
—**dap′per·ness,** *n.*

dap·ple (dap′əl) *adj., n., v.* **-pled, -pling.** —*adj.* spotted: *a dappled horse.*
—*n.* **1** a spotted appearance or condition. **2** an animal with a spotted or mottled skin.
—*v.* mark or become marked with spots. [cf. ON *depill* spot]

dap·pled (dap′əld) *adj.* spotted.

dap·ple–grey (dap′əl grā′) *adj.* grey with spots of darker grey. Also, **dapple-gray.**

darb (därb) *n. Cdn. Slang.* any thing or person thought to be especially large, good, etc. [origin uncertain]

Dar·by and Joan (där′bē ən jōn′) any old and devoted married couple. [from characters in an English ballad of the eighteenth century]

dare (der) *v.* **dared** or **durst, dared, dar·ing;** *n.* —*v.* **1** have courage; be bold; be bold enough to: *He doesn't dare dive from the bridge.* **2** have courage; not be afraid of; face or meet boldly: *The explorer dared the dangers of the Arctic.* **3** meet and resist; face and defy. **4** challenge: *I dare you to jump.*
I dare say, probably; maybe; perhaps: *I dare say his success was due to hard work.*
—*n.* a challenge. [OE *dearr* infinitive, *durran*)] —**dar′er,** *n.*
☛ *Syn.* **1. Dare, venture** = be courageous or bold enough to do something. **Dare** emphasizes the idea of meeting fearlessly any danger or trouble, especially in doing something that is or seems important: *Only one man dared to enter the burning building.* **Venture** emphasizes the idea of being willing to take chances: *He decided to venture into a new business.*

dare·dev·il (der′dev′əl) *n., adj.* —*n.* a recklessly adventurous person; one who does bold and dangerous things that are unnecessary. —*adj.* reckless: *a daredevil stunt.*

dar·ing (der′ing) *n., adj.* —*n.* the courage to take risks; boldness. —*adj.* courageous; bold. —**dar′ing·ly,** *adv.* —**dar′ing·ness,** *n.*

dark (därk) *adj., n.* —*adj.* **1** without light or with very little light: *the dark side of the moon. It was a dark, moonless night. I thought he must be in bed, because his window was dark.* **2** allowing only some light to pass through: *She was wearing her dark glasses.* **3** not light-complexioned: *a dark skin, dark good looks.* **4** deep in shade; closer in color to black than white: *dark green, a dark background, dark hair.* **5** secret; hidden: *He kept his past dark.* **6** evil; wicked: *a dark deed.* **7** gloomy and sad; dismal: *Those were dark days. Don't always look on the dark side of things.* **8** sullen or angry: *She gave him a dark look.* **9** hard to understand; obscure: *dark sayings.* **10** ignorant; unenlightened: *a culturally dark age.* **11** of radio or television stations, not broadcasting.
keep dark, keep silent; not tell about.
—*n.* **1 the dark,** the absence of light; darkness: *He's afraid of the dark. It was a shock to step from the dark of the cave into the sunlight.* **2** the time when the dark of night begins; nightfall: *The children are not allowed out after dark. They waited until dark to continue their journey.* **3** a dark color: *the darks and lights in a painting.*
in the dark, not knowing or understanding; in ignorance: *I'm still in the dark about what I'm supposed to do on the project.*
[OE *deorc*] —**dark′ly,** *adv.* —**dark′ness,** *n.*
☛ *Syn. adj.* **1. Dark, dim** = without light. **Dark** = without any light or with very little light: *The house is dark, not a light is on.* **Dim** = without enough light to see clearly or distinctly: *With only the fire burning, the room was dim.*

Dark Ages 1 the Middle Ages, especially the early part (from the 5th to the 11th centuries) so named from the idea that it was a time of economic and intellectual poverty in most parts of Europe. **2** any similar period.

Dark Continent a term applied to Africa.

dark·en (där′kən) *v.* make or become dark or darker.
—**dark′en·er,** *n.*

dark·ey (där′kē) *n., pl.* **-eys.** See **darky.**

dark horse *Informal.* **1** an unexpected winner about which little is known. **2** a person who is unexpectedly nominated for a political or other office.

dark·ish (där′kish) *adj.* rather dark. —**dark′ish·ness,** *n.*

dark lantern a lantern whose light can be hidden by a cover or dark glass.

dark·ling (därk′ling) *adv., adj.* —*adv. Poetic.* in the dark. —*adj.* dark; dim; obscure. [< *dark* + OE *-ling,* an adverbial suffix indicating state or manner]

dark·room (därk′rüm′ *or* -rùm′) *n.* a room arranged for developing or printing photographs, having no light or a light of a color that will not affect light-sensitive photographic materials.

dark·some (därk′səm) *adj. Poetic.* **1** dark. **2** gloomy.

dark·y (där′kē) *n., pl.* **dark·ies.** *Offensive.* a black; Negro. Also, **darkey.**

dar·ling (där′ling) *n., adj.* —*n.* **1** a person very dear to another; a person much loved. **2** a favorite: *He's the darling of the jet set.* —*adj.* **1** very dear; much loved. **2** *Informal.* very attractive; pleasing; charming: *a darling little shop.* [OE *dēorling* < *dēore* dear] —**dar′ling·ly,** *adv.* —**dar′ling·ness,** *n.*

darn¹ (därn) *v., n.* —*v.* mend by weaving rows of thread or yarn across a hole or torn place. —*n.* **1** the act of darning. **2** a place mended by darning. [< dial. F *darner* mend < *darne* piece < Breton *darn*]

darn² (därn) *interj., adj., adv., or n. Informal.* a mild form of the word **damn,** used to express annoyance, anger, surprise, etc.: *Darn! The window's frozen shut. He's a darn fool.* [< *damn;* influenced by *tarnal* (informal for *eternal*)]

darned (därnd) *adj. Informal.* damned.

dar·nel (där′nəl) *n.* any of several species of ryegrass, especially *Lolium temulentum,* a noxious weed found in grainfields in Europe and Asia. **Persian darnel** (*L. persicum*) is a common and troublesome Canadian weed introduced from Asia. [ME; cf. F dial. *darnelle*]

darn·er (där′nər) *n.* **1** a person who darns. **2** a darning needle.

darn·ing (där′ning) *n.* **1** the act of mending with stitches. **2** the articles darned or to be darned.

darning needle 1 a long needle with an eye large enough to take the heavy thread used for darning. **2** *Informal.* dragonfly.

dart (därt) *n., v.* —*n.* **1** a small, slender, pointed weapon usually having feathers at the back, for throwing by hand or shooting from a tube or gun. **2 darts,** an indoor game in which players throw darts at a round board marked off in concentric circles and numbered radiating sections (used with a singular verb). **3** a sudden quick movement: *He made a dart for the window.* **4** a sharp look, word, etc. **5** a tapered fold, or tuck, in a garment to shape it to a part of the body or to make it hang better: *Long, narrow sleeves usually have darts at the elbow.*
—*v.* **1** throw or shoot suddenly and quickly. **2** move suddenly and quickly: *She darted across the street.* **3** direct or send suddenly: *She darted an angry glance at her sister.* **4** sew darts in a garment. [ME < OF < Gmc.]

dart·er (där′tər) *n.* **1** any of a subfamily (Etheostomidae) of small, slender, freshwater fishes of E North America, some of which are brightly colored. **2** snakebird. **3** an animal, person, or thing that darts.

Dar·win·i·an (där win′ē ən) *adj., n.* —*adj.* **1** of or having to do with Charles Darwin (1809-1882), an English scientist. **2** of or having to do with his theory of evolution. —*n.* a person who believes in Darwinism.

Dar·win·ism (där′wən iz′əm) *n.* Charles Darwin's theory of evolution, that in successive generations all plants and animals tend to develop slightly varying forms. The forms that survive are those which through natural selection have adapted themselves to their environment better than the forms that become extinct.

dash (dash) *v., n.* —*v.* **1** throw: *We dashed water over him.* **2** splash: *She dashed some paint on the canvas.* **3** rush: *They dashed by in a car.* **4** strike violently against something. **5** smash: *He dashed the bowl to bits on a rock.* **6** ruin: *Our hopes were dashed.* **7** depress; discourage. **8** mix with a small amount of something else. **9** abash; confound: *He was dashed by the sudden questioning of the teacher.*
dash off, do, make, write, etc. quickly: *He dashed off a short letter to his friend.*

—*n.* **1** a splash. **2** a rush. **3** a smash. **4** anything that depresses or discourages; a check. **5** a small amount. **6** a short race: *the hundred-yard dash.* **7** a blow; a stroke. **8** a mark (—) used in writing or printing, especially to show a break in sense or in the structure of a sentence. **9** *Telegraphy.* a long sound or signal that represents a letter or part of a letter: *Morse code uses dots and dashes.* **10** dashboard (def. 1). **11** energy; spirit; liveliness. **12** showy appearance or behavior. [ME *dasche*(*n*); cf. Danish *daske* slap]

dash·board (dash′bôrd′) *n.* **1** a panel with controls and gauges, below the windshield and in front of the operator in an automobile, aircraft, etc. **2** a screen on the front of a wagon, boat, etc. to provide protection from splashing mud or water.

dash·er (dash′ər) *n.* **1** one that dashes. **2** a device with blades for stirring the cream in a churn or ice-cream freezer. **3** *Cdn.* the fence surrounding the ice of a hockey rink; the boards.

da·shi·ki (dä shē′kē) *n.* a loose-fitting, collarless, pullover robe or tunic, usually made of a brightly colored and patterned cotton. [of West African origin]

dash·ing (dash′ing) *adj.* **1** full of energy and spirit; lively. **2** having or showing a sense of style; showy. —**dash′ing·ly,** *adv.*

das·sie (das′ē) *n.* hyrax.

das·tard (das′tərd) *n.* **1** a mean coward; sneak. **2** (*adj.*) mean and cowardly; sneaking. [ME, originally, a dullard, apparently < *dazed*, pp. of *daze* + -*ard*, as in *dullard*, etc.] —**das′tard·ly,** *adj.* —**das′tard·li·ness,** *n.*

dat. dative.

da·ta (dā′tə *or* dat′ə) *n.* pl. of **datum.** facts or concepts presented in a form suitable for processing in order to draw conclusions: *All the data indicate the beginning of an economic boom.*
☞ *Usage.* **Data** is the plural of the seldom-used singular *datum.* Since its meaning is often collective, referring to a group of facts as a unit, **data** is often used with a singular verb in informal English: *The data you have collected is not enough to convince me.* Formal English continues to regard **data** as a plural rather than as a collective noun: *We will analyse the data that have been obtained.*

data bank a body of information stored and available for processing in a computer.

data processing the operations performed on data, especially by a computer, in order to derive information or to organize files. —**da′ta-pro·cess′ing,** *adj.*

date¹ (dāt) *n., v.,* **dat·ed, dat·ing.** —*n.* **1** the time when something happens. **2** a statement of time: *There is a date stamped on every piece of Canadian money.* **3** a period of time. **4** an appointment for a certain time, especially for a social engagement with a person of the opposite sex: *She's made a date with him for Saturday.* **5** the social engagement itself: *She said it was a boring date. He's out on a date.* **6** *Informal.* the person with whom one has such an engagement: *Who's your date for the dance?*
out of date, old-fashioned; not in present use: *That dress looks out of date.*
to date, till now; up to the present moment; yet: *There have been no replies to date.*
up to date, a to the present time. **b** modern; according to the latest style or idea; in fashion: *His clothes are always up to date.*
—*v.* **1** mark with a date; put a date on. **2** find out the date of; give a date to: *The scientist was unable to date the fossil.* **3** belong to a certain period of time; have its origin: (*usually used with* from): *That house dates from the late 18th century.* **4** make a social appointment with a person of the opposite sex: *He's been trying for months to date her.* **5** go out regularly with a particular person of the opposite sex; go on dates: *They've been dating for a long time. She dates a fellow from another school.* **6** be or become out of date. [ME < MF < Med.L *data,* pp. fem. of L *dare* give] —**dat′a·ble or date′a·ble,** *adj.*
☞ *Usage.* **Dates.** The usual Canadian method of writing dates is: *July 1, 1867; November 3, 1985.* However, in military use, and increasingly among scientists, the day of the month is placed first: *3 Nov. 1985.* Names of months having more than four letters are often abbreviated. In numeric dating, Canadian and British practice has been to indicate the day, month, and year in that order: 3/11/85. American practice is to put the month before the day: 11/3/85. To avoid confusion between these two systems, the preferred international system of numeric dating puts year, month, and day: *1985 11 03, 85 11 03,* or *85-11-03.* If required, such dates can be followed by the time, using the 24-hour clock: 85 11 03 21 05.

date² (dāt) *n.* **1** the oblong, fleshy, edible fruit of the date palm. **2** date palm. [ME < OF < L *dactylus* < Gk. *daktylos* date, finger. Doublet of DACTYL.]

dat·ed (dāt′id) *adj.* **1** marked with a date; showing a date. **2** out of date. —**dat′ed·ly,** *adv.* —**dat′ed·ness,** *n.*

date·less (dāt′lis) *adj.* **1** without a date; not dated. **2** endless; unlimited. **3** so old that it cannot be given a date. **4** old but still admirable, in good style, etc.

date line 1 an imaginary line agreed upon as the place where each calendar day first begins. It runs north and south through the Pacific, mostly along the 180th meridian. When it is Sunday just

hat, āge, fär; let, ēqual, tèrm; it, īce
hot, ōpen, ôrder; oil, out; cup, pút, rüle,
əbove, takən, pencəl, lemən, circəs

ch, child; ng, long; sh, ship
th, thin; ᴛʜ, then; zh, measure

east of the date line, it is Monday just west of it. **2** a line in a letter, newspaper, etc. giving the date and place of writing.

date palm a tall palm tree (*Phoenix dactylifera*) that bears dates. It is native to Syria but widely cultivated in tropical regions of the world.

date stamp 1 a rubber stamp for recording dates, having a series of numbers and, often, the names of the months on separate parallel rings of rubber that can be rotated to bring the desired numbers and names into alignment for any given date. **2** an inked impression made by such a stamp. —**date′-stamp′,** *v.*

da·tive (dā′tiv) *adj., n.* —*adj. Grammar.* of, having to do with, or being the grammatical case found in some languages (such as German and Latin), that shows that a noun, pronoun, or adjective is an indirect object of a verb or an object of any of certain prepositions. English has no dative case, but expresses such a grammatical relationship by prepositions such as *to* or *for* and through word order. —*n.* **1** the dative case. **2** a word or construction in the dative case. *Abbrev:* dat. [< L *dativus* of giving < *datus,* pp. of *dare* give]

da·tum (dā′təm *or* dat′əm) *n., pl.* **da·ta.** a fact from which conclusions can be drawn. [< L *datum* (thing) given, pp. neut. of *dare.* Doublet of DIE².]
☞ *Usage.* See note at **data.**

daub (dob *or* dôb) *v., n.* —*v.* **1** coat or cover with plaster, clay, mud, etc. **2** apply (greasy or sticky stuff). **3** make dirty; soil; stain. **4** paint unskilfully.
—*n.* **1** something used to daub. **2** a mark made by a daub; smear. **3** a crudely painted picture. [ME < OF *dauber* < L *dealbare* < *de-* + *albus* white] —**daub′er,** *n.*

daugh·ter (do′tər *or* dô′tər) *n.* **1** a female child (immediate descendant of her parents). **2** a female descendant. **3** a girl or woman thought of as related to something in the same way that a child is related to its parents: *a daughter of France.* **4** anything thought of as a daughter in relation to its origin: *Skill is the daughter of hard work.* [OE *dohtor*]

daughter element *Physics.* an element produced by the decay of a radio-active element.

daugh·ter–in–law (do′tər in lo′ *or* dô′tər in lô′) *n., pl.* **daugh·ters-in-law.** the wife of one's son.

daugh·ter·ly (do′tər lē *or* dô′tər lē) *adj.* **1** of a daughter. **2** like that of a daughter. **3** proper for a daughter.

daunt (dont *or* dônt) *v.* dismay or discourage. [ME < OF *danter* < L *domitare* < *domare* tame]

daunt·less (dont′lis *or* dônt′lis) *adj.* not to be frightened or discouraged; brave. —**daunt′less·ly,** *adv.* —**daunt′less·ness,** *n.*

dau·phin (do′fən *or* dô′fən; *French,* dō faɴ′) *n.* the title given to the oldest son of the king of France, from 1349 to 1830. [< F *dauphin,* originally a family name]

dau·phine (do′fēn *or* dô′fēn; *French,* dō fēn′) *n.* the wife of a dauphin. [< F. See DAUPHIN.]

dau·phin·ess (do′fən is *or* dô′fən is) *n.* dauphine.

dav·en·port (dav′ən pôrt′) *n.* **1** a large chesterfield, or sofa. **2** *Brit.* a writing desk with drawers and a hinged shelf to write on. [origin uncertain]

Da·vid (dā′vid) *n.* in the Bible, the second king of Israel, who organized the Jewish tribes into a national state.
David and Jonathan, any pair of devoted friends.

dav·it (dav′it *or* dā′vit) *n.* **1** one of a pair of cranelike devices projecting over the side of a ship, used especially for raising or lowering lifeboats or cargo. **2** a crane projecting over the bow of a ship, used for raising or lowering an anchor. [ME < AF *daviot*]

Da·vy Jones (dā′vē jōnz′) the evil spirit of the sea; the sailor's devil.

Davy Jones's locker the sea, especially as the grave of those who have drowned or been buried at sea.

daw (do *or* dô) *n.* jackdaw. [ME *dawe*]

daw·dle (do′dəl *or* dô′dəl) *v.,* **-dled, -dling;** *n.* —*v.* waste time; idle; loiter: *Don't dawdle over your work.* —*n.* **1** a person who dawdles. **2** the act of dawdling. [origin uncertain] —**daw′dler,** *n.*

dawn (don *or* dôn) *n., v.* —*n.* **1** the break of day; the first light in the east. **2** the beginning: *before the dawn of history.*
—*v.* **1** grow light: *The day dawned bright and clear.* **2** grow clear to

the eye or mind: *It dawned on me that she was expecting a gift.*
3 begin; appear: *A new era is dawning.* [ME *dawnen* < *dawning*
daybreak, probably < ON; replacing ME *dawen* < OE *dagian*
become day]
☛ *Hom.* **don** (don).

day (dā) *n.* **1** the time between sunrise and sunset. **2** the light of
day; daylight. **3** the 24 hours of day and night; the time it takes the
earth to turn once on its axis: *There are 31 days in January.*
4 *Astronomy.* the time needed by any celestial body to turn once on
its axis. **5** a certain day on which something happened, set aside for
a particular purpose or for celebration: *Christmas Day.* **6** the hours
for work: *She works a seven-hour day.* **7** a certain period of time:
the present day, in days of old. **8** a period of life, activity, power, or
influence: *He has had his day.* **9** the conflict or contest of a
particular day: *Our team won the day. The day is ours.*
call it a day, *Informal.* stop work: *I'm tired; let's call it a day.*
day by day, each day.
day in, day out, every day.
from day to day, each day.
pass the time of day, take part in small talk.
the time of day, a the time. **b** a greeting; salutation.
[OE *dæg*]
☛ *Hom.* **dey.**

day bed or **day·bed** (dā′bed′) *n.* a bed, usually narrow,
having a low headboard and a footboard of equal height. A day bed
can be used as a couch by day.

day book 1 *Bookkeeping.* a book in which a record is kept of
each day's business. **2** diary.

day·break (dā′brāk′) *n.* dawn; the time when it first begins to
get light in the morning.

day camp a summer camp for children in which they have
daytime activities as at a regular camp but return home for the
night.

day–care (dā′ker′) *adj., n.* —*adj.* of, having to do with, or
providing care and training for babies and preschool children
outside the home during the day: *She takes her baby to the
neighborhood day-care centre every morning on her way to work.*
—*n.* the care and training of babies and preschool children outside
the home during the day: *The ratepayers were asking for more
funds for day-care.*

day·dream (dā′drēm′) *n., v.* **-dreamed** or **-dreamt, -dream·ing.**
—*n.* **1** a dreamy thought about pleasant things. **2** a pleasant plan or
fancy, unlikely to come true. —*v.* think dreamily about pleasant
things. —**day′dream′er,** *n.*

day laborer or **labourer** an unskilled or manual worker who
is paid by the day.

day letter a telegram sent during the day for delivery later the
same day. Service is slower for a day letter than for a regular
telegram but cheaper.

day·light (dā′līt′) *n.* **1** the light of day. **2** the daytime. **3** dawn;
daybreak. **4** publicity; openness. **5** open space; a gap.
see daylight, *Informal.* **a** understand. **b** approach the end of a hard
or tiresome job.

daylight–saving time time that is one hour in advance of
standard time and gives more daylight after working hours. Clocks
are set ahead one hour in the spring and back one hour in the fall.

day lily 1 any of a genus (*Hemerocallis*) of plants of the lily
family native to Europe and Asia but widely cultivated for their
large yellow, orange, or red flowers that last about a day. **2** plantain
lily.

day·lin·er (dā′līʹnər) *n.* a railway train which runs express
between two cities, or between suburbs and a city during the day.

day·long (dā′long′) *adj. or adv.* through the whole day.

day nursery a nursery for the care of small children during the
day.

Day of Atonement Yom Kippur.

Day of Judgment the day of God's final judgment of mankind
at the end of the world.

day school 1 a school held in the daytime. **2** a private school for
students who live at home.

days of grace the extra days (usually three) allowed for
payment after a bill or note falls due.

day·spring (dā′spring′) *n. Poetic.* the dawn; daybreak.

day·star (dā′stär′) *n.* **1** the morning star. **2** *Poetic.* sun.

day·time (dā′tīm′) *n.* the time when it is day.

day–to–day (dā′ tə dā′) *adj.* ordinary or regular; everyday:
*Civil servants are involved in the day-to-day operation of
government.*

daze (dāz) *v.* **dazed, daz·ing;** *n.* —*v.* **1** confuse; bewilder; cause to
feel stupid; stun: *She was so dazed by her fall that she didn't know
where she was.* **2** dazzle. —*n.* a confused state of mind;
bewilderment. [ME *dase*(n) < ON; cf. Icelandic *dasask* become
weary]

daz·ed·ly (dā′zid lē) *adv.* in a dazed, confused, or stupid
manner.

daz·zle (daz′əl) *v.* **-zled, -zling;** *n.* —*v.* **1** confuse, dim, or
overpower (the eyes) with too bright light or with quick-moving
lights. **2** overcome (the sight or the mind) by brightness, display,
etc.: *The young pianist's performance dazzled the critics.* —*n.*
the act or fact of dazzling; a bewildering brightness. [< *daze*]
—**daz′zler,** *n.* —**daz′zling·ly,** *adv.*

D.B.E. Dame (Commander of the Order) of the British Empire.

dbl. double.

DC District of Columbia.

DC, D.C., or **d.c.** direct current.

D.C. 1 District of Columbia. **2** Doctor of Chiropractic. **3** *Music.*
return to beginning (for Ital. *da capo*).

D.C.L. 1 Doctor of Canon Law. **2** Doctor of Civil Law.

D.C.M. Distinguished Conduct Medal.

D.C.V.O. Distinguished Commander of the Victorian Order.

D.D. Doctor of Divinity.

D–day (dē′dā′) *n.* **1** the day when the Allies landed in France in
World War II; June 6, 1944. **2** the day on which a previously
planned military attack is to be made, or on which an operation is
to be started.

D.D.S. Doctor of Dental Surgery.

DDT (dē′dē tē′) *n.* a colorless, odorless crystalline compound that
is a very powerful and long-lasting poison, formerly much used as
an insecticide. *Formula:* $C_{14}H_9Cl_5$ [short for *d*ichloro - *d*iphenyl -
*t*richloroethane]

de– *prefix.* **1** do the opposite of, as in *decamp, deforest,
decentralize, demobilize.* **2** down, as in *depress, descend.* **3** away;
off, as in *deport, detract.* **4** cause to leave something, as in *derail.*
5 entirely; completely (intensive), as in *despoil.* **6** remove, as in
defrost. [< L *de-* < *de* from, away]

DE Delaware.

dea·con (dē′kən) *n.* **1** an officer of a church who helps the
minister in church duties other than preaching. **2** a member of the
clergy immediately below a priest in rank. [OE *diacon* < L
diaconus < Gk. *diakonos* servant]

dea·con·ess (dē′kən is) *n.* a woman who is an official assistant
in church work, especially in caring for the sick and the poor.

dea·con·ry (dē′kən rē) *n., pl.* **-ries. 1** the position of deacon.
2 deacons.

de·ac·ti·vate (dē ak′tə vāt′) *v.* **-at·ed, -at·ing.** make inoperative
or inactive: *to deactivate a bomb, to deactivate a military base.*
—**de·ac′ti·va′tion,** *n.* —**de·ac′ti·va′tor,** *n.*

dead (ded) *adj., adv., n.* —*adj.* **1** no longer living; that has died.
2 without life; inanimate. **3** like death: *in a dead faint.* **4** not active
or productive; dull, stagnant, quiet, etc. **5** without force, power,
spirit, or feeling: *a dead handshake. She spoke in a dead voice.* **6** no
longer having significance, power, or effect: *a dead issue.* **7** no
longer in use; obsolete: *a dead language.* **8** no longer functioning or
producing: *a dead battery.* **9** out of play; not in the game: *a dead
ball.* **10** *Informal.* very tired; worn-out. **11** sure; certain: *a dead shot,
a dead certainty.* **12** complete; absolute: *a dead loss, dead silence.*
13 not connected to a source of power: *a dead circuit. The
telephone line is dead.* **14** *Printing.* of type, etc., already used or no
longer needed.
—*adv.* **1** completely; absolutely: *The forecast was dead wrong. I'm
dead tired.* **2** directly, straight.
—*n.* **1** **the dead,** *pl.* those who are dead; all who no longer have life:
We remembered the dead of our wars on Remembrance Day. **2** the
time of greatest darkness, quiet, cold, etc.: *the dead of night.* [OE
dēad] —**dead′ness,** *n.*
☛ *Syn. adj.* **1, 2. Dead, deceased, lifeless** = without life. **Dead** applies
particularly to someone or something that was living or alive, but no longer is:
The flowers in my garden are dead. **Deceased,** a technical word, applies only to
a dead person: *The deceased man left no will.* **Lifeless** is used both of what now
is or seems to be without life and of things that never had life: *He lifted the
lifeless body.*

dead air 1 air that is trapped between two walls for insulation.
2 *Radio and television.* a period of no broadcasting.

dead·beat (ded′bēt′) *n.* **1** *Informal.* **a** a person who avoids
paying for what he gets. **b** a lazy person; loafer. **2** (*adj.*) of a needle
on a meter, etc., showing a steady reading; not oscillating.

dead centre in an engine, the position of the crank and
connecting rod at which the connecting rod has no power to turn
the crank. Dead centre occurs at each end of a stroke, when the
crank and the connecting rod are in the same straight line.

dead duck *Informal.* **1** a person or thing that is completely exhausted and without further strength or usefulness. **2** one whose fate is sealed: *The boss said, "Make another mistake like that, and you're a dead duck."*

dead·en (ded'ən) *v.* **1** make dull or weak; lessen the intenseness or force of. **2** reduce the sound of. —**dead'en·er,** *n.*

dead end 1 a street, passage, etc. closed at one end. **2** a point in a discussion, plan, etc. beyond which progress is impossible: *When the committee reached a dead end, they decided to drop the plan.*

dead–end (ded'end') *adj.* **1** closed at one end. **2** having no opportunity for progress, advancement, etc.; fruitless: *a dead-end job.*

dead·eye (ded'ī') *n.* a round, flat, wooden block used to fasten the shrouds of a ship.

dead·fall (ded'fol' *or* -fôl') *n.* **1** a trap for animals made so that a heavy weight falls upon and holds or kills the animal. **2** a mass of fallen trees and underbrush. **3** a dead tree that has been blown to the ground.

dead·head (ded'hed') *n., v.* —*n.* **1** *Informal.* a person who rides on a bus, sees a game, without paying. **2** *Informal.* a train, railway car, bus, etc. travelling without passengers or freight. **3** *Slang.* a stupid or dull person. **4** *Cdn.* a log or fallen tree partly or entirely submerged in a lake, etc., usually with one end embedded in the bottom.
—*v. Informal.* drive a train, bus, truck, etc. without passengers or freight.

dead heat a race that ends in a tie.

dead letter 1 an unclaimed letter; a letter that cannot be delivered or returned to the sender because the address is wrong, impossible to read, or incomplete. **2** a law, rule, etc. that is not enforced.

dead·line (ded'līn') *n.* **1** a time limit; the latest possible time to do something. **2** a line or boundary that must not be crossed.

dead load the constant, invariable load that a structure such as a bridge carries, that is due to the weight of the supported structures, permanent attachments, etc. Also called **dead weight.** Compare **live load.**

dead·lock (ded'lok') *n., v.* —*n.* a position in which it is impossible to act or continue because of disagreement: *Employers and strikers were at a deadlock.* —*v.* bring or come to such a position: *The talks were deadlocked for weeks.*

dead·ly (ded'lē) *adj.* **-li·er, -li·est;** *adv.* —*adj.* **1** causing death; liable to cause death; fatal: *a deadly wound.* **2** like death: *deadly paleness.* **3** filled with hatred that lasts till death: *deadly enemies.* **4** causing death of the spirit: *deadly sin.* **5** *Informal.* extreme; intense. **6** dull: *The party was a deadly affair.*
—*adv.* **1** *Informal.* extremely. **2** like death. **3** as if dead. —**dead'li·ness,** *n.*
☛ *Syn. adj.* **1.** See note at **fatal.**

deadly nightshade 1 black nightshade. **2** belladonna.

deadly sins the seven sins that can lead to damnation: pride, covetousness, lust, anger, gluttony, envy, and sloth.

dead march funeral march.

dead·pan (ded'pan') *adj., adv., n., v.* **-panned, -pan·ning.** —*adj.* showing no expression or emotion: *a deadpan face, deadpan humor.*
—*adv.* in a deadpan manner: *He told the whole ridiculous story deadpan.*
—*n.* a deadpan face or manner.
—*v.* express or act in a deadpan manner: *to deadpan a joke.*

dead point dead centre.

dead reckoning the calculation of the location of a ship or aircraft without observations of the sun, stars, etc. by using a compass and studying the record of the voyage.

Dead Sea Scrolls the name given to a number of parchment, leather, and copper scrolls found in 1947 and later in caves near the Dead Sea. They date approximately from between 100 B.C. and A.D. 100, and contain Hebrew and Aramaic texts of Biblical writings, explanation, etc.

dead weight 1 the heavy weight of anything inert. **2** a very great or oppressive burden. **3** the mass of a vessel or vehicle without a load. **4** freight chargeable by mass rather than by volume, or bulk. **5** dead load. —**dead'-weight',** *adj.*

dead·wood (ded'wùd') *n.* **1** dead branches or trees. **2** useless people or things. **3** wording that adds nothing to the meaning of a sentence.

deaf (def) *adj.* **1** not able to hear. **2** not able to hear well. **3** not willing to hear; heedless: *A miser is deaf to all requests for money.*
deaf and dumb, unable to hear and speak.
[OE *dēaf*] —**deaf'ly,** *adv.* —**deaf'ness,** *n.*

deaf·en (def'ən) *v.* **1** make deaf. **2** stun with noise. **3** drown out by a louder sound. **4** make soundproof. —**deaf'en·ing·ly,** *adv.*

hat, āge, fär; let, ēqual, tèrm; it, īce
hot, ōpen, ôrder; oil, out; cup, pùt, rüle,
above, takən, pencəl, lemən, circəs

ch, child; ng, long; sh, ship
th, thin; ŦH, then; zh, measure

deaf–mute (def'myüt') *n.* a person who is deaf and dumb.

deal¹ (dēl) *v.* **dealt, deal·ing;** *n.* —*v.* **1** have to do (*with*): *Arithmetic deals with numbers.* **2** occupy oneself; take action: *The courts deal with those who break the laws.* **3** act; behave: *Deal fairly with everyone.* **4** do business; buy and sell: *A butcher deals in meat.* **5** give: *One fighter dealt the other a blow.* **6** give a share of to each; distribute. **7** distribute (playing cards).
deal out, to give out or distribute.
—*n.* **1** *Informal.* a business arrangement; bargain. **2** *Informal.* a distribution; arrangement; plan: *a new deal.* **3** *Card games.* **a** the distribution of cards. **b** a player's turn to deal. **c** the time during which one deal of cards is being played. **d** the cards held by a player; hand. **4** a quantity; amount: *I took a deal of trouble.* **5** a dealing; distributing.
a good deal or **a great deal, a** a large part, portion, or amount: *She spends a great deal of her money on holiday trips.* **b** to a great extent or degree; much: *He smokes a good deal.*
a square deal, an honest business transaction; a fair arrangement. [OE *dælan*]

deal² (dēl) *n.* **1** a board of pine or fir wood, usually more than 7 inches wide and 6 feet long and less than 3 inches thick (about 180× 1800×76 mm). **2** pine or fir wood in the form of deals. **3** (*adj.*) made of deal: *a deal table.* [< MLG or MDu. *dele* plank]

deal·er (dēl'ər) *n.* **1** a person or group that trades; one engaged in buying and selling: *a car dealer.* **2** *Card games.* the person who distributes the cards to the players. **3** a person who deals, or acts, in a particular way: *a plain dealer.*

deal·er·ship (dē'lər ship') *n.* the business, franchise, or territory of a dealer (def. 1).

deal·ing (dēl'ing) *n.* **1** a way of doing business: *The storekeeper is respected for his honest dealing.* **2** a way of acting; behavior toward others. **3** the act or process of distributing. **4 dealings,** *pl.* **a** business relations: *The fur trader was honest in his dealings with the trappers.* **b** actions; behavior: *The teacher tried to be fair in all his dealings with students.*

dealt (delt) *v.* pt. and pp. of **deal¹.**

dean (dēn) *n.* **1** the head of a school or faculty in a university or college. **2** a member of the faculty of a university or college who has charge of the behavior or studies of the students. **3** a high official of a church, often in charge of a cathedral. **4** the member who has belonged to a group longest. [ME < OF *deien* < LL *decanus* master of ten < *decem* ten]

dean·er·y (dēn'ər ē) *n., pl.* **-er·ies. 1** the position or authority of a dean. **2** the residence of a dean.

dean·ship (dēn'ship) *n.* the position, office, or rank of a dean.

dear (dēr) *adj., n., adv., interj.* —*adj.* **1** much loved; precious. **2** much valued; highly esteemed. *Dear* is used as a form of polite address at the beginning of letters: *Dear Sir, Dear Isabel.* **3** high-priced; costly; expensive.
—*n.* a dear one.
—*adv.* **1** with affection; fondly: *He held his wife dear.* **2** at a high price; at a great cost.
—*interj.* an exclamation of surprise, trouble, etc. [OE *dēore*]
—**dear'ly,** *adv.* —**dear'ness,** *n.*
☛ *Hom.* **deer.**
☛ *Syn. adj.* **3.** See note at **expensive.**

dear·ie or **dear·y** (dēr'ē) *n., pl.* **dear·ies.** *Informal.* a dear one; darling.

dearth (dèrth) *n.* **1** a scarcity; lack; too small a supply. **2** a scarcity of food; famine. [ME *derthe* < *dere* hard, grievous < OE *dēor*]

death (deth) *n.* **1** the act or fact of dying; the end of life in human beings, animals, or plants. **2** the state or condition of being dead. **3** Often, **Death,** the power that destroys life, often represented as a skeleton dressed in black and carrying a scythe. **4** any ending that is like dying; total distruction: *the death of an empire, the death of all our hopes.* **5** any condition like being dead. **6** a cause of death: *Alcoholism was the death of her.* **7** bloodshed; murder.
at death's door, dying; almost to die; almost dead.
be death on, be very strongly opposed to: *He's death on all drugs.*
do to death, a kill; murder. **b** do, act, or say the same thing so often that it becomes boring.
put to death, kill or execute.

to death, almost beyond endurance; extremely: *She said she was bored to death.*

to the death, to the last resource; to the last extreme: *a fight to the death.* [OE *dēath*] —**death′like′,** *adj.*

death·bed (deth′bed′) *n.* **1** a bed on which a person dies. **2** the last hours of life. **3** (*adj*l.) during the last hours of life: *The murderer made a deathbed confession.*

death·blow (deth′blō′) *n.* **1** a blow that kills. **2** anything that puts an end (to something else).

death cup a very poisonous mushroom (*Amanita phalloides*) having a white, green, or brown cap and a bulbous base and appearing in woods in summer or early autumn.

death duty succession duty.

death·ful (deth′fəl) *adj.* **1** deadly. **2** like death. **3** like that of death. **4** mortal.

death·less (deth′lis) *adj.* never dying; living forever; immortal; eternal. —**death′less·ness,** *n.*

death·ly (deth′lē) *adj., adv.* —*adj.* **1** like that of death: *Her face was a deathly white.* **2** causing death; deadly. **3** *Poetic.* of death. —*adv.* **1** as if dead. **2** extremely: *deathly ill.*

death mask a clay, wax or plaster likeness of a person's face made from a cast taken after his death.

death penalty punishment by death.

death rate the proportion of the number of deaths per year to the total population or to some other stated number.

death sand *Military.* radio-active dust that may be scattered over vast areas. It would kill all, or most, of the life it touched.

death's–head (deths′hed′) *n.* a human skull, used as a symbol of death.

death·trap (deth′trap′) *n.* **1** an unsafe building or structure where the risk of fire or other hazard is great. **2** a very dangerous situation.

death warrant an official order for a person's death.

death·watch (deth′woch′) *n.* **1** a watch kept beside a dying or dead person. **2** a guard for a person about to be put to death. **3** a small destructive beetle that lives in wood and makes a ticking sound that is supposed to be an omen of death.

deb (deb) *n. Informal.* debutante.

de·ba·cle (dā bä′kəl *or* di bak′əl) *n.* **1** a disaster; overthrow; downfall. **2** the breaking up of ice in a river. **3** a violent rush of waters carrying debris. [< F *débâcle* < *débâcler* free *dé-* un- + *bâcler* to bar]

de·bar (di bär′) *v.* -**barred,** -**bar·ring.** bar out; shut out; prevent; prohibit. [< F *débarrer* < LL *debarrare* < L *de-* from + *barrare* bar] —**de·bar′ment,** *n.*

de·bark[1] (di bärk′) *v.* go or put ashore from a ship or aircraft; disembark. [< F *débarquer* < *dé-* from + *barque* bark[3] < LL *barca*]

de·bark[2] (dē bärk′) *v.* remove bark from (a tree). [< *de-* + *bark*[1]] —**de·bark′er,** *n.*

de·bar·ka·tion (dē′bär kā′shən) *n.* debarking or being debarked; a landing from a ship or aircraft.

de·base (di bās′) *v.* -**based,** -**bas·ing.** **1** make low in quality or character; dishonor or cheapen: *to debase oneself by a mean act.* **2** lower the exchange value of currency: *Poor management by a country of its financial affairs will generally debase its currency on world markets.* **3** lower the content value of a coin or coinage by increasing the proportion of base metal in it. [< *de-* down + (*a*)*base*] —**de·base′ment,** *n.* —**de·bas′er,** *n.*

de·bat·a·ble (di bāt′ə bəl) *adj.* **1** capable of being debated; open to debate. To be debatable, a topic must have at least two sides. **2** not decided; in dispute.

de·bate (di bāt′) *v.* -**bat·ed,** -**bat·ing;** *n.* —*v.* **1** discuss reasons for and against (something). **2** argue about (a question, topic, etc.) in a public meeting. **3** think over in one's mind; consider. —*n.* **1** a discussion of reasons for and against. **2** a public argument for and against a question in a meeting. A formal debate is a contest between two sides to see which one has more skill in speaking and reasoning. **3** in Parliament, the discussion of a motion that is to be voted on. [ME < OF *debatre* < VL *debattere* < L *de-* (intensive) + *battuere* beat] —**de·bat′er,** *n.*

☞ *Syn. v.* **1.** See note at **discuss.**

de·bauch (di boch′ *or* di bôch′) *v., n.* —*v.* **1** lead away from virtue or morality; corrupt morally or seduce: *debauched by bad companions.* **2** corrupt or spoil the senses, taste, judgment, etc.: *a mind debauched by prejudice.* —*n.* **1** a bout or period of debauchery. **2** debauchery. [< F *débaucher* entice from duty] —**de·bauch′er,** *n.* —**de·bauch′ment,** *n.*

deb·au·chee (deb′o chē′ *or* deb′ô chē′, deb′o shē′ *or* deb′ô shē′) *n.* an intemperate, dissipated, or depraved person.

de·bauch·er·y (di boch′ər ē *or* di bôch′ər ē) *n., pl.* -**er·ies.** **1** too much indulgence in sensual pleasures; dissipation. **2** a seduction from virtue or morality.

de·ben·ture (di ben′chər) *n.* a bond, especially one issued by a corporation rather than a government and backed by the general assets of the corporation. [ME < L *debentur* there are owing, 3rd person pl., present passive, of *debere*]

de·bil·i·tate (di bil′ə tāt′) *v.* -**tat·ed,** -**tat·ing.** weaken: *A hot wet climate is often debilitating to people not accustomed to it.* [< *debilitare* < *debilis* weak] —**de·bil′i·ta′tion,** *n.*

de·bil·i·ty (di bil′ə tē) *n., pl.* -**ties.** weakness. [ME < OF *debilite* < L *debilitas* < *debilis* weak]

deb·it (deb′it) *n., v.* —*n.* **1** *Accounting.* **a** the entry of something owed in an account. **b** the left-hand side of an account where such entries are made. **c** the amount entered or shown on this side. **2** the money owed by a person on an account. —*v.* **1** enter on the debit side of an account. **2** charge with or as a debt: *Debit his account $500.* **3** enter as a debit in a bank account, etc. [< L *debitum* (thing) owed, pp. neut. of *debere.* Doublet of DEBT.]

deb·o·nair *or* **deb·o·naire** (deb′ə ner′) *adj.* **1** especially of a man, suave; elegant and refined. **2** lighthearted and cheerful. **3** having pleasant manners; courteous. [ME < OF *debonaire* < *de bon aire* of good disposition] —**deb′o·nair′ly,** *adv.*

de·bouch (di büsh′) *v.* **1** come out from a narrow or confined place into open country: *The soldiers debouched from the gorges into the plain.* **2** come out; emerge; issue: *A horde of children debouched from the bus.* [< F *déboucher* < *dé-* from + *bouche* mouth < L *bucca*]

de·bouch·ment (di büsh′mənt) *n.* **1** an act of debouching. **2** a mouth; outlet: *the debouchment of a river.*

de·brief (dē brēf′) *v.* question a combat pilot, intelligence agent, etc. immediately on return from a mission to find out the results of the mission and anything else the person learned while on the mission.

de·brief·ing (dē brē′fing) *n.* the action or process of questioning a combat pilot, etc. on return from a mission.

de·bris *or* **dé·bris** (də brē′, dā′brē, *or* deb′rē; *French,* dā brē′) *n.* **1** scattered fragments; ruins; rubbish: *Debris from the explosion was scattered all over the street.* **2** *Geology.* a mass of fragments of rock, etc.: *the debris left by a glacier.* [< F *débris* < OF *debrisier* < *de-* away + *brisier* break]

debt (det) *n.* **1** something owed to another. **2** a liability or obligation to pay or render something: *to be in debt to the grocer, to get out of debt.* **3** the state or condition of being under such an obligation. **4** a sin. **5** *Cdn.* **a** a credit given at a trading post to hunters and trappers in the form of supplies to be paid for out of the next season's catch. **b** the amount of credit given. **c** in the North, credit taken at any store. [ME < OF *dette* < L *debitum* (thing) owed, pp. neut. of *debere.* Doublet of DEBIT.]

debt of honor *or* **honour** a betting or gambling debt.

debt·or (det′ər) *n.* **1** a person who owes something to someone else. **2** *Cdn.* a person owing or taking debt at a trading post, store, etc.

de·bug (dē bug′) *v.* -**bugged,** -**bug·ging.** **1** locate and remove errors or malfunctions in: *to debug a computer program.* **2** locate and remove hidden microphones in (a room, etc.). **3** remove insects from.

de·bunk (di bungk′) *v.* **1** expose as false, exaggerated, empty, etc.: *to debunk a theory. She wrote an article debunking the manufacturer's claims.* **2** expose the false reputation of: *to debunk a hero.* —**de·bunk′er,** *n.*

de·but *or* **dé·but** (dā′byü *or* dā byü′) *n.* **1** a first public appearance: *an actor's debut on the stage; the debut of a new magazine.* **2** a first formal appearance in society. [< F *début* < *débuter* make the first stroke < *de-* from + *but* mark (in game or sport)]

deb·u·tante *or* **dé·bu·tante** (deb′yə tänt′ *or* deb′yə tänt′, dā′byü tänt′ *or* dā′byü tänt′) *n.* a young woman making her debut into upper-class society, especially at a formal ball. [< F *débutante,* ppr. fem. of *débuter.* See DEBUT.]

dec. **1** deceased. **2** declension. **3** decrease.

Dec. December.

deca– *SI prefix.* ten: *A decagram is ten grams. Symbol:* da [< Gk. combining form *deka-* < *deka* ten]

dec·ade (dek′ād) *n.* **1** a period of ten years. **2** a group of ten. [< F < LL *decas, decadis* < Gk. *dekas* group of ten < *deka* ten]

de·ca·dence (dek′ə dəns) *n.* a falling off; decline; decay: *the*

decadence of manners. [< F < Med.L *decadentia* < L *de-* down + *cadere* fall]

de·ca·dent (dek′ə dənt) *adj., n.* —*adj.* falling off; declining; growing worse. —*n.* a decadent person. —**de′ca·dent·ly,** *adv.*

de·caf·fein·ate (dē kaf′ə nat′) *v.* **-at·ed, -at·ing.** remove the caffeine from: *They drink only decaffeinated coffee.*

dec·a·gon (dek′ə gon′) *n.* a polygon having 10 sides. [< Med.L *decagonum* < Gk. *dekagonon* < *deka* ten + *gōnia* corner, angle]

dec·a·he·dron (dek′ə hē′drən) *n., pl.* **-drons, -dra** (-drə) a polyhedron having ten faces. [< NL < Gk. *deka* ten + Gk. *hedra* base]

de·cal (dē′kal, dek′əl *or* di kal′) *n.* decalcomania.

de·cal·co·ma·ni·a (di kal′kə mā′nē ə) *n.* **1** a design or picture treated so that it will stick to glass, wood, etc. **2** a process of decorating glass, wood, etc. by applying these designs or pictures. [< F *décalcomanie* < *décalquer* transfer a tracing + *manie* mania]

Dec·a·logue (dek′ə lôg′) *n.* in the Bible, the Ten Commandments (Exod. 20:2-17). Also, **Decalog.** [< F *décalogue* < LL < Gk. *dekalogos* < *deka* ten + *logos* word]

de·camp (di kamp′) *v.* **1** depart quickly, secretly, or without ceremony. **2** leave a camp. [< F *décamper* < *dé-* departing from + *camp* camp] —**de·camp′ment,** *n.*

dec·a·nal (dek′ə nəl *or* di kā′nəl) *adj.* of a dean or deanery. [< LL *decanus* dean]

de·cant (di kant′) *v.* **1** pour off (liquor or a solution) gently without disturbing the sediment. **2** pour from one container to another. [< Med.L *decanthare* < *de-* from + *canthus* lip (of container) < Gk. *kanthos* corner of the eye] —**de′can·ta′tion,** *n.*

de·cant·er (di kan′tər) *n.* a glass bottle with a stopper, used for serving wine or liquor.

de·cap·i·tate (di kap′ə tāt′) *v.* **-tat·ed, -tat·ing.** cut off the head of; behead. [< LL *decapitare* < L *de-* away + *caput, capitis* head] —**de·cap′i·ta′tion,** *n.* —**de·cap′i·ta′tor,** *n.*

dec·a·pod (dek′ə pod′) *n.* **1** any of an order (Decapoda) of crustaceans having five pairs of appendages with one or more pair modified into pincers. Lobsters, shrimps, and crab are decapods. **2** any of an order (Decapoda) of cephalopod molluscs having 10 arms, including squid and cuttlefish. **3** (*adj.*) of, having to do with, or designating a decapod. [< *deca-* ten + Gk. *pous, podos* foot]

de·car·bon·ate (dē kär′bə nāt′) *v.* **-at·ed, -at·ing.** remove carbon dioxide or carbonic acid from. —**de·car′bon·a′tor,** *n.*

de·car·bon·ize (dē kär′bə nīz′) *v.* **-ized, -iz·ing.** remove carbon from: *Iron is decarbonized in making steel.* —**de·car′bon·iz′er,** *n.*

dec·a·syl·lab·ic (dek′ə sə lab′ik) *adj., n.* —*adj.* having ten syllables. —*n.* decasyllable.

dec·a·syl·la·ble (dek′ə sil′ə bəl) *n.* a line of verse having ten syllables.

de·cath·lon (di kath′lon) *n.* an athletic contest consisting of 10 separate events for the competitor, in which the winner is the person who has the highest total of points from all the events. The decathlon consists of the 100-metre, 400-metre, and 1500-metre runs, and the long jump, high jump, pole vault, shot put, javelin and discus throws, and 110-metre hurdles. [< *deca-* + Gk. *athlon* contest]

de·cay (di kā′) *v., n.* —*v.* **1** become rotten: *The fruit and vegetables began to decay.* **2** cause to rot. **3** grow less in power, strength, wealth, beauty, etc. —*n.* **1** a rotting condition. **2** a loss of power, strength, wealth, beauty, etc. **3** *Physics.* a loss in quantity of a radio-active substance through disintegration of its component nuclei. [ME < OF *decair* < *de-* down + *cair* < L *cadere* fall]

☛ *Syn. v.* **1. Decay, rot, decompose** = change from a good or healthy condition to a bad. **Decay** emphasizes the idea of changing little by little through natural processes: *Some diseases cause the bones to decay.* **Rot,** more emphatic, emphasizes the idea of spoiling, and applies especially to plant and animal matter: *The fruit rotted on the vines.* **Decompose** emphasizes the idea of breaking down into original parts, by natural or chemical processes: *Bodies decompose after death.*

de·cease (di sēs′) *n., v.* **-ceased, -ceas·ing.** —*n.* death: *His decease was unexpected.* —*v.* die. [ME < OF *deces* < L *decessus* < *decedere* < *de-* away + *cedere* go]

de·ceased (di sēst′) *adj., n.* —*adj.* dead (*used of persons*). —*n.* **the deceased,** a particular person or persons who have died recently: *a memorial service for the deceased.*

☛ *Syn. adj.* See note at **dead.**

de·ce·dent (di sē′dənt) *n.* *Law. Esp.U.S.* deceased person: *The decedent's will was read in court.* [< L *decedens, -entis,* ppr. of *decedere.* See DECEASE.]

de·ceit (di sēt′) *n.* **1** the act or practice of making a person believe as true something that is false. **2** a dishonest trick; a lie spoken or acted. **3** the quality of being deceitful; deceitfulness: *He*

hat, āge, fär; let, ēqual, tèrm; it, īce
hot, ōpen, ôrder; oil, out; cup, pût, rüle,
əbove, takən, pencəl, lemən, circəs

ch, child; ng, long; sh, ship
th, thin; ᴛʜ, then; zh, measure

was so full of deceit that he believed his own lies. [ME < OF *deceite* < *deceveir.* See DECEIVE.]

☛ *Syn.* **1. Deceit, deception, guile** =false or misleading representation. **Deceit** suggests a habit of trying to mislead others by covering up or twisting the truth and giving wrong ideas of things: *The trader was truthful and without deceit.* **Deception** applies to the act that gives a false or wrong idea, but does not always suggest a dishonest purpose: *A magician uses deception.* **Guile** suggests craftiness and slyness and deception by means of tricks: *He got what he wanted by guile, not work.*

de·ceit·ful (di sēt′fəl) *adj.* **1** ready or willing to deceive or lie: *a deceitful person.* **2** meant to deceive: *a deceitful friendliness.* **3** tending to deceive; deceptive: *a deceitful mildness in the air.* —**de·ceit′ful·ly,** *adv.* —**de·ceit′ful·ness,** *n.*

de·ceive (di sēv′) *v.* **-ceived, -ceiv·ing.** **1** cause to accept as true something that is not true; mislead. **2** use deceit. [ME < OF *deceveir* < L *decipere* < *de-* away + *capere* take] —**de·ceiv′a·ble,** *adj.* —**de·ceiv′er,** *n.* —**de·ceiv′ing·ly,** *adv.*

☛ *Syn.* **1.** See note at **cheat.**

de·cel·er·ate (dē sel′ər āt′) *v.* **-at·ed, -at·ing.** decrease the velocity of; slow down. [< *de-* + (ac)*celerate*] —**de·cel′er·a′tion,** *n.* —**de·cel′er·a′tor,** *n.*

De·cem·ber (di sem′bər) *n.* the twelfth and last month of the year. It has 31 days. [ME < OF *decembre* < L *December* < *decem* ten; because it was the tenth month in the early Roman calendar]

de·cem·vir (di sem′vər) *n., pl.* **-virs, -vi·ri** (-və rī′ *or* -və rē′). **1** in ancient Rome, a member of a council of ten men. The decemvirs in 451 and 450 B.C. prepared the earliest Roman law code. **2** a member of a council of ten. [< L *decemvir,* sing. of *decemviri* < *decem* ten + *viri* men]

de·cem·vi·rate (di sem′vər it *or* di sem′və rāt′) *n.* **1** the office or government of decemvirs. **2** a group or council of ten men or decemvirs.

de·cen·cy (dē′sən sē) *n., pl.* **-cies.** **1** the quality or state of being decent; conforming to accepted standards of behavior, good taste, courtesy, etc.: *Common decency requires that you pay for the window you broke.* **2 decencies,** *pl.* **a** the generally accepted standards of behavior; proper and suitable actions: *She tried hard to observe the decencies although the situation was unfamiliar to her.* **b** things needed for a proper standard of living.

de·cen·ni·al (di sen′ē əl) *adj., n.* —*adj.* **1** of or for ten years. **2** happening every ten years. —*n.* a tenth anniversary. [< L *decennium* decade < *decem* ten + *annus* year]

de·cent (dē′sənt) *adj.* **1** proper and right: *a decent burial. The decent thing to do is to apologize.* **2** not vulgar, immodest or obscene: *decent language. His stories are usually decent.* **3** conformity to generally accepted standards of honesty, goodness, sincerity, etc.: *decent people.* **4** meeting at least the minimum standards of quality, etc.; reasonably good; adequate: *a decent wage. You can't even get a decent meal in this town.* **5** not severe; rather kind: *His boss was very decent about his being late for work.* **6** *Informal.* properly dressed to be seen in public: *Are you decent, or shall I wait outside?* [< L *decens, -entis* becoming, fitting, ppr. of *decere*] —**de′cent·ly,** *adv.* —**de′cent·ness,** *n.*

de·cen·tral·i·za·tion (dē sen′trəl ə zā′shən *or* dē sen′trəl ī zā′shən) *n.* the act of decentralizing or the state of being decentralized.

de·cen·tral·ize (dē sen′trəl īz′) *v.* **-ized, -iz·ing.** **1** spread or distribute (authority, power, etc.) among several groups or local governments. **2** reorganize (a large industry, business, etc.) into smaller units of management and operation: *decentralize a department store.*

de·cep·tion (di sep′shən) *n.* **1** the act of deceiving. **2** the state of being deceived. **3** something that deceives; an illusion. **4** a trick meant to deceive; fraud; sham. [< LL *deceptio, -onis* < *decipere.* See DECEIVE.]

☛ *Syn.* **1.** See note at **deceit.**

de·cep·tive (di sep′tiv) *adj.* **1** tending to deceive; misleading: *a deceptive calm before the storm.* **2** meant to deceive; deceiving: *the deceptive mildness of his manner did not fool them for long.* —**de·cep′tive·ly,** *adv.* —**de·cep′tive·ness,** *n.*

dé·charge (dā shärzh′) *n. Cdn.* a shallow stretch in a water course, where it is necessary to unload a canoe, etc. in order to make way by tracking or paddling.

make a décharge, unload in order to pass through a shallow stretch of water.
[< Cdn.F < *décharger* unload]

deci– *SI prefix.* tenth: *A decimetre is one tenth of a metre.* *Symbol*: d

dec·i·bel (des′ə bel′) *n.* a unit for comparing levels of power, based on a logarithmic scale. Although the bel is the basic unit, the decibel is the unit most often used, especially for expressing the intensity of sound. [< *deci-* + *bel,* a unit of measure in physics, after A. G. *Bell* (1847-1922), the inventor of the telephone]

de·cide (di sīd′) *v.* **-cid·ed, -cid·ing.** **1** settle (a question, dispute, etc.) by giving victory to one side; give a judgment or the decision. **2** make up one's mind; resolve. **3** cause (a person) to reach a decision. [< L *decidere* cut off < *de-* away + *caedere* cut] —**de·cid′er,** *n.*

☛ *Syn.* **2. Decide, determine, resolve** = make up one's mind. **Decide** emphasizes the idea of coming to a conclusion after some talk or thinking over: *I decided to take the position at the bank.* **Determine** suggests fixing one's mind firmly and unalterably on doing something: *I am determined to make a success of it.* **Resolve** = make up one's mind positively to do or not to do something: *He resolved to do good work.*

de·cid·ed (di sīd′id) *adj.* **1** clear; definite; unquestionable. **2** firm; determined. —**de·cid′ed·ness,** *n.*

☛ *Usage.* **Decided, decisive.** There is a distinction between **decided,** meaning definite or unquestionable, and **decisive,** meaning having or giving a clear result: *His height gave him a decided advantage. In World War II the Battle of El Alamein was a decisive victory.*

de·cid·ed·ly (di sīd′id lē) *adv.* **1** clearly; definitely; unquestionably. **2** firmly; in a determined manner.

de·cid·u·ous (di sij′ü əs) *adj.* **1** falling off at a particular season or stage of growth: *deciduous leaves, deciduous horns.* **2** of trees, shrubs, etc., shedding leaves annually. Maples, elms, and most oaks are deciduous trees. [< L *deciduus < decidere < de-* + *cadere* fall] —**de·cid′u·ous·ly,** *adv.* —**de·cid′u·ous·ness,** *n.*

de·cil·lion (di sil′yən) *n.* **1** in Canada, the United States, and France, a numeral consisting of 1 with 33 zeros following it. **2** in the English and German numerical systems, a numeral consisting of 1 with 60 zeros following it. [< *deci-* < (*mi*)*llion*]

dec·i·mal (des′ə məl) *adj., n.* —*adj.* based on or having to do with the number 10. The metric system is a decimal system of measurement. —*n.* **1** a numeral having a decimal point; decimal number: *The numerals 23.6, 3.09, and 0.728 are decimals.* **2** decimal point: *Put the decimal between the units and the tenths.* [< L *decimus* tenth]

decimal fraction **1** a decimal number. **2** a decimal number less than one.

dec·i·mal·ize (des′ə mə līz′) *v.* **-ized, -iz·ing.** change (a number, system, etc.) to a decimal form or system: *Britain decimalized her currency in the early 1970's.*

dec·i·mal·ly (des′ə məl ē) *adv.* **1** by means of decimals. **2** by tens.

decimal number a number including a fraction whose denominator is 10, 100, 1000, etc., usually written in decimal form. *Examples*: 0.2, 9.93, 4.1.

decimal point the period between the units and the tenths of a decimal fraction. The decimal point separates the whole number from the fractional part of a decimal number.

dec·i·mate (des′ə māt′) *v.* **-mat·ed, -mat·ing.** **1** destroy much of; kill a large part of: *War had decimated the tribe.* **2** select by lot and execute every tenth man of. **3** take or destroy one tenth of. [< L *decimare* take a tenth, ult. < *decem* ten] —**dec′i·ma′tion,** *n.* —**dec′i·ma′tor,** *n.*

dec·i·me·tre (des′ə mē′tər) *n.* an SI unit for measuring length, equal to one tenth of a metre or 10 centimetres. One cubic decimetre is equal to one litre. *Symbol*: dm Also, **decimeter.** [< F *décimètre*]

de·ci·pher (di sī′fər) *v.* **1** make out the meaning of something that is not clear: *trying to decipher poor handwriting, to decipher a mystery.* **2** interpret secret writing by using a key; change something in cipher or code to ordinary language. —**de·ci′pher·a·ble,** *adj.* —**de·ci′pher·er,** *n.*

de·ci·sion (di sizh′ən) *n.* **1** the act of making up one's mind; resolution. **2** the deciding or settling of a question, dispute, etc. by giving judgment to one side. **3** a judgment reached or given. **4** firmness; determination: *A man of decision makes up his mind what to do and then does it.* **5** *Boxing.* the winning of a match on points or by the verdict of the referee and judges, rather than by a knockout. [< L *decisio, -onis < decidere.* See DECIDE.]

de·ci·sive (di sī′siv) *adj.* **1** having or giving a clear result; settling something beyond question. **2** having or showing decision: *a*

decisive answer. —**de·ci′sive·ly,** *adv.* —**de·ci′sive·ness,** *n.*
☛ *Usage.* See note at **decided.**

deck (dek) *n., v.* —*n.* **1** a floor or platform extending from side to side of a ship. Often the upper deck has no roof over it. **2** a raised floor or platform against an outside wall of a house or cottage, usually having no roof, used for sunbathing, etc. **3** any floor, platform, or shell resembling the deck of a ship. **4** a pack of playing cards.

clear the deck or **decks,** **a** remove unnecessary objects from the decks of a warship to prepare for action. **b** make ready for any action.

on deck, *Informal.* **a** ready for work, etc.; on hand: *We were all on deck for the cleanup.* **b** next in line, especially for batting in baseball.

stack the deck, *Informal.* **a** arrange a pack of cards dishonestly. **b** prepare circumstances in advance.

—*v.* **1** provide with a deck. **2** decorate or trim: *The hall was decked with flags.* **3** dress splendidly or elegantly (*used with* out): *She was all decked out in blue satin.*

deck out, dress; adorn: *Grace was decked out in white linen.* [< MDu. *dek* roof]

deck chair a light folding chair, usually having a canvas cover, for use in the open air.

deck·er (dek′ər) *n. Cdn. Baseball.* a catcher's mitt.

deck hand a sailor who works on deck; an ordinary sailor.

deck·house (dek′hous′) *n.* a cabin or compartment built on the deck of a ship.

deck·le (dek′əl) *n.* **1** a detachable frame around the outside of a mould used in making paper by hand. **2** either of two bands along the edge of the wire of a paper-making machine that regulate the width of the web. **3** deckle edge. [< G *Deckel,* dim. of *Decke* cover]

deckle edge **1** the rough edge of untrimmed paper made on a deckle. **2** an imitation of it. —**deck′le·edged′,** *adj.*

deck tennis a game similar to tennis, usually played on board a passenger ship, in which a ring of hope, rubber, etc. is tossed back and forth over a net.

de·claim (di klām′) *v.* **1** recite in public; make a formal speech. **2** speak in a loud and emotional manner; speak or write for effect. [< L *declamare < de-* (intensive) + *clamare* cry] —**de·claim′er,** *n.*

dec·la·ma·tion (dek′lə mā′shən) *n.* **1** the act or art of reciting in public; making a formal speech or speeches. **2** a selection of poetry, prose, etc. for reciting; formal speech. **3** the act of talking loudly and emotionally. **4** loud and emotional talk.

de·clam·a·to·ry (di klam′ə tô′rē) *adj.* **1** having to do with declamation. **2** loud and emotional.

dec·la·ra·tion (dek′lə rā′shən) *n.* **1** the act of declaring: *a declaration of love.* **2** a public statement or formal announcement: *a declaration of war.* **3** a document containing a declaration. **4** a statement acknowledging possession of income, goods, etc. for purposes of taxation, customs charges, etc. **5** a strong statement. **6** *Bridge.* a bid, especially the winning bid. **7** *Cricket.* a tactical decision by one side to close its innings.

Declaration of Independence in the United States, the public statement adopted by the Continental Congress on July 4, 1776, in which the American colonies were declared free and independent of Great Britain.

de·clar·a·tive (di klar′ə tiv *or* di kler′ə tiv) *adj.* making a statement. —**de·clar′a·tive·ly,** *adv.*
☛ *Usage.* **Declarative sentences,** as opposed to imperative, interrogative, and exclamatory sentences, make statements: *That was the most delicious breakfast we had ever tasted.*

de·clar·a·to·ry (di klar′ə tôr′ē *or* di kler′ə tôr′ē) *adj.* declarative.

de·clare (di kler′) *v.* **-clared, -clar·ing.** **1** announce publicly and formally; make known; proclaim: *Parliament has the power to declare war. That company has just declared a dividend on its stock.* **2** say strongly; assert: *She declared that she would solve the problem if it took her all night.* **3** state one's opinion or decision; proclaim oneself for or against something (*used with a pronoun ending in -self*): *They declared themselves against the use of violence.* **4** acknowledge being in possession of (income, assets, goods, etc.) for income tax, customs charges, etc. **5** *Bridge.* announce what suit will be played as trumps. [ME < L *declarare < de-* (intensive) + *clarare* make clear < *clarus* clear] —**de·clar′er,** *n.*
☛ *Syn.* **1.** See note at **announce. 2 Declare, assert** = say something positively. **Declare** = state something openly, strongly, and confidently, sometimes in spite of possible contradiction: *The weather bureau declares that the rain will stop.* **Assert** = state something positively, usually without proof and sometimes in spite of proof that one is wrong: *He asserts that he was not there, but ten people saw him.*

de·clas·si·fy (dē klas′ə fī′) *v.* **-fied, -fy·ing.** remove (documents, codes, etc.) from the list of restricted, confidential, or secret information.

de·clen·sion (di klen′shən) *n.* **1** *Grammar.* in certain languages:

a a variation in the form of nouns, pronouns, and adjectives according to their case. **b** a class of nouns, etc. having similar forms for the different cases. Latin nouns are usually grouped in five declensions. **c** the act of giving the variant forms of a word. **2 a** a downward movement, bend, or slope. **b** a sinking or falling into a lower or inferior condition; deterioration or decline. [irregularly < OF < L *declinatio, -onis* < *declinare*. See DECLINE.]

de·clin·a·ble (di klīn′ə bəl) *adj.* that can be declined; especially, in grammar, having different forms to show different cases: *German nouns are declinable.*

dec·li·na·tion (dek′lə nā′shən) *n.* **1** a downward bend or slope. **2** a polite refusal. **3** the deviation of the needle of a compass from true north or south. **4** *Astronomy.* the angular distance of a star, planet, etc. from the celestial equator. The declination of a star is used to locate its north or south position in the heavens. **5** a turning aside; deviation from a standard.

de·cline (di klīn′) *v.* **-clined, -clin·ing;** *n.* —*v.* **1** refuse, especially politely, to accept or to do (something): *The man declined my offer of help.* **2** bend or slope down: *The hill declines to a fertile valley.* **3** grow less in strength, power, value, etc.; grow worse; decay: *Great nations have risen and declined.* **4** *Grammar.* give or list the cases or case endings of (a noun, pronoun, or adjective). —*n.* **1** falling or sinking to a lower level: *the decline of the sun to the horizon, a decline in prices.* **2** growing worse; a losing of strength, power, value, etc.: *the decline of a person's strength, the decline of the Roman Empire.* **3** the last part of anything: *in the decline of a person's life.* **4** a wasting disease; consumption; tuberculosis of the lungs. **5** a downward slope. [< L *declinare* < *de-* from + *clinare* bend] —**de·clin′er,** *n.*
☛ *Syn. v.* **1.** See note at **refuse.**

de·cliv·i·tous (di kliv′ə təs) *adj.* rather steep.

de·cliv·i·ty (di kliv′ə tē) *n., pl.* **-ties.** a downward slope. [< L *declivitas* < *declivus* sloping downward < *de-* down + *clivus* slope]

de·clutch (dē kluch′) *v.* disengage the clutch of a car, truck, etc.

de·coct (di kokt′) *v.* extract desired substances from (herbs, etc.) by boiling. [< L *decoctus,* pp. of *decoquere* < *de-* away + *coquere* cook]

de·coc·tion (di kok′shən) *n.* **1** the act of boiling to extract some desired substance. **2** a preparation made by boiling a substance in water or other liquid; an extract obtained by boiling.

de·code (dē kōd′) *v.* **-cod·ed, -cod·ing.** translate (coded messages) into ordinary language. —**de·cod′er,** *n.*

dé·colle·tage (dā′kol ə täzh′; *French,* dā kôl tȧzh′) *n.* **1** the neckline of a dress, blouse, etc. that is cut revealingly low. **2** a dress, blouse, etc. cut with such a neckline. [< F]

dé·colle·té (dā′kol ə tā′; *French,* dā kôl tā′) *adj.* **1** of a dress, blouse, etc., low-necked. **2** wearing a low-necked dress, blouse, etc. [< F *décolleté,* pp. of *décolleter* bare the neck of]

de·col·o·nize (dē kol′ə nīz′) *v.* **-ized, iz·ing.** give independence to (a colony). —**de·col′o·niz·a′tion,** *n.*

de·col·or or **de·col·our** (dē kul′ər) *v.* decolorize.

de·col·or·ant (dē kul′ər ənt) *adj., n.* —*adj.* able to decolorize. —*n.* a substance that decolorizes.

de·col·or·ize or **de·col·our·ize** (dē kul′ər īz′) *v.* **-ized, -iz·ing.** remove color from, as by bleaching.

de·com·pose (dē′kəm pōz′) *v.* **-posed, -pos·ing. 1** decay; rot or become rotten. **2** separate (a substance) into what it is made of: *A prism decomposes sunlight into its many colors.* **3** of a substance, become separated into its parts. —**de′com·pos′er,** *n.*
☛ *Syn.* **1.** See note at **decay.**

de·com·po·si·tion (dē′kom pə zish′ən) *n.* **1** the act or process of decomposing. **2** decay; rot.

de·com·press (dē′kəm pres′) *v.* **1** release from pressure. **2** remove pressure from (a diver, etc.) gradually by means of an air lock or decompression chamber.

de·com·pres·sion (dē′kəm presh′ən) *n.* the removal or lessening of pressure, especially of air pressure.

decompression chamber an airtight compartment used for the gradual readjustment of persons from abnormal to normal air pressure or for the simulation of low air pressure in training flyers for high-altitude flight.

decompression sickness a disorder characterized by severe headache, pain in muscles and joints, cramp, and difficulty in breathing, due to the formation of nitrogen bubbles in body tissues and caused by too sudden and substantial a decrease in atmospheric pressure, as when a person returns too rapidly to normal atmospheric pressure from high underwater pressure or when a person ascends too rapidly to a high altitude in an unpressurized aircraft.

de·con·ges·tant (dē′kən jest′ənt) *n.* a drug used to relieve congestion of the mucous membranes in the nose.

de·con·tam·i·nate (dē′kən tam′ə nāt′) *v.* **-nat·ed, -nat·ing.**

hat, āge, fär; let, ēqual, tėrm; it, īce
hot, ōpen, ôrder; oil, out; cup, pút, rüle,
əbove, takən, pencəl, lemən, circəs

ch, child; ng, long; sh, ship
th, thin; ᴛʜ, then; zh, measure

1 make free from poison gas or harmful radio-active agents. **2** free from any sort of contamination. —**de′con·tam′i·na′tion,** *n.*

de·con·trol (dē′kən trōl′) *v.* **-trolled, -trol·ling;** *n.* —*v.* remove controls from: *to decontrol the price of meat.* —*n.* a removing of controls.

dé·cor or **de·cor** (dā kôr′) *n.* **1** decoration. **2** the overall style and arrangement of the furnishings of a room, etc. **3** a stage setting. [< F *décor* < *décorer* decorate]

dec·o·rate (dek′ə rāt′) *v.* **-rat·ed, -rat·ing. 1** furnish with ornamental things, especially for a particular occasion: *to decorate a Christmas tree. The room was decorated with flowers for the reception.* **2** plan the style, color, and arrangement of interior furnishings, wallpaper, etc. **3** paint or paper a room, house, etc. **4** give a medal, ribbon, etc. to (a person) as a mark of honor: *The firefighter was decorated for bravery.* [< L *decorare* < *decus, decoris* adornment]
☛ *Syn.* **1. Decorate, ornament, adorn** = add something to give or increase beauty. **Decorate** = put on ornaments or other trimming to add finish, color, or a festive appearance to something: *We decorated the Christmas tree.* **Ornament** suggests adding, often permanently, something that especially suits a thing and adds to its general effect and beauty: *Stained glass windows ornament the church.* **Adorn** suggests adding something that is beautiful itself and therefore increases the beauty of a thing or person: *She adorned her hair with flowers.*

dec·o·ra·tion (dek′ə rā′shən) *n.* **1** the act or process of decorating. **2** anything used to add beauty; ornament. **3** a medal, ribbon, etc. awarded as a mark of honor: *The general wore many decorations.*

dec·o·ra·tive (dek′ə rə tiv or dek′ə rā′tiv) *adj.* decorating; helping to adorn; ornamental: *The flowered curtains were highly decorative.* —**dec′o·ra·tive·ly,** *adv.* —**dec′o·ra·tive·ness,** *n.*

dec·o·ra·tor (dek′ə rā′tər) *n.* **1** a person who decorates, especially one who specializes in designing color schemes and the style and arrangement of furnishings for rooms, etc. **2** (*adj.*) designed for use in the decoration of rooms, etc.: *decorator fabrics, decorator colors.*

dec·o·rous (dek′ə rəs or di kô′res) *adj.* well-behaved; acting properly; in good taste; dignified. [< L *decorus* < *decor* seemliness, comeliness] —**dec′o·rous·ly,** *adv.* —**dec′o·rous·ness,** *n.*

de·co·rum (di kô′rəm) *n.* **1** propriety of action, speech, dress, etc.: *You behave with decorum when you do what is proper.* **2** an observance or requirement of polite society. [< L *decorum,* neut. of *decorus* seemly]

de·coy (*v.* di koi′; *n.* dē′koi or di koi′) *v., n.* —*v.* **1** lure wild birds, animals, etc. into a trap or within gunshot. **2** lead or tempt into danger. **3** *Cdn.* deke. —*n.* **1** an artificial bird used to lure real birds into a trap or within range of a hunter's gun. **2** a bird or other animal trained to lure others of its kind into a trap. **3** any place into which wild birds or animals are lured. **4** any person or thing used to lead or tempt into danger. [< MDu. *de kooi* the cage < L *cavea* cave] —**de·coy′er,** *n.*

de·crease (*v.* di krēs′; *n.* dē′krēs or di krēs′) *v.* **-creased, -creas·ing;** *n.* —*v.* **1** become less: *Hunger decreases as one eats.* **2** make less: *to decrease prices.* —*n.* **1** the process of becoming less: *A decrease in humidity made the hot weather more bearable.* **2** the amount by which a thing becomes or is made less. **on the decrease,** decreasing. [ME < OF *de(s)creiss-,* a stem of *descreistre* < L *decrescere* < *de-* down + *crescere* grow] —**de·creas′ing·ly,** *adv.*
☛ *Syn. v.* **1, 2. Decrease, diminish, dwindle** = become or make less. **Decrease** suggests steadily going down little by little: *The output of the factory is decreasing.* **Diminish** suggests becoming smaller in size, amount, or importance because someone or something keeps taking away a part: *The medical bills during his long sickness have diminished his savings.* **Dwindle** emphasizes the idea of wasting away, or becoming smaller and smaller until almost nothing is left: *Our savings have dwindled.*

de·cree (di krē′) *n., v.* **-creed, -cree·ing.** —*n.* **1** a decision or order made by a government, court, church, etc. **2** something foreordained. —*v.* order or determine by or as if by decree: *The government decreed that the election would take place July 8.* [ME < OF *decre,* var. of *decret* < L *decretum,* pp. neut. of *decernere* < *de-* from + *cernere* sift, decide] —**de·cree′er,** *n.*

decree ni·si (nī′sī or nē′sē) *Law.* a conditional granting of a divorce. The decree becomes final, or absolute, after a given period unless cause to the contrary is shown in the interim. [< L *nisi* unless]

dec·re·ment (dek′rə mənt) *n.* **1** a gradual decrease; slow loss. **2** the amount lost by gradual decrease. **3** *Mathematics.* the amount by which a variable decreases. [< L *decrementum* < *decrescere*. See DECREASE; compare INCREMENT.]

de·crep·it (di krep′it) *adj.* broken down or weakened by old age; old and feeble. [< L *decrepitus* broken down < *de-* + *crepare* creak] —**de·crep′it·ly,** *adv.*

de·crep·i·tude (di krep′ə tyüd′ *or* di krep′ə tüd′) *n.* feebleness, usually from old age, a decrepit condition; weakness.

decresc. decrescendo.

de·cre·scen·do (dē′krə shen′dō *or* dā′krə shen′dō) *n., pl.* **-dos;** *adj., adv. Music.* —*n.* **1** a gradual decrease in force or loudness; diminuendo. The sign for a decrescendo is >. **2** a passage to be played or sung with a decrescendo. —*adj. or adv.* with a gradual decrease in force or loudness. *Abbrev.:* decresc. [< Ital.]

de·cre·tal (di krē′təl) *n. Roman Catholic Church.* a papal decree or reply settling some question of doctrine or ecclesiastical law. [ME < OF < Med.L *decretale,* ult. < L *decretum.* See DECREE.]

de·cri·al (di krī′əl) *n.* the act of decrying.

de·crim·i·nal·ize (dē krim′ə nəl īz′) *v.* **-ized, -iz·ing.** remove (a specific act, etc.) from the category of criminal offence: *to decriminalize the possession of marijuana.* —**de·crim′i·nal·i·za′tion,** *n.*

de·cry (di krī′) *v.* **-cried, -cry·ing. 1** condemn: *The minister decried gambling in all its forms.* **2** make little of; try to lower the value of: *The lumber dealer decried the use of concrete for houses.* [< F *decrier* < *de-* away, apart + *crier* cry < L *quiritare*] —**de·cri′er,** *n.*

de·cum·bent (di kum′bənt) *adj.* **1** of stems, branches, etc., lying or trailing on the ground with the end tending to climb. **2** lying down; reclining. [< L *decumbens, -entis,* ppr. of *decumbere* lie down]

de·cur·rent (di kėr′ənt) *adj. Botany.* especially of a leaf, extending downward from the base as two wings along the stem. The common thistle (*Cirsium vulgare*) has decurrent leaves. [< L *decurrens, -entis,* ppr. of *decurrere* < *de-* down + *currere* run]

ded·i·cate (ded′ə kāt′) *v.* **-cat·ed, -cat·ing. 1** set apart for a sacred or solemn purpose; consecrate: *The new altar was dedicated at a special service.* **2** give up wholly or earnestly to some person or purpose: *The minister dedicated his life to the service of God.* **3** address (a book, poem, etc.) to a friend or patron as a mark of affection, respect, gratitude, etc. **4** celebrate the opening of (a bridge, institution, meeting, etc.) with an official ceremony. [< L *dedicare* proclaim, affirm < *de-* (intensive) + *dicare* proclaim] —**ded′i·ca′tor,** *n.*
☞ *Syn.* **2.** See note at **devote.**

ded·i·ca·tion (ded′ə kā′shən) *n.* **1** setting apart or being set apart for a sacred or solemn purpose: *the dedication of a church.* **2** very great and constant interest; close attachment; complete loyalty (to some person or purpose): *a dedication to music, a dedication to one's country.* **3** the words dedicating a book, poem, etc. to a friend or patron. **4** a ceremony attending the official opening of something, as a building, institution, or convention: *the dedication of a new library wing.*

ded·i·ca·tive (ded′ə kə tiv *or* ded′ə kā′tiv) *adj.* dedicatory.

ded·i·ca·to·ry (ded′ə kə tô′rē) *adj.* of dedication; as a dedication.

de·duce (di dyüs′ *or* di düs′) *v.* **-duced, -duc·ing. 1** infer from a general rule or principle; reach (a conclusion) by reasoning: *After looking at the evidence, the firemen deduced the cause of the fire.* **2** trace the course, descent, or origin of. [< L *deducere* < *de-* down + *ducere* lead]

de·duc·i·ble (di dyüs′ə bəl *or* di düs′ə bəl) *adj.* capable of being deduced or inferred.

de·duct (di dukt′) *v.* take away; subtract. [< L *deductus,* pp. of *deducere.* See DEDUCE.]
☞ *Syn.* See note at **subtract.**

de·duct·i·ble (di duk′tə bəl) *adj.* that can be deducted.

de·duc·tion (di duk′shən) *n.* **1** the act of taking away; subtraction: *No deduction in pay is made for absence due to illness.* **2** the amount deducted. **3** *Logic.* the act of reaching a conclusion by reasoning; inference. A person using deduction reasons from general laws to particular cases. *Example: All animals die; a cat is an animal; therefore, a cat will die.* **4** a conclusion reached by this method of reasoning.
☞ *Usage.* **Deduction** and **induction** are the names of two opposite processes of logical reasoning. **Deduction** is the process by which one starts with a general principle, or premise, applies it to a particular case, and arrives at a conclusion that is true provided the premise is true: *All animals die; this is an animal; therefore, this will die.* **Induction** applies to the process by which one collects many particular cases, finds out by experiment which is common to all of them, and forms a general rule or principle that is probably true of the whole class: *Every animal I have tested died; therefore, all animals die.*

de·duc·tive (di duk′tiv) *adj.* of or using deduction; reasoning by deduction. —**de·duc′tive·ly,** *adv.*

deed (dēd) *n., v.* —*n.* **1** something done; act. **2** a brave, skilful, or unusual act. **3** an action; doing; performance. **4** a written or printed document, sealed and signed, containing some contract. A buyer of real estate receives a deed legally transferring the ownership. **in deed,** in fact; actually.
—*v.* transfer by deed. [OE *dæd*]

deed poll *Law.* a deed involving only one party, consisting of a formal declaration of an act. A legal name change is made by deed poll. [from the original practice of 'polling', or cutting even, the edge of such a deed, rather than indenting it, as was done for deeds made in two or more copies. 16c.]

dee·jay (dē′jā′) *n. Informal.* disc jockey. [abbrev. of *disc jockey*]

deem (dēm) *v.* think; believe; consider: *The lawyer deemed it unwise to take the case to court.* [OE *dēman* < *dōm* judgment]

de–em·pha·size (dē em′fə sīz′) *v.* **-ized, -iz·ing.** reduce emphasis on; make less prominent; play down: *They agreed to de-emphasize the contentious points.*

deep (dēp) *adj., adv., n.* —*adj.* **1** going far down or back: *a deep well, a deep recess.* **2** from far down or back: *Take a deep breath.* **3** far down or back: *a deep cut.* **4** far on. **5** in depth: *a tank two metres deep.* **6** low in pitch: *a deep voice.* **7** strong and dark in color: *a deep red.* **8** strong; great; intense; extreme: *deep sorrow, a deep sleep.* **9** requiring or showing much thought and study: *a deep book.* **10** immersed or involved: *deep in thought, deep in debt.* **11** wise; shrewd. **12** sly; crafty. **13** extreme: *He's in deep trouble.* —*adv.* **1** far down or back: *The men dug deep before they found water.* **2** of time, far on: *He studied deep into the night.* —*n.* **1** a deep place. **2** the most intense part: *the deep of winter.* **3 the deep,** the sea. [OE *dēop*] —**deep′ly,** *adv.* —**deep′ness,** *n.*

deep–chest·ed (dēp′ches′tid) *adj.* having a thick chest.

deep·en (dēp′ən) *v.* make or become deeper.

deep–freeze (*n.* dēp′frēz′; *v.* dēp′frēz′) *n., v.* **-froze or -freezed, -fro·zen or -freezed, -freez·ing.** —*n.* **1** a freezer cabinet or chest for freezing foods rapidly and storing them frozen for long periods. **2** the state of being deep-frozen: *The government kept the controversial report in deep-freeze.* —*v.* **1** freeze (food) rapidly for storage in a deep-freeze. **2** keep as if frozen: *to deep-freeze a plan.* —**deep′-freez′er,** *n.*

deep–fry (dēp′frī′) *v.* **-fried, -fry·ing.** fry in deep fat or oil. —**deep′-fry′er,** *n.*

deep–laid (dēp′lād′) *adj.* planned secretly and carefully: *deep-laid schemes.*

deep–root·ed (dēp′rüt′id) *adj.* **1** deeply rooted. **2** firmly fixed: *deep-rooted traditions, a deep-rooted dislike.*

deep–sea (dēp′sē′) *adj.* of or in the deeper parts of the sea: *a deep-sea diver.*

deep–seat·ed (dēp′sēt′id) *adj.* **1** far below the surface. **2** firmly fixed: *The disease was so deep-seated that it could not be cured.*

deep–set (dēp′set′) *adj.* **1** set deeply. **2** firmly fixed.

deep South *or* **Deep South** in the United States, generally, Georgia, Alabama, Mississippi, Louisiana, and part of South Carolina.

deep structure *Linguistics.* **1** the underlying pattern of relationships linking the elements of meaning of a sentence. **2** a formal representation of this, showing the relationships symbolically but without the grammatical indicators used to show them in the actual sentence. Compare **surface structure.**

deep–wat·er (dēp′wo′tər *or* -wô′tər) *adj.* of or having to do with deep water; deep-sea.

deer (dēr) *n., pl.* **deer. 1** any of various cud-chewing animals (family Cervidae) having long, slender legs with small, split hoofs, the males (and, in some species, some females) having solid, bony antlers that are shed each year. See **white-tailed deer, mule deer, fallow deer, red deer, roe deer, musk deer. 2** any member of the family Cervidae, including the moose, elk, and caribou. **3** *Cdn. North.* caribou. [OE *dēor* animal]
☞ *Hom.* **dear.**

deer fly any of a genus (*Chrysops*) of small horseflies having dark markings on the wings.

deer·hound (dēr′hound′) *n.* a breed of large dog resembling a greyhound, but larger and having shaggy hair. The deerhound comes from Scotland, where it was originally bred for hunting deer.

deer lodge a lodge or camp to accommodate deer hunters,

especially one that may be rented by hunters visiting the area during the open season.

deer mouse any of several New World mice (genus *Peromyseus*) usually having brownish fur with white underparts and feet.

deer·skin (dēr′skin′) *n.* **1** the hide of a deer. **2** leather made from it: *deerskin moccasins.* **3** deerskins, *pl.* clothing made from this leather.

deer·stalk·er (dēr′stok′ər *or* -stôk′ər) *n.* **1** a person who hunts deer by stalking. **2** a close-fitting cap with earflaps, originally worn by hunters.

de-es·ca·late (dē es′kə lāt′) *v.* **-lat·ed, -lat·ing.** stop or reverse growth or expansion: *to de-escalate a war.* **—de-es′ca·la′tion,** *n.*

def. **1** definition; defined. **2** defendant. **3** deferred. **4** defective.

de·face (di fās′) *v.* **-faced, -fac·ing.** spoil the appearance of; mar. [< obs. F *defacer* < *de-* away, apart + *face* face < L *facies* form] **—de·fac′er,** *n.*

☛ *Syn.* **Deface, disfigure** = spoil the appearance of someone or something. **Deface** = spoil the surface of something by blotting out an important detail, by scratching something in, etc.: *Scribbled pictures and remarks defaced the pages of the library book.* **Disfigure** suggests spoiling the beauty of a person or thing by permanent injury too deep or serious to remove: *The accident left her face disfigured.*

de·face·ment (di fās′mənt) *n.* **1** the act of defacing. **2** the state of being defaced. **3** anything that defaces.

de fac·to (dē′fak′tō *or* dā′fak′tō) **1** in fact; in reality. **2** actually existing, whether legal or not: *a de facto government.* [< L *de facto* from the fact]

de·fal·cate (di fal′kāt, di fol′kāt, *or* di fôl′kāt) *v.* **-cat·ed, -cat·ing.** steal or misuse money trusted to one's care. [< Med.L *defalcare*, literally, to cut off with a sickle < *de-* away + *falx, -cis* sickle] **—de·fal′ca·tor,** *n.*

de·fal·ca·tion (dē′fal kā′shən, dē′fol kā′shən, *or* dē′fôl kā′shən) *n.* **1** the theft or misuse of money entrusted to one's care. **2** the amount stolen or misused.

def·a·ma·tion (def′ə mā′shən *or* dē′fə mā′shən) *n.* a defaming or being defamed; slander; libel.

de·fam·a·to·ry (di fam′ə tô′rē) *adj.* defaming; slanderous.

de·fame (di fām′) *v.* **-famed, -fam·ing.** attack the good name of; harm the reputation of; speak evil of; slander; libel: *Men in public life are sometimes defamed by opponents.* [ME < OF *diffamer* < L *diffamare* damage by rumor < *de-* down, from (confused with *dis-*) + *fama* rumor] **—de·fam′er,** *n.*

de·fault (di folt′ *or* -fôlt′) *n., v.* **—n.** **1** a failure to do something or to appear somewhere when due; neglect. If, in any contest, one side does not appear, it loses by default. **2** a failure to pay when due. **3** *Law.* a failure to appear in court at the time specified for a legal proceeding.
in default of, in the absence of; lacking: *In default of tools, she used a hairpin and a needle.*
—v. **1** fail to do something or appear somewhere when due. **2** fail to pay when due. **3** *Law.* **a** fail to appear in court at a specified time. **b** declare (a person) in default. **c** lose a case by default. [ME < OF *defaute* < *defaillir* < *de-* de- + *faillir*, ult. < L *fallere* deceive]

de·fault·er (di fol′tər *or* -fôl′tər) *n.* **1** a person who defaults. **2** a person who steals or misuses money trusted to his care.

de·feat (di fēt′) *v., n.* **—v.** **1** win a victory over; overcome: *to defeat an opposing team, to defeat an enemy.* **2** bring to nothing; prevent the success of; frustrate or thwart: *to defeat someone's plans, to defeat a bill in Parliament.* **3** *Law.* make null and void; annul.
—n. **1** defeating or being defeated: *the defeat of all our hopes, the defeat of an army.* **2** an instance of defeating: *It was a humiliating defeat.* [ME < OF *de(s)fait,* pp. of *desfaire* < LL *diffacere* < L *dis-un-* + *facere* do] **—de·feat′er,** *n.*

☛ *Syn.* *v.* **1. Defeat, conquer, overcome** = win a victory over someone or something. **Defeat** = win a victory, at least for the moment: *We defeated Laurier Collegiate in basketball yesterday.* **Conquer,** more formal, emphasizes the idea of winning control over people, things, or feelings: *Some countries may be defeated, but never conquered.* **Overcome** emphasizes the idea of getting the better of things or, especially, feelings: *He could not overcome his dislike for that man.*

de·feat·ism (di fēt′iz əm) *n.* the attitude or behavior of a defeatist.

de·feat·ist (di fēt′ist) *n., adj.* **—n.** a person who tends to expect, or readily accepts defeat. **—adj.** characteristic of a defeatist: *a defeatist attitude.*

def·e·cate (def′ə kāt′) *v.* **-cat·ed, -cat·ing.** have a movement of the bowels. [< L *defaecare* < *de-* from + *faeces,* pl. dregs, solid excrement] **—def′e·ca′tion,** *n.*

de·fect (*n.* dē′fekt *or* di fekt′; *v.* di fekt′) *n., v.* **—n.** **1** a fault; blemish; imperfection. **2** the lack of something essential to completeness; a falling short. **—v.** forsake one's own country, group, etc. for another, especially another that is opposed to it in

hat, āge, fär; let, ēqual, tėrm; it, īce
hot, ōpen, ôrder; oil, out; cup, pùt, rüle,
əbove, takən, pencəl, lemən, circəs
ch, child; ng, long; sh, ship
th, thin; ŦH, then; zh, measure

political or social doctrine. [< L *defectus* want < *deficere* fail. See DEFICIENT.] **—de·fec′tor,** *n.*

☛ *Syn.* **1. Defect, flaw** = an imperfection or fault. **Defect** is the general word, applying to any imperfection on the surface or in the make-up of a person or thing: *A hearing aid helps to overcome defects in hearing. No person is without defects.* **Flaw** applies to a defect in structure, suggesting a crack or break when used literally, a fault in character when used figuratively: *That bubble is a flaw in the glass. Jealousy is the great flaw in his character.*

de·fec·tion (di fek′shən) *n.* **1** a falling away from loyalty, duty, religion, etc.; desertion. **2** failure.

de·fec·tive (di fek′tiv) *adj.* **1** having a serious flaw or blemish; faulty: *His hearing is defective. We returned the toaster because it was defective.* **2** *Grammar.* lacking one or more of the usual forms of inflection. *Ought* is a defective verb. **3** of a person, below normal in intelligence.
—n. a defective person or thing; especially, a person having subnormal intelligence. **—de·fec′tive·ly,** *adv.* **—de·fec′tive·ness,** *n.*

de·fence (di fens′ *or, for def. 4,* dē′fens) *n.* **1** the act of defending or protecting; a guarding against attack or harm: *The armed forces are responsible for the defence of the country.* **2** anything that defends or protects; something used to guard against attack or harm: *A wall around a city used to be a defence against enemies. A well-built house or a warm coat is a defence against cold weather.* **3** *Boxing or fencing.* the act of defending oneself. **4** the team or players defending a goal in a game. **5** an action, speech, or writing in favor of something. **6** *Law.* **a** the arguments, etc. presented by a defendant or his lawyer in contesting a case. **b** a defendant and his lawyers collectively. Also, **defense.** [ME < OF < L *defensa* < *defendere* ward off]

de·fence·less (di fens′lis) *adj.* having no defence; unprotected; helpless against attack or harm: *A baby is defenceless.* Also, **defenseless. —de·fence′less·ly,** *adv.* **—de·fence′less·ness,** *n.*

de·fence·man (di fens′mən) *n., pl.* **-men.** *Sports.* a player whose job is to prevent the opposing players from approaching the goal. Also, **defenseman.**

defence mechanism **1** any self-protective reaction by an organism. **2** *Psychology.* an unconscious adjustment of behavior or mental attitude designed to shut out unpleasant emotions.

de·fend (di fend′) *v.* **1** guard from attack or harm; protect. **2** *Sports.* **a** try to keep an opponent away from: *to defend a goal.* **b** maintain one's position as champion by playing or fighting against a challenger: *He will forfeit his title unless he defends it within a year.* **3** justify or maintain against opposition, criticism, etc.: *to defend one's argument. She defended their conduct in a letter to the editor.* **4** *Law.* **a** act as counsel for in a court of law: *He has hired a well-known lawyer to defend him.* **b** resist or deny the claim of a plaintiff; contest a lawsuit or charge: *Is she going to defend the speeding charge?* [ME < OF < L *defendere* ward off]
—de·fend′a·ble, *adj.*

☛ *Syn.* **1.** See note at **guard.**

de·fen·da·ble (di fen′də bəl) *adj.* defensible.

de·fend·ant (di fen′dənt) *n.* **1** a person against whom an action is brought in a court of law. Compare **accused.** **2** a person charged with a criminal offence in a court of law.

de·fend·er (di fen′dər) *n.* **1** a protector or guardian. **2** *Sports.* the holder of a championship who is defending it by playing or fighting against a challenger.

de·fense (di fens′) See **defence.**

de·fense·less (di fens′lis) See **defenceless.**

de·fense·man (di fens′mən) *n., pl.* **-men.** See **defenceman.**

de·fen·si·bil·i·ty (di fen′sə bil′ə tē) *n.* the quality or state of being defensible.

de·fen·si·ble (di fen′si bəl) *adj.* **1** capable of being defended. **2** justifiable; proper. **—de·fen′si·bly,** *adv.*

de·fen·sive (di fen′siv) *adj., n.* **—adj.** **1** ready to defend; defending. **2** for defence: *Their team had a good defensive strategy.* **3** of defence: *a defensive attitude.*
—n. **1** a position or attitude of defence. **2** anything that defends.
on the defensive, ready to defend, apologize, or explain: *She has been criticized so much that she is always on the defensive.*
—de·fen′sive·ly, *adv.* **—de·fen′sive·ness,** *n.*

de·fer[1] (di fėr′) *v.* **-ferred, -fer·ring.** put off; delay. [< L *differe.* Doublet of DIFFER.]
☛ *Syn.* See note at **delay.**

de·fer[2] (di fėr′) v. **-ferred, -fer·ring.** yield; submit to another's judgment, opinion, or wishes: *He deferred to his sister's wishes.* [< F *déférer* < L *deferre* < *de-* down + *ferre* carry]

def·er·ence (def′ər əns) n. **1** a yielding to the judgment or opinion of another; courteous submission. **2** respect; regard. **in deference to,** out of respect or regard for: *In deference to his father's wishes,* he worked hard at his studies.
☛ *Syn.* 2. See note at **honor.**

def·er·ent (def′ər ənt) adj. deferential.

def·er·en·tial (def′ər en′shəl) adj. showing defence; respectful. —**def′er·en′tial·ly,** adv.

de·fer·ment (di fėr′mənt) n. a putting off; delay.

de·ferred (di fėrd′) adj. **1** postponed. **2** with benefits withheld for a certain time. **3** *Esp.U.S.* exempted for a time from induction into the armed forces.

de·fi·ance (di fī′əns) n. **1** the act or an instance of openly resisting or opposing: *Rebellion always involves defiance against authority.* **2** intent or willingness to openly resist or oppose: *Her defiance showed clearly on her face. He shouted his defiance.* **in defiance of,** in open opposition to; showing contempt or disregard for: *She took the car in defiance of her father's wishes.*

de·fi·ant (di fī′ənt) adj. showing defiance; challenging; openly resisting or offering a challenge; hostile. [< F *défiant,* ppr. of *défier* defy] —**de·fi′ant·ly,** adv. —**de·fi′ant·ness,** n.

de·fi·cien·cy (di fish′ən sē) n., pl. **-cies. 1** a lack or absence of something needed or required; incompleteness. **2** the amount by which something falls short or is too small.

de·fi·cient (di fish′ənt) adj., n. —adj. **1** incomplete; defective. **2** not sufficient in quantity, force, etc.; lacking: *His diet is deficient in protein.* —n. a person or thing that is deficient: *a mental deficient.* [< L *deficiens, -entis* failing, ppr. of *deficere* < *de-* from + *facere* make, do] —**de·fi′cient·ly,** adv.

def·i·cit (def′ə sit) n. the amount by which a sum of money falls short; shortage: *Since the club owed $15 and had only $10 in the treasury, there was a deficit of $5.* [< L *deficit* it is wanting. See DEFICIENT.]

de·fi·er (di fī′ər) n. a person who defies.

de·file[1] (di fīl′) v. **-filed, -fil·ing. 1** make filthy or dirty; make disgusting in any way. **2** destroy the purity or cleanness of; corrupt. **3** violate the sanctity of: *During the war many shrines and churches were defiled by marauding raiders.* **4** stain; dishonor: *Charges of corruption defiled the reputation of the government.* [alteration of ME *defoul* (< OF *defouler* trample down, violate) after obs. *file befoul* < OE *fȳlan* < *fūl* foul] —**de·fil′er,** n.

de·file[2] (di fīl′ or dē′fīl) v. **-filed, -fil·ing;** n. —v. march in a line. —n. **1** a narrow way or passage through which troops can march only in narrow columns. **2** a steep and narrow valley. [< F *défilé,* special use of pp. of *défiler* march by files < *dé-* off + *file* file[1]]

de·file·ment (di fīl′mənt) n. **1** the act of defiling. **2** the state of being defiled. **3** something that defiles. [< *defile*[1]]

de·fine (di fīn′) v. **-fined, -fin·ing. 1** make clear the meaning of; explain: *A dictionary defines words.* **2** make clear; make distinct. **3** fix; settle. **4** settle the limits of. **5** be a distinguishing feature of; characterize: *Perseverance usually defines success.* [ME < OF < L *definire* to limit < *de-* from + *finis* boundary] —**de·fin′a·ble,** adj. —**de·fin′er,** n.

def·i·nite (def′ə nit) adj. **1** clear and exact in meaning or expression; free of ambiguity or doubt: *He wouldn't give a definite answer. She was very definite about the time of the shot. Is it definite that we're going?* **2** precisely defined; having exact limits; fixed: *a definite area, a definite number of players.* **3** See **definite article.** [< L *definitus,* pp. of *definire.* See DEFINE.] —**def′i·nite·ness,** n.
☛ *Usage.* **Definite, definitive** are not synonyms, although both suggest "leaving no doubt." **Definite** is a synonym of *distinct* and means "perfectly clear and exact," leaving no doubt about either what is meant or what is not meant: *I expect a definite answer, either yes or no.* **Definitive** is a synonym of *decisive,* and means "final and complete," putting an end to doubt or uncertainty: *We have appealed to the Supreme Court for a definitive answer.*

definite article *Grammar.* in English, the word *the,* used before nouns to designate a specific or previously identified person, thing, etc.

def·i·nite·ly (def′ə nit lē or def′nət lē) adv. **1** in a definite manner. **2** certainly: *Will you go? Definitely.*

def·i·ni·tion (def′ə nish′ən) n. **1** the act or process of explaining or making clear the meaning of a word or group of words. **2** a statement that makes clear the meaning of a word or group of words; explanation. **3** the power of making clear and distinct. The capacity of a lens to give a clear, distinct image of an object is called its definition. **4** clearness or distinctness of detail, etc. in the

reproduction of sound or images on a recording, photograph, television screen, etc.

def·i·ni·tion·al (def′ə nish′ə nəl) adj. of or having to do with definition.

de·fin·i·tive (di fin′ə tiv) adj., n. —adj. **1** conclusive; final. **2** authoritative; completely reliable: *That book is the definitive work on marine biology.* **3** designating a type of postage stamp issued in various denominations and available for a certain length of time in all post offices for regular use. Canadian definitive stamps usually feature the Queen or a series of related designs for the various denominations.
—n. **1** *Grammar.* a word that limits or defines a noun, such as *the, this, all,* and *none.* **2** a definitive stamp. —**de·fin′i·tive·ly,** adv. —**de·fin′i·tive·ness,** n.
☛ *Usage.* See note at **definite.**

de·flate (di flāt′) v. **-flat·ed, -flat·ing. 1** let air or gas out of (a balloon, tire, football, etc.). **2** reduce the amount of; reduce: *to deflate prices, to deflate currency.* **3** become reduced. **4** injure or destroy the conceit or confidence of: *Our laughter soon deflated him.* [< L *deflare* < *de-* off + *flare* blow] —**de·fla′tor,** n.

de·fla·tion (di flā′shən) n. **1** the act of deflating: *the deflation of a tire, the deflation of a prig.* **2** a reduction. **3** the reduction of the amount of available money in circulation so that prices go down. **4** *Geology.* the removal of solid particles by the wind, leaving the rocks exposed to the weather.

de·fla·tion·ar·y (di flā′shən er′ē) adj. of or having to do with deflation.

de·flect (di flekt′) v. bend or turn aside; change the direction of. [< L *deflectere* < *de-* away + *flectere* bend] —**de·flec′tor,** n.

de·flec·tion (di flek′shən) n. **1** a bending or turning aside. **2** the amount of bending or turning. **3** a bending downward. **4** *Physics.* the movement of the needle or indicator of a scientific instrument from its zero or normal position.

de·flec·tive (di flek′tiv) adj. **1** causing deflection. **2** tending to deflect.

de·flex·ion (di flek′shən) *Esp.Brit.* See **deflection.**

de·flo·ra·tion (dē′flôr ā′shən or def′lə rā′shən) n. the act of deflowering.

de·flow·er (dē flou′ər) v. **1** end the virginity of (a girl or woman). **2** mar the beauty or innocence of; spoil. **3** strip flowers from. —**de·flow′er·er,** n.

de·fo·li·ant (dē fō′lē ənt) n. a chemical agent that defoliates.

de·fo·li·ate (dē fō′lē āt′) v. **-at·ed, -at·ing.** remove the leaves from (a plant or plants), especially by means of a chemical spray. —**de·fo′li·a′tion,** n. —**de·fo′li·a′tor,** n.

de·for·est (dē fôr′ist) v. clear of trees: *The land had to be deforested before the settlers could farm it.* —**de·for′est·a′tion,** n. —**de·for′est·er,** n.

de·form (di fôrm′) v. **1** spoil the form or shape of: *Shoes that are too tight deform the feet.* **2** make ugly; disfigure: *a face deformed by rage.* **3** become altered in shape or form. **4** *Physics.* change the shape of by stress. —**de·form′er,** n.

de·for·ma·tion (dē′fôr mā′shən or def′ər mā′shən) n. **1** deforming or being deformed. **2** a change of form. **3** a changed form. **4** *Physics.* a change in the shape or dimensions of a body, resulting from stress; strain. **5** *Geology.* **a** any change in the original state or size of rock masses, especially as produced by faulting. **b** an instance of this.

de·formed (di fôrmd′) adj. especially of the body or a part of it, not properly formed; distorted or misshapen: *a deformed foot.*

de·form·i·ty (di fôr′mə tē) n., pl. **-ties. 1** a part that is not properly formed. **2** the condition of being improperly formed. **3** an improperly formed person or thing. **4** ugliness.

de·fraud (di frod′ or -frôd′) v. take money, rights, etc. away from by fraud; cheat: *The dishonest lawyer defrauded the widow of her savings.* [ME < MF < L *defraudare* < *de-* completely + *fraus, fraudis* fraud] —**de·fraud′er,** n.

de·fray (di frā′) v. pay (costs or expenses): *The expenses of national parks are defrayed by the taxpayers.* [< F *défrayer* < *de-* (intensive) + *frai* cost] —**de·fray′er,** n.

de·fray·al (di frā′əl) n. a payment (of expenses, etc.).

de·fray·ment (di frā′mənt) n. defrayal.

de·frock (dē frok′) v. unfrock (def. 2).

de·frost (dē frost′) v. **1** remove frost or ice from. **2** thaw out (frozen foods).

de·frost·er (dē fros′tər) n. a device that removes ice, either through heat or mechanically. Defrosters are used on automobile windshields and in refrigerators.

deft (deft) adj. skilful; nimble: *the deft fingers of a violinist or a surgeon.* [var. of *daft*] —**deft′ly,** adv. —**deft′ness,** n.
☛ *Syn.* See note at **dexterous.**

de·funct (di fungkt′) *adj., n.* —*adj.* dead; extinct. —*n.*
the defunct, the dead person. [< L *defunctus,* pp. of *defungi* finish < *de-* (intensive) + *fungi* perform]

de·fuse (di fyüz′) *v.* —**fused, —fus·ing. 1** remove the fuse or triggering device from (a bomb, etc.). **2** remove or neutralize a potential source of trouble or friction in: *to defuse a tense situation.*

de·fy (di fī′) *v.* -**fied, -fy·ing. 1** resist boldly or openly. **2** withstand; resist: *This strong fort defies capture.* **3** challenge (a person) to do or prove something. [ME < OF *de(s)fier* < VL < L *dis-* away, apart + *fidus* faithful]

deg. degree(s).

de·gauss (di gous′, di gos′, *or* di gôs′) *v.* **1** neutralize the magnetic field of (a steel ship) by means of electric coils carrying currents producing an opposing magnetic field. **2** demagnetize. [< Karl Friedrich *Gauss* (1777-1855), a German mathematician]

de·gen·er·a·cy (di jen′ər ə sē) *n.* a degenerate condition.

de·gen·er·ate (*v.* di jen′ər āt′; *adj. and n.* di jen′ər it) *v.* -**at·ed, -at·ing;** *adj., n.* —*v.* **1** decline in physical, mental, or moral qualities; grow worse. **2** *Biology.* **a** of an organism, become less specialized and simpler in structure. **b** of a structure or part in an organism, become functionally useless.
—*adj.* that has degenerated.
—*n.* a person who shows degraded and debased physical, mental, or moral qualities: *Only a degenerate could have committed such a horrible crime.* [< L *degenerare,* ult. < *de-* down + *genus* race, kind] —**de·gen′er·ate·ly,** *adv.*

de·gen·er·a·tion (di jen′ər ā′shən) *n.* **1** the process of degenerating. **2** a degenerate condition. **3** *Medicine.* a deterioration in tissues or organs caused by disease, injury, etc. **4** *Biology.* evolution or development toward simpler structures or toward the disappearance of structures or functions.

de·gen·er·a·tive (di jen′ər ə tiv *or* di jen′ər ā′tiv) *adj.* **1** tending to degenerate. **2** characterized by degeneration; showing degeneration.

de·glu·ti·tion (dē′glü tish′ən *or* deg′lü tish′ən) *n.* the act or power of swallowing. [< F *déglutition* < L *deglutire* swallow down]

deg·ra·da·tion (deg′rə dā′shən) *n.* **1** degrading or being degraded: *Failure to obey orders caused the captain's degradation to the rank of a private.* **2** a degraded condition: *The drunkard, filthy and half-starved, lived in degradation.* **3** *Geology.* the wearing down of land, rocks, etc. by erosion.

de·grade (di grād′) *v.* -**grad·ed, -grad·ing. 1** reduce to a lower rank; take away a position, an honor, etc. from. **2** make bad; lower in value; debase: *You degrade yourself when you tell a lie.* **3** *Geology.* wear down by erosion. **4** *Biology.* reduce to a lower classification. **5** *Chemistry.* reduce systematically the molecule of (a compound) into others of less complex structure. [ME < OF *degrader* < LL *degradare* < L *de-* down + *gradus* step, grade] —**de·grad′a·ble,** *adj.* —**de·grad′er,** *n.*

de·gree (di grē′) *n.* **1** a stage or step in a scale or process. **2** a step in direct line of descent: *a cousin two degrees removed.* **3** the amount, intensity, or extent of an action or condition: *To what degree is he interested in reading?* **4** a unit for measuring temperature. The boiling point of water is 100 degrees Celsius. *Symbol:* ° **5** a unit used with the SI for measuring plane angles, especially in navigation, surveying, etc. There are 360 degrees in a circle and 90° in a right angle. One degree is equal to (π ÷ 180) radians. *Symbol:* ° **6** rank: *A princess is a lady of high degree.* **7** a rank or title given by a university or college to a student whose work fulfils certain requirements, or to a person as an honor: *an M.A. degree, a D.D. degree.* **8** *Grammar.* one of the three stages in the comparison of adjectives or adverbs. *Fast* is the positive degree; *faster,* the comparative degree; *fastest,* the superlative degree. **9** *Algebra.* the rank as determined by an exponent or sum of exponents. a^3 and a^2b are terms of the third degree. $x^2y^2z^3$ is a term of the seventh degree. **10** *Law.* a measure of the seriousness of a crime: *first-degree murder.* **11** *Music.* **a** an interval between any note of the scale and the next note. **b** a line or space on the staff showing the position of the notes. **c** the interval between two of these. **12** a relative condition, manner, way, or respect: *A bond and a stock may both be wise investments, each in its degree.*
by degrees, gradually.
to a degree, a to a large amount; to a great extent. **b** somewhat; rather.
[ME < OF *degre* < VL *degradus* < *degradare* divide into steps < L *de-* down + *gradus* step, grade]
☛ *Usage.* Degrees. Academic degrees, when given with a person's name, are separated from the name by a comma: *Harry James, M.A.; Harry Paynter, D.Sc.* When the institution granting the degree is named or when the year of granting is given, the following forms are used: *George Smith, B.A. (Alberta), M.A. (McGill), Ph.D. (Toronto); Helen Lawrence, B.A. '35, M.A. '38.*

degree Celsius a unit used with the SI for measuring temperature. On a thermometer, zero degrees Celsius (0°C) is the temperature at which water freezes, and one hundred degrees Celsius (100°C) is the temperature at which water boils. A

hat, āge, fär; let, ēqual, tėrm; it, īce
hot, ōpen, ôrder; oil, out; cup, pùt, rüle,
əbove, takən, pencəl, lemən, circəs

ch, child; ng, long; sh, ship
th, thin; ŦH, then; zh, measure

temperature interval of one degree Celsius is equal to one kelvin (1°C = 1K). *Symbol:* °C

de·hisce (dē his′) *v.* -**hisced, -hisc·ing.** of a mature fruit, anther, etc., burst open along a definite line, discharging seeds or pollen. [< L *dehiscere,* ult. < *de-* down + *hiare* gape]

de·his·cence (dē his′əns) *n.* the bursting open of a mature fruit, anther, etc. to discharge seeds of pollen.

de·his·cent (dē his′ənt) *adj.* of certain fruits, anthers, etc., splitting or bursting open along one or more definite lines when mature to release seeds or pollen.

de·horn (dē hôrn′) *v.* remove the horns from.

de·hu·man·ize (dē hyü′mən īz′) *v.* -**ized, -iz·ing.** deprive of human qualities, interest, sympathy, etc. —**de·hu′man·i·za′tion,** *n.*

de·hy·drate (dē hī′drāt) *v.* -**drat·ed, -drat·ing. 1** deprive (a chemical compound) of water or the elements of water. **2** remove water or moisture from; dry. **3** lose water or moisture.

de·hy·dra·tion (dē′hī drā′shən) *n.* **1** the removal or loss of water from a chemical compound or from vegetables, fruits, etc. **2** an excessive loss of body fluids.

de–ice (dē īs′) *v.* -**iced, -ic·ing.** prevent formation of ice on; remove ice from (an aircraft, etc.). —**de·ic′er,** *n.*

de·i·fi·ca·tion (dē′ə fə kā′shən) *n.* defying or being defied.

de·i·fy (dē′ə fī′) *v.* -**fied, -fy·ing. 1** make a god of. **2** worship or regard as a god. [ME < OF *deifier* < LL *deificare* < *deus* god + *deus* god + *facere* make] —**de′i·fi′er,** *n.*

deign (dān) *v.* **1** condescend; think fit: *So conceited a man would never deign to notice us.* **2** condescend to give (an answer, a reply, etc.). [ME < OF *deignier* < L *dignari* < *dignus* worthy]

De·i gra·ti·a (dē′ī grä′shē ē *or* dā′ē grä′tē ə) *Latin.* by the grace of God.

de·ism (dē′iz əm) *n.* **1** a belief that God exists entirely apart from our world and does not influence the lives of human beings. **2** a belief in God without accepting any particular religion. [< L *deus* god]

de·ist (dē′ist) *n.* a person who believes in deism.

de·i·ty (dē′ə tē) *n., pl.* -**ties. 1** a god or goddess. **2** a divine nature; the state of being a god. **3 the Deity,** God. [ME < OF *deite* < L *deitas* < *deus* god]

dé·jà vu (dā zhä vy) *French.* the feeling or sense that one has already experienced something that is in fact a new situation or happening.

de·ject·ed (di jek′tid) *adj.* in low spirits; sad; discouraged. —**de·ject′ed·ly,** *adv.* —**de·ject′ed·ness,** *n.*
☛ *Syn.* See note at **sad.**

de·jec·tion (di jek′shən) *n.* lowness of spirits; sadness; discouragement: *Her face showed her dejection at missing the party.* [< L *dejectio, -onis* < *dejicere* < *de-* down + *jacere* throw]

dé·jeu·ner (dā zhœ nā′) *n. French.* **1** breakfast. **2** luncheon.

de ju·re (dē jür′ē *or* dā jür′ā) *Latin.* by right; according to law.

deka– *U.S.* See **deca–.**

deke (dēk) *n., v.* **deked, dek·ing.** —*n. Hockey. Cdn.Slang.* a fake shot or movement intended to draw a defending player out of position. —*v.* **1** draw (a defending player) out of position by faking a shot or movement. **2** manoeuvre (oneself or the puck) by feinting so as to outsmart a defending player. [< *decoy*]

del. 1 delete. **2** delegate. **3** delivery.

Del. Delaware.

de·lay (di lā′) *v., n.* —*v.* **1** put off till a later time: *We will delay the party for a week.* **2** make late; keep waiting; hinder the progress of: *The accident delayed the train for two hours. Ignorance delays progress.* **3** go or act slowly or with pauses, etc.: *Don't delay; they're waiting for you.*
—*n.* **1** the act of delaying. **2** the fact of being delayed. [ME < OF *delaier* postpone < *de-* away + *laier* leave, let, probably < Celtic] —**de·lay′er,** *n.* —**de·lay′ing·ly,** *adv.*
☛ *Syn. v.* **1. Delay, defer, postpone** = put off doing something. **Delay** emphasizes the idea of putting off, and suggests either holding off for some reason but planning to act at some later time or, often, putting off indefinitely: *I delayed seeing the dentist.* **Defer** usually suggests deciding to put off until a better time, with the intention of acting then: *I deferred going until I had more time.* **Postpone** suggests deferring until a definite time, after something has been done, learned, etc.: *I postponed going until next week.*

de·le (dē′lē) v. **-led, -le·ing.** *Printing.* cross out; delete. [< L *dele*, imperative of *delere* delete]

de·lec·ta·ble (di lek′tə bəl) *adj.* very pleasing; delightful. [ME < OF < L *delectabilis* < *delectare*. See DELIGHT.]
—**de·lec′ta·ble·ness**, n. —**de·lec′ta·bly**, *adv.*

de·lec·ta·tion (dē′lek tā′shən) n. delight; pleasure; entertainment: *The magician did many tricks for our delectation.*

del·e·ga·cy (del′ə gə sē) n., pl. **-cies.** delegation.

del·e·gate (n. del′ə git *or* del′ə gāt′; v. del′ə gāt′) n., v. **-gat·ed, -gat·ing.** —n. a person given power or authority to act for others; representative. —v. **1** appoint or send (a person) as a delegate: *Each club delegated one member to attend the provincial meeting.* **2** give over (one's power or authority) to another as agent or deputy: *The provinces have delegated some of their rights to the Federal Government.* [< L *delegatus*, pp. of *delegare* < *de-* (intensive) + *legare* send with a commission]

del·e·ga·tion (del′ə gā′shən) n. **1** delegating or being delegated: *the delegation of authority.* **2** a group of delegates: *Each province sent a delegation to the national convention.*

de·lete (di lēt′) v. **-let·ed, -let·ing. 1** strike out or take out (anything written or printed); remove; cross out. **2** erase; wipe out: *Shock deleted all recollection of the accident from her mind.* [< L *deletus*, pp. of *delere* destroy]

del·e·te·ri·ous (del′ə tēr′ē əs) *adj.* harmful; injurious. [< NL *deleterius* < Gk. *dēlētērios*, ult. < *dēleesthai* hurt]
—**del′e·te′ri·ous·ly**, *adv.*

de·le·tion (di lē′shən) n. **1** the act of deleting. **2** the fact of being deleted. **3** a deleted part.

delft (delft) n. **1** a kind of earthenware made in the Netherlands, having an opaque white glaze and decorated, usually, in blue. **2** any pottery having a similar glaze and color. [< *Delft*, a city in the SW Netherlands]

delft·ware (delft′wer′) n. delft.

de·lib·er·ate (adj. di lib′ər it; v. di lib′ər āt′) adj., v. **-at·ed, -at·ing.** —adj. **1** carefully thought out; made or done on purpose: *His excuse was a deliberate lie.* **2** slow and careful in deciding what to do: *A deliberate person takes a long time to make up his mind.* **3** slow, but firm and purposeful: *They advanced with deliberate steps.*
—v. **1** think over carefully; consider. **2** discuss reasons for and against something; debate. [< L *deliberatus*, pp. of *deliberare* < *de-* (intensive) + *librare* weigh] —**de·lib′er·ate·ly**, *adv.*
—**de·lib′er·ate·ness**, n. —**de·lib′er·a′tor**, n.
☛ *Syn.* See note at **slow.**

de·lib·er·a·tion (di lib′ər ā′shən) n. **1** careful thought. **2** a discussion of reasons for and against something; debate: *the deliberations of the Legislative Assembly.* **3** slowness and care: *The hunter aimed his gun with great deliberation.*

de·lib·er·a·tive (di lib′ər ə tiv *or* di lib′ər ā′tiv) *adj.* **1** for deliberation; having to do with deliberation; discussing reasons for and against something: *Parliament is a deliberative body.* **2** characterized by deliberation; coming as a result of deliberation. —**de·lib′er·a′tive·ly**, *adv.*

del·i·ca·cy (del′ə kə sē) n., pl. **-cies. 1** a delicate quality or nature; slightness and grace: *the delicacy of lace, the delicacy of a flower, the delicacy of a baby's skin.* **2** fineness of feeling for small differences; sensitiveness: *delicacy of hearing or touch.* **3** need of care, skill, or tact: *a matter of great delicacy.* **4** thought or regard for the feelings of others. **5** a shrinking from what one considers offensive or not modest. **6** weakness; the condition of being easily hurt or made ill: *The child's delicacy was a worry to his parents.* **7** a choice kind of food; a dainty.

del·i·cate (del′ə kit) *adj.* **1** light and pleasant to taste or smell: *delicate foods, a delicate fragrance.* **2** soft or fine in structure or make: *delicate features, delicate silks for blouses.* **3** easily crushed, broken, or torn; fragile: *a delicate flower, a delicate china cup.* **4** requiring skill and care in handling: *a delicate situation, a delicate heart operation.* **5** of a color, pale; not intense: *a delicate shade of green.* **6** capable of responding to very slight changes of condition; very sensitive: *delicate instruments, a delicate sense of touch.* **7** easily hurt or made ill: *a delicate child. She has a delicate constitution.* **8** very subtle; marked by fine distinctions: *delicate shades of meaning, delicate irony.* **9** having or showing consideration for the feelings of others: *a delicate approach.* **10** excessively refined or sensitive. [ME < L *delicatus* pampered]
—**del′i·cate·ly**, *adv.* —**del′i·cate·ness**, n.
☛ *Syn.* **1, 2. Delicate, dainty** = fine in quality and pleasing to the senses and taste. **Dainty** emphasizes smallness: *The child wore a dainty dress.* **Delicate** suggests fineness of quality without regard to size: *a delicate perfume from a dainty flower. He does delicate woodcarving.*

del·i·ca·tes·sen (del′ə kə tes′ən) n. **1** a store that sells prepared foods, such as cooked meats, smoked fish, cheese, salads, pickles, etc. **2** the foods sold at such a store. [< G *Delikatessen*, pl. of *Delikatesse* delicacy < F]
☛ *Usage.* **Delicatessen** = a store that sells prepared foods, is singular in use: *The delicatessen closes at nine o'clock.* When *delicatessen* means the foods sold at such a store, it is usually plural in use: *Delicatessen usually require little preparation for serving.*

de·li·cious (di lish′əs) *adj.* **1** very pleasing to taste or smell. **2** very pleasing; delightful: *a delicious color combination.* **3 Delicious,** a kind of red or yellow apple having a fine flavor. [ME < OF *delicieus* < LL *deliciosus* < *delicae* delight < *delicere* entice. See DELIGHT.] —**de·li′cious·ly**, *adv.* —**de·li′cious·ness**, n.
☛ *Syn.* **1. Delicious, luscious** = delighting the senses. **Delicious** is used chiefly to mean pleasing in flavor, less often in fragrance or aroma: *This dessert is delicious. The coffee smells delicious.* **Luscious** adds to *delicious* the suggestion of richness or sweetness and, when applied to fruit, ripeness or juiciness: *She makes luscious apple pie.*

de·light (di līt′) n., v. —n. **1** great pleasure; joy. **2** something that gives great pleasure. —v. **1** please greatly. **2** have great pleasure: *Children delight in surprises.* [ME < OF *delit* < *delitier* < L *delectare* to charm < *delicere* entice < *de-* (intensive) + *lacere* entice; spelling influenced by *light*] —**de·light′er**, n.
☛ *Syn. n.* **1.** See note at **pleasure.**

de·light·ed (di līt′id) *adj.* greatly pleased; joyful; glad.
—**de·light′ed·ly**, *adv.*

de·light·ful (di līt′fəl) *adj.* very pleasing; giving joy.
—**de·light′ful·ly**, *adv.* —**de·light′ful·ness**, n.

de·light·some (di līt′səm) *adj.* delightful. —**de·light′some·ly**, *adv.* —**de·light′some·ness**, n.

De·li·lah (di lī′lə) n. **1** in the Bible, the Philistine woman who was loved by Samson and who betrayed him. See **Samson. 2** any false, treacherous woman.

de·lim·it (di lim′it) v. fix the limits of; mark the boundaries of.
—**de·lim′i·ta′tion**, n.

de·lin·e·ate (di lin′ē āt′) v. **-at·ed, -at·ing. 1** trace the outline of. **2** draw; sketch. **3** describe in words. [< L *delineare* < *de-* (intensive) + *linea* line] —**de·lin′e·a′tor**, n.

de·lin·e·a·tion (di lin′ē ā′shən) n. **1** a drawing; sketch. **2** description.

de·lin·quen·cy (di ling′kwən sē) n., pl. **-cies. 1** the failure to do what is required by law or duty; guilt. **2** a fault; offence. **3** the condition or habit of behaving unlawfully: *Juvenile delinquency is greatly increased by wartime conditions.*

de·lin·quent (di ling′kwənt) adj., n. —adj. **1** failing to do what is required by law or duty; guilty of a fault or an offence. **2** due and unpaid; overdue: *The owner lost his house when it was sold for delinquent taxes.* **3** having to do with delinquents.
—n. a delinquent person; offender; criminal. [< L *delinquens, -entis,* ppr. of *delinquere* fail < *de-* down + *linquere* leave]
—**de·lin′quent·ly**, *adv.*

del·i·quesce (del′ə kwes′) v. **-quesced, -quesc·ing.** become liquid by absorbing moisture from the air. [< L *deliquescere* < *de-* + *liquescere* become fluid < *liquere* be liquid]

del·i·ques·cence (del′ə kwes′əns) n. the act or process of deliquescing.

del·i·ques·cent (del′ə kwes′ənt) *adj.* becoming liquid by absorbing moisture from the air.

de·lir·i·ous (di lir′ē əs) *adj.* **1** temporarily out of one's senses; wandering in mind; raving. **2** wildly excited: *delirious with joy.* **3** caused by delirium. —**de·lir′i·ous·ly**, *adv.* —**de·lir′i·ous·ness**, n.

de·lir·i·um (di lir′ē əm) n., pl. **-lir·i·ums, -lir·i·a** (-lir′ē ə). **1** a temporary disorder of the mind that occurs during fevers, insanity, drunkenness, etc. Delirium is characterized by excitement, irrational talk, and hallucinations. **2** any wild excitement that cannot be controlled. [< L *delirium* < *delirare* rave, be crazy < *de lira* (*ire*) (go) out of the furrow in (ploughing)]

delirium tre·mens (trē′mənz) delirium characterized by violent tremblings and terrifying hallucinations, usually caused by prolonged excessive consumption of alchoholic drinks. *Abbrev.:* d.t.'s [< NL *delirium tremens* trembling delirium]

de·list (dē list′) v. remove from a list, catalogue, etc.

de·liv·er (di liv′ər) v. **1** carry and give out; distribute: *to deliver mail.* **2** hand over; give up: *to deliver a fort to the enemy.* **3** give forth in words: *The traveller delivered an interesting talk about his journey. The jury delivered its verdict.* **4** strike; throw: *to deliver a blow.* **5** set free; rescue; save from evil or trouble: *"Deliver us from evil."* **6** help give birth: *The farmer delivered his prize cow of a calf.* **7** help in the birth of: *The doctor delivered the baby at noon.* **deliver oneself of,** a speak; give out: *He delivered himself of a carefully prepared statement to the press.* b unburden oneself of (ideas, feelings, etc.)
[ME < OF *delivrer* < L *deliberare* set free < *de-* (intensive) + *liber* free] —**de·liv′er·a·ble**, *adj.* —**de·liv′er·er**, n.
☛ *Syn.* **5.** See note at **rescue.**

de·liv·er·ance (di liv′ər əns *or* di liv′rəns) *n.* **1** the act of setting free or the state of being set free; a rescue; release. **2** a formal opinion or judgment.

de·liv·er·y (di liv′ər ē *or* di liv′rē) *n., pl.* **-er·ies. 1** the act of carrying and handing over letters, goods, etc.; the act of distributing: *The mail delivery was late today.* **2** a giving up; handing over: *The captive was released upon the delivery of his ransom.* **3** a manner of speaking; way of giving a speech, lecture, etc.: *Our minister has an excellent delivery.* **4** an act or way of striking, throwing, etc. **5** a rescue; release. **6** the act of giving birth; childbirth: *a difficult delivery.* **7** the act of assisting at a birth. **8** anything that is delivered; goods to be delivered.

dell (del) *n.* a small, sheltered glen or valley, usually with trees in it. [OE]

de·louse (dē lous′ *or* -louz′) *v.* **-loused, -lous·ing.** remove lice from.

Del·phi (del′fī) *n.* a town in ancient Greece where a famous oracle of Apollo was located.

Del·phi·an (del′fē ən) *adj.* Delphic.

Del·phic (del′fik) *adj.* **1** having to do with the oracle of Apollo at Delphi. **2** obscure; having a double meaning.

Delphic oracle the oracle of Apollo at Delphi. The oracle often gave ambiguous answers to questions.

del·phin·i·um (del fin′ē əm) *n.* any of a genus (*Delphinium*) of annual and perennial herbs of the buttercup family found in temperate regions of the northern hemisphere. Many species are cultivated in gardens for their tall spikes of blue, purple, pink, or white flowers. [< NL < Gk. *delphinion* < *delphin* dolphin; from the shape of the nectar gland of the flower]

del·ta (del′tə) *n.* **1** a deposit of earth and sand, usually three-sided, that collects at the mouths of some rivers. **2** the fourth letter of the Greek alphabet (δ, Δ). **3** any triangular space or figure. [< Gk.]

Del·ta·wing *or* **del·ta·wing** (del′tə wing′) *adj.* of an aircraft, having wings in the shape of a Greek delta or triangle.

del·toid (del′toid) *adj., n.* —*adj.* **1** shaped like the Greek delta (Δ); triangular. **2** of or having to do with the deltoid muscle. —*n.* the deltoid muscle. [< NL *deltoides* < Gk. *deltoeidēs* < *delta* delta + *eidos* form]

deltoid muscle *Physiology.* a large, triangular muscle of the shoulder. It lifts the arm away from the side of the body.

de·lude (di lüd′) *v.* **-lud·ed, -lud·ing.** mislead; deceive: *He deluded himself into believing he would pass his examinations without studying.* [< L *deludere* < *de-* (to the detriment of) + *ludere* play] —**de·lud′er,** *n.* —**de·lud′ing·ly,** *adv.*

del·uge (del′yüj) *n., v.* **-uged, -ug·ing.** —*n.* **1** a great flood. **2** a heavy fall of rain. **3** any overwhelming rush: *Most stores have a deluge of orders just before Christmas.* **4** the **Deluge,** in the Bible, the great flood in the days of Noah (Genesis 7). —*v.* **1** flood. **2** overwhelm as if by a flood: *The movie star was deluged with requests for his autograph.* [ME < OF < L *diluvium* < *diluere* < *dis-* away + *luere* wash]
☛ *Syn. n.* **1.** See note at **flood.**

de·lu·sion (di lü′zhən) *n.* **1** the act of deluding or the state of being deluded: *In his delusion, he has expected his friends to come to his rescue.* **2** a false notion or belief: *The voyages of Columbus disproved the common delusion of his time that the earth was flat.* **3** *Psychiatry.* a fixed belief maintained in spite of all evidence from one's own senses and the objective world that true believes is false: *The old man suffered from the delusion that his food was being poisoned.* [ME < LL *delusio, -onis* < *deludere.* See DELUDE.]
☛ *Syn.* **3.** See note at **illusion.**

de·lu·sive (di lü′siv) *adj.* misleading; deceptive; false. —**de·lu′sive·ly,** *adv.* —**de·lu′sive·ness,** *n.*

de·lu·so·ry (di lü′sə rē) *adj.* delusive; deceptive.

de·luxe *or* **de luxe** (də lùks′ *or* də luks′) *adj.* of exceptionally fine or luxurious quality; elegant and costly. [< F]

delve (delv) *v.* **delved, delv·ing. 1** search carefully for information: *The scholar delved in many libraries for facts.* **2** *Archaic or dialect.* dig. [OE *delfan*] —**delv′er,** *n.*

de·mag·net·ize (dē mag′nə tīz′) *v.* **-ized, -iz·ing.** deprive of magnetism. —**de·mag′net·i·za′tion,** *n.*

dem·a·gog (dem′ə gog′) *Esp.U.S.* See **demagogue.**

dem·a·gog·ic (dem′ə goj′ik *or* dem′ə gog′ik) *adj.* **1** of or having to do with a demagogue. **2** like a demagogue or demagogues.

dem·a·gogue (dem′ə gog′) *n.* a popular leader who stirs up the people by appealing to their emotions and prejudices, especially a person whose aim is personal advancement or power. [< Gk. *dēmagōgos* < *dēmos* people + *agōgos* leader < *agein* lead]

dem·a·gogu·er·y (dem′ə gog′ər ē) *n.* **1** the principles and

practices of a demagogue. **2** government by a demagogue. **3** demagogues as a group.

dem·a·go·gy (dem′ə gō′jē, dem′ə goj′ē, *or* dem′ə gog′ē) *n.* demagoguery.

de·mand (di mand′) *v., n.* —*v.* **1** ask for with authority or claim as a right: *to demand a trial, to demand payment of a debt. The police officer demanded his driver's licence.* **2** ask urgently or insistently: *"What have you done with my hockey stick?" she demanded.* **3** call for; require; need: *Training a puppy demands patience.* —*n.* **1** an urgent or insistent request: *a demand for an answer.* **2** the thing demanded: *His demand was the immediate release of all the prisoners.* **3** a claim; call: *With two jobs to look after, he has many demands on his time.* **4** a seeking or being sought after; request or need: *Because of the large crop, the supply of apples was greater than the demand. Taxis are in great demand on rainy days.* **on demand,** as and when requested: *a loan payable on demand.* [ME < OF < L *demandare* < *de-* from + *mandare* to order] —**de·mand′er,** *n.*
☛ *Syn.* **v. 1, 4. Demand, claim, require** =ask or call for something as a right or need. **Demand** emphasizes insisting, sometimes in a domineering way, on getting something a person or thing has the authority, right, or need to call for: *I demand an answer immediately.* **Claim** emphasizes having, or stating one has, the right to get what is demanded: *He claimed the inheritance.* **Require** emphasizes the need for what is demanded: *This letter requires an answer.*

de·mand·ing (di man′ding) *adj.* exacting: *a demanding person, a demanding job.*

de·mar·cate (dē′mär kāt′ *or* di mär′kāt) *v.* **-cat·ed, -cat·ing. 1** set and mark the limits of. **2** separate; distinguish. [< *demarcation*] —**de′mar·ca′tor,** *n.*

de·mar·ca·tion (dē′mär kā′shən) *n.* **1** the act of setting and marking the limits. **2** a separation; distinction. [< Sp. *demarcación* < *de-* off + *marcar* mark]

de·mean¹ (di mēn′) *v.* lower in dignity or standing; humble: *The prince demeaned himself by mixing with thieves and robbers.* [< *de-* down + *mean²*; formed after *debase*]

de·mean² (di mēn′) *v.* behave or conduct oneself (in a certain manner): *He demeaned himself well.* [ME < OF *demener* < *de-* (intensive) + *mener* lead < L *minare* drive]

de·mean·or *or* **de·mean·our** (di mēn′ər) *n.* the way a person looks and acts; behavior; conduct; manner. [ME *demenure* < *demenen* behave < OF *demener.* See DEMEAN².]

de·ment·ed (di men′tid) *adj.* insane; crazy. [< L *dementare* < *demens* mad < *de-* out of + *mens, mentis* mind] —**de·ment′ed·ly,** *adv.* —**de·ment′ed·ness,** *n.*

de·men·tia (di men′shə) *n.* a condition characterized by a partial or complete deterioration of mental powers, the ability to reason, etc.

dementia prae·cox (prē′koks *or* prī′koks) *Obsolete.* schizophrenia. [< L *dementia praecox* precocious insanity]

de·mer·it (dē mer′it) *n.* **1** a fault; defect. **2** a mark against a person's record given for unsatisfactory performance or behavior or for violation of a rule or law, and entailing a loss of privileges or other punishment upon accumulation of a certain number of marks. Many provinces have a system of demerits for certain driving offences. **3** (*adj.*) of, having to do with, or designating a system that uses demerits to record offences.

de·mesne (di mān′ *or* di mēn′) *n.* **1** *Law.* the possession of land as one's own. **2** the land or land and buildings possessed as one's own; real estate. **3** the house and land belonging to a lord and used by him. **4** domain; realm. **5** region. [ME < AF *demesne,* a respelling of OF *demeine* domain. Doublet of DOMAIN.]

De·me·ter (di mē′tər) *n. Greek mythology.* the goddess of agriculture and of the fruitful earth, corresponding to the Roman goddess Ceres.

De Meurons (də mü′rənz) a group of disbanded mercenaries belonging to a Swiss-German regiment, many of whom settled in Lord Selkirk's Red River Colony in 1820. [< Col. de *Meuron,* commander of the regiment]

demi- *prefix.* **1** half: *demigod = half god.* **2** smaller than usual in size, power, etc.: *demitasse = a small cup.* [< F *demi* half < VL < L *dimidius* < *dis-* apart + *medius* middle]

dem·i·god (dem′ē god′) *n.* **1** *Mythology.* **a** a god that is partly human; the offspring of a god or goddess and a human being:

Hercules was a demigod. **b** a minor or lesser god. **2** a person who is so outstanding in some way that he seems to be godlike: *The famous hockey player was a demigod to his young fans.*

dem·i·john (dem′ē jon′) *n.* a large bottle of glass or earthenware enclosed in wicker. [< F *dame-jeanne* Lady Jane, playful personification]

de·mil·i·tar·ize (dē mil′ə tə rīz′) *v.* -ized, -iz·ing. free from military control. —**de·mil′i·ta·ri·za′tion,** *n.*

dem·i·monde (dem′ē mond′ *or* dem′ē mônd′) *n.* **1** a class of women who, though not socially respectable, maintain a position on the fringes of society because they are supported by wealthy lovers. **2** any social group considered not entirely respectable. [< F *demi-monde* half-world]

de·mise (di mīz′) *n., v.* -mised, -mis·ing. —*n.* **1** death. **2** *Law.* the transfer of an estate by a will or lease. **3** the transfer of royal power by death or abdication.
—*v.* **1** *Law.* transfer (an estate) by a will or lease. **2** transfer (royal power) by death or abdication. [apparently < AF *demise,* pp. of *desmettre* put away < *des-* away + *mettre* put < L *mittere* let go, send]

dem·i·sem·i·qua·ver (dem′ē sem′ē kwä′vər) *n. Music.* a thirty-second note.

dem·i·tasse (dem′ē tas′) *n.* **1** a small cup for serving black coffee. **2** a small cup of black coffee. [< F *demi-tasse* half-cup]

de·mo·bi·lize (dē mō′bə līz′) *v.* -lized, -liz·ing. **1** disband: *After the war, it took several months to demobilize the armed forces.* **2** discharge from one of the armed forces. —**de·mo′bi·li·za′tion,** *n.*

de·moc·ra·cy (di mok′rə sē) *n., pl.* -cies. **1** a government that is periodically elected and thus controlled by the people who live under it. Under a democracy, the people rule either by direct vote at public meetings or indirectly through the election of certain representatives to govern them. **2** the ideals and principles of such a government, such as equality of rights and opportunities and the rule of the majority. **3** a country, state, or community having such a government. **4** the treatment of others as one's equals. [< F *démocratie* < Gk *dēmokratia* < *dēmos* people + *kratos* rule]

dem·o·crat (dem′ə krat′) *n.* **1** a person who believes that a government should be run by the people who live under it. **2** a person who treats other people as equals. **3** a light, four-wheeled carriage drawn by two horses, having two double seats, one behind the other. **4 Democrat,** *U.S.* a member of the Democratic Party.

dem·o·crat·ic (dem′ə krat′ik) *adj.* **1** of or like a democracy. **2** treating other people as one's equals: *She was very democratic in her treatment of the employees.* **3 Democratic,** *U.S.* of or having to do with the Democratic Party. —**dem′o·crat′i·cal·ly,** *adv.*

Democratic Party one of the two main political parties of the United States.

de·moc·ra·tize (di mok′rə tīz′) *v.* -tized, -tiz·ing. make or become democratic. —**de·moc′ra·ti·za′tion,** *n.*

de·mod·u·late (dē moj′ə lāt′) *v.* -lat·ed, -lat·ing. *Electronics.* separate an output signal from a modulated carrier wave.

de·mod·u·la·tion (dē moj′ə lā′shən) *n. Electronics.* the process of separating information (the output signal) from a modulated carrier wave.

de·mod·u·la·tor (dē moj′ə lā′tər) *n. Electronics.* a device used for demodulation.

de·mo·graph·ic (dē′mə graf′ik *or* dem′ə graf′ik) *adj.* of or having to do with demography. —**de′mo·graph′i·cal·ly,** *adv.*

de·mog·ra·phy (di mog′rə fē) *n.* the science dealing with the statistics of births, deaths, diseases, etc. of a community. —**de·mog′ra·pher,** *n.*

dem·oi·selle (dem′wä zel′) *n.* **1** damsel. **2** a crane of Asia, Europe, and N Africa, having long white plumes behind the eyes. **3** a type of dragonfly. **4** hoodoo (def. 3). [< F < OF *dameisele.* Doublet of DAMSEL.]

de·mol·ish (di mol′ish) *v.* **1** pull or tear down; wreck; raze: *The old train station will be demolished this summer.* **2** break into pieces; smash or crush: *The whole pile of books fell on the door and demolished it.* **3** show to be false or weak; ruin or discredit: *The government's arguments for the new bill were demolished by the opposition.* [< F *démolis-,* a stem of *démolir* < L *demoliri* tear down < *de-* down + *moles* mass] —**de·mol′ish·er,** *n.* —**de·mol′ish·ment,** *n.*
☛ *Syn.* See note at **destroy.**

dem·o·li·tion (dem′ə lish′ən *or* dē′mə lish′ən) *n.* destruction; ruin.

demolition bomb a bomb with a relatively large explosive

charge, used especially for destroying buildings and other important objects.

de·mon (dē′mən) *n.* **1** an evil spirit; devil; fiend. **2** a very wicked or cruel person. **3** an evil or undesirable influence or condition: *The demon of greed ruined the miser's happiness.* **4** a person who has great energy, vigor, or skill: *He's a demon for work.* **5** Usually spelled **daemon, a** an attendant or guardian spirit. **b** *Greek mythology.* a supernatural being halfway between a god and a human being. [< L < Gk. *daimonion* divine (thing); in Christian writings, evil spirit < *daimōn* divinity, spirit]

de·mon·e·tize (dē mon′ə tīz′ *or* -mun′ə tīz′) *v.* -tized, -tiz·ing. **1** deprive of its standard value as money. **2** withdraw from use as money. —**de·mon′e·ti·za′tion,** *n.*

de·mo·ni·ac (di mō′nē ak′) *adj., n.* —*adj.* **1** of demons. **2** devilish; fiendish. **3** raging; frantic. **4** possessed by an evil spirit. —*n.* a person supposed to be possessed by an evil spirit.

de·mo·ni·a·cal (dē′mo·nī′ə kəl) *adj.* demoniac. —**de′mo·ni·a·cal·ly,** *adv.*

de·mon·ic (di mon′ik) *adj.* **1** of evil spirits; caused by evil spirits. **2** influenced by a guiding spirit; inspired.

de·mon·ism (dē′mən iz′əm) *n.* **1** belief in demons. **2** the worship of demons.

de·mon·ol·a·try (dē′mən ol′ə trē) *n.* the worship of demons.

de·mon·ol·o·gy (dē′mən ol′ə jē) *n.* the study of demons or of beliefs about demons.

de·mon·stra·bil·i·ty (di mon′strə bil′ə tē *or* dem′ən strə bil′ə tē) *n.* the quality or state of being demonstrable.

de·mon·stra·ble (di mon′strə bəl *or* dem′ən strə bəl) *adj.* capable of being proved.

de·mon·stra·bly (di mon′strə blē *or* dem′ən strə blē) *adv.* **1** in a manner that can be proved; clearly. **2** by demonstration.

dem·on·strate (dem′ən strāt′) *v.* -strat·ed, -strat·ing. **1** establish the truth of; prove. **2** explain and illustrate with the aid of examples, experiments, etc.: *We watched the lab instructor demonstrate the process of electrolysis.* **3** try to prove the quality, usefulness, etc. of a product to a prospective buyer or buyers by showing it in use: *The salesman demonstrated the electric drill for her by drilling holes in thick steel.* **4** show clearly and openly: *She demonstrated her love for her niece by giving her a big hug.* **5** publicly show feeling or views about a particular person, issue, etc.: *An angry crowd demanding better police protection demonstrated in front of the city hall.* [< L *demonstrare* < *de-* (intensive) + *monstrare* show]

dem·on·stra·tion (dem′ən strā′shen) *n.* **1** a clear proof: *a demonstration of the defendant's guilt, a demonstration that the earth is round.* **2** an explanation with the use of examples, experiments, etc.: *a demonstration of weaving techniques.* **3** a showing of a product in use to illustrate its merits to a prospective buyer or buyers: *the demonstration of a new overhead projector.* **4** an open show or expression of feeling: *a demonstration of joy.* **5** a public show of feelings or views about a person, cause, etc. by many people in a parade or meeting. **6** *Logic.* an argument or series of propositions that leads to a conclusion. **7** *Mathematics.* the process of proving that certain assumptions necessarily produce a certain result.

de·mon·stra·tive (di mon′strə tiv) *adj., n.* —*adj.* **1** expressing one's affections freely and openly: *The girl's demonstrative greetings embarrassed her shy brother.* **2** showing clearly; explanatory. **3** giving proof; conclusive. **4** *Grammar.* pointing out the one or ones referred to as distinct from others of the same group or class. The adjective *this* in *this book* is a demonstrative adjective which serves to distinguish one particular book from all others.
—*n. Grammar.* a pronoun or adjective that points out: *That* and *these* are demonstratives. —**de·mon′stra·tive·ly,** *adv.* —**de·mon′stra·tive·ness,** *n.*
☛ *Usage. This, that, these, those* are called **demonstrative adjectives** or **pronouns** according to their use in a sentence. Adjective: *This car we bought in May.* Pronoun: *This costs a good bit more than those.*

dem·on·stra·tor (dem′ən strā′tər) *n.* **1** a person who demonstrates a process, procedure, or product for an audience, such as one who shows a medical or dental procedure or conducts a laboratory experiment for students, or one who shows how a machine or apparatus is used. **2** a person who takes part in a demonstration of protest or demand: *Several demonstrators were hurt in a scuffle with guards.* **3** a sample product used by a seller to demonstrate the merits of the product: *She got a very good deal on her new car because it was a demonstrator.*

de·mor·al·ize (di môr′əl īz′) *v.* -ized, -iz·ing. **1** corrupt the morals of: *The drug habit demoralizes people.* **2** weaken the spirit, courage, or discipline of; dishearten: *Lack of food and ammunition demoralized the besieged soldiers.* **3** throw into confusion or disorder: *Threats of war demoralized the stock market.*
—**de·mor′al·i·za′tion,** *n.* —**de·mor′a·liz′er,** *n.*

de·mote (di mōt′) v. **-mot·ed, -mot·ing.** put back to a lower grade; reduce in rank. [< *de-* + (*pro*)*mote*]

de·mot·ic (di mot′ik) adj., n. **—adj.** of the common people; popular. **—n.** a simplified form of ancient Egyptian writing. [< Gk. *demotikos* < *dēmos* the people]

de·mo·tion (di mō′shən) n. **1** the act of demoting. **2** the fact of being demoted.

de·mount (dē mount′) v. remove from a mounting.

de·mount·a·ble (dē moun′tə bəl) adj. that can be removed: *a demountable wheel rim.*

de·mul·cent (di mul′sənt) adj., n. **—adj.** soothing. **—n.** a soothing ointment or medicine. [< L *demulcens, -entis,* ppr. of *demulcere* < *de-* + *mulcere* soothe]

de·mur (di mėr′) v. **-murred, -mur·ring;** n. **—v. 1** object: *The clerk demurred at working overtime.* **2** Law. present a demurrer. **—n.** objection. [< OF *demurer* < L *demorari* < *de-* (intensive) + *morari* delay]

de·mure (di myůr′) adj. **-mur·er, -mur·est. 1** quiet and modest in behavior: *a demure young lady.* **2** artificially proper; assuming an air of modesty; coy: *the demure smile of a flirt.* [< obs. *mure,* adj., demure < OF *meür* < L *maturus* mature] **—de·mure′ly,** adv. **—de·mure′ness,** n.
☛ **Syn. 1.** See note at **modest.**

de·mur·rage (di mėr′ij) n. **1** the failure to load or unload a ship, railway car, etc. within the time specified. **2** the payment made for this failure. [< *demur*]

de·mur·rer (di mėr′ər) n. an objection by one party to a lawsuit that although the facts are as presented by the opposite party, the first party does not have to answer the claim. A person sued for an old debt might present a demurrer, claiming that the statute of limitations prohibits the suit.

de·my·thol·o·gize (dē′mi thol′ə jīz′) v. **-ized, —iz·ing. 1** remove the mythological elements from (especially the Bible) in order to disclose the underlying meaning. **2** remove mythical or mystical elements from; make rational, realistic, or commonplace: *to demythologize Hollywood.*

den (den) n., v. **denned, den·ning. —n. 1** a wild animal's home; lair: *The bear's den was in a cave.* **2** a room in a home where a person can read, work, or think in privacy: *There is a small, cosy den off the living room.* **3** a small, dirty, unattractive room, house, etc.: *The beggars lived in dens along the waterfront.* **4** a place used as a hideout or for secret activities: *a den of thieves.* **5** a group of eight to ten Wolf Cubs.
—v. 1 live in or retire to a den. **2** escape into or hide in a den. [OE *denn*] **—den′like′,** adj.

Den. Denmark.

de·nar·i·us (di ner′ē əs) n. **-nar·i·i** (-ner′ē ī′ or -ner′ē ē′). in ancient Rome: **1** a silver coin. **2** a gold coin. [< L *denarius* containing ten (here, ten times the value of an *as²*) < *deni* ten at a time. Doublet of DINAR, DENIER².]

de·na·tion·al·ize (dē nash′ən əl īz′ or -nash′nəl īz′) v. **-ized, -iz·ing. 1** deprive of national rights, scope, or character. **2** of industries, return from national to private control or ownership. **—de·na′tion·al·i·za′tion,** n.

de·nat·u·ral·ize (dē nach′ə rəl īz′ or -nach′rəl īz′) v. **-ized, -iz·ing. 1** make unnatural. **2** withdraw citizenship from (a naturalized citizen). **—de·nat′u·ral·i·za′tion,** n.

de·na·ture (dē nā′chər) v. **-tured, -tur·ing. 1** change the nature of. **2** make (alcohol, food, etc.) unfit for drinking or eating without destroying its usefulness for other purposes. **—de·na′tur·a′tion,** n.

de·na·zi·fy (dē nät′sə fī′ or -nat′sə fī′) v. **-fied, -fy·ing.** rid of Nazi doctrines or Nazi influences. **—de·na′zi·fi·ca′tion,** n.

den·drite (den′drīt) n. **1** Geology. **a** a stone or mineral with branching, tree-like markings. **b** a tree-like marking. **2** Anatomy. the branching part at the receiving end of a nerve cell. [< Gk. *dendrītēs* of a tree < *dendron* tree]

den·dro·chro·no·log·i·cal (den′drō kron′ə loj′ə kəl) adj. of or having to do with dendrochronology.

den·dro·chro·nol·o·gy (den′drō krə nol′ə jē) n. the science or technique of dating past events, archeological sites, etc. by studying the growth of rings of timber.

den·dro·log·i·cal (den′drə loj′ə kəl) adj. of or having to do with dendrology. **—den·dro·log′i·cal·ly,** adv.

den·drol·o·gist (den drol′ə jist′) n. a person trained in dendrology, especially one whose work it is.

den·drol·o·gy (den drol′ə jē) n. the branch of botany dealing with trees and shrubs.

De·ne (den′ē or den′ā) n.pl., adj. **—n.** the Athapascan Indian peoples of the Northwest Territories. **—adj.** of, having to do with, or designating the Dene. [< F *déné* < Athapascan *dene* people, men]

hat, āge, fär; let, ēqual, tėrm; it, īce
hot, ōpen, ôrder; oil, out; cup, půt, rüle,
ə above, takən, pencəl, lemən, circəs

ch, child; ng, long; sh, ship
th, thin; ŦH, then; zh, measure

Den·eb (den′eb) n. a first magnitude star in the constellation Cygnus. [< Arabic *dhanab* tail]

Dene Nation *Cdn.* the official organization representing the Athapascan peoples of the Northwest Territories. The Dene Nation was formerly called the Northwest Territories Indian Brotherhood.

de·neu·tral·ize (dē nyü′trəl īz′ or -nü′trəl īz′) v. **-ized, -iz·ing.** abolish the neutral status of (a country, territory, etc.). **—de·neu′tral·i·za′tion,** n.

den·gue (deng′gā or deng′gē) n. an infectious fever with skin rash and severe pain in the joints and muscles. [< Sp. < Swahili *kidinga popo*]

de·ni·al (di nī′əl) n. **1** an assertion that something is not true or real: *a denial that ghosts exist.* **2** an assertion that one does not believe or accept something: *Galileo was required to give a public denial of his theories.* **3** the act of refusing to satisfy a request, etc. **4** refusal to acknowledge a person or thing; a disowning. **5** self-denial.

de·ni·er¹ (di nī′ər) n. a person who denies. [< *deny*]

den·ier² (den′yər or də nēr′ for 1; də nēr′ for 2 and 3) n. **1** a unit of mass for measuring the fineness of silk, rayon, or nylon yarn. One denier equals a yarn weighing one gram for each 9000 metres. **2** Historical. a small coin of France and other W European countries. [< OF < L *denarius.* Doublet of DINAR, DENARIUS.]

den·i·grate (den′ə grāt′) v. **-grat·ed, -grat·ing. 1** defame; blacken the reputation of (someone). **2** make black; blacken. [< L *denigrare* blacken thoroughly < *de-* (intensive) + *nigrare* blacken < *niger* black]

den·i·gra·tion (den′ə grā′shən) n. the act of blackening a reputation; defamation.

den·im (den′əm) n. **1** a heavy, coarse cotton cloth with a diagonal weave, usually woven with a colored wrap and white filling threads. Denim is used mainly for work and casual clothes, upholstery, etc. **2 denims,** pl. pants or overalls made of denim, usually blue. [short for F *serge de Nîmes* serge of Nîmes]

de·ni·tri·fy (dē nī′trə fī′) v. **-fied, -fy·ing.** Chemistry. **1** remove nitrogen or its compounds from. **2** change (nitrates) by reduction into nitrites, nitrogen, or ammonia.

den·i·zen (den′ə zən) n. **1** an inhabitant; occupant: *Fish are denizens of the sea.* **2** a foreigner who is given certain rights of citizenship. **3** a foreign word, plant, animal, etc. that has been naturalized: *The common English sparrow is a denizen of North America; it was first brought from Europe about 1850.* [ME < AF *denzein* < *denz* within < LL < L *de* from + *intus* within]

de·nom·i·nate (v. di nom′ə nāt′; adj. di nom′ə nit′ or -nom′ə nāt′) v. **-nat·ed, -nat·ing;** adj. **—v.** give a specific name to. **—adj.** designating a number that represents a quantity in terms of a unit of a unit of measurement. 7 m and 18 kg are denominate numbers. [< L *denominare* < *de-* (intensive) + *nomen* name]

de·nom·i·na·tion (di nom′ə nā′shən) n. **1** a name for a group or class of things; name. **2** a religious group, usually represented by a number of local churches. Presbyterian and Baptist are two large Protestant denominations. **3** a class or kind of units: *The Canadian coin of lowest denomination is a cent.* **4** the act of naming.

de·nom·i·na·tion·al (di nom′ə nā′shən əl or di nom′ə nāsh′nəl) adj. having to do with some religious denomination or denominations; controlled by a religious denomination; sectarian. **—de·nom′i·na′tion·al·ly,** adv.

de·nom·i·na·tion·al·ism (di nom′ə nā′shən əl iz′əm or di nom′ə nāsh′nəl iz′əm) n. **1** denominational principles. **2** a division into denominations.

de·nom·i·na·tive (di nom′ə nə tiv or -nom′ə nā′tiv) adj., n. **—adj. 1** giving a distinctive name; naming. **2** Grammar. formed from a noun or an adjective. *Centre* and *whiten* are denominative verbs. **—n.** Grammar. a word formed from a noun or an adjective. **—de·nom′i·na′tive·ly,** adv.

de·nom·i·na·tor (di nom′ə nā′tər) n. **1** Mathematics. the number below the line in a fraction, stating the size of the parts in their relation to the whole. In 3/4, 4 is the denominator, and 3 is the numerator. **2** a person or thing that names.

de·no·ta·tion (dē′nō tā′shən) n. **1** a meaning, especially the exact, literal meaning. Compare **connotation. 2** an indication; a denoting or marking out. **3** a mark or sign; symbol. **4** Logic. **a** the

class, type, or number of things included in a given term; extension. **b** a value, quantity, etc. represented by a symbol.

de·note (di nōt′) v. **-not·ed, -not·ing. 1** be the sign of; indicate: *A fever usually denotes sickness.* **2** be a name for; mean. **3** stand for as a symbol: *The sign 'x' denotes multiplication.* [< F *dénoter* < L *denotare* < *de-* down + *nota* mark]

de·noue·ment or **dé·noue·ment** (dā nü′moN; *French,* dā nü mäN′) n. the solution or unravelling of a plot in a play, a story, etc.; outcome; end. [< F *dénouement* < *dénouer* untie < L *de* down from + *nodare* tie]

de·nounce (di nouns′) v. **-nounced, -nounc·ing. 1** condemn publicly; express strong disapproval of. **2** inform against; accuse: *He denounced his own brother to the military police as a spy.* **3** give formal notice of the termination of (a treaty, etc.). [ME < OF *denouncier* < L *denuntiare* < *de-* (intensive) + *nuntius* messenger] —**de·nounc′er,** n.

de·nounce·ment (di nouns′mənt) n. the act of denouncing; denunciation.

de nou·veau (də nü vō′) *French.* again; afresh; anew.

de no·vo (dē nō′vō) *Latin.* anew; starting again.

D. en Ph. Docteur en Philosophie (Doctor of Philosophy).

dense (dens) adj. **den·ser, dens·est. 1** closely packed together; thick: *a dense fog.* **2** profound; intense; impenetrable: *dense ignorance.* **3** stupid; dull; slow-thinking: *His dense look showed he did not understand the problem.* **4** *Photography.* (of a developed negative) relatively opaque, with strong contrasts of light and shade. [< L *densus*] —**dense′ly,** adv. —**dense′ness,** n.

den·si·ty (den′sə tē) n., pl. **-ties. 1** a dense condition or quality; having parts very close together; compactness; thickness: *The density of the forest prevented us from seeing more than a little way ahead.* **2** the quantity of anything per unit area: *population density.* **3** *Physics.* the quantity of matter in a particular unit of volume; the ratio of the mass of a given volume of a substance to that of an equal volume of a standard substance. A cubic metre of lead has more mass than a cubic metre of wood, so we say lead has a greater density than wood. Water is the standard of density for solids and liquids, and air for gases. **4** *Electricity.* **a** the quantity of electricity per unit of area on a charged surface. **b** current density. **5** *Photography.* the relative opaqueness of a developed negative. **6** stupidity.

dent¹ (dent) n., v. —n. **1** a hollow made by a blow or pressure; a dint: *Bullets had made dents in the soldier's steel helmet.* **2** an impression, especially one that weakens or damages: *The new TV set made a bad dent in our bank account.* —v. **1** make a dent in. **2** become dented. [ME *dente,* var. of *dint*]

dent² (dent) n. **1** a toothlike part, as in a gearwheel, comb, etc. **2** a notch; indentation. [< OF *dent* tooth < L *dens, dentis*]

den·tal (den′təl) adj., n. —adj. **1** of or for the teeth. **2** of, by, or for dentistry. **3** *Phonetics.* of speech sounds, produced by placing the tip of the tongue against or near the back of the upper front teeth: *French speakers pronounce the consonants* (t) *and* (d) *as dental sounds, whereas in English* (t) *and* (d) *are alveolar.* —n. *Phonetics.* a consonantal sound produced by placing the tip of the tongue against or near the back of the upper front teeth. [< L *dens, dentis* tooth]

dental floss a thin, strong, smooth thread used to remove plaque and food particles from between the teeth.

den·ta·li·um (den tā′lē əm) n. any of a genus (*Dentalium*) of burrowing molluscs found along seashores, having an elongated, tapering shell that is open at both ends. Dentalium shell was traditionally used by North American Indian peoples of the West Coast to make decorations for clothing, etc.

den·tate (den′tāt) adj. **1** having teeth or pointed, toothlike projections. **2** of leaves, having a toothed margin. [< L *dentatus* < *dens, dentis* tooth]

den·ti·care (den′tə ker′) n. a government-sponsored program of dental insurance for all people.

den·ti·frice (den′tə fris) n. a paste, powder, or liquid for cleaning the teeth. [< F < L *dentifricium* < *dens, dentis* tooth + *fricare* rub]

den·tin (den′tin) n. dentine.

den·tine (den′tēn or den′tin) n. the hard, bony material beneath the enamel of a tooth, forming the main part of a tooth. [< L *dens, dentis* tooth]

den·tist (den′tist) n. a person who is qualified to practise the prevention and treatment of tooth decay and other problems and diseases of the teeth and gums, and to fit patients with false teeth. [< F *dentiste* < *dent* tooth < L *dens, dentis*]

den·tist·ry (den′tis trē) n. the art or profession of a dentist.

den·ti·tion (den tish′ən) n. **1** the growth of teeth; teething. **2** the kind, number, and arrangement of the teeth: *Dogs and wolves have the same dentition.* [< L *dentitio, -onis* < *dens, dentis* tooth]

den·toid (den′toid) adj. like a tooth.

den·ture (den′chər) n. Usually, **dentures,** pl. a group of false teeth set in a plate to fit over the gum, especially a full set of upper and lower teeth. [< F *denture* < *dent* tooth < L *dens, dentis*]

den·tur·ist (den′chər ist) n. a person trained to make and fit dentures.

de·nu·da·tion (dē′nyü dā′shən or den′yə dā′shən) n. **1** a denuding. **2** a denuded condition. **3** *Geology.* the laying bare of rock, especially by erosion.

de·nude (di nyüd′ or -nüd′) v. **-nud·ed, -nud·ing. 1** make bare; strip of clothing, covering, etc.: *trees denuded of leaves.* **2** *Geology.* lay (rock) bare by removing what lies above, especially by erosion. [< L *denudare* < *de-* (intensive) + *nudus* bare]

de·nun·ci·a·tion (di nun′sē ā′shən) n. **1** public condemnation; expression of strong disapproval. **2** the act of informing against; accusation. **3** a formal notice of the intention to end a treaty, etc. **4** a declaration of a curse, revenge, etc.; warning; threat. [< L *denuntiatio, -onis* < *denuntiare.* See DENOUNCE.] —**de·nun′ci·a′tor,** n.

de·nun·ci·a·to·ry (di nun′sē ə tô′rē or di nun′shē ə tô′rē) adj. condemning; accusing; threatening.

Den·ver sandwich (den′vər) western sandwich. [< *Denver,* the capital of Colorado]

de·ny (di nī′) v. **-nied, -ny·ing. 1** declare (something) is not true: *The prisoner denied the charges against him. They denied the existence of disease in the town.* **2** say that one does not hold to or accept: *to deny a political party.* **3** refuse: *I could not deny her so small a favor.* **4** refuse to acknowledge; disown: *He denied his signature.*

deny (oneself), do without the things one wants.

deny (oneself) **to,** refuse to see: *Illness forced Mrs. Smith to deny herself to all callers.* [< F *dénier* < L *denegare* < *de-* completely + *negare* say no] ☛ *Syn.* **1. Deny, contradict** = declare something not true. **Deny** = state definitely or emphatically that something is untrue or cannot be true: *He denied the accusation.* **Contradict** suggests arguing forcefully against what has been said, whether it is true or not: *He contradicts everything I say, even if he has to insist that black is white.*

de·o·dar (dē′ə där′) n. a cedar of the Himalayas, having drooping branches. It is cultivated for shade. [< Hind. < Skt. *devadaru* wood of the gods]

de·o·dor·ant (dē ō′dər ənt) n., adj. —n. a preparation that destroys, prevents, or masks an undesirable odor, especially a powder, liquid, or salve used on the body. —adj. capable of destroying, preventing, or masking undesirable odors.

de·o·dor·ize (dē ō′dər īz′) v. **-ized, -iz·ing.** remove undesirable odors from: *to deodorize a bathroom.* —**de·o′dor·i·za′tion,** n.

de·o·dor·iz·er (dē ō′dər īz′ər) n. a substance used to destroy or mask odors, especially in a room, on articles of furniture, etc.: *He bought some deodorizer for the dog's bed.*

De·o gra·ti·as (dē′ō grā′shē as or grä′tē əs) *Latin.* thanks to God.

De·o vo·len·te (dē′ō vō len′tē or vō len′tā) *Latin.* if God is willing. *Abbrev.:* D.V.

de·ox·i·dize (dē ok′sə dīz′) v. **-dized, -diz·ing.** remove oxygen from. —**de·ox′i·di·za′tion,** n. —**de·ox′i·diz′er,** n.

de·ox·y·gen·ate (dē ok′sə jə nāt′) v. **-at·ed, -at·ing.** remove oxygen from; deoxygenize. —**de·ox′y·gen·a′tion,** n.

de·ox·y·ri·bo·nu·cle·ic acid (dē ok′sə rī′bō nyü klē′ik or -nü klē′ik) DNA, an essential component of all living matter, that in higher organisms contains the genetic codes determining heredity. [< *de-* from, away + *oxy*(gen) + *ribonucleic acid*]

dep. 1 deputy. **2** department. **3** deponent. **4** deposit. **5** depot.

de·part (di pärt′) v. **1** go away; leave: *The train departs at 6:15.* **2** turn away; change (*from*): *to depart from one's usual way of doing things.* **3** quit or leave (now used especially in **depart this life**): *She departed this life at the age of seventy.* **4** die. [ME < OF < LL *departire* divide < L *de-* away + *pars, partis* part] ☛ *Syn.* **1. Depart, withdraw, retire** = go away or leave; all are formal words in this sense. **Depart** suggests parting or separating oneself from a person, place, or thing: *He departed from his home.* **Withdraw** and **retire** = go apart or remove oneself from a place or someone's presence, usually for a good reason: *I withdrew* (retired) *while they discussed my qualifications.*

de·part·ed (di pär′tid) n.sing. or pl., adj. —n. a dead person or persons. —adj. **1** dead. **2** gone; past.

de·part·ment (di pärt′mənt) n. **1** a separate part or division of a larger unit, such as a government, business, school, etc.: *the city fire department, the furniture department of a store, the department of external affairs of the federal government, the English department of a school.* **2** a field or range of activity or influence: *He said that handling complaints from customers was not his*

department. 3 in France and some Latin American countries, an administrative district similar to a province.

de·part·men·tal (dē′pärt men′təl) *adj.* 1 having to do with a department. 2 divided into departments. —**de′part·men′tal·ly,** *adv.*

de·part·men·tal·ize (dē′pärt men′tə līz′) *v.* **-ized, -iz·ing.** 1 divide into departments. 2 arrange, classify, or restrict as if in departments. —**de′part·men′ta·li·za′tion,** *n.*

department store a store that is organized into departments where many different kinds of merchandise and services are sold.

de·par·ture (di pär′chər) *n.* 1 the act of going away; the act of leaving. 2 a turning away; change: *a departure from our old custom.* 3 a starting on a new course of action or thought. 4 death.

de·pend (di pend′) *v.* 1 rely; trust: *You can depend on this timetable from the depot.* 2 get support; rely for help: *Children depend on their parents.* 3 be a result of; be controlled or influenced by: *The success of our picnic depends partly on the weather.* 4 hang down.
that depends or **it depends,** the answer will be determined by certain conditions or actions that are not yet definitely known or understood: *"That depends," answered the cook.*
[ME < OF *dependre* < L *dependere* < *de-* from + *pendere* hand] —**de·pend′er,** *n.*
☛ *Syn.* 1, 2. See note at **rely.**

de·pend·a·bil·i·ty (di pen′də bil′ə tē) *n.* reliability; trustworthiness.

de·pend·a·ble (di pen′də bəl) *adj.* reliable; trustworthy. —**de·pend′a·ble·ness,** *n.* —**de·pend′a·bly,** *adv.*

de·pend·ant (di pen′dənt) *n., adj.* —*n.* a person who depends on someone else for support: *He has a younger brother living with him as a dependant.* —*adj.* Rare. See **dependent.**
☛ *Usage.* See note at **dependent.**

de·pend·ence (di pen′dəns) *n.* 1 reliance on another for support or help. 2 reliance; trust. 3 the condition of being a result of another thing; the fact of being controlled or influenced by something else: *the dependence of crops on the weather.* 4 a person or thing relied on.

de·pend·en·cy (di pen′dən sē) *n., pl.* **-cies.** 1 a country or territory controlled by another country: *Gibraltar is a dependency of the United Kingdom.* 2 dependence. 3 a thing that depends on another for existence or help.

de·pend·ent (di pen′dənt) *adj., n.* —*adj.* 1 relying on another for support or help: *A child is dependent on its parents.* 2 resulting from another thing; controlled or influenced by something else: *Good crops are dependent on the right kind of weather.* 3 hanging down. 4 *Grammar.* subordinate: *a dependent clause.* —*n.* See **dependant.** —**de·pend′ent·ly,** *adv.*
☛ *Usage.* **Dependant, dependent.** Although some people use these two forms interchangeably, most writers use *dependant* for the noun and *dependent* for the adjective.

de·per·son·al·ize (dē pėr′sən əl īz′) *v.* **-ized, -iz·ing.** take away subjective or personal elements from; make impersonal: *Too much bureaucracy depersonalizes the relationship between government and the people. The song tells of his own experience, but the experience has been depersonalized.* —**de·per′son·al·i·za′tion,** *n.*

de·pict (di pikt′) *v.* 1 represent by drawing, painting or carving; picture. 2 describe in words: Who Has Seen the Wind *depicts life on the Prairies during the Depression.* [< L *depictus,* pp. of *depingere* < *de-* + *pingere* paint] —**de·pict′er,** *n.*

de·pic·tion (di pik′shən) *n.* 1 the act or process of depicting. 2 a picture, sculpture, description, etc.

dep·i·late (dep′ə lāt′) *v.* **-lat·ed, -lat·ing.** remove hair from. [< L *depilare* < *de-* from + *pilus* hair] —**dep′i·la′tion,** *n.*

de·pil·a·to·ry (di pil′ə tô′rē) *adj., n.* **-ries.** —*adj.* capable of removing hair. —*n.* a paste, liquid, or other preparation for removing hair.

de·plane (dē plān′) *v.* **-planed, -plan·ing.** leave an airplane: *It was raining when we deplaned at Dorval Airport.*

de·plete (di plēt′) *v.* **-plet·ed, -plet·ing.** empty; exhaust: *The traveller went home because his funds were depleted.* [< L *depletus,* pp. of *deplere* empty < *de-* + *-plere* fill]

de·ple·tion (di plē′shən) *n.* 1 a depleting. 2 the state of being depleted.

de·plor·a·ble (di plôr′ə bəl) *adj.* 1 to be deplored; regrettable; lamentable: *a deplorable accident.* 2 wretched; miserable. —**de·plor′a·ble·ness,** *n.* —**de·plor′a·bly,** *adv.*

de·plore (di plôr′) *v.* **-plored, -plor·ing.** be very sorry about; regret deeply; lament. [< L *deplorare* < *de-* + *plorare* weep]

de·ploy (di ploi′) *v.* 1 spread out (troops, military units, etc.) from a column into a long battle line. 2 distribute (personnel, resources, etc.) in convenient positions for future use. [< F *déployer* < *dé-* + *ployer* < L *plicare* fold] —**de·ploy′ment,** *n.*

hat, āge, fär; let, ēqual, tėrm; it, īce
hot, ōpen, ôrder; oil, out; cup, pút, rüle,
əbove, takən, pencəl, lemən, circəs
ch, child; ng, long; sh, ship
th, thin; ŦH, then; zh, measure

de·po·lar·ize (dē pō′lər īz′) *v.* **-ized, -iz·ing.** destroy or neutralize the polarity or polarization of. —**de·po′lar·i·za′tion.** *n.*

de·pone (di pōn′) *v.* **-poned, -pon·ing.** testify in writing under oath. [< L *deponere* put down (in Med.L, testify) < *de-* down + *ponere* put]

de·po·nent (di pō′nənt) *n., adj.* —*n.* 1 a person who testifies, especially in writing, under oath. 2 *Greek and Latin grammar.* a verb passive in form but active in meaning. —*adj.* having passive form but active meaning. [< L *deponens, -entis,* ppr. of *deponere* < *de-* away, down + *ponere* put]

de·pop·u·late (dē pop′yə lāt′) *v.* **-lat·ed, -lat·ing.** deprive of inhabitants: *The conquerors depopulated the enemy's country, driving the inhabitants away or killing them.* —**de·pop′u·la′tor,** *n.*

de·pop·u·la·tion (dē pop′yə lā′shən) *n.* depopulating or being depopulated.

de·port (di pôrt′) *v.* 1 banish; expel; remove. When an alien is deported, he is sent out of the country, usually back to his native land. 2 behave or conduct (oneself) in a particular manner: *The boys were trained to deport themselves like gentlemen.* [< F *déporter* < L *deportare* < *de-* away + *portare* carry] —**de·port′er,** *n.*
☛ *Syn.* 1. See note at **banish.**

de·por·ta·tion (dē′pôr tā′shən) *n.* banishment; expulsion; removal: *Deportation of criminals from England to Australia was once common.*

de·port·ment (di pôrt′mənt) *n.* 1 the way a person acts; behavior; conduct: *A gentleman is known by his deportment.* 2 good bearing; graceful movement: *Young ladies once took lessons in deportment as a part of their regular studies.*

de·pos·al (di pōz′əl) *n.* deposing; deposition.

de·pose (di pōz′) *v.* **-posed, -pos·ing.** 1 put out of office or a position of authority: *The king was deposed by the revolution.* 2 *Law.* declare under oath, especially when making a statement for later use as evidence in court; testify: *He deposed that he had seen the prisoner on the day of the murder.* [ME < OF *deposer* < *de-* down (< L) + *poser* put. See POSE¹.] —**de·pos′able,** *adj.* —**de·pos′er,** *n.*

de·pos·it (di poz′it) *v., n.* —*v.* 1 put down; lay down; leave lying: *The flood deposited a layer of mud in the streets.* 2 put in a place for safe-keeping: *People deposit money in banks.* 3 pay as a pledge to do something or to pay more later. If you deposit part of the price, most stores will keep an article for you until you can pay the rest.
—*n.* 1 the material laid down or left lying by natural means: *a deposit of mud and sand at the mouth of a river.* 2 something put in a place for safe-keeping: *Money put in a bank is a deposit.* 3 a sum of money paid as a pledge or security: *In the election, one of the candidates lost his deposit.* 4 the act of depositing. 5 a mass of some mineral in rock or in the ground.
on deposit, a in a place for safe-keeping. **b** in a bank.
[< L *depositus,* pp. of *deponere* < *de-* away + *ponere* put]

dep·o·si·tion (dē′pə zish′ən or dep′ə zish′ən) *n.* 1 the act of putting out of office or a position of authority. 2 *Law.* **a** the act of testifying under oath. **b** testimony given under oath; especially, such testimony taken down in writing to be used as evidence later in court: *The witness made a deposition because she was not able to testify in court.* 3 the act or process of depositing: *the deposition of sediment at the mouth of a river.* 4 something deposited; deposit.

de·pos·i·tor (di poz′ə tər) *n.* a person who deposits, especially one who deposits money in a bank.

de·pos·i·to·ry (di poz′ə tô′rē) *n., pl.* **-ries.** a place where a thing is put for safekeeping or storage; storehouse.

dep·ot (dep′ō or de′pō) *n.* 1 a bus or railway station. 2 a storehouse, especially for military supplies. 3 a military recruiting and distribution centre. [< F *dépôt* < L *depositum* < *deponere.* See DEPOSIT.]

de·prave (di prāv′) *v.* **-praved, -prav·ing.** make bad; corrupt: *Too much liquor often depraves a person's character.* [ME < L *depravare* < *de-* + *pravus* crooked, wrong] —**de·pra·va′tion,** *n.* —**de·prav′er,** *n.*

de·praved (di prāvd′) *adj.* corrupt; perverted.
☛ *Syn.* See note at **corrupt.**

de·prav·i·ty (di prav′ə tē) *n., pl.* **-ties.** 1 wickedness; corruption. 2 a corrupt act; bad practice.

dep·re·cate (dep′rə kāt′) v. -cat·ed, -cat·ing. express strong disapproval of; plead against; protest against: *Lovers of peace deprecate war.* [< LL *deprecari* plead in excuse, avert by prayer < *de-* + *precari* pray] —**dep′re·cat′ing·ly,** *adv.* —**dep′re·ca′tor,** *n.*
☛ *Usage.* **Deprecate, depreciate.** Do not confuse **deprecate** = express strong disapproval of, with **depreciate** =lessen in value or price: *I feel I must deprecate the course the club is following. Naturally a car depreciates after a number of years of service.*

dep·re·ca·tion (dep′rə kā′shən) n. a strong expression of disapproval; a pleading or protesting against something.

dep·re·ca·to·ry (dep′rə kə tô′rē) adj. 1 deprecating. 2 *Informal.* apologetic.

de·pre·ci·ate (di prē′shē āt′) v. -at·ed, -at·ing. 1 lessen the value or price of. 2 lessen in value: *Certain goods depreciate if they are kept very long.* 3 speak slightingly of; belittle: *He depreciates the value of exercise.* [< L *depretiare* < *de-* + *pretium* price] —**de·pre′ci·at′ing·ly,** *adv.* —**de·pre′ci·a′tor,** *n.*
☛ *Usage.* See note at **deprecate.**

de·pre·ci·a·tion (di prē′shē ā′shən) n. 1 a lessening or lowering in value: *Machinery undergoes depreciation as it is used or becomes obsolete.* 2 the amount of such loss of value, or the allowance made for it in accounting. 3 a speaking slightingly of; belittling.

de·pre·ci·a·to·ry (di prē′shē ə tô′rē) adj. tending to depreciate, disparage, or undervalue.

dep·re·da·tion (dep′rə dā′shən) n. the act of plundering; robbery; a ravaging. [< L *depraedatio, -onis* < *depraedare* pillage < *de-* + *praeda* booty]

de·press (di pres′) v. 1 make sad or gloomy; cause to have low spirits: *She was depressed by the bad news from home.* 2 press down; push down; lower: *depress the keys of a piano.* 3 lower in amount or value. 4 reduce the activity of; weaken: *Some medicines depress the action of the heart.* [< OF *depresser* < L *depressus,* pp. of *deprimere* < *de-* + *premere* press] —**de·press′ing·ly,** *adv.* —**de·press′or,** *n.*

de·pres·sant (di pres′ənt) adj., n. —adj. decreasing the rate of vital activities; quieting. —n. a medicine that lessens pain or excitement; sedative or tranquillizer.

de·pressed (di prest′) adj. 1 gloomy; low-spirited; sad. 2 pressed down; lowered. 3 *Botany and zoology.* flattened down; broader than high.
☛ *Syn.* 1. See note at **sad.**

depressed area a region characterized by unemployment, poverty, etc.

de·pres·sion (di presh′ən) n. 1 the state of feeling sad or gloomy; low spirits. 2 *Psychology.* a condition in which a person has continual feelings of sadness or hopelessness not directly caused by real events. 3 the action of pressing down: *Depression of the gas pedal causes an automobile to accelerate.* 4 a lowering of amount, force, activity, or quality: *A rapid depression of the mercury in a barometer usually indicates a storm.* 5 a low place or part; hollow: *Depressions in the lawn were filled with water after the rain.* 6 a period of low economic activity, accompanied by high levels of unemployment. 7 **the Depression,** the severe economic depression of the 1930's. 8 *Meteorology.* an area of low barometric pressure; low.

dep·ri·va·tion (dep′rə vā′shən) n. 1 the act of depriving. 2 the state of being deprived; loss; privation.

de·prive (di prīv′) v. -prived, -priv·ing. 1 take away from by force: *The people deprived the cruel tyrant of his power.* 2 keep from having or doing: *Worrying deprived him of sleep.* [ME < OF *depriver* < *de-* (intensive) + *priver* deprive < L *privare,* originally, exempt] —**de·priv′er,** *n.*

de pro·fun·dis (dē′prō fun′dis or dā′prō fūn′dis) *Latin.* from the depths (of sorrow, misery, despair, etc.). [initial words of Psalm CXXX]

dept. 1 department. 2 deputy.

depth (depth) n. 1 the quality of being deep; deepness. 2 the distance from top to bottom: *the depth of a hole.* 3 the distance from front to back: *The depth of our house is 40 metres.* 4 a deep place. 5 the deepest part: *in the depths of the earth.* 6 the most central part; middle: *in the depth of the forest.* 7 intensity (of feelings, etc.). 8 profoundness: *A philosopher should have depth of mind.* 9 lowness of pitch. 10 intensity of color, etc.
out of (one's) **depth, a** in water so deep that one cannot touch bottom. **b** in a situation too difficult to understand or cope with: *He was out of his depth in the mathematics class.*
[ME *depth(e)* < OE *dēop* deep]

depth bomb depth charge.

depth charge an explosive charge dropped from a ship or airplane and set to explode at a certain depth under water.

dep·u·ta·tion (dep′yə tā′shən) n. 1 the act of deputing. 2 a group of persons appointed to act for others.

de·pute (di pyüt′) v. -put·ed, -put·ing. 1 appoint (someone) to do one's work or to act in one's place: *The teacher deputed a pupil to take charge of the room while she was gone.* 2 give (work, authority, etc.) to another. [ME < OF < LL *deputare* assign < L *deputare* consider as < *de-* + *putare* think, count]

dep·u·tize (dep′yə tīz′) v. -tized, -tiz·ing. 1 appoint as deputy. 2 act as deputy.

dep·u·ty (dep′yə tē) n., pl. -ties. 1 a person appointed to do the work of or to act in the place of another: *A deputy minister is an assistant to a minister in the cabinet.* 2 a representative to or in certain assemblies. In Quebec, the members of the National Assembly are often called deputies. 3 (*adjl.*) acting as a deputy. [< F *député,* originally pp. of *députer* < LL *deputare.* See DEPUTE.]

deputy minister in Canada, a senior civil servant who acts as assistant to a cabinet minister.

deputy returning officer in Canada, an official appointed by the returning officer of a constituency to look after the procedure of voting at a particular polling station: *The deputy returning officer is in charge of counting the ballots. Abbrev.:* DRO

der. 1 derivation; derivative; derived.

de·rac·i·nate (dē ras′ə nāt′) v. -at·ed, -at·ing. 1 tear up by the roots. 2 displace from one's home or one's normal environment: *deracinated refugees.*

de·rail (dē rāl′) v. 1 cause (a train, etc.) to run off the rails. 2 run off the rails. —**de·rail′ment,** *n.*

de·range (di rānj′) v. -ranged, -rang·ing. 1 disturb the order or arrangement of; throw into confusion. 2 make insane. [< F *déranger* < *dé-* away + *ranger* range]

de·range·ment (di rānj′mənt) n. 1 a disturbance of order or arrangement. 2 a mental disorder; insanity.

der·by (dėr′bē; *esp.Brit.* där′bē *for 1 and 2*) n., pl. -bies. 1 **Derby, a** a famous horse race in England, founded by the Earl of Derby in 1780 and run every year at Epsom Downs, near London. **b** any of several annual horse races of similar importance: *the Kentucky Derby.* 2 any contest or race: *a fishing derby, a dog derby, a bicycle derby.* 3 a man's stiff hat having a rounded crown and narrow brim; bowler. See **hat** for picture.

der·e·lict (der′ə likt′) adj., n. —adj. 1 abandoned; deserted; forsaken: *a derelict ship.* 2 failing in one's duty; negligent. —n. 1 a ship abandoned at sea. 2 any despised, deserted person or thing: *The ragged old derelict was begging for money to buy a meal.* [< L *derelictus,* pp. of *derelinquere* abandon < *de-* (intensive) + *re-* behind + *linquere* leave]

der·e·lic·tion (der′ə lik′shən) n. 1 a failure in one's duty; negligence. 2 an abandonment; desertion; forsaking.

de·ride (di rīd′) v. -rid·ed, -rid·ing. make fun of; laugh at in scorn; ridicule with contempt. [< L *deridere* < *de-* down + *ridere* laugh] —**de·rid′er,** *n.* —**de·rid′ing·ly,** *adv.*
☛ *Syn.* See note at **ridicule.**

de ri·gueur (də rē gœr′) *French.* required by etiquette; according to custom; proper.

de·ri·sion (di rizh′ən) n. 1 scornful laughter; ridicule; contempt. 2 an object of ridicule. [< L *derisio, -onis* < *deridere.* See DERIDE.]

de·ri·sive (di rī′siv) adj. mocking; ridiculing. —**de·ri′sive·ly,** *adv.* —**de·ri′sive·ness,** *n.*

de·ri·so·ry (di rī′sə rē) adj. 1 derisive. 2 laughable; deserving contempt.

deriv. derivation; derivative.

der·i·va·tion (der′ə vā′shən) n. 1 the act or process of deriving. 2 the state of being derived. 3 the source; origin: *The celebration of Halloween is of Scottish derivation. Many English words are of French derivation.* 4 the formation of a new word from an existing word or base, especially by the addition of an affix other than an inflectional ending. *Example: quickness = quick + -ness* (a suffix). 5 a statement of how a word was formed.

der·i·va·tive (di riv′ə tiv) adj., n. —adj. derived; not original. —n. 1 something derived. Words formed by adding prefixes and suffixes, etc. to other words are called derivatives. 2 *Chemistry.* a substance obtained from another by modification or by partial substitution of components. —**de·riv′a·tive·ly,** *adv.*

de·rive (di rīv′) v. -rived, -riv·ing. 1 receive or obtain from a particular source: *He derives a great pleasure from music. Gasoline is derived from petroleum.* 2 come from a source or origin; originate or develop: *Our word table derives from Latin tabula.* 3 make or create new words by adding suffixes or prefixes: *The words kindness, kinder, and unkind are derived from kind.* 4 trace the development or origin of a custom, condition, word. etc.: *Scholars derive many modern English words from Old French. He derives all*

his present troubles from the loss of his job years ago. **5** obtain by reasoning; deduce: *He derived his conclusion from the large amount of data he had collected.* **6** obtain (a chemical compound) from another by substituting a different element. [< MF < LL *derivare* lead off, draw off < L *de-* from + *rivus* stream]
—**de·riv′a·ble,** *adj.* —**de·riv′er,** *n.*

derived word a word formed by adding one or more prefixes or suffixes to an existing word or root.

der·ma (dėr′mə) *n.* **1** the sensitive layer of skin beneath the epidermis. See **epidermis** for picture. **2** the skin. [< Gk. *derma* skin]

der·mal (dėr′məl) *adj.* of the skin.

der·ma·ti·tis (dėr′mə tī′tis) *n.* inflammation of the skin.

der·ma·to·log·i·cal (dėr′mə tə loj′ə kəl) *adj.* of or having to do with dermatology.

der·ma·tol·o·gist (dėr′mə tol′ə jist) *n.* a person trained in dermatology, especially one whose work it is.

der·ma·tol·o·gy (dėr′mə tol′ə jē) *n.* the science that deals with the skin and its diseases.

der·ma·to·sis (dėr′mə tō′sis) *n.* any skin disease. [< Gk. *derma, -atos* skin + E *-osis*]

der·mis (dėr′mis) *n.* derma.

der·o·gate (der′ə gāt′) *v.* **-gat·ed, -gat·ing. 1** take away; detract: *The king felt that summoning a parliament would derogate from his authority.* **2** become worse; degenerate. [< L *derogare* < *de-* down from + *rogare* ask]

der·o·ga·tion (der′ə gā′shən) *n.* **1** a lessening or impairment (of power, law, position, etc.); detraction. **2** the state of becoming worse; deterioration; debasement.

de·rog·a·tive (di rog′ə tiv) *adj.* derogatory. —**de·rog′a·tive·ly,** *adv.*

de·rog·a·to·ry (di rog′ə tô′rē) *adj.* **1** disparaging; belittling; showing an unfavorable opinion of some person or thing: *The word skinny has a derogatory connotation, but slender has not.* **2** lessening the value; detracting. —**de·rog′a·to′ri·ly,** *adv.*

der·rick (der′ik) *n.* **1** a machine for lifting and moving heavy objects. A derrick has a long arm that swings at an angle from the base of an upright post or frame. **2** a towerlike framework over an oil well, gas well, etc. which holds the drilling and hoisting machinery. [after *Derrick,* a 17th-century hangman at Tyburn, London]

der·ri·ère or **der·ri·ere** (der′ē er′) *n.* buttocks.

der·ring-do (der′ing dü′) *n. Archaic.* heroic daring; daring deeds. [alteration of ME *dorryng don* daring to do]

der·rin·ger (der′in jər) *n.* a short pistol of relatively large calibre. [after H. *Derringer,* an American inventor]

der·ris (der′is) *n.* any of a genus (*Derris*) of tropical woody climbing plants of the pea family, including some species whose roots yield the compound rotenone, used as an insecticide and fish poison. [< NL *Derris* < Gk. *derris* leather cover]

der·vish (dėr′vish) *n.* a member of any of several Moslem religious orders dedicated to a life of poverty and chastity. The dervishes of some orders practise religious rites that include whirling, dancing, etc. [< Turkish *dervīsh* < Persian *darvīsh*]

de·sal·i·nate (dē sal′ə nāt′) *v.* **-nat·ed, -nat·ing.** remove salt from, especially from sea water. —**de·sal′i·na′tion,** *n.*

des·cant (*v.* des kant′; *n.* des′kant) *n., v.* —*n.* **1** *Music.* **a** a separate melody or counterpoint sung above the basic melody. **b** the highest part or melody in harmonic music; soprano or treble. **2** any song or melody. **3** an extended comment; discourse. —*v.* **1** talk at great length; discourse freely: *to descant upon the wonders of nature.* **2** *Music.* sing or play a melody with one or more additional melodies. [ME < OF *deschanter* < Med.L *discantare* < L *dis-* away + *cantus* song < *canere* sing]

de·scend (di send′) *v.* **1** go or come down from a higher place to a lower place: *The river descends to the sea.* **2** pass from an earlier to a later time: *We still have many superstitions descended from the Middle Ages.* **3** go in sequence from greater to smaller, or higher to lower: *The numerals 100, 75, 50, 25 form a series arranged in descending order.* **4** extend or slope downward: *The road descended in a winding path to the sea.* **5** make a sudden appearance or attach (used with **on** or **upon**): *The wolves descended on the sheep and killed them. Many tourists descended upon the town during the exhibition.* **6** be handed down from parent to child; pass by inheritance: *The land has descended in the family for 150 years.* **7** come down from a source, especially an ancestor (*usually used after the verb* be): *John is descended from a pioneer family.* **8** lower oneself; stoop: *He descended to cheating in an effort to win the scholarship.* [ME < OF < L *descendere* < *de-* down + *scandere* climb]

de·scend·ant (di sen′dənt) *n., adj.* —*n.* **1** a person born of a certain family or group: *a descendant of the United Empire Loyalists.* **2** an offspring; child; great-grandchild, etc. You are a

hat, āge, fär; let, ēqual, tėrm; it, īce
hot, ōpen, ôrder; oil, out; cup, pút, rüle,
əbove, takən, pencəl, lemən, circəs

ch, child; ng, long; sh, ship
th, thin; ₮H, then; zh, measure

direct descendant of your parents, grandparents, great-grandparents, etc. —*adj.* descending; going or coming down.

de·scend·ent (di sen′dənt) *adj.* descending.

de·scent (di sent′) *n.* **1** the act or process of coming down or going down from a higher to a lower place: *the balloon made a rapid descent.* **2** a downward slope: *the sharp descent of the ground to the sea.* **3** a way or passage down; a means of descending: *We took the steep descent carefully.* **4** a family line; ancestry: *Our family is of Turkish descent. They can trace their descent back to the eighteenth century.* **5** a transmitting or handing down of property, qualities, etc. from parent to child; transmission through inheritance: *The estate was acquired by descent. We can trace the descent of red hair in our family through five generations.* **6** a sinking to a lower condition or quality; a decline: *a descent to bigotry and racism.* **7** a sudden attack or unexpected appearance: *The descent of the invaders on the town led to the slaughter of many people.* [ME < OF *descente* < *descendre* < L *descendere.*] See DESCEND.
➤ Hom. **dissent.**

de·scribe (di skrīb′) *v.* **-scribed, -scrib·ing. 1** tell or write about: *The reporter described the accident in detail.* **2** give a picture of in words, music, etc. **3** draw the outline of; trace: *The skater described a figure 8.* [< L *describere* < *de-* from + *scribere* write] —**de·scrib′a·ble,** *adj.* —**de·scrib′er,** *n.*

de·scrip·tion (di skrip′shən) *n.* **1** the act of describing; the act of giving a picture or account in words. **2** a composition or account that describes. **3** a picture in words, music, etc. **4** a kind or sort: *In the crowd there were people of every description.* **5** the act of tracing; the act of drawing in outline.

de·scrip·tive (di skrip′tiv) *adj.* **1** describing; that tells about by using description. **2** *Grammar.* **a** describing. In the phrase *cold water, cold* is a descriptive adjective. **b** adding descriptive detail; non-restrictive. **3** of or having to do with an objective, factual description: *descriptive biology, descriptive linguistics.* —**de·scrip′tive·ly,** *adv.* —**de·scrip′tive·ness,** *n.*

de·scry (di skrī′) *v.* **-scried, -scry·ing.** catch sight of; be able to see; make out: *The shipwrecked sailor at last descried an island far away on the horizon.* [ME < MF *descrier* proclaim < *des-* away + *crier* cry < L *quiritare*]

des·e·crate (des′ə krāt′) *v.* **-crat·ed, -crat·ing.** treat or use without respect; disregard the sacredness of: *The enemy desecrated the church by using it as a stable.* [< *de-* (do the opposite of) + (con)secrate] —**des′e·crat′er** or **des′e·cra′tor,** *n.*

des·e·cra·tion (des′ə krā′shən) *n.* **1** the act of desecrating: *The Puritans thought that work or amusement on Sundays was a desecration of the Sabbath.* **2** the fact or state of being desecrated.

de·seg·re·gate (dē seg′rə gāt′) *v.* **-gat·ed, -gat·ing.** abolish any law or practice that requires the members of a particular race or particular races to be isolated for any purpose from the rest of the population: *to desegregate the schools.*

de·seg·re·ga·tion (dē seg′rə gā′shən) *n.* **1** the act or process of desegregating. **2** the state of being desegregated.

de·sen·si·tize (dē sen′sə tīz′) *v.* **-tized, -tiz·ing. 1** make less sensitive. **2** *Photography.* make less sensitive to light. —**de·sen′si·ti·za′tion,** *n.* —**de·sen′si·tiz′er,** *n.*

des·ert¹ (dez′ərt) *n.* **1** a dry, barren region, usually sandy and without trees. **2** (*adj.*) dry; barren. **3** a region that is not inhabited or cultivated; wilderness. **4** (*adj.*) not inhabited or cultivated; wild: *Robinson Crusoe was shipwrecked on a desert island.* **5** a place or environment that provides no stimulus to the intellect or imagination. [ME < OF < LL *desertum* (thing) abandoned, pp. neut. of *deserere.* See DESERT².]
➤ **Syn. 1, 2. Desert, wilderness** = an uninhabited or uncultivated region. **Desert** emphasizes dryness and barrenness and applies to a region that is usually sandy and without water, trees, or inhabitants: *Great sections of desert in Arizona and California have been turned into rich agricultural areas by irrigation.* **Wilderness** emphasizes lack of trails and roads and applies particularly to a region where few men have ever been and that is covered with dense vegetation: *Large areas in northern Ontario are wilderness.*

de·sert² (di zėrt′) *v.* **1** go away and leave; abandon; forsake: *The man was guilty of deserting his family.* **2** run away from duty. **3** leave military service without permission and with no intention of returning: *The soldier who had deserted was caught and court-martialled.* **4** fail; leave: *The boy's courage deserted him when he*

met the angry dog. [< F < LL *desertare* < L *deserere* abandon < *de-* dis- + *serere* join] **—de·sert′er,** *n.*

☛ *Hom.* desert[3], dessert.

☛ *Syn.* **1. Desert, forsake, abandon** = leave someone or something completely. **Desert** emphasizes breaking a promise, oath, etc. or running away from a duty, and therefore implies blame: *He deserted his country and helped the enemy.* **Forsake** emphasizes breaking off sentimental attachments and thus has emotional connotations, but does not necessarily suggest blame: *He forsook the country village for a career in banking.* **Abandon** emphasizes that the action is final and complete, though it may be voluntary or involuntary, necessary or resulting from a desire to avoid duty: *They abandoned the wrecked plane.*

de·sert[3] (di zèrt′) *n.* Usually, **deserts,** *pl.* what is deserved; a suitable reward or punishment: *The robber got his just deserts when he was sentenced to five years in prison.* [ME < OF *deserte,* pp. of *deservir* < L *deservire.* See DESERVE.]

☛ *Hom.* desert[2], dessert.

de·ser·tion (di zèr′shən) *n.* **1** deserting or being deserted. **2** *Law.* a deliberate abandoning of one's husband or wife and of the related moral and legal obligations. **3** a running away from duty. **4** the leaving of military service without permission.

de·serve (di zèrv′) *v.* **-served, -serv·ing. 1** have a claim or right to; be worthy of: *Good work deserves good pay.* **2** be worthy: *He deserves well.* [ME < OF < L *deservire* serve well < *de-* (intensive) + *servire* serve] **—de·serv′er,** *n.*

de·serv·ed·ly (di zèr′vid lē) *adv.* according to what is deserved; justly; rightly: *deservedly punished.*

de·serv·ing (di zèr′ving) *adj.* **1** that deserves; worthy (of something). **2** worth helping. **—de·serv′ing·ly,** *adv.*

des·ha·bille (dez′ə bēl′; *French,* dā zä bē′) *n.* dishabille.

des·ic·cate (des′ə kāt′) *v.* **-cat·ed, -cat·ing. 1** dry thoroughly. **2** make dry. **3** preserve by drying thoroughly. **4** make or become intellectually or emotionally dry. [< L *desiccare* < *de-* out + *siccus* dry] **—des′ic·ca′tion,** *n.* **—des′ic·ca′tor,** *n.*

☛ *Usage.* Desiccate. Observe the proper meaning of this word. Because desiccated foods have often been cut into small pieces, people sometimes suppose that *desiccate* means "cut up or shred."

de·sid·er·a·ta (di sid′ər ā′tə *or* di sid′ər at′ə) *n.* pl. of **desideratum.**

de·sid·er·a·tive (di sid′ər ə tiv *or* di sid′ər ā′tiv) *adj., n.* **—adj.** expressing, implying, or having desire. **—n.** *Grammar.* expressing the desire to perform the action signified by another verb from which it is derived.

de·sid·er·a·tum (di sid′ər ā′təm *or* di sid′ər at′əm) *n., pl.* **-ta.** something desired or needed: *His consent is a desideratum.* [< L *desideratum,* pp. neut. of *desiderare* long for]

de·sign (di zīn′) *n., v.* **—n. 1** a drawing, plan, or sketch made to serve as a pattern from which to work: *a design for a machine, a dress design.* **2** in painting, weaving, building, etc., an arrangement of detail, form, and color: *a wallpaper design in tan and brown.* **3** the art of making designs, patterns, or sketches: *Architects are skilled in design.* **4** a piece of artistic work. **5** a plan in mind to be carried out. **6** a scheme of attack; evil plan: *The thief had designs upon the safe.* **7** a purpose; aim; intention: *Whether by accident or design, he overturned the lamp.* **8** the underlying plan or conception; organization of parts in relation to the whole and to its purpose: *the evidence of design in a communication satellite, unity of design in a novel.*

by design, on purpose; by intention.
—v. 1 make a first sketch of; plan out; arrange the form and color of; draw in outline: *to design a dress.* **2** make drawings, sketches, plans, etc.: *He designs for a firm of dressmakers.* **3** plan out; form in the mind; contrive: *The author designed an exciting plot.* **4** have in mind to do; purpose: *Did you design this, or did it just happen?* **5** set apart; intend: *His parents designed him for the ministry.* [MF *dessein,* n., and F *désigner,* v., both < earlier *desseigner* < L *designare* < *de-* (intensive) + *signum* mark]

☛ *Syn. n.* **5.** See note at **plan. 7.** See note at **intention.**

des·ig·nate (*v.* dez′ig nāt′; *adj.* dez′ig nit *or* dez′ig nāt′) *v.* **-nat·ed, -nat·ing.** **—v. 1** mark out; point out; indicate definitely: *Red lines designate main roads on this map. His uniform designates his rank.* **2** name; entitle: *The ruler of the country was designated king.* **3** select for duty, office, etc.; appoint: *That is the man designated as the new Governor General.*
—adj. appointed; selected. [< L *designare.* See DESIGN.] **—des′ig·na′tor,** *n.*

des·ig·na·tion (dez′ig nā′shən) *n.* **1** the act of marking out; the act of pointing out; a definite indication: *The designation of places on a map should be clear.* **2** a descriptive title; name: *"Your Majesty" is a designation given to the Queen.* **3** the appointment or selection for a duty, office, position, etc.: *The designation of Cabinet officers is one of the powers of the Prime Minister.*

de·sign·ed·ly (di zīn′id lē) *adv.* purposely; intentionally.

de·sign·er (di zīn′ər) *n.* **1** a person who designs: *The dress designer completed his patterns and sketches for his spring showing of women's clothes.* **2** plotter; schemer.

de·sign·ing (di zīn′ing) *adj., n.* **—adj.** scheming; plotting: *a designing rogue.* **—n.** the art of making designs, patterns, sketches, etc.: *She studies dress designing at school.* **—de·sign′ing·ly,** *adv.*

de·sir·a·bil·i·ty (di zīr′ə bil′ə tē) *n.* the state or quality of being desirable.

de·sir·a·ble (di zīr′ə bəl) *adj.* worth wishing for; worth having; pleasing; good; excellent. **—de·sir′a·ble·ness,** *n.* **—de·sir′a·bly,** *adv.*

de·sire (di zīr′) *v.* **-sired, -sir·ing;** *n.* **—v. 1** long for; wish strongly for. **2** express a wish for; ask for or request, especially in a formal manner: *The Governor General desires your presence.*
—n. 1 a strong wish; a longing: *His desire is to travel.* **2** an expressed wish; request. **3** something desired. **4** sensual appetite; lust. [ME < OF *desirer* < L *desiderare* long for] **—de·sir′er,** *n.*

☛ *Syn. v.* **1.** See note at **wish. -n. 1. Desire, longing, craving** = a strong wish. **Desire** applies to any strong wish, good or bad, for something a person thinks or hopes he can get: *His desire is to travel.* **Longing** applies to an earnest desire, sometimes for something a person thinks he can get if he tries or wishes hard enough, but often for something that seems beyond reach: *His longing for a bicycle is pathetic.* **Craving** applies to a desire so strong that it amounts to a need or hunger: *She has a craving for candy.*

de·sir·ous (di zīr′əs) *adj.* having or showing desire or longing; strongly wishing: *desirous of fame, desirous to learn all one can. He was desirous that his true identity be concealed.*

de·sist (di sist′ *or* di zist′) *v.* stop; cease: *The judge ordered him to desist from fighting.* [< MF *desister* < L *desistere* < *de-* from + *sistere* stop]

desk (desk) *n.* **1** a piece of furniture with one or more drawers and a flat or sloping top on which to write or to rest books, papers, etc. **2** a department of work at a certain location or at a desk: *the information desk of a library, the copy desk of a newspaper office.* [< Med.L *desca* < Ital. *desco* < L *discus* quoit, dish < Gk. *diskos.* Doublet of DAIS, DISCUS, DISH, and DISK.]

D. ès L. Docteur ès Lettres; Doctor of Letters.

des·o·late (*adj.* des′ə lit; *v.* des′ə lāt′) *adj., v.* **-lat·ed, -lat·ing. —adj. 1** laid waste; devastated; barren: *desolate land.* **2** not lived in; deserted: *a desolate house.* **3** left alone; solitary; lonely. **4** unhappy; wretched; forlorn: *The ragged, hungry child looked desolate.* **5** dreary; dismal: *a desolate life.*
—v. 1 make unfit to live in; lay waste: *The Vikings desolated the land they attacked.* **2** deprive of inhabitants. **3** make lonely, unhappy, or forlorn: *He was desolated to hear that his old friend was going away.* [ME < L *desolatus,* pp. of *desolare* < *de-* completely + *solus* alone] **—des′o·late·ly,** *adv.* **—des′o·late·ness,** *n.* **—des′o·lat′er, des′o·la′tor,** *n.*

☛ *Syn. adj.* **4. Desolate, disconsolate** = unhappy and forlorn. **Desolate** = unhappy because feeling left alone, deserted by everyone or, especially, separated from someone: *She was desolate when he went away.* **Disconsolate** = wretched because broken-hearted, without hope, and unable to be consoled or comforted: *She was disconsolate when her former boy friend married another girl.*

des·o·la·tion (des′ə lā′shən) *n.* **1** the action of making desolate: *the desolation of a vast area by fire.* **2** the condition of being desolated; devastation: *the desolation left by the forest fire.* **3** the condition of being solitary, deserted, or uninhabited: *the desolation of the Barren Ground.* **4** a lonely or isolated place. **5** lonely sorrow or misery; grief: *There was desolation in the eyes of the condemned man.*

de·spair (di sper′) *n., v.* **—n. 1** a complete loss of hope; the state of being without hope; a feeling that nothing good can happen: *Despair seized us as we felt the boat sinking. In despair, he took his own life.* **2** a person or thing that causes hopelessness: *She was the despair of her parents.* **—v.** lose or give up hope: *The doctors despaired of saving the sick man's life.* [ME < OF *despeir* < *desperer* < L *desperare* < *de-* out of, without + *sperare* to hope]

☛ *Syn. n.* **1. Despair, desperation** = hopelessness. **Despair** emphasizes loss of hope and usually suggests sinking into a state of discouragement: *In his despair over losing his job he sold all his precious possessions and left town.* **Desperation** suggests a recklessness that is caused by despair and is expressed in rash or frantic action as a last resort: *He had no job and no money, and in desperation he robbed a bank.*

de·spair·ing (di sper′ing) *adj.* feeling, showing, or expressing despair; hopeless. **—de·spair′ing·ly,** *adv.* **—de·spair′ing·ness,** *n.*

☛ *Syn.* See note at **hopeless.**

des·patch (dis pach′) See dispatch.

des·patch·er (dis pach′ər) See dispatcher.

des·per·a·do (des′pə rä′dō *or* des′pə rā′dō) *n., pl.* **-does or -dos.** a bold or reckless criminal; a dangerous outlaw. [< OSp. *desperado* < L *desperatus.* Doublet of DESPERATE.]

des·per·ate (des′pər it *or* des′prit) *adj.* **1** having lost all hope: *She would have to be desperate before she asked for help.* **2** made reckless or violent through loss of hope: *a desperate criminal.* **3** resulting from loss of hope; showing recklessness caused by

despair: *a last, desperate bid for freedom.* **4** giving little or no hope of improvement; very dangerous or serious: *a desperate illness. The situation is desperate.* **5** having an extreme need or desire: *desperate for affection. After a week of being cooped up in the cabin, he was desperate for something to do.* **6** extreme: *in desperate need of assistance.* [ME < L *desperatus,* pp. of *desperare.* See DESPAIR. Doublet of DESPERADO.] —**des′per·ate·ly,** *adv.* —**des′per·ate·ness,** *n.*

☛ *Syn.* **4.** See note at **hopeless.**

des·per·a·tion (des′pər ā′shən) *n.* recklessness caused by despair; willingness to do anything, regardless of risks or consequences: *Desperation finally made her give herself up. He saw that the stairs were on fire and in desperation he jumped out of the window.*

☛ *Syn.* See note at **despair.**

des·pic·a·ble (des pik′ə bəl *or* des′pi kə bəl) *adj.* fit to be despised; contemptible: *Cowards and liars are despicable.* [< LL *despicabilis* < L *despicari* despise] —**des·pic′a·ble·ness,** *n.* —**des·pic′a·bly,** *adv.*

de·spise (di spīz′) *v.* -**spised,** -**spis·ing.** look down on; feel contempt for; scorn: *Most people despise a traitor.* [ME < OF *despis-,* a stem of *despire* < L *despicere* < *de-* down + *specere* look at] —**de·spis′er,** *n.*

de·spite (di spīt′) *prep., n.* —*prep.* in spite of: *The boys went for a walk despite the rain.*
—*n.* **1** insult; injury. **2** *Archaic.* malice; spite. **3** *Archaic.* contempt; scorn.
in despite of, in spite of.
[ME < OF *despit* < L *despectus* a looking down upon < *despicere* < *de-* down + *specere* look at]

de·spite·ful (di spīt′fəl) *adj. Archaic.* spiteful; malicious. —**de·spite′ful·ly,** *adv.* —**de·spite′ful·ness,** *n.*

de·spoil (di spoil′) *v.* rob; plunder. [ME < OF *despoillier* < L *despoliare* < *de-* completely + *spolium* armor, booty]

de·spoil·ment (di spoil′mənt) *n.* despoliation.

de·spo·li·a·tion (di spō′lē ā′shən) *n.* robbery; pillage.

de·spond (di spond′) *v., n.* —*v.* lose heart, courage, or hope.
—*n. Archaic.* despondency. [ME < L *despondere* < *de-* away + *spondere* lose heart] —**de·spond′ing·ly,** *adv.*

de·spond·ence (di spon′dəns) *n.* despondency.

de·spond·en·cy (di spon′dən sē) *n., pl.* -**cies.** loss of courage or hope; discouragement; dejection.

de·spond·ent (di spon′dənt) *adj.* without courage or hope; discouraged; dejected. —**de·spond′ent·ly,** *adv.*

des·pot (des′pot *or* des′pət) *n.* **1** a tyrant; oppressor. **2** a monarch having unlimited power; an absolute ruler. **3** any person who uses his power to get his own way: *Some fathers are despots in the eyes of their children.* **4** in medieval Italy, a noble, prince, or military leader in Italian cities. [< MF < Gk. *despotēs* master]

des·pot·ic (des pot′ik) *adj.* of a despot; tyrannical; having unlimited power.

des·pot·i·cal·ly (des pot′ik lē) *adv.* in a despotic manner; with absolute power.

des·pot·ism (des′pət iz′əm) *n.* **1** tyranny; oppression. **2** government by a monarch having unlimited power. **3** despotic rule or control.

des·sert (di zėrt′) *n.* **1** a course served at the end of a meal. **2** a food, such as fruit, cake, or ice cream, served at this course. [< F *dessert* < *desservir* clear the table < *des-* from + *servir* serve < L *servire*]

☛ *Hom.* **desert², desert³.**

des·sert·spoon (di zėrt′spün′) *n.* a spoon larger than a teaspoon and smaller than a tablespoon.

des·sert·spoon·ful (di zėrt′spün′fül) *n., pl.* -**fuls.** the amount that a dessertspoon can hold.

des·ti·na·tion (des′tə nā′shən) *n.* **1** a place to which a person or thing is going or is being sent. **2** a setting apart for a particular purpose or use; intention.

des·tine (des′tən) *v.* -**tined,** -**tin·ing.** **1** set apart for a particular purpose or use; intend: *The prince was destined from birth to a be a king.* **2** cause by fate: *My letter was destined never to reach him.*
destined for, **a** intended to go to; bound for: *ships destined for England.* **b** intended for: *My brother is destined for the ministry.* [ME < OF < L *destinare* make fast < *de-* (intensive) + *stare* stand]

des·ti·ny (des′tə nē) *n., pl.* -**nies.** **1** one's lot or fortune; what becomes of a person or thing in the end. **2** what is predetermined to happen in spite of all efforts to change or prevent it. **3** the power that foreordains; overruling necessity; fate: *Do you believe in destiny?*

☛ *Syn.* **1.** See note at **fate.**

des·ti·tute (des′tə tyüt′ *or* des′tə tüt′) *adj.* **1** lacking necessities

hat, āge, fär; let, ēqual, tėrm; it, īce
hot, ōpen, ôrder; oil, out; cup, pút, rüle,
əbove, takən, pencəl, lemən, circəs
ch, child; ng, long; sh, ship
th, thin; ŦH, then; zh, measure

such as food, clothing, and shelter: *The family is destitute and needs help.* **2** not having; being without, especially something desirable or needed (*used with* of): *a region destitute of trees. The tyrant was destitute of pity.* [< L *destitutus,* pp. of *destituere* forsake < *de-* away + *statuere* put, place]

des·ti·tu·tion (des′tə tyü′shən *or* des′tə tü′shən) *n.* **1** a destitute conditon; extreme poverty. **2** the state of being without; lack.

☛ *Syn.* **1.** See note at **poverty.**

de·stroy (di stroi′) *v.* **1** ruin or wreck by tearing down, breaking, etc. or as if by tearing down, breaking, etc.; demolish: *Hail destroyed their crop. Many paintings were destroyed in the flood. His reputation has been destroyed by his involvement in the scandal.* **2** defeat completely: *The enemy was destroyed.* **3** put an end to; bring to nothing: *A heavy rain destroyed all hope of a picnic. Repeated failures have destroyed her confidence.* **4** kill: *The injured dog had to be destroyed.* **5** counteract the effect of; make void. [ME < OF *destruire* < VL < L *destruere* < *de-* un- + *struere* pile, build]

☛ *Syn.* **1. Destroy, demolish** = ruin. **Destroy** suggests bringing to nothing or making useless by breaking to pieces, taking apart, killing, or other means: *Some children destroy all their toys.* **Demolish** = tear down, and applies only to things thought of as having been built up, such as buildings or, figuratively, arguments and theories: *The city demolished many buildings to make room for the speedway.*

de·stroy·er (di stroi′ər) *n.* **1** a person or thing that destroys. **2** a small, fast warship equipped with guns, torpedoes, and other weapons: *In wartime, the Royal Canadian Navy used destroyers for hunting submarines.*

de·struct·i·bil·i·ty (di struk′tə bil′ə tē) *n.* the quality of being destructible.

de·struct·i·ble (di struk′tə bəl) *adj.* capable of being destroyed. —**de·struct′i·ble·ness,** *n.*

de·struc·tion (di struk′shən) *n.* **1** the act or process of destroying. **2** the condition or fact of being destroyed; ruin. **3** anything that destroys; the causes or means of destruction: *That letter was the destruction of all her hopes.* [ME < OF < L *destructio, -onis* < *destruere* destroy. See DESTROY.]

☛ *Syn.* **4.** See note at **ruin.**

de·struc·tive (di struk′tiv) *adj.* **1** tending to destroy; liable to cause destruction: *Termites are destructive insects.* **2** destroying; causing destruction. **3** guilty of destroying; in the habit of causing destruction: *Destructive children should be corrected.* **4** not helpful; not constructive: *His criticism was destructive because it showed what was wrong, but did not show how to correct it.*
—**de·struc′tive·ly,** *adv.* —**de·struc′tive·ness,** *n.*

des·ue·tude (des′wə tyüd′ *or* des′wə tüd′) *n.* disuse: *Many words once commonly used have fallen into desuetude.* [< F < L *desuetudo* < *de-* dis- + *suescere* accustom]

des·ul·to·ry (des′əl tô′rē) *adj.* jumping from one thing to another; unconnected; without aim or method: *The careful and systematic study of a few books is better than the desultory reading of many.* [< L *desultorius* of a leaper, ult. < *de-* down + *salire* leap] —**des′ul·to′ri·ly,** *adv.* —**des′ul·to′ri·ness,** *n.*

de·tach (di tach′) *v.* **1** loosen and remove; unfasten; separate: *She detached a charm from her bracelet.* **2** separate a number of men, ships, tanks, etc. from the main body for some special duty: *One squad of soldiers was detached to guard the camp.* [< F *détacher,* formed with *dé-* away + OF *tache* nail] —**de·tach′a·ble,** *adj.* —**de·tach′er,** *n.*

de·tached (di tacht′) *adj.* **1** separate from others; isolated: *A detached house is not in a solid row with others.* **2** not influenced by one's interests and prejudices, or those of others; impartial; aloof. —**de·tach′ed·ly** (di tach′id lē), *adv.* —**de·tach′ed·ness** (di tach′id nis), *n.*

de·tach·ment (di tach′mənt) *n.* **1** separation. **2** standing apart; aloofness. **3** a freedom from prejudice or bias; impartial attitude: *Students were surprised at the professor's air of detachment in talking about his own books.* **4** *Military.* **a** troops, ships, tanks, etc. sent on or assigned to some special duty: *He belonged to the machine-gun detachment.* **b** the state of being on special duty: *a platoon of soldiers on detachment.* **5** the smallest unit in the organization of the Royal Canadian Mounted Police or other police force. Some rural detachments of the RCMP have only one or two officers.

de·tail (dē′tāl *or* di tāl′) *n., v.* —*n.* **1** a small part of something; a

particular item that is not of great importance in itself: *Their stories were alike in every detail.* 2 dealing with or showing things individually or one by one: *He doesn't care for the detail involved in accounting. This new map has more detail than the old one.* 3 any of the small parts that go to make up a painting, etc.: *The details are beautifully painted, but the general effect is dull.* 4 a reproduction of a part of a painting or other work of art: *The picture on the card is a detail of a painting by Leonardo da Vinci.* 5 *Esp.Military.* a a small group selected for or sent on some special duty: *The captain sent a detail of six soldiers to guard the road.* b the task or duty itself.

go into detail, give all the parts or particulars separately: *There was no time to go into detail, so she just gave them a general outline of the situation.*

in detail, part by part; giving all the particulars: *She described the inside of the airplane in detail.*

—*v.* 1 give the particulars of; report or tell in full: *She detailed all the things she had seen and done on her trip. The particulars are detailed in the enclosed brochure.* 2 select for or send on special duty: *Policemen were detailed to hold back the crowd watching the parade.* [< F *détail* < *détaillir* cut in pieces < *de-* completely + *tailler* cut] —**de·tail′er,** *n.*

☛ *Syn. n.* **1.** See note at **item.**

☛ *Pronun.* **Detail.** The noun may be pronounced in two ways: (dē′tāl *or* di tāl′). The second is older; the first especially common in situations where the word is used a great deal (army life, architecture, etc.). The pronunciation (dē′tāl) is also frequently used for def. 2 of the verb.

de·tailed (dē′tāld *or* di tāld′) *adj.* having much detail: *a detailed description, a detailed map.*

de·tain (di tān′) *v.* 1 hold back; keep from going; delay. 2 keep in custody; confine: *The police detained the suspected thief for further questioning.* 3 *Archaic.* withhold. [ME < OF *detenir* < L *detinere* < *de-* away + *tenere* hold]

de·tain·ee (dē tā′nē′) *n.* a person held in custody; prisoner.

de·tain·ment (di tān′mənt) *n.* detention.

de·tect (di tekt′) *v.* 1 find out; discover or reveal: *to detect a crime.* 2 discover the existence or presence of: *to detect an odor: She detected a note of sadness in his voice.* 3 *Electronics.* demodulate. [< L *detectus,* pp. of *detegere* < *de-* un- + *tegere* cover]

de·tect·a·ble (di tek′tə bəl) *adj.* capable of being detected.

de·tect·i·ble (di tek′tə bəl) See **detectable.**

de·tec·tion (di tek′shən) *n.* 1 the act or process of detecting or the fact of being detected: *the detection of a crime.* 2 *Electronics.* demodulation.

de·tec·tive (di tek′tiv) *n.* 1 a police officer whose work is investigating crimes. 2 a person who works for a company or organization as an investigator. 3 (*adj.*) having to do with detectives and their work: *detective stories.* 4 (*adj.*) designed for or used in detecting something: *detective devices.*

de·tec·tor (di tek′tər) *n.* 1 a device or instrument for detecting or measuring the presence of electricity, radio-activity, heat, etc. 2 *Electronics.* demodulator. 3 any person or thing that detects.

dé·tente (dā tänt′) *n. French.* the easing of tensions, especially between nations or political groups: *a détente in the cold war.*

de·ten·tion (di ten′shən) *n.* 1 the act of detaining or holding back; especially, keeping in custody: *A jail is used for the detention of persons who have been arrested.* 2 the state of being detained; delay. [< LL *detentio, -onis* < L *detinere.* See DETAIN.]

de·ter (di tèr′) *v.* **-terred, -ter·ring.** discourage; keep back; hinder: *The extreme heat deterred us from going downtown.* [< L *deterrere* < *de-* from + *terrere* frighten]

de·ter·gent (di tèr′jənt) *n., adj.* —*n.* 1 a chemical compound that acts like a soap, used for cleansing: *Detergents are usually preferred to soap for most laundry and for dishes because they keep dirt particles suspended in the water.* 2 any substance for cleansing: *Soap is a detergent.* —*adj.* cleansing: *the detergent action of suds.* [< L *detergens, -entis,* ppr. of *detergere* < *de-* off + *tergere* wipe]

de·te·ri·o·rate (di tèr′ē ə rāt′) *v.* **-rat·ed, -rat·ing.** 1 become worse; lessen in value; depreciate: *Machinery deteriorates if it is not given good care.* 2 make worse. [< L *deteriorare* < *deterior* worse]

de·te·ri·o·ra·tion (di tèr′ē ə rā′shən) *n.* 1 a deteriorating. 2 the condition of having deteriorated.

de·ter·ment (di tèr′mənt) *n.* 1 a deterring. 2 something that deters.

de·ter·mi·na·ble (di tèr′mə nə bəl) *adj.* 1 capable of being settled or decided. 2 capable of being found out exactly.

de·ter·mi·nant (di tèr′mə nənt) *n., adj.* —*n.* 1 something that determines. 2 *Mathematics.* the sum of all the products that can be

formed according to special laws from a certain number of quantities arranged in a square block. —*adj.* determining.

de·ter·mi·nate (di tèr′mə nit) *adj.* 1 with exact limits; fixed; definite. 2 settled; positive. 3 determined; resolute. 4 *Botany.* designating an inflorescence in which each floral stem ends in a single flower; cymose. —**de·ter′mi·nate·ly,** *adv.* —**de·ter′mi·nate·ness,** *n.*

de·ter·mi·na·tion (di tèr′mə nā′shən) *n.* 1 the act of formally setting or deciding a question, problem, controversy, etc.: *the determination of the boundary lines of the provinces.* 2 the result of settling or deciding; settlement or decision: *They were unable to come to any determination on the question of inheritance.* 3 the act of finding out the exact amount, position, or kind by calculating, measuring, etc.: *the determination of the amount of gold in a sample of ore.* 4 the result of finding out by calculating, etc.; conclusion or solution: *Their research was based on earlier scientific determinations.* 5 the result of coming to a decision; a fixed purpose: *She left with the determination to find out who her real parents were.* 6 great firmness in carrying out a purpose; the quality of being determined: *The boy's determination was not weakened by the difficulties he met.* 7 *Logic.* **a** the making of an idea, concept, etc. more concise in its outline by the addition of restrictive attributes or other qualifying features. **b** the defining of a concept by specifying its parts.

de·ter·mi·na·tive (di tèr′mə nə tiv *or* di tèr′mə nā′tiv) *adj., n.* —*adj.* determining. —*n.* something that determines. —**de·ter′mi·na·tive·ly,** *adv.* —**de·ter′mi·na·tive·ness,** *n.*

de·ter·mine (di tèr′mən) *v.* **-mined, -min·ing.** 1 make up one's mind firmly; resolve: *He determined to become the best Scout in his troop.* 2 settle; decide. 3 find out exactly; fix: *The captain determined the latitude and longitude of his ship's position.* 4 *Geometry.* fix the position of. 5 be the deciding factor in reaching a certain result; bring about a certain result: *Tomorrow's events will determine whether we are to go or stay.* 6 fix or settle beforehand. 7 give an aim to; direct; impel: *Let hope determine your thinking.* 8 limit; define: *The meaning of a word is partly determined by its use in a particular sentence.* 9 put an end to; conclude. 10 come to an end. [ME < OF < L *determinare* set limits to < *de-* completely + *terminus* end]

☛ *Syn.* **1.** See note at **decide.**

de·ter·mined (di tèr′mənd) *adj.* 1 with one's mind firmly made up; resolved: *The determined explorer kept on his way in spite of the storm.* 2 firm; resolute: *His determined look showed that he had made up his mind.*

de·ter·mined·ly (di tèr′mənd lē *or* di tèr′mən id lē) *adv.* in a determined manner.

de·ter·min·er (di tèr′mə nər) *n.* a person or thing that determines; especially: *Grammar.* a specifying word such as *the, a, her,* or *this,* that comes before a noun or before an adjective followed by a noun.

de·ter·min·ism (di tèr′mən iz′əm) *n.* 1 the doctrine that human actions are the necessary results of antecedent causes. 2 the doctrine that all events are determined by antecedent causes.

de·ter·min·ist (di tèr′mən ist) *n.* a person who believes in determinism.

de·ter·rence (di ter′əns) *n.* 1 the act or process of deterring. 2 something that deters; a restraint.

de·ter·rent (di tèr′ənt *or* di ter′ənt) *adj., n.* —*adj.* deterring; restraining. —*n.* something that deters: *Fear of consequences is a common deterrent from wrongdoing.*

de·test (di test′) *v.* dislike very much; hate. [< F *détester* < L *detestari* curse while calling the gods to witness < *de-* (intensive) + *testari* to witness] —**de·test′er,** *n.*

☛ *Syn.* See note at **hate.**

de·test·a·ble (di tes′tə bəl) *adj.* deserving to be detested; hateful. —**de·test′a·ble·ness,** *n.* —**de·test′a·bly,** *adv.*

de·tes·ta·tion (dē′tes tā′shən) *n.* 1 a very strong dislike; hatred. 2 a detested person or thing.

de·throne (di thrōn′) *v.* **-throned, -thron·ing,** deprive of the power to rule; remove from a throne; depose.

de·throne·ment (di thrōn′mənt) *n.* dethroning or being dethroned.

det·o·nate (det′ə nāt′) *v.* **-nat·ed, -nat·ing.** 1 cause to explode with a loud noise: *The workmen detonated the dynamite.* 2 explode with a loud noise: *The bomb detonated.* [< L *detonare* < *de-* (intensive) + *tonare* thunder]

det·o·na·tion (det′ə nā′shən) *n.* 1 an explosion with a loud noise. 2 a loud noise.

det·o·na·tor (det′ə nā′tər) *n.* 1 a fuse, percussion cap, etc. used to set off an explosive. 2 any explosive.

de·tour (dē′tür *or* di tür′) *n., v.* —*n.* 1 a road that is used when the main road or direct road cannot be travelled. 2 a roundabout

way. —v. **1** use a roundabout way; make a detour: *We detoured around the flooded part of the highway.* **2** cause to use a detour. [< F *détour* < *détourner* turn aside < *de-* away from + *tourner* turn]

de·tox·i·cate (dē tok′sə kāt′) v. **-cat·ed, -cat·ing.** detoxify. —**de·tox′i·ca′tion,** n.

de·tox·i·fy (dē tok′sə fī′) v. **-fied, -fy·ing.** remove a poison or toxic substance, or its effect from: *to detoxify an alcoholic.* —**de·tox′i·fi·ca′tion,** n.

de·tract (di trakt′) v. take away quality, value, etc. (*from*): *The ugly frame detracts from the picture.* [< L *detractus,* pp. of *detrahere* < *de-* away + *trahere* draw]

de·trac·tion (di trak′shən) n. **1** the act of speaking evil; belittling. **2** a taking away; detracting.

de·trac·tive (di trak′tiv) adj. **1** tending to detract. **2** speaking evil; belittling. —**de·trac′tive·ly,** adv.

de·trac·tor (di trak′tər) n. a person who speaks evil of or belittles another.

de·train (dē trān′) v. **1** get off a railway train. **2** put off from a railway train.

det·ri·ment (det′rə mənt) n. **1** damage; injury; harm: *He continued working long hours, apparently without detriment to his health.* **2** something that causes damage or harm. [ME < L *detrimentum* < *deterere* < *de-* away + *terere* wear]

det·ri·men·tal (det′rə men′təl) adj. damaging; injurious; harmful: *Lack of sleep is detrimental to one's health.* —**det′ri·men′tal·ly,** adv.

de·tri·tus (di trī′təs) n. **1** particles of rock or other material worn away from a mass. **2** any disintegrated material; debris: *The detritus left by the flood covered the highway.* [< L *detritus* a rubbing away]

de trop (də trō′) French. **1** too much; too many. **2** unwelcome; in the way.

deuce¹ (dyüs or düs) n. **1** a playing card marked with a 2. **2** Dice. **a** the side of a die having two spots. **b** a throw of two. **3** Tennis. a tie score at 40 each in a game, or five games each in a set. [< OF *deus* two < L *duos,* accus. of *duo* two]

deuce² (dyüs or düs) interj. Informal. a mild oath used to express annoyance or surprise: *What the deuce does he want now?* [probably < LG *duus* deuce¹, an unlucky throw at dice]

deu·ced (dyüst or düst, dyü′sid or dü′sid) adj., adv. Informal. —adj. devilish; excessive. —adv. devilishly; excessively.

deu·ced·ly (dyü′sid lē or dü′sid lē) adv. Informal. devilishly; excessively.

de·us ex ma·chi·na (dē′əs eks mak′ə nə) Latin. **1** a person, god, or event that comes just in time to solve a difficulty in a story, play, etc. **2** a person or event that solves any difficulty in a dramatic manner. [literally, god from the machinery (with reference to a stage device in the ancient theatre)]

Deut. Deuteronomy.

deu·te·ri·um (dyü tēr′ē əm or dü tēr′ē əm) n. an isotope of hydrogen having a mass double that of ordinary hydrogen; heavy hydrogen. Symbol: D or ²H [< NL < Gk. *deutereion,* neut., having second place < *deuteros* second]

deuterium oxide heavy water. Formula: D_2O

deu·ter·on (dyü′tə ron′ or dü′tə ron′) n. Chemistry. the nucleus of a deuterium atom, consisting of one proton and one electron. [< *deuterium* + *-on,* as in *proton*]

Deu·ter·on·o·my (dyü′tər on′ə mē or dü′tər on′ə mē) n. the fifth book of the Bible. [< L < Gk. *Deuteronomion* < *deuteros* second + *nomos* law]

deu·to·plasm (dyü′tə plaz′əm or dü′tə plaz′əm) n. Biology. the yolk or other material that provides nourishment for the embryo in an egg or cell. [< Gk. *deuteros* second + *plasma.* See PLASMA.]

Deutsche Mark (doi′chə) **1** the basic unit of money in the Federal Republic of Germany (West Germany), divided into 100 pfennigs. See table at **money. 2** a coin worth one Deutsche Mark. Also, **deutsche mark.**

de·val·u·ate (dē val′yü āt′) v. **-at·ed, -at·ing.** devalue.

de·val·u·a·tion (dē val′yü ā′shən) n. devaluating or being devalued.

de·val·ue (dē val′yü) v. **-val·ued, -val·u·ing. 1** officially reduce the value of currency in relation to other currencies or to gold. **2** lessen or take away the importance or value of.

dev·as·tate (dev′əs tāt′) v. **-tat·ed, -tat·ing.** make desolate; destroy; ravage: *A long war devastated the border towns.* [< L *devastare* < *de-* (intensive) + *vastus* waste] —**dev′as·tat′or,** n.

dev·as·ta·tion (dev′əs tā′shən) n. devastating or being devastated: *The people were shocked at the devastation caused by the forest fire.*

de·vel·op (di vel′əp) v. **1** come into being gradually through successive stages of growth and change: *Many plants develop from*

hat, āge, fär; let, ēqual, tėrm; it, īce
hot, ōpen, ôrder; oil, out; cup, put, rüle,
above, takən, pencəl, lemən, circəs

ch, child; ng, long; sh, ship
th, thin; ᴛʜ, then; zh, measure

seeds. *Land animals are believed to have developed from sea animals.* **2** bring into being through successive stages: *The modern power loom was developed from a simple hand loom.* **3** go from earlier to later stages, especially by a natural process of growth and change; become gradually bigger, fuller, more mature, etc.: *He is developing into a fine, healthy child. The idea had been developing in his mind for some time.* **4** cause to grow and mature: *Exercise and wholesome food develop healthy bodies.* **5** come to have; acquire bit by bit: *to develop an aversion for seafood. He has developed an interest in stamp collecting.* **6** work out in more and more detail; make bigger, better, fuller, etc.: *to develop an argument. Gradually they developed their plans for the Boys' Club.* **7** make or become known; reveal: *No new facts developed from the detective's inquiry.* **8** change, especially by means of construction work, from a natural or near natural state to one that serves another purpose: *The plan to develop the park area was strongly opposed by the public. The government is developing the water power of the northern rivers for industry.* **9** make more urban, more up-to-date, or more industrialized: *They have developed the old downtown area.* **10** become more industrialized, etc.: *the developing nations.* **11** Photography. **a** treat with chemicals to bring out the image recorded on a photographic plate or film: *The film was developed commercially but she made the prints herself.* **b** of an image, be brought out; become visible: *We watched the picture develop.* [< F *développer* unwrap]

de·vel·op·er (di vel′əp ər) n. **1** a person whose business is developing real estate on a large scale: *A developer buys a tract of land and builds an office complex, an apartment building, houses, etc. on it for the purpose of selling them.* **2** Photography. a chemical used to bring out the picture on an exposed film, plates, etc. **3** any person or thing that develops.

de·vel·op·ment (di vel′əp mənt) n. **1** the act of working out in great detail: *The development of a feasible plan took many hours of work.* **2** the process of developing; growth: *The parents followed their child's development with pride.* **3** a happening; an outcome or result; news: *Newspapers give information about the latest developments in world affairs.* **4** bringing into being through successive stages: *the development of a new kind of motor.* **5** progression through successive stages by a natural process of growth and change: *the development of a caterpillar into a butterfly.* **6** changing something from a natural or older state for a particular purpose: *the development of the waterfront for industry.* **7** the product or result of developing in this way: *The old farm is now a large housing development.* **8** a group of buildings constructed by the same person or company: *The new development will have business offices and stores.* **9** Photography. the developing of a film.

de·vel·op·men·tal (di vel′əp men′təl) adj. having to do with development.

development road Cdn. in the North, a road or one of a system of access roads intended to help the exploitation of natural resources.

de·vi·ance (dē′vē əns) n. **1** the quality or state of being deviant. **2** deviant behavior: *the problem of controlling deviance.*

de·vi·ant (dē′vē ənt) adj., n. —adj. deviating from an accepted standard of behavior. —n. a person who is deviant, especially in sexual behavior.

de·vi·ate (v. dē′vē āt′; n. dē′vē ət or dē′vē āt′) v. **-at·ed, -at·ing;** n. —v. **1** turn aside (from a way, course, rule, truth, etc.); diverge: *His statements sometimes deviated slightly from the truth.* **2** cause to turn aside. —n. an individual who shows a marked deviation from the norm. [< LL *deviare* < *de-* aside + *via* way] —**de′vi·a′tor,** n.

➤ Syn. See note at diverge.

de·vi·a·tion (dē′vē ā′shən) n. a turning aside from a way, course, rule, truth, etc.; divergence: *No deviation from the rules was allowed. The deviation of the compass needle was caused by the iron on the ship.*

de·vi·a·tion·ism (dē′vē ā′shə niz′əm) n. a turning aside from strict principles, especially from official Communist policy.

de·vi·a·tion·ist (dē′vē ā′shən ist) n. a person who turns aside from strict principles, especially from official Communist policy.

de·vice (di vīs′) n. **1** a mechanical invention used for a special purpose; machine; apparatus: *a device for lighting a gas stove.* **2** a plan; scheme; trick: *By some device or other he got the boy to let*

him into the house. **3** a drawing or figure used in a pattern or as an ornament. **4** *Literature or music.* a stylistic or technical feature introduced to achieve a particular effect. **5** a picture or design on a coat of arms, often accompanied by a motto. **6** motto.

leave to (one's) own devices, leave to do as one thinks best: *The teacher left us to our own devices in choosing a book for our report.* [fusion of ME *devis* separation, talk + *devise* design, emblem, plan; both < OF < L *divisus,* pp. of *dividere* divide]

☞ *Usage.* **Device, devise.** Do not confuse **device**, meaning a mechanical invention or a scheme or trick, with **devise**, meaning "think out": *By one unfair device after another, he amassed a huge fortune. Ann devised a new plan for the organization.*

dev·il (dev′əl) *n., v.* **-illed** or **-iled, -il·ling** or **-il·ing; interj.** —*n.*
1 the Devil, the supreme spirit of evil; the enemy of goodness; Satan. **2** an evil spirit; fiend, demon. **3** a wicked or cruel person. **4** a very dashing, energetic, or reckless person. **5** an unfortunate or wretched person: *The poor devil didn't even hear the warning.*
6 *Informal.* something that is hard to handle, solve, understand, etc.: *That last problem was a real devil.* **7** something very bad; an evil influence or power: *the devil of greed.* **8** *Historical.* printer's devil. **9** a person who does literary work for another, for which the latter gets the credit or pay. **10** any of various machines for tearing or shredding paper, rags, etc.
between the devil and the deep (blue) sea, between two equally dangerous and unpleasant alternatives; in a dilemma.
devil of a, *Informal.* **a** very difficult, awkward, complicated, etc.: *We had the devil of a time getting the piano into the basement.*
b very: *She's done a devil of a fine job.*
give the devil his due, be fair even to a bad or disliked person.
go to the devil, go to ruin, degenerate morally.
raise the devil, *Slang.* make a great disturbance.
the devil take the hindmost, do not worry about what happens to the slowest or last one.
the devil to pay, much trouble ahead.
—*v.* **1** tease; bother; harass. **2** prepare (food) with hot seasoning: *to devil ham, devilled eggs.* **3** tear (rags, etc.) to pieces with a devil; subject to the cleaning action of a devil.
—*interj.* **the devil!** exclamation used to express disgust, anger, surprise, etc. [OE *deofol* < L < Gk. *diabolos* slanderer < *diaballein* slander < *dia-* across, against + *ballein* throw]

dev·il·fish (dev′əl fish′) *n., pl.* **-fish** or **-fish·es. 1** any of a family (Mobulidae) of very large rays found in warm seas. **2** any large cephalopod, especially an octopus.

de·vil·ish (dev′əl ish *or* dev′lish) *adj., adv.* —*adj.* **1** of, having to do with, like, or worthy of a devil or devils; cruel, wicked, mischievous, etc.: *a devilish scheme for getting the inheritance.*
2 *Informal.* very great; extreme: *She's always in such a devilish hurry.* —*adv. Informal.* very; extremely: *They worked devilish hard.*
—**dev′il·ish·ly,** *adv.* —**dev′il·ish·ness,** *n.*

dev·il–may–care (dev′əl mā ker′) happy-go-lucky or reckless: *She showed a devil-may-care attitude toward authority.*

dev·il·ment (dev′əl mənt) *n.* **1** an evil action; wicked behavior. **2** daring behavior. **3** mischief.

devil ray devilfish.

dev·il·ry (dev′əl rē) *n., pl.* **-ries.** deviltry.

devil's advocate 1 in the Roman Catholic Church, an official appointed to argue against a proposed beatification or canonization. **2** a critic who argues either against a popular cause or for an unpopular cause.

devil's club a spiny shrub (*Oplopanax horridus*) of the same family as ivies and ginseng found in W North America, having very large, maple-like leaves, small, greenish-white flowers, and scarlet berries.

devil's darning needle dragonfly.

devil's food cake a rich, dark, chocolate cake.

dev·il·try (dev′əl trē) *n., pl.* **-tries. 1** an evil action; wicked behavior. **2** daring behavior. **3** mischief. **4** great cruelty or wickedness.

de·vi·ous (dē′vē əs) *adj.* **1** winding; twisting; round-about: *We took a devious route through side streets and alleys to avoid the crowded main streets.* **2** straying from the right course; not straightforward; going astray: *His devious nature was shown in half lies and acts of petty dishonesty.* [< L *devius* < *de-* out of + *via* the way] —**de′vi·ous·ness,** *n.* —**de′vi·ous·ly,** *adv.*

de·vise (di vīz′) *v.* **-vised, -vis·ing;** *n.* —*v.* **1** think out; plan; contrive; invent: *The boys devised a scheme for earning money during the summer vacation.* **2** *Law.* give or leave (land, buildings, etc.) by a will.
—*n. Law.* **1** a giving or leaving of land, buildings, etc. by a will. **2** a will or part of a will doing this. **3** land, buildings, etc. given or left

in this way. [ME < OF *deviser* dispose in portions, arrange, ult. < L *dividere* divide] —**de·vis′a·ble,** *adj.*
☞ *Usage.* See note at **device.**

de·vis·ee (di vīz′ē′ *or* dev′ə zē′) *n. Law.* a person to whom land, buildings, etc. are given or left by a will.

de·vis·er (di vīz′ər) *n.* one who devises; an inventor.

de·vi·sor (di vī′zər *or* di vī′zôr) *n. Law.* a person who gives or leaves land, buildings, etc. by a will.

de·vi·tal·i·za·tion (dē vī′təl ə zā′shən *or* dē vī′təl ī zā′shən) *n.* devitalizing or being devitalized.

de·vi·tal·ize (dē vī′təl īz′) *v.* **-ized, -iz·ing. 1** kill; take the life of. **2** weaken; exhaust; make less vital.

de·void (di void′) *adj.* not having; lacking (*used with* **of**): *a speech completely devoid of humor.* [ME; originally *devoided,* pp. of *devoid* cast out < OF *desvoidier* < *des-* away + *voidier* to empty < *voide* empty, ult. < var. of L *vacuus*]

de·voir (də vwär′) *n.* **1** Usually, **devoirs,** *pl.* formal acts of courtesy or respect. **2** *Archaic.* duty.

dev·o·lu·tion (dev′ə lü′shən *or* dē′və lü′shən) *n.* **1** a progression from stage to stage. **2** the transmitting or passing of property from person to person; the passing on to a successor of an unexercised right. **3** the delegating of duty, responsibility, etc.) to another. **4** *Biology.* evolution toward simpler structures or toward the disappearance of structures or functions; degeneration. **5** the decentralizing of authority; transfer of power from a central government to regional or local governments. [< Med.L *devolutio, -onis* < *devolvere.* See DEVOLVE.]

de·volve (di volv′) *v.* **-volved, -volv·ing. 1** transfer (duty, work, etc.) to someone else. **2** be handed down to someone else; be transferred: *If the president is unable to handle his duties, they devolve upon the vice-president.* [< L *devolvere* < *de-* down + *volvere* roll]

De·vo·ni·an (də vō′nē ən) *adj., n.* —*adj.* **1** of or having to do with Devonshire, a county in SW England. **2** *Geology.* of or having to do with a period of the Paleozoic era. —*n.* **1** a native of Devonshire, England. **2** *Geology.* **a** the period of the Paleozoic era coming between the Carboniferous and the Silurian. See chart at **geology. b** the rocks formed during this period.

Devonshire cream (dev′ən shər) a rich, thickened cream; clotted cream.

de·vote (di vōt′) *v.* **-vot·ed, -vot·ing. 1** give up (oneself, one's money, time, or efforts) to some person, purpose, or service: *The mother devoted herself to her children.* **2** set apart and consecrate to God or to a sacred purpose. **3** set apart from any particular purpose: *That museum devotes one wing to modern art.* [< L *devotus,* pp. of *devovere* < *de-* entirely + *vovere* vow. Doublet of DEVOUT.]
☞ *Syn.* **1. Devote, dedicate, consecrate** = give something or someone up to a purpose. **Devote** emphasizes giving up seriously to a single purpose, shutting out everything else: *He devoted his time to study.* **Dedicate** emphasizes giving up or setting apart earnestly or solemnly for a serious or sacred use: *He dedicated his life to science. They dedicated the hospital.* **Consecrate** = set a person or thing apart as sacred or glorified, by a solemn vow or ceremony: *A bishop consecrated the burial ground.*

de·vot·ed (di vōt′id) *adj.* **1** loyal; faithful: *a devoted friend.* **2** set apart for some purpose; dedicated; consecrated. —**de·vot′ed·ly,** *adv.* —**de·vot′ed·ness,** *n.*

dev·o·tee (dev′ə tē′) *n.* **1** a person deeply devoted to something. **2** a person earnestly devoted to religion.

de·vo·tion (di vō′shən) *n.* **1** a deep, steady affection; a feeling of loyalty; faithfulness: *the devotion of a lifelong friend.* **2** the act of devoting or the state of being devoted: *the devotion of much time to study.* **3** earnestness in religion; devoutness. **4** religious worship or observance; divine worship. **5 devotions,** *pl.* religious worship or prayers: *He was at his devotions.*

de·vo·tion·al (di vō′shən əl) *adj.* having to do with devotion; used in worship. —**de·vo′tion·al·ly,** *adv.*

de·vour (di vour′) *v.* **1** of animals, eat. **2** eat hungrily or greedily: *They devoured their meal in about ten minutes.* **3** consume; destroy: *The fire quickly devoured the whole building.* **4** swallow up; engulf. **5** take in with eyes or ears in a hungry, greedy way: *devour a new book.* **6** completely absorb the attention or emotions of: *devoured by curiosity, devoured by envy.* [ME < OF *devorer* < L *devorare* < *de-* down + *vorare* gulp] —**de·vour′er,** *n.* —**de·vour′ing·ly,** *adv.*

de·vout (di vout′) *adj.* **1** active in worship and prayer; religious. **2** showing devotion: *a devout prayer.* **3** earnest; sincere; hearty: *devout thanks, a devout follower.* [ME < OF *devot* < L *devotus,* pp. of *devovere.* Doublet of DEVOTE.] —**de·vout′ly,** *adv.*
—**de·vout′ness,** *n.*
☞ *Syn.* **1.** See note at **pious.**

dew (dyü *or* dü) *n., v.* —*n.* **1** the moisture from the air that condenses and collects in small drops on cool surfaces during the night. **2** moisture in small drops. **3** anything fresh like dew.
—*v.* make wet with dew; moisten. [OE *dēaw*] —**dew′less,** *adj.*
☞ *Hom.* **do** (dü), **due.**

dew·ber·ry (dyü′ber′ē *or* dü′-) *n., pl.* **-ries. 1** any trailing blackberry, including numerous species and cultivated varieties. The northern dewberry (*Rubus flagellarius*) is a North American species found from Nova Scotia and Quebec west to Minnesota and south to Texas. **2** the fruit of any of these plants.

dew·claw (dyü′klo′ *or* -klô′, dü′klo′ *or* -klô′) *n.* a small, useless hoof or toe on the feet of deer, pigs, dogs, etc.

dew·drop (dyü′drop′ *or* dü′-) *n.* a drop of dew.

Dew·ey decimal system (dyü′ē *or* dü′ē) a system for classifying books, pamphlets, etc. in libraries. Each subject and its subdivisions are assigned specific numbers and decimals. *Examples:* Literature 800, History 900, Canadian History 971, Canadian Northwest History 971.2. [< Melvil *Dewey* (1851-1931), an American librarian, who devised the system]

dew·lap (dyü′lap′ *or* dü′-) *n.* **1** a loose fold of skin under the throat of cattle and some other animals. **2** a similar fold of skin under the throat of certain birds. [< *dew* (origin and meaning uncertain) + *lap* < OE *læppa* pendulous piece]

dew point the temperature at which the water vapor in air that is cooling begins to condense as dew.

dew–worm (dyü′wèrm′ *or* dü′-) *n. Cdn.* any large earthworm that comes to the surface at night when there is dew on the grass. Dew-worms are often used as fishing bait.

dew·y (dyü′ē *or* dü′ē) *adj.* **dew·i·er, dew·i·est. 1** wet with dew. **2** of dew. **3** like dew; refreshing; sparkling; coming gently; vanishing quickly. —**dew′i·ly,** *adv.* —**dew′i·ness,** *n.*

Dex·e·drine (dek′sə drēn′) *n. Trademark.* dextroamphetamine.

dex·ter (deks′tər) *adj.* **1** of or on the right-hand side. **2** *Heraldry.* situated on that part of an escutcheon to the right of the bearer, and hence to the left of the observer. [< L *dexter* right]

dex·ter·i·ty (deks ter′ə tē) *n.* **1** skill in using the body, especially the hands. **2** skill in using the mind; cleverness.

dex·ter·ous (deks′tər əs *or* deks′trəs) *adj.* **1** having or showing skill in using the body, especially the hands. **2** having or showing skill in using the mind; clever. Also, **dextrous.** —**dex′trous·ly,** *adv.* —**dex′ter·ous·ness,** *n.*

☞ *Syn.* **1. Dexterous, deft, adroit** (def. 2) = skilful in using the hands and body. **Dexterous** suggests easy, quick, smooth movements and lightness and sureness of touch coming from practice: *Mary is a dexterous pianist.* **Deft** adds to **dexterous** the idea of neatness and exceptional lightness and swiftness: *A surgeon has to be deft.* **Adroit** adds to **dexterous** the idea of being quick-witted and is sometimes reserved for mental skill or resourcefulness: *The adroit lawyer got the truth out of the witness.*

dex·tral (deks′trəl) *adj.* **1** of the right hand; right-hand. **2** right-handed. **3** having the spire or whorl rising from left to right when viewed from above, as with most snail shells.

dex·tran (deks′tran) *n. Chemistry.* a white, slimy carbohydrate, produced in sugar solutions by bacterial action. It is administered instead of blood plasma to persons in a state of shock. [< L *dexter* right hand, from its plane of polarization]

dex·trin (deks′trin) *n.* a gummy substance obtained from starch, used as an adhesive, for sizing paper, etc. [< F]

dex·trine (deks′trin *or* deks′trēn) *n.* dextrin.

dex·tro·am·phet·a·mine (dek′strō am fet′ə mēn′ *or* -min) *n.* a form of amphetamine used in medicine as a stimulant, etc.

dex·trose (deks′trōs) *n.* a sugar that is less sweet than cane sugar; a form of glucose. *Formula:* $C_6H_{12}O$ [< *dexter* + (*gluc*)*ose*]

dex·trous (deks′trəs) *adj.* dexterous.

dey (dā) *n., pl.* **deys.** *Historical.* a title for rulers of Algiers, Tunis, and Tripoli. [< F < Turkish *dāī,* originally, maternal uncle] ☞ *Hom.* **day.**

D.F. Defender of the Faith.

D.F.C. Distinguished Flying Cross.

D.F.M. Distinguished Flying Medal.

D.G. 1 Dei gratia. **2** Deo gratias.

dhar·ma (där′mə) *n.* **1** *Buddhism.* law. **2** *Hinduism.* virtue; righteousness; correct behavior. [< Skt. *dharma* decree, custom, right course of conduct]

dhole (dōl) *n., pl.* **dholes** *or* **dhole.** an Asian wild animal (*Cuon alpinus*) of the dog family having a reddish-brown coat and rounded ears. Dholes usually hunt in packs. [native name]

dho·ti (dō′tē) *n.* **1** a garment for the lower body worn especially by Hindu men, consisting of a single, large unstitched piece of cloth tied around the waist and loosely wrapping the legs down to the ankles. **2** a fabric used for dhotis. [< Hind.]

dhow (dou) *n.* a lateen-rigged sailing ship that is used along the coasts of the Arabian peninsula and E Africa. [cf. Arabic *dāw*]

di-¹ *prefix.* twice; double; twofold, as in *dioxide, dicotyledon.* Also, **dis-,** before *s.* [< Gk. *di-* < *dis*]

di-² the form of **dis-¹** before *b, d, l, m, n, r, s, v,* and sometimes before *g* and *j,* as in *direct, divert.*

hat, āge, fär; let, ēqual, tèrm; it, īce
hot, ōpen, ôrder; oil, out; cup, put, rüle,
əbove, takən, pencəl, lemən, circəs
ch, child; ng, long; sh, ship
th, thin; ᴛʜ, then; zh, measure

di-³ the form of **dia-** before vowels, as in *diorama.*

dia- *prefix.* through; across; thoroughly, as in *diaphragm.* Also, **di-** before vowels. [< Gk. *dia- < dia,* prep.]

di·a·be·tes (dī′ə bē′tis *or* dī′ə bē′tēz) *n.* any of several diseases characterized by an excessive quantity of urine and abnormal thirst, especially diabetes mellitus. [NL < Gk. *diabētēs* a passer-through < *dia-* through + *bainein* go]

diabetes mel·li·tus (mel′ē′təs *or* mel ī′təs) a form of diabetes characterized by excessive sugar in the urine and by the inability of the body to absorb normal amounts of sugar and starch. [NL *diabetes mellitus* honey diabetes]

di·a·bet·ic (dī′ə bet′ik *or* dī′ə bē′tik) *adj., n.* —*adj.* **1** of or having to do with diabetes. **2** having diabetes. —*n.* a person having diabetes.

di·a·ble·rie (dē ä′blə rē) *n.* **1** diabolic magic or art; sorcery; witchcraft. **2** deviltry; reckless mischief. **3** a domain or realm of devils. [< F]

di·a·bol·ic (dī′ə bol′ik) *adj.* **1** devilish; like the Devil; very cruel or wicked; fiendish. **2** having to do with the Devil or devils. [< LL *diabolicus* < Gk. *diabolikos* < *diabolos.* See DEVIL.] —**di′a·bol′i·cal·ly,** *adv.*

di·a·bol·i·cal (dī′ə bol′ə kəl) *adj.* diabolic.

di·ab·o·lism (dī ab′ə liz′əm) *n.* **1** sorcery; witchcraft. **2** a diabolical action; deviltry. **3** belief in or worship of a devil or devils. **4** the character or condition of a devil.

di·a·chron·ic (dī′ə kron′ik) *adj.* of or concerned with the occurrence and development of phenomena, especially of language, over time: *diachronic linguistics.* Compare **synchronic.** —**di′a·chron′i·cal·ly,** *adv.*

di·a·chron·i·cal·ly (dī′ə kron′ə klē) *adv.* in a diachronic manner; chronologically.

di·ac·o·nal (dī ak′ə nəl) *adj.* of or having to do with a deacon. [< Med.L *diaconalis* < L *diaconus.* See DEACON.]

di·ac·o·nate (dī ak′ə nit *or* dī ak′ə nāt′) *n.* **1** the rank or position of a deacon. **2** a group of deacons.

di·a·crit·ic (dī′ə krit′ik) *adj., n.* —*adj.* diacritical. —*n.* a diacritical mark. [< Gk. *diakritikos* < *diakrinein* < *dia-* apart + *krinein* separate]

di·a·crit·i·cal (dī′ə krit′ə kəl) *adj.* **1** serving to distinguish; marking a distinction. **2** capable of seeing distinctions: *a man of superior diacritical powers.* —**di′a·crit′i·cal·ly,** *adv.*

diacritical mark a mark like ″ ˆ ˜ ′ *or* ` placed over or under a letter to indicate pronunciation, etc.

di·a·dem (dī′ə dem′) *n.* **1** a crown. **2** an ornamental band of cloth formerly worn as a crown. **3** royal power, authority, or dignity. [< L < Gk. *diadēma* < *diadeein* < *dia-* across + *deein* bind]

di·aer·e·sis (dī er′ə sis) *n., pl.* **-ses** (-sēz′). See **dieresis.**

di·ag·nose (dī′əg nōs′ *or* dī′əg nōz′) *v.* **-nosed, -nos·ing.** make a diagnosis of; find out the nature of by an examination: *The doctor diagnosed the child's disease as measles.*

di·ag·no·sis (dī′əg nō′sis) *n., pl.* **-ses** (-sēz). **1** the act or process of finding out what disease a person or animal has by examination and careful study of the symptoms: *The doctor used X-rays and blood tests in his diagnosis.* **2** a careful study of the facts about something to find out its essential features, faults, etc. **3** a decision reached after a careful study of symptoms or facts. **4** *Biology.* a description that classifies precisely; the scientific determination of a genus, species, etc. [< NL < Gk. *diagnōsis* < *diagignōskein* < *dia-* apart + *gignōskein* learn to know]

di·ag·nos·tic (dī′əg nos′tik) *adj.* **1** of or having to do with diagnosis: *a diagnostic survey of the problem.* **2** helping in diagnosis: *diagnostic tests.* —**di·ag·nos′ti·cal·ly,** *adv.*

di·ag·nos·ti·cian (dī′əg nos tish′ən) *n.* a person who is expert in making diagnoses.

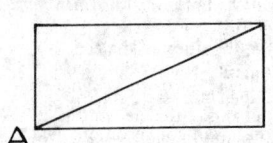

Line AB is a diagonal.

di·ag·o·nal (dī ag′ə nəl) *adj., n.* —*adj.* **1** *Geometry.* joining any

two non-adjacent angles or vertices of a polygon or polyhedron. **2** slanting; oblique. **3** having slanting parts, lines, etc.: *a diagonal weave.*
—*n.* **1** *Geometry.* a diagonal line or plane. **2** a diagonal direction, line, pattern, etc. **3** something set or placed on a slant. [< L *diagonalis* < Gk. *diagōnios* from angle to angle < *dia-* across + *gōnia* angle]

di·ag·o·nal·ly (dī ag′ə nəl ē) *adv.* in a diagonal direction.

di·a·gram (dī′ə gram′) *n., v.* **-grammed** or **-gramed, gram·ming** or **gram·ing.** —*n.* a drawing or sketch showing important parts of a thing. A diagram may be an outline, a plan, a drawing, a figure, a chart, or a combination of any of these, made to show clearly what a thing is or how it works: *He drew a diagram to show us how to get to his house. The engineer drew a diagram of the bridge.* —*v.* put on paper, a blackboard, etc. in the form of a drawing or sketch; make a diagram of. [< L < Gk. *diagramma* < *dia-* apart, out + *graphein* mark]

di·a·gram·mat·ic (dī′ə grə mat′ik) *adj.* **1** in the form of a diagram. **2** in outline only; sketchy.

di·a·gram·mat·i·cal (dī′ə grə mat′ə kəl) *adj.* diagrammatic.

di·a·gram·mat·i·cal·ly (dī′ə grə mat′ik lē) *adv.* in the form of a diagram.

di·al (dī′əl *or* dīl) *n., v.* **-alled** or **-aled, -al·ling** or **-al·ing.** —*n.* **1** a marked surface on which a moving pointer indicates a measurement of some kind. The face of a clock or of a compass is a dial. A dial may show the amount of water in a tank or the amount of steam pressure in a boiler. **2** the plate or disk on a radio or television set marked with numbers to identify the station frequencies, and having a moveable indicator connected to a tuning knob for tuning in different stations. **3** a disk on a telephone that is rotated in order to make connection with another telephone line. **4** the control knob in the centre of the face of a combination lock, that must be rotated through a particular sequence of numbers in order to open the lock. —*v.* use a dial in order to operate, select, etc.: *to dial a combination on a lock, to dial a favorite program. Dial carefully when you use the phone. He dialled a wrong number.* [apparently < Med.L (*rota*) *dialis* daily (wheel) < L *dies* day]

dial. dialect; dialectal.

di·a·lect (dī′ə lekt′) *n.* **1** a form of speech characteristic of a fairly definite region or class: *the Scottish dialect, the dialect spoken in Lunenberg, Nova Scotia.* **2** one of a group of closely related languages: *Some of the Romance dialects* (*all descended from Latin*) *are French, Italian, Spanish, and Portuguese.* **3** the jargon (def. 3) of a profession or other group: *thieves' dialect.* **4** (*adj.*) of or having to do with a dialect: *a dialect dictionary.* [< L *dialectus* < Gk. *dialektos*, ult. < *dia-* between + *legein* speak]
☞ **Syn. 1.** See note at **language.**
☞ *Usage.* **Dialects** exist because of the separation of groups of speakers either regionally or socially. Where several regional dialects exist, one may attain the highest status because it may be spoken in the area which contains the centre of government, education, or trade. A dialect is a valid form of a language; it is not to be confused with a misuse of a standard form.

di·a·lec·tal (dī′ə lek′təl) *adj.* of or having to do with a dialect; like that of a dialect. —**di′a·lec′tal·ly,** *adv.*

di·a·lec·tic (dī′ə lek′tik) *n., adj.* —*n.* **1** the art or practice of logical discussion employed in finding out the truth of a theory or opinion. **2** logical argumentation; a discussion of the logical truth of an opinion or theory. **3** *Logic.* a branch that consists of formal rhetorical reasoning. **4** *Logic.* a method based on the resolution of contradictory opposites, thesis and antithesis, leading to synthesis. —*adj.* **1** having to do with logical discussion: *dialectic criticism.* **2** dialectal.

di·a·lec·ti·cal (dī′ə lek′tə kəl) *adj.* dialectic.

dialectical materialism a socialist doctrine formulated by Karl Marx and Friedrich Engels, using the philosopher Hegel's dialectic method, that advocates a classless society emerging as the result of a long struggle between economic classes. It is the official communist philosophy.

di·a·lec·ti·cian (dī′ə lek tish′ən) *n.* **1** a person skilled in dialectic; logician. **2** dialectologist.

di·a·lec·tics (dī′ə lek′tiks) *n.* dialectic.

di·a·lec·tol·o·gist (dī′ə lek tol′ə jist) *n.* a person trained in dialectology, especially one whose work it is.

di·a·lec·tol·o·gy (dī′ə lek tol′ə jē) *n.* the study of dialects.

di·a·log (dī′ə log′) *Esp. U.S.* See **dialogue.**

di·a·logue (dī′ə log′) *n., v.* **-logued, -logu·ing.** —*n.* **1** conversation between two or more persons. **2** the element of a story, play, motion picture, etc. that consists of conversation: *The play has clever dialogue. Dialogue is difficult for some novelists.* **3** communication or interchange of ideas or opinions, especially

between individuals or groups having opposing or very different viewpoints. **4** *Music.* a composition for two voices or instruments or two groups of voices or instruments, thought of as resembling a conversation. **5** a literary work in the form of a conversation.
—*v.* **1** take part in an interchange of ideas or opinions. **2** express in the form of a dialogue. [ME < OF *dialoge* < L < Gk. *dialogos* < *dia-* between + *logos* speech]

dial tone the humming sound that is heard in a telephone receiver when the receiver is lifted, indicating that the line is in service and open for use.

di·a·lyse or **di·a·lyze** (dī′ə līz′) *v.* **-lysed** or **-lyzed, -lys·ing** or **-lyz·ing.** *Chemistry.* **1** apply dialysis to. **2** separate or procure by dialysis. —**di′a·lys′er** or **di′a·lyz′er,** *n.*

di·al·y·sis (dī al′ə sis) *n., pl.* **-ses** (-sēz′). **1** *Chemistry.* the separation of crystalloids from colloids in solution by the application of the principle that crystalloids diffuse readily through a membrane, and colloids not at all or very slightly. **2** *Medicine.* hemodialysis. [< Gk. *dialysis* < *dia-* apart + *lyein* loose]

di·a·lyt·ic (dī′ə lit′ik) *adj.* having to do with or like dialysis.

diam. diameter.

di·a·mag·net·ic (dī′ə mag net′ik) *adj., n.* —*adj.* repelled by a magnet; taking a position at right angles to the lines of force of a magnet. —*n.* a diamagnetic body or substance. —**di′a·mag·net′i·cal·ly,** *adv.*

di·a·mag·net·ism (dī′ə mag′nə tiz′əm) *n.* **1** a diamagnetic quality. **2** diamagnetic phenomena. **3** the science dealing with diamagnetic phenomena.

di·a·man·té (dyä mäⁿ tā′) *n., adj.* —*n.* French. a fabric set with rhinestones, paste, etc. so that it sparkles. —*adj.* set with diamonds or diamond chips: *diamanté buttons.*

di·am·e·ter (dī am′ə tər) *n.* **1** a straight line passing from one side to the other through the centre of a circle, sphere, etc. **2** the length of such a line, especially a measurement of width or thickness through the centre of a round object such as a ball, tree trunk, etc. [< OF *diametre* < L < Gk. *diametros* < *dia-* across + *metron* measure]

di·a·met·ric (dī′ə met′rik) *adj.* **1** of or along a diameter. **2** direct; absolute; exactly opposite.

di·a·met·ri·cal (dī′ə met′rə kəl) *adj.* diametric.

di·a·met·ri·cal·ly (dī′ə met′rik lē) *adv.* **1** as a diameter. **2** directly; exactly; entirely.

diametrically opposed, directly opposite; exactly contrary.

di·a·mond (dī′mənd *or* dī′ə mənd) *n.* **1** a colorless or tinted precious stone, formed of pure carbon in crystals. Diamond is the hardest substance known. **2** a piece of this stone, or a gem made from it. Inferior diamonds are used to cut glass. **3** (*adj.*) made of or containing diamond or a diamond: *a diamond ring.* **4** a tool with a diamond tip for cutting. **5** a plane figure shaped like this ◆. **6 a** a playing card with one or more red diamond-shaped designs on it. **b diamonds,** *pl.* the suit of cards marked with this design. **7** *Baseball.* the space inside the lines that connect the bases.

diamond cut diamond, a dispute or struggle between two well-matched opponents.

diamond in the rough or **rough diamond,** a person who has good qualities but poor manners.
[ME < OF *diamant* < Med.L *diamas, -antis,* alteration of L *adamas, -antis* adamant]

diamond anniversary a 60th or, sometimes, 75th anniversary.

di·a·mond·back (dī′mənd bak′ *or* dī′ə mənd-) *n.* a large, very dangerous rattlesnake (*Crotalus adamanteus*) of the S United States, having cream-and-grey diamond-shaped markings.

diamondback terrapin an edible aquatic turtle (*Malaclemys terrapin*) of the salt marshes and coasts of the E United States having a raised pattern of diamond-shaped markings on its shell.

diamond hitch a hitch used in fastening a load to a pack-animal, in which the rope is thrown back and forth across the animal in such a way that it forms a diamond pattern on top of the pack.

diamond jubilee the celebration of a 60th or, sometimes, 75th anniversary.

diamond wedding the 60th or, sometimes, 75th anniversary of a wedding.

diamond willow *Cdn.* willow wood having a diamond-patterned grain, resulting from an abnormal growth of the stems that may occur in any species of willow. It is prized for making lamps, walking-sticks, ornaments, etc.

Di·an·a (dī an′ə) *n.* **1** *Roman mythology.* the goddess who was the protector and helper of women. She was also the goddess of the moon and of hunting and corresponds to the Greek goddess Artemis. **2** *Poetic.* moon.

di·an·thus (dī an′thəs) *n.* any of a genus (*Dianthus*) of annual and perennial herbs of the pink family, including the carnation,

sweet william, and pink. [< NL *Dianthus* < Gk. *Dios*, genitive of *Zeus* Zeus + *anthos* flower]

di·a·pa·son (dī′ə pā′zən *or* dī′ə pā′sən) *n.* **1** *Poetic.* harmony. **2** melody; strain. **3** a swelling musical sound. **4** the whole range of a voice or instrument. **5** range; gamut; entire scope: *the diapason of emotional experience.* **6** a fixed standard of pitch. **7** a tuning fork. **8** in an organ, either of two principal stops: **a open diapason,** a stop giving full, majestic tones. **b stopped diapason,** a stop giving powerful flutelike tones. **9** *Greek music.* octave. [< L < Gk. *diapasōn* octave < *dia pasōn (chordōn)* across all (the notes of the scale)]

A diaper design used for a 19th-century Canadian patchwork quilt

di·a·per (dī′ə pər *or* dī′pər) *n., v.* —*n.* **1** a piece of cloth folded up, or a pad of other absorbent material, as underpants for a baby; napkin. **2** an allover pattern of small repeated geometric figures, especially diamonds. **3** a white cotton or linen cloth woven with such a pattern. Babies' diapers were originally made of such material. —*v.* **1** put a diaper on: *to diaper a baby.* **2** ornament with a diaper pattern. [ME < OF *diapre,* var. of *diaspre* < Med.Gk. *diaspros* < *dia-* (intensive) + *aspros* white]

di·aph·a·nous (dī af′ə nəs) *adj.* transparent: *Gauze is a diaphanous fabric.* [< Med.L *diaphanus* < Gk. *diaphanēs* < *dia-* through + *phainein* show] —**di·aph′a·nous·ly,** *adv.* —**di·aph′a·nous·ness,** *n.*

di·a·pho·re·sis (dī′ə fə rē′sis) *n. Medicine.* perspiration, especially when artificially induced. [< LL < Gk. *diaphorēsis* < *dia-* through + *phorein* carry]

di·a·pho·ret·ic (dī′ə fə ret′ik) *adj., n.* —*adj.* causing perspiration. —*n.* a drug or other agent causing perspiration.

di·a·phragm (dī′ə fram′) *n.* **1** a partition of muscles and tendons separating the cavity of the chest from the cavity of the abdomen. **2** a thin partition in some shellfish, etc. **3** a thin disk or cone that moves rapidly to and fro when sounds or electrical signals are directed at it, used in telephone receivers, microphones, earphones, and in similar instruments. **4** a device for controlling the amount of light entering a camera, microscope, etc. **5** a contraceptive device, consisting of a flexible, moulded cap, usually made of thin rubber, that is fitted over the entrance to the uterus to prevent the entry of sperm. [< LL < Gk. *diaphragma* < *dia-* across + *phragma* fence < *phrassein* to fence]

di·a·phrag·mat·ic (dī′ə frag mat′ik) *adj.* having to do with a diaphragm; like a diaphragm.

di·ar·chy (dī′är kē) *n., pl.* **-chies.** government by two people or two ruling authorities. Also, **dyarchy.** [< Gk. *di-* twice + *archos* ruler (< *archein* to rule) + E -*y³*]

di·a·rist (dī′ə rist) *n.* a person who keeps a diary.

di·ar·rhe·a *or* **di·ar·rhoe·a** (dī′ə rē′ə) *n.* the condition of having too many and too loose movements of the bowels. [< LL *diarrhoea* < Gk. *diarrhoia* < *dia-* through + *rheein* flow]

di·a·ry (dī′ə rē) *n., pl.* **-ries. 1** an account written down each day, of what one has done, thought, etc. during the day. **2** a book for keeping such an account. [< L *diarium* < *dies* day]

Di·as·po·ra (dī as′pə rə) *n.* **1** the scattering of the Jews after their captivity in Babylon. **2** the Jews thus scattered. **3** the early Jewish Christians living outside Palestine. **4** Jews living outside modern Israel. [< Gk. *diaspora* a scattering < *dia-* through + *speirein* sow]

di·a·stase (dī′ə stās′) *n.* an enzyme that changes starch into dextrine and maltose during digestion, germination of seeds, etc. [< F < Gk. *diastasis* separation < *dia-* apart + *sta-* stand]

di·as·to·le (dī as′tō lē′) *n.* the normal, rhythmical dilation of the heart, especially that of the ventricles. [< LL < Gk. *diastolē* expansion < *dia-* apart + *stellein* send]

di·as·tol·ic (dī′əs tol′ik) *adj.* having to do with diastole.

di·a·ther·mic (dī′ə thėr′mik) *adj.* having to do with diathermy. [< F *diathermique* < Gk. *dia-* through + *thermē* heat]

di·a·ther·my (dī′ə thėr′mē) *n.* a method of treating disease by heating the tissues beneath the skin with an electric current.

di·a·tom (dī′ə tom′) *n.* any of numerous microscopic, unicellular, aquatic algae that have hard shells composed mostly of silica. [<

hat, āge, fär; let, ēqual, tėrm; it, īce
hot, ōpen, ôrder; oil, out; cup, pùt, rüle,
əbove, takən, pencəl, lemən, circəs
ch, child; ng, long; sh, ship
th, thin; ŦH, then; zh, measure

NL *Diatoma,* genus name < Gk. *diatomos* cut in half < *diatemnein* cut through]

di·a·to·ma·ceous (dī′ə tə mā′shəs) *adj.* of or having to do with diatoms; consisting of or containing diatoms or their fossil remains: *diatomaceous earth.*

di·a·tom·ic (dī′ə tom′ik) *adj. Chemistry.* **1** containing only two atoms. **2** containing two replaceable atoms. **3** bivalent.

di·a·ton·ic (dī′ə ton′ik) *adj. Music.* of or using only the eight tones of a standard major or minor scale. [< L *diatonicus* < Gk. *diatonikos* < *dia-* through + *tonos* tone]

diatonic scale *Music.* a standard major or minor scale of eight tones in the octave.

di·a·tribe (dī′ə trīb′) *n.* a bitter and violent denunciation of some person or thing. [< L *diatriba* < Gk. *diatribē* pastime, study, discourse < *dia-* away + *tribein* wear]

dib (dib) *n.* **1** a small marble, usually made of clay: *He bought some dibs at the store.* **2 dibs,** *pl.* the game played with such marbles. **3 dibs,** *pl. Slang.* **a** money made, especially in small amounts. **b** one's share or shares in any profitable venture. [origin uncertain]

di·ba·sic (dī bā′sik) *adj. Chemistry.* having two hydrogen atoms that can be replaced by two atoms or radicals of a base in forming salts.

dib·ble (dib′əl) *n., v.* **-bled, -bling.** —*n.* a pointed tool that makes holes in the ground for seeds, young plants, etc. —*v.* **1** make a hole in (the soil) with or as if with a dibble. **2** sow or plant (seeds, etc.) in this way. [origin uncertain]

dice (dīs) *n. pl.* of **die³;** *v.* **diced, dic·ing.** —*n.* **1** small cubes with a different number of spots (one to six) on each side, used in playing games and gambling. **2** *Informal.* a single one of these cubes; die³. **3** a game of chance played with such cubes (*used with a singular verb*). **4** small cubes of food. —*v.* **1** play dice, tossing them to see how many spots there will be on the sides turned up. **2** lose by gambling with dice (*used with* **away**): *She diced away her inheritance.* **3** take serious risks: *dicing with death.* **4** cut (vegetables, etc.) into small cubes: *to dice carrots.* —**dic′er,** *n.*

dic·ey (dī′sē) *adj. Slang.* **1** chancy; risky; uncertain. **2** on the point of erupting into a dangerous situation.

di·chlo·ride (dī klô′rīd *or* -klô′rid) *n.* a compound composed of chlorine and one other element or a radical, with two atoms of chlorine for every atom of the other element or radical.

di·chot·o·mous (dī kot′ə məs) *adj.* **1** divided or dividing into two parts. **2** *Botany.* branching by repeated divisions into two.

di·chot·o·my (dī kot′ə mē) *n., pl.* **-mies. 1** a division into two parts. **2** *Botany.* branching by repeated divisions into two parts. **3** *Zoology.* a form of branching in which each successive axis divides into two. **4** *Logic.* classification by division, or by successive subdivison, into two groups or sections: *the dichotomy in the universe of the living and the nonliving.* [< Gk. *dichotomia* a cutting in half < *dicha* in two + *temnein* cut]

di·chro·mate (dī krō′māt) *n.* a chromate whose molecules have two atoms of chromium; bichromate.

di·chro·mat·ic (dī′krō mat′ik) *adj.* **1** having two colors. **2** *Zoology.* showing two color phases independent of phases correlated with age, sex, or season. **3** of, having to do with, or affected with dichromatism (def. 2).

di·chro·ma·tism (dī krō′mə tiz′əm) *n.* **1** a dichromatic quality or condition. **2** color blindness in which a person can distinguish only two of the primary colors. [see DI-¹, CHROMATIC]

dick (dik) *n. Slang.* detective. [shortened form of *detective*]

dick·cis·sel (kik sis′əl) *n.* a brownish-grey finch (*Spiza americana*) that breeds in central North America and winters in N South America. The adult male in breeding plumage looks like a tiny meadowlark.

dick·ens (dik′ənz) *n., interj.* —*n.* the devil; deuce. —*interj.* **the dickens!** an exclamation expressing surprise or annoyance.

Dick·en·si·an (di ken′zē ən *or* di ken′sē ən) *adj., n.* —*adj.* **1** of or having to do with Charles Dickens (1812-1870), an English novelist. **2** of or suggestive of his style, writings, characters, etc. —*n.* a person who studies or admires Charles Dickens or his works.

dick·er (dik′ər) *v., n.* —*v.* trade by barter or by petty bargaining.

—*n.* **1** a petty bargain. **2** the act of bargaining. [< *dicker*, n., a lot of ten hides]

dick·ey[1] (dik′ē) *n., pl.* **-eys. 1** a shirt front that can be detached. **2** a high collar on a shirt. **3** a child's bib or pinafore. **4** vestee. **5** the driver's seat on the outside of a carriage. **6** a seat at the back of a carriage for servants. **7** a small bird. **8** donkey. [< *Dick*, proper name]

dick·ey[2] (dik′ē) *n., pl.* **-eys.** *Cdn.* a pull-over garment for the upper body, having a hood and made of duffle or skins; parka; atigi (def. 2). Also, **dickie, dicky.** [< Eskimo *atigi*]

dick·ie (dik′ē) *n., pl.* **-ies.** See **dickey**[2].

dick·y (dik′ē) *n., pl.* **—ies.** See **dickey**[2].

di·cot (dī′kot) *n.* dicotyledon.

di·cot·y·le·don (dī kot′ə lē′dən) *n.* any flowering plant having two seed leaves (cotyledons) in the embryo, including the hardwood trees and most cultivated plants. Dicotyledons and monocotyledons constitute the two main groups of angiosperms. See also **monocotyledon.**

di·cot·y·le·don·ous (dī kot′ə lē′dən əs) *adj.* having two seed leaves; belonging to the dicotyledons.

dict. 1 dictionary. **2** dictator.

dic·ta (dik′tə) *n.* a pl. of **dictum.**

Dic·ta·phone (dik′tə fōn′) *n. Trademark.* an instrument that records and reproduces sounds, used for dictating and transcribing. [< *dicta(te)* + *-phone*]

dic·tate (*v.* dik′tāt or dik tāt′; *n.* dik′tāt) *v.* **-tat·ed, -tat·ing;** *n.* —*v.* **1** say or read (something) aloud for another person or other persons to write or type: *to dictate a letter, to dictate a spelling list.* **2** command with authority; give orders that must be obeyed: *No one is going to dictate to me.* —*n.* a direction or order that is to be carried out or obeyed: *An honest man follows the dictates of his conscience.* [< L *dictare* say often < *dicere* tell, say]

dic·ta·tion (dik tā′shən) *n.* **1** the act of saying or reading (something) aloud for another person or other persons to write or type: *The pupils wrote to the teacher's dictation.* **2** the words said or read aloud to be written down: *We have dictation during the first five minutes of our French class.* **3** the act of commanding with authority; act of giving orders that must be obeyed: *The slave acted at the dictation of his master.*

dic·ta·tor (dik′tā tər or dik tā′tər) *n.* **1** a person exercising absolute authority; especially, a person who, without having any claim through inheritance or free popular election, seizes control of a government: *The dictator of the country had complete power over its people.* **2** a person whose authority is widely accepted in some special field: *a dictator of men's fashions.* **3** a person who dictates words or sentences for someone else to record.

dic·ta·to·ri·al (dik′tə tô′rē əl) *adj.* **1** of or like that of a dictator: *dictatorial government.* **2** imperious; domineering; overbearing: *The soldiers disliked the dictatorial manner of the new officer.* —**dic′ta·to′ri·al·ly,** *adv.*

dic·ta·tor·ship (dik′tā tər ship′ or dik tā′tər ship′) *n.* **1** the position or rank of a dictator. **2** the period during which a dictator rules. **3** absolute authority; the power to give orders that must be obeyed. **4** a country under the rule of a dictator.

dic·tion (dik′shən) *n.* **1** the manner of expressing ideas in words; style of speaking or writing. Good diction implies grammatical correctness, a wide vocabulary, and skill in the choice and arrangement of words. **2** pronunciation and enunciation in speaking or singing: *clear diction.* [< L *dictio, -onis* saying < *dicere* say]

☛ *Syn.* **Diction, phraseology, wording** = words and the way of using them. **Diction** applies to words and emphasizes the choice of words used to express ideas and feelings and the way in which they convey meaning: *John's diction is poor; he uses too much slang and too many colorless words.* **Phraseology** applies to the grouping of words, particularly in the way peculiar to a person, group, profession, etc.: *I don't understand legal phraseology.* **Wording** applies to words and grouping but emphasizes their special suitability for a purpose: *I like the wording of that greeting.*

dic·tion·ar·y (dik′shən er′ē) *n., pl.* **-ar·ies. 1** a book of words arranged alphabetically, with information about their meanings, forms, and, usually, pronunciation and history. Some dictionaries also give information on how words are used in sentences and idiomatic expressions. **2** a book of names or words of some special subject or activity, arranged alphabetically, with information on meanings, uses, etc.: *a law dictionary, a dictionary of trade names.* **3** a book of alphabetically arranged words of one language with equivalent words or meanings in another language: *an English-Czech dictionary, a French-English dictionary.* [< Med.L *dictionarium* < L *dictio.* See DICTION.]

Dic·to·graph (dik′tə graf′) *n. Trademark.* a telephone with a very sensitive transmitter, used for secretly listening to or obtaining a record of conversation. [< L *dictum* (thing) said + E *-graph*]

dic·tum (dik′təm) *n., pl.* **-tums** or **-ta. 1** a formal comment; an authoritative opinion: *The dictum of the critics was that the play was excellent.* **2** maxim; saying. [< L *dictum* (thing) said, pp. neut. of *dicere* say]

did (did) *v.* pt. of **do**[1].

di·dac·tic (dī dak′tik or di dak′tik) *adj.* **1** intended to instruct: *The fables of Aesop are didactic stories; each one has an instructive moral.* **2** inclined to instruct others; teacherlike: *The older brother was called "Professor" because of his didactic manner.* [< Gk. *didaktikos* < *didaskein* teach] —**di·dac′ti·cal·ly,** *adv.*

di·dac·ti·cal (dī dak′tə kəl or di dak′tə kəl) *adj.* didactic.

di·dac·ti·cism (dī dak′tə siz′əm or di dak′tə siz′əm) *n.* a didactic quality, character, or manner.

di·dac·tics (dī dak′tiks or di dak′tiks) *n.* the science or art of giving instruction.

did·dle (did′el) *v.* **-dled, -dling.** *Informal.* **1** cheat; swindle. **2** waste (time). **3** ruin. [origin uncertain]

did·n't (did′ənt) did not.

di·do (dī′dō) *n., pl.* **-dos** or **-does.** *Informal.* a prank; trick; a mischievous or disorderly action. [origin uncertain]

didst (didst) *v. Archaic and poetic.* 2nd pers. sing. past tense of **do**[1]. *Thou didst* means *You* (sing.) *did.*

die[1] (dī) *v.* **died, dy·ing. 1** cease to live; stop living; become dead. **2** come to an end; lose force or strength; stop. **3** *Informal.* want very much; long keenly (*used in a progressive tense, followed by* **to** or **for**): *I'm dying to go to the Rockies. She was dying for a cold drink.*

die away or **down,** stop or end little by little; lose force or strength gradually: *The music died away.*

die hard, struggle until death; resist to the very end; refuse to give in.

die off, die one after another until all are dead: *The whole herd of cattle died off in the epidemic.*

die out, a stop or end little by little. **b** cease or end completely. [OE *dīegan*]

☛ *Hom.* dye.

☛ *Syn.* **1, 2. Die, perish** = stop living or existing. **Die,** the general word meaning "to stop living," is also used figuratively of things that have been active in any way: *The noisy conversation of the class died down suddenly when the teacher came into the room.* **Perish,** more formal or literary than **die,** emphasizes losing life through violence or hardship, and used figuratively means "to go out of existence permanently": *Many perished in the great fire. The forces of evil may cause civilization to perish.*

☛ *Usage.* **Die** is generally used with *of* before an illness: *He died of* (not *from* or *with*) *cancer.*

die[2] (dī) *n., pl.* **dies. 1** any tool or apparatus for shaping, cutting, or stamping things, usually under pressure. A die is usually a metal block or plate cut in a certain way. **2** a tool for cutting threads on pipes, bolts, etc. [< *die*[3]]

☛ *Hom.* dye.

die[3] (dī) *n., pl.* **dice.** a small cube marked with a different number of spots (from one to six) on each face, used for gambling and playing certain games: *Dice are often used in pairs.* See also **dice. the die is cast,** the decision is made and cannot be changed. [ME < OF *de* < L *datum* (thing) given (i.e., by fortune), pp. neut. of *dare* give. Doublet of DATUM.]

☛ *Hom.* dye.

die·back (dī′bak′) *n.* a disease of trees and other woody plants in which the twigs and tips of branches die first.

die-cast (dī′kast′) *adj.* made by the process of die-casting: *a die-cast engine block.*

die caster a person who makes die castings.

die casting 1 a process by which metal is cast to a desired shape by being forced into a mould, or die, when molten. **2** a metal object made in this way.

di·e·cious (dī ē′shəs) See **dioecious.**

die-hard (dī′härd′) *adj., n.* —*adj.* resisting to the very end; refusing to give in. —*n.* a person who refuses to give in.

di·e·lec·tric (dī′i lek′trik) *adj., n.* —*adj.* non-conducting. —*n.* a dielectric substance, such as glass, rubber, or wood.

di·er·e·sis or **di·aer·e·sis** (dī er′ə sis) *n., pl.* **-ses** (-sēz′). two dots (¨) placed over the second of two consecutive vowels to indicate that the second vowel is to be pronounced in a separate syllable. *Example:* naïve. [< L *diaeresis* < Gk. *diairesis* separation, division < *diaireein* divide < *dia-* apart + *haireein* take]

die·sel (dē′zəl or dē′səl) *n.* **1** diesel engine. **2** a vehicle powered by a diesel engine. **3** (*adj.*) powered by a diesel engine: *a diesel train.* **4** (*adj.*) of or for diesel engines: *diesel fuel.*

diesel engine an internal-combustion engine that burns fuel oil which is ignited by heat from compressed air instead of by an electric spark, as in a gasoline engine. [after R. *Diesel* (1858-1913), its inventor]

diesel motor diesel engine.

diesel oil a light fuel oil burned by diesel engines and obtained from crude oil after the distillation of gasoline and kerosene.

die·sink·er (dī′singk′ər) *n.* a person who makes dies for shaping or stamping.

Di·es I·rae (dī′ēz ī′rē *or* dē′ās ē′rī) **1** a medieval Latin hymn describing the Day of Judgment and usually sung at masses for the dead. **2** a musical setting for such a hymn. [< L *dies irae* day of wrath]

di·et[1] (dī′ət) *n., v.* **-et·ed, -et·ing.** —*n.* **1** the usual food and drink for a person or animal. **2** a special selection of food and drink eaten during illness or in an attempt to lose or gain weight. **3** something provided habitually or repeatedly: *a steady diet of good advice.* —*v.* eat or cause to eat special food and drink. [ME < OF *diete(r)* < L < Gk. *diaita* way of life] —**di′et·er,** *n.*

di·et[2] (dī′ət) *n.* **1** a formal assembly. **2** the national lawmaking body in certain countries. [< Med.L *dieta* day's work, session of councillors, ult. identical with *diet*[1] but influenced by L *dies* day]

di·e·tar·y (dī′ə ter′ē) *adj., n., pl.* **-tar·ies.** —*adj.* of or having to do with diet: *Dietary rules tell what food to eat for healthy living and how to prepare it.* —*n.* **1** a system of rules for eating and drinking. **2** a daily allowance of food in a prison, hospital, etc.

di·e·tet·ic (dī′ə tet′ik) *adj.* of or having to do with diet. —**di·e·tet′i·cal·ly,** *adv.*

di·e·tet·ics (dī′ə tet′iks) *n.* the science that deals with the amount and kinds of food needed by the body (*used with a singular verb*).

di·e·ti·tian *or* **di·e·ti·cian** (dī′ə tish′ən) *n.* a person trained to plan meals that have the proper proportion of various kinds of food.

dif– the form of **dis-**[1] before *f*, as in *diffuse.*

diff. difference; different.

dif·fer (dif′ər) *v.* **1** be unlike; be different. **2** have or express a different opinion; disagree. [ME < OF < L *differre* set apart, differ < *dis-* apart + *ferre* carry. Doublet of DEFER[1].]

☛ *Usage.* Differ is followed by *from* when it means "be unlike or different": *My answers to the algebra problems differed from Mary's.* When the meaning is "disagree," *differ* is followed by *with* or *from: I differed from him in the solution he offered. She never differs with my plans.*

dif·fer·ence (dif′rəns *or* dif′ər əns) *n.* **1** the condition of being different. **2** the way of being different; point in which people or things are different. **3** what is left after subtracting one number from another: *The difference between 6 and 15 is 9.* **4** the amount or extent by which one thing differs from another: *The difference in size between Nova Scotia and Ontario is great.* **5** the condition of having a different opinion; disagreement. **6** a dispute.
make a difference, a give or show different treatment. **b** matter; be important; have an effect or influence.
split the difference, a divide what is left in half. **b** meet halfway; compromise.

☛ *Syn. n.* **1. Difference, discrepancy, disparity** = unlikeness between two things. **Difference** applies to lack of sameness or any unlikeness, large or small, in a detail, quality, etc.: *There is a difference in John's and Mary's heights.* **Discrepancy** applies to a lack of agreement between things that should be alike or balance: *There was a discrepancy between the two reports of the accident.* **Disparity** applies to a lack of equality: *There is a disparity between my expenses and my income.*

dif·fer·ent (dif′rənt *or* dif′ər ənt) *adj.* **1** not alike; not like. **2** not the same; separate; distinct: *I saw her three different times today.* **3** not like others or most others; unusual. —**dif′fer·ent·ly,** *adv.*

☛ *Usage.* **Different.** In formal English, the standard idiom is *different from: His second book was entirely different from his first.* Informal usage is divided, using *from* occasionally, sometimes *to* (which is a common British idiom), and more often *than: She was different than any other girl he had ever known. Different than* is becoming more common when the object is a clause: *The house was a good deal different than he remembered it.*

dif·fer·en·ti·a (dif′ər en′shē ə) *n., pl.* **-ti·ae** (-shē ē′ *or* -shē ī′). *Logic.* the quality or condition that distinguishes one species from all the others of the same genus or class. [< L *differentia* difference]

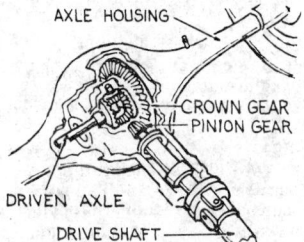

AXLE HOUSING
CROWN GEAR
PINION GEAR
DRIVEN AXLE
DRIVE SHAFT
The rear-axle assembly of an automobile, showing the differential

dif·fer·en·tial (dif′ər en′shəl) *adj., n.* —*adj.* **1** of a difference;

hat, āge, fär; let, ēqual, tèrm; it, īce
hot, ōpen, ôrder; oil, out; cup, pút, rüle,
əbove, takən, pencəl, lemən, circəs

ch, child; ng, long; sh, ship
th, thin; ŦH, then; zh, measure

showing a difference; depending on a difference: *Differential duties, rates, charges, etc. are those that differ according to circumstances.* **2** distinguishing; distinctive. **3** having to do with distinguishing characteristics or specific differences: *A differential diagnosis attempts to distinguish between two similar diseases or objects of natural history.* **4** *Mathematics.* having to do with or involving differentials. **5** *Physics and mechanics.* concerning the difference of two or more motions, pressures, etc. **6** *Geology.* producing different or selective effects on formations or constituents of rocks, soils, etc.: *differential erosion, differential weathering.*
—*n.* **1** a differential duty or rate; the difference involved.
2 *Mathematics.* an infinitesimal difference between consecutive values of a variable quantity. **3** in an automobile, an arrangement of gears that allows one of the rear wheels to turn faster than the other in going round a corner or curve. —**dif′fer·en′tial·ly,** *adv.*

differential calculus the branch of mathematics dealing with differentials and their relations. Compare **integral calculus.**

dif·fer·en·ti·ate (dif′ər en′shē āt′) *v.* **-at·ed, -at·ing. 1** show or mark a difference between or in: *an act of kindness that differentiates real consideration for others from mere politeness.* **2** recognize or see a distinction; discriminate: *The twins were so much alike that it was almost impossible to differentiate between them.* **3** become different in character: *The words* metal *and* mettle *have the same origin but have differentiated over the centuries to become two separate words.* —**dif′fer·en′ti·a′tor,** *n.*
☛ *Syn.* 1, 2. See note at **distinguish.**

dif·fer·en·ti·a·tion (dif′ər en′shē ā′shən) *n.* the act or process of differentiating; alteration; modification; distinction.

dif·fi·cult (dif′ə kult′ *or* dif′ə kəlt) *adj.* **1** hard to do or understand: *Cutting down the tree was difficult. Mathematics is difficult for some people.* **2** hard to deal with, get along with, or please: *The secretary found her new employer difficult.*

dif·fi·cul·ty (dif′ə kul′tē *or* dif′ə kəl tē) *n., pl.* **-ties. 1** the fact or condition of being difficult: *the difficulty of a job.* **2** hard work; much effort. **3** trouble. **4** financial trouble. **5** something that is difficult; something in the way; an obstacle. **6** a disagreement; quarrel.
in difficulties, in trouble, especially money trouble: *Our spendthrift friend is in difficulties again.*
make difficulties, cause trouble; hinder by raising objections: *We will get the meeting finished quickly if no one makes difficulties.*
[ME < L *difficultas* < *difficilis* hard < *dis-* not + *facilis* easy]

dif·fi·dence (dif′ə dəns) *n.* lack of self-confidence; shyness.

dif·fi·dent (dif′ə dənt) *adj.* lacking in self-confidence; shy. [< L *diffidens, -entis,* ppr. of *diffidere* < *dis-* away + *fidere* trust] —**dif′fi·dent·ly,** *adv.*

dif·fract (di frakt′) *v.* break up by diffraction. [< L *diffractus,* pp. of *diffringere* < *dis-* up + *frangere* break]

dif·frac·tion (di frak′shən) *n. Physics.* **1** a breaking up of a ray of light into a series of light and dark bands or into the colored bands of the spectrum. **2** a similar breaking up of sound waves, electricity, etc.

dif·frac·tive (di frak′tiv) *adj.* having to do with diffraction; tending to diffract. —**dif·frac′tive·ly,** *adv.* —**dif·frac′tive·ness,** *n.*

dif·fuse (*v.* di fyüz′; *adj.* -fyüs′) *v.* **-fused, -fus·ing;** *adj.* —*v.* **1** spread out so as to cover a larger space or surface; scatter widely. **2** *Physics.* mix together by spreading into one another, as one gas with another or one liquid with another; spread by diffusion. —*adj.* **1** not concentrated at a single point; spread out: *diffuse light.* **2** using many words where a few would do: *a diffuse writer.* [ME < L *diffusus,* pp. of *diffundere* < *dis-* in every direction + *fundere* pour] —**dif·fuse′ly,** *adv.* —**dif·fuse′ness,** *n.* —**dif·fus′er,** *n.*

dif·fus·i·ble (di fyü′zə bəl) *adj.* capable of being diffused.

dif·fu·sion (di fyü′zhən) *n.* **1** the act or fact of diffusing; a spreading widely; a scattering: *The invention of printing greatly increased the diffusion of knowledge.* **2** being widely spread or scattered; a diffused condition. **3** *Physics.* a mixing together of the molecules or atoms of gases or of liquids by spreading into one another. **4** the use of too many words; wordiness.

dif·fu·sive (di fyü′siv) *adj.* **1** tending to diffuse. **2** showing diffusion. **3** using too many words; wordy. —**dif·fu′sive·ly,** *adv.* —**dif·fu′sive·ness,** *n.*

dig (dig) *v.* **dug** *or* (*archaic*) **digged, dig·ging;** *n.* —*v.* **1** use a shovel, spade, hands, claws, or snout to make a hole or to turn over

ground: *After digging for three hours, they were still only one metre down. She's out in the garden digging for earthworms.* **2** make or form by removing earth or other material: *to dig a hole, to dig a basement.* **3** prepare by turning over ground: *to dig a garden.* **4** make a way by digging: *to dig through a snowbank, to dig under a fence.* **5** get by digging: *to dig potatoes, to dig clams.* **6** make a careful search or inquiry for information, or into a book, etc.: *We will really have to dig for that information.* **7** make a thrust or stab into; prod: *The rider dug her spurs into the horse.* **8** *Slang.* understand or appreciate: *Do you dig what they're talking about?* **9** *Slang.* like or admire: *I don't dig rock music.*

dig in, a work hard. **b** make a protective trench. **c** secure one's position: *He has really dug in at the factory.* **d** *Informal.* eat heartily.

dig into, *Informal.* work hard at.

dig up, a unearth. **b** excavate. **c** find out.

—*n.* **1** the act of digging. **2** *Informal.* an archaeological excavation. **3** *Informal.* a thrust or poke: *a dig in the ribs.* **4** *Informal.* a sarcastic remark: *He made several nasty little digs about their escapade.* **5 digs,** *pl. Esp.Brit. Informal.* lodgings; quarters; diggings (def. 3). [ME *dygge(n)*, probably < MF *diguer* < Gmc.]

di·gam·ma (dī gam′ə) *n.* a letter in the early Greek alphabet (*F*), with the phonetic value of English (w).

Dig·by chicken (dig′bē) *Cdn.* a small smoke-cured herring. [< *Digby*, N.S.]

di·gest (*v.* dī jest′ *or* di jest′; *n.* dī′jest) *v., n.* —*v.* **1** change (food) in the stomach and intestines so that it can be taken into the blood and used as nourishment. **2** undergo this process; be digested: *Some foods digest more quickly than others.* **3** understand and absorb mentally; arrange in the mind: *It often takes a long time to digest new ideas.* **4** condense and arrange according to some system; summarize. **5** endure; tolerate: *I find it difficult to digest his bad manners.* **6** *Chemistry.* soften or decompose by means of heat, moisture, or chemicals.

—*n.* **1** information condensed according to some system; a summary: *a digest of law.* **2** a periodical, etc. containing a collection of summaries: *a book-review digest.* [ME < L *digestus*, pp. of *digerere* separate, dissolve < *dis-* apart + *gerere* carry]

☛ *Syn. n.* See note at **summary.**

di·gest·er (dī jes′tər *or* di jes′tər) *n.* **1** a person who makes a digest. **2** a heavy, covered kettle, etc. for softening or dissolving a substance by heat and moisture.

di·gest·i·bil·i·ty (dī jes′tə bil′ə tē *or* di jes′tə bil′ə tē) *n.* the quality of being digestible.

di·gest·i·ble (dī jes′tə bəl *or* di jes′tə bəl) *adj.* capable of being digested; easily digested. —**di·gest′i·ble·ness,** *n.* —**di·gest′i·bly,** *adv.*

di·ges·tion (dī jes′chən *or* di jes′chən) *n.* **1** the digesting of food. **2** the ability to digest food. **3** the act of digesting books, etc.

di·ges·tive (dī jes′tiv *or* di jes′tiv) *adj., n.* —*adj.* **1** of or for digestion: *Saliva is one of the digestive juices.* **2** helping digestion. —*n.* something that aids digestion. —**di·gest′ive·ly,** *adv.*

dig·ger (dig′ər) *n.* **1** a person that digs. **2** the part of a machine that turns up the ground. **3** any tool for digging. **4** Usually, **Digger,** *Informal.* an Australian or New Zealander.

digger wasp any of various solitary wasps (family Sphecidae) that dig into the ground to make their nests, stocking the nests with paralyzed insects or spiders for their larvae to feed on.

dig·gings (dig′ingz) *n.pl.* **1** a mine or place where digging is being done: *The archaeologists examined the new diggings.* **2** the material that is dug out. **3** *Informal.* a place to live.

dight (dīt) *v.* **dight** *or* **dight·ed, dight·ing.** *Archaic.* **1** dress; adorn. **2** equip. [OE *dihtan* compose, arrange < L *dictare* dictate]

dig·it (dij′it) *n.* **1** a finger or toe. **2** any of the figures 0, 1, 2, 3, 4, 5, 6, 7, 8, 9. Sometimes 0 is not called a digit but is known as a cipher. [ME < L *digitus* finger]

dig·it·al (dij′ə təl) *adj., n.* —*adj.* **1** of or having to do with the fingers or toes. **2** of or having to do with numerals (digits) or calculation by numerals. **3** of, having to do with, or providing information in the form of numerals. A digital clock shows the time in the form of changing numerals rather than by hands moving over a dial. —*n.* a key of an organ, piano, etc. played with the finger.

digital computer a type of electronic calculating machine using numbers expressed as digits of some numerical system to solve problems that can be expressed mathematically.

dig·i·tal·is (dij′ə tal′is *or* dij′ə tā′lis) *n.* **1** a medicine used for stimulating the heart, obtained from the dried leaves of the purple foxglove. **2** foxglove. [< L *digitalis* pertaining to the finger < *digitus* finger; from the shape of the corolla]

dig·i·tate (dij′ə tāt′) *adj.* **1** having fingers or toes. **2** *Botany.* having radiating divisions like fingers. **3** *Zoology.* having digits or digitlike parts. —**dig′i·tate·ly,** *adv.*

dig·i·ti·grade (dij′ə tə grād′) *n., adj.* —*n.* an animal having feet shaped so that the toes are on the ground, but not the heels. Dogs, cats, and horses are digitigrades. —*adj.* having feet like this. [F < L *digitus* finger, toe + *gradi* walk]

dig·i·tize (dij′ə tīz′) *v.* **-ized, -iz·ing.** express (data, etc.) in a digital form of notation for direct processing by a computer. —**dig′i·ti·za′tion,** *n.* —**dig′i·tiz′er,** *n.*

dig·ni·fied (dig′nə fīd′) *adj.* having or showing dignity; noble or stately. —**dig′ni·fied′ly,** *adv.*

dig·ni·fy (dig′nə fī′) *v.* **-fied, -fy·ing.** **1** give dignity to; make noble, worth-while, or worthy: *The little farmhouse was dignified by the great elms around it.* **2** give a high-sounding name to. [< OF *dignifier* < LL *dignificare* < L *dignus* worthy + *facere* make]

dig·ni·tar·y (dig′nə ter′ē) *n., pl.* **-tar·ies.** a person who has a position of honor: *A bishop is a dignitary of the church.*

dig·ni·ty (dig′nə tē) *n., pl.* **-ties. 1** a proud and self-respecting manner; stateliness and formality: *He replied with dignity that he was not interested in their scheme. She had great dignity of bearing.* **2** self-respect; self-esteem: *She maintained that lying about the matter would be beneath her dignity.* **3** high rank, office, or position or the honor or esteem attached to it: *He felt that casual dress was not in keeping with the dignity of his position as director.* **4** the quality of being worthy of honor or esteem; true worth, nobility, or excellence: *The dignity of labor.* **5** *Archaic.* dignitary. [ME < OF *dignete* < L *dignitas* < *dignus* worthy. Doublet of DAINTY.]

di·graph (dī′graf) *n.* two letters used together to spell a single sound. *Examples: ea* in *each, th* in *with, sh* in *shop.* Compare **ligature.** [< *di-¹* double, twice + Gk. *graphē* a writing]

di·gress (dī gres′ *or* di gres′) *v.* turn aside; get off the main subject in talking or writing. [< L *digressus*, pp. of *digredi* deviate < *dis-* aside < *gradi* to step] —**di·gress′er,** *n.*

☛ *Syn.* See note at **diverge.**

di·gres·sion (dī gresh′ən *or* di gresh′ən) *n.* a turning aside; a getting off the main subject in talking or writing.

di·gres·sive (dī gres′iv *or* di gres′iv) *adj.* tending to digress; digressing. —**di·gres′sive·ly,** *adv.* —**di·gres′sive·ness,** *n.*

di·he·dral (dī hē′drəl) *adj., n.* —*adj.* **1** having or formed by two intersecting planes: *a dihedral angle.* **2** of aircraft wings, not horizontal, but inclined to each other so as to form a dihedral angle. **3** of an aircraft, having such wings. —*n.* **1** a figure formed by two intersecting planes; a dihedral angle. **2** the angle between an upwardly or downwardly inclined aircraft wing and the horizontal plane of its axis. [< *di-¹* two + Gk. *hedra* seat; base + E *-al¹*]

dike¹ (dīk) *n., v.* **diked, dik·ing.** —*n.* **1** a bank of earth or a dam built as a defence against flooding. **2** a ditch or channel for water. **3** a bank of earth thrown up in digging. **4** a low wall of earth or stone; causeway. **5** a barrier; obstacle. **6** *Geology.* a long, usually narrow mass of igneous rock that was thrust, while molten, into a fissure in older rock. —*v.* **1** provide with a dike or dikes. **2** drain with a ditch or channel for water. Also, **dyke.** [ME < ON *dik.* Akin to DITCH.]

dike² (dīk) *n. Slang.* a lesbian. Also, **dyke.** [origin uncertain]

dike·land (dīk′lənd) *n.* land, usually below sea level, that is protected from flooding by a system of embankments.

di·lan·tin (dī lan′tin) *n.* a white, powdery drug used in treating epilepsy. [*di*phenyl/hyd*antoin* sodium]

dilantin sodium dilantin.

di·lap·i·dat·ed (di lap′ə dāt′id) *adj.* falling to pieces; partly ruined or decayed through neglect: *a dilapidated house.* [< L *dilapidatus*, pp. of *dilapidare* demolish, destroy (with stones) < *dis-* (intensive) + *lapis, lapidis* stone]

di·lap·i·da·tion (di lap′ə dā′shən) *n.* a falling to pieces; decay; ruin; tumble-down condition: *The house was in the last stage of dilapidation.*

dil·a·ta·tion (dī′lə tā′shən *or* dil′ə tā′shən) *n.* dilation.

di·late (dī lāt′ *or* di lāt′) *v.* **-lat·ed, -lat·ing. 1** make or become larger or wider: *The pupils of John's eyes dilated when the light dimmed.* **2** speak or write in a very complete or detailed manner. [< L *dilatare* < *dis-* apart + *latus* wide]

☛ *Syn.* **1.** See note at **expand.**

di·lat·ed (dī lāt′id *or* di lāt′id) *adj.* widened; expanded.

di·la·tion (dī lā′shən *or* di lā′shən) *n.* **1** the act of dilating; enlargement; widening. **2** a dilated condition. **3** a dilated part.

di·la·tor (dī lā′tər *or* di lā′tər) *n.* **1** a person or thing that dilates. **2** *Physiology.* a muscle that dilates some part of the body. **3** a surgical instrument for dilating wounds, canals of the body, etc.

dil·a·to·ry (dil′ə tô′rē) *adj.* **1** tending to delay; not prompt. **2** causing delay. [< L *dilatorius* < *dilator* delayer < *dilatus,* pp. to *differre* defer, delay. See DIFFER.] —**dil′a·to′ri·ly,** *adv.* —**dil′a·to′ri·ness,** *n.*

dil·do (dil′dō) *n.* a device shaped like an erect penis, used for sexual stimulation. [of unknown origin. 17c.]

di·lem·ma (di lem′ə) *n.* **1** a situation requiring a choice between two things when either one is unpleasant or undesirable; a difficult choice: *Her dilemma was that she would have to give up her holiday trip or miss playing in the basketball finals.* **2** an argument forcing an opponent to choose one of two alternatives equally unfavorable to him. [< LL < Gk. *dilemma* < *di-* two + *lemma* premise]
☛ *Syn.* **1.** See note at **predicament.**

dil·et·tan·te (dil′ə tan′tē *or* dil′ə tänt′) *n., pl.* **-tes** (-tēz) *or* **-ti** (-tē). **1** a lover of the fine arts. **2** a person who is interested in some art or other subject only as an amusement, a dabbler or trifler. [< Ital. *dilettante* < *dilettare* < L *delectare.* See DELIGHT.]

dil·et·tan·te·ism (dil′ə tan′tē iz′əm *or* dil′ə tän′tē iz′əm) *n.* dilettantism.

dil·et·tan·ti (dil′ə tan′tē *or* dil′ə tän′tē) *n.* a pl. of **dilettante.**

dil·et·tant·ism (dil′ə tan′tiz əm *or* dil′ə tän′tiz əm) *n.* the quality or practice of a dilettante.

dil·i·gence¹ (dil′ə jəns) *n.* the quality of being diligent; careful effort; the ability to work hard and steadily; industry: *The student's diligence was rewarded with high marks.* [< F < L *diligentia* < *diligere.* See DILIGENT.]

dil·i·gence² (dil′ə jəns) *n.* a public stagecoach formerly used in some parts of Europe. [special use of *diligence¹*]

dil·i·gent (dil′ə jənt) *adj.* **1** hard-working; industrious. **2** careful and steady. [< L *diligens, -entis,* ppr. of *diligere* value highly, love < *dis-* apart + *legere* choose] —**dil′i·gent·ly,** *adv.*
☛ *Syn.* **1.** See note at **busy.**

dill (dil) *n.* **1** a tall herb (*Anethum graveolens*) of the parsley family having finely divided leaves and flat clusters of small yellow flowers. The aromatic leaves, immature flower clusters, and seeds are used to flavor soups, stews, salads, and cucumber pickles. **2** the seeds or leaves of this plant. **3** dill pickle: *Dills are my favorite pickles.* [OE *dile*]

dill pickle a cucumber pickle flavored with dill.

dil·ly (dil′ē) *n., pl.* **-lies.** *Slang.* a person or thing thought of as extraordinary, unique, odd, outstanding, etc.: *a dilly of a game.* [apparently < *de*lightful + *-y²*]

dil·ly-dal·ly (dil′ē dal′ē) *v.* **-lied, -ly·ing.** waste time; loiter; trifle.

di·lute (di lüt′ *or* dī lüt′) *v.* **-lut·ed, -lut·ing;** *adj.* —*v.* **1** make weaker or thinner by adding water or some other liquid. **2** lessen the force, effect, or value of. **3** become diluted. —*adj.* **1** diluted. **2** present in solution, especially a weak solution: *a dilute acid.* [< L *dilutus,* pp. of *diluere* < *dis-* apart + *luere* wash]

di·lu·tion (di lü′shən *or* dī lü′shən) *n.* **1** the act of diluting. **2** the fact or state of being diluted. **3** something diluted.

di·lu·vi·al (di lü′vē əl *or* dī lü′vē əl) *adj.* **1** of or having to do with a flood. **2** made up of debris left by a flood or glacier. [< L *diluvialis* < *diluvium.* See DELUGE.]

di·lu·vi·an (di lü′vē ən *or* dī lü′vē ən) *adj.* diluvial.

dim (dim) *adj.* **dim·mer, dim·mest;** *v.* **dimmed, dim·ming.** —*adj.* **1** not bright, clear, or distinct: *a dim light, a dim outline.* **2** not clearly or completely perceived or distinguished; vague: *He had a dim memory of the event.* **3** not able to see or perceive clearly and distinctly: *Her eyesight was getting dim.* **4** not likely to have a good result or outcome: *Her future looks dim.* **5** without lustre; dull. **6** *Informal.* unfavorable: *He takes a dim view of his chances of winning the race.*
take a dim view of, disapprove of; look on with disfavor: *He takes a dim view of practical jokes.*
—*v.* **1** make or become dim: *The theatre lights were dimmed.* **2** change the headlights of a motor vehicle to the low beam.
dim out, make nearly but not absolutely dark, by allowing light to appear only through slits, by use of blue lights, etc.: *to dim out the lights on stage.*
[OE *dimm*] —**dim′ly,** *adv.* —**dim′ness,** *n.*
☛ *Syn. adj.* **1.** See note at **dark.**

dim. **1** diminuendo. **2** diminutive.

dime (dīm) *n.* a coin of Canada or the United States, equal to one tenth of a dollar; a ten-cent coin.
a dime a dozen, *Informal.* cheap and commonplace: *Those comic T-shirts are a dime a dozen.*
[< OF *disme* < L *decima (pars)* tenth (part) < *decem* ten]

dime novel a sensational or melodramatic novel, usually published as a cheap paperback: *Dime novels are all he ever reads.*

di·men·sion (di men′shən *or* dī men′shən) *n.* **1** the measurement

hat, āge, fär; let, ēqual, tèrm; it, īce
hot, ōpen, ôrder; oil, out; cup, pút, rüle,
əbove, takən, pencəl, lemən, circəs

ch, child; ng, long; sh, ship
th, thin; ᴛʜ, then; zh, measure

of length, breadth, or thickness: *The dimensions of my room are 4.2 metres by 3.1 metres.* **2** the size; extent: *It was a project of large dimensions.* **3** element, factor, or characteristic: *His latest work adds a new dimension to the art of film.* [ME < MF < L *dimensio, -onis* < *dis-* out + *metiri* measure]

di·men·sion·al (di men′shən əl *or* dī men′shən əl) *adj.* having to do with dimension or dimensions. —**di·men′sion·al·ly,** *adv.*

di·mer (dī′mər) *n. Chemistry.* a compound in which two molecules of the same substance are present, especially as produced by polymerization. [< *di-¹* two + Gk. *meros* part]

dim·er·ous (dim′ə rəs) *adj.* consisting of two parts, divisions, or members.

dime store a store selling a large variety of articles in a low price-range.

dim·e·ter (dim′ə tər) *n.* a line of verse having two metrical feet. *Examples:* The hóoded bát/Twirls sóftly bý (Walter de la Mare). [< L *dimetrus* < Gk. *dimetros* < *di-* two + *metron* meter]

dimin. **1** diminuendo. **2** diminutive.

di·min·ish (di min′ish) *v.* **1** make or become smaller in size, amount, or importance; lessen; reduce: *The heat diminished as the sun went down.* **2** *Music.* reduce a minor interval by a half-tone. [blend of *diminue* (< L *diminuere* < *dis-* (intensive) + *minuere* lessen) and *minish* (< OF *menuisier* make small < VL *minutiare,* ult. < L *minutus* small)] —**di·min′ish·ing·ly,** *adv.*
☛ *Syn.* See note at **decrease.**

di·min·u·en·do (di min′yü en′dō) *n., pl.* **-dos;** *adj., adv., v. Music.* —*n.* **1** a gradual decrease of loudness. The sign in music for a diminuendo is >. **2** a passage to be played or sung with a diminuendo.
—*adj. or adv.* with a diminuendo.
—*v.* decrease gradually in force or loudness. *Abbrev.:* dim. or dimin. [< Ital. *diminuendo,* ppr. of *diminuire* diminish]

dim·i·nu·tion (dim′ə nyü′shən *or* dim′ə nü′shən) *n.* diminishing; lessening; reduction; decrease. [ME < OF < L *diminutio, -onis*]

di·min·u·tive (di min′yə tiv) *adj., n.* —*adj.* **1** small; little; tiny. **2** expressing smallness. —*n.* **1** a small person or thing. **2** *Grammar.* a word or part of a word expressing smallness, as the suffixes *-let* and *-kin.* [< Med.L *diminutivus* < L *diminutus,* pp. of *diminuere* lessen] —**di·min′u·tive·ly,** *adv.* —**di·min′u·tive·ness,** *n.*
☛ *Syn. adj.* **1.** See note at **little.**

dim·i·ty (dim′ə tē) *n., pl.* **-ties.** a thin cloth, usually of cotton, woven with heavy threads at intervals in a striped or cross-barred arrangement, used for dresses, curtains, etc. [ME < Ital. *dimito* < Gk. *dimitos* of double thread < *di-* double + *mitos* warp thread]

dim·mer (dim′ər) *n.* **1** a device for dimming an electric light: *We have a dimmer for the light in our dining room.* **2** a switch for changing the headlights of a motor vehicle to the low beam. **3** any person or thing that dims.

di·mor·phic (dī môr′fik) *adj.* occurring in two distinct forms: *Some aquatic plants have dimorphic leaves; the floating leaves are different from the lower submerged leaves.*

di·mor·phism (dī môr′fiz əm) *n.* **1** the occurrence within one type, species, etc. of two distinct forms or two distinct types of individual. **2** the property of certain substances of crystallizing in two distinct forms.

di·mor·phous (dī môr′fəs) *adj.* **1** of a chemical compound, crystallizing in two distinct forms. **2** dimorphic.

dim·out (dim′out′) *n.* a lessening or concealing of light at night.

dim·ple (dim′pəl) *n., v.* **-pled, -pling.** —*n.* **1** a small natural hollow on the surface of a plump part of the body, such as on the cheek, the chin, or the back of the hand. **2** any small, hollow place: *A golf ball has dimples.* —*v.* **1** make dimples in: *The rain dimpled the smooth surface of the pond.* **2** have or form dimples: *Her cheeks dimple when she smiles.* [ME *dympull,* cognate with MHG *tümpfil* pool]

dim·wit (dim′wit′) *n. Informal.* a stupid person; fool or simpleton.

dim·wit·ted (dim′wit′əd) *adj. Informal.* not intelligent; stupid: *a dimwitted person.*

din (din) *n., v.* **dinned, din·ning.** —*n.* a loud, confused noise that lasts for some time.

—*v.* **1** make a din. **2** strike with a din. **3** say over and over: *He was always dinning into our ears the importance of hard work.* [OE *dynn*; cf. ON *dynr*]
► *Syn. n.* See note at **noise**.

di·nar (dē när′) *n.* **1** the basic unit of money in certain countries: in Algeria, divided into 100 centimes; in Bahrain, Iraq, Jordan, Kuwait, and the People's Republic of Yemen, divided into 1000 fils; in Libya, divided into 1000 millemes; in Tunisia, divided into 1000 millimes; in Yugoslavia, divided into 100 paras. See table at **money**. **2** a unit of money in Iran, equal to ⅟₁₀₀ of a rial. **3** a unit of money in the United Arab Emirates, equal to ⅟₁₀ of a dirham. **3** a coin worth one dinar. **5** any of various gold coins used in ancient Arab countries. [< Arabic or Persian < LGk. *denarion* < L *denarius*]

dine (dīn) *v.* **dined, din·ing. 1** eat dinner. **2** give a dinner to or for. **dine out,** eat dinner away from home. [ME < OF *disner* < VL *disjejunare* to breakfast < *dis* apart (cessation) + *jejunium* fast²]

din·er (dī′nər) *n.* **1** a person who is eating dinner. **2** dining car. **3** a restaurant shaped like such a car. **4** a small eating place, usually near a main highway.

di·nette (dī net′) *n.* a small dining room.

ding (ding) *v., n.* —*v.* **1** make a sound like a bell; ring continuously. **2** *Informal.* say over and over. —*n.* the sound made by a bell. [imitative]

ding–a–ling (ding′ə ling′) *n. Slang.* fool; nitwit; oaf.

ding·bat (ding′bat′) *n. Slang.* **1** a stupid, silly, or crazy person. **2** any thing, gadget, or device; dingus. [origin uncertain]

ding–dong (ding′dong′) *n., adj.* —*n.* **1** the sound made by a bell or anything like a bell with alternating strokes; any persistent or monotonous ringing. **2** a jingle; rhyme in verse or song. —*adj.* **1** ringing with alternating strokes. **2** *Informal.* in which each side has the advantage in turns; closely contested: *a ding-dong contest, a ding-dong race.* [imitative]

din·ghy (ding′gē *or* ding′ē) *n., pl.* **-ghies. 1** a small rowboat. **2** a small boat used as a tender or lifeboat by a large boat. **3** a small sailboat. [< Hind. *dingi*]

din·gle (ding′gəl) *n.* a small, deep, shady valley. [origin uncertain]

din·go (ding′gō) *n., pl.* **-goes.** a wolflike wild dog (*Canis dingo*) of Australia. [< native Australian name]

din·gus (ding′əs) *n. Slang.* a thing, gadget, or device of which the name is unknown, unfamiliar, or forgotten. [< Du. *dinges* < *ding* thing, object]

din·gy (din′jē) *adj.* **-gi·er, -gi·est.** dirty-looking; not bright and fresh; dull. [origin uncertain] —**din′gi·ly,** *adv.* —**din′gi·ness,** *n.*

dining car a railway car in which meals are served.

dining room a room in which dinner and other meals are served.

dink·ey (dingk′ē) *n., pl.* **-eys.** *Informal.* a small locomotive, used for pulling freight cars around in a railway yard, for hauling logs, etc. [< *dinky*]

dink·y (dingk′ē) *adj.* **dink·i·er, dink·i·est.** *Slang.* small; insignificant; cute. [< Scottish or N. English dial. *dink* trim + *-y*]

din·ner (din′ər) *n.* **1** one of the three main meals of the day, especially the largest meal. Some people have dinner at noon; others have a lunch at noon and dinner in the evening. **2** a formal social event including dinner: *They're having a dinner to celebrate their parents' wedding anniversary.* **3** the food served at dinner. **4** a packaged, prepared meal, designed for quick and convenient preparation: *a TV dinner.* [ME < OF *disner* dine; infinitive used as noun] —**din′ner·less,** *adj.*

dinner jacket tuxedo (def. 1).

din·ner·time (din′ər tīm′) *n.* the time at which dinner is eaten.

din·ner·ware (din′ər wer′) *n.* plates, serving dishes, etc. for serving dinner.

di·no·saur (dī′nə sôr′ *or* din′ə sôr′) *n.* any of a group of extinct reptiles constituting two separate orders, the reptilelike Saurischia and the birdlike Ornithischia, which dominated the earth during the Mesozoic era. Some of the later dinosaurs were gigantic, the largest land animals that have ever lived on earth. [< NL *dinosaurus* < Gk. *deinos* terrible + *sauros* lizard]

di·no·sau·ri·an (dī′nə sô′rē ən *or* din′ə sô′rē ən) *adj., n.* —*adj.* of or like a dinosaur. —*n.* dinosaur.

dint (dint) *n., v.* —*n.* **1** a hollow made by the force of a blow or by pressure; dent. **by dint of,** by the force of; by means of: *By dint of hard work the job was completed on schedule.* —*v.* **1** make a dent in. **2** become dented. [OE *dynt*; cf. ON *dyntr*]

di·oc·e·san (dī os′ə sən *or* dī′ə sē′sən) *adj., n.* —*adj.* of or having to do with a diocese. —*n.* a bishop of a diocese.

di·o·cese (dī′ə sis *or* dī′ə sēs′) *n.* the district over which a bishop has authority. [ME < OF *diocise* < L < Gk. *dioikēsis* province, diocese < *oikeein* inhabit]

di·ode (dī′ōd) *n.* **1** an electronic device or component consisting of a semiconductor and two attached electrodes, used especially as a rectifier, converting alternating current to direct current. Also called **semiconductor diode. 2** a simple electron tube having only two electrodes (an anode and a cathode),formerly widely used as a rectifier but now largely replaced by the semiconductor diode. [< *di-²* + electrode. 20c.]

di·oe·cious (dī ē′shəs) *adj. Botany.* having male and female flowers in separate plants. Also, **diecious.** [< NL *dioecia,* genus name < Gk. *di-* double + *oikos* house]

Di·o·nys·i·a (dī′ə nish′ē ə *or* dī′ə nis′ē ə) *n.pl.* a set of festivals in honor of the Greek god Dionysus.

Di·o·nys·i·ac (dī′ə nis′ē ak′) *adj.* Dionysian.

Di·o·ny·sian (dī′ə nish′ən *or* dī′ə nis′ē ən) *adj.* **1** of or having to do with Dionysus. **2** highly exuberant; frenzied.

Di·o·ny·sus (dī′ə nī′səs) *n. Greek mythology.* the god of wine, corresponding to the Roman god Bacchus.

di·o·ram·a (dī′ə ram′ə) *n.* **1** a picture that is usually looked at through a small opening. It is lighted in such a way as to be very realistic. **2** a scene to be viewed through a window-like opening, showing a painted background and a foreground occupied by sculptured figures (life-size or smaller) of animals, people, etc. and appropriate accessory objects. [< F < Gk. *dia-* through + *horama* sight]

di·o·rite (dī′ə rīt′) *n.* a coarse-grained igneous rock consisting essentially of hornblende and feldspar. [< F *diorite* < Gk. *diorizein* distinguish (< *dia-* through + *orizein* mark a boundary) + F *-ite* ite¹]

Di·os·cu·ri (dī′əs kyür′ī *or* dī′əs kyü′rē) *n.pl.* the twins Castor and Pollux. [< Gk. *Dioskouroi* < *Dios,* gen. of *Zeus* Zeus + *kouros* boy, son]

di·ox·ide (dī ok′sīd *or* -ok′sid) *n. Chemistry.* an oxide having two atoms of oxygen per molecule.

di·ox·in (dī ok′sən) *n.* any of a family of 75 aromatic hydrocarbons, some of which are highly toxic, that are produced as industrial by-products in the manufacture of chlorinated phenols and are also believed to be formed through combustion; especially, one such hydrocarbon, the most toxic manmade chemical. Dioxins, known chemically as chlorinated dibenzo-*p*-dioxins, have the general formula $C_{12}H_nCl_{8-n}O_2$; the most toxic form is 2,3,7,8-tetrachlorodibenzo-*p*-dioxin.

dip (dip) *v.* **dipped** *or* **dipt, dip·ping;** *n.* —*v.* **1** put under water or any liquid and lift quickly out again: *Mary dipped her hand into the pool.* **2** go under water and come quickly out again. **3** dye by dipping in a liquid. **4** wash or clean by dipping in a liquid. **5** immerse in a solution for plating or galvanizing. **6** make (a candle) by putting a wick into hot tallow or wax. **7** take up in the hollow of the hand or with a pail, pan, or other container: *to dip up water from a well, to dip up a sample of wheat.* **8** put (one's hand, a spoon, etc.) into to take out something. **9** lower and raise again quickly: *The ship's flag was dipped as a salute.* **10** sink or drop down: *The bird dipped in its flight.* **11** slope downward:*The road dips.* **12** of an aircraft, make a short, sudden dive to gain momentum for a climb. **13** read or look at for a short time (*used with* **into**): *to dip into a magazine while waiting.* **14** inquire into superficially; dabble (*used with* **into**): *to dip into the arts for a time.* —*n.* **1** a dipping of any kind, especially a plunge into and out of a tub of water, the ocean, etc. **2** a liquid in which to dip something: *sheep dip.* **3** a candle made by dipping. **4** that which is taken out or up by dipping. **5** a creamy mixture of foods eaten by dipping into it with a cracker, piece of bread, etc.: *a cheese dip.* **6** a sudden drop. **7** the degree of slope down. **8** a sinking down and out of sight; setting: *the dip of the sun.* **9** the angular distance of the visible horizon below the horizontal plane through the observer's eye. **10** the downward inclination of the magnetic needle at any particular place; the angle which the direction of the needle makes with the horizontal. **11** *Slang.* pickpocket. [OE *dyppan.* Cognate with DEEP.]
► *Syn. v.* **1. Dip, plunge, immerse** = put into a liquid. **Dip** emphasizes taking right out again after putting or lowering partly in or wholly under: *I dipped my handkerchief in the cool water.* **Plunge** emphasizes throwing or putting completely under, suddenly or with force: *I plunged the vegetables into boiling water.* **Immerse** emphasizes keeping completely under long enough to get thoroughly soaked: *I immersed my clothes in the soapy water.*

Dip. Ed. Diploma in Education.

diph·the·ri·a (dif thēr′ē ə *or* dip thēr′ē ə) *n.* an acute, infectious disease of the throat, usually accompanied by a high fever and by the formation of membranes that hinder breathing. [< F *diphthérie* < Gk. *diphthera* hide, leather; with reference to the tough membrane developed on the affected parts]

diph·the·ri·al (dif thēr′ē əl *or* dip thēr′ē əl) *adj.* having to do with diphtheria; diphtheritic.

diph·the·rit·ic (dif′thə rit′ik *or* dip′thə rit′ik) *adj.* **1** of diphtheria; like diphtheria. **2** suffering from diphtheria.

diph·thong (dif′thong *or* dip′thong) *n.* **1** *Phonetics.* a vowel sound made up of two identifiable vowel sounds in immediate sequence and pronounced in one syllable, as *ou* in *house, oi* in *noise.* **2** two vowel letters representing a single vowel sound, properly called a digraph, as *ea* in *eat.* **3** several letters joined together in printing, such as *ffi, æ,* and *œ,* properly called a ligature. [< F *diphthongue* < LL < Gk. *diphthongos* < *di-* double + *phthongos* sound]
☛ *Spelling, Pronun.* Sometimes a **diphthong** is represented by only one letter, as *i* in *ice* or *u* in *abuse.* The commonest English diphthongs are: ī (ä + i), oi (ō + i), ou (ä + ů), and yü (i + ü) or (y + ü).

diph·thon·gal (dif thong′gəl *or* dip thong′gəl) *adj.* of or like a diphthong.

diph·thong·ise (dif′thong īz′ *or* dip′thong īz′) *v.* **-ised, -is·ing.** See **diphthongize.**

diph·thong·ize (dif′thong īz′ *or* dip′thong īz′) *v.* **-ized, iz·ing.** **1** change (a vowel or vowels) into a diphthong. **2** become a diphthong.

dip·loid (dip′loid) *adj., n.* —*adj.* **1** double or twofold. **2** designating a nucleus, cell, or organism having paired homologous chromosomes (twice the haploid number of chromosomes). —*n.* a diploid nucleus, cell, or organism. Compare **haploid.** [< Gk. *diploos* double + E *-oid,* or taken from G. 20c. Cf. HAPLOID]

di·plo·ma (də plō′mə) *n., pl.* **-mas** *or* **-ma·ta** (-mə tə). **1** a certificate given by a school, college, or university to its graduating students. **2** any certificate that bestows certain rights, privileges, honors, etc. [< L *diplōma* paper folded double, ult. < *diploos* double]

di·plo·ma·cy (də plō′mə sē) *n., pl.* **-cies.** **1** the management of relations between nations. The making of treaties, international agreements, etc. is an important part of diplomacy. **2** skill in managing such relations. **3** skill in dealing with others; tact: *Our son showed diplomacy in being very helpful at home the day he wanted to use the car.* [< F *diplomatie* < *diplomate* diplomat]

dip·lo·mat (dip′lə mat′) *n.* **1** a person employed in diplomacy, especially a representative of a nation who is located in a foreign country with the duty of looking after the interests of his own nation in the foreign country. **2** a person who is skilful in dealing with others; a tactful person. [back-formation < F *diplomatique.* See DIPLOMATIC.]

dip·lo·mat·ic (dip′lə mat′ik) *adj.* **1** of or having to do with the management of relations between nations or with the people conducting such relations: *diplomatic immunity. Ambassadors and high commissioners are the highest-ranking members of the diplomatic service.* **2** having or showing skill in dealing with others; tactful: *a diplomatic policeman. He gave a diplomatic answer to avoid hurting his friend's feelings.* [< NL *diplomaticus,* F *diplomatique* < Gk. *diplōma, -atos.* See DIPLOMA.]

dip·lo·mat·i·cal·ly (dip′lə mat′ik lē) *adv.* in a diplomatic manner; with diplomacy.

diplomatic corps all of the ambassadors, ministers, etc. of foreign nations at the capital of a country.

di·plo·ma·tist (de plō′mə tist) *n.* diplomat.

di·plo·pi·a (di plō′pē ə) *n.* a visual disorder or defect in which single objects are seen in duplicate; double vision. [< NL < *diplo-* double + Gk. *ōps eye*]

di·plop·ic (di plop′ik *or* di plō′pik) *adj.* of or having to do with diplopia.

di·po·lar (dī pō′lər) *adj.* of, having to do with, or being a dipole.

di·pole (dī′pōl′) *n.* **1** two opposite, equal electric charges or magnetic poles separated by a small distance. **2** a molecule in which the centres of positive and negative charge are separated. **3** a radio or television antenna consisting of a straight metal rod divided at the centre point, with the connecting wire fixed at this point.

dip·per (dip′ər) *n.* **1** a long-handled utensil for dipping liquids, similar to a ladle but having a larger, deeper, usually flat-bottomed, cup. **2** any of a genus (*Cinclus*) of diving birds that feed on insects, etc. in fast-flowing streams. The American dipper (*C. mexicanus*) is a fairly small, grey bird found around western mountain streams from Alaska and the Yukon south to Panama. **3 Dipper,** *Astronomy.* See **Big Dipper** and **Little Dipper.** **4** any person or thing that dips.

dipping needle a magnetic needle balanced to swing vertically and indicate by its dip the direction of the earth's magnetic field.

dip·py (dip′ē) *adj.* **-pi·er, -pi·est.** *Slang.* **1** foolish; half-witted. **2** light-headed; giddy; intoxicated.

dip·so·ma·ni·a (dip′sə mā′nē ə) *n.* an abnormal, uncontrollable craving for alcoholic liquor. [< NL < Gk. *dipsa* thirst + *mania* mania]

dip·so·ma·ni·ac (dip′sə mā′nē ak′) *n.* a person who has dipsomania.

hat, āge, fär; let, ēqual, tèrm; it, īce
hot, ōpen, ôrder; oil, out; cup, pût, rüle,
əbove, takən, pencəl, lemən, circəs
ch, child; ng, long; sh, ship
th, thin; ᴛʜ, then; zh, measure

dip·stick (dip′stik′) *n.* a rod for measuring the level of liquid in a container, such as the oil in the crankcase of a car.

dip·sy-do *or* **dip·sy-doo** (dip′sē dü′) *n. Slang.* **1** *Baseball.* a curved ball that is hard to hit. **2** tricky or complicated manoeuvring: *the dipsy-do of a magician.*

dip·sy-doo·dle (dip′sē dü′dəl) *n., v.* **-dled, -dling.** *Slang.* —*n.* **1** *Baseball.* **a** a dipsy-do. **b** a pitcher who is expert at throwing a dipsy-do. **2** a deceptive person; tricky thing. —*v.* deceive; trick.

dipt (dipt) *v.* a pt. and a pp. of **dip.**

dip·ter·an (dip′tə rən) *n., adj.* —*n.* any dipterous insect. —*adj.* dipterous.

dip·ter·ous (dip′tər əs) *adj.* of, having to do with, or belonging to a large order (Diptera) of insects characterized by a single pair of wings and sucking or piercing mouthparts. Members of this order are also called **two-winged flies** and include houseflies, mosquitoes, and midges. [< NL *dipterus* two-winged < Gk. *dipteros* < *di-* two + *pteron* wing]

dip·tych (dip′tik) *n.* **1** an ancient writing tablet consisting of two pieces of wood or ivory hinged together along one side, like a book, and having the inner surfaces waxed for writing on with a stylus. **2** a pair of paintings or carvings on two panels hinged together. **3** anything folded so as to have two matching parts. [< LL *diptycha,* neut. pl. < Gk. *diptychos* folded double < *di-* twice + *ptychē* fold]

dire (dīr) *adj.* **dir·er, dir·est.** **1** causing great fear or suffering; terrible: *a dire flood, a dire enemy.* **2** desperate; urgent; extreme: *dire poverty. They were in dire distress.* [< L *dirus*] —**dire′ly,** *adv.* —**dire′ness,** *n.*
☛ *Hom.* dyer.

di·rect (di rekt′ *or* dī rekt′) *v., adj., adv.* —*v.* **1** manage; control; guide: *The teacher directs the work of the pupils.* **2** plan, guide, and rehearse the staging of a play, opera, motion picture, television or radio program, etc. See **director** (def. 3). **3** order; command: *The captain directed his men to advance.* **4** tell or show the way; give information about where to go, what to do, etc.: *Can you direct me to the railway station?* **5** point (to); aim (at): *We should direct our efforts to a useful end.* **6** put the address on (a letter, package, etc.). **7** address (words, etc.) to a person: *to direct a request to the king.* **8** point, aim, or project (something) in a particular direction or course: *The firefighter directed his hose at the flames.*
—*adj.* **1** proceeding in a straight line; without a stop or turn; straight: *a direct route.* **2** in an unbroken line of descent: *a direct descendant of Queen Victoria.* **3** immediate: *He took direct charge of the library.* **4** without anyone or anything in between; by oneself or itself; not through others: *a direct tax.* **5** straightforward; frank; plain; truthful: *a direct answer. He made a direct denial of the charge of cheating.* **6** exact; absolute: *the direct opposite.*
—*adv.* directly. [< L *directus,* pp. of *dirigere* set straight < *dis-* apart + *regere* guide] —**di·rect′ing·ly,** *adv.* —**di·rect′ness,** *n.*
☛ *Syn. v.* **1.** See note at **manage.** *adj.* **1. Direct, immediate** = proceeding from one to another without a break. **Direct** = going straight from one to another in an unbroken line, though there may be many steps between: *Overwork and too much strain were the direct cause of his death.* **Immediate** = going from one thing to the next, without anything between: *A heart attack was the immediate cause of his death.*
☛ *Usage.* **Direct address.** The name or descriptive term by which one addresses a person or persons: *My friends, I wish you would forget this night. It's all right, Mrs. Williams, for you to come in now.* As these examples show, the term denoting the person or persons addressed is set off from the rest of the sentence by a comma, or, if it is in the middle of the sentence, by two commas.

direct current a steady electric current that flows in one direction. *Abbrev.:* DC, D.C., or d.c.

direct discourse discourse in which the exact words of a speaker are quoted. *Example: "I'll think it over," he replied.* compare **indirect discourse.**

di·rec·tion (di rek′shən *or* dī rek′shən) *n.* **1** guidance; management; control: *The school is under the direction of a good principal.* **2** an order; command. **3** a knowing or telling what to do, how to do, where to go, etc.; instruction: *Can you give me directions how to reach Montreal?* **4** the address on a letter or package. **5** the course taken by a moving body, such as a ball or a bullet. **6** any way in which one may face or point. **7** a line of action, tendency, etc.: *The town shows improvement in many directions.* **8** *Music.* a word, phrase, or sign indicating the tempo or style in which a score or part of a score should be played.

☛ *Syn.* **7. Direction, trend, tendency** = line or course of action. **Direction** applies to the line followed in the course of progress or an aim guiding the course of action: *The crime investigation has taken a new direction.* **Trend** applies particularly to a general direction of custom or preference: *The trend is toward fewer required subjects in school.* **Tendency** applies to natural movement in a certain direction or an inclination to act in a definite direction: *The tendency is toward higher taxes.*

di·rec·tion·al (di rek′shən əl *or* dī rek′shən əl) *adj.* **1** of or having to do with direction in space. **2** *Radio.* fitted for determining the direction from which signals come, or for sending signals in one direction only. **3** having to do with direction: *a directional tendency, directional signals.*

direction finder a receiving device, usually having a loop aerial, by which the direction of incoming radio signals may be determined.

di·rec·tive (di rek′tiv *or* dī rek′tiv) *n., adj.* —*n.* an order or instruction as to procedure. —*adj.* directing. —**di·rec′tive·ly,** *adv.* —**di·rec′tive·ness,** *n.*

di·rect·ly (di rekt′lē *or* dī rekt′lē) *adv.* **1** in a direct line or manner; straight. **2** exactly; absolutely: *directly opposite.* **3** immediately; at once.

direct object *Grammar.* a term for a word showing the person or thing undergoing the action expressed by the verb. In "The car struck me," *me* is the direct object.

Di·rec·toire (dē rek twär′) *n., adj.* —*n.* the Directory. —*adj.* **1** of the time of the Directory. **2** of or resembling the ornate styles of the Directory period: *a Directoire table, Directoire dresses.*

di·rec·tor (di rek′tər *or* dī rek′tər) *n.* **1** a person who leads or controls; manager: *the director of a private school, the director of a building restoration project.* **2** one of a group of persons chosen to direct the overall affairs of a company or institution: *She is on the board of directors of a large corporation.* **3** a person who plans, guides, and rehearses the staging of a play, opera, motion picture, etc. **4** *Music.* a person who leads a choir, orchestra, etc.; conductor.

☛ *Usage.* **Director** (def. 3), **producer.** Usually, the **producer** initiates a show and controls the business side of the production, while the **director** has overall responsibility for the creative side. The **producer** is sometimes called an *impresario.*

di·rec·tor·ate (di rek′tər it *or* dī rek′tər it) *n.* **1** the position of a director. **2** a group of directors.

di·rec·to·ri·al (di rek′tô′rē əl *or* dī′rek tô′rē əl) *adj.* having to do with a director or directorate.

di·rec·tor·ship (di rek′tər ship′ *or* dī rek′tər ship′) *n.* the position or term of office of a director.

di·rec·to·ry (di rek′tə rē *or* dī rek′tə rē) *n., pl.* **-ries;** *adj.* —*n.* **1** a list of names and addresses: *A telephone book is one kind of directory.* **2** a book of rules or instructions. **3** a group of directors; directorate. **4 Directory,** a group of five men that governed France 1795-1799. —*adj.* directing; advisory: *legislation of a directory character.*

direct question a question quoted directly. *Example:* She asked, *"When did they arrive?"* Compare **indirect question.**

direct tax a tax demanded of the persons who must pay it. Income taxes, property taxes, and succession duties are direct taxes. The federal sales tax is an indirect tax.

dire·ful (dīr′fəl) *adj.* dire; dreadful; terrible. —**dire′ful·ly,** *adv.* —**dire′ful·ness,** *n.*

dirge (dėrj) *n.* **1** a song or hymn of lamentation for a person's death, especially one that is part of a funeral rite. **2** any slow, sad, solemn song, tune, or poem. [contraction of L *dirige* direct (imperative of *dirigere*), first word in office for the dead]

dir·ham (də ram′) *n.* **1** the basic unit of money in Morocco, divided into 100 centimes. **2** the basic unit of money in the United Arab Emirates, divided into 10 dinar and 1000 fils. See table at **money.** **3** a coin or note worth one dirham. [< Arabic *dirham* < L < Gk. *drachmē*]

dir·i·gi·bil·i·ty (dir′ə jə bil′ə tē) *n.* the fact or quality of being dirigible.

dir·i·gi·ble (dir′ə jə bəl *or* di rij′ə bəl) *n., adj.* —*n.* a kind of aircraft having a long, gas-filled hull that keeps it up in the air and a steering and propelling mechanism underneath the hull; airship. Some dirigibles have a rigid hull; in others the hull is non-rigid. —*adj.* capable of being steered. [< L *dirigere* direct]

dirk (dėrk) *n., v.* —*n.* dagger. —*v.* stab with a dirk. [origin unknown]

dirn·dl (dėrn′dəl) *n.* **1** an Alpine peasant girl's costume consisting of a blouse, a tight bodice, and a full, bright-colored skirt, gathered at the waist. **2** a dress imitating such a costume. **3** a skirt of this type. [< South G dial. *Dirndl* girl, dim. of *Dirne* maid]

dirt (dėrt) *n.* **1** mud, dust, earth, or anything of this nature. Dirt soils whatever it gets on. **2** loose earth; soil. **3** lewdness of speech or thought. **4** nastiness, meanness, or corruption. **5** *Informal.* anything worthless or contemptible: *She had treated them like dirt.* **6** malicious gossip: *He delighted in spreading all the latest dirt.* **7** *Mining.* the earth, gravel, or other material from which gold is separated by washing.

eat dirt, *Informal.* submit to a humiliating experience, such as making an apology or taking back something one has said. [ME *drit* < ON *drit* excrement] —**dirt′less,** *adj.*

dirt bike a motorcycle that is designed for riding over rough ground and that cannot be licensed for use on roads.

dirt–cheap (dėrt′chēp′) *adj.* very cheap.

dirt farmer *Informal.* a person who does his own farming.

dirt·y (dėr′tē) *adj.* **dirt·i·er, dirt·i·est;** *v.* **dirt·ied, dirt·y·ing.** —*adj.* **1** soiled by dirt; unclean. **2** that makes dirty; soiling: *a dirty job.* **3** unpleasant; disagreeable: *to hire someone to do the dirty work.* **4** not clear or pure in color; clouded: *a dirty red.* **5** low; mean; vile: *a dirty trick.* **6** not decent; lewd or obscene: *a dirty joke.* **7** stormy; windy: *dirty weather.* **8** causing a great amount of radio-active fallout: *a dirty bomb.* —*v.* **1** make dirty; soil. **2** become dirty. —**dirt′i·ness,** *n.*

☛ *Syn. adj.* **1. Dirty, filthy, foul** = unclean. **Dirty** = soiled in any way: *Children playing in mud get dirty.* **Filthy,** often expressing a disgusted attitude toward a person or thing, emphasizes the idea of being too dirty: *In some cities and towns the streets are filthy.* **Foul,** expressing a strong reaction of disgust, suggests being filled or covered with filth or something unhealthy, impure, or rotten: *The water in the swamp is foul.*

dirty linen private or intimate matters that are slightly shameful or reprehensible, causing embarrassment if made public.

wash (one's) **dirty linen in public,** make a public spectacle of family quarrels, etc.

dirty pool conduct or an action that is mean, dishonest, or unfair.

Dirty Thirties *or* **dirty thirties** *Historical.* the drought years of the 1930's, which coincided with the Great Depression. [from the dust storms resulting from the prairie drought]

Dis (dis) *n.* **1** *Roman mythology.* the god of the lower world, corresponding to the Greek god Pluto. **2** the lower world; Hades.

dis-¹ *prefix.* **1** the opposite of, as in *discontent.* **2** do the reverse of, as in *disentangle.* **3** apart; away, as in *dispel.* **4** not, as in *dishonest.* **5** completely (intensive), as in *disembowel.* Also, **di-,** before *b, d, l, m, n, r, s, v,* and sometimes before *g* and *j;* **dif-** before *f.* [< L]

dis-² a form of **di-¹** before *s,* as in *dissyllable.*

dis·a·bil·i·ty (dis′ə bil′ə tē) *n., pl.* **-ties. 1** the condition of being disabled: *an accident resulting in permanent disability.* **2** something that disables: *Paralysis is a physical disability.* **3** *Law.* something that disqualifies: *Her relationship to the accused was a disability that disqualified her from serving on the jury at his trial.*

dis·a·ble (dis ā′bəl) *v.* **-bled, -bling. 1** deprive of ability or power; make useless; cripple. **2** disqualify legally. —**dis·a′ble·ment,** *n.*

☛ *Syn.* **1.** See note at **cripple.**

dis·a·bled (dis ā′bəld) *adj.* deprived of ability or power; crippled.

dis·a·buse (dis′ə byüz′) *v.* **-bused, -bus·ing.** free from deception or error: *Education should disabuse people of prejudice.*

dis·ac·cord (dis′ə kôrd′) *v., n.* —*v.* disagree; be out of harmony. —*n.* disagreement; lack of harmony.

dis·ad·van·tage (dis′əd van′tij) *n.* **1** a lack of advantage; unfavorable condition: *The deaf child was at a disadvantage in school.* **2** harm; loss: *The candidate's enemies spread rumors to his disadvantage.*

dis·ad·van·taged (dis′əd van′tijd) *adj.* **1** suffering from severe economic or social disadvantage. **2** (*noml.*) **the disadvantaged,** *pl.* all those who are disadvantaged.

dis·ad·van·ta·geous (dis ad′vən tā′jəs) *adj.* causing disadvantage; unfavorable. —**dis·ad′van·ta′geous·ly,** *adv.* —**dis·ad′van·ta′geous·ness,** *n.*

dis·af·fect·ed (dis′ə fek′tid) *adj.* **1** unfriendly; discontented. **2** no longer loyal; disloyal: *a disaffected Communist.*

dis·af·fec·tion (dis′ə fek′shən) *n.* **1** unfriendliness; discontent: *Lack of food and supplies caused disaffection among the soldiers.* **2** disloyalty; desertion: *The government party was seriously weakened by the disaffection of many of its members.*

dis·af·fil·i·ate (dis′ə fil′ē āt′) *v.* **-at·ed, -at·ing.** end an affiliation; dissociate. —**dis·af·fil′i·a′tion,** *n.*

dis·a·gree (dis′ə grē′) *v.* **-greed, -gree·ing. 1** fail to agree; differ: *The witness disagreed with the lawyer about the time of the accident.* **2** quarrel; dispute. **3** have a bad effect; be harmful: *Strawberries disagree with him.*

dis·a·gree·a·ble (dis′ə grē′ə bəl) *adj.* **1** not to one's liking;

unpleasant. 2 bad-tempered; cross. —**dis′a·gree′a·ble·ness**, *n.*
—**dis′a·gree′a·bly**, *adv.*

dis·a·gree·ment (dis′ə grē′mənt) *n.* **1** a failure to agree; difference of opinion. **2** a quarrel or dispute. **3** a difference; unlikeness: *There is a striking disagreement between the two species.*

dis·al·low (dis′ə lou′) *v.* **1** refuse to allow; deny the truth or value of. **2** *Law.* reject: *The request for a new trial was disallowed.* **3** *Cdn.* of the Federal Government, nullify an act of a provincial legislature.

dis·al·low·ance (dis′ə lou′əns) *n.* **1** a disallowing: *The trial proceeded after the disallowance of the Crown Attorney's request.* **2** *Cdn.* the power of the Federal Government to annul provincial legislation. **3** *Cdn.* an act of the Federal Government exercising this power.

dis·ap·pear (dis′ə pēr′) *v.* **1** pass from sight. **2** pass from existence; be lost. —**dis′ap·pear′er**, *n.*
☛ *Syn.* **1. Disappear, vanish, fade** = pass from sight. **Disappear** is the general word, meaning pass out of sight, whether slowly or quickly, gradually or suddenly: *He disappeared into the night.* **Vanish** = disappear without a trace, usually suddenly, often in some strange or mysterious way: *The stranger vanished from the town.* **Fade** = disappear slowly: *The ship faded into the fog.*

dis·ap·pear·ance (dis′ə pēr′əns) *n.* the act of disappearing.

dis·ap·point (dis′ə point′) *v.* **1** fail to satisfy or please; leave (one) wanting or expecting something. **2** fail to keep a promise to (someone). **3** keep from happening; oppose and defeat. —**dis′ap·point′er**, *n.*

dis·ap·point·ment (dis′ə point′mənt) *n.* **1** the state of being or feeling disappointed. **2** a person or thing that causes disappointment. **3** the act or fact of disappointing.

dis·ap·pro·ba·tion (dis′ap rə bā′shən) *n.* disapproval.

dis·ap·prov·al (dis′ə prüv′əl) *n.* **1** an opinion or feeling against; an expression of an opinion against; dislike. **2** a refusal to consent; rejection.

dis·ap·prove (dis′ə prüv′) *v.* **-proved, -prov·ing. 1** have or express an opinion against. **2** show dislike (*of*): *The boy disapproved of going to school in the summer.* **3** refuse consent to; reject: *The judge disapproved the verdict.* —**dis′ap·prov′ing·ly**, *adv.*

dis·arm (dis ärm′) *v.* **1** take weapons away from: *The police captured the bandits and disarmed them.* **2** stop having armed forces; reduce or limit the size of the armed forces. **3** remove suspicion from; make friendly; calm the anger of: *The speaker's frankness disarmed the angry mob, and they soon began to cheer him.* **4** make harmless: *The soldiers disarmed the big bomb.* —**dis·arm′er**, *n.* —**dis·arm′ing·ly**, *adv.*

dis·ar·ma·ment (dis är′mə mənt) *n.* **1** the act of disarming. **2** the reduction or limitation of armed forces and their equipment.

dis·ar·range (dis′ə rānj′) *v.* **-ranged, -rang·ing.** disturb the arrangement of; put out of order: *The wind disarranged her hair.* —**dis·ar·range′ment**, *n.* —**dis·ar·rang′er**, *n.*

dis·ar·ray (dis′ə rā′) *n., v.* —*n.* **1** a disorder; confusion. **2** a disorder of clothing. —*v.* **1** put into disorder or confusion. **2** *Archaic.* undress; strip.

dis·as·sem·ble (dis′ə sem′bəl) *v.* **-bled, -bling.** take apart.

dis·as·so·ci·ate (dis′ə sō′shē āt′) *v.* **-at·ed, -at·ing.** dissociate.

dis·as·ter (də zas′tər) *n.* an event that causes much suffering or loss; great misfortune: *A destructive fire, flood, earthquake, or shipwreck is a disaster.* [< F *désastre* < Ital. *disastro* (lack of a lucky star) < *dis-* without + *astrum* star < Gk. *astron*]
☛ *Syn.* **Disaster, calamity, catastrophe** = a great misfortune. **Disaster** applies to an event that happens suddenly or unexpectedly and causes much loss and suffering: *The lack of rain for so many weeks was a disaster for the farmers.* **Calamity** applies to a disaster that causes intense suffering and grief, often to a great number: *The flooding of the river last year was a calamity.* **Catastrophe** suggests a disaster that is final and complete, causing loss that can never be made up: *A nuclear war would be a catastrophe.*

disaster area 1 an area that has suffered a disaster. **2** an area that, having suffered some severe disaster, becomes entitled to special government assistance: *The flooded section of the province was designated a disaster area.*

dis·as·trous (di zas′trəs) *adj.* bringing disaster; causing great danger, suffering, loss, pain, or sorrow. —**dis·as′trous·ly**, *adv.*

dis·a·vow (dis′ə vou′) *v.* deny that one knows about, approves of, or is responsible for; disclaim: *The prisoner disavowed the confession bearing his signature.*

dis·a·vow·al (dis′ə vou′əl) *v.* a disavowing; denial of knowledge, approval, or responsibility.

dis·band (dis band′) *v.* **1** dismiss from service: *Most of the army was disbanded after the war.* **2** break ranks; become scattered. —**dis·band′ment**, *n.*

dis·bar (dis bär′) *v.* **-barred, -bar·ring.** deprive (a lawyer) of the right to practise his profession. —**dis·bar′ment**, *n.*

hat, āge, fär; let, ēqual, tèrm; it, īce
hot, ōpen, ôrder; oil, out; cup, pút, rüle,
above, takən, pencəl, lemən, circəs
ch, child; ng, long; sh, ship
th, thin; ŦH, then; zh, measure

dis·be·lief (dis′bi lēf′) *n.* a lack of belief; refusal to believe.
☛ *Syn.* See note at **unbelief.**

dis·be·lieve (dis′bi lēv′) *v.* **-lieved, -liev·ing.** have no belief in. —**dis′be·liev′er**, *n.*

dis·bur·den (dis bėr′dən) *v.* relieve of a burden: *The boy disburdened his mind to his brother by confessing what he had done.*

dis·burse (dis bėrs′) *v.* **-bursed, -burs·ing.** pay out; expend. [MF < OF *desbourser* < *des-* away from + *bourse* purse < LL *bursa* < Gk. *byrsa* leather, wineskin] —**dis·burs′er**, *n.*
☛ *Syn.* See note at **spend.**

dis·burse·ment (dis bėrs′mənt) *n.* **1** the act of paying out: *Our treasurer attends to the disbursement of funds.* **2** the money paid out; expenditure.

disc (disk) *n., v.* —*n.* **1** a phonograph record. **2** any of the round, concave blades of a disc harrow. **3** disc harrow. **4** See **disk.** —*v.* cultivate with a disc harrow. Also, **disk.**

disc. **1** discount. **2** discovered.

dis·card (*v.* dis kärd′; *n.* dis′kärd) *v., n.* —*v.* **1** give up as useless or worn out; throw aside. **2** *Card games.* **a** get rid of (useless or unwanted playing cards) by throwing them aside or playing them. **b** play (a card) that is neither a trump nor of the suit led. **c** throw out an unwanted card.
—*n.* **1** the act of throwing aside as useless. **2** something thrown aside as useless or not wanted: *That old book is a discard from the library.* **3** *Card games.* the unwanted cards thrown aside; a card played as useless. [< *dis-¹* + *card¹*] —**dis·card′er**, *n.*

dis·cern (di sėrn′ *or* di zėrn′) *v.* perceive; see clearly; distinguish; recognize. [ME < OF *discerner* < L *discernere* < *dis-* off + *cernere* separate] —**dis·cern′er**, *n.*

dis·cern·i·ble (di sėr′nə bəl *or* di zėr′nə bəl) *adj.* capable of being discerned. —**dis·cern′i·bly**, *adv.*

dis·cern·ing (di sėr′ning *or* di zėr′ning) *adj.* shrewd; acute; discriminating. —**dis·cern′ing·ly**, *adv.*

dis·cern·ment (di sėrn′mənt *or* di zėrn′mənt) *n.* **1** keenness in perceiving and understanding; good judgment; shrewdness. **2** the act of discerning.
☛ *Syn.* **1.** See note at **insight.**

dis·charge (*v.* dis chärj′; *n.* dis chärj *or* dis′chärj) *v.* **-charged, -charg·ing;** *n.* —*v.* **1** unload (a ship); unload (cargo) from a ship; unload. **2** fire; shoot: *to discharge a gun.* **3** release; let go; dismiss: *to discharge a patient from a hospital, to discharge a committee.* **4** dismiss from a job; fire: *He was discharged for incompetence.* **5** give off; let out: *The wound was still discharging pus.* **6** come or pour forth: *The river discharged into a bay.* **7** rid of an electric charge; withdraw electricity from. **8** pay; settle: *to discharge a debt.* **9** release from an obligation; exempt: *to discharge a debtor from his debts.* **10** perform; carry out: *to discharge one's duty.* **11** *Law.* cancel or set aside (a court order or an obligation). **12** remove or bleach (a dye or color) from a textile, cloth, etc.
—*n.* **1** an unloading. **2** a firing off of a gun, a blast, etc.: *The noise of the discharge could be heard for blocks.* **3** a release; the act of letting go; a dismissing: *the discharge of a convict from prison.* **4** a piece of writing that shows a person's release or dismissal; certificate of release: *Members of the armed services got discharges when the war ended.* **5** a giving off; a letting out: *His father explained that lightning is a discharge of electricity from the clouds.* **6** something given off or let out: *the watery discharge from a sore.* **7** the rate of flow: *The discharge from the pipe is 45 cubic decimetres per second.* **8** the transference of electricity between two charged bodies when placed in contact or near each other. **9** payment. **10** carrying out; performance: *A public official should be honest in the discharge of his duties.* [< *dis-¹* + *charge*] —**dis·charg′er**, *n.*
☛ *Syn. v.* **10.** See note at **perform.**

disc harrow a harrow that turns and loosens soil by means of one or more rows of revolving saucer-shaped blades set at an angle.

dis·ci·ple (də sī′pəl) *n.* **1** a person who believes in and helps to spread the ideas and teachings of another; follower. **2** one of the followers of Jesus, especially one of the twelve Apostles. **3 Disciple,** a member of the Disciples of Christ. [ME < OF < L *discipulus* pupil (*discere* learn)]
☛ *Syn.* **1.** See note at **follower.**

dis·ci·ple·ship (di sī′pəl ship′) *n.* 1 the state of being a disciple. 2 the time during which one is a disciple.

Disciples of Christ a religious sect founded in U.S. in 1809, that rejects all creeds and seeks to unite Christians on the basis of the New Testament alone.

dis·ci·plin·a·ble (dis′ə plin ə bəl) *adj.* 1 that can be disciplined. 2 deserving discipline.

dis·ci·pli·nar·i·an (dis′ə plə ner′ē ən) *n., adj.* —*n.* a person who enforces discipline or who believes in strict discipline. —*adj.* disciplinary.

dis·ci·pli·nar·y (dis′ə plə ner′ē) *adj.* 1 of or having to do with discipline. 2 for discipline; intended to improve discipline: *disciplinary measures.*

dis·ci·pline (dis′ə plin) *n., v.* —**plined, -plin·ing.** —*n.* 1 training, especially of the mind or character. 2 the training effect of experience, misfortune, etc. 3 a trained condition of order and obedience. 4 order among school pupils, members of the armed forces, or members of any group. 5 a particular system of rules for conduct. 6 the methods or rules for regulating the conduct of members in a church. 7 the control exercised over members of a church. 8 punishment; chastisement. 9 a branch of instruction or education; a field of study: *the discipline of science.* —*v.* 1 train; bring to a condition of order and obedience; bring under control: *A good officer must know how to discipline men.* 2 punish: *The rebellious convicts were severely disciplined.* [ME < OF < L *disciplina* < *discipulus.* See DISCIPLE.] —**dis′ci·plin·er,** *n.*

disc jockey *Informal.* a person who chooses, plays, and introduces popular recorded music for a radio program, dance or other social functoin, etc. Also, **disk jockey.**

dis·claim (dis klām′) *v.* 1 refuse to recognize as one's own; deny connection with: *The motorist disclaimed responsibility for the accident.* 2 give up all claim to: *She disclaimed any share in the invention.*

dis·claim·er (dis klām′ər) *n.* 1 denial or repudiation. 2 a written statement of denial or repudiation.

dis·close (dis klōz′) *v.* —**closed, -clos·ing.** 1 open to view; uncover. 2 make known; reveal. —**dis·clos′er,** *n.*
☛ *Syn.* 2. See note at **reveal.**

dis·clo·sure (dis klō′zhər) *n.* 1 the act of disclosing. 2 the thing disclosed.

dis·co (dis′kō) *n., v.* —*n.* 1 discothèque. 2 the style of music or dancing characteristic of discothèques. 3 (*adj.*) of, having to do with, or characteristic of discothèques or their styles of music or dancing. —*v.* go to or dance at a discothèque.

dis·cog·ra·pher (dis kog′rə fər) *n.* a person who compiles discographies.

dis·cog·ra·phy (dis kog′rə fē) *n.* 1 a list of phonograph records, classified according to performer, musical category, date of release, etc. 2 the history or study of phonograph records.

dis·coid (dis′koid) *adj., n.* —*adj.* 1 like a disk in shape. 2 *Botany.* of a composite flower head, composed of only disk flowers. —*n.* a disklike object.

dis·col·or or **dis·col·our** (dis kul′ər) *v.* 1 change or spoil the color of; stain: *Smoke had discolored the new paint work.* 2 become changed in color.

dis·col·or·a·tion or **dis·col·our·a·tion** (dis kul′ər ā′shən) *n.* 1 discoloring or being discolored. 2 a discolored spot: *There was a slight discoloration at the bottom of the curtain.*

dis·com·bob·u·late (dis′kəm bob′yə lāt′) *v.* —**lat·ed, -lat·ing.** *Informal.* disconcert; confuse. —**dis′com·bob′u·la′tion,** *n.*

dis·com·fit (dis kum′fit) *v.* 1 overthrow completely; defeat; rout. 2 defeat the plans or hopes of; frustrate. 3 embarrass greatly; confuse; disconcert. [ME < OF *desconfit,* pp. of *desconfire* < *des-* away + *confire* make, accomplish < L *conficere*] —**dis·com′fit·er,** *n.*

dis·com·fi·ture (dis kum′fi chər) *n.* 1 a complete overthrow; defeat; rout. 2 the defeat of plans or hopes; frustration. 3 confusion.

dis·com·fort (dis kum′fərt) *n., v.* —*n.* 1 a lack of comfort; a feeling of uneasiness: *He felt considerable discomfort after the operation.* 2 a feeling of embarrassment, confusion, etc.: *Her discomfort increased as her guilt became more and more evident.* 3 something that causes discomfort. —*v.* make uncomfortable or uneasy.

dis·com·pose (dis′kəm pōz′) *v.* —**posed, -pos·ing.** disturb the self-possession of; make uneasy; bring into disorder.

dis·com·po·sure (dis′kəm pō′zhər) *n.* the state of being disturbed; uneasiness; embarrassment.

dis·con·cert (dis′kən sèrt′) *v.* 1 disturb the self-possession of; embarrass greatly; confuse: *The policeman was disconcerted at finding that he had arrested the wrong man.* 2 upset; disorder: *The chairman's plans were disconcerted by the late arrival of the speaker.* —**dis′con·cert′ing·ly,** *adv.*
☛ *Syn.* 1. See note at **confuse.**

dis·con·cert·ed (dis′kən sèr′tid) *adj.* disturbed; confused. —**dis′con·cert′ed·ly,** *adv.* —**dis′con·cert′ed·ness,** *n.*

dis·con·nect (dis′kə nekt′) *v.* undo or break the connection of; unfasten; separate: *He disconnected the electric fan by pulling out the plug.*

dis·con·nect·ed (dis′kə nek′tid) *adj.* 1 not connected; separate. 2 without order or connection; incoherent; broken: *The injured man could give only a disconnected account of the accident.* —**dis′con·nect′ed·ly,** *adv.* —**dis′con·nect′ed·ness,** *n.*

dis·con·nec·tion (dis′kə nek′shən) *n.* 1 the act of disconnecting. 2 the state of being disconnected; separation.

dis·con·nex·ion (dis′kə nek′shən) *Esp.Brit.* See **disconnection.**

dis·con·so·late (dis kon′sə lit) *adj.* without hope; forlorn; unhappy; cheerless. [ME < Med.L *disconsolatus* < L *dis-* not + *consolatus,* pp. of *consolari* < *com-* together + *solari* soothe] —**dis·con′so·late·ly,** *adv.* —**dis·con′so·late·ness,** *n.*
☛ *Syn.* See note at **desolate.**

dis·con·tent (dis′kən tent′) *n., adj., v.* —*n.* lack of contentment; restlessness or dissatisfaction. —*adj.* discontented. —*v.* make discontented.

dis·con·tent·ed (dis′kən ten′tid) *adj.* not contented; not satisfied; displeased and restless; disliking what one has and wanting something different: *She was discontented with life in the country.* —**dis′con·tent′ed·ly,** *adv.* —**dis′con·tent′ed·ness,** *n.*

dis·con·tent·ment (dis′kən tent′mənt) *n.* discontent.

dis·con·tin·u·ance (dis′kən tin′yü əns) *n.* stopping or being stopped.

dis·con·tin·u·a·tion (dis′kən tin′yü ā′shən) *n.* 1 a breaking off; stopping; ceasing. 2 a break; interruption.

dis·con·tin·ue (dis′kən tin′yü) *v.* —**tin·ued, -tin·u·ing.** 1 cause to cease; put an end or stop to: *The morning train has been discontinued. After the patient got well, the doctor discontinued his visits.* 2 cease from; cease to take, use, etc. 3 *Law.* terminate (a lawsuit) at the request of the plaintiff or by his failure to continue it. —**dis′con·tin′u·er,** *n.*

dis·con·ti·nu·i·ty (dis′kon tə nyü′ə tē *or* -kon tə nü′ə tē) *n.* lack of connection and unity: *The discontinuity of the plot made the novel clumsy and hard to understand.*

dis·con·tin·u·ous (dis′kən tin′yü əs) *adj.* not continuous; broken, interrupted. —**dis′con·tin′u·ous·ly,** *adv.*

dis·co·phile (dis′kə fīl′) *n.* a connoisseur and collector of phonograph records.

dis·cord (dis′kôrd) *n.* 1 a difference of opinion; unfriendly relations; a disagreement. 2 *Music.* a a lack of harmony in tones sounded at the same time. b an inharmonious combination of tones. 3 harsh, clashing sounds. [ME < OF *discord* < *discorder* < L *discordare* < *discors, -cordis* discordant < *dis-* apart + *cor, cordis* heart]

dis·cord·ance (dis kôr′dəns) *n.* 1 a discord of sounds. 2 disagreement.

dis·cord·an·cy (dis kôr′dən sē) *n.* discordance.

dis·cord·ant (dis kôr′dənt) *adj.* 1 not in harmony: *a discordant note in music.* 2 not in agreement; not fitting together: *Many discordant views were expressed.* 3 harsh; clashing: *The sound of some automobile horns is discordant.* —**dis·cord′ant·ly,** *adv.*

disc·o·thèque (dis′kə tek′) *n.* a type of night club where one may listen and dance to music on records. [< F; originally, record library]

dis·count (*v.* dis′kount *or* dis kount′; *n.* dis′kount) *v., n.* —*v.* 1 deduct (a certain percentage) of the amount or cost: *The store discounts 3 percent on all bills when due.* 2 allow for exaggeration, prejudice, or inaccuracy in; believe only part of. 3 make less effective by anticipation: *The price of the stock fell before its dividend was reduced, for the reduction had already been discounted.* 4 buy, sell, or lend money on (a note, bill of exchange, etc.), deducting a certain percentage to allow for unpaid interest. 5 lend money, deducting the interest in advance. 6 sell goods at a discount. —*n.* 1 a deduction from the amount or cost: *During the sale the dealer allowed a 10 percent discount on all cash purchases.* 2 (*adj.*) having or referring to a price less than the current average retail price: *discount merchandise, discount prices.* 3 a percentage charged for buying, selling, or lending money on (a note, bill of exchange, etc.). 4 the interest deducted in advance. 5 the act of discounting.

at a discount, a at less than the regular price; below par. **b** easy to get because not in demand.
[< MF *desconter* < *des-* away + *conter* count < L *computare*]
—**dis′count·a·ble**, *adj.* —**dis′count·er**, *n.*

dis·coun·te·nance (dis koun′tə nəns) *v.* -**nanced, -nanc·ing.**
1 refuse to approve; discourage: *This school discountenances secret societies.* **2** abash; disconcert.

discount house 1 discount store. **2** *Esp.Brit.* a financial firm which trades in discounted rates, loans, etc.

discount rate the percentage charged for discounting notes.

discount store a retail store that sells merchandise for less than the current average retail price, making its profit from a big sales volume with low overhead.

dis·cour·age (dis kėr′ij) *v.* -**aged, -ag·ing. 1** take away the courage of; lessen the hope or confidence of: *Repeated failures discouraged him.* **2** try to prevent by disapproving; frown upon. **3** prevent or hinder through fear, loss of incentive, etc.: *Lack of recognition discouraged him from writing more novels.* **4** make unattractive; make to seem not worthwhile: *The chill of winter soon discouraged our picnics.* [ME < OF *descoragier* < *des-* away + *corage*. See COURAGE.] —**dis·cour′ag·er**, *n.* —**dis·cour′ag·ing·ly**, *adv.*

dis·cour·age·ment (dis kėr′ij mənt) *n.* **1** the state of being or feeling discouraged. **2** the thing that discourages. **3** the act of discouraging.

dis·course (*n.* dis′kôrs; *v.* dis kôrs′) *n., v.* -**coursed, -cours·ing.**
—*n.* **1** a formal speech or writing: *Lectures and sermons are discourses.* **2** a conversation; talk. —*v.* **1** speak or write formally. **2** converse; talk. [< F *discours* < Med.L < L *discursus* < *dis-* in different directions + *currere* run] —**dis·cours′er**, *n.*

dis·cour·te·ous (dis kėr′tē əs) *adj.* not courteous; rude; impolite. —**dis·cour′te·ous·ly**, *adv.* —**dis·cour′te·ous·ness**, *n.*

dis·cour·te·sy (dis kėr′tə sē) *n., pl.* -**sies. 1** lack of courtesy; rudeness; impoliteness. **2** a rude or impolite act.

dis·cov·er (dis kuv′ər) *v.* **1** see or learn of for the first time; find out. **2** *Archaic.* make known; reveal. [ME < OF *descovrir* < *des-* away + *covrir* cover < L *cooperire*] —**dis·cov′er·a·ble**, *adj.*
—**dis·cov′er·er**, *n.*

dis·cov·er·y (dis kuv′ər ē *or* dis kuv′rē) *n., pl.* -**er·ies. 1** the act of discovering. **2** the thing discovered. **3** a person whose special talent has just been discovered, especially an actor, writer, athlete, etc.

dis·cred·it (dis kred′it) *v., n.* —*v.* **1** destroy trust in; show to be unworthy of belief or trust: *to discredit a witness. Science has discredited the theory that the earth is flat.* **2** refuse to believe; give no credit to: *I see no reason to discredit his statement.* **3** damage the reputation of; disgrace.
—*n.* **1** reason for disbelief; doubt; distrust: *The new evidence throws discredit on her testimony.* **2** loss of good name or standing: *His conduct brought discredit on his firm.* **3** a person or thing that causes loss of good name or standing; disgrace: *Her behavior was a discredit to the school.*

dis·cred·it·a·ble (dis kred′ə tə bəl) *adj.* bringing discredit.
—**dis·cred′it·a·bly**, *adv.*

dis·creet (dis krēt′) *adj.* **1** prudent and tactful in speech or behavior; restrained: *a discreet servant. A lawyer must be discreet and not violate the confidence of a client.* **2** showing prudence and tact; polite: *The salesman maintained a discreet distance while they discussed their finances. Her criticism was so discreet that he was not offended.* **3** not lavish or ostentatious; modest: *discreet elegance.* [ME < OF *discret* < Med.L < L *discretus* separated, pp. of *discernere*. Doublet of DISCRETE. See DISCERN.] —**dis·creet′ly**, *adv.*
—**dis·creet′ness**, *n.*
☛ *Hom.* discrete.

dis·crep·an·cy (dis krep′ən sē) *n., pl.* -**cies. 1** lack of consistency; difference; disagreement. **2** an example of inconsistency: *The lawsuit was lost because of discrepancies in the statements of the witnesses.*
☛ *Syn.* **1**. See note at **difference.**

dis·crep·ant (dis krep′ənt) *adj.* differing; disagreeing; different; inconsistent. [< L *discrepans, -antis,* ppr. of *discrepare* < *dis-* differently + *crepare* sound] —**dis·crep′ant·ly**, *adv.*

dis·crete (dis krēt′) *adj.* **1** separate; distinct. **2** consisting of distinct parts. [ME < L *discretus,* separated, pp. of *discernere.* Doublet of DISCREET. See DISCERN.] —**dis·crete′ly**, *adv.*
—**dis·crete′ness**, *n.*
☛ *Hom.* discreet.

dis·cre·tion (dis kresh′ən) *n.* **1** the freedom to judge or choose: *Making final plans was left to the president's discretion.* **2** the quality of being discreet; good judgment; carefulness in speech or action; wise caution.

dis·cre·tion·ar·y (dis kresh′ən er′ē) *adj.* with freedom to decide or choose; left to one's own judgment.

hat, āge, fär; let, ēqual, tėrm; it, īce
hot, ōpen, ôrder; oil, out; cup, pút, rüle,
ə above, takən, pencəl, lemən, circəs
ch, child; ng, long; sh, ship
th, thin; ᴛʜ, then; zh, measure

dis·crim·i·nate (*v.* dis krim′ə nāt′; *adj.* dis krim′ə nit) *v.*
-**nat·ed, -nat·ing. 1** note or see a difference; make a distinction (*between*): *It is often difficult to discriminate between a mere exaggeration and a deliberate falsehood.* **2** make a distinction: *The law ought not to discriminate against any race, creed, or color.*
3 see the difference in or between; distinguish with the mind: *The study of literature helps a person discriminate good writing from poor writing.* [< L *discriminare* < *discrimen* separation < *discernere.* See DISCERN.] —**dis·crim′i·nate·ly**, *adv.*
—**dis·crim′i·na′tor**, *n.*
☛ *Syn. v.* **1, 3.** See note at **distinguish.**

dis·crim·i·nat·ing (dis krim′ə nāt′ing) *adj.* **1** having or showing the ability to discriminate well: *a discriminating judgment. A discriminating buyer will be able to see that this fabric is inferior.*
2 that discriminates: *The discriminating mark of measles is a rash on the skin.* **3** *Business.* differential. —**dis·crim′i·nat′ing·ly**, *adv.*

dis·crim·i·na·tion (dis krim′ə nā′shən) *n.* **1** the act of making or recognizing differences and distinctions. **2** the ability to make fine distinctions: *Her discrimination in such matters is well-known.* **3** the act or practice of making or showing a difference based on prejudice: *He was happy to work for a firm in which there was no discrimination.*

dis·crim·i·na·tive (dis krim′ə nə tiv *or* dis krim′ə nā′tiv) *adj.*
1 that distinguishes; discriminating. **2** discriminatory; biassed: *a discriminative tax.*

dis·crim·i·na·to·ry (dis krim′ə nə tô′ rē) *adj.* marked by or showing partiality or prejudice; biassed: *discriminatory laws.*

dis·crown (dis kroun′) *v.* deprive of royal power; depose.

dis·cur·sive (dis kėr′siv) *adj.* wandering or shifting from one subject to another; rambling: *His carefully planned speech was not discursive, but developed one topic.* —**dis·cur′sive·ly**, *adv.*
—**dis·cur′sive·ness**, *n.*

dis·cus (dis′kəs) *n., pl.* -**cus·es** *or* -**ci** (-kī *or* -kē). **1** a heavy, circular plate of stone or metal, used in athletic games as a test of skill and strength in throwing. **2** the act of throwing the discus. [< L < Gk. *diskos* quoit. Doublet of DAIS, DESK, DISH, and DISK.]

dis·cuss (dis kus′) *v.* **1** talk about together, bringing in various points of view; talk over informally. **2** explain in detail; expound in speech or writing: *Her new book discusses the future of the publishing industry in Canada.* [ME < L *discussus,* pp. of *discutere* < *dis-* apart + *quatere* shake] —**dis·cuss′er**, *n.*
☛ *Syn.* **Discuss, argue, debate** = talk something over with others. **Discuss** emphasizes considering all sides of a question: *We discussed the best road to take.* **Argue** suggests taking one side and bringing forward facts and reasons for it and against the others: *I argued for taking the new highway.* **Debate** suggests more formal arguing, often publicly, between clearly drawn up sides: *The Oxford students debated against two Canadian students in Toronto last week.*

dis·cus·sant (dis kus′ənt) *n.* a person who takes part in a panel discussion, symposium, etc.

dis·cus·sion (dis kush′ən) *n.* **1** talking about together; going over the reasons for and against; the act of discussing things informally. **2** a formal, detailed presentation of a topic in speech or writing; discourse: *He concluded his talk with a discussion of the social implications of a guaranteed annual wage.*

dis·dain (dis dān′) *v., n.* —*v.* look down on; consider beneath oneself; scorn: *He took a taxi, disdaining to go by bus.* —*n.* contempt; scorn. [ME < OF *desdeignier* < *des-* away + *deignier* deign < L *dignari*]
☛ *Syn. n.* See note at **scorn.**

dis·dain·ful (dis dān′fəl) *adj.* feeling or showing disdain.
—**dis·dain′ful·ly**, *adv.* —**dis·dain′ful·ness**, *n.*

dis·ease (də zēz′) *n.* **1** a condition in which an organ, system, or part does not function properly; sickness; illness: *People, animals, and plants are all liable to suffer from disease.* **2** any particular illness: *Chicken pox is an infectious disease.* **3** a disordered or bad condition of mind, morals, public affairs, etc. [ME < OF *desaise* < *des-* away + *aise* ease, opportunity < VL *adjacens* neighbourhood < L *adjacens* adjacent] —**dis·ease′ful**, *adj.*

dis·eased (də zēzd′) *adj.* **1** having a disease; showing signs of sickness or illness; being diseased: *a diseased hand.* **2** disordered: *a diseased mind.*

dis·em·bark (dis′em bärk′) *v.* **1** go ashore from a ship or leave

an aircraft: *We disembarked at Montreal.* 2 unload from a ship or aircraft: *to disembark passengers.*

dis·em·bar·ka·tion (dis′em bär kā′shən) *n.* disembarking or being disembarked.

dis·em·bar·rass (dis′em bar′əs *or* dis′em ber′əs) *v.* 1 free from something that holds back or entangles; disengage. 2 relieve; rid. 3 free from embarrassment or uneasiness.

dis·em·bod·y (dis′em bod′ē) *v.* -**bod·ied**, -**bod·y·ing**. separate (a soul, spirit, etc.) from the body: *Ghosts are usually thought of as disembodied spirits.* —**dis′em·bod′i·ment,** *n.*

dis·em·bow·el (dis′em bou′əl) *v.* -**elled** *or* -**eled**, -**el·ling** *or* -**el·ing.** take or rip out the bowels of. —**dis′em·bow′el·ment,** *n.*

dis·en·chant (dis′en chant′) *v.* free from a magic spell or illusion. —**dis′en·chant′er,** *n.* —**dis′en·chant′ing·ly,** *adv.* —**dis′en·chant′ment,** *n.*

dis·en·cum·ber (dis′en kum′bər) *v.* free from a burden, annoyance, or trouble.

dis·en·fran·chise (dis′en fran′chīz) *v.* -**chised**, -**chis·ing.** disfranchise.

dis·en·fran·chise·ment (dis′en fran′chiz mənt) *n.* disfranchisement.

dis·en·gage (dis′en gāj′) *v.* -**gaged**, -**gag·ing.** 1 free from an engagement, pledge, obligation, etc. 2 detach; loosen: *The mother disengaged her hand from that of the sleeping child.* 3 *Military.* go away from combat or contact with (an enemy). —**dis′en·gage′ment,** *n.*

dis·en·gaged (dis′en gājd′) *adj.* 1 not busy; free from appointments. 2 released; detached.

dis·en·tan·gle (dis′en tang′gəl) *v.* -**tan·gled**, -**tan·gling.** free from tangles or complications; untangle. —**dis′en·tan′gle·ment,** *n.*

dis·en·throne (dis′en thrōn′) *v.* -**throned**, -**thron·ing.** dethrone.

dis·en·twine (dis′en twīn′) *v.* -**twined**, -**twin·ing.** disentangle.

dis·es·tab·lish (dis′es tab′lish) *v.* deprive of the character of being established; especially, withdraw state recognition or support from (a church). —**dis′es·tab′lish·ment,** *n.*

dis·es·teem (dis′es tēm′) *v. or n.* scorn; dislike.

dis·fa·vor *or* **dis·fa·vour** (dis fā′vər) *n., v.* —*n.* 1 unfavorable opinion; disapproval: *The employees looked with disfavor on any attempt to change their cafeteria.* 2 the state or condition of having lost favor or trust; being regarded with disapproval: *The ambassador was in disfavor with the government at home.* —*v.* view with disapproval; withhold favor from.

dis·fig·ure (dis fig′ər *or* -fig′yər) *v.* -**ured**, -**ur·ing.** spoil the appearance of; mar the beauty of: *Large billboards disfigured the countryside.* —**dis·fig′ur·er,** *n.*
☛ *Syn.* See note at **deface.**

dis·fig·ure·ment (dis fig′ər mənt *or* -fig′yər mənt) *n.* 1 the act of disfiguring. 2 a disfigured condition. 3 something that disfigures; a defect.

dis·fran·chise (dis fran′chīz) *v.* -**chised**, -**chis·ing.** 1 take the rights of citizenship away from. A disfranchised person cannot vote or hold office. 2 take a right or privilege from. Also, **disenfranchise.**

dis·fran·chise·ment (dis fran′chiz mənt) *n.* disfranchising or being disfranchised. Also, **disenfranchisement.**

dis·gorge (dis gôrj′) *v.* -**gorged**, -**gorg·ing.** 1 throw up (what has been swallowed); vomit forth. 2 pour forth; discharge: *Swollen streams disgorged their waters into the river.* 3 give up unwillingly: *The robbers were forced to disgorge their plunder.* [ME < OF *desgorger* < *des-* reverse of + *gorge* < LL *gurges* throat, jaws < L *gurges* abyss, whirlpool] —**dis·gorg′er,** *n.*

dis·grace (dis grās′) *n., v.* -**graced**, -**grac·ing.** —*n.* 1 a loss of respect or honor: *The boy's disgrace was deeply felt by his family.* 2 a person or thing that causes dishonor or shame: *To be put in prison is usually considered a disgrace.* 3 the state or condition of having fallen from honor and good repute: *The girl was in disgrace with her teachers and friends for having cheated on an exam.* —*v.* 1 cause to lose honor or respect; bring shame upon: *He disgraced his family by his behavior.* 2 treat with disfavor; humiliate: *The cowardly officer was disgraced for failing to do his duty.* [< F *disgrâce* < Ital. *disgrazia* < *dis-* opposite of + *grazia* grace < L *gratia*] —**dis·grac′er,** *n.*
☛ *Syn. n.* 1. **Disgrace, dishonor, ignominy** = loss of good name or respect. **Disgrace** suggests losing the respect and approval of others: *He was in disgrace after his ungentlemanly behavior.* **Dishonor** suggests losing one's honor or reputation, or having that taken from one: *For neglect of duty he was stripped of his rank with dishonor.* **Ignominy** means public disgrace or dishonor and suggests being put to shame and held in contempt: *He brought on himself the ignominy of being caught cheating in the game.*

dis·grace·ful (dis grās′fəl) *adj.* causing loss of honor or respect; shameful. —**dis·grace′ful·ly,** *adv.* —**dis·grace′ful·ness,** *n.*

dis·grun·tle (dis grun′təl) *v.* -**tled**, -**tling.** put in bad humor; dissatisfy: *a disgruntled customer.* [< *dis-¹* apart + obs. *gruntle,* frequentative of *grunt*]

dis·grun·tled (dis grun′təld) *adj.* in bad humor; discontented; disgusted; displeased. [< *dis-* + obs. *gruntle* grunt, grumble]

dis·guise (dis gīz′) *v.* -**guised**, -**guis·ing;** *n.* —*v.* 1 make changes in clothes or appearance of (someone) for concealment or for looking like someone else: *The spy disguised himself as an old man.* 2 hide what (something) really is; make (something) seem like something else: *The pirates had disguised their ship. He disguised his handwriting. He disguised his hate by a show of friendliness.* —*n.* 1 the use of a changed or unusual dress and appearance in order not to be recognized: *The criminal resorted to disguise to escape from jail.* 2 clothes, actions, etc. used to hide who one really is or to make a person look like someone else: *Woman's clothes and a wig formed his disguise.* 3 a false or misleading appearance; deception; concealment. 4 the state or condition of being disguised. [ME < OF *desguiser* < *des-* down + *guise* guise < Gmc.] —**dis·guis′ed·ly,** *adv.* —**dis·guise′ment,** *n.* —**dis·guis′er,** *n.*

dis·gust (dis gust′) *n., v.* —*n.* 1 a strong, sickening dislike; loathing: *Bad odors or tastes can arouse disgust. Many people wrote to express their disgust at the newspaper's sensational account of the murder trial.* 2 weary indignation or dissatisfaction: *His excuses for not helping out were so silly that she finally hung up in disgust.* —*v.* 1 arouse loathing in; be very offensive to. 2 cause weary indignation or dissatisfaction in. [< MF *desgoust,* n., *desgouster,* v. < *des-* apart + *goust* taste < L *gustus*] —**dis·gust′ing·ly,** *adv.*
☛ *Syn. n.* See note at **dislike.**

dis·gust·ed (dis gus′tid) *adj.* 1 filled with disgust. 2 *Informal.* fed up; tired: *She said she was disgusted with their constant quarrelling.* —**dis·gust′ed·ly,** *adv.* —**dis·gust′ed·ness,** *n.*

dis·gust·ing (dis gus′ting) *adj.* that disgusts; unpleasant; distasteful. —**dis·gust′ing·ly,** *adv.*

dish (dish) *n., v.* —*n.* 1 any vessel or container, usually shallow and flat-bottomed, used for holding or serving food. 2 **dishes,** *pl.* cups, saucers, glasses, plates, bowls, etc. together: *It's your turn to wash the dishes.* 3 the amount of food served in a dish. 4 a particular kind of food: *My favorite dish is sliced peaches and cream.* 5 something shallow and hollow like a dish. 6 *Slang.* an attractive person. 7 *Slang.* something that one really likes; a favorite thing: *That kind of music is just my dish.* —*v.* 1 put (food) into a dish ready for serving or eating (often used with **out** *or* **up**): *You may dish the dinner now.* 2 shape like a dish; make concave. 3 ruin or defeat. 4 present (facts, etc.) neatly and attractively (used with **up**): *to dish up a good argument.* 5 *Informal.* give or dispense, especially very freely or indiscriminately (used with **out**): *to dish out punishment, dishing out compliments.*
dish it out, *Slang.* abuse or punish someone physically or verbally: *He can dish it out, but he can't take it.*
[OE *disc* < L *discus* dish, discus < Gk. *diskos.* Doublet of DAIS, DESK, DISCUS, and DISK.]

dis·ha·bille (dis′ə bēl′) *n.* 1 informal, careless dress. 2 a garment or costume worn carelessly. 3 the condition of being only partly dressed. Also, **deshabille.** [< F *déshabillé,* pp. of *déshabiller* < *dés-* away + *habiller* dress]

dis·har·mo·ny (dis här′mə nē) *n., pl.* -**nies.** lack of harmony; discord.

dish·cloth (dish′kloth′) *n.* a cloth to wash dishes with.

dis·heart·en (dis här′tən) *v.* discourage; depress: *A long drought disheartens a farmer.* —**dis·heart′en·ing·ly,** *adv.* —**dis·heart′en·ment,** *n.*

di·shev·el (də shev′əl) *v.* -**elled** *or* -**eled**, -**el·ling** *or* -**el·ing.** disarrange or rumple (hair, clothing, etc.).

di·shev·elled *or* **di·shev·eled** (də shev′əld) *adj.* 1 rumpled; mussed; disordered; untidy: *a dishevelled appearance.* 2 hanging loosely or in disorder: *dishevelled hair.* [ME < OF *descheveler* < *des-* away + *chevel* hair < L *capillus*]

dish·ful (dish′fül) *n., pl.* -**fuls.** as much as a dish can hold.

dis·hon·est (dis on′ist) *adj.* 1 lacking honesty or integrity; inclined to cheat, steal, deceive, etc.: *You cannot expect a fair deal from a dishonest merchant.* 2 showing falseness or deceit: *a dishonest advertisement, a dishonest account of the accident.* 3 arranged to work or function in an unfair way: *a dishonest card game, dishonest scales.* —**dis·hon′est·ly,** *adv.*

dis·hon·es·ty (dis on′is tē) *n., pl.* -**ties.** 1 lying, cheating, or stealing; lack of honesty. 2 a dishonest act.

dis·hon·or *or* **dis·hon·our** (dis on′ər) *n., v.* —*n.* 1 a loss of honor or reputation; shame; disgrace. 2 the cause of dishonor. 3 a refusal or failure to pay a cheque, bill, etc. —*v.* 1 cause or bring dishonor to. 2 refuse or fail to pay (a cheque,

bill, etc.). —**dis·hon′or·er** or **dis·hon′our·er**, *n.*
☞ *Syn. n.* **1.** See note at **disgrace.**

dis·hon·or·a·ble or **dis·hon·our·a·ble** (dis on′ər ə bəl) *adj.*
1 causing loss of honor; shameful; disgraceful. **2** without honor.
—**dis·hon′or·a·ble·ness** or **dis·hon′our·a·ble·ness**, *n.*
—**dis·hon′or·a·bly** or **dis·hon′our·a·bly**, *adv.*

dis·hon·our (dis on′ər) See **dishonor.**

dish·pan (dish′pan′) *n.* a large pan or basin in which to wash
dishes.

dish·rag (dish′rag′) *n.* dishcloth.

dish·tow·el (dish′tou′əl) *n.* a cloth for drying dishes; tea towel.

dish·wash·er (dish′wosh′ər) *n.* **1** a machine for washing,
rinsing, and drying dishes in one continuous operation. **2** a person
who washes dishes, especially one employed by a restaurant,
hospital, etc.

dish·wa·ter (dish′wot′ər *or* -wô′tər) *n.* water in which dishes are
being or have been washed.

dis·il·lu·sion (dis′i lü′zhən) *v., n.* —*v.* free from illusion: *He
thought he could trust everyone; but soon he was disillusioned.* —*n.*
freeing or being freed from illusion.

dis·il·lu·sion·ment (dis′i lü′zhən mənt) *n.* disillusioning or
being disillusioned.

dis·in·cen·tive (dis′in sen′tiv) *n.* deterrent.

dis·in·cli·na·tion (dis in′klə nā′shən) *n.* unwillingness.

dis·in·cline (dis′in klīn′) *v.* **-clined, -clin·ing.** make or be
unwilling.

dis·in·clined (dis′in klīnd′) *adj.* unwilling.

dis·in·fect (dis′in fekt′) *v.* destroy potentially harmful
micro-organisms or on: *Surgical instruments are disinfected
before they are used.* —**dis′in·fec′tor**, *n.*

dis·in·fect·ant (dis′in fek′tənt) *n., adj.* —*n.* an agent that
disinfects, especially a chemical substance such as alcohol,
chlorine, and carbolic acid. —*adj.* that disinfects.

dis·in·fec·tion (dis′in fek′shən) *n.* the destruction of disease
germs.

dis·in·gen·u·ous (dis′in jen′yü əs) *adj.* insincere, not frank.
—**dis′in·gen′u·ous·ly**, *adv.* —**dis′in·gen′u·ous·ness**, *n.*

dis·in·her·it (dis′in her′it) *v.* prevent from inheriting; deprive of
an inheritance: *to disinherit one's children.*

dis·in·her·it·ance (dis′in her′ə təns) *n.* the act of disinheriting
or the state of being disinherited.

dis·in·te·grate (dis in′tə grāt′) *v.* **-grat·ed, -grat·ing. 1** break up;
separate into small parts or bits: *Time had caused the old books to
disintegrate into a pile of fragments and dust.* **2** *Physics.* change in
nuclear structure through bombardment by charged particles.

dis·in·te·gra·tion (dis in′tə grā′shən) *n.* **1** a breaking up;
separation into small parts or bits: *Rain and frost had caused the
gradual disintegration of the rock.* **2** *Physics.* the emission of an
alpha or beta particle by the nucleus of a radio-active element.

dis·in·te·gra·tor (dis in′tə grā′tər) *n.* **1** a person or thing that
causes disintegration. **2** a machine for disintegrating a substance.

dis·in·ter (dis′in tėr′) *v.* **-terred, -ter·ring. 1** take out of a grave
or tomb; dig up. **2** bring to light; discover and reveal.

dis·in·ter·est (dis in′trist *or* -in′tər ist) *n.* lack of interest;
indifference.

dis·in·ter·est·ed (dis in′tris tid *or* -in′tər es′tid) *adj.* not having
or showing selfish motives; not concerned with one's own interests;
impartial; fair. —**dis·in′ter·est·ed·ly**, *adv.* —**dis·in′ter·est·ed·ness**, *n.*
☞ *Usage.* **Disinterested** and **uninterested** should not be confused. **Disinterested**
= having no selfish interest or personal feelings in a matter and therefore
having no reason or desire to be anything but strictly impartial and fair: *A
judge should be disinterested.* **Uninterested** = not interested in any way, having
no concern or feelings about the matter and paying no attention: *An
uninterested boy can spoil a class.*

dis·in·ter·ment (dis′in tėr′mənt) *n.* **1** the act of disinterring or
the state of being disinterred. **2** something disinterred.

dis·join (dis join′) *v.* separate; keep from joining; prevent from
being joined.

dis·joint (dis joint′) *v.* **1** take apart at the joints: *disjoint a
chicken.* **2** break up; disconnect; put out of order: *The boy's speech
was stumbling and disjointed.* **3** put out of joint; dislocate. **4** come
apart; be put out of joint.

dis·joint·ed (dis join′tid) *adj.* **1** taken apart at the joints.
2 broken up; disconnected; incoherent. **3** out of joint.
—**dis·joint′ed·ly**, *adv.* —**dis·joint′ed·ness**, *n.*

disjoint set *Mathematics.* one of two or more sets having no
numbers in common.

dis·junc·tion (dis jungk′shən) *n.* **1** the act of disjoining or state

hat, āge, fär; let, ēqual, tėrm; it, īce
hot, ōpen, ôrder; oil, out; cup, pút, rüle,
above, takən, pencəl, lemən, circəs

ch, child; ng, long; sh, ship
th, thin; ᴛʜ, then; zh, measure

of being disjoined; a separation. **2** *Logic.* the relation between the
terms of a disjunctive proposition.

dis·junc·tive (dis jungk′tiv) *adj., n.* —*adj.* **1** causing separation;
separating. **2** *Grammar.* showing a choice or contrast between two
ideas, words, etc. *Either... or, but, yet,* etc. are disjunctive
conjunctions. *Otherwise, else,* etc. are disjunctive adverbs. **3** *Logic.*
involving alternatives. A disjunctive proposition asserts that one or
the other of two things is true but both cannot be true.
—*n.* **1** *Logic.* a statement involving alternatives. **2** *Grammar.* a
disjunctive conjunction. —**dis·junc′tive·ly**, *adv.*

disk (disk) *n., v.* —*n.* **1** a round, thin, flat object. **2** a round, flat or
apparently flat, surface: *the sun's disk.* **3** the round central part of
the flower head of most composite plants: *The daisy has a yellow
disk.* **4** *Anatomy.* any round, flat part or structure, especially the
masses of fibrous cartilage between the bodies of the vertebrae. **5** a
round, thin, flat plate coated with a magnetic substance, used for
storing data for a computer. **6** See **disc.**
—*v.* See **disc.** Also, **disc.** [< L *discus* discus < Gk. *diskos.* Doublet
of DAIS, DESK, DISCUS, and DISH.] —**disk′like′** or **disc′like′**, *adj.*
—**disk′er** or **disc′er**, *n.*

disk flower any of the tiny flowers that make up the central disk
of the flower head of a composite plant. The ox-eye daisy has
yellow disk flowers and white ray flowers. See **composite** for
picture.

disk harrow See **disc harrow.**

disk jockey See **disc jockey.**

dis·like (dis līk′) *n., v.* **-liked, -lik·ing.** —*n.* a feeling of not liking;
a feeling against. —*v.* not like; object to; having a feeling against.
☞ *Syn. n.* **Dislike, distaste, disgust** = a feeling of not liking someone or
something. **Dislike** is the general word, applying to any degree of this feeling:
Bob has a dislike for study and would rather play baseball. **Distaste** applies to a
fixed dislike for something one finds unpleasant or disagreeable: *He has a
distaste for chocolate.* **Disgust** applies to a strong dislike for something that is
disagreeable, sickening, or bad: *We feel disgust for bad odors and tastes.*

dis·lo·cate (dis′lō kāt′) *v.* **-cat·ed, -cat·ing. 1** cause one or more
of the bones of a joint to be shifted out of place: *The football player
dislocated his shoulder when he fell.* **2** put out of order; disturb;
upset: *Our plans for the picnic were dislocated by the bad weather.*
—**dis′lo·ca′tor**, *n.*

dis·lo·ca·tion (dis′lō kā′shən) *n.* the act of dislocating or the
state of being dislocated.

dis·lodge (dis loj′) *v.* **-lodged, -lodg·ing. 1** drive or force out of a
place, position, etc.: *The workman used a crowbar to dislodge a
heavy stone from the wall. Heavy gunfire dislodged the enemy from
the fort.* **2** leave a lodging place.

dis·lodg·ment (dis loj′mənt) *n.* the act of dislodging or the state
of being dislodged.

dis·loy·al (dis loi′əl) *adj.* not loyal; unfaithful: *A disloyal servant
let the thieves into the house.* —**dis·loy′al·ly**, *adv.*

dis·loy·al·ty (dis loi′əl tē) *n., pl.* **-ties. 1** lack of loyalty;
unfaithfulness: *The traitor was shot for disloyalty to his country.* **2** a
disloyal act.
☞ *Syn.* **1. Disloyalty, treachery, treason** = faithlessness. **Disloyalty** =
unfaithfulness, felt or shown, to anyone or anything to whom one owes
allegiance or is bound by promises, love, or friendship: *Refusing to defend
parents, school, or country is disloyalty.* **Treachery** = dishonest faithlessness,
and suggests some definite act of betraying trust while pretending to be loyal:
Secretly working to the detriment of a friend is treachery. **Treason** applies to
treachery to one's country, shown by doing something specifically to help the
enemy: *Deliberately broadcasting enemy propaganda to our troops is treason.*

dis·mal (diz′məl) *adj.* **1** dark; gloomy: *Damp caves or rainy days
are dismal.* **2** dreary; miserable: *Sickness often makes a person feel
dismal.* [ME *dismall* < AF *dis mal* evil days < L *dies mali*]
—**dis′mal·ly**, *adv.*

dis·man·tle (dis man′təl) *v.* **-tled, -tling. 1** strip of covering,
equipment, furniture, guns, rigging, etc.: *The warship was
dismantled before the hull was sold for scrap metal.* **2** pull down or
take apart: *We had to dismantle the bookcases to move them.* [<
MF *desmanteler* < *des-* away + *mantel* mantle < L *mantellum*]

dis·mast (dis mast′) *v.* take the mast or masts from; break down
the mast or masts of: *The storm dismasted the ship.*

dis·may (dis mā′) *n., v.* —*n.* a loss of courage because of fear of
what is about to happen. —*v.* trouble greatly; make afraid: *The
thought that she might fail the history test dismayed her.* [ME <
OF *desmaier* < VL *dismagare* deprive of strength < L *dis-*

(reverse) + Frankish **magan* have strength] —**dis·may′ing·ly,** *adv.*
☛ *Syn. n.* **Dismay, consternation** = a feeling of being unnerved or overwhelmed by the thought of what is going to happen next. **Dismay** suggests loss of ability to face or handle something frightening, baffling, or upsetting that comes as a surprise or shock: *The mother was filled with dismay when her son confessed he had robbed a store.* **Consternation** = dismay and dread so great that a person cannot think clearly or, sometimes, move: *To our consternation the child darted out in front of the speeding car.*

dis·mem·ber (dis mem′bər) *v.* **1** pull apart; cut to pieces; separate or divide into parts: *The Austro-Hungarian Empire was dismembered after the First World War.* **2** cut or tear the limbs from. —**dis·mem′ber·ment,** *n.*

dis·miss (dis mis′) *v.* **1** send away; allow to go: *At noon the teacher dismissed the class.* **2** remove from a position or office; discharge; fire: *The clerk was dismissed because he was always late for work.* **3** put out of mind; stop thinking about or considering: *Dismiss your troubles and be happy. She dismissed the magazine article with a laugh.* **4** *Law.* refuse to consider (a complaint, plea, etc.) in a court: *to dismiss a charge.* [< L *dismissus,* var. of *dimissus* < *dis-* away + *missus,* pp. of *mittere* send]

dis·miss·al (dis mis′əl) *n.* **1** the act of dismissing or the state or fact of being dismissed. **2** a written or spoken order dismissing someone.

dis·mis·sion (dis mish′ən) *n.* dismissal.

dis·mount (dis mount′) *v.* **1** get off a horse, bicycle, etc. **2** knock, throw, or otherwise remove from a horse; unhorse. **3** take (a thing) from its setting or support: *The cannon was dismounted for shipping to another fort.* **4** take apart; take to pieces. **5** deprive (troops) of horses or mounts: *The Indians dismounted the troops by stealing their horses.*

dis·o·be·di·ence (dis′ə bē′dē əns *or* dis′ə bē′dyəns) *n.* a refusal to obey; failure to obey.

dis·o·be·di·ent (dis′ə bē′dē ənt *or* dis′ə bē′dyənt) *adj.* refusing to obey; failing to obey. —**dis′o·be′di·ent·ly,** *adv.*

dis·o·bey (dis′ə bā′) *v.* fail to follow orders or rules; refuse to obey. —**dis′o·bey′er,** *n.*

dis·o·blige (dis′ə blīj′) *v.* **-bliged, -blig·ing.** **1** neglect to oblige; refuse to oblige; refuse to do a favor for. **2** give offence to.

dis·or·der (dis ôr′dər) *n., v.* —*n.* **1** a lack of order; confusion: *The room was in such disorder that it was impossible to find anything.* **2** a public disturbance; riot. **3** a sickness; disease: *a disorder of the stomach.*
—*v.* **1** destroy the order of; throw into confusion. **2** upset the functions of; cause sickness in: *Such food is likely to disorder the stomach.*

dis·or·dered (dis ôr′dərd) *adj.* **1** not in order; disturbed. **2** sick.

dis·or·der·ly (dis ôr′dər lē) *adj., adv.* —*adj.* **1** not orderly; in confusion: *The books and papers lay in a disorderly pile on the floor.* **2** causing disorder; making a disturbance; breaking rules; unruly: *a disorderly mob.* **3** *Law.* acting against public peace and order: *disorderly conduct.*
—*adv. Archaic.* in a disorderly manner. —**dis·or′der·li·ness,** *n.*

dis·or·gan·ize (dis ôr′gən īz′) *v.* **-ized, -iz·ing.** throw into confusion and disorder; upset the order and arrangement of: *Heavy snowstorms disorganized the train schedule.* —**dis·or′gan·i·za′tion,** *n.*

dis·o·ri·ent (dis ôr′ē ent′) *v.* disorientate.

dis·o·ri·en·tate (dis ôr′ē en tāt′) *v.* cause to lose sense of direction or time; mix up; disconcert: *His sudden rise to fame and fortune disorientated him at first.* —**dis·o·ri·en·ta′tion,** *n.*

dis·own (dis ōn′) *v.* refuse to recognize as one's own; cast off: *He disowned his disobedient son. The politician disowned his former views on the subject.*

dis·par·age (dis par′ij *or* dis per′ij) *v.* **-aged, -ag·ing.** **1** speak slightingly of; try to lessen the importance or value of; belittle: *The coward disparaged the hero's brave attempt to rescue the drowning child.* **2** lower the reputation of; discredit. [ME < OF *desparagier* match unequally < *des-* apart + *parage* rank, lineage < L *par* equal] —**dis·par′ag·er,** *n.* —**dis·par′ag·ing·ly,** *adv.*

dis·par·age·ment (dis par′ij mənt *or* dis per′ij mənt) *n.* **1** the act of disparaging. **2** something that lowers a thing or person in worth or importance. **3** a lessening in esteem or standing: *Say nothing that will be to Joe's disparagement.*

dis·pa·rate (dis′pə rit) *adj.* distinct in kind; essentially different; unlike. [< L *disparatus,* pp. of *disparare* < *dis-* apart + *parare* get] —**dis′pa·rate·ly,** *adv.* —**dis′pa·rate·ness,** *n.*

dis·par·i·ty (dis par′ə tē *or* dis per′ə tē) *n., pl.* **-ties.** inequality; difference: *There will be disparities in the accounts of the same event given by several people.*
☛ *Syn.* See note at **difference.**

dis·part (dis pärt′) *v.* separate; divide into parts.

dis·pas·sion (dis pash′ən) *n.* freedom from emotion or prejudice; calmness; impartiality.

dis·pas·sion·ate (dis pash′ən it) *adj.* free from emotion or prejudice; calm; impartial: *To a dispassionate observer, the drivers of both cars seemed equally at fault.* —**dis·pas′sion·ate·ly,** *adv.* —**dis·pas′sion·ate·ness,** *n.*

dis·patch *or* **des·patch** (dis pach′) *v., n.* —*v.* **1** send off to some place or for some purpose: *He dispatched a messenger to tell the general what had happened.* **2** get (something) done promptly or speedily. **3** give the death blow to; kill. **4** *Informal.* eat up. **5** dismiss; send away; get rid of: *The housewife dispatched the salesman.*
—*n.* **1** a sending off (of a letter, a messenger, etc.): *Please hurry up the dispatch of this telegram.* **2** a written message such as a news report or a report to a government by an ambassador or other official: *This dispatch has been two days on the way.* **3** promptness; speed. **4** a putting to death; killing. **5** an agency for conveying goods, etc.
mention in dispatches, *Military.* **a** commend (someone) for bravery, distinguished service, etc. in the official report of an action. **b** the fact of being commended in this way: *He was promoted twice and received three mentions in dispatches.*
[< Ital. *dispacciare* hasten or Sp. *despachar*]

dispatch box dispatch case.

dispatch case a usually flat, stiff case for carrying documents or other papers.

dis·patch·er *or* **des·patch·er** (dis pach′ər) *n.* a person who dispatches: *He is a dispatcher for a taxi company.*

dis·pel (dis pel′) *v.* **-pelled, -pel·ling.** drive away and scatter; disperse: *The captain's cheerful laugh dispelled our fears.* [< L *dispellere* < *dis-* away + *pellere* drive] —**dis·pel′ler,** *n.*
☛ *Syn.* See note at **scatter.**

dis·pen·sa·ble (dis pen′sə bəl) *adj.* **1** that may be done without; unimportant. **2** capable of being dispensed or administered. —**dis·pen′sa·ble·ness,** *n.*

dis·pen·sa·ry (dis pen′sə rē) *n., pl.* **-ries.** **1** a place where medicines and medical advice are given free or for a small charge. **2** that part of a hospital where medicines are prepared and stored.

dis·pen·sa·tion (dis′pən sā′shən) *n.* **1** the act of giving out; act of distributing: *the dispensation of charity to the poor.* **2** the thing given out or distributed: *They gave thanks for the dispensations of Providence.* **3** rule; management: *England under the dispensation of Elizabeth I.* **4** the management or ordering of the affairs of the world by Providence or Nature. **5** a religious system: *the Christian dispensation.* **6** *Roman Catholic Church.* **a** official permission to disregard a law, obligation, etc. without penalty. **b** the writing giving such permission.

dis·pen·sa·to·ry (dis pen′sə tô′rē) *n., pl.* **-ries.** **1** a book that tells how to prepare and use medicines. **2** *Archaic.* dispensary.

dis·pense (dis pens′) *v.* **-pensed, -pens·ing.** **1** give out; distribute: *The Red Cross dispensed food and clothing to the refugees.* **2** carry out; put in force; apply: *Judges and courts of law dispense justice.* **3** prepare and give out: *Druggists dispense medicines.* **4** exempt or excuse (*from*): *They were dispensed from their oath.*
dispense with, **a** get rid of; make unnecessary: *The new evaluation system dispenses with the need for oral examinations.* **b** get along without; do without: *He found he could dispense with rich food when he began to eat properly.*
[ME < OF *despenser* < L *dispensare* weigh out < *dis-* out < *pendere* weigh]
☛ *Syn.* **1.** See note at **distribute.**

dis·pens·er (dis pens′ər) *n.* **1** a device, often automatic and often coin-operated, which is made to release its contents one at a time or in measured amounts: *There are dispensers for gum, chocolate bars, coffee, sandwiches, cigarettes, paper cups, etc.* **2** a container, such as a spray bottle or aerosol can, that sprays or feeds out its contents in a convenient form and amount.

dis·peo·ple (dis pē′pəl) *v.* **-pled, -pling.** deprive of all or many people or inhabitants.

dis·per·sal (dis pėr′səl) *n.* a dispersion; the act of scattering or state of being scattered: *the dispersal of a crowd.*

dis·perse (dis pėrs′) *v.* **-persed, -pers·ing.** **1** send in different directions; scatter: *The police dispersed the rioters.* **2** go in different directions: *The crowd dispersed when the game was over.* **3** distribute; circulate: *Children went through the crowd dispersing handbills.* **4** disappear or cause to disappear; dispel; dissipate: *The swelling on his arm was dispersed by cold compresses.* **5** *Physics.* divide (white light) into its colored rays. **6** *Chemistry.* scatter (the particles of a colloid) throughout another substance or a mixture. [ME < MF *disperser* < L *dispersus,* pp. of *dispergere* < *dis-* in every direction + *spargere* scatter]
☛ *Syn.* **1.** See note at **scatter.**

dis·per·sion (dis pėr′zhən *or* dis pėr′shən) *n.* **1** dispersing or being dispersed. **2** *Physics.* **a** the separation of light into its different colors. **b** a similar separation of electromagnetic waves, etc. **3** *Chemistry.* **a** a substance that has been dispersed. **b** the system consisting of the dispersed colloidal particles and the medium in which they are dispersed.

dis·per·sive (dis pėr′siv) *adj.* dispersing; tending to disperse.

dis·pir·it (dis pir′it) *v.* depress; discourage; dishearten. —**dis·pir′it·ed·ly,** *adv.* —**dis·pir′it·ed·ness,** *n.*

dis·place (dis plās′) *v.* **-placed, -plac·ing. 1** put something else in the place of; take the place of: *The automobile has displaced the horse and buggy.* **2** remove from a position of authority. **3** put out of place; move from its usual place or position: *A floating body displaces its own weight of liquid.*

displaced person a person forced out of his own country by war, famine, political disturbance, etc. *Abbrev.:* DP *or* D.P.

dis·place·ment (dis plās′mənt) *n.* **1** displacing or being displaced. **2** the volume or mass of a fluid displaced by something floating in it; especially, the volume or mass of water displaced by a ship. **3** the volume in a pump or engine cylinder displaced by a stroke of the piston. **4** *Geology.* the distance of movement of rock or strata on one side of a fault in relation to the corresponding rock or strata on the other side.

dis·play (dis plā′) *v., n.* —*v.* **1** expose to view, especially in such a way so as to show to advantage: *Many ancient weapons are displayed in the museum.* **2** make plain or clear; show: *He displayed great tact in his handling of a delicate situation.* **3** spread out; unfold or unfurl: *to display a flag, to display a newspaper.* **4** *Electronics.* present (electronic signals) in visual form, as on a cathode-ray tube. **5** *Zoology.* of a bird, etc., make a breeding display. —*n.* **1** a planned showing of something for some special purpose; exhibit: *Our class had a display of drawings at the Exhibition.* **2** an obvious showing or revealing; making plain or clear: *a shocking display of bad temper, a display of courage.* **3** a showing off; ostentation: *Her fondness for display led her to buy showy clothes.* **4** *Printing.* the choice and arrangement of type so as to make certain words or parts prominent. **5** *Electronics.* **a** a device for presenting computerized information or electronic signals visually, such as a cathode-ray tube. **b** the information so presented. **6** *Zoology.* especially among certain birds, a pattern of movement resembling a kind of dance, performed by the males just prior to breeding. [ME < OF *despleier* < L *displicare* scatter < *dis-* apart + *plicare* fold]
☛ *Syn.* **1. Display, exhibit, evince** = show. **Display** = put out in view for others, especially the public, to look at: *The stores are displaying new spring clothes.* **Exhibit** = show as something especially worth looking at in a way that draws attention: *She exhibited her wedding presents on the table.* **Evince** = show in some way something that cannot be seen with the eyes, such as a feeling or quality: *He evinced obvious displeasure when he learned he would have to stay after school.* -n. **1.** See note at **show.**

dis·please (dis plēz′) *v.* **-pleased, -pleas·ing.** offend, annoy, or be disagreeable to: *She was displeased by their apparent lack of respect. The new furnishings displeased him.* —**dis·pleas′ing·ly,** *adv.*

dis·pleas·ure (dis plezh′ər) *n.* **1** the feeling of being displeased; annoyance or disapproval. **2** *Archaic.* discomfort; uneasiness. **3** *Archaic.* offence; injury.

dis·port (dis pôrt′) *v., n.* —*v.* amuse (oneself); sport, play: *People laughed at the clumsy bears disporting themselves in the water.* —*n. Archaic.* a pastime; amusement. [ME < OF *desporter* < *des-* away from + *porter* carry < L *portare*]

dis·pos·a·ble (dis pōz′ə bəl) *adj.* **1** capable of being disposed of. **2** at one's disposal; available.

dis·pos·al (dis pōz′əl) *n.* **1** the act or process of getting rid of something: *The city looks after the disposal of garbage.* **2** the act or process of selling or giving away to another: *She arranged for the disposal of her property in her will.* **3** a final arranging of matters; a settling of affairs: *The chairman's disposal of the difficulty satisfied everybody.* **4** the act or process of putting in a certain order or position: *The disposal of the chairs around the sides of the room left plenty of space in the middle.* **5** sale.
at (someone's) **disposal,** ready for one's use or service at any time; under one's control or management: *She put all her books at her guests' disposal. Does he have a car at his disposal?*

dis·pose (dis pōz′) *v.* **-posed, -pos·ing. 1** put in a certain order or position; arrange: *The battleships were disposed in a straight line.* **2** arrange (matters); settle (affairs); determine. **3** make ready or willing; incline: *More pay and shorter hours of work disposed him to take the new job.* **4** make liable or subject to: *Getting your feet wet disposes you to catching cold.*
dispose of, a to dispose of a lot of old papers. **b** sell or give away: *to dispose of one's property.* **c** eat or drink up: *We disposed of a whole watermelon.* **d** arranged; settle: *The club disposed of its business in an hour.*

hat, āge, fär; let, ēqual, tėrm; it, īce
hot, ōpen, ôrder; oil, out; cup, pùt, rüle,
əbove, takən, pencəl, lemən, circəs
ch, child; ng, long; sh, ship
th, thin; ŦH, then; zh, measure

[ME < OF *disposer* < *dis-* variously + *poser* place. See POSE¹.] —**dis·pos′er,** *n.*

dis·posed (dis pōzd′) *adj.* having a particular disposition or attitude: *How were they disposed toward the plan? He was a well-disposed young man—friendly and sympathetic.*
disposed to, inclined; tending: *He is always disposed to get angry at the least little thing.*

dis·po·si·tion (dis′pə zish′ən) *n.* **1** one's habitual ways of acting toward others or of thinking about things; nature: *a cheerful disposition, a selfish disposition.* **2** a tendency; inclination: *a disposition to argue.* **3** the act or process of putting in order or position; orderly arrangement: *the disposition of troops in battle.* **4** final arrangement; settlement: *the satisfactory disposition of a difficult problem.* **5** the act or process of getting rid of, giving away, selling, etc.: *the disposition of nuclear wastes. The court will look after the disposition of the property of the deceased.*
☛ *Syn.* **1. Disposition, temperament, temper** = the qualities that characterize a person as an individual. **Disposition** applies to the controlling mental or emotional quality that determines a person's natural or usual way of thinking and acting: *He has a quarrelsome disposition.* **Temperament** applies to the combined physical, emotional, and mental qualities that determine a person's whole nature: *He has an artistic temperament.* **Temper** applies to the combined natural and acquired qualities that determine the state of mind in which a person meets problems and troubles: *He is calm in temper.* **Temper** may also be applied to a more temporary state: *I found him in a good temper.*

dis·pos·sess (dis′pə zes′) *v.* **1** force to give up the possession of a house, land, etc.; oust: *The farmer was dispossessed for not paying his rent.* **2** deprive: *Fear dispossessed him of his senses.* —**dis′pos·ses′sion,** *n.* —**dis′pos·ses′sor,** *n.*

dis·praise (dis prāz′) *v.* **-praised, -prais·ing;** *n.* —*v.* express disapproval of; speak against; blame. —*n.* an expression of disapproval; blame. —**dis·prais′er,** *n.*

dis·prize (dis prīz′) *v.* **-prized, -priz·ing.** *Archaic.* disdain.

dis·proof (dis prüf′) *n.* **1** a disproving; refutation. **2** a fact, reason, etc. that disproves something.

dis·pro·por·tion (dis′prə pôr′shən) *n., v.* —*n.* a lack of proportion; lack of proper proportion; lack of symmetry. —*v.* make disproportionate.

dis·pro·por·tion·al (dis′prə pôr′shən əl) *adj.* not in proportion; disproportionate.

dis·pro·por·tion·al·ly (dis′prə pôr′shən ə lē) *adv.* without proportion; unequally.

dis·pro·por·tion·ate (dis′prə pôr′shən it) *adj.* out of proportion; lacking in proper proportion: *a disproportionate amount of time spent on details.*

dis·pro·por·tion·ate·ly (dis′prə pôr′shən it lē) *adv.* in a disproportionate degree; inadequately or excessively.

dis·prove (dis prüv′) *v.* **-proved, -prov·ing.** prove false or incorrect; refute. —**dis·prov′a·ble,** *adj.*

dis·put·a·ble (dis pyüt′ə bəl *or* dis′pyə tə bəl) *adj.* liable to be disputed; uncertain; questionable.

dis·pu·tant (dis′pyə tənt *or* dis pyüt′ənt) *n.* a person who takes part in a dispute or debate.

dis·pu·ta·tion (dis′pyə tä′shən) *n.* **1** a debate; controversy. **2** a dispute.

dis·pu·ta·tious (dis′pyə tā′shəs) *adj.* fond of disputing; inclined to argue. —**dis′pu·ta′tious·ly,** *adv.* —**dis′pu·ta′tious·ness,** *n.*

dis·put·a·tive (dis pyüt′ə tiv) *adj.* disputatious.

dis·pute (dis pyüt′) *v.* **-put·ed, -put·ing;** *n.* —*v.* **1** discuss; argue; debate. **2** quarrel. **3** disagree with (a statement); declare not true; call in question: *The insurance company disputed his claim for damages.* **4** fight against; oppose; resist: *disputing the enemy troops' advance.* **5** fight or contend for; try to win: *The brothers were disputing ownership of the house. The troops had to dispute every patch of ground as they advanced.*
—*n.* **1** an argument; debate. **2** a quarrel.
beyond dispute, a not to be disputed. **b** final; settled.
in dispute, being disputed.
[< L *disputare* examine, discuss, argue < *dis-* item by item + *putare* calculate] —**dis·put′er,** *n.*
☛ *Syn. n.* **1.** See note at **argument.**

dis·qual·i·fi·ca·tion (dis kwol′ə fə kā′shən) *n.* **1** disqualifying or being disqualified. **2** something that disqualifies.

dis·qual·i·fy (dis kwol′ə fī′) v. **-fied, -fy·ing. 1** make unfit; make unable to do something: *His injury disqualified him from playing football.* **2** declare unfit or unable to do something; deprive of a right or privilege: *He was disqualified from voting because he was in jail.* **3** *Sports, etc.* without the right to play or the right to win a competition: *The hockey team was disqualified by the referee for refusing to come out on the ice.*

dis·qui·et (dis kwī′ət) v., n. —v. make uneasy or anxious; disturb: *Rumors of a revolution disquieted the dictator.* —n. uneasiness; anxiety.

dis·qui·et·ing (dis kwī′ə ting) adj. disturbing.

dis·qui·e·tude (dis kwī′ə tyüd′ or -kwī′ə tüd′) n. uneasiness; anxiety.

dis·qui·si·tion (dis′kwə zish′ən) n. a long or formal speech or writing about a subject. [< L *disquisitio, -onis*, ult. < *dis-* (intensive) + *quaerere* seek]

dis·re·gard (dis′ri gärd′) v., n. —v. **1** pay no attention to; take no notice of: *Disregarding his clothing, he jumped into the lake to save the child.* **2** treat without proper regard or respect; slight. —n. **1** lack of attention; neglect: *a disregard for fame and fortune, disregard of traffic laws.* **2** a lack of proper regard or respect: *Her action showed a shocking disregard for the feelings of others.* —**dis·re·gard′er,** n.

dis·re·gard·ful (dis′ri gärd′fəl) adj. lacking in regard; neglectful; careless.

dis·rel·ish (dis rel′ish) v. or n. dislike.

dis·re·mem·ber (dis′ri mem′bər) v. *Informal.* fail to remember; forget.

dis·re·pair (dis′ri per′) n. a bad condition; need of repairs: *The house was in disrepair.*

dis·rep·u·ta·ble (dis rep′yə tə bəl) adj. **1** having a bad reputation; shady: *a disreputable dance hall.* **2** not respectable; dishonorable: *disreputable conduct, a disreputable politician.* **3** shabby; much worn: *a disreputable old hat.* —**dis·rep′u·ta·bly,** adv.

dis·re·pute (dis′ri pyüt′) n. disgrace; discredit; disfavor: *Many remedies formerly used are now in disrepute.*

dis·re·spect (dis′ri spekt′) n. a lack of respect; rudeness; impoliteness: *Older people disliked the boy because of his disrespect toward his parents.*

dis·re·spect·ful (dis′ri spekt′fəl) adj. rude; showing no respect; lacking in courtesy to elders or superiors. —**dis′re·spect′ful·ly,** adv. —**dis′re·spect′ful·ness,** n.

dis·robe (dis rōb′) v. **-robed, -rob·ing.** undress. —**dis·rob′er,** n.

dis·rupt (dis rupt′) v. break up; split: *A violent quarrel disrupted the meeting.* [< L *disruptus*, pp. of *disrumpere* < *dis-* apart + *rumpere* break] —**dis·rup′tion,** n.

dis·rup·tive (dis rup′tiv) adj. tending to break up; causing disruption: *a disruptive influence.*

dis·sat·is·fac·tion (dis′sat is fak′shən) n. discontent; displeasure.

dis·sat·is·fac·to·ry (dis′sat is fak′tə rē or -sat is fak′trē) adj. causing discontent; unsatisfactory.

dis·sat·is·fied (dis sat′is fīd′) adj. **1** discontented; displeased. **2** showing discontent or displeasure.

dis·sat·is·fy (dis sat′is fī′) v. **-fied, -fy·ing.** fail to satisfy; make discontented; displease.

dis·sect (dis sekt′ or dī sekt′) v. **1** cut in pieces; divide into parts. **2** cut up or separate the parts of (an animal, plant, etc.) in order to examine or study the structure. **3** examine carefully part by part; analyse: *The lawyer dissected the testimony to show where the witnesses had contradicted themselves.* [< L *dissectus*, pp. of *dissecare* < *dis-* apart + *secare* cut]

dis·sect·ed (di sek′tid or dī sek′tid) adj. cut or divided into many parts: *These plants have dissected leaves.*

dis·sec·tion (di sek′shən or dī sek′shən) n. **1** the act of separating or dividing an animal or plant into parts in order to examine or study its structure. **2** an animal, plant, etc. that has been dissected. **3** an analysis; consideration of something in detail or point by point.

dis·sec·tor (di sek′tər or dī sek′tər) n. **1** a person who dissects. **2** an instrument used in dissecting.

dis·sem·ble (di sem′bəl) v. **-bled, -bling. 1** disguise or hide (one's real feelings, thoughts, plans, etc.): *She dissembled her anger with a smile.* **2** conceal one's motives, etc.; be a hypocrite. **3** pretend; feign: *The bored listener dissembled an interest he didn't feel.* **4** pretend not to see or notice; disregard; ignore. [alteration,

after *resemble*, of obs. *dissimule* dissimulate < OF *dissimuler* < L *dissimulare*] —**dis·sem′bler,** n. —**dis·sem′bling·ly,** adv.

dis·sem·i·nate (di sem′ə nāt′) v. **-nat·ed, -nat·ing.** scatter or spread widely: *to disseminate knowledge.* [< L *disseminare* < *dis-* in every direction + *semen* seed] —**dis·sem′i·na′tion,** n. —**dis·sem′i·na′tor,** n.

dis·sen·sion (di sen′shən) n. a disputing; quarrelling; hard feelings caused by a difference in opinion: *Their political disagreement caused dissension.*

dis·sent (di sent′) v., n. —v. **1** differ in opinion; disagree: *Two of the judges dissented from the decision of the other three.* **2** refuse to conform to the rules and beliefs of an established church. —n. **1** a difference of opinion; disagreement: *Dissent among the members broke up the club meeting.* **2** a refusal to conform to the rules and beliefs of an established church: *The Puritans' dissent caused their separation from the Church of England.* [ME < L *dissentire* < *dis-* differently + *sentire* think, feel] —**dis·sent′ing·ly,** adv. ☛ *Hom.* **descent.**

dis·sent·er (di sen′tər) n. **1** a person who dissents. **2 Dissenter,** in England and Scotland, a Protestant who belongs to some church other than the state church.

dis·sen·tient (di sen′shənt) adj., n. —adj. dissenting, especially from the opinion of the majority. —n. a person who dissents.

dis·ser·ta·tion (dis′ər tā′shən) n. a formal discussion of a subject, especially a thesis submitted by a candidate for a doctoral or other higher degree; treatise. [< L *dissertatio, -onis* < *dissertare*, frequentative of *disserere* < *dis-* apart (distribution) + *serere* join words]

dis·serv·ice (dis sèr′vis or di sèr′vis) n. a bad treatment; harm; injury.

dis·sev·er (di sev′ər) v. sever; separate.

dis·si·dence (dis′ə dəns) n. disagreement; dissent.

dis·si·dent (dis′ə dənt) adj., n. —adj. disagreeing; dissenting. —n. a person who disagrees or dissents. [< L *dissidens, -entis*, ppr. of *dissidere* < *dis-* apart + *sedere* sit]

dis·sim·i·lar (dis sim′ə lər) adj. not similar; unlike; different. —**dis·sim′i·lar·ly,** adv.

dis·sim·i·lar·i·ty (dis sim′ə lar′ə tē or di sim′ə ler′ə tē) n., pl. **-ties.** lack of similarity; unlikeness; difference.

dis·sim·i·late (dis sim′ə lāt′) v. **-lated, -lating.** make or become unlike.

dis·sim·i·la·tion (di sim′ə lā′shən) n. **1** the act or process of making or becoming unlike. **2** *Biology.* the breaking down of organic substances into simpler ones; catabolism. **3** *Phonetics.* the changing of one of two similar, neighboring speech sounds so that one becomes unlike the other. *Example:* The Latin word *peregrinus* became Italian *pellegrino*, changing the first (r) to (l). See the etymologies for *peregrine* and *pilgrim*.

dis·si·mil·i·tude (dis′sə mil′ə tyüd or -sə mil′ə tüd′) n. unlikeness; difference.

dis·sim·u·late (di sim′yə lāt′) v. **-lat·ed, -lat·ing.** disguise or hide under a pretence; dissemble. [< L *dissimulare*] —**dis·sim′u·la′tor,** n.

dis·sim·u·la·tion (di sim′yə lā′shən) n. the act of dissembling; hyprocrisy; pretence; deceit.

dis·si·pate (dis′ə pāt′) v. **-pat·ed, -pat·ing. 1** spread in different directions; scatter: *The crowd soon dissipated.* **2** disappear: *The fog had dissipated by mid morning.* **3** cause to disappear; dispel: *The sun dissipated the mists.* **4** spend foolishly; waste on things of little value: *The extravagant son soon dissipated his father's fortune.* **5** indulge too much in foolish or harmful pleasures. [< L *dissipare* < *dis-* in different directions + *sipare* throw]

dis·si·pat·ed (dis′ə pāt′id) adj. **1** indulging too much in evil or foolish pleasures; dissolute: *a dissipated youth.* **2** scattered. **3** wasted.

dis·si·pa·tion (dis′ə pā′shən) n. **1** dissipating or being dissipated. **2** an amusement; diversion, especially harmful amusements. **3** too much indulgence in foolish pleasures; intemperance.

dis·so·ci·ate (di sō′shē āt′) v. **-at·ed, -at·ing. 1** break the connection or association with; separate: *When the man discovered that his companions were dishonest, he soon dissociated himself from them.* **2** *Chemistry.* separate or decompose by dissociation. [< L *dissociare* < *dis-* apart + *socius* ally]

dis·so·ci·a·tion (di sō′sē ā′shən or di sō′shē ā′shən) n. **1** the act of dissociating or state of being dissociated. **2** *Chemistry.* **a** separation of molecules of an electrolyte into constituent ions; ionization. Sodium and chlorine ions are formed by the dissociation of sodium chloride molecules in water. **b** reversible decomposition. Dissociation occurs when water is heated so that it decomposes into hydrogen and oxygen; when the temperature is lowered again, the elements recombine into water. **3** *Psychology.* the separation

of an idea or feeling from the main stream of consciousness.

dis·so·ci·a·tive (di sō′shē ə tiv *or* di sō′shē ā′tiv) *adj.* having to do with or causing dissociation.

dis·sol·u·bil·i·ty (di sol′yə bil′ə tē) *n.* the fact or quality of being dissoluble.

dis·sol·u·ble (di sol′yə bəl) *adj.* capable of being dissolved. —**dis·sol′u·ble·ness,** *n.*

dis·so·lute (dis′ə lüt′) *adj.* living an immoral life. [< L *dissolutus,* pp. of *dissolvere.* See DISSOLVE.] —**dis′so·lute·ly,** *adv.*

dis·so·lu·tion (dis′ə lü′shən) *n.* **1** a breaking up; termination: *The partners arranged for the dissolution of their partnership.* **2** the ending of an assembly, especially of a parliament prior to an election. **3** ruin; destruction. **4** death. **5** a breaking down; decomposition: *the dissolution of water by electrolysis.* **6** the act or process of changing into a liquid state. **7** the state of being liquid.

dis·solve (di zolv′) *v.* **-solved, -solv·ing;** *n.* —*v.* **1** make or become liquid, especially by putting or being put into water; form into a solution in a liquid: *Salt or sugar will dissolve in water.* **2** break up; end: *to dissolve a partnership.* **3** dismiss or end (an assembly, especially a parliament before an election). **4** fade away: *The dream dissolved when she woke up.* **5** solve; explain; clear up. **6** separate into parts; decompose. **7** *Motion pictures and television.* fade or cause to fade gradually from the screen while the succeeding scene slowly appears.
dissolved in tears, shedding many tears.
—*n. Motion pictures and television.* the gradual disappearing of the figures of a scene while those of a succeeding scene slowly take their place. [ME < L *dissolvere* < *dis-* (intensive) + *solvere* loose] —**dis·solv′a·ble,** *adj.* —**dis·solv′er,** *n.*
▶ *Syn. v.* **1.** See note at **melt.**

dis·so·nance (dis′ə nəns) *n.* **1** a combination of sounds that is not harmonious; harshness and unpleasantness of sound; discord. Compare **consonance. 2** disagreement; lack of harmony. **3** *Music.* the relationship or sound of two or more tones in a combination which is conventionally considered to be in a condition of unrest needing resolution or completion; discord.

dis·so·nant (dis′ə nənt) *adj.* **1** harsh in sound; clashing; not harmonious. **2** out of harmony with other views or persons; disagreeing: *Her dissonant views always made the meetings unpleasant.* [ME < L *dissonans, -antis,* ppr. of *dissonare* < *dis-* differently + *sonare* sound] —**dis′so·nant·ly,** *adv.*

dis·suade (di swād′) *v.* **-suad·ed, -suad·ing.** persuade not to do something (*used with* **from**): *The father dissuaded his son from leaving school.* [ME < L *dissuadere* < *dis-* against + *suadere* to urge]

dis·sua·sion (di swā′zhən) *n.* the act of dissuading.

dis·sua·sive (di swā′siv) *adj.* attempting to dissuade; tending to dissuade. —**dis·sua′sive·ly,** *adv.* —**dis·sua′sive·ness,** *n.*

dis·syl·lab·ic (dis′ə lab′ik) *adj.* disyllabic.

dis·syl·la·ble (dis′sil′ə bəl *or* di sil′ə bəl) *n.* disyllable. [< F *dissylabe* < L < Gk. *disyllabos* < *di-* two + *syllabē* syllable]

dist. **1** district. **2** distance. **3** distinguish; distinguished.

dis·taff (dis′taf) *n.* **1** a stick, split at the tip, to hold wool, flax, etc. so that it may be spun into thread. **2** the staff on a spinning wheel for holding flax. **3** woman's work or affairs. **4** the female sex; woman or women. **5** the female branch of a family. [OE *distæf* < *dis-* (akin to MLG *dise* bunch of flax on a distaff) + *stæf* staff]

distaff side the maternal side or branch of a family. Compare **spear side.**

dis·tain (dis tān′) *v. Archaic.* **1** discolor; stain. **2** dishonor; disgrace. [ME < OF *desteindre* < *des-* apart + *teindre* dye, color < L *tingere*]

dis·tal (dis′təl) *adj. Anatomy.* away from the place of attachment or origin; terminal: *Fingernails are at the distal ends of fingers.* [< *distant*]

dis·tance (dis′təns) *n., v.* **-tanced, -tanc·ing.** —*n.* **1** the space in between; the extent of separation in space: *Is the theatre within walking distance? The distance from here to town is five kilometres.* **2** a long way; far away: *The farm is situated quite a distance from the highway.* **3** a place far away: *a light in the distance.* **4** the time in between; interval. **5** *Music.* the interval or difference between two tones. **6** a lack of friendliness or familiarity; coolness of manner; reserve. **7** *Painting.* **a** the distant part of a landscape: *One sees cattle grazing in the distance.* **b** the part of a picture that represents this: *There is no distance in his paintings, which are all flat and two-dimensional.* **8** *Horse racing.* a space measured back from the winning post. In order to qualify for further heats, a horse must be within this space when the winner finishes.
go the distance, *Sports.* **a** play an entire game without substitution. **b** of a boxer, fight or last an entire match without being knocked out.
keep at a distance, refuse to be friendly or familiar with; treat with

hat, āge, fär; let, ēqual, tėrm; it, īce
hot, ōpen, ôrder; oil, out; cup, pút, rüle,
above, takən, pencəl, lemən, circəs

ch, child; ng, long; sh, ship
th, thin; ŦH, then; zh, measure

reserve: *We tried to be friendly but she kept us at a distance.*
keep (one's) distance, a remain some distance away: *The dog might be dangerous, so keep your distance.* **b** be not too friendly or familiar; be or stay aloof: *She prefers to keep her distance with her employees.*
—*v.* **1** leave far behind; do much better than. **2** *Horse racing.* beat by a distance. [ME < MF *destance* < L *distantia* < *distare.* See DISTANT.]

dis·tant (dis′tənt) *adj.* **1** far away in space: *Vancouver is distant from Quebec City. The moon is distant from the earth.* **2** away: *The town is three kilometres distant.* **3** far apart in time, relationship, likeness, etc.; not close: *A third cousin is a distant relative.* **4** not friendly: *She gave him only a distant nod.* [ME < MF < L *distans, -antis,* ppr. of *distare* < *dis-* off + *stare* stand] —**dis′tant·ly,** *adv.*
▶ *Syn.* **1, 2.** Distant, far, remote = not near. **Distant** = standing away in space, and suggests a considerable space unless the exact measure is stated: *He lives in a distant city. Kingston is 255 kilometres distant from Toronto.* **Far** = a long way off: *the far North is not so remote as it used to be.* **remote** = far removed, especially from the centre of things: *The far North is not so remote as it used to be.*

dis·taste (dis tāst′) *n.* dislike; aversion: *His distaste showed plainly on his face.*
▶ *Syn.* See note at **dislike.**

dis·taste·ful (dis tāst′fəl) *adj.* unpleasant; disagreeable; offensive. —**dis·taste′ful·ly,** *adv.* —**dis·taste′ful·ness,** *n.*

dis·tem·per[1] (dis tem′pər) *n., v.* —*n.* **1** an infectious disease of dogs and other animals, accompanied by a short, dry cough and a loss of strength. **2** any sickness of the mind or body; disorder; disease. **3** disturbance.
—*v.* make unbalanced; disturb; disorder. [ME < LL *distemperare* mix improperly < L *dis-* not + *temperare* mix in proper proportion]

dis·tem·per[2] (dis tem′pər) *n., v.* —*n.* **1** a method or process of painting in which powdered colors are mixed with glue or other sizing, used especially for painting interior walls, scenes for theatre sets, etc. Distemper is a kind of tempera. **2** the paint used in distemper painting. **3** a painting done in distemper.
—*v.* **1** mix (ingredients) to produce distemper. **2** paint with such a mixture. [< OF *destemprer* soak < LL *distemperare* mix thoroughly < L *dis-* completely + *temperare* mix]

dis·tend (dis tend′) *v.* stretch out; swell out; expand: *His cheeks distended when he blew his bugle. The pouter pigeon can distend its crop.* [< L *distendere* < *dis-* apart + *tendere* stretch]

dis·ten·si·ble (dis ten′sə bəl) *adj.* capable of being distended.

dis·ten·sion *or* **dis·ten·tion** (dis ten′shən) *n.* the act of distending or the state of being distended.

dis·tich (dis′tik) *n., pl.* **-tichs.** two lines of verse forming a stanza, and usually making complete sense; couplet. *Example:*

  Those who in quarrels interpose
  Must often wipe a bloody nose.

[< L < Gk. *distichon* < *di-* two + *stichos* line]

dis·til *or* **dis·till** (dis til′) *v.* **-tilled, -til·ling. 1** heat (a liquid or other substance) and condense the vapor given off. Distilled water is pure because the impurities in the original water do not vaporize when the water does. See **distillation** for picture. **2** obtain by distilling: *Gasoline is distilled from crude oil.* **3** extract; refine: *A jury must distil the truth from the testimony of the witnesses.* **4** give off in drops: *Flowers distil nectar.* **5** fall or let fall in drops; drip. **6** undergo distillation. [< L *distillare* < *de-* down + *stilla* drop]

dis·til·late (dis′tə lit *or* dis′tə lāt′) *n.* a distilled liquid; something obtained by distilling.

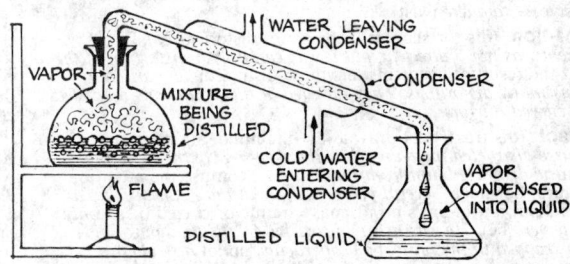

WATER LEAVING CONDENSER
CONDENSER
VAPOR
MIXTURE BEING DISTILLED
COLD WATER ENTERING CONDENSER
FLAME
VAPOR CONDENSED INTO LIQUID
DISTILLED LIQUID

dis·til·la·tion (dis′tə lā′shən) *n.* **1** the act or process of distilling.

2 something distilled; extract; essence: *Kerosene is a distillation of petroleum.*

dis·tilled (dis tild′) *adj.* obtained by distilling.

dis·till·er (dis til′ər) *n.* a person or thing that distils, especially a person or company that makes whisky, rum, brandy, etc.

dis·till·er·y (dis til′ər ē *or* dis til′rē) *n., pl.* **-er·ies.** a place where distilling is done, especially of whisky, rum, brandy, etc.

dis·tinct (dis tingkt′) *adj.* **1** not the same; separate: *There are two distinct questions to be considered.* **2** different in quality or kind: *Mice are distinct from rats.* **3** clear; plain: *distinct writing.* **4** unmistakable; definite; decided: *a distinct lisp, a distinct advantage.* [< L *distinctus,* pp. of *distinguere.* See DISTINGUISH.] **—dis·tinct′ness,** *n.*

dis·tinc·tion (dis tingk′shən) *n.* **1** the act of making a difference; distinguishing from others: *He treated all alike, without distinction.* **2** the quality or state of being distinguishable; difference: *What is the distinction between ducks and geese?* **3** a point of difference; a distinguishing quality or feature: *There are only minor distinctions between our house and the others on the block.* **4** honor or esteem: *The title is given as a mark of distinction.* **5** a mark or sign of honor. **6** excellence that distinguishes one from others; superiority: *a man of distinction. The novel has true distinction. The soldier had served with distinction.*

distinction without a difference, a false distinction; artificial difference.

dis·tinc·tive (dis tingk′tiv) *adj.* **1** clearly distinguishing from others; special; characteristic: *Police officers wear a distinctive uniform.* **2** designating one of a set of speech sounds in a given language that serve to distinguish words. The difference between *p* and *b* is distinctive in English because it alone distinguishes words such as *pat* from *bat.* **—dis·tinc′tive·ly,** *adv.* **—dis·tinc′tive·ness,** *n.*

dis·tinct·ly (dis tingkt′lē) *adv.* **1** clearly; plainly: *Speak distinctly.* **2** unmistakably; decidedly: *The prisoner was distinctly unhappy.*

dis·tin·gué (dis′tang gā′ *or* dis tang′gā; *French* dis taɴ gā′) *adj.* looking important or superior; distinguished. [< F]

dis·tin·guish (dis ting′gwish) *v.* **1** tell apart; see or show the difference between. **2** see or show the difference (*often used with* **between** *or* **among**): *I find it hard to distinguish between Maria's handwriting and her sister's.* **3** see or hear clearly; make out plainly: *It is much too dark for me to distinguish the outline of the house.* **4** make different; be a special quality or feature of: *The ability to talk distinguishes human beings from animals.* **5** make famous or well known: *She distinguished herself by winning all three prizes.* **6** separate into different groups; classify. [< L *distinguere* mark with a prick < *dis-* between + *stinguere* to prick]
☛ *Syn.* **1. Distinguish, differentiate, discriminate** = see or show the differences in or between things. **Distinguish** = see and know the qualities and features of a thing that give it its special character and set it off from others: *He distinguished the violins in the orchestra.* **Differentiate** = show the exact differences between one thing and others of the same class: *The teacher differentiated between Shakespeare's sonnets and Milton's.* **Discriminate** = see the fine shades of difference between things: *Sometimes only experts can discriminate between counterfeit bills and genuine money.*

dis·tin·guish·a·ble (dis ting′gwish ə bəl) *adj.* capable of being separated or differentiated. **—dis·tin′guish·a·bly,** *adv.*

dis·tin·guished (dis ting′gwisht) *adj.* **1** having or showing excellence, honor, or greatness: *She is a distinguished artist. He received a medal for distinguished conduct.* **2** suited for or having the appearance of a great or honored person: *a distinguished profile. He was tall and distinguished.*
☛ *Syn.* **1.** See note at **eminent.**

dis·tort (dis tôrt′) *v.* **1** pull or twist out of shape; change the normal appearance of: *Rage distorted his face.* **2** change from the truth; twist the meaning of: *The man distorted the facts of the accident to escape blame.* [< L *distortus,* pp. of *distorquere < dis-* (intensive) + *torquere* twist]

dis·tor·tion (dis tôr′shən) *n.* **1** the act of distorting: *The statement was not a direct lie but it was certainly a distortion of the truth.* **2** the result of distorting; anything distorted: *The article contains many distortions. They laughed at the distortions produced by the curved mirrors.*

dis·tract (dis trakt′) *v.* **1** draw away (the mind, attention, etc.): *The nurse distracted the baby while the doctor gave the injection. The music distracted him from his studies.* **2** confuse the attention of; disturb; bewilder: *Several people talking at once can distract a listener.* **3** put out of one's mind; make frantic or crazed (*used only after the verb* **be**): *He was nearly distracted by the thought of his brother trapped in the mine.* [< L *distractus,* pp. of *distrahere < dis-* away + *trahere* draw] **—dis·tract′ible,** *adj.* **—dis·tract′ing·ly,** *adv.*

dis·tract·ed (dis trak′təd) *adj.* **1** confused; bewildered: *She looked about her in a distracted way, trying to remember what she had come into the room for.* **2** in a frenzy; frantic; crazed: *He stood on the roof of the burning building, distracted with terror.* **—dis·tract′ed·ly,** *adv.*

dis·trac·tion (dis trak′shən) *n.* **1** distracting or being distracted: *In their distraction, the parents of the missing child hardly knew what they were doing.* **2** anything that draws away the attention, mind, etc.: *Noise can be a distraction when you are studying.* **3** something that relieves the mind or spirit; a relief from continued thought, effort, grief, etc.: *Movies are a convenient and popular distraction.*

dis·train (dis trān′) *v. Law.* seize (goods) for unpaid rent or other debts. [ME < OF *destreindre* < L *distringere < dis-* apart + *stringere* draw] **—dis·train′er** *or* **dis·train′or,** *n.*

dis·traint (dis trānt′) *n. Law.* an act of distraining.

dis·trait (dis trā′) *adj.* not paying attention; absent-minded. [< F *distrait,* pp. of *distraire* distract]

dis·traught (dis trot′ *or* dis trôt′) *adj.* **1** in a state of mental conflict and confusion. **2** crazed. [var. of obs. *distract,* adj. See DISTRACT.]

dis·tress (dis tres′) *n., v.* **—n.** **1** great mental or physical pain; trouble. **2** misfortune: *economic distress.* **3** a dangerous or desperate situation: *A ship sinking or burning at sea is in distress.*
—v. **1** cause pain, grief, or suffering to; make miserable or troubled. **2** subject to pressure, stress, or strain. [ME < OF *distrece,* ult. < L *districtus,* pp. of *distringere < dis-* apart + *stringere* draw] **—dis·tress′ing·ly,** *adv.*
☛ *Syn.* **n. 1.** See note at **sorrow.**

distressed area a region characterized by an abnormally low standard of living because of unemployment, poverty, etc.

dis·tress·ful (dis tres′fəl) *adj.* **1** causing distress; painful. **2** feeling or showing distress; suffering. **—dis·tress′ful·ly,** *adv.* **—dis·tress′ful·ness,** *n.*

dis·trib·ute (dis trib′yüt) *v.* **-ut·ed, -ut·ing.** **1** give (some of) to each; divide and give out in shares: *to distribute candy.* **2** spread; scatter: *Distribute the paint evenly over the wall.* **3** divide into parts: *The children were distributed into three groups for the tour.* **4** arrange; classify. **5** *Logic.* use (a term) so that it includes every member of a class. *Example:* dogs in the sentence *All dogs are animals.* **6** *Printing.* take apart and return (composed type) to the proper compartments in the case. [< L *distributus,* pp. of *distribuere < dis-* individually + *tribuere* assign]
☛ *Syn.* **1. Distribute, dispense** = give out shares. **Distribute** = divide the amount one has into shares, usually definite but not necessarily equal, and give them out according to some plan: *The teacher distributed paper to the class.* **Dispense** = give to each of a group the amount that has been measured out as his right or proper share: *The club dispensed new clothing to the children in the orphanage.*

dis·tri·bu·tion (dis′trə byü′shən) *n.* **1** the act or process of distributing: *Everyone was waiting for the distribution of the prizes.* **2** the position, arrangement, or spread of anything over an area or space or a period of time: *an even distribution of paint. Caribou have a wide distribution in the North.* **3** anything distributed. **4** *Economics.* the marketing of products; the process by which goods get to the consumers: *She is in charge of distribution for the company.* **5** division and arrangement; classification. **6** *Statistics.* a systematic arrangement of numerical data.

dis·tri·bu·tion·al (dis′trə byü′shə nəl) *adj.* of or having to do with distribution.

dis·trib·u·tive (dis trib′yə tiv) *adj., n.* **—adj.** **1** of or having to do with distribution; distributing. **2** *Mathematics.* designating a property of an operation by which the operation has the same result when applied to a set of quantities as it has when applied to individual members of the set. Multiplication is distributive over addition since $a(b + c)$ is the same as $ab + ac.$ **3** *Grammar.* designating each individual of a group considered separately. *Each, every, either* and *neither* are distributive words.
—n. a distributive word. **—dis·trib′u·tive·ly,** *adv.* **—dis·trib′u·tive·ness,** *n.*

distributive curve *Statistics.* a graph showing how the frequencies expressed are distributed.

dis·trib·u·tor (dis trib′yə tər) *n.* **1** a person or thing that distributes. **2** a person or company that distributes to consumers the goods grown or made by producers. **3** a part of a gasoline engine that distributes electric current to the spark plugs.

dis·trict (dis′trikt) *n., v.* **—n.** **1** a part of a larger area; region: *Northern Ontario is the leading gold-mining district in Canada. They lived in a fashionable district of the city.* **2** a part of a country, a province, or a city marked off for a special purpose, such as providing schools, electing officials, etc.: *a school district, a local improvement district. The Northwest Territories are divided into three districts: Mackenzie, Keewatin, and Franklin.* **—v.** divide into districts. [< LL *districtus* district < L *distringere.* See DISTRESS.]

district attorney *U.S.* a lawyer who is the prosecuting officer for a federal or state judicial district.

dis·trust (dis trust′) *v., n.* —*v.* not trust; have no confidence in; be suspicious of. —*n.* a lack of trust or confidence; suspicion: *She could not overcome her distrust of the stranger.*
☛ *Syn. n.* See note at **suspicion.**

dis·trust·ful (dis trust′fəl) *adj.* not trusting; suspicious. **distrustful of,** lacking confidence in. —**dis·trust′ful·ly,** *adv.* —**dis·trust′ful·ness,** *n.*

dis·turb (dis tėrb′) *v.* 1 destroy the peace, quiet, or rest of: *The noise of the road construction disturbed us so much that we couldn't sleep.* 2 break in upon with noise or change; interrupt: *Don't disturb him now; he's studying.* 3 put out of order: *Someone has disturbed all my papers.* 4 make uneasy; trouble: *The party officials were disturbed by the results of the survey.* 5 inconvenience: *Don't disturb yourself; I can do it.* [< L *disturbare* < *dis-* (intensive) + *turba* commotion] —**dis·turb′er,** *n.* —**dis·turb′ing·ly,** *adv.*

dis·turb·ance (dis tėr′bəns) *n.* 1 disturbing or being disturbed. 2 anything that disturbs. 3 confusion; disorder: *The police were called to quell the disturbance.* 4 uneasiness; trouble; worry.

di·sul·phide or **di·sul·fide** (dī sul′fīd or -sul′fid) *n. Chemistry.* a compound consisting of two atoms of sulphur combined with another element or radical. Also, **bisulphide.**

dis·un·ion (dis yün′yən) *n.* 1 a separation; division. 2 a lack of unity; disagreement.

dis·u·nite (dis′yə nīt′) *v.* -nit·ed, -nit·ing. 1 separate; divide. 2 destroy the unity of; cause to disagree.

dis·u·ni·ty (dis yü′nə tē) *n.* lack of unity; disunion.

dis·use (*n.* dis yüs′; *v.* dis yüz′) *n., v.* -used, -us·ing. —*n.* lack of use; not being used: *The old tools were rusted from disuse. Many words common in Shakespeare's time have fallen into disuse.* —*v.* stop using.

di·syl·lab·ic (dī′si lab′ik or dis′i lab′ik) *adj.* having two syllables: *Ditto is a disyllabic word.*

di·syl·la·ble (dī′sil ə bəl or dī sil′ə bəl, dis′il ə bəl or di sil′ə bəl) *n.* a word having two syllables.

ditch (dich) *n., v.* —*n.* a long, narrow trench dug in the earth, usually used to carry off water. —*v.* 1 make a ditch or ditches. 2 make a ditch or ditches in. 3 drive (a vehicle) into a ditch: *He ditched his car.* 4 land (an aircraft not equipped for the purpose) on water. 5 abandon (especially an aircraft in flight): *The pilot ditched the airplane because two engines were on fire.* 6 *Slang.* a get rid of. b leave in the lurch. [OE *dīc*] —**ditch′er,** *n.*

ditch·dig·ger (dich′dig′ər) *n.* a person or machine that digs ditches.

ditch·dig·ging (dich′dig′ing) *n., adj.* —*n.* the job of digging ditches. —*adj.* of or for the digging of ditches.

dith·er (diŦH′ər) *n., v.* —*n. Informal.* a state of quivering excitement or hesitation: *We were all in a dither, waiting for the results of the competition.* —*v. Informal.* act nervously or indecisively; hesitate. [origin uncertain]

dith·y·ramb (dith′ə ram′ or dith′ə ramb′) *n.* 1 a Greek choral song in honor of Dionysus. 2 a poem that is full of wild emotion, enthusiasm, etc. 3 any speech or writing like this. [< L < Gk. *dithyrambos*]

dith·y·ram·bic (dith′ə ram′bik) *adj.* 1 of or like a dithyramb. 2 wildly enthusiastic.

dit·to (dit′ō) *n., pl.* -tos; *adv., v.* -toed, -to·ing; *interj.* —*n.* 1 the same; exactly the same as appeared before. 2 inverted commas or apostrophes (") that stand for ditto; ditto mark. 3 a copy; duplicate. —*adv. Informal.* as said or done before; likewise. —*v.* 1 copy or repeat: *She simply dittoed what I had said.* 2 make a copy or copies of on a duplicating machine: *to ditto a memo.* —*interj. Informal.* the same; "I agree!" [< Ital. *ditto* said < L *dictus,* pp. of *dicere* say]

ditto mark a small mark (") used in lists, tables, etc. directly under something written to show that it is repeated. *Example:*
　10 copies at 10¢ each = $1.00
　40　 "　 "　5¢　" = $2.00

dit·ty (dit′ē) *n., pl.* -ties. a short, simple song or poem. [ME < OF *dite* < L *dictatum* (thing) dictated, pp. neut. of *dictare* dictate]

ditty bag a small bag, used especially by sailors, to hold sewing things and other odds and ends. [origin uncertain]

ditty box a small box used as a ditty bag.

di·u·ret·ic (dī′yə ret′ik) *adj.; n.* —*adj.* causing an increase in the flow of urine. —*n.* any drug that causes an increase in the flow of urine. [ME < LL *diureticus* < Gk. *diourētikos* < *dia-* through + *ourein* urinate]

di·ur·nal (dī ėr′nəl) *adj.* 1 occurring every day; daily. 2 of or

hat, āge, fär; let, ēqual, tėrm; it, īce
hot, ōpen, ôrder; oil, out; cup, pút, rüle,
above, takən, pencəl, lemən, circəs
ch, child; ng, long; sh, ship
th, thin; ŦH, then; zh, measure

belonging to the daytime. 3 *Zoology.* active during the day and not at night: *Most birds are diurnal.* 4 *Botany.* opening during the day and closing at night. 5 lasting a day. [ME < LL *diurnalis* < L *dies* day. Doublet of JOURNAL.] —**di·ur′nal·ly,** *adv.*

div. 1 dividend. 2 division; divided.

di·va (dē′və) *n., pl.* -vas. a prima donna; famous woman opera singer. [< Ital. < L *diva* goddess]

di·va·gate (dī′və gāt′) *v.* -gat·ed, -gat·ing. wander; stray. [< L *divagari* < *dis-* about + *vagari* wander]

di·va·ga·tion (dī′və gā′shən) *n.* a wandering.

di·va·lent (dī vā′lənt) *adj. Chemistry.* having a valence of two.

di·van (dī′van or də van′) *n.* 1 a long, low, usually backless and armless couch. 2 in Turkey and other Middle Eastern countries: a a court or council. b a council chamber. 3 a smoking room. [< Turkish *divan* < Persian *dēvān* (now *dīwān*) collection of written sheets, book or set of accounts, hence accounting office, treasury, council chamber; 16c.]

dive (dīv) *v.* dived or dove, dived, div·ing; *n.* —*v.* 1 plunge headfirst into the water. 2 go down or out of sight suddenly: *He dived into an alley.* 3 plunge the hand suddenly into anything: *He dived into his pocket and fished out a dollar.* 4 of an aircraft, missile, etc., plunge downward at a steep angle. 5 of a submarine, submerge. 6 penetrate with the mind: *John has been diving into the history of the Incas.* —*n.* 1 the act of diving. 2 the downward plunge of an aircraft, missile, submarine, etc. 3 *Informal.* a cheap, disreputable place for drinking and gambling. [OE *dȳfan*]
☛ *Usage.* **Dived, dove.** Both forms are used in Canadian English for the past tense, though **dived** seems to be more widely preferred in writing and in formal English. However, **dove** (< OE *dūfan*) is the standard form for many people.

dive-bomb (dīv′bom′) *v.* bomb at close range using a dive bomber.

dive bomber a bomber that releases its bomb load just before it pulls out of a dive toward the target.

div·er (dīv′ər) *n.* 1 a person or thing that dives. 2 a person whose occupation is to work under water. 3 a diving bird: *The loon is a well-known Canadian diver.*

di·verge (di vėrj′ or dī vėrj′) *v.* -verged, -verg·ing. 1 move or lie in different directions from one point; branch off: *Their paths diverged at the fork in the road.* 2 differ or vary: *They usually agreed, but their opinions diverged on this matter.* 3 turn away from a set course; deviate. 4 cause to diverge. 5 *Mathematics.* (of a series) increase indefinitely as more terms are added. [< LL *divergere* < *dis-* in different directions + *vergere* slope]
☛ *Syn.* 1. **Diverge, deviate, digress** = turn or move in a different direction. **Diverge** = branch out in different directions like a Y from a main or old path or way: *Our paths diverged when we left school.* **Deviate** = turn aside in one direction from a normal or regular path, way of thinking or acting, rule, etc.: *The teacher deviated from her custom and gave us no homework.* **Digress** applies chiefly to turning aside from the main subject while speaking or writing: *I lose interest if an author digresses too much.*

di·ver·gence (di vėr′jəns or dī vėr′jəns) *n.* 1 the act or state of diverging; difference: *The committee couldn't come to any agreement because of the wide divergence of opinion among its members.* 2 *Mathematics.* the fact of diverging.

di·ver·gen·cy (di vėr′jən sē or dī vėr′jən sē) *n., pl.* -cies. divergence.

di·ver·gent (di vėr′jənt or dī vėr′jənt) *adj.* 1 diverging; different. 2 causing divergence. —**di·ver′gent·ly,** *adv.*

di·vers (dī′vərz) *adj.* several different; various: *She leafed through divers books in the library.* [ME < OF < L *diversus,* pp. of *divertere.* See DIVERT.]

di·verse (di vėrs′, dī vėrs′, or dī′vėrs) *adj.* 1 different; completely unlike. 2 varied: *A person of diverse interests can talk on many subjects.* [var. of *divers*; now regarded as immediately from L *diversus*] —**di·verse′ness,** *n.*

di·verse·ly (di vėrs′lē or dī vėrs′lē) *adv.* in different ways or directions; differently; variously.

di·ver·si·fi·ca·tion (di vėr′sə fə kā′shən or dī vėr′sə fə kā′shən) *n.* the act or process of diversifying or the state of being diversified.

di·ver·si·fy (di vėr′sə fī′ or dī vėr′sə fī′) *v.* -fied, -fy·ing. 1 give variety to; vary: *He joined a travel club to diversify his interests.*

2 expand or extend business activities into different fields: *The company has recently diversified and now produces a whole range of cleaning products.* 3 distribute (investments, etc.) among several different securities in order to reduce risk. [< Med.L *diversificare* < L *diversus* diverse + *facere* make] —**di·ver′si·fi′er,** *n.*

di·ver·sion (di vėr′zhən *or* dī vėr′zhən) *n.* 1 a manoeuvre intended to draw attention away from a planned activity or attack; feint. 2 an amusement; entertainment; pastime: *Golf is my father's favorite diversion.* 3 a turning aside: *High tariffs often cause a diversion of trade from one country to another.*

di·ver·sion·ar·y (di vėr′zhən er′ē *or* dī vėr′zhən er′ē) *adj.* of or like a diversion or feint, especially in military tactics.

di·ver·si·ty (di vėr′sə tē *or* dī vėr′sə tē) *n., pl.* **-ties.** 1 complete difference; unlikeness. 2 variety: *Diversity of opinion is encouraged in a democracy.*
☛ *Syn.* 2. See note at **variety.**

di·vert (di vėrt′ *or* dī vėrt′) *v.* 1 turn aside: *A ditch diverted water from the stream into the fields.* 2 amuse; entertain: *She browsed through the bookstore, looking for something to divert her during the flight.* [< MF *divertir* < L *divertere* < *dis-* aside + *vertere* turn]

di·ver·ti·men·to (di ver′tē men′tō) *n., pl.* **-ti** (-tē). *Music.* 1 an instrumental composition, usually in several movements, intended to amuse and entertain. 2 an instrumental composition, usually light and entertaining, consisting of variations on a previously existing theme. [< Ital.]

di·ver·tisse·ment (dē ver tēs män′) *n.* 1 an amusement; entertainment. 2 a short ballet. 3 *Music.* **a** a collection of songs and dances inserted into an opera, ballet, etc. **b** divertimento. **c** a light, entertaining composition for use between the acts of an opera, ballet, etc. [< F]

Dives (dī′vēz) *n.* 1 in the Bible, the rich man in the parable of the rich man and the beggar (Luke 16:19-31). 2 any rich man.

di·vest (di vest′ *or* dī vest′) *v.* 1 strip; rid; free: *The police divested the impostor of his stolen uniform and fake decorations.* 2 force to give up; deprive: *Citizens were divested of their right to vote.* 3 *Law.* take away (property). [< Med.L *divestire* < OF *desvestir* < *des-* away + *vestir* < L *vestire* clothe]

di·vide (di vīd′) *v.* **-vid·ed, -vid·ing;** *n.* —*v.* 1 separate into parts: *A brook divides the field. The river divides and forms two streams.* 2 *Mathematics.* separate into equal parts: *Divide 8 by 2, and you get 4.* Symbol: ÷ 3 give some of to each; share: *The children divided the candy among them.* 4 disagree or cause to disagree; differ or cause to differ in feeling, opinion, etc.: *The school divided on the choice of a motto. Jealousy divided us.* 5 separate or cause to separate into two groups in voting. 6 mark off in parts; graduate (a scale, instrument, etc.).
—*n.* a ridge of land separating the regions drained by two different river systems. [ME < L *dividere*]
☛ *Syn. v.* 1. See note at **separate.**

di·vid·ed (di vīd′id) *adj.* 1 separated. 2 of a leaf, cut to the base so as to form distinct portions.
☛ *Usage.* **Divided usage.** Usage is said to be *divided* when two or more forms of a word are used more or less equally by the members of a speech community. **Divided usage** is not applied, for example, to localisms, like *coulee, gulch, ravine* (when referring to the same object), or to differences, such as *ain't* and *isn't,* that belong to separate levels of the language. It applies to spellings, pronunciations, or constructions on which speakers and writers of similar education might differ. The two pronunciations of *either* (ē′ͭHər and ī′ͭHər), the two spellings of *honor* (*honor* and *honour*) and the two past tenses of *dive* (*dived* and *dove*) are examples of divided usage.

divided highway a road, such as an expressway, having a median strip or boulevard between lanes of traffic going in opposite directions.

divided skirt a woman's garment that looks like a flared skirt but is divided and sewn in the manner of trousers.

div·i·dend (div′ə dend′) *n.* 1 *Mathematics.* a number or quantity to be divided by another: *In 8 ÷ 2, 8 is the dividend.* 2 money to be shared by those to whom it belongs. If a company makes a profit, it declares a dividend to the owners of the company. 3 a share of such money. 4 a part of the profits of an insurance company given to a person holding an insurance policy. [< L *dividendum* (thing) to be divided]

di·vid·er (di vīd′er) *n.* 1 a person or thing that divides. 2 a device for partitioning an area into several sections. 3 a piece of cardboard for separating sections of a notebook. 4 **dividers,** *pl.* an instrument for measuring distances, dividing lines, etc.; compasses.

div·i·na·tion (div′ə nā′shən) *n.* 1 the art or act of foreseeing the future or revealing the unknown by supernatural means. 2 a skilful guess or prediction.

di·vin·a·to·ry (də vin′ə tôr′ē *or* də vin′ə tə rē) *adj.* of or having to do with divination.

di·vine (di vīn′) *adj., n., v.* **-vined, -vin·ing.** —*adj.* 1 of God or a god. 2 by or from God. 3 to or for God; sacred; holy. 4 like God or a god; heavenly. 5 *Informal.* delightful; excellent; unusually good: *"What a divine hat!" cried Sue.*
—*n.* a person who knows much about theology, especially a minister or priest.
—*v.* 1 find out or foretell by supernatural means. 2 find out by intuition or by guessing. *She divined their plan and immediately set out to stop them.* 3 locate water, minerals, etc. underground by using a divining rod. [ME < OF < L *divinare*) < L *divinus* of a deity < *divus* deity] —**di·vine′ness,** *n.*

di·vine·ly (di vīn′lē) *adv.* 1 in a divine or godlike manner. 2 by the agency or influence of God. 3 supremely: *The orchestra played divinely at its first concert.*

di·vin·er (di vīn′ər) *n.* a person who divines, especially one who foresees the future or perceives the unknown, or professes to do these things.

divine right of kings the right to rule, thought to have been given to kings by God.

diving bell a large, hollow, bell-shaped container open at the bottom, used since ancient times as a chamber for people to work in under water. A diving bell is supplied with air through a hose; the pressure of the air keeps the water out.

diving suit a waterproof suit with a helmet into which air can be pumped through a tube. Diving suits are worn by persons working under water.

divining rod a forked stick, usually of willow or hazel, supposed to indicate the location of water or metal underground by bending downward.

di·vin·i·ty (di vin′ə tē) *n., pl.* **-ties.** 1 a divine being; a god or goddess. 2 **the Divinity,** God. 3 divine nature or quality: *The divinity of Jesus is accepted by Christians.* 4 theology: *a student of divinity.* 5 a creamy fudge.

di·vis·i·bil·i·ty (di viz′ə bil′ə tē) *n.* the quality of being divisible.

di·vis·i·ble (di viz′ə bəl) *adj.* 1 capable of being divided. 2 capable of being divided without leaving a remainder: *Any even number is divisible by 2.*

di·vi·sion (di vizh′ən) *n.* 1 dividing or being divided. 2 the act or process of giving some to each; distribution: *a division of labor.* 3 *Mathematics.* the process of dividing one number by another. 4 something that divides, such as a boundary or a partition. 5 one of the parts, sections, or groups into which something is divided. 6 *Military.* a major formation or unit under single command, including administrative services, arms, etc. 7 *Biology.* a major category in the classification of plants, corresponding to the phylum in the classification of animals. This category is more specific than the kingdom and more general than the class. See chart at **classification.** 8 a difference of opinion or interest; disagreement. 9 the process of separating into two groups for voting in a legislative body. [< L *divisio, -onis* < *dividere* divide]

di·vi·sion·al (di vizh′ən əl) *adj.* of, having to do with, or belonging to a division: *a divisional commander.*

division of labor or **labour** 1 a condition under which the work of a society is divided among various trades and professions, as those of priest, soldier, shoemaker, etc. 2 a distribution of separate small parts of a process among many workers, as in a modern shoe factory.

di·vi·sive (di vī′siv) *adj.* 1 tending or serving to divide, disunite, etc. 2 causing or tending to cause strife, disunity, etc. —**di·vi′sive·ly,** *adv.* —**di·vi′sive·ness,** *n.*

di·vi·sor (di vī′zər) *n.* 1 a number or quantity by which another is divided: *In 8 ÷ 2, 2 is the divisor.* 2 a number or quantity that divides another without a remainder.

di·vorce (di vôrs′) *n., v.* **-vorced, -vorc·ing.** —*n.* 1 the legal ending of a marriage. 2 complete separation: *The pamphlet advocated the divorce of church and state.*
—*v.* 1 legally dissolve the marriage contract between. 2 end marriage with (one's spouse) by getting a divorce: *Mrs. Smith divorced her husband.* 3 separate or detach something (from): *She led a lonely life, divorced from all her childhood friends and pleasures.* [ME < OF < L *divortium* separation < *divertere.* See DIVERT.] —**di·vorc′er,** *n.*

di·vor·cé (di vôr′sā′) *n.* a divorced man.

di·vor·cee (di vôr′sā′) *n.* a divorced person.

di·vor·cée (di vôr′sā′) *n.* a divorced woman.

di·vorce·ment (di vôrs′mənt) *n.* divorce.

div·ot (div′ət) *n.* a small piece of turf or earth dug up by a golf club in making a stroke. [origin uncertain]

di·vulge (di vulj′ *or* dī vulj′) *v.* **-vulged, -vulg·ing.** reveal (something secret); make known; make public: *The traitor*

divulged secret plans to the enemy. [< L *divulgare* publish < *dis-away* + *vulgus* common people] **—di·vulg′er,** *n.*

div·vy (div′ē) *v.* **div·vied, div·vy·ing;** *n. Slang.* —*v.* divide or share.

divvy up, make a division into shares.
—*n.* a share or portion. [var. of *divide*]

dix (dēs) *n.* **1** in bezique and some card games, the lowest trump. **2** in pinochle, a score of ten points. [< F *dix* ten]

Dix·ie (dik′sē) *n.* the southern states of the United States, especially those that united to form the Confederacy in 1860-61.

Dix·ie·land or **dix·ie·land** (dik′sē land′) *n.* a style of orchestral jazz with a strong rhythm in ⁴/₄ time, usually played by a small band, with improvisation often by several instruments at the same time.

diz·en (diz′ən or dī′zən) *v. Archaic.* bedizen. [cf. MDu. *disen* wind up flax, MLG *dise* bunch of flax on distaff]

diz·zy (diz′ē) *adj.* **-zi·er, -zi·est;** *v.* **-zied, -zy·ing.** —*adj.* **1** having a sensation that things about one are whirling or spinning around and that one is about to fall: *Most of the midway rides make me dizzy.* **2** confused; bewildered. **3** causing or likely to cause dizziness: *The mountaineer climbed to a dizzy height.* **4** *Informal.* foolish; silly: *What a dizzy thing to do!*
—*v.* make dizzy: *The ride on the merry-go-round had dizzied her.* [OE *dysig* foolish] **—diz′zi·ly,** *adv.* **—diz′zi·ness,** *n.*

DJ or **D.J. 1** disc jockey. **2** dinner jacket.

djinn (jin) See **jinn.**
☛ *Hom.* **gin.**

D.Litt. Doctor of Letters or of Literature (for L *Doctor Lit(t)erarum*).

D.L.S Doctor of Library Science.

dm decimetre(s).

DM Deutsche Mark.

DNA any of various acids that are an essential component of all living matter and that in higher organisms contain the genetic codes determining heredity. [abbrev. of *d*eoxyribo*nucleic a*cid]

DNB Dictionary of National Biography.

DND or **D.N.D.** Department of National Defence.

do¹ (dü) *v. pres. sing.* **1 do, 2 do, 3 does;** *pl.* **do;** *pt.* **did;** *pp.* **done;** *ppr.* **do·ing;** *n.* —*v.* **1** carry out; perform: *That's easier said than done. She did her work.* **2** act; work: *Do or die.* **3** complete; finish; end: *My assignment is done.* **4** make; produce: *Walt Disney did a movie about wild life in the Arctic.* **5** be the cause of; bring about: *Do good. Your work does you credit.* **6** act; behave: *Do wisely.* **7** render: *to do homage, to do justice.* **8** deal with as the case may require; take care of: *to do the dishes, to do one's hair; to have one's hair done.* **9** get along; manage; fare: *How are they doing?* **10** be satisfactory; be enough; serve: *He said any kind of paper would do.* **11** work out; solve: *to do a puzzle, to do a sum.* **12** cook: *The roast will be done in an hour.* **13** cover; traverse: *We did 100 kilometres in an hour.* **14** *Informal.* cheat; trick. **15 Do** is also used in certain constructions where it has a grammatical function (as an auxiliary verb) but no special meaning in itself: **a** in asking questions: *Do you like milk?* **b** to emphasize a verb: *I do want to go.* **c** to stand for a verb already used: *My dog goes where I do.* **d** in negative statements that contain **not:** *I do not think they will come. He enjoyed the movie but she did not.* **e** in inverted constructions after the adverbs *rarely, hardly, little,* etc.: *Rarely did she laugh.*

do away with, a abolish: *do away with a rule.* **b** kill.

do by, act or behave toward; treat.

do for, a look after the needs of, as housekeeper, etc: *Who did for her while she was sick?* **b** *Informal.* ruin, destroy, or kill: *That job almost did for me.*

do in, *Informal.* **a** ruin or kill: *That exercise is enough to do anybody in.* **b** tire out: *I'm all done in.*

do (one's) bit See **bit².**

do up, a close or fasten a zipper, buttons, laces, etc.: *Do up your shoe laces.* **b** have trouble doing up the top button. **b** close the fastenings of: *to do up a coat.* **c** wrap up: *to do up a package.* **d** clean and get ready for use: *to do up a room.* **c** *Informal.* wear out; exhaust.

do without, get along without the thing mentioned or implied: *We can do without luxuries if we have to.*

have to do with, relate to; deal with: *Abstract art has little to do with everyday experience.*

how do you do? How are you? (*used as a greeting*).

it isn't done, it is not considered good manners, good taste, etc.
—*n. Informal.* celebration: *They had a big do for us when we got back.* [OE *dōn*]
☛ *Hom.* **dew, due.**
☛ *Syn.* **1. Do, perform, accomplish** = carry out work, etc. **Do** is the general word and may be used, at least informally, of every kind of act: *He did nothing today.* **Perform,** the formal word, often interchangeable with **do,** particularly means carry an action through to the end, and often suggests regular activities:

hat, āge, fär; let, ēqual, tèrm; it, īce
hot, ōpen, ôrder; oil, out; cup, put, rüle,
əbove, takən, pencəl, lemən, circəs

ch, child; ng, long; sh, ship
th, thin; ŦH, then; zh, measure

He performed none of his duties today. **Accomplish** = carry out successfully to the desired end: *He worked hard but accomplished very little.*

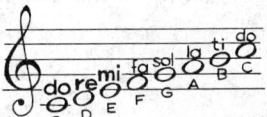

The diatonic (eight-tone) major scale, with C as the first tone

do² (dō) *n. Music.* **1** the first and last tones of an eight-tone major scale: *do, re, mi, fa, sol, la, ti, do.* **2** the tone C. [substituted for *ut.* See GAMUT.]
☛ *Hom.* **doe, dough.**

do. ditto.

DOA dead on arrival.

do·a·ble (dü′ə bəl) *adj.* that can be done.

dob·bin (dob′ən) *n.* a farm horse, especially a quiet plodding one. [var. of *Robin,* traditional name for a farm horse]

Do·ber·man pin·scher (dō′bər mən pin′shər) a breed of fairly large, slender, short-haired dog originally developed in Germany. Doberman pinschers are often trained as watchdogs. [< Ludwig *Doberman,* a German dog breeder + G *Pinscher* terrier]

dob·son·fly (dob′sən flī′) *n., pl.* **-flies.** any of a family (Corydalidae) of insects found in many parts of the world, especially *Corydalis cornutus,* whose large, carnivorous, aquatic larva, called a hellgrammite, is used as fishing bait. Also, **dobson fly.** [origin uncertain]

do·cent (dō′sənt) *n.* **1** *U.S.* a lecturer, especially at a college or university. **2** a person trained as a guide and lecturer to conduct groups through a picture gallery, museum, etc. [< G < L *docens, -entis,* ppr. of *docere* teach]

do·cile (dō′sīl, dos′īl, or dos′əl) *adj.* **1** easily managed; obedient. **2** easily taught; willing to learn. [ME < L *docilis* < *docere* teach] **—do′cile·ly,** *adv.*
☛ *Syn.* **1.** See note at **obedient.**

do·cil·i·ty (dō sil′ə tē) *n.* a docile quality.

dock¹ (dok) *n., v.* —*n.* **1** a large basin equipped with floodgates to receive ships for loading, unloading, and repairs. **2** a platform, wharf, etc. for loading or unloading cargo or freight. **3** the water between two piers, permitting the entrance of ships. **4** drydock. —*v.* **1** bring (a ship) alongside a dock: *The sailors docked the ship and began to unload it.* **2** come into a dock. **3** join spacecraft together in space. [< MDu. or MLG *docke*]

dock² (dok) *n., v.* —*n.* **1** the solid, fleshy part of an animal's tail. **2** the part of a tail left after cutting or clipping. —*v.* **1** cut short; cut the end off: *Horses' and dogs' tails are sometimes docked.* **2** cut down; take away part of: *The company docked the employees' wages when they came late to work.* [OE *-docca,* as in *finger-docca* finger muscle]

dock³ (dok) *n.* the place where an accused person stands in criminal court. [cf. Flemish *dok* pen]

dock⁴ (dok) *n.* any of numerous herbs (genus *Rumes*) of the buckwheat family, some of which are troublesome weeds. [OE *docce*]

dock·age¹ (dok′ij) *n.* **1** a place to dock ship. **2** a charge for using a dock. **3** the docking of ships. [< *dock¹*]

dock·age² (dok′ij) *n.* **1** an act of cutting down or cutting off. **2** a cut or deduction made, as from wages. **3** easily removable foreign material that is added to grain in processing. [< *dock²*]

dock·er¹ (dok′ər) *n. Esp.Brit.* a laborer who works on a dock; longshoreman.

dock·er² (dok′ər) *n.* a person or thing that docks, cuts off, or cuts short.

dock·et (dok′it) *n., v.* —*n.* **1** a list of cases to be tried by a court: *There are 12 cases on this morning's docket.* **2** a summary or list of decisions made in a court of law. **3** any list of matters to be considered by some group of people; agenda. **4** a label or ticket giving the contents of a package, document, etc. —*v.* **1** enter on a docket. **2** make a summary or list of (judgments, documents, etc.). **3** mark with a docket. [origin uncertain]

dock·yard (dok′yärd′) *n.* a place where ships are built,

equipped, and repaired. A dockyard contains docks, workshops, and warehouses for supplies.

doc·tor (dok′tər) *n., v.* —*n.* **1** a person who is qualified to treat diseases and physical or mental disorders and who makes this his or her work; a physician, surgeon, psychiatrist, or veterinarian. **2** dentist. **3** any person who treats diseases: *a witch doctor.* **4** a person who has received the highest degree possible in a university: *a Doctor of Laws, a Doctor of Philosophy.* **5** *Archaic.* a learned man; teacher. **6** any of various mechanical devices, especially one designed to remedy something. **7** a brightly-colored artificial fishing fly. *Abbrevs.:* Dr. (defs 1 and 2); D. (def. 4).
—*v.* **1** give medical treatment to; try to heal: *She doctors her children when they have colds or stomach aches.* **2** *Informal.* practise medicine. **3** tamper with: *The whisky had been doctored with water. The dishonest cashier doctored the accounts.* **4** alter or weaken, especially for a bad purpose: *The whisky had been doctored with water. The dishonest teller doctored the accounts.* **5** mend; repair, especially machinery, etc. [ME < OF *doctour* < L *doctor* teacher < *docere* teach]

doc·tor·al (dok′tər əl) *adj.* of or having to do with a doctor or doctorate.

doc·tor·ate (dok′tər it) *n.* the degree of Doctor given by a university.

doc·tri·naire (dok′trə ner′) *n., adj.* —*n.* an impractical theorist; a person who tries to apply a theory rigidly, without considering the actual circumstances or consequences. —*adj.* characteristic of a doctrinaire; theoretical and impractical: *a doctrinaire approach.*

doc·tri·nal (dok′trī′nəl *or* dok′trə nəl) *adj.* of, characterized by, or having to do with doctrine: *a doctrinal sermon.* —**doc·tri′nal·ly,** *adv.*

doc·trine (dok′trən) *n.* **1** what is taught as the belief of a church, nation, or group of persons. **2** what is taught; teachings. **3** a belief, especially a religious one. [ME < OF < L *doctrina* < *doctor.* See DOCTOR.]

doc·u·dra·ma *or* **doc·u·dra·ma** (dok′yə dram′ə) *n.* a film that is basically factual but which contains fictional elements for added dramatic interest.

doc·u·ment (*n.* dok′yə mənt; *v.* dok′yə ment′) *n., v.* —*n.* something written, printed, etc. that gives information or proof of some fact; any original or official paper that can be used as evidence. Letters, maps, and pictures are documents.
—*v.* **1** provide with original or official papers. **2** prove or support by means of such papers. **3** provide with references to authoritative material and original sources that support a claim, argument, or theory: *Her article on the effects of artificial lighting is well documented.* **4** demonstrate or illustrate in a book, motion picture, etc.: *The film documents the changing face of the North.* [< L *documentum* example, proof < *docere* show] —**doc′u·men·ta′tion,** *n.*

doc·u·men·ta·ry (dok′yə men′tə rē *or* dok′yə men′trē) *adj., n., pl.* **-ries.** —*adj.* **1** consisting of documents; in writing, print, etc.: *The man's own letters were documentary evidence of his guilt.* **2** presenting or recording factual information in an artistic fashion: *a documentary film.* —*n.* a documentary book, motion picture, radio or television program.

dod·der¹ (dod′ər) *v.* **1** shake; tremble. **2** move unsteadily; totter: *The man dodders about as if he were ninety years old.* [origin uncertain] —**dod′der·er,** *n.*

dod·der² (dod′ər) *n.* any of a genus (*Cuscuta*) of annual plants of the morning-glory family, having no leaves, chlorophyl, or roots when mature, and living as parasites by twining around other plants and drawing food from them through suckers. [ME *doder*]

do·dec·a·gon (dō dek′ə gon′) *n.* a polygon having 12 sides. [< Gk. *dōdekagonon* < *dōdeka* twelve + *gōnia* angle]

do·dec·a·he·dron (dō′dek ə hē′drən) *n., pl.* **-drons, -dra** (-drə). a polyhedron having 12 faces. The faces of a regular dodecahedron are regular pentagons. [< Gk. *dōdekaedron* < *dōdeka* twelve + *hedra* seat, base]

dodge (doj) *v.* **dodged, dodg·ing;** *n.* —*v.* **1** move quickly to one side: *He dodged into the shadow of the house.* **2** move quickly in order to get away from (a person, a blow, or something thrown): *He dodged the ball as it came flying toward his head.* **3** get away from or avoid an obligation, problem, etc. by trickery, cunning, or evasion; evade: *She is trying to dodge her responsibilities as leader by not taking a stand on the issue.*
—*n.* **1** a sudden movement to one side. **2** *Informal.* a trick or scheme: *a clever dodge.* [origin uncertain]

dodge·ball (doj′bol′ *or* -bôl′) *n.* a game in which players forming a circle or two opposite lines try to hit opponents in the centre with a large ball.

dodg·er (doj′ər) *n.* **1** a person who dodges, especially one who uses tricky or cunning devices. **2** a small handbill.

do·do (dō′dō) *n., pl.* **-dos** *or* **-does. 1** either of two extinct species of large heavy bird (genus *Raphus*) having a large hooked bill, short legs, and small wings that were useless for flying. The dodos, believed to be most closely related to the pigeon family, were found on islands in the Indian Ocean. **2** *Informal.* a person who is hopelessly old-fashioned. **3** *Informal.* a stupid person; dolt.
dead as a dodo, defunct or obsolete, with no chance or revival: *That issue is dead as a dodo.*
[< Pg. *doudo* fool]

doe (dō) *n.* the female of a deer, antelope, rabbit, hare, and of most other animals whose male is called a buck. See also **hind.** [OE dā]
☛ *Hom.* do², dough.

Doe (dō) *n.* See **John Doe.**

doe-eyed (dō′īd′) *adj.* having eyes as naïve, shy, and soft as those of a doe.

do·er (dü′ər) *n.* a person who does something, especially with energy and enthusiasm.

does (duz) *v.* 3rd pers. sing., present tense, of **do¹.**

doe·skin (dō′skin′) *n.* **1** the skin of a female deer. **2** a very soft leather made from this skin. **3** a smooth, soft woolen cloth with a short nap, used for suits, sportswear, etc.

does·n't (duz′ənt) *v.* does not.

do·est (dü′ist) *v. Archaic.* 2nd pers. sing., present tense, of **do¹.** *Thou doest* means *you* (sing.) *do.*

do·eth (dü′ith) *v. Archaic.* 3rd pers. sing., present tense, of **do¹.** *She doeth* means *she does.*

doff (dof) *v.* **1** take off; remove: *to doff one's clothes.* **2** take off or lift one's hat in greeting: *He doffed his hat to her.* **3** get rid of; throw aside. [originally a 14c. contraction of *do off* take or put off, remove] [contraction of *do off*]

dog (dog) *n., v.* **dogged, dog·ging.** —*n.* **1** a domesticated, meat-eating mammal (*Canis familiaris*), kept as a pet or used for such purposes as guarding people or property, hunting, or leading the blind. Two breeds of dog are the cocker spaniel and the greyhound. **2** (*adj.*) designating the family (Canidae) of meat-eating animals that includes the dog as well as wolves, coyotes, jackals, and foxes. **3** a male dog, fox, wolf, etc. **4** any of various animals resembling a dog in some way, such as the prairie dog. **5** a mean, contemptible man. **6** *Informal.* a person or thing that is inferior or unattractive. **7** *Informal.* a man; fellow: *You're a lucky dog.* **8** any of various simple mechanical devices for holding or gripping. **9** a firedog; andiron.
every dog has his day, everyone gets some attention or luck sometime in his life.
go to the dogs, be ruined; deteriorate rapidly.
let sleeping dogs lie, don't stir up unnecessary trouble; let well enough alone.
put on the dog, *Informal.* behave or dress in a showy, affected manner.
teach an old dog new tricks, get an older person to accept new ideas or ways of doing things.
—*v.* **1** hunt or follow like a dog: *The police dogged the thief's footsteps until they caught him.* **2** worry as if by a dog; beset: *The company was dogged by financial crises for several years.* **3** fasten or secure (a log, etc.) by means of a dog (def. 8). [OE *docga*] —**dog′like,** *adj.*

do·gan (dō′gən) *n. Cdn. Slang.* a Roman Catholic, especially one of Irish background. [origin uncertain]

dog·bane (dog′bān′) *n.* **1** any of a genus (*Apocynum*) of mainly tropical plants having clusters of small, white, or pink, bell-shaped flowers. Some dogbanes are poisonous. **2** (*adj.*) designating the family (Apocynaceae) of herbs, shrubs, and trees that includes dogbanes and periwinkles.

dog·ber·ry (dog′ber′ē) *n., pl.* **-ries. 1** any of various plants having berrylike fruit, such as the European dogwood, mountain ash, or wild gooseberry. **2** the fruit of any of these plants.

dog·cart (dog′kärt′) *n.* **1** a small cart pulled by a dog or dogs. **2** a small, open, usually two-wheeled carriage with two seats that are back to back.

dog·catch·er (dog′kach′ər) *n.* a person whose job is to pick up stray dogs and take them to the pound.

dog days in the northern hemisphere, a period of very hot, humid, and uncomfortable weather during July and August. [with reference to the rising of Sirius, the Dog Star]

doge (dōj; *Italian,* dō′jā) *n.* the chief magistrate of Venice or Genoa when they were republics. [< Venetian Ital. < L *dux* leader. Doublet of DUCE, DUKE.]

dog-ear (dog′ēr′) *n., v.* —*n.* a folded-down corner of a page in a

book: *I made a dog-ear to mark the page where I stopped reading.* —*v.* fold down the corner of. Also, **dog's-ear.**

dog–eared (dog′ērd′) *adj.* **1** having a dog-ear: *Find the dog-eared page.* **2** having many pages with dog-ears: *a dog-eared old schoolbook.* **3** looking much used; shabby: *Almost everything in the room is dog-eared.*

dog–eat–dog (dog′ēt′dog′) *adj.* marked by ruthless or vicious competition: *a dog-eat-dog society.*

dog·fight (dog′fīt′) *n., v.* **-fought, -fight·ing.** *Informal.* —*n.* **1** a fight between dogs. **2** any rough fight or uproar. **3** a combat between individual fighter planes. —*v.* engage in a dogfight.

dog·fish (dog′fish′) *n., pl.* **-fish** or **-fishes. 1** any of several species of small shark found in temperate and warm seas, especially the **spiny dogfish** (*Squalus acanthias*), having a spine in front of each back fin. **2** bowfin.

dog·ged (dog′id) *adj.* stubborn; persistent; not giving up: *In spite of failures, he kept on with dogged determination.* [< *dog*] —**dog′ged·ly,** *adv.* —**dog′ged·ness,** *n.*

dog·ger¹ (dog′ər) *n.* **1** a person who dogs. **2** *Logging.* a workman who ties dogs or hooks to a log for hauling by cable.

dog·ger² (dog′ər) *n.* a broad boat with two masts, used by fishermen in the North Sea. [ME; origin uncertain]

dog·ger·el (dog′ər əl) *n., adj.* —*n.* poor poetry; poetry that is trivial and not well written: *Doggerel is often written for a comic effect.* —*adj.* having to do with or designating such poetry. [ME; origin uncertain]

dog·gie (dog′ē) *n.* a child's word or a pet name for a dog.

doggie bag a bag given to a patron by a restaurant for the purpose of carrying home food left over from the patron's meal. [from the idea of taking leftover food, especially meat, home to one's pet]

dog·gone (dog′gon) *adj., adv., v.* **-goned, -gon·ing.** *Slang.* —*adj.* darned; damned. —*adv.* very; much. —*v.* darn; damn.

dog·gy (dog′ē) *adj.* **-gi·er, -gi·est;** *n., pl.* **-gies.** —*adj.* **1** of or like a dog: *There's a doggy smell in the car.* **2** *Informal.* outwardly showy. —*n.* See **doggie.**

dog·house (dog′hous′) *n.* a small house or shelter for a dog. **be in the doghouse,** *Slang.* be in disfavor with somebody.

do·gie (dō′gē) *n.* in the western parts of Canada and the United States, a motherless calf on the range or in a range herd. Also, **dogy.** [origin uncertain]

dog in the manger a person who prevents others from using or enjoying something of no value to himself (from the fable of the dog that would not let the ox eat the hay in the manger). —**dog–in–the–man′ger,** *adj.*

dog·leg (dog′leg′) *n., v.* **-legged, -leg·ging.** —*n.* **1** a sharp angle or bend like that of a dog's hind leg: *a dogleg in a road.* **2** something having a sharp angle or bend. **3** (*adj.*) of or shaped like a dogleg. —*v.* follow or have a course with a sharp angle: *The street doglegs before it crosses the railway.*

dog·ma (dog′mə) *n., pl.* **-mas, -ma·ta** (-mə tə). **1** a belief or body of beliefs authorized by a church. **2** a doctrine or belief. **3** an opinion asserted in a positive manner as if it were authoritative. [< L < Gk. *dogma* opinion < *dokeein* think]

dog·mat·ic (dog mat′ik) *adj.* **1** having to do with dogma; doctrinal. **2** asserting opinions as if one were the highest authority; positive; overbearing. **3** asserted without proof. —**dog·mat′i·cal·ly,** *adv.*

dog·mat·i·cal (dog mat′ə kəl) *adj.* dogmatic.

dog·ma·tism (dog′mə tiz′əm) *n.* a positive or authoritative assertion of opinion.

dog·ma·tist (dog′mə tist) *n.* **1** a person who asserts opinions as if they were authoritative. **2** a person who states dogmas.

dog·ma·tize (dog′mə tīz′) *v.* **-tized, -tiz·ing. 1** assert opinions in a positive or authoritative manner. **2** express as a dogma.

do–good·er (dü′gùd′ər) *n. Informal.* a person who is too eager to correct or set things right.

Dog·rib (dog′rib) *n., pl.* **-rib** or **-ribs;** *adj.* —*n.* **1** a member of an Amerindian people who live in the Northwest Territories. The Dogrib traditionally occupied the region between Great Bear Lake and Great Slave Lake. **2** the Athapascan language of the Dogrib. —*adj.* of or having to do with the Dogrib or their language.

dog rose a wild rose (*Rosa canina*) native to Europe, having white or pink flowers.

dog salmon chum, a species of Pacific salmon.

dog's-ear (dogz′ēr′) *n., v.* dog-ear.

hat, āge, fär; let, ēqual, tėrm; it, īce
hot, ōpen, ôrder; oil, out; cup, pùt, rüle, above, takən, pencəl, lemən, circəs
ch, child; ng, long; sh, ship
th, thin; ᴛн, then; zh, measure

dog·sled (dog′sled′) *n. Cdn.* a sled that is pulled by dogs. See **sled** for picture.

dog–sledge (dog′slej′) *n. Cdn.* dogsled.

dog's life a miserable life.

Dog Star 1 Sirius. **2** Procyon.

dog's–tooth violet (dogz′tüth′) *n.* dogtooth violet.

dog tag *Informal.* **1** an identification disk worn on a neck chain by a member of the armed forces. **2** a metal disk attached to a dog's collar.

dog–team (dog′tēm′) *n.* a number of dogs trained as a team for use in pulling a vehicle, especially a sled: *They had travelled the entire distance by dog-team.*

dog–tired (dog′tīrd′) *adj.* very tired.

dog·tooth violet (dog′tüth′) any of a genus (*Erythronium*) of plants of the lily family, having yellow, white, or purple lily-like flowers and long, pointed oval-shaped leaves; especially a species (*E. americanum*) with yellow flowers found in the woods of E North America, also called adder's-tongue.

dog–train (dog′trān′) *n. Cdn.* a sled pulled by a team of dogs.

dog·trot (dog′trot′) *n.* a gentle, easy trot.

dog·watch (dog′woch′) *n.* a two-hour period of work on a ship. There are two dogwatches a day, one from 4 to 6 p.m. and the other from 6 to 8 p.m.

dog·wood (dog′wùd′) *n.* **1** any of a genus (*Cornus*) of trees, shrubs, and herbs having clusters of small flowers, often surrounded by showy, petal-like bracts, and red, dark blue, or white fruit. The blossom of the western flowering dogwood is the floral emblem of British Columbia. **2** the heavy, hard wood of any of these trees or shrubs. **3** (*adj.*) designating a family (Cornaceae) of shrubs, trees, or herbs found throughout the world. The dogwood family consists of about 100 species, including the flowering dogwoods and the bunchberry.

do·gy (dō′gē) *n., pl.* **-gies.** See **dogie.**

doh (dō) See **do².**

doi·ly (doi′lē) *n., pl.* **-lies. 1** a small piece of linen, lace, or paper used on or under plates, vases, etc. **2** a small dessert napkin. [after a 17th-century London dry-goods dealer]

do·ings (dü′ingz) *n.pl.* **1** things done; actions. **2** social activities or behavior.

doit (doit) *n.* **1** a former Dutch copper coin worth about ¼ cent. **2** a small sum; trifle; bit: *No one cares a doit what he thinks.* [< Du. *duit*]

do–it–your·self (dü′it yər self′) *adj.* designed for use, construction, or assembly by amateurs: *a do-it-yourself construction kit.*

do·jo (dō′jō) *n.* a gymnasium or studio where karate, judo, etc. are taught.

dol·ce (dōl′chä) *adj. Italian.* sweet; soft.

dol·ce far nien·te (dōl′chä fär nyen′tä) *Italian.* pleasant idleness (literally, sweet to do nothing).

dol·drums (dol′drəmz *or* dōl′-) *n.pl.* **1** certain regions of the ocean near the equator where the wind is very light or constantly shifting. Sailing ships caught in the doldrums were often unable to move for days. **2** the calm or windless weather characteristic of these regions. **3** dullness; a gloomy feeling; low spirits: *The whole family was in the doldrums because of the rainy weather.* [probably related to *dull*]

dole¹ (dōl) *n., v.* **doled, dol·ing.** —*n.* **1** a portion of money, food, etc. given in charity. **2** a small portion. **3** the relief money given by a government to unemployed people: *Many people received the dole during the Depression.* **4** *Archaic.* lot; fate. **go** or **be on the dole,** receive relief money from the government. —*v.* **1** deal out in portions to the poor. **2** give in small portions. [OE *dāl* part. Related to DEAL¹.]

dole² (dōl) *n. Archaic.* sorrow; grief. [ME < OF *doel* < VL *dolus* grief < L *dolere* grieve]

dole·ful (dōl′fəl) *adj.* sad; mournful; dreary; dismal. —**dole′ful·ly,** *adv.* —**dole′ful·ness,** *n.*

dole·some (dōl′səm) *adj. Archaic.* doleful.

dol·i·co·ce·phal·ic (dol′ə kō sə fal′ik) *adj.* having a skull

whose breadth is less than eighty percent of its length; long-headed. Compare **brachycephalic.**

doll (dol) *n., v.* —*n.* **1** a child's plaything made to look like a baby, child, or grown person. **2** a pretty child, girl, or woman. **3** *Slang.* a very attractive or likable person.
—*v. Slang.* dress in a stylish or showy way. (*used with* **up**): *They were all dolled up for the party.* [pet name for *Dorothy*]
—**doll′-like′,** *adj.*

dol·lar (dol′ər) *n.* **1** the basic unit of money in Australia, Bahamas, Barbados, Bermuda, Canada, Guyana, Hong Kong, Jamaica, Liberia, New Zealand, Singapore, Trinidad and Tobago, United States, West Indies (Leeward Islands, Windward Islands), and Zimbabwe, divided into 100 cents. *Symbol:* $ See table at **money. 2** a note or coin worth one dollar. [earlier *daler* < LG < G (*Joachims*)*thaler* coin of St. Joachim's valley (in Bohemia)]

dollar crisis the situation arising when a country's reserve of dollars becomes dangerously low through failure to balance its imports from the United States by its exports.

dollar diplomacy *Informal.* a rich country's use of economic aid to needy nations in order to advance its own financial interests or to gain allies for its foreign policy.

dollar gap the shortage of dollars (for exchange) in a country suffering from a dollar crisis.

dollar imperialism the extending of control and authority into foreign countries through the buying power of the dollar.

dollar sign or **mark** the symbol $, meaning dollar or dollars: *Five dollars can be written $5.*

dol·lop (dol′əp) *n., v.* —*n. Informal.* a portion or serving, large or small: *a dollop of ice cream.* —*v.* apply or spread on heavily. [? < Scand.; cf. Norwegian *dolp* lump]

dol·ly (dol′ē) *n., pl.* **doll·ies. 1** a child's name for a doll. **2** a small, low frame on wheels, used to move heavy objects: *the fridge was moved on a dolly.* **3** a small truck on which a motion-picture or television camera can be moved about. **4** a small locomotive run on narrow-gauge tracks, used in switching, construction jobs, etc. **5** *Mining.* a device for shaking and washing ore in a vessel. **6** a bar with a flat or cup-shaped piece set at an angle on one end, used to form or hold the head of a rivet. **7** a block placed on the top of a pile while it is being driven. [< *doll*]

Dolly Var·den (vär′dən) **1** a char (*Salvelinus malma*) native to NW North America and NE Asia, having small red, orange, or yellow spots on the sides and back. **2** *Historical.* a long flower-printed dress having the skirt tied in loops to show the petticoat. **3** *Historical.* a woman's wide-brimmed hat trimmed with flowers and turned down at one side. [< *Dolly Varden*, a character in Dickens' *Barnaby Rudge*]

dol·man (dol′mən *or* dōl′mən) *n., pl.* **-mans. 1** a woman's coat with capelike flaps instead of sleeves. **2** a long Turkish robe, open at the front. **3** a hussar's gold-braided uniform jacket worn like a cape with the sleeves hanging free. [ult. < Turkish *dōlāmān*]

dolman sleeve a sleeve that tapers from narrow at the wrist to wide at the shoulder.

A dolmen on the downs in Wiltshire, England

dol·men (dol′mən) *n.* a prehistoric monument, generally regarded as a tomb, consisting of a large, flat stone laid across upright stones. [< F < Breton *tol* table + *men* stone]

dol·o·mite (dol′ə mīt′) *n.* **1** a rock consisting mainly of calcium and magnesium carbonate. Much so-called white marble is really dolomite. **2** calcium and magnesium carbonate. *Formula:* $CaCO_3$·$MgCO_3$ [after D. G. de *Dolomieu* (1750-1801), a French geologist]

dol·o·mit·ic (dol′ə mit′ik) *adj.* containing or consisting of dolomite.

do·lor or **do·lour** (dō′lər) *n. Poetic.* sorrow; grief. [ME < OF < L *dolor*]

do·lo·ro·so (dō′lō rō′sō) *adj. Music.* plaintive, soft, sorrowful. [< Ital.]

dol·or·ous (dol′ər əs *or* dō′lər əs) *adj.* **1** mournful; sorrowful. **2** grievous; painful. —**dol′or·ous·ly,** *adv.* —**dol′or·ous·ness,** *n.*

do·lour (dō′lər) See **dolor.**

dol·phin (dol′fən) *n.* **1** any of various small toothed whales (family Delphinidae) having a snout shaped like a beak. Dolphins are often trained to perform in aquariums. **2** (*adj.*) designating the family that includes the dolphins and the killer whale. **3** porpoise. **4** either of two large, edible, saltwater fishes (genus *Coryphaena*) remarkable for their changes of color when taken from the water. **5** a buoy or piling used to mark a channel for ships. [ME < OF *daulphin* < L < Gk. *delphis*]

dolphin striker on a ship, a small spar under the bowsprit that helps support the jib boom.

dolt (dōlt) *n.* a dull, stupid person. [apparently a var. of obs. *dold*, pp. of ME **dole(n)* to dull, OE *dol* dull]

dolt·ish (dōl′tish) *adj.* dull and stupid.

–dom *noun-forming suffix.* **1** the position, rank, or realm of a —: *kingdom = realm of a king.* **2** the condition of being —: *martyrdom = condition of being a martyr.* **3** all those who are —: *heathendom = all those who are heathen.* [OE *-dōm* state, condition < *dōm.* See **DOOM.**]

dom. **1** domestic. **2** dominion.

Dom. **1** Dominion. **2** Dominican.

do·main (dō mān′) *n.* **1** the territory under the control of one ruler or government. **2** the land owned by one person; an estate. **3** a field of thought, action, etc.: *the domain of science, the domain of politics.* [< F *domaine* < OF < L *dominium* < *dominus*, lord, master < *domus* house. Doublet of **DEMESNE.**]

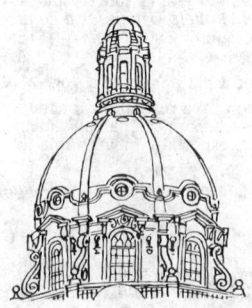

The dome of the Alberta legislature

dome (dōm) *n., v.* **domed, dom·ing.** —*n.* **1** *Architecture.* a large, rounded roof or ceiling on a circular or many-sided base. **2** anything that is or appears high and rounded: *the dome of the sky, the dome of a hill.* **3** *Crystallography.* a prism whose faces meet in a horizontal edge, like the roof of a house. **4** *Geology.* an anticlinal formation, circular or elliptical in structure, characteristic of oil and salt deposits, extrusions of volcanic lava, etc. **5** *Slang.* the head. —*v.* **1** cover with a dome. **2** form into the shape of a dome. **3** rise or swell like a dome. [< F *dôme* < Provençal *doma* < LL *doma* roof, house < Gk.] —**dome′like′,** *adj.*

dome car a railway car having a glass-enclosed upper level that resembles a dome and affords a wide view.

dome fastener *Cdn.* a metal or plastic fastener consisting of two parts, one with a small, rounded projection in the centre that snaps into a socket in the centre of the other.

Domesday Book (dümz′dā′) a record of the value and ownership of the lands in England, made in 1086 at the order of William the Conqueror.

do·mes·tic (də mes′tik) *adj., n.* —*adj.* **1** of the home, household, or family affairs: *domestic cares, a domestic scene.* **2** fond of home and family life. **3** of animals, not wild; tame: *Cats, dogs, cows, horses, sheep, and pigs are domestic animals.* **4** of one's own country; not foreign: *domestic news, domestic affairs.* **5** made in one's own country; native: *domestic cheese.*
—*n.* a servant in a household: *Cooks, butlers, and maids are domestics.* [< L *domesticus* < *domus* house] —**do·mes′ti·cal·ly,** *adv.*

do·mes·ti·cate (də mes′tə kāt′) *v.* **-cat·ed, -cat·ing. 1** change (animals or plants) from a wild to a tame or cultivated state; tame. **2** make fond of home and family life. **3** bring (a foreign word, custom, etc.) into accepted use in a region or country; adopt.

do·mes·ti·ca·tion (də mes′tə kā′shən) *n.* domesticating or being domesticated.

do·mes·tic·i·ty (dō′mes tis′ə tē) *n., pl.* **-ties. 1** home and family life. **2** fondness for home and family life. **3** domesticities, *pl.* domestic affairs.

domestic science home economics.

dom·i·cile (dom′ə sil′ *or* dom′ə səl) *n., v.* **-ciled, -cil·ing.** —*n.* **1** a dwelling place; home; residence. **2** *Law.* a place of permanent residence. One may have several residences, but only one legal domicile at a time. —*v.* settle in a domicile. [ME < MF < L *domicilium* < *domus* house]

dom·i·cil·i·ar·y (dom′ə sil′ē er′ē) *adj.* having to do with a domicile.

dom·i·nance (dom′ə nəns) *n.* a being dominant; rule; control.

dom·i·nan·cy (dom′ə nən sē) *n., pl.* **-cies.** dominance.

dom·i·nant (dom′ə nənt) *adj., n.* —*adj.* **1** controlling, ruling, or governing; strongest and most influential: *The dominant influence in her life has been her grandmother.* **2** rising high above its surroundings; towering: *The window looked out on the dominant hills to the west.* **3** *Music.* based on or having to do with the fifth note in a standard major or minor scale. **4** *Biology.* of or designating a gene in one of a pair of chromosomes that dominates over the corresponding gene in the other chromosome and is therefore expressed as a trait in an organism. If one of such a pair of genes inherited by a person is for brown eyes and the other is for blue, the person will have brown eyes because that gene is dominant. Compare **recessive.** —*n. Music.* the fifth tone in an eight-tone scale. G is the dominant in the key of C. [< F < L *dominans, -antis,* ppr. of *dominari.* See DOMINATE.] —**dom′i·nant·ly,** *adv.*
☛ *Syn. adj.* **1. Dominant, predominant, paramount** = uppermost. **Dominant** = ruling, and therefore having the most influence, power, or authority: *Efficiency is the dominant idea in many businesses.* **Predominant** = before others in influence, power, authority, and therefore principal or superior: *Love of liberty is predominant in struggles for independence.* **Paramount** = first in importance, authority, or rank, and therefore supreme: *It is of paramount importance that we finish the work on time.*

dom·i·nate (dom′ə nāt′) *v.* **-nat·ed, -nat·ing. 1** control or rule by strength or power: *A person of strong will often dominates others. Dandelions will dominate over lawn grass if they are not kept out.* **2** rise high above; tower over: *The mountain dominates the harbor.* **3** have the foremost place or the greatest influence in: *The new hockey team already dominates the league. Their products dominate the market.* [< L *dominari* < *dominus* lord, master] —**dom′i·na′tor,** *n.*

dom·i·na·tion (dom′ə nā′shən) *n.* dominating or being dominated; control; rule: *The country was under the domination of a tyrant for many years.*

dom·i·neer (dom′ə nēr′) *v.* rule (over) at one's own will; tyrannize; be overbearing in asserting one's authority. [< Du. *domineren* < F < L *dominari.* See DOMINATE.]

dom·i·neer·ing (dom′ə nēr′ing) *adj.* inclined to domineer; overbearing: *a domineering attitude, a domineering person.* —**dom′i·neer′ing·ly,** *adv.*

Do·min·i·can (də min′ə kən) *adj., n.* —*adj.* **1** of Saint Dominic or the religious orders founded by him. **2** of or having to do with the Dominican Republic. —*n.* **1** a friar or nun belonging to the Dominican order. **2** a native or inhabitant of the Dominican Republic.

dom·i·nie (dom′ə nē *for 1*; dom′ə nē *or* dō′mə nē *for 2*) *n.* **1** *Esp.Scottish.* schoolmaster. **2** *Informal.* clergyman. [< L *domine* (vocative) lord, master]

do·min·ion (də min′yən) *n.* **1** supreme authority; rule; control. **2** a territory or country under the control of one ruler or government: *The old king divided his dominion between his sons.* **3 Dominion, a** a name used for certain self-governing countries in the Commonwealth of Nations: *the Dominion of Canada, the Dominion of New Zealand.* **b** (*adj.*) in Canada, under the control or authority of the federal government: *the Dominion Fire Commissioner.* **c** (*adj.*) in Canada, relating to the country as a whole; national in scope: *the Dominion Drama Festival.* [< obs. F < Med.L *dominio, -onis,* alteration of L *dominium* ownership]

Dominion Day a national holiday commemorating the establishment of the Dominion of Canada on July 1, 1867; Canada Day.

dom·i·no (dom′ə nō′) *n., pl.* **-noes** *or* **-nos. 1** dominoes, a game played with flat, black, oblong pieces of wood, bone, etc. that are either blank or marked with dots on one side (*used with a singular verb*). **2** one of the pieces used in playing this game. **3** a long, loose, hooded cloak and a mask for the upper part of the face, worn as a disguise, especially at masquerades. **4** a mask, usually black, for the upper part of the face. **5** a person wearing a domino. [< F < L *domino* (dative of *dominus* master), short for some such phrase, jestingly used, as *benedicamus Domino* let us praise the Lord]

don¹ (don *or* dōn) *n.* **1 Don,** a Spanish title meaning Mr. or Sir: *Don Felipe.* **2** a Spanish gentleman; Spaniard. **3** in England, a university teacher, especially a head, fellow, or tutor of a college of Oxford or Cambridge. **4** in some Canadian universities and colleges, an official in charge of a student residence. **5** *Archaic.* a person of rank or distinction. [< Sp. < L *dominus* lord, master]
☛ *Hom.* **dawn** (don).

don² (don) *v.* **donned, don·ning.** put on. [contraction of *do on*]
☛ *Hom.* **dawn.**

Do·ña (don′yä *or* dō′nyä) *n.* **1** a Spanish title meaning Lady or Madam. **2** a Spanish lady. [< Sp. < L *domina* mistress. Doublet of DONNA.]

hat, āge, fär; let, ēqual, tèrm; it, īce
hot, ōpen, ôrder; oil, out; cup, pùt, rüle,
above, takən, pencəl, lemən, circəs

ch, child; ng, long; sh, ship
th, thin; ᴛʜ, then; zh, measure

do·nate (dō′nāt *or* dō nāt′) *v.* **-nat·ed, -nat·ing.** give; contribute, especially to an institution or public service: *My mother donates blood regularly. He donated fifty dollars to the church.* [< L *donare* < *donum* gift] —**do·nat′or,** *n.*

do·na·tion (dō nā′shən) *n.* **1** the act of giving or contributing. **2** a gift; contribution.

done (dun) *adj., v.* —*adj.* **1** completed; finished; ended; through. **2** *Informal.* worn out; exhausted. **3** cooked; cooked enough: *Are the potatoes done?* **4** proper; fitting; conforming to custom or convention: *This is the done thing. Eating peas with a knife is not done.* —*v.* pp. of **do¹.**
☛ *Hom.* **dun.**
☛ *Usage.* **Done with** is used in informal speech to mean finished, completed: *I'd like to get done with this.*

dong (dong) *n., pl.* **dong. 1** the basic unit of money in Vietnam, divided into 100 hao. See table at **money. 2** a note worth one dong.

don·jon (dun′jən *or* don′jən) *n.* the large, strongly fortified inner tower of a castle; keep. [var. of *dungeon*]
☛ *Hom.* **dungeon** (dun′jən).

Don Juan (don wän′, don hwän′, *or* don jü′ən) **1** a legendary Spanish nobleman who led a dissolute and immoral life. **2** any person leading an immoral life; libertine.
☛ *Pronun.* **Don Juan.** This name is usually pronounced (don wän′) or (don hwän′) in imitation of the Spanish pronunciation (dōng ʜwän′), but Byron's poem *Don Juan* and its hero are always pronounced (don jü′ən).

don·key (dong′kē *or* dung′kē) *n., pl.* **-keys. 1** a domestic animal descended from the wild ass of Africa (*Equus asinus*), resembling a horse but smaller and having longer ears, a shorter neck and mane, and smaller hooves. **2** a stubborn person. **3** a silly or stupid person. **4** donkey engine. [? a nickname form of *Duncan*]

donkey engine a small steam engine. Donkey engines are used on ships for hoisting anchor, etc.

donkey's years *Informal.* a very long time: *We haven't had a family reunion in donkey's years.*

don·na (don′ə; *Italian,* dôn′nä) *n.* **1** lady. **2 Donna,** an Italian title meaning Lady or Madam. [< Ital. < L *domina* mistress. Doublet of DOÑA.]

don·nish (don′ish) *adj.* of or like a type of university don; pedantic; formal. —**don′nish·ly,** *adv.* —**don′nish·ness,** *n.*

Don·ny·brook (don′ə brùk′) *n. Informal.* a riot; a brawl: *The players engaged in a terrific Donnybrook after the hockey game.* Also, **donnybrook.** [< Donnybrook, a town in the Irish Republic, site of an annual fair. The 1855 fair was suppressed because of wild brawls.]

do·nor (dō′nər) *n.* a person who contributes; giver: *The Canadian Red Cross Society welcomes blood donors.* [ME < AF *donour* < L *donator* < *donare.* See DONATE.]

do-noth·ing (dü′nuth′ing) *n.* **1** one who does nothing; idler. **2** a person unwilling to take action because it may upset the existing order.

Don Qui·xo·te (don kē hō′tē *or* don kwik′sət; *Spanish,* dōn kē ʜō′tā) **1** the hero of a story by Cervantes that satirizes chivalric romances, published in two parts in 1605 and 1615. Don Quixote is chivalrous and idealistic but ridiculously impractical. **2** any person of high but impractical ideas.

don't (dōnt) do not.
☛ *Usage.* **Don't** is universally used in conversation and often in informal writing when *do not* would seem too emphatic or when rhythm seems more comfortable with the shorter form. The use of **don't** in place of *does not* is substandard.

doo·dad (dü′dad) *n. Informal.* a fancy, trifling ornament.

doo·dle (dü′dəl) *v.* **-dled, -dling;** *n.* —*v.* make drawings or marks of any kind while thinking of something else; drawing absent-mindedly: *He doodled while he was talking on the telephone.* —*n.* a drawing or mark made absent-mindedly.

doo·dle·bug (dü′dəl bug′) *n.* **1** *Informal.* a small car or other vehicle. **2** any of various devices with which it is claimed mineral and oil deposits can be located. **3** *Informal.* buzz bomb. **4** *U.S.* **a** the larva of the ant lion. **b** any of various similar larvae. [< *doodle* simpleton + *bug*]

doo·hick·ey (dü′hik ē) *n. Informal.* **1** any small mechanical device; gadget. **2** any small device, whose name has been

temporarily forgotten: *Pass that doohickey for opening windows.* [a humorous coinage based on *do*]

doom (düm) *n., v.* —*n.* **1** fate. **2** an unhappy or terrible fate; ruin; death: *The soldiers marched to their doom in battle.* **3** judgment; sentence: *The judge pronounced the guilty man's doom.* **4** the end of the world; God's final judgment of mankind.
—*v.* **1** make a bad or undesirable outcome certain: *The weather doomed our hopes for a picnic.* **2** destine to an unhappy or terrible fate: *the doomed men.* **3** condemn (to punishment): *The prisoner was doomed to death.* [OE *dōm* law, judgment]
☛ *Syn. n.* **1.** See note at **fate.**

dooms·day (dümz′dā′) *n.* the end of the world; day of God's final judgment of mankind.

Doomsday Book Domesday Book.

door (dôr) *n.* **1** a movable structure of wood, metal, glass, etc. intended for closing up an entrance to a building or room: *Doors usually swing or slide open and shut.* **2** a similar structure designed to close off an opening giving access to a cupboard, closet, etc.: *a bookcase with sliding glass doors.* **3** an opening where a door is; doorway: *I saw him just as he came through the door.* **4** the room or building to which a particular door belongs: *His house is three doors down the street.* **5** any means by which to go in or out; a way to get something; access: *an open door to the Yukon.*
close, shut, or **slam the door,** reject or exclude; make something impossible: *The car accident slammed the door on our hopes of a summer trip.*
lay at the door of, blame for.
show (someone) **the door,** ask or order a person to leave.
[OE *duru*] —**door′like′,** *adj.*

door·bell (dôr′bel′) *n.* a bell inside the house to be rung by pressing a button or pulling a handle on the outside of a door as a signal that someone has arrived.

door·jamb (dôr′jam′) *n.* the upright piece forming the side of a doorway.

door·keeper (dôr′kēp′ər) *n.* **1** a person who guards a door or entrance. **2** doorman.

door·knob (dôr′nob′) *n.* a knob on a door that releases the latch of the door when turned.

door·man (dôr′mən *or* -man′) *n., pl.* **-men. 1** a person whose work is opening the door of a hotel, store, apartment house, etc. for people going in or out. **2** a person who guards a door.

door·mat (dôr′mat′) *n.* **1** a mat for wiping dirt off shoes, usually placed at an outside door of a house. **2** *Informal.* a person who is easily imposed upon. **3** knotgrass.

door·nail (dôr′nāl′) *n.* a nail with a large head.
dead as a doornail, entirely dead.

door·plate (dôr′plāt′) *n.* a metal plate on a door with a name, number, etc. on it.

door·post (dôr′pōst′) *n.* doorjamb.

door·sill (dôr′sil′) *n.* threshold.

door·step (dôr′step′) *n.* a step leading from an outside door to the ground.

door·stop (dôr′stop′) *n.* a device to hold a door open or to prevent it from opening too far.

door-to-door (dôr′tə dôr′) *adj., adv.* —*adj.* **1** making a call, often uninvited, at each residential or business address in turn in a particular area or district: *a door-to-door salesman, a door-to-door canvasser.* **2** made or done by going from one address to the next: *door-to-door selling.* **3** going from the original starting point to the final destination: *The courier service offers door-to-door delivery.*
—*adv.* **1** at or to each address in turn: *She went door-to-door, campaigning for the election.* **2** from starting point to destination: *The taxi cost us six dollars door-to-door.*

door·way (dôr′wā′) *n.* an entrance to be closed by a door.

door·yard (dôr′yärd′) *n.* a yard near the door of a house; yard around a house.

doo·zer (dü′zər) *n. Slang.* doozy.

doo·zy (dü′zē) *n. Slang.* an outstanding person or thing: *Their new camper is a doozy.*

dope (dōp) *n., v.* **doped, dop·ing.** —*n.* **1** *Slang.* a harmful narcotic drug, such as heroin or opium. **2** oil, grease, etc., used to make machinery run smoothly. **3** a varnish formerly put on the cloth parts of an airplane to make them stronger, waterproof, and airtight. **4** *Slang.* facts; information: *What's the latest dope on the scandal?* **5** *Slang.* a forecast; prediction. **6** *Slang.* a very stupid person. **7** *Slang.* a stimulating drug illegally given to a horse before a race. —*v.* **1** *Slang.* apply or give dope to: *The doctor doped her before setting her broken leg.* **2** use dope. **3** *Slang.* work out; forecast;

predict. [< Du. *doop* dipping sauce < *doopen* dip] —**dop′er,** *n.*

dope·ster (dōp′stər) *n. Slang.* a person who claims to be in the know, especially in sports, politics, etc., and makes forecasts about future events.

dope·y or **dop·y** (dōp′ē) *adj. Slang.* **1** drugged; drowsy; as if affected by drugs. **2** very stupid.

dop·pel·gäng·er (dup′əl geng′ər) *n.* a ghostly double of a living person. [< G < *doppel* double + *Gänger* goer]

dop·pler or **Dop·pler** (dop′lər) *adj.* of or having to do with the Doppler effect.

Doppler effect *Physics.* the apparent shift in the frequency of sound, light, and other waves caused by relative movement between the source and the observer. [< Christian *Doppler* (1803-1853), an Austrian physicist]

Doppler shift Doppler effect.

dor (dôr) *n.* a kind of large beetle. [OE *dora*]

do·ré (dô′rā *or* dô′rē) *n. Cdn.* walleye (def. 7). [Cdn.F *(poisson) doré* golden (fish)]

Do·ri·an (dô′rē ən) *adj., n.* —*adj.* of or having to do with Doris or its inhabitants; Doric. —*n.* a native or inhabitant of Doris.

Dor·ic (dôr′ik) *adj., n.* —*adj.* **1** *Architecture.* of, having to do with, or designating the earliest of the three orders of ancient Greek architecture. The characteristic Doric column is eight diameters high and has a tapering shaft with shallow flutes and a plain, rounded capital. The Parthenon in Athens, dedicated to the goddess Athena, is a Doric temple. See **order** for picture. **2** of or having to do with Doris, a small region in the central part of ancient Greece, its people, or their language. —*n.* a dialect of ancient Greek spoken especially in the Peloponnesus.

Dor·king (dôr′king) *n.* a breed of chicken having a long, heavy body and five toes on each foot. [after *Dorking*, a town in Surrey, England]

dorm (dôrm) *n. Informal.* dormitory.

dor·man·cy (dôr′mən sē) *n.* a dormant condition.

dor·mant (dôr′mənt) *adj.* **1** sleeping or apparently sleeping: *Bears are dormant during the winter.* **2** in a state of rest or inactivity: *a dormant volcano. Plant bulbs are dormant during the cold of winter.* [ME < OF *dormant*, ppr. of *dormir* sleep < L *dormire*]
☛ *Syn.* **3.** See note at **inactive.**

Dormers on a 19th-century mansion designed by Sir Charles Barry, in Guelph, Ontario

dor·mer (dôr′mər) *n.* **1** a small, gablelike structure projecting from a sloping roof, having a window set vertically into the outer end. **2** the window itself. [originally, a sleeping room; < OF *dormeor* < L *dormitorium.* Doublet of DORMITORY.]

dormer window dormer.

dor·mi·to·ry (dôr′mə tô′rē) *n., pl.* **-ries. 1** a sleeping room containing a number of beds. **2** a building with sleeping and living accommodation for many people; a residence, as for students at a university. **3** (*adj.*) of or designating a community serving as a residential satellite to a nearby city. [< L *dormitorium* < *dormire* sleep. Doublet of DORMER.]

dor·mouse (dôr′mous′) *n., pl.* **-mice.** any of numerous small, mouselike rodents of the Old World, especially *Muscardinus avellanarius*, having fine, soft fur, large black eyes, and a very long furry tail. [apparently < E dial. *dorm* sleep, doze (< F *dormir* < L *dormire*) + mouse]

dor·sal (dôr′səl) *adj.* of, on, or near the back: *a dorsal fin.* [< LL *dorsalis* < L *dorsum* back] —**dor′sal·ly,** *adv.*

Dor·set (dôr′sit) *n.* an Eskimo culture of northeastern Canada and N Greenland, lasting from approximately 900 B.C. to A.D. 1000, characterized by skill in carving and by the hunting of seal and caribou. [< Cape *Dorset*, Baffin Island]

do·ry¹ (dô′rē) *n., pl.* **-ries.** a rowboat with a flat bottom and high sides, often used by ocean fishermen. [< Central Am.Ind. *dóri* dugout]

do·ry² (dô′rē) *n., pl.* **-ries.** *Cdn.* **1** John Dory, an edible sea fish. **2** walleye (def. 7); doré. [< doré]

dos·age (dōs′ij) *n.* **1** the size and frequency of a dose. **2** the

giving of medicine in doses. **3** the intensity or length of application of X-rays in certain methods of therapy.

dose (dōs) *n., v.* **dosed, dos·ing.** —*n.* **1** the amount of a medicine to be taken at one time. **2** a portion; the amount of anything given at one time as a remedy, treatment, etc.: *a dose of flattery.* **3** a certain amount of brandy, sugar etc. added to wine to give it strength or flavor.
—*v.* **1** give medicine to in doses; treat with medicine: *The doctor dosed the boy with quinine.* **2** add syrup, etc. to (wine) during bottling to increase flavor or strength. [< F < LL < Gk. *dosis* a giving < *didonai* give] —**dos′er,** *n.*

do·sim·e·ter (dō sim′ə tər) *n.* a device for measuring the dosage or amount of radiation received over a given period of time. [< Gk. *dosis* dose + E -*meter*]

doss (dos) *n., v.* —*n. Slang.* **1** a bed in a cheap lodging house. **2** a doss house. **3** sleep.
—*v.* **1** bed down in any convenient spot; sleep. [probably < F *dos* the back < VL *dossum* < L *dorsum*]

doss house *Slang.* a cheap lodging house.

dos·si·er (dos′ē ā *or* dos′ē ər) *n.* a collection of papers or documents about some subject or person. [< F]

dost (dust) *v. Archaic.* doest.

dot¹ (dot) *n., v.* **dot·ted, dot·ting.** —*n.* **1** a tiny, round mark; a very small spot; point. **2** a small round spot: *a blue necktie with white dots.* **3** *Music.* **a** a tiny, round mark after a note or rest that makes it half again as long. **b** a similar mark placed over or under a note to indicate that it is to be played or sung staccato. **4** a short sound used in sending messages by telegraph or radio.
on the dot, *Informal.* at exactly the right time; at the specified time.
—*v.* **1** mark with a dot or dots: *He never dots his i's when he writes.* **2** be here and there in; give variety to: *Trees and bushes dotted the broad lawn.*
dot (one's) i's and cross (one's) t's *or* **dot the i's and cross the t's,** be very accurate or meticulous.

dot² (dot) *n.* dowry. [< F < L *dos, dotis*]

DOT *or* **D.O.T.** Department of Transport.

dot·age (dōt′ij) *n.* an enfeebled and childish mental condition that sometimes accompanies old age. [< *dote*]

do·tard (dō′tərd) *n.* a person who is mentally enfeebled and childish because of old age; one in his dotage. [< *dote*]

dote (dōt) *v.* **dot·ed, dot·ing. 1** be feeble-minded and childish because of old age. **2** be foolishly fond of; be too fond (*used with* **on** *or* **upon**): *He dotes on his daughter.* [ME *doten*] —**dot′er,** *n.*

doth (duth) *v. Archaic.* doeth.

dot·ted (dot′id) *adj.* **1** marked with or as with a dot or dots. **2** formed of dots: *Sign on the dotted line.* **3** *Music.* of a note or rest, followed by a dot, thus making it half again as long: *a dotted eighth.*

dotted swiss a kind of swiss (a fine, sheer, crisp fabric) having a pattern of woven or flocked dots. [< *Swiss* (muslin)]

dot·ter·el (dot′ər əl) *n.* **1** a rare Eurasian plover (*Eudromias morinellus*) having a mottled brown back and reddish-brown belly. **2** any of various other birds of the same family (Charadriidae, especially genus *Charadrius*). **3** *Brit. Dialect.* a stupid person who is easily fooled or cheated. [< *dote*]

dot·tle (dot′əl) *n.* the plug of tobacco left in a pipe after smoking. [ME *dottel* a plug, ? dim. of *dot* small piece]

dot·ty (dot′ē) *adj.* **-ti·er, -ti·est. 1** *Informal.* feeble-minded or mentally unbalanced. **2** *Informal.* unsteady; shaky; feeble. **3** *Informal.* very enthusiastic. **4** full of dots. —**dot′ti·ness,** *n.*

Dou·ay Bible (dü′ā) an English translation of the Latin Vulgate Bible, made by a group of Roman Catholic scholars. The New Testament was published at Reims in 1582, the Old Testament at Douai in 1609-1610. The Douay Bible is the version traditionally used by English-speaking Roman Catholics. [< *Douai*, a town in N France]

Douay Version Douay Bible.

dou·ble (dub′əl) *adj., adv., n., v.* **-bled, -bling.** —*adj.* **1** twice as much, as many, as large, as strong, etc.: *double pay, a double letter.* **2** for two: *a double bed.* **3** made of two similar parts; in a pair: *double doors.* **4** made of two unlike parts; combining two in one. *Bear* has a double meaning: *carry* and a certain animal. **5** insincere; deceitful; false: *a double tongue.* **6** *Botany.* having more than one set of petals: *Some roses are double, others are single.* **7** *Music.* **a** having two beats or a multiple of two beats to the measure. **b** (of an instrument) producing a tone an octave lower than the ordinary instrument: *a double trumpet.*
—*adv.* **1** twice. **2** two (of everything) instead of one: *The blow made him see double.*
—*n.* **1** a number or amount that is twice as much. **2** a person or thing just like another: *I saw your double in the streetcar yesterday. She always uses a double to do the stunts for her in her films.* **3** a fold; bend. **4** a sharp backward bend or turn; shift. **5** *Baseball.* the

hat, āge, fär; let, ēqual, tèrm; it, īce
hot, ōpen, ôrder; oil, out; cup, pùt, rüle,
above, takən, pencəl, lemən, circəs
ch, child; ng, long; sh, ship
th, thin; ⱦH, then; zh, measure

hit by which a batter gets to second base. **6** *Bridge.* the act of doubling a bid. **7** **doubles,** *pl.* game with two players on each side.
on the double, a quickly; at a run. **b** in double time.
—*v.* **1** make twice as much or twice as many. **2** become twice as much or as many. **3** be used for another; be the double of. **4** take another's place: *Tom doubled for me when I couldn't get to the meeting.* **5** serve two purposes; play two parts: *The maid doubled as cook.* **6** fold; bend: *He doubled his fists in anger.* **7** turn suddenly and sharply; turn back on one's own trail: *The fox doubled back on its track to get away from the dogs.* **8** go around: *The ship doubled the Cape.* **9** *Bridge.* increase the points or penalties of (an opponent's bid). **10** turn at the run: *We doubled over to the barracks.* **11** make move at the run: *The corporal doubled his men around the building.* **12** *Baseball.* make a two-base hit.
double back, a fold over: *She doubled back the cloth to make a hem.* **b** go back the same way that one came: *He decided he must have passed the house, so he doubled back.*
double up, a fold back; fold up: *He doubled up the dollar bill and put it in his pocket.* **b** draw the knees up toward the chest; bend the upper part of the body toward the lower part: *She doubled up in pain.* **c** share a room, a bed, etc. with another: *When guests came, the two brothers had to double up.* **d** move at the double; run. [ME < OF < L *duplus.* Doublet of DUPLE.] —**dou′bler,** *n.*
☛ *Usage.* **Double letter.** In abbreviations, a double letter often indicates plurality: *pp.* = *pages; LL.B.* = *Bachelor of Laws.*
☛ *Usage.* **Double negative.** The use of two negatives for one is no longer acceptable in formal or informal educated usage, though it is often found in substandard speech and writing. Substandard: *There wasn't no answer to my call.* Formal and informal: *There was no answer to my call. There wasn't any answer to my call.* But two negatives cancelling each other out may be used for special effects: *He isn't unaware of it.*

double agent a person who is ostensibly working as a secret agent for one side but is in fact working for the other. A double agent may even be deceiving both sides.

double bar *Music.* a double line on a staff that marks the end of a movement or of an entire piece of music.

dou·ble–bar·relled *or* **dou·ble–bar·reled** (dub′əl bar′əld *or* dub′əl ber′əld) *adj.* **1** having two barrels: *a double-barrelled shotgun.* **2** having a two-fold purpose. **3** having a double meaning: *a double-barrelled question.*

A double bass

double bass a stringed instrument with a deep bass tone, the largest member of the modern violin family, played standing upright on the floor with the player standing behind it. The double bass, which has five or six strings, is derived directly from one of the seventeenth-century viols, not from the violins.

double bassoon a large bassoon, an octave lower in pitch than the ordinary bassoon.

double bill two plays, movies, etc. presented on one program.

double boiler a pair of pans, one of which fits down into the other. The food in the upper pan is cooked gently by the heat from the boiling water in the lower pan.

dou·ble–breast·ed (dub′əl bres′tid) *adj.* of clothing, overlapping enough to make two thicknesses cross the breast and having two rows of buttons.

dou·ble–check (dub′əl chek′) *v., n.* —*v.* check twice: *The police double-checked the vagrant's story before releasing him.* —*n.* a checking of something twice.

double chin a soft fold of flesh under the chin.

double cross *Informal.* an act of treachery.

dou·ble–cross (dub'əl krös') *v. Informal.* promise to do one thing and then do another; be treacherous to. —**dou'ble-cross'er,** *n.*

double dagger a mark (‡) used for reference from one place in a book to another.

dou·ble–deal·er (dub'əl dēl'ər) *n.* a person guilty of double-dealing.

dou·ble–deal·ing (dub'əl dēl'ing) *n. or adj.* pretending to do one thing and then doing another; deceiving.

double–deck (dub'əl dek') *adj., v.* —*adj.* having or consisting of two decks, floors, levels, sections, etc.: *double-deck beds.* —*v.* arrange or construct in two decks, floors, etc.

dou·ble–deck·er (dub'əl dek'ər) *n.* 1 a structure having two decks, floors, levels, sections, etc.: *Some railway cars are double-deckers.* 2 a sandwich having two layers of filling between three slices of bread.

dou·ble–edged (dub'əl ejd') *adj.* 1 two-edged. 2 as much against as for: *a double-edged compliment.*

dou·ble–en·ten·dre (du'bəl on ton'drə; *French,* dü blän täN'drə) *n.* a word or expression with two meanings. One is often indelicate or improper. [< obs. F *double entendre,* literally, to be taken two ways]

double entry a system of bookkeeping in which each transaction is written down twice, once on the credit side of the account and once on the debit side.

dou·ble–faced (dub'əl fāst') *adj.* 1 having two faces or aspects. 2 of cloth, having a nap or finish on both sides. 3 two-faced.

double feature a motion-picture program with two full-length films.

dou·ble–head·ed (dub'əl hed'id) *adj.* 1 two-fold; double. 2 having two heads: *a double-headed tool.* 3 having both good and bad qualities.

dou·ble–head·er (dub'əl hed'ər) *n.* 1 two baseball games between the same teams on the same day, one right after the other. 2 a railway train pulled by two engines.

double indemnity in life insurance, a clause binding the insurance company to pay twice the face value of the policy in case of the accidental death of the insured.

dou·ble–joint·ed (dub'əl join'tid) *adj.* having very flexible joints that allow fingers, arms, legs, etc. to bend in unusual ways.

double knit a knitted fabric made on a machine with a double set of needles to produce a double thickness of cloth: *Double knits are often reversible.*

double–knit (dub'əl nit') *adj.* knitted on a machine with a double set of needles: *double-knit jersey.*

dou·ble–park (dub'əl pärk') *v.* park (a car, etc.) beside another car that is occupying the area where parking is allowed: *It is usually illegal to double-park.*

double play *Baseball.* a play in which two base runners are put out. —**double'-play',** *adj.*

dou·ble–quick (dub'əl kwik') *n., adj., adv., v.* —*n.* in marching, the next quickest step to a run.
—*adj.* very quick.
—*adv.* in double-quick time.
—*v.* march in double-quick step.

dou·ble–reed (dub'əl rēd') *adj. Music.* having two reeds bound together and made to vibrate against each other. The oboe and the bassoon are double-reed instruments.

double sharp *Music.* a sign (× or ⊗) to indicate that a note must be raised two half tones above the natural pitch.

dou·ble·speak (dub'əl spēk') *n.* double talk.

double star two stars so close together that they look like one to the naked eye.

A doublet of the
early 17th century

dou·blet (dub'lit) *n.* 1 a short, close-fitting jacket with or without

sleeves, worn by European men from about the 15th to the 17th century. 2 a pair of two similar or equal things. 3 one of a pair. 4 one of two or more words in a language, derived from the same original source but coming by different routes. *Example: fragile* and *frail.*

double tackle a pulley with two grooved wheels.

dou·ble–take (dub'əl tāk') *n.* a delayed reaction to a situation, joke, etc., often used for comic effect by actors.

double talk talk that is purposely made confusing so as to cloak ignorance or deceit.

dou·ble–think (dub'əl thingk') *n.* the simultaneous acceptance or putting forth of ideas, concepts, or principles that are in fact contradictory. Doublethink may be unconscious, or it may be deliberate and intended to mislead. [coined by George Orwell in his novel *1984,* pub. 1949]

double time 1 payment at twice the normal rate: *They get double time for working on Sundays or holidays.* 2 a rate of marching in which 180 paces, each of about 90 cm, are taken in a minute. 3 double-quick.

dou·ble·tree (dub'əl trē') *n.* a crossbar on a carriage, wagon, plough, etc. When two horses are used, the singletrees of their harness are attached to this crossbar.

double window a window together with a storm window, made either in one piece or as separate structures.

dou·bloon (dub lün') *n.* a former Spanish gold coin. Its value varied from about $5 to about $16. [< F *doublon* or < Sp. *doblón* < *doble* double]

dou·bly (dub'lē) *adv.* 1 twice; twice as. 2 two at a time. 3 *Archaic.* deceitfully.

doubt (dout) *v., n.* —*v.* 1 not believe; not to be sure of; feel uncertain about. 2 be uncertain. 3 *Archaic.* be afraid; fear; suspect: *They doubted a sinister motive in the king's friendliness.*
—*n.* 1 a lack of belief or sureness; uncertainty. 2 a feeling of uncertainty. 3 an uncertain condition or situation: *In such a case, the defendant is entitled to the benefit of the doubt.*
beyond doubt, surely; certainly.
in doubt, not sure; uncertain.
no doubt, a surely; certainly: *No doubt we will win in the end.*
b probably: *Even if he had money, he'd no doubt expect me to pay the bill.*
without doubt, without question; certainly: *He will pass the test without doubt.*
[ME < OF *douter* < L *dubitare*] —**doubt'er,** *n.* —**doubt'ing·ly,** *adv.*

☛ *Syn. n.* 1. See note at **suspicion.**

☛ *Usage.* In negative statements the verb **doubt** is followed by *that: I don't doubt that she is clever.* In positive statements use *whether* (in formal use) or *if* (informal) to show uncertainty: *I doubt whether she can pass the exam.* To show real lack of belief, use *that: I doubt that she can answer this question.*

doubt·ful (dout'fəl) *adj.* 1 unclear; not distinct; not certain: *a doubtful advantage. It is doubtful whether he ever saw his friend again.* 2 full of doubt; feeling uncertain: *He looked doubtful.* 3 open to question or suspicion: *Her sly answers made her sincerity doubtful.* —**doubt'ful·ly,** *adv.* —**doubt'ful·ness,** *n.*

doubting Thomas (tom'əs) a person who doubts everything. [< St. *Thomas,* the disciple who doubted Christ's resurrection (John 20: 24-29).]

doubt·less (dout'lis) *adv.* 1 surely; certainly. 2 probably. —**doubt'less·ly,** *adv.* —**doubt'less·ness,** *n.*

douche (düsh) *n., v.* **douched, douch·ing.** —*n.* 1 a jet of water applied on or into any part of the body: *A douche of salt water up my nose helped relieve my cold in the head.* 2 an application of a douche. 3 a spray, syringe, or other device for applying a douche.
—*v.* 1 apply a douche to. 2 take a douche. [< F < Ital. *doccia,* ult. < L *ducere* lead]

dough (dō) *n.* 1 a soft, thick mixture of flour, liquid, and other ingredients for baking. Bread, biscuits, cake, pie crust, etc. are made from dough. 2 any soft, thick mass like this. 3 *Informal.* money. [OE *dāg*] —**dough'like',** *adj.*

dough·boy (dō'boi') *n. U.S. Informal.* an infantryman in the United States army.

dough·nut (dō'nut') *n.* a small cake, often ring-shaped, fried in deep fat.

dough·ty (dou'tē) *adj.* **-ti·er, -ti·est.** *Archaic.* brave; valiant; strong: *doughty knights.* [OE *dohtig < dugan* be good] —**dought'i·ly,** *adv.* —**dough'ti·ness,** *n.*

dough·y (dō'ē) *adj.* **dough·i·er, dough·i·est.** of or like dough; soft and thick or pale and flabby.

Doug·las fir (dug'ləs) 1 any of a small genus (*Pseudotsuga*) of trees of the pine family native to W North America and E Asia; especially, *P. menziesii,* one of the most important timber trees of North America, having long, narrow, hanging cones and flat needles

growing singly along the stem. This species occurs in two forms: a very tall coastal form with yellowish-green needles, usually growing to more than 50 metres high, and a smaller, inland form with bluish-green needles. 2 the hard, strong wood of this tree. [after David *Douglas* (1798-1834), a Scottish botanist and explorer]

Douk (dūk) *n. Slang.* Doukhobor.

Douk·ho·bor or **Douk·ho·bour** (dü′kə bôr′) *n.* a member of a 200-year-old Christian sect originally from Russia, that traditionally believes that every person knows what is right and must be guided by this knowledge rather than by any outside authority. Several thousand Doukhobors left Russia in 1898 and settled in western Canada. [< Russian *dukhoborcy* < *dukh* spirit + *borcy* wrestlers]

Dou·ma (dü′mä) See **Duma.**

dour (dür *or* dour) *adj.* 1 gloomy; sullen. 2 stern; severe. 3 stubborn. [< L *durus* hard, stern] —**dour′ly,** *adv.* —**dour′ness,** *n.*

douse (dous) *v.* **doused, dous·ing.** 1 plunge or be plunged into water or any other liquid. 2 throw water over; drench. 3 *Informal.* put out (a light); extinguish: *We doused the candles.* 4 lower or slacken (a sail) in haste. 5 close (a porthole). [origin uncertain] —**dous′er,** *n.*

dove[1] (duv) *n.* 1 any of various species of pigeon, especially any of several of the smaller, wild species. 2 **Dove,** the Holy Ghost. 3 a person who tends to favor compromise of conciliation in disputes or controversial issues, especially one who opposes war or a policy of military strength. Compare **hawk**[1] (def. 3). 4 a gentle, innocent, or loving person. [OE *dūfe.* Related to DIVE.]

dove[2] (dōv) *v.* a pt. of **dive.**
☛ *Usage.* See note at **dive.**

dove·cot (duv′kot′) *n.* dovecote.

dove·cote (duv′kōt′) *n.* a small house or shelter for doves or pigeons.

dove·kie (duv′kē) *n.* 1 a small, black-and-white auk (*Plautus alle*) of the North Atlantic, which breeds in the Arctic and winters farther south. It is common as a migrant along the eastern Canadian coasts from Baffin Island south to the Maritimes. Also, **dovekey.** 2 the black guillemot. See **guillemot.** [Scottish dim. of *dove*[1]]

dove·tail (duv′tāl′) *n., v.* —*n.* 1 a wedge-shaped projection at the end of a piece of wood, metal, etc. that can be fitted into a corresponding opening at the end of another piece to form a joint. 2 the joint formed in this way. —*v.* 1 fasten, join, or fit together with projections that fit into openings. 2 fit together exactly: *The various bits of evidence dovetailed so completely that the mystery was solved at once.*

dow·a·ger (dou′ə jər) *n.* 1 a woman who holds some title or property from her dead husband: *The queen and her mother-in-law, the queen dowager, were both present.* 2 *Informal.* a dignified, elderly woman. [< OF *douagere* < *douage* dower < *douer* endow < L *dotare*]

dow·dy (dou′dē) *adj.* **-di·er, -di·est;** *n., pl.* **-dies.** —*adj.* 1 dressed in a dull or unimaginative way: *a dowdy person.* 2 not stylish; shabby: *The old lady wore a dowdy coat and a shapeless hat.* —*n.* a woman whose clothes are dowdy. [origin uncertain] —**dow′di·ly,** *adv.* —**dow′di·ness,** *n.*

dow·el (dou′əl) *n., v.* **-elled** or **-eled, -el·ling** or **-el·ing.** —*n.* a peg or pin fitted into corresponding holes in two pieces of wood, etc. so as to form a joint holding the two pieces or parts together. See **joint** for picture. —*v.* fasten or furnish with dowels. [probably akin to MLG *dovel,* G *Döbel* plug, tap (of a cask)]

dow·er (dou′ər) *n., v.* —*n.* 1 *Law.* a widow's share of her dead husband's property. 2 *Archaic or poetic.* dowry. 3 a natural gift, talent, or quality; endowment. —*v.* provide with a dower; endow. [ME < OF *douaire* < Med.L *dotarium* < L *dotare* endow < *dos, dotis* dowry] —**dow′er·less,** *adj.*

dow·itch·er (dou′ə chər) *n.* either of two very similar and closely related species (*Limnodromus griseus* and *L. scolopaceus*) of shore bird belonging to the same family as sandpipers and snipes, having a very long, straight bill and a white lower back and rump. They breed in arctic and subarctic regions of North America and winter as far south as Central and South America.

down[1] (doun) *adv., prep., adj., v., n.* —*adv.* 1 from a higher to a lower place or condition: *The soldiers laid down their arms. They ran down from the top of the hill.* 2 in a lower place or condition: *Down in the valley the fog still lingers.* 3 to or in a place or condition thought of as lower: *down river; down East. He lives in the Yukon, but goes down to Vancouver every winter.* 4 to a position or condition that is difficult, dangerous, etc.: *The dogs ran the fox down.* 5 from an earlier to a later time or person: *The house was handed down from father to son.* 6 from a larger to a smaller amount, degree, station, etc.: *everyone from the hotel manager down to the shoeshine boy. The temperature has gone down.* 7 actually; really: *Stop talking, and get down to work.* 8 on paper; in

hat, āge, fär; let, ēqual, tėrm; it, īce
hot, ōpen, ôrder; oil, out; cup, pút, rüle,
əbove, takən, pencəl, lemən, circəs
ch, child; ng, long; sh, ship
th, thin; ℸн, then; zh, measure

writing: *Take down what I say.* 9 when bought: *You can pay part of the price down and the rest later.* 10 into a heavier or more concentrated form: *to boil down to a thick syrup.*
down with, a put down. **b** get rid of.
down with (someone or something)! an exclamation used to express a strong desire for the removal or end of somebody or something: *Down with the King! Down with TV!*
—*prep.* down along, through, or into: *to ride down a hill, to walk down a street, to sail down a river.*
—*adj.* 1 in a lower place or condition. 2 going or pointed down: *the down escalator.* 3 sick; ill: *She is down with a cold.* 4 sad; discouraged: *He felt down about his failure.* 5 *Football.* no longer in play. 6 behind an opponent by a certain number. 7 *Baseball.* out.
down and out, a completely without health, money, friends, etc. **b** *Boxing.* knocked out.
down on, *Informal.* **a** angry at; having a grudge against. **b** attacking; criticizing.
—*v.* 1 put down; get down: *He downed the medicine at one swallow.* 2 defeat: *to down the favorite team.* 3 lie down: *Down, Fido!*
—*n.* 1 a downward movement. 2 a period of bad luck or unhappiness: *the ups and downs of life.* 3 *Football.* a chance to move the ball forward. In Canadian football, a team is allowed three downs in which to move the ball forward ten yards. 4 *Informal.* a grudge: *to have a down on someone.* [var. of *adown,* OE *adūne,* earlier *of dūne* from (the) hill. Cf. *down*[3].]

down[2] (doun) *n.* 1 the short, soft, fluffy feathers beneath the outer feathers of adult birds, and forming the plumage of young birds. Down is used in pillows and as a lightweight insulation for winter clothing, etc. 2 soft hair or fluff; fuzz: *The down on a boy's chin develops into a beard.* [ME < ON *dúnn*]

down[3] (doun) *n.* Usually, **downs,** *pl.* a stretch of high, rolling, grassy land. [OE *dūn* hill]

down·beat (doun′bēt′) *n., adj.* —*n. Music.* 1 the first beat in a measure. 2 the downward gesture of the conductor's hand to indicate this beat. —*adj. Informal.* 1 casual and relaxed: *an official tour with a downbeat approach.* 2 depressing or depressed.

down·cast (doun′kast′) *adj., n.* —*adj.* 1 directed downward: *Ashamed of his mistake, he stood with downcast eyes.* 2 dejected; sad; discouraged: *She was downcast by her failure to make the team.* —*n.* a ventilation shaft in a mine.

down·er (dou′nər) *n. Slang.* 1 a depressant drug, such as a tranquillizer or barbiturate. 2 a depressing experience or situation: *That interview was a downer.*

down·fall (doun′fol′ *or* -fôl′) *n.* 1 a coming to ruin; sudden overthrow of a great person, institution, or nation through a change in fortune: *the downfall of a hero, the downfall of an empire.* 2 a heavy fall of rain or snow; a downpour.

down·fall·en (doun′fol′ən *or* -fôl′ən) *adj.* fallen; overthrown; ruined.

down–filled (doun′fild′) *adj.* filled or insulated with down from birds: *Down-filled pillows are very soft. Down-filled clothing is very light and warm.*

down·fold (doun′fōld′) *n. Geology.* a downward fold or depression; syncline.

down·grade (doun′grād′) *n., v.* **-grad·ed, -grad·ing.** —*n.* 1 a downward slope. 2 a going down toward an inferior state or condition: *He's been on the downgrade since he missed that promotion.* —*v.* 1 lower the status and rate of pay of a job or person: *The position has been downgraded.* 2 reduce in value or esteem: *a downgraded reputation.* 3 think of or refer to in a slighting way; belittle: *Don't downgrade the novel; it was a first attempt.*

down·heart·ed (doun′här′tid) *adj.* discouraged; dejected; depressed. —**down′heart′ed·ly,** *adv.* —**down′heart′ed·ness,** *n.*

down·hill (doun′hil′) *adv., adj.* —*adv.* 1 down the slope of a hill; toward the bottom of a hill. 2 toward a worse condition or state (used especially in the expression **go downhill**): *Her business has been going downhill for some time.*
—*adj.* 1 sloping or going downward: *a downhill run.* 2 of or designating the sport of skiing down hillsides or mountainsides, usually on prepared slopes, the top of which are reached by means of some sort of mechanical lift. Downhill skiing requires more rigid boots and bindings than cross-country skiing. Also called **alpine.**

3 for use in downhill skiing: *downhill skis.* **4** *Informal.* proceeding smoothly and without effort; easy: *After we got the members signed up, the rest of the planning was all downhill.*

Down·ing Street (doun′ing) **1** in London, a street where several important offices of the British government are located, including the official residence (at No. 10) of the Prime Minister. **2** the British government.

down payment in instalment buying, a deposit or initial payment made at the time of a purchase.

down·pour (doun′pôr′) *n.* a heavy rainfall.

down·right (doun′rīt′) *adj., adv.* —*adj.* **1** thorough; complete: *a downright thief, a downright lie.* **2** plain; positive: *His downright answer left no doubt as to what he thought.* **3** plain and direct in speech or behavior: *a downright person.* —*adv.* **1** thoroughly; completely: *He was downright rude to me.* **2** plainly; definitely. —**down′right·ly,** *adv.* —**down′right′ness,** *n.*

down·spout (doun′spout′) *n.* a vertical pipe attached to an eavestrough for carrying rainwater down to the ground.

Down's syndrome (dounz) mongolism.

down·stage (doun′stāj′) *adj. or adv.* in a theatre, toward or at the front of the stage.

down·stairs (doun′sterz′) *adv., adj., n.* —*adv.* **1** down the stairs: *Bill slipped and fell downstairs.* **2** on a lower floor: *I looked downstairs but couldn't find it.* **3** to a lower floor: *I went downstairs for breakfast.* —*adj.* on a lower floor: *The downstairs rooms are dark.* —*n.* the lower floor or floors: *The downstairs is usually much warmer.*

down·stream (doun′strēm′) *adv., adj.* —*adv.* in the direction of the current of a stream or river. —*adj.* farther along in the direction of a stream or river: *The sawmill was downstream from the town.*

down·time (doun′tīm′) *n.* a period during normal working hours when a machine, department, or factory is shut down for repairs, etc.: *attempts to reduce downtime.*

down-to-earth (doun′tə ėrth′) *adj.* practical; realistic: *He would rather have down-to-earth planning than visionary theories.*

down·town (doun′toun′) *adv., adj., n.* —*adv. or adj.* **1** to, toward, or in the lower part of a town. **2** to or in the main part or business section of a town: *His office is in downtown Vancouver. She likes working downtown.* —*n.* the business section or main part of a town.

down·trod (doun′trod′) *adj.* downtrodden.

down·trod·den (doun′trod′ən) *adj.* **1** tyrannized over; oppressed. **2** trodden down.

down under the region of Australia, New Zealand, etc. [with reference to the antipodes, in relation to the British Isles]

down·ward (doun′wərd) *adv. or adj.* **1** toward a lower place or condition. **2** from an earlier to a later time: *downward through history.* **3** toward a lower or worse condition or state: *There is a downward trend in the economy.* —**down′ward·ly,** *adv.* —**down′ward·ness,** *n.*

down·wards (doun′wərdz) *adv.* downward.

down·y (doun′ē) *adj.* **down·i·er, down·i·est. 1** of soft feathers or hair. **2** covered with soft feathers or hair. **3** like down; soft; fluffy. —**down′i·ly,** *adv.* —**down′i·ness,** *n.*

dow·ry (dou′rē) *n., pl.* **-ries. 1** the money, property, etc. that a bride brings to her husband. **2** a natural gift, talent, or quality; endowment from nature: *a dowry of good health and intelligence.* Also, **dower.** [ME < AF *dowarie* < OF *douaire.* See DOWER.]

dowse (douz) *v.* **dowsed, dows·ing.** use a divining rod to locate water, minerals, etc. [< Brit. dial. (SW England) ? < ME *dushen* push down; 17c.] / —**dows′er,** *n.*

dox·ol·o·gy (doks ol′ə jē) *n., pl.* **-gies.** a hymn or statement praising God. One of the best-known doxologies begins: "Glory to God in the highest." [< Med.L. < Gk. *doxologia* < *doxologos* < *doxa* glory, praise + *logos* speaking]

dox·y¹ (dok′sē) *n. Informal.* a doctrine or belief. [abstracted from *orthodoxy, heterodoxy,* etc.]

dox·y² (dok′sē) *n. Slang.* a prostitute or mistress. [origin uncertain]

doy·en (doi′ən *or* dwä′yən; *French,* dwä yaɴ′) *n.* a leader or senior member of a group. [< F *doyen* dean < OF *deien.* See DEAN.]

doy·enne (doi yen′ *or* dwä yen′; *French,* dwä yen′) *n.* a woman who is a leader or senior member of a group: *the doyenne of popular singers.*

doy·ley (doi′lē) See **doily.**

doz. dozen; dozens.

doze (dōz) *v.* **dozed, doz·ing;** *n.* —*v.* **1** sleep lightly; be half asleep: *I was dozing on the chesterfield when I heard a light knock on the door.* **2** fall into a light sleep (*used with* **off**): *He dozed off during the news broadcast.* —*n.* a light sleep; a nap. [< Scand.; cf. Danish *döse* make dull] —**doz′er,** *n.*

doz·en (duz′ən) *n., pl.* **-ens** or (*after a number*) **-en.** a group of 12. [ME < OF *dozeine* < *douse* twelve < L *duodecim*]

doz·enth (duz′ənth) *adj.* the twelfth.

doz·er (dō′zər) *n. Informal* bulldozer.

doz·y (dō′zē) *adj.* **doz·i·er, doz·i·est.** drowsy; sleepy. —**doz′i·ly,** *adv.* —**doz′i·ness,** *n.*

DP or **D.P.** displaced person.

D.Paed. Doctor of Paedagogy (for L *Doctor Paedagogiae*).

D.Péd. Docteur de Pédagogie.

DPH Department of Public Health.

D.P.H. Diploma of Public Health.

D.Phil. Doctor of Philosophy.

dpt. 1 department. **2** deponent.

dr. 1 dram(s). **2** debtor. **3** drawer. **4** debit.

Dr. or **Dr 1** Doctor. **2** Drive.

drab¹ (drab) *adj.* **drab·ber, drab·best;** *n.* —*adj.* **1** dull; monotonous; unattractive: *the drab houses of the mining town.* **2** dull brownish-grey. —*n.* **1** a dull brownish-grey. **2** a khaki drill uniform: *The soldiers wore drab on manoeuvres.* [apparently var. of *drap* cloth < F. See DRAPE.] —**drab′ly,** *adv.* —**drab′ness,** *n.*

drab² (drab) *n.* **1** a dirty, untidy woman. **2** prostitute. [cf. Irish *drabóg* slattern]

drab³ (drab) *n.* See **dribs and drabs.**

drachm (dram) See **dram.**

drach·ma (drak′mə) *n., pl.* **-mas** or **-mae** (-mē). **1** the basic unit of money in Greece, divided into 100 lepta. See table at **money.** **2** a coin worth one drachma. **3** an ancient Greek silver coin. **4** an ancient Greek unit of mass. [< L *drachma* < Gk. *drachmē* handful]

Dra·co (drā′kō) *n.* a northern constellation, a part of which forms a semicircle around the Little Dipper. [< L *Draco* dragon]

dra·co·ni·an (drā kō′nē ən) *adj.* Often, **Draconian. 1** of or having to do with Draco, an Athenian legislator of the 7th century B.C., or his harsh code of laws. **2** harsh or cruel: *draconian security procedures.*

dra·con·ic (drā kon′ik) *adj.* Sometimes, **Draconic,** draconian. —**dra·con′i·cal·ly,** *adv.*

drae·ger·man (drag′ər mən *or* drā′gər-) *n., pl.* **-men.** *Cdn.* especially in the Maritimes, a coal miner trained in underground rescue work and the use of special oxygen equipment effective in gas-filled mines. [< Alexander B. Dräger (1870-1928), a German scientist who devised the special equipment used by these men + *man*]

draft (draft) *n., v.* —*n.* **1** a current of air inside a building or other enclosed space. **2** a device for regulating a current of air: *When I opened the draft of the furnace the fire burned faster.* **3** a plan; sketch. **4** a rough, unpolished version of a piece of writing. The first draft of an essay is often quite different from the finished work. **5** a selection of persons or things from a group for some special purpose. **6** the persons or things selected. **7** *Esp.U.S.* **a** a system for selecting persons for compulsory military service. **b** a group of persons selected in this way. **8** the act of pulling loads. **9** the quantity or thing pulled. **10** (*adj.*) used for pulling loads: *Draft horses are bigger and stronger than horses used for riding.* **11** the act of pulling in a net to catch fish. **12** the quantity of fish caught in a net at one time. **13** a written order requiring the payment of a stated amount of money, especially a cheque drawn by one branch of a bank on another. **14** a heavy demand or drain on anything: *Her long illness was a draft on her resources.* **15** the depth of water that a ship draws or needs for floating, especially when loaded. **16** the act or an instance of drinking or inhaling: *He emptied the glass at one draft.* **17** the amount drunk or inhaled: *She took in a large draft of fresh air.* **18** the act of drawing beer, ale, etc. from a keg or other container. **19** the amount drawn at one time: *a draft of ale.* **20** (*adj.*) drawn from a keg, etc. when ordered: *Some people prefer draft beer to bottled beer.* **21** beer, ale, etc. drawn from a keg, etc. when ordered: *Do they sell draft there?*

on draft, of beer, ale, etc., available for drawing directly from a keg, etc. when ordered: *Most taverns have beer on draft.*

—*v.* **1** make up or prepare a plan, sketch, or rough version of: *to draft new legislation. She drafted the letter to the editor in the bus on her way home.* **2** select from a group for some special purpose, such as for military service for the special duty in the armed forces: *Ten men from the battalion were drafted for guard duty.* **3** draw off or away. [var. of *draught*] —**draft′er,** *n.*

☛ *Usage.* **Draft** has become the preferred spelling for all senses, though

draught is still widely used for such meanings as in *a draught of fish, a ship's draught,* or *beer on draught.*

draft–dodg·er (draft'doj'ər) *n.* a person who evades compulsory military service, especially in the United States.

draft·ee (draf tē') *n. U.S.* a person who is drafted for military service.

draft horse a large, strong, heavily built horse used for hauling heavy loads, pulling a plough, etc. Draft horses are now bred mainly for show.

drafts·man (drafts'mən) *n., pl.* **-men. 1** a person who makes plans or sketches. A draftsman draws designs or diagrams from which buildings and machines are made. **2** a person who draws up legal or official documents. Also, **draughtsman. 3** an artist who is especially skilled in drawing.
☛ *Usage.* See note at **draft.**

drafts·man·ship (drafts'mən ship') *n.* the work of a draftsman. Also, **draughtsmanship.**

draft·y (draf'tē) *adj.* **draft·i·er, draft·i·est.** having, letting in, or exposed to currents of air: *a drafty room, a drafty window.* Also, **draughty. —draft'i·ly,** *adv.* **—draft'i·ness,** *n.*

drag (drag) *v.* **dragged, drag·ging;** *n.* —*v.* **1** pull or move along heavily or slowly; pull or draw along the ground: *A team of horses dragged the big log out of the forest.* **2** go too slowly: *Time drags when you have nothing to do.* **3** trail along the ground: *Your scarf is dragging.* **4** pull a net, hook, harrow, etc. over or along for some purpose: *to drag a lake for fish or for a drowned person's body.* **5** use a drag. **6** *Slang.* take part in a drag race. **7** *Slang.* puff on a cigarette, etc. **8** bring (something irrelevant) into a discussion (*used with* **in**): *Whatever we're talking about, he drags in stamp-collecting.* **drag out** or **on,** make or be too slow or long: *She dragged her story out to take up the whole coffee break.*
drag (one's) **feet** or **heels,** *Informal.* act or work slowly on purpose.
—*n.* **1** a net, hook, etc. used in dragging. **2** the act of dragging. **3** anything dragged. **4** any person or thing that holds back; an obstruction or hindrance: *outworn ideas that are a drag on progress. A lazy player is a drag on a hockey team.* **5** a low, strong sled for carrying heavy loads; stoneboat. **6** a big coach with seats inside and on top. **7** a heavy harrow or other implement drawn over land to level it and break up clods. **8** a device used to retard motion or action, such as a sea anchor or a brake on a fishing reel or the wheel of a vehicle. **9** the force acting on a body in motion through a fluid in a direction opposite to the body's motion and produced by friction. **10** a pull on a fishing line caused by a water current. **11** *Hunting.* **a** an animal's trail or scent. **b** an artificial scent dragged on the ground to leave a trail for hounds. **c** a drag hunt. **12** *Slang.* social or political influence: *He's got a lot of drag at city hall.* **13** *Slang.* a puff on a cigarette, etc.: *She took a final drag and put out the cigarette.* **14** *Slang.* a boring person or situation: *That party was a drag.* **15** *Slang.* street: *That's the main drag.* **16** *Slang.* women's clothing worn by a man (*used especially in the phrase* **in drag**). [ME < ON *draga,* if not a dial. var. of **draw,** OE *dragan*]
☛ *Syn. v.* **1.** See note at **draw.**

drag·ger (drag'ər) *n.* **1** a person or thing that drags. **2** a boat used in fishing; trawler.

drag·gle (drag'əl) *v.* **-gled, -gling. 1** make wet or dirty by dragging through mud, water, dust, etc. **2** trail along the ground. **3** follow slowly; lag behind; straggle.

drag·hound (drag'hound') *n.* a hound trained to follow an artificial scent or drag.

drag hunt a hunt using an artificial scent or drag.

drag·line (drag'līn') *n.* **1** a rope dragging from something, such as the guide line on a dirigible. **2** an excavating or dredging machine having an endless belt of scoops or buckets that are drawn towards the machine in the digging operation. **3** a rope for pulling anything.

drag·net (drag'net') *n.* **1** a net pulled over the bottom of a river, pond, etc. or along the ground: *Fish and small birds can be caught in a dragnet.* **2** an extensive search or hunt to catch or round up criminals, etc.: *They were arrested in the police dragnet.*

drag·o·man (drag'ə mən) *n., pl.* **-mans** or **-men.** in the Near East, an interpreter. [< F < Med.Gk. *dragomanos* < Arabic *targumān*]

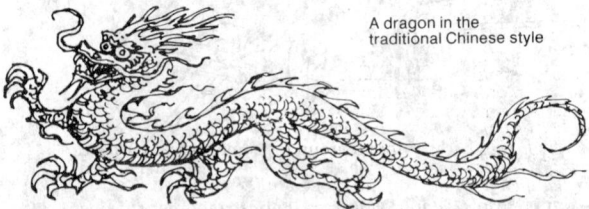
A dragon in the traditional Chinese style

drag·on (drag'ən) *n.* **1** *Folklore and legend.* a monster, usually

hat, āge, fär; let, ēqual, tėrm; it, īce
hot, ōpen, ôrder; oil, out; cup, pùt, rüle,
əbove, takən, pencəl, lemən, circəs
ch, child; ng, long; sh, ship
th, thin; ⱦH, then; zh, measure

conceived of as a huge, fierce, lizardlike or snakelike creature, often having wings like a bat and often capable of breathing out fire and smoke. **2** a fierce, belligerent, or extremely stern person, especially a woman. **3** any of numerous small, brilliantly colored tree lizards (genus *Draco*) of S Asia and the East Indies having winglike membranes. [ME < OF < L *draco* < Gk. *drakōn*] **—drag'on-like',** *adj.*

drag·on·fly (drag'ən flī') *n., pl.* **-flies.** any of a suborder (Anisoptera) of insects having a long, slender body, large head with large eyes, and four long, iridescent, membranous wings which are held straight out from the body when at rest. Dragon flies are harmless and even beneficial to man because they eat many other insects considered harmful.

drag·on·nade (drag'ə näd') *n.* **1** the persecution of the French Protestants by the troops of Louis XIV. **2** any persecution by soldiers. [< F *dragonnade* < *dragon.* See DRAGOON.]

dra·goon (drə gün') *n., v.* —*n.* **1** *Historical.* a soldier who was mounted on a horse and was armed with a heavy musket. **2** a soldier in any of several cavalry regiments. Most dragoon regiments are now equipped with tanks or other armed vehicles. —*v.* **1** oppress or persecute by dragoons. **2** force by violence; bully or oppress: *He was dragooned into signing a false statement.* [< F *dragon* dragon, pistol, (later) soldier]

drag race a contest with motor vehicles to see which can accelerate fastest.

drag·ster (drag'stər) *n. Slang.* a car used in a drag race.

drag strip a straight stretch of asphalt or concrete road set aside or built for drag races.

drain (drān) *v., n.* —*v.* **1** draw a liquid off slowly: *A ditch drains water from a swamp.* **2** flow off gradually: *The water drains into a river.* **3** draw water or other liquid from; empty or dry by draining: *They drained the swamp to get more land for crops.* **4** dry; lose moisture by dripping or flowing: *I left the umbrella outside to drain.* **5** take away from slowly; use up little by little; deprive: *The long war had drained the country of its young people and its resources.* **6** empty by drinking; drink dry: *He drained his glass.*
—*n.* **1** a means, such as a channel or pipe, for carrying off water or other liquid. **2** a slow taking away or withdrawing; a gradual outflow or lessening: *Lack of opportunity at home caused a serious drain of talent to other regions.* **3** anything that causes such an overflow or lessening: *The big car soon became a drain on her budget.*
down the drain, to nothing: *His savings went down the drain on a bad investment.*
[OE *drēahnian.* Related to DRY.]

drain·age (drān'ij) *n.* **1** the act or process of draining; a gradual flowing off. **2** a system of channels or pipes for carrying off water or waste of any kind. **3** what is drained off. **4** the area that is drained.

drainage basin the area that is drained by a river and its tributaries.

drain·board (drān'bôrd') *n.* **1** a board set at a downward angle into one side of a sink for draining off the water from washed dishes. **2** a rubber mat or tray used for the same purpose.

drain·er (drān'ər) *n.* **1** a person who makes channels or lays pipes for draining land. **2** a pan, vat, etc. for draining off liquid.

drain·pipe (drān'pīp') *n.* a pipe for carrying off water or other liquid.

drake (drāk) *n.* the adult male of a duck. [OE *draca* < L *draco.* Doublet of DRAGON.]

dram¹ (dram) *n.* **1** in apothecaries' weight, a unit equal to 60 grains or ⅛ ounce (about 3.89 g). **2** in avoirdupois weight, a unit equal to 27.34 grains or ¹⁄₁₆ ounce (about 1.77 g). **3** a small drink of alcoholic liquor. **4** a small amount of anything. Also, *Brit.* **drachm.** [ME < OF *drame* < L *drachma.* Doublet of DRACHMA.]

dram² (dram) *n. Cdn. Historical. Logging.* a section of a timber raft, made up of several cribs lashed together. [origin uncertain]

dra·ma (dram'ə *or* drä'mə) *n.* **1** a story written to be acted out by actors on a stage or on film, etc.; a play. **2** a series of happenings suggesting a play: *The history of Arctic exploration is a great and thrilling drama.* **3** the art of writing, acting, or producing plays; the branch of literature having to do with plays: *He is studying drama.* [< LL < Gk. *drama* play, deed < *draein* do]

Dram·a·mine (dram'ə mēn') *n. Trademark.* a drug used against seasickness, airsickness, etc. It is also useful against hives.

dra·ma·tic (drə mat′ik) *adj.* **1** of or having to do with plays. **2** seeming like a drama or play; full of action or feeling; exciting: *There was a dramatic pause and then he leaped onto the stage.* —**dra·mat′i·cal·ly,** *adv.*

☛ *Syn.* **2.** Dramatic, theatrical, melodramatic, as applied to situations in real life, mean "having qualities suitable to plays or the stage." **Dramatic** emphasizes genuineness, and suggests exciting the imagination as well as moving the feelings: *The reunion of the veterans with their wives was dramatic.* **Theatrical** emphasizes show and unreality, and suggests artificial or cheap effects calling directly on the feelings: *Her show of gratitude was theatrical.* **Melodramatic** emphasizes falseness and exaggeration, especially in trying to stir up the feelings: *The paper gave a melodramatic account of the child's murder.*

dra·mat·ics (drə mat′iks) *n.pl.* **1** the art or practice of acting or producing plays (*usually used with a singular verb*): *She is studying dramatics.* **2** dramatic productions. **3** exaggerated emotional behavior or expression: *Don't pay any attention to his dramatics.*

dram·a·tis per·so·nae (dram′ə tis pər sō′nē or pər sō′nī) the characters or actors in a play. [< L]

dram·a·tist (dram′ə tist) *n.* a writer of plays; playwright.

dram·a·ti·za·tion (dram′ə tə zā′shən or dram′ə tī zā′shən) *n.* **1** the act of dramatizing. **2** what is dramatized.

dram·a·tize (dram′ə tīz′) *v.* **-tized, -tiz·ing. 1** make a drama of; arrange in the form of a play: *to dramatize a novel.* **2** show or express in a dramatic way; make exciting and thrilling. —**dram′a·tiz′er,** *n.*

dram·a·turge (dram′ə tėrj′) *n.* a dramatist, especially one employed by a theatre company.

dram·a·tur·gic (dram′ə tėr′jik) *adj.* having to do with dramaturgy. —**dram′a·tur′gi·cal·ly,** *adv.*

dram·a·tur·gy (dram′ə tėr′jē) *n.* the art of writing or producing dramas. [< Gk. *dramatourgia* < *drama* drama + *-ourgos* making < *ergon* work]

drank (drangk) *v.* pt. and a pp. of **drink.**

drape (drāp) *v.* **draped, drap·ing;** *n.* —*v.* **1** cover or hang with cloth falling loosely in graceful folds, especially as a decoration: *The buildings were draped with red, white, and blue bunting.* **2** arrange (clothes, hangings, etc.) in graceful folds: *The designer draped the robe around the model's shoulders.* **3** fall in graceful folds: *Soft fabrics drape well.* **4** stretch out loosely or lazily: *He draped his legs over the arm of the chesterfield.*
—*n.* **1 drapes,** *pl.* large curtains that are made to hang in folds; draperies: *There are drapes on the large windows in the living room.* **2** arrangement of cloth in folds: *The bodice of the dress has a soft drape.* **3** the way a garment hangs on the body: *I don't like the drape of the skirt.* [ME < OF *draper* < *drap* cloth < LL *drappus*]

drap·er (drāp′ər) *n. Esp.Brit.* a dealer in cloth or dry goods.

drap·er·y (drā′pər ē or drāp′rē) *n., pl.* **-per·ies. 1** clothing or hangings arranged in graceful folds, especially on figures in paintings or sculpture. **2** the graceful arrangement of hangings or clothing. **3** cloth or fabric. **4 draperies,** *pl.* drapes.

dras·tic (dras′tik) *adj.* **1** acting with force or violence; forceful and violent: *The general was a drastic man who showed no mercy.* **2** extreme; severe; harsh: *The police took drastic measures to put a stop to the crime wave.* [< Gk. *drastikos* effective < *draein* do] —**dras′ti·cal·ly,** *adv.*

draught (draft) See **draft.** [ME *draht* < OE *dragan* draw] —**draught′er,** *n.*

☛ *Usage.* See note at **draft.**

☛ *Spelling.* Compounds and derivatives beginning with **draught-** are entered under their **draft-** form.

draughts (drafts) *n.pl. Brit.* the game of checkers.

Dra·vid·i·an (drə vid′ē ən) *n., adj.* —*n.* **1** a family of about 20 languages spoken by the traditional inhabitants of central and S India, N Sri Lanka, and some parts of Pakistan. **2** a member of any of the Dravidian-speaking peoples. —*adj.* of, having to do with, or designating the Dravidian-speaking peoples or their languages.

draw (dro or drô) *v.* **drew, drawn, draw·ing;** *n.* —*v.* **1** pull; drag: *The horse drew the wagon.* **2** pull out; pull up; pull back: *He drew the cork from the bottle.* **3** bring out; take out; get out: *Draw a pail of water from the well.* **4** take out a pistol, sword, etc. for action. **5** take; get; receive: *I drew another idea from the story. He draws his pay each Friday.* **6** make; cause; bring: *Your actions draw praise or blame on yourself.* **7** move; come; go: *We drew near the fire to get warm.* **8** attract; cause to come: *A parade draws a crowd.* **9** make a picture or likeness of with pencil, pen, chalk, crayon, etc.; represent by lines. **10** make pictures or likenesses with pen, pencil, chalk, crayon, etc.; make drawings: *He draws very well for a six-year-old.* **11** describe; depict: *The characters in this novel are not fully drawn; they seem unreal.* **12** write out in proper form; frame; draft (*usually used with* up): *The will was drawn up by a lawyer.* **13** write (an order to pay money): *to draw a cheque.* **14** obtain

resources or assistance, etc. from: *You can always draw on your savings if you have to. He had a vast store of knowledge to draw on.* **15** make a current of air to carry off smoke: *A chimney draws.* **16** breathe in; inhale; take in: *to draw a breath.* **17** of time, etc., come or go gradually but steadily: *The day drew to a close. Night draws on. Death was drawing nigh her.* **18** make the same score in (a game); finish with either side winning. **19** pull out to make tense; extend completely; stretch: *The men drew the rope taut.* **20** make or become small or smaller; shrink. **21** of a ship or boat, sink to a depth of; need for floating: *A ship draws more water when it is loaded than when it is empty. The big ship draws 8.5 metres of water.* **22** take out the insides of; eviscerate. **23** make (tea) by extracting the essence. **24** find out by reasoning; infer: *to draw a conclusion.* **25** draw by lot; get by chance. **26** empty; drain: *to draw a lake.* **27** *Curling.* slide a stone so that it comes to rest within the target area without hitting another stone.

draw a blank, fail completely to get what one wants: *He tried to get information from their neighbors but drew a blank.*

draw (oneself) **up,** stand up straight.

draw out, a extend too much; prolong: *Don't draw out the story so much. The movie was long and drawn out.* **b** persuade to talk; get to respond freely: *We tried to draw him out because we knew he was just shy.*

draw the line, set a limit, especially for behavior: *She doesn't know where to draw the line in playing pranks.*

draw up, a arrange in order: *to draw up a squad on the parade square.* **b** come or bring to a stop: *A taxi drew up at the entrance.*
—*n.* **1** the act of drawing. **2** anything that attracts. **3** *Sports and games.* tie: *If neither side wins, it is a draw.* **4** a lottery; a drawing of lots. **5** the lot drawn. **6** a part of a drawbridge that can be moved. **7** a small land basin into or through which water drains; valley: *The rancher found his strayed cattle grazing in a draw.* **8** *Curling.* a shot in which the stone comes to rest within the target area without hitting another stone. [OE *dragan*]

☛ *Syn. v.* **1.** Draw, drag, haul = pull. **Draw** suggests smoothness or ease of movement: *He drew a chair to the table.* **Drag** suggests resistance and means to pull with force, sometimes slowly: *He dragged the couch across the room.* **Haul** suggests pulling or dragging something very heavy, slowly and with great effort: *Two engines are needed to haul trains over the mountains.*

draw·back (dro′bak′ or drô′-) *n.* **1** something that lessens satisfaction or success; a disadvantage or hindrance: *Our trip was interesting, but the rainy weather was a drawback.* **2** a refund of duty paid on imported goods that are later exported or used to produce something for export.

draw·bridge (dro′brij′ or drô′-) *n.* a bridge that can be wholly or partly lifted, lowered, or moved to one side in order to prevent passage across it or to enable large boats to pass along the river beneath it.

draw·ee (dro ē′ or drô ē′) *n.* a person for whom an order to pay money is written.

draw·er (dro′ər or drô′ər *for 1-4;* drôr *for 5;* drôrz *for 6*) *n.* **1 a** person who draws liquor, as at a bar. **2** draftsman. **3** a person who writes an order to pay money. **4** any person or thing that draws. **5** a box built to slide in and out of a table, dresser, desk, etc.: *He kept his shirts in a drawer in the dresser.* **6 drawers,** *pl.* an undergarment for the lower part of the body, fitting around the waist and having long or short legs; underpants.

draw·ing (dro′ing or drô′-) *n.* **1** the art or act of making a picture or design with lines drawn on a surface, especially without the use of color. **2** a picture or design made in this way.

drawing board 1 a board used as a support for drawing or drafting on paper. **2** the planning stage: *The new fighter plane is still on the drawing board. The scheme failed completely and they were forced to go back to the drawing board.*

drawing knife drawknife.

draw·ing-pin (dro′ing pin′ or drô′-) *n. Esp.Brit.* thumbtack.

drawing room 1 a room for receiving or entertaining guests; parlor. **2** a private compartment in a passenger car of a train, including beds for one or more persons, toilet, etc., and often specially made up to order for a person or group. **3** *Historical.* a levee or formal reception, especially at court. [for *withdrawing room*]

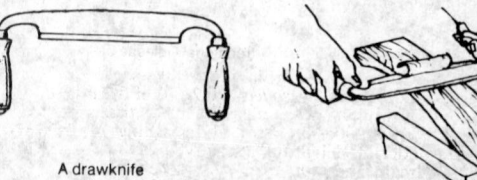

A drawknife

draw·knife (dro′nīf′ or drô′-) *n., pl.* **-knives.** a tool for shaving wood, consisting of a long blade with a handle at either end, set at

right angles to the blade. The blade is always drawn toward the user.

drawl (drol *or* drôl) *v., n.* —*v.* talk in a slow way, making the vowels of words very long: *He drawled a lazy answer.* —*n.* a way of speaking in which the vowels of words are made long: *English speakers in some regions speak with a drawl.* [apparently related to *draw*] —**drawl′er,** *n.* —**drawl′ing·ly,** *adv.*

draw·mas·ter (dro′mas′tər *or* drô′-) *n. Curling.* the official in charge of organizing a bonspiel, drawing teams, arranging schedules of play, etc.

drawn (dron *or* drôn) *v.* pp. of **draw.**

drawn work ornamental work done by drawing threads from a fabric, the remaining portions usually being formed into patterns by needlework.

draw·shave (dro′shăv′ *or* drô′-) *n.* drawknife.

draw·string (dro′string′ *or* drô′-) *n.* a cord, ribbon, or string running through a hem, eyeholes, etc. so that it can be drawn tight: *a hood with a drawstring, a drawstring at the top of a duffel bag.*

dray (drā) *n., v.* —*n.* a low, strong cart for hauling heavy loads. —*v.* transport or carry on a cart. [OE *dræge* dragnet < *dragan* draw]

dray·age (drā′ij) *n.* **1** the act of hauling a load on a dray. **2** a charge for hauling a load on a dray.

dray·man (drā′mən) *n., pl.* **-men.** a man who drives a dray.

DRB *or* **D.R.B.** Defence Research Board.

dread (dred) *v., n., adj.* —*v.* **1** look forward to with fear or extreme uneasiness or reluctance: *He dreaded the long walk back home in the dark. She dreaded the interview.* **2** feel great fear. **3** *Archaic.* regard with awe. —*n.* **1** fear, especially of something that will or may happen: *The old man lived in dread of winter.* **2** a person or thing inspiring fear. —*adj.* **1** dreaded; dreadful: *a dread tyrant.* **2** held in awe; awe-inspiring. [OE *drædan*]
☛ *Syn. n.* **1.** See note at **fear.**

dread·ful (dred′fəl) *adj.* **1** causing dread; terrible or awe-inspiring: *The dragon was a dreadful creature.* **2** *Informal.* very bad; very unpleasant: *I have a dreadful cold.* —**dread′ful·ness,** *n.*

dread·ful·ly (dred′fəl ē) *adv.* **1** in a dreadful manner. **2** *Informal.* very; exceedingly: *He was dreadfully upset.*

dread·nought *or* **dread·naught** (dred′not′ *or* -nôt′) *n.* a big, powerful battleship with heavy armor and large guns. [< *Dreadnought,* the first such ship, built in 1906]

dream (drēm) *n., v.* **dreamed** *or* **dreamt, dream·ing.** —*n.* **1** something thought, felt, seen, or heard during sleep. **2** something unreal, like a dream: *The boy had dreams of being a hero.* **3** the state in which a person has dreams. **4** something having great beauty or charm. **5** a daydream; reverie.
like a dream, very easily, smoothly, etc.; without any problems, complications, setbacks, etc.: *My new typewriter works like a dream. The interview went like a dream.*
—*v.* **1** have a dream or dreams: *He dreamed he was a Mountie.* **2** have daydreams: *The girl dreamed of being a famous scientist.* **3** think of (something) as possible; suppose in a vague way; imagine: *We never dreamed that he'd actually believe it.* **4** spend in dreaming (*usually used with* **away**): *He dreamed the afternoon away.*
dream up, *Informal.* devise or conceive (an idea, invention, etc.) in the mind; think up: *She was always dreaming up fanciful machines.* [OE *dréam* joy, music; meaning influenced by ON *draumr* dream] —**dream′less,** *adj.* —**dream′like′,** *adj.*

dream·boat (drēm′bōt′) *n. Slang.* **1** a very imaginative invention, idea, etc.: *Today's commonplaces are often yesterday's dreamboats.* **2** a very attractive person.

dream·er (drēm′ər) *n.* **1** a person who has dreams. **2** a person whose ideas do not fit real conditions; impractical person.

dream·land (drēm′land′) *n.* **1** a place where a person seems to be when he is dreaming. **2** a beautiful and desirable place. **3** an ideal place existing only in the imagination. **4** sleep.
in dreamland, asleep.

dreamt (dremt) *v.* a pt. and a pp. of **dream.**

dream·y (drēm′ē) *adj.* **dream·i·er, dream·i·est. 1** like something in a dream; vague; dim: *a dreamy recollection.* **2** full of dreams: *a dreamy sleep.* **3** fond of thinking about pleasant things that are unreal; impractical: *a dreamy person.* **4** soft and soothing: *dreamy songs.* **5** *Informal.* wonderful, delightful, attractive, etc. —**dream′i·ly,** *adv.* —**dream′i·ness,** *n.*

drear (drēr) *adj. Poetic.* dreary.

drear·y (drēr′ē) *adj.* **drear·i·er, drear·i·est. 1** dull; gloomy; cheerless; depressing. **2** *Archaic.* sad; sorrowful. **3** uninteresting;

hat, āge, fär; let, ēqual, tèrm; it, īce
hot, ōpen, ôrder; oil, out; cup, pút, rüle,
ə above, takən, pencəl, lemən, circəs

ch, child; ng, long; sh, ship
th, thin; ᴛʜ, then; zh, measure

boring: *We heard a dreary sermon last Sunday.* [OE *dréorig*] —**drear′i·ly,** *adv.* —**drear′i·ness,** *n.*

dredge¹ (drej) *n., v.* **dredged, dredg·ing.** —*n.* **1** a machine with a scoop, series of buckets, etc. for removing mud, sand, or other materials from the bottom of a river, harbor etc. **2** an apparatus with a net, used for gathering oysters, etc. It is dragged along the bottom of the sea.
—*v.* **1** clean out or deepen (a channel, harbor, etc.) with a dredge; use a dredge. **2** bring up or gather with a dredge. **3** dig up; gather: *The lawyer dredged up all the facts he could find to support his case.* [ME *dreg.* Related to DRAG.] —**dredg′er,** *n.*

dredge² (drej) *v.* **dredged, dredg·ing.** sprinkle: *to dredge meat with flour.* [apparently < *dredge,* n., grain mixture < OF *dragie* < L < Gk. *tragēmata* spices] —**dredg′er,** *n.*

DREE (drē) *Cdn.* Department of Regional Economic Expansion.

dregs (dregz) *n.pl.* **1** the solid bits of matter that settle to the bottom of a liquid: *After pouring the tea, she rinsed the dregs out of the teapot.* **2** the most worthless part: *the dregs of society.* [ME < Scand.; cf. Icel. *dreggjar*]

drench (drench) *v., n.* —*v.* **1** wet thoroughly; soak: *We were drenched in the cloudburst.* **2** give a dose of medicine to (an animal). —*n.* **1** a thorough wetting; soaking. **2** a dose of liquid medicine put down the throat of an animal. [OE *drencan* < *drincan* drink] —**drench′er,** *n.* —**drench′ing·ly,** *adv.*
☛ *Syn. v.* See note at **wet.**

Dresden (drez′dən) *n.* **1** a kind of fine porcelain, noted for its delicacy of design. **2** something made of this porcelain. [< *Dresden,* a city in East Germany, near which this ware was originally made]

dress (dres) *n., v.* **dressed** *or* **drest, dress·ing.** —*n.* **1** an outer garment consisting of a bodice and skirt, usually in one piece, worn by women and girls. **2** (*adjl.*) of or for a dress: *dress fabric.* **3** an outer covering or appearance: *The trees were in their summer dress.* **4** clothes: *They care very little about dress.* **5** formal clothes. **6** (*adjl.*) of or characterized by formal dress: *It was a dress occasion.* **7** (*adjl.*) worn on formal occasions: *a dress suit.* **8** clothes suitable for or characteristic of a certain time or occasion: *formal dress, casual dress. The play was performed in modern dress.*
—*v.* **1** put clothes on. **2** wear clothes properly and attractively: *Her sister really knows how to dress.* **3** put formal clothes on: *They always dress for dinner.* **4** decorate; trim; adorn: *The store windows were dressed for Christmas.* **5** make ready for use; prepare: *The butcher dressed the chickens by pulling out the feathers, cutting off the head and feet, and taking out the insides.* **6** arrange (the hair) by curling, combing, etc.: *She just had her hair dressed.* **7** put a medicine, bandage, etc. on (a wound or sore): *The nurse dressed the wound every day.* **8** form in a straight line: *The captain ordered the soldiers to dress their ranks.* **9** smooth or finish: *to dress leather.*
dress down, scold or rebuke severely.
dress up, a put on one's best clothes. **b** put on formal clothes. [ME < OF *dresser* arrange, ult. < L *directus* straight. See DIRECT.]
☛ *Syn. n.* **3. Dress, apparel, attire** = clothing. **Dress** is the general word for outer clothing, dresses and suits, etc.: *I can't go camping without the proper dress.* **Apparel,** more formal and impersonal, applies to outer clothing for men, women, or children: *You can't buy underwear in that store; it carries only apparel.* **Attire,** rather formal, emphasizes the general impression made by clothes: *We need neat, not fine, attire.* —*v.* **1.** See note at **dress.**

dres·sage (dres′ij; *French,* dre säzh′) *n.* the process of guiding a horse without reins through various manoeuvres, the rider using barely perceptible signals of leg pressure, body weight, etc. [< F]

dress coat a man's coat with an open front and two long tails, worn on formal occasions, especially in the evening.

dress·er¹ (dres′ər) *n.* **1** a person who dresses another person, especially one whose work is helping actors or entertainers dress for their performances. **2** a person whose work is decorating and arranging displays in store windows. **3** a person who dresses attractively or in a particular way: *He's a smart dresser.* **4** a tool or machine to prepare things for use. [< *dress*]

dress·er² (dres′ər) *n.* **1** a piece of furniture with drawers for clothes and, usually, a mirror. **2** a piece of furniture with shelves for dishes. **3** a table on which to get food ready for serving. [ME < OF. See DRESS.]

dress·ing (dres′ing) *n.* **1** what is put on or in something to prepare it for use. **2** a sauce for salads, fish, meat, etc. **3** a stuffing of bread crumbs, seasoning, etc. for roast chicken, turkey, etc.

4 the medicine, bandage, etc. put on a wound or sore. **5** fertilizer. **6** formation: *The soldiers are noted for their dressing on parade.* **7** preparations before and during getting dressed: *She took care with her dressing before the dance.* **8** preparation for display: *the dressing of a store window.*

dress·ing–down (dres'ing doun') *n.* a severe scolding.

dressing gown a loose robe worn while dressing or resting.

dressing room a room for getting dressed in, especially a room behind the stage in a theatre, in which actors dress.

dressing table a table with a mirror at which one can sit to put on cosmetics, brush or arrange the hair, etc.

dress·mak·er (dres'māk'ər) *n.* **1** a person whose work is making clothes, especially for women. **2** (*adj.*) of women's clothing, having soft or flowing lines and fine decoration: *a dressmaker suit.* Compare **tailored**.

dress·mak·ing (dres'māk'ing) *n.* the act or occupation of making dresses, etc.

dress parade a formal military parade in dress uniform.

dress rehearsal a rehearsal of a play with costumes and scenery just as for a regular performance.

dress suit a suit worn by men on formal occasions, especially in the evening.

dress·y (dres'ē) *adj.* **dress·i·er, dress·i·est. 1** stylish and formal; not casual: *That outfit is too dressy for a wiener roast.* **2** fond of wearing showy clothes. —**dress'i·ness,** *n.*

drest (drest) *v.* a pt. and pp. of **dress.**

drew (drü) *v.* pt. of **draw.**

drib·ble (drib'əl) *v.* **-bled, -bling;** *n.* —*v.* **1** flow or let flow in drops, small amounts, etc.; trickle: *Gasoline dribbled from the leak in the tank.* **2** let saliva run from the mouth. **3** move (a ball) along by bouncing it or giving it short kicks. —*n.* **1** a dropping; dripping; trickle. **2** a very light rain. **3** the act of dribbling a ball. [< *drib,* var. of *drip*] —**drib'bler,** *n.*

drib·let (drib'lit) *n.* a small amount: *He paid off the debt in driblets, a dollar or two a week.*

dried (drīd) *v.* pt. and pp. of **dry.**

dri·er (drī'ər) *adj., n.* —*adj.* comparative of **dry.** —*n.* **1** Also, **dryer,** a substance added to oil paint, varnish, etc. to make it dry faster. **2** See **dryer.**

drift (drift) *v., n.* —*v.* **1** carry or be carried along by currents of water or air: *The wind drifted the boat onto rocks. A raft drifts if it is not steered.* **2** move or appear to move aimlessly: *People drifted in and out of the meeting.* **3** go along without knowing or caring where one is going: *Some people have a purpose in life; others just drift.* **4** pass without special intention. **5** move or appear one at a time or in small groups as drift does on a beach: *The students drifted into class.* **6** heap or be heaped up by the wind: *The wind is so strong it's drifting the snow. The snow is drifting badly.* —*n.* **1** a drifting: *the drift of an iceberg.* **2** the direction of drifting. **3** a tendency; trend. *The drift of opinion was against war.* **4** the meaning; direction of thought: *I caught the drift of his speech, but I couldn't understand all the details.* **5** snow, sand, etc. heaped up by the wind. **6** floating matter driven by currents of water, as a log or a mass of wood. **7** a slow current of water, especially a slow ocean current. **8** the sideways movement of an aircraft or ship off its projected course due to crosscurrents of air or water. **9** the distance that a ship or aircraft is off its course because of currents. **10** *Geology.* sand, gravel, rocks, etc. moved from one place and left in another by a river, glacier, etc. **11** an almost horizontal passageway in a mine along a vein of ore, coal, etc. [ME *drift* a driving < OE *drīfan* drive. Related to DRIVE.] —**drift'ing·ly,** *adv.*

drift·age (drif'tij) *n.* **1** a drifting. **2** the distance drifted. **3** what has drifted; material that drifts around in water or is washed up on the shore.

drift·wood (drift'wůd') *n.* wood drifting in the water or washed ashore.

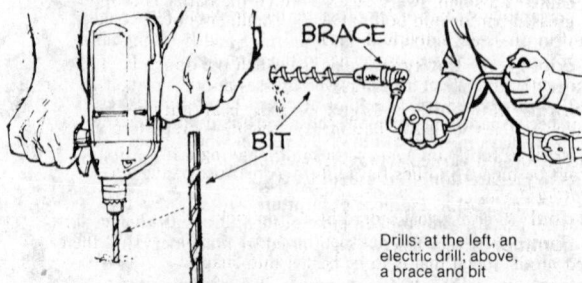

BRACE

BIT

Drills: at the left, an electric drill; above, a brace and bit

drill¹ (dril) *n., v.* —*n.* **1** an implement or machine for boring holes.

2 group instruction and training in physical exercises or in marching, handling a rifle, etc. **3** the process of teaching or training by having the learners do a thing over and over again: *The teacher gave the class plenty of drill in arithmetic.* **4** *Informal.* a correct or approved procedure for doing something: *This leaflet gives the drill for putting the machine together.* **5** a snail that bores into and destroys oysters. —*v.* **1** bore a hole in; pierce with a drill. **2** teach by having learners do a thing over and over again. **3** be taught or trained in this way. **4** do or cause to do physical or military exercises. [< MDu. *dril* (n.) < *drillen* (v.) bore] —**drill'er,** *n.*

☛ *Syn. n.* **3.** See note at **exercise.**

drill² (dril) *n., v.* —*n.* **1** a machine for planting seeds in rows. It makes a small furrow, drops the seed, and then covers the furrow. **2** a small furrow to plant seeds in. **3** a row of planted seeds. —*v.* plant in small furrows. [origin uncertain]

drill³ (dril) *n.* a strong, twilled cotton cloth similar to denim, used for overalls, uniforms, ticking, etc. [short for *drilling* < G *Drillich* < L *trilix* of three threads < *tri-* three + *licium* thread]

drill⁴ (dril) *n.* a baboon (*Mandrillus leucophaeus*) of W Africa, closely related to the mandrill but smaller. [probably < African name]

drill·ing (dril'ing) *n.* drill³.

drill·mas·ter (dril'mas'tər) *n.* an instructor who teaches by drilling, especially one who drills soldiers in marching, handling guns, etc.

dri·ly (drī'lē) See **dryly.**

drink (dringk) *v.* **drank, drunk** or (*sometimes*) **drank, drink·ing;** *n.* —*v.* **1** swallow (liquid). **2** swallow the liquid contents of: *She drank the whole glass.* **3** take and hold; absorb: *The dry ground drank up the rain.* **4** drink liquor: *Does he drink?* **5** drink liquor to excess. **6** drink in honor of: *They drank his health.*

drink in, take in eagerly with the senses.

drink to, drink in honor of; drink with good wishes for. —*n.* **1** any liquid swallowed or to be swallowed. **2** liquor. **3** excessive drinking of liquor. **4** *Slang.* a body of water; ocean, lake, pool, etc. [OE *drincan*] —**drink'less,** *adj.*

☛ *Syn. v.* **1. Drink, sip, imbibe** = swallow a liquid. **Drink** is the general word: *A person or animal must drink water in order to stay alive.* **Sip** = drink little by little in very small quantities: *One should sip, not gulp, very cold or hot liquids.* **Imbibe,** formal, is now for the most part used humorously in the literal sense of drinking; used figuratively, it means "absorb": *His one desire is to imbibe more knowledge.*

☛ *Usage.* **Drunk, drank.** Although **drunk** is the usual past participle, many educated North Americans use **drank** in speech: *He's drank several glasses of milk already.* In writing, **drunk** should be used, except perhaps when writing dialogue. **Drank** is now the proper form for the past tense.

☛ *Usage.* See note at **drunk.**

drink·a·ble (drink'ə bəl) *adj., n.* —*adj.* fit to drink. —*n.* something to drink.

drink·er (dringk'ər) *n.* a person who drinks, especially one who drinks liquor as a habit or to excess.

drip (drip) *v.* **dripped** or **dript, drip·ping;** *n.* —*v.* **1** fall or let fall in drops. **2** be so wet that drops fall. —*n.* **1** a falling in drops. **2** the liquid that falls in drops. **3** a part that projects to keep water off the parts below. **4** *Slang.* a person considered to be objectionable. [OE *dryppan* < *dropa* a drop]

drip–dry (drip'drī') *adj., v.* **-dried, -dry·ing.** —*adj.* made to be dried by being let drip after washing, then needing little or no ironing: *drip-dry curtains.* —*v.* let drip until dry.

drip·ping (drip'ing) *n.* **1** liquid that has dripped down. **2** the melted fat and juice that drip down from meat while roasting: *Some people like beef dripping spread on bread.*

dripping pan a pan put under roasting meat to catch the dripping.

dript (dript) *v.* a pt. and a pp. of **drip.**

drive (drīv) *v.* **drove, driv·en, driv·ing;** *n.* —*v.* **1** make go; cause to move: *Drive the dog away.* **2** make go by hitting; propel: *to drive a spike.* **3** force into or out of some place, condition, act, etc.: *That dog's barking drives me crazy. Hunger drove him to steal.* **4** manage; operate; guide by steering: *to drive a car, to drive a motorboat.* **5** go or travel in a car or other vehicle: *We drove out into the country for the afternoon.* **6** travel over or across in a car, etc.; cover: *We drove 300 kilometres without stopping.* **7** carry or transport in a car or other vehicle: *The truck driver drove the boys all the way to Toronto.* **8** bring about or obtain by being clever, shrewd, forceful, etc.: *He drove a good bargain when he bought his bicycle.* **9** compel (oneself or another) to work very hard: *He drove himself to complete the project on schedule.* **10** dash or rush with force: *The ship drove on the rocks.* **11** set in motion; supply power for: *The wind drives the windmill.* **12** *Mining.* excavate horizontally; make a drift. **13** go through an area and herd or direct (game) toward waiting hunters with guns. **14** *Sports.* hit very hard and fast: *to drive a golf ball.* **15** aim; strike. **16** get or make by drilling.

boring, etc.: *to drive a well.* **17** move (logs) in large numbers down a river: *The loggers drove the logs to the mill.*

drive at, mean; intend: *I didn't understand what he was driving at.*
let drive, aim; strike: *The boxer let drive a left to the jaw.*
—*n.* **1** a trip, usually short, taken in a car or other vehicle: *a Sunday drive.* **2** a road (*used mainly in street names*): *Winona Drive.* **3** a driveway (def. 1): *He left his car in the drive all night.* **4** capacity for hard work; forceful action; energy: *Her success was largely due to her great drive.* **5** an impelling force; pressure: *The craving for approval is a strong drive in mankind.* **6** a special effort of a group for some purpose: *The town had a drive to get money for charity.* **7** a very hard, fast hit. **8** a military attack, often a large-scale, forceful attack. **9** the act or process of moving a herd of cattle or sheep overland. **10** the act or process of floating a great many logs down a river: *Drives are held when the ice melts in spring.* **11** a great many logs floating down a river. **12** a thing or things driven: *a drive of logs.* **13** a part that drives machinery: *a chain drive.* **14** the special way in which a motor, transmission, etc. generates or controls a vehicle's power or motion: *fluid drive, four-wheel drive.* **15** *Mining.* a horizontal or inclined tunnel or passage. [OE *drīfan*]
☛ *Syn. n.* **1.** See note at **ride.**

drive-in (drīv'in') *n.* a place where customers may make purchases, eat, or attend movies, etc. while seated in their cars.

driv·el (driv'əl) *v.* **-elled** or **-eled, -el·ling** or **-el·ing**; *n.* —*v.* **1** let saliva run from the mouth. **2** flow like saliva running from the mouth. **3** talk or say in a stupid, foolish manner; talk silly nonsense. **4** waste (time, energy, etc.) in a stupid, foolish way.
—*n.* **1** saliva running from the mouth. **2** stupid, foolish talk. [OE *dreflian*]

driv·el·ler or **driv·el·er** (driv'əl ər) *n.* a person who drivels.

driv·en (driv'ən) *v., adj.* —*v.* pp. of **drive.** —*adj.* carried along and gathered into heaps by the wind; drifted.

driv·er (drīv'ər) *n.* **1** a person or thing that drives. **2** a person who directs the movement of an engine, automobile, horses, etc. **3** a person who makes the people under him work very hard. **4** a golf club with a large wooden head, used in hitting the ball from the tee. **5** a part of a machine, such as a gear or wheel, that transmits the motion to another part or parts. —**driv'er·less,** *adj.*

drive shaft a shaft that transmits power or motion, such as the shaft in a motor vehicle that connects the transmission to the axle of the driving wheels.

drive·way (drīv'wā') *n.* **1** a private road. A driveway usually leads from a house to the public street or road. **2** *Cdn.* a road, especially one that is lined with trees and lawns.

driz·zle (driz'əl) *v.* **-zled, -zling;** *n.* —*v.* **1** rain in very small drops resembling mist. **2** fall in very small drops. **3** shed or let fall in very small drops.
—*n.* rain that falls in very small drops. [? < ME *drese* to fall < OE *drēosan*]

driz·zly (driz'lē) *adj.* drizzling.

DRO deputy returning officer.

drogue (drōg) *n.* **1** a device shaped like a large funnel at the end of the hose used to refuel airplanes in flight. The pilot of the plane being refuelled guides the nose of his plane into the drogue. **2** a small parachute that springs open when a parachute pack is opened and helps to draw out the main parachute. **3** a similar device attached to a space capsule, etc. to stabilize it or slow it down. **4** sea anchor. [? var. of *drag*, n.]

droit (droit; *French,* drwä) *n.* **1** *Law.* a right or claim. **2** something to which a person has a right or claim; a due.

droll (drōl) *adj., n., v.* —*adj.* amusingly odd; humorously quaint; laughable: *We smiled at the monkey's droll tricks.*
—*n.* a funny person; jester; buffoon.
—*v.* joke; jest. [< F *drôle* (originally n.) good fellow < Du. *drol* little fat fellow]

droll·er·y (drōl'ər ē or drōl'rē) *n., pl.* **-er·ies. 1** something odd and amusing; a laughable trick. **2** quaint humor. **3** jesting.

drom·e·dar·y (drom'ə der'ē or drum'ə der'ē) *n., pl.* **-dar·ies.** a swift camel raised for racing and riding, especially the one-humped Arabian camel. [ME < OF *dromedaire* < LL *dromedarius* < Gk. *dromas, -ados* runner]

drone¹ (drōn) *n., v.* **droned, dron·ing.** —*n.* **1** a male bee, especially a male honeybee. Drones do not sting, gather honey, or help in the upkeep of a hive; their sole function is to mate with the queen. **2** a person not willing to work; idler; loafer. **3** a pilotless aircraft, missile, or vessel directed by remote control.
—*v.* spend time idly; loaf. [OE *drān*]

drone² (drōn) *v.* **droned, dron·ing;** *n.* —*v.* **1** make a deep, continuous, humming sound: *Bees droned among the flowers.* **2** talk or say in a monotonous voice: *to drone a prayer.* —*n.* **1** a deep, continuous, humming sound: *the drone of airplane motors.* **2** any of

hat, āge, fär; let, ēqual, tėrm; it, īce
hot, ōpen, ôrder; oil, out; cup, put, rüle,
əbove, takən, pencəl, lemən, circəs

ch, child; ng, long; sh, ship
th, thin; ᴛʜ, then; zh, measure

the pipes on a bagpipe that sound a continuous tone. [related to DRONE¹]

drool (drül) *v., n.* —*v.* **1** let saliva run from the mouth as a baby does. **2** *Informal.* make an excessive show of pleasure or enthusiasm (*often used with* over): *drooling over the rock group's latest recording.* —*n.* **1** saliva running from the mouth. **2** *Slang.* foolish talk. [contraction of *drivel*]

droop (drüp) *v., n.* —*v.* **1** hang down; bend down. **2** become weak; lose strength and energy. **3** become discouraged or depressed; be sad and gloomy.
—*n.* a bending position; the act or condition of hanging down. [ME < ON *drūpa*] —**droop'ing·ly,** *adv.* —**droop'y,** *adj.*

drop (drop) *n., v.* **dropped, drop·ping.** —*n.* **1** a small, roundish mass of liquid, usually formed in falling: *a drop of rain, a drop of blood.* **2** something small and roundish, resembling such a mass: *a cough drop, a lemon drop. Some earrings are called drops.* **3** a very small amount of liquid: *Drink a drop of this.* **4** a very small amount of anything: *a drop of kindness.* **5** a sudden fall or decrease: *a drop in temperature, a drop in prices.* **6** the distance down; the length of fall: *a drop of ten metres.* **7** something arranged to fall or let fall: *A letter drop is a slot, usually with a hinged cover.* **8** *Baseball.* a pitch that suddenly dips downward as it reaches the plate. **9** the act of letting bombs, supplies, etc. fall from an aircraft. **10 drops,** *pl.* liquid medicine given in drops.
at the drop of a hat, a when a signal is given. **b** at once; willingly.
drop in the bucket, a very small amount compared to the rest.
get or **have the drop on,** *Slang.* **a** point a gun at (a person) before he can point one at you. **b** get or have an advantage over.
—*v.* **1** fall or let fall in small masses of liquid: *Rain drops from the sky. He had to drop some medicine into his sore eye.* **2** take a sudden fall or decrease: *The price of tomatoes always drops in August.* **3** let fall: *He dropped the package.* **4** cause to fall: *The boxer dropped his opponent with one hard punch.* **5** fall dead or wounded: *The soldier dropped when the bullet hit him.* **6** fall from exhaustion: *I'm so tired, I could drop.* **7** cause to fall dead or wounded; kill: *The hunter dropped the deer with one shot.* **8** go lower; sink: *The sun dropped below the horizon.* **9** make lower; cause to become lower: *Drop your voice.* **10** pass into a less active or worse condition: *She finally dropped into a coma.* **11** let go; dismiss: *Members who do not pay will be dropped from the club.* **12** leave out; omit: *Drop the "e" in "drive" before adding "ing."* **13** stop; end; close: *They agreed to let the quarrel drop.* **14** write and send (a letter, etc.): *Drop me a note when you get there.* **15** pay a casual or unexpected visit (*used with* in, by, over, *etc.*): *We dropped in at my brother's last night.* **16** give or express casually: *to drop a hint.* **17** go along gently with the current or tide: *The raft dropped down the river.* **18** set down from a ship, automobile, carriage, etc.: *The taxi driver dropped his passengers at the corner.* **19 a** *Rugger.* make (a goal) by a drop kick. **b** *Football.* drop-kick (a ball). **20** *Slang.* lose: *The team dropped four straight games.*
drop behind or **back,** lag behind; fall behind: *He started out strongly in the race but soon dropped back to fourth place.*
drop off, a go to sleep. **b** become less; decrease: *sales of chewing gum have dropped off.* **c** stop: *I think I'll drop off at the grocery store.*
drop out, leave school, a training program, etc. without completing the course.
[OE *dropa*] —**drop'like',** *adj.*

drop cake 1 a small, sweet cake for which the batter is dropped onto a greased pan or into boiling oil. **2** a small, sweet cake baked in a muffin tin as an individual serving.

drop cookie or **cooky** a cookie for which the dough is dropped onto a flat sheet for baking.

drop–forge (drop'fôrj') *v.* **-forged, -forg·ing.** beat (hot metal) into shape with a very heavy hammer or weight. —**drop'-forg'er,** *n.*

drop–front (drop'frunt') *adj.* of furniture, having a front that opens out on hinges and lies flat to form a shelf or writing surface: *a drop-front desk.*

drop goal *Rugger.* a goal scored by a drop kick.

drop hammer a very heavy weight lifted by machinery and then dropped on the metal that is to be beaten into shape.

drop–in centre (drop'in') an informal place, often run by a church or social service organization, for young people to come to for help, recreation, or companionship.

drop kick a kick given to a football just as it touches the ground after being dropped from the hands.

drop-kick (drop′kik′) *v.* give (a football) a drop kick. —**drop′-kick′er**, *n.*

drop leaf a hinged section of the surface of a table. Such a leaf can be folded down when not in use.

drop-leaf (drop′lēf′) *adj.* having a drop leaf: *a drop-leaf dining table.*

drop·let (drop′lit) *n.* a tiny drop.

drop light an electric or gas lamp connected with a fixture above by a tube or wire.

drop-off (drop′ôf′) *n.* 1 a lessening or decline: *a drop-off in sales.* 2 a sudden, sharp slope.

drop-out (drop′out′) *n.* 1 a person who leaves school, a training program, etc. without completing the course. 2 the act or fact of dropping out. 3 (*adj.*) of or having to do with drop-outs or dropping out: *the drop-out generation, a low drop-out rate.*

drop·per (drop′ər) *n.* 1 a person or thing that drops. 2 a small glass or plastic tube with a hollow rubber cap at one end and a small opening at the other end from which a liquid can be made to fall in drops.

drop·pings (drop′ingz) *n.pl.* 1 what is dropped. 2 the dung of animals and birds.

drop·si·cal (drop′sə kəl) *adj.* 1 of or like dropsy. 2 having dropsy.

drop·sy (drop′sē) *n.* an abnormal accumulation of watery fluid in certain tissues or cavities of the body. [ME, var. of *hydropsy* < OF *idropisie* < L *hydropisis* < Gk. *hydrōps* < *hydōr* water]

dropt (dropt) *v.* a pt. and a pp. of **drop.**

drosh·ky or **dros·ky** (drosh′kē) *n., pl.* **-kies.** a low, open, four-wheeled Russian carriage. [< Russian *drozhki,* dim. of *drogi* wagon]

dro·soph·i·la (drō sof′ə lə) *n., pl.* **-lae** (-lē′ *or* -lī′). any of a genus (*Drosophila*) of small, two-winged flies, most of which feed on ripe or rotting fruit, etc. Some species, especially *D. melanogaster,* are widely used in laboratory genetic research. [< NL < Gk. *drosos* dew + *philos* loving]

dross (dros) *n.* 1 the waste or scum that comes to the surface of molten metals; slag. 2 waste material; rubbish. [OE *drōs*]

drought (drout) *n.* 1 a long period of dry weather; continued lack of rain. 2 a prolonged shortage of anything. 3 *Archaic or dialect.* thirst. [OE *drūgath.* Related to DRY.]
☛ *Usage.* **Drought, drouth.** Both forms are in good use, though **drought** is more usual in formal English.

drought·y (drout′ē) *adj.* showing or suffering from drought.

drouth (drouth) *n.* drought.
☛ *Usage.* See note at **drought.**

drouth·y (drouth′ē) *adj.* droughty.

drove[1] (drōv) *v.* pt. of **drive.**

drove[2] (drōv) *n.* 1 a group of cattle, sheep, pigs, etc. moving or driven along together; a herd or flock. 2 many people moving along together; a crowd. [OE *drāf*]

dro·ver (drō′vər) *n.* 1 a person who drives cattle, sheep, pigs, etc. to market. 2 a dealer in cattle.

drown (droun) *v.* 1 suffocate under water or other liquid. 2 kill by keeping under water or some other liquid. 3 cover with water; flood. 4 be stronger or louder than; keep from being heard (*usually used with* **out**): *The boat's whistle drowned out what she was trying to tell us.* 5 get rid of: *He tried to drown his sorrow in drink.* [OE *druncnian.* Related to DRINK.] —**drown′er**, *n.* —**drown′ing·ly**, *adv.*

drowse (drouz) *v.* **drowsed, drows·ing;** *n.* —*v.* 1 be sleepy or half asleep; doze: *drowsing in a hammock.* 2 make or be inactive or dull, as if asleep. 3 pass (time) in drowsing (*used with* **away**): *She drowsed the day away.*
—*n.* the state of being sleepy or half asleep. [OE *drūs(i)an* sink, become slow]

drow·sy (drou′zē) *adj.* **-si·er, -si·est.** 1 half asleep; sleepy. 2 causing sleepiness or half sleep; lulling. 3 inactive; lethargic. —**drow′si·ly**, *adv.* —**drow′si·ness**, *n.*
☛ *Syn.* 1. See note at **sleepy.**

drub (drub) *v.* **drubbed, drub·bing.** 1 beat with a stick; thrash; whip soundly. 2 in a fight, game, contest, etc., defeat by a large margin. [? < Arabic *daraba* beat] —**drub′ber**, *n.*

drudge (druj) *n., v.* **drudged, drudg·ing.** —*n.* a person who does hard, tiresome, or disagreeable work. —*v.* do hard, tiresome, or disagreeable work. [ME *drugge(n);* probably related to OE *drēogan* work, suffer]

drudg·er·y (druj′ər ē *or* druj′rē) *n., pl.* **-er·ies.** hard, uninteresting, or disagreeable work.

drug (drug) *n., v.* **drugged, drug·ging.** —*n.* 1 a substance (other than food) used as a medicine or as a component of a medicine, especially one listed in an official pharmacopoeia. Such a substance increases or retards the activity of the cells, organs, etc. that it affects. 2 a substance that brings drowsiness or sleep, or lessens pain by dulling the nerves; narcotic: *Opium is a habit-forming drug.*
drug on the market, an article that is too abundant, is no longer in demand, or has too slow a sale.
—*v.* 1 give drugs to, particularly drugs that are harmful or cause sleep. 2 put a harmful or poisonous drug in (food or drink). 3 affect or overcome (the body or senses) as if by a drug: *The wine drugged him. She was drugged by the soothing music.* [ME < MF *drogue* < MLG *droge-fate* dry barrels, with *droge-* wrongly taken as the name of the contents] —**drug′less**, *adj.*

drug·get (drug′it) *n.* 1 a coarse, thick woollen fabric used for rugs. 2 a rug or carpet made of this fabric. 3 a woollen or mixed fabric used for clothing. [< F *droguet*]

drug·gist (drug′ist) *n.* 1 a person who sells drugs, medicines, etc. 2 a person licensed to fill prescriptions; pharmacist.

drug·store (drug′stôr′) *n.* a store where drugs and other medicines are sold. A drugstore often sells soft drinks, cosmetics, magazines, etc. as well as drugs.

Dru·id or **dru·id** (drü′id) *n.* a member of a religious order of priests, prophets, poets, etc. among the ancient Celts of Britain, Ireland, and Gaul where they were powerful as leaders and judges until the advent of the Christian religion. [< F *druide* < L *druidae,* pl. < Gaulish; cf. Old Irish *drui* sorcerer]

Dru·id·ess or **dru·id·ess** (drü′ə dis) *n.* a female Druid; a Druidic prophetess.

Dru·id·ic or **dru·id·ic** (drü id′ik) *adj.* of or having to do with the Druids.

dru·id·i·cal (drü id′ə kəl) *adj.* druidic.

Dru·id·ism (drü′ə diz′əm) *n.* the religion of the Druids, or their beliefs and practices.

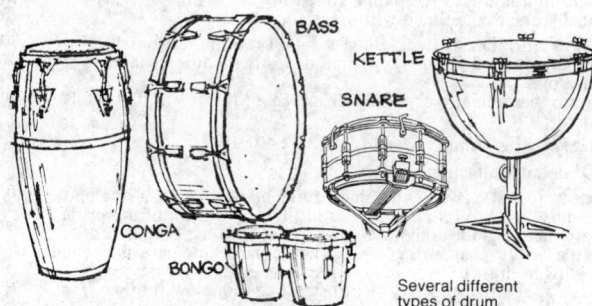

Several different types of drum

drum (drum) *n., v.* **drummed, drum·ming.** —*n.* 1 a musical percussion instrument that makes a sound when it is beaten, tapped, or brushed. A drum is usually a hollow cylinder with a covering stretched tightly over each end. 2 the sound made when a drum is beaten; any sound like this. 3 anything shaped somewhat like a drum. 4 the part around which something is wound in a machine. 5 a drum-shaped container to hold oil, food, etc. 6 eardrum. 7 *Architecture.* a a circular or polygonal structure upon which a dome is erected. b the block of stone making up one section of the shaft of a column. 8 a natural organ by which an animal produces a loud or bass sound. 9 drumfish.
beat the drums for, *Informal.* support vigorously; promote; advocate.
—*v.* 1 beat or play a drum; make a sound like this. 2 beat, tap, or strike again and again: *Stop drumming on the table with your fingers.* 3 force into one's mind by repeating over and over: *Algebra had to be drummed into me because I didn't understand it.* 4 sound like a drum; resound: *The noise drummed in his ears.* 5 (of birds and insects) make a hollow, reverberating sound, as by quivering the wings: *The gnats drummed around him.* 6 call or summon by or as if by beating a drum.
drum out of, send away from in disgrace.
drum up, a call together: *We could not drum up enough players for our game.* **b** get by asking again and again: *to drum up support for a project.*

[< *drumslade* drummer < Du. or LG *trommelslag* drumbeat]
—**drum′like′**, *adj.*

drum·beat (drum′bēt′) *n.* the sound made when a drum is beaten.

drum dance *Cdn.* **1** an Inuit dance consisting of expressive body movements and gestures, performed to the accompaniment of drums and with the dancer or dancers singing as they dance. **2** any of various Indian dances accompanied by drums.

drum·fish (drum′fish′) *n., pl.* **-fish** or **-fish·es.** any of various carnivorous fishes (family Sciaenidae) found mainly along the warm and tropical western shores of the Atlantic. Most drumfishes can make a drumming sound by moving certain muscles attached to the air bladder.

drum·head (drum′hed′) *n.* the parchment or membrane stretched tightly over the end of a drum.

drumhead court–martial a court-martial on the battlefield or while troops are moving, held in order to try offenders without delay.

drum·lin (drum′lən) *n.* a ridge or oval hill formed by deposit from a glacier. [for *drumling,* dim. of *drum* ridge < Irish and Scots Gaelic *druim* ridge]

drum major the leader or director of a marching band.

drum ma·jo·rette (mā′jə ret′) a girl who accompanies a marching band, twirling a baton.

drum·mer (drum′ər) *n.* **1** a person who plays a drum, especially a skilled player. **2** *Informal.* sales representative.

drum·stick (drum′stik′) *n.* **1** a stick for beating a drum. **2** the lower, meaty part of the leg of a cooked chicken, turkey, or other edible bird.

drunk (drungk) *adj., n., v.* —*adj.* **1** overcome by liquor; intoxicated. **2** very much excited or affected: *drunk with success.* —*n. Slang.* **1** a person who is often drunk; a drunkard. **2** a spell of drinking liquor; drinking spree: *a three-day drunk.* —*v.* pp. and archaic pt. of **drink.** *He had drunk all the milk.*
☞ *Usage.* **Drunk, drunken.** As an adjective standing before the noun, the form **drunken** is preferred.

drunk·ard (drungk′ərd) *n.* a person who is often drunk; a person who frequently drinks too much liquor.

drunk·en (drungk′ən) *adj., v.* —*adj.* **1** drunk. **2** caused by or resulting from being drunk. **3** from drinking too much liquor. —*v. Archaic.* a pp. of **drink.** —**drunk′en·ly,** *adv.* —**drunk′en·ness,** *n.*
☞ *Usage.* See note at **drunk.**

drunk·om·e·ter (drungk om′ə tər) *n.* breathalyzer.

dru·pa·ceous (drü pā′shəs) *adj. Botany.* **1** like a drupe. **2** producing drupes.

drupe (drüp) *n.* a soft, fleshy fruit having a thin, skinlike covering and, in the centre, a hard pit or stone containing the seed. Cherries and peaches are drupes. [< NL *drupa* < L < Gk. *dryppa* very ripe olive]

drupe·let (drüp′lit) *n.* a small drupe. A raspberry or blackberry is a mass of drupelets.

Druse (drüz) *n.* a member of a sect in Syria and Lebanon whose secret, basically Moslem religion contains Christian elements. [< Arabic *Durūz,* pl.]

druth·ers (druᴛн′ərz) *n.pl. Informal or dialect.* a free choice: *If I had my druthers, I'd quit tomorrow.*

dry (drī) *adj.* **dri·er, dri·est;** *v.* **dried, dry·ing;** *n., pl.* **drys.** —*adj.* **1** not wet; not moist. **2** having little or no rain: *a dry climate.* **3** not giving milk: *That cow has been dry for a month.* **4** containing no water or other liquid. **5** not shedding tears or accompanied by tears: *a dry sob.* **6** wanting a drink; thirsty. **7** not under, in, or on water: *dry land.* **8** not liquid; solid: *dry measure.* **9** causing thirst: *Cutting the lawn is dry work.* **10** apparently matter-of-fact but actually ironic: *dry humor.* **11** not interesting; dull: *a dry speech.* **12** without butter: *dry toast.* **13** free from sweetness or fruity flavor: *dry wine.* **14** *Informal.* having or favoring laws against making and selling alcoholic beverages. **15** abstaining from drinking alcoholic beverages. **16** bald; plain; unadorned: *a list of dry facts.* —*v.* make or become dry.

dry out, a make or become completely dry: *He laid his socks on a rock to dry out.* **b** *Informal.* take or cause to take treatment for alcoholism.

dry up, a of water of a body of water, etc., disappear as a result of evaporation, drainage, or cutting off of the source of supply: *The creek dried up last summer.* **b** lose all moisture: *The paint dried up because someone left the top off the jar.* **c** *Slang.* stop talking: *Why don't you dry up?* —*n. Informal.* a person who favors laws against making and selling alcoholic drinks. [OE *drȳge*] —**dry′ness,** *n.*
☞ *Syn. adj.* **1. Dry, arid** = without moisture. **Dry** is the general word, meaning "not wet, or moist": *This bread is dry.* **Arid** = completely dry or dried out,

hat, āge, fär; let, ēqual, tėrm; it, īce
hot, ōpen, ôrder; oil, out; cup, pút, rüle,
əbove, takən, pencəl, lemən, circəs

ch, child; ng, long; sh, ship
th, thin; ᴛн, then; zh, measure

and adds the idea of barrenness, particularly when applied to land: *No crops will grow in this arid soil.*

dry·ad or **Dry·ad** (drī′əd *or* drī′ad) *n., pl.* **-ads, -a·des** (-ə dēz′). *Greek mythology.* a nymph that lives in a tree; wood nymph. [< L < Gk. *Dryades,* pl. < *drys* tree]

dry battery 1 a set of dry cells connected to produce electric current. **2** a dry cell.

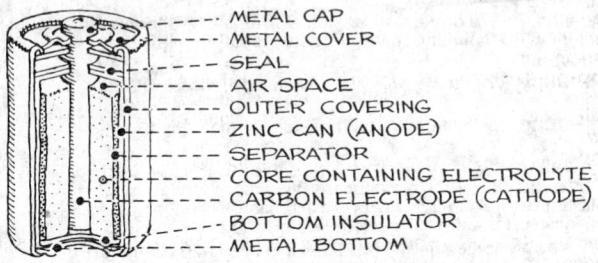

METAL CAP
METAL COVER
SEAL
AIR SPACE
OUTER COVERING
ZINC CAN (ANODE)
SEPARATOR
CORE CONTAINING ELECTROLYTE
CARBON ELECTRODE (CATHODE)
BOTTOM INSULATOR
METAL BOTTOM

A carbon-zinc dry cell: a flashlight battery. The electrolyte, a paste of ammonium chloride, zinc chloride, manganese dioxide, and carbon, reacts with the zinc, causing it to become negatively charged. When the zinc anode and the carbon cathode are connected by a conducting wire, electrons flow from the anode to the cathode, producing an electric current.

dry cell an electrochemical cell in which the electrolyte is in the form of a paste so that it cannot spill.

dry cereal any breakfast cereal that does not require cooking and is sold ready for eating.

dry–clean (drī′klēn′) *v.* clean clothes, drapes, etc. by dry cleaning.

dry–clean·a·ble (drī′klēn′ə bəl) *adj.* that can be dry-cleaned: *Most fabrics are dry-cleanable.*

dry cleaner a person or company that does dry cleaning.

dry cleaning 1 the cleaning of fabrics without water, using a solvent. Most commercial dry cleaning today is done with synthetic or petroleum-base solvents. **2** something that is to be or has been dry-cleaned: *I have to pick up the dry cleaning on my way home today.*

dry dock an area set between two piers, built watertight so that water may be pumped out or kept high. Dry docks are used for building or repairing ships.

dry–dock (drī′dok′) *v.* **1** place in a dry dock. **2** go into dry dock.

dry·er (drī′ər) *n.* **1** an appliance or machine for drying things quickly, especially by heat or blowing air: *A clothes dryer dries clothes by blowing air over them as they are tumbled in a revolving drum.* **2** a stand or rack for hanging clothes up to dry. **3** See **drier** (def. 1). **4** any person or thing that dries.

dry–eyed (drī′īd′) *adj.* not weeping; not shedding tears: *He remained dry-eyed at the funeral.*

dry–farm (drī′färm′) *v.* farm (land) where there is no irrigation and little rain.

dry farmer a person who engages in dry farming.

dry farming a way of farming land in dry regions where there is no irrigation, using methods that save soil moisture and raising crops that survive drought.

dry fly an artificial fishing lure made to resemble a fly or other insect floating on the water.

dry goods cloth, ribbon, lace, etc.

Dry Ice *Trademark.* a very cold, white solid formed when carbon dioxide is compressed and then cooled. It is used for cooling because it changes from solid back to gas without becoming liquid.

dry law a law prohibiting the making and selling of alcoholic liquor.

dry·ly or **dri·ly** (drī′lē) *adv.* in a dry manner: *He spoke dryly of his experiences at election time.*

dry measure a system of units for measuring such things as

grain, flour, or fruit. One bushel is equal to about 36.4 dm³.
　2 pints　= 1 quart
　8 quarts = 1 peck
　4 pecks　= 1 bushel

dry nurse a nurse who takes care of a baby, but does not suckle
it.

dry-nurse (drī′nèrs′) v. **-nursed, -nurs·ing.** act as dry nurse to.

dry point 1 a picture made from a copper plate into which lines
have been engraved with a hard needle without using acid. 2 the
needle used. 3 this method of engraving.

dry rot 1 the decay of seasoned wood, causing it to crumble to a
dry powder by the action of various fungi. 2 a disease of plants
caused by the fungi that produce dry decay. 3 any of these fungi.
4 inner decay: *Lack of new people and new ideas often causes dry
rot in an organization.*

dry run 1 a practice test or session. 2 *Military.* any simulated
firing practice, bombing approach, etc. without use of live
ammunition.

dry-shod (drī′shod′) adj. or adv. having dry shoes; without
getting the feet wet.

dry-stone (drī′stōn′) adj. built of stone without the use of
mortar.

dry·wall (drī′wol′ or -wəl′) n., v. —n. 1 a construction method
for interior walls, using plasterboard instead of wet plaster.
2 plasterboard. 3 (adjl.) made of plasterboard: *drywall panelling.*
—v. construct a wall with plasterboard instead of wet plaster.

dry wash clothes, linens, etc. that have been washed and dried,
but not ironed.

d.s. 1 daylight saving. 2 *Business.* days after sight.

DS *Typing.* double space.

D.S. or **d.s.** *Music.* repeat from the point indicated (for Ital. *dal
segno* from the sign).

D.Sc. Doctor of Science (for L *Doctor Scientiae*).

D.S.C. Distinguished Service Cross.

D.S.M. Distinguished Service Medal.

D.S.O. Distinguished Service Order.

D.S.T. or **DST** Daylight Saving Time.

D.Th. or **D.Theol.** Doctor of Theology (for L *Doctor
Theologiae*).

d.t.'s delirium tremens.

Du. Dutch.

du·al (dyü′əl or dü′əl) adj., n. —adj. 1 of two; showing two.
2 consisting of two parts; double; twofold: *The airplane had dual
controls, one set for each pilot.* 3 *Grammar.* signifying or denoting
reference to two. Some languages have a **dual number** for nouns,
pronouns, verbs, etc. distinct in form from singular and plural.
—n. *Grammar.* 1 the dual number. 2 a word or construction in the
dual number. [< L *dualis* < *duo* two]
☛ *Hom.* **duel.**

du·al·ism (dyü′əl iz′əm or dü′əl iz′əm) n. 1 a dual conditon;
duality. 2 *Philosophy.* the doctrine that all the phenomena of the
universe can be explained by two separate and distinct substances
or principles, such as mind and matter. 3 *Theology.* **a** the doctrine
that Christ consisted of two personalities. **b** the doctrine that two
distinct elements are constituted in man, as body and spirit.

du·al·ist (dyü′əl ist or dü′əl ist) n. a believer in dualism.

du·al·is·tic (dyü′əl is′tik or dü′əl is′tik) adj. 1 having to do with
dualism; based on dualism. 2 dual. —**du′al·is′ti·cal·ly,** adv.

du·al·i·ty (dyü al′ə tē or dü al′ə tē) n., pl. **-ties.** a dual condition
or quality.

du·al–pur·pose (dyü′əl pèr′pəs or dü′əl-) adj. having, serving,
or designed for two functions.

dub¹ (dub) v. **dubbed, dub·bing.** 1 make (a person) a member of
an order of knighthood by striking his shoulder lightly with a sword:
He was dubbed a knight. 2 give a title to; call; name: *Because of his
very blond hair, the boys dubbed him 'Whitey'.* 3 smooth or dress
(wood, leather, etc.) by rubbing, scraping, etc. [OE *dubbian*]

dub² (dub) n., v. **dubbed, dub·bing.** *Slang.* —n. 1 a clumsy,
unskilful person. 2 *Sports.* an awkward, clumsy player. —v. do or
play awkwardly; bungle. [? related to *dub¹*]

dub³ (dub) v. **dubbed, dub·bing;** n. —v. 1 push; thrust. 2 beat a
drum. —n. 1 a thrust or push. 2 the beat of a drum. [origin
uncertain]

dub⁴ (dub) v. **dubbed, dub·bing;** n. —v. 1 add music, voices, or
sound effects to (a motion-picture film, a radio or television
broadcast, a recording, etc.) by making a new sound track: *The*

Italian film was dubbed with English dialogue. 2 add (sounds) to.
3 make a record of (a previously made recording).
—n. the sounds added. [short for *double*]

du·bi·e·ty (dyü bī′ə tē or dü bī′ə tē) n., pl. **-ties.** 1 doubtfulness;
uncertainty. 2 something that is doubtful.

du·bi·ous (dyü′bē əs or dü′bē əs) adj. 1 doubtful; uncertain: *a
dubious compliment, dubious authorship, a dubious friend.* 2 of
questionable character; probably bad: *a dubious scheme for making
money.* [< L *dubiosus* < *dubius* doubtful < *du-* two]
—**du′bi·ous·ly,** adv. —**du′bi·ous·ness,** n.

du·cal (dyü′kəl or dü′kəl) adj. of or having to do with a duke or
dukedom. [< LL *ducalis* < L *dux, ducis* leader]

duc·at (duk′ət) n. 1 a gold or silver coin formerly used in some
European countries. 2 *Slang.* a ticket. [ME < Ital. *ducato* < Med.L
< L *dux, ducis* leader]

du·ce (dü′chä) n. *Italian.* 1 leader. 2 **Duce,** the title given to
Benito Mussolini (1883-1945), dictator of Italy from 1922 to 1943. [<
Ital. < L *dux, ducis* leader. Doublet of DOGE, DUKE.]

duch·ess (duch′is) n. 1 the wife or widow of a duke. 2 a woman
with a rank equal to that of a duke. [ME < OF *duchesse* < *duc*
duke. See DUKE.]

duch·y (duch′ē) n., pl. **duch·ies.** the territory under the rule of a
duke or duchess; a dukedom.

duck¹ (duk) n. 1 any of numerous small or medium-sized aquatic
birds (family Anatidae) having a thick body, short neck and legs,
flat bill, and webbed feet. 2 the adult female of a duck. Compare
drake. 3 the flesh of a duck used for food. 4 *Informal.* a darling;
pet. 5 *Slang.* a person, especially one considered strange but
harmless: *He's a queer old duck.*
like water off a duck's back, without having any effect.
make ducks and drakes of or **play ducks and drakes with,** handle
recklessly; squander foolishly.
[OE *dūce.* Related to DUCK².] —**duck′like′,** adj.

duck² (duk) v., n. —v. 1 dip or plunge suddenly under water and
out again. 2 lower the head or bend the body suddenly to keep from
being hit, seen, etc. 3 lower (the head) or bend (the body) suddenly.
4 *Informal.* get or keep away from; avoid: *He is always ducking his
responsibilities.* 5 *Informal.* escape; make off (*often used with* **out**):
She ducked out when she heard they were coming.
—n. the act or an instance of ducking. [ME *duke(n)*] —**duck′er,** n.

duck³ (duk) n. 1 a strong cotton or linen cloth with a lighter and
finer weave than canvas. Duck is used to make small sails and
clothes for sailors or people living in hot climates. 2 **ducks,** pl.
Informal. trousers made of duck. [< Du. *doek* cloth]

duck⁴ (duk) n. a military vehicle that resembles a truck, but has a
watertight body so that it may move through the water like a boat.
[for DUKW, its code name]

duck·bill (duk′bil′) n. platypus.

duckbilled platypus platypus.

duck·board (duk′bôrd′) n. Usually, **duckboards,** pl. a platform
of slats laid on a muddy, wet, or cold surface to form a floor or
path.

ducking stool *Historical.* a stool on which a person was tied
and ducked into water as a punishment.

duck·ling (duk′ling) n. a young duck.

duck·pins (duk′pinz′) n. a game that resembles bowling but is
played with smaller balls and pins.

duck soup *Slang.* something that is easily done; a cinch: *This
job will be duck soup to us.*

duck·weed (duk′wēd′) n. 1 any of a genus (*Lemna*) of tiny
floating aquatic plants found in ponds and also in stagnant water.
2 (adjl.) designating a family (Lemnaceae) of tiny, stemless, aquatic
plants, including the duckweeds, that float freely on or in the water,
having no real foliage, but consisting only of a frond or fronds, with
one or more roots growing from the bottom, and minute flowers
from the top or edge. Members of the duckweed family are the
simplest flowering plants.

duct (dukt) n. 1 a tube, pipe, or channel for carrying liquid, air,
wires, etc. 2 a tube in the body for carrying a bodily fluid: *tear
ducts.* [< L *ductus* < *ducere* lead] —**duct′less,** adj.

duc·tile (duk′tīl or duk′təl) adj. 1 capable of being hammered out
thin or drawn out into a wire: *Gold and copper are ductile metals.*
2 easily moulded or shaped: *Wax is ductile.* 3 easily managed or
influenced; docile. [< F < L *ductilis* < *ducere* lead]

duc·til·i·ty (duk til′ə tē) n., pl. **-ties.** a ductile quality.

ductless gland a gland without a duct whose secretion passes
directly into the blood or lymph circulating through it; endocrine
gland. The thyroid, the spleen, and the thymus are ductless glands.

dud (dud) n., adj. *Informal.* —n. 1 a person or thing that is useless
or unsatisfactory; a failure, misfit, etc.: *The novel proved to be a*

dud. **2** a shell or bomb that fails to explode. **3 duds,** *pl.* **a** clothes. **b** possessions; personal belongings.
—*adj.* worthless, useless, or unsatisfactory: *a dud cheque.* [ME *dudde*; of unknown origin]

dude (dyüd *or* düd) *n.* **1** in the western parts of Canada and the United States, a city-bred person, especially one who spends a holiday on a ranch. **2** a man who pays too much attention to his clothes; dandy. [origin unknown]

dude ranch a ranch that is run as a tourist resort.

dudg·eon (duj'ən) *n. Archaic.* anger; resentment.
in high dudgeon, very angry; resentful. [origin unknown]

dud·ish (dyüd'ish *or* düd'ish) *adj.* like that of a dude.

due (dyü *or* dü) *adj., n., adv.* —*adj.* **1** owed as a debt; to be paid or given to as a right: *Money is due to him for his work. Respect is due to older people.* **2** proper; suitable; rightful: *Good deeds deserve due reward; bad deeds deserve due punishment.* **3** as much as needed; enough: *Use due care when crossing streets.* **4** promised to come or be ready; looked for; expected: *The train is due at noon. Your report is due tomorrow.* **5** of notes, bills, etc., becoming payable; having reached maturity; mature. **6** of dates, on which notes, bills, etc. become mature.
become due, be required to be paid.
due to, caused by: *The accident was due to his careless use of the gun.*
fall due, be required to be paid.
—*n.* **1** something owed as a debt or to be paid or given as a right: *Courtesy is a person's due as long as he is your guest.* **2 dues,** *pl.* **a** the amount of money owed or to be paid; a fee; tax. **b** the amount of money owed or to be paid to a club, etc. by a member.
give a person his due, be fair to a person.
—*adv.* straight; directly; exactly: *The wind is due east.* [ME < OF *deü,* pp. of *devoir* owe < L *debere*]
☞ *Hom.* **dew, do¹** (dü).
☞ *Usage.* **Due** was originally used only as an adjective, and therefore in formal English many writers use **due** only to introduce an adjective phrase (one modifying a noun): *Her success was due to hard work* (modifies *success*). In informal English **due** is often used to introduce an adverb phrase: *Due to her hard work, she succeeded.* However, many people do not approve of this construction. To avoid it, use **because of** or **on account of**: *She succeeded because of her hard work. On account of her hard work, she succeeded.*

du·el (dyü'əl *or* dü'əl) *n., v.* **-elled** *or* **-eled, -el·ling** *or* **-el·ing.** —*n.* **1** a formal fight between two men armed with swords or firearms. Duels were arranged to settle quarrels, avenge insults, etc., and were fought in the presence of witnesses, called seconds. **2** any fight or contest between two opponents: *a duel of wits.* —*v.* fight in a duel or duels. [< Med.L *duellum* a combat between two < L *duellum* (early form of *bellum*) war]
☞ *Hom.* **dual.**

du·el·list *or* **du·el·ist** (dyü'əl ist *or* dü'əl ist) *n.* a person who fights a duel or duels.

du·en·na (dyü en'ə *or* dü en'ə) *n.* **1** an elderly woman who is the governess and chaperone of young girls in a Spanish or Portuguese family. **2** a governess; chaperone. [< Sp. *dueña* < L *domina* mistress]

du·et (dyü et' *or* dü et') *n.* **1** a piece of music to be sung or played by two people. **2** two singers or players performing together. [< Ital. *duetto,* dim. of *duo.* See DUO.]

duff¹ (duf) *n.* a flour pudding boiled in a cloth bag: *plum duff.* [var. of *dough*]

duff² (duf) *n.* the decaying vegetable matter that covers the ground in a forest. [origin uncertain]

duff³ (duf) *n. Slang.* buttocks. [origin uncertain]

duf·fel *or* **duf·fle** (duf'əl) *n.* **1** a coarse woollen cloth having a thick nap. **2** the personal belongings of a hunter, camper, soldier, etc. **3** duffel sock. **4** duffel bag. [< Du. < *Duffel,* a town near Antwerp]

duffel bag *or* **duffle bag** **1** a large bag of heavy cloth or canvas, used by campers, hunters, soldiers, etc. for carrying personal belongings. **2** any bag of stout material.

duffel coat *or* **duffle coat** a knee-length, usually hooded coat made of duffel.

duffel sock *or* **duffle sock** in the North: **1** one of a pair of wrap-around leggings made of long strips of duffel or blanketing, worn as a protection against intense cold. **2** an outer sock or liner made of duffel, worn between a sock and a boot or mukluk, etc.

duff·er (duf'ər) *n. Informal.* a useless, clumsy, or stupid person. [origin uncertain]

duf·fle (duf'əl) See **duffel.**

dug¹ (dug) *v.* pt. and pp. of **dig.**

dug² (dug) *n.* a teat or nipple of a female animal. [< Scand.; cf. Danish *dægge,* Swedish *dägga* suckle]

du·gong (dü'gong) *n.* a large, whalelike marine mammal (*Dugong dugon*) found in shallow coastal waters of E Africa, the Philippines,

hat, āge, fär; let, ēqual, tėrm; it, īce
hot, ōpen, ôrder; oil, out; cup, pùt, rüle,
əbove, takən, pencəl, lemən, circəs

ch, child; ng, long; sh, ship
th, thin; ℞H, then; zh, measure

New Guinea, and N Australia, having flipperlike forelimbs and a paddlelike, slightly forked tail. The dugong is the only living member of the family Dugongidae. [< Malay *dūyong*]

dug·out (dug'out') *n.* **1** a rough shelter made by digging into the side of a hill, trench, etc. During war, soldiers use dugouts for protection against bullets and bombs. **2** a small shelter at the side of a baseball field, used by players who are not at bat or not in the game. **3** a boat made by hollowing out a large log. **4** *Cdn.* especially on the Prairies, a large excavation used to hold water collected there from the spring thaw and from rainfall: *Some dugouts are used for watering livestock; others are used for watering land.*

du·i (dyü'ē *or* dü'ē) *n.* a pl. of **duo.**

duke (dyük *or* dük) *n.* **1** a nobleman ranking next below a prince and above a márquis. **2** a prince who rules a small state or country called a duchy. **3 dukes,** *pl. Slang.* hands; fists. [ME < OF *duc* < L *dux, ducis* leader. Doublet of DOGE, DUCE.]

duke·dom (dyük'dəm *or* dük'-) *n.* **1** the territory under the rule of a duke or duchess; duchy. **2** the title or rank of a duke.

Duk·ho·bor (dü'kə bôr') *n.* Doukhobor.

dul·cet (dul'sit) *adj.* soothing, especially to the ear; sweet; pleasing. [< F *doucet,* dim. of *doux,* earlier *dulz* sweet < L *dulcis*]

dul·ci·mer (dul'sə mər) *n.* a musical instrument with metal strings, played by striking the strings with two hammers. [< MF *doulcemer,* var. of *doulcemele* < L *dulcis* sweet + *melos* song (< Gk.)]

Dul·cin·e·a *or* **dul·cin·ea** (dul sin'ē ə *or* dul'sə nē'ə) *n.* any idolized sweetheart. [< *Dulcinea,* the peasant girl who is Don Quixote's sweetheart and whom he idolizes as a fine and beautiful lady; from Sp. *dulce* sweet]

dull (dul) *adj., v.* —*adj.* **1** not sharp or pointed: *a dull knife.* **2** not bright or clear: *dull eyes, a dull day.* **3** slow in understanding; stupid: *a dull mind.* **4** showing a lack of liveliness in the senses or feelings. **5** not interesting; tiresome; boring: *a dull book.* **6** having little life, energy, or spirit; not active: *Business is dull these days.* **7** not felt sharply: *a dull pain.*
—*v.* make or become dull. [ME *dul*] —**dull'ly,** *adv.* —**dull'ness** *or* **dul'ness,** *n.*
☞ *Syn. adj.* **1.** Dull, blunt = with the edge or point not sharp. **Dull** suggests that the object described has lost the sharpness it had or is not as sharp as it should be: *This knife is dull.* **Blunt** suggests that the edge or point is not intended to be sharp or keen: *The blunt side of a knife will not cut meat. The weapon used by the murderer was a blunt instrument, possibly a poker.* **3.** See note at **stupid.**

dull·ard (dul'ərd) *n.* a person who is stupid and who learns very slowly.

dull·ish (dul'ish) *adj.* rather dull.

dull·ly (dul'lē) *adv.* in a dull manner.

dulse (duls) *n.* a large, edible, reddish seaweed (*Rhodymenia palmata*) found along the American and European coasts of the North Atlantic. [< Irish and Scots Gaelic *duileasg*]

du·ly (dyü'lē *or* dü'lē) *adv.* **1** according to what is due; properly; rightfully: *The documents were duly signed before a lawyer.* **2** as much as is needed; enough. **3** when due; at the proper time: *The debt was duly paid.*

Du·ma (dü'mä) *n.* in Imperial Russia, the national lawmaking body, established in 1905 and discontinued in 1917. Also, **Douma.** [< Russian *duma* thought, counsel, ult. < Gmc. Related to DEEM, DOOM.]

dumb (dum) *adj.* **1** not having the power of speech: *Animals are dumb.* **2** suffering from an inability to speak as a result of sickness, injury, etc.; mute: *deaf and dumb.* **3** silenced for the moment by fear, surprise, shyness, etc.: *The poor child was dumb with embarrassment.* **4** not expressed in words: *dumb astonishment, dumb grief.* **5** unwilling to speak; silent: *They questioned him repeatedly, but he remained dumb.* **6** *Informal.* stupid; unintelligent, or foolish: *He's pretty dumb. Dialling the wrong number is a dumb thing to do.* [< (defs. 1-3) OE *dumb;* (def. 4) influenced by G *dumm* stupid] —**dumb'ly,** *adv.* —**dumb'ness,** *n.*
☞ *Syn.* **1.** Dumb, mute, speechless = without speech. **Dumb** = without the power of speech, and although often used interchangeably with **mute** and **speechless,** it is the term applied particularly to animals: *Even intelligent animals are dumb.* **Mute** emphasizes being silent for some strong reason, and applies particularly to people who have never been able to speak because they were born deaf or became deaf in very early life and have never or almost never heard sounds: *Many mute children are now taught to speak.* **Speechless** =

without speech, usually temporarily and as the result of emotion, surprise, etc.: *I was speechless with rage.*

dumb–bell (dum′bel′) *n.* **1** a short bar of wood or iron with large, heavy, round ends. Dumb-bells are generally used in pairs and are lifted or swung around to exercise the muscles of the arms, back, etc. **2** *Slang.* a stupid person.

dumb·found (dum′found′) See **dumfound.**

dumb show gestures without words; pantomime: *He indicated by dumb show that he wanted to speak to me privately.*

dumb·struck (dum′struk′) *adj.* made speechless through amazement.

dumb·wait·er (dum′wāt′ər) *n.* **1** a small box with shelves, pulled up and down a shaft like an elevator to send dishes, food, rubbish, etc. from one floor to another. **2** a small stand placed near a dining table, for holding dishes, etc.

dum·dum (dum′dum) *n.* a soft-nosed bullet that spreads out when it strikes, causing a large, jagged wound. [< *Dum Dum,* a town near Calcutta, India, where it was first made]

dumdum bullet dumdum.

dum·found (dum′found′) *v.* amaze to the point of making unable to speak; bewilder utterly. [< *dumb* + con*found*]

dum·my (dum′ē) *n., pl.* **-mies;** *adj.* —*n.* **1** a figure of a person, used to display clothing in store windows, to shoot at in rifle practice, to tackle in football, etc. **2** an empty or imitation package or article used for display or advertisement: *All the articles in this window are dummies.* **3** *Informal.* a stupid person; blockhead. **4** an imitation; counterfeit. **5** a person supposedly acting for himself, but really acting for another. **6** a person who has nothing to say or who takes no active part in affairs. **7** *Card games.* **a** a player whose cards are laid face up on the table and played by his partner. **b** a hand of cards played in this way. **8** *Printing.* **a** a sample volume bound or unbound, and usually either blank or only partly printed, to show the size and general appearance of a book, etc. in preparation (in Great Britain called a *size copy*). **b** a format for parts or the whole of a magazine, book, etc. made up of printer's proofs pasted down upon empty pages to show the general arrangement of the material; layout.
—*adj.* **1** made to resemble the real thing; make-believe; imitation; counterfeit: *The children played soldier with dummy swords made of wood.* **2** acting for another while supposedly acting for oneself. **3** *Card games.* played with a hand of cards exposed. [< *dumb* + -*y¹*]

dump (dump) *v., n.* —*v.* **1** empty out; throw down; unload in a mass: *The truck backed up to the curb and dumped the topsoil on the driveway.* **2** unload rubbish. **3** put (goods) on the market in large quantities and at a low price; especially, do so in a foreign country at a price below that in the home country. **4** *Slang.* get rid of; abandon; reject: *to dump an unpopular candidate.* **5** *Slang.* express strong disapproval or contempt; disparage or malign (*used with* **on**): *She dumped on the government's foreign policy in a letter to the editor.*
—*n.* **1** a place for unloading rubbish. **2** a heap of rubbish. **3** a place for storing military supplies: *an ammunition dump.* **4** *Slang.* a shabby, ill-kept, untidy or otherwise depressing house, town, or locality: *Life in this dump is unbearable.* **5** *Logging.* a place at water's edge where cut logs are piled before being rolled into the water and driven downstream. **6** *Placer mining.* a pile of dirt waiting to be put through the sluice box to separate any gold that may be there. [ME ? < Scand; cf. Danish *dumpe* fall with a thud]

dump car or **truck** a vehicle that opens at the bottom or tips to dump its contents.

dump·ling (dump′ling) *n.* **1** a rounded piece of dough, boiled or steamed and served with meat. **2** a small pudding made by enclosing fruit in a piece of dough and baking or steaming it. **3** a dumpy animal or person, short and of rounded outlines. [< *dump* a badly shaped piece + -*ling*]

dumps (dumps) *n.pl. Informal.* low spirits; gloomy feelings. **(down) in the dumps,** feeling gloomy or sad. [prob. < Du. *domp* haze, dullness. Related to DAMP.]

dump·y (dump′ē) *adj.* **dump·i·er, dump·i·est.** short and fat. —**dump′i·ly,** *adv.* —**dump′i·ness,** *n.*

dun¹ (dun) *v.* **dunned, dun·ning;** *n.* —*v.* demand payment of a debt from (someone) again and again. —*n.* **1** a demand for payment, especially of a debt. **2** a person constantly demanding payment of a debt. [var. of *din,* with reference to making a din for money due] ☛ *Hom.* **done.**

dun² (dun) *n.* or *adj.* dull greyish-brown. [OE *dunn*] ☛ *Hom.* **done.**

Duncan Phyfe (dung′kən fīf′) **1** of, like, or having to do with a style of gracefully proportioned and soundly constructed furniture.

2 this style of furniture. **3** a piece of furniture of this style. [after *Duncan Phyfe* (1768-1854), an American furniture designer]

dunce (duns) *n.* **1** a child slow at learning his lessons in school. **2** a stupid person. [< *Duns*(man), name applied by his attackers to any follower of *Duns Scotus,* a medieval theologian]

dunce cap or **dunce's cap** a tall, cone-shaped cap formerly worn as a punishment by a child who was slow in learning his lessons in school.

dun·der·head (dun′dər hed′) *n.* a stupid, foolish person; dunce; blockhead. [dunder of uncertain origin] —**dun′der·head′ed·ness,** *n.*

dune (dyün *or* dün) *n.* a mound or ridge of loose sand heaped up by the wind. [< F < MDu. *dune.* Akin to DOWN³.]

dune buggy a small, usually roofless vehicle, often a converted car, for use on sand dunes or rough terrain.

dung (dung) *n., v.* —*n.* waste matter from the bowels of animals; manure: *Dung is much used as a fertilizer.* —*v.* put dung on as a fertilizer. [OE]

dun·ga·ree (dung′gə rē′ *or* dung′gə rē′) *n.* **1** a coarse cotton cloth, used for work clothes, sails, etc., especially blue denim. **2 dungarees,** *pl.* trousers or clothing made of this cloth. [< Hindi. *dungrī* a coarse calico cloth. 17c.]

dung beetle 1 any of various scarab beetles that feed on dung both as adults and larvae. **2** any of various other dung-eating beetles.

dun·geon (dun′jən) *n., v.* —*n.* **1** a dark underground room to keep prisoners in. **2** donjon. —*v.* confine in a dungeon; imprison. [ME < OF *donjon* < Gmc.] ☛ *Hom.* **donjon.**

dung·hill (dung′hil′) *n.* **1** a heap of dung. **2** a vile place or person.

dunk (dungk) *v.* **1** dip (something to eat) into a liquid: *to dunk doughnuts in coffee.* **2** *Informal.* push somebody into water. [< LG *dunken* dip] —**dunk′er,** *n.*

Dunk·ard (dungk′ərd) *n.* a member of the Church of the Brethren. [variant of *Dunker* < Pennsylvania Du. *Dunker* < LG *dunken* dip, baptize]

Dunk·er (dungk′ər) *n.* Dunkard.

dun·lin (dun′lən) *n., pl.* **-lin** or **-lins.** a small sandpiper (*Calidris alpina*) having a downward-curving bill and grey plumage that in breeding season becomes reddish on the back and black on the belly. Dunlins breed in the Arctic and winter on seacoasts farther south. [dim. of *dun²*]

dun·nage (dun′ij) *n.* **1** personal belongings; kit; baggage. **2** branches, mats, etc. placed around a cargo to protect it from damage by water or chafing. [origin uncertain]

du·o (dyü′ō *or* dü′ō) *n., pl.* **duos, dui. 1** *Music.* a duet. **2** *Informal.* a pair. [< Ital. < L *duo* two]

du·o·dec·i·mal (dyü′ō des′ə məl *or* dü′ō-) *adj., n.* —*adj.* having to do with twelfths or twelve; proceeding by twelves. —*n.* **1** a twelfth part. **2 duodecimals,** *pl. Mathematics.* a system of numbering or computing, using twelve as a base instead of ten as in the decimal system.

du·o·dec·i·mo (dyü′ō des′ə mō′ *or* dü′ō-) *n., pl.* **-mos. 1** the page size of a book in which each leaf is one twelfth of a whole printer's sheet of paper, or about 12.5 x 19 centimetres. **2** a book having pages of this size. [< L *in duodecimo* in a twelfth]

du·o·de·nal (dyü′ō dē′nəl *or* dü′ō-) *adj.* of or in the duodenum: *a duodenal ulcer.*

du·o·de·num (dyü′ō dē′nəm *or* dü′ō-) *n., pl.* **-na** (-nə). the first part of the small intestine, just below the stomach. See **alimentary canal** for picture. [ME < Med.L < L *duodeni* twelve each; with reference to its length, about twelve finger breadths]

du·o·tone (dyü′ə tōn′ *or* dü′ə tōn′) *adj., n.* —*adj. Printing.* printed in two tones of the same color. —*n.* a method by which illustrations are reproduced in two tones of the same color. [< L *duo* two + E *tone*]

dup. duplicate.

dupe (dyüp *or* düp) *n., v.* **duped, dup·ing.** —*n.* **1** a person easily deceived or tricked. **2** one who is being deluded or tricked: *The young politician's inexperience is making him the dupe of some unscrupulous schemers.* —*v.* deceive; trick. [< F < OF *duppe,* earlier *d'uppe* < L *upupa* hoopee (a bird thought to be stupid)] —**dup′er,** *n.*

du·ple (dyü′pəl *or* dü′pəl) *adj.* **1** double. **2** *Music.* having two or a multiple of two beats to the measure. [< L *duplus* double. Doublet of DOUBLE.]

du·plet (dyü′plit *or* dü′plit) *n. Chemistry.* a pair of electrons that is shared by two atoms.

duple time two-part time.

du·plex (dyü′pleks *or* dü′pleks) *adj., n.* —*adj.* double; twofold. —*n.* **1** *Cdn.* a building consisting of two dwellings under one roof,

either side by side or one above the other: *Most of the houses on this street are duplexes.* 2 *Cdn.* one of the dwellings of such a building. 3 *U.S.* duplex apartment. [< L *duplex* < *du-* two + *plicare* fold]

duplex apartment *U.S.* a self-contained apartment with rooms on two floors.

du·pli·cate (*adj., n.* dyü′plə kit *or* dü′plə kit; *v.* dyü′plə kāt′ *or* dü′plə kāt′) *adj., n., v.* **-cat·ed, -cat·ing.** —*adj.* **1** exactly alike; corresponding exactly: *We have duplicate keys for the front door.* **2** having or consisting of two similar or corresponding parts: *A person's lungs are duplicate.* **3** designating a card game in which identical hands are played by a second set of players in order to compare scores: *duplicate bridge.* —*n.* **1** an exact copy; reproduction; replica: *He made a duplicate of his letter to the editor of the newspaper.* **2** a counterpart; double: *This chair is a duplicate of one we have at home.* **in duplicate,** in two copies exactly alike: *This application must be made out in duplicate.* —*v.* **1** make an exact copy of; repeat exactly. **2** make double or twofold; double. [< L *duplicatus,* pp. of *duplicare* to double < *du-* two + *plicare* fold]

du·pli·ca·tion (dyü′plə kā′shən *or* dü′plə kā′shən) *n.* **1** duplicating or being duplicated. **2** a duplicate copy.

du·pli·ca·tor (dyü′plə kā′tər *or* dü′plə kā′tər) *n.* a machine for making many exact copies of anything written or typed; a duplicating machine.

du·plic·i·ty (dyü plis′ə tē *or* dü plis′ə tē) *n., pl.* **-ties.** deceitfulness; treachery; secretly acting one way and openly acting another in order to deceive. [< LL *duplicitas* doubleness < L *duplex.* See DUPLEX.]

du·ra·bil·i·ty (dyür′ə bil′ə tē *or* dür′ə bil′ə tē) *n., pl.* **-ties.** lasting quality; ability to stand wear.

du·ra·ble (dyür′ə bəl *or* dür′ə bəl) *adj.* able to last a long time; not soon injured or worn out. [ME < OF < L *durabilis* < *durare* to last, harden < *durus* hard] —**du′ra·ble·ness,** *n.* —**du′ra·bly,** *adv.*

Du·ral·u·min (dyü ral′yə min′ *or* dü ral′yə min′) *n.* *Trademark.* a light, strong, hard metal that is an alloy of aluminum containing copper, manganese, and magnesium. [< *durable* + *aluminum*]

du·rance (dyür′əns *or* dür′əns) *n.* imprisonment. [< MF *durance* duration]

du·ra·tion (dyü rā′shən *or* dü rā′shən) *n.* length of time; the time during which something lasts: *The strike was expected to be of short duration.*
for the duration, until the end, especially of a war. [ME < LL *duratio, -onis* < L *durare* to last]

dur·bar (dèr′bär) *n.* in India: **1** an official court or audience chamber. **2** any formal reception or assembly held by a governmental authority. **3** *Historical.* in British India, a formal assembly held to mark special occasions such as the proclamation of Queen Victoria as Empress of India. [< Hind., Persian *darbār* court]

du·ress (dyü res′ *or* dü res′, dyür′es *or* dür′es) *n.* **1** compulsion. A person cannot be legally forced to fulfil a contract signed under duress. **2** imprisonment. [ME < OF *duresse* < L *duritia* hardness < *durus* hard]

Dur·ham (dèr′əm) *n.* shorthorn. [< *Durham,* a county in England, where this breed originated]

Durham boat a large boat much used in the early nineteenth century on the St. Lawrence and its tributaries for carrying freight and passengers. It could be propelled by sails or poles. [after Robert Durham, an 18th-century American boat builder]

Durham report, the *Report on the Affairs of British North America,* issued in 1839 by Lord Durham (1792-1840), Governor-in-Chief of British North America from May to December, 1838. The report led to the union of Upper and Lower Canada in 1841 and to the introduction of responsible government and municipal government in Canada.

dur·ing (dyür′ing *or* dür′ing) *prep.* **1** throughout; through the entire time of: *The old man stays in the house during the day, but usually goes for a walk in the evening. The children played tag during recess.* **2** at some time in; in the course of: *They're going to drop in and see us sometime during the day.* [ppr. of obs. *dure* endure < OF < L *durare*]

Du·roc (dyür′ok *or* dür′ok) *n.* a breed of large, red pigs developed in the United States. [after the name of a horse owned by the developer of this breed. 19c.]

Du·roc-Jer·sey (dyür′ok jėr′zē *or* dür′ok-) *n.* Duroc.

dur·ra (dür′ə) *n.* a variety of sorghum raised for grain. [< Arabic *dhura*]

durst (dėrst) *v.* a pt. of **dare.**

du·rum (dyür′əm *or* dür′əm) *n.* a species of wheat (*Triticum*

hat, āge, fär; let, ēqual, tèrm; it, īce
hot, ōpen, ôrder; oil, out; cup, pùt, rüle,
əbove, takən, pencəl, lemən, circəs

ch, child; ng, long; sh, ship
th, thin; ᴛʜ, then; zh, measure

durum) having a high gluten content, used especially in making pastas, such as macaroni and spaghetti. [< L *durum,* neut. of *durus* hard]

durum wheat durum.

dusk (dusk) *n., adj., v.* —*n.* **1** the time just before dark; twilight. **2** shade; gloom.
—*adj.* *Poetic.* dusky.
—*v.* make or become dusky or shadowy. [var. of OE *dux, dox* dark]

dusk·y (dus′kē) *adj.* **dusk·i·er, dusk·i·est.** **1** somewhat dark; dark colored. **2** dim; obscure. —**dusk′i·ly,** *adv.* —**dusk′i·ness,** *n.*
☛ *Syn.* **1. Dusky, swarthy** = rather dark. **Dusky,** the general word, means rather dark and dim, but not completely without light or color: *It was dusky in the old warehouse.* **Swarthy** = very dark colored, and applies only to complexion: *He has a swarthy skin.*

dust (dust) *n., v.* —*n.* **1** fine, dry earth. **2** any fine powder. **3** the earth, especially as a place of burial. **4** what is left of a dead body after decay. **5** a low or humble condition. **6** a worthless thing. **7** a cloud of dust floating in the air: *The car raised a great dust.* **8** confusion; disturbance; turmoil: *to raise a dust about nothing.* **9** *Brit.* ashes or refuse.
bite the dust, *Slang.* fall dead or wounded: *A shot rang out and one of the outlaws bit the dust.*
lick the dust, humble oneself slavishly.
shake the dust off (one's) **feet,** go away feeling angry or scornful.
throw dust in (someone's) **eyes,** deceive or mislead a person: *The escape plan depended on his success in throwing dust in the eyes of the police.*
—*v.* **1** remove dust from furniture, etc.: *Be careful when you dust the figurines. I spent two hours dusting.* **2** make free of dust or other loose dirt (used with **off**): *He picked up his fallen hat, dusted it off, and left.* **3** bring back to use; revive (used with **off**): *She dusted off an old manuscript and sent it to a publisher.* **4** sprinkle with dust, powder, etc.: *to dust crops with an insecticide.* **5** *Archaic.* soil with dust. [OE *dūst*] —**dust′like′,** *adj.*

dust·bin (dust′bin′) *n.* *Brit.* a receptacle for refuse or trash; garbage can.

dust bowl especially in the western parts of Canada and the United States, a region that suffers from severe dust storms due to long periods of drought.

dust devil a small whirlwind that stirs up a column of dust, leaves, etc. as it moves along.

dust·er (dus′tər) *n.* **1** a person or thing that dusts, especially a cloth, brush, etc. used to get dust off things. **2** a contrivance for removing dust by sifting; sieve. **3** an apparatus for sifting or blowing dry poisons on plants to kill insects. **4** a light dress or robe that opens down the front, usually without a belt and worn especially when doing light household chores. **5** a lightweight coat worn over the clothes to protect them from dust. **6** *Informal.* a dust storm.

dusting powder **1** an antiseptic powder for dusting over wounds, etc. **2** a fine, usually perfumed, powder for dusting on the body after a bath, etc.

dust jacket a removable paper cover for a book, folded over the cover to protect it and to display the book effectively for selling purposes.

dust·less (dust′lis) *adj.* **1** without dust. **2** not causing dust.

dust·pan (dust′pan′) *n.* a flat pan, shaped like a short, broad shovel with a straight edge, for sweeping dust or debris into from the floor.

dust·proof (dust′prüf′) *adj.* impervious to dust.

dust sheet a large sheet to protect articles of furniture from dust.

dust storm a strong wind carrying clouds of dust across or from a dry region.

dust·up (dust′up′) *n.* *Slang.* a violent quarrel; commotion; disturbance.

dust·y (dus′tē) *adj.* **dust·i·er, dust·i·est.** **1** covered with or full of dust. **2** like dust; dry and powdery. **3** having the color of dust; greyish: *a dusty pink.* —**dust′i·ly,** *adv.* —**dust′i·ness,** *n.*

Dutch (duch) *adj., n.* —*n.* **1** the Dutch, *pl.* **a** the people of the Netherlands, a small country in W Europe. **b** *Esp.U.S.* the Pennsylvania Dutch. **c** *Obsolete.* the people of Germany, including the Netherlands. **2** the official language of the Netherlands.

3 *Obsolete.* the language of Germany and the Netherlands.
beat the Dutch, *Informal.* be very strange or surprising; outdo anything considered remarkable.
in Dutch, *Slang.* in trouble or disgrace: *He's in Dutch with his sister.*
—*adj.* **1** of or having to do with the Netherlands, its people, or their language. **2** *Esp.U.S.* Pennsylvania Dutch. **3** *Obsolete.* German.
go Dutch, *Informal.* have each person pay for himself.
[< MDu. *dutsch* Dutch, German]
☛ *Usage.* The numerous derogatory expressions compounded of **Dutch,** such as **Dutch courage** and **Dutch uncle,** are a legacy from the Dutch-English commercial rivalry of the 17th and 18th centuries.

Dutch courage *Informal.* courage brought on by alcohol.

Dutch door a door that is divided into an upper and lower section, each of which may be opened separately.

Dutch elm disease a killing disease of elm trees, caused by fungus and carried by insects.

Dutch·man (duch′mən) *n., pl.* **-men. 1** a native or inhabitant of the Netherlands. **2** a Dutch ship. **3** *Informal.* a German.

Dutch·man's-breech·es (duch′mənz brich′iz) *n.sing. or pl.* a spring-flowering perennial herb (*Dicentra cucullaria*) of the eastern woodlands of North America, closely related to the bleeding heart, having fernlike leaves and hanging, or nodding, double-spurred flowers that resemble upside-down breeches.

Dutch oven 1 a large, heavy metal pot with a high, rounded lid, used for cooking roasts, etc. in the oven. **2** a metal box with an open side, used for roasting meat, etc. before an open fire: *The open side of the Dutch oven faces toward the fire.* **3** a brick oven in which the walls are first heated, and food is put in to cook after the fire goes out or is removed.

Dutch treat *Informal.* a meal or entertainment in which each person pays for himself.

Dutch uncle *Informal.* a person who sternly or severely criticizes or scolds another.

du·te·ous (dyü′tē əs *or* dü′tē əs) *adj.* dutiful; obedient.
—**du′te·ous·ly,** *adv.* —**du′te·ous·ness,** *n.*

du·ti·a·ble (dyü′tē ə bəl *or* dü′tē ə bəl) *adj.* on which a duty or tax must be paid: *Perfumes imported into Canada are dutiable goods.*

du·ti·ful (dyü′tə fəl *or* dü′tə fəl) *adj.* **1** doing the duties required of one; obedient: *a dutiful daughter.* **2** required by duty; proceeding from or expressing a sense of duty: *dutiful words.* —**du′ti·ful·ly,** *adv.* —**du′ti·ful·ness,** *n.*

du·ty (dyü′tē *or* dü′tē) *n., pl.* **-ties. 1** the thing that a person ought to do; something that is right to do: *It is your duty to obey the laws.* **2** the feeling of having to do what is right: *He acted from a sense of duty, although he was afraid.* **3** the thing that a person has to do in his work; action required by one's occupation or position: *One of his duties as a reporter is to cover the meetings of the city council.* **4** the proper behavior owed to an older or superior person; obedience; respect. **5** a tax due to the government, especially on goods brought into or taken out of a country. **6** a tax on the performance of certain transactions, the execution of various deeds and documents, etc.
do duty for, serve in place of.
in duty bound, compelled to do something as a duty.
off duty, away from one's work or occupation: *He's off duty till six o'clock.*
on duty, at or to one's work or occupation: *She goes on duty at midnight.*
[ME < AF *duete* < *du,* var. of OF *deü.* See DUE.]
☛ *Syn.* **1. Duty, obligation** = what a person ought to do. **Duty** applies to what a person ought to do because conscience, piety, or law demands it: *I have a duty to help my parents.* **Obligation** applies to something incidental to social living, to specific actions demanded by usage, customs, etc.: *I have obligations to my neighbors.*

duty-bound (dyü′tē bound′ *or* dü′tē-) *adj.* bound by duty; obligated: *He was duty-bound to pay his share of the cost.*

duty-free (dyü′tē frē′ *or* dü′tē-) *adj.* exempt from custom duty.

du·um·vir (dyü um′vər *or* dü um′vər) *n., pl.* **-virs, -vi·ri** (-və rī or -və rē). in ancient Rome, either of two men who shared the same governmental position. [< L *duumvir* man of two]

du·um·vir·ate (dyü um′vər it *or* dü um′vər it) *n.* **1** a governmental position shared by two men simultaneously: *The consulship in ancient Rome was a duumvirate.* **2** a union or partnership of two men.

du·vet (dyü′vā *or* dü′vā) *n.* a down-filled quilt or comforter with a removable cover, used instead of a top sheet and blanket.

du·ve·tyn (dü′və tēn′) *n.* a soft, closely woven woollen cloth having a velvety finish. [< *duvet* down quilt < F]

D.V. 1 Deo volente. **2** Douai Version.

DVA Department of Veterans Affairs.

D.V.M. Doctor of Veterinary Medicine.

dwarf (dwôrf) *n., pl.* **dwarfs** *or* **dwarves** (dwôrvz); *v.* —*n.* **1** a person, animal, or plant much smaller than the usual size for its kind. **2** in fairy tales, a tiny, often ugly, person who has magic powers. **3** (*adj.*) much smaller than the usual size of its kind; checked in growth.
—*v.* **1** keep from growing large; check in growth. **2** cause to seem small by contrast or by distance: *That tall building dwarfs the other.* [OE *dweorg*]
☛ *Syn. n.* **1. Dwarf, midget, pygmy** = a person very much smaller than normal. **Dwarf** applies particularly to a very small person whose growth has been stunted, usually by glandular deficiency, and who often has a head large enough for a normal person of his age, or larger, or a body deformed in some way. **Dwarf** may be applied to a stunted animal or plant. With plants, however, **dwarf** usually refers not to the individual but to a *kind* or *variety* smaller than related varieties, either because of natural differentiation or because of breeding: *dwarf marigolds, the dwarf birch.* **Midget** applies to a tiny person who is perfectly shaped and normal in every way except size. A **pygmy** is one of a diminutive race found in Africa; but the word may be used as a synonym for both **dwarf** and **midget.**

dwarf·ish (dwôr′fish) *adj.* like a dwarf; smaller than usual.
—**dwarf′ish·ly,** *adv.* —**dwarf′ish·ness,** *n.*

dwell (dwel) *v.* **dwelt** *or* **dwelled, dwell·ing. 1** *Formal or poetic.* make one's home; live. **2** keep the attention fixed; think, write, or speak at length or insistently (*used with* **on** *or* **upon**): *to dwell on one's misfortunes.* [OE *dwellan* delay]

dwell·er (dwel′ər) *n.* a person who lives in a place: *a city dweller.*

dwell·ing (dwel′ing) *n. Formal or poetic.* a place used, or meant to be used, to live in; residence; abode: *a two-family dwelling.*

dwelling place dwelling.

dwelt (dwelt) *v.* a pt. and a pp. of **dwell.**

dwin·dle (dwin′dəl) *v.* **-dled, -dling.** make or become smaller and smaller; shrink; diminish. [dim. of obs. *dwine* < OE *dwīnan* waste away]
☛ *Syn.* See note at **decrease.**

dwt. pennyweight(s).

DWT *or* **dwt** dead-weight tonnage.

DX *or* **D.X.** *Radio.* distance; distant.

Dy dysprosium.

Dy·ak (dī′ak) *n.* a member of an Indonesian people living in central Borneo.

dyb·buk (dib′uk) *n. Jewish folklore.* a spirit, either a demon or the soul of a dead person, that takes possession of a living human being. Also, **dibbuk.** [< Hebrew *dibbuq,* originally, cement, glue]

dye (dī) *n., v.* **dyed, dye·ing.** —*n.* **1** a coloring matter used to color cloth, hair, etc., or a liquid containing it: *Some dyes are vegetable, others chemical.* **2** a color produced by treatment with such coloring matter; tint; hue: *A good dye will not fade.*
of deepest *or* **blackest dye,** of the lowest or vilest kind.
—*v.* **1** color (cloth, hair, etc.) by dipping into or treating with a liquid containing coloring matter: *to have a dress dyed.* **2** color; stain: *The spilled grape juice dyed the tablecloth purple.* **3** become colored when treated with a dye: *This material dyes evenly.* [OE *dēag*]
☛ *Hom.* **die.**

dyed-in-the-wool (dīd′in ℞ə wül′) *adj.* **1** of people, thorough-going, especially in a political sense; unchanging: *a dyed-in-the-wool conservative.* **2** of materials, dyed before being woven into cloth.

dye·ing (dī′ing) *n.* the coloring of fabrics with dye.

dy·er (dī′ər) *n.* a person whose business is dyeing fabrics.

dye·stuff (dī′stuf′) *n.* any substance, such as indigo or cochineal, yielding a dye or used as a dye.

dy·ing (dī′ing) *adj., n., v.* —*adj.* **1** about to die. **2** coming to end. **3** of death; at death.
—*n.* death.
—*v.* ppr. of **die¹.**

dyke (dīk) *n., v.* **dyked, dyk·ing.** See **dike.**

dy·nam·ic (dī nam′ik) *adj., n.* —*adj.* **1** of or having to do with energy or force in motion. **2** of or having to do with dynamics. **3** active; energetic; forceful: *Many successful salesmen have dynamic personalities.*
—*n.* **1 dynamics, a** the branch of physics that deals with the study of the motion of bodies (kinematics) and the relation between motion and the forces producing it (kinetics). **b** kinetics. **c** mechanics (def. 1), including kinetics, kinematics, and statics. **2** Often, **dynamics,** *pl.* a force or set of forces producing change, growth, or interaction: *the dynamics of glacier motion, the dynamics of family life, the values that constitute the dynamic of a civilization.* **3** Usually, **dynamics,** *pl.* a branch of study dealing with

such forces: *He is an expert on population dynamics.* **4 dynamics,** *pl. Music.* the effect of variation and contrast in force or loudness. [< Gk. *dynamikos* < *dynamis* power]

dy·nam·i·cal (dī nam′ə kəl) *adj.* dynamic.

dy·nam·i·cal·ly (dī nam′ik lē) *adv.* in a dynamic manner.

dy·na·mism (dī′nə miz′əm) *n.* **1** any of various doctrines or philosophical systems which seek to explain the phenomena of nature by the action of some force. **2** dynamic quality; energetic quality.

dy·na·mist (dī′nə mist) *n.* a person who believes in dynamism.

dy·na·mite (dī′nə mīt′) *n., v.* **-mit·ed, -mit·ing.** —*n.* a powerful explosive often used in blasting rock, tree stumps, etc., made of nitroglycerine mixed with an absorbent material and pressed into round sticks. —*v.* **1** blow up or destroy with dynamite. **2** mine or charge with dynamite. [< Gk. *dynamis* power; named by Alfred Nobel (1833-1896), the inventor] —**dy′na·mit′er,** *n.*

dy·na·mo (dī′nə mō′) *n., pl.* **-mos. 1** generator (def. 1). **2** a very energetic and forceful person. [short for *dynamo-electric machine*]

dy·na·mo–e·lec·tric (dī′nə mō i lek′trik) *adj.* having to do with the transformation of mechanical energy into electric energy, or electric energy into mechanical energy. [< *dynamo-* (< Gk. *dynamis* power) + *electric*]

dy·na·mom·e·ter (dī′nə mom′ə tər) *n.* an apparatus for measuring force or power, especially one for measuring the power of an engine. [< F *dynamomètre*]

dy·na·mom·e·try (dī′nə mom′ə trē) *n.* the art or process of measuring forces.

dy·na·mo·tor (dī′nə mō′tər) *n.* a combined electric motor and dynamo for changing the voltage of an electric current.

dy·nast (dī′nast *or* din′ast) *n.* **1** a member of a dynasty; hereditary ruler. **2** any ruler. [< L < Gk. *dynastēs* < *dynasthai* be powerful]

dy·nas·tic (dī nas′tik *or* di nas′tik) *adj.* of or having to do with a dynasty. —**dy·nas′tic·al·ly,** *adv.*

dy·nas·ty (dī′nəs tē *or* din′əs tē) *n., pl.* **-ties. 1** a succession of rulers who belong to the same family: *The Bourbon dynasty ruled France for more than 200 years.* **2** the period of time during which a dynasty rules.

dy·na·tron (dī′nə tron′) *n.* **1** a vacuum tube that uses the secondary emission of electrons caused by an increase in the plate voltage to decrease the plate current. Dynatrons are often used in radio as oscillators. **2** *Physics.* meson. [< Gk. *dyna*mis + elec*tron.* See DYNAMIC, ELECTRIC.]

dyne (dīn) *n.* a unit of force equal to ten micronewtons. [< F < Gk. *dynamis* power < *dynasthai* be powerful]

hat, āge, fär; let, ēqual, tèrm; it, īce
hot, ōpen, ôrder; oil, out; cup, pût, rüle,
əbove, takən, pencəl, lemən, circəs

ch, child; ng, long; sh, ship
th, thin; ₮H, then; zh, measure

dys·en·ter·y (dis′ən ter′ē *or* dis′ən trē) *n.* a painful disease of the intestines, producing diarrhea with blood and mucus. [ME < OF *dissenterie* < L Gk. *dysenteria* < *dys-* bad + *entera* intestines]

dys·func·tion (dis fungk′shən) *n.* a functional abnormality or impairment, as of a body organ. [< Gk. *dys-* bad + E function]

dys·func·tion·al (dis fungk′shə nəl) *adj.* **1** having to do with dysfunction. **2** performing badly or improperly; malfunctioning.

dys·gen·ic (dis jen′ik) *adj.* having to do with or causing degeneration in the type of offspring produced; opposed to *eugenic*. [< Gk. *dys-* bad + *gen-* produce]

dys·lex·i·a (dis lek′sē ə) *n.* an impairment of the ability to read. [< NL < Gk. *dys-* faulty, bad + *lexia* < Gk. *lexis* speech. 19c.]

dys·lex·ic (dis lek′sik) *adj.* of or having to do with dyslexia.

dys·pep·si·a (dis pep′sē ə *or* dis pep′shə) *n.* poor digestion; indigestion. [< L < Gk. *dyspepsia* < *dys-* bad + *pep-* cook, digest]

dys·pep·tic (dis pep′tik) *adj., n.* —*adj.* **1** having to do with or causing dyspepsia. **2** suffering from dyspepsia. **3** gloomy; pessimistic. —*n.* a person who has dyspepsia. —**dys·pep′ti·cal·ly,** *adv.*

dys·pha·si·a (dis fā′zē ə *or* dis fā′zhə) *n.* difficulty in speaking or in understanding speech, as a result of brain damage. [< NL < Gk. *dys-* bad + *-phasis*. See APHASIA.]

dys·pho·ri·a (dis fôr′ē ə) *n. Medicine.* a chronic feeling of general discontent and illness. [< Gk. *dysphoria* discomfort, ult. < *dys-* ill, bad + *phorein* to bear, suffer]

dys·pro·si·um (dis prō′sē əm *or* dis prō′shē əm) *n.* a rare chemical element, the most magnetic substance known. *Symbol:* Dy; *at.no.* 66; *at.wt.* 162.50. [< NL < Gk. *dysprositos* hard to get at]

dys·to·pi·a (dis tō′pē ə) *n.* an imaginary place or state where everything is bad and people lead a wretched life. [<NL *dys-* bad + *-topia* as in *utopia*. Coined by J.S. Mill. 19c.]

dys·to·pi·an (dis tō′pē ən) *adj.* of, having to do with, or being a dystopia.

dys·tro·phy (dis′trə fē) *n. Medicine.* **1** defective nutrition. **2** defective development or degeneration: *muscular dystrophy.* [< Gk. *dys-* bad + *trophē* nourishment]

dz. dozen(s).

Ee

e or **E** (ē) *n., pl.* **e's** or **E's. 1** the fifth letter of the English alphabet. **2** any speech sound represented by this letter. **3** a person or thing identified as *e*, especially the fifth in a series. **4** *Music.* **a** the third tone of the scale of C major. **b** a symbol representing this tone. **c** a key or string that produces this tone. **d** the scale or key that has E as its keynote. **5** E, something shaped like the letter E. **6** *Mathematics.* the base of the system of natural logarithms, having an approximate numerical value of 2.718 28. **7** (*adjl.*) of or being an E or e.

e 1 *Physics.* erg. **2** *Baseball.* error.

e– *prefix.* out of; from, as in *educe, emerge, erase, evoke.* It is the form of **ex-¹** used before consonants except *c, f, p, q, s, t.*

E excellent.

E or **E. 1** east; eastern. **2** English. **3** earth.

E. 1 Earl. **2** engineer; engineering.

ea. each.

EA educational age.

each (ēch) *adj., pron., adv.* **—adj.** every one of two or more persons or things considered separately or one by one: *Each dog has a name.*
—pron. 1 every single one: *He gave a pencil to each.* **2** all of a group, thought of as individuals: *We each have our work to do.*
—adv. for each; to each; apiece: *These pencils cost ten cents each.* [OE ǣlc < ā ever + gelīc alike]
☛ *Syn. adj.* **Each, every** = one and all (of a number or group). **Each** emphasizes that one and all of a number, or one and the other of two, are thought of singly, as individuals: *Each dog has a name* means that, as individuals, all the dogs in the group have names of their own. **Every,** relating to a group, means that one and all are included, with no exceptions: *Every dog has a name* = none of the dogs was left without a name. In a more inclusive sense, **every** refers to one and all everywhere: *Every dog has his day.*
☛ *Usage.* As a pronoun, **each** is singular: *Each of the four players has seven cards.* When **each** is used as an adjective modifying a noun, however, it is the noun that decides whether a following verb or pronoun is singular or plural: *Each player looks at his seven cards.* (sing.) *The four players each look at their seven cards.* (pl.)

each other 1 each of two in an action or relation that is common to both: *They struck each other* (that is, they struck, *each* striking *the other*). **2** one another: *The three boys struck at each other.*
☛ *Usage.* **Each other** is in good use for more than two, although formal usage frequently has *one another.* General: *The boys in the class were shouting to each other.* Formal: *The boys in the class were shouting to one another.*

ea·ger (ē'gər) *adj.* **1** wanting very much; desiring strongly; impatient to do or get something: *The child is eager to have the candy.* **2** characterized by or showing keenness of desire or feeling: *eager looks.* [ME < OF *aigre* keen < L *acer, acris*] **—ea'ger·ly,** *adv.* **—ea'ger·ness,** *n.*
☛ *Syn.* **1. Eager, keen, anxious** = desirous, or wanting very much. **Eager** suggests enthusiasm with a touch of impatience: *The boys were eager to start building the clubhouse.* **Keen** suggests intensity of desire and quickness in action: *keen on learning golf.* **Anxious** implies desire overhung with fear about what may happen: *They were anxious to do their best.*

eager beaver *Informal.* an especially hard-working person.

ea·gle (ē'gəl) *n.* **1** any of a number of large, strong birds of prey (family Accipitridae), having very keen eyes and powerful wings. Eagles eat small animals, fish, or other birds. **2** a standard bearing the figure of an eagle as an emblem. **3** *Golf.* two strokes less than par for any hole on a course. [ME < OF *aigle* < L *aquila*]

eagle eye 1 keen vision. **2** careful watch; lookout: *keeping an eagle eye on the prisoners, keeping an eagle eye out for bargains.*

ea·gle–eyed (ē'gəl īd') *adj.* able to see far and clearly.

ea·glet (ē'glit) *n.* a young eagle. [< F *aiglette*, dim. of *aigle* eagle]

ear¹ (ēr) *n.* **1** the organ of hearing and balance in the higher vertebrates. In man and other mammals it consists typically of three parts: the **external ear, middle ear,** and **inner ear. 2** the external, visible part of the ear in man and most mammals. **3** the sense of hearing. **4** the ability to distinguish small differences in sounds: *That musician has a very good ear for pitch and tone.* **5** attention, especially favorable attention; heed: *to give ear to a request. He has the ear of the director.* **6** something resembling an external ear in shape or position, such as the handle of a cup.
all ears, *Informal.* listening attentively or eagerly.
believe (one's) **ears,** credit what one hears.

bend (someone's) **ear,** *Slang.* talk to someone at great length.
by ear, without memorizing written music: *He can't read music but he can play almost anything by ear.*
fall on deaf ears, receive no attention; be ignored.
go in one ear and out the other, be heard but make no impression: *Their warning to him simply went in one ear and out the other.*
have or **keep an ear to the ground.** *Informal.* pay attention to what people are thinking and saying so that one can act accordingly.
lend an ear, listen; pay attention.
play it by ear, *Informal.* proceed instinctively or spontaneously, without a plan.
set by the ears, cause to disagree or quarrel; stir up trouble between.
set (something) **on its ear,** *Informal.* put into a state of excitement or upheaval: *a young designer setting the fashion world on its ear.*
turn a deaf ear, refuse to listen; pay no attention.
up to the ears, *Informal.* deeply taken up; thoroughly involved; almost overcome.
wet behind the ears, *Informal.* inexperienced; not yet able to cope; quite immature.
[OE ēare] **—ear'less,** *adj.* **—ear'like',** *adj.*

ear² (ēr) *n., v.* **—n.** the mature spike of cereal plants, containing the seeds, or kernels. An ear of corn consists of rows of kernels surrounding the outside of a long, thick, woody cob. **—v.** of such plants, develop ears; mature: *Soon the corn will ear.* [OE ēar]

ear·ache (ēr'āk') *n.* pain in the ear.

ear·drop (ēr'drop') *n.* earring, especially one with a hanging ornament.

ear·drum (ēr'drum') *n.* the thin membrane that stretches across the middle ear and vibrates when sound waves strike it; tympanic membrane. See **ear¹** for picture.

eared *adj.* **1** having ears or earlike parts. **2** having an ear or ears of a specific number or kind (*used in compounds*): *a mangy, one-eared dog.*

eared seal any of a family (Otariidae) of seals having short, pointed external ears, thick fur, and hind limbs that can turn forward to support the body for locomotion on land.

ear·flap (ēr'flap') *n.* a part of a cap that can be turned down over the ear to keep it warm.

earl (ėrl) *n.* **1** in the United Kingdom, a nobleman ranking below a marquis and above a viscount. The wife or widow of an earl is called a countess. **2** *Historical.* In England, a noble who was the governor of a county or shire. **3** the title of an earl. [OE *eorl*]

ear·lap (ēr'lap') *n.* **1** an earflap. **2** the lobe of the ear. **3** the external ear; visible part of the ear.

earl·dom (ėrl'dəm) *n.* **1** the territory under the rule of an earl. **2** the rank or dignity of an earl.

ear·ly (ėr'lē) *adv., adj.* **-li·er, -li·est. —adv. 1** near the beginning: *The sun is not hot early in the day.* **2** before the usual, normal, or expected time: *We got there 15 minutes early.* **3** long ago; far back in time; in ancient times: *The plough was invented early in the history of man.* **4** before very long; in the near future; soon.
early on, at an early stage: *They learned early on not to push him.*
—adj. 1 that happens or arrives before the usual, normal, or

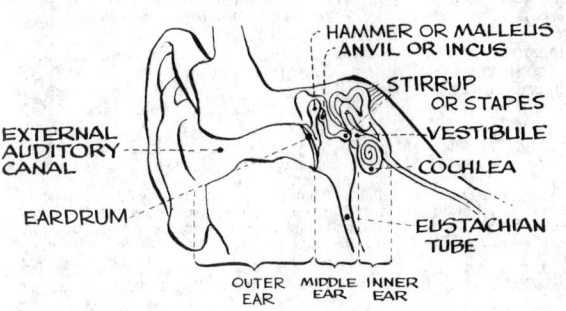

HAMMER OR MALLEUS
ANVIL OR INCUS
STIRRUP OR STAPES
VESTIBULE
COCHLEA
EUSTACHIAN TUBE
EXTERNAL AUDITORY CANAL
EARDRUM
OUTER EAR   MIDDLE EAR   INNER EAR

The human ear

expected time: *an early dinner, an early spring.* **2** of or occurring in the first part: *In his early years he liked ships.* **3** happening far back in time. **4** occurring in the near future: *Let us have an early reply.* [OE *ǣrlīce* < *ǣr* ere + -*līce* -ly[1]] —**ear′li·ness,** *n.*

early bird a person who gets up or arrives early.

ear·mark (ēr′märk′) *n., v.* —*n.* **1** *Informal.* a mark made on the ear of an animal to show who owns it. **2** a special mark, quality, or feature that identifies or gives information about a person or thing; sign.
—*v.* **1** make an earmark on. **2** identify or give information about: *Careful work earmarks a good student.* **3** set aside for some special purpose: *Five hundred dollars is earmarked to buy books for the library.*

ear·muffs (ēr′mufs′) *n.pl.* a pair of coverings to put over the ears to keep them warm.

earn (ėrn) *v.* **1** receive for work or service; be paid: *She earns ten dollars a day.* **2** do enough work for; deserve; be worth: *He is paid more than he really earns.* **3** bring or get as deserved: *Her unselfish acts earned her the respect of all who knew her.* **4** gain as a profit or return: *Money well invested earns good interest.* [OE *earnian*]
—**earn′er,** *n.*
☛ *Hom.* urn.

ear·nest[1] (ėr′nist) *adj., n.* —*adj.* **1** sincerely zealous; strong and firm in purpose; serious. **2** important; to be taken seriously: *"Life is real, life is earnest." —n.*
in earnest, a seriously: *I speak in earnest.* **b** sincerely zealous; serious.
[OE *eornost*] —**ear′nest·ly,** *adv.* —**ear′nest·ness,** *n.*

ear·nest[2] (ėr′nist) *n.* **1** the part given or done in advance as a pledge for the rest: *Take this as an earnest of what is to come.* **2** anything that shows what is to come; pledge; token. [ME *ernes,* apparently alteration (by association with -*ness*) of *erres* < OF *erres,* pl. < L *arra* < Gk. *arrhabōn* < Hebrew *'ērābōn*]

earnest money money paid as a pledge.

earn·ings (ėr′ningz) *n.pl.* money earned; wages; profits.

ear·phone (ēr′fōn′) *n.* a receiver for a radio, telephone, hearing aid, etc. that fits over or is inserted into the ear: *Many portable radios have earphones for private listening.*

ear·piece (ēr′pēs′) *n.* **1** a part of something that is connected to, held to, or supported by the ear: *the earpiece of a telephone.* **2** earflap.

ear·plug (ēr′plug′) *n.* a round piece of pliable material such as wax, rubber, or plastic, for insertion into the outer ear to keep out water or noise.

ear·ring (ēr′ring′) *n.* an ornament for the lobe of the ear, held in place either by a wire or post passed through a hole pierced in the lobe or by a screw or clip.

ear·shot (ēr′shot′) *n.* the distance at which a sound can be heard; range of hearing: *He was out of earshot and could not hear our shouts.*

earth (ėrth) *n., v.* —*n.* **1** the planet on which we live; the third planet from the sun, and the fifth in size. **2** all the people who live on this planet. **3** this world (often in contrast to heaven and hell). **4** dry land. **5** ground; soil; dirt: *The earth in the garden is soft.* **6** the ground: *The arrow fell to earth 100 metres away.* **7** the hole of a fox or other burrowing animal. **8** worldly matters. **9** *Chemistry.* a metallic oxide from which it is difficult to remove the oxygen, such as alumina. **10** *Electricity.* the connection of a conductor with the earth.
come back to earth, stop dreaming and get back to practical matters.
down to earth, seeing things as they really are; practical.
on earth, ever (*an intensifier used with* **how, what,** etc.): *How on earth can we get all this in the car? What on earth is he talking about?*
run to earth, a hunt or chase until caught. **b** look for until found.
—*v.* **1** connect (an electrical wire or other conductor) with the earth; ground. **2** cover with soil: *to earth up a plant or its roots.* **3** drive (a fox, etc.) to its burrow. **4** of a hunted fox, etc., hide in its burrow. [OE *eorthe*]
☛ *Syn. n.* **1, 3.** Earth, world, globe = the planet on which we live. **Earth** applies to this planet in contrast to the other planets and sun, stars, etc. or, sometimes, to heaven and hell. **World** applies to the earth as the home of man, usually suggesting all mankind and human affairs. In the works of older writers, **world** sometimes means the visible universe, including sun, stars, etc. **Globe** applies to the earth as our world, and emphasizes its roundness: *Nowadays everyone on earth should try to understand the people of the world all over the globe.*

earth·born (ėrth′bôrn′) *adj.* **1** sprung from the earth. **2** human; mortal.

earth·bound (ėrth′bound′) *adj.* bound or limited to this earth.

earth·en (ėr′thən) *adj.* **1** made of earth. **2** made of baked clay.

earth·en·ware (ėr′thən wer′) *n.* **1** an opaque, somewhat porous type of pottery fired at a relatively low temperature. Earthenware must be glazed to make it non-porous. Compare **porcelain, stoneware. 2** any pottery. **3** articles made of earthenware. **4** (*adj.*) made of earthenware: *an earthenware jug.*

earth·ling (ėrth′ling) *n.* **1** an inhabitant of the earth; human being. **2** a worldly person.

earth·ly (ėrth′lē) *adj.* -**li·er,** -**li·est. 1** having to do with the earth, man's world, and not with heaven. **2** possible; conceivable: *That rubbish is of no earthly use.* —**earth′li·ness,** *n.*
☛ *Syn.* **1. Earthly, terrestrial, worldly** = having to do with the earth. **Earthly** describes things connected with life in this world, in contrast to heavenly things: *He thinks only of earthly affairs.* **Terrestrial** is the formal word, contrasted with **celestial,** and is used particularly to describe things on the earth regarded as a planet: *Of all terrestrial beings man is the most adaptable.* **Worldly,** in contrast to **spiritual,** emphasizes thinking only of human affairs, especially pleasures, success, vanity, etc.: *She enjoys parties, dances, and other worldly pleasures.*

earth·man (ėrth′man′ or ėrth′mən) *n.* -**men.** a person considered as an inhabitant of the planet earth; human being.

earth·nut (ėrth′nut′) *n.* **1** the underground part of certain plants, such as root, tuber, or underground pod: *Peanuts are earthnuts.* **2** a plant producing such a root, tuber, etc.

earth·quake (ėrth′kwāk′) *n.* a shaking of the earth's surface, caused by the sudden movement of masses of rock or by changes beneath the earth's surface.

earth science any of a group of sciences concerned with the origin and physical features of the earth. *Examples:* geology, geography, seismology.

earth–shak·ing (ėrth′shāk′ing) *adj.* of extreme importance or significance.

earth tide a modification of the earth's crust, similar to the ocean tide, due to gravitation. The rigidity of the earth can be calculated from the distortions thus caused in solid rock.

earth·ward (ėrth′wərd) *adv. or adj.* toward the earth.

earth·wards (ėrth′wərdz) *adv.* earthward.

earth·work (ėrth′wėrk′) *n.* **1** a bank of earth piled up for a fortification. **2** the moving of earth in engineering operations.

earth·worm (ėrth′wėrm′) *n.* any of various round, segmented worms (class Oligochaeta) that live in soil, especially any of the genus *Lumbricus,* which are valued in gardens, etc. because they help to aerate and fertilize the soil.

earth·y (ėr′thē) *adj.* **earth·i·er, earth·i·est. 1** of earth or soil. **2** like earth or soil. **3** not spiritual; worldly. **4** not refined; coarse. **5** natural; simple and frank; unsophisticated. —**earth′i·ly,** *adv.* —**earth′i·ness,** *n.*

ear trumpet a trumpet-shaped instrument held to the ear as an aid in hearing.

ear·wax (ēr′waks′) *n.* the sticky, yellowish substance that collects in the canal of the outer ear.

ear·wig (ēr′wig′) *n.* any of numerous insects (order Dermaptera) having long, jointed antennae and a long, slender body, with a pair of appendages at the tail end that are like forceps. [OE *ēarwicga* < *ēare* ear + *wicga* beetle, worm]

ease (ēz) *n., v.* **eased, eas·ing.** —*n.* **1** freedom from pain or trouble; comfort. **2** freedom from trying hard; lack of effort: *He enjoyed the ease of his part-time job.* **3** freedom from constraint; natural or easy manner.
at ease, a free from pain or trouble; comfortable. **b** with the hands behind the back, the feet apart, and the body somewhat relaxed: *The soldiers stood at ease.*
take (one's) ease, make oneself comfortable; rest.
with ease, without having to try hard; with little effort: *He learned to spell with ease.*
—*v.* **1** make free from pain or trouble; give relief or comfort to. **2** lessen; lighten: *This medicine eased my pain.* **3** make easy; loosen: *The belt is too tight; ease it a little.* **4** move slowly and carefully: *He eased the big box through the narrow door.* **5** become less rapid, less tense, etc. **6** make (money, credit, etc.) available at low rates of interest. **7** of securities, goods, etc., tend to decline in prices.
ease in, break in with light work.
ease off or **up, a** lessen; lighten. **b** loosen.
ease out, dismiss from or leave quietly (a job, an office, etc.).
[ME < OF *aisier* < *aise* comfort, elbow-room < VL *adjacens* neighborhood < L *adjacens* adjacent. Doublet of ADJACENT.]
☛ *Syn. n.* **1. Ease, comfort** = freedom from strain. **Ease** = freedom from hard work, trouble, pain, or any pressure, and suggests being relaxed or at rest: *When the holidays come, I am going to live a life of ease.* **Comfort** = freedom from all strain, pain, hardship, and unhappiness, and emphasizes feeling well and perfectly content: *Let others have money and fame; I want only comfort.*

ea·sel (ē′zəl) *n.* a support or frame for holding an artist's canvas,

a blackboard, etc. upright. [< Du. *ezel* easel, literally, ass < L *asinus*]

ease·ment (ēz′mənt) *n.* **1** *Law.* a right held by one person in land owned by another. **2** an easing; relief: *an easement of political tension.* **3** convenience.

eas·i·ly (ē′zə lē) *adv.* **1** in an easy manner; without difficulty or great effort: *He solved the puzzle easily.* **2** without pain or trouble; comfortably: *The patient was resting easily.* **3** smoothly; freely. **4** by far; beyond question: *She is easily the best singer in the choir.* **5** very likely: *A war may easily begin.*

eas·i·ness (ē′zē nis) *n.* **1** the quality, condition, or state of being easy. **2** carelessness; indifference.

east (ēst) *n., adj., adv.* —*n.* **1** the direction of the sunrise; point of the compass to the right as one faces north. **2** Also, **East,** the part of any country toward the east. **3 the East, a** the eastern part of Canada and the United States. **b** the countries in Asia; the Orient. **c** the Soviet Union and the countries allied with it; the communist world. **d** the Eastern Roman Empire.
back East or **down East,** *Cdn.* **a** any point to the east of Winnipeg, especially that part east of Quebec: *He's from down East.* **b** in or towards any place east of Winnipeg, especially that part east of Quebec: *Western Canadians speak of Ontario as being back East.* —*adj.* **1** toward the east. **2** from the east. **3** in the east.
east of, farther east than.
—*adv.* toward the east: *They travelled east.* [OE *ēast*]

east·bound (ēst′bound′) *adj.* going toward the east.

East·er (ēs′tər) *n., adj.* —*n.* **1** the yearly Christian celebration commemorating Christ's rising from the dead. In most churches, Easter comes between March 21 and April 26, on the first Sunday after the first full moon after March 21. **2** the season of Easter. —*adj.* of or for Easter: *Easter music.* [OE *ēastre*, originally, the name of a dawn goddess < *ēast* east]

Easter egg a colored egg, either real or made of chocolate, glass, etc. used as a gift or ornament at Easter.

Easter lily any of several cultivated lilies having large, waxy, white trumpet-shaped flowers, especially *Lilium longiflorum*, often grown for Easter.

east·er·ly (ēs′tər lē) *adj. or adv.* **1** toward the east. **2** from the east: *an easterly wind.*

east·ern (ēs′tərn) *adj.* **1** toward the east. **2** from the east. **3** of or in the east; of or in the eastern part of the country. **4** of or in the Orient, or Asia; Oriental. **5** of or having to do with the Soviet Union and its East European satellites.

Eastern Church 1 *Historical.* the Christian church in the eastern Roman Empire that separated from the Western Church in the 9th century. **2** Orthodox Eastern Church. **3** Uniat Church.

East·ern·er (ēs′tər nər) *n.* a native or inhabitant of the eastern part of the country: *In the West, Ontario people are referred to as Easterners. In Ontario, Maritimers are referred to as Easterners.*

east·ern·most (ēs′tərn mōst′) *adj.* farthest east.

eastern red cedar red juniper.

Eastern rite the liturgy and organization of the Orthodox Eastern Church or any of the Uniat churches.

Eastern Townships most of that part of Quebec lying south of the St. Lawrence River Valley and west of a line drawn southeast from Quebec City to the United States border. The Eastern Townships were first settled by United Empire Loyalists.

eastern white cedar a medium-sized arborvitae (*Thuja occidentalis*) found especially in eastern Canada and the United States, having a tapered trunk and a dense, narrow, conical crown. Because the wood of this tree is extremely light in mass and resistant to decay, it is valuable for poles, shingles, canoes, etc.

East·er·tide (ēs′tər tīd′) *n.* Easter time.

East Germanic a subdivision of the Germanic languages. The only East Germanic language of which there are written records is Gothic.

East Indian *n., adj.* —*n.* **1** a native or inhabitant of the Indian subcontinent. **2** a person of East Indian descent. **3** *Historical.* a native or inhabitant of the East Indies. —*adj.* of or having to do with the Indian subcontinent, the East Indies, or East Indians.

East Indies *Historical.* the name that was given to the region of S Asia that includes India and SE Asia, to distinguish it from the newly discovered West Indies: *Indonesia was once called the Dutch East Indies.*

East·main (ēst′mān′) *n. Cdn.* the eastern shore of Hudson Bay.

east–north·east (ēst′north′ēst′) *n., adj., adv.* —*n.* a direction or compass point midway between east and northeast. —*adj. or adv.* in, toward, or from this direction.

east–south·east (ēst′south′ēst′) *n., adj., adv.* —*n.* a direction or compass point midway between east and southeast. —*adj. or adv.* in, toward, or from this direction.

hat, āge, fär; let, ēqual, tèrm; it, īce
hot, ōpen, ôrder; oil, out; cup, pút, rüle,
əbove, takən, pencəl, lemən, circəs

ch, child; ng, long; sh, ship
th, thin; ŦH, then; zh, measure

east·ward (ēst′wərd) *adj., adv., n.* —*adj.* toward the east; east: *an eastward slope.*
—*adv.* toward the east; east: *to ride eastward.*
—*n.* an eastward part, direction, or point.

east·ward·ly (ēst′wərd lē) *adj. or adv.* **1** toward the east. **2** of winds, from the east.

east·wards (ēst′wərdz) *adv.* eastward.

eas·y (ē′zē) *adj.* **eas·i·er, eas·i·est;** *adv.* —*adj.* **1** requiring little effort; not hard: *easy work.* **2** free from pain, discomfort, trouble, or worry: *an easy life.* **3** giving comfort or rest: *an easy chair.* **4** fond of comfort or rest; lazy. **5** not harsh; not severe; not strict: *easy terms.* **6** not hard to influence; ready to agree with, believe in, or help anyone: *Choose whichever one you wish: I'm easy.* **7** smooth and pleasant; not awkward: *easy manners.* **8** not tight; loose: *an easy fit.* **9** not fast; slow: *an easy pace.* **10** not much in demand; not hard to get. **11** of a money market, favorable to borrowers. **12** of aces or honors in card games, divided evenly between the competing sides.
on easy street, in comfortable circumstances.
—*adv. Informal.* in an easy manner; with ease. [ME < OF *aisie*, pp. of *aisier* set at ease. See EASE.]
☛ *Syn. adj.* **1. Easy, simple, effortless** = requiring little effort. **Easy** = not hard because not too much work is needed: *Dinner was easy to prepare.* **Simple** = not complicated: *I can work out simple crossword puzzles.* **Effortless** = without effort, but suggests seeming to be easy or simple either by nature or by training: *Watch the effortless movements of a cat.*

easy chair a comfortable chair, usually having arms and cushions.

eas·y·go·ing (ē′zē gō′ing) *adj.* usually taking matters easily; tending not to worry: *an easygoing person.*

easy mark *Informal.* a person who is easily imposed on.

eat (ēt) *v.* **ate, eat·en, eat·ing. 1** take into the mouth and swallow, especially solid food that needs at least some chewing: *He ate slowly. I don't eat meat.* **2** have a meal: *Where shall we eat?* **3** destroy, use up, or waste by or as if by eating (*usually used with* **up, through, into,** *etc.*): *Termites have eaten through the posts. Extravagant spending soon ate up his inheritance. The acid has eaten into the metal.* **4** make by or as if by eating: *Moths had eaten holes in the sweater.* **5** *Informal.* make annoyed or anxious: *What's eating her?*
eat (one's) heart out, be consumed with longing; pine.
eat (one's) words, *Informal.* take back what one has said; retract.
eat out of (someone's) hand, be completely submissive to someone.
eat up, a eat all of: *The dog still hasn't eaten up the food we put out.* **b** *Informal.* finish eating: *Eat up, we've got to go.* **c** *Informal.* receive eagerly or greedily: *They showered him with attention and he just ate it up.*
[OE *etan*] —**eat′er,** *n.*
☛ *Usage.* **Eat.** The principal parts of *eat* are: *eat* (ēt), *ate* (āt), *eaten* (ē′tən). The British pronunciation of **ate** (et) is rarely heard in Canada.

eat·a·ble (ē′tə bəl) *adj., n.* —*adj.* fit to eat; edible. —*n.* Usually, **eatables,** *pl.* food.

ea·ten (ē′tən) *v.* pp. of **eat.**

eat·er·y (ē′tər ē) *n., pl.* **-er·ies.** *Informal.* restaurant.

Eau de Co·logne (ō′ də kə lōn′) *Trademark.* cologne. [< F *eau de Cologne* water of Cologne, Germany, where it was first made]

eau de vie (ō′ də vē′) *French.* brandy; literally, water of life.

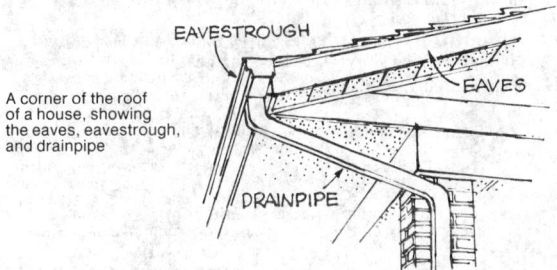

EAVESTROUGH
EAVES
DRAINPIPE

A corner of the roof of a house, showing the eaves, eavestrough, and drainpipe

eaves (ēvz) *n.pl.* the lower edges of a roof projecting beyond the wall of a building. [OE *efes*]

☞ *Usage.* **Eaves,** originally singular, is now understood as plural, and a new singular, *eave,* is sometimes found.

eaves·drop (ēvz′drop′) *v.* **-dropped, -drop·ping.** listen to what one is not supposed to hear; listen secretly to private conversation. [OE *efesdrype* the dripping of water from the eaves, the ground on which the water drips; hence to stand there, especially to listen to private conversation] **—eaves′drop′per,** *n.*

eaves·trough (ēvz′trof′) *n.* a channel placed along the eaves of a roof to catch rainwater and carry it away.

ebb (eb) *n., v.* **—n. 1** a flowing of the tide away from the shore; fall of the tide. **2** a growing less or weaker; decline. **3** a point of decline: *His fortunes were at their lowest ebb.*
—v. 1 flow out; fall: *We waded farther out as the tide ebbed.*
2 grow less or weaker; decline: *His courage began to ebb as he neared the haunted house.* [OE *ebba*]

ebb and flow 1 the falling and rising of the tide. **2** constantly changing circumstances; a period of growth followed by a period of decline: *The ebb and flow of business.*

ebb tide the flowing of the tide away from the shore.

eb·on (eb′ən) *n. Archaic or poetic.* ebony.

eb·on·ite (eb′ən īt′) *n.* a hard, black substance made by heating rubber together with a large quantity of sulphur; vulcanite. Ebonite is used in making combs and buttons and for electric insulation. [< *ebony* + *-ite*[1]]

eb·on·y (eb′ən ē) *n., pl.* **-on·ies. 1** the hard, heavy, usually almost black wood of any of various tropical Old World trees (genus *Diospyros*), used especially for decorative woodwork, carvings, etc. **2** any tree that yields ebony. **3** (*adjl.*) made of or resembling ebony. **4** (*adjl.*) designating a family (Ebonaceae) of tropical trees and shrubs, including the ebonies and persimmons. [ME *hebeny* < L *ebeninus* of ebony < Gk. < Egyptian]

e·bul·lience (i bul′yəns *or* i bul′ē əns) *n.* **1** an overflow of excitement, liveliness, etc.; great enthusiasm. **2** a bubbling up like a boiling liquid: *the ebullience of the river below the falls.*

e·bul·lient (i bul′yənt *or* i bul′ē ənt) *adj.* **1** overflowing with excitement, liveliness, etc.; very enthusiastic. **2** boiling; bubbling. [< L *ebulliens, -entis,* ppr. of *ebullire* < *ex-* out + *bullire* boil] **—e·bul′lient·ly,** *adv.*

eb·ul·li·tion (eb′ə lish′ən) *n.* **1** boiling; bubbling up. **2** an outburst (of feeling, etc.).

ec- the form of **ex-**[2] before consonants, as in *eccentric, eclectic, ecstasy.*

é·car·té (ā′kär tā′) *n.* a card game for two people, played with 32 cards. [< F *écarté,* pp. of *écarter* discard < *é-* out + *carte* card[1]]

ec·ce ho·mo (ek′sē hō′mō *or* ek′e) **1** Latin for "Behold the man!" (John 19:5). **2** a picture, statue, etc. of Christ crowned with thorns.

ec·cen·tric (ek sen′trik) *adj., n.* **—adj. 1** out of the ordinary; odd, peculiar: *eccentric clothes, eccentric habits.* **2** of circles, spheres, etc., not having the same centre. Compare **concentric.** **3** not having a circular path or shape: *the eccentric orbit of a planet.* **4** off centre; having its axis set off centre: *an eccentric wheel.*
—n. 1 a person who behaves in an unusual manner. **2** a disk or wheel set off centre so that it can change circular motion into back-and-forth motion. [< Med.L *eccentricus* < L *eccentrus* < Gk. *ekkentros* < *ek-* out + *kentron* centre] **—ec·cen′tri·cal·ly,** *adv.*

ec·cen·tric·i·ty (ek′sen tris′ə tē) *n., pl.* **-ties. 1** something queer or out of the ordinary; oddity; peculiarity. **2** an eccentric condition; the state of being unusual or out of the ordinary. **3** the length of the back-and-forth stroke of an eccentric (def.2). **4** *Astronomy.* the amount of deviation of the orbit of a planet from a perfect circle.

ec·cle·si·as·tic (i klē′zē as′tik) *n., adj.* **—n.** clergyman. **—adj.** ecclesiastical. [< LL *ecclesiasticus* < Gk., ult. < *ekklēsia* church. See ECCLESIASTES.]

ec·cle·si·as·ti·cal (i klē′zē as′tə kəl) *adj.* of or having to do with the church or the clergy. **—ec·cle′si·as′ti·cal·ly,** *adv.*

ECG electrocardiogram.

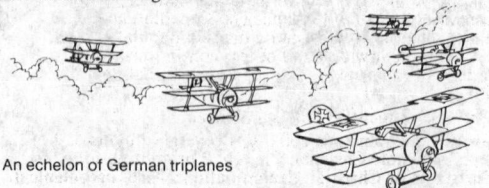

An echelon of German triplanes

ech·e·lon (esh′ə lon′) *n., adj., v.* **—n. 1** an arrangement of

troops, ships, etc. in a steplike formation. **2** the level of command. **3** a unit performing a special task or stationed in a certain position: *a maintenance echelon, a support echelon.*
—adj. of, having to do with, or in the form of an echelon.
—v. form into a steplike arrangement. [< F *échelon* rung of a ladder < *échelle* ladder < L *scala*]

e·chid·na (i kid′nə) *n., pl.* **-nas, -nae** (-nē *or* -nī). either of two species of egg-laying mammal (*Zaglossus bruijni* of New Guinea and *Tachyglossus aculeatus* of Australia) both having a spine-covered back, a long, narrow snout, and a long, sticky tongue for catching ants and termites, on which they feed. The echidnas constitute the family Tachyglossidae. [< L < Gk. *echidna* viper]

e·chi·no·derm (i kī′nə dėrm′ *or* ek′ə nə dėrm′) *n.* any of a phylum (Echinodermata) of invertebrate animals that live on the sea bottom, including starfish, sea urchins, and sea cucumbers. Echinoderms have a radially symmetrical body. [< NL *Echinodermata* < Gk. *echinos* sea urchin, originally, hedgehog + *derma* skin]

e·chi·nus (i kī′nəs) *n., pl.* **-ni** (-nī *or* -nē). **1** any of a genus (*Echinus*) of sea urchins, such as an edible species (*E. esculentus*) of the Mediterranean. **2** *Architecture.* the rounded moulding forming part of the capital of a Doric column. See **order** for picture. [< L < Gk. *echinos* sea urchin, originally hedgehog]

ech·o (ek′ō) *n., pl.* **ech·oes;** *v.* **ech·oed, ech·o·ing. —n. 1** a sounding again; repeating of a sound. An echo is heard when a sound is sent back by a cliff or hill. **2** a person who repeats the words or imitates the feelings, acts, etc. of another. **3** the act of repeating the words or imitating the feelings, acts, etc. of another. **4** a sympathetic response: *Patriotic sentiments evoke an echo in every breast.* **5** *Music.* **a** a very soft repetition of a phrase. **b** a stop of an organ for producing soft or echo-like tones. **6** a cardplayer's response to a signal from his partner or by a signal to his partner's lead. **7** a radio wave which has been reflected. Such echoes are the basis of radar, sonar, etc.
—v. 1 send back or repeat (sound): *The hills echoed the sound of the explosion.* **2** be repeated in sound; resound: *The boom echoed through the valley.* **3** repeat (the words) or imitate (the feelings, acts, etc.) of another: *That girl is always echoing her mother.* [ME < L < Gk.; cf. *ēchē* sound] **—ech′o·er,** *n.* **—ech′o·like′,** *adj.*

Ech·o (ek′ō) *n. Greek legend.* a nymph who pined away with love for Narcissus until only her voice was left.

e·cho·ic (e kō′ik) *adj.* **1** like an echo. **2** in imitation of natural sounds; onomatopoeic. *Buzz, caw,* and *moo* are echoic words.

ech·o·ism (ek′ō iz′əm) *n.* onomatopoeia.

ech·o·lo·ca·tion (ek′ō lō kā′shən) *n.* the determination of the position of a distant or invisible object by means of the reflection of sound waves from it, based on the determination of the length of time required for the sound waves, or echo, to return and the direction from which they return. Bats use echolocation to navigate.

é·clair (ē kler′ *or* ā kler′) *n.* an oblong piece of puff pastry filled with whipped cream or custard and covered with icing. [< F *éclair,* literally, lightning < *éclairer* lighten < L *exclarare* < *ex-* out + *clarus* clear]

é·clat (ā klä′) *n.* **1** a brilliant success. **2** fame; glory. **3** a burst of applause or approval. [< F *éclat* < *éclater* burst out]

ec·lec·tic (ek lek′tik) *adj., n.* **—adj. 1** selecting and using what seems best from various sources. **2** made up of such selections. **—n.** a follower of an eclectic method. [< Gk. *eklektikos* < *eklegein* < *ek-* out of + *legein* pick] **—ec·lec′ti·cal·ly,** *adv.*

ec·lec·ti·cism (ek lek′tə siz′əm) *n.* **1** the use or advocacy of an eclectic method. **2** an eclectic system of philosophy, medicine, etc.

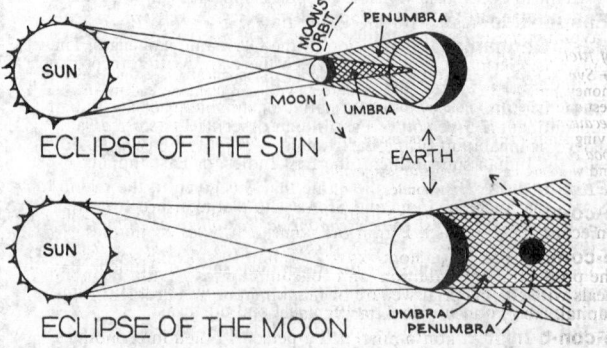

ECLIPSE OF THE SUN

ECLIPSE OF THE MOON

e·clipse (i klips′) *n., v.* **e·clipsed, e·clips·ing. —n. 1** a darkening

of the sun, moon, etc. when some other heavenly body is in a position that partly or completely cuts off its light as seen from some part of the earth's surface. A **solar eclipse** occurs when the moon passes between the sun and the earth. A **lunar eclipse** occurs when the moon enters the earth's shadow. 2 a loss of importance or reputation; failure for a time: *The former champion has suffered an eclipse.* —*v.* 1 cut off or obscure the light from; darken. 2 obscure the importance or reputation of; make less outstanding by comparison; surpass: *Napoleon eclipsed all the other generals of his time.* [ME < OF < L < Gk. *ekleipsis* < *ek-* out + *leipein* leave] —**e·clips′er**, *n.*

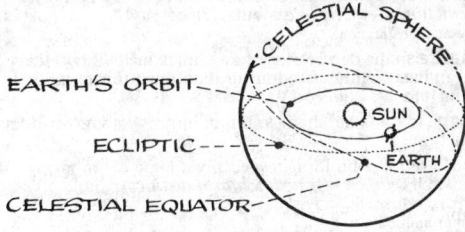

e·clip·tic (i klip′tik) *n., adj.* —*n.* the great circle on the celestial sphere that is the apparent annual path of the sun around the earth. It is the plane that contains the orbit of the earth. —*adj.* of or having to do with the ecliptic or an eclipse.

e·clip·ti·cal (i klip′tə kəl) *adj.* ecliptic.

ec·logue (ek′log) *n.* a short poem about country life, often written as a dialogue between shepherds. [< L *ecloga* < Gk. *eklogē* a selection < *eklegein*. See ECLECTIC.]

ECM European Common Market.

eco- *combining form.* of or having to do with the environment or habitat; ecological: *ecosystem.*

é·cole (ā kol′) *n.* French. school.

ec·o·log·i·cal (ek′ə loj′ə kəl *or* ē′kə loj′ə kəl) *adj.* of or having to do with ecology. —**ec′o·log′i·cal·ly**, *adv.*

e·col·o·gist (ē kol′ə jist) *n.* a person trained in ecology, especially one whose work it is.

e·col·o·gy (ē kol′ə jē) *n.* 1 the branch of biology that deals with the relation of living organisms to their environment and to each other. 2 the branch of sociology that deals with the relations between human beings and their environment. [< Gk. *oikos* house + E -*logy*]

econ. economic; economics; economy.

e·con·o·met·ric (i kon′ə met′rik) *adj.* of or having to do with econometrics. —**e·con′o·met′ri·cal·ly**, *adv.*

e·con·o·met·rics (i kon′ə met′riks) *n.* (used with a singular verb) the use of mathematics and statistics to verify economic theories, make economic forecasts, etc.

e·co·nom·ic (ē′kə nom′ik *or* ek′ə nom′ik) *adj.* 1 having to do with economics. Economic problems have to do with the production, distribution, and consumption of wealth. 2 having to do with the management of the income, supplies, and expenses of a household, community, government, etc. 3 having to do with the material welfare of a community or nation; practical; utilitarian: *economic geography.* 4 economical; saving; thrifty.
☛ *Usage.* **Economic, economical.** Although the meanings and uses of these two words often overlap, careful writers distinguish between them, using **economic** to refer to economics and the economy, and **economical** to refer to saving, or thrift: *There is danger of an economic crisis. We are going to buy a more economical car.*

e·co·nom·i·cal (ē′kə nom′ə kəl *or* ek′ə nom′ə kəl) *adj.* 1 avoiding waste; saving; thrifty: *An efficient engine is economical of fuel.* 2 having to do with economics.
☛ *Syn.* 1. **Economical, frugal, thrifty** = saving. **Economical** = avoiding waste of money, time, work, or any other resources by careful planning and making the best and fullest possible use of what is spent: *He does more than others because he is economical of time and energy.* **Frugal** emphasizes saving by living simply and needing or using little: *The frugal widow bought and used food carefully.* **Thrifty** = avoiding waste by planning well, spending carefully, and working hard: *Successful farmers are thrifty.*
☛ *Usage.* See note at **economic.**

e·co·nom·i·cal·ly (ē′kə nom′ik lē *or* ek′ə nom′ik lē) *adv.* 1 in an economical manner. 2 from the point of view of economics.

e·co·nom·ics (ē′kə nom′iks *or* ek′ə nom′iks) *n.* the science of the production, distribution, and consumption of wealth. Economics deals with the material welfare of mankind and the problems of capital, labor, wages, prices, tariffs, taxes, etc.

e·con·o·mist (i kon′ə mist) *n.* 1 a person trained in economics, especially one whose work it is. 2 *Archaic.* an economical person.

e·con·o·mize (i kon′ə mīz′) *v.* -**mized**, -**miz·ing.** 1 manage so as

hat, āge, fär; let, ēqual, tèrm; it, īce
hot, ōpen, ôrder; oil, out; cup, pút, rüle,
əbove, takən, pencəl, lemən, circəs
ch, child; ng, long; sh, ship
th, thin; ᴛʜ, then; zh, measure

to avoid waste; use to the best advantage. 2 cut down expenses. —**e·con′o·miz′er**, *n.*

e·con·o·my (i kon′ə mē) *n., pl.* -**mies.** 1 making the most of what one has; freedom from waste in the use of anything; thrift. 2 an instance of this; saving: *Many little economies were necessary.* 3 the managing of affairs and resources to the best advantage; management. 4 an efficient arrangement of parts; organization; system. 5 a system of managing the production, distribution, and consumption of goods: *feudal economy.* [< L < Gk. *oikonomia* < *oikos* house + *nemein* manage]

e·co·spe·cies (ē′kō spē′sēz *or* ek′ō-, ē′kō spē′shēz *or* ek′ō-) *n., pl.* -**cies.** a group of organisms within a taxonomic species that have become modified structurally and physiologically by their environment but that can still interbreed with other groups in the species to produce fertile offspring. [< *ecology* + *species.* 20c.]

e·co·sphere (ē′kō sfēr′ *or* ek′ō sfēr′) *n.* the parts of the universe that can support life, especially the biosphere of the earth.

e·co·sys·tem (ē′kō sis′təm *or* ek′ō sis′təm) *n.* the system formed by the interaction of all the living things of a particular environment with one another and with their habitat.

ec·ru *or* **é·cru** (ek′rü *or* ā′krü) *n. or adj.* very pale brown; the color of unbleached linen. [< F *écru* raw, unbleached, var. of *cru* raw < L *crudus*]

ec·sta·sy (ek′stə sē) *n., pl.* -**sies.** 1 state of great joy; thrilling or overwhelming delight; rapture: *Speechless with ecstasy, the little boy gazed at the toys.* 2 any strong feeling that completely absorbs the mind; uncontrollable emotion. 3 trance. [< L *extasis* < Gk. *ekstasis* trance, distraction < *existanai* < *ek-* out + *histanai* to place]

ec·stat·ic (ek stat′ik) *adj., n.* —*adj.* 1 full of ecstasy; showing ecstasy. 2 caused by ecstasy. 3 likely to show ecstasy. —*n.* 1 a person subject to fits of ecstasy. 2 **ecstatics,** *pl.* fits of ecstasy; raptures. —**ec·stat′i·cal·ly**, *adv.*

ecto- *combining form.* to or on the outside: *Ectoderm = the outer cellular layer of an embryo.* [< Gk. *ekto-* < *ektos* outside]

ec·to·derm (ek′tə dèrm′) *n. Biology.* the outer layer of cells formed during the development of the embryos of animals. Skin, hair, nails, the enamel of teeth, and essential parts of the nervous system, grow from the ectoderm. [< *ecto-*+-*derm* skin (< Gk. *derma*)]

ec·to·morph (ek′tə môrf′) *n.* 1 a human body type characterized by a light frame, medium to tall stature, long limbs, and long, thin, tight muscles. It is one of three basic body types. Compare **endomorph, mesomorph.** 2 a person having such a body structure.

ec·to·mor·phic (ek′tə môr′fik) *adj.* of, having to do with, or being an ectomorph.

–ectomy *combining form.* indicating surgical removal of a part or organ of the body, as in *tonsillectomy.* [< NL -*ectomia* < Gk. *ek-* out + -*tomos* a cutting < *temnein* to cut]

ec·to·plasm (ek′tə plaz′əm) *n.* 1 *Biology.* the outer portion of the cytoplasm of a cell. 2 a supposed emanation from the body of a medium in a trance. [< *ecto-*+-*plasm* something moulded (< Gk. *plasma*)]

é·cu (ā kʏ′). *n., pl.* **é·cus** (ā kʏ′). French. 1 in the Middle Ages, a short triangular shield carried by a mounted soldier. 2 any of several French gold or silver coins of varying value, in use from the 13th century on, especially a silver coin of the 17th and 18th centuries.

Ec·ua·do·re·an *or* **Ec·ua·do·ri·an** (ek′wə dôr′ē ən) *n., adj.* —*n.* a native or inhabitant of Ecuador, a country in NW South America. —*adj.* of or having to do with Ecuador or its people. a

ec·u·mene (ek′yə mēn′) *n.* the permanently settled portion of a country, continent, etc.; inhabited land. The Canadian ecumene consists of three separate blocs of fairly densely populated land connected by a continent-wide band of less continuously settled land called a **broken ecumene.** [< Gk. *oikoumenē* inhabited, ult. < *oikos* dwelling, habitation]

ec·u·men·ic (ek′yə men′ik) *adj.* ecumenical.

ec·u·men·i·cal (ek′yə men′ə kəl) *adj.* 1 general; universal. 2 of or representing the whole Christian Church. 3 promoting unity among all Christians or Christian denominations. Also, **oecumenical.** [< L < Gk. *oikoumenikos* < *oikoumenē (gē)* inhabited (world), ult. < *oikos* dwelling] —**ec′u·men′i·cal·ly**, *adv.*

ec·u·me·nism (ek′yə mə niz′əm) *n.* ecumenical principles or a church movement in support of them.

ec·ze·ma (ek′sə mə *or* eg zē′mə) *n.* an inflammation of the skin with redness, itching, and the formation of patches of scales. [< NL < Gk. *ekzema* < *ek-* out + *zeein* to boil]

–ed¹ *suffix.* forming the past tense of most English verbs. [OE *-de, -ede, -ode, -ade*]
☛ *Pronun.* **-ed.** Pronounced as a separate syllable (id) after (t) or (d): *wanted, loaded*; otherwise, as (d) after a vowel or voiced consonant: *vowed, lagged*; and as (t) after a voiceless consonant: *dressed, washed.*

–ed² *suffix.* **1** forming the past participle. **2** with various meanings: **a** having; supplied with, as in *bearded, long-legged, pale-faced, tender-hearted.* **b** having the characteristics of, as in *honeyed.* [OE *-ed, -od, -ad*]
☛ *Pronun.* **-ed.** Pronunciation as for **-ed¹** except that, in certain participles used adjectivally, **-ed²** may be pronounced (id) instead of (d) or (t): *aged* (ā′jid), *learned* (lėrn′id), *crooked* (krúk′id).

ed. **1** editor; edition; edited. **2** educated at.

E.D. (Canadian) Efficiency Decoration (for officers of Military Auxiliary Forces).

E·dam (ē′dam *or* ē′dəm) *n.* Edam cheese.

Edam cheese 1 a round, yellow cheese made in the Netherlands, and usually having red wax on the outside. **2** any cheese resembling this. [< a village in the Netherlands]

E.D.C. or **EDC 1** European Defence Community (France, Italy, West Germany, and Benelux united for mutual defence). **2** *Cdn.* Export Development Corporation.

Ed·da (ed′ə) *n., pl.* **Ed·das.** either of two Icelandic literary works written about 1200 to 1230, one in prose, the other in verse. They relate some of the old Norse myths and legends and give rules for the writing of poetry. [< ON *ōthr* poetry < Gmc. **wōth-* exaltation of spirits, poetry, song]

ed·dy (ed′ē) *n., pl.* **-dies;** *v.* **-died, -dy·ing.** —*n.* **1** water, air, etc. moving against the main current, especially when having a whirling motion; small whirlpool or whirlwind. **2** any similar current, as of fog or dust, or of thought or opinion: *Eddies of controversy grew around the new theory.* —*v.* **1** move against the main current in a whirling motion; whirl: *The water eddied down the drain.* **2** move in circles. [? < OE *ed-* turning + *ēa* stream]

e·del·weiss (ā′dəl vīs′) *n.* a small Alpine plant (*Leontopodium alpinum*) of the composite family, having heads of very small, yellow flowers in the centre of star-shaped clusters of fuzzy leaves. [< G *Edelweiss* < *edel* noble + *weiss* white]

e·de·ma (i dē′mə) *n., pl.* **-ma·ta** (-mə tə). a swelling caused by an abnormal accumulation of watery fluid in the tissues of the body. [< NL < Gk. *oidēma* < *oidos* tumor]

E·den (ē′dən) *n.* **1** in the Bible, the garden where Adam and Eve lived at first. **2** a delightful spot; paradise. [< Hebrew *'ēdēn*, literally, pleasure, delight]

e·den·tate (ē den′tāt) *n., adj.* —*n.* any of an order (Edentata) of New World mammals having only cheek teeth or no teeth at all, including sloths, anteaters, and armadillos. —*adj.* **1** of, having to do with, or belonging to the order Edentata. **2** lacking teeth. [< L *edentatus* < *ex-* without + *dens, dentis* tooth]

edge (ej) *n., v.* **edged, edg·ing.** —*n.* **1** a line or place where something ends; part farthest from the middle; side. **2** a brink; verge. **3** a thin, sharp side that cuts. The blade of a knife, axe, or razor has an edge. **4** sharpness; keenness. **5** *Informal.* an advantage: *We have a slight edge on the second team in the league.*
on edge, a disturbed; nervous; tense. **b** tense with eagerness; anxious; impatient: *We were all on edge until we arrived at the station.*
set on edge, a disturb; cause to feel excited or irritable. **b** make eager, anxious, or impatient.
take the edge off, deprive of force, strength, or enjoyment.
—*v.* **1** put an edge on; form an edge on. **2** move in a sideways manner: *She edged through the crowd.* **3** move little by little: *He edged his chair nearer to the fire.* **4** *Informal.* win a narrow victory over: *Our team edged the visitors 3-2.* **5** tilt a ski so that the edge cuts the snow.
edge in, manage to get in.
edge out, *Informal.* win by a narrow margin: *Montreal edged out Toronto in the playoffs.*
[OE *ecg*] —**edg′er,** *n.*

edge·ways (ej′wāz′) *adv.* with the edge forward; in the direction of the edge.
get a word in edgeways, manage to say something to a talkative person or in a talkative group.

edge·wise (ej′wīz′) *adv.* edgeways.

edg·ing (ej′ing) *n.* **1** anything forming an edge or put on along an edge. **2** a border or trimming for an edge.

edg·y (ej′ē) *adj.* **edg·i·er, edg·i·est. 1** having an edge; sharp; sharply defined: *edgy outlines.* **2** impatient; irritable. —**edg′i·ly,** *adv.* —**edg′i·ness,** *n.*

ed·i·bil·i·ty (ed′ə bil′ə tē) *n.* fitness for eating.

ed·i·ble (ed′ə bəl) *adj., n.* —*adj.* fit to eat; eatable: *Not all mushrooms are edible.* —*n.* Usually, **edibles,** *pl.* things fit to eat; food. [< LL *edibilis* < L *edere* eat]

e·dict (ē′dikt) *n.* a public order or command by some authority; decree. [< L *edictum* < *edicere* < *ex-* out + *dicere* say]
☛ *Syn.* See note at **proclamation.**

Edict of Nantes the decree signed at Nantes in 1598 by Henry IV of France, giving religious freedom to the French Protestants. It was repealed in 1685 by Louis XIV.

ed·i·fi·ca·tion (ed′ə fə kā′shən) *n.* moral improvement; spiritual benefit; instruction.

ed·i·fice (ed′ə fis) *n.* a building, especially a large or imposing building. [ME < OF *edifice* < L *aedificium* < *aedificare* build < *aedis* temple (pl., house) + *facere* make]
☛ *Syn.* See note at **building.**

ed·i·fy (ed′ə fī′) *v.* **-fied, -fy·ing.** improve morally; benefit spiritually; instruct. [ME < OF *edifier* < L *aedificare* build (up). See EDIFICE.]

e·dile (ē′dīl) See **aedile.**

ed·it (ed′it) *v.* **1** prepare for publication, correcting errors, checking facts, etc. **2** have charge of (a newspaper, magazine, dictionary, etc.) and decide what shall be printed in it. **3** revise or give final form to (motion-picture film, tape recordings, etc.) by such means as cutting and splicing. [< L *editus,* pp. of *edere* < *ex-* out + *dare* give; partly < *editor*]

edit. edition; edited; editor.

e·di·tion (i dish′ən) *n.* **1** all the copies of a book, newspaper, etc. printed alike and issued at or near the same time: *In the second edition of the book many of the errors in the first edition had been corrected.* **2** the form in which a book is printed or published: *The reading matter in the cheap one-volume edition was exactly the same as in the three-volume edition. Some books appear in pocket editions.* **3** an issue of the same newspaper, book, etc. published at different times with additions, changes, alterations, etc.: *the afternoon edition, a foreign edition.*

ed·i·tor (ed′ə tər) *n.* **1** a person who edits, especially one whose occupation is preparing material for publication or broadcasting. **2** a person who is responsible for the content of a periodical or newspaper, or for a particular section or department of one: *a sports editor.* **3** a device used for editing motion-picture films, magnetic tape, etc., including a splicer, etc. [< L]

ed·i·to·ri·al (ed′ə tô′rē əl) *n., adj.* —*n.* an article in a newspaper or magazine, or a comment in a radio or television broadcast, giving the opinion or attitude of the publisher, editor, speaker, etc. regarding some subject. —*adj.* of, having to do with, or by an editor.

ed·i·to·ri·al·ist (ed′ə tô′rē ə list) *n.* a person who writes editorials.

ed·i·to·ri·al·ize (ed′ə tô′rē ə līz′) *v.* **-ized, -iz·ing. 1** write news articles as if they were editorials, including comment and criticisms in the articles. **2** write an editorial.

ed·i·to·ri·al·ly (ed′ə tô′rē ə lē) *adv.* **1** in an editorial manner. **2** in an editorial.

ed·i·tor-in-chief (ed′ə tər in chēf′) *n., pl.* **ed·i·tors-in-chief.** the person who is the head of the editorial staff of a publication or publishing house.

ed·i·tor·ship (ed′ə tər ship′) *n.* the position, duties or authority of an editor.

E·dom (ē′dəm) *n.* in the Bible, a region in Palestine south of the Dead Sea (Num. 20: 14-21).

E·dom·ite (ē′dəm īt′) *n.* a native or inhabitant of Edom.

E.D.P. or **EDP** electronic data processing.

EDT, E.D.T., or **e.d.t.** Eastern Daylight Time.

ed·u·ca·ble (ej′ə kə bəl) *adj.* capable of being educated, taught, or trained.

ed·u·cate (ej′ə kāt′) *v.* **-cat·ed, -cat·ing. 1** develop in knowledge, skill, ability, or character by training, study, or experience; teach; train. **2** send to school. [< L *educare* bring up, raise; related to *educere.* See EDUCE.]

ed·u·ca·tion (ej′ə kā′shən) *n.* **1** a development in knowledge, skill, ability, or character by teaching, training, study, or experience; teaching; training. **2** the knowledge, skill, ability, or character developed by teaching, training, study, or experience.

3 the science and art that deals with the principles, problems, etc. of teaching and learning.

☛ *Syn.* **2. Education, enlightenment, culture** = the qualities and knowledge a person gets from study, teaching, and experience. **Education** emphasizes the training, knowledge, and abilities a person gets through teaching and study: *A person with education knows how to speak, write, and read well.* **Enlightenment** emphasizes the insight and understanding that make a person free from prejudice and ignorance: *A person with enlightenment knows the value of education.* **Culture** applies to the combination of enlightenment and fineness of feeling and taste that results from complete education: *A person of culture appreciates music and art.*

ed·u·ca·tion·al (ej′ə kā′shən əl *or* ej′ə kāsh′nəl) *adj.* **1** of or having to do with education: *an educational association.* **2** giving education; tending to educate: *an educational motion picture.*
—**ed′u·ca′tion·al·ly,** *adv.*

ed·u·ca·tion·al·ist (ej′ə kā′shə nə list) *n.* an expert on the methods and principles of education; educator.

ed·u·ca·tion·ist (ej′ə kā′shə nist) *n.* educationalist.

ed·u·ca·tive (ej′ə kā′tiv) *adj.* **1** that educates; instructive. **2** of or having to do with education.

ed·u·ca·tor (ej′ə kā′tər) *n.* **1** a person whose profession is education; teacher. **2** a leader in education; authority on methods and principles of education.

e·duce (i dyüs′ *or* i düs′) *v.* **e·duced, e·duc·ing.** bring out; draw forth; elicit; develop. [< L *educere* < *ex-* out + *ducere* lead]

Ed·war·di·an (ed wôr′dē ən *or* ed wär′dē ən) *adj.* **1** of or having to do with King Edward VII or his reign. **2** like or characteristic of this age, especially as marked by material wealth, luxury, and complacency.

–ee *noun-forming suffix.* **1** a person who is ——: *absentee* = *person who is absent.* **2** a person who is ——ed: *appointee* = *person who is appointed.* **3** a person to whom something ——ed: *mortgagee* = *person to whom something is mortgaged.* **4** a person who ——s: *standee* = *a person who stands.* [< F *-é,* masc. pp. ending]

E.E. Electrical Engineer.

EEC European Economic Community.

EEG *Medicine.* electroencephalogram.

eel (ēl) *n.* **1** any of an order (Apodes) of long, snakelike, usually scaleless fishes having a smooth, slimy skin and no pelvic fins. **2** any of various other fishes that are similar in shape, such as the electric eel or the lamprey. [OE *ǣl*] —**eel′-like′,** *adj.*

eel·grass (ēl′gras′) *n.* **1** a perennial marine plant (*Zostera marina*) growing under water along the Atlantic and Pacific coasts of North America, having very long, tapelike leaves. **2** tape grass.

eel·pout (ēl′pout′) *n.* **1** a small, eel-like saltwater fish. **2** burbot. [OE *ǣlepūte*]

e′en (ēn) *adv. Poetic.* even.

e′er (er) *adv. Poetic.* ever.
☛ *Hom.* air, err, ere, heir.

–eer *suffix.* **1** a person who is concerned with, works with, or deals with, as in *auctioneer, charioteer.* **2** a person who produces, as in *pamphleteer, sonneteer.* **3** be concerned or deal with, as in *electioneer.* [< F *-ier*]

ee·rie (ēr′ē) *adj.* **-ri·er, -ri·est. 1** causing fear; strange; weird: *an eerie scream.* **2** timid because of superstition. [ME *eri,* var. of *erg,* OE *earg* cowardly] —**ee′ri·ness,** *n.*
☛ *Hom.* eyrie.
☛ *Syn.* **1.** See note at **weird.**

ee·ri·ly (ēr′ə lē) *adv.* in an eerie way; in a way that causes fear: *The shutters in the old, deserted house creaked eerily.*

ee·ry (ēr′ē) *adj.* **-ri·er, -ri·est.** See **eerie.**

ef– the form of **ex-**¹ before *f,* as in *effect.*

EFC Eastern Football Conference.

ef·face (ə fās′) *v.* **-faced, -fac·ing. 1** rub out; blot out; do away with; destroy; wipe out: *The inscriptions on many ancient monuments have been effaced by time. It takes many years to efface the unpleasant memories of a war.* **2** keep (oneself) from being noticed; make inconspicuous: *The shy boy effaced himself by staying in the background.* [< F *effacer* < *es-* away + *face* face < L *facies* form] —**ef·face′a·ble,** *adj.* —**ef·fac′er,** *n.*
☛ *Syn.* **1.** See note at **erase.**

ef·face·ment (ə fās′mənt) *n.* effacing or being effaced.

ef·fect (i fekt′) *n., v.* —*n.* **1** whatever is produced by a cause; something made to happen by a person or thing; result. **2** the power to produce results; force; validity. **3** influence: *The medicine had an immediate effect.* **4** the impression produced. **5** the combination of color or form in a picture, etc.: *Sunshine coming through leaves creates a lovely effect.* **6** purport; intent; meaning. **7** **effects,** *pl.* personal property; belongings; goods.
for effect, for show; to impress or influence others.
give effect to, put in operation, make active.

hat, āge, fär; let, ēqual, tèrm; it, īce
hot, ōpen, ôrder; oil, out; cup, pùt, rüle,
above, takən, pencəl, lemən, circəs

ch, child; ng, long; sh, ship
th, thin; ᴛʜ, then; zh, measure

in effect, a in result; in fact; really. **b** in operation; active: *The new rules are now in effect.*

into effect, in operation; in action; in force.

of no effect, with no results; useless.

take effect, begin to operate; become active: *The new prices will take effect on January 1st.*

to the effect, with the meaning or purpose.
—*v.* **1** produce as an effect; make happen; get done; bring about. **2** *Rare.* make; construct. [ME < L *effectus* < *efficere* < *ex-* out + *facere* make]
☛ *Syn. n.* **1. Effect, consequence, result** = something produced by a cause. **Effect** applies to whatever is produced by a cause, particularly what happens or occurs directly and immediately: *The effect of raising the speed limit was a number of bad accidents.* **Consequence** applies to something that follows, but is not always closely or directly connected with the cause: *As a consequence, there was a provincial investigation of highway conditions.* **Result** applies to what happens as a final effect or consequence: *The result was a new set of traffic regulations.* **7.** See note at **property.**
☛ *Usage.* **Effect, affect.** Because these words sound similar, they are often confused in writing. Most commonly, **effect** is a noun, meaning "result", and **affect** is a verb, meaning "to influence": *We don't know what effect the new rule will have. The new rule will affect everybody.* However, in formal English **effect** is also used as a verb meaning "get done, bring about": *He effected an improvement in the working conditions.* Thus *to affect a proposal* means to influence it or make a change in it, while *to effect a proposal* means to get it done or bring it to completion.

ef·fec·tive (i fek′tiv) *adj., n.* —*adj.* **1** producing an effect. **2** producing the desired effect. **3** in operation; active: *These laws will become effective on New Year's Day.* **4** striking; impressive. **5** actual or real, not theoretical or nominal (*used only before a noun*): *one's effective income after deductions.* **6** of a soldier, military force, etc., equipped and ready for action.
—*n.* a soldier, military unit, etc. equipped and ready for action.
—**ef·fec′tive·ly,** *adv.* —**ef·fec′tive·ness,** *n.* —**ef·fect′less,** *adj.*
☛ *Syn. adj.* **1. Effective, effectual, efficient** = producing an effect. **Effective,** usually describing things, emphasizes producing a wanted or expected effect: *Several new drugs are effective in treating serious diseases.* **Effectual,** describing people or things, emphasizes having produced or having the power to produce the exact effect or result intended: *His efforts are more energetic than effectual.* **Efficient,** often describing people, emphasizes being able to produce the effect wanted or intended without wasting energy, time, etc.: *A skilled surgeon is highly efficient.*

ef·fec·tor (ə fek′tər) *n. Physiology.* **1** a muscle or gland capable of responding to a nerve impulse. **2** the part of a nerve that transmits an impulse.

ef·fec·tu·al (i fek′chü əl) *adj.* **1** producing the effect desired; capable of producing the effect desired: *Quinine is an effectual preventive of malaria.* **2** valid. —**ef·fec′tu·al·ness,** *n.*
☛ *Syn.* **1.** See note at **effective.**

ef·fec·tu·al·ly (i fek′chü əl ē) *adv.* with a desired effect; thoroughly.

ef·fec·tu·ate (i fek′chü āt′) *v.* **-at·ed, -at·ing.** cause; make happen; bring about; accomplish. [< F *effectuer* < L *effectus.* See EFFECT.]

ef·fem·i·na·cy (ə fem′ə nə sē) *n.* lack of manly qualities; unmanly weakness or delicacy.

ef·fem·i·nate (ə fem′ə nit) *adj.* lacking in manly qualities; showing weakness or delicacy. [< L *effeminatus,* pp. of *effeminare* make a woman out of < *ex-* out + *femina* woman]
—**ef·fem′i·nate·ly,** *adv.* —**ef·fem′i·nate·ness,** *n.*

ef·fen·di (ə fen′dē) *n., pl.* **-dis.** in Turkey: **1** a title of respect similar to "Sir" or "Master." **2** a person having this title; doctor, official, scholar, etc. [< Turkish *efendi* < Gk. *authentēs* master, doer < *auto-* by oneself + *hentēs* one who acts]

ef·fer·ent (ef′ər ənt) *adj., n.* —*adj.* of nerves, blood vessels, etc., conveying outward from a central organ or point. Efferent nerves carry impulses from the brain to the muscles. Compare **afferent.**
—*n.* an efferent nerve. [< L *efferens, -entis,* ppr. of *efferre* < *ex-* out + *ferre* carry]

ef·fer·vesce (ef′ər ves′) *v.* **-vesced, -vesc·ing. 1** give off bubbles of gas; bubble: *Ginger ale effervesces.* **2** be lively and gay; be excited. [< L *effervescere* boil up < *ex-* out + *fervescere* begin to boil < *fervere* be hot]

ef·fer·ves·cence (ef′ər ves′əns) *n.* **1** the act or process of bubbling. **2** liveliness; gaiety.

ef·fer·ves·cent (ef′ər ves′ənt) *adj.* **1** giving off bubbles of gas; bubbling. **2** lively; gay. —**ef′fer·ves′cent·ly,** *adv.*

ef·fete (i fēt′) *adj.* no longer able to produce; worn out; exhausted. [< L *effetus* worn out by bearing < *ex-* out + *fe-* breed, bear] —**ef·fete′ly,** *adv.* —**ef·fete′ness,** *n.*

ef·fi·ca·cious (ef′ə kā′shəs) *adj.* producing the desired results; effective: *Vaccination for smallpox is efficacious.* —**ef′fi·ca′cious·ly,** *adv.* —**ef′fi·ca′cious·ness,** *n.*

ef·fi·ca·cy (ef′ə kə sē) *n., pl.* **-cies.** the power to produce a desired effect or result; effectiveness. [< L *efficacia* < *efficere* accomplish. See EFFICIENT.]

ef·fi·cien·cy (ə fish′ən sē) *n., pl.* **-cies.** 1 the ability to produce the effect wanted without waste of time, energy, etc. 2 efficient operation: *Friction lowers the efficiency of a machine.*

efficiency expert a person whose profession is to devise more effective, economical methods of doing things in factories, offices, etc.

ef·fi·cient (ə fish′ənt) *adj.* 1 able to produce the effect wanted without waste of time, energy, etc. 2 actually producing an effect: *Heat is the efficient cause in changing water to steam.* [< L *efficiens, -entis,* ppr. of *efficere* < *ex-* out of + *facere* do, make] —**ef·fi′cient·ly,** *adv.*
☛ *Syn.* 1. See note at **effective.**

ef·fi·gy (ef′ə jē) *n., pl.* **-gies.** a statue, etc. of a person; image: *The dead man's monument bore his effigy.*
burn or **hang** (someone) **in effigy,** burn or hang an image of a person to show hatred or contempt.
[< F *effigie* < L *effigies* < *effingere* < *ex-* out + *fingere* form]

ef·flo·resce (ef′lə res′) *v.* **-resced, -resc·ing.** 1 burst into bloom; blossom out. 2 *Chemistry.* **a** change either throughout or on the surface to a powder by loss of water of crystallization when exposed to air. **b** become covered with a crusty deposit when water evaporates. [< L *efflorescere* < *ex-* out + *flos, floris* flower]

ef·flo·res·cence (ef′lə res′əns) *n.* 1 the act or process of blooming; flowering. 2 the period or state of flowering: *The efflorescence of Romantic music occurred during the nineteenth century.* 3 a mass of flowers. 4 anything resembling a mass of flowers. 5 *Chemistry.* **a** a change that occurs when crystals lose their water of crystallization and become powder. **b** a powder formed in this way. **c** a deposit formed in this way. **d** the formation of a crusty deposit when water evaporates from a solution. 6 an eruption on the skin; rash.

ef·flo·res·cent (ef′lə res′ənt) *adj.* 1 blooming; flowering. 2 *Chemistry.* **a** that changes from crystals into powder by losing water of crystallization when exposed to air. **b** covered with a deposit formed by efflorescence.

ef·flu·ence (ef′lü əns) *n.* 1 an outward flow. 2 the thing that flows out; emanation.

ef·flu·ent (ef′lü ənt) *adj., n.* —*adj.* flowing out or forth. —*n.* 1 a stream flowing out of another stream, lake, etc. 2 liquid industrial waste, sewage, etc., especially when causing pollution. 3 something that flows out or forth; effluence; emanation. [< L *effluens, -entis,* ppr. of *effluere* < *ex-* out + *fluere* flow]

ef·flu·vi·a (i flü′vē ə) *n.* a pl. of effluvium.

ef·flu·vi·al (i flü′vē əl) *adj.* of or having to do with effluvia.

ef·flu·vi·um (i flü′vē əm) *n., pl.* **-vi·a** or **-vi·ums.** 1 an unpleasant vapor or odor. 2 a vapor; odor. [< L *effluvium* a flowing out < *effluere.* See EFFLUENT.]

ef·fort (ef′ərt) *n.* 1 the use of energy and strength to do something; a trying hard: *Climbing a steep hill takes effort.* 2 a hard try; strong attempt. 3 the result of effort; anything done with effort; achievement. Works of literature or art are often called literary or artistic efforts. [< F < OF *esfort* < *esforcier* force, exert < L *ex-* out + *fortis* strong]
☛ *Syn.* 1. **Effort, endeavor, application** = active use of physical or mental power to do something. **Effort** emphasizes using energy and strength and trying hard, but usually suggests a single act or action: *John made an effort to finish his work today.* **Endeavor,** more formal, applies to sincere and serious effort continued over some time: *By constant endeavor, he realized his ambition.* **Application** emphasizes continued effort and close attention to what one is doing: *By application to his work he makes good grades.*

ef·fort·less (ef′ərt lis) *adj.* requiring or involving no effort; easy. —**ef′fort·less·ly,** *adv.* —**ef′fort·less·ness,** *n.*
☛ *Syn.* See note at **easy.**

ef·fron·ter·y (ə frun′tər ē *or* ə frun′trē) *n., pl.* **-ter·ies.** shameless boldness; impudence: *The politician had the effrontery to ask the people he had insulted to vote for him.* [< F *effronterie* < OF < LL *effrons* barefaced, shameless < *ex-* without + *frons, frontis* forehead, ability to blush, hence, without blushing]

ef·ful·gence (i ful′jəns) *n.* brightness; radiance.

ef·ful·gent (i ful′jənt) *adj.* shining brightly; radiant. [< L

ef·ful·gens, -entis, ppr. of *effulgere* < *ex-* forth + *fulgere* shine] —**ef·ful′gent·ly,** *adv.*

ef·fuse (i fyüz′) *v.* **-fused, -fus·ing.** pour out; spill; shed. [< L *effusus,* pp. of *effundere* < *ex-* out + *fundere* pour]

ef·fu·sion (i fyü′zhən) *n.* 1 a pouring out: *the effusion of blood.* 2 an unrestrained expression of feeling, etc. in talking or writing.

ef·fu·sive (i fyü′siv) *adj.* showing too much feeling; too emotional in expression. —**ef·fu′sive·ly,** *adv.* —**ef·fu′sive·ness,** *n.*

eft[1] (eft) *n.* 1 a newt in the land stage. 2 formerly, a small newt or lizard. [OE *efete.* Cf. NEWT.]

eft[2] (eft) *adv.* Obsolete. again. [OE]

eft·soon (eft sün′) *adv.* Archaic. 1 soon afterward. 2 again. [OE *eftsōna* < *eft* again + *sōna* at once]

eft·soons (eft sünz′) *adv.* Archaic. eftsoon.

e.g. for example (for L *exempli gratia*).
☛ *Usage.* **E.g.** is not usually italicized, that is, not underlined in writing, but should always have abbreviation periods. In all but expository prose or technical writing, the English phrase "for example" is stylistically preferable. In formal writing *e.g.* is preceded by some punctuation mark.

e·gad (ē gad′) *interj.* a mild oath, like "by Jove." [alteration of *a God!* Oh God!]

e·gal·i·tar·i·an (ē gal′ə ter′ē ən) *n., adj.* —*n.* a person who believes in equality, especially in social equality. —*adj.* of or relating to equality, especially social equality.

e·gal·i·tar·i·an·ism (ē gal′ə ter′ē ə niz′əm) *n.* belief in equality, especially in social equality.

egg[1] (eg) *n.* 1 a roundish body, covered with a shell or membrane, that is laid by the female of birds, fishes, and other animals that do not bring forth their young. 2 *Biology.* a female reproductive cell. 3 anything shaped like a hen's egg. 4 *Slang.* an aerial bomb.
have or **put all** (one's) **eggs in one basket,** risk everything that one has on one chance.
bad egg, a person or plan that comes to no good.
good egg, a promising person or thing.
[ME < ON] —**egg′less,** *adj.* —**egg′like′,** *adj.*

egg[2] (eg) *v.* urge; encourage (*on*): *The other boys egged him on to fight.* [ME < ON *eggja* < *egg* edge, point]

egg·beat·er (eg′bē′tər) *n.* 1 a kitchen utensil for beating or whipping eggs, cream, etc., especially a hand-operated one with rotary blades. 2 *Slang.* helicopter.

egg cell a mature female reproductive cell; ovum.

egg·head (eg′hed′) *n. Informal. Often derogatory.* an intellectual, especially one who is committed to cultural and intellectual interests and who pays no attention to popular fads; highbrow.

egg·nog (eg′nog′) *n.* a drink made of eggs beaten up with milk and sugar, often containing whisky, brandy, or wine. [< *egg*[1] + *nog* strong ale]

egg·plant (eg′plant′) *n.* 1 a plant (*Solanum melongena*) bearing a large, egg-shaped fruit, used as a vegetable and having a glossy purple skin when ripe. 2 the fruit of this plant.

egg roll a small, filled pastry containing bean sprouts or other vegetables and, often, pieces of chicken, shrimp, etc. Egg rolls are fried in deep fat.

egg·shell (eg′shel′) *n., adj.* —*n.* the shell covering an egg. —*adj.* like an eggshell; very thin and delicate.

e·gis (ē′jis) *n.* aegis.

eg·lan·tine (eg′lən tīn′ *or* eg′lən tēn′) *n.* sweetbrier. [< F *eglantine,* dim. of OF *aiglent* < VL *aculentus* < L *acus* needle]

e·go (ē′gō *or* eg′ō) *n., pl.* **e·gos.** 1 the individual as a whole in his capacity to think, feel, and act; self. 2 *Informal.* conceit. 3 *Philosophy.* the element of being that consciously and continuously enables an individual to think, feel, and act. 4 *Psychoanalysis.* the part of the personality that is conscious of the environment and adapts itself to it. [< L *ego* I]

e·go·cen·tric (ē′gō sen′trik *or* eg′ō-) *adj., n.* —*adj.* looking upon oneself as the focus and object of all experience and events; seeing everything in relation to oneself; self-centred; egoistic. —*n.* an egocentric person.

e·go·ism (ē′gō iz′əm *or* eg′ō iz′əm) *n.* 1 the state of seeking the welfare of oneself only; selfishness. 2 talking too much about oneself; conceit. 3 the ethical doctrine that morality lies in the pursuit of individual self-interest, and that self-interest motivates all conduct.
☛ *Syn.* See note at **egotism.**

e·go·ist (ē′gō ist *or* eg′ō ist) *n.* 1 a person who seeks the welfare of himself only; selfish person. 2 a person who talks too much about himself; conceited person. 3 a believer in egoism as a principle of human conduct.

e·go·is·tic (ē′gō is′tik *or* eg′ō is′tik) *adj.* 1 seeking the welfare

of oneself only; selfish. **2** talking too much about oneself; conceited. —**e′go·is′ti·cal·ly**, *adv.*

e·go·ma·ni·a (ē′gō mā′nē ə *or* eg′ō-) *n.* the quality or state of being extremely self-centred and conceited.

e·go·ma·ni·ac (ē′gō mā′nē ak′ *or* eg′ō-) *n.* a person characterized by egomania.

e·go·ma·ni·a·cal (ē′gō mə nī′ə kəl *or* eg′ō-) *adj.* of, having to do with, or characterized by egomania. —**e′go·ma·ni′a·cal·ly**, *adv.*

e·go·tism (ē′gə tiz′əm *or* eg′ə tiz′əm) *n.* **1** the excessive use of *I, my,* and *me*; habit of thinking, talking, or writing too much of oneself. **2** self-conceit. **3** selfishness. [< *ego* + *-t* + *-ism*]
➤ *Syn.* **Egotism, egoism** = a habit of thinking too much about self. **Egotism** emphasizes conceit, boasting, and selfishness, and means always talking about oneself and one's own affairs and trying to get attention: *Henry's egotism drives away friends.* **Egoism** emphasizes being self-centred and looking at everyone and everything only as it affects oneself and one's own welfare, but does not suggest boasting or annoying conceit, nor always selfishness: *We forget the natural egoism of a genius if he is charming.*

e·go·tist (ē′gə tist *or* eg′ə tist) *n.* **1** a person who thinks and talks about himself a great deal; conceited, boastful person. **2** a selfish person.

e·go·tis·tic (ē′gə tis′tik *or* eg′ə tis′tik) *adj.* **1** characterized by egotism; conceited. **2** selfish. —**e′go·tis′ti·cal·ly**, *adv.*

e·go·tis·ti·cal (ē′gə tis′tə kəl *or* eg′ə tis′tə kəl) *adj.* egotistic.

ego trip *Informal.* an experience or act whose primary value or purpose is to enhance the self-satisfaction of the person involved: *His newspaper column was just an ego trip.*

e·go-trip (ē′gō trip′) *v.* **-tripped, -trip·ping.** *Informal.* indulge in an ego trip. —**e′go-trip′per**, *n.*

e·gre·gious (i grē′jəs) *adj.* **1** remarkably or extraordinarily bad; outrageous; flagrant: *an egregious lie.* **2** remarkable; extraordinary. [< L *egregius* < *ex-* out + *grex, gregis* herd, flock] —**e·gre′gious·ly**, *adv.*

e·gress (ē′gres) *n.* **1** a going out: *The enemy blocked the narrow pass so that no egress was possible for our soldiers.* **2** a way out; exit. **3** the right to go out. [< L *egressus* < *egredi* < *ex-* out + *gradi* step, go]

e·gret (ē′gret *or* eg′ret) *n.* any of various herons that in mating season grow tufts of beautiful, long plumes, which were formerly much used as ornaments for the head. [< F *aigrette*]

E·gyp·tian (i jip′shən) *n., adj.* —*n.* **1** a native or inhabitant of Egypt, a country in NE Africa. **2** the Afro-Asiatic language of the ancient Egyptians. **3** *Obsolete.* Gypsy. —*adj.* of or having to do with Egypt or its people.

Egyptian cotton a type of cotton having long fibres, much grown in Egypt.

E·gyp·tol·o·gist (ē′jip tol′ə jist) *n.* a person trained in Egyptology, especially one whose work it is.

E·gyp·tol·o·gy (ē′jip tol′ə jē) *n.* the science or study of the monuments, history, language, etc. of ancient Egypt.

eh (ā) *interj.* **1** an exclamation expressing doubt, surprise, or failure to hear exactly. **2** an exclamation suggesting "Yes" for an answer or assuming that the answer will be affirmative: *You're going home now, eh?*

EIB Export-Import Bank.

ei·der (ī′dər) *n.* **1** any of several large sea ducks (especially of genus *Somateria*) that breed in the Arctic. **2** eiderdown. [< Icel. *æthr*]

ei·der·down (ī′dər doun′) *n.* **1** the soft feathers from the breasts of eiders, used to stuff pillows, bed quilts, as trimming, etc. **2** a quilt stuffed with these feathers.

eider duck eider (def. 1).

eight (āt) *n., adj.* —*n.* **1** one more than seven; 8. **2** the numeral 8: *He makes his eights with two circles.* **3** the eighth in a set or series; especially a playing card having eight spots: *the eight of diamonds.* **4** *Rowing.* **a** a crew of eight rowers. **b** the boat they use. **5** any set or series of eight persons or things: *The computer was programmed to count in eights.*
—*adj.* **1** being one more than seven. **2** being eighth in a set or series (*used mainly after the noun*): *Section Eight is missing.* [OE *eahta*]

eight ball *Pool.* a black ball bearing a figure 8, which in certain varieties of the game carries a penalty if hit or pocketed.
behind the eight ball, *Slang.* in an unfavorable position; an awkward or threatening situation.

eight·een (ā′tēn′) *n., adj.* —*n.* **1** eight more than ten; 18. **2** the numeral 18: *The 18 is not in line with the other figures in the column.* **3** the eighteenth in a set or series. **4** a set or series of eighteen persons or things.
—*adj.* being eighteen in a set or series (*used after the noun*): *Chapter Eighteen.* [OE *eahtatēne*]

eight·eenth (ā′tēnth′) *adj. or n.* **1** next after the 17th; last in a series of eighteen; 18th. **2** one, or being one, of 18 equal parts.

hat, āge, fär; let, ēqual, tèrm; it, īce
hot, ōpen, ôrder; oil, out; cup, pút, rüle,
əbove, takən, pencəl, lemən, circəs

ch, child; ng, long; sh, ship
th, thin; ͭн, then; zh, measure

eighth (ātth) *adj., n.* —*adj.* **1** next after the seventh; last in a series of eight; 8th. **2** being one of 8 equal parts.
—*n.* **1** the next after the seventh; last in a series of eight; 8th. **2** one of 8 equal parts. **3** *Music.* one octave.

eighth note *Music.* a short note; one eighth of a whole note; quaver. See **note** for picture.

eighth rest *Music.* a rest, or sign for silence, equal in duration to an eighth note.

eight·i·eth (ā′tē ith) *adj. or n.* **1** next after the 79th; last in a series of 80; 80th. **2** one, or being one, of 80 equal parts.

eight·y (ā′tē) *n., pl.* **eight·ies;** *adj.* —*n.* **1** eight times ten; 80. **2 eighties,** *pl.* the years from eighty through eighty-nine, especially of a century or of a person's life: *My great-grandmother is in her eighties.* —*adj.* eight times ten; 80. [OE *eahtatig*]

ei·kon (ī′kon) See **icon.**

Einstein equation (īn′stīn) an equation expressing the relation of mass and energy: E = MC². E is the energy in joules; M is the mass in grams; C is the velocity of light in centimetres per second.

ein·stein·i·um (īn stīn′ē əm) *n.* a rare, artificial chemical element that is radio-active and is produced as a by-product of nuclear fission. *Symbol:* Es; *at.no.* 99; *at.wt.* (254); *half-life* 276 days. [after Albert *Einstein*]

eis·tedd·fod (ā stech′vod) *n., pl.* **eis·tedd·fod·au** (ā′stechˈvodˈī). an annual assembly of Welsh poets and musicians. [< Welsh *eisteddfod* session < *eistedd* sit, akin to E *sit*]

ei·ther (ē′ͭнər *or* ī′ͭнər) *adj., pron., adv., conj.* —*adj.* **1** one or the other of two: *Either hat is becoming.* **2** each of two: *On either side of the river lie cornfields.*
—*pron.* one or the other of two: *Either of the hats is becoming.*
—*adv.* **1** any more than another; also: *If you don't go, I won't go either.* **2** *Informal.* a word used to strengthen a negative in contradiction or retraction: *I have the keys with me—no, I don't either.*
—*conj.* one or the other of two: *Either come in or go out.* [OE *ǣgther* < *ǣghwæther* each of two < *ā* always + *gehwæther* each of two]
➤ *Usage.* In formal writing, **either** is always construed as singular (though its informal use as a plural is increasing): *Either is good enough for me. Either Grace or Phyllis is expected.*

e·jac·u·late (i jak′yə lāt′) *v.* **-lat·ed, -lat·ing. 1** say suddenly and briefly; exclaim. **2** eject; discharge. [< L *ejaculari* < *ex-* out + *jaculum* javelin < *jacere* throw]

e·jac·u·la·tion (i jak′yə lā′shən) *n.* **1** something said suddenly and briefly; exclamation. **2** an ejection; discharge.

e·jac·u·la·to·ry (i jak′yə lə tô′rē) *adj.* **1** said suddenly and briefly; containing exclamations. **2** ejecting; discharging.

e·ject (i jekt′) *v.* **1** throw out: *The volcano ejected lava and ashes.* **2** force out; expel: *The landlord ejected the tenant who did not pay his rent.* [< L *ejectus,* pp. of *ejicere* throw out < *ex-* out + *jacere* throw]

e·jec·tion (i jek′shən) *n.* **1** ejecting or being ejected. **2** something ejected: *Lava is a volcanic ejection.*

ejection capsule a cockpit or cabin that can be ejected from an airplane and parachuted to earth.

ejection seat in an aircraft, a seat that, with its occupant, can be instantly ejected and parachuted to earth.

e·ject·ment (i jekt′mənt) *n.* an ejecting; a dispossessing; an ousting.

e·jec·tor (i jek′tər) *n.* a person or thing that ejects.

eke¹ (ēk) *v.* **eked, ek·ing.** *Archaic or dialect.* increase; enlarge; lengthen.
eke out, a supply what is lacking to; supplement: *The clerk eked out his regular wages by working evenings and Sundays.* **b** barely make (a living) by various schemes or makeshifts. [dial. var. of obs. *eche* augment, OE *ēcan* < OE *ēaca* addition]

eke² (ēk) *adv. or conj. Archaic.* also; moreover. [OE *ēac*]

EKG electrocardiogram.

e·kis·tic (i kis′tik) *adj.* of or having to do with ekistics.

e·kis·ti·cal (i kis′tə kəl) *adj.* ekistic.

e·kis·tics (i kis′tiks) *n.* (*used with a singular verb*) the study of the ecology of human beings in settlements or communities. [< Gk.

oikistiké (< *oikistés* settler < *oikos* house) + E *-ics*. 20c.]

el (el) *n.* **1** *Informal.* an elevated railway. **2** the letter L (or l) or something shaped like a capital L. **3** See **ell²**.

e·lab·o·rate (*adj.* i lab′ə rit *or* i lab′rit; *v.* i lab′ə rāt′) *adj., v.* **-rat·ed, -rat·ing.** —*adj.* worked out with great care; having many details; complicated.
—*v.* **1** work out with great care; add details to: *The inventor spent months in elaborating his plans for a new engine.* **2** talk, write, etc. in great detail; give added details: *The witness was asked to elaborate upon one of his statements.* **3** make with labor; produce. [< L *elaboratus*, pp. of *elaborare* < *ex-* out + *labor* work]
—**e·lab′o·rate·ly,** *adv.* —**e·lab′o·rate·ness,** *n.* —**e·lab′o·rat·or,** *n.*
▸ *Syn. adj.* **Elaborate, studied, labored** = worked out in detail. **Elaborate** emphasizes the idea of details, and means having many details all worked out with great care and exactness: *The scientists made elaborate preparations for studying the eclipse.* **Studied** emphasizes care in working out details, and means being thought out beforehand and done on purpose: *His studied politeness was insulting.* **Labored** emphasizes great effort to work out details, and means showing effort by being strained and unnatural: *The boy gave a labored excuse for arriving late at school.*

e·lab·o·ra·tion (i lab′ə rā′shən) *n.* **1** elaborating or being elaborated. **2** something elaborated.

E·lam·ite (ē′ləm īt′) *n.* a native or inhabitant of Elam, an ancient country in what is now W Iran, just east of ancient Babylonia.

é·lan (ā lon′; *French,* ā län′) *n.* liveliness or enthusiasm combined with flair. [< F *élan* < *élancer* dart]

e·land (ē′lənd) *n.* either of two large, oxlike antelopes (*Taurotragus oryx* and *T. derbianus*) of central and southern Africa, having straight, spiral horns. [< Du. *eland* elk]

e·lapse (i laps′) *v.* **e·lapsed, e·laps·ing.** slip away; glide by; pass: *Hours elapsed while he slept like a log.* [< L *elapsus*, pp. of *elabi* < *ex-* away + *labi* glide]

e·las·mo·branch (i las′mə brangk′ *or* i laz′mə brangk′) *n.* any of a subclass (Elasmobranchii; also called Euselachii) of fishes having a cartilaginous skeleton and five to seven pairs of gill slits opening directly to the outside from the pharynx. [< NL *Elasmobranchii*, pl. < Gk. *elasmos* metal plate + *branchia* gills]

e·las·tic (i las′tik) *adj., n.* —*adj.* **1** having the quality of springing back to its original size, shape, or position after being stretched, squeezed, bent, etc.: *Toy balloons, sponges, and steel springs are elastic.* **2** springing back; springy: *an elastic step.* **3** being able to recover quickly from weariness, low spirits, or misfortune; buoyant: *His elastic spirits never let him be discouraged for long.* **4** easily altered to suit changed conditions; flexible; adaptable.
—*n.* **1** tape or fabric woven partly of rubber threads. **2** a rubber band. [< NL *elasticus* < Gk. *elastikos* driving, propulsive < *elaunein* drive] —**e·las′ti·cal·ly,** *adv.*

e·las·tic·i·ty (i las′tis′ə tē *or* ē′las tis′ə tē) *n.* **1** an elastic quality: *Rubber has great elasticity.* **2** flexibility: *Good and evil are words having great elasticity of meaning.*

e·las·ti·cized (i las′ti sīzd′) *adj.* woven or made with elastic: *The dress has an elasticized belt.*

e·las·to·mer (i las′tə mər) *n.* an elastic substance, such as natural rubber, synthetic rubber, or any of various rubberlike plastics. [< *elastic* + Gk. *meros* part]

e·las·to·mer·ic (ē las′tə mer′ik) *adj.* of, having to do with, or being an elastomer: *elastomeric vinyl.*

e·late (i lāt′) *v.* **e·lat·ed, e·lat·ing.** put in high spirits; make joyful or proud. [< L *elatus* < *ex-* out, away + *latus*, pp. to *ferre* carry]

e·lat·ed (i lāt′id) *adj.* in high spirits; joyful; proud. —**e·lat′ed·ly,** *adv.* —**e·lat′ed·ness,** *n.*

e·la·tion (i lā′shən) *n.* high spirits; joyous pride; exultant gladness.

E layer the Heaviside layer.

el·bow (el′bō) *n., v.* —*n.* **1** the joint between the upper arm and forearm. **2** the outer part of this joint, especially the point formed when the arm is bent. See **arm** for picture. **3** a joint in the forelimb of a four-legged animal that corresponds to the human elbow. **4** the part of a sleeve covering the elbow. **5** something resembling a bent elbow, such as a sharp bend in a road or river or a short, sharply bent piece of pipe used to join pipes at an angle.
at (someone's) **elbow,** near at hand; close by: *When John did his homework, his dictionary was always at his elbow.*
out at (the) elbows, ragged or very poor.
rub elbows with, mingle with (people, especially of a different social level).
up to the elbows in, deeply involved in or occupied with.
—*v.* **1** push with the elbow: *Somebody elbowed him off the sidewalk.* **2** make (one's) way by pushing: *He elbowed his way*

through the crowd. [OE *elnboga* < *eln* length of lower arm + *boga* bow²]

elbow grease *Informal.* hard work; energy.

elbow room or **el·bow·room** (el′bō rüm′ *or* -rùm′) *n.* plenty of room; enough space to move or work in.

eld (eld) *n. Archaic.* **1** old age. **2** old times; former times. [OE *eldo* < *eald* old]

eld·er¹ (el′dər) *adj., n.* —*adj.* **1** born, produced, or formed before something else; older; senior: *my elder brother, an elder statesman.* **2** prior in rank, validity, etc.: *an elder title to an estate.* **3** earlier; former: *in elder times.*
—*n.* **1** an older person: *The children showed respect for their elders.* **2** an aged person. **3** an ancestor. **4** one of the older and more influential men of a tribe or community; a chief, ruler, member of council, etc. **5** any of various important officers of certain churches. [OE *eldra*, comparative of *eald* old]
▸ *Usage.* **Elder, eldest.** These forms of *old* survive in formal English and are used, when speaking of persons, chiefly for members of the same family: *the elder brother, our eldest daughter,* and in some phrases: *the elder statesman.*

el·der² (el′dər) *n.* any of a genus (*Sambucus*) of shrubs or small trees of the honeysuckle family having clusters of small, white or pink flowers and edible red, purple, or black berries. [OE *ellærn*]

el·der·ber·ry (el′dər ber′ē) *n., pl.* **-ries. 1** the edible fruit of an elder, used for jam, wine, etc. **2** elder².

eld·er·ly (el′dər lē) *adj., n.* —*adj.* somewhat old; beyond middle age; near old age. —*n.*
the elderly, people who are old.
▸ *Syn.* See note at **old.**

eld·er·ship (el′dər ship′) *n.* **1** the office or position of an elder in a church. **2** a group or court of elders; presbytery.

eld·est (el′dist) *adj.* oldest. [OE *eldest(a)*, superlative of *eald* old]
▸ *Usage.* See note at **elder.**

El·do·ra·do (el′də rä′dō) *n., pl.* **-dos. 1** a legendary city of great wealth sought by early explorers in South America. **2** any fabulously wealthy place. Also, **El Dorado.** [< Sp. *El Dorado* the gilded]

elec. or **electr.** electricity; electrical; electrician.

e·lect (i lekt′) *v., adj.* —*v.* **1** choose or select for an office by voting: *The club members elect a new president each year.* **2** choose; select: *We elected to play baseball.* **3** *Theology.* of God, select for salvation and eternal life.
—*adj.* **1** elected but not yet in office (*used after a noun*): *the chairman elect.* **2** specially chosen; selected or elite. **3** *Theology.* chosen by God for salvation and eternal life. **4** (*noml.*) **the elect,** *pl.* **a** a group of people who have special rights and privileges. **b** *Theology.* those who have been chosen by God for salvation and eternal life. [< L *electus*, pp. of *eligere* < *ex-* out + *legere* choose]

e·lec·tion (i lek′shən) *n.* **1** a choice. **2** a choosing by vote. **3** a selection by God for salvation. **4** a general election.

e·lec·tion·eer (i lek′shən ēr′) *v.* work for the success of a candidate or party in an election. —**e·lec′tion·eer′er,** *n.*

e·lec·tive (i lek′tiv) *adj., n.* —*adj.* **1** chosen by an election: *Aldermen are elective officials.* **2** filled by an election: *an elective office.* **3** having the right to vote in an election. **4** having to do with the principle of electing to office. **5** *Chemistry.* tending to combine with certain substances in preference to others. **6** open to choice; not required: *German is an elective subject in many high schools.*
—*n.* a subject or course of study that may be taken, but is not required. —**e·lec′tive·ly,** *adv.* —**e·lec′tive·ness,** *n.*

e·lec·tor (i lek′tər) *n.* **1** a person who has the right to vote in an election. **2** *U.S.* a member of the electoral college. **3** one of the princes who had the right to elect the emperor of the Holy Roman Empire.

e·lec·tor·al (i lek′tər əl) *adj.* **1** of electors. **2** of or having to do with an election. —**e·lec′tor·al·ly,** *adv.*

electoral college *U.S.* a group of people chosen by the voters to elect the President and Vice-President of the United States.

e·lec·tor·ate (i lek′tər it) *n.* **1** the persons having the right to vote in an election. **2** a territory under the rule of an elector of the Holy Roman Empire. **3** the rank of an elector of the Holy Roman Empire.

electr. electrical; electricity; electrician.

E·lec·tra (i lek′trə) *n. Greek legend.* the daughter of Agamemnon and Clytemnestra. Electra urged her brother, Orestes, to kill their mother and her lover in order to avenge the murder of their father.

Electra complex *Psychiatry.* the repressed desire of a daughter for her father, parallel to the Oedipus complex in males.

e·lec·tric (i lek′trik) *adj., n.* —*adj.* **1** of or having to do with electricity; electric current. **2** producing or carrying an electric current: *an electric wire, an electric generator.* **3** produced by electricity: *an electric shock, an electric fire.* **4** operated by

electricity: *an electric shaver.* **5** of a musical instrument, using electronic amplification: *an electric guitar.* **6** thrilling or exciting: *an electric atmosphere, an electric performance.*
—*n.* **1** *Informal.* an electric train, car, etc. **2** *Archaic.* a nonconducting substance, such as amber or glass, used to excite or store electricity. [< NL *electricus* < LGk. *ēlektron* amber (which, under friction, has the property of attracting)]

e·lec·tri·cal (i lek′trə kəl) *adj.* electric.

e·lec·tri·cal·ly (i lek′trik lē) *adv.* by electricity.

electrical storm electric storm

electrical transcription **1** the system of radio broadcasting from a special phonograph record. **2** a special phonograph record used for such broadcasting.

electric brain electronic brain.

electric chair a chair used in electrocuting criminals.

electric eel a large, eel-like, freshwater fish (*Electrophorus electricus*) of South America having an electric organ in its tail which can produce a shock strong enough to stun a person.

electric eye photo-electric cell.

electric field the space surrounding an electrically charged body within which it produces electric force.

electric heater a portable device that furnishes heat by means of small electric coils.

e·lec·tri·cian (i lek′trish′ən *or* ē′lek trish′ən) *n.* a person whose work is installing or repairing electric wires, lights, motors, etc.

e·lec·tric·i·ty (i lek′tris′ə tē *or* ē′lek tris′ə tē) *n.* **1** a form of energy that can produce light, heat, magnetism, and chemical changes, and that can be generated by friction, induction, or chemical changes. **2** an electric current; flow of electrons. **3** the branch of physics that deals with electricity.

electric light bulb the glass bulb and the enclosed filament by which electricity is converted to light for illumination.

electric ray any of a family (Torpedinidae) of rays found in warm seas, having an electric organ in each wing which can produce shocks used by the rays to stun prey and also used for defence.

electric storm *or* **electrical storm** a storm accompanied by thunder and lightning.

e·lec·tri·fi·ca·tion (i lek′trə fə kā′shən) *n.* electrifying or being electrified.

e·lec·tri·fy (i lek′trə fī′) *v.* **-fied, -fy·ing. 1** charge with electricity. **2** equip to use electricity: *Some railways once operated by steam are now electrified.* **3** give an electric shock to. **4** excite; thrill. **5** provide with electric power service: *Many rural areas will soon be electrified.*

electro– *combining form.* **1** electric, as in *electromagnet.* **2** electrically, as in *electropositive.* **3** electricity. [< Gk. *ēlektron* amber]

e·lec·tro·bi·ol·o·gy (i lek′trō bī ol′ə jē) *n.* the branch of biology that deals with electrical phenomena in living organisms.

e·lec·tro·car·di·o·gram (i lek′trō kär′dē ə gram′) *n.* a tracing made by an electrocardiograph. *Abbrev.*: ECG, EKG

e·lec·tro·car·di·o·graph (i lek′trō kär′dē ə graf′) *n.* an instrument that records the electric current produced by the action of the heart muscle, used in the diagnosis and treatment of heart disease.

e·lec·tro·chem·i·cal (i lek′trō kem′ə kəl) *adj.* of, having to do with, or involving the principles or processes of electrochemistry.

electrochemical cell a device capable of producing an electric current by means of chemical action, consisting of a container with two electrodes of different metals in a paste or liquid that will conduct electricity. An electrochemical cell generates a current when the electrodes are connected by a conducting wire. A flashlight battery is an electrochemical cell.

e·lec·tro·chem·is·try (i lek′trō kem′is trē) *n.* the branch of chemistry that deals with chemical changes produced by electricity and the production of electricity by chemical changes.

e·lec·tro·cute (i lek′trə kyüt′) *v.* **-cut·ed, -cut·ing.** kill by an electric current. [< *electro-* + exe*cute*]

e·lec·tro·cu·tion (i lek′trə kyü′shən) *n.* killing by electricity.

e·lec·trode (i lek′trōd) *n.* a conductor through which an electric current enters or leaves a conducting medium such as an electrolyte, gas, or vacuum in a battery, electron tube, etc. [< *electro-* + Gk. *hodos* way]

e·lec·tro·dy·nam·ic (i lek′trō dī nam′ik) *adj.* **1** of or having to do with the force of electricity in motion. **2** of or having to do with electrodynamics. —**e·lec′tro·dy·nam′i·cal·ly,** *adv.*

e·lec·tro·dy·nam·ics (i lek′trō dī nam′iks) *n.* the branch of

hat, āge, fär; let, ēqual, tèrm; it, īce
hot, ōpen, ôrder; oil, out; cup, pùt, rüle,
əbove, takən, pencəl, lemən, circəs
ch, child; ng, long; sh, ship
th, thin; ᴛʜ, then; zh, measure

physics that deals with the action of electricity or with electric currents.

e·lec·tro·en·ceph·a·lo·gram (i lek′trō en sef′ə lə gram′) *n.* a tracing made by an electroencephalograph. *Abbrev.*: EEG

e·lec·tro·en·ceph·a·lo·graph (i lek′trō en sef′ə lə graf′) *n.* an instrument for measuring the electrical activity of the brain, used in the diagnosis and treatment of brain disorders.

e·lec·tro·lier (i lek′trə lēr′) *n.* a chandelier or other support for electric lights. [< *electro-* + chande*lier*]

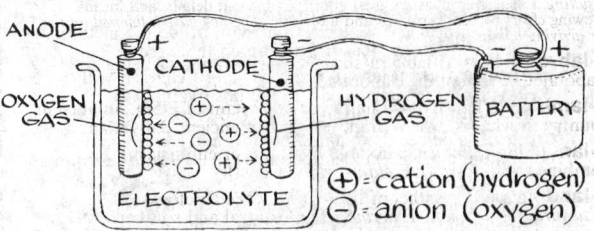

The electrolysis (def. 1) of water. the electrolyte is water with salt (or sulphuric acid, etc.) added to ionize it.

e·lec·trol·y·sis (i lek′trol′ə sis *or* ē′lek trol′ə sis) *n.* **1** the chemical decomposition of an electrolyte (a conducting solution or molten salt) by the passage of an electric current through it. Electrolysis is used for electroplating metals and also to produce chemicals, such as chlorine. **2** the destruction of body tissues, such as hair roots or moles, by means of an electric current. [< *electro-* + *-lysis* a loosing (< Gk. *lysis* < *lyein* loose)]

e·lec·tro·lyte (i lek′trə līt′) *n.* **1** a solution or molten substance that conducts an electric current, becoming decomposed in the process. In an electrolyte the current is carried by ions moving in the electric field between electrodes, not by free electrons, as in metals. See **dry cell** and **electrolysis** for pictures. **2** a compound which, in solution or in the molten state, will conduct an electric current. [< *electro-* + Gk. *lytos* loosed < *lyein* loose]

e·lec·tro·lyt·ic (i lek′trə lit′ik) *adj.* of or having to do with electrolysis or with an electrolyte. —**e·lec′tro·lyt′i·cal·ly,** *adv.*

electrolytic cell any device which uses electrolysis to produce chemical changes or an electric current.

e·lec·tro·lyze (i lek′trə līz′) *v.* **-lyzed, -lyz·ing.** decompose by electrolysis. —**e·lec′tro·ly·za′tion,** *n.* —**e·lec′tro·lyz′er,** *n.*

e·lec·tro·mag·net (i lek′trō mag′nit) *n.* a strong temporary magnet made by coiling wire around an iron core and passing an electric current through the wire. The current causes the iron to become magnetized.

e·lec·tro·mag·net·ic (i lek′trō mag net′ik) *adj.* of, having to do with, or caused by electromagnetism. —**e·lec′tro·mag·net′i·cal·ly,** *adv.*

electromagnetic radiation radiation consisting of electromagnetic waves. See also **photon.**

electromagnetic spectrum the whole range of wavelengths (or frequencies) of electromagnetic waves, from the longest radio waves (wavelength 10^5 metres) to the shortest cosmic rays (wavelength 10^{-17} metre).

electromagnetic wave a wave of energy resulting from periodic variations in the intensity of electric and magnetic fields vibrating at right angles to each other. Electromagnetic waves can travel through space or matter and include radio waves, infrared radiation, light waves, X rays, gamma rays, and cosmic rays.

e·lec·tro·mag·net·ism (i lek′trō mag′nə tiz′əm) *n.* **1** the magnetism produced by a current of electricity. **2** the branch of physics that deals with this.

e·lec·tro·me·chan·i·cal (i lek′trō mə kan′ə kəl) *adj.* of, having to do with, or being a mechanical device or process that is electrically activated or controlled.

e·lec·trom·e·ter (i lek′trom′ə tər *or* ē′lek trom′ə tər) *n.* an instrument for measuring differences in electrical charge or potential.

e·lec·tro·mo·tive (i lek′trə mō′tiv) *adj.* **1** producing a flow of electricity. **2** of or having to do with electromotive force.

electromotive force the amount of energy derived from an electric source in one second when one unit of current is passing through the source, commonly measured in volts. Electromotive force is produced by differences in electrical charge or potential. *Abbrev.*: EMF, e.m.f., or emf

electromotive series *Chemistry.* an arrangement of the metallic elements so that each is positive with reference to those that follow it and negative with reference to those that precede it.

e·lec·tro·mo·tor (i lek′trə mō′tər) *n.* **1** a machine producing electric current. **2** a motor run by electricity.

e·lec·tron (i lek′tron) *n.* an elementary particle present in all atoms, consisting of a negative electric charge of about 1.602×10^{-19} coulombs. It has a mass of about 9.11×10^{-31} kilograms when at rest. [< Gk. *ēlektron*. See ELECTRIC.]

electron beam a stream of electrons moving in the same direction at the same speed. The electron beam inside the picture tube of a television set inscribes the picture on the screen.

e·lec·tro·neg·a·tive (i lek′trō neg′ə tiv) *adj.* **1** charged with negative electricity. **2** tending to pass to the positive pole in electrolysis. **3** non-metallic; acid.

electron gun a device that guides the flow and greatly increases the speed of atomic particles. Electron guns are used in oil refining and in various other industries.

e·lec·tron·ic (i lek′tron′ik *or* ē′lek tron′ik) *adj.* of or having to do with an electron or electrons. —**e·lec′tron′i·cal·ly,** *adv.*

electronic brain computer (def. 1). Also, **electric brain.**

electronic music music created, usually on magnetic tape, from sound made by electronic generators and filters.

e·lec·tron·ics (i lek′tron′iks *or* ē′lek tron′iks) *n.* the branch of physics that deals with the production, activity, and effects of electrons in motion (*used with a singular verb*). Radar, radio, television, etc. are based on the principles of electronics.

electron microscope a microscope that uses beams of electrons instead of beams of light, and has much higher power than any ordinary microscope. Its enlarged images are now observable directly by the eye, but are projected upon a fluorescent surface or photographic plate.

electron tube a device for producing a controlled flow of electrons, consisting of a sealed glass or metal tube, etc., either having a vacuum inside or containing a gas at low pressure through which the electrons can move readily to carry current between the electrodes inside the tube. Microwave tubes and cathode-ray tubes are two kinds of electron tube.

e·lec·tron·volt (i lek′tron vōlt′) *n.* a unit used with the SI for measuring the kinetic energy of electrons. One electronvolt is equal to the energy acquired by an electron when it is accelerated through a potential difference of one volt (equivalent to 1.602×10^{-19} joules). *Symbol*: eV

e·lec·troph·o·rus (i lek′trof′ə rəs *or* ē′lek trof′ə rəs) *n., pl.* **-ri** (-rī′ *or* -rē′). a simple device for producing charges of electricity by means of induction. [< NL *electrophorus* < *electro-* + Gk. *-phoros* bearing]

e·lec·tro·plate (i lek′trə plāt′) *v., n.* **-plat·ed, -plat·ing;** *n.* —*v.* cover with a coating of metal by means of electrolysis. —*n.* **1** silverware, etc., covered in this way. **2** *Printing.* a plate made by this process. —**e·lec′tro·plat′er,** *n.*

e·lec·tro·pos·i·tive (i lek′trō poz′ə tiv) *adj., n.* —*adj.* **1** charged with positive electricity. **2** tending to pass to the negative pole (cathode) in electrolysis. **3** metallic; basic. —*n.* an electropositive substance.

e·lec·tro·scope (i lek′trə skōp′) *n.* any of various devices or instruments for detecting the presence of a minute electric charge on a body and showing whether the charge is positive or negative.

e·lec·tro·stat·ic (i lek′trə stat′ik) *adj.* having to do with electricity at rest or with stationary electric charges. —**e·lec′tro·stat′i·cal·ly,** *adv.*

e·lec·tro·stat·ics (i lek′trə stat′iks) *n.* the branch of physics that deals with objects charged with electricity.

e·lec·tro·ther·a·py (i lek′trō ther′ə pē) *n.* the treatment of disease by electricity.

e·lec·tro·type (i lek′trə tīp′) *n., v.* **-typed, -typ·ing.** —*n.* **1** *Printing.* a metal or composition plate. **2** a print made from such a plate. —*v.* make such a plate or plates of. —**e·lec′tro·typ′er,** *n.*

e·lec·tro·va·lence (i lek′trō vā′ləns) *n.* the number of electrons

gained or lost by an atom when it becomes an ion in a compound. —**e·lec′tro·va′lent,** *adj.*

e·lec·trum (i lek′trəm) *n.* a pale-yellow alloy of gold and silver, used by the ancients. [< L < Gk. *ēlektron*]

e·lec·tu·ar·y (i lek′chü er′ē) *n., pl.* **-ar·ies.** a medicinal paste of powdered drugs and syrup or honey. [ME < LL *electuarium* < Gk. *ekleikton* < *ekleichein* lick out < *ex-* out + *leichein* lick]

el·ee·mos·y·nar·y (el′ə mos′ə ner′ē *or* el′ē mos′ə ner′ē) *adj.* **1** of or for charity; charitable. **2** provided by charity; free. **3** dependent on charity; supported by charity. [< LL *eleemosynarius* < L *eleemosyna* < Gk. *eleēmosynē* compassion < *eleos* mercy]

el·e·gance (el′ə gəns) *n.* **1** refined grace and richness; luxury free from coarseness. **2** something elegant.

el·e·gan·cy (el′ə gən sē) *n., pl.* **-cies.** elegance.

el·e·gant (el′ə gənt) *adj.* **1** having or showing good taste; gracefully and richly refined: *The palace had elegant furnishings.* **2** expressed with taste; correct and polished in expression or arrangement: *an elegant speech.* **3** *Informal.* fine; excellent; superior. [< F < L *elegans, -antis*] —**el′e·gant·ly,** *adv.*
➤ *Syn.* **1.** See note at *fine.*

el·e·gi·ac (el′ə jī′ək) *adj., n.* —*adj.* **1** of or suitable for an elegy. **2** sad; mournful; melancholy. **3** written in elegiacs. —*n.* *Classical prosody.* a dactylic hexameter couplet, the second line having only a long or accented syllable in the third and sixth feet like this:
ART
ART

el·e·gize (el′ə jīz′) *v.* **-gized, -giz·ing. 1** write an elegy about. **2** write an elegy; lament.

el·e·gy (el′ə jē) *n., pl.* **-gies. 1** a mournful or melancholy poem; poem that is a lament for the dead. Milton's *Lycidas* and Shelley's *Adonais* are elegies. **2** a poem written in elegiac verses. [< F *élégie* < L < Gk. *elegeia*, ult. < *elegos* mournful poem]

elem. 1 element(s); elementary.

el·e·ment (el′ə mənt) *n.* **1** one of the simple substances, such as gold, iron, carbon, sulphur, oxygen, and hydrogen, that have not yet been separated into simpler parts by chemical means; a substance composed of atoms that are chemically alike. See chart of elements on the following page. **2** one of the parts of which anything is made up: *Honesty, industry, and kindness are elements of good living.* **3** one of the four substances—earth, water, air, and fire—that were once thought to make up all other things. **4** the place, condition, activities, etc. best suited to or preferred by a person or thing: *She was in her element tinkering with old clocks.* **5** a unit, such as a military formation, that is part of a larger group. **6** the **elements,** *pl.* **a** the simple, necessary parts to be learned first; first principles. **b** the atmospheric forces: *The storm seemed a war of the elements.* **c** bread and wine used in the Eucharist. [< L *elementum* rudiment, first principle]
➤ *Syn.* **2. Element, component, constituent** = one of the parts of which something is made up. **Element** is the general word, applying to a part of any thing, but sometimes suggests an essential or basic part: *Kindness is an element of courtesy.* **Component** = a part of something that is put together as a compound or mixture: *Ice cream and syrup are components of a sundae.* **Constituent,** often used interchangeably with *component,* differs in suggesting active helping to form the whole instead of just being a part: *Syrup is a necessary constituent of a sundae.*

el·e·men·tal (el′ə men′təl) *adj.* **1** of the four elements — earth, water, air, and fire. **2** of the forces of nature: *Primitive peoples usually worship elemental gods, such as the sun, earth, thunder, etc.* **3** as found in nature; simple but powerful: *Survival is an elemental instinct.* **4** being a necessary or essential part. **5** elementary. —**el′e·men′tal·ly,** *adv.*

el·e·men·ta·ry (el′ə men′tə rē *or* el′ə men′trē) *adj.* **1** of or dealing with the simple, necessary parts to be learned first; having to do with first principles; introductory. **2** *Chemistry.* **a** made up of only one chemical element; not a compound: *Silver is an elementary substance.* **b** having to do with a chemical element or elements. **3** elemental. **4** of or having to do with elementary schools. —**el′e·men′tar·i·ly,** *adv.*
➤ *Syn.* **1. Elementary, rudimentary, primary** = having to do with the beginnings of something. **Elementary** emphasizes the idea of basic things and means having to do with the first steps or beginning facts and principles of anything: *John learned simple addition and subtraction when he began elementary arithmetic.* **Rudimentary** is a formal word emphasizing the idea of an undeveloped beginning and used particularly to mean "consisting of the first parts and principles of knowledge or of a subject studied": *She has only a rudimentary knowledge of mathematics.* **Primary** emphasizes coming first in order or time: *Children attend primary school before high school.*

elementary school a school of six, seven, or eight grades for children aged six and over, which is followed by high school or junior high school. Some elementary schools also include kindergarten.

el·e·men·toid (el′ə men′toid) *adj.* having the appearance of an element: *an elementoid compound.*

PERIODIC TABLE OF THE ELEMENTS

	Ia	IIa	IIIb	IVb	Vb	VIb	VIIb		VIIIb		Ib	IIb	IIIb	IVa	Va	VIa	VIIa	0
1	1* H																1* H	2 He
2	3 Li	4 Be			KEY	79 Au	← Atomic number ← Symbol						5 B	6 C	7 N	8 O	9 F	10 Ne
3	11 Na	12 Mg											13 Al	14 Si	15 P	16 S	17 Cl	18 Ar
4	19 K	20 Ca	21 Sc	22 Ti	23 V	24 Cr	25 Mn	26 Fe	27 Co	28 Ni	29 Cu	30 Zn	31 Ga	32 Ge	33 As	34 Se	35 Br	36 Kr
5	37 Rb	38 Sr	39 Y	40 Zr	41 Nb	42 Mo	43 Tc	44 Ru	45 Rh	46 Pd	47 Ag	48 Cd	49 In	50 Sn	51 Sb	52 Te	53 I	54 Xe
6	55 Cs	56 Ba	57 La	72 Hf	73 Ta	74 W	75 Re	76 Os	77 Ir	78 Pt	79 Au	80 Hg	81 Tl	82 Pb	83 Bi	84 Po	85 At	86 Rn
7	87 Fr	88 Ra	89 Ac	104 Rf	105 Ha													

*Hydrogen is usually placed in both groups Ia and VIIa because it shares some characteristics with the elements of each group.

58 Ce	59 Pr	60 Nd	61 Pm	62 Sm	63 Eu	64 Gd	65 Tb	66 Dy	67 Ho	68 Er	69 Tm	70 Yb	71 Lu
90 Th	91 Pa	92 U	93 Np	94 Pu	95 Am	96 Cm	97 Bk	98 Cf	99 Es	100 Fm	101 Md	102 No	103 Lr

ALPHABETICAL LIST OF THE ELEMENTS, WITH THEIR SYMBOLS AND ATOMIC NUMBERS

actinium	Ac	89	europium	Eu	63	molybdenum	Mo	42	scandium	Sc	21
aluminum	Al	13	fermium	Fm	100	neodymium	Nd	60	selenium	Se	34
americium	Am	95	fluorine	F	9	neon	Ne	10	silicon	Si	14
antimony	Sb	51	francium	Fr	87	neptunium	Np	93	silver	Ag	47
argon	Ar	18	gadolinium	Gd	64	nickel	Ni	28	sodium	Na	11
arsenic	As	33	gallium	Ga	31	niobium	Nb	41	strontium	Sr	38
astatine	At	85	germanium	Ge	32	nitrogen	N	7	sulfur	S	16
barium	Ba	56	gold	Au	79	nobelium	No	102	tantalum	Ta	73
berkelium	Bk	97	hafnium	Hf	72	osmium	Os	76	technetium	Tc	43
beryllium	Be	4	hahnium	Ha	105	oxygen	O	8	tellurium	Te	52
bismuth	Bi	83	helium	He	2	palladium	Pd	46	terbium	Tb	65
boron	B	5	holmium	Ho	67	phosphorus	P	15	thallium	Tl	81
bromine	Br	35	hydrogen	H	1	platinum	Pt	78	thorium	Th	90
cadmium	Cd	48	indium	In	49	plutonium	Pu	94	thulium	Tm	69
calcium	Ca	20	iodine	I	53	polonium	Po	84	tin	Sn	50
californium	Cf	98	iridium	Ir	77	potassium	K	19	titanium	Ti	22
carbon	C	6	iron	Fe	26	praseodymium	Pr	59	tungsten	W	74
cerium	Ce	58	krypton	Kr	36	promethium	Pm	61	uranium	U	92
cesium	Cs	55	lanthanum	La	57	protactinium	Pa	91	vanadium	V	23
chlorine	Cl	17	lawrencium	Lr	103	radium	Ra	88	xenon	Xe	54
chromium	Cr	24	lead	Pb	82	radon	Rn	86	ytterbium	Yb	70
cobalt	Co	27	lithium	Li	3	rhenium	Re	75	yttrium	Y	39
copper	Cu	29	lutetium	Lu	71	rhodium	Rh	45	zinc	Zn	30
curium	Cm	96	magnesium	Mg	12	rubidium	Rb	37	zirconium	Zr	40
dysprosium	Dy	66	manganese	Mn	25	ruthenium	Ru	44			
einsteinium	Es	99	mendelevium	Md	101	rutherfordium	Rf	104			
erbium	Er	68	mercury	Hg	80	samarium	Sm	62			

el·e·phant (el′ə fənt) *n., pl.* **-phants** or *(esp. collectively)* **-phant.** either of two huge mammals (family Elephantidae) of Africa and Asia having thick, tough, almost hairless, grey skin, a thickset body, thick legs, and a flexible, muscular proboscis called a trunk, that is a prolongation of the nose and upper lip and is used for conveying food and water to the mouth. These animals, the **African elephant** (*Loxodonta africana*) and the **Indian elephant** (*Elephas maximus*), are the only living representatives of the order Proboscidea. [ME < OF *olifant* < L < Gk. *elephas, -antis* elephant, ivory, probably < Egyptian]

el·e·phan·ti·a·sis (el′ə fan tī′ə sis) *n.* a disease in which parts of the body, usually the legs, become greatly enlarged and the skin thickened and broken. It is caused by parasitic worms that block the flow of lymph. [< L < Gk. *elephantiasis* < *elephas, -antis* elephant]

el·e·phan·tine (el′ə fan′tīn or el′ə fan′tēn) *adj.* **1** like an elephant; huge; heavy; clumsy; slow. **2** of elephants.

elephant seal either of two enormous hair seals, the **northern elephant seal** (*Mirounga angustirostris*) and the **southern elephant seal** (*M. leonina*), having a thick, heavy body and a large head with a long, broad snout, the adult male also having a long proboscis which, when inflated, curves downward into the mouth. Elephant seals are the largest pinnipeds.

el·e·phant's–ear (el′ə fənts ēr′) *n.* any of a genus (*Colocasia*) of tropical Old World plants of the arum family having very large, heart-shaped leaves, especially *C. esculenta*, cultivated in several varieties as an ornamental plant and also (especially in the Far East and the South Pacific) for its starchy rootstocks. See also **taro.**

El·eu·sin·i·an mysteries (el′yə sin′ē ən) in ancient Greece, the secret, religious ceremonies held yearly at Eleusis in honor of the goddesses Demeter and Persephone.

E·leu·sis (i lü′sis) *n.* a city in ancient Greece, near Athens.

el·e·vate (el′ə vāt′) *v.* **-vat·ed, -vat·ing. 1** lift up; raise. **2** raise in rank or station: *The soldier was elevated to knighthood for bravery.* **3** raise in quality: *Good books elevate the mind.* **4** put in high spirits; make joyful or proud; elate. [< L *elevare* < *ex-* out + *levare* lighten, raise]
☛ *Syn.* 2, 3. See note at **raise.**

el·e·vat·ed (el′ə vāt′id) *adj., n.* **—adj. 1** lifted up; raised; high. **2** dignified; lofty; noble. **3** in high spirits; joyful; proud. **—n.** *Informal.* elevated railway.

elevated railway a railway raised above the ground on a supporting frame high enough for streetcars, automobiles, etc. to pass underneath.

el·e·va·tion (el′ə vā′shən) *n.* **1** a raised place; high place: *A hill is an elevation.* **2** the height above the earth's surface: *The airplane fell from an elevation of 1000 metres.* **3** the height above sea level: *The elevation of Calgary is 1045 metres.* **4** dignity; loftiness; nobility. **5** raising; lifting up: *the elevation of Caesar to be the ruler of Rome.* **6** being raised or lifted up. **7** a flat drawing of the front, rear, or side of a building. **8** *Astronomy.* the altitude of the pole or of any heavenly body above the horizon. **9** *Surveying.* the angular distance of an object above the horizontal plane through the point of observation.

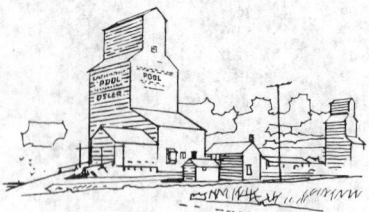

A Prairie elevator

el·e·va·tor (el′ə vā′tər) *n.* **1** anything that raises or lifts. **2** a moving platform or cage to carry people and freight up and down in a building, mine, etc. **3** a building for storing grain. **4** a horizontal, flat, hinged piece on an aircraft, usually on the tail, that is lowered or raised to make the aircraft climb or descend. See **airplane** for picture. [< LL]

elevator shaft a vertical passageway for an elevator.

e·lev·en (i lev′ən) *n., adj.* **—n. 1** one more than ten; 11. **2** the numeral 11: *That looks like an 11.* **3** the eleventh in a set or series. **4** *Cricket, soccer, etc.* a team of eleven players: *This year our school has the best eleven ever.* **5** any set or series of eleven persons or things.
—adj. 1 being one more than ten. **2** being eleventh in a set or series (*after the noun*): *Chapter Eleven.* [OE *endleofan* one left (over

e·lev·enth (i lev′ənth) *adj. or n.* **1** next after the 10th; last in a series of 11. **2** one, or being one, of 11 equal parts.

eleventh hour the latest possible moment; time just before it is too late.

elf (elf) *n., pl.* **elves. 1** a tiny, mischievous fairy. **2** a small, mischievous person. [OE *ælf*] **—elf′like′,** *adj.*

elf·in (el′fən) *adj. —adj.* of or suitable for elves; like an elf's: *The child's elfin smile was very charming.* **—n.** elf.

elf·ish (el′fish) *adj.* elflike; elfin; mischievous. **—elf′ish·ly,** *adv.* **—elf′ish·ness,** *n.*

elf·lock (elf′lok′) *n.* a tangled lock of hair, supposedly caused by elves.

e·lic·it (i lis′it) *v.* draw forth: *to elicit a reply, to elicit applause, to elicit the truth.* [< L *elicitus,* pp. of *elicere* < *ex-* out + *lacere* entice] **—e·lic′it·or,** *n.*
☛ *Hom.* **Illicit. Illicit** is a formal adjective meaning unlawful or improper: *The police are trying to stop the illicit sale of drugs.*

e·lic·i·ta·tion (i lis′ə tā′shən) *n.* a drawing forth or being drawn forth.

e·lide (i līd′) *v.* **-lid·ed, -lid·ing. 1** omit or slur over (a syllable or vowel) in pronunciation. The *e* in *the* is elided in *th' inevitable hour.* **2** omit or cancel (a written word, passage, etc.). **3** ignore or suppress. [< L *elidere* < *ex-* out + *laedere* dash]

e·li·gi·bil·i·ty (el′ə jə bil′ə tē) *n., pl.* **-ties.** fitness; qualification; desirability.

el·i·gi·ble (el′ə jə bəl) *adj., n.* **—adj. 1** fit or proper to be chosen; desirable: *an eligible bachelor.* **2** properly qualified; meeting all requirements set by law or rule: *Players had to pass in all subjects to be eligible for the school team.* **—n.** an eligible person. [< F < LL < L *eligere* pick out, choose. See ELECT.] **—el′i·gi·ble·ness,** *n.* **—el′i·gi·bly,** *adv.*

e·lim·i·nate (i lim′ə nāt′) *v.* **-nat·ed, -nat·ing. 1** get rid of; remove: *The new bridge over the railway tracks eliminated the danger in crossing.* **2** pay no attention to; leave out of consideration; omit: *The architect eliminated furniture, rugs, etc. in figuring the cost of the house.* **3** *Mathematics.* get rid of (an unknown quantity) by combining algebraic equations. **4** put out of a championship competition by reason of defeat: *The Toronto team was eliminated in the first round of the hockey playoffs.* **5** expel (waste) from the body; excrete. [< L *eliminare* < *ex-* out + *limen* threshold] **—e·lim′i·na·tor,** *n.*
☛ *Syn.* 1. See note at **exclude.**

e·lim·i·na·tion (i lim′ə nā′shən) *n.* eliminating or being eliminated.

E·lis (ē′lis) *n.* an ancient division of W Greece. Olympic games were held on the plains of Olympia in Elis.

e·li·sion (i lizh′ən) *n.* **1** the slurring or suppression of a vowel or a syllable in pronouncing. Elision is often used in poetry, and generally consists in cutting off a vowel at the end of one word when the next begins with a vowel. **2** omission or cancellation. [< L *elisio, -onis* < *elidere.* See ELIDE.]

e·lite or **é·lite** (i lēt′ or ā lēt′) *n., adj.* **—n. 1** the part of a community or group regarded as being the most distinguished, gifted, intelligent, rich, etc. (*sometimes used as a plural*). **2** a size of typewriter type having 12 characters to the inch (2.54 cm). **—adj. 1** of or having to do with an elite. **2** choice; superior; distinguished. **3** of or having to do with elite type. [< F *élite,* fem. pp. of *élire* pick out < L *eligere.* See ELECT.]

e·lit·ism or **é·lit·ism** (i lēt′iz əm or ā lēt′ism) *n.* **1** control or leadership by an elite. **2** belief in or support of such control or leadership. **3** awareness of belonging to an elite.

e·lit·ist or **é·lit·ist** (i lēt′ist or ā lēt′ist) *adj., n. —adj.* of, having to do with, or characterized by elitism. **—n.** a person who believes in elitism or considers himself a member of an elite.

e·lix·ir (i lik′sər) *n.* **1** a substance supposed to have the power of changing lead, iron, etc. into gold or of lengthening life indefinitely, sought by the alchemists of the Middle Ages. **2** a universal remedy; cure-all. **3** a medicine made of drugs or herbs mixed with alcohol and syrup. **4** the quintessence of a thing; chief principle. [ME < Med.L < Arabic *al-iksīr* (def. 1), probably < Gk. *xērion* drying powder used on wounds < *xēros* dry]

E·liz·a·be·than (i liz′ə bē′thən) *adj., n. —adj.* of or having to do with the time of Queen Elizabeth I (1533-1603). **—n.** a person, especially a writer, of the time of Queen Elizabeth I.

Elizabethan sonnet a type of sonnet used by Shakespeare and many other Elizabethans. It has a rhyme scheme *abab cdcd efef gg.*

elk (elk) *n., pl.* **elks** or *(esp. collectively)* **elk. 1** a large North American mammal (*Cervus canadensis*), the second largest member of the deer family, having a light or dark-brown coat with a light-colored rump patch, long, shaggy, dark-brown hair covering the neck and shoulders, and, in the adult male, large antlers, usually with five tines; wapiti. Some authorities consider the elk to be of

the same species as the European red deer. **2** a large deer (*Alces alces*) of Europe and Asia, considered by many authorities to be of the same species as the North American moose. The elk closely resembles the moose, but is considerably smaller. **3** any of several other large deer of Asia. **4** a soft leather made from elk hide, or from calfskin or cowhide in imitation of this. [apparently < AF form of OE *eolh*]

elk·hound (elk'hound') *n.* Norwegian elkhound.

ell¹ (el) *n.* an old measure of length, chiefly used in measuring cloth. In England it was equal to 45 inches (about 115 cm). [OE *eln* length of lower arm]

ell² (el) *n.* **1** an extension of a building at one end and usually at right angles to it. **2** a pipe or tube with a right-angled bend.

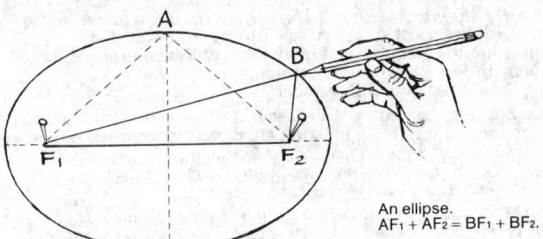

An ellipse.
$AF_1 + AF_2 = BF_1 + BF_2$.

el·lipse (i lips') *n. Geometry.* an oval having both ends alike. It is the path of a point that moves so that the sum of its distances from two fixed points remains the same. Any conic section formed by a cutting plane inclined to the base but not passing through the base is an ellipse. [< L *ellipsis.* See ELLIPSIS.]

el·lip·ses (i lip'siz *for 1;* i lip'sēz *for 2) n.* **1** pl. of **ellipse.** **2** pl. of **ellipsis.**

el·lip·sis (i lip'sis) *n., pl.* **-ses** (-sēz). **1** *Grammar.* the omission of a word or words that could complete the construction of a sentence. *Example:* In She is as tall as her brother, *there is a permissible* ellipsis of *is tall* after *brother.* **2** in writing or printing, marks (. . . or * * *) used to show an omission. [< L < Gk. *elleipsis* < *elleipein* come short, leave out]

el·lip·soid (i lip'soid) *n., adj.* —*n. Mathematics.* **1** a solid of which all plane surfaces are ellipses or circles. **2** any such surface. —*adj.* of or in the form of an ellipsoid.

el·lip·tic (i lip'tik) *adj.* elliptical.

el·lip·ti·cal (i lip'tə kəl) *adj.* **1** having to do with or shaped like an ellipse. **2** having to do with or marked by ellipsis. **3** of speech or writing, extremely concise or economical of words, often to the point of obscurity. —**el·lip'ti·cal·ly,** *adv.*

elm (elm) *n.* **1** any of a genus (*Ulmus*) of tall trees native mainly to north temperate regions, valued as shade and timber trees. **2** the hard wood of an elm. **3** (*adjl.*) designating the family (Ulmaceae) of trees that includes the elms and hackberries. [OE]

el·o·cu·tion (el'ə kyü'shən) *n.* **1** the art of speaking or reading clearly and effectively in public; art of public speaking, including the correct use of the voice, gestures, etc. **2** a manner of speaking or reading in public. [< L *elocutio, -onis* < *eloqui* < *ex-* out + *loqui* speak]

el·o·cu·tion·ar·y (el'ə kyü'shən er'ē) *adj.* of or having to do with elocution.

el·o·cu·tion·ist (el'ə kyü'shən ist) *n.* **1** a person skilled in elocution. **2** a teacher of elocution.

E·lo·him (e lō'him) *n.* a Hebrew name for God. [< Hebrew *elohim,* pl.]

e·lon·gate (i long'gāt) *v.* **-gat·ed, -gat·ing;** *adj.* —*v.* lengthen; extend; stretch: *A rubber band can be elongated to several times its normal length.* —*adj.* **1** lengthened. **2** long and thin: *the elongate leaf of a willow.* [< L *elongare* < *ex-* out + *longus* long]

e·lon·ga·tion (ē'long gā'shən) *n.* **1** a lengthening; extension. **2** a lengthened part; continuation.

e·lope (i lōp') *v.* **e·loped, e·lop·ing. 1** run away with a lover. **2** run away; escape. [< AF *aloper,* ? < ME *lope(n)* run, probably < ON *hlaupa* leap] —**e·lope'ment,** *n.* —**e·lop'er,** *n.*

el·o·quence (el'ə kwəns) *n.* **1** a flow of speech that has grace and force: *The eloquence of the speaker moved all hearts.* **2** the power to win by speaking; the art of speaking so as to stir the feelings.

el·o·quent (el'ə kwənt) *adj.* **1** having eloquence. **2** highly expressive: *an eloquent gesture. His frown was eloquent of his displeasure.* [ME < OF < L *eloquens, -entis,* ppr. of *eloqui* < *ex-* out + *loqui* speak] —**el'o·quent·ly,** *adv.*

else (els) *adj., adv.* —*adj.* **1** other; different; instead: *What else*

hat, āge, fär; let, ēqual, tėrm; it, īce
hot, ōpen, ôrder; oil, out; cup, pūt, rüle,
əbove, takən, pencəl, lemən, circəs

ch, child; ng, long; sh, ship
th, thin; ŦH, then; zh, measure

could I say? **2** in addition: *The Browns are here; do you expect anyone else?* —*adv.* **1** differently: *How else can it be done?* **2** otherwise; if not: *Hurry, else you will be late.*

or else, *Informal.* or suffer for it; or pay a penalty: *You'd better return my bike, or else.* [OE *elles*]

► **Usage.** The possessive ending is transferred to **else** when this word follows a pronoun: *someone else's,* (not *whose else*).

else·where (els'wer' *or* -hwer') *adv.* somewhere else; in or to some other place.

else·whith·er (els'wiŦH'ər *or* -hwiŦH'ər) *adv. Archaic.* elsewhere.

e·lu·ci·date (i lü'sə dāt') *v.* **-dat·ed, -dat·ing.** make clear; explain: *The scientist elucidated his theory by a few simple experiments.* [< LL *elucidare* < L *ex-* out + *lucidus* bright] —**e·lu'ci·da'tor,** *n.*

e·lu·ci·da·tion (i lü'sə dā'shən) *n.* a making clear; explanation.

e·lude (i lüd') *v.* **e·lud·ed, e·lud·ing. 1** slip away from; avoid or escape by cleverness, quickness, etc.: *The sly fox eluded the dogs.* **2** escape discovery by; baffle: *The cause of cancer will not long elude research.* [< L *eludere* < *ex-* out + *ludere* play] —**e·lud'er,** *n.*

► **Syn. 1.** See note at **escape.**

► **Usage.** Do not confuse **elude** with **allude. Elude** = avoid or escape from: *The thief eluded his pursuers.* **Allude** = mention or refer to: *She alluded briefly to the minister's speech.*

E·lul (e lül') *n.* in the Hebrew calendar, the sixth month of the ecclesiastical year and the twelfth month of the civil year.

e·lu·sion (i lü'zhən) *n.* an eluding; clever avoidance. [< Med.L *elusio, -onis* < *eludere.* See ELUDE.]

e·lu·sive (i lü'siv) *adj.* **1** hard to describe or understand; baffling. **2** tending to elude: *The elusive fox got away from the hunters.* —**e·lu'sive·ly,** *adv.* —**e·lu'sive·ness,** *n.*

e·lu·so·ry (i lü'sə rē) *adj.* elusive.

e·lu·vi·um (i lü'vē əm) *n., pl.* **-vi·a** (-vē ə). *Geology.* a deposit of debris and dust produced by the erosion and disintegration of rock, that has remained in its place of origin. [< NL < L *ex* out + *luere* wash]

el·ver (el'vər) *n.* a young eel, just past the larval stage. [var. of *eelfare,* the passing of young eels up a stream < *eel + fare* journey (blend of OE *fær* and *faru*)]

elves (elvz) *n.* pl. of **elf.**

elv·ish (el'vish) *adj.* elfish; elflike.

E·lys·i·an (i liz'ē ən *or* i lizh'ən) *adj.* **1** of or having to do with Elysium. **2** happy; delightful.

Elysian Fields *Greek mythology.* Elysium.

E·lys·i·um (i liz'ē əm *or* i lizh'əm) *n.* **1** *Greek mythology.* a place where heroes and virtuous people lived after death. **2** any place or condition of perfect happiness; paradise. [< L < Gk. *Elysion (pedion)* Elysian (field)]

el·y·tra (el'ə trə) *n.* pl. of **elytron.**

el·y·tron (el'ə tron') *n., pl.* **-tra.** either of the hardened front wings of beetles and some other insects, that form a protective covering for the hind pair. [< NL < Gk. *elytron* sheath < *elyein* roll around]

em¹ (em) *n., pl.* **ems. 1** the letter M, m. **2** *Printing.* the square of any size of type; unit for measuring the amount of print in a line, page, etc. It was originally the portion of a line occupied by the letter *m.*

'em or **em²** (əm) *pron.pl. Informal.* them. [probably < OE *hem* them]

em-¹ the form of **en-¹** before *b, p,* and sometimes *m,* as in *embark, employ.*

em-² the form of **en-²** before *b, m, p, ph,* as in *emblem, emphasis.*

E.M. 1 Efficiency Medal. **2** Edward Medal.

e·ma·ci·ate (i mā'shē āt' *or* i mā'sē āt') *v.* **-at·ed, -at·ing.** make unnaturally thin; cause to lose flesh or waste away: *A long illness had emaciated the invalid.* [< L *emaciare* < *ex-* (intensive) + *macies* leanness]

e·ma·ci·a·tion (i mā'shē ā'shən *or* i mā'sē ā'shən) *n.* an unnatural thinness from loss of flesh; wasting away.

em·a·nate (em′ə nāt′) v. -nat·ed, -nat·ing. come forth: *Fragrance emanated from the flowers. The rumor emanated from Ottawa.* [< L *emanare* < *ex-* out + *manare* flow]
☛ *Syn.* See note at **issue.**

em·a·na·tion (em′ə nā′shən) n. 1 a coming forth. 2 anything that comes forth from a source: *Light and heat are emanations from the sun.* 3 *Chemistry.* a gas given off by a disintegrating radio-active substance.

e·man·ci·pate (i man′sə pāt′) v. -pat·ed, -pat·ing. release from slavery or restraint; set free. [< L *emancipare* < *ex-* away + *manceps* purchaser < *manus* hand + *capere* take]
—**e·man′ci·pa′tion,** n. —**e·man′ci·pa′tor,** n.

e·mas·cu·late (v. i mas′kyə lāt′; adj. i mas′kyə lit or i mas′kyə lāt′) v. -lat·ed, -lat·ing; adj. —v. 1 remove the male glands of; castrate. 2 destroy the force of; weaken: *The editor emasculated the speech by cutting out its strongest passages.* —adj. deprived of vigor; weakened; effeminate. [< L *emasculare* < *ex-* away + *masculus* male] —**e·mas′cu·la′tion,** n. —**e·mas′cu·la′tor,** n.

em·balm (em bom′ or em bäm′) v. 1 treat (a dead body) with drugs, chemicals, etc. to keep it from decaying. 2 keep in memory; preserve: *Many fine sentiments are embalmed in poetry.* 3 fill with sweet scent; perfume: *Roses embalmed the June air.* Also, **imbalm.** [ME < OF *embaumer* < *en-* in + *baume* balm < L *balsamum*] —**em·balm′er,** n. —**em·balm′ment,** n.

em·bank (em bangk′) v. protect, enclose, or confine with a raised bank of earth, stones, etc.

em·bank·ment (em bangk′mənt) n. 1 a raised bank of earth, stones, etc., used to hold back water, support a roadway, etc. 2 a protecting, enclosing, or confining with a bank of this kind.

em·bar·go (em bär′gō) n. -goes; v. -goed, -go·ing. —n. 1 an order of a government forbidding ships to enter or leave its ports: *During the war, an embargo was placed on certain vessels.* 2 any restriction put on commerce by law. 3 a restriction; restraint; hindrance.
—v. lay an embargo on; forbid to enter or leave port. [< Sp. *embargo* < *embargar* restrain < VL *in-* in + *barra* bar]

em·bark (em bärk′) v. 1 go on board ship: *Many people embark for Europe in Montreal.* 2 enter a plane, bus, train, etc. as a passenger. 3 put on board ship: *The general embarked his troops.* 4 set out; start: *After leaving university, the young man embarked on a business career.* 5 involve (a person) in an enterprise; invest (money) in an enterprise: *He foolishly embarked much money in the swindler's scheme and so lost it all.* [< F *embarquer* < *en-* in + *barque* bark³] —**em′bar·ka′tion,** n.

em·bar·rass (em bar′əs or em ber′əs) v. 1 disturb (a person); make self-conscious: *Meeting strangers embarrassed the shy boy so that he blushed and stammered.* 2 complicate; mix up; make difficult: *He embarrasses discussion of the simplest subject by use of technical terms.* 3 involve in difficulties; hinder: *Heavy equipment embarrassed the army's movements.* 4 burden with debt; involve in financial difficulties. [< F *embarrasser,* literally, to block < Ital. *imbarazzare* (< VL *barra* bar), literally, put a block into]
☛ *Syn.* 1. See note at **confuse.**

em·bar·rass·ing (em bar′əs ing or em ber′əs ing) adj. that embarrasses. —**em′bar′rass·ing·ly,** adv.

em·bar·rass·ment (em bar′əs mənt or em ber′əs mənt) n. 1 embarrassing or being embarrassed. 2 something that embarrasses: *The bad-mannered boy was an embarrassment to his parents.*

em·bas·sa·dor (em bas′ə dər or em bas′ə dôr′) n. ambassador.

em·bas·sy (em′bə sē) n., pl. -sies. 1 an ambassador and his staff of assistants. An embassy ranks next above a legation. 2 the official residence, office, etc. of an ambassador in a foreign country. 3 the position or duties of an ambassador. 4 a person or group officially sent to a foreign government with a special errand. 5 a special errand; important mission; official message. [< OF *ambassee* < Ital. < Provençal < Gmc; cf. Gothic *andbahti* service]

em·bat·tle¹ (em bat′əl) v. -tled, -tling. 1 prepare for battle; form into battle order. 2 fortify (a town, etc.). [ME < OF *embatailler* < *en-* into + *bataille* battle < L *battuere* beat]

em·bat·tle² (em bat′əl) v. -tled, -tling. provide with battlements; fortify. [< *em-¹* + obs. *battle,* v., furnish with battlements]

em·bay (em bā′) v. 1 put or bring into a bay for shelter; force into a bay. 2 shut in; surround.

em·bed (em bed′) v. -bed·ded, -bed·ding. 1 plant in a bed: *He embedded the bulbs in a box of sand.* 2 fix or enclose in a surrounding mass: *Precious stones are found embedded in rock.* 3 fix firmly (in the mind): *Every detail of the accident is embedded in my memory.* Also, **imbed.**

em·bel·lish (em bel′ish) v. 1 decorate; adorn; ornament. 2 make more interesting by adding real or imaginary details; elaborate: *He embellished the old stories so that they sounded new.* [ME < OF *embelliss-,* a stem of *embellir* < *en-* in (intensive) + *bel* handsome < L *bellus*]

em·bel·lish·ment (em bel′ish mənt) n. 1 a decoration; adornment; ornament. 2 a detail, often imaginary, added to make a story, account, etc. more interesting.

em·ber¹ (em′bər) n. 1 a piece of wood or coal still glowing in the ashes of a fire. 2 **embers,** pl. ashes in which there is still some fire. [OE *æmerge*]

em·ber² (em′bər) adj. having to do with the Ember days. [OE *ymbren, ymbryne* course, literally, running around < *ymb* around + *ryne* a running]

Ember day *Roman Catholic and Anglican churches.* one of four series of three days each set apart for fasting and prayer. The Ember days are the Wednesday, Friday, and Saturday following the first Sunday in Lent, following Whitsunday, and including or following September 14 and December 13.

em·bez·zle (em bez′əl) v. -zled, -zling. steal by putting to one's own use money held in trust for some other person or group of persons: *The treasurer embezzled $2000 from the club's funds.* [< AF *enbesiler* < OF *besillier* maltreat, of uncertain origin] —**em·bez′zle·ment,** n. —**em·bez′zler,** n.

em·bit·ter (em bit′ər) v. make bitter; make more bitter: *The old man was embittered by the loss of his money.* —**em·bit′ter·ment,** n.

em·bla·zon (em blā′zən) v. 1 display conspicuously; picture in bright colors. 2 decorate; adorn: *The knight's shield was emblazoned with his coat of arms.* 3 praise highly; honor publicly; make known the fame of: *King Arthur's exploits were emblazoned in song and story.* —**em·bla′zon·er,** n. —**em·bla′zon·ment,** n.

em·bla·zon·ry (em blā′zən rē) n., pl. -ries. 1 a brilliant decoration; adornment; conspicuous display. 2 a display of coats of arms, etc.; heraldic decoration.

em·blem (em′bləm) n. 1 an object or representation that stands for an invisible quality, idea, etc. by some connection of thought; sign of an idea; symbol: *The dove is an emblem of peace.* 2 a heraldic device. 3 a picture suggesting a moral, often with an accompanying explanation, proverb, etc. [< L *emblema* inlaid work < Gk. *emblēma* insertion < *en-* in + *ballein* throw]
☛ *Syn.* 1. **Emblem, symbol** = an object or sign that represents something else. The two words are interchangeable in current usage; but **symbol** strictly means something naturally associated in the mind with the thing symbolized: *The crown is the symbol of kingship.* **Emblem** is usually something that is chosen arbitrarily to represent the nature of the object in mind: *The beaver and the maple leaf are both emblems of Canada.*

em·blem·at·ic (em′blə mat′ik) adj. used as an emblem; symbolical: *The Cross is emblematic of Christianity.*

em·blem·at·i·cal (em′blə mat′ə kəl) adj. emblematic. —**em′blem·at′i·cal·ly,** adv.

em·bod·i·ment (em bod′ē mənt) n. 1 embodying or being embodied. 2 that in which something is embodied; person or thing symbolizing some idea, quality, etc. 3 something embodied.

em·bod·y (em bod′ē) v. -bod·ied, -bod·y·ing. 1 put into visible form; express in definite form: *The building embodied the idea of the architect.* 2 bring together and include in a single book, law, system, etc.; organize: *The British North America Act embodies the conditions of Confederation.* 3 make part of an organized book, law, system, etc.; incorporate: *The new engineer's suggestions were embodied in the revised plan of the bridge.*

em·bold·en (em bōl′dən) v. make bold; encourage. —**em·bold′en·er,** n.

em·bol·ic (em bol′ik) adj. 1 of or caused by an embolus or embolism. 2 *Biology.* pushing or growing inwards.

em·bo·lism (em′bə liz′əm) n. 1 the obstruction of a blood vessel by an embolus. 2 embolus. [< L < Gk. *embolismos < emballein < en-* in + *ballein* throw]

em·bo·lus (em′bə ləs) n., pl. -li (-lī or -lē′). a particle of foreign matter, such as a detached blood clot, air bubble, or mass of bacteria, that has been carried along in the bloodstream until it has become lodged so as to obstruct the flow of blood. [< L < Gk. *embolos* peg; < *emballein* put in. See EMBOLISM.]

em·bon·point (än bôn pwan′) n. *French.* fatness; plumpness.

em·bos·om (em bùz′əm or em bü′zəm) v. 1 surround; enclose; envelop. 2 embrace; cherish.

em·boss (em bos′) v. 1 decorate with a design, pattern, etc. that stands out from the surface, made by pressing or moulding: *Canadian coins are embossed with letters and figures.* 2 cause to stand out from the surface: *He ran his finger over the letters to see if they had been embossed.* [ME < OF *embocer < en-* in + *boce* swelling, boss²]

em·boss·ment (em bos′mənt) n. 1 an embossing. 2 a figure carved or moulded in relief. 3 a part that sticks out; bulge.

em·bou·chure (äm′bü shür′) *n.* **1** the mouth of a river. **2** the widening of a river valley into a plain. **3** *Music.* **a** the mouthpiece of a wind instrument. **b** the shaping and use of the lips, tongue, etc. in playing such an instrument; lip. [< F *embouchure* < *emboucher* put into or discharge from a mouth < *en-* + *bouche* mouth < L *bucca*]

em·bow·er (em bou′ər) *v.* enclose in a shelter of leafy branches.

em·brace (em brās′) *v.* **-braced, -brac·ing;** *n.* —*v.* **1** clasp or hold in the arms to show love or friendship; hug. **2** hug one another: *The two lovers embraced.* **3** take up or accept, especially willingly or gladly: *to embrace an opportunity, to embrace a cause.* **4** include as an integral part: *The collection embraces all his early writings.* **5** surround; enclose: *A high wall embraced the garden.* —*n.* **1** the act of clasping or holding in the arms. **2** encirclement or grasp: *The small firm now found itself in the embrace of a multinational corporation.* **3** close association. [ME < OF *embracer* take into one's arms < VL < L *in-* in + *brachium* arm < Gk. *brachion*] —**em·brace′a·ble,** *adj.*

em·bra·sure (em brā′zhər) *n.* **1** an opening in a wall for a gun, with sides that spread outward to permit the gun to swing through a greater arc. See *fort* for picture. **2** *Architecture.* a slanting of the wall at an oblique angle on the inner sides of a window or door. [< F *embrasure* < *embraser* widen an opening]

em·bro·cate (em′brō kāt′) *v.* **-cat·ed, -cat·ing.** bathe and rub with liniment or lotion. [< LL *embrocare* < *embroc(h)a* < Gk. *embrochē* lotion < *en-* in + *brechein* wet]

em·bro·ca·tion (em′brō kā′shən) *n.* **1** a bathing and rubbing with liniment or lotion. **2** the liniment or lotion used.

em·broi·der (em broi′dər) *v.* **1** ornament (cloth, leather, etc.) with a raised design or pattern made with a needle and thread. **2** make (a design, pattern, etc.) on cloth, leather, etc. with stitches: *She embroidered flowers around the edge of the collar.* **3** do embroidery. **4** add imaginary details to; exaggerate: *He didn't exactly tell lies, but he did embroider his stories.* [< *em-¹* + *broider* < *embroider* < OF *broder*] —**em·broi′der·er,** *n.*

EMBROIDERY

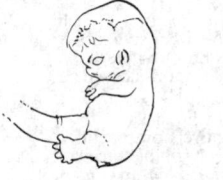

EMBROIDERY IN CROSS-STITCH

FAGGOTING USED TO FORM THE SEAMS OF A SHIRT

EMBROIDERED FLOWER WITH AN EYELET CENTRE

EMBROIDERY IN SATIN STITCH

HEMSTITCHING

FEATHERSTITCHING ALONG THE SEAMS OF A QUILT

em·broi·der·y (em broi′dər ē *or* em broi′drē) *n., pl.* **-der·ies.** **1** the act or art of embroidering. **2** raised and ornamental designs in cloth, leather, etc. sewn with a needle; embroidered work or material. **3** imaginary details; exaggeration.

em·broil (em broil′) *v.* **1** involve (a person, country, etc.) in a quarrel: *He did not wish to become embroiled in the dispute.* **2** throw (affairs, etc.) into a state of confusion. [< F *embrouiller* < *en-* in + *brouiller* to disorder] —**em·broil′er,** *n.* —**em·broil′ment,** *n.*

em·brown (em broun′) *v.* tan; darken.

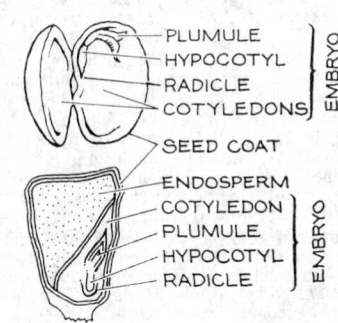

PLUMULE
HYPOCOTYL
RADICLE
COTYLEDONS
EMBRYO

SEED COAT

ENDOSPERM
COTYLEDON
PLUMULE
HYPOCOTYL
RADICLE
EMBRYO

A human embryo, above, about 6 weeks old.

Plant embryos, at right: a bean seed (top) and a corn seed (bottom)

em·bry·o (em′brē ō) *n., pl.* **-bry·os. 1** the unborn young of a vertebrate, especially a mammal, and especially during the earliest

hat, āge, fär; let, ēqual, tèrm; it, īce
hot, ōpen, ôrder; oil, out; cup, put, rüle,
above, taken, pencəl, lemən, circəs

ch, child; ng, long; sh, ship
th, thin; ғн, then; zh, measure

stage of its development; the term is used for a human offspring in the womb up to about the end of the ninth week after conception. Compare **fetus. 2** the undeveloped plant within a seed, usually consisting of a radicle, plumule, and cotyledons. **3** a beginning or undeveloped state of something. **4** (*adj.*) embryonic.
in embryo, in an undeveloped state.
[< Med.L < Gk. *embryon* < *en-* in + *bryein* swell]

em·bry·o·log·ic (em′brē ə loj′ik) *adj.* embryological.

em·bry·o·log·i·cal (em′brē ə loj′ə kəl) *adj.* of or having to do with embryology.

em·bry·ol·o·gist (em′brē ol′ə jist) *n.* a person trained in embryology, especially one whose work it is.

em·bry·ol·o·gy (em′brē ol′ə jē) *n.* the branch of biology that deals with the formation and development of embryos.

em·bry·on·ic (em′brē on′ik) *adj.* **1** of the embryo. **2** undeveloped; not mature. —**em·bry·on′i·cal′ly,** *adv.*

em·cee (*n.* em′sē′; *v.* em′sē′) *n., v.* **-ceed, -cee·ing.** *Informal.* —*n.* master of ceremonies. —*v.* act as master of ceremonies of; be master of ceremonies. Also, **M.C.**

e·mend (i mend′) *v.* suggest changes to free (a faulty text, document, etc.) from errors; correct. [< L *emendare* < *ex-* out of + *mendum, menda* fault. Doublet of AMEND.] —**e·mend′a·ble,** *adj.* —**e·mend′er,** *n.*

e·men·date (ē′men dāt′) *v.* **-dat·ed, -dat·ing.** emend.

e·men·da·tion (ē′men dā′shən *or* em′en dā′shən) *n.* **1** a correction; improvement. **2** a suggested change to free a faulty text, document, etc. from errors.

em·er·ald (em′ər əld *or* em′rəld) *n., adj.* —*n.* **1** a bright-green precious stone; transparent green beryl. **2** a piece of this stone or a gem made from it. **3** a bright green. **4** *Printing.* a size of type; 6½ point.
—*adj.* bright-green. [ME < OF *esmeralde* < L < Gk. *smaragdos*]

Emerald Isle *Poetic.* Ireland.

e·merge (i mèrj′) *v.* **-merged, -merg·ing. 1** come out; come up; come into view: *The sun emerged from behind a cloud.* **2** become known: *Many facts emerged as a result of the investigation.* [< L *emergere* < *ex-* out + *mergere* dip]
☞ *Syn.* See note at **issue.**

e·mer·gence (i mèr′jəns) *n.* the act or fact of emerging; coming into view.

e·mer·gen·cy (i mèr′jən sē) *n., pl.* **-cies. 1** a sudden need for immediate action: *I keep a fire extinguisher in my car for use in an emergency.* **2** (*adj.*) for a time of sudden need: *an emergency brake.* **3** (*adj.*) carried out or performed in a situation requiring immediate action: *an emergency operation.*
☞ *Syn.* **Emergency, crisis** = a trying or dangerous time or state of affairs. **Emergency** suggests a sudden or unexpected happening or situation that calls for action without delay: *The failure of the city's electric power caused an emergency.* **Crisis** emphasizes the life-or-death nature of a happening or situation that marks a turning point in the life of a person, country, etc.: *The floods brought a crisis into the lives of the valley's inhabitants.*
☞ *Usage.* See note at **crisis.**

emergency brake an auxiliary brake, usually hand-operated, to hold a vehicle in place when parked, stopped on a hill, etc.

e·mer·gent (i mèr′jənt) *adj.* emerging.

e·mer·i·tus (i mer′ə təs) *adj., n.* —*adj.* retired from an office or position but retaining one's rank and title as an honor: *a professor emeritus.* —*n.* a person holding such an honorary title and rank. [< L *emeritus,* pp. of *emerere* + *ex-* to the end + *merere* serve]

e·mer·sion (i mèr′zhən *or* i mèr′shən) *n.* an emerging. [< L *emersio, -onis* < *emergere.* See EMERGE.]

em·er·y (em′ər ē *or* em′rē) *n.* a hard, dark mineral, an impure corundum, used for grinding, smoothing, and polishing. [< F *émeri* < Ital. < VL *smericulum* < Med.Gk. *smēris* < Gk. *smyris* abrasive powder]

e·met·ic (i met′ik) *adj., n.* —*adj.* causing vomiting. —*n.* something that causes vomiting. [< L < *emeticus* < Gk. *emetikos* < *emeein* vomit]

EMF, emf, or **E.M.F.** electromotive force.

em·i·grant (em′ə grənt) *n., adj.* —*n.* a person who leaves his own country or region to settle in another. Compare **immigrant.** —*adj.* leaving one's own country or region to settle in another.

em·i·grate (em′ə grāt′) v. **-grat·ed, -grat·ing.** leave one's own country or region to settle in another: *Many people emigrated from Russia during the revolution.* Compare **immigrate.** [< L *emigrare* < *ex-* out + *migrare* move]

em·i·gra·tion (em′ə grā′shən) n. **1** the act of leaving one's own country or region to settle in another: *In recent years there has been much emigration from Europe to Canada.* **2** a movement of emigrants.

é·migré (em′ə grā′; *French,* ā mē grā′) n., pl. **-grés** (-grāz′; *French,* -grā′). *French.* **1** an emigrant. **2** a royalist refugee from France during the French Revolution. **3** a refugee from Russia during and after the Russian Revolution.

em·i·nence (em′ə nəns) n. **1** a rank or position above all or most others; high standing; greatness; fame. **2** a high place; lofty hill. **3 Eminence,** *Roman Catholic Church.* the title of honor given to a cardinal.

é·mi·nence grise (ā mē näns grēz′) n., pl. **é·mi·nences grises** (ā mē näns grēz′) *French.* a person who exercises power unofficially or behind the scenes. [literally, grey eminence, a nickname of Père Joseph (died 1638), a French monk who was private secretary to Cardinal Richelieu.]

em·i·nent (em′ə nənt) adj. **1** distinguished; exalted: *The Governor General is an eminent man.* **2** conspicuous; noteworthy: *The judge was a man of eminent fairness.* **3** high; lofty. **4** prominent; projecting. [< L *eminens, -entis,* ppr. of *eminere* be prominent < *ex-* out + *minere* jut] **—em′i·nent·ly,** adv.

☛ *Syn.* **2. Eminent, prominent, distinguished** = well-known. **Eminent** = standing high among or above all others of the same kind because of excellence in something: *Wolfe and Montcalm were eminent generals.* **Prominent** = standing out from the crowd, and suggests being well-known at least locally: *The president of that bank is a prominent man in his home town.* **Distinguished** = set off from others of the same kind because of outstanding qualities, and suggests being well-known to the public: *Lieutenant-generals are distinguished officers.*

☛ *Usage.* Do not confuse **eminent** and **imminent.**

eminent domain *Law.* the right of the government to take private property for public use. The owner must be paid for the property taken.

e·mir (ə mēr′) n. **1** a Moslem title given to rulers, governors, and military and naval commanders. **2** a title of dignity given to the descendants of Mohammed. Also, **amir.** [< Arabic *amir* commander]

e·mir·ate (ə mēr′it) n. **1** the rank or authority of an emir. **2** the territory governed by an emir.

em·is·sar·y (em′ə ser′ē) n., pl. **-sar·ies.** a person sent on a mission or errand, especially one sent secretly. [< L *emissarius* < *emittere.* See EMIT.]

e·mis·sion (i mish′ən) n. **1** the act or fact of emitting. **2** the thing emitted. **3** *Electronics.* **a** the streaming out of electrons from the heated cathode of a vacuum tube. **b** the streaming out of electrons from an electrode subjected to irradiation or to the impact of electrons or ions. [< L *emissio, -onis* < *emittere.* See EMIT.]

e·mis·sive (i mis′iv) adj. emitting.

e·mit (i mit′) v. **e·mit·ted, e·mit·ting. 1** give off; send out; discharge: *The sun emits light and heat. Volcanoes emit lava.* **2** put into circulation; issue. **3** utter; express: *The trapped lion emitted roars of rage.* [< L *emittere* < *ex-* out + *mittere* send]

e·mit·ter (i mit′ər) n. **1** the electrode in a transistor that is the source of electrons. **2** a substance that emits radio-active particles: *a beta emitter.* **3** any person or thing that emits.

Em·man·u·el (i man′yü əl) n. Christ. Also, **Immanuel.**

Em·men·ta·ler (em′ən tä′lər) n. a pale-yellow Swiss cheese made from whole milk. [< G *Emmentaler* < *Emmenthal,* a town in Switzerland]

Em·men·thal (em′ən täl′) n. Emmentaler.

em·met (em′it) n. *Archaic.* ant. [OE *æmete*]

Em·my (em′ē) n., pl. **-mies.** an annual award presented in the United States by the Academy of Television Art and Sciences for outstanding achievement in the field of television. The Emmy is a gold-plated statuette. [origin uncertain]

EMO Emergency Measures Organization.

e·mol·lient (i mol′yənt *or* i mol′ē ənt) adj., n. **—**adj. softening; soothing. **—**n. something that softens and soothes: *Cold cream is an emollient for the skin. His encouragement was an emollient to her troubled mind.* [< L *emolliens, -entis,* ppr. of *emollire* soften < *ex-* (intensive) + *mollis* soft]

e·mol·u·ment (i mol′yə mənt) n. the profit from a job, office, or position; salary; fee. [< L *emolumentum* profit, ult. < *ex-* out + *molere* grind]

e·mote (i mōt′) v. **e·mot·ed, e·mot·ing.** *Informal.* **1** act, especially in an exaggerated manner. **2** show emotion. **—e·mot′er,** n.

e·mo·tion (i mō′shən) n. **1** feeling as opposed to reason: *Fear, anger, love, joy, and grief are emotions.* **2** a strong feeling; a subjective reaction involving psychological and physical changes; excitement or agitation: *a voice choked with emotion, an emotion-charged meeting.* [< F *émotion* (after *motion*) < *émouvoir* stir up < L *emovere* < *ex-* out + *movere* move]

☛ *Syn.* See **feeling.**

e·mo·tion·al (i mō′shən əl *or* i mōsh′nəl) adj. **1** of or having to do with the emotions. **2** showing emotion. **3** appealing to the emotions: *The guest speaker made an emotional plea for money to help crippled children.* **4** easily affected by emotion: *Emotional people are likely to cry if they hear sad music or read sad stories.* **—e·mo′tion·al·ly,** adv.

e·mo·tion·al·ism (i mō′shən əl iz′əm *or* i mōsh′nəl iz′əm) n. **1** an emotional quality or character. **2** an appeal to the emotions. **3** a tendency to display emotion too easily.

e·mo·tion·al·ist (i mō′shə nə list *or* i mōsh′nə list) n. **1** a person whose emotions are easily aroused. **2** a person who uses the emotions to try to influence others. **3** a person who bases theories of conduct on the emotions.

e·mo·tive (i mō′tiv) adj. **1** showing or causing emotion. **2** having to do with the emotions. **—e·mo′tive·ly,** adv. **—e·mo′tive·ness,** n.

em·pan·el (em pan′əl) v. **-elled** or **-eled, -el·ling** or **-el·ing.** impanel.

em·pa·thet·ic (em′pə thet′ik) adj. of, having to do with, or characterized by empathy.

em·path·ic (em path′ik) adj. empathetic.

em·pa·thize (em′pə thīz′) v. **—ized, —iz·ing.** feel empathy: *to emphathize with someone's aspirations.*

em·pa·thy (em′pə thē) n. *Psychology.* the quality or process of entering fully, through imagination, into another's feelings or motives, into the meaning of a work of art, etc. [< Gk. *empatheia* < *en-* in + *pathos* feeling]

em·pen·nage (em pen′ij) n. *Aeronautics.* the tail assembly of an aircraft. [< F *empennage* feathering of an arrow < OF *empenner* to feather (an arrow)]

em·per·or (em′pər ər) n. a man who is the sovereign ruler of an empire. [ME < OF *empereor* < L *imperator* commander < *imperare* command < *in-* in + *parare* order]

em·pha·sis (em′fə sis) n., pl. **-ses** (-sēz′). **1** special force; stress; importance: *emphasis on scientific studies.* **2** special force or loudness given to particular syllables, words, or phrases; stress. [< L < Gk. < *emphainein* indicate < *en-* in + *phainein* show]

em·pha·size (em′fə sīz′) v. **-sized, -siz·ing. 1** give special force to; stress; make important: *He emphasized that word by saying it very loudly.* **2** call attention to: *Accidents emphasize the need for careful driving.*

em·phat·ic (em fat′ik) adj. **1** spoken or done with force or stress; strongly expressed: *Her answer was an emphatic "No!"* **2** speaking with force or stress; expressing oneself strongly: *The emphatic speaker kept pounding the table and shouting.* **3** attracting attention; very noticeable; striking: *The club made an emphatic success of their party.* [< Gk. *emphatikos* < *emphainein.* See EMPHASIS.] **—em·phat′i·cal·ly,** adv.

em·phy·se·ma (em′fə sē′mə) n. a condition especially of the lung, in which body tissue becomes bloated by air. [< NL < Gk. *emphysēma* bodily inflation] **—em′phy·se·mat′ic,** adj.

em·pire (em′pīr) n. **1** a group of countries or states under the same ruler or government, one country having some measure of control over the rest: *the British Empire.* **2** a country ruled by an emperor or empress: *the Japanese Empire.* **3** absolute power; supreme authority. [ME < OF < L *imperium*]

Em·pire (em′pīr) adj. **1** of or having to do with the first French Empire (1804-1815). **2 a** of, like, or having to do with a style of massive, ornate furniture in fashion during the Empire period. **b** of, like, or having to do with a style of high-waisted, short-sleeved woman's dress in fashion during this period.

em·pir·ic (em pir′ik) n., adj. **—**n. **1** a person who lacks theoretical or scientific knowledge and relies entirely on practical experience. **2** a person without regular or proper training; quack. **—**adj. empirical. [< L *empiricus* < Gk. *empeirikos* < *en-* in + *peira* experience, experiment]

em·pir·i·cal (em pir′ə kəl) adj. **1** based on experiment and observation: *Chemistry is largely an empirical science.* **2** based entirely on practical experience, without regard to science or theory: *The quack doctor had only an empirical knowledge of medicine.* **—em·pir′i·cal·ly,** adv.

em·pir·i·cism (em pir′ə siz′əm) n. **1** the use of methods based on experiment and observation, especially as practised in the natural sciences. **2** *Philosophy.* the theory that all knowledge is

based on experience. **3** reliance on experience without the aid of science; unscientific practice or quackery.

em·pir·i·cist (em pir′ə sist) *n.* a person who practises or advocates empiricism.

em·place·ment (em plās′mənt) *n.* **1** a space or platform for a heavy gun or guns. **2** a placing in position: *the emplacement of windows into a wall.*

em·plane (em plān′) *v.* **-planed, -plan·ing.** **1** get on an airplane. **2** put (someone or something) on an airplane.

em·ploy (em ploi′) *v., n.* —*v.* **1** use the services of; give work and pay to: *That big factory employs many workers.* **2** use: *You employ a knife, fork, and spoon in eating.* **3** engage the attention of; keep busy; occupy: *Instead of wasting time, she employed herself in reading.* —*n.* being employed; service for pay; employment: *There are many workers in the employ of the government.* [< F *employer* < L *implicare* < *in-* in + *plicare* fold. Doublet of IMPLICATE, IMPLY.] —**em·ploy′a·ble,** *adj.*
☛ *Syn. v.* **1. Employ, hire** = give work and pay to someone. **Employ** emphasizes a certain regularity and dignity in the work even though it is done for pay: *The steel mill employs most of the men in the town.* **Hire,** the more everyday word, emphasizes the fact of the work being paid: *She hired a man to mow the lawn.* **2.** See note at **use.**

em·ploy·e or **em·ploy·é** (em ploi′ē or em′ploi ē′) See **employee.**

em·ploy·ee (em ploi′ē or em′ploi ē′) *n.* a person who works for some person or firm for pay. [< F *employé,* pp. of *employer* employ]

em·ploy·er (em ploi′ər) *n.* **1** a person or firm that employs one or more persons. **2** user.

em·ploy·ment (em ploi′mənt) *n.* **1** employing or being employed. **2** what a person does for a living; work. **3** use: *There is a clever employment of color in that painting.*
☛ *Syn.* **2.** See note at **occupation.**

em·po·ri·um (em pô′rē əm) *n., pl.* **-ri·ums, -ri·a** (-rē ə). **1** a centre of trade; market place. **2** a large store selling many different things. [< L < Gk. *emporion* < *emporos* merchant, traveller < *en-* on + *poros* voyage]

em·pow·er (em pou′ər) *v.* **1** give power or authority to: *The secretary was empowered to sign certain contracts.* **2** enable; permit: *Man's erect position empowers him to use his hands freely.* Also, **impower.**

em·press (em′pris) *n.* **1** the wife of an emperor. **2** a woman who is the sovereign ruler of an empire.

em·prise or **em·prize** (em prīz′) *n. Archaic.* **1** an adventure; daring undertaking. **2** knightly daring. [ME < OF *emprise,* originally fem. pp. of *emprendre* undertake < *en-* in + *prendre* take < L *prehendere*]

emp·ty (emp′tē) *adj.* **-ti·er, -ti·est;** *v.* **-tied, -ty·ing;** *n., pl.* **-ties.** —*adj.* **1** with nothing or no one in it: *The birds had gone and their nest was empty.* **2** vacant; unoccupied: *an empty room or house.* **3** having no cargo; unloaded: *an empty ship.* **4** not real; meaningless: *An empty promise is insincere. An empty threat has no force behind it.* **5** lacking knowledge or sense; foolish; frivolous. **6** *Informal.* hungry.
empty of, without; lacking.
—*v.* **1** pour out or take out the contents of; make empty: *Empty the box of rubbish into the fire.* **2** become empty: *The hall emptied as soon as the concert was over.* **3** flow out; discharge: *The St. Lawrence River empties into the Gulf of St. Lawrence.* —*n. Informal.* something that is empty; an empty bottle, container, freight car, etc. [OE *æmtig* < *æmetta* leisure] —**emp′ti·ly,** *adv.* —**emp′ti·ness,** *n.*

emp·ty-hand·ed (emp′tē han′did) *adj.* having nothing in the hands; bringing or taking nothing: *We expected our uncle to bring a present for each of us, but he arrived empty-handed.*

emp·ty-head·ed (emp′tē hed′id) *adj.* silly; stupid.

empty set *Mathematics.* a set that has no members.

em·pur·pled (em pėr′pəld) *adj.* made purple; colored with purple.

em·pyr·e·al (em pir′ē əl, em pīr′ē əl, *or* em′pə rē′əl) *adj.* of the empyrean; celestial; heavenly.

em·py·re·an (em′pī rē′ən *or* em′pə rē′ən) *n., adj.* —*n.* **1** the highest heaven; region of pure light. **2** the sky; firmament; the vault of the heavens. —*adj.* empyreal. [< LL *empyreus* < Gk. *empyrios,* *empyros* < *en-* in + *pyr* fire]

e·mu (ē′myü) *n.* a very large flightless bird (*Dromaius novae hollandiae*) of Australia, the only living member of the family Dromaiidae, resembling an ostrich but smaller. [< Pg. *ema* ostrich, crane]

e.m.u., emu, or **E.M.U.** electromagnetic unit.

em·u·late (em′yə lāt′) *v.* **-lat·ed, -lat·ing.** try to equal or excel:

hat, āge, fär; let, ēqual, tėrm; it, īce
hot, ōpen, ôrder; oil, out; cup, pút, rüle,
əbove, takən, pencəl, lemən, circəs
ch, child; ng, long; sh, ship
th, thin; ŦH, then; zh, measure

The proverb tells us to emulate the industry of the ant. [< L *aemulari* < *aemulus* striving to equal] —**em′u·la′tor,** *n.*

em·u·la·tion (em′yə lā′shən) *n.* imitation in order to equal or excel; ambition or desire to equal or excel.

em·u·la·tive (em′yə lə tiv *or* em′yə lā′tiv) *adj.* **1** tending to emulate. **2** of or caused by emulation. —**em′u·la·tive·ly,** *adv.*

em·u·lous (em′yə ləs) *adj.* wishing to equal or excel. [< L *aemulus*] —**em′u·lous·ly,** *adv.* —**em′u·lous·ness,** *n.*

e·mul·si·fi·ca·tion (i mul′sə fə kā′shən) *n.* emulsifying or being emulsified.

e·mul·si·fy (i mul′sə fī′) *v.* **-fied, -fy·ing.** make into an emulsion. —**e·mul′si·fi′er,** *n.*

e·mul·sion (i mul′shən) *n.* **1** a mixture of liquids that do not dissolve in each other. In an emulsion very fine drops of one of the liquids are evenly distributed throughout the other. **2** *Pharmacy.* a milky liquid containing very tiny drops of fat, oil, etc. Cod-liver oil is made into an emulsion to improve its taste. **3** a light-sensitive coating on a camera film, plate, etc. [< NL *emulsio, -onis* < L *emulgere* < *ex-* out + *mulgere* milk]

en (en) *n.* **1** the letter N, n. **2** *Printing.* half the width of an em.

en-[1] *prefix.* **1** cause to be; make, as in *enable, enfeeble.* **2** put in; put on, as in *encircle, enthrone.* **3** other meanings, as in *enact, encourage, entwine.* The addition of *en-* rarely changes the meaning of a verb except to make it more emphatic. Also, **em-,** before *b, p,* and sometimes *m.* [< OF < L *in-* < *in* in, into]

en-[2] *prefix.* in; on, as in *energy.* Also, **em-,** before *b, m, p, ph.* [< Gk.]

-en[1] *suffix.* **1** cause to be; make, as in *blacken, sharpen.* **2** cause to have, as in *heighten, strengthen.* **3** become, as in *sicken, soften.* **4** come to have; gain, as in *lengthen.* [OE *-nian*]

-en[2] *suffix.* made of, as in *silken, wooden, woollen.* [OE]

-en[3] *suffix.* -en (or -n) ends the past participles of many strong verbs, as in *fallen, shaken, written, sworn.* [OE]

-en[4] *suffix.* -en is used to form the plural of a few nouns, as in *children, oxen.* [OE -an]

en·a·ble (en ā′bəl) *v.* **-bled, -bling.** give ability, power, or means to; make able: *Airplanes enable people to travel through the air.*

en·act (en akt′) *v.* **1** pass (a bill) giving it validity as law; make into a law. **2** decree; order. **3** play the part of; act out; play: *In his time, the famous actor had enacted many characters from Shakespeare.*

en·act·ment (en akt′mənt) *n.* **1** enacting or being enacted. **2** law.

e·nam·el (i nam′əl) *n., v.* **-elled** or **-eled, -el·ling** or **-el·ing.** —*n.* **1** a glasslike substance melted and then cooled to make a smooth, hard surface. Different colors of enamel are used to cover or decorate metal, pottery, etc. **2** a paint or varnish used to make a smooth, hard, glossy surface. **3** the smooth, hard, glossy outer layer of the teeth. **4** anything covered or decorated with enamel. **5** any smooth, hard, shiny coating or surface. —*v.* **1** cover or decorate with enamel. **2** form an enamel-like surface upon. **3** adorn with various colors; decorate as if with enamel. [ME < AF *enamayller* < *en-* on + *amayl* enamel < Gmc.] —**e·nam′el·ler** or **e·nam′el·er,** *n.*

e·nam·el·ware (i nam′əl wer′) *n.* pots, pans, etc. that are made of metal coated with enamel.

en·am·or or **en·am·our** (en am′ər) *v.* arouse to love; cause to fall in love; charm: *Her beauty enamored the prince.* [< OF *enamourer* < *en-* in + *amour* love < L *amor*]

en·am·ored or **en·am·oured** (en am′ərd) *adj.* very much in love; captivated; charmed (*usually used with* of): *He was enamored of the boss's daughter.*

en a·vant (äN nä väN′) *French.* forward.

en bloc (en′blok′ *or* äN′blok′; *French,* äN blôk′) all together; in one lump. [< F]

en·camp (en kamp′) *v.* **1** make a camp: *It took the soldiers only an hour to encamp.* **2** stay in a camp: *They encamped there for three weeks.* **3** put in a camp: *They were encamped in tents.* —**en·camp′ment,** *n.*

en·cap·su·late (en kap′sə lāt′ *or* en kap′syə lāt′) *v.* **-lat·ed, -lat·ing.** **1** enclose or be enclosed in or as if in a capsule: *The book encapsulates a vanishing way of life.* **2** condense; abridge.

en·case (en kās′) v. **-cased, -cas·ing.** incase.

en·caus·tic (en kos′tik or en kôs′tik) n., adj. Ceramics, etc. —n. **1** the method or process of burning in colors. **2** a work produced by this method. —adj. decorated by burning in colors. Encaustic tile is decorated by burning in colored clays.

–ence suffix. **1** the act, fact, quality, or state of ——ing, as in abhorrence, dependence, indulgence. **2** the quality or state of being ——ent, as in absence, confidence, competence, independence, prudence. See also **-ency.** [< L -entia]

en·ceinte (en sent′; French, än sant′) adj. pregnant. [< F]

en·ce·phal·ic (en′sə fal′ik) adj. of or having to do with the brain. [< Gk. enkephalos brain]

en·ceph·a·lit·ic (en sef′ə lit′ik) adj. having to do with or suffering from encephalitis.

en·ceph·a·li·tis (en sef′ə lī′tis) n. an inflammation of the brain caused by injury, infection, poison, etc. Sleeping sickness is one kind of encephalitis. [< NL < Gk. enkephalos brain + Gk. -itis]

en·ceph·a·lo·gram (en sef′ə lə gram′) n. an X-ray photograph of the brain.

en·ceph·a·lo·my·e·li·tis (en sef′ə lō mī′ə lī′təs) n. an inflammation of the brain and spine, found in humans and certain animals, especially horses.

en·ceph·a·lon (en sef′ə lon′) n. brain. [< NL < Gk. enkephalos < en- in + kephalē head]

en·chain (en chān′) v. **1** put in chains; fetter. **2** attract and fix firmly; hold fast: The speaker's earnestness enchained the attention of his audience.

en·chant (en chant′) v. **1** use magic on; put under a spell: The witch enchanted the princess. **2** delight greatly; charm. [< F enchanter < L incantare < in- against + cantare chant] —**en·chant′er,** n.

en·chant·ing (en chant′ing) adj. **1** very delightful; charming. **2** bewitching.

en·chant·ment (en chant′mənt) n. **1** the use of magic; the act of putting under a spell. **2** the condition of being put under a magic spell. **3** a magic spell. **4** delight; rapture. **5** something that delights or charms; great delight; charm.

en·chan·tress (en chan′tris) n. **1** a woman who makes magic spells; witch. **2** a very delightful, charming woman.

en·chase (en chās′) v. **-chased, -chas·ing. 1** engrave: His initials were enchased on the back of the watch. **2** ornament with engraved designs; decorate with gems, inlay, etc.: The shield was enchased with gold and silver. **3** place in a setting; mount; frame. [< F enchâsser < en- in + châsse frame, case < L capsa box]

en·chi·la·da (en′chi lä′də) n. a tortilla rolled around a filling of meat, cheese, etc., served with a peppery sauce. [< Mexican Sp., ult. < Sp. en- in + Nahuatl chili chili]

en·cir·cle (en sèr′kəl) v. **-cled, -cling. 1** form a circle around; surround: Trees encircled the pond. **2** go in a circle around: The moon encircles the earth.

en·cir·cle·ment (en sèr′kəl mənt) n. encircling or being encircled.

en·clave (en′klāv) n. **1** a country or district surrounded by the territory of another country. **2** a separate or distinct unit enclosed within a larger one. [< F enclave < enclaver enclose]

en·clit·ic (en klit′ik) n. a word or contraction that, having no stress, is pronounced as part of the preceding word. Examples: not in I cannot tell; s in Bert's here (= Bert is here). [< LL encliticus < Gk. enklitikos < enklinein lean on < en- in, on + klinein lean, incline]

en·close (en klōz′) v. **-closed, -clos·ing. 1** shut in on all sides; surround. **2** put a wall or fence around. **3** include in an envelope or package along with something else: A cheque was enclosed with the letter. Also, **inclose.** [< en-¹ in + close, v., ME, after OF enclos, pp. of enclore]

en·clo·sure (en klō′zhər) n. **1** enclosing or being enclosed. **2** something that encloses, such as a wall or fence. **3** an enclosed place or area: The cows were herded into the enclosure. **4** something enclosed, especially additional material enclosed in an envelope with a letter. Also, **inclosure.**

en·code (en kōd′) v. **-cod·ed, -cod·ing.** put into code: The spy encoded his message before mailing it. —**en·cod′er,** n.

en·co·mi·ast (en kō′mi ast′) n. a writer or speaker of encomiums; eulogist. [< Gk. enkōmiastēs < enkōmion. See ENCOMIUM.]

en·co·mi·um (en kō′mē əm) n., pl. **-mi·ums, -mi·a** (-mē ə). an elaborate expression of praise; high praise; eulogy. [< LL < Gk. enkōmion, neut., laudatory < en- in + kōmos revelry]

en·com·pass (en kum′pəs) v. **1** surround completely; shut in on all sides; encircle: The atmosphere encompasses the earth. **2** enclose; contain. —**en·com′pass·ment,** n.

en·core (ong′kôr or on′kôr) interj., n., v. **-cored, -cor·ing.** —interj. once more; again. —n. **1** an extra performance or appearance by a musician, entertainer, etc. in response to audience demand. **2** a demand by an audience for such a performance or appearance. —v. call for a repetition of a song, etc., or the reappearance of a performer, etc.: The audience encored the singer by applauding. [< F]

en·coun·ter (en koun′tər) v., n. —v. **1** meet unexpectedly: I encountered an old friend on the train. **2** meet with (difficulties, opposition, etc.); be faced with. **3** meet as an enemy; meet in a fight or battle. —n. **1** a meeting; unexpected meeting. **2** a meeting of two opposed forces, teams, etc.; a fight; battle. [ME < OF encontrer < VL < L in- in + contra against]

en·cour·age (en kèr′ij) v. **-aged, -ag·ing. 1** give courage to; increase the hope or confidence of; urge on: Success encourages you to go ahead and do better. **2** be favorable to; help; support: High prices for farm products encourage farming. [ME < OF encoragier < en- in + corage courage, ult. < L cor heart] —**en·cour′ag·er,** n. —**en·cour′ag·ing·ly,** adv.

en·cour·age·ment (en kèr′ij mənt) n. **1** encouraging. **2** the state of being or feeling encouraged. **3** something that encourages.

en·croach (en krōch′) v. **1** go beyond proper or usual limits: The sea encroached upon the shore and submerged the beach. **2** trespass upon the property or rights of another; intrude: He is a good salesman and will not encroach upon his customer's time. [< OF encrochier < en- in + croc hook < Gmc.] —**en·croach′er,** n.

☛ Syn. **2.** See note at **intrude.**

en·croach·ment (en krōch′mənt) n. **1** encroaching. **2** something taken by encroaching.

en·crust (en krust′) v. incrust.

en·crus·ta·tion (en′krus tā′shən) n. incrustation.

en·cum·ber (en kum′bər) v. **1** hold back (from running, doing, etc.); hinder; hamper: Heavy shoes encumber the wearer in the water. **2** make difficult to use; fill; obstruct: Rubbish and old boxes encumbered the fire escape. **3** weigh down; burden: The farm was encumbered with a heavy mortgage. Also, **incumber.** [ME < OF encombrer < en- in + combre barrier, probably < Celtic]

en·cum·brance (en kum′brəns) n. **1** anything that encumbers; a hindrance; obstruction. **2** an annoyance; trouble; burden. **3** a dependent person; child. **4** Law. a claim, mortgage, etc. on property. Also, **incumbrance.**

–ency noun-forming suffix. **1** the act, fact, quality, or state of ——ing, as in dependency. **2** the quality or state of being ——ent, as in clemency, frequency. **3** other meanings, as in agency, currency. See also **-ence.** [< L -entia]

encyc. or **ency.** encyclopedia.

en·cyc·li·cal (en sik′lə kəl or en sī′klə kəl) n., adj. —n. Roman Catholic Church. a letter from the Pope to his clergy. —adj. intended for wide circulation. [< LL encyclicus < Gk. enkyklios < en- in + kyklos circle]

en·cy·clo·pe·di·a or **en·cy·clo·pae·di·a** (en sī′klə pē′dē ə) n. **1** a book or series of books giving information, usually arranged alphabetically, on all branches of knowledge. **2** a book treating one subject very thoroughly, with its articles arranged alphabetically: a medical encyclopedia. [< LL encyclopaedia < Gk. enkyklopaideia, for enkyklios paideia well-rounded education]

en·cy·clo·pe·dic or **en·cy·clo·pae·dic** (en sī′klə pē′dik) adj. **1** covering a wide range of subjects; possessing wide and varied information. **2** of or having to do with an encyclopedia. —**en·cy′clo·pe′dic·al·ly,** adv.

en·cy·clo·pe·dist or **en·cy·clo·pae·dist** (en sī′klə pē′dist) n. a person who makes or compiles an encyclopedia.

en·cyst (en sist′) v. enclose or become enclosed in a cyst or sac. —**en·cyst′ment,** n.

end (end) n., v. —n. **1** the last part; conclusion: He read through to the end of the book. **2** the edge or outside limit of an object or area; boundary: Those trees mark the end of their property. **3** the point where something that has length stops or ceases to be: Every stick has two ends. **4** a purpose; object: The end of work is to get something done. **5** a result; outcome: It is hard to tell what the end will be. **6** death; destruction: He met his end in the accident. **7** a cause of death or destruction. **8** a part left over; remnant; fragment. **9** Football. the player at either end of the line. **10** the furthest or most distant part; extreme point: The police will hunt the murderer to the ends of the earth. **11** Curling. one of the divisions of a game: Our team was beaten in the last end.

loose ends, a not settled or established. **b** in confusion or disorder.

end to end, with the end of one object set next to the end of

another; endways: *The dominoes were arranged end to end on the table.*

jump or **go off the deep end,** *Slang.* act suddenly and rashly without deliberation.

keep or **hold** (one's) **end up,** sustain one's part or bear one's share fully in an undertaking or performance.

make an end of, stop; do no more.

make both ends meet, a spend no more than one has. **b** just manage to live on what one has.

no end, *Informal.* very much; very many: *We had no end of trouble with that car.*

on end, a upright in position: *He stood the dominoes on end.* **b** one after another: *It snowed for days on end.*

put an end to, stop; do away with; destroy; kill.
—*v.* **1** have a boundary: *Their property ends here.* **2** bring or come to an end; stop; finish: *Let us end this fight.* **3** form the end of; be the end of: *This chapter ends the book.* **4** destroy; kill. **5** surpass: *It was a holiday to end all holidays.* **6** arrive at a particular final stage, condition, rank, etc. (*used with* **up**): *She ended up a judge. You'll end up in the water if you keep rocking the boat.* [OE *ende*]
—**end′er,** *n.*

☛ *Syn. v.* **1. End, conclude, finish** = bring or come to a close. **End** suggests a sudden stop or natural close: *My holidays ended when school started.* **Conclude** is a formal word and suggests a formal ending of a speech, essay, action, piece of business, etc.: *Singing the national anthem will conclude the meeting.* **Finish** suggests ending only after getting everything done that should be done: *I never finish my homework on time.*

end-all (end′ol′ *or* -ôl′) *n.* the ultimate; the end of everything.

en·dan·ger (en dān′jər) *v.* cause danger to; expose to loss or injury: *Fire endangered the hotel's guests, but no lives were lost.*

en·dear (en dēr′) *v.* make dear: *Her kindness endeared her to all of us.* —**en·dear′ing·ly,** *adv.*

en·dear·ment (en dēr′mənt) *n.* **1** endearing. **2** the thing that endears. **3** an act or word showing love or affection; caress.

en·deav·or or **en·deav·our** (en dev′ər) *v., n.* —*v.* try hard; attempt earnestly; make an effort; strive. —*n.* an earnest attempt; effort. [ME < *en-¹* + *devoir* < *dever* duty < OF *deveir* < L *debere* owe] —**en·deav′or·er** or **en·deav·our·er,** *n.*

☛ *Syn. v.* See note at **try.** —*n.* See note at **effort.**

en·dem·ic (en dem′ik) *adj., n.* —*adj.* regularly found in a particular people or locality: *Cholera is endemic in India.* —*n.* an endemic disease. [< Gk. *endēmos* native < *en-* in + *dēmos* people] —**en·dem′i·cal·ly,** *adv.*

en dés·ha·bil·lé (äN dā zä bē yā′) *French.* partly or carelessly dressed.

end·ing (en′ding) *n.* **1** the last part; end. **2** death. **3** *Grammar.* a letter or syllable added to a word or stem to change its meaning or to show how it is used in relation to other words. The common plural ending in English is *-s* or *-es,* as in *kings, dresses.*

en·dive (en′dīv *or* on′dīv; *French,* äN dēv′) *n.* **1** a kind of chicory having finely divided, curly leaves, used for salads. **2** a kind of chicory that has broad leaves and looks like smooth white celery, also used for salads; escarole. [ME < OF < Med.L *endivia* < L *intibus* < Gk. *entybon*]

end·less (end′lis) *adj.* **1** having no end; never stopping; lasting or going on forever: *the endless motion of the stars.* **2** appearing to have no end; seeming never to stop: *an endless task.* **3** with the ends joined; continuous: *A bicycle chain is an endless chain.* —**end′less·ly,** *adv.* —**end′less·ness,** *n.*

end man 1 the man at the end of a row or line. **2** in a minstrel show, a man at either end of a line of performers.

end·most (end′mōst′) *adj.* nearest to the end; last; farthest.

endo– *combining form.* within; inside; inner, as in *endocarp, endoderm, endogamy.* [< Gk. *endo-* < *endon*]

en·do·car·di·al (en′dō kär′dē əl) *adj.* **1** in the heart. **2** of or having to do with the endocardium.

en·do·car·di·um (en′dō kär′dē əm) *n.* the delicate, smooth membrane that lines the chambers of the heart. [< NL *endocardium* + Gk. *endon* within + *kardia* heart]

en·do·carp (en′dō kärp′) *n. Botany.* the inner layer of a fruit or ripened ovary of a plant. A peach stone is an endocarp. [< *endo-* + Gk. *karpos* fruit]

en·do·crine (en′dō krīn′, en′dō krin, *or* en′dō krēn′) *adj., n.* —*adj.* **1** producing secretions that pass directly into the blood or lymph instead of into a duct. The thyroid is an endocrine gland. **2** of or having to do with the endocrine glands or the hormones they secrete. —*n.* **1** endocrine gland. **2** its secretion. [< *endo-* + Gk. *krinein* separate]

endocrine gland any of various ductless glands that secrete hormones that influence other organs in the body.

en·do·derm (en′dō dėrm′) *n. Biology.* the inner layer of cells formed during development of animal embryos. The lining of the

hat, āge, fär; let, ēqual, tėrm; it, īce
hot, ōpen, ôrder; oil, out; cup, pút, rüle,
above, takən, pencəl, lemən, circəs

ch, child; ng, long; sh, ship
th, thin; ᵺ, then; zh, measure

organs of the digestive system develops from the endoderm. [< *endo-* + Gk. *derma* skin]

en·do·don·tics (en′dō don′tiks) *n.* (*used with a singular verb*) the branch of dentistry dealing with the diagnosis and treatment of disorders of the pulp of the teeth. [< NL *endodontia* < Gk. *endo-* within + *odōn* tooth. 19c.]

en·do·don·tist (en′dō don′tist) *n.* a dentist who specializes in endodontics; a root-canal specialist.

end of steel *Cdn.* **1** the limit to which tracks have been laid for a railway. **2** a town at the end of a railway line; the terminus of a northern railway: *A road will soon connect us with the end of steel.*

en·dog·a·mous (en dog′ə məs) *adj.* of or having to do with endogamy.

en·dog·a·my (en dog′ə mē) *n.* **1** the custom of marrying within one's own group, tribe, etc. **2** pollination of a flower by pollen from another flower on the same plant. [< *endo-* + *-gamy*]

en·dog·e·nous (en doj′ə nəs) *adj. Biology.* growing from the inside, originating within. [< *endo-* + *-genous* born, produced (< Gk. *-genēs*)]

en·dog·e·ny (en doj′ə nē) *n. Biology.* a growing from within, as in cell formation.

en·do·lymph (en′dō limf′) *n.* the fluid of the inner ear.

en·do·morph (en′də môrf′) *n.* **1** a human body type characterized by a heavy frame, relatively short stature with short limbs, and the capacity for great muscular development. It is one of three basic body types. Compare **ectomorph, mesomorph.** **2** a person having such a body structure.

en·do·mor·phic (en′də môr′fik) *adj.* of, having to do with, or being an endomorph.

end–on (end′on′) *adj.* of or on the end: *an end-on collision.*

en·do·plasm (en′dō plaz′əm) *n. Biology.* the inner portion of the cytoplasm of a cell. [< *endo-* + Gk. *plasma* something formed or moulded]

en·dor·sa·tion (en′dôr sā′shən) *n. Cdn.* approval; support: *The mayor's proposals received wide endorsation.*

en·dorse (en dôrs′) *v.* **-dorsed, -dors·ing. 1** write one's name, instructions, etc. on the back of (a cheque, money order, or other document): *He had to endorse the cheque before the bank would cash it.* **2** approve; support: *Parents heartily endorsed the plan for a school playground.* Also, **indorse.** [alteration of ME *endoss(n)* < OF *endosser* < *en-* on + *dos* back < L *dorsum*] —**en·dors′able,** *adj.* —**en·dors′er,** *n.*

en·dor·see (en′dôr sē′ *or* en′dôr sē′) *n.* a person to whom a cheque, note, or other document is assigned by endorsement. Also **indorsee.**

en·dorse·ment (en dôrs′mənt) *n.* **1** the act of writing on the back of a cheque or other document. **2** a name, comment, or instructions, etc. written on the back of a cheque or other document. **3** approval; support: *The proposal for a new stadium has our endorsement.* **4** an additional provision or clause in an insurance contract by which the coverage described in the contract may be increased or diminished. Also, **indorsement.**

en·do·skel·e·ton (en′dō skel′ə tən) *n.* the internal supporting structure of all vertebrates and some other groups of animals such as starfish, sea urchins, and some varieties of coral. Compare **exoskeleton.**

en·do·sperm (en′dō spėrm′) *n. Botany.* nourishment for the embryo enclosed with it in the seed of a plant. See **embryo** for picture.

en·dow (en dou′) *v.* **1** give money or property to provide an income for: *The rich man endowed the college he had attended.* **2** furnish at birth; provide with some ability, quality, or talent; favor: *Nature endowed her with both beauty and brains.* [ME < OF *endouer* < *en-* in + *douer* endow < L *dotare*] —**en·dow′er,** *n.*

en·dow·ment (en dou′mənt) *n.* **1** the money or property given to provide an income: *This college has a large endowment.* **2** a gift from birth; ability; talent: *A good sense of rhythm is a natural endowment.* **3** the act of endowing.

end·pa·per (end′pā′pər) *n.* a folded sheet of paper half of which is pasted to the inside of either cover of a book, the other half acting as a flyleaf.

end product 1 the part remaining after something is processed. 2 *Nuclear physics.* the last stable member of a series of isotopes, each produced by the radio-active decay of the preceding isotope.

en·due (en dyü′ *or* en dü′) *v.* **-dued, -du·ing.** 1 provide with a quality or power; furnish; supply: *The wisest man is not endued with perfect wisdom.* 2 put on. 3 clothe. Also, **indue.** [ME < OF *enduire* < L *inducere* lead into; confused with L *induere* put on]

en·dur·ance (en dyür′əns *or* en dür′əns) *n.* 1 the power to last or keep on: *A person must have great endurance to run in a marathon.* 2 the power to put up with, bear, or stand: *His endurance of the pain was remarkable.* 3 an act or instance of enduring pain, hardship, etc.

en·dure (en dyür′ *or* en dür′) *v.* **-dured, -dur·ing.** 1 keep on; last: *These statues have endured for a thousand years.* 2 undergo; bear; tolerate: *Those brave people endured much pain.* [ME < OF *endurer* < L *indurare* make hard < *in-* in (causative) + *durus* hard] **—en·dur′a·ble,** *adj.* **—en·dur′a·bly,** *adv.* **—en·dur′er,** *n.*
☛ *Syn.* 2. See note at **bear.**

en·dur·ing (en dyür′ing *or* en dür′ing) *adj.* lasting; permanent. **—en·dur′ing·ly,** *adv.*
☛ *Syn.* See note at **lasting.**

end use the particular function that a manufactured product serves or to which it is limited.

end·ways (end′wāz′) *adv.* 1 on end; upright. 2 with the end forward; in the direction of the end. 3 lengthwise. 4 end to end.

end·wise (end′wīz′) *adv.* endways.

En·dym·i·on (en dim′ē ən) *n. Greek mythology.* a beautiful youth loved by Selene, the goddess of the moon.

end zone 1 *Football.* the part of the field between each goal line and the corresponding end of the field. 2 *Hockey.* the ice between each blue line and the corresponding end of the rink.

ENE *or* **E.N.E.** east-northeast, a direction halfway between east and northeast.

en·e·ma (en′ə mə) *n., pl.* **en·e·mas, en·em·a·ta** (i nem′ə tə). 1 an injection of liquid into the rectum to flush the bowels. 2 the apparatus used. [< Gk. *enema* < *en-* in + *hienai* send]

en·e·my (en′ə mē) *n., pl.* **-mies;** *adj.* **—***n.* 1 a person or group that hates and tries to harm another. 2 a hostile force, nation, fleet, army, or air force; person, ship, etc. of a hostile nation. 3 anything harmful: *Frost is an enemy of plants.*
—*adj.* of an enemy. [ME < OF *enemi* < L *inimicus* < *in-* not + *amicus* friendly]
☛ *Syn. n.* 1, 2. **Enemy, foe** = a hostile person, group, country, army, etc. **Enemy** is the common and general word, applying to any person or group who wants or tries to harm another person or group in any way: *Because of his unfair methods that businessman has many enemies.* **Foe,** now chiefly poetic or literary, means a very dangerous and actively opposed enemy.

en·er·get·ic (en′ər jet′ik) *adj.* 1 full of energy; eager to work. 2 full of force; active. **—en′er·get′i·cal·ly,** *adv.*

en·er·gize (en′ər jīz′) *v.* **-gized, -giz·ing.** give energy to; make active.

en·er·giz·er (en′ər jī′zər) *n.* 1 any one of several drugs used to give energy or to relieve severe mental depression. 2 a device that stores chemical energy and can operate small mechanisms.

en·er·gy (en′ər jē) *n., pl.* **-gies.** 1 active strength or force; healthy power; vigor: *Young people usually have more energy than old people.* 2 strength; force; power. 3 *Physics.* the capacity for doing work, such as lifting or moving an object. Energy is measured in joules. [< LL < Gk. *energeia* < *energos* active < *en-* in + *ergon* work]

en·er·vate (en′ər vāt′) *v.* **-vat·ed, -vat·ing.** lessen the vigor or strength of; weaken: *A hot, damp climate enervates people who are not used to it.* [< L *enervare* < *ex-* away + *nervus* sinew, nerve] **—en′er·va′tion,** *n.* **—en′er·va′tor,** *n.*

en fa·mille (äN fȧ mē′) *French.* with one's family; at home; informally.

en·fant (äN fäN′) *n. French.* child.

en·fant ter·ri·ble (äN fäN te rē′blə) *French.* 1 a child whose behavior, questions, remarks, etc. embarrass older people. 2 a person who is indiscreet or lacks a sense of responsibility.

en·fee·ble (en fē′bəl) *v.* **-bled, -bling.** make feeble; weaken. **—en·fee′ble·ment,** *n.* **—en·fee′bler,** *n.*

en·fi·lade (en′fə lād′) *n., v.* **-lad·ed, -lad·ing. —***n.* gunfire directed from the side at a line of troops or a position held by them. **—***v.* fire guns at (a line of troops or the position held by them) from the side. [< F *enfilade* < *enfiler* thread, pierce < *en-* on + *fil* thread < L *filum*]

en·fold (en fōld′) *v.* 1 fold in; wrap up: *The old lady was enfolded*

in a shawl. 2 embrace; clasp: *The mother enfolded her baby in her arms.* Also, **infold.**

en·force (en fôrs′) *v.* **-forced, -forc·ing.** 1 force obedience to; put into force: *Policemen and judges enforce the laws.* 2 force; compel: *The robbers enforced obedience to their demand by threats of violence.* 3 urge with force; emphasize: *The teacher enforced the principle by examples.* [ME < OF *enforcier*, ult. < L *in-* + *fortis* strong] **—en·force′a·ble,** *adj.* **—en·forc′er,** *n.*

en·force·ment (en fôrs′mənt) *n.* an enforcing; putting into force: *Strict enforcement of the laws against speeding will reduce automobile accidents.*

en·fran·chise (en fran′chīz) *v.* **-chised, -chis·ing.** 1 give the right to vote: *For federal elections, Canadian citizens are enfranchised at the age of 18.* 2 set free; release from slavery or restraint. **—en·fran′chis·er,** *n.*

en·fran·chise·ment (en fran′chiz mənt) *n.* enfranchising or being enfranchised.

eng. 1 engineer; engineering. 2 engraving; engraved; engraver.

Eng. 1 England; English. 2 Engineer.

en·gage (en gāj′) *v.* **-gaged, -gag·ing.** 1 keep busy; occupy: *Work engages much of his time.* 2 keep oneself busy; be occupied; be active; take part: *He engages in politics. His wife engages in social work.* 3 hire; employ: *She engaged a cook for the summer.* 4 arrange to secure for occupation or use; reserve: *We engaged a room in the hotel.* 5 bind by a promise or contract; pledge: *I will engage to be there on time.* 6 promise or pledge to marry: *John and Mary are engaged. John is engaged to Mary.* 7 catch and hold; attract: *Bright colors engaged the baby's attention.* 8 fit into; lock together; interlock: *The teeth of one gear engage with the teeth of another. The teeth engage each other.* 9 come into contact with in battle; attack: *Our soldiers engaged the enemy.* [< F *engager* < *en gage* under pledge] **—en·gag′er,** *n.*

en·ga·gé (äN gä zhā′) *n. Cdn. Historical.* one hired by a fur company for inland service in the trade. [< Cdn.F < F *engagé* enlisted]

en·gaged (en gājd′) *adj.* 1 promised or pledged to marry. 2 busy; occupied: *Engaged in conversation, they did not see us.* 3 taken for use or work; hired. 4 fitted together. 5 involved in a fight or battle.

en·gage·ment (en gāj′mənt) *n.* 1 the act of engaging. 2 the fact or condition of being engaged. 3 a promise; pledge: *An honest person fulfils all his engagements.* 4 the time between becoming pledged to marry and the actual wedding: *They got married after an engagement of six months.* 5 a meeting with someone at a certain time; appointment. 6 the period of being hired; time of use or work. 7 a fight; battle.
☛ *Syn.* 7. See note at **battle.**

en·gag·ing (en gāj′ing) *adj.* very attractive; pleasing; charming. **—en·gag′ing·ly,** *adv.* **—en·gag′ing·ness,** *n.*

En·gel·mann spruce (eng′gəl mən) 1 a tall spruce (*Picea engelmannii*) found throughout the interior mountain regions of British Columbia and Alberta, having oval cones and curved bluish-green needles often covered with a whitish, powdery coating called a bloom. 2 the light, soft wood of this tree. [< George Engelmann (1809-1884), a German-born physicist and botanist]

en·gen·der (en jen′dər) *v.* bring into existence; produce; cause: *Filth engenders disease.* [ME < OF *engendrer* < L *ingenerare* < *in-* in + *generare* create]

en·gine (en′jən) *n.* 1 a machine that applies power to some work, especially a machine that can start others moving. 2 a machine that pulls a railway train. 3 a machine; device, instrument: *Those big guns are engines of war.* [ME < OF *engin* < L *ingenium* inborn qualities, talent < *in-* in + *gen-*, root of *gignere* create, produce, beget. Related to GENIUS.]

en·gi·neer (en′jə nēr′) *n., v.* **—***n.* 1 a person who takes care of or runs engines: *The driver of a locomotive is an engineer.* 2 a person trained in a branch of engineering, especially one whose profession it is. 3 a member of the armed forces trained in military construction work. 4 a person who originates and skilfully carries through a plan or enterprise.
—*v.* 1 plan, build, direct, or work as a professional engineer. 2 manage; guide: *Although many opposed his plan, he engineered it through to final approval.*

en·gi·neer·ing (en′jə nēr′ing) *n.* 1 the application of science to such practical uses as the design and building of structures and machines, and the making of many products of modern technology: *Knowledge of engineering is needed in building railways, bridges, and dams.* 2 the act of managing, contriving, or manoeuvring.

engine house a station for a fire engine.

en·gin·er·y (en′jən rē) *n.* engines; machines.

Eng·land·er (ing′glən dər) *n.* an English person.

Eng·lish (ing′glish) *n., adj., v.* **—***n.* 1 **the English,** *pl.* **a** the people of England. **b** *Cdn.* English Canadians. 2 the English language,

belonging to the West Germanic branch of the Indo-European language family; it is the traditional and official language of England, one of the official languages of Canada, and also the language of most other Commonwealth countries and the United States. It is usually divided into three main historical periods: Old English or Anglo-Saxon (before 1100), Middle English (about 1100-1500), and Modern English (from about 1500). **3** a large size of type formerly used in printing, about equal to 14 point. **4** Often, **english,** a spinning motion imparted to a ball by hitting on one side of its centre.
—*adj.* **1** of or having to do with England, its people, or the language English. **2** *Cdn.* of or having to do with Canadian English or English Canadians.
—*v.* **1** translate into or express in English. **2** Often, **english,** give a spinning motion to a (billiard ball, etc.). [OE *Englisc* < *Engle* the English people] —**Eng′lish·ness,** *n.*

English Canadian a Canadian of English ancestry or whose principal language is English, especially as opposed to French. —**Eng′lish-Ca·na′di·an,** *adj.*

English cocker spaniel a breed of hunting dog, resembling the cocker spaniel but larger, an adult weighing between 12 and 15 kg.

English horn a wooden musical instrument resembling an oboe, but larger and having a lower tone. [a mistranslation of F *cor anglé* angled, cornered horn, *anglé* being confused with *anglais* English]

Eng·lish·man (ing′glish mən) *n., pl.* **-men. 1** a man who is a native or inhabitant of England. **2** a man of English descent.

English setter a breed of setter, having black and white markings, and sometimes tan spots.

English sonnet Elizabethan sonnet.

English sparrow a small weaverbird (*Passer domesticus*) native to the Old World but now also common throughout North America and Australia, having streaked brown plumage and, in the male, a black bib. Also called **house sparrow.**

English walnut a Eurasian walnut (*Juglans regia*) long cultivated in England before being introduced to North and South America, valued as an ornamental tree and for its edible nuts and its timber.

Eng·lish·wom·an (ing′glish wùm′ən) *n., pl.* **-wom·en. 1** a woman who is a native or inhabitant of England. **2** a woman of English descent.

en·gorge (en gôrj′) *v.* **-gorged, -gorg·ing. 1** swallow greedily. **2** glut; gorge. **3** feed greedily. **4** *Medicine.* congest with blood.

engr. 1 engineer. **2** engraved; engraver; engraving.

en·graft (en graft′) *v.* **1** insert or graft a shoot from one tree or plant into or on another: *Peach trees can be engrafted on plum trees.* **2** add permanently; implant: *Honesty and thrift are engrafted in his character.* Also, **ingraft.**

en·grave (en grāv′) *v.* **-graved, -grav·ing. 1** cut in; carve artistically; decorate by engraving: *The jeweller engraved the boy's initials on the back of the watch.* **2** *Printing.* **a** cut in lines on a metal plate, block of wood, etc., for printing. **b** print from such a plate, block, etc. **3** impress deeply; fix firmly: *His mother's face was engraved on his memory.* [< *en-¹* + *grave³*]

en·grav·er (en grāv′ər) *n.* a person who engraves metal plates, blocks of wood, etc. for printing.

en·grav·ing (en grāv′ing) *n.* **1** the art of an engraver; cutting lines in metal plates, blocks of wood, etc. for printing. **2** a picture printed from an engraved plate, block, etc. **3** an engraved plate, block, etc.; engraved design or pattern.

en·gross (en grōs′) *v.* **1** occupy wholly; take up all the attention of: *She was engrossed in a story.* **2** copy or write in large letters; write a beautiful copy of. **3** write out in formal style; express in legal form. **4** *Business.* buy all or much of (the supply of some commodity) so as to control prices. [(defs. 1,4) < *in gross* < F *en gros* in a lump, in large amounts; (defs. 2, 3) < AF *engrosser* < *en-* in + *grosse* large writing, document] —**en·gross′er,** *n.* —**en·gross′ment,** *n.*

en·gulf (en gulf′) *v.* swallow up; overwhelm; submerge: *A wave engulfed the small boat.* Also, **ingulf.**

en·hance (en hans′) *v.* **-hanced, -hanc·ing.** make greater; add to; heighten: *The gardens enhanced the beauty of the house.* [ME < AF *enhauncer* raise, ult. < L *altus* high. Related to HAWSER.] —**en·hance′ment,** *n.*

en·har·mon·ic (en′här mon′ik) *adj. Music.* **1** having to do with or designating a scale, a style of music, or an instrument employing intervals smaller than a semitone, especially quarter tones. **2** of different notes on the scale that have the same tone or key on an instrument. *Example:* C sharp and D flat.

en haut (än ō′) *French.* above; on high.

e·nig·ma (i nig′mə) *n.* **1** a puzzling statement; riddle: *To most of*

hat, āge, fär; let, ēqual, tèrm; it, īce
hot, ōpen, ôrder; oil, out; cup, pùt, rüle,
əbove, takən, pencəl, lemən, circəs
ch, child; ng, long; sh, ship
th, thin; ᴛн, then; zh, measure

the audience the philosopher seemed to speak in enigmas. **2** a baffling or puzzling problem, situation, person, etc.: *The queer behavior of the child was an enigma even to its parents.* [< L < Gk. *ainigma* < *ainissesthai* speak darkly < *ainos* fable]

en·ig·mat·ic (en′ig mat′ik *or* ē′nig mat′ik) *adj.* enigmatical.

en·ig·mat·i·cal (en′ig mat′ə kəl *or* ē′nig mat′ə kəl) *adj.* like a riddle; baffling; puzzling; mysterious. —**en′ig·mat′i·cal·ly,** *adv.*

en·jamb·ment *or* **en·jambe·ment** (en jam′mənt *or* en jamb′mənt; *French,* än zhänb män′) *n. Prosody.* the continuation of a sentence without pause from one line or couplet to the next. [< F *enjambement* < MF *enjamber* encroach, stride < *en-* on + OF *jambe* leg < L *gamba*]

en·join (en join′) *v.* **1** order; direct; urge: *Parents enjoin good behavior on their children.* **2** *Law.* issue an authoritative command. Through an injunction a judge may enjoin a person not to do some act. [ME < OF *enjoindre* < L *injungere* attack, charge < *in-* on + *jungere* join] —**en·join′er,** *n.* —**en·join′ment,** *n.*

en·joy (en joi′) *v.* **1** have or use with joy; be happy with; take pleasure in. **2** have as an advantage or benefit: *He enjoyed good health.* **3** be happy; have a good time (*used with a reflexive pronoun*): *Did you enjoy yourself at the party?* [ME < OF *enjoir* < *en-* in (intensive) + *joir* rejoice < L *gaudere*] —**en·joy′er,** *n.*

en·joy·a·ble (en joi′ə bəl) *adj.* capable of being enjoyed; giving enjoyment; pleasant. —**en·joy′a·bly,** *adv.*

en·joy·ment (en joi′mənt) *n.* **1** enjoying. **2** something enjoyed. **3** joy; happiness; pleasure. **4** the condition of having as an advantage or benefit; possession; use: *Laws protect the enjoyment of our rights.*

en·kin·dle (en kin′dəl) *v.* **-dled, -dling. 1** arouse; excite; stir up. **2** light up; brighten.

en·lace (en lās′) *v.* **-laced, -lac·ing. 1** wind about; encircle; enfold. **2** twine together; interlace. [< F *enlacer*]

en·large (en lärj′) *v.* **-larged, -larg·ing. 1** make or become larger; increase in size. **2** talk or write in greater detail; elaborate (*used with on or upon*): *The reporter asked him to enlarge on his earlier statement.* [ME < OF *enlarger* < *en-* in (causative) + *large* large < L *largus* copious] —**en·larg′er,** *n.*
☛ *Syn.* **1.** See note at **increase.**

en·large·ment (en lärj′mənt) *n.* **1** enlarging or being enlarged. **2** anything that is an enlarged form of something else. **3** *Photography.* a print that is made larger than the negative. **4** anything that enlarges something else; an addition.

en·light·en (en līt′ən) *v.* give the light of truth and knowledge to; free from prejudice, ignorance, etc. —**en·light′en·er,** *n.*

en·light·en·ment (en līt′ən mənt) *n.* **1** an enlightening of the mind. **2** the fact or state of being enlightened.
☛ *Syn.* See note at **education.**

En·light·en·ment (en līt′ən mənt) *n.* a philosophical movement in Europe in the 18th century, characterized by rationalism, by scepticism about existing political and social beliefs, and by emphasis on intellectual freedom.

en·list (en list′) *v.* **1** get someone to join a branch of the armed forces. **2** enrol in some branch of the armed forces. **3** induce to join in some cause or undertaking; secure the help or support of: *The mayor enlisted the churches of our city to work for more parks.* **4** join in some cause or undertaking; give help or support. —**en·list′er,** *n.*

enlisted man *Esp.U.S.* a member of the armed forces who is not a commissioned officer or cadet.

en·list·ment (en list′mənt) *n.* **1** enlisting or being enlisted. **2** the time for which a person enlists.

en·liv·en (en līv′ən) *v.* make lively, active, gay, or cheerful: *The speaker enlivened his talk with humor. Bright curtains enliven a room.* —**en·liv′en·er,** *n.* —**en·liv′en·ing·ly,** *adv.*

en masse (on′ mas′ *or* en′ mas′; *French,* än mäs′) in a group; all together. [< F]

en·mesh (en mesh′) *v.* catch in a net; enclose in meshes; entangle. —**en·mesh′ment,** *n.*

en·mi·ty (en′mə tē) *n., pl.* **-ties.** the feeling that enemies have for

each other; hatred. [ME < OF *ennemistie* < VL < L *inimicus*. See ENEMY.]

en·no·ble (en nō′bəl) *v.* **-bled, -bling. 1** give a title or rank of nobility to; raise to the rank of nobleman. **2** raise in the respect of others; dignify; exalt: *A good deed ennobles the person who does it.* **3** make finer or more noble in nature: *His character had been ennobled through suffering.* —**en·no′ble·ment,** *n.* —**en·no′bler,** *n.*

en·nui (on′wē; *French,* än nYē′) *n.* a feeling of weariness and discontent from lack of occupation or interest; boredom. [< F. Related to ANNOY.]

e·nor·mi·ty (i nôr′mə tē) *n., pl.* **-ties. 1** extreme wickedness; outrageousness: *The murderer finally realized the enormity of his crime.* **2** an extremely wicked crime; outrageous offence.

e·nor·mous (i nôr′məs) *adj.* **1** extremely large; huge: *Long ago enormous animals lived on the earth.* **2** extremely wicked; outrageous. [< L *enormis* < *ex-* out of + *norma* pattern] —**e·nor′mous·ness,** *n.*
☛ *Syn.* **1.** See note at **huge.**

e·nor·mous·ly (i nôr′məs lē) *adv.* in or to an enormous degree; extremely; vastly; beyond measure.

e·nough (i nuf′) *adj., n., adv., interj.* —*adj.* as much or as many as needed or wanted: *Buy enough food for the picnic.* —*n.* an adequate quantity or number: *I have had enough to eat.* —*adv.* **1** sufficiently; adequately: *Have you played enough?* **2** quite; fully: *He is willing enough to take a tip.* **3** rather; fairly: *She talks well enough for a baby.* —*interj.* stop! no more! [OE *genōg*]
☛ *Syn. adj.* **Enough, sufficient, adequate** = as much as is needed. **Enough** is the general word, and is often used interchangeably with **sufficient,** but it means "as much as is needed to satisfy a desire": *A growing boy never has enough time to play.* **Sufficient** = as much as is required to satisfy a need: *She is not getting sufficient food.* **Adequate** = as much as is needed to meet special, sometimes minimum, requirements: *To be healthy one must have an adequate diet.*
☛ *Usage.* **Enough.** There is a strong tendency to place the adjective **enough** after a noun it modifies, and the adverb **enough** must be placed after an adjective or adverb it modifies: *We have room enough. Martha's sewing is good enough for me. You don't get up early enough.*

e·nounce (i nouns′) *v.* **e·nounced, e·nounc·ing. 1** proclaim; make a public or formal statement. **2** speak; pronounce; enunciate.

e·now (i nou′) *adj., n. or adv. Archaic.* enough.

en pas·sant (än pä sän′) *French.* in passing; by the way; incidentally.

en·quire (en kwīr′) *v.* **-quired, -quir·ing.** inquire.

en·quir·y (en kwīr′ē *or* en′kwə rē) *n., pl.* **-quir·ies.** inquiry.

en·rage (en rāj′) *v.* **-raged, -rag·ing.** put into a rage; make very angry; make furious. [< OF *enrager* < *en-* in (causative) + *rage* rage < VL *rabia* < L *rabies*]

en rap·port (än rä pôr′) *French.* in sympathy; in agreement.

en·rapt (en rapt′) *adj.* rapt; filled with great delight.

en·rap·ture (en rap′chər) *v.* **-tured, -tur·ing.** fill with great delight; entrance: *The audience was enraptured by the singer's beautiful voice.*

en·rich (en rich′) *v.* **1** make rich or richer: *An education enriches your mind. Decorations enrich a room. Fertilizers enrich the soil.* **2** raise the nutritive value of (a food) by adding vitamins and minerals in processing. **3** make (a radio-active element) more fissionable by increasing the content of fissionable material: *Uranium that has its content of the isotope U235 increased is called enriched uranium.* **4** *Education.* expand the range or content of a course of study: *an enriched program.* [ME < OF *enrichir* < *en-* in (causative) + *riche* rich] —**en·rich′er,** *n.*

en·rich·ment (en rich′mənt) *n.* **1** enriching or being enriched. **2** anything that enriches.

en·rol *or* **en·roll** (en rōl′) *v.* **-rolled, -rol·ling. 1** write in a list. **2** have one's name written in a list. **3** make a member. **4** become a member. **5** enlist. [ME < OF *enroller* < *en-* in + *rolle* roll, *n.*, ult. < L *rota* wheel]

en·rol·ment *or* **en·roll·ment** (en rōl′mənt) *n.* **1** an enrolling. **2** the number enrolled: *The school has an enrolment of 200 students.*

en route (on rüt′; *French,* än rüt′) on the way: *We shall stop at Toronto en route from Montreal to Winnipeg.* [< F]

en·sam·ple (en sam′pəl) *n. Archaic.* example.

en·san·guine (en sang′gwin) *v.* **-guined, -guin·ing.** stain with blood.

en·sconce (en skons′) *v.* **-sconced, -sconc·ing. 1** shelter safely; hide: *The soldiers were ensconced in strongly fortified trenches.*

2 settle comfortably and firmly: *The cat ensconced itself in the armchair.* [< *en-¹* + *sconce* fortification, probably < Du. *schans*]

en·sem·ble (on som′bəl) *n.* **1** all the parts of a thing considered together; general effect. **2** *Music.* **a** a united performance of the full number of singers, instrumentalists, etc.: *After the solo all the singers joined in the ensemble.* **b** a group of musicians or the musical instruments used in taking part in such a performance: *Two violins, a cello, and a harp made up the string ensemble.* **3** a set of clothes of which each item is chosen to match or complement the others; a complete, harmonious costume. [< F < VL < L *in-* + *simul* at the same time]

en·shrine (en shrīn′) *v.* **-shrined, -shrin·ing. 1** enclose in a shrine: *A fragment of the Cross is enshrined in the cathedral.* **2** keep sacred; cherish: *Memories of happier days were enshrined in the old man's heart.*

en·shrine·ment (en shrīn′mənt) *n.* **1** enshrining. **2** anything that enshrines or surrounds.

en·shroud (en shroud′) *v.* cover; hide; veil: *Fog enshrouded the ship, but we could hear its siren.*

en·sign (en′sīn *or* en′sən for 1, 3, and 4; en′sən for 2) *n.* **1** a flag; banner: *the Red Ensign.* **2** the lowest commissioned officer in the United States navy. **3** *Historical.* a British army officer whose duty was carrying the flag. **4** the sign of one's rank, position, or power; symbol of authority. [ME < OF *enseigne* < L *insignia* insignia. Doublet of INSIGNIA.]

en·sign·ship (en′sən ship′) *n.* the rank or position of an ensign.

en·si·lage (en′sə lij) *n.* **1** the preservation of green fodder by packing it in a silo or pit. **2** green fodder preserved in this way. Ensilage is used to feed cattle in winter. [< F]

en·slave (en slāv′) *v.* **-slaved, -slav·ing.** reduce to slavery; subjugate or dominate: *an enslaved people. She was enslaved by alcohol.*

en·slave·ment (en slāv′mənt) *n.* enslaving or being enslaved.

en·snare (en sner′) *v.* **-snared, -snar·ing.** catch in a snare; trap. —**en·snare′ment,** *n.* —**en·snar′er,** *n.* Also, **insnare.**

en·sue (en sü′ *or* en syü′) *v.* **-sued, -su·ing. 1** come after; follow: *The ensuing year means the next year.* **2** happen as a result: *In his anger he hit the man, and a fight ensued.* [ME < OF *ensuivre* < L *insequi* < *in-* upon + *sequi* follow]
☛ *Syn.* See note at **follow.**

en·sure (en shür′) *v.* **-sured, -sur·ing. 1** make sure or certain: *Careful planning and hard work ensured the success of the party.* **2** make sure of getting; secure: *A letter of introduction will ensure you an interview.* **3** make safe; protect: *Proper clothing ensured us against the cold.* [< AF *enseurer* < *en-* in (causative) + *seür* sure < L *securus*]
☛ *Usage.* **Ensure, insure. Ensure** is the usual spelling for 'make sure or certain'; **insure,** for 'arrange for money payment in case of loss, accident, or death': *Check your work to ensure its accuracy. They insured their house against fire.*

-ent *suffix.* **1** —ing, as in *absorbent, indulgent, coincident.* **2** one that —s, as in *correspondent, president, superintendent.* **3** other meanings, as in *competent, confident.* [< L *-ens, -entis*]

en·ta·bla·ture (en tab′lə chür′ *or* en tab′lə chər) *n. Architecture.* a horizontal band forming the top of a wall or storey, supported by columns or pilasters. In classical architecture, the entablature consists of a cornice, a frieze, and an architrave. See **column** for picture. [< Ital. *intavolatura* < *in-* on + *tavola* board, tablet < L *tabula*]

en·tail (en tāl′) *v., n.* —*v.* **1** impose; require: *Owning an automobile entailed greater expense than he had expected.* **2** limit the inheritance of (property, etc.) to a specified line of heirs so that it cannot be left to anyone else. An entailed estate usually passes to the eldest son. —*n.* **1** entailing. **2** an entailed inheritance. **3** the order of descent specified for an entailed estate. [ME < *en-¹* + OF *taille* cutting, tax < *taillier* cut] —**en·tail′er,** *n.*

en·tail·ment (en tāl′mənt) *n.* entailing or being entailed.

en·tan·gle (en tang′gəl) *v.* **-gled, -gling. 1** get twisted up and caught; tangle: *Loose string is easily entangled.* **2** get into difficulty; involve: *The villain tried to entangle the hero in an evil scheme.* **3** perplex; confuse. —**en·tan′gler,** *n.* —**en·tan′gling·ly,** *adv.*

en·tan·gle·ment (en tang′gəl mənt) *n.* **1** entangling or being entangled. **2** anything that entangles: *The trench was protected by a barbed-wire entanglement.*

en·tente (on tont′; *French,* än tänt′) *n.* **1** an understanding; agreement between two or more governments. **2** the parties to an understanding; governments that have made an agreement.

en·tente cor·diale (än tänt′ kôr dyäl′) *French.* a friendly understanding or agreement.

en·ter (en′tər) *v.* **1** go or come into: *She entered the house. They*

entered the yard. **2** go or come in: *Let them enter.* **3** become a part or member of; join: *He entered the armed forces when he was 18.* **4** cause to join; enrol; obtain admission for: *Parents enter their children in school.* **5** begin; start (*often used with* **on** *or* **upon**): *to enter the practice of law.* **6** become involved; begin to take part (*often used with* **into**): *to enter a contest, to enter into the spirit of the game, to enter into conversation with someone.* **7** write or print in a book, list, etc.: *A dictionary enters words in alphabetical order.* **8** come into or take possession of (*usually used with* **upon**). **9** put formally on record: *to enter a complaint in court.* **10** form a part of (*used with* **into**): *The possibility of failure didn't even enter into her calculations.* **11** consider (*used with* **into**): *The book does not enter into the issue of morality at all.* **12** *Theatre.* come on stage (*used as a stage direction*): *Enter Ghost.* **13** report (a ship or its cargoes) at the custom house. [ME < OF *entrer*, ult. < L *intra* within] —**en′ter·er,** *n.*

en·ter·ic (en ter′ik) *adj.* intestinal. [< Gk. *enterikos* < *entera* intestines]

enteric fever typhoid fever.

en·ter·i·tis (en′tər ī′tis) *n.* an inflammation of the intestines, usually accompanied by diarrhea, fever, etc. [< Gk. *entera* intestines + E *-itis*]

en·ter·prise (en′tər prīz′) *n.* **1** an important, difficult, or dangerous undertaking. **2** an undertaking; project: *a business enterprise.* **3** readiness to start projects; courage and energy in starting projects. **4** the carrying on of enterprises; taking part in enterprises. See **private enterprise.** [ME < OF *entreprise* < *entre-* between + *prendre* take < L *prehendere*]

en·ter·pris·ing (en′tər prīz′ing) *adj.* ready to try new, important, difficult, or dangerous plans; courageous and energetic in starting projects.

en·ter·tain (en′tər tān′) *v.* **1** amuse; please; interest: *The circus entertained the children.* **2** have as a guest: *She entertained ten people at dinner.* **3** have guests; invite people to one's home: *She entertains a great deal.* **4** take into the mind; consider: *to entertain an idea.* **5** hold in the mind; maintain: *Even after failing twice, we still entertained a hope of success.* [< F *entretenir* < *entre-* among + *tenir* hold < L *tenere*] —**en·ter·tain·a·ble,** *adj.*

☛ *Syn.* 1. See note at **amuse.**

en·ter·tain·er (en′tər tān′ər) *n.* **1** a person who entertains. **2** a singer, musician, reciter, etc. who takes part in public entertainments.

en·ter·tain·ing (en′tər tān′ing) *adj.* very interesting; pleasing; amusing. —**en′ter·tain′ing·ly,** *adv.*

en·ter·tain·ment (en′tər tān′mənt) *n.* **1** entertaining or being entertained. **2** something that interests, pleases, or amuses. A show or play is an entertainment. **3** hospitality; the act or practice of paying attention to the comfort and desires of guests: *The hostess devoted herself to the entertainment of her guests.*

en·thal·py (en thal′pē *or* en′thal pē) *n. Physics.* the heat content per unit mass of substance. [< Gk. *enthalpein* to warm in]

en·thral or **en·thrall** (en throl′ *or* -thrôl′) *v.* **-thralled, -thrall·ing.** **1** captivate; fascinate; charm: *The explorer enthralled the audience with the story of his exciting adventures.* **2** make a slave of; enslave. Also **inthral** or **inthrall.** —**en·thral′ment** or **en·thrall′ment,** *n.*

en·throne (en thrōn′) *v.* **-throned, -thron·ing.** **1** set on a throne. **2** place highest of all; exalt: *"Mercy is enthroned in the hearts of men."* **3** invest with authority, especially as a sovereign or as a bishop. Also, **inthrone.** —**en·throne′ment,** *n.*

en·thuse (en thūz′ *or* en thyūz′) *v.* **-thused, -thus·ing.** *Informal.* **1** show enthusiasm. **2** fill with enthusiasm. [< *enthusiasm*]

☛ *Usage.* Although many people object to **enthuse,** it is now often heard in the U.S. and, less often, in Canada. It is wise to avoid the word in formal writing.

en·thu·si·asm (en thū′zē az′əm *or* en thyūz′ē az′əm) *n.* eager interest; zeal: *The great leader filled his followers with enthusiasm.* [< LL *enthusiasmus* < Gk. *enthousiasmos* < *entheos* god-possessed < *en-* in + *theos* god]

en·thu·si·ast (en thū′zē ast′ *or* en thyūz′ē ast′) *n.* **1** a person who is filled with eager interest or zeal: *a baseball enthusiast.* **2** a person who is carried away by his feelings for a cause.

en·thu·si·as·tic (en thū′zē as′tik *or* en thyūz′ē as′tik) *adj.* full of enthusiasm; eagerly interested. —**en·thu′si·as′ti·cal·ly,** *adv.*

en·tice (en tīs′) *v.* **-ticed, -tic·ing.** tempt by arousing hopes or desires; attract by offering some pleasure or reward: *The robber enticed his victims into a cave by promising to show them a gold mine.* [ME < OF *enticier* stir up, incite ? < *en-* in + L *titio* firebrand] —**en·tic′er,** *n.* —**en·tic′ing·ly,** *adv.*

☛ *Syn.* See note at **lure.**

en·tice·ment (en tīs′mənt) *n.* **1** enticing or being enticed. **2** anything that entices.

en·tire (en tīr′) *adj.* **1** having all the parts or elements; whole;

hat, āge, fär; let, ēqual, tėrm; it, īce
hot, ōpen, ôrder; oil, out; cup, pút, rüle,
əbove, takən, pencəl, lemən, circəs

ch, child; ng, long; sh, ship
th, thin; ᴛʜ, then; zh, measure

complete: *The entire platoon was wiped out.* **2** not broken; in one piece. **3** of leaves, not indented. **4** not castrated or gelded: *an entire horse.* [ME < OF *entier* < L *integer* < *in-* not + *tag-* a base of *tangere* touch. Doublet of INTEGER.]

☛ *Syn.* 1. See note at **complete.**

en·tire·ly (en tīr′lē) *adv.* **1** wholly; completely; fully. **2** solely.

en·tire·ty (en tīr′tē *or* en tīr′ə tē) *n., pl.* **-ties. 1** wholeness; completeness. **2** a complete thing; the whole.

in its entirety, wholly; completely: *He enjoyed the concert in its entirety.*

en·ti·tle (en tī′təl) *v.* **-tled, -tling. 1** give the title of; call by the name of: *She read a poem entitled "Trees."* **2** give a claim or right to; provide with a reason to ask or get something: *Their age and experience entitle old people to the respect of young people.* Also, **intitle.** [ME < OF *entituler* < LL *intitulare* < L *in-* in + *titulus* title]

en·ti·tle·ment (en tī′təl mənt) *n.* something to which one is entitled.

en·ti·ty (en′ti tē) *n., pl.* **-ties. 1** something that has a real and separate existence either actually or in the mind; anything real in itself: *Persons, mountains, languages, and beliefs are entities.* **2** a state of being; existence. [< LL *entitas* < L *ens, entis,* ppr. of *esse* be]

en·tomb (en tüm′) *v.* **1** place in a tomb; bury. **2** shut up as if in a tomb. Also, **intomb.** [ME < OF *entomber* < *en-* in + *tombe* tomb < LL *tumba* < Gk. *tymbos*] —**en·tomb′ment,** *n.*

en·to·mo·log·ic (en′tə mə loj′ik) *adj.* entomological.

en·to·mo·log·i·cal (en′tə mə loj′ə kəl) *adj.* of or having to do with entomology.

en·to·mol·o·gist (en′tə mol′ə jist) *n.* a person trained in entomology, especially one whose work it is.

en·to·mol·o·gy (en′tə mol′ə jē) *n.* the branch of zoology that deals with insects. [< Gk. *entomon* insect + E *-logy*]

en·tou·rage (on′tü räzh′) *n.* a group of attendants or people usually accompanying a person. [< F *entourage* < *entourer* surround]

en·tr'acte (än trakt′) *n.* **1** an interval between two acts of a play, ballet, opera, etc. **2** the music, dancing, or any entertainment performed during this interval. [< F *entr'acte* between-act]

en·trails (en′trālz *or* en′trəlz) *n.pl.* **1** the inner parts of a man or animal. **2** the intestines; bowels. **3** any inner parts. [ME < OF *entrailles* < LL *intralia* < L *interanea* < *inter* within]

en·train (en trān′) *v.* **1** get on a train. **2** put on a train: *The soldiers were entrained at night.*

en·trance¹ (en′trəns) *n.* **1** the act of entering: *The actor's entrance was greeted with applause.* **2** a place by which to enter; door, passageway, etc. **3** the freedom or right to enter; permission to enter. [< MF *entrance* < *entrer* enter < L *intrare.* See ENTER.]

en·trance² (en trans′) *v.* **-tranced, -tranc·ing. 1** put into a trance. **2** fill with joy; delight; charm. [< *en-¹* + *trance*] —**en·tranc′ing·ly,** *adv.*

en·trance·ment (en trans′mənt) *n.* **1** entrancing or being entranced. **2** something that entrances.

en·trance·way (en′trəns wā′) *n.* a place by which to enter.

en·trant (en′trənt) *n.* **1** a person who enters. **2** a new member in a profession, club, association, etc. **3** a person who takes part in a contest. [< F *entrant,* ppr. of *entrer* enter]

en·trap (en trap′) *v.* **-trapped, -trap·ping. 1** catch in a trap. **2** bring into difficulty or danger; deceive; trick: *By clever questioning, the lawyer entrapped the witness into contradicting himself.* —**en·trap′ment,** *n.* [< MF *entrapre* < *en-* in (intensive) + *trape* trap]

en·treat (en trēt′) *v.* ask earnestly; beg and pray; implore: *The captives entreated the savages not to kill them.* Also, **intreat.** [ME < OF *entraitier* < *en-* in (intensive) + *traitier* treat < L *tractare*] —**en·treat′er,** *n.* —**en·treat′ing·ly,** *adv.*

en·treat·y (en trēt′ē) *n., pl.* **-treat·ies.** an earnest request; prayer: *The savages paid no attention to their captives' entreaties for mercy.*

en·tre·chat (än trə shä′) *n. Ballet.* a vertical leap in which the

dancer's calves are beaten together as the feet, pointed downwards, cross. Several beats may be performed in one leap. [< F *entrechat*, a respelling of Ital. (*capriola*) *intrecciata* complicated (leap) < *intrecciare* intertwine < *in-* in + *treccia* tress, plait]

en·tree or **en·trée** (on′trā; *French*, än trā′) *n.* **1** the freedom or right to enter; access. **2** the main dish of food at dinner or lunch. **3** a dish of food served before the roast or between the main courses at dinner. [< F *entrée*, fem. pp. of *entrer* enter]

en·trench (en trench′) *v.* **1** surround with a trench; fortify with trenches. **2** establish firmly: *Exchanging gifts at Christmas is a custom entrenched in people's minds.* **3** trespass; encroach; infringe: *Do not entrench upon the rights of others.* Also, **intrench.**

en·trench·ment (en trench′mənt) *n.* **1** entrenching. **2** an entrenched position. **3** a defence consisting of a trench and a rampart of earth or stone. Also, **intrenchment.**

en·tre nous (än trə nü′) *French.* between ourselves; confidentially.

en·tre·pôt (on′trə pō′) *n.* **1** a place where goods are stored; warehouse. **2** a place where goods are sent for distribution; commercial centre. [< F]

en·tre·pre·neur (on′trə prə nėr′) *n.* a person who organizes and manages a business or industrial enterprise, attempting to make a profit but taking the risk of a loss. [< F *entrepreneur* < *entreprendre* undertake]

en·tre·pre·neur·i·al (on′trə prə nėr′ē əl) *adj.* of or having to do with an entrepreneur or entrepreneurs, especially when involving strong initiative and opportunism.

en·tre·pre·neur·ship (on′trə prə nėr′ship) *n.* **1** the existence or activity of entrepreneurs. **2** the qualities or function of an entrepreneur.

en·tre·sol (en′tər sol′ *or* on′trə sol′) *n.* a low storey between the first two floors of a building; mezzanine. [< F]

en·tro·py (en′trə pē) *n.* **1** *Physics.* **a** in a thermodynamic system, a measure of the energy that is not available for conversion into mechanical work. **b** a measure of the degree of molecular disorder in a system. **2 a** the tendency of the universe toward increasing disorder. **b** the probable outcome of this tendency. **3** *Communications.* a statistical measure of the predictable accuracy of a system in transmitting information. [< G *Entropie*, probably influenced by Gk. *entropia* a turning in < *en-* + *tropē* a turning < *trepein* to turn]

en·trust (en trust′) *v.* **1** charge with a trust; trust: *The club entrusted the newly elected treasurer with all its money.* **2** give the care of; hand over for safekeeping: *While travelling, they entrusted their son to his grandparents.* Also, **intrust.**
☛ *Syn.* **2.** See note at **commit.**

en·try (en′trē) *n., pl.* **-tries. 1** the act of entering. **2** a place by which to enter; a way to enter. A vestibule is an entry. **3** something written or printed in a book, list, etc. Each word explained in a dictionary is an entry. A bookkeeper makes entries in a ledger. **4** a person or thing that takes part in a contest. **5** *Law.* the act of taking possession of lands or buildings by entering or setting foot on them. **6** a giving of an account of a ship's cargo at a custom house to obtain permission to land the goods. [ME < OF *entree* < *entrer*. See ENTER.]

entry word **1** in a dictionary, a word listed in alphabetical order and followed by information concerning its pronunciation, meanings, etc. Entry words are printed in heavy black type. **2** in other reference books, a word giving the subject of the following article. **3** the word under which a book, pamphlet, etc. is entered in a list or catalogue.

en·twine (en twīn′) *v.* **-twined, -twin·ing. 1** twine together. **2** twine around: *Roses entwined the little cottage.* —**en·twine′ment,** *n.*

en·twist (en twist′) *v.* twist together.

e·nu·mer·ate (i nyü′mər āt′ *or* i nü′mər āt′) *v.* **-at·ed, -at·ing. 1** name one by one; give a list of: *He enumerated the provinces of Canada.* **2** count. **3** *Cdn.* make up or enter in a list of voters in an area. [< L *enumerare* < *ex-* out + *numerus* number]

e·nu·mer·a·tion (i nyü′mər ā′shən *or* i nü′mər ā′shən) *n.* **1** an enumerating; listing; counting. **2** a list.

e·nu·mer·a·tive (i nyü′mər ə tiv *or* i nü′mər ə tiv, i nyü′mər ā′tiv *or* i nü′mər ā′tiv) *adj.* that enumerates; having to do with enumeration.

e·nu·mer·a·tor (i nyü′mər ā′tər *or* i nü′mər ā′tər) *n.* **1** *Cdn.* a person appointed to list, prior to an election, the eligible voters in a polling area. **2** any person or thing that lists or counts.

e·nun·ci·ate (i nun′sē āt′ *or* i nun′shē āt′) *v.* **-at·ed, -at·ing.**

1 pronounce (words): *He is a well-trained actor and enunciates very distinctly.* **2** state definitely; announce: *After performing many experiments, the scientist enunciated a new theory.* [< L *enuntiare* < *ex-* out + *nuntius* messenger] —**en·nun′ci·a·tor,** *n.*

e·nun·ci·a·tion (i nun′sē ā′shən) *n.* **1** one's manner of pronouncing words. **2** a definite statement; announcement: *the enunciation of a set of rules.*

en·ure (in yür′) See **inure.**

en·u·re·sis (en′yə rē′sis) *n.* involuntary passing of urine, especially during sleep.

en·vel·op (en vel′əp) *v.* **-oped, -op·ing. 1** wrap; cover. **2** surround: *Our soldiers enveloped the enemy and captured them.* **3** hide; conceal: *Fog enveloped the village.* [ME < OF *enveloper* < *en-* in (intensive) + *voloper* wrap]

en·ve·lope (en′və lōp′ *or* on′və lōp′) *n.* **1** a paper cover in which a letter or anything flat and fairly thin can be mailed, filed, etc. It can usually be folded over and sealed by wetting a gummed edge. **2** a covering; wrapper. **3** *Botany.* a surrounding or enclosing part, as of leaves. **4** *Biology.* any enclosing covering, such as membrane or shell; integument. **5** *Geometry.* a curve or surface touching a continuous series of curves or surfaces. **6** *Astronomy.* a nebulous mass surrounding the nucleus of a comet on the side nearest the sun. **7** a bag that holds the gas in a balloon or airship. **8** the outer covering of a rigid airship. [< F *enveloppe* < *envelopper* envelop]

en·vel·op·ment (en vel′əp mənt) *n.* **1** enveloping or being enveloped. **2** something that envelops; wrapping; covering.

en·ven·om (en ven′əm) *v.* **1** make poisonous. **2** fill with bitterness, hate, etc: *The wicked boy envenomed his father's mind against his half brother.* [ME < OF *envenimer* < *en-* in + *venim* venom < L *venenum*]

en·vi·a·ble (en′vē ə bəl) *adj.* to be envied; desirable; worth having: *She has an enviable school record.* —**en′vi·a·ble·ness,** *n.* —**en′vi·a·bly,** *adv.*

en·vi·ous (en′vē əs) *adj.* full of envy; feeling or showing envy. [ME < AF *envious,* var. of OF *envieus* < *envie.* See ENVY.] —**en′vi·ous·ly,** *adv.* —**en′vi·ous·ness,** *n.*

en·vi·ron (en vī′rən) *v.* surround; enclose. [ME < OF *environner* < *environ* around · < *en-* in + *viron* circle]

en·vi·ron·ment (en vī′rən mənt) *n.* **1** all the surrounding conditions and influences that affect the development of a living thing. Differences in environment often account for differences in the same kind of plant found in different places. **2** surroundings: *an environment of poverty. Banff has a beautiful environment.*

en·vi·ron·men·tal (en vī′rən men′təl) *adj.* having to do with environment.

en·vi·ron·men·tal·ism (en vīr′ən men′təl iz′əm) *n.* **1** *Psychology.* the theory that environment is more influential than heredity in the development of an individual. **2** emphasis on the protection of the natural environment and the preservation of ecological balance.

en·vi·ron·men·tal·ist (en vī′rən men′təl əst) *n., adj.* —*n.* **1** a person who believes in and advocates the protection of the natural environment against pollution, etc. and the preservation of ecological balance. **2** *Psychology.* an advocate of the theory of environmentalism. —*adj.* of or having to do with environmentalists or environmentalism.

en·vi·rons (en vī′rənz) *n.pl.* surrounding districts; suburbs.

envisage (en viz′ij) *v.* **-aged, -ag·ing. 1** foresee; visualize: *I envisage no difficulty with our plans.* **2** *Archaic.* look in the face of; confront: *He finally envisaged the realities of the situation.* [< F *envisager* < *en-* in + *visage* face]

en·vi·sion (en vizh′ən) *v.* have a mental picture of; imagine, especially something that does not yet exist; picture to oneself; look forward to: *It is difficult to envision a state of permanent peace.*

en·voy[1] (en′voi) *n.* **1** messenger. **2** a diplomat ranking next below an ambassador and next above a minister. [< F *envoyé,* pp. of *envoyer* send < OF *envoier.* See ENVOY[2].]

en·voy[2] (en′voi) *n.* **1** a short stanza ending a poem. **2** a postscript to a literary work, often addressed to a friend or patron of the author. [ME < OF *envoy* < *envoier* send < VL < L *in via* on the way]

en·vy (en′vē) *n., pl.* **-vies;** *v.* **-vied, -vy·ing.** —*n.* **1** discontent or ill will at another's good fortune because one wishes it were one's own; dislike for a person who has what one wants. **2** the object of such feeling: *She was the envy of the younger girls in the school.* —*v.* **1** feel envy toward: *Some people envy the rich.* **2** feel envy because of: *James envied his friend's success.* [ME < OF *envie* < L *invidia,* ult. < *invidere* look with enmity at < *in-* against + *videre* see]

☞ *Usage.* **Envy** (def. 1), **covet**. **Envy** = feel discontent, jealousy, or sometimes, hatred or resentment toward a person who has something one wishes one had oneself: *John envies famous people.* **Covet** = feel a great desire for something, especially something belonging to someone else: *He covets his neighbor's new car.*

en·womb (en wüm′) *v.* enclose in, or as if in, a womb.

en·wrap (en rap′) *v.* **-wrapped, -wrap·ping.** enclose; envelop; wrap. Also, **inwrap.**

en·wreathe (en rēᴛH′) *v.* **-wreathed, -wreath·ing.** wreathe around; encircle; surround. Also, **inwreathe.**

en·zy·mat·ic (en′zī mat′ik *or* en′zi mat′ik) *adj.* of, having to do with, or produced by enzymes.

en·zyme (en′zīm *or* en′zim) *n.* a chemical substance, produced in living cells, that can cause changes in other substances within the body without being changed itself. Pepsin is an enzyme. [< Med.Gk. *enzymos* leavened < *en-* in + *zymē* leaven]

en·zy·mol·o·gist (en′zī mol′ə jist *or* en′zi mol′ə jist) *n.* a person trained in enzymology, especially one whose work it is.

en·zy·mol·o·gy (en′zī mol′ə jē *or* en′zi mol′ə jē) *n.* the study of enzymes.

E·o·cene (ē′ə sēn′) *n., adj. Geology.* —*n.* **1** the earliest division of the Tertiary period, beginning approximately 60 million years ago, when the lowest rocks were formed. **2** the rocks formed during this period. See chart at **geology.** —*adj.* having to do with this period or group of rocks. [< Gk. *ēōs* dawn + *kainos* recent]

e·o·hip·pus (ē′ō hip′əs) *n.* any of an extinct genus (*Hyracotherium*) of animals of the Eocene epoch, the earliest known stage in the evolution of the horse. These dog-sized animals had forefeet with four toes and hind feet with two. [< NL *Eohippus* < Gk. *ēōs* dawn + *hippos* horse]

E·o·li·an (ē ō′lē ən) See **Aeolian.**

e·o·lith (ē′ə lith′) *n.* a roughly-shaped stone tool belonging to a very early stage of human culture. [< Gk. *ēōs* dawn + *lithos* stone]

e·o·lith·ic or **E·o·lith·ic** (ē′ə lith′ik) *adj., n.* —*adj.* of or having to do with a very early stage of human culture, characterized by the use of the most primitive stone instruments. —*n.* this stage, the earliest part of the Stone Age.

e·on (ē′ən *or* ē′on) *n.* a very long period of time; many thousands of years: *Eons passed before life existed on the earth.* Also, **aeon.** [< L *aeon* < Gk. *aiōn* lifetime, age]

E·os (ē′os) *n. Greek mythology.* the goddess of the dawn. Eos corresponds to the Roman goddess Aurora. [< L < Gk.]

e·o·sin (ē′ə sin) *n.* **1** a rose-red dye or stain made from coal tar. *Formula:* $C_{20}H_8Br_4O_5$ **2** its reddish-brown potassium or sodium salt. [< Gk. *ēōs* dawn]

E·o·zo·ic (ē′ə zō′ik) *n., adj.* —*n. Geology.* **1** the era in which living things first appeared. See chart at **geology.** **2** the rocks formed during this era. —*adj.* of or having to do with this era or the rocks formed during it. [< Gk. *ēōs* dawn + *zōē* life + E *-ic*]

ep- form of **epi-** before vowels and *h*, as in *epode, ephemeral.*

Ep. Epistle(s).

EP of phonograph records, extended play.

ep·au·lette or **ep·au·let** (ep′ə let′) *n.* an ornamental tab or piece on the shoulder of a uniform. [< F *épaulette,* dim. of *épaule* shoulder]

é·pée (ā pā′) *n.* a sword used in fencing, especially one with a sharp point and no cutting edge. [< F *épée* < OF *espee* < L *spatha* < Gk. *spathē* blade, sword]

e·phah (ē′fə) *n.* an ancient Hebrew unit of dry measure equal to about 35 litres. [< Hebrew]

e·phed·rin (i fed′rin; *in chemistry,* ef′ə drin) *n.* ephedrine.

e·phed·rine (i fed′rin; *in chemistry also,* ef′ə drēn′ *or* ef′ə drin) *n.* a drug used to relieve hay fever, asthma, head colds, etc. It is a plant alkaloid. *Formula:* $C_{10}H_{15}ON$ [< NL *ephedra* < L *ephedra* horsetail (a plant) < Gk.]

e·phem·er·a (i fem′ər ə) *n., pl.* **-er·ae** (-ə rē′ *or* -ə rī′) *or* **-er·as.** **1** any short-lived or transitory person or thing: *Of the many books published in a year, the majority are ephemerae.* **2** an emphemerid; May fly. **3** a brief fever. [< Gk. *ephēmeros* living only a day < *epi-* upon + *hēmera* day]

e·phem·er·al (i fem′ər əl) *adj.* lasting for only a day; lasting for only a very short time; very short-lived. [< Gk. *ephēmeros* lasting only a day < *epi-* upon, over + *hēmera* day]

e·phem·er·id (i fem′ər id) *n.* mayfly.

E·phe·sian (i fē′zhən) *n., adj.* —*n.* a native or inhabitant of Ephesus, an ancient Greek city in W Asia Minor. —*adj.* of Ephesus or its people.

eph·od (ef′od *or* ē′fod) *n.* a vestment worn in ancient times by

Hebrew priests when performing sacred duties. [< Hebrew]

eph·or (ef′ôr *or* ef′ər) *n., pl.* **-ors, -o·ri** (-ə rī′ *or* -ə rē′). in ancient Sparta, one of the five leading magistrates, elected yearly by the people to advise the king. [< L < Gk. *ephoros* < *epi-* over + *horaein* see]

epi- *prefix.* on; over; upon; in addition; to; among, as in *epidemic.* Also, **ep-,** before vowels and *h*. [< Gk. *epi-* < *epi,* prep., adv.]

ep·ic (ep′ik) *n., adj.* —*n.* **1** a long poem that tells of the adventures of one or more great heroes. An epic is written in a dignified, majestic style, and often gives expression to the ideals of a nation or race. *Beowulf,* the *Iliad,* and *Paradise Lost* are epics. **2** any writing having the qualities of an epic. **3** any story or series of events worthy of being the subject of an epic. **4** *Informal.* a spectacular motion picture or other entertainment. —*adj.* **1** of or having to do with an epic. **2** like an epic; grand in style; heroic. [< L *epicus* < Gk. *epikos* < *epos* word, story] —**ep′i·cal·ly,** *adv.*

ep·i·cal (ep′ə kəl) *adj.* epic.

ep·i·ca·lyx (ep′ə kā′liks *or* -kal′iks) *n. Botany.* a ring of bracts at the base of a flower that looks like an outer calyx.

ep·i·carp (ep′ə kärp′) *n.* the outer layer of the pericarp of a fruit. The epicarp forms the skin of a pear or peach. [< *epi-* on + Gk. *karpos* fruit]

ep·i·cene (ep′ə sēn′) *adj., n.* —*adj.* **1** *Grammar.* **a** having only one gender for both sexes. The Latin noun *leo* is epicene, for it is masculine in gender but stands for both *lion* and *lioness.* **b** of common gender. English nouns such as *fish, human,* etc. are epicene. **2** belonging to or having the characteristics of both sexes. **3** not clearly of either sex; sexless. **4** effeminate. —*n.* **1** an epicene person. **2** an epicene noun. [< L < Gk. *epikoinos* common gender < *epi-* upon + *koinos* common]

ep·i·cen·tre (ep′ə sen′tər) *n.* **1** the point from which earthquake waves seem to go out. It is situated directly above the true centre of the earthquake. **2** any point of great tension, disturbance, etc.: *the epicentre of a revolt.* Also, **epicenter.**

ep·i·cot·yl (ep′ə kot′əl) *n.* the part of a plant embryo stem above the cotyledons.

ep·i·cure (ep′ə kyur′) *n.* a person who has a refined taste in eating and drinking and cares much about foods and drinks. [Anglicized var. of *Epicurus*]

ep·i·cu·re·an (ep′ə kyə rē′ən) *adj., n.* —*adj.* **1** like an epicure; fond of pleasure and luxury. **2** fit for an epicure. **3 Epicurean,** of Epicurus or his philosophy. —*n.* **1** a person fond of pleasure and luxury; epicure. **2 Epicurean,** a believer in the philosophy of Epicurus.

Ep·i·cu·re·an·ism (ep′ə kyə rē′ən iz′əm) *n.* **1** the philosophy or principles of Epicurus (342?-270 B.C.), a Greek philosopher who taught that pleasure is the highest good and that virtue alone produces pleasure. **2** Also, **epicureanism,** the belief in or practice of this philosophy.

ep·i·dem·ic (ep′ə dem′ik) *n., adj.* —*n.* **1** a rapid spreading of a disease so that many people have it at the same time: *All the schools in the city were closed because of an epidemic of scarlet fever.* **2** the rapid spread of an idea, fashion, etc. —*adj.* affecting many people at the same time; widespread: *an epidemic disease. The wild rumors had reached epidemic proportions.* [< F *épidémique* < *épidémie* < Med.L < Gk. *epidēmia* stay, visit, prevalence (of a disease) < *epi-* among + *dēmos* people]

ep·i·dem·i·cal (ep′ə dem′ə kəl) *adj.* epidemic. —**ep·i·dem′i·cal·ly,** *adv.*

ep·i·de·mi·o·log·ic (ep′ə dē′mē ə loj′ik *or* ep′ə dem′ē-) *adj.* of or having to do with epidemiology. —**ep′i·de·mi·o·log′i·cal,** *adj.* —**ep′i·de·mi·o·log′i·cal·ly,** *adv.*

ep·i·de·mi·ol·o·gist (ep′ə dē′mē ol′ə jist *or* ep′ə dem′ē-) *n.* a person trained in epidemiology, especially one whose work it is.

ep·i·de·mi·ol·o·gy (ep′ə dē′mē ol′ə jē *or* ep′ə dem′ē-) *n.* the branch of medicine dealing with the occurrence, transmission, and control of infections and epidemic diseases.

ep·i·der·mal (ep′ə dèr′məl) *adj.* of or having to do with the epidermis.

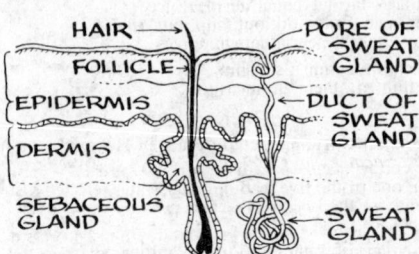

The layers of human skin as seen through a microscope

ep·i·der·mis (ep′ə dėr′mis) *n.* **1** the outer layer of the skin of vertebrates. **2** the outer covering on the shells of many molluscs. **3** any of various other outer layers of invertebrates. **4** a skinlike layer of cells in seed plants and ferns. [< LL < Gk. *epidermis* < *epi-* on + *derma* skin]

ep·i·dote (ep′ə dōt′) *n.* a mineral consisting chiefly of aluminium, iron, and lime silicate. [< F *épidote* < Gk. *epididonai* to increase < *epi-* over + *didonai* give (because it is longer in the base of the crystal than allied materials)]

ep·i·glot·tis (ep′ə glot′is) *n.* a thin, triangular plate of cartilage that covers the entrance to the windpipe during swallowing, so that food, etc. does not get into the lungs. See **windpipe** for picture. [< LL < Gk. *epiglottis* < *epi-* on + *glotta* tongue]

ep·i·gram (ep′ə gram′) *n.* **1** a short, pointed, witty saying. *Example: "The only way to get rid of temptation is to yield to it."* **2** a short poem ending in a witty or clever turn of thought. *Example:*

"Here lies our Sovereign Lord the King
Whose word no man relied on,
Who never said a foolish thing,
Nor ever did a wise one."

[< L < Gk. *epigramma* < *epigraphein* < *epi-* on + *graphein* write]
☛ *Usage.* **Epigrams.** An **epigram** is a short, pointed, witty saying. A special type of epigram is the **paradox**, which makes a statement that, as it stands, contradicts fact or common sense or itself, and yet suggests a truth or at least a half truth: *All generalizations are false, including this one.* Closely related to epigrams are **aphorisms**—pithy statements but more likely to be abstract and not necessarily witty: *A living dog is better than a dead lion.* **Proverbs** are the often quoted, concrete expressions of popular wisdom. They are likely to make observations on character or conduct: *Still waters run deep.*

ep·i·gram·mat·ic (ep′ə grə mat′ik) *adj.* **1** of epigrams; full of epigrams. **2** like an epigram; terse and witty. —**ep′i·gram·mat′i·cal·ly,** *adv.*

ep·i·graph (ep′ə graf′) *n.* **1** an inscription on a building, monument, tomb, etc. **2** a quotation or motto at the beginning of a book or chapter. [< Gk. *epigraphē* inscription < *epigraphein* < *epi-* on + *graphein* write]

e·pig·ra·phy (i pig′rə fē) *n.* **1** inscriptions. **2** the branch of knowledge that deals with the deciphering and interpretation of inscriptions. [< *epigraph* inscription < Gk. *epigraphē* < *epigraphein.* See EPIGRAM.]

ep·i·lep·sy (ep′ə lep′sē) *n.* a chronic disorder of the central nervous system characterized by attacks involving partial or complete loss of consciousness and, usually, mild or severe convulsions. [< LL < Gk. *epilepsia* seizure, ult. < *epi-* on + *lambanein* take]

ep·i·lep·tic (ep′ə lep′tik) *adj., n.* —*adj.* **1** of or having to do with epilepsy: *Most epileptic seizures can be controlled with drugs.* **2** affected with epilepsy. —*n.* a person affected with epilepsy.

ep·i·logue (ep′ə log′) *n.* **1** a concluding section added to a novel, poem, etc. and serving to round out or interpret the work. **2** a speech or poem after the end of a play, addressed to the audience and spoken by one of the actors. **3** the actor who speaks an epilogue. [< F *épilogue* < L < Gk. *epilogos,* ult. < *epi-* in addition + *legein* speak]

ep·i·neph·rine (ep′ə nef′rin or ep′ə nef′rēn) *n.* adrenalin. [< *epi-* + Gk. *nephros* kidney + E *-ine²*]

E·piph·a·ny (i pif′ə nē) *n.* **1** the yearly Christian celebration commemorating the coming of the Wise Men to Christ at Bethlehem; in most Christian churches, January 6. **2 epiphany,** a moment or experience of revelation. [ME < OF < LL < LGk. *epiphania,* ult. < Gk. *epi-* to + *phainein* show]

ep·i·phyte (ep′ə fīt′) *n.* any plant, such as Spanish moss or certain orchids, that grows on or is attached to another plant for support but does not derive its nourishment from its host; air plant. [< *epi-* on + Gk. *phyton* plant]

ep·i·phyt·ic (ep′ə fit′ik) *adj.* being an epiphyte; having the characteristics of an epiphyte. —**ep′i·phyt′i·cal·ly,** *adv.*

Epis. **1** Episcopal; Episcopalian. **2** Epistle.

Episc. Episcopal; Episcopalian.

e·pis·co·pa·cy (i pis′kə pə sē) *n., pl.* -**cies. 1** the government of a church by bishops. **2** bishops as a group. **3** the position, rank, or term of office of a bishop; episcopate.

e·pis·co·pal (i pis′kə pəl) *adj.* **1** of or having to do with bishops. **2** governed by bishops. **3 Episcopal,** of or having to do with the Church of England, the Anglican Church of Canada, the Protestant Episcopal Church in the United States, etc. [< LL *episcopalis* < L *episcopus* bishop < Gk. *episkopos* overseer < *epi-* on, over + *skopos* watcher. See BISHOP.]

E·pis·co·pa·lian (i pis′kə pāl′yən *or* i pis′kə pā′lē ən) *n., adj.* —*n.* a member of the Protestant Episcopal Church. —*adj.* Episcopal.

E·pis·co·pa·lian·ism (i pis′kə pāl′yə niz′əm) *n.* **1** the doctrines, ceremonies, etc. of Episcopalians. **2** adherence to the Episcopal Church or Episcopal principles.

e·pis·co·pate (i pis′kə pit *or* i pis′kə pāt′) *n.* **1** the position, rank, or term of office of a bishop. **2** a district under the charge of a bishop; bishopric. **3** bishops as a group.

ep·i·sode (ep′ə sōd′) *n.* **1** an incident or experience that stands out from others: *The year he spent in France was an important episode in the artist's life.* **2 a** a set of events or actions separate from the main plot of a novel, story, etc. **b** *Music.* a similar digression in a composition. **3** in classical Greek tragedy, the part between two choric songs. [< Gk. *epeisodion,* neut., coming in besides, ult. < *epi-* on + *eis* into + *hodos* way]

ep·i·sod·ic (ep′ə sod′ik) *adj.* **1** like an episode; incidental; occasional. **2** consisting of a series of episodes: *His new novel is loosely episodic.* —**ep′i·sod′i·cal·ly,** *adv.*

ep·i·sod·i·cal (ep′ə sod′ə kəl) *adj.* episodic.

e·pis·te·mo·log·i·cal (i pis′tə mə loj′ə kəl) *adj.* of or having to do with epistemology. —**e·pis′te·mo·log′i·cal·ly,** *adv.*

e·pis·te·mol·o·gist (i pis′tə mol′ə jist) *n.* a person knowledgable about or studying epistemology.

e·pis·te·mol·o·gy (i pis′tə mol′ə jē) *n.* the part of philosophy that deals with the origin, nature, and limits of knowledge. [< Gk. *epistēmē* knowledge + E *-logy*]

e·pis·tle (i pis′əl) *n.* **1** a letter, especially an instructive or a formal one. **2** a literary work, usually in verse, written in the form of a letter. **3 Epistle, a** a letter written by one of Christ's Apostles. The Epistles make up 21 books of the New Testament. **b** a selection from one of these, read as part of certain Christian church services. [OE *epistole* < L < Gk. *epistolē,* ult. < *epi-* to + *stellein* send]
☛ *Syn.* **1.** See note at **letter.**

e·pis·to·lar·y (i pis′tə ler′ē) *adj.* **1** carried on by letters; contained in letters. **2** of letters; suitable for writing letters.

ep·i·style (ep′i stīl′) *n. Architecture.* the part of a building resting directly on top of columns; architrave. [< L < Gk. *epistylion* < *epi-* on + *stylos* pillar]

ep·i·taph (ep′ə taf′) *n.* **1** a short statement in memory of a dead person, usually put on his tombstone. **2** any brief writing resembling such an inscription. [< L < Gk. *epitaphion* funeral oration < *epi-* at + *taphos* tomb]

ep·i·tha·la·mi·um (ep′ə thə lā′mē əm) *n., pl.* -**mi·ums, -mi·a** (-mē ə). a poem or song in honor of a bride, bridegroom, or newly married couple. [< L < Gk. *epithalamion* < *epi-* at + *thalamos* bridal chamber]

ep·i·the·li·al (ep′ə thē′lē əl) *adj.* of the epithelium.

ep·i·the·li·um (ep′ə thē′lē əm) *n., pl.* -**li·ums, -li·a** (-lē ə). *Biology.* a thin layer of cells forming a tissue that covers surfaces and lines hollow organs. [< NL < Gk. *epi-* on + *thēlē* nipple]

ep·i·thet (ep′ə thet′) *n.* **1** a descriptive expression; an adjective or noun, or sometimes a clause, expressing some quality or attribute. In *crafty Ulysses* and *Richard the Lion-Hearted* the epithets are *crafty* and *the Lion-Hearted.* **2** a word or phrase (sometimes highly insulting) used in place of a person's name. **3** that part of the scientific name of an animal or plant which denotes a species, variety, or other division of a genus. [< L < Gk. *epitheton* added < *epi-* on + *tithenai* place]

e·pit·o·me (i pit′ə mē′) *n.* **1** a condensed account; summary. An epitome contains only the most important points of a literary work, subject, etc. **2** a person or thing that is typical or representative of a quality; an ideal or typical example: *Solomon is spoken of as the epitome of wisdom.* [< L < Gk. *epitomē* < *epitemnein* cut short < *epi-* into + *temnein* cut]

e·pit·o·mize (i pit′ə mīz′) *v.* -**mized, -miz·ing.** make an epitome of; summarize.

ep·i·zo·ot·ic (ep′ə zō ot′ik) *adj., n.* —*adj.* temporarily prevalent

among animals. —*n.* an epizootic disease. [< *epi-* among < Gk. *zōion* animal]

ep·och (ē′pok *or* ep′ək) *n.* **1** a period of time; era. **2** a period of time in which striking things happened. **3** the starting point of such a period: *The invention of the steam engine marked an epoch in the evolution of industry.* **4** one of the divisions of time into which a geological period is divided: *the Recent epoch of the Quarternary period.* [< Med.L < Gk. *epochē* a stopping, fixed point in time < *epechein* < *epi-* up + *echein* hold]

ep·och·al (ep′ək əl *or* ē′pok əl) *adj.* **1** having to do with an epoch. **2** epoch-making.

ep·och–mak·ing (ē′pok māk′ing *or* ep′ək–) *adj.* beginning an epoch; causing important changes.

ep·ode (ep′ōd) *n. Greek prosody.* **1** a lyric poem in which a long line is followed by a shorter one. **2** a part of a lyric ode following the strophe and antistrophe. [< F < L *epodos* < Gk. *epoidos* < *epi-* after + *aidein* sing]

ep·o·nym (ep′ō nim′) *n.* **1** a person from whom a nation, tribe, place, etc. gets or are reputed to get its name: *Romulus is the eponym of Rome.* **2** a person whose name is a synonym for something: *Ananias is the eponym of liar.* [< Gk. *epōnymos* < *epi-* to + *onyma* (dial.) name]

ep·on·y·mous (ep on′ə məs) *adj.* giving one's name to a nation, tribe, place, etc.

ep·ox·y (ep ok′sē) *adj., n., pl.* **-ox·ies.** —*adj.* containing oxygen as a bond between two different atoms already united in another way. Epoxy resins are extremely durable plastics used for adhesives, varnishes, etc. —*n.* an epoxy resin. [< *ep-* + *oxy*gen]

ep·si·lon (ep′sə lon′ *or* ep sī′lən) *n.* the fifth letter of the Greek alphabet (E, ε), corresponding to *e* (as in *get*) in English. [< Med.Gk. *epsilon* < Gk. *e psilon* simple *e*]

Epsom Downs (ep′səm) the track near the town of Epsom where England's famous horse race, the Derby, is run.

Epsom salt *or* **salts** hydrated magnesium sulphate, a bitter, white, crystalline powder used in medicine, especially as a laxative. *Formula:* MgSO$_4$·7H$_2$O [< *Epsom*, a town in SE England]

eq. **1** equal; equation. **2** equivalent. **3** equator.

eq·ua·bil·i·ty (ek′wə bil′ə tē *or* ē′kwə–) *n.* an equable condition or quality.

eq·ua·ble (ek′wə bəl *or* ē′kwə bəl) *adj.* changing little; uniform; even; tranquil. [< L *aequabilis* < *aequare* make uniform < *aequus* even, just] —**eq′ua·bly,** *adv.* —**eq′ua·ble·ness,** *n.*
☞ *Syn.* See note at **even.**

e·qual (ē′kwəl) *adj., n., v.* **e·qualled** *or* **e·qualed, e·qual·ling** *or* **e·qual·ing.** —*adj.* **1** the same in amount, size, number, value, degree, rank, nature, quality, etc. as another: *Ten dimes are equal to one dollar. The two roasts were almost equal in size.* **2** the same throughout; even; uniform. **3** evenly matched; with no advantage on either side: *an equal contest.* **4** having the strength, capacity, ability, etc. necessary for a task or situation (*used with* **to**): *She proved to be equal to the task.* **5** *Archaic.* just; fair.
—*n.* a person or thing that is equal to another: *We are all equals here. In swimming she had no equal.* 7 + 3 is the equal of 5 × 2.
—*v.* **1** be the same as: *Four times five equals twenty.* Symbol: = **2** make or do something equivalent to; match: *He tried hard to equal the scoring record.* —**e′qual·ly,** *adv.* [< L *aequalis* < *aequus* even, just]
☞ *Syn. adj.* **1. Equal, equivalent, tantamount** = as much as another or each other. **Equal** = exactly the same in size, amount, value, or any quality that can be measured or weighed: *The pieces of pie are equal.* **Equivalent,** applying to things otherwise different, means equal in value or in a quality that cannot be physically measured, such as meaning, importance, effect, etc.: *A Grade XIII course in high school may be regarded as equivalent to a first year course in university.* **Tantamount,** a formal word, applying only to immaterial things, means equivalent to another in effect: *His answer was tantamount to an insult.*

e·qual·i·ty (i kwol′ə tē) *n., pl.* **-ties.** being equal; sameness in amount, size, number, value, degree, rank, etc.

e·qual·i·za·tion (ē′kwəl ə zā′shən *or* ē′kwəl ī zā′shən) *n.* **1** the act of equalizing or the state of being equalized. **2** *Cdn.* the principle or practice of the federal government paying money to the poorer provinces in order to bring their standard of living nearer to that of the wealthier provinces.

e·qual·ize (ē′kwəl īz′) *v.* **-ized, -iz·ing. 1** make the same. **2** make even or uniform.

e·qual·iz·er (ē′kwə lī′zər) *n.* **1** a person or thing that equalizes. **2** a device for equalizing strain, pressure, etc. **3** *Electricity.* **a** any network of coils, resistors, or capacitors introduced into a circuit to change its response, especially its frequency response. **b** a conductor of low resistance used to equalize voltages.

e·qual–sign (ē′kwəl sīn′) *n.* the sign (=), used in equations.

equals sign equal-sign.

e·qua·nim·i·ty (ē′kwə nim′ə tē *or* ek′wə–) *n.* evenness of mind

hat, āge, fär; let, ēqual, tèrm; it, īce
hot, ōpen, ôrder; oil, out; cup, pút, rüle,
əbove, takən, pencəl, lemən, circəs
ch, child; ng, long; sh, ship
th, thin; ᴛʜ, then; zh, measure

or temper; calmness: *A wise man bears misfortune with equanimity.* [< L *aequanimitas* < *aequus* even + *animus* mind, temper]

e·quat·a·ble (i kwā′tə bəl) *adj.* that can be equated. —**e·quat′a·bil′i·ty,** *n.*

e·quate (i kwāt′) *v.* **e·quat·ed, e·quat·ing. 1** state to be equal; put in the form of an equation. **2** consider, treat, or represent as equal. **3** make equal. **4** reduce to an average. [< L *aequare* make equal < *aequus* equal]

e·qua·tion (i kwā′zhən *or* i kwā′shən) *n.* **1** a statement of equality between two quantities. *Examples:* (4 × 8) + 12 = 44; C = 2πr. **2** an expression using chemical formulas and symbols showing the substances used and produced in a chemical reaction. *Example:* HCl + NaOH = NaCl + H$_2$O. **3** equating or being equated.

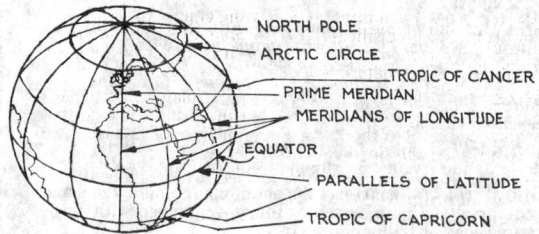

NORTH POLE
ARCTIC CIRCLE
TROPIC OF CANCER
PRIME MERIDIAN
MERIDIANS OF LONGITUDE
EQUATOR
PARALLELS OF LATITUDE
TROPIC OF CAPRICORN

e·qua·tor (i kwā′tər) *n.* **1** an imaginary circle around the middle of the earth, halfway between the North Pole and the South Pole. **2** a similarly situated circle on any heavenly body. **3** a great circle (**celestial equator**) of the celestial sphere, the plane of which is perpendicular to the axis of the earth. See *ecliptic* for picture. [< Med.L *aequator (diei et noctis)* equalizer (of day and night) < L *aequare* make equal. See EQUATE.]

e·qua·to·ri·al (ē′kwə tô′rē əl *or* ek′wə–) *adj.* **1** of, at, or near the equator: *equatorial countries.* **2** similar to conditions at or near the equator.

eq·uer·ry (ek′wər ē) *n., pl.* **-ries. 1** an officer of a royal or noble household who has charge of the horses or who accompanies his master's carriage. **2** an attendant on a royal or noble person. [short for *groom of the equerry*; < F *écurie* stable < Gmc.; influenced by L *equus* horse]

e·ques·tri·an (i kwes′trē ən) *adj., n.* —*adj.* **1** of horsemen or horsemanship; having to do with horseback riding: *Jockeys need to have equestrian skill.* **2** on horseback; mounted on horseback. An equestrian statue shows a person riding a horse. —*n.* a rider or performer on horseback. [< L *equestris* of a horseman < *equus* horse]

e·ques·tri·enne (i kwes′trē en′) *n.* a woman rider or performer on horseback. [< F]

equi– *combining form.* **1** equal, as in *equivalence.* **2** equally, as in *equiangular, equidistant.* [< L *aequus* equal]

e·qui·an·gu·lar (ē′kwē ang′gyə lər) *adj.* having all angles equal: *A square is equiangular.*

e·qui·dis·tant (ē′kwə dis′tənt) *adj.* equally distant: *All points of the circumference of a circle are equidistant from the centre.* —**e′qui·dis′tant·ly,** *adv.*

e·qui·lat·er·al (ē′kwə lat′ər əl) *adj., n.* —*adj.* designating a geometric figure having all its sides equal in length. —*n.* **1** a geometric figure having all its sides equal in length. **2** a side equal in length to others. [< LL *aequilateralis* < L *aequus* equal + *latus, lateris* side] —**e′qui·lat′er·al·ly,** *adv.*

e·quil·i·brant (i kwil′ə brənt) *n. Physics.* a force able to balance a specified force or set of forces.

e·qui·li·brate (ē′kwə lī′brāt *or* i kwil′ə brāt′) *v.* **-brat·ed, -brat·ing.** balance. [< LL *aequilibratus* in equilibrium < L *aequus* equal + *libra* balance] —**e′qui·li·bra′tion,** *n.* —**e′qui·li·bra′tor,** *n.*

e·qui·lib·ri·um (ē′kwə lib′rē əm *or* ek′wə–) *n.* **1** a state of balance; condition in which opposing forces exactly balance or equal each other: *Scales are in equilibrium when the weights on each side are equal.* **2** the state of a chemical system when no further change occurs in it. **3** a condition of balance between powers of any kind. **4** mental poise: *She is a sensible person and*

will not let petty annoyances upset her equilibrium. [< L *aequilibrium,* ult. < *aequus* equal + *libra* balance]

e·qui·mo·lec·u·lar (ē′kwə mə lek′yə lər) *adj.* having an equal number of molecules.

e·quine (ē′kwīn *or* ek′wīn) *adj., n.* —*adj.* of horses; like a horse; like that of a horse. —*n.* a horse. [< L *equinus* < *equus* horse]

e·qui·noc·tial (ē′kwə nok′shəl *or* ek′wə-) *adj., n.* —*adj.* 1 having to do with either equinox. Equinoctial points are the two imaginary points in the sky where the sun crosses the celestial equator. 2 occurring at or near the equinox: *equinoctial gales.* 3 at or near the earth's equator: *Borneo is an equinoctial island.* —*n.* 1 the celestial equator. 2 a storm occurring at or near the equinox.

equinoctial line the celestial equator. See **equator** (def. 3).

e·qui·nox (ē′kwə noks′ *or* ek′wə-) *n.* either of the two times in the year when the centre of the sun crosses the celestial equator, and day and night are of equal length all over the earth. The **vernal** (spring) **equinox** occurs about March 21, the **autumnal equinox** about September 22. [< Med.L *equinoxium* < L *aequinoctium* < *aequus* equal + *nox* night]

e·quip (i kwip′) *v.* **e·quipped, e·quip·ping.** furnish with all that is needed; fit out; provide: *The fort was equipped with guns, ammunition, and food. He was equipped with a good mind and a keen sense of humor.* [< F *équipper* < OF *esquiper* < ON *skipa* man (a ship) < *skip* ship. Akin to SHIP.]
☛ *Syn.* See note at **furnish.**

eq·ui·page (ek′wə pij) *n.* 1 a carriage. 2 a carriage with its horses, driver, and servants. 3 equipment; outfit.

equip·ment (i kwip′mənt) *n.* 1 the act of equipping. 2 the state of being equipped. 3 what a person or thing is equipped with; an outfit. 4 knowledge or skill; ability.

e·qui·poise (ē′kwə poiz′ *or* ek′wə-) *n.* 1 a state of balance. 2 a balancing force; counterbalance.

eq·ui·se·tum (ek′wə sē′təm) *n., pl.* **-tums, -ta** (-te). 1 a genus of plants with jointed, green, cylindrical stems, either simple or branched, rough to the touch, and having leaves reduced to scales. 2 horsetail. [< NL < L *equisaetum* < *equus* horse + *saeta* (coarse) hair]

eq·ui·ta·ble (ek′wə tə bəl) *adj.* 1 fair; just: *Paying a person what he has earned is equitable.* 2 *Law.* having to do with or dependent upon equity; valid in equity, as distinguished from common law and statute law. —**eq′ui·ta·ble·ness,** *n.* —**eq′ui·ta·bly,** *adv.*

eq·ui·ta·tion (ek′wə tā′shən) *n.* horseback riding; horsemanship. [< L *equitatio, -onis,* ult. < *equus* horse]

eq·ui·tes (ek′wə tēz′) *n.pl.* in ancient Rome: 1 originally, the class of citizens serving in the cavalry. 2 later, a privileged class of citizens. [< L *equites,* pl. of *eques* horseman, knight < *equus* horse]

eq·ui·ty (ek′wə tē) *n., pl.* **-ties.** 1 fairness; justice. 2 what is fair and just. 3 *Law.* **a** a system of rules and principles based on fairness and justice. Equity covers cases in which fairness and justice require a settlement not covered by common law. **b** a claim or right according to equity. 4 the amount that a property, business, etc. is worth beyond what is owed on it. [< L *aequitas* < *aequus* even, just]

e·quiv·a·lence (i kwiv′ə ləns *or* i kwiv′ləns) *n.* 1 a being equivalent; equality in value, force, significance, etc. 2 *Chemistry.* **a** the quality of having equal valence. **b** valence. 3 *Geometry.* the fact of being equal in extent, but not in form.

e·quiv·a·lent (i kwiv′ə lənt *or* i kwiv′lənt) *adj., n.* —*adj.* 1 equal in value, measure, force, effect, meaning, etc.: *Nodding one's head is equivalent to saying yes.* 2 *Chemistry.* equal in combining or reacting value to a (stated) quantity of another substance. 3 having the same extent: *A triangle and a square may be equivalent in area.* —*n.* 1 something equivalent: *He accepted the equivalent of his wages in groceries.* 2 a word, expression, sign, etc. of equal meaning or import. [< LL *aequivalens, -entis,* ppr. of *aequivalere* < L *aequus* equal + *valere* be worth] —**e·quiv′a·lent·ly,** *adv.*

e·quiv·o·cal (i kwiv′ə kəl) *adj.* 1 having two or more meanings; intentionally vague or ambiguous: *His equivocal answer left us uncertain as to his real opinion.* 2 undecided; uncertain: *The result of the experiment was equivocal.* 3 questionable; rousing suspicion: *The stranger's equivocal behavior made everyone distrust him.* [< LL *aequivocus* ambiguous < L *aequus* equal + *vocare* call] —**e·quiv′o·cal·ly,** *adv.* —**e·quiv′o·cal·ness,** *n.*

e·quiv·o·cate (i kwiv′ə kāt′) *v.* **-cat·ed, -cat·ing.** use expressions of double meaning in order to mislead. [< LL

aequivocare call by the same name < *aequivocus* ambiguous. See EQUIVOCAL.] —**e·quiv′o·cat′ing·ly,** *adv.* —**e·quiv′o·ca′tor,** *n.*

e·quiv·o·ca·tion (i kwiv′ə kā′shən) *n.* 1 the use of equivocal expressions in order to mislead. 2 an equivocal expression.

–er[1] *noun-forming suffix.* 1 a person or thing that —s: *admirer* = *a person who admires; burner* = *a thing that burns.* 2 a native or inhabitant of — : *Newfoundlander* = *a native or inhabitant of Newfoundland; villager* = *a native or inhabitant of a village.* 3 a person that makes or works with —: *hatter* = *a person who makes hats.* 4 a person or thing that is or has —: *six-footer* = *a person who is six feet tall.* [OE *-ere,* ult. < L *-arius*]
☛ *Usage.* **-er, -or.** Names of persons or things performing an act (nouns of agent) and some other nouns are generally formed in English by adding **-er** to a verb (*doer, killer, painter, heater, thinker*), but many, chiefly nouns taken from Latin or French (*assessor, prevaricator*), end in **-or.** With a few words (*exhibitor,* or *exhibiter, adviser* or *advisor*) either ending may be used.

–er[2] *suffix.* a person or thing connected with —, as in *officer.* [< AF, OF < L *-arius, -arium*]

–er[3] *suffix forming the comparative degree.* 1 of certain adjectives, as in *softer, smoother.* 2 of certain adverbs, as in *slower.* [OE *-ra* (masc.), *-re* (fem., neut.), adj. OE *-or,* adv.]
☛ *Usage.* See notes at **adjective** and **adverb.**

–er[4] *suffix.* frequently; again and again, as in *flicker, patter.* [OE *-rian*]

Er erbium.

E.R. Queen Elizabeth (for L *Elizabeth Regina*).

e·ra (ēr′ə) *n.* 1 a historical period distinguished by certain important or significant happenings; an age in history. The decade from 1929 to 1939 is often called the Depression Era. 2 a period of time starting from some important or significant happening, date, etc.: *the A-bomb era.* 3 a system of reckoning time from some important or significant happening, given date, etc. The Christian era is the period of time reckoned from about four years after the Birth of Christ. 4 one of five very extensive periods of time in geological history. See chart at **geology.** [< LL *era,* var. of *aera* number, epoch; probably same word as L *aera* counters (for reckoning), pl. of *aes* brass]

e·rad·i·ca·ble (i rad′ə kə bəl) *adj.* that can be eradicated.

e·rad·i·cate (i rad′ə kāt′) *v.* **-cat·ed, -cat·ing.** 1 get rid of entirely; destroy completely: *Yellow fever has been eradicated in many countries.* 2 pull out by the roots: *to eradicate weeds from a garden.* [< L *eradicare* < *ex-* out + *radix, radicis* root] —**e·rad′i·ca′tor,** *n.*

e·rad·i·ca·tion (i rad′ə kā′shən) *n.* an eradicating; complete destruction.

e·rase (i rās′) *v.* **e·rased, e·ras·ing.** 1 rub out; scrape out: *He erased the wrong answer and wrote in the right one.* 2 remove all trace of; blot out: *The blow on his head erased from his memory the details of the accident.* [< L *erasus,* pp. of *eradere* < *ex-* out + *radere* scrape] —**e·ras′a·ble,** *adj.*
☛ *Syn.* 1, 2. **Erase, expunge, efface** = remove everything from a record of some kind. **Erase** = remove all trace of something by scraping or rubbing, literally as from paper or figuratively as from memory: *I erased him from my mind.* **Expunge** = blot out so that the thing seems never to have existed: *The judge ordered certain charges expunged from the record.* **Efface** = wipe out identity or existence by or as if by rubbing away the face: *Rain and wind effaced the inscription on the monument.*

e·ras·er (i rās′ər) *n.* a piece of rubber or any other substance for erasing marks made with pencil, ink, chalk, etc.

e·ra·sure (i rā′shər *or* i rā′zhər) *n.* 1 erasing. 2 an erased word, letter, etc. 3 a place where a word, letter, etc. has been erased.

Er·a·to (er′ə tō′) *n. Greek mythology.* the Muse of lyric poetry.

er·bi·um (ėr′bē əm) *n.* a rare metallic chemical element of the yttrium group. Symbol: Er; *at.no.* 68; *at.wt.* 167.26. [< NL *erbium* < Ytt*erby,* a town in Sweden]

ere (er) *prep., conj. Archaic.* —*prep.* before. —*conj.* 1 before. 2 sooner than; rather than. [OE ǣr]
☛ *Hom.* **air, e'er, err, heir.**

Er·e·bus (er′ə bəs) *n. Greek mythology.* a dark, gloomy place through which the dead passed on their way to Hades.

e·rect (i rekt′) *adj., v.* —*adj.* 1 straight up; upright: *That flagpole stands erect.* 2 raised; bristling: *The cat faced the dog with fur erect.* —*v.* 1 put straight up; set upright: *They erected a television antenna on the roof. The mast was erected on a firm base.* 2 build; put up: *That house was erected forty years ago.* 3 put together; set up: *When the missing parts arrived, we erected the machine.* [ME < L *erectus,* pp. of *erigere* < *ex-* up + *regere* direct] —**e·rect′ly,** *adv.* —**e·rect′ness,** *n.* —**e·rect′or,** *n.*
☛ *Syn. adj.* 1. See note at **upright.**

e·rec·tile (i rek′tīl) *adj.* of body tissue or an organ, capable of becoming rigid or erect when filled with blood.

e·rec·tion (i rek′shən) *n.* 1 the act of erecting or the state of

being erected; construction: *the erection of a building.* **2** something erected; a building or other structure. **3** the enlarged, rigid state or condition of erectile tissue or an organ, especially of the penis or clitoris when filled with blood due to sexual excitement. **4** an erect penis.

ere·long (er′lông′) *adv. Archaic.* before long; soon.

er·e·mite (er′ə mīt′) *n. Archaic.* hermit. [ME < L *eremita* < Gk. *erēmitēs* dweller in a desert < *erēmos* uninhabited. Doublet of HERMIT.]

ere·while (er′wīl′ *or* -hwīl′) *adv. Archaic.* a while before; a short time ago.

erg (ėrg) *n.* a unit for measuring work or energy, equal to 0.1 microjoules. *Abbrev.:* e [< Gk. *ergon* work]

er·go (ėr′gō) *adv. or conj. Latin.* therefore.

er·gom·e·ter (ėr gom′ə tər) *n.* an instrument for measuring the work done, or energy produced, by a muscle or group of muscles. [< Gk. *ergon* work + E *-meter.* 20c.]

er·go·nom·ic (ėr gə nom′ik) *adj.* of or having to do with ergonomics.

er·go·nom·ics (ėr gə nom′iks) *n. (used with a singular verb)* the scientific study of the relationship between human beings and their working environment with a view to increasing efficiency. [< Gk. *ergon* work + E *economics.* 20c.]

er·gon·o·mist (ėr gon′ə mist′) *n.* a person trained in ergonomy, especially one whose work it is.

er·got (ėr′gət *or* ėr′got) *n.* **1** a disease of rye and other cereals in which the grains are replaced by blackish fungus growths. **2** any fungus producing this disease. **3** the growth produced by this disease. **4** a medicine made from these growths, used to stop bleeding and to contract muscles. [< F < OF *argot* cock's spur]

E·rie (ēr′ē) *n., pl.* **E·rie** *or* **E·ries. 1** a member of an Amerindian people living along the southern and eastern shores of Lake Erie. **2** the language of the Erie.

Er·in (er′ən) *n. Poetic.* Ireland.

E·rin·y·es (i rin′ē ēz′) *n. pl.* of **Erinys.** *Greek mythology.* the Furies, also called Eumenides.

E·rin·ys (i rin′is *or* i rī′nis) *n., pl.* **E·rin·y·es.** one of the Erinyes.

erl·king (ėrl′king′) *n. Germanic mythology.* a spirit or personification of natural forces, such as cold, storm, etc. that does harm, especially to children. [< G *Erlkönig* alder-king, a mistranslation of Danish *ellerkonge* king of the elves]

er·mine (ėr′mən) *n., pl.* **-mines** *or* **(esp. collectively) -mine. 1** a small carnivorous mammal (*Mustela erminea*) of northern and arctic regions closely related to the weasels, having thick, soft fur which in summer is brown on the upper parts of the body and creamy white on the under parts, but which in winter in the most northerly regions changes to pure white except for the tip of the tail, which remains black. **2** any northern weasel in its white winter coat. **3** the highly valued fur of an ermine, traditionally used to trim the ceremonial or official robes of a judge, monarch, etc. **4** the position or rank of a judge, noble, or monarch. [ME < OF < Gmc. or < L *Armenius* (*mus*) Armenian (rat)]

Er·mite (ėr′mīt) *n. Cdn.* a type of sharp, salty blue cheese made in the Eastern townships of Quebec. [< Cdn F < F *ermite* hermit, because made by Benedictine monks.]

erne (ėrn) *n.* a sea eagle, especially *Haliaetus albicilla* of Europe. [OE *earn*]

e·rode (i rōd′) *v.* **e·rod·ed, e·rod·ing. 1** eat into; eat or wear away gradually: *Running water erodes soil and rocks. The channel had probably eroded for a million years.* **2** form by a gradual eating or wearing away: *The stream eroded a channel in the solid rock.* [< L *erodere* < *ex-* away + *rodere* gnaw]

e·rog·e·nous (ə roj′ə nəs) *adj.* of or designating any area of the body that can produce sexual excitement when stimulated.

E·ros (ėr′os *or* er′os) *n. Greek mythology.* the god of love, son of Aphrodite. Eros corresponds to the Roman god Cupid.

e·ro·sion (i rō′zhən) *n.* **1** a gradual eating or wearing away by glaciers, running water, waves, or wind: *By absorbing water, trees help prevent the erosion of soil.* **2** the condition of being eaten or worn away. [< L *erosio, -onis* < *erodere.* See ERODE.]

e·ro·sive (i rō′siv) *adj.* eroding; causing erosion.

e·rot·ic (i rot′ik) *adj., n.* —*adj.* **1** of, having to do with, or arousing sexual desire. **2** characterized by strong sexual desire or sensitivity to sexual stimulation. —*n.* an erotic person. [< Gk. *erōtikos* of Eros] —**e·rot′i·cal·ly,** *adv.*

e·rot·i·ca (i rot′i kə) *n.* erotic literature, art, etc.

e·rot·i·cism (i rot′i siz′əm) *n.* **1** an erotic quality, theme, or character. **2** sexual arousal or desire.

err (ėr *or* er) *v.* **1** go wrong; make mistakes: *Everyone errs at some time or other.* **2** be wrong; be mistaken or incorrect. **3** do wrong;

hat, āge, fär; let, ēqual, tėrm; it, īce
hot, ōpen, ôrder; oil, out; cup, pút, rūle,
above, takən, pencəl, lemən, circəs
ch, child; ng, long; sh, ship
th, thin; ᴛʜ, then; zh, measure

sin: *To err is human; to forgive, divine.* [ME < OF < L *errare* wander]

☛ *Hom.* **air, e'er, ere,** and **heir** (for 2nd pronun. of **err**).

☛ *Pronun.* **Err.** In the past regularly pronounced (ėr); but there is a growing tendency to pronounce it (er), probably by analogy with *error* (er′ər).

er·rand (er′ənd) *n.* **1** a trip to do something for someone else: *The little boy goes to the stores and runs other errands for his parents.* **2** what one is sent to do. **3** the purpose or object of a trip. [OE *ǣrende*]

errand boy 1 a boy who does errands. **2** *Informal.* a person who acts entirely under others, without using his own initiative or intelligence.

er·rant (er′ənt) *adj.* **1** travelling in search of adventure; wandering; roving. **2** of thoughts, conduct, etc., straying from the regular path. [< F *errant,* ppr. of OF *errer* travel, blended with F *errant,* ppr. of *errer* err]

er·rant·ry (er′ənt rē) *n., pl.* **-ries.** the conduct or action of a knight-errant.

er·ra·ta (ə rä′tə *or* ə rā′tə) *n. pl.* of **erratum.**

er·rat·ic (ə rat′ik) *adj., n.* —*adj.* **1** not steady; uncertain; irregular: *An erratic mind jumps from one idea to another.* **2** odd; unusual: *erratic behavior.* —*n.* **1** *Geology.* a boulder or mass of rock transported from its original site, especially by glacial action. **2** an erratic person or thing. [< L *erraticus* < *errare* err]

er·rat·i·cal·ly (ə rat′ik lē) *adv.* in an erratic manner.

er·ra·tum (ə rä′təm *or* ə rā′təm) *n., pl.* **-ta. 1** an error in printing or writing. **2** Usually, **errata,** *pl.* a list of errors in a printed work, included with the work on a separate page. [< L *erratum,* neut. pp. of *errare* err]

er·ro·ne·ous (ə rō′nē əs) *adj.* wrong; mistaken; incorrect: *Years ago many people held the erroneous belief that the earth was flat.* [< L *erroneus* < *errare* err] —**er·ro′ne·ous·ly,** *adv.* —**er·ro′ne·ous·ness,** *n.*

er·ror (er′ər) *n.* **1** something wrong; what is incorrect; a mistake: *A false belief is an error.* **2** wrongdoing; sin. **3** *Baseball.* a faulty play that permits the batter to remain at bat or allows a runner who should have been put out to advance. **4** in measurements or calculations, the difference between the observed or approximate amount and the correct amount.

in error a wrong or mistaken: *The teacher was in error.* **b** by mistake: *He got on the westbound bus in error.* [ME < OF < L *error* < *errare* err]

☛ *Syn.* **1. Error, mistake** = something incorrect or wrong. **Error** implies a straying or deviation from a rule or course of action: *I failed my test because of errors in spelling.* **Mistake** applies to an error in judging or understanding, usually due to taking one thing for another: *I used your towel by mistake.*

er·satz (er′zäts *or* er′zats) *adj. or n.* substitute. [< G]

Erse (ėrs) *n., adj.* —*n.* **1** the Celtic language of the Scottish Highlanders. **2** the Celtic language of Ireland or of the Isle of Man. —*adj.* of either of these languages.

☛ *Usage.* The terms **Gaelic** (for the Scottish language), **Irish,** and **Manx** are now preferred to **Erse.**

erst (ėrst) *adv. Archaic.* formerly; long ago. [OE *ǣrst,* superlative of *ǣr* ere]

erst·while (ėrst′wīl′ *or* -hwīl′) *adv., adj.* —*adv. Archaic.* some time ago; in time past; formerly. —*adj.* former; past.

e·ru·cic acid (i rū′sik) a fatty acid found especially in rapeseed. *Formula:* $C_{22}H_{42}O_2$

e·ruct (i rukt′) *v.* belch. [< L *eructare* < *ex-* out + *ructare* belch]

e·ruc·tate (i ruk′tāt) *v.* **-tat·ed, -tat·ing.** belch.

e·ruc·ta·tion (i ruk′tā′shən *or* ē′ruk tā′shən) *n.* **1** belching. **2** that which is belched up.

er·u·dite (er′yə dīt′ *or* er′ə dīt′) *adj.* scholarly; learned. [< L *eruditus,* pp. of *erudire* instruct < *ex-* away + *rudis* rude] —**er′u·dite′ly,** *adv.* —**er′u·dite′ness,** *n.*

er·u·di·tion (er′yə dish′ən *or* er′ə dish′ən) *n.* acquired knowledge; scholarship; learning.

e·rupt (i rupt′) *v.* **1** burst forth: *Hot water erupted from the geyser.* **2** throw forth: *The volcano erupted lava and ashes.* **3** break out in a rash: *Her skin erupted when she had measles.* **4** break through the gums: *When the baby was seven months old, its teeth started to erupt.* [< L *eruptus,* pp. of *erumpere* < *ex-* out + *rumpere* burst]

e·rup·tion (i rup′shən) *n.* **1** a bursting forth. **2** a throwing forth of lava, etc. from a volcano or of hot water from a geyser. **3** *Medicine.* **a** a breaking out in a rash: *When a person has measles, his skin is in a state of eruption.* **b** red spots on the skin; rash: *Scarlet fever causes an eruption on the body.* **4** a breaking through of the gums: *The eruption of teeth made the baby fretful.* **5** an outbreak; outburst: *eruptions of racial or national hatred.*

e·rup·tive (i rup′tiv) *adj., n.* —*adj.* **1** bursting forth; tending to burst forth. **2** causing the skin to break out: *Measles is an eruptive disease.* **3** *Geology.* of or formed by volcanic eruptions. —*n. Geology.* a rock formed or forced up by eruption.

-ery *noun-forming suffix. noun-forming suffix.* **1** a place for ——ing, as in *cannery, hatchery.* **2** a place for ——s, as in *nunnery.* **3** the occupation or business of a ——, as in *cookery.* **4** the state or condition of a ——, as in *slavery.* **5** the qualities, actions, etc. of a ——, as in *knavery.* **6** ——s as a group, as in *machinery.* [< OF *-erie* < *-ier* (< L *-arius*) + *-ie* (< LL *-ia* < Gk. *-ia*)]

er·y·sip·e·las (er′ə sip′ə ləs *or* ēr′ə sip′ə ləs) *n.* **1** an acute infectious disease characterized by fever and a deep-red inflammation of the skin. **2** an acute or chronic bacterial disease of swine, and less commonly of turkeys and sheep, characterized by enteritis, red patches on the skin, and arthritis. [< Gk.]

e·ryth·ro·my·cin (i rith′rō mī′sin) *n.* an antibiotic drug related to streptomycin, used for treating infections caused by certain gram-positive bacteria. Formula: $C_{37}H_{67}NO_{13}$ [< Gk. *erythros* red + *mykēs* fungus]

Es einsteinium.

-es¹ *noun plural suffix.* a form of **-s** used for nouns ending in *s, z, sh, ch,* or a final *y* that changes to *i* in the plural, for some nouns ending in a vowel, and for nouns ending in *f* that changes to *v* in the plural. *Examples: masses, fuzzes, bushes, churches, families, tomatoes, scarves.*

-es² *verb suffix.* a form of **-s** used for verbs ending in *s, z, sh, ch,* or a final *y* that changes to *i,* and for some verbs ending in a vowel. *Examples: blesses, buzzes, flashes, teaches, flies, goes.*

E·sau (ē′so *or* ē′sô) *n.* in the Bible, the older son of Isaac and Rebecca, who sold his birthright to his brother Jacob (Genesis 25:21-34).

es·ca·drille (es′kə dril′) *n. Historical.* **1** a squadron of usually six aircraft, especially in the French armed forces in World War I. **2** a small fleet of ships. [< F *escadrille,* dim. of *escadre* squadron; form influenced by Sp. *escuadrilla,* dim. of *escuadra*]

es·ca·lade (es′kə lād′) *n., v.* —*n.* the climbing of the walls of a fortified place with the help of ladders. —*v.* scale or attack over (a wall, rampart, etc.) by means of ladders. [< F < Ital. *scalata,* ult. < L *scala* ladder]

es·ca·late (es′kə lāt′) *v.* **-lat·ed, -lat·ing.** increase or expand by stages in amount, intensity, extent, etc.: *escalating costs. Small battles can easily escalate into major wars.* [back formation < *escalator*] —**es′ca·la′tion,** *n.*

es·ca·la·tor (es′kə lā′tər) *n.* a continuous moving stairway. Many department stores have escalators to carry the customers from one floor to another. [< *Escalator,* a blend of *escalade* and *elevator,* a trademark]

escalator clause a provision in a contract allowing an increase or decrease in wages, royalties, etc. under specified conditions.

es·cal·lop (es kol′əp *or* es kal′əp) *v., n.* —*v.* bake in a cream sauce or with bread crumbs. —*n.* **1** food cooked in this way: *escallop of veal.* **2** a scallop (def. 1). [(originally n.) < OF *escalope* shell < Gmc.]

es·ca·pade (es′kə pād′ *or* es′kə pād′) *n.* **1** a breaking loose from rules or restraint. **2** a wild adventure or prank. [< F < Ital. *scappata < scappare* escape]

es·cape (es kāp′) *v.* **-caped, -cap·ing;** *n., adj.* —*v.* **1** get free; get out and away: *to escape from prison.* **2** get free from: *He thinks he will never escape hard work.* **3** keep free or safe from; avoid: *We all escaped the measles.* **4** avoid capture, trouble, etc.: *The thief has escaped.* **5** come out of without being intended: *A cry escaped her lips.* **6** fail to be noticed or remembered by: *I knew his face, but his name escaped me.*
—*n.* **1** escaping. **2** a way of escaping: *There was no escape from the trap.* **3** relief from boredom, trouble, etc.: *to find escape in mystery stories.* **4** an outflow or leakage of gas, water, etc.
—*adj.* providing a way of escape or avoidance. [ME < AF *escaper,* ult. < L *ex-* out + *cappa* cloak]
☛ *Syn. v.* **3.** Escape, evade, elude = keep free from someone or something. **Escape** = miss possible or threatened unpleasantness or danger by being out of its way or by managing to keep free: *He escaped being killed in the blast because he had not gone to work.* **Evade** emphasizes cleverness or trickery in managing to stay free: *Some children try to evade doing chores around the*

home. **Elude** suggests slipperiness and quickness in getting away from trouble that is close or in keeping free: *The bandit eluded the posse that was following him.*

escape clause a clause that frees a signer of a contract from certain responsibilities under specified circumstances.

es·cap·ee (i skā pē′) *n.* a person who has escaped, especially one who has escaped from prison.

escape mechanism **1** *Psychiatry.* a thought or action, usually unconscious, that permits avoidance of an unpleasant reality. **2** any device or apparatus, such as an ejection seat in an aircraft, designed to permit escape or release in an emergency.

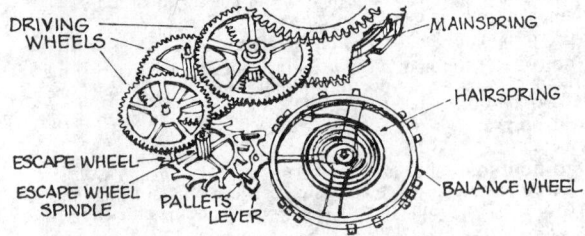

The balance wheel and lever escapement of a mainspring-driven mechanical watch. The mainspring turns the escape wheel through a series of driving wheels. The balance wheel and lever control the movement of the escape wheel by allowing it to turn through only one notch at a time.

es·cape·ment (es kāp′mənt) *n.* **1** a device in a timepiece consisting of a notched wheel and a lever or catch, by which the clockwork is controlled and which transmits energy from the source of power to the pendulum or balance wheel. **2** the mechanism that controls the movement of a typewriter carriage.

escape velocity *Physics.* the minimum speed an object must attain to get free of a gravitational field. An escape velocity of approximately 40 320 km/h is needed to overcome the gravitational pull of the earth.

es·cap·ism (es kāp′iz əm) *n.* a habitual avoidance of unpleasant realities by recourse to imagination or to entertainment.

es·cap·ist (es kāp′ist) *n., adj.* —*n.* a person who seeks escape from reality in daydreams, amusements, etc. —*adj.* providing a way of escaping from reality: *escapist literature.*

es·ca·role (es′kə rōl′) *n.* a kind of endive that has broad leaves, used for salads. [< F]

es·carp (es kärp′) *n.* escarpment.

es·carp·ment (es kärp′mənt) *n.* **1** a steep slope; cliff. **2** the ground made into a steep slope as part of a fortification. [< F *escarpement < escarper* form into a steep slope < *escarpe* a steep slope < Ital. *scarpa* < Gmc.]

es·cha·to·log·i·cal (es′kə tə loj′ə kəl) *adj.* of or having to do with eschatology.

es·cha·tol·o·gy (es′kə tol′ə jē) *n.* **1** the body of doctrines concerning the four last things: death, judgment, heaven, and hell. **2** the branch of theology that deals with these things. [< Gk. *eschatos* last, final + E *-logy*]

es·cheat (es chēt′) *n., v.* —*n. Law.* **1** a reverting of the ownership of property to the state or to the lord of a manor when there are no legal heirs. **2** the property whose ownership has so reverted. —*v. Law.* **1** revert to the state or the lord of the manor. **2** confiscate; transfer (the ownership of property) to the state. [ME < OF *eschete,* ult. < L *ex-* out + *cadere* fall]

es·chew (es chü′) *v.* avoid; shun; keep away from: *A wise person eschews bad company.* [ME < OF *eschiver* < Gmc.] —**es·chew′er,** *n.*

Es·co·ri·al (es kô′rē əl) *n.* a huge structure near Madrid, containing a palace and tomb for the kings of Spain, a church, a college, and a monastery.

es·cort (*n.* es′kôrt; *v.* es kôrt′) *n., v.* —*n.* **1** a person or a group of persons going with another to give protection, show honor, etc.: *an escort of ten Mounties.* **2** a man or boy who accompanies a woman or girl on a walk, to a dance, etc.: *Her escort to the party was a tall young man.* **3** one or more ships, aircraft, etc. serving as a guard: *During World War II Canada's destroyers served as escorts to many convoys.* **4** the act of going with another as an escort.
—*v.* accompany as an escort: *Warships escorted the royal yacht. Four policemen escorted the dangerous criminal to prison. John escorted Mary to the movies.* [< F *escorte* < Ital. *scorta* < *scorgere* guide < L *ex-* out + *corrigere* set right]
☛ *Syn. v.* See note at **accompany.**

es·cri·toire (es′krə twär′ *or* es′krə twär′) *n.* a writing desk. [< F < LL *scriptorium* < L *scribere* write]

es·crow (es′krō *or* es krō′) *n. Law.* a deed, bond, or other written agreement put in charge of a third person until certain conditions are fulfilled by two other parties.
in escrow, held by a third party in accordance with an agreement. [< AF var. of OF *escroue* scrap, scroll < Gmc.]

es·cu·do (es kü′dō) *n., pl.* **-dos. 1** the basic unit of money in Portugal and Mozambique, divided into 100 centavos. See table at **money. 2** a unit of money in Chile, equal to 1/1000 of a peso. **3** a coin worth one escudo. **3** any of various gold or silver coins formerly used in Spain, Portugal, and their colonies. [< Pg. < L *scutum* shield]

es·cu·lent (es′kyə lənt) *adj.* suitable for food; edible. [< L *esculentus* < *esca* food]

Es·cu·ri·al (es kyür′ē əl) *n.* Escorial.

es·cutch·eon (es kuch′ən) *n.* **1** a shield or shield-shaped surface on which a coat of arms is put. **2** a protective metal plate around a keyhole. **3** the panel on a ship's stern bearing her name.
blot on the escutcheon, a disgrace to honor or reputation. [< ONF *escuchon* < L *scutum* shield]

–ese *suffix.* **1** of, belonging to, or having to do with: *Japanese = of, belonging to, or having to do with Japan.* **2** a native or inhabitant of: *Portuguese = a native or inhabitant of Portugal.* **3** the language of: *Chinese = the language of China.* **4** the typical style or vocabulary of: *journalese = newspaper style.* [< OF *-eis* < L *-ensis*]

ESE *or* **E.S.E.** east-southeast, a direction halfway between east and southeast.

es·ker (es′kər) *n.* a winding ridge of sand, gravel, etc. believed to have been deposited by meltwater streams flowing inside the retreating glaciers of the Ice Age. Also, **eskar.** [< Irish *eiscir*]

Es·ki·mo (es′kə mō′) *n., pl.* **-mos** *or* **-mo. 1** a member of a group of peoples living in northern Canada, Alaska, Greenland, and NE Asia. **2** the language of these peoples; Inuktitut. [< Danish < F < Algonquian *eskimantsis* eaters of raw flesh]

Eskimo dog *Cdn.* a breed of large, very strong dog native to the North, long used by the Inuit for pulling sleds and for hunting. An Eskimo dog can go for several days without food and still pull a load of 50 kg.

Eskimo pie a chocolate-coated ice-cream bar.

e·so·phag·e·al (ē′sə faj′ē əl) *adj.* of, having to do with, or connected with the esophagus.

e·soph·a·gus (ē sof′ə gəs *or* i sof′ə gəs) *n., pl.* **-gi** (-jī *or* -gē). the passage for food from the mouth to the stomach; gullet. Also **oesophagus.** See *alimentary canal* for picture. [< NL < Gk. *oisophagos* < *oiso-* carry + *phagein* eat]

es·o·ter·ic (es′ə ter′ik) *adj.* **1** understood only by the select few; intended for an inner circle of disciples, scholars, etc. **2** private; secret; confidential; opposed to *exoteric.* [< Gk. *esōterikos*, ult. < *esō* within] —**es′o·ter′i·cal·ly,** *adv.*

esp. *or* **espec.** especially.

E.S.P. *or* **ESP** extrasensory perception.

es·pal·ier (es pal′yər) *n., v.* —*n.* **1** a framework of stakes upon which fruit trees and shrubs are trained. **2** a plant or row of plants trained to grow in this way. —*v.* trail or furnish with an espalier. [< F < Ital. *spalliera* support < *spalla* shoulder]

Es·pa·ña (es pä′nyä) *n. Spanish.* Spain.

es·par·to (es pär′tō) *n.* either of two grasses (*Stipa tenacissima* or *Lygeum spartum*) native to Spain and N Africa used for making baskets, rope, and paper. [< Sp. < L < Gk. *spartos*]

espec. especially.

es·pe·cial (es pesh′əl) *adj.* special; particular; exceptional: *my especial friend, of no especial value.* [ME < OF < L *specialis* belonging to a particular species. Doublet of SPECIAL.]

es·pe·cial·ly (es pesh′əl ē *or* es pesh′lē) *adv.* particularly; chiefly; unusually.
► *Syn.* **Especially, particularly, principally** = in a special manner or degree, first or most of all. **Especially** emphasizes the idea of over and above all others: *This book is designed especially for young students.* **Particularly** singles out the foremost case or example from others of the same class or kind: *All my arithmetic problems are hard, but particularly this one.* **Principally** emphasizes the idea of before all others or for the most part: *Robberies occur principally at night.*
► *Usage.* **Especially, specially. Especially** = pre-eminently or exceptionally. **Specially** = for that purpose and no other. You should say, *I came specially to see John;* but, *I came especially to see John* if you would see others after seeing John, or if you have other business in mind besides visiting. A parallel distinction exists between **especial** and **special,** although the latter word now replaces **especial** for most purposes.

Es·pe·ran·to (es′pə rän′tō *or* es′pə ran′tō) *n.* an artificial language for international use, whose vocabulary and grammar are based on forms common to the principal European languages. [<

hat, āge, fär; let, ēqual, tèrm; it, īce
hot, ōpen, ôrder; oil, out; cup, pút, rüle, əbove, takən, pencəl, lemən, circəs
ch, child; ng, long; sh, ship
th, thin; ŦH, then; zh, measure

the pseudonym "*Dr. Esperanto*" used by its inventor, Dr. Zamenhof]

es·pi·al (es pī′əl) *n.* **1** the act of spying. **2** the act of watching. **3** discovery.

es·pi·o·nage (es′pē ə nij *or* es′pē ə näzh′) *n.* the use of spies, especially the use of spies by one country to find out the military, political, etc. secrets of another; spying. [< F *espionnage* < *espionner* to spy < *espion* spy < Ital. *spione* < *spia* spy < Gmc.]

es·pla·nade (es′plə näd′ *or* es′plə näd′) *n.* **1** any open, level space used for public walks or drives. **2** an open space separating a fortress from the houses of a town. [< F < Sp. *esplanada* < *esplanar* < L *explanare* < *ex-* out + *planus* level]

es·pous·al (es pouz′əl) *n.* **1** espousing; adoption (of a cause, etc.). **2** the ceremony of becoming engaged or married. **3** espousals, *pl.* **a** a betrothal; betrothal ceremony. **b** a marriage; wedding. [ME < OF *espousailles*, pl. < L *sponsalia*, neut. pl. of *sponsalis* having to do with betrothal < *sponsus* betrothed. See ESPOUSE.]

es·pouse (es pouz′) *v.* **-poused, -pous·ing. 1** marry. **2** take up or make one's own: *Late in life he espoused a new religion.* [ME < OF *espouser* < L *sponsare* < *sponsus* betrothed, pp. of *spondere* betroth] —**es·pous′er,** *n.*

es·pres·so (es pres′ō) *n., pl.* **-sos.** a very strong coffee made from dark-roasted, finely powdered beans and brewed under steam pressure. [< Ital. *espresso,* pp. of *esprimere* < L *exprimere.* See EXPRESS.]

espresso bar a coffee shop that specializes in espresso.

es·prit (es prē′) *n.* lively wit; spirit. [< F *esprit* < L *spiritus* spirit, originally, breath < *spirare* breathe. Doublet of SPIRIT, SPRITE.]

esprit de corps (es prē′də kôr′) *French.* a sense of union and of common interests and responsibilities in some group: *The regiment has a strong esprit de corps.*

es·py (es pī′) *v.* **-pied, -py·ing.** see or catch sight of something, especially something far away, small, or partly hidden. [ME < OF *espier* < Gmc.]

Esq. Esquire.
► *Usage.* **Esq., Esquire.** Written after a man's name in the inside and outside address of a letter. **Esq.** or **Esquire** is formal and is no longer widely used in Canada except in official and professional circles. Many people consider the usage British, archaic, or both. No other title (such as *Mr., Dr., Hon.*) should be used with the word: *Harry A. Kinne, Esq.*

–esque *suffix.* **1** in the ——style; resembling the ——style, as in *Romanesque.* **2** like a ——; like that of a ——, as in *statuesque.* [< F < Ital. *-esco* < Gmc. Akin to -ISH.]

Es·qui·mau (es′kə mō′) *n., pl.* **-maux** (-mō′ *or* -mōz′). Eskimo.

es·quire (es kwīr′ *or* es′kwīr) *n.* **1** in the Middle Ages, a young man of noble family who attended a knight until he himself was made a knight. **2** an Englishman ranking next below a knight. **3** *Archaic.* an English country gentleman; squire. **4 Esquire,** a title of respect (for birth, position or education) placed after a man's last name instead of placing *Mr.* before the name: *John Jones, Esquire = Mr. John Jones.* [ME < OF *esquier* < L *scutarius* shieldbearer < *scutum* shield]
► *Usage.* See note at Esq.

ess (es) *n.* **1** the 19th letter of the alphabet (S, s). **2** anything shaped like an S.

–ess *suffix.* female, as in *heiress, hostess, lioness.* [< F *-esse* < L < Gk. *-issa*]

es·say (*n.* es′ā *for 1 and 2,* es′ā *or* e sā′ *for 3; v.* e sā′) *n., v.* —*n.* **1** a literary composition on a certain subject. An essay is usually shorter and more personal, but less methodical than a treatise. **2** a written composition, theme, term paper, etc. assigned as an exercise in a high school, college, etc. **3** a try; attempt. —*v.* try; attempt: *He essayed a very difficult jump.* [< OF *essai* < L *exagium* a weighing] —**es·say′er,** *n.*

es·say·ist (es′ā ist) *n.* a writer of essays.

es·sence (es′əns) *n.* **1** that which makes a thing what it is; the necessary part or parts; important feature or features: *Kindness is the essence of politeness.* **2** any concentrated substance that has the characteristic flavor, fragrance, or effect of the plant, fruit, etc. from which it is obtained. Atropine is the essence of the belladonna plant. **3** a solution of such a substance in alcohol. Essence of peppermint is oil of peppermint dissolved in alcohol. **4** a perfume.

5 something that is, especially a spiritual or immaterial entity. [ME < OF < L *essentia* < *esse* be]

es·sen·tial (ə sen′shəl) *adj., n.* —*adj.* **1** needed to make a thing what it is; basic; necessary: *Good food and enough rest are essential to good health.* **2** of, like, or constituting the essence of a substance. **3** being or containing the essence, or fragrance, flavor, and medicinal qualities, of a plant or other material: *essential odors.* **4** being such by its essence or very nature, or in the highest sense: *essential happiness, essential poetry.* —*n.* an absolutely necessary element or quality; a basic part; fundamental feature: *Learn the essentials first; then learn the details.* [ME < Med.L *essentialis* < L *essentia*. See ESSENCE.] —**es·sen′tial·ly,** *adv.*
☛ *Syn. adj.* **1.** See note at **necessary.**

essential oil a volatile oil having the characteristic fragrance or flavor of the plant or fruit from which it is extracted. It is used in making perfumes and in flavoring.

-est *suffix forming the superlative degree.* **1** of adjectives, as in *warmest.* **2** of adverbs, as in *slowest.* [OE *-est, -ost*]
☛ *Usage.* See notes at **adjective** and **adverb.**

est. 1 established. **2** estate. **3** estuary.

EST or **E.S.T.** Eastern Standard Time.

es·tab·lish (i stab′lish) *v.* **1** set up permanently: *to establish a government or a business.* **2** settle in a position; set up in a business: *He established himself in the most comfortable chair. A new doctor has established himself on this street.* **3** bring about permanently; cause to be accepted: *to establish a custom.* **4** show beyond dispute; prove: *to establish a fact.* **5** make (a church) a national institution recognized and supported by the government. [ME < OF *establiss-,* a stem of *establir* < L *stabilire* make stable < *stabilis* stable] —**es·tab′lish·er,** *n.*
☛ *Syn.* **1.** See note at **fix.**

established church a church that is a national institution, recognized and supported by the government.

es·tab·lish·ment (i stab′lish mənt) *n.* **1** the act of establishing or the state of being established: *the establishment of a scholarship fund.* **2** something established, such as a household, business, church, army, or code of laws. **3 the Establishment, a** the Church of England and the Presbyterian Church of Scotland. **b** the people having the greatest social and political influence in a country and generally being opposed to change and the influence of other groups. **4** the number of people in a regiment, a ship's company, etc., as set by regulations: *The regiment needed three officers to complete its establishment.*

es·tab·lish·men·tar·i·an (i stab′lish mən ter′ē ən) *adj., n.* —*adj.* of, having to do with, or supporting the Establishment. —*n.* a person who belongs to or supports the Establishment. —**es·tab′lish·men·tar′i·an·ism,** *n.*

es·tate (i stāt′) *n.* **1** a large piece of land belonging to a person; landed property: *He has a beautiful estate with a country house and a swimming pool on it.* **2** what a person owns; property; possessions. Land and buildings are real estate. When a person dies, his estate is divided up among those to whom he has left it. **3** a condition or stage in life: *He will receive his inheritance when he reaches man's estate.* **4** a class or order of persons within a nation. The traditional estates (called **the three estates**) making up the body politic in European countries were the nobility, the clergy, and the commons (the third estate), each with different political rights. See also **fourth estate.** [ME < OF *estat* < L *status* state. Doublet of STATE.]

Es·tates–Gen·er·al (i stāts′jen′ər əl *or* -jen′rəl) *n.* States-General (def. 1).

es·teem (i stēm′) *v., n.* —*v.* **1** have a very favorable opinion of; regard highly: *We esteem people of good character.* **2** think; consider: *Men have often esteemed happiness the greatest good.* —*n.* a very favorable opinion; high regard: *Courage is held in esteem.* [ME < OF *estimer* < L *aestimare* value]
☛ *Syn. v.* **1.** See note at **value.**

es·ter (es′tər) *n.* a compound resulting from the reaction of an acid with an alcohol, so that the acid hydrogen of the acid is replaced by the hydrocarbon radical of the alcohol. Animal and vegetable fats and oils are esters. [coined by L. Gmelin (1788-1853), a German chemist]

Es·ther (es′tər) *n.* in the Bible, a Jewish woman, the wife of a Persian king, who saved her people from massacre. Her story is told in the Book of Esther.

es·thete (es′thēt *or* ēs′thēt) *n.* aesthete.

es·thet·ic (es thet′ik *or* ēs thet′ik) *adj.* aesthetic. —**es·thet′i·cal·ly,** *adv.*

es·thet·i·cism (es thet′ə siz′əm *or* ēs thet′ə siz′əm) *n.* aestheticism.

es·thet·ics (es thet′iks *or* ēs thet′iks) *n.* aesthetics.

Es·tho·ni·an (es thō′nē ən) *n. or adj.* Estonian.

es·ti·ma·ble (es′tə mə bəl) *adj.* **1** worthy of esteem; deserving high regard. **2** capable of being estimated or calculated. —**es′ti·ma·bly,** *adv.*

es·ti·mate (*n.* es′tə mit *or* es′tə māt′; *v.* es′tə māt′) *n., v.* -**mat·ed, -mat·ing.** —*n.* **1** a judgment or opinion about how much, how many, how good, etc.: *My estimate of the length of the room was 7 metres; it actually measured 6 metres 56 centimetres.* **2** a statement of what a certain job will cost, made by one willing to do the work: *The painter's estimate for painting the house was $1500.* —*v.* **1** form a judgment or opinion about (how much, how many, how good, etc.). **2** fix the work, size, amount, etc., especially in a rough way; calculate approximately. **3** draw up or submit a statement of the cost of doing a specified piece of work or the price at which a contractor is prepared to undertake it. [< L *aestimatus,* pp. of *aestimare* value] —**es′ti·ma′tor,** *n.*
☛ *Syn. v.* **1. Estimate, appraise, evaluate** = judge the measure, weight, or value of someone or something. **Estimate** suggests an opinion based on personal knowledge, experience, or taste, and emphasizes that the result given may not be correct: *Without measuring, I would estimate the length of the room as five metres.* **Appraise** emphasizes expert opinion, and suggests that the result given is correct or cannot be questioned: *to appraise property for taxation.* **Evaluate** especially suggests trying to find the value or amount of a thing or person in terms of something besides money: *She evaluates people by their clothes.*

es·ti·ma·tion (es′tə mā′shən) *n.* **1** judgment; opinion: *In my estimation, your plan will not work.* **2** esteem; respect; regard: *to hold in high estimation.* **3** the act or process of estimating.

es·ti·val (es′tə vəl *or* es tī′vəl) *adj.* of or having to do with summer. Also, **aestival.** [< L *aestivalis* < *aestivus,* adj. of *aestas* summer]

es·ti·vate (es′tə vāt′) *v.* -**vat·ed, -vat·ing. 1** spend the summer. **2** *Zoology.* spend the summer in a dormant or torpid condition. Some snakes estivate. Also, **aestivate.**

es·ti·va·tion (es′tə vā′shən) *n.* **1** *Zoology.* the state of being in a dormant or torpid condition during the summer. **2** *Biology.* the arrangement of the parts of a flower in the bud.

Es·to·ni·an (es tō′nē ən) *n., adj.* —*n.* **1** a native or inhabitant of Estonia, a republic in the W Soviet Union. **2** a person of Estonian descent. **3** the Finno-Ugric language of the Estonians. —*adj.* of or having to do with Estonia, its people or their language. Also, **Esthonian.**

es·top (es top′) *v.* -**topped, -top·ping. 1** *Law.* prevent from asserting or doing something contrary to a previous assertion or act. **2** *Archaic.* stop; bar; obstruct. [< OF *estoper* < *estoupe* tow < L *stuppa*]

es·top·pel (es top′əl) *n.* estopping.

es·trange (es trānj′) *v.* -**tranged, -trang·ing. 1** turn (a person) from affection to indifference, dislike, or hatred; make unfriendly; separate: *A quarrel had estranged him from his family.* **2** keep apart; keep away. [ME < OF *estranger* < L *extraneare* < *extraneus* strange, foreign. Related to STRANGE.] —**es·trang′er,** *n.*

es·trange·ment (es trānj′mənt) *n.* **1** estranging. **2** being estranged: *A misunderstanding between the two friends had caused their estrangement.*

es·tray (es trā′) *n.* a stray person, animal, or thing.

es·tro·gen (es′trə jən) *n.* any of three hormones that induce a series of physiological changes in females, especially in the reproductive or sexual organs. [< L *oestrus* frenzy + E *-gen* producing]

es·trous cycle (es′trəs *or* ē′strəs) the hormonally controlled reproductive cycle of the female of all mammals except the higher primates, from the beginning of one period of estrus, or heat, to the beginning of the next.

es·trus (es′trəs *or* ē′strəs) a condition or period in the sexual cycle of all female mammals except the higher primates in which they are receptive to copulation with males and are capable of conceiving; heat.

es·tu·ar·y (es′chü er′ē) *n., pl.* -**ar·ies. 1** a broad mouth of a river flowing into the sea, where its current meets the tide and is influenced by it. **2** an inlet of the sea. [< L *aestuarium* < *aestus* tide] —**es′tu·ar′i·al,** *adj.*

-et *suffix.* —little: *owlet* = little owl; *islet* = little isle. [< OF]

e·ta (ā′tə *or* ē′tə) *n.* the seventh letter of the Greek alphabet (H, η).

ETA estimated time of arrival.

et al. and others (for L *et alii*).

etc. et cetera.
☛ *Usage.* **Etc.** is usually read "and so forth". For example, the definition of *equality* reads "exact likeness in size, number, value, rank, etc." **Etc.** in such

definitions shows that the meaning applies to many items similar to the ones mentioned.

et·cet·er·a (et set′ər ə *or* set′rə) **1** and others or the rest; and so forth. **2** or the like; or something similar. [ME < L *et* and + *cetera* the other (things)]

☛ *Usage.* Et cetera is a Latin phrase meaning "and so forth". Since the *et* itself means "and", there is no need to put *and* before it. It is wrong to write *and et cetera* or *and etc.*

et·cet·er·as (et set′ər əz *or* -set′rəz) *n.pl.* usual additions or extra things.

etch (ech) *v.* **1** engrave by using acid to eat a drawing or design into a metal plate, glass, etc. **2** engrave a drawing or design on (a plate, etc.) by means of acid: *to etch a copper plate.* **3** practise this art. **4** impress vividly: *The scene was etched on his mind.* [< Du. *etsen* < G *ätzen.* Akin to EAT.] —**etch′er,** *n.*

etch·ing (ech′ing) *n.* **1** a picture or design printed from an etched plate. **2** an etched plate; an etched drawing or design. **3** the art of an etcher; the process of engraving a drawing or design on a metal plate, glass, etc. by means of acid.

e·ter·nal (i tėr′nəl) *adj.* **1** without beginning or ending; lasting throughout all time. **2** always and forever the same. **3** seeming to go on forever; occurring very frequently. **4** (*noml.*) **the Eternal,** God. [ME < OF < L *aeternalis,* ult. < *aevum* age]

☛ *Syn. adj.* **1. Eternal, everlasting** = lasting forever. **Eternal** emphasizes having neither a beginning nor an end: *God is eternal.* **Everlasting** emphasizes having no end, but going on and on forever: *We wish for everlasting peace.*

Eternal City Rome.

e·ter·nal·ly (i tėr′nəl ē) *adv.* **1** without beginning or ending; throughout all time. **2** always and forever. **3** constantly; incessantly.

eternal triangle a situation involving conflict arising from the emotional, usually sexual, relationships among either two men and one woman or two women and one man.

e·ter·ni·ty (i tėr′nə tē) *n., pl.* **-ties. 1** time without beginning or ending; all time. **2** an eternal quality; endlessness. **3** the endless period after death. **4** a seemingly endless period of time. [ME < OF *eternite* < L *aeternitas* < *aeternus* eternal, ult. < *aevum* age]

e·ter·nize (i tėr′nīz) *v.* **-nized, -niz·ing.** make eternal; perpetuate; immortalize. —**e·ter′ni·za′tion,** *n.*

eth·ane (eth′ān) *n.* colorless, odorless, flammable hydrocarbon of the methane series, present in natural gas and coal gas. *Formula:* C_2H_6 [< *ether*]

eth·a·nol (eth′ə nōl′ *or* eth′ə nol′) *n.* ethyl alcohol. [< *ethane* + *alcohol*]

e·ther (ē′thər) *n.* **1** a colorless, strong-smelling liquid that burns and evaporates readily. Its fumes cause unconsciousness when deeply inhaled. Ether is used as an anesthetic, a solvent for fats and resins, etc. *Formula:* $(C_2H_5)_2O$ **2** the upper regions of space beyond the earth's atmosphere; clear sky. **3** the invisible, elastic substance formerly supposed to be distributed evenly through all space and to conduct light waves, electric waves, etc. Also, **aether** (for defs. 2 and 3). [< L *aether* < Gk. *aithēr* upper air]

e·the·re·al (i thēr′ē əl) *adj.* **1** light; airy; delicate: *Her ethereal beauty made her seem more like a spirit than a human being.* **2** not of the earth; heavenly. **3** of or having to do with the upper regions of space. **4** of or having to do with the ether diffused through space. Also, **aethereal.** —**e·the′re·al·ly,** *adv.*

e·the·re·al·ize (i thēr′ē əl īz′) *v.* **-ized, -iz·ing.** make ethereal.

e·ther·i·za·tion (ē′thər ə zā′shən *or* ē′thər ī zā′shən) *n.* **1** being or becoming etherized. **2** a giving of ether as an anesthetic.

e·ther·ize (ē′thər īz′) *v.* **-ized, -iz·ing. 1** make unconscious with ether fumes. **2** change into ether.

eth·ic (eth′ik) *adj., n.* —*adj.* ethical. —*n.* ethics; a system of ethics. [< L *ethicus* < Gk. *ēthikos* < *ēthos* moral character]

eth·i·cal (eth′ə kəl) *adj.* **1** having to do with standards of right and wrong; of ethics or morality. **2** in accordance with formal or professional rules of right and wrong: *It is not considered ethical for a doctor to disclose a patient's confidences.* —**eth′i·cal·ly,** *adv.*

☛ *Syn.* **1.** See note at **moral.**

eth·ics (eth′iks) *n.* **1** the study of standards of right and wrong; that part of science and philosophy dealing with moral conduct, duty, and judgment (*used with a singular verb*). **2** formal or professional rules of right and wrong; system of conduct or behavior (*used with a plural verb*): *Medical ethics do not permit doctors to advertise.*

E·thi·op (ē′thē op′) *adj. or n.* Ethiopian.

E·thi·o·pi·an (ē′thē ō′pē ən) *n., adj.* —*n.* **1** a native or inhabitant of Ethiopia, a country in NE Africa. **2** *Archaic.* a black African. —*adj.* **1** of or having to do with Ethiopia or its people. **2** *Archaic.* black African.

E·thi·op·ic (ē′thē op′ik *or* ē′thē ō′pik) *n., adj.* —*n.* the ancient Semitic language of Ethiopia. —*adj.* of or having to do with this language or the church using it.

hat, āge, fär; let, ēqual, tėrm; it, īce
hot, ōpen, ôrder; oil, out; cup, pút, rüle,
əbove, takən, pencəl, lemən, circəs

ch, child; ng, long; sh, ship
th, thin; ŦH, then; zh, measure

eth·moid (eth′moid) *adj., n.* —*adj.* having to do with certain bones situated in the walls and septum of the nose and containing numerous perforations for the filaments of the olfactory nerve. —*n.* an ethmoid bone. [< Gk. *ēthmoeidēs* < *ēthmos* sieve + *eidos* form]

eth·nic (eth′nik) *adj., n.* —*adj.* **1** of or having to do with various groups of people and their characteristics, customs, and languages. **2** *Cdn.* of or having to do with immigrants who are not native speakers of English or French: *ethnic dances, the ethnic vote.* **3** heathen or pagan. —*n. Cdn. Informal.* an immigrant who is not a native speaker of English or French; a person of foreign birth or descent: *There are ethnics in Toronto from many parts of Europe.* [< L *ethnicus* < Gk. *ethnikos* < *ethnos* nation]

☛ *Usage.* **Ethnic,** *adj.* (def. 2) and *n.* This use of **ethnic** has become established in Canada and is spreading to the United States, though many people consider it unacceptable. While the word is useful in that it recognizes that different nationalities have individual qualities and customs, it becomes insulting if it is used to refer scornfully to people not of English or French descent.

eth·ni·cal (eth′nə kəl) *adj.* ethnic.

eth·nic·i·ty (eth nis′ə tē) *n.* ethnic quality, character, or status.

ethno– *combining form.* race; nation, as in *ethnology.* [< Gk. *ethno-* < *ethnos*]

eth·no·cen·tric (eth′nō sen′trik) *adj.* characterized by preoccupation with one's own cultural or national group and belief in its superiority over all others.

eth·no·cen·tric·i·ty (eth′nō sen tris′ə tē) *n.* ethnocentrism.

eth·no·cen·trism (eth′nō sen′triz əm) *n.* the quality or condition of being ethnocentric.

eth·nog·ra·pher (eth nog′rə fər) *n.* a person trained in ethnography, especially one whose work it is.

eth·no·graph·ic (eth′nə graf′ik) *adj.* having to do with ethnography. —**eth′no·graph′i·cal·ly,** *adv.*

eth·nog·ra·phy (eth nog′rə fē) *n.* the scientific description and classification of the various cultural groups of people.

eth·no·log·ic (eth′nə loj′ik) *adj.* ethnological.

eth·no·log·i·cal (eth′nə loj′ə kəl) *adj.* having to do with ethnology.

eth·no·log·i·cal·ly (eth′nə loj′ik lē) *adv.* from the point of view of ethnology.

eth·nol·o·gist (eth nol′ə jist) *n.* a person trained in ethnology, especially one whose work it is.

eth·nol·o·gy (eth nol′ə jē) *n.* the branch of anthropology that deals with the various cultural groups of people, their origin, distribution, and characteristics.

e·tho·log·i·cal (eth′ə loj′i kəl) *adj.* of or having to do with ethology. —**eth′o·log′i·cal·ly,** *adv.*

e·thol·o·gist (ē thol′ə jist) *n.* a person trained in ethology, especially one whose work it is.

e·thol·o·gy (ē thol′ə jē) *n.* the scientific study of the behavior of animals, especially of wild animals in their natural environment.

e·thos (ē′thos) *n.* the essential and distinctive character or spirit of a race, or people, or of a system, culture, institution, etc. [< NL < Gk. *ēthos* character, nature]

eth·yl (eth′əl) *n.* **1** a univalent radical present in many organic compounds. Ordinary alcohol contains ethyl. *Formula:* C_2H_5 **2 Ethyl,** *Trademark.* **a** a poisonous, colorless lead compound used in gasoline to reduce knocking; tetraethyl lead. *Formula:* $Pb (C_2H_5)_4$ **b** a gasoline containing this compound. [< *ether*]

ethyl alcohol ordinary alcohol, made by the fermentation of grain, sugar, etc. *Formula:* C_2H_5OH

eth·yl·ene (eth′ə lēn′) *n.* a colorless, inflammable gas with an unpleasant odor, used as an anesthetic, in making organic compounds, and for coloring and ripening citrus fruits. *Formula:* C_2H_4

e·ti·o·late (ē′tē ə lāt′) *v.* **-lat·ed, -lat·ing. 1** *Botany.* make (a plant) pale or colorless by depriving of light; blanch. **2** of a plant, become pale or colorless through lack of sunlight. **3** make weak, dull, colorless: *His literary style was bland and etiolated.* [< F *étioler* blanch + E *-ate*] —**e′ti·o·la′tion,** *n.*

e·ti·ol·o·gy (ē′tē ol′ə jē) *n.* **1** the assigning of a cause. **2** the science that deals with origins or causes. **3** the theory of the causes

of disease. Also, **aetiology.** [< L *aetiologia* < Gk. *aitiologia* < *aitia* cause + *-logos* treating of]

et·i·quette (et′ə ket′ *or* et′ə kət) *n.* **1** the conventional rules for conduct or behavior in polite society. **2** the formal rules or conventions governing conduct in a profession, official ceremony, etc.: *medical etiquette.* [< F < Gmc.]

Eton collar a broad, stiff collar worn outside the coat collar. See **collar** for picture.

Eton jacket a short, black coat with broad lapels. The jacket comes to the waist and is not made to button.

E·tru·ri·an (i trür′ē ən) *adj. or n.* Etruscan.

E·trus·can (i trus′kən) *n.* **1** a native or inhabitant of Etruria. **2** the language of Etruria. —*adj.* of or having to do with Etruria, an ancient country in W Italy, its people, their language, art, or customs. [< L *Etruscus*]

et seq. and the following; and that which follows. [for L *et sequens*].

–ette *noun-forming suffix.* **1** small, as in *kitchenette, statuette.* **2** female, as in *farmerette, suffragette.* **3** a substitute for; imitation, as in *leatherette.* [< F *-ette*, fem. of *-et* -et]

é·tude (ā tyüd′ *or* ā tüd′) *n.* **1 a** a study. **2 a** a piece of music intended to develop skill in technique. **b** a composition of a similar type, having artistic quality, and intended for public performance: *Chopin's etudes.* [< F *étude* study < L *studium.* Doublet of STUDIO, STUDY.]

et·y·mo·log·i·cal (et′ə mə loj′ə kəl) *adj.* of or having to do with the origin and history of words. —**et′y·mo·log′i·cal·ly,** *adv.*

et·y·mol·o·gist (et′ə mol′ə jist) *n.* a person trained in etymology, especially one whose work it is.

et·y·mol·o·gy (et′ə mol′ə jē) *n., pl.* **-gies. 1** an explanation of the origin of a word and a description of the changes it has gone through in its history. **2** the branch of linguistics dealing with word origins. [< L < Gk. *etymologia* < *etymon* the original sense or form of a word (neut. of *etymos* true, real) + *-logos* treating of]

et·y·mon (et′ə mon′) *n.* the original form of a word that is the basis of later derivatives. [< Gk. *etymon* (neut. adj.) what is true]

eu– *prefix.* good; well, as in *eulogy, euphony.* [< Gk.]

Eu europium.

eu·ca·lypt (yü′kə lipt′) *n.* eucalyptus.

eu·ca·lyp·tus (yü′kə lip′təs) *n.* **-tus·es, -ti** (-tī *or* -tē). any of a genus (*Eucalyptus*) of mainly Australian evergreen trees of the myrtle family cultivated for their wood, gum, and resin, and the oil that can be extracted from the leaves. Also, **eucalypt.** [< NL < Gk. *eu-* well + *kalyptos* covered; with reference to bud covering]

Eu·cha·rist (yü′kə rist) *n.* **1** the Christian sacrament of the Lord's Supper; Holy Communion. **2** the consecrated bread and wine used in this sacrament. [< LL < Gk. *eucharistia* thankfulness, the Eucharist]

Eu·cha·ris·tic (yü′kə ris′tik) *adj.* having to do with the Eucharist.

eu·chre (yü′kər) *n., v.* **-chred, -chring.** —*n.* **1** a simple card game for two, three, or four players, using the 32 (or 28, or 24) highest cards in the pack. **2** a social gathering during which people play euchre. **3** the failure of the side that declared the trump to win three tricks.
—*v.* **1** defeat (the side that declared the trump) at euchre. **2** *Informal.* outwit; defeat. [origin uncertain]

Eu·clid·e·an *or* **Eu·clid·i·an** (yü klid′ē ən) *adj.* **1** of or having to do with Euclid, a Greek mathematician who wrote a book on geometry about 300 B.C. **2** of or about his principles of geometry.

eu·gen·ic (yü jen′ik) *adj.* **1** having to do with improvement of the race; improving the race; improving the offspring produced: *eugenic breeding.* **2** coming of good stock. [< Gk. *eugenēs* well-born < *eu-* well + *genos* birth]

eu·gen·i·cal·ly (yü jen′ik lē) *adv.* in a eugenic manner; with respect to racial improvement.

eu·gen·ics (yü jen′iks) *n.sing. or pl.* **1** the science of improving the human race by a careful selection of parents in order to develop healthier and more intelligent children. **2** the science of improving offspring.

eu·la·chon (yü′lə kən) *n.* oolichan.

eu·lo·gist (yü′lə jist) *n.* a person who eulogizes.

eu·lo·gis·tic (yü′lə jis′tik) *adj.* praising highly.

eu·lo·gis·ti·cal (yü′lə jis′tə kəl) *adj.* eulogistic.
—**eu′lo·gis′ti·cal·ly,** *adv.*

eu·lo·gi·um (yü lō′jē əm) *n., pl.* **-gi·ums, -gi·a** (-jē ə).

eulogy; praise. [< Med.L *eulogium*, var. of L *eulogia* < Gk. *eulogia.* See EULOGY.]

eu·lo·gize (yü′lə jīz′) *v.* **-gized, -giz·ing.** praise very highly.
—**eu′lo·giz′er,** *n.*

eu·lo·gy (yü′lə jē) *n., pl.* **-gies. 1** a speech or writing in praise of a person, action, etc.: *He pronounced a eulogy upon the hero.* **2** high praise. [< Gk. *eulogia* < *eu-* well + *legein* speak]

Eu·men·i·des (yü men′ə dēz′) *n.pl. Greek mythology.* the Furies; Erinyes. Literally, the kindly (goddesses), a name used for the Furies to avoid offending them.

eu·nuch (yü′nək) *n.* **1** a castrated man. **2** a castrated man in charge of a harem or the household of an Oriental ruler. [< L *eunuchus* < Gk. *eunouchos* < *eunē* bed + *echein* keep]

eu·pep·si·a (yü pep′sē ə *or* yü pep′shə) *n.* good digestion; opposed to *dyspepsia.* [< NL < Gk. *eupepsia* < *eupeptos* having a good digestion < *eu-* well + *peptein* digest]

eu·pep·tic (yü pep′tik) *adj.* **1** having good digestion. **2** aiding digestion.

eu·phe·mism (yü′fə miz′əm) *n.* **1** the use of a mild or indirect expression instead of one that is harsh or unpleasantly direct. **2** a mild or indirect expression used in this way. *Pass away* is a common euphemism for *die.* The name *Eumenides,* meaning *kindly goddesses,* was a euphemism for the Furies. [< Gk. *euphēmismos* < *euphemizein* speak with fair words < *eu-* good + *phēmē* speaking]

eu·phe·mist (yü′fə mist) *n.* a person who uses euphemisms.

eu·phe·mis·tic (yü′fə mis′tik) *adj.* of or showing euphemism; containing a euphemism.

eu·phe·mis·ti·cal·ly (yü′fə mis′tik lē) *adv.* by way of euphemism; using euphemism.

eu·phon·ic (yü fon′ik) *adj.* **1** having to do with euphony. **2** euphonious.

eu·pho·ni·ous (yü fō′nē əs) *adj.* sounding well; pleasing to the ear; harmonious. —**eu·pho′ni·ous·ly,** *adv.* —**eu·pho′ni·ous·ness,** *n.*

eu·pho·ni·um (yü fō′nē əm) *n.* a brass musical instrument resembling a tuba and having a loud, deep tone. [< NL < Gk. *euphōnos* well-sounding < *eu-* good + *phōnē* sound]

eu·pho·ny (yü′fə nē) *n., pl.* **-nies. 1** agreeableness of sound; pleasing effect to the ear; harmony of speech sounds as uttered or combined in utterance. **2** a tendency to change sounds so as to favor ease of utterance. [< LL < Gk. *euphōnia* < *eu-* good + *phōnē* sound]

eu·phor·bi·a (yü fôr′bē ə) *n.* any of a genus (*Euphorbia*) of plants of the spurge family, including the spurges and poinsettia, all having a milky juice or latex which in some species is poisonous. [< L *euphorbea* < *Euphorbus,* a Greek physician]

eu·pho·ri·a (yü fō′rē ə) *n. Psychology.* a feeling of well-being. [< NL < Gk. *euphoria* < *eu-* good + *pherein* bear]

eu·phor·ic (yü fôr′ik) *adj.* having to do with or characterized by euphoria.

eu·phu·ism (yü′fyü iz′əm) *n.* **1** an affected style of speaking and writing English that was fashionable around 1600, characterized by long series of antitheses, frequent similes, and alliteration. *Example*: *"...the milk of the Tygresse, that the more salt there is thrown into it the fresher it is."* **2** any affected, elegant style of writing; flowery, artificial language. [< *Euphues,* the main character in two works of John Lyly, a 16th-century English dramatist and romance writer]

eu·phu·ist (yü′fyü ist) *n.* a person who uses euphuism.

eu·phu·is·tic (yü′fyü is′tik) *adj.* using or containing euphuism; like euphuism. —**eu′phu·is′ti·cal·ly,** *adv.*

Eur. Europe; European.

Eur·a·sian (yür ā′zhən *or* yür ā′shən) *adj., n.* —*adj.* **1** of or having to do with Europe and Asia or its people. **2** of mixed European and Asian parentage. —*n.* a person of mixed European and Asian parentage.

Eur·at·om (yür at′əm) *n.* an organization to pool the nuclear-power research and developments of six European countries (France, West Germany, Italy, Belgium, the Netherlands, and Luxembourg); European Atomic Energy Community.

eu·re·ka (yü rē′kə) *interj.* an exclamation of triumph about a discovery or a solution to a problem. [< Gk. *heurēka* I have found (it) < *heuriskein* to find; the exclamation traditionally attributed to the ancient Greek mathematician Archimedes, on making a discovery] [< Gk.]

eu·rhyth·mic (yü riⱦн′mik *or* yü rith′mik) *adj.* **1** of or having to do with eurhythmics. **2** pleasingly proportioned. Also, **eurythmic.** —**eu·rhyth′mi·cal·ly,** *adv.*

eu·rhyth·mics (yü riⱦн′miks *or* yü rith′miks) *n.* a system for the development of rhythm and grace by the performing of bodily movements in response to music.

eu·ro (yür′ō) *n.* wallaroo.

Euro– *combining form.* **1** Europe or European, as in *Eurodollar, Eurocanadian.* **2** Europe, or European, and —, as in *Eurasian.* Also, before vowels, **Eur-**.

Eu·ro·com·mu·nism (yür′ō kom′yə niz′əm) *n.* Communism as practised by the Communist Parties of W Europe, especially as it differs from the policies, doctrines, and practices of the Soviet Union. —**Eu′ro·com′mu·nist′**, *n., adj.*

Eu·ro·crat (yür′ə krat′) *n.* a member of the administration of the European Economic Community.

Eu·ro·dol·lar (yür′ō dol′ər) *n.* a United States dollar held in a bank, etc. in Europe.

Eu·ro·mart (yür′ō märt′) *n.* the European Economic Community.

Eu·ro·pe·an (yür′ə pē′ən) *adj., n.* —*adj.* **1** of or having to do with Europe or its inhabitants. **2** of or designating a major race of mankind that includes the traditional inhabitants of Europe, the Middle East, and N Africa, distinguished by a combination of biological characteristics, including generally lighter skin than any other major racial group.
—*n.* **1** a native or inhabitant of Europe. **2** a person whose recent ancestors came from Europe. **3** a member of the European race.

European Common Market European Economic Community.

European Economic Community a trading and political association of W European countries for eliminating tariffs between each other and working toward a complete economic union. The original member countries, all joining in 1958, were Belgium, France, Italy, Luxembourg, the Netherlands, and W Germany. The United Kingdom, the Irish Republic, and Denmark joined in 1973.

Eu·ro·pe·an·ize (yür′ə pē′ən īz′) *v.* **-ized, -z·ing.** make European in appearance, habit, way of life, etc.

European plan a hotel system by which guests pay for only room and service, meals being extra; opposed to *American plan.*

eu·ro·pi·um (yü rō′pē əm) *n.* a rare, metallic chemical element of the same group as cerium. *Symbol:* Eu; *at.no.* 63; *at.wt.* 151.96. [< NL < L *Europa* Europe < Gk.]

eu·ryth·mic (yü riᴛн′mik *or* yü rith′mik) See **eurhythmic.**

eu·ryth·mics (yü riᴛн′miks *or* yü rith′miks) See **eurhythmics.**

Eu·sta·chi·an tube (yü stā′kē ən *or* yü stā′shən) a slender canal between the pharynx and the middle ear, which equalizes the air pressure on the two sides of the eardrum. See **ear** for picture. [< Bartolommeo *Eustachio*, a 16th-century Italian anatomist]

eu·tha·na·sia (yü thə nā′zē ə *or* yü′thə nā′zhə) *n.* **1** an easy, painless death. **2** a painless killing, especially to end a painful and incurable disease; mercy killing. [< Gk. *euthanasia* < *eu-* easy + *thanatos* death]

eu·then·ics (yü then′iks) *n.* the science of improving biologically the human race by controlling the environment or living conditions. [< Gk. *euthēnia* well-being]

eu·troph·ic (yü trof′ik *or* yü trō′fik) *adj.* of a lake or river, having excessive plant growth due to a high concentration of nutrients (such as phosphates), resulting in a decrease in oxygen, and hence a decrease in the number of fish, etc. Compare **oligotrophic.** [< Gk. *eu-* good, well + *trophikos* nourishing < *trophē* food, nourishment] —**eu·troph′i·ca′tion,** *n.*

eu·troph·y (yü′trə fē) *n.* the condition of being eutrophic.

eV electronvolt.

e·vac·u·ant (i vak′yü ənt) *adj., n.* —*adj. Medicine.* producing evacuation; cathartic; purgative. —*n.* an evacuant medicine, drug, etc., especially a purgative.

e·vac·u·ate (i vak′yü āt′) *v.* **-at·ed, -at·ing. 1** leave empty; withdraw from: *The soldiers evacuated the fort.* **2** withdraw; remove: *to evacuate all foreign residents from the war zone.* **3** make empty: *to evacuate the bowels.* [< L *evacuare* < *ex-* out + *vacuus* empty] —**e·vac′u·a′tor,** *n.*

e·vac·u·a·tion (i vak′yü ā′shən) *n.* **1** a leaving empty; a withdrawal from occupation or possession; the act or process of evacuating. **2** removal. **3** making empty. **4** a discharge.

e·vac·u·ee (i vak′yü ē′ *or* i vak′yü ē′) *n.* one who is removed to a place of greater safety.

e·vade (i vād′) *v.* **e·vad·ed, e·vad·ing. 1** get away from by trickery; avoid by cleverness. **2** avoid the truth by indefinite or misleading statements. [< L *evadere* < *ex-* away + *vadere* go] ☛ *Syn.* **1.** See note at **escape.**

e·vad·er (i vād′ər) *n.* one who evades.

e·val·u·ate (i val′yü āt′) *v.* **-at·ed, -at·ing. 1** judge the worth, quality, or importance of: *to evaluate a statement, to evaluate a new data processing system.* **2** find or decide the value of: *An*

hat, āge, fär; let, ēqual, tèrm; it, īce
hot, ōpen, ôrder; oil, out; cup, pút, rüle,
əbove, takən, pencəl, lemən, circəs

ch, child; ng, long; sh, ship
th, thin; ᴛн, then; zh, measure

expert evaluated the old clock at $900. [< F *évaluer*] —**e·val′u·a′tor,** *n.*
☛ *Syn.* See note at **estimate.**

e·val·u·a·tion (i val′yü ā′shən) *n.* **1** an evaluating. **2** an estimate of worth or quality: *The coach made too high an evaluation on the centre's ability to score.*

e·val·u·a·tive (i val′yü ā′ tiv *or* i val′yü ə tiv) *adj.* of or having to do with evaluation.

ev·a·nesce (ev′ə nes′) *v.* **-nesced, -nes·cing.** disappear gradually; fade away; vanish. [< L *evanescere* < *ex-* out + *vanescere* vanish < *vanus* insubstantial]

ev·a·nes·cence (ev′ə nes′əns) *n.* **1** a gradual disappearance; a fading away; vanishing. **2** a tendency to disappear or fade away; inability to last long.

ev·a·nes·cent (ev′ə nes′ənt) *adj.* tending to disappear or fade away; able to last only a short time.

e·van·gel (i van′jəl) *n.* **1** the Gospel; good news of the saving of mankind through Christ. **2** good news. **3** evangelist. **4 Evangel,** in the Bible, one of the four gospels; Matthew, Mark, Luke, or John. [< L *evangelium* < Gk. *euangelion* good tidings, ult. < *eu-* good + *angellein* announce]

e·van·gel·ic (ē′van jel′ik *or* ev′ən jel′ik) *adj.* evangelical.

e·van·gel·i·cal (ē′van jel′ə kəl *or* ev′ən jel′ə kəl) *adj.* **1** of, concerning, or according to the four Gospels of the New Testament. **2** of or having to do with the Protestant churches that emphasize Christ's atonement and salvation by faith as the most important parts of Christianity. Methodists and Baptists are evangelical; Unitarians and Universalists are not. **3** evangelistic.
4 Evangelical, a designating those Protestant churches deriving from Lutheranism, rather than Calvinism. Compare **Reformed. b** (in some parts of Europe) Protestant. —**e·van′gel′i·cal·ly,** *adv.*

e·van·gel·i·cal·ism (ē′van jel′ə kəl iz′əm *or* ev′ən jel′ə kəl iz′əm) *n.* **1** the doctrines of an evangelical church. **2** the adherence to such doctrines.

e·van·gel·ism (i van′jə liz′əm) *n.* **1** a preaching of the Gospel; earnest effort for the spread of the Gospel. **2** the work of an evangelist. **3** the belief in the doctrines of an evangelical church or party.

e·van·gel·ist (i van′jə list) *n.* **1** a preacher of the Gospel. **2** a travelling preacher who stirs up religious feeling in revival services or camp meetings. **3 Evangelist,** any one of the four apostles, Matthew, Mark, Luke, or John, who wrote the Gospels bearing their names.

e·van·gel·is·tic (i van′jə lis′tik) *adj.* **1** of the Evangelists. **2** of or by evangelists. —**e·van′gel·is′ti·cal·ly,** *adv.*

e·van·gel·ize (i van′jə līz′) *v.* **-ized, -iz·ing. 1** preach the Gospel to. **2** convert to Christianity by preaching. —**e·van′gel·i·za′tion,** *n.*

e·vap·o·rate (i vap′ə rāt′) *v.* **-rat·ed, -rat·ing. 1** change into a vapor: *Boiling water evaporates rapidly. Some solids, such as moth balls and Dry Ice, evaporate without melting.* **2** remove moisture, especially water, from: *Heat is used to evaporate milk.* **3** give off moisture. **4** vanish; disappear; fade away: *His good resolutions evaporated soon after New Year's Day.* [< L *evaporare* < *ex-* out + *vapor* vapor]

evaporated milk whole milk that has been concentrated, by evaporation of some of its water, to one half or less of its original bulk, sealed in tins, and sterilized by treating.

e·vap·o·ra·tion (i vap′ə rā′shən) *n.* **1** a changing of a liquid or solid into vapor. **2** a being changed into vapor. **3** the removal of water or other liquid. **4** disappearance.

e·vap·o·ra·tor (i vap′ə rā′tər) *n.* an apparatus for evaporating water or other liquid.

e·va·sion (i vā′zhən) *n.* **1** getting away from something by trickery; avoiding by cleverness: *Evasion of one's duty is contemptible.* **2** an attempt to escape an argument, a charge, a question, etc.: *The prisoner's evasions of the lawyer's questions convinced the jury of his guilt.* **3** a means of evading; trick or excuse used to avoid something. [ME < OF < LL *evasio, -onis* < L *evadere.* See **EVADE.**]

e·va·sive (i vā′siv *or* i vā′ziv) *adj.* tending or trying to evade: *Perhaps is an evasive answer.* —**e·va′sive·ly,** *adv.* —**e·va′sive·ness,** *n.*

eve (ēv) *n.* **1** the evening or day before a holiday or some other special day: *Christmas Eve.* **2** the time just before: *Everything was quiet on the eve of the battle.* **3** *Poetic.* evening. [var. of *even²*]

Eve (ēv) *n.* in the Bible, the first woman. Tempted by Satan, she ate the forbidden fruit and afterwards induced Adam, her husband, to do the same (Genesis 2:21-25; 3:20).
daughter of Eve, any woman.

e·ven¹ (ē'vən) *adj., v., adv.* —*adj.* **1** level; flat; smooth: *Even country has no hills.* **2** at the same level; in the same plane or line: *The snow was even with the window.* **3** always the same; regular; uniform: *An even motion does not change.* **4** equal: *They divided the money into even shares.* **5** See **even number.** **6** neither more nor less; exact: *Twelve apples make an even dozen.* **7** owing nothing: *When he had paid all of his debts, he was even.* **8** not easily disturbed or angered; calm: *A person with an even temper is seldom excited.* **9** not favoring one more than another; fair: *Justice is even treatment.*
be even, **a** owe nothing. **b** have revenge.
—*v.* **1** make equal; tie: *to even the score.* **2** make level or of similar length: *She evened the edges by trimming them.*
—*adv.* **1** in an even manner. **2** just; exactly: *She left even as you came.* **3** indeed: *He is ready, even eager, to go.* **4** fully; quite: *He was faithful even unto death.* **5** though one would not expect it; as one would not expect: *Even the least noise disturbs her.* **6** still; yet: *You can do even better if you try.*
break even, *Informal.* have equal gains and losses.
even if, in spite of the fact that; although.
even though, although.
get even, **a** owe nothing. **b** have revenge.
[OE *efen*] —**e'ven·er,** *n.* —**e'ven·ly,** *adv.* —**e'ven·ness,** *n.*
☛ *Syn. adj.* **3. Even, uniform, equable** = always the same. **Even** emphasizes being regular and steady, never changing in motion, action, quality, etc.: *The even hum of the motor stopped.* **Uniform** emphasizes being always the same in form or character, never changing from the normal or regular: *We should have uniform traffic laws.* **Equable** is a formal word used interchangeably with **even,** but suggesting a quality in the thing or person that makes it likely to be even or uniform: *She has an equable temperament.*

e·ven² (ē'vən) *n. Poetic.* evening. [OE *æfen*]

e·ven–hand·ed (ē'vən han'did) *adj.* impartial; fair; just: *The judge meted out even-handed justice to all.* —**e'ven-hand'ed·ly,** *adv.* —**e'ven-hand'ed·ness,** *n.*

eve·ning (ēv'ning) *n., adj.* —*n.* **1** the last part of day and early part of night; the time between day and night. **2** the time between sunset and bedtime. **3** the last part: *Old age is the evening of life.* —*adj.* in the evening; of the evening; for the evening. [OE *æfnung* < *æfnian* become evening < *æfen* evening]

evening dress formal clothes worn in the evening.

evening gown a woman's evening dress.

evening primrose **1** any of a genus (*Oenothera*) of New World herbs having spirally arranged leaves and fragrant flowers, especially a common wildflower (*O. biennis*) whose yellow flowers open in the evening. **2** (*adj.*) **evening-primrose,** designating the family (Onagraceae) of plants that includes the fireweed, fuchsia, and evening primrose.

evening star a bright planet seen in the western sky after sunset. Venus is often the evening star.

even number a number that has no remainder when divided by 2: *The even numbers are 4, 6, 8, etc.*

e·ven·song (ē'vən song') *n.* **1** in certain Christian churches, service said or sung in the late afternoon or early evening; vespers. **2** *Archaic.* evening. [OE *æfensang*]

e·vent (i vent') *n.* **1** a happening; *current events.* **2** an important happening: *The discovery of oil in Alberta was certainly an event.* **3** the result; outcome: *We made careful plans and awaited the event.* **4** an item or contest in a program of sports: *The broad jump was the last event.*
at all events or **in any event,** in any case; whatever happens.
in the event of, in case of; if there is; if there should be: *In the event of rain the party will be held indoors.*
in the event that, if it should happen that; supposing: *In the event that the roads are icy, we will not come.*
[< L *eventus* < *evenire* < *ex-* out + *venire* come]
☛ *Syn.* **1. Event, incident, occurrence** = happening. **Event** applies particularly to a happening of some importance, usually resulting from what has gone before: *Graduation from high school is an event that most students eagerly look forward to.* **Incident** applies to a less important happening taking place between events, but not always in connection with them: *The unexpected meeting with a boy I used to know was an amusing incident.* **Occurrence** is the general word for any happening, event, or incident: *Going to school is an everyday occurrence.*

e·ven–tem·pered (ē'vən tem'pərd) *adj.* not easily disturbed or angered; calm.

e·vent·ful (i vent'fəl) *adj.* **1** full of events; having many unusual events: *Our day at the fall fair was highly eventful.* **2** having important results; important: *July 1, 1867, Dominion Day, was an eventful day for Canada.* —**e·vent'ful·ly,** *adv.* —**e·vent'ful·ness,** *n.*

e·ven·tide (ē'vən tīd') *n. Poetic.* evening.

e·ven·tu·al (i ven'chü əl) *adj.* coming in the end; final: *His eventual success after several failures surprised us.* —**e·ven'tu·al·ly,** *adv.*

e·ven·tu·al·i·ty (i ven'chü al'ə tē) *n., pl.* **-ties.** a possible occurrence or condition; possibility: *We hope for rain but are ready for the eventuality of drought.*

e·ven·tu·ate (i ven'chü āt') *v.* **-at·ed, -at·ing.** come out in the end; happen finally; result. —**e·ven'tu·a'tion,** *n.*

ev·er (ev'ər) *adv.* **1** at any time: *Is she ever at home?* **2** at all times; always: *ever at your service.* **3** at all; by any chance; in any case: *What did you ever do to make him so angry?*
ever so, *Informal.* very.
for ever and a day, always.
[OE *æfre*]

ev·er·glade (ev'ər glād') *n. U.S.* a large tract of low wet ground partly covered with tall grass; a large swamp or marsh.

ev·er·green (ev'ər grēn') *adj., n.* —*adj.* **1** remaining green all year: *evergreen leaves.* **2** having leaves or needles all year: *evergreen tree.* **3** enduring: *an evergreen hope.*
—*n.* **1** an evergreen tree, shrub, or herb. **2** conifer: *a stand of evergreens.* **3** **evergreens,** *pl.* evergreen twigs or branches used for decoration, especially at Christmas.

ev·er·last·ing (ev'ər las'ting) *adj., n.* —*adj.* **1** lasting forever; never ending or stopping. **2** lasting a long time. **3** lasting too long; repeated too often; tiresome: *his everlasting complaints.*
—*n.* **1** an eternity. **2** any of numerous plants of the composite family having papery flowers that are used for winter bouquets and decorations because they keep their form and in many cases their color when they are dry. One of the most widely grown of the everlastings is the strawflower. **3** any of various other plants with similar characteristics, such as amaranths or any of several grasses with showy spikes or pannicles. **4** **the Everlasting,** God. —**ev'er·last'ing·ly,** *adv.* —**ev'er·last'ing·ness,** *n.*
☛ *Syn. adj.* **1.** See note at **eternal.**

ev·er·more (ev'ər môr') *adv.* or *n.* always; forever.

e·ver·sion (i vėr'zhən *or* i vėr'shən) *n.* **1** a turning of an organ, structure, etc. inside out. **2** a being turned inside out. [< L *eversio, -onis* < *evertere.* See EVERT.]

e·vert (i vėrt') *v.* turn inside out. [< L *evertere* < *ex-* out + *vertere* turn]

eve·ry (ev'rē) *adj.* **1** all, regarded singly or separately; each and all: *Every written word is made of letters.* **2** all possible; complete: *We showed him every consideration.*
every now and then, from time to time: *Every now and then we have a frost that ruins the crop.*
every other, each first, third, fifth, etc., or second, fourth, sixth, etc.: *The milkman makes deliveries every other day.*
every which way, *Informal.* in all directions; helter-skelter: *He had packed his suitcase every which way.*
[OE *æfre* ever+ *ælc* each]
☛ *Syn.* **1.** See note at **each.**

eve·ry·bod·y (ev'rē bud'ē *or* -bod'ē) *pron.* every person; everyone: *Everybody likes the new minister.*
☛ *Usage.* **Everybody, everyone. a** Both these pronouns are grammatically singular: *Everybody was thrilled when our troops marched past. Everyone who wishes to attend is invited.* Sometimes, however, a following pronoun may be plural: *Everyone was dressed in their best clothes.* In this example *everyone* is thought of as referring to a number of people, and the use of *their* avoids distinguishing between *his* and *her.* To make such expressions accord with formal written usage, it is often better to change the **everybody** or **everyone** to a more specific plural or collective than to change the later pronoun. **b** The pronoun **everybody** is always written as one word.

eve·ry·day (ev'rē dā') *adj.* **1** of every day; daily: *Accidents are everyday occurrences.* **2** for every ordinary day; not for Sundays or holidays: *She wears everyday clothes to work.* **3** not exciting or unusual; ordinary: *He's just an everyday writer.*
☛ *Usage.* **Everyday** is written as one word when it is an adjective, but as two words when **day** is a noun modified by **every:** *This was an everyday occurrence. Every day seemed a year.*

Every·man (ev'rē man') *n.* **1** an early sixteenth-century morality play symbolizing man's journey through life. **2** the chief character in this play, personifying humanity. **3** the average man; a typical human being.

eve·ry·one (ev'rē wun' *or* ev'rē wən) *pron.* every person; everybody: *Everyone took his purchases home.* Also, **every one.**
☛ *Usage.* **Everyone. a** See note at **everybody. b** Everyone is usually one word, but when **one** is stressed or emphasized, it is written as two words: *Everyone wants to attend the concert. Winning this game depends upon every one of you.*

eve·ry·thing (ev'rē thing') *pron., n.* —*pron.* every thing; all

things. —*n.* something extremely important; a very important thing: *This news means everything to us.*

☛ *Usage.* **Everything** is written as one word when it is a noun or pronoun, but as two words when **thing** is a noun modified by **every:** *Everything has its proper place. There is a noun for every thing or idea you can name.*

eve·ry·where (ev′rē wer′ *or* -hwer′) *adv.* in every place; in all places: *We looked everywhere for our lost dog.*

e·vict (i vikt′) *v.* 1 expel by a legal process from land, a building, etc.; eject (a tenant): *Because he had not paid his rent, the tenant was evicted by the sheriff.* 2 expel or put out by force: *The soldiers evicted the enemy from the occupied building.* [< L *evictus,* pp. of *evincere.* See EVINCE.] —**e·vic′tor,** *n.*

e·vic·tion (i vik′shən) *n.* evicting or being evicted; explusion.

ev·i·dence (ev′ə dəns) *n., v.* **-denced, -denc·ing.** —*n.* 1 whatever makes clear the truth or falsehood of something: *The evidence showed that he had not been near the place of the crime.* 2 *Law.* **a** facts established and accepted in a court of law. Before deciding a case, the judge or jury hears all the evidence given by both sides. **b** a person who gives testimony in a court of law: *queen's evidence.* 3 an indication; sign: *A smile gives evidence of pleasure.*
in evidence, easily seen or noticed: *A crying baby is much in evidence.*
—*v.* make easy to see or understand; show clearly; prove: *His smiles evidenced his pleasure.*
☛ *Syn.* **n. 1. Evidence, testimony, proof** = something that makes clear that a thing is true or false. **Evidence** applies to any facts that point toward, but do not fully prove, the truth or falsehood of something: *Running away was evidence of his guilt.* **Testimony** = something said or done to show or prove something true or false: *His speech was clear testimony of his good intentions.* **Proof** = complete evidence that leaves no doubt: *His actions were proof that he was telling the truth.*

ev·i·dent (ev′ə dənt) *adj.* easy to see or understand; clear; plain: *He has brought Betty a kitten, to her evident joy.* [< L *evidens, -entis* < *ex-* out + *videns,* ppr. of *videre* see]
☛ *Syn.* See note at **obvious.**

ev·i·den·tial (ev′ə den′shəl) *adj.* 1 serving as evidence; of evidence; based on evidence. 2 like evidence; giving evidence.

ev·i·dent·ly (ev′ə dənt lē) *adv.* plainly; clearly; apparently.

e·vil (ē′vəl) *adj., n.* —*adj.* 1 morally bad; wrong; sinful; wicked: *an evil life, an evil character.* 2 causing harm or injury: *an evil plan.* 3 unfortunate. 4 due to bad character or conduct: *an evil reputation.* —*n.* 1 something bad; sin; wickedness. 2 something that causes harm or injury; something that takes away happiness and prosperity: *War is a great evil.* [OE *yfel*] —**e′vil·ly,** *adv.* —**e′vil·ness,** *n.*
☛ *Syn. adj.* **1.** See note at **bad.**

e·vil·do·er (ē′vəl dü′ər) *n.* a person who does evil.

e·vil·do·ing (ē′vəl dü′ing) *n.* the doing of evil.

evil eye the power that some people are supposed to have of causing harm or bringing bad luck to others by looking at them. —**e′vil-eyed′,** *adj.*

e·vil–mind·ed (ē′vəl mīn′did) *adj.* having an evil mind; wicked; malicious.

Evil One the Devil; Satan.

e·vince (i vins′) *v.* **e·vinced, e·vinc·ing.** 1 show clearly: *The dog evinced its dislike of strangers by growling.* 2 show that one has (a certain quality, trait, etc.). [< LL *evincere* claim for oneself < *ex-* out + *vincere* conquer] —**e·vince′ment,** *n.*
☛ *Syn.* **1.** See note at **display.**

e·vin·ci·ble (i vin′sə bəl) *adj.* able to be proved; demonstrable.

e·vis·cer·ate (i vis′ər āt′) *v.* **-at·ed, -at·ing.** 1 remove the bowels from; disembowel. 2 deprive of something essential: *The abridgment leaves the book somewhat eviscerated.* [< L *eviscerare* < *ex-* out + *viscera* viscera] —**e·vis′cer·a′tion,** *n.*

e·vo·ca·tion (ev′ō kā′shən) *n.* an evoking.

e·voc·a·tive (i vok′ə tiv) *adj.* tending to produce or arouse an emotional response. —**e·voc′a·tive·ly,** *adv.* —**e·voc′a·tive·ness,** *n.*

e·voke (i vōk′) *v.* **e·voked, e·vok·ing.** call forth; bring out: *A good joke evokes a laugh.* [< L *evocare* < *ex-* out + *vocare* call] —**e·vok′er,** *n.*

ev·o·lu·tion (ev′ə lü′shən *or* ē′və lü′shən) *n.* 1 any process of formation or growth; gradual development: *the evolution of the modern steamship from the first crude boat.* 2 something evolved; a product of development; not a sudden discovery or creation. 3 the theory that all living things developed from a few simple forms of life or from a single form. 4 a movement of ships or soldiers, planned beforehand. 5 a movement that is a part of a definite plan, design, or series: *the graceful evolutions of a ballet dancer.* 6 a releasing; giving off; setting free: *the evolution of heat from burning coal.* 7 *Mathematics.* the extraction of roots from powers. [< L *evolutio, -onis* < *evolvere.* See EVOLVE.]

ev·o·lu·tion·al (ev′ə lü′shən əl *or* ē′və lü′shən əl) *adj.* evolutionary.

hat, āge, fär; let, ēqual, tėrm; it, īce
hot, ōpen, ôrder; oil, out; cup, put, rüle,
above, takən, pencəl, lemən, circəs

ch, child; ng, long; sh, ship
th, thin; ᴛн, then; zh, measure

ev·o·lu·tion·ar·y (ev′ə lü′shən er′ē *or* ē′və lü′shən er′ē) *adj.* 1 having to do with evolution or development. 2 in accordance with the theory of evolution. 3 performing evolutions; having to do with evolutions.

ev·o·lu·tion·ist (ev′ə lü′shən ist *or* ē′və lü′shən ist) *n.* a student of, or believer in, the theory of evolution.

e·volve (i volv′) *v.* **e·volved, e·volv·ing.** 1 develop gradually; work out: *The boys evolved a plan for earning money during their summer vacation.* 2 *Biology.* develop by a process of growth and change to a more highly organized condition. 3 release; give off; set free. 4 be developed by evolution. [< L *evolvere* < *ex-* out + *volvere* roll] —**e·volv′er,** *n.*

e·volve·ment (i volv′mənt) *n.* evolving or being evolved.

ev·zone (ev′zōn) *n.* a member of an elite Greek infantry corps that is famous for its valor. [< Gk. *euzōnos* dressed for exercise < *eu-* well + *zōnē* girdle]

ewe (yü) *n.* a female sheep. [OE *ēowu*]
☛ *Hom.* yew, you.

ew·er (yü′ər) *n.* a large water jug with a wide mouth and spout. [ME < AF var. of OF *eviere, aiguiere* < VL *aquaria* < L *aquarius* of or for water < *aqua* water]

ex¹ (eks) *prep.* 1 out of. *Ex elevator* means free of charges until the time of removal from the grain elevator. 2 without; not including. *Ex-dividend* stocks are stocks on which the purchaser will not receive the next dividend to be paid. [< L]

ex² (eks) *n.* 1 the 24th letter of the alphabet (X, x). 2 anything shaped like an X.

ex³ (eks) *n. Informal.* a former spouse, boyfriend, girlfriend, etc.: *She saw her ex downtown yesterday.*

Ex (eks) *n. Informal.* an exhibition, especially the Canadian National Exhibition held annually in Toronto.

ex-¹ *prefix.* 1 out of, from, or out, as in *express, exit, export.* 2 utterly or thoroughly, as in *exterminate, exasperate.* 3 former or formerly, as in *ex-president, ex-member.* Also: **e-,** before consonants except *c, f, p, q, s, t;* **ef-,** before *f.* [< L *ex-* < *ex* out of]

ex-² *prefix.* from, out, as in *exodus.* Also, **ec-,** before consonants. [< Gk.]

ex. 1 example. 2 examined. 3 exchange. 4 exercise.

Ex. Exodus.

ex·ac·er·bate (eg zas′ər bāt′ *or* eks as′ər bāt′) *v.* **-bat·ed, -bat·ing.** 1 make worse; aggravate (pain, disease, anger). 2 irritate (a person's feelings). [< L *exacerbare* < *ex-* completely + *acerbus* harsh, bitter]

ex·ac·er·ba·tion (eg zas′ər bā′shən *or* eks as′ər bā′shən) *n.* 1 aggravation. 2 irritation.

ex·act (eg zakt′) *adj., v.* —*adj.* 1 without any error or mistake; strictly correct; accurate; precise: *an exact measurement, the exact amount.* 2 strict; severe, rigorous. 3 characterized by or using strict accuracy: *A scientist should be an exact thinker.*
—*v.* 1 demand and get; force to be paid: *If he does the work, he can exact payment for it.* 2 call for; need; require: *A hard piece of work exacts effort and patience.* [< L *exactus,* pp. of *exigere* weigh accurately < *ex-* out + *agere* weigh] —**ex·act′a·ble,** *adj.*
—**ex·act′ness,** *n.* —**ex·act′or,** *n.*
☛ *Syn. adj.* **1.** See note at **correct.**

ex·act·ing (eg zak′ting) *adj.* 1 requiring much; making severe demands; hard to please: *an exacting employer.* 2 requiring effort, care, or attention: *Flying an airplane is exacting work.*
—**ex·act′ing·ly,** *adv.* —**ex·act′ing·ness,** *n.*

ex·ac·tion (eg zak′shən) *n.* 1 an exacting; a demanding and getting; an enforcing of a payment considered arbitrary: *The ruler's exactions of money left the people very poor.* 2 being exacted; extortion. 3 thing exacted. Taxes, fees, etc., forced to be paid, are exactions.

ex·act·i·tude (eg zak′tə tyüd′ *or* eg zak′tə tüd′) *n.* exactness.

ex·act·ly (eg zakt′lē) *adv.* 1 in an exact manner; accurately; precisely. 2 just so; quite right.

exact science a science in which facts can be accurately observed and results can be accurately predicted. Mathematics and physics are exact sciences.

ex·ag·ger·ate (eg zaj′ər āt′) *v.* **-at·ed, -at·ing.** 1 make

(something) greater than it is; overstate: *He exaggerated the dangers of the trip in order to frighten them into not going.* 2 increase or enlarge abnormally. 3 say or think something is greater than it is; go beyond the truth: *He always exaggerates when he tells about things he has done.* [< L *exaggerare* < *ex-* out, up + *agger* heap] —**ex·ag′ger·a′tor,** *n.*

ex·ag·ger·a·tion (eg zaj′ər ā′shən) *n.* 1 a statement that goes beyond the truth: *It is an exaggeration to say that you would rather die than touch a snake.* 2 the act of going beyond the truth: *His constant exaggeration made people distrust him.* 3 being exaggerated.

ex·alt (eg zolt′ *or* eg zôlt′) *v.* 1 place high or raise in rank, honor, power, character, quality, etc.: *We exalt a man when we elect him to high office.* 2 fill with pride, joy, or noble feeling. 3 praise, honor; glorify. [< L *exaltare* < *ex-* out, up + *altus* high]

ex·al·ta·tion (eg′zol tā′shən *or* eg′zôl tā′shən) *n.* 1 exalting or being exalted. 2 an elation of mind or feeling; rapture.

ex·am (eg zam′) *n. Informal.* examination.

ex·am·i·na·tion (eg zam′ə nā′shən) *n.* 1 a careful test; inspection: *The doctor made a careful examination of my eyes.* 2 a set of questions to test knowledge or skill; a formal test: *an examination in arithmetic.* 3 a written set of answers given in such a test: *The examinations have still not been marked.* 4 *Law.* an interrogation, especially of a witness.
☛ *Syn.* 1. See note at **investigation**.

ex·am·ine (eg zam′ən) *v.* -ined, -in·ing. 1 look at closely and carefully. 2 test the knowledge or qualifications of; ask questions of; test. 3 question (a witness) formally. [< F *examiner* < L *examinare* < *examen* a weighing < *exigere.* See EXACT.] —**ex·am′in·a·ble,** *adj.* —**ex·am′in·er,** *n.*

ex·am·i·nee (eg zam′ə nē′) *n.* a person who is being examined.

ex·am·ple (eg zam′pəl) *n.* 1 one thing taken to show what others are like; a case that shows something; sample: *Vancouver is an example of a busy city.* 2 a model; pattern of something to be imitated or avoided: *That father is a good example to his sons.* 3 an instance or sample that serves to illustrate a way of doing or making something: *The problems in the arithmetic textbook were accompanied by examples.* 4 an instance or case, especially of punishment intended as a warning to others: *As an example, the captain made the shirkers clean up the camp.*
for example, as an illustration or illustrations; for instance: *Children play many games, for example, baseball.*
make an example of, treat sternly, or punish, as a sample of the result of misbehavior: *The teacher made an example of John by making him write "I won't talk in class" one hundred times.*
set an example, behave so that others may profitably imitate; be a model or pattern of conduct.
without example, with nothing like it before.
[ME < OF *essample* < L *exemplum,* originally, that which is taken out (i.e., a sample) < *eximere.* See EXEMPT.]
☛ *Syn.* 1. **Example, sample** = a part or thing taken to show the nature of something. **Example** applies to an individual thing, fact, happening, situation, etc. that shows what the type or kind is like or how a general rule works: *This chair is an example of period furniture.* **Sample** applies to a part taken out of a thing or class to show the quality of the whole, which is considered to be exactly like it: *She looked carefully at all the samples of material before buying any. The doctor examined a sample of her blood.* 2. See note at **model**.

ex·as·per·ate (eg zas′pər āt′) *v.* -at·ed, -at·ing. irritate very much; annoy extremely; make angry: *The child's endless questions exasperated her father.* [< L *exasperare* < *ex-* thoroughly + *asper* rough] —**ex·as′per·at′ed·ly,** *adv.* —**ex·as′per·at′er,** *n.*
☛ *Syn.* See note at **irritate**.

ex·as·per·a·tion (eg zas′pər ā′shən) *n.* 1 the act of exasperating. 2 extreme annoyance, irritation, or anger.

exc. except.

Exc. Excellency.

Ex·cal·i·bur (eks kal′ə bər) *n. Arthurian legend.* the magic sword of King Arthur. [ME < OF *escalibor* < Med.L *Caliburnus,* probably < Celtic]

ex ca·the·dra (eks′kə thē′drə *or* kath′ə drə) 1 with authority; from the seat of authority. 2 spoken with authority; authoritative. [< L *ex cathedra* from the chair]

ex·ca·vate (eks′kə vāt′) *v.* -vat·ed, -vat·ing. 1 make a hole by removing dirt, sand, rock, etc.: *The construction company will begin to excavate tomorrow.* 2 make by digging; dig: *The tunnel was excavated through solid rock.* 3 dig out; scoop out: *Steam shovels excavated the dirt.* 4 get or uncover by digging: *They excavated the ancient buried city.* [< L *excavare* < *ex-* out + *cavus* hollow]

ex·ca·va·tion (eks′kə vā′shən) *n.* 1 a digging; a digging out or up. 2 a hole or hollow made by digging.

ex·ca·va·tor (eks′kə vā′tər) *n.* a person or thing that excavates. A steam shovel is an excavator.

ex·ceed (ek sēd′) *v.* 1 go beyond; be more or greater than; do more than; surpass: *The sum of 5 and 7 exceeds 10.* 2 be more or greater than others. [< F < L *exedere* < *ex-* out + *cedere* go]
☛ *Syn.* 1. See note at **excel**.

ex·ceed·ing (ek sēd′ing) *adj., adv.* —*adj.* surpassing; very great; unusual; extreme. —*adv. Archaic.* exceedingly.

ex·ceed·ing·ly (ek sēd′ing lē) *adv.* extremely; unusually; very: *Yesterday was an exceedingly hot day.*

ex·cel (ek sel′) *v.* -celled, -cel·ling. 1 be better than; do better than: *He excelled his classmates in history.* 2 be better than others; do better than others: *excel in wisdom.* [< F < L *excellere*]
☛ *Syn.* 1, 2. **Excel, surpass, outdo** = be better in quality or action. **Excel** emphasizes standing out above others in fineness, merit, or doing things: *He excels in mathematics.* **Surpass** = be better in comparison with others or a definite standard: *Mary surpassed all the previous school records for the high jump.* **Outdo** emphasizes doing more or better than others, especially more or better than has been done before: *The runner outdid all other contestants for the athlete-of-the-year award.*

ex·cel·lence (ek′sə ləns) *n.* 1 being better than others; superiority: *the pursuit of excellence.* 2 an unusually good quality: *The inn was famous for the excellence of its food.* 3 **Excellence,** Excellency; Your Excellency.

ex·cel·len·cy (ek′sə lən sē) *n., pl.* -cies. 1 excellence. 2 **Excellency,** a title of honor used in speaking to or of the Governor General, an ambassador, a bishop, etc. *Abbrev.:* Exc.

ex·cel·lent (ek′sə lənt) *adj.* unusually good; better than others; first-class: *She is an excellent golfer.* [< L *excellens, -entis,* ppr. of *excellere* excel] —**ex′cel·lent·ly,** *adv.*

ex·cel·si·or (*adj.* ek sel′sē ôr; *n.* ek sel′sē ər) *adj., n.* —*adj. Latin.* ever upward; higher. —*n.* 1 short, fine, curled shavings of soft wood used as a packing material or as stuffing. 2 a size of printing type (3 point). This sentence is set in excelsior. [< L *excelsior,* comparative of *excelsus* high, pp. of *excellere* excel]

ex·cept (ek sept′) *prep., conj., v.* —*prep.* leaving out; but; other than: *every day except Sunday.* —*conj.* 1 *Informal.* unless (*often used with* **that**): *I'd like to go with you except that I can't swim.* 2 with any purpose other than; otherwise than: *He hardly ever goes out except to visit his brother.* 3 *Archaic.* unless: *except you repent.* —*v.* take out or leave out; exclude: *All the children, the baby excepted, were helping to clean up the backyard.*
except for, leaving out; other than: *It's a good movie, except for a few boring scenes near the beginning.*
[< L *exceptus,* pp. of *excipere* < *ex-* out + *capere* take]
☛ *Syn. prep.* **Except, but** = leaving out. **Except** emphasizes the idea of leaving out, keeping out, or even shutting out: *Everyone was invited to the party except me.* **But** is unemphatic, and suggests more the idea of not taking in than of keeping out: *Everyone was invited but me.*
☛ *Usage.* See note at **accept**.

ex·cept·ing (ek sep′ting) *prep., conj.* —*prep.* except; leaving out; other than. —*conj. Archaic.* unless.

ex·cep·tion (ek sep′shən) *n.* 1 the act of leaving out or excluding: *I like all the paintings, with the exception of this one. They said they could make no exception, and that everyone would have to pay the full fee.* 2 an unusual instance; a case that does not follow the rule: *She usually comes on time; today was an exception.*
take exception, object or protest: *He took exception to the editorial, and wrote a letter to the newspaper about it.*

ex·cep·tion·a·ble (ek sep′shən ə bəl) *adj.* liable to objection; objectionable.

ex·cep·tion·al (ek sep′shən əl) *adj.* out of the ordinary; unusual: *This warm weather is exceptional for January.* —**ex·cep′tion·al·ly,** *adv.*

ex·cerpt (*n.* ek′sèrpt; *v.* ek sèrpt′) *n., v.* —*n.* a selected passage; quotation; extract: *The article included excerpts from several medical books.* —*v.* take out; select (passages) from; quote; make extracts from. [< L *excerptum,* pp. of *excerpere* < *ex-* out + *carpere* pluck]

ex·cess (ek ses′ *or, esp. for 4,* ek′ses) *n.* 1 the action or an instance of going beyond what is usual, enough, or right: *The excesses of the last city council were exposed in the report. He was opposed to all excess in eating and drinking.* 2 an amount or degree beyond what is usual, enough, or right: *an excess of grief. She said he never drank to excess.* 3 the amount by which one quantity or thing is more than another: *She had to pay for an excess of five kilograms on her luggage.* 4 (*adj.*) more than the usual permitted, or proper amount: *Airlines charge for excess baggage.*
in excess of, more than; over: *They expect the contributions to be in excess of $5000.*
[ME < OF < L *excessus* < *excedere.* See EXCEED.]

ex·ces·sive (ek ses′iv) *adj.* too much; too great; going beyond what is necessary or right: *She didn't buy the couch because she felt the price was excessive.* —**ex·cess′ive·ly,** *adv.* —**ex·cess′ive·ness,** *n.*

Syn. Excessive, exorbitant, inordinate = too much or too great. **Excessive** = going beyond what is right or normal in amount or extent: *Mary spends an excessive amount of time telephoning.* **Exorbitant** also = excessive, beyond what is proper or reasonable, and particularly describes demands: *He asked an exorbitant rent for the house.* **Inordinate** = going beyond what is in order, and suggests a lack of restraint: *He has an inordinate appetite.*

ex·change (eks chānj′) *v.* **-changed, -chang·ing;** *n.* —*v.* **1** give (for something else): *She would not exchange her house for a palace.* **2** give in trade for something regarded as equivalent: *I will exchange ten dimes for a dollar.* **3** give and receive (things of the same kind): *to exchange letters.* **4** replace or have replaced (a purchase): *We cannot exchange swimsuits.* **5** make an exchange. **6** pass or be taken in exchange or as an equivalent.
—*n.* **1** an exchanging; giving and receiving: *Ten dimes for a dollar is a fair exchange.* **2** something that has been given, received, or offered in an exchange. **3** a place where things are exchanged or traded. Stocks are bought, sold, and traded in a stock exchange. **4** a central telephone office. **5** a system of settling accounts in different places by exchanging bills of exchange that represent money instead of exchanging money itself. **6** the changing of the money of one country into the money of another. **7** a fee charged for settling accounts or changing money. **8** the rate of exchange; varying rate or sum in one currency given for a fixed sum in another currency. [ME < OF *eschangier* < VL *excambiare* < *ex-* out + *cambiare* change (< Celtic)] —**ex·chang′er,** *n.*
Syn. v. **2.** Exchange, interchange = give and take. **Exchange** emphasizes the idea of trading, or giving one thing and getting back another: *We exchanged souvenirs.* **Interchange** emphasizes the idea of an even exchange, of taking turns giving and receiving or of giving back something equal in value or amount: *Delegates from different countries interchanged ideas.*

ex·change·a·bil·i·ty (eks chān′jə bil′ə tē) *n.* the quality or condition of being exchangeable.

ex·change·a·ble (eks chān′jə bəl) *adj.* capable of being exchanged.

exchange reaction *Chemistry.* a process in which atoms of the same element exchange positions within a molecule or between molecules.

ex·cheq·uer (eks chek′ər) *n.* **1** a treasury, especially the treasury of a state or nation. **2** *Informal.* finances; funds. **3 Exchequer, a** the department of the British government in charge of its finances and the public revenues. **b** the offices of this department of the British government. **c** the funds of the British government. [ME < OF *eschequier* chessboard; because accounts were kept on a table marked in squares]

Exchequer Court a court having jurisdiction to hear legal actions brought by or against the Federal Government, absorbed in 1971 by the Federal Court of Canada.

ex·cise¹ (ek′sīz *or* ek sīz′) *n.* a tax on the manufacture, sale, or use of certain articles made, sold, or used within a country. There is an excise on tobacco. [apparently < MDu. *excijs* < OF *acceis* tax, ult. < L *ad-* to + *census* tax]

ex·cise² (ek sīz′) *v.* **-cised, -cis·ing.** remove by or as if by cutting out: *to excise a tumor, to excise a passage from a book.* [< L *excisus,* pp. of *excidere* < *ex-* out + *caedere* cut]

ex·ci·sion (ek sizh′ən) *n.* the action or process of excising.

ex·cit·a·bil·i·ty (ek sīt′ə bil′ə tē) *n.* the quality or state of being excitable.

ex·cit·a·ble (ek sīt′ə bəl) *adj.* **1** easily stirred up and aroused: *Our dog is excitable and will bark at anything.* **2** capable of responding to stimuli: *an excitable nerve.* —**ex·cit′a·ble·ness,** *n.* —**ex·cit′a·bly,** *adv.*

ex·cit·ant (ek sī′tənt) *n., adj.* —*n.* **1** something that arouses or excites; stimulant. **2** the liquid that produces a magnetic field in an electric cell. —*adj.* stimulating; tending to arouse or excite.

ex·ci·ta·tion (ek′sī tā′shən) *n.* exciting or being excited, especially the production of a magnetic field by means of electricity or the raising of an atom or nucleus to a higher level of energy.

ex·cite (ek sīt′) *v.* **-cit·ed, -cit·ing.** **1** stir up the feelings of; move to strong emotion: *It excited her just to think of what she would do with the money.* **2** arouse: *His new jacket excited envy in some of the other boys.* **3** stir to action or activity: *Don't excite the dogs.* **4** produce or increase a response in (an organ, tissue, organism, etc.); stimulate: *to excite a nerve.* **5** produce a magnetic field in (the coils of a generator, etc.). **6** raise (an atom, nucleus, or molecule) to a higher level of energy. [ME < L *excitare,* ult. < *ex-* out + *ciere* set in motion] —**ex·cit′ed·ly,** *adv.*

ex·cit·ed (ek sīt′id) *adj.* **1** stirred up; aroused: *He was so excited he couldn't sleep.* **2** *Physics.* raised to a higher level of energy: *an excited atom.* —**ex·cit′ed·ly,** *adv.*

ex·cite·ment (ek sīt′mənt) *n.* **1** an exciting; arousing: *the excitement of nations to war.* **2** the state of being excited. **3** something that excites. **4** noisy activity; commotion; ado: *What's all the excitement?*

hat, āge, fär; let, ēqual, tėrm; it, īce
hot, ōpen, ôrder; oil, out; cup, půt, rüle,
əbove, takən, pencəl, lemən, circəs

ch, child; ng, long; sh, ship
th, thin; ŦH, then; zh, measure

ex·cit·er (ek sī′tər) *n.* **1** a person or thing that excites. **2** *Electricity.* **a** a dynamo, battery, etc. used to produce a magnetic field in another dynamo or motor. **b** a device for producing Hertzian waves.

ex·cit·ing (ek sī′ting) *adj.* producing excitement: *an exciting piece of news, an exciting game.*

ex·claim (eks klām′) *v.* say or speak suddenly in surprise or strong feeling; cry out. [< F < L *exclamare* < *ex-* + *clamare* cry out]

ex·cla·ma·tion (eks′klə mā′shən) *n.* **1** exclaiming. **2** something exclaimed. *Ah!* and *oh!* are exclamations.
Usage. An exclamation may be any statement or command that would be spoken with special force or emphasis. It may also be a sentence in which a special structure or word order indicates force or emphasis: *What a fine house you have! How comfortable it looks!*

exclamation mark *or* **exclamation point** a mark of punctuation (!) used after a word or sentence to show that it is an exclamation. The exclamation mark is also used, within square brackets or, informally, parentheses, to suggest that some statement or situation is remarkable, absurd, or the like.
Usage. Take care not to overuse exclamation marks. If too many are used in a piece of writing, they quickly lose their effectiveness. Except in very familiar writing, don't use more than one exclamation mark after any one word, phrase, or sentence.

ex·clam·a·to·ry (eks klam′ə tô′rē) *adj.* using, containing, or expressing exclamation: *an exclamatory sentence.*

ex·clude (eks klüd′) *v.* **-clud·ed, -clud·ing.** **1** shut out; keep out: *Blinds exclude light. Faith excludes doubt.* **2** keep from a place, privilege, activity, etc.; keep from including or considering: *Professional players are excluded from the competition. The invitation excludes children.* [ME < L *excludere* < *ex-* out + *claudere* shut] —**ex·clud′er,** *n.*
Syn. **1.** Exclude, eliminate = keep out. **Exclude** emphasizes keeping someone or something from coming in to a place, thought, rights, etc.: *Closing the windows excludes street noises.* **Eliminate** emphasizes putting out something already in, by getting rid of it or shutting it off from attention: *He eliminated fear from his thinking.*

ex·clud·ing (eks klü′ding) *prep.* except for; with the exception of; not counting: *All the neighbors, excluding those away on holidays, will be at the picnic.*

ex·clu·sion (eks klü′zhən) *n.* the act of excluding or the state of being excluded.
to the exclusion of, so as to exclude: *She worked away at her science project, to the exclusion of everything else.*
[< L *exclusio, -onis* < *excludere.* See EXCLUDE.]

ex·clu·sive (eks klü′siv *or* eks klü′ziv) *adj., n.* —*adj.* **1** each shutting out the other. *Baby* and *adult* are exclusive terms since a person cannot be both. **2** shutting out all or most other things, considerations, etc.: *He demanded our exclusive attention. She has an exclusive interest in sports.* **3** not divided or shared with others; single; sole: *A patent gives an inventor the exclusive right for a certain number of years to make what he has invented.* **4** excluding certain people or groups for social, financial, or other reasons: *an exclusive club, an exclusive school.* **5** selling only expensive items: *an exclusive boutique.* **6** not available elsewhere or to anyone else: *an exclusive design, an exclusive interview.*
exclusive of, excluding; leaving out; not counting or considering: *There are 26 days in that month, exclusive of Sundays. The label says the dress is all cotton, exclusive of trimmings.*
—*n.* something exclusive, especially an article, news story, etc. published by only one periodical. —**ex·clu′sive·ly,** *adv.* —**ex·clu′sive·ness,** *n.*

ex·clu·siv·i·ty (ek′sklü siv′ə tē) *n.* **1** the quality or state of being exclusive; exclusiveness. **2** exclusive rights.

ex·com·mu·ni·cate (eks′kə myü′nə kāt′) *v.* **-cat·ed, -cat·ing.** cut off from membership in a church; expel formally from the fellowship of a church; prohibit from participating in any of the rites of a church. [< LL *excommunicare,* literally, put out of the fellowship (of the Church) < L *ex-* out of + *communis* common]

ex·com·mu·ni·ca·tion (eks′kə myü′nə kā′shən) *n.* **1** a formal expulsion from the fellowship of a church; prohibition from participating in any of the rites of a church. **2** the formal, official statement announcing excommunication. **3** the condition or state of a person who has been excommunicated.

ex·co·ri·ate (eks kô′rē āt′) *v.* **-at·ed, -at·ing.** **1** strip or rub off the skin of; make raw and sore. **2** denounce violently. [< LL

excoriare < *ex-* off + *corium* hide, skin] —**ex·co′ri·a′tion,** *n.*

ex·cre·ment (eks′krə mənt) *n.* waste matter discharged from the bowels; feces. [< L *excrementum,* ult. < *excernere* < *ex-* out + *cernere* sift]

ex·cre·men·tal (eks′krə men′təl) *adj.* of or like excrement.

ex·cres·cence (eks kres′əns) *n.* **1** an unnatural or disfiguring growth or addition, such as a wart or bunion. **2** any abnormal increase or outgrowth.

ex·cres·cent (eks kres′ənt) *adj.* **1** forming an unnatural growth or a disfiguring addition. **2** *Phonetics.* of a sound, present for no historical or grammatical reason, as *b* in *thimble,* derived from Old English *thymle.* [< L *excrescens, -entis,* ppr. of *excrescere* < *ex-* out + *crescere* grow]

ex·cre·ta (eks krē′tə) *n.pl.* waste matter discharged from the body, such as sweat or urine. [< L *excreta,* neut. pl. of *excretus,* pp. of *excernere.* See EXCREMENT.]

ex·crete (eks krēt′) *v.* **-cret·ed, -cret·ing.** discharge (waste matter) from the body; separate (waste matter) from the blood or tissues. The skin excretes sweat. [< L *excretus,* pp. of *excernere.* See EXCREMENT.]

ex·cre·tion (eks krē′shən) *n.* **1** the discharge of waste matter from the body; the separation of waste matter from the blood or tissues. **2** the waste matter discharged from the body; waste matter separated from the blood or tissues. Sweat is an excretion.

ex·cre·tive (eks krē′tiv) *adj.* excreting; serving to excrete.

ex·cre·to·ry (eks′krə tô′rē *or* eks krē′tə rē) *adj.* of or having to do with excretion; that excrete: *The kidneys are excretory organs.*

ex·cru·ci·at·ing (eks krü′shē āt′ing) *adj.* very painful; torturing; causing great suffering. [< L *excruciate* crucify, torture < L *excruciare* < *ex-* utterly + *cruciare* torture, crucify < *crux, crucis* cross] —**ex·cru′ci·at′ing·ly,** *adv.*

ex·cul·pate (eks′kəl pāt′ *or* eks kul′pāt) *v.* **-pat·ed, -pat·ing.** free from blame; prove innocent. [< Med.L **exculpare* < L *ex-* out + *culpa* guilt]

ex·cul·pa·tion (eks′kəl pā′shən) *n.* **1** freeing from blame; proving innocent. **2** a vindication; proof of innocence; excuse.

ex·cul·pa·to·ry (eks kul′pə tôr′ē) *adj.* tending to exculpate or capable of exculpating.

ex·cur·sion (eks kėr′zhən *or* eks kėr′shən) *n.* **1** a short journey made with the intention of returning; a pleasure trip: *Our club went on an excursion to the mountains.* **2** a round trip at a reduced fare, usually involving a restriction on the length of time spent on the trip, dates of travel, etc. **3** a group of people who go on an excursion. **4** a wandering from the subject; deviation; digression. **5** *Obsolete.* a raid or attack. [< L *excursio, -onis* < *excurrere* < *ex-* out + *currere* run]

ex·cur·sion·ist (eks kėr′zhən ist *or* eks kėr′shən ist) *n.* a person who goes on an excursion.

ex·cur·sive (eks kėr′siv) *adj.* off the subject; wandering; rambling. —**ex·cur′sive·ly,** *adv.*

ex·cus·a·ble (ek skyü′zə bəl) *adj.* that can or ought to be excused: *Her anger was excusable since they had been so rude.* —**ex·cus′a·bly,** *adv.*

ex·cuse (*v.* eks kyüz′; *n.* eks kyüs′) *v.* **-cused, -cus·ing;** *n.* —*v.* **1** overlook (a fault, etc.); pardon; forgive. **2** give a reason or apology for; try to clear of blame: *She excused her own faults by blaming others.* **3** be a reason or explanation for; clear of blame: *Sickness excused his absence from school.* **4** free from duty or obligation; let off: *Those who passed the first test are excused from the second one.* **5** not demand or require; dispense with: *We will excuse your presence.* **6** seek or obtain exemption or release for. **excuse oneself, a** ask to be pardoned. **b** ask permission to leave. —*n.* **1** a real or pretended reason or explanation. **2** an apology given. **3** the act of excusing. [ME < OF < L *excusare* < *ex-* away + *causa* cause] —**ex·cus′er,** *n.*

☛ *Syn. v.* **1. Excuse, pardon, forgive** = free from blame or punishment. **Excuse** = overlook, or let off with only disapproval, less important errors and faults: *This time he excused my carelessness.* **Pardon,** more formal in tone, means free from punishment due for serious faults, wrongdoing, or crimes: *The governor pardoned the thief.* **Forgive** suggests more personal feeling, and emphasizes giving up all wish to punish for a wrong done: *He forgave his brother for leaving home.* —*n.* **2. Excuse, apology** = something said to explain an offence or failure. **Excuse** suggests trying to justify a mistake or failure or to make it seem less serious, in order to escape being blamed or punished: *He is always late, and always has an excuse.* **Apology** suggests admitting that one has, or seems to have, done or been wrong and expressing regret: *He offered his apology for damaging my car.*

☛ *Usage.* **Excuse, pardon. Pardon me** is sometimes considered more elegant than **Excuse me** in upper-class social situations. **I beg (your) pardon** is a standard formula meaning "I didn't hear what you said"; it can also be a sarcastic retort to a stupid or incredible statement. **Excuse** has the special meaning of "give permission to leave."

exec. executive; executor.

ex·e·cra·ble (ek′sə krə bəl) *adj.* **1** abominable; detestable: *an execrable crime.* **2** *Informal.* very bad: *execrable taste in art.* —**ex′e·cra·ble·ness,** *n.* —**ex′e·cra·bly,** *adv.*

ex·e·crate (ek′sə krāt′) *v.* **-crat·ed, -crat·ing. 1** express or feel extreme loathing for; abhor: *The former leader's cruelty was execrated by his disillusioned followers.* **2** curse. [< L *ex(s)ecrare* < *ex-* completely + *sacer* accursed] —**ex′e·crat′or,** *n.* —**ex′e·cra′tion,** *n.*

ex·e·cute (ek′sə kyüt′) *v.* **-cut·ed, -cut·ing. 1** carry out; do: *The nurse executed the doctor's orders.* **2** put into effect; enforce: *to execute a law.* **3** put to death according to law: *The convicted murderer was executed.* **4** make according to a plan or design: *The tapestry was executed with great skill.* **5** perform or play (a piece of music). **6** *Law.* make (a deed, lease, contract, will, etc.) complete or valid by signing, sealing, or doing whatever is necessary. [ME < OF < Med.L *ex(s)ecutare* < L *ex(s)ecutus,* pp. of *exsequi* < *ex* out + *sequi* follow]

☛ *Syn.* **1.** See note at **perform.**

ex·e·cu·tion (ek′sə kyü′shən) *n.* **1** a carrying out; doing, performing, or producing: *the execution of one's duties, the execution of a statue in marble.* **2** putting into effect; enforcing: *the execution of a law.* **3** the manner of carrying out or doing something: *The pianist's execution was flawless.* **4** putting to death according to law. **5** making according to a plan or design. **6** *Law.* making complete or valid by signing, sealing, or doing what is necessary. **7** a written order from a court directing a judgment to be carried out.

do execution, *Archaic.* have an effective, especially a destructive, action.

ex·e·cu·tion·er (ek′sə kyü′shən ər *or* ek′sə kyüsh′nər) *n.* **1** a person who carries out the death penalty according to law. **2** any person who puts another to death.

ex·ec·u·tive (eg zek′yə tiv) *adj., n.* —*adj.* **1** having to do with carrying out or managing affairs: *an executive committee. The head of a school has an executive position.* **2** suitable or designed for executives: *an executive suite, executive toys.* **3** having the duty and power of putting the laws into effect: *The Cabinet is the executive branch of our government.* **4** involving or having to do with a group of people responsible for running the affairs of a society, association, or club: *There's an executive meeting this afternoon.* —*n.* **1** a person who carries out or manages affairs: *The president of a company is an executive.* **2** a person, group, or branch of government that has the duty and power of putting the laws into effect. **3** a group of people responsible for running the affairs of a society, association, or club. —**ex·ec′u·tive·ly,** *adv.*

Executive Council in Canada, the cabinet of a provincial government, consisting of the Premier and his ministers.

ex·ec·u·tor (eg zek′yə tər *for 1;* ek′sə kyü′tər *for 2*) *n.* **1** a person named in a will to carry out the provisions of the will. Compare **administrator** (def. 2). **2** a person who performs or carries out things. [ME < AF *executour* < L *ex(s)ecutor* < *exsequi.* See EXECUTE.]

ex·ec·u·trix (eg zek′yə triks′) *n.* a female executor.

ex·e·ge·sis (ek′sə jē′sis) *n., pl.* **-ses** (-sēz). **1** a scholarly explanation or interpretation of the Bible or of a passage in the Bible: *The minister gave an exegesis of the parable of the Good Samaritan.* **2** an explanation or interpretation of a word, sentence, etc.; explanatory note. [< Gk. *exēgēsis* < *ex-* out + *hēgeesthai* lead, guide]

ex·e·get·ic (ek′sə jet′ik) *adj.* having to do with exegesis; expository.

ex·e·get·i·cal (ek′sə jet′ə kəl) *adj.* exegetic.

ex·em·plar (eg zem′plər *or* eg zem′plär) *n.* **1** a person or thing worth imitating; an ideal model or pattern: *They looked on him as the exemplar of courage.* **2** a typical case; example: *She was belligerent and defensive, the exemplar of the insecure child.* [ME < L *exemplar* < *exemplum.* See EXAMPLE.]

ex·em·pla·ry (eg zem′plə rē *or* eg′zəm pler′ē) *adj.* **1** worth imitating; being a good model or pattern: *exemplary conduct. She showed exemplary courage.* **2** of a penalty or punishment, serving as a warning or deterrent: *a sentence of exemplary severity.* **3** serving as an example; typical: *exemplary passages from a book.* [< L *exemplaris* < *exemplum.* See EXAMPLE.]

ex·em·pli·fi·ca·tion (eg zem′plə fə kā′shən) *n.* **1** showing by example; being an example. **2** something that serves to illustrate; example: *The sudden price increases were an exemplification of the law of supply and demand.*

ex·em·pli·fy (eg zem′plə fī′) *v.* **-fied, -fy·ing.** show by example; be an example of: *The knights exemplified courage and courtesy.* [< Med.L *exemplificare* < L *exemplum* example + *facere* make]

ex·em·pli gra·ti·a (eg zem′plī grä′shē ə *or* eg zem′plē gra′tē ə) *Latin.* for example; for instance. *Abbrev.:* e.g.

ex·empt (eg zempt') *v., adj., n.* —*v.* make free (from a duty, obligation, rule, etc.); release: *Students who get very high marks will be exempted from the final examination.*
—*adj.* freed from a duty, obligation, rule, etc.; released: *Food is exempt from sales tax.*
—*n.* a person who has been exempted. [ME < OF < L *exemptus*, pp. of *eximere* < *ex*- out + *emere* take]

ex·emp·tion (eg zemp'shən) *n.* 1 exempting or being exempted; freedom from a duty, obligation, rule, etc.; immunity: *Churches have exemption from taxes.* 2 something that is exempted, especially a part of a person's income that does not have to be taxed: *There is a basic tax exemption that can be claimed by everyone.*
☛ *Syn.* 2. **Exemption, immunity** = freedom from obligation or duty. **Exemption** emphasizes freeing a person or thing from some obligation, rule, etc. required of or applied to others: *Churches have exemption from taxes.* **Immunity** emphasizes being protected from obligations, restrictions, and penalties to which other people are liable: *Members of Parliament have immunity from jury duty.*

ex·er·cise (ek'sər sīz') *n., v.* **-cised, -cis·ing.** —*n.* 1 activity to train or develop the body or keep it healthy: *Running and playing volleyball are forms of exercise.* 2 a particular activity or series of activities designed to develop or train the body or develop some skill or faculty: *He does exercises every morning. There is an exercise at the end of each lesson.* 3 active use or practice; employment: *the exercise of one's right to vote, the exercise of care to promote safety.* 4 the performance of duties, functions, etc.
5 **exercises,** *pl.* a formal activity, ceremony: *the opening exercises in a Sunday school.*
—*v.* 1 take part or cause to take part in an activity to keep fit or to train or develop some part of the body: *singing scales to exercise the voice. She exercises every other day at a fitness club.* 2 use actively; employ: *to exercise one's mind or imagination, to exercise care in crossing the street.* 3 carry out in action; perform or fulfil: *to exercise the duties of one's office.* 4 have as an effect: *What others think exercises a great influence on most of us.* 5 occupy the attention of, especially so as to worry, trouble, or annoy (*usually used in the passive*): *The city council has been greatly exercised by the problem of inflation.* [ME < OF *exercice* < L *exercitium* < *exercere* not allow to rest < *ex*- + *arcere* keep away]
—**ex'er·cis'er,** *n.*
☛ *Syn.* 1. **Exercise, practice, drill** = active use of physical or mental power for training or improvement. **Exercise** emphasizes repeated use of mental or physical powers to develop strength, health, and energy: *Exercise of the mind increases its power.* **Practice** applies to action repeated often and regularly to develop skill or gain perfection, especially in the use of a particular power: *Learning to play the piano well takes much practice.* **Drill** = constant repetition of a particular kind of exercise to discipline the body or mind and develop correct habits: *Children need drill in spelling.*

ex·ert (eg zėrt') *v.* 1 put forth; exercise or bring to bear: *to exert effort, to exert one's authority.* 2 try hard; strive (*used with a reflexive pronoun*): *We're going to have to exert ourselves to make the deadline.* [< L *ex(s)ertus,* pp. of *ex(s)erere* thrust out < *ex*- out + *serere* attach]

ex·er·tion (eg zėr'shən) *n.* 1 effort: *The exertion of moving the piano was too much for him and he collapsed. It was through the exertions of many volunteers that the fair succeeded.* 2 putting into action; active use; use: *an exertion of authority.*

ex·e·unt (ek'sē ənt *or* ek'sē ünt) *v. Latin.* in stage directions, the signal for actors to leave the stage. It is the plural of **exit** and means "They go out."

ex·ha·la·tion (eks'hə lā'shən) *n.* 1 exhaling. Breathing out is an exhalation of air. 2 something exhaled; air, vapor, smoke, odor, etc.

ex·hale (eks hāl') *v.* **-haled, -hal·ing.** 1 breathe out: *to exhale air from the lungs. The doctor told him to exhale completely.* 2 give off (air, vapor, smoke, odor, etc.). 3 pass off as vapor; rise like vapor: *Sweet odors exhale from the flowers.* [< F < L *exhalare* < *ex*- out + *halare* breathe]

ex·haust (eg zost' *or* eg zôst') *v., n.* —*v.* 1 empty completely: *to exhaust a well.* 2 use up: *to exhaust one's money.* 3 tire very much: *The climb up the hill exhausted us.* 4 drain of strength, resources, etc.: *The long war exhausted the country.* 5 draw off: *to exhaust the air in a jar.* 6 leave nothing important to be found out or said about; study or treat thoroughly: *Her book about tulips exhausted the subject.* 7 be discharged; go forth: *Gases from an automobile exhaust through a pipe.* 8 deprive wholly of useful or essential properties: *to exhaust the soil.* 9 deprive of ingredients by the use of solvents.
—*n.* 1 the escape of used steam, gasoline, etc. from a machine. 2 a means or way for used steam, gasoline, etc. to escape from an engine. 3 the used steam, gasoline, etc. that escapes. [< L *exhaustus,* pp. of *exhaurire* < *ex*- out, off + *haurire* draw]
—**ex·haust'er,** *n.*

ex·haust·ed (eg zost'tid *or* eg zôst'tid) *adj.* 1 used up. 2 worn out; very tired. —**ex·haust'ed·ly,** *adv.*
☛ *Syn.* 2. See note at **tired.**

ex·haust·i·bil·i·ty (eg zos'tə bil'ə tē *or* eg zôs'tə bil'ə tē) *n.*

hat, āge, fär; let, ēqual, tėrm; it, īce
hot, ōpen, ôrder; oil, out; cup, pút, rüle,
əbove, takən, pencəl, lemən, circəs
ch, child; ng, long; sh, ship
th, thin; ŦH, then; zh, measure

the quality of being exhaustible; capability of being exhausted.

ex·haust·i·ble (eg zos'tə bəl *or* eg zôs'tə bəl) *adj.* capable of being exhausted.

ex·haus·tion (eg zos'chən *or* eg zôs'chən) *n.* 1 exhausting or being exhausted. 2 extreme fatigue.

ex·haus·tive (eg zos'tiv *or* eg zôs'tiv) *adj.* leaving out nothing important; thorough; comprehensive: *Her conclusions are based on an exhaustive study of the subject.* —**ex·haust'ive·ly,** *adv.*
—**ex·haust'ive·ness,** *n.*
☛ *Usage.* Do not confuse **exhaustive,** meaning "thorough," with **exhausting,** meaning "very tiring." An *exhaustive* lecture on Vitamin A would be *exhausting* to an eighth-grade class, but appropriate in a medical school.

ex·haust·less (eg zost'lis *or* eg zôst'lis) *adj.* that cannot be exhausted.

ex·hib·it (eg zib'it) *v., n.* —*v.* 1 show; display. 2 show publicly. 3 show in court as evidence; submit for consideration or inspection.
—*n.* 1 a show; display. 2 the thing or things shown publicly. 3 a small exhibition or a part of a large exhibition: *Have you seen the art exhibit in the Jubilee Building?* 4 a document or other thing shown in court and referred to in written evidence. [< L *exhibitus,* pp. of *exhibere* < *ex*- out + *habere* hold]
☛ *Syn. v.* 1. See note at **display.** *-n.* 2, 3. **Exhibit, exhibition** = a public show. **Exhibit** applies particularly to an object or collection of things put on view at a fair, exhibition, or other public show: *His lambs were part of the school's exhibit at the county fair.* **Exhibition** applies to a public show of works of art, rare objects of any kind, commercial objects, etc.: *The city holds an exhibition of all its different products every year.*

ex·hi·bi·tion (ek'sə bish'ən) *n.* 1 the act of showing; display: *He said he had never seen such an exhibition of bad manners.* 2 a public show: *The art school holds an exhibition every year.* 3 a thing or things shown publicly. 4 a public showing of livestock, produce, manufactured goods, etc., accompanied by amusements such as sideshows, rides, games, and other forms of entertainment; a big fair: *the Canadian National Exhibition.*
☛ *Syn.* 2. See note at **exhibit.**

ex·hi·bi·tion·ism (ek'sə bish'ən iz'əm) *n.* 1 an excessive tendency to seek attention or to show off one's abilities. 2 a compulsive tendency to expose the genitals in public. 3 an instance of such exposure.

ex·hi·bi·tion·ist (ek'sə bish'ən ist) *n.* 1 a person who tends to seek attention or show off his abilities excessively. 2 a person given to compulsive exposure of the genitals in public.

ex·hib·i·tor (eg zib'ə tər) *n.* a person, company, or group that exhibits.

ex·hil·a·rate (eg zil'ə rāt') *v.* **-rat·ed, -rat·ing.** 1 refresh; invigorate: *The girls were exhilarated by their early-morning swim.* 2 make merry or lively; put into high spirits: *He was exhilarated by the prospect of getting home a day early.* [< L *exhilarare* < *ex*- thoroughly + *hilaris* merry] —**ex·hil'a·rat'or,** *n.*

ex·hil·a·ra·tion (eg zil'ə rā'shən) *n.* 1 an exhilarated feeling or condition; high spirits; stimulation. 2 the act of exhilarating.

ex·hort (eg zôrt') *v.* urge strongly; advise or warn earnestly: *The preacher exhorted his congregation to live better lives.* [< L *exhortari* < *ex*- + *hortari* urge strongly] —**ex·hort'er,** *n.*

ex·hor·ta·tion (eg'zôr tā'shən *or* ek'sôr tā'shən) *n.* 1 a strong urging; earnest advice or warning. 2 a speech, sermon, etc. that exhorts.

ex·hor·ta·tive (eg zôr'tə tiv) *adj.* exhortatory.

ex·hor·ta·to·ry (eg zôr'tə tô'rē) *adj.* urging; intended to exhort; admonitory.

ex·hu·ma·tion (eks'hyü mā'shən) *n.* an exhuming.

ex·hume (eks hyüm' *or* eg zyüm') *v.* **-humed, -hum·ing.** 1 take out of a grave or out of the ground; dig up. 2 reveal. [< Med.L *exhumare* < L *ex*- out of + *humus* ground]

ex·i·gence (ek'sə jəns) *n.* exigency.

ex·i·gen·cy (eg zij'ən sē *or* ek'sə jən sē) *n., pl.* **-cies.** 1 the state or quality of being urgent: *The exigency of the case justified his rudeness.* 2 **exigencies,** *pl.* urgent needs; requirements of a particular situation: *The exigencies of business kept her from attending the conference.* 3 a situation demanding immediate action or attention; urgent case.

ex·i·gent (ek'sə jənt) *adj.* 1 demanding immediate action or attention; urgent: *The exigent pangs of hunger sent him on a search*

for food. **2** demanding a great deal; exacting. [< L *exigens, -entis,* ppr. of *exigere.* See EXACT.]

ex·i·gu·i·ty (ek′sə gyü′ə tē) *n.* scantiness; smallness.

ex·ig·u·ous (eg zig′yü əs *or* ek sig′yü əs) *adj.* scanty; small. [< L *exiguus* scanty, originally, weighed out (sparingly) < *exigere.* See EXACT.] —**ex·ig′u·ous·ly,** *adv.* —**ex·ig′u·ous·ness,** *n.*

ex·ile (eg′zīl *or* ek′sīl) *v.* **-iled, -il·ing;** *n.* —*v.* force (a person) to leave his country or home; banish: *After the revolution many people were exiled from the country.*
—*n.* **1** being exiled; banishment: *Napoleon's exile to Elba was brief.* **2** an exiled person. **3** any prolonged absence from one's own country. [ME < OF *exilier* < LL *exiliare* < L *ex(s)ilium*]
☞ *Syn. v.* See note at **banish.**

ex·im·port (eks′im pôrt) *n.* Cdn. in professional football, a non-Canadian, who, after playing in the country for a certain number of years, qualifies as a Canadian player.

ex·ist (eg zist′) *v.* **1** have actual existence; be; be real. **2** continue to be: *The problem still exists.* **3** live; have life: *A person cannot exist without air.* **4** occur or be recorded: *Such cases exist in medicine, but they are rare.* [< F *exister* < L *ex(s)istere* < *ex-* forth + *sistere* stand]

ex·ist·ence (eg zis′təns) *n.* **1** real or actual being; being: *to come into existence, to question the existence of ghosts.* **2** way of life; life: *Many bush pilots lead a dangerous existence.* **3** an occurrence; presence. **4** all that exists. **5** something that exists.

ex·ist·ent (eg zis′tənt) *adj.* **1** existing. **2** existing now; of the present time.

ex·is·ten·tial (eg′zis ten′shəl *or* ek′sis ten′shəl) *adj.* **1** of or having to do with existence. **2** of or having to do with existentialism: *an existential play.* —**ex′is·ten′tial·ly,** *adv.*

ex·is·ten·tial·ism (eg′zis ten′shəl iz′əm *or* ek′sis ten′shəl iz′əm) *n.* a system of philosophy that avoids thought-out theories on life and holds that man is free, and responsible to himself alone, and that reality consists in living.

ex·is·ten·tial·ist (eg′zis ten′shə list *or* ek′sis ten′shə list) *adj., n.* —*adj.* having to do with or resembling existentialism. —*n.* a person who supports or follows the philosophy of existentialism.

ex·it (eg′zit *or* ek′sit) *n., v.* —*n.* **1** a way out: *The theatre had six exits.* **2** a going out; departure. **3** *Theatre.* the departure of an actor from the stage: *a graceful exit.* **4** death.
—*v.* **1** make an exit; go out or away, or die. **2** *Theatre.* go off stage (*used as a stage direction*): *Exit Hamlet.* [< L *exit* goes out; also < L *exitus* a going out; both < *ex-* out + *ire* go]

ex li·bris (eks′lī′bris *or* lē′bris) *Latin.* **1** from the library (*of*); an inscription used on a bookplate, followed by the name of the book's owner. **2** bookplate.

ex·o·bi·ol·o·gist (ek′sō bī ol′ə jist′) *n.* a person trained in exobiology, especially one whose work it is.

ex·o·bi·ol·o·gy (ek′sō bī ol′ə jē) *n.* the study of life on other planets or celestial bodies. [< Gk. *exō-* outside + E *biology*]

ex·o·carp (ek′sō kärp′) *n.* epicarp. [< Gk. *exō-* outside + *karpos* fruit]

Exod. Exodus.

ex·o·dus (ek′sə dəs) *n.* **1** going out; departure, especially of a large number of people: *Every summer there is an exodus from the city.* **2** Often, **Exodus,** the departure of the Israelites from Egypt under Moses. **3 Exodus,** the second book of the Bible, containing an account of this departure. [< L < Gk. *exodos* < *ex-* out + *hodos* way]

ex of·fi·ci·o (ěks′ ə fĭsh′ē ō) because of one's office: *The secretary is, ex officio, a member of all committees.* [< L]

ex·og·a·my (ek sog′ə mē) *n.* **1** the custom or law requiring marriage to a person outside one's own group, tribe, clan, etc. **2** reproduction by the fusion of gametes from distantly related or unrelated parents.

ex·og·e·nous (eks oj′ə nəs) *adj.* **1** of, having to do with, or originating from external causes: *an exogenous infection.* **2** *Botany.* designating stems that increase in thickness by the addition of annual layers on the outside of the wood, inside the bark. [< NL *exogenus* growing on the outside < Gk. *exō-* outside + *genēs* born, produced]

ex·on·er·ate (eg zon′ər āt′) *v.* **-at·ed, -at·ing. 1** free from blame; prove or declare innocent: *Witnesses of the accident completely exonerated the driver of the truck.* **2** relieve from a duty, task, obligation, etc. [< L *exonerare* < *ex-* off + *onus, oneris* burden] —**ex·on′er·a′tion,** *n.* —**ex·on′er·a′tor,** *n.*

ex·or·bi·tance (eg zôr′bə təns) *n.* being exorbitant.

ex·or·bi·tant (eg zôr′bə tənt) *adj.* going far beyond what is customary, right, or reasonable; grossly excessive: *exorbitant prices, an exorbitant demand.* [< L *exorbitans, -antis,* ppr. of *exorbitare* go out of the track < *ex-* out of + *orbita* track]
☞ *Syn.* See note at **excessive.**

ex·or·bi·tant·ly (eg zôr′bə tənt lē) *adv.* **1** extravagantly. **2** in an excessive degree or amount; beyond reasonable limits.

ex·or·cise (ek′sôr sīz′) *v.* **-cised, -cis·ing. 1** drive out (an evil spirit) by prayers, ceremonies, etc. **2** free (a person or place) from an evil spirit. [< LL *exorcizare* < Gk. *exorkizein* bind by oath, conjure, exorcise < *ex-* + *horkos* oath] —**ex′or·cis′er,** *n.*

ex·or·cism (ek′sôr siz′əm) *n.* **1** the act of exorcising. **2** the prayers, ceremonies, etc. used in exorcising.

ex·or·cist (ek′sôr sist) *n.* a person who exorcises.

ex·or·cize (ek′sôr sīz′) *v.* **-cized, -ciz·ing.** See exorcise.

ex·or·di·um (eg zôr′dē əm *or* ek sôr′dē əm) *n., pl.* **-di·ums, -di·a** (-dē ə). **1** the beginning. **2** the introductory part of a speech, treatise, etc. [< L *exordium* < *ex-* + *ordiri* begin, originally, begin a web]

ex·o·skel·e·tal (ek′sō skel′ə təl) *adj.* of or having to do with the exoskeleton.

ex·o·skel·e·ton (ek′sō skel′ə tən) *n.* the hard, external structure that protects or supports the bodies of many invertebrates, such as oysters, lobsters, or insects. Compare **endoskeleton.** [< Gk. *exo-* outside + E *skeleton*]

ex·o·sphere (eks′ō sfēr′) *n.* the outermost rim of the earth's atmosphere; the layer of the atmosphere in which the ionosphere begins to merge with interplanetary space.

ex·o·ter·ic (ek′sə ter′ik) *adj.* **1** capable of being understood by the general public. **2** not belonging to an inner circle of disciples, scholars, etc. **3** popular; well-known; commonplace; opposed to *esoteric.* [< LL *exotericus* < Gk. *exōterikos* < *exō-* outside < *ek* out of]

ex·ot·ic (eg zot′ik) *adj., n.* —*adj.* **1** foreign; not native: *Many exotic plants are grown in Canada as house plants.* **2** strange or unusual in a way that is fascinating or beautiful; strikingly unusual: *an exotic glamor.* **3** *Informal.* beautiful or fascinating because of strangeness.
—*n.* something exotic. [< L *exoticus* < Gk. *exōtikos* < *exō-* outside < *ek* out of] —**ex·ot′i·cal·ly,** *adv.*

ex·ot·i·ca (ek zot′i kə) *n.pl.* exotic things, especially things that are different, strange, or unusual in an intriguing or exciting way: *He has interested himself in such exotica as undersea aquariums and geodesic houseboats.*

exotic dancer a striptease dancer.

ex·ot·i·cism (eg zot′ə siz′əm) *n.* **1** the state or quality of being exotic. **2** something such as a foreign word or phrase.

exp. 1 export; exportation. **2** express. **3** expenses. **4** expired.

ex·pand (ek spand′) *v.* **1** increase in size; enlarge; swell: *The balloon expanded as it filled with air.* **2** spread out; open out; unfold; extend: *A bird expands its wings before flying.* **3** express in greater detail; enlarge upon: *She expanded on the theme in the second chapter.* **4** *Mathematics.* express (a quantity) as a sum of terms, product of terms, etc. [< L *expandere* < *ex-* out + *pandere* spread. Doublet of SPAWN.] —**ex·pand′er,** *n.* —**ex·pand′ing·ly,** *adv.*
☞ *Syn.* **1. Expand, swell, dilate** = make or become larger. **Expand** emphasizes spreading out or opening out in any or all directions: *Our interests expand as we grow.* **Swell** emphasizes growing bigger, getting higher or bigger around than normal, usually from pressure inside or from having something added: *His abscessed tooth made his face swell.* **Dilate** = widen, and applies particularly to circular or hollow things: *The pupils of her eyes dilated in the darkness.*

ex·pan·da·ble (ek span′də bəl) *adj.* expansible.

ex·panse (ek spans′) *n.* a large, unbroken space or stretch; wide, spreading surface: *The Pacific Ocean is a vast expanse of water.* [< L *expansum,* pp. neut. of *expandere.* See EXPAND.]

ex·pan·si·bil·i·ty (ek span′sə bil′ə tē) *n.* a capacity for expanding.

ex·pan·si·ble (ek span′sə bəl) *adj.* capable of being expanded.

ex·pan·sile (ek span′sīl *or* ek span′səl) *adj.* **1** capable of expanding; of such a nature as to expand. **2** of or having to do with expansion.

ex·pan·sion (ek span′shən) *n.* **1** spreading out so as to occupy more space: *Heat caused the expansion of the gas in the balloon.* **2** growing larger; swelling: *The expanding gas caused the expansion of the balloon.* **3** being expanded; increase in size, volume, etc.: *The expansion of the factory doubled the amount of goods it produced.* **4** the amount or degree of expansion. **5** a part or thing that is the result of expanding: *The thesis is an expansion of a paper he wrote last year.* **6** in an engine, the increase in volume of the working fluid which takes place in a cylinder. **7** *Mathematics.* the expression of a quantity as a sum of terms, product of terms, etc. [< LL *expansio, -onis* < *expandere.* See EXPAND.]

ex·pan·sion·ar·y (ek span′shə ner′ē) *adj.* **1** having to do with or tending to expansion or expansionism. **2** inflationary.

ex·pan·sion·ism (ek span′shə niz′əm) *n.* a policy of territorial or commercial expansion, usually at the expense of weaker rivals.

ex·pan·sion·ist (ek span′shən ist) *n., adj.* —*a* a supporter or advocate of expansionism. —*adj.* of, having to do with, or favoring expansionism.

ex·pan·sive (ek span′siv) *adj.* **1** capable of expanding or tending to expand. **2** wide; spreading. **3** taking in much or many things; broad; extensive. **4** showing one's feelings freely and openly; demonstrative: *He is a very expansive and hospitable person.* —**ex·pan′sive·ly,** *adv.* —**ex·pan′sive·ness,** *n.*

ex par·te (eks′ pär′tē) *Latin.* **1** *Law.* of a legal proceeding, from or in the interest of one side or party only. **2** partisan.

ex·pa·ti·ate (ek spā′shē āt′) *v.* **-at·ed, -at·ing. 1** write or talk much (*on*): *She expatiated on the thrills of her trip.* **2** roam or wander freely. [< L *ex(s)patiari* walk about < *ex-* out + *spatium* space] —**ex·pa′ti·a′tor,** *n.*

ex·pa·ti·a·tion (ek spā′shē ā′shən) *n.* **1** the act of writing or talking much. **2** an extended talk, description, etc.

ex·pa·tri·ate (*v.* eks pā′trē āt′; *adj., n.* eks pā′trē it or eks pā′trē āt′) *v.* **-at·ed, -at·ing; adj., n.** —*v.* **1** banish; exile. **2** withdraw (oneself) from one's country; renounce one's citizenship.
—*adj.* expatriated: *There are many expatriate Canadians in New York.*
—*n.* an expatriated person; exile or emigrant. [< LL *expatriare* < L *ex-* out of + *patria* fatherland]

ex·pa·tri·a·tion (eks pā′trē ā′shən) *n.* **1** a banishment; exile. **2** a withdrawal from one's country; renunciation of one's citizenship.

ex·pect (ek spekt′) *v.* **1** look forward to; think likely to come or happen. **2** look forward to with reason or confidence; desire and feel sure of getting: *They expect to be married in April. He's expecting a bonus from his company.* **3** count on as reasonable, necessary, or right: *A soldier is expected to be properly dressed. He expected a reward for finding and returning the dog.* **4** *Informal.* think; suppose; guess: *I expect they'll be coming by car.* [< L *ex(s)pectare* < *ex-* out + *specere* look] —**ex·pect′a·ble,** *adj.* —**ex·pect′a·bly,** *adv.*

ex·pect·ance (ek spek′təns) *n.* expectation.

ex·pect·an·cy (ek spek′tən sē) *n., pl.* **-cies. 1** expecting or being expected. **2** what is expected, especially the expected amount based on statistical information: *a life expectancy of 67 years.*

ex·pect·ant (ek spek′tənt) *adj., n.* —*adj.* having or showing expectation: *He opened his Christmas present with an expectant smile.*
expectant mother, a woman who is pregnant.
—*n.* a person who expects something. —**ex·pect′ant·ly,** *adv.*

ex·pec·ta·tion (ek′spek tā′shən) *n.* **1** the act or state of expecting something to come or happen; anticipation: *Contrary to expectation, he turned out to be an excellent student.* **2** something expected; the thing looked forward to. **3** Usually, **expectations,** *pl.* a reason for expecting something; a prospect, especially of advancement or prosperity: *They say she has great expectations.*
in expectation (of), expecting: *It was only in expectation of a reward that he returned the wallet.*

expectation of life the average number of years that a person of a certain age can expect to live.

ex·pect·ing (ek spek′ting) *adj. Informal.* pregnant.

ex·pec·to·rant (ek spek′tə rənt) *adj., n.* —*adj.* causing or helping the discharge of phlegm, etc. —*n.* a medicine that promotes expectoration.

ex·pec·to·rate (ek spek′tə rāt′) *v.* **-rat·ed, -rat·ing.** cough up and spit out (phlegm, etc.); spit. [< L *expectorare* < *ex-* out of + *pectus, pectoris* breast] —**ex·pec′to·ra′tor,** *n.*

ex·pec·to·ra·tion (ek spek′tə rā′shən) *n.* **1** the act of expectorating. **2** the expectorated matter.

ex·pe·di·ence (ek spē′dē əns) *n.* expediency.

ex·pe·di·en·cy (ek spē′dē ən sē) *n., pl.* **-cies. 1** usefulness; suitability for bringing about a desired result; desirability or fitness under the circumstances. **2** personal advantage; self-interest: *Her offer to help was prompted by expediency, not kindness.*

ex·pe·di·ent (ek spē′dē ənt) *adj., n.* —*adj.* **1** fit for bringing about a desired result; desirable or suitable under the circumstances; useful: *She decided it would be expedient to take an umbrella.* **2** prompted by a concern for personal advantage; based on self-interest; polite. —*n.* a means of bringing about a desired result: *Having no ladder or rope, the prisoner tied sheets together and escaped by this expedient.* [< L *expediens, -entis,* ppr. of *expedire* free from a net, set right < *ex-* out + *pes, pedis* foot] —**ex·pe′di·ent·ly,** *adv.*

ex·pe·dite (ek′spə dīt′) *v.* **-dit·ed, -dit·ing. 1** make easy and quick; speed up: *If everyone will help, it will expedite matters.* **2** do quickly. [< L *expeditus,* pp. of *expedire.* See EXPEDIENT.]

hat, āge, fär; let, ēqual, tėrm; it, īce
hot, ōpen, ôrder; oil, out; cup, put, rüle,
above, takən, pencəl, lemən, circəs

ch, child; ng, long; sh, ship
th, thin; ℱH, then; zh, measure

ex·pe·dit·er (ek′spə dīt′ər) *n.* a person who expedites, especially one employed to look after supplying raw materials or delivering finished products on schedule.

ex·pe·di·tion (ek′spə dish′ən) *n.* **1** a journey for some special purpose. A voyage of discovery or a military march against the enemy is an expedition. **2** the group of people, ships, etc. that make such a journey. **3** efficient and prompt action; speed: *He completed his work with expedition.*

ex·pe·di·tion·ar·y (ek′spə dish′ən er′ē) *adj.* of, concerning, or making up an expedition.

ex·pe·di·tious (ek′spə dish′əs) *adj.* quick; speedy; efficient and prompt. —**ex′pe·di′tious·ly,** *adv.* —**ex′pe·di′tious·ness,** *n.*

ex·pel (ek spel′) *v.* **-pelled, -pel·ling. 1** force out; force to leave: *When the gunpowder exploded, the bullet was expelled from the gun.* **2** put out; dismiss permanently: *A troublesome pupil may be expelled from school.* [< L *expellere* < *ex-* out + *pellere* drive] —**ex·pel′ler,** *n.*

ex·pel·lant or **ex·pel·lent** (ek spel′ənt) *adj., n.* —*adj.* tending to force out or expel. —*n.* an expellant medicine.

ex·pend (ek spend′) *v.* spend; use up. [< L *expendere* < *ex-* out + *pendere* weigh, pay. Doublet of SPEND.] —**ex·pend′er,** *n.*
☛ *Syn.* See note at **spend.**

ex·pend·a·ble (ek spen′də bəl) *adj., n.* —*adj.* **1** normally consumed or used up in service: *Pencils, paper, stamps, etc. are expendable items.* **2** that may be sacrificed if necessary; more convenient, economical, etc. to sacrifice in certain situations than to rescue or protect: *People don't usually like to think of themselves as being expendable in their jobs.* —*n.* Usually, **expendables,** *pl.* expendable persons or things.

ex·pend·i·ture (ek spen′də chür′ or ek spen′də chər) *n.* **1** spending; using up: *Such a complicated enterprise requires the expenditure of much money, time, and effort.* **2** the amount of money, time, energy, etc. spent or used up: *Limit your expenditures to what is necessary.*

ex·pense (ek spens′) *n.* **1** the cost; charge: *The expense of the trip was slight. He travelled at his uncle's expense. They had many a laugh at his expense.* **2** a cause of spending: *Running a car is an expense.* **3** an expending; the paying out of money; outlay: *Her time at university put her father to considerable expense.* **4** loss; sacrifice. **5 expenses,** *pl.* **a** the charges incurred in running one's business or doing one's job. **b** the money to repay such charges: *Because she has to travel a lot as a consultant, she gets expenses besides her salary.*
at the expense of, with the loss or sacrifice of: *He achieved the prosperity he had desired, but it was at the expense of his health.* [ME < AF < LL *expensa* < L *expensus,* pp. of *expendere.* See EXPEND.]

ex·pen·sive (ek spen′siv) *adj.* costly; high-priced. —**ex·pen′sive·ly,** *adv.* —**ex·pen′sive·ness,** *n.*
☛ *Syn.* **Expensive, costly, dear** = costing much. **Expensive,** the general word, means "high-priced," sometimes suggesting more than a person can afford, sometimes more than a thing is worth, and applies to cost in money or in time, effort, etc.: *He had a very expensive pocketknife.* **Costly** = of very high price, but usually because rare, precious, luxurious, etc., and is often used to refer to great effort, sacrifice, etc.: *a costly jewel, a costly victory.* **Dear** = too expensive: *Meat is dear this week.*

ex·pe·ri·ence (ek spēr′ē əns) *n., v.* **-enced, -enc·ing.** —*n.* **1** something that has happened to one; what is or has been met with, felt, done, seen, etc. on a particular occasion: *The expedition through the jungle was an exciting experience for her.* **2** of living through something; observing or taking part in events: *He has learned a lot by experience.* **3** everything gone through that makes up the life of a person, community, race, etc.: *No parallel for such wickedness can be found in human experience.* **4** skill, practical knowledge, or wisdom gained by observing, doing, or living through things: *a person of wide experience. Have you had any experience in this kind of work?*
—*v.* have happen to one; meet with; feel; live through: *Visiting the Calgary Stampede was the greatest thrill I ever experienced.* [ME < OF < L *experientia* < *experiri* test, try out] —**ex·pe′ri·enc·er,** *n.*
☛ *Syn. v.* **Experience, undergo** = go through something in life. **Experience** emphasizes having something happen to one, but does not suggest whether it is pleasant or unpleasant, brief or long-lasting, important or unimportant: *Visiting the Calgary Stampede was the greatest thrill I ever experienced.* **Undergo** suggests having to suffer or live through something unpleasant, painful, or

dangerous: *I had to undergo many disappointments and failures before experiencing success.*

ex·pe·ri·enced (ek spēr´ē ənst) *adj.* skilful or wise because of much experience in a particular field or activity; expert; practised: *an experienced nurse, an experienced driver.*

ex·pe·ri·en·tial (ek spēr´ē en´shəl) *adj.* having to do with experience; based on or coming from experience.

ex·per·i·ment (*v.* ek sper´ə ment´; *n.* ek sper´ə mənt) *v., n.* —*v.* try in order to find out; make trials or tests: *He has been experimenting with dyes to get the color he wants.* —*n.* **1** a test or trial to find out something new or to demonstrate something that is known: *a cooking experiment to test a new kind of flour. We did an experiment in school today to show how electricity produces magnetism.* **2** a conducting of such tests or trials; experimentation: *Scientists test out theories by experiment.* [< L *experimentum* < *experiri*. See EXPERIENCE.] —**ex·per´i·ment´er,** *n.*
☛ *Syn. n.* **1.** See note at **trial.**

ex·per·i·men·tal (ek sper´ə men´təl) *adj.* **1** based on experiments: *Chemistry is an experimental science.* **2** used for or specializing in experimentation: *an experimental farm.* **3** based on experience, not on theory or authority. **4** for testing or trying out: *They are growing an experimental variety of wheat at the university farm.* **5** tentative: *The new drug is still in the experimental stage.* —**ex·per´i·men´tal·ly,** *adv.*

ex·per·i·men·tal·ism (ek sper´ə men´tə liz´əm) *n.* the use or advocacy of experimentation.

ex·per·i·men·tal·ist (ek sper´ə men´tə list´) *n.* a person who conducts scientific experiments.

ex·per·i·men·ta·tion (ek sper´ə men tā´shən) *n.* the act or process of experimenting or making experiments: *More experimentation is needed to confirm the results.*

ex·pert (*n.* ek´spèrt; *adj.* ek´spèrt *or* ek spèrt´) *n., adj.* —*n.* a very skilful person; person who knows a great deal about some special thing or topic. —*adj.* **1** very skilful; knowing a great deal about some special field of knowledge. **2** from an expert; requiring or showing knowledge about some special field of knowledge. [< L *expertus,* pp. of *experiri* test. See EXPERIENCE.] —**ex´pert·ly or ex·pert´ly,** *adv.* —**ex·pert´ness,** *n.*
☛ *Syn. adj.* **1. Expert, proficient, skilled** = having the training and knowledge to do a special thing well. **Expert** = having mastery or unusual ability as the result of experience in addition to training and practice: *He is an expert chemist.* **Proficient** = very good at doing something, especially as the result of training and practice: *She is proficient at sewing.* **Skilled** = knowing thoroughly how to do something and being unusually proficient at doing it: *He is a skilled mechanic.*

ex·per·tise (ek´spər tēz´) *n.* **1** an overall grasp of a subject, process, etc., produced by ability, experience, and skill. **2** the state or quality of being an expert; skill. [< F]

ex·pi·a·ble (ek´spē ə bəl) *adj.* that can be expiated.

ex·pi·ate (ek´spē āt´) *v.* **-at·ed, -at·ing.** make amends for (a wrong, sin, etc.); atone for: *The young king tried to expiate injustices of his uncle's rule.* [< L *expiare* < *ex-* completely + *piare* appease < *pius* devout] —**ex´pi·a´tor,** *n.*

ex·pi·a·tion (ek´spē ā´shən) *n.* **1** making amends for a wrong, sin, etc.; atonement: *He made a public apology in expiation of his error.* **2** amends; a means of atonement.

ex·pi·a·to·ry (ek´spē ə tô´rē) *adj.* intended to expiate; expiating; atoning.

ex·pi·ra·tion (ek´spə rā´shən) *n.* **1** coming to an end: *the expiration of a lease.* **2** breathing out: *the expiration of used air from the lungs.* **3** the sound made in breathing out.

ex·pir·a·to·ry (ek spīr´ə tô´rē) *adj.* having to do with breathing out air from the lungs.

ex·pire (ek spīr´) *v.* **-pired, -pir·ing. 1** come to an end: *You must obtain a new automobile licence before your old one expires.* **2** die. **3** breathe out: *to expire used air from the lungs.* [< L *ex(s)pirare* < *ex-* out + *spirare* breathe] —**ex·pir´er,** *n.*

ex·pi·ry (ek spī´rē *or* ek´spə rē) *n., pl.* **-ries.** expiration.

ex·plain (ek splān´) *v.* **1** make clear or understandable; tell what something means or how something is done, organized, formed, used, etc.: *The teacher explained how a generator works. Can you explain what refraction is? I explained the paragraph to her.* **2** tell the significance of; interpret: *to explain a dream. Nobody could explain his strange behavior.* **3** give an acceptable reason for; excuse or justify: *She couldn't explain her absence.* **4** give an explanation: *Wait! Let me explain!*
explain away, get rid of or make insignificant by giving reasons or as if by giving reasons: *to explain away someone's fears. There is a lot of evidence against her that cannot be explained away.*
explain (oneself), a make one's meaning clear: *I guess I didn't explain myself very well because nobody understood.* **b** justify or give reasons for one's conduct: *Why did you go off and leave your little brother alone? Explain yourself.*
[< L *explanare* < *ex-* out + *planus* flat] —**ex·plain´a·ble,** *adj.* —**ex·plain´er,** *n.*
☛ *Syn.* **1. Explain, interpret** = make plain or understandable. **Explain** = make clear and plain something that is not understood: *He explained all the difficult mathematical problems to me.* **Interpet** = explain or bring out the meaning of something especially difficult, by using special knowledge or, sometimes, unusual understanding or imagination: *She interpreted the symbolism of the poem for us.*

ex·pla·na·tion (ek´splə nā´shən) *n.* **1** the act or process of explaining: *His explanation of electricity was easy to follow. Their attitude toward the new members requires explanation.* **2** something that explains: *That book was a good explanation of the principle of atomic fission.*

ex·plan·a·to·ry (ek splan´ə tô´rē) *adj.* explaining; serving or helping to explain: *Read the explanatory part of the lesson before you try to do the problems.*

ex·ple·tive (ek´splə tiv *or* ek splē´tiv) *n., adj.* —*n.* **1** an oath or exclamation that has no meaning other than as an expression of surprise, anger, annoyance, etc.: *The expressions* Damn! *and* My goodness! *are expletives.* **2** a syllable, word, or phrase added to fill out a line of verse, etc. without adding anything to the sense. **3** *Grammar.* a word used in a sentence to take the normal place of the subject or object, which is identified later. *There* and *it* in the following sentences are expletives: *There is a book on the table. It is too bad that the book has no pictures. They thought it terrible that the book should cost so much.* —*adj.* serving to fill out, without adding meaning. [< LL *expletivus* < *expletus,* pp. of *explere* < *ex-* out + *plere* fill]

ex·pli·ca·ble (ek splik´ə bəl *or* ek´splə kə bəl) *adj.* capable of being explained. [< L *explicabilis* < *explicare.* See EXPLICIT.]

ex·pli·cate (ek´splə kāt´) *v.* **-cat·ed, -cat·ing. 1** develop the meaning or implication of (a principle, doctrine, etc.); analyse logically. **2** explain. [< L *explicare.* See EXPLICIT.] —**ex´pli·ca´tor,** *n.*

ex·pli·ca·tion (ek´splə kā´shən) *n.* **1** explanation. **2** a detailed statement or description.

ex·pli·ca·to·ry (ek´splə kə tô´rē) *adj.* that explains.

ex·plic·it (ek splis´it) *adj.* **1** clearly expressed; distinctly stated; definite and unambiguous: *an explicit statement of intentions. He gave such explicit directions that everyone understood them.* Compare **implicit. 2** clear and unreserved in expression; frank; outspoken: *The description of the accident victim's injuries was so explicit that it shocked some people.* [< L *explicitus,* pp. of *explicare* unfold, explain < *ex-* un- + *plicare* fold] —**ex·plic´it·ly,** *adv.* —**ex·plic´it·ness,** *n.*

ex·plode (ek splōd´) *v.* **-plod·ed, -plod·ing. 1** burst violently and noisily because of pressure from within; blow up: *The building was destroyed when the defective boiler exploded.* **2** undergo an uncontrolled chemical or nuclear reaction that produces a violent expansion of gases, along with noise, heat, light, etc.: *The bomb exploded.* **3** cause to explode; set off: *to explode dynamite.* **4** react suddenly with noise or violence: *The speaker's mistake was so funny the audience exploded with laughter.* **5** cause to be rejected; destroy belief in: *Columbus helped to explode the theory that the earth was flat.* **6** increase rapidly in an uncontrolled way: *an exploding population.* **7** *Phonetics.* **a** end the articulation of (a stop) by audibly releasing the breath. The first *p* in *pop* is always exploded, the final *p* is often not. **b** of a stop, be articulated with such a release of breath. [< L *explodere* drive out by clapping < *ex-* out + *plaudere* clap] —**ex·plod´er,** *n.*

ex·plod·ed (ek splō´dəd) *adj.* designating a diagram showing the parts of a machine, apparatus, etc. separated from each other, as if by an explosion, but in the correct position in relation to each other: *The manual has an exploded view of the universal joint.*

ex·ploit (*n.* eks´ploit *or* eks ploit´; *v.* ek sploit´) *n., v.* —*n.* a bold, unusual act; daring deed: *Old stories tell about the exploits of famous heroes.* —*v.* **1** make use of; turn to practical account: *A mine is exploited for its minerals.* **2** make unfair or selfish use of: *Nations sometimes exploit their colonies, taking as much wealth out of them as they can.* [ME < OF *esploit* < VL *explicitum* achievement < L *explicitum,* pp. neut. of *explicare* unfold, settle. See EXPLICIT.] —**ex·ploit´a·ble,** *adj.* —**ex·ploit´er,** *n.*
☛ *Syn. n.* **Exploit, feat, achievement** = a great or unusual deed. **Exploit** emphasizes daring or great courage or bravery in accomplishing something in the face of danger or against odds: *The pilot won the Victoria Cross for his exploits in the Battle of Britain.* **Feat** emphasizes use of great skill or strength in accomplishing something unusual: *Climbing Mount Everest is a tremendous feat.* **Achievement** emphasizes continued hard work in spite of difficulties and obstacles in accomplishing something outstanding: *Two Canadians, F.G. Banting and J.J.R. Macleod, won the Nobel Prize in 1923 for their achievements in medicine.*

ex·ploi·ta·tion (ek´sploi tā´shən) *n.* **1** use. **2** selfish or unfair use.

ex·ploit·a·tive (ek sploi′tə tiv′) *adj.* of, having to do with, or characterized by exploitation, especially when selfish or unfair.

ex·ploit·ive (ek sploi′tiv) *adj.* exploitative.

ex·plo·ra·tion (ek′splə rā′shən) *n.* the act or circumstance of exploring: *exploration for oil, the exploration of new territory.*

ex·plor·a·tive (ek splôr′ə tiv) *adj.* **1** exploratory. **2** inclined to make explorations.

ex·plor·a·to·ry (ek splôr′ə tô′rē) *adj.* of, having to do with, or related to exploration: *exploratory surgery, exploratory travels.*

ex·plore (ek splôr′) *v.* **-plored, -plor·ing. 1** go or travel over land or water for the purpose of finding out about geographical features, natural resources, etc.: *Champlain explored the Ottawa River and Georgian Bay.* **2** go or search through a place, etc., in order to find out about it: *to explore one's surroundings. They explored the abandoned house.* **3** look into closely and carefully; investigate: *We will have to explore all the possibilities before deciding on a course of action.* **4** examine carefully, especially by touch: *She explored the wall with her fingers, searching for the light switch. The doctor explored the wound.* [< L *explorare* investigate, spy out; originally, cry out (at sight of game or enemy) < *ex-* out + *plorare* weep] **—ex·plor′ing·ly,** *adv.*
☛ *Syn.* **2.** See note at **search.**

ex·plor·er (ek splôr′ər) *n.* **1** a person who explores. **2** any instrument for exploring a wound, a dental cavity, etc.

ex·plo·sion (eks plō′zhən) *n.* **1** blowing up; bursting with a loud noise: *the explosion of a bomb.* **2** a loud noise caused by something blowing up: *People 10 kilometres away heard the explosion.* **3** a noisy bursting forth: *an explosion of laughter.* **4** *Phonetics.* the sudden audible release of the breath at the end of the articulation of a stop. **5** an outbreak or bursting forth of anything capable of development: *an explosion of anger, the population explosion.* [< L *explosio, -onis* < *explodere.* See EXPLODE.]

ex·plo·sive (eks plō′siv *or* ek splō′ziv) *adj., n.* **—adj. 1** capable of exploding; likely to explode: *Gunpowder is explosive.* **2** tending to burst forth noisily: *The irritable old man had an explosive temper.* **3** *Phonetics.* pronounced with a slight pop or sudden release of breath. The consonants *p, b, t, d, k,* and *g* (as in *go*) are explosive. **4** of or having to do with sudden outbursts: *explosive evolution, an explosive situation.*
—n. 1 a substance that is capable of exploding: *Explosives are used in making fireworks.* **2** a projectile, firework, etc. containing such a substance and designed to explode under certain conditions. **3** *Phonetics.* an explosive consonant. **—ex·plo′sive·ly,** *adv.* **—ex·plo′sive·ness,** *n.*

ex·po·nent (ek spō′nənt) *n.* **1** a person or thing that explains, interprets, etc. **2** a person who favors or speaks for (*used with* **of**): *She is an exponent of the guaranteed annual wage.* **3** a person or thing that stands as an example, type, or symbol of something: *This man is a famous exponent of self-education.* **4** *Algebra.* an index or small number written above and to the right of a symbol or quantity to show how many times the symbol or quantity is to be used as a factor. *Examples:* $2^2 = 2 \times 2$; $a^3 = a \times a \times a$. [< L *exponens, -entis,* ppr. of *exponere.* See EXPOUND.]

ex·po·nen·tial (ek′spō nen′shəl) *adj.* having to do with algebraic exponents; involving unknown or variable quantities as exponents. **—ex′po·nen′tial·ly,** *adv.*

ex·port (*v.* ek spôrt′ *or* ek′spôrt; *n.* ek′spôrt) *v., n.* **—v.** send (articles or goods) out of one country for sale and use in another: *Canada exports millions of tonnes of wheat each year.* **—n. 1** the act of selling or shipping articles or goods to another country. **2** the goods or articles so sold and shipped: *Asbestos is an important export of Quebec.* **3** (*adj.*) of a kind or quality suitable for export: *export liquors. Export quality is usually higher than the regular domestic quality.* **4** (*adj.*) of or having to do with exports or exporting: *export duty.* [< L *exportare* < *ex-* away + *portare* carry] **—ex′por·ta′tion,** *n.*

ex·port·er (ek spôr′tər *or* ek′spôr tər) *n.* a person or company whose business is exporting goods.

ex·pose (ek spōz′) *v.* **-posed, -pos·ing. 1** lay open; leave unprotected; uncover: *The soldiers in the open field were exposed to the enemy's gunfire. His foolish actions exposed him to ridicule.* **2** lay open to view, especially something that was hidden; display or make visible: *to expose a card in a card game. They stripped off the paint around the fireplace, exposing the original tile surface.* **3** make known; show up; reveal: *to expose a murderer. The investigators exposed the takeover plot.* **4** *Photography.* allow light to reach and act on a sensitive film, plate, or paper. **5** put out without shelter; abandon: *The ancient Spartans used to expose babies that they did not want.* [< OF *exposer* < *ex-* forth (< L *ex-*) + *poser* put. See POSE¹.] **—ex·pos′er,** *n.*

ex·po·sé (ek′spō zā′) *n.* the showing up of a crime, of dishonesty, fraud, etc. [< F *exposé,* originally pp. of *exposer* expose]

hat, āge, fär; let, ēqual, tèrm; it, īce
hot, ōpen, ôrder; oil, out; cup, pùt, rüle,
əbove, takən, pencəl, lemən, circəs

ch, child; ng, long; sh, ship
th, thin; ᴛʜ, then; zh, measure

ex·posed (ek spōzd′) *adj.* **1** uncovered or unprotected: *These flowers should not be planted in an exposed location.* **2** open to view; not concealed: *an exposed card.* **3** of a photographic film or plate, acted on by light; used and ready to develop.

ex·po·si·tion (ek′spə zish′ən) *n.* **1** a public show or exhibition. The Canadian National Exhibition is a well-known annual exposition. **2** a detailed explanation: *the exposition of a scientific theory.* **3** a speech or a piece of writing explaining a process or idea. **4** *Music.* **a** the first section of a movement, as of a sonata, in which the principal and secondary subjects are presented. **b** the first entry, in a fugue, of the theme or themes in each part or voice.

ex·pos·i·tor (ek spoz′ə tər) *n.* a person who explains or expounds; interpreter or commentator. [< LL < L *exponere.* See EXPOUND.]

ex·pos·i·to·ry (ek spoz′ə tô′rē) *adj.* of, having to do with, or including exposition: *expository writing.*

ex post fac·to (eks′ pōst′ fak′tō) made or done after something, but applying to it. An **ex post facto law** applies to actions done before the law was passed. [< Med.L *ex post facto* from what is done afterwards]

ex·pos·tu·late (eks pos′chə lāt′) *v.* **-lat·ed, -lat·ing.** reason earnestly with a person, protesting against something he means to do or has done; remonstrate (*with*): *They expostulated with their son about the foolishness of leaving school.* [< L *expostulare* < *ex-* (intensive) + *postulare* demand] **—ex·pos′tu·la′tor,** *n.*

ex·pos·tu·la·tion (eks pos′chə lā′shən) *n.* an earnest protest; remonstrance: *Expostulations having failed, the teacher resorted to threats.*

ex·pos·tu·la·to·ry (eks pos′chə lə tô′rē) *adj.* of or characteristic of expostulation.

ex·po·sure (eks pō′zhər) *n.* **1** the act or instance of exposing: *The exposure of the real criminal cleared the innocent man. Anyone would dread public exposure of all his faults.* **2** the condition or an instance of being exposed: *Years of exposure to the rain had ruined the machinery.* **3** appearance in public, as on television, etc.: *His campaign manager thought he needed more television exposure.* **4** a position in relation to the sun and wind. A house with a southern exposure is open to sun and wind from the south. **5** *Photography.* **a** the time during which light reaches and acts on a film or plate. **b** the part of a film used for one picture. **c** the total amount of light on a film in making a picture.

exposure meter *Photography.* a device for measuring the intensity of light, used to indicate the correct exposure needed for taking a photograph under particular light conditions. Some cameras have a built-in exposure meter.

ex·pound (eks pound′) *v.* **1** make clear; explain or interpret. **2** set forth or state in detail. [ME < OF *espondre* < L *exponere* < *ex-* forth + *ponere* put]

ex·press (eks pres′) *v., adj., n.* **—v. 1** put into words: *Express your ideas clearly.* **2** show by look, voice, or action; reveal: *Your smile expresses joy.* **3** show by a sign, figure, etc.; indicate: *The sign × expresses multiplication.* **4** send by express. **5** press out; squeeze out: *The juice is expressed from grapes to make wine.* **6** say what one thinks (*used with a reflexive verb*): *A good speaker expresses himself clearly.*
—adj. 1 clear; plain; definite: *It was his express wish that we should go without him.* **2** for a particular purpose; special: *She came for the express purpose of seeing you.* **3** exact: *He is the express image of his father.*
—n. 1 a special messenger or message sent for a particular purpose. **2** a quick or direct means of sending things. Packages and money can be sent by express in trains or airplanes. **3** a system or company for sending parcels, money, etc.: *Canadian National Express.* **4** (*adj.*) having to do with express: *An express agency or company is in the express business.* **5** things sent by express. **6** (*adv.*) by express; directly. **7** (*adj.*) travelling fast and making few stops: *an express train.* **8** a train, bus, elevator, etc. travelling fast and making few stops. **9** (*adj.*) for fast travelling: *an express highway.* [< L *expressus,* pp. of *exprimere* < *ex-* out + *premere* press] **—ex·press′er,** *n.*

ex·press·age (eks pres′ij) *n.* **1** the business of carrying parcels, money, etc. by express. **2** a charge for carrying parcels, etc. by express.

ex·press·i·ble (eks pres′ə bəl) *adj.* capable of being expressed.

ex·pres·sion (eks presh′ən) *n.* **1** putting into words: *Clarity of expression is important in style.* **2** a word or group of words used as a unit: *"Wise guy" is a slang expression.* **3** showing by look, voice, or action: *Her sigh was an expression of sadness.* **4** an indication of feeling, spirit, character, etc.; look that shows feeling: *He had a silly expression on his face.* **5** a bringing out the meaning or beauty of something read, spoken, played, sung, etc.: *Try to read with more expression.* **6** a showing by a sign, figure, etc. **7** a symbol or group of symbols expressing some mathematical process or quantity. **8** a pressing out: *the expression of oil from plants.*

ex·pres·sion·ism (eks presh′ən iz′əm) *n.* **1** a movement in art and literature in the late 19th and 20th centuries, marked by the attempt to express the artist's subjective feelings without regard to accepted forms or tradition. It began as a revolt against naturalism and impressionism. **2** a similar movement in music.

ex·pres·sion·ist (eks presh′ə nist) *n., adj.* —*n.* a writer, artist, etc. who follows the principles of expressionism. —*adj.* of, like, or having to do with expressionism.

ex·pres·sion·is·tic (eks presh′ə nis′tik) *adj.* of or having to do with expressionism or expressionists.

ex·pres·sion·less (eks presh′ən lis) *adj.* without expression: *an expressionless face, an expressionless voice.*

ex·pres·sive (eks pres′iv) *adj.* **1** serving as a sign or indication; representing (*used with* **of**): *Alas is a word expressive of sadness.* **2** full of expression; having or showing much feeling, meaning, etc.: *an expressive pause. He has a very expressive face.* **3** of or having to do with expression: *She is a writer of great expressive power.* —**ex·pres′sive·ly,** *adv.* —**ex·pres′sive·ness,** *n.*
☛ *Syn.* **2. Expressive, significant, suggestive** = full of meaning. **Expressive** emphasizes showing a meaning or feeling in a strikingly clear or lively way: *An expressive shrug revealed his contempt.* **Significant** emphasizes being full of meaning, which may be expressed, but often is only pointed to: *Graduation Day is a significant event in every student's life.* **Suggestive** emphasizes conveying meaning in an indirect way, as by expressing part of the meaning or by hinting: *The teacher gave an interesting and suggestive list of composition topics.*

ex·press·ly (eks pres′lē) *adv.* **1** clearly; plainly; definitely: *You were expressly forbidden to touch it.* **2** specially; for the particular purpose: *She came expressly to see you.*

ex·press·way (eks pres′wā′) *n.* a divided highway for fast driving; a highway that stretches for long distances with few intersections. Most interchanges on expressways are built on two levels so that vehicles do not have to cross in front of each other on the highway.

ex·pro·pri·ate (eks prō′prē āt′) *v.* **-at·ed, -at·ing. 1** take (property) away from an owner, especially for public use: *The provincial government expropriated 50 000 square metres of land for a public housing development.* **2** put (a person) out of possession; dispossess. [< Med.L *expropriare* < *ex-* away from + *proprius* one's own] —**ex·pro′pri·a′tion,** *n.* —**ex·pro′pri·a′tor,** *n.*

ex·pul·sion (eks pul′shən) *n.* an expelling or being expelled: *expulsion of air from the lungs. The threat of expulsion from school did not help.* [< L *expulsio, -onis* < *expellere.* See EXPEL.]

ex·pul·sive (eks pul′siv) *adj.* expelling or having the power to expel: *the expulsive power of steam under pressure.*

ex·punge (eks punj′) *v.* **-punged -pung·ing.** remove completely; blot out; erase: *The secretary was directed to expunge certain accusations from the record.* [< L *expungere* < *ex-* out + *pungere* prick] —**ex·pung′er,** *n.*
☛ *Syn.* See note at **erase.**

ex·pur·gate (eks′pər gāt′) *v.* **-gat·ed, -gat·ing.** remove objectionable passages or words from (a book, letter, etc.); purify. [< L *expurgare* < *ex-* out + *purgare* purge] —**ex′pur·ga·tor,** *n.*

ex·pur·ga·tion (eks′pər gā′shən) *n.* the removing or removal from a book, etc. of something that seems objectionable.

ex·qui·site (eks′kwi zit *or* eks kwiz′it) *adj.* **1** very lovely in a delicate way: *exquisite lace. Violets are exquisite flowers.* **2** of highest excellence; most admirable: *an exquisite painting technique, exquisite taste.* **3** keenly sensitive: *an exquisite ear for music.* **4** sharp; intense: *exquisite pain, exquisite joy.* [< L *exquisitus,* pp. of *exquirere* < *ex-* out + *quaerere* seek] —**ex′qui·site·ly,** *adv.* —**ex′qui·site·ness,** *n.*

ex–serv·ice (eks′sèr′vis) *adj.* having formerly served in the armed forces.

ex–serv·ice·man (eks′sèr′vis mən) *n., pl.* **-men.** a man who formerly served in the armed forces.

ex·tant (eks′tənt *or* eks tant′) *adj.* still in existence; currently existing: *Some of Captain Vancouver's charts are extant.* [< L *ex(s)tans, -antis,* ppr. of *ex(s)tare* < *ex-* out, forth + *stare* stand]

ex·tem·po·ral (eks tem′pə rəl) *adj. Archaic.* extemporaneous.

ex·tem·po·ra·ne·ous (eks tem′pə rā′nē əs) *adj.* **1** spoken or done without preparation; impromptu: *an extemporaneous speech.* **2** made for the occasion; makeshift: *an extemporaneous shelter against a storm.* **3** inclined and able to make speeches without preparation: *an extemporaneous speaker.* [< LL *extemporaneus* < L *ex tempore* according to the moment] —**ex·tem′po·ra′ne·ous·ly,** *adv.* —**ex·tem′po·ra′ne·ous·ness,** *n.*

ex·tem·po·rar·y (eks tem′pə rer′ē) *adj.* extemporaneous. —**ex·tem′po·rar′i·ly,** *adv.*

ex·tem·po·re (eks tem′pə rē *or* eks tem′pə rā) *adj. or adv.* on the spur of the moment; without preparation; offhand or impromptu: *Each pupil will be called on to speak extempore.* [< L *ex tempore* according to the moment]

ex·tem·po·rize (eks tem′pə rīz′) *v.* **-rized, -riz·ing. 1** speak, play, sing, or dance, composing as one proceeds: *The pianist was extemporizing.* **2** compose offhand; make for the occasion: *The campers extemporized a shelter for the night.* —**ex·tem′po·ri·za′tion,** *n.* —**ex·tem′po·riz′er,** *n.*

ex·tend (eks tend′) *v.* **1** stretch out: *She extended her hand to the visitor.* **2** continue in time, space, or direction: *The beach extended for more than a kilometre in each direction.* **3** straighten out: *Extend your arms in front of you.* **4** lengthen: *to extend a deadline. They have extended the ski trail another three kilometres.* **5** enlarge or broaden: *to extend a gym, to extend one's knowledge.* **6** become longer or larger: *The competition was not strong enough to extend him.* **7** give; grant: *to extend help to someone in need, to extend credit.* **8** exert (oneself); strain. **9** cause to put out greater or maximum effort: *The competition was not strong enough to extend him.* [< L *extendere* < *ex-* out + *tendere* stretch] —**ex·tend′er,** *n.*
☛ *Syn.* **4.** See note at **lengthen.**

ex·tend·ed (eks ten′did) *adj.* **1** extensive; widespread. **2** stretched out; prolonged. **3** widened. **4** spread out; outstretched.

ex·tend·i·ble (ek sten′də bəl) *adj.* extensible. —**ex·tend′i·bil′i·ty,** *n.*

ex·ten·si·bil·i·ty (ek sten′sə bil′ə tē) *n.* the quality of being extensible.

ex·ten·si·ble (eks ten′sə bəl) *adj.* capable of being protruded, stretched, or opened out: *an extensible tongue.*

ex·ten·sile (eks ten′sīl *or* eks ten′səl) *adj.* extensible.

ex·ten·sion (eks ten′shən) *n.* **1** extending or being extended: *The extension of one's right hand is a sign of friendship.* **2** an extended part; addition: *The new extension to the school will have several classrooms and a gym.* **3** an extra telephone connected to a line: *He heard it all because he was listening in on the extension.* **4** an increase in time, especially in the time allowed for something: *I got an extension on my essay deadline because I had been sick.* **5** an educational program provided by a university for people who cannot take regular courses: *People who have full-time jobs can upgrade their education by taking evening classes through extension.* **6** (*adj.*) of, in, or designating such a program: *She's taking an extension course.* **7** range; extent. **8** *Physics.* that property of a body by which it occupies a portion of space. **9** the straightening of a part by the action of an extensor muscle. **10** the condition of being straightened in this way. **11** the pulling or stretching of a fractured or dislocated part to enable the bones to be restored to their natural relative positions. [< LL *extensio, -onis* < L *extendere.* See EXTEND.] —**ex·ten′sion·less,** *adj.*

extension cord an electrical cord having a plug at one end and a socket at the other, used to lengthen the cord attached to an electrical appliance.

extension ladder a ladder having a movable part or parts enabling it to be extended to varying heights as needed.

ex·ten·si·ty (eks ten′sə tē) *n.* spatial quality.

ex·ten·sive (eks ten′siv) *adj.* **1** of great extent; wide; broad; large: *an extensive park. She has extensive knowledge in several branches of science.* **2** far-reaching; affecting many things; comprehensive: *extensive change.* **3** depending on the use of large areas: *extensive agriculture.* —**ex·ten′sive·ly,** *adv.* —**ex·ten′sive·ness,** *n.*

ex·ten·sor (eks ten′sər *or* eks ten′sôr) *n. Physiology.* a muscle that extends or straightens out a limb or other part of the body. [< LL *extensor* one who stretches]

ex·tent (eks tent′) *n.* **1** the size, space, length, amount, or degree to which a thing extends: *Railways carry people and goods through the whole extent of the country. The extent of a judge's power is limited by law.* **2** something extended; an extended space: *a vast extent of prairie.* **3** *Physics.* anything that has extension; an object or body having length, area, or volume. **4** *Mathematics.* a continuous magnitude of dimensions: *A plane figure is 2-extent.* **5** *Logic.* extension. [< AF *extente, estente,* fem. pp., used as a noun, of *estendre* extend < L *extendere.* See EXTEND.]

ex·ten·u·ate (eks ten′yū āt′) *v.* **-at·ed, -at·ing. 1** make (guilt, a fault, an offence, etc.) seem less; excuse in part: *She claimed there*

were extenuating circumstances for their rude behavior. **2** Archaic. make thin or weak. [< L *extenuare* < *ex*- out + *tenuis* thin] —**ex·ten′u·at′ing·ly,** *adv.* —**ex·ten′u·a·tor,** *n.*

ex·ten·u·a·tion (eks ten′yü ā′shən) *n.* **1** extenuating: *The lawyer pleaded his client's youth in extenuation of the crime.* **2** extenuated condition. **3** something that lessens the seriousness of guilt, a fault, an offence, etc.; a partial excuse.

ex·te·ri·or (eks tēr′ē ər) *n., adj.* —*n.* **1** an outer surface or part; outward appearance; outside: *The exterior of the house was of brick. The gruff old man has a harsh exterior but a kind heart.* **2** an outdoor scene on the stage. **3** a motion picture made outdoors. —*adj.* **1** on the outside; outer: *The skin of an apple is its exterior covering.* **2** coming from without; happening outside: *exterior influences.* [< L *exterior*, comparative of *exterus* outside < *ex*- out of]

exterior angle Geometry. **1** any of the four angles formed on the outer sides of two parallel lines by a straight line cutting through the parallel lines. **2** the angle formed on the outside of a polygon between one of its sides and an extension of a side next to it. Compare **interior angle.** See **triangle** for picture.

ex·ter·mi·nate (eks tėr′mə nāt′) *v.* **-nat·ed, -nat·ing.** destroy completely: *This poison will exterminate rats.* [< LL *exterminare* destroy < L *exterminare* drive out < *ex*- out of + *terminus* boundary]

ex·ter·mi·na·tion (eks tėr′mə nā′shən) *n.* complete destruction: *This poison is useful for the extermination of rats.*

ex·ter·mi·na·tor (eks tėr′mə nā′tər) *n.* a person or thing that exterminates, especially a person whose business is exterminating cockroaches, bedbugs, rats, etc.

ex·ter·nal (eks tėr′nəl) *adj., n.* —*adj.* **1** on the outside; outer: *the external wall of a house.* **2** to be used on the outside of the body: *Liniment and rubbing alcohol are external remedies.* **3** entirely outside; coming from without: *external air. External influences affect our lives.* **4** having existence outside one's mind: *external reality.* **5** for outward appearance; superficial: *His politeness is only external.* **6** not essential or basic: *His decision was influenced too much by external factors.* **7** having to do with international affairs; foreign: *external affairs. War affects a nation's external trade.* —*n.* **1** an outer surface or part; outside. **2 externals,** *pl.* clothing, manners, outward acts, or appearances: *He judges people by such externals as clothing and length of hair.* [< L *externus* outside < *exterus* outside < *ex*- out of] —**ex·ter′nal·ly,** *adv.*

external ear the fleshy part of the ear next to the head, including the opening to the vestibule.

ex·ter·nal·ise (eks tėr′nə līz′) See **externalize.**

ex·ter·nal·i·ty (eks′tər nal′ə tē) *n., pl.* **-ties. 1** the quality of being external. **2** an external thing.

ex·ter·nal·ize (eks tėr′nə līz′) *v.* **-ized, iz·ing.** give shape or form to; make external. Also, **externalise.**

ex·tinct (eks tingkt′) *adj.* **1** no longer in existence: *The dinosaur is an extinct animal.* **2** no longer active; extinguished: *an extinct volcano.* [< L *ex(s)tinctus,* pp. of *ex(s)tinguere.* See EXTINGUISH.]

ex·tinc·tion (eks tingk′shən) *n.* **1** extinguishing or being extinguished: *The sudden extinction of the lights left the room in darkness.* **2** being or becoming extinct: *The caribou was once threatened with extinction.* **3** a suppression; a doing away with completely; wiping out; destruction: *The war caused the extinction of many pacifist organizations.*

ex·tin·guish (eks ting′gwish) *v.* **1** put out; quench: *Water extinguished the fire.* **2** put an end to; do away with; wipe out; destroy: *One failure after another extinguished her hope.* **3** eclipse or obscure by superior brilliancy. [< L *ex(s)tinguere* < *ex*- out + *stinguere* quench] —**ex·tin′guish·able,** *adj.* ☞ *Syn.* **2.** See note at **abolish.**

ex·tin·guish·er (eks ting′gwi shər) *n.* **1** a person or thing that extinguishes. **2** a device for quenching fires.

ex·tir·pate (eks′tər pāt′ *or* eks tėr′pāt) *v.* **-pat·ed, -pat·ing. 1** remove or destroy completely; abolish or exterminate: *to extirpate a prejudice.* **2** tear up the roots. [< L *ex(s)tirpare* < *ex*- out + *stirps* root] —**ex′tir·pa′tor,** *n.*

ex·tir·pa·tion (eks′tər pā′shən) *n.* **1** complete removal or destruction. **2** a tearing up by the roots.

ex·tir·pa·to·ry (ek stėr′pə tôr′ē) *adj.* extirpating; serving to root out or destroy.

ex·tol *or* **ex·toll** (eks tōl′) *v.* **-tolled, -tol·ling.** praise highly. [< L *extollere* < *ex*- up + *tollere* raise]

ex·tort (eks tôrt′) *v.* **1** obtain (something, such as money, a favor, or a promise) from a person by threats, criminal accusations, or violence. **2** obtain (something) by persistent demands or arguments, cajoling, etc.: *children extorting a promise of a picnic from their*

hat, āge, fär; let, ēqual, tėrm; it, īce
hot, ōpen, ôrder; oil, out; cup, pút, rüle,
əbove, takən, pencəl, lemən, circəs

ch, child; ng, long; sh, ship
th, thin; ŦH, then; zh, measure

parents. [< L *extortus,* pp. of *extorquere* < *ex*- out + *torquere* twist] —**ex·tort′er,** *n.*
☞ *Syn.* See note at **extract.**

ex·tor·tion (eks tôr′shən) *n.* **1** the act or an instance of inducing or attempting to induce someone to do something by threats, real or false criminal accusations, or violence: *Extortion is an indictable offence in Canada.* **2** the demanding of an exorbitant price.

ex·tor·tion·ar·y (eks tôr′shən er′ē) *adj.* characterized by or given to extortion.

ex·tor·tion·ate (eks tôr′shən it) *adj.* **1** characterized by extortion: *extortionate demands.* **2** much too great; exorbitant: *an extortionate price.* —**ex·tor′tion·ate·ly,** *adv.*

ex·tor·tion·er (eks tôr′shən ər) *n.* a person who is guilty of extortion.

ex·tor·tion·ist (eks tôr′shən ist) *n.* extortioner.

ex·tra (eks′trə) *adj., n., adv.* —*adj.* more, greater, or better than what is usual, expected, or needed: *extra pay, an extra workload. Do you have an extra pencil?* —*n.* **1** something for which an additional charge is made: *The rear window defroster is an extra. Her bill for extras was $30.* **2** something in addition to what is usual, expected, or needed. **3** a special edition of a newspaper. **4** an extra worker, especially a person hired by the day to act in crowd scenes, etc. in a motion picture. —*adv.* more than usually: *The quality is extra fine. They like their coffee extra strong.* [probably short for *extraordinary*]

extra– *prefix.* outside, beyond, besides, as in *extraordinary.* [< L]

ex·tract (*v.* eks trakt′; *n.* eks′trakt) *v., n.* —*v.* **1** pull out or draw out, usually with some effort: *to extract a tooth.* **2** obtain by pressing, distilling, etc., or by a chemical process: *to extract oil from olives.* **3** draw out or obtain against a person's will: *to extract payment, to extract a confession.* **4** deduce: *to extract a principle from a collection of facts.* **5** derive: *to extract pleasure from a situation.* **6** take out; select (a passage) from a book, speech, etc. **7** Mathematics. calculate or find (the root of a number). —*n.* **1** something drawn out or taken out; a passage taken from a book, speech, etc. **2** a concentrated preparation of a substance. *Vanilla extract,* made from vanilla beans, is often used as a flavoring in ice cream. [< L *extractus,* pp. of *extrahere* < *ex*- out + *trahere* draw] —**ex·trac′tor,** *n.*
☞ *Syn. v.* **1. Extract, extort** = draw out with force. **Extract** emphasizes pulling out something hard to get loose: *The dentist extracted her wisdom tooth.* **Extort** suggests wringing something from a person who does not want to give it up: *Not even torture could extort from him the names of his companions.*

ex·tract·a·ble (eks trak′tə bəl) *adj.* capable of being extracted.

ex·tract·i·ble (eks trak′tə bəl) *adj.* extractable.

ex·trac·tion (eks trak′shən) *n.* **1** extracting or being extracted: *the extraction of a tooth.* **2** descent; origin: *Ms. Del Rio is of Spanish extraction.*

ex·trac·tive (eks trak′tiv) *adj.* **1** extracting; tending to extract. **2** capable of being extracted.

ex·tra·cur·ric·u·lar (eks′trə kə rik′yə lər) *adj.* outside the regular course of study: *Football and debating are extra-curricular activities in high school.*

ex·tra·dit·a·ble (eks′trə dīt′ə bəl) *adj.* **1** that can be extradited. A person accused of murder in the United States is extraditable if he is caught in Canada. **2** for which a person can be extradited: *Murder is extraditable.*

ex·tra·dite (eks′trə dīt′) *v.* **-dit·ed, -dit·ing. 1** give up or deliver (a fugitive or prisoner) to another nation or legal authority for trial or punishment: *If an escaped prisoner from Canada is caught in the United States, he can be extradited to Canada.* **2** obtain the extradition of (such a person). [< *extradition*]

ex·tra·di·tion (eks′trə dish′ən) *n.* the surrender of a fugitive or prisoner by one state, nation, or legal authority to another for trial or punishment. [< F < L *ex*- out + *traditio* a delivering up < *tradere* hand over]

ex·tra·le·gal (eks′trə lē′gəl) *adj.* beyond the control or influence of law.

ex·tra·mar·i·tal (eks′trə mar′ə təl *or* -mer′ə təl) *adj.* outside the limits or bonds of marriage.

ex·tra·mu·ral (eks′trə myür′əl) *adj.* **1** occurring or done outside the boundaries of a school or college: *extramural activities.* **2** between schools or colleges: *extramural hockey.* **3** of, having to do with, or taking part in studies outside the normal program of a university, college, etc. **4** beyond the boundaries or walls of a city. [< L *extra muros* outside the walls + E *-al*]

ex·tra·ne·ous (eks trā′nē əs) *adj.* **1** coming from outside; foreign: *Sand or some other extraneous matter had got into the butter.* **2** not essential to what is under consideration; irrelevant: *In her talk on conservation, she made several interesting but extraneous remarks about wildlife photography.* [< L *extraneus* < *extra* outside < *ex* out of. Doublet of STRANGE.]

ex·traor·di·nar·i·ly (eks trôr′də ner′ə lē *or* eks′trə ôr′də ner′ə lē) *adv.* in an extraordinary manner; to an extraordinary degree; most unusually.

ex·traor·di·nar·y (eks trôr′də ner′ē *or* eks′trə ôr′də ner′ē) *adj.* **1** far beyond what is ordinary; most unusual; very remarkable: *Two metres is an extraordinary height for a woman. He is an extraordinary child.* **2** outside of or additional to the regular class of officials; special. An **envoy extraordinary** is an envoy sent on a special mission; he ranks below an ambassador. [< L *extraordinarius* < *extra ordinem* out of the (usual) order]

ex·tra·po·late (ek strap′ə lāt′ *or* eks′trə pə lāt′) *v.* **-lat·ed, -lat·ing. 1** *Mathematics.* project new values or terms of a series from those already known. **2** infer something by projecting from known facts on the assumption that they form part of a series. [< *extra* + inter*polate*] —**ex′tra·po·la′tion,** *n.* —**ex′trap′o·la′tor,** *n.*

ex·tra·sen·so·ry (eks′trə sen′sər ē) *adj.* beyond the normal scope or range of the senses: *Mental telepathy is one kind of extrasensory perception.*

extrasensory perception the perceiving of thoughts, actions, etc. in other than a normal fashion; mental telepathy.

ex·tra·ter·res·tri·al (ek′strə tə res′trē əl) *adj.* coming from or existing beyond the limits of the earth's atmosphere: *extra-terrestrial life.*

ex·tra·ter·ri·to·ri·al (eks′trə ter′ə tô′rē əl) *adj.* **1** outside the laws of the country that a person is living in. Any ambassador to a foreign country has certain extra-territorial privileges. **2** beyond territorial limits or jurisdiction.

ex·trav·a·gance (eks trav′ə gəns) *n.* **1** careless and lavish spending; wastefulness: *His extravagance kept him always in debt.* **2** going beyond the bounds of reason; excess: *The extravagance of the sales rep's claims caused us to doubt the worth of his product.* **3** an extravagant action, idea, purchase, etc.

ex·trav·a·gant (eks trav′ə gənt) *adj.* **1** spending carelessly and lavishly; wasteful: *An extravagant person usually has extravagant tastes and habits.* **2** beyond the bounds of reason; excessive: *People laughed at the inventor's extravagant praise of his invention. He refused to buy the ring because of its extravagant price.* [< Med.L *extravagans, -antis,* ppr. of *extravagari* < L *extra-* outside + *vagari* wander] —**ex·trav′a·gant·ly,** *adv.*

ex·trav·a·gan·za (eks trav′ə gan′zə) *n.* a lavish or spectacular play, piece of music, literary composition, etc. Musical comedies having elaborate scenery, gorgeous costumes, etc. are extravaganzas. [< Ital. *stravaganza* peculiar behavior, influenced by E *extra*]

ex·treme (eks trēm′) *adj.* **-trem·er, -trem·est;** *n.* —*adj.* **1** much more than usual; very great; very strong. **2** very severe or harsh: *The government took extreme measures to crush the revolt.* **3** farthest from the centre; outermost: *the extreme outlying districts of the city.* **4** farthest from the centre in political opinion, etc.; in favor of strong measures; not moderate: *She's a member of the extreme right.* **5** far from the usual or ordinary: *an extreme mode of dress.*
—*n.* **1** something extreme; one of two things as far or as different as possible from each other: *Love and hate are two extremes of feeling.* **2** an extreme degree or condition: *Joy is happiness in the extreme.* **3** *Mathematics.* the first or last term in a proportion or series: *In the proportion, 2 is to 4 as 8 is to 16, 2 and 16 are the extremes; 4 and 8 are the means.*
go to extremes, do or say too much; resort to extreme measures. [< L *extremus,* superlative of *exterus* outside < *ex-* out of] —**ex·treme′ness,** *n.*
☛ *Usage.* **Extreme.** Although *extremer* and *extremest* are used as the comparative and superlative of *extreme, more extreme* and *most extreme* are found more frequently in general usage.

ex·treme·ly (eks trēm′lē) *adv.* much more than usual; very.

extremely high frequency the highest range of frequencies in the radio spectrum, between 30 and 300 gigahertz. Extremely high frequency is the range next above superhigh frequency.

extremely low frequency the lowest range of frequencies in the radio spectrum, between 30 and 300 hertz.

extreme unction *Roman Catholic Church.* the sacrament given by a priest to a dying person or one in danger of death.

ex·trem·ist (eks trēm′ist) *n., adj.* —*n.* a person who goes to extremes, especially one who takes an extreme view or position in politics; a radical. —*adj.* having or showing extreme views or ideas; radical: *an extremist position. He is too extremist ever to get elected in this riding.*

ex·trem·i·ty (eks trem′ə tē) *n., pl.* **-ties. 1** the very end; the farthest possible place; the last part or point. **2** an extreme need, danger, suffering, etc.: *In their extremity the people on the sinking ship bore themselves bravely.* **3** the highest degree; the ultimate: *Joy is the extremity of happiness.* **4** an extreme action: *The soldiers were forced to the extremity of firing their rifles to scatter the angry mob.* **5 the extremities,** *pl.* the hands and feet.

ex·tri·ca·ble (eks′trə kə bəl) *adj.* capable of being extricated.

ex·tri·cate (eks′trə kāt′) *v.* **-cat·ed, -cat·ing.** set free (from entanglements, difficulties, embarrassing situations, etc.); release: *Tom extricated his younger brother from the barbed-wire fence.* [< L *extricare* < *ex-* out of + *tricae* perplexities] —**ex′tri·ca′tion,** *n.*

ex·trin·sic (eks trin′sik) *adj.* **1** not essential or inherent; caused by external circumstances. **2** being, coming, or acting from outside of a thing: *extrinsic aid, an extrinsic stimulus.* [< later L *extrinsecus* outer < earlier L *extrinsecus* from outside < OL **extrim* from outside + *secus* following]

ex·trin·si·cal·ly (eks trin′sik lē) *adv.* in an extrinsic manner; from without; externally.

extro– *prefix.* outward or outside, as in *extrovert.* [var. of L *extra-*]

ex·trorse (eks trôrs′) *adj. Botany.* turned or facing outward. [< LL *extrorsus* in an outward direction < *extra-* outside + *versus* towards]

ex·tro·ver·sion (eks′trə vėr′zhən *or* -ver′shən) *n.* the tendency to be more interested in other persons and in what is going on around one than in one's own thoughts and feelings. Compare **introversion.**

ex·tro·vert (eks′trə vėrt′) *n.* a person more interested in other persons and in what is going on around him than in his own thoughts and feelings; a person who is active and expressive rather than thoughtful. Compare **introvert.** [< *extro-* outside (var. of *extra-*) + L *vertere* turn]

ex·trude (eks trüd′) *v.* **-trud·ed, -trud·ing. 1** squeeze, force, or push out. **2** shape (metal, plastic, etc.) by forcing through a die. **3** protrude; project. [< L *extrudere* < *ex-* out + *trudere* thrust]

ex·tru·sion (eks trü′zhən) *n.* **1** the act or process of extruding. **2** something produced by this process: *plastic extrusions.* **3** a being extruded. [< L *extrudere.* See EXTRUDE.]

ex·tru·sive (eks trü′siv) *adj.* tending to extrude.

ex·u·ber·ance (eg zü′bər əns) *n.* **1** the fact, quality, state, or condition of being exuberant. **2** great abundance. **3** luxurious growth.

ex·u·ber·an·cy (eg zü′bər ən sē) *n., pl.* **-cies.** exuberance.

ex·u·ber·ant (eg zü′bər ənt) *adj.* **1** having or showing high spirits and unrestrained joy: *She gave us an exuberant welcome.* **2** too elaborate or lavish: *an exuberant use of metaphors.* **3** very abundant; overflowing: *exuberant good health.* **4** profuse in growth; luxuriant: *the exuberant vegetation of the jungle.* [< L *exuberans, -antis,* ppr. of *exuberare* grow luxuriantly < *ex-* thoroughly + *uber* fertile] —**ex·u′ber·ant·ly,** *adv.*

ex·u·da·tion (eks′yə dā′shən) *n.* **1** exuding. **2** something exuded, such as sweat.

ex·ude (eks yüd′ *or* eg züd′) *v.* **-ud·ed, -ud·ing. 1** come or send out in drops; ooze: *Sweat exudes from the skin.* **2** show conspicuously or abundantly: *She exudes self-confidence.* [< L *ex(s)udare* < *ex-* out + *sudare* sweat]

ex·ult (eg zult′) *v.* be very glad; rejoice greatly: *The winners exulted in their victory.* [< L *ex(s)ultare,* frequentative of *exsilire* leap out or up < *ex-* forth + *salire* leap]

ex·ult·ant (eg zul′tənt) *adj.* rejoicing greatly; exulting; triumphant: *He gave an exultant shout.*

ex·ul·ta·tion (eg′zul tā′shən *or* ek′sul tā′shən) *n.* the act of exulting; great rejoicing; triumph: *There was exultation over the army's victory.*

ex·urb (ek′sėrb) *n.* an exurban area. [< *ex-*[1] out of + *suburb,* coined in 1955 by A.C. Spectorsky (1910-1972), U.S. author and editor]

ex·ur·ban (eks′ėr′bən) *adj.* of, having to do with, or in a residential region or area outside the suburbs of a major city, especially one inhabited by well-to-do or wealthy people.

ex·ur·ban·ite (eks′ėr′bən īt′) *n.* a person living in an exurban area, especially one who commutes to the city.

-ey *adjective-forming suffix.* full of; containing; like, as in *clayey, skyey,* etc. [var. of *-y¹*]

ey·as (ī′əs) *n.* **1** a young hawk taken from the nest for training as a falcon. **2** nestling. [ME *a nyas* (mistaken as *an eyas*) < OF *niais,* literally, fresh from the nest; ult. < L *nidus* nest]

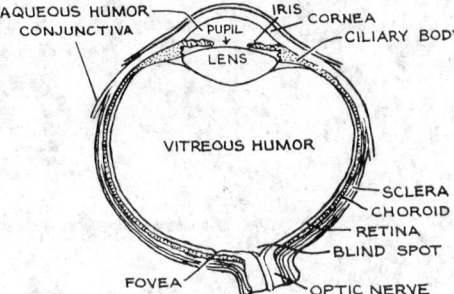

A diagram of the human eye, shown from above

eye (ī) *n., v.* **eyed, ey·ing** or **eye·ing.** —*n.* **1** either of the two organs of the body by which people and animals see; organ of sight. **2** the colored part of this organ; iris: *He has brown eyes.* **3** this organ and all the visible structures on and around it, including the eyelids, eyelashes, etc.: *The blow gave him a black eye.* **4** any organ that is sensitive to light. **5** Often, **eyes,** *pl.* the sense of seeing; vision; sight: *She has very good eyes.* **6** the ability to see small differences in things: *A good artist must have an eye for color.* **7** a look; glance: *He cast an eye in her direction.* **8** a watchful look. **9** Often, **eyes,** *pl.* a way of thinking or considering; view; opinion; judgment: *She can do no wrong in his eyes. Beauty is in the eye of the beholder.* **10** something like or suggesting an eye: *the eye of a needle, the eye of a potato.* **11** the calm, clear area at the centre of a hurricane, cyclone, etc.
an eye for an eye, punishment or revenge as severe as the offence or injury.
be all eyes, watch eagerly and attentively: *The children were all eyes as he began to open the box.*
catch (someone's) **eye,** attract someone's attention: *A notice in the newspaper caught his eye.*
eyes right or **eyes left,** a military order to turn the head to the right or to the left as a salute while marching.
have an eye for, be a sound and appreciative judge of: *She has an eye for a good painting.*
have an eye to, look out for; pay attention to.
in the public eye, often seen in public or often mentioned in newspaper or magazine articles, etc.: *She is very much in the public eye since her record-breaking swim.*
keep an eye on, watch; take care of: *Keep an eye on the baby.*
make eyes at, look at in a flirtatious or loving way.
my eye, *Slang.* an exclamation used to express disagreement or contradiction: *Tired, my eye! She's just lazy.*
open (someone's) **eyes,** make a person see what is really happening: *That experience opened our eyes to what he was really like.*
see eye to eye, agree entirely; have exactly the same opinion: *They often don't see eye to eye, but they never actually fight.*
set eyes on, see; look at: *I knew who he was the minute I set eyes on him.*
shut (someone's) **eyes to,** refuse to see or consider: *You can't shut your eyes to the problem forever.*
with an eye to, for; considering.
—*v.* **1** fix the gaze on; look at: *He sat there, curiously eyeing everything in the room.* **2** look at watchfully or sharply: *The dog eyed the stranger.* [OE *ēage*] —**eye′like′,** *adj.*
► *Hom.* aye², 1.

eye·ball (ī′bol′ or -bôl′) *n., v.* —*n.* the ball-shaped part of the eye without the lids and bony socket. —*v. Slang.* look at closely or intently.
eyeball to eyeball, *Informal.* face to face.

eye·brow (ī′brou′) *n.* **1** the arch of hair above the eye. **2** the bony ridge that it grows on.
raise eyebrows or **an eyebrow,** arouse interest or excitement; cause a mild sensation: *His outlandish get-up raised a few eyebrows, but that was all.*
raise an eyebrow or (one's) **eyebrows,** look surprised: *She raised her eyebrows at his outburst.*

eye–catch·er (ī′kach′ər) *n. Informal.* anything striking; an attraction.

hat, āge, fär; let, ēqual, tėrm; it, īce
hot, ōpen, ôrder; oil, out; cup, put, rüle,
above, takən, pencəl, lemən, circəs
ch, child; ng, long; sh, ship
th, thin; ϴ, then; zh, measure

eye–catch·ing (ī′kach′ing) *adj. Informal.* **1** striking; appealing. **2** conspicuous; clearly visible.

eye·cup (ī′kup′) *n.* a small cup with a rim shaped to fit over the eye, used in washing the eyes or putting medicine in them.

eyed (īd) *adj.* **1** having an eye or eyes. **2** having an eye or eyes of a specific kind, color, number, etc. (*used in compounds*): *a one-eyed pirate, a dark-eyed girl.*

eye·drop·per (ī′drop′ər) *n.* dropper (def. 2).

eye·ful (ī′fül) *n.* **1** as much as the eye can see at one time. **2** *Informal.* a good look. **3** *Slang.* a person who is unusually good-looking.

eye·glass (ī′glas′) *n.* **1** a lens for aiding or correcting vision, especially a monocle. **2** eyecup. **3** eyepiece. **4 eyeglasses,** *pl.* a pair of glass or plastic lenses held in a frame and worn in front of the eyes to aid or correct vision; spectacles.

eye·hole (ī′hōl′) *n.* **1** the bony socket for the eyeball. **2** a hole to look through. **3** a round opening for a pin, hook, rope, etc. to go through.

eye·lash (ī′lash′) *n.* **1** one of the hairs on the edge of the eyelid. **2** one row or fringe of such hairs.
by an eyelash, by a narrow margin; by very little.

eye·less (ī′lis) *adj.* blind or without eyes.

eye·let (ī′lit) *n.* **1** a small, round hole for a lace or cord to go through. **2** a metal ring that is set around such a hole to strengthen it; grommet. **3** a hole to look through. **4** a small, round hole edged with fine stitches, used as a decorative pattern in embroidery. **5** cloth having an allover pattern of such eyelets. [< OF *œillet,* dim. of *œil* eye < L *oculus;* influenced by E *eye* and *-let*]
► *Hom.* islet.

eye·lid (ī′lid′) *n.* the movable fold of skin over the eye.

eye·lin·er (ī′lī′nər) *n.* a colored cosmetic applied as a fine line on the eyelids along the base of the lashes to emphasize the contour of the eyes.

eye–o·pen·er (ī′ō′pən ər or ī′ōp′nər) *n.* **1** a happening or discovery that comes as a revelation: *Her behavior during the trial was an eye-opener; I had no idea she could be so cool-headed.* **2** a drink of liquor taken early in the day.

eye–o·pen·ing (ī′ō′pə ning or -ōp′ning) *adj.* enlightening or revealing: *an eye-opening experience.*

eye·piece (ī′pēs′) *n.* the lens or set of lenses nearest to the eye of the user in a telescope, microscope, etc.

eye·shade (ī′shād′) *n.* **1** a visor to shield the eyes in bright light. **2** eye shadow.

eye shadow a cosmetic in any of various colors applied to the eyelids to accent the eye.

eye·shot (ī′shot′) *n.* the range of vision.

eye·sight (ī′sīt′) *n.* **1** the power of seeing; sight. **2** the range of vision; view.

eye socket the bony cavity in which the eyeball is set.

eye·sore (ī′sôr′) *n.* something unpleasant to look at: *An untidy garbage heap is an eyesore.*

eye·spot (ī′spot′) *n.* the simplest kind of organ for seeing found in many invertebrates, consisting of a spot of pigment that is sensitive to light.

eye·stalk (ī′stok′ or -stôk′) *n. Zoology.* the stalk or peduncle upon which the eye is borne in lobsters, shrimp, etc.

eye·strain (ī′strān′) *n.* a tired or weak condition of the muscles of the eye caused by overuse or by an uncorrected defect, such as shortsightedness.

eye·tooth (ī′tüth′) *n., pl.* **-teeth.** either of the two pointed, upper teeth between the incisors and the bicuspids; upper canine tooth.
give (one's) **eyeteeth for,** *Informal.* go to great lengths to get or achieve: *I'd give my eyeteeth for a piano like that.*

eye·wash (ī′wosh′) *n.* **1** a liquid preparation to clean or heal the eyes. **2** *Slang.* deceiving flattery. **3** *Slang.* nonsense.

eye·wit·ness (ī′wit′nis) *n.* a person who actually sees or has seen some act or happening, and thus can give testimony concerning it.

ey·rie (ir′ē *or* ēr′ē) *n., pl.* **-ries. 1** the nest of an eagle or other bird of prey high on a mountain or cliff. **2** a house, castle, etc. built in a high place. Also, **aerie.** [< Med.L *aeria* < OF *aire* air < L *ager* field; different spellings influenced by L *aer* air and ME *ey* egg] ☛ *Hom.* **eerie** (ēr′ē).

ey·rir (ā′rir) *n., pl.* **au·rar** (ou′rär). a unit of money in Iceland, equal to ¹/₁₀₀ of a krona. [< ON, prob. < L *aureus* a gold coin]

Ff

f or **F** (ef) *n., pl.* **f's** or **F's. 1** the sixth letter of the English alphabet. **2** any speech sound represented by this letter. **3** a person or thing identified as *f*, especially the sixth in a series. **4 F, a** a grade rating a person's work or performance as too poor to be accepted; failing grade. **b** a person receiving such a rating. **5** *Music.* **a** the fourth tone in the scale of C major. **b** a symbol representing this tone. **c** a key, string, etc. that produces this tone. **d** the scale or key that has F as its keynote. **6** something shaped like the letter F. **7** (*adj.*) of or being an F or f.

f. 1 female; feminine. **2** forte. **3** franc. **4** *Mathematics.* function. **5** *Photography.* f number. **6** folio. **7** frequency. **8** the following page, line, etc.: *P. 83f. means page 83 and the following page.* **9** frame.

F fluorine.

F. or **F 1** Fahrenheit. **2** French. **3** Friday. **4** February.

fa (fä) *n. Music.* **1** the fourth tone of an eight-tone major scale. **2** the tone F. See **do²** for picture. [See GAMUT.]

fab (fab) *adj. Slang.* fabulous.

Fa·bi·an (fā′bē ən) *adj., n.* —*adj.* **1** using or designating a strategy of delay and avoidance of direct confrontation to wear out an opponent; cautious and circumspect. **2** of or having to do with the Fabian Society. —*n.* a member or supporter of the Fabian Society. [< *Fabius Maximus*, a Roman general who successfully harassed Hannibal's army without risking a battle]

Fa·bi·an·ism (fā′bē ən iz′əm) *n.* **1** especially in politics, the practice of using delay and avoidance of direct confrontation to wear out an opponent. **2** a moderate form of socialism; the principles and methods of the Fabian Society.

Fabian Society an English socialist society, founded in 1884, that favors the adoption of socialism by gradual reform rather than by revolution.

fa·ble (fā′bəl) *n., v.* **-bled, -bling.** —*n.* **1** a story made up to teach a lesson. **2** an untrue story; falsehood. **3** a legend; myth. —*v.* tell or write fables. [ME < OF < L *fabula* < *fari* speak] ☞ *Usage.* See note at **allegory.**

fa·bled (fā′bəld) *adj.* **1** told about in fables, legends, or myths. **2** having no real existence; made up; fictitious.

fab·li·au (fab′lē ō′) *n., pl.* **-aux** (-ōz′). a medieval poem, usually French or English, relating a short tale that deals with real or possible (often comic) incidents of ordinary human life. [< F *fabliau*, dim. of *fable* fable]

fab·ric (fab′rik) *n.* **1** any woven, knitted, or pressed material; cloth. Velvet, canvas, linen, felt, and flannel are fabrics. **2** the texture or quality of such material. Cloth may have a smooth or rough fabric. **3** a structure; something constructed of combined parts; framework: *the fabric of society.* [< F *fabrique* < L *fabrica* workshop. Doublet of FORGE¹.]

fab·ri·cate (fab′rə kāt′) *v.* **-cat·ed, -cat·ing. 1** build; construct; manufacture. **2** make by fitting together standardized parts: *Automobiles are fabricated from parts made in different factories.* **3** make up; invent (stories, lies, excuses, etc.). **4** forge (a document). [< L *fabricare* build < *fabrica* workshop] —**fab′ri·ca′tor,** *n.*

fab·ri·ca·tion (fab′rə kā′shən) *n.* **1** manufacture; fabricating. **2** something fabricated, especially a story, lie, excuse, etc.

fab·u·list (fab′yə list) *n.* **1** a person who tells, writes, or makes up fables. **2** liar.

fab·u·lous (fab′yə ləs) *adj.* **1** not believable; amazing; exaggerated: *That antique shop charges fabulous prices.* **2** of or belonging to a fable; imaginary: *The phoenix is a fabulous bird.* **3** like a fable. **4** *Informal.* wonderful; exciting: *We had a fabulous time at the party.* [< L *fabulosus* < *fabula.* See FABLE.] —**fab′u·lous·ly,** *adv.* —**fab′u·lous·ness,** *n.*

fa·çade (fə säd′) *n.* **1** the front part of a building. **2** any side of a building that faces a street or other open space. **3** a front or outward part or appearance of anything, especially when thought of as concealing something: *a façade of honesty.* Also, **facade.** [< F *façade* < *face.* See FACE.]

face (fās) *n., v.* **faced, fac·ing.** —*n.* **1** the front part of the head, from forehead to chin: *a beautiful face, a wide face.* **2** an expression or look: *His face was sad.* **3** a distortion of the face, usually

expressing annoyance, disgust, etc. or meant to amuse: *He made a face and said he didn't like the coat. A little girl on the bus was making faces at people.* **4** outward appearance or aspect: *On the face of it, he seems to have a good chance to win. We have new information that puts a different face on the matter.* **5** the upper or outer surface of something: *the face of the earth.* **6** the front or main side of something: *the face of a clock, the face of a playing card.* **7** *Mathematics.* one of the plane surfaces of a solid: *A cube has six faces.* **8** *Mining.* the surface at the end of a tunnel, drift, or excavation where work is in progress. **9** *Printing.* typeface. **10** dignity, self-respect, or prestige: *To some people, loss of face is a disaster. She tried to save face by changing the subject.* **11** gall; nerve; impudence: *I didn't think she would have the face to come back after being asked to leave.*

face to face, a with faces toward each other: *The skaters were lined up face to face.* **b** in person; personally: *I never expected to meet him face to face.* **c** in the actual presence (used with **with**): *The wounded soldier knew he was face to face with death.*

in the face of, a in the presence of: *She showed no fear in the face of danger.* **b** in spite of: *He has succeeded in the face of tremendous difficulties.*

pull a long face, look unhappy or disapproving.

put a good (or **brave,** etc.) **face on,** make the best of; face cheerfully, bravely, etc.

set (one's) **face against,** oppose and resist: *He has set his face against any kind of change.*

show (one's) **face,** appear; be seen.

to (someone's) **face,** boldly or impudently, in the presence of: *He repeated the gossip to the teacher's face.*

—*v.* **1** have the face toward: *The dancers stood facing each other. Our house faces east.* **2** turn the face toward: *He was told to face the wall.* **3** be opposite to: *Look at the picture facing page 60.* **4** meet bravely or boldly; confront: *The mayor went out to face the angry demonstrators. She has the courage to face her problems.* **5** present itself to: *Another problem now faced us. They were faced with a difficult decision.* **6** cover the surface of with a layer of different material: *a wooden house faced with brick.* **7** apply a facing to a garment, etc. **8** smooth the surface of (stone, etc.). **face off,** *Cdn. Sports.* put a puck, ball, etc. into play by dropping it between the sticks of two players facing each other: *The referee starts a hockey game by facing off the puck at centre ice.*

face up to, meet bravely and boldly: *to face up to a difficult situation, to face up to an enemy.*

[< F *face* < VL *facia* < L *facies* form]

☞ *Syn. n.* **1. Face, countenance, visage** = the front part of the head. **Face** is the common word, but especially emphasizes the physical nature or the features: *That girl has a pretty face.* **Countenance** is formal and emphasizes the looks, especially as they show a person's thoughts, feelings, or character: *He has a cheerful countenance.* **Visage** is a literary word meaning either face or countenance, but emphasizing the general look of the face: *The countries were awed by the emperor's sombre visage.*

face card a playing card that is a king, queen, or jack.

face·cloth (fās′kloth′) *n.* a small cloth, usually made of towelling, for washing the face or body.

–faced having a specific kind of face or number of faces: *sad-faced, round-faced, two-faced, satin-faced.*

face·less (fās′lis) *adj.* **1** without a face: *a faceless clock.* **2** anonymous; without individual character.

face-lift (fās′lift′) *n., v.* —*n.* **1** an operation designed to improve the appearance of a face by tightening the skin, removing wrinkles, etc. **2** *Informal.* a change in appearance or manner of operation, designed to improve or bring up-to-date: *The whole company needs a facelift.* —*v.* give a facelift to. —**face′lift′er,** *n.*

face-off (fās′of′) *n. Sports.* the act of putting the puck, ball, etc. into play; a facing off: *The last goal was scored from the face-off.*

fac·er (fās′ər) *n.* **1** one that faces. **2** a blow in the face. **3** a violent check; a sudden serious difficulty.

face-sav·ing (fās′sā′ving) *adj.* that preserves or is intended to preserve one's dignity, self-respect, etc.: *That was just a face-saving gesture.*

fac·et (fas′it) *n., v.* **-et·ted** or **-et·ed, -et·ting** or **-et·ing.** —*n.* **1** any of the small, flat, polished surfaces of a cut gem. **2** any of the segments of a compound eye of an insect, etc. **3** the flat, narrow surface between the flutes of a column. **4** a view or aspect, as of a

character or personality: *Selfishness was a facet of his character that we seldom saw.*
—*v.* cut facets on. [< F *facette*, dim. of *face*. See FACE.]

fa·ce·tious (fə sē′shəs) *adj.* **1** having the habit of joking. **2** said in fun; not to be taken seriously. [< L *facetia* jest < *facetus* witty] —**fa·ce′tious·ly**, *adv.* —**fa·ce′tious·ness**, *n.*

face value **1** the value stated on a bond, cheque, coin, bill, etc.: *He paid much more than the face value for the silver quarters in his collection.* **2** the apparent worth or meaning: *He took the compliment at face value and did not worry about any hidden meaning.*

fa·cia (fā′shē ə *or* fā′shə) See fascia.

fa·cial (fā′shəl) *adj.*, *n.* —*adj.* **1** of the face: *facial features, facial expression.* **2** for the face: *a facial treatment, facial tissue.* —*n. Informal.* a massage or cosmetic treatment of the face.

fac·ile (fas′īl, fas′ēl, *or* fas′əl) *adj.* **1** easily done, used, etc.: *a facile task, facile methods.* **2** moving, acting, working, etc. with ease; fluent or ready: *a facile hand, a facile tongue, a facile pen.* **3** showing little thought, effort, depth, etc.; superficial or insincere: *facile answers to complex questions, facile repentance.* **4** *Archaic.* of easy manners or temper; agreeable; mild: *Her facile nature adapted itself to any company.* [< L *facilis* easy < *facere* do] —**fac′ile·ly**, *adv.* —**fac·ile′ness**, *n.*
☛ *Usage.* In defs. 1 and 2 as well as 3, *facile* can have a pejorative meaning: *facile methods* could be naïve and superficial; *a facile tongue* could refer to a way of speaking that seemed too smooth and charming to be convincing or sincere.

fa·cil·i·tate (fə sil′ə tāt′) *v.* **-tat·ed, -tat·ing.** make easy; lessen the labor of; help forward; assist: *A vacuum cleaner facilitates housework.*

fa·cil·i·ty (fə sil′ə tē) *n.*, *pl.* **-ties.** **1** the absence of difficulty; ease: *The facility of communication is far greater now than it was a hundred years ago.* **2** the ability to do anything easily, quickly, or smoothly; fluency or skill. **3** Usually, **facilities**, *pl.* something, such as equipment, furnishings, etc., that makes an action or activity possible or easier: *The library provides facilities for studying. The school has excellent sports facilities.* **4** *Archaic.* the quality of being mild or easy-going.

fac·ing (fās′ing) *n.* **1** a layer of different material covering a surface, used for protection or ornament: *The front of the courthouse has a marble facing.* **2** a lining along the inside edges of the front opening, neckline, etc. of a garment in the same or a contrasting fabric: *A facing is often meant to be turned back, as a collar or cuff.* **3 facings**, *pl.* the cuffs, collar, and trimmings of a military or military-style coat, usually in a contrasting color.

facsim. facsimile.

fac·sim·i·le (fak sim′ə lē) *n.*, *v.* **-led** (-lid), **-le·ing.** —*n.* **1** an exact copy or likeness; a perfect reproduction. **2** a process for transmitting printed matter and photographs by radio and reproducing them on paper at the receiving set.
in facsimile, exactly.
—*v.* make a facsimile of. [< L *fac* (imperative) make + *simile* (neut.) like]

fact (fakt) *n.* **1** anything known to be true or to have really happened; something that has or had actual existence: *historical facts, the fact of the existence of gravity. It is a fact that he was there, because several people identified him. Space travel is a fact.* **2** the quality of being real; the state of things as they are or have happened; reality; truth: *The fact of the matter is, he never wanted to go. I want fact, not fantasy.* **3** something said or believed to be true or to have really happened: *Check your facts before you present your argument.* **4** an actual deed or act, especially a criminal act: *She was charged with being an accessory after the fact.* **5** *Law.* anything that is known or alleged to have occurred in connection with a case (as distinguished from a principle or rule): *A question of fact is decided by the jury, a question of law by the court.*
as a matter of fact, **in fact**, or **in point of fact**, in truth; actually: *He hasn't had much education; in fact, he never got past grade five.* [< L *factum* (thing) done, pp. neut. of *facere* do. Doublet of FEAT.]
☛ *Usage.* **Fact.** *The fact that* is very often a circumlocution for which *that* alone would be more direct and more acceptable stylistically: *He was quite conscious (of the fact) that his visitor had some special reason for coming.*

fact–find·ing (fakt′fīn′ding) *n.* **1** the determination of the facts or realities of a case or situation. **2** (*adjl.*) engaged in or having the purpose of finding facts: *a fact-finding committee, an arbitrator engaged on a fact-finding mission.* —**fact′-find′er**, *n.*

fac·tion (fak′shən) *n.* **1** a group of people in a political party, church, club, etc. acting together, usually in opposition to another such group or the main body: *A faction often seeks to promote only its own interests at the expense of the group as a whole.* **2** strife or

quarrelling among the members of a political party, church, club, etc. [< L *factio, -onis* party, originally, a doing < *facere* do. Doublet of FASHION.]

fac·tion·al (fak′shən əl) *adj.* **1** of or having to do with factions; partisan. **2** causing faction.

fac·tion·al·ism (fak′shən əl iz′əm) *n.* a condition or situation characterized by faction: *a democracy threatened by regional, linguistic, and religious factionalism.*

fac·tious (fak′shəs) *adj.* **1** fond of causing strife or faction. **2** of or caused by strife or faction. [< L *factiosus* < *factio*. See FACTION.] —**fac′tious·ly**, *adv.* —**fac′tious·ness**, *n.*

fac·ti·tious (fak tish′əs) *adj.* developed by effort; not natural; artificial: *Extensive advertising can cause a factitious demand for an article.* [< L *facticius* artificial < *facere* do, make. Doublet of FETISH.] —**fac·ti′tious·ly**, *adv.* —**fac·ti′tious·ness**, *n.*

fac·ti·tive (fak′tə tiv) *adj. Grammar.* **1** denoting a verb that takes a direct object and an objective complement. *Examples:* They *made* him captain. They *called* him a fool. **2** of or having to do with such a verb. [< NL *factitivus* < L *factitare* make or declare to be < *factare* make (frequentative) < *facere* make, do] —**fac′ti·tive·ly**, *adv.*

fact of life **1** a part of life or existence that cannot be changed or ignored, especially an unpleasant or harsh part. **2 facts of life**, *pl. Informal.* information about human sexual functions.

fac·tor (fak′tər) *n.*, *v.* —*n.* **1** any element, condition, quality, etc. that helps to bring about a result: *Endurance is an important factor of success in sports.* **2** *Mathematics.* any of the numbers, algebraic expressions, etc. that produce a given number or quantity when multiplied together: 5, 3, and 4 *are factors of* 60. **3** a person who acts as a representative of a company; agent: *The Hudson's Bay Company formerly employed many factors, now usually called managers, in its fur-trading posts throughout the Northland.* **4** a finance company, bank, etc. that buys the debts owing to another firm at a discount in order to make a profit by collecting them. **5** *Obsolete.* gene.
—*v.* **1** *Mathematics.* separate into factors. **2** act as a factor. [< L *factor* doer < *facere* do]

fac·tor·age (fak′tər ij) *n.* **1** the business of a factor or agent; buying and selling on commission. **2** a commission paid to a factor or agent.

fac·tor·i·al (fak tôr′ē əl) *n.*, *adj.* —*n. Mathematics.* the product of a given integer and all the positive integers below it down to one. *Example:* Factorial 4 = 4×3×2×1× = 24 *Symbol:* *n!* or ⃞ (where *n* is the given integer). —*adj.* of or having to do with factors or factorials.

fac·tor·ize (fak′tə rīz′) *v.* **-rized, -riz·ing.** *Mathematics.* separate into factors.

fac·to·ry (fak′tə rē *or* fak′trē) *n.*, *pl.* **-ries.** **1** a building or group of buildings where things are manufactured. **2** *Historical.* a trading post: *Moose Factory, Ontario.* [< Med.L *factoria* < L *factor.* See FACTOR.]

fac·to·tum (fak tō′təm) *n.* a person employed to do all kinds of work. [< Med.L < L *fac* (imperative) do + *totum* (the whole)]

fac·tu·al (fak′chü əl) *adj.* of, containing, or consisting of fact or facts: *The newspaper simply gave a factual report on the fire, without speculating on possible causes.* —**fac′tu·al·ly**, *adv.* —**fac′tu·al·ness**, *n.*

fac·ul·ty (fak′əl tē) *n.*, *pl.* **-ties.** **1** a power of the mind or body: *the faculty of hearing, the faculty of memory. She is over ninety years old, but she still has all her faculties.* **2** the power to do some special thing, especially a power of the mind: *Nell has a remarkable faculty for arithmetic.* **3** the teaching staff of a university or college. **4** a department of learning in a university: *the faculty of theology, the faculty of law.* **5** the members of a profession: *The medical faculty is made up of doctors, surgeons, etc.* [< L *facultas* < *facilis.* See FACILE.]

fad (fad) *n.* something everybody is very much interested in for a short time; a craze; rage: *Crossword puzzles became a fad several years ago.* [origin uncertain]

fad·dish (fad′ish) *adj.* **1** inclined to follow fads. **2** like a fad. —**fad′dish·ly**, *adv.* —**fad′dish·ness**, *n.*

fad·dist (fad′ist) *n.* a person devoted to a fad or one who readily takes up fads.

fade (fād) *v.* **fad·ed, fad·ing.** **1** lose color or brightness: *The bedroom curtains have faded a lot.* **2** lose freshness or strength; wither: *Most of the garden flowers had faded by September.* **3** die away; disappear: *The sound of the train faded in the distance.* **4** cause to fade: *Sunlight will fade the colors in some fabrics.*
fade in, of a motion-picture image or electronic signal, slowly become more distinct or louder.
fade out, of a motion-picture image or electronic signal, slowly becomes less distinct or quieter.
[ME < OF *fader* < *fade* pale, weak < VL *fatidus* < L *fatuus* silly,

tasteless; influenced by L *sapidus* (cf. OF *sade*) tasty]
☛ *Syn.* **3.** See note at **disappear.**

fade–in (fād′in′) *n.* in motion pictures, radio, or television, a gradual increase in brightness, distinctness, or sound.

fade·less (fād′lis) *adj.* not fading; permanent.

fade–out (fād′out′) *n.* **1** in motion pictures, radio, or television, a gradual decrease in brightness, distinctness, or sound. **2** a gradual disappearance.

fae·cal (fē′kəl) See **fecal.**

fae·ces (fē′sēz) See **feces.**

fa·er·ie (fā′ər ē *or* fer′ē) *n., pl.* **-ies;** *adj. Archaic.* —*n.* **1** fairyland. **2** fairy. —*adj.* fairy. [var. of *fairy*]
☛ *Hom.* **fairy, ferry** (fer′ē).

fa·er·y (fā′ər ē *or* fer′ē) See **faerie.**

fag¹ (fag) *v.* **fagged, fag·ging;** *n.* —*v.* **1** work hard or until wearied: *Tom fagged away at his arithmetic.* **2** tire by work: *The horse was fagged.* **3** *Brit.* act as a servant of an older boy in a public school. —*n.* **1** a hard, uninteresting job; drudgery. **2** a person who does hard work; drudge. **3** *Brit.* a boy who acts as a servant of an older boy in a public school. [origin uncertain]

fag² (fag) *n. Esp.Brit. Slang.* cigarette. [origin uncertain]

fag³ (fag) *n. Slang.* a male homosexual. [shortened form of *faggot²*]

fag end 1 the last and poorest part of anything; remnant. **2** the coarse, unfinished end of a piece of cloth. **3** an untwisted end of rope.

fag·got¹ or **fag·ot** (fag′ət) *n., v.* —*n.* **1** a bundle of sticks or twigs tied together: *He built the fire with faggots.* **2** a bundle of iron rods or pieces of iron or steel to be welded. —*v.* **1** tie or fasten together into bundles; make into a faggot. **2** ornament with faggoting. [< OF]

fag·got² (fag′ət) *n. Slang.* a male homosexual. [origin unknown]

fag·got·ing or **fag·ot·ing** (fag′ət ing) *n.* **1** a style of embroidery in which a group of crosswise threads is pulled out of a fabric and the lengthwise threads thus exposed are tied together in groups resembling faggots. **2** a decorative openwork method of joining two finished edges. See **embroidery** for picture.

fag·ot (fag′ət) See **faggot¹.**

fag·ot·ing (fag′ət ing) See **faggoting.**

Fahr. Fahrenheit.

Fahr·en·heit (far′ən hīt′ *or* fer′ən hīt′) *adj.* of, based on, or according to the Fahrenheit scale for measuring temperature, on which 32 degrees marks the freezing point of water and 212 degrees the boiling point. *Abbrev.:* F, F, or Fahr. [< Gabriel Daniel *Fahrenheit* (1686-1736), the German physicist who introduced this scale]

fai·ence (fī ons′ *or* fä äns′; *French*, fä yäns′) *n.* a glazed earthenware or porcelain, usually of fine quality. [< F; said to be named after and to have been invented in *Faenza,* Italy, in 1299]

fail (fāl) *v., n.* —*v.* **1** not succeed; fall short of success: *He tried hard, but failed to achieve his goal.* **2** be unsuccessful in an examination, course of study, etc.; receive a mark of failure: *She failed her first year.* **3** give a mark of failure to: *The teacher failed a third of the class.* **4** fall far short of what is wanted or expected; come to nothing: *The project failed. The crops failed again this year.* **5** decrease to the point of not being enough; run out: *A rescue party found them just before their supplies failed.* **6** not remember or choose to do; neglect: *He failed to follow our advice.* **7** not be able (*to*): *I fail to understand why she didn't even show up.* **8** be of no use to, when needed: *Words failed her and she could think of nothing to say. His friends failed him when he was in trouble.* **9** stop performing or operating: *We were still far from home when the engine failed.* **10** lose strength; become weak or weaker: *The sick man's heart was failing.* **11** not make enough profit to stay in business; go bankrupt: *That company will fail.* —*n. Archaic* (except in **without fail**). failure.
without fail, without failing to do, happen, etc.; surely; certainly. [ME < OF *faillir,* ult. < L *fallere* deceive] —**fail′er,** *n.*

fail·ing (fāl′ing) *n., prep.* —*n.* **1** failure. **2** a fault; weakness; defect. —*prep.* in the absence of; in default of; lacking: *Failing good weather, the party will be held indoors.*
☛ *Syn. n.* **2.** See note at **fault.**

faille (fīl *or* fāl) *n.* a soft, ribbed cloth of silk, rayon, acetate, etc. [< F < MDu. *falie* scarf]

fail–safe (fāl′sāf′) *adj.* of a mechanism or system, incorporating an element that enables it to return automatically to a safe condition in the event of a breakdown or malfunction.

fail·ure (fāl′yər) *n.* **1** a falling short of success; lack of success. **2** the fact of not being successful in an examination, course, etc. **3** a not doing; neglecting. **4** a falling short of what is wanted or expected: *the failure of crops.* **5** a loss of strength; becoming weak;

---

hat, āge, fär; let, ēqual, tėrm; it, īce
hot, ōpen, ôrder; oil, out; cup, pút, rüle,
above, takən, pencəl, lemən, circəs

ch, child; ng, long; sh, ship
th, thin; ŦH, then; zh, measure

dying away. **6** not making enough profit to stay in business; becoming bankrupt: *the failure of a company.* **7** a person or thing that has failed: *The picnic was a failure because it rained.*

fain (fān) *adv., adj. Archaic.* —*adv.* by choice; gladly; willingly. —*adj.* **1** willing, but not eager; willing under the circumstances: *She did not care for life in the city but was fain to make the best of it.* **2** glad; willing. **3** eager; desirous. [OE *fægen*]
☛ *Hom.* **feign.**

faint (fānt) *adj., n., v.* —*adj.* **1** not clear or plain; dim: *faint idea, faint colors. We could see a faint outline of trees through the fog.* **2** weak; exhausted; feeble: *a faint voice.* **3** done feebly or without zest: *a faint attempt.* **4** ready to faint; about to faint: *I feel faint.* **5** lacking courage; cowardly. —*n.* a condition in which a person is unconscious for a short time, caused by an insufficient flow of blood to the brain: *She fell to the floor in a faint.* —*v.* **1** lose consciousness temporarily. **2** *Archaic.* grow weak; lose courage: *"Ye shall reap, if ye faint not."* [ME < OF *faint, feint,* pp. of *faindre, feindre.* See FEIGN.] —**faint′ly,** *adv.* —**faint′ness,** *n.*
☛ *Hom.* **feint.**

faint·heart (fānt′härt′) *n. Archaic or poetic.* a faint-hearted person.

faint–heart·ed (fānt′här′tid) *adj.* lacking courage; cowardly; timid. —**faint′-heart′ed·ly,** *adv.* —**faint′-heart′ed·ness,** *n.*

fair¹ (fer) *adj., adv., n.* —*adj.* **1** not favoring one more than the other or others; just; honest: *a fair judge.* **2** according to the rules: *fair play.* **3** pretty good; not bad; average: *She has a fair understanding of the subject. There is only a fair crop of wheat this year.* **4** favorable; likely; promising: *He is in a fair way to succeed.* **5** not dark; blond: *fair hair, a fair complexion.* **6** not cloudy or stormy; clear; sunny: *The weather will be fair today.* **7** pleasing to the eye or mind; beautiful: *a fair lady. He spoke fair words.* **8** of good size or amount; ample: *They own a fair piece of property.* **9** clean or pure; without blemishes: *fair water, a fair copy.* **10** easily read; plain: *fair handwriting.* **11** favorable; helpful, especially to a ship's course: *We had fair winds all the way.* **12** seeming good at first, but not really so: *His fair promises proved false.*
fair and square, *Informal.* just; honest.
fair to middling, moderately good; average.
—*adv.* **1** in an honest, straightforward manner; honestly: *fair-spoken, to play fair.* **2** directly; straight: *The stone hit him fair on the head.*
bid fair, seem likely; have a good chance.
—*n. Archaic.* a woman, especially a sweetheart. [OE *fæger*]
—**fair′ness,** *n.*
☛ *Hom.* **fare.**
☛ *Syn. adj.* **1. Fair, just, impartial** = not showing favor in making judgments. **Fair** emphasizes putting all on an equal footing: *He is fair even to people he dislikes.* **Just** emphasizes paying attention only to what is right or lawful: *Our teacher is always just in her grading.* **Impartial** emphasizes complete absence of favor or feeling for or against either side: *We need someone impartial to settle this quarrel.*

fair² (fer) *n.* **1** a gathering of people for the purpose of showing goods, products, etc.: *the Royal Winter Fair. At the county fair last year, prizes were given for the best farm products and livestock.* **2** a gathering of people to buy and sell, often held in a certain place at regular times during the year: *a trade fair.* **3** an entertainment and sale of articles; bazaar: *Our church held a fair to raise money.* [ME < OF *feire* < LL *feria* holiday]
☛ *Hom.* **fare.**

fair ball *Baseball.* a batted ball that is not a foul.

fair game 1 animals or birds that it is lawful to hunt. **2** a person or thing that is considered a suitable or legitimate pursuit or attack: *She was fair game for political cartoonists because of her odd way of dressing.*

fair·ground (fer′ground′) *n.* an outdoor space, usually having equipment for exhibitions and entertainment, where fairs are held.

fair–haired (fer′herd′) *adj.* having light-colored hair.

fair–haired boy *Informal.* a favorite.

fair·ing (fer′ing) *n.* a structure fitted around a part of an aircraft, spacecraft, motor vehicle, etc. to make a smooth outline and thus reduce drag: *landing gear fairings.*

fair·ish (fer′ish) *adj.* fairly good, well, or large.

fair·ly (fer′lē) *adv.* **1** in a fair manner. **2** to a fair degree. **3** justly;

honestly. **4** rather; somewhat: *The pay was fairly good.* **5** actually or really: *He fairly beamed when he saw his picture in the paper.* **6** clearly.

fair–mind·ed (fer′mīn′did) *adj.* not prejudiced; just; impartial. **—fair′-mind′ed·ly,** *adv.* **—fair′-mind′ed·ness,** *n.*

fair play 1 an abiding by the rules of a game; fair dealings in any contest. **2** just and equal treatment of all.

fair sex women, collectively.

fair shake *Esp.U.S. Informal.* an honest arrangement; fair treatment.

fair–spo·ken (fer′spō′kən) *adj.* speaking smoothly and pleasantly; civil; courteous.

fair–way (fer′wā′) *n.* **1** an unobstructed passage or way. The fairway in a harbor is the channel for ships. **2** the part in a golf course where the grass is kept short, between the tee and the putting green.

fair–weath·er (fer′weтн′ər) *adj.* **1** of or fitted for fair weather. **2** weakening or failing in time of need: *He is only a fair-weather friend.*

fair·y (fer′ē) *n., pl.* **fair·ies;** *adj.* **—n. 1** a supernatural being of folklore and mythology having magical powers and able to help or harm human beings. In recent legend, fairies have been pictured as very small, and sometimes very lovely and delicate. In medieval story, however, fairies were often of full human size. **2** *Slang.* a male homosexual. **—adj. 1** of fairies. **2** like a fairy; lovely; delicate: *wings of fairy gossamer.* [ME < OF *faerie* < *fae.* See FAY¹.] **—fair′y-like′,** *adj.* ☛ *Hom.* **faerie, ferry.**

fair·y·land (fer′ē land′) *n.* **1** the imaginary place where the fairies live. **2** any charming and pleasant place.

fairy ring a ring of mushrooms and darker grass, etc. growing around the edge of a body of underground fungi. It used to be thought that fairy rings were made by fairies when dancing.

fairy tale 1 a story about fairies or other beings with magic powers. **2** an untrue story, especially one intended to deceive; lie. **—fair′y-tale′,** *adj.*

fait ac·com·pli (fet′ə kom′plē; *French,* fe tä kôn plē′) something done and so no longer worth opposing. [< F]

faith (fāth) *n., interj.* **—n. 1** a believing without proof; trust. **2** belief in God, religion, or spiritual things. **3** what is believed. **4** religion. **5** a being faithful; loyalty: *Good faith is honesty of intention; bad faith is intent to deceive.* **6** a promise to remain loyal: *The captured soldiers refused to break faith even under torture.* **in bad faith,** dishonestly or insincerely. **in faith,** truly; indeed. **in good faith,** honestly; sincerely: *Although the boys had done the wrong thing, they had acted in good faith.* **keep faith,** keep one's promise. **—interj.** *Archaic.* truly; indeed. [ME < OF *feid* < L *fides.* Doublet of FAY².] ☛ *Syn. n.* **1.** See note at **conviction. 3.** See note at **belief.**

faith·ful (fāth′fəl) *adj., n.* **—adj. 1** worthy of trust; doing one's duty; keeping one's promise; loyal: *a faithful friend, a faithful servant.* **2** true; accurate: *The witness gave a faithful account of what happened.* **3** *Archaic.* full of faith. **—n. the faithful,** a true believers. **b** loyal followers or supporters. **—faith′ful·ly,** *adv.* **—faith′ful·ness,** *n.* ☛ *Syn. adj.* **1. Faithful, loyal, constant** = true to a person or thing. **Faithful** emphasizes being true to a person, group, belief, duty, or trust to which one is bound by a promise, pledge, honor, or love: *He is a faithful friend.* **Loyal** adds to faithful the idea of wanting to stand by and fight for the person or thing, even against heavy odds: *She was loyal during his trial.* **Constant** emphasizes steadfast devotion to friends or loved ones: *One could not find a more constant friend.*

faith·less (fāth′lis) *adj.* **1** unworthy of trust; failing in one's duty; breaking one's promise; not loyal: *A traitor is faithless.* **2** not reliable. **3** without faith; unbelieving. **—faith′less·ly,** *adv.* **—faith′less·ness,** *n.*

fake (fāk) *v.* **faked, fak·ing;** *n., adj.* **—v. 1** make to seem satisfactory; falsify; counterfeit: *The picture was faked by pasting together two photographs.* **2** intentionally give a false appearance of; simulate: *to fake an illness.* **—n.** a fraud; deception: *The beggar's limp was a fake.* **—adj.** intended to deceive; false: *a fake testimonial.* [origin uncertain] **—fak′er,** *n.*

fak·er·y (fā′kər ē) *n.* fraud or deceit.

fa·kir (fā′kər or fə kēr′) *n.* **1** a Moslem holy man who lives by begging, such as a dervish. **2** a Hindu ascetic, such as a yogi. [< Arabic *faqir* poor]

Fa·lange (fā′lanj or fə lanj′; *Spanish,* fä läng′нä) *n.* the political

party holding power in Spain since the Civil War (1936-1939). [< Sp. < L *phalanx* phalanx < Gk.]

Fa·lan·gist (fə lan′jist) *n.* a member of the Falange.

fal·cate (fal′kāt) *adj.* curved like a sickle; hooked. [< L *falcatus* < *falx, falcis* sickle]

fal·chion (fol′chən or fôl′chən) *n.* **1** a medieval sword having a broad, short blade with an edge that curves to a point. **2** *Poetic.* any sword. [ME < OF Ital. *falcione,* ult. < L *falx, falcis* sickle]

fal·con (fol′kən, fal′kən, or fôl′kən) *n.* **1** any of a family (Falconidae) of birds of prey that are active during the day; especially, any of the genus *Falco,* including the peregrine falcon, gyrfalcon, and North American sparrow hawk, having long pointed wings and a strong, hooked bill with a toothlike projection on the side of the upper part. **2** any of various falcons or hawks trained for use in falconry, especially a female peregrine. Compare **tercel.** [ME < OF < LL *falco, -onis* for L *falx, falcis* sickle; from the hooked talons]

fal·con·er (fol′kən ər or fôl′kən ər) *n.* **1** a man who hunts with falcons. **2** a breeder and trainer of falcons.

fal·con·ry (fol′kən rē or fôl′kən rē) *n.* **1** the sport of hunting with falcons. **2** the training of falcons to hunt.

fal·de·ral (fol′də rol′) *n.* **1** a flimsy thing, a trifle. **2** nonsense; rubbish. **3** a meaningless refrain in songs. Also, **falderol, folderol.**

fall (fol or fôl) *v.* **fell, fall·en, fall·ing;** *n.* **—v. 1** drop or come down from a higher place: *The snow is falling fast. The leaves are falling from the trees.* **2** come down suddenly from an erect position: *He fell on his knees.* **3** hang down: *Her curls fell upon her shoulders.* **4** droop: *His spirits fell when he heard they weren't going.* **5** yield to temptation: *He was tempted and fell.* **6** lose position, power, dignity, etc.: *The dictator fell from the people's favor.* **7** be captured, overthrown, or destroyed: *The fort fell to the enemy.* **8** drop wounded or dead; especially, be killed in battle: *The plaque carried the names of those who fell in the last war.* **9** pass into a certain condition; become: *He fell asleep. The rent falls due on Monday.* **10** come; arrive: *When night falls, the stars appear.* **11** come by chance or lot: *Our choice fell on him.* **12** come to pass; happen; occur: *Christmas falls on Sunday this year.* **13** pass by inheritance: *The money fell to the only son.* **14** be placed: *The principal stress of farmer falls on the first syllable.* **15** become lower or less: *Prices fell sharply. The water in the river has fallen 80 centimetres. Her voice fell.* **16** be divided: *The story falls into five parts.* **17** look sad or disappointed: *His face fell at the bad news.* **18** slope downward: *The land falls gradually to the beach.* **19** be directed: *The light falls on my book.* **20** *Lumbering.* cut down; fell.

fall across, or **among,** come upon or among by chance; meet with.

fall apart, crumble; break down; disintegrate.

fall away, **a** withdraw support or allegiance. **b** become bad or worse. **c** be overthrown or destroyed. **d** become thin.

fall back, retreat; go toward the rear: *The soldiers fell back to a stronger position.*

fall back on, **a** go back to for safety. **b** turn to for help or support: *He knew he could fall back on his father.*

fall behind, fail to keep up; drop back: *Before the race was half over, the slow runners had fallen a lap behind.*

fall down on, *Informal.* prove a failure at.

fall flat, fail completely; have no effect or interest: *The poor performance fell flat.*

fall for, *Slang.* **a** be deceived by. **b** fall in love with.

fall foul (of or **upon), a** become entangled. **b** come into conflict; quarrel with. **c** come into collision, as ships.

fall from, *Obsolete.* **a** disagree with. **b** forsake allegiance to. **c** give up.

fall from grace, **a** *Informal.* lose favor. **b** revert to sin or evildoing; backslide.

fall heir to, inherit.

fall in, **a** collapse; cave in: *The roof fell in from the weight of the snow.* **b** *Military.* take one's place in line; line up in the correct formation.

fall in with, **a** meet by chance: *On our trip, we fell in with some interesting people.* **b** agree: *They fell in with our plans.*

fall off, **a** drop; become less: *Attendance at baseball games falls off late in the season.* **b** (of health) deteriorate.

fall on, **a** attack: *Thieves fell on the man and stole his money.* **b** come across; light on.

fall out, a *Military.* leave one's place in line. **b** stop being friends; quarrel. **c** turn out; happen.

fall short (of), a fail. **b** fail to equal: *Income fell short of expenditures.*

fall through, fail: *His plans fell through.*

fall to, a begin to fight or attack: *The swordsman fell to with great enthusiasm.* **b** begin to eat: *The girls fell to as soon as they sat down.* **c** go into place; close by itself: *The lid of the chest fell to.*

fall under, belong under; be classified as.

fall upon, attack.

—n. 1 a falling; dropping from a higher place. **2** the amount that falls: *We had a very heavy fall of snow last winter.* **3** the distance

that anything falls. **4** waterfall. **5** a coming down suddenly from an erect position: *The child had a bad fall when he tripped on the step.* **6** a hanging down; dropping. **7** a giving in to temptation. **8** a loss of position, power, dignity, etc. **9** a capture; overthrow; destruction. **10** the proper place: *the fall of a stress.* **11** a lowering; becoming less. **12** a downward slope. **13** the season of the year between summer and winter; autumn. **14** *Wrestling.* **a** being thrown on one's back. **b** a contest. **15** **falls,** *pl.* **a** a waterfall; cataract; cascade. **b** an apparatus used in lowering and raising a ship's boat. **16 the Fall,** in the Bible, the sin of Adam and Eve in yielding to temptation and eating the forbidden fruit. **17** a long, full woman's hairpiece that hangs freely.

ride for a fall, act so as to be in danger or get into trouble. [OE *feallan*]

☞ *Usage.* **Falls** is treated as singular and as plural. We speak of *a falls* but ordinarily use it with a plural verb: *The falls are almost dry in August.* When *falls* is part of a place name, the name is used with a singular verb: *Niagara Falls is receding.*

fal·la·cious (fə lā′shəs) *adj.* **1** deceptive; misleading: *fallacious hopes for a lasting peace.* **2** containing or being a fallacy; logically unsound: *fallacious reasoning.* —**fal·la′cious·ly,** *adv.* —**fal·la′cious·ness,** *n.*

fal·la·cy (fal′ə sē) *n., pl.* **-cies. 1** a false idea; mistaken belief; error: *It is a fallacy to suppose that riches always bring happiness.* **2** a mistake in reasoning; misleading or unsound argument. **3** unsoundness; falsity; delusive character. [< L *fallacia* < *fallax* deceptive < *fallere* deceive]

fal·lal (fal′lal′) *n.* a useless bit of finery. [coined word]

fall·en (fol′ən *or* fôl′ən) *v., adj.* —*v.* pp. of **fall.** —*adj.* **1** dropped: *They picked up some fallen apples.* **2** on the ground; down flat: *a fallen tree.* **3** degraded. **4** overthrown; destroyed. **5** (*noml.*) **the fallen,** *pl.* all those killed in battle: *The memorial commemorates the fallen of the First World War.* **6** shrunken; decreased: *fallen cheeks.*

fall·er (fol′ər *or* fôl′ər) *n. Logging.* a person whose work is to fell trees.

fall fair *Cdn.* a fair held in the fall in a community for the exhibiting and judging of livestock, produce, and crafts, often with horse races, dances, and other forms of entertainment.

fall guy *Slang.* **1** the member of a comic act who takes all the knocks. **2** any person left in a difficult situation, especially a scapegoat.

fal·li·bil·i·ty (fal′ə bil′ə tē) *n.* a fallible quality or nature.

fal·li·ble (fal′ə bəl) *adj.* **1** liable to be deceived or mistaken; liable to err. **2** liable to be erroneous, inaccurate, or false. [< Med.L *fallibilis* < *fallere* deceive]

falling sickness epilepsy.

falling star meteor.

fall line a line that marks the end of layers of hard rock of a plateau and the beginning of a softer rock layer of a coastal plain. Many falls and rapids mark this line.

Fal·lo·pi·an tubes (fə lō′pē ən) a pair of slender tubes through which ova from the ovaries pass to the uterus. [after *Fallopius,* a 16th-century Italian anatomist]

fall-out (fol′out′ *or* fôl′-) *n.* **1** the radio-active particles or dust that fall to the earth after a nuclear explosion. **2** any incidental result or side-effect.

fal·low¹ (fal′ō *or, esp. in the Prairie Provinces,* fol′ō) *adj., n., v.* —*adj.* of land, ploughed and left unseeded for a season or more: *a fallow field.*

lie fallow, a of land, be left ploughed and unseeded. **b** remain inactive, unproductive, etc.: *bonds lying fallow in a safety deposit box.*

—*n.* land or ground left fallow; summer fallow.
—*v.* plough and harrow (land) and leave unseeded. [OE *fealg*]

fal·low² (fal′ō) *n. or adj.* pale yellowish brown. [OE *fealu*]

fallow deer either of two species of small deer (*Dama dama* of S Europe and *D. mesopotamica* of SW Asia) having flattened, palmate antlers and a coat ranging in color from pale yellow to reddish, with white or brown spots in summer.

false (fols *or* fôls) *adj.* **fals·er, fals·est;** *adv.* —*adj.* **1** not true; not correct; wrong: *false statements, false testimony.* **2** not truthful; lying. **3** not loyal; not faithful: *a false friend.* **4** made or done so as to deceive: *The fugitive left a false trail for his pursuers. The dishonest butcher used false scales.* **5** *Music.* not true in pitch: *a false note.* **6** not real; artificial: *false diamonds.* **7** based on wrong notions; ill-founded: *false pride, a false sense of security.* **8** *Biology.* improperly called or named. The false acacia is really a locust tree. —*adv.* in a false manner.

play false, deceive; cheat; trick; betray.
[< L *falsus* < *fallere* deceive] —**false′ly,** *adv.* —**false′ness,** *n.*

☞ *Syn. adj.* **6.** *False, counterfeit* = not real or genuine. *False,* describing something made to look like the real thing, emphasizes pretending to be what it really is not, and sometimes suggests being intended to deceive others: *Most*

hat, āge, fär; let, ēqual, tèrm; it, īce
hot, ōpen, ôrder; oil, out; cup, put, rüle,
above, takən, pencəl, lemən, circəs

ch, child; ng, long; sh, ship
th, thin; ₮H, then; zh, measure

false teeth really look natural. **Counterfeit** emphasizes passing as the real thing, and always suggests being meant to deceive or cheat: *Counterfeit money occasionally gets into circulation.*

false alarm 1 a warning signal, such as a fire alarm, air raid siren, etc., given when no danger exists. **2** a situation that arouses some strong reaction, as of hope, fear, etc., which proves to be unjustified.

false bottom the bottom of a trunk, suitcase, drawer etc., that forms a secret or a supplementary compartment.

false colors or **colours 1** a flag of another country, used for deception: *The raiding ship was flying false colors.* **2** false pretences.

false face a funny or ugly mask; mask.
put on a false face, assume a certain appearance or behavior in order to deceive.

false·hood (fols′hud *or* fôls′-) *n.* **1** lack of truth or accuracy; falsity. **2** a false idea, theory, etc. **3** the practice of making false statements; lying. **4** a false statement; lie.
☞ *Syn.* **4.** See note at **lie.**

false pride a pride based on mistaken ideas.

false ribs the ribs not attached to the breastbone. Human beings have five pairs of false ribs.

false step 1 a wrong step; stumble: *One false step and the climber would fall to his death.* **2** a mistake or blunder: *The police were waiting for the suspect to make a false step.*

false teeth artificial teeth used after the real teeth have been removed.

fal·set·to (fol set′ō *or* fôl set′ō) *n., pl.* **-tos;** *adv.* —*n.* **1** an adult male voice pitched artificially high, especially a singing voice that goes above the normal full tenor range. **2** a singer who uses falsetto. —*adv.* in falsetto: *He sang the part falsetto.* [< Ital. *falsetto,* dim. of *falso* false < L *falsus.* See FALSE.]

false·work (fols′werk′ *or* fôls′-) *n.* a temporary structure that supports a bridge, etc. until the main structure is completed.

fal·sies (fol′sēz *or* fôl′sēz) *n.pl. Informal.* a type of padded brassiere, worn to give a full-bosomed appearance.

fal·si·fi·ca·tion (fol′sə fə kā′shən *or* fôl′sə fə kā′shən) *n.* falsifying or being falsified.

fal·si·fy (fol′sə fī′ *or* fôl′sə fī′) *v.* **-fied, -fy·ing. 1** make false; change in order to deceive; misrepresent. **2** make false statements; lie. **3** prove to be false; disprove. [< LL *falsificare* < L *falsificus* acting falsely < *falsus* (see FALSE) + *facere* make] —**fal′si·fi′er,** *n.*

fal·si·ty (fol′sə tē *or* fôl′sə tē) *n., pl.* **-ties. 1** being false; incorrectness: *the falsity of his smile. Education showed him the falsity of his superstitions.* **2** something false; lie. **3** untruthfulness; deceitfulness; treachery.

Fal·staff·i·an (fol staf′ē ən *or* fôl staf′ē ən) *adj.* **1** of or having to do with Falstaff, a soldier in Shakespeare's *Henry IV* and *Merry Wives of Windsor,* or his group of ragged soldiers. **2** fat, jolly, and brazen, as Falstaff was.

fal·ter (fol′tər *or* fôl′tər) *v., n.* —*v.* **1** lose courage; draw back; hesitate; waver: *The soldiers faltered for a moment as their captain fell.* **2** move unsteadily; stumble; totter. **3** speak in hesitating, broken words; stammer: *Greatly embarrassed, he faltered out his thanks.* **4** come forth in hesitating, broken sounds: *His voice faltered.*
—*n.* **1** the act of faltering. **2** a faltering sound. [ME *falteren;* cf. ON *faltrask* be burdened] —**fal′ter·er,** *n.*
☞ *Syn. v.* **1.** See note at **hesitate.**

fame (fām) *n.* **1** the condition of being very well known; having much said or written about one. **2** what is said about one; reputation. [< obs. F < L *fama* < *fari* speak]

famed (fāmd) *adj.* famous; celebrated; well-known.

fa·meuse (fə myüz′; *French,* fä mœz′) *n. Cdn.* snow apple. [< F *fameuse*]

fa·mil·ial (fə mil′yəl *or* fə mil′ē əl) *adj.* **1** of, having to do with, or characteristic of a family. **2** tending to occur in or be transmitted within a family: *a familial snub nose.*

fa·mil·iar (fə mil′yər) *adj., n.* —*adj.* **1** often seen or experienced; well-known; common: *a familiar tune, a familiar face. A knife is a familiar tool.* **2** well acquainted: *He is familiar with French.* **3** close; personal; intimate: *familiar friends.* **4** not formal; friendly. **5** too

friendly; presuming; forward: *They didn't like his familiar manner.*
—*n.* **1** a close friend. **2** a spirit or demon supposed to serve a particular person. A witch is traditionally supposed to have a familiar in the shape of a black cat. **3** *Roman Catholic Church.* a person who belongs to the household of a bishop, and renders domestic, though not menial, service. **4** an officer of the Inquisition whose chief duty was to arrest the accused or suspected. [ME < OF < L *familiaris* < *familia.* See FAMILY.] —**fa·mil′iar·ly**, *adv.*

☛ *Syn. adj.* **3. Familiar, intimate, confidential** = personally near or close. **Familiar** suggests the free and easy relationsihp that comes when people are closely acquainted or have known each other a long time: *I am not familiar with my cousin.* **Intimate** suggests a close relationship that develops when people know each other and each other's thoughts and feelings very well: *They are intimate friends.* **Confidential** emphasizes the trust people place in each other, and suggests that neither will divulge the other's secrets and private affairs: *She is the manager's confidential secretary.*

fa·mil·iar·i·ty (fə mil′yar′ə tē *or* fa mil yer′ə tē, fə mil′ē ar′ə tē *or* fa mil′ē er′ə tē) *n., pl.* **-ties. 1** close acquaintance. **2** a freedom of behavior suitable only to friends; lack of formality or ceremony. **3** an instance of such behavior: *She dislikes such familiarities as the use of her first name by people she has just met.*

fa·mil·iar·ize (fə mil′yər īz′) *v.* **-ized, -iz·ing. 1** make well acquainted: *Before playing the new game, familiarize yourself with the rules.* **2** make well-known: *The publicity given to nuclear research has familiarized a whole new vocabulary.* —**fa·mil′iar·i·za′tion**, *n.*

fam·i·ly (fam′ə lē *or* fam′lē) *n., pl.* **-lies. 1** a father, mother, and their children. **2** the children of a father and mother: *Do they have a family?* **3** one's spouse and children: *She says her family doesn't want to move.* **4** a group of related people living in the same house. **5** all of a person's relatives. **6** a group of related people; tribe. **7** *Biology.* a major category in the classification of plants and animals, more specific than the order and more general than the genus. Lions, tigers, and leopards belong to the cat family. The prairie lily, dogtooth violet, and trillium belong to the lily family. See chart at **classification. 8** *Linguistics.* a group of related languages descending from a single language. English, French, German, Hindi, Italian, and Russian are some of the languages belonging to the Indo-European family. **9** any group of related or similar things. [< L *familia* household < *famulus* servant]

☛ *Usage.* **Family**, though singular, may take a plural verb when the emphasis is on the individual members: *Her family is opposed to the marriage. The family were gathered in the living room.*

family allowance 1 an allowance paid to members of the armed forces, often to cover living expenses overseas. **2** an allowance paid by a government to parents for each of their children under a stipulated age. **3 Family Allowance,** in Canada, an allowance paid by the Federal Government for children under the age of 18 who are maintained by parents and guardians. Provincial governments can vary the rates within certain limits, and a few provinces have their own program to supplement the federal one.

family circle the immediate members of a family; adults and children of a particular household.

Family Compact in Canada, the name applied to the governing class of Upper Canada before 1837, and, in particular, to the executive and legislative councils of Upper Canada.

family man 1 a man who has a family. **2** a man who takes pleasure in his family and enjoys domestic life.

family name surname; last name.

family skeleton a cause of shame that a family tries to keep secret: *They tried to ignore their family skeleton, the desertion of their grandfather to the enemy.*

family tree 1 a diagram showing the relationships and descent of all the members and ancestors of a family; genealogical chart. **2** all the members of a family line.

fam·ine (fam′ən) *n.* **1** starvation. **2** a lack of food in a place; time of starving: *Many people have died during famines in India.* **3** a very great shortage of anything: *a coal famine.* [< F *famine* < *faim* hunger < L *fames*]

fam·ish (fam′ish) *v.* be or make extremely hungry; make or become weak from hunger.

be famished or **famishing,** *Informal.* be very hungry: *Let's eat; I'm famished.* [ME *famen* famish < OF *afamer* < L *ad* (intensive) + *fames* hunger; modelled after verbs in *-ish*]

☛ *Syn.* See note at **hunger.**

fa·mous (fā′məs) *adj.* **1** very well known; noted: *a famous general.* **2** *Informal.* first-rate; excellent. [< AF < L *famosus* < *fama.* See FAME.] —**fa′mous·ly,** *adv.*

☛ *Syn.* **1. Famous, renowned, noted** = very well known. **Famous** applies to a person, place, thing, or happening widely known to the public either during or after its lifetime or existence, always in a good way if still living: *A great crowd of people greeted the famous cosmonaut.* **Renowned** suggests great or

long-lasting fame, often great praise and honor: *Shakespeare is renowned.* **Noted** = well known for a particular thing, but not always for something good or for a long time: *The noted gangster was deported.*

fan¹ (fan) *n., v.* **fanned, fan·ning.** —*n.* **1** an instrument or device with which to stir the air in order to cool or ventilate a room, to cool one's face, or to blow dust away. **2** anything spread out like an open fan. **3** of machinery: **a** any of various devices consisting essentially of a series of radiating flat or curved blades attached to and revolving with a central hublike part. **b** such a device turned by a belt from the driveshaft for cooling the radiator of an automobile. **c** such a device turned by an electric motor for cooling a room. **4** a winnowing machine.
—*v.* **1** make a current of (air) with a fan, etc. **2** direct a current of air toward with a fan, etc.: *Fan the fire to make it burn faster.* **3** drive away with a fan, etc.: *She fanned the flies from the sleeping child.* **4** stir up; arouse: *Cruel treatment fanned their dislike into hate.* **5** spread out like an open fan. **6** blow gently and refreshingly upon; cool: *The breeze fanned their hot faces.* **7** winnow. **8** *Baseball. Slang.* strike out: *He fanned three times in one game. The pitcher fanned five batters.* [OE *fann* < L *vannus* fan for winnowing grain] —**fan′like**, *adj.* —**fan′ner**, *n.*

fan² (fan) *n. Informal.* **1** a person extremely interested in a sport, one of the performing arts, etc., especially as a spectator: *a hockey fan, a movie fan.* **2** an admirer of an actor, writer, etc. [short for *fanatic*]

fa·nat·ic (fə nat′ik) *n., adj.* —*n.* a person who is carried away beyond reason by his feelings or beliefs. —*adj.* enthusiastic or zealous beyond reason. [< L *fanaticus* inspired by divinity < *fanum* temple]

fa·nat·i·cal (fə nat′ə kəl) *adj.* unreasonably enthusiastic; extremely zealous. —**fa·nat′i·cal·ly**, *adv.*

fa·nat·i·cism (fə nat′ə siz′əm) *n.* an unreasonable enthusiasm; extreme zeal.

fan·cied (fan′sēd) *adj.* imagined; imaginary.

fan·ci·er (fan′sē ər) *n.* a person who is especially interested in and knowledgeable about something, especially the growing or breeding of particular kinds of plants or animals: *She's a dog fancier.*

fan·ci·ful (fan′sē fəl) *adj.* **1** marked by fancy or caprice; quaint; whimsical: *fanciful designs or decorations.* **2** influenced by fancy; indulging in fancies: *He was in a fanciful mood when he wrote this delightful story.* **3** suggested by fancy; imaginary; unreal: *He gave a fanciful account of the events.* —**fan′ci·ful·ly**, *adv.* —**fan′ci·ful·ness**, *n.*

fan·cy (fan′sē) *n., pl.* **-cies;** *v.* **-cied, -cy·ing;** *adj.* **-ci·er, -ci·est.** —*n.* **1** one's power to imagine; imagination, especially for a decorative, whimsical, or playful kind: *Poetic fancy has produced some great works of literature.* **2** something imagined or supposed; something unreal: *Is it just fancy, or do I hear a sound?* **3** an idea or notion: *He had a sudden fancy to go for a swim.* **4** a liking or fondness based mainly on whim: *They took a fancy to each other right away.*
—*v.* **1** form an idea of; imagine: *Can you fancy yourself living in that house?* **2** have an idea; suppose; guess: *I fancy she is about sixty.* **3** like or be fond of: *He fancied the idea of having a reunion.* **fancy oneself,** think highly of oneself: *That girl really fancies herself.* —*adj.* **1** having or showing great technical skill and grace: *He showed us some fancy dancing.* **2** not plain or simple; decorated, ornamental, or elaborate; showy: *a fancy table setting, a fancy costume.* **3** of high quality: *These canned peaches are labelled fancy.* **4** extravagant, especially of prices: *It's a nice place, but they also have fancy prices.* **5** of an animal or plant, bred for special ornamental or odd qualities that have no practical function. [contraction of *fantasy*]

☛ *Syn. n.* **1.** See note at **imagination.**

fancy dress a costume for a masquerade, especially one representing an animal, a person from history or fiction, etc.

fan·cy–free (fan′sē frē′) *adj.* **1** not in love. **2** carefree; not restrained.

fancy man *Slang.* a man who is supported by a woman, especially by a prostitute.

fancy woman *Slang.* a mistress or prostitute.

fan·cy·work (fan′sē wèrk′) *n.* ornamental needlework; embroidery, crocheting, etc.

F. and A. M. Free and Accepted Masons.

fan·dan·go (fan dang′gō) *n., pl.* **-gos. 1** a lively Spanish dance in three-quarter time. **2** the music for such a dance. [< Sp.]

fane (fān) *n. Archaic or poetic.* temple; church. [< L *fanum* temple]

fan·fare (fan′fer) *n.* **1** a short tune or call sounded by trumpets, bugles, hunting horns, etc. **2** a loud show of activity, talk, etc.; showy flourish. [< F *fanfare* < *fanfarer* blow a fanfare < Sp. < Arabic *farfâr* talkative]

fang (fang) *n.* **1** a long, sharp tooth by which certain animals, such as dogs, wolves, etc. seize and hold prey; canine tooth: *The hungry wolf buried its fangs in the caribou's neck.* **2** a hollow or grooved tooth by which a poisonous snake injects poison into its prey. **3** a long, slender, tapering part of anything, such as the root of a tooth or the prong of a fork. [OE]

fan hitch *Cdn.* a method of harnessing sled dogs first used by Eskimos, with a lead dog up in front and others on shorter traces fanning out behind him.

fan·light (fan′līt′) *n.* **1** a semicircular window with bars spread out like an open fan. **2** any semicircular or other window over a door.

fan mail the mail received by a celebrity from fans.

fan·ny (fan′ē) *n., pl.* **fan·nies.** *Slang.* buttocks.

fan·tail (fan′tāl′) *n.* **1** a tail, end, or part spread out like an open fan. **2** a breed of domestic pigeon having a large tail that spreads out like a fan. **3** any of various birds, fish, etc. having a fan-shaped tail. **4** *Architecture.* a fan-shaped structure or part.

fan-tan (fan′tan′) *n.* **1** a Chinese gambling game played by betting on the number of coins under a bowl. **2** a card game in which the player who gets rid of his cards first wins the game. [< Chinese *fan t'an* repeated divisions]

fan·ta·si·a (fan tā′zhē ə, fan tā′zhə, *or* fan tä′zē ə) *n. Music.* **1** a composition in which form depends on the composer's fancy. **2** a medley of popular tunes with interludes. [< Ital. *fantasia* < L < Gk. *phantasia.* Doublet of FANTASY.]

fan·ta·sist (fan′tə sist′) *n.* a person who creates fantasies.

fan·ta·size (fan′tə sīz′) *v.* **-sized, -siz·ing.** indulge in vivid and often extravagant daydreams or fantasies: *He often fantasized about living the life of a rock star.*

fan·tas·tic (fan tas′tik) *adj.* **1** very fanciful; capricious; eccentric; irrational: *The idea of space travel seemed fantastic a hundred years ago.* **2** existing only in the imagination; unreal: *There are many fantastic creatures in* The Wizard of Oz. **3** very odd or queer; wild and strange in shape; showing unrestrained fancy: *The firelight cast weird, fantastic shadows on the walls.* **4** *Informal.* unbelievably good, quick, high, etc.: *That store charges fantastic prices.* [ME < OF < LL < Gk. *phantastikos* < *phantazesthai* appear] **—fan·tas′ti·cal·ly,** *adv.*

fan·tas·ti·cal (fan tas′tə kəl) *adj.* fantastic.

fan·ta·sy (fan′tə sē *or* fan′tə zē) *n., pl.* **-sies.** **1** the play of the mind; imagination or fancy: *The idea of space travel was once pure fantasy.* **2** a fanciful or fantastic idea or notion; a caprice or whim: *It was a mere fantasy, not to be taken seriously.* **3** wild imagining or day-dreaming; the creation of unrealistic or far-fetched mental images to satisfy desires not fulfilled in real life: *living in a world of fantasy.* **4** such an idea or mental image: *fantasies about sudden wealth and fame.* **5** fiction featuring strange and grotesque characters and fantastic acts or events in a coherent setting: The Lord of the Rings *is a fantasy.* **6** *Music.* fantasia. Also, **phantasy.** [ME < OF *fantasie* < L < Gk. *phantasia* appearance, image, ult. < *phainein* show. Doublet of FANTASIA.]

fan tracery *Architecture.* tracery used in fan vaulting.

fan vaulting *Architecture.* a style of vaulting in which the ribs flare out like those of a fan.

fan·wise (fan′wīz′) *adv.* as a fan; spread out like an open fan.

FAO in the United Nations, Food and Agricultural Organization.

far (fär) *adj.* **far·ther** *or* **fur·ther, far·thest** *or* **fur·thest;** *adv.* —*adj.* **1** distant; not near: *a far country.* **2** more distant: *the far side of the hill.* **3** extending to a great distance; long: *a far look ahead, a far journey.*
—*adv.* **1** a long way off in time or space: *far distant.* **2** very much: *It is far better to be overcautious than to be careless in driving.* **3** to an advanced point, distance, or degree: *He studied far into the night. The explorers penetrated far into the jungle.*
as far as, to the distance, point, or degree that.
by far, very much: *He was by far the better swimmer.*
far and away, very much: *He was far and away the best student.*
far and near, everywhere.
far and wide, everywhere; even in distant parts.
far be it from me, I do not dare or want.
far from it, by no means; not at all: *Agree with you? Far from it!*
far out, *Slang.* **a** fine; excellent. **b** very advanced and different; avant-garde: *His taste in art is far out.*
go far, a last long: *That new shampoo doesn't go very far.* **b** tend very much. **c** get ahead: *She shows great promise; she should go far.*
how far, to what distance, point, or degree.
in so far as, to the extent that.
so far, a to this or that point: *He accepts teasing just so far and then he gets angry.* **b** until now or then: *Our team has won every game so far this season.*
so far as, to the extent that.

hat, āge, fär; let, ēqual, tėrm; it, īce
hot, ōpen, ôrder; oil, out; cup, pút, rüle,
above, takən, pencəl, lemən, circəs
ch, child; ng, long; sh, ship
th, thin; ᴛʜ, then; zh, measure

so far so good, until now everything has been safe or satisfactory. [OE *feorr*]
☛ *Syn. adj.* **1.** See note at **distant.**

far·ad (far′əd *or* fer′əd) *n.* an SI unit of electrical capacity. A farad is the capacity of a condenser having a charge of one coulomb when the potential across the plate is one volt. *Symbol:* F. [after Michael *Faraday.* See FARADAY.]

far·a·day (far′ə dā′ *or* fer′ə dā′) *n.* a unit of electricity equal to about 96 500 coulombs. In electrolysis, it is the amount needed to deposit one gram atom of a univalent element. [< Michael *Faraday* (1791-1867), an English physicist and chemist]

fa·rad·ic (fə rad′ik *or* fə red′ik) *adj.* of or having to do with induced currents of electricity.

far·an·dole (far′ən dōl′ *or* fer′ən dōl′) *n.* **1** a fast Provençal dance in six-eight time, in which the dancers join hands to form a chain, following a leader in a winding course. **2** the music for this dance. [< F < Provençal *farandoulo*]

far·a·way (fär′ə wā′) *adj.* **1** distant; far away: *faraway countries.* **2** dreamy: *A faraway look in her eyes showed that she was thinking of something else.*

farce (färs) *n., v.* —*n.* **1** a play intended merely to make people laugh, full of ridiculous happenings, absurd actions, and improbable situations. **2** such plays as a class; branch of drama concerned with such plays. **3** the kind of humor found in such plays; broad humor. **4** ridiculous mockery; absurd pretence: *The trial was a mere farce.* —*v.* spice (a composition or speech); season: *He farced his essay with anecdotes.* [< F *farce,* literally, stuffing < *farcir* < L *farcire* stuff; originally applied to comic interludes]

far·ceur (fär sèr′) *n.* **1** a writer or performer of farces. **2** a wag; joker. [< F]

far·ci·cal (fär′sə kəl) *adj.* of or like a farce; ridiculous; absurd; improbable. **—far′ci·cal·ly,** *adv.* **—far′ci·cal·ness,** *n.*

far cry a long way.

far·del (fär′dəl) *n. Archaic.* bundle; burden. [ME < OF *fardel,* dim. of *farde* bundle < Arabic *farda*]

fare (fer) *n., v.* **fared, far·ing.** —*n.* **1** the sum of money paid to ride in an aircraft, a train, car, bus, etc. **2** the passenger on an aircraft, a train, car, bus, etc. **3** food provided or eaten: *dainty fare.*
—*v.* **1** eat food; be fed. **2** get along; do: *If you fare well, you have good luck or success.* **3** turn out; happen: *It will fare hard with the thief if he is caught.* **4** *Archaic.* go; travel. [OE *faran*] **—far′er,** *n.*
☛ *Hom.* **fair.**

Far East China, Japan, and other parts of E Asia.

fare·well (*interj.* fer′wel′; *n.* fer′wel′ *for 1-3,* fer′wel′ *for 4*) *interj., n.* —*interj.* **1** an expression of good wishes at parting. **2** goodbye; good luck.
—*n.* **1** an expression of good wishes at parting. **2** goodbye; good luck. **3** a departure; leave-taking. **4** (*adj.*) of farewell; parting; last: *The singer gave a farewell performance.*

far-fetched (fär′fecht′) *adj.* not likely; hard to believe; forced; strained: *a far-fetched excuse.*

far-flung (fär′flung′) *adj.* widely spread; covering a large area.

fa·ri·na (fə rē′nə) *n.* **1** flour or meal made from any grain or root, especially cornmeal or coarse wheat flour used for puddings or as a breakfast cereal. **2** starch, especially from potatoes. [< L *farina* < *far* grits]

far·i·na·ceous (far′ə nā′shəs *or* fer′ə nā′shəs) *adj.* consisting of flour or meal; starchy; mealy. Cereals, bread, and potatoes are farinaceous foods.

farm (färm) *n., v.* —*n.* **1** a tract of land together with the buildings on it, where agricultural crops or domestic livestock or birds are raised. **2** a tract of land or water where a specific thing is raised for market. See **fish farm, oyster farm.** **3** *Sports.* a farm club. **4** *Archaic.* **a** a fixed yearly amount payable in the form of rent, taxes, etc. **b** a fixed yearly amount accepted from a person instead of taxes, or the like, that he is authorized to collect. **5 a** the letting out of the collection of public taxes. **b** the condition of being let out at a fixed amount: *a district in farm.* **c** a district let out for the collection of taxes.
—*v.* **1** raise crops or animals on a farm: *Mary and her brother farm for a living.* **2** cultivate land: *They farm 100 hectares.* **3** take proceeds or profits of (a tax, undertaking, etc.) on paying a fixed sum. **4** let out (taxes, revenues, an enterprise, etc.) to another for a

fixed sum or percentage. **5** let the labor or services of (a person) for hire. **6** contract for the maintenance of (paupers, children, etc.).
farm out, a *Sports.* send a professional athlete to a less advanced league so that he can gain experience. **b** turn over to a person, company, etc. for a special purpose: *He farms out the right to pick berries on his land.*
[ME < OF *ferme* lease, leased farm < *fermer* make a contract < L *firmare* < *firmus* firm]

farm club or **team** *Sports.* a minor-league team that trains players for the major leagues.

farm·er (fär′mər) *n.* **1** a person who raises crops or animals on a farm. **2** a person who takes a contract for the collection of taxes by agreeing to pay a certain sum to the government.

farm·er·ette (fär′mər et′) *n. Informal.* a woman or girl who works on a farm.

farm hand a person employed to work on a farm.

farm·house (färm′hous′) *n.* the dwelling on a farm.

farm·ing (fär′ming) *n.* **1** the business of raising crops or animals on a farm; agriculture. **2** the practice of letting out the collection of a public revenue. **3** the condition of being let out at a fixed sum.

farm·land (färm′land′ *or* färm′lənd) *n.* land suitable for or used for raising crops or grazing.

farm·out (färm′out′) *n.* a sublease for drilling oil, granted by one company to another.

farm·stead (färm′stəd) *n.* a farm with its buildings.

farm system *Sports.* an organization of clubs or teams that train players for a major-league club.

farm·yard (färm′yärd′) *n.* the yard connected with the buildings of a farm or enclosed by them.

Far North in Canada, the Arctic and sub-Arctic regions; the territories lying north of the provinces.

far·o (fer′ō) *n.* a gambling game played by betting on the order in which certain cards will appear. [apparently alteration of *Pharoah*]

far–off (fär′of′) *adj.* distant; far away: *far-off lands.*

far–out (fär′out′) *adj., interj.—adj.* eccentric or avant-garde: *far-out ideas.—interj.* an expression of delighted amazement.

far·ra·go (fə rä′gō *or* fə rä′gō) *n., pl.* **-goes.** a confused mixture; hodgepodge; jumble. [< L *farrago* mixed fodder, ult. < *far* grits]

far–rang·ing (fär′rān′jing) *adj.* **1** able to travel over a great length or distance: *far-ranging missiles.* **2** covering a wide area (of thought, influence, subject matter, etc.): *a far-ranging debate, a far-ranging inspection.*

far–reach·ing (fär′rēch′ing) *adj.* having a wide influence or effect; extending far.

far·ri·er (far′ē ər *or* fer′ē ər) *n.* **1** a blacksmith who shoes horses. **2** *Archaic.* a horse doctor; veterinarian. [< MF *ferrier* < L *ferrarius* < *ferrum* iron]

far·ri·er·y (far′ē ər ē *or* fer′ē ər ē) *n., pl.* **-er·ies. 1** the work of a farrier. **2** the place where a farrier works. **3** *Archaic.* the care and treatment of horses.

far·row (far′ō *or* fer′ō) *n., v.—n.* a litter of pigs.—*v.* give birth to a litter of pigs: *The sow farrowed yesterday. She farrowed a litter of six.* [OE *fearh*]

far·ru·ca (fär rü′kä) *n.* an Andalusian gypsy dance. [< Sp., ultimately < a dim. of *Francisco* Francis]

far–see·ing (fär′sē′ing) *adj.* **1** able to see far. **2** looking ahead; planning wisely for the future.

far–sight·ed (fär′sīt′id) *adj.* **1** having a condition of the eyes in which the visual images of nearby objects come to a focus behind the retina, so that they are not clear. A far-sighted person has better vision for distant objects than for near objects; able to see far. Compare **near-sighted. 2** looking ahead; planning wisely for the future.—**far′-sight′ed·ly,** *adv.*—**far′-sight′ed·ness,** *n.*

fart (färt) *v., n. Slang.—v. Vulgar.* emit intestinal gas through the anus.—*n. Vulgar.* such an emission of gas.
[ME *ferten* < OE *feortan,* related to OHG *ferzan* and Skt. *pardatē*]

far·ther (fär′FHər) *adj., adv.* (a comparative of **far).**—*adj.* more distant: *Three kilometres is farther than two.*
—*adv.* **1** at or to a greater distance: *Go no farther.* **2** at or to a more advanced point: *He has investigated the subject farther than most people.* **3** in addition; also. [ME *ferther*]

☛ *Usage.* **Farther, further.** In formal English **farther** is used for physical distance and **further** for abstract and metaphysical senses: *We have moved our campsite farther from the road. His criticisms of the school went further than mine.* Informally, **further** is often used in all senses.

far·ther·most (fär′FHər mōst′) *adj.* most distant; farthest.

far·thest (fär′FHist) *adj., adv.* (a superlative of **far).**—*adj.* **1** most distant. **2** longest: *His last trip was the farthest he had ever undertaken.*—*adv.* **1** to or at the greatest distance. **2** most. [ME *ferthest*]

far·thing (fär′FHing) *n.* **1** a former British coin worth a fourth of a penny. **2** something having little value. [OE *feothung* < *feortha* fourth]

A farthingale of the mid 18th century. The framework of cane and whalebone, attached to a corselet, is shown on the right.

far·thin·gale (fär′FHing gāl′) *n.* a hoop skirt or framework for extending a woman's skirt at the hip line, worn in England from about 1550 to about 1650. [< MF *verdugale* < Sp. *verdugado* < *verdugo* rod, ult. < L *viridis* green]

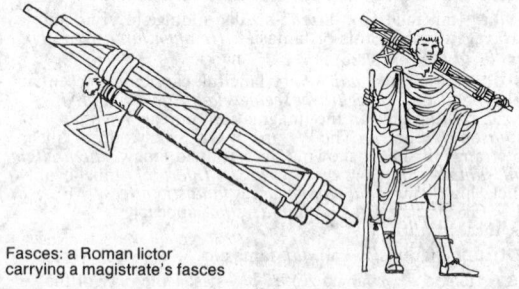

Fasces: a Roman lictor carrying a magistrate's fasces

fas·ces (fas′ēz) *n. pl.* of **fas·cis** (fas′is). in ancient Rome, a bundle of rods or sticks containing an axe with the blade projecting, carried before a magistrate as a symbol of authority. [< L *fasces,* pl. of *fascis* bundle]

fas·ci·a (fash′ē ə *or* fā′shə *for 1, 3, 4;* fash′ē ə *or* fash′ə *for 2) n., pl.* **-ci·ae** (-ē ē′ *or* -ē ī′). **1** a long, flat band or surface, such as a horizontal band forming part of a cornice or architrave, or a flat surface above a shop window, often carrying the name of the shop. **2** a sheet of connective tissue beneath the skin, enclosing and separating groups and layers of muscle. **3** a broad band of contrasting color. **4** *Brit.* dashboard. [< L]

fas·ci·cle (fas′ə kəl) *n.* **1** a small bundle; especially, in botany, a small cluster of flowers, leaves, roots, etc. **2** one of the parts of a book published in instalments. [< L *fasciculus,* dim. of *fascis* bundle]

fas·ci·cule (fas′ə kyül′) *n.* fascicle.

fas·ci·nate (fas′ə nāt′) *v.* **-nat·ed, -nat·ing. 1** attract very strongly; enchant by charming qualities: *The actress's charm and beauty fascinated everyone.* **2** hold motionless by strange power, terror, etc.: *Snakes are said to fascinate small birds.* [< L *fascinare* < *fascinum* spell]

fas·ci·nat·ing (fas′ə nāt′ing) *adj.* captivating; enchanting; charming.—**fas′ci·nat′ing·ly,** *adv.*

fas·ci·na·tion (fas′ə nā′shən) *n.* **1** fascinating or being fascinated. **2** a very strong attraction; charm; enchantment.

fas·ci·na·tor (fas′ə nā′tər) *n.* **1** a long, lightweight scarf, usually knitted or crocheted, worn by women over the head or around the neck. **2** a person who fascinates.

fas·cine (fa sēn′) *n.* **1** a bundle of sticks tied together, formerly used to fill ditches, strengthen earthworks, etc. **2** *Cdn.* a large, circular trap, resembling a palisade enclosure, for catching fish. [< F < L *fascina* bundle of sticks < *fascis* bundle]

fas·cism (fash′iz əm) *n.* **1** Also, **Fascism,** the doctrines, principles, or methods of Fascists. **2** any system of government in which property is privately owned, but in which all industry and labor are regulated by a strong national government, while all opposition is rigorously suppressed. [< Ital. *fascismo* < *fascio* bundle (as political emblem) < L *fascis*]

☛ *Usage.* **Fascism, Fascist** are capitalized when they refer to the Italian movement or party, as we capitalize *Liberal* and *Conservative* in this country.

When the word refers to a movement in another country in which the party has a different name, it need not be capitalized but often is. When it refers to the general idea of fascist politics, or an unorganized tendency, it is not capitalized. Compare **Nazi.**

fas·cist (fash′ist) *n., adj.* —*n.* **1 Fascist,** a member of a strongly nationalistic political party that seized control of the Italian government in 1922 under the leadership of Mussolini. **2** Also, **Fascist,** a member of any similar political party in other countries. **3** a person who favors and supports fascism. —*adj.* Also, **Fascist,** of or having to do with fascism or fascists. ☛ *Usage.* See note at **fascism.**

fash·ion (fash′ən) *n., v.* —*n.* **1** a manner; way: *Crabs walk in a peculiar fashion.* **2** the prevailing style; current custom in dress, manners, speech, etc. **3** a garment in the current style: *That shop carries all the latest fashions.* **4** (*adj.*) of or concerned with fashion or fashions: *a fashion magazine, a fashion designer.* **5** social prominence or standing, as shown by dress or way of life: *a man of fashion.*
after or **in a fashion,** in some way or other; not very well.
set the fashion, fix the fashion, method, etc. for others to follow.
—*v.* make; shape; form: *She fashioned a whistle out of the stick.* [ME < AF *fashion* < L *factio* a doing or making. Doublet of **FACTION.**]
☛ *Syn. n.* 2. **Fashion, style** = custom in dress, manners, living, speech, etc. **Fashion** applies to the custom prevailing at a particular time or among a particular group: *She likes to read about the latest fashions.* **Style** is often used in place of *fashion,* but now particularly emphasizes good taste, regardless of the fashion: *That dress is such good style that it will last for years.* —*v.* See note at **make.**

fash·ion·a·ble (fash′ən ə bəl *or* fash′nə bəl) *adj.* **1** following the fashion; in fashion; stylish. **2** of, like, or used by people of fashion. —**fash′ion·a·ble·ness,** *n.*

fash·ion·a·bly (fash′ən ə blē *or* fash′nə blē) *adv.* in a fashionable manner.

–fashioned *combining form.* in fashion or style: *old-fashioned* = *old in fashion or style.*

fast¹ (fast) *adj., adv.* —*adj.* **1** quick; rapid; swift: *a fast runner.* **2** indicating a time ahead of the correct time: *My watch is fast.* **3** too free; wild; not restrained in pleasures: *He led a fast life, drinking and gambling.* **4** firm; secure; tight: *a fast hold on a rope.* **5** loyal; steadfast: *They have been fast friends for years.* **6** not fading easily: *This cloth is dyed with fast color.* **7** adapted for speed; helping to produce or increase speed: *a fast track.* **8** with greater than average speed, force, etc.: *a fast pitcher.* **9** firmly fixed or attached; tightly shut or locked: *a fast window or door.* **10** *Photography.* (of a film, lens, etc.) making a short exposure possible.
—*adv.* **1** quickly; rapidly; swiftly. **2** firmly; securely; tightly. **3** thoroughly; completely; soundly: *He was fast asleep.* **4** *Archaic.* close; near.
play fast and loose, be tricky, insincere, or unreliable: *to play fast and loose with the truth.*
[OE *fæst*]
☛ *Syn. adj.* 1. See note at **quick.**

fast² (fast) *v., n.* —*v.* go without food; eat little or nothing; go without certain kinds of food. Members of some religious faiths fast on certain days. —*n.* **1** a fasting. **2** a day or period of fasting.
break (one's) fast, eat the first meal of the day. [OE *fæstan*]

fast·back (fast′bak′) *n.* **1** an automobile roof that slopes downward in a long curve to the back. **2** an automobile with such a roof.

fast·ball (fast′bol′ *or* -bôl′) *n.* a variety of softball having a number of features to add speed and action, making the game more like baseball.

fast day a day observed by fasting, especially a day regularly set apart by a religious organization.

fas·ten (fas′ən) *v.* **1** fix firmly in place; tie, lock, or shut: *to fasten a dress, to fasten a door.* **2** impose; impute: *He tried to fasten the blame upon his companions.* **3** direct; fix: *The dog fastened his eyes on the stranger.* **4** become fixed in place: *The door wouldn't fasten properly.*
fasten on or **upon,** take hold of; seize.
[OE *fæstnian* < *fæst* fast¹]

fas·ten·er (fas′ən ər) *n.* **1** a person who fastens. **2** an attachment, device, etc. used to fasten a door, garment, etc.

fas·ten·ing (fas′ən ing) *n.* a device used to fasten things together: *Locks, bolts, clasps, hooks, buttons, etc. are all fastenings.*

fas·tid·i·ous (fas tid′ē əs *or* fas tid′yəs) *adj.* hard to please; extremely refined or critical; easily disgusted: *a fastidious eater. He's fastidious about clothes.* [< L *fastidiosus* < *fastidium* loathing] —**fas·tid′i·ous·ly,** *adv.* —**fas·tid′i·ous·ness,** *n.*

fast·ness (fast′nis) *n.* **1** a strong, safe place; stronghold: *The bandits hid in their mountain fastness.* **2** being fast.

hat, āge, fär; let, ēqual, tèrm; it, īce
hot, ōpen, ôrder; oil, out; cup, pút, rüle,
əbove, takən, pencəl, lemən, circəs

ch, child; ng, long; sh, ship
th, thin; ŦH, then; zh, measure

fast talk smooth, persuasive patter, often designed to prevent or overcome suspicion.

fast–talk (fast′tok′ *or* -tôk′) *v.* gain (something) or persuade (a person) by means of fast talk: *He fast-talked his way into the job.*

fast time *Informal.* daylight-saving time.

fat (fat) *n., adj.* **fat·ter, fat·test;** *v.* **fat·ted, fat·ting.** —*n.* **1** any of various kinds of white or yellow oily substance formed in the bodies of animals and also in some seeds. **2** any animal tissue mainly composed of such a substance. **3** *Chemistry.* any of a class of organic compounds of which the natural fats are mixtures. **4** the richest, best, or most nourishing part of anything. **5** *Cdn. Seal hunting.* **a** seal blubber. **b** sealskins with attached blubber. **c** seals, especially whitecoats, as the object of the hunt.
chew the fat, *Slang.* talk casually together; chat.
in or **into the fat,** *Cdn. Seal hunting.* among the seal herd: *The hunt began yesterday, with all 11 ships in the fat.*
the fat is in the fire, it is too late to prevent unpleasant results; matters have been made worse.
live off the fat of the land, have the best of everything.
—*adj.* **1** consisting of or containing fat; oily: *fat meat.* **2** abounding in some element; fertile: *fat land.* **3** yielding much money; profitable: *a fat job.* **4** affording good opportunities. **5** full of good things; plentifully supplied; plentiful. **6** fleshy; plump; round and well-fed: *He has got quite fat.* **7** thick; broad. **8** dull; stupid. **9** too fat; corpulent; obese. **10** *Slang.* not much; little; small: *A fat chance you have of catching him now. A fat lot of help you are to me.*
—*v.* make or become fat; fatten. [OE *fætt,* originally pp., fatted] —**fat′like′,** *adj.* —**fat′ly,** *adv.* —**fat′ness,** *n.*
☛ *Syn. adj.* 6, 9. **Fat, stout, portly** = having too much flesh. **Fat** is the general word, in common use applying to any degree from healthy, well-fed plumpness to ugly, unhealthy obesity: *That boy is too fat.* **Stout** emphasizes thickness and bulkiness, but sometimes suggests firm rather than flabby flesh and is often used as a euphemism for too fat: *She calls herself stylishly stout.* **Portly** = stout and stately: *The retired admiral is a portly old gentleman.*

fa·tal (fā′təl) *adj.* **1** causing death: *fatal accidents.* **2** causing destruction or ruin: *The loss of all our money was fatal to our plans.* **3** decisive; fateful: *At last the fatal day for the contest arrived.* **4** influencing fate: *Fates, the three goddesses who controlled the fate of mankind, were sometimes called the fatal sisters.* [ME < L *fatalis* < *fatum.* See **FATE.**]
☛ *Syn.* 1. **Fatal, deadly, mortal,** and **lethal** can all mean "causing death." **Fatal** is used of something that has caused death or is sure to cause it: *a fatal disease.* **Deadly** refers to something likely to cause death: *a deadly weapon.* **Mortal** is used to refer to a state, event, etc. but not to a weapon: *a mortal wound.* **Lethal** is used of something sure to kill and designed or intended to do so: *a lethal dose.*

fa·tal·ism (fā′təl iz′əm) *n.* **1** the belief that fate controls everything that happens. **2** submission to everything that happens as inevitable.

fa·tal·ist (fā′təl ist) *n.* a believer in fatalism.

fa·tal·is·tic (fā′təl is′tik) *adj.* **1** of or having to do with fatalism. **2** believing that fate controls everything; accepting things and events as inevitable. —**fa·tal·is′ti·cal·ly,** *adv.*

fa·tal·i·ty (fə tal′ə tē *or* fā tal′ə tē) *n., pl.* **-ties. 1** a fatal accident or happening; death: *There were several fatalities on the highways last weekend.* **2** a person killed in such an accident or happening: *Even good drivers can become fatalities.* **3** a fatal influence or effect; deadliness: *The fatality of many types of cancer has been reduced.* **4** the condition of being controlled by fate; inevitable necessity: *a vain struggle against fatality.* **5** fatalism.

fa·tal·ly (fā′təl ē) *adv.* **1** in a manner leading to death or disaster: *He was fatally wounded.* **2** according to fate.

Fatal Sisters the Fates.

Fa·ta Mor·ga·na (fā′tə môr gä′nə) Morgan le Fay, the fairy half-sister of King Arthur.

fat cat *Slang.* a person who is rich, privileged, and powerful or influential.

fate (fāt) *n.* **1** a power that determines and controls everything that is or happens; destiny: *Fate is beyond human control. He does not believe in fate.* **2** what is caused by fate. **3** one's lot or fortune. **4** what becomes of a person or thing: *The jury settled the fate of the accused.* **5** death; ruin. **6 Fates,** *pl. Greek and Roman mythology.* the three goddesses believed to control human life. They were Clotho, who spins the thread of life; Lachesis, who decides how long it shall be; and Atropos, who cuts it off. [ME < L *fatum*

(thing) spoken (i.e., by the gods), pp. neut. of *fari* speak]
☞ *Hom.* fete.
☞ *Syn.* **1, 3. Fate, destiny, doom** = a person's fortune or lot in life. **Fate** suggests some power or force that determines what becomes of a person or thing, and emphasizes an outcome that cannot be avoided, escaped, or changed: *World history describes the fate of many nations.* **Destiny,** often used interchangeably with **fate,** emphasizes a fate all prearranged and not to be altered: *Death is every man's destiny.* **Doom** applies to an unhappy or awful end: *The condemned man went to his doom.*

fat·ed (fāt′id) *adj.* **1** controlled by fate. **2** destined; predestined.

fate·ful (fāt′fəl) *adj.* **1** controlled by fate. **2** determining what is to happen; decisive. **3** showing what fate decrees; prophetic. **4** causing death, destruction, or ruin; disastrous. **—fate′ful·ly,** *adv.* **—fate′ful·ness,** *n.*

fat·head (fat′hed′) *n. Slang.* a dolt; a stupid or slow person.

fa·ther (fo′ᵺər) *n., v.* **—n. 1** a male parent. **2** a person who is like a father. **3** a male ancestor; forefather. **4** a person who helped to make something; founder, leader, inventor, author, oldest member, etc.: *Fathers of Confederation. Alexander Graham Bell was the father of the telephone.* **5** a title of respect used in addressing priests or other clergymen. **6** a clergyman having this title. **7** a title of respect to an old man. **8** in ancient Rome, a senator. **9 the Father,** God. **10 the fathers,** *pl.* the chief writers and teachers of the Christian Church during the first six centuries A.D. **—v. 1** produce or bring forth, as a father; beget: *He has fathered three children.* **2** take care of as a father does; act as a father to. **3** make; originate. **4** acknowledge oneself as the father of. [OE *fæder*]

father confessor 1 a priest who hears confessions. **2** a person to whom one confides everything.

fa·ther·hood (fo′ᵺər húd′) *n.* the condition of being a father.

fa·ther–in–law (fo′ᵺər in lo′ *or* -lô′) *n., pl.* **fa·thers-in-law.** the father of one's husband or wife.

fa·ther·land (fo′ᵺər land′) *n.* one's native country; the land of one's ancestors.

fa·ther·less (fo′ᵺər lis) *adj.* **1** without a father living. **2** without a known father.

fa·ther·ly (fo′ᵺər lē) *adj.* **1** of or belonging to a father: *fatherly responsibilities.* **2** like a father; kindly. **—fa′ther·li·ness,** *n.*

Fathers of Confederation the men, led by Sir John A. Macdonald, who brought about the confederation of the original provinces of Canada in 1867.

fath·om (faᵺ′əm) *n., pl.* **fath·oms** or (*esp. collectively*) **fath·om;** *v.* **—n.** a unit of measure equal to six feet (about 1.83 m), used mostly in measuring the depth of water and the length of ships' ropes, cables, etc. **—v. 1** measure the depth of; sound. **2** get to the bottom of; understand fully. [OE *fæthm* width of the outstretched arms]

fath·om·a·ble (faᵺ′əm ə bəl) *adj.* **1** that can be measured. **2** understandable.

fath·om·less (faᵺ′əm lis) *adj.* **1** too deep to be measured. **2** impossible to be fully understood.

fa·tigue (fə tēg′) *n., v.* **-tigued, -ti·guing;** *adj.* **—n. 1** physical or mental weariness. **2** any task or exertion producing weariness: *The doctor has not yet recovered from the fatigues of the epidemic.* **3** a weakening (of metal) caused by long-continued use or strain. **4** *Physiology.* a temporary decrease in the capacity of an organ or cell to function after excessive activity. **5** fatigue duty. **6 fatigues,** *pl.* clothes worn during fatigue duty. **—v. 1** cause fatigue in; weary. **2** weaken (metal) by much use or strain. **—adj.** having to do with fatigue. [< F *fatigue* < *fatiguer* < L *fatigare* tire]

fatigue duty non-military work done by members of the armed forces. Cleaning up the camp or repairing roads is fatigue duty.

Fa·ti·ma (fə tē′mə *or* fat′ə mə) *n.* A.D. 606?-632, the favorite daughter of Mohammed.

fat·ling (fat′ling) *n.* a calf, lamb, kid, or pig fattened to be killed for food.

fat·ten (fat′ən) *v.* **1** make (a stock animal, etc.) fat or fleshy (*often used with* **up**): *The hogs were being fattened for market.* **2** enrich (soil). **3** make richer or fuller; swell. **4** become fat or fatter. **—fat′ten·er,** *n.*

fat·tish (fat′ish) *adj.* somewhat fat.

fat·ty (fat′ē) *adj.* **-ti·er, -ti·est. 1** of fat; containing fat: *fatty tissues.* **2** like fat; oily; greasy. **—fat′ti·ly,** *adv.* **—fat′ti·ness,** *n.*

fatty acid *Chemistry.* any of a group of organic acids, some of which, such as stearic acid, are found in animal and vegetable fats and oils. *Formula:* $C_nH_{2n}O_2$

fa·tu·i·ty (fə tyü′ə tē *or* fə tü′ə tē) *n., pl.* **-ties.** self-satisfied stupidity; folly; silliness. [< L *fatuitas* < *fatuus* foolish]

fat·u·ous (fach′ü əs) *adj.* stupid but self-satisfied; foolish; silly. [< L *fatuus* foolish] **—fat′u·ous·ly,** *adv.* **—fat′u·ous·ness,** *n.*
☞ *Syn.* See note at **foolish.**

fau·bourg (fō′bür *or* fō′bürg; *French,* fō bür′) *n.* **1** suburb. **2** a district in a city.

fau·cal (fo′kəl *or* fô′kəl) *adj., n.* **—adj.** of, having to do with, or produced in fauces. **—n.** *Phonetics.* a sound produced in fauces. [< L *fauces* throat + E -*al*]

fau·ces (fo′sēz *or* fô′sēz) *n.pl.* the cavity at the back of the mouth, leading into the pharynx. [< L]

fau·cet (fo′sit *or* fô′sit) *n.* **1** a device for controlling the flow of water or other liquid in a pipe, tank, barrel, etc.; tap. **2** the enlarged end of a pipe into which the end of another pipe fits. [< F *fausset* < *fausser* bore through, originally, break < L *falsare* corrupt]

faugh (fo *or* fô) *interj.* an exclamation of disgust.

fault (folt *or* fôlt) *n., v.* **—n. 1** something that is not as it should be; a flaw; defect. **2** a mistake. **3** a cause for blame; responsibility: *Whose fault was it?* **4** *Geology.* a break in a mass of rock with the segment on one side of the break pushed up or down. **5** *Tennis, etc.* a failure to serve the ball into the right place. **6** an accidental defect in an electric circuit.
at fault, a deserving blame; wrong. **b** puzzled; perplexed.
find fault, pick out faults; complain: *The boy said that his father was always finding fault.*
find fault with, object to; criticize: *The teacher was always finding fault with badly done homework.*
in fault, deserving blame; wrong.
to a fault, too much; very.
—v. 1 *Tennis, etc.* fail to serve the ball into the right place. **2** find fault with: *Her work could not be faulted.* **3** *Geology.* (of rock strata) cause or undergo a fault or faults. [ME < OF *faute,* ult. < L *fallere* deceive]
☞ *Syn.* **1. Fault, failing** = a defect in character, mental attitude, emotional make-up, conduct, or habits. **Fault** particularly suggests a lack of something essential to perfection, but, not necessarily a cause for blame: *Sloppiness is his greatest fault.* **Failing** suggests a falling short of perfection, and applies particularly to a weakness in character, often excusable: *Extravagance is her failing.*

fault·find·er (folt′fīn′dər *or* fôlt′-) *n.* **1** a person who finds fault; complainer. **2** a device for locating defects, as in an electric circuit.

fault·find·ing (folt′fīn′ding *or* fôlt′-) *n. or adj.* finding fault; complaining; pointing out faults.

fault·less (folt′lis *or* fôlt′-) *adj.* without a single fault; free from blemish or error; perfect. **—fault′less·ly,** *adv.* **—fault′less·ness,** *n.*

fault·y (fol′tē *or* fôl′tē) *adj.* **fault·i·er, fault·i·est.** having faults; containing blemishes or errors; wrong; imperfect. **—fault′i·ly,** *adv.* **—fault′i·ness,** *n.*

faun (fon *or* fôn) *n. Roman mythology.* one of a class of minor rural deities originally represented as men with the horns and tail of a goat, but later partially assimilated with the Greek satyrs and, like them, represented as having a goat's hind legs and a lustful character. [ME < L *Faunus* a rural deity]
☞ *Hom.* fawn.

fau·na (fo′nə *or* fô′nə) *n.* all the animals of a particular region or time: *the fauna of Australia, the fauna of the carboniferous age.* [< NL *Fauna* a rural goddess, wife of Faunus] **—faun′al,** *adj.*

Faust (foust) *n. German legend.* an old philosopher who sells his soul to the devil in return for having everything that he wants on earth. The story of Faust has inspired many literary and musical works since medieval times. **—Faust′i·an,** *adj.*

Faust·us (fous′təs) *n.* Faust. Marlowe's play on Faust is called *The Tragedy of Dr. Faustus.*

Fauves (fōvz) *n.pl.* a group of French painters, including Henri Matisse, whose work in the period from 1905 to 1920 is characteristic of Fauvism. [< F *fauves* wild beasts]

Fau·vism (fō′viz əm) *n. Painting.* a style that was an extreme form of expressionism, developed in France in the early 20th century and characterized by simplicity and boldness of design, vivid clashing colors, and individuality of approach.

faux pas (fō′ pä′ *or* fō′ pä′) *pl.* **faux pas** (fō′ päz′ *or* fō′ päz′). a slip in speech, conduct, manners, etc.; breach of etiquette; blunder. [< F]

fa·vor *or* **fa·vour** (fā′vər) *n., v.* **—n. 1** an act of kindness: *Will you do me a favor?* **2** liking; approval: *They are sure to look with favor on your plan.* **3** the condition of being liked or approved: *A fashion in favor this year may be out of favor next year.* **4** the favoring of one or some more than others; favoritism. **5** a gift or token: *The knight wore his lady's favor on his arm.* **6** a small gift, especially one given as a souvenir at a party. **7** *Now rare.* a letter; note: *We acknowledge your favor of the 15th.*
in favor of, a on the side of; supporting. **b** to the advantage of;

helping. **c** to be paid to: *Make the cheque out in favor of the company, not the sales representative.*
in (someone's) **favor,** for someone's benefit.
—*v.* **1** show kindness to. **2** like; approve. **3** give more than fair treatment to. **4** be on the side of; support: *to favor legal reform.* **5** be to the advantage of; help. **6** treat gently: *The dog favors his sore foot when he walks.* **7** look like: *She favors her mother.* [ME < OF < L *favor* < *favere* show kindness to] —**fa′vor·er or fa′vour·er,** *n.*
☛ *Syn. n.* 2. **Favor, good will** = kindly or friendly feeling. **Favor** emphasizes having kindly or friendly thoughts or giving approval: *The manager looked on the new clerk with favor.* **Good will** emphasizes greater friendliness and desire or effort to be helpful: *The audience showed its good will toward the singer by its applause.*

fa·vor·a·ble or **fa·vour·a·ble** (fā′vər ə bəl *or* fāv′rə bəl) *adj.* **1** favoring; approving. **2** being to one's advantage; helping: *a favorable wind.* **3** boding well; promising. —**fa′vor·a·ble·ness or fa′vour·a·ble·ness,** *n.* —**fa′vor·a·bly or fa′vour·a·bly,** *adv.*
☛ *Syn.* 3. **Favorable, auspicious** = promising or giving signs of turning out well. **Favorable** = promising because conditions or people having to do with an event or situation show they will be helpful: *It was a favorable time for our trip, since business was light.* **Auspicious** = promising because all the signs point to a lucky or successful outcome: *The popularity of his first book was an auspicious beginning of his career.*

fa·vored or **fa·voured** (fā′vərd) *adj.* **1** treated with favor. **2** having special advantages; talented.

fa·vor·ite or **fa·vour·ite** (fā′vər it *or* fāv′rit) *adj., n.* —*adj.* liked better than others; liked very much.
—*n.* **1** a person or thing liked better than others; one liked very much: *Hank is a favorite with everybody.* **2** a person treated with special favor. **3** *Sports.* a person, horse, etc. expected to win a contest. [ME < MF *favorit* (fem. *favorite*) < Ital. *favorito,* ult. < *favore* favor < L *favor*]

fa·vor·it·ism or **fa·vour·it·ism** (fā′vər ə tiz′əm *or* fāv′rə tiz′əm) *n.* **1** a favoring of one or some more than others; having favorites. **2** the state of being a favorite.

fa·vour (fā′vər) See **favor.**

fawn¹ (fon *or* fôn) *n., adj., v.* —*n.* **1** a young deer less than a year old. **2** a light, slightly greyish, brown color.
—*adj.* having the color fawn.
—*v.* of deer, give birth to young. [ME < OF *faon,* ult. < L *fetus* fetus] —**fawn′like′,** *adj.*
☛ *Hom.* **faun.**

fawn² (fon *or* fôn) *v.* **1** cringe and bow to get favor or attention; act slavishly: *Flattering relatives fawned on the rich old man.* **2** of dogs, etc., show fondness by crouching, wagging the tail, licking the hand, etc. [OE *fagnian* < *fægen* fain] —**fawn′er,** *n.* —**fawn′ing·ly,** *adv.*
☛ *Hom.* **faun.**

fay¹ (fā) *n.* fairy. [ME < OF *fae, fee,* ult. < L *fatum.* See FATE.]

fay² (fā) *n. Archaic.* faith: *By my fay!* [ME < OF *fei* < L *fides.* Doublet of FAITH.]

faze (fāz) *v.* **fazed, faz·ing.** *Informal.* disturb; worry; bother; put out. [var. of *feeze,* OE *fesian* drive]
☛ *Hom.* **phase.**
☛ *Usage.* **Faze,** an informal term meaning "worry, bother, or disturb," is almost always used negatively: *His original failure did not faze him. Nothing we said fazed her — she did just as she pleased.*

FBI *U.S.* Federal Bureau of Investigation.

F clef *Music.* the bass clef. See **clef** for picture.

F.D. Fire Department.

Fe iron. [< L *ferrum*]

F.E. Forest Engineer.

fe·al·ty (fē′əl tē) *n., pl.* **-ties. 1** in the Middle Ages, the loyalty and duty owed by a vassal to his feudal lord: *The nobles swore fealty to the king.* **2** loyalty; faithfulness; allegiance. [ME < OF *feaulte* < L *fidelitas.* Doublet of FIDELITY.]

fear (fēr) *n., v.* —*n.* **1** being afraid; wanting to escape from a danger, pain, or evil that one feels is near; dread: *In spite of his fear, he opened the door and stepped out into the dark.* **2** a cause for fear; danger: *There is no fear of our losing.* **3** an uneasy feeling or anxious thought; concern: *He had no fear of opposition.* **4** a feeling of awe and reverence.
for fear of, in order to prevent: *We went as quietly as we could, for fear of arousing the dog.*
without fear or favor, impartially; justly.
—*v.* **1** feel fear. **2** feel fear of. **3** have an uneasy feeling or anxious thought; feel concern. **4** have awe and reverence for: *to fear God.* [OE *fær* peril]
☛ *Syn. n.* 1. **Fear, dread, alarm** = the disagreeable feeling that comes over a person when danger or harm threatens. **Fear** is the general word, meaning "being afraid": *The knight felt no fear in the midst of battle.* **Dread** applies to the fear that comes from knowing something unpleasant or frightening will happen or from expecting danger, often unknown or uncertain: *He has a constant dread of losing his job.* **Alarm** applies to startled or excited fear,

hat, āge, fär; let, ēqual, tėrm; it, īce
hot, ōpen, ôrder; oil, out; cup, pùt, rüle,
əbove, takən, pencəl, lemən, circəs

ch, child; ng, long; sh, ship
th, thin; ᴛʜ, then; zh, measure

coming from the sudden appearance of danger: *The explosion caused widespread alarm.*

fear·ful (fēr′fəl) *adj.* **1** causing fear; terrible; dreadful: *The conflagration was a fearful sight.* **2** full of fear; afraid: *fearful of the dark.* **3** showing or caused by fear: *She cast a fearful glance about her.* **4** *Informal.* very bad, unpleasant, etc.: *a fearful cold.* —**fear′ful·ly,** *adv.* —**fear′ful·ness,** *n.*

fear·less (fēr′lis) *adj.* without fear; afraid of nothing; brave; daring. —**fear′less·ly,** *adv.* —**fear′less·ness,** *n.*

fear·some (fēr′səm) *adj.* **1** causing fear; frightful: *a fearsome sight.* **2** timid; afraid: *fearsome of danger.* —**fear′some·ly,** *adv.* —**fear′some·ness,** *n.*

fea·sance (fē′zəns) *n. Law.* the doing or performance of a condition, obligation, duty, etc.

fea·si·bil·i·ty (fē′zə bil′ə tē) *n.* the quality of being easily done or carried out.

fea·si·ble (fē′zə bəl) *adj.* **1** capable of being done or carried out easily; practicable: *The committee selected the plan that seemed most feasible.* **2** likely; probable: *The witness's explanation of the accident sounded feasible.* **3** suitable; convenient: *The road was too rough to be feasible for travel by automobile.* [ME < OF *faisable,* ult. < L *facere* do] —**fea′si·ble·ness,** *n.* —**fea′si·bly,** *adv.*
☛ *Syn.* 1. See note at **possible.**

feast (fēst) *n., v.* —*n.* **1** an elaborate meal prepared for a number of guests on some special occasion. **2** an unusually delicious or abundant meal. **3** something that gives pleasure or joy; a special treat: *a feast for the eyes.* **4** a religious festival or celebration: *Christmas and Easter are the most important Christian feasts.*
—*v.* **1** have a feast. **2** provide with a feast: *The queen feasted the ambassadors.* **3** give pleasure or joy to: *We feasted our eyes on the magnificent view.* [ME < OF < L *festa* festal ceremonies] —**feast′er,** *n.*
☛ *Syn. n.* 1. **Feast, banquet** = an elaborate meal with many guests. **Feast** emphasizes the abundance, fineness, and richness of the food and drink, served to a large number in celebration of a special occasion: *We went to the family feast.* **Banquet** emphasizes the formality of the celebration and applies particularly to a formal dinner given in rich surroundings: *A banquet was given by the town to honor the returning hero.*

feast day a day set aside as a celebration of some religious festival, or in honor of some person, event, or thing.

feat (fēt) *n.* a great or unusual deed; an act showing great skill, daring, strength, etc. [ME < OF *fait* < L *factum* (thing) done. Doublet of FACT.]
☛ *Hom.* **feet.**
☛ *Syn.* See note at **exploit.**

feath·er (feᴛʜ′ər) *n., v.* —*n.* **1** one of the light, thin growths that cover a bird's skin. Because they are soft and light, feathers are often used to fill pillows. **2** something like a feather in shape or lightness. **3** the act of feathering an oar. **4** *Archery.* **a** a feather or something like it attached to the end of an arrow to direct its flight.
feather in one's cap, something to be proud of.
in feather, covered with feathers.
in fine (or **high** or **good**) **feather,** in very good humor; exuberantly happy: *We were all in fine feather the first day on the trail.*
—*v.* **1** supply or cover with feathers. **2** grow like feathers. **3** move like feathers. **4** turn (an oar) after a stroke so that the blade is flat and keep it that way until the next stroke begins. **5** turn (the blade of an airplane propeller) to decrease wind resistance. **6** touch or apply pressure lightly: *The driver feathered his brakes to slow down on the slippery road.* **7** touch (the strings of a violin, etc.) very lightly with a bow.
feather (one's) nest, take advantage of chances to get rich. [OE *fether*] —**feath′er·less,** *adj.* —**feath′er·like′,** *adj.*

feather bed a soft, warm mattress filled with feathers.

feath·er·bed·ding (feᴛʜ′ər bed′ing) *n.* the requiring of an employer to pay more employees than he considers are needed, or to pay full wages for unnecessary work or for restricted output.

feath·er·brain (feᴛʜ′ər brān′) *n.* a silly, foolish, weak-minded person.

feath·er·brained (feᴛʜ′ər brānd′) *adj.* silly; foolish; scatterbrained: *That was a featherbrained thing to do!*

feath·ered (feᴛʜ′ərd) *adj.* **1** having feathers; covered with feathers. **2** equipped and supplied with feathers: *a feathered dart.* **3** swift; rapid: *birds in their feathered flight.*

feath·er·edge (feᴛн′ər ej′) *n.* a very thin edge.

feath·er·edged (feᴛн′ər ejd′) *adj.* having a very thin edge.

feath·er·stitch (feᴛн′ər stich′) *n., v.* —*n.* a zigzag embroidery stitch. —*v.* **1** make zigzag embroidery stitches. **2** decorate with such stitches.

feath·er·weight (feᴛн′ər wāt′) *n., adj.* —*n.* **1** a very light thing or person. **2** a boxer who weighs between 55 and 57 kilograms. **3** an unimportant person or thing: *He is a featherweight on the political scene.*
—*adj.* **1** very light. **2** of or having to do with featherweights. **3** unimportant.

feath·er·y (feᴛн′ər ē) *adj.* **1** having feathers; covered with feathers. **2** like feathers; soft, light, etc. —**feath′er·i·ness,** *n.*

feat·ly (fēt′lē) *adv. Archaic.* **1** nimbly; skilfully. **2** suitably; properly. **3** neatly; elegantly.

fea·ture (fē′chər) *n., v.* **-tured, -tur·ing.** —*n.* **1** a part of the face. The eyes, nose, mouth, chin, and forehead are features. **2 features,** *pl.* the face. **3** a distinct part or quality; something that stands out and attracts attention. **4** a main attraction, especially a full-length motion picture. **5** a special article, comic strip, etc. in a newspaper or magazine.
—*v.* **1** make a feature of; give special prominence to: *The movie featured an outstanding actor. The store was featuring radios in its sale.* **2** be featured; have a prominent part (*in*): *She features in several recent films.* **3** *Informal.* be like in features. [ME < OF *feture* < L *factura* < *facere* do]
☛ *Syn. n.* **3. Feature, characteristic, trait** = a quality of a person or thing. **Feature** applies to a quality or detail that stands out and attracts attention: *The main features of the resort are its climate and scenery.* **Characteristic** applies to a quality or feature that expresses or shows the character or nature of a person, thing, or class or distinguishes it from others: *Ruggedness was a characteristic of the early pioneers in Canada.* **Trait** applies particularly to a distinguishing feature of the character or mind of a person: *Cheerfulness is his outstanding trait.*
☛ *Usage.* The term **feature article** or **feature story** is often used for a newspaper or magazine article that gives the writer's feelings and opinions about an event or situation, as opposed to a **news story,** which gives the facts without personal comment.

fea·tured (fē′chərd) *adj.* **1** having a certain kind of facial feature (*used only in compounds*): *a hard-featured man.* **2** shown or advertised as a special feature: *The featured entertainers this week are a group from Winnipeg.*

fea·ture·less (fē′chər lis) *adj.* without striking features; not distinctive or impressive: *a featureless landscape.*

Feb. February.

feb·ri·fuge (feb′rə fyüj′) *n., adj.* —*n.* **1** a medicine to reduce fever. **2** a cooling drink. —*adj.* curing or lessening fever. [< F. Cf. FEVERFEW.]

fe·brile (fē′brīl or fē′brəl, feb′rīl or feb′rəl) *adj.* **1** of fever; feverish. **2** caused by fever. [< Med.L *febrilis* < *febris* fever]

Feb·ru·ar·y (feb′rü er′ē or feb′yü er′ē) *n., pl.* **-ar·ies.** the second month of the year. It has 28 days except in leap years, when it has 29. [< L *Februarius* < *februa,* pl., the feast of purification celebrated on Feb. 15]

fe·cal (fē′kəl) *adj.* having to do with feces. Also, **faecal.**

fe·ces (fē′sēz) *n.pl.* the waste matter discharged from the intestines. Also, **faeces.** [< L *faeces,* pl., dregs]

feck·less (fek′lis) *adj.* futile; ineffective. [< *feck* vigor, var. of *fect* < *effect*]

fe·cund (fē′kənd or fek′ənd) *adj.* fruitful; productive; fertile: *Edison had a fecund mind.* [< F < L *fecundus*]

fe·cun·di·ty (fi kun′də tē) *n.* fruitfulness; fertility.

fed¹ (fed) *v.* pt. and pp. of **feed.**

fed² (fed) *n. Slang.* **1** a member or official of the federal government. **2 the feds,** *pl.* the federal government. **3** *U.S.* an agent or official of the F.B.I.

Fed·a·yeen (fed′ä yēn′) *n., pl.* **-yeen.** in Egypt, a commando or guerrilla fighter. [< colloquial Arabic *fidā'iyīn,* pl. of literary Arabic *fidā'ī* (literally) one who sacrifices himself < *fidā'* redemption; sacrifice]

fed·er·al (fed′ər əl or fed′rəl) *adj., n.* —*adj.* **1** formed by an agreement between groups establishing a central organization to handle their common affairs while the parties to the agreement keep control of local affairs: *The Canadian Federation of Agriculture is a federal organization of farm representatives.* **2** of or having to do with the central government formed in this way: *Parliament is the federal lawmaking body of Canada.* **3** Also, **Federal,** of or having to do with the central government. **4 Federal,** in the United States: **a** of or having to do with the Federal Party. **b** supporting the central government during the Civil War.

—*n.* **Federal,** in the United States, a supporter or soldier of the central government during the Civil War. [< L *foedus, foederis* compact] —**fed′er·al·ly,** *adv.*

Federal Bureau of Investigation a United States government bureau that investigates violations of federal laws, except those concerning postal service, currency, taxes, etc., which are under the jurisdiction of other federal agencies.

Federal Court of Canada a court with trial and appeal divisions, that deals with cases involving revenues of the Crown, claims in relation to patent, copyright, or trademark, claims under maritime law, and other specialized matters, and that has exclusive jurisdiction over suits against the Crown in federal affairs.

Federal Government 1 the government of Canada, located in Ottawa. Its responsibilities are specified by the British North America Act. **2** the Prime Minister and his Cabinet. Also, **federal government.**

fed·er·al·ism (fed′ər əl iz′əm or fed′rəl iz′əm) *n.* the federal principle of government.

fed·er·al·ist (fed′ər əl ist or fed′rəl ist) *n.* a person who favors the federal principle of government.

fed·er·al·ize (fed′ər əl īz′ or fed′rəl īz′) *v.* **-ized, -iz·ing. 1** put under the control of the federal government. **2** unite into a federal union. —**fed′er·al·i·za′tion,** *n.*

fed·er·ate (*v.* fed′ər āt′; *adj.* fed′ər it or fed′rit) *v.* **-at·ed, -at·ing;** *adj.* —*v.* join in a league, federal union, etc. —*adj.* formed into a federation; federated. [< L *foederare* league together < *foedus, -deris* compact]

fed·er·a·tion (fed′ər ā′shən) *n.* **1** the act or process of federating, especially the formation of a federal union. **2** a nation formed by federation; a union of a number of separate provinces, states, etc.: *Canada and the United States are both federations.* **3** a union formed by agreement of organizations, states, or nations; league: *a federation of student groups.*

fed·er·a·tive (fed′ər ə tiv or fed′ər ā′tiv) *adj.* of, like, or forming a federation.

fe·do·ra (fi dô′rə) *n.* a man's soft felt hat with a curved brim and a crown creased lengthwise. [apparently from the play *Fédora* by the French playwright Sardou]

fee (fē) *n., v.* **feed, fee·ing.** —*n.* **1** a sum of money asked or paid for a service or privilege; charge: *Doctors and lawyers get fees for their services.* **2 fees,** *pl.* the money paid for instruction at a school or university. **3** in a feudal society, land held by a vassal on condition of homage and service to a superior lord who has actual ownership of it; fief. **4** an inherited or heritable estate in land. See also **fee simple** and **fee tail. 5** *Obsolete.* gratuity; tip.
hold in fee, have absolute legal possession of.
—*v. Rare.* give a fee to. [ME < AF var. of OF *fieu* < Med.L *feudum* fief? < Gmc.; cf. OE *feoh* money, cattle]

fee·ble (fē′bəl) *adj.* **-bler, -blest. 1** lacking strength; weak: *a feeble old man.* **2** weak intellectually or morally: *a feeble mind.* **3** lacking in force; ineffective: *a feeble attempt.* **4** lacking in volume, brightness, etc.: *a feeble cry.* [ME < OF *feble* < L *flebilis* lamentable < *flere* weep] —**fee′ble·ness,** *n.* —**fee′bly,** *adv.*

fee·ble–mind·ed (fē′bəl mīn′did) *adj.* weak in mind; lacking normal intelligence. —**fee′ble–mind′ed·ly,** *adv.* —**fee′ble–mind′ed·ness,** *n.*

feed (fēd) *v.* **fed, feed·ing;** *n.* —*v.* **1** give food to. **2** give as food to: *Feed this grain to the chickens.* **3** of animals, eat: *Don't disturb the cows while they're feeding.* **4** supply with material: *to feed a machine; to feed a furnace.* **5** relay (radio or television signals) to a transmitting station for broadcast. **6** satisfy; gratify: *Praise fed his vanity.* **7** nourish: *He fed his anger with thoughts of revenge.* **8** *Theatre.* supply (another actor) with cues. **9** *Sports.* pass or give (the puck, ball, etc.) to a teammate.
fed up, *Slang.* **a** fed too much. **b** bored; tired.
feed on or **upon, a** live at the expense of; prey on. **b** derive satisfaction, support, etc. from.
—*n.* **1** food for livestock, especially a prepared mixture of grain, etc. **2** an allowance or amount of such food given at one time. **3** *Informal.* a meal, especially a large one: *They gave us a good feed.* **4** the action or process of feeding, especially supplying material to a machine. **5** the material supplied. **6** the mechanism or system by which something is fed, as material for a machine, radio signals, etc. **7** *Theatre.* **a** a line or cue to which a comedian replies with a line that gets a laugh. **b** a person who gives such cues. **8** *Sports.* the act or an instance of passing a puck, ball, etc. [OE *fēdan* < *fōda* food]
☛ *Syn. n.* **1. Feed, fodder** = food for animals and fowls: *Give the chicken their feed.* **Fodder** applies to coarse or dried feed, like alfalfa, hay, corn, or other plants fed to horses, cattle, pigs, or sheep: *Put some fodder in the bins.*

feed·back (fēd′bak′) *n.* **1** the return to a system, machine, etc. of part of its output in order to change or control future output. **2** the modification of a biological or psychological reaction or

process by the activity of some of its products. 3 *Informal.* information on the results of one's actions that will influence one's future decisions or actions.

feed·bag (fēd′bag′) *n.* a bag that can be hung over a horse's head for holding oats, etc.; nose bag.
put on the feedbag, *Slang.* eat.

feed·box (fēd′boks′) *n.* 1 a box used to hold food for livestock. 2 a box containing the mechanism for feeding a machine.

feed·er (fēd′ər) *n.* 1 a person or thing that feeds. 2 a device that supplies food to a person or animal: *a bird feeder.* 3 anything that supplies something else with material. A brook is a feeder for a river. A branch that brings traffic to the main line is a feeder. 4 *Electricity.* a wire or cable used to conduct electricity from a source to a distribution point.

feeder line a branch airline, railway, pipeline, etc.

feed·lot (fēd′lot) *n.* a plot of land for feeding and fattening livestock for the market.

feel (fēl) *v.* **felt, feel·ing;** *n.* —*v.* 1 touch: *Feel this cloth.* 2 try to find or make (one's way) by touch: *He felt his way across the room when the lights went out.* 3 test or examine by touching: *to feel a person's pulse, to feel a child's forehead to see if he has a fever.* 4 search by touch; grope: *He felt in his pockets for a dime.* 5 find out by touching: *Feel how cold my hands are.* 6 be aware of: *to feel the cool breeze.* 7 having the feeling of being; be: *She feels well.* 8 give the feeling of being; seem: *The air feels cold.* 9 have in one's mind; experience: *He feels joy.* 10 have pity or sympathy: *She feels for all who suffer.* 11 be influenced or affected by: *The ship feels her helm.* 12 think; believe; consider: *I feel that we will win.*
feel like, *Informal.* **a** have a desire for; want: *I feel like an ice-cream cone.* **b** seem as if it is going to: *It feels like rain.* **c** seem like to the sense of touch: *the cat's fur felt like silk.*
feel out, find out about in a cautious way.
—*n.* 1 the touch: *I like the feel of silk.* 2 the way in which something feels to the touch: *Wet soap has a greasy feel.* 3 the sense of touch. 4 the act of feeling. [OE *fēlan*]

feel·er (fēl′ər) *n.* 1 a special part of an animal's body for touching with. An insect's antennae are its feelers. 2 a suggestion, remark, hint, question, etc. made to find out what others are thinking or planning. 3 a person or thing that feels.

feel·ing (fēl′ing) *n., adj.* —*n.* 1 the sense of touch: *By feeling we can distinguish between something hard and something soft.* 2 a sensation experienced through this sense: *a feeling of pain.* 3 the ability or power to experience physical sensation: *She had no feeling in her left hand.* 4 emotion: *Joy, sorrow, fear, and anger are feelings.* 5 the capacity for emotion; sensibility: *She was guided by feeling rather than thought.* 6 sensitivity to the higher or more refined emotions: *His work shows both feeling and taste.* 7 pity; sympathy. 8 an opinion; sentiment: *Her feeling was that right would win.* 9 the quality felt to belong to anything: *There is a weird feeling about the place.* 10 **feelings,** *pl.* susceptibilities: *You hurt her feelings with that remark.*
—*adj.* full of feeling; sensitive, emotional. —**feel′ing·ly,** *adv.*
☛ *Syn. n.* 4. Feeling, emotion, passion = a pleasant or painful mental state produced in a person in reaction to a stimulus of some kind. **Feeling** is the general word: *He had a vague feeling of hope.* **Emotion** = a strong and moving feeling, such as love, fear, sorrow, joy, etc.: *She was so overwhelmed with emotion that she couldn't speak for a moment.* **Passion** = violent emotion, usually overcoming the power to think clearly and taking complete possession of a person: *In a passion of rage he smashed the watch.*

fee simple *Law.* an estate in land without any limitation on inheritance or transfer of ownership; in Canada it denotes full ownership, subject to the rights of the Crown.

feet (fēt) *n.* pl. of **foot.**
carry off one's feet, **a** make very enthusiastic. **b** impress.
sit at one's feet, be a pupil or admirer of.
stand on one's own feet, be independent.
☛ *Hom.* **feat.**

fee tail *Law.* an estate in land subject to specified restrictions on who may inherit it.

feign (fān) *v.* 1 put on a false appearance of; pretend: *Some animals feign death when in danger.* 2 make up with intent to deceive; invent falsely: *to feign an excuse.* 3 *Archaic.* represent fictitiously. 4 *Archaic.* imagine: *The phoenix is a feigned bird.* [ME < OF *feign-,* a stem of *feindre* < L *fingere* form] —**feign′er,** *n.*
☛ *Hom.* **fain.**

feigned (fānd) *adj.* 1 imagined; not real. 2 pretended: *a feigned attack.* 3 invented to deceive: *a feigned headache.* —**feign′ed·ly,** *adv.*

feint (fānt) *n., v.* —*n.* 1 a movement intended to deceive; pretended blow; sham attack. 2 a false appearance; pretence. —*v.* make a pretended blow or sham attack: *The fighter feinted with his right hand and struck with his left.* [< F *feinte* < *feindre* feign]
☛ *Hom.* **faint.**

feist·y (fīs′tē) *adj.,* **feist·i·er, feist·i·est.** *Slang.* 1 aggressively energetic and exuberant. 2 touchy or quarrelsome. —**feist′i·ness,** *n.*

---

hat, āge, fär; let, ēqual, tèrm; it, īce
hot, ōpen, ôrder; oil, out; cup, pùt, rüle,
abŏve, takən, pencəl, lemən, circəs

ch, child; ng, long; sh, ship
th, thin; ᴛʜ, then; zh, measure

feld·spar (feld′spär′) *n.* any of several crystalline minerals composed mostly of aluminum silicates. Also **felspar.** [< *feld-* (< G *Feldspar,* literally, field spar) + *spar³*]

fe·lic·i·tate (fə lis′ə tāt′) *v.* **-tat·ed, -tat·ing.** formally express good wishes to; congratulate: *John's friends felicitated him on his good fortune.* [< LL *felicitare* < *felix* happy]

fe·lic·i·ta·tion (fə lis′ə tā′shən) *n.* a formal expression of good wishes; congratulation.

fe·lic·i·tous (fə lis′ə təs) *adj.* 1 well chosen for the occasion; unusually appropriate: *The poem was full of striking and felicitous similes.* 2 having a gift for apt speech. —**fe·lic′i·tous·ly,** *adv.* —**fe·lic′i·tous·ness,** *n.*

fe·lic·i·ty (fə lis′ə tē) *n., pl.* **-ties.** 1 happiness; bliss. 2 good fortune; blessing. 3 a pleasing aptness in expression; appropriateness; grace: *The famous writer phrased his ideas with felicity.* 4 a happy turn of thought; well-chosen phrase. [ME < OF < L *felicitas* < *felix* happy]
☛ *Syn.* 1. See note at **happiness.**

fe·line (fē′līn) *adj.* —*adj.* 1 of or having to do with the cat family. 2 catlike; stealthy; sly: *The hunter stalked the deer with noiseless feline movements.* —*n.* any animal belonging to the cat family. Lions, tigers, and panthers are felines. [< L *felis* cat]

fell¹ (fel) *v.* pt. of **fall.**

fell² (fel) *v., n.* —*v.* 1 cause to fall; knock down: *One blow felled him to the ground.* 2 cut down (a tree). 3 turn down and stitch one edge of (a seam) over the other.
—*n.* 1 all the trees cut down in one season. 2 a seam made by felling. [OE *fellan < feallan* fall]

fell³ (fel) *adj.* 1 cruel; fierce; terrible: *a fell blow.* 2 deadly; destructive: *a fell disease.* [ME < OF *fel* < VL *fello.* See FELON¹.]

fell⁴ (fel) *n.* the skin or hide of an animal. [OE. Related to FILM.]

fell⁵ (fel) *n.* 1 a stretch of high moorland. 2 a hill; mountain. [< ON *fiall*]

fel·la (fel′ə) *n. Slang.* fellow.

fel·la·gha (fə lä′gə) *n., pl.* **-ghas** or **-gha.** an Arab guerrilla fighting in Algeria or Tunisia. [< Arabic *fallaq* (literally) outlaw]

fel·lah¹ (fel′ə) *n., pl.* **fel·la·hin** (fel′ə hēn′). a peasant or farm laborer in Egypt and other Arabic-speaking countries. [< Arabic *fallāh* husbandman]

fel·lah² (fel′ə) *n. Slang.* fellow.

fell·er¹ (fel′ər) *n.* 1 a person or thing that fells. 2 a part attached to a sewing machine to fell seams.

fell·er² (fel′ər) *n. Slang.* fellow.

fel·loe (fel′ō) *n.* the circular rim of a wheel into which the outer ends of the spokes are inserted. Also, **felly.** See **wheel** for picture. [var. of FELLY]

fel·low (fel′ō; *for defs. 1 to 4, often* fel′ə) *n.* 1 *Informal.* a man or boy (*often used as a familiar form of address*): *There were three fellows in the car. Never mind, old fellow! 2 Informal.* boyfriend: *She's got a new fellow.* 3 a companion or associate. 4 one of the same class or rank; equal: *The world has not his fellow.* 5 the other one of a pair; mate. 6 a graduate student who has a fellowship in a university or college. 7 an honored member of a learned society. 8 (*adj.*) belonging to the same class; united by the same work, interests, aims, etc.; being in the same or a like condition: *fellow citizens, fellow sufferers.*
hail fellow well met, very friendly.
[OE *fēolaga* < ON *fēlagi* partner (literally, fee-layer)]

fellow feeling sympathy.

fellow man or **fel·low-man** (fel′ō man′) *n.* a fellow human being; another human being or human beings in general, thought of as one's comrades or peers.

fel·low·ship (fel′ō ship′) *n.* 1 companionship; friendliness. 2 a taking part with others; sharing. 3 a group of people having similar tastes, interests, etc.; brotherhood; corporation. 4 a position or sum of money given to a person, such as a graduate student, to enable him to go on with his studies. 5 the relationship existing among those holding the same religious beliefs; communion.

fellow traveller or **traveler** a person sympathizing with, though not a member of, a political movement or party, especially the Communist Party.

fel·ly (fel′ē) n., pl. -lies. felloe. [OE felg]

fel·on[1] (fel′ən) n., adj. —n. a person who has committed a felony. —adj. Archaic. wicked or cruel. [ME < OF felon < L; ultimate origin uncertain]

fel·on[2] (fel′ən) n. a painful, usually pus-filled infection on a finger or toe, especially near the nail; whitlow. [origin uncertain]

fe·lo·ni·ous (fə lō′nē əs) adj., adv. —adj. 1 that is a felony; criminal. 2 wicked; villainous. —fe·lo′ni·ous·ly, adv. —fe·lo′ni·ous·ness, n.

fel·o·ny (fel′ə nē) n., pl. -nies. a crime regarded by the law as grave, or major, such as arson, rape, or murder. The equivalent in Canadian law of the term felony is indictable offence.

fel·spar (fel′spär′) n. feldspar.

felt[1] (felt) v. pt. and pp. of feel.

felt[2] (felt) n., v. —n. 1 a kind of cloth that is not woven but is made by rolling and pressing together wool, hair, or fur, used to make hats, slippers, and pads. 2 something made of felt. 3 (adjl.) made of felt: a felt hat. 4 Papermaking. a belt, usually of textile material, that carries the freshly formed paper through the machine. —v. 1 make into felt. 2 cover with felt. 3 of fibres, become pressed or matted together like felt. [OE]

felt pen a pen similar to a ballpoint, but having a point or tip made of felt and using a more liquid ink.

fe·luc·ca (fə luk′ə) n. a long, narrow, lateen-rigged ship similar to a galley, formerly used especially by privateers because of its speed. [< Ital. < Arabic fulk ship]

fem. female; feminine.

fe·male (fē′māl) n., adj. —n. 1 a woman or girl. 2 an animal belonging to the sex that gives birth to young or produces eggs. 3 Botany. **a** a flower having a pistil or pistils and no stamens. **b** a plant bearing only flowers with pistils. —adj. 1 of or having to do with women or girls. 2 belonging to the sex that gives birth to young or produces eggs. 3 Botany. **a** designating or having to do with any reproductive structure that produces or contains elements that need fertilization from the male element. **b** bearing flowers that contain a pistil or pistils but no stamens: a female plant. 4 of pipe fittings, etc., having a hollow part into which a corresponding male part fits. [ME < OF < femelle < L femella, dim. of femina woman; form influenced by male]

fem·i·nine (fem′ə nin) adj., n. —adj. 1 like a woman or women; having qualities considered characteristic of women. 2 suited to women: feminine fashions. 3 effeminate. 4 Grammar. belonging to or designating the grammatical gender that includes some words for female persons and animals as well as a wide variety of other kinds of referents. In French, the words femme (woman), maison (house), and lune (moon) are feminine; in German, the words Frau (woman), Tür (door), and Sonne (sun) are feminine. Compare **masculine**, **neuter**. —n. Grammar. 1 the feminine gender. 2 a word or form in the feminine gender. [ME < OF < L femininus < femina woman] —fem′i·nine·ly, adv. —fem′i·nine·ness, n.

feminine rhyme a rhyme of two syllables of which the second is unstressed (as, motion, notion), or of three syllables of which the second and third are unstressed (as, happily, snappily).

fem·i·nin·i·ty (fem′ə nin′ə tē) n. 1 a feminine quality or condition. 2 women.

fem·i·nism (fem′ə niz′əm) n. a doctrine that favors increased rights and activities for women.

fem·i·nist (fem′ə nist) n. a person who believes in or favors feminism.

femme fa·tale (fäm′ fä täl′) pl. femmes fa·tales (fäm′ fä täl′). French. a disastrously seductive woman; siren.

fem·o·ral (fem′ə rəl) adj. of the femur. [< L femur, femoris thigh]

fe·mur (fē′mər) n., pl. fe·murs, fem·o·ra (fem′ə rə). thighbone. [< L femur thigh]

fen[1] (fen) n. Brit. a marsh; swamp; bog. [OE fenn]

fen[2] (fen) n., pl. fen. 1 a unit of money in the People's Republic of China, equal to ⅟₁₀₀ of a yuan or ⅟₁₀ of a chiao. 2 a coin worth one fen. [< Chinese]

fence (fens) n., v. fenced, fenc·ing. —n. 1 a railing, wall, or other means of enclosing a yard, garden, field, farm, etc. to show where the property ends or to keep people or animals out or in. 2 a person who buys and sells stolen goods. 3 a place where stolen goods are bought and sold. 4 a guard, guide, or gauge designed to regulate the movements of a tool or machine.

mend (one's) **fences**, Informal. **a** look after one's political interests

at home, as in preparation for renomination. **b** improve one's relations and popularity in any area.

on the fence, Informal. not having made up one's mind which side to take; doubtful. —v. 1 put a fence around; enclose with a fence; keep out or in with a fence. 2 separate as by a fence; keep apart or at a distance: The patents were used to fence in and block off other manufacturers. 3 fight, now only in sport, with long, slender swords called foils; compete in fencing (def. 1). 4 use evasive tactics, as in debate; parry or quibble. 5 buy and sell stolen goods. [var. of defence]

fenc·er (fen′sər) n. 1 a person who fences with a sword or foil. 2 a person who makes or mends fences.

fenc·ing (fen′sing) n. 1 the art of fighting, now only as a sport, with swords or foils. 2 the act or practice of parrying the points of one's opponent in a debate, discussion, or argument. 3 the material for making fences. 4 fences.

fend (fend) v. 1 Archaic. defend. 2 resist.

fend for (oneself), Informal. provide for oneself; get along by one's own efforts.

fend off, ward off; keep off. [var. of defend]

fend·er (fen′dər) n. 1 a curved protective covering over the wheels of an automobile, truck, etc.; mudguard. 2 a guard, made of rubber, rope, plastic, etc., hung over the sides of a boat or attached to a dock to protect the boat in docking. 3 a device such as a frame attached to the front of a locomotive, streetcar, etc. to reduce injury to an animal or person in case of a collision. 4 a metal guard, frame, or screen in front of a fireplace to keep hot coals and sparks from the room. 5 anything that keeps or wards something off. [var. of DEFENDER.]

fen·es·tra·tion (fen′is trā′shən) n. 1 the arrangement of windows in a building. 2 Medicine. the operation of making an opening into the labyrinth or semicircular canal of the ear to eliminate deafness caused by obstruction of sound waves. [< L fenestrare provide with windows < fenestra window]

Fe·ni·an (fē′nē ən or fēn′yən) n., adj. —n. 1 a member of an Irish secret organization founded in the United States about 1858 for the purpose of overthrowing English rule in Ireland. 2 a member of a group of warriors in Irish legend. —adj. of or having to do with the Fenians. [< OIrish fēne, a name of the ancient inhabitants of Ireland, confused with Irish fianna, a legendary body of warriors]

fen·nel (fen′əl) n. a perennial European herb (Foeniculum vulgare) of the parsley family cultivated for its aromatic seeds and leaves which are used to flavor food. [OE fenol < VL *fenuclum, ult. < L fenum hay]

fen·ny (fen′ē) adj. 1 marshy; swampy; boggy. 2 growing or living in fens. [OE fennig < fenn fen]

feoff (fef) See fief.

fe·ral[1] (fēr′əl) adj. 1 wild; untamed. 2 brutal; savage. [< L fera beast]

fe·ral[2] (fē′rəl) adj. 1 deadly or fatal: a feral disease. 2 gloomy; funereal. [< L feralis of the dead, of funeral rites]

fer·ma·ta (fer mah′tə) n. Music. a pause (def. 4).

fer·ment (v. fər ment′; n. fėr′ment) v., n. —v. 1 undergo a gradual chemical change, giving off bubbles of gas, and changing in character. Vinegar is formed when cider ferments. 2 cause this chemical change in (something). 3 cause unrest in; excite; agitate. 4 be excited; seethe with agitation or unrest. —n. 1 a substance or organism that causes fermentation: Yeast is used as a ferment in brewing beer. 2 excitement; agitation; unrest. [< L fermentare < fermentum leaven < fervere boil] —fer·ment′a·ble, adj. —fer·ment′er, n.

fer·men·ta·tion (fėr′men tā′shən) n. 1 the act or process of fermenting. 2 excitement; agitation; unrest: There was a long period of fermentation before the outbreak of revolution. 3 a chemical change caused by a ferment.

fer·mi·um (fėr′mē əm) n. an artificial, radio-active, metallic element. Symbol: Fm; at.no. 100; at.wt. (257); half-life approx. 80 days. [< Enrico Fermi, an Italian-born American physicist]

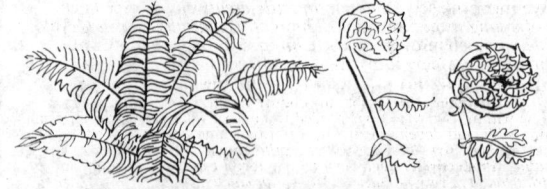

An ostrich fern, common in the Maritimes, with fiddleheads of this fern shown at the right

fern (fėrn) n. any of a class (Polypodiopsida, also called Filicinae)

of flowerless vascular plants reproducing by means of spores. [OE *fearn*] —**fern′like′**, *adj.*

fern·er·y (fėr′nər ē *or* fėrn′rē) *n., pl.* **-er·ies. 1** a place where ferns are grown for ornament. **2** a container in which ferns are grown for ornament.

fern·y (fėr′nē) *adj.* of, like, or overgrown with ferns.

fe·ro·cious (fə rō′shəs) *adj.* savage; fierce. [< L *ferox, -ocis* fierce] —**fe·ro′cious·ly**, *adv.*
☛ *Syn.* See note at **fierce.**

fe·ro·cious·ness (fə rō′shəs nəs) *n.* ferocity.

fe·roc·i·ty (fə ros′ə tē) *n., pl.* **-ties.** savage behavior; fierceness. [< L *ferocitas* < *ferox* fierce]

–ferous *suffix.* producing; containing; conveying, as in *metalliferous.* [< *-fer* (< *ferre* bear) + E *-ous*]

fer·ret (fer′it) *n., v.* —*n.* **1** a domesticated albino form of the European polecat used especially for hunting rodents. **2** black-footed ferret.
—*v.* **1** hunt with ferrets. **2** drive out of hiding (*usually used with* **out**): *to ferret out a criminal.* **3** find or find out by persistent searching (*usually used with* **out**): *to ferret out the truth of the matter.* [ME < OF *fuiret*, ult. < L *fur* thief]

fer·ric (fer′ik) *adj.* of or containing iron, especially trivalent iron. [< L *ferrum* iron]

ferric oxide a reddish-brown compound of iron and oxygen found naturally as hematite and produced chemically as a powder for use as a pigment, abrasive, etc. *Formula:* Fe_2O_3

Fer·ris wheel (fer′is) a large, revolving framework of steel like an upright wheel, equipped with swinging seats that hang from its rim: *Ferris wheels are found in the amusement areas of fairs, exhibitions, and carnivals.* [< G. W. G. Ferris (1859-1896), an American engineer, the inventor]

ferro– *combining form.* iron; derivation from iron, as in *ferrochromium.* [< L *ferrum* iron]

fer·ro·chro·mi·um (fer′ō krō′mē əm) *n.* an alloy of iron and chromium.

fer·ro·con·crete (fer′ō kon′krēt *or* -kon krēt′) *n.* concrete strengthened by a metal framework embedded in it; reinforced concrete.

fer·ro·man·ga·nese (fer′ō mang′gə nēz′ *or* -mang′gə nēs′) *n.* an alloy of iron, manganese, and sometimes carbon, used for making tough steel.

fer·rous (fer′əs) *adj.* of or containing divalent iron. [< L *ferrum* iron]

fer·ru·gi·nous (fə rü′jə nəs) *adj.* **1** of or containing iron; like that of iron. **2** reddish brown like rust. [< L *ferruginus* < *ferrugo* iron rust < *ferrum* iron]

fer·rule (fer′əl *or* fer′əl) *n.* a metal ring or cap put around the end of a cane, wooden handle, umbrella, etc. to strengthen and protect it. Also, **ferule.** [earlier *verrel*, < OF *virelle* < L *viriola*, dim. of *viriae* bracelets; form influenced by L *ferrum* iron]

fer·ry (fer′ē) *n., pl.* **-ries;** *v.* **-ried, -ry·ing.** —*n.* **1** a boat that carries people and goods back and forth across a river or narrow stretch of water. **2** a place where a ferry operates. **3** delivering aircraft to a destination for flying them.
—*v.* **1** carry (people and goods) back and forth on a ferry, etc., especially as a regular service: *Hundreds of cars are ferried across Northumberland Strait every day.* **2** cross on a ferry: *They ferried to Wolfe Island last Sunday.* **3** carry back and forth across a wide stretch of water in an aircraft. **4** fly an aircraft to a destination for delivery. [OE *ferian* < *fær* fare]
☛ *Hom.* **faery, fairy.**

fer·ry·boat (fer′ē bōt′) *n.* ferry (def. 1).

fer·ry·man (fer′ē mən) *n., pl.* **-men. 1** a person who owns or has charge of a ferry. **2** a person who works on a ferry.

fer·tile (fėr′tīl *or* fėr′təl) *adj.* **1** capable of reproduction; able to produce seeds, fruit, young, etc. **2** of soil, capable of producing plants, crops, etc.: *Sand is not very fertile.* **3** capable of producing many young; prolific: *Rabbits are fertile creatures for they have litters of young more often than many other animals.* **4** productive of many ideas; inventive: *a fertile mind.* **5** *Biology.* capable of developing into a new individual; fertilized: *Chicks hatch from fertile eggs.* [< L *fertilis* < *ferre* bear] —**fer′tile·ness**, *n.*
☛ *Syn.* **1. Fertile, productive** = able to produce much. **Fertile** emphasizes containing within itself the things needed to nourish what is brought forth and maintain its life and development, and describes things in which seeds or ideas can take root and grow: *The seed fell on fertile ground. He has a fertile imagination.* **Productive** emphasizes bringing forth, especially in abundance: *Those fruit trees are very productive. He is a productive writer.*

Fertile Crescent a fertile, crescent-shaped strip of land on the eastern shore of the Mediterranean. See **Babylonia** for map.

fer·til·i·ty (fėr til′ə tē) *n.* the condition of being fertile.

fer·ti·li·za·tion (fėr′tə lə zā′shən *or* fėr′tə lī zā′shən) *n.* **1** the

hat, āge, fär; let, ēqual, tėrm; it, īce
hot, ōpen, ôrder; oil, out; cup, pùt, rüle,
əbove, takən, pencəl, lemən, circəs

ch, child; ng, long; sh, ship
th, thin; ŦH, then; zh, measure

application of fertilizer. **2** *Biology.* the union of male and female reproductive cells to form a cell that will develop into a new individual.

fer·ti·lize (fėr′tə līz′) *v.* **-lized, -liz·ing. 1** make fertile; make able to produce much: *A crop of alfalfa fertilized the soil by adding nitrates to it.* **2** put fertilizer on. **3** *Biology.* of a male reproductive cell, or sperm, unite with (an egg cell) in fertilization; impregnate.

fer·ti·liz·er (fėr′tə līz′ər) *n.* a person or thing that fertilizes, especially a substance put on land to make it able to produce more. Manure is a common fertilizer.

fer·ule¹ (fer′ül *or* fer′əl) *n., v.* **-uled, -ul·ing.** —*n.* a stick or ruler used for punishing children by striking them, especially on the hand. —*v.* punish with a stick or ruler. [< L *ferula* rod]

fer·ule² (fer′ül *or* fer′əl) See **ferrule.**

fer·ven·cy (fėr′vən sē) *n.* great warmth of feeling; intensity; ardor.

fer·vent (fėr′vənt) *adj.* **1** showing warmth of feeling; ardent; intense: *a fervent plea.* **2** hot; glowing. [< L *fervens, -entis,* ppr. of *fervere* boil] —**fer′vent·ly**, *adv.* —**fer′vent·ness**, *n.*

fer·vid (fėr′vid) *adj.* **1** showing great warmth of feeling; intensely emotional. **2** intensely hot. [< L *fervidus* < *fevere* boil] —**fer′vid·ly**, *adv.* —**fer′vid·ness**, *n.*

fer·vor *or* **fer·vour** (fėr′vər) *n.* **1** great warmth of feeling; intense emotion: *The patriot's voice trembled from the fervor of his emotion.* **2** intense heat. [ME < OF < L *fervor* < *fervere* boil]

fes·cue (fes′kyü) *n.* **1** any of a genus (*Festuca*) of grasses native to temperate and cold regions of the northern hemisphere, some of which are widely cultivated as pasture and fodder grasses and for use in lawn mixtures. **2** a small stick, etc. used as a pointer in teaching children to read. [ME < OF *festu* < L *festuca*]

fess *or* **fesse** (fes) *n. Heraldry.* a wide, horizontal band across the middle of a shield. [ME < OF *fesse, faisse* < L *fascia* band]

fes·ta (fes′tə) *n. Italian.* a holiday; feast; festival; party.

fes·tal (fes′təl) *adj.* of a feast, festival, or holiday; gay; joyous; festive: *A wedding or a birthday is a festal occasion.* [< MF < LL < L *festum* feast]

fes·ter (fes′tər) *v., n.* —*v.* **1** form pus: *The neglected wound festered and became very painful.* **2** cause pain or suffering. **3** cause pain or bitterness; rankle: *Resentment festered in his heart.* **4** decay; rot. —*n.* a sore that forms pus; small ulcer. [ME < OF *festre* < L *fistula* pipe, ulcer. Doublet of FISTULA.]

fes·ti·val (fes′tə vəl) *n.* **1** a day or special time of rejoicing or feasting, often in memory of some great happening: *Christmas and Easter are two festivals of the Christian Church.* **2** a celebration; entertainment: *Every year the city has a music festival during the first week in May.* **3** a competition among drama groups, orchestras, etc. for recognition as the best in the region: *the Dominion Drama Festival.* **4** merry-making; revelry. **5** (*adj.*) having to do with a festival. [< Med.L *festivalis*, ult. < L *festum* feast]

fes·tive (fes′tiv) *adj.* of or for a feast, festival, or holiday; gay; joyous; merry: *A birthday or wedding is a festive occasion.* —**fes′tive·ly**, *adv.* —**fes′tive·ness**, *n.*

fes·tiv·i·ty (fes tiv′ə tē) *n., pl.* **-ties. 1** a festive activity; something done to celebrate: *Are you attending the festivities tonight?* **2** gaiety; merriment. **3** festival.

fes·toon (fes tün′) *n., v.* —*n.* **1** a hanging curve of flowers, leaves, ribbons, etc.: *The flags were hung on the wall in colorful festoons.* **2** a carved or moulded ornament like this on furniture, pottery, etc. —*v.* **1** decorate with festoons: *The Christmas tree was festooned with tinsel.* **2** form into festoons; hang in curves: *Draperies were festooned over the window.* [< F *feston* < Ital. *festone* < *festa* festival, feast]

fet·a (fet′ə) *n.* a firm, crumbly, white Greek cheese made from sheep's or goat's milk.

fe·tal *or* **foe·tal** (fē′təl) *adj.* of, having to do with, or like a fetus.

fetch (fech) *v., n.* —*v.* **1** go and get; bring. *He's gone to fetch the newspaper.* **2** cause to come; succeed in bringing. **3** be sold for: *Eggs were fetching a good price that year.* **4** *Informal.* attract; charm: *Flattery will fetch her.* **5** *Informal.* hit; strike: *He fetched him one on the nose.* **6** give (a groan, sigh, etc.). **7** reach; arrive

at: *They tried to fetch the harbor but the storm broke too soon.* **8** of ships, take a course; move; go: *The boat was fetching to windward.* **fetch and carry,** do small jobs.
fetch up, arrive; stop.
—*n.* **1** the act of fetching. **2** a trick. [OE *feccan*] —**fetch′er,** *n.*

fetch·ing (fech′ing) *adj. Informal.* attractive; charming. —**fetch′ing·ly,** *adv.*

fete or **fête** (fāt′; French, fet) *n., v.* **fet·ed** or **fêt·ed, fet·ing** or **fêt·ing.** —*n.* a festival; a gala entertainment or celebration, usually held outdoors: *A large fete was given for the benefit of the town hospital.* —*v.* honor with a fete; entertain: *The engaged couple were feted by their friends.* [< F *fête* feast]
☛ *Hom.* fate (fāt′).

fet·ich (fet′ish or fē′tish) See **fetish.**

fet·id (fet′id or fē′tid) *adj.* smelling very bad; stinking. [< L *foetidus* < *foetere* to smell. —**fet′id·ly,** *adv.* —**fet′id·ness,** *n.*

fet·ish (fet′ish or fē′tish) *n.* **1** a material object believed to contain a spirit or to have magical powers. **2** anything regarded with unreasoning reverence or devotion: *Some people make a fetish of style.* **3** a condition in which sexual excitement is derived from an object or a non-sexual part of the body. **4** an object or non-sexual body part giving such excitement. [< F *fétiche* < Pg. *feitiço* charm, originally adj., artificial < L *facticius.* Doublet of FACTITIOUS.]

fet·ish·ism (fet′ish iz′əm or fē′tish iz′əm) *n.* **1** a belief in fetishes; worship of fetishes. **2** behavior characterized by a fetish (def. 3).

fet·ish·ist (fet′ish ist′) *n.* a person who worships or is obsessed by a fetish; one who practices fetishism.

fet·lock (fet′lok) *n.* **1** the tuft of hair above a horse's hoof on the back part of the leg. **2** the part of a horse's leg where this tuft grows. See **horse** for picture. **3** the joint at this spot. [ME *fetlok*]

fe·tor (fē′tər) *n.* a strong, offensive smell. [< L *foetor* < *foetere* to smell]

fet·ter (fet′ər) *n., v.* —*n.* **1** a chain or shackle for the feet to prevent escape. **2** Usually **fetters,** *pl.* anything that shackles or binds; restraint. —*v.* **1** bind with fetters; chain the feet of. **2** bind; restrain: *The boy had to learn to fetter his temper.* [OE *feter.* Related to FOOT.]

fet·tle (fet′əl) *n.* condition; trim: *The horse is in fine fettle and should win the race.* [? < ME *fettel(en)* gird up < OE *fetel* belt]

fe·tus or **foe·tus** (fē′təs) *n.* the unborn young of a vertebrate, especially a mammal, and especially during the later period of its development when it begins to clearly resemble the newborn of its species; the term is used for a human offspring in the womb from about nine weeks after conception. Compare **embryo.** [< L]

feud¹ (fyüd) *n., v.* —*n.* **1** a long and deadly quarrel between families, tribes, etc., often passed down from generation to generation. **2** continued strife between two persons, groups, etc. **3** a quarrel. —*v.* engage in a deadly quarrel, especially one involving families: *They have been feuding with their neighbors for years.* [var. of ME *fede* < OF *fe(i)de* < OHG *fehida* enmity]
☛ *Syn.* **3.** See note at **quarrel.**

feud² (fyüd) *n.* a feudal estate; fief. [< Med.L *feudum* < Gmc.]

feu·dal (fyü′dəl) *adj.* **1** of or having to do with feudalism. **2** of or having to do with feuds or fiefs. [< Med.L *feudalis* < *feudum.* See FEUD².]

feu·dal·ism (fyü′dəl iz′əm) *n.* **1** the social, economic, and political system of Western Europe in the Middle Ages. Under this system vassals gave military and other services to a lord in return for protection and the use of land owned by the lord. **2** any social, economic, or political system that suggests or resembles this.

feu·dal·is·tic (fyü′dəl is′tik) *adj.* **1** of or having to do with feudalism. **2** tending toward or favoring feudalism.

feu·dal·i·ty (fyü dal′ə tē) *n., pl.* **-ties. 1** feudalism. **2** a feudal estate; fief.

feudal system feudalism.

feu·da·to·ry (fyü′də tô′rē) *adj., n., pl.* **-ries.** —*adj.* **1** owing feudal services (to). **2** holding or held as a feudal estate or fief. —*n.* **1** a feudal vassal: *The duke summoned his feudatories to aid him in war.* **2** a feudal estate; fief.

feu de joie (fœ də zhwä′) *pl.* **feux de joie. 1** a salute made by a line of troops firing their rifles in rapid succession. **2** *French.* bonfire. [< F, literally, fire of joy]

feud·ist (fyüd′ist) *n.* a person engaging in a feud.

fe·ver (fē′vər) *n., v.* —*n.* **1** an unhealthy condition of the body in which the temperature is higher than normal. **2** any of various

diseases that cause fever, such as scarlet fever and typhoid fever. **3** an excited, restless condition. **4** a current fad or enthusiasm for something or for some person.
—*v.* affect with fever or excite as if with fever. [OE *fefer* < L *febris*] —**fe′ver·less,** *adj.*

fe·vered (fē′vərd) *adj.* **1** having fever; hot with fever: *a fevered brow.* **2** excited; restless.

fe·ver·few (fē′vər fyü′) *n.* a perennial European plant (*Chrysanthemum parthenium*) of the composite family having small, daisylike flowers. Feverfew, formerly widely believed to be useful in reducing a fever, is still often cultivated as a garden flower. [OE *feferfūg(i)e* < LL *febrifug(i)a* < L *febris* fever + *fugare* drive away]

fe·ver·ish (fē′vər ish or fēv′rish) *adj.* **1** having fever, especially a slight fever. **2** caused by fever: *feverish thirst, feverish dreams.* **3** causing fever: *a feverish climate.* **4** infested with fever: *a feverish swamp.* **5** excited; restless. —**fe′ver·ish·ly,** *adv.* —**fe′ver·ish·ness,** *n.*

fe·ver·ous (fē′vər əs or fēv′rəs) *adj.* feverish.

fever pitch a state of intense excitement or frenzied activity.

fe·ver–root (fē′və rüt′) *n.* feverwort.

fever sore a cold sore.

fe·ver·wort (fē′vər wèrt′) *n.* any of several perennial herbs (genus *Triosteum*) of the honeysuckle family formerly used in medicine.

few (fyü) *adj., n.* —*adj.* not many: *There are few women more than 185 centimetres tall.* —*n.* **1** a small number: *Only a few of the boys had bicycles.* **2 the few,** the minority, especially a small, privileged group.
quite a few, *Informal.* a good many: *We caught ten fish, but quite a few got away.*
[OE *fēawe*] —**few′ness,** *n.*
☛ *Usage.* **fewer, less.** Fewer refers only to number and to things that are counted: *Fewer cars were on the road. There were fewer than sixty present.* In formal usage less refers only to amount or quantity and to things that are measured: *There was a good deal less tardiness in the second term. There was even less hay than the summer before.*

fez (fez) *n., pl.* **fez·zes.** a felt cap, usually red, having a high crown with a flat top and ornamented with a long, black tassel. It was formerly the national headdress of Turkish men. See **cap** for picture. [< Turkish; after *Fez,* Morocco]

ff fortissimo.

ff. 1 and the following pages, sections, etc.: *P. 26 ff. means page 26 and the following few pages.* **2** folios.

F.I. Falkland Islands.

fi·a·cre (fi ä′kər; French, fyä′ᴋʀ) *n.* a small four-wheeled horse-drawn hackney coach. [< St. *Fiacre,* the name of the hotel in Paris where they were first hired]

fi·an·cé (fē′än sā′ or fē′än sā′) *n.* a man to whom a woman is engaged to be married. [< F *fiancé,* pp. of *fiancer* betroth]

fi·an·cée (fē′än sā′ or fē′än sā′) *n.* a woman to whom a man is engaged to be married. [< F]

fi·as·co (fē as′kō) *n., pl.* **-cos** or **-coes.** a failure; breakdown. [< F < Ital. *fiasco,* literally, flask; development of meaning uncertain]

fi·at (fī′ət or fī′at, fē′ət or fē′at) *n.* **1** an authoritative order or command; decree. **2** sanction: *He acted under the fiat of the king.* [< L *fiat* let it be done]

fib (fib) *n., v.* **fibbed, fib·bing.** —*n.* a lie about some small matter; a trivial lie. —*v.* tell such a lie. [? < *fibble-fable* < *fable*] —**fib′ber,** *n.*
☛ *Syn.* See note at **lie.**

fi·ber (fī′bər) See **fibre.**

Fi·ber·glas (fī′bər glas′) *n. Trademark.* fibreglass.

fi·bre (fī′bər) *n.* **1** one of the threadlike cells or structures that combine with others to form certain plant or animal tissues. **2** tissue formed in this way: *muscle fibre. Hemp fibre is used to make rope or cloth.* **3** a slender, threadlike root of a plant. **4** a long, slender filament of wool, cotton, glass, rayon, nylon, asbestos, etc. used especially for making yarn or cloth. **5** a yarn or cloth made of such fibres. **6** texture: *cloth of coarse fibre.* **7** essential nature or character: *a strong moral fibre. The very fibre of his being was stirred.* Also, **fiber.** [< F *fibre* < L *fibra*]

fi·bre·board (fī′bər bôrd′) *n.* a building material made by compressing fibrous materials, such as wood or cane fibre or straw, into flat, semirigid sheets. It is used in the construction of interior walls, as sheathing for the inside of exterior walls, etc. Also, **fiberboard.**

fi·bre·glass (fī′bər glas′) *n., v.* —*n.* **1** glass drawn and spun into fine threads or fibres. **2** a thick material consisting of matted fibreglass, used for insulation. **3** textile fabric woven from fibreglass, used for curtains, etc. **4** a moulded or pressed material consisting of plastic mixed with fibreglass, used for making boat

hulls, automobile bodies, etc. **5** (*adjl.*) made of fibreglass.
—*v.* form or shape with fibreglass. Also, **fiberglass.**

fibre optics **1** the technology of using a very long, fine, flexible glass or acrylic fibre or a bundle of such fibres for transmitting light or optical images by total internal reflection or refraction. **2** (*adjl.*) designating such a fibre or a bundle of such fibres forming part of a telecommunications system, optical instrument, etc.

fi·bril (fī′brəl) *n.* **1** a small or very slender fibre. **2** one of the hairs on the roots of some plants. [< NL *fibrilla* < L *fibra* fibre]

fi·bril·late (fī′brə lāt′ *or* fib′rə-) *v.* **-lat·ed, -lat·ing. 1** of a muscle or muscle fibre, undergo or exhibit fibrillation. **2** break up or form into fibrils.

fi·bril·la·tion (fī′brə lā′shən *or* fib′rə-) *n.* **1** the act or process of splitting or forming into fibrils. **2** irregular, usually rapid, twitching of individual muscle fibres within a muscle. **3** rapid, irregular contractions or twitchings in the muscular wall of the heart, interfering with or replacing the normal rhythmical contractions of the heart.

fi·brin (fī′brən) *n.* a tough, elastic, insoluble protein forming the fibrous network of a blood clot. Fibrin is formed from fibrinogen by the action of an enzyme in the blood. [< L *fibra* fibre]

fi·brin·o·gen (fī brin′ə jen′) *n.* a soluble protein found especially in blood plasma, that is converted into fibrin by the action of an enzyme when blood clots. [< *fibrin* + *-gen*]

fi·bri·no·sis (fī′brə nō′sis) *n.* a condition marked by too much fibrin in the blood.

fi·brin·ous (fī′brə nəs) *adj.* of or like fibrin.

fi·broid (fī′broid) *adj.,* *n.* —*adj.* made up of fibres or of fibrelike structure. —*n.* a tumor made up of fibres or fibrous tissue.

fi·bro·sis (fī brō′sis) *n.* an excessive growth of fibrous connective tissue in the body. [< NL *fibrosis* < L *fibra* fibre + *-osis* -osis]

fi·bro·si·tis (fī′brə sī′tis) *n.* inflammation of fibrous tissue in the muscle sheaths.

fi·brous (fī′brəs) *adj.* made up of fibres; having fibres; like fibre. —**fi′brous·ly,** *adv.*

fib·u·la (fib′yə lə) *n., pl.* **-lae** (-lē′) *or* **-las. 1** the outer, thinner of the two bones in the human lower leg, extending from the knee to the ankle. **2** the corresponding bone in the hind leg of an animal. **3** a clasp or brooch, often highly ornamented, used by the ancient Greeks and Romans: *A fibula resembles a safety pin.* [< L *fibula* clasp, brooch]

fib·u·lar (fib′yə lər) *adj.* of or having to do with the fibula.

–fic *adjective-forming suffix.* causing, as in *scientific, terrific.* [< L *-ficus* < *facere* do, make]

–fication *noun-forming suffix.* a making or doing; corresponding to verbs ending in *-fy;* as in *falsification, purification.* [< L *-ficatio, -onis* < *-ficare* < *facere* do, make]

fich·u (fish′ü) *n.* a three-cornered piece of muslin, lace, or other soft material worn by women about the neck, with the ends drawn together or crossed on the breast. [< F]

fick·le (fik′əl) *adj.* likely to change without reason; changing; not constant: *fickle fortune, a fickle friend.* [OE *ficol* deceitful] —**fick′le·ness,** *n.*

fic·tion (fik′shən) *n.* **1** novels, short stories, and other prose writings that tell about imaginary, and sometimes real, people and happenings. Both characters and events in fiction may sometimes be partly real. **2** what is imagined or made up; imaginary happenings; make-believe: *The explorer exaggerated so much in telling about his adventures that it was impossible to separate fact from fiction.* **3** an imaginary account or statement; made-up story. **4** an inventing of imaginary accounts, stories, etc.; a feigning. **5** *Law.* something acted upon as a fact, in spite of its possible falsity. It is a legal fiction that a corporation is a person. [< L *fictio, -onis* < *fingere* to form, fashion]

fic·tion·al (fik′shən əl) *adj.* of or having to do with fiction. —**fic′tion·al·ly,** *adv.*

fic·ti·tious (fik tish′əs) *adj.* **1** not real; imaginary; made-up: *Characters in novels are usually entirely fictitious.* **2** assumed in order to deceive; false: *The criminal used a fictitious name.* [< L *ficticius* artificial < *fingere* form, fashion] —**fic·ti′tious·ly,** *adv.* —**fic·ti′tious·ness,** *n.*

fid (fid) *n.* **1** a square wooden or iron bar used to support a topmast. **2** a round, tapering pin, usually of hardwood, used for separating strands of rope in splicing. It has a groove along one side for feeding a strand to be tucked between the separated strands. [origin uncertain]

–fid *adjective-forming suffix.* split; cleft; lobed, as in *bifid.* [< L *-fidus* < *findere* cleave, split]

fid·dle (fid′əl) *n., v.* **-dled, -dling.** —*n.* **1** *Informal.* an instrument of the violin or viol family, especially a violin. **2** on a ship, a low

hat, āge, fär; let, ĕqual, tèrm; it, īce
hot, ōpen, ôrder; oil, out; cup, pùt, rüle,
əbove, takən, pencəl, lemən, circəs

ch, child; ng, long; sh, ship
th, thin; ₮H, then; zh, measure

railing on the edge of a table to prevent dishes, etc. from sliding off when the ship rolls or pitches. **3** *Slang.* deception or fraud.
fit as a fiddle, in excellent physical condition.
play second fiddle, take a secondary part.
—*v.* **1** *Informal.* play on a violin. **2** make aimless movements; play nervously or restlessly; toy: *Instead of answering, the embarrassed boy just fiddled with his jacket.* **3** spend time idly or aimlessly: *fiddling around in his workshop.* **4** tamper or interfere: *Don't fiddle with the controls.* **5** *Slang.* swindle; cheat. [OE *fithele* (recorded in *fithelere* fiddler); probably akin to Med.L *vitula.* See VIOL.]
—**fid′dler,** *n.*

fid·dle–de–dee (fid′əl dē dē′) *n. or interj.* nonsense.

fid·dle–fad·dle (fid′əl fad′əl) *n., interj., v.* **-idled, -idling.** *Formal.* —*n.* trifling speech or action.
—*interj.* nonsense.
—*v.* busy oneself about trivial things. [? reduplication of *fiddle*]

fid·dle·head (fid′əl hed′) *n.* **1** one of the young, curled fronds of certain ferns (such as the ostrich fern), that are eaten as a delicacy. Fiddleheads are eaten especially in Nova Scotia and New Brunswick. See **fern** for picture. **2** a scroll-shaped ornament on a ship's bow, resembling the head of a violin.

fid·dle·neck (fid′əl nek′) *n.* fiddlehead.

fiddler crab a small burrowing crab common along the Atlantic Coast of the United States.

fid·dle·stick (fid′əl stik′) *n., interj.* —*n.* **1** *Archaic.* a violin bow. **2** a mere nothing; trifle. —*interj.*
fiddlesticks, *pl.* nonsense! rubbish!

fid·dle·sticks (fid′əl stiks′) *interj.* nonsense! rubbish!

Fi·de·i De·fen·sor (fī dē ī *or* fē′dā ē di fen′sôr) *Latin.* Defender of the Faith, one of the titles of the British Sovereign.

fi·del·i·ty (fə del′ə tē *or* fī del′ə tē) *n., pl.* **-ties. 1** faithfulness to a trust or vow; steadfast faithfulness; loyalty. **2** strictness or thoroughness in the performance of duty: *His fidelity and industry brought him speedy promotion.* **3** exactness, as in a copy; accuracy: *The reporter wrote his story with absolute fidelity.* **4** the ability of a device, as a radio transmitter or receiver, to transmit or reproduce an electric signal or sound accurately. [< L *fidelitas,* ult. < *fides* faith. Doublet of FEALTY.]

fidg·et (fij′it) *v., —v.* **1** move about restlessly; be uneasy: *A child fidgets if he has to sit still for a long time.* **2** make uneasy. —*n.* **1** the condition of being restless or uneasy. **2** a person who moves about restlessly. **3 the fidgets,** *pl.* a fit of restlessness or uneasiness. [< obs. *fidge* move restlessly]

fidg·et·y (fij′ə tē) *adj.* restless; uneasy.

fi·du·ci·ar·y (fə dyü′shē er′ē *or* fə dü′shē er′ē) *adj., n., pl.* **-ar·ies.** —*adj.* **1** held in trust: *fiduciary estates.* **2** holding in trust. A fiduciary possessor is legally responsible for what belongs to another. **3** of a trustee; of trust and confidence: *A guardian acts in a fiduciary capacity.* **4** depending upon public trust and confidence for its value. Paper money that cannot be redeemed in gold or silver is fiduciary currency.
—*n.* a trustee. [< L *fiduciarius* < *fiducia* trust]

fie (fī) *interj.* for shame! shame! [< OF]
☛ *Usage.* The disgust, disapproval, or impatience conveyed by this word is now often ironical.

fief (fēf) *n.* in feudal times, a piece of land held from a lord in return for military and other services as required; feudal estate. Also, **feoff.** [< F < Gmc.]

field (fēld) *n., v.* —*n.* **1** a piece of land used for crops or pasture: *a wheat field.* **2** land with few or no trees. **3** a piece of land used for some special purpose: *a playing field.* **4** land yielding some product: *a coal field.* **5** *Military.* **a** the place where a battle is or has been fought. **b** a battle: *The English won the field at Poitiers.* **c** a region where certain military operations are carried on. **6** *Sports.* **a** an area for athletics, games, etc. **b** the part of this area used for contests in jumping, etc. **c** the sports contested in this area. **d** all those participating in a game, contest, or outdoor sport: *At the halfway mark in the marathon, a Canadian was leading the field.* **e** all those participating in a game or contest except one or more specified: *to bet on one horse against the field.* **f** a defensive football, baseball, etc. team. **7** *Baseball.* **a** the playing field, including both infield and outfield. **b** the outfield. **8** a range of opportunity or interest; sphere of activity or operation: *the field of science.* **9** a large, flat space;

broad surface: *a field of ice.* **10** the surface on which some emblem is pictured or painted: *the field of a coat of arms.* **11** the ground of each division of a flag. **12** *Physics.* the space throughout which a force operates. A magnet has a magnetic field about it. **13** the space or area in which things can be seen through a telescope, microscope, etc. without moving it: *the field of vision.* **14** *Television.* the entire screen area occupied by an image.

play the field,   a *Informal.* take a broad sphere of action or operation. **b** *Slang.* go out with many different persons of the opposite sex.

take the field, begin a battle, campaign, game, etc.

—*v.* **1** *Baseball, cricket, etc.* **a** stop or catch and return (a ball). **b** act as a fielder. **2** put into the field; bring in or have as player, candidate, etc.: *to field a good baseball team. The party fielded only a handful of candidates.* **3** *Informal.* answer skilfully (difficult or controversial questions). **4** protect; defend: *He fielded his political position gracefully.* [OE *feld*]

field artillery artillery mounted on carriages for easy movement by armies in the field.

field day 1 a day set aside for athletic contests and outdoor sports. **2** a day when soldiers perform drills, mock fights, etc. **3** a day of unusual activity, display, or success.

field·er (fēl′dər) *n.* **1** *Baseball.* a player who is stationed around or outside the diamond to stop the ball and throw it in. **2** *Cricket.* a person playing a similar position.

field event any one of the events at an athletic meet that are held on the field as opposed to on the track. Jumping, pole-vaulting, shot-putting, and discus-throwing are field events.

field·fare (fēld′fer′) *n.* a European thrush having a grey head, black tail, and brown-and-white body. [OE *feldefare*]

field glasses or **field glass** binoculars.

field goal *Football.* a goal counting three points scored by kicking the ball between the uprights and above the bar of the goal post.

field gun an artillery gun.

field hockey a game played on a grass field by two teams whose players, except the goalie, use curved sticks and try to drive a ball into the opposing team's goal.

field hospital a temporary hospital near a battlefield.

field house a building near an athletic field, used for storing equipment, for dressing rooms, etc.

field jacket a light, waterproof cotton jacket designed to be worn by soldiers in combat.

field kitchen a portable kitchen that can be set up in the open to cook food for a large number of people, such as an army unit.

field magnet an electromagnet used in a generator or motor to make a strong electrical field.

field·man (fēld′man′ or fēld′mən) *n., pl.* **-men.** a sales representative, researcher, or government agent who has direct contact with customers, research subjects, etc. and usually works at a distance from his head office.

field marshal the officer of the highest rank in the armies of certain countries, ranking above a general. *Abbrev.:* F.M.

field mouse 1 any of various voles, especially a medium-sized species (*Microtus pennsylvanicus*) found throughout most of Canada and the northern United States. **2** any of a genus (*Apodemus*) of nocturnal, burrowing Old World mice found in Europe, Asia, and N Africa.

field officer any commissioned officer senior to a captain and junior to a brigadier-general.

field of fire the area that a gun or battery covers effectively. galf0434a

field·piece (fēld′pēs′) *n.* field gun.

field·stone (fēld′stōn′) *n., adj.* —*n.* rough stones used for houses, walls, etc. especially when found in the area near the construction site. —*adj.* of or resembling fieldstone.

field test a test made of a new product, system, etc. in the environment or by the users for which it is intended, to determine its durability, efficiency, acceptability, etc.

field–test (fēld′test′) *v.* conduct a field test of: *Their new elementary reading program was field-tested in several provinces before being published.*

field trial 1 a test of the performance of hunting dogs in the field. **2** a test of a new product under actual conditions of use.

field trip a trip to give students special opportunities for observing facts relating to a particular field of study.

field work the scientific or technical work done in the field by surveyors, geologists, linguists, sociologists, etc.

field·work (fēld′wèrk′) *n.* a temporary fortification for defence made by soldiers in the field.

field·work·er (fēld′wèrk′ər) *n.* one engaged in field work. Also, **field worker.**

fiend (fēnd) *n.* **1** an evil spirit; devil. **2** an extremely wicked or cruel person. **3 the Fiend,** the Devil. **4** *Informal.* a person who indulges excessively in some habit, practice, game, etc.: *He is a fiend for work.* [OE *feond*, originally ppr. of *feogan* hate] —**fiend′like′,** *adj.*

fiend·ish (fēn′dish) *adj.* extremely cruel or wicked; devilish: *fiendish tortures, a fiendish yell.* —**fiend′ish·ly,** *adv.* —**fiend′ish·ness,** *n.*

fierce (fèrs) *adj.* **fierc·er, fierc·est. 1** savage; wild: *a fierce lion.* **2** raging; violent: *a fierce wind.* **3** very eager or active; ardent: *a fierce determination to win.* **4** *Informal.* intense; extreme: *The heat was fierce.* [ME < OF *fers, fiers* < L *ferus* wild] —**fierce′ly,** *adv.* —**fierce′ness,** *n.*

▸ **Syn. 1. Fierce, ferocious, savage** = wild and harsh. **Fierce** emphasizes having a pitiless or unfeeling nature, showing a readiness to harm or kill, or being given to wild rage, especially in manner or actions: *He was a fierce fighter.* **Ferocious** suggests being wildly fierce or cruel, or showing wild force, especially in looks, disposition, or actions: *That man looks ferocious.* **Savage** adds the idea of showing an uncivilized lack of restraint on the emotions or passions and an inhuman lack of feeling for pain caused to others: *He has a savage temper.*

fier·y (fīr′ē or fī′ər ē) *adj.* **fier·i·er, fier·i·est. 1** consisting of fire; containing fire; burning; flaming. **2** like fire; very hot, brilliant, or glowing: *a fiery red.* **3** full of feeling or spirit; ardent: *a fiery speech.* **4** easily aroused or excited: *a fiery temper.* **5** inflamed: *a fiery sore.* —**fier′i·ly,** *adv.* —**fier′i·ness,** *n.*

fi·es·ta (fē es′tə) *n.* **1** a religious festival; saint's day. **2** a holiday; festivity. [< Sp. *fiesta* feast]

fife (fīf) *n., v.* **fifed, fif·ing.** —*n.* a small, shrill musical instrument like a flute: *Fifes and drums are used in playing marches.* —*v.* play on a fife. [< G *Pfeife* pipe] —**fif′er,** *n.*

fif·teen (fif′tēn′) *n., adj.* —*n.* **1** five more than ten; 15. **2** the numeral 15: *The 15 refers to the song number, not the page.* **3** the fifteenth in a set or series. **4** a set or series of fifteen persons or things.

—*adj.* **1** five more than ten; 15: *Fifteen people answered the ad.* **2** being fifteenth in a set or series (*used after the noun*): *Chapter Fifteen.* [OE *fiftēne*]

fif·teenth (fif′tēnth′) *adj. or n.* **1** next after the 14th; last in a series of fifteen; 15th. **2** one, or being one, of 15 equal parts.

fifth (fifth) *adj., n.* —*adj.* **1** next after the fourth; last in a series of five; 5th. **2** being one of 5 equal parts.

—*n.* **1** the next after the fourth; last in a series of five; 5th. **2** one of 5 equal parts. **3** *Music.* **a** the fifth tone from the keynote of a scale; the dominant. **b** the interval between such tones. **c** a combination of such tones. **4** *Slang.* a bottle of liquor containing 25.6 fluid ounces (about 0.8 dm³), which is one fifth of a U.S. gallon. [alteration of OE *fifta*]

fifth column any persons within a country who secretly aid its enemies. Originally, the term was applied to the Franco supporters in Madrid during the Spanish Civil War, who constituted an additional, or fifth, column to the four military columns that attacked the city from outside.

fifth columnist a member of the fifth column.

fifth·ly (fifth′lē) *adv.* in the fifth place.

fifth wheel *Informal.* a person or thing that is not needed.

fif·ti·eth (fif′tē ith) *adj. or n.* **1** next after the 49th; last in a series of fifty; 50th. **2** one, or being one, of 50 equal parts.

fif·ty (fif′tē) *n., pl.* **-ties;** *adj.* —*n.* **1** five times ten; 50. **2** the numeral 50. **3** the fiftieth in a set or series. **4** a 50-dollar bill: *She asked the teller for two fifties.* **5 fifties,** *pl.* the years from fifty through fifty-nine, especially of a century or of a person's life: *Her grandfather is in his fifties.* **6** a set or series of fifty persons or things.

—*adj.* **1** five times ten; 50. **2** being fiftieth in a set or series (*used after the noun*): *Chapter Fifty.* [OE *fiftig*]

fif·ty–fif·ty (fif′tē fif′tē) *adv. or adj. Informal.* half-and-half; in or with equal shares.

fig¹ (fig) *n.* **1** any of a genus (*Ficus*) of tropical and subtropical trees and shrubs of the mulberry family bearing seedlike fruits in a fleshy, pear-shaped receptacle. **2** the receptacle of any of these trees or shrubs, especially the soft, sweet, edible receptacle, commonly called a fruit, of *F. carica*. Figs are eaten fresh or dried. **3** something of little or no value; trifle (*used with a negative*): *I don't care a fig for your opinion.* [ME < OF *figue* < Provençal *figa*, ult. < L *ficus* fig]

fig² (fig) *n. Informal.* dress; equipment. **in full fig,** fully dressed or equipped. [origin uncertain]

fig. 441 **file**

fig. figure; figurative; figuratively.

fight (fīt) *n., v.* **fought, fight·ing.** —*n.* **1** a struggle; battle; conflict; combat; contest. **2** an angry dispute. **3** the power or will to fight.
show fight, resist; be ready to fight: *The hunted animal was too weary to show fight.*
—*v.* **1** take part in a fight. **2** take part in a fight against; war against. **3** carry on (a fight, conflict, etc.). **4** get or make by fighting. **5** cause to fight. **6** disagree angrily; quarrel: *The brothers were always fighting about one thing or another.*
fight back, offer resistance; show fight: *They had no heart to fight back.*
fight it out, fight until one side wins.
fight off, a turn back; repel: *Fight off an enemy attack.* **b** overcome; stop the progress of: *to fight off a cold.*
fight on, continue struggling.
fight shy of, keep away from; avoid.
[OE *feoht,* n., *feohtan,* v.]
☛ *Syn. n.* **1. Fight, combat, conflict** = battle or struggle. **Fight** = a struggle for victory or mastery between two or more peoples, animals, or forces, and particularly suggests hand to hand fighting: *When boys fight, they often hurt one another.* **Combat** applies particularly to a battle between two armed men or forces: *The gladiators were ordered into combat in the arena.* **Conflict** emphasizes clashing, and applies to a battle or fight or to a mental or moral struggle between two beliefs, duties, etc.: *We all undergo mental conflicts.*

fight·er (fī′tər) *n.* **1** one that fights. **2** a professional boxer. **3** fighter plane.

fight·er–bomb·er (fī′tər bom′ər) *n.* an aircraft used both as a fighter and as a bomber.

fighter plane a highly manoeuvrable and heavily armed airplane used mainly for attacking enemy aircraft or strafing ground forces.

fighting chance *Informal.* the possibility of success after a long, hard struggle.

fighting cock 1 gamecock. **2** *Informal.* a pugnacious person.

fig·ment (fig′mənt) *n.* something imagined; a made-up story. [< L *figmentum* < *fingere* form, fashion]

fig·ur·ate (fig′ər it *or* fig′yər it) *adj.* **1** having a characteristic or well-defined form, shape, or pattern. **2** *Music.* full of embellishments; ornate.

fig·ur·a·tion (fig′ər ā′shən *or* fig′yər ā′shən) *n.* **1** a form; shape. **2** a forming; shaping. **3** a representation by a likeness or symbol. **4** the act of marking or adorning with figures or designs. **5** *Music.* **a** the use of transitional tones, ornaments, etc. that are essential to the harmony. **b** the indicating of harmonics with figures above the bass part.

fig·ur·a·tive (fig′ər ə tiv *or* fig′yər ə tiv) *adj.* **1** in writing or speech, using words out of their literal meaning to add beauty or force. **2** having many figures of speech. Much poetry is figurative. **3** representing by a likeness or symbol: *A globe is a figurative model of the world.* —**fig′ur·a·tive·ly,** *adv.* —**fig′ur·a·tive·ness,** *n.*

fig·ure (fig′ər *or* fig′yər) *n., v.* **-ured, -ur·ing.** —*n.* **1** a symbol for a number. The symbols 1, 2, 3, etc. are called figures. **2** an amount or value given in figures: *The price is too high; ask a lower figure.* **3** a form or shape: *In the darkness she saw dim figures moving.* **4** a form enclosing a surface or space: *Circles, triangles, squares, cubes, and spheres are geometrical figures.* **5** a person; character: *Samuel de Champlain is a great figure in Canadian history.* **6** a human form; a person considered from the point of view of appearance, manner, etc.: *The poor old woman was a figure of distress.* **7** an artificial representation of the human form in sculpture, painting, drawing, etc., usually of the whole or greater part of the body. **8** an image; likeness. **9** a picture; drawing; diagram; illustration: *This dictionary makes use of many figures to help explain the meaning of words.* **10** a design; pattern: *Cloth or wallpaper often has figures on it.* **11** *Music.* a motif (def. 3). **12** an outline traced by movements: *figures made by an airplane.* **13** *Dancing or skating.* a set of movements. **14** a figure of speech. **15** *Logic.* any of the forms of a syllogism that differ only in the position of the middle term. **16 figures,** calculations using figures, arithmetic: *She was never very good at figures.*
—*v.* **1** use figures to find the answer to a problem; reckon, compute; show by figures. **2** be conspicuous; appear: *The names of great leaders figure in the story of human progress.* **3** show by a figure; represent in a diagram. **4** decorate with a figure or pattern. **5** think; consider. **6** *Informal.* make sense: *That figures.* **7** *Music.* **a** write figures over and under (the bass) to indicate the intended harmony. **b** use transitional tones, ornaments, etc. in; embellish. **8** picture mentally; imagine: *Figure to yourself a happy family, secure in their own home.*
figure on, *Informal.* **a** depend on; rely on. **b** consider as part of a plan or undertaking.
figure out, *Informal.* **a** find out by using figures: *She soon figured out how much it would cost.* **b** think out; understand: *She couldn't figure out what was meant.*
[< F < L *figura* < *fingere* form] —**fig′ur·er,** *n.*
☛ *Syn. n.* **3.** See note at **form.**

fig·ured (fig′ərd *or* fig′yərd) *adj.* **1** decorated with a design or pattern; not plain. **2** shown by a figure, diagram, or picture. **3** formed; shaped: *figured in bronze.* **4** *Music.* **a** ornamented; florid. **b** having accompanying chords of the bass part indicated by figures.

fig·ure·head (fig′ər hed′ *or* fig′yər-) *n.* **1** a person who is the head in name only, and has no real authority or responsibility. **2** a statue or carving decorating the bow on a ship.

figure of speech an expression in which words are used out of their literal meaning or in exceptional combinations to add beauty or force. Similes and metaphors are figures of speech.

figure skate a skate for use in figure skating.

fig·ure–skate (fig′ər skāt′ *or* fig′yər-) *v.* **-skat·ed, -skat·ing.** engage in figure skating.

fig·ure–skat·er (fig′ər skā′ter *or* fig′yər-) *n.* a person who figure-skates.

figure skating the art or practice of performing figures and balletic programs on ice skates, often to music.

fig·ur·ine (fig′ər ēn′ *or* fig′yər ēn′) *n.* a small ornamental figure made of stone, pottery, metal, etc.; statuette. [< F < Ital. *figurina,* dim. of *figura* figure]

fig·wort (fig′wèrt′) *n.* **1** any of a genus (*Scrophularia*) of plants found in north temperate regions, having small greenish or purplish flowers. **2** (*adj.*) designating the family of plants that includes the figworts, speedwells, and mulleins.

Fi·ji (fē′jē) *n.* a native of the Fiji Islands, a group of islands in the S Pacific.

Fi·ji·an (fē′jē ən *or* fi jē′ən) *n., adj.* —*n.* **1** a native or inhabitant of the Fiji Islands, a group of islands in the S Pacific. **2** the Malayo-Polynesian language of the Fijians. —*adj.* of or having to do with the Fiji Islands, their people, or their language.

fil·a·ment (fil′ə mənt) *n.* **1** a very fine thread. **2** a very slender, threadlike part. The wire that gives off light in an electric light bulb is a filament. **3** *Botany.* the stalklike part of a stamen that supports the anther. See **flower** for picture. **4** the wire in a vacuum tube through which current passes to generate the heat necessary for electrons to be emitted. In some vacuum tubes, the filament also acts as the cathode. **5** a continuous strand of yarn of a synthetic, as acetate, which may be used in weaving without spinning. [< LL *filamentum* < L *filum* thread]

fil·a·men·tous (fil′ə men′təs) *adj.* **1** threadlike. **2** having filaments.

fil·bert (fil′bərt) *n.* **1** hazelnut. **2** any of several hazels cultivated for their edible nuts, especially a European species (*Corylus maxima*). [after St. *Philibert,* because the nuts ripen about the time of his day, August 22]

filch (filch) *v.* steal in small quantities; pilfer: *He filched pencils from the teacher's desk.* [origin uncertain] —**filch′er,** *n.*
☛ *Syn.* See note at **steal.**

file¹ (fīl) *n., v.* **-filed, -fil·ing.** —*n.* **1** a place for keeping papers in order. **2** a set of papers kept in order. **3** a line of persons, animals, or things one behind another. **4** a small detachment of soldiers. **5** one of the lines of squares extending across a chessboard, checkerboard, etc. from player to player. **6** a collection of news stories sent by wire.
in file, one after another; in succession: *We walked in file.*
on file, kept in order in a file: *All the reports are on file.*
—*v.* **1** put away (papers), in order. **2** march or move in a file. **3** make application. **4** send (a news story) by wire: *The reporter immediately filed his story of the explosion.* [< F *fil* thread (< L *filum*) and F *file* row (ult. < LL *filare* spin a thread)] —**fil′er,** *n.*

Files

file² (fīl) *n., v.* **filed, fil·ing.** —*n.* a steel tool with many small ridges or teeth on it: *The rough surface of a file is used to cut through or wear away hard materials or to make rough materials*

hat, āge, fär; let, ēqual, tèrm; it, īce
hot, ōpen, ôrder; oil, out; cup, pùt, rüle,
above, takən, pencəl, lemən, circəs
ch, child; ng, long; sh, ship
th, thin; ₮н, then; zh, measure

smooth. —*v.* smooth or wear away with a file. [OE *fīl*] —**fil′er**, *n.*

file clerk a person whose work is taking care of the files in an office.

file·fish (fīl′fish′) *n., pl.* **-fish** or **-fish·es.** any of various tropical marine fishes (family Balistidae) having a rough skin and a very long dorsal spine.

fi·let (fi lā′, fil′ā or fē′lā) *n.* **1** a net or lace having a square mesh. **2** fillet (def. 3). [< F. See FILLET.]

filet mignon a small, round, thick piece of choice beef, cut from the tenderloin.

fil·i·al (fil′ē əl) *adj.* of a son or daughter; due from a son or daughter: *The children treated their parents with filial respect.* [< LL *filialis* < L *filius* son, *filia* daughter] —**fil′i·al·ly,** *adv.*

fil·i·bus·ter (fil′ə bus′tər) *n., v.* —*n.* **1 a** the deliberate hindering of the passage of a bill in a legislature by long speeches or other means of delay. **b** a member of a legislature who hinders the passage of a bill by such means. **2** a person who fights against another country without the authorization of his government; freebooter. —*v.* **1** deliberately hinder the passage of a bill by long speeches or other means of delay. **2** fight against another country without the authorization of one's government; act as a freebooter. [< Sp. *filibustero* < Du. *vrijbuiter.* See FREEBOOTER.] —**fil′i·bus′ter·er,** *n.*

fil·i·gree (fil′ə grē′) *n., v.* **-greed, -gree·ing;** *adj.* —*n.* **1** very delicate, lacelike ornamental work of gold or silver wire. **2** a lacy, delicate, or fanciful pattern in any material: *The frost made a beautiful filigree on the window pane.* —*v.* decorate with or form into filigree. —*adj.* ornamented with filigree; made into filigree. [for *filigrane* < F < Ital. *filigrana* < L *filum* thread + *granum* grain]

filing cabinet a set of steel or wooden drawers for storing files of letters or other papers, records, etc.

fil·ings (fīl′ingz) *n.pl.* the small pieces of iron, wood, etc. that have been removed by a file.

Fil·i·pine (fil′ə pēn′) See **Philippine.**

Fil·i·pi·no (fil′ə pē′nō) *n., pl.* **-nos;** *fem.* **Filipina, -nas;** *adj.* —*n.* a native or inhabitant of the Philippines, a country consisting of about 7 000 islands in the W Pacific Ocean; *adj.* of or having to do with the Philippines or its inhabitants; Philippine.

fill (fil) *v., n.* —*v.* **1** put into until there is room for no more; make full: *to fill a cup.* **2** become full: *The hall filled rapidly.* **3** take up all the space in: *The crowd filled the hall.* **4** satisfy the hunger or appetite of. **5** supply what is needed for: *A store fills orders, prescriptions, etc.* **6** stop up or close by putting something in: *A dentist fills decayed teeth.* **7** hold and do the duties of (a position, office, etc.). **8** supply a person for or appoint a person to (a position, office, etc.).
fill in, a fill with something put in. **b** complete by filling. **c** put in to complete something. **d** acquaint with; bring up to date: *Could you fill me in as to what happened during my absence?*
fill out, a make larger; grow larger; swell. **b** make rounder, grow rounder. **c** complete by filling. **d** complete (a questionnaire, etc.), enter requested information on a form.
fill the bill, come up to requirements.
fill up, fill; fill completely.
—*n.* **1** enough to fill something. **2** all that is needed or wanted: *Eat and drink your fill; there is plenty for all of us.* **3** something that fills: *Earth or rock used to make uneven land level is called fill.* [OE *fyllan* < *full* full]

fill·er (fil′ər) *n.* **1** a person or thing that fills. **2** an implement used to fill something, such as a funnel. **3** anything put in to fill something. A pad of paper for a notebook, a preparation put on wood before painting it, and the tobacco inside cigars are all fillers. **4** something used to fill an empty space.

fil·lér (fel′ler) *n.* a unit of money in Hungary, equal to ¹⁄₁₀₀ of a forint. [< Hungarian]

fil·let (fil′it; *n.* 3 *and v.* 2, *usually* fi lā′) *n., v.* —*n.* **1** a narrow band, ribbon, etc. put around the head to keep the hair in place or as an ornament. **2** a narrow band or strip of any material. Fillets are often used between mouldings, the flutes of a column, etc. **3** a slice of fish, meat, etc. without bones or fat; filet. —*v.* **1** bind or decorate with a narrow band, ribbon, strip, etc. **2** cut (fish, meat, etc.) into fillets. [< F *filet,* dim. of *fil* < L *filum* thread]

fill-in (fil′in′) *n.* **1** a person or thing used to fill a vacancy or omission. **2** an activity that occupies spare time between more important events. **3** information that brings (someone) up to date on a situation; a briefing.

fill·ing (fil′ing) *n.* **1** anything put in to fill something. A dentist puts a filling in a decayed tooth. **2** the threads running from side to side across a woven fabric. **3** a making full; becoming full.

filling station a place where gasoline and oil for motor vehicles are sold.

fil·lip (fil′əp) *v., n.* —*v.* **1** strike with the fingernail as it is snapped quickly outwards after being bent and held back against the thumb. **2** toss or cause to move by striking in this way: *He filliped a coin into the beggar's cup.* **3** rouse; revive; stimulate. —*n.* **1** a quick, light blow given by striking with the fingernail as it is snapped quickly outwards after being bent and held back against the thumb. **2** anything that rouses, revives, or stimulates: *Relishes serve as fillips to the appetite.* [probably imitative]

fil·ly (fil′ē) *n., pl.* **-lies.** **1** a young female horse; a mare that is less than four or five years old. **2** *Informal.* a lively girl. [< ON *fylja.* Akin to FOAL.]

film (film) *n., v.* —*n.* **1** a very thin layer, sheet, surface, or coating: *a film of dew. Oil poured on water will spread and make a film.* **2** a thin, flexible strip or sheet of cellulose material coated on one side with a light-sensitive emulsion and used in making photographic negatives or transparencies. **3** motion picture. **4** a very thin sheet or leaf of metal or other material.
—*v.* **1** cover or become covered with a film: *Her eyes filmed with tears.* **2** make a motion picture after or from: *to film a scene, to film a novel.* **3** be suitable for a motion picture: *Battle scenes usually film well.* **4** make a motion picture: *They're filming on location next week.* [OE *filmen.* Related to FELL⁴.] —**film′like′,** *adj.*

film·go·er (film′gō′ər) *n.* a person who goes to see motion pictures, especially one who does so regularly or habitually.

film·ic (fil′mik) *adj.* of, having to do with, or like a motion picture or motion pictures.

film·mak·er (film′mā′kər) *n.* a person who makes motion pictures.

film·mak·ing (film′mā′king) *n.* the art or process of making motion pictures.

film·strip (film′strip′) *n.* a series of still pictures on one theme or subject, put on film to be projected in sequence.

film·y (fil′mē) *adj.* **film·i·er, film·i·est. 1** of or like a film; very thin. **2** covered with or as if with a film. —**film′i·ly,** *adv.* —**film′i·ness,** *n.*

fils (fils) *n., pl.* **fils. 1** a unit of money in Bahrain, Iraq, Jordan, Kuwait, and the People's Democratic Republic of Yemen, equal to ¹⁄₁₀₀₀ of a dinar. **2** a unit of money in the United Arab Emirates equal to ¹⁄₁₀₀ of a dinar and ¹⁄₁₀₀₀ of a dirham. **3** a coin worth one fils. [Arabic]

fil·ter (fil′tər) *n., v.* —*n.* **1** a device for straining out substances from a liquid or gas by passing it slowly through felt, paper, sand, charcoal, etc. A filter is used to remove impurities from drinking water. **2** the felt, paper, sand, charcoal, or other porous material used in such a device. **3** any of various devices for removing dust, smoke, germs, etc. from the air. **4** a device for controlling certain light rays, electric currents, etc. Putting a yellow filter in front of a camera lens causes less blue light to reach the film.
—*v.* **1** pass through a filter; strain. **2** act as a filter for. **3** pass or flow very slowly: *Water filters through the sandy soil and into the well.* **4** remove or control by a filter: *Filter out all the dirt before using this water.* [< Med.L *filtrum* felt < Gmc.] —**fil′ter·er,** *n.*

fil·ter·a·ble (fil′tər ə bəl) *adj.* **1** that can be filtered. **2** capable of passing through a filter that arrests bacteria: *a filterable virus.*

filter tip 1 a cigarette with an attached filter, for removing impurities from the smoke before it is inhaled. **2** the filter itself.

filth (filth) *n.* **1** foul, disgusting dirt: *The alley was littered with garbage and other filth.* **2** obscene words or thoughts; vileness; moral corruption. [OE *fylth* < *fūl* foul]

filth·y (fil′thē) *adj.* **filth·i·er, filth·i·est. 1** disgustingly dirty; foul. **2** vile. —**filth′i·ly,** *adv.* —**filth′i·ness,** *n.*
☛ *Syn.* See note at **dirty.**

fil·tra·ble (fil′trə bəl) *adj.* filterable.

fil·trate (fil′trāt) *n., v.* **-trat·ed, -trat·ing.** —*n.* liquid that has been passed through a filter. —*v.* pass through a filter.

fil·tra·tion (fil trā′shən) *n.* filtering or being filtered.

fin (fin) *n.* **1** a movable winglike part of a fish's body. Moving the fins enables the fish to swim, guide, and balance itself in the water. See **fish** for picture. **2** something like a fin in shape or use, as: **a** a fixed or movable piece attached to aircraft to provide stability in flight. See **airplane** for picture. **b** any of the thin, flat, lateral projections on a radiator, engine cylinder, etc., designed to dissipate heat. **c** flipper (def. 2). [OE *finn*] —**fin′less,** *adj.* —**fin′like′,** *adj.*
☛ *Hom.* **Finn.**

fi·na·gle (fə nā′gəl) *v.* **-gled, -gling.** *Informal.* **1** manage craftily or cleverly: *He finagled his way into the job.* **2** cheat; swindle. [var. of Brit. dial. *fainaigue* renege at cards; origin uncertain] —**fi·na′gler,** *n.*

fi·nal (fī′nəl) *adj., n.* —*adj.* **1** at the end; last; with no more after it. **2** deciding; settling the question; not to be changed: *The*

decisions of the judge will be final. **3** having to do with purpose: *a final clause.*
—*n.* **1** something final: *The last examination of a school term is a final.* **2 finals,** *pl.* the last or deciding set in a series of contests, examinations, etc. [ME < L *finalis* < *finis* end]
☞ *Syn. adj.* **1.** See note at **last**[1].

fi·na·le (fə nal′ē *or* fə nä′lē) *n.* **1** the last part of a piece of music or a play. **2** the last part; end. [< Ital. *finale* final]

fi·nal·ist (fī′nəl ist) *n.* a person who takes part in the last or deciding set in a series of contests, etc.

fi·nal·i·ty (fī nal′ə tē *or* fə nal′ə tē) *n.,* *pl.* **-ties. 1** being final, finished, or settled: *He spoke with an air of finality.* **2** something final; a final act, speech, etc.

fi·nal·ize (fī′nəl īz′) *v.* bring to a conclusion; complete or finish in such a manner as to be final: *The committee hopes to finalize its report next week.*
☞ *Usage.* This word, though well established, is considered jargon by many people.

fi·nal·ly (fī′nəl ē) *adv.* **1** at the end; at last. **2** so as to decide or settle the question.

fi·nance (fī′nans, fə nans′, *or* fī nans′) *n.,* *v.* **-nanced, -nanc·ing.**
—*n.* **1** money matters. **2** the management of large sums of public or private money. **Public finance** is the management of government revenue and expenditure. **3 finances,** *pl.* money matters; money; funds; revenues.
—*v.* **1** provide money for: *His friends helped him finance a new business.* **2** manage the finances of. [ME < OF *finance* ending, settlement of a debt, ult. < *fin* end < L *finis.* Related to FINE[2].]

finance company a firm whose business is lending money for repayment by instalments with interest.

fi·nan·cial (fī nan′shəl *or* fə nan′shəl) *adj.* **1** having to do with money matters. **2** having to do with the management of large sums of public or private money. —**fi·nan′cial·ly,** *adv.*
☞ *Syn.* **1. Financial, monetary, fiscal** = having to do with money. **Financial** = having to do with money matters in general: *His financial affairs are in bad condition.* **Monetary** = of or directly connected with money itself: *His work brought him fame, but little monetary reward.* **Fiscal** = having to do with the funds and financial affairs of a government, institution, or corporation: *The fiscal year of the Canadian government begins on April 1.*

fin·an·cier (fī′nən sēr′, fin′ən sēr′, *or* fə nan′sēr) *n.* **1** a person skilled in finance. **2** a person who is active in matters involving large sums of money. [< F]

fin·back (fin′bak′) *n.* rorqual.

finch (finch) *n.* any of a family (Fringillidae) of songbirds having a short, strong, conical bill for crushing seeds. Some common finches are the goldfinches, grosbeaks, buntings, and cardinals. [OE *finc*]

find (fīnd) *v.* **found, find·ing;** *n.* —*v.* **1** come upon; happen on; meet with: *He found a silver dollar in the road.* **2** look for and get: *Please find my hat for me.* **3** discover; learn: *We found that he could not swim.* **4** see; know; feel; perceive: *He found that he was growing sleepy.* **5** get; get the use of: *Can you find time to do this?* **6** arrive at; reach: *Water finds its level.* **7** *Law.* decide and declare: *The jury found the accused man guilty.* **8** provide; supply: *to find food and lodging for a friend.* **9** come to have; receive: *The book found many readers.*
find oneself, learn one's abilities and make good use of them.
find out, learn about; come to know; discover.
—*n.* **1** finding. **2** something found, especially something exciting or valuable. [OE *findan*]

find·er (fīn′dər) *n.* **1** a person or thing that finds. **2** a small extra lens on the outside of a camera that shows what is being photographed. **3** a small telescope attached to a larger one to help find objects more easily.

fin de siè·cle (fan də sye′kl) *French.* the end of the century. From about 1880 to 1910, *fin de siècle* was used to mean "up-to-date," connoting also "over-elegant" or "decadent."

find·ing (fīn′ding) *n.* **1** discovering. **2** the thing found. **3** Often, **findings,** *pl.* the decision or conclusion reached after an examination of facts, data, etc. by a commission, judge, scholar, etc.: *The Commission will publish its findings next spring.* **4 findings,** *pl.* the tools and supplies, other than the main materials, used by a shoemaker, dressmaker, or other artisan: *A jeweller's findings include swivels, clasps, and wire.*

fine[1] (fīn) *adj.* **fin·er, fin·est;** *adv.,* *v.* **fined, fin·ing.** —*adj.* **1** of very high quality; very good; excellent: *a fine sermon, a fine view, a fine young man.* **2** very small or thin: *fine wire.* **3** in very small particles: *fine sand.* **4** sharp: *a tool with a fine edge.* **5** not coarse or heavy; delicate: *fine linen.* **6** refined; elegant: *fine manners.* **7** subtle: *The law makes fine distinctions.* **8** too highly decorated; showy: *fine language or writing.* **9** handsome; good-looking: *a fine horse.* **10** clear; pleasant; bright: *fine weather.* **11** without impurities: *Fine gold is gold not mixed with any other metal.* **12** having a stated

hat, āge, fär; let, ēqual, tèrm; it, īce
hot, ōpen, ôrder; oil, out; cup, pùt, rüle,
əbove, takən, pencəl, lemən, circəs

ch, child; ng, long; sh, ship
th, thin; ᴛʜ, then; zh, measure

proportion of gold or silver in it. A gold alloy that is 925/1000 fine is 92.5 percent gold. **13** well; in good health: *I feel fine.*
—*adv.* *Informal.* very well; excellently.
—*v.* make fine or finer; become fine or finer. [ME < OF *fin,* ult. < L *finire* finish] —**fine′ly,** *adv.*
☞ *Syn. adj.* **1. Fine, choice, elegant** = very high quality. **Fine** is the general word: *He does fine work.* **Choice** = of fine or the best quality, usually carefully picked by or for a taste that can tell and appreciate differences in quality or value: *He selected a choice piece of jade.* **Elegant** = showing fine taste, rich or luxurious but graceful and refined: *She selected elegant drapes.*

fine[2] (fīn) *n.,* *v.* **fined, fin·ing.** —*n.* a sum of money paid as a punishment.
in fine, a finally. **b** in a few words; briefly.
—*v.* cause to pay a fine. [ME < OF *fin* < L *finis* end; in Med.L. settlement, payment]

fi·ne[3] (fē′nā) *n.* *Music.* a direction marking the end of a passage that has to be repeated. [< Ital.]

fine arts the arts depending upon taste and appealing to the sense of beauty; painting, drawing, sculpture, and architecture. Literature, music, dancing, and acting are also usually included in the fine arts.

fine–drawn (fīn′dron′ *or* -drôn′) *adj.* **1** drawn out until very small or thin. **2** very subtle: *Fine-drawn distinctions are difficult to understand.*

fine–grained (fīn′grānd′) *adj.* having a fine, close grain: *Mahogany is a fine-grained wood.*

fine·ness (fīn′nis) *n.* **1** being fine. **2** the proportion of gold or silver in an alloy.

fin·er·y (fīn′ər ē) *n.,* *pl.* **-er·ies.** showy clothes, ornaments, etc. [< FINE[1]]

fine–spun (fīn′spun′) *adj.* **1** spun or drawn out until very small or thin. **2** very subtle.

fi·nesse (fə nes′) *n.,* *v.* **-nessed, -ness·ing.** —*n.* **1** delicacy of execution; skill: *That artist shows wonderful finesse.* **2** the skilful handling of a delicate situation to one's advantage; craft; stratagem: *a master of finesse.* **3** *Bridge, whist, etc.* an attempt to take a trick with a lower card while holding a higher card, in the hope that the card or cards between may not be played.
—*v.* **1** use finesse. **2** bring or change by finesse. **3** make a finesse with (a card). [< F *finesse* < *fin* fine[1]]

fine–toothed (fīn′tütht′) *adj.* having fine, very closely set teeth: *a fine-toothed saw.*
go over with a fine-toothed comb, examine carefully.

fin·ger (fing′gər) *n.,* *v.* —*n.* **1** one of the five end parts of the hand, especially the four besides the thumb. **2** the part of a glove that covers a finger. **3** anything shaped or used like a finger. **4** the breadth of a finger (about 2 cm). **5** the length of a finger (about 11.5 cm).
burn (one's) **fingers,** get into trouble by meddling.
have a finger in the pie, a take part or have a share in doing something. **b** meddle; interfere.
put (one's) **finger on,** point out exactly.
put the finger on, *Slang.* single out for slaying (by a gang).
twist around (one's) **little finger,** manage easily; control completely.
—*v.* **1** touch or handle with the fingers; use the fingers on. **2** perform or mark (a passage of music) with a certain fingering. **3** pilfer; filch; steal. **4** *Slang.* point out; betray; inform upon. **5** make vague grasping movements with the fingers. **6** point or extend like a finger. [OE] —**fin′ger·er,** *n.*

finger board **1** a strip of wood on the neck of a violin, guitar, etc. against which the strings are pressed by the fingers of the player. **2** the keyboard on a piano or organ.

finger bowl a small bowl to hold water for rinsing the fingers during or after a meal.

fin·ger·hold (fing′gər hōld′) *n.* **1** anything that offers a grip for the fingers. **2** a grip using the fingers only. **3** a weak support or grip.

fin·ger·ing (fing′gər ing *or* fing′gring) *n.* **1** a touching or handling with the fingers; way of using the fingers. In playing certain musical instruments the fingering is important. **2** the signs marked on a piece of music to show which fingers are to be used in playing particular notes.

fin·ger·ling (fing′gər ling) *n.* **1** a young fish; a fry, especially late in the first year. **2** something very small.

fin·ger·mark (fing′gər märk′) *n.* a smudge or stain left by a finger.

fin·ger·nail (fing′gər nāl′) *n.* the hard layer of hornlike substance at the end of a finger.

fin·ger·paint (fing′gər pānt′) *v.* paint with the fingers, palms, etc. instead of with brushes.

finger paint any of various thickened water colors used in finger painting.

finger painting 1 a technique of applying paint using fingers, palms, etc. instead of brushes. 2 a design or picture so painted.

finger post a guidepost having a sign shaped like a finger or hand to show the direction.

fin·ger·print (fing′gər print′) *n., v.* —*n.* an impression of the markings on the inner surface of the last joint of a finger or thumb. Fingerprints are unique to an individual and so are used for identification. —*v.* take the fingerprints of.

fin·ger·tip (fing′gər tip′) *n.* the very end or tip of the finger.

fin·i·al (fin′ē əl or fī′nē əl) *n.* 1 *Architecture.* an ornament on the top of a roof, the corner of a tower, the end of a pew in church, etc. 2 the highest point. [< Med.L *finium* final settlement (probably originally, end) < L *finis*]

fin·i·cal (fin′ə kəl) *adj.* finicky. [apparently < *fine*[1]] —**fin′i·cal·ly**, *adv.*

fin·ick·ing (fin′ə king) *adj.* finicky.

fin·ick·y (fin′ə kē) *adj.* too dainty or particular; too precise or fussy: *He's terribly finicky about his food.* [< *finical*]

fin·is (fin′is) *n.* end. [< L]

fin·ish (fin′ish) *v., n.* —*v.* 1 bring (action, speech, etc.) to an end; end. 2 bring (work, affairs, etc.) to completion; complete: *He started the race but did not finish it.* 3 come to an end: *There was so little wind that the sailing race didn't finish until after dark.* 4 use up completely: *to finish a spool of thread.* 5 *Informal.* overcome completely: *My answer finished him.* 6 *Informal.* destroy; kill: *to finish a wounded animal.* 7 perfect; polish. 8 prepare the surface in some way: *to finish cloth with nap.*
finish off, a complete. **b** overcome completely; destroy; kill.
finish up, a complete. **b** use up completely.
finish with, a complete. **b** stop being friends with; have nothing to do with. **c** finish using; come to the end of one's need of: *Have you finished with my book yet?*
—*n.* 1 the end. 2 a polished condition or quality; perfection. 3 the way in which a surface is prepared. 4 something used to finish something else. 5 cultivated manners or speech; social polish. 6 the work done on a building after the main structure is finished, such as the window and door trim, etc. 7 the material used for such work.
in at the finish, present at the end.
[ME < OF *feniss*-, a stem of *fenir* < L *finire*] —**fin′ish·er**, *n.*
☛ *Hom.* **Finnish.**
☛ *Syn. v.* 1. See note at **end.**

fin·ished (fin′isht) *adj.* 1 ended. 2 completed. 3 *Informal.* exhausted; defeated; completely overcome: *By the third round the boxer was finished.* 4 perfected; polished.

finishing school a private school that prepares young women for social life rather than for business or a profession.

fi·nite (fī′nīt) *adj., n.* —*adj.* 1 having limits or bounds; not infinite: *Death ends our finite existence.* 2 *Grammar.* designating a verb inflected for features such as person, number, and tense. In the sentence *Before going to the game, she stopped to mail the letter, stopped* is the finite verb, *going* is a participle, and *to mail* is an infinitive. 3 *Mathematics.* **a** of a number, capable of being reached or passed in counting. **b** of a magnitude, less than infinite and greater than infinitesimal.
—*n.* something finite. [< L *finitus,* pp. of *finire* finish]

fink (fingk) *n. Slang.* 1 informer. 2 strikebreaker. 3 any unpleasant person.

Finn (fin) *n.* 1 a native or inhabitant of Finland, a country in N Europe. 2 a person of Finnish descent. 3 a member of any of the peoples speaking Finnic languages.
☛ *Hom.* **fin.**

fin·nan had·die (fin′ən had′ē) smoked haddock. [for *Findhorn haddock;* from the name of a town in Scotland]

Finn·ic (fin′ik) *n., adj.* —*n.* a branch of the Finno-Ugric family of languages, including Finnish, Estonian, and Lapp. —*adj.* of or having to do with this group of languages or the Finns.

Finn·ish (fin′ish) *n., adj.* —*n.* the Finnic language of the Finns. —*adj.* of or having to do with Finland, its people, or their language.
☛ *Hom.* **finish.**

Finn·mark (fin′märk′) *n.* markka.

Fin·no·U·gric (fin′ō yü′grik *or* -ü′grik) *n., adj.* —*n.* a family of languages spoken primarily in N and E Europe and W Asia, including Finnish, Estonian, Hungarian, and Lapp. —*adj.* of or having to do with any of the peoples speaking these languages.

fin·ny (fin′ē) *adj.* 1 abounding with fish: *The sea is sometimes called the finny deep.* 2 having fins. 3 like a fin.

fin whale rorqual.

fiord (fyôrd) *n.* a long narrow bay of the sea between high banks or cliffs. Norway has many fiords. Also, **fjord.** [< Norwegian *fiord,* earlier *fjorthr.* Akin to FIRTH.]

fir (fėr) *n.* 1 any of a genus (*Abies*) of evergreen trees of the pine family found throughout the north temperate regions of the world, having leaves shaped like flattened needles and upright cones. The four species of the fir native to Canada are balsam fir, alpine fir, amabilis fir, and grand fir. 2 the wood of any of these trees. [OE *fyrh* (cf. *furhwudu* fir-wood) or < ON *fyri*]
☛ *Hom.* **fur.**

fire (fīr) *n., v.* **fired, fir·ing.** —*n.* 1 the flame, heat, and light caused by something burning. 2 a burning mass of fuel: *Put more wood on the fire.* 3 fuel arranged for burning: *A fire was laid in the fireplace.* 4 a destructive burning: *A great fire destroyed the furniture factory.* 5 a preparation that will burn: *Red fire is used in signalling.* 6 something that suggests a fire because it is hot, glowing, brilliant, or light: *the fire of lightning, an insane fire in his eye, the fire in a diamond.* 7 any feeling that suggests fire; passion, fervor, enthusiasm, excitement, etc. 8 a burning pain; fever; inflammation: *the fire of a wound.* 9 a severe trial or trouble. 10 the shooting or discharge of guns, etc.: *enemy fire.*
between two fires, attacked from both sides.
catch fire, begin to burn: *Be careful that the curtains don't catch fire from the lamp.*
go through fire and water, endure many troubles or dangers.
hang fire, a be slow in going off. **b** be slow in acting. **c** be delayed.
lay a fire, build a fire so that it is ready to be lit.
on fire, a burning. **b** full of a feeling or spirit like fire; excited: *The troops were on fire with the desire for victory.*
play with fire, meddle with something dangerous.
set fire to, cause to burn.
set on fire, a cause to burn. **b** fill with a feeling or spirit like fire.
take fire, begin to burn.
under fire, a exposed to shooting from enemy guns. **b** attacked; blamed.
—*v.* 1 cause to burn. 2 begin to burn; burst into flame. 3 supply fuel to; tend: *The men fired the steamship's huge furnaces.* 4 dry with heat; bake: *Bricks are fired to make them hard.* 5 grow or make hot, red, glowing, etc. 6 arouse; excite; inflame: *Stories of adventure fire the imagination.* 7 discharge (a gun, bomb, gas mine, etc.). 8 discharge or propel a missile, etc. from or as if from a gun; shoot: *to fire a rocket. The soldiers fired from the fort. The hunter fired small shot.* 9 *Informal.* dismiss from a job, etc. 10 of grain, turn yellow before ripening as a result of drought or disease. 11 of pottery, etc., respond in a specified manner to baking in a kiln: *This clay fires a deep red.*
fire away, *Informal.* begin; start; go ahead.
fire up, a start a fire in a furnace, boiler, etc: *The men did not have time to fire up.* **b** become angry, lose one's temper. **c** set a machine or other device in operation.
[OE *fȳr*] —**fir′er,** *n.*

fire alarm 1 the signal that a fire has broken out. 2 a device that gives such a signal.

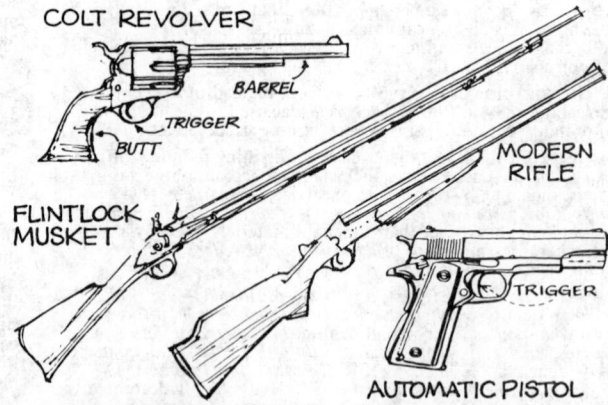

COLT REVOLVER   BARREL   TRIGGER   BUTT

FLINTLOCK MUSKET

MODERN RIFLE

TRIGGER

AUTOMATIC PISTOL

fire·arm (fīr′ärm′) *n.* rifle, pistol, or other weapon to shoot with, usually such as a person can carry.

fire·ball (fîr′bol′ *or* -bôl′) *n.* **1** anything that looks like a ball of fire, such as a ball of lightning. **2** a large, brilliant meteor. **3** the great billowing mass of fire produced by an atomic explosion. **4** *Baseball.* a very fast pitch to the batter. **5** *Informal.* a person who possesses great energy and enthusiasm.

fire·boat (fîr′bōt′) *n.* a boat equipped with apparatus for putting out fires on a dock, ship, etc.

fire·bomb (fîr′bom′) *n., v.* —*n.* an incendiary bomb. —*v.* attack or destroy with a firebomb or firebombs.

fire·bomb·er (fîr′bom′ər) *n.* **1** a person who attacks or destroys with firebombs. **2** water bomber.

fire·bomb·ing (fîr′bom′ing) *n.* **1** the act or an instance of using an incendiary bomb to attack or destroy: *Several people have been arrested in connection with the firebombing.* **2** the use of a water bomber to fight a forest fire.

fire·box (fîr′boks′) *n.* **1** the place for the fire in a furnace, boiler, etc. **2** the furnace of a steam boiler, especially that of a steam locomotive.

fire·brand (fîr′brand′) *n.* **1** a piece of burning wood. **2** a person who stirs up unrest, strife, rebellion, etc.; hothead.

fire·break (fîr′brāk′) *n.* a strip of land that has been cleared of trees or on which the sod has been turned over so as to prevent the spreading of a forest fire or a prairie fire.

fire·brick (fîr′brik′) *n.* a brick capable of standing great heat, and used to line furnaces and fireplaces.

fire brigade 1 a body of men organized, often privately or temporarily, to fight fires. **2** *Esp.Brit.* a fire department.

fire·bug (fîr′bug′) *n. Informal.* a person who has a mania for setting houses or property on fire; pyromaniac.

fire clay clay capable of resisting high temperatures, used for making crucibles, firebricks, etc.

fire company a group of men organized to put out fires.

fire·crack·er (fîr′krak′ər) *n.* a paper roll containing gunpowder and a fuse: *A firecracker explodes with a loud noise.*

fire·damp (fîr′damp′) *n.* a mixture of gases, consisting mainly of methane, that forms in coal mines. It is dangerously explosive when mixed with certain proportions of air.

fire department a municipal department in charge of the fighting and preventing of fires.

fire·dog (fîr′dog′) *n.* andiron.

fire drill drill for firemen, a ship's crew, pupils in a school, etc. to train them for duties or for orderly exit in case of fire.

fire–eat·er (fîr′ēt′ər) *n.* **1** an entertainer who pretends to eat fire. **2** a person who is too ready to fight or quarrel.

fire engine a truck with a machine for throwing water, chemicals, etc. and with ladders and other equipment to put out fires.

fire escape a stairway, ladder, etc. in or on a building, to use in case of fire.

fire extinguisher a container filled with chemicals that can be sprayed upon fire to extinguish it.

fire·fight·er (fîr′fīt′ər) *n.* **1** a member of a fire department. **2** a person who fights forest fires.

fire·fight·ing (fîr′fīt′ing) *n.* the act or process of fighting fires.

fire–find·er (fîr′fīn′dər) *n.* an instrument consisting of a sighting device and a map, for finding the position of a forest fire.

fire·fly (fîr′flī′) *n., pl.* **-flies. 1** any of a family (Lampyridae) of small nocturnal beetles having an abdominal organ by means of which they produce flashes of light. Firefly larvae and the adult wingless females of some species are called glow-worms. **2** any of various other beetles having luminescent organs, especially some tropical members of the family Elateridae.

fire·guard (fîr′gärd′) *n.* **1** fire screen. **2** fire break.

fire hall 1 *Cdn.* a building in which firefighting equipment is kept. **2** the headquarters of a fire department: *Permits for burning rubbish may be obtained at the fire hall.*

fire insurance insurance against damage or loss caused by fire.

fire irons tools, such as a poker, tongs, and shovel, needed for tending a fire.

fire·less (fîr′lis) *adj.* **1** without a fire. **2** without enthusiasm or animation.

fire·light (fîr′līt′) *n.* the light from a fire.

fire line 1 firebreak. **2** the front edge of a forest fire or a prairie fire.

fire·lock (fîr′lok′) *n.* an old type of gun, fired by a spark falling on the gunpowder; flintlock.

fire·man (fîr′mən) *n., pl.* **-men. 1** a man whose work is putting

hat, āge, fär; let, ēqual, tėrm; it, īce
hot, ōpen, ôrder; oil, out; cup, pút, rüle,
əbove, takən, pencəl, lemən, circəs
ch, child; ng, long; sh, ship
th, thin; ŦH, then; zh, measure

out fires. **2** a man whose work is taking care of the fire in a furnace, boiler, locomotive, etc.

fire·place (fîr′plās′) *n.* a place built in the wall of a room or out of doors to hold a fire.

fire plug hydrant.

fire pot the part of a stove, furnace, etc. that holds the fire.

fire·pow·er (fîr′pou′ər) *n.* **1** the amount of fire delivered by a military unit, by a particular weapon, etc. **2** the ability to deliver fire.

fire·proof (fîr′prüf′) *adj., v.* —*adj.* that will not burn; almost impossible to burn: *A building made entirely of steel and concrete is fireproof.* —*v.* make fireproof.

fire–rang·er (fîr′rān′jər) *n.* a government employee engaged in preventing and putting out forest fires on Crown lands.

fire–reels (fîr′rēlz′) *n. Cdn. Esp.Ontario* fire engine.

fire sale a sale of goods damaged as a result of a fire.

fire screen a screen to be placed in front of a fire as protection against heat or flying sparks.

fire ship a ship loaded with explosives and inflammable materials, set adrift among enemy ships.

fire·side (fîr′sīd′) *n., adj.* —*n.* **1** the space around a fireplace or hearth. **2** the home. **3** home life. —*adj.* beside the fire.

fire–spot·ter (fîr′spot′ər) *n.* a person who works as an agent of the firefighting authorities by watching for and locating forest fires.

fire station fire hall.

fire tower a tower from which to keep watch for forest fires.

fire·trap (fîr′trap′) *n.* **1** a building hard to get out of in case of fire. **2** a building that will burn very easily.

fire·truck fire engine.

fire wall 1 a fireproof wall for confining a possible fire. **2** a fireproof plate or shield behind the engine of an automobile or airplane.

fire·ward·en (fîr′wôr′dən) *n.* an official whose duty is preventing and putting out fires in forests, camps, etc.

fire·wa·ter (fîr′wo′tər *or* -wô′tər) *n. Humorous.* any strong alcoholic drink: *The North American Indians called whisky, gin, rum, etc. firewater.*

fire·weed (fîr′wēd′) *n.* **1** any of several plants (genus *Epilobium*) of the evening-primrose family, especially a tall species (*E. angustifolium*) of north temperate regions, that flourishes especially in newly burned areas, having long, showy spikes of purplish-pink flowers. The fireweed is the floral emblem of the Yukon. **2** any of several other plants that commonly grow in burned areas.

fire·wood (fîr′wúd′) *n.* wood for burning in a stove, fireplace, etc.

fire·work (fîr′wėrk′) *n.* **1** a firecracker, bomb, rocket, etc. that makes a loud noise or a beautiful, fiery display, especially at night. **2 fireworks,** a firework display.

firing line 1 any line where soldiers are stationed to shoot at the enemy, a target, etc. **2** the soldiers on such a line. **3** the foremost position in a controversy, campaign for a cause, etc.

firing range 1 an area used for shooting practice. **2** the distance within which specific weapons are effective: *The robber was within firing range.*

firing squad 1 a small detachment of troops assigned to shoot to death a condemned person. **2** a detachment assigned to fire a salute.

fir·kin (fėr′kən) *n.* **1** a quarter of a barrel, used as a measure of capacity. **2** a small wooden cask for butter, etc. [ME *ferdekyn* < MDu. *verdelkijn,* dim. of *verdel,* literally, fourth part]

firm[1] (fėrm) *adj., v.* —*adj.* **1** not yielding easily to pressure or force; solid; hard: *firm flesh.* **2** not easily moved or shaken; tightly fastened or fixed: *a tree firm in the earth.* **3** steady in motion or action: *a firm step, a firm grasp.* **4** not easily changed; determined; resolute; positive: *a firm purpose.* **5** not changing; staying the same; steady: *a firm price.*
—*v.* make or become firm. [< L *firmus*] —**firm′ly,** *adv.* —**firm′ness,** *n.*

☛ *Syn. adj.* **1. Firm, hard, solid** = not yielding easily to pressure or force. **Firm** = so strong, tough, or compact in composition or structure that it is not easy to squeeze or pull out of shape, bend, or dig or cut into: *His muscles are firm.* **Hard** = so strong, stiff, or thick as to be almost impossible to squeeze, pull,

etc.: *The ground is too hard to dig.* **Solid** = so strongly built, uniformly dense, firm, or hard as to withstand all pressure or force: *We build houses on solid ground.*

firm² (fèrm) *n.* a company or partnership of two or more persons in business together: *an old and trusted friend.* [< Ital. < Sp., Pg. *firma* signature, ult. < L *firmus* firm¹]

fir·ma·ment (fèr′mə mənt) *n.* the arch of the heavens; sky. [< L *firmamentum,* ult. < *firmus* firm¹]

firn (fèrn) *n.* névé. [< G *firn* of last year]

first (fèrst) *adj., adv., n.* —*adj.* **1** coming before all others; 1st: *John is first in his class.* **2** *Music.* **a** highest in pitch. **b** playing or singing the part highest in pitch.
in the first place, first; firstly; before anything else.
(the) first thing, at the earliest possible moment: *He is going first thing in the morning.*
—*adv.* **1** before all others; before anything else: *Women and children go first.* **2** before some other thing or event: *First bring me the chalk.* **3** for the first time: *when I first visited Italy.* **4** rather; sooner: *I'll go to jail first.*
—*n.* **1** a person, thing, place, etc. that is first. **2** the winning position in a race, etc. **3** the beginning. **4** in an automobile or similar machine, the first, or lowest, gear; low. **5** **firsts,** *pl.* articles of the best quality.
at first, in the beginning: *At first John did not like school.*
first and last, taking all together.
from the first, since the beginning. [OE *fyrst*]
☛ *Usage.* **First. a** When used with a numeral, **first** precedes the numeral: *For tomorrow I want you to do the first six problems.* **b first, last, latest. First** and **last** refer to items in a series, usually of more than two: *His first act in office was to appoint a new secretary. We felt let down at the end of the last act.* **Latest** refers to a series that is still continuing: *Have you read the latest instalment of the new serial story?* **Last** refers either to the final item of a completed series or to the most recent item of a continuing series: *His last jump proved fatal. I was pleased with the last election.*

first aid the emergency treatment given to an injured person before a doctor comes. —**first′-aid′,** *adj.*

first base **1** *Baseball.* the base that must be touched first by a runner. **2** a first baseman.
get to first base, *Informal.* make the first step toward success: *The new secretary will never get to first base if she is not punctual.*

first-born (fèrst′bôrn′) *adj., n.* —*adj.* born first; oldest. —*n.* the first-born child.

first-class (fèrst′klas′) *adj., adv.* —*adj.* **1** of the highest class or best quality; excellent. **2** of or having to do with the class of mail that includes letters, post cards, etc.: *It would be expensive to send a heavy parcel by first-class mail.* —*adv.* **1** on a first-class ship, train, airplane, etc.; in or on the first-class section. **2** by first-class mail.

first day Sunday.

first-day cover (fèrst′dā′) *Philately.* an envelope bearing a commemorative stamp, cancelled on its first day of issue by the post office that issued it.

first finger the finger next to the thumb.

first fruits **1** the earliest fruits of the season. **2** the first products or results.

first-hand (fèrst′hand′) *adj. or adv.* from the original source; direct: *first-hand information. He got the information first-hand.*

first lieutenant *Military.* a commissioned officer junior to a captain and senior to a second lieutenant.

first-ling (fèrst′ling) *n.* **1** the first of its kind. **2** the first product or result. **3** the first offspring of an animal.

first-ly (fèrst′lē) *adv.* in the first place; first.

First Meridian *Cdn.* the basic north-south line from which lands were surveyed in the Northwest Territories and are now surveyed in the Prairie Provinces. The First Meridian is located just west of Winnipeg.

first name a person's first given name or, sometimes, the second (or third) given name if that is what the person is usually known by.

first person *Grammar.* the form of a pronoun or verb used to refer to the speaker and those he includes with himself. *I, me, mine,* and *we, us, ours* are pronouns of the first person.

first quarter **1** the period between the new moon and the first half moon. **2** the phase of moon represented by the first half moon after the new moon.

first-rate (fèrst′rāt′) *adj., adv.* —*adj.* **1** of the highest class. **2** *Informal.* excellent; very good. —*adv. Informal.* excellently; very well.

firth (fèrth) *n.* especially in Scotland, a narrow arm of the sea; estuary of a river. [< ON *fjörthr.* Akin to FIORD.]

fisc (fisk) *n.* a royal or state treasury; exchequer. [< L *fiscus* purse]

fis·cal (fis′kəl) *adj., n.* —*adj.* **1** financial. **2** having to do with a treasury or exchequer: *Important changes were made in the government's fiscal policy.* —*n.* in some countries, a public prosecutor. [< L *fiscalis* < *fiscus* purse] —**fis′cal·ly,** *adv.*
☛ *Syn. adj.* **1.** See note at **financial.**

fiscal year the time between one yearly settlement of financial accounts and another. The fiscal year of the Canadian government ends March 31.

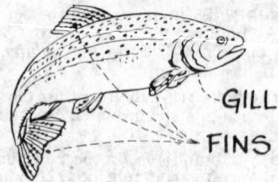
Fish: a rainbow trout—
about 36 cm long
including the tail
GILL
FINS

fish (fish) *n., pl.* **fish** or (esp. for different species) **fish·es;** *v.* —*n.* **1** any of a large group of cold-blooded aquatic vertebrates that breathe by means of gills and most of which have fins and scales. Living fishes are divided into three taxonomic classes: the jawless fishes (Agnatha), including lampreys and hagfishes; the cartilaginous fishes (Chondrichthyes), including sharks and rays; and the bony fishes (Osteichthyes), including sturgeons, salmon and trout, perches, smelts, tunas, flatfishes, and drumfishes. **2** any of various other aquatic creatures (*usually used in compounds*): *starfish, crayfish, jellyfish.* **3** the flesh of fish used for food. **4** *Informal.* a person, especially when thought of as being disadvantaged or lacking some desirable human trait: *a queer fish. The poor fish was caught red-handed.* **5** a long strip of iron, wood, etc. used to strengthen a joint, etc. **6** the **Fishes,** *pl. Astronomy* or *astrology.* Pisces.
a fish out of water, a person who is uncomfortable or ill at ease as a result of being out of his usual environment.
have other fish to fry, *Informal.* have other, especially more important, things to do.
—*v.* **1** try to catch fish. **2** try to catch fish in: *to fish a pool.* **3** try to pick up as if with a hook, etc. (*used with* for): *He fished for the quarter with a bent wire.* **4** search by groping inside something: *She fished in her purse for a coin.* **5** take or pull out, as if fishing: *I fished the map from the back of the drawer.* **6** try to get, especially by indirect means (*used with* for): *fishing for compliments.*
fish in troubled waters, take advantage of confusion or trouble to get what one wants.
fish out, exhaust the supply of fish in (a lake, etc.) by fishing. [OE *fisc*] —**fish′less,** *adj.* —**fish′like′,** *adj.*

fish and chips pieces of fish fried in a batter and served with French fried potatoes.

fish eagle osprey.

fish·er (fish′ər) *n.* **1** a North American animal (*Martes pennanti*) of the weasel family closely related to and resembling the marten, but larger and less arboreal. Fishers are found in the forests of Canada and the N United States. **2** the thick, dark greyish-brown fur of a fisher. **3** *Archaic.* fisherman.
☛ *Hom.* **fissure.**

fish·er·man (fish′ər mən) *n., pl.* **-men. 1** a man who fishes for a living or for pleasure. **2** a ship used in fishing.

fish·er·y (fish′ər ē) *n., pl.* **-er·ies. 1** the business or industry of catching fish. **2** a place for catching fish: *Salmon is the main catch in the Pacific fisheries.*

fish-eye lens (fish′ī′) a wide-angle photographic lens that covers a field of vision of about 180 degrees, producing a circular image with distortion similar to that of a reflection on a globe.

fish farm a place where fish are bred and raised for the market.

fish flake a slatted platform used for drying fish: *Fish flakes are a familiar sight in Newfoundland fishing villages.*

fish flour a tasteless, odorless, high-protein flour produced by pulverizing dried fish.

fish glue a strong glue made from waste parts of fish.

fish hawk *n.* osprey.

fish-hook (fish′hùk′) *n.* a hook used for catching fish.

fish house a hut or small building on the shore, where fishermen store their gear, catch, etc. Fish houses are sometimes used also for smoking and curing fish.

fish·ing (fish′ing) *n.* the catching of fish for a living or for pleasure.

fishing ground a place where fish are plentiful.

fishing hole a hole cut through the ice of a lake, river, etc. to catch fish in winter.

fishing line a line used in fishing.

fishing pole fishing rod.

fishing rod a slender rod, made of bamboo, plastics, etc. for fishing.

fishing smack a small ship used in fishing at sea.

fishing tackle rods, lines, hooks, etc. used in catching fish.

fish ladder fishway.

fish line fishing line.

fish meal ground-up dried fish used as feed for livestock, etc. or as fertilizer.

fish·mon·ger (fish′mung′gər *or* -mong′gər) *n. Esp.Brit.* a dealer in fish.

fish oil oil obtained from fish.

fish pass fishway.

fish·plate (fish′plāt′) *n.* a plate used to fasten two rails or beams together end to end. The rails of a railway track are usually joined by fishplates.

fish pole fishing rod.

fish·pond (fish′pond′) *n.* a pond in which there are fish, especially an ornamental pool where fish, such as goldfish, are kept in captivity.

fish stick **1** frozen fish fillets packaged in the form of a short, oblong stick for ease in shipping and handling: *Each year, thousands of fish sticks are shipped from the Maritimes to markets in Central Canada.* **2** a portion of fish, often breaded and pre-cooked, frozen and packaged for retail sale.

fish story *Informal.* an exaggerated, unbelievable story.

fish·tail (fish′tāl′) *adj., v. —adj.* like a fish's tail in shape or action. *—v.* **1** swing the tail of an airplane from side to side to reduce its speed. **2** of a motor vehicle, etc., have the rear end swing from side to side out of control.

fish·way (fish′wā′) *n.* a waterway built as an ascending series of little pools to enable fish to pass over a dam or falls on their way to spawning grounds upstream.

fish·wife (fish′wīf′) *n., pl.* **-wives.** **1** a woman who sells fish. **2** a woman who uses coarse and abusive language.

fish·y (fish′ē) *adj.* **fish·i·er, fish·i·est.** **1** like a fish in smell, taste, or shape. **2** of fish. **3** full of fish. **4** *Informal.* unlikely; suspicious. **5** without expression or lustre; dull. **—fish′i·ly,** *adv.* **—fish′i·ness,** *n.*

fis·sile (fis′il *or* fis′əl) *adj.* **1** easily split. **2** capable of nuclear fission. [< L *fissilis* < *findere* cleave]

fis·sion (fish′ən) *n.* **1** a splitting apart; division into parts. **2** *Biology.* a method of reproduction in which the body of the parent divides for two or more independent individuals. Many simple plants and animals reproduce by fission. **3** the splitting that occurs when the nucleus of an atom under bombardment absorbs a neutron. Nuclear fission releases tremendous amounts of energy when heavy elements, especially plutonium and uranium, are involved. [< L *fissio, -onis* < *findere* cleave]

fis·sion·a·ble (fish′ən ə bəl) *adj.* capable of nuclear fission.

fission bomb an atomic bomb that derives its force solely from the splitting of atoms. The original atomic bombs were fission bombs; hydrogen bombs are fusion bombs.

fis·sure (fish′ər) *n., v.* **-sured, -sur·ing.** *—n.* **1** a split or crack; a long, narrow opening: *a fissure in a rock.* **2** a splitting apart; a division into parts. **3** a natural cleft or opening in an organ or part of the body. *—v.* split apart; divide into parts; become split. [< F < L *fissura* < *findere* cleave]

☛ *Hom.* **fisher.**

fist (fist) *n.* **1** the hand closed tightly. **2** *Informal.* the hand. **3** *Informal.* handwriting. **4** *Printing.* a symbol (☛). [OE *fȳst*] **—fist′like′,** *adj.*

–fisted *combining form.* having ——fists: *quick-fisted = having quick fists.*

fist·ful (fist′fül′) *n., pl.* **fist·fuls.** as much as a closed hand can hold.

fist·ic (fis′tik) *adj. Informal.* having to do with fighting with the fists; done with the fists.

fist·i·cuffs (fis′ti kufs′) *n.pl.* **1** a fight with the fists. **2** blows with the fists: *It soon came to fisticuffs between them.*

fist·note (fist′nōt′) *n.* in printed texts, a special note preceded by a fist (def. 4).

fis·tu·la (fis′chə lə) *n., pl.* **-las, -lae** (-lē′ *or* -lī′). **1** a tube or pipe. **2** a tubelike sore connecting the surface of the body with an internal organ or cavity. [< L *fistula* pipe, ulcer. Doublet of FESTER, *n.*]

hat, āge, fär; let, ēqual, tèrm; it, īce
hot, ōpen, ôrder; oil, out; cup, pút, rüle,
əbove, takən, pencəl, lemən, circəs

ch, child; ng, long; sh, ship
th, thin; ŦH, then; zh, measure

fis·tu·lar (fis′chə lər) *adj.* **1** tubelike; tubular. **2** made up of tubelike parts. **3** having to do with a fistula.

fit¹ (fit) *adj.* **fit·ter, fit·test;** *v.* **fit·ted, fit·ting;** *n. —adj.* **1** suitable or appropriate: *a dress fit for a queen. The movie isn't fit for children. Grass is fit food for cattle; it is not fit for human beings.* **2** having the necessary or proper qualifications: *They were declared fit for active service. He's not fit to run his own business.* **3** prepared for something or to do or undergo something; ready: *fit to receive visitors. I was almost fit to scream.* **4** in good physical condition; healthy: *They exercise daily to keep fit.*

see *or* **think fit,** consider it suitable, right, etc. (to): *She may see fit to ignore the whole incident.*

—v. **1** be suited or suitable to; be fit for: *Let the punishment fit the crime.* **2** make right, proper, or suitable: *to fit the action to the word.* **3** have the right size or shape (for): *The last piece of the puzzle didn't fit. The dress fits her well.* **4** supply with something needed or wanted; equip (*often used with* out *or* up): *The car is fitted with radial tires.* **5** put (something) on or in, making necessary adjustments: *to fit a slipcover on a chesterfield.* **6** make ready or competent; prepare: *They are receiving preliminary training to fit them for the expedition.* **7** accommodate: *to fit another appointment into a busy schedule.* **8** correspond or agree with: *Her story doesn't fit the facts.*

—n. **1** the manner in which one thing fits another: *the fit of a coat, a tight fit.* **2** something that fits: *This coat is a good fit.* [ME *fyt;* origin uncertain] **—fit′ness,** *n.*

☛ *Syn. adj.* **1. Fit, suitable, appropriate** = have the right qualities for something. **Fit** =having the qualities needed for the purpose, work, or use of the person or thing: *That shack is not fit to live in.* **Suitable** = having the qualities right or proper for a definite occasion, purpose, position, condition, or situation: *The lawyer found a suitable office.* **Appropriate** = unusually fit or suitable for the particular person, purpose, position, occasion, etc.: *A tailored suit is appropriate for a secretary.*

fit² (fit) *n.* **1** a sudden, sharp attack of illness: *a fit of colic.* **2** a sudden attack of illness characterized by loss of consciousness or by convulsions: *a fainting fit, a fit of epilepsy.* **3** any sudden, sharp attack: *In a fit of anger he hit his friend.* **4** a short period of doing one thing: *a fit of laughter.*

by fits and starts, irregularly; starting, stopping, beginning again, and so on. [OE *fitt* conflict]

fitch (fich) *n.* **1** the European polecat. **2** the dark-brown fur of a polecat. [? < MDu. *fisse*]

fitch·et (fich′it) *n.* fitch.

fitch·ew (fich′ü) *n.* fitch.

fit·ful (fit′fəl) *adj.* going on and then stopping awhile; irregular: *a fitful sleep, a fitful conversation.* [< fit²] **—fit′ful·ly,** *adv.* **—fit′ful·ness,** *n.*

fit·ly (fit′lē) *adv.* **1** in a suitable manner. **2** at a proper time.

fit·ter (fit′ər) *n.* **1** a person who fits. **2** a person who fits dresses, suits, etc. on people. **3** a man who adjusts parts of machinery. **4** a man who supplies and fixes anything necessary for some purpose: *a pipe fitter.*

fit·ting (fit′ing) *adj., n. —adj.* right; proper; suitable. *—n.* **1** a trying on of unfinished clothes to see if they will fit. **2** **fittings,** *pl.* furnishings; fixtures. **—fit′ting·ly,** *adv.*

☛ *Syn. adj.* **Fitting, becoming, seemly** = suitable. **Fitting** = suiting the purpose or nature of a thing, character or mood of a person, atmosphere or spirit of a time, place, or occasion, etc.: *It is a fitting evening for a dance.* **Becoming** = fitting or suitable in conduct or speech, suiting a person's character, position, or personal standards: *Gentleness is becoming in a nurse.* **Seemly** = pleasing and fitting or becoming, as judged by rules for conduct or behavior as well as by good taste: *Swearing is not seemly in a child.*

five (fīv) *n., adj. —n.* **1** one more than four; 5: *I counted only five.* **2** the numeral 5: *I think it's a five, but I'm not sure.* **3** the fifth in a set or series; especially, a playing card or side of a die having five spots: *a pair of fives.* **4** a five-dollar bill: *She gave me two fives.* **5** a set or series of five persons or things: *The Romans counted in fives.* **6 fives,** an English ball game similar to squash, played in a walled court with bats or hands (*used with a singular verb*).

—adj. **1** being one more than four; 5: *We ordered five tickets.* **2** being fifth in a set or series (*used mainly after the noun*): *Lesson Five is easier than Lesson Four.* [OE *fīf*]

five·fold (fīv′fōld′) *adj., adv. —adj.* **1** five times as much or as many. **2** having five parts. *—adv.* five times as much or as many.

Five Nations a former confederacy of Iroquois Indian tribes,

consisting of the Mohawks, Oneidas, Onondagas, Cayugas, and Senecas. Members of the Five Nations (now the Six Nations) lived in Ontario and Quebec.

five·pin (fīv′pin′) *n.* **1 fivepins,** a bowling game in which a heavy ball is rolled along a long indoor alley with the aim of knocking over the five bottle-shaped wooden pins arranged upright at the other end (*used with a singular verb*): *Fivepins is a popular Canadian game.* **2** one of the pins used in this game.

Five–Year Plan 1 in the Soviet Union, any of the six government plans for the economic development of the country, the first of which was adopted in 1928. **2** any similar plan in various other countries.

fix (fiks) *v.* **fixed, fix·ing;** *n.* —*v.* **1** make firm; become firm; fasten tightly; be fastened tightly: *We fixed the post in the ground.* **2** settle; set: *He fixed the price at one dollar.* **3** direct or hold steady (eyes, attention, etc.); be directed or held steadily. **4** attract and hold (the eye, attention, etc.). **5** make or become rigid. **6** put definitely: *She fixed the blame on the leader.* **7** treat to keep from changing or fading: *A dye or photograph is fixed with chemicals.* **8** mend; repair. **9** *Informal.* put in order; arrange. **10** *Informal.* put in a condition or position favorable to oneself or unfavorable to one's opponents; bribe. **11** *Informal.* get revenge upon; get even with; punish. **12** *Chemistry.* make stable; change into a more permanent form or state. **13** prearrange or influence the outcome of a game, race, trial, etc. by payment or other inducement: *The jury had been fixed.*
fix on or **upon,** decide on; choose; select.
fix up, *Informal.* **a** mend; repair. **b** put in order; arrange. **c** provide with something needed: *I will fix you up in that house.*
—*n. Informal.* **1** a position hard to get out of; awkward state of affairs. **2** the position of a ship, aircraft, radio transmitter, etc. as determined by obtaining radio signals or other signals from two or more given points. **3** an arrangement for dodging the law, especially one made by bribery. **4** money thus paid. **5** a sports contest whose outcome is prearranged. **6** a dose of a narcotic. [< F *fixer,* ult. < L *fixus,* pp. of *figere* fix] —**fix′a·ble,** *adj.*
► *Syn. v.* **1, 2. Fix, establish, settle** = set someth...ng or someone firmly in position. **Fix** emphasizes setting so firmly, solidly, or definitely in a position, place, or condition that it is hard to change or move: *We fixed the stove in place.* **Establish** emphasizes making firm, steady and lasting, and means "set up or fix firmly or permanently": *They established a partnership.* **Settle** = put in a steady, ordered, or permanent position, place, or condition: *He settled his daughter in a business of her own.*

fix·a·tion (fiks ā′shən) *n.* **1** the act of fixing or condition of being fixed. **2** a treatment to keep something from changing or fading: *the fixation of a photographic film.* **3** *Chemistry.* the process of changing into a more stable form. **4** a morbid attachment or prejudice.

fix·a·tive (fik′sə tiv) *n., adj.* —*n.* a substance used to keep something from fading or changing. —*adj.* that prevents fading or change.

fixed (fikst) *adj.* **1** not movable; firm. **2** settled; set; definite: *fixed charges for taxicabs.* **3** steady; not moving. **4** made stiff or rigid. **5** *Informal.* prearranged privately or dishonestly: *a fixed horse race.* **6** *Chemistry.* **a** entering into a stable compound. **b** not volatile: *a fixed acid.*

fix·ed·ly (fik′sid lē) *adv.* in a fixed manner; without change; intently: *to stare fixedly.*

fix·ed·ness (fik′sid nis) *n.* a being fixed; intentness.

fixed star a star whose position in relation to other stars appears not to change.

fix·er (fik′sər) *n.* **1** fixative. **2** *Informal.* a person who arranges deals, negotiations, political favors, etc., especially underhandedly or illegally.

fix·ings (fik′singz) *n.pl. Informal.* **1** furnishings; trimmings. **2** ingredients.

fix·i·ty (fik′sə tē) *n., pl.* **-ties. 1** a fixed condition or quality; permanence; steadiness; firmness. **2** something fixed.

fix·ture (fiks′chər) *n.* **1** something put in place to stay: *bathroom fixtures, electric-light fixtures.* **2** a person or thing that stays in one place, job, etc.: *After twenty-five years of service, he is considered a fixture in the factory.* **3** a game or some other sports event for which a date has been fixed. [var. of obs. *fixure* (< L *fixura* a fastening < *figere* fasten); influenced by *mixture*]

fiz (fiz) *v.* **fizzed, fiz·zing;** *n.* See **fizz.**

fizz (fiz) *v., n.* —*v.* make a hissing sound. —*n.* **1** a hissing sound. **2** a bubbling drink, such as champagne, soda water, etc. [imitative]

fiz·zle (fiz′əl) *v.* **-zled, -zling;** *n.* —*v.* **1** hiss or sputter weakly: *The firecracker fizzled instead of exploding with a bang.* **2** *Informal.* fail.
fizzle out, end in failure.
—*n.* **1** a hissing; sputtering. **2** *Informal.* failure. [< obs. *fise* the breaking of wind; cf. OE *fisting*]

fizz·y (fiz′ē) *adj.* **fizz·i·er, fizz·i·est.** that fizzes.

fjord (fyôrd) See **fiord.**

fl. 1 fluid. **2** flourished. **3** florin. **4** floor. **5** *Music.* flute.

FL Florida.

F.L. or **F/L** Flight Lieutenant.

Fla. Florida.

flab (flab) *n.* excess fat or loose flesh on the body, resulting from overeating, poor muscle tone, etc. [back formation from *flabby;* 20c.]

flab·ber·gast (flab′ər gast′) *v. Informal.* make speechless with surprise; astonish greatly; amaze. [? blend of *flap* or *flabby* + *aghast*]

flab·by (flab′ē) *adj.* **-bi·er, -bi·est.** lacking firmness or force; soft; weak: *flabby cheeks.* [var. of earlier *flappy* < *flap*] —**flab′bi·ly,** *adv.* —**flab′bi·ness,** *n.*
► *Syn.* See note at **limp².**

flac·cid (flak′sid) *adj.* limp; weak: *flaccid muscles, a flaccid will.* [< L *flaccidus* < *flaccus* flabby] —**flac′cid·ly,** *adv.*

flac·cid·i·ty (flak sid′ə tē) *n.* a flaccid quality or condition.

flack¹ (flak) *n., v. Slang.* —*n.* **1** a publicity or press agent. **2** public relations material; publicity. —*v.* **1** act as a publicity agent: *flacking for a well-known author.* **2** put out as publicity material. [origin uncertain]

flack² (flak) See **flak.**

fla·con (flä kon′; *French,* flä kôn′) *n.* a small bottle with a stopper, used for perfume, smelling salts, etc. [< F < OF *flascon.* See FLAGON.]

flag¹ (flag) *n., v.* **flagged, flag·ging.** —*n.* **1** a piece of cloth, often rectangular, that shows the emblem of a country, of a unit of the armed forces, or of some other organization: *the Canadian flag, the regimental flag.* **2** a piece of cloth, often rectangular and of a bright color, used as a decoration: *The hall was decorated with many flags.* **3** a piece of cloth of a certain shape, color, or design that has a special meaning: *A red flag is often a sign of danger, a white flag of surrender, a black flag of disaster.* **4** something that suggests a flag. The tail of a deer or of a setter dog is a flag. **5** something like a flag. **6** a large cloth used to keep lights from interfering with a television camera. **7 flags,** *pl.* **a** the feathers on the second joint of a bird's wing. **b** the long feathers on the lower parts of certain birds' legs.
—*v.* **1** put a flag or flags over or on; decorate with flags. **2** stop or signal, especially by waving a flag: *to flag a train.* **3** communicate by a flag: *to flag a message.* **4** decoy (game) by waving a flag or something like it to excite attention or curiosity. [? < *flag³*]

flag² (flag) *n.* **1** any of various plants having sword-like leaves, such as the blue flag (a wild iris) or the sweet flag (an arum). **2** the leaf of any of these plants. [cf. Danish *flæg*]

flag³ (flag) *v.* **flagged, flag·ging.** get tired; grow weak; droop: *After doing the same thing for a long time, one's interest flags.* [cf. earlier Du. *vlaggheren* flutter]

flag⁴ (flag) *n., v.* **flagged, flag·ging.** —*n.* flagstone. —*v.* pave with flagstones. [? var. of *flake*]

flag·el·lant (flaj′ə lənt or flə jel′ənt) *n., adj.* —*n.* **1** a person who whips or is whipped. **2** a religious fanatic who whips himself for religious discipline or for penance. —*adj.* having the habit of whipping.

flag·el·late (flaj′ə lāt′) *v.* **-lat·ed, -lat·ing;** *adj.* —*v.* whip; flog. —*adj.* **1** long, slender, and flexible, as a flagellum or whiplash. **2** having flagella. **3** *Botany.* having runners or runnerlike branches. [< L *flagellare* < *flagellum,* dim. of *flagrum* whip] —**flag′el·la′tor,** *n.*

flag·el·la·tion (flaj′ə lā′shən) *n.* a whipping; flogging.

fla·gel·lum (flə jel′əm) *n., pl.* **-la** (-lə) or **-lums. 1** *Biology.* a long, whiplike tail or part, which is an organ of locomotion in certain cells, bacteria, protozoa, etc. **2** a whip. **3** *Botany.* a runner of a plant. [< L *flagellum,* dim. of *flagrum* whip]

flag·eo·let (flaj′ə let′) *n.* a small wind musical instrument resembling a flute, with a mouthpiece at one end, six main finger holes, and sometimes keys. [< F *flageolet,* dim. of OF *flajol* flute, ult. < L *flare* blow]

flag football a game following the rules of Canadian football but in which tackling is outlawed, the ball carrier being stopped in his advance when a handkerchief is snatched from his back pocket.

flag·ging¹ (flag′ing) *adj.* drooping; tired; weak. [< *flag³*]

flag·ging² (flag′ing) *n.* **1** flagstones. **2** a pavement made of flagstones. [< *flag⁴*]

fla·gi·tious (flə jish′əs) *adj.* scandalously wicked; shamefully vile. [< L *flagitiosus* < *flagitium* shame] —**fla·gi′tious·ly,** *adv.* —**fla·gi′tious·ness,** *n.*

flag·man (flag′mən) *n., pl.* **-men. 1** a person who has charge of or

carries a flag. **2** a person who signals with a flag or lantern at a railway crossing, etc.

flag officer a naval officer having a rank of rear-admiral or above and entitled to display a flag on his ship indicating his rank or command.

flag of truce a white flag used as a sign of surrender or of a desire to confer with the enemy.

flag·on (flag′ən) *n.* **1** a container for liquids, usually having a handle and a spout, and often a cover. **2** a large bottle, holding about two litres. **3** the contents of a flagon. [ME < OF *flascon*. Akin to FLASK.]

flag·pole (flag′pōl′) *n.* a pole from which a flag is flown.

fla·gran·cy (flā′grən sē) *n.* a flagrant nature or quality.

fla·grant (flā′grənt) *adj.* notorious; outrageous; scandalous. [< L *flagrans, -antis,* ppr. of *flagrare* burn] —**fla′grant·ly,** *adv.*

fla·gran·te de·lic·to (flə gran′tä di lik′tō) *Law.* in the very act of committing the crime; in the performance of the deed. [< L *in flagrante delicto,* literally, while the crime is blazing]

flag·ship (flag′ship′) *n.* the ship that carries the officer in command of a fleet or squadron and displays his flag.

flag·staff (flag′staf′) *n.* a pole from which a flag is flown.

flag station or **stop** a railway station where trains stop only when a signal is given.

flag·stone (flag′stōn′) *n.* a large, flat stone, used for paving walks, patios, etc.

flail (flāl) *n., v.* —*n.* an instrument for threshing grain by hand. A flail consists of a wooden handle with a short, heavy stick fastened at one end by a thong. —*v.* **1** strike with a flail. **2** beat; thrash. [OE *fligel.* Related to FLY², v.]

flair (fler) *n.* **1** a keen perception: *That trader had a flair for bargains.* **2** a natural talent: *The poet had a flair for making clever rhymes.* [< F *flair* scent < *flairer* smell < L *flagrare*] ☛ Hom. **flare.**

flak (flak) *n.* **1** gunfire from the ground, directed against aircraft. **2** anti-aircraft guns. **3** *Informal.* continuing, insistent criticism, complaints, etc.: *She got a lot of flak for what she said on television.* [for *Fl.A.K.,* an abbreviation of G *Fliegerabwehrkanone* anti-aircraft gun]

flake¹ (flāk) *n., v.* **flaked, flak·ing.** —*n.* **1** a small, light mass; a soft, loose bit: *a flake of snow.* **2** a thin, flat piece or layer: *flakes of rust, flakes of ice floating on the pond, corn flakes.* —*v.* **1** come off in flakes; take off, chip, or peel in flakes: *Dirty spots showed where the paint had flaked off.* **2** break or separate into flakes. **3** cover or mark with flakes; make spotted. **4** form into flakes. **flake out,** *Slang.* drop with exhaustion; lose consciousness. [ME ? < Scand.; cf. ON *flaki*] —**flake′like′,** *adj.* —**flak′er,** *n.*

flake² (flāk) *n.* a slatted platform used for drying fish; fish flake. [ME < ON *flake, fleke* a hurdle, wicker shield]

flak·y (flā′kē) *adj.* **flak·i·er, flak·i·est. 1** consisting of flakes: *Mica is a flaky substance.* **2** easily broken or separated into flakes. —**flak′i·ly,** *adv.* —**flak′i·ness,** *n.*

flam·bé (fläm bā′; *French,* flän bā′) *adj., v.* **-béd** or **-béed, -bé·ing.** —*adj.* of food, served with alcoholic liquor that has been poured over it and set alight (*used after a noun*): *peach flambé.* —*v.* pour liquor over and set aflame. [< F]

flam·beau (flam′bō) *n., pl.* **-beaux** (-bōz) **or -beaus. 1** a flaming torch. **2** a large, decorated candlestick. [< F < OF *flambe* flame, ult. < L *flamma*]

flam·boy·ance (flam boi′əns) *n.* a flamboyant nature or quality.

flam·boy·ant (flam boi′ənt) *adj., n.* —*adj.* **1** gorgeously brilliant; flaming: *flamboyant colors.* **2** very ornate; excessively decorated: *flamboyant architecture.* **3** given to display; ostentatious; showy: *a flamboyant person.* **4** having wavy lines or flamelike curves: *flamboyant designs.* —*n.* royal poinciana. Also called **flamboyant tree.** [< F *flamboyant,* ppr. of *flamboyer* flame] —**flam·boy′ant·ly,** *adv.*

flame (flām) *n., v.* **flamed, flam·ing; adj.** —*n.* **1** one of the glowing red or yellow tongues of light that shoot out from a blazing fire. **2** a burning gas or vapor. **3** a burning with flames; blaze. **4** a thing or condition, such as love or anger, that suggests flame. **5** a bright light. **6** a patch or streak of color. **7** a burning feeling; ardor; zeal. **8** *Informal.* sweetheart. **9** a bright reddish yellow or reddish orange. —*v.* **1** burn with flames; blaze. **2** grow hot, red, etc.: *Her cheeks flamed.* **3** shine brightly; give out a bright light. **4** have or show a burning feeling. **5** burst out quickly and hotly; be or act like a flame. **flame out, up,** or **forth, a** burst out quickly and hotly. **b** of jet engines, fail to function. —*adj.* a bright reddish yellow or reddish orange. [ME < OF < L *flamma*] —**flame′less,** *adj.* —**flame′like′,** *adj.* ☛ **Syn.** *n.* **1, 3. Flame, blaze** = a bright burning or fire. **Flame** applies to either a single glowing tongue of fire, such as from a candle, or to a fire burning

hat, āge, fär; let, ēqual, tèrm; it, īce
hot, ōpen, ôrder; oil, out; cup, put, rüle,
əbove, takən, pencəl, lemən, circəs
ch, child; ng, long; sh, ship
th, thin; ŦH, then; zh, measure

brightly and quickly, and is often used in the plural to suggest a fire with many bright tongues darting or shooting up: *The dying fire suddenly burst into flame. The house burst into flames.* **Blaze** applies to a hotter, brighter, and steadier fire: *The whole room was lighted by the blaze in the fireplace.*

fla·men (flā′men) *n., pl.* **fla·mens** or **flam·i·nes** (flam′ə nēz′). a priest devoted to one particular Roman god: *a flamen of Jupiter.* [< L]

fla·men·co (flə meng′kō) *n.* **1** a style of Spanish Gypsy dance performed with castanets to fast, fiery, vigorous rhythms. **2** a song or piece of music in this style, or for such a dance. [< Sp. *flamenco* Flemish (applied to the Gypsies' dance celebrating their departure from Germany, later confused with Flanders)]

flame·out (flām′out′) *n.* the sudden failure of a jet engine to function, especially while the aircraft containing it is in flight.

flame·proof (flām′prüf′) *adj.* **1** not liable to combustion. **2** not liable to burn when in contact with flames: *flame-proof curtains.*

flame–re·sist·ant (flām′ri zis′tənt) *adj.* resistant to flame; not easily burned.

flame thrower 1 a weapon or device that directs a jet of burning gasoline mixture, napalm, etc. through the air. **2** a person who operates such a weapon or device. [translation of G *Flammenwerfer*]

flam·ing (flām′ing) *adj.* **1** burning with flames. **2** like a flame; very bright; brilliant. **3** showing or arousing strong feeling; violent; vehement.

fla·min·go (flə ming′gō) *n., pl.* **-gos** or **-goes.** any of a family (Phoenicopteridae) of large, mostly tropical, wading birds having a very long neck and legs, a large, broad, downward-curving bill, and plumage ranging from pale pink to scarlet, with black wing tips. [< Pg. < Sp. *flamenco* < Provençal *flamenc* < *flama* < L *flamma* flame]

Fla·min·i·an Way (flə min′ē ən) an old Roman road leading north from Rome, built in 220 B.C.

flam·ma·bil·i·ty (flam′ə bil′ə tē) *n.* the quality of being flammable.

flam·ma·ble (flam′ə bəl) *adj.* easily set on fire; inflammable. ☛ *Usage.* **Flammable** and **inflammable** mean the same, but **inflammable** is sometimes confusing because it looks like a negative. Even so, **inflammable** is more usual in Canada—except in science and industry, where care is taken to use **flammable.** Whichever form is used, the opposite is **nonflammable,** not **non-inflammable.**

flan (flan) *n.* **1** *Brit.* a tart or open pastry filled with fruit, custard, etc. **2** a blank piece of metal, ready to be stamped and made into a coin. [< MF *flaon* tart < Gmc.]

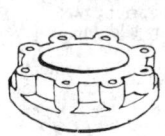 

A flange for attaching
a pipe to a surface

The wheel of a railway car,
having a flange on the inner edge

flange (flanj) *n., v.* **flanged, flang·ing.** —*n.* a projecting edge, rim, collar, etc. on an object for keeping it in place, attaching it to another object, strengthening it, etc. Railway cars and locomotives have wheels with flanges to keep them on the track. —*v.* provide with a flange. [var. of *flanch,* n., < *flanch,* v., < OF *flanchir* bend]

flank (flangk) *n., v.* —*n.* **1** the fleshy part of the side between the ribs and the hip, especially on a four-footed animal. **2** a cut of beef from the flank. See **beef** for picture. **3** the side of a mountain, building, etc. **4** the far right or left side of an army, fleet, etc. —*v.* **1** be at the side of: *High buildings flanked the dark, narrow alley.* **2** get around the far right or the far left side of. **3** attack from or on the side. **4** occupy a position on the flank or side. **5** present the flank or side. [ME < OF *flanc* < Gmc.] —**flank′er,** *n.*

flan·nel (flan′əl) *n., adj.* —*n.* **1** a soft, warm woollen cloth.

2 flannelette. **3** a face-cloth. **4 flannels,** *pl.* **a** clothes, especially trousers, made of flannel. **b** woollen underwear.
—*adj.* made of flannel.

flan·nel·ette (flan′əl et′) *n.* a soft, warm, cotton cloth with a fuzzy nap, that looks like flannel.

flap (flap) *v.* **flapped, flap·ping;** *n.* —*v.* **1** swing or sway about loosely: *The curtains flapped in the open windows.* **2** cause to swing or sway loosely: *The breeze noisily flapped the sheets on the clothes line.* **3** move (wings, arms, etc.) up and down. **4** fly by moving wings up and down: *The large bird flapped away.* **5** strike noisily with something broad and flat. **6** *Slang.* become excited, confused, or alarmed.
—*n.* **1** a flapping motion. **2** a noise caused by flapping. **3** a blow from something broad and flat. **4** a broad, flat piece, usually hanging or fastened at one edge only: *His coat had flaps on the pockets.* **5** a small, movable section of an airplane wing near the fuselage that is lowered to increase lift at low air speeds. **6** *Slang.* excitement or anger; commotion. **7** *Surgery.* a piece of flesh partially detached from adjacent tissue as for later use in grafting. **8** *Phonetics.* a type of trill in which the vibrating organ gives only a single tap, as in some British pronunciations of *merry, very,* etc. [ME; probably imitative] —**flap′like′,** *adj.*

flap·doo·dle (flap′dü′dəl) *n. Slang.* nonsense; rubbish; humbug. [a coined word]

flap·jack (flap′jak′) *n.* a pancake; griddlecake.

flap·per (flap′ər) *n.* **1** something broad and flat to strike with. **2** a broad, flat, hanging piece; flap. **3** a young bird just able to fly. **4** *Informal.* especially, in the 1920's, a young girl; girl who is rather forward and unconventional.

flare (fler) *v.* **flared, flar·ing;** *n.* —*v.* **1** flame up briefly or unsteadily, sometimes with smoke: *A gust of wind made the torches flare.* **2** signal by lights: *The rockets flared a warning.* **3** spread or cause to spread outward from a narrower part, somewhat like a bell: *a flared skirt. The sides of a ship flare from the keel to the deck.* **4** blaze suddenly (*often used with* **up**): *The dying fire flared up briefly.* **5** break out suddenly (*usually used with* **up** *or sometimes,* **out**): *The fighting has flared up again in spite of the peace talks. His temper flared up and he struck out with his fist.*
—*n.* **1** a bright, unsteady light or blaze that lasts only a short time: *The flare of a match showed us his face.* **2** a dazzling light that burns for a short time, used for signalling, lighting up a battlefield, etc. **3** a sudden outburst. **4** a spreading out into a bell shape. **5** a part that spreads out: *the flare of a skirt.* [cf. Norwegian *flara* blaze] ☛ *Hom.* **flair.**

flare·pot (fler′pot′) *n.* a metal sphere, usually containing kerosene, that may be lit as a warning signal.

flare–up (fler′up′) *n.* **1** an outburst of flame. **2** *Informal.* a sudden outburst of anger, violence, etc.

flar·ing (fler′ing) *adj.* **1** flaming. **2** gaudy. **3** spreading gradually outward in form or shape.

flash (flash) *n., v., adj.* —*n.* **1** a sudden brief light or flame: *a flash of lightning.* **2** a sudden, brief feeling, outburst, or display: *a flash of hope, a flash of temper, a flash of wit.* **3** a very brief time; instant. **4** a brief news report, usually received by teletype, or given over the radio or television. **5** a showy display. **6** a small piece of colored ribbon, etc., worn on clothing as an insignia or emblem. **flash in the pan,** a sudden, showy attempt or effort that often fails or is not followed by further efforts.
in a flash, in a very short time: *It all happened in a flash.*
—*v.* **1** give out a sudden, brief light or flame. **2** come suddenly; pass quickly. **3** cause to flash. **4** give out or send out like a flash. **5** communicate by flashes; send by telegraph, radio, etc. **6 a** a rush of water, as produced by a dam or sluiceway, used to float a boat over shoals or for other purposes. **b** the device, as a lock or sluice, used for this purpose. **7** *Informal.* show off.
—*adj.* flashy. [apparently imitative] —**flash′er,** *n.*
☛ *Syn. n.* **1. Flash, glitter, sparkle** = a sudden or unsteady light. **Flash** = a sudden, bright light that disappears immediately: *We saw a single flash of light from the signal tower.* **Glitter** = a bright and wavering light that off and on sends out brilliant flashes as light is reflected from a shining, hard surface: *We saw the glitter of swords in the moonlight.* **Sparkle** = light shooting out in many tiny, brief, brilliant flashes like sparks: *We looked at the sparkle of the little dancing waves in the sunlight.*

flash–back (flash′bak′) *n.* **1** in a novel, play, movie, etc., the introduction of some event or scene that took place or is supposed to have taken place at an earlier time. **2** the scene thus introduced.

flash bulb **1** a bulb, often containing magnesium, used to give a bright light for taking photographs indoors, in shadow, or at night. **2** a portable electric device used to make bright flashes for taking photographs.

flash burn a severe burn caused by instantaneous thermal radiation, such as that from an atomic bomb.

flash card one of a set of cards displaying letters, words, figures, pictures, etc., intended to be shown briefly for drills in reading arithmetic, and other school subjects, or to be used for various other purposes.

flash cube a cube-shaped device containing four flash bulbs, that can be attached to certain kinds of cameras so that four flash pictures can be taken without having to change bulbs.

flash flood a very sudden, violent flooding of a river, stream, etc.

flash gun *Photography.* an apparatus for holding and setting off a flash bulb.

flash·i·ness (flash′ē nis) *n.* a flashy quality.

flash·ing (flash′ing) *n.* **1** the pieces of sheet metal used to cover and protect the joints and angles of a building to make them watertight. **2** the process of suddenly letting in a rush of water so as to produce an artificial flood, as for cleaning a sewer.

flash·light (flash′līt′) *n.* **1** a light that flashes, used in a lighthouse or for signalling. **2** a portable electric light, usually operated by batteries. **3** flash bulb.

flash·point (flash′point′) *n.* **1** the lowest temperature at which vapor from a combustible substance such as gasoline will ignite if exposed to flame. **2** the point at which anger, indignation, etc. bursts out into action or violence.

flash·y (flash′ē) *adj.* **flash·i·er, flash·i·est. 1** very bright for a short time; flashing. **2** showy; gaudy. —**flash′i·ly,** *adv.*

flask (flask) *n.* **1** any bottle-shaped container, especially one having a narrow neck: *Flasks of thin glass are used in chemical laboratories for heating liquids.* **2** a small glass, plastic or metal bottle with flat sides, made to be carried in the pocket. **3** a box or frame for holding the sand, etc. used as a mould in a foundry. [OE *flasce*; cf. LL *flasca* < Gmc.]

flat¹ *adj.* **flat·ter, flat·test;** *n., adv., v.* **flat·ted, flat·ing.** —*adj.* **1** smooth and level; even: *flat land.* **2** spread out; at full length: *The storm left the trees flat.* **3** not very deep or thick: *A plate is flat.* **4** with little air in it: *a flat tire.* **5** not to be changed; positive: *A flat refusal is complete. A flat rate involves no extra charges.* **6** without much life, interest, flavor, etc.; dull: *flat food, a flat voice, flat beer.* **7** not shiny or glossy: *a flat yellow.* **8** not clear or sharp in sound. **9** *Music.* **a** below the true pitch. **b** one half step or half note below natural pitch. **c** marked with or having flats. **10** of feet, having the arches fallen.
that's flat, I mean it.
—*n.* **1** something flat. **2** flatboat. **3** a shallow box or basket. **4** flatcar. **5** a piece of theatrical scenery. **6** *Informal.* a tire with little air in it. **7** a flat part: *The front of an open hand is the flat.* **8** flat land. **9** land covered with shallow water; marsh; swamp. **10** *Music.* **a** a tone or note that is one half step or half note below natural pitch. **b** the sign ♭ that shows such a tone or note. **11** *Horse racing.* **a** a race on a flat course in contrast to a steeplechase or other jumping race. **b** flat racing, on a track without jumps or obstacles.
—*adv.* **1** *Music.* below the true pitch. **2** in a flat manner; flatly: *Bill fell flat on the floor.* **3** in or into a flat position; horizontally. **4** directly; exactly.
fall flat, fail completely; have no effect or interest.
flat out, at maximum speed or effort.
—*v.* **1** make or become flat. **2** *Music.* make or sound flat. [ME < ON *flatr*] —**flat′ly,** *adv.* —**flat′ness,** *n.*

flat² (flat) *n.* an apartment or set of rooms on the same floor and not generally self-contained. [alteration of *flet,* OE *flett*]

flat·boat (flat′bōt′) *n., v.* —*n.* a large boat with a flat bottom, often used for carrying goods on a river or canal. —*v.* transport in a flatboat.

flat·bot·tomed (flat′bot′əmd) *adj.* of a boat, having a flat bottom.

flat·car (flat′kär′) *n.* a railway freight car without a roof or sides.

flat·chest·ed (flat′ches′təd) *adj.* of a woman, having extremely small or shrunken breasts.

flat·fish (flat′fish′) *n., pl.* **-fish** or **-fish·es.** any of an order (Heterosomata; also called Pleuronectiformes) of spiny-finned marine fishes having a very compressed (flattened) body and both eyes on one side, which is kept uppermost as the fish swim along the bottom of the sea.

flat·foot (flat′füt′) *n., pl.* **-feet. 1** a foot with a flattened arch. **2** a condition in which the feet have flattened arches. **3** *Slang.* policeman.

flat–foot·ed (flat′füt′id) *adj.* **1** having feet with flattened arches. **2** *Informal.* not to be changed or influenced; firm; uncompromising. —**flat′foot′ed·ly,** *adv.* —**flat′foot′ed·ness,** *n.*

Flat·head (flat′hed′) *n.* a member of an Amerindian people living in W Montana. [from their supposed practice of flattening the heads of their children]

flat·i·ron (flat'ī'ərn) *n.* an iron with a flat surface, which, when heated, is used for smoothing wrinkles out of cloth.

flat·ten (flat'ən) *v.* make or become flat.
flatten out, a spread out flat. **b** *Aeronautics.* return to a level position from a dive or climb; level off.
—**flat'ten·er,** *n.*

flat·ter (flat'ər) *v.* **1** praise too much or beyond what is true; praise insincerely. **2** show to be better looking than is actually the case: *This picture flatters her.* **3** try to please or win over by flattering. **4** cause to be pleased or feel honored.
flatter oneself, a be pleased to know or think. **b** overestimate oneself.
[? extended use of ME *flateren* float. Related to FLUTTER.]
—**flat'ter·er,** *n.* —**flat'ter·ing·ly,** *adv.*

flat·ter·y (flat'ər ē) *n., pl.* **-ter·ies. 1** the act of flattering. **2** words of praise, usually untrue or overstated.

flat·tish (flat'ish) *adj.* somewhat flat.

flat·top (flat'top') *n.* **1** *Esp.U.S. Informal.* an aircraft carrier. **2** a haircut similar to a crew cut but completely flat across the top.

flat·u·lence (flach'ə ləns) *n.* **1** gas in the stomach or intestines. **2** pompous speech or behavior; vanity; emptiness.

flat·u·lent (flach'ə lənt) *adj.* **1** having gas in the stomach or intestines. **2** causing gas in the stomach or intestines. **3** pompous in speech or behavior; vain; empty. [< F < L *flatus* a blowing < *flare* blow]

fla·tus (flā'təs) *n., pl.* **-tus·es.** gas in the stomach, intestines, etc. [< L]

flat·ware (flat'wer') *n.* **1** knives, forks, and spoons. **2** plates, platters, saucers, etc.

flat·ways (flat'wāz') *adv.* with the flat side forward, upward, or touching.

flat·worm (flat'wėrm') *n.* any of a phylum (Platyhelminthes) of invertebrates having an unsegmented, usually flat body, including some, such as tapeworms and flukes, that are parasites in man and animals.

flaunt (flont *or* flônt) *v., n.* —*v.* **1** show off. **2** wave proudly: *banners flaunting in the breeze.* —*n.* a flaunting. [? < Scand.; cf. Norwegian *flanta* gad about] —**flaunt'er,** *n.* —**flaunt'ing·ly,** *adv.*

flau·tist (flo'tist *or* flô'tist) *n.* flutist.

fla·vor *or* **fla·vour** (flā'vər) *n., v.* —*n.* **1** a taste, especially a characteristic taste: *Chocolate and vanilla have different flavors.* **2** anything used to give a certain taste to food or drink; flavoring. **3** a characteristic quality: *Many stories by Joseph Conrad have a flavor of the sea.* **4** an aroma; odor.
—*v.* **1** give an added taste to; season: *We use salt, pepper, and spices to flavor food.* **2** give a characteristic quality to: *Many exciting adventures flavor an explorer's life.* [ME < OF *flaur*, ult. < L *fragrare* emit odor] —**fla'vor·er** *or* **fla'vour·er,** *n.* —**flav'or·less** *or* **fla'vour·less,** *adj.*
☛ *Syn. n.* **1.** See note at **taste.**

fla·vor·ing *or* **fla·vour·ing** (flā'vər ing *or* flāv'ring) *n.* something used to give a certain taste to food or drink: *vanilla flavoring, chocolate flavoring.*

fla·vour (flā'vər) See **flavor.**

flaw[1] (flo *or* flô) *n., v.* —*n.* **1** a defective place; crack: *A flaw in the dish caused it to break.* **2** a fault; defect. —*v.* make or become defective; crack. [ME < Scand.; cf. Swedish *flaga*]
☛ *Syn. n.* **2.** See note at **defect.**

flaw[2] (flo *or* flô) *n.* a gust of wind; sudden squall. [< Scand.; cf. Norwegian *flaga* gust]

flaw·less (flo'lis *or* flô'lis) *adj.* perfect; without a flaw.
—**flaw'less·ly,** *adv.* —**flaw'less·ness,** *n.*

flax (flaks) *n.* any of a genus (*Linum*) of annual herbs, especially *L. usitatissimum,* which has been cultivated in several varieties since ancient times for its seeds and fibre. The seeds (flaxseed) yield linseed oil and the fibre of the stems is processed to make linen thread, which is woven into linen cloth. The stem fibre of flax, especially when prepared for spinning into thread. [OE *fleax*]

flax·en (flak'sən) *adj.* **1** made of flax. **2** like the color of flax; pale yellow: *flaxen hair.*

flax·seed (flaks'sēd') *n.* the seed of flax; linseed: *Flaxseed is used to make linseed oil and some medicines.*

flay (flā) *v.* **1** strip the skin or outer covering from by whipping or lashing: *The tyrant had his enemies flayed alive.* **2** scold severely; criticize without pity or mercy: *The angry man flayed his servant with his tongue.* **3** rob; cheat. [OE *flēan*] —**flay'er,** *n.*

fld. field.

flea (flē) *n.* any of a large order (Siphonaptera) of small, wingless, jumping insects with mouthparts adapted for sucking blood. Fleas are parasitic on mammals and birds.

hát, āge, fär; let, ēqual, tėrm; it, īce
hot, ōpen, ôrder; oil, out; cup, pút, rüle,
above, takən, pencəl, lemən, circəs
ch, child; ng, long; sh, ship
th, thin; ŦH, then; zh, measure

flea in one's ear, a a severe scolding; rebuff. **b** a sharp hint. [OE *flēah*]
☛ *Hom.* **flee.**

flea·bane (flē'bān') *n.* **1** any of a genus (*Erigeron*) of plants of the composite family found throughout the world, traditionally believed to ward off fleas. Several fleabanes are common Canadian weeds; other species are cultivated as garden flowers. **2** any of various other similar composite plants.

flea–bite (flē'bīt') *n.* **1** the bite of a flea or the itchy red spot left by such a bite. **2** a small pain or annoyance.

flea–bit·ten (flē'bit'ən) *adj.* **1** bitten by fleas. **2** having reddish-brown spots on a light-colored hide: *a flea-bitten horse.* **3** *Informal.* wretched; shabby.

flea market a market selling a mixture of cheap or odd items, junk, antiques, etc.

fleck (flek) *n., v.* —*n.* **1** a spot or patch of color, light, etc.: *Freckles are brown flecks on the skin.* **2** a small particle; flake. —*v.* sprinkle with spots or patches of color, light, etc.; speckle: *Sunlight coming through the branches flecked the shadow cast by the tree.* [ME < ON *flekkr*]

flecked (flekt) *adj.* sprinkled with spots or patches of color, light, etc.; speckled: *The bird's breast is flecked with brown.*

flec·tion (flek'shən) *n.* **1** a bending: *Every flection of his arm caused the muscles to bulge.* **2** a bent part; bend. **3** *Grammar.* inflection. **4** *Physiology.* flexion. Also, *esp.Brit.* **flexion.** [< L *flexio, -onis < flectere* bend]

fled (fled) *v.* pt. and pp. of **flee.**

fledge (flej) *v.* **fledged, fledg·ing. 1** grow the feathers needed for flying. **2** bring up (a young bird) until it is able to fly. **3** provide or cover with feathers. [cf. OE *unflicge* unfledged, unfit to fly]

fledg·ling *or* **fledge·ling** (flej'ling) *n.* **1** a young bird just able to fly. **2** a young, inexperienced person.

flee (flē) *v.* **fled, flee·ing. 1** run away; try to get away by running. **2** run away from; try to get away from by running. **3** go quickly; move swiftly: *The clouds are fleeing before the wind.* **4** pass away; cease; vanish: *The shadows flee as day breaks.* [OE *flēon*] —**fle'er,** *n.*
☛ *Hom.* **flea.**

fleece (flēs) *n., v.* **fleeced, fleec·ing.** —*n.* **1** the wool that covers a sheep or similar animal. **2** the quantity of wool shorn from a sheep at one time. **3** something like a fleece: *a fleece of hair, the fleece of new-fallen snow.* **4** a fabric with a soft, silky pile, used for lining outer garments. **5** the pile of such a fabric. —*v.* **1** cut the fleece from. **2** strip of money or belongings; rob; cheat: *The gamblers fleeced him of a large sum.* [OE *flēos*] —**fleec'er,** *n.* —**fleece'like,** *adj.*

fleec·y (flēs'ē) *adj.* **fleec·i·er, fleec·i·est. 1** like a fleece; soft and white: *Fleecy clouds floated in the blue sky.* **2** covered with fleece. **3** made of fleece. —**fleec'i·ly,** *adv.* —**fleec'i·ness,** *n.*

fleer (flēr) *v. or n.* jeer; sneer; jibe. [ME *flery(e)*, *flire*; cf. Norwegian *flira* grin]

fleet[1] (flēt) *n.* **1** a group of warships under one command; navy: *the Canadian fleet.* **2** a group of boats, aircraft, automobile, etc. moving or working together: *a fleet of trucks.* [OE *flēot* ship, vessel < *flēotan* float]

fleet[2] (flēt) *adj., v.* —*adj.* swift; rapid. —*v.* pass swiftly; move rapidly. [OE *flēotan,* v.; adj. < ON *fljótr.* Akin to FLOAT.] —**fleet'ly,** *adv.* —**fleet'ness,** *n.*

fleet·ing (flē'ting) *adj.* passing swiftly; moving rapidly; soon gone. —**fleet'ing·ly,** *adv.*

Fleet Street in London, England: **1** a very old street, now the location of many newspaper offices. **2** the newspaper industry.

Flem·ing (flem'ing) *n.* **1** a native of Flanders, a region on the North Sea extending from NE France to the SW Netherlands. **2** a Belgian whose native language is Flemish.

Flem·ish (flem'ish) *n.* **1** the language of the Flemings, a Germanic language very similar to Dutch. It is one of the two official languages of Belgium. **2** the **Flemish,** *pl.* Flemish-speaking people collectively; the Flemings. —*adj.* of or having to do with Flanders, the Flemings, or their language.

flense (flens) *v.* **flensed, flens·ing.** strip skin or blubber from a seal

or whale. [< Du. *flensen* or Danish and Norwegian *flense*] —**flens′er**, *n.*

flesh (flesh) *n., v.* —*n.* **1** the soft substance of a human or animal body that covers the bones and is covered by skin. Flesh consists mostly of muscles and fat. **2** the tissue or muscles of animals. **3** fatness. **4** meat, especially of a sort not usually eaten by human beings. **5** the body, not the soul or spirit. **6** the physical side of human nature, as distinguished from the spiritual or moral side. **7** the human race; people as a group. **8** all living creatures. **9** one's family or relatives by birth. **10** the soft or edible part of fruits or vegetables: *The McIntosh apple has crisp, juicy, white flesh.* **11** the color of a white person's skin; pinkish white with a little yellow. **in the flesh, a** alive. **b** in person. —*v.* **1** plunge (a weapon) into the flesh. **2** feed (a hound or hawk) with flesh. **3** excite to passion, bloodshed, etc.) by a foretaste. **4** remove flesh, tissue, etc. from (hides). **5** make or become fleshy (*often used with* out): *Sam was always skinny, but he has fleshed out lately.* **6** fill up or out as if with flesh; give body or substance to (*usually used with* out): *to flesh out a bare plot outline.* [OE *flæsc*] —**flesh′less,** *adj.* —**flesh′er,** *n.*

flesh and blood **1** the body; the material composing man's physical frame. **2** an individual person or persons. **3** human nature: *The temptation was more than flesh and blood could resist.* **4** one's family or relatives by birth; a child or relative by birth.

flesh-and-blood (flesh′ən blud′) *adj.* having human existence; real: *a flesh-and-blood heroine.*

flesh–col·ored or **–col·oured** (flesh′kul′ərd) *adj.* pinkish white with a tinge of yellow.

–fleshed *combining form.* having ——flesh: *solid-fleshed* = having solid flesh.

flesh fly any of a family (Sarcophagidae) of two-winged flies resembling houseflies, including many species that are scavengers and others that are parasites in living animals.

flesh·ly (flesh′lē) *adj.* **-li·er, -li·est. 1** of the flesh; bodily. **2** sensual. **3** of or having to do with the material body; mortal; human. **4** worldly. —**flesh′li·ness,** *n.*

flesh·pot (flesh′pot′) *n.* **1 fleshpots,** *pl.* good food and bodily comfort; luxury. **2** Usually, **fleshpots,** *pl.* a place or establishment offering luxurious, sensual living or entertainment: *visiting the fleshpots of the city.*

flesh wound a wound that merely injures the flesh; slight wound.

flesh·y (flesh′ē) *adj.* **flesh·i·er, flesh·i·est. 1** having much flesh: *The calf is the fleshy part of the lower leg.* **2** plump; fat. **3** of flesh; like flesh. **4** pulpy. —**flesh′i·ly,** *adv.* —**flesh′i·ness,** *n.*

Two styles of fleur-de-lis. The one on the left is from the Canadian coat of arms.

fleur–de–lis (flèr′də lē′ *or* flèr′də lēs′) *n., pl.* **fleurs-de-lis** (flèr′də lēz′ *or* flèr′də lē′). **1** *Heraldry.* a design or device representing a lily. **2** the former royal coat of arms of France. **3** the unofficial emblem of the province of Quebec. **4** iris. [< F *fleur-de-lis* lily flower]

flew (flü) *v.* pt. of **fly²**.
☛ Hom. **flu, flue.**

flews (flüz) *n.pl.* the overhanging part of the lip of certain dogs, especially hounds. [origin uncertain]

flex (fleks) *v., n.* —*v.* **1** bend: *He slowly flexed his stiff arm.* **2** of muscles, tighten and relax alternately. —*n.* **1** flexibility. **2** a bend or contraction of a muscle. **3** *Esp.Brit.* flexible insulated wire used to connect electric appliances or lamps; cord. [< L *flexus,* pp. of *flectere* bend]

flex·i·bil·i·ty (flek′sə bil′ə tē) *n.* a flexible quality.

flex·i·ble (flek′sə bəl) *adj.* **1** easily bent; not stiff; bending without breaking: *Leather, rubber, and wire are flexible materials.* **2** easily adapted to fit various uses, purposes, etc.: *flexible plans. The actor's flexible voice accommodated itself to every emotion.* **3** easily managed; willing to yield to influence or persuasion. [< F < L < *flexibilis* < *flexus.* See FLEX.] —**flex′i·bly,** *adv.*
☛ Syn. **1, 3. Flexible, pliant, limber** = easily bent. **Flexible** = capable of being bent or twisted easily and without breaking, or, used figuratively of people and their minds, etc., capable of being turned or managed with little trouble if handled skilfully: *Great thinkers have flexible minds.* **Pliant,** literally and

figuratively, emphasizes having the quality of bending or adapting itself easily rather than of being easily affected by outside force: *English is a pliant language.* **Limber,** used chiefly of the body, means "having flexible muscles and joints": *A jumper has limber legs.*

flex·ile (flek′səl) *adj.* flexible.

flex·ion (flek′shən) *n.* **1** *Physiology.* **a** a bending of some part of the body by the action of flexors. **b** a being bent in this way. **2** *Esp.Brit.* flection (def. 3). [var of *flection*]

flex·or (flek′sər) *n. Physiology.* any muscle that bends some part of the body. [< NL]

flex·time (fleks′tīm′) *n.* a flexible system of working hours, whereby employees can choose their starting and finishing times.

flex·ure (flek′shər) *n.* **1** bending; curving. **2** a bend; curve. [< L *flexura* < *flexus.* See FLEX.]

flib·ber·ti·gib·bet (flib′ər tē jib′it) *n.* **1** a frivolous, flighty person. **2** chatterbox. —**flib′ber·ti·gib′bet·y,** *adj.*

flick¹ (flik) *n., v.* —*n.* **1** a quick, light blow; sudden, snapping stroke: *By a flick of his whip, he drove the fly from the horse's head.* **2** the light, snapping sound of such a blow or stroke. **3** a sudden jerk; a short, quick movement: *The fisherman made a short cast with a flick of his wrist.* **4** a streak; splash; fleck. **5** *Slang.* movie. —*v.* **1** strike lightly with a quick, snapping blow: *He flicked the dust from his shoes with a handkerchief.* **2** make a sudden, snapping stroke with: *The boys flicked wet towels at each other.* **3** flutter; move quickly and lightly. [probably imitative]

flick² (flik) *n. Slang.* motion picture.

flick·er¹ (flik′ər) *v., n.* —*v.* **1** shine with a wavering light; burn with an unsteady flame: *A dying fire flickered on the hearth.* **2** move quickly and lightly in and out or back and forth: *The tongue of a snake flickers.* **3** cause to flicker: *There was just enough breeze to flicker the candle.* —*n.* **1** a wavering, unsteady light or flame. **2** a brief flame; spark. **3** a quick, light movement. [OE *flicorian*]

flick·er² (flik′ər) *n.* any of several North American woodpeckers (genus *Colaptes*) having a brown back barred with black, a conspicuous white rump, and pale, black-spotted underparts. The **yellow-shafted flicker** (*Colaptes auratus*), common in many parts of Canada, has yellow on the underside of wings and tail. [? imitative of its note]

fli·er (flī′ər) See **flyer.**

flight¹ (flīt) *n.* **1** the act or manner of flying. **2** the distance a bird, bullet, aircraft, etc. can fly. **3** a group of things flying through the air together: *a flight of six birds.* **4** an air-force unit of either planes or personnel. **5** a trip in an aircraft. **6** a swift movement. **7** a soaring above or beyond what is ordinary. **8** a set of stairs or steps between landings or storeys of a building. [OE *flyht.* Related to FLY².]

flight² (flīt) *n.* **1** the act of fleeing or running away: *The defeated army was in flight.* **2** escape: *The flight of the prisoners was soon discovered.*
put to flight, force to flee.
take to flight, flee.
[ME *fliht* < OE *flēon* flee]

flight attendant a person employed by an airline to look after passengers during a flight.

flight bag a small, lightweight bag of vinyl, canvas, etc. having a zippered closing and designed to be carried as hand luggage on an airplane, etc.

flight deck **1** a separate compartment in some aircraft for the pilot and crew. **2** the uppermost deck on an aircraft carrier, which functions as a takeoff and landing area.

flight·less (flīt′lis) *adj.* unable to fly.

flight lieutenant an air-force officer ranking next above a flying officer and below a squadron leader. *Abbrev.:* F/L., F.L., or Flt.Lt.

flight·path (flīt′path′) *n.* **1** the course taken by an aircraft, missile, etc. **2** a course indicated by an electronic beam as a navigation aid.

flight sergeant an air-force non-commissioned officer ranking next above a sergeant and below a warrant officer. *Abbrev.:* Flt. Sgt.

flight·y (flī′tē) *adj.* **flight·i·er, flight·i·est. 1** likely to have sudden fancies; full of whims; frivolous. **2** slightly crazy; light-headed. —**flight′i·ly,** *adv.* —**flight′i·ness,** *n.*

flim·flam (flim′flam′) *n., v.* **-flammed, -flam·ming.** *Informal.* —*n.* **1** nonsense; rubbish. **2** deception; a low trick. —*v.* cheat (a person) out of money; trick. —**flim′flam′mer,** *n.*

flim·sy (flim′zē) *adj.* **-si·er, -si·est;** *n., pl.* **-sies.** —*adj.* **1** light and thin; frail: *Muslin is too flimsy to be used for sails.* **2** not serious or convincing; inadequate: *a flimsy excuse.* —*n.* **1** a thin paper used by reporters. **2** a newspaper report on this paper. **3** a sheet of very thin paper for typing or writing. [? <

alteration of *film* + *-sy*; adj. suffix] —**flim′si·ly,** *adv.* —**flim′si·ness,**
n.

flinch (flinch) *v., n.* —*v.* draw back from difficulty, danger, or
pain; shrink. —*n.* **1** a drawing back: *He took his punishment
without a flinch.* **2** a game played with cards bearing numbers from
1 to 14. [probably < OF *flenchir* < Frankish **hlankjan* bend; cf. G
lenken] —**flinch′ing·ly,** *adv.*
☛ *Syn. v.* See note at **shrink.**

flin·ders (flin′dərs) *n.pl.* small pieces; fragments; splinters: *The
box was smashed into flinders.* [cf. Norwegian *flindra*]

fling (fling) *v.* **flung, fling·ing;** *n.* —*v.* **1** throw forcefully; hurl
violently: *The angry man flung his hat on the floor.* **2** move rapidly;
rush; flounce: *She flung angrily out of the room.* **3** plunge; kick.
4 put suddenly or violently: *Fling him into jail.* **5** move (a part of
the body) in an impulsive, unrestrained way: *The girl happily flung
her arms around her mother's neck.*
—*n.* **1** a violent throw. **2** a plunge; kick. **3** a time of doing as one
pleases: *He had his fling when he was young; now he must work.*
4 a lively Scottish dance: *the Highland fling.*
have or **take a fling at,** *Informal.* **a** try; attempt. **b** make scornful
remarks about.
[? akin to ON *flengja* flog]

flint (flint) *n.* **1** a very hard grey or brown stone, a kind of quartz,
that makes a spark when struck against steel. **2** a piece of this stone
used with steel to light fires, explode gunpowder, etc. **3** anything
very hard or unyielding: *He had a heart of flint.* [OE]

flint glass a brilliant glass containing lead, potassium or sodium,
and silicon. It is used for lenses, dishes, etc.

flint·lock (flint′lok′) *n.* **1** a gunlock in which a flint striking
against steel makes sparks that explode the gunpowder. Flintlocks
were used on guns from the 1600's to the 1800's. **2** a gun with such
a gunlock.

flint·y (flin′tē) *adj.* **flint·i·er, flint·i·est.** **1** containing flint: *a flinty
rock formation.* **2** hard like flint: *The boys were tired after walking
over the flinty asphalt.* **3** hard; unyielding: *The sergeant had flinty
eyes.* —**flint′i·ly,** *adv.* —**flint′i·ness,** *n.*

flip¹ (flip) *v.* **flipped, flip·ping;** *n., adj.* **flip·per, flip·pest.** —*v.* **1** toss
or move with a snap of a finger and thumb: *He flipped a coin on the
counter.* **2** flip a coin in the air to decide something by chance: *They
flipped to see who would pay for the coffee.* **3** jerk; turn or move
with a jerk; flick: *She flipped her fan shut. The branch flipped back.
The driver flipped his whip at a fly.* **4** turn over quickly: *He flipped
the pages of the magazine. She flipped the eggs before serving
them.*
—*n.* **1** a smart tap; snap; a sudden jerk: *The cat gave the kitten a
flip on the ear.* **2** a quick overturning: *The airplane took a flip just
before it crashed.*
—*adj. Informal.* flippant. [probably imitative]

flip² (flip) *n.* a hot drink containing beer, ale, cider, or the like,
with sugar and spice. [nominal use of *flip¹, v.*]

flip³ (flip) *adj. Informal.* flippant.

flip·pan·cy (flip′ən sē) *n., pl.* **-cies.** **1** being flippant. **2** flippant
speech or conduct.

flip·pant (flip′ənt) *adj.* smart or pert in speech; not respectful: *a
flippant answer.* [? < *flip¹* + *-ant*] —**flip′pant·ly,** *adv.*

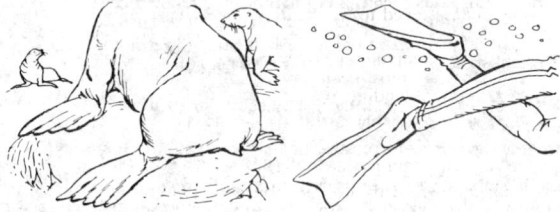

The flippers of a seal   Rubber flippers for the feet

flip·per (flip′ər) *n.* **1** a broad, flat fin especially adapted for
swimming: *Seal flippers are a popular food in Newfoundland.* **2** a
piece of rubber or plastic that fits onto the foot and has a broad, flat
blade extending from the toe, used by swimmers to give extra
power, especially when swimming underwater: *A pair of flippers is
part of every skindiver's equipment.* **3** a person or thing that flips: *a
pancake flipper.* **4** a stabilizing fin on an ocean liner. **5** *Slang.* the
hand.

flip side the reverse side of a phonograph record, especially the
less well-known or popular side.

flirt (flėrt) *v., n.* —*v.* **1** try to win the attention and affection of
someone by amorous behavior of a playful or frivolous kind.
2 trifle; toy: *He flirted with the idea of going to Europe, though he*

---

flinch   **453**   **flock**

hat, āge, fär; let, ēqual, tėrm; it, īce
hot, ōpen, ôrder; oil, out; cup, pùt, rüle,
əbove, takən, pencəl, lemən, circəs

ch, child; ng, long; sh, ship
th, thin; ᴛʜ, then; zh, measure

couldn't afford it. **3** move quickly to and fro; flutter: *She flirted her
fan impatiently.* **4** toss; jerk.
—*n.* **1** a person who flirts. **2** a quick movement or flutter: *With a
flirt of its tail, the bird flew away.* **3** a toss; jerk. [ult. imitative (see
v. def. 4)] —**flirt′er,** *n.*

flir·ta·tion (flėr tā′shən) *n.* **1** a pretending to be in love with
someone. **2** a love affair that is not serious. **3** flirting or toying.

flir·ta·tious (flėr tā′shəs) *adj.* **1** inclined to flirt. **2** having to do
with flirtation. —**flir·ta′tious·ly,** *adv.* —**flir·ta′tious·ness,** *n.*

flit (flit) *v.* **flit·ted, flit·ting;** *n.* —*v.* **1** fly lightly and quickly; flutter:
Birds flitted from tree to tree. **2** pass lightly and quickly: *Many idle
thoughts flitted through his mind as he lay in the sun.* —*n.* a light,
quick movement. [ME < ON *flytja.* Akin to FLEET².] —**flit·ter,** *n.*

flitch (flich) *n.* a side of a pig salted and cured; side of bacon. [OE
flicce]

flit·ter (flit′ər) *v. or n.* flutter. [< *flit*]

fliv·ver (fliv′ər) *n. Slang.* a small, cheap automobile. [origin
unknown]

float (flōt) *v., n.* —*v.* **1** stay on top of or be held up by air, water,
or other liquid. **2** move with a moving liquid; drift: *The boat floated
out to sea.* **3** rest or move in a liquid, the air, etc. **4** cause to float.
5 cover with liquid; flood. **6** sell (securities): *to float an issue of
stock.* **7** launch or set up (a company, etc.), especially by issuing
and selling securities. **8** launch or initiate (a plan, idea, etc.).
9 move about aimlessly or effortlessly: *He floats from job to job.*
10 of currency, interest rates, etc., be allowed to find a level on the
market based on supply and demand, without restrictions or
artificial support.
—*n.* **1** anything that stays up or holds up something else in water,
such as a raft. **2** a cork on a fish line. **3** an air-filled organ that
supports a fish. **4** an air-filled, water-tight part on an aircraft for
landing or floating on water; pontoon. **5** a hollow, metal ball that
regulates the level, supply, or outlet of a liquid. **6** a flat board of a
water wheel or paddle wheel. **7** a low, flat car that carries
something to be shown in a parade. **8** a drink consisting of ginger
ale or a similar beverage with ice cream in it. **9** *Geology.*
a fragments of rock, mineral, or ore loosened from their source and
deposited elsewhere: *iron ore float.* **b** fine mineral particles floating
in water: *They have located the source of the float coal.* **10 floats,** in
the theatre, footlights. [OE *flotian* < *flēotan.* Related to FLEET².]
—**float′a·ble,** *adj.*

float·er (flō′tər) *n.* **1** a person or thing that floats. **2** *Informal.* a
person who often changes his place of living, working, etc.
3 *Sports.* a ball thrown or hit so as to travel slowly and appear to
hang in the air, usually on a slightly arched course. **4** an insurance
policy covering a category of goods, as household furnishings,
rather than specific items, as a particular gem.

float·ing (flō′ting) *adj.* **1** that floats. **2** not fixed; not staying in
one place; moving around. **3** in use or circulation; not permanently
invested. **4** not funded; changing: *The floating debt of a business
consists of notes, drafts, etc. payable within a short time.*
5 *Medicine.* not in the normal position; displaced: *a floating kidney.*
6 of or having to do with a machine part, such as a connecting rod
or coupler, that is connected or hung in such a way that it functions
without causing vibration. —**float′ing·ly,** *adv.*

floating ribs the ribs not attached to the breastbone; last two
pairs of ribs.

float plane a seaplane equipped with two floats, or pontoons, on
which it lands, rests, and takes off.

float·stone (flōt′stōn′) *n.* **1** a stone used to smooth the surface of
bricks used in curved work. **2** a whitish-grey spongy variety of opal,
light enough to float.

floc·cu·lent (flok′yə lənt) *adj.* **1** like bits of wool. **2** made up of
soft, woolly masses. **3** covered with a soft, woolly substance. [< L
floccus tuft of wool]

flock¹ (flok) *n., v.* —*n.* **1** animals of one kind that feed and move
about in a group, especially sheep, goats, or birds. **2** a large group;
crowd. **3** people of the same church group; band; company.
—*v.* go or gather in a flock; come crowding: *The children flocked
around the Christmas tree.* [OE *flocc*]

flock² (flok) *n., v.* —*n.* **1** a tuft of wool. **2** waste wool or cotton
used to stuff mattresses and cushions. **3** finely powdered or very

short fibres of wool, etc. used to form a velvety raised pattern on wallpaper or fabric.
—v. **1** stuff with flock. **2** cover or coat with flock. [ME < OF *floc* < L *floccus*]

floe (flō) *n.* **1** a field or sheet of floating ice. **2** a floating piece broken off from such a field or sheet. [? < Norwegian *flo*]
☛ *Hom.* **flow.**

flog (flog) *v.* **flogged, flog·ging. 1** whip very hard; beat with a whip, stick, etc. **2** *Slang.* sell or try to sell.
flog a dead horse, pursue a futile argument or a lost cause.
flog to death, be too persistent in trying to persuade or convince someone of (something), causing the person to lose interest: *It wasn't a bad idea, but he flogged it to death.*
[? English school slang for L *flagellare* whip] —**flog′ger,** *n.*

flood (flud) *n., v.* —*n.* **1** a flow of water over what is usually dry land. **2** *Poetic.* a large amount of water; ocean; sea; lake; river. **3** a great outpouring of anything: *a flood of light, a flood of words.* **4** a flowing of the tide toward the shore; rise of the tide. **5 the Flood,** in the Bible, the water that deluged the earth in the time of Noah. (Genesis 7).
in flood, filled to overflowing with an unusual amount of water: *The river was in flood.*
—*v.* **1** flow over or into: *When the snows melted last spring, the river rose and flooded our fields.* **2** fill much fuller than usual. **3** become covered or filled with water: *During the thunderstorm, our cellar flooded.* **4** cover the surface of something with water: *The attendants flooded the ice before every hockey game.* **5** pour out or stream like a flood: *Sunlight flooded into the room.* **6** fill, cover or overcome like a flood: *The rich man was flooded with requests for money.* **7** flow like a flood. **8** cause or allow too much fuel into (a carburetor) so that it fails to start; receive too much fuel into the carburetor. [OE *flōd*] —**flood′er,** *n.*
☛ *Syn. n.* **1. Flood, deluge, inundation** = a great flow of water. **Flood** applies particularly to a great flow of water over land usually dry, caused by the rising and overflowing of a river or other body of water: *Floods followed the melting of mountain snow.* **Deluge** applies to a great flood that washes away everything in its path, or, sometimes, to a heavy, continuous rain that causes a flood: *Livestock drowned in the deluge.* **Inundation,** formal, means an overflow covering everything around: *Crops were destroyed by the inundation of the fields.*

flood control the control of floods and the prevention of damage caused by them, by means of dams, levees, dikes, extra outlets, reforestation, etc.

flood·gate (flud′gāt′) *n.* **1** a gate in a canal, river, stream, etc. to control the flow of water. **2** something that controls any flow or passage.

flood·light (flud′līt′) *n., v.* **-light·ed** or. **-lit, -light·ing.** —*n.* **1** a lamp that gives a broad beam of light: *Several floodlights were used to illuminate the stage.* **2** the broad beam of light from such a lamp. —*v.* illuminate with floodlights.

flood plain a plain bordering a river and made of soil deposited by floods.

flood tide the flowing of the tide toward the shore; the rise of the tide.

floor (flôr) *n., v.* —*n.* **1** the inside bottom covering of a room. **2** a storey of a building. **3** a flat surface at the bottom of anything. **4** the part of a room or hall where members of a lawmaking body, etc. sit and from which they speak: *the floor of the House of Commons.* **5** the right or privilege to speak in a lawmaking body, etc.: *The chairman decides who has the floor.* **6** the main part of an exchange, where buying and selling of stocks, bonds, etc. is done. **7** *Informal.* of prices, amounts, etc., the lowest level. **8** *Mining.* an underlying stratum on which a seam of coal, etc. lies.
—*v.* **1** put a floor in or over. **2** knock down. **3** *Informal.* defeat. **4** *Informal.* confuse or puzzle completely: *The last question on the exam floored us all.* **5** place upon a floor; base. [OE *flōr*] —**floor′er,** *n.*

floor·board (flôr′bôrd′) *n.* **1** one of the strips of wood used in a wooden floor. **2** Usually, **floorboards,** *pl.* the floor of an automobile.

floor hockey an indoor game derived from hockey, in which the players use a long stick to carry and pass a plastic puck or a ring resembling a quoit or rope or felt.

floor·ing (flôr′ing) *n.* **1** a floor. **2** floors collectively. **3** material for making floors.

floor price a minimum price set by the government on a commodity to protect the producer against sudden declines in price.

floor show an entertainment consisting of music, singing, dancing, etc. presented at a night club, hotel, etc.

floor·walk·er (flôr′wok′ər or -wôk′ər) *n.* a person employed in a large store to oversee sales, direct customers, etc.

flooz·ie or **flooz·y** (flü′zē) *n., pl.* **flooz·ies.** *Slang.* a woman or

girl, especially one of loose morals, such as a prostitute. [? variant of *Flossie,* a nickname for *Florence,* a woman's name]

flop (flop) *v.* **flopped, flop·ping;** *n.* —*v.* **1** move loosely or heavily; flap around clumsily: *The fish flopped helplessly on the deck.* **2** fall, drop, throw, or move heavily or clumsily: *He flopped down into a chair.* **3** change or turn suddenly. **4** *Informal.* fail.
—*n.* **1** flopping. **2** the sound made by flopping. **3** *Informal.* a failure: *The new play was a flop.* [imitative var. of *flap*] —**flop′per,** *n.*

flop·house (flop′hous′) *n.* a cheap, run-down hotel or rooming house, especially one used by down-and-outs.

flop·py (flop′ē) *adj.* **-pi·er, -pi·est.** *Informal.* flopping; tending to flop: *She bought a sunhat with a floppy brim.* —**flop′pi·ly,** *adv.* —**flop′pi·ness,** *n.*

flo·ra (flô′rə) *n.* **1** the plants of a particular region or time: *the flora of the West Indies.* **2** a work that systematically describes such plants. [< L]

Flo·ra (flô′rə) *n. Roman mythology.* the goddess of flowers and spring.

flo·ral (flô′rəl) *adj.* **1** of or having to do with flowers: *floral decorations.* **2** resembling flowers: *a floral design.*

floral envelope *Botany.* the floral leaves (petals or sepals, or both) of a flower, collectively.

Flor·ence flask (flôr′əns) **1** a thin glass bottle with a long neck, usually covered with straw or something similar, for holding olive oil or wine. **2** a bottle of this shape used in a laboratory for heating chemicals.

Flor·en·tine (flôr′ən tēn′) *adj., n.* —*adj.* of or having to do with Florence, a city in Italy. —*n.* **1** a native or inhabitant of Florence. **2 florentine,** a twilled silk cloth, used for wearing apparel.

flo·res·cence (flô res′əns) *n.* **1** the act of blossoming. **2** the condition of blossoming. **3** the period of blossoming. [< NL *florescentia,* ult. < L *florere* flourish]

flo·res·cent (flô res′ənt) *adj.* blossoming.

flo·ret (flô′rit) *n.* **1** a small flower. **2** *Botany.* one of the small flowers in a flower head of a composite plant, such as an aster. [< OF *florete,* dim. of *flor* flower < L *flos, floris*]

flor·i·bun·da (flôr′ə bun′də) *n.* a variety of hybrid cultivated rose producing a number of flowers on a single stem, each flower often as large as tea roses. [< NL *floribunda* < L *flos, floris* flower]

flo·ri·cul·ture (flôr′ə kul′chər) *n.* the cultivation of flowering plants.

flor·id (flôr′id) *adj.* **1** highly colored; ruddy: *a florid complexion.* **2** elaborately ornamented; flowery; showy; ornate. [< L *floridus* < *flos, floris* flower] —**flor′id·ly,** *adv.* —**flor′id·ness,** *n.*

flor·in (flôr′ən) *n.* **1** a former British coin worth two shillings. **2** a gold coin issued at Florence in 1252. **3** gulden. **4** any of various gold or silver coins used at different times in European countries. [< F < Ital. *fiorino* a Florentine coin marked with a lily < *fiore* flower < L *flos, floris*]

flo·rist (flô′rist) *n.* a person who raises or sells flowers.

floss (flos) *n., v.* —*n.* **1** short, loose silk fibres. **2** a soft, shiny, untwisted silk or cotton thread used for embroidery. **3** dental floss. **4** soft, silky fluff or fibres, such as the fibres inside milkweed pods.
—*v.* use dental floss to clean teeth. [apparently related to FLEECE]

floss·y (flos′ē) *adj.* **floss·i·er, floss·i·est. 1** of floss; like floss. **3** *Informal.* fancy; glamorous; highly decorated. —**floss′i·ness,** *n.*

flo·ta·tion (flō tā′shən) *n.* **1** floating or launching. **2** getting started or established. **3** selling or putting on sale. [var. of *floatation* < *float,* v.]

flo·til·la (flō til′ə) *n.* **1** a small fleet. **2** a fleet of small ships. [< Sp., dim. of *flota* fleet < F < ON *floti* fleet]

flot·sam (flot′səm) *n.* the wreckage of a ship or its cargo found floating on the sea.
flotsam and jetsam, a wreckage or cargo found floating on the sea or washed ashore. **b** odds and ends; useless things. **c** people without steady work or permanent homes.
[< AF *floteson* < *floter* float. Akin to FLOAT.]

flounce[1] (flouns) *v.* **flounced, flounc·ing;** *n.* —*v.* **1** go with an angry or impatient movement of the body: *She flounced out of the room in a rage.* **2** twist; jerk; turn. **3** an angry or impatient fling or turn of the body. **2** a twist; turn; jerk. [? < Scand.; cf. Swedish *flunsa* plunge]

flounce[2] (flouns) *n., v.* **flounced, flounc·ing.** —*n.* a wide strip of cloth, gathered along the top edge and sewed to a dress, skirt, etc. as trimming; a wide ruffle. —*v.* trim with a flounce or flounces. [var. of *frounce* < OF *fronce* wrinkle < Gmc.]

flounc·ing (floun′sing) *n.* **1** fabric for flounces. **2** a flounce or flounces.

floun·der[1] (floun′dər) *v., n.* —*v.* **1** struggle awkwardly without making much progress; plunge about: *Men and horses were floundering in the deep snowdrifts.* **2** be clumsy or confused and

make mistakes: *The frightened girl could only flounder through her song.* —*n.* a floundering. [? blend of *founder*[1] and *blunder*]

floun·der[2] (floun′dər) *n., pl.* **-der** or **-ders.** any of numerous flatfishes constituting two families (Pleuronectidae and Bothidae), including some very important food fishes, such as plaice, halibut, and turbot. [< AF *floundre* < Scand.; cf. Swedish *flundra*]

flour (flour) *n., v.* —*n.* **1** a fine, powdery substance made by grinding and sifting wheat or other grain. **2** any fine soft powder. —*v.* **1** cover with flour. **2** grind and sift (grain) into flour. [special use of *flower*, i.e., the flower (best) of the meal]

flour·ish (flėr′ish) *v., n.* —*v.* **1** grow or develop with vigor; thrive; do well. **2** be in the best time of life or activity. **3** wave (a sword, stick, arm, etc.) in the air. **4** make a showy display. —*n.* **1** a waving in the air. **2** a showy decoration in handwriting. **3** *Music.* a showy trill or passage: *a flourish of trumpets.* **4** a showy display of enthusiasm, heartiness, etc. **5** an expression used for effect in speech or writing. **6** the state of being in the best time of life: *in full flourish.* [ME < OF *floriss-,* a stem of *florir* < L *florere* bloom < *flos, floris* flower] —**flour′ish·ing·ly,** *adv.*

flour mill **1** a machine for grinding wheat or other grain into flour. **2** a place or establishment where there is such a machine or machines.

flour·y (flour′ē) *adj.* **1** of or like flour. **2** covered or white with flour.

flout (flout) *v., n.* —*v.* **1** treat with contempt or scorn; mock; scoff at: *The disobedient boy flouted his mother's advice.* **2** show contempt or scorn; scoff. —*n.* a contemptuous speech or act; insult; mockery; scoffing. [var. of *flute,* v.] —**flout′er,** *n.* —**flout′ing·ly,** *adv.*

flow (flō) *v., n.* —*v.* **1** run like water; move in a current or stream. **2** pour out; pour along. **3** move easily or smoothly; glide. **4** hang loosely and waving. **5** be plentiful; be full and overflowing: *a land flowing with milk and honey.* **6** flow in; rise. —*n.* **1** the act or way of flowing. **2** any continuous movement like that of water in a river: *a rapid flow of speech.* **3** the rate of flowing. **4** something that flows; current; stream. **5** the flowing of the tide toward the shore; rise of the tide. **6** *Physics.* the directional movement in a current or stream that is a characteristic of all fluids as air or electricity. [OE *flōwan*]
☛ *Hom.* **floe.**
☛ *Syn. v.* **Flow, gush, stream** = run or pour out or along. **Flow** emphasizes the continuous forward movement of running or pouring water, whether fast or slow, in great or small quantity: *Water flowed in the streets.* **Gush** = rush out or flow forth suddenly in considerable quantity from an opening: *Oil gushed from the new well.* **Stream** = pour forth steadily from a source or flow steadily, always in the same direction: *Rain streamed down the gullies.*

flow·age (flō′ij) *n.* **1** a flowing or flooding. **2** the state of being flooded. **3** the liquid that flows or floods. **4** the rate at which a liquid flows or floods. **5** *Physics.* the gradual structural alteration of a solid, such as asphalt, by intermolecular movement.

flow chart a diagram showing sequence of operations and the relationship between different elements of a complex system or process, as in manufacturing or data processing.

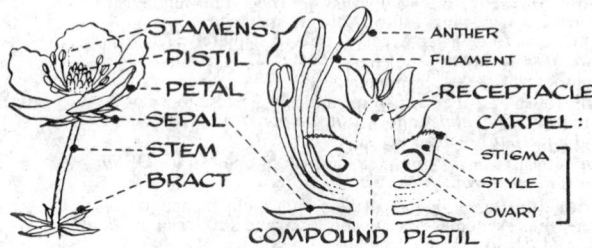

Flower: the parts of a buttercup

flow·er (flou′ər) *n., v.* —*n.* **1** the often showy and brightly colored part of an angiosperm plant that appears before the fruit and includes the reproductive organs and surrounding structures, such as petals and sepals and the receptacle on which they are borne. **2** a showy part of such a plant made up of a group of flowers or flowers and surrounding, petal-like bracts. The flower of a daisy is composed of central disk flowers surrounded by petal-like ray flowers. The flower of the dogwood and poinsettia consists of tiny, inconspicuous flowers surrounded by colored, petal-like bracts. **3** a plant that bears flowers, especially a herbaceous plant: *The rose is a common garden flower.* **4** a flowerlike reproductive structure on a flowerless plant, such as a moss. **5** the finest part: *The flower of the country's youth was killed in the war.* **6** the time of being at one's best: *a man in the flower of life.* **7** an embellishment or decoration: *flowers of speech.* **8 flowers,** *pl. Chemistry.* a fine powder produced by sublimation or condensation: *flowers of sulphur.*
in flower, flowering: *Our apple tree is in flower.*

hat, āge, fär; let, ēqual, tėrm; it, īce
hot, ōpen, ôrder; oil, out; cup, pút, rüle,
əbove, takən, pencəl, lemən, circəs
ch, child; ng, long; sh, ship
th, thin; ŦH, then; zh, measure

in full flower, at the peak of attainment: *in the full flower of her career.*
—*v.* **1** have or produce flowers: *Our lilac didn't flower this year.* **2** reach or be at one's best. **3** cause to blossom or bloom. **4** decorate with flowers or a floral design. [ME < OF *flour* < L *flos, floris*] —**flow′er·er,** *n.* —**flow′er·less,** *adj.* —**flow′er·like′,** *adj.*

flow·ered (flou′ərd) *adj.* **1** having flowers. **2** covered or decorated with flowers.

flow·er·et (flou′ər it) *n.* **1** a small flower. **2** floret.

flower head a bloom, or blossom, composed of many tiny flowers grouped together so that they appear to be a single flower; compound flower: *Composite plants, such as the daisy and dandelion, have flower heads.* See **composite** for picture.

flow·er·ing (flou′ər ing) *adj.* having flowers.

flowering quince any of a genus (Chaenomeles) of Asian shrubs and small trees of the rose family, widely cultivated for their showy, usually red, flowers.

flow·er·pot (flou′ər pot′) *n.* a pot to hold earth for a plant to grow in.

flow·er·y (flou′ər ē) *adj.* **-er·i·er, -er·i·est. 1** having many flowers. **2** containing many fine words and fanciful expressions. —**flow′er·i·ly,** *adv.* —**flow′er·i·ness,** *n.*

flow·ing (flō′ing) *adj.* **1** moving in a current or stream: *flowing water.* **2** moving easily or smoothly: *flowing words.* **3** hanging loosely: *flowing robes.* —**flow′ing·ly,** *adv.* —**flow′ing·ness,** *n.*

flow·me·ter (flō′mē′tər) *n.* any apparatus designed to measure and record the rate of flow of a liquid or gas.

flown (flōn) *v.* pp. of **fly**[2].

FLQ or **F.L.Q.** Front de Libération du Québec.

Flt.Lt. Flight Lieutenant.

Flt.Sgt. Flight Sergeant.

flu (flü) *n. Informal.* influenza.
☛ *Hom.* **flew, flue.**

flub (flub) *v.* **flubbed, flub·bing;** *n.* —*v.* do (something) very clumsily; make a mess of. —*n.* a failure in performance; botch; mistake; error.

fluc·tu·ate (fluk′chü āt′) *v.* **-at·ed, -at·ing. 1** rise and fall; change continually; vary irregularly: *The temperature fluctuates from day to day.* **2** move in waves. [< L *fluctuare* < *fluctus* wave]

fluc·tu·a·tion (fluk′chü ā′shən) *n.* **1** a rising and falling; continual change; irregular variation. **2** a wavelike motion.

flue (flü) *n.* **1** a tube, pipe, or other enclosed passage for conveying smoke, hot air, etc.: *Our chimney has several flues.* **2** flue pipe. **3** the air passage in such a pipe. [origin uncertain]
☛ *Hom.* **flew, flu.**

flue-cured (flü′kyürd′) *adj.* of tobacco, cured by being hung for several days in a place heated through flues, without smoke.

flu·en·cy (flü′ən sē) *n.* **1** a smooth, easy flow: *The orator had great fluency of speech.* **2** easy, rapid speaking or writing.

flu·ent (flü′ənt) *adj.* **1** flowing smoothly or easily: *Long practice had enabled the traveller to speak fluent French.* **2** speaking or writing easily and rapidly. **3** not fixed or stable; fluid. [< L *fluens, -entis,* ppr. of *fluere* flow] —**flu′ent·ly,** *adv.*
☛ *Syn.* **2. Fluent, glib, voluble** = speaking easily. **Fluent** suggests being knowledgeable or well prepared and speaking or writing easily and rapidly: *He is a fluent lecturer.* **Glib** = speaking too easily and smoothly, suggesting a lack of sincerity behind the words or superficial talk: *He is a glib liar.* **Voluble** = speaking fluently and continuously, often suggesting an uncheckable flood of words: *Detained by my voluble friend, I was late.*

flue pipe in an organ, a pipe in which the sound is made by a current of air striking its mouth or opening.

fluff (fluf) *n., v.* —*n.* **1** soft, light, downy particles: *Woollen blankets often have fluff on them.* **2** a soft, light, downy mass: *The little kitten looked like a ball of fluff.* **3** *Slang.* a mistake in reading, speaking, etc. on the stage or on radio or television.
—*v.* **1** shake up into a soft, light, downy mass: *I fluffed the pillows when I made the bed.* **2** become fluffy. **3** move or float softly like fluff. **4** *Slang.* make a mistake in reading one's lines, etc. [apparently var. of *flue* downy matter: OE *flug-* in *flugol* fleeting, related to *flēogan* to fly; influenced by *puff*]

fluff·y (fluf′ē) *adj.* **fluff·i·er, fluff·i·est. 1** soft and light like fluff:

Whipped cream is fluffy. **2** covered with fluff; downy: *fluffy baby chicks.* —**fluff′i·ly,** *adv.* —**fluff′i·ness,** *n.*

flü·gel·horn or **flu·gel·horn** (flü′gəl hôrn′) *n.* one of several brass wind instruments similar in design to a cornet but having a more mellow tone. [< G *Flügelhorn* < *Flügel* wing + *Horn* horn]

flu·id (flü′id) *n., adj.* —*n.* any liquid or gas; any substance that flows: *Water, mercury, air, and oxygen are fluids.* —*adj.* **1** in the state of a fluid; like a fluid; flowing. **2** of or having to do with fluids. **3** changing easily; not fixed. [< L *fluidus* < *fluere* flow] —**flu′id·ly,** *adv.* —**flu′id·ness,** *n.*
☛ *Syn. n.* See note at **liquid.**

fluid dram one-eighth of a fluid ounce (about 3.6 cm³).

flu·id·ic (flü id′ik) *adj.* of or having to do with fluidics.

flu·id·ics (flü id′iks) *n.* (*used with a singular verb*) the technology and use of systems or devices that depend for their operation on the flow and pressure of a fluid in a channel, instead of electronic or mechanical elements.

flu·id·i·ty (flü id′ə tē) *n.* a fluid condition or quality.

flu·id·ize (flü′ə dīz′) *v.* **-ized, -iz·ing.** make fluid; especially, make (a solid) like a fluid by pulverizing it and suspending the particles in a stream of gas so that the whole can be transported as a fluid.

fluid ounce a unit for measuring liquids, equal to one-twentieth of a pint, or about 28.4 cm³.

fluke¹ (flük) *n.* **1** the pointed part of an anchor that catches in the ground. See **anchor** for picture. **2** the barbed head or barb of an arrow, harpoon, etc. **3** either half of a whale's tail. [? special use of *fluke³*]

fluke² (flük) *n., v.* **fluked, fluk·ing.** *Informal.* —*n.* **1** *Billiards or pool.* a lucky shot. **2** a lucky chance; fortunate accident. —*v.* **1** *Billiards or pool.* make or hit by a lucky shot. **2** get by chance or accident. [origin uncertain]

fluke³ (flük) *n.* **1** any of numerous parasitic flatworms constituting two classes (Monogenea and Digenea, formerly placed in the single class Trematoda). Some flukes have very complex life cycles, requiring three different types of host. **2** a flatfish, especially any of various flounders. [OE *flōc*]

fluk·ey or **fluk·y** (flük′ē) *adj.* **fluk·i·er, fluk·i·est.** *Informal.* **1** obtained by chance rather than by skill. **2** uncertain: *flukey weather.*

flume (flüm) *n.* **1** a deep, narrow valley with a stream running through it. **2** a large, inclined trough or chute for carrying water. Flumes are used to transport logs and to furnish water for power or irrigation. [ME < OF *flum* < L *flumen* river < *fluere* flow]

flum·mer·y (flum′ər ē) *n., pl.* **-mer·ies. 1** pudding made of milk, eggs, flour, sugar, etc. **2** an empty compliment; empty trifling; nonsense. [< Welsh *llymru*]

flum·mox (flum′əks) *v. Informal.* confuse; bewilder; confound. [? < dial. *flummocks* to maul, mangle] —**flum′mox·er,** *n.*

flung (flung) *v.* pt. and pp. of **fling.**

flunk (flungk) *Informal. v., n.* —*v.* **1** fail in school work: *He flunked his chemistry examination but passed all the others.* **2** cause to fail. **3** mark or grade as having failed. **4** give up; back out. **flunk out,** dismiss or be dismissed from school, college, etc. because of inferior work. —*n.* a failure. [origin uncertain]

flunk·ey (flungk′ē) *n., pl.* **-eys. 1** a man servant who wears livery; footman. **2** a flattering, fawning person. **3** *Dialect.* a farm hand; cook's assistant. Also, **flunky.** [? alteration of *flanker* one posted on the flank of a person or group < *flank*, v. < *flank*, n. < OF *flanc* < Gmc.]

flunk·y (flungk′ē) *n., pl.* **flunk·ies.** See **flunkey.**

flu·or (flü′ôr) *n.* fluorite. [< L *fluor* a flowing < *fluere* flow]

fluo·resce (flür es′, flôr es′, or flü′ə res′) *v.* **-resced, -resc·ing.** give off light by fluorescence. [< *fluorescence*]

fluo·res·cence (flür es′əns, flôr es′əns, or flü′ə res′əns) *n.* **1** a giving off of light from a substance while exposed to certain rays (X rays and ultraviolet rays). **2** the property of a substance that causes this. Fluorescence is an ability to transform light so as to emit rays of a different wave length or color. **3** the light given off in this way. [< *fluor* (spar) + *-escence*, as in *phosphorescence*]

fluo·res·cent (flür es′ənt, flôr es′ənt, or flü′ə res′ənt) *adj.* that gives off light by fluorescence. Fluorescent substances glow in the dark when exposed to X rays.

fluorescent lamp a type of electric lamp, usually a cathode-ray tube containing a gas or vapor that produces light (**fluorescent light**) when acted on by an electric current.

fluor·ic (flü ôr′ik) *adj.* of, having to do with, or obtained from fluorite or fluorine.

fluor·i·date (flür′ə dāt′ or flôr′ə dāt′) *v.* **-dat·ed, -dat·ing.** add small amounts of fluoride to drinking water, especially to prevent tooth decay in children. [back formation < *fluoridation*]

fluor·i·da·tion (flür′ə dā′shən or flôr′ə dā′shən) *n.* the act or process of fluoridating. [< *fluoride*]

fluor·ide (flür′īd, flôr′īd, or flü′ə rīd′) *n.* a compound of fluorine and another element or radical.

fluor·ine (flür′ēn or -in, flôr′ēn or -in, flü′ər ēn or -in) *n.* a poisonous, greenish-yellow gaseous chemical element similar to chlorine. *Symbol:* F; *at.no.* 9; *at.wt.* 18.9984. [< *fluor*(ite); because found in *fluorite*]

fluor·ite (flür′īt, flôr′īt, or flü′ə rīt′) *n.* a transparent, crystalline mineral that occurs in many colors; calcium fluoride. It is used for fusing metals, making glass, etc. *Formula:* CaF₂ [< *fluor*]

fluor·o·car·bon (flür′ō kär′bən, flôr′ō-, or flü′ər ō-) *n.* any of a group of synthetic compounds derived from hydrocarbons, in which some or all the hydrogen atoms have been replaced by flourine atoms. Fluorocarbons are usually nonflammable, nontoxic, and resilient to chemical change; they are used for making resins and plastics and as refrigerants and solvents.

fluor·o·scope (flür′ə skōp′ or flôr′ə skōp′) *n.* a device containing a fluorescent screen for examining objects exposed to X rays or other radiations. The parts of the object not penetrated by the rays cast shadows on the screen. [< *fluor*(escence) + *-scope*]

fluor·o·scop·ic (flür′ə skop′ik or flôr′ə skop′ik) *adj.* of or having to do with the fluoroscope or with fluoroscopy. —**fluor′o·scop′i·cal·ly,** *adv.*

fluor·spar (flür′spär, flôr′spär, or flü′ər spär′) *n.* fluorite.

flur·ry (flėr′ē) *n., pl.* **-ries;** *v.* **-ried, -ry·ing.** —*n.* **1** a sudden gust of wind: *A flurry upset the small sailboat.* **2** a light fall of snow or, less usually, rain: *snow flurries.* **3** a sudden excitement, confusion, or disturbance. —*v.* excite; confuse; disturb: *Noise in the audience flurried the actor so that he forgot his lines.* [? blend of *flutter* and *hurry*]

flush¹ (flush) *v., n.* —*v.* **1** blush; glow. **2** cause to blush or glow: *Exercise flushed his face.* **3** flush suddenly; flow rapidly: *Embarrassment caused the blood to flush to her cheeks.* **4** wash or cleanse with a rapid flow of water: *The city streets were flushed every night.* **5** empty out; drain: *flush water from flooded land.* **6** make joyful and proud; excite: *The team was flushed with its first victory.* **7** of a plant, send out shoots. —*n.* **1** a blush; glow. **2** a sudden rush; rapid flow. **3** an excited condition or feeling; sudden rush of joyous pride, etc. **4** a sudden, fresh growth: *April brought the first flush of grass.* **5** glowing vigor; freshness: *the first flush of youth.* **6** a fit of feeling very hot. [? blend of *flash* and *blush*]

flush² (flush) *adj., adv., v.* —*adj.* **1** even; level: *The edge of the new shelf must be flush with the old one.* **2** well supplied; having plenty: *The rich man was always flush with money.* **3** abundant; plentiful: *Money is flush when times are good.* **4** liberal; lavish. **5** prosperous. **6** glowing; ruddy. **7** direct; square. —*adv.* **1** so as to be level; evenly. **2** directly; squarely: *The fighter hit him flush on the nose.* —*v.* make even; level. [? extended use of *flush¹*]

flush³ (flush) *v.* **1** fly or start up suddenly. **2** cause to fly or start up suddenly: *The hunter's dog flushed a partridge in the woods.* [origin uncertain] —**flush′er,** *n.*

flush⁴ (flush) *n. Card games.* a hand all of one suit. [< OF *flus, flux* < L *fluxus* flow]

flus·ter (flus′tər) *v., n.* —*v.* make nervous and excited; confuse. —*n.* nervous excitement; confusion. [< Scand.; cf. Icelandic *flaustr* bustle and *flaustra* be flustered]

A flute

flute (flüt) *n., v.* **flut·ed, flut·ing.** —*n.* **1** a reedless woodwind instrument consisting of a long, slender tube of metal or wood, with holes stopped by fingers or keys for producing the different tones, and a mouth hole in the side near one end. A flute has a range of three octaves upward from middle C. **2** a long, rounded groove, as in the shaft of a column, etc. —*v.* **1** play on a flute. **2** make high-pitched, melodious sounds

similar to those of a flute. 3 make long, rounded grooves in. [ME < OF *fleüte, flaüte* < Provençal *flauta*, ult. < L *flatus* pp. of *flare* blow] —**flute′like′**, *adj.*

flut·ed (flü′təd) *adj.* 1 having long, rounded grooves: *a fluted column.* 2 sounding like a flute: *speaking in fluted tones.*

Fluting used to decorate the mantel around a fireplace

flut·ing (flü′ting) *n.* a type of decoration consisting of long, round grooves.

flut·ist (flü′tist) *n.* a person who plays a flute, especially a skilled player. Also, **flautist.**

flut·ter (flut′ər) *v., n.* —*v.* 1 wave back and forth quickly and lightly. 2 flap the wings; flap. 3 come or go with a fluttering motion. 4 move about restlessly; flit. 5 be in a state of excitement: *The crowd fluttered with expectation.* 6 beat feebly and irregularly: *Her pulse fluttered.* 7 confuse, excite.
—*n.* 1 the action of fluttering. 2 a confused or excited condition: *The appearance of the Queen caused a great flutter in the crowd.* 3 unstable vibration of some part of an aircraft: *wing flutter.* 4 in high-fidelity sound reproduction, a change in pitch caused by variations in the speed of a record turntable or reel of tape. Also, **flitter.** [ME *floteren* < OE *flotorian* float. Related to FLEET[1].] —**flut′ter·er,** *n.* —**flut′ter·ing·ly,** *adv.*

flu·vi·al (flü′vē əl) *adj.* of, found in, or produced by a river: *A delta is a fluvial deposit.* [< L *fluvialis* < *fluvius* river]

flux (fluks) *n., v.* —*n.* 1 a flow; flowing. 2 a flowing in of the tide. 3 continuous change: *New words and meanings keep the English language in a state of flux.* 4 an unnatural discharge of blood or liquid matter from the body. 5 a substance used to help metals or minerals fuse together: *Rosin is used as a flux in soldering.* 6 the rate of flow of a fluid, heat, etc. across a certain surface or area.
—*v.* 1 cause an unnatural discharge of blood or liquid matter in; purge. 2 fuse together; melt. 3 heat with a substance that helps metals or minerals fuse together. [< L *fluxus* < *fluere* flow]

flux·ion (fluk′shən) *n.* 1 a flowing; flow. 2 a discharge. 3 *Mathematics.* the rate of change of a continuously varying quantity; differential.

fly[1] (flī) *n., pl.* **flies.** 1 any of a large order (Diptera) of two-winged insects, especially the housefly and related, stout-bodied insects. 2 any of various other winged insects (*usually used in compounds*): *dragonfly, firefly, caddis fly.* 3 a fishing lure consisting of a fish-hook with feathers, silk, tinsel, etc. attached to make it resemble an insect.
fly in the ointment, a small thing that spoils something else or lessens its value.
[OE *flēoge* < *flēogan* fly[2]]

fly[2] (flī) *v.* **flew, flown, fly·ing** for 1-12; **flied, fly·ing** for 13; *n., pl.* **flies.** —*v.* 1 move through the air with wings. 2 float or wave in the air. 3 cause to float or wave in the air: *to fly a kite.* 4 travel through the air in an aircraft. 5 manage an aircraft: *The pilot has to fly long hours.* 6 move through the air in bits or shreds: *The bottle flew into a thousand pieces.* 7 **a** hunt with a falcon. **b** attack by flying, as a hawk does. 8 travel over in an aircraft. 9 manage (an aircraft). 10 carry in an aircraft. 11 move swiftly; go rapidly. 12 run away; flee; flee from; shun. 13 *Baseball.* hit a ball high into the air with a bat.
fly at, attack violently.
fly in the face of, disobey openly; defy.
fly off, leave suddenly; break away.
fly off the handle, get very excited.
fly up, be promoted from Brownie to Girl Guide.
let fly, a aim; shoot; throw: *The hunter let fly an arrow.* **b** say violently.
—*n.* 1 Also, *esp.Brit.,* **flies,** *pl.* a flap or opening in a garment, especially in the front of trousers. 2 a piece of canvas that serves as an outer flap or roof for a tent. 3 the length of an extended flag from the staff to the outer edge. 4 the outer edge of a flag. 5 *Baseball.* a ball hit high into the air with a bat. 6 **flies,** *pl.* in a theatre, the space above a stage.
on the fly, a while still in the air; before touching the ground. **b** without stopping or interrupting what one is doing: *We worked all day, eating snacks on the fly.*
[OE *flēogan*]

fly·a·way (flī′ə wā′) *adj.* 1 fluttering; streaming. 2 frivolous;

hat, āge, fär; let, ēqual, tèrm; it, īce
hot, ōpen, ôrder; oil, out; cup, put, rüle,
above, takən, pencəl, lemən, circəs

ch, child; ng, long; sh, ship
th, thin; ₮H, then; zh, measure

flighty. 3 produced and packaged for shipment by air: *flyaway supplies.*

fly·blown (flī′blōn′) *adj.* 1 tainted by the eggs or larvae of flies. 2 spoiled. 3 covered with fly specks.

fly–by–night (flī′bī nīt′) *adj., n.* —*adj.* not reliable; not to be trusted. —*n. Informal.* 1 a person who avoids paying his debts by leaving secretly at night. 2 an unreliable or irresponsible person.

fly·catch·er (flī′kach′ər) *n.* 1 any of an Old World subfamily (Muscicapinae, of the family Muscicapidae) of small songbirds characterized by the habit of darting out from a perch to catch flying insects. 2 any of a New World family (Tyrannidae) of songbirds, such as the kingbirds or phoebes, having similar habits.

fly·er or **fli·er** (flī′ər) *n.* 1 a person or thing that flies. 2 pilot. 3 a very fast train, ship, bus, etc. 4 *Slang.* a reckless financial venture. 5 *Informal.* a try; an experimental venture into something. 6 a small handbill, used for advertising. 7 one step of a straight flight of stairs.

fly·fish (flī′fish′) *v.* fish with flies, natural or artificial, as bait.

fly·fish·ing (flī′fish′ing) *n.* fishing with natural or artificial flies as bait.

fly–in (flī′in′) *adj.* designed for flying into; having landing facilities: *a fly-in fishing camp.*

fly-in camp *Cdn.* a fishing or hunting camp that is accessible only by airplane.

fly·ing (flī′ing) *adj.* 1 that flies; moving through the air. 2 floating or waving in the air. 3 swift. 4 short and quick; hasty: *Aunt Mary paid us a flying visit last week.* 5 of cattle brands, wavy.
with flying colors or **colours,** successfully; triumphantly: *He passed the examination with flying colors.*

flying boat a type of seaplane having a boatlike hull.

flying buttress an arched support or brace built between the wall of a building and a supporting column to bear some of the weight of the roof. See **buttress** for picture.

Flying Dutchman 1 a legendary Dutch sea captain condemned to sail the seas until the day of judgment. 2 his ghostlike ship, supposed to appear at sea and to be a bad omen.

flying fish any of a family (Exocoetidae) of marine fishes found in warm and tropical seas, having large, winglike pectoral fins by means of which they can glide some distance through the air after leaping from the water.

flying jib a small, triangular sail set in front of the regular jib.

flying machine aircraft.

flying officer an air-force officer ranking next above a pilot officer and below a flight lieutenant. *Abbrev.:* F.O. or F/O.

flying saucer a disklike object that some people claim to have seen flying in the sky at great speed over various parts of the world.

flying spot *Television.* a moving beam of light that produces a succession of thin lines against a surface containing an image. The areas of lightness and darkness are electronically picked up and transmitted to receiving sets where the image is reproduced.

flying squirrel any of a subfamily (Petaurinae) of nocturnal squirrels of North America, Asia, and Europe, having a fold of fur-covered skin along each side joining the front and hind legs, which is stretched taut when the animals spread out their legs, permitting them to glide through the air.

flying wing 1 *Cdn. football.* a player whose position is variable behind the line of scrimmage: *There is no flying wing on American football teams.* 2 a type of aircraft in which the motors, fuselage, etc. are inside the wing structure.

fly·leaf (flī′lēf′) *n., pl.* **-leaves.** a blank sheet of paper at the beginning or end of a book, pamphlet, etc.

fly·man (flī′mən) *n., pl.* **-men.** *Theatre.* a stagehand who works in the flies above the stage.

fly·o·ver (flī′ō′vər) *n.* 1 flypast. 2 *Esp.Brit.* a highway overpass.

fly·pa·per (flī′pā′pər) *n.* a paper coated with a sticky substance to catch flies.

fly·past (flī′past′) *n.* a display in which aircraft in formation fly over a reviewing stand located on the ground: *We enjoyed the flypast at the air show.*

fly specks the tiny, dark spots left by flies on windows, light bulbs, etc.; fly dung.

fly swatter a device for killing flies, usually consisting of a long wooden or wire handle to which is attached a broad, flat piece of perforated rubber, plastic, etc.

fly·trap (flī′trap′) n. 1 a plant that traps insects. 2 a trap to catch flies.

fly–up (flī′up′) n. a ceremony at which Brownies are promoted to Girl Guides.

fly·way (flī′wā′) n. an established route followed by migrating birds.

fly·weight (flī′wāt′) n. a boxer who weighs between 49 and 51 kilograms.

fly·wheel (flī′wēl′ or -hwēl′) n. a heavy wheel attached to machinery to keep the speed even.

fm. fathom.

Fm fermium.

FM or **F.M.** frequency modulation.

F.M. field-marshal.

f number Photography. the number obtained by dividing the focal length of a lens by its effective diameter.

foal (fōl) n., v. —n. a young horse, donkey, etc.; colt or filly. **in** or **with foal**, of a mare, pregnant.
—v. give birth to (a foal). [OE fola]

foam (fōm) n., v. —n. 1 a mass of very small bubbles. 2 a frothy mass formed in the mouth as saliva or on the skin of animals as sweat: The dog with foam around its mouth is suffering from rabies. 3 a spongy, flexible material made from plastics, rubber, etc.
—v. 1 form or gather foam. 2 cause to foam. 3 break into foam: The stream foams over the rocks. 4 cover with foam.
foam at the mouth, be greatly enraged.
[OE fám] —**foam′less,** adj. —**foam′like′,** adj.

foam rubber a firm, spongy foam of natural or synthetic rubber, used especially for mattresses, and upholstery.

foam·y (fō′mē) adj. foam·i·er, foam·i·est. 1 covered with foam; foaming. 2 made of foam. 3 like foam. —**foam′i·ly,** adv. —**foam′i·ness,** n.

fob¹ (fob) n. 1 a small pocket in trousers to hold a watch, etc. 2 a short watch chain, ribbon, etc. that hangs out of a watch pocket. 3 an ornament worn at the end of such a chain, ribbon, etc. [cf. dial. HG fuppe pocket]

fob² (fob) v. fobbed, fob·bing; n. —v. trick; deceive; cheat.
fob off, a put off or deceive by a trick. **b** palm off or get rid of by a trick.
—n. a trick. [? extended use of fob¹]

f.o.b. or **F.O.B.** free on board.

fo·cal (fō′kəl) adj. of, having to do with, or situated at a focus.

focal length the distance of a focus from the optical centre of a lens or concave mirror.

fo·cal·ize (fō′kəl īz′) v. -ized, -iz·ing. 1 focus. 2 bring or come into focus. —**fo′cal·i·za′tion,** n.

fo·ci (fō′sī or fō′sē) n. a pl. of focus.

fo·cus (fō′kəs) n., pl. -cus·es or -ci; v. -cus·ses or -cus·es, -cussed or -cused, -cus·sing or -cus·ing. —n. 1 a point at which rays of light, heat, etc. meet or from which they diverge or seem to diverge after being reflected by a mirror or refracted by a lens. 2 focal length. 3 the correct adjustment of a lens, the eye, etc. to make a clear image: to bring a telescope into focus. 4 the central point of attention, activity, disturbance, etc.: The focus of a disease is the part of the body where it is most active. 5 Geometry. a either of two fixed points used in determining an ellipse. b a point used in determining some other curve.
in focus, clear; distinct.
out of focus, blurred; indistinct.
—v. 1 bring (rays of light, heat, etc.) to a point. 2 adjust (a lens, the eye, etc.) to make a clear image: A near-sighted person cannot focus accurately on distant objects. 3 make (an image, etc.) clear by adjusting a lens, the eye, etc. 4 concentrate: When studying, he focussed his mind on his lessons. [< L focus hearth] —**fo′cus·ser** or **fo′cus·er,** n.

fod·der (fod′ər) n., v. —n. coarse food for horses, cattle, etc.: Hay and cornstalks are fodder. —v. give fodder to (horses, cattle, etc.). [OE fōdor < fōda food]
☛ Syn. See note at feed.

foe (fō) n. an enemy. [OE fāh hostile]
☛ Syn. See note at enemy.

foehn (fān; German, fœn) n. Meteorology. a warm, dry wind that blows down the slopes of a mountain and across a valley, especially in the Alps. Also, **föhn.** [< dial. G föhn, ult. < L Favonius the west wind]

foe·man (fō′mən) n., pl. -men. Archaic. enemy.

foe·tal (fē′təl) See fetal.

foe·tus (fē′təs) See fetus.

fog (fog) n., v. fogged, fog·ging. —n. 1 a cloud of fine drops of water that forms just above the earth's surface; thick mist. 2 a darkened condition; dim, blurred state. 3 a confused or puzzled condition: His mind was in a fog during most of the examination. —v. 1 cover with fog. 2 darken; dim; blur. 3 become covered or filled with fog. 4 confuse; puzzle. [< foggy]

fog bank a dense mass of fog.

fog·bound (fog′bound′) adj. kept from travelling, especially from sailing, by fog.

fo·gey (fō′gē) n., pl. -geys. one who is behind the times or lacks enterprise. Also, **fogy.** [origin uncertain]

fog·gy (fog′ē) adj. -gi·er, -gi·est. 1 having much fog; misty. 2 not clear; dim; blurred: His understanding of geography was rather foggy. 3 confused; puzzled. [< fog long grass; originally, marshy] —**fog′gi·ly,** adv. —**fog′gi·ness,** n.

fog·horn (fog′hôrn′) n. 1 a horn or siren used in foggy weather to warn ships of danger from rocks, collision, etc. 2 a loud, harsh voice.

fo·gy (fō′gē) n., pl. -gies. See fogey.

foi·ble (foi′bəl) n. a weak point; a weakness in character: Talking too much is one of her foibles. [< F foible, older form of modern faible feeble]

foie gras (fwä grä′) French. See pâté de foie gras.

foil¹ (foil) v. 1 prevent (someone) from carrying out (plans, attempts, etc.); get the better of; turn aside or hinder: The hero foiled the villain. 2 prevent (a scheme, plan, etc.) from being carried out or from succeeding. 3 spoil (a trace or scent) by crossing it. [< OF fouler trample, full (cloth) < VL fullare < L fullo a fuller; with reference to spoiling a trace or scent by crossing it]

foil² (foil) n., v. —n. 1 metal beaten, hammered, or rolled into a very thin sheet: tin foil, aluminum foil. 2 anything that makes something else look or seem better by contrast. 3 a very thin layer of polished metal, placed under a gem to give it more color or sparkle. 4 Architecture. a leaflike ornament; arc or rounded space between cusps.
—v. 1 coat or back with foil. 2 set off by contrast. [ME < OF < L folia leaves]

foil³ (foil) n. 1 a long, narrow sword with a knob or button on the point to prevent injury, used in fencing. 2 foils, pl. fencing. [origin uncertain]

foist (foist) v. 1 palm off as genuine; impose slyly: The dishonest shopkeeper foisted inferior goods on his customers. 2 put in secretly or slyly: The author discovered that the translator had foisted several passages into his book. [probably < dial. Du. vuisten take in hand < vuist fist]

fol. 1 folio. 2 following.

fold¹ (fōld) v., n. —v. 1 bend or double over on itself. 2 bring together with the parts in or around one another. 3 bring close to the body. 4 put the arms around and hold tenderly. 5 wrap; enclose. 6 Informal. bring or come to a halt; close up; terminate: They folded the business after only two months and with great loss.
fold in, add to a mixture in cooking by gently turning one part over another with strokes of a spoon: Fold in beaten egg whites.
fold up, a make or become smaller by folding. **b** break down; collapse. **c** Informal. fail.
—n. 1 a layer of something folded. 2 a hollow place made by folding. 3 something that is or can be folded. 4 the act or process of folding. 5 Geology. a bend in a layer of rock. [OE fealdan]

fold² (fōld) n., v. —n. 1 a pen to keep sheep in. 2 sheep kept in a pen. 3 a church group; congregation; church.
return to the fold, a return to active membership of one's church. **b** return to the place or group of people to which one naturally belongs.
—v. put or keep (sheep) in a pen. [OE falod]

–fold suffix. 1 times as many; times as great, as in tenfold. 2 formed or divided into—parts, as in manifold. [OE -feald. Related to FOLD¹.]

fold·er (fōl′dər) n. 1 a person or thing that folds. 2 a holder for papers, made by folding a piece of cardboard. 3 a pamphlet made of one or more folded sheets.

fol·de·rol (fol′də rol′) See falderal.

folding doors doors having one part hinged to another so that they can open and close by folding and unfolding.

folding money Informal. paper money, as opposed to coins.

fo·li·a·ceous (fō′lē ā′shəs) adj. 1 leaflike; leafy. 2 made of

leaflike plates or thin layers. [< L *foliaceus* < *folia* leaves]

fol·i·age (fō′lē ij) *n.* **1** the leaves of a plant, especially of a tree. **2** a decoration made of carved or painted leaves, flowers, etc. [alteration of F *feuillage* < *feuille* leaf < L *folia* leaves]

fo·li·ate (*adj.* fō′lē it *or* fō′lē āt′; *v.* fō′lē āt′) *adj., v.* **-at·ed, at·ing.** —*adj.* **1** having leaves; covered with leaves. **2** resembling a leaf; leaflike.
—*v.* **1** put forth leaves. **2** split into leaflike plates or thin layers. **3** shape like a leaf. **4** decorate with leaflike ornaments. [< L *foliatus* < *folia* leaves]

fo·li·a·tion (fō′lē ā′shən) *n.* **1** a growing of leaves; putting forth of leaves: *foliation of trees in the spring.* **2** being in leaf. **3** a decoration with leaflike ornaments or foils. **4** *Geology.* **a** the property of splitting up into leaflike layers. **b** the leaflike plates or layers into which crystalline rocks are divided.

folic acid (fō′lik) *Biochemistry.* a crystalline compound of the vitamin complex, found in green leaves, mushrooms, and some animal tissue and used in the treatment of anemia. *Formula:* $C_{19}H_{19}N_7O_6$ [< L *folium* leaf + E *-ic*]

fo·li·o (fō′lē ō′) *n., pl.* **-li·os;** *v.* —*n.* **1** a large sheet of paper folded once to make two leaves, or four pages, of a book, etc. **2 a** a book of the largest size, having pages made by folding large sheets of paper once; large volume. A folio is usually any book more than 11 inches (about 28 cm) in height. **b** the size of a folio book. **3** (*adj.*) of the largest size; made of large sheets of paper folded once: *The encyclopedia was in twenty volumes folio.* **4** *Printing.* **a** page number of a book, etc. **5** a leaf of a book, manuscript, etc. numbered on the front side only. **6** a case for loose papers, etc.
in folio, of folio size or form.
—*v.* number the pages or folios of (a book, etc.); page. [< L *folio,* ablative of *folium* leaf]

folk (fōk) *n., pl.* **folk** *or* **folks;** *adj.* —*n.* **1** people as a group: *Most city folk know very little about farming.* **2** a tribe; nation. **3 folks,** *pl.* **a** people. **b** *Informal.* the members of one's own family; one's relatives. **4** folk music (def. 2).
—*adj.* **1** of or having to do with the common people, their beliefs, legends, customs, etc. **2** of or having to do with folk songs or folk music: *a folk festival.* [OE *folc*]

folk·a·thon (fōk′ə thon′) *n. Slang.* a gathering for the singing of folk songs for a long period of time. [< *folk* songs + mar*athon*]

folk dance **1** a dance originating and handed down among the common people. **2** the music for such a dance.

folk etymology popular misconception of the origin of a word that often results in a modification of its sound or spelling. Thus, ME *crevice* became E *crayfish,* influenced by *fish.*

folk·lore (fōk′lôr′) *n.* the beliefs, legends, customs, etc. of a people, tribe, etc.

folk·lor·ic (fōk′lôr′ik) *adj.* of, having to do with, or characteristic of folklore.

folk·lor·ist (fōk′lôr′ist) *n.* a person who studies or knows much about folklore.

folk music **1** music originating among the common people and passed on from generation to generation, especially by oral tradition. **2** any of many kinds of modern popular music, usually similar in style to traditional folk music.

folk·nik (fōk′nik) *n. Slang.* a person keen on singing or listening to folk songs. [< *folk* songs + beat*nik*]

folk–rock (fōk′rok′) *n.* rock-and-roll music with folk-song themes or lyrics.

folk singer a person who sings folk songs.

folk song **1** a song originating, as a rule, among the common people and handed down from generation to generation: *"Alouette" is a well-known French-Canadian folk song.* **2** a modern song imitating or similar to a traditional folk song.

folk·sy (fōk′sē) *adj.* **-si·er, -si·est.** *Informal.* **1** friendly; social: *It was just a nice, folksy evening.* **2** plain and unpretentious. **3** artificially or affectedly simple or familiar: *The movie was full of folksy stupidity.* —**folk′si·ness,** *n.*

folk tale a story or legend originating among the common people and handed down from generation to generation.

folk·way (fōk′wā′) *n.* a traditional custom of a people or a social group.

fol·li·cle (fol′ə kəl) *n.* **1** a small cavity, sac, or gland. Hair grows from follicles. **2** a one-celled seed vessel. It is a dry fruit that splits open along one seam only. Milkweed pods are follicles. [< L *folliculus,* dim. of *follis* bellows]

fol·lic·u·lar (fə lik′yə lər) *adj.* **1** of or resembling a follicle or follicles. **2** *Medicine.* affecting the follicles: *follicular tonsillitis.*

fol·low (fol′ō) *v., n.* —*v.* **1** go or come after: *Night follows day. He leads; we follow.* **2** result from; result: *Misery follows war. If you eat too much candy, a stomach ache will follow.* **3** go along:

---

hat, āge, fär; let, ēqual, tėrm; it, īce
hot, ōpen, ôrder; oil, out; cup, pút, rüle,
əbove, takən, pencəl, lemən, circəs
ch, child; ng, long; sh, ship
th, thin; ᴛʜ, then; zh, measure

Follow this road to the corner. **4** go along with; accompany: *My dog followed me to school.* **5** pursue: *The hounds followed the fox.* **6** act according to; take as a guide; use; obey: *Follow her advice.* **7** accept (a person) as a guide or leader; accept the authority or example of. **8** keep the eyes or attention on: *I could not follow that bird's flight.* **9** keep the mind on; keep up with and understand: *He found it hard to follow the conversation.* **10** take as one's work or profession; be concerned with: *He expects to follow the law.*
as follows, the following: *The duties of the various officers are as follows.*
follow out, carry out to the end.
follow through, **a** continue a stroke or motion through to the end: *Most golfers follow through after hitting the ball.* **b** carry out fully; complete: *When one begins a job, one should try to follow it through.*
follow up, **a** follow closely and steadily. **b** carry out to the end. **c** increase the effect by further action: *He followed up his first request by asking again a week later.*
—*n.* **1** the act of following. **2** *Billiards.* a stroke that causes the player's ball to roll on after the ball is struck by it. [OE *folgian*]
☛ **Syn.** *v.* **1, 2. Follow, succeed, ensue** = come after. **Follow** is the general word meaning "come or go after": *He has come to take up his new position, but his wife will follow later.* **Succeed** = come next in order of time, and usually suggests taking the place of someone or something: *He succeeded his father as president of the company.* **Ensue,** formal, means "follow as a result or conclusion": *A lasting friendship ensued from our working together during the war.*

fol·low·er (fol′ō ər) *n.* **1** a person who follows the ideas or beliefs of another; adherent: *a follower of Socrates.* **2** an attendant or supporter. **3** a person or thing that follows, or comes after. **4** a part of a machine that takes its motion from another part.
☛ **Syn.** **2. Follower, adherent, disciple** = someone who follows another, his beliefs, a cause, etc. **Follower** is the general word: *Men who promise security always find followers among unthinking people.* **Adherent** means a faithful follower who gives active and loyal support to a belief, cause, party, or leader: *Socialized medicine has many adherents.* **Disciple** emphasizes both devotion to a person as leader and teacher and firm belief in his teachings: *He is a disciple of Einstein.*

fol·low·ing (fol′ō ing) *n., adj.* —*n.* **1** followers; attendants. **2 the following,** the persons, things, items, etc. now to be named, related, described, etc. —*adj.* that follows; next after.

follow–through (fol′ō thrü′) *n.* **1** *Sports.* the smooth completion of a movement, especially of a stroke in golf or tennis after the ball has been hit. **2** any logical continuation and completion.

fol·low–up (fol′ō up′) *n., adj.* —*n.* **1** the act of following up. **2** any action or thing, such as a second or third visit, appeal, letter, etc., designed to be a further effort in achieving some goal. —*adj.* sent or used as a follow-up: *a follow-up circular.*

fol·ly (fol′ē) *n., pl.* **-lies. 1** a being foolish; lack of sense; unwise conduct. **2** a foolish act, practice, or idea; something silly. **3** a costly but foolish undertaking. [ME < OF *folie* < *fol* foolish. See FOOL.]

fo·ment (fō ment′) *v.* **1** promote; foster (trouble, rebellion, etc.). **2** apply warm water, hot cloths, etc. to (a hurt or pain). [< LL *fomentare* < *fomentum* a warm application < L *fovere* warm] —**fo·ment′er,** *n.*

fo·men·ta·tion (fō′men tā′shən) *n.* **1** a stirring up; instigation; encouragement. **2** the application of moist heat. **3** a hot, moist application.

fond (fond) *adj.* **1** loving; liking: *a fond look.* **2** loving foolishly or too much. **3** cherished: *fond hopes.* **4** *Archaic.* foolish; foolishly ready to believe or hope.
be fond of, **a** having a liking for: *My uncle is fond of children.* **b** like to eat: *Most cats are fond of fish.*
[ME *fonned,* pp. of *fonne(n)* be foolish; origin uncertain] —**fond′ly,** *adv.* —**fond′ness,** *n.*

fon·dant (fon′dənt) *n.* **1** a creamy sugar candy used as a filling or coating for other candies. **2** a candy consisting mainly of fondant. [< F *fondant,* literally, melting, ppr. of *fondre* melt. See FOUND³.]

fon·dle (fon′dəl) *v.* **-dled, -dling.** pet; caress lovingly: *Mothers like to fondle their babies.* [< *fond,* v., special use of *fond,* adj.] —**fon′dler,** *n.*

fon·due (fon′dü *or* fon dü′) *n.* **1** a dish usually consisting of melted Swiss cheese, white wine, seasonings, and, often, brandy, into which cubes of bread are dipped and then eaten. **2** any of various similar dishes consisting of small pieces of food dipped into

a hot liquid at the table. [< F *fondue*, fem. pp. of *fondre* melt. See FOUND[3].]

font[1] (font) *n.* **1** a basin holding water for baptism. **2** a basin for holy water. **3** *Poetic or archaic.* fountain or source: *the font of truth.* [ML *fons, fontis* spring]

font[2] (font) *n. Printing.* a complete set of type of one size and style. [< F *fonte* < *fondre* melt. See FOUND[3].]

fon·ta·nel (fon′tə nel′) *n.* a membrane-covered spot on the growing skull of an infant or fetus. [< F *fontanelle*, dim. of *fontaine*. See FOUNTAIN.]

food (füd) *n.* **1** what an animal or plant takes in to enable it to live and grow. **2** what is eaten: *Give him food and drink.* **3** a particular kind or article of food. **4** what helps anything to live and grow. **5** what sustains or serves for consumption in any way: *food for thought.* [OE *fōda*]

☛ *Syn.* **1.** Food, provisions, rations = what human beings and animals eat. **Food** is the general word for what is taken in by people, animals, or plants to keep them alive and help them grow: *Milk is a valuable food.* **Provisions** = a supply of food, either for immediate use or stored away: *I must buy provisions for the holidays.* **Rations** = fixed allowances of food set for one day's use or allowed under some system of rationing: *The survivors lived for three days on small rations of water and chocolate.*

food poisoning sickness from eating contaminated or poisonous food, usually characterized by vomiting, diarrhea, etc.; also, in certain acute types of poisoning, by prostration, respiratory paralysis, etc.

food processor a kitchen appliance having a number of interchangeable blades and other attachments for performing a variety of functions in the preparation of food, such as slicing, grating, dicing, chopping, mixing, and blending.

food·stuff (füd′stuf′) *n.* **1** any material for food: *Grain and meat are foodstuffs.* **2** any nutritionally valuable element in food, as protein or carbohydrate.

foo·fa·raw or **foo·fe·raw** (fü′fə rô′ *or* -rô′) *n.* **1** unnecessary ornamentation, as frills, fringes, bows, etc. **2** *Slang.* a loud disturbance caused by something of no importance. [origin uncertain]

fool (fül) *n., v.* —*n.* **1** a person without sense; unwise or silly person. **2** *Historical.* a clown kept by a king or lord to amuse people; jester. **3** a person who has been deceived or tricked; dupe. —*v.* **1** act like a fool for fun; play; joke: *The teacher told him not to fool during class.* **2** make a fool of; deceive; trick.
fool around, *Informal.* waste time foolishly.
fool away, *Informal.* waste foolishly.
fool with, *Informal.* meddle foolishly with.
[ME < OF *fol* madman, probably < LL *follis* empty-headed < L *follis* bag, bellows]

☛ *Syn. n.* **1.** Fool, idiot, imbecile, in non-technical use, mean "a foolish person." **Fool** suggests absence of intelligence, and expresses contempt for someone who acts without good sense or judgment: *She is a fool to leave school when her grades are so high.* **Idiot** is used of someone acting as if he were totally feeble-minded: *She was such an idiot that she walked in the deep snow without her boots.* **Imbecile** is used of someone the speaker considers half-witted: *Look at that imbecile grinning at nothing.*

fool·er·y (fül′ər ē) *n., pl.* **-er·ies.** a foolish action.

fool·har·dy (fül′här′dē) *adj.* **-di·er, -di·est.** foolishly bold; rash.
—**fool′har′di·ness,** *n.*

fool hen any of various grouse, especially the spruce grouse, which has never learned to fear man and therefore can be easily captured or killed. Fool hens have often been killed with a stick or stone.

fool·ish (fül′ish) *adj.* **1** like a fool; without sense; unwise; silly. **2** ridiculous. —**fool′ish·ly,** *adv.* —**fool′ish·ness,** *n.*

☛ *Syn.* **1.** Foolish, silly, fatuous = without sense. **Foolish** = like a fool, showing lack of common sense and judgment: *The foolish girl insists on having her own way.* **Silly** = seeming weakminded, doing and saying things without sense or point, often making oneself ridiculous: *It is silly to giggle at everything.* More contemptuous, **fatuous** = silly, empty-headed, and stupid, but also self-satisfied: *After his boring speech, the fatuous speaker waited for applause.*

fool·proof (fül′prüf′) *adj.* so safe or simple that even a fool can use or do it: *The car had a foolproof safety catch on the door.*

fool's cap 1 a cap or hood worn by the fool or jester of a king or lord. **2** a dunce cap.

fools·cap (fülz′skap′) *n.* writing paper in sheets usually about 21 cm wide by 35 cm long. [from the watermark]

fool's errand a foolish or useless undertaking.

fool's gold a mineral that looks like gold; iron pyrites or copper pyrites.

fool's paradise a condition of happiness based on false beliefs or hopes.

foot (füt) *n., pl.* **feet;** *v.* —*n.* **1** the end part of a leg; the part that a

person, animal, or thing stands on. **2** the part near the feet; the end toward which the feet are put. **3** the lowest part; bottom; base. **4** the part of a stocking, etc. that covers the foot. **5** soldiers that go on foot; infantry. **6** a unit for measuring length, equal to 12 inches or one third of a yard (30.48 cm). *Symbol:* ′ **7** one of the parts into which a line of verse is divided. This line has four feet: The boy | stood on | the burn | ing deck. **8** the last of a list or series.
on foot, a standing or walking. **b** going on; in progress.
put (one's) best foot forward, *Informal.* **a** do one's best. **b** try to make a good impression.
put (one's) foot down, *Informal.* make up one's mind and act firmly.
put (one's) foot in it, *Informal.* get into trouble by meddling; blunder.
under foot, a in the way. **b** in one's power; in subjection.
with one foot in the grave, almost dead; dying.
—*v.* **1** make or renew the foot of (a stocking, etc.). **2** walk. **3** dance. **4** add. **5** *Informal.* pay (a bill, etc.). [OE *fōt*]

foot·age (füt′ij) *n.* **1** the length in feet. **2** quantity of lumber expressed in board feet.

foot–and–mouth disease a dangerous, contagious virus disease of cattle and some other animals, causing blisters in the mouth and around the hoofs.

foot·ball (füt′bol′ *or* -bôl′) *n.* **1** an outdoor game played by two teams, in which each side tries to kick, pass, or carry a ball across the opposing team's goal line. Canadian and American football have different regulations with regard to size of field, number of players, number of downs, rules of play, etc. **2** the oval, air-filled, usually leather ball used in playing this game. **3** *Brit.* **a** soccer. **b** the round, air-filled, usually leather ball used in soccer; a soccer ball.

foot·board (füt′bôrd′) *n.* **1** a board or small platform to be used as a support for the feet. **2** an upright piece across the foot of a bed.

foot·bridge (füt′brij′) *n.* a bridge for pedestrians only.

foot–can·dle (füt′kan′dəl) *n.* a unit for measuring illumination, equal to about 10.8 lux. It is the amount of light produced by a standard candle at a distance of one foot.

foot·ed (füt′əd) *adj.* **1** having a foot or feet: *a footed wine glass.* **2** having a foot or feet of a specific kind, number, etc. (*used in compounds*): *swift-footed, flat-footed, a four-footed animal.*

–footer *combining form.* a person or thing—feet in height or length: *six-footer = a person or thing six feet in height or length.*

foot·fall (füt′fol′ *or* -fôl′) *n.* **1** the sound of steps coming or going. **2** footstep.

foot fault *Tennis.* a failure to keep both feet behind the base line when serving, or to keep one foot on the ground.

foot·gear (füt′gēr′) *n.* shoes, boots, etc.

foot·hill (füt′hil′) *n.* a low hill at the base of a mountain or mountain range: *We visited a cattle ranch in the foothills of the Rockies.*

foot·hold (füt′hōld′) *n.* **1** a place to put a foot; support for the feet; surface to stand on: *He climbed the steep cliff by finding footholds in cracks in the rock.* **2** a firm footing or position: *It is hard to break a habit that has gained a foothold.*

foot·ing (füt′ing) *n.* **1** a firm placing or position of the feet: *He lost his footing and fell down on the ice.* **2** the position of the feet: *When he changed his footing, he lost his balance.* **3** a place to put a foot; a support for the feet; surface to stand on: *The steep cliff gave us no footing.* **4** a firm place or position: *The newly rich family struggled for a footing in society.* **5** a basis of understanding; relationship: *Canada and the United States are on a friendly footing.* **6** an adding. **7** the amount found by adding; sum; total. **8** the act of moving on the feet; walking, dancing, etc. **9** the manner of placing or using the feet; footwork. **10 footings,** *pl.* the concrete foundations of a building, wall, etc.

foot·less (füt′lis) *adj.* **1** without a foot or feet. **2** without support; not substantial. **3** *Informal.* awkward; helpless; inefficient.
—**foot′less·ly,** *adv.* —**foot′less·ness,** *n.*

foot·let (füt′lit) *n.* a very short type of sock sometimes worn by women.

foot·lights (füt′līts′) *n.pl.* **1** a row of lights at the front of a stage. **2** the profession of acting; stage; theatre.

foot·loose (füt′lüs′) *adj. Informal.* free to go anywhere or do anything.

foot·man (füt′mən) *n., pl.* **-men. 1** a male servant who answers the bell, waits on table, goes with an automobile or carriage to open the door, etc. Footmen, who usually wear special uniforms, are now found mainly in royal palaces. **2** *Archaic.* foot soldier.

foot·mark (füt′märk′) *n.* footprint.

foot·note (füt′nōt′) *n.* a note at the bottom of a page about something in the text.

foot·pace (füt′pās′) *n.* walking pace; speed of ordinary walking.

foot·pad (füt′pad′) *n. Archaic.* a highway robber who goes on foot only.

foot·path (fút′path′) *n.* a path for pedestrians only.

foot–pound (fút′pound′) *n.* a unit for measuring energy, equal to the energy needed to raise a weight of one pound to a height of one foot (about 1.36J). *Abbrev.:* F.P., f.p., or fp

foot·print (fút′print′) *n.* the mark made by a foot.

foot·race (fút′rās′) *n.* a race run on foot, as distinguished from one on horseback, etc.

foot·rest (fút′rest′) *n.* a support on which to rest the feet.

foot rule a wooden or metal ruler one foot long.

foot·sie (fút′sē) *n. Informal.* foot (*especially a child's term*).
play footsie, *Informal.* **a** touch feet, knees, etc. in a flirtatious way, especially while sitting at a table, **b** toy or flirt with, especially in a secretive or ambiguous way: *Some government MPs were playing footsie with the opposition.*

foot·slog (fút′slog′) *v.* **-slogged, -slog·ging.** march or plod, especially a long distance, or through difficult terrain. —**foot′slog′ger,** *n.*

foot soldier a soldier who fights on foot; infantryman.

foot·sore (fút′sôr′) *adj.* having sore feet, especially from much walking.

foot·stalk (fút′stok′ *or* -stôk′) *n.* **1** the stem of a leaf, flower, or flower cluster. **2** a stemlike part of an animal, by which it is supported or attached to something.

foot·step (fút′step′) *n.* **1** a person's step. **2** the distance covered in one step. **3** the sound of steps coming or going. **4** the mark made by a foot; footprint. **5** a step on which to go up or down.
follow in someone's footsteps, do as another has done.

foot·stool (fút′stül′) *n.* a low stool on which to rest the feet when one is sitting in a chair, etc.

foot·way (fút′wā′) *n.* a path for pedestrians only; sidewalk.

foot·wear (fút′wer′) *n.* shoes, slippers, stockings, etc.

foot·work (fút′werk′) *n.* the way of using the feet: *Footwork is important in boxing and dancing.*

foot·worn (fút′wôrn′) *adj.* **1** worn by feet: *a footworn path.* **2** having tired feet.

foo·zle (fü′zəl) *v.* **-zled, -zling;** *n.* —*v.* do clumsily; bungle (a golf stroke, etc.). —*n.* a clumsy failure, especially a badly played stroke in golf. [cf. dial. G *fuseln* work badly or slowly]

fop (fop) *n.* a vain man who is very fond of fine clothes and has affected manners; empty-headed dandy. [origin uncertain]

fop·per·y (fop′ər ē) *n., pl.* **-per·ies.** foppish behavior; fine clothes, affected manners, etc. suitable for a fop.

fop·pish (fop′ish) *adj.* **1** of a fop; suitable for a fop. **2** vain; empty-headed; affected. —**fop′pish·ly,** *adv.* —**fop′pish·ness,** *n.*

for (fôr; *unstressed,* fər) *prep., conj.* —*prep.* **1** in place of: *We used boxes for chairs.* **2** in support of; in favor of: *He voted for Laurier.* **3** representing; in the interest of: *A lawyer acts for his client.* **4** in return for; in consideration of: *These apples are five for a dollar. We thanked him for his kindness.* **5** with the object or purpose of taking, achieving, or obtaining: *He went for a walk. He is looking for a job.* **6** in order to become, have, keep, etc.: *The navy trains men for sailors. He ran for his life.* **7** in search of: *She is hunting for her cat.* **8** in order to get to: *He has just left for Toronto.* **9** meant to belong to or with, or to be used by or with; suited to: *a box for gloves, books for children.* **10** because of; by reason of: *to shout for joy. He was punished for stealing.* **11** in honor of: *A party was given for her.* **12** with a feeling toward: *She has an eye for beauty. We longed for home.* **13** with respect or regard to: *It is warm for April. Eating too much is bad for one's health.* **14** as far or as long as; throughout; during: *We walked for four kilometres. He worked for an hour.* **15** as being: *They know it for a fact.* **16** in spite of: *For all his faults, we like him still.* **17** in proportion to: *For every poisonous snake there are many harmless ones.* **18** to the amount of: *His father gave him a cheque for $20.* **Oh! for,** I wish that I might have: *Oh! for the wings of a bird!* —*conj.* because: *We can't go, for it is raining.* [OE]
☛ *Hom.* fore, four.
☛ *Usage.* **For.** A comma is usually needed between two co-ordinate clauses joined by **for;** without it the **for** might be read as a preposition: *He was glad to go, for Mrs. Crane had been especially good to him.* (not: *He was glad to go for Mrs. Crane....*)
☛ *Syn.* See another note at **because.**

for– *prefix.* away; opposite; completely, as in *forbid, forswear.* [OE]

for. **1** foreign. **2** forestry.

for·age (fôr′ij) *n., v.* **-aged, -ag·ing.** —*n.* **1** food for horses, cattle, etc. **2** the act of hunting or searching for anything, especially food: *We went on a forage for supplies.* —*v.* **1** supply with food; feed. **2** hunt or search for anything, especially food: *The boys foraged in the kitchen till they found some cookies. The man made a living by foraging for old metal.* **3** get by hunting or searching about. **4** get or take food from. **5** plunder: *The*

hat, āge, fär; let, ēqual, tèrm; it, īce
hot, ōpen, ôrder; oil, out; cup, pút, rüle,
əbove, takən, pencəl, lemən, circəs
ch, child; ng, long; sh, ship
th, thin; ŦH, then; zh, measure

soldiers foraged the villages near their camp. [ME < OF *fourrager* < *fuerre* fodder < Gmc.] —**for′ag·er,** *n.*

fo·ra·men (fō rā′mən *or* fō rä′mən) *n., pl.* **-ra·mens** (-rā′mənz) or **-ra·mi·na** (-rä′mə nə). *Biology.* a small hole or hollow, especially a natural cavity in a bone. [< L]

for·a·min·i·fer (fôr′ə min′ə fər) *n.* any of an order (Foraminifera) of protozoans having a calcareous shell that in many species has many tiny holes through which slender processes protrude for locomotion and feeding. [< NL < L *foramen* a small opening + *ferre* bear]

for·as·much as (fôr′əz much′) in view of the fact that; because; since.

for·ay (fôr′ā) *n., v.* —*n.* a raid for plunder. —*v.* plunder; lay waste; pillage. [ME < OF *fourrier* < *fuerre* fodder. See FORAGE.]

for·bade (fər bad′ *or* fər bād′) *v.* pt. of **forbid.**

for·bear[1] (fôr ber′) *v.* **-bore, -borne, -bear·ing. 1** hold back; keep from doing, saying, using, etc.: *The boy forbore to hit back because the other boy was smaller.* **2** be patient; control oneself. [OE *forberan*] —**for·bear′er,** *n.* —**for·bear′ing·ly,** *adv.*

for·bear[2] (fôr′ber) See **forebear.**

for·bear·ance (fôr ber′əns) *n.* **1** the act of forbearing. **2** patience; self-control.
☛ *Syn.* **2.** See note at **patience.**

for·bid (fər bid′) *v.* **-bade** or **-bad, -bid·den** or **-bid, -bid·ding. 1** order (someone) not to do something; make a rule against; prohibit. **2** keep from happening; prevent: *God forbid!* **3** command to keep away from; exclude from: *I forbid you the house.* [OE *forbēodan*]
☛ *Syn.* **1. Forbid, prohibit** = order not to do something. **Forbid** = give an order, often directly or personally, or make a rule that something must not be done, and suggests that obedience is expected: *His father forbade him, to smoke.* **Prohibit** is formal, and means "to make a formal regulation against something," usually by law or official action, and suggests power to enforce it: *Smoking is often prohibited in theatres.*

for·bid·den (fər bid′ən) *adj., v.* —*adj.* not allowed; against the law or rules. —*v.* pp. of **forbid.**

for·bid·ding (fər bid′ing) *adj.* **1** causing fear or dislike; hostile; grim: *The enemy soldier's look was forbidding.* **2** looking dangerous or unpleasant; threatening: *The coast was rocky and forbidding.* —**for·bid′ding·ly,** *adv.* —**for·bid′ding·ness,** *n.*

for·bore (fôr bôr′) *v.* pt. of **forbear**[1].

for·borne (fôr bôrn′) *v.* pp. of **forbear**[1].

for·by (fôr bī′) *Scottish and archaic. prep., adv.* —*prep.* **1** besides. **2** close by; near. —*adv.* besides.

force (fôrs) *n., v.* **forced, forc·ing.** —*n.* **1** active power or strength; energy: *the force of running water.* **2** strength used against a person or thing; violence or constraint: *to rule by force. The rebels took the village by force.* **3** the power to control, influence, persuade, convince, etc.; effectiveness; vividness: *He writes with force.* **4** a group of people working or acting together: *our office force.* **5** a body of persons organized for or assigned to a military or policing function. **6 forces,** *pl.* the whole military strength of a nation or state; armed forces. **7** *Physics.* any cause that produces, changes, or stops the motion of a body. **8** an agency, influence or source of power likened to a physical force: *social forces.* **9** the precise meaning or import (of a word, etc.): *What is the force of that question?* **10** binding power; validity, as of a law or contract: *The force of some laws has to be tested in court.*
by force of, by means of: *by force of argument.*
in force, a in effect or operation; binding; valid. **b** with full strength or in great numbers: *The press turned out in force to the news conference.*
—*v.* **1** use force on. **2** make or drive by force. **3** get or take by force. **4** put by force. **5** impose or impress by force: *to force one's views on another.* **6** break open or through by force. **7** overpower by force. **8** urge to violent effort. **9** make by an unusual or unnatural effort; strain. **10** hurry the growth or development of: *He forced his rhubarb by growing it in a dark, warm place.* **11** *Baseball.* compel (a player) to leave one base and try in vain to reach the next. [< F, ult. < L *fortis* strong] —**force′less,** *adj.* —**forc′er,** *n.*
☛ *Syn. n.* **1.** See note at **power.**

forced (fôrst) *adj.* **1** made, compelled, or driven by force: *The work of slaves is forced labor.* **2** made by an unusual or unnatural effort: *She hid her dislike for him with a forced smile.*

forced march an unusually long, fast march.

force–feed (fôrs′fēd′) v. **-fed, -feed·ing. 1** feed (an animal or person) by forcible means, as by passing a tube through the mouth into the stomach: *Geese were formerly often fattened by force-feeding.* **2** force (someone) to accept or take in (ideas, etc.).

force·ful (fôrs′fəl) *adj.* full of force; strong; powerful; vigorous; effective: *a forceful manner.* —**force′ful·ly,** *adv.* —**force′ful·ness,** *n.*
☛ *Syn.* **Forceful, forcible.** Both terms mean "showing force, powerful", but only **forcible** (def. 1) means "done with force, or violence": *a forceful style* but *a forcible entry.*

force·meat (fôrs′mēt′) *n.* chopped and seasoned meat, used for stuffing, etc. [< *force,* var. of obs. *farce* stuffing + *meat*]

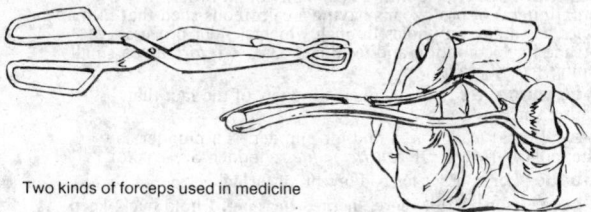

Two kinds of forceps used in medicine

for·ceps (fôr′seps *or* fôr′səps) *n., pl.* **-ceps.** a pair of small pincers or tongs used by surgeons, dentists, etc. for seizing, holding, and pulling. [< L *forceps* < *formus* hot + *capere* take]

force pump a pump with a valveless piston whose action forces liquid through a pipe; any pump which delivers liquid under pressure.

for·ci·ble (fôr′sə bəl) *adj.* **1** made or done by force; using force: *a forcible entry into a house.* **2** having or showing force; strong; powerful; effective; convincing: *a forcible speaker.*
—**for′ci·ble·ness,** *n.* —**for′ci·bly,** *adv.*
☛ *Syn.* See note at **forceful.**

ford (fôrd) *n., v.* —*n.* a place where a river or stream is shallow enough to be crossed by walking or driving through the water. —*v.* cross (a river, etc.) by walking or driving through the water: *They spent an hour looking for a place to ford the river.* [OE]
—**ford′a·ble,** *adj.*

for·done (fôr dun′) *adj. Archaic.* worn out; exhausted.

fore¹ (fôr) *adj., adv., n.* —*adj. or adv.* at the front; toward the beginning or front; forward. —*n.* the forward part; front, especially of a ship or boat.
to the fore, a in or into full view; in or into a conspicuous place or position. **b** at hand; ready. **c** alive.
[*adj.* < *fore-*; *adv.* < OE]
☛ *Hom.* **for, four.**

fore² (fôr) *interj. Golf.* a shout of warning to persons ahead on the fairway who are liable to be struck by the ball. [? for *before*]
☛ *Hom.* **for, four.**

fore– *prefix.* **1** front; in front; at or near the front, as in *forecastle, foremast.* **2** before; beforehand, as in *foreknow, foresee.* [OE *fore* before]

fore and aft 1 at or toward both bow and stern of a ship. **2** on a ship, lengthwise; from bow to stern; placed lengthwise.

fore–and–aft (fôr′ənd aft′ *or* fôr ən aft′) *adj.* lengthwise on a ship; from bow to stern; placed lengthwise. A fore-and-aft-rigged ship has the sails set lengthwise.

fore·arm¹ (fôr′ärm′) *n.* the part of the arm between the elbow and wrist.

fore·arm² (fôr ärm′) *v.* prepare for trouble ahead of time; arm beforehand.

fore·bear (fôr′ber) *n.* an ancestor; forefather. Also, **forbear.** [< *fore- + be + -er*]

fore·bode (fôr bōd′) *v.* **-bod·ed, -bod·ing. 1** give warning of; predict: *Black clouds forebode a storm.* **2** have a feeling that something bad is going to happen. —**fore·bod′er,** *n.*

fore·bod·ing (fôr bō′ding) *n.* **1** a prediction; warning. **2** a feeling that something bad is going to happen: *As the lights went out, we were filled with foreboding.*

fore·brain (fôr′brān′) *n.* the front section of the brain, consisting of the cerebrum, the pituitary gland, and the pineal body.

fore·cast (fôr′kast′) *v.* **-cast·ed, -cast·ed, -cast·ing.** —*v.*
1 prophesy; predict: *Cooler weather is forecast for tomorrow.* **2** be a prophecy or prediction of. **3** foresee; plan ahead.
—*n.* **1** a prophecy; prediction. **2** a planning ahead; foresight.
—**fore′cast′er,** *n.*

fore·cas·tle (fōk′səl *or* fôr′kas′əl) *n.* **1** the upper deck in front of the foremast of a ship or boat. **2** the sailors' quarters in a merchant ship, formerly in the forward part of the ship.

fore·check (fôr′chek′) *v. Hockey.* check an opposing player in his own defensive zone. —**fore′check′er,** *n.*

fore·close (fôr klōz′) *v.* **-closed, -clos·ing. 1** shut out; prevent; exclude. **2** *Law.* **a** take away the right to redeem (a mortgage): *When the conditions of a mortgage are not met, the holder can foreclose and have the property sold to satisfy his claim.* **b** take away the right of (a mortgager) to redeem his property. [ME < OF *forclos,* pp. of *forclore* exclude < *for-* out (< L *foris*) + *clore* shut < L *claudere*]

fore·clo·sure (fôr klō′zhər) *n.* the foreclosing of a mortgage.

fore·court (fôr′kôrt′) *n.* **1** an enclosed space in front of a building. **2** *Tennis, badminton, etc.* the area at the front of the court, especially the area near the net.

fore·done (fôr dun′) *adj. or v. Archaic.* exhausted.

fore·doom (fôr düm′) *v.* doom beforehand.

fore·fa·ther (fôr′fo′ᴛʜər) *n.* ancestor.

fore·fend (fôr fend′) *v.* See **forfend.**

fore·fin·ger (fôr′fing′gər) *n.* the finger next to the thumb; first finger; index finger.

fore·foot (fôr′fut′) *n., pl.* **-feet. 1** one of the front feet of an animal. **2** the forward end of a ship's keel.

fore·front (fôr′frunt′) *n.* **1** the place of greatest importance, activity, etc. **2** foremost part.

fore·gath·er (fôr gaᴛʜ′ər) See **forgather.**

fore·go¹ (fôr gō′) *v.* **-went, -gone, -go·ing.** do without; give up: *She decided to forego the movies and do her essay.* Also, **forgo.** [OE *foregān*] —**fore·go′er,** *n.*

fore·go² (fôr gō′) *v.* **-went, -gone, -go·ing.** precede; go before. [OE *foregān*] —**fore·go′er,** *n.*

fore·go·ing (fôr′gō′ing) *adj.* preceding; previous.

fore·gone (*adj.* fôr′gon *or* fôr gon′; *v.* fôr gon′) *adj.,* —*adj.* that has gone before; previous. —*v.* pp. of **forego.**

foregone conclusion a fact or result that was expected with certainty; inevitable result: *It was a foregone conclusion that there would be traffic jams while the road was being repaired.*

fore·ground (fôr′ground′) *n.* the part of a picture or scene nearest the observer; part toward the front.
in the foreground, conspicuous.

fore·hand (fôr′hand′) *adj., n.* —*adj.* made with the palm of the hand turned forward. —*n.* **1** *Tennis, etc.* a stroke made with the palm of the hand turned forward. **2** a position in front or above; advantage.

fore·hand·ed (fôr′han′did) *adj.* **1** providing for the future; prudent; thrifty. **2** done beforehand; early; timely.
—**fore′hand′ed·ness,** *n.*

fore·head (fôr′hed′ *or* fôr′id) *n.* **1** the part of the face above the eyes. **2** a front part. [OE *forhēafod*]

for·eign (fôr′ən) *adj.* **1** outside one's own country: *She has travelled much in foreign countries.* **2** of, characteristic of, or coming from outside one's own country: *a foreign ship, a foreign language, foreign money.* **3** having to do with other countries; carried on or dealing with other countries: *foreign trade.* **4** not belonging; not related: *Sitting still all day is foreign to a healthy boy's nature.* **5** not related to the matter that is being discussed or considered. **6** *Law.* falling outside the jurisdiction of a particular country. **7** not belonging naturally to the place where found: *a foreign object in the eye, a foreign substance in the blood.* [ME < OF *forain,* ult. < L *foras* outside] —**for′eign·ness,** *n.*

foreign affairs a country's relations with other countries.

for·eign–born (fôr′ən bôrn′) *adj.* born in another country.

for·eign·er (fôr′ən ər) *n.* **1** a person from another country; alien. **2** *Informal.* a person strange to one's own customs, ideas, etc. **3** a foreign ship.

foreign legion part of any army made up largely of soldiers who are volunteers from other countries: *the French Foreign Legion.*

Foreign Office *Brit.* the government department in charge of foreign affairs.

fore·judge (fôr juj′) *v.* **-judged, -judg·ing.** judge beforehand.

fore·knew (fôr nyü′ *or* -nü′) *v.* pt. of **foreknow.**

fore·know (fôr nō′) *v.* **-knew, -known, -know·ing.** know beforehand.

fore·knowl·edge (fôr′nol′ij) *n.* knowledge of a thing before it happens.

fore·known (fôr nōn′) *v.* pp. of **foreknow.**

fore·la·dy (fôr′lā′dē) *n., pl.* **-dies.** forewoman (def. 1).

fore·land (fôr′land′) *n.* a cape; headland; promontory.

fore·leg (fôr′leg′) *n.* one of the front legs of an animal.

fore·lock (fôr′lok′) *n.* a lock of hair that grows just above the forehead.

take time by the forelock, act promptly.

fore·man (fôr′mən) *n., pl.* **-men. 1** the man in charge of a group of workers or of some part of a factory. **2** the chairman of a jury.

fore·mast (fôr′mast *or* fôr′məst) *n.* on a ship, the mast nearest the bow.

fore·men·tioned (fôr men′shənd *or* fôr′men′shənd) *adj.* mentioned previously; aforementioned.

fore·most (fôr′mōst′) *adj., adv.* —*adj.* **1** first. **2** chief; leading; most notable. —*adv.* first: *He stumbled and fell head foremost.* [OE *formest*; double superlative of *forma* first, superlative of *fore* before]

fore·name (fôr′nām′) *n.* the first name.

fore·noon (fôr′nün′) *n., adj.* —*n.* the time between early morning and noon. —*adj.* between early morning and noon.

fo·ren·sic (fə ren′sik) *adj., n.* —*adj.* of or suitable for a law court or public debate. —*n.* a spoken or written exercise in argumentation, as in a college or high-school class in speech or rhetoric. [< L *forensic* < *forum* forum]

forensic medicine the application of medical science to problems of law; medical jurisprudence.

fore·or·dain (fôr′ôr dān′) *v.* ordain beforehand; predestine.

fore·or·di·na·tion (fôr′ôr də nā′shən) *n.* an ordaining beforehand; predestination.

fore·part (fôr′pärt′) *n.* the front part.

fore·paw (fôr′pô′ *or* -pô′) *n.* front paw.

fore·piece (fôr′pēs′) *n.* the front or first piece of something.

fore·quar·ter (fôr′kwôr′tər) *n.* a front leg, shoulder, and nearby ribs of beef, lamb, pork, etc.; front quarter.

fore·ran (fôr ran′) *v.* pt. of forerun.

fore·reach (fôr rēch′) *v.* **1** move ahead quickly, as a ship does after coming into the wind. **2** move ahead of; pass. **3** get the better of.

fore·run (fôr run′) *v.* **-ran, -run, -run·ning. 1** precede. **2** be a sign or warning of (something to come). **3** forestall.

fore·run·ner (fôr′run′ər) *n.* **1** a person going before or sent before to show that someone or something else is coming; herald. **2** a sign or warning of something to come: *Black clouds are often the forerunners of a storm.* **3** a predecessor; ancestor.

fore·sail (fôr′sāl′ *or* fôr′səl) *n.* **1** the principal sail on the foremast of a schooner. **2** the lowest sail on the foremast of a square-rigged ship.

fore·saw (fôr so′ *or* -sô′) *v.* pt. of foresee.

fore·see (fôr sē′) *v.* **-saw, -seen, -see·ing.** see or know beforehand: *Mother put up a big picnic lunch, because she foresaw how hungry we would be.* [OE *forsēon*] —**fore·see′a·ble,** *adj.* —**fore·see′a·bly,** *adv.*

fore·seen (fôr sēn′) *v.* pp. of foresee.

fore·shad·ow (fôr shad′ō) *v.* indicate beforehand; be a warning of: *Black clouds foreshadow a storm.*

fore·shank (fôr′shangk′) *n.* the upper part of the foreleg of an animal, or a cut of meat from this part.

fore·sheet (fôr′shēt′) *n.* **1** one of the ropes used to hold a foresail in place. **2 foresheets,** *pl.* the space in the forward part of an open boat.

fore·shore (fôr′shôr′) *n.* the part of the shore between the high-water mark and low-water mark.

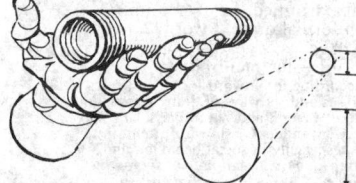

Foreshortening.
The hand and the cylinder are both foreshortened to suggest depth in the drawing.

fore·short·en (fôr shôr′tən) *v.* in a drawing or painting, represent (lines, etc.) as of less than true length in order to give the proper impression to the eye.

fore·show (fôr shō′) *v.* **-showed, -shown, -show·ing.** show beforehand; foretell; foreshadow. [OE *forescēawian*]

fore·shown (fôr shōn′) *v.* pp. of foreshow.

fore·sight (fôr′sīt′) *n.* **1** the power to see or realize beforehand

hat, āge, fär; let, ēqual, tèrm; it, īce
hot, ōpen, ôrder; oil, out; cup, put, rüle,
əbove, takən, pencəl, lemən, circəs
ch, child; ng, long; sh, ship
th, thin; ŦH, then; zh, measure

what is likely to happen. **2** careful thought for the future; prudence. **3** a looking ahead; a view into the future.
☞ *Syn.* 2. See note at **prudence.**

fore·sight·ed (fôr′sīt′id *or* fôr′sīt′id) *adj.* having or showing foresight. —**fore′sight·ed·ness,** *n.*

fore·skin (fôr′skin′) *n.* the fold of skin that covers the end of the penis.

for·est (fôr′ist) *n., v.* —*n.* **1** a large area of land covered with trees; thick woods, woodland. **2** the trees themselves. **3** (*adj.*) of or in a forest: *forest fires.* —*v.* plant with many trees; make into a forest. [ME < OF *forest,* ult. < L *foris* out of doors] —**for′est·less,** *adj.*

fore·stall (fôr stol′ *or* -stôl′) *v.* **1** prevent by acting first: *The mayor forestalled a riot by having the police ready.* **2** deal with (a thing) in advance; anticipate; be ahead of. **3** buy up (goods, etc.) in advance in order to increase the price. [ME *forstalle(n)* < OE *foresteall* prevention] —**fore·stall′er,** *n.*

for·est·a·tion (fôr′is tā′shən) *n.* the planting or taking care of forests.

fore·stay (fôr′stā′) *n.* the rope or cable reaching from the top of a ship's foremast to the bowsprit. The forestay helps to support the foremast.

for·est·er (fôr′is tər) *n.* **1** a person trained in forestry, especially one whose work it is. **2** forest ranger. **3** a person, bird, or animal that lives in a forest.

forest preserve a forest protected by the government from wasteful cutting, fires, etc.

forest ranger a government official in charge of patrolling and guarding a public forest or section of forest and its wildlife.

for·est·ry (fôr′is trē) *n.* the science and art of cultivating, caring for, managing, and utilizing forests.

fore·taste (*n.* fôr′tāst′; *v.* fôr tāst′) *n., v.* **-tast·ed, -tast·ing.** —*n.* a preliminary taste; anticipation: *The boy got a foretaste of business life by working during his vacation.* —*v.* taste beforehand; anticipate.

fore·tell (fôr tel′) *v.* **-told, -tell·ing.** tell or show beforehand; predict; prophesy: *Who can foretell what a baby will do next?* —**fore·tell′er,** *n.*

fore·thought (fôr′thot′ *or* -thôt′) *n.* **1** previous thought or consideration; planning. **2** careful thought for the future; prudence; foresight: *A little forethought will often prevent mistakes.*

fore·to·ken (*v.* fôr tō′kən; *n.* fôr′tō′kən) *v.* indicate beforehand; be an omen of. —*n.* an indication of something to come; omen. [OE *foretācn*]

fore·told (fôr tōld′) *v.* pt. and pp. of foretell.

fore·top (fôr′top′ *or* fôr′təp) *n.* a platform at the top of the foremast.

fore–top·gal·lant (fôr′top gal′ənt *or* -tə gal′ənt) *adj.* of or being the mast, sail, yard, etc. next above the fore-topmast.

fore–top·mast (fôr′top′mast′ *or* -top′məst) *n.* the mast next above the foremast.

fore–top·sail (fôr′top′sāl′ *or* -top′səl) *n.* the sail set on the fore-topmast and next above the foresail.

for·ev·er (fər ev′ər) *adv., n.* —*adv.* **1** for always; without ever coming to an end. **2** all the time; always: *That woman is forever talking.* —*n. Informal.* an excessively long time; an eternity: *He is taking forever to write that book.*

for·ev·er·more (fər ev′ər môr′) *adv.* forever.

fore·warn (fôr wôrn′) *v.* warn beforehand: *The dark clouds forewarned us of a thunderstorm.*

fore·went (fôr went′) *v.* pt. of forego.

fore·wing (fôr′wing′) *n.* the front wing of an insect.

fore·wom·an (fôr′wum′ən) *n., pl.* **-wom·en. 1** a woman who supervises a group of workers, as in a factory, etc. **2** a chairwoman of a jury.

fore·word (fôr′wèrd′) *n.* a short preface to a book or other writing, especially an introductory note on the work of the author by a distinguished writer, scholar, public figure, etc.
☞ *Syn.* See note at **introduction.**

for·feit (fôr′fit) *v., n., adj.* —*v.* lose or have to give up as a

penalty for some act, neglect, fault, etc.: *He forfeited his deposit when he lost the library book.*
—*n.* **1** something lost or given up because of some act, neglect, or fault; penalty; fine: *A headache was the forfeit he paid for staying up late.* **2** the loss or giving up of something as a penalty.
—*adj.* lost or given up as a penalty; forfeited. [ME < OF *forfait* < *forfaire* transgress < *for-* wrongly (< L *foris* outside) + *faire* do < L *facere*] —**for′feit·a·ble,** *adj.* —**for′feit·er,** *n.*

for·fei·ture (fôr′fi chər) *n.* **1** the loss or giving up of something as a penalty; a forfeiting. **2** the thing forfeited; penalty; fine.

for·fend (fôr fend′) *v. Archaic.* ward off; avert; prevent. Also **forefend.**

for·gat (fər gat′) *v. Archaic.* a pt. of **forget.**

for·gath·er (fôr gaᴛн′ər) *v.* **1** gather together; assemble; meet. **2** meet by accident. **3** be friendly; associate. Also, **foregather.**

for·gave (fər gāv′) *v.* pt. of **forgive.**

forge[1] (fôrj) *n., v.* **forged, forg·ing.** —*n.* **1** a furnace or open fireplace where metal is heated to a high temperature before being hammered into shape: *The blacksmith took the white-hot horseshoe out of the forge.* **2** a blacksmith's shop; smithy. **3** a place where iron or other metal is melted and refined.
—*v.* **1** heat (metal) to a high temperature and then hammer it into shape. **2** make; shape or form: *They forged a strong and lasting friendship.* **3** make or write a fraudulent or counterfeit imitation of: *to forge a signature. The supposed will of the dead man had been forged.* **4** make a fraudulent imitation of another person's signature on (a cheque, etc.): *He was sent to jail for forging cheques.* [ME < OF *forge,* ult. < L *fabrica* workshop. Doublet of FABRIC.] —**forg′er,** *n.*

forge[2] (fôrj) *v.* **forged, forg·ing.** move forward slowly but steadily: *to forge ahead.* [origin uncertain]

for·ger·y (fôr′jər ē) *n., pl.* **-ger·ies. 1** the act of forging a signature, etc. **2** something made or written falsely to deceive: *The painting was a forgery. The signature on the cheque was not mine but a forgery.*

for·get (fər get′) *v.* **-got, -got·ten** or **-got, -get·ting. 1** let go out of the mind; be unable to remember; be unable to remember: *I couldn't introduce her because I had forgotten her name.* **2** omit or neglect without meaning to: *She said she would not forget to send him a postcard.* **3** leave behind unintentionally: *She had to return home because she had forgotten her purse.*
forget (oneself), a not think of oneself and one's interests; be unselfish. **b** fail to consider what one should do or be; say or do something improper: *He forgot himself and blurted out the name.* [OE *forgietan* < *for-* (opposite) + ON *geta* get] —**for·get′ta·ble,** *adj.* —**for·get′ter,** *n.*

for·get·ful (fər get′fəl) *adj.* **1** apt to forget; having a poor memory. **2** heedless: *forgetful of danger.* **3** *Poetic.* causing to forget. —**for·get′ful·ly,** *adv.* —**for·get′ful·ness,** *n.*

for·get-me-not (fər get′mē not′) *n.* any of a genus (*Myosotis*) of low-growing herbs of the borage family having blue or white flowers. Some species are cultivated as garden flowers.

forg·ing (fôr′jing) *n.* something forged; a piece of metal that has been forged.

for·give (fər giv′) *v.* **-gave, -giv·en, -giv·ing. 1** give up the wish to punish or get even with; pardon; excuse; not have hard feelings about or toward. **2** give up all claim to; not demand payment for: *to forgive a debt.* [OE *forgiefan* < *for-* away + *giefan* give] —**for·giv′a·ble,** *adj.* —**for·giv′a·bly,** *adv.*
☛ *Syn.* **1.** See note at **excuse.**

for·giv·en (fər giv′ən) *v.* pp. of **forgive.**

for·give·ness (fər giv′nis) *n.* **1** the act of forgiving; pardon. **2** willingness to forgive.

for·giv·ing (fər giv′ing) *adj.* that forgives; willing to forgive. —**for·giv′ing·ly,** *adv.* —**for·giv′ing·ness,** *n.*

for·go (fôr gō′) *v.* **-went, -gone, -go·ing.** See **forego.**

for·gone (fôr gon′) *v.* pp. of **forgo.**

for·got (fər got′) *v.* a pt. and a pp. of **forget.**

for·got·ten (fər got′ən) *v.* a pp. of **forget.**

for·int (fôr′int) *n.* **1** the basic unit of money in Hungary, divided into 100 fillér. See table at **money. 2** a coin worth one forint. [< Hungarian *forint,* prob. < Ital. *fiorino* florin]

fork (fôrk) *n., v.* —*n.* **1** an instrument having a handle and two or more long, pointed prongs, or tines, at one end: *a table fork, a garden fork.* **2** anything shaped like a fork, such as a tuning fork or a divining rod. **3** the place where a tree, road, or stream divides into two branches: *They parted at the fork of the road.* **4** one of the branches into which anything is divided.

—*v.* **1** lift, throw, or dig with a fork. **2** make in the shape or form of a fork. **3** have a fork or forks; divide into branches.
fork up, out or **over,** *Slang.* hand over; pay out.
[OE *forca* < L *furca*] —**fork′less,** *adj.* —**fork′like′,** *adj.*

forked (fôrkt; *archaic or poetic,* fôr′kid) *adj.* **1** having a fork or forks; divided into branches. **2** zigzag: *forked lightning.*
speak with a forked tongue, speak untruths; tell lies.

fork·lift (fôrk′lift′) *n.* a self-propelled vehicle having a power-operated horizontal forklike device that can be raised and lowered for lifting and moving heavy objects.

for·lorn (fôr lôrn′) *adj.* **1** left alone; neglected; deserted: *The lost kitten, a forlorn little animal, was wet and dirty.* **2** wretched in feeling or looks; unhappy. **3** hopeless; desperate. **4** bereft (*of*): *forlorn of hope.* [OE *forloren* lost, pp. of *forlēosan*] —**for·lorn′ly,** *adv.* —**for·lorn′ness,** *n.*

forlorn hope 1 a desperate enterprise. **2** an undertaking almost sure to fail. **3** a party of soldiers engaged in a very dangerous job. [alteration of Du. *verloren hoop* lost troop]

form (fôrm) *n., v.* —*n.* **1** appearance apart from color or materials; shape. **2** a shape of body; body of a person or animal. **3** something that gives shape to something else: *A mould is a form.* **4** an orderly arrangement of parts: *The effect of a work of literature, art, or music comes from its form as well as its content.* **5** a way of doing something; manner; method: *He is a fast runner, but his form in running is bad.* **6** a set way of doing something; behavior according to custom or rule; formality; ceremony: *Shaking hands is a form. Many forms have little or no real meaning.* **7** a set order of words; formula: *A written agreement to buy, sell, or do something follows a certain form.* **8** a document with printing or writing on it and blank spaces to be filled in: *To get a licence, you must fill out a form.* **9** the way in which a thing exists, takes shape, or shows itself; condition; character; manifestation: *Water appears also in the forms of ice, snow, and steam.* **10** kind; sort; variety: *Heat, light, and electricity are forms of energy.* **11** a good condition of body or mind: *Athletes exercise to keep in form.* **12** *Grammar.* any of the ways in which a word is spelled or pronounced to express different ideas and relationships. *Boys* is the plural form of *boy. Saw* is the past form of *see. My* and *mine* are the possessive forms of *I.* **13** a grade in school, especially in high school. **14** a long seat; bench. **15** *Printing.* type fastened in a frame ready for printing or making plates. **16** *Philosophy.* the element or quality in a thing that makes it what it is.
bad form, behavior contrary to accepted customs.
good form, behavior in accord with accepted customs.
—*v.* **1** give shape to; make: *The cook formed the dough into loaves.* **2** be formed; take shape: *Clouds form in the sky.* **3** become: *Water forms ice when it freezes.* **4** make up; compose: *Parents and children form a family.* **5** organize; establish: *We formed a club.* **6** develop: *Form good habits while you are young.* **7** arrange in some order: *The soldiers formed themselves into lines.* [ME < OF < L *forma,* mould] —**form′a·ble,** *adj.*
☛ *Syn. n.* **1. Form, shape, figure** = the appearance of something apart from the color or the material of which it is made. **Form** particularly suggests that there is substance or structure under the surface, giving rise to the special appearance seen: *There have been many improvements in the form of airplanes.* **Shape,** more informal, emphasizes definiteness of form and solidness of body or substance, and means the whole outline or mould of the person or thing: *His head has a strange shape.* **Figure** applies only to the outline of a form: *He drew figures of animals.*

-form *suffix.* **1** having the form of —, as in *cruciform.* **2** having — form or forms, as in *multiform.* [< L *-formis* < *forma* form]

for·mal (fôr′məl) *adj., n.* —*adj.* **1** with strict attention to outward forms and ceremonies; not familiar and homelike; stiff: *The judge always had a formal manner in court.* **2** according to set customs or rules. **3** done with the proper forms; clear and definite: *A written contract is a formal agreement to do something.* **4** very regular; symmetrical; orderly. **5** having to do with the form, not the content. **6** of language, conforming to a studied style in vocabulary, syntax, and pronunciation, as accepted for dignified use.
—*n.* **1** a social gathering at which formal dress is worn. **2** a gown worn to formal social gatherings: *She was dressed in her first formal.* [< L *formalis* < *forma* form] —**for′mal·ly,** *adv.*
☛ *Syn.* **1, 2. Formal, conventional** = according to outward forms and rules. **Formal** = showing strict attention to rules and set ways of doing things, and implies correctness, stiffness, and lack of warmth and naturalness: *The judge always had a formal manner in court.* **Conventional** = showing attention to generally accepted forms and customs, especially in social behavior, and emphasizes lack of originality: *She wrote a conventional note of sympathy.*
☛ *Usage.* Do not confuse **formally** with **formerly.**
☛ *Usage.* See note at **informal.**

form·al·de·hyde (fôr mal′də hīd′) *n.* a colorless gas with a sharp, irritating odor, used in solution as a disinfectant and preservative. *Formula:* CH_2O [< *form(ic acid)* + *aldehyde*]

for·ma·lin (fôr′mə lin) *n.* a solution for formaldehyde in water.

for·mal·ism (fôr′məl iz′əm) *n.* strict attention to outward forms and ceremonies.

for·mal·ist (fôr′məl ist) *n.* a person inclined to formalism.

for·mal·is·tic (fôr′məl is′tik) *adj.* of formalism or formalists.

for·mal·i·ty (fôr mal′ə tē) *n., pl.* **-ties.** **1** a procedure required by custom or rule; outward form; ceremony. **2** attention to forms and customs: *Visitors at the court of a king are received with formality.* **3** stiffness of manner, behavior, or arrangement.

for·mal·ize (fôr′məl īz′) *v.* **-ized, -iz·ing.** **1** make formal. **2** give a definite form to. —**for′mal·i·za′tion,** *n.* —**for′mal·iz·er,** *n.*

formal logic the branch of logic that deals with the structure or form of propositions (apart from their content) and the process of deductive reasoning by which conclusions are drawn.

for·mat (fôr′mat) *n.* **1** the shape, size, and general arrangement of a book, magazine, etc. **2** the design, plan, or arrangement of anything: *the format of a legislative program, television show, etc.* [< F < L (*liber*) *formatus* (book) formed (in a special way)]

for·ma·tion (fôr mā′shən) *n.* **1** forming or being formed: *Heat causes the formation of steam from water. The formation of words is a fascinating study.* **2** the way in which a thing is arranged; arrangement; order: *troops in battle formation. There was an interesting formation of ice crystals on the window.* **3** the thing formed: *Clouds are formations of tiny drops of water in the sky.* **4** *Geology.* a series of layers or deposits of the same kind of rock or mineral.

form·a·tive (fôr′mə tiv) *adj.* **1** having to do with formation or development; forming; moulding: *Home and school are the chief formative influences in a child's life.* **2** *Grammar.* used to form words. Words may be made from other words by adding formative endings, such as *-ly* and *-ness.* **3** *Biology.* that can produce new cells or tissues: *formative tissue, formative yolk.* —**for′ma·tive·ly,** *adv.* —**for′ma·tive·ness,** *n.*

for·mer¹ (fôr′mər) *adj.* **1** first of two. In Jack and Jim, Jack is the former. **2** earlier; past; long past: *In former times people lived in caves.* **3** (*noml.*) **the former,** the first of two: *When Sue is offered ice cream or pie, she always chooses the former.* [ME *formere,* comparative back-formation from *formest.* See FOREMOST.]

for·mer² (fôr′mər) *n.* a person or thing that forms. [< *form*]

for·mer·ly (fôr′mər lē) *adv.* in the past; some time ago: *Mrs. Smith was formerly known as Miss Snell.*
☛ *Usage.* Do not confuse **formerly** with **formally.**

For·mi·ca (fôr mī′ka) *n. Trademark.* a laminated plastic material with a hard, smooth, shiny, heat-resistant surface, used mainly for counter and table tops.

for·mic acid (fôr′mik) a colorless liquid that is irritating to the skin. It occurs in ants, spiders, nettles, etc. and is used in dyeing, finishing textiles, etc. *Formula:* CH_2O_2 [< L *formica* ant]

for·mi·da·ble (fôr′mə də bəl) *adj.* hard to overcome; hard to deal with; to be dreaded. [< L *formidabilis* < *formidare* dread] —**for′mi·da·ble·ness,** *n.* —**for′mi·da·bly,** *adv.*

form·less (fôrm′lis) *adj.* without definite or regular form; shapeless. —**form′less·ly,** *adv.* —**form′less·ness,** *n.*

form letter a letter so phrased that it may be sent to many different people; a letter copied from a pattern.

form sheet **1** a detailed information sheet having the names of the horses and jockeys in the day's races, records of past performances, weights carried, etc. **2** a list giving the records of participants in any match, contest, etc.

for·mu·la (fôr′myə lə) *n., pl.* **-las** or **-lae** (-lē′ *or* -lī′). **1** a set form of words, especially one that by much use has partly lost its meaning: *"How do you do?" is a formula of greeting.* **2** a statement of religious belief or doctrine: *The Apostles' Creed is a formula of the Christian faith.* **3** a rule for doing something, especially as used by those who do not know the reason on which it is based. **4** a recipe; prescription: *a formula for making soup.* **5** a mixture, especially one for feeding a baby, made according to a recipe or prescription. **6** *Chemistry.* an expression showing by symbols and figures the composition of a compound: *The formula for water is* H_2O. **7** an expression showing by algebraic symbols a rule, principle, etc. $(a + b)^2 = a^2 + 2ab + b^2$ is an algebraic formula. [< L *formula,* dim. of *forma* form]

for·mu·lae (fôr′myə lē *or* fôr′myə lī′) *n.* a pl. of **formula.**

for·mu·lar·y (fôr′myə ler′ē) *n., pl.* **-lar·ies;** *adj.* —*n.* **1** a collection of formulas. **2** a set form of words; formula. **3** *Pharmacy.* a book of formulas for standard preparations used in medicines. —*adj.* having to do with formulas.

for·mu·late (fôr′myə lāt′) *v.* **-lat·ed, -lat·ing.** **1** state definitely; express in systematic form: *Our ideas of fair treatment for all Canadians are formulated in a Bill of Rights.* **2** express in a formula; reduce to a formula. —**for′mu·la·tor,** *n.*

for·mu·la·tion (fôr′myə lā′shən) *n.* **1** a definite statement; an expression in systematic form. **2** expression in a formula.

for·mu·lism (fôr′myə liz′əm) *n.* **1** reliance on, or adherence to, formulas. **2** a group or set of formulas.

hat, āge, fär; let, ēqual, tèrm; it, īce
hot, ōpen, ôrder; oil, out; cup, put, rüle,
əbove, takən, pencəl, lemən, circəs
ch, child; ng, long; sh, ship
th, thin; ŦH, then; zh, measure

for·ni·cate (fôr′nə kāt′) *v.* **-cat·ed, -cat·ing.** commit fornication. [< Ecclesiastical L *fornicari* < *fornix* brothel] —**for′ni·ca·tor,** *n.*

for·ni·ca·tion (fôr′nə kā′shən) *n.* voluntary sexual intercourse other than between a married couple, especially where either person or both persons are unmarried.

for·sake (fôr sāk′) *v.* **-sook, -sak·en, -sak·ing.** give up; leave alone; abandon. [OE *forsacan* < *for-* away + *sacan* dispute, deny]
☛ *Syn.* See note at **desert²**.

for·sak·en (fôr sāk′ən) *v., adj.* —*v.* pp. of **forsake.** —*adj.* deserted; abandoned: *a forsaken house.* —**for·sak′en·ly,** *adv.*

for·sook (fôr suk′) *v.* pt. of **forsake.**

for·sooth (fôr süth′) *adv. Archaic.* in truth; indeed. [OE *forsōth* < *for* for + *sōth* sooth, truth]

for·swear (fôr swer′) *v.* **-swore, -sworn, -swear·ing.** **1** renounce on oath; swear or promise solemnly to give up. **2** deny solemnly or on oath. **3** be untrue to one's sworn word or promise; perjure (oneself). [OE *forswerian*]

for·swore (fôr swôr′) *v.* pt. of **forswear.**

for·sworn (fôr swôrn′) *adj., v.* —*adj.* untrue to one's sworn word or promise; perjured. —*v.* pp. of **forswear.**

for·syth·i·a (fôr sith′ē ə *or* fôr sī′thē ə) *n.* any of a genus (*Forsythia*) of European and Asian shrubs of the olive family having yellow flowers that appear early in spring, before the leaves. Forsythias are widely cultivated. [< NL; after William *Forsyth* (1737-1804), a British horticulturist]

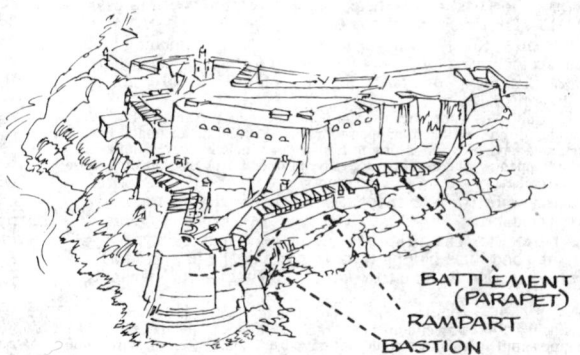

El Morro, a Spanish fort commanding the harbor of San Juan, Puerto Rico. The fort was built in 1584.

fort (fôrt) *n.* **1** a strong building or place that can be defended against an enemy. **2** *Historical.* a trading post. In the early days of the fur trade, these posts were usually fortified: *Winnipeg is built on the site of Fort Garry, an old Hudson's Bay Company post.*
hold the fort, make a defence.
[< F < L *fortis* strong]

forte¹ (fôrt) *n.* something a person does very well; strong point: *Cooking is her forte.* [< F *forte,* fem. of *fort* strong < L *fortis*]

for·te² (fôr′tā) *adj., adv., n. Music.* —*adj.* or *adv.* loud. —*n.* a loud passage or tone. [< Ital. *forte* strong < L *fortis*]

forth (fôrth) *adv.* **1** forward; onward. **2** into view or consideration; out. **3** away.
and so forth, and so on; and the like: *We ate cake, candy, nuts, and so forth.*
[OE]

forth·com·ing (fôrth′kum′ing *or* fôrth kum′ing) *adj., n.* —*adj.* **1** about to appear; approaching: *The forthcoming week will be busy.* **2** ready when wanted: *She needed help, but none was forthcoming.* **3** ready to meet or make advances; accommodating. —*n.* an appearance; approach.

forth·right (*adj.* fôrth′rīt′; *adv. also* fôrth′rīt′) *adj., adv.* —*adj.* frank and outspoken; straightforward; direct. —*adv.* **1** straight ahead; directly forward. **2** at once; immediately. —**forth′right′ly,** *adv.* —**forth′right′ness,** *n.*

fort hunter *Historical.* a hunter, usually an Indian, employed by a fur company to provide meat for a trading post, or fort.

forth·with (fôrth′with′ *or* -wiᴛʜ′) *adv.* at once; immediately: *She said she would be there forthwith.*

for·ti·eth (fôr′tē ith) *adj. or n.* **1** next after the 39th; last in a series of forty; 40th. **2** one, or being one, of 40 equal parts.

for·ti·fi·ca·tion (fôr′tə fə kā′shən) *n.* **1** a fortifying: *Soldiers were busy with the fortification of the village.* **2** anything used in fortifying; a fort, wall, ditch, etc. **3** a fortified place. **4** the enriching of foods with vitamins and minerals.

for·ti·fy (fôr′tə fī′) *v.* **-fied, -fy·ing. 1** build forts, walls, etc.; strengthen against attack; provide with forts, walls, etc. **2** give support to; strengthen. **3** add something that strengthens or enriches: *Alcohol is used to fortify port wine. Refined foods are often fortified with vitamins and minerals.* [ME < OF *fortifier* < LL *fortificare,* ult. < L *fortis* strong + *facere* make] —**for′ti·fi·er,** *n.*

for·tis·si·mo (fôr tis′ə mō′) *adj., adv., n. Music.* —*adj. or adv.* very loud.
—*n.* a very loud passage or tone. *Abbrev.:* ff [< Ital. *fortissimo,* superlative of *forte* strong]

for·ti·tude (fôr′tə tyüd′ *or* fôr′tə tüd′) *n.* courage in facing pain, danger, or trouble; firmness of spirit. [< L *fortitudo* < *fortis* strong] ☛ *Syn.* See note at **patience.**

for·ti·tu·di·nous (fôr′tə tyü′də nəs *or* fôr′tə tü′də nəs) *adj.* having or characterized by fortitude: *a fortitudinous display of character.*

fort·night (fôrt′nīt) *n.* two weeks. [ME *fourtenight,* contraction of OE *fēowertēne niht* fourteen nights]

fort·night·ly (fôrt′nīt lē) *adv., adj., n.* —*adv.* once every two weeks.
—*adj.* appearing or happening once in every two weeks.
—*n.* a periodical published every two weeks.

FOR·TRAN (fôr′tran) *n.* a high-level computer programming language used especially in scientific and mathematical fields. [< *for*mula *tran*slation. 20c.]

for·tress (fôr′tris) *n.* a fortified place; large and well-protected fort. [ME < OF *forteresse* < *fort* strong < L *fortis*]

for·tu·i·tous (fôr tyü′ə təs *or* fôr tü′ə təs) *adj.* happening by chance; accidental: *a fortuitous meeting, a fortuitous acquaintance.* [< L *fortuitus,* ult. < *fors, fortis* chance] —**for·tu′i·tous·ly,** *adv.* —**for·tu′i·tous·ness,** *n.*
☛ *Syn.* **Fortuitous** is sometimes used to refer to events that, besides being accidental and unintentional, happen to be providential or fortunate. **Fortuitous** and **fortunate** have a common origin: L *fors, fortis* luck. However, not every **fortunate** happening may be correctly referred to as **fortuitous,** but only those that are accidentally so.

for·tu·i·ty (fôr tyü′ə tē *or* fôr tü′ə tē) *n., pl.* **-ties.** chance; accident.

for·tu·nate (fôr′chə nit) *adj.* **1** having good luck; lucky. **2** bringing good luck; having favorable results. [< L *fortunatus,* pp. of *fortunare* assign fortune to < *fortuna* fortune] —**for′tu·nate·ly,** *adv.*
☛ *Syn.* **1, 2. Fortunate, lucky** = having or bringing good luck. **Fortunate** suggests being favored by circumstances strongly to one's advantage or helpful in bringing about success that could not have been counted on or in bringing something wholly unexpected: *He made a fortunate decision when he went into advertising.* **Lucky** is less formal and emphasizes the idea of accident or pure chance: *It was lucky that he missed his train the day it was wrecked.*

for·tune (fôr′chən) *n.* **1** a great deal of money or property; riches; wealth. **2** what is going to happen to a person; fate: *Gypsies often claim that they can tell people's fortunes.* **3** good luck; prosperity; success. **4** what happens; luck; chance: *Fortune was against us; we lost.* [ME < OF < L *fortuna*]

fortune hunter 1 a person who tries to get a fortune by marrying someone rich. **2** anybody who seeks wealth.

for·tune·tell·er (fôr′chən tel′ər) *n.* a person who claims to be able to tell what is going to happen to other people.

for·ty (fôr′tē) *n., pl.* **-ties;** *adj.* —*n.* **1** four times ten; 40. **2 forties** *pl.* the years from forty through forty-nine, especially of a century or of a person's life: *She achieved success as a playwright in her forties.* —*adj.* four times ten; 40. [OE *fēowertig*]

For·ty-Nin·er (fôr′tē nīn′ər) *n.* a person who went to California to seek gold in 1849. It had been discovered there in 1848.

forty winks *Informal.* a short nap.

fo·rum (fô′rəm) *n.* **1** the public square or market place in ancient Rome. The forum in Rome was used for public assemblies and business. **2** an assembly for discussing questions of public interest. **3** a law court; tribunal. [< L]

for·ward (fôr′wərd) *adv., adj., v., n.* —*adv.* **1** ahead; onward: *The men marched forward.* **2** toward the front. **3** out; into view or consideration: *In his talk he brought forward several new ideas.* —*adj.* **1** toward the front: *the forward part of a ship.* **2** far ahead; advanced: *A child of four years that can read is forward for his age.* **3** ready; eager: *He knew his lesson and was forward with his answers.* **4** pert; bold.

—*v.* **1** send on further: *Please forward my mail to my new address.* **2** help along: *He did all he could to forward his friend's plan.*
—*n. Sports.* a player whose position is in the front line. [OE *forweard*] —**for′ward·er,** *n.* —**for′ward·ly,** *adv.*
☛ *Syn. adj.* **4.** See note at **bold.**

for·ward·ness (fôr′wərd nis) *n.* **1** readiness; eagerness. **2** pertness; boldness.

forward pass the throwing of a football to a player on the same team in the direction of the opponent's goal.

for·wards (fôr′wərdz) *adv.* forward.

for·went (fôr went′) *v.* pt. of **forgo.**

fos·sa (fos′ə) *n.* **fos·sae** (fos′ē *or* fos′ī). *Anatomy.* a shallow depression or cavity in a bone, etc. [< L *fossa* ditch]

fosse (fos) *n.* a ditch; trench; canal; moat. [ME < OF < L *fossa* ditch]

fos·sil (fos′əl) *n.* **1** the remains of prehistoric animals or plants preserved in rocks where they have become petrified: *Bone fossils of dinosaurs have been discovered in Alberta.* **2** traces of animal life preserved in ancient rocks: *fossils of footprints.* **3** (*adj.*) forming or having the characteristics of a fossil: *fossil remains.* **4** (*adj.*) derived from the remains of living things: *fossil resins. Coal, oil, and natural gas are fossil fuels. Fossils of ferns are often found in coal.* **5** a very old-fashioned person, set in his ways. **6** (*adj.*) belonging to the outworn past: *fossil ideas.* [< F < L *fossilis* dug up < *fodere* dig] —**fos′sil-like′,** *adj.*

fos·sil·if·er·ous (fos′ə lif′ər əs) *adj.* containing fossils.

fos·sil·ize (fos′ə līz′) *v.* **-ized, -iz·ing. 1** make into a fossil; change into a fossil; turn into stone. **2** make or become antiquated, set, stiff, or rigid. —**fos′sil·i·za′tion,** *n.*

fos·ter (fos′tər) *v., adj.* —*v.* **1** help the growth or development of; encourage: *Ignorance fosters superstition.* **2** care for fondly; cherish. **3** bring up; rear.
—*adj.* **1** of or involved in a relationship like that between parent and child or between siblings, although not closely related by birth or bound by legal adoption: *a foster child, a foster mother.* **2** designating a home where one or more children of other parents are given parental care, often temporary: *The baby was in a foster home for a year before being adopted.* [OE *fōstrian* nourish, *fōster* nourishment. Related to FOOD.]
☛ *Syn. v.* **2.** See note at **cherish.**

fou·droy·ant (fü droi′ənt) *adj.* **1** striking like lightning; suddenly overwhelming. **2** *Medicine.* starting suddenly and severely: *a foudroyant TB case.* [< F *foudroyant* < *foudroyer* strike like lightning < OF *foudre* lightning < LL *fulgere* < L *fulgur* lightning]

fouet·té (fwe tā′) *n., v.* **-téd, -té·ing.** *Ballet.* —*n.* a quick turn in which one leg acts as a pivot as the other leg is thrown sideways and then bent in with the toes pointing toward the other knee. —*v.* perform a fouetté. [< F *fouetté,* literally, a whipped step, pp. of *fouetter* whip, beat]

fought (fot *or* fôt) *v.* pt. and pp. of **fight.**

foul (foul) *adj., v., n., adv.* —*adj.* **1** very dirty; impure; nasty; smelly; containing or covered with filth: *Open the windows and let out the foul air.* **2** very wicked; vile: *Murder is a foul crime.* **3** obscene; indecent: *foul language.* **4** against the rules; unfair. **5** hitting against: *One boat was foul of the other.* **6** tangled up; caught: *The sailor cut the foul rope.* **7** clogged up: *The fire will not burn because the chimney is foul.* **8** of a ship, having the bottom covered with seaweed, barnacles, etc. **9** unfavorable; stormy: *Foul weather delayed the ship.* **10** contrary: *a foul wind.* **11** *Informal.* very unpleasant or objectionable. **12** *Baseball.* of or having to do with foul balls or foul lines.
—*v.* **1** make dirty or impure; pollute; soil; defile: *Exhaust fumes fouled the air.* **2** become dirty or impure: *Spark plugs foul if not cared for properly.* **3** dishonor; disgrace: *a name fouled by misdeeds.* **4** make a foul, make a foul against. **5** *Baseball.* hit a ball so that it falls outside the foul lines. **6** hit against: *One boat fouled the other.* **7** get tangled up with; catch: *The rope fouled the anchor chain.* **8** clog up: *Grease fouled the drain.* **9** cover (a ship's bottom) with seaweed, barnacles, etc.
foul out, a *Baseball.* be put out by hitting a ball that is caught outside the foul lines. **b** *Basketball.* be put out of a game for having committed too many fouls.
foul up, *Informal.* make a mess of; bungle.
—*n.* **1** something done contrary to the rules; unfair play. **2** *Baseball.* a foul ball.
—*adv.*
go, fall, or **run foul of, a** hit against and get tangled up with. **b** get into trouble or difficulties with.
[OE *fūl*] —**foul′ly,** *adv.* —**foul′ness,** *n.*
☛ *Hom.* **fowl.**
☛ *Syn. adj.* **1.** See note at **dirty.**

fou·lard (fü lärd′) *n.* **1** a soft, thin fabric made of silk, rayon, or cotton, usually with a printed pattern. It is used for neckties, dresses, etc. **2** a necktie or handkerchief made from this material.

[< F < Swiss F *foulat* cloth that has been cleansed and thickened]

foul ball *Baseball.* a ball hit so that it falls outside the foul lines.

foul line 1 *Baseball.* either the line from home to first base, or from home to third base, with their marked or unmarked continuations. **2** *Basketball.* a line within the circle in front of each basket from which foul shots are made. **3** a line or mark which may not be stepped on or over in making a broad jump, throwing the javelin, etc.

foul-mouthed (foul′mouᵀʜd′ *or* -moutht′) *adj.* habitually using vile, offensive language.

foul play 1 unfair play; a thing or things done against the rules. **2** treachery; violence.

foul shot *Basketball.* **1** a free shot awarded to one team for a foul by the opponent's team. **2** a score of one point for putting such a shot into the basket.

foul tip *Baseball.* a ball deflected by the bat back to the catcher.

foul-up (foul′up′) *n. Slang.* a disorder or muddle that interferes with a project or operation: *There was a last minute foul-up in the sports program.*

found¹ (found) *v.* pt. and pp. of **find.**

found² (found) *v.* **1** establish; set up: *Champlain founded Quebec in 1608.* **2** rest for support; base: *He founded his claim on facts.* [ME < OF *fonder* < L *fundare* < *fundus* bottom]

found³ (found) *v.* melt and mould (metal); make of molten metal; cast. [< F *fondre* < L *fundere* pour]

foun·da·tion (foun dā′shən) *n.* **1** the part on which the other parts rest for support; base: *the foundation of a house.* **2** the basis of a belief, idea, argument, etc.: *The report has no foundation in fact.* **3** founding or being founded. **4** an institution founded and endowed: *a charitable foundation.* **5** a fund given to support an institution. **6** a part over which something is laid: *Her full skirt swirled over a foundation of starched cotton petticoats.* **7** a foundation garment. **8** a cream or liquid cosmetic applied on the face as a base for rouge, powder, etc. **9** (*adj.*) of, having to do with, for, or serving as a foundation: *a foundation plan, foundation planting.* —**foun·da·tion·al,** *adj.* —**foun·da·tion·al·ly,** *adv.*
☛ *Syn.* **1.** See note at **base¹.**

foundation garment a woman's corset, girdle, etc., usually having a brassiere attached.

foun·der¹ (foun′dər) *v.* **1** fill with water and sink: *The ship foundered in the storm.* **2** break down; go lame; stumble: *His horse foundered.* **3** become worn out; fail. **4** cause to fill with water and sink. **5** cause (a horse) to break down, fall lame, etc. **6** *Golf.* hit (the ball) into the ground. [ME < OF *fondrer,* ult. < L *fundus* bottom]

found·er² (foun′dər) *n.* a person who founds or establishes something. [< *found²*]

found·er³ (foun′dər) *n.* a person who casts metals. [< *found³*]

found-in (found′in′) *n. Cdn.* a person arrested for being present in a brothel, in an illegal drinking or gambling establishment, etc.

found·ling (found′ling) *n.* a baby or child found abandoned. [ME *fundeling.* Related to FIND.]

found·ry (foun′drē) *n., pl.* -ries. **1** a place where metal is melted and moulded; place where things are made of molten metal. **2** the melting and moulding of metal; process of making things of molten metal. **3** things made of molten metal; castings. [< F *fonderie* < *fondre* found³]

fount (fount) *n.* **1** fountain. **2** source: *He is a fount of knowledge.* [< L *fons, fontis* spring]

foun·tain (foun′tən) *n.* **1** a stream or spray of water rising into the air. **2** a decorative structure through which water is forced into the air in a stream or spray. **3** a spring of water. **4** a device by which a jet of water is forced upward so that people may get a drink: *a drinking fountain.* **5** soda fountain. **6** a source; origin: *Solomon was a fountain of wisdom.* **7** a container to hold a steady supply of ink, oil, etc. [ME < OF *fontaine* < LL *fontana,* originally fem. of *fontanus* of a spring < L *fons, fontis* spring]

foun·tain·head (foun′tən hed′) *n.* **1** the source of a stream. **2** an original source.

Fountain of Youth a legendary spring whose waters were supposed to cure any sickness and restore youth.

fountain pen a pen for writing that automatically supplies liquid ink to the nib from a rubber or plastic tube inside.

four (fôr) *n., adj.* —*n.* **1** one more than three; 4: *There are four left in the box.* **2** the numeral 4: *She crossed the 3 out and put a 4 in its place.* **3** the fourth in a set or series; especially a playing card or side of a die having four spots: *He threw a four.* **4** *Rowing.* **a** a crew of four rowers. **b** the boat they use. **5** *Cricket.* a hit for which four runs are scored. **6** any set or series of four persons or things: *They set up a four to play cards.*
on all fours, a on all four feet. **b** on hands and knees.
—*adj.* **1** being one more than three. **2** being fourth in a set or series

hat, āge, fär; let, ēqual, tėrm; it, īce
hot, ōpen, ôrder; oil, out; cup, pút, rüle,
əbove, takən, pencəl, lemən, circəs
ch, child; ng, long; sh, ship
th, thin; ᴛʜ, then; zh, measure

(*used mainly after the noun*): *I don't understand Section Four of the manual.* [OE *fēower*]
☛ *Hom.* **for, fore.**

four flush 1 *Poker.* a four-card suit (instead of the five needed for a flush). **2** *Slang.* false pretence; bluff.

four-flush·er (fôr′flush′ər) *n. Slang.* a person who pretends to be more or other than he really is; bluffer.

four·fold (fôr′fōld′) *adj., adv.* —*adj.* **1** four times as much or as many. **2** having four parts. —*adv.* four times as much or as many.

four-foot·ed (fôr′fút′id) *adj.* having four feet.

four-four (fôr′fôr′) *adj. Music.* indicating or having four quarter notes in a bar or measure, the first and third of which are accented.

four freedoms freedom of speech, freedom of worship, freedom from want, and freedom from fear, set forth in 1941 by President Franklin D. Roosevelt of the United States.

four-hand·ed (fôr′han′did) *adj.* **1** having four hands. **2** for four players.

Four-H clubs or **4-H clubs** a national system of clubs to teach rural children agriculture and home economics. Their purpose is the improvement of head, heart, hands, and health.

Four Horsemen of the Apocalypse in the Bible, the riders of four different colored horses, seen in a prophetic vision, the red horse representing War, the black horse, Famine, the pale horse, Death and Pestilence, the white horse, Christ or Victory (Rev. 6:1-8).

four-in-hand (fôr′in hand′) *n.* **1** a necktie tied in a slip knot with the ends left hanging. **2** a carriage pulled by four horses driven by one person. **3** a team of four horses.

four-letter word (fôr′let′ər) any of a group of one-syllable words referring to sexual organs or acts or to excretory functions, often used as expletives and generally thought of as obscene or vulgar.

four-o'clock (fôr′ə klok′) *n.* a small plant having red, white, or yellow trumpet-shaped flowers that open late in the afternoon and close in the morning.

four of a kind *Poker.* a hand having four cards of the same value.

four·score (fôr′skôr′) *adj. or n.* four times twenty; 80.

four·some (fôr′səm) *n.* **1** a group of four people. **2** a game played by four people, two on each side. **3** the players.

four·square (*adj.* fôr′skwer′; *n.* fôr′skwer′) *adj., n.* —*adj.* **1** square. **2** frank; outspoken. **3** not yielding; firm. —*n.* a square.

four·teen (fôr′tēn′) *n., adj.* —*n.* **1** four more than ten; 14. **2** the numeral 14: *That should be a 14, not a 15.* **3** the fourteenth in a set or series. **4** a set or series of fourteen persons or things. —*adj.* **1** being four more than ten; 14. **2** being fourteenth in a set or series (*used after the noun*): *Lesson Fourteen.* [OE *fēowertēne*]

four·teenth (fôr′tēnth′) *adj. or n.* **1** next after the 13th; last in a series of fourteen; 14th. **2** one, or being one, of 14 equal parts.

fourth (fôrth) *adj., n.* —*adj.* **1** next after the third; last in a series of four; 4th. **2** being one of 4 equal parts. —*n.* **1** the next after the third; last in a series of four; 4th. **2** one of 4 equal parts. **3** in automobiles and similar machines, the forward gear next above third; high gear in a four-gear system. **4** *Music.* **a** the fourth tone from the keynote of a scale. **b** the interval between such tones. **c** a combination of such tones.

fourth dimension a dimension in addition to length, breadth, and depth: *Time has been thought of as a fourth dimension.*

fourth estate the press; newspapers and those who work for them. See **estate** (def.4).

fourth·ly (fôrth′lē) *adv.* in the fourth place.

Fourth of July in the United States, a holiday in memory of the adoption of the Declaration of Independence on July 4, 1776.

four-wheeled (fôr′wēld′ *or* -hwēld′) *adj.* having four wheels; running on four wheels.

fowl (foul) *n., pl.* **fowls** or (*esp. collectively*) **fowl;** *v.* —*n.* **1** a chicken or domestic turkey. **2** any of various other birds of the same order (Galliformes), especially those hunted as game. **3** the

flesh of a fowl used for food. **4** *Archaic.* (*except in compounds*). any bird: *waterfowl.*
—*v.* hunt, shoot, catch, or trap wildfowl. [OE *fugol*]
☛ *Hom.* foul.

fowl·er (foul′ər) *n.* a person who hunts, shoots, catches, or traps wild birds.

fowling piece a light gun for shooting wild birds.

fox (foks) *n., v.* —*n.* **1** any of various carnivorous mammals (genera *Vulpes, Alopex,* etc.) of the dog family that do not hunt in packs and that have large, pointed ears, and a slender, pointed muzzle, and a bushy tail. Foxes are famous for their cunning, especially in escaping hunters. **2** the fur of a fox. **3** a sly, cunning person.
—*v.* **1** *Informal.* trick in a sly and crafty way. **2** of beer, turn sour. **3** make (beer) sour. **4** discolor; stain (the pages of a book). **5** become discolored or stained. **6** make or repair (a boot, shoe, etc.) by covering with or adding upper leather. **7** hunt the fox. [OE]
—**fox′like′,** *adj.*

Fox (foks) *n., pl.* **Fox·es** or **Fox. 1** a member of an Amerindian people formerly living in the Fox River valley in Wisconsin. **2** the Algonquian language of the Fox and Sauk peoples.

fox·ber·ry (foks′ber′ē) *n. Cdn.* mountain cranberry.

fox·glove (foks′gluv′) *n.* any of a genus (*Digitalis*) of biennial and perennial herbs of the figwort family native to Europe and Asia, especially *D. purpurea,* cultivated for its showy spikes of tubular purple or white flowers or for its leaves, which are a source of the drug digitalis. [OE *foxes glōfa*]

fox·hole (foks′hōl′) *n.* a hole in the ground for protection against enemy fire.

fox·hound (foks′hound′) *n.* either of two breeds of large, short-haired hound (the American foxhound and the English foxhound) trained especially for hunting foxes.

fox hunt a sport in which hunters on horseback follow dogs that find and chase a fox.

fox–hunt (foks′hunt′) *v.* pursue or hunt foxes with hounds.
—**fox′-hunt′er,** *n.*

fox–hunt·ing (foks′hun′ting) *n., adj.* —*n.* the sport of hunting foxes with hounds. —*adj.* **1** having to do with the hunting of foxes. **2** having the habits and preferences of a fox hunter.

fox·tail (foks′tāl′) *n.* **1** any grass of two genera (*Setaria* and *Alopecurus*) having soft, round, bushlike spikes of flowers. **2** a wild barley (*Hordeum jubatum*) having a bushy, tassle-like flower spike. Often called **foxtail barley.** **3** the tail of a fox.

fox terrier either of two breeds of terrier (**wire-haired fox terrier** and **smooth fox terrier**) having a white-and-black or white-and-brown coat, originally bred in England for driving foxes from their holes.

fox trot 1 a dance in 2/4 or 4/4 time with short, quick steps. **2** the music for this dance.

fox–trot (foks′trot′) *v.* **-trot·ted, -trot·ting.** dance the fox trot.

fox·y (fok′sē) *adj.* **fox·i·er, fox·i·est. 1** like a fox; sly; crafty. **2** discolored; stained. —**fox′i·ly,** *adv.* —**fox′i·ness,** *n.*

foy·er (foi′ər *or* foi′ā) *n.* **1** an entrance hall used as a lounging room in a theatre or hotel; lobby. **2** an entrance hall. [< F, ult. < L *focus* hearth]

F.P., f.p., or **fp 1** foot-pound. **2** freezing point.

fpm or **f.p.m.** feet per minute

fps or **f.p.s.** feet per second

fr. 1 franc. **2** from. **3** fragment.

Fr francium.

Fr. 1 France; French. **2** Father. **3** Friday. **4** Friar.

Fra (frä) *n.* Brother. It is used as the title of a monk or friar. [< Ital. *fra,* abbreviation of *frate* brother < L *frater*]

fra·cas (frā′kəs) *n.* a noisy quarrel or fight; disturbance; uproar; brawl. [< F < Ital. *fracasso < fracassare* smash]

frac·tion (frak′shən) *n.* **1** *Mathematics.* **a** one or more of the equal parts of a whole. ½, ⅔, ¾, ⅚, and ⅞ are fractions. **b** a division of one mathematical expression by another, indicated by a line with one quantity above it and another below it. **2** a very small part, amount, etc.; fragment. **3** breaking. **4** *Chemistry.* any of the components of a substance separated by distillation, crystallization, etc. [< LL *fractio, -onis* < L *frangere* break]

frac·tion·al (frak′shən əl) *adj.* **1** having to do with fractions. **2** forming a fraction: *440 metres is a fractional part of a kilometre.* **3** very small; insignificant. **4** *Chemistry.* of or designating a method for separating a mixture into its component parts based on certain differences in boiling points, solubility, etc. of these parts:

fractional crystallization, fractional oxidation. **5** in stock exchanges, being less than the amount used as a standard unit of measurement, as less than 100 shares of stock, or $10 000 of bonds.
—**frac′tion·al·ly,** *adv.*

frac·tion·ate (frak′shə nāt′) *v.* **-at·ed, -at·ing. 1** *Chemistry.* separate a mixture into components or properties by distillation, crystallization, etc. **2** acquire or obtain by this process.
—**frac′tion·a′tion,** *n.*

frac·tious (frak′shəs) *adj.* **1** cross; fretful; peevish. **2** hard to manage; unruly. [< *fraction* (in obs. sense of discord, brawling), on the model of *captious,* etc.] —**frac′tious·ly,** *adv.* —**frac′tious·ness,** *n.*

frac·ture (frak′chər) *v.* **-tured, -tur·ing;** *n.* —*v.* break; crack: *The boy fell from a tree and fractured his arm.*
—*n.* **1** a break; crack. **2** breaking or being broken. **3** a breaking of a bone or cartilage. **4** the surface of a freshly broken mineral. [< F < L *fractura < frangere* break]

frae (frā) *Scottish. prep., adv.* —*prep.* from. —*adv.* fro.

frag·ile (fraj′il *or* fraj′əl) *adj.* easily broken, damaged, or destroyed; delicate; frail. [< L *fragilis* (related to *frangere* break). Doublet of FRAIL.] —**frag′ile·ly,** *adv.* —**frag′ile·ness,** *n.*

fra·gil·i·ty (frə jil′ə tē) *n.* a fragile quality.

frag·ment (*n.* frag′mənt; *v.* frag ment′) *n., v.* —*n.* **1** a broken piece; part broken off. **2** an incomplete or disconnected part: *He could hear only fragments of the conversation.* **3** a part of an incomplete or unfinished work.
—*v.* break or divide into fragments. [< L *fragmentum < frangere* break]

frag·men·tal (frag men′təl) *adj.* **1** fragmentary. **2** *Geology.* formed from older rocks.

frag·men·tar·y (frag′mən ter′ē) *adj.* **1** made up of fragments; incomplete; disconnected: *fragmentary remains of a temple, fragmentary evidence, a fragmentary account.* **2** *Geology.* fragmental.

frag·men·ta·tion (frag′mən tā′shən) *n.* the actual process of breaking into many pieces.

fragmentation bomb a bomb, grenade, etc. that throws bits of metal in all directions as it bursts.

fra·grance (frā′grəns) *n.* a sweet smell; pleasing odor.

fra·grant (frā′grənt) *adj.* having or giving off a pleasing odor; sweet-smelling. [< L *fragrans, -antis,* ppr. of *fragrare* emit odor] —**fra′grant·ly,** *adv.*

frail (frāl) *adj.* **1** not very strong; weak; physically delicate: *a frail child.* **2** easily broken, damaged, or destroyed; fragile: *Be careful, those branches are a very frail support.* **3** morally weak; liable to yield to temptation. [ME < OF *fraile* < L *fragilis* fragile. Doublet of FRAGILE.] —**frail′ly,** *adv.* —**frail′ness,** *n.*

frail·ty (frāl′tē) *n., pl.* **-ties. 1** being frail. **2** moral weakness; liability to yield to temptation. **3** a fault or sin caused by moral weakness.

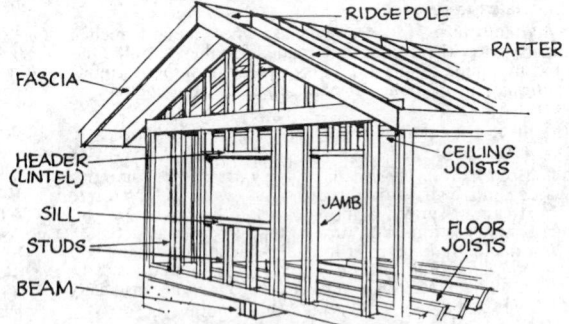

Part of the frame of a house

frame (frām) *n., v.* **framed, fram·ing.** —*n.* **1** a supporting structure over which something is stretched or built: *the frame of a house.* **2** anything made of parts fitted and joined together; structure. **3** the body; bodily structure: *a man of heavy frame.* **4** skeleton. **5** the way in which a thing is put together. **6** an established order; plan; system. **7** a shape; form. **8** the border in which a thing is set: *a window frame, a picture frame.* **9** one of a series of pictures on a strip of film. **10** one image transmitted by television. **11** one turn at bowling. **12** in programmed learning, a single item or statement presented at one time. **13** *Pool, snooker.* **a** the triangular form used to arrange the balls at the start of a game. **b** the triangle of balls thus placed. **c** the period of play between the placing of the balls.

—*v.* **1** shape; form: *to frame one's life according to a noble pattern.*
2 put together; plan; make: *Laws are framed in Parliament.* **3** put a
border around; enclose with a frame. **4** *Slang.* prearrange falsely;
make seem guilty. [OE *framian* to profit < *fram* forth] **—fram′er,** *n.*

frame house a house made of a wooden framework covered
with boards.

frame of mind a way of thinking or feeling; disposition; mood.

frame-up (frām′up′) *n. Slang.* **1** a secret and dishonest
arrangement made beforehand. **2** a prearranged scheme made to
have a person falsely accused.

frame·work (frām′wèrk′) *n.* **1** an open frame or skeletal
structure over which something is stretched or built or in which
something is encased. **2** the way in which a thing is put together;
structure; system. **3** the larger branches of a tree.

franc (frangk) *n.* **1** the basic unit of money in Belgium, Benin,
Burundi, Cameroon, Central African Republic, Chad, Congo
Republic, France, Gabon, Ivory Coast, Luxembourg, Madagascar,
Mali, Niger, Rwanda, Senegal, Switzerland, Togo, and Upper
Volta, divided into 100 centimes. See table at **money. 2** a coin worth
one franc. [ME < OF *franc* < *Francorum Rex* king of the Franks,
on an early gold coin first struck in 1360]
☛ *Hom.* **frank.**

fran·chise (fran′chīz) *n., v.* **-ised, -is·ing.** —*n.* **1** a privilege or
right granted by a government: *The city granted the company a
franchise to operate buses on the city streets.* **2** the right to vote: *A
Canadian citizen receives the federal franchise at the age of 18.*
3 the privilege, often exclusive, of selling the products of a
manufacturer or providing a company's service in a given area.
—*v.* **1** give (a person, company, etc.) a franchise. **2** make (a
product, service, etc.) available as a franchise. [ME < OF *franchise*
a freeing < *franc* free. See FRANK.]

Fran·cis·can (fran sis′kən) *n., adj.* —*n.* a member of a religious
order founded by Saint Francis of Assisi (1182-1226) in 1209. —*adj.*
of or having to do with this religious order.

fran·ci·um (fran′sē əm) *n.* a rare radio-active chemical element.
Symbol: Fr; *at.no.* 87; *at.wt.* (223); *half-life* 22 minutes. [< NL;
after *France*]

fran·ci·za·tion or **fran·ci·sa·tion** (fran′sə zā′shən *or* fran′sī
zā′shən) *n. Cdn.* the act or process of making or becoming French
or French-speaking: *the francization of industry in Quebec.*

fran·cize or **fran·cise** (fran′sīz) *v.* **-cized, -ciz·ing; -cised,
-cis·ing.** *Cdn.* make or become French or French-speaking.

Fran·co– *combining form.* **1** French or French-speaking, as in
Francophile. **2** French and ——: *the Franco-Prussian war.*
3 French-Canadian: *Franco-Albertan.*

fran·co·phile (frang′kə fīl′) *n.* **1** a person who greatly admires
France, its people, and its culture. **2** in Canada, a
non-French-Canadian who shows particular sympathy with the
policies and culture of French-speaking Canada.

Fran·co·phone (frang′kə fōn′) *n. Cdn.* **1** a person in a bilingual
or multilingual country whose native or principal language is
French. **2** (*adj.*) of, having to do with, or made up of people whose
native or principal language is French: *a Francophone riding,
Francophone Africa.*

franc–ti·reur (frän tē rœr′) *n., pl.* **francs-ti·reurs** (frän tē rœr′).
French. **1** a member of an irregular light-infantry corps. **2** a guerrilla
fighter or sniper. [literally, freeshooter < *franc* free + *tireur*
shooter]

fran·gi·ble (fran′jə bəl) *adj.* breakable. [< F < L *frangere* break]

fran·gi·pan·i (fran′jə pan′ē) *n., pl.* **-pan·is** or **-pan·i. 1** any of
various tropical American shrubs or small trees (genus *Plumeria*) of
the dogbane family having large, very fragrant flowers. **2** a perfume
made from the flowers of a frangipani or imitating their odor. [<
Muzio *Frangipani*, a 16th-century Italian marquis, supposed
inventor of the perfume]

Fran·glais (fräng glä′) *n.* French spoken with many English
words and expressions. [< F *français* French + *anglais* English]

frank¹ (frangk) *adj., v., n.* —*adj.* **1** free in expressing one's real
thoughts, opinions, and feelings; not hiding what is in one's mind;
not afraid to say what one thinks. **2** clearly manifest; undisguised;
plain; downright: *frank mutiny.*
—*v.* **1** send (a letter, package, etc.) without charge. **2** mark (a
letter, package, etc.) for free mailing.
—*n.* **1** a mark to show that a letter, package, etc. is to be sent
without charge. **2** the right to send letters, packages, etc. without
charge. **3** a letter, package, etc. sent without charge. [< OF *franc*
free, sincere (originally, a Frank, freedom in early France being
confined to the Franks, the dominant tribe) < Gmc.] **—frank′ly,**
adv. **—frank′ness,** *n.*
☛ *Hom.* **franc.**
☛ *Syn. adj.* **1. Frank, outspoken, candid** = not afraid to say what one thinks or
feels. **Frank** = free in expressing or showing, by manner or looks or actions,
one's real thoughts and feelings: *His eyes are frank and honest.* **Outspoken** =

hat, āge, fär; let, ēqual, tèrm; it, īce
hot, ōpen, ôrder; oil, out; cup, put, rüle,
above, takən, pencəl, lemən, circəs
ch, child; ng, long; sh, ship
th, thin; ŦH, then; zh, measure

speaking out frankly and openly, hiding or keeping back nothing even when it
involves giving offence: *He was outspoken in his criticism.* **Candid** = frank and
sincere and, above all, completely truthful and impartial: *His candid account of
his best friend's dishonesty surprised some people.*

frank² (frangk) *n. Informal.* frankfurter.
☛ *Hom.* **franc.**

Frank (frangk) *n.* a member of a group of West Germanic peoples
who crossed the Rhine and invaded the Roman Empire in the 4th
century A.D., gradually conquering most of Gaul and Germany. The
Frankish empire was at its height under Charlemagne. [? named for
their national weapon; cf. OE *franca* spear]

Frank·en·stein (frangk′ən stīn′) *n.* **1** in a novel by Mary Shelley
(1797-1851), a man who creates a monster that he cannot control.
2 Also, **Frankenstein's monster,** a thing that causes the ruin of its
creator. **3** monster.

frank·furt (frangk′fərt) *n.* frankfurter; wiener.

frank·furt·er (frangk′fèr′tər) *n.* wiener. [< G *Frankfurter* of
Frankfurt]

frank·in·cense (frangk′in sens′) *n.* a fragrant resin from certain
Asiatic or African trees that gives off a sweet, spicy odor when
burned. [ME < OF *franc encens* pure incense]

Frank·ish (frangk′ish) *adj., n.* —*adj.* of or having to do with the
Franks. —*n.* the language of the Franks (def. 1).

frank·lin (frangk′lən) *n. Historical.* a landowner of free but not
noble birth in 14th and 15th century England. [ME *francoleyn,* ult.
< Med.L *francus* free < Gmc.]

fran·tic (fran′tik) *adj.* **1** wild with fright, pain, rage, or frustration.
2 marked by wild, uncontrolled action or activity: *He made a
frantic effort to stop the car.* **3** *Archaic.* insane. [ME < OF
frenetique < L < Gk. Doublet of PHRENETIC.] **—fran′ti·cal·ly,** *adv.*

frap·pé (fra pā′) *adj., n.* —*adj.* iced; cooled. —*n.* **1** fruit juice
sweetened and frozen. **2** any frozen or iced food or drink. [< F
frappé, pp. of *frapper* chill, beat]

fra·ter·nal (frə tèr′nəl) *adj.* **1** brotherly. **2** of, having to do with,
or being a fraternity, society, or guild. **3** of twins, developing from
two separately fertilized egg cells. Compare **identical** (def. 3). [< L
fraternus brotherly < *frater* brother] **—fra·ter′nal·ly,** *adv.*

fra·ter·ni·ty (frə tèr′nə tē) *n., pl.* **-ties. 1** a male students' society
in a university or college, basically a social club, usually having
secret rites and a name made up of Greek letters. Compare **sorority.**
2 a society, guild, or order of people, especially men, with common
interests or a common goal. **3** people having similar interests, work,
etc.: *The publishing fraternity.* **4** fraternal feeling brotherhood. [< L
fraternitas brotherhood]

frat·er·nize (frat′ər nīz′) *v.* **-nized, -niz·ing. 1** associate in a
brotherly way; be friendly. **2** associate in a friendly way with
citizens of a hostile nation during occupation of their territory.
—frat′er·ni·za′tion, *n.* **—frat′er·niz′er,** *n.*

frat·ri·cid·al (frat′rə sīd′əl) *adj.* of, having to do with, or
involving fratricide.

frat·ri·cide (frat′rə sīd′) *n.* **1** the act of killing one's brother or
sister. **2** a person who commits fratricide. [< L *fratricidium* the
murder of one's brother < *frater* brother + *-cidium* act of killing
(for def. 1); < L *fratricida* one who murders his brother < *frater* +
-cida killer (for def. 2)]

Frau (frou) *n., pl.* **Frau·en** (frou′ən). *German.* **1** Mrs. **2** wife.

fraud (frod *or* frôd) *n.* **1** deceit; cheating; dishonesty: *Any intent to
deceive is considered as fraud.* **2** a dishonest act, statement, etc.;
something done to deceive or cheat; trick. **3** *Informal.* a person who
is not what he pretends to be. [ME < OF *fraude* < L *fraus, fraudis*
cheating]

fraud·u·lence (froj′ə ləns *or* frôj′ə ləns) *n.* being fraudulent.

fraud·u·len·cy (froj′ə lən sē *or* frôj′ə lən sē) *n., pl.* **-cies.**
fraudulence.

fraud·u·lent (froj′ə lənt *or* frôj′ə lənt) *adj.* **1** deceitful; cheating;
dishonest. **2** intended to deceive. **3** done by fraud; obtained by
trickery. [ME < OF < L *fraudulentus*] **—fraud′u·lent·ly,** *adv.*

fraught (frot *or* frôt) *adj.* loaded; filled: *A battlefield is fraught
with horror.* [pp. of obs. *fraught* load, verbal use of noun, < MDu.
or MLG *vracht* freight]

Fräu·lein (froi′līn) *n., pl.* **Fräu·lein.** *German.* **1** Miss. **2** an
unmarried woman or girl.

fray[1] (frā) *n.* a noisy quarrel; fight. [var. of *affray*]

fray[2] (frā) *v.* 1 separate into threads; make or become ragged or worn along the edge. 2 wear away; rub. [< F *frayer* < L *fricare* rub]

fra·zil (fraz′əl *or* frə zil′) *n. Cdn.* ice crystals or flakes formed in the turbulent waters of rivers, rapids, etc. and often accumulating as icebanks along the shore. Also, **frazil ice.** [< Cdn.F < F *fraisil* coal cinders, ult. < L *fax, facis,* torch]

fraz·zle (fraz′əl) *v.* **-zled, -zling;** *n. Informal.* —*v.* 1 tear to shreds; fray; wear out. 2 tire out; weary. —*n.* a frazzled condition. [blend of *fray*[2] and obs. *fazle,* ME *faselyn* unravel < OE *fæs* a fringe]

freak (frēk) *n., v.* —*n.* 1 an event, object, etc. that is very strange or unusual: *a freak of nature.* 2 (*adj.*) very strange or unusual: *a freak storm.* 3 a person or animal having some extreme abnormality or deformity; monstrosity. 4 *Slang.* enthusiast; buff: *a hockey freak.* 5 a sudden change or turn of mind without reason; an odd notion or fancy; caprice.
—*v.*
freak out, *Slang.* **a** experience or cause to experience the disorientation, altered perception, hallucinations, etc. brought on by psychedelic drugs. **b** react or cause to react strongly to any experience; make or become extremely excited, angry, etc.: *The new amusement park really freaked him out.* [cf. OE *frīcian* dance]

freak·ish (frē′kish) *adj.* like, characteristic of, or full of freaks; strange, unusual, or capricious. —**freak′ish·ly,** *adv.* —**freak′ish·ness,** *n.*

freak·out (frēk′out′) *n. Slang.* the act or an instance of freaking out.

freak·y (frē′kē) *adj.* 1 freakish. 2 *Slang.* very odd or unconventional; bizarre; outlandish: *freaky clothes, a freaky rock group.*

freck·le (frek′əl) *n., v.* **-led, -ling.** —*n.* a small, light-brown spot on the skin. —*v.* 1 make freckles on; cover with freckles: *The sun freckles the skin of some people.* 2 become marked or spotted with freckles. [probably alteration of *frecken* < ON *freknur,* pl.]

freck·ly (frek′lē) *adj.* covered with freckles.

free (frē) *adj.* **fre·er, fre·est;** *adv., v.* **freed, free·ing.** —*adj.* 1 not under another's control; having liberty; able to do, act, or think as one pleases. 2 showing liberty; caused by liberty. 3 not held back, fastened, or shut up; released; loose. 4 not hindered. 5 clear (*of* or *from*); exempt from; not marred or bothered by: *free of error, free from taxes. The whole community was free of disease.* 6 allowed; permitted (*to*): *You are free to speak.* 7 clear; open. 8 open to all: *a free port.* 9 without cost or payment. 10 without paying a tax or duty. 11 generous: *I appreciated his free offer to carry my suitcase.* 12 giving or using much. 13 abundant. 14 not following rules, forms, or words, exactly; not strict. 15 saying what one thinks; frank. 16 not restrained enough by manners or morals. 17 *Chemistry.* not combined with something else: *Oxygen exists free in the atmosphere.*
free and easy, paying little attention to rules or customs; unrestrained.
free from or **of,** without; lacking.
free with, giving or using freely.
make free with, use as if one owned or had complete rights; act uninhibitedly.
set free, make free; let loose; release.
—*adv.* 1 without cost or payment. 2 in a free manner.
—*v.* 1 relieve from any kind of burden, bondage, or slavery; make free: *The prisoner was freed early for good behavior.* 2 let loose; release: *to free a boat from weeds.* 3 clear: *He will have to free himself of this charge of stealing.* [OE *frēo, frīo*] —**free′ly,** *adv.* —**free′ness,** *n.*
☛ *Syn. v.* 2. See note at **release.**

free·bie (frē′bē) *n. Slang.* something free, especially a gift offered as a perquisite or a promotional gimmick.

free·board (frē′bôrd′) *n.* 1 that part of a ship's side between the water line and the deck or gunwale. 2 the distance between the ground and the under part of the frame of an automobile.

free·boot (frē′büt′) *v.* act as a freebooter; plunder.

free·boot·er (frē′büt′ər) *n.* a pirate; buccaneer. [< Du. *vrijbuiter* < *vrij* free + *buit* booty]

free·boot·ing (frē′büt′ing) *n.* piracy; buccaneering.

free·born (frē′bôrn′) *adj.* 1 born free, not in slavery. 2 of or suitable for people born free.

Free Church a Presbyterian church, known as the "Free Church of Scotland" that seceded from the established Presbyterian Church in 1843.

free city a city forming an independent state.

freed·man (frēd′mən) *n., pl.* **-men.** a man freed from slavery.

free·dom (frē′dəm) *n.* 1 the state or condition of being free. 2 the condition of not being under another's control; power to do, say, or think as one pleases; liberty. 3 free use: *We give all guests the freedom of our home.* 4 lack of restraint; frankness. 5 ease of movement or action.

freedom of the seas, the right of ships to come and go on the high seas, no state having any jurisdiction over foreign vessels except within its own territorial waters. [OE *frēodōm*]
☛ *Syn.* 2. Freedom, liberty, independence = not being under the rule or control of another. **Freedom** emphasizes the power to make one's own laws, impose one's own restraints, control one's own life. **Liberty** emphasizes the right or power to do as one pleases, without restraint: *Freedom of speech does not mean liberty to gossip or tell lies.* **Independence** emphasizes the power to stand alone, not subject to or dependent on someone or something else: *Parents generally try to teach their children independence.*

Free·dom·ite (frē′dəm īt′) *n.* a member of the Sons of Freedom, a Doukhobor sect.

freed·wom·an (frēd′wum′ən) *n., pl.* **-wom·en.** a woman freed from slavery.

free enterprise an economic system based on the right of a private individual to run a business for profit, with a minimum of government control.

free fall 1 the fall of a body when it is unrestrained by anything except gravity. 2 the period in a parachute jump between jumping off and the opening of a parachute.

free–for–all (frē′fər ol′ *or* -ôl′) *adj., n.* —*adj.* open to all. —*n.* a fight, race, etc. open to all or in which everybody participates.

Free French the French people who continued resistance to the Nazis during World War II after the Franco-German armistice of 1940.

free–hand (frē′hand′) *adj.* done by hand without using instruments, measurements, etc.: *freehand drawing.*

free hand the authority to act as one sees fit; carte blanche: *The committee was given a free hand, with no questions asked about how they spent the money.*

free–hand·ed (frē′han′did) *adj.* generous; liberal.

free·hold (frē′hōld′) *n. Law.* 1 a piece of land held for life or with the right to transfer it to one's heirs. 2 the holding of land in this way.

free·hold·er (frē′hōl′dər) *n.* a person who has a freehold.

free lance 1 a writer, artist, etc. who works independently and sells his work to anyone who will buy it. 2 in the Middle Ages, a soldier who fought for any person, group, or state that would pay him. 3 a person who fights or works for any cause that he chooses.

free–lance (frē′lans′) *adj., v.* **-lanced, -lanc·ing.** —*adj.* working as a free lance. —*v.* work as a free lance. —**free′-lanc′er,** *n.*

free·load or **free–load** (frē′lōd′) *v. Slang.* 1 attend a party, convention, etc. chiefly for the free food and drink. 2 take liberally, without contributing anything of one's own. —**free′load′er,** *n.*

free·man (frē′mən) *n., pl.* **-men.** 1 a person who is not a slave or a serf. 2 a person who has civil or political freedom; citizen.

free·mar·tin (frē′mär′tən) *n.* a sterile female calf born as a twin to a male calf. [origin unknown; 17c.]

free·ma·son (frē′mā′sən) *n.* 1 *Historical.* a member of a guild of itinerant skilled stoneworkers in the Middle Ages, who had passwords and secret signs by which they recognized each other. 2 **Freemason,** a member of the Ancient Free and Accepted Masons, a world-wide fraternal society pledged to brotherliness, mutual aid, and charity; Mason.

free·ma·son·ry (frē′mā′sən rē) *n.* 1 **Freemasonry,** the principles, doctrines, etc. of the society of Freemasons; Masonry. 2 the members of this society; Freemasons collectively. 3 natural or instinctive understanding and sympathy.

free on board delivered free of charge on a train, ship, etc. *Abbrev.:* f.o.b. or F.O.B.

free port 1 a port open to traders of all countries on the same conditions. 2 a port where no taxes or duties have to be paid.

free press a press not censored or controlled by the government of the country where it operates.

free·sia (frē′zhə) *n.* any of a genus (Freesia) of S African plants of the iris family having fragrant red, yellow, white, or pink flowers. Freesias are widely cultivated as greenhouse plants. [< NL; after F. H. T. *Freese* (1795?-1876), a German botanist]

free–spo·ken (frē′spō′kən) *adj.* speaking freely; saying what one thinks; frank.

free·stone (frē′stōn′) *n.* 1 any stone, such as limestone or sandstone, that can easily be cut without splitting. 2 a fruit stone, or

pit, that can be easily separated from the pulp. **3** a fruit having such a stone. **4** (*adj.*) having such a stone: *freestone peaches.*

free·style (frē′stīl′) *adj., n.* —*adj.* of or designating a performance, event, etc., as in a sports competition, in which the performer or contestant is not confined to a specific style or bound by the usual rules of execution. —*n.* a freestyle performance, event, etc.

free·think·er (frē′thingk′ər) *n.* a person who forms his religious opinions independently of authority or tradition.

free thought religious opinions formed independently of authority or tradition.

free trade 1 international trade free from protective duties and subject only to tariffs for revenue. **2** the system, principles, or practice of maintaining such trade. **3** trade unrestricted by taxes, customs, duties, or differences of treatment.

free·trad·er (frē′trād′ər) *n.* **1** a person who favors the system of free trade. **2** *Cdn. Historical.* a man who traded in furs independently of such companies as the Hudson's Bay Company.

free verse poetry not restricted by the usual conventions of metre, rhyme, etc.

free·way (frē′wā′) *n. Esp.U.S.* a high-speed highway on which no tolls are charged.

free·wheel (frē′wēl′ or -hwēl′) *n., v.* —*n.* **1** in the transmission of an automobile, etc., a device that permits the drive shaft to run freely when it is turning faster than the engine shaft. **2** on a bicycle, a device that enables the wheels to continue turning while the pedals are held still. —*v.* coast.

free·wheel·ing (frē′wēl′ing or -hwēl′ing) *adj.* **1** using or having a freewheel. **2** independent or unhampered: *a freewheeling operator.*

free·will (frē′wil′) *adj.* voluntary: *a freewill offering.*

free will a voluntary choice; freedom of decision.

free world the non-communist nations. —**free′-world′**, *adj.*

freeze (frēz) *v.* **froze, fro·zen, freez·ing;** *n.* —*v.* **1** turn into ice; harden by cold: *to freeze ice cream. The water in the pond has frozen.* **2** cause something to become hard and stiff by lowering the temperature to below the freezing point (0°C): *By freezing meat we can keep it from spoiling.* **3** feel or be very cold: *You'll freeze if you don't have a good sleeping bag.* **4** be of the degree of cold at which water becomes ice: *It is freezing tonight.* **5** kill or damage by frost. **6** be killed or damaged by frost. **7** freeze over. **8** become clogged by pieces of ice: *The car stalled because the gas line froze.* **9** fix or become fixed to something by freezing. **10** make or become stiff and unfriendly. **11** chill or be chilled with fear, etc. **12** become suddenly motionless: *The cat froze as soon as it saw the bird. He heard a step behind him and froze with fear.* **13** fix (prices, wages, etc.) at a definite amount, usually by governmental decree. **14** make (funds, bank balances, etc.) unusable and inaccessible by governmental decree. **15** prohibit the further use of (a raw material) in any way: *Cobalt was frozen during the war.* **16** make numb by injecting or applying an anesthetic: *to freeze the gum before extracting a tooth.* **freeze on to,** *Informal.* hold on tightly to. **freeze out,** *Informal.* force out; exclude: *The clique's unfriendliness froze out all newcomers.* —*n.* **1** a state of extreme coldness; frost; freezing: *The freeze last night damaged the apple trees.* **2** a period during which there is freezing weather. [OE *frēosan*] ☞ *Hom.* **frieze.**

freeze–dry (frēz′drī′) *v.* **-dried, -dry·ing.** preserve (food, vaccine, etc.) by quick-freezing it and then evaporating the frozen moisture content in a high vacuum. Freeze-dried substances keep for a long period without refrigeration.

freez·er (frē′zər) *n.* **1** an insulated cabinet, compartment, or room maintained at a temperature at least several degrees below the freezing point, for freezing perishable foods and storing them in the frozen state. **2** a device for making ice cream.

freeze–up (frēz′up′) *n. Cdn.* the time of year when rivers and lakes freeze over; onset of winter: *Freeze-up came late last year.*

freez·ing (frē′zing) *n., adj.* —*n.* freezing point, especially that of water: *It's below freezing outside.* —*adj. Informal.* very cold: *It's freezing in here.*

freezing point the temperature at which a liquid freezes. The freezing point of water at sea level is zero degrees Celsius. *Abbrev.:* F.P., f.p., or fp

F region the part of the ionosphere comprising the two layers above the E layer. The two sections, both of which reflect radio waves, are known as the *F 1 layer* and *F 2 layer.*

freight (frāt) *n., v.* —*n.* **1** the load of goods carried on a train, ship, etc.: *It took a whole day to unload the freight.* **2** the carrying of goods on a train, ship, etc. **3** the charge for this. **4** anything carried for pay by land, water, or air; goods in transit. **5** a train for carrying goods. **6** a load; burden. —*v.* **1** load with freight. **2** carry as freight. **3** send as freight. **4** load; burden. [ME < MDu. or MLG *vrecht*]

hat, āge, fär; let, ēqual, tèrm; it, īce
hot, ōpen, ôrder; oil, out; cup, put, rüle,
əbove, takən, pencəl, lemən, circəs

ch, child; ng, long; sh, ship
th, thin; ŦH, then; zh, measure

freight·age (frāt′ij) *n.* **1** the carrying of goods on a train, ship, etc. **2** charge for this. **3** freight; cargo.

freight car a railway car for carrying freight.

freight·er (frāt′ər) *n.* a ship or aircraft for carrying freight.

French (french) *adj., n.* —*adj.* **1** of or having to do with France, its people, or language. **2** French Canadian; of or having to do with French Canada, French Canadians, or their language. —*n.* **1** the people of France. **2** the people of French Canada. **3** the French language: *The kind of French spoken in Canada is called Canadian French.* [OE *Frencisc* < *Franca* Frank]

French and Indian War the part of the Seven Years' War fought in North America between Great Britain and France, with Indian allies (1754-1763).

French Canada 1 French Canadians as a group; all French Canadians. **2** the part of Canada inhabited mainly or entirely by French Canadians, especially the province of Quebec.

French Canadian 1 a Canadian whose ancestors came from France. **2** of or having to do with French Canada or French Canadians. **3** the language of the French Canadians; Canadian French.

French chalk talc used for marking lines on cloth or removing grease.

French Community an association formed in 1958 of France and her dependent territories, and many of her former colonies.

French cuff a sleeve cuff that is folded back at the wrist and fastened with a cuff link instead of a button.

French doors a pair of doors hinged at the sides and opening in the middle. They have panes of glass like a window.

French dressing a salad dressing made of olive oil, vinegar, salt, spices, etc.

French fact *Cdn.* the existence of French Canada as a distinct cultural entity.

French fry a strip of potato that has been **French fried,** that is, fried in deep fat until brown and crisp on the outside; chip (def. 4).

A French horn

French horn a brass wind instrument that has a mellow tone.

French·ie (fren′chē) *Derogatory slang.* a French Canadian.

French·i·fy (fren′chə fī′) *v.* **-fied, -fy·ing.** make French or like the French.

French leave 1 the act of leaving without ceremony, permission, or notice; secret or hurried departure. **2** originally, the custom of going away from a reception, etc., without taking leave of the host or hostess.

French·man (french′mən) *n., pl.* **-men. 1** a native or inhabitant of France. **2** a citizen of France. **3** a French Canadian.

French pastry 1 small, individual, rich cakes, tarts, eclairs, etc. **2** one of these cakes.

French Provincial 1 of, like, or having to do with a style of furniture, architecture, or fabric design that originated in the 17th and 18th century French provinces. **2** this style of furniture.

French Revolution the revolution in France from 1789 to 1799, which ousted the monarchy and set up a republic.

French seam a seam stitched first on the right side of the material, then on the wrong side, to cover the raw edges.

French Shore *Cdn.* **1** the west coast of Newfoundland, where the French held fishing and other rights from 1713 till 1904. **2** an area originally settled by the Acadian French, located on the southwest coast of Nova Scotia.

French toast slices of bread dipped in a mixture of egg and milk and then fried in a small quantity of fat.

French windows a pair of long windows like doors, hinged at the sides and opening in the middle.

French·wom·an (french′wŭm′ən) *n., pl.* **-wom·en. 1** a woman who is a native or inhabitant of France. **2** a French-Canadian woman.

fre·net·ic (frə net′ik) *adj.* frenzied; frantic. [var. of *phrenetic*] **—fre·net′i·cal·ly,** *adv.*

fre·num (frē′nəm) *n., pl.* **-na** or **-nums.** a fold of mucous membrane serving to support and restrain the movement of a movable organ or part, such as the membrane under the tongue.

fren·zied (fren′zēd) *adj.* greatly excited; frantic. **—fren′zied·ly,** *adv.*

fren·zy (fren′zē) *n., pl.* **-zies. 1** a state of near madness: *She was in a frenzy of grief when she heard of her son's death.* **2** a state of very great excitement: *The spectators were in a frenzy after the home team scored the winning goal.* [ME < OF *frenesie* < L *phrenesis,* ult. < Gk. *phrēn* mind]

Fre·on (frē′on) *n. Trademark.* any of a group of nonflammable, inert gaseous or liquid fluorocarbons used especially as refrigerants and as propellants for aerosol sprays.

fre·quen·cy (frē′kwən sē) *n., pl.* **-cies. 1** *Physics.* **a** the number of times that any regularly repeated event, as a vibration, occurs in a given unit of time. **b** the rate of occurrence. **2** a frequent occurrence. **3** the number of complete cycles per second of an alternating current or any type of wave motion: *Different radio stations broadcast at different frequencies so that their signals can be heard distinctly.* **4** *Mathematics.* the ratio of the number of times an event actually occurs to the number of times it might occur in a given period. **5** *Statistics.* the number of cases of the data under consideration falling within a particular class interval.

frequency band *Television, radio, etc.* a certain range of wave lengths; channel.

frequency modulation *Radio.* **1** a method of transmitting the sound signals of a broadcast by changing the frequency of the carrier waves to match the sound signals. **2** a broadcasting system that uses frequency modulation. Compare **amplitude modulation.** *Abbrev:* FM or F.M.

fre·quent (*adj.* frē′kwənt; *v.* fri kwent′) *adj., v. —adj.* **1** occurring often, near, together, or every little while. **2** regular; habitual: *He is a frequent caller at our house.* **—v.** go often to; be often in: *Frogs frequent ponds, streams, and marshes.* [< L *frequens, -entis* crowded]

fre·quen·ta·tive (fri kwen′tə tiv) *adj., n. —adj. Grammar.* expressing frequent repetition of an action. *Waggle* is a frequentative verb from *wag.* **—n.** a frequentative verb.

fre·quent·er (fri kwen′tər) *n.* a habitual visitor.

fre·quent·ly (frē′kwənt lē) *adv.* often, repeatedly; every little while.

☛ *Syn.* See note at **often.**

fres·co (fres′kō) *n., pl.* **-coes** or **-cos;** *v.* **-coed, -co·ing. —n. 1** the act or art of painting with water colors on damp, fresh plaster. **2** a picture or design so painted. **—v.** paint in fresco. [< Ital. *fresco* cool, fresh]

fresh (fresh) *adj.* **1** newly made, arrived, or obtained: *fresh footprints.* **2** not known, seen, or used before; new; recent. **3** additional; further; another: *After her failure she made a fresh start.* **4** not salty: *There is fresh water in the Great Lakes.* **5** not spoiled; newly grown, produced, or gathered; not stale. **6** not artificially preserved. **7** not wearied; vigorous; lively. **8** not faded or worn; bright. **9** looking healthy or young. **10** clean; newly washed: *a fresh shirt.* **11** pure; cool; refreshing: *a fresh breeze.* **12** fairly strong; brisk: *a fresh wind.* **13** not experienced. **14** *Slang.* too bold; impudent. [OE *fersc;* but influenced in form by OF *fresche,* fem. of *freis* < Gmc.] **—fresh′ly,** *adv.* **—fresh′ness,** *n.*

fresh·en (fresh′ən) *v.* **1** make new, pure, or bright: *He thought it would be a good idea to freshen the paint on the house.* **2** become stronger: *The wind freshened at sunset.*
freshen up, do something to make, or feel, fresh: *He freshened up by taking a bath and changing his clothes.*

fresh·et (fresh′it) *n.* **1** a flood caused by heavy rains or melted snow. **2** a rush of fresh water flowing into the sea. [< *fresh* flood, stream, or pool of fresh water + *-et*]

fresh·ette (fresh et′) *n.* a girl student in the first year of a university course.

fresh·man (fresh′mən) *n., pl.* **-men. —n. 1** a student in the first year of a university course. **2** beginner. **3** (*adj.*) of or having to do with freshmen.

fresh·wa·ter (fresh′wo′tər *or* -wô′tər) *adj.* **1** of, having to do with, or living in water that is not salty: *The catfish is a freshwater fish.* **2** not used to sailing on the sea: *a freshwater sailor.*

fres·no (frez′nō) *n., pl.* **fres·noes.** buck scraper. [< *Fresno Agricultural Works, California*]

fret¹ (fret) *v.* **fret·ted, fret·ing;** *n. —v.* **1** be peevish, unhappy, discontented, or worried: *A baby sometimes frets in hot weather. Don't fret about your mistake.* **2** make peevish, unhappy, discontented, or worried. **3** eat away; wear; rub. **4** roughen; disturb. **—n.** a peevish complaining; worry; a discontented condition. [OE *fretan* eat] **—fret′ter,** *n.*

fret² (fret) *n., v.* **fret·ted, fret·ting. —n.** an ornamental pattern made of straight lines bent or combined at angles. **—v.** decorate with fretwork. [ME < OF *frete* trellis work]

fret³ (fret) *n.* one of a series of ridges of wood, ivory, or metal on a guitar, banjo, etc. to show where to put the fingers to produce particular tones. [origin uncertain]

fret·ful (fret′fəl) *adj.* **1** inclined to fret; peevish; unhappy; discontented. **2** agitated; seething: *the fretful sea.* **3** gusty: *the fretful wind.* **—fret′ful·ly,** *adv.* **—fret′ful·ness,** *n.*

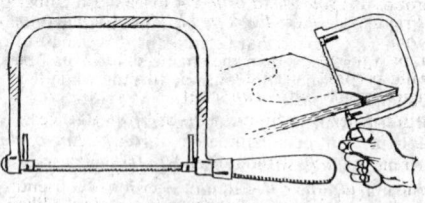

A fret saw

fret saw a saw with a very narrow, fine blade set in a U-shaped frame, used for cutting open designs in thin wood. Fret saws usually have between seven and 14 teeth per centimetre. Compare **coping saw.**

fret·ted (fret′id) *adj., v. —adj.* having frets. **—v.** pt. and pp. of **fret¹** and **fret².**

Traditional fretwork on the gable of a house in rural Ontario

fret·work (fret′wèrk′) *n.* ornamental openwork or carving.

Freud·i·an (froi′dē ən) *adj., n. —adj.* of or having to do with Sigmund Freud (1856-1939), an Austrian physician, who developed a theory and technique of psychoanalysis, or with his teachings. **—n.** a person who believes in Freud's teachings or follows his technique of psychoanalysis.

Freud·i·an·ism (froi′dē ə niz′əm) *n.* **1** the teachings of Freud. **2** a Freudian quality or character.

F.R.G.S. Fellow of the Royal Geographical Society.

Fri. Friday.

fri·a·bil·i·ty (frī ə bil′ə tē) *n.* the state of being friable.

fri·a·ble (frī′ə bəl) *adj.* easily crumbled: *Dry soil is friable.* [< L *friabilis* < *friare* crumble]

fri·ar (frī′ər) *n.* a member of certain religious orders, especially the Roman Catholic mendicant orders, the Franciscans, Dominicans, Carmelites, and Augustinians. [ME < OF *frere* < L *frater* brother]

fri·ar·y (frī′ər ē) *n., pl.* **-ar·ies. 1** a building or buildings where friars live; monastery. **2** a brotherhood of friars.

fric·an·deau (frik′ən dō′) *n.* veal or other meat larded, braised, or fried, and served with a sauce. [< F *fricandeau,* related to *fricassée.* See FRICASSEE.]

fric·as·see (frik′ə sē′) *n., v.* **-seed, -see·ing. —n.** meat cut up, stewed, and served in a sauce made with its own gravy. **—v.** prepare (meat) in this way. [< F *fricassée* < *fricasser* mince and cook in sauce]

fric·a·tive (frik′ə tiv) *adj., n. —adj. Phonetics.* of consonants, pronounced by forcing the breath through a narrow opening. The English fricative consonants are (f), (v), (th), (ŦH), (s), (z), (sh), (zh),

and (h). —*n.* a fricative consonant. [< NL < L *fricare* to rub]

fric·tion (frik′shən) *n.* **1** a rubbing of one object against another; rubbing: *Matches are lighted by friction.* **2** *Physics.* the resistance to motion of surfaces that touch; resistance of a moving body to water, air, etc. through which it travels or to the surface on which it moves: *A sled moves more easily on smooth ice than on rough ground because there is less friction.* **3** conflict of differing ideas, opinions, etc.; disagreement: *Political differences caused friction between the two countries.* [< L *frictio, -onis* < *fricare* rub]

fric·tion·al (frik′shən əl) *adj.* having to do with friction; caused by friction. —**fric′tion·al·ly,** *adv.*

Fri·day (frī′dē *or* frī′dā) *n.* **1** the sixth day of the week, following Thursday. **2** the servant of Robinson Crusoe. **3** any faithful servant or devoted friend. [OE *Frīgedæg* Frigg's day < gen. of *Frīg* + *dæg* day; based on L *dies Veneris* Venus' day]

fridge (frij) *n. Informal.* refrigerator. Also, **frig.** [shortening of *refrigerator* or *Frigidaire* (a trademark)]

fried (frīd) *adj., v.* —*adj.* cooked in fat. —*v.* pt. and pp. of **fry**[1].

fried cake a small cake fried in deep fat; doughnut or cruller.

friend (frend) *n.* **1** a person who knows and likes another. **2** a person who favors and supports. **3** a person who belongs to the same side or group: *Are you friend or foe?* **4 Friend,** a member of the Society of Friends; Quaker: *The Friends favor simplicity in clothes and manners.*
be friends with, be a friend of.
make friends with, become a friend of.
[OE *frēond,* originally ppr. of *frēogan* love]

friend at court a person who can help one to influence others; influential friend.

friend·less (frend′lis) *adj.* without friends. —**friend′less·ness,** *n.*

friend·ly (frend′lē) *adj.* **-li·er, -li·est;** *adv.* —*adj.* **1** of a friend; having the attitude of a friend; kind: *a friendly greeting.* **2** like a friend; like a friend's. **3** on good terms; not hostile: *friendly relations between countries.* **4** wanting to be a friend: *a friendly dog.* **5** favoring and supporting; favorable: *a friendly breeze.* —*adv.* in a friendly manner; as a friend. [OE *frēondlīc*] —**friend′li·ness,** *n.*

friend·ship (frend′ship) *n.* **1** the state of being friends. **2** a liking between friends. **3** a friendly feeling; friendly behavior: *His smile radiated friendship.*

fries (frīz) *n.pl.* French fries.

frieze[1] (frēz) *n.* **1** a horizontal band of decoration around a room, building, mantel, etc. **2** *Architecture.* a horizontal band forming part of the upper section of a wall, often ornamented with sculpture. The frieze is the part of an entablature between the cornice and architrave. See **column** for picture. [< F *frise* < Med.L *frisium* < L *Phrygium* of Phrygia]
☛ *Hom.* **freeze.**

frieze[2] (frēz) *n., v.* —*n.* a thick woollen cloth with a shaggy nap on one side. —*v.* raise a nap on (cloth). [ME < OF (*drap de*) *frise* Frisian (cloth)]
☛ *Hom.* **freeze.**

frig (frij) *n. Informal.* refrigerator.

frig·ate (frig′it) *n.* **1** a modern warship larger than a corvette and smaller than a destroyer, used especially as an escort vessel. **2** *Historical.* a three-masted sailing warship of medium size. [< F *frégate* < Ital. *fregata*]

frigate bird any of a genus (*Fregata*, constituting the family Fregatidae) of tropical and subtropical sea birds having mainly black plumage, long, slender, strong wings, a long forked tail, and a long bill that curves downward at the tip. Frigate birds are noted for robbing other birds of their fish.

Frigg (frig) *n. Norse mythology.* the wife of Odin and goddess of the sky.

fright (frīt) *n., v.* —*n.* **1** sudden fear; sudden terror. **2** *Informal.* a person or thing that is ugly, shocking, or ridiculous: *She looked a fright in that hat.* —*v. Poetic.* frighten. [OE *fryhto*]

fright·ed (frīt′id) *adj.* frightened; terrified.

fright·en (frīt′ən) *v.* **1** fill with fright; make afraid; scare. **2** become afraid. —**fright′en·er,** *n.*
☛ *Syn.* **1. Frighten, scare, alarm** = fill with fear. **Frighten** is the general word: *The rattlesnake frightened me.* **Scare** particularly suggests suddenly giving sharp fear or terror to a timid person or animal: *The firecrackers scared the puppy.* **Alarm** = fill with intense fear and anxiety: *Her failure to come home at midnight alarmed us.*

fright·ened (frīt′ənd) *adj.* filled with fright; afraid.
☛ *Syn.* See note at **afraid.**

fright·en·ing (frīt′ning *or* frīt′ən ing) *adj.* capable of causing fright or fear: *a frightening experience.* —**fright′en·ing·ly,** *adv.*

fright·ful (frīt′fəl) *adj.* **1** causing fright or horror; dreadful; terrible: *a frightful thunderstorm.* **2** ugly; shocking. **3** *Informal.* very great. —**fright′ful·ly,** *adv.* —**fright′ful·ness,** *n.*

hat, āge, fär; let, ēqual, tèrm; it, īce
hot, ōpen, ôrder; oil, out; cup, pút, rüle,
above, takən, pencəl, lemən, circəs

ch, child; ng, long; sh, ship
th, thin; ₮н, then; zh, measure

frig·id (frij′id) *adj.* **1** very cold: *a frigid climate.* **2** cold in feeling or manner; stiff; chilling: *a frigid reception.* [< L *frigidus* < *frigere* be cold < *frigus* cold] —**frig′id·ly,** *adv.* —**frig′id·ness,** *n.*

fri·gid·i·ty (fri jid′ə tē) *n.* being frigid.

Frigid Zone either of two regions comprising the high latitudes, north of the Arctic Circle in the northern hemisphere and south of the Antarctic Circle in the southern hemisphere, forming part of a now obsolete classification system for world climate zones. See also **Temperate Zone, Torrid Zone.**

frill (fril) *n., v.* —*n.* **1** a ruffle. **2** *Informal.* anything added merely for show; useless ornament; affectation of dress, manner, speech, etc. **3** a fringe of feathers, hair, etc. around the neck of a bird or animal.
—*v.* **1** decorate with a ruffle; adorn with ruffles. **2** form into a ruffle. [origin uncertain]

fril·ly (fril′ē) *adj.* **1** having ruffles or frills. **2** like frills.

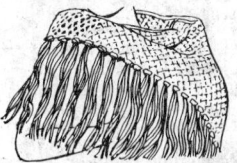

A shawl with a fringe

fringe (frinj) *n., v.* **fringed, fring·ing.** —*n.* **1** a border or trimming made of threads, cords, etc., either loose or tied together in small bunches: *The chesterfield had a fringe along the bottom edge.* **2** anything like this; border: *A fringe of hair over her forehead.* **3** anything thought of as marginal rather than central: *He belongs to the radical fringe of the labor movement.* **4** (*adj.*) of the border or outside. **5** (*adj.*) apart from the main purpose; secondary: *They didn't want to spend too much time on fringe issues.*
—*v.* **1** make a border for. **2** be a border for; border: *Bushes fringed the road.* [ME < OF *frenge* < L *fimbria*]

fringe benefit any employment benefit given to an employee over and above his regular wages: *Pensions and medical insurance are fringe benefits.*

fringe land *Cdn.* in the North, land that is relatively far from a railway.

frip·per·y (frip′ər ē) *n., pl.* **-per·ies. 1** cheap, showy clothes; gaudy ornaments. **2** a cheap, showy article of clothing; gaudy ornament. **3** showing off; foolish display; pretended refinement: *Affectations of manner and speech are mere frippery.* [< F *friperie,* ult. < *frepe* rag]

Fris·bee (friz′bē) *n. Trademark.* a light disk, usually of plastic, that is shaped like an upside-down saucer with a flange turned inward at the bottom to facilitate throwing and catching. It is spun through the air in various ways. [Named after Mother Frisbie's Pie Company in Bridgeport, Connecticut, whose pie plates were formerly used in a similar way.]

Fri·sian (frizh′ən) *n., adj.* —*n.* **1** a native or inhabitant of Friesland, a district in N Netherlands, or certain nearby islands. **2** the language spoken in Friesland and certain nearby islands: *Frisian is a West Germanic dialect, closely akin to English.* —*adj.* of or having to do with Friesland, its people, or their language.

frisk (frisk) *v.* **1** run and jump about playfully; skip and dance joyously; frolic. **2** *Slang.* search (a person) for concealed weapons, stolen goods, etc. by running a hand quickly over the person's clothes. **3** *Slang.* steal from (a person) in this way. [originally *adj.*, < OF *frisque* < Gmc.; cf. G *frisch*]

frisk·y (fris′kē) *adj.* **frisk·i·er, frisk·i·est.** playful; lively. —**frisk′i·ly,** *adv.* —**frisk′i·ness,** *n.*

fris·son (frē sōN′) *n. French.* a shiver, as of pleasure or fear; thrill.

frith (frith) *n.* firth. [var. of *firth*]

frit·il·lar·y (frit′ə ler ē) *n., pl.* **-lar·ies. 1** any of a genus (*Fritillaria*) of plants of the lily family of north temperate regions having drooping, bell-shaped flowers often spotted or checkered with green or purple. **2** any of various butterflies (family Nymphalidae, especially of genera *Speyeria* and *Boloria*) having orange or brownish wings spotted with black and sometimes silver.

[< NL *fritillaria* < L *fritillus* dice box; with reference to the checkered markings on the petals]

frit·ter[1] (frit′ər) *v., n.* —*v.* **1** waste little by little. **2** cut or tear into small pieces; break into fragments. —*n.* a small piece; fragment. [< OF *freture, fraiture* < L *fractura*. See FRACTURE.] —**frit′ter·er**, *n.*

frit·ter[2] (frit′ər) *n.* a small cake of batter, sometimes containing fruit or other food, fried in fat: *corn fritters.* [ME < OF *friture*, ult. < L *frigere* fry]

fritz (frits) *n.*
on the fritz, *Slang.* out of order; not working or functioning: *The TV is on the fritz again.*

fri·vol·i·ty (fri vol′ə tē) *n., pl.* **-ties. 1** being frivolous. **2** frivolous act or thing.

friv·o·lous (friv′ə ləs) *adj.* **1** lacking in seriousness or sense; silly: *Frivolous behavior is out of place in church.* **2** of little worth or importance; trivial: *He wasted his time on frivolous matters.* [< L *frivolus*] —**friv′o·lous·ly,** *adv.* —**friv′o·lous·ness,** *n.*

frizz or **friz** (friz) *v.* **frizzed, friz·zing;** *n., pl.* **friz·zes.** —*v.* form into small, crisp curls; curl. —*n.* hair curled in small, crisp curls or a very close crimp. [apparently < G *friser*]

friz·zle[1] (friz′əl) *v.* **-zled, -zling;** *n.* —*v.* form into small, crisp curls; curl. —*n.* **1** being frizzled. **2** a small, crisp curl. [? related to OE *frīs* curly] —**friz′zler,** *n.*

friz·zle[2] (friz′əl) *v.* **-zled, -zling;** *n.* —*v.* **1** make a hissing, sputtering noise when cooking; sizzle. **2** fry or broil until crisp. —*n.* a sizzle. [? < *fry* and *sizzle*]

friz·zly (friz′lē) *adj.* **-zli·er, -zli·est.** full of small, crisp curls; curly.

friz·zy (friz′ē) *adj.* **-zi·er, -zi·est.** frizzly.

fro (frō) *adv.* from; back.
to and fro, first one way and then back again; back and forth. [< ON *frá.* Akin to FROM.]

frock (frok) *n., v.* —*n.* **1** a gown; dress. **2** a loose outer garment. **3** a robe worn by a clergyman.
—*v.* **1** clothe in a frock. **2** invest with clerical authority. [ME < OF *froc*]

frock coat a man's coat reaching approximately to the knees, and equally long in front and at the back.

frog[1] (frog) *n.* **1** any of a family (Ranidae) of small, squat, tailless amphibians having smooth, usually green or brown skin, and long, strong hind legs adapted for leaping. Compare **toad. 2** any of various other amphibians of the same order (Anura; also called Salientia), such as the tree frogs. **3** the arrangement of a rail where a railway track crosses or branches from another. **4** a pad of horny substance in the middle of the bottom of a foot of a horse, donkey, etc. **5** a small perforated or spiked device for holding flowers upright in a vase, bowl, etc. **6** *Derogatory slang.* a French Canadian or Frenchman.
frog in (one's) **throat,** *Informal.* a slight hoarseness caused by soreness or swelling in the throat.
[OE *frogga*]

A frog closing
on a jacket

frog[2] (frog) *n.* **1** an ornamental fastening for a coat or dress. **2** an attachment or loop on a belt, for carrying a sword, bayonet, etc. [? < Pg. *froco* < L *floccus* flock[2]]

frog kick *Swimming.* a movement of the legs in which the swimmer draws his knees forward and then kicks out to the sides and brings both legs together again. The frog kick is done in the breast stroke.

frog·man (frog′man′ or frog′mən) *n., pl.* **-men.** a skindiver, especially one in or working for the armed forces. Most of the world's navies now have frogmen.

frol·ic (frol′ik) *n., v.* **-icked, -ick·ing;** *adj.* —*n.* **1** a gay prank; fun. **2** a merry game or party. **3** *Historical.* a gathering for work, such as a husking bee or a barn raising.
—*v.* play; have fun; make merry.
—*adj.* full of fun; gay; merry. [< Du. *vrolijk* < MDu. *vrō* glad + *-lijk* -ly] —**frol′ick·er,** *n.*

frol·ic·some (frol′ik səm) *adj.* full of fun; gay; merry.

from (frum *or* from: *unstressed*, frəm) *prep.* **1** out of; of: *Bricks are made from clay.* **2** starting out from; beginning with: *the train from Montreal. Study the lesson from page 10 to page 15.* **3** originating in; having a source: *The river flows from the mountain. Much of our asbestos is from Quebec.* **4** caused by; because of; by reason of: *to act from a sense of duty.* **5** as being unlike: *Anyone can tell apples from oranges.* **6** off: *He took a book from the table.* **7** out of the control or possession of: *He took the knife from the baby.* [OE *fram, from*]

frond (frond) *n.* **1** a divided leaf of a fern, palm, etc. **2** a leaflike part of a seaweed, lichen, etc. [< L *frons, frondis* leaf]

front (frunt) *n., adj., v., adv.* —*n.* **1** the first part; foremost part: *the front of a car.* **2** the part that faces forward: *the front of a dress.* **3** something fastened or worn on the front. **4** *Military.* the area where active fighting is going on between opposing armies. **5** a sphere of activity combining different groups in a political or economic battle: *the labor front.* **6** the forces fighting for some political or social aim. **7** the land facing a street, river, lake, etc. **8** a manner of looking or behaving. **9** *Informal.* an outward appearance of wealth, importance, etc. **10** *Informal.* a person appointed to add respectability or prestige to an enterprise. **11** *Informal.* a person or thing that serves as a cover for illegal activities. **12** forehead. **13** the face. **14** *Cdn.* **a** the settled, civilized part of the country at the edge of the frontier. **b** in Newfoundland and Nova Scotia, the area where the spring seal hunt takes place, at the edge of the Arctic ice fields. **15** the dividing surface between two dissimilar air masses: *The weather report says there is a cold front approaching from the northwest.*
in front of, in a place or position before (a person or thing): *He stood in front of me.*
—*adj.* **1** of, on, in, or at the front. **2** *Phonetics.* pronounced by raising the tongue against or near the forward part of the hard palate. The *e* (ē) in *she* is a front vowel.
—*v.* **1** have the front toward; face. **2** be in front of. **3** furnish with a front. **4** meet face to face; defy; oppose. **5** *Informal.* serve as a cover for a pressure group, an illegal activity, or the like: *Some claimed that the dockers' union fronted for the smuggling ring.*
—*adv.*
eyes front! look forward! direct the eyes ahead!
[< L *frons, frontis,* literally, forehead]

front·age (frun′tij) *n.* **1** the front of a building or of a lot. **2** the length of this front. **3** the direction that the front of a building or lot faces. **4** the land facing a street, river, etc. **5** the land between a building and a street, river, etc.

frontage road a road paralleling an expressway or freeway to provide access for local traffic.

fron·tal (frun′təl) *adj., n.* —*adj.* **1** of, on, in, or at the front. **2** of the forehead. —*n.* a bone of the forehead. [< NL *frontalis* < L *frons, frontis,* literally, forehead] —**front′al·ly,** *adv.*

front bench 1 in a legislative chamber, the front seats on either side, reserved for the party leaders. **2** the party leaders.

front bencher in a legislative body, one of the leading members of a political party: *Cabinet ministers are the government front benchers.*

front-end loader (frunt′end) a tracked vehicle having a hydraulically operated scoop at the front, used for picking up a load of dirt, rocks, etc. from the ground and transferring it to a truck or dumping place.

fron·tier (fron tēr′, frun tēr′, *or* fron′tēr) *n.* **1** the farthest part of a settled country, where the wilds begin: *The Yukon is part of Canada's present-day frontier.* **2** a part of one country that touches on the border of another; boundary line or border between two countries. **3** an uncertain or undeveloped region: *the frontiers of science.* **4** (*adj.*) of, on, or like a frontier: *frontier life, the frontier spirit.* [ME < OF *frontiere* < *front* front < L *frons, frontis,* literally, forehead]

Frontier College a famous Canadian educational body serving isolated mining and logging camps.

fron·tiers·man (fron tērz′mən *or* frun tērz′-) *n., pl.* **-men.** a man who lives on the frontier.

fron·tis·piece (frun′tis pēs *or* fron′tis pēs′) *n.* **1** a picture facing the title page of a book or of a division of a book. **2** *Architecture.* **a** the main part or the decorated entrance of a building. **b** a pediment over a door, gate, etc. [< F *frontispice* < LL *frontispicium,* literally, looking at the forehead < L *frons, frontis* forehead + *specere* look]

front·let (frunt′lit) *n.* **1** a band or ornament worn on the forehead. **2** the forehead of an animal.

front line *Military.* the part of the front nearest to enemy positions in battle.

front man 1 one who officially represents a group or organization. **2** one who fronts for another: *The pleasant storekeeper was front man for a gang of jewel smugglers.*

front matter *Printing.* the pages of a book that precede the actual text. The preface and table of contents belong to the front matter.

front–page (frunt′pāj′) *adj., v.* **-paged, -pag·ing.** —*adj.* suitable for the front page of a newspaper; important: *front-page news.* —*v.* put on the front page; play up; emphasize.

frost (frost) *n., v.* —*n.* **1** a freezing condition; very cold weather; temperature below the point at which water freezes: *There was frost in the air last night.* **2** the moisture frozen on or in a surface; feathery crystals of ice that are formed when water vapor in the air condenses at a temperature below freezing: *frost on the grass, frost on windows.* **3** a coldness of manner or feeling. **4** *Slang.* failure. —*v.* **1** cover or become covered with frost. **2** cover with something that suggests frost; especially, cover with icing: *to frost a cake.* **3** kill or injure by frost. [OE] —**frost′less,** *adj.* —**frost′like′,** *adj.*

frost·bite (frost′bīt′) *n., v.* **-bit, -bit·ten, -bit·ing.** —*n.* an injury to a part of the body caused by severe cold. —*v.* injure (a part of the body) by severe cold.

frost·bit·ten (frost′bit′ən) *adj., v.* —*adj.* injured by severe cold. —*v.* pp. of **frostbite.**

frost boil a defective place in a paved road where the pavement has heaved as a result of the expansion of trapped moisture frozen during the cold weather; a frost heave.

frost·ed (fros′tid) *adj.* **1** covered with frost: *a frosted window.* **2** finished or decorated with a surface suggesting frost: *frosted glass.* **3** covered with icing: *a frosted cake.* **4** frozen.

frost heave frost boil.

frost·ing (fros′ting) *n.* **1** a mixture of sugar and some liquid, with flavoring, etc. used to cover and decorate a cake; icing. **2** a dull finish on glass, metal, etc.

frost·line (frost′līn′) *n. Geology.* the depth to which frost penetrates into the ground.

frost·y (fros′tē) *adj.* **frost·i·er, frost·i·est. 1** cold enough for frost; freezing: *a frosty morning.* **2** covered with frost: *The glass is frosty.* **3** covered with anything like frost. **4** cold in manner or feeling; unfriendly: *a frosty greeting.* **5** hoary or grey, as if covered with frost. —**frost′i·ly,** *adv.* —**frost′i·ness,** *n.*

froth (froth) *n., v.* —*n.* **1** a mass of very small bubbles; foam: *The bottle of pop had been shaken so much that it was half froth.* **2** foaming saliva coming from the mouth, caused by disease, exertion, etc. **3** something light and trifling; trivial notions, talk, etc. —*v.* **1** give out froth; foam. **2** cover with froth. **3** cause to foam by beating, pouring, etc. [ME < ON *frotha*]

froth·y (froth′ē) *adj.* **froth·i·er, froth·i·est. 1** of or like froth; foamy. **2** light; trifling, shallow, unimportant. —**froth′i·ly,** *adv.* —**froth′i·ness,** *n.*

frou–frou (frü′frü′) *n.* **1** a swishing sound; rustling, especially of a woman's clothes. **2** *Informal.* fancy or fussy trimmings; frills. [< F]

fro·ward (frō′wərd *or* frō′ərd) *adj.* not easily managed; willful; contrary. [< *fro* + *-ward*] —**fro′ward·ly,** *adv.* —**fro′ward·ness,** *n.*

frown (froun) *n., v.* —*n.* **1** a drawing together of the brows, usually in deep thought or disapproval. **2** any expression or show of disapproval. —*v.* **1** draw the brows together, as in deep or disapproval: *He frowned, trying to remember the name.* **2** show displeasure or anger. **3** express by frowning: *He frowned his annoyance.* **frown on,** disapprove of: *They frown on gambling.* [ME < OF *froignier* < Celtic] —**frown′ing·ly,** *adv.*
☛ *Syn. v.* **1, 2. Frown, scowl** = draw the eyebrows together, usually to express feeling or attitude. **Frown** = draw the eyebrows tightly together, sometimes in looking closely at or concentrating, but usually to express irritation or displeasure: *The teacher frowned when the boy came in late.* **Scowl** = look sullen or sour out of discontent or ill-temper: *He is a disagreeable person, always scowling.*

frowz·y (frou′zē) *adj.* **frowz·i·er, frowz·i·est. 1** slovenly; dirty; untidy. **2** smelling bad or stale; musty. Also, **frowsy.** [cf. obs. *frowze* frizz, ruffle, rumple, and dial. Brit. *frowsty* musty] —**frowz′i·ly,** *adv.* —**frowz′i·ness,** *n.*

froze (frōz) *v.* pt. of **freeze.**

fro·zen (frō′zən) *adj., v.* —*adj.* **1** turned into ice; hardened by cold: *a frozen dessert. The water in the pail was frozen.* **2** very cold: *the frozen north.* **3** kept at a temperature below freezing to prevent spoiling: *frozen foods.* **4** killed or injured by frost. **5** covered or clogged with ice: *a frozen lake, a frozen water main.* **6** too frightened or stiff to move; made motionless as if turned to ice: *frozen to the spot in horror.* **7** without affection or feeling: *a frozen heart.* **8** temporarily forbidden to be sold or exchanged: *frozen assets.* **9** of prices, wages, etc., fixed at a particular amount or level. —*v.* pp. of **freeze.**

F.R.S. Fellow of the Royal Society.

F.R.S.C. Fellow of the Royal Society of Canada.

front matter 475 **fruitcake**

hat, āge, fär; let, ēqual, tèrm; it, īce
hot, ōpen, ôrder; oil, out; cup, pút, rüle,
əbove, takən, pencəl, lemən, circəs
ch, child; ng, long; sh, ship
th, thin; ᴛʜ, then; zh, measure

frt. freight.

fruc·ti·fi·ca·tion (fruk′tə fə kā′shən) *n.* **1** a forming or bearing of fruit. **2** the fruit.

fruc·ti·fy (fruk′tə fī′) *v.* **-fied, -fy·ing. 1** bear fruit. **2** make fruitful; fertilize. [< F < L *fructificare* < *fructus* fruit + *facere* make]

fruc·tose (fruk′tōs) *n.* a sugar occurring in three different forms, especially the sweet form found in fruit juices, honey, etc. *Formula:* $C_6H_{12}O_6$ [< L *fructus* fruit]

fru·gal (frü′gəl) *adj.* **1** avoiding waste; saving; tending to avoid unnecessary spending: *A frugal housekeeper buys and uses food carefully.* **2** costing little; barely sufficient: *He ate a frugal supper of bread and milk.* [< L *frugalis,* ult. < *frux, frugis* fruit] —**fru′gal·ly,** *adv.*
☛ *Syn.* **1.** See note at **economical.**

fru·gal·i·ty (frü gal′ə tē) *n., pl.* **-ties.** thrift; avoidance of waste; a tendency to avoid unnecessary spending.

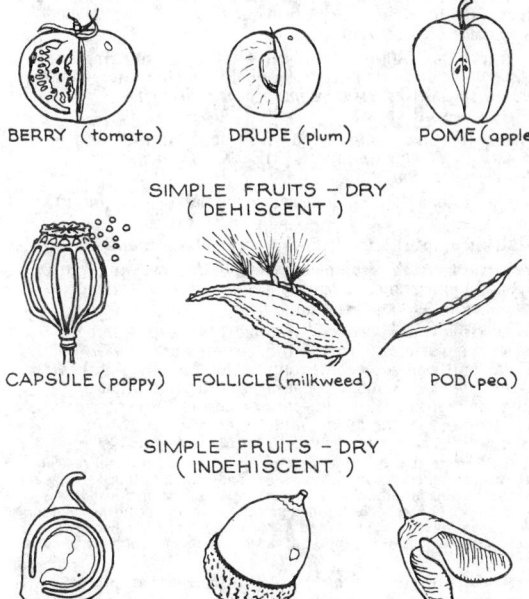

SIMPLE FRUITS – FLESHY
BERRY (tomato)   DRUPE (plum)   POME (apple)

SIMPLE FRUITS – DRY (DEHISCENT)
CAPSULE (poppy)   FOLLICLE (milkweed)   POD (pea)

SIMPLE FRUITS – DRY (INDEHISCENT)
ACHENE (buttercup)   NUT (oak)   SAMARA (maple)

Some types of simple fruit. Compound fruits include aggregate fruits (e.g. raspberry) and multiple fruits (e.g. pineapple).

fruit (früt) *n., v.* —*n.* **1** the sweet or tart, fleshy, edible, usually seed-bearing product of a flowering tree, shrub, or vine, usually eaten raw and as a dessert. Apples, oranges, raspberries, and saskatoons are fruits. **2** *Botany.* the part of a plant that contains the seeds. It is the ripened ovary of a flower and the tissues connected with the ovary. Pea pods, acorns, grains of wheat, cucumbers, tomatoes, etc. are fruits. **3** the useful product of plants: *the fruits of the earth.* **4** a product; result: *His invention was the fruit of much effort.* —*v.* produce or cause to produce fruit. [ME < OF < L *fructus* < *frui* enjoy] —**fruit′er,** *n.* —**fruit′like′,** *adj.*

fruit·age (früt′ij) *n.* **1** the bearing of fruit. **2** fruit; crop of fruit. **3** a product; result.

fruit·cake (früt′kāk′) *n.* **1** a rich cake containing preserved fruits, nuts, raisins, spices, etc. **2** *Slang.* a person considered to be weird or eccentric.

fruit cup mixed fruits served in a cup or glass as an appetizer or a dessert.

fruit·er·er (früt′ər ər) *n.* a dealer in fruit.

fruit fly 1 any of a family (Trypetidae) of small two-winged flies whose larvae feed on plant tissues. Many species are serious orchard pests because their larvae feed on fruits. 2 drosophila.

fruit·ful (früt′fəl) *adj.* 1 producing or bearing much fruit; productive or fertile: *a fruitful tree, a fruitful garden, fruitful soil.* 2 producing much of anything; especially producing good results: *a fruitful discussion. The trade mission proved to be fruitful.* 3 favorable to the growth of fruit or useful vegetation in general: *fruitful showers.* —**fruit′ful·ly,** *adv.* —**fruit′ful·ness,** *n.*

fru·i·tion (frü ish′ən) *n.* 1 the state of having results; fulfilment; realization: *Her plans have at last come to fruition.* 2 *Archaic.* the pleasure that comes from possession or use. 3 the bearing of fruit. [< LL fruitio, -onis < frui enjoy]

fruit·less (früt′lis) *adj.* 1 having no results; useless; unsuccessful. 2 producing no fruit; barren. —**fruit′less·ly,** *adv.*

fruit nappie or **fruit nappy** a small bowl or dish in which dessert such as fruit may be served.

fruit ranch a ranch or farm where fruit is raised.

fruit stand a small store or stand where fruit is sold.

fruit sugar 1 levulose. 2 a finely powdered form of cane sugar.

fruit tree any tree that bears edible fruit, especially a cultivated one.

fruit·wood (früt′wůd) *n., adj.* —*n.* the wood of fruit trees used in carvings, furniture, etc. —*adj* 1 of fruitwood. 2 related to the patterns or color of fruitwood.

fruit·y (früt′ē) *adj.* **fruit·i·er, fruit·i·est.** 1 tasting or smelling like fruit. 2 *Informal.* full of rich or strong quality; highly interesting, attractive, or suggestive: *His description was fruity but embarrassing.* —**fruit′i·ness,** *n.*

fru·men·ty (frü′mən tē) *n.* hulled wheat boiled in milk and flavored with sugar, cinnamon, etc. [ME < OF frumentee < frument < L frumentum grain]

frump (frump) *n.* a dowdy, unattractive woman or girl. [origin uncertain]

frump·ish (frump′ish) *adj.* frumpy. —**frump′ish·ly,** *adv.*

frump·y (frump′ē) *adj.* **frump·i·er, frump·i·est.** dowdy and out of style in general appearance: *a frumpy woman, a frumpy old coat.* —**frump′i·ly,** *adv.* —**frump′i·ness,** *n.*

frus·trate (frus′trāt) *v.* **-trat·ed, -trat·ing.** 1 bring to nothing; make useless or worthless: *Heavy rain frustrated our plan for a picnic.* 2 prevent from succeeding; oppose successfully; defeat: *to frustrate an opponent.* 3 make discouraged or discontented by preventing the realization of a purpose or desire: *It's very frustrating to stand in line for an hour to get into a movie and then not get seats.* [< L frustrari < frustra in vain] —**frus′trat·er,** *n.*
☛ *Syn.* 1, 2. **Frustrate, thwart, baffle** = keep from doing something. **Frustrate** emphasizes making all efforts and plans useless and vain, and thus keeping a person from achieving his aim: *The boy's waywardness frustrated his father's plans for his future.* **Thwart** = block someone's effort by some contrary action: *The sudden storm thwarted the men who were trying to reach the wrecked plane.* **Baffle** suggests causing confusion or bewilderment: *The absence of clues baffled the police.*

frus·trat·ed (frus′trā təd) *adj.* 1 foiled or defeated in one's chosen or desired goal: *He makes a good living as an accountant, but he's actually a frustrated painter.* 2 filled with frustration; feeling discontented or discouraged because of not being able to fulfil one's desires or purposes: *Everything had gone wrong that day, and by evening she was so frustrated, she couldn't enjoy the show. He's just a frustrated old busybody.*

frus·tra·tion (frus trā′shən) *n.* 1 the act of frustrating. 2 the state or condition of being frustrated: *After spending two hours trying to find the place, she gave up in frustration.* 3 a feeling of discontent or discouragement, because of not being able to achieve one's desires: *He takes out his frustrations on unsuspecting customers.* 4 something that frustrates: *the frustrations of city driving.*

frus·tum (frus′təm) *n.* **-tums, -ta** (-tə). 1 *Geometry.* the part of a cone-shaped solid left after the top has been cut off by a plane parallel to the base. 2 the part of a solid between two cutting planes, especially two parallel planes. [< L frustum piece]

fry¹ (frī) *v.* **fried, fry·ing;** *n., pl.* **fries.** —*v.* 1 cook in a pan or on a griddle over direct heat, usually in hot fat or oil. 2 undergo frying: *While the hamburgers were frying, he set the table.* —*n.* 1 fried food; a dish of fried meat, fish, etc. 2 a social gathering at which food is fried and eaten: *a fish fry.* [ME < OF frire < L frigere]

fry² (frī) *n., pl.* **fry.** 1 a young fish, from the time that it is hatched and free-swimming. 2 small adult fish, such as sardines, that live together in large schools. 3 the young of any of various other animals. 4 children. 5 See also **small fry.** [ME < ON frjó seed]

fry·er (frī′ər) *n.* 1 a chicken young and tender enough for frying. A fryer usually weighs less than 1.5 kg. 2 a deep utensil for deep-frying food.

frying pan a shallow pan with a long handle, used for frying food.
out of the frying pan into the fire, straight from one danger or difficulty into a worse one.

fry pan or **fry·pan** (frī′pan′) *n.* frying pan.

ft. 1 foot; feet. 2 fort.

fth. or **fthm.** fathom.

fuch·sia (fyü′shə) *n., adj.* —*n.* 1 any of a genus (Fuchsia) of mostly tropical shrubs of the evening-primrose family having showy, hanging flowers of pink, purple, or red. Fuchsias are widely cultivated as pot plants. 2 an intense purplish red or purplish pink. [< NL; after Leonard Fuchs (1501-1566), a German botanist]

fud·dle (fud′əl) *v.* **-dled, -dling.** 1 make stupid with alcohol; intoxicate. 2 confuse; muddle. [origin uncertain]

fud·dy-dud·dy (fud′ē dud′ē) *n., pl.* **-dies;** *adj. Informal.* —*n.* a fussy or stuffy old-fashioned person. —*adj.* obsolete; old-fashioned. [origin uncertain]

fudge¹ (fuj) *n.* a soft candy made of sugar, milk, butter, and a flavoring such as chocolate or caramel. [origin unknown]

fudge² (fuj) *n., interj., v.* **-fudged, fudg·ing.** —*n.* 1 an item of last-minute news or other material added to the type page or printing plate of a newspaper page. 2 nonsense; empty talk: *That's a lot of fudge.*
—*interj.* a word used to express annoyance or disbelief.
—*v.* 1 insert (an item of last-minute news, etc.) into a type page or printing plate. 2 avoid committing oneself on an issue or coming to grips with a problem; hedge; waffle: *Don't let him fudge on the issue.* 3 put together in a makeshift or dishonest way; fake. 4 cheat or welsh: *to fudge on a promise.* [? < obs. fadge make fit, adjust]

Fueh·rer (fyü′rər; *German,* fv′rər) See **Führer.**

fu·el (fyü′əl) *n., v.* **-elled** or **-eled, -el·ling** or **-el·ing.** —*n.* 1 something burned to provide heat or power: *Coal, wood, gas, and oil are fuels.* 2 a material from which atomic energy can be obtained, as in a reactor. 3 material that supplies nutrients for a living organism: *Your body needs fuel to live and grow.* 4 anything that keeps up or increases a feeling: *His insults were fuel to her hatred.*
—*v.* 1 supply with fuel. 2 get fuel. [ME < OF fouaille, ult. < L focus hearth]

fuel cell an electric cell that produces electrical energy directly from the oxidation of a fuel that is continuously added to the cell.

fu·gal (fyü′gəl) *adj.* of, having to do with or in the style of a fugue.

fu·gi·tive (fyü′jə tiv) *n., adj.* —*n.* a person who is fleeing or who has fled: *The murderer became a fugitive from justice.*
—*adj.* 1 fleeing; having fled; runaway. 2 lasting only a very short time; passing swiftly: *fugitive thoughts, the fugitive hours.* 3 of literary works, being of passing interest. 4 moving about; shifting or roving. [ME < OF < L fugitivus < fugere flee] —**fu′gi·tive·ly,** *adv.* —**fu′gi·tive·ness,** *n.*

fugue (fyüg) *n. Music.* a contrapuntal composition based on one or more short themes in which different voices or instruments repeat the same melody with slight variations. [< F < Ital. < L fuga flight]

Füh·rer (fyü′rər; *German,* fv′rər) *n. German.* the title given to Adolf Hitler (1889-1945), the German dictator. Führer means leader.

–ful *suffix.* 1 full of, as in *cheerful.* 2 characterized by or having the qualities of, as in *careful, masterful.* 3 having a tendency or the ability to, as in *forgetful, harmful, mournful.* 4 enough to fill, as in *cupful, handful.* [OE; representing full, adj.]

ful·crum (fůl′krəm or ful′krəm) *n., pl.* **-crums, -cra** (-krə). a support on which a lever turns or rests in moving or lifting something. [< L fulcrum bedpost < fulcire support]

ful·fil or **ful·fill** (fůl fil′) *v.* **-filled, -fill·ing.** 1 carry out (a promise, prophecy, etc.); cause to happen or take place. 2 do or perform (a duty); obey (a command, law, etc.). 3 satisfy (a requirement, condition, etc.); serve (a purpose): *to fulfil a need.* 4 finish; complete: *to fulfil a contract.* [OE fullfyllan] —**ful·fill′er,** *n.*

ful·fil·ment or **ful·fill·ment** (fůl fil′mənt) *n.* fulfilling or being fulfilled; completion; accomplishment: *Winning the race brought him a feeling of fulfilment.*

full¹ (fůl) *adj., adv., n.* —*adj.* 1 able to hold no more; with no empty space; filled: *a full cup.* 2 complete; entire: *a full supply, a full treatment. I waited a full hour.* 3 of the greatest size, amount, extent, development, etc.: *He was running at full speed. The rose is in full bloom.* 4 more than enough to satisfy: *She ate a full meal.*

5 having had enough food: *a full stomach. He was full after the first course.* 6 very: *He knew full well that he would have to go back.* 7 plump; round; well filled out: *a full face.* 8 having a large amount or number (*used with of*): *Her room was full of toys. The lake is full of fish.* 9 made with a large amount of material, in gathers, folds, pleats, etc.: *a full skirt, full sleeves.* 10 of the highest grade or rank: *a full professor.* 11 of sound, strong and deep; sonorous: *a full alto voice.* 12 completely taken up with; absorbed (*used with of*): *He's full of his latest project.*
—*adv.* 1 completely; entirely. 2 squarely; directly: *The blow hit him full in the face.*
—*n.*
the full, the greatest size, amount, etc.: *The moon is past the full. He was determined to satisfy his curiosity to the full.*
in full, a to or for the complete amount: *The account has been paid in full.* **b** written or said with all the words; not shortened: *Write your name in full.*
[OE]

full² (fùl) *v.* clean and thicken (cloth). [< *fuller*]

full·back (fùl′bak′) *n.* Football, etc. a player whose position is farthest behind the front line.

full blast *Informal.* in full operation; at highest speed or largest capacity.

full-blood·ed (fùl′blud′id) *adj.* 1 of pure race, breed, or strain; thoroughbred. 2 vigorous; hearty.

full-blown (fùl′blōn′) *adj.* 1 in full bloom. 2 completely developed or matured.

full-bod·ied (fùl′bod′ēd) *adj.* having considerable strength, flavor, etc.: *a full-bodied wine.*

full dress the formal clothes worn for important social or ceremonial occasions.

full-dress (fùl′dres′) *adj.* 1 having to do with or requiring full dress; formal: *a full-dress reception.* 2 utilizing all resources; all-out; exhaustive: *a full-dress report, a full-dress debate.*

full·er (fùl′ər) *n.* a person whose work is cleaning and thickening cloth. [OE *fullere* < L *fullo* fuller]

fuller's earth a soft, clay-like mixture used for removing grease from cloth and for purifying oil.

full-fash·ioned (fùl′fash′ənd) *adj.* knitted to fit the shape of the foot, leg, or body.

full-fledged (fùl′flejd′) *adj.* 1 fully developed. 2 of full rank or standing.

full-grown (fùl′grōn′) *adj.* fully grown; mature.

full house 1 Theatre, etc. the fact or state of every seat being occupied. 2 Poker. a hand made up of three cards of one kind and two of another, such as three sixes and two kings.

full-length (fùl′length′ or -lengkth′) *adj.* 1 showing or for the full length of the human figure: *a full-length portrait, a full-length mirror.* 2 reaching almost to the floor: *full-length windows, a full-length dress.* 3 of traditional or standard size, length, duration, etc.: *a full-length novel, a full-length chesterfield, a full-length coat.*

full moon 1 the moon seen with the whole disk illuminated. 2 the period when this occurs. See **moon** for picture.

full nelson *Wrestling.* a hold applied by hooking both arms under the opponent's with the hands gripped behind the opponent's neck.

full·ness (fùl′nis) *n.* the state or condition of being full. Also, **fulness.**
in the fullness of time, in due course.

full-rigged (fùl′rigd′) *adj.* 1 of a sailing ship, completely equipped with masts and sails. 2 completely equipped.

full sail 1 with all sails set. 2 with all possible power and energy.

full-scale (fùl′skāl′) *adj.* 1 made in the original or actual size: *a full-scale drawing, a full-scale working model.* 2 using or involving all available resources; total or all-out: *a full-scale investigation, full-scale fighting.*

full stop Punctuation. period.

full swing 1 full operation; vigorous activity or movement: *The party was in full swing.* 2 with vigor: *He ran full swing.*

full-throat·ed (fùl′thrōt′id) *adj.* 1 clamorous and loud; vociferous. 2 rich and full in sound; sonorous.

full-time (fùl′tīm′) *adj. or adv.* for the usual or normal length of time: *Full-time clerk wanted* (adj.). *The plant employs men full-time only* (adv.).

ful·ly (fùl′ē) *adv.* 1 in a full manner or degree; completely: *She was now fully awake. He could not fully describe what he had seen.* 2 abundantly; plentifully: *fully covered by insurance.* 3 at least: *It was fully three hours before they could reach her.*

ful·mar (fùl′mər) *n.* any of various heavily built, gull-like sea birds (family Procellariidae) of polar regions, especially an arctic

hat, āge, fär; let, ēqual, tèrm; it, īce
hot, ōpen, ôrder; oil, out; cup, pùt, rüle,
above, takən, pencəl, lemən, circəs

ch, child; ng, long; sh, ship
th, thin; ŦH, then; zh, measure

bird (*Fulmarus glacialis*) having two color phases: a mainly white phase with grey back and wings and a smoky grey phase. Fulmars belong to the same family as the shearwaters. [< ON *fúll* foul + *már* gull; from the foul-smelling liquid it ejects in self-defence]

ful·mi·nate (fùl′mə nāt′) *v.* **-nat·ed, -nat·ing;** *n.* —*v.* 1 thunder forth (censure, threats, decrees, etc.): *The churches and the newspapers fulminated against the crime wave.* 2 denounce violently; censure strongly. 3 explode violently. 4 of a disease, develop suddenly and severely. 5 thunder and lighten.
—*n.* 1 a violent explosive. 2 a salt of fulminic acid. The fulminates, chiefly mercury and silver, are very unstable compounds, exploding with great violence by percussion or heating. [< L *fulminare* < *fulmen* lightning] —**ful′mi·na′tor,** *n.*

ful·mi·na·tion (fùl′mə nā′shən) *n.* 1 a violent denunciation; strong censure. 2 a violent explosion.

fulminic acid *Chemistry.* an acid encountered only in its salts, the fulminates, which are highly explosive. *Formula:* CNOH

ful·ness (fùl′nis) See **fullness.**

ful·some (fùl′səm *or* fùl′səm) *adj.* 1 offensive or distasteful because of excessiveness, insincerity, etc.: *fulsome praise.* 2 abundant; profuse: *a fulsome harvest, fulsome detail.* 3 Archaic. loathsome. [< *full* + *-some¹*; influenced in meaning by *foul*] —**ful′some·ly,** *adv.* —**ful′some·ness,** *n.*

fu·ma·gil·lin (fyü′mə gil′in) *n.* an antibiotic derived from a fungus, used especially against amoebic infections. *Formula:* $C_{26}H_{34}O_7$

fu·ma·role (fyü′mə rōl′) *n.* in volcanic areas, an opening in the earth's crust from which steam and gases issue: *There are many fumaroles near Katmai volcano in Alaska.* [< F *fumarolle* < Ital. *fumaruolo* < LL *fumariolum* smoke hole, ult. < L *fumus* smoke]

fum·ble (fum′bəl) *v.* **-bled, -bling;** *n.* —*v.* 1 feel or grope about clumsily; search awkwardly: *He fumbled about in his pockets for the ticket. Jane fumbled for words to express her thanks.* 2 handle awkwardly: *He fumbled the introduction.* 3 Sports. fail to catch and hold (a ball).
—*n.* 1 an awkward groping or handling. 2 Sports. a failure to catch and hold a ball. [cf. LG *fummeln*] —**fum′bler,** *n.* —**fum′bling·ly,** *adv.*

fume (fyüm) *n., v.* **fumed, fum·ing.** —*n.* 1 Usually, **fumes,** *pl.* a vapor, gas, or smoke, especially if harmful, strong, or odorous: *The strong fumes of the acid nearly choked him.* 2 an angry or irritable mood: *She was obviously in a fume.*
—*v.* 1 give off fumes. 2 pass off in fumes. 3 be in a state of anger or great irritation: *By the time we got there he was fuming.* 4 treat with fumes. [ME < OF *fum* < L *fumus* smoke] —**fum′er,** *n.*

fumed oak oak darkened and colored by exposure to ammonia fumes.

fu·mi·gate (fyü′mə gāt′) *v.* **-gat·ed, -gat·ing.** expose to fumes in order to kill vermin or to disinfect: *The whole apartment building needs to be fumigated.* [< L *fumigare* to smoke < *fumus* smoke, *fume*] —**fu′mi·ga′tion,** *n.*

fu·mi·ga·tor (fyü′mə gā′tər) *n.* 1 a person who fumigates. 2 an apparatus for fumigating.

fun (fun) *n., v.* **funned, fun·ning.** —*n.* 1 lively play or playfulness; amusement: *an evening full of fun.* 2 a source of amusement: *That game is a lot of fun.* 3 (adjl.) Informal. amusing or entertaining: *It was a fun evening.* 4 ridicule: *He became a figure of fun.*
for fun or **in fun,** not seriously; as a joke; playfully: *The trick was meant in fun.*
make fun of or **poke fun at,** laugh at; ridicule.
—*v.* Informal. act or speak in fun. [? originally v., var. of obs. *fon* befool]

func·tion (fungk′shən) *n., v.* —*n.* 1 proper work; normal action or use; purpose: *The function of the stomach is to digest food.* 2 a formal public or social gathering for some purpose: *All the local dignitaries attended the great function to welcome the Queen.* 3 Mathematics. quantity whose value depends on, or varies with, the value given to one or more related quantities: *The volume of a sphere is a function of the radius.* 4 anything likened to a mathematical function. 5 Grammar. the position or positions in which a linguistic form occurs in an utterance.
—*v.* 1 work; be used; act: *My new pen does not function very well.* 2 have a function; serve (as): *That heavy old china ornament functions as a doorstop now.* [< L *functio, -onis* < *fungi* perform]

func·tion·al (fungk'shən əl) *adj.* **1** of or having to do with a function or functions. **2** having a function; working; acting. **3** stressing usefulness instead of beauty: *a functional approach to furniture design.* **4** designed or developed mainly from the point of view of usefulness: *functional clothing.* **5** *Medicine.* affecting the function of an organ or part of the body, but not its structure: *functional heart disease.* —**func'tion·al·ly,** *adv.*

functional illiterate a person whose ability to read is too poor for practical purposes.

func·tion·al·ism (fungk'shə nə liz'əm) *n. Architecture and design.* the principle that the design of a structure should be determined primarily by its purpose or function.

func·tion·ar·y (fungk'shən er'ē) *n., pl.* **-ar·ies;** *adj.* official.

fund (fund) *n., v.* —*n.* **1** a sum of money set aside for a special purpose: *The school has a fund of $1000 to buy books with.* **2** a stock or store ready for use; supply: *There is a fund of information in a dictionary.* **3** **funds,** *pl.* money available for use: *He had to cancel his trip because he ran out of funds.*
—*v.* **1** provide funds for: *A summer recreation program is being funded by the community association.* **2** set aside a sum of money to pay the interest on (a debt). **3** change (a debt) from a short term to a long term. **4** put into a fund or store; collect; store up. [< L *fundus* bottom, a piece of land]

fun·da·ment (fun'də mənt) *n. Usually facetious.* buttocks. [< L *fundamentum,* ult. < L *fundus* bottom]

fun·da·men·tal (fun'də men'təl) *adj., n.* —*adj.* **1** of or forming a foundation or basis; essential; basic: *the fundamental principles of design.* **2** involving or affecting a basic structure, function, etc.; radical: *a fundamental change of attitude.* **3** principal; main: *The fundamental purpose of her campaign is to block the legislation.* **4** *Music.* having to do with the lowest note of a chord.
—*n.* **1** a principle, rule, law, etc. that forms a foundation or basis; essential part: *the fundamentals of grammar.* **2** *Music.* the lowest note of a chord. **3** *Physics.* the component of a wave that has the greatest wave length. [< NL *fundamentalis* < L *fundamentum* foundation, ult. < L *fundus* bottom] —**fun'da·men'tal·ly,** *adv.*

fun·da·men·tal·ism (fun'də men'təl iz'əm) *n.* **1** the belief that the words of the Bible were inspired by God and should be believed and followed literally. **2** Often, **Fundamentalism,** a movement in certain churches upholding this belief.

fun·da·men·tal·ist (fun'də men'təl ist) *n.* a person who believes in fundamentalism. Fundamentalists refuse to accept any teaching that conflicts with the Bible.

fu·ner·al (fyü'nər əl *or* fyün'rəl) *n.* **1** the ceremonies that accompany the burial or burning of the dead, which usually include holding a religious service and taking the body to the place of burial. **2** the procession taking a dead person's body to the place where it is to be buried or burned. **3** (*adj.*) of or suitable for a funeral: *A funeral march is very slow.* [< LL *funeralis* of a funeral < L *funus, funeris* funeral, death]

funeral director a person who manages a funeral home; undertaker.

funeral home a business establishment that makes arrangements for or conducts funeral services and has facilities for preparing the bodies of the dead for burial or cremation.

funeral parlor *or* **parlour** funeral home.

fu·ner·ar·y (fyü'nər er'ē) *adj.* of a funeral or burial: *A funerary urn holds the ashes of a dead person's body.*

fu·ne·re·al (fyü nēr'ē əl) *adj.* **1** of or suitable for a funeral. **2** sad; gloomy; dismal. [< L *funereus* < *funus, -neris* funeral] —**fu·ne're·al·ly,** *adv.*

fun fair **1** a local fund-raising bazaar offering many attractions for children. **2** *Brit.* an amusement park.

fun·gal (fung'gəl) *adj., n.* —*adj.* fungous. —*n.* fungus.

fun·gi (fung'gī; fung'gē, fun'jī *or* fun'jē) *n. pl.* of **fungus.**

fun·gi·cid·al (fung'gə sīd'əl *or* fun'jə sīd'əl) *adj.* that destroys fungi.

fun·gi·cide (fung'gə sīd' *or* fun'jə sīd') *n.* any substance that destroys fungi. [< L *fungus* + E *-cide²*]

fun·goid (fung'goid) *adj.* resembling a fungus; having spongy, unhealthful growths.

fun·gous (fung'gəs) *adj.* **1** of a fungus or of fungi; like a fungus; spongy. **2** growing or springing up suddenly, but not lasting. **3** caused by a fungus. [< L *fungosos* < *fungus* fungus]

fun·gus (fung'gəs) *n., pl.* **fun·gi** *or* **fun·gus·es.** **1** any of a major group (Fungi) of plantlike organisms that lack chlorophyll and also lack the characteristic plant structures such as stems, leaves, and roots. The group includes yeasts, molds, rusts, mildews,

mushrooms, etc. It is usually classified as a division of the plant kingdom, but some taxonomists place the group in the kingdom Protista, along with the bacteria, protozoans, etc., while others propose classifying it as a separate kingdom. **2** something that grows or springs up rapidly like a mushroom. **3** a diseased, spongy growth on the skin. **4** (*adj.*) fungous. [< L; probably akin to Gk. *sphongos* sponge]

fu·nic·u·lar (fyü nik'yə lər) *adj.* of, hanging from, or operated by a rope or cable. A **funicular railway** is a railway system in which the cars are moved by cables. [< L *funiculus,* dim. of *funis* rope]

funk (fungk) *n., v. Informal.* —*n.* **1** a state of extreme fear; panic. **2** a depressed mood: *He's been in a funk since he and his girlfriend broke up.* **3** coward.
—*v.* **1** be afraid; shrink back or flinch. **2** frighten. [origin uncertain]

funk·y¹ (fungk'ē) *adj.* **funk·i·er, funk·i·est.** *Informal.* being in a state of panic or mental depression.

funk·y² (fungk'ē) *adj.* **funk·i·er, funk·i·est.** *Informal.* **1** *Music.* of or having an earthy, emotional blues style. **2** offbeat, especially in a campy or earthy way: *funky clothes, a funky restaurant.*

A funnel for pouring

fun·nel (fun'əl) *n., v.* **-nelled** *or* **-neled, -nel·ling** *or* **-nel·ing.** —*n.* **1** a tapering tube with a wide, cone-shaped mouth, used for pouring a liquid or powder into a container with a small opening: *He used a funnel to pour the gas into the tank.* **2** anything shaped like a funnel. **3** a cylindrical metal chimney; smokestack: *The steamship had two funnels.* **4** flue.
—*v.* pass or feed through or as if through a funnel. [ME < OF *fonel* < LL *fundibulum* < L *infundibulum* < *in-* in + *fundere* pour]

fun·ny (fun'ē) *adj.* **-ni·er, -ni·est;** *n., pl.* **-nies.** —*adj.* **1** causing laughter; amusing or comical: *a funny story, a funny accident. My little brother was very funny the first time he tried to skate.* **2** trying or intended to amuse: *She was just being funny.* **3** *Informal.* strange; peculiar; odd: *That's funny; I thought I left my wallet right here. He said he went home because his stomach was feeling funny.* **4** deceptive or tricky: *Don't try anything funny or you might get hurt.*
—*n.* **funnies,** *pl. Informal.* **a** comic strips. **b** a section of a newspaper devoted to comic strips: *Who's got the funnies?* [< *fun*] —**fun'ni·ly,** *adv.* —**fun'ni·ness,** *n.*

☛ *Syn. adj.* **1. Funny, laughable** = such as to cause laughter or amusement. **Funny** particularly suggests being unusual or extraordinary in a way that causes amusement or laughter: *The funny little man and his funny little children keep our neighborhood smiling.* **Laughable** is the general word meaning "ridiculous, fit to cause or causing laughter": *His fine airs are laughable.*

funny bone **1** the part of the elbow over which a nerve passes. When the funny bone is struck, a sharp, tingling sensation is felt in the arm and hand. **2** sense of humor: *The comment struck her funny bone and she burst out laughing.*

funny paper *or* **papers** the section of a newspaper containing the comic strips.

fur (fėr) *n., v.* **furred, fur·ring.** —*n.* **1** the thick covering of hair on the skin of certain animals. **2** skin with such hair on it: *Fur is used to make, cover, trim, or line clothing.* **3** (*adj.*) made of fur. **4** Usually, **furs,** *pl.* a garment made of fur. **5** a furlike coating, such as the whitish matter on the tongue during illness.
make the fur fly, *Informal.* cause trouble; quarrel; fight.
—*v.* **1** make, cover, trim, or line with fur. **2** coat or become coated with a furlike matter, such as on the tongue during illness. **3** fasten thin strips of wood to (beams, walls, etc.) to make a support for laths, etc. or to provide air spaces. [ME < OF *forrer* line, encase < *forre* sheath < Gmc.] —**fur'less,** *adj.*
☛ *Hom.* **fir.**

fur. **1** furlong. **2** furnished.

fur·be·low (fėr'bə lō') *n., v.* —*n.* a bit of elaborate trimming: *a dress with many frills and furbelows.* —*v.* trim in an elaborate way. [var., by folk etymology, of F dial. *ferbalaw, farbala,* var. of F *falbala*]

fur·bish (fėr'bish) *v.* **1** brighten by rubbing or scouring; polish: *He furbished up the rusty sword.* **2** restore to good condition; make usable again (*usually used with* **up**): *Before going to France, he furbished up his half-forgotten French.* [ME < OF *forbiss-,* a stem of *forbir* polish < Gmc.] —**fur'bish·er,** *n.*

fur brigade *Cdn. Historical.* a convoy of freight canoes, dogsleds, York boats, etc. that carried furs and other goods to and from remote trading posts.

fur·cate (fėr′kāt or fėr′kit) *adj.* forked. [< Med.L *furcatus* cloven < L *furca* fork]

fur·fur·al (fėr′fə ral′ or fėr′fə ral′) *n.* a liquid aldehyde made by distilling corn cobs, oat hulls, etc. It is used in manufacturing dyes and plastics, in refining oil, etc. *Formula:* $C_5H_4O_2$ [< *furfur*ane + *al*dehyde]

Fu·ries (fyür′ēz) *n.pl.* Greek and Roman mythology. the three spirits of revenge; Erinyes.

fu·ri·ous (fyür′ē əs) *adj.* 1 intensely violent; raging: *a furious storm.* 2 full of wild, fierce anger. 3 of unrestrained energy, speed, etc.: *furious activity.* [< L *furiosus* < *furia* fury] —**fu′ri·ous·ly,** *adv.* —**fu′ri·ous·ness,** *n.*

furl (fėrl) *v., n.* —*v.* roll up; fold up; curl: *to furl a sail, furl a flag.* —*n.* 1 the act of furling. 2 the manner in which a sail, flag, etc. is furled. 3 a roll, coil, or curl of anything furled. [< F *ferler* < OF *ferlir* < *fer* firm (< L *firmus*) + *lier* bind < L *ligare*] —**furl′er,** *n.*

fur·long (fėr′lông) *n.* a unit for measuring distance equal to one-eighth of a mile (about 0.2 km). *Abbrev.:* fur. [OE *furlang* < *furh* furrow + *lang* long]

fur·lough (fėr′lō) *n., v.* —*n.* a leave of absence, especially for a soldier. —*v.* give leave of absence to. [< Du. *verlof*]

fur·nace (fėr′nis) *n.* 1 an enclosed structure for providing heat for buildings by warming water or air that circulates through pipes and radiators, hot-air registers, etc. 2 an enclosed structure for providing intense heat for use in separating metal from ore, in treating metal, in producing coke, etc. 3 a very hot place: *The room was a furnace when the windows were closed.* 4 a severe test. [ME < OF *fornais, fornaise* < L *fornax, -acis* < *fornus* oven]

fur·nish (fėr′nish) *v.* 1 supply; provide: *The sun furnishes heat.* 2 supply (a room, house, etc.) with furniture, equipment, etc. [< OF *furniss-,* a stem of *furnir* accomplish < Gmc.] —**fur′nish·er,** *n.*

☞ *Syn.* 1, 2. **Furnish, equip** = provide or supply. **Furnish** = provide things or services necessary for existence or wanted for use or comfort: *We furnished the living room. The caterer furnished both food and waiters. Furnish one good reason.* **Equip** = fit out with what is needed to do work or to work with: *We equipped the kitchen. He is not equipped to translate Latin.*

fur·nish·ings (fėr′nish ingz) *n.pl.* 1 the furniture or equipment for a room, house, etc. 2 accessories of dress; articles of clothing: *That store sells men's furnishings.*

fur·ni·ture (fėr′nə chər) *n.* 1 the movable articles needed in a room, house, etc.: *Beds, chairs, tables, and desks are furniture.* 2 *Archaic.* articles needed; equipment: *The harness and ornamental coverings for a horse were called furniture in the Middle Ages.* 3 apparatus, appliances, or instruments for work, now especially the tools, utensils, rigging, stores, and tackle of a ship. 4 *Printing.* strips or blocks of wood or metal, lower than type-high, set in and about pages of type to fill out large white areas such as margins. [< F *fourniture*]

fu·ror (fyür′ôr) *n.* 1 an outburst of wild enthusiasm or excitement among a group; uproar: *There was a great furor in the crowd when the announcement was made.* 2 an inspired or excited mood: *He wrote the poem in a furor.* 3 fury; rage. [< F *fureur* < L *furor* < *furere* rage]

fu·rore (fyü′rôr or fyə rôr′ē) *n.* furor. [< Ital. *furore* < L *furor*]

furred (fėrd) *adj.* 1 having fur. 2 made, covered, trimmed, or lined with fur. 3 wearing fur. 4 coated with matter suggesting fur: *A furred tongue is a sign of illness.* 5 provided with furring strips: *a furred wall.*

fur·ri·er (fėr′ē ər) *n.* 1 a dealer in furs. 2 a person whose work is preparing furs or making and repairing fur garments.

fur·ri·er·y (fėr′ē ər ē) *n., pl.* **-er·ies.** 1 furs. 2 the business or work of a furrier.

fur·ring (fėr′ing) *n.* 1 fur used to make, cover, trim, or line clothing. 2 a coating of matter suggesting fur. 3 the application of thin strips of wood to beams, walls, etc. to make a level support for laths, etc. or to provide air spaces. 4 the strips used for this, also called **furring strips.**

fur·row (fėr′ō) *n., v.* —*n.* 1 a long, narrow groove or track cut in the ground by a plough. 2 any long, narrow groove or track: *Heavy trucks made deep furrows in the muddy road.* 3 a wrinkle. —*v.* 1 make furrows in. 2 wrinkle: *His face was furrowed with age.* [OE *furh*]

fur·ry (fėr′ē) *adj.* **-ri·er, -ri·est.** 1 consisting of fur. 2 covered with or wearing fur: *a little furry animal.* 3 looking or feeling like fur. 4 coated or covered as if with fur: *a furry tongue.* —**fur′ri·ness,** *n.*

fur seal any of various eared seals highly valued as a source of sealskin because of their thick coats with fine underfur. The **northern fur seal** (*Callorhinus ursinus*) of the N Pacific Ocean is one of the most important for the fur trade.

fur·ther (fėr′ᴛʜər) *adj., adv.* (a comparative of **far**); *v.* —*adj.*

---

hat, āge, fär; let, ēqual, tėrm; it, īce
hot, ōpen, ôrder; oil, out; cup, pùt, rüle,
əbove, takən, pencəl, lemən, circəs

ch, child; ng, long; sh, ship
th, thin; ᴛʜ, then; zh, measure

1 farther; more distant: *on the further side.* 2 more: *Have you any further need of me?* —*adv.* 1 at or to a greater distance. 2 to a greater extent. 3 moreover; furthermore; besides: *He said further that he would support us in any way he could.* —*v.* help forward; promote. [OE *furthra,* adj., *furthor,* adv. < *forth* forth]

☞ *Syn. v.* See note at **promote.**
☞ *Usage.* See note at **farther.**

fur·ther·ance (fėr′ᴛʜər əns) *n.* an act of furthering; helping forward; advancement; promotion.

fur·ther·more (fėr′ᴛʜər môr′) *adv.* moreover; also; besides.

fur·ther·most (fėr′ᴛʜər mōst′) *adj.* furthest.

fur·thest (fėr′ᴛʜist) *adv. or adj.* (a superlative of **far**). 1 to or at the greatest degree or extent. 2 to or at the greatest distance in space or time. [ME]

fur·tive (fėr′tiv) *adj.* 1 done stealthily; secret: *He made a furtive attempt to read his sister's letter.* 2 sly; stealthy; shifty: *The thief had a furtive manner.* [< L *furtivus* < *fur* thief] —**fur′tive·ly,** *adv.* —**fur′tive·ness,** *n.*

fu·run·cle (fyür′ung kəl) *n. Medicine.* a boil; inflammatory sore. [< L *furunculus,* dim. of *fur* thief]

fu·ry (fyür′ē) *n., pl.* **-ries.** 1 wild, fierce anger; a rage. 2 violence; fierceness. 3 a raging or violent person. 4 unrestrained energy, speed, etc.: *work with fury.* 5 **Fury,** *Greek and Roman mythology.* any one of the three spirits of revenge.
like fury, *Informal.* violently; very rapidly.
[< L *furia*]

☞ *Syn.* 1. See note at **rage.**

furze (fėrz) *n.* 1 a low, prickly, European evergreen shrub (*Ulex europaeus*) of the pea family having yellow flowers, common on wastelands; gorse. 2 any of several related plants. [OE *fyrs*]

fuse¹ (fyüz) *n., v.* **fused, fus·ing.** —*n.* 1 a wick or a long, narrow sheath filled with combustible powder used to ignite an explosive charge from a safe distance. 2 any of various mechanical or electrical devices for detonating a bomb, shell, etc. —*v.* fit or provide with a fuse. [< Ital. *fuso* < L *fusus* spindle]

fuse² (fyüz) *n., v.* **fused, fus·ing.** —*n.* a safety device in an electric circuit consisting of or containing a metal strip or wire that melts when the current exceeds a specific amperage, thus breaking the circuit.
—*v.* 1 melt or melt together, especially by the action of heat. 2 blend or unite as if by melting together. 3 cease or cause to cease functioning because of the melting of a fuse: *The lights fused when we turned on the heater.* [< L *fusus,* pp. of *fundere* pour, melt]

fu·see (fyü zē′) *n.* 1 a large-headed match that will burn in a wind. 2 a flare used by railways as a signal: *A fusee burns with a red or green light.* Also. **fuzee.** [< F *fusée* spindleful < OF *fus spindle < L *fusus*]

fu·se·lage (fyü′zə läzh′ or fyü′zə lij) *n.* the body of an aircraft that holds passengers, cargo, etc. The wings and tail are attached to the fuselage. See **airplane** for picture. [< F *fuselage* < *fuselé* spindle-shaped]

fu·sel oil (fyü′zəl) a sharp or bitter, poisonous, oily liquid that occurs in alcoholic liquors when they are not distilled enough. [*fusel* < G *Fusel* bad liquor]

fu·si·bil·i·ty (fyü′ze bil′ə tē) *n.* the quality of being fusible.

fu·si·ble (fyü′zə bəl) *adj.* that can be fused or melted. —**fus′si·ble·ness,** *n.*

fu·si·form (fyü′zə fôrm′) *adj.* rounded and tapering from the middle toward each end; spindle-shaped: *A milkweed pod is somewhat fusiform.* [< L *fusus* spindle + E *-form*]

fu·sil (fyü′zəl) *n.* a light flintlock musket. [< F *fusil* steel for tinder box, ult. < L *focus* hearth]

fu·sil·eer (fyü′zə lēr′) See **fusilier.**

fu·sil·ier (fyü′zə lēr′) *n.* 1 *Historical.* a soldier armed with a light flintlock musket called a fusil. 2 a private soldier in a regiment that used to be armed with fusils. [< F *fusilier* < *fusil* musket]

fu·sil·lade (fyü′zə lād′) *n., v.* **-lad·ed, -lad·ing.** —*n.* 1 a discharge of many firearms at the same time or in rapid succession. 2 something that resembles a fusillade: *The reporters greeted the*

mayor with a fusillade of questions. —*v.* attack or shoot down by a fusillade. [< F *fusillade* < *fusiller* shoot < *fusil* musket]

fu·sion (fyü′zhən) *n.* **1** a melting; melting together; fusing: *Bronze is made by the fusion of copper and tin.* **2** a blending; union: *A new party was formed by the fusion of two political groups.* **3** a fused mass. **4** *Nuclear physics.* the combining of two nuclei to create a nucleus of greater mass: *The fusion of atomic nuclei releases tremendous amounts of energy, which can be used in such things as the hydrogen or fusion bomb.* [< L *fusio, -onis* < *fundere* pour, melt]

fusion bomb a nuclear bomb using the principle of fusion, rather than fission, to produce an explosion. The hydrogen bomb is a fusion bomb.

fu·sion·ist (fyü′zhən ist) *n.* a person taking part in a union of political parties or factions.

fuss (fus) *n., v.* —*n.* **1** too much bother about small matters; useless talk and worry; attention given to something not worth it. **2** a person who fusses too much. —*v.* **1** make a fuss: *Nervously she fussed about her work.* **2** make nervous or worried; bother. [origin uncertain] —**fuss′er,** *n.*

fuss·y (fus′ē) *adj.* **fuss·i·er, fuss·i·est. 1** inclined to fuss; hard to please; very particular: *A sick person is sometimes fussy about his food.* **2** much trimmed; elaborately made: *fussy clothes.* **3** full of details; requiring much care: *a fussy job.* —**fuss′i·ly,** *adv.* —**fuss′i·ness,** *n.*

fus·tian (fus′chən) *n., adj.* —*n.* **1** a coarse, heavy cloth made of cotton and flax: *Fustian was used for clothing in Europe throughout the Middle Ages.* **2** a thick cotton cloth like corduroy. **3** pompous, high-sounding language; would-be eloquence. —*adj.* **1** made of fustian. **2** pompous high-sounding, but cheap. [ME < OF *fustaigne* < LL *fustaneum* < L *fustis* stick of wood]

fus·tic (fus′tik) *n.* **1** a tropical American tree of the mulberry family. **2** the wood of this tree. **3** the dye. [< F *fustoc* < Sp. < Arabic *fustuq.* Akin to PISTACHIO.]

fust·y (fus′tē) *adj.* **fust·i·er, fust·i·est. 1** having a stale smell; musty; mouldy; stuffy. **2** old-fashioned; out-of-date. [< *fust,* n., < OF *fust* wine cask < L *fustis* staff] —**fust′i·ly,** *adv.* —**fust′i·ness,** *n.*

fut. future.

fu·tile (fyü′tīl *or* fyü′təl) *adj.* **1** not successful; useless. **2** not important; trifling. **3** occupied with things of no value or importance; lacking in purpose: *a futile life.* [< L *futilis* pouring easily, worthless < *fundere* pour] —**fu′tile·ly,** *adv.* —**fu′tile·ness,** *n.* ☛ *Syn.* **1.** See note at **vain.**

fu·til·i·ty (fyü til′ə tē) *n., pl.* **-ties. 1** uselessness. **2** unimportance. **3** a useless or unimportant action, event, etc.

fut·tock (fut′ək) *n.* one of the curved timbers that form the middle of a rib in a ship. [? for *foot hook*]

fu·ture (fyü′chər) *n., adj.* —*n.* **1** the time to come; the days, years, etc. ahead: *He has not done very well so far but hopes to do better in the future.* **2** what is to come; what will be: *She claims she can foretell the future.* **3** a chance or expectation of success and prosperity: *a young man with a future.* **4** *Grammar.* **a** a future tense. **b** a verb form in this tense. **5 futures,** *pl.* commodities or stocks bought or sold to be received or delivered at a future date. —*adj.* **1** that is to come; that will be; coming. **2** *Grammar.* of, having to do with, or being a verb tense that indicates time to come. *Will go* is the future tense of *go.* [< L *futurus,* future participle of *esse* be] —**fu′ture·less,** *adj.*

future perfect 1 *Grammar.* a verb tense formed by adding *will have* or *shall have* to the past participle, to express action to be completed in the future: *By next week, he will have gone.* **2** designating this tense. **3** a very form or verb phrase in this tense.

fu·tur·ism (fyü′chər iz′əm) *n.* **1** a movement in art, literature, and music that began in Italy in the early 20th century, and that rejected traditional forms and methods in an attempt to express the violence, speed, and noise of contemporary civilization. **2** the practice or policy of concentrating on predictions of what will happen in the future as the basis for present-day decisions and actions.

fu·tur·ist (fyü′chər ist) *n., adj.* —*n.* a person who practises or studies futurism. —*adj.* of or having to do with futurism or the future.

fu·tur·is·tic (fyü′chə ris′tik) *adj.* **1** of or having to do with the future or what is thought of as characteristic of the future: *a futuristic movie, set in the year 2050. The display featured futuristic designs in furnishings.* **2** of or having to do with futurism. —**fu′tur·is′ti·cal·ly,** *adv.*

fu·tu·ri·ty (fyü tyür′ə tē *or* fyü tür′ə tē) *n., pl.* **-ties. 1** the time to come; future. **2** a future state or event. **3** the quality of being future.

fu·tur·ol·o·gist (fyü′chər ol′ə jist) *n.* a person who practises or studies futurology; futurist.

fu·tur·ol·o·gy (fyü′chər ol′ə jē) *n.* the profession or policy of using forecasts of the future as a basis for present-day decisions and actions; futurism (def. 2).

fu·zee (fyü zē′) See **fusee.**

fuzz (fuz) *n., v.* —*v.* **1** loose, fine, light fibres or hairs; fluff or down: *Peaches and some caterpillars are covered with fuzz.* **2** *Slang.* Usually, **the fuzz,** the police or a police officer. —*v.* make or become fuzzy: *The blanket is fuzzing.*

fuzz·y (fuz′ē) *adj.* **fuzz·i·er, fuzz·i·est. 1** of fuzz: *The baby's hair was just a fuzzy halo.* **2** like fuzz: *My hair gets fuzzy when it's humid outside.* **3** covered with fuzz: *a fuzzy caterpillar.* **4** not clear or distinct; blurred or imprecise: *Everything looks fuzzy when I don't have my glasses on. That argument is an example of fuzzy thinking.* —**fuzz′i·ly,** *adv.* —**fuzz′i·ness,** *n.*

fwd. forward.

–fy *verb-forming suffix.* **1** make or make into; cause to be, as in *simplify, intensify, pacify, horrify.* **2** become, as in *solidify, putrify.* **3** make like, as in *citify.* [< F *-fier* < *-ficare* < *facere* do, make]

FY fiscal year.

fyl·fot (fil′fot) *n.* swastika. [? < *fill foot,* a design for filling the foot of a painted window]

Gg

g or **G** (jē) *n., pl.* **g's** or **G's.** **1** the seventh letter of the English alphabet. **2** any speech sound represented by this letter. **3** a person or thing identified as *g*, especially the seventh in a series. **4** *Music.* **a** the fifth tone of the scale of C major. **b** a symbol representing this tone. **c** a key string, etc. of a musical instrument that produces this tone. **d** the scale or key that has G as its keynote. **5** *Physics.* a unit of acceleration equal to the force of gravity upon a body at rest, used to measure the force exerted on an accelerating body. **6** something shaped like the letter G. **7** (*adj.*) of or being a G or g.

g gram(s).

g. or **g** **1** gravity. **2** guinea. **3** gauge. **4** genitive. **5** gender. **6** goalkeeper.

G **1** German. **2** giga- (an SI prefix). **3** *Slang.* a grand; one thousand dollars.

G. **1** gravity. **2** German. **3** Gulf.

Ga gallium.

Ga. Georgia.

GA Georgia.

G.A. **1** in the United Nations, General Assembly. **2** General Agent.

gab (gab) *n., v.* **gabbed, gab·bing.** *Informal.* —*n.* chatter; gabble; idle talk.
gift of (the) gab, fluency of speech; glibness.
—*v.* talk too much; chatter; gabble. [probably imitative]

gab·ar·dine (gab′ər dēn′ or gab′ər dēn′) *n.* **1** a closely woven, woollen, cotton, or rayon cloth having small, diagonal ribs on its surface, used for raincoats, suits, etc. **2** a garment of gabardine. [var. of *gaberdine*]

gab·ble (gab′əl) *v.* **-bled, -bling;** *n.* —*v.* **1** make unintelligible or animal sounds: *They heard the geese gabbling in the yard.* **2** talk rapidly, without making much sense: *She was gabbling on excitedly about a fire she had seen.* —*n.* rapid, nonsensical talk or unintelligible sounds: *the gabble of geese.* [< *gab*, var. of *gob* < Gaelic *gob* mouth] —**gab′bler,** *n.*

gab·by (gab′ē) *adj.* **-bi·er, -bi·est.** *Informal.* very talkative.

gab·er·dine (gab′ər dēn′ or gab′ər dēn′) *n.* **1** a man's long, loose coat or cloak worn in the Middle Ages, especially by Jews. **2** See **gabardine.** [< Sp. *gabardina*]

gab·fest (gab′fest′) *n. Informal.* **1** a long conversation. **2** an informal gathering for conversation and discussion.

ga·bi·on (gā′bē ən) *n.* **1** *Military.* a cylinder of wicker filled with earth, formerly used as a defence. In modern warfare sandbags are used in place of gabions. **2** a similar cylinder made of metal, etc. and filled with stones, used in building dams, supporting bridge foundations, etc. [< F < Ital. *gabbione,* ult. < L *cavea* cage]

GABLE

Green Gables, the farm house near Cavendish, P.E.I. that is featured in *Anne of Green Gables,* by L. M. Montgomery

ga·ble (gā′bəl) *n.* **1** the end of a ridged roof, with the triangular upper part of the wall that it covers. **2** an end wall topped by a gable. **3** a triangular ornament or canopy over a door, window, etc. [ME < OF *gable* < ON *gafl*] —**ga′ble·like′,** *adj.*

ga·bled (gā′bəld) *adj.* built with a gable or gables; having or forming gables.

gable roof a roof that slopes down on either side from a single ridgepole, forming a gable at either end. See **roof** for picture.

gable window **1** a window in a gable (def. 1). **2** a window with an ornamental gable (def. 3) over it.

ga·by (gā′bē) *n., pl.* **-bies.** *Informal.* a fool; simpleton. [origin uncertain]

gad¹ (gad) *v.* **gad·ded, gad·ding;** *n.* —*v.* **1** go about looking for pleasure or excitement: *She was always gadding about town.* **2** move about restlessly. —*n.* **1** the act of gadding. **2** gadabout: *He*

is a born gad. [? back formation < obs. *gadling* companion < OE *gædeling* < *gæd* fellowship + *-ling*] —**gad′der,** *n.*

gad² (gad) *n., v.* **gad·ded, gad·ding.** —*n.* **1** a goad. **2** a pointed mining tool for breaking up rock, coal, ore, etc. —*v.* **1** goad. **2** break up (rock or ore) with a gad. [< Scand.; cf. Icelandic *gaddr*]

Gad or **gad³** (gad) *n. or interj. Archaic.* a word used as a mild oath, exclamation of surprise, etc. [euphemistic var. of *God*]

gad·a·bout (gad′ə bout′) *n. Informal.* a person who goes about looking for pleasure or excitement; person fond of going from place to place. [< *gad¹*]

gad·fly (gad′flī′) *n., pl.* **-flies.** **1** any of several large flies that sting cattle, horses, etc. The horsefly and botfly are gadflies. **2** a person who irritates others or rouses them from a state of self-satisfaction by calling attention to their faults, etc. [< *gad²* + *fly*]

gadg·et (gaj′it) *n. Informal.* a small mechanical, electrical or electronic device or contrivance; any ingenious device: *She's always buying gadgets for her car; the latest one is a coffee maker that plugs into the lighter.* [origin uncertain]

gadg·et·ry (gaj′ə trē) *n.* **1** gadgets: *electronic gadgetry.* **2** the inventing, making, and using of gadgets.

gad·o·lin·i·um (gad′ə lin′ē əm) *n.* a rare magnetic metallic chemical element. *Symbol:* Gd; *at.no.* 64; *at.wt.* 157.25. [after Johann *Gadolin* (1760-1852), a Finnish chemist]

gad·wall (gad′wol) *n.* a medium-sized duck (*Anas strepera*) found mainly around sloughs and shallow lake margins in W North America, Europe, and Asia, the male having mainly grey plumage, the female brownish. [origin unknown. 17c.]

Gae·a (jē′ə) *n. Greek mythology.* the goddess of the earth and mother of the Titans.

Gael (gāl) *n.* **1** a Scottish Highlander. **2** a Celt who is a native or inhabitant of Scotland, Ireland, or the Isle of Man. [< Scots Gaelic *Gaidheal* < OIrish *Goidhel*]

Gael·ic (gā′lik; *also, esp.Scottish,* gäl′ik) *adj., n.* —*adj.* of or having to do with the Gaels, especially the Scottish Highlanders, or their language. —*n.* the language of the Gaels. Gaelic is a Celtic language, related to Welsh.

gaff (gaf) *n., v.* —*n.* **1** a strong hook or barbed spear for pulling large fish out of the water. **2** a sharp metal spur fastened to the leg of a gamecock. **3** a spar or pole extending along the upper edge of a fore-and-aft sail. See **sloop** for picture. **4** something uncomfortable or hard to take. **5** *Slang.* a hoax, fraud, or trick.
blow the gaff, *Slang.* give away a secret.
stand the gaff, *Slang.* hold up well under strain or punishment of any kind.
—*v.* **1** hook or pull (a fish) out of the water with a gaff. **2** *Slang.* **a** deceive or trick. **b** fix for the purpose of cheating; rig: *to gaff the dice.* [< F *gaffe* < Celtic; cf. Irish Gaelic *gaf, gafa*]

gaffe (gaf) *n.* a tactless or indiscreet remark, action, etc.; faux pas. [< F]

gaf·fer (gaf′ər) *n. Informal.* an old man. [alteration of *godfather*]
☞ *Usage.* **Gaffer** is now normally used in a humorous or unfavorable sense; it is the masculine counterpart of **gammer,** an old gossip.

gaff·top·sail (gaf′top′sāl′ or -top′səl) *n.* a topsail set above a gaff.

gag (gag) *n., v.* **gagged, gag·ging.** —*n.* **1** something thrust into a person's mouth to keep him from talking, crying out, etc. **2** anything used to silence a person; a restraint or hindrance to free speech. **3** *Informal.* an amusing remark or trick; something said or done to cause a laugh; a joke: *The comedian's gags made the audience laugh.* **4** closure (def. 4).
—*v.* **1** keep from talking, crying out, etc. by means of a gag: *The bandits tied the watchman's arms and gagged him.* **2** force to keep silent; restrain or hinder from free speech. **3** say something to cause a laugh. **4** choke or strain in an effort to vomit. **5** cause to choke or strain in an effort to vomit. [probably imitative] —**gag′ger,** *n.*

ga·ga (gä′gä′) *adj. Slang.* **1** crazy or mentally confused. **2** wildly or foolishly enthusiastic: *They went quite gaga over the show.* [< F *gaga* old fool]

gage¹ (gāj) *n., v.* **gaged, gag·ing.** —*n.* **1** a pledge to fight; challenge: *The knight threw down his gauntlet as a gage of battle.* **2** something deposited as security; a pledge. —*v. Archaic.* offer as a

pledge or security; wager. [ME < OF *gage* < Frankish **wadja-*. Doublet of WAGE.]
☞ *Hom.* gauge.

gage² (gāj) *n., v.* **gaged, gag·ing.** See **gauge.** —**gage′a·ble,** *adj.* —**gag′er,** *n.*
☞ *Hom.* gauge.

gag·gle (gag′əl) *n., v.* **-gled, -gling.** —*n.* **1** a flock of geese. **2** *Informal.* a group or cluster of people: *A gaggle of autograph hunters waited outside the door.* **3** a gabbling or cackling sound, as that made by geese. —*v.* make gabbling or cackling sounds.

gag·man (gag′man′) *n., pl.* **-men.** a man who invents comic lines and situations for comedians.

gai·e·ty (gā′ə tē) *n., pl.* **-ties. 1** cheerful liveliness; merriment: *Her gaiety helped the party.* **2** lively entertainment. **3** bright appearance; showiness; finery: *gaiety of dress.* Also, **gayety.** [< F *gaieté*]

gai·ly (gā′lē) *adv.* **1** in a gay manner; happily; merrily: *She ran gaily to meet them. The children chattered gaily.* **2** brightly, showily: *The room was gaily decorated.* Also, **gayly.**

gain (gān) *v., n.* —*v.* **1** get; obtain; secure: *The king gained possession of more lands.* **2** get as an increase, addition, advantage, or profit. **3** make progress; advance; improve: *The sick child is gaining and will soon be well.* **4** win; be the victor in: *to gain the prize, to gain the battle.* **5** get to; arrive at; reach: *The swimmer gained the shore.* **6** of a timepiece, run too fast: *My watch gains about six minutes a week.* **7** come closer; begin to catch up or catch up on: *He saw that the second runner was gaining. The pirate ship was slowly gaining on them.*
—*n.* **1** an increase in profit or advantage: *He has made a substantial gain over his opponent in this competition.* **2** getting wealth: *Greed is love of gain.* **3** an increase in amount or degree: *a gain in speed, a gain of ten percent.* **4** *Electronics.* amplification of a radio signal, etc. **5** **gains,** *pl.* profits; earnings; winnings. [< F *gagner* < Gmc.]

gain·er (gā′nər) *n.* **1** one that gains. **2** *Swimming.* a fancy dive in which the diver turns a back somersault in the air.

gain·ful (gān′fəl) *adj.* bringing in money or advantage; profitable. —**gain′ful·ly,** *adv.*

gain·said (gān′sed′) *v.* a pt. and a pp. of **gainsay.**

gain·say (gān′sā′) *v.* **-said** or **-sayed, -saying.** *Archaic or poetic.* **1** deny; dispute: *The facts cannot be gainsaid.* **2** contradict; speak against: *to gainsay an opponent.* [< obs. *gain-* against + *say*] —**gain′say′er,** *n.*

gainst or **'gainst** (genst or gänst) *prep. or conj. Poetic.* against.

gait (gāt) *n.* **1** the kind of step used in walking or running. A gallop is one of the gaits of a horse. **2** a way of walking or running; carriage or bearing of the body in moving: *He has a lame gait because of an injured foot.* [ME < ON *gata* way]
☞ *Hom.* gate.

gait·ed (gā′tid) *adj.* having a certain gait: *heavy-gaited oxen.*

gai·ter (gā′tər) *n.* **1** a cloth or leather covering for the lower leg, buttoned or buckled on one side and extending from the instep up to the ankle, the calf, or the knee. **2** a similar covering extending only up to the ankle; spat. **3** an ankle-high shoe with an elastic insert in each side and no laces. Also called **gaiter shoe.** [< F *guêtre*]

gal¹ (gal) *n. Informal.* girl.

gal² (gal) a unit used in geodesy and geophysics for measuring acceleration due to gravity. It is equal to one centimetre per second per second (1 cm/s²). [after *Galileo* (1564-1642), Italian mathematician, astronomer, and physicist; 20c.]

gal. gallon(s).

ga·la (gā′lə or gal′ə) *n.* **1** a festive occasion; festival. **2** (*adj.*) of, for, or involving festivity: *a gala occasion.* [< F < Ital.; cf. OF *gale* merriment]

ga·lac·tic (gə lak′tik) *adj. Astronomy.* of or having to do with a galaxy of stars, especially the Milky Way. [< Gk. *galaktikos* < *gala, -aktos* milk]

galactic circle *Astronomy.* the great circle whose plane passes almost centrally along the Milky Way.

galactic cluster any diffuse group of stars, usually numbering over a hundred, such as the Pleiades.

Gal·a·had (gal′ə had′) *n.* **1** *Arthurian legend.* the noblest and purest knight of the Round Table. Sir Galahad was the only knight who was allowed to look into the Holy Grail. **2** any man considered to be very noble and pure.

gal·an·tine (gal′ən tēn′) *n.* veal, chicken, or other white meat boned, boiled, and seasoned, and then served cold in its own jelly. [< F]

Gal·a·te·a (gal′ə tē′ə) *n. Greek mythology.* an ivory statue of a maiden, carved by Pygmalion. When he fell in love with the statue, Aphrodite gave it life.

Ga·la·tian (gə lā′shən) *n., adj.* —*n.* a native or inhabitant of Galatia, an ancient country in central Asia Minor that later became a Roman province. —*adj.* of or having to do with Galatia or its people.

gal·ax·y (gal′ək sē) *n., pl.* **-ax·ies. 1** *Astronomy.* any of the many systems or groupings of stars making up the universe. A galaxy may contain millions or billions of stars. **2** **Galaxy,** the Milky Way, the faintly luminous band of countless stars that stretches across the sky. **3** a brilliant or splendid group: *The queen was followed by a galaxy of brave knights and fair ladies.* [< OF < LL < Gk. *galaxias* < *gala, -aktos* milk]

gale¹ (gāl) *n.* **1** a very strong wind. **2** *Meteorology.* a wind with a velocity of 50-88 km/h (28-47 knots). Winds of gale force are presented by numbers 7 to 9 on the Beaufort scale. **3** *Archaic or poetic.* breeze. **4** a noisy outburst: *gales of laughter.* [origin uncertain]

gale² (gāl) *n.* sweet gale (a shrub). [OE *gagel*]

ga·le·na (gə lē′nə) *n.* a grey metallic ore consisting of lead sulphide. It is the most important source of lead. *Formula:* PbS [< L]

ga·le·nite (gə lē′nīt) *n.* galena.

Ga·li·cian (gə lish′ən) *n., adj.* —*n.* **1** a native or inhabitant of Galicia, a region in central Europe, now divided between Poland and the Soviet Union. **2** a native or inhabitant of Galicia, a region and former kingdom in NW Spain. —*adj.* of or having to do with either Galicia.

Gal·i·le·an¹ (gal′ə lē′ən) *n., adj.* —*n.* **1** a native or inhabitant of Galilee, a region in N Palestine that was a Roman province in the time of Jesus. **2** a Christian. **3 the Galilean,** Jesus. —*adj.* of or having to do with Galilee or its people.

Gal·i·le·an² (gal′ə lē′ən or gal′ə lā′ən) *adj.* of or having to do with Galileo (1564-1642), the Italian mathematician, astronomer, and physicist who is regarded as the founder of modern experimental science.

gal·i·ot or **gal·li·ot** (gal′ē ət) *n.* **1** a small, fast galley equipped both with oars and sails that was used until the end of the 18th century. **2** a heavy, single-masted, Dutch cargo vessel or fishing boat. [ME < OF *galiote*, dim. of *galie* ult. < Med.Gk. *galea*]

gall¹ (gol or gôl) *n.* **1** bile, especially animal bile used in medicine, etc. **2** *Archaic.* gall bladder. **3** anything very bitter or harsh. **4** bitterness; hate: *His heart was filled with gall.* **5** *Informal.* excessive boldness; impudence: *He had a lot of gall to talk to his employer in such a nasty way.* [OE *gealla*]

gall² (gol or gôl) *v., n.* —*v.* **1** make or become sore by rubbing: *The rough strap galled the horse's skin.* **2** annoy; irritate. —*n.* **1** a sore spot on the skin caused by rubbing. **2** a cause of annoyance or irritation. [extended use of *gall¹*]

gall³ (gol or gôl) *n.* a growth, or tumor, on the leaves, stems, or roots of plants, caused by insects, fungi, bacteria, etc. The galls of oak trees contain tannic acid used in making ink, medicine, etc. [< F *galle* < L *galla*]

Gal·la (gal′ə) *n.* **1** a member of one of the Hamitic tribes of Ethiopia and other countries of northeast Africa. **2** the language of the Gallas.

gal·lant (*adj. 1-3* gal′ənt, *4, 5* gə lant′, gə lont′, or gal′ənt; *n.* gal′ənt, gə lont′, or gə lant′) *adj., n.* —*adj.* **1** noble; brave; daring: *King Arthur was a gallant knight. They made a gallant effort to save the building.* **2** grand; fine; stately: *a gallant ship.* **3** showy in dress or appearance. **4** very polite and attentive to women. **5** amorous.
—*n.* **1** *Archaic.* a man who wears showy clothes; man of fashion. **2** a man who is very polite and attentive to women. **3** lover. [ME < OF *galant*, ppr. of *galer* make merry < *gale.* See GALA.] —**gal′lant·ly,** *adv.* —**gal′lant·ness,** *n.*

gal·lant·ry (gal′ən trē) *n., pl.* **-ries. 1** noble spirit or conduct; bravery; dashing courage. **2** great politeness and chivalrous attention to women. **3** a gallant act or speech. **4** *Archaic.* a gay appearance; showy display.

gall bladder or **gall·blad·der** (gol′blad′ər or gôl′-) *n.* a sac attached to the liver, in which excess bile is stored until needed.

gal·le·ass (gal′ē as′) *n. Historical.* a heavy, low built warship larger than a galley and equipped with both oars and sails. It was used in the 16th and 17th centuries. [< MF *galeasse* < Ital. *galeazza* < *galea* < Med.Gk.]

gal·le·on (gal′yən *or* gal′ē ən) *n.* a large, heavy sailing ship, usually having three or four decks, used in Europe as a warship and armed trading ship, especially from the 15th to the end of the 16th century. The Spaniards used many galleons in the fleet of the Armada. [< Sp. *galeón* < *galea* < Med.Gk.]

gal·ler·y (gal′ər ē *or* gal′rē) *n., pl.* **-ler·ies. 1** a long, narrow platform or passage projecting from the wall of a building. **2** a projecting upper floor in a church, theatre, or hall, with seats or room for part of the audience; balcony. **3** the highest floor of this kind in a theatre. **4** the people who sit in the highest balcony of a theatre. **5** a group of people watching or listening; audience. **6** a long, narrow room or passage; hall. **7** a covered walk or porch. **8** an underground passage. **9** a room or building where works of art are shown. **10** a collection of works of art. **11** a room or building for use as a shooting range,etc.
play to the gallery, *Informal.* try to get the praise or favor of the common people by doing or saying what will please them, in the manner of actors who used to style their performance to suit the tastes of the people watching from the gallery. [< Ital. *galleria*]

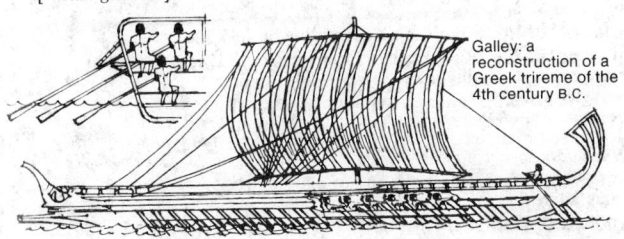

Galley: a reconstruction of a Greek trireme of the 4th century B.C.

gal·ley (gal′ē) *n., pl.* **-leys. 1** a long, low ship propelled mainly by one or more banks of oars, used in ancient and medieval times as a warship and a trading ship. Ancient galleys sometimes carried a square sail. The medieval Mediterranean galleys had a large lateen sail. **2** the kitchen of a ship or aircraft. **3** *Printing.* **a** a shallow oblong tray for holding type that has been set. **b** a proof taken from the type in a galley, used to make corrections before the type is made up into pages. [ME < OF *galee*, ult. < Med.Gk. *galea*]

galley proof *Printing.* galley (def. 3b).

galley slave 1 a person compelled or condemned to row a galley. **2** a drudge.

gall·fly (gol′flī′ *or* gôl′-) *n., pl.* **-flies.** any of various small insects that deposit their eggs on plants and cause galls that the larvae feed on.

gal·liard (gal′yərd) *n.* **1** a lively dance in triple time, popular in the 16th and 17th centuries. **2** the music for this dance. **3** *Archaic.* a strong, valiant, or gallant man.

gal·lic (gal′ik) *adj. Chemistry.* **1** of gallium. **2** containing gallium, especially with a valence of three.

Gal·lic (gal′ik) *adj.* **1** of or having to do with Gaul or its people. **2** French. [< L *Gallicus* < *Gallus* a Gaul]

gallic acid an acid obtained especially from galls on plants, used in making ink, dyes, etc. *Formula:* $C_7H_6O_5H_2O$

Gal·li·cism (gal′ə siz′əm) *n.* **1** a French idiom or expression. **2** such an idiom or expression literally translated into another language. *Example: that leaps to the eyes,* from French *ça saute aux yeux,* meaning "that is obvious." **3** a French trait or characteristic.

Gal·li·cize *or* **gal·li·cize** (gal′ə sīz′) *v.* **-cized, -ciz·ing.** make or become French in character, habits, language, etc. —**Gal′li·ci·za′tion** *or* **gal′li·ci·za′tion,** *n.*

gal·li·gas·kins (gal′ə gas′kinz) *n.pl.* **1** loose breeches. **2** leggings. [formerly *garragascoynes* < MF *garguesque,* var. of *(à la) greguesque* < Ital. *alla grechesca* in the Greek fashion < *greco* Greek < L *Graecus*; influenced by earlier *Gascoyne* Gascon]

gal·li·na·ceous (gal′ə nā′shəs) *adj.* of or having to do with an order (Galliformes) of heavy-bodied birds that nest on the ground and fly only short distances, including chickens, turkeys, pheasants, and grouse. [< L *gallinaceus* < *gallina* hen]

gall·ing (gol′ing *or* gôl′-) *adj.* bitterly disappointing; very annoying or irritating: *a galling defeat at the hands of an inferior opponent.*

gal·li·nule (gal′ə nyül′ *or* gal′ə nül′) *n.* any of several marsh birds of the rail family found throughout the world, having long thin toes and a fleshy shield on the forehead. The common gallinule (*Gallinula chloropus*), found in many parts of the world, occurs in Canada only in southern Ontario. [< NL *gallinula* < L *gallina* hen, ult. < *gallus* cock]

Gal·li·o (gal′ē ō′) *n.* **1** in the Bible, a Roman proconsul who,

hat, āge, fär; let, ēqual, tèrm; it, īce
hot, ōpen, ôrder; oil, out; cup, put, rüle,
əbove, takən, pencəl, lemən, circəs

ch, child; ng, long; sh, ship
th, thin; ᴛʜ, then; zh, measure

when the Jews accused St. Paul, refused to take action against him. **2** any person, especially an official, who avoids becoming involved in matters which are not his immediate concern; an easygoing, indifferent person.

gal·li·pot (gal′ə pot′) *n.* a small pot or jar of glazed earthenware. Gallipots were used by druggists to hold medicine, salve, etc. [< *galley + pot*]

gal·li·um (gal′ē əm) *n.* a shiny, soft, bluish-white metallic element similar to mercury, with a low melting point. Gallium is used as a substitute for mercury in thermometers. *Symbol:* Ga; *at.no.* 31; *at.wt.* 69.72. [< NL ? < L *gallus* cock, translation of *Lecoq* (de Boisbaudran), the discoverer]

gal·li·vant (gal′ə vant′) *v.* **1** travel or roam for pleasure: *They're gallivanting around Europe this summer.* **2** go about frivolously or indiscreetly with members of the opposite sex. [? < *gallant*]

gall·nut (gol′nut′ *or* gôl′-) *n.* a nutlike gall on plants.

gal·lon (gal′ən) *n.* a unit for measuring liquids, equal to 4 quarts. The traditional Canadian gallon was equal to about 4.55 dm³; the United States gallon is equal to about 3.79 dm³. *Abbrev.:* gal. [ME < ONF *galon*]

gal·loon (gə lün′) *n.* a narrow braid of gold, silver, or silk thread used in trimming uniforms, furniture, etc. [< F *galon* < *galonner* dress the hair with ribbons < OF *gale* merriment. See GALA.]

gal·lop (gal′əp) *n., v.* —*n.* **1** the fastest gait of horses and other four-footed animals. In a gallop, all four feet are off the ground together once in each stride. **2** a ride taken at this gait. **3** a fast pace or progression: *doing the chores at a gallop.* —*v.* **1** ride at a gallop: *The cowboy galloped along the trail.* **2** go at a gallop: *The pony galloped up to the fence.* **3** cause to gallop: *John galloped his horse down the road.* **4** go very fast; hurry: *She came galloping downstairs to tell us the news.* [< F *galoper* < Gmc.] —**gal′lop·er,** *n.*

gal·lous (gal′əs) *adj. Chemistry.* containing gallium, especially with a valence of two.

gal·lows (gal′ōz) *n., pl.* **-lows** *or* **-lows·es. 1** a wooden structure usually consisting of a crossbar on two upright posts, used for hanging criminals. **2** a structure like this, used for supporting or suspending something. **3 the gallows,** punishment by hanging: *Many people are against the gallows.*
cheat the gallows, escape the death penalty for a crime. [OE *galga*]

gallows bird *Informal.* a person who deserves to be hanged.

gall·stone (gol′stōn′ *or* gôl′-) *n.* a pebble-like mass that sometimes forms in the gall bladder or its duct. When one or more gallstones stop the flow of bile, a painful illness results.

Gal·lup poll (gal′əp) a poll or opinion on social and political issues, etc., taken from a selected group of people and intended to reflect the opinion of the general public. [< George *Gallup,* an American statistician, born 1901]

gal·op (gal′əp; *French,* gä lō′) *n., v.* —*n.* **1** a lively dance in two-four time. **2** the music for this dance. —*v.* dance a galop. [< F]

ga·lore (gə lôr′) *adj.* in abundance: *Over Christmas we had parties galore.* [< Irish *go leōr* to sufficiency]

ga·losh (gə losh′) *n.* a high overshoe having a rubber or plastic sole and a rubber, plastic, or fabric top, worn in wet or snowy weather (*usually used in the plural*): *I hate wearing galoshes.* [< F *galoche*]

ga·lumph (gə lumf′) *v.* move or run heavily or clumsily: *He went galumphing up the stairs in his great boots.* [blend of *gallop* and *triumphant*; coined by Lewis Carroll]

gal·van·ic (gal van′ik) *adj.* **1** producing a direct current of electricity, especially by chemical action. **2** of or caused by an electric current. **3** affecting as if by galvanism; startling or stimulating: *a galvanic personality.* **4** produced as if by an electric shock: *a galvanic reaction.* [< *galvanism*]

gal·va·nism (gal′və niz′əm) *n.* **1** a direct electric current, especially one produced by chemical action. **2** *Medicine.* the use of such electricity to stimulate muscles and nerves. **3** any power or quality that arouses a sudden or forceful reaction: *We were overwhelmed by the galvanism of the actor's performance.* [< F *galvanisme,* after Luigi *Galvani* (1737-98), an Italian physicist]

gal·va·nize (gal′və nīz′) *v.* **-nized, -niz·ing. 1** apply an electric current to. **2** arouse suddenly; startle. **3** cover (iron or steel) with a

thin coating of zinc to prevent rust. —**gal′va·ni·za′tion,** *n.*
—**gal′va·niz′er,** *n.*

galvanized iron iron covered with a thin coating of zinc, to resist rust.

gal·va·nom·e·ter (gal′və nom′ə tər) *n.* an instrument for detecting and measuring a small electric current. [< *galvano-*, combining form of *galvanic* + *-meter*]

gal·va·no·met·ric (gal′və nə met′rik or gal van′ə met′rik) *adj.* I having to do with a galvanometer. 2 measured by a galvanometer.

gal·va·nom·e·try (gal′və nom′ə trē) *n.* the detection, measurement, and determination of the direction of electric currents by a galvanometer.

gal·va·no·scope (gal′və nə skōp′ or gal van′ə skōp′) *n.* an instrument for detecting very small electric currents and showing their direction. [< *galvano-*, combining form of *galvanic* + *-scope*]

gam (gam) *n. Slang.* a leg, especially a woman's leg. [prob. < F dial. *gambe* < ONF; ult. < LL *gamba* leg]

gam·bit (gam′bit) *n.* 1 *Chess.* a way of opening a game by purposely risking a pawn or a piece to gain some advantage. 2 any rather risky move or stratagem intended to gain an advantage: *His opening gambit was to call for an investigation.* [< F < Provençal *cambi* an exchange < Ital. *cambio* < LL *cambiare* to change ? < Celtic]

gam·ble (gam′bəl) *v.* **-bled, -bling;** *n.* —*v.* 1 play games of chance for money or some other prize or stake. 2 take a risk in order to gain some advantage: *She decided to gamble by refusing the job offer and hoping for a better one.* 3 bet; wager. 4 lose or squander by gambling (used with **away**): *He gambled away his inheritance.* —*n. Informal.* 1 a risky venture or undertaking. 2 an act of gambling. [probably related to GAME, *v.*]

gam·bler (gam′blər) *n.* a person who gambles a great deal, especially one who lives on money won in games of chance.

gam·bling (gam′bling) *n.* 1 the playing of games of chance for money or some other prize or stake. 2 the taking of risks in order to gain some advantage.

gam·boge (gam bōj′ or gam büzh′) *n.* a gum resin from certain tropical trees, used as a yellow pigment and as a cathartic. [< NL *gambogium* < *Cambodia*]

gam·bol (gam′bəl) *n., v.* **-bolled** or **-boled, -bol·ling** or **-bol·ing.** —*n.* a playful running and jumping about; caper; frolic. —*v.* frisk about; run and jump about in play: *Lambs gambolled in the meadow.* [< F *gambade* < Ital. *gambata* < *gamba* leg]

gam·brel (gam′brəl) *n.* 1 the hock of a horse or other animal. 2 a gambrel roof. [< ONF *gamberel* < *gambe* leg < LL *gamba, camba* < Gk. *kampē* bend]

gambrel roof a two-sided roof having two slopes on each side, with the lower slope steeper than the upper one. See **roof** for picture.

game¹ (gām) *n., adj.* **gam·er, gam·est;** *v.* **gamed, gam·ing.** —*n.* I an activity done for entertainment or amusement; a way of playing: *Football, solitaire, and chess are games.* 2 the equipment, etc. necessary to play a particular game, especially any of various table games: *We got several games for Christmas.* 3 a physical or mental exercise with certain rules, played either alone or with another person or group, and often involving competition: *a game of tag. Are you going to the game tonight?* 4 any one of a number of contests making up a set or series: *The tennis champion won four games out of six.* 5 the condition of the score in a game: *At the end of the first period the game was 6 to 3 in our favor.* 6 the number of points required to win. 7 a particular manner of playing: *He plays a good game.* 8 any activity or undertaking that is carried on as if under set rules and that tests one's skill or endurance: *the game of life, the game of diplomacy.* 9 *Informal.* any business venture, profession, etc.: *the acting game.* 10 a plan; scheme: *He tried to trick us, but we saw through his game.* 11 what is hunted or pursued. 12 wild animals, birds, or fish hunted or caught for sport or for food. 13 flesh of wild animals or birds used for food.
ahead of the game, winning rather than losing.
be off (one's) **game,** play badly.
be on (one's) **game,** play well.
make game of, make fun of; laugh at; ridicule.
play the game, *Informal.* follow the rules; be a good sport.
the game is up, *Informal.* the plan or scheme has failed.
—*adj.* 1 having to do with game, hunting, or fishing: *Game laws protect wild life.* 2 brave; plucky: *The losing team put up a game fight.* 3 having spirit or will enough: *The explorer was game for any adventure.*
die game, die fighting; die bravely.
—*v.* gamble. [OE *gamen* joy] —**game′ly,** *adv.* —**game′ness,** *n.*
☛ *Syn. n.* 1. See note at **play.**

game² (gām) *adj. Informal.* lame; crippled; injured: *a game leg.* [origin uncertain]

game bag 1 a bag for carrying game that has been killed. 2 the amount of game killed.

game bird a bird hunted for sport or food.

game·cock (gām′kok′) *n.* a rooster bred and trained for cockfighting.

game fish a fish that fights to get away when hooked.

game fowl any of several breeds or strains of domestic fowl from which gamecocks are produced.

game·keep·er (gām′kēp′ər) *n.* a person employed to breed and look after game animals and birds on an estate and to prevent anyone from stealing them or killing them without permission.

game law a law made to restrict and regulate hunting and fishing in order to preserve or protect game animals, birds, and fish.

game misconduct *Hockey.* a penalty banishing a player from the ice for the remainder of the game, awarded for gross misconduct or after the player has received three major penalties in the same game.

game of chance any game depending on luck, not skill.

game preserve or **reserve** a large tract of land set aside by the government for the protection of wild life.

games·man·ship (gāmz′mən ship′) *n.* the art or practice of defeating an opponent, as in a game, by skilful but somewhat underhanded manoeuvres and ploys: *learning the fine points of political gamesmanship.*

game·some (gām′səm) *adj.* full of play; sportive; ready to play. —**game′some·ly,** *adv.*

game·ster (gām′stər) *n.* gambler.

gam·ete (gam′ēt or gə mēt′) *n.* a mature reproductive cell capable of uniting with another to form a fertilized cell that can develop into a new plant or animal. Gametes are produced by a special type of cell division called meiosis; each gamete has only half the number of chromosomes of other body cells. [< NL *gameta* < Gk. *gametē* wife, *gametēs* husband, ult. < *gamos* marriage]

ga·me·to·phyte (gə mē′tə fīt′) *n.* the gamete-producing form or generation of a plant that reproduces by alternation of generations. In lower plants, such as mosses, the gametophyte is the dominant form. Compare **sporophyte.** [< *gameto-*, combining form of *gamete* + *-phyte*]

game warden an official whose duty it is to enforce the game laws in a certain district.

gam·ey (gā′mē) See **gamy.**

gam·in (gam′ən) *n.* 1 a neglected boy left to roam about the streets; urchin. 2 any small, lively person. 3 (*adjl.*) like an urchin; impudent. [< F]

gam·ing (gā′ming) *n.* the playing of games of chance for money; gambling.

gam·ma (gam′ə) *n.* 1 the third letter of the Greek alphabet (Γ, γ = English G, g). 2 the third in any series or group.

gamma globulin the constituent of blood plasma that contains the most antibodies and is often used for temporary immunization against infectious diseases such as measles and hepatitis.

gamma rays electromagnetic radiation of very high frequency and great penetrating power, given off by radio-active substances. Gamma rays are similar to X rays, but shorter in wave length.

gam·mer (gam′ər) *n. Archaic.* an old woman. [alteration of *godmother*]
☛ *Usage.* See note at **gaffer.**

gam·mon¹ (gam′ən) *n., v.* —*n. Brit. Informal.* nonsense; humbug. —*v.* 1 talk nonsense, especially with intent to deceive. 2 deceive; hoax: *We were gammoned into sounding the fire alarm.* [cf. ME *gamen* game¹] —**gam′mon·er,** *n.*

gam·mon² (gam′ən) *n.* 1 the lower end of a side of bacon. 2 a smoked or cured ham. [< ONF *gambon* < *gambe* leg < LL *gamba.* See GAMBREL.]

gam·o·pet·al·ous (gam′ə pet′əl əs) *adj. Botany.* having the petals joined to form a tube-shaped corolla. [< Gk. *gamos* marriage + E *petal* + *-ous*]

gam·o·sep·al·ous (gam′ə sep′əl əs) *adj. Botany.* having the sepals joined together. [< Gk. *gamos* marriage + E *sepal* + *-ous*]

-gamous *combining form.* characterized by marriage or sexual union, as in *bigamous.* [< Gk. *-gamos* < *gamos* marriage + *-ous*]

gam·ut (gam′ət) *n.* 1 *Music.* **a** the whole series of recognized notes. **b** the complete scale of any key, especially the major scale. 2 the entire range of anything: *In one minute I ran the gamut of feeling from hope to despair.* [contraction of Med.L *gamma ut* < *gamma* G, the lowest tone, + *ut*, later *do*; notes of the scale were named from syllables in a Latin hymn: *Ut queant laxis resonare*

fibris, *Mira gestorum famuli tuorum, Solve polluti labii reatum, Sancte Iohannes*]

gam·y (gām′ē) *adj.*, **gam·i·er, gam·i·est. 1** having a taste or smell characteristic of the meat of wild animals or birds when it is too strong, as when the meat is tainted or improperly cooked. **2** especially of animals, brave or plucky. **3** scandalous or racy. Also, **gamey.** —**gam′i·fy,** *adv.* —**gam′i·ness,** *n.*

–gamy *combining form.* marriage or sexual union, as in *bigamy.* [< Gk. *-gamia* < *gamos* marriage]

gan or **'gan** (gan) *v. Archaic or poetic.* began, pt. of **gin⁴.**

gan·der (gan′dər) *n.* **1** an adult male goose. **2** a fool; simpleton. **3** *Slang.* a look: *Take a gander at that outfit.* [OE *gandra*]

gan·dy dancer (gan′dē) a member of a railway section gang, especially a seasonal or itinerant laborer. [? < former *Gandy Manufacturing Company of Chicago, Ill.* that made tools used by railway laborers]

gang¹ (gang) *n., v.* —*n.* **1** a group of people acting or going around together, especially for criminal or other purposes generally considered antisocial. **2** a group of people working together under one supervisor: *Two gangs of workmen were repairing the road.* **3** a group of people closely associated for social purposes: *Let's have the gang over for coffee after the show.* **4** a set of tools, machines, or components arranged to work together: *a gang plough.* —*v. Informal.* **a** form a gang. **b** attack in a gang.
gang up, come together into a group for some purpose: *We ganged up to give a party for our coach.*
gang up on, oppose as a group: *Let's gang up on that bully.* [OE *gang* a going]

gang² (gang) *v. Scottish.* go; walk.

gang·land (gang′land′) *n.* **1** the world of organized criminal gangs. **2** (*adj.*) of or having to do with this world: *a gangland slaying.*

gan·gli·a (gang′glē ə) *n.* pl. of **ganglion.**

gan·gling (gang′gling) *adj.* awkwardly tall and slender; lank and loosely built. [apparently ult. < *gang,* v.]

gan·gli·on (gang′glē ən) *n., pl.* **-gli·a** or **-gli·ons. 1** a mass of nerve cells forming a nerve centre outside of the brain or spinal cord. **2** a cyst on the sheath of a tendon or on the outer membrane of a joint. **3** a centre or concentration of force or energy. [< LL *ganglion* a type of swelling < Gk.]

gan·gly (gang′glē) *adj.* gangling.

gang·plank (gang′plangk′) *n.* a movable bridge used by persons or animals in getting on and off a ship, etc.

gang plough or **plow** a plough consisting of several shares for turning several furrows at a time.

gan·grene (gang′grēn *or* gang grēn′) *n., v.* **-grened, -gren·ing.** —*n.* the decay of tissue in a part of a living person or animal when the blood supply is interfered with by injury, infection, freezing, etc. —*v.* affect or become affected with gangrene: *The wounded leg gangrened and had to be amputated.* [< L *gangraena* < Gk. *gangraina*]

gan·gre·nous (gang′grə nəs) *adj.* of or having gangrene; decaying.

gang·ster (gang′stər) *n.* a member of an organized gang of criminals.

gang·ster·ism (gang′stə riz′əm) *n.* **1** the committing of crimes by members of an organized gang. **2** gangsters or their crimes: *The fight against gangsterism never stops.* **3** crime of the type committed by gangs or gangsters.

gang·way (gang′wā′) *n., interj.* —*n.* **1** passageway. **2** a passageway on a ship. **3** gangplank. —*interj. Informal.* get out of the way, please! stand aside and make room!

gan·net (gan′it) *n.* any of several large, white, fish-eating sea birds (family Sulidae) having long, black-tipped wings, a pointed bill and tail, and webbed feet. Gannets nest in colonies on cliffs. [OE *ganot*]

gan·oid (gan′oid) *adj., n.* —*adj.* **1** designating a type of fish scale that has a bright, enamel-like outer layer. **2** designating a fish or group of fishes having such scales: *The bowfin is a ganoid fish.* —*n.* a ganoid fish. [< Gk. *ganos* brightness]

gant·let (gont′lit *or* gônt′lit) See **gauntlet².**

gan·try (gan′trē) *n., pl.* **-tries. 1** a movable, bridgelike structure for carrying a travelling crane, consisting of side towers on parallel tracks that support a horizontal framework along which the crane moves. **2** a similar structure spanning several railway tracks, used to carry block signals. **3** a towerlike, movable framework with platforms at different levels, used for servicing a rocket on its launching pad. **4** a frame for supporting a barrel or cask on its side. [< ONF *gantier* < L *canterius* beast of burden, rafter, framework < Gk. *kanthēlios* pack ass]

hat, āge, fär; let, ēqual, tèrm; it, īce
hot, ōpen, ôrder; oil, out; cup, pùt, rüle,
əbove, takən, pencəl, lemən, circəs

ch, child; ng, long; sh, ship
th, thin; ŦH, then; zh, measure

Gan·y·mede (gan′ə mēd′) *n. Greek and Roman mythology.* a handsome youth, cupbearer to the gods of Olympus.

gaol (jāl) *Brit.* See **jail.**

gaol·er (jāl′ər) *Brit.* See **jailer.**

gap (gap) *n.* **1** a broken place; hole or opening, as in a fence, hedge, or wall. **2** an empty part; unfilled space; blank: *My diary is not complete; there are several gaps in it.* **3** a wide difference of opinion, character, etc; disparity: *the generation gap.* **4** a narrow way or route through or between something, as a mountain pass or as a channel between islands or an island and the mainland.
bridge, close, fill, or **stop a gap,** make up a deficiency. [ME < ON. Related to GAPE.]

gape (gāp) *v.* **gaped, gap·ing;** *n.* —*v.* **1** open wide: *A deep crevasse gaped before us.* **2** open the mouth wide, as when hungry or yawning. **3** stare with the mouth open: *The children gaped when they saw the huge birthday cake.*
—*n.* **1** a wide opening. **2** the act of opening the mouth wide. **3** an open-mouthed stare. **4 the gapes, a** a fit of yawning. **b** a disease of birds and poultry. [ME < ON *gapa*] —**gap′er,** *n.*

gar (gär) *n., pl.* **gar** or **gars. 1** any of a genus (*Lepisosteus*) making up a small family (Lepisosteidae) of mainly freshwater fishes of North and Central America having a long, slender, round body covered with an armor of very hard scales and a long, narrow, alligator-like snout with many needle-like teeth. **2** needlefish. [shortened form of *garfish*]

ga·rage (gə räzh′, gə raj′ *or* gə razh′) *n., v.* **-raged, -rag·ing.** —*n.* **1** a shelter for automobiles, trucks, etc.: *Their new house has a two-car garage.* **2** a commercial establishment for repairing and servicing automobiles, trucks, etc. —*v.* put or keep in a garage. [< F *garage* < *garer* put in shelter]

garage sale an informal sale of personal possessions, furniture, etc., usually held in a private garage or driveway and patronized mostly by neighbors and passers-by. See also **yard sale.**

garb (gärb) *n., v.* —*n.* **1** the way one is dressed; a characteristic style of clothing: *a doctor's garb, a painter's garb.* **2** the outward covering, form, or appearance. —*v.* clothe: *The doctor was garbed in white.* [< F *garbe* < Ital. *garbo* grace]

gar·bage (gär′bij) *n.* **1** waste animal or vegetable matter from a kitchen, store, etc. to be thrown away. **2** any worthless material: *We threw out several boxes of garbage when we cleaned out the attic.* **3** *Informal.* inferior, worthless, or offensive speech, writings, etc.: *That argument is a lot of garbage and shouldn't be taken seriously.* [ME, animal entrails; origin uncertain]

gar·ble (gär′bəl) *v.* **-bled, -bling. 1** make unfair or misleading selections from (facts, statements, writings, etc.), omit parts of, often in order to misrepresent: *Foreign newspapers gave a garbled account of the ambassador's speech.* **2** confuse or mix up (statements, words, etc.) unintentionally. [< Ital. *garbellare* < Arabic *gharbala* sift, probably < LL *cribellare,* ult. < *cribrum* sieve] —**gar′bler,** *n.*

gar·çon (gär sôN′) *n., pl.* **-çons** (-sôN′). *French.* **1** a young man or boy. **2** a male servant. **3** waiter.

gar·den (gär′dən) *n., v.* —*n.* **1** a piece of ground used for growing vegetables, herbs, flowers, or fruits. **2** (*adj.*) **a** growing or grown in a garden: *garden flowers.* **b** in or for a garden: *garden tools, a garden walk.* **3** a park or other place where plants or animals may be viewed by the public: *The city has a fine botanical garden.* **4** a fertile and delightful region or place. **5** (*adj.*) common or ordinary: *His jokes were all the common or garden variety.*
lead up (or **down**) **the garden path,** *Informal.* mislead or entice. —*v.* make, take care of, or work in a garden: *He loves to garden.* [ME < ONF *gardin* < Gmc.] —**gar′den·like,** *adj.*

garden cress an annual plant (*Lepidium sativum*) of the mustard family, native to Asia, but widely cultivated as a salad plant.

gar·den·er (gärd′nər *or* gär′də nər) *n.* **1** a person whose occupation is taking care of a garden, lawn, etc. **2** a person who makes a garden or works in a garden.

garden heliotrope 1 the common heliotrope (*Heliotropium arborescens*), a garden plant having wrinkled leaves and clusters of lilac or blue flowers with a fragrance like vanilla. **2** the common valerian (*Valeriana officinalis*), a garden plant having clusters of tiny, very fragrant, white or reddish flowers.

gar·de·nia (gär dēn′yə or gär dē′nē ə) n. 1 any of a large genus (*Gardenia*) of tropical and subtropical trees and shrubs of the madder family, having fragrant, roselike, white or yellow flowers with waxy petals. 2 a flower of any of these trees or shrubs, often worn as a corsage. [< NL; after Alexander *Garden* (1730-1791), an American botanist]

gar·fish (gär′fish′) n. gar. [< OE *gār* spear + *fisc* fish]

gar·gan·tu·an (gär gan′chü ən) adj. Sometimes, **Gargantuan**, enormous; gigantic: *a gargantuan meal, a gargantuan undertaking.* [< *Gargantua*, a good-natured giant of enormous appetite in a satire by Rabelais]

gar·get (gär′git) n. 1 in cattle and pigs, an inflamed condition of the head or throat. 2 in cows, ewes, etc., an inflammation of the udder. [< OF *gargate*]

gar·gle (gär′gəl) v. **-gled, -gling**; n. —v. 1 wash or rinse (the inside of the throat) with liquid kept in motion in the throat by the air that is slowly expelled from the lungs. 2 utter with a sound like gargling. —n. 1 a liquid used for gargling. 2 a sound like that produced by gargling. [probably imitative and influenced by OF *gargouiller* < *gargoule* throat < L *gurgulio* windpipe]

Gargoyles on the Peace Tower of the Houses of Parliament, Ottawa

gar·goyle (gär′goil) n. 1 a spout for carrying off rain water, projecting from the gutter of a building and usually having the form of a grotesque head or creature. Gargoyles are characteristic of Gothic architecture. 2 a projection or ornament on a building resembling a gargoyle. 3 a person having an extremely ugly face. [ME < MF *gargouille* (imitative); cf. L *gurgulio* gullet]

gar·ish (ger′ish or gar′ish) adj. 1 unpleasantly bright; glaring. 2 showy; gaudy. [ult. < obs. *gaure* stare] —**gar′ish·ly**, adv. —**gar′ish·ness**, n.

gar·land (gär′lənd) n., v. —n. 1 a wreath of flowers, leaves, etc. worn on the head or hung as a decoration. Garlands are often used as symbols of peace, victory, etc. 2 something like a garland. 3 a collection of short poems, ballads, etc.; anthology. 4 a collar or loop of rope on a ship's mast, used to hoist spars, etc. or to prevent chafing or fraying. —v. decorate with or form into a garland or garlands. [ME < OF *garlande*]

gar·lic (gär′lik) n. 1 a perennial plant (*Allium sativum*) of the lily family, widely grown for its strong-smelling and strong-tasting bulb. The bulb of garlic is made up of small sections called cloves. 2 a bulb or clove of this plant, used to season meats, salads, etc. [OE *gārlēac* < *gār* spear + *lēac* leek]

gar·lick·y (gär′lik ē) adj. smelling or tasting of garlic.

gar·ment (gär′mənt) n., v. —n. 1 any article of clothing. 2 an outer covering. —v. clothe. [ME < OF *garnement* < *garnir* fit out. See GARNISH.] —**gar′ment·less**, adj.

gar·ner (gär′nər) v., n. —v. 1 gather and store away: *Wheat is cut and garnered at harvest time. Squirrels garner nuts in the fall.* 2 earn. —n. 1 a storehouse for grain; granary. 2 a store of anything. [ME < OF *gernier, grenier* < L *granarium* < *granum* grain]

gar·net (gär′nit) n., adj. —n. 1 a brittle silicate mineral occurring mainly in red crystals. The transparent, deep-red variety of garnet is used as a semiprecious gemstone; other varieties are used as abrasives. 2 a gem cut from this mineral. 3 a deep red. —adj. deep red. [ME *gernet* < OF *grenat* grained (stone) < LL *granatum* < L *granum* grain, seed. See GRENADE.] —**gar′net·like′**, adj.

gar·nish (gär′nish) n., v. —n. 1 something laid on or around food as a decoration: *a garnish of parsley.* 2 a decoration; trimming. —v. 1 decorate (food). 2 decorate; trim. 3 Law. warn or notify by a garnishment. [ME < OF *garniss-*, a stem of *garnir* provide, defend < Gmc.] —**gar′nish·er**, n.

gar·nish·ee (gär′nish ē′) v. **-nish·eed, -nish·ee·ing**; n. Law. —v.

1 take (money or property) from a person by the authority of a court to pay a debt. If a creditor garnishees a debtor's salary, a certain portion of the salary is withheld and paid to the creditor. 2 notify (a person) not to hand over money or property belonging to the defendant in a lawsuit until the plaintiff's claims have been settled: *The debtor's employer was garnisheed.* —n. a person notified to hold the defendant's money or property as a trustee until the lawsuit is settled.

gar·nish·ment (gär′nish mənt) n. 1 decoration; trimming. 2 Law. a a legal notice warning a person to hold in his possession property that belongs to the defendant in a lawsuit until the plaintiff's claims have been settled. b a summons to a third person to appear in court while a lawsuit between others is being heard.

gar·ni·ture (gär′nə chər) n. decoration; trimming; garnish, especially of food. [< F]

ga·rotte (gə rot′ or gə rōt′) n., v. **-rot·ted, -rot·ting**. See **garrote**. —**ga·rot′ter**, n.

gar·pike (gär′pīk′) n. gar, especially a species (*Lepisosteus osseus*) found in eastern North America from southern Ontario and Quebec to the Gulf of Mexico, also called **longnose gar**.

gar·ret (gar′it or ger′it) n. 1 a space in a house just below a sloping roof; attic. 2 a room or apartment in such a place. [ME < OF *garite* watchtower < *garir* defend < Gmc.]

gar·ri·son (gar′ə sən or ger′ə sən) n., v. —n. 1 the soldiers stationed in a fort, town, etc., usually for the purpose of defending it. 2 a place where such troops are stationed. 3 (*adj.*) of, associated with, or having a garrison: *Kingston is a garrison town.* —v. 1 station troops in (a fort, town, etc.) to defend it. 2 take over or occupy (a fort, town, etc.) as a garrison. [ME < OF *garison* < *garir*. See GARRET.]

gar·rote (gə rot′ or gə rōt′) n., v. **-rot·ed, -rot·ing**. —n. 1 a method of execution formerly used in Spain, in which the person was strangled with an iron collar. 2 the iron collar used for this type of execution. 3 a cord, wire, etc. used for strangling in a robbery, a surprise attack on an enemy, etc. 4 strangulation, especially in order to rob. —v. 1 execute by garroting. 2 attack or kill with a garrote. Also, **garotte, garrotte**. [< Sp. *garrote* stick for twisting cord] —**gar·rot′er**, n.

gar·rotte (gə rot′ or gə rōt′) n., v. **-rot·ted, -rot·ting**. See **garrote**. —**gar·rot′ter**, n.

gar·ru·li·ty (gə rü′lə tē) n. the quality or state of being garrulous.

gar·ru·lous (gar′yə ləs or gar′ə ləs) adj. 1 talking too much about trifles. 2 using too many words. [< L *garrulus* < *garrire* chatter] —**gar′ru·lous·ly**, adv. —**gar′ru·lous·ness**, n.

gar·ter (gär′tər) n., v. —n. 1 a band or strap, usually of elastic, used to hold up a stocking or sock. 2 an elastic band worn around the arm to keep the sleeve pushed up. 3 **Garter**, a See **Order of the Garter**. b the badge of this order. c membership in it. —v. support or fasten with or as if with a garter. [ME < OF *gartier* < *garet* bend of the knee < Celtic]

garter snake any of various small, harmless, brownish or greenish snakes (genus *Thamnophis*) of North America having yellow or red stripes along the body.

gas¹ (gas) n., pl. **gas·es**; v. **gassed, gas·sing**. —n. 1 any fluid substance that can expand without limit; not a solid or liquid. Oxygen and nitrogen are gases. 2 any gas or mixture of gases except air. 3 any mixture of gases that can be burned, usually obtained from coal but occasionally from other substances. Gas was once much used for lighting, but is now used chiefly for cooking and heating. 4 any gas used as an anesthetic, such as nitrous oxide (laughing gas). 5 *Mining.* an explosive mixture of methane with air. 6 a substance that vaporizes and then poisons, suffocates, or stupefies: *The police used tear gas to dispel the mob.* 7 gas accumulated in or released from the stomach, usually as a result of indigestion or some other stomach disorder: *He suffers from gas pains.* 8 *Slang.* empty or boasting talk. 9 *Slang.* a person or thing that is very amusing, appealing, exciting, etc.: *The party was a gas.* —v. 1 supply with gas. 2 treat with gas; use gas on. Some kinds of seeds are gassed to hasten sprouting. 3 give off gas. 4 attack with gas; use gas on: *The police were forced to gas the violent criminals who refused to leave the building.* 5 *Slang.* talk idly, emptily, or boastfully. 6 *Slang.* excite, amuse, or appeal to greatly. [alteration of Gk. *chaos* chaos; coined by Jean B. van Helmont (1577-1644), a Flemish physicist] —**gas′less**, adj.

gas² (gas) n., v. **gassed, gas·sing**. Informal. —n. gasoline. **step on the gas, a** push down the accelerator of a motor vehicle. **b** go or act faster; hurry: *We'd better step on the gas and get these dishes done.* —v. fill the tank of a motor vehicle with gasoline (usually used with up): *We gassed up before we left the city.*

gas·bag (gas′bag′) n. 1 a container to hold gas. 2 an inflatable bag used to plug a gas pipe during repairs. 3 *Slang.* a person who talks too much; windbag.

gas burner the small nozzle of a gas fixture from which gas comes out and is burned.

Gas·con (gas′kən) *n., adj.* —*n.* **1** a native of Gascony, a region in SW France. Gascons were formerly noted for their boastfulness. **2 gascon,** a boastful, swaggering person. —*adj.* **1** of or having to do with Gascony or its people. **2 gascon,** boastful. [< F]

gas·con·ade (gas′kən ād′) *n., v.* **-ad·ed, -ad·ing.** —*n.* extravagant boasting. —*v.* boast extravagantly. [< F *gasconnade* < *gascon* Gascon]

gas·e·ous (gas′ē əs *or* gās′ē əs) *adj.* in the form of gas; of or like a gas: *Steam is water in a gaseous condition.*

gas fitter a person whose work is putting in and repairing pipes and fixtures for the use of gas in buildings.

gash (gash) *n., v.* —*n.* a long, deep cut or wound. —*v.* make a long, deep cut or wound in. [earlier *garsh* < ONF *garser* scarify]

gas·i·fy (gas′ə fī′) *v.* **-fied, -fy·ing.** change into a gas. —**gas′i·fi·ca′tion,** *n.* —**gas′i·fi′er,** *n.*

gas jet 1 a small nozzle or burner at the end of a gas fixture where the gas comes out. **2** a flame of gas.

gas·ket (gas′kit) *n.* **1** a ring or strip of rubber, metal, plaited hemp, etc. packed around a piston, pipe joint, etc. to make it leakproof. **2** a cord or small rope used to secure a furled sail on a yard. [origin uncertain]

gas·light (gas′līt′) *n.* **1** light made by burning gas. **2** a gas burner or gas jet.

gas main a large underground pipe to carry gas.

gas·man (gas′man′) *n., pl.* **-men. 1** a man whose work is to read consumers' gas meters and report the amount of gas used. **2** a man who manufactures or supplies gas. **3** a gas fitter. **4** a man who inspects coal mines for firedamp.

gas mantle a lacelike tube around a gas flame that glows and gives off light when heated.

gas mask a helmet or mask that covers the mouth and nose and is supplied with a filter containing chemicals to neutralize poisons. The wearer breathes only filtered air.

gas·o·hol (gas′ə hol′ *or* gas′ə hôl′) *n.* a mixture of gasoline and alcohol used as a fuel for motor vehicles. A mixture of about nine parts gasoline to one part alcohol can be used in a conventional vehicle without engine modification.

gas·o·line (gas′ə lēn′ *or* gas′ə lēn′) *n.* a colorless liquid consisting of a mixture of hydrocarbons, which evaporates and burns very easily and is made by distilling petroleum. Gasoline is used mainly as a fuel in internal-combustion engines. Also, **gasolene.** [< *gas* + *-ol,* suffix meaning "oil" (< L *oleum*) + *-ine²*]

gas·om·e·ter (gas om′ə tər) *n.* **1** a container for holding and measuring gas. **2** a gas tank. [< F *gazomètre* < *gaz* gas + *mètre* measure; influenced by *gas*]

gasp (gasp) *n., v.* —*n.* **1** a sudden, short intaking of breath through the mouth. A gasp often indicates suspense, shock, or fear. **2** one of a series of short breaths caused by having difficulty in breathing: *After her hard run, her breath came in gasps.* **at the last gasp, a** about to die. **b** at the final moment. —*v.* **1** catch the breath with difficulty. **2** breathe with gasps. **3** utter with gasps. **4** with (for); long (for). [ME < ON *geispa* yawn]

gasp·er (gas′pər) *n. Slang.* cigarette.

gas·pe·reau (gas′pə rō′) *n., pl.* **gas·pe·reaux.** *Cdn.* the alewife, an Atlantic food fish. [< Cdn.F]

Gas·pe·sian (gas pā′zhən *or* gas pē′zhən) *n., adj. Cdn.* —*n.* a native or inhabitant of the Gaspé Peninsula in E Quebec. [< Cdn.F *Gaspésien*] —*adj.* of or having to do with the Gaspé or its inhabitants.

gas·ser (gas′ər) *n.* **1** a person or thing that gasses. **2** a natural gas-well. **3** *Slang.* something of more than usual merit; a huge success.

gas station a place for supplying motor vehicles with gasoline, motor oil, water, etc.

gas·sy (gas′ē) *adj.* **-si·er, -si·est. 1** full of gas; containing gas. **2** like gas: *a gassy smell.*

gas·tric (gas′trik) *adj.* of, in, or near the stomach. [< Gk. *gastēr, gastros* stomach]

gastric juice the thin, nearly clear digestive fluid secreted by glands in the mucous membrane that lines the stomach. It contains pepsin and other enzymes and hydrochloric acid.

gas·trin (gas′trin) *n.* a hormone secreted by the mucous lining of the stomach and that stimulates the secretion of gastric juice.

gas·tri·tis (gas trī′tis) *n. Medicine.* an inflammation of the stomach, especially of its mucous membrane. [< Gk. *gastēr, gastros* stomach + E *-itis*]

gastro- *combining form.* **1** the stomach: *gastrotomy = surgical incision into the stomach.* **2** the stomach and ——: *gastrohepatic =*

hat, āge, fär; let, ēqual, tèrm; it, īce
hot, ōpen, ôrder; oil, out; cup, pút, rüle,
ə above, takən, pencəl, lemən, circəs
ch, child; ng, long; sh, ship
th, thin; ŦH, then; zh, measure

of or having to do with the stomach and liver. Also, **gastr-** before vowels. [< Gk. *gastēr, gastros*]

gas·tro·en·ter·i·tis (gas′trō en′tə rī′tis) *n. Medicine.* inflammation of the membranes of the stomach and intestines.

gas·tro·nome (gas′trə nōm′) *n.* a person who is expert in gastronomy; epicure. [< F *gastronome,* back formation < *gastronomie.* See GASTRONOMY.]

gas·tro·nom·ic (gas′trə nom′ik) *adj.* of or having to do with gastronomy.

gas·tro·nom·i·cal (gas′trə nom′ə kəl) *adj.* gastronomic.

gas·tron·o·my (gas tron′ə mē) *n.* the art or science of good eating. [< F < Gk. *gastronomia* < *gastēr, gastros* stomach + *nomos* law]

gas·tro·pod (gas′trə pod′) *n.* **1** any of a large class (Gastropoda) of molluscs having one-piece shells or no shells, and most of which move by means of a single, broad, disklike foot attached to the undersurface of their bodies. Snails, limpets, and slugs are gastropods. **2** (*adj.*) of, having to do with, or designating this class of molluscs. [< NL *Gastropoda,* pl. < Gk. *gastēr, gastros* stomach + *-podos* footed < *pous, podos* foot]

gas·tru·la (gas′trü lə) *n., pl.* **-lae** (-lē′ *or* -lī′). *Biology.* the stage in the development of all many-celled animals when the embryo is usually saclike and composed of two layers of cells. [< NL *gastrula,* dim. of Gk. *gastēr, gastros* stomach]

gat¹ (gat) *v. Archaic.* a pt. of **get.**

gat² (gat) *n. Obsolete slang.* pistol. [shortened form of *Gatling gun*]

gate (gāt) *n.* **1** a movable part or frame for closing an opening in a wall or fence. It turns on hinges or slides open and shut. **2** an opening in a wall, usually fitted with a door, turnstile, or some other barrier; gateway. **3** the part of a building containing the gate or gates, with the adjoining towers, walls, etc. **4** a way to go in or out; a way to get to something. **5** a barrier intended to prevent entrance, stop traffic, etc.: *Level crossings are often equipped with gates to keep cars off the track when a train is passing.* **6** a door, valve, etc. to stop or control the flow of water in a pipe, dam, lock, etc. **7** the number of people who pay to see a contest, exhibition, performance, etc. **8** the total amount of money received from these people: *The two teams divided a gate of $3250.* **get the gate,** *Slang.* be dismissed. **give the gate to,** *Informal.* **a** dismiss or turn away. **b** *Hockey.* award a player a penalty, thus putting him off the ice. [OE *gatu,* pl. of *geat*] —**gate′less,** *adj.* —**gate′like′,** *adj.*

gate·crash (gāt′krash′) *v. Slang.* attend a party, social function, or entertainment without being invited or without a ticket.

gate–crash·er (gāt′krash′ər) *n. Informal.* a person who attends parties, gatherings, etc. without an invitation; an uninvited guest.

gate·house (gāt′hous′) *n.* **1** a house at or over a gate, used as the keeper's quarters. See **castle** for picture. **2** a structure at the gate of a reservoir, dam, etc., with machinery for regulating the flow of water.

gate·keep·er (gāt′kē′pər) *n.* a person employed to guard a gate and control passage through it.

gate·post (gāt′pōst′) *n.* one of the posts on either side of a gate. A swinging gate is fastened to one gatepost and closes against the other.

gate·way (gāt′wā′) *n.* **1** an opening in a wall, fence, etc., fitted with a gate or some other barrier. **2** a way to go in or out; way to get to or attain something: *a gateway to success. Winnipeg was known as the Gateway to the West.* **3** the frame of a gate or a structure built over it.

gath·er (gaŦH′ər) *v., n.* —*v.* **1** bring into one place or group: *He gathered his books and papers and started off to school.* **2** come together; assemble: *A crowd gathered at the scene of the accident.* **3** get together gradually or from various sources: *to gather sticks for a fire.* **4** form a mass; collect: *Tears gathered in her eyes.* **5** pick and collect; take: *Farmers gather their crops.* **6** get or gain little by little: *The train gathered speed as it left the station.* **7** collect (oneself, one's strength, energies, thoughts, etc.) for an effort. **8** put together in the mind; conclude; infer: *I gathered from his words that he was really much upset.* **9** pull together in folds; wrinkle: *She gathered her brow in a frown.* **10** pull together in little folds and stitch: *The skirt is gathered at the waist.* **11** draw together

or closer: *Gather your robe around you.* **12** come to a head and form pus: *A boil is a painful swelling that gathers under the skin.* **13** *Bookbinding.* collect and place in order (the printed, folded sheets of a book).

gathered to (one's) **fathers,** dead and buried.

gather up, a pick up and put together. **b** pull together; bring into a smaller space.

—*n.* **1** one of the little folds between the stitches when cloth is pulled together in folds. **2** a contraction; drawing together. **3** *Glassmaking.* a blob of glass collected on the end of a blowpipe. [OE *gaderian* < *geador* (to)gether]

☛ *Syn. v.* **Gather, collect, assemble** = bring or come together. **Gather,** the general word, is interchangeable with **collect,** though the former is the more colloquial and idiomatic. **Collect** is of Latin origin and sometimes has a more professional air: *collect stamps, collect taxes;* but *gather wealth, gather honey.* **Assemble,** more formal, has the special sense of "bringing or coming together according to a definite plan or purpose": *assemble a watch. Parliament assembles.*

gath·er·ing (gaŦн′ər ing *or* gaŦн′ring) *n.* **1** the act of one that gathers. **2** that which is gathered. **3** a meeting; assembly; party; crowd. **4** a swelling that comes to a head and forms pus.

☛ *Syn.* **3.** See note at **meeting.**

Gat·ling gun (gat′ling) an early type of machine gun consisting of a revolving cluster of barrels around a central axis. [after Richard J. *Gatling* (1818-1903), an American inventor]

GATT General Agreement on Tariffs and Trade.

gauche (gōsh) *adj.* awkward or clumsy in social situations; tactless. [< F *gauche* left-handed] —**gauche′ly,** *adv.* —**gauche′ness,** *n.*

gau·che·rie (gō′shə rē′ *or* gō′shə rē′) *n.* **1** awkwardness in social situations; tactlessness. **2** an awkward or tactless movement, act, etc. [< F]

gau·cho (gou′chō) *n., pl.* **-chos.** a cowboy or herdsman of the southern plains of South America. [< Sp.]

gaud (god *or* gôd) *n.* a cheap, showy ornament; trinket: *beads, mirrors, and such gauds.* [apparently < AF *gaude* < *gaudir* rejoice < L *gaudere*]

☛ *Hom.* **god** (god).

gaud·y (god′ē *or* gôd′ē) *adj.* **gaud·i·er, gaud·i·est.** bright or ornate in a cheap and tasteless way: *gaudy jewellery.* —**gaud′i·ly,** *adv.* —**gaud′i·ness,** *n.*

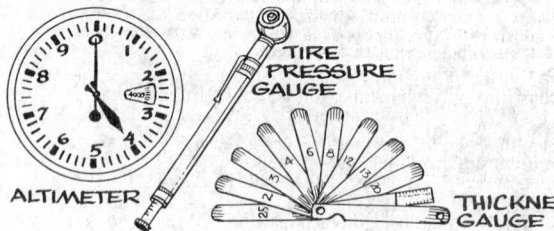

ALTIMETER · TIRE PRESSURE GAUGE · THICKNESS GAUGE

gauge (gāj) *n., v.* **gauged, gaug·ing.** —*n.* **1** a standard measure or scale of measurement to which something must conform. There are gauges of the capacity of a barrel, the thickness of sheet iron, the diameter of wire, etc. **2** an instrument for measuring. A **steam gauge** measures the pressure of steam. **3** a means of estimating or judging. **4** size, capacity, or extent. **5** the diameter of the bore of a firearm, especially a shotgun. **6** the distance between rails of a railway track or between the right and left wheels of a wagon, automobile, etc. standard gauge is 56½ inches (about 144 cm). Compare **broad-gauge** and **narrow-gauge.** **7** the position of one sailing ship with reference to another and to the wind. A ship having the weather gauge of another is to the windward of it. **8** the length of the exposed part of shingles, tiles, etc. when laid in rows. **9** a measure of the fineness of knitted fabric, expressed as the number of loops made per unit of width; the higher the number, the finer the texture.

—*v.* **1** measure accurately with a measuring device: *He had a special instrument to gauge the width of the metal strip.* **2** estimate; judge: *It is difficult to gauge the character of a stranger.* Also, **gage.** [ME < ONF] —**gauge′a·ble,** *adj.*

☛ *Hom.* **gage.**

gaug·er (gāj′ər) *n.* **1** a person or thing that gauges. **2** an official who measures the contents of barrels of taxable liquor. **3** a collector of excise taxes. Also, **gager.**

Gaul (gol *or* gôl) *n.* **1** one of the Celtic inhabitants of Gaul, an ancient country in W Europe. **2** Frenchman. [(def. 1) < F *Gaule* < L *Gallia* < *Gallus* a Gaul; (def. 2) < L *Gallus*]

Gau·lei·ter (gou′lī tər) *n.* **1** a high official in the Nazi party who acted as governor of a district in Germany or German-occupied territory. **2 gauleiter,** any subordinate who carries out harsh or criminal orders. [< G < *Gau* district + *Leiter* leader]

gaunt (gont *or* gônt) *adj.* **1** very thin and bony; with hollow eyes and a starved look: *Hunger and suffering make people gaunt.* **2** looking bare and gloomy; desolate, forbidding or grim: *The ancient castle stood gaunt on the hilltop.* [origin uncertain] —**gaunt′ly,** *adv.* —**gaunt′ness,** *n.*

☛ *Syn.* **1.** See note at **thin.**

gaunt·let¹ (gont′lit *or* gônt′lit) *n.* **1** a stout, heavy glove, usually of leather covered with plates of iron or steel, that was part of a knight's armor. See **armor** for picture. **2** a stout, heavy glove with a wide, flaring cuff, used for protection in industry, etc. **3** the wide, flaring cuff.

take up the gauntlet, a accept a challenge. **b** take up the defence of a person, opinion, etc.

throw down the gauntlet, challenge. [ME < OF *gantelet,* dim. of *gant* glove < Gmc.]

gaunt·let² (gont′lit *or* gônt′lit) *n. Historical.* a military punishment in which the offender had to run between two rows of men who struck him with clubs or other weapons as he passed.

run the gauntlet, a pass between two rows of men, each of whom strikes the runner as he passes. **b** carry out an action in spite of danger threatening on all sides: *During the war, convoys ran the gauntlet of enemy submarines.* **c** be exposed to unfriendly attacks, criticism, etc. Also, **gantlet.** [< Swedish *gatlopp* < *gata* lane + *lopp* course]

Gau·ta·ma (got′ə mə, gô′tə mə, *or* gou′tə mə) *n.* Buddha. Also, **Gotama.**

gauze (goz *or* gôz) *n.* **1** a very thin, light cloth of cotton, silk, etc., easily seen through. Cotton gauze is often used for bandages. **2** a thin haze. [< F *gaze;* after *Gaza,* the capital of the Gaza Strip, SW of Israel] —**gauze′like′,** *adj.*

gauz·y (goz′ē *or* gôz′ē) *adj.* **gauz·i·er, gauz·iest.** like gauze; thin and light as gauze. —**gauz′i·ly,** *adv.* —**gauz′i·ness,** *n.*

gave (gāv) *v.* pt. of **give.**

gav·el (gav′əl) *n.* a small mallet used by a presiding officer to signal for attention and order or by an auctioneer to announce that the bidding is over. [origin uncertain]

ga·vi·al (gā′vē əl) *n.* a crocodilian reptile (*Gavialis gangeticus*) of India, the only species in the family Gavialidae, resembling crocodiles and alligators but having a very long, slender snout. [< F < Hind. *ghariyāl*]

ga·votte (gə vot′) *n.* **1** a dance like a minuet but much more lively. **2** the music for this dance. [< F < Provençal *gavoto* < *Gavots,* Alpine people]

gawk (gok *or* gôk) *n., v.* —*n.* an awkward person; clumsy fool. —*v. Informal.* stare rudely or stupidly. [origin uncertain] —**gawk′er,** *n.*

gawk·y (gok′ē *or* gôk′ē) *adj.* **gawk·i·er, gawk·i·est.** awkward; clumsy. —**gawk′i·ly,** *adv.* —**gawk′i·ness,** *n.*

gay (gā) *adj.* **gay·er, gay·est.** —*adj.* **1** happy and full of fun: *gay laughter.* **2** bright-colored; showy: *gay decorations.* **3** fond of pleasures: *They had led a gay and wild life.* **4** dissolute or licentious: *a gay old dog.* **5** *Slang.* homosexual. —*n. Slang.* homosexual. [< F *gai*] —**gay′ness,** *n.*

☛ *Syn.* **1. Gay, merry** = lively and light-hearted. **Gay** emphasizes being free from care and full of life, joy, and high spirits; **merry** emphasizes being full of laughter and lively pleasure and fun: *The gay young people were merry as they danced.*

☛ *Usage.* Many people now avoid this use (def. 1) of **gay** because of the widespread use of the word (def. 5) to mean "homosexual."

gay·e·ty (gā′ə tē) *n., pl.* **-ties.** See **gaiety.**

gay·ly (gā′lē) See **gaily.**

gaz. gazette; gazetteer.

gaze (gāz) *v.* **gazed, gaz·ing;** *n.* —*v.* look long and steadily. —*n.* a long, steady look. [cf. Norwegian and Swedish dial. *gasa*] —**gaz′er,** *n.* —**gaz′ing·ly,** *adv.*

☛ *Syn. v.* **Gaze, stare** = look long and steadily at someone or something. **Gaze** emphasizes looking steadily and intently, chiefly in wonder, delight, or interest: *For hours he sat gazing at the stars.* **Stare** emphasizes looking with wide-open eyes steadily and directly at someone or something or off into space, chiefly in curiosity, rudeness, surprise, or stupidity: *The little girl stared at the stranger briefly before answering his question.*

ga·ze·bo (gə zē′bō) *n., pl.* **-bos** or **-boes.** a summerhouse, balcony, etc. that commands a wide view. [supposedly < *gaze,* on the pattern of Latin future tenses in *-bo*]

ga·zelle (gə zel′) *n.* any of a genus (*Gazella*) of small to medium-sized antelope of Africa and Asia, having a slender graceful body, long, thin legs, and lustrous eyes. [< F < Arabic *ghazāl*] —**ga·zelle′-like′,** *adj.*

ga·zette (gə zet′) *n., v.* **-zet·ted, -zet·ting.** —*n.* **1** newspaper. **2** an official government journal containing lists of appointments,

promotions, etc. —*v.* publish, list, or announce in a gazette. [< F < Ital. *gazzetta*, originally, coin; from the price of a paper]

gaz·et·teer (gaz′ə tēr′) *n.* **1** a dictionary of geographical names. **2** a writer for a gazette. **3** an official appointed to publish a gazette. [< F *gazettier*]

gaz·pa·cho (gäs pä′chō) *n.* a vegetable soup served cold, made with tomatoes, cucumbers, onions, peppers, olive oil, etc. [<Sp]

G.B. Great Britain.

G.B.E. (Knight or Dame) Grand (Cross or Order) of the British Empire.

G.C. George Cross.

G.C.B. (Knight) Grand Cross of the (Order of the) Bath.

GCD, G.C.D., or **g.c.d.** greatest common divisor.

GCF, G.C.F. or **g.c.f.** greatest common factor.

G clef *Music.* the treble clef.

GCM, G.C.M. or **g.c.m.** greatest common measure.

G.C.V.O. (Knight) Grand Cross of the (Royal) Victorian Order.

Gd gadolinium.

Ge germanium.

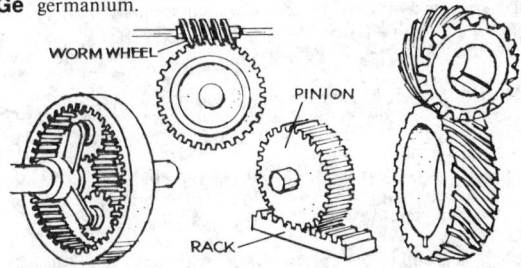

WORM WHEEL / PINION / RACK

Four types of gear assembly: from left to right, a planetary gear train, worm gear, rack and pinion, and helical gears

gear (gēr) *n., v.* —*n.* **1** a wheel having teeth that fit into the teeth of another wheel of the same kind. If the wheels are of different sizes, they will turn at different speeds. **2** an arrangement of fixed and moving parts for transmitting or changing motion; mechanism; machinery: *The car ran off the road when the steering gear broke.* **3** working order; adjustment: *His watch got out of gear and would not run.* **4** the equipment needed for some purpose. Harness, clothes, household goods, tools, tackle, and rigging are various kinds of gear.
in gear, a connected to the motor, etc. **b** in working order.
out of gear, disconnected from the motor, etc.
shift gears, change from one gear to another; connect a motor, etc. to a different set of gears.
—*v.* **1** connect by gears. An automobile moves when the motor is geared to the driving wheels. **2** fit or work together; mesh: *The cogs gear smoothly.* **3** provide with gear; equip; harness. **4** put into gear. **5** make subordinate to in order to serve: *The steel industry was geared to the needs of war.* [ME < ON *gervi*] —**gear′less,** *adj.*

gear·ing (gēr′ing) *n.* **1** a set of gears, chains, etc. for transmitting motion or power; gears. **2** the act of fitting a machine with gears. **3** the way in which a machine is fitted with gears.

gear·shift (gēr′shift′) *n.* a device for connecting a motor, etc. to any of several sets of gears.

gear·wheel (gēr′wēl′ or -hwēl′) *n.* a wheel having teeth that fit into the teeth of another wheel of the same kind.

geck·o (gek′ō) *n., pl.* **geck·os** or **geck·oes.** any of several small, soft-skinned, insect-eating lizards (family Gekkonidae) found in the tropics, having suction pads on its toes for climbing. [< Malay *gekok*; imitative of its cry]

gee[1] (jē) *interj., n., v.* **geed, gee·ing.** —*interj. or n.* a command to horses, oxen, etc. directing them to turn to the right. *Haw* is used for "left." —*v.* turn to the right.

gee[2] (jē) *interj.* an exclamation or mild oath. [a shortened form of *Jesus*]

geek (gēk) *n. Slang.* **1** a circus performer whose act consists of eating or biting the heads off live animals, such as chickens or snakes. **2** an odd or weird person, especially one considered repulsive.

geese (gēs) *n.* pl. of **goose.**

gee·zer (gē′zər) *n. Slang.* a fellow, usually an odd person and especially an elderly one. [dial. pronunciation of *guiser* someone in disguise, mummer]

Ge·hen·na (gə hen′ə) *n.* **1** hell. **2** a place of torment or misery. [< L < Gk. *geenna* hell < Hebrew *gê'hinnōm*, originally the valley of Hinnom where children had been burned in sacrifice]

Gei·ger counter (gī′gər) a device that counts and counts

hat, āge, fär; let, ēqual, tèrm; it, īce
hot, ōpen, ôrder; oil, out; cup, pút, rüle,
əbove, takən, pencəl, lemən, circəs
ch, child; ng, long; sh, ship
th, thin; ŦH, then; zh, measure

ionizing particles. It is used to measure radio-activity, test cosmic-ray particles, etc. [after Hans *Geiger*, a German physicist]

Geiger–Mül·ler counter (mul′ər; German, mYl′ər) an improved, more sensitive form of the Geiger counter.

gei·sha (gā′shə *or* gē′shə) *n., pl.* **-sha** or **-shas.** a Japanese girl specially trained in singing, dancing, the art of conversation, etc., in order to act as a hostess or companion for men. [< Japanese]

gel (jel) *n., v.* **gelled, gel·ling.** —*n.* a jelly-like or solid material formed from a colloidal solution. When glue sets, it forms a gel. —*v.* form a gel. Egg white gels when it is cooked. [shortened form of *gelatin*]

gel·a·tin (jel′ə tən) *n.* **1** an odorless, tasteless substance obtained by boiling animal tissues, bones, hoofs, etc. Gelatin dissolves easily in hot water and becomes jelly-like when cool; it is used in making jellied desserts, camera film, glue, etc. **2** any of various vegetable substances having similar properties. **3** a preparation or product in which gelatin is the basic constituent. [< F < Ital. *gelatina* < *gelata* jelly < L *gelare* freeze]

gel·a·tine (jel′ə tən *or* jel′ə tēn′) *n. Esp.Brit.* gelatin.

ge·lat·i·nous (jə lat′ə nəs) *adj.* **1** jelly-like; of the consistency of jelly. **2** of or containing gelatin.

geld (geld) *v.* **geld·ed** or **gelt, geld·ing.** remove the testicles of an animal, especially a horse; castrate. [ME < ON *gelda* castrate < *geldr* barren]

geld·ing (gel′ding) *n.* a gelded horse or other animal.

gel·id (jel′id) *adj.* cold as ice; frosty. [< L *gelidus* < *gelum* cold]

gel·ig·nite (jel′ig nīt′) *n.* a type of dynamite in which the absorbent base for the nitroglycerin consists mainly of wood pulp and a nitrate such as potassium nitrate.

gelt (gelt) *v.* a pt. and a pp. of **geld.**

gem (jem) *n., v.* **gemmed, gem·ming.** —*n.* **1** a precious stone; jewel. Diamonds and rubies are gems. **2** a person or thing that is very precious, beautiful, etc.: *The gem of his collection was a rare Persian stamp.* **3** a kind of muffin made of coarse flour. —*v.* set or adorn with gems, or set as if with gems: *Stars gem the sky.* [< F < L *gemma* gem, bud] —**gem′like′,** *adj.*

Ge·ma·ra (gə mä′rə *or* gə mô′rə) *n.* the second main part of the Talmud, consisting of a commentary on the first part, called the Mishnah. [< Aramaic *gemara* completion]

gem·i·nate (*v.* jem′ə nāt′; *adj.* jem′ə nit *or* jem′ə nāt′) *v.* **-nat·ed, -nat·ing;** *adj.* —*v.* make or become double; combine in pairs. —*adj.* combined in a pair or pairs; coupled. [< L *geminare* < *geminus* twin] —**gem′i·na′tion,** *n.*

Gem·i·ni (jem′ə nī′ *or* jem′ə nē′) *n.pl.* (*used with a singular verb*) **1** *Astronomy.* a northern constellation containing the two bright stars, Castor and Pollux. **2** *Astrology.* **a** the third sign of the zodiac. The sun enters Gemini about May 21. See **zodiac** for picture. **b** a person born under this sign. [< L *gemini* twins]

gem·ma (jem′ə) *n., pl.* **gem·mae** (jem′ē). **1** *Botany.* a bud. **2** *Biology.* a budlike growth that can develop into a new plant or animal. [< L *gemma* bud] —**gem·ma′tion,** *n.*

gem·mol·o·gist or **gem·ol·o·gist** (jem ol′ə jist) *n.* an expert in gemmology.

gem·mol·o·gy or **gem·ol·o·gy** (jem ol′ə jē) *n.* the study of gems, their origins, uses, etc.

gem·mule (jem′yül) *n.* a small gemma. [< L *gemmula,* dim. of *gemma* bud]

gems·bok (gemz′bok′) *n.* a large oryx (*Oryx gazella*) of S Africa. [< Afrikaans < G *Gemsbock* < *Gemse* chamois + *Bock* buck]

gem·stone (jem′stōn′) *n.* a precious or semiprecious stone, capable of being cut and polished to make a gem.

gen (jen) *n., v.* **genned, gen·ning.** *Slang.* —*n.* authentic, detailed information. —*v.* give authentic, detailed information to. [originally Royal Air Force slang, perhaps < *genuine* information]

–gen *suffix.* producing or produced, as in *antigen, nitrogen.* [< F < Gk. *-genēs,* ult. < *gignesthai* be born]

gen. **1** gender. **2** general. **3** genitive. **4** genus. **5** generator.

Gen. Genesis.

Gen. or **Gen** general.

gen·darme (zhon′därm; *French*, zhäɴ därm′) *n., pl.* **-darmes** (-därmz). **1** especially in France, one of a body of soldiers employed as armed police officers. **2** any police officer. [< F *gendarme* < *gens d'armes* men of arms]

gen·der (jen′dər) *n.* **1** *Grammar.* **a** a system of grouping words (such as nouns, pronouns, and adjectives) into two or more classes, either arbitrarily or according to certain features of structure or meaning, such as sex, social rank, shape, size, or kind of existence (living things as opposed to non-living). **b** any such category. **c** a form or inflection used to indicate such a category. **2** *Informal.* sex. [ME < OF *gendre* < L *genus, -neris* kind, sort]
☛ *Usage.* **Grammatical gender.** Many languages have special endings for masculine, feminine, and neuter nouns and for adjectives modifying them, but English lost such formal distinctions several hundred years ago. Now, except in pronouns and a few nouns borrowed from other languages (*actress, mistress, alumnus, alumna, aviatrix, blonde, masseur, masseuse*), gender is indicated only by the meaning of the word: *man—woman, nephew—niece, rooster—hen.*

gene (jēn) *n.* a part of a germ cell that occupies a fixed place on a chromosome and determines the nature and development of an inherited characteristic. The genes inherited from its parents determine what kind of plant or animal will develop from a fertilized egg cell. [< Gk. *genea* breed, kind]
☛ *Hom.* **jean.**

ge·ne·a·log·i·cal (jē′nē·ə·loj′ə·kəl *or* jen′ē·ə·loj′ə·kəl) *adj.* having to do with genealogy. A genealogical table or chart shows the descent of a person or family from an ancestor.
—**ge′ne·a·log′i·cal·ly,** *adv.*

ge·ne·al·o·gist (jē′nē·al′ə·jist *or* jē′nē·ol′ə·jist, jen′ē·al′ə·jist *or* jen′ē·ol′ə·jist) *n.* a person who traces genealogies; person who makes a study of genealogies.

ge·ne·al·o·gy (jē′nē·al′ə·jē *or* jē′nē·ol′ə·jē, jen′ē·al′ə·jē *or* jen′ē·ol′ə·jē) *n., pl.* **-gies. 1** an account or record of the descent of a person or family from an ancestor or ancestors. **2** the descent of a person or family from an ancestor; pedigree; lineage. **3** the study or investigation of lines of descent; study of pedigrees. [< L < Gk. *genealogia,* ult. < *genea* generation + *-logos* treating of]

gen·er·a (jen′ər·ə) *n.* pl. of **genus.**

gen·er·al (jen′ər·əl *or* jen′rəl) *adj., n.* —*adj.* **1** of all; for all; from all: *A government takes care of the general welfare.* **2** common to many or most; not limited to a few; widespread: *There is a general interest in sports.* **3** not specialized; not limited to one kind, class, departments, or use: *A general reader reads different kinds of books.* **4** not detailed; sufficient for practical purposes: *general instructions.* **5** indefinite; vague: *She referred to her trip in a general way.* **6** of or for all those forming a group: *The word* cat *can be used as a general term for cats, lions, and tigers.* **7** of highest rank; in chief: *a general manager, the solicitor general.*
—*n.* **1** *Canadian Forces.* the highest-ranking officer, next above a lieutenant-general. *Abbrev.:* Gen. *or* Gen **2** an officer of similar rank in the armed forces of other countries. **3** any officer ranking above a colonel and entitled to command a force larger than a regiment, such as a lieutenant-general. **4** any officer in command of many soldiers: *Sir Arthur Currie was a famous Canadian general.* **5** a general fact, idea, principle, or statement. **6** the head of a religious order. **7** *Archaic.* people as a group; the public.
in general, a referring to all those mentioned. **b** usually; for the most part: *In general, people get along fairly well together.* [< L *generalis* of a whole class < *genus, -neris* class, race]
☛ *Syn. adj.* **1, 2. General, common, popular** = belonging or relating to all. **General** = belonging to or existing among all, or almost all, of a group or class of people or things thought of as a whole: *Laws are made for the general good.* **Common** = shared by all the members of a group or class: *English is the common language in the United States.* **Popular** = belonging to, existing among, or representing the general public: *Various polls are devised to find out popular opinions.*

General Assembly the legislative body of the United Nations.

general delivery a department of a post office that handles mail which is not addressed to a street number or box number.

general election 1 an election involving all the voters of a country. **2** in Canada, an election in which either a new federal Parliament or a new provincial legislative assembly is elected.

gen·er·al·is·si·mo (jen′ər·əl·is′ə·mō *or* jen′rəl·is′ə·mō) *n., pl.* **-mos.** in certain countries: **1** the commander-in-chief of all the military forces of a country. **2** the commander-in-chief of several armies in the field. [< Ital. *generalissimo,* superlative of *generale* general]

gen·er·al·ist (jen′ər·əl·ist) *n.* a person who does not specialize in any one field of study but has a wide general knowledge.

gen·er·al·i·ty (jen′ər·al′ə·tē) *n., pl.* **-ties. 1** a general statement; a word or phrase not definite enough to have much meaning or value: *The candidate spoke only in generalities; not once did he mention definite laws that he and his party would try to pass.* **2** a general principle or rule: *"Nothing happens without a cause" is a*

generality. **3** the greater part; main body; mass: *The generality of people must work for a living.* **4** general quality or condition: *A rule of great generality has very few exceptions.*

gen·er·al·i·za·tion (jen′ər·ə·lə·zā′shən *or* jen′ər·əl·ī·zā′shən; jen′rəl·ə·zā′shən *or* jen′rəl·ī·zā′shən) *n.* **1** the act or process of generalizing. **2** a general idea, statement, principle, or rule: *Her argument was weakened by too many generalizations.*

gen·er·al·ize (jen′ər·əl·īz′ *or* jen′rəl·īz′) *v.* **-ized, -iz·ing. 1** make into one general statement; bring under a common heading, class, or law: *All men, women, and children can be generalized under the term "human being."* **2** infer (a general rule) from particular facts: *If you have seen cats, lions, leopards, and tigers eat meat, you can generalize that the cat family eats meat.* **3** state in a more general form; extend in application. The statement that $5 + 3 = 8$ and $50 + 30 = 80$ can be generalized to the form $5a + 3a = 8a.$ **4** talk indefinitely or vaguely; use generalities. **5** make general; bring into general use or knowledge. **6** make general inferences.
—**gen′er·al·iz′er,** *n.*

gen·er·al·ly (jen′ər·əl·ē *or* jen′rəl·ē) *adv.* **1** as a rule; in most cases; usually: *He is generally on time.* **2** by or to most people; commonly; widely: *It was once generally believed that the earth is flat.* **3** in a general way; without giving details; not specially: *Generally speaking, our coldest weather comes in January.*

General of the Army *U.S.* the highest-ranking officer in the army.

General Radio Service *Cdn.* a range of radio frequencies officially reserved for use by the general public for short-range, private communication. The U.S. name, widely used in Canada, is Citizens' Band.

gen·er·al·ship (jen′ər·əl·ship′ *or* jen′rəl-) *n.* **1** ability as a general; skill in commanding an army. **2** skilful management; leadership. **3** the rank, commission, authority, or term of office of a general.

general staff a group of high army officers who make plans of war or national defence.

general store a small store that carries a wide variety of goods for sale but is not divided into departments: *General stores are usually located in small communities and rural areas.*

gen·er·ate (jen′ər·āt′) *v.* **-at·ed, -at·ing. 1** produce; cause to be: *Rubbing generates heat. Steam can be used to generate power or electricity.* **2** produce (offspring). **3** *Mathematics.* form (a line, surface, figure, or solid) by moving a point, line, or plane. [< L *generare* < *genus, -neris* race]

gen·er·a·tion (jen′ər·ā′shən) *n.* **1** all the people born about the same time. Your parents and their friends belong to one generation; you and your friends belong to the following generation. **2** the average time from the birth of one generation to the birth of the next generation; about 30 years. **3** one step, or stage, in the history of a family: *The picture showed four generations—great-grandmother, grandmother, mother, and baby.* **4** the production of offspring. **5** production; a causing to be; generating: *Steam and water power are used for the generation of electricity.* **6** *Biology.* a form or stage of a plant or animal, with reference to its method of reproduction: *the asexual generation of a fern.* **7** one step, or stage, in the history or development of something: *an earlier generation of computers.* **8** *Mathematics.* the formation of a line, surface, figure, or solid by moving a point, line, or plane. —**gen′er·a′tion·al,** *adj.*

gen·er·a·tive (jen′ər·ə·tiv *or* jen′ər·ā′tiv) *adj.* **1** having to do with the production of offspring. **2** having the power of producing. —**gen′er·a·tive·ly,** *adv.* —**gen′er·a·tive·ness,** *n.*

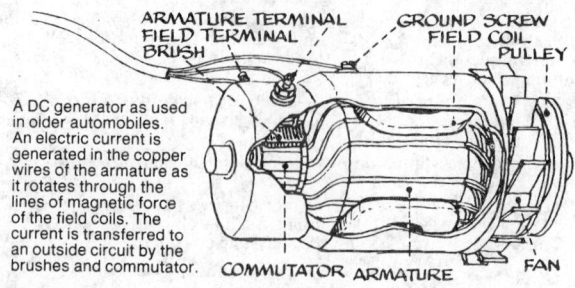

ARMATURE TERMINAL
FIELD TERMINAL
BRUSH
GROUND SCREW
FIELD COIL
PULLEY

A DC generator as used in older automobiles. An electric current is generated in the copper wires of the armature as it rotates through the lines of magnetic force of the field coils. The current is transferred to an outside circuit by the brushes and commutator.

COMMUTATOR ARMATURE FAN

gen·er·a·tor (jen′ər·ā′tər) *n.* **1** a machine that changes mechanical energy into electrical energy. **2** an apparatus for producing gas or steam. **3** any person or thing that generates; originator. [< L]

gen·er·a·trix (jen′ər·ā′triks) *n., pl.* **gen·er·a·tri·ces** (jen′ər·ə·trī′sēz). *Mathematics.* a point, line, etc. whose motion produces a line, surface, figure, or solid. [< L]

ge·ner·ic (jə ner′ik) *adj.* **1** having to do with or characteristic of a genus of plants or animals: *Cats and lions show generic differences.* **2** having to do with a class or group of similar things; inclusive; not specific: *Liquid is a generic term.* **3** applied to, or referring to, a group or class; general; not special. [< L *genus, generis* kind] —**ge·ner′i·cal·ly,** *adv.*

gen·er·os·i·ty (jen′ər os′ə tē) *n., pl.* **-ties. 1** a being generous; willingness to share with others; unselfishness. **2** nobleness of mind; absence of meanness. **3** a generous act.

gen·er·ous (jen′ər əs *or* jen′rəs) *adj.* **1** willing to share with others; unselfish. **2** having or showing a noble mind; willing to forgive; not mean: *a generous mind.* **3** large; plentiful: *A quarter of a pie is a generous serving.* **4** of wine, rich and full of flavor. [< L *generosus* of noble birth < *genus, -neris* race, stock] —**gen′er·ous·ly,** *adv.* —**gen′er·ous·ness,** *n.*

gen·e·sis (jen′ə sis) *n., pl.* **-ses** (-sēz). **1** origin; creation; coming into being. **2 Genesis,** the first book of the Bible. Genesis gives an account of the creation of the world. [< L < Gk.]

gen·et (jen′it) See **jennet.**

ge·net·ic (jə net′ik) *adj.* **1** having to do with origin and natural growth. **2** of or having to do with genetics. [< Gk. *genētikos* < *genesis* origin, creation]

ge·net·i·cal·ly (jə net′ik lē) *adv.* **1** with respect to genesis or origin. **2** according to the laws of genetics.

ge·net·i·cist (jə net′ə sist) *n.* a person trained in genetics, especially one whose work it is.

ge·net·ics (jə net′iks) *n.* **1** the branch of biology dealing with the principles of heredity and variation in animals and plants of the same or related kinds. **2** the genetic make-up of an individual organism or a type or group.

Ge·ne·va Convention (jə nē′və) an agreement between nations providing for the neutrality of the members and buildings of the medical departments on battlefields. It was first formulated at Geneva, Switzerland, in 1864.

Ge·ne·van (jə nē′vən) *n., adj.* —*n.* a native or inhabitant of Geneva, a city in SW Switzerland. —*adj.* of or having to do with Geneva or its people.

gen·ial (jē′nē əl *or* jēn′yəl) *adj.* **1** smiling and pleasant; cheerful and friendly; kindly: *a genial welcome.* **2** helping growth; pleasantly warming; comforting: *genial sunshine.* [< L *genialis,* literally, belonging to the genius < *genius.* See GENIUS.] —**gen′ial·ly,** *adv.* —**gen′ial·ness,** *n.*

ge·ni·al·i·ty (jē′nē al′ə tē) *n.* a genial quality.

gen·ic (jen′ik) *adj. Biology.* of, relating to, or like a gene; genetic.

–genic *combining form.* **1** producing; having to do with production: *carcinogenic = producing cancer.* **2** of or having to do with a gene or genes. **3** suitable for; suitable for production or reproduction by: *photogenic = suitable for photography.*

ge·nie (jē′nē) *n.* a spirit; jinni: *When Aladdin rubbed his lamp, the genie came and did whatever Aladdin asked.* [< F *génie*]

ge·ni·i (jē′nē ī′) *n.* a pl. of **genius.**

gen·i·tal (jen′ə təl) *adj.* of or having to do with sexual reproduction or the sex organs. [< L *genitalis,* ult. < *gignere* beget]

gen·i·tals (jen′ə təlz) *n.pl.* the external sex organs.

gen·i·ti·val (jen′ə tī′vəl) *adj.* of or in the genitive case.

gen·i·tive (jen′ə tiv) *adj., n.* —*adj.* of, having to do with, or being the grammatical case, found in many languages, that shows that a noun, pronoun, or adjective refers to the possessor or source of something or to a part of a larger whole. The genitive case in Latin and German corresponds roughly to the possessive form of a noun or pronoun in English (*his laugh, a bird's wing, the machine's inner workings*). —*n.* **1** the genitive case. **2** a word or construction in the genitive case. [< L *genitivus* of origin]

gen·ius (jē′nē əs *or* jēn′yəs) *n., pl.* **gen·ius·es** for 1-4, 7, **ge·ni·i** for 5, 6, 8. **1** very great natural power of mind. Genius is shown by extraordinary ability to think, invent, or create. **2** a person having such power: *Shakespeare was a genius.* **3** a great natural ability of some special kind: *Mozart played the piano well, but he had a genius for composing.* **4** the special character or spirit of a person, nation, age, language, etc.: *Shakespeare gave expression to the genius of Elizabethan England.* **5** a guardian spirit of a person, place, institution, etc.: *the genius of the hill.* **6** either of two spirits, one good and one evil, supposed to influence a person's fate. **7** a person who powerfully influences another. **8** a spirit; genie; jinni. [< L *genius* god presiding over birth, ult. < *genere* beget]

gen·o·cid·al (jen′ə sīd′əl) *adj.* of or having to do with genocide.

gen·o·cide (jen′ə sīd′) *n.* systematic measures for the extermination of a national, cultural, religious, or radical group. [< Gk. *genos* race + *-cide*; coined by R. Lemkin in 1944]

Gen·o·ese (jen′ō ēz′) *n., pl.* **-ese;** *adj.* —*n.* a native or inhabitant

of Genoa, a seaport in NW Italy. —*adj.* of or having to do with Genoa or its people.

hat, āge, fär; let, ēqual, tèrm; it, īce
hot, ōpen, ôrder; oil, out; cup, pùt, rüle,
əbove, takən, pencəl, lemən, circəs

ch, child; ng, long; sh, ship
th, thin; ŦH, then; zh, measure

gen·o·type (jen′ə tīp′) *n. Biology.* **1** the arrangement or combination of genes in an organism. **2** a group of organisms each having the same combinations of hereditary characteristics. [< Gk. *genos* race + E *type*]

gen·re (zhon′rə; *French,* zhäNR) *n.* kind; sort; style, especially of works of literature, art, etc.: *The novel and the drama are two literary genres.* [< F < L *genus* kind]

genre painting a style of painting that shows scenes from ordinary life.

gens[1] (jenz) *n., pl.* **gen·tes** (jen′tēz). **1** in ancient Rome, a group of families that claimed the same ancestor and were united by a common name and common religious ceremonies: *Julius Caesar was a member of the Julian gens.* **2** a tribe; clan. **3** *Ethnology.* a group or tribe of people descended through their fathers from a common ancestor. [< L]

gens[2] (zhäN) *n.pl. French.* any group of people following the same occupation, engaged in the same business, or inhabiting the same region. *Gens de chantier* are lumberjacks.

gent (jent) *n. Informal.* gentleman.

gen·teel (jen tēl′) *adj.* **1** belonging or suited to polite society. **2** polite; well-bred; fashionable; elegant. **3** trying to be aristocratic, but not really being so. [< F *gentil* < L *gentilis.* Doublet of GENTILE, GENTLE, JAUNTY.] —**gen·teel′ly,** *adv.* —**gen·teel′ness,** *n.*

gen·tian (jen′shən) *n.* **1** any of a genus (*Gentiana*) of mostly perennial plants having blue, white, red, or yellow funnel-shaped flowers and stemless leaves. **2** the dried rhizome and root of a yellow-flowered European gentian (*G. lutea*), which is used as a tonic. **3** (*adj.*) designating the family of plants (Gentianaceae) that includes the gentians. [< L *gentiana;* said to be named for *Gentius,* king of Illyria (ancient country on the Adriatic)]

gentian violet a crystalline derivative of aniline that forms a violet solution in water, used as a dye, chemical indicator, and antiseptic.

gen·tile or **Gen·tile** (jen′tīl) *n., adj.* —*n.* **1** a person who is not a Jew. **2** a heathen; pagan. **3** among Mormons or Moslems, a person who is not a Mormon or Moslem. —*adj.* **1** not Jewish. **2** heathen; pagan. **3** among Mormons or Moslems, of or having to do with those outside of the Mormon or Moslem community. [ME < LL *gentilis* foreign < L *gentilis* of a people, national. Doublet of GENTEEL, GENTLE, JAUNTY.]

gen·til·i·ty (jen til′ə tē) *n., pl.* **-ties. 1** membership in the aristocracy or upper class. **2** good manners; refinement: *The lady had an air of gentility.* **3** pretended refinement.

gen·tle (jen′təl) *adj.* **-tler, -tlest;** *v.* —*adj.* **1** not severe, rough, or violent; mild: *a gentle tap.* **2** soft; low: *a gentle sound.* **3** moderate: *gentle heat, a gentle slope.* **4** kindly; friendly: *a gentle disposition.* **5** easily handled or managed: *a gentle dog.* **6** of good family and social position; well-born. **7** honorable; good; superior. **8** *Archaic.* noble; gallant: *a gentle knight.* **9** refined; polite. —*v.* treat in a soothing way; make quiet or gentle: *The rider gentled his excited horse.* [ME < OF *gentil* < L *gentilis* of the (same) family, national < *gens, gentis* family, nation. Doublet of GENTEEL, GENTILE, JAUNTY.] —**gen′tle·ness,** *n.*

☛ *Syn.* **1. Gentle, mild, meek** = agreeable, not harsh, rough, or violent. **Gentle** emphasizes control of strength or force, and suggests being pleasant or pleasing or being soft, tender, calm, or kindly: *My nurse is gentle in touch, manner, and voice.* **Mild** emphasizes being by nature not disagreeable, lacking in harshness, severity, etc.: *He is a mild man and seldom gets angry.* **Meek,** applying only to people, and meaning mild or gentle in disposition, emphasizes being patient and humble: *This meek little clerk tries to please everyone.*

gen·tle·folk (jen′təl fōk′) *n.pl.* people of good family and social position.

gen·tle·man (jen′təl mən) *n., pl.* **-men. 1** a man of good family and social position. **2** a man who is honorable, polite, and considerate of others. **3** a man of independent means, who does not work at any occupation or profession. **4** a personal servant of a gentleman, used especially in the phrase *gentleman's gentleman.* **5** a polite term for any man, also used (in the plural) as a form of address: *Ask the gentleman to come in please. Ladies and gentlemen, please take your seats.* —**gen′tle·man·like′,** *adj.*

☛ *Usage.* See note at **man.**

gen·tle·man–in–wait·ing (jen′təl mən in wā′ting) *n.* a man of good family who attends a king or prince.

gen·tle·man·ly (jen′təl mən lē) *adj.* of, characteristic of, or suitable for a gentleman: *a gentlemanly bow, a gentlemanly sport.* —**gen′tle·man·li·ness,** *n.*

gentleman's agreement or **gentlemen's agreement** an unwritten agreement that is not legally binding but depends only on the honor of the people or countries that participate in it.

gen·tle·wom·an (jen′təl wùm′ən) *n., pl.* **-wom·en.** 1 a woman of good family and social position. 2 a woman who is courteous and cultured. 3 a woman attendant of a lady of rank. —**gen′tle·wom′an·ly,** *adv.*

gen·tly (jen′tlē) *adv.* 1 in a gentle way; tenderly; softly. 2 gradually: *a gently sloping hillside.*

gen·try (jen′trē) *n.* 1 people of good family and social position; formerly, in the British Isles, members of the class of wealthy landowners ranking just below the nobility. 2 people of a particular class: *the academic gentry.* [alteration of *gentrice* < OF *genterise,* ult. < *gentil.* See GENTLE.]

gen·u·flect (jen′yə flekt′) *v.* bend the knee as an act of reverence or worship. [< Med.L *genuflectere* < L *genu* knee + *flectere* bend]

gen·u·flec·tion (jen′yə flek′shən) *n.* a bending of the knee as an act of reverence or worship.

gen·u·flex·ion (jen′yə flek′shən) *n. Esp.Brit.* genuflection.

gen·u·ine (jen′yü ən) *adj.* 1 actually being what it seems or is claimed to be; real; true: *genuine leather, a genuine diamond.* 2 without pretence; sincere; frank: *genuine sorrow.* [< L *genuinus* native, natural, ult. < *gignere* beget] —**gen′u·ine·ly,** *adv.* —**gen′u·ine·ness,** *n.*

☞ *Syn.* 1. **Genuine, authentic** = what it is claimed to be. **Genuine** refers to something that is real, pure, actually having the nature or quality it is supposed to have: *The table is genuine mahogany, not wood stained to look like mahogany.* **Authentic** = of genuine origin or authorship: *That is his authentic signature, not a forgery.*

☞ *Pronun.* The pronunciation (jen′yü īn′) is frequently heard even among educated Canadians. However, many consider it a vulgarism.

ge·nus (jē′nəs *or* jen′əs) *n., pl.* **gen·er·a** *or* **ge·nus·es.** 1 *Biology.* a major category in the classification of plants and animals, more specific than the family and more general than the species. The prairie crocus (*Anemone patens*) and the Canada anemone (*Anemone canadensis*) belong to the same genus. The scientific name of every species of animal or plant is made up of the genus name (capitalized) followed by the species name (not capitalized). See chart at **classification.** 2 any kind or sort. 3 *Logic.* a class or group of individuals divided into subordinate groups called species. [< L]

geo– *combining form.* earth; land, as in *geocentric.* [< Gk. *geō* < *gē* earth]

ge·o·cen·tric (jē′ō sen′trik) *adj.* 1 as viewed or measured from the earth's centre. 2 having or representing the earth as a centre: *The people of medieval times had a geocentric view of the universe.* Compare **heliocentric.** [< *geo*- + Gk. *kentron* centre] —**ge′o·cen′tri·cal·ly,** *adv.*

ge·o·cen·tri·cal (jē′ō sen′trə kəl) *adj.* geocentric.

ge·ode (jē′ōd) *n.* 1 a rock having a cavity lined with crystals. 2 the cavity itself. [< F *géode* < L < Gk. *geōdēs* earthy < *gē* earth + *eidos* form]

ge·o·des·ic (jē′ə des′ik *or* jē′ə dē′zik) *n., adj.* —*n.* the shortest possible distance betwen two points along a surface, especially a curved surface. —*adj.* 1 of or having to do with geodesy or the geometry of curved lines. 2 *Architecture.* built with short, straight, lightweight struts forming a spherical grid of triangles: *A geodesic dome uses the minimum amount of material to produce a given volume.*

ge·od·e·sy (jē od′ə sē) *n.* the branch of applied mathematics dealing with the shape and dimensions of the earth or large areas on its surface, determining the exact position of points on the surface, and variations in the earth's gravity and magnetism. Geodesy is based on the notion of measuring a sphere by dividing its surface area into triangles. [< NL < Gk. *geodaisia* < *gē* earth + *daiein* divide]

ge·o·det·ic (jē′ə det′ik) *adj.* of, having to do with, or involving geodesy: *geodetic measurements, a geodetic project.* —**ge′o·det′i·cal·ly,** *adv.*

ge·og·no·sy (jē og′nə sē) *n.* the branch of geology that deals with the structure of the earth, its rocks and minerals, and the water and air surrounding it. [< F < Gk. *gē* earth + *gnōsis* knowledge]

ge·og·ra·pher (jē og′rə fər) *n.* a person trained in geography, especially one whose work it is.

ge·o·graph·ic (jē′ə graf′ik) *adj.* geographical.

ge·o·graph·i·cal (jē′ə graf′ə kəl) *adj.* of or having to do with geography. —**ge′o·graph′i·cal·ly,** *adv.*

geographical mile nautical mile.

ge·og·ra·phy (jē og′rə fē) *n., pl.* **-phies.** 1 the science that deals with the earth's surface and its division into continents and countries, and the climate, animal and plant life, peoples, resources, industries, and products of these divisions. 2 the surface features of a place or region. 3 a book about geography. [< L < Gk. *geōgraphia* < *gē* earth + *graphein* describe]

geol. geology; geologic.

ge·o·log·ic (jē′ə loj′ik) *adj.* geological.

ge·o·log·i·cal (jē′ə loj′ə kəl) *adj.* of or having to do with geology. —**ge′o·log′i·cal·ly,** *adv.*

ge·ol·o·gist (jē ol′ə jist) *n.* a person trained in geology, especially one whose work it is.

ge·ol·o·gy (jē ol′ə jē) *n., pl.* **-gies.** 1 the science that deals with the earth's crust, the layers of which it is composed, and their history. 2 the features of the earth's crust in a place or region; rocks, rock formation, etc. of a particular area. 3 a book about geology. [< NL *geologia* < Gk. *gē* earth + *-logos* treating of]

geom. geometry; geometric.

ge·o·mag·net·ic (jē′ō mag net′ik) *adj.* of or having to do with the magnetism of the earth.

ge·o·mag·net·ism (jē′ō mag′nə tiz′əm) *n.* 1 the magnetism of the earth. 2 the science concerned with the magnetism of the earth.

ge·om·e·ter (jē om′ə tər) *n.* geometrician. [< L < Gk. *geōmetrēs* < *gē* earth + *metrēs* measurer]

ge·o·met·ric (jē′ə met′rik) *adj.* 1 of geometry or according to its principles: *geometric proof.* 2 consisting of or characterized by straight lines, circles, triangles, etc.; regular and symmetrical: *a geometric design.*

ge·o·met·ri·cal (jē′ə met′rə kəl) *adj.* geometric. —**ge′o·met′ri·cal·ly,** *adv.*

ge·om·e·tri·cian (jē om′ə trish′ən *or* jē′ə mə trish′ən) *n.* a person trained in geometry, especially one whose work it is.

geometric progression a series, such as 2, 4, 8, 16, or 5, 1/5, 1/25, in which the ratio of each term to its predecessor is always constant. Compare **arithmetic progression.**

ge·om·e·trid (jē om′ə trid) *n.* any of a family (Geometridae) of medium-sized, grey or greenish moths whose larvae are called measuring worms or inchworms. [< NL *Geometridae,* pl. < L < Gk. *geōmetrēs.* See GEOMETER.]

ge·om·e·try (jē om′ə trē) *n., pl.* **-tries.** 1 the branch of mathematics that deals with lines, angles, surfaces, and solids. Geometry includes the definition, comparison, and measurement of squares, triangles, circles, cubes, cones, spheres, etc. 2 a book about geometry. [< L < Gk. *geōmetria* < *gē* earth + *-metria* measuring]

ge·o·mor·phic (jē′ə môr′fik) *adj.* of or having to do with the shape or the surface features of the earth or a heavenly body such as the moon.

ge·o·mor·pho·log·i·cal (jē′ə môr′fə loj′ə kəl) *adj.* of or having to do with geomorphology.

ge·o·mor·phol·o·gist (jē′ō môr fol′ə jist) *n.* a person trained in geomorphology, especially one whose work it is.

ge·o·mor·phol·o·gy (jē′ō môr fol′ə jē) *n.* the science that deals with the surface features of the earth or a heavenly body such as the moon, and with the origin and development of these features and their relationship with geological structures.

ge·o·phys·i·cal (jē′ō fiz′ə kəl) *adj.* of or having to do with geophysics.

ge·o·phys·i·cist (jē′ō fiz′ə sist′) *n.* a person trained in geophysics, especially one whose work it is.

ge·o·phys·ics (jē′ō fiz′iks) *n.* the science that deals with the relations between the features of the earth and the forces that produce them; the physics of the earth (*used with a singular verb*). Geophysics includes magnetism, meteorology, oceanography, seismology, etc.

ge·o·po·lit·i·cal (jē′ō pə lit′ə kəl) *adj.* of, having to do with, or involved in geopolitics. —**ge′o·po·lit′i·cal·ly,** *adv.*

ge·o·pol·i·ti·cian (jē′ō pol′ə tish′ən) *n.* a person who has special skill in, or knowledge of, geopolitics.

ge·o·pol·i·tics (jē′ō pol′ə tiks) *n.* the study of government and its policies as affected by physical geography.

George (jôrj) *n.* 1 a part of the insignia of the Order of the Garter, representing Saint George slaying the dragon. It may be a piece set

GEOLOGICAL TIME CHART

ERAS	PERIODS, EPOCHS, AND THEIR BEGINNINGS (years ago)		CHANGES AND CHARACTERISTICS
CENOZOIC ERA	Quaternary Period	Recent, or Holocene, Epoch (10 thousand)	Glaciers melt and Great Lakes are formed. Climate warm. Humans live in most parts of the earth, develop agriculture, use metals, domesticate animals.
		Pleistocene Epoch (1.5 million)	Great ice sheets cover northern hemisphere. Climate cool. Mountains continue to rise in western North America. Early humans reach Europe and North America.
	Tertiary Period	Pliocene Epoch (10 million)	Climate cooling. Mountains rising in western Canada. Many volcanoes. Birds and mammals spread around the world. Humans appear near end of epoch.
		Miocene Epoch (27 million)	Climate mild. Rocky Mountains and Sierra Nevadas forming. Flowering plants and trees resemble modern kinds.
		Oligocene Epoch (38 million)	Climate mild. Alps and Himalayas begin to rise. Many volcanoes. Oil and natural gas are formed.
		Eocene Epoch (50 million)	Climate mild. Seas flood shores of continents. Primitive apes, early horses, and elephants appear.
		Paleocene Epoch (65 million)	Mountains become higher. Climates less uniform. Mammals, flowering plants become common.
MEZOZOIC ERA	Cretaceous Period (130 million)		Seas spread over the land. Flowering plants appear. Dinosaurs die out. Most chalk deposits are made.
	Jurassic Period (180 million)		Shallow seas invade continents. Dinosaurs reach their largest size. First birds appear.
	Triassic Period (225 million)		Reptiles dominate the earth. First mammals appear.
PALEOZOIC ERA	Permian Period (270 million)		Ural Mountains are formed. Glaciers in southern hemisphere melt. Gas, oil, and salt are formed. Reptiles developing.
	Carboniferous Period —Pennsylvanian (310 million)		Appalachian Mountains are formed. Large amounts of coal are formed. First reptiles appear.
	—Mississippian (350 million)		Warm, moist climate produces great forests that later become coal beds. Fish and amphibians plentiful.
	Devonian Period (405 million)		Gas and oil are formed. Many kinds of fish in seas and fresh water. First insects appear.
	Silurian Period (435 million)		Coral reefs are formed. First amphibians and forests of fernlike trees appear.
	Ordovician Period (480 million)		Floods sometimes cover two-thirds of North America. Jawless fish appear. Algae become plentiful.
	Cambrian Period (575 million)		Seas spread across North America. First fishes appear. Greatest development of invertebrates.
PRECAMBRIAN TIME (4.5 billion?)			Cooling and melting of the earth's crust. Evidence of bacteria, the first known living things, about 3.5 billion years ago.

with jewels or a single carved gem. **2** *Brit. Slang.* the automatic pilot of an aircraft.

George Cross in the Commonwealth of Nations, the highest award for civilian courage, established by King George VI. See **medal** for picture. *Abbrev.*: G.C.

geor·gette (jôr jet′) *n.* a light, fine, sheer crepe fabric having a dull pebbled or crinkly surface. [from the name of a French modiste]

Geor·gian (jôr′jən) *adj., n.* —*adj.* **1** of, having to do with, or characteristic of the reigns of the four Georges, Kings of Great Britain and Ireland from 1714 to 1830: *Georgian architecture, Georgian furniture.* **2** of, having to do with, or characteristic of the reigns of King George V (1910-1936) and King George VI (1936-1952), especially of George V: *the Georgian poets.* **3** of or having to do with the Soviet Republic of Georgia, its people, or their language. **4** of or having to do with the state of Georgia in the United States.
—*n.* **1** a person, such as a writer, belonging to either of the Georgian periods in England. **2** a native or inhabitant of the Soviet Republic of Georgia. **3** the Caucasian language of the people of Georgia. **4** a native or inhabitant of the State of Georgia in the United States.

ge·o·sphere (jē′ə sfēr′) *n.* the solid matter that comprises the earth.

ge·o·trop·ic (jē′ə trop′ik) *adj. Biology.* affected by geotropism; responding to gravity. [< *geo-* + Gk. *tropikos* < *tropē* turning]

ge·ot·ro·pism (jē ot′rə piz′əm) *n. Biology.* a response to gravity. **Positive geotropism** is a tendency to move down into the earth, as roots do. **Negative geotropism** is a tendency to move upward.

ger. gerund.

Ger. **1** German; Germany. **2** Germanic.

ge·ra·ni·um (jə rā′nē əm *or* jə rān′yəm) *n.* **1** any of various cultivated plants (genus *Pelargonium*) native to S Africa, having showy clusters of pink, red, or white flowers. Geraniums are very popular house and garden plants. **2** any of a genus (*Geranium*) of plants found mainly in temperate regions, having divided leaves, pink or purple flowers, and long, pointed pods. **3** (*adj.*) designating the family (Geraniaceae) of plants that includes the genera *Pelargonium* and *Geranium.* [< L < Gk. *geranion* < *geranos* crane; from the resemblance of the pod to a crane's bill]

ger·bil (jėr′bəl) *n.* any of a subfamily (Gerbillinae, of the family Cricetidae) of small burrowing rodents native to the Old World, having large eyes and ears, soft, brown or greyish fur, and a long, hairy tail. Gerbils have been popular as cage pets in North America since the 1960's. [< F *gerbille* < NL *gerbillus*, dim. of *gerbo* jerboa]

ger·fal·con (jėr′fol′kən *or* -fôl′kən) *n.* See **gyrfalcon**. [ME < OF *gerfaucon* < Gmc.]

ger·i·at·rics (jer′ē at′riks) *n.* the branch of medicine that deals with the study of old age and its diseases. Compare **gerontology.** [< Gk. *gēras* old age + *iatreia* healing]

germ (jėrm) *n.* **1** a micro-organism, especially one that causes disease. **2** the earliest form of a living thing; seed; bud. **3** the beginning of anything; origin. [< F < L *germen* sprout] —**germ′less,** *adj.* —**germ′like′,** *adj.*

ger·man¹ (jėr′mən) *adj.* **1** having the same parents. Children of the same father and mother are **brothers-german** or **sisters-german.** **2** being a child of one's uncle or aunt. A **cousin-german** is a first cousin. [ME < OF *germain* < L *germanus*]

ger·man² (jėr′mən) *n.* **1** a dance with complicated steps and frequent changing of partners; cotillion. **2** a party at which it is danced. [short for *German cotillion*]

Ger·man (jėr′mən) *n., adj.* —*n.* **1** a native or inhabitant of West Germany (Federal Republic of Germany) or East Germany (German Democratic Republic) in central Europe. **2** a person of German descent. **3** the Germanic language of Germany and Austria and parts of Switzerland; especially, the standard form used in literature, on radio, television, and the stage, etc.
—*adj.* of or having to do with Germany, Germans, or German. [< L *Germanus*]

ger·man·der (jėr man′dər) *n.* any of a genus (*Teucrium*) of plants of the mint family found in all parts of the world, typically having spikes of small, two-lipped flowers with the lower lip more prominent than the upper. [< LL *germandra* < Gk. *chamaidryas*, alteration of *chamaidrys* ground oak]

ger·mane (jėr mān′) *adj.* closely connected; to the point; pertinent: *Your statement is not germane to the discussion.* [var. of *german¹*]

Ger·man·ic (jėr man′ik) *n., adj.* —*n.* a main branch of the Indo-European family of languages, including English, German, Dutch, Frisian, Flemish, Danish, Norwegian, Swedish, Icelandic, and Gothic, that have developed from a common language spoken in Europe up to about 2500 years ago.
—*adj.* **1** of, having to do with, or designating this group of languages or the language they descended from. **2** of, having to do with, or designating any of the peoples speaking these languages. **3** German.

ger·ma·ni·um (jėr mā′nē əm) *n.* a rare, greyish-white, brittle, metallic element. Germanium is used in making transistors. *Symbol*: Ge; *at.no.* 32; *at.wt.* 72.59. [< NL < L *Germania* Germany]

German measles a contagious virus disease resembling measles, but much less serious.

German shepherd a breed of large, intelligent dog developed in Germany, often trained to work with soldiers and police, to guide the blind, etc.; Alsatian.

German silver nickel silver.

germ cell one of the reproductive cells in a sexually reproducing animal or plant which undergo meiosis to produce gametes (egg or sperm cells). Compare **somatic cell.**

ger·mi·cid·al (jėr′mə sīd′əl) *adj.* capable of killing germs.

ger·mi·cide (jėr′mə sīd′) *n.* any substance that kills germs, especially disease germs. [< *germ* + *-cide²*]

ger·mi·nal (jėr′mə nəl) *adj.* **1** of, like, or characteristic of germs or germ cells. **2** in the earliest stage of development; embryonic.

ger·mi·nate (jėr′mə nāt′) *v.* **-nat·ed, -nat·ing.** **1** grow or sprout, or cause to grow or sprout: *Seeds germinate in the spring. Warmth and moisture germinate seeds.* **2** start growing or developing: *An idea was germinating in his head.* [< L *germinare* < *germen* sprout] —**ger′mi·na′tion,** *n.* —**ger′mi·na′tor,** *n.*

germ plasm a substance in germ cells that transmits hereditary characteristics to the offspring.

germ warfare the spreading of germs to produce disease among the enemy in time of war.

ger·on·tol·o·gy (jer′ən tol′ə jē) *n.* the branch of science that studies the aging process and the problems of old people. Compare **geriatrics.**

ger·ry·man·der (ger′ē man′dər *or* jer′ē-) *n., v.* —*n.* an arrangement of the political boundaries of a riding, constituency, etc. that gives the party in power an undue advantage in an election. —*v.* **1** arrange the political boundaries of a riding, constituency, etc. so as to give the party in power an undue advantage in an election. **2** manipulate unfairly. [< *Gerry* + sala*mander*; Governor Gerry's party rearranged the districts of Massachusetts in 1812, and Essex County was divided so that one district became roughly salamander-shaped]

ger·und (jer′ənd) *n. Grammar.* a verb form used as a noun. *Abbrev.*: ger. [< LL *gerundium*, ult. < L *gerere* bear]
☛ *Usage.* The English **gerund** ends in *-ing.* It has the same form as the present participle but differs in use. Gerund: *Running a hotel appealed to him.* Participle: *Running around the corner, he bumped into a cop.* A gerund may take an object (*running a hotel*) or a complement (*being a hero*), and it may serve in any of the functions of a noun: Subject: *Looking for an apartment always fascinated her.* Object: *He taught dancing.* Predicate noun: *Seeing is believing.* Adjectival use: *a fishing boat* (a boat for fishing, not a boat that fishes). Object of a preposition: *a great day for hiking.*

ge·run·di·al (jə run′dē əl) *adj.* **1** of a gerund. **2** used as a gerund.

ge·run·dive (jə run′div) *n.* a Latin verb form used as an adjective, frequently expressing the idea of necessity.

gest *or* **geste** (jest) *n. Archaic.* **1** a story or romance in verse. **2** a story; tale. **3** a deed; exploit. [ME < OF < L *gesta* deeds < *gerere* carry on, accomplish]

Ge·stalt (gə shtält′) *n. Psychology.* the total structure or pattern of various acts, experiences, and elements, so integrated as to constitute a whole that is greater than the sum of its parts. [< G *Gestalt* form, configuration]

Ge·sta·po (gə stäp′ō *or* gə stä′pō) *n.* in Nazi Germany, an official organization of secret police and detectives. [< G *Geheime Staats Polizei* secret state police]

ges·ta·tion (jes tā′shən) *n.* **1** the act or period of carrying young in the uterus from conception to birth; pregnancy. **2** the formation and development of a project, etc. in the mind. [< L *gestatio, -onis* < *gestare* carry]

ges·tic·u·late (jes tik′yə lāt′) *v.* **-lat·ed, -lat·ing.** make or use gestures, especially vehement gestures. [< L *gesticulari*, ult. < *gestus* gesture] —**ges·tic′u·la′tor,** *n.*

ges·tic·u·la·tion (jes tik′yə lā′shən) *n.* **1** the act of gesticulating. **2** gesture.
☛ *Syn.* **2.** See note at **gesture.**

ges·tic·u·la·tive (jes tik′yə lə tiv *or* jes tik′yə lā′tiv) *adj.* making or using gestures.

ges·ture (jes′chər) *n., v.* **-tured, -tur·ing.** —*n.* **1** a movement of the hands, arms, or any part of the body, used instead of words or with words to help express an idea or feeling: *a gesture of dismissal. His speech was accompanied by many gestures.* **2** any action made for effect or to impress others: *Her refusal was merely a gesture; she really wanted to go.* —*v.* make or use gestures: *She gestured sharply, to silence him.* [< Med.L *gestura* < L *gerere* to bear, conduct]

☞ *Syn. n.* **1. Gesture, gesticulation** = movement of the head, shoulders, hands, or arms to express thought or feeling. **Gesture** applies to any such movement or motion used to take the place of words or add to the meaning expressed by the words: *He did not speak, but with a gesture indicated that I should follow him.* **Gesticulation** applies only to wild, excited, or clumsy gestures: *His gesticulations suggested he was losing his temper rapidly.*

get (get) *v.* **got, got** or **got·ten, get·ting. 1** come to have; obtain; receive; gain: *I got a new coat yesterday. He got first prize in the spelling contest.* **2** reach; *I got home early last night. Your letter got here yesterday.* **3** catch; get hold of: *I have got a bad cold.* **4** cause to be or do: *He got his hair cut yesterday. They got the fire under control.* **5** *Informal.* be obliged (*used with some form of* **have**): *We have got to win.* **6** become: *to get sick, to get old.* **7** be: *Don't get nervous when you have to take the test.* **8** arrive (at) or come (to): *We should get to Yellowknife by noon. Call me when you get there.* **9** persuade; influence: *We got him to speak.* **10** prepare: *Will you help me get dinner?* **11** begin; start: *We soon got talking about our days at camp.* **12** possess; have (*used with some form of* **have**): *She has got black hair.* **13** usually of animals, beget. **14** *Informal.* hit; strike: *The bullet got the soldier in the arm.* **15** *Informal.* kill. **16** *Informal.* puzzle; annoy. **17** *Informal.* understand: *I don't get what you mean.*

get about, a go from place to place. **b** spread, become widely known.
get across (to), *Informal.* **a** make understand; communicate: *You can't get anything across to her when she's in that mood.* **b** become clear or understood: *It finally got across to him that he wasn't welcome.*
get after, a scold. **b** urge.
get ahead, advance one's position, career, etc.; be successful.
get along, a go away. **b** advance. **c** manage. **d** succeed; prosper. **e** be on good terms: *He doesn't get along with his neighbors.*
get around, a go from place to place. **b** become widely known; spread. **c** overcome opposition by charm, flattery, etc.; win over: *Her winning smile often helped her to get around her father.* **d** deceive; trick.
get at, a reach. **b** find out: *Try to get at the truth.* **c** *Informal.* tamper with; influence with money or threats.
get away, a leave: *I won't be able to get away from here until after lunch.* **b** escape: *She got away, through the window. The dog got away from him.* **c** set out; start: *The last car got away at 10 o'clock.*
get away with, *Informal.* succeed in taking or doing something and escaping safely: *He thought he could get away with being late but he was caught.*
get back, a return. **b** recover.
get back at, *Slang.* get revenge on.
get behind, a support; endorse. **b** fail to keep up to schedule.
get by, *Informal.* **a** pass. **b** not be noticed or caught. **c** do well enough; manage all right: *They got by on his small salary.*
get (someone) down, make downhearted; discourage; depress: *The hot weather was getting him down.*
get down to, a begin: *It took him a long time to get down to work.* **b** reach by removing what stands in the way: *After much questioning of the witness, the lawyer got down to the truth.*
get even, a pay back for a wrong done; obtain revenge: *He promised to get even with his sister for twisting his arm.* **b** win back what was lost: *After he had lost twenty marbles, he played all afternoon trying to get even.*
get in, a go in. **b** put in. **c** arrive. **d** become friendly or familiar (*with*).
get into, a find out about. **b** get control of. **c** come to be in; result in being in: *get into trouble.*
get it, *Informal.* be reprimanded or punished: *I'll get it if I'm late again.*
get off, a come down from or out of. **b** take off. **c** escape the full punishment deserved: *The naughty boy got off with a scolding.* **d** help to escape. **e** start. **f** put out; issue. **g** say or express (a joke or funny remark). **h** deliver (a speech).
get on, a go up on or into. **b** put on. **c** advance. **d** manage. **e** succeed. **f** agree.
get on to, a learn; grasp. **b** communicate with.
get out, a go out. **b** take out. **c** go away. **d** escape. **e** help to escape. **f** become known. **g** publish. **h** find out.
get over, a recover from: *He was a long time getting over his illness.* **b** overcome. **c** *Slang.* make clear or convincing. **d** *Slang.* succeed.
get over with, come to grips with and dispose of (something unpleasant).
get set, get ready; prepare.
get there, succeed.

hat, āge, fär; let, ēqual, tèrm; it, īce
hot, ōpen, ôrder; oil, out; cup, pùt, rüle,
əbove, takən, pencəl, lemən, circəs
ch, child; ng, long; sh, ship
th, thin; ₮н, then; zh, measure

get through, a get to the end of; finish: *She always gets through her homework quickly.* **b** complete or cause to complete successfully: *He got through the test. His friend's help got him through.* **c** make or get a telephone connection: *I tried to phone you but I couldn't get through.* **d** make oneself understood; succeed in communicating: *No one can get through to her when she's angry.*
get together, *Informal.* **a** bring or come together; meet; assemble. **b** come to an agreement: *The workers and their employer couldn't get together about wages.*
get up, a get out of bed, etc. **b** stand up. **c** prepare; arrange: *He spent all evening getting up the next day's lesson.* **d** dress up. **e** go ahead.

[ME *gete*(n) < ON *geta*]

☞ *Syn.* **1. Get, obtain, acquire** = come to have something. **Get** = come to have something in some way or by some means, whether or not one wants or tries to gain it: *I got a new car. He got a bad reputation.* **Obtain** usually suggests working hard or trying to get something one wants: *I obtained permission to go.* **Acquire** emphasizes getting possession of something, usually by one's own efforts or actions: *I acquired a reading knowledge of German.*

☞ *Usage.* **Get** is increasingly used as an informal emphatic passive auxiliary: *We all got punished.*

☞ *Usage.* **Get up.** See note at **rise.**

get·a·way (get′ə wā′) *n. Informal.* **1** the act of getting away; escape. **2** the start of a race.

Geth·sem·a·ne (geth sem′ə nē) *n.* in the Bible, a garden near Jerusalem, the scene of Jesus' agony, betrayal, and arrest (Matt. 26:36). [< Gk. *Gethsēmanē* < Aramaic]

getter (get′ər) *n.* **1** one that gets. **2** a chemically active substance such as magnesium, used in vacuum tubes to clear gases. **3** a sire, especially a begetter of superior offspring. **4** *Cdn.* poisoned bait used in exterminating wolves, gophers, etc.

get-to·geth·er (get′tə geтн′ər) *n. Informal.* an informal social gathering or party.

get-up (get′up′) *n. Informal.* **1** the way a thing is put together; arrangement; style. **2** dress; costume.

get-up-and-go (get′up′ən gō′) *Informal. n., adj.* —*n.* energy; initiative. —*adj.* full of energy and initiative; enterprising.

GeV gigaelectronvolt; one billion electronvolts.

gew·gaw (gü′go *or* gü′gô) *n., adj.* —*n.* a showy trifle; gaudy, useless ornament or toy; bauble. —*adj.* showy but trifling.

gey·ser (gī′zər, gī′sər, *or* gā′zər) *n., v.* **1** a spring that sends a column of hot water and steam into the air at intervals. **2** anything that spurts or gushes like a geyser. —*v.* spurt or cause to spurt like a geyser. [< Icel. *Geysir*, the name of a spring in Iceland < *geysa* gush]

Gha·nai·an or **Gha·ni·an** (gä′nē ən) *adj., n.* —*adj.* of or having to do with Ghana or its people. —*n.* a native or inhabitant of Ghana.

ghast·ly (gast′lē) *adj.* **-li·er, -li·est;** *adv.* —*adj.* **1** horrible: *Murder is a ghastly crime.* **2** like a dead person or ghost; deathly pale: *The sick man's face was ghastly.* **3** *Informal.* shocking: *a ghastly failure.* —*adv.* in a ghastly manner. [OE *gāstlic* < *gāst* ghost + *-lic* -ly] —**ghast′li·ness,** *n.*

☞ *Syn. adj.* **1. Ghastly, grisly, horrible** refer to something that causes terror or horror. **Ghastly** suggests a connection or association with death, and emphasizes the frightening or horrifying appearance or nature of what is described: *We saw a ghastly accident.* **Grisly** emphasizes being so ghastly or horrible, and sometimes unearthly or weird, as to cause a person to shudder with horror or dread: *Robbing graves is a grisly occupation.* **Horrible** emphasizes the feeling of horror or abhorrence caused by what is described: *It was a horrible murder.*

ghat or **ghaut** (got *or* gôt) *n.* in India: **1** steps or a stairway leading down to a river; landing place. **2** a mountain pass. [< Hind.]

ghee (gē) *n.* a semiliquid butter clarified by boiling; it is made especially in India, with butter from the milk of cows or buffaloes. [< Hind.]

gher·kin (gėr′kən) *n.* **1** the small, prickly, cucumberlike fruit of an annual vine (*Cucumis anguria*) of the gourd family, used for pickles. **2** the vine itself. **3** the small, immature fruit of a cucumber when pickled. [< earlier Du. *agurkje*, dim. of *agurk* < G < Slavic < Med.Gk., ult. < Persian *angorah* watermelon]

ghet·to (get′ō) *n., pl.* **-tos. 1** a part of a city inhabited mainly or entirely by a minority group that is obliged to live there for reasons of poverty, prejudice, or government policy. **2** *Historical.* a part of a European city where Jews were obliged to live. [< Ital.]

ghost (gōst) *n., v.* —*n.* **1** the spirit of a dead person. It is supposed to live in another world and appear to living people as a

pale, dim, shadowy form. **2** anything pale, dim, or shadowy like a ghost; a faint image; the slightest suggestion: *the ghost of a smile, not a ghost of a chance.* **3** *Informal.* ghost writer. **4** *Television.* a secondary or multiple image resulting from the reflection of a transmitted signal.

give up the ghost, die.

—*v.* **1** *Informal.* write (a book, etc.) or work as a ghost writer: *His autobiography was ghosted by a journalist. The journalist had ghosted for several other public figures.* **2** haunt as a ghost does. [OE *gāst*] —**ghost′like′**, *adj.*

☞ *Syn. n.* **1. Ghost, spectre, apparition** = an appearance or visible form of someone or something not really present. **Ghost** applies chiefly to the spirit of a dead person: *He saw his father's ghost.* **Spectre** applies to a ghostly, mysterious, usually frightening shape, something appearing as if by magic: *A spectre flitted through the graveyard.* **Apparition** applies especially to an appearance, often of someone dead or about to die, seeming very real to the person seeing it and impossible to explain or understand: *The apparition of his mother startled him.*

ghost·ly (gōst′lē) *adj.* **-li·er, -li·est. 1** like a ghost; pale, dim, and shadowy: *In the darkness he seemed to see ghostly forms.* **2** of or having to do with a ghost. **3** *Archaic.* spiritual; religious. —**ghost′li·ness,** *n.*

ghost town a town that has become empty and lifeless: *When the gold rush was over, the once-flourishing community became a ghost town.*

ghost-write (gōst′rīt′) *v.* **-wrote, -writ·ten, -writ·ing.** write (something) for another who is nominally the author.

ghost writer a person who writes something for another who is nominally the author.

ghoul (gül) *n.* **1** in Oriental stories, a horrible demon, believed to feed on corpses. **2** a person who robs graves or corpses. **3** a person who enjoys what is revolting, brutal, and horrible. [< Arabic < *ghūl* ogre, monster]

ghoul·ish (gü′lish) *adj.* like a ghoul; revolting, brutal, and horrible. —**ghoul′ish·ly,** *adv.* —**ghoul′ish·ness,** *n.*

GHQ General Headquarters.

G.I. or **GI** (jē′ī′) *adj., n., pl.* **G.I.'s, GI's,** or **GIs** (jē′īz′). *U.S.* —*adj.* **1** government issue: *G.I. shoes, G.I. socks.* **2** *Informal.* conforming to regulations; standard: *G.I. uniform.* —*n. Informal.* soldier. [short for Government *I*ssue]

gi·ant (jī′ənt) *n., adj.* —*n.* **1** a legendary being having human form, but superhuman size and strength. **2** a person or thing of unusual size, strength, importance, etc. —*adj.* like a giant; unusually big and strong; huge. [ME < OF *geant* < L *gigas, gigantis* < Gk.]

giant arborvitae or **giant cedar** western red cedar.

gi·ant·ess (jī′ən tis) *n.* a female giant.

giant panda panda (def. 1).

giant powder an explosive resembling dynamite, used in blasting.

giaour (jour) *n.* a Moslem term for a person who does not believe in the Moslem religion. [< Turkish *giaur* < Persian *gaur*]

gib·ber (jib′ər *or* gib′ər) *v.* —*v.* chatter senselessly; talk rapidly and indistinctly: *The monkeys gibbered angrily at each other.* —*n.* senseless chattering; rapid indistinct talking. [imitative]

gib·ber·ish (jib′ər ish *or* gib′ər ish) *n.* meaningless chatter or unintelligible language: *the gibberish of monkeys.*

gib·bet (jib′it) *n., v.* **-bet·ed, -bet·ing.** —*n.* **1** an upright post with a projecting arm at the top, from which the bodies of criminals were hung after execution. **2** gallows.
—*v.* **1** hang on a gibbet. **2** hold up to public scorn or ridicule. **3** put to death by hanging. [ME < OF *gibet,* dim. of *gibe* club]

gib·bon (gib′ən) *n.* any of a genus (*Hylobates*) of small, long-armed, manlike apes found in the forests of S and SE Asia. Gibbons live mainly in trees but on the ground they walk upright. [< F]

gib·bous (gib′əs) *adj.* **1** curved out; bulging. **2** referring to the moon or a planet in the phase during which more than half the disk is illuminated, but less than the whole disk. See **moon** for picture. **3** humpbacked. [< L *gibbosus* < *gibbus* hump] —**gib′bous·ly,** *adv.* —**gib′bous·ness,** *n.*

gibe or **jibe** (jīb) *v.* **gibed, gib·ing;** *n.* jeer; scoff; sneer. [? < OF *giber* handle roughly < *gibe* staff] —**gib′er,** *n.* —**gib′ing·ly,** *adv.*

gib·let (jib′lit) *n.* **1** giblets, *pl.* the heart, liver, and gizzard of a fowl. **2** (*adjl.*) made from giblets: *giblet gravy.* [< OF *gibelet* stew of game]

Gi·bral·tar (jə brol′tər *or* jə brôl′tər) *n.* a strongly fortified place; impregnable stronghold. [< *Gibraltar,* a British fortress built on the Rock of Gibraltar, a huge hill of rock at the southern tip of Spain.]

gid·dy (gid′ē) *adj.* **-di·er, -di·est. 1** having a confused, whirling feeling in one's head; dizzy. **2** likely to make dizzy; causing

dizziness: *a giddy height.* **3** rarely or never serious; flighty; heedless: *Nobody can tell what that giddy girl will do next.* [OE *gydig* mad, possessed (by an evil spirit) < *god* a god] —**gid′di·ly,** *adv.* —**gid′di·ness,** *n.*

gift (gift) *n.* **1** something given; a present: *a Christmas gift.* **2** the act of giving: *The house came to him by gift from an uncle.* **3** the power or right of giving: *The job is within his gift.* **4** a natural ability; special talent: *a gift for painting.* [ME < ON *gipt.* Akin to GIVE.]

gift·ed (gif′tid) *adj.* having natural ability or special talent: *a gifted musician.*

gift horse **look a gift horse in the mouth,** question the value of a gift.

gift-wrap (gift′rap′) *v.* **-wrapped, -wrap·ping;** *n.* —*v.* wrap for presentation as a gift, using decorative paper, ribbon, etc. —*n.* decorative paper, etc. suitable for wrapping gifts.

A gig (def. 1)

gig¹ (gig) *n., v.* **gigged, gig·ging.** —*n.* **1** a light, open, two-wheeled carriage drawn by one horse. **2** a light, narrow ship's boat moved by oars or sails, often for the use of the captain in going to and from shore. **3** a long, light rowboat used especially for racing. **4** a machine for raising nap on cloth.
—*v.* **1** travel in a gig. **2** raise the nap of (cloth) with a gig. [origin uncertain]

gig² (gig) *n., v.* **gigged, gig·ging.** —*n.* a fish spear; harpoon. —*v.* spear (fish) with a gig. [short for *fishgig,* ult. < Sp. *fisga* harpoon]

gig³ (gig) *n. Slang.* an engagement for a band, singer, etc. to perform, especially for one night only.

giga- (gig′ə; *sometimes,* jig′ə) *SI prefix.* billion: *A gigametre is one billion metres.* *Symbol:* G

gi·gan·tic (jī gan′tik) *adj.* **1** like a giant: *Paul Bunyan was a gigantic lumberjack.* **2** huge; enormous: *a gigantic building project.* [< L *gigas, gigantis* giant. See GIANT.] —**gi·gan′ti·cal·ly,** *adv.*

gi·gan·tism (jī gan′tiz əm) *n.* **1** abnormal growth or size. **2** *Medicine.* pathological overdevelopment caused by malfunction of the pituitary gland; acromegaly.

gig·gle (gig′əl) *v.* **-gled, -gling;** *n.* —*v.* laugh in a silly or nervous way. —*n.* a silly or nervous laugh. [imitative] —**gig′gler,** *n.* —**gig′gling·ly,** *adv.*

gig·gly (gig′lē) *adj.* having a tendency to giggle.

gig·let (gig′lit) *n.* a flighty, giggly girl.

gig·o·lo (jig′ə lō′) *n., pl.* **-los.** a man who is paid for being a dancing partner or escort for a woman. [< F]

gig·ot (jig′ət) *n.* **1** a leg-of-mutton sleeve. **2** a leg of mutton, veal, etc. [< F]

Gi·la monster (hē′lə) a large, poisonous lizard (*Heloderma suspectum*) found in the SW United States and N Mexico, having a stout body with black-and-pink, or black-and-orange, beadlike scales. It grows to about 50 cm long. [after *Gila* River, Arizona]

gild¹ (gild) *v.* **1** cover with a thin layer of gold or gold-colored material; make golden. **2** make (something) shine as if with gold: *The light from the setting sun gilded the windows.* **3** make (something) seem better than it is.
gild the lily, a adorn something that is beautiful enough not to need adornment; adorn unnecessarily. **b** praise something fine or beautiful excessively or unnecessarily.
[OE *gyldan* < *gold* gold]
☞ *Hom.* guild.

gild² (gild) See **guild.**

gild·ing (gil′ding) *n.* **1** a thin layer of gold or gold-colored material with which a thing is gilded. **2** an attractive outer appearance hiding an unattractive or unpleasant reality or fact.

gil·guy (gil′gī) *n.* **1** a temporary rope or rigging on a ship. **2** a gaudy, useless trinket; gimcrack. [? < *guy¹*]

gill¹ (gil) *n., v.* —*n.* **1** an organ of aquatic animals such as fish, tadpoles, or crabs, that enables them to obtain oxygen from the

water. See **fish** for picture. **2** any of the thin, leaflike radiating structures on the underside of the cap of a mushroom. **3 gills,** *pl.* **a** the red, hanging flesh under the throat of a fowl; wattle. **b** the flesh below a person's jaws.
—*v.* **1** catch (fish) by the gills in a gill net. **2** clean (fish). **3** cut away the gills of (a mushroom). [ME < ON; cf. Swedish *gäl*]

gill² (jil) *n.* a unit for measuring liquids, equal to one fourth of a pint (about 142 mL). [ME < OF *gille* wine measure]

gil·lie (gil′ē) *n.* **1** in the Scottish Highlands, a man who acts as an attendant or guide for a hunter or fisherman. **2** *Historical.* a male servant or attendant to a Highland chief. [< Scots Gaelic *gille* lad]

gill net a net suspended upright in the water, for catching fish by entangling their gills in its meshes.

gill·net (gil′net′) *v.* **-net·ted, -net·ting.** catch fish by using a gill net.

gill·net·ter (gil′net′ər) *n.* **1** a person who fishes with a gill net. **2** a boat used for gillnetting.

gil·ly (gil′ē) *n., pl.* **-lies.** See **gillie.**

gil·ly·flow·er (gil′ē flou′ər) *n.* any of various clove-scented flowers, especially the clove pink, stock, or wallflower. [ME < OF *gilofre* < L < Gk. *karyophyllon* clove tree < *karyon* clove + *phyllon* leaf]

gilt (gilt) *adj., n.* —*adj.* gilded. —*n.* a thin layer of gold or gold-colored material with which a thing is gilded; gilding.
gilt on the gingerbread, an additional adornment to something that is already sufficiently attractive.
☛ *Hom.* **guilt.**

gilt-edged (gilt′ejd′) *adj.* **1** having gilded edges. **2** of the very best quality: *gilt-edged stocks and securities.*

gim·bals (jim′bəlz *or* gim′bəlz) *n.pl.* an arrangement for keeping an object horizontal. A ship's compass is supported on gimbals made of a pair of rings pivoted to swing, one within the other, on axes at right angles to each other. [ult. < OF *gemel* twin < L *gemellus*]

gim·crack (jim′krak′) *n., adj.* —*n.* a showy, useless trifle. —*adj.* showy but useless. [origin uncertain]

gim·let¹ (gim′lit) *n.* a small hand tool for boring small holes in wood, consisting of a shaft having a screw point and attached to a crosswise handle. [ME < OF *guimbelet*]

gim·let² (gim′lit) *n.* a cocktail made with vodka or gin, lime-juice, and sugar. [< *gimlet¹*, coined on model of *screwdriver*, another cocktail]

gim·let-eyed (gim′lit īd′) *adj.* having sharp and piercing eyes.

gim·mick (gim′ik) *n., v.* —*n.* **1** *Slang.* any small device, especially one used secretly or in a tricky manner. **2** a deceptive thing or quality; trick. **3** something to attract attention; stunt.
—*v.* fit with gimmicks or gadgets. [origin uncertain] —**gim′mick·y,** *adj.*

gimp (gimp) *n.* a braidlike trimming made of silk, worsted, or cotton, sometimes stiffened with wire, used on garments, curtains, furniture, etc. [< F *guimpe* < OF < Gmc. Doublet of GUIMPE.]
☛ *Hom.* **guimpe.**

gin¹ (jin) *n.* a strong, colorless alcoholic drink, made from grain and usually flavored with juniper berries. [shortened form of *geneva* liquor]

gin² (jin) *n., v.* **ginned, gin·ning.** —*n.* **1** a machine for separating cotton from its seeds. **2** a trap; snare. —*v.* **1** separate (cotton) from its seeds. **2** trap; snare. [ME < OF *(en)gin* engine] —**gin′ner,** *n.*

gin³ (jin) *n.* gin rummy.

gin⁴ (jin) *v.* **gan, gun, gin·ning.** *Archaic or poetic.* begin. [OE *ginnan,* short for *aginnan,* var. of *onginnan*]

gin·ger (jin′jər) *n., adj., v.* —*n.* **1** the aromatic, hot-tasting underground stem of an East Indian plant (*Zingiber officinale*) used as a spice, sweetmeat (preserved with sugar or syrup), or flavoring for beverages, and also used in medicine. **2** the perennial, reedlike plant which produces this underground stem, cultivated throughout the tropics. **3** *(adj.)* designating the family (Zingiberaceae) of plants that includes ginger and cardamom. **5** *Informal.* liveliness; energy: *That horse has plenty of ginger.* **6** a light, reddish-brown color.
—*adj.* having the color ginger: *ginger hair.*
—*v.* **1** treat or flavor with ginger. **2** *Informal.* make spirited or enliven: *The new manager soon gingered up the company.* [OE *gingiber* < LL < L *zinziber* < Gk. *zingiberis* > Prakrit *singabēra* ? < Malayalam *inchi-ver*]

ginger ale a non-alcoholic, sweetened, carbonated drink flavored with ginger.

ginger beer a drink similar to ginger ale, but made with fermenting ginger.

gin·ger·bread (jin′jər bred′) *n.* **1** a cake flavored with molasses

hat, āge, fär; let, ēqual, tèrm; it, īce
hot, ōpen, ôrder; oil, out; cup, put, rüle,
əbove, takən, pencəl, lemən, circəs

ch, child; ng, long; sh, ship
th, thin; ᴛʜ, then; zh, measure

and ginger. **2** a kind of cookie made of similar ingredients, usually cut into various shapes and often decorated with icing. **3** intricate wooden decoration, such as fretwork or carving on the gables of houses, etc. Many old houses, especially in central and eastern Canada, are trimmed with gingerbread. **4** *(adj.)* of or designating such decoration. **5** *(adj.)* of ornamentation on furniture, etc., tasteless and gaudy.

gin·ger·ly (jin′jər lē) *adv. or adj.* with extreme care or caution. —**gin′ger·li·ness,** *n.*

gin·ger·snap (jin′jər snap′) *n.* a thin, crisp, cookie flavored with ginger and molasses.

gin·ger·y (jin′jər ē) *adj.* **1** like ginger; hot and sharp; spicy. **2** light reddish or brownish yellow. **3** alert; full of vigor.

ging·ham (ging′əm) *n.* **1** a plain-woven fabric usually of cotton or a cotton blend and usually having a woven two-color pattern of checks or stripes. **2** *(adj.)* made of gingham: *a gingham dress.* [< F *guingan* < Malay *ginggang,* originally, striped]

gin·gi·val (jin′jə vəl *or* jin jī′vəl) *adj.* **1** of or having to do with the gums. **2** *Phonetics.* referring to the ridge behind and above the upper front teeth; alveolar. [< NL *gingivalis* < L *gingiva* gum]

gin·gi·vi·tis (jin′jə vī′tis) *n.* inflammation of the gums.

gink·go (ging′kō *or* jing′kō) *n., pl.* **-goes.** a large deciduous tree (*Ginkgo biloba*) native to China but widely cultivated in temperate regions as an ornamental tree, having fan-shaped leaves and yellow fruit. The ginkgo, the only living species of the order Ginkgoales, is often called a "living fossil" because it does not exist in the wild; it has apparently escaped extinction because since ancient times it has been cultivated in Chinese temple gardens. [< Japanese]

gin rummy (jin) a kind of rummy in which players form sequences and matching combinations and lay down their hands when having ten or fewer points. [origin uncertain]

gin·seng (jin′seng) *n.* **1** either of two herbs (*Panax schinseng* of China and *P. quinquefolius* of North America) having leaves with five lobes, scarlet berries, and a thick, forked, aromatic root used in medicine, especially in China. **2** the root of this plant. **3** *(adj.)* designating the family (Araliaceae) of plants that includes the ginsengs and ivy. [< Chinese *jên shên* (*jên* man, from a frequent shape of the root)]

Gi·o·con·da (jē′ə kon′də′; *Italian,* jō kōn′dä) *n.* La Gioconda, a famous portrait usually called the Mona Lisa, painted by Leonardo da Vinci (1452-1519), Italian painter and scientist.

Gip·sy *or* **gip·sy** (jip′sē) *n., pl.* **-sies;** *adj.* See **Gypsy.**

gipsy moth gypsy moth.

gi·raffe (jə raf′) *n.* a large, hoofed, cud-chewing, African mammal (*Giraffa camelopardalis*) having a very long neck and legs and a beige coat with reddish-brown spots. It is the tallest of all living mammals, reaching a height of 5.5 metres or more. [< F < Arabic *zarāfah*]

gir·an·dole (jīr′ən dōl′) *n.* **1** a decorative branched candlestick. **2** a rotating jet of water. **3** a rotating firework. [< F *girandole* < Ital. *girandola* fireworks circle, dim. of *giranda* fire circle < *girare* turn in a circle < LL *gyrare* turn < Gk. *gyros* ring]

gird¹ (gėrd) *v.* **girt** *or* **gird·ed, gird·ing.** **1** put a belt or band around. **2** fasten with a belt or band. **3** surround; enclose. **4** get ready for action: *They girded themselves for battle.* **5** clothe; furnish; equip, etc. [OE *gyrdan*]

gird² (gėrd) *v. or n.* jeer; sneer; scoff. [origin uncertain]

gird·er (gėr′dər) *n.* a main supporting beam, usually horizontal. Steel girders are often used to make the framework of bridges and tall buildings. [< *gird¹*]

gir·dle (gėr′dəl) *n., v.* **-dled, -dling.** —*n.* **1** a belt, sash, cord, etc. worn around the waist. **2** anything that surrounds or encloses: *a girdle of trees around the pond.* **3** a support like a corset worn about the hips or waist. **4** a ring made around a tree trunk, etc. by cutting the bark.
—*v.* **1** form a girdle around; encircle: *Wide roads girdle the city.* **2** cut away the bark so as to make a ring around (a tree, branch, etc.). **3** put a girdle on or around. [OE *gyrdel* < *gyrdan* gird¹] —**gir′dler,** *n.*

girl (gėrl) *n.* **1** a female child. **2** a young, unmarried woman. **3** a female servant. **4** *Informal.* sweetheart. **5** *Informal.* a woman of any age. [ME *gurle, girle* child, young person; origin uncertain]

girl Friday a female assistant or aid.

girl·friend (gèrl'frend') *n.* **1** a female companion of a boy or man; sweetheart or lover: *Does he have a girlfriend?* **2** a girl who is one's friend.

Girl Guides **1** a nonpolitical, nondenominational organization for girls and young women whose aim is to help them to learn co-operation, leadership, self-reliance, and consideration for others, and to develop physical fitness and spiritual values, in order to become responsible, resourceful, and happy members of society. The Girl Guides of Canada has five programs for different ages: Brownies, Guides, Pathfinders, Cadets, and Rangers. **2 Girl Guide**, a member, aged nine to twelve, of the Girl Guides.

girl·hood (gèrl'hùd) *n.* the time or condition of being a girl: *The old woman recalled her girlhood with pleasure.*

girl·ie (gèr'lē) *n. Informal.* a girl or woman.

girl·ish (gèr'lish) *adj.* **1** of a girl. **2** like that of a girl. **3** proper or suitable for girls: *She thought she was too old now for such girlish games.* —**girl'ish·ly,** *adv.* —**girl'ish·ness,** *n.*

Gi·ron·dist (jə ron'dist) *n.* a member of a French political party of moderate republicans from 1791 to 1793.

girt[1] (gèrt) *v.* a pt. and a pp. of **gird**[1].

girt[2] (gèrt) *v.* **1** put a belt, girdle, or girth around; gird. **2** fasten with a belt, girdle, or girth.

girth (gèrth) *n., v.* —*n.* **1** the measure around anything: *a man of large girth, the girth of a tree.* **2** a strap or band that keeps a saddle, pack, etc. in place on a horse's back. See **harness** and **saddle** for pictures. —*v.* **1** measure in girth. **2** fasten with a strap or band. [ME < ON *gjörth* girdle. Akin to GIRD[1].]

gist (jist) *n.* the essential part; real point or main idea; the substance of an argument. [< OF *gist* (it) consists (in), depends (on) < L *jacet* it lies]

git·tern (git'ərn) *n.* an old musical instrument with wire strings, resembling a guitar. [ME < OF *guiterne*]

give (giv) *v.* **gave, giv·en, giv·ing;** *n.* —*v.* **1** hand over as a present; make a present of: *My brother gave me his watch.* **2** hand over; deliver: *to give a person into custody, to give one's word. Please give me a drink.* **3** hand over in return for something: *I gave it to him for $5.* **4** let have; cause to have: *Give me permission to leave.* **5** deal; administer: *He gives hard blows even in play. She gave the ball a kick.* **6** offer; present: *This newspaper gives a full story of the game.* **7** put forth; make; do; utter: *He gave a cry of pain.* **8** furnish; supply: *to give aid to the enemy.* **9** produce; yield; deliver: *to give a lecture.* **10** cause; create: *Don't give the teacher any trouble.* **11** relinquish; surrender: *to give ground.* **12** yield to pressure or force: *The lock gave when he battered the door.* **13** provide a view or passage; open; lead: *This window gives upon the courtyard.*
give and take, exchange evenly or fairly.
give away, *Informal.* **a** give as a present. **b** give as a bride: *The bride's father gave her away.* **c** cause to become known; reveal; betray: *The spy gave away secrets to the enemy.*
give back, return: *Give back the book you borrowed.*
give in, a stop fighting and admit defeat; yield. **b** hand in: *He gave in his history project when it was due.*
give it to, *Informal.* **a** beat; punish. **b** scold.
give off, send out; put forth.
give or take, add or subtract (a few): *The distance is two kilometres, give or take a few metres.*
give out, a send out; put forth: *The roses gave out a sweet smell.* **b** distribute: *The boys gave out the handbills.* **c** make known: *The news was given out at midnight.* **d** become used up: *The food gave out during the famine.* **e** become worn out or exhausted: *The old man's strength gave out during the long walk.*
give over, a hand over; deliver. **b** stop.
give up, a hand over; deliver; surrender. **b** stop having or doing. **c** stop trying: *Don't give up now; we're almost there.* **d** have no more hope for: *They've given him up as dead.* **e** devote entirely: *He gave himself up to his studies.*
—*n.* a yielding to force or pressure; elasticity: *You need a fabric with give for this pattern.* [ME *give(n)* < *yive(n)*; initial g in ME form influenced by ON *gefa* give] —**giv'er,** *n.*
☞ *Syn. v.* **Give, present, confer** = hand over or bestow something as a gift. **Give** is the general word: *He gave me these books.* **Present** = give in a formal way, often with ceremony: *The Board of trade presented a trophy to the football team.* **Confer** = give in a kindly or courteous way, as to an inferior, or to present as an honor or favor: *She conferred her smiles on the admiring crowd.*

give–and–take (giv'ən tāk') *n.* **1** an even or fair exchange; mutual concession. **2** good-natured banter; exchange of talk.

give·a·way (giv'ə wā') *n. Informal.* **1** an unintentional revelation; exposure; betrayal. **2** a radio or television show in which contestants participate and receive prizes. **3** anything given away or sold at a cheap price to promote business, good relations, etc.

giveaway show or **program** giveaway (def. 2).

giv·en (giv'ən) *adj., v.* —*adj.* **1** stated; fixed; specified: *You must finish the test in a given time.* **2** assigned as a basis of calculating, reasoning, etc.: *Given that the radius is 19 cm, find the circumference.* —*v.* pp. of **give**.
given to, inclined or disposed towards: *The old soldier was given to boasting.*

given name a personal name given to a person as a child, usually by the parents or godparents, and used especially by the person's friends and family: *Gordon and Charles are the given names of Gordon Charles McRae; McRae is his surname, or last name.*

giz·zard (giz'ərd) *n.* **1** a bird's second stomach, where the food from the first stomach is ground up fine. **2** a muscular organ in insects and earthworms that is posterior to the crop and serves to grind the food. [ME < OF *gister*, ult. < L *gigeria* cooked entrails of a fowl]

Gk. Greek.

gla·brous (glā'brəs) *adj.* without hair or down; smooth: *Nasturtiums have glabrous stems.* [< L *glaber* smooth]

gla·cé (gla sā') *adj.* **1** coated with a glaze of sugar. **2** frozen. **3** finished with a glossy surface: *glacé silk.* [< F *glacé*, pp. of *glacer* impart a gloss to]

gla·cial (glā'shəl) *adj.* **1** of ice or glaciers; having much ice or many glaciers. **2** relating to a glacial epoch or period. **3** made by the pressure and movement of ice or glaciers: *a glacial plain.* **4** like ice; very cold; icy: *She gave him a glacial stare.* [< L *glacialis* < *glacies* ice] —**gla'cial·ly,** *adv.*

glacial epoch or **period** ice age.

gla·ci·ate (glā'shē āt') *v.* **-at·ed, -at·ing. 1** cover with ice or glaciers. **2** expose to or change by the action of glaciers. **3** freeze. —**gla'ci·a'tion,** *n.*

gla·cier (glā'shər *or* glās'yər) *n.* a large mass of ice formed from snow on high ground wherever winter snowfalls exceeds summer melting. It moves very slowly down a mountain or along a valley. [< F *glacier* < *glace* ice < L *glacies*]

glacier lily *Cdn.* a plant (*Erythronium grandiflorum*) of the lily family found in the mountains of W North America, having yellow flowers that appear in May and June, often before the snow has disappeared; snow lily.

gla·ci·o·log·i·cal (glā'shē ə loj'ə kəl *or* glā'sē ə loj'ə kəl) *adj.* of or having to do with glaciers or glaciology.

gla·ci·ol·o·gist (glā'shē ol'ə jist *or* glā'sē ol'ə jist) *n.* a person trained in glaciology, especially one whose work it is.

gla·ci·ol·o·gy (glā'shē ol'ə jē *or* glā'sē ol'ə jē) *n.* the science that deals with glaciers and glaciation. [< F < L *glacies* + E *-logy*]

gla·cis (glā'sis, glas'is, *or* glas'ē) *n.* **1** a gentle slope. **2** in fortification, a bank of earth in front of a counterscarp, having a gradual slope toward the field or open country. [< F *glacis*, originally, slippery place < *glacer* freeze, make icy < *glace* ice]

glad[1] (glad) *adj.* **glad·der, glad·dest. 1** happy; experiencing joy: *I'm glad you could come. I'll be glad when exams are over.* **2** bringing joy; very pleasant: *glad news.* **3** caused by or expressing happiness: *We heard her glad shout when she saw us.* **4** very willing: *I'd be glad to help out.* **5** bright and cheerful. [OE *glæd* bright, shining] —**glad'ly,** *adv.* —**glad'ness,** *n.*
☞ *Syn.* **1. Glad, happy** = feeling pleasure or joy. **Glad,** which is not used before the noun when describing people (as distinct from their looks, etc.), particularly suggests feeling contented and filled with pleasure or delight: *She was glad to see him.* **Happy** particularly suggests feeling deeply and fully contented or satisfied and at peace, or filled with joy: *He will never be happy until he has paid all his debts.*

glad[2] (glad) *n. Informal.* gladiola.

glad·den (glad'ən) *v.* make or become glad: *His heart was gladdened by the good news.* —**glad'den·er,** *n.*
☞ *Syn.* See note at **cheer.**

glade (glād) *n.* an open space in a wood or forest. [probably related to GLAD[1]]

glad·i·a·tor (glad'ē ā'tər) *n.* **1** in ancient Rome, a slave, captive, or paid fighter who fought at the public shows. **2** a person who argues, fights, wrestles, etc. with great skill. [< L *gladiator* < *gladius* sword]

glad·i·a·to·ri·al (glad'ē ə tô'rē əl) *adj.* of or having to do with gladiators.

glad·i·o·la (glad'ē ō'lə) *n., pl.* **-la** *or,* formerly, **-li** (-lī *or* -lē). any of a genus (*Gladiolus*) of plant of the iris family that grow from bulblike underground stems, having stiff, sword-shaped leaves and spikes of large, showy flowers all growing on one side of the stem. Gladiola are widely grown for their flowers.

glad·i·o·lus (glad'ē ō'ləs) *n.* gladiola. [< L *gladiolus*, dim. of

gladius sword]

glad rags *Slang.* one's best clothes.

glad·some (glad′səm) *adj.* **1** glad; joyful; cheerful. **2** causing gladness; pleasant; delightful. —**glad′some·ly,** *adv.* —**glad′some·ness,** *n.*

Glad·stone bag (glad′stōn *or* glad′stən) a travelling bag that opens flat into two equal compartments. [after William Ewart *Gladstone* (1809-1898), a British statesman]

glair (gler) *n.* **1** the raw white of an egg or any similar viscous substance. **2** a glaze or size made from it. [ME < OF *glaire,* ult. < L *clarus* clear]

glaive (glāv) *n. Archaic.* a sword; broadsword. [ME < OF < L *gladius* sword]

glam·or (glam′ər) See **glamour.**

glam·or·ize (glam′ər īz′) *v.* **-ized, -iz·ing.** make someone or something glamorous. Also, **glamourize.** —**glam′or·i·za′tion,** *n.*

glam·or·ous (glam′ər əs *or* glam′rəs) *adj.* full of glamour; fascinating; charming. —**glam′or·ous·ly,** *adv.*

glam·our (glam′ər) *n.* **1** a romantic or exciting fascination; alluring charm: *the glamour of show business. The mysterious stranger had a glamour about him.* **2** a magic spell or influence. Sometimes, **glamor.** [alteration of *grammar* or its var. *gramarye* occult learning; originally, a spell]
➥ *Spelling.* See note at **-or.**

glam·our·ize (glam′ər īz′) *v.* glamorize.

glance (glans) *n., v.* **glanced, glanc·ing.** —*n.* **1** a quick look. **2** a flash of light; gleam: *eyes glancing.* **3** a glancing off; deflected motion; swift, oblique movement. **4** a passing reference; brief allusion.
—*v.* **1** look quickly; cause to look quickly. **2** flash with light; gleam: *eyes glancing.* **3** hit and go off at a slant: *The spear glanced off his armor and hit the wall.* **4** make a short reference and go on to something else. [var. of ME *glace(n)* strike a glancing blow < OF *glacier* to slip, ult. < L *glacies* ice] —**glanc′ing·ly,** *adv.*
➥ *Usage. n.* **Glance** and **glimpse** should not be confused. **Glance** applies to a look directed at someone or something: *I gave him only a glance.* **Glimpse** applies to what is seen, a short, quick, imperfect view such as can be seen in a glance: *I caught a glimpse of him as he turned the corner.*

gland (gland) *n.* **1** an organ in the body by which certain substances are separated from the blood and changed into some secretion for use in the body, such as bile, or into a product to be discharged from the body, such as sweat. The liver, the kidneys, the pancreas, and the thyroid are glands. **2** any of various structures similar to glands such as the lymph nodes. **3** *Botany.* a secreting organ or structure, generally on or near a surface. [< F *glande* < OF *glandre* < L *glandula,* dim. of *glans, glandis* acorn]

glan·ders (glan′dərz) *n.* a serious contagious disease of horses, mules, etc., accompanied by swellings beneath the lower jaw and a profuse discharge from the nostrils. [< OF *glandre* gland < L *glandula.* See GLAND.]

glan·du·lar (glan′jə lər *or* glan′dyə lər) *adj.* of or like a gland; having glands; made up of glands. —**glan′du·lar·ly,** *adv.*

glan·du·lous (glan′jə ləs *or* glan′dyə ləs) *adj.* glandular.

glare[1] (gler) *n., v.* **glared, glar·ing.** —*n.* **1** a strong, bright light; light that shines so brightly that it hurts the eyes: *The glare from the ice made his eyes sore.* **2** a fierce, angry stare. **3** too great brightness and showiness.
—*v.* **1** give off a strong, bright light; shine so brightly as to hurt the eyes. **2** stare fiercely and angrily: *The angry man glared at his defiant son.* **3** express by a fierce, angry stare. **4** be too bright and showy. [ME *glaren;* cf. OE *glæren* glassy]

glare[2] (gler) *n., adj.* —*n.* a bright, smooth surface.
glare ice, *Cdn.* ice that has a smooth, glassy surface. —*adj.* bright and smooth. [extended use of *glare*[1]]

glar·ing (gler′ing) *adj.* **1** very bright; shining so brightly as to hurt the eyes; dazzling: *glaring headlights.* **2** too bright and showy: *glaring colors.* **3** very easily seen; conspicuous: *a glaring error in spelling.* —**glar′ing·ly,** *adv.* —**glar′ing·ness,** *n.*

glar·y (gler′ē) *adj.* glaring.

glass (glas) *n., v.* —*n.* **1** a hard, brittle substance that is usually transparent, made by fusing sand with soda, potash, lime, or other substances. *Windows are made of glass.* **2** a tumbler or similar drinking vessel made of glass, plastic, etc.: *He knocked a glass off the table.* **3** the amount that a glass can hold: *to drink a glass of water.* **4 glasses,** *pl.* **a** a pair of glass or plastic lenses together with the frame that holds them in place, worn to correct defective vision or to protect the eyes; eyeglasses; spectacles. **b** binoculars. **5** a piece of glass used for a particular purpose, such as a windowpane or a plate of glass covering a picture. **6** mirror. **7** barometer. **8** an optical lens or instrument, such as a telescope, magnifying glass, or monocle. **9** (*adj.*) made of glass: *a glass dish.* **10** (*adj.*) having to do with glass or the manufacture of glass: *the glass industry.*

hat, āge, fär; let, ēqual, tėrm; it, īce
hot, ōpen, ôrder; oil, out; cup, pút, rüle,
above, takən, pencəl, lemən, circəs
ch, child; ng, long; sh, ship
th, thin; ᴛʜ, then; zh, measure

see through rose-colored glasses, be very, often unduly, optimistic about something.
—*v.* **1** enclose or protect with glass (*often used with* **in**): *to glass in a porch.* **2** fit or provide with glass. **3** reflect; mirror. **4** make or become glassy. [OE *glæs*]

glass blower a person who shapes glass by blowing it while it is still hot and soft.

glass blowing the art or process of shaping glass by blowing it while it is still hot and soft.

glass·ful (glas′fùl) *n., pl.* **-fuls.** as much as a drinking glass holds.

glass·house (glas′hous′) *n.* a greenhouse; hothouse.

glass·ine (gla sēn′) *n.* a thin, tough, glazed, almost transparent paper, used in packaging.

glass·ware (glas′wer′) *n.* articles made of glass.

glass wool glass spun in very fine threads, with a texture resembling loose fibres of wool, used for insulation, etc.

glass·work (glas′wėrk′) *n.* **1** the manufacture of glass or glassware. **2** objects or articles made of glass; glassware. **3** the fitting of window glass; glazing.

glass·wort (glas′wėrt′) *n.* any of a genus (*Salicornia*) of annual plants of the goosefoot family native to European saltwater marshes, having fleshy stems with leaves reduced to scalelike sheaths. Glasswort ashes were formerly used as a source of soda for glassmaking.

glass·y (glas′ē) *adj.* **glass·i·er, glass·i·est.** **1** like glass; smooth or easily seen through: *glassy water.* **2** having a fixed, expressionless stare: *The dazed man's eyes were glassy.* —**glass′i·ly,** *adv.* —**glass′i·ness,** *n.*

Glau·ber's salt (glou′bərz, glo′bərz, *or* glô′bərz) sodium sulphate, used as a cathartic, etc. [after Johann R. *Glauber* (1604-1668), a German chemist]

glau·co·ma (glo kō′mə, glô kō′mə, *or* glou kō′mə) *n.* a disease of the eye, characterized by hardening of the eyeball and gradual loss of sight. [< Gk. *glaukoma* < *glaukos* grey]

glau·cous (glo′kəs *or* glô′kəs) *adj.* **1** light bluish-green. **2** covered with whitish powder as plums and grapes are. [< L *glaucus* < Gk. *glaukos* grey]

glaze (glāz) *v.* **glazed, glaz·ing;** *n.* —*v.* **1** put glass in; cover with glass. Pieces of glass cut to the right size are used to glaze windows and picture frames. **2** make a smooth, glassy surface or glossy coating on (china, food, etc.). **3** become smooth, glassy, or glossy. —*n.* **1** a smooth, glassy surface or glossy coating: *the glaze on a china cup, a glaze of ice.* **2** a substance used to make such a surface or coating on things. [ME *glase(n)* < *glas* glass, OE *glæs*] —**glaz′er,** *n.*

gla·zier (glā′zhər *or* glā′zhē ər) *n.* a person whose work is putting glass in windows, picture frames, etc. [ME *glasier* < *glas* glass, OE *glæs*]

glaz·ing (glāz′ing) *n.* **1** the work of a glazier. **2** glass set or to be set in frames. **3** a substance used to make a smooth, glassy surface or glossy coating on things. **4** such a surface or coating.

gleam (glēm) *n., v.* —*n.* **1** a flash or beam of light. **2** a short or faint light. **3** a short appearance; faint show: *After one gleam of hope, they all became discouraged.*
—*v.* **1** flash or beam with light: *A cat's eyes gleam in the dark.* **2** shine with a short or faint light. **3** appear suddenly; be shown briefly. [OE *glæm*]
➥ *Syn. n.* **2. Gleam, glimmer** (def. 1) = a brief, unsteady, or not bright light. **Gleam** applies to a light that comes out of the darkness and disappears soon, or is softened or toned down: *We saw the gleam of headlights through the rain.* **Glimmer** applies to a faint light, a light shining feebly or with varying intensity: *We saw the glimmer of a distant light through the trees.*

glean (glēn) *v.* **1** gather (grain) left on a field by reapers. **2** gather little by little or slowly: *The spy gleaned information from the soldier's talk.* [ME < OF *glener* < LL *glennare* < Celtic] —**glean′er,** *n.*

glebe (glēb) *n.* **1** *Poetic.* soil; earth; field. **2** a portion of land assigned to a clergyman as part of his living. [< L *gleba*]

glee (glē) *n.* **1** joy; delight; mirth. **2** a song for three or more usually male voices each singing a different part. A glee is usually sung without accompaniment. [OE *glēo*]

glee club a society or group organized for singing glees or other part songs.

glee·ful (glē′fəl) *adj.* filled with glee; merry; joyous. —**glee′ful·ly**, *adv.* —**glee′ful·ness**, *n.*

glee·man (glē′mən) *n., pl.* -**men.** *Archaic.* a singer; minstrel.

glee·some (glē′səm) *adj.* gleeful.

glen (glen) *n.* a small, narrow valley. [< Scots Gaelic *gleann*]

glen·gar·ry (glen gar′ē *or* glen ger′ē) *n., pl.* -**ries.** a Scottish cap with straight sides and a lengthwise crease in the top, often having short ribbons at the back. See **cap** for picture. [after *Glengarry,* a valley in Scotland]

glib (glib) *adj.* **glib·ber, glib·best. 1** speaking or spoken too smoothly and easily to be sincere: *a glib sales talk. No one believed his glib excuses.* **2** without depth; not thought out; superficial: *a glib solution.* [short for *glibbery* slippery; cf. Du. *glibberig*] —**glib′ly**, *adv.* —**glib′ness**, *n.*
☛ *Syn.* **1.** See note at **fluent.**

glide (glīd) *v.* **glid·ed, glid·ing;** *n.* —*v.* **1** move along smoothly, evenly, and easily. Birds, ships, dancers, and skaters glide. **2** pass gradually, quietly, or imperceptibly: *The years glided past.* **3** of an aircraft, come down slowly at a slant without using a motor. Under favorable circumstances, an airplane can glide about 1.5 km for every 300 m that it is above the ground. **4** *Music.* pass from one tone to another with a break; slur. **5** *Phonetics.* produce a glide. —*n.* **1** a smooth, even, easy movement. **2** of an aircraft, a coming down slowly at a slant without using a motor. **3** *Music.* a slur. **4** *Phonetics.* **a** a sound made in passing from one speech sound to another, such as the *y* often heard between the *i* and *r* in *hire.* **b** a semivowel. **5** *Dancing.* **a** a step made by sliding rather than raising the foot. **b** a waltz or other dance using such steps. **6** a metal or plastic attachment under a piece of furniture to make it easy to move. [OE *glīdan*]
☛ *Syn. v.* **1.** See note at **slide.**

glid·er (glīd′ər) *n.* a person or thing that glides, especially an aircraft resembling an airplane but without a motor. A glider has very long wings in proportion to the body, and is kept up in the air by rising air currents.

glim (glim) *n. Slang.* a light; lamp; candle. [related to GLEAM, GLIMMER]

glim·mer (glim′ər) *n., v.* —*n.* **1** a faint or unsteady light. **2** a vague idea or feeling; a faint glimpse: *The doctor's report gave us only a glimmer of hope.* —*v.* **1** shine with a faint or unsteady light: *The candle glimmered and went out.* **2** appear faintly or dimly. [ME. Related to GLEAM.]
☛ *Syn. n.* **1.** See note at **gleam.**

glim·mer·ing (glim′ər ing *or* glim′ring) *n.* glimmer.

glimpse (glimps) *n., v.* **glimpsed, glimps·ing.** —*n.* **1** a short, quick view: *I caught a glimpse of the falls as our train went by.* **2** a short, faint appearance. —*v.* **1** catch a short quick view of. **2** look quickly; glance. [ME. Related to GLIM, GLIMMER.]
☛ *Syn. n.* **1.** See note at **glance.**

glint (glint) *v. or n.* gleam; flash: *His eyes glinted fiercely in the light.* (v.) *There was a glint of steel as the man swung his axe.* (n.) [cf. dial. Swedish *glinta*]

glis·sade (gli sad′ *or* gli säd′) *n., v.* -**sad·ed, -sad·ing.** —*n.* **1** *Ballet.* a gliding step, often ending in a leap. **2** a sliding down any smooth, sloping surface. —*v.* perform a glissade; slide. [< F *glissade* < *glisser* slide]

glis·san·do (gli sän′dō) *adj., n. pl.* -**di** (dē). *Music.* —*adj.* performed with a gliding effect. A pianist plays a glissando passage by running the fingers rapidly over the keys. —*n.* **1** a gliding effect. **2** a glissando passage. [in imitation of Italian, < F *glissant*, ppr. of *glisser* slide]

glis·ten (glis′ən) *v. or n.* sparkle; shine. [OE *glisnian*]

glis·ter (glis′tər) *v. or n. Archaic.* glisten; glitter; sparkle. [? < *glisten*; cf. MDu. *glisteren*]

glit·ter (glit′ər) *v., n.* —*v.* **1** glisten, sparkle; shine with a bright, sparkling light: *Jewels and new coins glitter.* **2** be bright and showy. **3** become covered with ice after a freezing rain. —*n.* **1** a bright, sparkling light. **2** brightness; showiness; a bright display. **3** the bright, sparkling ice that forms on everything outdoors after a rain that freezes. [ME < ON *glitra*] —**glit′ter·er**, *n.*
☛ *Syn. n.* **1.** See note at **flash.**

glit·ter·y (glit′ər ē) *adj.* glittering.

gloam·ing (glōm′ing) *n.* evening twilight; dusk. [OE *glōmung* < *glōm* twilight; influenced by *glow*]

gloat (glōt) *v.* gaze intently; ponder with pleasure; stare: *The miser gloated over his gold.* [cf. ON *glotta* smile scornfully] —**gloat′er**, *n.* —**gloat′ing·ly**, *adv.*

glob·al (glōb′əl) *adj.* **1** of the earth as a whole; worldwide: *the threat of global war.* **2** shaped like a globe. —**glob′al·ly**, *adv.*

glo·bate (glō′bāt) *adj.* shaped like a globe.

globe (glōb) *n., v.* **globed, glob·ing.** —*n.* **1** anything round like a ball; sphere. **2** the earth; world. **3** a sphere with a map of the earth or sky on it. **4** anything rounded like a globe. An electric light bulb is a globe. —*v.* gather or form into a globe. [< F < L *globus*]
☛ *Syn. n.* **2.** See note at **earth.**

globe·fish (glōb′fish′) *n., pl.* -**fish** *or* -**fish·es.** puffer.

globe·flow·er (glōb′flou′ər) *n.* any of a genus (*Trollius*) of plants of the buttercup family having globe-shaped, usually yellow, flowers.

globe·trot·ter (glōb′trot′ər) *n.* a person who travels widely over the world, especially for pleasure.

globe·trot·ting (glōb′trot′ing) *n.* travelling widely throughout the world, especially as a tourist.

glo·bose (glō′bōs *or* glō bōs′) *adj.* globular. [< L *globosus* < *globus* globe]

glob·u·lar (glob′yə lər) *adj.* **1** shaped like a globe or globule; round; spherical. **2** consisting of globules. —**glob′u·lar·ly**, *adv.*

glob·ule (glob′yəl) *n.* a very small ball; tiny drop: *globules of sweat.* [< F < L *globulus*, dim. of *globus* globe]

glob·u·lin (glob′yə lin) *n.* any of a group of proteins, found in plant and animal tissues, that are soluble in weak salt solutions but insoluble in water.

glock·en·spiel (glok′ən spēl′) *n.* a musical instrument consisting of a graduated series of small, tuned bells, metal bars, or tubes mounted in a frame and struck by two little hammers. [< G *Glockenspiel* < *Glocke* bell + *Spiel* play]

glom·er·ate (glom′ər it) *adj.* clustered together; collected into a rounded mass. [< L *glomeratus*, pp. of *glomerare* < *glomus, -meris* ball]

glom·er·ule (glom′ər ül′) *n.* any compact cluster. [< NL *glomerulus*, dim. of L *glomus* ball]

gloom (glüm) *n., v.* —*n.* **1** deep shadow; darkness; dimness. **2** low spirits; sadness. **3** a dejected or sad look. —*v.* **1** be or become dark, dim, or dismal. **2** be in low spirits; feel miserable. **3** look sad or dismal. [ME *gloume(n)* look sullen, lower²; origin uncertain]

gloom·y (glü′mē) *adj.* **gloom·i·er, gloom·i·est. 1** dark; dim: *a gloomy winter day.* **2** in low spirits; sad; melancholy: *a gloomy mood.* **3** causing low spirits; discouraging; dismal: *a gloomy book.* [< *gloom, v.*] —**gloom′i·ly**, *adv.* —**gloom′i·ness**, *n.*

glo·ri·a (glô′rē ə) *n.* **1** a Christian song of praise to God, or its musical setting. **2 Gloria,** one of three Christian songs of praise to God, beginning "Glory be to God on high," "Glory be to the Father," and "Glory be to Thee, O Lord." **3** halo. **4** a fabric made of silk and some other material, used for umbrellas. [< L]

glo·ri·fi·ca·tion (glô′rə fə kā′shən) *n.* **1** glorifying or being glorified. **2** an embellished version of something. **3** *Brit. Informal.* celebration.

glo·ri·fy (glô′rə fī′) *v.* -**fied, -fy·ing. 1** give glory to; make glorious. **2** praise; honor; worship. **3** exalt to the glory of heaven. **4** cause to seem more splendid, important, etc. than is actually the case: *I'm just a glorified handyman around the place. She glorified the essay by calling it a monograph.* [ME < OF *glorifier* < L *glorificare* < *gloria* glory + *facere* make] —**glo′ri·fi′er**, *n.*

glo·ri·ous (glô′rē əs) *adj.* **1** having or deserving glory; illustrious. **2** giving glory; worthy of high praise: *a glorious victory.* **3** magnificent; splendid: *a glorious pageant.* **4** *Informal.* admirable; delightful; fine: *have a glorious time. Isn't it a glorious day?* [ME < AF < L *gloriosus* < *gloria* glory] —**glo′ri·ous·ly**, *adv.*

glo·ry (glô′rē) *n., pl.* -**ries;** *v.* -**ried, -ry·ing.** —*n.* **1** great praise and honor; fame; renown. **2** that which brings praise and honor; a source of pride and joy: *Her real glory was not her beauty but her success as a doctor.* **3** adoring praise and thanksgiving. **4** radiant beauty; brightness; magnificence; splendor. **5** a condition of magnificence, splendor, or greatest prosperity. **6** the splendor and bliss of heaven; heaven. **7** halo.
go to glory, die.
in (one's) **glory,** *Informal.* in a state of greatest satisfaction or enjoyment: *He's in his glory with a dish of ice cream.* —*v.* be proud; rejoice.
glory in, take great pride or delight in: *Her father gloried in her success as a pianist.* [ME < OF *glorie* < L *gloria*]

gloss¹ (glos) *n., v.* —*n.* **1** a smooth, shiny surface; lustre: *Varnished furniture has a gloss.* **2** an outward appearance or surface that covers faults underneath. —*v.* put a smooth, shiny surface on.
gloss over, smooth over or explain away (a fault, error, etc.): *He tried to gloss over his negligence.* [cf. ON *glossi* flame]

gloss² (glos) *n., v.* —*n.* **1** an explanation; comment. **2** glossary.

3 a translation inserted between the lines of a text printed in a foreign language.
—*v.* comment on; explain. [< L < Gk. *glōssa*, literally, tongue]
—**gloss′er,** *n.*

glos·sar·i·al (glo ser′ē əl) *adj.* having to do with a glossary; like a glossary.

glos·sa·ry (glos′ə rē) *n., pl.* **-ries.** a list of special, technical, or difficult words with explanations or comments: *a glossary to Shakespeare's plays, a glossary of terms used in chemistry. Textbooks sometimes have glossaries at the end.* [< L *glossarium* < *glossa.* See GLOSS².]

gloss·y (glos′ē) *adj.* **gloss·i·er, gloss·i·est;** *n.* —*adj.* smooth and shiny. —*n. Informal.* a photograph printed on glossy paper.
—**gloss′i·ly,** *adv.* —**gloss′i·ness,** *n.*

glot·tal (glot′əl) *adj.* **1** of the glottis. **2** *Phonetics.* produced in the glottis. *H* in *hope* is often a glottal sound.

glot·tis (glot′is) *n.* the opening in the upper part of the windpipe, between the vocal cords. See **windpipe** for picture. [< NL < Gk. *glōttis,* ult. < *glōtta* tongue]

glove (gluv) *n., v.* **gloved, glov·ing.** —*n.* **1** a covering for the hand, having separate sections for each of the four fingers and the thumb. **2** a padded covering to protect the hand: *a hockey glove, a baseball glove.*
fit like a glove, fit perfectly or tightly.
hand in glove, in an intimate relationship.
handle with (kid) gloves, treat gently or carefully.
—*v.* **1** cover or provide with a glove or gloves. **2** *Baseball.* catch a ball. [OE *glōf*] —**glove′less,** *adj.*

glov·er (gluv′ər) *n.* a person who makes or sells gloves.

glow (glō) *n., v.* —*n.* **1** the shine from something that is red-hot or white-hot. **2** any similar shine: *The firefly's glow was fascinating.* **3** brightness: *the glow of sunset.* **4** a warm feeling or color of the body: *the glow of health on his cheeks.* **5** an eager look on the face: *a glow of interest or excitement.*
—*v.* **1** shine as if hot or white-hot. **2** show a warm color; look warm; be red or bright: *Her cheeks glowed as she danced.* **3** be hot; burn. **4** be eager or animated. [OE *glōwan*]

glow·er (glou′ər) *v., n.* —*v.* stare angrily; scowl: *The fighters glowered at each other.* —*n.* an angry or sullen look. [? < obs. *glow,* v., stare] —**glow′er·ing·ly,** *adv.*

glow·ing (glō′ing) *adj.* **1** shining from something that is red-hot or white-hot. **2** bright: *glowing colors.* **3** showing a warm color: *glowing cheeks.* **4** eager; animated: *a glowing description.*
—**glow′ing·ly,** *adv.*

glow–worm (glō′wėrm′) *n.* any of various insect larvae or wingless adult insects that emit a glow from the abdomen, either continuously or for prolonged periods; especially, a larva or wingless adult female of any of the fireflies.

glox·in·i·a (glok sin′ē ə) *n.* any of several plants (genus *Sinningia*) native to tropical South America, especially *S. speciosa,* widely cultivated as a pot plant, having large, bell-shaped, velvety flowers that are usually mainly red or purple. [< NL; after Benjamin P. *Gloxin,* a German botanist]

gloze (glōz) *v.* **glozed, gloz·ing. 1** smooth or gloss (over): *His friends glozed over his faults.* **2** *Obsolete.* make glosses upon. [ME < OF *gloser* < *glose* < L *glossa.* See GLOSS².]

glu·cose (glü′kōs) *n.* **1** a kind of sugar occurring naturally in fruits. It is about half as sweet as cane sugar. *Formula:* $C_6H_{12}O_6$ **2** a syrup made from starch. [< F < Gk. *glykys* sweet]

glue (glü) *n., v.* **glued, glu·ing.** —*n.* **1** a substance used to stick things together, often made by boiling the hoofs, skins, and bones of animals in water. **2** any similar sticky substance made of casein, rubber, etc.; adhesive. Glues are stronger than pastes.
—*v.* **1** stick together with glue. **2** fasten tightly; attach firmly: *During the ride down the mountain his hands were glued to the steering wheel.* **3** regard or look at fixedly: *He walked on, his eyes glued to the road.* [ME < OF *glu* < LL *glus, glutis*] —**glu′er,** *n.*

glu·ey (glü′ē) *adj.* **glu·i·er, glu·i·est. 1** like glue; sticky. **2** full of glue; smeared with glue.

glum (glum) *adj.* **glum·mer, glum·mest.** gloomy; dismal; sullen: *a glum look.* [cf. LG *glum* tubid, muddy. Akin to GLOOM.] —**glum′ly,** *adv.*
☛ *Syn.* See note at **sullen.**

glume (glüm) *n.* either of two dry bracts at the base of a spikelet on the head of a grass such as wheat. [< L *gluma* husk, related to L *glubere* to peel, remove the husk from. 18c.]

glut (glut) *v.* **glut·ted, glut·ting;** *n.* —*v.* **1** fill full; feed or satisfy fully: *Years of war had glutted his appetite for adventure.* **2** fill too full; supply too much for: *The prices for wheat dropped when the market was glutted with it.* —*n.* **1** a full supply; great quantity. **2** too great a supply. [< obs. *glut,* n., glutton < OF]

hat, āge, fär; let, ēqual, tėrm; it, īce
hot, ōpen, ôrder; oil, out; cup, pút, rüle,
ə above, takən, pencəl, lemən, circəs

ch, child; ng, long; sh, ship
th, thin; ŦH, then; zh, measure

glu·tam·ic acid (glü tam′ik) a white crystalline amino acid obtained from proteins. *Formula:* $C_5H_9NO_4$ [*glut*en + *am*ide + *-ic*]

glu·ta·mine (glü′tə mēn′ *or* glü′tə min) *n.* a crystalline amine derived from glutamic acid. *Formula:* $C_5H_{10}N_2O_3$ [< *glutam*ic acid + *ine²*]

glu·ten (glü′tən) *n.* a tough, sticky substance that remains in flour when the starch is taken out. [< L *gluten* glue]

glu·te·nous (glü′tə nəs) *adj.* **1** like gluten. **2** containing much gluten.
☛ *Hom.* glutinous.

glu·ti·nous (glü′tə nəs) *adj.* sticky. —**glu′ti·nous·ly,** *adv.*
—**glu′ti·nous·ness,** *n.*
☛ *Hom.* glutenous.

glut·ton¹ (glut′ən) *n.* **1** a greedy eater; a person who eats too much. **2** a person who never seems to have enough of something: *That boxer is a glutton for punishment.* [ME < OF *glouton* < L *glutto*]

glut·ton² (glut′ən) *n.* wolverine. [translation of G *Vielfrass,* literally, great eater, derived by popular etymology from Swedish *fjällfräs* mountain cat]

glut·ton·ous (glut′ən əs) *adj.* **1** greedy about food; having the habit of eating too much. **2** greedy. —**glut′ton·ous·ly,** *adv.*
—**glut′ton·ous·ness,** *n.*

glut·ton·y (glut′ən ē) *n., pl.* **-ton·ies.** greediness about food; the habit of eating too much.

glyc·er·in (glis′ər in) *n.* a colorless, syrupy, sweet liquid obtained from fats and oils, used in ointments, lotions, antifreeze solutions, explosives, etc. *Formula:* $C_3H_8O_3$ Also, **glycerine** (glis′ər in *or* glis′ər ēn′). [< F *glycérine* < Gk. *glykeros* sweet]

glyc·er·ol (glis′ər ōl′ *or* glis′ər ol′) *n.* glycerin.

gly·co·gen (glī′kə jən) *n.* a starchlike substance in the liver and other animal tissues that is changed into glucose when needed. [< Gk. *glykys* sweet + E *-gen*]

gly·col (glī′kol *or* glī′kōl) *n. Chemistry.* **1** a colorless liquid obtained from certain ethylene compounds and used as an antifreeze, solvent, etc. *Formula:* $C_2H_6O_2$ **2** any of a similar group of alcohols. [< *glyc*erin + *-ol*]

G.M. George Medal.

G–man (jē′man′) *n., pl.* **-men.** *U.S. Informal.* a special agent of the United States Department of Justice; an agent of the FBI. [for *Government man*]

Gmc. Germanic.

G.M.T. *or* **GMT** Greenwich mean time.

gnarl (närl) *n., v.* —*n.* a knot in wood; hard, rough lump. Wood with gnarls is hard to cut. —*v.* make knotted and rugged like an old tree; contort; twist. [< *gnarled*]

gnarled (närld) *adj.* **1** having many knots or hard, rough lumps; knotty and twisted: *a gnarled old cypress.* **2** rough and hard; rugged and sinewy, as the hands of a person who has done much hard, rough manual work. [var. of *knurled*]

gnash (nash) *v.* **1** grind (the teeth) together. **2** bite by gnashing the teeth. [var. of ME *gnast,* apparently < ON *gnastan* a gnashing]

gnat (nat) *n.* any of various small two-winged flies that bite, such as black-flies. [OE *gnætt*] —**gnat′like′,** *adj.*

gnaw (no *or* nô) *v.* **gnawed, gnawed** *or* **gnawn, gnaw·ing. 1** wear away by biting: *to gnaw a bone. The mouse has gnawed right through the oatmeal box.* **2** make by biting: *A rat gnaws a hole.* **3** wear away; consume or corrode. **4** torment: *A feeling of guilt gnawed my conscience.* [OE *gnagan*] —**gnaw′er,** *n.* —**gnaw′ing·ly,** *adv.*

gnawn (non *or* nôn) *v.* a pp. of **gnaw.**

gneiss (nīs) *n.* a metamorphic rock composed of quartz, feldspar, and mica or hornblende. It is distinguished from granite by its layered structure. [< G]
☛ *Hom.* nice.

gnome (nōm) *n.* **1** *Folklore.* a dwarf that lives underground and guards treasures of precious metals and stones. **2** an odd-looking, dwarfish person: *a little gnome of a man.* [< F < NL *gnomus;* invented by Paracelsus (16th c.)]

gno·mic (nō'mik *or* nom'ik) *adj.* full of maxims or instructive sayings; aphoristic. [< Gk. *gnōmikos* < *gnōmē* judgment, opinion]

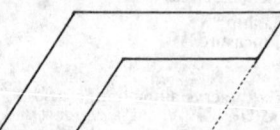

The solid outline is a gnomon (def. 2).

gno·mon (nō'mon) *n.* **1** a rod, pointer, or triangular piece on a sundial, etc. that shows the time of day by casting its shadow on a marked surface. **2** *Geometry.* what is left of a parallelogram after a similar parallelogram has been taken away at one corner. [< Gk. *gnōmōn* indicator < *gignōskein* know]

gno·mon·ic (nō mon'ik) *adj.* **1** of or having to do with a gnomon or sundial. **2** having to do with the measuring of time, etc. by a sundial.

gnos·tic (nos'tik) *adj.* of, having to do with, or possessing knowledge, especially of spiritual things. [< *Gnostic*]

Gnos·tic (nos'tik) *n., adj.* —*n.* a believer in Gnosticism. —*adj.* of Gnosticism or Gnostics. [< Gk. *gnōstikos* of knowledge < *gignōskein* know]

Gnos·ti·cism (nos'tə siz'əm) *n.* a mystical religious and philosophical doctrine of pre-Christian and early Christian times.

GNP *or* **G.N.P.** gross national product.

gnu (nyü *or* nü) *n., pl.* **gnu** *or* **gnus.** either of two large African antelopes (*Connochaetes taurinus* and *C. gnou*) having an oxlike head, curved horns, and a long, tufted tail; wildebeest. [< Hottentot]
☛ *Hom.* **knew, new.**

go (gō) *v.* **went, gone, go·ing;** *n., pl.* **goes;** *adj.* —*v.* **1** move along: *Go straight home.* **2** move away; leave: *It is time for us to go.* **3** be in motion; act; work; run: *Does your watch go well?* **4** get to be; become: *to go mad.* **5** be habitually; be: *to go hungry.* **6** proceed; advance: *to go to Edmonton.* **7** attend on a regular basis: *He goes to the vocational school.* **8** be current: *A rumor went through the town.* **9** be known: *She went under a false name.* **10** put oneself: *Don't go to any trouble for me.* **11** extend; reach: *His memory does not go back that far.* **12** pass: *The summer holidays go quickly.* **13** be given: *First prize goes to the winner.* **14** be sold: *The painting goes to the highest bidder.* **15** tend; lead: *This goes to show that you must work harder.* **16** turn out; have a certain result: *How did the game go?* **17** have its place; belong: *This book goes on the top shelf.* **18** make a certain sound: *The cork went "Pop!"* **19** have certain words; be said: *How does that poem go?* **20** refer; appeal; *go to court.* **21** stop being; be given up, used up, or lost: *His eyesight is going.* **22** die: *His wife went first.* **23** break down; give way: *The engine in the old car finally went.* **24** *Informal.* put up with; stand: *I can't go tea.*

as people (*or* **things**) **go,** considering how others are.
go about, a be busy at; work on. **b** move from place to place. **c** turn around; change direction.
go ahead, a proceed without hesitating; carry on: *He went ahead with his plan in spite of their objections.* **b** advance or improve one's position.
go all out, strive to the utmost extent.
go along, agree; co-operate.
go around, a move from place to place. **b** be enough to give some to all.
go at, a attack: *With a snarl, the dog went at the intruder.* **b** *Informal.* make a start on: *The boys went at the dinner as if they were starving.*
go back on See **back.**
go by, a pass. **b** be guided by; follow: *He promised to go by the rules.* **c** be controlled by. **d** be known by: *She goes by the nickname of "Slim."*
go down, a descend; decline; sink. **b** be defeated; lose. **c** lose violence; subside: *The wind went down in the evening.* **d** be accepted by: *His motion did not go down with the assembly.* **e** in contract bridge, fail to fulfill one's contract.
go for, *Informal.* **a** try to get. **b** favor; support. **c** be attracted to. **d** attack.
go in for, *Informal.* try to do; take part in; spend time and energy at: *She used to go in for basketball.*
go into, a *Arithmetic.* be contained in: *3 goes into 9 three times.* **b** investigate.
go in with, join; share with.
go it, *Informal.* go fast.
go it alone, act without assistance; act independently or solely.
go off, a leave; depart. **b** be fired; explode: *The gun went off*

accidentally. **c** stop functioning; cease working: *The hydro went off during the storm.* **d** lose quality; deteriorate. **e** take place; happen.
go on, a go ahead; go forward. **b** start functioning: *The radio goes on when you turn this switch.* **c** manage. **d** behave: *If you go on that way, you'll get into trouble.* **e** happen: *What goes on here?*
go one better, a outdo or excel to some extent in quality or fitness of action. **b** accept a bet and offer to increase it by a unit in kind.
go out, a leave a room, one's home, etc.: *She went out at eight o'clock.* **b** stop burning: *Don't let the candle go out.* **c** go dark: *The lights went out during the storm.* **d** go to parties, movies, about town, etc.: *They don't go out much.* **e** date; keep company: *Are she and Rocco still going out?* **f** of the heart, feelings, etc., feel sympathy for a person or persons: *His heart went out to them.* **g** go on strike. **h** cease to be fashionable. **i** *Golf.* play the first nine holes of a course.
go over, *Informal.* **a** look at carefully. **b** do again. **c** read again. **d** succeed. **e** change sides, political party, etc. **f** *Slang.* beat up.
go through, a go to the end of; do all of; finish: *I went through two books over the weekend.* **b** undergo; experience: *She went through some hard times.* **c** search: *He went through his pockets to find a nickel.* **d** use up; spend; exhaust: *She went through all her money.* **e** be accepted or approved: *The new schedule did not go through.*
go through with, complete; carry out to the end: *He disliked the job so much that he refused to go through with it.*
go together, keep steady company.
go under, a be overwhelmed or sunk. **b** be ruined; fail.
go up, a ascend; rise. **b** increase: *The price went up.* **c** be built; be raised: *New houses are going up quickly. The curtain goes up at 7 p.m.*
go with, a accompany. **b** keep company with: *He's been going with Peg for a long time.* **c** be in harmony with: *That tie goes with your suit.*
go without, do without the thing stated or implied.
let go, a allow to escape. **b** give up one's hold. **c** give up. **d** fail to keep in good condition.
let (oneself) **go, a** give way to one's feelings or desires. **b** fail to keep oneself in good condition.
to go, of prepared food, for taking away from the place where it was bought, to be eaten elsewhere: *She ordered two hamburgers to go.* —*n.* **1** the act of going. **2** *Informal.* spirit; energy. **3** *Informal.* the state of affairs; way things are. **4** *Informal.* a fashion; style; rage. **5** *Informal.* a try; attempt; chance: *Let's have another go at this problem.* **6** something successful; a success: *He seems to be making a go of his new store.* **7** *Informal.* a bargain; anything agreed on: *It's a go.*
no go, *Informal.* not to be done or had; impossible; useless; worthless.
on the go, *Informal.* always moving or acting: *He is so busy that he's on the go from morning till night.*
—*adj. Slang.* in the launching of space capsules, missiles, etc., in perfect order and ready to proceed; A-one: *All systems are go.* [OE *gān*] —**go'er,** *n.*
☛ *Syn.* v. **2. Go, leave** = move away from a point or place. **Go,** the opposite of *come,* emphasizes the movement involved: *He comes and goes as he pleases.* **Leave** emphasizes the departure from the place where one is (or has been): *He has left home. The boat left yesterday.*
☛ *Usage.* **Go and** is used informally to introduce or emphasize a verb: *Go and try it yourself* (no actual movement meant). *She went and shot the bear herself.* Sometimes the phrase suggests criticism of the action referred to: *He went and bought that rusty old car.* Though **go and** is appropriate in writing dialogue and in some narration, it should be omitted in exposition and in all formal writing.

goad (gōd) *n., v.* —*n.* **1** a sharp-pointed stick for driving cattle, etc.; gad. **2** anything that drives or urges one on. —*v.* drive or urge on; act as a goad to: *Hunger goaded him to steal a loaf of bread.* [OE *gād*]

go-a·head (gō'ə hed') *Informal. n.* **1** the action of going forward; ambition; spirit. **2** authority to proceed. **3** (*adj.*) disposed to push ahead; ambitious. **4** (*adj.*) giving authority to proceed: *a go-ahead signal.*

goal (gōl) *n.* **1** *Sports.* **a** the space between two posts into which a player tries to shoot a puck, kick a ball, etc. in order to score. **b** the act of scoring in such a manner. **c** the point or points counted for scoring a goal; a score: *Our team won, four goals to three.* **d** the position of goalkeeper. **2** the finish line of a race. **3** something for which an effort is made; something wanted; one's aim or object in doing something: *His goal was to be a great doctor.*
play goal, *Informal.* be the goalie.
[ME *gol*; origin uncertain] —**goal'·less,** *adj.*

goal·er (gō'lər) *n.* goalie.

goal·ie (gō'lē) *n. Sports.* the player who guards the goal to prevent scoring; goalkeeper.

goal·keep·er (gōl'kēp'ər) *n.* goalie.

goal line the line marking the goal in a game.

goal-mouth (gōl'mouth') *n. Sports.* the area just in front of the goal.

goal post *Sports.* one of a pair of posts with a bar across them, forming a goal.

goal tender goalie.

goat (gōt) *n., pl.* **goat** or **goats.** 1 any of a genus (*Capra*) of bovid mammals with backward-curving horns, native to stony and mountainous regions of Europe, Asia, and N Africa, and including numerous domestic breeds and varieties raised for milk, meat, and wool. Goats are most closely related to sheep, but are lighter in build, stronger, and more agile. 2 *Informal.* scapegoat. 3 **Goat,** *Astronomy or astrology.* Capricorn.
get (someone's) goat, *Informal.* make someone annoyed or angry. [OE *gāt*] —**goat′like′,** *adj.*

goat·ee (gō tē′) *n.* a small pointed beard on a man's chin. See **beard** for picture.

goat·herd (gōt′hėrd′) *n.* a person who tends goats.

goat·skin (gōt′skin′) *n.* 1 the hide of a goat. 2 leather made from the hide of goats. 3 something made of goatskin, such as a container for wine or water.

goat·suck·er (gōt′suk′ər) *n.* any of a family (Caprimulgidae) of nocturnal insect-eating birds having long, slender wings, a very short bill, an enormous mouth, and soft, mottled plumage resembling that of owls. Two goatsuckers found in Canada are the whippoorwill and the nighthawk. [so called from an ancient belief that these birds with their enormous mouths sucked milk from goats in pastures; the birds often fly about grazing animals at night, catching insects on the wing]

gob[1] (gob) *n. Informal.* a lump; mass: *She put a big gob of honey on her bread.* [apparently < OF *gobe*]

gob[2] (gob) *n. U.S. Slang.* a sailor in the United States navy. [origin uncertain]

gob·bet (gob′it) *n.* a lump; mass. [ME < OF *gobet,* dim. of *gobe* gobe[2]]

gob·ble[1] (gob′əl) *v.* **-bled, -bling.** 1 eat fast and greedily; swallow quickly in big pieces. 2 *Informal.* seize upon eagerly (*used with* **up**): *He gobbled up every piece of information he could find on the rock group.* [< gob[2]]

gob·ble[2] (gob′əl) *v.* **-bled, -bling;** *n.* —*v.* make the throaty sound that a male turkey does. —*n.* the throaty sound that a turkey makes. [imitative]

gob·ble·dy·gook or **gob·ble·de·gook** (gob′əl dē gŭk′) *n. Informal.* speech or writing that is unnecessarily complicated or involved: *Official documents are often full of gobbledygook.* [coined by Maury Maverick, U.S. Congressman, in 1944]

gob·bler (gob′lər) *n.* a male turkey.

Gob·e·lin (gob′ə lin) *adj.* 1 made at the factory of the Gobelins in Paris: *Gobelin tapestry or upholstery.* 2 of or having to do with such tapestry or upholstery.

go–be·tween (gō′bi twēn′) *n.* a person who goes back and forth between others with messages, proposals, suggestions, etc.; intermediary: *He acted as a go-between in the settlement of the strike.*

gob·let (gob′lit) *n.* 1 a drinking glass with a base and stem. 2 *Archaic.* a hollow dish to drink from, usually without a handle. [ME < OF *gobelet,* dim. of *gobel* cup]

gob·lin (gob′lən) *n. Folklore.* an ugly sprite that is mischievous or evil. [ME < MF *gobelin* ? < MHG *kobold* sprite]

go·by (gō′bē) *n., pl.* **-by** or **-bies.** any of a large family (Gobiidae) of small, mainly marine fishes having a large head and two spiny dorsal fins and with the pelvin fins united to form a kind of suction cup which permits the fishes to cling to rocks, etc. [< L *gobius, cobius,* a kind of fish < Gk. *kōbios*]

go–by (gō′bī′) *n. Informal.* a going by or casting off; a slight; intentional neglect: *He gave her the go-by.*

go·cart or **go–cart** (gō′kärt′) *n.* 1 a low seat on wheels to take a small child around on. 2 a small framework with casters in which children sometimes learn to walk. 3 a light carriage. 4 go-kart.

god (god) *n., interj.* —*n.* 1 **God,** in the Christian, Jewish, Moslem, and certain other religions, the creator and ruler of the universe; the Supreme Being, perfect in goodness, knowledge and power. 2 a being thought of as superior to nature and to human beings and considered worthy of worship. 3 a male god. 4 an image of a god; idol. 5 a person or thing intensely admired and respected: *His father was a god to him.*
—*interj.* Often, **God,** *Slang.* an exclamation or oath, often regarded as blasphemous or improper, expressing surprise, admiration, dismay, irritation, etc.; often used in expressions such as **My God!** or **God in Heaven!** [OE]
☞ *Hom.* **gaud.**

hat, āge, fär; let, ēqual, tèrm; it, īce
hot, ōpen, ôrder; oil, out; cup, pùt, rüle,
ə above, takən, pencəl, lemən, circəs

ch, child; ng, long; sh, ship
th, thin; ŦH, then; zh, measure

god–aw·ful (god′ô′fəl *or* -ô′fəl) *adj. Slang.* terrible; dreadful: *a god-awful performance.*

god·child (god′chīld′) *n., pl.* **-chil·dren.** a child for whom an adult takes vows at its baptism.

god–daugh·ter (god′dò′tər *or* -dô′tər) *n.* a female godchild.

god·dess (god′is) *n.* 1 a female god. 2 a very beautiful or charming woman.

go–dev·il (gō′dev′əl) *n.* 1 *Mining and lumbering.* a type of sleigh used to move ore, logs, etc. 2 a stoneboat or drag. 3 a device flushed through a pipeline to clean the inside of the pipe.

god·fa·ther (god′fo′ŦHər) *n.* a man who takes vows for a child when it is baptized.

god–for·sak·en (god′fər sāk′ən) *adj.* 1 Often, **Godforsaken,** apparently forsaken by God. 2 completely given over to evil; totally depraved. 3 desolate; wretched.

God–giv·en (god′giv′ən) *adj.* 1 given by God. 2 very welcome and suitable.

God·head (god′hed′) *n.* 1 God. 2 **godhead,** divine nature; divinity.

god·hood (god′hùd′) *n.* divine character; divinity.

god·less (god′lis) *adj.* 1 not believing in God; not religious. 2 wicked; evil. —**god′less·ly,** *adv.* —**god′less·ness,** *n.*

god·like (god′līk′) *adj.* 1 like God or a god; divine. 2 suitable for God or a god.

god·ly (god′lē) *adj.* **-li·er, -li·est.** 1 obeying God's laws; religious; pious; devout. 2 *Archaic.* of or from God; divine. —**god′li·ness,** *n.*

god·moth·er (god′muŦH′ər) *n.* a woman who takes vows for a child when it is baptized.

god·par·ent (god′per′ənt) *n.* a godfather or godmother.

God's acre a churchyard with graves in it; a burial ground; cemetery.

god·send (god′send′) *n.* something unexpected and very welcome, as if sent from God.

god·son (god′sun′) *n.* a male godchild.

God·speed (god′spēd′) *n.* a wish of success to a person starting on a journey or undertaking.

god·wit (god′wit′) *n.* any of a genus (*Limosa*) of large shore birds having a long, upturned bill and long legs. Godwits belong to the same family (Scolopacidae) as snipes and sandpipers. [origin uncertain]

goe·thite or **go·thite** (gō′tīt *or* gœ′tīt) *n.* a mineral consisting of a hydrous oxide of iron. [< Johann W. von *Goethe* (1749-1832), German writer, noted also for studies in mineralogy]

go–get·ter (gō′get′ər) *n. Slang.* an aggressive person who tries hard for, and usually gets, what he wants.

gog·gle (gog′əl) *v.* **-gled, -gling;** *n.* —*v.* 1 stare with wide-open or bulging eyes: *We all goggled at the huge dog.* 2 of the eyes, bulge or open very wide: *The children's eyes goggled as the magician pulled a rabbit out of the empty hat.* 3 be goggle-eyed with surprise, wonder, or disbelief. 4 (*adj.*) bulging: *the goggle eyes of a frog.*
—*n.* Usually, **goggles,** *pl.* a pair of large, close-fitting spectacles to protect the eyes from light, dust, etc.: *He wore goggles while welding the broken steel rod.* [ME *gogel(en);* origin uncertain]

gog·gle–eyed (gog′əl īd′) *adj.* having rolling, bulging, or staring eyes.

go–go (gō′gō′) *adj.* 1 of, having to do with, or designating a type of dance characterized by rapid, rhythmic body movements and performed either alone or without body contact between partners. 2 performing such a dance, especially in a discothèque: *a go-go dancer.*

Goid·el (goi′dəl) *n.* 1 any member of the Gaelic branch of the Celts. 2 a speaker of a Goidelic language.

Goid·el·ic (goi del′ik) *adj., n.* —*adj.* 1 of or having to do with the Goidels. 2 of, having to do with, or denoting the Celtic language group to which Scots Gaelic, Irish, and Manx belong. —*n.* one of the two main divisions of the Celtic language (the other being *Brythonic*), including Scots Gaelic, Irish, and Manx.

go·ing (gō′ing) *n., adj.* —*n.* 1 a going away; leaving: *His going was sudden.* 2 the condition of the ground or road for walking, riding, etc.: *The going is bad on a muddy road.*

—*adj.* **1** moving; acting; working; running. **2** that goes; that can or will go. **3** in existence; existing; current: *the going price for gold.* **be going to,** will; be about to: *It is going to rain soon.* **going on,** almost; nearly: *It is going on four o'clock.*

going concern a company, store, etc. that is doing good business.

go·ing-o·ver (gō'ing ō'vər) *n.* **1** *Informal.* a thorough study; intense and critical examination. **2** *Slang.* **a** a scolding. **b** a beating.

go·ings-on (gō'ing zon') *n.pl.* actions or behavior, especially when viewed with disapproval or suspicion: *Her parents were unhappy about the goings-on at the party.*

goi·tre (goi'tər) *n.* chronic enlargement of the thyroid gland, usually producing a large swelling in the throat. Goitres may be caused by inadequate iodine in the diet, or they may be caused or accompanied by hyperthyroidism or hypothyroidism. Also, **goiter.** [< F *goitre,* ult. < L *guttur* throat]

go-kart (gō'kärt') *n.* a small four-wheeled racing vehicle that consists of a bare chassis and a low-powered engine.

Gol·con·da (gol kon'də) *n.* a mine or source of wealth. [after an ancient city in S India, famed for its wealth and for its diamond cutting]

gold (gōld) *n., adj.* —*n.* **1** a shiny, yellow, non-rusting, metallic chemical element that is a precious metal used especially for making jewellery and coins. *Symbol:* Au (for L *aurum*); *at.no.* 79; *at.wt.* 196.967. **2** coins made of gold. **3** money in large sums; wealth; riches. **4** a bright, beautiful, or precious thing or material: *prairie gold. He has a heart of gold.* **5** a deep, slightly brownish yellow. —*adj.* **1** made of gold: *gold coins, a gold bracelet.* **2** resembling gold; having the metallic color of gold: *a book bound in dark blue, with gold lettering.* **3** deep slightly brownish yellow: *a gold carpet.* [OE]

gold·beat·er (gōld'bēt'ər) *n.* a person whose work is beating gold into very thin sheets.

gold brick *Informal.* anything that looks good at first, but turns out to be worthless.

gold-brick (gōld'brik') *v., n. Slang.* —*v.* **1** swindle, as by means of a gold brick. **2** pretend illness to avoid duties. —*n.* a person, especially in the armed forces, who avoids duty or shirks work. —**gold'-brick'er,** *n.*

gold digger 1 a person who digs for or mines gold. **2** *Slang.* a woman who is interested in men for what she can get out of them.

gold dust very tiny bits of gold; gold in a fine powder.

gold·en (gōl'dən) *adj.* **1** made or consisting of gold: *golden earrings.* **2** resembling gold; having the metallic color of gold: *a golden buckle.* **3** shining or lustrous like gold: *The windows were golden from the light of the setting sun.* **4** deep, slightly brownish yellow: *golden velvet upholstery.* **5** blond: *golden hair.* **6** most excellent or precious; extremely valuable, important, etc.: *golden deeds.* **7** extremely favorable or advantageous: *a golden opportunity.* **8** very happy and prosperous; flourishing: *the golden days of youth, a golden age.* **9** having to do with the fiftieth year or event in a series: *a golden wedding anniversary.*

Golden Age 1 *Greek and Roman mythology.* the first age of mankind, an era of perfect prosperity, happiness, and innocence. **2** a legendary and imaginary age, long past, of perfect human happiness and innocence. **3** **golden age,** a period of great progress, cultural achievement, etc.

golden calf 1 in the Bible, an idol made of gold, set up by the Israelites in the wilderness. **2** wealth too highly esteemed.

golden eagle a large, mainly dark-brown eagle (*Aquila chrysaetos*) of the northern hemisphere having golden brown feathers on the back of the head and neck, legs that are feathered to the toes, and a large bill.

gold·en·eye (gōl'dən ī') *n., pl.* **-eye** or **-eyes.** either of two northern diving ducks having black-and-white plumage and yellow eyes: *the* **common goldeneye** (*Bucephala clangula*) and **Barrow's goldeneye** (*B. islandica*).

Golden Fleece *Greek mythology.* a fleece of gold that hung in a sacred grove, where it was guarded by a dragon until Jason and the Argonauts carried it away with the help of Medea.

golden mean the avoidance of extremes; a safe, sensible way of doing things; moderation.

golden retriever a breed of medium-sized retriever having a golden, water-resistant coat often trained to retrieve game, especially waterfowl.

gold·en·rod (gōl'dən rod') *n.* any of a genus (*Solidago*) of mostly perennial plants of the composite family having toothed leaves and spikes or pannicles of tiny flower heads that are composed of both disk and ray flowers. **Canada goldenrod** (*S. canadensis*) is a common Canadian weed.

golden rule a rule of conduct common to most great religions that a person should behave toward others as he would want them to behave toward him.

golden wedding the 50th anniversary of a wedding.

gold·eye (gōld'ī') *n., pl.* **-eye** or **-eyes.** *Cdn.* an edible freshwater fish (*Hiodon alosoides*) native to rivers and lakes from Ontario to the Northwest Territories and south to Oklahoma and Mississippi. Goldeye is smoked and dyed for marketing as a table delicacy.

gold-filled (gōld'fild') *adj.* made of cheap metal covered with a layer of gold.

gold·finch (gōld'finch') *n.* **1** any of several small North American songbirds (genus *Spinus*) especially *S. tristis,* the male of which has bright-yellow and black plumage in breeding season. **2** a small European songbird (*Carduelis carduelis*) often kept as a cage bird, the male of which has a red-and-white head, mainly black body, and gold patches on the wings. [OE *goldfinc*]

gold·fish (gōld'fish') *n., pl.* **-fish** or **-fish·es.** a thick-bodied freshwater fish (*Carassius auratus*) of the same family as minnows and carps, native to E Asia but widely raised in many different breeds as an ornamental fish for aquariums and ponds. In the wild, goldfish are usually olive green but as ornamental fish they are selectively bred for a golden or orange color.

gold·i·locks (gōl'də loks') *n.* **1** a person, especially a girl, with blond hair. **2** a yellow-flowered Eurasian plant (*Aster linosyris*) of the composite family.

gold leaf gold beaten into very thin sheets.

gold mine 1 a mine where ore yielding gold is obtained. **2** the source of something of great value: *His special knowledge made him a gold mine of information. His real-estate business is a gold mine.*

gold-plate (gōld'plāt') *v.* **-plat·ed, -plat·ing.** coat (another metal or a metal object) with gold, especially by electroplating: *Gold-plated silver is called vermeil.*

gold rush a sudden movement of people to a place where gold has just been found.

gold·smith (gōld'smith') *n.* a person whose work is making articles of gold. [OE]

gold standard the use of gold as the standard of value for the money of a country. The nation's unit of money value is declared by the government to be equal to and exchangeable for a certain amount of gold.

golf (golf) *n., v.* —*n.* an outdoor game played with a small, hard ball and a set of long-handled clubs having wooden or iron heads. The player tries to drive his ball into each of a number of holes with as few strokes as possible. —*v.* play the game of golf: *He golfs every Saturday.* [origin uncertain] —**golf'er,** *n.*

golf club 1 a long-handled club having a wooden or iron head, used in playing golf. **2** a group of people joined together for the purpose of playing golf. **3** the buildings, land, etc. used by such a group.

golf course a place where golf is played, having tees, greens, and fairway.

golf links golf course.

Gol·go·tha (gol'gə thə *or* gol goth'ə) *n.* **1** the place of Christ's crucifixion; Calvary. **2** a place of burial. [< Gk. < Aramaic *gūlgūlthā* place of skulls < Hebrew]

Go·li·ath (gə lī'əth) *n.* **1** in the Bible, a giant whom David killed with a stone from a sling (I Sam. 17:4-51). **2** any huge, extremely strong man.

gol·li·wog (gol'ē wog') *n.* a black-faced rag doll.

gol·ly (gol'ē) *interj.* a word used to express surprise, etc.

go·losh (gə losh') See **galosh.**

Go·mor·rah or **Go·mor·rha** (gə môr'ə) *n.* **1** in the Bible, a wicked city destroyed, together with Sodom, by fire from heaven (Gen. 18 and 19). **2** any extremely wicked place.

gon·ad (gō'nad *or* gon'ad) *n.* an organ in which reproductive cells develop. Ovaries and testes are gonads. [< NL < Gk. *gonē* seed < *gignesthai* be produced]

gon·do·la (gon'də lə) *n.* **1** a long, narrow, flat-bottomed boat with a high peak at each end, used on the canals of Venice. **2** a large flat-bottomed river boat with rounded ends. **3** a freight car that has low sides and no top. **4** a car that hangs under a dirigible and holds the motors, passengers, etc. **5** *Cdn.* a broadcasting booth built up near the roof of a hockey arena. **6** a car that hangs from and moves along a cable: *We went up the mountain in the gondola.* [< dial. Ital. *gondola* < *gondolare* to rock]

gon·do·lier (gon'də lēr') *n.* a man who rows or poles a gondola. [< F < Ital. *gondoliere* < *gondola* gondola]

gone (gon) *adj., v.* —*adj.* **1** moved away; left. **2** lost: *a gone case.* **3** dead. **4** used up. **5** failed; ruined. **6** weak; faint: *a gone feeling.*

7 *Slang.* **a** very good; great: *the gone blues sung by Bessie Smith.* **b** that carries strong feeling; transported; inspired: *a gone look on his face, gone music.*
far gone, much advanced; deeply involved.
gone on, *Informal.* in love with.
—*v.* pp. of **go.**

gon·er (gon′ər) *n. Informal.* a person or thing that is dead, ruined, past help, etc.

gon·fa·lon (gon′fə lən) *n.* a flag or banner hung from a crossbar instead of a pole, often having several streamers. Gonfalons were used by certain medieval Italian republics. [< Ital. *gonfalone,* ult. < OHG *gundfano,* literally, war banner]

gong (gong) *n.* **1** a percussion instrument consisting of a platelike metal disk with a turned-up rim that is struck with a usually soft-headed hammer, producing a hollow, bell-like sound of indefinite pitch. **2** a similar metal disk or hemisphere producing a tone when struck with a hammer, used as a signalling device, alarm, etc. [< Malay]

gon·or·rhe·a or **gon·or·rhoe·a** (gon′ə rē′ə) *n.* a contagious venereal disease that causes inflammation of the genital, urinary, and certain other organs. [< LL < Gk. *gonorrhoia* < *gonos* seed + *rhoia* flow]

goo (gü) *n. Slang.* any thick, sticky substance. [origin uncertain] —**goo′ey,** *adj.*

good (gud) *adj.* **bet·ter, best;** *n., interj.* —*adj.* **1** having the right qualities; admirable; desirable: *a good book, a good game.* **2** as it ought to be; right; proper: *Do what seems good to you.*
3 well-behaved: *a good boy.* **4** kind; friendly: *Say a good word for me.* **5** benevolent; gracious: *a good king.* **6** honorable; worthy: *my good friend.* **7** reliable; dependable: *good judgment.* **8** real; genuine: *It is hard to tell counterfeit money from good money.* **9** agreeable; pleasant: *Have a good time.* **10** beneficial; advantageous; useful: *drugs good for a fever.* **11** well-suited to its purpose: *A craftsman insists on good tools.* **12** satisfying; sufficient in size and quality: *a good meal.* **13** not spoiled; sound: *a good apple.* **14** thorough; complete: *to do a good job.* **15** skilful; clever: *a good manager, to be good at arithmetic.* **16** fairly great; more than a little: *a good while.*
as good as, almost the same as; almost; practically: *The day is as good as over.*
feel good, *Informal.* feel well or elated.
good and, *Informal.* very; extremely: *She was good and angry.*
good for, a able to do, live, or last. **b** able to pay. **c** worth: *a coupon good for a free ride.*
make good, a make up for; give or do in place of; pay for: *He made good the damage done by his car.* **b** fulfil; carry out: *to make good a promise.* **c** succeed in doing. **d** succeed; prosper: *His parents expected him to make good.* **e** prove.
—*n.* **1** benefit; advantage; use: *work for the common good.* **2** that which is good: *He always looked for the good in people.* **3** a good thing. **4** good people.
for good or **for good and all,** forever; finally; permanently: *He has left Canada for good.*
to the good, on the side of profit or advantage; in one's favor.
—*interj.* that is good! [OE *gōd*]
☛ *Usage.* **good, well.** Careful speakers maintain the distinction between **good** and **well,** using the former as adjective only: *Her playing is good (adj.) She plays well (adv.).* Both terms are used as adjectives to mean "fit, in good health": *I feel good. I feel well.* While both these sentences are acceptable, many people prefer *I feel well* to be used in writing.

Good Book the Bible.

good-bye or **good-bye** (gud′bī′) *interj.* or *n., pl.* **-byes.** an expression of good wishes on parting or ending a telephone conversation; farewell. Sometimes, **good-by.** [contraction of *God be with ye*]

good cheer 1 feasting and merrymaking. **2** good food and drink. **3** a spirit of optimism and courage: *Be of good cheer.*

good day a form of greeting or farewell said in the daytime.

good deal 1 much; many: *It cost a good deal more than I expected.* **2** *Informal.* a favorable business transaction; bargain: *It was a good deal all around.*

good evening a form of greeting or farewell said in the evening.

good-for-noth·ing (gud′fər nuth′ing) *adj., n.* —*adj.* worthless; useless. —*n.* a person who is worthless or useless.

Good Friday the Friday before Easter, observed by Christians in commemoration of Christ's crucifixion.

good-heart·ed (gud′här′tid) *adj.* kind and generous. —**good′-heart′ed·ly,** *adv.* —**good′heart′ed·ness,** *n.*

good humor or **humour** a cheerful, pleasant disposition or mood.

good-hu·mored or **good-hu·moured** (gud′hyü′mərd or gud′yü′mərd) *adj.* cheerful; pleasant. —**good′-hu′mored·ly** or **good′-hu′moured·ly,** *adv.* —**good′-hu′mored·ness** or **good′-hu′moured·ness,** *n.*

hat, āge, fär; let, ēqual, tèrm; it, īce
hot, ōpen, ôrder; oil, out; cup, put, rüle,
əbove, takən, pencəl, lemən, circəs

ch, child; ng, long; sh, ship
th, thin; ᴛʜ, then; zh, measure

good·ish (gud′ish) *adj. Informal.* **1** pretty good. **2** fairly great; considerable: *There was a goodish amount of work involved.*

good-look·er (gud′lük′ər) *adj. Informal.* a person or animal of attractive or handsome appearance.

good-look·ing (gud′lük′ing) *adj.* having a pleasing appearance; handsome; attractive: *a good-looking woman.*

good looks a handsome or pleasing personal appearance.

good·ly (gud′lē) *adj.* **-li·er, -li·est. 1** considerable: *a goodly quantity.* **2** *Archaic.* **a** excellent; fine: *a goodly land.* **b** good-looking: *goodly youth.* —**good′li·ness,** *n.*

good·man (gud′mən) *n., pl.* **-men.** *Archaic.* **1** the master of a household; husband. **2** a title for a man ranking below a gentleman: *Goodman Brown.*

good morning a form of greeting or farewell said in the morning.

good nature pleasant or kindly disposition; amiability.

good-na·tured (gud′nā′chərd) *adj.* pleasant; kindly; cheerful; agreeable. —**good′-na′tured·ly,** *adv.* —**good′-na′tured·ness,** *n.*

good·ness (gud′nis) *n., interj.* —*n.* **1** the quality or state of being good. **2** excellence; virtue. **3** kindness; friendliness. **4** the valuable quality; best part.
—*interj.* an exclamation of surprise.
☛ *Syn. n.* **2.** Goodness, virtue = excellence in character. Goodness applies to the inner quality in a person that makes him kind, generous, fair, sympathetic, and otherwise acceptable in character and conduct: *His goodness is shown by the many kind deeds he does.* Virtue applies to moral excellence that is acquired by consciously developing particular qualities of character, such as moral courage, justice, wise judgment, etc., or by consciously following the principles of right and wrong: *He is a man of the highest virtue.*

good night a form of farewell said at night.

goods (gudz) *n.pl.* **1** personal property; belongings. **2** things for sale; wares. **3** material for clothing; cloth. **4** *Slang.* what is needed to do something. **5** *Brit.* freight.
catch with the goods, a catch with stolen goods. **b** catch in the act of committing a crime.
deliver the goods, *Slang.* do what is expected or wanted.
get or **have the goods on,** *Slang.* find out or know something bad about.
☛ *Syn.* **1.** See note at **property.**

Good Samaritan 1 in the Bible, a traveller who rescued and cared for another traveller who had been beaten and robbed by thieves (Luke 10:30-37). **2** any person who is unselfish in helping others.

good-sized (gud′sīzd′) *adj.* large or somewhat large; ample: *a good-sized helping.*

good speed a farewell expressing a wish for success or good luck.

goods train *Brit.* freight train.

good-tem·pered (gud′tem′pərd) *adj.* easy to get along with; cheerful; agreeable. —**good′-tem′pered·ly,** *adv.*

good turn a kind or friendly act; favor.

good-wife (gud′wīf′) *n., pl.* **-wives.** *Archaic.* **1** the mistress of a household. **2** a title for a woman ranking below a lady: *Goodwife Brown.*

good will 1 a kindly or friendly feeling. **2** cheerful consent; willingness. **3** the reputation and steady trade that a business has with its customers.
☛ *Syn.* **1.** See note at **favor.**

good·y¹ (gud′ē) *n., pl.* **good·ies;** *interj., adj. Informal.* —*n.* **1** something very good to eat; a piece of candy or cake: *There were lots of goodies at the party.* **2** anything desirable, pleasurable, or attractive: *a list of election goodies.*
—*interj.* an exclamation of pleasure.
—*adj.* making too much of being good; goody-goody. [< *good*]

good·y² (gud′ē) *n., pl.* **good·ies.** an old woman of humble station. [var. of *goodwife*]

good·y-good·y (gud′ē gud′ē) *adj., n., pl.* **-good·ies.** —*adj.* making too much of being good; good in an affected, prim, or weak way. —*n.* a person who makes too much of being good.

goof (güf) *n., v. Slang.* —*n.* **1** a stupid or foolish person. **2** a blunder; an obvious or careless error. —*v.* **1** make a mistake; blunder. **2** make a complete hash of (something undertaken); bungle

(*used with* **up**): *Don't ask him to do it, because he's sure to goof it up.*

goof off, waste time; loaf; shirk work or duty.
[apparently < dial. var. of earlier *goof* dunce]

goof·ball (güf′bol′ *or* -bôl′) *n. Slang.* 1 a barbiturate pill, especially one taken with alcohol. 2 an odd, peculiar, or crazy person.

goo·gol (gü′gəl) *n.* a number represented by one followed by a hundred zeros; 10¹⁰⁰. [coined by Dr. Edward Kasner (1878-1955), an American mathematician, on the basis of a child's word for a very large number]

goo·gol·plex (gü′gəl pleks′) *n.* a number represented by one followed by googol zeros; 10¹⁰^¹⁰⁰.

goon (gün) *n. Slang.* 1 a ruffian hired to disrupt labor disputes. 2 a stupid person. [from semihuman characters in a comic strip of the 1930's]

goose (güs) *n., pl.* **geese** for 1-4, **goos·es** for 5, 6; *v.* —*n.* 1 any of various large, long-necked, web-footed waterfowl belonging to the same family (Anatidae) as ducks and swans. Geese are intermediate in size between ducks and swans and are less aquatic than either of these groups. 2 a female goose as distinguished from the male (gander). 3 the flesh of a goose. 4 a silly person: *What a goose you are!* 5 a tailor's smoothing iron with a long, curved handle like a goose's neck. 6 *Slang.* a sudden prod in the buttocks.
cook (someone's) goose, *Informal.* ruin someone's chances, plans, etc.
kill the goose that lays the golden eggs, sacrifice future good or profit to satisfy present needs or greed.
—*v. Slang.* 1 prod (a person) suddenly in the buttocks. 2 feed gasoline suddenly to (an engine). [OE *gōs*] —**goose′like′,** *adj.*

goose·ber·ry (güs′ber′ē *or* güz′-) *n., pl.* **-ries.** 1 any of various shrubs (genus *Ribes*) of the northern hemisphere bearing yellowish-green or reddish-purple acid berries, some of which have prickly skins. 2 the fruit of any of these trees, used especially in pies, jellies, and preserves. [? alteration of F *groseille* + E *berry*]

goose flesh skin that has become rough like that of a plucked goose, from cold or fright.

goose·foot (güs′füt′) *n., pl.* **-foots.** 1 any of a genus (*Chenopodium*) of weedy plants having small, greenish flowers, dry, seedlike fruits, and, in some species, leaves shaped like the foot of a goose. 2 (*adj.*) designating the family of herbs, shrubs, and small trees that includes the goosefoots and also the common vegetables beets and spinach.

goose·herd (güs′hèrd′) *n.* a person who tends geese.

goose·neck (güs′nek′) *n.* anything long and curved like a goose's neck, such as an iron hook, a movable support for a lamp, or a curved, connecting pipe.

goose pimples goose flesh.

goose step a marching step in which the leg is swung high with straight, stiff knee.

goose–step (güs′step′) *v.* **-stepped, -step·ing.** march with a goose step.

go·pher (gō′fər) *n.* 1 a buff-colored, burrowing ground squirrel (*Spermophilus richardsonii*) found in the central plains of North America, having short legs, short, rounded ears, small pouches inside the cheeks, and a slightly bushy tail about one third as long as the body. The gopher is one of the commonest mammals of the Canadian Prairies. 2 any of various other ground squirrels. 3 pocket gopher. [prob. < N.Am. F *gaufre* honeycomb, a reference to the animals' tunnels in the ground; possibly also influenced by *gopher* (earlier *magofer*) the name of a burrowing land tortoise of S United States. 19c.]

Gor·di·an knot (gôr′dē ən) 1 a knot tied by Gordius, King of Phrygia, to be undone only by the person who should rule Asia. Alexander the Great cut the knot with his sword after failing to untie it. 2 an intricate or baffling problem.
cut the Gordian knot, solve an intricate or vexing problem by some quick and drastic means.

Gor·don setter (gôr′dən) a breed of setter developed in Scotland, having a black coat with tan markings. [after 4th Duke of *Gordon* (1743-1827), Scottish nobleman and sportsman. 19c.]

gore[1] (gôr) *n.* blood that is shed; thick blood; clotted blood: *The battlefield was covered with gore.* [OE *gor* dirt, dung]

gore[2] (gôr) *v.* **gored, gor·ing.** wound with a horn or tusk: *The savage bull gored the farmer to death.* [ME *gorre(n)*; origin uncertain]

gore[3] (gôr) *n., v.* **gored, gor·ing.** —*n.* 1 a tapering or triangular piece of cloth put or made in a skirt, sail, etc. to give greater width or change the shape. 2 *Cdn.* an unassigned tract of land remaining after the surveying and marking out of a township into lots. —*v.* put or make a gore in. [OE *gāra* point < *gār* spear]

gorge (gôrj) *n., v.* **gorged, gorg·ing.** —*n.* 1 a deep, narrow valley, usually steep and rocky. 2 a gorging; gluttonous meal. 3 the contents of a stomach. 4 a feeling of disgust, indignation, resentment, etc. 5 a narrow rear entrance from a fort into an outwork or outer part. 6 a mass stopping up a narrow passage: *An ice gorge blocked the river.* 7 *Archaic.* the throat; gullet.
—*v.* 1 eat greedily until full; stuff with food. 2 fill full; stuff. [ME < OF *gorge* throat, ult. < LL *gurges* throat, jaws < L *gurges* abyss, whirlpool] —**gorg′er,** *n.*

gor·geous (gôr′jəs) *adj.* richly colored; splendid: *a gorgeous sunset.* [< OF *gorgias* fashionable, with reference to the ruff for the throat < *gorge* throat. See GORGE.] —**gor′geous·ly,** *adv.* —**gor′geous·ness,** *n.*

gor·get (gôr′jit) *n.* 1 a piece of armor for the throat. See **armor** for picture. 2 a covering for the neck and breast, formerly worn by women. [< OF *gorgete*, dim. of *gorge*. See GORGE.]

Gor·gon (gôr′gən) *n.* 1 *Greek mythology.* any of three horrible sisters who had snakes for hair and whose look turned the beholder to stone. Medusa is the best-known of the three Gorgons. 2 **gorgon,** any very ugly or terrible woman. [< L *Gorgo, -onis* < Gk. *Gorgō* < *gorgos* terrible]

Gor·gon·zo·la (gôr′gən zō′lə) *n.* a strong, white Italian cheese that looks and tastes much like Roquefort cheese. [< *Gorgonzola*, a town in Italy]

go·ril·la (gə ril′ə) *n.* 1 the largest and most powerful anthropoid ape (*Gorilla gorilla*), found in the forests of central Africa. 2 *Slang.* a strong and brutal man. [< NL < Gk. < W African word, according to a traveller in the 5th c. B.C.]
☛ *Hom.* guerrilla.

gor·mand (gôr′mənd) *n.* gourmand.

gor·mand·ize (gôr′mən dīz′) *v.* **-ized, -iz·ing.** stuff oneself with food; eat very greedily; gorge. [originally n., < F *gourmandise* gluttony] —**gor′mand·iz′er,** *n.*

gorse (gôrs) *n.* furze. [OE *gorst*]

gor·y (gôr′ē) *adj.* **gor·i·er, gor·i·est.** 1 very bloody. 2 characterized by violence, bloodshed, etc. —**gor′i·ly,** *adv.* —**gor′i·ness,** *n.*

gosh (gosh) *interj.* an exclamation or mild oath.
by gosh, by God. [euphemism for *God*]

gos·hawk (gos′hok′ *or* -hôk′) *n.* any of several short-winged hawks (genus *Accipiter*), especially *A. gentilis*, a large, mainly grey hawk of the northern hemisphere, formerly used in falconry. [OE *gōshafoc* < *gōs* goose + *hafoc* hawk]

Go·shen (gō′shən) *n.* 1 in the Bible, a fertile part of Egypt where the Israelites were permitted to live (Exod. 8:20-22). 2 a land of plenty and comfort.

gos·ling (goz′ling) *n.* a young goose.

go–slow (gō′slō′) *n. Informal.* 1 a change, development, etc. that progresses at a slow pace. 2 a deliberate slowing down of the rate of work, production, etc.; slowdown.

gos·pel (gos′pəl) *n.* 1 the teachings of Jesus and the Apostles. 2 Usually, **Gospel, a** any one of the first four books of the New Testament, by Matthew, Mark, Luke, and John. **b** a part of one of these books read during a religious service. 3 *Informal.* anything earnestly believed or taken as a guide for action. 4 the absolute truth. [OE *gōdspel* good tidings (i.e., of the Nativity) < *gōd* good + *spel* spell[2]]

gos·sa·mer (gos′ə mər *or* goz′ə mər) *n., adj.* —*n.* 1 a film or thread of cobweb. 2 a very thin, light cloth. 3 a thin, light, waterproof cloth or coat. 4 anything very light and thin. —*adj.* like gossamer; very light and thin; filmy. [ME, prob. < *gossomer* goose summer, a name for Indian summer, referring to a time of year when goose was eaten and cobwebs were plentiful]

gos·san (gos′ən *or* goz′ən) *n. Mining.* decomposed rock that often indicates an ore-bearing vein, because of its rusty-red color resulting from oxidized iron pyrites. [< Cornish *gossen* < *gōs* blood]

gos·sip (gos′ip) *n., v.* **-siped, -sip·ing.** —*n.* 1 idle talk, not always truthful, about people and their affairs. 2 a person who gossips a good deal. 3 *Archaic.* friend. 4 *Archaic.* godparent.
—*v.* repeat what one knows, or the idle talk that one hears, about people and their affairs. [OE *godsibb*, originally, godparent < *god* God + *sibb* relative] —**gos′sip·er,** *n.*

gos·sip·mon·ger (gos′ip mung′gər *or* -mong′gər) *n.* a person who spreads gossip.

gos·sip·y (gos′ip ē) *adj.* 1 fond of gossip. 2 full of gossip.

gos·soon (go sün′) *n. Irish.* a boy, especially one who is a servant. [an Irish alteration of F *garçon*]

got (got) *v.* pt. and a pp. of **get.**

☞ *Usage.* **Got** is frequently used as a way of intensifying have in the sense of "possess" or "be obligated": *Have you got a pencil? I've got to study now.* However, this usage is inappropriate in formal English. See also **gotten.**

Go·ta·ma (go'tə mə *or* gô'tə mə) *n.* Gautama or Buddha.

Goth (goth) *n.* **1** a member of a Germanic people that overran the Roman Empire in the third, fourth, and fifth centuries A.D. The Goths settled in S and E Europe. **2** an uncivilized person; barbarian. [ME < LL *Gothi,* pl.]

𝔚𝔥𝔞𝔫𝔫𝔢 𝔱𝔥𝔞𝔱 𝔄𝔭𝔯𝔦𝔩𝔩𝔢 𝔀𝔦𝔱𝔥 𝔥𝔦𝔰 𝔰𝔥𝔬𝔲𝔯𝔢𝔰 𝔰𝔬𝔱𝔢
𝔗𝔥𝔢 𝔡𝔯𝔬𝔤𝔥𝔱𝔢 𝔬𝔣 𝔐𝔞𝔯𝔠𝔥𝔢 𝔥𝔞𝔱𝔥 𝔭𝔢𝔯𝔠𝔢𝔡 𝔱𝔬 𝔱𝔥𝔢 𝔯𝔬𝔱𝔢

𝔥𝔬𝔪𝔢 𝔖𝔴𝔢𝔢𝔱 𝔥𝔬𝔪𝔢

Gothic (def. 3a): two samples of Old English, a style of Gothic used in early English printing and still often used for diplomas, etc. Shown at the top is the beginning of Chaucer's *Canterbury Tales;* below, a typical example of a modern use of the type.

Goth·ic (goth'ik) *n., adj.* —*n.* **1** *Architecture.* a style characterized by pointed arches and high, steep roofs, developed in W Europe during the Middle Ages. **2** the East Germanic language of the Goths. **3** Often, **gothic,** *Printing.* **a** a family of heavy, angular typefaces or lettering styles based on medieval scripts and used especially by the earliest European printers, characterized by thick-and-thin lines and thin serifs; black letter. Gothic was used in Germany until about the 1930's. **b** sans-serif. —*adj.* **1** of or having to do with the Goths or their language. **2** of or designating the style of architecture called Gothic. **3** crude or barbarous. **4** medieval. **5** of or designating a style of literature that emphasizes the supernatural and the grotesque, usually having a medieval setting. [< LL *Gothicus*]

got·ten (got'ən) *v.* a pp. of **get.**

☞ *Usage.* Both **got** and **gotten** are accepted as the past participle of the verb **get.** Some people use only one or the other; others use either one, depending on the rhythm of the sentence. However, only **got** is used in the sense of "possess": *She's got nice clothes. She has gotten* (or *got*) *a new dress.*

gouache (gwäsh) *n.* **1** a method of painting with opaque water colors obtained by mixing pigments with water and gum. **2** a color made in this way. **3** a painting using this medium. [< F *gouache* < Ital. *guazzo* water colors, mire; earlier; watering place < L *aquatio* watering place]

Gou·da (gou'də *or* gü'də) *n.* a mild, yellow cheese made in Holland. [< *Gouda,* a city in the Netherlands]

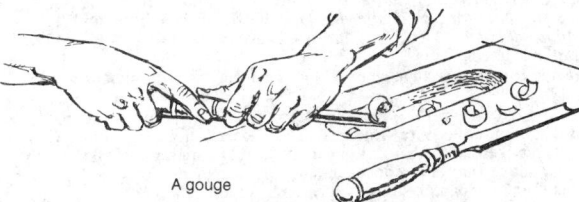

A gouge

gouge (gouj) *n., v.* **gouged, goug·ing.** —*n.* **1** a chisel with a concave blade used for cutting round grooves or holes in wood, stone, etc. **2** a groove, trench, or hole made by gouging: *There was a long gouge in the desk top.* **3** *Informal.* a cutting with or as if with a gouge. **4** *Informal.* a trick; cheat; swindle. —*v.* **1** cut with a gouge or something like it: *to gouge a piece of wood.* **2** make by gouging: *to gouge a channel.* **3** dig or tear (*out*): *to gouge out dirt.* **4** *Informal.* overcharge or swindle. [< F < LL *gulbia*] —**goug'er,** *n.*

gou·lash (gü'lash) *n.* a highly seasoned stew made of beef or veal and vegetables. It is usually seasoned with paprika. [< Hungarian *gulyás* (*hús*) herdsman's (meat)]

gou·ra·mi (gùr'ə mē *or* gù rä'mē) *n., pl.* **-mis.** any of various tropical freshwater fishes (family Anabantidae) of SE Asia, including some brightly colored species that are popular for home aquariums. [< Malay *gurami*]

gourd (gôrd *or* gürd) *n.* **1** the hard-shelled, inedible fruit of any of various vines (genera *Cucurbita* and *Lagenaria*), often dried and used for ornament or for making bowls, cups, etc. **2** any of the plants that bear such fruit. **3** (*adj.*) designating the family (Cucurbitaceae) of climbing or trailing plants that includes the gourds as well as cucumbers, pumpkins, muskmelons, and squashes. **4** the hard-shelled fruit of any of various other plants, such as calabash, that is dried and used for utensils, etc. **5** a bowl, bottle, etc. made from the dried shell of a gourd. [ME < F *gourde* < OF *cohorde* < L *cucurbita*]

gourde (gürd) *n.* **1** the basic unit of money in Haiti, divided into 100 centimes. See table at **money. 2** a note worth one gourde. [< F]

hat, āge, fär; let, ēqual, tèrm; it, īce
hot, ōpen, ôrder; oil, out; cup, pùt, rüle,
əbove, takən, pencəl, lemən, circəs
ch, child; ng, long; sh, ship
th, thin; ŦH, then; zh, measure

gour·mand (gür'mənd) *n.* **1** a person who is fond of good eating. **2** a person who is greedy; glutton. Also **gormand.** [< F *gourmand* gluttonous < *gourmet* gourmet]

gour·met (gür'mā) *n.* a person who is expert in judging and choosing fine foods, wines, etc.; epicure. [< F < OF *gourmet, groumet* wine taster < *gromet* servant]

gout (gout) *n.* **1** a painful disease of the joints, often characterized by a painful swelling of the big toe. **2** a drop; splash; clot: *gouts of blood.* [ME < OF *goute* < L *gutta* a drop, with reference to the medieval theory of the flow of body humors]

goût (gü) *n. French.* taste.

gout·y (gout'ē) *adj.* **gout·i·er, gout·i·est. 1** swollen with gout: *a gouty toe.* **2** of or like gout. **3** causing or caused by gout. **4** having or tending to have gout. —**gout'i·ly,** *adv.* —**gout'i·ness,** *n.*

Gov. or **gov. 1** governor. **2** government.

gov·ern (guv'ərn) *v.* **1** rule; control; manage: *to govern a country, to govern one's temper.* **1** exercise a directing or restraining influence over; determine: *the motives governing a person's decision.* **3** hold back; restrain; check. **4** be a rule or law for: *the principles governing a case.* **5** *Grammar.* require (a word) to be in a certain case, number, or mood; require (a certain case, number, or mood). [ME < OF *governer* < L *gubernare* < Gk. *kybernaein* steer] —**gov'ern·a·ble,** *adj.*

☞ *Syn.* **1.** See note at **rule.**

gov·ern·ance (guv'ər nəns) *n.* government; rule; control.

gov·ern·ess (guv'ər nis) *n.* a woman who teaches children in a private house.

gov·ern·ment (guv'ərn mənt *or* guv'ər mənt) *n.* **1** the rule or authority over a country, province, district, etc.; direction of the affairs of state. **2** the person or persons ruling a country, state, district, etc.; administration. **3** a system of ruling: *Canada has a democractic government.* **4** the country, province, district, etc. ruled. **5** rule; control. **6** *Grammar.* the relationship by which one word determines the case, number, or person of another depending on it.

gov·ern·men·tal (guv'ərn men'təl *or* guv'ər men'təl) *adj.* of or having to do with government. —**gov'ern·men'tal·ly,** *adv.*

Government House *Cdn.* **1** the official residence of the Governor General in Ottawa, also known as Rideau Hall. **2** in some provinces, the official residence of the lieutenant-governor.

gov·er·nor (guv'ər nər) *n.* **1** the appointed ruler of a colony; the representative of a monarch in a colony. **2** an official appointed to govern a province, city, fort, etc. **3** in the United States, an official elected as the executive head of a state. **4** a person who manages or directs a club, society, institution, etc. A club often has a board of governors. **5** an automatic device that controls the supply of steam, gas, etc. and keeps a machine going at a certain speed. [ME < OF *governeor* < L *gubernator* steersman]

governor general *pl.* **governors general. 1** a governor who has subordinate or deputy governors under him. **2 Governor General, a** in Canada, the representative of the Crown, appointed on the advice of the prime minister for a term of five years. **b** the representative of the Crown in certain other independent countries of the Commonwealth of Nations. Also, **governor- general.**

gov·er·nor·ship (guv'ər nər ship' *or* guv'nər ship') *n.* the position or term of office of governor.

Govt. or **govt.** government.

gow·an (gou'ən) *n. Scottish.* any of various white or yellow wildflower, especially a daisy. [< dial. *gowlan,* var. of *golding* gold-colored]

gown (goun) *n., v.* —*n.* **1** a woman's dress, especially a formal or evening dress. **2** a loose outer garment with very wide sleeves, such as those worn by judges, clergy, members of a university, and students graduating from university to show their position, profession, etc. **3** a nightgown or dressing gown. **4** the members of a university: *arguments between town and gown.* —*v.* put a gown on; dress in a gown. [ME < OF *goune* < LL *gunna*] —**gown'less,** *adj.*

gowns·man (gounz'mən) *n., pl.* **-men. 1** a person such as a lawyer or member of the clergy who wears a gown as a mark of his profession. **2** a member of a university; wearer of an academic gown.

goy (goi) *n., pl.* **goy·im.** *Yiddish. Derogatory.* **1** a non-Jew; gentile. **2** a Jew who does not observe the law. [originally < Hebrew]

gp. group(s).

G.P. *Medicine.* general practitioner.

GPM, gpm, or **g.p.m.** gallons per minute.

G.P.O. General Post Office.

gr. **1** grain(s). **2** gross. **3** grade. **4** grammar. **5** group. **6** great.

Gr. Greek; Greece.

G.R. King George (for L *Georgius Rex*).

grab (grab) *v.* **grabbed, grab·bing;** *n.* —*v.* **1** seize suddenly; snatch: *The dog grabbed the meat and ran.* **2** take possession of in an unscrupulous manner: *to grab land.* **3** *Informal.* capture; arrest: *The police grabbed the robbers after a long chase.* **4** get or take in a hurry: *to grab a sandwich.* —*n.* **1** the act of snatching; a sudden seizing: *She made a grab for the apple.* **2** that which is grabbed. **3** a mechanical device for firmly holding something that is to be lifted or raised. [cf. MDu. *grabben*] —**grab′ber,** *n.*

grab bag **1** a bag or other receptacle filled with an assortment of articles, one of which may be selected, sight unseen, by a person paying a certain price. **2** *Informal.* any varied assortment.

grace (grās) *n., v.* **graced, grac·ing.** —*n.* **1** beauty of form, movement, or manner; a pleasing or agreeable quality. **2** mercy; pardon. **3** *Theology.* **a** God's free and undeserved favor to and love for mankind; the influence of God operating in man to improve or strengthen him. **b** the condition of being influenced and favored by God. **4** a short prayer of thanks said before or after a meal. **5** the favor shown by granting a postponement: *The bank gave him three days' grace.* **7** virtue; merit; excellence. **8** Usually, **Grace,** a title used in speaking to or of a duke, duchess, or archbishop: *He spoke a few words to his Grace the Duke of Bedford.* **9** a grace note. **10 Graces,** *pl.* three Greek sister goddesses controlling beauty and charm in people and in nature.
have the grace, have the goodness or courtesy: *He had the grace to say he was sorry.*
in (someone's) bad graces, out of favor with or disliked by (someone): *She was in the teacher's bad graces for a week after that episode.*
in (someone's) good graces, favored or liked by (someone).
with bad grace, unpleasantly; unwillingly.
with good grace, pleasantly; readily.
—*v.* **1** give or add grace to; set off with grace. **2** do a favor or honor to: *The Queen graced the ball with her presence.* **3** *Music.* add grace notes to. [< F < L *gratia* < *gratus* pleasing]

grace·ful (grās′fəl) *adj.* having or showing grace; beautiful in form, movement, or manner; pleasing; agreeable: *A good dancer must be graceful. She thanked him with a graceful speech.* —**grace′ful·ly,** *adv.* —**grace′ful·ness,** *n.*

grace·less (grās′lis) *adj.* **1** without grace. **2** not caring for what is right and proper: *That boy is a graceless rascal.* —**grace′less·ly,** *adv.* —**grace′less·ness,** *n.*

grace note *Music.* a note or group of notes added for ornament and not essential to the harmony or melody. It is written in as a small note, with a slur leading to the following note.

gra·cious (grā′shəs) *adj., interj.* —*adj.* **1** pleasant; kindly; courteous: *The bride's gracious manner pleased everyone.* **2** pleasant, kindly, and courteous to people of lower social position: *The Queen greeted the crowd with a gracious smile.* **3** of God, merciful; kindly. —*interj.* an exclamation of surprise. [ME < OF < L *gratiosus*] —**gra′cious·ly,** *adv.* —**gra′cious·ness,** *n.*

grack·le (grak′əl) *n.* any of several large American blackbirds having dark, iridescent plumage. The common grackle (*Quiscalus quiscula*) is found throughout Canada east of the Rockies. [< L *graculus* jackdaw]

grad. graduate; graduated.

gra·da·tion (grā dā′shən *or* grə dā′shən) *n.* **1** a change by steps or stages; gradual change: *Our acts show gradation between right and wrong.* **2** Usually, **gradations,** *pl.* a step, stage, or degree in a series: *There are many gradations between poverty and wealth. The rainbow shows gradations of color.* **3** the act or process of grading. [< L *gradatio, -onis* < *gradus* step, degree]

grade (grād) *n., v.* **grad·ed, grad·ing.** —*n.* **1** in schools: **a** any one division, or class, arranged according to the pupil's progress. **b** the pupils in any such division. **2** a step or stage in a course or process. **3** a degree in a scale of rank, quality, value, etc.: *grade A milk.* **4** a group of people or things having the same rank, quality, value, etc. **5 the grades,** *U.S.* elementary school. **6** a number or letter that shows how well one has done: *Her grade in English is B.* **7** the

slope of a road, railway track, etc. **8** the amount of slope. **9** *Stock breeding.* an animal having one purebred parent.
at grade, on the same level.
down grade, a a going down. **b** getting worse.
make the grade, a ascend a steep slope. **b** overcome difficulties.
up grade, a a going up. **b** getting better.
—*v.* **1** arrange in classes; arrange according to size, value, etc; sort: *These apples are graded by size.* **2** be of a particular grade or quality. **3** give a grade to: *The teacher graded the papers.* **4** *Stock breeding.* improve (stock) by breeding with purebred stock (*often used with up*). **5** make more nearly level: *The workmen graded the land around the new house.* **6** change gradually; go through a series of steps, stages, or degrees: *Red and yellow grade into orange.* [< F < L *gradus* step, degree]

grade crossing level crossing.

grad·er (grād′ər) *n.* **1** a person or thing that grades, especially a machine for levelling earth. **2** *Esp.U.S.* a person who is in a certain grade in elementary or secondary school (*used only in compounds*): *a sixth-grader.*

grade school *U.S.* elementary school.

gra·di·ent (grā′dē ənt) *n., adj.* —*n.* **1** the rate at which a road, railway track, etc. rises. **2** the sloping part of a road, etc. **3** *Physics.* the rate at which temperature or pressure changes. **4** a curve or graph representing such a rate.
—*adj.* **1** going up or down gradually. **2** moving by taking steps; walking. [< L *gradiens, -entis,* ppr. of *gradi* walk, go < *gradus* step, degree]

grad·u·al (graj′ü əl) *adj.* occurring, developing, etc. by degrees too small to be separately noticed; little by little: *a gradual increase in sound. The hill had a gradual slope.* [< Med.L *gradualis* < L *gradus* step, degree] —**grad′u·al·ly,** *adv.*

grad·u·and (graj′ü and′) *n. Esp.Cdn.* a student who is about to graduate. [< Med.L *graduandus* < *graduare.* See GRADUATE.]

grad·u·ate (*v.* graj′ü āt′; *n.* graj′ü it′ *or* graj′ü āt) *v.* **-at·ed, -at·ing;** *n.* —*v.* **1** finish a course of study at a school, college, or university and receive a diploma or paper saying one has done so: *Mary's brother graduated from university last year.* **2** give a diploma to for finishing a course of study. **3** mark with degrees for measuring: *A thermometer is graduated.* **4** arrange in regular steps, stages, or degrees: *An income tax is graduated so that the people who make the most money pay the highest rate of taxes.* **5** change gradually.
—*n.* **1** a person who has graduated. **2** a container marked with degrees for measuring. **3** (*adj.*) of, having to do with, or for graduates: *a graduate dinner.* **4** (*adj.*) **a** being a person who has received a first degree from a university: *A graduate student is one who is studying for an advanced degree.* **b** of or for such persons: *graduate school.* [< Med.L *graduare* < L *gradus* step, degree] —**grad′u·a·tor,** *n.*
☛ *Pronun.* The pronunciation (graj′ü āt′) for the noun is most commonly heard among Westerners.

grad·u·a·tion (graj′ü ā′shən) *n.* **1** graduating or being graduated from a school, college, or university. **2** the ceremony of graduating; graduating exercises. **3** a marking with degrees for measuring. **4** a mark or set of marks to show degrees for measuring. **5** an arrangement in regular steps, stages, or degrees.

graf·fi·ti (grə fē′tē) *n. pl.* of **graffito.** verses, sayings, or pictures drawn, scribbled, or scratched on a public surface such as a wall or fence. Graffiti are usually anonymous and are often cleverly done. [< Ital. *graffito* scribbling < *graffio* a scratch, scribble < Gk. *graphein* draw, write]

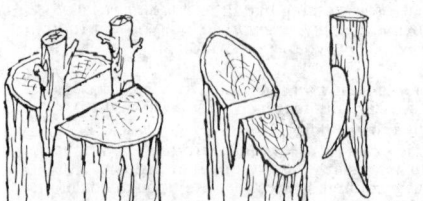

Three kinds of plant graft. The pieces are tied or taped together and kept moist until the grafted part begins to grow.

graft¹ (graft) *v., n.* —*v.* **1** insert (a shoot, bud, etc.) from one tree or plant into a slit in another so that it will grow there permanently. **2** produce or improve (a fruit, flower etc.) by grafting. **3** do grafting on. **4** transfer (a piece of skin, bone, etc.) from one part of the body to another so that it will grow there permanently. **5** insert or fix as if by grafting. **6** become grafted.
—*n.* **1** the shoot, bud, etc. used in grafting. **2** the place on a tree or plant where the shoot, bud, etc. is inserted. **3** the tree or plant that has had a shoot, bud, etc. grafted on it. **4** the act of grafting. **5** a

piece of skin, bone, etc. transferred in grafting. [earlier *graff* < OF *grafe* < L *graphium* < Gk. *grapheion* stylus (< *graphein* write); from similarity of shape] —**graft′er,** *n.*

graft² (graft) *n., v.* —*n.* **1** the taking of money dishonestly, especially in connection with city or government business; political dishonesty, corruption, etc. **2** a method of getting money dishonestly. **3** money dishonestly taken or obtained. —*v. Informal.* make money dishonestly through one's job, especially in political positions. [origin uncertain] —**graft′er,** *n.*

gra·ham (grā′əm) *n. (adj.)* designating or made from a finely ground, unsifted, whole-wheat flour: *graham crackers.* [after Sylvester *Graham* (1794-1851), an American reformer of dietetics]

Grail (grāl) *n.* the cup or dish supposed to have been used by Christ at the Last Supper, in which one of His followers received the last drops of blood from Christ's body on the cross; Holy Grail. [ME < OF *graal* < Med.L *gradale* plate, or VL *cratale* < *crater* bowl < Gk. *kratēr*]

grain (grān) *n., v.* —*n.* **1** a single seed or seedlike fruit of wheat, oats, and similar cereal grasses. **2** the seeds or seedlike fruits of such plants in the mass. **3** the plants that these seeds or seedlike fruits grow on. **4** a tiny, hard particle of sand, salt, sugar, etc. **5** a unit for measuring mass, equal to about 0.065 grams. The grain is the smallest unit in avoirdupois, troy, and apothecaries' weight. **6** the smallest possible amount; tiniest bit: *a grain of truth.* **7** the arrangement or direction of fibres in wood, layers in stone, etc. Wood and stone split along the grain. **8** the little lines and other markings in wood, marble, etc. **9** the rough surface of leather, originally, the hairy side of the skin. **10 a** the plane of cleavage in coal, stone, etc.; lamination. **b** the directions in which cleavage occurs in diamond polishing. **11** the quality of a substance due to the size, character, or arrangement of its constituent particles; texture: *a stone or salt of coarse grain.* **12** natural character; disposition: *Laziness was against the grain for her.* **13** *Photography.* any of the small, separate particles of light-sensitive material emulsified and deposited on photographic film. The size of the particle limits the possible enlargement of the image and affects the speed of exposure. —*v.* **1** form into grains. **2** paint in imitation of the grain in wood, marble, etc. **3** remove the hair from (a skin or skins). **4** soften and raise the grain of (leather). [ME < OF < L *granum* grain, seed] —**grain′less,** *adj.*

grain alcohol ethyl alcohol, often made from grain.

grained (grānd) *adj.* **1** having little lines and markings. **2** painted in imitation of the grain in wood, marble, etc. **3** with the hair removed; roughened on the surface.

grain elevator a building for storing grain.

grain·field (grān′fēld′) *n.* a field in which grain grows.

grain·ing (grān′ing) *n.* painting in imitation of the grain in wood, marble, etc.

gram (gram) *n.* an SI unit for measuring mass, equal to one one-thousandth of a kilogram: *A nickel has a mass of about five grams.* Symbol: g Also, **gramme.** [< F *gramme* < LL < Gk. *gramma* small marked weight < *graphein* mark, write]

–gram¹ *combining form.* something written; message, as in *cablegram, telegram, monogram.* [< Gk. *-gramma* something written, ult. < *graphein* write]

–gram² or **–gramme** *combining form.* grams; of a gram, as in *kilogram, milligram.* [see GRAM]

gra·mer·cy (grə mėr′sē *or* gram′ər sē) *interj. Archaic.* **1** many thanks; thank you. **2** an exclamation of surprise. [ME < OF *grant merci* (God give you) great reward]

gram·mar (gram′ər) *n.* **1** the scientific study and classification of a language with reference to the sounds and forms of words and the structure of sentences. **2** a systematic study comparing the forms and constructions of two or more languages. **3** a systematic study comparing present with past forms and usage of a language. **4** a treatise or book on any of these subjects. **5** the system of the forms and uses of words in a particular language: *Grammar is often thought of as a set of rules.* **6** the use of words according to this system: *Good grammar is important in formal writing.* **7** the elements of any subject: *the grammar of painting.* [ME < OF *grammaire* < L *grammatica* < Gk. *grammatikē (technē)* (art) of letters, ult. < *graphein* write]

gram·mar·i·an (grə mer′ē ən) *n.* a person knowledgable about or studying grammar.

grammar school **1** a public school having the grades between primary school and high school. **2** in the United Kingdom, a secondary school that prepares students for university.

gram·mat·i·cal (grə mat′ə kəl) *adj.* **1** according to the grammar (def. 5) of a particular language: *Our French teacher speaks grammatical English but has a French accent.* **2** of or having to do with grammar: *a grammatical error.*

hat, āge, fär; let, ēqual, tèrm; it, īce
hot, ōpen, ôrder; oil, out; cup, put, rüle,
əbove, takən, pencəl, lemən, circəs
ch, child; ng, long; sh, ship
th, thin; ᴛʜ, then; zh, measure

gram·mat·i·cal·ly (grə mat′ik lē) *adv.* according to the principles and rules of grammar; as regards grammar.

gramme (gram) See **gram.**

gram–mo·lec·u·lar (gram′mə lek′yə lər) *adj.* of or having to do with gram-molecular weight.

gram–molecular weight the mass of one molecule of an element or compound, expressed in grams.

gram–neg·a·tive or **Gram–neg·a·tive** (gram′neg′ə tiv) *adj.* designating bacteria that do not retain the violet color when stained by Gram's method. See **Gram's method.**

gram·o·phone (gram′ə fōn′) *n.* record player; phonograph. [Inversion of *phonogram* < Gk. *phōnē* sound + *-gram¹*]

gram–pos·i·tive (gram′poz′ə tiv) *adj.* designating bacteria that retain the violet color when stained by Gram's method. See **Gram's method.**

gram·pus (gram′pəs) *n.* **1** a large grey dolphin (*Grampus griseus*) found in the Atlantic and Pacific oceans. **2** any of various other relatively small cetaceans, such as the killer whale. [*graundepose* < earlier *grapeys* < OF *graspeis* < L *crassus piscis* fat fish]

Gram's method (gramz) *Bacteriology.* a technique for classifying bacteria, by which they are stained with gentian violet and then treated with a decolorizing agent. Certain species (called gram-positive bacteria) retain the violet stain after this treatment, while others (gram-negative bacteria) lose it.

gran·a·ry (grā′nə rē, grān′rē, *or* gran′ə rē) *n., pl.* **-ries. 1** a place or building where grain is stored. **2** a region in which much grain is grown. [< L *granarium* < *granum* grain]

grand (grand) *adj., n.* —*adj.* **1** large and of fine appearance: *grand mountains.* **2** fine; noble; dignified; stately; splendid: *grand music, a grand old man.* **3** highest or very high in rank; chief: *a grand duke, a grand master in chess.* **4** great; important; main: *the grand staircase.* **5** complete; comprehensive: *grand total.* **6** *Informal.* very pleasing: *a grand time.* **7** in names of relationship, in the second degree of ascent or descent: *grandmother, grandson.* —*n.* **1** *Slang.* a thousand dollars. **2** grand piano. [< MF *grant, grand* < L *grandis* big] —**grand′ly,** *adv.* —**grand′ness,** *n.*

☛ *Syn. adj.* **2. Grand, stately, noble** = great, dignified, fine, and impressive. **Grand** emphasizes greatness that makes the person or thing described stand out, and suggests impressive dignity or splendor: *Under the leadership of that grand old man, the nation withstood its peril.* **Stately** emphasizes impressive dignity, sometimes also appearance: *He was moved by the stately rhythm of processional music.* **Noble** emphasizes an imposing greatness, splendor, or stateliness in appearance: *The Rocky Mountains are a noble sight.*

gran·dad or **grand·dad** (gran′dad′ *or* grand′dad′) *n. Informal.* grandfather (def. 1).

gran·dam (gran′dam) *n. Archaic.* **1** grandmother. **2** an old woman. [ME < AF *graund dame*]

gran–dame (gran′dām) *n. Archaic.* grandam.

grand–aunt (grand′ant′) *n.* an aunt of one's father or mother; great-aunt.

grand·child (gran′chīld′ *or* grand′-) *n., pl.* **-chil·dren.** a child of one's son or daughter.

grand·daugh·ter (gran′do′tər *or* gran′dô′tər) *n.* a daughter of one's son or daughter.

grand duchess **1** the wife or widow of a grand duke. **2** a lady equal in rank to a grand duke. **3** in Russia before 1917, a princess of the ruling house.

grandy duchy the territory under the rule of a grand duke or grand duchess.

grand duke **1** a prince who rules a small state or country called a grand duchy. A grand duke ranks just below a king. **2** in Russia before 1917, a prince of the ruling house.

gran·dee (gran dē′) *n.* **1** in Spain or Portugal, a nobleman of the highest rank. **2** a person of high rank or great importance. [< Sp., Pg. *grande*]

gran·deur (gran′jər) *n.* greatness; majesty; nobility; dignity; splendor. [< F *grandeur* < *grand* grand]

grand·fa·ther (gran′fo′ᴛʜər *or* grand′-) *n.* **1** the father of one's father or mother. **2** forefather.

grandfather clock or **grandfather's clock** a clock in a tall, wooden case that stands on the floor.

grand·fa·ther·ly (gran'fo'тнər lē or grand'-) adj. 1 of a grandfather. 2 like or characteristic of a grandfather.

gran·di·flo·ra (gran'də flôr'ə) n., adj. —n. a variety of hybrid cultivated rose developed from crosses of floribunda and tea roses, and combining attributes of both. —adj. bearing large flowers (used especially in specific names of plants). [< NL Grandiflora < L grandis grand + flos, floris flower]

gran·dil·o·quence (gran dil'ə kwəns) n. the use of lofty or pompous words.

gran·dil·o·quent (gran dil'ə kwənt) adj. using lofty or pompous words. [< L grandiloquus < grandis grand + loqui speak; influenced by the form of E eloquent] —**gran·dil'o·quent·ly**, adv.

gran·di·ose (gran'dē ōs') adj. 1 grand in an imposing or impressive way; magnificent. 2 grand in an affected or pompous way; trying to seem magnificent. [< F < Ital. grandioso] —**gran'di·ose·ly**, adv.

grand jury a special jury called to examine a charge against a person to determine if there is sufficient evidence to warrant bringing the accused to trial on that charge. Grand juries have been abolished in most of the Canadian provinces that had them.

Grand Lama Dalai Lama.

grand larceny U.S. in some States, a theft in which the value of the property taken equals or is more than a specified sum ($50 in many of the States, but varying considerably from State to State). Compare **petty larceny.**

grand·ma (gran'mä', gram'mä', or grand'mä') n. Informal. grandmother.

grand march a ceremony at a ball in which the guests march around the ballroom in couples.

grand master 1 the head of a military order of knighthood, of a lodge, etc. 2 an expert chess player who has consistently done well in international championships.

grand·moth·er (gran'muтн'ər or grand'-) n. 1 the mother of one's father or mother. 2 a female ancestor.

grand·moth·er·ly (gran'muтн'ər lē or grand'-) adj. 1 of a grandmother. 2 like or characteristic of a grandmother.

grand·neph·ew (gran'nef'yü or grand'-) n. the son of one's nephew or niece.

grand·niece (gran'nēs' or grand'-) n. the daughter of one's nephew or niece.

grand opera a musical drama, having a serious and often tragic theme, in which all the speeches are sung or recited to the accompaniment of an orchestra.

grand·pa (gran'pä', gram'pä', or grand'pä') n. Informal. grandfather.

grand·par·ent (gran'per'ənt or grand'-) n. a grandfather or grandmother.

grand piano a large, harp-shaped piano with horizontal frame and strings. Compare **upright piano.**

grand·sire (gran'sīr' or grand'-) n. Archaic. 1 grandfather. 2 forefather. 3 an old man.

grand slam Bridge. the winning of all the tricks in a hand.

grand·son (gran'sun' or grand'-) n. a son of one's son or daughter.

grand·stand (gran'stand' or grand'-) n. the main seating place for people at an athletic field, race track, parade, etc., usually having a roof.

grand·un·cle (grand'ung'kəl) n. great-uncle.

grange (grānj) n. 1 a farm with its buildings; farmstead. 2 the Grange, U.S. a an organization of farmers to promote agricultural interests, founded in 1867. b a local branch of this organization. [ME < OF < VL granica < L granum grain]

grang·er (grān'jər) n. 1 farmer. 2 Granger, a member of the Grange.

gran·ite (gran'it) n. a hard igneous rock consisting chiefly of quartz and feldspar. Granite is much used for buildings and monuments. [< Ital. granito grained, pp. of granire < grano grain < L granum]

gran·ite·ware (gran'it wer') n. ironware covered with grey enamel.

gra·nit·ic (grə nit'ik) adj. of or like granite.

gran·nie or **gran·ny** (gran'ē) n., pl. -nies. Informal. 1 grandmother. 2 an old woman. 3 a fussy person.

grannie knot or **granny knot** a knot differing from a square knot in having the ends crossed the wrong way. A grannie knot is not as secure as a square knot. See **knot** for picture.

grant (grant) v., n. —v. 1 give what is asked; allow: to grant a request, to grant permission. 2 admit to be true; accept with proof; concede: I grant that you are right. 3 bestow or confer (a right, etc.) by formal act; transfer or convey (the ownership of property), especially by deed or writing.

take for granted, assume to be true; accept as proved or as agreed to.

—n. 1 something granted, such as a privilege, right, sum of money, or tract of land: The companies that built the railways received large grants of land from the government. 2 the act of granting. [ME < OF graanter, var. of creanter, promise, authorize, ult. < L credens, ppr. of credere trust] —**grant'a·ble**, adj. —**grant'er**, n.

grant·ee (gran'tē') n. a person to whom a grant is made.

grant·or (gran'tər or gran'tôr') n. a person who makes a grant.

gran·u·lar (gran'yə lər) adj. 1 consisting of or containing grains or granules. 2 resembling grains or granules. —**gran'u·lar·ly**, adv.

gran·u·late (gran'yə lāt') v. -lat·ed, -lat·ing. 1 form into grains or granules. 2 roughen on the surface. 3 become granular; develop granulations. Wounds granulate in healing. —**gran'u·la'tor**, n.

gran·u·lat·ed (gran'yə lāt'id) adj. 1 formed into grains or granules: granulated sugar. 2 roughened on the surface. 3 having granulations.

gran·u·la·tion (gran'yə lā'shən) n. 1 a formation into grains or granules. 2 a roughening on the surface. 3 a granule on a roughened surface. 4 the formation of small, grainlike bodies, especially in the process of healing. 5 a small, grainlike body or elevation, especially one of those that form on the surface of wounds during healing.

gran·ule (gran'yül) n. 1 a small grain. 2 a small bit or spot like a grain. [< LL granulum, dim. of granum grain]

gran·u·lose (gran'yə lōs') n. that part of a starch granule on which diastase and saliva act.

grape (grāp) n. 1 a small, round, juicy, thin-skinned fruit that grows in bunches on grapevines and is eaten as a fruit, either fresh or dried, used for making jellies, or fermented to make wine. Grapes may be greenish white, red, or purple. 2 grapevine. 3 (adj.) designating the family (Vitaceae) of mainly tropical, climbing shrubs that includes grapes and the Virginia creeper. 4 a bluish-purple color; violet. 5 **the grape**, wine. 6 grapeshot. [ME < OF grape bunch of grapes < graper pick grapes < grape hook < Gmc.] —**grape'like'**, adj.

grape·fruit (grāp'früt') n., pl. -fruit or -fruits. 1 a large, edible citrus fruit with a thick yellow rind and juicy, acid, yellow or pink pulp. 2 the tropical and subtropical evergreen tree (Citrus paradisi) of the rue family that bears such fruit.

grape·shot (grāp'shot') n. a cluster of small iron balls formerly used as a charge for cannon.

grape sugar a sugar formed in all green plants, but especially in grapes; dextrose.

grape·vine (grāp'vīn') n. 1 any of numerous vines (genus Vitis) of the grape family native to north temperate regions, especially an E Asian species, V. Vinifera, which has been cultivated in many varieties since ancient times for its fruit, called grapes. 2 Informal. a means of circulating information, etc. unofficially or secretly from person to person.

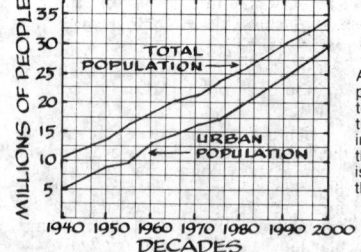

A graph of Canadian population trends projected to the year 2000. It shows that the total population is increasing, and also that the urban population is increasing relative to the rural.

graph (graf) n., v. —n. 1 a line or diagram showing how one quantity depends on or changes with another. 2 Mathematics. any line or lines representing the relations of equations or functions. —v. draw such a line or diagram; draw a line representing some change, equation, or function. [for graphic formula. See GRAPHIC.]

–graph combining form. 1 make a picture, draw, or write, as in photograph. 2 a machine that makes a picture, draws, or writes, as in seismograph. 3 drawn or written, as in autograph. 4 something drawn or written, as in lithograph. [< Gk. -graphos < graphein write]

graph·ic (graf'ik) adj. 1 lifelike; vivid: a graphic account of the battle. 2 of or about diagrams and their use. 3 shown by a graph: a graphic record of school attendance for a month. 4 of or about drawing, painting, engraving, or etching: the graphic arts. 5 of or

used in handwriting: *graphic symbols*. **6** written; inscribed. [< L
graphicus < Gk. *graphikos* < *graphein* write]

graph·i·cal (graf′ə kəl) *adj*. graphic.

graph·i·cal·ly (graf′ik lē) *adv*. **1** by a diagram or pictures.
2 vividly.

graphic arts drawing, painting, engraving, etching, etc.

graph·ite (graf′īt) *n*. a soft, black form of carbon found in nature,
having a metallic lustre, used for pencil leads, electrodes, and
crucibles, as a lubricant for machinery, and as a moderator in
nuclear reactors. [< G *Graphit* < Gk. *graphein* write]

graph·o·log·i·cal (graf′ə loj′ə kəl) *adj*. of or having to do with
graphology: *graphological analysis*.

graph·ol·o·gist (gra fol′ə jist) *n*. a person trained in graphology,
especially one whose work it is.

graph·ol·o·gy (gra fol′ə jē) *n*. the study of handwriting,
especially as a means of analysing a person's character. [< Gk.
graphē writing + E *-logy*]

-graphy *combining form*. **1** a writing, describing, or recording, as
in *telegraphy*. **2** a descriptive science, as in *geography*. [< Gk.
-graphia < *graphein* write]

grap·nel (grap′nəl) *n*. **1** an instrument with one or more hooks for
seizing and holding something. **2** a small anchor with three or more
hooks. See **anchor** for picture. [ME *grapenel*, dim. of OF *grapin*
hook, dim. of *grape* hook < Gmc. Related to GRAPE.]

grap·ple (grap′əl) *v*. **-pled, -pling;** *n*. —*v*. **1** seize and hold fast;
grip or hold firmly. **2** struggle; fight: *The wrestlers grappled in the
centre of the ring*. **3** use a grappling iron; search with a grappling
iron.
—*n*. **1** a seizing and holding fast; a firm grip or hold. **2** an iron bar
with hooks at one end for seizing and holding fast an object;
grappling iron; grapnel. [< OF *grapil* hook < Gmc. Related to
GRAPE.] —**grap′pler,** *n*.

grappling iron grapnel.

grasp (grasp) *v., n*. —*v*. **1** seize and hold fast by closing the
fingers around. **2** seize greedily: *to grasp an opportunity*.
3 understand.
grasp at, a try to grasp; try to take hold of. **b** accept eagerly: *Joan
grasped the opportunity*.
—*n*. **1** a seizing and holding tightly; clasp of the hand. **2** the power
of seizing and holding; reach: *He has a strong grasp. Success is
within his grasp*. **3** control; possession. **4** understanding: *He has a
good grasp of mathematics*. [ME *graspe(n)*. Related to GROPE.]
—**grasp′a·ble,** *adj*. —**grasp′er,** *n*.
☞ *Syn*. *v*. **1**. See note at **seize**.

grasp·ing (gras′ping) *adj*. eager to get all that one can; greedy.
—**grasp′ing·ly,** *adv*. —**grasp′ing·ness,** *n*.

grass (gras) *n., v*. —*n*. **1** non-woody green plants that grow in
pastures and meadows and are suitable for food for grazing animals:
Horses, cows, and sheep eat grass. **2** any of a large family
(Gramineae) of plants having jointed, non-woody stems, long,
narrow leaves, and flowers in spikelets. Wheat, corn, sugar cane,
and bamboo are grasses. **3** land covered with grass: *There was a
sign saying "Keep off the grass."* **4** pasture. **5** *Slang*. marijuana.
at grass, a out to pasture. **b** out of work; at leisure.
go to grass, a graze; go to pasture. **b** take a rest.
let the grass grow under (one's) **feet,** waste time; lose chances.
put, send, or **turn out to grass, a** turn (an animal) out to pasture.
b *Informal*. force (a person) into retirement.
—*v*. **1** seed to grass; grow grass over or on. **2** feed on grass: *to
grass livestock*. [OE *gærs, græs*. Related to GREEN, GROW.]
—**grass′less,** *adj*. —**grass′like′,** *adj*.

grass hockey *Cdn*. field hockey.

grass·hop·per (gras′hop′ər) *n*. **1** any insect belonging to the
orthopteran families Acrididae and Tettigoniidae, having biting
mouthparts, two pairs of wings, and long, strong hind legs adapted
for jumping. Grasshoppers eat plants and are often serious pests in
grainfields. **2** a cocktail made of crème de menthe, crème de cacao,
and cream.

grass·land (gras′land′) *n*. land with grass on it, used for pasture.

grass roots 1 *Politics*. people and party organizations at the
local level, especially in rural communities. **2** soil near or at the
surface. **3** the beginning or source. —**grass-roots,** *adj*.

grass snake any of various harmless snakes (family
Colubridae), such as garter snakes or water snakes.

grass widow 1 a woman whose husband is temporarily away.
2 a woman who is divorced or separated from her husband.
[originally, an unmarried woman who had lived with a man, prob.
from the idea of a bed of grass or straw typifying such a
relationship]

grass·y (gras′ē) *adj*. **grass·i·er, grass·i·est. 1** covered with grass:
a grassy meadow. **2** of or like grass. —**grass′i·ness,** *n*.

grate¹ (grāt) *n., v*. **grat·ed, grat·ing.** —*n*. **1** a framework of iron

hat, āge, fär; let, ēqual, tèrm; it, īce
hot, ōpen, ôrder; oil, out; cup, pút, rüle,
əbove, takən, pencəl, lemən, circəs
ch, child; ng, long; sh, ship
th, thin; ᴛʜ, then; zh, measure

bars to hold a fire. A coal furnace has a grate. **2** fireplace. **3** a
framework of bars over a window or opening; grating. **4** *Mining*. a
screen used for separating or grading ore.
—*v*. furnish with a grate or grating. [< Med.L *grata* < L *cratis*
hurdle] —**grate′like′,** *adj*.
☞ *Hom*. **great**.

grate² (grāt) *v*. **grat·ed, grat·ing. 1** have an annoying or
unpleasant effect; annoy: *His rude manners grate on other people*.
2 rub harshly together: *to grate the teeth*. **3** make a grinding sound;
sound harshly. **4** move with a harsh sound: *The door grated on its
old, rusty hinges*. **5** wear down or grind off in small pieces: *to grate
cheese*. **6** *Archaic*. wear away by rubbing. [< OF *grater* < Gmc.]
☞ *Hom*. **great**.

grate·ful (grāt′fəl) *adj*. **1** feeling gratitude; thankful. **2** pleasing;
welcome: *a grateful breeze*. [< obs. *grate* agreeable (< L *gratus*) +
-ful] —**grate′ful·ly,** *adv*. —**grate′ful·ness,** *n*.
☞ *Syn*. **1**. Grateful, thankful = feeling or expressing gratitude. **Grateful**
emphasizes recognizing and gladly acknowledging favors or kindness shown to
one by others: *I am grateful to the friends who have helped me*. **Thankful,**
often used as if it were a less formal substitute for **grateful**, emphasizes giving
or feeling thanks for one's good fortune: *I am thankful that I have good
friends*.

grat·er (grā′tər) *n*. a device with a rough surface for wearing
vegetables, cheese, etc. down into shreds or particles.

grat·i·fi·ca·tion (grat′ə fə kā′shən) *n*. **1** gratifying or being
gratified: *The gratification of every wish of every person is not
possible*. **2** something that satisfies or pleases.

grat·i·fy (grat′ə fī′) *v*. **-fied, -fy·ing. 1** give pleasure or
satisfaction to; please: *Flattery gratifies a vain person*. **2** satisfy;
indulge: *to gratify a craving for chocolate*. [< F < L *gratificari* <
gratus pleasing + *facere* make, do] —**grat′i·fi′er,** *n*.
—**grat′i·fy′ing·ly,** *adv*.
☞ *Syn*. **2**. See note at **humor**.

grat·ing¹ (grāt′ing) *n*. a framework of bars over a window or
opening. [< *grate¹*]

grat·ing² (grāt′ing) *adj*. **1** unpleasant; annoying; irritating. **2** harsh
or jarring in sound: *a grating voice*. [< *grate²*]

grat·is (grat′is *or* grā′tis) *adv. or adj*. for nothing; free of charge.
[< L *gratis*, ult. < *gratia* favor]

grat·i·tude (grat′ə tyüd′ *or* grat′ə tüd′) *n*. a kindly feeling
because of a favor received; desire to do a favor in return;
thankfulness. [< LL *gratitudo* < *gratus* thankful]

gra·tu·i·tous (grə tyü′ə təs *or* grə tü′ə təs) *adj*. **1** freely given or
obtained; free. **2** without reason or cause; unnecessary; uncalled
for: *a gratuitous insult*. —**gra·tu′i·tous·ly,** *adv*.
—**gra·tu′i·tous·ness,** *n*.

gra·tu·i·ty (grə tyü′ə tē *or* grə tü′ə tē) *n., pl*. **-ties. 1** a present,
usually of money, given in place of or in addition to a fee, in return
for a service; tip. Gratuities are given to waiters, porters, servants,
etc.; they are voluntary but usually expected. **2** a payment given to
members of the armed forces on being discharged or at retirement.
[< Med.L *gratuitas* gift, apparently < L *gratuitus* free]

grat·u·late (grach′ə lāt′) *v*. **-lat·ed, -lat·ing.**
Archaic. **1** congratulate. **2** greet with joy. [< L *gratulatus*, ult. <
gratus pleasing, thankful. 16c.] —**grat′u·la′tion,** *n*.

grat·u·la·to·ry (grach′ə lə tôr′ē) *adj. Archaic*. congratulatory.

gra·va·men (grə vā′mən) *n., pl*. **-vam·i·na** (-vam′ə nə).
1 grievance. **2** *Law*. the part of an accusation that weighs most
heavily against the accused. [< L *gravamen* < *gravare* load <
gravis heavy]

grave¹ (grāv) *n*. **1** a hole dug in the ground in which a dead body
is to be buried. **2** a mound or monument over it. **3** any place that
becomes the receptacle of what is dead: *a watery grave*. **4** death.
make (someone) **turn over in his grave,** say or do something that
someone who is dead would have objected to strongly while alive.
one foot in the grave, near death.
secret as the grave, kept as a close secret. [OE *græf*. Related to
GRAVE³.]

grave² (grāv *for adj. 1-4;* gräv *or* grăv *for adj. 5, n.*) *adj*. **grav·er,
grav·est;** *n*. —*adj*. **1** important; weighty; momentous: *It was a grave
decision to make*. **2** serious; threatening: *grave questions, doubts,
symptoms, news*. **3** dignified; sober; solemn: *a grave face, a grave
ceremony*. **4** sombre: *grave colors*. **5** *Phonetics*. **a** low in pitch; not

acute. **b** having a grave accent. —*n.* a grave accent. [< F < L *gravis* serious] —**grave′ly,** *adv.* —**grave′ness,** *n.*

➤ *Syn. adj.* **3. Grave, serious, sober** = thoughtful and free from frivolity or gaiety in mood, looks, behavior, etc. **Grave** emphasizes dignity and lack of gaiety, especially in looks, behavior, and attitude, and suggests having a great problem on one's mind: *His expression was grave.* **Serious** emphasizes being thoughtful, concerned with important things, and free from frivolity or giddiness, especially in disposition and manner: *He became serious when he spoke of finding a job.* **Sober** suggests a settled or self-restrained seriousness or gravity, especially in looks, behavior, and speech: *His words were sober and wise.*

grave³ (grāv) *v.* **graved, graved** or **grav·en, grav·ing. 1** *Archaic.* engrave; carve; sculpture. **2** impress deeply; fix firmly. [OE *grafan*] —**grav′er,** *n.*

grave⁴ (grāv) *v.* **graved, grav·ing.** clean (the bottom of a wooden ship) and cover with tar. [origin uncertain]

gra·ve⁵ (grä′vā) *adj., adv. Music.* —*adj.* slow and solemn in tempo. —*adv.* slowly and solemnly. [< Ital. *grave,* learned borrowing from L *gravis* serious, heavy]

grave accent a mark (`) placed over a vowel to indicate stress, pitch, quality of sound (as in French *père*), or syllabic value (as in *belovèd*).

grave·dig·ger (grāv′dig′ər) *n.* a person whose work is digging graves.

grav·el (grav′əl) *n., v.* **-elled** or **-eled, -el·ling** or **-el·ing.** —*n.* **1** pebbles and pieces of rock coarser than sand. Gravel is much used for roads and walks. **2** a road surfaced with gravel. **3** small concretions formed in the kidneys or bladder. —*v.* **1** cover with gravel: *to gravel a road.* **2** puzzle; perplex. [ME < OF *gravele,* dim. of *grave* sand, seashore < Celtic]

grav·el·ly (grav′əl ē) *adj.* **1** having much gravel. **2** consisting of or like gravel. **3** rough; rasping; grating: *a gravelly voice.*

gra·ven (grā′vən) *adj.* —*adj.* **1** engraved; carved; sculptured. **2** deeply impressed; firmly fixed. —*v.* a pp. of **grave³.**

graven image 1 statue. **2** idol.

grav·er (grā′vər) *n.* **1** a tool for cutting, engraving, etc. **2** engraver.

grave·stone (grāv′stōn′) *n.* a stone that marks a grave.

grave·yard (grāv′yärd′) *n.* **1** a place for burying the dead; cemetery; burial ground. **2** a lot, yard, etc. in which old or useless objects are discarded. **3** *Slang.* graveyard shift: *He has been working on graveyard for a month now.*

graveyard shift *Slang.* the working hours between midnight and the morning shift.

gra·vim·e·ter (grə vim′ə tər) *n.* a device used to measure gravity at the earth's surface; a gravity meter. [< F *gravimètre* < L *gravis* heavy + F *mètre* measure]

grav·i·met·ric (grav′ə met′rik) *adj.* **1** of or having to do with gravimetry. **2** *Chemistry.* of or having to do with measurement by weight. **3** of or having to do with the use of gravity measurements to calculate distances and draw maps.

gra·vim·e·try (grə vim′ə trē) *n.* the measurement of weight, specific gravity, or density.

grav·i·tate (grav′ə tāt′) *v.* **-tat·ed, -tat·ing. 1** move or tend to move by gravitation. **2** settle down; sink; fall: *The sand and dirt in the water gravitated to the bottom of the bottle.* **3** tend to go; be strongly attracted. [< NL *gravitare,* ult. < L *gravis* heavy]

grav·i·ta·tion (grav′ə tā′shən) *n.* **1** *Physics.* the fact that the earth pulls any object toward it and that the sun, moon, stars, and other such bodies in the universe do the same; the force or pull that makes bodies in the universe tend to move toward one another. **2** a moving or tendency to move caused by this force. **3** a settling down; sinking; falling. **4** a natural tendency toward some point or object of influence: *the gravitation of population to the cities.*

grav·i·ta·tion·al (grav′ə tā′shən əl or grav′ə tāsh′nəl) *adj.* of gravitation; having to do with gravitation. —**grav′i·ta′tion·al·ly,** *adv.*

grav·i·ty (grav′ə tē) *n., pl.* **-ties. 1 a** the natural force that causes objects to move or tend to move toward the centre of the earth or moon, or a planet. The gravity is slightly less at the top of a high mountain than at sea level. **b** the natural force that makes objects move or tend to move toward each other; gravitation. **2** (*adj.*) of or having to do with gravity or gravitation or the effect of either. **3** heaviness; weight (*used especially in* **centre of gravity**): *The toy was hard to tip over because it had a low centre of gravity.* **4** a serious or solemn manner or behavior: *a look of gravity.* **5** a serious or critical character: *When he had explained the gravity of the situation, they were all willing to help.* [< L *gravitas* < *gravis* heavy]

gra·vure (grə vyür′ or grā′vyür) *n.* **1** photogravure. **2** a plate or print produced by photogravure. [< F *gravure* < *graver* engrave < Gmc.]

gra·vy (grā′vē) *n., pl.* **-vies. 1** a sauce for meat, potatoes, etc. made from the juice that comes out of meat in cooking. **2** the juice itself. **3** *Slang.* easy gain or profit over and above what would normally be expected: *We've covered all our expenses; the rest is gravy.* [ME *grave,* a misreading of OF *grané* sauce, originally, properly grained, seasoned, ult. < L *granum* grain]

gravy train *Slang.* a situation in which good profits can be realized with little effort.

ride a gravy train, a realize easy profits. **b** enjoy an easy life.

gray (grā) See **grey.**

gray·beard (grā′bērd′) See **greybeard.**

gray–head·ed (grā′hed′id) See **grey-headed.**

gray·ish (grā′ish) See **greyish.**

gray jay Canada jay.

gray·lag (grā′lag′) See **greylag.**

gray·ling (grā′ling) *n.* **1** any of a genus (*Thymallus*) making up a subfamily (Thymallinae) of freshwater fishes found in the cold, clear streams of northern North America, Europe, and Asia, famous as a food and game fish and also for their beautiful coloring and the smell of wild thyme that freshly caught specimens have. Some authorities place the graylings in a distinct family (Thymallidae). **2** any of various greyish or brownish butterflies (family Satyridae), especially a European species, *Hipparchia semele.*

graze¹ (grāz) *v.* **grazed, graz·ing;** *n.* —*v.* **1** feed on growing grass. Cattle and sheep graze. **2** put (cattle, sheep, etc.) to feed on growing grass or a pasture. **3** tend or look after (cattle, sheep, etc.) while they are grazing. —*n.* a grazing or feeding on grass. [OE *grasian* < *græs* grass] —**graz′er,** *n.*

graze² (grāz) *v.* **grazed, graz·ing;** *n.* —*v.* **1** touch lightly in passing; rub lightly (against). **2** scrape the skin from: *The bullet grazed his shoulder.* —*n.* **1** a slight wound made by grazing. **2** the act of grazing. [origin uncertain]

gra·zier (grā′zhər) *n.* a person who grazes cattle for market.

gra·zing (grāz′ing) *n.* the growing grass that cattle, sheep, etc. feed on; pasture.

Gr.Brit. or **Gr.Br.** Great Britain.

grease (grēs) *n., v.* **greased, greas·ing.** —*n.* **1** animal fat that has been melted and then allowed to cool to a soft solid. **2** any thick, oily substance, especially one used as a lubricant. **3** shorn, uncleaned, wool. **4** the natural oil in raw wool. **5** *Hunting.* the fat or fatness of deer, etc. Animals fat enough for killing are said to be **in grease,** or **in pride** or **prime of grease.** —*v.* **1** smear with grease; put grease on or in: *Long-distance swimmers grease their bodies for protection against the cold water.* **2** lubricate with grease: *He took his car to have it greased.* **3** *Slang.* give money to as a bribe or tip. [ME < OF *graisse* < L *crassus* fat] ➤ *Hom.* **Greece.**

grease cup a small cup to hold oil or grease, fastened on machinery to supply grease to parts that need it.

grease gun a device, usually consisting of a grease-filled cylinder with a plunger at one end and a nozzle at the other, for lubricating bearings, etc.

greas·er (grē′sər) *n.* **1** one that greases. **2** *U.S. Derogatory slang.* a Mexican or Spanish American.

grease·wood (grēs′wùd′) *n.* **1** a low, spiny shrub (*Sarcobatus vermiculatus*) of the goosefoot family found in alkaline regions in the western parts of Canada and the United States. **2** any of various similar or related shrubs.

greas·y (grē′sē) *adj.* **greas·i·er, greas·i·est. 1** smeared with grease; having grease on it. **2** containing much grease: *greasy food.* **3** like grease; smooth; slippery: *The roads were greasy after the snowfall.* **4** disagreeably unctuous; oily in manner, expression, etc. —**greas′i·ly,** *adv.* —**greas′i·ness,** *n.*

greasy spoon *Slang.* a small, cheap restaurant having an unsanitary appearance.

great (grāt) *adj., n.* —*adj.* **1** big; large: *a great house, a great crowd.* **2** more than usual; much: *great ignorance.* **3** important; remarkable; famous: *a great composer.* **4** most important; main; chief: *the great seal.* **5** noble; generous: *a great heart.* **6** much in use; favorite: *That is a great habit of his.* **7** very much of a: *a great talker.* **8** *Informal.* very good; fine: *We had a great time at the party.* **9** *Informal.* skilful; expert: *He's great at skiing.* **10** in names of relationship, of the next generation before or after: *great-grandmother, great-grandson.*

go great guns, *Slang.* move vigorously ahead; advance at full speed. —*n.* Usually, **greats,** *pl. Informal.* a great or outstanding person; celebrity: *All the greats of show business have appeared at the Palace.* [OE *grēat*] —**great′ly,** *adv.* —**great′ness,** *n.*

➤ *Hom.* **grate.**

Syn. 1, 2. Great, large, big = above average in size or measure. **Great** chiefly means "more than usual" (in degree), but sometimes is used to describe physical size that is impressive in some way: *We saw the great redwoods* (size). *They are trees of great age* (degree). **Large** = of great size, amount, etc. but never degree: *We saw many large trees.* **Big** particularly emphasizes weight and bulk: *A redwood is a big tree, very heavy and thick.*

great–aunt (grāt′ant′) *n.* an aunt of one's father or mother; grandaunt.

Great Bear *Astronomy.* Ursa Major.

great circle **1** any circle on the surface of a sphere having its plane passing through the centre of the sphere. The equator is one of the great circles of the earth. **2** an arc of such a circle; the line of shortest distance between two points on the earth's surface.

great·coat (grāt′kōt′) *n.* a heavy overcoat, especially one worn by members of the armed forces.

Great Dane a breed of large, rangy, powerful dog with a smooth, short coat.

Great Dog *Astronomy.* Canis Major.

great–grand·child (grāt′gran′chīld′ *or* -grand′-) *n., pl.* -chil·dren. a grandchild of one's son or daughter.

great–grand·daugh·ter (grāt′gran′do′tər *or* -gran′dô′tər) *n.* a granddaughter of one's son or daughter.

great–grand·fa·ther (grāt′gran′fo′ŦHər *or* -grand′-) *n.* a grandfather of one's father or mother.

great–grand·moth·er (grāt′gran′muŦH′ər *or* -grand′-) *n.* a grandmother of one's father or mother.

great–grand·par·ent (grāt′gran′per′ənt *or* -grand′-) *n.* a grandfather or grandmother of one's mother or father.

great–grand·son (grāt′gran′sun′ *or* -grand′-) *n.* a grandson of one's son or daughter.

great grey owl a very large owl (*Strix nebulosa*) of coniferous forests of the northern hemisphere, having a round head with a very large face, yellow eyes, a long tail, and grey plumage. It is the largest North American owl.

great–heart·ed (grāt′här′tid) *adj.* **1** noble; generous. **2** brave; fearless. —**great′-heart′ed·ness,** *n.*

great horned owl a large owl (*Bubo virginianus*) of the New World having mottled brown-and-white plumage and large, hornlike tufts of feathers on the head.

great·ly (grāt′lē) *adv.* to a great degree; very much.

Great Mogul the emperor of Delhi, of the Mogul dynasty that ruled over a large part of India from 1526 to 1857.
great mogul, a great or important person, especially a tycoon.

great–neph·ew (grāt′nef′yū) *n.* a son of one's nephew or niece; grandnephew.

great–niece (grāt′nēs′) *n.* a daughter of one's nephew or niece; grandniece.

Great Russians a Slavic people living in central northern and NE Russia.

great seal the most important seal of a country, province, etc. stamped on official documents as proof of their approval by the government.

Great Spirit a deity worshipped by certain tribes or groups of North American Indians.

great–un·cle (grāt′ung′kəl) *n.* an uncle of one's father or mother; granduncle.

Great Wall of China a huge stone wall on the boundary between northern and northwestern China and Mongolia, about 2400 kilometres long. It was begun in the third century B.C. for the defence of China against attack by nomads from the north.

Great War the First World War, from 1914 to 1918.

Great White Way the brightly lighted theatre district along Broadway, a street in New York City.

greave (grēv) *n.* a piece of armor for the front of the leg below the knee (*usually used in the plural*). See **armor** for picture. [ME < OF *greves,* pl.; origin uncertain]

grebe (grēb) *n.* any of a family (Podicipitidae) of swimming and diving birds resembling loons, having lobed toes and a pointed bill. Most grebes have crests or ruffs during the nesting season. [< F *grèbe*]

Gre·cian (grē′shən) *adj., n.* —*adj.* **1** of architecture, art, facial features, etc., conforming to the styles or forms of ancient Greece: *a Grecian profile, a façade of Grecian elegance.* **2** Greek. —*n.* **1** a Greek. **2** a person skilled in the Greek language or literature.

Grecian nose a straight nose; a nose that does not dip at the forehead.

Greco– *combining form.* **1** Greece; Greek things: *Grecophile = a lover of Greece or Greek things.* **2** Greek and —: *Greco-Roman = Greek and Roman.* [< L *Graeco-* < Gk. *Graikos* a Greek]

hat, āge, fär; let, ēqual, tėrm; it, īce
hot, ōpen, ôrder; oil, out; cup, pút, rüle,
above, takən, pencəl, lemən, circəs
ch, child; ng, long; sh, ship
th, thin; ŦH, then; zh, measure

Gre·co·phile (grē′kō fīl′ *or* grē′kō fil) *n.* a person who loves Greece and Greek things.

Gre·co–Ro·man (grē′kō rō′mən) *adj.* Greek and Roman.

greed (grēd) *n.* the wanting of more than one's share; extreme or excessive desire: *a miser's greed for money.* [< *greedy*]

greed·y (grē′dē) *adj.* **greed·i·er, greed·i·est.** **1** wanting to get more than one's share; having a very great desire to possess something. **2** wanting to eat or drink a great deal in a hurry; piggish. [OE *grǣdig*] —**greed′i·ly,** *adv.* —**greed′i·ness,** *n.*

Greek (grēk) *n., adj.* —*n.* **1** a native or inhabitant of Greece. **2** a person of Greek descent. **3** the Indo-European language of the Greeks. **Ancient Greek** is the language used from prehistoric times until about A.D. 200; **late Greek,** the language from about A.D. 200 until about 700; **medieval Greek,** the language during the Middle Ages until about A.D. 1500; **modern Greek,** the language from about 1500 on. **4** a member of the Greek Orthodox Church.
it's Greek to me, I can't understand it.
—*adj.* **1** of or having to do with Greece, its people, or their language. **2** *Architecture.* of or having to do with a style developed by the ancient Greeks, characterized by symmetry and graceful proportion, plain or fluted pillars, and pediments. **3** of or having to do with the Greek Orthodox Church. **4** of or having to do with the Orthodox Eastern Church. [OE *grēcas* (earlier *Crēcas*), pl. < L *Graeci,* pl. of *Graecus* a Greek < Gk. *Graikos*]

Greek Catholic **1** a member of a small Eastern rite church within the Catholic Church, originating in SE Europe and now active especially in Greece and Turkey. **2** a member of the Greek Orthodox Church. **3** of or having to do with Greek Catholics or their churches.

Greek cross a cross whose four arms are of the same length and form right angles. See **cross** for picture.

Greek fire a substance used in warfare by the Byzantine Greeks, probably a petroleum-based mixture that apparently burst into flame spontaneously when wet and that could not be put out with water.

Greek gift a gift offered to conceal treachery or as part of a treacherous plan. [< the story of the Trojan horse]

Greek Orthodox Church **1** the established church of Greece, a member of the Orthodox Eastern Church. **2** Orthodox Eastern Church.

green (grēn) *n., adj., v.* —*n.* **1** the color of most growing plants, grass, and leaves; the color in the spectrum between yellow and blue. **2** green coloring matter, dye, paint, etc. **3** green cloth or clothing. **4** grassy land or a plot of grassy ground. **5** putting green. **6 greens,** *pl.* **a** green leaves and branches used for decoration, wreaths, garlands, etc. **b** leaves and stems of plants used as food: *salad greens.*
the Green, the national color of the Irish Republic. —*adj.* **1** having the color green. **2** covered with growing plants, grass, leaves, etc.: *green fields.* **3** characterized by growing grass, etc.: *a green Christmas.* **4** undecayed: *green old age.* **5** not dried, cured, seasoned, or otherwise prepared for use: *green tobacco.* **6** not ripe; not fully grown: *green peaches.* **7** not trained or experienced; not mature in age, judgment, etc.: *a green girl.* **8** easily fooled; easy to trick or cheat. **9** recent; fresh; new: *a green wound.* **10** having a pale, sickly color because of fear, jealousy, or sickness.
—*v.* make or become green. [OE *grēne.* Related to GRASS, GROW.] —**green′ness,** *n.*

green·back (grēn′bak′) *n.* **1** *U.S.* a piece of United States paper money having the back printed in green. **2** *Slang.* paper money.

green bean any of various cultivated varieties of bean whose green pods with the seeds inside are used as a vegetable when still young and tender.

green·bri·er (grēn′brī′ər) *n.* any of several climbing plants (genus *Smilax*) of the lily family having prickly stems and greenish flowers.

Green Chamber a name given to the Canadian House of Commons because of the color of the rugs, draperies, etc. in the room in which the House meets.

green corn ears of sweet corn in the young, tender, milky stage, suitable for eating roasted or boiled.

green·er·y (grēn′ər ē *or* grēn′rē) *n., pl.* -er·ies. **1** green plants,

grass, or leaves; verdure. **2** a place where green plants are grown or kept.

green–eyed (grēn′īd′) *adj.* **1** having green eyes. **2** jealous.

green·gage (grēn′gāj′) *n.* a large plum having a light-green skin and pulp. [after Sir William *Gage*, who introduced it into England c. 1725]

green·gro·cer (grēn′grō′sər) *n. Brit.* a person who sells fresh vegetables and fruit.

green·gro·cer·y (grēn′grō′sər ē *or* -grōs′rē) *n., pl.* **-cer·ies.** *Brit.* a store that sells fresh vegetables and fruit.

green·heart (grēn′härt′) *n.* **1** a large, tropical American tree (*Ocotea rodioei*, also classified as *Nectandra rodioei*) of the laurel family valued especially for its timber and also for the quinine-like alkaloid obtained from its bark. **2** the strong, dense, durable, greenish wood of this tree. **3** any of various similar trees or their wood.

green·horn (grēn′hôrn′) *n. Informal.* **1** a person without experience. **2** a person easy to trick or cheat. [with reference to the green horns of young oxen]

green·house (grēn′hous′) *n.* a building with transparent or translucent glass or plastic roof and sides, used for growing and displaying plants in a controlled atmosphere.

green·ing (grēn′ing) *n.* an apple having a yellowish-green skin when ripe.

green·ish (grēn′ish) *adj.* somewhat green.

Green·land whale (grēn′lənd) bowhead.

green light *Informal.* permission to proceed on a particular task or undertaking.

green manure 1 green, leafy plants ploughed under to enrich the soil. **2** manure that has not decayed.

green onion a young onion pulled before it is mature. Its thin, tender green leaves and small, undeveloped bulb are eaten raw, as in salads, or cooked.

green·room (grēn′rüm′ *or* -rum′) *n. Theatre.* a room for the use of actors and actresses when not on the stage.

green·stone (grēn′stōn′) *n.* **1** *Geology.* any of various igneous rocks having a greenish color. **2** a variety of jade. **3** a piece of this stone.

green·sward (grēn′swôrd′) *n.* growing grass; turf.

green tea tea made from leaves that have been steamed and then crushed and dried in ovens. Green tea has not been fermented like black tea.

green thumb a remarkable ability to grow flowers, vegetables, etc., especially as a hobby: *When Aunt Mary saw our garden, she said Mother must certainly have a green thumb.*

green turtle a large, edible sea turtle (*Chelonia mydas*) found in warm coastal waters throughout the world, having greenish flesh that is especially valued for turtle soup.

Green·wich mean time (grin′ij, grin′ich, *or* gren′ich) the basis for setting standard time in England and elsewhere, reckoned from the meridian passing through Greenwich. Greenwich mean time is the basic time used in sea navigation. Also, **Greenwich Time.** *Abbrev.:* GMT or G.M.T.

Greenwich Village (gren′ich) a section of New York City, famous as a district where artists, writers, etc. live.

green·wood (grēn′wúd′) *n.* the forest in spring and summer when the trees are green with leaves.

greet (grēt) *v.* **1** speak or write to in a friendly, polite way; address in welcome. **2** address; salute: *She greeted him sternly.* **3** receive: *His speech was greeted with cheers.* **4** present itself to; meet: *A strange sight greeted her eyes.* [OE *grētan*] —**greet′er,** *n.*

greet·ing (grēt′ing) *n.* **1** the act or words of a person who greets another; welcome. **2 greetings,** *pl.* friendly wishes on a special occasion: *Christmas greetings.*

gre·gar·i·ous (grə ger′ē əs *or* grə gar′ē əs) *adj.* **1** living in flocks, herds, or other groups: *Sheep and cattle are gregarious.* **2** fond of being with others. **3** of or having to do with a flock or crowd. [< L *gregarius* < *grex, gregis* flock] —**gre·gar′i·ous·ly,** *adv.* —**gre·gar′i·ous·ness,** *n.*

Gre·go·ri·an (grə gô′rē ən) *adj.* **1** of or having to do with Pope Gregory I, pope from A.D. 590 to 604: *Gregorian music.* **2** of or introduced by Pope Gregory XIII, pope from 1572 to 1585.

Gregorian calendar the calendar now in use in most countries, introduced by Pope Gregory XIII in 1582 as an improvement on the Julian calendar.

Gregorian chant vocal music having free rhythm and a limited scale, introduced by Pope Gregory I, 540?-604, and still used in the Roman Catholic Church. It is usually sung without an accompaniment.

grem·lin (grem′lən) *n.* an imaginary mischievous spirit or goblin, especially one supposed to trouble airplane pilots. [origin uncertain]

gre·nade (grə nād′) *n.* **1** a small bomb, usually thrown by hand: *The soldiers threw grenades into the enemy's trenches.* **2** a round, glass bottle filled with chemicals that scatter as the glass breaks. Fire grenades are thrown on fires to extinguish them. [< F < OF (*pume*) *grenate* pomegranate, fruit full of seeds; ult. < L *granum* seed, grain]

gren·a·dier (gren′ə dēr′) *n.* **1** originally, a soldier who threw grenades. **2** today, a soldier in any one of several infantry regiments. [< F *grenadier* < *grenade.* See GRENADE.]

gren·a·dine¹ (gren′ə dēn′ *or* gren′ə dēn′) *n.* a thin, openwork fabric used for women's dresses. [< F, ? named for *Granada,* Spain]

gren·a·dine² (gren′ə dēn′ *or* gren′ə dēn′) *n.* a syrup made from pomegranate or currant juice. [< F *grenadin* < *grenade.* See GRENADE.]

Gret·na Green (gret′nə) a village in S Scotland in which many runaway couples from England used to be married.

grew (grü) *v.* pt. of **grow.**

grew·some (grü′səm) *adj.* gruesome. —**grew′some·ness,** *n.*

grey (grā) *n., adj., v.* —*n.* **1** the color made by mixing black and white. **2** something having this color, as: **a** a grey cloth or clothing. **b** a grey horse. —*adj.* **1** having a color between black and white: *Ashes are grey.* **2** having grey hair: *He's very grey.* **3** old; ancient. **4** dark; gloomy; dismal: *a grey day.* **5** being intermediate or indeterminate in character, condition, or situation: *There are too many grey areas in our club's constitution.* —*v.* make or become grey. Also, **gray.** [OE *græg*] —**grey′ly,** *adv.* —**grey′ness,** *n.*

grey·beard (grā′bērd′) *n.* an old man. Also, **graybeard.**

Grey Cup *Cdn.* **1** a trophy awarded to the champion professional football team each year in Canada. It is competed for annually in a single game by the winning teams of the Eastern Football Conference and the Western Football Conference. **2** the game played to decide the winner of this trophy. [< Earl *Grey,* Governor General of Canada 1904-1911, who first presented the cup in 1909]

grey eminence éminence grise.

Grey Friar a Franciscan friar.

grey–head·ed (grā′hed′id) *adj.* having grey hair. Also, **gray-headed.**

grey·hound (grā′hound′) *n.* a breed of tall, slender, swift dog having a smooth coat and sharp sight. [OE *grīghund*; not connected with *grey*; cf. ON *greyhunda* < *grey* bitch]

grey·ish (grā′ish) *adj.* somewhat grey. Also, **grayish.**

grey jay Canada jay.

grey·lag (grā′lag′) *n.* a large, grey goose (*Anser anser*) common in Europe and Asia.

grey matter 1 the greyish tissue in the brain and spinal cord that contains nerve cells and some nerve fibres. **2** *Informal.* intelligence; brains.

grey mullet mullet (def. 1).

grey seal a large, silvery to dusky grey or brownish hair seal (*Halichoerus grypus*) found along the temperate coasts of the Atlantic Ocean.

grey squirrel a common arboreal squirrel (*Sciurus carolinensis*) native to E North America from the Gulf of Mexico north to the Great Lakes region, and now also found in Europe. The typical color of this squirrel is grizzled grey, but there is a common black phase, especially in the northern part of its range.

grey wolf timber wolf.

grid (grid) *n.* **1** a framework of parallel iron bars; grating; gridiron. **2** *Military.* the numbered squares drawn on maps and used for map references. **3** *Surveying.* **a** the system of survey lines running parallel to lines of latitude and longitude, used in the division of an area into counties, sections, lots, etc. **b** one of these lines. **4** the lead plate in a storage battery. **5** an electrode in a vacuum tube that controls the flow of current between the filament and the plate. **6** a network of electric lines and connections. **7** *Theatre.* a framework above the stage, from which scenery, light, etc. are hung and manipulated. [shortened form of *gridiron*]

grid·dle (grid′əl) *n., v.* **-dled, -dling.** —*n.* a heavy flat plate of metal or soapstone, used for cooking bacon, pancakes, etc. —*v.* cook on a griddle. [ME < OF **gredil* (cf. OF *grediller* singe) < L *craticulum.* See GRILL.]

grid·dle·cake (grid′əl kāk′) *n.* a thin, flat cake of batter cooked on a griddle; pancake; flapjack.

grid·i·ron (grid′ī′ərn) *n.* **1** grill (def. 1). **2** a framework or network resembling a grill. **3** a football field. **4** *Theatre.* grid. [ME *gredire* griddle, var. of *gredile* < OF * *gredil* (see GRIDDLE); final element assimilated to *iron*]

grid leak a very high resistance placed in a vacuum tube to permit the escape of excess electrons.

grid road *Cdn.* a municipal road that follows a grid line established by survey. In Saskatchewan, these roads are built two miles (about 3.2 km) apart from north to south and one mile (about 1.6 km) from east to west.

grief (grēf) *n.* **1** deep sadness caused by trouble or loss; heavy sorrow. **2** a cause of sadness or sorrow: *Her son's incurable illness was a great grief to her.*
come to grief, have trouble; fail: *Although he worked hard, his plan came to grief.* [ME < OF *grief* < *grever.* See GRIEVE.]
☛ *Syn.* **1.** See note at **sorrow.**

griev·ance (grēv′əns) *n.* a real or imagined wrong; reason for being angry or annoyed; cause for complaint.

grieve (grēv) *v.* **grieved, griev·ing. 1** feel grief; be very sad: *She grieved over her kitten's death.* **2** cause to feel grief; make very sad; afflict. [ME < OF *grever,* ult. < L *gravis* heavy] —**griev′er,** *n.* —**griev′ing·ly,** *adv.*

griev·ous (grēv′əs) *adj.* **1** hard to bear; causing great pain or suffering: *grievous cruelty.* **2** flagrant; atrocious: *Wasting food when people are starving is a grievous wrong.* **3** causing grief: *a grievous loss.* **4** full of grief; showing grief: *a grievous cry.* —**griev′ous·ly,** *adv.* —**griev′ous·ness,** *n.*

grif·fin (grif′ən) *n.* a mythical creature with the head, wings, and forelegs of an eagle, and the body, hind legs, and tail of a lion. Also, **griffon, gryphon.** [ME < OF *grifon* < L *gryphus,* var. of *gryps* < Gk.]

grif·fon¹ (grif′ən) *n.* either of two breeds of dog: the **Brussels griffon,** a terrier-like toy dog with a smooth or wiry coat, originally from Belgium; and the **wire-haired pointing griffon,** a medium-sized sporting dog with a wiry, grey-and-chestnut coat, originally from the Netherlands. [< F *griffon,* an English breed of dog < OF *grifon.* See GRIFFIN.]

grif·fon² (grif′ən) See **griffin.**

grift·er (grif′tər) *n. Slang.* a swindler, especially one who operates a dishonest game of chance at a fair, circus, etc. [perhaps var. of *grafter*]

grig (grig) *n. Dialect.* **1** a small or young eel. **2** cricket or grasshopper. **3** a cheerful, lively person. [ME *grege,* originally meaning dwarf; origin uncertain. 14c.]

grill (gril) *n., v.* —*n.* **1** a cooking utensil consisting of a framework of thin metal bars on which meat, fish, etc. are placed to be cooked by a fire or electric heating element. **2** food that is cooked in this way. **3** a restaurant or dining room specializing in broiled meat, fish, etc.
—*v.* **1** cook by direct heat, as on a grill; broil. **2** torture or torment with heat: *grilled by the hot desert sun.* **3** question severely and persistently: *The detectives grilled the prisoner until he confessed.* [< F *gril* < OF *greil,* earlier *grail* < L *craticulum,* var. of *craticula* gridiron, dim. of *cratis* latticework. Doublet of GRIDDLE.] —**grill′er,** *n.*

grille (gril) *n.* an ornamental metal grating used as a barrier or screen. The grille on the front of a car protects the radiator. [< F < L *cracticula* < *cratis* hurdle]

grill·room (gril′rüm′ or -rüm′) *n.* grill (def. 3).

grilse (grils) *n., pl.* **grilse** or **gril·ses.** a salmon that is returning from the sea to fresh water for the first time. [ME; ? var. of *grisle* greyish]

grim (grim) *adj.* **grim·mer, grim·mest. 1** without mercy; stern; harsh; fierce. **2** not yielding; not relenting. **3** looking stern, fierce, or harsh. **4** horrible; ghastly: *He made grim jokes about death and ghosts.* [OE *grimm* fierce] —**grim′ly,** *adv.* —**grim·ness,** *n.*

gri·mace (grə mās′ or grim′is) *n., v.* **-maced, -mac·ing.** —*n.* a twisting of the face; an ugly or funny smile. —*v.* make grimaces. [< F < Sp. *grimazo* panic] —**gri·mac′er,** *n.*

gri·mal·kin (grə mal′kən) *n.* **1** cat. **2** an old female cat. **3** a spiteful old woman. [probably < *grey* + *Malkin,* dim. of *Maud,* proper name]

grime (grīm) *n., v.* **grimed, grim·ing.** —*n.* dirt rubbed deeply and firmly into a surface: *the grime on a coal miner's hands.* —*v.* cover with grime; make very dirty. [? OE *grīma* mask]

grim·y (grīm′ē) *adj.* **grim·i·er, grim·i·est.** covered with grime; very dirty. —**grim′i·ly,** *adv.* —**grim′i·ness,** *n.*

grin (grin) *v.* **grinned, grin·ning;** *n.* —*v.* **1** smile broadly. **2** show, make or express by smiling broadly: *He grinned approval.* **3** draw back the lips and show the teeth in anger, pain, scorn, etc.: *A snarling dog grins.*
—*n.* **1** a broad smile. **2** the act of showing the teeth in anger, pain, scorn, etc. [OE *grennian*] —**grin′ner,** *n.*

hat, āge, fär; let, ēqual, tèrm; it, īce
hot, ōpen, ôrder; oil, out; cup, pút, rüle,
əbove, takən, pencəl, lemən, circəs
ch, child; ng, long; sh, ship
th, thin; ℲH, then; zh, measure

grind (grīnd) *v.* **ground** or *(rare)* **grind·ed, grind·ing;** *n.* —*v.* **1** crush into bits or into powder: *Our back teeth grind food. Wheat is ground into flour in a mill.* **2** produce or make by grinding: *to grind flour.* **3** crush by harshness or cruelty: *The slaves were ground down by their masters.* **4** sharpen, smooth, or wear by rubbing on something rough: *An axe is ground on a grindstone.* **5** rub harshly (on, into, against, or together): *to grind one's heel into the earth, to grind one's teeth in anger.* **6** work by turning a crank: *to grind a coffee mill.* **7** produce by turning a crank: *to grind out music on a hand organ.* **8** *Informal.* work or study long and hard.
—*n.* **1** the act of grinding. **2** a grinding sound. **3** *Informal.* long, hard work or study. **4** a dull and laborious task. **5** *Informal.* a person who works long and hard at his studies. [OE *grindan*]

grind·er (grīn′dər) *n.* **1** a person or thing that grinds: *a coffee grinder.* **2** a man or machine that sharpens tools. **3** a back tooth for grinding food; molar.

grind·stone (grīn′stōn′ or grīnd′-) *n.* a flat, round stone set in a frame and turned by a crank, treadle, etc. It is used to sharpen tools, such as axes and knives, or to smooth and polish things.
have, keep or **put** (one's) **nose to the grindstone,** work long and hard.

grin·go (gring′gō) *n., pl.* **-gos.** *Informal. Often derogatory.* a white foreigner; especially, as used in Mexico and N South America, an American. [< Mexican Spanish, possibly an alteration of *griego* Greek]

grip (grip) *n., v.* **gripped, grip·ping.** —*n.* **1** a firm hold; seizing and holding tight; tight grasp. **2** the power of gripping: *a healthy grip.* **3** the manner or style of holding something, such as a golf club or tennis racket. **4** a tool or device for grasping and holding something. **5** a part to take hold of; handle: *the grip of a suitcase.* **6** a special way of shaking hands, as used by members of a secret society to identify each other. **7** a small suitcase; travelling bag. **8** firm control or mastery: *in the grip of fear, to get a grip on oneself. The country is in the grip of winter.* **9** mental grasp. **10** a sudden, sharp pain. **11** a stagehand or a member of a film production crew who adjusts sets or scenery and props.
come to grips (with), a attempt to deal or cope with (a problem, situation, etc.). **b** engage in combat with (an enemy).
—*v.* **1** take a firm hold on; seize and hold tight. **2** get and keep the interest and attention of: *An exciting story grips the reader.* [OE *gripe* < *grīpan* grasp] —**grip′less,** *adj.* —**grip′per,** *n.*

gripe (grīp) *v.* **griped, grip·ing;** *n.* —*v.* **1** *Informal.* complain, especially continually and in an ill-tempered manner: *What's he griping about now?* **2** cause a sudden, sharp pain in the bowels of (a person). **3** experience such pain. **4** *Archaic.* clutch; grip. **5** *Archaic.* oppress or distress.
—*n.* **1** *Informal.* a grievance or complaint. **2** Usually, **gripes,** *pl.* colic. **3** *Archaic.* the act of clutching or gripping. **4** *Archaic.* grasp; control: *The empire held very small nations in its gripe.* [OE *grīpan*] —**grip′er,** *n.*

grippe (grip) *n.* a contagious disease like a very severe cold with fever; influenza. [< F < Russian *khrip* hoarseness]

grip·ping (grip′ing) *adj.* that grips; especially, that holds the attention or interest. —**grip′ping·ly,** *adv.*

Gri·sel·da (grə zel′də) *n.* a very, meek, patient woman. [< *Griselda,* the heroine of several medieval romances, including Chaucer's *Clerk's Tale,* famed for her meekness and patience when cruelly treated by her husband]

gri·sette (gri zet′) *n.* a French working girl, especially a flirtatious seamstress or shop assistant. [< F *grisette* < *gris* grey; from usual color of their dresses]

gris·ly (griz′lē) *adj.* **-li·er, -li·est.** frightful; horrible; ghastly. [OE *grislic*] —**gris′li·ness,** *n.*
☛ *Hom.* **grizzly.**
☛ *Syn.* See note at **ghastly.**

grist (grist) *n.* **1** grain to be ground. **2** grain that has been ground; meal or flour.
grist to (someone's) **mill,** source of profit to someone. [OE *grīst* < *grindan* grind]

gris·tle (gris′əl) *n.* cartilage; firm, tough, elastic tissue. Babies have gristle instead of bone in some parts of the skull. [OE]

gris·tly (gris′lē) *adj.* **-tli·er, -tli·est.** of, containing, or like gristle.

grist mill a mill for grinding grain.

grit (grit) *n., v.* **grit·ted, grit·ting.** —*n.* **1** very fine bits of gravel or sand: *There was grit in the spinach.* **2** a coarse sandstone. **3** the

grain or texture of a stone with respect to fineness, coarseness, etc. **4** the abrasive quality of a sanding disk, cloth, paper, etc. **5** *Informal.* courage; pluck: *The fighter showed plenty of grit.* **6 Grit,** *Cdn. Informal.* **a** a member of the Liberal party in Canada. **b** (*adj.*) of or associated with the Liberals. —*v.* **1** grate; grind: *He gritted his teeth and plunged into the cold water.* **2** cover or spread with grit. **3** make or cause to make a grating or gritty sound. [OE *grēot*]

grits (grits) *n.pl.* **1** coarsely ground corn, oats, etc., with the husks removed. **2** *U.S.* coarse hominy. [OE *grytte*]

grit·ty (grit′ē) *adj.* **-ti·er, -ti·est. 1** of or containing grit; like grit; sandy. **2** *Informal.* courageous; plucky. —**grit′ti·ly,** *adv.* —**grit′ti·ness,** *n.*

griz·zle¹ (griz′əl) *n., adj., v.* -**zled, -zling.** —*n.* **1** greying hair. **2** wig. **3** the color grey. **4** a grey animal, especially a horse. —*adj.* grey; grizzled. —*v.* make or become grey. [ME < MF *grisel,* dim. of *gris* grey < Gmc.]

griz·zle² (griz′əl) *v.* -**zled, -zling.** *Brit.* especially of a child, fret or whine.

griz·zled (griz′əld) *adj.* **1** grey; greyish. **2** grey-haired.

griz·zly (griz′lē) *adj.* -**zli·er, -zli·est;** *n., pl.* -**zlies.** —*adj.* grizzled. —*n.* **1** grizzly bear. **2** *Mining.* a screening device made of iron bars or rails and used to separate ore from gravel. ☛ Hom. grisly.

grizzly bear a large bear, a subspecies of the brown bear found in the alpine and arctic tundra and subalpine forests of W North America. Most of the grizzlies in the Rocky Mountains are dark brown with long, white-tipped hairs on the shoulders and back; in the arctic tundra, however, many have a cream-colored back with reddish-brown underparts and legs.

groan (grōn) *n., v.* —*n.* a deep-throated sound expressing grief, pain, or disapproval; deep, short moan. —*v.* **1** give a groan or groans. **2** be loaded or overburdened: *The table groaned with food.* **3** express by groaning. **4** suffer greatly. [OE *grānian*] —**groan′er,** *n.* ☛ Hom. grown.

☛ **Syn.** *n.* **Groan, moan** = a low sound expressing painful feelings. **Groan** suggests a heavier sound than **moan** and implies suffering too hard to bear and, often, rebelliousness: *the groans of people caught in the wreckage; the groans of slaves under a yoke.* **Moan** implies a more continuous and involuntary cry of pain or some similar sound: *the moan of the wind.*

groat (grōt) *n.* **1** an old English silver coin worth about six cents. **2** a very small sum. [< MDu. *groot,* literally, thick (coin)]

groats (grōts) *n.pl.* hulled grain; hulled and crushed grain. [OE *grotan,* pl.]

gro·cer (grō′sər) *n.* a merchant who sells food and household supplies. [ME < OF *grossier,* originally, one who sells in bulk; ult. < L *grossus* thick] ☛ Hom. grosser.

gro·cer·y (grō′sər ē or grōs′rē) *n., pl.* -**cer·ies. 1** a store that sells food and household supplies. **2 groceries,** *pl.* commodities sold by a grocer, especially food. **3** the business or trade of a grocer.

gro·ce·te·ri·a (grō′sə tēr′ē ə) *n.* a self-service grocery store. [*grocery* + cafe*teria*]

grog (grog) *n.* **1** a drink made of rum or any other strong alcoholic liquor diluted with water. **2** any strong alcoholic liquor. [short for *grogram,* nickname of British Admiral Vernon, from his *grogram* cloak]

grog·gy (grog′ē) *adj.* **-gi·er, -gi·est.** *Informal.* **1** shaky; unsteady. **2** drunk; intoxicated. —**grog′gi·ly,** *adv.* —**grog′gi·ness,** *n.*

grog·ram (grog′rəm) *n.* a coarse cloth made of silk, wool, or combinations of these with mohair. [< F *gros grain* coarse grain]

grog·shop (grog′shop′) *n.* *Esp.Brit.* saloon.

groin (groin) *n.* **1** the hollow on either side of the body where the thigh joins the abdomen. **2** *Architecture.* a curved edge or line where two vaults of a roof intersect. See **vault¹** for picture. [ME *grynde,* influenced by *loin*]

grom·met (grom′it) *n.* **1** a metal eyelet. **2** a ring of rope, used as an oarlock, to hold a sail on its stays, etc. [< obs. F *gromette* curb of bridle < *gourmer* curb]

groom (grüm) *n., v.* —*n.* **1** a man or boy who has charge of horses. **2** a man just married or about to be married; bridegroom. **3** in England, any of several officers of the royal household. **4** *Archaic.* manservant. —*v.* **1** feed and take care of (horses); rub down and brush. **2** take care of the appearance of; make neat and tidy. **3** prepare (a person) to run for a political office. [ME *grom(e)* boy; origin uncertain; cf. OF *gromet* servant] —**groom′er,** *n.*

grooms·man (grümz′mən) *n., pl.* -**men.** the man who attends the bridegroom at a wedding.

groove (grüv) *n., v.* **grooved, groov·ing.** —*n.* **1** a long, narrow channel or furrow, especially one cut by a tool: *The plate rests in a groove on the rack.* **2** any similar channel; rut: *Wheels leave grooves in a dirt road.* **3** a fixed way of doing things: *It is hard to get out of a groove.* **in the groove,** *Slang.* **a** *Music.* playing or played smoothly and with great skill. **b** excellent or excellently. —*v.* **1** make a groove or grooves in. **2** *Slang.* feel enjoyment or excitement, especially as a result of being in tune with the surrounding atmosphere or stimuli (*often used with* **on**): *He grooves on classical jazz.* [< MDu. *groeve* furrow, ditch] —**groov′er,** *n.*

groov·y (grü′vē) *adj.* *Slang.* **1** fashionable and exciting: *a groovy new singer. They thought it would be groovy to live in a van.* **2** wonderful; marvellous.

grope (grōp) *v.* **groped, grop·ing;** *n.* —*v.* **1** feel about with the hands: *He groped for a flashlight when the lights went out.* **2** search blindly and uncertainly: *The detectives groped for some clue to the murder.* **3** find by feeling about with the hands; feel (one's way) slowly: *The blind man groped his way to the door.* —*n.* the act of groping. [OE *grāpian.* Related to GRASP, GRIP, GRIPE.] —**grop′er,** *n.* —**grop′ing·ly,** *adv.*

gros·beak (grōs′bēk′) *n.* any of various North American or European finches having a large, strong, cone-shaped bill. Common Canadian grosbeaks are the **rose-breasted grosbeak** (*Pheucticus ludovicianus*), **evening grosbeak** (*Hesperiphona vespertina*), and **pine grosbeak** (*Pinicola enucleator*). [< F *grosbec* < *gros* large + *bec* beak]

gro·schen (grō′shən) *n.* a unit of money in Austria, equal to ¹⁄₁₀₀ of a schilling. [< G < ML (*denarius*) *grossus* thick denarius]

gros·grain (grō′grān′) *n., adj.* —*n.* a closely woven silk or rayon cloth with heavy cross threads and a dull finish. —*adj.* having heavy cross threads and a dull finish. [var. of *grogram*]

gros point (grōs′point′; *French,* grō pwan′) *n.* a coarse cross-stitch used for needlepoint embroidery. [< F *gros* large + *point* stitch]

gross (grōs) *adj., n., pl.* **gross·es** for 1, **gross** for 2; *v.* —*adj.* **1** with nothing taken out; whole; entire. The gross receipts are all the money taken in before costs are deducted. **2** obviously bad; glaring: *gross misconduct. She makes gross errors in pronunciation.* **3** coarse; vulgar: *Her manners are too gross for a lady.* **4** too big and fat; overfed. **5** thick; heavy; dense: *the gross growth of a jungle.* **6** concerned with large masses or outlines; general. —*n.* **1** the whole sum; total amount. **2** a unit consisting of twelve dozen; 144. **in the gross, a** as a whole; in bulk. **b** wholesale. —*v.* make a gross profit of; earn a total of: *He grosses $20 000 per year.* [ME < OF *gros* < L *grossus* thick] —**gross′er,** *n.* —**gross′ly,** *adv.*

gross national product the total market value of a nation's goods and services, before allowances or deductions. *Abbrev.:* GNP or G.N.P.

gross·ness (grōs′nis) *n.* being gross.

gross profit the difference between the cost and the selling price of goods, before deductions.

gross ton long ton.

gross weight the total weight, including wastage, packaging, etc.

grosz (grosh) *n., pl.* **gro·szy** (grosh′ē). a unit of money in Poland, equal to ¹⁄₁₀₀ of a zloty. [< Polish]

grot (grot) *n.* *Poetic.* grotto.

gro·tesque (grō tesk′) *adj., n.* —*adj.* **1** odd or unnatural in shape, appearance, manner, etc.; fantastic; queer: *The book had pictures of hideous dragons and other grotesque monsters.* **2** ridiculous; absurd: *The monkey's grotesque antics made the children laugh.* **3** of painting, etc., combining designs, ornaments, figures, etc. in a fantastic or unnatural way. —*n.* a painting, etc. combining designs, ornaments, figures, etc. in a fantastic or unnatural way. [< F < Ital. *grottesco* < *grotta.* See GROTTO.] —**gro·tesque′ly,** *adv.* —**gro·tesque′ness,** *n.*

grot·to (grot′ō) *n., pl.* -**toes** or -**tos. 1** a cave. **2** an artificial cave made for coolness or pleasure. **3** a shrine in or like a cave. [< Ital. *grotta* < L *crypta* < Gk. *kryptē* vault. Doublet of CRYPT.]

grot·ty (grot′ē) *adj.* **-ti·er, -ti·est.** *Slang.* unpleasant, ugly, or nasty. [< *grotesque.* 20c.] —**grot′ti·ness,** *n.*

grouch (grouch) *v., n. Informal.* —*v.* be sulky or ill-tempered; complain. —*n.* **1** a sulky person. **2** a sulky, discontented feeling. [var. of obs. *grutch* < OF *groucher* murmur, grumble. Doublet of GROUSE², GRUDGE.]

grouch·y (grouch′ē) *adj.* **grouch·i·er, grouch·i·est.**

Informal. sulky; sullen; discontented. **—grouch′i·ly,** *adv.*
—grouch′i·ness, *n.*

ground¹ (ground) *n., adj., v.* **—n. 1** the solid part of the earth's surface: *Snow covered the ground.* **2** earth; soil; dirt: *The ground was hard.* **3** a particular piece of land; land for some special purpose: *The Cariboo was his favorite hunting ground.* **4** the foundation for what is said, thought, claimed, or done; basis; reason. **5** underlying surface; background: *The cloth has a blue pattern on a white ground.* **6 grounds,** *pl.* **a** land or area for some purpose or special use. **b** the land, lawns, and gardens around a house, school, etc. **7 grounds,** *pl.* the small bits that sink to the bottom of a drink such as coffee or tea; dregs; sediment. **8 grounds,** *pl.* foundation or basis: *no grounds for complaint.* **9** the connection of an electrical conductor with the earth. **10** in a radio, television set, etc., the connection for the conductor that leads to the ground.
above ground, alive.
break ground, a dig; plough. **b** begin building.
break new ground, a do something for the first time. **b** do something in a new and original manner.
cover ground, a go over a certain distance or area. **b** travel. **c** do a certain amount of work, etc.
cut the ground from under (someone's) **feet,** spoil a person's defence or argument by meeting it in advance.
fall to the ground, fail; be given up.
from the ground up, completely; entirely; thoroughly: *He learned his father's business from the ground up.*
gain ground, a go forward; advance; progress: *During the second day of fighting, the army began to gain ground.* **b** become more common or widespread.
give ground, retreat; yield: *Under our attack the enemy was forced to give ground.*
hold (one's) **ground,** keep one's position; not retreat or yield.
lose ground, a retreat; yield. **b** fall back; give up what has been gained: *As soon as the runner became tired, he began to lose ground.* **c** become less common or widespread.
on the grounds of, because of; by reason of.
run into the ground, *Informal.* overdo.
shift (one's) **ground,** change one's position; use a different defence or argument.
stand (one's) **ground,** keep one's position; refuse to retreat or yield: *Even though the boxer was hurt, he stood his ground.*
—adj. of, on, at, or near the ground; living or growing in, on, or close to the ground.
—v. 1 put on the ground; cause to touch the ground. **2** run aground; hit the bottom or shore: *The boat grounded in shallow water.* **3** put on a firm foundation or basis; establish firmly. **4** instruct in the first principles or elements: *The class is well grounded in grammar.* **5** furnish with a background. **6** connect (an electric wire or other conductor) with the earth. **7** prohibit (an aviator or an aircraft) from flying. **8** *Baseball.* hit a grounder. [OE *grund* bottom]

ground² (ground) *v.* pt. and pp. of **grind.**

ground crew 1 the non-flying personnel responsible for the conditioning and maintenance of airplanes. **2** any group of men responsible for maintaining a baseball field or other playing field.

ground·er (groun′dər) *n. Baseball.* a ball hit or thrown so as to bound or roll along the ground.

ground·fish (ground′fish′) *n.* any fish that lives at or near the bottom of the sea, such as cod or haddock.

ground floor 1 the first floor of a building. **2** the beginning of a venture: *to get in on the ground floor.* **3** *Informal.* the best position in relation to a business deal, etc.

ground glass 1 glass with the surface roughened so that it is not transparent. **2** glass that has been ground to powder.

ground hemlock a common low-growing shrub (*Taxus canadensis*), a species of yew found in forests from Newfoundland to Manitoba and the NE United States.

ground·hog (ground′hog′) *n.* a marmot (*Marmota monax*) found across most of Canada south of the Barren Land and in the NE United States, having a thickset body, a flat head on a very short neck, and short, rounded ears. Also called **woodchuck.**

Groundhog Day February 2, when the groundhog is supposed to come out of his burrow to see whether the sun is shining; if the sun is shining and he sees his shadow, he returns to his burrow for six more weeks of winter; if the sky is overcast, he expects an early spring.

ground ice 1 ice formed below the surface of a body of water, either at the bottom or attached to submerged objects. Also called **anchor ice. 2** ice spread throughout the soil in permafrost.

ground·less (ground′lis) *adj.* without foundation, basis, or reason. **—ground′less·ly,** *adv.* **—ground′less·ness,** *n.*

ground·ling (ground′ling) *n.* **1** a plant or animal that lives close to the ground. **2** a fish that lives at the bottom of the water. **3** a spectator or reader who has poor taste. **4** *Historical.* a spectator of a play who sat or stood in the pit.

hat, āge, fär; let, ēqual, tėrm; it, īce
hot, ōpen, ôrder; oil, out; cup, pùt, rüle,
əbove, takən, pencəl, lemən, circəs
ch, child; ng, long; sh, ship
th, thin; ₮H, then; zh, measure

ground·nut (ground′nut′) *n.* **1** any of various plants having edible tubers or nutlike underground seeds, such as the peanut. **2** the edible tuber, pod, etc. of such a plant.

ground pine 1 any of several North American club mosses, (genus *Lycopodium*) having creeping stems and erect branches with needlelike leaves. **2** a European and N African plant (*Ajuga chamaepitys*) of the mint family having a pinelike smell when crushed.

ground plan 1 the plan of a floor of a building. **2** the first or fundamental plan.

ground rule one of a set of basic rules or principles for action or procedure.

ground·sel (ground′səl *or* groun′-) *n.* any of several plants (genus *Senecio*) of the composite family having chiefly yellow flower heads, especially *S. vulgaris,* a common weed of Europe and Asia. [OE *g(r)undeswelge < grund* ground or *gund* pus + *swelgan* swallow¹; variously explained as meaning "ground-swallower" because it spreads rapidly, or "pus absorber" because it was used to reduce abcesses]

ground·sheet (ground′shēt′) *n.* a waterproof sheet, as of rubber or plastic, used under a tent, sleeping bag, etc. to protect against damp from the ground.

ground·sill (ground′sil′) *n.* a horizontal timber used as a foundation; lowest part of a wooden framework; sill. [ME *gronsel < OE grund* ground + *syll(e)* sill; the modern form has been influenced by its components *ground* and *sill*]

ground squirrel 1 any of a genus (*Spermophilus,* also classified as genus *Citellus*) of small, burrowing rodents of North America, Europe, and Asia belonging to the same family as squirrels, including some, such as the prairie gopher, that are pests in grainfields. **2** any of various other rodents of the same family (Sciuridae), such as chipmunks.

ground swell 1 the broad, deep waves caused by a distant storm, earthquake, etc. **2** a great rise or increase in the amount, degree, or force of anything.

ground water water that flows or seeps through the ground into springs and wells.

ground wire a wire connecting electric wiring, a radio, etc. with the ground.

ground·work (ground′wėrk′) *n.* a foundation; basis.

ground zero the exact point where a bomb strikes the ground or, in an atomic explosion, the area directly beneath the core of radiation.

group (grüp) *n., v.* **—n. 1** a number of persons or things together: *A group of children were playing tag.* **2** a number of persons or things belonging or classed together: *Wheat, rye, and oats belong to the grain group.* **3** an air force unit larger than a squadron, and smaller than a wing.
—v. 1 form into a group. **2** bring together; put in a group. **3** arrange in groups. [< F < Ital. *gruppo* < Gmc.]

group captain an air-force officer ranking next above a wing commander and below an air commodore. *Abbrev:* G.C. or G/C

group·er (grüp′ər) *n., pl.* **-er** or **-ers.** any of numerous large-mouthed food fishes (family Serranidae, especially genera *Epinephelus* and *Mycteroperca*) found in warm seas, including some very large species that reach a length of two metres and a mass of 225 kilograms. Groupers belong to the same family as the sea basses. [< Pg. *garupa*]

group·ie (grü′pē) *n. Slang.* **1** a female fan who follows male members of touring musical groups, sports teams, etc., especially one who seeks sexual intimacy with them. **2** any avid fan or follower; hanger-on.

group·ing (grüp′ing) *n.* a placing or manner of being placed in a group or groups.

grouse¹ (grous) *n., pl.* **grouse.** any of numerous birds (family Tetraonidae) hunted as game, having a plump body and feathered legs and mainly brownish plumage. Some Canadian grouse are the ruffed grouse, spruce grouse, and prairie chicken; the largest grouse is the Old World capercaillie. [origin uncertain]

grouse² (grous) *v.* **groused, grous·ing;** *n. Informal.* **—v.** grumble; complain. **—n. 1** complaint. **2** a person who complains;

grumbler. [apparently < OF *groucer*, var. of *groucher* murmur, grumble. Doublet of GROUCH, GRUDGE.]

grous·er[1] (grou′sər) *n. Informal.* a grouch or complainer.

grous·er[2] (grou′sər) *n.* **1** a pole driven into a river bottom, etc. to keep a boat or other floating object in place. **2** on a tractor, one of a set of cleats attached to a wheel or track to prevent slipping. [origin unknown]

grout (grout) *n., v.* —*n.* thin mortar used to fill cracks, etc. —*v.* fill up or finish with this mortar. [OE *grūt*]

grove (grōv) *n.* a group of trees standing together. An orange grove is an orchard of orange trees. [OE *grāf*]

grov·el (grov′əl *or* gruv′əl) *v.* -elled or -eled, -el·ling or -el·ing. **1** lie or crawl face downward at someone's feet; humble oneself: *The frightened slaves grovelled before their cruel master.* **2** enjoy low, mean or contemptible things. [back formation from ME *grovelinge* (adv.) on the face < *on grufe* prone < ON *á grúfu*] —**grov′el·ler** or **grov′el·er,** *n.*

grow (grō) *v.* **grew, grown, grow·ing. 1** become bigger by taking in food, as plants and animals do. **2** exist; sprout; spring; arise: *a tree growing only in the tropics.* **3** become greater; increase: *His fame grew.* **4** become gradually attached or united by growth: *The vine has grown fast to the wall.* **5** become: *to grow cold, to grow rich.* **6** cause to grow; produce; raise: *to grow corn.* **7** allow to grow: *to grow a beard.* **8** develop.
grow on or **upon,** have an increasing effect or influence on: *The habit grew on me.*
grow up, a advance to or arrive at full growth and maturity. **b** come into being; be produced; develop.
[OE *grōwan.* Related to GRASS, GREEN.]

grow·er (grō′ər) *n.* **1** a person who grows something: *a fruit grower.* **2** a plant that grows in a certain way: *a quick grower.*

growing pains 1 pains during childhood and youth, supposed to be caused by growing. **2** troubles that arise when something new is just developing.

growl (groul) *v., n.* —*v.* **1** make a deep, low, angry sound: *The dog growled at the tramp.* **2** express by growling: *He growled his thanks.* **3** complain angrily: *The soldiers growled about the poor food.* **4** rumble.
—*n.* **1** a deep, low, angry sound; deep, warning snarl. **2** an angry complaint. **3** a rumble. [probably imitative]

growl·er (groul′ər) *n.* **1** a person or animal that growls. **2** a floating piece of ice resembling a small iceberg, broken off from a glacier or larger iceberg.

grown (grōn) *adj., v.* —*adj.* **1** arrived at full growth. **2** covered with a growth. —*v.* pp. of **grow.**
☛ *Hom.* **groan.**

grown-up (grōn′up′) *adj., n.* —*adj.* **1** adult. **2** characteristic of or suitable for adults. —*n.* an adult: *The boy went to church with the grown-ups.*

growth (grōth) *n.* **1** the process of growing; development. **2** the amount of growing or developing; increase: *one year's growth.* **3** what has grown or is growing: *A thick growth of bushes covered the ground.* **4** an unhealthy mass of tissue formed in or on the body. Cancer causes a growth.

GRS *Cdn.* General Radio Service; CB.

grub (grub) *n., v.* **grubbed, grub·bing.** —*n.* **1** a wormlike form or larva of an insect. A grub is usually the smooth, thick larva of a beetle. **2** a drudge. **3** *Slang.* food.
—*v.* **1** dig: *Pigs grub for roots.* **2** root out of the ground; dig up: *It took the farmer weeks to grub the stumps on his land.* **3** rid (ground) of roots, etc. **4** drudge; toil. **5** search or rummage. **6** *Slang.* eat. [ME *grubbe(n);* related to OE *grafan,* OHG *grubilōn* to dig] —**grub′ber,** *n.*

grub·by (grub′ē) *adj.* **-bi·er, -bi·est. 1** dirty; grimy: *grubby hands.* **2** mean or contemptible: *a grubby little con artist.* **3** infested with grubs. —**grub′bi·ness,** *n.*

grub·stake (grub′stāk′) *n., v.* **-staked, -stak·ing.** —*n.* **1** the food, outfit, money, etc. supplied to a prospector on the condition of sharing in whatever he finds. **2** the arrangement by which this is done. **3** *Cdn.* the money or the means to buy food and other provisions for a certain period. **4** *Cdn.* a store of food or provisions. —*v.* provide with a grubstake. —**grub′stak′er,** *n.*

Grub Street 1 a former street in London where poor, struggling writers lived. **2** writers of little ability who write merely to earn money; hack writers.

grudge (gruj) *n., v.* **grudged, grudg·ing.** —*n.* ill will; a sullen feeling against; dislike of long standing.
bear a grudge, have and keep a grudge.
—*v.* **1** feel anger or dislike toward (a person) because of (something); envy the possession of: *He grudged me my little prize*

even though he had won a bigger one. **2** give or let have unwillingly: *The mean man grudged his horse the food that it ate.* [earlier meaning, grumble, complain; var. of obs. *grutch* < OF *groucher* murmur, grumble. Doublet of GROUCH, GROUSE[2].]
☛ *Syn. n.* **1.** See note at **spite.**

grudg·ing·ly (gruj′ing lē) *adv.* unwillingly.

gru·el (grü′əl) *n., v.* **-elled** or **-eled, -el·ling** or **-el·ing.** —*n.* a thin, almost liquid food made by boiling oatmeal, etc. in water or milk. Gruel is often given to those who are sick or old. —*v. Informal.* tire out completely; exhaust. [ME < OF *gruel,* ult. < Gmc.]

gru·el·ing (grü′əl ing) See **gruelling.**

gru·el·ling (grü′əl ing) *adj., n. Informal.* —*adj.* exhausting; very tiring: *a gruelling contest.* —*n.* an exhausting or very tiring experience.

grue·some (grü′səm) *adj.* horrible; frightful; revolting. Also, **grewsome.** [< *grue* shudder; cf. MDu., MLG *gruwen*] —**grue′some·ly,** *adv.* —**grue′some·ness,** *n.*

gruff (gruf) *adj.* **1** deep and harsh; hoarse. **2** rough; rude; unfriendly; bad-tempered: *a gruff manner.* [< MDu. *grof*] —**gruff′ly,** *adv.* —**gruff′ness,** *n.*

grum·ble (grum′bəl) *v.* **-bled, -bling;** *n.* —*v.* **1** mutter in discontent; complain in a bad-tempered way. **2** express by grumbling. **3** rumble: *His stomach was grumbling from hunger.* —*n.* **1** a mutter of discontent; bad-tempered complaint. **2** a rumble. [related to OE *grymettan* roar, and *grim*] —**grum′bler,** *n.*
☛ *Syn. v.* **1, 2.** See note at **complain.**

grump·y (grump′ē) *adj.* **grump·i·er, grump·i·est.** surly; ill-humored; gruff: *The grumpy old man found fault with everything.* [origin uncertain] —**grump′i·ly,** *adv.* —**grump′i·ness,** *n.*

Grun·dy (grun′dē) *n.* **Mrs. Grundy,** a character who personifies prudish or narrow-minded disapproval of manners, actions, etc.: *What would Mrs. Grundy say to such brief swimsuits?* [from a person often referred to by the characters in Thomas Morton's play *Speed the Plough* (1798)]

grun·gy (grun′jē) *adj. Slang.* unkempt, unattractive, dirty, etc.: *a grungy hotel in the old part of town.*

grunt (grunt) *n., v.* —*n.* **1** the deep, hoarse sound that a pig makes. **2** a sound like this: *The old man got out of his chair with a grunt.* **3** any of various marine fishes (family Pomadasyidae) found mostly in tropical coastal waters, that can produce a grunting sound with their teeth. Some authorities classify the grunts with the drumfishes in the family Sciaenidae.
—*v.* **1** make the deep, hoarse sound of a pig. **2** say with a sound like this: *The sullen boy grunted his apology.* [OE *grunnettan* < *grunian* grunt] —**grunt′er,** *n.*

Gru·yère (gri yer′ *or* grü yer′) *n.* a variety of firm, light-yellow cheese made from whole milk. [< *Gruyère,* a district in Switzerland]

gryph·on (grif′ən) See **griffin.**

G.S. General Staff.

G string 1 on a musical instrument, a string tuned to G. **2** a narrow loincloth held up by a cord around the waist. **3** a similar covering worn by striptease artists. **4** a single-wire method of television transmission.

gt. 1 great. **2** *Pharmacy.* drop (for L *gutta*).

Gt.Br. or **Gt.Brit.** Great Britain.

gtd. guaranteed.

guai·a·cum (gwī′ə kəm) *n.* **1** any of a genus (*Guaiacum*) of tropical American evergreen trees, such as the lignum vitaes, having bluish flowers, capsular fruit, and pinnate leaves. **2** the hard, heavy, greenish-brown wood of any of these trees, especially a lignum vitae. **3** a resin obtained from a lignum vitae, used in making varnishes and formerly also used in medicine. [< NL *Guaiacum* the genus name < Sp. *guayacán* < Arawak (West Indies) *guayacan*]

GU Guam.

gua·na·co (gwä nä′kō) *n., pl.* **-cos.** a South American wild mammal (*Lama guanicoe*) belonging to the same family as the camel, having a thick, soft, pale-brown coat. The guanaco is closely related to the vicuña, llama, and alpaca. [< Sp. < Quechua (Indian lang. of Peru) *huancau*]

gua·no (gwä′nō) *n., pl.* **-nos. 1** the manure of sea birds, found especially on islands near Peru. Guano is an excellent fertilizer. **2** an artificial fertilizer made from fish. [< Sp. < Quechua (Indian lang. of Peru) *huanu*]

gua·ra·ni (gwär′ə nē) *n.* **1** the basic unit of money in Paraguay, divided into 100 centimos. See table at **money. 2** a coin worth one guarani. [< *Guaraní,* a group of Indians from Central South America]

guar·an·tee (gar′ən tē′, ger′ən tē′, *or* gär′ən tē′) *n., v.* **-teed, -tee·ing.** —*n.* **1** a promise to pay or do something if another fails; a pledge to replace goods if they are not as represented; backing. **2** a

person who so promises. **3** one to whom such a pledge is made. **4** something given or taken as security; guaranty. **5** an assurance; promise: *Wealth is not a guarantee of happiness.*
—*v.* **1** stand behind; give a guarantee for; assure genuineness or permanence of; answer for fulfilment of (a contract, etc.): *This company guarantees its clocks for a year. The father guaranteed his son's future behavior.* **2** undertake to secure for another: *He will guarantee us possession of the house by May.* **3** secure (*used with* **against** *or* **from**): *His insurance guaranteed him against money loss in case of fire.* **4** promise (to do something): *I will guarantee to prove every statement I made.* **5** pledge that (something) has been or will be: *The advance payment of money guarantees the good faith of the purchaser.* **6** make sure or certain: *Wealth does not guarantee happiness.* [probably var. of *guaranty*]

guar·an·tor (gar'ən tôr' *or* ger'ən tôr') *n.* a person who makes or gives a guarantee.

guar·an·ty (gar'ən tē *or* ger'ən tē) *n.*, *pl.* **-ties**; *v.* **-tied**, **-ty·ing**.
—*n.* **1** the act or fact of giving security. **2** a pledge or promise given as security; security. —*v.* guarantee. [< OF *guarantie* < *guarantir* to warrant < *guarant* a warrant < Gmc. Doublet of WARRANTY.]

guard (gärd) *v.*, *n.* —*v.* **1** keep safe; watch over carefully; take care of: *The dog guards the house.* **2** defend; protect: *The goalie guards the goal.* **3** keep from escaping: *The soldiers guarded the prisoners day and night.* **4** keep in check; hold back; keep under control: *Guard your tongue.* **5** take precautions (against).
guard against, avoid or prevent by being careful: *His mother told him to guard against getting his feet wet.*
—*n.* **1** a person or group that guards. A soldier or group of soldiers guarding a person or place is a guard. **2** anything that gives protection; contrivance or appliance to protect against injury, loss, etc.: *A guard was placed in front of the fire.* **3** a careful watch: *A soldier kept guard over the prisoners.* **4** a picked body of soldiers: *a guard of honor.* **5** defence; protection. **6** *Boxing, fencing, or cricket.* a position of defence. **7** arms or weapons held in a position of defence. **8** *Football.* a player on either side of the centre. **9** *Basketball.* either of the two players serving as defencemen. **10** *Brit.* a person in charge of a railway train; brakeman. **11** *Historical.* the man in charge of a stagecoach. **12 the Guards, a** certain British regiments whose duties include guarding the sovereign. **b** certain Canadian regiments: *the Governor General's Horse Guards.*
off guard, unready; unprepared: *He caught the goalie off guard and scored.*
off (one's) guard, off guard.
on guard, ready to defend or protect; watchful: *A dog stood on guard near the door.*
stand guard, do sentry duty: *The soldier stood guard at the gate of the fort.*
[< F *garder* (earlier *guarder*), *v.*, *garde* (earlier *guarde*), *n.* < Gmc. Doublet of WARD.] —**guard'er,** *n.*
☛ *Syn. v.* **1. Guard, defend, protect** = keep safe. **Guard** = keep safe by watching over carefully: *The dog guarded the child night and day.* **Defend** = guard from harm by keeping away, turning aside, or resisting danger or attack: *He defended the child against the big boys.* **Protect** = keep safe by means of something that serves as a shield and keeps away danger or harm: *Proper food protects a person's health.*

guard·ed (gär'did) *adj.* **1** kept safe; carefully watched over; protected. **2** careful; cautious: *"Maybe" is a guarded answer to a question.* —**guard'ed·ly,** *adv.* —**guard'ed·ness,** *n.*

guard·ed·ly (gär'did lē) *adv.* in a guarded manner.

guard·house (gärd'hous') *n.* **1** a building used as a jail for soldiers. **2** a building used by soldiers on guard.

guard·i·an (gär'dē ən *or* gärd'yən) *n.*, *adj.* —*n.* **1** a person who takes care of another or of some special thing. **2** a person appointed by law to take care of the affairs of someone who is young or cannot take care of them himself. —*adj.* protecting: *a guardian angel.* [ME < AF *gardein,* var. of OF *g(u)arden* < *guarde* < Gmc. Doublet of WARDEN.]

guard·i·an·ship (gär'dē ən ship') *n.* the position or care of a guardian.

guard·rail (gärd'rāl') *n.* a rail or railing for protection.

guard·room (gärd'rüm' *or* -rùm') *n.* **1** a room used by soldiers on guard. **2** a room used as a jail for soldiers.

guards·man (gärdz'mən) *n.*, *pl.* **-men.** **1** a guard. **2** a private in any one of the Guards regiments. **3** any man serving in such a regiment.

gua·va (gwä'və) *n.* **1** any of several tropical American trees and shrubs (genus *Psidium*) of the myrtle family, especially *P. guajava,* widely cultivated in tropical regions for its sweet, edible pear-shaped fruit. **2** the fruit of a guava, used especially for jams, jellies, and preserves. [< Sp. *guayaba* < native name]

gu·ber·na·to·ri·al (gyü'bər nə tô'rē əl *or* gü'bər nə tô'rē əl) *adj.* *Esp.U.S.* of a governor; having to do with a governor. [< L *gubernator,* originally, pilot < *gubernare.* See GOVERN.]

hat, āge, fär; let, ēqual, tėrm; it, īce
hot, ōpen, ôrder; oil, out; cup, pùt, rüle,
əbove, takən, pencəl, lemən, circəs

ch, child; ng, long; sh, ship
th, thin; ᴛʜ, then; zh, measure

guck (guk) *n.* *Informal.* anything oozy, slimy, or similarly distasteful. [? < goo + *muck*]

gudg·eon (guj'ən) *n.* **1** a small freshwater fish (*Gobio gobio*) of the minnow and carp family found in Europe and N Asia, having a barbel on each side of the mouth. Gudgeons are used for food and also for fishing bait. **2** any of various other small fishes. **3** a person easily fooled or cheated. [ME < OF *goujon,* ult. < L *gobius* a kind of fish < Gk.]

guer·don (gėr'dən) *n. or v.* *Poetic.* reward. [ME < OF *guerdon,* var. of *werdon* < Med.L *widerdonum* < OHG *widarlōn* repayment, influenced by L *donum* gift]

gue·ril·la (gə ril'ə) See **guerrilla.**

Guern·sey (gėrn'zē) *n.*, *pl.* **-seys.** **1** a breed of dairy cattle originally from the island of Guernsey, resembling Jersey cattle, but somewhat larger. **2 guernsey,** a close-fitting, woollen sweater worn especially by sailors, originating on the island of Guernsey.

guer·ril·la (gə ril'ə) *n.*, *adj.* —*n.* **1** a member of a small independent band of fighters who harass the enemy by sudden raids, ambushes, etc. **2** warfare carried on by such fighters. —*adj.* of or by guerillas: *a guerilla attack.* [< Sp. *guerrilla,* dim. of *guerra* war]
☛ *Hom.* **gorilla.**

guess (ges) *v.*, *n.* —*v.* **1** form an opinion (of) without really knowing: *to guess the height of a tree.* **2** get right or find out by guessing: *to guess a riddle.* **3** think; believe; suppose.
—*n.* **1** an opinion formed without really knowing. **2** a guessing. [n. < v.; ME; cf. Swedish *gissa*] —**guess'er,** *n.*
☛ *Syn. v.* **1. Guess, conjecture, surmise** = form an opinion without knowing enough. **Guess,** the least formal word, suggests forming an opinion on the basis of what one thinks likely, without really knowing for certain: *He guessed the distance to the nearest town.* **Conjecture** suggests having some evidence, but not enough for proof: *Scientists conjecture the value of a new drug.* **Surmise** = form a conjecture more on what one suspects might be true than on facts one knows: *He surmised her thoughts.*

guess·ti·mate (*n.* ges'tə mət, *v.* ges'tə māt') *n.*, *v.* **-mat·ed, -mat·ing.** *Slang.* —*n.* an informal estimate based mainly on guesswork. —*v.* make a guesstimate of.

guess·work (ges'wėrk') *n.* work, action, or result based on guessing; guessing: *There is a lot of guesswork involved in buying a used car.*

guest (gest) *n.*, *adj.*, *v.* —*n.* **1** a person who is received and entertained at another's home, club, etc. **2** a person who is not a regular member; visitor. **3** a person staying at a hotel, motel, boarding house, etc.
be my guest, *Informal.* you are welcome to do as you wish; help yourself: *"May I use your phone?" "Certainly; be my guest."*
—*adj.* **1** of or for guests: *a guest room, guest towels.* **2** being a guest: *a guest conductor, a guest lecturer.*
—*v.* be or appear as a guest: *He guested on the new talk show last night.* [OE *giest* stranger (friend or foe)? < ON *gestr.* Akin to HOST².]
☛ *Syn. n.* **1.** See note at **visitor.**

guff (guf) *n.* *Informal.* foolish talk, especially when used in an attempt to hide the real facts. [probably imitative]

guf·faw (gu fo' *or* gu fô') *n.*, *v.* —*n.* a loud, coarse burst of laughter. —*v.* laugh loudly and coarsely. [imitative]

guid·ance (gī'dəns) *n.* **1** a guiding; leadership; direction: *Under her mother's guidance Nan learned to cook.* **2** something that guides. **3** *Education.* studies and counselling intended to help students understand their school environment, make the most of their opportunities, and plan for the future. **4** *Aeronautics.* the regulation of the path of rockets, missiles, etc. in flight.

guide (gīd) *v.* **guid·ed, guid·ing;** *n.* —*v.* **1** show the way; lead; conduct; direct. **2** manage; control; regulate.
—*n.* **1** a person or thing that shows the way, leads, conducts, or directs: *Tourists and hunters sometimes hire guides.* **2** a part of a machine for directing or regulating motion or action. **3** guidebook. **4 Guide,** Girl Guide. [ME < OF *guider* < Gmc.] —**guid'er,** *n.* —**guide'less,** *adj.*
☛ *Syn. v.* **1. Guide, lead, conduct** = show the way. **Guide** emphasizes knowing the way and all the points of interest or danger along it, and means to go along to point these out: *The Indian guided the hunters.* **Lead** emphasizes going ahead to show the way, expecting the person or thing to follow: *The dog led his master to the injured man.* **Conduct** emphasizes going with the person or thing to guide or assist him: *He conducted a party of tourists to Europe.*

guide·board (gīd′bôrd′) n. a board or sign with directions for travellers, often attached to a guidepost.

guide·book (gīd′buk′) n. a book of directions and information, especially one for travellers, tourists, etc.

guided missile a missile whose course may be controlled during flight, usually by means of radio signals.

guide·line (gīd′līn′) n. a principle or instruction set forth as a guide.

guide·post (gīd′pōst′) n. a post with signs and directions on it for travellers. A guidepost where roads meet tells travellers what places each road goes to and how far it is to each place.

Guid·er (gī′dər) n. an adult who is associated in some way with the Girl Guides or Brownies.

guide rope 1 a rope that is used to steady and guide something. 2 a long rope hanging from a dirigible or balloon for regulating its speed and altitude.

guide word in dictionaries and similar reference works, either of two words appearing at the top of a page, one indicating the first entry word on the page and the other showing the last entry word on the page.

gui·don (gī′dən or gī′don) n. 1 a small flag or streamer carried as a guide by soldiers, or used for signalling. 2 a soldier who carries the guidon. [< F < Ital. *guidone*]

guild (gild) n. 1 a society for mutual aid or for some common purpose: *the Canadian Guild of Potters.* 2 in the Middle Ages, a union of the men in one trade, formed to keep standards high and to protect their common interests: *the guild of silversmiths.* [ME < ON *gildi*]
☛ Hom. **gild.**

guil·der (gil′dər) n. 1 the basic unit of money in Surinam, divided into 100 cents. See table at **money.** 2 gulden. 3 a note worth one guilder. [alteration of *gulden*]

guild·hall (gild′hol′ or -hôl′) n. 1 the hall in which a guild meets. 2 a town hall; city hall.

guilds·man (gildz′mən) n., pl. **-men.** a member of a guild.

guile (gīl) n. crafty deceit; craftiness; sly tricks: *A swindler uses guile; a robber uses force.* [ME < OF < Gmc. Akin to WILE.]
☛ Syn. See note at **deceit.**

guile·ful (gīl′fəl) adj. crafty and deceitful; sly and tricky.
—**guile′ful·ly,** adv. —**guile′ful·ness,** n.

guile·less (gīl′lis) adj. without guile; honest; frank; sincere.
—**guile′less·ly,** adv. —**guile′less·ness,** n.

guil·le·mot (gil′ə mot′) n. 1 any of a genus (*Cepphus*) of black-and-white northern sea birds of the auk family having a straight, pointed, black bill. 2 *Esp.Brit.* murre (def. 1). [< F *guillemot*, probably < *Guillaume* William]

guil·lo·tine (n. gil′ə tēn′; v. gil′ə tēn′) n., v. **-tined, -tin·ing.**
—n. 1 a machine for beheading persons by means of a heavy blade that slides down between two grooved posts. The guillotine was much used during the French Revolution. 2 a machine for cutting paper. —v. 1 behead with a guillotine. 2 cut with a guillotine. [< F, after Joseph I. *Guillotin* (1738-1814), a French physician and advocate of its use] —**guil′lo·tin′er,** n.

guilt (gilt) n. 1 the fact or state of having done wrong; being guilty; being blameworthy. 2 guilty action or conduct; a crime; offence. [OE *gylt* offence]
☛ Hom. **gilt.**

guilt·less (gilt′lis) adj. not guilty; free from guilt; innocent.
☛ Syn. See note at **innocent.**

guilt·y (gil′tē) adj. **guilt·i·er, guilt·i·est.** 1 having done wrong; deserving to be blamed and punished: *The jury pronounced the prisoner guilty of murder.* 2 knowing or showing that one has done wrong: *The one who did the crime had a guilty conscience and a guilty look.* [OE *gyltig*] —**guilt′i·ly,** adv. —**guilt′i·ness,** n.

guimpe (gimp or gamp) n. a blouse worn under a dress and showing at the neck or at the neck and arms. [< F < Gmc. Doublet of GIMP.]
☛ Hom. **gimp** (gimp).

guin·ea (gin′ē) n. 1 an amount equal to 21 shillings (£1.05), formerly used in the British Isles in stating prices, fees, etc. 2 a former British gold coin worth 21 shillings. [< *Guinea* (Pg. *Guiné,* F *Guinée*) in W Africa, since the coin was originally made of gold from there; 17c.]

guinea fowl a domestic fowl (*Numida meleagris*) resembling a pheasant, having dark-grey plumage with small white spots, and a naked head and neck. It is native to Africa, but raised for food in many parts of the world. [< *Guinea.* See GUINEA.]

guinea hen 1 guinea fowl. 2 a female guinea fowl.

guinea pig 1 a plump-bodied, short-eared, short-tailed rodent (*Cavia cobaya*) often kept as a cage pet and extensively used in scientific research. 2 any person or thing serving as a subject for experiment or testing. [< *Guinea,* in the sense of coming from a distant country; the animal actually came from South America. See GUINEA.]

Guin·e·ver (gwin′ə vər) n. See **Guinevere.**

Guin·e·vere (gwin′ə vēr′) n. *Arthurian legend.* Arthur's wife, who became the mistress of Lancelot.

guise (gīz) n. 1 a style of dress; garb: *The soldier went into the village in the guise of a monk so that he would not be recognized.* 2 external appearance; aspect; semblance: *His theory is nothing but an old idea in a new guise.* 3 an assumed appearance; pretence: *Under the guise of friendship he plotted treachery.* [ME < OF < Gmc. Akin to WISE².]

Guitars: a Spanish guitar and an electric guitar

gui·tar (gə tär′) n. a musical instrument having usually six strings that are plucked or strummed with the fingers or a pick, a flat face and back, and a long neck with frets, serving as a fingerboard. [< Sp. *guitarra* < Gk. *kithara* cithara. oublet of CITHARA and ZITHER.]

gulch (gulch) n. a deep, narrow ravine with steep sides, especially one marking the course of a stream or torrent. [origin unknown]

gul·den (gul′dən) n., pl. **-dens** or **-den. 1** the basic unit of money in the Netherlands, divided into 100 cents. See table at **money.** 2 a coin or note worth one gulden. Also called **guilder.** [< Du. and G. *Gulden,* literally, golden]

gules (gyūlz) n. or adj. *Heraldry.* red. [ME < OF *goules* red fur neck-piece (originally, pieces of neck fur) < *goule* throat < L *gula*]

gulf (gulf) n. 1 a large bay; an arm of an ocean or sea extending into the land. 2 a very deep break or cut in the earth. 3 any wide separation: *The quarrel left a gulf between the two friends.* 4 something that swallows up; whirlpool. [ME < OF *golfe* < Ital. *golfo,* ult. < Gk. *kolpos,* originally, bosom] —**gulf′like′,** adj.

gulf·weed (gulf′wēd′) n. any of a genus (*Sargassum*) of brown seaweeds, especially a tropical American species (*S. bacciferum*) having many berry-like sacs that keep it afloat.

gull¹ (gul) n. any of numerous aquatic birds (family Laridae, especially genus *Larus*) having long wings, webbed feet, a strong, slightly hooked bill, and mainly white plumage with some grey and black, especially on the wings and back. [ME ? < Welsh *gwylan*]

gull² (gul) v., n. —v. deceive; cheat. —n. a person who is easily deceived or cheated. [origin uncertain]

Gul·lah (gul′ə) n. 1 a member of a group of black people living along the coast of South Carolina and Georgia and on the islands off the coast. 2 the dialect of English spoken by the Gullahs, characterized by elements of various African languages.

gull·er·y (gul′ər ē) n. a breeding place of gulls.

gul·let (gul′it) n. 1 a passage for food from the mouth to the stomach; esophagus. 2 the throat. [ME < OF *goulet,* ult. < L *gula* throat]

gul·li·bil·i·ty (gul′ə bil′ə tē) n. being gullible; tendency to be easily deceived or cheated.

gul·li·ble (gul′ə bəl) adj. easily deceived or cheated. [< *gull²*] —**gul′li·bly,** adv.

gul·ly (gul′ē) n., pl. **-lies;** v. **-lied, -ly·ing.** —n. 1 a narrow gorge; a small ravine. 2 a channel or ditch made by heavy rains or running water: *After the storm, the newly-seeded lawn was covered with gullies.* 3 *Cricket.* the part of the playing field behind the slips. b a fielder stationed in the gully.
—v. make gullies in. [? var. of *gullet*]

gulp (gulp) v., n. —v. 1 swallow eagerly or greedily. 2 keep in; choke back; repress: *The disappointed boy gulped down a sob.* 3 gasp; choke.
—n. 1 the act of swallowing. 2 the amount swallowed at one time; mouthful. [imitative] —**gulp′er,** n.

gum¹ (gum) n., v. **gummed, gum·ming.** —n. 1 a sticky juice, obtained from or given off by certain trees and plants, that hardens

in the air and dissolves in water. Gum is used to make glue, drugs, candy, etc. **2** any similar secretion, such as resin, gum resin, etc. **3** a preparation of such a substance for use in industry or the arts. **4** chewing gum. **5** the substance on the back of a stamp, the flap of an envelope, etc.; mucilage; glue. **6** rubber. **7** gum tree.
—*v.* **1** smear, stick, stick together, or stiffen with gum. **2** give off gum; form gum. **3** make or become sticky; clog with something sticky.
gum up, *Slang.* mess up; put out of order. [ME < OF *gomme* < L *gummi* < Gk. *kommi*]

gum² (gum) *n.* Often, **gums**, *pl.* the flesh around the teeth. [OE *gōma* palate]

gum ammoniac a natural mixture of gum and resin, used in medicine; ammoniac.

gum arabic the gum obtained from acacia trees, used in making candy, medicine, mucilage, etc.

gum·bo (gum′bō) *n., pl.* **-bos. 1** the pods of the okra plant. **2** the plant itself. **3** soup thickened with okra pods: *chicken-gumbo soup.* **4** soil that contains much silt and becomes very sticky when wet, especially that found on the western prairies. [of African origin]

gum·boil (gum′boil′) *n.* a small abscess on the gum.

gum·boot (gum′büt′) *n.* a high rubber boot.

gum·drop (gum′drop′) *n.* a stiff, jelly-like piece of candy made of gum arabic, gelatin, etc. sweetened and flavored.

gum·my (gum′ē) *adj.* **-mi·er, -mi·est. 1** sticky; like gum. **2** covered with gum. **3** giving off gum. —**gum′mi·ness,** *n.*

gump·tion (gump′shən) *n. Informal.* **1** initiative; energy; resourcefulness. **2** common sense; good judgment. [< Scots dial.; origin uncertain]

gum resin a natural mixture of gum and resin, obtained from certain plants.

gum·shoe (gum′shü′) *n., v.* **-shoed, shoe·ing.** —*n.* **1** a rubber overshoe. **2** gumshoes, *pl.* sneakers. **3** *Slang.* detective.
—*v. Slang.* go around quietly and secretly.

gum tree any of various trees, such as the sweet gum and eucalyptus, that yield gum.

gum·wood (gum′wůd′) *n.* the wood of a gum tree, especially the sweet gum.

gun¹ (gun) *n., v.* **gunned, gun·ning.** —*n.* **1** a weapon with a long metal tube for shooting shells, bullets, shot, etc. An artillery piece or a cannon is properly a gun; rifles, pistols, and revolvers are commonly called guns. **2** (*adj.*) of or involving a gun or guns: *a gun barrel, a gun battle.* **3** the firing of a gun as a signal or salute. **4** *Slang.* gunman. **5** a hunter or member of a shooting party. **6** a device for ejecting or discharging something: *a spray gun, an electron gun, a grease gun.* **7** See **big gun.**
beat or **jump the gun, a** of a competitor in a race, etc., start before the signal is given. **b** act prematurely or before the expected or permitted time.
give it the gun, *Informal.* speed up greatly; suddenly go, act, etc. much faster.
spike (someone's) guns See **spike¹.**
stick to (one's) guns, keep one's position under opposition or attack; refuse to retreat or yield.
under the gun, *Informal.* in a difficult position; having to defend one's position, actions, etc.
—*v.* **1** hunt or hunt (*for*) with a gun. **2** shoot (someone) with a gun (*usually used with* **down**): *He was gunned down as he left his car.* **3** go after, with intent to hurt, destroy, etc. (*used with* **for**): *They'll be gunning for you when they read the report.* **4** try hard (*used with* **for**): *gunning for a victory.* **5** cause to accelerate suddenly and fast: *He gunned the engine to pass.* [ME ? < ON *Gunna*, shortened form of *Gunnhildr*, a woman's name applied to engines of war]

gun² (gun) *v. Archaic or poetic.* pp. of **gin⁴.**

gun barrel the metal tube of a gun.

gun·boat (gun′bōt′) *n.* a small warship, often one that can be used in shallow water.

gun carriage a structure on which a gun is mounted or moved and on which it is fired.

gun·cot·ton (gun′kot′ən) *n.* cellulose nitrate, especially when highly nitrated for use as an explosive.

gun·dog (gun′dog′) *n.* a dog trained to locate, flush, or retrieve game for hunters who use guns. Pointers, setters, and retrievers are breeds commonly trained as gundogs.

gun·fight (gun′fīt′) *n.* a fight in which guns are used.

gun·fire (gun′fīr′) *n.* the shooting of a gun or guns.

gung–ho (gung′hō′) *adj. Slang.* full of unrestrained energy and enthusiasm; eager to begin, carry on, take part, etc.: *He's just starting out in business and is terribly gung-ho.*

gunk (gungk) *n. Informal.* any unpleasant, heavy, oil or sticky matter; guck.

hat, āge, fär; let, ēqual, tėrm; it, īce
hot, ōpen, ôrder; oil, out; cup, půt, rüle,
 əbove, takən, pencəl, lemən, circəs

ch, child; ng, long; sh, ship
th, thin; ŦH, then; zh, measure

gunk hole (gungk) *Cdn.* a tiny, rocky-sided cove with deep water, making an excellent fishing spot.

gun·lock (gun′lok′) *n.* the part of a gun by which the charge is fired.

gun·man (gun′mən) *n., pl.* **-men. 1** a man who uses a gun to rob or kill. **2** a man noted for his skill in using a gun.

gun·met·al (gun′met′əl) **1** any of various dark-grey alloys used for chains, buckles, handles, etc. **2** a dark, somewhat bluish grey. **3** a kind of bronze formerly used for making guns. **4** (*adj.*) of, having to do with, or resembling gunmetal.

gun·nel¹ (gun′əl) See **gunwale.**

gun·nel² (gun′əl) *n.* any of a family (Pholidae) of eel-like marine fishes of northern coastal regions. [origin uncertain]

gun·ner (gun′ər) *n.* **1** a person trained to fire artillery pieces; a soldier, airman, etc. who handles and fires guns. **2** a naval officer in charge of a ship's guns. **3** a person, especially a private, serving in the artillery. **4** a person who hunts with a gun.

gun·ner·y (gun′ər ē) *n.* **1** the art and science of constructing and managing big guns. **2** the use of guns; the shooting of guns. **3** guns collectively.

gun·ning (gun′ing) *n.* the act of shooting with a gun; hunting with a gun.

gun·ny (gun′ē) *n., pl.* **-nies. 1** a strong, coarse fabric used for sacks, bags, etc. **2** a sack, bag, etc. made of this fabric. [< Hind. *goni*]

gunny sack a sack or bag made of gunny.

gun pit an excavation where artillery is placed.

gun·point (gun′point′) *n.* the tip or point of a gun barrel.
at gunpoint, being threatened by a gun; having a gun pointed at one.

gun·pow·der (gun′pou′dər) *n.* a powder that explodes with force when brought into contact with fire. Gunpowder is used in guns, fireworks, and blasting. One kind of gunpowder is made of saltpetre, sulphur, and charcoal.

gun room **1** a room where guns are kept. **2** a room for junior officers of a warship.

gun·run·ning (gun′run′ing) *n.* the bringing of guns and ammunition into a country illegally.

gun·shot (gun′shot′) *n.* **1** a shot fired from a gun. **2** the shooting of a gun. **3** the distance that a gun will shoot.

gun·sight (gun′sīt′) *n.* a device on a gun to help in taking aim.

gun·sling·er (gun′sling′ər) *n. Slang.* gunman.

gun·smith (gun′smith′) *n.* a person whose work is making or repairing small guns.

gun·stock (gun′stok′) *n.* the wooden support or handle to which the barrel of a gun is fastened.

Gun·ter's chain (gun′tərz) *Surveying.* a measuring chain 66 feet long (about 20 metres). [named after Edmund *Gunter* (1581-1626), an English mathematician]

gun·wale (gun′əl) *n.* the reinforced top edge of the side of a boat, designed to add strength and rigidity and to provide support for a rowlock or tholepins. Also, **gunnel¹.** See **rowboat** for picture. [< *gun¹* + *wale* a plank; because formerly used to support guns]

gup·py (gup′ē) *n., pl.* **-pies.** a small, brightly colored, freshwater fish (*Lebistes reticulatus*) native to NE South America and the West Indies, that bears live young instead of laying eggs as most fish do. Guppies are popular for home aquariums. [after Robert J. L. *Guppy* of Trinidad, who supplied the first specimens]

gur·gle (gėr′gəl) *v.* **-gled, -gling;** *n.* —*v.* **1** flow or run with a bubbling sound: *Water gurgles when it is poured out of a bottle or when it flows over stones.* **2** make a bubbling sound: *The baby gurgled happily.* **3** express with a gurgle.
—*n.* a bubbling sound. [? imitative]

Gurk·ha (gür′kə) *n.* a member of a Nepalese Hindu people famous for its soldiers.

gur·nard (gėr′nərd) *n.* sea robin; especially, any of several European species. [ME < OF *gornart* grunter < *grognier* to grunt < L *grunnire*]

gu·ru (gü′rü *or* gů rü′) *n.* **1** *Hinduism.* a personal religious adviser or teacher. **2** a person who guides others, especially in a spiritual way. [< Hind. *gurū*]

gush (gush) v., n. —v. 1 rush out suddenly; pour out. 2 *Informal.* talk in a silly way about one's affections or enthusiasms. 3 give forth suddenly or very freely. 4 have an abundant flow of blood, tears, etc.
—n. 1 a rush of water or other liquid from an enclosed place: *If you get a deep cut, there is usually a gush of blood.* 2 *Informal.* silly, emotional talk. 3 a sudden and violent outbreak; burst: *a gush of anger.* [probably imitative]
☛ *Syn. v.* 1. See note at **flow.**

gush·er (gush′ər) n. 1 an oil well that flows copiously without being pumped. 2 *Informal.* a gushy person.

gush·ing (gush′ing) adj. 1 that gushes. 2 effusive.

gush·y (gush′ē) adj. **gush·i·er, gush·i·est.** showing one's feelings in a silly way; effusive; sentimental. —**gush′i·ly,** adv. —**gush′i·ness,** n.

gus·set (gus′it) n. 1 a triangular piece of material inserted in a dress, etc. to give greater strength or more room. 2 a bracket or plate used to reinforce the joints of a structure. [ME < OF *gousset* < *gousse* husk]

gus·sy (gu′sē) v. *Slang.* make seemly or attractive; spruce (up): *The girls gussied themselves up for the party.* [origin uncertain]

gust (gust) n. 1 a sudden, violent rush of wind: *A gust upset the small sailboat.* 2 a sudden burst of rain, smoke, sound, etc. 3 an outburst of anger, enthusiasm, etc. [< ON *gustr*]

gus·ta·to·ry (gus′tə tô′rē) adj. of the sense of taste; having to do with tasting: *Eating fine foods gives gustatory pleasure.* [< L *gustatus,* pp. of *gustare* taste]

gus·to (gus′tō) n., pl. **-tos.** 1 keen relish; hearty enjoyment: *The hungry boy ate his dinner with gusto.* 2 a liking or taste. [< Ital. *gusto,* originally, taste < L *gustus*]

gust·y (gus′tē) adj. **gust·i·er, gust·i·est.** 1 coming in gusts; windy; stormy. 2 marked by outbursts: *gusty laughter.* —**gust′i·ly,** adv. —**gust′i·ness,** n.

gut (gut) n., v. **gut·ted, gut·ting;** adj. —n. 1 intestine. 2 **guts,** pl. entrails; bowels. 3 catgut. 4 a narrow channel or gully. 5 **guts,** pl. *Informal.* **a** courage or forcefulness. **b** the inner or essential part: *the guts of a car, the guts of the problem.* 6 (adjl.) *Informal.* **a** essential or basic: *the gut issues in a campaign.* **b** arising from deep, basic feelings; instinctive: *a gut reaction.*
—v. 1 remove the entrails of; disembowel. 2 plunder or destroy the inside of: *Fire gutted the building and left only the brick walls standing.*
—adj. *Slang.* vital; basic: *The gut issue is the demand for higher wages.* [OE *guttas,* pl.]

gut·sy (gut′sē) adj. **-si·er, -si·est.** *Slang.* courageous or forceful; having guts: *a gutsy political leader.*

gut·ta–per·cha (gut′ə pèr′chə) n. a substance resembling rubber, obtained from the thick milky juice (latex) of any of several Malaysian trees of the sapodilla family, used in dentistry, for insulating electric wires, etc. [< Malay]

gut·ter (gut′ər) n., v. —n. 1 a channel or ditch along the side of a street or road to carry off water; the low part of a street beside the sidewalk. 2 eavestrough. 3 any channel or groove, such as the channel along each side of a bowling lane. 4 **the gutter,** a wretched, poverty-stricken, or depraved environment: *a child of the gutter.* 5 (adjl.) having to do with, characteristic of, or associated with a wretched or depraved environment: *gutter language, gutter journalism.* 6 *Printing.* the white space formed by the inner margins of two facing pages of a book.
—v. 1 form gutters in. 2 flow or melt in streams: *A candle gutters when the melted wax runs down its sides.* 3 become channelled. [ME < AF *gotere,* ult. < L *gutta* drop]

gut·ter·snipe (gut′ər snīp′) n. *Informal.* 1 an urchin who lives in the streets. 2 any ill-bred person.

gut·tur·al (gut′ər əl or gut′rəl) adj., n. —adj. 1 of the throat. 2 formed in the throat; harsh: *The man spoke in a guttural voice.* 3 *Phonetics.* formed between the back of the tongue and the soft palate, or velum; velar. The *g* in *go* is sometimes called a guttural sound.
—n. *Phonetics.* a sound formed between the back of the tongue and the soft palate. [< NL *gutturalis* < L *guttur* throat] —**gut′tur·al·ly,** adv. —**gut′tur·al·ness,** n.

guy[1] (gī) n., v. **guyed, guy·ing.** —n. a rope, chain, wire, etc. attached to something to steady or secure it. —v. steady or secure with a guy or guys. [< OF *guie* < *guier* to guide, ult. < Gmc.]

guy[2] (gī) n., v. **guyed, guy·ing.** —n. 1 *Slang.* fellow; chap. 2 *Esp.Brit.* a queer-looking or oddly dressed person. —v. *Informal.* make fun of; tease. [< *Guy Fawkes,* a leader of the Gunpowder Plot (1605) to blow up the British king and parliament]

Guy·a·nese (gī′ə nēz′) n., pl. **-ese;** adj. —n. a native or inhabitant of Guyana, a country in South America, formerly British Guiana. —adj. of or having to do with Guyana.

guy rope one of several ropes attached to a tent, marquee, etc. for pegging it to the ground as a means of support.

guz·zle (guz′əl) v. **-zled, -zling.** drink greedily; drink too much. [probably < OF *gosiller* vomit (? originally, pass through the throat); cf. F *gosier* throat] —**guz′zler,** n.

gym (jim) n. gymnasium.

gym·na·si·a (jim nā′zē ə)ˉn. a pl. of **gymnasium.**

gym·na·si·um (jim nā′zē əm) n., pl. **-si·ums** or **si·a.** a room, building, etc. fitted up for physical exercise or training and for indoor athletic sports. [< L < Gk *gymnasion* < *gymnazein* exercise (naked) < *gymnos* naked]

Gym·na·si·um (jim nā′zē əm; *German,* gym nä′zē ùm) n. in Germany, etc., a secondary school that prepares students for the universities.

gym·nast (jim′nast) n. an expert in gymnastics. [< Gk. *gymnastēs* < *gymnazein* exercise. See GYMNASIUM.]

gym·nas·tic (jim nas′tik) adj. having to do with bodily exercise or activities. —**gym·nas′ti·cal·ly,** adv.

gym·nas·tics (jim nas′tiks) n.pl. physical exercises for developing the muscles, such as are performed in a gymnasium.

gym·no·sperm (jim′nə spèrm′) n. any of a division (Gymnospermae; also called Pinophyta) of plants producing seeds that are exposed, not enclosed in an ovary. Many gymnosperms, such as pines, spruces, firs, junipers, and cedars, bear their seeds on cones. [< NL < Gk. *gymnospermos* < *gymnos* naked + *sperma* seed]

gym·no·sper·mous (jim′nə spèr′məs) adj. belonging to the gymnosperms; having the seeds exposed.

gy·nae·col·o·gist (gī′nə kol′ə jist, jī′nə kol′ə jist, or jin′ə kol′ə jist) See **gynecologist.**

gy·nae·col·o·gy (gī′nə kol′ə jē, jī′nə kol′ə jē, or jin′ə kol′ə jē) See **gynecology.**

gy·nan·drous (ji nan′drəs or jī nan′drəs) adj. *Botany.* having stamens and pistil joined as one, as in an orchid. [< Gk. *gynandros* of doubtful sex < *gynē* woman + *anēr, andros* man]

gy·ne·co·log·ic (gī′nə kə loj′ik, jī′nə kə loj′ik or jin′ə kə loj′ik) adj. of or having to do with gynecology. —**gy′ne·co·log′i·cal·ly,** adv.

gy·ne·col·o·gist (gī′nə kol′ə jist, jī′nə kol′ə jist, or jin′ə kol′ə jist) n. a physician who specializes in gynecology. Also, **gynaecologist.**

gy·ne·col·o·gy (gī′nə kol′ə jē, jī′nə kol′ə jē, or jin′ə kol′ə jē) n. the branch of medicine dealing with the diseases and reproductive functions specific to women. Also, **gynaecology.** [< Gk. *gynē, gynaikos* woman + E *-logy*]

gy·noe·ci·um (jī nē′sē əm or jə nē′sē əm) n., pl. **-ci·a** (-sē ə). *Botany.* the pistil or pistilis of a flower. [< NL < Gk. *gynē* woman + *oikion* house]

–gynous combining form. female; woman; female organs: *misogynous = hating women.* [< Gk. *-gynos* < *gynē* woman]

gyp (jip) v. **gypped, gyp·ping;** n. *Slang.* —v. cheat; swindle: *He gypped me out of three dollars.* —n. 1 a swindle; fraud: *That show was a big gyp; it wasn't anything like the ad.* 2 a cheat; swindler. [shortened form of *gypsy*] —**gyp′per,** n.

gyp·sif·er·ous (jip sif′ər əs) adj. having or yielding gypsum.

gyp·soph·i·la (jip sof′ə lə) n. any of a genus (Gypsophila) of Old World plants of the pink family, such as baby's breath, having many small, white or pink flowers on delicate branching stems with few leaves. [< NL < Gk. *gypsos* gypsum + *philos* fond of]

gyp·sum (jip′səm) n. a mineral used for making plaster of Paris, fertilizer, etc.; hydrated calcium sulphate. Alabaster is one form of gypsum. *Formula:* $CaSO_4 \cdot 2H_2O$ [< L < Gk. *gypsos* chalk, plaster]

gypsum board plasterboard.

Gyp·sy (jip′sē) n., pl. **-sies;** adj. —n. 1 Sometimes, **gypsy,** a member of a wandering people having dark skin and black hair who originally migrated to Europe from N India in the 15th and 16th

centuries. They have continued to live a nomadic life in Europe and North America. **2** Romany, the language of the Gypsies. **3 gypsy,** a person who looks like a Gypsy or leads a wandering life.
—*adj.* **gypsy,** of, having to do with, or like a Gypsy or the Gypsies: *a gypsy girl, gypsy music.* Also **Gipsy, gipsy.** [< *Egyptian,* since the Gypsies were thought to have originated in Egypt; 16c.]

gypsy moth a European moth (*Porthetria dispar*), a kind of tussock moth introduced into North America in the 19th century. Its hairy, greyish-brown larvae eat the leaves of trees and have become a serious pest in North America.

gy·rate (jī′rāt *or* jī rāt′) *v.* **-rat·ed, -rat·ing.** move in a circle or spiral; whirl; rotate: *A top gyrates.* [< L *gyrare* < *gyrus* circle < Gk. *gyros*] **—gy·ra′tor,** *n.*

gy·ra·tion (jī rā′shən) *n.* a circular or spiral motion; whirling; rotation.

gy·ra·to·ry (jī′rə tô′rē) *adj.* gyrating.

gyr·fal·con (jèr′fol′kən *or* -fôl′kən) *n.* the largest falcon (*Falco rusticolus*), found mainly in arctic and subarctic regions, varying in color from almost pure white with black streaks and speckles to dark greyish-brown.

gyro– *combining form.* circle; spiral, as in *gyroscope.* [< Gk. *gyro-* < *gyros*]

gy·ro·com·pass (jī′rō kum′pəs) *n.* a compass using a motor-driven gyroscope instead of a magnetic needle to point to the north. It points to the geographic North Pole instead of to the magnetic pole.

gy·ro·pi·lot (jī′rō pī′lət) *n. Aeronautics.* a device that automatically keeps an aircraft on course; automatic pilot.

gy·ro·plane (jī′rō plān′) *n.* an aircraft that is kept in the air by means of horizontal blades rapidly rotating around a vertical axis.

hat, āge, fär; let, ēqual, tèrm; it, īce
hot, ōpen, ôrder; oil, out; cup, put, rüle,
əbove, takən, pencəl, lemən, circəs

ch, child; ng, long; sh, ship
th, thin; ŦH, then; zh, measure

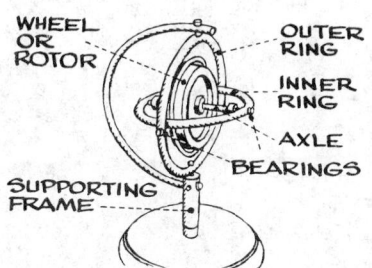

WHEEL OR ROTOR
OUTER RING
INNER RING
AXLE
BEARINGS
SUPPORTING FRAME

A gyroscope. Once it is set spinning rapidly, it will continue to rotate in the same plane regardless of magnetic forces and no matter which way the supporting frame is turned.

gy·ro·scope (jī′rə skōp′) *n.* a heavy wheel or disk mounted so that its axis can turn freely in one or more directions. A spinning gyroscope tends to resist change in the direction of its axis, and is used to keep ships and aircraft balanced.

gy·ro·scop·ic (jī′rə skop′ik) *adj.* having to do with a gyroscope.

gy·ro·sta·bi·liz·er (jī′rə stā′bə līz′ər) *n.* a gyroscopic device for stabilizing a seagoing vessel by counteracting its rolling motion.

gy·ro·stat·ics (jī′rə stat′iks) *n.* the branch of physics that deals with the laws governing the rotation of solid bodies.

gyve (jīv) *n., v.* **gyved, gyv·ing.** —*n.* fetter; shackle, especially for the leg. —*v.* put fetters or shackles on. [ME; origin uncertain] ☛ *Hom.* jive.

Hh

h or **H** (āch) *n., pl.* **h's** or **H's. 1** the eighth letter of the English alphabet. **2** any speech sound represented by this letter. **3** a person or thing identified as *h*, especially the eighth in a series. **4 H**, a symbol used on pencils to indicate the degree of hardness of the lead: *A 2H pencil is hard; 4H is very hard.* Compare **B** and **HB**. **5** something shaped like the letter H. **6** (*adj.*) of or being an H or h.

h 1 hour. **2** hecto- (an SI prefix).

h. or **h** *Baseball.* hit(s).

h. or **H 1** harbor. **2** hard; hardness. **3** high; height. **4** hundred. **5** husband.

H 1 hydrogen. **2** *Physics.* **a** intensity of magnetic field. **b** the earth's horizontal component of magnetic field. **3** *Electricity.* henry. **4** *Slang.* heroin.

ha (ho, hä, or ha) *interj.* **1** an exclamation of surprise, joy, triumph, etc.: *"Ha! I've caught you!" cried the giant to Jack.* **2** in writing, a way of indicating laughter: *"Ha! ha! ha!" laughed the boys.*

ha hectare.

Ha hahnium.

ha·be·as cor·pus (hā'bē əs kôr'pəs) *Law.* a writ or order requiring that a prisoner be brought before a judge or into court to decide whether he is being held lawfully. The right of habeas corpus is a protection against unjust imprisonment. [< L *habeas corpus* you may have the person]

hab·er·dash·er (hab'ər dash'ər) *n.pl.* **1** a dealer in men's furnishings, such as hats, ties, shirts, socks, etc. **2** a dealer in small articles, such as buttons, needles, and trimmings. [? < AF *hapertas*, a kind of cloth]

hab·er·dash·er·y (hab'ər dash'ər ē *or* hab'ər dash'rē) *n., pl.* **-er·ies. 1** the articles sold by a haberdasher. **2** the shop of a haberdasher.

hab·er·geon (hab'ər jən) *n.* **1** a short coat of mail without sleeves. Also, **haubergeon. 2** hauberk. [ME < OF *haubergeon*, dim. of *hauberc.* See HAUBERK.]

ha·bil·i·ment (hə bil'ə mənt) *n.* **1 habiliments,** *pl.* articles of clothing. **2** dress; attire. [ME < OF *(h)abillement* < *abiller* prepare, fit out; originally, reduce (a tree) to a trunk by stripping off branches < *bille* long stock, log < Celtic]

hab·it (hab'it) *n., v.* —*n.* **1** a tendency to act in a certain way or do certain things: *She has an irritating habit of drumming her fingers on the desk. His habit is to do the hardest job first.* **2** disposition or character: *a man of morose habit.* **3** a pattern of behavior acquired by repetition and that is regularly followed in certain circumstances or situations, often one that has become automatic: *the habit of brushing one's teeth. It is her habit to check all the doors and windows before going to bed.* **4** addiction. **5** the distinctive dress or costume worn by members of some religious orders: *The Grey Nuns traditionally wore a grey habit.* **6** a costume worn for riding; riding habit. **7** the characteristic form, mode of growth, etc., of an animal or plant: *The honeysuckle is of a twining habit.* **8** *Archaic.* clothing.
take the habit, become a nun.
—*v.* clothe. [ME < OF < L *habitus* < *habere* hold, live in, stay]
☛ **Syn. Habit** and **custom** both refer to an established practice. **Habit** refers more to a personal practice, something one does without thinking about it: *Biting one's fingernails is a bad habit.* **Custom** refers especially to practice adopted by a group of people or an individual and continued over a long period of time: *It was a custom in her family to play euchre every Friday evening.*

hab·it·a·ble (hab'ə tə bəl) *adj.* fit to live in. —**hab'it·a·ble·ness,** *n.* —**hab'it·a·bly,** *adv.*

hab·it·ant (*n. 1* hab'ə tənt; *n. 2, adj.* hab'ə tont'; *French,* ä bē tän') *n., adj.* —*n.* **1** inhabitant. **2** *Cdn.* a French-Canadian farmer. —*adj. Cdn.* of or having to do with French Canadians or French Canada, especially with regard to country life. [< Cdn.F < F < L *habitans, -antis,* ppr. of *habitare* live in < *habere*]

hab·i·tat (hab'ə tat') *n.* **1** the place where an animal or plant naturally lives or grows: *The jungle is the habitat of tigers.* **2** a place of living; dwelling place. [< L *habitat* it inhabits]

hab·i·ta·tion (hab'ə tā'shən) *n.* **1** a place to live in; home; dwelling. **2** an inhabiting.

ha·bit·u·al (hə bich'ü əl) *adj.* **1** done by habit; caused by habit: *a habitual smile, habitual courtesy.* **2** being or doing something by habit: *A habitual reader reads a great deal.* **3** often done, seen, or used; usual; customary: *Ice and snow are a habitual sight in arctic regions.* —**ha·bit'u·al·ly,** *adv.* —**ha·bit'u·al·ness,** *n.*

ha·bit·u·ate (hə bich'ü āt') *v.* **-at·ed, -at·ing. 1** make used (*to*); accustom: *Loggers are habituated to hard work.* **2** go to (a place) frequently. [< LL *habituari* be in a state of, be characterized by (? passive of **habituare* bring into a state) < L *habitus* condition (*see* HABIT); influenced in meaning by E *habit*] —**ha·bit'u·a'tion,** *n.*

hab·i·tude (hab'ə tyüd' *or* hab'ə tüd') *n.* **1** a characteristic condition of body or mind. **2** a habit; custom; practice. [< F < L *habitudo* condition]

ha·bit·u·é (he bich'ü ā' *or* hə bich'ü ā') *n.* a person who has the habit of going to a place frequently: *a habitué of the theatre.* [< F *habitué,* pp. of *habituer* accustom]

Habs·burg (haps'bėrg; *German,* häps'bürk) See **Hapsburg.**

ha·ci·en·da (hä'sē en'də) *n. Spanish American.* a large ranch; landed estate; country house. [< Sp. < L *facienda* (things) to be done < *facere* do]

hack¹ (hak) *v., n.* —*v.* **1** cut with repeated rough or uneven blows: *She hacked the crate apart with an old axe. He hacked away at the tree.* **2** make (one's way) by cutting away vegetation: *hacking our way through the underbrush.* **3** *Slang.* handle (something) successfully; cope or tolerate (*often used with* **it**): *He couldn't hack the long hours. It takes a special kind of person to hack it in this business.* **4** cough in short, dry bursts. **5** *Basketball.* commit the foul of hitting the arm of (an opponent who has the ball).
—*n.* **1** a rough cut. **2** a tool or instrument for hacking or cutting, such as an axe, pick, hoe, etc. **3** *Curling.* a notch cut in the ice at one end of a rink, used as a foothold when a player throws his rock. **4** a short dry cough. **5** *Basketball.* a personal foul committed by striking the arm of a player who has the ball. [OE *haccian*] —**hack'er,** *n.*
☛ *Syn. v.* **1.** See note at **cut.**

hack² (hak) *n., v., adj.* —*n.* **1** a carriage for hire. **2** *Informal.* taxi. **3** an old or worn-out horse. **4** a horse for ordinary riding. **5** a person hired to do routine literary work; drudge. **6** a plodding, faithful, but undistinguished worker in an organization, as a political party: *an old party hack.*
—*v.* **1** ride on horseback over roads. **2** *Informal.* drive a taxi. **3** write or act as a hack.
—*adj.* working or done merely for money; hired; drudging. [short for *hackney*]

hack·a·more (hak'ə môr') *n.* a halter (def. 1). [< Sp. *jáquima*]

hack·ber·ry (hak'ber'ē) *n., pl.* **-ries. 1** any of a genus (*Celtis*) of trees and shrubs of the elm family found mainly in temperate and tropical regions, having small, edible, cherrylike fruits. **2** the fruit of any of these trees. **3** the soft wood of any of these trees. [var. of *hagberry* < Scand.; cf. Danish *hæggebær*]

hack·le¹ (hak'əl) *n., v.* **-led, -ling.** —*n.* **1** a comb used in dressing flax, hemp, etc. **2** one of the long, slender feathers on the neck of certain male birds. **3** the neck plumage of certain birds. **4** *Fishing.* **a** the part of an artificial fly corresponding to the legs of an insect, made from feathers from the neck of a rooster. **b** a hackle fly. **5 hackles,** *pl.* the erectile hairs on the back of a dog's neck.
raise the hackles, *Informal.* arouse suspicion or anger.
—*v.* comb (flax, hemp, etc.) with a hackle. [ME *hakell.* Related to HECKLE.]

hack·le² (hak'əl) *v.* **-led, -ling.** cut roughly; hack; mangle. [< *hack¹*]

hackle fly a wingless artificial fly used in fishing.

hack·man (hak'mən) *n., pl.* **-men.** the driver of a hack or carriage for hire.

hack·ma·tack (hak'mə tak') *n. Cdn.* any of various evergreens, especially the tamarack. [< Algonquian]

hack·ney (hak'nē) *n., pl.* **-neys;** *adj., v.* **-neyed, -ney·ing.** —*n.* **1** a horse for ordinary riding. **2** a carriage for hire.
—*adj.* hired; let out, employed, or done for hire.
—*v.* use too often; make commonplace. [ME *hakeney* < *Hackney,* a town in England]

hack·neyed (hak'nēd) *adj.* used too often; commonplace: *"White as snow" is a hackneyed comparison.*

hack·saw (hak'sô' *or* -sô') *n.* a saw for cutting metal, having a narrow, fine-toothed blade fixed under tension in a frame. See **saw**[1] for picture.

hack·work (hak'wėrk') *n.* **1** routine literary work done by a hack. **2** any similar work of a routine or unstimulating nature.

had (had; *unstressed,* həd *or* əd) *v.* pt. and pp. of **have.**
☛ *Usage.* **Had better, had rather. Had better** is the usual idiom for giving advice or making an indirect command: *You had better take cover before she sees you.* Informally, a shorter form without *had* is common, but this should not be used in formal writing: *If he asks you to do it, you better do it.*

had·dock (had'ək) *n., pl.* **-dock** *or* **-docks.** an important food fish (*Melanogrammus aeglefinus*) of the northern Atlantic, related to and resembling the cod, but smaller. [ME *haddok*; origin uncertain]

Ha·des (hā'dēz) *n.* **1** *Greek mythology.* **a** the home of the dead, below the earth. **b** the god of the lower world, also called Pluto. **2 hades,** *Informal.* hell. [< Gk. *Haidēs*]

had·n't (had'ənt) had not.

had·ron (had'ron) *n.* any of a class of particles, including protons and neutrons, that are capable of taking part in strong nuclear reactions and whose constituent particles are quarks.

hadst (hadst) *v. Archaic.* 2nd pers. sing., past tense, of **have.** *Thou hadst* means *you* (sing.) *had.*

haema– *combining form.* hema-.
☛ *Spelling.* Words beginning with **haem-** or **haema-** are entered under their **hem-** and **hema-** forms.

haf·ni·um (haf'nē əm) *n.* a rare chemical element somewhat like zirconium. *Symbol:* Hf; *at.no.* 72; *at.wt.* 178.49. [< *Hafnia,* L name for Copenhagen]

haft (haft) *n., v.* —*n.* the handle of a knife, sword, dagger, etc.). —*v.* furnish with a handle or hilt; set in a haft. [OE *hæft*]

hag (hag) *n.* **1** a very ugly old woman, especially one who is vicious or malicious. **2** witch. [ME *hagge,* related to OE *hægtesse* witch, fury]

Ha·gen (hä'gən) *n.* in the *Nibelungenlied,* the murderer of Siegfried. [< G]

hag·fish (hag'fish') *n., pl.* **-fish** *or* **-fish·es.** any of about 20 species of primitive, eel-like, marine vertebrates constituting the family Myxinidae, having a round sucking mouth surrounded by thick barbels, and horny teeth which they use to bore into the bodies of fish they feed on, eating them from inside.

Hag·ga·dah *or* **Hag·ga·da** (hə gä'də) *n., pl.* **-doth** (-dôth'). **1** in the Talmud: **a** a story or legend that explains or illustrates the Jewish law. **b** the section containing such stories and legends. **2 a** the text of the Seder service on the first, or the first two, evenings of Passover. **b** a book containing this text. [< Hebrew *haggadah* story < *higgid* relate]

hag·gard (hag'ərd) *adj.* wild-looking from pain, fatigue, worry, hunger, etc.; gaunt; careworn. [< MF *hagard* of the hedges, untamed (hawk) ? < MHG *hag* hedge] —**hag'gard·ly,** *adv.* —**hag'gard·ness,** *n.*

hag·gis (hag'is) *n. Scottish.* the heart, lungs, and liver of a sheep mixed with suet and oatmeal and boiled in the stomach of the animal. [ME ? < Scottish *hag* chop; cf. ON *höggva.* Akin to HEW.]

hag·gle (hag'əl) *v.* **-gled, -gling;** *n.* —*v.* **1** dispute about a price or the terms of a bargain; wrangle. **2** mangle in cutting; hack. —*n.* the act of haggling; a wrangle or dispute about terms. [< Scottish *hag* chop, hack < ON *höggva*] —**hag'gler,** *n.*

hag·i·og·ra·pher (hag'ē og'rə fər *or* hä'jē og'rə fər) *n.* **1** a writer of lives of the saints. **2** any writer on sacred subjects.

hag·i·o·graph·ic (hag'ē ə graf'ik *or* hä'jē ə graf'ik) *adj.* of or having to do with hagiography.

hag·i·og·ra·phy (hag'ē og'rə fē *or* hä'jē og'rə fē) *n.* the writing of lives of the saints; hagiology. [< LL < Gk. *hagios* holy + *graphos* thing written]

hag·i·o·log·ic (hag'ē ə loj'ik *or* hä'jē ə loj'ik) *adj.* of or having to do with hagiology.

hag·i·ol·o·gy (hag'ē ol'ə jē *or* hä'jē ol'ə jē) *n., pl.* **-gies.** **1** literature that deals with the lives and legends of saints. **2** a book on this subject. **3** a list of saints. [< Gk. *hagios* holy + E *-logy*]

hag·rid·den (hag'rid'ən) *adj.* worried or tormented, as if by witches; harassed.

hah (hä) *interj.* ha.

hahn·i·um (hä'nē əm) a very unstable, artificially created element. *Symbol:* Ha; *at.no.* 105; *at.wt.* (262) or (260). [after Otto *Hahn* (1879-1968), a German physicist]
☛ *Usage.* No name has yet been officially adopted internationally for element 105. Scientists in the Soviet Union and the United States both claim priority in synthesizing this element. **Hahnium** is the name proposed by the U.S. group.

The Soviet group has proposed the name **nielsbohrium,** in honor of the Danish physicist *Niels Bohr* (1885-1962).

Hai·da (hī'də) *n., pl.* **Hai·da;** *adj.* —*n.* **1** a member of an Amerindian people of western British Columbia. **2** the language of the Haida. —*adj.* of or having to do with the Haida or their language.

hai·ku (hī'kü) *n.* a Japanese verse form consisting of three lines of five, seven, and five syllables respectively. [< Japanese]

hail[1] (hāl) *v., n., interj.* —*v.* **1** shout in welcome to; greet; cheer: *The crowd hailed the winner.* **2** greet as; call: *They hailed him leader.* **3** call loudly to; shout to: *The captain hailed the passing ship.*
hail from, come from.
—*n.* **1** a greeting; cheer; shout of welcome. **2** a loud call; shout.
within hail, near enough to hear a call or shout.
—*interj. Poetic.* greetings! welcome!: *Hail to the winner!*
hail fellow well met, very friendly.
[earlier *be hail!* < ON *heill* healthy] —**hail'er,** *n.*
☛ *Hom.* hale.

hail[2] (hāl) *n., v.* —*n.* **1** rounded lumps of ice, usually not much bigger than large raindrops, that fall instead of rain from cumulus clouds under certain meteorological conditions involving rising air currents (*used with a singular verb*): *The hail was coming down hard. Our garden was destroyed by hail.* **2** a fall or shower of such lumps of ice: *It was the first hail of the season.* **3** a penetrating or forceful rush or shower of something, having the effect of hail: *a hail of abuse. They were met by a hail of bullets.*
—*v.* **1** be the case that hail is falling (*used with the subject* **it**): *It hailed yesterday.* **2** pour down like hail: *The critics hailed scorn on his inept performance.*
hailed out, destroyed by hail: *Their crop was hailed out.*
[OE *hægel*]
☛ *Hom.* hale.

hail·stone (hāl'stōn') *n.* a piece of hail: *There were large hailstones all over the lawn.*

hail·storm (hāl'stôrm') *n.* a storm with hail.

hair (her) *n., adj.* —*n.* **1** a fine, threadlike outgrowth from the skin of human beings and animals. **2** a mass of such growths. **3** the hair of the human head: *I must get my hair cut.* **4** a fine, threadlike growth from the outer layer of plants. **5** a very narrow space; something very small; least degree: *He won the race by a hair.*
get in (someone's) **hair,** annoy; be a nuisance to.
let (one's) **hair down,** be informal or unconventional in behavior.
not turn a hair, not show any sign of being disturbed or embarrassed.
split hairs, make excessively fine distinctions.
to a hair, exactly; just right.
—*adj.* made of or with hair. [OE *ǣr*]
☛ *Hom.* hare, Herr.

hair·breadth (her'bredth' *or* -bretth') *adj., n.* —*adj.* very narrow; extremely close: *a hairbreadth escape.* —*n.* a very narrow space; a very small distance.

hair·brush (her'brush') *n.* a brush for the hair.

hair·cloth (her'kloth') *n.* a cloth made of horsehair or camel's hair, used to cover furniture, stiffen garments, etc.

hair·cut (her'kut') *n.* **1** the act or an instance of cutting the hair of the head: *I need a haircut.* **2** the result of cutting the hair; hairstyle.

hair·do (her'dü') *n., pl.* **-does.** the way in which the hair, especially of a woman, is arranged.

hair·dress·er (her'dres'ər) *n.* a person whose work is cutting and taking care of people's, especially women's, hair.

hair·dress·ing (her'dres'ing) *n.* **1** the act or process of cutting and arranging someone's hair. **2** the business or occupation of a hairdresser.

haired (herd) *adj.* having hair, especially of a specified kind (*usually used in compounds*): *dark-haired, curly-haired.*

hair·less (her'lis) *adj.* without hair.

hair·line (her'līn') *n.* **1** the natural irregular margin where hair growth ends on the head, especially the forehead. **2** a very thin line. **3** (*adj.*) very thin or narrow: *a hairline crack in a wall.* **4** *Printing.* a very fine line, especially a stroke or part of a letter thinner than other parts.

hair net a net worn to keep one's hair in place.

hair·piece (her'pēs') *n.* **1** a wing or section of real or artificial hair worn to cover baldness; toupee. **2** an extra length or section of real or artificial hair worn by women as part of a coiffure, to add bulk or length.

hair·pin (her'pin') *n., adj.* —*n.* **1** a pin, usually a U-shaped piece of wire, shell, or plastic, used by women to keep the hair in place. **2** a sharp bend in a road, river, etc., likened to a hairpin in shape. —*adj.* shaped like a hairpin; U-shaped: *a hairpin bend.*

hair-rais·ing (her'rāz'ing) *adj. Informal.* making the hair seem to stand on end; terrifying.

hair's-breadth or **hairs·breadth** (herz'bredth' *or* -bretth') *n. or adj.* hairbreadth.

hair seal any of a family (Phocidae) of seals highly specialized for an aquatic life, having hind limbs reduced to flippers that cannot be rotated forward, a broad head with large eyes and no external ears, and a coat consisting of stiff hair with only a thin undercoat. The harbor seal, ringed seal, and harp seal are hair seals.

hair shirt a rough shirt or girdle made of horsehair, worn as a penance.

hair·split·ting. (her'split'ing) *n., adj. —n.* the making of excessively fine distinctions. *—adj.* being excessively subtle.

hair·spring (her'spring') *n.* a very fine spiral spring that regulates the motion of the balance wheel in a watch or clock.

hair·style (her'stīl') *n.* a way of arranging or wearing the hair: *Her new hairstyle is very attractive.*

hair·styl·ist (her'stī'list) *n.* a hairdresser, especially one who creates hairstyles to suit individual customers.

hair trig·ger a trigger that operates by very slight pressure.

hair-trig·ger (her'trig'ər) *adj.* 1 having a hair trigger. 2 set off by the slightest pressure: *a hair-trigger temper.*

hair·y (her'ē) *adj.* **hair·i·er, hair·i·est.** 1 covered with hair; having much hair. 2 of or like hair. 3 *Slang.* difficult; disturbing; dismaying: *a hairy situation.* **—hair'i·ly,** *adv.* **—hair'i·ness,** *n.*

Hai·sla (hī'slə) *n., pl.* **Hai·sla** or **Hai·slas.** 1 a group of Kwakiutl Indians of the northern branch, living in British Columbia. 2 a member of this group.

Hai·ti·an (hā'shon *or* hā'tē ən) *n., adj. —n.* 1 a native or inhabitant of Haiti, a republic in the West Indies. 2 Haitian Creole. *—adj.* of or having to do with Haiti, its people, or their language.

Haitian Creole the language of the majority of Haitians, based on French, but incorporating features of various West African languages.

hak·a·pik (hak'ə pik) *n.* a long pole having a hammer head and a spike at one end, used in killing seals. [< Norwegian]

hake (hāk) *n., pl.* **hake** or **hakes.** any of several marine food fishes (genera *Merluccius* and *Urophycis*) of the cod family having an elongated body and large head. Some authorities classify hakes as a separate family, Merlucciidae. [dial. var. of *hook*; from the hooklike growth under the lower jaw; cf. Norwegian *hakefisk*]

ha·kim¹ (hə kēm') *n.* in Moslem countries, a physician. [< Arabic *hakīm* wise man]

ha·kim² (hä'kim) *n.* in Moslem countries, a ruler; judge or governor. [< Arabic *hākim* ruler]

ha·la·la (hə lä'lə) *n.* a unit of money in Saudi Arabia, equal to ¹⁄₁₀₀ of a rial. [< Arabic]

hal·berd (hal'bərd) *n.* a weapon that was both a spear and a battle-axe, used in warfare in the 15th and 16th centuries. [< F *hallebarde* < Ital. *alabarda* < Gmc.]

hal·berd·ier (hal'bər dēr') *n. Historical.* a soldier armed with a halberd.

hal·bert (hal'bərt) *n.* halberd.

hal·cy·on (hal'sē ən) *adj., n. —adj.* 1 calm; peaceful; happy. 2 of or having to do with the halcyon. *—n. Archaic or poetic.* a bird that was supposed to calm the waves; kingfisher. [< L < Gk. *halkyon,* var. of *alkyon* kingfisher]

hale¹ (hāl) *adj.* **hal·er, hal·est.** strong and well; healthy. [OE *hāl*] **—hale·ness,** *n.*
☞ *Hom.* hail.

hale² (hāl) *v.* **haled, hal·ing.** 1 drag by force. 2 compel to go: *The man was haled into court.* [ME < OF *haler* < Gmc. Doublet of HAUL.]
☞ *Hom.* hail.

ha·ler (hä'lər) *n., pl.* **-lers** or **-le·ru** (-lə rü'). a unit of money in Czechoslovakia, equal to ¹⁄₁₀₀ of a koruna.

half (haf) *n., pl.* **halves;** *adj., adv. —n.* 1 one of two equal parts. 2 in certain games, one of two equal periods. 3 *Golf.* a score equal to that of one's opponent, on any hole or on a round. 4 one of two nearly equal parts: *Which is the bigger half?* 5 *Football.* a halfback.
by half, by far.
—adj. 1 forming a half; being or making half of. 2 not complete; being only part of: *A half-truth is often no better than a lie.*
—adv. 1 to half of the full amount or degree: *a glass half full of milk.* 2 party: *speak half aloud.* 3 almost: *The beggar was half dead from hunger.*
half past, thirty minutes after a specified hour: *It's half past four.*
not half, a to a very slight extent. **b** *Informal.* not at all; the reverse of: *not half bad.*
[OE *healf*]

hat, āge, fär; let, ēqual, tèrm; it, īce
hot, ōpen, ôrder; oil, out; cup, pùt, rüle,
əbove, takən, pencəl, lemən, circəs
ch, child; ng, long; sh, ship
th, thin; ŦH, then; zh, measure

half-and-half (haf'ənd haf') *adj., adv., n. —adj.* 1 half one thing and half another. 2 not clearly one thing or the other. *—adv.* in two equal parts. *—n.* 1 a mixture of milk and cream. 2 *Brit.* a beverage consisting of two drinks, especially ale and porter, mixed together.

half·back (haf'bak') *n. Sports.* a player whose position is behind the forward line.

half-baked (haf'bākt') *adj.* 1 not cooked enough. 2 *Informal.* not fully worked out; incomplete. 3 *Informal.* not experienced; showing poor judgment.

half blood the relationship between persons who are related through one parent only.

half-blood (haf'blud') *n.* 1 half-breed. 2 a person related to another through one parent only.

half-blood·ed (haf'blud'id) *adj.* 1 having parents of different races. 2 related through only one parent.

half boot a boot reaching about halfway to the knee.

half-breed (haf'brēd') *n., adj. —n.* 1 a person whose parents are of different races. 2 Métis. *—adj.* of or having to do with half-breeds.

half brother a brother related through one parent only.

half-caste (haf'kast') *n.* a person whose parents belong to different races, especially an offspring of a European father and an Asiatic mother.

half cock the position of the hammer of a gun when it is pulled back halfway. At half cock the trigger is locked and the gun cannot be fired.
go off at half cock, a fire too soon. **b** act or speak without sufficient thought or preparation.

half crown *Historical.* a British silver coin worth two shillings and sixpence.

half-assed (haf'ast') *adj. Slang.* incompetent, inefficient, or ineffective: *a half-assed philosopher. She does her work in a half-assed sort of way.*

half eagle a former gold coin of the United States, worth $5.

half-heart·ed (haf'här'tid) *adj.* lacking interest or enthusiasm; not earnest: *a half-hearted attempt.* **—half'-heart'ed·ly,** *adv.* **—half'-heart'ed·ness,** *n.*

half hitch a knot formed by passing the end of a rope under and over its standing part and then inside the loop. See **knot** for picture.

half-hour (haf'our') *n.* 1 thirty minutes; half an hour: *It took us a half-hour to get there.* 2 the halfway point in one of the 24 hours of the day: *The bus goes every 30 minutes, on the hour and the half-hour.* 3 (*adj.*) of, having to do with, or lasting a half-hour: *a half-hour wait, the half-hour chime of a clock.* **—half'-hour'ly,** *adv.*

half-life (haf'līf') *n. Nuclear physics.* the time in which half of the original radiant energy of a radio-active substance is given off, used to distinguish one substance from another and as a measurement of radio-activity.

half-light (haf'līt') *n.* a dim light, as of early evening.

half-mast (haf'mast') *n., v. —n.* a position halfway or part way down from the top of a mast, staff, etc.: *When the Governor General died, flags were lowered to half-mast as a mark of respect.* *—v.* put (a flag) at half-mast: *They have half-masted the flag.*

half moon 1 the moon when only half of its surface appears bright. See **moon** for picture. 2 something shaped like a half moon or crescent.

half nelson *Wrestling.* a hold, applied by hooking one arm under an opponent's armpit and putting a hand on the back of his neck.

half note *Music.* a note held half as long as a whole note; minim. See **note** for picture.

half-pence (hā'pəns) *n.pl.* a pl. of **halfpenny.**

half·pen·ny (hā'pə nē *or* hāp'nē) *n., pl.* **half·pen·nies** (hā'pə nēz *or* hāp'nēz) or **half·pence.** 1 a small British coin worth half a penny, or one two-hundredths of a pound. 2 a former British coin in use before 1971, worth half an old penny, or one twenty-fourth of a shilling. 3 (*adj.*) worth a halfpenny. 4 (*adj.*) having little value.

half rest *Music.* a rest lasting as long as a half note.

half sister a sister related through one parent only.

half·sole (haf′sōl′) v. -soled, -sol·ing. put a new half sole or half soles on (shoes, etc.).

half sole the sole of a shoe or boot from the toe to the instep.

half sovereign Historical. a British gold coin worth ten shillings.

half–staff (haf′staf′) n. or v. Esp.U.S. half-mast.

half step Music. the difference in pitch between two adjacent keys on a piano; a semitone.

half–tim·bered (haf′tim′bərd) adj. having walls of wooden framework with the spaces filled by plaster, stone, or brick.

half–time (haf′tīm′) n. 1 Sports. the interval between two halves of a game. 2 (adj.) having to do with this period: the half-time score.

half tone Music. an interval equal to half a tone on the scale; half step.

half–tone (haf′tōn′) n. 1 Photo-engraving. a a process used in making pictures for books and magazines. b a picture made by this process. 2 a tone in a painting, etc. halfway between the highlights and deep shades.

half–track or **half·track** (haf′trak′) n. an army motor vehicle that has wheels in front and short tracks in the rear for driving, used to carry personnel and weapons.

half–truth (haf′trüth′) n. an assertion or statement that is only partly true.

half·way (haf′wā′) adv., adj. —adv. half the way; half the required distance: The rope reached only halfway to the boat. **go** or **meet halfway,** do one's share toward reaching an agreement or toward patching up a quarrel.
—adj. 1 midway: The inn served as a halfway house between the two towns. 2 not going far enough; incomplete; inadequate: Halfway measures are never satisfactory.

halfway house 1 an inn or other resting place at a midway point on a route or journey. 2 a place or hostel offering a somewhat structured and sheltered environment designed to help recently released convicts, mental patients, etc. become gradually adjusted to society.

half–wit (haf′wit′) n. 1 a feeble-minded person. 2 a stupid, foolish person.

half–wit·ted (haf′wit′id) adj. 1 feeble-minded. 2 very stupid; foolish. —**half′-wit′ted·ly,** adv. —**half′-wit′ted·ness,** n.

hal·i·but (hal′ə bət) n., pl. -but or -buts. 1 a North Atlantic flatfish (Hippoglossus hippoglossus) highly valued as a commerical food fish. It is the largest flatfish, sometimes reaching a length of two metres and a mass of over 300 kilograms. 2 any of various similar and related flatfishes, such as the **Pacific halibut** (H. stenolepsis) or the **Greenland halibut** (Reinhardtius hippoglossoides). [ME halybutte < haly holy + butte flatfish; eaten on holy days]

hal·ide (hal′īd or hal′id, hā′līd or hā′lid) n., adj. —n. any compound of a halogen with another element or radical. Sodium chloride is a halide. —adj. haloid. [< hal(ogen) + ide]

hal·i·dom (hal′ə dəm) n. Archaic. 1 a holy place; sanctuary. 2 something regarded as holy; a holy relic. [OE hāligdōm < hālig holy + -dōm position, conditon]

hal·i·dome (hal′ə dōm′) n. Archaic. halidom.

Hal·i·go·ni·an (hal′i gō′nē ən) n., adj. —n. 1 a native or inhabitant of Halifax, Nova Scotia. 2 a native or inhabitant of Halifax, a city in Yorkshire, England. —adj. of or having to do with Halifax.

hal·ite (hal′īt or hā′līt) n. native rock salt. [< NL halites < Gk. hals salt]

hal·i·to·sis (hal′ə tō′sis) n. bad or offensive breath. [< NL < L halitus breath]

hall (hol or hôl) n. 1 a way to go through a building; passageway; corridor. 2 a passageway or room at the entrance of a building. 3 a large room for holding meetings, parties, banquets, etc. 4 a building for public business: The mayor's office is in the town hall. 5 a building of a school, college, or university. 6 a mansion, especially the manor of an estate. [OE heall]
☛ Hom. haul.

hal·le·lu·jah or **hal·le·lu·iah** (hal′ə lü′yə) interj., n. —interj. praise ye the Lord! —n. a song of praise to God. Also, **alleluia.** [< Hebrew halleluyah praise ye Yah (Jehovah)]

Halley's comet (hal′ēz) the comet that Halley predicted could be seen about every 75 years, last seen in 1910. [after Edmund Halley (1656-1742), an English astronomer]

hal·liard (hal′yərd) See **halyard.**

hall·mark (hol′märk′ or hôl′-) n., v. —n. 1 an official mark indicating standard of purity, put on gold and silver articles. 2 a mark or sign of genuineness or good quality: Courtesy and self-control are the hallmarks of a gentleman. —v. put a hallmark on. [from Goldsmiths' Hall in London, the seat of the Goldsmiths' Company, by whom the stamping was legally regulated in Britain]

hal·lo or **hal·loa** (hə lō′) See **hello.**

hal·loo (hə lü′) interj., n., pl. -loos; v. -looed, -loo·ing. —interj. 1 Hunting. a shout to make hounds run faster. 2 a call or shout to attract attention.
—n. 1 Hunting. a shout to make hounds run faster. 2 a call or shout to attract attention. 3 a shout; call.
—v. shout; call. [ME < OF halloer chase with shouts, var. of haler < hale, hare (the shout). Cf. HARASS.]

hal·low[1] (hal′ō) v. 1 make holy; make sacred. 2 honor as holy or sacred. [OE hālgian < hālig holy]

hal·low[2] (hə lō′) interj., n. or v. halloo.

hal·lowed (hal′ōd; in church use, often hal′ō id) adj. 1 made holy; sacred; consecrated: A churchyard is hallowed ground. 2 honored or observed as holy.

Hal·low·een or **Hal·low·e'en** (hal′ō ēn′, hal′ə wēn′, hol′ə wēn′, or hol′ō ēn′) n. the evening of October 31. The next day is Allhallows or All Saints' Day. [for Allhallow-even < all + obs. hallow (ME halwe < OE hālga saint) + even[2]. See HALLOW[1].]

Hal·low·mas (hal′ō məs or hol′ō məs, hal′ō mas′ or hol′ō mas′) n. a former name of the Christian church feast of Allhallows or All Saints' Day, observed on November 1.

hal·lu·ci·nate (hə lü′sə nāt′) v. -at·ed, -at·ing. experience hallucinations.

hal·lu·ci·na·tion (hə lü′sə nā′shən) n. 1 the perception of an external object that is not in fact present. Hallucination is characteristic of some mental illnesses and can be induced by hypnosis, fever, or drugs. 2 the object of such perception. 3 any false impression or notion; delusion. [< L hallucinatio, -onis < hallucinari wander (of the mind), ult. < Gk. haluein be beside oneself; form influenced by L vaticinari rave]

hal·lu·ci·na·to·ry (hə lü′sə nə tôr′ē) adj. of, having to do with, or characterized by hallucination.

hal·lu·cin·o·gen (hə lü′sə nə jən) n. a drug or substance that produces hallucinations.

hal·lu·cin·o·gen·ic (hə lü′sə nə jen′ik) adj. of, producing, or tending to produce, hallucinations: hallucinogenic drugs.

hall·way (hol′wā′ or hôl′-) n. 1 a way to go through a building; passageway; corridor. 2 a passageway or room at the entrance of a building.

ha·lo (hā′lō) n., pl. -los or -loes; v. -loed, -lo·ing. —n. 1 a series of colored rings appearing around the sun or moon when it is seen through a cloud or ice crystals suspended in the atmosphere. The colors of the halo range from a red inner ring to a blue outer ring. Compare **corona** (def. 1). 2 a ring or circle of light shown around the head of a saint or divine being in a painting, etc. to symbolize saintliness; nimbus. 3 a kind of splendor, glory, or glamor that surround an idealized person or thing: A halo of romance surrounds King Arthur and his knights.
—v. surround with a halo. [< L halo < Gk. halōs disk, threshing floor (with reference to circular path of the oxen)]

hal·o·gen (hal′ə jən or hāl′ə jən) n. any one of the chemical elements, iodine, bromine, chlorine, fluorine, and astatine, that combine directly with metals to form salts. The halogens are the most active elements. [< Gk. hals, halos salt + E -gen]

hal·oid (hal′oid or hā′loid) adj., n. —adj. 1 of or like a salt. 2 formed from a halogen. —n. halide. [< Gk. hals, halos salt + E -oid]

hal·o·thane (hal′ə thān′) n. a nonexplosive, volatile liquid, the vapor of which is inhaled to produce general anesthesia. Formula: $C_2HBrClF_3$

halt[1] (holt or hôlt) v., n., interj. —v. 1 stop for a time. 2 cause to stop for a time.
—n. a stop for a time; stopping.
call a halt, order a stop.
—interj. a command to stop or come to a halt. [< F halte < G halt < halten stop, hold]

halt[2] (holt or hôlt) v., adj., n. —v. 1 be in doubt; hesitate; waver: Shyness made her halt as she talked. 2 be faulty or imperfect: A poor argument halts. 3 Archaic. be lame or crippled; limp.
—adj. Archaic. lame; crippled; limping.
—n. 1 Archaic. lameness; crippled condition; limping walk. 2 **the halt,** persons who halt, limp, or hesitate. [OE healt, adj., haltian, v.] —**halt′ing·ly,** adv.

hal·ter (hol′tər or hôl′tər) n., v. —n. 1 a headstall with an attached strap or rope for leading a horse, cow, etc. 2 a rope for hanging a convicted criminal; noose. 3 death by hanging. 4 a

woman's top, consisting of a front bodice fastened behind the neck and at the back or waist, leaving the arms, shoulders, most of the back, and, sometimes, the midriff bare. 5 (*adj.*) designating a dress neckline or bodice like this.
—*v.* put a halter on (an animal) or tie (an animal) with a halter. [OE *hælftre*]

hal·vah or **hal·va** (häl vä′ or häl′vä) *n.* a confection of ground sesame seeds and honey, etc.

halve (hav) *v.* **halved, halv·ing. 1** divide into two equal parts; share equally: *The two girls agreed to halve expenses on their trip.* **2** reduce to half: *The new machine halves the time of doing the work by hand.* [< *half*]
☛ Hom. **have.**

halves (havz) *n.* pl. of **half.**
by halves, a not completely; partly. **b** in a half-hearted way.
go halves, share equally.

hal·yard (hal′yərd) *n.* on a ship, a rope or tackle used to raise or lower a sail, yard, flag, etc. Also, **halliard.** [ME *hallyer* < *hale*²; form influenced by *yard*²]

ham (ham) *n., v.* **hammed, ham·ming.** —*n.* **1** salted and smoked meat from the upper part of a pig's hind leg. **2** the upper part of an animal's hind leg, used for food. See **pork** for picture. **3** Often, **hams,** *pl.* the back of the thigh; thigh and buttock. **4** the part of the leg back of the knee. **5** *Informal.* **a** an actor who exaggerates his speeches, gestures, etc. in a play or film; one who overacts. **b** clumsy or exaggerated acting. **c** any person who behaves or poses in an exaggerated way before an audience, photographer, etc. **6** *Informal.* an amateur radio operator.
—*v. Informal.* exaggerate a dramatic part or behave in an exaggerated manner; overact. [OE *hamm*]

Ham (ham) *n.* in the Bible, the second son of Noah, supposed by legend to be the ancestor of the African races (Gen. 10:6-20).

ham·a·dry·ad (ham′ə drī′əd or ham′ə drī′ad) *n.* **1** *Greek and Roman mythology.* one of a class of wood nymphs, each inhabiting a tree of which she was the spirit, and dying when the tree died. **2** king cobra. **3** hamadryas. [< L < Gk. *Hamadryas, -adis* < *hama* together (with) + *drys* tree]

ham·a·dry·as (ham′ə drī′əs) *n.* a baboon (*Papio hamadryas*) of the savanna regions of S Arabia and NE Africa, the adult male having a grey coat with a long mane extending from the head to the middle of the back. The hamadryas, also called sacred **baboon,** was regarded as sacred by the ancient Egyptians.

ham·burg (ham′bėrg) *n.* hamburger.

ham·burg·er (ham′bėr′gər) *n.* **1** ground beef. **2** this meat shaped into flat cakes and fried or broiled, especially when served in a split roll. [< G *Hamburger* pertaining to Hamburg]

Hamburg steak or **hamburg steak** hamburger (def. 1).

hame (hām) *n.* either of two curved pieces on either side of the collar in a horse's harness. The traces are fastened to the hames. See **harness** for picture. [OE *hama* covering]

Ham·ite (ham′īt) *n.* **1** a descendant of Ham. **2** a member of various peoples in N and E Africa.

Ham·it·ic (ham it′ik or hə mit′ik) *adj.* **1** of or having to do with the Hamites. **2** of or having to do with a group of languages in N and E Africa, including ancient Egyptian, Berber, Ethiopian, etc.

ham·let (ham′lit) *n.* a small group of houses together with a few businesses and services such as stores and a post office, situated in the country and having no fixed boundaries. A hamlet is usually smaller than a village and has no local government of its own. [< OF *hamelet,* dim. of *hamel* village < Gmc. Akin to HOME.]

ham·mer (ham′ər) *n., v.* —*n.* **1** a tool with a metal head and a handle, used to drive nails and beat metal into shape. **2** a machine in which a heavy block of metal is used for beating, striking, etc.: *a steam hammer, trip hammer.* **3** a small mallet used by auctioneers to indicate by a rap the sale of an article. **4** one of the padded mallets for striking the string of a piano. **5** a lever with a hard head for striking a bell, as in a clock. **6** the part of the firing mechanism of a gun that is released by the tripper so that it strikes the percussion cap of a cartridge or pushes the firing pin and explodes the charge. **7** the malleus of the ear. **8** *Track and field.* a metal ball attached to a length of steel wire with a handle on the other end by which it is twirled around in a circle and thrown for distance. **9** anything shaped or used like a hammer.
come or **go under the hammer,** be sold at auction.
hammer and tongs, with all one's force and strength: *The two boys fought hammer and tongs.*
—*v.* **1** drive, hit, or work with a hammer. **2** beat into shape with a hammer. **3** fasten by using a hammer. **4** hit again and again. **5** force by many efforts. **6** work out with much effort.
hammer at, work hard at; keep working hard at.: *He hammered at his homework until it was finished.*
hammer away, a work hard at; keep working at: *She hammered away at her homework. He hammered away till the job was done.*

hat, āge, fär; let, ēqual, tèrm; it, īce
hot, ōpen, ôrder; oil, out; cup, pu̇t, rüle,
above, takən, pencəl, lemən, circəs
ch, child; ng, long; sh, ship
th, thin; ᴛʜ, then; zh, measure

b keep nagging; badger: *He hammered away at his mother till he got what he wanted.*
hammer out, a beat into shape with a hammer. **b** flatten or spread with a hammer. **c** remove with a hammer. **d** work out with much effort. **e** make clear by much thinking or talking: *The boys finally hammered out the plans for their clubhouse.* [OE *hamor*] —**ham′mer·er,** *n.* —**ham′mer·like′,** *adj.*

hammer and sickle the Soviet emblem of a crossed hammer and sickle, standing for the laborer and the farmer, that symbolizes Russian communism.

ham·mer·head (ham′ər hed′) *n.* any of a genus (*Sphyrna*) of sharks found in warm and temperate seas throughout the world, having a broad, flattened head resembling a double-headed hammer or a broad shovel. The hammerheads constitute the family Sphyrnidae.

ham·mer·less (ham′ər lis) *adj.* **1** having no hammer. **2** of firearms, having no visible hammer. A hammerless pistol has its hammer covered.

hammer lock *Wrestling.* a hold in which an opponent's arm is twisted and held behind his back.

ham·mock (ham′ək) *n.* a swinging bed or couch made of canvas, netted cord, etc. that is suspended at both ends. [< Sp. *hamaca* < Carib]

ham·per¹ (ham′pər) *v.* hold back; hinder: *The unwieldy bundle severely hampered his progress.* [ME *hampre(n);* origin uncertain]

ham·per² (ham′pər) *n.* a large container, often a wicker basket, usually having a cover: *a picnic hamper, a clothes hamper.* [var. of *hanaper* < OF *hanapier* < *hanap* cup < Gmc.]

ham·ster (ham′stər) *n.* any of various Old World rodents (family Cricetidae) having a short tail, stocky body, and large cheek pouches. Hamsters are often kept as cage pets. [< G]

ham·string (ham′string′) *n., v.* **-strung** or **(rare) -stringed, -string·ing.** —*n.* **1** in a human being, one of the tendons at the back of the knee. **2** in a four-footed animal, the great tendon at the back of the hock. —*v.* **1** cripple by cutting the hamstring. **2** cripple; disable; destroy the activity, efficiency, etc. of.

ham·strung (ham′strung′) *v.* pt. and pp. of **hamstring.**

hand (hand) *n., v., adj.* —*n.* **1** the end part of the arm; part that a person grasps and holds things with. **2** the end of any limb that grasps, holds, or clings. We call a monkey's feet hands. **3** something resembling a hand in shape, appearance, or use: *The hands of a clock or watch show the time.* **4** a hired worker who uses his hands: *a factory hand, a farm hand.* **5** a member of a ship's crew; sailor. **6** Usually, **hands,** *pl.* a possession; control: *The property is no longer in my hands.* **b** care or charge: *The baby-sitter was glad when the sick child was taken off his hands.* **7** a part or share in doing something: *He had no hand in the matter.* **8** side: *At her left hand stood two men.* **9** source: *She heard his story at first hand.* **10** one's style of handwriting: *He writes in a clear hand.* **11** a person's signature. **12** skill; ability: *The artist's work showed a master's hand.* **13** a person, with reference to action, skill, or ability: *She is a great hand at thinking up new games.* **14** a round of applause or clapping: *The crowd gave the winner a big hand.* **15** a promise of marriage. **16** a measure used in giving the height of horses, etc.; the breadth of a hand, about 10 centimetres: *This horse is 18 hands high.* **17** *Card games.* **a** the cards held by a player in one round of a card game. **b** one round of a card game. **c** a player in a card game.
all hands, a all sailors of a ship's crew. **b** *Informal.* all members of a group.
at first hand, from direct knowledge or experience.
at hand, a within reach; near; close. **b** ready.
at second hand, from a source other than the original source: *The story he had heard at second hand proved to be an exaggeration.*
at the hand (or **hands**) **of,** from (a person, as giver, doer, etc.): *We have received many favors at his hands.*
bear a hand, help.
by hand, by using the hands, not machinery.
change hands, pass from one person to another: *During the sale, a lot of money changed hands.*
clean hands, freedom from crime or dishonesty.
eat out of (one's) **hand,** follow one's ideas, leadership, etc.; submit to one's authority.

force (someone's) hand, a make a person do something. **b** make a person show what he is going to do.

from hand to mouth, without being able to put something aside for the future: *During the long strike, many men with families lived from hand to mouth.*

give a hand, assist; help: *Please give me a hand with this trunk.*

hand and glove (with), intimate; in close relations.

hand in glove (with), intimate; in close relations.

hand in hand, a holding hands. **b** together.

hands down, easily: *He won the contest hands down.*

hand to hand, close together; at close quarters: *to fight hand to hand.*

have (one's) hands full, be very busy; be able to do no more; have as much to do as one can manage.

in hand, a under control. **b** in possession. **c** going along; being done.

join hands, a become partners. **b** marry.

keep (one's) hand in, keep up one's skill; keep in practice.

lay hands on, a seize; take; get. **b** arrest. **c** attack; harm. **d** bless by touching with the hands.

lend a hand, help or assist: *He asked his brother to lend a hand with the chores.*

on hand, a within reach; near; close. **b** ready; in stock: *The supermarket has lots of oranges on hand.* **c** present: *I will be on hand again tomorrow.*

on the one hand, considering this side; from this point of view: *On the one hand I feel that to buy this house would be a good investment in the long run.*

on the other hand, considering the other side of the question or argument; from the opposite point of view: *I want the bicycle very much; on the other hand, I can't afford to buy it.*

out of hand, a out of control: *The angry crowd soon got out of hand.* **b** at once; without hesitation: *The boy was expelled out of hand.* **c** finished; done with.

show (one's) hand, reveal one's real intentions.

sit on (one's) hands, *Informal.* **a** applaud feebly; show little enthusiasm for a play, performance, etc. **b** do nothing.

take a hand, take part or make an attempt: *It looked so interesting that he was tempted to take a hand himself.*

take in hand, a bring under control: *That child should be taken in hand by someone.* **b** start to deal with: *The supervisor promised to take the matter in hand.*

tie (someone's) hands, make one unable to do something.

to hand, a within reach; near; close. **b** in one's possession.

try (one's) hand, try to do; test one's ability: *After trying his hand at politics, he soon went back into business.*

turn (one's) hand to, work at.

wait on hand and foot, serve diligently.

wash (one's) hands of, have no more to do with; refuse to be responsible for.

—*v.* **1** give with the hand; pass; pass along: *Please hand me the butter.* **2** help with the hand: *The hotel doorman handed the lady into her car.*

hand down, a pass along. **b** *Law.* announce (a decision, opinion, etc.).

hand in, give or pass to a person in authority: *The tests were handed in to the teacher.*

hand it to, *Informal.* acknowledge as superior: *You've got to hand it to him; he's quite a salesman.*

hand on, pass along: *He read the note and handed it on to the person next to him.*

hand out, give out; distribute: *The storekeeper handed out free suckers.*

hand over, give to another; deliver: *When John asked for his book, I handed it over.*

—*adj.* of, for, by, or in the hand. [OE] —**hand'like',** *adj.*

hand·bag (han'bag' *or* hand'-) *n.* **1** a woman's small bag for money, keys, cosmetics, etc.; purse. **2** a small travelling bag to hold clothes, etc.

hand·ball (han'bol' *or* hand'-, han'bôl' *or* hand'-) *n.* **1** a game in which two or four players use their hands, usually gloved, to hit a small, hard, rubber ball against a wall or board or against the walls of a court. **2** the ball used in this game.

hand·bar·row (han'bar'ō *or* hand'-, han'ber'ō *or* hand'-) *n.* **1** a frame with two handles at each end by which it is carried. **2** handcart.

hand·bell (hand'bel') *n.* a bell with a handle, to be rung by hand, especially one of a tuned set used for musical performances.

hand·bill (han'bil' *or* hand'-) *n.* a printed notice, announcement, advertisement, etc. to be handed out to people.

hand·book (han'bŭk' *or* hand'-) *n.* **1** a small book of directions or reference, especially in some field of study; manual: *a handbook of engineering.* **2** a guidebook for tourists. **3** a book for recording bets.

hand brake a brake operated by a manual lever. The emergency brake on some automobiles is a hand brake.

hand·breadth (han'bredth' *or* hand'-, han'bretth' *or* hand'-) *n.* the breadth of a hand, used as a measure. It varies from about 6 to 10 cm.

hand·car (hand'kär') *n.* a small car used on railway tracks by maintenance men and driven by a hand lever that is pumped up and down.

hand·cart (han'kärt' *or* hand'-) *n.* a small cart pulled or pushed by hand.

hand·clap (hand'klap') *n.* a striking together of the hands to signal, mark rhythm, applaud, etc.

hand·craft (hand'kraft') *n., v.* —*n.* handicraft. —*v.* make by hand or handicraft: *handcrafted furniture, a handcrafted shawl.*

hand·cuff (han'kuf' *or* hand'-) *n., v.* —*n.* Usually, **handcuffs,** *pl.* a device to secure a prisoner, usually consisting of a pair of metal rings or clasps joined by a short chain, that are fastened and locked about the wrists. —*v.* put handcuffs on: *The prisoner was handcuffed. They handcuffed him to a post.*

–handed *combining form.* **1** having a hand or hands. **2** having a certain kind or number of hands, as in *left-handed.* **3** using a certain number of hands: *a two-handed stroke.*

hand·ful (han'fŭl *or* hand'-) *n., pl.* **-fuls. 1** as much or as many as the hand can hold. **2** a small number or quantity. **3** *Informal.* a person or thing that is hard to handle or control: *That boy is quite a handful.*

hand grenade a small bomb designed to be thrown by hand.

hand·grip (hand'grip') *n.* **1** a grip or grasping of the hand, used in greeting. **2** a handle.

come to handgrips, get into a hand-to-hand fight.

hand·gun (han'gun' *or* hand'gun') *n.* a firearm that is held and fired with one hand: *A revolver is a handgun.*

hand·held (hand'held') *adj.* of an appliance, machine, etc., designed to be operated while being held in the hand: *a hand-held electric mixer.*

hand·hold (hand'hōld') *n.* a place to put the hands.

hand·i·cap (han'di kap' *or* han'dē-) *n., v.* **-capped, -cap·ping.** —*n.* **1** something that puts a person at a disadvantage; hindrance; mental or physical defect: *A sore throat is a handicap to a singer.* **2** a contest in which rules are applied to ensure that nobody has an unfair advantage or is at an unfair disadvantage. **3** the disadvantage or advantage given in such a contest or game: *If a runner has a handicap of 5 metres in a 100-metre dash, it means that he has to run either 95 metres or 105 metres.* —*v.* **1** put at a disadvantage as by a mental or physical defect; hinder: *The pitcher was handicapped by a lame arm.* **2** give a handicap to: *The Sports Committee handicapped me 5 metres.* [for *hand in cap;* apparently with reference to an old game] —**hand'i·cap'per,** *n.*

hand·i·craft (han'di kraft' *or* han'dē-) *n.* **1** skilful use of the hands: *The design on the leather purse showed fine handicraft.* **2** a trade or art requiring skill with the hands: *Basket weaving is a handicraft.* **3** an article made by hand, especially one requiring skill or imagination to make: *The display of handicrafts included wooden ware, pottery, and children's clothes.* [alteration of *handcraft,* patterned after *handiwork*]

hand·i·crafts·man (han'di krafts'mən *or* han'dē-) *n., pl.* **-men.** a person skilled with his hands in a trade or art; craftsman.

hand·i·work (han'di wĕrk' *or* han'dē-) *n.* **1** work done with the hands. **2** work that a person has done himself. **3** the result of a person's action. [OE *handgeweorc* handwork]

hand·ker·chief (hang'kər chif) *n.* **1** a piece of fine cotton, linen, silk, etc., generally square, used especially for wiping the nose. **2** a piece of cloth worn over the head or around the neck; kerchief.

han·dle (han'dəl) *n., v.* **-dled, -dling.** —*n.* **1** the part of a thing made to be held or grasped by the hand. **2** a chance; opportunity; occasion: *Don't let your conduct give any handle for gossip.* **3** *Slang.* a name or title.

fly off the handle, *Slang.* get angry or excited; lose one's temper or self-control.

handle to (one's) name, *Slang.* a title of nobility, etc.

—*v.* **1** touch, feel, hold, or move with the hand; use the hands on: *Don't handle the ornaments; they're very delicate.* **2** manage; direct; control: *The captain handles his soldiers well.* **3** behave or perform in a certain way when driven, managed, directed, etc.: *This car handles easily.* **4** deal with; treat: *The boy handled his kitten roughly.* **5** deal in; trade in: *The store handles meat and groceries.* [OE *handle < hand* hand]

han·dle·bars (han'dəl bärz') *n.pl.* the bars, usually curved, in front of the rider, by which a bicycle, etc. is guided.

–handled *combining form.* having a — handle: *a black-handled pot = a pot having a black handle.*

han·dler (han′dlər) *n.* **1** a person or thing that handles. **2** a person who helps to train a boxer, or who acts as his second during a boxing match. **3** a person who shows dogs or cats in a contest.

hand·made (han′mād′ *or* hand′-) *adj.* made by hand, not machinery; not machine-made.

hand·maid (han′mād′ *or* hand′-) *n.* **1** a female servant. **2** a female attendant.

hand·maid·en (han′mād′ən *or* hand′-) *n.* handmaid.

hand–me–down (hand′mē doun′) *n., adj. Informal.* —*n.* **1** a second-hand article, especially a garment, passed from one person to another. **2** any cheap, badly tailored coat, suit, etc. —*adj.* having been passed on or handed down.

hand organ a large music box that is made to play tunes by turning a crank.

hand·out (hand′out′) *n.* **1** a portion of food handed out: *The tramp was given a handout.* **2** a news story or piece of publicity issued to the press by a business organization, government agency, etc. **3** a set of mimeographed notes issued to students in connection with their courses, to people attending a public lecture, etc.

hand–picked (hand′pikt′ *or* hand′-) *adj.* **1** picked by hand. **2** carefully selected. **3** unfairly selected.

hand·rail (hand′rāl′) *n.* a railing used as a guard or support on a stairway, platform, etc.

hand·saw (han′so′ *or* hand′-, han′sô′- *or* hand′-) *n.* a saw used with one hand.

hand·sel (han′səl) *n., v.* **-selled** *or* **-seled, -sel·ling** *or* **-sel·ing.** —*n.* **1** a gift given in token of good wishes, as at New Year's, to one entering a new job or house, etc. **2** a first payment; the first money taken in by a dealer in the morning, or on opening a new store. **3** a first experience of anything; forestate. —*v.* **1** give a handsel to. **2** inaugurate. **3** be the first to use, try, taste, etc. Also, **hansel.** [OE *handselen* giving of the hand (i.e., to confirm a bargain)]

hand·set (hand′set′) *n.* a telephone that has the receiver and mouthpiece in the same unit.

hand·shake (han′shāk′ *or* hand′-) *n.* a clasping and shaking of hands by two people as a sign of friendship when meeting or parting, or to seal a bargain.

hand·some (han′səm) *adj.* **-som·er, -som·est. 1** good-looking; pleasing in appearance. We usually say that a man is handsome, but that a woman is pretty or beautiful. **2** fairly large: *Ten thousand dollars is a handsome amount of money.* **3** generous: *a handsome gift.* **4** gracious; proper. [ME *handsom* easy to handle, ready at hand < *hand + -some¹*] —**hand′some·ly,** *adv.* —**hand′some·ness,** *n.*

☛ *Syn.* **1.** See note at **beautiful.**

hand–spike (han′spīk′ *or* hand′-) *n.* a bar used as a lever, especially on a ship.

hand–spring (han′spring′ *or* hand′-) *n.* a somersault made from a standing position, in which the person comes down first on his hands, turning the body forward or backward in a full circle and landing again on his feet.

hand–stand (han′stand′ *or* hand′-) *n.* an act or feat of supporting the body on the hands alone, while the trunk and legs are stretched in the air.

hand–to–hand (han′tə hand′ *or* hand′-) *adj. or adv.* close together; at close quarters: *a hand-to-hand fight.*

hand–to–mouth (han′tə mouth′ *or* hand′-) *adj.* having nothing to spare; being unable to save or provide for the future; not thrifty.

hand·work (hand′wėrk′) *n.* work done by hand, not by machinery.

hand·wov·en (hand′wō′vən) *adj.* **1** woven on a loom operated by hand. **2** of basketwork, etc., woven by hand.

hand·writ·ing (hand′rīt′ing) *n.* **1** writing done by hand; writing done with pen, pencil, etc. **2** a manner or style of writing: *He recognized his mother's handwriting on the envelope.*

handwriting on the wall, a in the Bible, a cryptic handwriting seen by Belshazzar, King of Babylon, on the wall of his palace, which Daniel interpreted as a prophecy of the fall of Babylon (Daniel 5:26-28). **b** a portent of doom.

see *or* **read the handwriting on the wall,** a perceive that an institution, order, way of life, etc. is coming to an end. **b** see things as the really are.

hand·y (han′dē) *adj.* **hand·i·er, hand·i·est. 1** easy to reach or use; saving work; useful; convenient: *handy shelves, a handy tool.* **2** skilful with the hands: *She's handy with tools.* **3** easy to handle or manage. —**hand′i·ly,** *adv.* —**hand′i·ness,** *n.*

hand·y·man (han′dē man′) *n., pl.* **-men.** a man who does odd jobs.

---

hat, āge, fär; let, ēqual, tèrm; it, īce
hot, ōpen, ôrder; oil, out; cup, pút, rüle,
əbove, takən, pencəl, lemən, circəs

ch, child; ng, long; sh, ship
th, thin; ᵺ, then; zh, measure

hang (hang) *v.* **hung** *or* (*for defs. 3, 4*) **hanged, hang·ing;** *n.* —*v.* **1** fasten or be fastened to something above. **2** fasten or be fastened so as to swing or turn freely: *to hang a door on its hinges.* **3** put or be put to death by hanging with a rope around the neck: *He was hanged several weeks after being sentenced.* **4** die by hanging. **5** cover or decorate with things that hang: *to hang a window with curtains. The walls were hung with pictures.* **6** bend down; droop: *He hung his head in shame.* **7** fasten in position. **8** attach (paper, etc.) to walls. **9** depend. **10** be wearisome or tedious: *Time hangs on his hands.* **11** hold fast; cling. **12** be doubtful or undecided; hesitate; waver. **13** keep (a jury) from making a decision or reaching a verdict. One member can hang a jury by refusing to agree with the others. **14** loiter; linger: *Don't hang about!* **15** hover.

hang back, be unwilling to go forward; be backward.

hang it! an expression of annoyance.

hang on, a hold tight: *The dying man hung on to life for several days.* **b** be unwilling to let go, stop, or leave. **c** depend on. **d** consider or listen to very carefully: *She hung on the teacher's every word.*

hang out, a show by hanging outside. **b** lean out. **c** *Slang.* live; stay.

hang over, a be about to happen to; threaten: *The possibility of being punished hung over him for days.* **b** *Informal.* remain from an earlier time or condition.

hang together, a stick together. **b** be coherent or consistent: *The story does not hang together.*

hang up, a put on a hook, peg, etc. **b** put a telephone receiver back in place. **c** hold back; delay; detain. —*n.* the way that something hangs: *I don't like the hang of the skirt.*

get the hang of, *Informal.* a get the knack of; discover how to operate, do, etc.: *She had never used a calculator before, but it didn't take her long to get the hang of it.* **b** understand the meaning or significance of: *I didn't quite get the hang of what he said.*

give *or* **care a hang,** *Informal.* care or be concerned about (*usually used with a negative*): *He doesn't give a hang about anybody.* [OE *hōn* (with past *hēng*) suspend, and OE *hangian* be suspended, blended with ON *hengja* suspend]

☛ *Usage.* **Hanged, hung.** In formal English, the preferred form of the past tense and past participle for def. 3 only is **hanged:** *The murderer was hanged.* In informal English, however, **hung** is often used: *He was hung for his crimes.*

hang·ar (hang′ər) *n.* **1** a shed for aircraft. **2** a shed. [< F < Med. L *angarium* shed for shoeing horses, ? < Gmc.]

☛ *Hom.* **hanger.**

hang·bird (hang′bėrd′) *n.* any of various birds that build a hanging nest, especially the Baltimore oriole.

hang·dog (hang′dog′) *adj.* ashamed; sneaking; degraded.

hang·er (hang′ər) *n.* **1** a person who hangs things. A paperhanger puts on wallpaper. **2** a tool or machine that hangs things. **3** anything on which something else is hung: *a coat hanger.* **4** a loop, ring, etc. attached to something to hang it up by. **5** a kind of short, light sword formerly worn by sailors on their belts.

☛ *Hom.* **hangar.**

hang·er–on (hang′ər on′) *n., pl.* **hang·ers–on. 1** a follower; dependent. **2** an undesirable follower. **3** a person who often goes to a place.

hang–glid·er (hang′glī′dər) *n.* a large, flat, usually delta-shaped kite with an attached harness or seat, designed to carry a person through the air for a short while. The flyer runs into the wind toward the edge of a cliff and soars down to earth, suspended from the kite.

hang–glid·ing (hang′glī′ding) *n.* the sport of gliding through the air while suspended from a hang-glider.

hang·ing (hang′ing) *n., adj.* —*n.* **1** death by hanging with a rope around the neck. **2** Often, **hangings,** *pl.* something that hangs from a wall, bed, etc: *Curtains and valances are hangings.* —*adj.* **1** deserving to be punished by hanging: *a hanging crime.* **2** fastened to something above. **3** leaning over or down. **4** located on a height or steep slope.

hang·man (hang′mən) *n., pl.* **-men.** a man who hangs criminals who have been sentenced to death by hanging.

hang·nail (hang′nāl′) *n.* a bit of skin that hangs partly loose near a fingernail. [alteration of *agnail,* OE *angnægl* (< ang- compressed, painful + *nægl* nail, corn), under the influence of *hang*]

hang·out (hang′out′) *n. Slang.* **1** a place one lives in or goes to often. **2** a rendezvous, especially for criminals.

hang·o·ver (hang′ō′vər) *n.* **1** *Informal.* something that remains from an earlier time or condition. **2** *Slang.* a condition resulting from consumption of too much alcohol the previous night.

hang–up (hang′up′) *n. Slang.* a personal or emotional difficulty; an obsession or inhibition.

hank (hangk) *n.* **1** a coil; loop. **2** a loop or coil of yarn, especially one containing a definite length. [< ON *hönk*]

han·ker (hang′kər) *v.* wish; crave. [origin uncertain]

han·ker·ing (hang′kər ing *or* hang′kring) *n.* a longing; craving: *I have a hankering for a large, juicy steak.*

hank·y (hang′kē) *n., pl.* **-hank·ies.** *Informal.* handkerchief.

hank·y–pank·y (hang′kē pang′kē) *n. Slang.* underhand or questionable dealing or behavior; dishonest or illicit goings-on: *He denied that there was any hanky-panky involved in his getting the contract.*

Han·o·ve·ri·an (han′ō vēr′ē ən) *adj., n.* —*adj.* **1** of or having to do with Hanover, Germany. **2** of or having to do with Hanover, the English royal house from 1714 to 1901. —*n.* **1** a native or inhabitant of Hanover. **2** a supporter of the House of Hanover.

Han·sard (han′sərd) *n.* the printed record of the proceedings of the Canadian or British House of Commons. [after Luke *Hansard* (1752-1828), first compiler]

hanse (hans) *n.* in the Middle Ages, a merchant guild of a town. [ME < OF < MHG *hanse* merchants' guild < OHG *hansa* band]

Han·se·at·ic (han′sē at′ik) *adj.* of or having to do with the Hanseatic League.

Hanseatic League in the Middle Ages, a league of towns in Germany and nearby countries for the promotion and protection of commerce.

han·sel (han′səl) See **handsel.**

An English hansom cab, widely used for public transport in the second half of the 19th century

han·som cab (han′səm) *n.* a two-wheeled cab for two passengers drawn by one horse. [after Joseph *Hansom*, an early designer of such cabs]

Ha·nuk·kah *or* **Ha·nuk·ka** (hä′nü kä′; *Hebrew,* hä′nü kä′) *n.* the Feast of Dedication or the Feast of Lights, an eight-day Jewish festival, falling in December. Also, **Chanukah.** [< Hebrew *hannukah* dedication]

hap (hap) *n., v.* **happed, hap·ping.** *Archaic.* —*n.* chance; luck. —*v.* happen. [ME < ON *happ*]

hap·haz·ard (*n.* hap′haz′ərd; *adj. or adv.* hap′haz′ərd) *n., adj., adv.* —*n.* chance: *Events seemed to happen at haphazard.* —*adj.* random; casual; not planned: *Haphazard answers are usually wrong.* —*adv.* by chance; at random; casually: *He took a card haphazard from the pack.* —**hap′haz′ard·ly,** *adv.* —**hap′haz′ard·ness,** *n.* ☛ *Syn. adj.* See note at **random.**

hap·less (hap′lis) *adj.* unlucky; unfortunate. —**hap′less·ly,** *adv.* —**hap′less·ness,** *n.*

hap·loid (hap′loid) *adj., n.* —*adj.* designating a nucleus, cell, or organism possessing a single set of unpaired chromosomes. When a diploid germ cell undergoes meiosis, it becomes a haploid cell, or gamete. —*n.* a haploid nucleus, cell, or organism. Compare **diploid.** [< Gk. *haploeidēs* single-formed < *haplous* single + *eidos* form. 20c.]

hap·ly (hap′lē) *adv. Archaic.* perhaps; by chance.

hap·pen (hap′ən) *v.* **1** take place; occur: *Nothing interesting happens here.* **2** be or take place by chance: *Accidents will happen.* **3** have the fortune (*to*); chance: *I happened to sit next to a famous hockey player.* **4** be done (*to*); go wrong with: *Something has happened to this lock; the key won't turn.*

as it happens, by chance; as it turns out: *As it happens, I have no money with me.*

happen on *or* **upon, a** meet by chance. **b** find by chance: *She happened on a dime while looking for her ball.*

happen to, be the fate of; become of: *Nobody knew what happened to the last explorer.* [ME *happen*(n) < *hap*]

hap·pen·ing (hap′ən ing *or* hap′ning) *n.* anything that happens; event; occurrence.

hap·pen·stance (hap′ən stans′) *n. Informal.* a situation or circumstance that is the result of chance: *The success of the deal was more happenstance than shrewd bargaining.*

hap·pi·ly (hap′ə lē) *adv.* **1** in a happy manner; with pleasure, joy, and gladness: *She lives happily.* **2** luckily; fortunately: *Happily, he saved her from falling.* **3** aptly; appropriately.

hap·pi·ness (hap′ē nis) *n.* **1** being happy; gladness. **2** good luck; good fortune. **3** aptness.

☛ *Syn.* **1. Happiness, felicity, bliss** = a feeling of satisfaction and pleasure. **Happiness** is the general word, applying to a feeling of contentment coming from being and doing well or of satisfaction at having got what one wanted: *His promotion brought him happiness.* **Felicity,** formal, means great or joyous happiness: *May the couple live their lives together in health and felicity.* **Bliss** suggests feeling lifted to the heights of happiness or joy: *They are in a state of bliss now that they are engaged.*

hap·py (hap′ē) *adj.* **-pi·er, -pi·est. 1** feeling or showing pleasure and joy; glad; pleased; contented. **2** lucky, fortunate: *By a happy chance, I found the lost money.* **3** clever and fitting; apt; successful and suitable: *a happy way of expressing an idea.* [ME *happy* < *hap*] ☛ *Syn.* **1.** See note at **glad.**

hap·py–go–luck·y (hap′ē gō luk′ē) *adj.* taking things easily; trusting to luck.

happy hunting ground 1 the North American Indian paradise. **2** any paradise. **3** any pleasant place with which one is particularly associated: *He returns every summer to his happy hunting ground in California.*

Haps·burg (haps′bėrg; *German,* häps′bürk) *n.* a German princely family, prominent since about 1100. The Hapsburgs were rulers of the Holy Roman Empire from 1438 to 1806, of Austria from 1804 to 1918, of Hungary from 1526 to 1918, and of Spain from 1516 to 1700. Also, **Habsburg.** [< *Habsburg,* shortening of *Habichtsburg* (meaning hawk's castle), name of a castle in Aargau, Switzerland]

har·a–ki·ri (har′ə kēr′ē, her′ə-, *or* hä′rə-) *n.* suicide committed by ripping open the abdomen with a knife, the national form of honorable suicide in Japan. Also, **hara-kari** *or* **hari-kari.** [< Japanese < *hara* belly + *kiri* cutting]

ha·rangue (hə rang′) *n., v.* **-rangued, -rangu·ing.** —*n.* **1** a noisy speech. **2** a long, pompous speech. —*v.* **1** address in a harangue. **2** deliver a harangue. [ME < OF *arenge* < Gmc.] —**ha·rangu′er,** *n.*

har·ass (har′əs, her′əs, *or* hə ras′) *v.* **1** trouble by repeated attacks; harry: *Pirates harassed the villages along the coast.* **2** disturb; worry; torment. [< F *harasser* < OF *harer* set a dog on] ☛ *Syn.* **2.** See note at **worry.**

har·ass·ment (har′əs mənt, her′əs mənt, *or* hə ras′mənt) *n.* **1** harassing. **2** being harassed; worry. **3** something that harasses.

har·bin·ger (här′bin jər) *n., v.* —*n.* one that goes ahead to announce another's coming; forerunner: *The robin is a harbinger of spring.* —*v.* announce beforehand; announce. [ME < OF *herbergere* provider of shelter (hence, one who goes ahead), ult. < *herberge* lodging < Gmc. Akin to HARBOR.]

har·bor *or* **har·bour** (här′bər) *n., v.* —*n.* **1** a naturally or artificially sheltered area of deep water where ships may dock or anchor. A harbor may have loading and unloading facilities for passengers and cargo. **2** any place of shelter. —*v.* **1** give shelter to; give a place to hide: *The dog's shaggy hair harbors fleas.* **2** take shelter or refuge. **3** keep or nourish in the mind: *Don't harbor unkind thoughts.* [OE *hereborg* lodgings < *here* army + *beorg* shelter] —**har′bor·er** *or* **har′bour·er,** *n.* —**har′bor·less** *or* **har′bour·less,** *adj.*

☛ *Syn. n.* **1. Harbor, port** = place of shelter for ships. **Harbor** emphasizes shelter, and applies to a protected part of the sea, or other large body of water, where land or breakwaters shield against wind and heavy waves: *Many yachts are lying at anchor in the harbor.* **Port** emphasizes the idea of a place to put in to land or unload at the end of a voyage, and applies particularly to a harbor where commercial ships dock for loading and unloading: *The ship arrived in port.* *v.* **3.** See note at **cherish.**

har·bor·age *or* **har·bour·age** (här′bər ij *or* här′brij) *n.* **1** a shelter for ships and boats. **2** any shelter.

harbor master *or* **harbour master** an officer who has charge of a harbor or port and enforces its regulations.

harbor seal *or* **harbour seal** a hair seal (*Phoca vitulina*) found along the northern coasts of North America, Europe, and Asia in salt and inland waters, having a usually light or medium-brown coat with irregular, dark-brown spots or streaks.

har·bour (här′bər) See **harbor.**

hard (härd) *adj., adv.* —*adj.* **1** solid and firm to the touch; not soft: *Rocks are hard.* **2** firmly formed; tight: *His muscles were hard.* **3** needing much ability, effort, or time; difficult: *a hard problem.*

4 causing much pain, trouble, care, etc.; severe: *a hard illness.*
5 stern; unfeeling: *a hard master.* **6** not pleasant; harsh: *a hard face, a hard laugh.* **7** acting or done with energy, persistence, etc.: *a hard worker.* **8** vigorous; violent: *a hard storm, a hard run.* **9** containing mineral salts that interfere with the action of soap: *hard water.* **10** containing much alcohol: *hard liquor.* **11** of wheat, having a hard kernel and high gluten content. **12** *Informal.* real and significant: *hard facts, hard news.* **13** *Phonetics.* of the English consonants *c* and *g,* pronounced as stops, as in *corn* and *get,* rather than as fricatives or affricates, as in *city* and *gem.* Compare **soft** (def. 11). **14** of a drug, seriously addictive and harmful to health: *hard drugs such as heroin and cocaine.* Compare **soft** (def. 14). **15** of currency, fully backed by gold or silver and therefore stable and high in exchange value. Compare **soft** (def. 15).
hard and fast, that cannot be changed or broken; strict.
hard of hearing, rather deaf.
hard put to it, in much difficulty or trouble.
hard up, *Informal.* needing money or anything very badly: *He is always hard up the day before he is paid. It rained throughout our holiday, and we were hard up for things to do.*
—*adv.* **1** so as to be hard, solid, or firm: *frozen hard.* **2** firmly; tightly: *Don't hold hard.* **3** with difficulty: *to breathe hard.* **4** so as to cause trouble, pain, care, etc.: harshly; severely: *taxes that bear hard upon us.* **5** with steady effort or much energy: *Try hard.* **6** with vigor or violence: *He hit hard.* **7** earnestly; intently: *look hard at a person.* **8** to the extreme limit; fully.
hard by, near; close: *The house stands hard by the bridge.*
[OE *heard*] —**hard′ness,** *n.*
☛ *Syn.* See note at **firm.**

hard·back (härd′bak′) *n. or adj.* hardbound.

hard–bit·ten (härd′bit′ən) *adj.* stubborn; unyielding.

hard·board (härd′bôrd′) *n.* a thin, strong building board made in large sheets by compressing wood fibres and sawdust with a resinous or plastic binder under heat. Hardboard with a decorative surface finish, such as imitation woodgrain or brick, is often used for interior panelling.

hard–boiled (härd′boild′) *adj.* **1** boiled until hard: *hard-boiled eggs.* **2** *Informal.* not easily influenced by the feelings; tough; rough.

hard·bound (härd′bound′) *adj., n.* —*adj.* of a book or edition, having relatively rigid covers of board, cloth, leather, etc.; hardcover; hardback. —*n.* a book or edition bound in such a way.

hard cash **1** metal coins. **2** cash.

hard cider fermented cider, containing alcohol.

hard coal anthracite.

hard core the permanent or most lasting part of any thing or any group; the central or vital part.

hard–core (härd′kôr′) *adj.* **1** showing or describing explicit sex, often involving sadism or masochism: *hard-core pornography, hard-core movies.* **2** solidly or permanently established or committed: *hard-core disco fans.*

hard·cov·er (härd′kuv′ər) *adj. or n.* hardbound.

hard·en (här′dən) *v.* **1** make or become hard. **2** make or become capable of endurance. **3** make or become unfeeling or pitiless. **4** temper or make (metals and alloys, especially steel) hard by raising to a high temperature and then cooling in oil, water, or air. **5** of prices of stocks, commodities, etc., become higher; rise. —**hard′en·er,** *n.*

hard–fea·tured (härd′fē′chərd) *adj.* having stern or cruel features.

hard·hack (härd′hak′) *n.* a North American spiraea (*Spiraea tomentosa*) having tapering clusters of small pink or white flowers and woolly leaves and branches.

hard–hat or **hard hat** (härd′hat′) *n., adj.* —*n.* **1** Usually, **hard hat,** a rigid helmet, as of metal or fibreglass, worn by construction workers, miners, etc. for protection against falling objects. **2** *Informal.* a construction worker or miner, etc. or a person thought of as typical of such people. —*adj.*
hard-hat, *Informal.* of or having to do with such people or the conservative attitudes considered to be typical of them.

hard·head (härd′hed′) *n.* **1** a person not easily moved; a shrewd, unemotional person. **2** any of various fishes, such as the lake trout or alewife.

hard–head·ed (härd′hed′id) *adj.* **1** not easily excited or deceived; practical; shrewd. **2** stubborn; obstinate. —**hard′-head′ed·ly,** *adv.* —**hard′-head′ed·ness,** *n.*

hard–heart·ed (härd′härt′id) *adj.* without pity; cruel; unfeeling. —**hard′-heart′ed·ly,** *adv.* —**hard′-heart′ed·ness,** *n.*

har·di·hood (här′dē hud′) *n.* boldness; daring.

har·di·ness (här′dē nis) *n.* **1** endurance; strength. **2** hardihood.

hard labor or **labour** hard work in addition to imprisonment.

hard line a stern, aggressive, or uncompromising attitude or

hat, āge, fär; let, ēqual, tèrm; it, īce
hot, ōpen, ôrder; oil, out; cup, pút, rüle,
above, takən, pencəl, lemən, circəs

ch, child; ng, long; sh, ship
th, thin; ᴛʜ, then; zh, measure

policy: *taking a hard line against minority language rights.*
—**hard′-line′,** *adj.* —**hard′-lin′er,** *n.*

hard·ly (härd′lē) *adv.* **1** only just; barely: *We hardly had time for breakfast.* **2** not quite; not altogether: *hardly strong enough.* **3** most probably not: *He will hardly come now.* **4** with trouble or effort: *money hardly earned.* **5** in a hard manner; harshly; severely: *to deal hardly with a person.*
☛ *Syn.* **1. Hardly, barely, scarcely** = only just or almost not what is named or stated, and are often used interchangeably. But **hardly** = near or close to the minimum limit, with little to spare: *I had hardly reached there when it began to rain.* **Barely** = just enough, with nothing to spare: *He eats barely enough.* **Scarcely** = almost not at all: *He has scarcely anything to eat.*
☛ *Usage.* **Hardly** and **scarcely** are treated as negatives and so should not have another negative with them: *The film showed hardly anything that was new to them* (not *hardly nothing*). *I scarcely had enough money* (not *I didn't scarcely have*).

hard–nosed (härd′nozd′) *adj. Informal.* practical and unsentimental, often to the point of ruthlessness: *a hard-nosed businessman.*

hard palate the front, bony part of the roof of the mouth.

hard·pan (härd′pan′) *n.* hard, firm, underlying earth.

hard pressed confronted with the necessity to act or react quickly or to work intensively; subject to severe pressure, attack, etc.: *hard pressed to get the manuscript ready for the publisher.*

hard put having one's resources heavily taxed; barely able: *hard put to think of an excuse.*

hard·rock (härd′rok′) *n., adj. Cdn.* —*n* **1** *Mining.* rock, such as quartz, that can be removed only by drilling or blasting. **2** *Slang.* a strong, rough person. —*adj.* Often, **hard-rock.** **1** of or having to do with hardrock: *hardrock miners.* **2** *Slang.* characterized by hardness and strength: *That hockey player was feared for his hardrock checking.*

hard sauce a sauce made by creaming sugar, butter, and flavoring together, used on cakes, puddings, etc.

hard sell *Informal.* a forceful and direct method of advertising; aggressive high-pressure salesmanship: *The company is using the hard sell to promote its new products.* Compare **soft sell.** —**hard′-sell′,** *adj.*

hard–shell (härd′shel′) *adj.* **1** having a hard shell. **2** *Informal.* strict; uncompromising.

hard·ship (härd′ship′) *n.* something hard to bear; hard condition of living: *Hunger, cold and sickness are hardships.*

hard sledding difficult going; unfavorable conditions.

hard·tack (härd′tak′) *n.* a very hard, dry biscuit.

hard·top (härd′top′) *n. Informal.* an automobile, having a body design similar to that of a convertible except that the top is rigid.

hard·ware (härd′wer′) *n.* **1** articles made from metal: *Locks, hinges, nails, and tools are hardware.* **2** *Military.* manufactured equipment such as guns, tanks, aircraft, or missiles. **3** the mechanical, electronic, or structural parts of a computer, teaching machine, etc. Compare **software.**

hard wheat wheat having a hard kernel and high gluten content, used in making bread, macaroni, etc.

hard·wood (härd′wúd′) *n.* **1** any hard, compact wood. **2** *Forestry.* any tree that has broad leaves or does not have needles. **3** the wood of such a tree. Oak, cherry, maple, etc. are hardwoods; pine and fir are softwoods.

hard·work·ing (härd′wèr′king) *adj.* usually working hard; diligent: *She is a hardworking student.*

har·dy (här′dē) *adj.* **-di·er, -di·est. 1** able to bear hard treatment, fatigue, etc.; strong; robust. **2** able to withstand the cold of winter in the open air: *hardy plants.* **3** bold; daring. **4** too bold; rash. [ME < OF *hardi,* pp. of *hardir* harden < Gmc.] —**har′di·ly,** *adv.*

hare (her) *n., pl.* **hare** or **hares;** *v.* **hared, har·ing.** —*n.* any of several small mammals (family Leporidae, especially genus *Lepus*) resembling and related to rabbits, but generally larger and having longer ears and legs and whose young are born fully furred, with open eyes. —*v.* hurry; run: *They hared off after the thief.* [OE *hara*] —**hare′like′,** *adj.*
☛ *Hom.* hair, Herr.

hare·bell (her′bel′) *n.* bluebell (def. 1).

hare·brained (her′brānd′) *adj.* giddy; heedless; reckless.

hare·lip (her′lip′) *n.* **1** a deformity caused when parts of the lip fail to grow together before birth. **2** a lip that is deformed in this way. —**hare′lipped′,** *adj.*

har·em (her′əm) *n.* **1** the part of a Moslem house where the women live. **2** its occupants; the wives, female relatives, female servants, etc. of a Moslem household. **3** of fur seals, wild horses, and certain other animals, a number of females controlled by one male. [< Arabic *haram, harim* forbidden]

har·i·cot (har′ə kō′ *or* her′ə kō′) *n.* a string bean. [< F]

har·i–kar·i (har′ē kar′ē, her′ə-, *or* hä′rē-) *n.* hara-kiri.

hark (härk) *v.* listen.
hark back, a go back; turn back: *His ideas hark back twenty years.* **b** return to a previous point or subject; revert: *Whenever we chat together, he is always harking back to his time in the army.* [ME *herkien*]

hark·en (här′kən) See **hearken.**

Har·le·quin (här′lə kwin′ *or* här′lə kin′) *n.* **1** in traditional Italian comedy and in pantomime, the lover of Columbine. He is usually masked, wears a costume of varied colors, and carries a wooden sword. **2 harlequin,** a mischievous person; buffoon. **3** (*adj.*) varied in color; many-colored. [< F < OF var. of *Herlequin* < ME *Herle King* King Herla (mythical figure); modern meaning in French is from Ital. *arlecchino* < OF *Harlequin*]

har·le·quin·ade (här′lə kwi nād′ *or* här′lə ki nād′) *n.* **1** a pantomime or play in which the harlequin and the clown are the leading players. **2** buffoonery; clownish antics.

harlequin bug a brightly colored North American bug (*Murgantia histrionica*) that is a pest of vegetable crops such as cabbage.

har·lot (här′lət) *n.* prostitute. [ME < OF *harlot* vagabond]

har·lot·ry (här′lət rē) *n.* prostitution.

harm (härm) *n., v.* —*n.* **1** hurt; damage: *The accident did a lot of harm to the car.* **2** evil; wrong: *What harm is there in borrowing a friend's bicycle?* —*v.* damage; injure; hurt. [OE *hearm*] —**harm′er,** *n.*

☞ *Syn. v.* **Harm, damage** = hurt or injure a person or thing. **Harm** = injure, but is a more informal word, and especially suggests injuring a person or his mind, health, rights, business, etc. so as to cause pain, loss, or suffering of some kind: *Unfounded and malicious rumors harmed his reputation.* **Damage** = hurt or harm so as to lessen the value, usefulness, or appearance of a person or thing: *The furniture was damaged in the fire.*

harm·ful (härm′fəl) *adj.* causing harm; injurious; hurtful. —**harm′ful·ly,** *adv.* —**harm′ful·ness,** *n.*

harm·less (härm′lis) *adj.* causing no harm; that would not harm anyone or anything. —**harm′less·ly,** *adv.* —**harm′less·ness,** *n.*

har·mon·ic (här mon′ik) *adj., n.* —*adj.* **1** *Music.* **a** of or having to do with harmony as distinguished from melody and rhythm. **b** of or having to do with overtones that are heard along with the main tone. **c** musical. **2** having to do with or marked by harmony, agreement, or concord; concordant; consonant. **3** *Physics.* of or having to do with any of the frequencies making up a wave or alternating current, that are integral multiples of the fundamental frequency. **4** *Mathematics.* having relations similar in some way to those of musical concords, 1, ½, ⅓, ¼, etc. are in harmonic progression.
—*n.* **1** *Music.* **a** a tone produced on a stringed instrument by a light pressure at a point on a string. **b** an overtone whose rate of vibration is an integral multiple of the main tone. Harmonics have a higher pitch and lower volume than main tones. **2** a fainter and higher tone heard along with the main tone; overtone. [< L *harmonicus* < Gk. *harmonikos* harmonic, musical < *harmonia.* See HARMONY.]

har·mon·i·ca (här mon′ə kə) *n.* a small, oblong musical instrument having several metal reeds which are caused to vibrate by air from the player's mouth controlled by the tongue and lips; mouth organ. [< L *harmonica* fem. of *harmonicus.* See HARMONIC.]

har·mon·ics (här mon′iks) *n.* the science of musical sounds.

har·mo·ni·ous (här mō′nē əs) *adj.* **1** agreeing in feelings, ideas, or actions; getting along well together: *The children played together in a harmonious group.* **2** arranged so that the parts are orderly or pleasing; going well together: *This picture is remarkable for its harmonious colors.* **3** sweet-sounding; musical. —**har·mo′ni·ous·ly,** *adv.* —**har·mo′ni·ous·ness,** *n.*

har·mo·ni·um (här mō′nē əm) *n.* a small musical organ with metal reeds. [< F *harmonium* < *harmonie.* See HARMONY.]

har·mo·nize (här′mə nīz′) *v.* **-nized, -niz·ing. 1** bring into harmony or agreement: *to harmonize several different points of view.* **2** go or put together in a pleasing way: *The colors in the room harmonized.* **3** *Music.* add tones to (a melody) to make successive chords. —**har′mo·ni·za′tion,** *n.* —**har′mo·niz′er,** *n.*

har·mo·ny (här′mə nē) *n., pl.* **-nies. 1** an agreement of feeling, ideas, or actions; getting along well together: *The two brothers lived and worked in perfect harmony.* **2** an orderly or pleasing arrangement of parts; going well together: *a harmony of design and color.* **3** *Music.* **a** a sounding together of tones in a chord. **b** the study of chords and of relating them to successive chords. **4** a sweet or musical sound; music. **5** the act of harmonizing, especially of singing voices: *The quartet achieved excellent harmony.* **6** a grouping of passages on the same subject from different stories or accounts, showing their points of agreement: *a harmony of the Gospels.* [< F *harmonie* < L < Gk. *harmonia* concord, a joining < *harmos* joint]

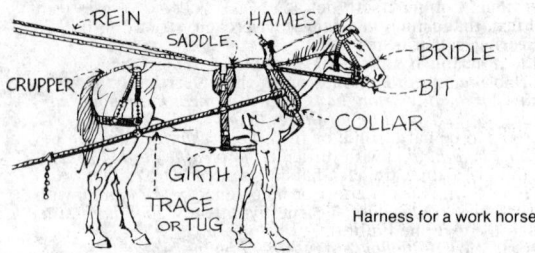

Harness for a work horse

har·ness (här′nis) *n., v.* —*n.* **1** the leather straps, bands, and pieces of various other shapes used to hitch a horse or other animal to a carriage, wagon, plough, etc. **2** an arrangement of straps to fasten or hold: *a parachute harness, a shoulder harness. We need a harness for the baby's crib.* **3** *Archaic.* the armor for a knight, soldier, or horse.
in harness, at one's regular work: *She was content to be back in harness after a good holiday.*
—*v.* **1** put harness on. **2** cause to produce power. Water in a stream is harnessed by allowing it to accumulate behind a dam and installing turbines that it can drive. **3** *Archaic.* put armor on. [ME < OF *harneis, ?* < Scand.]

A harp

harp (härp) *n., v.* —*n.* **1** a musical instrument with strings set in a triangular frame, played by plucking the strings with the fingers. **2** harp seal. —*v.* play on a harp.
harp on, keep on tiresomely talking or writing about; refer continually to.
[OE *hearpe*] —**harp′er,** *n.*

harp·ist (här′pist) *n.* a person who plays the harp, especially a skilled player.

har·poon (här pün′) *n., v.* —*n.* a barbed spear with a rope tied to it, used for catching whales and other sea animals. It is either hurled by the hand or fired from a gun. —*v.* strike, catch, or kill with a harpoon. [< F *harpon* < MF *harper* grip < Gmc.] —**har·poon′er** *or* **har′poon·eer′,** *n.*

harp seal a hair seal (*Pagophilus groenlandicus*) found in the arctic and subarctic waters of the Atlantic Ocean, mainly pale grey in color, with a dark-brown or black head and a large, irregular, horseshoe-shaped marking on its back.

harp·si·chord (härp′sə kôrd′) *n.* a stringed musical instrument resembling a piano, still played but used especially from about 1550 to 1750. It sounds somewhat like a harp because the strings are plucked by leather or quill points instead of being struck by hammers. [< obs. F *harpechorde* < *harpe* harp (< Gmc.) + *chorde* string of a musical instrument < L < Gk.]

Har·py (här′pē) *n., pl.* **-pies. 1** *Greek mythology.* any of several repulsive, filthy, greedy monsters having a woman's head and torso and a bird's wings, tail, and claws. **2 harpy,** a very greedy person who preys upon others. [< L *Harpyia* < Gk., probably related to *harpazein* snatch]

har·que·bus (här′kwə bəs) *n.* a form of portable firearm used

before muskets were invented. Also, **arquebus**. [< F (h)*arquebus* < Ital. *archibuso* < Du. *haakbus*, literally, hook gun]

har·ri·dan (har′ə dən *or* her′ə dən) *n.* a bad-tempered, disreputable old woman. [probably < F *haridelle* a worn-out horse]

har·ri·er[1] (har′ē ər *or* her′ē ər) *n.* **1** a breed of small hound resembling the English foxhound, used to hunt hares. **2** a cross-country runner. [apparently < *hare*]

har·ri·er[2] (har′ē ər *or* her′ē ər) *n.* **1** a person who harries. **2** a hawk that preys on small animals. [< *harry*]

Har·ris tweed (har′is *or* har′is) hand-woven tweed of very high quality, originally made on the Island of Harris in the Hebrides.

har·row (har′ō *or* her′ō) *n., v.* —*n.* a heavy frame with iron teeth or upright disks. Harrows are drawn over ploughed land to break up clods, cover seeds, etc.
—*v.* **1** draw a harrow over (land, etc.). **2** hurt; wound. **3** arouse uncomfortable feelings in; distress; torment. [ME *harwe*]
—**har′row·er**, *n.*

har·ry (har′ē *or* her′ē) *v.* **-ried, -ry·ing. 1** raid and rob with violence: *The pirates harried the towns along the coast.* **2** keep troubling; worry; torment: *He was harried by fear of losing his job.* [OE *hergian* < *here* army]

harsh (härsh) *adj.* **1** rough to the touch, taste, eye or ear; sharp and unpleasant: *a harsh voice, a harsh climate.* **2** without pity; cruel; severe: *a harsh man.* **3** stern; grim; forbidding: *a harsh expression.* [var. of ME *harsk*; cf. Danish *harsk* rancid] —**harsh′ly**, *adv.* —**harsh′ness**, *n.*

hart (härt) *n., pl.* **hart** *or* **harts.** an adult male deer, especially the male of the European red deer after its fifth year. [OE *heorot*]
☛ **Hom. heart.**

har·te·beest (här′tə bēst′ *or* härt′bēst′) *n., pl.* **-beest** *or* **-beests. 1** either of two large African antelopes (*Alcelaphus buselaphus* and *A. lichtensteini*) having a fawn-colored coat, a long, thin muzzle, and ringed, lyre-shaped horns. **2** any of several similar antelopes, such as *Damaliscus hunteri.* [< Afrikaans *hartebeest* hart beast]

harts·horn (härts′hôrn′) *n.* **1** ammonia dissolved in water. **2** smelling salts; sal volatile.

har·um–scar·um (her′əm sker′əm) *adj., adv., n.* —*adj.* reckless; rash; thoughtless: *What a harum-scarum child you are!*
—*adv.* recklessly; wildly: *He rushed harum-scarum down the main street.*
—*n.* a reckless person. [apparently < *hare* frighten + *scare*]

ha·rus·pex (hə rus′peks, har′əs peks′ *or* her′əs peks′) *n., pl.* **har·rus·pi·ces** (hə rus′pə sēz′). in ancient Rome, a member of a class of minor priests or soothsayers who made predictions by examining the entrails of animals killed in sacrifice, by observing lightning, etc. [< L *haruspex* < **haru-* entrails + *specere* inspect]

har·vest (här′vist) *n., v.* —*n.* **1** a reaping and gathering in of grain and other food crops, usually in the late summer or early autumn. **2** the time or season when grain, fruit, etc. are gathered in. **3** one season's yield of any natural product; a crop: *The oyster harvest was small this year.* **4** the result; consequences: *He is reaping the harvest of his mistakes.*
—*v.* **1** gather in for use: *to harvest wheat.* **2** gather a crop. **3** win or undergo as a result or consequence. [OE *hærfest*]
☛ *Syn. n.* **3.** See note at **crop.**

har·vest·a·ble (här′və stə bəl) *adj.* suitable or ready for harvesting.

har·vest·er (här′vis tər) *n.* **1** a person who works in a harvest field; reaper. **2** a machine for harvesting crops, especially grain.

harvest home 1 the end of harvesting. **2** a festival to celebrate the end of harvesting. **3** a harvest song.

harvest moon the full moon at harvest time, or about September 23.

harvest mouse 1 any of a genus (*Reithrodontomys*) of small, greyish, New World mice found in open, grassy areas from Canada south to N South America. **2** a very small Old World mouse (*Micromys minutus*) having reddish-brown fur, found in grain fields, etc.

has (haz; *unstressed,* həz *or* əz) *v.* 3rd pers. sing. present tense of **have.**

has–been (haz′bin′ *or* -bēn′) *n. Informal.* a person or thing whose best days are past.

hash[1] (hash) *n., v.* —*n.* **1** a mixture of cooked meat, potatoes, etc. chopped into small pieces and fried or baked. **2** a mixture; jumble. **3** a mess; muddle.
make a hash of, make a mess of: *She made a hash of mounting stamps in her album.*
settle (someone's) hash, *Informal.* subdue or silence someone completely; put an end to someone.
—*v.* **1** chop into small pieces. **2** make a mess or muddle of. **3** *Informal.* talk about in detail; discuss or review thoroughly (often

hat, āge, fär; let, ēqual, tèrm; it, īce
hot, ōpen, ôrder; oil, out; cup, put, rüle,
əbove, takən, pencəl, lemən, circəs

ch, child; ng, long; sh, ship
th, thin; ҭн, then; zh, measure

used with **over, through,** *etc.*): *The two leaders spent hours hashing over their problems.* [< F *hacher* < *hache* hatchet]

hash[2] (hash) *n. Slang.* hashish.

hash·eesh (hash′ēsh) *n.* hashish.

hash·ish (hash′ēsh *or* hash′ish) *n.* an extract from the dried flowers of the female hemp plant, that is smoked, chewed, or drunk for its intoxicating effect. [< Arabic *hashish* dried hemp leaves]

has·n't (haz′ənt) *v.* has not.

hasp (hasp) *n.* a clasp or fastening for a door, window, trunk, box, etc., especially a hinged metal clasp that fits over a staple or into a hole and is fastened by a peg, padlock, etc. [var. of OE *hæpse*]

has·sle (has′əl) *n., v.* **hassled, has·sling.** *Informal.* —*n.* **1** a struggle; argument: *There was a hassle about who was going to ride in the front seat of the car.* **2** trouble; annoyance; bother: *Driving in city traffic is too much of a hassle. Traffic jams create a lot of hassle.* —*v.* **1** struggle; argue. **2** worry; annoy; bother: *The film star was being hassled by newspaper reporters.* [origin uncertain]

has·sock (has′ək) *n.* **1** a padded footstool or thick cushion to rest the feet on, sit on, or kneel on. **2** a tuft or bunch of coarse grass. [OE *hassuc* coarse grass]

hast (hast) *v. Archaic.* 2nd pers. sing. present tense, of **have.** *Thou hast* means *you* (sing.)

has·tate (has′tāt) *adj.* shaped like the head of a spear. [< L *hastatus* < *hasta* spear]

haste (hāst) *n., v.* **hast·ed, hast·ing.** —*n.* **1** a trying to be quick; hurrying: *The king's business required haste.* **2** quickness without thought or care: *Haste makes waste.*
in haste, a in a hurry; quickly. **b** without careful thought; rashly.
make haste, hurry; be quick.
—*v. Poetic.* hasten. [ME < OF < Gmc.; cf. OE *hǣst* violence]
☛ *Syn. n.* **1.** See note at **hurry.**

has·ten (hās′ən) *v.* **1** cause to be quick; speed; hurry: *She hastened the children off to bed.* **2** be quick; go fast: *Let me hasten to explain.*

has·ten·er (hās′ən ər) *n.* a follow-up note or letter to hurry delivery of an order, payment of a bill, etc.

hast·y (hās′tē) *adj.* **hast·i·er, hast·i·est. 1** hurried; quick: *a hasty visit.* **2** not well thought out; rash: *His hasty decisions caused many mistakes.* **3** easily angered; quick-tempered: *He should not be so hasty.* —**hast′i·ly,** *adv.* —**hast′i·ness,** *n.*

hasty pudding 1 a mush of meal or flour made with boiling water (or milk) and seasoning. **2** *U.S.* a mush made with corn meal.

HATS

SHOVEL HAT

TOP HAT

SOMBRERO

DERBY

SOUTHWESTER

SHAKO

hat (hat) *n., v.* **hat·ted, hat·ting.** —*n.* **1** a covering for the head, usually with a crown and brim and usually worn outdoors. **2** *Roman Catholic Church.* **a** a red head covering worn by a cardinal. **b** the dignity or office of a cardinal.

hat in hand, with the head uncovered in respect; obsequiously; servilely.

pass the hat, take up a collection.

take off (one's) **hat to,** salute or honor by or as if by removing one's hat: *I take my hat off to anybody who can make that jump.*

talk through (one's) **hat,** talk without knowing what one is talking about; talk foolishly.

throw (one's) **hat into the ring,** *Informal.* enter a contest, especially for election to a public office.

under (one's) **hat,** *Informal.* as a secret; to oneself.
—*v.* cover or furnish with a hat. [OE *hætt*] —**hat′less,** *adj.* —**hat′like′,** *adj.*

hat·band (hat′band′) *n.* a band around the crown of a hat, just above the brim.

hatch[1] (hach) *v., n.* —*v.* **1** bring forth (young) from an egg or eggs: *A hen hatches chickens.* **2** keep (an egg or eggs) warm until the young come out: *The heat of the sun hatches turtles' eggs.* **3** come out from the egg: *Three chickens hatched today.* **4** produce living young: *Not all eggs hatch properly.* **5** arrange; plan, especially in secret; plot: *The robbers were hatching an evil scheme.*
—*n.* **1** the act of hatching. **2** the brood hatched. **3** something that is hatched. [ME *hæche(n)*] —**hatch′er,** *n.*

hatch[2] (hach) *n.* **1** an opening in a ship's deck through which the cargo is loaded. See **ship** for picture. **2** the trap door covering such an opening. **3** an opening in the floor or roof of a building, etc.: *an escape hatch.* **4** the lower half of a divided door. [OE *hæcc*]

hatch[3] (hach) *v., n.* —*v.* draw, cut, or engrave fine parallel lines on: *With a sharp pencil the artist hatched certain parts of the picture to darken and shade them.* —*n.* one of such a set of lines. See **crosshatch** for picture. [< F *hacher* chop, hatch. See HASH.]

hatch·back (hach′bak′) *n.* **1** a sloping back on a two-door or four-door automobile, the whole of which swings up like a hatch, giving access to the interior of the car. **2** an automobile having a hatchback.

hatch·el (hach′əl) *n., v.* **-elled** or **-eled, -el·ling** or **-el·ing.** —*n.* a comb used in cleaning flax, hemp, etc. —*v.* **1** comb (flax, hemp, etc.) with a hatchel. **2** annoy; torment; heckle. [var. of *hackle*[1]] —**hatch′el·ler** or **hatch′el·er,** *n.*

hatch·er·y (hach′ər ē or hach′rē) *n., pl.* **-er·ies.** a place for hatching eggs of fish, hens, etc.

hatch·et (hach′it) *n.* **1** a small axe with a short handle, for use with one hand. **2** tomahawk.

bury the hatchet, make peace.

dig up the hatchet, make war.

[ME < OF *hachette,* dim. of *hache* axe]

hatchet job *Informal.* a vicious or malicious attack in speech or writing.

hatchet man *Informal.* **1** a person who makes vicious or malicious attacks, especially one hired to do so. **2** a hired murderer.

hatch·ing (hach′ing) *n.* fine, parallel lines drawn, cut, or engraved close together. See **crosshatch** for picture. [< *hatch*[3]]

hatch·ment (hach′mənt) *n. Heraldry.* a square panel set diagonally, bearing the coat of arms of a recently deceased person, for temporary display of his house. [earlier *atcheament, achement,* contraction of *achievement*]

hatch·way (hach′wā′) *n.* **1** an opening in the deck of a ship to the lower part. **2** a similar opening in a floor, roof, etc.

hate (hāt) *v.* **hat·ed, hat·ing;** *n.* —*v.* **1** dislike very strongly; feel extreme hostility or aversion to: *a hated dictator. Many people hate snakes.* **2** dislike: *I hate that shade of blue.* —*n.* **1** a very strong dislike; hatred: *There was hate in his voice.* **2** an object of hatred. [OE *hatian*] —**hat′er,** *n.*

☛ *Syn. v.* **1.** Hate, detest, abhor = dislike someone or something very much. **Hate,** the general word, suggests very strong dislike and a feeling of hostility, often a desire to hurt or harm: *The prisoners hated the wicked guards.* **Detest** suggests strong or deep fixed dislike mixed with scorn for something or someone disagreeable or disgusting: *I detest a coward.* **Abhor** suggests a dislike that makes one shudder or shrink away from someone or something extremely disagreeable, disgusting, or shocking: *I abhor filth of any kind.*

hate·ful (hāt′fəl) *adj.* **1** causing hate; to be hated. **2** feeling hate; showing hate. —**hate′ful·ly,** *adv.* —**hate′ful·ness,** *n.*

☛ *Syn.* **1.** Hateful, odious, obnoxious = causing strong dislike or hate. **Hateful** emphasizes the hatred caused, a feeling of strong dislike and hostility combined with anger, fear, spite, a feeling of injury, etc.: *A bully does hateful things.* **Odious,** formal, emphasizes having qualities that cause hatred or strong dislike, and suggests being disagreeable, irritating, or disgusting: *Conditions in the slums are odious.* **Obnoxious** = being so disagreeable or annoying to a person that he cannot stand the sight or thought of what is described: *His disgusting table manners made him obnoxious to us.*

hat·ful (hat′fůl) *n.* **1** the amount a hat can hold. **2** a great deal; considerable amount.

hath (hath) *v. Archaic.* 3rd pers. sing. present tense, of **have.** *He hath* means *he has.*

hat·pin (hat′pin′) *n.* a long pin used by women to fasten a hat to the hair.

hat·rack (hat′rak′) *n.* a rack, shelf, or arrangement of hooks or pegs to put hats on.

ha·tred (hā′trid) *n.* very strong dislike; hate. [ME *hatred, hatreden* < *hate* hate + *-reden,* OE *ræden* condition, state]

hat·ter (hat′ər) *n.* a person who makes or sells hats.

hat trick 1 *Hockey and soccer.* three goals scored in a single game by the same player. **2** *Cricket.* the taking of three wickets with three successive balls. **3** *Informal.* any feat consisting of three or more victories in a row. [< the fact of a *hat* formerly being the prize for this feat in cricket]

hau·ber·geon (hô′bər jən or hô′bər jən) *n.* habergeon (def. 1).

hau·berk (hô′bèrk or hô′bèrk) *n.* a long coat of mail. [ME < OF *hauberc* < Gmc.; cf. OE *healsbeorg,* literally, neck cover]

haugh·ti·ness (hô′tē nis or hô′tē nis) *n.* a haughty manner or spirit; an arrogant looking down on other people.

haugh·ty (hô′tē or hô′tē) *adj.* **-ti·er, -ti·est. 1** too proud of oneself and too scornful of others. **2** showing too great pride of oneself and scorn for others: *a haughty smile.* [< *haught* or *haught* < OF *haut* < L *altus* high; French form influenced by OHG *hoh* high] —**haugh′ti·ly,** *adv.* —**haugh′ti·ness,** *n.*

☛ *Syn.* **1.** Haughty, arrogant = too proud. **Haughty** = feeling oneself superior to others and showing it by treating them with cold indifference and scorn: *A haughty girl is always unpopular at school.* **Arrogant** = thinking oneself more important than one is and showing it by treating others in a domineering and slighting manner: *He was so arrogant that he lost his job.*

haul (hôl or hôl) *v., n.* —*v.* **1** pull or drag with force: *The logs were hauled to the mill by horses.* **2** change; shift: *The wind hauled around to the east.* **3** of seals, come up out of the water onto land (used *with* out): *Harbor seals haul out at low tide to rest and sleep.*

haul off, a turn a ship away from an object. **b** draw away; withdraw. **c** *Informal.* draw back one's arm to give a blow.

haul on or **to the wind,** sail closer to the direction of the wind.

haul up, a turn a ship nearer to the direction of the wind. **b** change the course of (a ship).

—*n.* **1** the act of hauling; hard pull. **2** the load hauled: *Powerful trucks are used for heavy hauls.* **3** the distance that a load is hauled. **4** the amount won, taken, etc. at one time; catch: *a good haul of fish.* [< F *haler* < Gmc. Doublet of HALE[2].] —**haul′er,** *n.*

☛ *Hom.* **hall.**

☛ *Syn. v.* **1.** See note at **draw.**

haul·age (hol′ij or hôl′ij) *n.* **1** the act of hauling. **2** the force used in hauling. **3** a charge made for hauling.

haunch (honch or hônch) *n.* **1** the part of the body around the hip; the hip. **2** the hind quarter of an animal: *A dog sits on his haunches.* **3** a cut of meat consisting of the leg and loin of a deer, sheep, etc. [ME < OF *hanche* < Gmc.]

haunt (hont or hônt) *v., n.* —*v.* **1** of a ghost, appear frequently to a person or in a place; be continually present at a place: *People say ghosts haunt that old house.* **2** go often to; visit frequently: *They haunt the new bowling alley.* **3** be often with; come often to: *Memories of his youth haunted the old man.*

—*n.* **1** a place frequently gone to or often visited: *returning to their old haunts. The swimming pool was our favorite haunt in the summer.* **2** a place where wild animals habitually come to drink or feed. **3** *Dialect.* ghost. [ME < OF *hanter* < Gmc.; related to OE *hāmettan* shelter (cf. *home*)] —**haunt′er,** *n.* —**haunt′ing·ly,** *adv.*

haunt·ed (hon′tid or hôn′tid) *adj.* **1** visited by ghosts. **2** harried or harassed, as if by ghosts; troubled; worried.

Hau·sa (hou′sä) *n.* **1** a negroid people of the Sudan and northern Nigeria. **2** a member of this people. **3** the Chad language of this people.

haut·boy (hō′boi or ō′boi) *n.* oboe. [< F *hautbois* < *haut* high + *bois* wood; with reference to its high notes]

haute cou·ture (ōt kü tŷr′) *French.* **1** the best-known fashion houses and designers. **2** the clothes made by leading designers and dressmakers.

haute cui·sine (ōt kwē zēn′) *French.* **1** cooking as a fine art, especially as practised by acknowledged master chefs. **2** food that is prepared in this way.

hau·teur (hō tèr′ or ō tèr′) *n.* haughtiness; a haughty manner or spirit. [< F *hauteur* < *haut* high]

Ha·van·a (hə van′ə) *n.* a cigar made from Cuban tobacco. [< *Havana,* the capital of Cuba]

have (hav; *unstressed,* həv or əv; *before* 'to' *in def.* 6, *usually* haf) *v. pres.* **1** have, **2** have, **3** has, *pl.* have; *pt. and pp.* had; *ppr.* hav·ing. **1** hold: *I have a book in my hand.* **2** possess; own: *He has*

a big house and farm. **3** have as a part, quality, etc.: *The house has many windows. He has a pleasant face.* **4** cause to: *Have them send an extra copy.* **5** cause to be: *I'm having the dress made by a local dressmaker. He had his hair cut yesterday.* **6** be compelled or obliged: *We all have to eat. I had to explain it three times before he understood.* **7** obtain or receive: *Have a seat.* **8** show by action: *to have the courage to.* **9** experience: *to have a pain, to have fear.* **10** engage in; carry on; perform: *Have a talk with him.* **11** allow; permit (*used with a negative*): *They won't have any liquor in the house.* **12** maintain; assert: *They will have it so.* **13** keep; retain: *He has the directions in his mind.* **14** know; understand: *He has no Latin.* **15** hold in the mind: *to have an idea.* **16** be in a certain relation to: *She has three brothers.* **17** *Informal.* hold an advantage over: *You have him there.* **18** *Slang.* fool or cheat: *I think I've been had.* **19** become the parent of; bear or beget: *They plan to have children. She had her baby yesterday.* **20 have** is also used as an auxiliary for compound tenses expressing completed action: *They have arrived. She has already had four pieces of cake.*
have at, attack; hit.
have done, stop; be through.
have had it, *Slang.* **a** become disgusted; become fed up. **b** reach an end; lose something that one has had.
have it, a will; make happen: *As luck would have it, we missed the train.* **b** gain a victory or advantage. **c** receive a thrashing or punishment: *If he catches you, he'll let you have it.* **d** discover or hit upon an answer, solution, etc.: *Eureka! I have it!* **e** *Informal.* find oneself in certain (good or bad) circumstances: *You never had it so good.*
have it in for, *Informal.* have a grudge against; try to get revenge on.
have it out, fight or argue until a question is settled.
have nothing on, have no advantage of or superiority over.
have to, must: *All animals have to sleep. We will have to go now.*
have to do with, a be connected with; be related to. **b** be a companion, partner, or friend of; associate with.
to have and to hold, to keep and possess.
[OE *habban*]
☞ *Hom.* **halve.**
☞ *Syn.* **1. Have, hold, own** = possess or be in possession of something. **Have** is the general word: *He has many friends.* **Hold** emphasizes having control over or keeping: *He holds the office of treasurer. He cannot hold a friend long.* **Own** suggests having a right, especially a legal right, to hold a thing as property: *He owns a farm.*

have·lock (hav′lok) *n.* a white cloth covering for a cap. It falls over the back of the neck and gives protection against the sun. [after Henry *Havelock,* a British general]

ha·ven (hā′vən) *n., v.* —*n.* **1** a harbor, especially one providing shelter from a storm. **2** a place of shelter and safety. —*v.* shelter in a haven. [OE *hæfen*]

have–not (hav′not′) *n. Informal.* a person or country that has little or no property or wealth.

have·n't (hav′ənt) *v.* have not.

hav·er·sack (hav′ər sak′) *n.* a canvas bag with straps for wearing on the back or over one shoulder, used by soldiers, hikers, etc. for carrying food and equipment. [< F *havresac* < LG *Habersack* oat sack]

hav·oc (hav′ək) *n.* very great destruction or injury: *Tornadoes, severe earthquakes, and plagues create widespread havoc.*
play havoc with, injure severely; ruin; destroy.
[< AF var. of OF *havot* plundering, devastation (especially in phrase *crier havot* cry havoc) < Gmc.]

haw¹ (ho *or* hô) *n.* **1** the red berry of the hawthorn. **2** the hawthorn. [OE *haga*]

haw² (ho *or* hô) *interj., n., v.* —*interj. or n.* a stammering sound between words. —*v.* make this sound; stammer. [imitative]

haw³ (ho *or* hô) *interj., n., v.* —*interj. or n.* a command to horses, oxen, etc. directing them to turn to the left. *Gee* is used for "right." —*v.* turn to the left. [origin uncertain]

Ha·wai·ian (hə wī′yən) *n., adj.* —*n.* **1** a native or inhabitant of Hawaii, a group of islands in the Pacific Ocean, especially a person of Polynesian descent. **2** the Polynesian language of the Hawaiians. —*adj.* of or having to do with Hawaii, its people, or their language.

hawk¹ (hok *or* hôk) *n., v.* —*n.* **1** any of a genus (*Accipiter*) of small or medium-sized birds of prey that are active during the day, such as the goshawk and sparrow hawk. Hawks typically have short, rounded wings and a long tail. **2** any of various other related and similar birds of the family Accipitridae (kites, buzzards, etc.) or the family Falconidae (falcons). **3** a person who tends to take an aggressive or militant stand in controversial issues, especially one who favors war or a policy of military strength. Compare **dove¹** (def. 3). **4** a rapacious or grasping person.
—*v.* **1** hunt with trained hawks. **2** hunt or pursue like a hawk. [OE *hafoc*] —**hawk′like′,** *adj.*

hawk² (hok *or* hôk) *v.* **1** carry (goods) about for sale as a street peddler does. **2** advertise by shouting that goods are for sale. **3** spread (a report) around. [< *hawker¹*]

hat, āge, fär; let, ēqual, tèrm; it, īce
hot, ōpen, ôrder; oil, out; cup, put, rüle,
above, takən, pencəl, lemən, circəs
ch, child; ng, long; sh, ship
th, thin; ŦH, then; zh, measure

hawk³ (hok *or* hôk) *v., n.* —*v.* clear the throat noisily. —*n.* **1** a noisy effort to clear the throat. **2** the noise made in such an effort. [probably imitative]

hawk·er¹ (hok′ər *or* hôk′ər) *n.* a person who carries his wares around and offers them for sale by shouting; peddler. [probably < MLG *hoker.* Akin to HUCKSTER.]

hawk·er² (hok′ər *or* hôk′ər) *n.* a person who hunts with a hawk. [< *hawk¹*]

hawk–eyed (hok′īd′ *or* hôk′-) *adj.* having sharp eyes like a hawk.

hawk·ing (hok′ing *or* hôk′ing) *n.* the act of hunting with hawks; falconry.

hawk·ish (hok′ish *or* hôk′ish) *adj.* militant or aggressive; like or characteristic of a hawk (def. 3): *a hawkish policy, a hawkish atmosphere.*

hawk moth any of numerous large moths (family Sphingidae) having long, narrow forewings and short hindwings and a long, stout body.

hawk's–bill *or* **hawks·bill** (hoks′bil′ *or* hôks′-) *n.* hawk's-bill turtle.

hawk's–bill turtle a small, tropical sea turtle (*Eretmochelys imbricata*) having hooked jaws resembling the bill of a hawk. Tortoise-shell is made from the overlapping plates of its upper shell.

hawk·weed (hok′wēd′ *or* hôk′-) *n.* any of a large genus (*Hieracium*) of hairy plants of the composite family found in temperate regions of the world, having small, orange or yellow flower heads.

hawse (hoz *or* hôz, hos *or* hôs) *n.* **1** the part of a ship's bow where the hawseholes are located. **2** hawsepipe. **3** the distance between the bow of a moored ship and her anchor or anchors. [< ON *hals*]

hawse·hole (hoz′hōl′ *or* hôz′-, hos′hōl′ *or* hôs′-) *n.* a hole in the bow of a ship for a hawser or anchor chain to pass through.

hawse·pipe (hoz′pīp′ *or* hôz′-) *n.* a heavy iron or steel pipe lining a hawsehole. A hawsepipe has a curved rim that fits tightly against the edge of the hawsehole. See **ship** for picture.

haw·ser (ho′zər *or* hô′zər, ho′sər *or* hô′sər) *n.* a large, stout rope or a thin steel cable, used for mooring or towing ships. [ME < OF *haucier* hoist, ult. < L *altus* high]

haw·thorn (ho′thôrn *or* hô′-) *n.* any of a genus (*Crataegus*) of thorny shrubs and small trees of the rose family, having simple, usually toothed or lobed leaves, white or pink flowers, and small, usually red fruits called haws. Many hawthorns are cultivated as ornamental shrubs and trees. [OE *hagathorn* < *haga* hedge + *thorn* thorn]

hay (hā) *n., v.* —*n.* **1** grass, alfalfa, clover, etc. that has been cut and dried for use as food for cattle, horses, etc. **2** grass ready for mowing.
hit the hay, *Slang.* go to bed.
make hay, a cut and dry grass, alfalfa, clover, etc. for hay. **b** *Informal.* take advantage of some opportunity.
make hay while the sun shines, make hay (def. b).
—*v.* **1** cut and dry grass, alfalfa, clover, etc. for hay: *The men are haying in the east field.* **2** supply with hay. [OE *hēg.* Related to HEW.]
☞ *Hom.* **hey.**

hay·cock (hā′kok′) *n.* a small, cone-shaped pile of hay in a field.

hay·coil (hā′koil′) *n.* haycock.

hay fever an allergy affecting the respiratory tract and the eyes as a severe cold does, caused by the pollen of ragweed and other plants.

hay·field (hā′fēld′) *n.* a field where crops such as grass, alfalfa, or clover are grown or cut for hay.

hay·fork (hā′fôrk′) *n.* **1** pitchfork. **2** a mechanically operated device for loading hay into or out of a hayloft.

hay·loft (hā′loft′) *n.* the upper storey of a stable or barn, where hay is stored.

hay·mak·er (hā′māk′ər) *n.* **1** a person who tosses and spreads hay to dry after it is cut. **2** an apparatus for shaking up and drying hay. **3** *Slang. Boxing.* a hard, swinging, upward blow with the fist.

hay·mow (hā′mou′ *or* -mō′) *n.* **1** a place in a barn where hay is stored; hayloft. **2** a heap of hay stored in a barn.

hay·rack (hā′rak′) *n.* **1** a rack or frame used for holding hay to be eaten by cattle, horses, etc. **2** a framework on a wagon used in hauling hay, straw, etc. **3** the wagon and framework together.

hay·rick (hā′rik′) *n.* haystack.

hay·seed (hā′sēd′) *n.* **1** grass seed, especially that shaken out of hay. **2** the chaff that falls from hay. **3** *Slang.* a person from the country; farmer.

hay·stack (hā′stak′) *n.* a large pile of hay outdoors.

hay·wire (hā′wīr′) *n., adj.* —*n.* wire used to tie up bales of hay. —*adj.* **1** out of order; tangled up. **2** emotionally disturbed or upset. **3** *Slang.* shoddy; stop-gap; flimsy: *a haywire repair job.*
go haywire, get out of order; act in an excited or confused manner.

haz·ard (haz′ərd) *n., v.* —*n.* **1** a risk; danger; peril: *The life of an explorer is full of hazards.* **2** a chance. **3** *Golf.* any obstruction on a course that can trap a ball. **4** *Billiards.* a stroke by which the player sends the object ball or his own ball (after it hits another) into a pocket. **5** an old and complicated dice game from which craps developed.
at all hazards, whatever the risk; in spite of great danger or peril.
—*v.* **1** take a chance with; risk; venture: *I would hazard my life on his honesty.* **2** expose to risk. [ME < OF *hasard* < Arabic *al-zahr* the die²]

haz·ard·ous (haz′ər dəs) *adj.* dangerous; risky; perilous. —**haz′ard·ous·ly,** *adv.* —**haz′ard·ous·ness,** *n.*

haze¹ (hāz) *n.* **1** a small amount of mist, smoke, dust, etc. in the air: *A thin haze veiled the hills.* **2** vagueness of the mind during which one sees things indistinctly: *After he was hit on the head, everything was in a haze for him.* **3** general vagueness; a slight confusion of the mind. [origin uncertain; cf. E dial. *haze* drizzle, be foggy]

haze² (hāz) *v.* **hazed, haz·ing. 1** force to do unnecessary or ridiculous tasks; bully: *The freshmen resented being hazed by the older students.* **2** in western Canada and the United States, drive (cattle, horses, etc.) from horseback. [? < OF *haser* irritate, harass] —**haz′er,** *n.*

ha·zel (hā′zəl) *n., adj.* —*n.* **1** any of a genus (*Corylus*) of shrubs and small trees of the birch family bearing round, brown, edible nuts. **2** the wood of any of these trees. **3** hazelnut. **4** a greenish brown color. —*adj.* having the color hazel: *hazel eyes.* [OE *hæsel*]

ha·zel·nut (hā′zəl nut′) *n.* the round, brown, edible nut of a hazel; filbert.

ha·zy (hā′zē) *adj.* **-zi·er, -zi·est. 1** full of haze; misty; smoky: *hazy air.* **2** rather confused; vague; obscure: *hazy ideas.* —**ha′zi·ly,** *adv.* —**ha′zi·ness,** *n.*

HB a symbol used on pencils to indicate a medium degree of hardness of the lead. Compare **B** and **H**.

H.B.C. Hudson's Bay Company.

H–bomb (āch′bom′) *n.* hydrogen bomb.

H.C. House of Commons.

H.C.F., h.c.f., *or* **hcf** highest common factor.

h.c.l. *Informal.* high cost of living.

hd. head(s).

hdbk. handbook(s).

hdkf. handkerchief(s).

hdqrs. headquarters.

he (hē; *unstressed,* ē *or* i) *pron., subj.* **he,** *obj.* **him,** *poss.* **his,** *pl. subj.* **they,** *pl. obj.* **them,** *pl. poss.* **theirs;** *n., pl.* **he′s.** —*pron.* **1** a boy, man, or male animal: *John has to work hard, but he likes his job and it pays him well.* **2** anyone; a person: *He who hesitates is lost.* —*n.* a male human being or animal: *There were three he's and two she's in the litter of kittens.* [OE *hē*]

He helium.

HE *or* **H.E.** high explosive.

H.E. 1 His Eminence. **2** His Excellency.

head (hed) *n., pl.* **heads** (for 1-9, 11-25) *or* **head** (for 10); *adj., v.* —*n.* **1** the top part of the human body where the eyes, ears, and mouth are. **2** the corresponding part of an animal's body. **3** the top part of anything: *the head of a pin, the head of a page.* **4** the foremost part or end of anything; the front: *the head of a procession.* **5** a likeness of a head, especially as a work of art: *A marble head of the emperor was in the museum.* **6** Usually, **heads,** the side of a coin bearing the likeness of a head, especially that of a king, queen, president, etc.: *The tossed coin came up heads. The head of a Canadian coin carries a portrait of Queen Elizabeth II.*
7 the chief person; leader; commander; director. **8** the position of head; chief authority; leadership; command; direction. **9** a person; an individual: *Kings and queens are crowned heads.* **10** a unit, used in counting animals: *He sold fifty head of cattle and ten head of horses.* **11** anything rounded like a head: *a head of cabbage or lettuce.* **12** *Botany.* a cluster of small flowers growing closely together, as in composite plants or clover. **13** the part of a boil or pimple where pus is about to break through the skin. **14** the striking part of a tool or implement: *the head of a hammer.* **15** a piece of skin stretched tightly over the end of a drum, tambourine, etc. **16** either end of a barrel or cask. **17** the end of a bed, couch, etc. at which a person's head is placed. **18** mind; understanding; intelligence; intellect: *The old man has a wise head.* **19** a topic; point: *He arranged his speech under four main heads.* **20** a decisive point; crisis; conclusion: *His sudden refusal brought matters to a head.* **21** strength or force gained little by little: *As more people joined, the movement gathered head.* **22** pressure of water, steam, etc. **23** the source of a river or stream. **24** foam; froth. **25** *Nautical.* **a** the forward part of a ship. **b** a toilet.
come to a head, a of boils, pimples, etc., reach the stage where they are about to break through the skin. **b** reach a decisive stage: *The international crisis came to a head and war was declared.*
eat (one's) **head off, a** eat very much. **b** cost more to feed than one is worth.
give (someone) **his head,** let him go as he pleases.
go to (one's) **head, a** affect one's mind. **b** make one dizzy or intoxicated. **c** make one conceited.
hang (one's) **head,** be ashamed and show that one is so.
head over heels, a in a somersault. **b** hastily; rashly. **c** completely; thoroughly.
heads up, be careful; watch out: *Heads up! The Principal's coming.*
hide (one's) **head,** be ashamed and show that one is so.
keep (one's) **head,** not get excited; stay calm.
keep (one's) **head above water, a** stay afloat. **b** keep out of trouble or difficulty, especially financial difficulty: *He's finding it hard to keep his head above water these days.*
lay heads together, a confer; consult. **b** plot; conspire.
lose (one's) **head,** get excited; lose one's self-control.
make head, move forward; make progress; advance.
make head or tail of, understand.
on *or* **upon** (one's) **head,** on one's responsibility.
out of *or* **off** (one's) **head,** *Informal.* crazy; insane.
over (someone's) **head, a** beyond one's power to understand or manage. **b** to a person higher in authority: *He threatened to go to the manager over the foreman's head.* **c** so as to pass over or ignore a person who has a senior status, a prior claim, or a better right: *An outsider has now been promoted over their heads.*
put heads together, a confer; consult. **b** plot; conspire.
take it into (one's) **head, a** get the idea. **b** plan; intend.
talk (someone's) **head off,** talk endlessly.
turn (someone's) **head,** make someone conceited: *Her early success has not turned her head.*
—*adj.* **1** at the head, top, or front: *the head division of a parade.* **2** coming from in front: *a head wind.* **3** chief; leading; commanding; directing. **4** of, having to do with, or for the head.
—*v.* **1** be or go at the head, top, or front of: *to head a parade.* **2** cause to move or face in a certain direction: *to head a boat toward shore.* **3** move or go in a certain direction: *It's getting late; we'd better head for home.* **4** be the head or chief of; lead; command; direct: *to head a business.* **5** put a head on; furnish with a head. **6** form a head; come to a head. **7** cut off the head of.
head off, a get in front of and turn back or aside: *The cowboys tried to head off the stampeding herd.* **b** prevent; forestall: *He tried to head off possible trouble for himself by taking great care.*
head on, with the head or front first: *The car crashed head on into the wall.*
[OE *hēafod*] —**head′like′,** *adj.*

head·ache (hed′āk′) *n.* **1** pain in the head. **2** *Informal.* any thing, situation, etc. that is the cause of great bother, annoyance, etc.

head·band (hed′band′) *n.* **1** a band of cloth, ribbon, leather, etc. worn around the head to hold the hair in place or for ornament. **2** a flexible metal or plastic band that holds an earphone or earphones in place over the ear. **3** a decorative strip of material at the top and sometimes at the bottom of the spine of a book. **4** a decorative printed strip at the head of a page or chapter in a book.

head·board (hed′bôrd′) *n.* a board or frame that forms the head of a bed.

head·cheese (hed′chēz′) *n.* a jellied loaf formed of parts of the head and feet of pigs cut up, cooked, and seasoned.

head·dress (hed′dres′) *n.* **1** a covering or decoration for the head. **2** a way of wearing or arranging the hair.

head·ed (hed′id) *adj.* **1** having a head or heads. **2** having a head or heads of a specified kind or number (*used in compounds*): *pig-headed, bald-headed, light-headed.* **3** having a heading.

head·er (hed′ər) *n.* **1** a person, tool, or machine that puts on or takes off heads of grain, barrels, pins, etc. **2** *Informal.* a plunge or

dive headfirst: *He took a header into the water.* **3** *Masonry.* a brick or stone laid with its length across the thickness of a wall and its end facing the outer surface of the wall. Compare **stretcher. 4** *Carpentry.* **a** a beam set across and supporting the ends of joists, studs, or rafters to form one side of an opening in a wall, floor, or roof. **b** lintel. **5** *Soccer.* the act of hitting the ball with the head.

head·first (hed'fėrst') *adv.* **1** with the head first. **2** rashly.

head·fore·most (hed'fôr'mōst) *adv.* headfirst.

head·frame (hed'frām') *n. Mining.* the structure over a shaft to support the hoisting equipment.

head gate 1 an upstream gate of a lock in a canal or river. **2** the floodgate of a race, sluice, etc.

head·gear (hed'gēr') *n.* **1** a covering for the head; hat, cap, etc. **2** the harness for an animal's head.

head–hunt·er (hed'hun'tər) *n.* a person who practises head-hunting.

head–hunt·ing (hed'hunt'ing) *n., adj.* —*n.* the practice, among certain primitive tribes, of trying to get the heads of enemies as a sign of victory, manhood, etc. —*adj.* of or having to do with head-hunters.

head·ing (hed'ing) *n.* **1** the part forming the head, top, or front. **2** something written or printed at the top of a page. **3** the title of a page, chapter, etc.; topic.

head·lamp (hed'lamp') *n.* **1** a small lamp worn on the cap or the forehead. **2** a headlight on a train, automobile, etc.

head·land (hed'lənd *or* -land') *n.* a point of land jutting out into water; cape.

head·less (hed'lis) *adj.* **1** having no head. **2** without a leader. **3** without brains; stupid.

head·light (hed'līt') *n.* **1** of vehicles such as automobiles, one of two large lights at the front. **2** a large single light at the front of a locomotive, streetcar, etc. **3** on a ship, a light at a masthead.

head·line (hed'līn') *n., v.* **-lined, -lin·ing.** —*n.* **1** the words printed at the top of an article in a newspaper or magazine to indicate the topic dealt with. **2** a line printed at the top of a page giving the running title, page number, etc. **3 headlines,** publicity: *He's the kind of man who gets plenty of headlines.*
make headlines, receive publicity: *The new discovery made headlines everywhere.*
—*v.* furnish with a headline.

head·lock (hed'lok') *n. Wrestling.* a hold in which a person's head is held between the body and arm of his opponent.

head·long (hed'long') *adv. or adj.* **1** headfirst. **2** with great speed and force. **3** without stopping to think; in too great a rush: *rushing headlong into trouble.* [ME *hedlong,* alteration of earlier *hedlyng* < *hed* head + *-ling,* adv. suffix expressing direction, OE *-ling*]

head·man (hed'man' *or* hed'mən) *n., pl.* **-men.** a chief; leader.

head·mas·ter (hed'mas'tər) *n.* a person in charge of a school, especially of a private school; principal.

head·mas·ter·ship (hed'mas'tər ship') *n.* the position or authority of a headmaster.

head·most (hed'mōst') *adj.* first; most advanced.

head of steel *Cdn.* end of steel.

head–on (hed'on') *adj.* with the head or front first: *a head-on collision.*

head·phone (hed'fōn') *n.* a telephone or radio receiver held on the head, against the ears.

head·piece (hed'pēs') *n.* **1** a piece of armor for the head; helmet. **2** a hat, cap, or other covering for the head. **3** headphone. **4** *Informal.* the head; mind; intellect. **5** *Printing.* a decoration at the head of a page, chapter, etc.

head pin *Bowling and tenpins.* the front pin of the triangle of pins.

head·quar·ters (hed'kwôr'tərz) *n.pl. or sing.* **1** the place from which the chief or commanding officer of an army, police force, etc. sends out orders. **2** the centre from which any organization is controlled and directed; main office: *The headquarters of the Canadian Red Cross Society is in Toronto.*

head·rest (hed'rest') *n.* a support for the head: *The dentist's chair has a headrest.*

head·room (hed'rüm' *or* -rum') *n.* a clear space above; clearance; headway: *Some bridges do not have enough headroom to allow high trucks to pass underneath.*

head·set (hed'set') *n.* a pair of earphones.

head·ship (hed'ship) *n.* the position of head; chief authority.

head·shrink·er (hed'shring'kər) *n.* **1** *Slang.* psychiatrist. **2** a head-hunter who cuts off and shrinks the heads of his enemies.

heads·man (hedz'mən) *n., pl.* **-men.** a man who puts condemned persons to death by cutting off their heads.

hat, āge, fär; let, ēqual, tėrm; it, īce
hot, ōpen, ôrder; oil, out; cup, pùt, rüle,
əbove, takən, pencəl, lemən, circəs
ch, child; ng, long; sh, ship
th, thin; ŦH, then; zh, measure

head·stall (hed'stol' *or* -stôl') *n.* an arrangement of leather straps or rope that fits over the head of an animal, especially one that forms part of the bridle or halter of a horse.

head start 1 an advantage or lead allowed someone at the beginning of a race: *The smaller boy was given a head start.* **2** an advantage gained by beginning something before somebody else: *That team is playing better hockey than we are because they had a head start in practising.*

head·stock (hed'stok') *n.* **1** the part of a machine that contains the revolving or working parts. **2** the part of a lathe that holds the spindle.

head·stone (hed'stōn') *n.* **1** a stone set at the head of a grave; tombstone. **2** the principal stone in a foundation; cornerstone.

head·stream (hed'strēm') *n.* a stream that is the source of a larger stream.

head·strong (hed'strong') *adj.* **1** rashly or foolishly determined to have one's own way; hard to control or manage; obstinate. **2** showing rash or foolish determination to have one's own way: *a headstrong action.*

head tone 1 a note produced in the second or third register of the voice. **2** *Music.* a sung tone that causes vibration in the cavities of the head.

head·wait·er (hed'wāt'ər) *n.* a man in charge of the waiters in a restaurant, hotel, etc.

head·wa·ters (hed'wot'ərz *or* -wô'tərz) *n.pl.* the sources or upper parts of a river.

head·way (hed'wā') *n.* **1** forward motion: *The ship could make no headway against the strong wind and tide.* **2** progress with work, etc. **3** a clear space overhead in a doorway or under an arch, bridge, etc; clearance. **4** the interval of time between two trains, streetcars, ships, etc. going in the same direction over the same route.

head wind a wind blowing straight against the front of a ship, etc.

head·word (hed'wėrd') *n.* a word that is modified by another word or words; the main word of a phrase.

head·work (hed'wėrk') *n.* mental work; effort with the mind.

head·y (hed'ē) *adj.* **head·i·er, head·i·est. 1** hasty; rash. **2** apt to affect the head and make one dizzy; intoxicating. [ME *hevedi* headlong] —**head'i·ly,** *adv.* —**head'i·ness,** *n.*

heal (hēl) *v.* **1** make whole, sound, or well; bring back to health; cure (a disease or wound). **2** become whole or sound; get well; return to health; be cured: *His cut finger healed in a few days.* **3** free from anything bad. **4** get rid of (anything bad). [OE *hælan* < *hāl* well, whole] —**heal'er,** *n.*
☛ *Hom.* heel, he'll.
☛ *Syn.* 1. See note at **cure.**

health (helth) *n., interj.* —*n.* **1** being well; freedom from sickness. **2** a condition of body or mind: *She is in poor health.* **3** a toast drunk in honor of a person with a wish that he may be healthy and happy: *We all drank a health to the bride.* —*interj.*
your health, a phrase used in drinking a person's health.
[OE *hælth* < *hāl* well, whole]

health·ful (helth'fəl) *adj.* giving health; good for the health: *healthful exercise, a healthful diet.* —**health'ful·ly,** *adv.* —**health'ful·ness,** *n.*
☛ *Usage.* Healthful, healthy. Formal usage tends to distinguish between these words, using **healthful** to mean "giving health," and **healthy** to mean "having good health." Places and food are *healthful;* persons and animals are *healthy.*

healthy (hel'thē) *adj.* **health·i·er, health·i·est. 1** having good health: *a healthy baby.* **2** showing good health: *a healthy appearance.* **3** healthful. —**health'i·ly,** *adv.* —**health'i·ness,** *n.*
☛ *Syn.* 1, 2. **Healthy, wholesome** = having or showing health. **Healthy** emphasizes energy, strength, and freedom from sickness (physical or mental) both when used literally of people and when used figuratively of ideas, society, etc.: *He has a healthy appearance.* **Wholesome** emphasizes soundness and freedom from weakness, decay, or harmfulness physically or, particuarly, emotionally or morally: *Our uncle gave us some wholesome advice.*
☛ *Usage.* See note at **healthful.**

heap (hēp) *n., v.* —*n.* **1** a pile of many things thrown or lying together: *a heap of stones, a sand heap.* **2** *Informal.* a large amount. —*v.* **1** form into a heap; gather in heaps: *She heaped the dirty clothes beside the washing machine.* **2** give generously or in large amounts. **3** fill to the point of overflowing; load: *His mother heaped*

potatoes on his plate. His friends heaped praise on him after he won his victory. [OE *hēap*]

hear (hēr) *v.* **heard, hear·ing;** *interj.* —*v.* **1** perceive by the ear: *to hear sounds, to hear voices.* **2** be able to perceive by the ear: *He cannot hear well.* **3** listen to: *to hear a person's explanation.* **4** listen. **5** give a chance to be heard; give a formal hearing to, as a king, a judge, a teacher, or an assembly does. **6** find out by hearing: *to hear news.* **7** be told; receive news or information: *I don't know the plans for the meeting; I haven't heard yet.* **8** listen to with favor: *Lord, hear my prayer.*
hear from, a receive news or information from: *Have you heard from your friend?* **b** receive a reprimand from.
hear out, listen to till the end.
will not hear of it, will not listen to, think of, agree to, or allow it.
—*interj.*
hear! hear! shouts of approval; cheering.
[OE *hēran*] —**hear′er,** *n.*
☞ *Hom.* **here.**
☞ *Syn. v.* **1. Hear, listen** = perceive by the ear. **Hear** applies to the physical act of receiving sound through the ear: *Do you hear a noise?* **Listen** = pay attention to a sound and try to hear or understand it: *I heard him talking, but did not listen to what he said.*

heard (hèrd) *v.* pt. and pp. of **hear.**
☞ *Hom.* **herd.**

hear·ing (hēr′ing) *n.* **1** the sense by which sound is perceived: *The old man's hearing is poor.* **2** the act or process of perceiving sound: *Hearing the good news made him happy.* **3** a formal or official listening: *The Royal Commission has set a date for its next hearing.* **4** the trial of an action: *The judge gave both sides a hearing in court.* **5** a chance to be heard: *Give us a hearing.* **6** the distance that a sound can be heard: *to be within hearing of the baby, to talk freely in the hearing of others.*

hearing aid an electrical device to amplify sound, consisting usually of an earphone connected to a microphone and amplifier inside a small case.

heark·en (här′kən) *v. Archaic.* listen; listen attentively. Also, **harken.** [OE *hercnian, heorcnian*]

hear·say (hēr′sā′) *n.* common talk; gossip.

hearsay evidence *Law.* evidence based on the testimony of another person, rather than on the firsthand knowledge of the witness. Such evidence is usually not admissable.

hearse (hèrs) *n.* an automobile, carriage, etc. used in funerals to carry a dead person to his grave. [ME < OF *herce* < L *hirpex, -picis,* harrow; originally, a frame like a harrow]

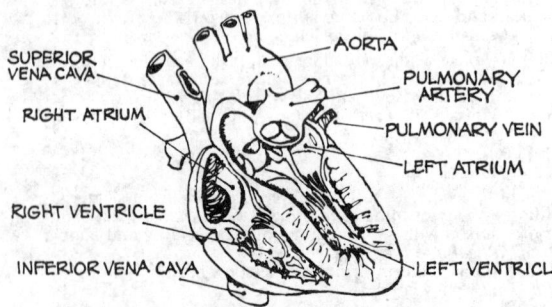

SUPERIOR VENA CAVA
RIGHT ATRIUM
RIGHT VENTRICLE
INFERIOR VENA CAVA
AORTA
PULMONARY ARTERY
PULMONARY VEIN
LEFT ATRIUM
LEFT VENTRICLE

The human heart, shown from the front

heart (härt) *n.* **1** a hollow, muscular organ that pumps the blood throughout the body by contracting and dilating. **2** the region of the heart; breast; bosom: *She clasped her hands to her heart.* **3** the feelings; mind; soul: *She has a kind heart.* **4** the source of the emotions, especially of love: *to give one's heart.* **5** a person, especially one who is loved or praised: *a group of stout hearts.* **6** kindness, sympathy: *to have no heart.* **7** spirit; courage; enthusiasm: *The losing team showed plenty of heart.* **8** the innermost part; middle; centre: *in the heart of the forest.* **9** the main part; vital or most important part: *the very heart of the matter.*

A heart (def. 10)

10 a figure shaped like a heart: *There was a big red heart on the*

front of the valentine. **11 a** a playing card with one or more red heart-shaped figures. **b hearts,** *pl.* a suit of playing cards with red heart-shaped designs on them. **c hearts,** a game in which the players try to get rid of cards of this suit (*used with a singular verb*).
after (one's) own heart, just as one likes it; pleasing one perfectly.
at heart, in one's deepest thoughts or feelings; really.
break the heart of, crush with sorrow or grief.
by heart, a by memory. **b** from memory.
eat (one's) heart out, feel great sorrow, grief, or worry.
from (one's) heart, with deepest feeling; sincerely.
get to the heart of, find out the secret or hidden meaning of.
have (one's) heart in (one's) boots or **mouth,** be very frightened.
have (one's) heart in the right place, mean well; have good intentions.
have the heart, a be courageous or spirited enough (to do something). **b** be hard-hearted enough: *He hadn't the heart to refuse his son's request.*
heart and soul, with all one's affections and energies.
heart of gold, an extremely kind, generous and sympathetic nature.
in (one's) heart of hearts, in one's deepest thoughts or feelings.
lay to heart, a keep in mind; remember. **b** think seriously about.
near (one's) heart, of great value or interest to one.
take heart, be encouraged.
take to heart, think seriously about or be deeply affected by.
to (one's) heart's content, as much as one wants.
wear (one's) heart on (one's) sleeve, show one's feelings too plainly.
with all (one's) heart, a sincerely. **b** gladly.
[OE *heorte*]
☞ *Hom.* **hart.**

heart·ache (härt′āk′) *n.* sorrow; grief.

heart attack a sudden instance of heart disease, especially a coronary thrombosis resulting in the destruction of an area of heart muscle.

heart·beat (härt′bēt′) *n.* a pulsation of the heart, including one complete contraction and dilation.

heart·break (härt′brāk′) *n.* a crushing sorrow or grief.

heart·break·ing (härt′brāk′ing) *adj.* crushing with sorrow or grief. —**heart′break·ing·ly,** *adv.*

heart·brok·en (härt′brō′kən) *adj.* crushed with sorrow or grief. —**heart′brok·en·ly,** *adv.* —**heart′brok·en·ness,** *n.*

heart·burn (härt′bèrn′) *n.* a burning sensation in the lower chest and the stomach, generally caused by digestive juices escaping from the stomach up into the esophagus.

heart·burn·ing (härt′bèr′ning) *n.* a feeling of envy or jealousy.

–hearted *combining form.* having a heart of a specified kind: *good-hearted, light-hearted.*

heart·en (här′tən) *v.* encourage; cheer up: *Good news heartens you.* —**heart·en·er,** *n.*

heart failure 1 a condition in which one or both sides of the heart are unable to pump enough blood to meet the needs of the body. **2** a sudden stopping of the heartbeat, resulting in death.

heart·felt (härt′felt′) *adj.* sincere; genuine.

hearth (härth) *n.* **1** the floor of a fireplace. **2** the home; fireside: *The soldier longed for his own hearth.* **3** the lowest part of a blast furnace. [OE *heorth*]

hearth·side (härth′sīd′) *n.* **1** the side of a hearth. **2** the home.

hearth·stone (härth′stōn′) *n.* **1** a stone forming a hearth. **2** the home; fireside.

heart·i·ly (här′tə lē) *adv.* **1** sincerely; genuinely; in a warm, friendly way: *to express good wishes very heartily.* **2** with enthusiasm; with a good will; vigorously: *to set to work heartily.* **3** with a good appetite. **4** very; completely; thoroughly.

heart·land (härt′land′) *n.* **1** any area or region that is the centre of, or vital to, an institution, industry, country, etc. **2** *Geopolitics.* an economically and militarily self-sufficient land mass, located centrally in and controlling the world island (Eurasia and Africa), and relatively invulnerable to attack.

heart·less (härt′lis) *adj.* **1** without kindness or sympathy; unfeeling; cruel. **2** *Archaic.* without courage, spirit, or enthusiasm. —**heart′less·ly,** *adv.* —**heart′less·ness,** *n.*

heart–lung machine or **pump** (härt′lung′) *Medicine.* a device used during heart surgery to pump blood through the body, thus temporarily taking the place of the heart.

heart–rend·ing (härt′ren′ding) *adj.* causing mental anguish; very distressing. —**heart′–rend·ing·ly,** *adv.*

hearts·ease or **heart's–ease** (härts′ēz′) *n.* **1** peace of mind. **2** wild pansy.

heart·sick (härt′sik′) *adj.* sick at heart; very much depressed; very unhappy.

heart·sore (härt′sôr′) *adj.* feeling or showing grief; grieved.

heart–strick·en (härt′strik′ən) *adj.* struck to the heart with grief; shocked with fear; dismayed.

heart·strings (härt′stringz′) *n.pl.* deepest feelings; strongest affections.

heart–throb (härt′throb′) *n.* 1 heartbeat. 2 *Informal.* a person with whom one is infatuated.

heart–to–heart (härt′tə härt′) *adj.* without reserve; frank; sincere.

heart–whole (härt′hōl′) *adj.* 1 not in love. 2 hearty; sincere.

heart·wood (härt′wŏd′) *n.* the hard, central wood of a tree.

heart·y (här′tē) *adj.* **heart·i·er, heart·i·est;** *n., pl.* **heart·ies.** —*adj.* 1 warm and friendly; genuine; sincere: *a hearty welcome.* 2 strong and well; vigorous: *The old man was still hale and hearty.* 3 full of energy and enthusiasm; not restrained: *He burst out in a loud, hearty laugh.* 4 with plenty to eat; nourishing: *A hearty meal satisfied his hunger.* 5 requiring or using much food: *a hearty eater.* —*n.* 1 a fellow sailor; a brave and good comrade. 2 an excessively hearty and effusive person; backslapper. [< *heart*] —**heart·i·ness,** *n.*

heat (hēt) *n., v.* —*n.* 1 the quality or state of being hot; hotness; high temperature. 2 the degree of hotness; temperature. 3 the sensation or perception of hotness or warmth. 4 *Physics.* a form of energy that consists of the motion of the molecules of a substance. The rate at which the molecules move determines the temperature. 5 the hot weather. 6 warmth or intensity of feeling; anger; violence; excitement; eagerness; ardor. 7 the hottest point; most violent or active state: *In the heat of the fight he lost his temper.* 8 *Slang.* pressure; coercion; torture. 9 one trial in a race: *He won the first heat, but lost the final race.* 10 one operation of heating in a furnace or a forge. 11 a periodically recurring condition of sexual excitement in female mammals. 12 the time during which this excitement lasts. **in heat,** in such a condition of excitement, and so able to be mated. —*v.* 1 make hot or warm; become hot or warm. 2 fill with strong feeling; inflame; excite; become excited. [OE *hǣtu.* Related to HOT.]

heat barrier See **thermal barrier.**

heat·ed (hē′təd) *adj.* angry or excited: *a heated debate, a heated reply.* —**heat·ed·ly,** *adv.*

heat·er (hēt′ər) *n.* a device that gives heat or warmth, especially one that is not part of a central heating system: *an electric baseboard heater. They have a block heater for their car.*

heat exchanger a device by means of which heat is transferred from one medium to another in order that it may be utilized as a source of power, as in an atomic power plant, certain gas turbine engines, etc.

heat exhaustion a condition due to prolonged exposure to heat, characterized by excessive sweating, faintness, dizziness, and, often, nausea. Compare **heatstroke.**

heath (hēth) *n.* 1 *Brit.* open wasteland, usually having sandy, acid soil and scrubby vegetation; moor. 2 any of a genus (*Erica*) of evergreen shrubs or trees having whorls of small, needlelike leaves and clusters of small, bell-shaped or tubular flowers. Heaths are common in much of Europe and Africa, especially on open wasteland with acid soil. 3 any of various other shrubs of similar habit and appearance, especially of the same family. 4 (*adj.*) designating the family (Ericaceae) of shrubs and trees that includes the heaths, heathers, rhododendrons, and blueberries. **(one's) native heath,** the place where one was born or brought up. [OE *hǣth*]

hea·then (hē′ℸən) *n., pl.* **-thens** or (*esp. collectively*) **-then.** 1 a person who does not believe in the God of the Bible; a person who is not a Christian, Jew, or Moslem. 2 (*adj.*) of or having to do with heathens or their religion or customs: *heathen temples.* 3 a person who is thought to have no religion or culture. 4 (*adj.*) not religious or cultured; unenlightened. [OE *hǣthen,* probably originally, heath dweller < *hǣth* heath]

☛ *Syn. n.* **Heathen, pagan** = unenlightened, unbelieving, as applied to people outside the Christian, Jewish, and Moslem faiths. But members of other established religions object to being called heathen or pagan. **Heathen** in particular, is sometimes used as a term of insult. Both words, therefore, are best used in historical contexts: *Julius Caesar was a pagan. The Goths were heathens.*

hea·then·dom (hē′ℸən dəm) *n.* 1 heathen worship or ways. 2 heathen lands or people.

hea·then·ish (hē′ℸən ish) *adj.* resembling or characteristic of the heathen; barbarous. —**hea′then·ish·ly,** *adv.* —**hea′then·ish·ness,** *n.*

hea·then·ism (hē′ℸən iz′əm) *n.* 1 heathen worship or ways. 2 the lack of religion or culture; barbarism.

heath·er (heℸ′ər) *n.* any of several species of heath, especially a plant (*Calluna vulgaris*) native to northern and alpine regions of Europe and Asia, and common in the British Isles, having clusters of tiny, bell-shaped, usually purplish-pink flowers. [? < *heath*]

heath·er·y (heℸ′ər ē) *adj.* 1 of or like heather. 2 covered with heather.

hat, āge, fär; let, ēqual, tèrm; it, īce
hot, ōpen, ôrder; oil, out; cup, pút, rüle,
above, takən, pencəl, lemən, circəs
ch, child; ng, long; sh, ship
th, thin; ℸн, then; zh, measure

heating element the part of an electrical heating device that gets hot.

heat lightning flashes of light without any thunder, seen near the horizon, especially on hot summer evenings.

heat pump a device using mechanical energy to transfer heat from one place or space to another one that is at a higher temperature. A heat pump can be used to heat a house in winter when the air is warmer inside, and to cool it in summer when the air is warmer outside.

heat shield a coating or covering of special material on the nose cone of a missile or spacecraft to protect it from the heat produced when it re-enters the earth's atmosphere.

heat·stroke (hēt′strōk′) *n.* a serious illness produced by long exposure to extreme heat and humidity, in which the body temperature rises dangerously high because the sweating system can no longer function to cool the body. Compare **heat exhaustion.**

heat wave a long period of very hot weather.

heave (hēv) *v.* **heaved** or (*esp. nautical*) **hove, heav·ing;** *n., interj.* —*v.* 1 lift with force or effort: *He heaved the heavy box into the wagon.* 2 lift and throw: *The sailors heaved the anchor overboard.* 3 pull with force or effort; haul: *They heaved on the rope.* 4 utter with effort: *He heaved a sigh of relief.* 5 rise and fall rhythmically: *the heaving sea.* 6 rise; swell or bulge: *The ground heaved during the earthquake.* 7 pant: *His chest was heaving from the exertion.* 8 try to vomit; retch. 9 of a ship, move in a certain direction: *A ship hove in sight.* 10 *Geology.* thrust (a vein, etc.) out of place horizontally. **heave in sight,** come into view. **heave to, a** stop (a ship) as by trimming the sails, etc. **b** of a ship, stop. —*n.* 1 the act or fact of heaving: *With a great heave, they got the dresser onto the truck.* 2 *Geology.* a horizontal displacement or dislocation of a vein or stratum at a fault. 3 **heaves,** a disease of horses characterized by difficult breathing, coughing, and heaving of the flanks (*used with a singular verb*). —*interj.* **heave ho!** a sailor's cry when pulling up the anchor, or pulling on any rope or cable. [OE *hebban*] —**heav′er,** *n.*

heav·en (hev′ən) *n.* 1 *Christianity and Judaism.* **a** the place where God and His angels live and where the blessed go after death, traditionally thought of as beyond the sky. Compare **hell** (def. 1). **b Heaven,** God; Providence: *They felt it was the will of Heaven.* 2 a place or condition of greatest happiness: *It was heaven just to be able to relax after the uproar.* 3 Usually, **heavens,** *pl.* the space that appears to be a dome over the earth, in which the sun, moon, and stars are seen; sky: *Millions of stars were shining in the heavens.* **for heaven's sake** or **good heavens!** an exclamation of surprise or protest. **move heaven and earth,** do everything possible. [OE *heofon*]

heav·en·ly (hev′ən lē) *adj.* 1 of or in heaven; divine; holy: *the heavenly Father, heavenly choirs.* 2 like or suitable for heaven; of more than human excellence: *heavenly peace.* 3 *Informal.* delightful; excellent: *a heavenly spot for a picnic, heavenly weather.* 4 of or in the heavens; in the sky: *The sun, moon, stars, planets, and comets are heavenly bodies.* —**heav′en·li·ness,** *n.*

heav·en·ward (hev′ən wərd) *adv.* toward heaven.

heav·en·wards (hev′ən wərdz) *adv.* heavenward.

Heav·i·side layer (hev′ē sīd′) 1 the second, or middle, layer of the ionosphere, which reflects radio waves of frequencies produced in short-wave broadcasting. 2 the ionosphere. [after Oliver Heaviside (1850-1925), a British physicist]

heav·y (hev′ē) *adj.* **heav·i·er, heav·i·est;** *n., pl.* **heav·ies;** *adv.* —*adj.* 1 hard to lift or carry; of great weight: *a heavy load.* 2 having much mass for its size; of great density: *heavy metal.* 3 of more than usual mass for its kind: *heavy silk.* 4 of great amount, force, or intensity; greater than usual; large: *a heavy vote, heavy strain, heavy sea, heavy sleep, heavy rain, heavy crop.* 5 being such to an unusual degree or extent: *a heavy buyer, a heavy smoker.* 6 hard to bear or endure: *heavy taxes.* 7 hard to deal with; trying or difficult in any way: *A heavy road is muddy, sandy, etc. and is thus hard to travel over. A heavy slope is a steep one. Heavy*

food is hard to digest. Heavy soil is hard to work. **8** weighted down; laden: *air heavy with moisture, eyes heavy with sleep.* **9** causing sorrow; sorrowful; gloomy: *heavy news.* **10** grave; serious; sober; sombre: *a heavy part in a play.* **11** cloudy: *a heavy sky.* **12** broad; thick; coarse: *a heavy line, heavy features.* **13** clumsy; sluggish; slow: *a heavy walk.* **14** ponderous; dull: *heavy reading.* **15** loud and deep: *the heavy roar of cannon.* **16** *Military.* **a** heavily armed or equipped: *heavy tanks.* **b** of large size: *heavy artillery.* **17** not risen enough: *heavy bread.* **18** *Physics.* designating an isotope possessing a greater atomic weight than the most abundant isotope of the same element: *heavy water.*
heavy with child, pregnant, especially in the last months of pregnancy.
—*n.* **1** a heavy person or thing. **2** *Informal. Theatre.* **a** the villain in a play. **b** an actor who plays villains or takes similar parts.
—*adv.* in a heavy manner; heavily.
hang heavy, of time, pass slowly and boringly: *He had nothing to do, and time was hanging heavy on his hands.*
[OE *hefig* < *hebban* heave] —**heav′i·ly,** *adv.* —**heav′i·ness,** *n.*
☛ *Syn. adj.* **1. Heavy, weighty, burdensome** = of great weight. **Heavy** emphasizes being hard to lift or carry, and used figuratively suggests something pressing down on or weighing down the mind or feelings: *He has heavy responsibilities.* **Weighty** = having great weight, but is used chiefly figuratively, applying to something of great importance: *He made a weighty announcement.* **Burdensome** suggests something very heavy that interferes with freedom of movement and puts a strain on the person or thing carrying it: *The extra work was burdensome.*

heav·y-armed (hev′ē ärmd′) *adj.* equipped with heavy weapons or armor.

heavy-duty (hev′ē dyü′tē *or* -dü′tē) *adj.* durably built to withstand unusual strain or very hard use: *a heavy-duty vacuum cleaner.*

heav·y-hand·ed (hev′ē han′did) *adj.* **1** clumsy; awkward: *Her heavy-handed attempts at humor were embarrassing.* **2** harsh; cruel.
—**heav′y-hand′ed·ly,** *adv.* —**heav′y-hand′ed·ness,** *n.*

heav·y-heart·ed (hev′ē här′tid) *adj.* sad; gloomy; in low spirits.

heavy hydrogen an isotope of hydrogen having a mass number of 2; deuterium. Heavy hydrogen has one proton and one neutron in its nucleus, while ordinary hydrogen has no neutrons. *Symbol:* D or ²H

heavy water water composed of oxygen and heavy hydrogen, represented by the formula D_2O, present in very small quantities in ordinary water. If ordinary water is electrolyzed, the percentage of heavy water in it is increased. Heavy water is used in nuclear power plants to moderate and control nuclear reactions. *Formula:* D_2O

heav·y-weight (hev′ē wāt′) *n.* **1** a person or thing of much more than average mass. **2** a boxer weighing more than 81 kilograms. **3** *Informal.* a person of great importance or influence: *a heavyweight in the political field.*

heb·dom·a·dal (heb dom′ə dəl) *adj.* weekly. [< LL *hebdomadalis* < *hebdomas, -adis* seven, seven days < Gk.]

He·be (hē′bē) *n.* Greek mythology. the goddess of youth, the daughter of Zeus and Hera. Hebe was the cupbearer to the gods before Ganymede was given that duty.

He·bra·ic (hi brā′ik *or* hē′brā′ik) *adj.* of or having to do with the Hebrews or their language or culture; Hebrew. [< LL *Hebraicus* < Gk. *Hebraikos*]

He·bra·ism (hē′brā iz′əm) *n.* **1** a linguistic structure or idiom peculiar to Hebrew. **2** such a structure or idiom translated literally into another language. **3** Hebrew character, spirit, thought, or practice.

He·bra·ist (hē′brā ist) *n.* **1** a scholar skilled in the Hebrew language and literature. **2** a person imbued with the Hebraic spirit.

He·bra·is·tic (hē′brā is′tik) *adj.* of or having to do with Hebraism or Hebraists; Hebraic.

He·brew (hē′brü) *n., adj.* —*n.* **1** a member of any of a group of Semitic peoples of ancient Palestine, especially an Israelite. **2** a descendant of any of these peoples, especially the Israelites. **3** the Semitic language of the ancient Hebrews. **4** the modern form of this language, one of the official languages of present-day Israel.
—*adj.* of or having to do with the Hebrews or their language. [ME < OF *Ebreu* < L *Hebraeus* < Gk. *Hebraios* < Aramaic *ʻebrai* < Hebrew *ʻibri,* literally one from beyond (the river)]

Hec·a·te (hek′ə tē *or, formerly,* hek′ət) *n.* Greek mythology. the goddess of the moon, earth, and realm of the dead. Hecate later came to be regarded as the goddess of witchcraft.

hec·a·tomb (hek′ə tōm′, -tüm′, *or* -tom′) *n.* **1** in ancient Greece and Rome, the sacrifice of 100 oxen at one time. **2** any great

slaughter. [< L < Gk. *hekatombē* sacrifice of 100 oxen < *hekaton* hundred + *bous* ox]

heck (hek) *interj., n. Informal.* a mild form of the word **hell,** used to express anger, annoyance, surprise, etc.: *Heck! I forgot the book. That's a heck of a thing to say.*

heck·le (hek′əl) *v.* **-led, -ling.** harass and annoy (a speaker, etc.) by asking bothersome questions, etc. [< *heckle* comb for flax or hemp, ME *hekele.* Related to HACKLE¹.] —**heck′ler,** *n.*

hect– (hekt) *SI prefix.* a form of **hecto-** used before a vowel.

hec·tare (hek′ter *or* hek′tär) *n.* a unit used with the SI for measuring land area, equal to 10 000 square metres. *Symbol:* ha [< F *hectare* < Gk. *hekaton* hundred + F *are* are²]

hec·tic (hek′tik) *adj., n.* —*adj.* **1** filled with or characterized by great excitement or confusion: *a hectic life. We spent three hectic days packing for the move.* **2** showing signs of a fever: *a hectic flush, hectic cheeks.* **3** of or designating the fever characteristic of such diseases as tuberculosis: *hectic fever, a hectic cough.* **4** consumptive.
—*n.* a flush or fever. [ME < OF *etique* < LL < Gk. *hektikos* habitual, consumptive < *hexis* habit]

hecto– *SI prefix.* hundred: *A hectometre is one hundred metres. Symbol:* h [< F < Gk. *hekaton*]

hec·to·graph (hek′tə graf′) *n., v.* —*n.* a machine for making many copies of a page of writing, a drawing, etc. The original writing is transferred to a surface coated with gelatin, and the copies are made from this. —*v.* make copies of with a hectograph.

hec·tor (hek′tər) *n., v.* —*n.* a bragging, bullying fellow. —*v.* bluster; bully. [< *Hector,* a Trojan hero]

he'd (hēd; *unstressed,* ĕd, id, *or* hid) **1** he had. **2** he would.
☛ *Hom.* heed.

hedge (hej) *n., v.* **hedged, hedg·ing.** —*n.* **1** a thick row of bushes or small trees, planted as a fence or boundary. **2** any barrier or boundary. **3** a means of protection or defence. **4** the act of hedging. —*v.* **1** enclose or separate with a hedge; put a hedge around or along: *to hedge a garden.* **2** avoid giving a direct answer; evade questions; avoid taking a definite stand: *Stop hedging and tell us what you want to do.* **3** protect oneself from losing money on (a bet, investment, etc.) by making other bets.
hedge in, **a** hem in; surround on all sides: *The town was hedged in by mountains and a forest.* **b** keep from getting away or moving freely.
[OE *hecg*] —**hedg′er,** *n.*

hedge·hog (hej′hog′) *n.* **1** any of a subfamily (Erinaceinae) of small mammals of Europe, Asia, and Africa, having a short tail, long nose, and short, thick, sharp spines on the back. When attacked or frightened, hedgehogs roll up into a bristling ball. **2** *Esp.U.S.* the porcupine of North America. **3** *Military.* **a** an X-shaped portable obstacle, usually laced with barbed wire. **b** an area defended by pillboxes, mines, and lanes for machine-gun fire.

hedge-hop (hej′hop′) *v.* **-hopped, -hop·ping.** fly an aircraft very low. —**hedge′-hop′per,** *n.*

hedge-hop·ping (hej′hop′ing) *n.* the act of flying an aircraft very low.

hedge·row (hej′rō′) *n.* a thick row of bushes or small trees forming a hedge.

hedge sparrow a small, sparrow-like, European songbird (*Prunella modularis*) that nests in hedges and other shrubbery.

he·don·ism (hē′dən iz′əm) *n.* the doctrine that pleasure or happiness is the highest good. [< Gk. *hēdonē* pleasure]

he·don·ist (hē′dən ist) *n.* a person who believes in or practises hedonism.

heed (hēd) *v., n.* —*v.* give careful attention to; take notice of: *Now heed what I say.* —*n.* careful attention; notice: *He went on as before, paying no heed to the warning signal.* [OE *hēdan*]
—**heed′er,** *n.*
☛ *Hom.* he'd.

heed·ful (hēd′fəl) *adj.* careful; attentive. —**heed′ful·ly,** *adv.* —**heed′ful·ness,** *n.*

heed·less (hēd′lis) *adj.* careless; thoughtless. —**heed′less·ly,** *adv.* —**heed′less·ness,** *n.*

hee-haw (hē′ho′ *or* -hô′) *n., v.* —*n.* **1** the braying sound made by a donkey. **2** a loud, coarse laugh. —*v.* **1** make the braying sound of a donkey. **2** laugh loudly and coarsely.

heel¹ (hēl) *n., v.* —*n.* **1** the back part of a person's foot, below the ankle. **2** the part of a stocking or shoe that covers the heel. **3** the part of a shoe or boot that is under the heel or raises the heel. **4** the part of an animal's hind leg that corresponds to a person's heel. **5** anything shaped, used, or placed at an end like a heel: *The end crust of a loaf of bread is sometimes called a heel.* **6** *Informal.* an untrustworthy or contemptible person.
at heel, near the heels; close behind.

cool (one's) heels, *Informal.* be kept waiting a long time: *She was left cooling her heels for an hour in the waiting room.*
down at the heel or **heels, a** of a shoe or shoes, with the heels worn down. **b** in a shabby or run-down condition: *The whole place looked very down at the heel.*
drag (one's) heels, a hold back or slow up on purpose. **b** agree reluctantly; work (at) without interest or enthusiasm.
kick up (one's) heels, behave in a merry and exuberant way; have fun: *He really kicked up his heels at the party.*
lay by the heels, put in prison or in stocks.
out at the heels, a with the heel of the stocking or shoe worn through. **b** shabby and run-down.
show a clean pair of heels, run away.
take to (one's) heels, run away.
to heel, a near a person's heels; close behind: *The dog walked to heel.* **b** under control: *He soon brought the mutineers to heel.*
—*v.* **1** follow closely behind someone: *I'm teaching my dog to heel.* **2** put a heel or heels on. **3** touch or drive forward with the heel or as if with the heel: *She heeled the horse.* **4** of dogs, follow one's master closely. **5** perform (a dance) with the heels. **6** *Golf.* strike (the ball) with the heel of the club. [OE *hēla*] —**heel′less,** *adj.*
☛ *Hom.* **heal.**

heel² (hēl) *v., n.* —*v.* lean over to one side; tilt; tip: *The ship heeled as it turned.* —*n.* the act of heeling. [alteration of earlier *heeld* < OE *h(i)eldan* < *heald* inclined]
☛ *Hom.* **heal.**

heeled (hēld) *adj.* **1** having a heel or heel-like projection. **2** *Slang.* **a** provided with money. **b** armed with a revolver or other weapon.

heel·er (hēl′ər) *n.* **1** a person who puts heels on shoes. **2** *Esp.U.S. Slang.* a follower or hanger-on of a political boss.

heel·tap (hēl′tap′) *n.* **1** a layer of leather, etc. in the heel of a shoe. **2** a small amount of liquor left in a glass after drinking.

heft (heft) *Informal. n., v.* —*n.* **1** mass or heaviness. **2** *Archaic.* the greater part; bulk. —*v.* **1** judge the mass or heaviness of by lifting: *She hefted the baseball bat to get the feel of it.* **2** lift; heave. [< *heave*]

heft·y (hef′tē) *adj.* **heft·i·er, heft·i·est.** *Informal.* **1** weighty; heavy: *a hefty load.* **2** large; considerable: *They got a hefty bill for repairs.* **3** big and strong. [< *heft*]

He·ge·li·an (hə gā′lē ən) *adj., n.* —*adj.* of, having to do with, or characteristic of Georg W.F. Hegel (1770-1831), a German philosopher, or his philosophy. —*n.* a follower of Hegel.

He·ge·li·an·ism (hə gā′lē ən iz′əm) *n.* the Hegelian philosophy, which maintains that facts and ideas merge in a total reality (the Absolute), and which incorporates a dialectic method of analysis by which a higher level of truth (synthesis) is arrived at through the resolution of logical opposites (thesis and antithesis).

he·gem·o·ny (hi jem′ə nē *or* hej′ə mō′nē) *n., pl.* **-nies.** political domination, especially, leadership or domination by one state over others in a group. [< Gk. *hēgemonia* < *hēgemōn* leader < *hēgeesthai* lead]

He·gi·ra (hi jī′rə *or* hej′ə rə) *n.* **1** the flight of Mohammed from Mecca to Medina in A.D. 622. The Moslems use a calendar reckoned from this date. **2** the Moslem era. **3** hegira, a journey, especially to escape; flight. Also, **Hejira.** [< Med.L < Arabic *hijrah* flight, departure]

heif·er (hef′ər) *n.* a young cow that has not yet had a calf. [OE *hēahfore*]

heigh (hī *or* hā) *interj.* a sound used to attract attention, give encouragement, express surprise, etc.

heigh–ho (hī′hō′ *or* hā′–) *interj.* an exclamation to express surprise, boredom, weariness, etc.

height (hīt) *n.* **1** the measurement from top to bottom; the tallness of anyone or anything; the point to which anything rises above ground: *My father's height is 187 centimetres.* **2** the distance above sea level. **3** a fairly great distance up: *rising at a height above the valley.* **4** a high point or place; hill: *the height overlooking the river, on the mountain heights.* **5** the highest part; top: *He had reached the height of his career by the age of forty.* **6** the highest point; greatest degree: *the height of folly.* **7** high rank; high degree. [OE *hīehthu* < *hēah* high]
☛ *Pronun.* The pronunciation (hītth) is heard in some dialects, but the standard form is (hīt).

height·en (hīt′ən) *v.* **1** make or become higher. **2** make or become stronger, greater, more intense, etc.: *The background music heightened the feeling of suspense.* —**height′en·er,** *n.*

height of land 1 a region higher than its surroundings. **2** *Cdn.* a watershed; divide: *A height of land marks the boundary between Labrador and Quebec.*

hei·nous (hā′nəs *or* hē′nəs) *adj.* very wicked; atrocious; abominable: *a heinous murder.* [ME < OF *haïnos,* ult. < *haïr* to hate < Gmc.] —**hei′nous·ly,** *adv.* —**hei′nous·ness,** *n.*

heir (er) *n.* **1** a person who receives, or has the right to receive,

hat, āge, fär; let, ēqual, tėrm; it, īce
hot, ōpen, ôrder; oil, out; cup, pùt, rüle,
əbove, takən, pencəl, lemən, circəs
ch, child; ng, long; sh, ship
th, thin; ᴛ‌н, then; zh, measure

someone's property or title after the death of its owner; a person who inherits property. **2** a person who inherits something; a person who receives or has something from someone who lived before him. [ME < OF < L *heres* heir]
☛ *Hom.* **air, e'er, ere, err** (er).

heir apparent *pl.* **heirs apparent.** a person who will be the first to succeed to a property or title. The Queen's oldest son, Prince Charles, is heir apparent to the throne.

heir·ess (er′is) *n.* **1** a female heir. **2** a female heir to great wealth.

heir·loom (er′lüm′) *n.* a possession handed down from generation to generation. [< *heir* + *loom,* originally, implement]

heir presumptive *pl.* **heirs presumptive.** a person who will be heir unless someone with a stronger claim is born.

heir·ship (er′ship) *n.* the position or rights of an heir; right of inheritance; inheritance.

heist (hīst) *v., n. Slang.* —*v.* rob or steal. —*n.* a theft or robbery. [alteration of *hoist*]

He·ji·ra (hi jī′rə *or* hej′ə rə) See **Hegira.**

Hel (hel) *n. Norse mythology.* **1** the goddess of death and of the lower world. **2** the lower world, inhabited by those who did not die in battle.

held (held) *v.* pt. and pp. of **hold¹.**

Hel·en of Troy (hel′ən) *Greek mythology.* a very beautiful Greek woman, the wife of King Menelaus of Sparta. Helen's abduction by Paris caused the Trojan War.

heli– *combining form.* the form of *helio-* used before vowels, as in *heliac.*

he·li·an·thus (hē′lē an′thəs) *n.* any of a genus (*Helianthus*) of plants of the composite family, including the sunflower and Jerusalem artichoke. [< NL < Gk. *hēlios* sun + *anthos* flower]

hel·i·cal (hel′ə kəl) *adj.* having to do with, or having the form of, a helix; spiral. —**hel′i·cal·ly,** *adv.*

hel·i·ces (hel′ə sēz′) *n.* a pl. of **helix.**

helico– *combining form.* of or shaped like a helix; spiral.

hel·i·coid (hel′ə koid′) *n., adj.* —*n. Geometry.* a surface generated by a straight line moving along a fixed helix and maintaining a constant angle with its axis. —*adj.* like a helix; spiral, as in certain univalve shells.

hel·i·con (hel′ə kon′ *or* hel′ə kən) *n.* a large bass tuba shaped in a large coil that passes round the player and over one shoulder. [< *helico-,* influenced by *Helicon*]

Hel·i·con (hel′ə kon′) *n. Greek mythology.* the mountain home of the Muses. [< Gk., the name of a mountain in Boeotia]

A helicopter

hel·i·cop·ter (hel′ə kop′tər *or* hē′lə kop′tər) *n., v.* —*n.* an aircraft having one or more horizontal propellers, or rotors, by means of which it can hover, take off and land vertically, and move forwards, backwards, or sideways in the air. —*v.* travel or carry by helicopter. [< F *hélicoptère* < Gk. *helix, -ikos,* spiral + *pteron* wing]

helio– *combining form.* the sun, as in *heliograph.* [< Gk. *hēlios* sun]

he·li·o·cen·tric (hē′lē ō sen′trik) *adj.* **1** viewed or measured from the centre of the sun. **2** having or representing the sun as a centre: *The Copernican system of astronomy is heliocentric.* Compare **geocentric.** [< *helio-* + Gk. *kentron* centre]

he·li·o·gram (hē′lē ə gram′) *n.* a message transmitted by heliograph.

he·li·o·graph (hē′lē ə graf′) *n., v.* —*n.* **1** a device for signalling by means of a movable mirror that flashes beams of light to a distance. The flashes of the mirror represent the dots and dashes of the Morse code. **2** an apparatus for taking photographs of the sun. —*v.* communicate or signal by heliograph.

He·li·os (hē′lē os′) *n. Greek mythology.* the god of the sun, corresponding to the Roman god Sol. Helios is represented as driving his chariot across the heavens every day.

he·li·o·scope (hē′lē ə skōp′) *n.* **1** a device for looking at the sun without injury to the eye. **2** a telescope having such a device.

he·li·o·ther·a·py (hē′lē ō ther′ə pē) *n.* the treatment of disease by means of sunlight.

he·li·o·trope (hē′lē ə trōp′ *or* hēl′yə-) *n., adj.* —*n.* **1** any of a genus (*Heliotropium*) of herbs or shrubs of the borage family having spikes or clusters of small white, lilac, or blue flowers that always turn to face the sun. The common heliotrope is a popular garden plant having oval, wrinkled leaves and clusters of lilac or blue flowers with a fragrance like vanilla. **2** the common valerian, also called garden heliotrope. **3** a reddish purple. **4** a bloodstone, a semiprecious stone.
—*adj.* reddish purple. [< L < Gk. *hēliotropion* < *hēlios* sun + *-tropos* turning]

he·li·ot·ro·pism (hē′lē ot′rə piz′əm) *n.* of certain plants and other organisms, a tendency to respond to sunlight by turning or bending toward it or away from it. Sunflowers exhibit positive heliotropism; that is, the flowers turn toward the sunlight. [< *heliotrope* any plant that turns toward the sun]

he·li·o·type (hē′lē ə tīp′) *n.* **1** a picture or print produced by a photomechanical process in which the impression in ink is taken directly from a prepared gelatin film that has been exposed under a negative. **2** such a process.

hel·i·port (hel′ə pôrt′) *n.* a place for helicopters to land or take off. Heliports are sometimes built on rooftops.

he·li·um (hē′lē əm) *n.* a rare, gaseous chemical element, first discovered in the sun's atmosphere. It is a very light, colorless, inert gas that will not burn, much used in balloons and dirigibles. *Symbol*: He; *at.no.* 2; *at.wt.* 4.0026. [< NL < Gk. *hēlios* sun]

he·lix (hē′liks) *n., pl.* **hel·i·ces** *or* **he·lix·es.** **1** a spiral shape or form. A screw thread and a watch spring are helices. **2** *Architecture.* an ornamental spiral, as on the capital of a Corinthian or Ionic column; volute. **3** the inward-curving rim of the outer ear. **4** *Geometry.* the curve traced by a straight line, on a plane that is wrapped around a cylinder, as the thread of a screw. [< L < Gk. *helix* a spiral]

hell (hel) *n., interj.* —*n.* **1** *Christianity and Judaism.* **a** the home of the Devil, where wicked persons suffer punishment after death, traditionally thought of as below or within the earth. Compare **heaven** (def. 1). **b** the powers of evil. **2** the abode of the dead; Hades. **3** a place or state of wickedness, torment, or misery: *War is hell.* **4** *Informal.* a severe scolding, punishment, etc.: *His mother gave him hell for being so rude.* **5** *Informal.* wild, mischievous spirits: *The kids were full of hell that day.*
come hell or high water, whatever difficulties or problems arise: *I'm going, come hell or high water.*
hell and high water, extreme difficulties or problems, whatever they may be: *He will keep his word through hell and high water.*
like hell, a *Informal.* very hard, fast, etc.: *I worked like hell.* **b** *Slang.* an exclamation expressing strong disagreement with a statement, proposal, etc.: *Like hell is he going to use my car!*
raise hell, *Informal.* cause trouble; make a disturbance: *The disgruntled prisoners started raising hell.*
—*interj. Slang.* an exclamation of annoyance, irritation, anger, or surprise: *Hell! There goes another fuse.* [OE]

he'll (hēl; *unstressed,* hil) he will.

hell·bent (hel′bent′) *adj., adv. Slang.* —*adj.* recklessly or stubbornly determined (*usually used with* **for** *or* **on**): *He was hellbent on spending all his money as soon as he got it.* —*adv.* recklessly or wildly: *She came tearing hellbent around the corner.*

hell·cat (hel′kat′) *n.* **1** a mean, spiteful woman. **2** witch.

hel·le·bore (hel′ə bôr′) *n.* **1** any of a genus (*Helleborus*) of poisonous plants of the buttercup family, especially the **black hellebore** (*H. niger*) an evergreen plant having showy white or pinkish flowers. **2** the dried underground stem of the black hellebore, or an extract from it, formerly used in medicine. **3** any of various poisonous, north temperate plants (genus *Veratrum*) of the lily family, especially *V. album*, having underground stems that yield alkaloids used to treat heart disease and also as an insecticide. **4** the dried underground stem of *V. album* or an extract from it. [< L < Gk. *helleboros*]

Hel·lene (hel′ēn) *n.* Greek. [back-formation singular of Gk.

Hellēnes, literally, descendants of Hellēn, mythical father of the Greeks]

Hel·len·ic (he len′ik *or* he lē′nik) *adj., n.* —*adj.* **1** Greek. **2** of Greek history, language, or culture from about 776 B.C. to the death of Alexander the Great in 323 B.C. —*n.* **1** the Greek language. **2** the branch of the Indo-European languages that includes the various dialects of Greek.

Hel·len·ism (hel′ən iz′əm) *n.* **1** the ancient Greek culture or ideals. **2** the adoption or imitation of Greek speech, ideals, etc. **3** an idiom or expression peculiar to the Greek language. **4** such an idiom or expression translated literally into another language.

Hel·len·ist (hel′ən ist) *n.* **1** a scholar skilled in the ancient Greek language, literature, and culture. **2** a person who uses or imitates Greek language, ideals, or customs.

Hel·len·is·tic (hel′ə nis′tik) *adj.* **1** of or having to do with Hellenists. **2** of or having to do with Greek history, language, and culture after the death of Alexander the Great in 323 B.C.

Hel·len·ize (hel′ən īz′) *v.* **-ized, -iz·ing.** **1** make Greek in character. **2** use or imitate the Greek language, ideals, or customs. —**Hel′len·i·za′tion,** *n.* —**Hel′len·iz′er,** *n.*

hel·ler¹ (hel′ər) *n.* **1** a unit of money in Czechoslovakia, worth 1/100 of a koruna. **2** a coin worth one heller. [< earlier *haller* < MHG *haller* or *häller,* supposedly from Schwäbisch*hall,* where hellers were first coined]

hel·ler² (hel′ər) *n. Slang.* a very mischievous or troublesome person; hellion: *She was a real heller as a child.*

hel·ler·y (hel′ə rē) *n. Slang.* mischief; wild behavior.

hell·fire (hel′fīr′) *n.* the fire of hell; punishment in hell.

hell·gram·mite (hel′grə mīt′) *n.* the larva of a dobsonfly, often used for fish bait. [origin uncertain]

hell·hole (hel′hōl′) *n. Informal.* a dreadful place; a place of great discomfort, filth, squalor, etc.

hell·hound (hel′hound′) *n.* **1** *Mythology.* Cerberus, the watchdog of Hades. **2** a dog or hound of hell. **3** a cruel, fiendish person.

hell·ion (hel′yən) *n. Informal.* a very mischievous or troublesome person. [origin uncertain]

hell·ish (hel′ish) *adj.* **1** fit to have come from hell; devilish; fiendish. **2** of hell. —**hell′ish·ly,** *adv.* —**hell′ish·ness,** *n.*

hel·lo (he lō′ *or* hə lō′) *interj., n., pl.* **-los;** *v.* **-loed, -lo·ing.**
—*interj.* an exclamation to attract attention or to express a greeting or surprise.
—*n.* a call of greeting or surprise, or to attract attention: *The girl gave a loud hello to tell us where she was.*
—*v.* shout; call. Also, **hallo, hollo, hullo.**

helm¹ (helm) *n.* **1** a handle or wheel by which a ship is steered. **2** a position of control or guidance: *The situation began to improve soon after the new director took over the helm.* [OE *helma*]
—**helm′less,** *adj.*

helm² (helm) *n., v. Archaic.* —*n.* helmet. —*v.* put a helmet on. [OE. Akin to HELMET.]

hel·met (hel′mit) *n.* **1** a covering to protect the head, usually made of a thick or rigid material, such as metal, fibreglass, or leather. Helmets are worn by soldiers, firefighters, football players, motorcyclists, etc. **2** the headpiece of ancient or medieval armor. See **armor** for picture. **3** something like a helmet, such as a hood-shaped part of the calyx or corolla of some flowers. [ME < OF *helmet,* dim. of *helme* helm² Gmc.]

hel·met·ed (hel′mə tid) *adj.* equipped with or wearing a helmet: *a helmeted motorcyclist.*

hel·minth (hel′minth) *n.* an intestinal worm, especially a roundworm or fluke. [< Gk. *helmins, -inthos*]

helms·man (helmz′mən) *n., pl.* **-men.** the person at the helm of a ship.

hel·ot (hel′ət *or* hē′lət) *n.* **1** Helot, a member of a class of serfs of ancient Sparta. **2** any slave or serf. [< L *Helotes,* pl. < Gk. *Heilōs,* probably related to Gk. *haliskesthai* be captured]

hel·ot·ism (hel′ət iz′əm *or* hē′lət iz′əm) *n.* serfdom like that of ancient Sparta.

hel·ot·ry (hel′ət rē *or* hē′lət rē) *n.* **1** helots; slaves. **2** serfdom; slavery.

help (help) *v., n.* —*v.* **1** provide with what is needed or useful: *to help a person with one's money.* **2** aid; assist: *to help someone with his work.* **3** give aid or assistance (*often used with* **out**): *We could finish the job faster if he would help.* **4** wait on or serve in a store, etc.: *"May I help you?" asked the clerk.* **5** make better; relieve: *This medicine should help your cough.* **6** prevent; stop: *It can't be helped.* **7** avoid; keep from: *He can't help yawning.* (See usage note). **8** serve with food (*usually used with a reflexive pronoun*): *He helped himself to a piece of cake. The host told them to help themselves.*

cannot help but, *Informal.* cannot avoid; cannot fail to: *I cannot help but admire her endurance.*

so help me or **so help me God,** as I solemnly promise; as I speak the truth.
—*n.* **1** anything done or given in helping: *Your advice is a great help.* **2** aid; assistance: *I need some help with my work.* **3** a person or thing that helps; helper. **4** a hired helper or group of hired helpers: *The storekeeper treats his help well.* **5** a means of making better; remedy: *The medicine was a help.* **6** a means of preventing or stopping. [OE *helpan*]

☞ *Usage.* **Can't help (but).** There are three possible idioms. General: *I can't help feeling sorry for him.* Formal: *I cannot but feel sorry for him.* Informal: *I can't help but feel sorry for him.* The last is an established idiom, though avoided by many writers.

☞ *Syn. v.* **1, 2. Help, aid, assist** = give support to someone or something by providing something needed or useful. **Help** emphasizes actively providing whatever physical, moral, or material support another needs for any purpose: *She helps her mother at home.* **Aid** particularly suggests helping in a less personal way or working together with another to do or get something: *She aids the children's hospital.* **Assist** suggests standing by to help or serve in any way needed or useful, especially in doing something: *A nurse assists a doctor.*

help·er (hel′pər) *n.* a person or thing that helps, especially a person who assits or supports another.

help·ful (help′fəl) *adj.* giving help; useful. —**help′ful·ly,** *adv.* —**help′ful·ness,** *n.*

help·ing (hel′ping) *n.* **1** the portion of food served to a person at one time. **2** a portion: *The program included a generous helping of contemporary music.*

help·less (help′lis) *adj.* **1** not able to help oneself; weak. **2** without help, protection, etc. —**help′less·ly,** *adv.* —**help′less·ness,** *n.*

help·mate (help′māt′) *n.* a companion and helper, especially a wife or husband.

help·meet (help′mēt′) *n.* helpmate. [from a misinterpretation of "an help meet for him" (Gen. 2:18, 20), in which *meet* = suitable]

hel·ter–skel·ter (hel′tər skel′tər) *adv., n., adj.* —*adv.* with headlong disorderly haste: *The children ran helter-skelter when the dog rushed at them.*
—*n.* noisy and disorderly haste, confusion, etc.
—*adj.* carelessly hurried; disorderly; confused.

helve (helv) *n.* the handle of an axe, hammer, etc. [OE *hielfe*]

hem[1] (hem) *n., v.* **hemmed, hem·ming.** —*n.* **1** a finished border or edge on an article of cloth; especially, an edge made by folding the cloth over and sewing it down. **2** any rim or margin. —*v.* **1** fold over and sew down the edge of (cloth). **2** border; edge.
hem in, around, or **about, a** surround on all sides. **b** keep from getting away or moving freely.
[OE *hemm*]

hem[2] (hem) *n., interj., v.* **hemmed, hem·ming.** —*n. or interj.* a word written to present the sound of clearing of the throat to attract attention or to show doubt or hesitation. —*v.* make a sound like that of clearing the throat: *"Uh...," she hemmed, and then kept quiet.*
hem and haw, hesitate in order to avoid committing oneself, stall: *The committee hemmed and hawed for several weeks and then turned the problem over to a subcommittee.* [imitative]

hem– *combining form.* the form of **hemo–** occurring before a vowel.

hema– *combining form.* hemo–. [< Gk. *haima, -atos* blood]

he–man (hē′man′) *Informal. n., adj.* —*n.* a virile, rugged man. —*adj.* tough; masculine; rugged.

hem·a·tite (hem′ə tīt′ or hē′mə tīt′) *n.* a naturally occurring mineral that is a valuable ore of iron, consisting of ferric oxide in a red earthy form or blackish crystalline form. *Formula:* Fe_2O_3 Also, **haematite.** [< L *haematites* < Gk. *haimatitēs* bloodlike < *haima, -matos* blood]

hemato– *combining form.* blood: *hematogenesis = the formation of blood.* [< Gk. *haima, -atos* blood]

hem·a·tol·o·gist (hem′ə tol′ə jist or hē′mə-) *n.* a person who studies blood, or an expert in the diseases of the blood. Also, **haematologist.**

hem·a·tol·o·gy (hem′ə tol′ə jē or hē′mə-) *n.* the branch of physiology that deals with the structure, function, and diseases of the blood. Also, **haematology.**

hemi– *prefix.* half, as in *hemisphere.* [< Gk.]

hem·i·mor·phite (hem′ə môr′fīt) *n.* a white crystalline mineral, hydrated zinc silicate, that is a common zinc ore. *Formula:* $Zn_4Si_2O_7(OH)_2 \cdot H_2O$

hem·i·ple·gi·a (hem′ə plē′jē ə) *n.* paralysis of one side of the body. [< Gk. *hēmi-* half + *plēgē* stroke]

hem·i·ple·gic (hem′ə plē′jik or -plej′ik) *adj., n.* —*adj.*

hat, āge, fär; let, ēqual, tèrm; it, īce
hot, ōpen, ôrder; oil, out; cup, pùt, rüle,
əbove, takən, pencəl, lemən, circəs

ch, child; ng, long; sh, ship
th, thin; ŦH, then; zh, measure

1 suffering from hemiplegia. **2** having to do with hemiplegia. —*n.* a person suffering from hemiplegia.

he·mip·ter·an (hi mip′tə rən) *n., adj.* —*n.* a hemipterous insect. —*adj.* of or designating the order (Hemiptera) comprising these insects.
☞ *Usage.* See note at **heteropterous.**

he·mip·ter·ous (hi mip′tər əs) *adj.* of or having to do with the insect order Hemiptera (usually called Heteroptera) that comprises the "true bugs".
☞ *Usage.* See note at **heteropterous.** [< *hemi–* + Gk. *pteron* wing]

hem·i·sphere (hem′ə sfēr′) *n.* **1** a half of a sphere or globe. **2** a half of the earth's surface. North America and South America are in the western hemisphere. Europe, Asia, Africa, and Australia are in the eastern hemisphere. All countries north of the equator are in the northern hemisphere. **3** a half of the celestial sphere, as divided by the celestial equator, the ecliptic, or the horizon. [< F < L < Gk. *hēmisphairion* < *hēmi-* half + *sphaira* sphere]

hem·i·spher·i·cal (hem′ə sfer′ə kəl) *adj.* **1** shaped like a hemisphere. **2** of a hemisphere.

hem·i·stich (hem′ə stik) *n.* half a line of verse, especially one separated from the rest of the line by a caesura. [< L < Gk. *hēmistichion* < *hēmi-* half + *stichos* line of verse]

hem·lock (hem′lok) *n.* **1** any of a genus (*Tsuga*) of evergreen trees of the pine family found in North America and E Asia, having hanging cones, needle-like leaves growing spirally along the stem, and bark that is rich in tannin. The three species of hemlock native to Canada are the western hemlock, mountain hemlock, and eastern hemlock. **2** the relatively hard wood of any of these trees. **3** a poisonous European plant (*Conium maculatum*) of the parsley family having spotted stems, finely divided leaves, and small, white flowers. **4** a poison made from this plant. [OE *hymlice*]

hem·mer (hem′ər) *n.* **1** a person or thing that hems. **2** an attachment to a sewing machine for hemming.

hemo– *combining form.* blood. [< Gk. *haima* blood]

he·mo·glo·bin (hē′mə glō′bən or hem′ə-) *n.* the protein matter in the red corpuscles of the blood, which carries oxygen from the lungs to the tissues and carbon dioxide from the tissues to the lungs. Also, **haemoglobin.** [for *hematoglobulin,* ult. < Gk. *haima* blood + L *globulus,* dim. of *globus* globe]

he·mo·phil·i·a (hē′mə fil′ē ə or hem′ə-) *n.* an inherited condition in which the blood does not clot normally. Excessive bleeding results from the slightest cut. Also, **haemophilia.** [< NL *haemophilia* < Gk. *haima* blood + *philia* affection, tendency]

he·mo·phil·i·ac (hē′mə fil′ē ak′ or hem′ə-) *n.* a person suffering from hemophilia. Also, **haemophiliac.**

hem·or·rhage (hem′ə rij or hem′rij) *n., v.* **-rhaged, -rhag·ing.** —*n.* a discharge of blood from the blood vessels, especially a heavy discharge. —*v.* suffer from a heavy or uncontrollable bleeding. Also, **haemorrhage.** [< L *haemorrhagia* < Gk. *haimorrhagia,* ult. < *haima* blood + *rhēgnynai* break, burst]

hem·or·rhoids (hem′ə roidz′) *n.pl.* swollen tissue near the anus caused by the dilation of blood vessels, often painful. Also, **haemorrhoids.** [< L *haemorrhoida* < Gk. *haimorrhois,* ult. < *haima* blood + *-rhoos* flowing]

hem·or·rhoi·dal (hem′ə roi′dəl) *adj.* **1** of or having to do with hemorrhoids. **2** suffering from hemorrhoids. Also, **haemorrhoidal.**

hemp (hemp) *n.* **1** a tall annual plant (*Cannabis sativa*) of the mulberry family native to Asia whose tough fibres are made into heavy string, rope, coarse cloth, etc. **2** hashish, marijuana, or some other drug obtained from the female hemp plant. **3** any of various other strong plant fibres or the plants yielding them, such as sisal hemp or Manila hemp. [OE *henep*]

hemp·en (hem′pən) *adj.* of, made of, or resembling hemp.

hemp nettle any of various plants (genus *Galeopsis*) of the mint family, especially a hairy, weedy plant (*G. tetrahit*) having toothed leaves and helmet-shaped flowers.

hem·stitch (hem′stich′) *n., v.* —*n.* **1** an ornamental stitch made by pulling out several parallel threads at or near a hem and gathering the remaining cross threads into small bunches. See **embroidery** for picture. **2** ornamental needlework made in this way. —*v.* hem or decorate with hemstitch.

hen (hen) *n.* **1** the adult female of the domestic fowl. **2** the adult

female of certain other birds and a few animals: *a hen sparrow, a hen lobster.* [OE *henn*] —**hen′like′**, *adj.*

hen·and·chick·ens (hen′ənd chik′ənz) *n.* (*used with a singular or plural verb*) any of various low-growing plants that spread by means of runners, especially the houseleek.

hen·bane (hen′bān′) *n.* a poisonous plant (*Hyoscyamus niger*) of the nightshade family native to Europe and Asia but now growing in North America, having large, sticky, hairy leaves and funnel-shaped yellowish flowers and having a strong, unpleasant smell. Henbane yields several powerful drugs used in medicine.

hence (hens) *adv., interj.* —*adv.* **1** as a result of this; therefore: *The attempts to raise money have failed; hence the project will have to be abandoned.* **2** from now; from this time onward: *A year hence, the incident will have been forgotten.* **3** *Archaic.* from here; away: *She went hence many years ago.* **4** *Archaic.* from this world or life. **5** *Archaic.* from this source or origin: *Hence came several problems.*
—*interj. Archaic.* go away! begone!
hence with, *Archaic.* away with; take away.
[ME *hennes* < OE *heonan* + *-s*, adv. ending]
☛ *Usage.* **Hence** is a formal or archaic word for the less formal **consequently** or **therefore** and the general **so that:** *He has not answered our last letter; hence it would seem he is not interested.* **Hence** is rare in current general writing.

hence·forth (hens′fôrth′) *adv.* from this time on; from now on.

hence·for·ward (hens′fôr′wərd) *adv.* henceforth.

hench·man (hench′mən) *n., pl.* **-men. 1** a follower or aide who obeys orders without scruple: *He had one of his henchmen collect the blackmail money.* **2** a trusted attendant or follower. [ME *henxtman* < OE *hengest* horse + *man* man; originally, a groom and, later, a page or squire. The derogatory sense of def. 1 seems to have developed in the 19c.]

hen·coop (hen′küp′) *n.* a coop for poultry.

hen·dec·a·gon (hen dek′ə gon′) *n.* a polygon having 11 angles. [< Gk. *hendeka* eleven + *gōnia* angle]

hen·e·quen or **hen·e·quin** (hen′ə kin) *n.* **1** an agave (*Agave fourcroydes*) native to Mexico. **2** a strong, yellowish fibre obtained from the leaves of this plant, used for making binder twine and rope and also coarse fabrics used for sacks, hammocks, etc. [< Sp. < native Yucatán word]

hen·house (hen′hous′) *n.* a house for poultry.

hen·na (hen′ə) *n., adj., v.* **-naed, -na·ing.** —*n.* **1** a small shrub (*Lawsonia inermis*) of the loosestrife family native to N Africa, the Mediterranean, Asia, and Australia, having small, fragrant white flowers and lance-shaped leaves which yield a dark orange-red dye. Henna is often grown as an ornamental. **2** the dye made from the leaves of this shrub. Henna has been used in different periods since ancient times to color fingernails, hair, beards, parts of the hands and feet, the manes and hoofs of horses, and also leather, wool, and silk. **3** a reddish brown.
—*adj.* reddish brown.
—*v.* color with henna: *hennaed hair.* [< Arabic *henna′*]

hen·ner·y (hen′ər ē) *n., pl.* **-ner·ies.** a place where poultry is kept.

hen party *Informal.* a social gathering of women.

hen·pecked (hen′pekt′) *adj. Informal.* domineered over by one's wife: *He's a tyrant at work, but henpecked at home.*

hen·ry (hen′rē) *n., pl.* **-ries** or **-rys.** an SI unit for measuring inductance. When a current varying at the rate of one ampere per second induces an electromotive force of one volt, the circuit has inductance of one henry. *Symbol:* H [after Joseph *Henry* (1797-1878), an American physicist]

hep (hep) *adj. Slang.* having intimate and informed up-to-date knowledge. [origin uncertain]

he·pat·ic (hi pat′ik) *adj., n.* —*adj.* **1** of, having to do with, or affecting the liver. **2** resembling the liver, especially in color. **3** *Botany.* of or designating the liverworts.
—*n.* **1** a medicine used in treating the liver. **2** liverwort. [< L < Gk. *hēpatikos* < *hēpar* liver]

he·pat·i·ca (hi pat′ə kə) *n.* any of a genus (*Hepatica*) of small, stemless plants of the buttercup family found in wooded areas of the temperate regions of the northern hemisphere, having lobed leaves and purple, blue, pink, or white flowers that bloom in early spring. [< NL, ult. < Gk. *hēpar* liver; the leaf is thought to resemble the liver in shape]

hep·a·ti·tis (hep′ə tī′tis) *n.* inflammation of the liver. [< Gk. *hēpar, hēpatos* liver + E *-itis*]

hep·cat (hep′kat′) *n. Slang.* **1** an informed admirer of swing music. **2** a performer in a swing band.

He·phaes·tus (hi fes′təs) *n. Greek mythology.* the god of fire and metalworking, corresponding to the Roman god Vulcan.

Hep·ple·white (hep′əl wīt′ or -hwīt′) *adj., n.* —*adj.* of, like, or having to do with a style of furniture having graceful curves and slender lines. —*n.* **1** this style of furniture. **2** a piece of furniture in this style. [after George *Hepplewhite* (?-1786), an English furniture designer]

hept– the form of **hepta-** before vowels, as in *heptarchy.*

hepta– *combining form.* seven, as in *heptagon.* [< Gk. *hepta*]

hep·ta·gon (hep′tə gon′) *n.* a polygon having seven sides. [< LL < Gk. *heptagonon* < *hepta* seven + *gōnia* angle]

hep·tag·o·nal (hep tag′ə nəl) *adj.* having the form of a heptagon.

hep·tam·e·ter (hep tam′ə tər) *n.* a line of verse having seven feet. *Example:*

And thrice | he rout | ed all | his foes, |

and thrice | he slew | the slain.

[< LL < Gk. *heptamētron* < *hepta* seven + *mētron* measure]

hep·tar·chy (hep′tär kē) *n., pl.* **-chies. 1** a government by seven persons. **2** a group of seven states, each under its own ruler. **3 the Heptarchy,** the seven principal Anglo-Saxon kingdoms between A.D. 449 and A.D. 838. [< hept- + Gk. *-archia* rule < *archos* ruler]

hep·ta·stich (hep′tə stik′) *n.* a group of seven lines forming a strophe, stanza, or poem. [< *hepta-* + Gk. *stichos* line of verse]

Hep·ta·teuch (hep′tə tyük′ or hep′tə tük′) *n.* the first seven books of the Bible.

her (hèr; *unstressed,* hər *or* ər) *pron., adj.* —*pron.* the objective form of **she:** *I like her.* —*adj.* **1** the possessive form of **she:** of, belonging to, or made or done by her or herself: *She raised her hand. Her graduation is next week. That's one of her paintings.* **2 Her,** a word used as part of any of certain formal titles when using the title to refer to the woman holding it: *Her Majesty the Queen.* [OE *hire*]
☛ *Usage.* **Her** and **hers** are possessive forms of **she. Her** is a determiner and is always followed by a noun: *This is her bicycle.* **Hers** is a pronoun and stands alone: *This bicycle is hers.*

her. heraldry; heraldic.

He·ra (hēr′ə) *n. Greek mythology.* the queen of the gods, the wife and sister of Zeus, who was also the special goddess of women and marriage. Hera corresponds to the Roman goddess Juno. Also, **Here.**

Her·a·cles (her′ə klēz′) *n.* Hercules.

her·ald (her′əld) *n., v.* —*n.* **1** in the Middle Ages, in western Europe, an officer who carried messages, made announcements, arranged and supervised tournaments and other public ceremonies, and regulated the use of armorial bearings. **2** a person who carries official messages, or makes important announcements. The word *Herald* is often used as the name of a newspaper. **3** a forerunner; harbinger: *Dawn is the herald of day.* **4** in Britain, an officer in charge of granting arms and recording arms and pedigrees, who also has important duties in various royal ceremonies.
—*v.* **1** give news of; announce or usher in: *The robins heralded the arrival of spring.* **2** greet enthusiastically; hail: *His election was heralded by the newspapers.* [ME < OF < W.Gmc. *heriwald* army chief]

he·ral·dic (he ral′dik) *adj.* of or having to do with heraldry or heralds.

her·ald·ry (her′əld rē) *n., pl.* **-ries. 1** the science or art dealing with coats of arms. Heraldry deals with a person's right to use a coat of arms, the tracing of family descent, the creating of a coat of arms for a new country, etc. **2** a heraldic device; collection of such devices. **3** coat of arms. **4** the ceremony or pomp connected with the life of noble families; pageantry.

herb (ėrb *or* hėrb) *n.* **1** any flowering plants whose stalk or stem lives only one season. Herbs do not form woody tissue as shrubs and trees do, though their roots may live many years. Peonies, buttercups, corn, wheat, cabbage, lettuce, etc. are herbs. **2** any of many herbaceous plants having aromatic leaves, roots, etc. that are used for flavoring food or in medicines or perfumes. Sage, mint, and lavender are herbs. [ME < OF < L *herba*]

her·ba·ceous (hèr bā′shəs) *adj.* **1** of or like an herb; having stems that are soft and not woody. **2** *Botany.* having the color, texture, etc. of a leaf: *a flower with herbaceous sepals.* [< L *herbaceus*]

herb·age (ėr′bij *or* hèr′bij) *n.* **1** herbs collectively, especially grass used for grazing. **2** the green leaves and soft stems of plants.

herb·al (hèr′bəl *or* ėr′bəl) *adj., n.* —*adj.* of, having to do with, or made of herbs: *herbal tea.* —*n.* a book about herbs, especially one that describes their uses as medicines.

herb·al·ist (hèr′bəl ist *or* ėr′bəl ist) *n.* a person who gathers herbs or deals in them.

her·bar·i·um (hèr ber′ē əm) *n., pl.* **-bar·i·ums, -bar·i·a** (-ber′ē ə). **1** a collection of dried plants systematically arranged. **2** a room

or building where such a collection is kept. [< LL *herbarium* < L *herba* herb. Doublet of ARBOR[1].]

her·bi·cide (hèr′bə sīd′) *n.* any chemical substance used to destroy plants or stop their growth. [< L *herba* herb + *-cidium* act of killing]

her·bi·vore (hèr′bə vôr′) *n.* any animal that feeds on plants, especially hoofed animals such as cows, horses, or deer.

her·biv·o·rous (hèr biv′ə rəs) *adj.* feeding on grass or other plants. Cattle are herbivorous animals. [< NL *herbivorus* < L *herba* herb + *vorare* devour]

herb·y (èr′bē *or* hèr′bē) *adj.* 1 having many herbs; grassy. 2 of or like herbs.

her·cu·le·an (hèr′kyə lē′ən *or* hèr kyü′lē ən) *adj.* 1 Herculean, of or having to do with Hercules or his labors. 2 having great strength or courage. 3 requiring or showing great strength or courage; very hard to do: *a herculean task, a herculean effort.*

Her·cu·les (hèr′kyə lēz′) *n.* 1 *Greek and Roman mythology.* a hero of immense strength who performed twelve extraordinary tasks or labors imposed on him by the goddess Hera. 2 *Astronomy.* a northern constellation. 3 any man of great strength. [< L < Gk. *Hēraklēs*, literally, the glory of Hera < *Hēra* + *kleos* glory]

herd (hèrd) *n., v.* —*n.* 1 a number of animals of one kind together: *a herd of cows, a herd of horses, a herd of elephants.* 2 people as a mass or mob; rabble: *the common herd.* 3 the keeper of a herd (*usually used in compounds*): *cowherd, goatherd.*
—*v.* 1 bring or come together in a herd or as if in a herd: *The cattle were herded into the corral. Many animals herd for protection.* 2 drive or take care of cattle, sheep, etc.: *His job is herding sheep.* [OE *heord*]
☞ *Hom.* **heard.**

herd·er (hèr′dər) *n.* herdsman.

herds·man (hèrdz′mən) *n., pl.* **-men.** a manager or keeper of a herd or herds of animals.

here (hèr) *adv., n., interj.* —*adv.* 1 in or at this place: *Put it down here. We have lived here for two years.* 2 to this place: *Come here.* 3 at this point in argument, conversation, etc.: *Here the speaker paused.* 4 a word used to call attention to the presence of a person or thing mentioned: *Here is your scarf. Al here could probably tell you where they are.* 5 on earth; in this life.
here and there, in various places; at scattered intervals: *Here and there we saw an early crocus blooming.*
here below, on earth; in this life.
here goes! *Informal.* announcement of something bold about to be done.
here's to, a wish for health, happiness, or success to.
here, there, and everywhere, in many different places: *There were toys here, there, and everywhere throughout the house.*
here you are, *Informal.* here is what you want.
neither here nor there, not to the point; off the subject; unimportant: *Why he took it is neither here nor there; what we want to know is what he did with it.*
—*n.* 1 this place: *Here is a good place to stop. Fill the bottle up to here.* 2 an answer showing that one is present when roll is called. 3 this life.
—*interj.* an exclamation expressing indignation, rebuke, etc.: *Here! Give me that! Here, that's not the way to talk!* [OE *hēr*]
☞ *Hom.* **hear.**

He·re (hèr′ē) *n.* Hera.

here·a·bout (hèr′ə bout′) *adv.* around here; about this place; near here.

here·a·bouts (hèr′ə bouts′) *adv.* herabout.

here·af·ter (hèr af′tər) *adv.* 1 after this; in the future. 2 in life after death. 3 (*noml.*) **the hereafter, a** the future. **b** life after death.

here·at (hèr at′) *adv. Archaic.* 1 when this happened; at this time. 2 because of this.

here·by (hèr bī′) *adv.* by this means; in this way: *I hereby certify that I am over 21 years of age.*

he·red·i·ta·ble (hə red′ə tə bəl) *adj.* that can be inherited.

he·red·i·tar·y (hə red′ə ter′ē) *adj.* 1 coming by inheritance: *Prince is a hereditary title.* 2 holding a position by inheritance: *The Queen is a hereditary ruler.* 3 *Biology.* transmitted or caused by heredity: *Color blindness is hereditary.* Compare **congenital.** 4 derived from one's parents or ancestors; established by tradition: *hereditary beliefs, a hereditary enemy.* 5 of or having to do with inheritance or heredity. [< L *hereditarius* < *hereditas.* See HEREDITY.]

he·red·i·ty (hə red′ə tē) *n., pl.* **-ties.** 1 *Biology.* the transmission of physical or mental characteristics or qualities from parent to offspring through elements called genes in the chromosomes of the germ cells that produce the offspring. 2 the qualities that have come to offspring from parents. 3 the tendency of offspring to be like the parents. 4 the transmission from one generation to another of property, titles, customs, etc. by inheritance or tradition.

hat, āge, fär; let, ēqual, tèrm; it, īce
hot, ōpen, ôrder; oil, out; cup, pùt, rüle,
əbove, takən, pencəl, lemən, circəs
ch, child; ng, long; sh, ship
th, thin; ŦH, then; zh, measure

Here·ford (her′ə fərd *or* hèr′fərd) *n.* a breed of beef cattle having a red body, white face, and white markings under the body. [< *Herefordshire,* England]

here·in (hèr in′) *adv.* 1 in this place, book, document, etc. 2 in this matter or way: *It is herein that the difference lies.*

here·in·af·ter (hèr′in af′tər) *adv.* afterward in this document, statement, etc.

here·in·be·fore (hèr in′bi fôr′) *adv.* before in this document, statement, etc.

here·in·to (hèr in′tü) *adv.* 1 into this place. 2 into this matter.

here·of (hèr ov′ *or* hèr uv′) *adv.* of or about this.

here·on (hèr on′) *adv.* 1 on this. 2 immediately after this.

her·e·sy (her′ə sē) *n., pl.* **-sies.** 1 a belief different from the accepted belief of a church, school, profession, etc. 2 the holding of such a belief. [ME < OF < LGk. *hairesis* a taking, choosing < *hairein* take]

her·e·tic (her′ə tik) *n., adj.* —*n.* a person who holds a belief that is different from the accepted belief of his church, school, profession, etc. —*adj.* holding such a belief. [< F *hérétique* < LL *haereticus* < Gk. *hairetikos* able to choose]

he·ret·i·cal (hə ret′ə kəl) *adj.* 1 of or having to do with heresy or heretics. 2 containing heresy; characterized by heresy.
—**he·ret′i·cal·ly,** *adv.*

here·to (hèr tü′) *adv.* to this place, thing, etc.

here·to·fore (hèr′tə fôr′) *adv.* before this time; until now.

here·un·der (hèr′un′dər) *adv. Formal.* 1 in a book, document, etc., below: *according to the terms specified hereunder.* 2 in accordance with or under the authority of this.

here·un·to (hèr′un tü′) *adv.* to this.

here·up·on (hèr′ə pon′) *adv.* 1 upon this. 2 immediately after this.

here·with (hèr wiŦH′ *or* -with′) *adv.* 1 with this. 2 by this means; in this way.

her·it·a·bil·i·ty (her′ə tə bil′ə tē) *n.* a heritable quality or condition.

her·it·a·ble (her′ə tə bəl) *adj.* 1 capable of being inherited. 2 capable of inheriting.

her·it·age (her′ə tij) *n.* 1 what is or may be handed on to a person from his ancestors; inheritance. 2 something that a person has as a result of having been born in a certain time, place, condition, etc.: *a heritage of violence. Their heritage was freedom.* [ME < OF *heritage* < *heriter* inherit < LL *hereditare,* ult. < L *heres, -redis* heir]

her·maph·ro·dite (hèr maf′rə dīt′) *n., adj.* —*n.* 1 an animal or plant having the reproductive organs of both sexes. 2 a person or thing that combines opposite qualities. 3 hermaphrodite brig.
—*adj.* of or like a hermaphrodite. [< L < Gk. *Hermaphroditos* Hermaphroditus, a son of Hermes and Aphrodite, who became united in body with a nymph]

hermaphrodite brig a sailing ship with two masts, square-rigged forward and schooner-rigged aft.

her·maph·ro·dit·ic (hèr maf′rə dit′ik) *adj.* of or like a hermaphrodite.

her·me·neu·tic (hèr′mə nyü′tik *or* hèr′mə nü′tik) *adj.* of or having to do with hermeneutics. —**her′me·neu′ti·cal·ly,** *adv.*

her·me·neu·ti·cal (hèr′mə nyu′tə kəl *or* her′mə nü′tə kəl) *adj.* hermeneutic.

her·me·neu·tics (hèr′mə nyü′tiks *or* hèr′mə nü′tiks) *n.* (*used with a singular verb*) the study of the principles of interpretation, especially of the Scriptures.

Her·mes (hèr′mēz) *n. Greek mythology.* a god who was the messenger of Zeus and the other gods, corresponding to the Roman god Mercury. Hermes was the god of boundaries and roads, of science and invention, of eloquence, luck, and cunning, and he was the patron of thieves.

her·met·ic (hèr met′ik) *adj.* 1 closed tightly so that air cannot get in; airtight. 2 of a poem, having a meaning that is difficult to decipher; obscure. 3 magical; alchemical. [< Med.L *hermeticus* < *Hermes* Trismegistus, supposed author of a work on magic and alchemy]

her·met·i·cal (hèr met'ə kəl) *adj.* hermetic. —**her·met'i·cal·ly**, *adv.*

her·mit (hèr'mit) *n.* **1** a person who goes away from other people and lives by himself in some lonely or out-of-the-way place, often for religious reasons. **2** a kind of spiced cookie made with molasses or brown sugar and usually containing raisins and nuts. [ME < OF < LL < Gk. *erēmitēs* < *erēmia* desert < *erēmos* uninhabited. Doublet of EREMITE.] —**her'mit·like'**, *adj.*

her·mit·age (hèr'mə tij) *n.* **1** the home of a hermit. **2** a place to live away from other people; retreat.

hermit crab any of various small, soft-bodied, decapod crustaceans resembling lobsters or crabs, that live in and carry around the empty shells of snails or other molluscs; especially, any of the genus *Pagurus* (family Paguridae), such as the common *P. bernhardus* of the coastal waters of North America and Europe.

hermit thrush a North American thrush (*Hylocichla guttata*) having a brownish back, reddish-brown tail, and spotted breast and noted for its beautiful, varied evening song.

her·ni·a (hèr'nē ə) *n., pl.* **-ni·as, -ni·ae** (-nē ē' *or* -nē ī'). the protrusion of a part of the intestine or some other organ through a break in its surrounding walls; a rupture. [< L]

her·ni·al (hèr'nē əl) *adj.* of or having to do with hernia.

he·ro (hēr'ō) *n., pl.* **-roes. 1** a person who does great and brave deeds and is admired for them: *the heroes of old.* **2** a person admired for contributing to a particular field: *a football hero, heroes of science.* **3** the most important male person in a story, play, motion picture, etc. **4** *Mythology and legend.* a man of more than human qualities, such as Hercules and Achilles. [ult. < L *heros* < Gk.]

He·ro (hēr'ō) *n.* *Greek mythology.* a priestess of Aphrodite, whose lover Leander swam the Hellespont every night to visit her. One night he drowned, and, on learning of his death, Hero killed herself.

he·ro·ic (hi rō'ik) *adj., n.* —*adj.* **1** like a hero or heroine in deeds or in qualities; brave; noble: *the heroic deeds of our firefighters.* **2** of or about heroes and their deeds: *The Iliad and the Odyssey are heroic poems.* **3** resembling the language or style of heroic poetry: *heroic prose.* **4** unusually daring or bold: *Only heroic measures could save the town from the flood.* **5** unusually large; larger than life size.
—*n.* **1** a heroic poem. **2 heroics,** *pl.* **a** high-sounding language. **b** words, feelings, or actions that seem grand or noble but are only for effect. **c** heroic verse. —**he·ro'i·cal·ly,** *adv.*

heroic age the period of the legendary heroes of a nation or folk: *the heroic age of Greece.*

he·ro·i·cal (hi rō'ə kəl) *adj.* heroic.

heroic couplet two successive and rhyming lines of verse in iambic pentameter.

heroic verse a poetic form used in heroic and other long poems. In English, German, and Italian, it is iambic pentameter. In French it is the Alexandrine. In Greek and Latin, it is dactylic hexameter.

her·o·in (her'ō in) *n.* a very powerful habit-forming sedative drug made from morphine. *Formula:* $C_{21}H_{23}NO_5$
☛ *Hom.* **heroine.**

her·o·ine (her'ō in) *n.* **1** a woman or girl admired for her bravery or great deeds: *Laura Secord and Madeleine de Verchères are Canadian heroines.* **2** the most important female person in story, play, motion picture, etc. **3** *Mythology and legend.* a woman or girl having more than human qualities. [< L < Gk. *hērōinē,* fem. of *hērōs* hero]
☛ *Hom.* **heroin.**

her·o·ism (her'ō iz'əm) *n.* **1** the actions and qualities of a hero or heroine; great bravery; daring courage. **2** a very brave act or quality.

her·on (her'ən) *n.* any of various wading birds (family Ardeidae) having a long neck that is doubled back in flight, long bill, long legs, and a short tail. The great blue heron (*Ardea herodias*) is the largest Canadian heron. [ME < OF *hairon* < Gmc.]

her·on·ry (her'ən rē) *n., pl.* **-ries.** a place where many herons come in the breeding season.

he·ro·wor·ship (hēr'ō wèr'ship) *v.* **-shipped** *or* **-shiped, -ship·ping** *or* **-ship·ing;** *n.* —*v.* idolize; worship as a hero. —*n.* Also, **hero worship, 1** in ancient Greece and Rome, the worship of ancient heroes as gods. **2** the idolizing of great men, or of persons thought of as heroes. —**he'ro·wor'ship·per** *or* **-wor'ship·er,** *n.*

her·pes (hèr'pēz) *n.* any of several virus diseases of the skin or mucous membranes, characterized by clusters of blisters. **Herpes simplex** is a type of herpes marked by watery blisters especially on the mouth, lips, or genitals. [< L < Gk. *herpēs* shingles < *herpein* creep]

her·pe·tol·o·gist (hèr'pə tol'ə jist) a person trained in herpetology, especially one whose work it is.

her·pe·tol·o·gy (hèr'pə tol'ə jē) *n.* the branch of zoology dealing with reptiles and amphibians. [< Gk. *herpeton* reptile (< *herpein* creep) + E *-logy*]

Herr (her) *n., pl.* **Her·ren** (her'ən). **1** a German title meaning Mr. or Sir. **2** a German gentleman.
☛ *Hom.* **hair, hare.**

her·ring (her'ing) *n., pl.* **-ring** *or* **-rings. 1** a small, silvery fish (*Clupea harengus*) of the North Atlantic and Pacific oceans that is one of the most important food fishes in the world. Herring are caught in huge quantities and sold fresh, salted, smoked, dried, or pickled, and are also canned, when they are called sardines. **2** any of a number of related fishes. **3** (*adj.*) designating a family (Clupeidae) of sea and freshwater fishes that includes the herring as well as the alewife, pilchard, and shad. **4** any of various other unrelated fishes, such as the lake herring (cisco) or the yellow herring (goldeye). [OE *hǣring*]

A band of decorative brickwork in a herringbone pattern on a house in Edam in the Netherlands

her·ring·bone (her'ing bōn') *n., v.* —*n.* **1** a zigzag pattern, resembling the spine of a herring. **2** cloth in a twill weave with a small, woven zigzag pattern: *He chose a herringbone for his suit.* **3** a zigzag arrangement of bricks, tiles, etc. **4** (*adj.*) of or designating a herringbone: *a herringbone tweed, a herringbone pattern.* **5** *Skiing.* a method of going up a slope by pointing the front of the skis outward and putting the weight on the inner side. —*v.* **1** produce a herringbone pattern. **2** *Skiing.* go up a slope by pointing the skis outward and putting one's weight on the inner side.

herringbone stitch *Embroidery.* a stitch consisting of crosses in a herringbone design.

herring choker *Cdn. Slang.* a person from the Maritime Provinces, especially one from New Brunswick.

herring gull a large gull (*Larus argentatus*) widely distributed throughout the northern hemisphere, the adults having white plumage with pearl-grey back and black wing tips. The herring gull is common in most of Canada, including the interior regions.

hers (herz) *pron.* a possessive form of **she:** that which belongs to her: *This money is hers. My answers were wrong, but hers were right.*
☛ *Usage.* See note at **her.**

her·self (hèr self'; *unstressed,* ər self') *pron.* **1** a reflexive pronoun, the form used instead of **she** or **her** when referring back to the subject of the sentence: *She asked herself if it was really worth all the trouble.* **2** a form of **she** or **her** used to make a statement stronger: *She brought the book herself. She herself did it.* **3** her usual self: *In those fits she is not herself.*

hertz (hèrtz) *n., pl.* **hertz.** an SI unit for measuring the frequency, or rate of occurrence, of waves and vibrations, equal to one cycle per second. The musical tone A above middle C on the piano has a frequency of 440 vibrations per second, or 440 hertz. Symbol: Hz [See HERTZIAN WAVES.]

Hertz·i·an waves (hèrt'sē ən) electromagnetic radiation, such as the waves used in communicating by radio. Hertzian waves are produced by irregular fluctuations of electricity in a conductor. [first investigated by Heinrich Rudolph *Hertz* (1857-1894), a German physicist]

he's (hēz; *unstressed,* ēz, iz, *or* hiz) **1** he is. **2** he has: *He's broken his hockey stick.*

Hesh·van (hesh'van) *n.* in the Hebrew calendar, the eighth month of the ecclesiastical year, and the second month of the civil year. Also **Heshwan, Hesvan.**

hes·i·tance (hez'ə təns) *n.* hesitancy.

hes·i·tan·cy (hez'ə tən sē) *n., pl.* **-cies.** hesitation; doubt; indecision.

hes·i·tant (hez'ə tənt) *adj.* hesitating; doubtful; undecided. —**hes'i·tant·ly,** *adv.*

hes·i·tate (hez'ə tāt') *v.* **-tat·ed, -tat·ing. 1** hold back because one feels doubtful; be undecided or uncertain: *He hesitated, wondering which road to take.* **2** be unwilling or reluctant because

of scruples: *I hesitated to ask you because you were so busy.* **3** stop for an instant; pause: *He hesitated before asking the question.* **4** speak with stops or pauses; stammer. [< L *haesitare* < *haerere* stick fast]

☛ *Syn.* **1. Hesitate, falter, waver** = show doubt or lack of firmness in deciding or acting. **Hesitate** emphasizes holding back, unable to make up one's mind firmly or to act promptly: *I hesitated about taking the position.* **Falter** suggests losing courage and hesitating or giving way after starting to act: *I went to apologize, but faltered at the door.* **Waver** suggests being unable to stick firmly to a decision and giving way or drawing back: *My confidence in him wavers.*

hes·i·tat·ing·ly (hez′ə tāt′ing lē) *adv.* with hesitation.

hes·i·ta·tion (hez′ə tā′shən) *n.* **1** the act or an instance of hesitating: *After some hesitation she decided to come with us.* **2** the state of being hesitant.

Hes·pe·ri·an (hes pēr′ē ən) *adj.* **1** western. **2** of or having to do with the Hesperides.

Hes·per·i·des (hes per′ə dēz′) *n.pl. Greek mythology.* **a** the four nymphs who guarded the golden apples of Hera. **b** the garden where these apples grew.

Hes·per·us (hes′pər əs) *n.* evening star, especially the planet Venus. [< L < Gk. *Hesperos,* originally adj., pertaining to the evening, western]

hes·sian (hesh′ən) *n.* a coarse fabric of jute and hemp, used in making bags, etc. [< *Hessian*]

Hes·sian (hesh′ən) *n., adj.* —*n.* **1** a native or inhabitant of Hesse, a district in West Germany. **2** a German mercenary soldier in the British army that fought against the Americans during the American Revolution. **3** a mercenary. —*adj.* of Hesse or its people. [< *Hesse,* a state in West Germany]

Hessian boots high boots with tassels, popular in England during the 19th century.

Hessian fly a small two-winged fly (*Mayetiola destructor*) whose larvae are destructive to wheat.

hest (hest) *n. Archaic.* behest; command. [alteration of OE *hǣs*]

Hes·ti·a (hes′tē ə) *n. Greek mythology.* the goddess of the hearth, corresponding to the Roman goddess Vesta.

Hes·van (hes′van) *n.* Heshvan.

he·tae·ra (hi tēr′ə) *n., pl.* **-tae·rae** (-tēr′ē or -tēr′ī). in ancient Greece, courtesan. [< Gk. *hetaira,* fem., companion]

he·tai·ra (hi tī′rə) *n., pl.* **-rai** (-rī). hetaera.

hetero– *combining form.* other; different, as in *heterogeneous.* [< Gk. *hetero- < heteros*]

het·er·o·dox (het′ər ə doks′ or het′rə-) *adj.* **1** contrary to or differing from an acknowledged standard; not orthodox: *a heterodox belief.* **2** rejecting the regularly accepted beliefs or doctrines: *a heterodox priest.* [< LL < Gk. *heterodoxos < heteros* other + *doxa* opinion]

het·er·o·dox·y (het′ər ə dok′sē or het′rə-) *n., pl.* **-dox·ies. 1** the quality or state of being heterodox. **2** a heterodox belief, doctrine, or opinion.

het·er·o·dyne (het′ər ə dīn′ or het′rə dīn′) *adj., v.* —*adj.* of or designating a strong, stable radio frequency called a beat, produced by combining the high unstable incoming frequency with another slightly different one given out by an oscillator in the receiver itself. The heterodyne frequency is the difference between the original two frequencies. —*v.* combine (two similar radio frequencies) to produce a beat. [< *hetero-* + *-dyne* force (< F < Gk. *dynamos* power)]

het·er·o·ge·ne·i·ty (het′ər ə jə nē′ə tē or het′rə-) *n., pl.* **-ties.** the quality or state of being heterogeneous; dissimilarity.

het·er·o·ge·ne·ous (het′ər ə jē′nē əs or het′rə-, het′ər ə jēn′yəs or het′rə-) *adj.* **1** different in kind; unlike; varied. **2** made up of unlike elements or parts; miscellaneous. Compare **homogeneous.** **3** *Mathematics.* of different kinds and having no common integral divison except 1. **4** of different degrees or dimensions. [< Med.L *heterogeneus,* ult. < Gk. *heteros* other + *genos* kind] —**het′er·o·ge′ne·ous·ly,** *adv.* —**het′er·o·ge′ne·ous·ness,** *n.*

het·er·o·gen·e·sis (het′ər ō jen′ə sis or het′rə-) *n.* alternation of generations.

het·er·o·nym (het′ər ə nim′ or het′rə nim) *n.* a word spelled the same as another but having a different sound and meaning. *Example: lead,* to conduct, and *lead,* a metal. [< *hetero-* + Gk. dial. *onyma* name; formed on the pattern of *homonym*]

het·er·op·ter·an (het′ə rop′tə rən) *n., adj.* —*n.* a heteropterous insect. —*adj.* of or designating the order (Heteroptera) comprising these insects.

☛ *Usage.* See note at **heteropterous.**

het·er·op·ter·ous (het′ə rop′tə rəs) *adj.* of or having to do with an insect order (Heteroptera) that comprises "true bugs" and includes the bedbug. Heteropterous insects usually have two pairs

hat, āge, fär; let, ēqual, tėrm; it, īce
hot, ōpen, ôrder; oil, out; cup, pùt, rüle,
above, takən, pencəl, lemən, circəs

ch, child; ng, long; sh, ship
th, thin; ᴛʜ, then; zh, measure

of wings, with the front pair thickened at the base; the wings are folded flat on the back when at rest.

☛ *Usage.* Some authorities classify all sucking insects as belonging to two separate orders: Heteroptera (also called Hemiptera), the "true bugs," including the bedbug, and Homoptera, including aphids, scale insects, etc.

het·er·o·sex·u·al (het′ər ə sek′shü əl or het′rə-) *adj., n.* —*adj.* **1** *Biology.* of or having to do with the different sexes. **2** of, having to do with, or characterized by sexual feeling for a person of the opposite sex. Compare **homosexual.** —*n.* a heterosexual person. —**het′er·o·sex′u·al·ly,** *adv.*

het·er·o·sex·u·al·i·ty (het′ər ə sek′shü al′ə tē or het′rə-) *n.* the quality or fact of being heterosexual.

het·man (het′mən) *n., pl.* **-mans.** a Cossack leader or chief. [< Polish < G *Hauptmann* chief < *Haupt* head + *Mann* man]

heu·ris·tic (hyü ris′tik) *adj.* **1** guiding or helping one to discover: *heuristic reasoning.* **2** *Education.* having to do with a method that encourages a student to use personal investigation, observation, etc. so that he may find things out for himself. [< Gk. *heuristein* to find + E *-ist* + *-ic*]

hew (hyü) *v.* **hewed, hewed** or **hewn, hew·ing. 1** cut with an axe, sword, etc.: *He hewed down the tree.* **2** cut into shape; form by cutting with an axe, adze, etc.: *to hew stone for building, to hew logs into beams.* **3** make or produce with cutting blows: *The knight hewed his way through the enemy.* **4** conform (to): *The newspaper hews strictly to the party line.* [OE *hēawan*]

☛ *Hom.* **hue.**

hew·er (hyü′ər) *n.* a person or thing that hews.

hewn (hyün) *v.* a pp. of **hew.**

hex (heks) *Informal. v., n.* —*v.* practise witchcraft on; bewitch. —*n.* **1** a witch. **2** a magic spell. [< Pennsylvania G < G *Hexe* witch]

hex– the form of **hexa-** before vowels.

hexa– *combining form.* six, as in *hexagon.* [< Gk. *hex* six]

hex·a·gon (hek′sə gon′) *n.* a polygon having six sides. [< L < Gk. *hexagōnon,* neut. of *hexagōnos* hexagonal, ult. < *hex* six + *gōnia* angle]

hex·ag·o·nal (heks ag′ə nəl) *adj.* **1** of or having the form of a hexagon. **2** having a hexagon as base or cross section. —**hex·ag′o·nal·ly,** *adv.*

hex·a·gram (hek′sə gram′) *n.* a six-pointed star formed of two equilateral triangles: ✡

hex·a·he·dral (hek′sə hē′drəl) *adj.* having six faces.

hex·a·he·dron (hek′sə hē′drən) *n., pl.* **-drons, -dra** (-drə). a polyhedron having six faces. See **polygon** for picture. [< Gk. *hexaedron,* neut. of *hexaedros < hex* six + *hedra* base, surface]

hex·am·e·ter (hek sam′ə tər) *n.* **1** a line of poetry consisting of six metrical feet. *Example:*

This is the| forest pri | mēval. The | murmuring |pines and the |hemlocks.

2 poetry consisting of hexameters. **3** (*adjl.*) of, having to do with, or consisting of hexameters. [< L < Gk. *hexametros < hex* six + *metron* measure]

hex·an·gu·lar (heks ang′gyə lər) *adj.* having six angles.

hex·a·pod (hek′sə pod′) *n.* an insect (def. 1); a member of the class Insecta. [< Gk. *hexapous, -podos < hex* six + *pous, podos* foot]

hex·a·stich (hek′sə stik′) *n.* a group of six lines forming a strophe, stanza, or a poem. [< *hexa-* + Gk. *stichos* line of verse]

hey (hā) *interj.* a sound made to attract attention, to express surprise or other feeling, or to ask a question.

☛ *Hom.* **hay.**

hey·day (hā′dā′) *n.* the period of greatest strength, vigor, spirits, prosperity, etc. [origin uncertain]

hf. half.

Hf hafnium.

HF, H.F., or **h.f.** high frequency.

hg. hectogram.

Hg mercury (for L *hydrargyrum*).

HG High German.

H.G. His Grace; Her Grace.

H.H. 1 His Highness; Her Highness. 2 His Holiness.

hhd. hogshead(s).

Hi (hī) *interj.* a call of greeting; hello.

HI Hawaii.

H.I. Hawaiian Islands.

hi·a·tus (hī ā′təs) *n., pl.* **-tus·es** or **-tus.** 1 an empty space; gap; a space that needs to be filled. 2 a slight pause between two vowels that come together in successive syllables or words. There is a hiatus between the *e's* in *pre-eminent.* [< L *hiatus* gap < *hiare* gape]

hi·ba·chi (hē bä′chē) *n.* a cast-iron or similar container in which charcoal is burnt for cooking, heating, etc. [< Japanese *hibachi* < *hi* fire + *bachi* bowl]

hi·ber·nal (hī bėr′nəl) *adj.* of or having to do with winter; wintry. [< L *hibernus* wintry]

hi·ber·nate (hī′bər nāt′) *v.* **-nat·ed, -nat·ing.** 1 spend the winter in sleep or in an inactive condition, as bears, groundhogs, and some other wild animals do. 2 be or become inactive: *I think I'll just hibernate for the first week of my holidays.* [< L *hibernare* < *hibernus* wintry]

hi·ber·na·tion (hī′bər nā′shən) *n.* the condition of hibernating.

Hi·ber·ni·a (hī bėr′nē ə) *n.* Poetic. Ireland. [< L] **—Hi·ber′ni·an,** *n., adj.*

Hi·ber·ni·an (hī bėr′nē ən) *adj., n.* —*adj.* Irish. —*n.* a native of Ireland; Irishman.

hi·bis·cus (hī bis′kəs *or* hə bis′kəs) *n.* any of a genus (*Hibiscus*) of herbs, shrubs, and small trees of the mallow family found in temperate and tropical regions around the world, often cultivated for their large, usually bell-shaped white, pink, red, blue, or yellow flowers. [< L]

hic·cough (hik′up) *n. or v.* hiccup.

hic·cup (hik′up *or* hik′əp) *n., v.* **hic·cupped, hic·cup·ping.** —*n.* 1 a sudden, involuntary contraction of the diaphragm that causes the glottis to close just when one is inhaling, producing a characteristic short clicking sound. 2 hiccups, *pl.* the state of having one hiccup after another: *I've got the hiccups.* —*v.* 1 make a hiccup or hiccups: *He hiccupped.* 2 say with a hiccup or hiccups: *She hiccupped her apologies.* [probably imitative]

hic ja·cet (hik jā′sit) 1 *Latin.* here lies. 2 epitaph.

hick (hik) *n., adj. Slang.* —*n.* 1 a farmer or farm worker. 2 an unsophisticated person. —*adj.* of or like hicks. [< *Hick,* a form of *Richard,* a man's name]

hick·ey (hik′ē) *n. Informal.* 1 a pimple or other blemish. 2 a gadget; dingus.

hick·o·ry (hik′ə rē *or* hik′rē) *n., pl.* **-ries.** —*n.* 1 any of a genus (*Carya*) of North American and Asian trees of the walnut family bearing egg-shaped nuts which in some species, such as the pecan, are edible. 2 the tough, hard wood of any of these trees. 3 a rod or switch made of this wood. 4 (*adj.*) made of this wood. [< Algonquian]

hid (hid) *v.* pt. and a pp. of **hide¹.**

hi·dal·go (hi dal′gō) *n., pl.* **-gos.** a Spanish nobleman of the second class, not as high in rank as a grandee. [< Sp. < OSp. *hijo de algo* son of someone (important)]

hid·den (hid′ən) *adj., v.* —*adj.* 1 concealed or secret: *a hidden staircase.* 2 mysterious or obscure: *a statement full of hidden meanings.* —*v.* a pp. of **hide¹.**

hide¹ (hīd) *v.* **hid, hid·den** *or* **hid, hid·ing.** 1 put out of sight; conceal: *She hid the presents in the attic. He hid his face in the pillow.* 2 shut off from sight; screen or obscure: *Clouds hid the moon.* 3 keep secret: *She hid her anxiety.* 4 conceal oneself: *The shy little boy hid behind his mother's skirt.*
hide out or **up,** remain concealed: *The bandits hid out for several weeks in a mountain shack.* [OE *hȳdan*] —**hid′er,** *n.*
☞ *Syn.* 1. **Hide, conceal** = put or keep out of sight. **Hide** is the general word: *I hid the present in my closet.* **Conceal** is more formal and usually suggests hiding with a purpose or keeping under cover: *She concealed the note in her dress.*

hide² (hīd) *n., v.* **hid·ed, hid·ing.** —*n.* 1 the skin of an animal, either raw or tanned. 2 a person's skin.
neither hide nor hair, nothing at all.
—*v. Informal.* beat; thrash. [OE *hȳd*]
☞ *Syn.* n. 1. See note at **skin.**

hide³ (hīd) *n. Historical.* an old English measure of land area varying from 60 to 120 acres (about 24 to 49 hectares). [OE *hīgid*]

hide-and-seek (hīd′ən sēk′) *n.* a children's game in which one player has to find all the others, who are hidden in different places.

The player who has to find the others is called "it." Also, **hide-and-go-seek.**

hide·a·way (hīd′ə wā′) *n.* 1 a place of concealment or hiding. 2 a quiet, restful place, especially one in an isolated area, for a person or small group of people to be alone.

hide·bound (hīd′bound′) *adj.* 1 of cattle, etc., with the skin sticking close to the bones. 2 narrow-minded and stubborn.

hid·e·ous (hid′ē əs) *adj.* 1 very ugly; frightful; horrible: *a hideous monster.* 2 terrible; revolting; abominable: *a hideous crime.* [ME < OF *hide* fear, horror] —**hid′e·ous·ly,** *adv.* —**hid′e·ous·ness,** *n.*

hide-out or **hide·out** (hīd′out′) *n.* a place for hiding or being alone.

hid·ey-hole or **hid·y-hole** (hī′dē hōl′) *n. Informal.* hideaway.

hid·ing¹ *n.* the condition of being hidden; concealment: *The bandits are still in hiding in the mountains. They went into hiding right after the robbery.* [< *hide¹*]

hid·ing² (hīd′ing) *n. Informal.* beating. [< *hide²*]

hid·ing-place (hīd′ing plās′) *n.* a place to hide: *We found a good hiding-place in the hedge.*

hie (hī) *v.* **hied, hie·ing** *or* **hy·ing.** *Archaic or poetic.* hasten; go quickly (*usually reflexive*): *He hied him to the rescue.* [OE *hīgian*]
☞ *Hom.* **hi, high.**

hi·er·arch (hī′ər ärk′) *n.* a chief priest.

hi·er·ar·chic (hī′ər är′kik) *adj.* hierarchical.

hi·er·ar·chi·cal (hī′ər är′kə kəl) *adj.* of, having to do with, or belonging to a hierarchy. —**hi′er·ar′chi·cal·ly,** *adv.*

hi·er·ar·chy (hī′ər är′kē) *n., pl.* **-chies.** 1 the order of higher and lower ranks in an organization or system. 2 church government by a hierarchy of priests or other clergy. 3 a body of clergy organized in orders or ranks, especially members of the highest orders. [< Med.L < Gk. *hierarchia* < *hieros* sacred + *archos* ruler]

hi·er·at·ic (hī′ər at′ik) *adj.* 1 having to do with the priestly caste; used by the priestly class; priestly. 2 designating or having to do with a form of Egyptian writing used by the early priests in their records. Hieratic writing is a simplified form of hieroglyphics. 3 of or having to do with certain styles in art, such as the Egyptian or Greek, in which earlier types or methods, fixed by religious tradition, are conventionally followed. [< *hieraticus* < Gk. *hieratikos,* ult. < *hieros* sacred]

hi·er·at·i·cal (hī′ər at′ə kəl) *adj.* hieratic. —**hi′er·at′i·cal·ly,** *adv.*

hi·er·o·glyph (hī′ər ə glif′) *n.* hieroglyphic.

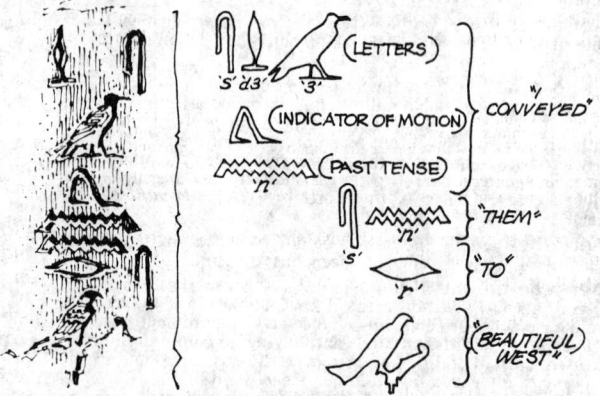

A section of a hieroglyphic inscription in the tomb of an official of the Egyptian Fifth Dynasty, c. 2350 B.C. The inscription describes the official's piety and devotion towards his parents, and his filial act in providing them with a proper burial. The part shown means "I conveyed them [his dead parents] to the [beautiful] West."

hi·er·o·glyph·ic (hī′ər ə glif′ik) *n., adj.* —*n.* 1 a picture of an object standing for a word, idea, or sound; a character or symbol standing for a word, idea, or sound. The ancient Egyptians used hieroglyphics instead of an alphabet like ours. 2 a secret symbol. 3 a letter or word that is hard to read. 4 **hieroglyphics,** *pl.* **a** any system of writing that uses hieroglyphics. **b** *Informal.* writing that is hard to read.
—*adj.* 1 of or written in hieroglyphics. 2 symbolical. 3 hard to read. [< LL < Gk. *hieroglyphikos* < *hieros* sacred + *glyphē* carving]

hi·er·o·glyph·i·cal (hī′ər ə glif′ə kəl) *adj.* hieroglyphic.
—**hi′er·o·glyph′i·cal·ly,** *adv.*

hi·er·o·phant (hī′ər ə fant′ *or* hī er′ə fant′) *n.* a demonstrator of sacred mysteries or religious knowledge. [< L < Gk. *hierophantes* < *hieros* sacred + *phainein* show]

hi–fi (*adj.* hī′fī′; *n.* hī′fī′) *adj., n. Informal.* —*adj.* high-fidelity. —*n.* high-fidelity reproduction of music, etc. or the equipment for such reproduction.

hig·gle (hig′əl) *v.* -**gled,** -**gling.** haggle. [? akin to HAGGLE.]

hig·gle·dy–pig·gle·dy (hig′əl dē pig′əl dē) *adv., adj., n.*
—*adv.* in jumbled confusion.
—*adj.* jumbled; confused.
—*n.* a jumble; confusion.

high (hī) *adj., adv., n.* —*adj.* **1** of more than usual height; tall: *a high building.* **2** being a specified distance or extent from top to bottom (*used following a noun*): *The mountain is 6100 metres high.* **3** far above the ground or some base: *an airplane high in the air.* **4** extending to or done from a height: *a high leap, a high dive.* **5** senior to others in rank or position: *a high official.* **6** superior; above others in personal qualities: *a person of high character.* **7** greater, stronger, or better than average; great: *high temperature.* **8** most important; chief; main: *the high altar.* **9** extreme of its kind: *high crimes.* **10** costly: *Strawberries are high in winter.* **11** above the normal pitch; shrill; sharp: *a high voice.* **12** advanced to its peak: *high summer.* **13** smelling bad as a result of decay; tainted: *Some people prefer to eat game after it has become high.* **14** haughty: *a high manner.* **15** *Slang.* excited by or as if by alcohol or drugs. **16** of a system of gears, having a driving gear larger than the driven gear, so as to cause the driven gear to revolve more rapidly than the other: *the high gear of an automobile.* **17** having extreme or rigid political or religious opinions, usually ultraconservative: *a high ritualist, a high Tory.* **18** *Biology.* highly developed; more advanced in structure, intelligence, etc.: *the higher algae, the higher apes.*
—*adv.* at or to a high point, place, rank, amount, degree, price, pitch, etc.: *The eagle flies high.*
fly high, have big ideas, plans, hopes, ambitions, etc.
high and dry, a out of the water; out of reach of the current or tide: *The fish was high and dry on the beach.* **b** all alone; without help: *He has left me high and dry with all this work to do.*
high and low, everywhere: *We looked high and low but couldn't find the letter.*
run high, a be strong or rough: *The tide runs high.* **b** become heated; reach a high pitch: *Tempers ran high at election time.*
—*n.* **1** something that is high. **2** in automobiles and similar machines, an arrangement of gears to give the greatest speed. **3** a high point, level, position, etc.: *Food prices reached a new high last month.* **4** *Meteorology.* an area of relatively high barometric pressure; anticyclone: *The weatherman reports that a high is approaching.* **5** *Slang.* a state of euphoria produced by or as if by drugs.
from on high, a from a high place or position. **b** from heaven.
on high, a in or to a high place or position; up in the air. **b** in or to heaven.
[OE *hēah*]
☛ *Hom.* hi, hie.
☛ *Syn. adj.* **1. High, tall, lofty** = of more than usual height. **High,** the general word, describes things, not people, that rise to more than usual height: *High hills surround the valley.* **Tall** = higher than the average of its kind, and is used to describe people or something that is or grows both high and narrow or slender: *He is a tall man. The corn grows tall here.* **Lofty,** more literally, means "very high, rising to an impressive height": *We saw the lofty Mount Robson, snow-capped and rising almost 4000 metres.*

High Arctic *Cdn.* the arctic islands and the northeastern part of the arctic mainland of Canada.

high·ball (hī′bol′ *or* -bôl′) *n., v.* —*n.* **1** a railway signal to proceed. **2** whisky, brandy, etc. mixed with soda water or ginger ale and served with ice in a tall glass. —*v. Slang.* **1** move or drive at high speed. **2** run on a speeded-up schedule.

high·born (hī′bôrn′) *adj.* of noble birth.

high·boy (hī′boi′) *n.* a tall chest of drawers on legs.

high·bred (hī′bred′) *adj.* **1** of superior breeding or stock. **2** well-mannered; very refined.

high·brow (hī′brou′) *n., adj. Informal.* —*n.* a person who has strong intellectual and cultural interests, especially one thought to have a feeling of superiority because of this. —*adj.* of, appealing to, or suitable for highbrows: *highbrow music, a highbrow discussion.*

High Church a party in the Anglican Communion, laying great stress on church authority, ceremonial observances, etc.

high–col·ored or **high–col·oured** (hī′kul′ərd) *adj.* **1** having a deep or vivid color. **2** florid; red.

high comedy comedy dealing with polite society and depending more on witty dialogue and well-drawn characters than on comic situations.

hat, āge, fär; let, ēqual, tèrm; it, īce
hot, ōpen, ôrder; oil, out; cup, pút, rüle,
əbove, takən, pencəl, lemən, circəs
ch, child; ng, long; sh, ship
th, thin; ᴛʜ, then; zh, measure

High Commission the embassy of one Commonwealth country in another.

High Commissioner the chief representative of one Commonwealth country in another. A High Commissioner has the status of an ambassador.

high–energy physics (hī′en′ər jē) the branch of physics that studies matter and energy in their most elementary forms, especially the study of particles that appear only at high speeds.

higher education education beyond the level of secondary school, especially university education.

higher mathematics mathematics that is more advanced and abstract than what is normally taught in secondary school.

high·er–up (hī′ər up′) *n. Informal.* a person occupying a superior position.

high–fa·lu·tin or **high–fa·lu·ting** (hī′fə lü′tən) *adj. Informal.* pompous; bombastic.

high–fi·del·i·ty (hī′fī del′ə tē *or* hī′fə del′ə tē) *adj.* **1** *Electronics.* indicating reproduction of the full audio range of a transmitted signal with a minimum of distortion. **2** of or having to do with high-fidelity reproduction, equipment, recordings, etc.

high·fli·er (hī′flī′ər) *n.* **1** a person or thing that flies high. **2** a person who is extravagant or has pretentious ideas, ambitions, etc.

high–flown (hī′flōn′) *adj.* **1** aspiring; extravagant. **2** attempting to be elegant or eloquent: *high-flown compliments.*

high–fly·er (hī′flī′ər) See **highflier.**

high frequency the range of radio frequencies between 3 and 30 megahertz. High frequency is the range next above medium frequency. *Abbrev:* HF, H.F., or h.f. —**high′–fre′quen·cy,** *adj.*

High German the literary and official language of Germany and Austria and one of the official languages of Switzerland. It developed from the dialects of the highlands in central and southern Germany.

high–grade (hī′grād′) *adj., n., v.* -**grad·ed, -grad·ing.** —*adj.* **1** of fine quality; superior: *high-grade bonds, a high-grade performance.* **2** *Mining.* designating or containing gold-bearing ore of a high assay value: *high-grade gold ore, high-grade dirt.* **3** of or having to do with high-grading.
—*n.* **1** gold nuggets or rich ore. **2** gold nuggets or rich ore stolen in small quantities from a mine.
—*v.* **1** steal small quantities of gold or ore from a mine. **2** *Logging.* take only the best timber from a stand. —**high′–grad′er,** *n.*

high–hand·ed (hī′han′did) *adj.* arbitrary or overbearing; disregarding the feelings of others: *a high-handed way of running things.* —**high′–hand′ed·ly,** *adv.* —**high′–hand′ed·ness,** *n.*

high hat a tall black silk hat; top hat.

high–hat (hī′hat′) *v.* -**hat·ted, -hat·ting;** *adj. Slang.* —*v.* treat as inferior; snub. —*adj.* putting on a superior, contemptuous air; snobbish.

high·jack (hī′jak′) See **hijack.** —**high′jack′er,** *n.*

high jinks (jingks) boisterous merrymaking; lively fun and sport.

high jump 1 an athletic contest or event in which the contestants try to jump as high as possible. **2** a jump of this kind.

high·land (hī′lənd) *n.* **1** a country or region that is higher and hillier than the neighboring country. **2** (*adj.*) of, having to do with, or in such country: *a highland meadow.* **3 the Highlands,** a hilly region in northern and western Scotland. **4** (*adj.*) **Highland,** of, having to do with, or in the Highlands.

Highland cattle a breed of small cattle from the Scottish Highlands, having shaggy fur and long, curved, widely set horns.

High·land·er (hī′lən dər) *n.* **1** a native or inhabitant of the Highlands of Scotland. **2** a soldier of a regiment from the Highlands of Scotland. **3** a soldier in an allied British or Canadian regiment.

Highland fling a lively dance originating in the Highlands of Scotland.

high·light (hī′līt′) *n., v.* -**light·ed, -light·ing.** —*n.* **1** the representation or effect of light falling on a particular part of something: *Rembrandt is famous for his use of dramatic highlights in his paintings. The photographer caught the highlight in the child's hair.* **2** the most interesting or most striking part, event, scene, etc.: *The highlight of our trip was the drive along the Cabot Trail.*

—*v.* **1** emphasize (a part of a painting, photograph, etc.) with lighting, light or bright color, etc. **2** make prominent: *The new product was highlighted in all the company's brochures.* **3** be the highlight of: *A spectacular acrobatic act highlighted the grandstand show.*

high·line (hī′līn′) *n.* highliner.

high·lin·er (hī′līn′ər) *n.* in a Maritime fishing fleet: **1** the boat making the largest catch within a specified time. **2** the captain of such a boat.

high·ly (hī′lē) *adv.* **1** in a high degree; very; very much. **2** favorably; with much approval; with great praise or honor. **3** at a high price.

High Mass a complete ritual of the Mass sung by the priest, with musical and choral accompaniment.

high·mind·ed (hī′mīn′did) *adj.* **1** having or showing high principles and feelings: *a high-minded person, a high-minded act of charity.* **2** *Archaic.* proud. —**high′mind′ed·ly**, *adv.* —**high′mind′ed·ness**, *n.*

high·ness (hī′nis) *n.* **1** being high; height. **2 Highness**, a title of honor given to members of royal families. The Prince of Wales is addressed as "Your Highness" and spoken of as "His Royal Highness."

high noon fully noon; exactly midday.

high·oc·tane (hī′ok′tān) *adj.* of gasoline, having a high percentage of octane or a high octane number.

high·pitched (hī′picht′) *adj.* **1** of high tone or sound; shrill: *a high-pitched whistle.* **2** of a roof, having a steep slope. **3** marked by or showing intense feeling; agitated: *the high-pitched excitement of the chase.*

high·pow·ered (hī′pou′ərd) *adj.* having much power or energy: *a high-powered car or rifle, a high-powered sales talk.*

high·pres·sure (hī′presh′ər) *adj., v.* **-sured, -sur·ing.** —*adj.* **1** having, involving, or requiring the use of a relatively high pressure: *a high-pressure cylinder, a high-pressure laminate.* **2** having or showing a high barometric pressure: *There is a high-pressure area just to the south.* **3** *Informal.* using or involving a strong, insistent approach or argument, especially in selling: *a high-pressured sales pitch.* **4** involving a lot of emotional tension or strain: *She has a high-pressure job.* —*v.* persuade or influence by using a strong, insistent approach or argument: *He was high-pressured into buying the more expensive rug.*

high·priced (hī′prīst′) *adj.* expensive.

high priest **1** a chief priest. **2** the head of the ancient Jewish priesthood.

high relief relief sculpture in which the modelled forms project well out from the background and parts may be undercut. See **relief** for picture.

high·rise (hī′rīz′) *adj., n.* —*adj.* having many storeys: *highrise apartment buildings.* —*n.* a building having many storeys: *He lives in a highrise downtown.*

high·road (hī′rōd′) *n.* **1** a main road; highway. **2** a direct and easy way: *There is no highroad to success.*

high school a school attended after the elementary or public school. Some provinces have junior high schools intermediate between elementary and high school. —**high′-school′**, *adj.*
➤ *Usage.* **High school.** Capitalize only when referring to a particular school: *He graduated from high school at seventeen. I graduated from Collins Bay High School in 1951.*

high seas the open ocean. The high seas are outside the jurisdiction of any country.

high·sound·ing (hī′soun′ding) *adj.* having an imposing or pretentious sound: *high-sounding words.*

high·spir·it·ed (hī′spir′ə tid) *adj.* having or showing a bold, proud, or energetic spirit: *a high-spirited horse. The team put up a high-spirited defence, even though they knew they were losing.* —**high′-spir′it·ed·ly**, *adv.* —**high′-spir′it·ed·ness**, *n.*

high spirits happiness; cheerfulness; gaiety.

high spot **1** the main part; the climax. **2** an attraction or place of interest for sightseers.

high·stick (hī′stik′) *v.* **high·sticked, high·sticking.** *Cdn. Hockey and lacrosse.* illegally strike or hinder an opposing player with one's stick raised above shoulder level.

high·stick·ing (hī′stik′ing) *n. Cdn. Hockey and lacrosse.* the act or practice of illegally striking or hindering an opposing player with one's stick carried above shoulder level: *He received a penalty for highsticking.*

high·strung (hī′strung′) *adj.* very sensitive; easily excited; nervous.

hight (hīt) *v. pt. and pp. Archaic.* named; called: *The knight was hight Gawain.* [OE *heht*, pt. of *hātan* be called]

high·tail (hī′tāl′) *v. Slang.* run away at full speed; hurry.
high-tail it, hurry or run fast.

high tech *Informal.* **1** designating a style of interior design that exploits the materials and structural features of industrial design. **2** high technology.

high technology advanced modern technology involving electronics, especially micro-electronics.

high·ten·sion (hī′ten′shən) *adj.* having or accommodating a high voltage: *high-tension wiring.*

high·test (hī′test′) *adj.* **1** passing very difficult requirements and tests. **2** of gasoline, vaporizing at a low temperature.

high tide **1** the highest level of the tide. **2** the time when the tide is highest. **3** the highest point; a culminating point.

high time **1** the time just before it is too late: *It is high time that we got ready to go.* **2** *Informal.* a lively, jolly time at a party, etc.

high·toned (hī′tōnd′) *adj.* **1** high in tone or pitch. **2** having a high character or high principles; dignified. **3** *Informal.* fashionable; stylish.

high treason treason against one's ruler, state, or government.

high water **1** the highest level of water. **2** high tide.

high·water mark **1** the highest level of water in a river or lake. **2** any highest point.

high·way (hī′wā′) *n.* **1** a public road. **2** a main road or route. **3** a direct line or way to some end.

high·way·man (hī′wā′mən) *n., pl.* **-men.** *Historical.* a man, usually on horseback who robbed travellers on a public road.

H.I.H. **1** His Imperial Highness. **2** Her Imperial Highness.

hi·jack (hī′jak′) *v.* **1** stop (a vehicle) in transit by force or threat in order to steal it or its cargo: *The truck was highjacked about 70 kilometres out of the city.* **2** steal (goods, etc.) by force or threat while they are being transported: *Several shipments have been highjacked.* **3** seize control of (an aircraft) in flight by force or threat in order to obtain money or some other concession. —**hi′jack′er**, *n.* [origin uncertain]

hi·jinks (hī′ jingks′) *n.* high jinks.

hike (hīk) *v.* **hiked, hik·ing;** *n. Informal.* —*v.* **1** take a long walk; tramp; march. **2** move, draw, or raise with a jerk: *He hiked himself up onto the platform.* **3** raise; increase: *The company is going to hike wages.*
—*n.* **1** a long walk; a march or tramp. **2** an increase: *a hike in prices.* [? related to HITCH] —**hik′er**, *n.*

hi·lar·i·ous (hə ler′ē əs) *adj.* **1** very merry; noisily cheerful: *It was a hilarious party.* **2** very funny: *The joke was hilarious.* [< L *hilaris.* See HILARITY.] —**hi·lar′i·ous·ly**, *adv.* —**hi·lar′i·ous·ness**, *n.*

hi·lar·i·ty (hə lar′ə tē *or* hə ler′ə tē) *n.* great mirth; noisy gaiety. [< L *hilaritas* < *hilaris, hilarus* gay < Gk. *hilaros*]

hill (hil) *n., v.* —*n.* **1** a raised part on the earth's surface, smaller than a mountain. **2** a heap, pile, or mound of earth, sand, etc.: *Moles had made hills all over the lawn. The potatoes were planted in hills.* **3** a plant or plants growing in a mound of earth: *a hill of corn.* **4** the Hill, *Cdn. Informal.* **a** Parliament Hill. **b** Parliament.
over the hill, *Informal.* past one's prime.
—*v.* **1** put a little heap of soil over and around. **2** form into a little heap. [OE *hyll*] —**hill′er**, *n.*

hill·bil·ly (hil′bil′ē) *n., pl.* **-lies;** *adj. Informal.* —*n.* a person who lives in the backwoods or a mountain region, especially in the S United States. —*adj.* of, having to do with, or characteristic of a hillbilly: *hillbilly music.*

hill·ock (hil′ək) *n.* a little hill.

hill·side (hil′sīd′) *n.* the side of a hill.

hill·top (hil′top′) *n.* the top of a hill.

hill·y (hil′ē) *adj.* **hill·i·er, hill·i·est.** **1** having many hills. **2** like a hill; steep. —**hill′i·ness**, *n.*

hilt (hilt) *n.* the handle of a sword, dagger, etc. See **sword** for picture.
up to the hilt, thoroughly; completely. [OE]

hi·lum (hī′ləm) *n., pl.* **-la** (-lə). *Botany.* the mark or scar on a seed at the point of attachment to the seed vessel. The eye of a bean is a hilum. [< L *hilum* trifle]

him (him; *unstressed,* im) *pron.* the objective case of **he**: *Take him home.* [OE *him*, dative of *hē* he]
➤ *Hom.* **hymn.**

H.I.M. His (or Her) Imperial Majesty.

Him·a·la·yan (him′ə lā′ən *or* hə mäl′yən) *adj.* of or having to do

with the Himalayas, a mountain range along the border between India and Tibet.

him·self (him self'; *unstressed*, im self') *pron.* **1** a reflexive pronoun, the form used instead of **he** or **him** when referring back to the subject of the sentence: *He cut himself. He asked himself what he really wanted. He kept the toy for himself.* **2** a form of **he** or **him** used to make a statement stronger: *Did you see Roy himself?* **3** his usual self: *He feels himself again.*

hind[1] (hīnd) *adj.* **hind·er, hind·most** or **hind·er·most.** back; rear: *The mule kicked up his hind legs.* [see HINDER[2]]

hind[2] (hīnd) *n., pl.* **hind** or **hinds.** a female deer, especially the female of the European red deer after its third year. [OE]

Hind. 1 Hindustan. **2** Hindustani. **3** Hindu. **4** Hindi.

hind·brain (hīnd'brān') *n.* the back of the brain, especially the part including the cerebellum and the medulla oblongata.

hin·der[1] (hin'dər) *v.* keep or hold back; get in the way of or make difficult: *recurring problems that hinder completion of a project. We were hindered by deep snow.* [OE *hindrian*]
—**hin'der·er,** *n.*
☛ *Syn.* See note at **prevent.**

hind·er[2] (hīn'dər) *adj.* hind; back; rear. [cf. OE *hinder* and *hindan* in back, behind]

hind·er·most (hīn'dər mōst') *adj.* hindmost.

Hin·di (hin'dē) *n.* the most widely spoken language of India, an Indo-European language that exists in several very different dialects as well as a standard literary form that is one of the official languages of India. [< Hind. *Hindī* < *Hind* India < Persian *Hind.* See HINDU.]

hind·most (hīnd'mōst') *adj.* farthest back; nearest the rear; last.

Hin·doo (hin'dü) *n., pl.* **-doos;** *adj.* See **Hindu.**

hind·quar·ter (hīnd'kwôr'tər) *n.* the hind leg and loin of a carcass of beef, lamb, etc.

hin·drance (hin'drəns) *n.* **1** a person or thing that hinders; obstacle. **2** the act of hindering.
☛ *Syn.* **1.** See note at **obstacle.**

hind·sight (hīnd'sīt') *n.* *Informal.* the ability to see, after the event is over, what should have been done.

Hin·du (hin'dü) *n., pl.* **-dus;** *adj.* —*n.* **1** a person who believes in Hinduism. **2** especially formerly, a native or inhabitant of India. —*adj.* **1** of or having to do with Hinduism or Hindus. **2** especially formerly, of or having to do with India. [< Persian *Hindū* < *Hind* India < OPersian *Hindu*]

Hindu. Hindustani.

Hin·du·ism (hin'dü iz'əm) *n.* a religion and way of life that is practised mainly in India, having an ancient tradition characterized by the doctrine of transmigration of souls, the worship of many gods who are all thought of as aspects of the one God, and, formerly, the support of a system of hereditary social classes generally called castes. The three great divinities of classical Hinduism are Vishnu, Shiva, and Shakti. A fourth divinity, Brahma, was widely worshipped for a time as the highest god.

Hin·du·sta·ni (hin'dù stä'nē *or* hin'dù stan'ē) *n., adj.* —*n.* a dialect of N India that was used as a common language of trade throughout India for a century and a half until 1947, when India was divided. Literary Hindi and Urdu both developed from Hindustani. —*adj.* of or having to do with Hindustan (India or N India), its people, or the language Hindustani. [< Hind., Persian *Hindūstānī* Indian < *Hindūstān* India < *Hindū* Hindu + *stan* place, country]

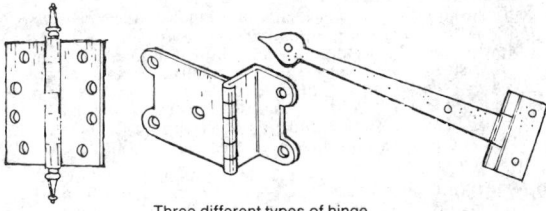

Three different types of hinge

hinge (hinj) *n., v.* **hinged, hing·ing.** —*n.* **1** a movable joint or mechanism by which a door, gate, cover, lid, etc. moves back and forth or up and down on its post, base, etc. **2** a natural joint that has a similar function: *the hinge of a clam shell.* **3** that on which something turns or depends; central principle or determining factor. —*v.* **1** furnish with or attach by a hinge or hinges. **2** depend (*used with* **on** *or* **upon**): *The success of the enterprise will hinge on the dedication of the people involved.* **3** hang or turn on a hinge. [ME *heng.* Related to HANG.]

hinged (hinjd) *adj.* having a hinge or hinges.

hin·ny (hin'ē) *n., pl.* **-nies.** the sterile offspring of a male horse and a female donkey. Compare **mule**[1]. [apparently dim. of ·hin < L *hinnus* (influenced by *hinnire* neigh) < Gk. *innos*]

hint (hint) *n., v.* —*n.* **1** a slight indication; clue: *A small black cloud gave a hint of the coming storm.* **2** a statement or action implying something that the person prefers not to say directly; an indirect suggestion: *When she stood up, he took it as a hint that the interview was over.* **3** a very small amount or suggestion: *The soup has just a hint of garlic.* **4** a piece of practical information: *helpful hints for the traveller.*
—*v.* give a hint (often used with **at**): *He tried to hint that she was tired by saying, "Do you often stay up this late?" The unsettled weather hinted at a storm.* [apparently < *hent*, v., seize, OE *hentan*] —**hint'er,** *n.* —**hint'ing·ly,** *adv.*
☛ *Syn. v.* **1. Hint, insinuate** = suggest indirectly. **Hint** = say something in a roundabout way, not openly, directly, or frankly: *She hinted that it was time to go to bed by saying, "Do you often stay up this late?"* **Insinuate** = suggest or hint something unkind or nasty in a sly or underhand way: *Are you insinuating that I am a liar?*

hin·ter·land (hin'tər land') *n.* **1** the country or region behind a coast; the inland region. **2** a region remote from and outside the influence of major urban centres; backwater. [< G]

hip[1] (hip) *n., v.* —*n.* **1** hipbone: *He broke his right hip when he fell.* **2** Usually, **hips,** *pl.* the part of the body between the waist and the thighs: *The skirt fits well over the hips.* **3** pelvis. **4** *Architecture.* the ridge formed by two sloping sides of a roof or by a sloping side meeting a sloping end.
on the hip, at a disadvantage.
—*v.* in architecture, form with a hip or hips. [OE *hype*] —**hip'less,** *adj.* —**hip'like',** *adj.*

hip[2] (hip) *n.* a pod containing the ripe seed of a rose bush. [OE *hēope*]

hip[3] (hip) *adj.* *Slang.* showing interest in and knowledge about the latest trends in fashion, music, etc.; aware; sophisticated. [var. of *hep*]

hip·bone (hip'bōn') *n.* **1** either of the large, irregular bones that form the main part of the pelvis in mammals. The hipbone is composed of the ilium, ischium, and pubis, which are fused into one bone in adults. **2** the rear, upper portion of either of these bones; ilium. See **pelvis** for picture.

hip joint the ball-and-socket joint formed by the top of the thighbone and the hipbone; the joint that connects the upper leg with the trunk.

hipped[1] (hipt) *adj.* **1** having a hip or hips. **2** having a hip or hips of a specified kind (*used in compounds*): *a narrow-hipped torso.* [< *hip*[1]]

hipped[2] (hipt) *adj.* *Slang.* obsessed. [var. of *hypt* < *hyp*, n., for *hypochondria*]

–hipped *combining form.* having — hips: *wide-hipped* = *having wide hips.*

hip·pie (hip'ē) *n.* *Slang.* **1** a person who rejects many of the customs and beliefs of conventional modern society and believes simply in freedom of expression and in love and fellowship; especially, any of the many young people of the 1960's who attempted to express such ideas through communal living, mysticism, the use of drugs, etc. **2** any person who defies convention by affecting an unkempt appearance, discourteous behavior, etc. [< *hip*[3] + *-ie*]
☛ *Usage.* Definition 2 is often used loosely as a term of disapproval, without regard for the full range of meaning involved in definition 1.

hip·po (hip'ō) *n.* *Informal.* hippopotamus.

Hip·po·crat·ic (hip'ə krat'ik) *adj.* of or having to do with Hippocrates (460?-377? B.C.), the ancient Greek physician who is called the father of medicine.

Hippocratic oath an oath describing the duties and obligations of a physician, usually taken by those about to become physicians.

Hip·po·crene (hip'ə krēn' *or* hip'ə krē'nē) *n.* a fountain on Mt. Helicon, sacred to the Muses and regarded as a source of poetic inspiration. [< L < Gk. *Hippokrēnē* < *hippos* horse + *krēnē* fountain]

hip·po·drome (hip'ə drōm') *n.* **1** in ancient Greece and Rome, an oval track for horse races and chariot races, surrounded by tiers of seats for spectators. **2** an arena or building for a circus, rodeo,

etc. [< L < Gk. *hippodromos* < *hippos* horse + *dromos* course]

Hip·pol·y·tus (hi pol′ə təs) *n. Greek mythology.* the son of Theseus. Falsely accused by his stepmother Phaedra, he was cursed by his father, and killed when his chariot overturned.

hip·po·pot·a·mus (hip′ə pot′ə məs) *n., pl.* **-mus·es, -mi** (-mī′ or -mē′) **1** a very large, plant-eating, hoofed mammal (*Hippopotamus amphibius*) found in and near lakes and rivers in tropical Africa, having thick, hairless skin, short legs, and a large head with an enormous mouth. Hippopotamuses may reach a length of about 4.5 metres and a mass of over 2 tonnes. **2** a smaller animal (*Choeropsis liberiensis*) of the same family (Hippopotamidae) of W Africa that reaches a length of about 1.5 metres. It is usually called the **pygmy hippopotamus.** [< L < Gk. *hippopotamus* < *hippos* horse + *potamos* river]

hip roof a roof with sloping ends and sides. See **roof** for picture.

hip·ster (hip′stər) *n. Slang.* **1** one who is unconventional in regard to music, sex, religion, the use of drugs, etc.; a person who is hep. **2** beatnik. **3** a jazz fan. [< *hip³* + *-ster*]

hip wader a long rubber boot reaching to the hip.

hir·cine (hėr′sīn or hėr′sən) *adj. Archaic.* **1** of or having to do with goats; resembling a goat, especially in having a strong, unpleasant odor. **2** lustful. [< L *hircinus* < *hircus* he-goat]

hire (hīr) *v.* **hired, hir·ing;** *n.* —*v.* **1** agree to pay for the temporary use of a thing or the work or services of a person: *He hired a car and a man to drive it.* **2** take on as an employee; engage: *The manager hired two more clerks last week.* **3** give the use of (a thing) or the work or services of (a person) in return for payment. **hire out,** give one's work in return for payment: *He hired out as a carpenter.*
—*n.* **1** payment for the use of a thing or the work or services of a person. **2** hiring.
for or **on hire,** available for use or work in exchange for payment: *They have boats for hire.* [OE *hȳr* (n.), *hȳrian* (v.)]
☛ *Syn. v.* **1.** See note at **employ.**

hire·ling (hīr′ling) *n.* a person available for hire, especially one who will follow anyone's orders and is interested only in the pay.

hir·sute (hėr′süt) *adj.* hairy. [< L *hirsutus*]

his (hiz; *unstressed,* iz) *adj., pron.* —*adj.* the possessive form of **he;** of, belonging to, or made or done by him or himself: *He shook his head. They attended his graduation. His novels are very good.*
—*pron.* **1** the posessive form of **he;** that which belongs to him: *The writing is his. Those tapes are his.* **2 His,** a word used as part of any of certain formal titles when using the title to refer to the man holding it: *His Majesty the King.* [OE *his,* genitive of *hē* he]

His·pa·ni·a (his pā′nē ə or his pā′nē ə) *n. Poetic.* Spain.

hiss (his) *v., n.* —*v.* **1** make a sound like that of the *s* in *see: The snake hissed as we approached.* **2** make this sound as a sign of disapproval. **3** force or drive by hissing: *They hissed him off the stage.* **4** utter by hissing or as if by hissing: *"Sit down and be quiet!" he hissed.*
—*n.* **1** the sound of hissing: *There was a loud hiss as the water boiled over onto the hot stove.* **2** the sound of hissing to express disapproval: *The actor was upset by the hisses of the crowd.* [imitative] —**hiss′er,** *n.*

hist (hist) *interj.* be still! listen!

hist. **1** history; historian. **2** histology.

his·ta·mine (his′tə mēn′ or his′tə min) *n.* an amine released by the body in allergic reactions. It lowers the blood pressure and is used in the diagnosis and treatment of various allergies. *Formula:* $C_5H_9N_3$ [< *hist*(*idine*), an amino acid (< Gk. *histion* tissue) + *amine*]

his·ti·dine (his′tə dēn′ or his′tə din) *n.* a basic amino acid found in many proteins. It is important in diet control. *Formula:* $C_6H_9N_3O_2$ [< Gk. *histion* tissue, web + *ide* + *-ine²*]

his·to·log·ic (his′tə loj′ik) *adj.* histological.

his·to·log·i·cal (his′tə loj′ə kəl) *adj.* of or having to do with histology. —**his′to·log′i·cal·ly,** *adv.*

his·tol·o·gist (his tol′ə jist) *n.* a person trained in histology, especially one whose work it is.

his·tol·o·gy (his tol′ə jē) *n.* **1** a branch of biology dealing with the structures of animal and plant tissues as seen through a microscope. **2** the tissue structure of an animal or plant. [< Gk. *histos* web + E *-logy*]

his·to·ri·an (his tô′rē ən) *n.* **1** a person who has much knowledge of history, especially one who writes or lectures about history. **2** a person who records events; chronicler.

his·tor·ic (his tôr′ik) *adj.* **1** famous or important in history:

Halifax and Kingston are historic cities. **2** historical (defs. 1-3).

his·tor·i·cal (his tôr′ə kəl) *adj.* **1** of or having to do with history: *a historical town.* **2** according to history; based on history. **3** known to be real or true; in history, not in legend. **4** historic (def. 1). [< L < Gk. *historikos* < *historia.* See HISTORY.] —**his·tor′i·cal·ly** (-ik lē), *adv.*

historical present the present tense used in describing past events to make them seem more vivid.

his·to·ri·og·ra·pher (hi stôr′ē og′rə fər) *n.* **1** a person specializing in historiography; one who studies the development, theory, and principles of historical writing. **2** a historian, especially one appointed to write the official history of an institution, etc. [< LL < Gk. *historiographos* < *historia* history + *graphein* write]

his·to·ri·og·ra·phy (hi stôr′ē og′rə fē) *n.* **1** the development, principles, and theory of the writing of history. **2** the writing of history, especially according to established principles of research and authentication of documentary evidence. **3** a body of historical writing.

his·to·ry (his′tə rē or his′trē) *n., pl.* **-ries. 1** a statement of what has happened. **2** systematic written account of a person, nation, movement, etc.: *a history of the fur trade.* **3** a known past: *This ship has an interesting history.* **4** all past events considered together; the course of human affairs: *one of the greatest achievements in history.* **5** the branch of knowledge or study that deals with the record and interpretation of past events: *a course in history.* **6** a statement or record of all the facts or events having to do with a person being treated by a doctor, social worker, etc.; a case history. **7** a textbook on history. **8** a historical play.
make history, **a** influence or guide the course of history. **b** do something spectacular or worthy of remembrance.
[< L *historia* < Gk. *historia* inquiry, record, history. Doublet of STORY¹.]

his·tri·on·ic (his′trē on′ik) *adj., n.* —*adj.* **1** theatrical and insincere; deliberately affected. **2** having to do with actors or acting; dramatic. —*n.* **histrionics,** *pl.* **1** a deliberately dramatic show of emotions, etc. for effect. **2** *Rare.* dramatics (*used with a singular verb*). [< L *histrionicus* < *histrio, -onis* actor] —**his′tri·on′i·cal·ly,** *adv.*

hit (hit) *v.* **hit, hit·ting;** *n.* —*v.* **1** give a blow to; strike; knock: *He hit the ball with the bat. He hit out against his opponents.* **2** get to (what is aimed at): *His second arrow hit the bull's-eye.* **3** discover, meet, or find, especially by chance or unexpectedly (*often used with* **on** or **upon**): *We happened to hit the right road in the dark. They've hit on a new idea for advertising the competition.* **4** have a painful or distressing effect on: *The death of his sister hit him hard. The province was hard hit by the drought.* **5** occur suddenly: *As he lifted the heavy box, a sharp pain hit him in the back. An idea just hit me.* **6** reach a certain point or place: *Prices hit a new high. The temperature hit an all-time low yesterday.* **7** attack or criticize sharply (*often used with* **at**): *The reviews hit the new play.* **8** please; appeal to: *This hits my fancy.* **9** *Baseball.* make a base hit: *She hit a double.*
hit below the belt, be unfair to an opponent.
hit it off, *Informal.* agree or get along well with someone: *Ron hit it off with his new neighbor right away.*
hit off, mimic or represent cleverly or accurately.
hit or miss, whether one succeeds or fails; regardless of results; by chance; at random.
hit the books, *Informal.* begin to study, especially very hard: *She decided it was time to hit the books.*
hit the nail on the head, be apt or to the point: *The solution he proposed hit the nail on the head.*
hit the roof or **ceiling,** *Informal.* react with a burst of anger: *When their father saw the condition of his car, he hit the roof.*
—*n.* **1** a blow; stroke. **2** a getting to what is aimed at. **3** a sharp attack or criticism. **4** a very successful or popular person or thing: *My brother was a big hit at my party. That new play is sure to be a hit.* **5** a stroke of luck. **6** *Baseball.* a successful hitting of the ball by a batter so that he can get at least to first base without the help of an error; base hit. [OE *hittan* < ON *hitta* meet with] —**hit′ter,** *n.*
☛ *Syn. v.* **1.** See note at **beat.**

hit–and–run (hit′ ən run′) *adj., n.* —*adj.* **1** of or caused by a driver who runs into another person or vehicle and drives away without stopping. **2** of or suggesting any similar act: *a hit-and-run attack.* —*n. Baseball.* a play in which the batter tries to hit the ball to protect a runner who has already left base.

hitch (hich) *v., n.* —*v.* **1** fasten with a hook, ring, rope, strap, etc.: *He hitched his horse to a post.* **2** harness to a wagon, carriage, etc.: *She hitched up the team and drove to town.* **3** become fastened or caught; fasten; catch. **4** move or pull with a jerk; move jerkily: *He hitched his chair nearer the fire.* **5** limp; hobble. **6** tie a hitch (def. 5): *He hitched a rope around the spar.* **7** *Informal.* obtain by hitchhiking: *She hitched a ride home.*
be or **get hitched,** *Slang.* be or get married.
—*n.* **1** a fastening; catch: *The hitch joining the plough to the tractor*

is broken. **2** a short, sudden pull or jerk; jerky movement: *The sailor gave his pants a hitch.* **3** a limp; hobble. **4** an obstacle; hindrance; a going wrong: *A hitch in their plans made them miss the train.* **5** a kind of knot used for temporary fastening: *He put a hitch in the rope.* **6** *Informal.* a free ride from a passing automobile. **7** *Slang.* a period of time, especially a period of service in the armed forces. **without a hitch,** smoothly; successfully.
[ME *hyche(n)*; origin uncertain] —**hitch′er,** *n.*

hitch·hike (hich′hīk′) *v.* **-hiked, -hik·ing;** *n. Informal.* —*v.* travel by asking for free rides from passing motorists: *They hitchhiked across the country last summer.* —*n.* a journey made in this way. —**hitch′hik′er,** *n.*

hitching post (hich′ing) a stand or post for hitching horses, etc.

hith·er (hiŦH′ər) *adv., adj.* —*adv.* to or toward this place; here. **hither and thither** or **hither and yon,** in all directions; this way and that: *The frightened chickens ran hither and thither.* —*adj.* on this side; nearer. [OE *hider.* Related to HERE.]

hith·er·most (hiŦH′ər mōst′) *adj.* nearest.

hith·er·to (hiŦH′ər tü′) *adv.* up to this time; until now.

hith·er·ward (hiŦH′ər wərd) *adv.* toward this place; hither.

hith·er·wards (hiŦH′ər wərdz) *adv.* hitherward.

Hit·ler·ism (hit′lər iz′əm) *n.* the totalitarian and nationalistic policies and beliefs of Adolf Hitler and the Nazi party in Germany (1933 to 1945).

hit list *Slang.* a list of people designated to be murdered by a particular person or group.

hit man *Slang.* a hired murderer.

hit-or-miss (hit′ər mis′) *adj.* showing a lack of care or planning; careless or haphazard: *He has always done his accounts in a hit-or-miss fashion.*

hit·ter (hit′ər) *n.* especially in sports, a person who hits: *He's a good hitter, but not much of a catcher.*

Hit·tite (hit′īt) *n., adj.* —*n.* **1** a member of an ancient people of Asia Minor and Syria. Their civilization existed from about 2000 B.C. until about 1200 B.C. **2** the Indo-European language of the Hittites. —*adj.* of or having to do with the Hittites or their language. [< Hebrew *Hittīm*]

hive (hīv) *n., v.* **hived, hiv·ing.** —*n.* **1** a house or box for bees to live in. **2** a large number of bees living together. **3** a busy place full of people: *On Saturdays, the department store is a hive.* **4** a swarming crowd. —*v.* **1** put (bees) in a hive. **2** of bees, enter a hive. **3** store up (honey) in a hive. **4** lay up for future use. **5** live close together like bees. [OE *hȳf*]

hives (hīvz) *n.* a condition characterized by small, very itchy, fluid-filled swellings on the skin, usually caused by an allergic reaction; uticaria. [Scottish; origin unknown]

H.J. hic jacet.

hkf. handkerchief(s).

hl. hectolitre(s).

h'm (həm) hem; hum.

hm. hectometre(s).

H.M. His Majesty; Her Majesty.

H.M.C.S. **1** His Majesty's Canadian Ship; Her Majesty's Canadian Ship: *H.M.C.S. St. Laurent.* **2** His Majesty's Canadian Service; Her Majesty's Canadian Service.

H.M.S. **1** His Majesty's Ship; Her Majesty's Ship. **2** His Majesty's Service; Her Majesty's Service.

ho (hō) *interj.* **1** an exclamation of surprise, joy, or scorn. **2** an exclamation used to attract attention: *Land ho!*
☛ *Hom.* hoe.

ho. house.

Ho holmium.

hoar (hôr) *adj.* hoary. [OE *hār*]
☛ *Hom.* whore.

hoard (hôrd) *n., v.* —*n.* what is saved and stored away; things stored. —*v.* save and store away: *A squirrel hoards nuts for the winter.* [OE *hord*] —**hoard′er,** *n.*
☛ *Hom.* horde.

hoard·ing (hôr′ding) *n.* **1** a temporary board fence put up around a construction site or a building that is being repaired. **2** *Brit.* billboard. [< *hoard* fence, apparently < AF *hurdis,* ult. < Gmc.]

hoar·frost (hôr′frost′) *n.* a film of tiny ice crystals that sometimes forms on a cold surface.

hoar·hound (hôr′hound′) See **horehound.**

hoarse (hôrs) *adj.* **hoars·er, hoars·est.** **1** rough and deep in sound; husky: *Her voice was hoarse from shouting at the game.* **2** having a

hat, āge, fär; let, ēqual, tèrm; it, īce
hot, ōpen, ôrder; oil, out; cup, pùt, rüle,
əbove, takən, pencəl, lemən, circəs
ch, child; ng, long; sh, ship
th, thin; ŦH, then; zh, measure

rough voice: *He's hoarse because of a cold.* [OE *hās;* influenced by ON **hârs*] —**hoarse′ly,** *adv.* —**hoarse′ness,** *n.*
☛ *Hom.* horse.

hoar·y (hôr′ē) *adj.* **hoar·i·er, hoar·i·est.** **1** of hair, grey or white. **2** having such hair; white or grey with age: *a hoary old man.* **3** very old; ancient. —**hoar′i·ness,** *n.*

hoar·y-head·ed (hôr′ē hed′id) *adj.* having white or grey hair.

hoary marmot *Cdn.* a large grey marmot (*Marmota caligata*) found in the mountains of western Canada; whistler. The hoary marmot is the largest North American marmot.

hoax (hōks) *n., v.* —*n.* a mischievous trick, especially one based on a made-up story: *The report of an attack from Mars was a hoax.* —*v.* play a mischievous trick on; deceive. [probably an alteration of *hocus*] —**hoax′er,** *n.*

hob¹ (hob) *n.* **1** a shelf at the back or side of a fireplace, used for keeping things warm. **2** a peg at which quoits, etc. are thrown. **3** a rotating device with a spiral cutting edge, used for cutting the teeth of worm gears, etc. [var. of *hub;* origin uncertain]

hob² (hob) *n.* **1** a hobgoblin; elf. **2** *Informal.* **play hob** or **raise hob,** cause trouble. [ME for *Rob* (*Robert* or *Robin*)]

hob·bit (hob′ət) *n.* a member of an imaginary race of small, good-natured people about half as tall as human beings, having beardless faces, curly hair, and woolly, leathery-soled feet. [created by J.R.R. Tolkien (1892-1973) in his books *The Hobbit* and *Lord of the Rings*]

hob·ble (hob′əl) *v.* **-bled, -bling;** *n.* —*v.* **1** walk or move awkwardly or unsteadily; limp: *She managed to hobble to the phone without using the crutches.* **2** cause to walk awkwardly or limp. **3** put a strap, rope, etc. around the legs of (an animal, especially a horse) so that it can move a little but not run away. **4** hinder. —*n.* **1** an awkward walk; limp. **2** a rope or strap used to hobble a horse, etc. [ME *hobelen;* cf. Du. *hobbelen* rock] —**hob′bler,** *n.*

hob·ble·de·hoy (hob′əl dē hoi′) *n.* a youth between boyhood and manhood, especially one who is clumsy or awkward. [origin uncertain]

hobble skirt a woman's skirt that is very narrow below the knees.

hob·by (hob′ē) *n., pl.* **-bies.** something a person especially likes to work at or study apart from his main business or occupation; any favorite pastime, topic of conversation, etc.
ride a hobby, give too much time or attention to one's hobby.
[ME *hobyn, hoby,* prob. from proper name *Robin.* See DOBBIN.] —**hob′by·ist,** *n.*

hob·by·horse (hob′ē hôrs′) *n.* **1** a stick with a horse's head, used as a toy by children. **2** a rocking horse. **3** a favorite idea or topic: *Father is again on his hobbyhorse of cutting costs.* [< *hobby;* orig. a small horse or figure of a horse. 16c.]

hob·gob·lin (hob′gob′lən) *n.* **1** a mischievous elf; goblin. **2** something imaginary that gives rise to fear. [< *hob²* + *goblin*]

hob·nail (hob′nāl′) *n.* a short nail with a large head used to protect the soles of heavy shoes or boots. [< *hob* peg + *nail*]

hob·nob (hob′nob′) *v.* **-nobbed, -nob·bing.** *Informal.* **1** associate intimately; talk together on familiar terms. **2** drink together. [from drinking phrase *hob or nob* give or take, ult. < OE *hæbbe* have + *næbbe* not have]

ho·bo (hō′bō) *n., pl.* **-bos** or **-boes.** a tramp. [origin uncertain]

Hob·son's choice (hob′sənz) the choice of taking the thing offered or nothing. [< Thomas *Hobson* (?-1631), an English stablekeeper, who would rent only the horse nearest his stable door or none]

hock¹ (hok) *n., v.* —*n.* **1** the joint in the hind leg of a horse, cow, etc. above the fetlock joint. See **horse** for picture. **2** the corresponding joint in the leg of a fowl. —*v.* cripple by cutting the tendons of the hock; hamstring. Also, **hough.** [OE *hōh*]

hock² (hok) *n. Esp.Brit.* a kind of white Rhine wine. [for *Hockamore,* alteration of *Hochheimer* (from *Hochheim,* Germany)]

hock³ (hok) *v., n. Slang.* —*v.* pawn: *He hocked his watch to buy a ticket.* —*n.* pawn.
in hock, a in another's possession as security; in pawn. **b** in debt.
out of hock, a no longer in another's possession as security. **b** no longer in debt.
[originally, *n.;* cf. Du. *hok* pen, jail]

hock·ey (hok′ē) *n.* **1** a game played on ice by two teams of six players wearing skates, in which the members of each team use hooked sticks to try to shoot a small, thick, black rubber disk (the puck) into the opposing team's goal. **2** field hockey. [< *hock* hooked stick, var. of *hook*]

hockey stick a hooked or curved stick used in playing hockey.

hock·shop (hok′shop′) *n. Informal.* a store where goods may be pawned.

ho·cus (hō′kəs) *v.* **-cussed** or **-cused, -cus·sing** or **-cus·ing. 1** play a trick on; hoax; cheat. **2** stupefy with drugs. **3** put drugs in (alcoholic drink). [short for *hocus-pocus*]

ho·cus–po·cus (hō′kəs pō′kəs) *n.* **1** sleight of hand; magic. **2** any meaningless or insincere talk or action designed to cover up a deception: *All his talk about our beautiful house and garden was just hocus-pocus.* **3** a typical formula for conjuring. [sham Latin used by jugglers, etc.; probably alteration of *hoc est corpus* (this is the Body) from the Eucharist]

hod (hod) *n.* **1** a trough or tray on a long handle, used for carrying bricks, mortar, etc. on the shoulder. **2** coal scuttle. [< MDu. *hodde*]

hod carrier a laborer who carries bricks, mortar, etc. in a hod.

hod·den (hod′ən) *n. Scottish.* a coarse cloth of undyed wool. [probably Northern dial. *hodden*, var. of *holden* (old pp. of *hold*) held, kept (at home, handed down)]

hodge·podge (hoj′poj′) *n.* a disorderly mixture; a mess or jumble. [var. of *hotchpotch*, var. of *hotchpot* < OF *hochepot* ragout < *hocher* shake (< Gmc.) + *pot* pot]

Hodg·kin's disease (hoj′kənz) a disease characterized by chronic enlargement of the lymph nodes, spleen, and, often, the liver. It often produces anemia and continuous or recurring fever.

hoe (hō) *n., v.* **hoed, hoe·ing. —***n.* an implement with a small blade set across the end of a long handle, used to loosen soil and cut weeds. —*v.* **1** loosen, dig, or cut with a hoe: *There are a lot of weeds to hoe again.* **2** work with a hoe: *He spent all morning hoeing.* [ME < OF *houe* < Gmc.] **—ho′er,** *n.*
☛ *Hom.* **ho.**

hoe·down (hō′doun′) *n.* **1** a lively dance, especially a square dance. **2** the music for such a dance. **3** a party featuring hoedowns: *There's a hoedown Saturday night.*

hog (hog) *n., v.* **hogged, hog·ging. —***n.* **1** a domestic pig, especially a full-grown, castrated male raised for meat. **2** *Informal.* a selfish, greedy person.
go the whole hog, go to the limit; do something thoroughly.
—*v. Slang.* take more than one's share of: *Don't hog the blanket.* [OE *hogg*]

hog·back (hog′bak′) *n.* **1** *Geology.* a low, sharp ridge with steep sides. **2** an arching back like that of a hog.

hog·gish (hog′ish) *adj.* very selfish, greedy, or filthy. **—hog′gish·ly,** *adv.* **—hog′gish·ness,** *n.*

hog·ma·nay (hog′mə nā′) *n.* in Scotland and northern England, New Year's eve, when children knock on doors for presents, cakes, etc. [origin uncertain]

hogs·head (hogz′hed′) *n.* **1** a large barrel or cask, especially one having a capacity of from 100 to 140 gallons (about 455 to 635 L). **2** a unit for measuring liquids, equal to 54 gallons (about 245 L). [? from shape of cask]

hog·wash (hog′wosh′) *n.* **1** refuse given to hogs; swill. **2** *Slang.* worthless stuff; nonsense.

hog–wild (hog′wīld′) *adj. Slang.* frenzied; wildly aroused; berserk.

Hoh·en·stau·fen (hō′ən stou′fən; *German*, hō′ən shtou′fən) *n.* a German princely family to which some of the German kings and Holy Roman emperors between 1138 and 1254 belonged.

Hoh·en·zol·lern (hō′ən zol′ərn; *German*, hō′ən tsôl′ərn) *n.* the German princely family that included the kings of Prussia from 1701 to 1918, and the emperors of Germany from 1871 to 1918.

hoi·den (hoi′dən) See **hoyden.**

hoi·den·ish (hoi′dən ish) See **hoydenish.**

hoi pol·loi (hoi′ pə loi′ *or* pol′oi) ordinary people; the general populace. [< Gk. *hoi polloi* the many]

hoist (hoist) *v., n.* —*v.* raise on high; lift up, often with ropes and pulleys: *hoist sails, hoist blocks of stone.*
hoist with (one's) own petard See **petard.**
—*n.* **1** a hoisting; lift. **2** an elevator or other apparatus for hoisting heavy loads. **3** the perpendicular height of a sail or flag on a ship. **4** a signal or message sent by means of flags hoisted. [earlier *hoise* < Du. *hijschen*] **—hoist′er,** *n.*

hoi·ty–toi·ty (hoi′tē toi′tē) *adj., n., interj.* —*adj.* **1** inclined to put on airs; haughty or pompous. **2** flighty or silly.
—*n.* hoity-toity behavior.
—*interj.* an exclamation of annoyed surprise at a display of haughtiness or arrogance.

ho·key–po·key (hō′kē pō′kē) *n.* **1** trickery; hocus-pocus. **2** a cheap kind of ice cream sold by street vendors.

ho·kum (hō′kəm) *n. Slang.* **1** pretentious nonsense; humbug; bunk. **2** elements such as crude comedy or maudlin sentiment introduced into a play, show, etc. merely for their immediate effect on the audience. [? < *hocus*]

hold¹ (hōld) *v.,* **held, held, hold·ing;** *n.* —*v.* **1** take in the hands or arms and keep; not let go; keep from getting away: *Please hold my hat. Hold my watch while I play this game.* **2** keep in some position or condition; force to keep: *He will hold the paper steady while you draw.* **3** keep from falling; support: *He held his head in his hands.* **4** not break, loosen, or give way: *The dike held during the flood.* **5** keep from acting; keep back: *Hold your breath.* **6** keep; retain: *This package will be held until called for.* **7** oblige (a person) to adhere to a promise, etc.: *They held him to his promise.* **8** keep by force against an enemy; defend: *Hold the fort.* **9** keep or have within itself; contain: *This theatre holds 500 people.* **10** have and keep as one's own; possess; occupy: *to hold an office.* **11** have and take part in; carry on together: *Shall we hold a meeting of the club?* **12** keep or have in mind: *to hold a belief.* **13** think; consider: *People once held that the earth was flat.* **14** remain faithful or firm: *He held to his promise.* **15** be true; be in force or effect: *The rule holds in all cases.* **16** keep on; continue: *The weather held warm.* **17** decide legally: *The court holds him guilty.* **18** *Music.* keep on singing or playing (a note).
hold back, a keep back; keep from acting. **b** avoid disclosing: *to hold back the truth.* **c** withhold money, wages, etc.
hold down, a keep down; keep under control. **b** *Slang.* have and keep: *to hold down a job.*
hold forth, a talk; preach (often used disparagingly). **b** offer.
hold in, a keep in; keep back. **b** restrain; control: *He was so angry he couldn't hold in his temper.*
hold off, a keep at a distance. **b** keep from acting or attacking.
hold on, a *Informal.* keep one's hold: *He held on to the overturned boat till help came.* **b** keep on; continue. **c** stop! wait a minute!
hold (one's) own, maintain one's strength or position in the face of opposition or difficulty.
hold out, a continue; last: *The water would not hold out much longer.* **b** stretch forth; extend: *Hold out your hand.* **c** keep resisting; not give in: *The company of soldiers held out for six days until help arrived.* **d** offer. **e** *Slang.* keep back (something expected or due).
hold over, a keep longer than originally scheduled: *The movie was so popular that it was held over for another week.* **b** postpone: *The game has been held over until next week.* **c** *Music.* hold (a tone) from one bar to the next.
hold up, a keep from falling; support. **b** show; display. **c** continue; last; endure. **d** stop: *The policeman held up the traffic.* **e** *Informal.* stop by force and rob.
hold with, a side with. **b** agree with. **c** approve of.
—*n.* **1** the act of holding: *to release one's hold.* **2** the manner of grasping or holding: *You must take a better hold if you are to pull your weight.* **3** something to hold by: *She looked for a hold on the smooth rock but couldn't find any.* **4** something to hold something else with. **5** a holding back; delay: *a hold in the launching of a missile.* **6** an order to delay or temporarily halt something. **7** a controlling force or influence: *A habit has a hold on you.* **8** *Wrestling.* a way of holding one's opponent. **9** *Music.* a sign for a pause. **10** a prison cell. **11** *Archaic.* a fort; stronghold.
lay or take hold of, a seize; grasp. **b** get control or possession. [OE *healdan*]
☛ *Syn. v.* **9.** See note at **contain. 10.** See note at **have.**

hold² (hōld) *n.* the interior of a ship below the deck. A ship's cargo is carried in its hold. [var. of *hole*]

hold·back (hōld′bak′) *n.* **1** something that holds back; restraint; hindrance. **2** an iron or strap on the shaft of a wagon or carriage to which the harness is attached, enabling a horse to stop or back the vehicle. **3** the act of holding back. **4** something held back.

hold·en (hōl′dən) *v. Archaic.* a pp. of **hold¹.**

hold·er (hōl′dər) *n.* **1** a person who holds a bill, note, cheque, etc. and is legally entitled to receive payment on it. **2** a person who owns or occupies property. **3** a device for holding something (*usually used in compounds*): *a cigarette holder, a potholder.* **4** any person or thing that holds.

hold·fast (hōld′fast′) *n.* anything used to hold something else in place. A catch, hook, or clamp is a holdfast.

hold·ing (hōl′ding) *n.* **1** land, especially a piece of land rented from someone else. **2** Usually, **holdings,** pl. property, especially in the form of stocks or bonds. **3** *Sports.* the illegal hindering of an opponent's movements.

holding company a company that owns stocks or bonds of other companies and thus often controls them.

hold·out (hōld′out′) *n. Informal.* **1** a person or group that refuses to submit or give in or accept an agreement. **2** refusal to settle or comply; continued resistance.

hold·o·ver (hōld′ō′vər) *n.* **1** a person or thing that is held over from another time or place: *He was a holdover from last year's team.* **2** a person who remains in office beyond the regular time.

hold·up (hōld′up′) *n.* **1** the act or an instance of forcibly stopping and robbing. **2** delay or hindrance: *She got out of her car to see what the holdup was.*

hole (hōl) *n., v.* **holed, hol·ing.** —*n.* **1** an opening in or through something, often a break or tear: *a hole in a stocking, a hole in a window. The calendar has a hole at the top to hang it up by.* **2** a hollow place; pit: *There's a hole in the lawn where the ground caved in.* **3** burrow: *Rabbits live in holes.* **4** a small, dark, dreary, or dirty place: *I wouldn't want to live in that hole.* **5** *Informal.* a flaw or defect: *That argument has several holes.* **6** *Informal.* an embarrassing, awkward, or difficult position: *He got himself into a hole, financially.* **7** *Golf.* **a** a small, round hollow to hit a ball into. **b** the part of a golf course leading from a tee to such a place. A regular golf course has 18 holes. **8** a small, narrow indentation in a coastline, especially in a bay or harbor (*often used in place names*).
burn a hole in (one's) **pocket,** of money, make one want badly to spend; be easily spent: *His Christmas gift is burning a hole in his pocket.*
in the hole, in debt or financial difficulties.
make a hole in, use up a large amount of: *The new radio made quite a hole in my savings.*
pick holes in, find fault with; criticize.
—*v.* **1** make a hole or holes in: *The side of the ship was holed by an iceberg.* **2** hit or drive into a hole.
hole out, hit a golf ball into a hole.
hole up, a of animals, go into a hole. **b** *Slang.* go into hiding for a time: *The robbers holed up in an old cabin.*
[OE *hol*]
☛ Hom. **whole.**
☛ *Syn. n.* **1, 2.** Hole, cavity = an open or hollow place in something. **Hole** is the common word applying to an opening in or through anything, or to a hollow space in something solid: *Fire burned a hole in the roof. He bored a hole in the tree.* **Cavity** is chiefly scientific or technical, and applies only to a hollow space inside a solid mass or body, often with an opening at the surface: *The dentist filled several cavities in my teeth.*

hole–and–cor·ner (hōl′ən kôr′nər) *adj. Informal.* furtive; underhand.

hole–in–the–wall (hōl′in ᴛʜə wol′ *or* -wôl′) *adj. Informal.* insignificant; shabby; grubby.

hol·ey (hō′lē) *adj.* having holes.
☛ *Hom.* **holy, wholly.**

hol·i·day (hol′ə dā′) *n., v.* —*n.* **1** a day free of work; day for pleasure and enjoyment. **2** a day on which, either by law or custom, general business is suspended: *Labor Day and July 1st are both holidays as specified by law.* **3** Often **holidays,** *pl.* vacation; period of rest or recreation: *the summer holidays. My mother gets three weeks of holidays a year.* **4** (*adj.*) suited to a holiday; festive: *in holiday spirits.* **5** a holy day; religious festival.
—*v.* take or have a holiday: *They are holidaying in the tropics.* [OE *hāligdæg* holy day]

ho·li·er–than–thou (hō′lē ər ᴛʜən ᴛʜou′) *adj., n. Informal.*
—*adj.* self-righteous. —*n.* a self-righteous person.

ho·li·ness (hō′lē nis) *n.* **1** being holy. **2 Holiness,** a title used in speaking to or of the Pope. [OE *hālignes*]

ho·lism (hō′liz əm) *n.* the philosophical theory that living nature consists of wholes that are greater than the sum of their parts.

ho·lis·tic (hō lis′tik) *adj.* **1** emphasizing the importance of the relationship between parts or elements and wholes: *holistic medicine.* **2** of or having to do with holism. —**ho·lis′ti·cal·ly,** *adv.*

hol·la (hə lä′ *or* hol′ə) *interj., n., or v.* hollo.

hol·land (hol′ənd) *n.* a linen, or linen and cotton cloth used for window shades, upholstery, etc. It is usually light-brown and sometimes glazed. [first made in *Holland*]

hol·lan·daise sauce (hol′ən dāz′) a creamy sauce made from egg yolks, butter, lemon juice, and seasoning, served with fish, vegetables, etc. [< F *hollandaise,* fem. of *hollandais* Dutch]

Hol·land·er (hol′ən dər) *n.* a native or inhabitant of the Netherlands; Dutchman.

Holland gin (hol′ənd) Hollands.

Hol·lands (hol′əndz) *n.* a strong gin made in the Netherlands. [< Du. *hollandsch* < *hollandsche genever* Dutch gin. 18c.]

hol·ler (hol′ər) *v., n. Informal.* —*v.* shout. —*n.* a loud cry or shout.

hol·lo (hə lō′ *or* hol′ō) *interj., n. pl.* **-los;** *v.* **-loed, -lo·ing.** —*interj.*

---

hat, āge, fär; let, ēqual, tèrm; it, īce
hot, ōpen, ôrder; oil, out; cup, pút, rüle,
əbove, takən, pencəl, lemən, circəs
ch, child; ng, long; sh, ship
th, thin; ᴛʜ, then; zh, measure

or n. **1** hello. **2** a shout of exultation or triumph. —*v.* hello. [var. of *halloo*]

hol·loa (hə lō′ *or* hol′ō) See **hollo.**

hol·low (hol′ō) *adj., n., v., adv.* —*adj.* **1** having a hole or cavity inside; not solid: *A tube or pipe is hollow. Some plants have hollow stems.* **2** shaped like a bowl or cup; having an inward curve; concave or sunken: *hollow cheeks. There is a large hollow place in the lawn where the earth has settled.* **3** sounding as if coming from something hollow; deep-toned and muffled: *a hollow voice, a hollow groan.* **4** lacking real worth, truth, or significance; worthless or false: *hollow promises, hollow joys, a hollow victory.* **5** empty or hungry: *a hollow stomach.*
—*n.* **1** a hollow place; a wide, shallow hole: *a hollow in the road.* **2** a small valley: *They built their house in a hollow.*
—*v.* **1** make or become hollow. **2** make or form by hollowing (*usually used with* out): *He hollowed out a canoe from a log.*
—*adv. Informal.* thoroughly or completely: *We beat their team hollow.* [OE *holh,* n.; influenced in use by *hol,* adj.] —**hol′low·ly,** *adv.* —**hol′low·ness,** *n.*

hol·low–eyed (hol′ō īd′) *adj.* **1** having eyes set deep in the head. **2** having dark shadows under the eyes: *hollow-eyed from lack of sleep.*

hol·ly (hol′ē) *n., pl.* **-lies. 1** any of a genus (*Ilex*) of trees and shrubs having thick, shiny leaves with spiny points along the edges, and clusters of bright-red berries. **2** the leaves and berries of a holly, used as Christmas decorations: *a wreath of holly.* **3** (*adj.*) designating the family (Aquifoliaceae) of trees and shrubs that includes the hollies. [OE *holegn*]

hol·ly·hock (hol′ē hok′) *n.* a tall perennial plant (*Althaea rosea*) of the mallow family native to China, but widely grown for its spikes of large, showy flowers. Hollyhock flowers are usually white, pink, red, or yellow. [ME *holihoc < holi* holy (OE *hālig*) + *hoc* mallow (OE *hocc*)]

Hol·ly·wood (hol′ē wùd′) *n.* the American motion-picture industry. [< *Hollywood,* a section of Los Angeles, California, centre of the United States motion-picture industry]

holm[1] (hōm) *n.* **1** low, flat land by a stream. **2** a small island in a river or lake near a large island or the mainland. [OE]
☛ *Hom.* **home.**

holm[2] (hōm) *n.* holm oak.
☛ *Hom.* **home.**

hol·mi·um (hōl′mē əm) *n.* a rare metallic chemical element belonging to the yttrium group. *Symbol:* Ho; *at.no.* 67; *at.wt.* 164.930. [< NL; < *Stockholm*]

holm oak an evergreen oak (*Quercus ilex*) of S Europe having leaves that look like holly. [OE *holegn* holly + *āc* oak]

hol·o·caust (hol′ə kost′ *or* hol′ə kôst′) *n.* **1** a sacrificial offering, all of which is burned. **2** great or total destruction of life, especially by fire. **3 the Holocaust,** the systematic killing of over six million Jews by the Nazi regime in Germany before and during World War II. [< L < Gk. *holokauston,* neut. of *holokaustos < holos* whole + *kaustos* burned]

Hol·o·cene (hol′ə sēn′) *adj., n. Geology.* Recent.

hol·o·gram (hol′ə gram′) *n.* a three-dimensional photograph obtained by exposing a photographic plate near an object illuminated by a laser beam.

hol·o·graph (hol′ə graf′) *adj., n.* —*adj.* wholly written in the handwriting of the person in whose name it appears: *a holograph will.* —*n.* a holograph manuscript, letter, document, etc. [< LL < Gk. *holographos < holos* whole + *graphē* writing] —**hol·o·graph·ic,** *adj.*

ho·log·ra·phy (hə log′rə fē) *n.* a photographic process for making three-dimensional pictures without the use of lenses, in which a split beam of laser light causes a diffraction pattern that is reconstructed in visible light.

holp (hōlp) *v. Archaic.* a pt. of **help.**

hol·pen (hōl′pən) *v. Archaic.* a pp. of **help.**

Hol·stein (hōl′stīn *or* hōl′stēn) *n.* a breed of large black-and-white dairy cattle, originating in Schleswig-Holstein, a state in West Germany.

Hol·stein–Frie·sian (hōl′stīn frē′zhən *or* hōl′stēn-) *n.* Holstein.

hol·ster (hōl′stər) *n.* a leather case for a pistol, usually attached to a belt. [< Du. *holster*]

ho·lus–bo·lus (hō′ləs bō′ləs) *adv. Informal.* all at once; altogether. [humorous Latinization of E *whole bolus*]

ho·ly (hō′lē) *adj.* **-li·er, -li·est;** *n., pl.* **-lies.** —*adj.* **1** belonging to or coming from God or a god; set apart for the service of God or a god; sacred: *the Holy Bible.* **2** perfect in nature and worthy of worship: *God is holy.* **3** pure in heart; godly: *a holy man.* **4** declared sacred by religious use and authority: *a holy day.* **5** worthy of deep respect and love: *the holy Cross.* —*n.* a holy place. [OE *hālig*]
☞ *Hom.* **holey, wholly.**

Holy Alliance a league formed by the rulers of Russia, Austria, and Prussia in 1815, supposedly uniting their governments in a Christian brotherhood.

Holy City **1** a city considered sacred by the adherents of a religion. Jerusalem, Rome, and Mecca are Holy Cities. **2** heaven.

Holy Communion in the Christian church, the commemoration of Christ's Last Supper, in which bread and wine are consecrated and taken as the body and blood of Christ or as symbols of them; the Eucharist.

holy day a religious festival, especially one not occurring on a Sunday. Ash Wednesday and Good Friday are holy days.

Holy Father a title of the Pope.

Holy Ghost **1** the spirit of God. **2** the third person of the Trinity.

Holy Grail Grail.

Holy Land Palestine.

Holy Office **1** *Roman Catholic Church.* the papal Congregation of the Holy Office, charged with the supervision and protection of Catholic faith and morals. **2** *Historical.* the Inquisition.

holy of holies **1** the inner shrine of the Jewish tabernacle and temple. **2** any place that is most sacred.

holy orders **1** the rite or sacrament of ordination. **2** the rank or position of an ordained Christian minister of priest. **3** *Roman Catholic and Anglican Churches.* the three higher ranks or positions of the clergy. Bishops, priests, and deacons are members of holy orders.
take holy orders, become ordained as a Christian minister or priest.

Holy Roman Empire an empire in western and central Europe regarded both as the continuation of the Roman Empire and as the temporal dominion of a universal dominion whose spiritual head was the Pope. It began in A.D. 962, or, according to some, in A.D. 800, and ended in 1806.

Holy Rood **1** the cross on which Jesus died. **2** a representation of it.

Holy Saturday the Saturday before Easter.

Holy Scripture Bible.

Holy See **1** the position or authority of the Pope. **2** the Pope's court.

Holy Spirit the spirit of God, the third person in the Trinity.

ho·ly·stone (hō′lē stōn′) *n., v.* **-stoned, -ston·ing.** —*n.* a piece of soft sandstone used for scrubbing the wooden decks of ships. —*v.* scrub with a holystone.

Holy Synod the church council that governs an Orthodox Church.

Holy Thursday **1** *Roman Catholic Church.* the Thursday before Easter. **2** *Anglican Church.* the 40th day after Easter; Ascension Day.

holy water water blessed by a priest.

Holy Week the week before Easter.

Holy Writ the Bible; the Scriptures.

hom. homonym.

hom·age (hom′ij) *n.* **1** respect; reverence; honor: *Everyone paid homage to the great leader.* **2** in feudal times: **a** a formal acknowledgment by a vassal that he owed loyalty and service to his lord. **b** anything done or given to show such acknowledgment. **3** a formal statement, or oath, of loyalty and service owed to one's sovereign. [ME < OF *homage* < *hom* man, vassal < L *homo*]
☞ *Syn.* **1.** See note at **honor.**

hom·bre (om′brā *or* om′brē; *Spanish,* ōm′brā) *n.* man. [< Sp.]

Hom·burg (hom′bérg) *n.* a man's felt hat having a slightly rolled brim and a crown creased lengthwise. [< *Homburg,* a German resort where it was first worn]

home (hōm) *n., v.* **homed, hom·ing.** —*n.* **1** the place where a person or family lives; one's own house. **2** the place where a person was born or brought up; one's own town or country. **3** (*advl.*) at, to, or toward one's own home: *He's not home. I want to go home.* **4** the social unit formed by a family, etc. living together in one house or apartment: *He comes from a broken home.* **5** a house, especially a new house built for occupation by one family: *luxury homes for sale.* **6** the natural habitat of an animal or plant: *The beaver makes its home in the water. The Canadian tundra is the home of the musk-ox.* **7** any place where a person can rest and be safe. **8** a place where people are homeless, poor, old, sick, blind, etc. may live. **9** *Games.* the objective or goal; especially, in baseball, home plate. **10** (*adjl.*) *Games.* **a** having to do with or situated at or near home. **b** reaching or enabling a player to reach home. **11** (*advl.*) **a** to the thing aimed at: *to drive a nail home.* **b** the heart or core; deep in: *His accusing words struck home and they were ashamed.* **c** successfully or effectively: *to speak home.* **12** (*adjl.*) of, having to do with, or coming from home: *one's home country, home remedies, a home game.*
at home, a in one's own home or country. **b** in a friendly place or familiar condition; at ease; comfortable. **c** ready to receive visitors. **d** a reception.
bring home to, make clear, emphatic, or realistic.
come home to, be understood or realized by.
home free, *Informal.* sure of success or victory: *One more game and then we're home free.*
see (someone) home, escort a person to that person's home: *He offered to see her home.*
—*v.* **1** go home. **2** bring, carry, or send home. **3** have a home. **4** furnish with a home.
home (in) on, be guided toward a goal or target by or as if by radar. [OE *hām*]
☞ *Hom.* **holm.**

home·bred (hōm′bred′) *adj., n.* —*adj.* **1** bred or reared at home; native; domestic. **2** not polished or refined; crude; unsophisticated. —*n. Slang. Sports.* homebrew.

home·brew (hōm′brü′) *n.* **1** an alcoholic liquor made at home, especially beer. **2** *Cdn. Slang.* **a** in Canadian professional football, a native-born player. **b** a local player in any sport; a player trained by the team for which he plays. **c** any person or thing of native origin.

home·com·ing (hōm′kum′ing) *n.* **1** a coming home. **2** an annual celebration held at many universities and colleges for alumni.

home economics the science and art that deals with the management of a household.

home–guard Indian *Cdn. Historical.* an Indian who was employed at a fur-trading post.

home Indian home-guard Indian.

home·land (hōm′land′) *n.* one's own or native land.

home·less (hōm′lis) *adj.* having no home. —**home′less·ness,** *n.*

home·like (hōm′līk′) *adj.* like home; friendly; familiar; comfortable. —**home′like′ness,** *n.*

home·ly (hōm′lē) *adj.* **-li·er, -li·est.** **1** not good-looking; plain: *His homely face lit up in a smile.* **2** suited to home life; simple; everyday: *homely pleasures, homely food.* —**home′li·ness,** *n.*
☞ *Syn.* **3.** See note at **ugly.**

home·made (hōm′mād′) *adj.* made at home.

home·mak·er (hōm′māk′ər) *n.* a person who manages a home, especially a woman who is a wife and mother.

home·mak·ing (hōm′māk′ing) *n.* the art or practice of managing a home and looking after a family.

ho·me·o·path (hō′mē ə path′ *or* hom′ē ə path′) *n.* a person who practises homeopathy.

ho·me·o·path·ic (hō′mē ə path′ik *or* hom′ē ə path′ik) *adj.* of or having to do with homeopathy or homeopaths. —**ho′me·o·path′i·cal·ly,** *adv.*

ho·me·op·a·thist (hō′mē op′ə thist *or* hom′ē op′ə thist) *n.* homeopath.

ho·me·op·a·thy (hō′mē op′ə thē *or* hom′ē op′ə thē) *n.* a system of treating disease by giving very small doses of a drug that in large quantities would produce symptoms of the disease in healthy persons. It is based on the theory that making the symptoms more intensive will stimulate the body to do what it does in fighting disease. [< Gk. *homoios* similar + E *-pathy*]

ho·me·o·sta·sis (hō′mē ō stā′sis) *n.* **1** the state of equilibrium between the different body activities of an organism, or the tendency to return to or compensate for loss of equilibrium. **2** the maintenance of or return to equilibrium between interdependent elements of a group, society, etc.

ho·me·o·stat·ic (hō′mē ō stat′ik) *adj.* of, having to do with, or showing homeostasis.

home–own·er (hōm′ōn′ər) *n.* a person who owns his own home.

home plate *Baseball.* the block or slab beside which a player stands to hit the ball, and to which he must return, after hitting the ball and rounding the bases, in order to score.

hom·er (hōm′ər) *n., v. Informal.* —*n.* **1** *Baseball. Informal.* home run. **2** *Slang.* a referee, umpire, etc. who favors, or is said to favor, the home team. **3** *Slang.* a supporter of the home-town team. **4** *Slang.* a player or team that plays well in home games. —*v. Baseball. Informal.* hit a home run.

Ho·mer·ic (hō mer′ik) *adj.* **1** by Homer, the epic poet of Ancient Greece. **2** of or having to do with Homer or his poems. **3** in the style of Homer; having some characteristics of Homer's poems. **4** of or having to do with age in Greek life from about 1200 to about 800 B.C.

Homeric laughter loud, hearty laughter.

home·room (hōm′rüm′) *n.* **1** the classroom in a school where a given class meets first every day to be checked for attendance, hear announcements, etc. **2** the classroom in a school, especially an elementary school, where a given class is taught most subjects, usually by the same teacher. **3** the period during which a class meets in the homeroom. **4** the students of a given homeroom. **5** (*adj.*) of or having to do with a homeroom or homerooms: *a homeroom plan. My homeroom teacher taught French.* Also, **home room.**

home rule the management of the affairs of a country, district, or city by its own people; local self-government.

home run *Baseball.* a run made by a player on a hit that enables him, without aid from fielding errors of the opponents, to make the entire circuit of the bases without a stop.

home·sick (hōm′sik′) *adj.* ill or depressed because one is away from home; longing for home. —**home′·sick′ness,** *n.*

home·spun (hōm′spun′) *adj., n.* —*adj.* **1** spun or made at home. **2** made of homespun cloth. **3** not polished; plain; simple: *homespun manners.* —*n.* **1** cloth made of yarn spun at home. **2** a strong, loosely woven cloth similar to homespun.

home·stead (hōm′sted′) *n., v.* —*n.* **1** a house with its land and other buildings; a farm with its buildings. **2** *Cdn.* in the West, a parcel of public land, usually consisting of 160 acres (a quarter section, equal to about 65 hectares), granted to a settler under certain conditions by the federal government. —*v.* **1** settle on such land: *His grandfather homesteaded in Saskatchewan.* **2** settle and work (land, etc.): *They homesteaded a quarter section west of the river.*

Homestead Act the Act of 1872 under which settlers became homesteaders in the Canadian West.

home·stead·er (hōm′sted′ər) *n.* **1** a person who has a homestead. **2** a settler granted a homestead by the federal government.

home stretch 1 the part of a track over which the last part of a race is run. **2** the last part.

home town 1 the town or city where one grew up or spent most of his early life. **2** the town or city of one's principal residence. —**home·town,** *adj.*

home·ward (hōm′wərd) *adv. or adj.* toward home.

home·wards (hōm′wərdz) *adv.* homeward.

home·work (hōm′werk′) *n.* **1** a lesson or lessons to be studied or prepared outside the classroom. **2** any work done at home. **3** work done in preparation for something; background reading or research: *The interviewer's searching questions showed that she had done her homework.*

home·y (hōm′ē) *adj.* **hom·i·er, hom·i·est.** *Informal.* like home; cosy and comfortable: *The old inn had a very homey atmosphere.*

hom·i·cid·al (hom′ə sīd′əl *or* hō′mə sīd′əl) *adj.* **1** of or having to do with homicide. **2** murderous. —**hom′i·cid′al·ly,** *adv.*

hom·i·cide[1] (hom′ə sīd′ *or* hō′mə sīd′) *n.* the killing of one human being by another. Intentional homicide is murder. [ME < OF < L *homicidium* < *homo* man + *-cidium* act of killing]

hom·i·cide[2] (hom′ə sīd′ *or* hō′mə sīd′) *n.* a person who kills a human being. [ME < OF < L *homicida* < *homo* man + *-cida* killer]

hom·i·let·ic (hom′ə let′ik) *adj.* having to do with sermons or the art of preaching. [< LL < Gk. *homilētikos* affable, ult. < *homileein* associate with < *homilos.* See HOMILY.]

hom·i·let·ics (hom′ə let′iks) *n.* the art of composing and preaching sermons.

hom·i·ly (hom′ə lē) *n., pl.* **-lies. 1** a sermon, usually based on some part of the Bible. **2** a serious moral talk or writing. [ME < OF *omelie* < LL < Gk. *homilia* < *homilos* throng < *homou* together + *ilē* crowd]

hom·i·nes (hom′ə nēz′) *n. pl.* of **homo.**

homing pigeon a pigeon trained to fly home from great distances. Homing pigeons are often used in racing or for carrying written messages.

hom·i·nid (hom′ə nid) *n., adj.* —*n.* any of a family (Hominidae)

hat, āge, fär; let, ēqual, tèrm; it, īce
hot, ōpen, ôrder; oil, out; cup, pùt, rüle,
əbove, takən, pencəl, lemən, circəs

ch, child; ng, long; sh, ship
th, thin; ŦH, then; zh, measure

of primate mammals, including modern man (*Homo sapiens*), the only surviving member of the group. —*adj.* of, having to do with, or belonging to the family Hominidae. [< NL *Hominidae,* the family name]

hom·i·noid (hom′ə noid′) *adj., n.* —*adj.* like a man; of the form of a man. —*n.* a hominoid animal. [< L *homo, -inis* man + E *-oid*]

hom·i·ny (hom′ə nē) *n.* dried, hulled corn. **Hominy grits** is coarsely ground hominy that is boiled in water or milk for food. [< short for *rockahominy* < Algonquian]

ho·mo[1] (hō′mō) *n., pl.* **hom·i·nes** (hom′ə nēz′). man. [< L]

ho·mo[2] (hō′mō) *n. Informal.* homogenized whole milk.

homo– *combining form.* the same, as in *homopterous.* [< Gk. *homo-* < *homos* same]

ho·mo·ge·ne·i·ty (hō′mə jə nē′ə tē *or* hom′ə-) *n.* the state of being homogeneous.

ho·mo·ge·ne·ous (hō′mə jē′nē əs *or* hom′ə-, hō′mə jēn′yəs *or* hom′ə-) *adj.* **1** of the same kind; similar: *homogeneous interests.* **2** composed of similar elements or parts; of uniform nature or character throughout: *a homogeneous rock, a homogeneous community.* Compare **heterogeneous. 3** *Mathematics.* **a** of the same kind and commensurable. **b** of the same degree or dimensions. [< Med.L < Gk. *homogenēs* < *homos* same + *genos* kind] —**ho′mo·ge′ne·ous·ly,** *adv.*

ho·mog·e·nize (hə moj′ə nīz′) *v.* **-nized, -niz·ing. 1** make homogeneous. **2** break up the fat globules of (whole milk) into extremely small particles so that the fat remains emulsified and does not rise to the top to form cream. —**ho·mog′e·ni·za′tion,** *n.*

hom·o·graph (hom′ə graf′ *or* hō′mə-) *n.* one of two or more words having the same spelling but different meanings, origins, or pronunciations. *Mail,* meaning "letters", and *mail,* meaning "armor", are homographs. [< Gk. *homographos* < *homos* same + *graphē* writing]

ho·mol·o·gous (hō mol′ə gəs) *adj.* **1** corresponding in position, proportion, value, structure, etc. **2** *Biology.* corresponding in type of structure and in origin but not necessarily in function. The wing of a bird and the foreleg of a horse are homologous. **3** *Chemistry.* differing in composition successively by a constant amount of certain constituents, and showing a gradation of chemical and physical properties. [< Gk. *homologos* agreeing < *homos* same + *logos* reasoning, relation]

hom·o·logue (hom′ə log′) *n.* a homologous thing, organ, or part.

ho·mol·o·gy (hō mol′ə jē) *n., pl.* **-gies. 1** a correspondence or similarity in position, proportion, value, structure, etc. **2** *Biology.* correspondence in type of structure and in origin. **3** *Chemistry.* the relation of the compounds forming a homologous series. [< Gk. *homologia* agreement < *homologos.* See HOMOLOGOUS.]

hom·o·nym (hom′ə nim′ *or* hō′mə nim′) *n.* **1** homophone (def. 1). **2** one of two or more words having the same pronunciation and spelling but different meanings and origins. *Rose,* past tense of the verb *rise,* and *rose,* meaning the flower, are homonyms. [< L < Gk. *homonymos* < *homos* same + dial. *onyma* name]

ho·mon·y·mous (hō mon′ə məs) *adj.* **1** of the nature of homonyms; alike in spelling and sound but not in meaning. **2** having, or being called by, the same name.

ho·mo·phile (hō′mə fīl′ *or* hom′ə-) *n. or adj.* homosexual.

hom·o·phone (hom′ə fōn′ *or* hō′mə-) *n.* **1** one of two or more words having the same pronunciation but different meanings, origins, and, sometimes, spellings. *Pear, pair,* and *pare* are homophones. **2** one of two or more letters or symbols having the same sound. The letters *c* and *k* are homophones in the word *cork.* [< Gk. *homophonos* < *homos* same + *phōnē* sound]

hom·o·phon·ic (hom′ə fon′ik *or* hō′mə-) *adj.* **1** having the same sound. **2** *Music.* **a** in unison. **b** having one part or melody predominating.

ho·moph·o·nous (hō mof′ə nəs) *adj.* homophonic.

ho·moph·o·ny (hō mof′ə nē *or* hom′ə fō′nē) *n.* **1** sameness of sound. **2** homophonic music.

ho·mop·ter·an (hō mop′tə rən) *n., adj.* —*n.* a homopterous insect. —*adj.* of or designating the order (Homoptera) comprising these insects.

☛ *Usage.* See note at **heteropterous.**

ho·mop·ter·ous (hō mop′tər əs) *adj.* of or having to do with an order (Homoptera) of sucking insects that feed on plants, including aphids, cicadas, and scale insects. Most homopterous insects have two pairs of wings, with the front pair of the same thickness throughout, either all leathery or all thin and membranous; the wings at rest are usually sloped upward in a tentlike position over the body.
☛ *Usage.* See note at **heteropterous.** [< *homo-* + Gk. *pteron* wing]

Ho·mo sa·pi·ens (hō′mō sā′pē enz *or* sap′ē enz) the specific name given to modern man, including all existing races, in the standard biological taxonomy. The species includes extinct types of man as well, such as Cro-Magnon man. [< L *homo sapiens,* literally, man having wisdom]

ho·mo·sex·u·al (hō′mə sek′shü əl *or* hom′ə-) *adj., n.* —*adj.* of, having to do with, or showing sexual desire for one of the same sex. Compare **heterosexual.** —*n.* a homosexual person. —**ho′mo·sex′u·al·ly,** *adv.*

ho·mo·sex·u·al·i·ty (hō′mə sek′shü al′ə tē *or* hom′ə-) *n.* the fact or quality of being homosexual.

ho·mun·cu·lus (hō mung′kyə ləs) *n., pl.* **-li** (-lī′ *or* -lē′). **1** a little man; dwarf. **2** a model of a little man used for demonstrating anatomy, etc. [< L *homunculus,* dim. of *homo* man]

hon. 1 honorary. **2** honorable or honourable.

Hon. 1 Honourable or Honorable. **2** Honorary. **3** Honors or Honours.

hon·cho (hon′chō) *n., pl.* **-chos.** *Slang.* boss or leader; bigwig: *Send your job application to the top honcho.* [< Japanese *hanchō* squad leader < *han* squad + *chō* head]

hone (hōn) *n., v.* **honed, hon·ing.** —*n.* a fine-grained whetstone on which to sharpen cutting tools, especially razors. —*v.* sharpen on a hone. [OE *hān* a stone]

hon·est (on′ist) *adj.* **1** not lying, cheating, or stealing; fair and upright; truthful: *an honest person.* **2** obtained by fair and upright means; without lying, cheating, or stealing: *honest profits.* **3** not hiding one's real nature; frank; open: *honest opposition. I would like your honest opinion.* **4** not mixed with something of less value; genuine; pure: *honest goods.* **5** *Archaic.* chaste; virtuous. [ME < OF < L *honestus* < *honos* honor] —**hon′est·ly,** *adv.*

hon·est-to-good·ness (on′is tə güd′nis) *adj. Informal.* sincere; genuine.

hon·es·ty (on′is tē) *n.* **1** fairness and uprightness. **2** truthfulness. **3** freedom from deceit or fraud. **4** a garden herb of the mustard family, with large, purple flowers and flat, round, semitransparent, satiny pods. **5** *Archaic.* chastity.
☛ *Syn.* **1. Honesty, integrity** = the quality of being honorable and upright in character and actions. **Honesty** emphasizes fairness and uprightness in relations with others, and refusal to steal, lie, cheat, or misrepresent: *He shows honesty in all his business affairs.* **Integrity** applies more directly to character than to actions, and means soundness of character, having very high standards of right and wrong, and refusing to do anything that does not measure up to them: *A man of integrity can be trusted.*

hon·ey (hun′ē) *n., pl.* **hon·eys;** *v.* **hon·eyed** *or* **hon·ied, hon·ey·ing.** —*n.* **1** a thick, sweet, liquid that bees make out of the nectar they collect from flowers. **2** any of various substances similar in taste, texture, etc., especially the nectar of flowers. **3** (*adj.*) of, having to do with, or like honey. **4** sweetness. **5** darling; sweetheart. **6** (*adj.*) lovable; dear. **7** *Informal.* a person or thing that is very attractive, pleasing, etc.: *He's a honey. That's a honey of a boat.* —*v.* **1** sweeten with or as with honey. **2** talk sweetly; flatter. [OE *hunig*] —**hon′ey·like′,** *adj.*

honey bag *Cdn. Slang.* a heavy plastic bag used in a toilet as a receptacle for human waste.

hon·ey·bee (hun′ē bē′) *n.* any of various social bees that produce honey, especially the common hive bee (*Apis mellifera*), widely kept for its honey and wax.

honey bucket *Cdn. Slang.* a bucket or pail used in a toilet as a receptacle for human waste.

hon·ey·comb (hun′ē kōm′) *n., v.* —*n.* **1** a structure of wax containing rows of six-sided cells made by bees, in which they store honey, pollen, and their eggs. **2** anything like this. **3** (*adj.*) like a honeycomb: *a honeycomb weave of cloth, a honeycomb pattern in knitting.* —*v.* **1** make or decorate like a honeycomb. **2** pierce with many holes or tunnels: *The rock was honeycombed with passages.* **3** weaken or harm by spreading through: *That city is honeycombed with crime.* [OE *hunigcamb*]

hon·ey·dew (hun′ē dyü′ *or* -dü′) *n.* **1** a sweet substance that oozes from the leaves of certain plants in hot weather. **2** a sweet, sticky substance excreted especially by aphids or scale insects, found as a deposit on the leaves and stems of plants. **3** honeydew melon.

honeydew melon a variety of muskmelon having sweet, green flesh and a smooth, whitish skin.

hon·eyed *or* **hon·ied** (hun′ēd) *adj.* **1** sweetened with honey. **2** laden with honey. **3** sweet as honey.

honey locust a tall, thorny North American tree (*Gleditsia triacanthos*) of the pea family having long compound leaves, small, greenish-white flowers, and large, flat, reddish-brown pods containing a sweet pulp.

hon·ey·moon (hun′ē mün′) *n., v.* —*n.* **1** the holiday spent together by a newly married couple. **2** the initial period of marriage. **3** the initial period of any new agreement, arrangement, etc., when things are harmonious and peaceful.
—*v.* spend or have a honeymoon. —**hon′ey·moon′er,** *n.*

hon·ey·suck·le (hun′ē suk′əl) *n.* **1** any of a genus (*Lonicera*) of shrubs or vines found in temperate regions, many of which are cultivated for their showy, often fragrant, tubular flowers. **2** (*adj.*) designating a family (Caprifoliaceae) of plants, mostly shrubs and vines, found in many parts of the world, but especially in north temperate regions, and including the honeysuckles, elders, and viburnums. **3** any of various plants similar to the honeysuckles, having flowers rich in nectar. [ME *hunisuccle,* dim. of OE *hunisūce* privet, literally, honey-suck < *hunig* honey + *sūcan* suck]

hon·ied (hun′ēd) *v., adj.* —*v.* a pt. and a pp. of **honey.** —*adj.* honeyed.

honk (hongk) *n., v.* —*n.* **1** the cry of the wild goose. **2** any similar sound: *the honk of a car horn.* —*v.* **1** make the cry of a wild goose or a similar sound. **2** cause to make a sound similar to that of a goose: *to honk a horn.* [imitative] —**honk′er,** *n.*

honk·er (hong′kər) *n. Cdn. Informal.* Canada goose.

honk·y-tonk (hong′kē tongk′) *Slang. n., adj.* —*n.* **1** a cheap bar or drinking place. **2** a low-class dance hall, night club, etc. —*adj.* of or having to do with the entertainment or music in a low-class dance hall, etc. [? imitative of the music typically found there]

hon·or *or* **hon·our** (on′ər) *n.* **1** glory; fame; renown. **2** credit for acting well; good name: *It was greatly to his honor that he refused the reward.* **3 honors** *or* **honours,** *pl.* a special favors or courtesies. **b** a special mention, grade, or credit given to a student for unusually excellent work. **c** an honors course. **d** *Bridge.* the ace, king, queen, jack, and ten of trumps, or the four aces in no-trump. **4** a source of credit; cause of honor. **5** a clear sense of what is right or proper; sticking to action that is right or that is usual and expected. **6** great respect; high regard: *Our Queen is held in honor. We pay honor to heroes.* **7** an act of respect: *funeral honors.* **8** rank; dignity; distinction: *Knighthood is an honor.* **9 Honor** *or* **Honour,** a title used in speaking to or of a judge, mayor, etc. **10** chastity; virtue. **11** *Golf.* the privilege of teeing off first, awarded to the player or side winning the previous hole.
do honor *or* **honour to,** a show honor to; treat with great respect. **b** cause honor to; bring honor to.
do the honors *or* **honours,** act as host or hostess.
on *or* **upon (one's) honor,** pledged to do what is expected; on the pledge of one's word: *He was on his honor not to divulge the secret.*
—*v.* **1** respect greatly; regard highly. **2** show respect to. **3** confer dignity upon; be an honor to; favor: *to be honored by a royal visit.* **4** accept and pay (a bill, draft, note, etc.) when due. [ME < OF < L *honos, honor*] —**hon′or·er** *or* **hon′our·er,** *n.*
☛ *Syn. n.* **5. Honor, deference, homage** = respect shown to someone. **Honor** = respect felt or shown in acknowledgment or appreciation of a person's high character or position or something he has done with high courage or ability: *We pay honor to heroes.* **Deference** = respect shown a person, or his age, position, or accomplishments, by putting his wishes or opinions before one's own: *In deference to his mother's wishes, he stopped smoking at the table.* **Homage** applies to honor paid with reverence: *He bowed in homage to the Unknown Soldier.*

hon·or·a·ble *or* **hon·our·a·ble** (on′ər ə bəl) *adj.* **1** having or showing a sense of what is right and proper; honest; upright. **2** causing honor; bringing honor to the one that has it; suffered under creditable circumstances. **3** accompanied by honor or honors: *an honorable burial, an honorable discharge.* **4** worthy of honor; to be respected; noble. **5** showing honor or respect. **6** having a title, rank, or position of honor. **7 Honorable,** See **Honourable.**
—**hon′or·a·ble·ness** *or* **hon′our·a·ble·ness,** *n.* —**hon′or·a·bly** *or* **hon′our·a·bly,** *adv.*

hon·o·rar·i·um (on′ə rer′ē əm) *n., pl.* **-rar·i·ums, -rar·i·a** (-rer′ē ə). an honorary fee for professional services on which no fixed price is set: *The guest speaker received an honorarium.* [< L *honorarium,* originally neut. of *honorarius* honorary]

hon·or·ar·y (on′ər er′ē) *adj.* **1** given as or done as an honor. **2** as an honor only; without pay or regular duties. Some associations have honorary secretaries, etc. as well as those who are regularly employed. **3** of an obligation, depending on one's honor for fulfillment, but not enforceable otherwise. [< L *honorarius* < *honos, honor* honor]

hon·or·if·ic (on′ər if′ik) *adj., n.* —*adj.* doing or giving honor;

showing respect or deference. —*n.* a title of respect. *Sir* is an honorific.

honors course or **honours course** a university program of study, usually taking a year or more longer than a general course, offered to superior scholars for specialization in certain major subjects.

honors degree or **honours degree** the university degree awarded to candidates successful in an honors course.

honors list or **honours list** **1** a list of persons receiving special honors or recognition. **2** *Esp.Brit.* a list of persons honored by the sovereign with titles or other distinctions.

honors of war or **honours of war** special favors or courtesies shown to a brave but defeated enemy.

honor system or **honour system** in schools and other institutions, a system of trusting people to obey the rules and do their work without being watched or forced.

hon·our (on′ər) See **honor.**

Hon·our·a·ble or **Hon·or·a·ble** (on′ər ə bəl) *adj.* **1** in Canada, a title given to members of the Privy Council (which includes the Federal Cabinet), to the Speakers of both the House of Commons and the provincial legislative assemblies, and to certain senior judges. **2** in Great Britain and elsewhere, a title of respect used under various conditions.
▸ *Usage.* **Honourable, Honorable.** The spelling *Honourable* is usually retained in Canada as an official title for Cabinet ministers, etc. *Abbrev.:* Hon.

hooch (hüch) See **hootch.**

hood¹ (hůd) *n., v.* —*n.* **1** a soft, loose, covering for the head and neck, either separate or as part of a cloak. **2** anything like a hood in shape or use. **3** a metal covering over the engine of an automobile. **4** *Falconry.* a cover for the head of a hawk, used to blind the hawk when not pursuing game. **5** a fold of cloth worn over an academic gown, having a band or bands of color to indicate the degree held and the university or college of the wearer. **6** a crest or other part on a bird's or animal's head that suggests a hood in shape, color, etc. **7** hood seal.
—*v.* cover or furnish with a hood. [OE *hōd*] —**hood′less,** *adj.* —**hood′like′,** *adj.*

hood² (hůd or hüd) *n. Slang.* **1** hoodlum (def. 1). **2** a criminal, especially one who uses force; thug; gunman; gangster.

–hood *noun-forming suffix.* **1** the state or condition of being, as in *boyhood, likelihood.* **2** the character or nature of, as in *manhood, sainthood.* **3** a group, body of, as in *priesthood, a sisterhood of noble women.* [OE *-hād* < *hād* state]

hood·ed (hůd′id) *adj.* **1** having a hood. **2** shaped like a hood.

hooded seal a large, grey hair seal (*Cystophora cristata*) of the North Atlantic and Arctic oceans, the adult males having a large nasal cavity that can be inflated to form a "hood" on top of the snout. Also called **hood seal.**

hood·lum (hüd′ləm) *n. Informal.* **1** a young rowdy; street ruffian. **2** a criminal, especially one who uses force; gangster. [probably < G (Bavarian dial.) *Hodalum, Huddellump*]

hoo·doo (hü′dü) *n., pl.* **-doos;** *v.* **-dooed, -doo·ing.** —*n.* **1** voodoo. **2** *Informal.* a person or thing that brings bad luck. **3** a natural pillar of rock, cemented gravel, or clay caused by erosion and often having a fantastic shape, found in western North America. Hoodoos are common in the Alberta badlands. **4** *Informal.* bad luck.
—*v. Informal.* bring or cause bad luck to. [? < var. of *voodoo*]

hood seal *Cdn.* hooded seal.

hood·wink (hůd′wingk′) *v.* **1** mislead by a trick; deceive. **2** *Archaic.* blindfold. [< *hood* + *wink,* make one wink (close the eyes) by covering with a hood] —**hood′wink·er,** *n.*

hoof (hüf or hůf) *n., pl.* **hoofs** or *(rare)* **hooves;** *v.* —*n.* **1** a hard, horny covering on the feet of horses, cattle, sheep, pigs, and some other animals. See **horse** for picture. **2** the whole foot of such animals. **3** *Slang.* the human foot.
on the hoof, of beef cattle, etc. alive; not killed and butchered.
—*v.* Also, **hoof it. 1** *Informal.* walk. **2** *Slang.* dance. **3** strike with the hoof. [OE *hōf*] —**hoof′less,** *adj.* —**hoof′like′,** *adj.*

hoof·beat (hüf′bēt′ or hůf′-) *n.* the sound made by an animal's hoofs.

hoofed (hüft or hůft) *adj.* having hoofs.

hoof·er (hüf′ər or hůf′ər) *n. Slang.* a professional dancer.

hook (hůk) *n., v.* —*n.* **1** a piece of metal, wood, or other stiff material, curved or having a sharp angle for catching, holding, or fastening something or for hanging things on: *a fishook, a clothes hook.* **2** a curved piece of wire, usually with a barb at the end, for catching fish. **3** a snare; trap. **4** anything curved or bent like a hook. **5** a large, curved knife for cutting down grass or grain. **6** a sharp bend. **7** a point of land. **8** the act of hooking. **9** *Sports.* the flight of a ball curving across the body of the person propelling it. Compare **slice** (def. 4). **10** *Boxing.* a short, swinging blow. **11** *Hockey.* an instance of hooking. **12** *Music.* a line on the stem of certain notes.

hat, āge, fär; let, ēqual, tėrm; it, īce
hot, ōpen, ôrder; oil, out; cup, půt, rüle,
ə above, takən, pencəl, lemən, circəs

ch, child; ng, long; sh, ship
th, thin; ŦH, then; zh, measure

by hook or by crook, in any way at all; by fair means or foul.
get the hook, *Slang.* be dismissed; lose one's job.
off the hook, *Informal.* free of responsibility; out of a predicament.
on (one's) own hook, *Informal.* independently.
—*v.* **1** attach or fasten with a hook or hooks. **2** join; fit; be fastened. **3** catch or take hold of with a hook. **4** catch (fish) with a hook. **5** give the form of a hook to. **6** be curved or bent like a hook. **7** catch by a trick. **8** *Informal.* steal. **9** make (rugs, etc.) by pulling loops of yarn or strips of cloth through canvas, burlap, etc. with a hook. **10** *Sports.* hit or throw (a ball) so that it curves across the body of the person propelling it. Compare **slice** (def. 7). **11** *Boxing.* hit with a short, swinging blow. **12** *Hockey.* impede the progress of a puck-carrier illegally by catching at his body from the side or rear with one's hockey stick.
hook it, *Slang.* run away.
hook up, a attach or fasten with a hook or hooks. **b** connect an electric light or appliance, or arrange and connect the parts of a radio set, telephone, etc.
[OE *hōc*] —**hook′like′,** *adj.*

hook·a (hůk′ə) See **hookah.**

hook·ah (hůk′ə) *n.* a tobacco pipe with a long tube by which the smoke is drawn through water for cooling; water pipe. Hookahs are used in the Orient. [< Arabic *huqqah* vase, pipe]

hook and eye a fastener for a garment, etc., consisting of a loop or bar and a hook that catches on it.

hooked (hůkt) *adj.* **1** curved or bent like a hook. **2** having hooks: *a hooked fastening on a dress.* **3** made with a hook; made by hooking: *A hooked rug is made by pulling yarn or strips of cloth through canvas, etc. with a hook.* **4** addicted, especially to drugs.

hook·er¹ (hůk′ər) *n.* **1** a person or thing that hooks. **2** *Informal.* thief; pilferer. **3** a drink of liquor: *a hooker of whisky.* **4** *Slang.* prostitute.

hook·er² (hůk′ər) *n.* **1** a small fishing boat. **2** an old-fashioned or clumsy ship. [apparently < Du. *hoeker, hoeckerschip* < *hoeck* hook; allusion uncertain]

hook·up (hůk′up′) *n.* the arrangement and connection of the parts of a radio or television set, telephone, broadcasting facilities, etc.

hook·worm (hůk′wėrm′) *n.* **1** any of various parasitic roundworms (family Ancylostomatidae) having hooked mouthparts by means of which they attach themselves to the intestinal lining to feed on blood and body fluids. The two species most commonly infesting man are *Necator americanus* of the S United States and Africa and *Ancylostoma duodenale* of Europe and Asia. **2** infestation with hookworms, producing anemia, fatigue and dullness, malnutrition, etc.

hook·y (hůk′ē) *n.* **play hooky,** *Informal.* stay away from school without permission; play truant.

hoo·li·gan (hü′lə gən) *n. Informal.* one of a gang of street ruffians; hoodlum. [? < an Irish surname]

hoo·li·gan·ism (hü′lə gən iz′əm) *n. Informal.* rough, noisy behavior; lawless fun.

hoop (hüp) *n.* **1** a ring or flat band in the form of a circle: *A hoop holds together the staves of a barrel.* **2** a large wooden, metal or plastic ring used as a toy: *The boy rolled his hoop along the sidewalk.* **3** a circular frame formerly used to spread out a woman's skirt. **4** *Croquet.* one of the metal arches through which players try to hit the balls. **5** anything shaped like a hoop.
—*v.* bind or fasten together with a hoop or hoops. [OE *hōp*] —**hoop′like′,** *adj.*
▸ *Hom.* **whoop.**

hoop·er (hüp′ər) *n.* a man who makes or repairs hoops on casks, barrels, etc.; cooper.

hoop·la (hüp′lä) *n. Slang.* **1** uproar; hullabaloo. **2** sensational advertising; ballyhoo. [originally, a coach driver's exclamation]

hoo·poe (hü′pü) *n.* a bird (*Upupa epops*) of S Europe, Africa, and Asia having pinkish-brown plumage with black-and-white wings, a fanlike crest, and a long, downward curving bill. It is the only member of its family (Upupidae). [earlier *hoop* < F *huppe* < L *upupa* (imitative of its call)]

hoop skirt a skirt worn over a framework of connected flexible hoops that make it spread out.

hoo·ray (hů rā′) *interj., n., or v.* hurrah.

hoose·gow (hüs′gau) *n. Slang.* jail. [< Mexican Sp. *juzgado* tribunal < pp. of *juzgar* to judge]

hoot (hüt) *n., v.* —*n.* **1** the sound that an owl makes. **2** a sound like that made by an owl: *the hoot of an automobile horn.* **3** a sound to show disapproval or scorn. **4** *Informal.* a tiny amount; a bit (*used only in the negative*): *He doesn't give a hoot what happens. That show wasn't worth a hoot.* **5** *Informal.* something causing laughter: *His clown costume was a hoot.*
—*v.* **1** make the sound that an owl makes or one like it. **2** show disapproval, scorn, or enjoyment by hooting: *The audience hooted the speaker's words. We hooted with laughter.* **3** force or drive by hooting: *They hooted her off the platform.* **4** say or show by hooting: *They hooted their scorn.* [ME *hute*(*n*); ? imitative] —**hoot′er,** *n.*

hootch (hüch) *n.* **1** hootchinoo. **2** *Slang.* any alcoholic liquor, especially cheap whisky. [shortening of *hootchinoo*]

hoo·tchi·noo (hü′chi nü′) *n.* in the Yukon and Alaska, a potent alcoholic liquor distilled illegally. [< *Hootchinoo*, an Indian people of S. Alaska < Tlingit *khutsnuwu* (literally, grizzly bear fort)]

hoo·te·nan·ny (hüt′nan′ē) *n., pl.* **-nies.** an informal party or jamboree featuring folk-singing. [developed from *hoot*]

hooves (hüvz *or* hùvz) *n.* a pl. of **hoof.**

hop¹ (hop) *v.* **hopped, hop·ping;** *n.* —*v.* **1** spring, or move by springing, on one foot. **2** spring, or move by springing, with both or all feet at once: *Many birds hop.* **3** jump over: *to hop a ditch.* **4** *Informal.* get on or in (a train, car, etc.): *I can just hop a bus and be there in 20 minutes.* **5** move or jump quickly onto, out of, etc.: *He hopped onto his bicycle and rode off. She hopped off the bus.* **6** *Informal.* fly across in an aircraft.
hop it, *Slang.* depart; go away.
—*n.* **1** a hopping; spring. **2** *Informal.* a flight in an airplane. **3** *Informal.* a dancing party: *the annual spring hop.* [OE *hoppian*]

hop² (hop) *n., v.* **hopped, hop·ping.** —*n.* **1** a vine (*Humulus lupulus*) of the mulberry family having flower clusters that look like small pine-cones. **2 hops,** *pl.* the dried, ripe, flower clusters of the hop vine, used to flavor beer and other malt drinks. —*v.* **1** pick hops. **2** flavor with hops. [< MDu. *hoppe*]

hope (hōp) *n., v.* **hoped, hop·ing.** —*n.* **1** an expectation that what one desires will happen. **2** a person or thing in which one places hope: *He is the hope of the family.* **3** something hoped for. **4** *Archaic.* trust; reliance.
—*v.* **1** wish and expect. **2** *Archaic.* trust; rely.
hope against hope, keep on hoping even though there is no good reason to have hope.
[OE *hopa*]

hope chest a chest in which a young woman collects articles that will be useful after she marries.

hope·ful (hōp′fəl) *adj., n.* —*adj.* **1** feeling or showing hope: *a hopeful smile. They were all in a hopeful frame of mind by morning.* **2** giving or inspiring hope: *The lessening of the fever was a hopeful sign.* —*n.* a person who expects or is likely to achieve something: *The room was filled with young hopefuls waiting for auditions.* —**hope′ful·ness,** *n.*

hope·ful·ly (hōp′fül ē) *adv.* **1** in a hopeful manner: *I went hopefully to my father.* **2** *Informal.* it is to be hoped: *Hopefully the weather will improve.*
☛ *Usage.* The use of **hopefully** (def. 2) to modify the idea behind a sentence rather than the actual verb is deplored by many critics and should be avoided in formal writing.

hope·less (hōp′lis) *adj.* **1** feeling no hope. **2** giving no hope: *a hopeless illness.* —**hope′less·ly,** *adv.* —**hope′less·ness,** *n.*
☛ *Syn.* **1. Hopeless** (def. 1), **desperate, despairing** = without hope. **Hopeless** suggests giving up completely: *He had been disappointed so often that he felt hopeless.* **Desperate** suggests a rash hopelessness, being without real hope but willing to run any risk to improve the situation: *The desperate gunman tried to shoot his way out of the trap.* **Despairing** = completely hopeless because unable to think of anything else to do or anywhere else to look for help: *Despairing of saving his business, he shot himself.*

Ho·pi (hō′pē) *n., pl.* **-pis. 1** a tribe of Pueblo Indians living mainly in stone-built towns in N Arizona. **2** a member of this tribe. **3** the language of this tribe.

hop·lite (hop′līt) *n.* in ancient Greece, a heavily armed foot soldier. [< Gk. *hoplitēs* < *hopla* arms]

hopped–up (hopt′up′) *adj. Slang.* **1** exhilarated; excited. **2** stimulated by drugs; high. **3** of engines, supercharged.

hop·per (hop′ər) *n.* **1** a person or thing that hops. **2** a grasshopper or other hopping insect. **3** a container, usually funnel-shaped, into which grain, corn, etc. is poured in order to be fed evenly into another container or a machine for grinding, mixing, etc.: *Some cement mixers are equipped with hoppers.*

hop·scotch (hop′skoch′) *n.* a children's game in which the players hop over the lines of a figure drawn on the ground. [< *hop¹* + *scotch* a scratch, line]

ho·ra (hôr′ə) *n.* **1** a Romanian and Israeli folk dance with a lively, syncopated rhythm. **2** the music for such a dance.

Ho·ra·tian (hə rā′shən) *adj.* of, like, or having to do with the Roman poet and satirist Horace (65-8 B.C.) or his poetry.

Ho·ra·tius (hə rā′shəs) *n. Roman legend.* a Roman hero who held back an invading Etruscan army until a bridge behind him was destroyed.

horde (hôrd) *n., v.* —*n.* **1** a crowd; swarm. **2** a wandering tribe or troop: *Hordes of Mongols and Turks invaded Europe during the Middle Ages.* —*v.* gather in a horde; live in a horde. [< F < G < Polish < Turkish *ordu* camp]
☛ *Hom.* **hoard.**

hore·hound (hôr′hound′) *n.* **1** a tall, Eurasian perennial herb (*Marrubium vulgare*) of the mint family having small white flowers and downy leaves. Also called **white horehound. 2** an extract from the leaves or flowers of this plant, used as a flavoring and also formerly in medicine. **3** candy or cough medicine flavored with this extract. **4** a Eurasian perennial herb (*Ballota nigra*), also of the mint family, having purple flowers and hairy leaves and an unpleasant smell. Also called **black horehound.** Also, **hoarhound.** [OE *hārhūne* < *hār* hoar + *hūne*, the name of a plant]

ho·ri·zon (hə rī′zən) *n.* **1** the line where the earth and sky seem to meet. You cannot see beyond the horizon. **2** Usually, **horizons,** pl. the limit of one's thinking, experience, interest, or outlook. **3** the actual or imaginary horizontal line in perspective drawing, etc., toward which receding parallel lines converge. It represents the eye level of the observer. **4** *Geology.* a distinct layer or group of layers of rock or soil. [ME < OF *orizonte* < L < Gk. *horizōn* (*kyklos*) bounding (circle), ult. < *horos* limit] —**ho·ri′zon·less,** *adj.*

VERTICAL
HORIZONTAL

hor·i·zon·tal (hôr′ə zon′təl) *adj., n.* —*adj.* **1** parallel to the horizon; at right angles to a vertical line. **2** flat; level: *You need a horizontal surface to work on.* **3** placed, acting, or working wholly or mainly in a horizontal direction: *A helicopter has horizontal rotors.* **4** of or having to do with the horizon; on, at, or near the horizon. **5** so organized as to include only one stage in production or one group of people or crafts: *a horizontal union, horizontal trusts.*
—*n.* something that is horizontal, such as a line, plane, direction, or position. —**hor′i·zon′tal·ly,** *adv.*

horizontal bar *Gymnastics.* a bar hung horizontally about 250 cm from the floor for chinning and other exercises.

hor·mone (hôr′mōn) *n.* **1** *Physiology.* a substance formed in certain parts of the body, which enters the blood stream and influences the activity of some organ. Adrenalin and insulin are hormones. **2** *Botany.* a substance carried in the sap of plants that acts similarly. **3** a synthetic substance that has the effect of a hormone. [< Gk. *hormōn* setting in motion, ult. < *hormē* impulse] —**hor·mo′nal,** *adj.*

horn (hôrn) *n., v.* —*n.* **1** a hard growth, usually curved and pointed, on the heads of cattle, sheep, goats, and certain other animals. **2** one of a pair of branching growths on the head of a deer, which fall off and grow afresh each year. **3** the tough fibrous material that horns are made of. A person's fingernails, the beaks of birds, the hoofs of horses, and tortoise shells are all made of horn. **4** anything that sticks up on the head of an animal: *a snail's horns, an insect's horns.* **5** something made, or formerly made, of horn. **6** a container made by hollowing out a horn: *a drinking horn, a powder horn.* **7** (*adj.*) made of horn. **8** a musical instrument shaped like a horn and formerly made of horn, sounded by blowing into the smaller end: *The brass section of an orchestra includes several kinds of horn.* **9** a device sounded as a warning signal: *a foghorn, an automobile horn.* **10** anything that projects like a horn or is shaped like a horn: *a saddle horn, the horn of a bay.* **11** either pointed tip of a new of old moon, or of some other crescent.
draw or **pull in** (one's) **horns, a** restrain oneself. **b** back down; withdraw.
horns of a dilemma, two unpleasant choices, one of which must be taken.
—*v.* **1** hit or wound with horns; gore. **2** furnish with horns.
horn in, *Slang.* meddle or intrude: *He kept trying to horn in on our conversation.*
[OE] —**horn′less,** *adj.* —**horn′like′,** *adj.*

horn·beam (hôrn′bēm′) *n.* any of a genus (*Carpinus*) of trees of the birch family found in north temperate regions, having smooth, grey bark and very hard white wood.

horn·bill (hôrn′bil′) *n.* any of a tropical Old World family

(Bucerotidae) of birds having a large bill which in some species has a bony lump, or casque, on the top of it.

horn·blende (hôrn'blend') *n.* a common black, dark-green, or brown mineral found in granite and other rocks. [< F]

horn·book (hôrn'bŏók') *n.* **1** a page with the alphabet, etc. on it, covered with a sheet of transparent horn and fastened in a frame with a handle, formerly used in teaching children to read. **2** an elementary treatise.

horned (hôrnd) *adj.* having a horn or horns.

horned lark a brown-and-white lark (*Eremophila alpestris*) found throughout much of the northern hemisphere, having black head and throat patches and small black tufts of feathers on either side of the head, resembling horns. The horned lark is found in open terrain throughout Canada, from the Arctic tundra south.

horned toad any of several small insect-eating lizards (genus *Phrynosoma*) of North America, having a broad, flat body, short tail, and many spines on the back and tail.

hor·net (hôr'nit) *n.* any of several large wasps (family Vespidae), mostly dark-colored, with white or yellow markings, that live in colonies above ground, in large roundish nests made of a papery material. Hornets often build their nests under the eaves of buildings. [OE *hyrnet(u)*; form influenced by E *horn*]

hornet's nest trouble in store; a situation likely to be troublesome.

stir up a hornet's nest, cause an outburst or angry reaction.

horn of plenty cornucopia (def. 2).

horn·pipe (hôrn'pīp') *n.* **1** a lively dance done by one person, formerly popular among sailors. **2** the music for it. **3** a musical wind instrument consisting of a wooden pipe with a bell-shaped end, used to accompany this dance.

horn·worm (hôrn'wèrm') *n.* a caterpillar of a hawk moth, having a smooth body and a hornlike projection at the back end.

horn·y (hôr'nē) *adj.* **horn·i·er, horn·i·est. 1** made of horn or a substance like it. **2** hard like horn: *The farmer's hands were horny from work.* **3** having a horn or horns. **4** *Slang.* sexually eager or excited; randy.

hor·o·loge (hôr'ə lōj' *or* hôr'ə loj') *n.* a timepiece; clock, sundial, hourglass, etc. [ME < OF *orloge* < L < Gk. *hōrologion* < *hōra* hour + *-logos* -telling]

ho·rol·o·ger (hō rol'ə jər) *n.* horologist.

ho·rol·o·gist (hō rol'ə jist) *n.* a person skilled in horology.

ho·rol·o·gy (hō rol'ə jē) *n.* **1** the science of measuring time. **2** the art of making timepieces. [< Gk. *hōra* time + E *-logy*]

hor·o·scope (hôr'ə skōp') *n. Astrology.* **1** the position of the planets and stars relative to each other at the hour of a person's birth, regarded as influencing his life. **2** a diagram of the heavens at given times, used in telling fortunes by the planets and the stars. **3** a fortune told by this means.

cast a horoscope, discover the influence that the stars and planets are supposed to have upon a person's life. [< L < Gk. *hōroskopos* < *hōra* time + *skopos* watcher]

ho·ros·co·py (hō ros'kə pē) *n.* **1** the practice of casting horoscopes. **2** the position of the planets, especially at a person's birth.

hor·ren·dous (hō ren'dəs) *adj.* horrible; terrible; frightful. [< L *horrendus*] —**hor·ren'dous·ly,** *adv.*

hor·ri·ble (hôr'ə bəl) *adj.* **1** causing horror; terrible; dreadful; frightful; shocking: *a horrible crime, a horrible disease.* **2** *Informal.* extremely unpleasant or amazing; *a horrible noise.* [ME < OF < L *horribilis* < *horrere* bristle] —**hor'ri·ble·ness,** *n.* —**hor'ri·bly,** *adv.*
☛ **Syn. 1.** See note at **ghastly.**

hor·rid (hôr'id) *adj.* **1** terrible; frightful. **2** *Informal.* very unpleasant: *a horrid little boy, a horrid day.* [< L *horridus*] —**hor'rid·ly,** *adv.* —**hor'rid·ness,** *n.*

hor·rif·ic (hō rif'ik) *adj.* producing horror; horrifying.

hor·ri·fy (hôr'ə fī') *v.* **-fied, -fy·ing. 1** cause to feel horror. **2** *Informal.* shock very much. [< L *horrificare*]

hor·ror (hôr'ər) *n.* **1** a shivering, shaking fear and dislike; terror and disgust caused by something frightful or shocking. **2** a very strong dislike; very great disgust. **3** the quality of causing horror. **4** a cause of horror. **5** *Informal.* something very bad or unpleasant. **the horrors,** *Informal.* **a** a fit of horror, as in delirium tremens. **b** extreme depressions; the blues.
[ME < OF < L *horror* < *horrere* bristle]

hors de com·bat (ôr də kôn bä') *French.* out of the fight; disabled.

hors d'oeu·vre (ôr' dèrv'; *French,* ôr dœ'vr) *pl.* **hors d'oeu·vres** (dèrvz'; *French,* dœ'vr). a relish or light food served before the regular courses of a meal: *Olives, celery, anchovies, etc. are often served as hors d'oeuvres.* [< F *hors d'œuvre,* literally, apart from (the main) work]

hat, āge, fär; let, ēqual, tèrm; it, īce
hot, ōpen, ôrder; oil, out; cup, pùt, rüle,
above, takən, pencəl, lemən, circəs
ch, child; ng, long; sh, ship
th, thin; ʈʜ, then; zh, measure

Horses: a draft horse (at left) and a racehorse

horse (hôrs) *n., pl.* **hors·es** *or* (*esp. collectively*) **horse;** *v.* **horsed, hors·ing.** —*n.* **1** a large four-legged animal (*Equus caballus*) with solid hoofs and a mane and tail of long, coarse hair. Horses have been used from very early times for riding and for carrying and pulling loads. **2** a full-grown male horse. **3** (*adj.*) designating a family (Equidae) of hoofed mammals, including the living and extinct horses, and the ass, onager, and zebras. **4** *Zoology.* any member of the horse family. **5** (*adj.*) of or having to do with horses. **6** soldiers on horses; cavalry: *a troop of horse.* **7** (*adj.*) on horses. **8** a piece of gymnasium apparatus to jump or vault over. **9** a frame with legs to support something; trestle.

a horse of a different color, something different.

hold (one's) horses, *Informal.* restrain oneself: *Hold your horses till we get there.*

on (one's) high horse, *Informal.* behaving in an arrogant or pretentious way: *He got up on his high horse and said he wasn't used to being treated that way.*

the horse's mouth, the original source; a well-informed source: *news straight from the horse's mouth.*

to horse! mount horses! get on horseback!
—*v.* **1** provide with a horse or horses. **2** put or go on horseback. **3** *Slang.* perform boisterously, as a part or a scene in a play. **horse around,** *Slang.* fool round; get into mischief. [OE *hors*]
☛ *Hom.* **hoarse.**

horse-and-bug·gy (hôrs' ən bug'ē) *adj.* outdated; old-fashioned: *horse-and-buggy ideas.*

horse·back (hôrs'bak') *n., adv.* —*n.* the back of a horse. —*adv.* on the back of a horse.

horse·boat (hôrs'bōt') *n. Historical.* a kind of ferry boat propelled by a paddle wheel that was turned by horses walking a treadmill on the boat. Horse-boats were used in Canada in the nineteenth century.

horse·car (hôrs'kär') *n.* **1** a streetcar pulled by a horse or horses. **2** a car used for transporting horses.

horse chestnut 1 a large tree (*Aesculus hippocastanium*) native to Europe and Asia, widely used in North America for ornament and shade, having showy spikes of white flowers and leaves made up of leaflets radiating out from the tip of the leaf stalk. The shiny brown seeds of the horse chestnut resemble chestnuts, but they are bitter and poisonous. **2** (*adj.*) designating the family (Hippocastanaceae) of trees and shrubs that includes the horse chestnut and the buckeyes.

horse·draw·ing (hôrs'dro'ing *or* -drô'ing) *n.* a contest in which horses or teams of horses draw increasingly heavier loads on a stoneboat until all but the strongest are eliminated. Also, **horsehauling.**

horse·flesh (hôrs'flesh') *n.* **1** horses for riding, driving, and racing. **2** meat from horses.

horse·fly (hôrs'flī') *n., pl.* **-flies.** any of a family (Tabanidae) of large, two-winged flies that suck the blood of horses, cattle, etc.

horse gentian feverwort.

horse·hair (hôrs'her') *n.* **1** the hair from the mane or tail of a horse. **2** a stiff fabric made of this hair. **3** (*adj.*) made of or stuffed with horsehair: *a horsehair sofa.*

horse·haul·ing (hôrs'hol'ing *or* -hôl'ing) *n.* horsedrawing.

horse·hide (hôrs′hīd′) *n.* **1** the hide of a horse. **2** leather made from this hide.

horse latitudes two regions where there is often very calm weather and that extend around the world at about 30° north and 30° south of the equator.

horse laugh *Informal.* a loud, boisterous laugh; guffaw.

horse·leech (hôrs′lēch′) *n.* **1** any of several large leeches (genus *Haemopis*) formerly thought to attach themselves to mouths of horses as they drank. **2** *Archaic.* veterinarian.

horse·less (hôrs′lis) *adj.* **1** without a horse. **2** not requiring a horse; self-propelled: *Automobiles used to be called horseless carriages.*

horse·man (hôrs′mən) *n., pl.* **-men.** **1** a man who rides on horseback. **2** a man skilled in riding or managing horses. **3** *Cdn. Slang.* a member of the Royal Canadian Mounted Police.

horse·man·ship (hôrs′mən ship′) *n.* the art of riding on horseback; skill in riding or managing horses.

horse marine *Humorous.* **1** a member of an imaginary corps of marines mounted on horseback, or cavalrymen doing duty on shipboard. **2** a person out of his natural surroundings.

horse·meat (hôrs′mēt′) *n.* the meat or flesh of a horse, especially when used for food.

horse opera *Slang.* a motion picture, radio or television drama, etc. about cowboys, horses, etc.; western.

horse pistol a large pistol formerly carried by horsemen.

horse·play (hôrs′plā′) *n.* rough, boisterous fun.

horse·pow·er (hôrs′pou′ər) *n.* a unit of power equal to 746 watts, used for measuring the power of engines, motors, etc.: *One horsepower is about three-quarters of a kilowatt; therefore, a 40 hp outboard motor would be about equal to a 30 kW outboard motor.* Symbol: hp

horse·rad·ish (hôrs′rad′ish) *n.* **1** a tall perennial herb (*Armoracia rusticana*) of the mustard family native to Europe and Asia, but widely cultivated for its pungent, thick, white root. **2** the root of this plant or a condiment made from it, used especially with beef.

horse sense *Informal.* common sense; plain, practical good sense.

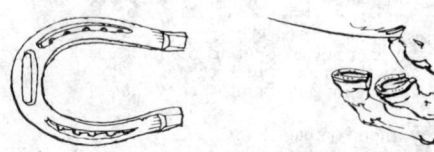

Horseshoes

horse·shoe (hôrs′shü′ or hôrsh′-) *n., v.* **-shoed, -shoe·ing.** —*n.* **1** a U-shaped metal plate nailed to a horse's hoof to protect it. **2** anything shaped like a horseshoe: *a horseshoe of flowers.* **3 horseshoes,** a game in which the players try to throw horseshoes over or near a stake 40 feet (about 12 m) away (*used with a singular verb*).
—*v.* put a horseshoe or horseshoes on.
☛ *Usage.* **Horseshoes** (def. 3), is plural in form and singular in use: *Horseshoes is often played by men.*

horseshoe crab **1** any of a genus (*Limulus*) of marine arthropods (order Xiphosura) found in shallow water along the east coasts of North America and Asia, having a body covered by a broad, rounded, domed carapace, and a long, slender tail spine. **2** any of various other living or extinct arthropods of the same order.

horse·tail (hôrs′tāl′) *n.* **1** any of a genus (*Equisteum*) of rushlike, perennial flowerless plants having hollow jointed stems surrounded by whorls of scalelike leaves. Horsetails are the only living members of the class Sphenopsida and belong to the same plant division as ferns and club mosses. **2** a horse's tail. **3** *Historical.* a stylized horsetail used as the emblem of a pasha in the Ottoman Empire.

horse trader **1** a buyer or seller of horses. **2** a shrewd negotiator.

horse·whip (hôrs′wip′ or -hwip′) *n., v.* **-whipped, -whip·ping.** —*n.* a whip for driving or controlling horses. —*v.* beat with a horsewhip.

horse·wom·an (hôrs′wùm′ən) *n., pl.* **-wom·en.** **1** a woman who rides on horseback. **2** a woman skilled in riding or managing horses.

hors·y (hôr′sē) *adj.* **hors·i·er, hors·i·est.** **1** of, like, or having to do with horses. **2** fond of horses or horse racing. **3** dressing or talking like people who spend much time with horses. **4** *Slang.* large and awkward in appearance. —**hors′i·ly,** *adv.* —**hors′i·ness,** *n.*

hor·ta·tive (hôr′tə tiv) *adj., n.* —*adj.* tending to exhort or encourage; hortatory. —*n.* an exhortation. —**hor′ta·tive·ly,** *adv.*

hor·ta·to·ry (hôr′tə tô′rē) *adj.* serving to urge or encourage; giving advice; exhorting. [< LL *hortatorius* < L *hortari* exhort]

hor·ti·cul·tur·al (hôr′tə kul′chər əl) *adj.* of or having to do with the growing of flowers, fruits, vegetables, plants, etc. —**hor′ti·cul′tur·al·ly,** *adv.*

hor·ti·cul·ture (hôr′tə kul′chər) *n.* the art or science of growing flowers, fruits, vegetables, etc. [< L *hortus* garden + E *culture*]

hor·ti·cul·tur·ist (hôr′tə kul′chər ist) *n.* a person trained in horticulture, especially one whose work it is.

Ho·rus (hô′rəs) *n.* a sun god of ancient Egypt, son of Osiris and Isis. Horus was represented as having the head of a hawk.

ho·san·na (hō zan′ə) *interj. or n.* **1** a shout of praise to the Lord. **2** a shout or praise, adoration, etc. [< LL < Gk. < Hebrew *hoshi'ahnna* save now, we pray]

hose (hōz) *n.pl.* (defs. 1 and 2), *n.sing., pl.* **hos·es** (def. 3); *v.* **hosed, hos·ing.** —*n.* **1** stockings or socks. **2** an outer garment formerly worn by men, extending from the waist to the knees or to the toes and covering each leg separately. Hose were attached to the doublet by laces or ribbons called points. **3** a tube made of rubber, plastic, canvas, or other material that will bend, used to carry water or other liquids for short distances.
—*v.* **1** put water on with a hose (*often used with* **down**): *She hosed down the lawn furniture.* **2** *Slang.* get the better of, especially by unfair means; cheat: *He said the team was tired of being hosed by the officials in the league.* [OE *hosa*]

ho·sen (hō′zən) *n.* archaic pl. of **hose** (def. 1).

ho·sier (hō′zhər) *n.* a person who makes or sells hosiery.

ho·sier·y (hō′zhər ē *or* hōzh′rē) *n.* **1** hose; stockings. **2** the business of a hosier.

hos·pice (hos′pis) *n.* **1** a house where travellers can lodge, especially such a house kept by monks. **2** an institution providing care for the terminally ill. [< F < L *hospitium* < *hospes, -pitis* guest, host[1]]

hos·pi·ta·ble (hos′pi tə bəl *or* hos pit′ə bəl) *adj.* **1** giving or liking to give a welcome, food and shelter, and friendly treatment to guests or strangers: *a hospitable family, reception, etc.* **2** willing and ready to consider; favorably receptive or open: *a person hospitable to new ideas.* [ME < L *hospitari* stay as a guest < *hospes, -pitis* guest, host[1]] —**hos′pi·ta·bly,** *adv.* —**hos′pi·ta·ble·ness,** *n.*

hos·pi·tal (hos′pi təl) *n.* **1** a place where sick or injured people are treated and cared for. **2** a similar place for sick or injured animals.
in hospital or **in the hospital,** in a hospital as a patient: *Two of the accident victims are in hospital with serious injuries.*
[ME < OF < Med.L *hospitale* inn, sing. of L *hospitalia* guest rooms, ult. < *hospes, -pitis* guest, host[1]. Doublet of HOSTEL, HOTEL.]

Hos·pi·tal·er (hos′pi tə lər) *n.* See **Hospitaller.**

hos·pi·tal·i·ty (hos′pə tal′ə tē) *n., pl.* **-ties.** friendly, generous reception and treatment of guests or strangers. [< L *hospitalitas* < *hospes* guest, host[1]]

hospitality suite *Cdn.* at a convention, conference, etc., a room or suite where free refreshments are offered, especially alcoholic drinks.

hos·pi·tal·ize (hos′pi təl īz′) *v.* **-ized, -iz·ing.** put in a hospital to be treated or cared for. —**hos′pi·tal·i·za′tion,** *n.*

Hos·pi·tal·ler or **Hos·pi·tal·er** (hos′pi tə lər) *n.* **1** a member of a military religious order, the Knights of the Hospital of St. John of Jerusalem (also called Knights Hospitallers), founded by crusaders in the 11th century. **2** a member of any religious order founded to take care of the sick, or for other charitable purposes.

hoss (hos) *n. Dialect.* horse.

host[1] (hōst) *n., v.* —*n.* **1** a person who receives another at his house as his guest. **2** the keeper of an inn or hotel. **3** *Biology.* a plant or animal in or on which a parasite lives: *The oak tree is the host of the mistletoe that grows on it.*
reckon without (one's) **host, a** overlook the chances of one's plans going wrong. **b** calculate one's bill or score without consulting the host or landlord.
—*v.* act as host. [ME < OF < L *hospes, -pitis* guest, host]

host[2] (hōst) *n.* **1** a large number; multitude: *A host of stars glittered in the sky.* **2** army. [ME < OF < LL *hostis* army < L *hostis* enemy (originally, stranger)]

Host (hōst) *n. Roman Catholic Church.* the bread or wafer used in the Mass. [ME < OF *oiste* < L *hostia* animal sacrificed; form influenced by *host*[1]]

hos·tage (hos′tij) *n.* **1** a person given up to another or held by an enemy as a pledge that certain promises, agreements, etc. will be carried out. **2** the state or condition of such a person. **3** a pledge; security.
give hostages to fortune, have persons or things that one may lose. [ME < OF *hostage, ostage* status of guest, status of hostage, *hostage < oste* guest < L *hospes, -pitis*]

hos·tel (hos′təl) *n.* **1** a lodging place, especially a supervised lodging place for young travellers, students, or vagrants. **2** an inn; hotel. [ME < OF *hostel, ostel* < Med.L *hospitale* inn. Doublet of HOSPITAL, HOTEL.]

hos·tel·ry (hos′təl rē) *n., pl.* **-ries.** an inn; hotel.

hostel school *Cdn. North.* residential school.

host·ess (hōs′tis) *n., v.* —*n.* **1** a woman who receives another person as her guest. **2** a woman who keeps an inn or hotel, or helps her husband to do so. **3** a woman who greets customers in a restaurant, night club, etc. and, usually, shows them to a table. **4** a woman who looks after passengers on an airplane, train, etc. —*v.* act as a hostess.

hos·tile (hos′til *or* hos′təl) *adj.* **1** of or having to do with an enemy or enemies: *the hostile army.* **2** opposed; unfriendly: *a hostile look.* **3** unfavorable; harsh: *a hostile climate.* [< L *hostilis* < *hostis* enemy] —**hos′tile·ly,** *adv.*
☛ *Syn.* **2. Hostile, unfriendly, inimical** = not friendly or favorable. **Hostile,** describing people or things, emphasizes being opposed, either actively unfriendly in purpose or spirit or openly acting against a person or thing: *Their hostile looks showed that he was unwelcome.* **Unfriendly** places less emphasis on active ill will, and suggests being unwilling to be agreeable, kindly, helpful, or encouraging in any way: *A cold, damp climate is unfriendly to tuberculosis.* **Inimical,** a formal word meaning "hostile," particularly suggests having harmful effects: *Jealousy is inimical to friendship.*

hos·til·i·ty (hos til′ə tē) *n., pl.* **-ties. 1** the feeling that an enemy has; the state of being an enemy; unfriendliness. **2** the state of being at war. **3** opposition; resistance. **4** a hostile act. **5 hostilities,** *pl.* acts of war; warfare; fighting.

hos·tler (os′lər *or* hos′lər) *n.* a person who takes care of horses at an inn or stable. Also, **ostler.** [var. of *ostler* < OF *hostelier* < *hostel.* See HOSTEL.]

hot (hot) *adj.* **hot·ter, hot·test;** *adv.* —*adj.* **1** much warmer than the body; having much heat: *That fire is hot.* **2** having a relatively high temperature: *This food is too hot to eat.* **3** giving or capable of giving a feeling of bodily heat: *a hot flush. This coat is too hot for summer wear.* **4** full of any strong feeling; passionate, violent, angry, etc.: *hot with rage.* **5** full of great interest or enthusiasm; very eager. **6** intense; violent: *a hot fight.* **7** new; fresh: *a hot scent or trail.* **8** near or approaching an object or answer sought. **9** following closely: *in hot pursuit.* **10** radio-active: *hot debris left by a nuclear explosion.* **11** electrically charged. **12** of jazz, played or playing with exciting variations from the score. **13** open and ready for instantaneous use: *the hot line between the White House and the Kremlin.* **14** *Slang.* obtained illegally; stolen: *hot diamonds.* **15** *Slang.* wanted by the police. **16** *Slang.* likely to win or succeed; difficult to beat, stop, or hinder: *a hot favorite, a hot team.*
make it hot for, *Informal.* make trouble for; make things unpleasant or uncomfortable for.
—*adv.* in a hot manner: *The sun beats hot upon the sand.*
blow hot and cold, waver in mind or opinion; vacillate.
[OE *hāt*] —**hot′ly,** *adv.* —**hot′ness,** *n.*

hot air *Slang.* empty, pompous talk or writing.

hot·bed (hot′bed′) *n.* **1** a bed of earth covered with glass and kept warm for the growing of plants. **2** any place favorable to rapid growth: *These slums are a hotbed of crime.*

hot·blood·ed (hot′blud′id) *adj.* **1** easily excited or angered. **2** rash; reckless. **3** passionate.

hot·box (hot′boks′) *n.* an overheated bearing on a shaft or axle.

hot cake a flapjack or pancake.
go or **sell like hot cakes, a** be sold quickly. **b** be in great demand.

hotch·potch (hoch′poch′) *n.* hodgepodge.

hot cross bun a bun marked with a cross, eaten during Lent, especially on Good Friday.

hot dog 1 wiener. **2** a sandwich made of a hot wiener enclosed in a long roll and usually served with mustard, relish, etc.

ho·tel (hō tel′) *n.* **1** a building where rooms may be rented and meals bought on a day-to-day basis. **2** *Cdn. Informal.* a place where beer and wine are sold for drinking on the premises; beer parlor. [< F *hôtel* < OF *hostel* < Med.L *hospitale* inn. Doublet of HOSPITAL, HOSTEL.]

hô·tel de ville (ō tel də vēl′) *French.* city hall; town hall.

ho·tel·ier (hō tel′yā *or* hō tel′yər) *n.* the owner or manager of a hotel.

hot·foot (hot′fut′) *adv., v. Informal.* —*adv.* in great haste: *She went hotfoot up the stairs with me after her.* —*v.* go in great haste; hurry (*usually used with* **it**): *We hotfooted it out to the airport.*

hat, āge, fär; let, ēqual, tèrm; it, īce
hot, ōpen, ôrder; oil, out; cup, pút, rüle,
əbove, takən, pencəl, lemən, circəs
ch, child; ng, long; sh, ship
th, thin; ᴛʜ, then; zh, measure

hot–head (hot′hed′) *n.* a hot-headed person.

hot–head·ed (hot′hed′id) *adj.* **1** having a fiery temper; easily angered. **2** impetuous; rash. —**hot′-head′ed·ly,** *adv.*
—**hot′-head′ed·ness,** *n.*

hot–house (hot′hous′) *n.* **1** a greenhouse that is heated for growing plants out of season or for growing tropical plants in a colder climate. **2** (*adj.*) grown in a hothouse: *hothouse tomatoes.* **3** (*adj.*) needing nurturing or careful handling, as if in a hothouse; delicate or sensitive: *She's no hothouse creature.*

hot–line or **hot-line** (hot′līn′) *n.* **1** a direct means of communication for use in emergencies, especially between heads of state of different countries. **2** (*adj.*) of, having to do with, or being a radio or television show which broadcasts the comments of members of the public who phone in to express their views, especially on a controversial subject. **3** a hot-line radio or television show.

hot–lin·er or **hot-lin·er** (hot′līn′ər) *n.* a person who conducts, or hosts, a hot-line show on radio or television.

hot pepper 1 any of various strong peppers, especially chili. **2** a plant producing hot peppers.

hot plate 1 a small, portable, gas or electric stove for cooking. **2** a heated metal plate for cooking food or keeping it hot.

hot potato *Slang.* something too controversial or too complex to handle.

hot·press (hot′pres′) *n.* a machine in which heat and pressure are applied together.

hot rod *Slang.* a rebuilt or modified automobile with a supercharged engine.

hot rodder (rod′ər) *Slang.* a person who drives a hot rod.

hot seat 1 *Slang.* electric chair. **2** an embarrassing predicament. **3** the chair occupied by the victim of an aggressive type of interview.
in the hot seat, in a situation in which one is subject to aggressive and searching questioning.

hot·shot (hot′shot′) *n. Slang.* **1** a person who is skilful or competent in a flashy and often aggressive way. **2** (*adj.*) of or characteristic of a hotshot: *a hotshot young politician.*

hot spot 1 an exciting and fashionable nightclub, resort, etc. **2** a local place or region of potential or actual unrest or violence. **3** a local area showing significant radio-activity.

hot spring Usually, **hot springs,** *pl.* a natural spring whose water has a higher temperature than the average temperature of its locality, especially one having water above 37°C.

hot·spur (hot′spèr′) *n.* an impetuous or reckless person. [< *Hotspur,* the nickname of Sir Henry Percy (1364-1403), portrayed as an impetuous character in Shakespeare's *Henry IV,* Part I]

hot–tem·pered (hot′tem′pərd) *adj.* having a quick temper; easily angered.

Hot·ten·tot (hot′ən tot′) *n.* **1** a member of a people of southern Africa. **2** the language of the Hottentots. —*adj.* of or having to do with the Hottentots or their language. [native word]

hot war a war involving actual fighting. Compare **cold war.**

hot water *Informal.* trouble.

hou·dah (hou′də) See **howdah.**

hough (hok) See **hock¹.**

hound (hound) *n., v.* —*n.* **1** any of various breeds of hunting dog, most of which hunt by scent and have large, drooping ears and short hair. **2** any dog. **3** *Slang.* a person who is very keen about pursuing or getting something: *an autograph hound, a news hound.* **4** a contemptible person.
follow the hounds or **ride to hounds,** go hunting on horseback with hounds.
—*v.* **1** keep on chasing or driving: *The police hounded the thief until they caught him.* **2** urge (on) continually or repeatedly; keep urging or pestering: *His parents hounded him to do his homework.* [OE *hund*]

hound's tooth or **hounds–tooth** (houndz′tüth′) *adj.* of textiles, having a pattern of broken checks.

hour (our) *n.* **1** a unit used with the SI for measuring time, equal to 3600 seconds or 60 minutes: *There are 24 hours in a day. Symbol:* h **2** one of the 12 points that measure time from noon to

midnight and from midnight to noon: *Some clocks strike the hours and the half-hours.* **3** the time of day: *The hour is 7:30.* **4** a particular or fixed time: *Our breakfast hour is at seven o'clock.* **5** a short or limited space of time: *After his hour of glory, he was soon forgotten.* **6** a period in a classroom, often less than a full hour. **7** the present time: *questions of the hour, the man of the hour.* **8** 15 degrees of longitude. **9** hours, *pl.* **a** the time for work, study, etc.: *Our school hours are 9 to 12 and 1 to 4.* **b** the usual times for going to bed and getting up. **c** seven special times of the day set aside for prayer and worship. **d** the prayers or services for these times. **e** **Hours,** the Greek goddesses of the seasons, orderliness, justice, and peace.

in an evil hour, at a bad or unlucky time.
[ME < OF *hure* < L < Gk. *hōra* season, time, hour]
☛ *Hom.* **our.**
☛ *Usage.* **Hours.** In very formal writing, hours are written in words: *four o'clock.* In most informal writing, figures are used with the abbreviations "a.m." and "p.m.," especially if several times are mentioned.

hour·glass (our′glas′) *n.* **1** a device for measuring time, consisting of two glass bulbs joined by a very narrow neck and containing a quantity of fine sand or other material that takes one hour to run from the upper bulb through the neck to the lower one. When the contents have run through, the hourglass can be reversed. **2** (*adj.*) resembling an hourglass in shape, with a very narrow central section: *an hourglass figure.*

hour hand the short hand on a clock or watch, which moves around the whole dial once in twelve hours.

hou·ri (hür′ē or hou′rē) *n., pl.* **-ris.** **1** one of the young, eternally beautiful maidens promised in the Koran to the faithful in paradise. **2** a beautiful and alluring woman. [< F < Persian *huri* < Arabic *haura* (*hawira* with eyes like gazelle's)]

hour·ly (our′lē) *adj., adv.* —*adj.* **1** done, happening, or counted every hour: *hourly news reports, an hourly wage.* **2** coming very often; frequent. —*adv.* **1** every hour; hour by hour. **2** very often; frequently.

house (*n.* hous; *v.* houz) *n., pl.* **hous·es** (houz′iz); *v.* **housed, hous·ing.** —*n.* **1** a building designed for people to live in, especially one for a single family. **2** the people living in a house; household: *The whole house was awake by 7 o'clock.* **3** an abode; habitation. **4** a building to hold anything: *an engine house.* **5** an assembly for making laws and considering questions of government; lawmaking body: *the House of Commons.* **6** the building in which such an assembly meets. **7** a place of business. **8** a business firm. **9** a place of entertainment; theatre. **10** an audience; attendance: *A large house heard the singer.* **11** a family regarded as consisting of ancestors, descendants, and kindred, especially a noble or royal family: *He was a prince of the house of Hanover.* **12** a religious order. **13** *Curling.* the goal or target.

bring down the house, *Informal.* be loudly applauded.
clean house, a set a house in order. **b** get rid of bad conditions; set a business, institution, etc. in order.
keep house, manage a home and its affairs.
on the house, free; paid for by the owner of the business: *After visiting the candy factory, we were each given a box of chocolates on the house.*
put or **set** (one's) **house in order,** arrange one's affairs in good order.
—*v.* **1** put or receive into a house; provide with a house: *Where can we house all these children?* **2** give shelter to; lodge. **3** place in a secure or protected position. **4** take shelter. [OE *hūs*]

house·boat (hous′bōt′) *n.* a boat that can be used as a place to live in.

house·bound (hous′bound′) *adj.* confined to the house; not able to leave one's house: *He is housebound because of his arthritis.*

house·break·er (hous′brāk′ər) *n.* a person who breaks into a house to steal or commit some other crime.

house·break·ing (hous′brāk′ing) *n.* *Law.* the act of breaking and entering a dwelling for an unlawful purpose. —**house′break′er,** *n.*

house·bro·ken (hous′brō′kən) *adj.* of a pet such as a dog or cat, trained to urinate and defecate only outdoors or in a special place indoors.

house·coat (hous′kōt′) *n.* a woman's loose, informal garment, usually having a long skirt, for wearing at home.

house·fly (hous′flī′) *n., pl.* **-flies.** a two-winged fly (*Musca domestica*) that lives around and in houses, feeding on food and garbage. Its larvae (maggots) develop in decaying organic matter.

house·hold (hous′hōld′) *n.* **1** all the people living in a house; family; family and servants. **2** a home and its affairs. **3** (*adj.*) of or having to do with a household; domestic: *household expenses, household cares.* **4** (*adj.*) common or familiar: *a household word.*

house·hold·er (hous′hōl′dər) *n.* **1** a person who owns or lives in a house. **2** the head of a family.

household word any very familiar word or phrase.

house·keep·er (hous′kēp′ər) *n.* a woman who manages a home and its affairs and does the housework, especially one hired to do so.

house·keep·ing (hous′kēp′ing) *n.* **1** the managing of a home and its affairs. **2** the internal operations and management of an organization or business.

house·leek (hous′lēk′) *n.* any of a genus (*Sempervivum*) of Old World plants having thick, fleshy leaves growing in rosettes around the stems, especially a pink-flowered species (*S. tectorum*) often grown as a garden plant. Houseleeks spread by means of runners.

house·maid (hous′mād′) *n.* a female servant who does housework.

housemaid's knee an inflammation near the knee, usually caused by much kneeling.

house·mas·ter (hous′mas′tər) *n.* a teacher in charge of a residence hall in a boarding school.

house·moth·er (hous′muᴛн′ər) *n.* a woman who supervises and takes care of a group of people living together as a family.

House of Assembly in Newfoundland, the provincial legislature consisting of 36 elected members.

house of cards anything that can be easily knocked down; flimsy structure.

House of Commons **1** in Canada, the elected representatives who meet in Ottawa to make laws and debate questions of government. There are 282 members of the House of Commons. **2** the chamber in which the representatives, or members, meet. **3** in the United Kingdom, the elected members of Parliament. **4** the buildings in which these members meet.

house of correction *Archaic.* any of various institutions for the confinement of juvenile offenders or other persons who have committed minor offences, such as a training school or reformatory.

house of God a place of worship; church; temple.

House of Lords in the United Kingdom, the upper, non-elective branch of the lawmaking body, composed of nobles and clergymen of high rank.

House of Representatives **1** in the United States: **a** the lower branch of the federal lawmaking body. **b** the chamber in which the representatives meet. **c** the lower branch of the lawmaking body of certain states. **2** the lower branch of the Parliament of Australia, or of the General Assembly of New Zealand.

house·par·ent (house′per′ənt) *n.* one of a married couple in charge of a residence at a school, college, or other institution.

house party **1** the entertainment of guests in a home, especially for a few days. **2** a group of guests thus entertained.

house physician a resident physician of a hotel, hospital, etc.

house plant a plant grown indoors in a pot or planter. Tropical plants, such as African violets and philodendrons, are popular as house plants in colder climates.

house–proud (hous′proud′) *adj.* proud of the appearance of one's house, especially to the point of being too fussy or fastidious.

house·room (hous′rüm′ *or* -rüm′) *n.* room or space in a house.

house sparrow English sparrow.

house-to-house (hous′tə hous′) *adv., adj.* from one house to the next, stopping at each in turn: *a house-to-house campaign.*

house·top (hous′top′) *n.* the top of a house; roof.

house·wares (hous′werz′) *n.pl.* equipment, etc. for a household, especially dishes, kitchen utensils and tools, small appliances, etc.

house·warm·ing (hous′wôr′ming) *n.* a party given when a person or family moves into a new residence.

house·wife (hous′wīf′ *for* 1; huz′if *for* 2) *n., pl.* **-wives** (huz′ifs *for* 2). **1** a woman who manages a home and its affairs for her husband, children, etc. **2** a small case for needles, thread, etc.

house·wife·ly (hous′wīf′lē) *adj.* of or like a housewife; thrifty or skilled in household affairs.

house·wif·er·y (hous′wīf′ər ē *or* -wīf′rē) *n.* the work of a housewife; housekeeping.

house·work (hous′wėrk′) *n.* the work to be done in housekeeping, such as washing, ironing, cleaning, and cooking.

hous·ing[1] (houz′ing) *n.* **1** the act of sheltering; providing houses as homes. **2** houses. **3** a shelter; covering. **4** a frame or plate for holding together and protecting the parts of a machine.

hous·ing[2] (houz′ing) *n.* an ornamental covering for a horse:

Under the saddle was a housing of red velvet. [< *house* covering < OF *houce* < Gmc.]

hove (hōv) *v.* a pt. and a pp. of **heave.**

hov·el (hov′əl *or* huv′əl) *n.* **1** a house that is small, crude, and unpleasant to live in. **2** an open shed for sheltering cattle, storing tools, etc. [ME; origin uncertain]

hov·er (hov′ər *or* huv′ər) *v.* **1** stay in or near one place in the air: *The humming bird hovered in front of the flower.* **2** stay in or near one place; wait nearby: *The dogs hovered around the kitchen door at mealtime.* **3** be in an uncertain condition; waver: *The sick man hovered between life and death.* [ME *hover(en)* < *hoven* hover; origin uncertain]

hov·er·craft (hov′ər kraft′ *or* huv′ər-) *n.* **1** a motorized vehicle capable of travelling just above the surface of water or land on a cushion of air created by powerful fans. **2 Hovercraft,** *Trademark.* a make of such a vehicle.

how (hou) *adv., n.* —*adv.* **1** in what way; by what means: *Tell her how to do it.* **2** to what degree, extent, etc.: *How long will it take you to do this?* **3** at what price: *How do you sell these apples?* **4** in what state or condition: *Tell me how Mrs. Jones is.* **5** for what reason; why: *How is it you are late?* **6** to what effect; with what meaning; by what name: *How do you mean?*
how come? *Informal.* What is the reason or cause? Why: *How come you didn't call last night?*
how now? what does this mean?
how so? why is it so?
how then? what does this mean?
—*n.* a way or manner of doing: *She considered all the hows and wherefores.* [OE *hū*]

how·be·it (hou bē′it) *adv. Archaic.* however it may be; nevertheless; however.

how·dah (hou′də) *n.* a seat for riding on an elephant's back, usually having a canopy and seating two or more persons. Also, **houdah.** [< Hind. *haudah* < Arabic *haudaj*]

how·e'er (hou er′) *conj. or adv. Poetic.* however.

how·ev·er (hou ev′ər) *conj., adv.* —*conj.* nevertheless; yet; in spite of that: *It is his; however, you may borrow it.* —*adv.* **1** to whatever extent, degree, or amount; no matter how: *However you do it, the effect will be the same.* **2** in whatever way; by whatever means: *However did you manage to get here?*
☛ *Syn. conj.* See note at **but.**

how·itz·er (hou′it sər) *n.* a short artillery piece for firing shells in a high curve. [earlier *howitz* < Du. < G *Haubitze* < Czech *houfnice* catapult]

howl (houl) *v., n.* —*v.* **1** give a long, loud, mournful cry: *Dogs and wolves howl.* **2** give a long, loud cry of pain, rage, distress, etc. **3** yell; shout: *It was so funny that we howled with laughter.* **4** force or drive by howling: *The angry mob howled the speaker off the platform.*
howl down, drown out the words of by howling.
—*n.* **1** a long, loud, mournful cry. **2** a loud cry of pain, rage, etc. **3** a yell of scorn, amusement, etc. **4** a yell; shout. **5** *Informal.* something causing laughter: *The skit by the teachers was a howl.* [ME *houle(n)*]

howl·er (houl′ər) *n.* **1** a person or thing that howls. **2** *Informal.* a ridiculous mistake; stupid blunder.

how·so·ev·er (hou′sō ev′ər) *adv.* **1** to whatever extent, degree, or amount; however. **2** in whatever way; by whatever means; however.

hoy·den (hoi′dən) *n.* a boisterous, romping girl; tomboy. Also, **hoiden.** [origin uncertain]

hoy·den·ish (hoi′dən ish) *adj.* of or like a hoyden; boisterous; romping. Also, **hoidenish.**

Hoyle (hoil) *n.* a book of rules and instructions for playing card games.
according to Hoyle, according to the rules or customs; fair; correct. [< Edmond *Hoyle* (1672-1769), an English writer on card games]

hp horsepower.

HP, H.P., *or* **h.p. 1** high pressure. **2** horsepower.

HQ headquarters.

hr. hour.

h.r. *Baseball.* home run.

HRC *or* **H.R.C.** Humanities Research Council.

H.R.H. His Royal Highness; Her Royal Highness.

H.S. *or* **HS** High School.

ht. 1 height. **2** heat.

Hts. Heights.

hub (hub) *n.* **1** the central part of a wheel. See **wheel** for picture. **2** any centre of interest, importance, activity, etc.: *London is the hub of the Commonwealth.* [var. of *hob¹*; origin uncertain]

hat, āge, fär; let, ēqual, tèrm; it, īce
hot, ōpen, ôrder; oil, out; cup, put, rüle,
əbove, takən, pencəl, lemən, circəs

ch, child; ng, long; sh, ship
th, thin; ᴛʜ, then; zh, measure

hub·ble (hub′əl) *n.* a small hump. [< *hubbly* rough, uneven, var. of E dial. *hobbly* < *hobble,* in the meaning "move unsteadily up and down"]

hub·bub (hub′ub) *n.* a noisy tumult; uproar. [imitative]

hu·bris (hyü′bris) *n.* insolence; arrogance; wanton or contemptuous pride. [< Gk. *hybris*]

huck·a·back (huk′ə bak′) *n.* a heavy, coarse, linen or cotton cloth with a rough surface, used for towels. [origin uncertain]

huck·le·ber·ry (huk′əl ber′ē) *n., pl.* **-ries. 1** any of a genus (*Gaylussacia*) of New World shrubs of the heath family bearing sweet, edible, dark-blue berries resembling blueberries. **2** the berry of any of these shrubs. [apparently alteration of *hurtleberry* < *hurtle* (dim. of E dial. *hurt,* OE *horte* whortleberry) + *berry*]

huck·ster (huk′stər) *n., v.* —*n.* **1** peddler. **2** a person who sells small articles. **3** *Esp.U.S. Informal.* a person who is in the advertising business. **4** a mean and unfair trader.
—*v.* sell; peddle; haggle. [cf. MDu. *hokester,* originally fem. Akin to HAWKER¹.]

hud·dle (hud′əl) *v.* **-dled, -dling;** *n.* —*v.* **1** crowd close: *The sheep huddled in a corner of the pen.* **2** crowd or put close together: *She huddled all four boys into one bed.* **3** curl oneself up: *The rescued swimmer sat huddled in a blanket by the fire.* **4** of football players, group together behind the line of scrimmage to receive signals.
—*n.* **1** a confused heap or mass of people or things crowded together. **2** *Football.* a grouping of players behind the line of scrimmage to receive signals, plan the next play, etc. **3** *Informal.* a secret conference: *The management has gone into a huddle about a new pricing policy.* **4** confusion. [cf. ME *hodre(n),* of the same meaning]

Hudson's Bay Company a trading company chartered by Charles II in 1670, as the Company of Adventurers of England trading into Hudson's Bay, to carry on the fur trade with the Indians of North America. The Hudson's Bay Company played a great part in the exploration and development of Canada's Northwest. [< Henry *Hudson,* died 1611, an English navigator and explorer]

Hudson seal muskrat fur that is dyed and processed to look like seal.

hue¹ (hyü) *n.* **1** that property of color by which it can be distinguished from grey of equal brightness; color; shade; tint: *all the hues of the rainbow.* **2** a variety of a color; a particular color. [OE *hīw*]
☛ *Hom.* **hew.**
☛ *Syn.* See note at **color.**

hue² (hyü) *n. Archaic* (except in **hue and cry**). shouting.
hue and cry, a shouts of alarm or protest. **b** an outcry or alarm formerly raised to call people to pursue a criminal, in which they were obliged by law to join. **c** the pursuit of a criminal in this way. [< F *hu* < *huer* shout]
☛ *Hom.* **hew.**

huff (huf) *n., v.* —*n.* a fit of anger or peevishness. —*v.* **1** make angry; offend. **2** *Dialect.* puff; blow. [imitative]

huff·y (huf′ē) *adj.* **huff·i·er, huff·i·est. 1** offended. **2** tending to be easily offended; touchy. —**huff′i·ly,** *adv.* —**huff′i·ness,** *n.*

hug (hug) *v.* **hugged, hug·ging;** *n.* —*v.* **1** put the arms around and hold close, especially in affection; embrace: *She hugged her sister and wished her good luck.* **2** squeeze tightly between the forelegs, as a bear does. **3** cling firmly or fondly to: *They still hug their belief in his story.* **4** keep close to: *The boat hugged the shore.*
—*n.* **1** a tight clasp with the arms. **2** a tight squeeze with the arms especially as a grip in wrestling. [apparently < ON *hugga* to comfort]

huge (hyüj) *adj.* **hug·er, hug·est. 1** extremely large in size, quantity, etc.: *A whale or an elephant is a huge animal.* **2** unusually great in extent, scope, degree, or capacity: *a huge undertaking.* [ME < OF *ahuge*] —**huge′ly,** *adv.* —**huge′ness,** *n.*
☛ *Syn.* **Huge, enormous, immense. Huge** is the most general word: *A St. Bernard is a huge dog.* **Enormous** implies "abnormally or excessively large or great": *enormous dimensions.* **Immense** often carries the original sense of being so large or great as to be impossible to measure by ordinary standards: *an immense body of water.*

hug·ger-mug·ger (hug′ər mug′ər) *n., adj., adv. Informal.* —*n.* confusion; disorder.
—*adj.* confused, disorderly.

—*adv.* in a confused, disorderly manner. [origin uncertain]

Hu·gue·not (hyü′gə not′ *or* hyü′gə nō′) *n.* **1** a Calvinistic French Protestant of the 16th and 17th centuries. **2** any member of a church founded by John Calvin. [< F *huguenot*, earlier *eigenot* (< Swiss G *Eidgenoss* confederate < *Eid* oath + *Genoss* comrade), influenced by the name of *Hugues* Besançon, a party leader; originally applied to Genevans who were partisans against the Duke of Savoy]

huh (hu) *interj.* a sound made to express surprise, contempt, etc., or to ask a question.

hu·la (hü′lə) *n.* **1** a native Hawaiian dance characterized by rhythmic movement of the hips and hand gestures that tell a story. **2** the music for this dance. [< Hawaiian]

hula hoop a plastic hoop designed to be rotated around the body by swinging the hips.

hu·la–hu·la (hü′lə hü′lə) *n.* hula.

hulk (hulk) *n., v.* —*n.* **1** the body of an old or worn-out ship. **2** a ship used as a prison. **3** a big, clumsy ship. **4** a big, clumsy person or thing.
—*v.* **1** be bulky or unwieldy; loom bulkily. **2** lounge or slouch clumsily or boorishly. [OE *hulc*, ? < Med.L < Gk. *holkas* merchant ship]

hulk·ing (hul′king) *adj.* big and clumsy.

hull¹ (hul) *n., v.* —*n.* **1** the outer covering of a seed. **2** the calyx of some fruits: *We call the green leaves at the stem of a strawberry its hull.* **3** any outer covering. —*v.* remove the hull or hulls from: *to hull strawberries, to hull grain.* [OE *hulu*] —**hull′er**, *n.*

hull² (hul) *n., v.* —*n.* **1** the body or frame of a ship. Masts, sails, and rigging are not part of the hull. **2** the main body or frame of a seaplane, airship, etc.
hull down, of ships, so far away that the hull is below the horizon. —*v.* strike or pierce the hull of (a ship) with a shell, torpedo, etc. [? extended use of *hull¹*]

hul·la·ba·loo (hul′ə bə lü′) *n.* a loud noise or disturbance; uproar. [imitative, probably < reduplication of *hullo*]

hul·lo (hə lō′) *interj., n. pl.* **-los;** *v.* **-loed, -lo·ing.** hello.

hum (hum) *v.* **hummed, hum·ming;** *n., interj.* —*v.* **1** make a continuous murmuring sound like that of a bee or of a spinning top: *The sewing machine hums busily.* **2** make a low sound like that symbolized by the letter *m*, in hesitation, embarrassment, dissatisfaction, etc. **3** sing with closed lips, not sounding words. **4** put or bring by humming: *The mother hummed her baby to sleep.* **5** *Informal.* be busy and active: *The new president made things hum.* —*n.* **1** a continuous murmuring sound: *the hum of the bees, the hum of the city street.* **2** a low sound like that symbolized by the letter *m*, to express hesitation, disagreement, etc. **3** a singing with closed lips, not sounding words.
—*interj.* a low sound like that symbolized by the letter *m*, used to express hesitation, disagreement, etc. [imitative] —**hum′mer**, *n.*

hu·man (hyü′mən) *adj., n.* —*adj.* **1** of, having do to do with, or belonging to mankind: *human nature, human affairs. To know the future is beyond human power.* **2** consisting of people: *the human race.* **3** having or showing qualities, good or bad, natural to people, as opposed to machines, animals, or divine beings: *human error. After all, he's only human.* **4** warm, open, responsive, etc.: *She's becoming more human as she gets to know us.*
—*n.* a human being; person. [ME < OF *humain* < L *humanus*]
☞ *Usage.* Do not confuse **human** (*adj.* 3) and **humane** (def. I). **Human** describes or suggests any quality, good or bad, belonging specially to man as distinct from animals or God, but particularly suggests his feelings or faults: *He is a very human person, warm and understanding and not too perfect.* **Humane** chiefly suggests man's tender and compassionate feelings and actions toward animals or people who are helpless, troubled, or suffering: *A humane person will not condone the torture of prisoners.*

human being a man, woman, or child; person.

hu·mane (hyü mān′) *adj.* **1** kind; merciful; not cruel or brutal. **2** tending to humanize and refine: *humane studies.* [var. of *human*] —**hu·mane′ly**, *adv.* —**hu·mane′ness**, *n.*
☞ *Usage.* See note at **human.**

hu·man·ism (hyü′mən iz′əm) *n.* **1** any system of thought or action mainly concerned with human interests. **2** the study of the humanities; literary culture. Humanism spread throughout Europe in the Middle Ages when scholars began to study Latin and Greek culture. As a result there was the great revival of art and learning that is called the Renaissance.

hu·man·ist (hyü′mən ist) *n.* **1** a follower of any philosophy or field of study mainly concerned with human interests and values. **2** a student of the humanities or of Latin and Greek culture.

hu·man·is·tic (hyü′mən is′tik) *adj.* of humanism or humanists.

hu·man·i·tar·i·an (hyü man′ə ter′ē ən) *adj., n.* —*adj.* **1** helpful to humanity; philanthropic. **2** of or having to do with humanitarianism, especially in theology. —*n.* **1** a person who is devoted to the welfare of all human beings. **2** a believer in theological or ethical humanitarianism. [< *humanity*; patterned after *unitarian*, etc.]

hu·man·i·tar·i·an·ism (hyü man′ə ter′ē ən iz′əm) *n.* **1** humanitarian principles or practices. **2** *Theology.* the doctrine that Jesus Christ was human, not divine. **3** the ethical doctrine that man's obligations are concerned wholly with human relations and the welfare of the human race.

hu·man·i·ty (hyü man′ə tē) *n., pl.* **-ties. 1** human beings taken as a group; people: *Advances in medical science help all humanity.* **2** the fact of being human; human character or quality. **3** the fact of being humane; humane treatment; kindness; mercy: *Treat animals with humanity.* **4 the humanities, a** the Latin and Greek languages and literatures. **b** languages, literatures, philosophies, art, etc. **c** the branches of learning concerned with human ideas and their values. [< F *humanité* < L *humanitas*]

hu·man·ize (hyü′mən īz′) *v.* **-ized, -iz·ing. 1** make human; give a human character or quality to. **2** make humane; cause to be kind or merciful. —**hu′man·i·za′tion,** *n.* —**hu′man·iz′er,** *n.*

hu·man·kind (hyü′mən kīnd′) *n.* the human race; mankind.

hu·man·ly (hyü′mən lē) *adj.* **1** in a human manner. **2** by human means or powers: *The task is humanly impossible.* **3** according to human knowledge, experience, or viewpoint.

hu·man·oid (hyü′mə noid′) *adj., n.* —*adj.* having human characteristics; resembling a human being: *humanoid robots.* —*n.* **1** one of the earliest ancestors of mankind. **2** any creature closely resembling a human being: *Science fiction often deals with humanoids from other planets.*

human rights the rights of an individual, such as the right to justice, equality of opportunity, and religious freedom, that are considered basic to life in any human society.

hum·ble (hum′bəl) *adj.* **-bler, -blest;** *v.* **-bled, -bling.** —*adj.* **1** low in position or condition; not important or grand: *A one-room cabin is a humble place in which to live.* **2** having or showing a feeling that one is unimportant, weak, poor, etc.; modest in spirit; not proud. **3** deeply or courteously respectful: *in my humble opinion.* —*v.* **1** make humble; bring down. **2** make lower in position, condition, or pride. [ME < OF < L *humilis* low < *humus* ground] —**hum′ble·ness,** *n.* —**hum′bler,** *n.* —**hum′bly,** *adv.*
☞ *Syn. adj.* **2. Humble, lowly, meek** = not proud in spirit or behavior. **Humble** in a good sense means modest, "without wrongful pride in oneself or one's accomplishments," but now chiefly suggests "feeling inferior and belittling oneself": *Defeat and failure make people humble.* **Lowly,** more literary, means "humble" in the good sense, but is now seldom used to describe people: *The saint had a lowly heart.* **Meek** = patient and mild in disposition, but now often suggests "being without proper pride or spirit, submitting tamely to abuse": *The little fellow was meek when the other boys made fun of him.*

hum·ble·bee (hum′bəl bē′) *n.* bumblebee. [ME *humbylbee*, ult. < *hum*]

humble pie an inferior pie made of the inward parts of an animal, formerly served to the huntsmen and servants after a hunt.
eat humble pie, a be forced to do something very disagreeable and humiliating. **b** admit one's mistakes and apologize.
[var. of *umble pie* < *umbles*, var. of *numbles* entrails < OF, pl. < L *lumbulus*, dim. of *lumbus* loin]

hum·bug (hum′bug′) *n., v.* **-bugged, -bug·ging.** —*n.* **1** a person who pretends to be what he is not; fraud. **2** a cheat. **3** pretence; sham. **4** nonsense; foolishness: *Dad says our argument is humbug.* **5** a hard candy, usually brown with light stripes.
—*v.* deceive with a sham; cheat. [origin unknown] —**hum′bug′ger,** *n.*

hum·ding·er (hum′ding′ər) *n. Slang.* a person or thing that is first-rate, extraordinary, or striking: *a humdinger of a car. Her retort was a humdinger.*

hum·drum (hum′drum′) *adj., n.* —*adj.* without variety; commonplace; dull.
—*n.* **1** a humdrum routine. **2** anything that is dull or tiresome. **3** a dull person. [varied reduplicaton of *hum*, v.]

hu·mer·al (hyü′mər əl) *adj.* **1** of or near the humerus. **2** of or near the shoulder.

hu·mer·us (hyü′mər əs) *n., pl.* **-mer·i** (-mər ī′ *or* -mər ē′). the long bone in the upper part of the forelimb or arm, reaching from the shoulder to the elbow. See **arm** for picture. [< L *umerus*]

hu·mid (hyü′mid) *adj.* moist; damp: *The air is very humid here.* [< L *umidus* < *umere* be moist] —**hu′mid·ly,** *adv.* —**hu′mid·ness,** *n.*
☞ *Syn.* See note at **damp.**

hu·mi·dex (hyü′mi deks′) *n. Cdn.* an index of discomfort resulting from a combination of humidity and heat. The humidex is calculated by adding a given value based on the dew point level to the temperature of the atmosphere (1 for a dew point of 10°, 6 for a

dew point of 18°, etc.). Thus, at a temperature of 25°C, the humidex is 26 when the dew point is 10° and 31 when the dew point is 18°.

Humidex	Level of discomfort
20-29	comfortable
30-39	varying degrees of discomfort
40-45	almost everyone feels uncomfortable
46 and over	many types of work must be discontinued

[< *humidity* + ind*ex*; first used by the Toronto Weather Office in 1965]

hu·mid·i·fi·ca·tion (hyü mid′ə fə kā′shən) *n.* a humidifying.

hu·mid·i·fi·er (hyü mid′ə fī′ər) *n.* a device for keeping air moist.

hu·mid·i·fy (hyü mid′ə fī′) *v.* **-fied, -fy·ing.** make humid or more humid.

hu·mid·i·ty (hyü mid′ə tē) *n.* **1** the state of the atmosphere with respect to the amount of water vapor present in it. See **relative humidity** and **absolute humidity.** **2** moisture, especially of the atmosphere: *The humidity today is worse than the heat.*

hu·mi·dor (hyü′mə dôr′) *n.* **1** a box, jar, etc. for keeping tobacco moist. **2** any similar device.

hu·mil·i·ate (hyü mil′ē āt′) *v.* **-at·ed, -at·ing.** lower the pride, dignity, or self-respect of; make ashamed. [< L *humiliare* < *humilis.* See HUMBLE.] —**hu·mil′i·at′ing·ly,** *adv.* —**hu·mil′i·a·tor,** *n.*
☞ *Syn.* See note at **ashamed.**

hu·mil·i·a·tion (hyü mil′ē ā′shən) *n.* a lowering of pride, dignity, or self-respect; making or being made ashamed.

hu·mil·i·ty (hyü mil′ə tē) *n., pl.* **-ties.** humbleness of mind; lack of pride; meekness. [< F *humilité* < *humilitas*]

hum·ming·bird (hum′ing bėrd′) *n.* any of a family (Trochilidae) of tiny New World birds having brightly colored, iridescent plumage, a long, slender bill, and long, narrow wings, and noted for their ability to hover in the air as they feed on the nectar of flowers and also for the characteristic humming sound made by their rapidly beating wings. The commonest Canadian species is the ruby-throated hummingbird (*Archilochus colubris*).

hum·mock (hum′ək) *n.* **1** a very small, rounded hill; knoll; hillock. **2** a bump or ridge in a field of ice. [origin unknown]

hum·mock·y (hum′ək ē) *adj.* **1** full of hummocks. **2** like a hummock.

hu·mor or **hu·mour** (hyü′mər or yü′mər) *n., v.* —*n.* **1** a funny or amusing quality: *I see no humor in your tricks.* **2** the ability to see or show the funny or amusing side of things. **3** speech, writing, etc. showing this ability. **4** a state of mind; mood; disposition: *Success puts you in good humor.* **5** a fancy; whim. **6** any of various body fluids formerly supposed to determine a person's health and disposition. They were blood, phlegm, choler (yellow bile), and melancholy (black bile).
out of humor or **humour,** angry; displeased; in a bad mood.
sense of humor or **humour,** the ability to see the amusing side of things.
—*v.* **1** give in to the fancies or whims of (a person); indulge. **2** adapt oneself to; act so as to agree with. [ME < AF < L *umor* fluid] —**hu′mor·less** or **hu′mour·less,** *adj.*
☞ *Syn. n.* **2.** See note at **wit.** —*v.* **1. Humor, indulge, gratify** = give someone what he wants. **Humor** = give in to someone's whims, changing moods, unreasonable demands, or purely imaginary desires, in order to quiet or comfort him: *Unless the little boy is humored, he has tantrums.* **Indulge** = give way, often too easily, to someone's wishes, especially ones that should not be granted, in order to please: *Many parents indulge their children by giving them too much candy and ice cream.* **Gratify** = make someone happy by providing what he likes or longs for: *Praise gratifies most people.*

hu·mor·esque (hyü′mər esk′) *n.* a light, playful, or humorous piece of music. [< G *Humoreske*]

hu·mor·ist (hyü′mər ist or yü′mər ist) *n.* **1** a person with a strong sense of humor. **2** a humorous talker or writer; a person who tells or writes jokes and funny stories.

hu·mor·ous (hyü′mər əs or yü′mər əs) *adj.* full of humor; funny; amusing. —**hu′mor·ous·ly,** *adv.* —**hu′mor·ous·ness,** *n.*

hu·mour (hyü′mər or yü′mər) See **humor.**

hump (hump) *n., v.* —*n.* **1** a rounded lump that sticks out: *Some camels have two humps on their backs.* **2** a mound; a hill. **3** a long, gradual hill in a railway yard where cars are uncoupled and allowed to roll down into the classification yard, where switches sort them out onto different tracks.
over the hump, past a difficult period or crucial test.
—*v.* **1** raise or bend up into a hump: *The cat humped her back when she saw the dog.* **2** move (a railway car) over the hump for sorting in the classification yard. **3** *Slang.* exert oneself; make an effort. [cf. Du. *homp* lump]

hump·back (hump′bak′) *n.* **1** hunchback. **2** a large baleen whale (*Megaptera novaeangliae*) found in all oceans, belonging to the same family (Balaenopteridae) as the rorquals but having a shorter and stouter body and a rounded back that shows as a hump above the water just before the whale sounds. Also called **humpback whale. 3** pink salmon. Also called **humpback salmon.**

hat, āge, fär; let, ēqual, tèrm; it, īce
hot, ōpen, ôrder; oil, out; cup, pút, rüle,
əbove, takən, pencəl, lemən, circəs

ch, child; ng, long; sh, ship
th, thin; ᴛʜ, then; zh, measure

hump·backed (hump′bakt′) *adj.* hunchbacked.

humph (humpf) *interj. or n.* an exclamation expressing doubt, disgust, contempt, etc.

hump·y (hump′ē) *adj.* **hump·i·er, hump·i·est. 1** full of humps. **2** humplike.

hu·mus (hyü′məs) *n.* the dark-brown or black part of soil formed from decayed leaves and other vegetable matter. Humus contains valuable plant foods. [< L *humus* earth]

Hun (hun) *n.* **1** a member of an Asiatic people who, under the leadership of Attila, overran much of eastern and central Europe between about A.D. 375 and 450. **2** Often, **hun,** a barbarous, destructive person. **3** *Derogatory.* **a** a German. **b** the German forces, used especially during World War I. **4** *Cdn.* Hungarian partridge. [OE (pl.) *Hūne, Hūnas*; probably < the native name of the people]

hunch (hunch) *v., n.* —*v.* **1** hump. **2** draw, bend, or form into a hump: *He sat hunched up with his chin on his knees.* **3** move, push, or shove by jerks.
—*n.* **1** a hump. **2** *Informal.* a vague feeling or suspicion: *I had a hunch we would win the game.* **3** a thick slice or piece; chunk. [origin unknown]

hunch·back (hunch′bak′) *n.* **1** a person with a crooked back that forms a hump at the level of the shoulders. **2** a crooked back that has a hump at the shoulders.

hunch·backed (hunch′bakt′) *adj.* having a hunchback.

hun·dred (hun′drəd) *n., pl.* **-dreds** or (after a number, etc.) **-dred;** *adj.* —*n.* **1** ten times ten; 100: *five hundred.* **2** a 100-dollar bill. **3 hundreds,** *pl.* the numbers between 100 and 999. **4** *Historical.* a division of an English county.
—*adj.* being ten times ten: *a hundred men.* [OE *hund* 100 + *red* reckoning]

Hundred Days the period of Napoleon's return to power in France in 1815, between his escape from Elba and his defeat, abdication, and final exile.

hun·dred·fold (hun′drəd fōld′) *adj., adv. or n.* a hundred times as much or as many.

hun·dredth (hun′drədth) *adj. or n.* **1** next after the 99th; last in a series of 100; 100th. **2** one, or being one, of 100 equal parts.

hun·dred·weight (hun′drəd wāt′) *n., pl.* **-weights** or (after a number, etc.) **-weight.** a unit for measuring mass equal to 100 pounds (about 45 kg) in Canada and 112 pounds (about 50 kg) in the British Isles.

Hundred Years' War a series of wars between England and France from 1337 to 1453.

hung (hung) *v.* a pt. and a pp. of **hang.**
☞ *Usage.* See note at **hang.**

Hun·gar·i·an (hung ger′ē ən) *n., adj.* —*n.* **1** a native or inhabitant of Hungary, a country in central Europe. **2** a person of Hungarian descent. **3** Finno-Ugric language of Hungary; Magyar.
—*adj.* of or having to do with Hungary, its people, or their language.

Hungarian partridge *Cdn.* a partridge (*Perdix perdix*) introduced to North America from Europe as a game bird. Many of the first such birds to be brought over came from Hungary.

hun·ger (hung′gər) *n., v.* —*n.* **1** an uncomfortable or painful feeling or a weak condition caused by lack of food. **2** a desire or need for food. **3** a strong desire; longing: *a hunger for kindness.*
—*v.* **1** feel hunger; be hungry. **2** *Archaic.* starve. **3** have a strong desire. [OE *hungor*] —**hun′ger·er,** *n.*
☞ *Syn.* See note at **famish.**

hunger strike a refusal to eat until certain demands are granted.

hun·gry (hung′grē) *adj.* **-gri·er, -gri·est. 1** feeling a desire or need for food: *I'm hungry.* **2** showing hunger: *a hungry look.* **3** causing hunger: *This is hungry work.* **4** having a strong desire or craving; eager: *hungry for knowledge.* **5** not rich or fertile: *hungry soil.* [OE *hungrig*] —**hun′gri·ly,** *adv.* —**hun′gri·ness,** *n.*
☞ *Syn.* **1. Hungry, famished** = needing food. **Hungry** is the general word: *Boys are always hungry.* **Famished** = brought to a serious state of physical exhaustion, sometimes even to the point of dying, by lack of food: *We try to feed and save famished war orphans.* But in informal use, it often means no more than "very hungry."

hunk (hungk) *n. Informal.* a big lump, piece, or roughly cut slice. [cf. Flemish *hunke* hunk]

hun·ker (hung'kər) *v.* squat on one's haunches. [origin uncertain]

hun·kers (hung'kərs) *n.pl.* haunches.

hunk·y¹ (hung'kē) *adj. Slang.* all right; safe and sound.

hunk·y² (hung'kē) *n. Slang. Usually derogatory.* a central European immigrant, especially a Hungarian. [prob. < earlier *hunk* foreigner < *Bohunk*]

hunk·y–do·ry (hung'kē dôr'ē) *adj. Slang.* fine, just right; satisfactory.

hunt (hunt) *v., n.* —*v.* 1 go after wild animals, game birds, etc. to catch or kill them for food or sport. 2 search through (a region) in pursuit of game. 3 use (horses or dogs) in the chase. 4 drive (out, away); pursue; harry; persecute. 5 try to find: *to hunt a clue.* 6 look thoroughly; search carefully: *to hunt through drawers.*
hunt down, a hunt for until caught or killed. **b** look for until found.
hunt out, seek and find.
hunt up, a look carefully for. **b** find by search.
—*n.* 1 the act of hunting: *Our gear for the duck hunt is all ready.* 2 a group of persons hunting together. 3 an attempt to find something; thorough look; careful search. [OE *huntian*]

hunt·er (hun'tər) *n.* 1 a person who hunts. 2 a horse or dog trained for hunting.

hunt·ing (hun'ting) *n.* the act of a person or animal that hunts, especially the pursuit of game: *They went hunting last weekend.*

hunting case a watchcase with a hinged cover to protect the crystal.

hunting ground 1 a place or region for hunting. 2 See **happy hunting ground.**

hunting horn a horn used in a hunt.

hunt·ress (hun'tris) *n.* a woman who hunts.

hunts·man (hunts'mən) *n., pl.* **-men.** 1 hunter. 2 the manager of a hunt.

hur·dle (hėr'dəl) *n., v.* **-dled, -dling.** —*n.* 1 in a race, a barrier for people or horses to jump over. 2 **hurdles,** *pl.* a race in which the runners jump over hurdles. 3 an obstacle, difficulty, etc. 4 a frame made of sticks used as a temporary fence. 5 *Brit.* a portable frame resembling a stoneboat or sled, formerly used for dragging traitors to a place of execution.
—*v.* 1 jump over: *The horse hurdled both the fence and the ditch.* 2 overcome (an obstacle, difficulty, etc.). 3 enclose with a frame of sticks. [OE *hyrdel*]

hur·dler (hėr'dlər) *n.* a person who jumps over hurdles in a race.

hur·dy (hėr'dē) *n. Slang.* hurdy-gurdy girl.

hur·dy–gur·dy (hėr'dē gėr'dē) *n., pl.* **-dies.** 1 a hand organ played by turning a handle. 2 *Historical.* an instrument shaped like a guitar, played by turning a wheel. [probably imitative]

hurdy–gurdy girl *Cdn. Historical.* a dancing girl, especially one of a number of young women imported into British Columbia mining communities as dancing partners.

hurl (hėrl) *v., n.* —*v.* 1 throw with much force: *The man hurled his spear at one bear; the dogs hurled themselves at the other.* 2 speak with strong feeling; utter violently: *He hurled insults at me.* —*n.* a forcible or violent throw. [cf. LG *hurreln*] —**hurl'er,** *n.*

hurl·y–burl·y (hėr'lē bėr'lē) *n., pl.* **-burl·ies.** disorder and noise; tumult. [< earlier *hurling and burling,* varied reduplication of *hurling* in obs. sense of "commotion" < *hurl*]

Hu·ron (hyür'ən) *n., adj.* —*n.* 1 a member of an Amerindian people formerly living in the region between Lake Huron and Lake Ontario. The Hurons were organized in a confederacy of four separate tribes. 2 the Iroquoian language of the Hurons. —*adj.* of or having to do with the Hurons or their language. [< F *huron* unkempt person, ruffian < *hure* dishevelled head of hair; a name applied to these Indians from about 1600]

Hu·ro·ni·an (hyü rō'nē ən) *adj., n. Geology.* —*adj.* 1 of or having to do with a rock system north of Lake Huron. 2 or or having to do with the period of the Proterozoic era in which these rocks originated. See chart at **geology.** —*n.* 1 a geological period of the Proterozoic era. 2 the rocks formed during this period.

hur·rah (hə rä' *or* hə ro') *interj., n., v.* —*interj. or n.* a shout of joy, approval, etc.
—*v.* shout hurrahs; cheer. Also, **hooray.**

hur·ray (hə rā') *interj., n., v.* hurrah.

hur·ri·cane (hėr'ə kān') *n.* 1 a tropical cyclone that forms over the Atlantic Ocean, with winds of more than 120 kilometres per hour and, usually, very heavy rain. Hurricanes sometimes move into temperate regions. 2 any wind with a speed of more than 120

kilometres per hour. 3 a sudden, violent outburst or commotion: *a hurricane of cheers.* [< Sp. *huracán* < Carib]

hurricane deck the upper deck on a river boat, etc.

hur·ried (hėr'ēd) *adj.* 1 done or made in a hurry; hasty: *a hurried reply.* 2 forced to hurry. —**hur'ried·ly,** *adv.*

hur·ry (hėr'ē) *v.* **-ried, -ry·ing.** *n., pl.* **-ries.** —*v.* 1 drive, carry, send, or move quickly. 2 move or act with more than an easy or natural speed. 3 urge to act or move quickly; hasten; urge to great speed: *Don't hurry the driver.* 4 cause to go on or occur more quickly; hasten.
—*n.* 1 a hurried movement or action. 2 an eagerness to have quickly or do quickly. 3 need of haste: *There is no hurry for this.* [origin uncertain]
☛ *Syn. n.* **1. Hurry, haste, speed** = quickness or swiftness in action or movement. **Hurry** = action that is quicker than is easy or natural, sometimes quicker than necessary, and often suggests bustling or rushing: *In her hurry she dropped the eggs.* **Haste** emphasizes trying to be quick, and often suggests hurried or rushed action, sometimes too rushed to get the desired results: *All this haste was of no use.* **Speed** = swift or rapid movement of people or things: *They did the work with speed.*

hur·ry–scur·ry *or* **hur·ry–skur·ry** (hėr'ē skėr'ē) *n., pl.* **-ries;** *adj., adv. Informal.* —*n.* a hurrying and confusion.
—*adj.* hurried and confused.
—*adv.* with hurrying and confusion.

hurt (hėrt) *v.* **hurt, hurt·ing;** *n.* —*v.* 1 cause pain, harm, or damage: *Falling on concrete hurts. My new shoes hurt.* 2 cause pain to; give a wound to; injure: *I hurt my arm when I fell.* 3 feel pain; suffer: *He said he hurt all over after his fall. My sprained ankle hurts terribly.* 4 have a bad effect on; do damage or harm to: *Will it hurt this hat if it gets wet? The scandal has hurt his chances of getting elected.* 5 grieve; distress: *He hurt his mother's feelings.*
—*n.* 1 a wound or injury: *It was just a small hurt.* 2 a bad effect; damage or harm: *The failure was a great hurt to her pride.* [apparently < OF *hurter* strike < Gmc.] —**hurt'er,** *n.*
☛ *Syn. v.* **2, 4.** See note at **injure.**

hurt·ful (hėrt'fəl) *adj.* causing pain, harm, distress, or damage; injurious: *a mean and hateful remark.* —**hurt'ful·ly,** *adv.*

hur·tle (hėr'təl) *v.* **-tled, -tling;** *n.* —*v.* 1 dash or drive violently; come or fling suddenly: *The car hurtled across the road into a fence. The impact of the crash hurtled the driver against the windshield of the car.* 2 move with a clatter; rush noisily or violently: *The express train hurtled past.* 3 *Rare.* collide (*used with* **against** *or* **together**).
—*n.* the act or fact of hurtling; clash; clatter. [ME, frequentative of *hurten* strike < OF < Gmc.; cf. ON *hrutr* a ram]

hus·band (huz'bənd) *n., v.* —*n.* 1 a married man, especially when considered with reference to the woman he is married to. 2 *Archaic.* manager.
—*v.* 1 manage carefully; be saving of: *A sick person must husband his strength.* 2 *Archaic.* of a woman, marry. 3 *Archaic.* till (soil); cultivate (plants). [OE *hūsbonda* < *hūs* house + *bonda* head of family (< ON *bóndi*)]

hus·band·ly (huz'bənd lē) *adj.* of, like, or befitting a husband.

hus·band·man (huz'bənd mən) *n., pl.* **-men.** *Archaic.* farmer.

hus·band·ry (huz'bənd rē) *n.* 1 careful management; thrift. 2 *Rare.* the management of one's affairs or resources. 3 farming, especially as a science or art.

hush (hush) *v., n., interj.* —*v.* 1 stop making a noise; make or become silent or quiet. 2 soothe; calm.
hush up, a keep from being told; stop discussion of. **b** *Informal.* be silent.
—*n.* a stopping of noise; silence; quiet.
—*interj.* stop the noise! be silent! keep quiet! [ME *hussht* silent, originally interj., silence!]

hush–hush (hush'hush') *adj. Informal.* secret; confidential: *hush-hush plans.*

hush money *Informal.* money paid to keep a person from telling something.

husk¹ (husk) *n., v.* —*n.* 1 the dry outer covering of certain seeds or fruits. The husk surrounding an ear of corn is made up of modified leaves. 2 the dry or worthless outer covering of anything.
—*v.* remove the husk from. [ME *huske,* origin uncertain; cf. MDu. *huyskijn,* dim. of *huus* house] —**husk'er,** *n.*

husk² (husk) *n.* a husky condition or quality of the voice. [back formation from *husky*]

husk·y¹ (hus'kē) *adj.* **husk·i·er, husk·i·est.** 1 dry in the throat; hoarse; rough of voice: *A cold sometimes causes a husky cough.* 2 of, like, or having husks. 3 big and strong: *a husky young man.* [< *husk¹,* n.] —**husk'i·ly,** *adv.* —**husk'i·ness,** *n.*

husk·y² (hus'kē) *n., pl.* **-ies.** 1 Siberian husky. 2 any northern work dog. 3 Husky, *Cdn. Slang.* especially in the North: **a** a member of the Inuit. **b** the language of the Inuit. [abbrev. of an early variant of *Eskimo.* 19c.]

hus·sar (hu̇ zär') *n.* 1 a light-armed cavalry soldier. 2 a member

of certain armored regiments. [< Hungarian *huszár*, originally, freebooter < Old Serbian *husar*, var. of *kursar* < Ital. *corsaro* runner < VL *cursarius* < L *cursus* a run. Doublet of CORSAIR.]

Huss·ite (hus′īt) *n., adj.* —*n.* a follower of John Huss (1369?-1415), a Bohemian religious reformer and martyr. —*adj.* of or having to do with John Huss or his teachings.

hus·sy (huz′ē or hus′ē) *n., pl.* **-sies. 1** a bold or bad-mannered girl. **2** a promiscuous woman or one who disregards moral conventions. [<E *huswif* housewife]

hus·tings (hus′tingz) *n.pl. or sing.* **1** in Great Britain, a platform from which candidates for Parliament were formerly nominated and from which they addressed the voters. **2** a platform from which speeches are made in a political campaign. **3** the proceedings at an election. [OE < ON *hústhing* council < *hús* house + *thing* assembly]

hus·tle (hus′əl) *v.* **-tled, -tling;** *n.* —*v.* **1** hurry. **2** force hurriedly or roughly: *The police hustled the tramps out of town.* **3** push or shove roughly; jostle rudely: *The other boys hustled him along the street.* **4** *Informal.* go or work quickly or with tireless energy: *He had to hustle to earn enough money to support his family.* **5** *Slang.* sell or solicit, especially in an aggressive or deceitful way. —*n.* **1** a hurry. **2** a rough pushing or shoving; rude jostling. **3** *Informal.* tireless energy. [< MDu. *hutselen* shake] —**hus′tler,** *n.*

hut (hut) *n.* **1** a small, roughly built house; a small cabin. **2** a temporary wooden or metal structure for quartering troops. [< F *hutte* < MHG *hütte*] —**hut′like′,** *adj.*

hutch (hutch) *n., v.* —*n.* **1** a pen for rabbits, etc. **2** a box, chest, or bin. **3** a cupboard, open or with glass doors, having shelves for dishes, etc. and set on a buffet. **4** a high cupboard with usually open shelves on the upper part; china cabinet. —*v.* put or keep in a hutch. [ME < OF *huche* < Med.L *hutica* chest]

Hut·ter·ite (hut′ər īt′) *n., adj.* —*n.* a member of an originally Austrian religious and ethnic group living mainly in Alberta and Manitoba. —*adj.* of or having to do with these people: *Hutterite communities.* [< Jacob *Hutter* (? -1536), who founded the group in 1528 + *-ite¹*]

huz·za (hə zä′) *interj., n. pl.* **-zas;** *v.* **-zaed, -za·ing.** —*interj. or n.* a loud shout of joy, encouragement, or applause; hurrah. —*v.* shout huzzas; cheer.

H.V., h.v., or **hv** high voltage.

h.w. high water.

hwan (hwän or wän) *n.* **1** a unit of money in Korea, revalued in 1962. **2** a coin worth one hwan. [< Korean]

hy·a·cinth (hī′ə sinth′) *n.* **1** any of a genus (*Hyacinthus*) of plants of the lily family, especially *H. orientalis*, cultivated in many varieties for its spikes of small, fragrant, bell-shaped flowers. **2** the flower or flower spike of a hyacinth. Hyacinths are usually blue, pink, or white. **3** a reddish-orange gem; a variety of zircon. **4** a purplish blue. [< L *hyacinthus* < Gk. *hyakinthos*, a kind of flower. Doublet of JACINTH.]

hy·a·cin·thine (hī ə sin′thən or hī′ə sin′thīn) *adj.* **1** of or like the hyacinth. **2** adorned with hyacinths.

Hy·a·des (hī′ə dēz′) *n.pl.* **1** *Astronomy.* a group of stars in the constellation Taurus. In ancient times, they were supposed to be a sign of rain when they rose with the sun. **2** *Greek mythology.* the daughters of Atlas, nymphs who supplied the earth with moisture and who were placed in the sky by Zeus.

hy·ae·na (hī ē′nə) See **hyena.**

hy·a·line (hī′ə lin or hī ə lin′) *adj., n.* —*adj.* glassy; transparent. A hyaline cartilage contains little fibre. —*n.* something glassy or transparent. [< LL *hyalinus* < Gk. *hyalinos* < *hyalos* glass]

hy·a·lite (hī′ə līt′) *n.* a colorless variety of opal, sometimes transparent like glass and sometimes whitish and translucent. [< Gk. *hyalos* glass]

hy·a·loid (hī′ə loid′) *adj.* glassy; transparent; crystalline.

hy·brid (hī′brid) *n., adj.* —*n.* **1** the offspring of two animals or plants of different species, varieties, etc. **2** anything of mixed origin. **3** a word formed of parts from different languages. *Example: starvation* (E *starve* + L *-ation*). —*adj.* **1** bred from two different species, varieties, etc.: *A mule is a hybrid animal.* **2** of mixed origin. [< L *hybrida,* var. of *ibrida* mongrel, *hybrid*]

hy·brid·ism (hī′brid iz′əm) *n.* **1** the production of hybrids; crossbreeding. **2** a hybrid character, nature, or condition.

hy·brid·i·za·tion (hī′brid ə zā′shən or hī′brid ī zā′shən) *n.* the production of hybrids; crossing of different species.

hy·brid·ize (hī′brid īz′) *v.* **-ized, -iz·ing. 1** cause to produce hybrids; crossbreed. Botanists hybridize different kinds of plants to get new varieties. **2** produce hybrids. —**hy′brid·iz′er,** *n.*

hybrid tea rose any of numerous relatively hardy varieties of bush rose developed from crosses of tea roses with other hybrids

hat, āge, fär; let, ēqual, tèrm; it, īce
hot, ōpen, ôrder; oil, out; cup, pút, rüle,
əbove, takən, pencəl, lemən, circəs

ch, child; ng, long; sh, ship
th, thin; ᴛʜ, then; zh, measure

and valued for their large, profuse blooms which occur in a wide range of colors and scents and also include many scentless varieties.

Hyde (hīd) *n.* **Mr.** See **Jekyll.**

hydr– *combining form.* the form of **hydro-** before vowels, as in *hydraulic.*

hy·dra (hī′drə) *n., pl.* **-dras, -drae** (-drē or -drī). **1 Hydra, a** *Greek mythology.* a monstrous serpent having nine heads, each of which, after being cut off, was replaced by two heads unless the wound was cauterized. The Hydra was slain by Hercules. **b** *Astronomy.* a southern constellation represented as a serpent. **2** any persistent evil. **3** a kind of freshwater polyp, so called because when the tubelike body is cut into pieces, each piece forms a new individual. [< L < Gk. *hydra* water serpent < *hydōr* water]

hy·dran·gea (hī drān′jə) *n.* any of a genus (*Hydrangea*) of shrubs or woody vines of the saxifrage family, several of which are cultivated in gardens and greenhouses for their large, showy clusters of small white, pink, or blue flowers. [< NL < Gk. *hydōr* water + *angeion* vessel, capsule; with reference to its cup-shaped seed capsule]

hy·drant (hī′drənt) *n.* a large, upright pipe with a valve for drawing water directly from a water main. Hydrants are used to get water to put out fires, to wash the streets, etc. [< Gk. *hydōr* water]

hy·drate (hī′drāt) *n., v.* **-drat·ed, -drat·ing.** —*n.* a compound produced when any of certain other substances unite with water, represented in formulas as containing molecules of water. Washing soda ($Na_2CO_3 \cdot 10H_2O$) is a hydrate. —*v.* become or cause to become a hydrate; combine with water to form a hydrate. Blue vitriol is hydrated copper sulphate. [< Gk. *hydōr* water]

hy·dra·tion (hī drā′shən) *n.* the act or process of combining with water, especially to form a hydrate.

hy·drau·lic (hī dro′lik or hī drô′lik) *adj.* **1** having to do with water or other liquid in motion. **2** operated by the pressure of water or other liquid: *a hydraulic press, hydraulic brakes.* **3** hardening under water: *hydraulic cement.* **4** of or having to do with hydraulics: *a hydraulic engineer.* —**hy·drau′li·cal·ly,** *adv.* [< L *hydraulicus* < Gk. *hydraulikos*, ult. < *hydōr* water + *aulos* pipe]

hy·drau·lics (hī dro′liks or hī drô′liks) *n.* the branch of science dealing with water and other liquids in motion, their uses in engineering, the laws of their actions, etc. (*used with a singular verb*).

hy·dra·zine (hī′drə zēn′ or hī′drə zin) *n.* **1** *Chemistry.* a colorless, fuming, toxic liquid in organic synthesis, and as rocket fuel. *Formula:* N_2H_4 **2** any of various compounds obtained from this liquid by replacing one or more hydrogen atoms with an organic radical.

hy·dric (hī′drik) *adj.* of or containing hydrogen.

hy·dride (hī′drīd or hī′drid) *n.* *Chemistry.* a compound of hydrogen with another element or radical.

hy·dri·od·ic (hī′dri od′ik) *adj.* containing hydrogen and iodine. Hydriodic acid (HI) is a colorless gas with a suffocating odor.

hy·dro (hī′drō) *n. Cdn.* **1** hydro-electric power: *Niagara Falls provides hydro for many factories.* **2** electricity as a utility distributed by a power company or commisson: *The hydro was off for two hours during the storm.* **3 Hydro,** a company or commission producing and distributing electricity as a utility.

hydro– *combining form.* **1** of or having to do with water, as in *hydrometer, hydrostatics.* **2** combined with hydrogen, as in *hydrochloric, hydrosulphuric.* Also, **hydr-,** before vowels. [< Gk. *hydro-* < *hydōr* water]

hy·dro·car·bon (hī′drō kär′bən) *n.* any of a class of compounds containing only hydrogen and carbon. Methane benzene, and acetylene are hydrocarbons. Gasoline is a mixture of hydrocarbons.

hy·dro·ceph·al·ic (hī′drə sə fal′ik) *adj.* affected with or having to do with hydrocephalus.

hy·dro·ceph·a·lous (hī′drə sef′ə ləs) *adj.* hydrocephalic.

hy·dro·ceph·a·lus (hī′drō sef′ə ləs) *n.* an accumulation of fluid within the cranium, especially in infancy, often causing great enlargement of the head. [< *hydro-* + Gk. *kephalē* head]

hy·dro·chlo·ric (hī′drə klô′rik) *adj.* containing hydrogen and chlorine.

hydrochloric acid a clear, colorless solution of hydrogen

chloride, that has a strong, sharp odor and is highly corrosive. Hydrochloric acid is present in a dilute form in gastric juice and is used in various industrial processes, in dyeing, and in medicine. *Formula*: HCl

hy·dro·cor·ti·sone (hī′drō kôr′tə zōn′) *n.* an adrenal hormone similar to cortisone, used in treating arthritis.

hy·dro·cy·an·ic (hī′drō sī an′ik) *adj.* containing hydrogen and cyanogen.

hydrocyanic acid a colorless, volatile solution of hydrogen cyanide, that has an odor like that of bitter almonds and is highly poisonous; prussic acid. It is used as a fumigant and in the manufacture of dyes, plastics, etc. *Formula*: HCN

hy·dro·dy·nam·ic (hī′drō dī nam′ik) *adj.* of or having to do with the force or motion of fluids, or with hydrodynamics.

hy·dro·dy·nam·ics (hī′drō dī nam′iks) *n.* the branch of physics dealing with the forces that water and other liquids exert; hydraulics.

hy·dro·e·lec·tric (hī′drō′i lek′trik) *adj.* of or having to do with the generation of elecricity by water power, or by the friction of water or steam: *There is a large hydro-electric power plant on the St. Lawrence Seaway.*

hy·dro·e·lec·tric·i·ty (hī′drō i lek′tris′ə tē) *n.* electricity produced from water power, etc.

hy·dro·flu·or·ic (hī′drō flü ôr′ik) *adj.* containing hydrogen and fluorine.

hydrofluoric acid a colorless, corrosive, volatile solution of hydrogen fluoride, used for etching glass. *Formula*: HF

hy·dro·foil (hī′drə foil′) *n.* **1** one of a set of blades or fins attached to the hull of a boat at an angle so that the boat, when moving, is lifted just clear of the water. Hydrofoils reduce friction and thus increase speed. **2** a boat equipped with hydrofoils.

hy·dro·gen (hī′drə jən) *n.* a colorless, odorless, gaseous chemical element, that burns easily and weighs less than any other known element. Hydrogen combines chemically with oxygen to form water. *Symbol*: H; *at.no.* 1; *at.wt.* 1.00797. [< F *hydrogène*, ult. < Gk. *hydōr* water + *-genēs* born]

hy·dro·gen·ate (hī′drə jən āt′ *or* hī droj′ən āt′) *v.* **-at·ed, -at·ing.** combine or treat with hydrogen; especially, combine an unsaturated organic compound with hydrogen. Vegetable oils are hydrogenated to produce solid fats.

hy·dro·gen·a·tion (hī′drə jə nā′shən) *n.* the process of combining with hydrogen.

hydrogen bomb a bomb that uses the fusion of atoms to cause an explosion of tremendous force. It is many times more powerful than an atomic bomb.

hydrogen chloride a colorless, strong-smelling, poisonous gas, a compound of hydrogen and chlorine. It is soluble in water, forming hydrochloric acid. *Formula*: HCl

hydrogen cyanide a colorless, highly poisonous gas, a compound of hydrogen and cyanogen. It has an odor of bitter almonds and dissolves in water to form hydrocyanic acid. *Formula*: HCN

hydrogen fluoride a colorless, corrosive, poisonous liquid or gas, a compound of hydrogen and fluorine. It is soluble in water, forming hydrofluoric acid. *Formula*: HF

hy·dro·gen·ize (hī′drə jən īz′ *or* hī droj′ən īz′) *v.* **-ized, -iz·ing.** hydrogenate.

hy·drog·e·nous (hī droj′ə nəs) *adj.* of or containing hydrogen.

hydrogen peroxide a colorless, unstable liquid often used in dilute solution as an antiseptic, a bleaching agent, etc. *Formula*: H_2O

hydrogen sulphide *or* **sulfide** a flammable, poisonous gas having a strong, offensive odor, found especially in mineral waters and decaying matter. *Formula*: H_2S

hy·dro·graph (hī′drə graf′) *n.* a hydrographic diagram, chart, or record.

hy·drog·ra·pher (hī drog′rə fər) *n.* a person trained in hydrography, especially one whose work it is.

hy·dro·graph·ic (hī′drə graf′ik) *adj.* of or having to do with hydrography. —**hy′dro·graph′i·cal·ly,** *adv.*

hy·drog·ra·phy (hī drog′rə fē) *n.* **1** the study, measurement and description of oceans, lakes, rivers, etc., especially with reference to their use for navigation and commerce. **2** oceans, lakes, rivers, etc., especially as dealt with on a map of a certain region, or in treatises or surveys: *the hydrography of northern Saskatchewan.*

hy·droid (hī′droid) *n.* a very simple form of hydrozoan that grows into branching colonies by budding; polyp. [< *hydra*]

hy·dro·ki·net·ic (hī′drō ki net′ik) *adj.* of or having to do with hydrokinetics.

hy·dro·ki·net·ics (hī′drō ki net′iks) *n.* the branch of physics dealing with the motion, or kinetics, of fluids; hydraulics.

hy·dro·log·ic (hī′drə loj′ik) *adj.* an expert in hydrology.

hy·drol·o·gist (hī drol′ə jist) *n.* a person trained in hydrology, especially one whose work it is.

hy·drol·o·gy (hī drol′ə jē) *n.* the branch of physical geography that deals with the laws, properties, distribution, etc. of water.

hy·drol·y·sis (hī drol′ə sis) *n., pl.* **-ses** (-sēz′). a chemical decomposition that changes a compound into other compounds by taking up the elements of water. [< *hydro-* + Gk. *lysis* a loosening]

hy·dro·lyze (hī′drə līz′) *v.* **-lyzed, -lyz·ing. 1** decompose by hydrolysis. **2** undergo hydrolysis. —**hy′dro·ly·za′tion,** *n.*

hy·dro·me·chan·ics (hī′drō mə kan′iks) *n.* the branch of physics dealing with the mechanics of fluids, or of their laws of equilibrium or motion.

hy·drom·e·ter (hī drom′ə tər) *n.* a graduated instrument for finding the specific gravities of liquids.

hy·dro·met·ric (hī′drə met′rik) *adj.* **1** of or having to do with hydrometry. **2** of or having to do with a hydrometer.

hy·dro·met·ri·cal (hī′drə met′rə kəl) *adj.* hydrometric.

hy·drom·e·try (hī drom′ə trē) *n.* the determinaton of specific gravity, purity, etc. by means of a hydrometer.

hy·dro·path·ic (hī′drə path′ik) *adj., n.* —*adj.* of or using hydropathy. —*n.* a sanitarium that specializes in hydropathy.

hy·drop·a·thy (hī drop′ə thē) *n.* the treatment of disease by using quantities of water externally and internally.

hy·dro·pho·bi·a (hī′drə fō′bē ə) *n.* **1** a morbid dread of water. **2** rabies, especially in human beings. Rabies in people is called hydrophobia because one of the symptoms is a dislike and fear of water and other liquids.

hy·dro·pho·bic (hī′drə fō′bik) *adj.* **1** of or having to do with hydrophobia. **2** suffering from hydrophobia. **3** not easily mixed with or made wet by water.

hy·dro·phone (hī′drə fōn′) *n.* **1** an instrument for detecting the position and source of sounds under water. **2** an instrument detecting water flowing in a pipe, used in finding leaks. **3** *Medicine.* a listening instrument for detecting sounds through a column of water.

hy·dro·phyte (hī′drə fīt′) *n.* any plant that can grow only in water or very wet soil. Most algae are hydrophytes.

hy·dro·plane (hī′drə plān′) *n.* **1** a light speedboat with hydrofoils or a bottom shaped so that the hull will rise out of the water at high speeds. **2** hydrofoil. **3** seaplane.

hy·dro·pon·ic (hī′drə pon′ik) *adj.* of, produced, or grown by hydroponics.

hy·dro·pon·ics (hī′drə pon′iks) *n.* the growing of plants in water containing the necessary nutrients instead of in soil. [< *hydro-* + L *ponere* to place]

hy·dro·qui·none (hī′drō kwi nōn′ *or* -kwin′ōn) *n.* a white, sweetish, crystalline compound, used in photographic developers and in medicine. *Formula*: $C_6H_4(OH)_2$

hy·dro·sol (hī′drə sol′ *or* -sōl′) *n. Chemistry.* a colloid in a water solution.

hy·dro·sphere (hī′drə sfēr′) *n.* **1** the water on the surface of the globe. **2** the water vapor in the atmosphere.

hy·dro·stat (hī′drə stat′) *n.* **1** any of various devices for preventing injury to a steam boiler as a result of lack of water. **2** an electrical device for detecting the presence of water from overflow, leakage, etc. [< *hydro-* + Gk. *-statos* that stands]

hy·dro·stat·ic (hī′drə stat′ik) *adj.* of or having to do with hydrostatics.

hy·dro·stat·ics (hī′drə stat′iks) *n.* the branch of physics that deals with the equilibrium and pressure of water and other liquids.

hy·dro·ther·a·peu·tics (hī′drō ther′ə pyü′tiks) *n.* hydropathy.

hy·dro·ther·a·py (hī′drō ther′ə pē) *n.* the treatment of various diseases by means of water; hydropathy.

hy·dro·trop·ic (hī′drə trop′ik) *adj.* having the tendency to turn or move toward, or away from, water.

hy·drot·ro·pism (hī drot′rə piz′əm) *n.* a tendency to turn or move toward or away from water. Hydrotropism causes roots to grow toward water.

hy·drous (hī′drəs) *adj.* containing water, usually in combination. A hydrous salt is a crystalline compound. [< Gk. *hydōr* water]

hy·drox·ide (hī drok′sīd *or* hī drok′sid) *n. Chemistry.* any compound consisting of an element or radical combined with one or

more hydroxyl radicals. Hydroxides of metals are bases; those of non-metals are acids.

hy·drox·yl (hī drok′səl) *n. Chemistry.* a univalent radical, —OH. It is found in all hydroxides.

hy·dro·zo·an (hī′drə zō′ən) *n.* any of a class (Hydrozoa) of invertebrate water animals having a simple body consisting of two layers of cells and a mouth that opens into the body, including hydras, polyps, many jellyfishes, etc. [< NL *Hydrozoa,* the genus name < Gk. *hydōr* water + *zōon* animal]

hy·e·na (hī ē′nə) *n.* any of a very small family (Hyaenidae) of wolflike carnivorous animals of Africa and Asia that live mainly as scavengers, having short hind legs and a large head with very powerful jaws and teeth. The spotted, or laughing, hyena is noted for a kind of howl that sounds like demented laughter. [< L *hyaena* < Gk. *hyaina* < *hys* pig]

Hy·ge·ia (hī jē′ə) *n. Greek mythology.* the goddess of health.

hy·giene (hī′jēn) *n.* **1** the principles of keeping well and preventing disease; the science of health. **2** practices such as cleanliness that help to preserve health: *personal hygiene.* [< F < NL (*ars*) *hygieina* the healthful art < Gk. *hygieinē* < *hygiēs* healthy]

hy·gien·ic (hī jē′nik *or* hī jen′ik) *adj.* **1** healthful; sanitary. **2** having to do with health or hygiene. —**hy′gi·en′i·cal·ly,** *adv.*

hy·gien·ist (hī′jē nist, hī jē′nist, *or* hī jen′ist) *n.* a person trained in hygiene, especially one whose work it is.

hygro– *combining form.* wet; moist; moisture, as in *hygrometer.* [< Gk. *hygro–* < *hygros* wet]

hy·grom·e·ter (hī grom′ə tər) *n.* any of several kinds of instrument for determining the amount of moisture in the air.

hy·gro·met·ric (hī′grə met′rik) *adj.* of or having to do with the measurement of moisture in the air.

hy·grom·e·try (hī grom′ə trē) *n.* the measurement of the amount of moisture in the air.

hy·gro·scope (hī′grə skōp′) *n.* an instrument that shows the changes in the humidity of the air.

hy·gro·scop·ic (hī′grə skop′ik) *adj.* **1** having to do with or perceptible by the hygroscope. **2** absorbing or attracting moisture from the air.

hy·ing (hī′ing) *v.* ppr. of **hie.**

Hyk·sos (hik′sos *or* hik′sōs) *n.pl.* Shepherd Kings, the foreign rulers of Egypt from about 1750 B.C. to about 1600 B.C.

hy·la (hī′lə) *n.* any of a genus (*Hyla*) of tree frogs. [< NL < Gk. *hylē* wood]

Hy·men (hī′mən) *n. Greek mythology.* the god of marriage.

hy·men (hī′mən) *n. Anatomy.* a fold of mucous membrane extending partly across the opening of the vagina and that is usually ruptured the first time sexual intercourse takes place. [<LL < Gk. *humēn* membrane. 17c.]

hy·me·ne·al (hī′mə nē′əl) *adj., n.* —*adj.* having to do with marriage. —*n.* a wedding song.

hy·me·nop·ter·an (hī′mə nop′tə rən) *n., adj.* —*n.* a hymenopterous insect. —*adj.* hymenopterous.

hy·me·nop·ter·ous (hī′mə nop′tər əs) *adj.* of or belonging to an order (Hymenoptera) of insects that includes ants, bees, and wasps. Winged hymenopterous insects have four membranous wings. [< Gk. *hymenopteros* < *hymēn* membrane + *pteron* wing]

hymn (him) *n., v.* —*n.* **1** a song of praise to God, especially one sung as part of a religious service. **2** any song of praise. —*v.* praise or honor with a hymn. [< L < Gk. *hymnos*] —**hymn′like′,** *adj.*
☛ *Hom.* **him.**

hym·nal (him′nəl) *n.* a book of religious hymns.

hym·nar·y (him′ner′ē *or* him′nər ē) *n., pl.* **-ies.** hymnal.

hym·nol·o·gist (him nol′ə jist) *n.* **1** a person knowledgable in or studying hymnology. **2** a composer of hymns.

hym·nol·o·gy (him nol′ə jē) *n.* **1** the study of hymns, their history, classification, etc. **2** hymns collectively. **3** the composing of hymns.

hy·oid (hī′oid) *n.* **1** a U-shaped bone that supports the tongue in man, lying at the base of the tongue above the thyroid cartilage. **2** a corresponding bone or group of bones in other vertebrates. [< F < NL < Gk. *hyoeidēs* U-shaped < *υ* (upsilon) + *eidos* form]

hyp. **1** hypothesis. **2** hypotenuse.

hype (hīp) *Slang. n., v.* —*n.* **1** exaggerated or sensational promotion or advertising: *There has been a lot of hype lately about customized cosmetics.* **2** drug addict. —*v.* **1** promote or advertise extravagantly (*often used with* **up**). **2** excite, enliven, or stimulate in an artificial way (*often used with* **up**): *to hype one's followers, to hype up a dull program.*

hat, āge, fär; let, ēqual, tèrm; it, īce
hot, ōpen, ôrder; oil, out; cup, pút, rüle,
əbove, takən, pencəl, lemən, circəs

ch, child; ng, long; sh, ship
th, thin; ᴛʜ, then; zh, measure

hyp·er (hī′pər) *adj. Slang.* overwrought or over-excited: *We were all pretty hyper after winning the third straight game.*

hyper– *prefix.* over; above; beyond; exceedingly; to excess, as in *hyperacidity, hypersensitive.* [< Gk. *hyper–* < *hyper*]

hy·per·a·cid·i·ty (hī′pər ə sid′ə tē) *n.* more than the normal amount of acid, especially in the stomach juices.

hy·per·ac·tive (hī′pər ak′tiv) *adj.* of, having to do with, or characterized by hyperactivity: *a hyperactive child.*

hy·per·ac·tiv·i·ty (hī′pər ak tiv′ətē) *n.* excessive or exaggerated activity or extreme restlessness, associated with physical or psychological disorders, especially in children.

hy·per·bo·la (hī pèr′bə lə) *n., pl.* **-las.** *Geometry.* a curve formed when a cone is cut by a plane making a larger angle with the base than the side of the cone makes. See **cone** for picture. [< NL < Gk. *hyperbolē,* ult. < *hyper–* beyond + *ballein* throw]

hy·per·bo·le (hī pèr′bə lē) *n.* exaggeration for effect. *Example*: *Waves high as mountains broke over the reef.* [< L < Gk. *hyperbolē.* See HYBERBOLA.]

hy·per·bol·ic (hī′pər bol′ik) *adj.* **1** of, like, or using hyperbole; exaggerated; exaggerating. **2** of or having to do with hyperbolas. —**hy′per·bol′i·cal·ly,** *adv.*

Hy·per·bo·re·an (hī′pər bô′rē ən) *n., adj.* —*n.* **1** *Greek legend.* one of a group of people described as living in a land of perpetual sunshine and plenty beyond the north wind. **2 hyperborean,** an inhabitant of the far north. —*adj.* **hyperborean,** of the far north; arctic; frigid. [< LL *Hyperboreanus* < L *Hyperboreus* < Gk. *Hyperboreos* beyond the north < *hyper–* beyond + *boreios* northern < *boreas* the north wind]

hy·per·crit·i·cal (hī′pər krit′ə kəl) *adj.* excessively critical. —**hy′per·crit′i·cal·ly,** *adv.*

hy·per·gly·ce·mi·a (hī′pər glī sē′mē ə) *n.* an abnormally high concentration of sugar in the blood. Also, **hyperglycaemia.** —**hy′per·gly·ce′mic,** *adj.*

Hy·pe·ri·on (hī pēr′ē ən) *n. Greek mythology.* **1** a Titan, father of the sun god Helios. **2** Helios. **3** Apollo.

hy·per·o·pi·a (hī′pər ō′pē ə) *n.* far-sightedness. [< NL < Gk. *hyper–* beyond + *ōps* eye]

hy·per·op·ic (hī′pər op′ik) *adj.* far-sighted.

hy·per·sen·si·tive (hī′pər sen′sə tiv) *adj.* excessively sensitive. —**hy′per·sen′si·tive·ness,** *n.*

hy·per·sen·si·tiv·i·ty (hī′pər sen′sə tiv′ə tē) *n.* excessive sensitivity.

hy·per·son·ic (hī′pər son′ik) *adj.* **1** of or denoting speed five or more times faster than that of sound. **2** able to travel at this speed.

hy·per·ten·sion (hī′pər ten′shən) *n.* an abnormally high blood pressure.

hy·per·thy·roid (hī′pər thī′roid) *n., adj.* —*n.* **1** an overactive thyroid gland. **2** a person having such a gland. —*adj.* relating to an overactive thyroid gland.

hy·per·tro·phy (hī pèr′trə fē) *n., pl.* **-phies;** *v.* **-phied, -phy·ing.** —*n.* the enlargement of a part or organ; growing too big. —*v.* grow too big. [< NL *hypertrophia* < Gk. *hyper–* over + *trophē* nourishment]

hy·phen (hī′fən) *n., v.* —*n.* a mark (-) used: **1** to connect words to form certain compounds (*double-dealer, light-hearted, door-to-door*). **2** to separate certain affixes to indicate special meaning (*re-creation* vs. *recreation*) or facilitate recognition of word elements for purposes of pronunciation, etc. (*re-enter*). **3** to indicate a break in a word at the end of a line of printing or writing. —*v.* hyphenate. [< LL < Gk. *hyphen* in one, hyphen < *hypo–* under + *hen* one]

hy·phen·ate (hī′fən āt′) *v.* **-at·ed, -at·ing.** connect by a hyphen; write or print with a hyphen.

hy·phen·a·tion (hī′fən ā′shən) *n.* the act of connecting by or writing with a hyphen.

hyp·nol·o·gy (hip nol′ə jē) *n.* the branch of science dealing with the phenomena of sleep.

hyp·no·sis (hip nō′sis) *n., pl.* **-ses** (-sēz). a state resembling deep sleep, but more active, in which a person has little will of his own and little feeling, and acts according to the suggestions of the person who induced the hypnosis. [< NL]

hyp·no·ther·a·pist (hip′nō ther′ə pist′) *n.* a person trained in hypnotherapy, especially one whose work it is.

hyp·no·ther·a·py (hip′nō ther′ə pē) *n.* the use of hypnotism to treat disorders, especially emotional, behavioral, or psychiatric disorders.

hyp·not·ic (hip not′ik) *adj., n.* —*adj.* 1 of, having to do with, or producing hypnosis. 2 easily hypnotized. 3 causing or tending to cause sleep: *the hypnotic monotone of his voice.*
—*n.* 1 a person under hypnosis or one who is easily hypnotized. 2 a drug or other means of causing sleep. [< LL *hypnoticus* < Gk. *hypnotikos* putting to sleep < *hypnoein* put to sleep < *hypnos* sleep]

hyp·not·i·cal·ly (hip not′ik lē) *adv.* in a hypnotic manner.

hyp·no·tism (hip′nə tiz′əm) *n.* 1 the inducing of hypnosis; hypnotizing. 2 the study of hypnosis.

hyp·no·tist (hip′nə tist) *n.* a person who hypnotizes.

hyp·no·tize (hip′nə tīz′) *v.* -tized, -tiz·ing. 1 put into a hypnotic state; cause hypnosis. 2 *Informal.* dominate or control the will of by suggestion. —**hyp′no·tiz′a·ble,** *adj.* —**hyp′no·ti·za′tion,** *n.* —**hyp′no·tiz′er,** *n.*

hy·po¹ (hī′pō) *n.* a colorless crystalline salt used as a fixing agent in photography; sodium thiosulphate or sodium hyposulphite. *Formula:* Na₂S₂O₃·5H₂O [short for *hyposulphite*]

hy·po² (hī′pō) *n., pl.* -pos. *Informal.* hypodermic.

hypo– *prefix.* 1 under; beneath; below, as in *hypodermic.* 2 less than; less than normal, as in *hypothyroid.* [< Gk. *hypo- < hypo*]

hy·po·chlo·rite (hī′pə klô′rīt) *n.* a salt of hypochlorous acid.

hy·po·chlo·rous acid (hī′pə klô′rəs) a yellow solution with an irritating odor, used as a bleach, disinfectant, etc. *Formula:* HClO

hy·po·chon·dri·a (hī′pə kon′drē ə) *n.* 1 unnatural anxiety about one's health; imaginary illness. 2 low spirits without any real reason. [< LL *hypochondria* abdomen < Gk. *hypochondria,* neut. pl. < *hypo-* under + *chondros* cartilage (of the breastbone); from the supposed seat of melancholy]

hy·po·chon·dri·ac (hī′pə kon′drē ak′) *n., adj.* —*n.* a person suffering from hypochondria. —*adj.* suffering from hypochondria.

hy·po·cot·yl (hī′pə kot′əl) *n.* the part of a plant embryo stem below the cotyledons. It produces the main root (radicle) at its lower end. See embryo for picture. [< *hypo-* + *cotyl(edon)*]

hy·poc·ri·sy (hi pok′rə sē) *n., pl.* -sies. 1 the act or fact of putting on a false appearance, especially of goodness or religion. 2 a pretending to be what one is not; pretence. [ME < OF *ypocrisie* < LL < Gk. *hypokrisis* acting, dissimulation, ult. < *hypo-* under + *krinein* judge]

hyp·o·crite (hip′ə krit′) *n.* a person who pretends to be what he is not, especially one who puts on an appearance of goodness or religion. [ME < OF *ypocrite* < L < Gk. *hypokritēs* actor. Related to HYPOCRISY.]

hyp·o·crit·i·cal (hip′ə krit′ə kəl) *adj.* of or like a hypocrite; insincere. —**hyp′o·crit′i·cal·ly,** *adv.*

hy·po·der·mic (hī′pə dèr′mik) *adj., n.* —*adj.* 1 under the skin. 2 injected or for injecting under the skin: *The doctor used a hypodermic needle.* —*n.* 1 a dose of medicine injected under the skin: *The doctor gave her a hypodermic to make her sleep.* 2 a syringe used to inject medicine under the skin. [< NL *hypoderma* < Gk. *hypo-* under + *derma* skin]

hy·po·der·mi·cal·ly (hī′pə dèr′mik lē) *adv.* by injection under the skin.

hypodermic injection an injection of medicine under the skin.

hy·po·gas·tric (hī′pə gas′trik) *adj.* of or having to do with the lower middle region of the abdomen.

hy·po·gly·ce·mi·a (hī′pō glī sē′mē ə) *n.* an abnormally low concentration of sugar in the blood. Also, **hypoglycaemia.** —**hy′po·gly·ce′mic,** *adj.*

hy·po·phos·phate (hī′pə fos′fāt) *n.* a salt of hypophosphoric acid.

hy·po·phos·phite (hī′pə fos′fīt) *n.* a salt of hypophosphorous acid, used in medicine as a tonic.

hy·po·phos·phor·ic (hī′pō fos fôr′ik) *adj.* of or having to do with an acid (H₄P₂O₆) produced by the slow oxidation of phosphorus in moist air.

hy·po·phos·pho·rous (hī′pə fos′fə rəs) *adj.* of or having to do with an acid of phosphorus (H₃PO₂) having salts which are used in medicine.

hy·poph·y·sis (hī pof′ə sis) *n., pl.* -ses (-sēz′). the pituitary gland. [< Gk. *hypophysis* attachment underneath < *hypo-* under + *physis* a growing < *phyein* cause to grow]

hy·po·sul·phite or **hy·po·sul·fite** (hī′pə sul′fīt) *n.* a salt of hyposulphurous acid.

hy·po·sul·phur·ous acid or **hy·po·sul·fur·ous acid** (hī′pō sul′fər əs, -sul′fyü rəs, *or* -sul fyür′əs) an unstable acid used as a reducing and bleaching agent. *Formula:* H₂S₂O₄

hy·pot·e·nuse (hī pot′ə nyüz′ *or* hī pot′ə nüz′, hī pot′ə nyüs′ *or* hī pot′ə nüs′) *n.* the side of a right-angled triangle opposite the right angle. See triangle for picture. [< LL *hypotenusa* < Gk. *hypoteinousa* subtending, ppr. of *hypoteinein* < *hypo-* under + *teinein* stretch]

hy·po·thal·a·mic (hī′pə thə lam′ik *or* hip′ə-) *adj.* of or having to do with the hypothalamus.

hy·po·thal·a·mus (hī′pə thal′ə məs *or* hip′ə-) *n.* the part of the brain beneath the thalamus. It controls hunger, thirst, temperature, and growth.

hy·poth·e·cate (hī poth′ə kāt′) *v.* -cat·ed, -cat·ing. pledge (property, stock, etc.) to a creditor as security for a loan or debt; mortgage. [< Med.L *hypothecare* < L < Gk. *hypothēkē* pledge < *hypo-* under + *tithenai* place] —**hy·poth′e·ca′tor,** *n.*

hy·poth·e·ca·tion (hī poth′ə kā′shən) *n.* 1 the act or fact of depositing as security. 2 a claim against property deposited as security.

hy·poth·e·nuse (hī poth′ə nyüz′ *or* hī pot′ə nüz′, hī poth′ə nyüs′ *or* hī poth′ə nüs′) *n.* hypotenuse.

hy·po·ther·mi·a (hī′pō thèr′mē ə) *n.* abnormally low body temperature. Hypothermia can be produced by exposure to cold air or water, leading to death in a matter of hours. Hypothermia is sometimes induced in medicine to slow a patient's metabolism, thus reducing the need for oxygen, especially during heart or brain surgery.

hy·poth·e·ses (hī poth′ə sēz′) *n.* pl. of hypothesis.

hy·poth·e·sis (hī poth′ə sis) *n., pl.* -ses. 1 something assumed because it seems likely to be a true explanation; theory. 2 a proposition assumed as a basis for reasoning. [< NL < Gk. *hypothesis* < *hypo-* under + *thesis* a placing]
☞ *Syn.* 1. See note at theory.

hy·poth·e·size (hī poth′ə sīz′) *v.* -sized, -siz·ing. 1 make a hypothesis. 2 assume; suppose.

hy·po·thet·ic (hī′pə thet′ik) *adj.* hypothetical.

hy·po·thet·i·cal (hī′pə thet′ə kəl) *adj.* 1 of or based on a hypothesis; assumed; supposed. 2 *Logic.* **a** of a proposition, involving a hypothesis or condition; conditional. **b** of a syllogism, having a hypothetical proposition for one of its premises. 3 fond of making hypotheses: *a hypothetical scientist.* [< L < Gk. *hypothetikos*] —**hy′po·thet′i·cal·ly,** *adv.*

hy·po·thy·roid (hī′pō thī′roid) *n., adj.* —*n.* 1 an underactive thyroid gland. 2 a person having such a gland. —*adj.* relating to an underactive thyroid gland.

hy·rax (hī′raks) *n.* any of an order (Hyracoidea) of small, agile, rodentlike mammals native to Africa and extreme SW Asia, having a plump body, short ears, tail, and neck, short, slender legs, and feet with pads on the soles and hooflike toes. [< NL *Hyrax* the generic name < Gk. *hyrax* shrew-mouse]

hy·son (hī′sən) *n.* a Chinese green tea. [< Chinese *hsi-ch'un* blooming spring]

hys·sop (his′əp) *n.* 1 a sweet-scented, perennial herb (*Hyssopus officinalis*) of the mint family native to Europe and Asia but widely cultivated as a garden herb, having evergreen leaves and spikes of small flowers used as flavoring for food and beverages and, formerly, as a medicine. 2 any of several related or similar plants. 3 a plant used in purification rites by the ancient Hebrews (Leviticus 14: 4, 6; Psalms 51: 7). [ME < OF < L < Gk. *hyssōpos* < Semitic]

hys·ter·ec·to·my (his′tə rek′tə mē) *n.* the surgical removal of the uterus. [< Gk. *hystera* uterus + E *-ectomy*]

hys·te·ri·a (his tēr′ē ə *or* his ter′ē ə) *n.* 1 a nervous disorder that causes violent fits of laughing and crying, imaginary or real illnesses, lack of self-control, etc. 2 a state of uncontrolled excitement, especially involving laughing or crying. [< NL < Gk. *hystera* uterus; because it was formerly thought that women are more often affected than men]

hys·ter·ic (his ter′ik) *adj., n.* —*adj.* hysterical. —*n.* a hysterical person.

hys·ter·i·cal (his ter′ə kəl) *adj.* 1 unnaturally excited. 2 showing an extreme lack of control; unable to stop laughing, crying, etc.; suffering from hysteria: *She was hysterical with grief.* [< L < Gk. *hysterikos* < *hystera* uterus] —**hys·ter′i·cal·ly,** *adv.*

hys·ter·ics (his ter′iks) *n.pl.* hysteria (def. 2).

I i

i or **I¹** (ī) *n.* **i's** or **I's. 1** the ninth letter of the English alphabet. **2** any speech sound represented by this letter. **3** a person or thing identified as *i*, especially the ninth in a series. **4** the Roman numeral for 1. **5** something shaped like the letter I. **6** (*adj.*) of or being an I or i.

I² (ī) *pron., subj.* **I,** *obj.* **me,** *poss.* **mine,** *pl. subj.* **we,** *pl. obj.* **us,** *pl. poss.* **ours,** *n., pl.* **I's.** *n., pl.* **I's.** the person who is speaking or writing. [OE *ic*]
☛ *Hom.* **aye, eye.**
☛ *Usage.* The pronoun *I* is written with a capital simply because in the old handwritten manuscripts a small *i* was likely to be lost or to get attached to a neighboring word, and a capital helped keep it a distinct word.

i– *prefix.* not; the form of **in-¹** before *gn,* as in *ignore.*
i. 1 intransitive. **2** island. **3** interest. **4** incisor.
I iodine.
I. 1 Island(s). **2** Isle(s). **3** *Politics.* Independent.
Ia. Iowa.
IA Iowa.
IAEA International Atomic Energy Agency (of the United Nations).
–ial *suffix.* a form of **-al,** used in *adverbial, facial,* etc.
i·amb (ī'amb *or* ī'am) *n.* an iambic foot or measure. [< F < L < Gk. *iambos*]
i·am·bic (ī am'bik) *adj., n. Prosody.* —*adj.* **1** of or designating a metrical foot consisting basically of two syllables, the first one having a weak stress and the second a strong stress. It has been by far the commonest metrical measure in English-language verse since the Middle Ages. *Example:*

   The sun | that brief | Decem | ber day

   Rose cheer | less o | ver hills | of gray.

2 in classical Latin and Greek verse, of or designating a metrical measure, or foot, consisting of two syllables, the first one short and the second one long. —*n.* **1** iamb. **2** Usually, **iambics,** *pl.* iambic verse.
iambic pentameter a poetic metre based on five iambic feet in a line of verse. Iambic pentameter was the standard metre for English verse from about the fifteenth century to the nineteenth.
i·am·bus (ī am'bəs) *n., pl.* **-bi** (-bī *or* -bē) **or bus·es.** iamb.
–ian *suffix.* a form of **-an,** used in certain words, such as *mammalian, Canadian,* etc.
–iana *suffix.* a form of *-ana,* as in *Canadiana.*
IATA International Air Transport Association.
i·at·ro·gen·ic (ī at'rə jen' ik) *adj.* of a disease or symptoms, caused or induced by a physician or medical treatment.
ib. ibid.
I·be·ri·an (ī bēr'ē ən) *n., adj.* —*n.* **1** a member of a group of peoples of European race, probably related to the peoples of N Africa, who inhabited the Iberian Peninsula (present-day Spain and Portugal) in ancient times. **2** any of the languages of the ancient Iberians. **3** a native or inhabitant of Spain or Portugal. **4** a native or inhabitant of an ancient region in W Asia, south of the Caucasus, called Iberia.
—*adj.* **1** of or having to do with the ancient Iberian Peninsula or ancient Iberia in Asia, or their peoples. **2** of or having to do with present-day Spain or Portugal or their inhabitants or languages.
i·bex (ī'beks) *n., pl.* **i·bex·es, ib·i·ces** (ib'ə sēz' *or* ī'bə sēz'), **or** *(esp. collectively)* **i·bex.** any of several wild goats (genus *Capra*) of Europe, Asia, and NE Africa having large horns that curve back in a semicircle and have broad ridges across the front surfaces. [< L]
ibid. in the same place (for L *ibidem*).
☛ *Usage.* **Ibid.** is used in a footnote to refer to the book, article, etc. mentioned in the immediately preceding footnote.
i·bis (ī'bis) *n., pl.* **i·bis·es** or *(esp. collectively)* **i·bis.** any of various medium-sized wading birds (family Threskiornithidae) of warm regions having a long, slender, downward-curved bill. The sacred ibis (*Threskiornis aethiopica*) of ancient Egypt, a black-and-white bird, is now found only south of the Sahara in Africa. The scarlet ibis (*Eudocimus ruber*) is found in tropical America. [< L < Gk. < Egyptian]
–ible *adjective-forming suffix.* that can be ——ed, as in

impressible, perfectible, reducible. [< OF < L *-ibilis*]
☛ *Usage.* See note at **-able.**
–ic *adjective-forming suffix.* **1** of or having to do with, as in *atmospheric, Icelandic.* **2** having the nature of, as in *artistic, heroic.* **3** constituting or being, as in *bombastic, monolithic.* **4** characterized by; containing; made up of, as in *alcoholic, iambic.* **5** made by; caused by, as in *phonographic.* **6** like; like that of; characteristic of, as in *meteoric, antagonistic, idyllic, sophomoric.* Many words ending in *-ic* have two or more of these meanings (1 to 6). **7** in chemical terms, *-ic* implies a smaller proportion of the element that *-ous* implies, as in *boric, chloric, ferric, sulphuric.* [< F *-ique* or L *-icus* or Gk. *-ikos*]
–ical *adjective-forming suffix.* **1** *-ic,* as in *geometrical, parasitical, hysterical.* **2** *-ic,* specialized or differentiated in meaning, as in *economical.* **3** *-ical* sometimes arises from *-al* added to nouns ending in *-ic,* as in *critical, musical.* [< L *-icalis*]
–ically *suffix. -ic* + *-ly.* Instead of *artistic-ly* we write *artistically;* instead of *alphabetic-ly* we write *alphabetically.* In speaking, the suffix is ordinarily pronounced in two syllables (-ik lē).
ICAO International Civil Aviation Organization (of the United Nations).
I·car·i·an (i ker'ē ən *or* ī ker'ē ən) *adj.* rash; carelessly bold. [< *Icarus*]
Ic·a·rus (ik'ə rəs *or* ī'kə rəs) *n. Greek mythology.* the son of Daedalus. When he and his father were escaping from Crete, using wings that Daedalus had made, Icarus flew so high that the sun melted the wax which held the wings on, and he fell to his death in the sea.
ICBM intercontinental ballistic missile.
ice (īs) *n., adj., v.* **iced, ic·ing.** —*n.* **1** water made solid by freezing; frozen water. **2** a layer or surface of ice. **3** a frozen area of sea or land: *Icebreakers cut through ice. Baby seals are found on the ice.* **4** a frozen surface for skating, curling, hockey, etc. **5 the ice,** *Cdn.* especially in Newfoundland, the edge of the Arctic ice fields where seal-hunting takes place. **6** something that looks or feels like ice: *camphor ice.* **7** a frozen dessert, usually made of sweetened fruit juice. **8** icing. **9** *Slang.* diamonds. **10** coldness of manner.
break the ice, *Informal.* **a** make a beginning; start something dangerous or difficult. **b** overcome first difficulties in taking or getting acquainted.
cut no ice, *Informal.* have little or no effect.
on thin ice, in a dangerous or difficult position.
—*adj.* **1** of ice; having to do with ice. **2** made or consisting of ice.
—*v.* **1** cool with ice; put ice in or around. **2** cover with ice. **3** turn to ice; freeze. **4** cover with icing. **5** *Hockey.* **a** shoot (a puck) from the defensive zone past the red line at the opposite end of the 'rink: *No player may ice the puck when his team is at full strength.* **b** put a team into play: *Our town iced a good hockey team.* [OE *īs*]
—**ice'less,** *adj.*
ice age 1 any of the times in geological history when much of the earth was covered with glaciers. **2** Often, **Ice Age,** the most recent such time, the Pleistocene epoch, when most of the northern hemisphere was covered by glaciers.
ice·berg (īs'bėrg') *n.* a large mass of ice floating in the sea. [? < Du. *ijsberg,* literally, ice mountain]
ice·boat (īs'bōt') *n.* **1** a light frame, often triangular, set on runners and fitted with sails or a propeller for skimming along the frozen surface of a lake, river, etc. **2** icebreaker.
ice·bound (īs'bound') *adj.* **1** held fast by ice; frozen in: *The ship was icebound for several weeks.* **2** shut in or obstructed by ice: *The port at Churchill is icebound for about 10 months of the year.*
ice–box or **ice·box** (īs'boks') *n.* **1** an insulated chest or box in which food is kept cool by ice. **2** refrigerator.
ice·break·er (īs'brāk'ər) *n.* a ship designed for breaking a passage through ice.
ice bridge 1 a winter road over a frozen river, lake, etc. **2** a bridge of ice formed by the jamming of ice in a river or other channel.
ice·cap (īs'kap') *n.* a permanent covering of ice over an area, sloping down on all sides from an elevated centre.

ice cream (īs'krēm' *or* īs'krēm') a frozen dessert made of cream or custard sweetened and flavored.

ice cube a small chunk of ice, usually having six sides, used for chilling drinks or food.

iced (īst) *adj.* **1** cooled with ice. **2** covered with ice. **3** covered with icing.

ice field 1 a large sheet of ice floating in the sea, larger than a floe. **2** a large sheet of ice on land.

ice-fish·er·man (īs'fish'ər mən) *n.* a person who goes ice fishing.

ice fishing *Cdn.* the act or practice of fishing through a hole or holes cut through ice.

ice hockey hockey.

ice·house (īs'hous') *n.* **1** a building where ice is stored and kept from melting. **2** a structure or pit having insulated walls and roof and used as a cold storage for meat and other perishables which are stored with blocks of ice or snow. **3** a snow house.

ice island a very large iceberg, often several kilometres across, having a flattish top.

ice–jam (īs'jam') *n., v.* **-jammed, -jam·ming.** —*n.* Also, **ice jam,** the damming up of a river or other watercourse with masses of ice that cannot float down owing to some obstruction. —*v.* block by an ice-jam.

Ice·land·er (īs'lan'dər *or* īs'lən dər) *n.* a native or inhabitant of Iceland, a large island in the N Atlantic.

Ice·lan·dic (īs lan'dik) *n., adj.* —*n.* the North Germanic language of Iceland. —*adj.* of or having to do with Iceland, its people, or their language.

Iceland moss a brownish or greyish lichen (*Cetraria islandica*) of arctic and northern alpine regions, an important food for caribou, muskoxen, etc. and also used in human food.

ice·man (īs'man' *or* īs'mən) *n., pl.* **-men** (-men' *or* -mən). a person who sells, delivers, or handles ice.

ice pack 1 a large expanse of floating ice, consisting of many small floes packed together. **2** a bag containing ice for application to the body.

ice pick a sharp-pointed tool for breaking up ice.

ice road ice bridge (def. 1).

ice sheet a broad, thick sheet of ice covering a very large area for a long time.

ice skate skate¹ (def. 1 and 2).

ice–skate (īs'skat') *v.* **-skat·ed, -skat·ing.** skate on ice. —**ice'-skat'er,** *n.*

ice storm a freezing rain that covers exposed surfaces with a layer of glistening ice; silver thaw (def. 1).

ice time 1 *Hockey.* the time actually spent on the ice by a player or players during a game. **2** the time during which the ice at a rink is available to a team or group.

ice water 1 water cooled with ice. **2** melted ice.

ice worm 1 *Cdn.* in the North: **a** a fictional creature, thought up as a joke. **b** ice-worm cocktail, a cocktail having bits of spaghetti in it. **2** a worm found on mountain snow and ice fields. [coined during the Klondike gold rush]

ich·neu·mon (ik nyü'mən *or* ik nü'mən) *n.* **1** a mongoose (*Herpestes ichneumon*) of Africa and S Europe. **2** ichneumon fly. [< L *ichneumon,* literally, searcher (supposedly of crocodile's eggs), ult. < *ichnos* track]

ichneumon fly any of a very large family (Ichneumonidae) of wasplike insects found in many parts of the world, including North America, whose larvae are parasites of many other insect larvae, especially caterpillars. Ichneumon flies are considered generally beneficial because they destroy insect pests.

i·chor¹ (ī'kôr *or* ī'kər) *n. Greek mythology.* the fluid supposed to flow in the veins of the gods. [< Gk.]

i·chor² (ī'kôr *or* ī'kər) *n.* an acrid, watery discharge from ulcers, wounds, etc. [< NL < Gk.]

ich·thy·ol·o·gist (ik'thē ol'ə jist) *n.* a person trained in ichthyology, especially one whose work it is.

ich·thy·ol·o·gy (ik'thē ol'ə jē) *n.* the branch of zoology dealing with fishes. [< Gk. *ichthys* fish + E *-logy*]

ich·thy·o·saur (ik'thē ə sôr') *n.* any of an order (Ichthyosauria) of extinct sea reptiles having a fishlike body, four flippers, and a long snout. [< NL *ichthyosaurus* < Gk. *ichthys* fish + *sauros* lizard] —**ich'thy·o·sau'ri·an,** *adj.*

ich·thy·o·sau·rus (ik'thē ə sô'rəs) *n., pl.* **-sau·ri** (-sô'rī or

-sô'rē). any of an order (Ichthyosauria) of extinct porpoiselike marine reptiles of the Mesozoic Era.

i·ci·cle (ī'si kəl) *n.* **1** a pointed, hanging stick of ice formed by the freezing of dripping water. **2** anything resembling this, such as tinsel for trimming a Christmas tree. **3** *Informal.* a cold or unemotional person. [ME *isykle* < OE *īs* ice + *gicel* icicle]

ic·ing (īs'ing) *n.* a sweet, creamy mixture used to cover cakes, etc., made of sugar and some liquid, flavoring, sometimes the beaten whites of eggs, etc.

icing sugar powdered sugar, usually containing a small amount of cornstarch. It is used in making icing, candy, etc.

i·con or **i·kon** (ī'kon) *n., pl.* **i·cons, i·co·nes** (ī'kə nēz'). **1** a sacred picture or image of Christ, an angel, a saint, etc. **2** any picture or image. Also, **eikon.** [< L < Gk. *eikōn*]

i·con·ic (ī kon'ik) *adj.* **1** of or having to do with icons or resembling an icon. **2** of memorial sculptures, etc., conventional in style.

i·con·o·clasm (ī kon'ə klaz'əm) *n.* the belief or practice of iconoclasts.

i·con·o·clast (ī kon'ə klast') *n.* **1** a person opposed to the use of images in religious worship. **2** a person who attacks cherished beliefs or institutions. [< Med.L *ikonoklastes* < Med.Gk. *eikonoklastēs* < Gk. *eikōn* image + *klaein* break]

i·con·o·clas·tic (ī kon'ə klas'tik) *adj.* of or having to do with iconoclasts.

i·co·nog·ra·phy (ī'kə nog'rə fē) *n., pl.* **-phies. 1** the art or study of illustrating by means of icons, symbols, etc. **2** the representation of an individual in portraits, statues, etc. [< Med.L < Gk. *eikonographia.* See icon, -graphy.]

–ics *suffix.* **1** facts, principles, science, as in *physics.* **2** methods, system, activities, as in *tactics.* [originally pl. of -ic < L -ica < Gk. *-ika,* neut. pl.]

ic·tas (ik'təs) *n.pl.* iktas.

ic·ter·ic (ik ter'ik) *n., adj.* —*n.* **1** a remedy for jaundice. **2** one who is affected with jaundice. —*adj.* of or having to do with icterus.

ic·ter·us (ik'tər əs) *n.* **1** jaundice. **2** *Botany.* the yellowing of certain plants, caused by too much cold or moisture. [< L *icterus* jaundice < Gk. *ikteros* a yellow bird believed to cure jaundice]

ic·tus (ik'təs) *n., pl.* **-tus·es** or **-tus.** rhythmical or metrical stress. [< L *ictus* a blow < *icere* to hit]

i·cy (ī'sē) *adj.* **i·ci·er, i·ci·est. 1** like ice; very cold: *an icy blast of wind.* **2** having much ice; covered with ice: *an icy road.* **3** of ice. **4** without warm feeling; cold and unfriendly: *an icy stare.* —**i'ci·ly,** *adv.* —**i'ci·ness,** *n.*

I'd (īd) **1** I would: *I'd leave tomorrow if I could.* **2** I had: *I'd better get back to work.*

id. idem.

ID Idaho.

Ida. Idaho.

ID card identification card.

–ide or **–id** *suffix.* compound of ——, as in *chloride, sulphide.* [< *oxide*]

i·de·a (ī dē'ə) *n.* **1** a mental concept or abstraction: *the idea of immortality.* **2** an opinion: *to force one's ideas on others.* **3** a plan, scheme, or design: *She told them her idea for the publicity campaign.* **4 ideas,** *pl.* resourcefulness; creative thinking: *a man of ideas, full of ideas.* **5** the point or purpose: *The idea of a vacation is to relax.* **6** a fancy or notion: *I had an idea you would be here for dinner.*

get ideas into (one's) **head,** expect too much.

the very idea, it is outrageous or ridiculous, etc.: *Crash the party? The very idea!*

[< L < Gk. *idea* form, kind < base *id-* see]

☞ **Syn. Idea, notion, thought** = something understood or formed in the mind. **Idea** is the general word applying to something existing in the mind as the result of understanding, thinking, reasoning, imagining, etc.: *Learn to express your ideas clearly.* **Notion** applies to an idea not fully, clearly, plainly, or completely formed or understood: *I have only a notion of what you mean.* **Thought** applies to an idea formed by reflection or reasoning, rather than by the imagination: *Tell me your thoughts on this proposal.*

i·de·al (ī dē'əl) *n., adj.* —*n.* a perfect type; model to be imitated; what one would wish to be: *Her mother is her ideal. Religion holds up high ideals for us to follow.*
—*adj.* **1** just as one would wish; perfect: *A warm, sunny day is ideal for a picnic.* **2** existing only in thought: *A point without length, breadth, or thickness is an ideal object.* **3** not practical; visionary. **4** having to do with ideas; representing an idea. [< LL *idealis* < L *idea.* See IDEA.] —**i·de'al·ism,** *n.*

i·de·al·ism (ī dē'əl iz'əm) *n.* **1** the practice of living or acting according to one's ideals or what ought to be, regardless of circumstances or of the approval or disapproval of others. **2** a

cherishing of fine ideals. **3** the imaginative or idealized treatment of things in art or literature as opposed to a faithful rendering of nature. **4** *Philosophy.* the belief that all our knowledge is a knowledge of ideas and that it is impossible to know whether there really is a world of objects on which our ideas are based. Idealism is opposed to materialism, which holds that objects really exist apart from our ideas about them.

i·de·al·ist (ī dē′əl ist) *n.* **1** a person who has high ideals and strives to act according to them. **2** a person who neglects practical matters in following ideals. **3** one who follows or practises idealism in art, literature, or philosophy.

i·de·al·is·tic (ī′dē əl is′tik *or* ī dē′əl is′tik) *adj.* **1** having high ideals and acting according to them. **2** forgetting or neglecting practical matters in trying to follow out one's ideals; not practical. **3** of or having to do with idealism or idealists. —**i·de′al·is′ti·cal·ly,** *adv.*

i·de·al·i·ty (ī′dē al′ə tē) *n., pl.* **-ties. 1** an ideal quality or character. **2** an ability to idealize. **3** something ideal or imaginary.

i·de·al·i·za·tion (ī dē′əl ə zā′shən *or* ī dē′əl ī zā′shən) *n.* **1** idealizing or being idealized. **2** the result of idealizing.

i·de·al·ize (ī dē′əl īz′) *v.* **-ized, -iz·ing.** make ideal; think of or represent as perfect rather than as is actually the case: *Douglas idealized his older sister and thought that everything she did was right.* —**i·de′al·iz′er,** *n.*

i·de·al·ly (ī dē′əl ē) *adv.* **1** according to an ideal; perfectly. **2** in idea or theory.

i·de·a·tion (ī′dē ā′shən) *n.* the formation of ideas.

i·de·a·tion·al (ī′dē ā′shən əl) *adj.* having to do with the process of forming ideas.

i·dée fixe (ē dā fēks′) *French.* a fixed idea; obsession.

idem (ī′dem *or* id′em) *pron. or adj. Latin.* the same as previously given or mentioned.

i·den·tic (ī den′tik) *adj.* identical.

i·den·ti·cal (ī den′tə kəl) *adj.* **1** the same: *Both events happened on the identical day.* **2** exactly alike: *Fifteen centimetres and 1.5 decimetres are identical amounts.* **3** of twins, developing from a single fertilized egg cell that split in two. Identical twins are always the same sex and usually resemble each other very closely. Compare **fraternal** (def. 3). [< Med.L *identicus* < L *idem* same] —**i·den′ti·cal·ly,** *adv.* **i·den′ti·cal·ness,** *n.*
☞ *Syn.* **1.** See note at **same.**

i·den·ti·fi·ca·tion (ī den′tə fə kā′shən) *n.* **1** an identifying or being identified. **2** something used to identify a person or thing: *She showed her driver's licence as identification.*

i·den·ti·fy (ī den′tə fī′) *v.* **-fied, -fy·ing. 1** recognize as being, or show to be, a certain person or thing; prove to be the same: *Fred identified the bag as his by what it contained.* **2** make the same; treat as the same: *The good king identified his people's welfare with his own.* **3** connect closely; link; associate: *He identified himself with the revolutionary movement.* —**i·den′ti·fi′able,** *adj.* —**i·den′ti·fi′er,** *n.*

i·den·ti·ty (ī den′tə tē) *n., pl.* **-ties. 1** being oneself or itself and not another; who or what one is: *The writer concealed his identity under an assumed name.* **2** exact likeness; sameness: *an identity of interests.* **3** the state or fact of being the same one or ones as described, mentioned, etc.: *They have established identity of these pearls with the ones reported missing.* [< LL *identitas,* ult. < L *idem* same]

ideo– *combining form.* idea: *ideogram = a written symbol that represents an idea.*

id·e·o·gram (id′ē ə gram′ *or* ī′dē ə-) *n.* a graphic symbol that represents a thing or an idea directly, without representing the sounds of the word for the thing or idea. Most Egyptian hieroglyphics and some Chinese characters are ideograms, as are numerals.

id·e·o·graph (id′ē ə graf′ *or* ī′dē ə-) *n.* ideogram.

i·de·o·log·i·cal (ī′dē ə loj′ə kəl *or* id′ē ə loj′ə kəl) *adj.* of or having to do with ideology. —**i·de·ol·og′i·cal·ly,** *adv.*

i·de·ol·o·gist (ī′dē ol′ə jist′ *or* id′ē ol′ə jist′) *n.* **1** a person who supports or expounds a particular ideology. **2** a person who studies ideologies or ideology. **3** a theorist, especially as opposed to a practical person.

i·de·o·logue (ī′dē ə log′ *or* id′dē ə log′) *n.* an ideologist, especially a person who supports or expounds a particular social or political ideology.

i·de·ol·o·gy (ī′dē ol′ə jē *or* id′ē ol′ə jē) *n., pl.* **-gies. 1** a body of doctrines or concepts, especially about social, political, or economic systems. **2** the combined doctrines, assertions, and intentions of a social or political movement. **3** abstract speculation, especially theorizing or speculation of a visionary or unpractical nature. **4** the study of ideas, their nature and origin.

---

hat, āge, fär; let, ēqual, tèrm; it, īce
hot, ōpen, ôrder; oil, out; cup, pùt, rüle,
above, takən, pencəl, lemən, circəs
ch, child; ng, long; sh, ship
th, thin; ᴛʜ, then; zh, measure

ides (īdz) *n.* in the ancient Roman calendar, the 15th day of March, May, July, and October, and the 13th day of the other months (*used with a singular or plural verb*). [< OF < L *idus*]

id·i·o·cy (id′ē ə sē) *n., pl.* **-cies. 1** the state of being an idiot. **2** an acting like an idiot. **3** very great stupidity or folly.

id·i·o·lect (id′ē ə lect′) *n.* the dialect of a person; the form of speech, including the sounds, grammar, usage, and vocabulary, used by an individual. [< idio– (< Gk. *idios* one's own) + (*dia*)*lect*]

id·i·om (id′ē əm) *n.* **1** a phrase or expression whose meaning cannot be understood from the ordinary meanings of its individual words: *"How do you do?" and "I have caught cold" are English idioms.* **2** dialect: *He speaks in the idiom of the Ottawa Valley.* **3** a people's way of expressing themselves: *In the French idiom, one can say "of a rapidity" for "rapid."* **4** *Music, arts, etc.* an individual manner of expression. [< LL < Gk. *idioma,* ult. < *idios* one's own]
☞ *Syn.* **2, 3.** See note at **language.**

id·i·o·mat·ic (id′ē ə mat′ik) *adj.* **1** using an idiom or idioms. **2** of or concerning idioms. **3** showing the individual character of a language; characteristic of a particular language. —**id′i·o·mat′i·cal·ly,** *adv.*

id·i·o·syn·cra·sy (id′ē ə sing′krə sē) *n., pl.* **-sies.** a personal peculiarity of taste, behavior, opinion, etc.: *He was an eccentric person with many idiosyncrasies.* [< Gk. *idiosynkrasia* < *idios* one's own + *synkrasis* temperament < *syn* together + *kerannynai* mix]

id·i·o·syn·crat·ic (id′ē ə sin krat′ik) *adj.* having to do with or due to idiosyncrasy.

id·i·ot (id′ē ət) *n.* **1** a person born with little ability to learn; a person who does not develop mentally. **2** a very stupid or foolish person: *He was an idiot to refuse that offer.* [< L < Gk. *idiōtēs,* originally, private person < *idios* one's own]
☞ *Syn.* See note at **fool.**

id·i·ot·ic (id′ē ot′ik) *adj.* of or like an idiot; very stupid or foolish. —**id′i·ot′i·cal·ly,** *adv.*

i·dle (ī′dəl) *adj.* **i·dler, i·dlest;** *v.* **i·dled, i·dling.** —*adj.* **1** doing nothing; not busy; not working: *idle hands.* **2** not willing to do things; lazy. **3** useless; worthless: *He wasted his time in idle pleasures.* **4** without any good reason, cause or foundation: *idle fears, idle rumors.*
—*v.* **1** be idle; waste time; do nothing: *Are you going to spend your whole vacation just idling?* **2** run slowly without transmitting power: *The motor of a car idles when it is out of gear and running slowly.* **3** spend (time) wastefully (*used with* away): *She idled away the hours.* **4** cause (a person or thing) to be idle; take out of work or use. [OE *īdel*] —**i′dle·ness,** *n.* —**i′dly,** *adv.*
☞ *Hom.* **idol, idyll.**
☞ *Syn. adj.* **1, 2. Idle, lazy, indolent** = not active or working. **Idle** = not busy or working at the moment, and does not always suggest cause for blame: *The long drought made many farm workers idle.* **Lazy,** usually suggesting cause for blame, means "not liking to work," and "not industrious when at work": *Lazy people are seldom successful.* **Indolent** = by nature or habit fond of ease and opposed to work or activity: *Too much idleness sometimes makes a man indolent.*

i·dler (ī′dlər) *n.* **1** a lazy person. **2** a device allowing a motor to idle. **3** an idle wheel.

idle wheel 1 a gear wheel placed between two others to transfer motion from one axis to another without change in direction or speed. **2** a pulley for taking up slack in a belt; idle pulley.

i·dol (ī′dəl) *n.* **1** an image or other object worshipped as a god. **2** in the Bible, a false god. **3** a person or thing worshipped or loved very much; object of extreme devotion. [ME < OF < L *idolum* < Gk. *eidōlon* image < *eidos* form]
☞ *Hom.* **idle, idyll.**

i·dol·a·ter (ī dol′ə tər) *n.* **1** a person who worships idols. **2** an admirer; adorer; devotee.

i·dol·a·tress (ī dol′ə tris) *n.* **1** a woman who worships idols. **2** an adorer; devotee.

i·dol·a·trous (ī dol′ə trəs) *adj.* **1** worshipping idols. **2** having to do with idolatry. **3** blindly adoring. —**i·dol′a·trous·ly,** *adv.*

i·dol·a·try (ī dol′ə trē) *n., pl.* **-tries. 1** the worship of idols. **2** worship of a person or thing; great love or admiration; extreme devotion. [< OF < L < Gk. *eidōlolatreia* < *eidōlon* image + *latreia* service]

i·dol·ize (ī′dəl īz′) v. **-ized, -iz·ing. 1** worship as an idol; make an idol of: *The ancient Hebrews idolized the golden calf.* **2** love or admire very much; be extremely devoted to: *The boy idolizes his mother.* —**i′dol·i·za′tion,** n.

i·dyll or **i·dyl** (ī′dəl or id′əl) n. **1** in poetry or prose, a short description of a simple and charming scene or event, especially one connected with country life. **2** a simple and charming scene, event, or experience suitable for such a description. **3** a short musical composition in a pastoral or sentimental mood. [< L *idyllium* < Gk. *eidyllion,* dim. of *eidos* form]
☛ *Hom.* **idle, idol** (ī′dəl).

i·dyl·lic (ī dil′ik or i dil′ik) adj. suitable for an idyll; simple and charming. —**i·dyl′li·cal·ly,** adv.

–ie suffix. little; darling, as in *dearie, lassie.* [var. of -y²]

i.e. that is (for L *id est*).

IE Indo-European.

–ier suffix. a person occupied or concerned with —, as in *financier, clothier.* [< F < L -*arius*]

if (if) conj., n. —conj. **1** supposing that; on condition that; in case that: *If you are going, leave now. I'll go if you will.* **2** whether: *I wonder if he will go.* **3** although; even though: *If he is little, he is strong.*
as if, as it would be if.
—n. a condition or supposition. [OE *gif*]
☛ *Usage.* **If, whether. If** is used to express conditions: *If the gasoline holds out, he will reach Jasper before dawn.* In formal usage **if** is not used with **or. Whether,** usually with **or,** is used, though not consistently, in: **a** conditions of two parts: *Whether it rains or not, they are determined to go.* **b** indirect questions: *He asked whether they should go or stay.* **c** expressions of doubt: *They wondered whether their decision had been wise.* In informal usage **if** would commonly take the place of **whether** in sentences **b** and **c** above.

IF, I.F., or **i.f.** intermediate frequency.

if·fy (if′ē) adj. *Informal.* uncertain, undecided, or risky: *an iffy proposition.*

I.F.S. or **IFS** Irish Free State.

i·gloo (ig′lü) n., pl. **-loos. 1** an Inuit dwelling, especially a domed structure built of blocks of snow. **2** any structure resembling this in shape. [< Eskimo *iglu, igdlu* abode, dwelling (irrespective of material and style of structure)]

ig·ne·ous (ig′nē əs) adj. **1** of or having to do with fire. **2** *Geology.* designating rock formed by the solidification of molten matter: *Granite is igneous rock.* [< L *igneus* < *ignis* fire]

ig·nis fat·u·us (ig′nis fach′ü əs) pl. **ig·nes fat·u·i** (ig′nēz fach′ü ī′ or fach′ü ē′). **1** a flitting phosphorescent light seen at night chiefly over marshy ground; will-o'-the-wisp. **2** something deluding or misleading. [< NL *ignis fatuus,* literally, foolish fire]

ig·nite (ig nīt′) v. **-nit·ed, -nit·ing. 1** set on fire. **2** make intensely hot; cause to glow with heat. **3** take fire; begin to burn. **4** *Chemistry.* heat to the point of combustion or chemical change. [< L *ignire* < *ignis* fire] —**ig·nit′er,** n.
☛ *Syn.* **1.** See note at **kindle.**

ig·ni·tion (ig nish′ən) n. **1** a setting on fire. **2** a catching fire. **3** a means of igniting or setting on fire. **4** the apparatus for igniting the explosive vapor in the cylinders of an internal-combustion engine. **5** any chemical or mechanical device used to ignite a rocket propellant or a fuel mixture in a jet engine.

ig·no·ble (ig nō′bəl) adj. **1** mean; base; without honor: *To betray a friend is ignoble.* **2** not of noble birth or position; humble: *Thomas Beckett came from an ignoble family.* [< L *ignobilis* < *in-* not + OL *gnobilis* noble] —**ig·no′ble·ness,** n. —**ig·no′bly,** adv.

ig·no·min·i·ous (ig′nə min′ē əs) adj. **1** shameful; disgraceful; dishonorable; humiliating. **2** contemptible. [< L *ignominiosus* < *ignominia.* See IGNOMINY.] —**ig′no·min′i·ous·ly,** adv. —**ig′no·min′i·ous·ness,** n.

ig·no·min·y (ig′nə min′ē) n., pl. **-min·ies. 1** loss of one's good name; public shame and disgrace; dishonor. **2** shameful action or conduct. [< L *ignominia* < *in-* not + *nomen* name; form influenced by OL *gnoscere* come to know]
☛ *Syn.* **1.** See note at **disgrace.**

ig·no·ra·mus (ig′nə rā′məs or ig′nə ram′əs) n., pl. **-mus·es.** an ignorant person. [< L *ignoramus* we do not know]

ig·no·rance (ig′nə rəns) n. a lack of knowledge; the quality or condition of being ignorant.

ig·no·rant (ig′nə rənt) adj. **1** knowing little or nothing; without knowledge: *A person who has not had much opportunity to learn may be ignorant without being stupid.* **2** caused by or showing lack of knowledge: *an ignorant remark.* **3** uninformed; unaware: *He was ignorant of the fact that his house had been burned.* [< L *ignorans, -antis,* ppr. of *ignorare* not know. See IGNORE.] —**ig′no·rant·ly,** adv.

☛ *Syn.* **1. Ignorant, illiterate, uneducated** = without knowledge. **Ignorant** = without general knowledge, sometimes without knowledge of some particular subject: *People who live in the city are often ignorant of farm life.* **Illiterate** = unable to read or write: *There are many illiterate people in the underdeveloped countries.* **Uneducated** = without systematic training or learning, in schools or from books: *Because of the shortage of schools many people in the world's backward countries are uneducated.*

ig·nore (ig nôr′) v. **-nored, -nor·ing.** pay no attention to; disregard. [< L *ignorare* not know < *ignarus* unaware < *in-* not + OL *gnarus* aware; form influenced by *ignotus* unknown]

i·gua·na (i gwä′nə) n. any of the larger lizards of the chiefly tropical American lizard family Iguanidae. The bright-green common iguana (*Iguana iguana*), found from Mexico south to N South America, often grows to a length of over 150 cm. [< Sp. < Carib]

IHS Jesus (a Christian emblem or monogram). [ME < LL, a misinterpretation of Gk. ΙΗΣ, the first three letters of the name Jesus]

i·ke·ba·na (ik′ə bä nə or ē′kə bä′nə) n. the Japanese art of flower arranging, which emphasizes a symmetrical balance and simplicity of design.

i·kon (ī′kon) See **icon.**

ik·tas (ik′täs) n.pl. *Cdn.* on the West Coast, goods or belongings; things: *We've got food and all the iktas we need for now.* [< Chinook Jargon]

il–¹ prefix. a form of **in-¹** occuring before *l,* as in *illegal.*

il–² prefix. a form of **in-²** occurring before *l,* as in *illuminate.*

IL Illinois.

il·e·ac (il′ē ak′) adj. of or having to do with the ileum.

il·e·i·tis (il′ē ī′tis) n. an inflammation of the ileum, due to infection, a tumor, etc. and involving partial or complete blocking of the passage of food through the small intestine.

il·e·um (il′ē əm) n. *Anatomy.* the lowest part of the small intestine. See **alimentary canal** for picture. [< LL *ileum,* var. of *ilium,* sing. of L *ilia* loins, entrails]
☛ *Hom.* **illium.**

i·lex (ī′leks) n. **1** holm oak. **2** holly. [< L]

il·i·ac (il′ē ak′) adj. of, having to do with, or near the ilium.

Il·i·ad (il′ē əd) n. a Greek epic poem, by Homer, about the siege of Ilium (Troy). [< L < Gk. *Ilias, -iados* < *Ilion* Ilium]

Il·i·on (il′ē ən) n. *Poetic.* Ilium.

il·i·um (il′ē əm) n., pl. **il·i·a** (il′ē ə). the broad, flat upper portion of the hipbone. See **pelvis** for picture. [< NL < LL *ilium,* sing. L *ilia* loins, entrails]
☛ *Hom.* **illeum.**

Il·i·um (il′ē əm) n. *Poetic.* ancient Troy.

ilk (ilk) adj., n. —adj. *Archaic.* same. —n. *Informal.* kind; sort.
of that ilk, *Informal.* **a** of the same place or name. **b** of that kind or sort.
[OE *īlca* same]

ill (il) adj. **worse, worst;** n., adv. —adj. **1** having some disease; not well; sick. **2** bad; evil; harmful: *an ill deed.* **3** unfavorable; unfortunate: *an ill wind.* **4** unkind; harsh; cruel.
ill at ease, uncomfortable.
—n. **1** a sickness; disease. **2** an evil; a harm; a trouble: *Poverty is an ill.*
—adv. **1** badly; harmfully. **2** unfavorably; unfortunately: *to fare ill.* **3** in an unkind manner; harshly; cruelly: *He speaks ill of his former friends.* **4** with trouble or difficulty; scarcely: *You can ill afford to waste your money.*
take ill, fall sick; become ill.
take (something) ill, take offence at or be offended by (something). [ME < ON *illr*]
☛ *Usage.* See note at **sick.**

I'll (īl) I will.

ill. illustration; illustrated.

Ill. Illinois.

ill–ad·vised (il′əd vīzd′) adj. acting or done without enough consideration; unwise.

ill–bred (il′bred′) adj. badly brought up; impolite; rude.

ill breeding bad manners; lack of a good upbringing; impoliteness; rudeness.

ill–con·sid·ered (il′kən sid′ərd) adj. not well considered; unwise; unsuitable.

ill–de·fined (il′di fīnd′) adj. not clear; not clearly indicated or explained; hazy.

ill–dis·posed (il′dis pōzd′) adj. unfriendly; unfavorable.

il·le·gal (i lē′gəl) adj. **1** prohibited by law: *illegal parking.* **2** prohibited by an accepted set of rules, especially in sports: *an illegal punch in boxing.* —**il·le′gal·ly,** adv.

il·le·gal·i·ty (il′ē gal′ə tē) *n., pl.* **-ties. 1** unlawfulness. **2** an illegal act; act contrary to law.

il·leg·i·bil·i·ty (i lej′ə bil′ə tē) *n., pl.* **-ties.** an illegible quality or condition.

il·leg·i·ble (i lej′ə bəl) *adj.* very hard or impossible to read. —**il·leg′i·ble·ness,** *n.* —**il·leg′i·bly,** *adv.*

il·le·git·i·ma·cy (il′ə jit′ə mə sē) *n., pl.* **-cies.** the fact or condition of being illegitimate.

il·le·git·i·mate (il′ə jit′ə mit) *adj.* **1** born of parents who are not married to each other. **2** not according to the law or the rules. **3** not logical; not properly deduced. —**il′le·git′i·mate·ly,** *adv.*

ill–fat·ed (il′fāt′id) *adj.* **1** sure to have a bad fate or end. **2** bringing bad luck; unlucky.

ill–fa·vored or **ill–fa·voured** (il′fā′vərd) *adj.* **1** not beautiful to look at; ugly. **2** unpleasant; offensive. —**ill′–fa′vored·ly,** or **ill′–fa′voured·ly,** *adv.* —**ill′–fa′vored·ness** or **ill′–fa′voured·ness,** *n.*

ill feeling dislike; mistrust: *There has been ill feeling between them since they quarrelled.*

ill–fit·ting (il′fit′ing) *adj.* fitting badly: *ill-fitting trousers.*

ill–found·ed (il′foun′did) *adj.* without a good reason or sound basis.

ill–got·ten (il′got′ən) *adj.* acquired by evil or unfair means; dishonestly obtained.

ill health poor health.

ill humor or **humour** a cross, unpleasant temper or mood.

ill–hu·mored or **ill–hu·moured** (il′hyü′mərd *or* -yü′mərd) *adj.* cross; unpleasant. —**ill′–hu′mored·ly** or **ill′–hu′moured·ly,** *adv.* —**ill′–hu′mored·ness** or **ill′–hu′moured·ness,** *n.*

il·lib·er·al (i lib′ər əl *or* i lib′rəl) *adj.* **1** not liberal; narrow-minded; prejudiced. **2** stingy; miserly. **3** without liberal culture; unscholarly; ill-bred.

il·lib·er·al·i·ty (i lib′ər al′ə tē) *n., pl.* **-ties.** being illiberal.

il·lic·it (i lis′it) *adj.* **1** not permitted or condoned by common custom: *an illicit love affair.* **2** illegal (def. 1): *illicit gambling.* —**il·lic′it·ly,** *adv.* —**il·lic′it·ness,** *n.*
☛ **Hom. elicit.**
☛ *Usage.* See note at **elicit.**

il·lim·it·a·ble (i lim′ə tə bəl) *adj.* limitless; boundless; infinite. —**il·lim′it·a·ble·ness,** *n.* —**il·lim′it·a·bly,** *adv.*

il·lit·er·a·cy (i lit′ər ə sē) *n., pl.* **-cies. 1** the quality or state of being illiterate, especially the inability to read or write. **2** an error in speaking or writing, suggesting a lack of education or knowledge.

il·lit·er·ate (i lit′ər it) *adj., n.* —*adj.* **1** unable to read or write. **2** unable to read or write as well as expected or required: *a newspaper editorial about illiterate university students.* **3** showing a lack of education; not cultured: *He writes in a very illiterate way.* —*n.* a person who is illiterate. —**il·lit′er·ate·ly,** *adv.* —**il·lit′er·ate·ness,** *n.*
☛ *Syn.* **1.** See note at **ignorant.**

ill–judged (il′jujd′) *adj.* unwise; rash.

ill–man·nered (il′man′ərd) *adj.* having or showing bad manners; impolite; rude. —**ill′–man′nered·ly,** *adv.* —**ill′–man′nered·ness,** *n.*

ill nature crossness; disagreeableness; spite.

ill–na·tured (il′nā′chərd) *adj.* cross; disagreeable; spiteful. —**ill′–na′tured·ly,** *adv.*

ill·ness (il′nis) *n.* **1** a sickness; disease. **2** poor health; a sickly condition: *She suffered from long periods of illness.*

il·log·i·cal (i loj′ə kəl) *adj.* **1** not according to the rules of logic. **2** not reasonable; foolish: *an illogical fear of the dark.* —**il·log′i·cal·ly,** *adv.* —**il·log′i·cal·ness,** *n.*

ill–spent (il′spent′) *adj.* spent badly; wasted; misspent.

ill–starred (il′stärd′) *adj.* unlucky; unfortunate; disastrous.

ill–suit·ed (il′süt′id) *adj.* poorly suited; unsuitable.

ill temper bad temper or disposition; crossness.

ill–tem·pered (il′tem′pərd) *adj.* having or showing a bad temper; cross. —**ill′–tem′pered·ly,** *adv.* —**ill′–tem′pered·ness,** *n.*

ill–timed (il′tīmd′) *adj.* done or happening at a bad time; inappropriate.

ill–treat (il′trēt′) *v.* treat badly or cruelly; do harm to; abuse.

ill treatment bad or cruel treatment; harm; abuse.

ill turn 1 an action that is unkind, unfriendly, or spiteful. **2** a change for the worse.

il·lume (i lüm′) *v.* **-lumed, -lum·ing.** *Poetic.* illuminate.

il·lu·mi·nant (i lü′mə nənt) *n.* something that gives light. Electricity and oil are illuminants.

il·lu·mi·nate (i lü′mə nāt′) *v.* **-nat·ed, -nat·ing. 1** light up; make

hat, āge, fär; let, ēqual, tèrm; it, īce
hot, ōpen, ôrder; oil, out; cup, put, rüle,
ə above, takən, pencəl, lemən, circəs

ch, child; ng, long; sh, ship
th, thin; ŦH, then; zh, measure

bright: *The room was illuminated by four large lamps.* **2** make clear; explain: *Our teacher could illuminate almost any subject we studied.* **3** decorate with lights: *The streets were illuminated for the celebration.* **4** decorate with gold, colors, pictures, and designs. In former times books and manuscripts were often illuminated. **5** enlighten; inform; instruct. **6** make illustrious. [< L *illuminare* < *in-* in + *lumen* light]

An illuminated initial letter from a Flemish manuscript of the Bible in Latin, dated A.D. 1148

il·lu·mi·na·tion (i lü′mə nā′shən) *n.* **1** an illuminating; a lighting up; a making bright. **2** the amount of light; light. **3** a making clear; explanation. **4** a decoration with lights. **5** the decoration of books and letters with gold, colors, pictures, and designs. **6** enlightenment.

il·lu·mi·na·tive (i lü′mə nə tiv *or* i lü′mə nā′tiv) *adj.* illuminating; tending to illuminate.

il·lu·mi·na·tor (i lü′mə nā′tər) *n.* **1** a person or thing that illuminates. **2** any instrument for illuminating, such as a lens for concentrating light or a mirror for reflecting light. **3** one who decorates manuscripts, books, etc. with color, gold, etc.

il·lu·mine (i lü′mən) *v.* **-mined, -min·ing.** make or become bright; illuminate; light up: *A smile can often illumine a homely face.* [< F *illuminer*]

illus. illustration; illustrated.

ill–us·age (il′yüs′ij *or* -yüz′ij) *n.* bad, cruel, or unfair treatment.

ill–use (*v.* il′yüz′; *n.* il′yüs′) *v.* **-used, -us·ing;** *n.* —*v.* treat badly, cruelly, or unfairly. —*n.* bad, cruel, or unfair treatment.

OPTICAL ILLUSIONS

A

B

Horizontal lines A and B are the same length but A appears shorter.

The three figures are the same size, but the lines suggesting perspective make the middle figure seem larger than the left one and smaller than the right one.

il·lu·sion (i lü′zhən) *n.* **1** an appearance or feeling that misleads because it is not real; something that deceives by giving a false idea: *an illusion of reality.* **2** a false impression or perception: *an optical illusion.* **3** a false idea, notion, or belief: *Many people have the illusion that wealth is the chief cause of happiness.* **4** a fine, delicate net fabric used especially for veils and trimmings. [< L *illusio, -onis* < *illudere* mock < *in-* at + *ludere* play]
☛ *Syn.* **1. Illusion, delusion** = something mistakenly or falsely believed to be true or real. **Illusion** applies to something appearing to be real or true, but actually not existing or being quite different from what it seems: *Good motion pictures create an illusion of reality.* **Delusion** applies to a false and often harmful belief about something that does exist: *The old woman had the delusion that the butcher was always trying to cheat her.*
☛ *Usage.* Do not confuse **illusion** and **allusion.** An **illusion** is a misleading appearance: *an illusion of wealth.* An **allusion** is an indirect reference or slight mention: *He made several allusions to recent novels.*

il·lu·sion·ist (i lü′zhən ist) *n.* **1** a person who produces illusions; conjurer. **2** a person who has illusions; dreamer.

il·lu·sive (i lü′siv) *adj.* illusory. —**il·lu′sive·ly,** *adv.* —**il·lu′sive·ness,** *n.*

il·lu·so·ry (i lü′sə rē) *adj.* due or resulting in an illusion; unreal or misleading.

illust. illustration; illustrated.

il·lus·trate (il′əs trāt′ *or* i lus′trāt) *v.* **-trat·ed, -trat·ing. 1** make clear or explain by stories, examples, comparisons, etc.: *The way that a pump works was used to illustrate the action of the heart in circulating blood through the body.* **2** provide with pictures, diagrams, maps, etc. that explain or decorate: *This book is well illustrated.* [< L *illustrare* light up, ult. < *in-* in + *lustrum*, originally, lighting]

il·lus·tra·tion (il′əs trā′shən) *n.* **1** a picture, diagram, map, etc. used to explain or decorate something. **2** a story, example, comparison, etc. used to make clear or explain something: *The teacher cut an apple into four equal pieces as an illustration of what "quarter" means.* **3** the act or process of illustrating.

il·lus·tra·tive (i lus′trə tiv *or* il′əs trā′tiv) *adj.* illustrating; used to illustrate; helping to explain: *A good teacher uses illustrative examples to explain difficult ideas.* —**il·lus′tra·tive·ly,** *adv.*

il·lus·tra·tor (il′əs trā′tər) *n.* a person or thing that illustrates, especially an artist who makes illustrations for books, magazines, etc.

il·lus·tri·ous (i lus′trē əs) *adj.* very famous; great; outstanding; eminent: *an illustrious statesman, an illustrious deed.* [< L *illustris* lighted up, bright] —**il·lus′tri·ous·ly,** *adv.* —**il·lus′tri·ous·ness,** *n.*

ill will unkind or unfriendly feeling; hostility; hate.

Il·lyr·i·a (i lir′ē ə) *n.* an ancient country in the region east of the Adriatic. —**Il·lyr′i·an,** *adj., n.*

il·men·ite (il′mə nīt′) *n.* a luminous black mineral consisting of iron, titanium, and oxygen. *Formula:* FeTiO₃ [< *Ilmen* Mountains in the Urals, where it was first discovered + *-ite¹*]

ILO in the United Nations, International Labor Organization.

ILS Instrument Landing System.

I'm (īm) I am.

im-¹ *prefix.* a form of **in-¹** occurring before *b, m, p,* as in *imbalance, immoral, impatient.*

im-² *prefix.* a form of **in-²** occurring before *b, m, p,* as in *imbibe, immure, impart.*

im·age (im′ij) *n., v.* **-aged, -ag·ing.** —*n.* **1** an artificial likeness or representation of a person or thing, especially a statue: *an image of a god.* **2** a person or thing resembling another; counterpart: *She is the very image of her mother.* **3** a picture in the mind; idea: *Your memory or imagination forms images of people and things that you do not actually see.* **4** a description or figure of speech that helps the mind to form forceful or beautiful pictures. Poetry often contains images. **5** public personality; the way a person, group, nation, etc. is regarded by the world at large or by clients, customers, etc.: *Canada's foreign image. He drives a conservative car because he feels it is good for his image.* **6** the impression of something produced optically, as by a lens or mirror. A **real image** is projected by a lens (by refraction) and a **virtual image** is reflected in a mirror. **7** the optical impression of something produced by an electronic device: *an image on a television screen.* —*v.* **1** make or form an image of. **2** reflect as a mirror does. **3** picture in one's mind; imagine. **4** describe with images. [ME < OF < L *imago*]

im·age·ry (im′ij rē) *n., pl.* **-ries. 1** pictures in the mind; things imagined. **2** descriptions and figures of speech that help the mind to form forceful or beautiful pictures. **3** images; statues.

i·mag·i·na·ble (i maj′ə nə bəl *or* i maj′nə bəl) *adj.* that can be imagined; possible. —**i·mag′i·na·bly,** *adv.*

i·mag·i·nar·y (i maj′ə ner′ē) *adj.* existing only in the imagination; not real: *Elves are imaginary. The equator is an imaginary line circling the earth midway between the North and South Poles.*

i·mag·i·na·tion (i maj′ə nā′shən) *n.* **1** an imagining; the power of forming in the mind pictures of things not present to the senses. **2** the ability to create new things or ideas or to combine old ones in new forms. **3** a creation of the mind; fancy.
☛ *Syn.* **1, 2. Imagination, fancy, fantasy** = the creative power of forming ideas or pictures in the mind. **Imagination** emphasizes the power to combine and shape ideas in new ways: *Poets, artists, and inventors make use of their imagination.* **Fancy** applies especially to the ability to develop original, often light-hearted ideas: *The playwright's comic fancy leads her to invent outrageous situations.* **Fantasy** emphasizes the unreality or incredibility of the ideas: *Her short stories owed more to fantasy than to the observation of reality.*

i·mag·i·na·tive (i maj′ə nə tiv *or* i maj′ə nā′tiv) *adj.* **1** showing imagination: *Fairy tales are imaginative.* **2** having a good imagination; able to imagine well; fond of imagining: *The imaginative child made up fairy stories.* **3** of imagination.
—**i·mag′i·na·tive·ly,** *adv.* —**i·mag′i·na·tive·ness,** *n.*

i·mag·ine (i maj′ən) *v.* **-ined, -in·ing. 1** picture in one's mind;

form an image or idea of: *We can hardly imagine life without electricity.* **2** suppose; guess: *I cannot imagine what you mean.* **3** think; believe: *She imagined someone was watching her.* [ME < OF < L *imaginari* < *imago, -ginis* image]
☛ *Syn.* **1. Imagine, conceive** = form in the mind. **Imagine** = form a clear and definite picture of something in the mind: *I like to imagine myself flying a plane.* **Conceive** = bring an idea into existence and give it an outline or pattern or shape in the mind: *The Wright brothers conceived the first successful motor-powered airplane.*

im·ag·ism (im′ə jiz′əm) *n.* an early 20th-century movement in poetry that advocates the use of clear and precise imagery and opposes symbolism and conventional metrical rhythm.

im·ag·ist (im′ə jist′) *n.* a poet who practises imagism. Most imagists use free verse.

im·ag·is·tic (im′ə jis′tik) *adj.* of, having to do with, or characteristic of imagism: *imagistic verse.*

i·ma·go (i mā′gō) *n., pl.* **i·ma·gos, i·mag·i·nes** (i maj′ə nēz′). **1** an insect in the final adult, especially winged, stage. **2** *Psychoanalysis.* an unconscious childhood concept of a parent or other person, carried over unchanged into adulthood. [< L *imago* image]

i·mam (i mäm′) *n.* **1** a Moslem priest. **2** a Moslem leader, chief, etc. [< Arabic *imam* < *amma* go before]

i·mam·ate (i mä′māt) *n.* **1** the rank or office of an imam. **2** the territory governed by an imam.

im·bal·ance (im bal′əns) *n.* **1** the state or condition of lacking balance or of being out of balance. **2** *Medicine.* a lack or defect of co-ordination in glands, muscles, etc.

im·balm (im bom′ *or* -bäm′) *v.* embalm.

im·be·cile (im′bə səl) *n., adj.* —*n.* **1** a person who has a weak mind and can learn to do only very simple tasks. **2** a very stupid or foolish person: *Don't be an imbecile.* —*adj.* **1** very weak in the mind. **2** very stupid or foolish: *an imbecile question.* [< F < L *imbecillus* weak, ult. < *in-* without + *baculum* staff]
☛ *Syn. n.* **2.** See note at **fool.**

im·be·cil·i·ty (im′bə sil′ə tē) *n., pl.* **-ties. 1** feebleness of mind; mental weakness. **2** great stupidity or dullness. **3** a very stupid or foolish action, remark, etc.

im·bed (im bed′) *v.* **-bed·ded, -bed·ding.** embed.

im·bibe (im bīb′) *v.* **-bibed, -bib·ing. 1** drink; drink in. **2** absorb: *The roots of a plant imbibe moisture from the earth.* **3** take into one's mind: *Children often imbibe superstitions that last all their lives.* [< L *imbibere* < *in-* in + *bibere* drink] —**im·bib′er,** *n.*
☛ *Syn.* **1.** See note at **drink.**

im·bri·cate (*v.* im′brə kāt′; *adj.* im′brə kit *or* im′brə kāt′) *v.* **-cat·ed, -cat·ing;** *adj.* —*v.* overlap as tiles or shingles do. —*adj.* **1** like roof tiles in shape, composition, etc. **2** like the pattern of overlapping tiles. [< L *imbricare* cover with tiles < *imbrex, -ricis* hollow tile]

im·bri·cat·ed (im′brə kāt′id) *adj.* overlapping.

im·bri·ca·tion (im′brə kā′shən) *n.* **1** an overlapping like that of tiles, shingles, etc. **2** a decorative pattern in imitation of this.

im·bro·glio (im brōl′yō) *n., pl.* **-glios. 1** a complicated or difficult situation. **2** a complicated misunderstanding or disagreement. [< Ital.]

im·brue (im brü′) *v.* **-brued, -bru·ing.** wet; stain: *His sword was imbrued with blood.* [ME < OF *embreuver* give to drink, ult. < L *bibere* drink]

im·bue (im byü′) *v.* **-bued, -bu·ing. 1** fill; inspire: *He imbued his son's mind with the ambition to succeed.* **2** fill with moisture or color. [< L *imbuere*]

IMF International Monetary Fund.

im·i·ta·ble (im′ə tə bəl) *adj.* that can be imitated.

im·i·tate (im′ə tāt′) *v.* **-tat·ed, -tat·ing. 1** try to be or act like; follow the example of: *The little boy imitated his father.* **2** make or do something like; copy: *A parrot imitates the sounds it hears.* **3** act like, especially for amusement: *He made us laugh by imitating a bear.* **4** be or look like; resemble: *Plastic is often made to imitate wood.* [< L *imitari*]
☛ *Syn.* **2.** See note at **copy.**

im·i·ta·tion (im′ə tā′shən) *n.* **1** the act or an instance of imitating: *We learn many things by imitation.* **2** something produced in this way; a copy or counterfeit: *He gave an imitation of a rooster crowing. This is an imitation of an 18th- century chair.* **3** (*adj.*) made to look like something else, especially something better, rarer, etc.: *imitation pearls, imitation leather.* **4** *Music.* the repetition of a melodic phrase or theme of a different pitch or key from the original, or in a different voice part, or with modifications of rhythm or intervals that do not destroy the resemblance.
in imitation of, imitating; in order to be like or look like.

im·i·ta·tive (im′ə tā′tiv) *adj.* **1** fond of imitating; likely or inclined to imitate others: *Monkeys are imitative.* **2** imitating;

showing imitation. *Bang* and *whizz* are imitative words. **3** not real. —**im′i·ta′tive·ly,** *adv.* —**im′i·ta′tive·ness,** *n.*

im·i·ta·tor (im′ə tā′tər) *n.* a person or animal that imitates.

im·mac·u·late (i mak′yə lit) *adj.* **1** without spot or stain; absolutely clean: *The newly laundered shirts were immaculate.* **2** without fault; in perfect order: *His appearance was immaculate.* **3** without sin; pure. **4** *Biology.* without colored marks or spots; unspotted. [< L *immaculatus* < *in-* not + *macula* spot] —**im·mac′u·late·ly,** *adv.* —**im·mac′u·late·ness,** *n.*

Immaculate Conception *Roman Catholic Church.* **1** the doctrine that the Virgin Mary was conceived free from original sin. **2** a festival observed on December 8 commemorating the Immaculate Conception.

im·ma·nence (im′ə nəns) *n.* the state of being immanent.

im·ma·nen·cy (im′ə nən sē) *n.* immanence.

im·ma·nent (im′ə nənt) *adj.* remaining within; inherent. [< L *immanens, -entis,* ppr. of *immanere* < *in-* in + *manere* stay]

Im·man·u·el (i man′yü əl) *n.* Christ. Also, **Emmanuel.** [< Hebrew *'Immānū'ēl,* literally, God with us]

im·ma·ter·i·al (im′ə tēr′ē əl) *adj.* **1** not important; insignificant. **2** not material; spiritual rather than physical. —**im′ma·te′ri·al·ly,** *adv.* —**im′ma·te′ri·al·ness,** *n.*

im·ma·ture (im′ə chúr′ *or* im′ə tyür′) *adj.* not mature; not ripe; not full-grown; not fully developed. —**im′ma·ture′ly,** *adv.*

im·ma·tu·ri·ty (im′ə chúr′ə tē *or* im′ə tyür′ə tē) *n.* the state of being immature.

im·meas·ur·a·ble (i mezh′ər ə bəl) *adj.* too vast to be measured; boundless; without limits. —**im·meas′ur·a·bly,** *adv.*

im·me·di·a·cy (i mē′dē ə sē) *n., pl.* **-cies. 1** the state or condition of being immediate. **2** topical significance; immediate importance.

im·me·di·ate (i mē′dē it) *adj.* **1** coming at once; without delay: *an immediate reply.* **2** with nothing between: *in immediate contact.* **3** direct: *the immediate result.* **4** closest; nearest: *my immediate neighbor.* **5** close; near: *the immediate neighborhood.* **6** having to do with the present: *our immediate plans.* **7** *Philosophy.* directly or intuitively perceived or known: *an immediate inference.* [< LL *immediatus,* ult. < L *in-* not + *medius* in the middle] —**im·me′di·ate·ness,** *n.*

☛ *Syn.* 3. See note at **direct.**

im·me·di·ate·ly (i mē′dē it lē) *adv., conj.* —*adv.* **1** at once; without delay: *I need an answer immediately because I have to leave.* **2** with nothing between; next. **3** directly. —*conj.* as soon as.

☛ *Syn.* 1. **Immediately, instantly, presently** = with little or no delay. **Immediately** = without delay, with no noticeable time in between: *Please close your books immediately and answer these questions.* **Instantly** = right now, without a second's delay: *The driver was killed instantly.* **Presently,** less common, means "soon, before very long": *I will do the dishes presently, but I want to finish this story first.*

im·med·i·ca·ble (i med′ə kə bəl) *adj.* incapable of being healed; incurable: *immedicable wounds, immedicable wrongs.*

im·me·mo·ri·al (im′ə mô′rē əl) *adj.* extending back beyond the bounds of memory; extremely old: *time immemorial.* —**im′me·mo′ri·al·ly,** *adv.*

im·mense (i mens′) *adj.* **1** very big; huge; vast: *The Pacific Ocean is an immense body of water.* **2** *Slang.* very good; fine; excellent. [< L *immensus* < *in-* not + *mensus* pp. of *metiri* measure] —**im·mense′ness,** *n.*

☛ *Syn.* 1. See note at **huge.**

im·mense·ly (i mens′lē) *adv.* very greatly.

im·men·si·ty (i men′sə tē) *n., pl.* **-ties. 1** a very great or boundless extent; vastness. **2** an infinite space or existence.

im·merge (i mèrj′) *v.* **-merged, -merg·ing.** immerse. [< L *immergere.* See IMMERSE.]

im·merse (i mèrs′) *v.* **-mersed, -mers·ing. 1** dip or lower into a liquid until covered by it. **2** baptize by dipping under water. **3** involve deeply; absorb: *immersed in business affairs, immersed in debts.* [< L *immersus,* pp. of *immergere* < *in-* in + *mergere* plunge]

☛ *Syn.* 1. See note at **dip.**

im·mers·i·ble (i mèr′sə bəl) *adj.* that can be immersed without damage; especially, of an electric appliance, that can be immersed in water without damage to the electric element: *an immersible fry pan.*

im·mer·sion (i mèr′zhən *or* i mèr′shən) *n.* **1** immersing or being immersed. **2** a baptism by dipping a person under water. **3** a method of teaching a foreign or additional language to a person by means of intensive exposure to and practice in the language. **4** (*adj.*) designating a course, school, etc. incorporating or employing such a method.

im·mi·grant (im′ə grənt) *n., adj.* —*n.* a person who comes into a country or region to live: *Canada has many immigrants from Europe.* Compare **emigrant.** —*adj.* **1** immigrating or recently

hat, āge, fär; let, ēqual, tèrm; it, īce
hot, ōpen, ôrder; oil, out; cup, pút, rüle,
əbove, takən, pencəl, lemən, circəs
ch, child; ng, long; sh, ship
th, thin; ‡H, then; zh, measure

immigrated: *an immigrant family.* **2** of or having to do with immigrants or immigration: *an immigrant visa.*

☛ *Usage.* See note at **emigrate.**

im·mi·grate (im′ə grāt′) *v.* **-grat·ed, -grat·ing.** come into a country or region to live. Compare **emigrate.** [< L *immigrare* < *in-* into + *migrare* move] —**im′mi·gra′tor,** *n.*

☛ *Usage.* See note at **emigrate.**

im·mi·gra·tion (im′ə grā′shən) *n.* **1** coming into a country or region to live: *There has been immigration to Canada from most of the countries of the world.* **2** immigrants: *The immigration of 1956 included many people from Hungary.*

im·mi·nence (im′ə nəns) *n.* **1** the state or fact of being imminent. **2** something that is imminent, especially something dangerous or evil.

im·mi·nen·cy (im′ə nən sē) *n.* imminence.

im·mi·nent (im′ə nənt) *adj.* likely to happen soon; about to occur: *The rapidly approaching black clouds show that a storm is imminent.* [< L *imminens, -entis,* ppr. of *imminere* overhang] —**im′mi·nent·ly,** *adv.*

☛ *Syn.* **Imminent, impending** =likely to happen soon. **Imminent,** chiefly describing danger, death, etc., suggests "hanging threateningly over a person" and means "likely to happen any minute without further warning": *Swept along by the swift current, he was in imminent danger of going over the falls.* **Impending** suggests hanging over one, often indefinitely, and keeping him in suspense, and means "near and about to take place": *impending disaster.*

☛ *Usage.* Do not confuse **imminent** with **eminent.**

im·mis·ci·ble (i mis′ə bəl) *adj.* incapable of being mixed: *Water and oil are immiscible.*

im·mo·bile (i mō′bīl *or* -mō′bəl) *adj.* **1** not movable; firmly fixed. **2** not moving; not changing; motionless.

im·mo·bil·i·ty (im′ō bil′ə tē) *n.* being immobile.

im·mo·bi·lize (i mō′bə līz′) *v.* **-lized, -liz·ing.** make immobile or almost immobile: *an immobilized truck. She has been immobilized by a severe back injury.* —**im·mo′bi·li·za′tion,** *n.*

im·mod·er·ate (i mod′ər it) *adj.* not moderate; too much; going too far; extreme; more than is right or proper. —**im·mod′er·ate·ly,** *adv.* —**im·mod′er·ate·ness,** *n.* —**im·mod′er·a′tion,** *n.*

im·mod·est (i mod′ist) *adj.* **1** bold or rude. **2** indecent or improper. —**im·mod′est·ly,** *adv.*

im·mod·es·ty (i mod′is tē) *n.* lack of modesty; boldness, impudence, or impropriety.

im·mo·late (im′ə lāt′) *v.* **-lat·ed, -lat·ing. 1** kill as a sacrifice. **2** sacrifice. [< L *immolare* sacrifice; originally, sprinkle with sacrificial meal < *in-* on + *mola* sacrificial meal]

im·mo·la·tion (im′ə lā′shən) *n.* a sacrifice.

im·mo·la·tor (im′ə lā′tər) *n.* a person who offers sacrifice.

im·mor·al (i môr′əl) *adj.* **1** morally wrong; wicked: *Lying and stealing are immoral.* **2** lewd; unchaste. —**im·mor′al·ly,** *adv.*

im·mo·ral·i·ty (im′ə ral′ə tē) *n., pl.* **-ties. 1** wickedness; wrongdoing; vice. **2** lewdness; unchastity. **3** an immoral act.

im·mor·tal (i môr′təl) *adj., n.* —*adj.* **1** living forever; never dying; everlasting. **2** of or having to do with immortal beings or immortality; divine. **3** likely to be remembered or famous forever. —*n.* **1** a person living forever. **2** immortals, *pl.* the gods of ancient Greek and Roman mythology. **3** a person likely to be remembered or famous forever: *Shakespeare is one of the immortals.* —**im·mor′tal·ly,** *adv.*

im·mor·tal·i·ty (im′ôr tal′ə tē) *n.* **-ties. 1** endless life; the fact or condition of living forever. **2** fame that is likely to last forever.

im·mor·tal·ize (i môr′təl īz′) *v.* **-ized, iz·ing. 1** make immortal. **2** give everlasting fame to. —**im·mor′tal·i·za′tion,** *n.* —**im·mor′tal·iz′er,** *n.*

im·mor·telle (im′ôr tel′) *n.* any of various everlastings, especially those species grown by florists and often dyed in different colors when they are dry, such as *Xeranthemum annuum* and species of *Anaphilis.* [< F *immortelle* immortal]

im·mov·a·bil·i·ty (i müv′ə bil′ə tē) *n.* being immovable.

im·mov·a·ble (i müv′ə bəl) *adj., n.* —*adj.* **1** that cannot be moved; firmly fixed. **2** not moving; not changing position; motionless. **3** firm; steadfast; unyielding. **4** unfeeling; impassive.

—*n.* **immovables,** *pl.* land, buildings, and other property that cannot be carried from one place to another. —**im·mov′a·bly,** *adv.*

im·mune (i myün′) *adj.* **1** protected from or resistant to disease, poison, etc.; not susceptible; having immunity: *Some people are immune to poison ivy; they can touch it without getting a rash.* **2** free from some duty or obligation, or from something unpleasant; exempt: *immune from taxes. Nobody is immune from criticism.* [< L *immunis,* originally, free from obligation]

im·mu·ni·ty (i myü′nə tē) *n., pl.* **-ties. 1** resistance to disease, poison, etc.: *One attack of measles often gives a person immunity to that disease for a number of years.* **2** freedom; protection: *The law gives schools and churches immunity from taxation.* [< L *immunitas < immunis.* See IMMUNE.]
☛ *Syn.* 2. See note at **exemption.**

im·mu·nize (im′yə nīz′) *v.* **-nized, -niz·ing.** give immunity to; make immune: *Vaccination immunizes people against smallpox.* —**im′mu·ni·za′tion,** *n.*

im·mu·nol·o·gist (im′yə nol′ə jist) *n.* a person trained in immunology, especially one whose work it is.

im·mu·nol·o·gy (im′yə nol′ə jē) *n.* the branch of biological science dealing with the nature and causes of resistance to disease.

im·mure (i myür′) *v.* **-mured, -mur·ing. 1** imprison. **2** confine closely. [< Med.L *immurare < L in-* in + *murus* wall] —**im·mure′ment,** *n.*

im·mu·ta·bil·i·ty (i myü′tə bil′ə tē) *n.* being immutable.

im·mu·ta·ble (i myü′tə bəl) *adj.* never changing; unchangeable. —**im·mu′ta·ble·ness,** *n.* —**im·mu′ta·bly,** *adv.*

imp (imp) *n.* **1** a young or small devil or demon. **2** a mischievous child. [OE *impe* a shoot, graft, ult. < VL *imputus* < Gk. *emphytos* engrafted]

imp. 1 imperative. **2** import; imported. **3** imperfect. **4** imprimatur. **5** imperial. **6** imprimis.

im·pact (*n.* im′pakt; *v.* im pakt′) *n., v.* —*n.* **1** a striking (of one thing against another); collision: *The impact of the two swords broke both of them.* **2** *Physics.* the single instantaneous blow of a moving body when it meets another body. **3** a forceful effect; dramatic effect: *the impact of automation on society.* —*v.* drive or press closely or firmly into something; pack in. [< L *impactus* struck against, pp. of *impingere.* See IMPINGE.]

im·pact·ed (im pak′tid) *adj.* **1** firmly wedged in place. **2** of a tooth, pressed between the jawbone and another tooth. **3** closely packed; driven or pressed tightly together.

im·pair (im per′) *v.* make worse; damage; weaken: *Poor food impaired his health.* [ME < OF *empeirer,* ult. < L *in-* + *pejor* worse]
☛ *Syn.* See note at **injure.**

im·paired (im perd′) *Law.* of a driver of a motor vehicle, under the influence of alcohol or any narcotic or hallucinogenic drug: *an impaired driver. She was charged with driving while impaired.*

impaired driving *Cdn. Law.* being in control of a motor vehicle while the ability to drive is weakened by alcohol or narcotics: *He was fined $200 on a charge of impaired driving.*

im·pair·ment (im per′mənt) *n.* **1** impairing or being impaired. **2** an injury; damage.

im·pa·la (im pal′ə *or* im pä′lə) *n., pl.* **-las** or (*esp. collectively*) **-la.** a medium-sized, slender, reddish-brown antelope (*Aepyceros melampus*) of the savannah and bush country of S and E Africa, the adult males having long, slender horns that curve in an S, so that from the front the two horns form the outline of a lyre. [< Zulu]

im·pale (im pāl′) *v.* **-paled, -pal·ing. 1** pierce through with something pointed; fasten upon something pointed: *The butterflies were impaled on small pins stuck in a sheet of cork.* **2** torture or punish by thrusting upon a pointed stake. **3** make helpless as if by piercing: *The teacher impaled the cheeky student with a look of ice.* [< F *empaler,* ult. < L *in-* on + *palus* stake] —**im·pale′ment,** *n.*

im·pal·pa·ble (im pal′pə bəl) *adj.* **1** that cannot be perceived by the sense of touch: *Sunbeams are impalpable. A thread of a spider's web is so thin as to be almost impalpable.* **2** very hard for the mind to grasp: *impalpable distinctions.* —**im·pal′pa·bly,** *adv.*

im·pan·el (im pan′əl) *v.* **-elled** or **-eled, -el·ling** or **-el·ing. 1** put on a list for duty on a jury. **2** select (a jury) from the list. Also, **empanel.**

im·par·a·dise (im par′ə dīs′ *or* im per′ə dīs′) *v.* **-dised, -dis·ing. 1** put in paradise; make supremely happy. **2** make a paradise of.

im·part (im pärt′) *v.* **1** give a part or share of; give: *The furnishings imparted an air of elegance to the room.* **2** communicate; tell: *The interview asked her to impart the secret of*

her success. [< L *impartire < in-* in + *pars, partis* part]
☛ *Syn.* See note at **communicate.**

im·par·tial (im pär′shəl) *adj.* showing no more favor to one side than to the other; fair; just. —**im·par′tial·ly,** *adv.*
☛ *Syn.* See note at **fair.**

im·par·ti·al·i·ty (im′pär shē al′ə tē) *n.* fairness; justice.

im·pass·a·bil·i·ty (im pas′e bil′ə tē) *n.* the state of being impassable.

im·pass·a·ble (im pas′ə bəl) *adj.* not passable; so that one cannot go around or across: *Deep mud made the road impassable.* —**im·pass′a·ble·ness,** *n.* —**im·pass′a·bly,** *adv.*

im·passe (im pas′ *or* im′pas) *n.* **1** a position from which there is no escape; a problem with no apparent solution; deadlock. **2** a road or way closed at one end; blind alley. [< F]

im·pas·si·bil·i·ty (im pas′ə bil′ə tē) *n.* the condition or quality of being impassible.

im·pas·si·ble (im pas′ə bəl) *adj.* **1** unable to suffer or feel pain. **2** that cannot be harmed. **3** without feeling; impassive. [< L *impassibilis,* ult. < *in-* not + *pati* suffer] —**im·pass′i·bly,** *adv.*

im·pas·sioned (im pash′ənd) *adj.* full of strong feeling; ardent; rousing: *an impassioned speech.*

im·pas·sive (im pas′iv) *adj.* **1** not showing any feeling or emotion; expressionless: *He listened with an impassive face.* **2** not feeling any emotion; placid or apathetic. **3** not feeling pain or injury; insensible: *The soldier lay as impassive as if he were dead.* —**im·pas′sive·ly,** *adv.* —**im·pas′sive·ness,** *n.*

im·pas·siv·i·ty (im′pa siv′ə tē) *n.* being impassive.

im·pas·to (im päs′tō) *n.* **1** a painting technique in which the paint is thickly applied, often with a palette knife. **2** the paint thus applied. [< Ital. *impasto < impastare* beplaster]

im·pa·tience (im pā′shəns) *n.* the quality or state of being impatient.
☛ *Hom.* impatiens.

im·pa·tiens (im pā′shəns) *n.* any of a genus (*Impatiens*) of annual and biennial plants having spurred or pouch-shaped flowers and seed pods that burst open when ripe; especially, a common garden plant (*I. petersiana*) cultivated in many varieties for its bright red, pink, white, or variegated flowers.
☛ *Hom.* impatience.

im·pa·tient (im pā′shənt) *adj.* **1** not patient; not willing to bear delay, opposition, pain, bother, etc.: *It took him so long to make up his mind that the salesclerk began to get impatient.* **2** restless; anxious: *They were impatient to see the new puppy.* **3** caused by or showing lack of patience: *an impatient answer.*
impatient of, unwilling to endure; not liking or wanting.
—**im·pa′tient·ly,** *adv.*

im·peach (im pēch′) *v.* **1** call in question; cast doubt on: *to impeach a person's honor, to impeach the testimony of a witness.* **2** charge with wrongdoing; accuse. **3** bring a (public official) to trial before a special court or tribunal for wrong conduct during office: *The judge was impeached for taking a bribe.* [ME < OF *empeechier* hinder < LL *impedicare < L in-* on + *pedica* shackle]

im·peach·a·ble (im pēch′ə bəl) *adj.* **1** liable to be impeached. **2** likely to cause impeachment: *an impeachable offence.*

im·peach·ment (im pēch′mənt) *n.* impeaching or being impeached.

im·pearl (im pėrl′) *v.* **1** form into pearl-like drops. **2** adorn with pearls or pearl-like drops.

im·pec·ca·bil·i·ty (im pek′ə bil′ə tē) *n.* an impeccable quality; faultlessness.

im·pec·ca·ble (im pek′ə bəl) *adj.* **1** faultless. **2** sinless. [< LL *impeccabilis < in-* not + *peccare* sin] —**im·pec′ca·bly,** *adv.*

im·pe·cu·ni·ous (im′pi kyü′nē əs) *adj.* having little or no money; penniless; poor. [< *in-* not + L *pecuniosus* rich < *pecunia* money < *pecu* head of cattle] —**im·pe·cu′ni·ous·ly,** *adv.*

im·ped·ance (im pēd′əns) *n.* **1** *Electricity.* the apparent resistance in an alternating-current circuit, made up of two components, reactance and true or ohmic resistance. **2** *Physics.* the ratio of pressure in a sound wave to the product of the particle velocity and the area of a cross section of the wave at a given point.

im·pede (im pēd′) *v.* **-ped·ed, -ped·ing.** hinder; obstruct. [< L *impedire < in-* on + *pes, pedis* foot] —**im·ped′er,** *n.*
☛ *Syn.* See note at **prevent.**

im·ped·i·ment (im ped′ə mənt) *n.* **1** a hindrance; obstruction. **2** a defect in speech: *Stuttering is an impediment.* **3** *Law.* a bar to the making of a valid marriage contract. [< L *impedimentum*]

im·ped·i·men·ta (im ped′ə men′tə) *n. pl.* **1** travelling equipment or baggage, especially the military supplies carried along with an army. **2** any equipment, belongings, etc. that one carries and that obstruct one or hinder progress. **3** *Law.* obstacles; hindrances. [< L]

im·pel (im pel′) v. -**pelled, -pel·ling. 1** drive; force; cause: *Hunger impelled the lazy man to work.* **2** cause to move; drive forward; push along: *The wind impelled the boat to shore.* [< L *impellere* < *in-* on + *pellere* push]
➤ *Syn.* **1.** See note at **compel.**

im·pel·lent (im pel′ənt) adj., n. —adj. tending to impel; impelling. —n. a person, force, or thing that impels.

im·pel·ler (im pel′ər) n. **1** a person or thing that impels. **2** the rotating blades of a centrifugal pump or blower.

im·pend (im pend′) v. **1** be likely to happen soon; be ready to occur; be near: *When war impends, wise men try to prevent it.* **2** hang; hang threateningly. [< L *impendere* < *in-* over + *pendere* hang]

im·pend·ent (im pen′dənt) adj. impending.

im·pend·ing (im pen′ding) adj. **1** likely to happen soon; about to occur (*used especially of something unpleasant*): *She dreaded the impending exams.* **2** overhanging: *Above him were impending cliffs.*
➤ *Syn.* **1.** See note at **imminent.**

im·pen·e·tra·bil·i·ty (im pen′ə trə bil′ə tē) n. being impenetrable.

im·pen·e·tra·ble (im pen′ə trə bəl) adj. **1** that cannot be entered, pierced, or passed: *A thick sheet of steel is impenetrable by an ordinary bullet.* **2** not open to ideas, influences, etc. **3** impossible to explain or understand; inscrutable: *an impenetrable mystery.* **4** *Physics.* of a body, excluding all other bodies from the space it occupies. —**im·pen′e·tra·bly,** adv.

im·pen·i·tence (im pen′ə təns) n. a lack of any sorrow or regret for doing wrong.

im·pen·i·tent (im pen′ə tənt) adj. not penitent; feeling no sorrow or regret for having done wrong. —**im·pen′i·tent·ly,** adv.

imper. imperative.

im·per·a·tive (im per′ə tiv) adj., n. —adj. **1** not to be avoided; urgent; necessary: *It is imperative that a very sick child stay in bed.* **2** expressing a command; commanding. **3** *Grammar.* denoting the mood of a verb that expresses a command, request, or advice. "Go!" and "Stop, look, listen!" are in the imperative mood. —n. **1** a command: *The great imperative is "Love thy neighbor as thyself."* **2** *Grammar.* **a** the imperative mood. **b** a verb form in this mood. *Abbrev.:* imp. *or* imper. [< L *imperativus< imperare* command] —**im·per′a·tive·ly,** adv. —**im·per′a·tive·ness,** n.

im·pe·ra·tor (im′pə rā′tər) n. **1** an absolute or supreme ruler. **2** in ancient Rome: **a** a victorious military commander. **b** the emperor. [< L *imperator < imperare* command]

im·per·cep·ti·ble (im′pər sep′tə bəl) adj. **1** very slight; gradual. **2** that cannot be perceived or felt. —**im′per·cep′ti·ble·ness,** n. —**im′per·cep′ti·bly,** adv.

imperf. imperfect.

im·per·fect (im pėr′fikt) adj., n. —adj. **1** not perfect; having some defect or fault. **2** not complete; lacking some part. **3** *Grammar.* expressing continued or customary action in the past. **4** *Music.* **a** denoting a major or minor third or sixth. **b** of an interval, diminished. —n. *Grammar.* **1** the imperfect tense. English has no imperfect, but such forms as *was studying* and *used to study* are similar to the imperfect in other languages. **2** a verb form in this tense. *Abbrev.:* imp., imperf. —**im·per′fect·ly,** adv. —**im·per′fect·ness,** n.

im·per·fec·tion (im′pər fek′shən) n. **1** a lack of perfection; imperfect condition or character. **2** a fault; defect: *an emerald with imperfections.*

im·per·fo·rate (im pėr′fə rit *or* im pėr′fə rāt′) adj. **1** not pierced through with holes. **2** of stamps, not separated from other stamps by perforations; having the margins whole. —**im·per′fo·ra′tion,** n.

im·pe·ri·al (im pėr′ē əl) adj., n. —adj. **1** of or having to do with an empire or its ruler. **2** of or having to do with the rule or authority of one country over other countries and colonies. **3** having the rank of an emperor. **4** supreme; majestic; magnificent. **5** of larger size or better quality. **6** designating a system of weights and measures traditionally used in Britain. Many units of the traditional systems of Canada and other countries are equivalent or nearly equivalent to those of the imperial system. See table at **measurement.** —n. **1** a small, pointed beard growing beneath the lower lip. See **beard** for picture. **2** a size of paper, 58.4 × 78.7 cm (in Britain, 55.9 × 76.2 cm). [< L *imperialis < imperium* empire] —**im·pe′ri·al·ly,** adv.

imperial gallon the traditional British gallon, equal to 160 fluid ounces (about 4.55 dm³). It is almost identical with the traditional Canadian gallon; both the imperial and Canadian gallons are about 20 percent bigger than the U.S. gallon.

im·pe·ri·al·ism (im pėr′ē əl iz′əm) n. **1** the policy of extending the rule or authority of one country over other countries and territories. **2** an imperial system of government. **3** the dominating of

---

hat, āge, fär; let, ēqual, tèrm; it, īce
hot, ōpen, ôrder; oil, out; cup, pút, rüle,
əbove, takən, pencəl, lemən, circəs
ch, child; ng, long; sh, ship
th, thin; ℉, then; zh, measure

another nation's economic, political, and even military structure without actually taking governmental control.

im·pe·ri·al·ist (im pėr′ē əl ist) n., adj. —n. a person who favors imperialism. —adj. imperialistic.

im·pe·ri·al·is·tic (im pėr′ē əl is′tik) adj. **1** of imperialism or imperialists. **2** favoring imperialism. —**im·pe′ri·al·is′ti·cal·ly,** adv.

Imperial Order Daughters of the Empire an organization of women founded in 1900, whose purpose is to stimulate patriotism and promote good citizenship.

im·per·il (im per′əl) v. -**illed** *or* -**iled, -il·ling** *or* -**il·ing.** put in danger.

im·pe·ri·ous (im pėr′ē əs) adj. **1** haughty; arrogant; domineering; overbearing. **2** imperative; necessary; urgent. [< L *imperiosus* commanding] —**im·pe′ri·ous·ly,** adv. —**im·pe′ri·ous·ness,** n.

im·per·ish·a·bil·i·ty (im per′ish ə bil′ə tē) n. the quality or state of being imperishable; enduring quality.

im·per·ish·a·ble (im per′ish ə bəl) adj. everlasting; not perishable; indestructible. —**im·per′ish·a·bly,** adv.

im·pe·ri·um (im pėr′ē əm) n., pl. -**pe·ri·a** (-pėr′ē ə). **1** command; supreme power; empire. **2** *Law.* the right to use the force of the state in order to enforce the law. [< L]

im·per·ma·nence (im pėr′mə nəns) n. the state or condition of being impermanent.

im·per·ma·nent (im pėr′mə nənt) adj. not lasting; temporary. —**im·per′ma·nent·ly,** adv.

im·per·me·a·bil·i·ty (im pėr′mē ə bil′ə tē) n. an impermeable quality or condition.

im·per·me·a·ble (im pėr′mē ə bəl) adj. **1** that cannot be passed through; impassable. **2** not permitting the passage of fluid through the pores, interstices, etc.

impers. impersonal.

im·per·son·al (im pėr′sən əl *or* im pėrs′nəl) adj. **1** referring to all or any persons, not to any special one: *"First come, first served" is an impersonal remark. In the expression* One must do his best, *the word* one *is impersonal.* **2** not affected by personal feelings; objective: *an impersonal approach to the case.* **3** having no existence as a person: *Electricity is an impersonal force.* **4** *Grammar.* of a verb, having nothing but an indefinite *it* for a subject. *Example:* rained in *It rained yesterday.* —**im·per′son·al·ly,** adv.

im·per·son·al·i·ty (im pėr′sən al′ə tē) n., pl. -**ties. 1** the quality or state of being impersonal; absence of personal quality. **2** an impersonal thing, force, etc.

impersonal pronoun any of the words *it, one, they,* or *you* when used to refer to a person or thing not named or identified: *It is cold today. One must do his best. They say that life begins at forty. You should be careful when crossing the street.*

im·per·son·ate (im pėr′sən āt′) v. -**at·ed, -at·ing. 1** pretend to be; mimic the voice, appearance, and manners of, especially in trying to deceive: *The thief impersonated a policeman.* **2** act the part of: *to impersonate Hamlet.* **3** *Archaic.* represent in personal form; personify; typify: *To many people Henry Hudson impersonates the spirit of adventure.* —**im·per′son·a′tion,** n.

im·per·son·a·tor (im pėr′sən ā′tər) n. one who impersonates, especially an actor who impersonates particular persons or types; professional mimic.

im·per·ti·nence (im pėr′tə nəns) n. **1** impudence; insolence. **2** a lack of pertinence; irrelevance. **3** an impertinent act or speech.

im·per·ti·nen·cy (im pėr′tə nən sē) n., pl. -**cies.** impertinence.

im·per·ti·nent (im pėr′tə nənt) adj. **1** saucy; impudent; insolent; rude. **2** not pertinent; not to the point; out of place. —**im·per′ti·nent·ly,** adv.
➤ *Syn.* **1. Impertinent, impudent, saucy** = showing lack of proper respect. **Impertinent** = showing lack of respect for others' privacy or rights: *Talking back to older people is impertinent.* **Impudent** adds the idea of shamelessness and defiance: *The impudent boy made faces at the teacher.* **Saucy** suggests a disrespectful attitude shown by light and flippant manner or speech: *The saucy girl tossed her head when her father scolded her.*

im·per·turb·a·bil·i·ty (im′pər tėr′bə bil′ə tē) n. being imperturbable; calmness.

im·per·turb·a·ble (im′pər tėr′bə bəl) adj. characterized by great

calmness and steadiness; not readily perturbed.
—im′per·turb′a·bly, *adv.*

im·per·vi·ous (im pèr′vē əs) *adj.* **1** not letting anything pass through; not allowing passage: *Rubber cloth is impervious to moisture.* **2** not open to or affected by argument, suggestions, etc.: *She is impervious to all the gossip about her.* —**im·per′vi·ous·ly**, *adv.* —**im·per′vi·ous·ness**, *n.*

im·pe·ti·go (im′pə tī′gō) *n.* an infectious skin disease causing pimples filled with pus. [< L *impetigo* < *impetere* attack < *in-* + *petere* aim for]

im·pet·u·os·i·ty (im pech′ü os′ə tē) *n., pl.* **-ties. 1** sudden or rash energy; violence; ardor: *The impetuosity of the speaker stirred the audience.* **2** an impetuous action.

im·pet·u·ous (im pech′ü əs) *adj.* **1** acting hastily, rashly, or with sudden feeling: *Children are usually more impetuous than adults.* **2** moving with great force or speed: *the impetuous rush of water over Niagara Falls.* [< LL *impetuosus* < L *impetus* attack] —**im·pet′u·ous·ly**, *adv.* —**im·pet′u·ous·ness**, *n.*

im·pe·tus (im′pə təs) *n.* **1** the force with which a moving body tends to maintain its velocity and overcome resistance: *the impetus of a moving automobile.* **2** a driving force; incentive: *Ambition is an impetus that impels some people toward success.* [< L *impetus* attack < *impetere* attack < *in-* + *petere* aim for]

imp. gal. imperial gallon.

im·pi·e·ty (im pī′ə tē) *n., pl.* **-ties. 1** lack of piety or reverence for God; wickedness. **2** lack of dutifulness or respect. **3** an impious act.

im·pinge (im pinj′) *v.* **-pinged -ping·ing. 1** hit; strike: *Rays of light impinge on the eye.* **2** encroach; infringe. [< L *impingere* + *in-* on + *pangere* strike]

im·pinge·ment (im pinj′mənt) *n.* an impinging.

im·pi·ous (im′pē əs *or* im pī′əs) *adj.* not pious; not having or not showing reverence for God; wicked; profane. —**im′pi·ous·ly**, *adv.* —**im′pi·ous·ness**, *n.*

imp·ish (imp′ish) *adj.* of or like an imp; especially mischievous: *an impish grin, an impish trick.* —**imp′ish·ly**, *adv.* —**imp′ish·ness**, *n.*

im·plac·a·bil·i·ty (im plak′ə bil′ə tē *or* im plā′kə bil′ə tē) *n.* the quality of being implacable.

im·plac·a·ble (im plak′ə bəl *or* im plā′kə bəl) *adj.* that cannot be placated, pacified, or appeased; relentless. —**im·pla′ca·bly**, *adv.*

im·plant (*v.* im plant′; *n.* im′plant) *v., n.* —*v.* **1** instil; fix deeply: *A good teacher implants high ideals in children.* **2** insert: *A steel tube is then implanted in the socket.* **3** set in the ground; plant. **4** graft or set (a piece of skin, bone, etc.) into the body. —*n.* **1** tissue grafted into the body. **2** a small radio-active tube or needle inserted into the body, especially to treat cancer.

im·plan·ta·tion (im′plan tā′shən) *n.* **1** implanting. **2** the state of being implanted.

im·plau·si·bil·i·ty (im plo′zə bil′ə tē *or* im plô′zə bil′ə tē) *n.* the quality or condition of being implausible.

im·plau·si·ble (im plo′zə bəl *or* im plô′zə bəl) *adj.* not plausible; lacking the appearance of truth or trustworthiness. —**im·plau′si·bly**, *adv.*

im·ple·ment (*n.* im′plə mənt; *v.* im′plə ment′) *n., v.* —*n.* a useful piece of equipment; tool; instrument; utensil: *Ploughs, axes, shovels, can openers, and brooms are all implements.* —*v.* **1** provide with implements or other means to carry out a task. **2** provide the power and authority necessary to accomplish or put (something) into effect: *to implement an order.* **3** carry out; get done: *Do not undertake a project unless you can implement it.* [< LL *implementum*, literally, that which fills a need < L *implere* < *in-* in + *-plere* fill] —**im′ple·men·ta′tion**, *n.*
☞ *Syn.* See note at **tool**.

im·pli·cate (im′plə kāt′) *v.* **-cat·ed, -cat·ing. 1** show to have a part in or to be connected with a crime, fault, etc.; involve: *The thief's confession implicated two other people.* **2** involve as a consequence; imply. **3** *Archaic.* entangle; fold or twist together. [< L *implicare* < *in-* in + *plicare* fold. Doublet of EMPLOY, IMPLY.]
☞ *Syn.* **1.** See note at **involve**.

im·pli·ca·tion (im′plə kā′shən) *n.* **1** implying or being implied. **2** something implied; an indirect suggestion; hint: *There was no implication of dishonesty in his failure in business.* **3** implicating or being implicated.

im·plic·it (im plis′it) *adj.* **1** without doubting, hesitating, or asking questions; absolute: *implicit trust, implicit obedience.* **2** meant, but not clearly expressed or distinctly stated; implied: *Her silence gave implicit consent.* Compare **explicit. 3** involved as a necessary part or

condition. [< L *implicitus*, pp. of *implicare.* See IMPLICATE.]
☞ *Syn.* See note at **explicit**.

im·plic·it·ly (im plis′it lē) *adv.* **1** unquestioningly. **2** by implication.

im·plied (im plīd′) *adj.* involved, indicated, suggested, or understood without a clear statement: *an implied contract, an implied rebuke.*

im·pli·ed·ly (im plī′id lē) *adv.* by implication.

im·plode (im plōd′) *v.* **-plod·ed, -plod·ing. 1** burst or cause to burst inward: *External pressure can cause a vacuum tube to implode.* **2** *Phonetics.* pronounce (a consonant) by implosion.

im·plore (im plôr′) *v.* **-plored, -plor·ing. 1** beg earnestly for. **2** beg (a person to do something). [< L *implorare*, originally, invoke with weeping < *in-* toward + *plorare* cry] —**im·plor′er**, *n.* —**im·plor′ing·ly**, *adv.*
☞ *Syn.* **1.** See note at **beg**.

im·plo·sion (im plō′zhən) *n.* **1** the action of imploding. **2** *Phonetics.* the suction of air into the pharynx in pronouncing an inhaled stop.

im·ply (im plī′) *v.* **-plied, -ply·ing. 1** indicate without saying outright; express indirectly; suggest: *Silence often implies consent. Her smile implied that she had forgiven us.* **2** involve as a necessary part or condition: *Speech implies the existence of a speaker.* [ME < OF *emplier* involve, put (in) < L *implicare.* Doublet of EMPLOY, IMPLICATE.]
☞ *Usage.* See note at **infer**.

im·po·lite (im′pə līt′) *adj.* not polite; having or showing bad manners; rude. —**im′po·lite′ly**, *adv.* —**im′po·lite′ness**, *n.*

im·pol·i·tic (im pol′ə tik′) *adj.* not politic; not expedient; unwise: *It is impolitic to offend people who could be of help to you.*

im·pon·der·a·ble (im pon′dər ə bəl) *adj., n.* —*adj.* that cannot be explained, or measured exactly: *Faith and love are imponderable forces.* —*n.* something imponderable. —**im·pon′der·a·bly**, *adv.*

im·port (*v.* im pôrt′ *or* im′pôrt; *n.* im′pôrt) *v., n.* —*v.* **1** bring in from a foreign country for sale or use: *Canada imports coffee from Brazil.* **2** mean; signify: *Tell me what your remark imports.* **3** be of importance or consequence. —*n.* **1** anything imported: *Rubber is a useful import.* **2** an importing; importation: *The import of diseased animals is forbidden.* **3** meaning; significance: *What is the import of your remark?* **4** importance: *It is a matter of great import.* **5** *Cdn.* **a** in professional football, a non-Canadian player who has played less than five years in Canada. **b** in other sports, a player who is not a native of the country or area in which he is playing. [< L *importare* < *in-* in + *portare* carry] ·

im·por·tance (im pôr′təns) *n.* being important; consequence; significance; value.
☞ *Syn.* **Importance, consequence** = the quality of having much value, meaning, influence, etc. **Importance**, the general word, emphasizes being of great value, meaning, etc. in itself: *Anybody can see the importance of good health.* **Consequence** emphasizes having, or being likely to have, important or far-reaching results or effects: *The discovery of insulin was an event of great consequence for diabetics.*

im·por·tant (im pôr′tənt) *adj.* **1** meaning much; worth noticing or considering; having value or significance. **2** having social position or influence. **3** acting as if important; seeming to be important; self-important: *He rushed around in an important manner, giving orders.* [< F < Med.L *importans, -antis*, ppr. of *importare* be significant < L *importare* bring on or in. See IMPORT.]
—**im·por′tant·ly**, *adv.*

im·por·ta·tion (im′pôr tā′shən) *n.* **1** the act of importing. **2** something imported.

im·port·er (im pôr′tər *or* im′pôr tər) *n.* a person or company whose business is importing goods.

im·por·tu·nate (im pôr′chə nit) *adj.* asking repeatedly; annoyingly persistent; urgent. —**im·por′tu·nate·ly**, *adv.* —**im·por′tu·nate·ness**, *n.*

im·por·tune (im′pôr tyün′ *or* im′pôr tün′) *v.* **-tuned, -tun·ing.** ask urgently or repeatedly; trouble with demands. [< MF < L *importunus* inconvenient] —**im′por·tune′ly**, *adv.* —**im′por·tun′er**, *n.*

im·por·tu·ni·ty (im′pôr tyü′nə tē *or* im′pôr tü′nə tē) *n., pl.* **-ties.** persistence in asking; the act of demanding again and again.

im·pose (im pōz′) *v.* **-posed, -pos·ing. 1** put (a burden, tax, punishment, etc.) on: *The judge imposed a fine of $500 on the convicted man.* **2** force or thrust one's authority or influence on another or others. **3** force or thrust (oneself or one's company) on another or others; obtrude; presume. **4** pass off (a thing upon a person) to deceive. **5** *Printing.* arrange (pages of type) in the correct order.
impose on *or* **upon, a** take advantage of; use in a selfish way: *to impose on the good nature of others.* **b** deceive; cheat; trick. [< F *imposer* < *in-* on + *poser* put, place] —**im·pos′er**, *n.*

im·pos·ing (im pōz′ing) *adj.* impressive because of size, appearance, or dignity; commanding attention: *The Peace Tower of the Parliament Buildings is an imposing landmark.* —**im·pos′ing·ly,** *adv.*

im·po·si·tion (im′pə zish′ən) *n.* **1** the act or fact of imposing. **2** a tax, duty, task, burden, etc. **3** an unfair tax, etc. **4** an imposing upon a person by taking advantage of his good nature: *Would it be an imposition to ask you to mail this parcel?* **5** a deception; fraud; trick. **6** a ceremonial laying on of hands in confirmation or ordination. **7** *Printing.* the act or process of arranging pages of type.

im·pos·si·bil·i·ty (im pos′ə bil′ə tē *or* im pos′ə bil′ə tē) *n., pl.* **-ties.** **1** the quality of being impossible. **2** something impossible.

im·pos·si·ble (im pos′ə bəl) *adj., n.* —*adj.* **1** that cannot be reached, done, or fulfilled; hopeless: *an impossible task, an impossible plan.* **2** that cannot be or happen: *It is impossible for two and two to be six.* **3** that cannot be true: *an impossible story.* **4** not able to be tolerated; very objectionable: *an impossible person.* —*n.* **1** something that is or seems impossible: *The sergeant always demanded the impossible of his men.* **2** an impossibility: *His statement is in the nature of an impossible.* —**im·pos′si·bly,** *adv.* —**im·pos′si·ble·ness,** *n.*

im·post¹ (im′pōst) *n.* **1** a tax on goods brought into a country; customs duty. **2** a tax; tribute. **3** *Racing.* the weight that a horse must carry in a handicap, assigned on the basis of age. [< OF, ult. < L *in-* on + *ponere* place, put]

im·post² (im′pōst) *n. Architecture.* the uppermost part of a column, etc. on which the end of an arch rests. See **arch** for picture. [< F < Ital. *imposta,* ult. < L *in-* on + *ponere* place, put]

im·pos·tor (im pos′tər) *n.* **1** a person who assumes a false name or character. **2** a deceiver; cheat. [< F *imposteur* < LL *impostor* < L *imponere* impose < *in* on + *ponere* place, put]

im·pos·ture (im pos′chər) *n.* the act or practice of deceiving by assuming a false character or name. [< F < LL *impostura* < L *imponere* impose]

im·po·tence (im′pə təns) *n.* a lack of power; helplessness; the condition or quality of being impotent.

im·po·ten·cy (im′pə tən sē) *n.* impotence.

im·po·tent (im′pə tənt) *adj.* **1** not having power or strength; helpless: *an impotent rage, a law against strikes that rendered the trade unions impotent.* **2** incapable of having sexual intercourse; especially, in a male, because of an inability to have an erection. —**im′po·tent·ly,** *adv.*

im·pound (im pound′) *v.* **1** shut up in or as if in a pen or pound: *to impound stray animals.* **2** take and hold in the custody of the law: *to impound documents for use as evidence in court.* **3** collect and confine (water) in a reservoir or behind a dam, as for irrigation. —**im·pound′er,** *n.*

im·pov·er·ish (im pov′ər ish *or* im pov′rish) *v.* **1** make very poor. **2** exhaust the strength, richness, or resources of; *impoverish the soil.* [ME < OF *empoveriss-,* a stem of *empoverir,* ult. < L *in-* + *pauper* poor] —**im·pov′er·ish·er,** *n.* —**im·pov′er·ish·ment,** *n.*

im·pov·er·ished (im pov′ər isht *or* im pov′risht) *adj.* very poor. ▸ *Syn.* See note at **poor.**

im·pow·er (im pou′ər) *v.* empower.

im·prac·ti·ca·bil·i·ty (im prak′tə kə bil′ə tē) *n., pl.* **-ties. 1** the quality of being impracticable. **2** something impracticable.

im·prac·ti·ca·ble (im prak′tə kə bəl) *adj.* **1** impossible to be done or put into practice: *His suggestions were impracticable.* **2** that cannot be used: *an impracticable road.* **3** *Archaic.* very hard to manage; intractable. —**im·prac′ti·ca·bly,** *adv.* ▸ *Usage.* See note at **impractical.**

im·prac·ti·cal (im prak′tə kəl) *adj.* not practical; unrealistic: *To build a bridge across the Atlantic Ocean is an impractical scheme.* —**im·prac′ti·cal·ly,** *adv.*
▸ *Usage.* **Impractical, impracticable. Impractical** describes things that are useless or people who have a very unrealistic view of life or show little judgment or common sense in what they do: *Buying useless things because they are on sale is impractical.* **Impracticable** describes things that have been proved unusable in actual practice or that would be impossible to put into practice: *Most schemes to abolish poverty are impracticable.*

im·pre·cate (im′prə kāt′) *v.* **-cat·ed, -cat·ing.** call down (curses, evil, etc.): *The witch doctor imprecated ruin on his people's enemies.* [< L *imprecare* < *in-* on + *prex, precis* prayer] —**im′pre·ca′tor,** *n.*

im·pre·ca·tion (im′prə kā′shən) *n.* **1** the act of calling down curses, evil, etc. **2** a curse.

im·pre·cise (im′prə sīs′) *adj.* lacking precision; inexact. —**im′pre·ci′sion,** *n.*

im·preg·na·bil·i·ty (im preg′nə bil′ə tē) *n.* the quality of being impregnable.

im·preg·na·ble (im preg′nə bəl) *adj.* able to resist attack; not yielding to force, persuasion, etc.: *an impregnable fortress, an*

hat, āge, fär; let, ēqual, tėrm; it, īce
hot, ōpen, ôrder; oil, out; cup, pùt, rüle,
above, takən, pencəl, lemən, circəs

ch, child; ng, long; sh, ship
th, thin; ŦH, then; zh, measure

impregnable argument. [ME < OF *imprenable* < *in-* not + *prenable* pregnable] —**im·preg′na·bly,** *adv.*

im·preg·nate (im preg′nāt) *v.* **-nat·ed, -nat·ing;** *adj.* —*v.* **1** make pregnant. **2** *Biology.* fertilize: *to impregnate an egg cell.* **3** fill (with); saturate: *Sea water is impregnated with salt.* **4** instil into (the mind); inspire; imbue: *A great book impregnates the mind with new ideas.*
—*adj.* impregnated. [< LL *impraegnare* make pregnant < *in-* + *praegnans* pregnant] —**im·preg′na·tor,** *n.*

im·preg·na·tion (im′preg nā′shən) *n.* **1** impregnating or being impregnated. **2** the thing, influence, etc. with which anything is impregnated.

im·pre·sa·ri·o (im′prə se′rē ō′) *n., pl.* **-sa·ri·os.** a person who presents or manages a concert tour, an opera or ballet company, or other, especially musical, entertainment. [< Ital. *impresario* < *impresa* undertaking, ult. < L *in-* on + *prehendere* take]

im·pre·scrip·ti·ble (im′prē skrip′tə bəl) *adj.* existing independently of law or custom; not justly to be taken away or violated: *imprescriptible rights.*

im·press¹ (*v.* im pres′; *n.* im′pres) *v.* **-pressed, -press·ing;** —*v.* **1** have a strong effect on the mind or feelings of: *A hero impresses us with his courage.* **2** fix in the mind: *She repeated the words to impress them on her memory.* **3** make marks by pressing or stamping: *to impress wax with a seal.* **4** imprint; stamp.
—*n.* an impression; a special mark or quality; stamp: *An author leaves the impress of his personality on his work.* [ME < OF < L *impressus,* pp. of *imprimere* < *in-* in + *premere* press] —**im·press′er,** *n.*

im·press² (im pres′) *v.* **-pressed, -press·ing. 1** seize by force for public use: *The police impressed our car in order to pursue the escaping robbers.* **2** force into military service: *He was impressed into the navy as a young man.* **3** bring in and use. [< *in-²* + *press²*]

im·press·i·ble (im pres′ə bəl) *adj.* impressionable.

im·pres·sion (im presh′ən) *n.* **1** an effect produced on a person: *Punishment seemed to make little impression on the child.* **2** an idea; notion: *I have a vague impression that I left the house unlocked.* **3** something produced by pressure as a mark, stamp, print, etc.: *The thief left an impression of his feet in the garden.* **4** impressing or being impressed. **5** *Dentistry.* a mould of the teeth and the surrounding gums. **6** *Printing.* **a** the total number of copies of a book made at one time. **b** a printed copy.

im·pres·sion·a·bil·i·ty (im presh′ən ə bil′ə tē *or* im presh′nə bil′ə tē) *n.* an impressionable quality or condition.

im·pres·sion·a·ble (im presh′ən ə bəl *or* im presh′nə bəl) *adj.* sensitive to impressions; easily impressed or influenced.

im·pres·sion·ism (im presh′ən iz′əm) *n.* **1** Often, **Impressionism,** a school of painting developed by French painters of the late 19th century and characterized by the use of strong, bright unmixed colors applied in small dabs to suggest natural reflected light. **2** a style in literature characterized by subjective impressions of reality presented in vivid, colorful scenes. **3** a style in music characterized by the use of unusual and rich harmonies, tonal qualities, etc. to suggest the composer's impressions of nature, emotion, etc.

im·pres·sion·ist (im presh′ən ist) *n.* **1** Usually, **Impressionist,** a painter of the 19th-century French school of Impressionism. **2** Often, **Impressionist,** a painter, writer, or composer who follows a style that presents subjective, often emotional, impressions of nature, etc. **3** an entertainer who does impersonations or impressions, especially of famous persons.

im·pres·sion·is·tic (im presh′ən is′tik) *adj.* **1** of or characteristic of impressionism or impressionists. **2** giving only a general or hasty impression.

im·pres·sive (im pres′iv) *adj.* able to make an impression on the mind, feelings, conscience, etc.: *an impressive lecture, an impressive storm, an impressive ceremony.* —**im·pres′sive·ly,** *adv.* —**im·pres′sive·ness,** *n.*

im·press·ment (im pres′mənt) *n.* the act or practice of impressing men or property for public service or use.

im·pri·ma·tur (im′pri mā′tər) *n.* **1** an official licence to print or publish a book, etc., now generally used of works sanctioned by the Roman Catholic Church. **2** sanction; approval. [< NL *imprimatur* let it be printed]

im·pri·mis (im prī′mis) *adv. Latin.* in the first place; first.

im·print (*n.* im′print; *v.* im print′) *n.*, *v.* —*n.* **1** a mark made by pressure; print: *the imprint of a foot in the sand.* **2** an impression; mark: *Suffering left its imprint on her face.* **3** a publisher's name, with the place and date of publication, on the title page or at the end of a book; a printer's name and address as printed on his work. —*v.* **1** mark by pressing or stamping; print: *to imprint a postmark on an envelope, to imprint a letter with a postmark.* **2** press or to impress: *to imprint a kiss on someone's cheek, a scene imprinted on the memory.* —**im·print′er,** *n.*

im·pris·on (im priz′ən) *v.* **1** put in prison. **2** confine closely; restrain.

im·pris·on·ment (im priz′ən mənt) *n.* **1** putting or keeping in prison. **2** being put or kept in prison. **3** close confinement; restraint.

im·prob·a·bil·i·ty (im prob′ə bil′ə tē) *n.*, *pl.* **-ties. 1** being improbable; unlikelihood. **2** something improbable.

im·prob·a·ble (im prob′ə bəl) *adj.* **1** not probable; not likely to happen. **2** not likely to be true: *an improbable story.*

im·prob·a·bly (im prob′ə blē) *adv.* with little or no probability.

im·promp·tu (im promp′tyü *or* im promp′tü) *adj.*, *adv.*, *n.* —*adj.* or *adv.* without previous thought or preparation; offhand: *a speech made impromptu.* —*n.* an impromptu speech, performance, etc.; improvisation. [< L *in promptu* in readiness]

im·prop·er (im prop′ər) *adj.* **1** not according to rules of conduct; not decent or polite: *improper language.* **2** not suitable for the purpose or in the circumstances; inappropriate: *improper clothing for a hike.* **3** incorrect: *an improper conclusion.* **4** not properly so called: *an improper fraction.* —**im·prop′er·ly,** *adv.*

☛ *Syn.* **1, 3. Improper, indecent** = not right or fitting according to accepted standards. **Improper** describes something that goes against or fails to observe standards of manners, morals, health, etc. set by those who know what is right or fitting: *Talking in church is improper.* **Indecent** = contrary to standards of good taste in behavior, modesty, and morals: *That fat girl looks indecent in those tight clothes.*

improper fraction a fraction greater than 1. *Examples:* ³/₂, ⁴/₃, ²⁷/₄.

im·pro·pri·e·ty (im′prə prī′ə tē) *n.*, *pl.* **-ties. 1** a lack of propriety; the quality of being improper. **2** improper conduct. **3** an improper act, expression, etc. Using *learn* in speech or writing to mean *teach* is an impropriety.

im·prove (im prüv′) *v.* **-proved, -prov·ing. 1** make better: *You could improve your handwriting if you tried.* **2** become better: *His health is improving.* **3** increase the value of (land or property). **4** *Historical.* in Upper Canada, clear virgin land of trees, underbrush, etc. in preparation for seeding. **5** use well; make good use of: *Improve your time by studying.*
improve on, make better; do better than.
[< AF *emprouer* < OF *en-* in + *prou* profit] —**im·prov′a·ble,** *adj.* —**im·prov′er,** *n.*

im·prove·ment (im prüv′mənt) *n.* **1** a making better or becoming better. **2** an increase in value. **3** a change or addition that increases value: *An old house can be made to look modern by judicious improvements.* **4** a better condition; anything that is better than another; advance. **5** *Historical.* in Upper Canada: **a** the condition of land cleared of trees and underbrush in preparation for seeding. **b** a piece of land in this condition: *an improvement of 50 acres.* **6 improvements,** *pl.* buildings, fences, etc. added to land.

im·prov·i·dence (im prov′ə dəns) *n.* a lack of foresight or thrift; failure to look ahead; carelessness in providing for the future.

im·prov·i·dent (im prov′ə dənt) *adj.* lacking foresight or thrift; not looking ahead; not careful in providing for the future. —**im·prov′i·dent·ly,** *adv.*

im·pro·vi·sa·tion (im′prə vī zā′shən *or* im′prov ə zā′shən) *n.* **1** the act or art of improvising. **2** something improvised. —**im′pro·vi·sa′tion·al,** *adj.*

im·pro·vise (im′prə vīz′) *v.* **-vised, -vis·ing. 1** compose or sing, speak, recite, etc. without preparation. **2** make or provide offhand, using whatever materials, etc. happen to be available: *The girls improvised a tent out of two blankets. and some long poles.* [< F < Ital. *improvvisare,* ult. < L *in-* not + *pro-* beforehand + *videre* see] —**im′pro·vis′er,** *n.*

im·pru·dence (im prü′dəns) *n.* a lack of prudence; imprudent behavior.

im·pru·dent (im prü′dənt) *adj.* not prudent; rash; unwise: *an imprudent decision.* —**im·pru′dent·ly,** *adv.*

im·pu·dence (im′pyə dəns) *n.* **1** the quality or state of being impudent; insolence. **2** impudent conduct or language.

im·pu·dent (im′pyə dənt) *adj.* rudely bold; insolent; forward. [<

L *impudens, -entis,* ult. < *in-* not + *pudere* be modest] —**im′pu·dent·ly,** *adv.*
☛ *Syn.* See note at **impertinent.**

im·pugn (im pyün′) *v.* call in question; attack by words or arguments; challenge as false. [ME < OF < L *impugnare* assault < *in-* against + *pugnare* fight] —**im·pugn′a·ble,** *adj.*

im·pulse (im′puls) *n.* **1** a sudden, driving force or influence; thrust; push: *the impulse of a wave, the impulse of hunger.* **2** the effect of a sudden, driving force or influence. **3** a sudden inclination or tendency to act: *A mob is influenced more by impulse than by reasoning.* **4** the stimulating force of desire or emotion: *The murderer acted on impulse.* **5** *Physiology.* a stimulus that is transmitted, especially by nerve cells, and influences action in the muscle, gland, or other nerve cells that it reaches. **6** *Mechanics.* the product obtained by multiplying the value of a force by the time during which it acts. **7** *Electricity.* pulse\(def. 4). [< L *impulsus* < *impellere.* See IMPEL.]

im·pul·sion (im pul′shən) *n.* **1** an impelling; driving force. **2** impulse. **3** impetus.

im·pul·sive (im pul′siv) *adj.* **1** acting upon impulse; easily moved: *The impulsive child gave all his money to the beggar.* **2** coming from a sudden impulse: *an impulsive sneer.* **3** driving with sudden force; able to impel: *an impulsive force.* —**im·pul′sive·ly,** *adv.* —**im·pul′sive·ness,** *n.*

im·pu·ni·ty (im pyü′nə tē) *n.* freedom from punishment, injury, or other unpleasant consequences: *If laws are not enforced, crimes are committed with impunity.* [< L *impunitas,* ult. < *in-* without + *poena* punishment]

im·pure (im pyür′) *adj.* **1** not pure; dirty; unclean. **2** mixed with something, especially a substance of lower value; adulterated. **3** not of one color, style, etc.; mixed. **4** forbidden by religion as unclean. —**im·pure′ly,** *adv.* —**im·pure′ness,** *n.*

im·pu·ri·ty (im pyür′ə tē) *n.*, *pl.* **-ties. 1** a lack of purity; the state of being impure. **2** Often, **impurities,** *pl.* an impure thing or element; anything that makes something else impure: *Unfiltered water has impurities.*

im·pu·ta·tion (im′pyə tā′shən) *n.* **1** the act of imputing. **2** a charge or hint of wrongdoing: *No imputation has ever been made against his good name.*

im·pute (im pyüt′) *v.* **-put·ed, -put·ing.** consider as belonging; attribute; charge (a fault, etc.) to a person; blame: *I impute his failure to laziness.* [< L *imputare* < *in-* in + *putare* reckon] —**im·put′a·ble,** *adj.*

in (in) *prep., adv., adj., n.* **In** expresses inclusion, situation, presence, existence, position, and action within limits of space, time, state, circumstances, etc. —*prep.* **1** inside; within: *in an hour, in the box.* **2** into: *Put it in the fire.* **3** with; having; by: *to wrap in paper, dressed in blue; to be in trouble.* **4** of; made of; using: *a table in mahogany.* **5** surrounded by; amid: *in the dust, in cold water.* **6** from among; out of: *one in a hundred.* **7** because of; for: *to act in self-defence.* **8** about; concerning: *a book in Canadian history.* **9** at; during; after: *in the present time. I will be back in one hour.* **10** while; when: *in crossing the street.*
in that, because.
—*adv.* **1** in or into some place, position, condition, etc.: *to come in. A sheepskin coat has the woolly side in.* **2** present, especially in one's home or office: *The doctor is not in today.* **3** *Informal.* in fashion: *Cocktail parties are in again.*
in for, unable to avoid; sure to get or have: *We are in for a storm.*
in on, taking part; involved: *A lot of people were in on the planning.*
in with, a friendly with. **b** partners with.
—*adj.* **1** that is in; being in. **2** coming or going in. **3** *Informal.* fashionable: *Pistachio is the color this fall.*
—*n.* **1** *Informal.* **a** a way of approach: *an in to a career in business.* **b** a position of familiarity or influence: *an in with the company president.* **2 ins,** *pl.* the group in office or in power.
ins and outs, a the turns and twists; nooks and corners: *The ins and outs of the road.* **b** the different parts; details: *The manager knows the ins and outs of the business better than the owner.* [OE]
☛ *Hom.* **inn.**
☛ *Usage.* **In, into. In** generally shows location (literal or figurative); **into** generally shows direction: *He was in the house. He came into the house. He was in a stupor. He fell into a deep sleep.* Informally, **in** is often used for **into:** *He fell in the creek.*
☛ *Usage.* See **at** for another usage note.

in-¹ *prefix.* not, the opposite of, or the absence of, as in *inexpensive, inattention, inconvenient.* Also: **i-** (before *gn*) **il-** (before *l*), **im-** (before *b, m, p*) **ir-** (before *r*). [< L]
☛ *Usage.* **In-** or **un-** prefixed to many words gives them a negative meaning, as in *inconsiderate, incapable, uneven, unloved.* Some words take both prefixes and one of them may be the more current. Thus *indistinguishable* is preferred to *undistinguishable.*

in-² *prefix.* **1** in, into, on, or upon, as in *inhale, inscribe.* **2 in-** is also used to strengthen a meaning or change an intransitive verb to a transitive, usually with little change in meaning. Also,

il- (before *l*), **im-** (before *b, m, p*), **ir-** (before *r*). [< L *in-* < *in*, prep.]
☛ *Usage.* See note at **in-¹**.

-in *suffix.* a variant of *-ine²*, sometimes used in chemical terms to denote neutral substance, as in *albumin, stearin.* [< NL < L *-ina*, fem. suffix to abstract nouns]

in. inch(s).

In indium.

IN Indiana.

in·a·bil·i·ty (in′ə bil′ə tē) *n.* a lack of ability, power, or means, being unable.

in·ab·sen·tia (in ab sen′shə) *Latin.* while absent.

in·ac·ces·si·bil·i·ty (in′ak ses′ə bil′ə tē) *n.* a lack of accessibility; being inaccessible.

in·ac·ces·si·ble (in′ak ses′ə bəl) *adj.* **1** not accessible; that cannot be reached or entered. **2** hard to get at; hard to reach or enter: *The fort on top of the steep hill is inaccessible.* **3** that cannot be obtained; hard to obtain. —**in′ac·ces′si·bly,** *adv.*

in·ac·cu·ra·cy (in ak′yə rə sē) *n., pl.* **-cies. 1** a lack of accuracy; being inaccurate: *The inaccuracy of the report was not hard to prove.* **2** an error or mistake: *There are several inaccuracies in the statistics.*

in·ac·cu·rate (in ak′yə rit) *adj.* not accurate; faulty; containing mistakes: *an inaccurate report. His aim was inaccurate and he missed the target.* —**in·ac′cu·rate·ly,** *adv.*

in·ac·tion (in ak′shən) *n.* an absence of action; idleness.

in·ac·tive (in ak′tiv) *adj.* not active; idle; sluggish.
—**in·ac′tive·ly,** *adv.*

☛ *Syn.* **Inactive, inert, dormant** = not in action or showing activity. **Inactive** = not acting or working, and suggests nothing more: *He is an inactive member of the club.* **Inert** = having by nature, condition, or habit no power or desire to move or act, and suggests being hard or impossible to set in motion or moving slowly: *He dragged the inert, unconscious body from the water.* **Dormant** suggests being asleep, and means "temporarily inactive": *Some animals and plants are dormant during the winter.*

in·ac·tiv·i·ty (in′ak tiv′ə tē) *n.* an absence of activity; idleness; sluggishness.

in·ad·e·qua·cy (in ad′ə kwə sē) *n.* being inadequate.

in·ad·e·quate (in ad′ə kwit) *adj.* not adequate; not enough; not as much as is needed: *inadequate preparation for an examination.* —**in·ad′e·quate·ly,** *adv.*

in·ad·mis·si·bil·i·ty (in′əd mis′ə bil′ə tē) *n.* the quality of being inadmissible.

in·ad·mis·si·ble (in′əd mis′ə bəl) *adj.* **1** not allowable. **2** not to be admitted. —**in′ad·mis′si·bly,** *adv.*

in·ad·vert·ence (in′əd vėr′təns) *n.* **1** a lack of attention; carelessness. **2** an oversight; mistake.

in·ad·vert·en·cy (in′əd vėr′tən sē) *n., pl.* **-cies.** inadvertence.

in·ad·vert·ent (in′əd vėr′tənt) *adj.* **1** not attentive; heedless; negligent. **2** not done on purpose; caused by oversight.
—**in′ad·vert′ent·ly,** *adv.*

in·ad·vis·a·bil·i·ty (in′ad vī′zə bil′ə tē) *n.* the condition of being inadvisable.

in·ad·vis·a·ble (in′əd vīz′ə bəl) *adj.* not advisable; unwise; not prudent. —**in′ad·vis′a·bly,** *adv.*

in·al·ien·a·bil·i·ty (in ā′lē ən ə bil′ə tē *or* in āl′yən ə bil′ə tē) *n.* the quality of being inalienable.

in·al·ien·a·ble (in ā′lē ən ə bəl *or* in āl′yən ə bəl) *adj.* that cannot be given away or taken away: *Every person has the inalienable right of equality before the law.* —**in·al′ien·a·bly,** *adv.*

in·am·o·ra·ta (in am′ə rä′tə) *n., pl.* **-tas.** the girl or woman with whom one is in love; sweetheart. [< Ital. *innamorata* ult. < L *in-* + *amor* love]

in·ane (in ān′) *adj., n.* —*adj.* **1** silly or foolish; empty of meaning; senseless: *an inane thing to do, inane remarks.* **2** *Archaic.* empty; void. —*n. Archaic.* something empty or without substance, especially the void of space. [< L *inanis*] —**in·ane′ly,** *adv.*

in·an·i·mate (in an′ə mit) *adj.* **1** not having life; not animate; lifeless: *the inanimate desert. Stones are inanimate.* **2** not animated; dull: *an inanimate face.* **3** appearing lifeless. —**in·an′i·mate·ly,** *adv.* —**in·an′i·mate·ness,** *n.*

in·a·ni·tion (in′ə nish′ən) *n.* **1** emptiness. **2** weakness from lack of food. [< LL *inanitio, -onis* < L *inanire* to empty < *inanis* empty]

in·an·i·ty (in an′ə tē) *n., pl.* **-ties. 1** silliness; lack of sense. **2** a silly or senseless act, practice, remark, etc. **3** emptiness.

in·ap·pli·ca·bil·i·ty (in ap′lə kə bil′ə tē *or* in′ə plik′ə bil′ə tē) *n.* the quality of being inapplicable.

in·ap·pli·ca·ble (in ap′lə kə bəl *or* in′ə plik′ə bəl) *adj.*

hat, āge, fär; let, ēqual, tèrm; it, īce
hot, ōpen, ôrder; oil, out; cup, pút, rüle,
əbove, takən, pencəl, lemən, circəs
ch, child; ng, long; sh, ship
th, thin; ŦH, then; zh, measure

not applicable; not appropriate; not suitable. —**in·ap′pli·ca·bly,** *adv.*

in·ap·po·site (in ap′ə zit) *adj.* not pertinent; not suitable; inappropriate. —**in·ap′po·site·ly,** *adv.*

in·ap·pre·ci·a·ble (in′ə prē′shē ə bəl *or* in′ə prē′shə bəl) *adj.* too small to be noticed or felt; very slight. —**in′ap·pre′ci·a·bly,** *adv.*

in·ap·pro·pri·ate (in′ə prō′prē it) *adj.* not appropriate; not suitable; not fitting: *Jokes are inappropriate at a funeral.* —**in′ap·pro′pri·ate·ly,** *adv.* —**in′ap·pro′pri·ate·ness,** *n.*

in·apt (in apt′) *adj.* **1** not apt; not suitable. **2** unskilful; inept. —**in·apt′ly,** *adv.* —**in·apt′ness,** *n.*
☛ *Syn.* See note at **inept**.

in·ap·ti·tude (in ap′tə tyüd′ *or* in ap′tə tüd′) *n.* **1** unfitness. **2** lack of skill.

in·ar·tic·u·late (in′är tik′yə lit) *adj.* **1** not distinct; not like regular speech: *an inarticulate mutter or groan.* **2** unable to speak in words; unable to say what one thinks; dumb: *Cats and dogs are inarticulate.* **3** *Zoology.* not jointed: *A jellyfish's body is inarticulate.* [< LL *inarticulatus*] —**in′ar·tic′u·late·ly,** *adv.* —**in′ar·tic′u·late·ness,** *n.*

in·ar·tis·tic (in′är tis′tik) *adj.* **1** not following the principles of art. **2** lacking talent in or appreciation of art. —**in′ar·tis′ti·cal·ly,** *adv.*

in·as·much as (in′əz much′) because; since; in view of the fact that: *Inasmuch as he was smaller than the other boys, he was given a head start in the race.*

in·at·ten·tion (in′ə ten′shən) *n.* a lack of attention; heedlessness; negligence.

in·at·ten·tive (in′ə ten′tiv) *adj.* not attentive; careless; heedless; negligent. —**in′at·ten′tive·ly,** *adv.* —**in′at·ten′tive·ness,** *n.*

in·au·di·ble (in ô′də bəl *or* in ô′də bəl) *adj.* that cannot be heard. —**in·au′di·bly,** *adv.*

in·au·gu·ral (in ô′gyə rəl *or* in ô′gyə rəl) *adj., n.* —*adj.* of or for an inauguration: *an inaugural address.* —*n.* an inaugural address or speech. [< F *inaugural* < *inaugurer* inaugural]

in·au·gu·rate (in ô′gyə rāt′ *or* in ô′gyə rāt′) *v.* **-rat·ed, -rat·ing. 1** install in office with a ceremony: *The new mayor will be inaugurated at noon tomorrow.* **2** make a formal beginning of; begin: *The development of the airplane inaugurated a new era in transportation.* **3** open for public use with a ceremony or celebration. [< L *inaugurare* < *in-* for + *augur* taker of omens] —**in·au′gu·ra′tor,** *n.*

in·au·gu·ra·tion (in ô′gyə rā′shən *or* inô′gyə rā′shən) *n.* **1** the act or ceremony of installing a person in office. **2** a beginning, especially a formal one. **3** the opening or bringing into use of public buildings, etc. with a ceremony or celebration: *We were present at the inauguration of the new City Hall.*

in·aus·pi·cious (in′ôs pish′əs *or* in′ôs pish′əs) *adj.* showing signs of probable failure; unfavorable; unlucky. —**in′aus·pi′cious·ly,** *adv.* —**in′aus·pi′cious·ness,** *n.*

inbd. inboard.

in·be·tween (in′bi twēn′) *adj., adv., n.* —*adj.* **1** coming or belonging in the middle; relating to the space or time separating two things: *He is at that in-between age, neither boy nor man.* **2** being neither one thing nor another; neutral; indifferent.
—*adv.* between.
—*n.* a person or thing that is in-between.

in·board (in′bôrd′) *adv., adj., n.* —*adv.* or *adj.* inside the hull of a ship; in or toward the middle of a ship. —*n.* **1** a motorboat having its motor inside the hull. **2** the motor itself.

in·born (in′bôrn′) *adj.* born in a person; instinctive; natural: *an inborn sense of rhythm.*

in·bound (in′bound′) *adj.* inward bound.

in·bred (in′bred′) *adj.* **1** inborn; natural: *an inbred courtesy.* **2** bred for generations from ancestors closely related.

in·breed (in′brēd′ *or* in brēd′) *v.* **-bred, -breed·ing. 1** breed from closely related persons, animals, or plants. **2** engender.

in·breed·ing (in′brēd′ing) *n.* the practice of breeding from closely related stock in order to develop or preserve desirable characteristics.

inc. 1 incorporated. 2 inclosure. 3 including; included; inclusive. 4 increase.

In·ca (ing′kə) *n.* 1 a member of an Amerindian people of South America that held power in Peru before the Spanish conquest. 2 a ruler of the Incas. [< Sp. < Quechua (SAm.Ind.) *ynca* prince of the ruling family] —**In′can,** *n., adj.*

in·cal·cu·la·ble (in kal′kyə lə bəl) *adj.* 1 too great in number to be counted; numerous: *The sands of the beach are incalculable.* 2 not to be reckoned beforehand: *A flood in the valley would cause incalculable losses.* 3 not to be relied on; uncertain. —**in·cal′cu·la·bly,** *adv.*

in ca·me·ra (in kam′ər ə) 1 *Law.* in the privacy of a judge's chambers, rather than in open court. 2 behind closed doors; secret. [< L *in camera* in a room, chamber]

in·can·des·cence (in′kən des′əns) *n.* the quality or state of being incandescent.

in·can·des·cent (in′kən des′ənt) *adj.* 1 glowing with heat; red-hot or white-hot. 2 intensely bright; brilliant. 3 having to do with or containing a material that gives light by incandescence. An **incandescent lamp** is an electric lamp with a filament of very fine wire that becomes white-hot when current flows through it. [< L *incandescens, -entis,* ppr. of *incandescere* begin to glow < *in-* in + *candere* be gleaming white]

in·can·ta·tion (in′kan tā′shən) *n.* 1 a set of words spoken as a magic charm or to cast a magic spell. *Double, double, toil and trouble, Fire burn and cauldron bubble* is an incantation. 2 the use of such words. 3 magical ceremonies; magic; sorcery. [< L *incantatio, -onis* < *incantare* chant a magic formula against < *in-* against + *cantare* chant]

in·ca·pa·bil·i·ty (in′kā pə bil′ə tē) *n.* an incapacity; unfitness.

in·ca·pa·ble (in kā′pə bəl) *adj.* without ordinary ability; not efficient; not competent: *An employer cannot afford to hire incapable workers.*
incapable of, a without the ability, power, or fitness for: *His honesty made him incapable of lying.* **b** not legally qualified for: *Certain beliefs make a man incapable of serving on a jury.* **c** not susceptible to; not capable of receiving or admitting: *incapable of exact measurement.* [< LL *incapabilis*] —**in·ca′pa·bly,** *adv.*

in·ca·pac·i·tate (in′kə pas′ə tāt′) *v.* **-tated, -tating.** 1 deprive of ability, power, or fitness; disable: *The man's injury incapacitated him for working.* 2 legally disqualify. —**in′ca·pac′i·ta′tion,** *n.*

in·ca·pac·i·ty (in′kə pas′ə tē) *n., pl.* **-ties.** 1 a lack of ability, power, or fitness; disability. 2 a legal disqualification.

in·car·cer·ate (in kär′sər āt′) *v.* **-ated, -ating.** imprison. [< LL *incarcerare* < L *in-* in + *carcer* jail] —**in·car′cer·a·tor,** *n.*

in·car·cer·a·tion (in kär′sər ā′shən) *n.* imprisonment.

in·car·na·dine (in kär′nə dīn′, in kär′nə dēn′, *or* in kär′nə din) *adj., v.* **-dined, -dining.** —*adj.* 1 blood-red. 2 flesh-colored. —*v.* make blood-red or flesh-colored. [< F < Ital. *incarnadino,* ult. < L *in-* in + *caro, carnis* flesh]

in·car·nate (*adj.* in kär′nit *or* in kär′nāt; *v.* in kär′nāt) *adj., v.* **-nated, -nating.** —*adj.* 1 embodied in flesh, especially in human form: *The villain was an incarnate fiend.* 2 personified or typified: *evil incarnate.* 3 *Botany.* flesh-colored.
—*v.* 1 make incarnate; embody. 2 put into an actual form; realize: *The sculptor incarnated his vision in a beautiful statue.* 3 be the living embodiment of: *She incarnates all womanly virtues in her own person.* [< L *incarnatus,* pp. of *incarnare* < *in-* in + *caro, carnis* flesh]

in·car·na·tion (in′kär nā′shən) *n.* 1 the taking on of human form by a divine being. 2 embodiment. 3 a person or thing that represents some quality or idea: *A miser is an incarnation of greed.* 4 the **Incarnation,** the union of divine nature and human nature in the person of Jesus Christ; assumption of human form by the son of God.

in·case (in kās′) *v.* **-cased, -casing.** 1 put into a case. 2 cover completely; enclose: *Armor incased the knight's body.* Also, **encase.**

in·case·ment (in kās′mənt) *n.* 1 incasing or being incased. 2 something that incases.

in·cau·tious (in kô′shəs *or* in kô′shəs) *adj.* not cautious; heedless; reckless; rash. —**in·cau′tious·ly,** *adv.* —**in·cau′tious·ness,** *n.*

in·cen·di·a·rism (in sen′dē ə riz′əm) *n.* 1 the crime of maliciously setting fire to property. 2 the deliberate stirring up of strife or rebellion.

in·cen·di·a·ry (in sen′dē er′ē) *adj., n., pl.* **-ar·ies.** —*adj.* 1 having to do with the malicious setting on fire of property. 2 causing fires; used to start a fire: *The enemy town was set on fire* with incendiary shells and bombs. 3 deliberately stirring up strife or rebellion: *The agitator was arrested for making incendiary speeches.*
—*n.* 1 a person who maliciously sets fire to property. 2 a person who deliberately stirs up strife or rebellion. 3 a shell or bomb containing chemical agents that cause fire. [< L *incendiarius* < *incendium* fire]

in·cense¹ (in′sens) *n.* 1 a substance giving off a sweet smell when burned. 2 the perfume or smoke from it. 3 something sweet, such as the perfume of flowers, or the pleasure given by flattery or praise. [ME < OF < LL *incensus* < L *incendere* burn]

in·cense² (in sens′) *v.* **-censed, -cens·ing.** make very angry; fill with rage: *Cruelty incenses kind people.* [< L *incensus,* pp. of *incendere* kindle]

in·cen·tive (in sen′tiv) *n.* something that urges a person on; the cause of action or effort; a motive; stimulus. [< L *incentivus* < *incinere* sound, cause to sound < *in-* in + *canere* sing]

in·cep·tion (in sep′shən) *n.* a beginning; commencement. [ME < L *inceptio, -onis* < *incipere* begin < *in-* on + *capere* take]

in·cep·tive (in sep′tiv) *adj., n.* —*adj.* 1 beginning; initial. 2 *Grammar.* expressing the beginning of an action or state. *Phosphoresce* is an inceptive verb. All verbs ending *-esce* and adjectives ending in *-escent* are inceptives. —*n. Grammar.* an inceptive word or structure.

in·cer·ti·tude (in sèr′tə tyüd′ *or* in sèr′tə tüd′) *n.* uncertainty; doubt. [< LL *incertitudo*]

in·ces·sant (in ses′ənt) *adj.* never stopping; continued or repeated without interruption: *The roar of Niagara Falls is incessant. The incessant noise of traffic kept her awake all night.* [< LL *incessans, -antis* < L *in-* not + *cessare* cease] —**in·ces′sant·ly,** *adv.*

in·cest (in′sest) *n.* the crime of sexual intercourse between persons so closely related that their marriage is prohibited by law. [< L *incestum* < *incestus* unchaste < *in-* not + *castus* chaste]

in·ces·tu·ous (in ses′chü əs) *adj.* 1 involving incest. 2 guilty of incest. —**in·ces′tu·ous·ly,** *adv.* —**in·ces′tu·ous·ness,** *n.*

inch (inch) *n., v.* —*n.* 1 a unit for measuring length, equal to ¹⁄₁₂ of a foot (2.54 cm). *Symbol:* ″ 2 the smallest part, amount, or degree; very little bit: *(used only with negatives):* He would not yield an inch.
by inches *or* **inch by inch,** by degrees; gradually.
every inch, in every way; completely.
within an inch of, very near; very close to: *The man was within an inch of death.*
—*v.* move slowly or little by little: *The worm inched along.* [OE *ynce* < L *uncia,* originally, a twelfth. Doublet of OUNCE¹.]

inch·meal (inch′mēl′) *adv., adj.* —*adv.* little by little; slowly. —*adj.* very slow.
—*n.*
by inchmeal, little by little; slowly.
[ME *inch* + *-mele* < OE *mælum* by measures < *mæl* measure]

in·cho·ate (in kō′it) *adj.* just begun; in an early stage; incomplete; undeveloped. [< L *inchoatus,* var. of *incohatus,* pp. of *incohare* begin, originally, harness < *in-* on + *cohum* yoke fastener] —**in·cho′ate·ly,** *adv.* —**in·cho′ate·ness,** *n.*

in·cho·a·tive (in kō′ə tiv) *adj., n.* —*adj.* 1 inchoate. 2 *Grammar.* inceptive. —*n. Grammar.* an inceptive word or structure.

inch·worm (inch′wėrm′) *n.* measuring worm.

in·ci·dence (in′sə dəns) *n.* 1 the act or fact of coming in contact with, occurring, or influencing. 2 the manner, extent, or rate of occurrence or effect: *a high incidence of traffic accidents during the holiday weekend. In an epidemic, the incidence of a disease is widespread.* 3 **a** *Physics.* the falling of a line, or of something moving in a line, on a surface. **b** the direction such a line, etc. takes in falling on a surface. The angle of incidence of a ray of light falling on a surface in the angle between the ray and a line perpendicular to that surface.

in·ci·dent (in′sə dənt) *n., adj.* —*n.* 1 a happening; event. 2 an event that helps or adds to something else. 3 a distinct piece of action in a story, play, or poem.
—*adj.* 1 liable to happen; belonging: *Hardships are incident to the life of an explorer.* 2 falling or striking (upon): *rays of light incident upon a mirror.* [< L *incidens, -entis,* pp. of *incidere* happen < *in-* on + *cadere* to fall]
☛ *Syn. n.* 1. See note at **event.**

in·ci·den·tal (in′sə den′təl) *adj., n.* —*adj.* 1 happening or likely to happen along with something else more important: *Certain discomforts are incidental to camping out.* 2 occurring by chance.
—*n.* Often, **incidentals,** *pl.* something incidental: *On our trip we spent $89 for meals, room, and bus fare, and $6 for incidentals, such as candy, magazines, and stamps.*
☛ *Syn. adj.* 1. See note at **accidental.**

in·ci·den·tal·ly (in′sə dent′lē *or* in′sə den′təl ē) *adv.* 1 in an

incidental manner; as an incident along with something else: *She mentioned incidentally that she had had no dinner.* **2** accidentally; by chance.

incidental music music played as accompaniment to a motion picture, play, etc. to help evoke an appropriate emotional climate or mood.

in·cin·er·ate (in sin′ər āt′) v. **-at·ed, -at·ing.** burn or be burned to ashes. [< Med.L *incinerare* < L *in-* into + *cinis, -neris* ashes] **—in·cin′er·a′tion,** n.

in·cin·er·a·tor (in sin′ər ā′tər) n. a furnace or other arrangement for burning garbage, trash, etc. to ashes.

in·cip·i·ence (in sip′ē əns) n. the very beginning; the earliest stage.

in·cip·i·ent (in sip′ē ənt) adj. just beginning; in an early stage. [< L *incipiens, -entis,* ppr. of *incipere* begin < *in-* on + *capere* take] **—in·cip′i·ent·ly,** adv.

in·cise (in sīz′) v. **-cised, -cis·ing. 1** cut into. **2** carve; engrave. [< F *inciser* < L *incidere* < *in-* into + *caedere* cut]

in·cised (in sīzd′) adj. **1** cut into. **2** carved; engraved. **3** having notches around the edge: *an incised leaf.*

in·ci·sion (in sizh′ən) n. **1** a cut made in something; gash: *The doctor made a small incision to remove all the glass from her foot.* **2** the act of incising. **3** an incisive quality.

in·ci·sive (in sī′siv) adj. sharp; penetrating; piercing; keen: *an incisive criticism.* [< Med.L *incisivus* < L *incidere.* See INCISE.] **—in·ci′sive·ly,** adv. **—in·ci′sive·ness,** n.

in·ci·sor (in sī′zər) n. a tooth having a sharp edge for cutting; one of the front teeth between the canine teeth in either jaw: *Man has eight incisors in all.* See **tooth** for diagram. [< NL]

in·ci·ta·tion (in′sī tā′shən or in′sə tā′shən) n. inciting.

in·cite (in sīt′) v. **-cit·ed, -cit·ing.** urge on; stir up; rouse. [< L *incitare,* ult. < *in-* on + *ciere* cause to move] **—in·cit′er,** n. **—in·cit′ing·ly,** adv.

☛ *Syn.* **Incite, instigate** = stir up or urge on to action. **Incite** = stir someone up or urge him on to do something good or bad: *Their captain's example incited the men to fight bravely.* **Instigate** = stir up to do something bad, or, more often, to bring about something bad, such as a plot or rebellion, by inciting others to act: *The police never discovered who instigated the looting.*

in·cite·ment (in sīt′mənt) n. **1** something that urges on, stirs up, or rouses: *Extreme poverty was their incitement to rebellion.* **2** the act of urging on, stirring up, or rousing.

in·ci·vil·i·ty (in′sə vil′ə tē) n., pl. **-ties. 1** rudeness; lack of courtesy; impoliteness. **2** a rude or impolite act.

incl. 1 inclosure. **2** including; inclusive.

in·clem·en·cy (in klem′ən sē) n., pl. **-cies.** severity; harshness: *The inclemency of the weather kept us at home.*

in·clem·ent (in klem′ənt) adj. **1** rainy; rough and stormy. **2** severe; harsh: *an inclement ruler.* [< L *inclemens, -entis*] **—in·clem′ent·ly,** adv.

in·cli·na·tion (in′klə nā′shən) n. **1** a preference; liking: *a strong inclination for sports.* **2** tendency: *Many middle-aged people have an inclination to become fat.* **3** a leaning; bending; bowing: *A nod is an inclination of the head.* **4** a slope; slant: *the inclination of a roof.* **5** *Geometry.* the difference of direction of two lines, especially as measured by the angle between them. [< L *inclinatio, -onis* < *inclinare.* See INCLINE.]

in·cline (v. in klīn′; n. in′klīn or in klīn′) v. **-clined, -clin·ing;** n. —v. **1** be favorable or willing; tend: *Dogs incline to prefer meat as a food.* **2** make favorable or willing; influence: *Incline your hearts to obey God's laws.* **3** slope; slant. **4** lean; bend; bow. **incline one's ear,** listen favorably. —n. **1** a slope; slant: *There is quite an incline to that roof.* **2** a sloping surface: *The side of a hill is an incline.* [ME < OF < L *inclinare* < *in-* in + *clinare* bend]

in·clined (in klīnd′) adj. **1** favorable; willing; tending: *I am inclined to agree with you.* **2** sloping; slanting.

inclined plane a plane surface set at an oblique angle to a horizontal surface.

in·cli·nom·e·ter (in′klə nom′ə tər) n. **1** an instrument for measuring the slope of anything. **2** an instrument for measuring the angle that an aircraft makes with the horizontal. [< *incline* + *-meter*]

in·close (in klōz′) v. **-closed, -clos·ing.** enclose.

in·clo·sure (in klō′zhər) n. enclosure.

in·clude (in klüd′) v. **-clud·ed, -clud·ing. 1** put, hold, or enclose within limits: *The price includes both house and furniture.* **2** contain; comprise: *The farm includes about 65 hectares.* **3** put in a total, a class, or the like; reckon in a count: *All on board the ship were lost, including the captain.* [ME < L *includere* < *in-* in + *claudere* shut] **—in·clud′a·ble,** adj.

☛ *Syn.* **2. Include, comprise, comprehend** = contain or take in as a part or parts. **Include** emphasizes containing or taking in as an element or part of the

hat, āge, fär; let, ēqual, tèrm; it, īce
hot, ōpen, ôrder; oil, out; cup, pùt, rüle,
əbove, takən, pencəl, lemən, circəs

ch, child; ng, long; sh, ship
th, thin; ŦH, then; zh, measure

whole: *The list includes my name.* **Comprise** emphasizes being made up of parts, or going together to make up the whole: *The list comprises the names of those who passed.* **Comprehend,** formal and applying to ideas, statements, outlines, etc., emphasizes holding or taking within the limits or scope of the whole: *The examination comprehended the whole course.*

in·clu·sion (in klü′zhən) n. **1** including or being included. **2** the thing included. [< Med.L *inclusio, -onis* < *includere.* See INCLUDE.]

in·clu·sive (in klü′siv) adj. **1** including in consideration; including; comprising. *Read pages 10 to 20 inclusive* means *Read pages 10 and 20 and all those in between.* **2** including much; including everything concerned: *Make an inclusive list of your expenses.* **inclusive of,** including; taking in; counting on. **—in·clu′sive·ly,** adv. **—in·clu′sive·ness,** n.

in·cog (in kog′) adj., adv., n. *Informal.* incognito.

incog. incognito.

in·cog·ni·to (in kog′nə tō′ or in′kog nē′tō) adj., adv., n., pl. **-tos.** —adj. or adv. with one's name, character, rank, etc. concealed: *The prince travelled incognito to avoid crowds and ceremonies.* —n. **1** a person who is incognito. **2** a disguised state or condition: *His incognito was not successful and he was recognized almost immediately.* [< Ital. < L *incognitus* unknown < *in-* not + *cognitus,* pp. of *cognoscere* come to know]

in·co·her·ence (in′kō hēr′əns) n. **1** a failure to stick together; looseness. **2** a lack of logical connection. **3** disconnected thought or speech: *the incoherence of a madman.*

in·co·her·en·cy (in′kō hēr′ən sē) n., pl. **-cies.** incoherence.

in·co·her·ent (in′kō hēr′ənt) adj. **1** not sticking together. **2** disconnected; confused. **—in′co·her′ent·ly,** adv.

in·com·bus·ti·bil·i·ty (in′kəm bus′tə bil′ə tē) n. the quality of being incombustible.

in·com·bus·ti·ble (in′kəm bus′tə bəl) adj., n. —adj. that cannot be burned; fireproof. —n. an incombustible substance.

in·come (in′kum) n. what comes in from property, business, work, etc.; receipts; returns. A person's yearly income is all the money that he gets in a year.

income tax a government tax on a person's income.

in·com·ing (in′kum′ing) adj., n. —adj. coming in: *The incoming tenant will pay a higher rent.* —n. a coming in: *the incoming of the tide.*

in·com·men·su·ra·bil·i·ty (in′kə men′shə rə bil′ə tē or in′kə men′sə rə bil′ə tē) n. the quality of being incommensurable; absence of a common measure or standard of comparison.

in·com·men·su·ra·ble (in′kə men′shə rə bəl or in′kə men′sə rə bəl) adj. **1** that cannot be compared because not measurable in the same units or by the same scale: *Money and human life are incommensurable.* **2** *Mathematics.* having no common integral divisor except 1. *Examples:* 8, 17, 11. **—in′com·men′su·ra·bly,** adv.

in·com·men·su·rate (in′kə men′shə rit or in′kə men′sə rit) adj. **1** not in proportion; not adequate: *strength incommensurate to a task.* **2** having no common measure; incommensurable. **—in′com·men′su·rate·ly,** adv.

in·com·mode (in′kə mōd′) v. **-mod·ed, -mod·ing.** inconvenience; trouble. [< L *incommodare* < *incommodus* < *in-* not + *commodus* convenient]

in·com·mo·di·ous (in′kə mō′dē əs) adj. **1** not roomy enough. **2** inconvenient; uncomfortable. **—in·com·mo′di·ous·ly,** adv.

in·com·mu·ni·ca·ble (in′kə myü′nə kə bəl) adj. not capable of being communicated or told.

in·com·mu·ni·ca·do (in′kə myü′nə kä′dō) adj. deprived of communication with others: *The prisoner was being held incommunicado.* [< Sp *incomunicado*]

in·com·pa·ra·ble (in kom′pə rə bəl, in kom′prə bəl, or in′kəm per′ə bəl) adj. **1** without equal; matchless: *Helen of Troy had incomparable beauty.* **2** not to be compared; unsuitable for comparison. **—in·com′pa·ra·bly,** adv.

☛ *Pronun.* See note at **comparable.**

in·com·pat·i·bil·i·ty (in′kəm pat′ə bil′ə tē) n., pl. **-ties. 1** the quality of being incompatible; a lack of harmony. **2** an incompatible thing, quality, etc.

in·com·pat·i·ble (in′kəm pat′ə bəl) adj., n. —adj. **1** not able to live or act together peaceably; opposed in character: *My cat and my*

dog are incompatible. **2** inconsistent: *Late hours are incompatible with health.* **3** of or denoting drugs, blood types, etc. that cannot be combined or used together because of undesirable chemical or physiological reactions.
—*n.* an incompatible person or thing. —**in'com·pat'i·bly,** *adv.*

in·com·pe·tence (in kom'pə təns) *n.* **1** a lack of ability, power, or fitness. **2** a lack of legal qualification.

in·com·pe·ten·cy (in kom'pə tən sē) *n.* incompetence.

in·com·pe·tent (in kom'pə tənt) *adj., n.* —*adj.* **1** not competent; lacking ability, power, or fitness. **2** not legally qualified. —*n.* an incompetent person. —**in'com'pe·tent·ly,** *adv.*

in·com·plete (in'kəm plēt') *adj.* not complete; lacking some part; unfinished. [< LL *incompletus*] —**in'com·plete'ness,** *n.*

in·com·plete·ly (in'kəm plēt'lē) *adv.* not fully; imperfectly.

in·com·pre·hen·si·bil·i·ty (in'kom pri hen'sə bil'ə tē) *n.* the fact or quality of being incomprehensible.

in·com·pre·hen·si·ble (in'kom pri hen'sə bəl) *adj.* impossible to understand. —**in'com·pre·hen'si·bly,** *adv.*

in·com·pre·hen·sion (in'kom pri hen'shən) *n.* lack of comprehension.

in·com·press·i·bil·i·ty (in'kəm pres'ə bil'ə tē) *n.* an incompressible condition or quality.

in·com·press·i·ble (in'kəm pres'ə bəl) *adj.* not capable of being squeezed into a smaller size.

in·con·ceiv·a·bil·i·ty (in'kən sē'və bil'ə tē) *n.* the quality of being inconceivable.

in·con·ceiv·a·ble (in'kən sē'və bəl) *adj.* **1** impossible to imagine: *A circle without a centre is inconceivable.* **2** hard to believe; incredible: *The new jet can travel at an inconceivable speed.* —**in·con·ceiv'a·ble·ness,** *n.*

in·con·ceiv·a·bly (in'kən sē'və blē) *adv.* **1** in an inconceivable manner. **2** to an inconceivable degree.

in·con·clu·sive (in'kən klü'siv) *adj.* not convincing; not settling or deciding something doubtful: *The jury found the evidence against the prisoner inconclusive and acquitted him.* —**in'con·clu'sive·ly,** *adv.* —**in'con·clu'sive·ness,** *n.*

in·con·gru·i·ty (in'kən grü'ə tē) *n., pl.* **-ties. 1** unfitness; inappropriateness; being out of place. **2** a lack of agreement or harmony; inconsistency. **3** something that is incongruous.

in·con·gru·ous (in kong'grü əs) *adj.* **1** out of keeping; not appropriate; out of place: *Heavy walking shoes would be incongruous with evening dress.* **2** lacking in agreement or harmony; not consistent. [< L *incongruus*] —**in·con'gru·ous·ly,** *adv.* —**in·con'gru·ous·ness,** *n.*

in·con·nu (in'kə nyü' *or* in'kə nü') *n., pl.* **-nu** *or* **-nus.** *Cdn.* a whitefish (*Stenodus leucichthys*) of northwestern North America and parts of Northern Asia, generally valued as a food fish. [< F *inconnu* unknown, because little known to anglers]

in·con·se·quence (in kon'sə kwens' *or* in kon'sə kwəns) *n.* a lack of logic or logical sequence; irrelevance; being inconsequent.

in·con·se·quent (in kon'sə kwent' *or* in kon'sə kwənt) *adj.* **1** not logical; not logically connected: *an inconsequent argument.* **2** not to the point; off the subject: *an inconsequent remark.* **3** apt to think or talk without logical connection. —**in·con'se·quent·ly,** *adv.*

in·con·se·quen·tial (in'kon sə kwen'shəl *or* in kon'sə kwen'shəl) *adj.* **1** unimportant; trifling. **2** inconsequent. —**in'con·se·quen'tial·ly,** *adv.*

in·con·sid·er·a·ble (in'kən sid'ər ə bəl) *adj.* not worthy of consideration; not important. —**in'con·sid·er·a·ble·ness,** *n.* —**in'con·sid·er·a·bly,** *adv.*

in·con·sid·er·ate (in'kən sid'ər it) *adj.* **1** not thoughtful of the rights and feelings of others. **2** thoughtless; heedless. —**in'con·sid·er·ate·ly,** *adv.* —**in'con·sid·er·ate·ness,** *n.*

in·con·sist·en·cy (in'kən sis'tən sē) *n., pl.* **-cies. 1** a lack of agreement or harmony; variance. **2** a failure to keep to the same principles, course of action, etc.; changeableness. **3** the thing, act, etc. that is inconsistent.

in·con·sist·ent (in'kən sis'tənt) *adj.* **1** lacking in agreement or harmony; at variance: *The policeman's accepting the bribe was inconsistent with his reputation for honesty.* **2** lacking harmony between its different parts; not uniform. **3** failing to keep to the same principles, course of action, etc.; changeable: *An inconsistent person's opinions change frequently without reason.* —**in'con·sist'ent·ly,** *adv.*

in·con·sol·a·ble (in'kən sōl'ə bəl) *adj.* not to be comforted; broken-hearted. —**in'con·sol'a·bly,** *adv.*

in·con·so·nant (in kon'sə nənt) *adj.* not harmonious; not in agreement or accord. —**in·con'so·nant·ly,** *adv.*

in·con·spic·u·ous (in'kən spik'yü əs) *adj.* not conspicuous; attracting little or no attention. —**in'con·spic'u·ous·ly,** *adv.* —**in'con·spic'u·ous·ness,** *n.*

in·con·stan·cy (in kon'stən sē) *n.* a lack of constancy; changeableness; fickleness.

in·con·stant (in kon'stənt) *adj.* not constant; changeable; fickle. —**in·con'stant·ly,** *adv.*

in·con·test·a·ble (in'kən tes'tə bəl) *adj.* not to be disputed; unquestionable. —**in'con·test'a·bly,** *adv.*

in·con·ti·nence (in kon'tə nəns) *n.* **1** lack of self-restraint. **2** lack of chastity.

in·con·ti·nent (in kon'tə nənt) *adj.* **1** without self-restraint. **2** not chaste; licentious. **3** *Medicine.* unable to control natural evacuations. [< L *incontinens, -entis*] —**in·con'ti·nent·ly,** *adv.*

in·con·tro·vert·i·ble (in'kon trə vėr'tə bəl) *adj.* that cannot be disputed; too clear or certain to be argued about; unquestionable. —**in'con·tro·vert'i·bly,** *adv.*

in·con·ven·ience (in'kən vēn'yəns *or* in'kən vēn'ē əns) *n., v.* **-ienced, -ienc·ing.** —*n.* **1** lack of convenience or ease; trouble; bother. **2** a cause of trouble, difficulty, or bother. —*v.* cause trouble, difficulty, etc. to: *Would it inconvenience you to carry this package for me?*

in·con·ven·ient (in'kən vēn'yənt *or* in kən vēn'ē ənt) *adj.* not convenient; causing trouble, difficulty, or bother; troublesome. [< L *inconveniens, -entis*] —**in'con·ven'ient·ly,** *adv.*

in·con·vert·i·bil·i·ty (in'kən vėr'tə bil'ə tē) *n.* the condition of being inconvertible.

in·con·vert·i·ble (in'kən vėr'tə bəl) *adj.* not convertible; incapable of being converted or exchanged: *Paper money is inconvertible when it cannot be exchanged for gold or silver.*

in·cor·po·rate (*v.* in kôr'pə rāt'; *adj.* in kôr'pə rit) *v.* **-rat·ed, -rat·ing;** *adj.* —*v.* **1** make (something) a part of something else; join or combine (something) with something else: *We shall incorporate your suggestion into this new plan.* **2** form into a corporation: *When the business became large, the owners incorporated it.* **3** form a corporation. **4** unite or combine so as to form one body. **5** embody; give material form to: *to incorporate one's thoughts in an article.* —*adj.* united; combined; incorporated. [< L *incorporare* < *in-* into + *corpus, -poris* body]

in·cor·po·ra·tion (in kôr'pə rā'shən) *n.* **1** incorporating: *The incorporation of air bubbles in the glass spoiled it.* **2** being incorporated. Incorporation gives a company the power to act as one person.

in·cor·po·ra·tor (in kôr'pə rā'tər) *n.* **1** a person who incorporates. **2** one of the original members of a corporation.

in·cor·po·re·al (in'kôr pô'rē əl) *adj.* not made of any material substance; spiritual. —**in'cor·po're·al·ly,** *adv.*

in·cor·rect (in'kə rekt') *adj.* **1** containing errors or mistakes; wrong; faulty. **2** not proper. —**in'cor·rect'ly,** *adv.* —**in'cor·rect'ness,** *n.*

in·cor·ri·gi·bil·i·ty (in kôr'ə jə bil'ə tē) *n.* the quality of being incorrigible.

in·cor·ri·gi·ble (in kôr'ə jə bəl) *adj., n.* —*adj.* **1** so firmly fixed (in bad ways, a bad habit, etc.) that nothing else can be expected: *an incorrigible liar.* **2** so fixed that it cannot be changed or cured: *an incorrigible habit of wrinkling one's nose.* —*n.* an incorrigible person. —**in·cor'ri·gi·bly,** *adv.*

in·cor·rupt (in'kə rupt') *adj.* **1** not corruptible; honest. **2** free from decay; sound. **3** not marred by errors, alterations, etc.: *The manuscript appeared to be an incorrupt text of Chaucer's original poem.*

in·cor·rupt·i·ble (in'kə rup'tə bəl) *adj.* **1** not to be corrupted; honest: *The incorruptible judge could not be bribed.* **2** not capable of decay: *Diamonds are incorruptible.* —**in'cor·rupt'i·bly,** *adv.*

in·crease (*v.* in krēs'; *n.* in krēs) *v.* **-creased, -creas·ing;** *n.* —*v.* make or become greater in size, number, degree, etc.: *to increase the speed of a car. The flowers will increase every year if you don't thin them out. The leader sought to increase his power.* —*n.* **1** a gain in size, numbers, etc.; growth; multiplication by propagation. **2** an addition; the result of increasing; increased product. **3** the production of offspring. **4** offspring.
on the increase, increasing: *The movement of people to the cities is on the increase.*
[ME < AF *encress-*, var. of OF *encreiss-*, a stem of *encreistre* < L *increscere* < *in-* + *crescere* grow] —**in·creas'er,** *n.*

☛ **Syn.** *v.* **1, 2. Increase, enlarge, augment** = make or become greater. **Increase** = make or grow greater in amount, number, wealth, power, etc.: *His weight has increased by ten kilograms.* **Enlarge** = make or become larger, chiefly in size, extent, or capacity: *They enlarged the school auditorium.* **Augment,** more formal, means "increase by adding amounts or sums to what there is": *Many teachers do outside work to augment their salaries.*

in·creas·ing·ly (in krēs′ing lē) *adv.* more and more.

in·cred·i·bil·i·ty (in kred′ə bil′ə tē) *n.* the quality of being incredible.

in·cred·i·ble (in kred′ə bəl) *adj.* **1** unbelievable: *If the story had not been so well documented, it would have been incredible.* **2** *Informal.* extraordinary; so unusual as to seem impossible: *Her last race was incredible; I've never seen anything like it.* —**in·cred′i·ble·ness,** *n.* —**in·cred′i·bly,** *adv.*
☛ *Usage.* Do not confuse **incredible** and **incredulous. Incredible** = unbelievable; **incredulous** = not ready to believe or showing a lack or belief: *His story of having seen a ghost seemed incredible to his family. If they are incredulous, show them the evidence.*

in·cre·du·li·ty (in′krə dyü′lə tē *or* in′krə dü′lə tē) *n.* lack of belief; doubt.

in·cred·u·lous (in krej′ə ləs) *adj.* **1** not willing or likely to believe; not credulous; doubting: *Most people are incredulous about ghosts and witches.* **2** showing a lack of belief: *an incredulous smile.* —**in·cred′u·lous·ly,** *adv.* —**in·cred′u·lous·ness,** *n.*
☛ *Usage.* See note at **incredible.**

in·cre·ment (in′krə mənt *or* ing′krə mənt) *n.* **1** an increase; growth. **2** the amount by which something increases. **3** *Mathematics.* **a** the amount, positive or negative, by which the value of an independent variable changes. **b** the amount by which the dependent function changes as a result. [< L *incrementum* < *increscere.* See INCREASE.]

in·crim·i·nate (in krim′ə nāt′) *v.* **-nat·ed, -nat·ing.** accuse of a crime, show to be guilty: *In his confession the thief incriminated two of his accomplices.* [< LL *incriminare* < L *in-* against + *crimen, -minis* charge] —**in·crim′i·na′tion,** *n.* —**in·crim′i·na′tor,** *n.*

in·crim·i·na·to·ry (in krim′ə nə tô′rē) *adj.* tending to incriminate.

in·crust (in krust′) *v.* **1** cover with a crust or hard coating: *The inside of a kettle is incrusted with lime.* **2** form a crust (*on*); form into a crust: *The extremely cold weather during the night had incrusted the snow so that it was able to bear our weight.* **3** decorate with a layer of costly material: *The gold crown was incrusted with precious gems.* Also, **encrust.** [< L *incrustare* < *in-* on + *crusta* crust]

in·crus·ta·tion (in′krus tā′shən) *n.* **1** incrusting or being incrusted. **2** a crust or hard coating. **3** a decorative layer of costly material. Also, **encrustation.**

in·cu·bate (in′kyə bāt′ *or* ing′kyə bāt′) *v.* **-bat·ed, -bat·ing. 1** sit on (eggs, etc.) in order to hatch them; brood. **2** keep (an egg, embryo, etc.) under conditions that will enable it to hatch, develop, etc. **3** of a disease, go through incubation. **4** gradually develop or cause to develop or take form: *The writer's last great novel was incubating in her mind for several years.* [< L *incubare* < *in-* on + *cubare* lie]

in·cu·ba·tion (in′kyə bā′shən *or* ing′kyə bā′shən) *n.* **1** incubating or being incubated. **2** the stage of a disease from the time of infection until the appearance of the first symptoms.

in·cu·ba·tor (in′kyə bā′tər *or* ing′kyə bā′tər) *n.* **1** an apparatus for keeping eggs warm so that they will hatch. It has a box or chamber that can be kept at a certain temperature. **2** a similar apparatus for protecting babies born very small or prematurely. **3** an apparatus in which bacterial cultures are developed. **4** any person or thing that incubates: *the incubator of separatism.* [< L]

in·cu·bus (in′kyə bəs *or* ing′kyə bəs) *n., pl.* **-bi** (-bī′ *or* -bē′) *or* **-bus·es. 1** an evil spirit supposed to descend upon sleeping persons, especially women. **2** nightmare. **3** an oppressive or burdensome thing: *This debt will be an incubus until I have paid it.* [< Med.L (def. 1), LL (def. 2) < L *incubare* < *in-* on + *cubare* lie]

in·cu·des (in kyü′dēz) *n.* pl. of **incus.**

in·cul·cate (in kul′kāt *or* in′kul kāt′) *v.* **-cat·ed, -cat·ing.** impress by repetition; teach persistently. [< L *inculcare,* originally, trample in, ult. < *in-* in + *calx, calcis* heel] —**in·cul′ca·tor,** *n.*

in·cul·ca·tion (in′kul kā′shən) *n.* the act or process of impressing principles, etc. on the mind by persistent urging or teaching.

in·cul·pate (in kul′pāt *or* in′kul pāt′) *v.* **-pat·ed, -pat·ing. 1** blame; accuse. **2** involve in responsibility for wrongdoing; incriminate. [< LL *inculpare* < L *in-* in + *culpa* blame]

in·cum·ben·cy (in kum′bən sē) *n., pl.* **-cies.** the holding of an office, position, etc. and performance of its duties; term of office: *During my uncle's incumbency as mayor, the city prospered.*

in·cum·bent (in kum′bənt) *adj., n.* —*adj.* **1** lying, leaning, or pressing (*on*). **2** resting (on a person) as a duty: *She felt it incumbent upon her to answer the letter at once.* **3** currently holding office: *the incumbent minister.* **4** *Poetic.* overhanging. —*n.* a person holding an office, position, church living, etc. [< L *incumbens, -entis,* ppr. of *incumbere* lie down on]

in·cum·ber (in kum′bər) *v.* encumber.

hat, āge, fär; let, ēqual, tėrm; it, īce
hot, ōpen, ôrder; oil, out; cup, put, rüle,
ə*bove, tak*ə*n, penc*ə*l, lem*ə*n, circ*ə*s
ch, child; ng, long; sh, ship
th, thin; ₮H, then; zh, measure

in·cum·brance (in kum′brəns) *n.* encumbrance.

in·cu·nab·u·la (in′kyə nab′yə lə) *n.* pl. of **incunabulum** (in′kyə nab′yə ləm). **1** the earliest stages or first traces of anything; beginnings. **2** books printed before the year 1500. [< L *incunabula* swaddling clothes < *cunae* cradle]

in·cur (in kėr′) *v.* **-curred, -cur·ring.** run into or meet with (something unpleasant), bring on oneself: *to incur many expenses. The explorers incurred great danger when they tried to cross the rapids.* [< L *incurrere* < *in-* upon + *currere* run]

in·cur·a·bil·i·ty (in kyür′ə bil′ə tē) *n.* the quality of being incurable.

in·cur·a·ble (in kyür′ə bəl) *adj., n.* —*adj.* not capable of being cured or remedied: *an incurable invalid.* —*n.* a person having an incurable disease. —**in·cur′a·bly,** *adv.*

in·cu·ri·ous (in kyür′ē əs) *adj.* **1** not curious; inattentive; unobservant; indifferent. **2** deficient in interest or novelty. —**in·cu′ri·ous·ly,** *adv.*

in·cur·sion (in kėr′zhən *or* in kėr′shən) *n.* **1** an invasion; raid; sudden attack: *The pirates made incursions along the coast.* **2** a running or flowing in: *Dikes protected the lowland from incursions of the sea.* [ME < L *incursio, -onis* < *incurrere.* See INCUR.]

in·cur·sive (in kėr′siv) *adj.* making incursions.

in·curve (in′kėrv′) *n. Baseball.* a pitch that curves toward the batter.

in·cus (ing′kəs) *n., pl.* **in·cu·des.** *Anatomy.* the middle one of a chain of three small bones in the middle ear of man and other animals: *The incus is shaped somewhat like an anvil.* See **ear**[1] for picture. [< L *incus, -udis* anvil]

ind. 1 independent. **2** indicative. **3** industrial. **4** index. **5** indirect. **6** indigo.

Ind (ind) *n. Poetic.* **1** India. **2** Indies.

Ind. 1 Indiana. **2** India; Indian. **3** *Politics.* Independent.

in·debt·ed (in det′id) *adj.* in debt; obliged; owing money or gratitude: *We are indebted to scientists for many of our comforts.*

in·debt·ed·ness (in det′id nis) *n.* **1** the condition of being in debt. **2** the amount owed; debts.

in·de·cen·cy (in dē′sən sē) *n., pl.* **-cies. 1** lack of decency; the quality of being indecent. **2** an indecent act or word.

in·de·cent (in dē′sent) *adj.* not decent; unseemly, improper, or morally offensive: *an indecent lack of gratitude, an indecent haste to sell off his father's belongings.* —**in·de′cent·ly,** *adv.*
☛ *Syn.* See note at **improper.**

in·de·ci·pher·a·ble (in′di sī′fər ə bəl) *adj.* incapable of being deciphered; illegible.

in·de·ci·sion (in′di sizh′ən) *n.* lack of decision; a tendency to delay or to hesitate; tendency to put off deciding or to change one's mind.

in·de·ci·sive (in′di sī′siv) *adj.* **1** having the habit of hesitating and putting off decisions. **2** not deciding or settling the matter: *an indecisive battle, an indecisive answer.* —**in·de′ci·sive·ly,** *adv.* —**in·de′ci·sive·ness,** *n.*

in·de·clin·a·ble (in′di klīn′ə bəl) *adj.* of words, having the same form in all grammatical constructions. *None* is an indeclinable pronoun.

in·dec·o·rous (in dek′ə rəs *or* in′di kô′rəs) *adj.* not suitable; improper; unseemly. [< L *indecorus*] —**in·dec′o·rous·ly,** *adv.* —**in·dec′o·rous·ness,** *n.*

in·de·co·rum (in′di kô′rəm) *n.* **1** lack of decorum. **2** improper behavior, speech, dress, etc. [< L *indecorum,* originally, neut. of *indecorus* indecorous]

in·deed (in dēd′) *adv., interj.* —*adv.* in fact; really; truly; surely: *War is indeed terrible.* —*interj.* an expression of surprise, doubt, contempt, etc.: *Indeed! I would not have done it.*

indef. indefinite.

in·de·fat·i·ga·bil·i·ty (in′di fat′ə gə bil′ə tē) *n.* the quality of being indefatigable; tirelessness.

in·de·fat·i·ga·ble (in′di fat′ə gə bəl) *adj.* never getting tired or giving up; tireless. [< L *indefatigabilis* < *in-* not + *defatigare* tire out < *de-* completely + *fatigare* tire] —**in′de·fat′i·ga·bly,** *adv.*

in·de·fea·si·ble (in′di fē′zə bəl) *adj.* not to be annulled or made

void: *Kings were once believed to have an indefeasible right to rule.* [< *in-*[1] + *defeasible* that may be annulled < AF *defeasible* < OF *desfaire* undo < *des-* apart + *faire* < L *facere* do] —**in·de·fea′si·bly,** *adv.*

in·de·fen·si·ble (in′di fen′sə bəl) *adj.* **1** that cannot be defended: *an indefensible island.* **2** not justifiable: *an indefensible lie.* —**in′de·fen′si·ble·ness,** *n.* —**in′de·fen′si·bly,** *adv.*

in·de·fin·a·ble (in′di fīn′ə bəl) *adj.* that cannot be defined. —**in′de·fin′a·ble·ness,** *n.* —**in′de·fin′a·bly,** *adv.*

in·def·i·nite (in def′ə nit) *adj.* **1** not clearly defined; not precise; vague: *"Maybe" is a very indefinite answer.* **2** not limited: *We have an indefinite time to finish this work.* **3** not specifying precisely. An indefinite adjective, pronoun, etc. does not determine the person, thing, time, etc. to which it refers. *Some, many,* and *few,* are often indefinite pronouns. [< L *indefinitus*] —**in·def′i·nite·ly,** *adv.* —**in·def′i·nite·ness,** *n.*

in·de·his·cent (in′di his′ənt) *adj. Botany.* not opening at maturity: *Acorns are indehiscent fruits. See* **fruit** *for picture.*

in·del·i·bil·i·ty (in del′ə bil′ə tē) *n.* the quality of being indelible; permanence.

in·del·i·ble (in del′ə bəl) *adj.* **1** that cannot be erased or removed; permanent: *indelible ink. He left an indelible impression of greatness.* **2** capable of making an indelible mark: *an indelible pencil.* [< L *indelebilis* < *in-* not + *delebilis* able to be destroyed < *delere* destroy] —**in·del′i·bly,** *adv.*

in·del·i·ca·cy (in del′ə kə sē) *n., pl.* **-cies.** lack of delicacy; being indelicate.

in·del·i·cate (in del′ə kit) *adj.* **1** not delicate; coarse; crude. **2** improper; immodest. —**in·del′i·cate·ly,** *adv.*

in·dem·ni·fi·ca·tion (in dem′nə fə kā′shən) *n.* **1** indemnifying or being indemnified. **2** compensation; recompense.

in·dem·ni·fy (in dem′nə fī′) *v.* **-fied, -fy·ing. 1** repay; make good; compensate for damage, loss, or expense incurred: *He promised to indemnify me for my losses.* **2** secure against damage or loss; insure. [< L *indemnis* unhurt (< *in-* not + *damnum* damage) + E *-fy*] —**in·dem′ni·fi·er,** *n.*

in·dem·ni·ty (in dem′nə tē) *n., pl.* **-ties. 1** the payment for damage, loss, or expense incurred. Money demanded by a victorious nation at the end of a war as a condition of peace is an indemnity. **2** a security against damage or loss; insurance. **3** in Canada, the remuneration paid to an M.P. or M.L.A. [< LL *indemnitas* < L *indemnis* unhurt < *in-* not + *damnum* damage]

in·dent[1] (*v.* in dent′; *n.* in′dent *or* in dent′) *v., n.* —*v.* **1** make or form notches or jags in (an edge, line, border, etc.): *an indented coastline. The rim of the plate was indented.* **2** begin (a line) farther from the edge of a page than the other lines: *We usually indent the first line of a paragraph.* **3** order (goods, etc.) by an indent. **4** draw an order upon (a source of supply). —*n.* **1** a notch; indentation. **2** an official requisition for supplies. **3** an order for goods. [ME < OF *endenter,* ult. < L *in-* in + *dens, dentis* tooth]

in·dent[2] (in dent′) *v.* **1** make a dent in; mark with a dent. **2** press in; stamp. [< *in-*[2] + *dent*]

in·den·ta·tion (in′dən tā′shən) *n.* **1** indenting or being indented. **2** a dent; notch; cut. **3** indention.

in·den·tion (in den′shən) *n.* **1** a beginning of a line farther from the edge of a page than the other lines. **2** the blank space left by doing this. **3** indentation.

in·den·ture (in den′chər) *n., v.* **-tured, -tur·ing.** —*n.* **1** a written agreement. **2** Usually, **indentures,** *pl.* a contract by which a person is bound to serve someone else, especially as an apprentice. **3** indentation. —*v.* bind (a person) by indentures. [ME < MF *endenteüre* indentation < OF *endenter. See* INDENT[1].]

in·de·pend·ence (in′di pen′dəns) *n.* **1** the quality or state of being independent; freedom from dependence on or control by another: *independence from one's parents. Jamaica and Trinidad and Tobago achieved independence within the Commonwealth in 1962.* **2** *Archaic.* enough income to live on; competence. *independence from his rich uncle.*
☛ *Syn.* **1.** See note at **freedom.**

Independence Day. *U.S.* the Fourth of July.

in·de·pend·en·cy (in′di pen′dən sē) *n., pl.* **-cies. 1** independence. **2** an independent country, territory, etc.

in·de·pend·ent (in′di pen′dənt) *adj., n.* —*adj.* **1** not needing, wanting or getting help from others; not connected with others: *independent work, independent thinking.* **2** not influenced by others; thinking or acting for oneself: *An independent person votes as he pleases.* **3** guiding, ruling, or governing oneself; not under another's

rule: *Canada is an independent country within the Commonwealth of Nations.* **4** not depending on others: *Miss Jones has an independent fortune.* **5** not resulting from another thing; not controlled or influenced by something else; separate; distinct. **6** *Mathematics.* of a variable, that can be assigned any value. **independent of,** apart from; without regard to: *independent of the feelings of others.* —*n.* **1** a person who is independent in thought or behavior, especially one who votes without regard to party. **2 Independent,** a person who stands for election to, or is an elected member of, a legislature without being a representative of any political party. **3** a business that operates without any outside management or control by another company or companies.

in·de·pend·ent·ly (in′di pen′dənt lē) *adv.* in an independent manner.

independently of, apart from; without regard to.

in-depth (in′depth′) *adj.* going below the surface; deep; detailed: *an in-depth study.*

in·de·scrib·a·ble (in′di skrīb′ə bəl) *adj.* that cannot be described; beyond description. —**in′de·scrib′a·bly,** *adv.*

in·de·struct·i·bil·i·ty (in′di struk′tə bil′ə tē) *n.* the quality of being indestructible.

in·de·struct·i·ble (in′di struk′tə bəl) *adj.* that cannot be destroyed. —**in′de·struct′i·bly,** *adv.*

in·de·ter·mi·na·ble (in′di tėr′mə nə bəl) *adj.* **1** not capable of being settled or decided. **2** not capable of being found out exactly. —**in′de·ter′mi·na·bly,** *adv.*

in·de·ter·mi·nate (in′di tėr′mə nit) *adj.* not determined; not fixed; indefinite; vague. —**in′de·ter′mi·nate·ly,** *adv.*

in·de·ter·mi·na·tion (in′di tėr′mə nā′shən) *n.* **1** a lack of determination. **2** an unsettled state.

in·dex (in′deks) *n., pl.* **-dex·es** *or* **-di·ces;** *v.* —*n.* **1** a list of the contents of a book, giving page, paragraph, or section references for each of the subjects discussed. The index is usually put at the end of a book and is arranged in alphabetical order. **2** something that points out or shows; sign: *A person's face is often an index of his mood.* **3** index finger. **4** a pointer: *A dial or scale usually has an index.* **5** *Printing.* a sign (☞) used to point out a particular note, paragraph, etc. **6** a number or formula expressing some property, ratio, etc. **7** *Mathematics.* **a** an exponent. **b** the number indicating the root. In ³√764 the index is 3. **8** a number that indicates the amount of business activity in relation to past levels of business activity: *the cost-of-living index.* —*v.* **1** provide with an index. **2** enter in an index. **3** prepare an index. **4** serve to indicate. **5** make provision for (income, income tax, etc.) to be adjusted automatically according to changes in the cost of living: *an indexed pension.* —**in′dex·er,** *n.* [< L *index,* originally, that which points out < *in-* toward + *dic-* point]

in·dex·a·tion (in′dek sā′shən) *n.* the act or policy of indexing income, taxes, etc.

Index Ex·pur·ga·to·ri·us (eks pėr′gə tô′rē əs) a list of books that the Roman Catholic Church forbids its members to read until objectionable parts have been taken out or changed.

index finger the finger next to the thumb; forefinger.

Index Li·bro·rum Pro·hib·i·to·rum (lī brô′rəm prō hib′ə tô′rəm) a list of books that the Roman Catholic Church forbids its members to read.

India ink 1 a black pigment consisting of lampblack mixed with a binding material and moulded into sticks or cakes. India ink is made chiefly in China and Japan. **2** a liquid ink prepared from this pigment.

In·di·a·man (in′dē ə mən) *n., pl.* **-men.** *Historical.* a ship in the trade with India, especially a large one belonging to the East India Company.

In·di·an (in′dē ən) *n., adj.* —*n.* **1** a member of any of the peoples who are the original inhabitants of the western hemisphere south of the Arctic coast region; Amerindian. **2** *Informal.* any of the languages spoken by any of these peoples. **3** a native or inhabitant of the Republic of India. **4** a native or inhabitant of the Indian subcontinent. —*adj.* **1** of or having to do with the Amerindian peoples or their languages. **2** of or having to do with the inhabitants of India or the Indian subcontinent. **3** made of corn or cornmeal: *Indian meal, Indian pudding.*

Indian agent in Canada, an official of the federal government who looks after Indian affairs on a reservation, etc.

Indian club a bottle-shaped wooden club that is swung for exercise.

Indian corn corn[1] (defs. 1, 2); maize.

Indian devil 1 the carcajou or wolverine. **2** a malevolent spirit; werewolf.

Indian file single file.

Indian giver *Informal.* a person who, when offended, takes back a gift after having bestowed it.
☛ *Usage.* Based on the idea that an Indian giving a gift expected another in return, this term is insulting to Indians and should be avoided.

Indian hall *Cdn. Historical.* a building or room where Indians bringing fur and other goods for sale were received.

Indian hemp **1** a North American dogbane (*Apocynum cannabinum*) having tough stem fibres that were used by Amerindian peoples to make cordage. **2** hemp.

Indian horse or **pony** a smallish type of horse bred by the western Indians; cayuse.

Indian ink India ink.

Indian list *Cdn.* **1** the official register of treaty Indians. **2** *Informal.* the list of persons barred by a legal interdict from buying liquor.
be on the Indian list, *Informal.* **a** be barred by law from buying liquor. **b** be blacklisted.

Indian meal meal made from Indian corn; corn meal.

Indian paintbrush any of various plants (genus *Castilleja*) of the figwort family having spikes of flowers and showy, bright scarlet or orange leaves just below the flowers.

Indian pipe a whitish or pinkish North American and Asian woodland plant (*Monotropa uniflora*) that lacks clorophyll, getting its nourishment from the remains of dead plants, and that has scalelike leaves and a single drooping flower at the top of the stem, giving the plant the appearance of a pipe.

Indian summer a time of mild, dry, hazy weather that sometimes occurs in October or early November, after the first frosts of autumn.

Indian tobacco a North American wild lobelia (*Lobelia inflata*) having small, pale-blue flowers and toothed leaves, formerly used in medicine but now regarded as poisonous.

Indian turnip jack-in-the-pulpit.

Indian wrestling any of several forms of wrestling formerly used as trials of strength by the Indians.

India paper **1** a thin, tough paper, used for Bibles, prayer books, etc. **2** a thin, soft paper, used for the first or finest impressions of engravings, etc.

India rubber or **india rubber** a substance of great elasticity obtained from the coagulated, milky juice of various tropical plants; rubber.

indic. indicative.

Indic (in′dik) *adj.* **1** of or having to do with India; Indian. **2** denoting or having to do with the Indian branch of the Indo-Iranian languages. [< L *Indicus* < Gk. *Indikos* < *India*]

in·di·cate (in′də kāt′) *v.* **-cat·ed, -cat·ing. 1** point out; point to: *The arrow on the sign indicates the right way to go.* **2** show; make known: *A thermometer indicates temperature.* **3** be a sign or hint of: *The haze indicated heat.* **4** give a sign or hint of: *A dog indicates its feelings by growling, whining, barking, or wagging its tail.* **5** *Medicine.* **a** show to be needed as a remedy or treatment: *The examination indicated surgery.* **b** show the presence of (a disease). [< L *indicare* < *index, -dicis.* See INDEX.]

in·di·ca·tion (in′də kā′shən) *n.* **1** indicating. **2** something that indicates; a sign: *There was no indication that the house was occupied.* **3** the amount or degree indicated: *The speedometer indication was 80 kilometres.*

in·dic·a·tive (in dik′ə tiv) *adj., n.* —*adj.* **1** pointing out; showing; being a sign (*of*); suggestive: *A headache is sometimes indicative of eye strain.* **2** *Grammar.* expressing or denoting a state, act, or happening as actual; asking a question of simple fact. In *I go* and *Did I go?* the verbs are in the indicative mood. —*n. Grammar.* **a** the indicative mood. **b** a verb form in this mood. —**in·dic′a·tive·ly,** *adv.*

in·di·ca·tor (in′də kā′tər) *n.* **1** a person or thing that indicates. **2** the pointer on the dial of an instrument that measures something. **3** a measuring or recording instrument. **4** a substance used to indicate chemical conditions or changes: *Litmus is an indicator.*

in·di·ces (in′də sēz′) *n.* a pl. of **index.**

in·dict (in dīt′) *v.* **1** charge with an offence or crime; accuse. **2** of a grand jury, find enough evidence against (an accused person) to justify a trial. [ME < AF *enditer* < OF. See INDITE.] —**in·dict′er** or **in·dict′or,** *n.*

in·dict·a·ble (in dīt′ə bəl) *adj.* **1** making a person liable to be indicted: *an indictable offence.* **2** liable to be indicted.

indictable offence a crime, such as armed robbery or murder, that is more serious than a summary offence. A person charged with an indictable offence in Canada may be arrested without a warrant and may be fingerprinted and photographed for police records.

in·dict·ment (in dīt′mənt) *n.* **1** the formal, written charge made against a person accused of a serious criminal offence. In Canada,

hat, āge, fär; let, ēqual, tèrm; it, īce
hot, ōpen, ôrder; oil, out; cup, pût, rüle,
əbove, takən, pencəl, lemən, circəs
ch, child; ng, long; sh, ship
th, thin; ŦH, then; zh, measure

an indictment is issued for any offence not punishable by summary conviction. **2** accusation.

in·dif·fer·ence (in dif′rəns or in dif′ər əns) *n.* **1** a lack of interest or attention. **2** little or no importance: *Where we ate was a matter of indifference to us.*
☛ *Syn.* **1.** Indifference, unconcern, apathy = lack of interest. **Indifference** emphasizes not caring one way or the other, showing no interest: *A lazy, careless person treats his work with indifference.* **Unconcern** emphasizes not caring enough to take a natural or proper interest, and suggests being unaware of any cause for anxiety or need for personal attention: *Nobody understands the unconcern of her parents.* **Apathy** suggests indifference to everything except one's own troubles, sorrow, or pain: *We have been worried about her apathy since her husband died.*

in·dif·fer·ent (in dif′rənt or in dif′ər ənt) *adj.* **1** having no feeling for or against; having or showing no interest: *indifferent to an admirer.* **2** impartial; neutral; without preference: *an indifferent decision.* **3** unimportant; not mattering much: *The time for starting is indifferent to me.* **4** not bad, but less than good; just fair: *an indifferent ballplayer.* **5** rather bad. **6** neutral in chemical, electrical, or magnetic quality.

in·dif·fer·ent·ly (in dif′rənt lē or in dif′ər ənt lē) *adv.* **1** with indifference. **2** without distinction; equally. **3** moderately; tolerably; passably. **4** poorly; badly; in an inferior manner: *He did his work indifferently.*

in·di·gence (in′də jəns) *n.* poverty.

in·dig·e·nous (in dij′ə nəs) *adj.* **1** originating or produced in a particular country; growing or living naturally in a certain region, soil, climate, etc.; native: *Musk-oxen are indigenous to Canada.* **2** innate; inherent. [< L *indigena* a native] —**in·dig′e·nous·ly,** *adv.*

in·di·gent (in′də jənt) *adj., n.* —*adj.* very poor and needy. —*n.* an indigent person. [< L *indigens, -entis,* ppr. of *indigere* need] —**in′di·gent·ly,** *adv.*

in·di·gest·i·bil·i·ty (in′də jes′tə bil′ə tē or in′dī jes′tə bil′ə tē) *n.* an indigestible nature or quality.

in·di·gest·i·ble (in′də jes′tə bəl or in′dī jes′tə bəl) *adj.* that cannot be properly digested; hard to digest. —**in′di·gest′i·bly,** *adv.*

in·di·ges·tion (in′də jes′chən or in′dī jes′chən) *n.* inability to digest food properly; difficulty in digesting food.

in·dig·nant (in dig′nənt) *adj.* angry at something unworthy, unjust, or mean. [< L *indignans, -antis,* ppr. of *indignari* be indignant (at), regard as unworthy < *indignus* unworthy < *in-* not + *dignus* worthy] —**in·dig′nant·ly,** *adv.*

in·dig·na·tion (in′dig nā′shən) *n.* anger at something unworthy, unjust, or mean; anger mixed with scorn; righteous anger: *Cruelty to animals arouses our indignation.*
☛ *Syn.* See note at **anger.**

in·dig·ni·ty (in dig′nə tē) *n., pl.* **-ties.** an injury to dignity; lack of respect or proper treatment; insult. [< L *indignitas*]
☛ *Syn.* See note at **insult.**

in·di·go (in′də gō′) *n., pl.* **-gos** or **-goes;** *adj.* —*n.* **1** a blue dyestuff that can be obtained from certain plants, but is now usually made artificially. **2** any of a genus (*Indigofera*) of plants of the pea family from which indigo is obtained. **3** a deep violet blue. —*adj.* deep violet blue. [< Sp. < L < Gk. *indikon,* originally *adj.,* Indian (dye)]

indigo bunting a bunting (*Passerina cyanea*) of central and E North America, the adult male having violet-blue plumage during the breeding season and brownish plumage, similar to that of the female, the rest of the year.

in·di·rect (in′də rekt′ or in′dī rekt′) *adj.* **1** not direct; not straight: *an indirect route.* **2** not directly connected; secondary: *Happiness is an indirect consequence of doing one's work well.* **3** not straightforward and to the point: *The witness gave an indirect answer to the lawyer's question instead of a frank "Yes" or "No."* **4** dishonest; deceitful: *indirect methods.* —**in′di·rect′ly,** *adv.* —**in′di·rect′ness,** *n.*

indirect discourse discourse in which a speaker's words are reported indirectly. *Example: He replied that he would think it over.*

in·di·rec·tion (in′də rek′shən or in′dī rek′shən) *n.* **1** a roundabout act, means, or method. **2** dishonesty; deceit.

indirect object the person or thing that is indirectly affected by the action of the verb. In English, the indirect object usually comes

before the direct object and shows to whom or for whom something is done. *Example: In* I gave John a book, John *is the indirect object, and* book *is the direct object.*

indirect question a question reported indirectly. *Example: She asked when they had arrived.* Compare **direct question.**

indirect tax a tax paid indirectly by the consumer and included in the price of an article.

in·dis·cern·i·ble (in′də sėr′nə bəl *or* in′də zėr′nə bəl) *adj.* not discernible; imperceptible. —**in·dis·cern′i·bly,** *adv.*

in·dis·creet (in′dis krēt′) *adj.* not discreet; not wise and judicious; imprudent: *The boy's indiscreet remark made the stranger feel insulted.* —**in′dis·creet′ly,** *adv.* —**in′dis·creet′ness,** *n.*

in·dis·cre·tion (in′dis kresh′ən) *n.* **1** being indiscreet; lack of good judgment; imprudence. **2** an indiscreet act.

in·dis·crim·i·nate (in′dis krim′ə nit) *adj.* **1** confused: *He tipped everything out of his suitcase in an indiscriminate mass.* **2** not discriminating; with no feeling for differences: *He is an indiscriminate reader and likes both good books and bad ones.* —**in′dis·crim′i·nate·ly,** *adv.* —**in′dis·crim′i·na′tion,** *n.*
☛ *Syn.* **2.** See note at **miscellaneous.**

in·dis·pen·sa·bil·i·ty (in′dis pen′sə bil′ə tē) *n.* the state or quality of being indispensable; absolute necessity.

in·dis·pen·sa·ble (in′dis pen′sə bəl) *adj.* absolutely necessary: *Air is indispensable to life.*
☛ *Syn.* See note at **necessary.**

in·dis·pen·sa·bly (in′dis pen′sə blē) *adv.* to an indispensable degree; necessarily.

in·dis·pose (in′dis pōz′) *v.* **-posed, -pos·ing. 1** make unwilling; make averse: *Hot weather indisposes a person to work hard.* **2** make slightly ill. **3** make unfit or unable.

in·dis·posed (in′dis pōzd′) *adj.* **1** slightly ill. **2** unwilling; without inclination; averse: *The men were indisposed to work nights.*

in·dis·po·si·tion (in′dis pə zish′ən) *n.* **1** a disturbance of health; slight illness. **2** an unwillingness; disinclination; aversion.

in·dis·put·a·bil·i·ty (in′dis pyüt′ə bil′ə tē *or* in dis′pyə tə bil′ə tē) *n.* being indisputable.

in·dis·put·a·ble (in′dis pyüt′ə bəl *or* in dis′pyə tə bəl) *adj.* not to be disputed; undoubtedly true; unquestionable. —**in′dis·put′a·bly,** *adv.*

in·dis·sol·u·bil·i·ty (in′di sol′yə bil′ə tē) *n.* being indissoluble; stability.

in·dis·sol·u·ble (in′di sol′yə bəl) *adj.* not capable of being dissolved, undone, or destroyed; lasting; firm. —**in′dis·sol′u·bly,** *adv.*

in·dis·tinct (in′dis tingkt′) *adj.* not distinct; not clear to the eye, ear, or mind; confused. [< L *indistinctus*] —**in′dis·tinct′ly,** *adv.* —**in′dis·tinct′ness,** *n.*

in·dis·tin·guish·a·ble (in′dis ting′gwish ə bəl) *adj.* that cannot be distinguished. —**in′dis·tin′guish·a·bly,** *adv.*

in·dite (in dīt′) *v.* **-dit·ed, -dit·ing.** put in words or writing; compose: *indite a letter.* [ME < OF *enditer* make known < L *in-* in + *dictare* dictate, express in writing. Cf. INDICT.]

in·di·um (in′dē əm) *n.* a rare metallic chemical element that is soft, white, malleable, and easily fusible. *Symbol:* In; *at.no.* 49; *at.wt.* 114.82. [< NL < L *indicum.* See INDIGO.]

in·di·vid·u·al (in′də vij′ü əl) *n., adj.* —*n.* **1** person: *She is a clever individual.* **2** a single or distinct person, animal, or thing: *She tries to remain an individual. The herd of giraffes consisted of thirty individuals.*
—*adj.* **1** single; particular; separate: *an individual question.* **2** for one only: *We use individual salt-cellars.* **3** having to do with or peculiar to one person or thing: *individual tastes.* **4** marking off one person or thing specially: *Each girl has an individual style of arranging her hair.* [< Med.L *individualis* < L *individuus* < *in-* not + *dividuus* divisible]
☛ *Syn.* See note at **person.**

in·di·vid·u·al·ism (in′də vij′ü əl iz′əm) *n.* **1** a theory that individual freedom is as important as the welfare of the community or group as a whole. **2** any ethical, economic, or political theory that emphasizes the importance of individuals. **3** each for himself; the absence of co-operation; wanting a separate existence for oneself. **4** individuality.

in·di·vid·u·al·ist (in′də vij′ü əl ist) *n.* **1** one who goes his own way, independent of the views or interests of others. **2** a supporter of individualism.

in·di·vid·u·al·is·tic (in′də vij′ü əl is′tik) *adj.* of individualism or individualists. —**in′di·vid′u·al·is′ti·cal·ly,** *adv.*

in·di·vid·u·al·i·ty (in′də vij′ü al′ə tē) *n., pl.* **-ties. 1** individual character; the sum of the qualities that make one person or thing different from another. **2** the condition of being individual; existence as an individual. **3** an individual person or thing.
☛ *Syn.* **1.** See note at **character.**

in·di·vid·u·al·ize (in′də vij′ü əl īz′) *v.* **-ized, -iz·ing. 1** make individual; cause to be different from others; give a distinctive character to. **2** consider as individuals; list one by one; specify. —**in′di·vid′u·al·i·za′tion,** *n.*

in·di·vid·u·al·ly (in′də vij′ü əl ē) *adv.* **1** personally; one at a time; as individuals: *The teacher helps us individually.* **2** each from the others: *People differ individually.*

in·di·vis·i·bil·i·ty (in′də viz′ə bil′ə tē) *n.* the state or quality of being indivisible.

in·di·vis·i·ble (in′də viz′ə bəl) *adj.* **1** not capable of being divided. **2** not capable of being divided without a remainder. —**in′di·vis′i·bly,** *adv.*

Indo– *combining form.* **1** Indian; of India or the East Indies; *Indo-Aryan* = of or having to do with the Aryans of India. **2** Indian and: *Indo-European* = of India and Europe.

In·do–Ar·yan (in′dō er′ē ən *or* -är′yən) *adj. or n.* Indic.

In·do–Chi·nese (in′dō chī nēz′) *n., adj.* —*n.* **1** a native or inhabitant of Indochina, a historical name for either the peninsula south of China that includes Burma, Thailand, Laos, Kampuchea, and Vietnam, or the eastern part of this peninsula, formerly under French control, including Vietnam, Laos, and Kampuchea. **2** Sino-Tibetan. —*adj.* of or having to do with Indochina or the Indo-Chinese.

in·doc·tri·nate (in dok′trə nāt′) *v.* **-nat·ed, -nat·ing. 1** teach a doctrine, belief, or principle to. **2** teach. [probably < Med.L *indoctrinare* < *in-* in + *doctrinare* teach < L *doctrina* doctrine] —**in·doc′tri·na′tion,** *n.* —**in·doc′tri·na′tor,** *n.*

In·do–Eu·ro·pe·an (in′dō yür′ə pē′ən) *adj., n.* —*adj.* **1** of India and Europe. **2** of or having to do with a group of related languages spoken in India, W Asia, and Europe. English, German, Latin, Greek, Persian, and Sanskrit are Indo-European languages. —*n.* **1** this group of languages. **2** the reconstructed prehistoric language from which they are derived; Aryan. **3** a member of an ethnological group that speaks an Indo-European language.

In·do–Ger·man·ic (in′dō jər man′ik) *adj. or n.* Indo-European.

In·do–I·ra·ni·an (in′dō ī rä′nē ən) *adj., n.* —*adj.* of or having to do with a division of the Indo-European family of languages that comprises the Indic and Iranian branches. —*n.* this division.

in·do·lence (in′də ləns) *n.* laziness; dislike of work; idleness.

in·do·lent (in′də lənt) *adj.* lazy; disliking work. [< LL *indolens, -entis* < L *in-* not + *dolens,* ppr. of *dolere* be in pain] —**in′do·lent·ly,** *adv.*
☛ *Syn.* See note at **idle.**

in·dom·i·ta·bil·i·ty (in dom′ə tə bil′ə tē) *n.* the quality or state of being indomitable.

in·dom·i·ta·ble (in dom′ə tə bəl) *adj.* unconquerable; unyielding: *indomitable courage.* [< LL *indomitabilis,* ult. < L *in-* not + *domare* tame] —**in·dom′i·ta·bly,** *adv.*

In·do·ne·sian (in′dō nē′zhən *or* in′dō nē′shən) *n., adj.* —*n.* **1** a native or inhabitant of the Republic of Indonesia, a country in SE Asia. **2** Bahasa Indonesia, the official language of Indonesia. **3** a member of a people believed to have been dominant on the Malay Archipelago before the Malays.
—*adj.* of or having to do with Indonesia, its people, or their language. [< Gk. *Indos* Indian + *nēsos* island]

in·door (in′dôr′) *adj.* **1** done, played, used, etc, in a house or building: *indoor tennis, indoor skating.* **2** that is indoors: *an indoor rink.*

in·doors (in′dôrz′) *adv.* in or into a house or building: *go indoors.*

in·dorse (in dôrs′) *v.* **-dorsed, -dors·ing.** endorse.

in·dor·see (in′dôr sē′) *n.* endorsee.

in·dorse·ment (in dôrs′mənt) *n.* endorsement.

In·dra (in′drə) *n. Hinduism.* the principal deity of the Rig-Veda, god of war and storm.

in·draft (in′draft′) *n.* **1** a drawing in. **2** an inward flow or current of water, air, etc.

in·drawn (in′drôn′ *or* -drôn′) *adj.* **1** drawn in. **2** preoccupied; introspective.

in·du·bi·ta·ble (in dyü′bə tə bəl *or* in dü′bə tə bəl) *adj.* not to be doubted; certain. —**in·du′bi·ta·ble·ness,** *n.* —**in·du′bi·ta·bly,** *adv.*

in·duce (in dyüs′ *or* in düs′) *v.* **-duced, -duc·ing. 1** lead on; influence; persuade: *Advertising induces people to buy.* **2** cause; bring about: *Some drugs induce sleep.* **3** produce (an electric

current, electric charge, or magnetic change) without direct contact. **4** infer by reasoning from particular facts to a general rule or principle. [< L *inducere* < *in-* in + *ducere* lead] —**in·duc′er**, *n.*

in·duce·ment (in dyüs′mənt *or* in düs′mənt) *n.* something that influences or persuades; incentive: *Prizes are inducements to try hard to win.*

in·duct (in dukt′) *v.* **1** bring in; introduce (into a place, seat, position, office, etc.). **2** put formally into a position, office, etc.: *They proposed to induct him as secretary.* **3** *U.S.* take into or enroll in military service. **4** initiate. [< L *inductus*, pp. of *inducere*. See INDUCE.]

in·duct·ance (in duk′təns) *n.* **1** the property of an electrical conductor or circuit that makes induction possible. **2** a circuit or a device having this property. **3** the lag in an electric circuit when the current goes on or off.

in·duc·tee (in′duk tē′) *n.* a person who is soon to be inducted, especially, in the United States, into military service.

in·duc·tile (in duk′til *or* in duk′təl) *adj.* not ductile.

in·duc·tion (in duk′shən) *n.* **1** the process by which electrical or magnetic properties are transferred from one circuit or object to another, without direct contact between the two. **2** the act of reasoning from particular facts to a general rule or principle. **3** the conclusion reached in this way. **4** the act of inducting; act or ceremony of installing a person in office. **5** the act of bringing into existence or operation; producing; causing; inducing: *induction of a hypnotic state.* **6** the drawing of the fuel mixture into the cylinder or cylinders of an internal-combustion engine.
☛ *Usage.* See note at **deduction.**

induction coil a device for producing a high, pulsating voltage from a current of low, steady voltage, such as that from a battery.

in·duc·tive (in duk′tiv) *adj.* **1** of or using induction; reasoning by induction. **2** having to do with electrical or magnetic induction. —**in·duc′tive·ly**, *adv.*

in·duc·tiv·i·ty (in′duk tiv′ə tē) *n.*, *pl.* **-ties.** an inductive property; capacity for induction.

in·duc·tor (in duk′tər) *n.* **1** a person who inducts another into office. **2** a part of an electrical apparatus that works or is worked by induction.

in·due (in dyü′ *or* in dü′) *v.* **-dued, -du·ing.** endue. [< L *induere* put on]

in·dulge (in dulj′) *v.* **-dulged, -dulg·ing.** **1** yield to the wishes of; humor: *We often indulge a sick person.* **2** give in to one's pleasures; let oneself have, use, or do what one wants: *He indulges in tobacco.* **3** give in to; let oneself have, use, or do: *She indulged her fondness for candy by eating a whole box.* [< L *indulgere*] —**in·dulg′ing·ly**, *adv.*
☛ *Syn.* **1.** See note at **humor.**

in·dul·gence (in dul′jəns) *n.* **1** yielding to the wishes of another or allowing oneself one's own desires. **2** something indulged in. **3** a favor; privilege. **4** *Roman Catholic Church.* **a** remission of the punishment still due for a sin, after the guilt has been forgiven. **b** dispensation.

in·dul·gent (in dul′jənt) *adj.* indulging or showing indulgence; lenient and agreeable; often excessively so: *an indulgent parent, an indulgent smile.* —**in·dul′gent·ly**, *adv.*

in·du·rate (*v.* in′dyü rāt′ *or* in′dü rāt′; *adj.* in′dyü rit *or* in′dü rit) *v.* **-rat·ed, -rat·ing;** *adj.* —*v.* **1** harden. **2** make or become unfeeling. —*adj.* **1** hardened. **2** unfeeling. [< L *indurare* < *in-* + *durus* hard] —**in′du·ra′tion**, *n.*

in·dus·tri·al (in dus′trē əl) *adj.*, *n.* —*adj.* **1** of or resulting from industry or productive labor: *industrial products.* **2** having to do with or connected with an industry or industries: *an industrial exhibition, industrial workers.* **3** for use in industry. **4** of or having to do with the workers in industries: *industrial insurance.* —*n.* a stock, bond, etc. of an industrial enterprise. [earlier < Med.L *industrialis* < L *industria* diligence; later < F *industriel* < L *industria*] —**in·dus′tri·al·ly**, *adv.*

in·dus·tri·al·ism (in dus′trē əl iz′əm) *n.* a system of social and economic organization in which large industries are very important and industrial activities or interests prevail.

in·dus·tri·al·ist (in dus′trē əl ist) *n.* **1** a person who conducts or owns an industrial enterprise. **2** an industrial worker.

in·dus·tri·al·i·za·tion (in dus′trē əl ə zā′shən *or* in dus′trē əl ī zā′shən) *n.* the development of large industries as an important feature in a country or a social or economic system.

in·dus·tri·al·ize (in dus′trē əl īz′) *v.* **-ized, -iz·ing.** **1** make industrial; develop industry in. **2** organize as an industry.

Industrial Revolution the change from an agricultural to an industrial civilization, especially that which took place in England from about the middle of the 18th century to the middle of the 19th century.

in·dus·tri·ous (in dus′trē əs) *adj.* working hard and steadily: *an*

hat, āge, fär; let, ēqual, tėrm; it, īce
hot, ōpen, ôrder; oil, out; cup, put, rüle,
above, takən, pencəl, lemən, circəs

ch, child; ng, long; sh, ship
th, thin; ᴛн, then; zh, measure

industrious student. [< L *industriosus*] —**in·dus′tri·ous·ly**, *adv.* —**in·dus′tri·ous·ness**, *n.*
☛ *Syn.* See note at **busy.**

in·dus·try (in′dəs trē) *n.*, *pl.* **-tries.** **1** any branch of business, trade, or manufacture: *the steel industry, the automobile industry.* **2** all such enterprises taken collectively: *Canadian industry is expanding.* **3** systematic work or labor. **4** steady effort; close attention to work: *Industry and thrift favor success.* [< L *industria*]

in·dwell·ing (in′dwel′ing) *adj.* dwelling within.

–ine[1] *suffix.* of; like; like that of; characteristic of; having the nature of; being, as in *crystalline, elephantine.* [< L *-inus,* sometimes < Gk. *-inos*]

–ine[2] *suffix.* used especially in the names of some chemicals, as in *chlorine, aniline.* [< F (< L *-ina*) or directly < L *-ina*]

in·e·bri·ate (*v.* in ē′brē āt′; *n., adj.* in ē′brē it) *v.* **-at·ed, -at·ing;** *n., adj.* —*v.* make drunk; intoxicate. —*n.* a habitual drunkard; intoxicated person. —*adj.* intoxicated; drunk. [< L *inebriare* < *in-* + *ebrius* drunk]

in·e·bri·a·tion (in ē′brē ā′shən) *n.* drunkenness; intoxication.

in·e·bri·e·ty (in′i brī′ə tē) *n.* drunkenness.

in·ed·i·ble (in ed′ə bəl) *adj.* not fit to eat: *Some toadstools are inedible.*

in·ed·u·ca·ble (in ej′ə kə bəl) *adj.* incapable of being educated.

in·ef·fa·ble (in ef′ə bəl) *adj.* **1** not to be expressed in words; too great to be described in words. **2** that must not be spoken. [< L *ineffabilis*, ult. < *in-* not + *ex-* out + *fari* speak] —**in·ef′fa·ble·ness**, *n.* —**in·ef′fa·bly**, *adv.*

in·ef·face·a·ble (in′ə fās′ə bəl) *adj.* that cannot be rubbed out or wiped out. —**in′ef·face′a·bly**, *adv.*

in·ef·fec·tive (in′ə fek′tiv) *adj.* **1** not effective; of little or no use: *An ineffective medicine fails to cure a disease or relieve pain.* **2** unfit for work; incapable. —**in′ef·fec′tive·ly**, *adv.* —**in′ef·fec′tive·ness**, *n.*

in·ef·fec·tu·al (in′ə fek′chü əl) *adj.* **1** failing to have the effect wanted; useless. **2** not able to produce the effect wanted. —**in′ef·fec′tu·al·ly**, *adv.*

in·ef·fi·ca·cious (in′ef ə kā′shəs) *adj.* not efficacious; not able to produce the effect wanted.

in·ef·fi·ca·cy (in ef′ə kə sē) *n.* a lack of efficacy; inability to produce the effect wanted.

in·ef·fi·cien·cy (in′ə fish′ən sē) *n.* a lack of efficiency; inability to get things done.

in·ef·fi·cient (in′ə fish′ənt) *adj.* **1** not efficient; not able to produce an effect without waste of time, energy, etc.; wasteful: *A machine that uses too much power is inefficient.* **2** incapable; not able to get things done: *an inefficient housekeeper.* —**in′ef·fi′cient·ly**, *adv.*

in·e·las·tic (in′i las′tik) *adj.* not elastic; stiff; inflexible; unyielding.

in·e·las·tic·i·ty (in′i las tis′ə tē) *n.* a lack of elasticity.

in·el·e·gance (in el′ə gəns) *n.* **1** a lack of elegance; lack of good taste. **2** something that is not elegant or graceful.

in·el·e·gan·cy (in el′ə gən sē) *n., pl.* **-cies.** inelegance.

in·el·e·gant (in el′ə gənt) *adj.* not elegant; not in good taste; crude; vulgar. —**in·el′e·gant·ly**, *adv.*

in·el·i·gi·bil·i·ty (in el′ə jə bil′ə tē) *n.* a lack of eligibility; being ineligible.

in·el·i·gi·ble (in el′ə jə bəl) *adj., n.* —*adj.* not suitable; not qualified: *His youth makes him ineligible for the post.* —*n.* a person who is not suitable or not qualified. —**in·el′i·gi·bly**, *adv.*

in·e·luc·ta·ble (in′i luk′tə bəl) *adj.* unable to be avoided; inevitable. [< L *ineluctabilis* < *eluctari* < *ex-* out + *luctari* struggle] —**in′e·luc′ta·bly**, *adv.*

in·ept (in ept′) *adj.* **1** not suitable; out of place: *He would be an inept choice as captain.* **2** awkward; clumsy; incompetent: *That was an inept performance.* **3** absurd; foolish: *inept ideas.* [< L *ineptus* < *in-* not + *aptus* apt] —**in·ept′ly**, *adv.* —**in·ept′ness**, *n.*
☛ *Syn.* **1, 2. Inapt** and **inept** have similar meanings, but only **inept** (def. 3) = foolish, absurd.

in·ept·i·tude (in ep′tə tyüd′ *or* in ep′tə tüd′) *n.* **1** unfitness; foolishness. **2** a silly or inappropriate act or remark.

in·e·qual·i·ty (in′ē kwol′ə tē) *n., pl.* **-ties. 1** lack of equality; the state or condition of being unequal in amount, size, value, rank, etc. **2** a lack of evenness, regularity, or uniformity. **3** *Mathematics.* an expression showing that two quantities are not equal, such as $a < b$ (*a* is smaller than *b*) or $a \neq b$ (*a* is not equal to *b*).

in·e·qua·tion (in′ē kwā′zhən) *n.* an algebraic statement showing that one quantity is greater (or smaller) than another. *Example: a > b (a is greater than b), c < d (c is smaller than or equal to d).*

in·eq·ui·ta·ble (in ek′wə tə bəl) *adj.* unfair; unjust. —**in·eq′ui·ta·bly,** *adv.*

in·eq·ui·ty (in ek′wə tē) *n., pl.* **-ties. 1** unfairness; injustice. **2** an unfair or unjust act.

in·e·rad·i·ca·ble (in′i rad′ə kə bəl) *adj.* that cannot be rooted out or got rid of. —**in′e·rad′i·ca·bly,** *adv.*

in·ert (in ėrt′) *adj.* **1** having no inherent power to move or act; lifeless: *A stone is an inert mass of matter.* **2** inactive; slow; sluggish. **3** *Chemistry.* with few or no active properties: *Helium and neon are inert gases.* [< L *iners, inertis* idle, unskilled < *in-* without + *ars, artis* art, skill] —**in·ert′ly,** *adv.* —**in·ert′ness,** *n.*
☛ *Syn.* **2.** See note at **inactive.**

in·er·tia (in ėr′shə) *n.* **1** a tendency to remain in the state one is in and not start changes. **2** *Physics.* the tendency of all objects and matter in the universe to stay still if still, or if moving, to go on moving in the same direction unless acted on by some outside force. [< L *inertia* < *iners.* See INERT.]

in·er·tial (in ėr′shəl) *adj.* resembling inertia: *Inertial navigation is made possible by gyroscopic control.*

in·es·cap·a·ble (in′is kāp′ə bəl) *adj.* that cannot be escaped or avoided. —**in′es·cap′a·bly,** *adv.*

in·es·ti·ma·ble (in es′tə mə bəl) *adj.* too good, great, valuable, etc. to be measured or estimated: *Freedom is an inestimable privilege.* —**in·es′ti·ma·bly,** *adv.*

in·ev·i·ta·bil·i·ty (in ev′ə tə bil′ə tē) *n.* the quality of being inevitable.

in·ev·i·ta·ble (in ev′ə tə bəl) *adj.* not avoidable; sure to happen; certain to come. [< L *inevitabilis* < *in-* not + *evitabilis* avoidable < *evitare* avoid < *ex-* + *vitare* avoid] —**in·ev′i·ta·bly,** *adv.*

in·ex·act (in′ig zakt′) *adj.* not exact; with errors or mistakes; not just right. —**in′ex·act′ly,** *adv.* —**in′ex·act′ness,** *n.*

in·ex·cus·a·ble (in′ik skyü′zə bəl) *adj.* that ought not to be excused; that cannot be justified. —**in′ex·cus′a·bly,** *adv.*

in·ex·haust·i·bil·i·ty (in′ig zos′tə bil′ə tē *or* in′ig zôs′tə bil′ə tē) *n.* an inexhaustible nature or quality.

in·ex·haust·i·ble (in′ig zos′tə bəl *or* in′ig zôs′tə bəl) *adj.* **1** that cannot be exhausted; very abundant. **2** tireless. —**in′ex·haust′i·bly,** *adv.*

in·ex·o·ra·bil·i·ty (in ek′sə rə bil′ə tē) *n.* an inexorable nature or quality.

in·ex·o·ra·ble (in ek′sə rə bəl) *adj.* relentless; unyielding; not influenced by prayers or entreaties: *The forces of nature are inexorable.* [< L *inexorabilis* < *in-* not + *ex-* (intensive) + *orare* entreat] —**in·ex′o·ra·bly,** *adv.*
☛ *Syn.* See note at **inflexible.**

in·ex·pe·di·en·cy (in′ik spē′dē ən sē) *n.* lack of expediency; being inexpedient.

in·ex·pe·di·ent (in′ik spē′dē ənt) *adj.* not expedient; not practicable, suitable, or wise.

in·ex·pen·sive (in′ik spen′siv) *adj.* not expensive; cheap; low-priced. —**in′ex·pen′sive·ly,** *adv.* —**in′ex·pen′sive·ness,** *n.*
☛ *Syn.* See note at **cheap.**

in·ex·pe·ri·ence (in′ik spėr′ē əns) *n.* lack of experience or practice; lack of skill or wisdom gained from experience.

in·ex·pe·ri·enced (in′ik spėr′ē ənst) *adj.* not experienced; without practice; lacking the skill and wisdom gained by experience.

in·ex·pert (in ek′spėrt *or* in′ik spėrt′) *adj.* not expert; unskilled. —**in·ex′pert·ly,** *adv.* —**in·ex′pert·ness,** *n.*

in·ex·pi·a·ble (in ek′spē ə bəl) *adj.* that cannot be atoned for: *Murder is an inexpiable crime.* [< L *inexpiabilis*]

in·ex·pli·ca·bil·i·ty (in′ik splik′ə bil′ə tē *or* in ek′splə kə bil′ə tē) *n.* an unexplainable nature or quality.

in·ex·pli·ca·ble (in′ik splik′ə bəl *or* in ek′splə kə bəl) *adj.* impossible to explain or understand; mysterious. [< L *inexplicabilis*] —**in·ex′pli·ca·bly,** *adv.*

in·ex·press·i·ble (in′ik spres′ə bəl) *adj.* that cannot be expressed; beyond expression. —**in′ex·press′i·bly,** *adv.*

in·ex·pres·sive (in′ik spres′iv) *adj.* not expressive; lacking in expression. —**in′ex·pres′sive·ly,** *adv.* —**in′ex·pres′sive·ness,** *n.*

in ex·ten·so (in ik sten′sō) at full length; in full. [< L *in extenso*, literally, in an extended (state)]

in·ex·tin·guish·a·ble (in′ik sting′gwish ə bəl) *adj.* that cannot be put out or stopped: *An inextinguishable fire keeps on burning.* —**in′ex·tin′guish·a·bly,** *adv.*

in ex·tre·mis (in ik strē′mis) at the point of death. [< L *in extremis*, literally, amid the final things]

in·ex·tri·ca·ble (in ek′strə kə bəl) *adj.* **1** that one cannot get out of. **2** that cannot be disentangled or solved. —**in·ex′tri·ca·bly,** *adv.*

inf. 1 infantry. **2** infinitive. **3** inferior. **4** below (for L *infra*). **5** information.

Inf. infantry.

in·fal·li·bil·i·ty (in fal′ə bil′ə tē) *n.* absolute freedom from error: *The infallibility of the Pope when speaking officially on matters of faith and morals was proclaimed by the Vatican Council in 1870.*

in·fal·li·ble (in fal′ə bəl) *adj.* **1** free from error; that cannot be mistaken: *an infallible rule.* **2** absolutely reliable; sure: *infallible obedience.* **3** *Roman Catholic Church.* incapable of error in the exposition of doctrine on faith and morals (said of the Pope as head of the Church). —**in·fal′li·bly,** *adv.*

in·fa·mous (in′fə məs) *adj.* **1** deserving or causing a very bad reputation; shamefully bad; extremely wicked. **2** having a very bad reputation; in public disgrace: *an infamous traitor.* [< Med.L *infamosus*, in L *infamis*] —**in′fa·mous·ly,** *adv.* —**in′fa·mous·ness,** *n.*

in·fa·my (in′fə mē) *n., pl.* **-mies. 1** a very bad reputation; public disgrace: *His act brought infamy to his family and himself.* **2** shameful badness; extreme wickedness. **3** a shamefully bad or extremely wicked act. [< L *infamia* < *in-* without + *fama* (good) reputation]

in·fan·cy (in′fən sē) *n., pl.* **-cies. 1** the condition or time of being an infant; babyhood; early childhood. **2** an early stage; beginning of development: *Space travel is in its infancy.* **3** the condition of being under the legal age of responsibility (in common law, under 21).

in·fant (in′fənt) *n., adj.* —*n.* **1** a baby; very young child. **2** a person under the legal age of responsibility; minor. —*adj.* **1** of or for an infant. **2** in an early stage; just beginning to develop. [< L *infans, infantis,* originally, not speaking < *in-* not + *fari* speak]

in·fan·ta (in fan′tə) *n.* **1** a daughter of a king of Spain or Portugal. **2** the wife of an infante. [< Sp., Pg. *infanta,* fem.]

in·fan·te (in fan′tā) *n.* a son of a king of Spain or Portugal, but not the heir to the throne. [< Sp., Pg.]

in·fan·ti·cide (in fan′tə sīd′) *n.* **1** the act of killing a baby. **2** a person who kills a baby. [< L *infanticidium* the killing of a baby < *infans, -antis* infant + *-cidium* act of killing (for def. 1); < L *infanticida* one who kills a baby < *infans, -antis* + *-cida* killer (for def. 2)]

in·fan·tile (in′fən tīl′ *or* in′fən təl) *adj.* **1** of an infant or infants; having to do with infants: *infantile diseases.* **2** like an infant; babyish; childish: *infantile behavior.* **3** in an early stage; just beginning to develop.

infantile paralysis poliomyelitis; polio.

in·fan·ti·lism (in fan′tə liz′əm) *n.* an abnormal persistence or appearance of childish traits in adults.

in·fan·tine (in′fən tīn′ *or* in′fən tin) *adj.* infantile; babyish; childish.

in·fan·try (in′fən trē) *n., pl.* **-tries. 1** soldiers trained, equipped, and organized to fight on foot. **2** the branch of an army made up of such soldiers. [< F *infanterie* < Ital. *infanteria* < *infante, fante* foot soldier; originally, a youth < L *infans, -fantis.* See INFANT.]

in·fan·try·man (in′fən trē mən) *n., pl.* **-men.** a soldier who fights on foot.

in·farct (in′färkt) *n.* an area of dead tissue resulting from obstruction of the blood supply to that area by a blood clot, air bubble, or other material.

in·farc·tion (in färk′shən) *n.* **1** a stoppage or sudden insufficiency of the blood supply due to a blood clot, air bubble, etc. in a vein or artery that results in the death of a portion of tissue or organ. **2** infarct.

in·fat·u·ate (*v.* in fach′ü āt′; *adj.* in fach′ü it *or* in fach′ü āt′) *v.* **-at·ed, -at·ing;** *adj.* —*v.* **1** make foolish. **2** inspire with a foolish or unreasoning passion. —*adj.* infatuated. [< L *infatuare* < *in-* in + *fatuus* foolish]

in·fat·u·at·ed (in fach′ü āt′id) *adj.* extremely adoring; foolishly in love: *He is infatuated with the girl.*

in·fat·u·a·tion (in fach′ū ā′shən) *n.* **1** infatuating or being infatuated. **2** a foolish love; unreasoning fondness.

in·fect (in fekt′) *v.* **1** cause illness in (a person, animal, etc.) by the action of disease-producing organisms: *A person who has influenza may infect other people.* **2** contaminate (the air, etc.) with such organisms. **3** produce infection in: *Dirt may infect an open wound.* **4** influence in a bad way; corrupt. **5** affect with a particular character, mood, belief, etc., as if by contagion: *The soldiers were infected with their captain's courage.* [< L *infectus*, pp. of *inficere* dye, originally, put in < *in-* in + *facere* make] —**in·fec′tor,** *n.*

in·fec·tion (in fek′shən) *n.* **1** the multiplication of harmful micro-organisms within the body: *The wound was cleaned to avoid infection.* **2** the condition produced by the establishment of such organisms in the body: *The pain was caused by a gum infection.* **3** an infectious disease. **4** the communication of ideas, feelings, etc. by persuasion, example, etc.

in·fec·tious (in fek′shəs) *adj.* **1** of a disease, communicable by infection, with or without direct contact. Compare **contagious.** **2** capable of producing an infection: *infectious agents such as viruses.* **3** designating a disease caused by a micro-organism: *infectious hepatitis.* **4** capable of readily affecting others; spreading easily or rapidly; catching: *She has an infectious laugh. Their enthusiasm was infectious.* —**in·fec′tious·ly,** *adv.* —**in·fec′tious·ness,** *n.*

in·fec·tive (in fek′tiv) *adj.* infectious.

in·fe·lic·i·tous (in′fə lis′ə təs) *adj.* **1** unsuitable; not appropriate. **2** unfortunate; unhappy.

in·fe·lic·i·ty (in′fə lis′ə tē) *n., pl.* **-ties. 1** unsuitability; inappropriateness. **2** a misfortune; unhappiness. **3** something unsuitable; inappropriate word, remark, etc.

in·fer (in fėr′) *v.* **-ferred, -fer·ring. 1** find out by reasoning; conclude: *Seeing the frown on my face, the boy inferred that I was displeased.* **2** indicate; imply: *Ragged clothing infers poverty.* **3** draw inferences. [< L *inferre* < *in-* in + *ferre* bring]
☛ *Usage.* **Infer, imply.** Though **infer** (def. 3) sometimes means **imply,** careful writers do not confuse the two words. A writer or speaker **implies** something in his words or manner; a reader or listener **infers** something from what he reads, sees, or hears: *She implied by the look in her eyes that she did not intend to keep the appointment. We inferred from the principal's announcement that he already knew who had broken the window.*

in·fer·ence (in′fər əns) *n.* **1** the process of inferring: *What happened is only a matter of inference; no one saw the accident.* **2** that which is inferred; conclusion: *What inference do you draw from smelling smoke?*

in·fer·en·tial (in′fər en′shəl) *adj.* having to do with or depending on inference. —**in′fer·en′tial·ly,** *adv.*

in·fe·ri·or (in fėr′ē ər) *adj., n.* —*adj.* **1** low in quality; below average: *an inferior grade of coffee.* **2** lower in importance, quality, merit, etc.: *This fabric is inferior to silk in strength. He has always felt inferior to his brothers.* **3** lower in position, rank, or importance: *an inferior officer. A lieutenant is inferior to a captain.* **4** *Botany.* **a** growing below some other organ. **b** belonging to the part of the flower that is farthest from the main stem. **5** *Zoology.* below or posterior to others of the same kind, or to the usual or normal position: *the inferior vena cava.* **6** *Printing.* set below the main line of type, as letters or numerals in chemical formulas: *In* H_2O, *the 2 is inferior.* —*n.* **1** a person who is lower in rank or station. **2** an inferior thing. [< L *inferior,* comparative of *inferus,* adj., situated below]

in·fe·ri·or·i·ty (in fėr′ē ôr′ə tē) *n.* an inferior condition or quality.

inferiority complex an abnormal or morbid feeling of being inferior to other people resulting in timidity in certain cases and in aggressiveness in others.

in·fer·nal (in fėr′nəl) *adj.* **1** of hell; having to do with the lower world. **2** hellish; diabolical: *infernal heat.* **3** *Informal.* abominable; outrageous. [< LL *infernalis,* ult. < L *inferus* below] —**in·fer′nal·ly,** *adv.*

infernal machine *Archaic.* a disguised bomb or other explosive apparatus intended for the malicious destruction of life and property.

in·fer·no (in fėr′nō) *n., pl.* **-nos. 1** hell. **2** a place or thing that seems to be like hell: *Within half an hour of the start of the fire, the whole building was a raging inferno.* [< Ital.]

in·fer·tile (in fėr′tīl *or* in fėr′təl) *adj.* not fertile; not fruitful; sterile.

in·fer·til·i·ty (in′fėr til′ə tē) *n.* a lack of fertility; being infertile.

in·fest (in fest′) *v.* trouble or disturb frequently or in large numbers: *Swamps are often infested by mosquitoes.* [< L *infestare* attack < *infestus* hostile]

in·fes·ta·tion (in′fes tā′shən) *n.* **1** infesting. **2** the condition of being infested.

in·fi·del (in′fə dəl) *n., adj.* —*n.* **1** a person who does not believe

hat, āge, fär; let, ēqual, tėrm; it, īce
hot, ōpen, ôrder; oil, out; cup, put, rüle,
above, takən, pencəl, lemən, circəs

ch, child; ng, long; sh, ship
th, thin; ᴛʜ, then; zh, measure

in religion. **2** *Esp.Historical.* a person who rejects or opposes a particular faith, especially Christianity or Islam. —*adj.* **1** being an infidel. **2** of, having to do with, or characteristic of infidels. [< L *infidelis* < *in-* not + *fidelis* faithful < *fides* faith]

in·fi·del·i·ty (in′fə del′ə tē) *n., pl.* **-ties. 1** lack of religious faith. **2** lack of belief in Christianity. **3** unfaithfulness, especially of husband or wife; disloyalty. **4** an unfaithful or disloyal act.

in·field (in′fēld′) *n.* **1** *Baseball.* **a** the part of the field within the base lines; diamond (def. 7). **b** the first, second, and third basemen and shortstop of a team: *That team has a good infield.* **2** the part of farm lands nearest the buildings.

in·field·er (in′fēl′dər) *n. Baseball.* a player of the infield.

in·fight·ing (in′fīt′ing) *n.* **1** *Informal.* internal dissension or conflict: *Infighting among salesmen lost their company the contract.* **2** *Boxing.* fighting at close quarters.

in·fil·trate (in fil′trāt *or* in′fil trāt′) *v.* **-trat·ed, -trat·ing. 1** pass into or through by, or as by, filtering: *Enemy troops infiltrated the front lines.* **2** filter into or through; permeate or cause to permeate.

in·fil·tra·tion (in′fil trā′shən) *n.* **1** an infiltrating or the condition of being infiltrated. **2** something that infiltrates. **3** a method of attack in which small groups of men penetrate the enemy's lines at various weak points.

infin. infinitive.

in·fi·nite (in′fə nit) *adj., n.* —*adj.* **1** without limits or bounds; endless: *the infinite extent of space.* **2** extremely great: *Teaching little children takes infinite patience.* **3** *Mathematics.* **a** greater than any assignable quantity or magnitude of the sort in question **b** beyond any finite magnitude, extending to infinity. —*n.* **1** that which is infinite. **2** *Mathematics.* an infinite quantity or magnitude. **3 the Infinite,** God. [< L *infinitus* < *in-* not + *finis* boundary] —**in′fi·nite·ness,** *n.*

in·fi·nite·ly (in′fə nit lē) *adv.* **1** to an infinite degree. **2** *Informal.* very or very much: *I'm infinitely obliged to you.*

in·fin·i·tes·i·mal (in′fi nə tes′ə məl) *adj., n.* —*adj.* **1** so small as to be almost nothing: *A millionth of a centimetre is an infinitesimal length.* **2** *Mathematics.* less than any assignable quantity or magnitude of the sort in question. —*n.* **1** an infinitesimal amount. **2** *Mathematics.* a variable continually approaching zero as a limit. [< NL *infinitesimus* the "nth" < L *infinitus.* See INFINITE.] —**in′fi·ni·tes′i·mal·ly,** *adv.*

in·fin·i·tive (in fin′ə tiv) *n.* a form of a verb, not limited by person and number. *Examples: Let him go. We want to go now. Abbrev.:* infin. [< LL *infinitivus* < L *infinitus* unrestricted. See INFINITE.]
☛ *Usage.* **infinitive.** The infinitive is the simple form of the verb, often preceded by *to: I want to buy a hat. Let him leave if he wants to leave.* Infinitives are used as: **a** nouns: *To swim across the English Channel is his ambition.* **b** adjectives: *He had money to burn.* **c** adverbs: *He went home to rest.* **d** part of verb phrases: *Henry will do most of the work.*
☛ *Usage.* See also note at **split infinitive.**

in·fin·i·tude (in fin′ə tyüd′ *or* in fin′ə tüd′) *n.* **1** the state of being infinite. **2** an infinite extent, amount, or number.

in·fin·i·ty (in fin′ə tē) *n., pl.* **-ties. 1** the state of being infinite: *the infinity of space.* **2** an infinite distance, space, time, or quantity. **3** an infinite extent, amount, or number: *the infinity of God's mercy.* **4** *Mathematics.* an infinite quantity or magnitude.
to infinity, without limits or bounds; endlessly. [< L *infinitas*]

in·firm (in fėrm′) *adj.* **1** weak; feeble. **2** weak in will or character; not steadfast. **3** not firm; not stable. —**in·firm′ly,** *adv.* —**in·firm′ness,** *n.*

in·fir·ma·ry (in fėr′mə rē) *n., pl.* **-ries.** a place for the care of the sick or injured, especially a small hospital or dispensary in a school or other institution.

in·fir·mi·ty (in fėr′mə tē) *n., pl.* **-ties. 1** weakness; feebleness. **2** a sickness; illness. **3** a moral weakness or failing.

in·flame (in flām′) *v.* **-flamed, -flam·ing. 1** arouse to violent emotion or action: *Her impassioned accusations inflamed the crowd.* **2** make more violent or intense: *to inflame a hatred.* **3** become aroused to violent emotion or action. **4** produce inflammation in: *The smoke had inflamed the fireman's eyes.* **5** of an organ or tissue in the body, become inflamed. [ME < OF *enflamer* < L *inflammare* < *in-* in + *flamma* flame]

in·flam·ma·bil·i·ty (in flam′ə bil′ə tē) *n.* an inflammable quality or condition.

in·flam·ma·ble (in flam′ə bəl) *adj., n.* —*adj.* **1** easily set on fire: *Paper and gasoline are inflammable.* **2** easily excited or aroused. —*n.* something inflammable. —**in·flam′ma·bly,** *adv.*
☛ *Usage.* See note at **flammable.**

in·flam·ma·tion (in′flə mā′shən) *n.* **1** a diseased condition of some part of the body, marked by heat, redness, swelling, and pain. **2** inflaming. **3** the condition of being inflamed.

in·flam·ma·to·ry (in flam′ə tô′rē) *adj.* **1** tending to excite or arouse: *The leader of the opposition made an inflammatory speech attacking the government.* **2** of, causing, or accompanied by inflammation: *an inflammatory condition of the tonsils.*

in·flate (in flāt′) *v.* -**flat·ed,** -**flat·ing.** **1** blow out or swell with air or gas: *to inflate a balloon.* **2** swell or puff out: *to inflate with pride.* **3** increase (prices or currency) beyond a reasonable or normal amount. [< L *inflatus,* pp. of *inflare* < *in-* into + *flare* blow] —**in·flat′a·ble,** *adj.* —**in·flat′er** or **in·fla′tor,** *n.*

in·fla·tion (in flā′shən) *n.* **1** a swelling (with air, gas, pride, etc.) **2** a swollen state; excessive expansion. **3** an increase of the currency of a country by issuing much paper money. **4** a sharp and sudden rise of prices resulting from too great an increase in the supply of paper money or bank credit.

in·fla·tion·ar·y (in flā′shən er′ē) *adj.* of or having to do with inflation; tending to inflate.

in·fla·tion·ist (in flā′shən ist) *n.* a person who favors inflation.

in·flect (in flekt′) *v.* **1** change the tone or pitch of (the voice). **2** *Grammar.* vary the form of (a word) to show case, number, gender, person, tense, mood, comparison, etc. By inflecting *who,* we have *whose* and *whom.* **3** undergo such variations: *Latin nouns inflect for case and number.* **4** bend; curve. [< L *inflectere* < *in-* in + *flectere* bend]

in·flec·tion (in flek′shən) *n.* **1** a change in the tone or pitch of the voice: *We end certain questions with a rising inflection.* **2** *Grammar.* **a** a variation in the form of a word to show case, number, gender, person, tense, mood, or comparison. **b** a suffix or other element used to indicate such a variation. **3** a bending; curving. **4** a bend; curve.

in·flec·tion·al (in flek′shən əl) *adj.* of, having to do with, or showing grammatical inflection.

in·flex·i·bil·i·ty (in flek′sə bil′ə tē) *n.* lack of flexibility; the state or quality of being inflexibile.

in·flex·i·ble (in flek′sə bəl) *adj.* **1** firm; unyielding; steadfast: *inflexible determination.* **2** that cannot be changed; unalterable. **3** not easily bent; stiff; rigid: *an inflexible steel rod.* —**in·flex′i·bly,** *adv.*
☛ *Syn.* **1. Inflexible, inexorable, unrelenting** = unyielding in character or purpose. **Inflexible** = unbending, holding fast or doggedly to what one has made up one's mind to do, think, or believe: *It is a waste of time to argue with someone whose attitude is inflexible.* **Inexorable** = not to be influenced or affected by begging or pleading, but firm and pitiless: *The principal was inexorable in his decision.* **Unrelenting** = not softening in force, harshness, or cruelty: *He was unrelenting in his hatred.*

in·flex·ion (in flek′shən) *n. Esp.Brit.* inflection.

in·flict (in flikt′) *v.* **1** cause to have or suffer; give a blow, wound, pain, etc. **2** impose (a burden, suffering, anything unwelcome, etc.): *to inflict a penalty. Mrs. Jones inflicted herself upon her relatives for a long visit.* [< L *inflictus,* pp. of *infligere* < *in-* on + *fligere* dash]

in·flic·tion (in flik′shən) *n.* **1** the act of inflicting. **2** something inflicted; pain; suffering; burden; punishment.

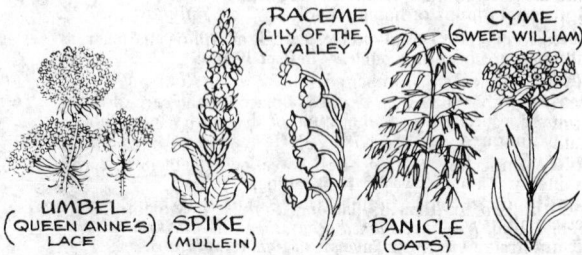

RACEME
(LILY OF THE VALLEY)

CYME
(SWEET WILLIAM)

UMBEL
(QUEEN ANNE'S LACE)

SPIKE
(MULLEIN)

PANICLE
(OATS)

Five common types of inflorescence

in·flo·res·cence (in′flô res′əns) *n.* **1** the flowering stage.

2 *Botany.* **a** the arrangement of flowers on the stem or axis. **b** a flower cluster. [< NL *inflorescentia* < L *in-* in + *flos, floris* flower]

in·flo·res·cent (in′flô res′ənt) *adj.* showing inflorescence; flowering.

in·flow (in′flō′) *n.* **1** a flowing in or into. **2** that which flows in.

in·flu·ence (in′flü əns) *n., v.* -**enced, -enc·ing.** —*n.* **1** the power of persons or things to act on others, seen only in its effects: *the influence of the moon on the tides.* **2** the power to produce an effect without using force: *A person may have influence by his ability, personality, position, or wealth.* **3** a person or thing that has such power. **4** *Electricity.* induction, especially electrostatic induction. **5** *Astrology.* the supposed power of the stars over the characters and destinies of human beings.
—*v.* have power over; change the nature or behavior of: *The moon influences the tides.* [ME < OF < Med.L *influentia,* originally, a flowing in < L *in-* in + *fluere* flow]
☛ *Syn. n.* **1.** See note at **authority.**

in·flu·en·tial (in′flü en′shəl) *adj.* **1** having much influence; having influence: *Influential friends helped him to get a job.* **2** using influence; producing results.

in·flu·en·za (in′flü en′zə) *n.* an acute contagious virus disease, occasionally resembling a severe cold in some of its symptoms, but much more dangerous and exhausting; flu. [< Ital. *influenza* influence]

in·flux (in′fluks) *n.* **1** a flowing in; steady flow: *the influx of immigrants into a country.* **2** the point where a river or stream flows into another river, a lake, or the sea; mouth. [< LL *influxus,* ult. < L *in-* in + *fluere* flow]

in·fo (in′fō) *n. Slang.* information.

in·fold (in fōld′) *v.* enfold.

in·form (in fôrm′) *v.* **1** give knowledge, facts, or news to: *The club secretary sent out letters informing members of a special meeting.* **2** give information about an offender or illegal or criminal activity to the police or some other authority; act as an informer (usually used with **against** or **on**). **3** inspire; animate: *God informed their hearts with pity.* [< L *informare* < *in-* in + *forma* form]
☛ *Syn.* **1. Inform, acquaint, notify** = tell or let someone know something. **Inform** emphasizes telling or passing along directly to a person facts or knowledge of any kind: *Her letter informed us how and when she expected to arrive.* **Acquaint** emphasizes introducing someone to facts or knowledge that he has not known before: *He acquainted us with his plans.* **Notify** = inform someone, by an official announcement or formal notice, of something he ought to or needs to know: *The university notified him that he was awarded a scholarship.*

in·for·mal (in fôr′məl) *adj.* **1** not formal; not in the regular or prescribed manner: *informal proceedings.* **2** without ceremony; casual: *an informal party, informal clothes.* **3** used in general, everyday English, but not used in formal speech or writing: *Using the term* kids *in place of* children *or* students *is informal.*
—**in·for′mal·ly,** *adv.*
☛ *Syn.* See note at **colloquial.**
☛ *Usage.* **Informal** English is the kind of English used by people in everyday speaking and writing; it ranges in style from the familiar, or casual, to the careful and precise. **Formal** English is used in lectures, speeches, learned articles, legal documents, and so on. As a usage label in this dictionary, **Informal** is used to mean "acceptable in everyday use, but not appropriate in situations requiring precise or formal language."

in·for·mal·i·ty (in′fôr mal′ə tē) *n., pl.* -**ties. 1** the quality of being informal; lack of ceremony. **2** an informal act.

in·form·ant (in fôr′mənt) *n.* a person who gives information to another: *My informant saw the accident happen.*

in·for·ma·tion (in′fər mā′shən) *n.* **1** knowledge; facts; news: *A dictionary gives information about words. The general sent information of his victory to headquarters.* **2** informing: *A guidebook is for the information of travellers.* **3** a person or office whose duty is to answer questions. **4** an accusation or complaint against a person. **5** any message or part of a message in coded form assembled by or fed to a computer.
☛ *Syn.* **1.** See note at **knowledge.**

in·for·ma·tion·al (in′fər mā′shən əl *or* in′fər mäsh′nəl) *adj.* giving information; instructive.

information theory the study of the efficiency of any communications system.

in·form·a·tive (in fôr′mə tiv) *adj.* giving information; instructive. —**in·form′a·tive·ly,** *adv.* —**in·form′a·tive·ness,** *n.*

in·form·er (in fôr′mər) *n.* **1** a person who gives information about an offender or illegal or criminal activity to the police or some other authority; especially one who does so for money or some other reward. **2** any person who provides information: *a financial informer.*

in·fra (in′frə) *adv. or prep. Latin.* beneath; below.

infra– *prefix.* below; beneath, as in *infra-red.* [< L *infra,* adv., prep.]

in·frac·tion (in frak′shən) *n.* a breaking of a law or obligation;

violation: *Reckless driving is an infraction of the law.* [< L *infractio, -onis* < *infringere.* See INFRINGE.]

in·fran·gi·ble (in fran′jə bəl) *adj.* **1** unable to be broken; unbreakable: *the infrangible laws of nature.* **2** inviolable: *an infrangible rule.* —**in·fran′gi·bly,** *adv.*

in·fra–red (in′frə red′) *adj.* of or having to do with the long, invisible light waves just beyond the red end of the color spectrum. Most of the heat from sunlight, incandescent lamps, carbon arcs, resistance wires, etc. is from infra-red rays.

in·fra·struc·ture (in′frə struk′chər) *n.* the essential elements of a system or structure.

in·fre·quence (in frē′kwəns) *n.* infrequency.

in·fre·quen·cy (in frē′kwən sē) *n.* scarcity; rarity.

in·fre·quent (in frē′kwənt) *adj.* not frequent; occurring seldom or far apart; scarce; rare. [< L *infrequens, -entis*] —**in·fre′quent·ly,** *adv.*

in·fringe (in frinj′) *v.* **-fringed, -fring·ing. 1** act contrary to or violate (a law, obligation, right, etc.): *A false label infringes the laws relating to food and drugs.* **2** trespass; encroach (*used with* **on** or **upon**): *to infringe upon the rights of another.* [< L *infringere* < *in-* in + *frangere* break] —**in·fring′er,** *n.* —**in·fringe′ment,** *n.*

in·fu·ri·ate (in fyúr′ē āt′) *v.* **-at·ed, -at·ing.** fill with extreme anger; make furious; enrage. [< Med.L *infuriare* < L *in-* into + *furia* fury] —**in·fu′ri·at′ing·ly,** *adv.* —**in·fu′ri·a′tion,** *n.*

in·fuse (in fyüz′) *v.* **-fused, -fus·ing. 1** permeate or fill with (a principle, quality, idea, etc.); impart: *The captain infused his own courage into his soldiers.* **2** inspire: *He infused the soldiers with his courage.* **3** steep or soak in a liquid to draw out flavor, minerals, etc. or to make a drink, drug, or other preparation: *We infuse tea leaves in hot water to make tea.* [< L *infusus,* pp. of *infundere* < *in-* in + *fundere* pour] —**in·fus′er,** *n.*

in·fu·si·ble (in fyü′zə bəl) *adj.* that cannot be fused or melted.

in·fu·sion (in fyü′zhən) *n.* **1** the act or process of infusing. **2** something poured in or mingled; infused element. **3** a liquid extract obtained by steeping or soaking.

in·fu·so·ri·an (in′fyə sô′rē ən) *n., adj.* —*n.* one of a group of one-celled animals that move by vibrating filaments. —*adj.* of or belonging to this group. [< NL *Infusoria,* genus name < L *infusus,* pp. of *infundere* pour in. See INFUSE.]

–ing[1] *suffix.* **1** the action, result, product, material, etc. of some verb, as in *hard thinking, the art of painting, a beautiful drawing, fine sewing, a blue lining, rich trimming.* **2** an action, result, product, material, etc. of some other part of speech, as in *lobstering, smoking, shirting.* **3** of one or more that ——: *The smoking habit is the habit of one who smokes.* [ME *-ing,* OE *-ing, -ung*]

–ing[2] *suffix.* **1** an element forming the present participle of verbs, as in *raining, staying, talking.* **2** that ——s: *Lasting happiness is happiness that lasts.* [ME *ing*(e), var. of *-ind*(e), *-end*(e), OE *-ende*]

in·ge·ni·ous (in jē′nē əs *or* in jēn′yəs) *adj.* **1** clever; skilful in planning or making: *The ingenious boy made a radio set.* **2** cleverly planned or made: *This mousetrap is an ingenious device.* [< L *ingeniosus* < *ingenium* natural talent] —**in·gen′ious·ly,** *adv.* —**in·gen′ious·ness,** *n.*

☛ *Syn.* **1.** See note at **clever.**
☛ *Usage.* Do not confuse **ingenious** and **ingenuous. Ingenious** = clever; skilful; **ingenuous** = frank; sincere; simple: *Fay is so ingenious that she is sure to think of some way of doing this work more easily. The ingenuous child had never thought of being suspicious of what others told her.*

in·gé·nue (on′zhə nü′; *French,* AN zhā NY′) *n., pl.* **-nues. 1** a simple, innocent girl or young woman, especially as represented on the stage, in films, etc. **2** an actress who plays such a part. [< F *ingénue,* originally fem. adj., ingenuous]

in·ge·nu·i·ty (in′jə nyü′ə tē *or* in′jə nü′ə tē) *n., pl.* **-ties. 1** skill in planning, inventing, etc.; cleverness. **2** a cleverly planned act, device, etc. [< L *ingenuitas* frankness < *ingenuus* ingenuous; influenced by association with *ingenious*]

in·gen·u·ous (in jen′yü əs) *adj.* **1** frank; open; sincere. **2** simple; natural; innocent. [< L *ingenuus,* originally, native, free bo┐ ┌] —**in·gen′u·ous·ly,** *adv.* —**in·gen′u·ous·ness,** *n.*

☛ *Usage.* See note at **ingenious.**

in·gest (in jest′) *v.* **1** take (food, etc.) into the body for digestion. **2** take in: *He ingested the new idea slowly.* [< L *ingestus,* pp. of *ingerere* < *in-* in + *gerere* carry] —**in·gest′ion,** *n.*

in·gle (ing′gəl) *n.* **1** fireplace. **2** a fire burning on the hearth. [? < Scots Gaelic *aingeal* fire]

in·gle·nook (ing′gəl núk′) *n.* a corner by the fire.

in·glo·ri·ous (in glô′rē əs) *adj.* **1** bringing no glory; shameful; disgraceful. **2** having no glory; not famous. —**in·glo′ri·ous·ness,** *n.*

in·got (ing′gət) *n.* a mass of metal, such as gold, silver or steel, cast into a block or bar. [OE *in-* in + *goten,* pp. of *gēotan* pour]

hat, āge, fär; let, ēqual, tèrm; it, īce
hot, ōpen, ôrder; oil, out; cup, pút, rüle,
əbove, takən, pencəl, lemən, circəs

ch, child; ng, long; sh, ship
th, thin; ŦH, then; zh, measure

in·graft (in graft′) *v.* engraft.

in·grain (*v.* in grān′; *adj., n.* in′grān′) *v., adj., n.* —*v.* **1** fix deeply and firmly; make an integral part of: *Certain habits are ingrained in one's nature.* **2** dye fibre before it is spun or woven. —*adj.* **1** dyed before manufacture. **2** made of yarn dyed before weaving: *an ingrain rug.*
—*n.* yarn, wool, etc. dyed before manufacture.

in·grate (in′grāt) *n., adj.* —*n.* an ungrateful person. —*adj. Archaic.* ungrateful. [< L *ingratus* < *in-* not + *gratus* thankful]

in·gra·ti·ate (in grā′shē āt′) *v.* **-at·ed, -at·ing.** bring (oneself) into favor: *He tried to ingratiate himself with the teacher by giving her presents.* [apparently < Ital. *ingraziare,* ult. < L *in gratiam* into favor] —**in·gra′ti·at′ing·ly,** *adv.*

in·grat·i·tude (in grat′ə tyüd′ *or* in grat′ə tüd′) *n.* a lack of gratitude or thankfulness; being ungrateful.

in·gre·di·ent (in grē′dē ənt) *n.* one of the parts of a mixture: *the ingredients of a cake.* [< L *ingrediens, -entis,* ppr. of *ingredi* < *in-* in + *gradi* go]

in·gress (in′gres) *n.* **1** a going in: *A high fence prevented ingress to the field.* **2** a way in; entrance. **3** a right to go in. [< L *ingressus* < *ingredi.* See INGREDIENT.]

in–group (in′grüp′) *n.* a group of people sharing interests, aims, and a sense of being exclusive, especially such a group having power or prestige.

in·grow·ing (in′grō′ing) *adj.* **1** growing within; growing inward. **2** growing into the flesh: *an ingrowing toenail.*

in·grown (in′grōn′) *adj.* **1** grown within; grown inward. **2** grown into the flesh.

in·gui·nal (ing′gwə nəl) *adj.* of the groin; in or near the groin. [< L *inguinalis* < *inguen* groin]

in·gulf (in gulf′) *v.* engulf.

in·hab·it (in hab′it) *v.* **1** live in (a place, region, house, cave, tree, etc.): *Fish inhabit the sea. Thoughts inhabit the mind.* **2** live; dwell. [< L *inhabitare* < *in-* in + *habitare* dwell < *habere* have, dwell]

in·hab·it·a·ble (in hab′ə tə bəl) *adj.* **1** capable of being inhabited. **2** fit to live in; habitable.

in·hab·it·ant (in hab′ə tənt) *n.* a person or animal that lives in a place. [< L *inhabitans, -antis,* ppr. of *inhabitare.* See INHABIT.]

in·hal·ant (in hāl′ənt) *n., adj.* —*n.* **1** a medicine to be inhaled. **2** an apparatus for inhaling it. —*adj.* used for inhaling.

in·ha·la·tion (in′hə lā′shən) *n.* **1** the act of inhaling. **2** a medicine to be inhaled.

in·ha·la·tor (in′hə lā′tər) *n.* an apparatus for inhaling anesthetics, medicine, etc.

in·hale (in hāl′) *v.* **-haled, -hal·ing.** draw into the lungs; breathe in (air, gas, fragrance, tobacco smoke, etc.). [< L *inhalare* < *in-* in + *halare* breathe]

in·hal·er (in hāl′ər) *n.* **1** an apparatus used in inhaling medicine, a gas, etc. **2** an apparatus for filtering dust, gases, etc. from air. **3** a person who inhales.

in·har·mon·ic (in′här mon′ik) *adj.* not harmonic; not musical.

in·har·mo·ni·ous (in′här mō′nē əs) *adj.* not harmonious; discordant; disagreeing. —**in′har·mo′ni·ous·ly,** *adv.*

in·here (in hēr′) *v.* **-hered, -her·ing.** exist; belong to as a quality or attribute: *Greed inheres in human nature. Power inheres in that ruler.* [< L *inhaerere* < *in-* in + *haerere* stick]

in·her·ence (in hēr′əns *or* in her′əns) *n.* the quality of being inherent.

in·her·ent (in hēr′ənt *or* in her′ənt) *adj.* existing as a natural or basic quality of a person or thing: *inherent honesty, the inherent sweetness of sugar.* [< L *inhaerens, -entis,* ppr. of *inhaerere.* See INHERE.]

in·her·ent·ly (in hēr′ənt lē *or* in her′ənt lē) *adv.* by its own nature; essentially.

in·her·it (in her′it) *v.* **1** get or have after another person dies; receive as an heir: *Mrs. Chan's nephew inherited the farm.* **2** succeed as an heir to property, a right, title, privilege, etc.: *When the old bachelor dies, his nephew will inherit.* **3** get or possess from one's ancestors: *Mary has inherited her father's blue eyes.* **4** receive

(anything) as by succession from predecessors: *When we took the house, we inherited the previous owner's carpets. The new government inherited a financial crisis.* [ME < OF *enheriter* < LL *inhereditare* < L *in-* in, + *heres, -redis* heir]

in·her·it·a·ble (in her′ə təl) *adj.* **1** capable of being inherited. **2** capable of inheriting; qualified to inherit.

in·her·it·ance (in her′ə təns) *n.* **1** the act of inheriting: *He obtained his house by inheritance from an aunt.* **2** the right of inheriting. **3** anything inherited: *Good health is a fine inheritance.*

inheritance tax succession duty.

in·her·i·tor (in her′ə tər) *n.* one who inherits; heir.

in·hib·it (in hib′it) *v.* **1** check; hold back; hinder or restrain: *The soldier's sense of duty inhibited his impulse to desert.* **2** prohibit; forbid. [< L *inhibitus,* pp. of *inhibere* < *in-* in + *habere* hold]

in·hi·bi·tion (in′ə bish′ən or in′hi bish′ən) *n.* **1** the act of inhibiting. **2** the state of being inhibited. **3** an idea, emotion, attitude, habit, or other inner force that restrains natural impulses.

in·hib·i·tive (in hib′ə tiv) *adj.* inhibitory.

in·hib·i·tor (in hib′ə tər) *n.* **1** a person or thing that inhibits. **2** *Chemistry.* anything that checks or interferes with a chemical reaction: *Antifreeze is an inhibitor.*

in·hib·i·to·ry (in hib′ə tô′rē) *adj.* inhibiting; tending to inhibit.

in·hos·pi·ta·ble (in hos′pi tə bəl *or* in′hos pit′ə bəl) *adj.* **1** not hospitable. **2** providing no shelter; barren: *The colonists encountered a rocky, inhospitable shore.* —**in·hos′pi·ta·ble·ness,** *n.* —**in·hos′pi·ta·bly,** *adv.*

in·hos·pi·tal·i·ty (in hos′pə tal′ə tē) *n.* a lack of hospitality; inhospitable behavior.

in·hu·man (in hyü′mən) *adj.* **1** without kindness; brutal; cruel. **2** not human; having or showing qualities not considered natural to a human being: *almost inhuman powers of endurance, an inhuman coldness of manner.* **3** not up to normal standards for human beings: *inhuman living conditions.* [ME < MF *inhumain* < L *inhumanus* < *in-* not + *humanus* human; later influenced in spelling by L *inhumanus*] —**in·hu′man·ly,** *adv.*

in·hu·mane (in′hyü mān′) *adj.* not humane; lacking in compassion, humanity, or kindness. —**in·hu·mane′ly,** *adv.*

in·hu·man·i·ty (in′hyü man′ə tē) *n., pl.* **-ties. 1** an inhuman quality; lack of feeling; cruelty; brutality. **2** an inhuman, cruel, or brutal act.

in·im·i·cal (in im′ə kəl) *adj.* **1** unfriendly; hostile. **2** adverse; unfavorable; harmful: *Lack of ambition is inimical to success.* [< LL *inimicalis* < L *inimicus* < *in-* not + *amicus* friendly] —**in·im′i·cal·ly,** *adv.*

☛ *Syn.* **1.** See note at **hostile.**

in·im·i·ta·bil·i·ty (in im′ə tə bil′ə tē) *n.* the fact or quality of being inimitable.

in·im·i·ta·ble (in im′ə tə bəl) *adj.* that cannot be imitated or copied; matchless. —**in·im′i·ta·bly,** *adv.*

in·iq·ui·tous (in ik′wə təs) *adj.* very unjust; wicked. —**in·iq′ui·tous·ly,** *adv.* —**in·iq′ui·tous·ness,** *n.*

in·iq·ui·ty (in ik′wə tē) *n., pl.* **-ties. 1** very great injustice; wickedness. **2** a wicked or unjust act. [< L *iniquitas* < *iniquus* < *in-* not + *aequus* just]

i·ni·tial (i nish′əl) *adj., n., v.* **-tialled** *or* **-tialed, -tial·ling** *or* **-tial·ing.** —*adj.* occurring at the beginning; first; earliest. —*n.* **1** the first letter of a word or name. **2** an extra large letter often decorated at the beginning of a chapter or other division of a book or illuminated manuscript. **3 initials,** the first letters of one's surname and one or more given names used instead of one's signature. —*v.* mark or sign with initials: *John Allen Smith initialled the note J.A.S.* [< L *initialis* < *initium* beginning < *inire* begin < *in-* in + *ire* go]

i·ni·tial·ly (i nish′əl ē) *adv.* at the beginning.

i·ni·ti·ate (*v.* i nish′ē āt′; *n., adj.* i nish′ē it *or* i nish′ē āt′) *v.* **-at·ed, -at·ing. 1** be the first one to start; begin. **2** admit (a person) by special forms or ceremonies (into mysteries, secret knowledge, or a society). **3** help to get a first understanding; introduce into the knowledge of some art or subject: *to initiate a person into business methods.* —*n.* a person who is initiated. —*adj.* initiated. [< L *initiare* < *initium* beginning < *inire* begin. See INITIAL.] —**i·ni′ti·a′tor,** *n.*

i·ni·ti·a·tion (i nish′ē ā′shən) *n.* **1** the act or process of initiating; beginning: *the initiation of the free concerts.* **2** being initiated. **3** a formal admission into a group or society. **4** the ceremonies by which one is admitted to a group or society.

i·ni·ti·a·tive (i nish′ē ə tiv, i nish′ə tiv *or* i nish′ē ā′tiv) *n.* **1** the active part in taking the first steps in any undertaking; the lead: *She is shy and does not take the initiative in making acquaintances.* **2** the readiness and ability to be the one to start something; enterprise: *A good leader must have initiative.* **3** the right to be the first to act, legislate, etc.

i·ni·ti·a·to·ry (i nish′ē ə tô′rē) *adj.* **1** first; beginning; introductory. **2** of initiation.

in·ject (in jekt′) *v.* **1** force (liquid) into a passage, cavity, or tissue: *to inject cortisone into a muscle, to inject fuel into an engine.* **2** fill (a cavity, etc.) with fluid forced in. **3** throw in; introduce: *The stranger injected a remark into their conversation.* [< L *injectus,* pp. of *inicere* < *in-* in + *jacere* throw] —**in·jec′tor,** *n.*

in·jec·tion (in jek′shən) *n.* **1** the act or process of injecting: *Drugs are given by injection as well as through the mouth.* **2** something injected.

in·ju·di·cious (in′jü dish′əs) *adj.* showing lack of judgment; unwise; not prudent. —**in′ju·di′cious·ly,** *adv.* —**in′ju·di′cious·ness,** *n.*

in·junc·tion (in jungk′shən) *n.* **1** a command; order: *Injunctions of secrecy did not prevent the news from leaking out.* **2** *Law.* a formal order issued by a court or judge ordering a person or group to refrain from doing something; a prohibition. **3** the act of commanding or authoritatively directing. [< LL *injunctio, -onis* < L *injungere* enjoin < *in-* in + *jungere* join. Related to ENJOIN.]

in·jure (in′jər) *v.* **-jured, -jur·ing. 1** cause damage to; wound, hurt, or harm: *She injured her arm when she fell. The fruit trees were injured by the frost. Her pride has been injured.* **2** do wrong to: *You injure him when you doubt his ability.* [< *injury*]

☛ *Syn.* **1. Injure, hurt, impair** = do harm or damage to someone or something. **Injure** is a general word meaning "to do something that harms, reduces, or takes away strength, health, perfection, rights, value, usefulness, etc.": *Dishonesty injures a business.* **Hurt,** a less formal substitute for **injure,** particularly means "to cause physical injury to a person or thing, or bodily or mental pain": *He hurt my hand by twisting it.* **Impair** = injure by weakening, diminishing, or decreasing strength or value: *Poor eating habits impair health.*

in·ju·ri·ous (in jür′ē əs) *adj.* **1** causing injury; harmful: *Hail is injurious to crops.* **2** unfair; unjust; wrongful. —**in·ju′ri·ous·ly,** *adv.* —**in·ju′ri·ous·ness,** *n.*

in·ju·ry (in′jər ē) *n., pl.* **-ju·ries. 1** a hurt or loss caused to or endured by a person or thing; damage; harm: *She escaped from the train wreck without injury.* **2** a wound; hurt; an act that harms or damages: *He received a serious injury in the accident. The accident will certainly be an injury to the reputation of the airline.* **3** unfairness; injustice; wrong: *You did me an injury when you said I lied.* [< L *injuria* < *in-* not + *jus, juris* right]

in·jus·tice (in jus′tis) *n.* **1** a lack of justice; being unjust. **2** an unjust act: *To send an innocent man to jail is an injustice.*

ink (ingk) *n., v.* —*n.* **1** a colored substance, usually a liquid, used for writing, printing, or drawing. **2** a dark liquid thrown out for protection by cuttlefish, squids, etc. —*v.* put ink on; mark or stain with ink. [ME < OF *enque* < LL < Gk. *enkauston* < *en* in + *kaiein* burn] —**ink′er,** *n.* —**ink′like′,** *adj.*

ink·horn (ingk′hôrn′) *n. Archaic.* a small container formerly used to hold ink, often made of horn.

ink·ling (ingk′ling) *n.* a slight suggestion; vague notion; hint. [ME *inclen* whisper, hint < OE *inca* doubt]

ink·stand (ingk′stand′) *n.* **1** a stand to hold ink and pens. **2** a container used to hold ink.

ink·well (ingk′wel′) *n.* a container used to hold ink on a desk or table.

ink·y (ingk′ē) *adj.* **ink·i·er, ink·i·est. 1** dark or black, like ink: *inky shadows.* **2** covered with ink; marked or stained with ink. **3** of ink. —**ink′i·ly,** *adv.* —**ink′i·ness,** *n.*

in·laid (in′lād′) *adj., v.* —*adj.* **1** set in the surface as a decoration or design: *The desk had an inlaid design of light wood in dark.* **2** decorated with a design or material set in the surface: *The box had an inlaid cover.* —*v.* pt. and pp. of **inlay.**

in·land (*adj.* in′lənd; *n., adv.* in′land′ *or* in′lənd) *adj., n., adv.* —*adj.* **1** away from the coast or the border; having to do with or situated in the interior: *an inland sea.* **2** domestic; not foreign: *inland trade.* —*n.* the interior of a country; land away from the border or the coast. —*adv.* in or toward the interior.

inland boat *Cdn. Historical.* York boat.

in-law (in′lo′ or in′lô′) *n. Informal.* a relative by marriage.

in·lay (in′lā′) *v.* **-laid, -lay·ing;** *n.* —*v.* **1** set as a decoration or design into a shallow recess in a surface: *to inlay strips of gold.* **2** decorate with something set into the surface: *to inlay a wooden box with silver.* —*n.* **1** an inlaid decoration, design, or material. **2** a shaped piece of

gold, porcelain, etc. cemented in a tooth as a filling. **3** a graft made by inlaying. —**in'lay'er,** *n.*

in·let (in'let' *or* in'lət) *n.* **1** a narrow strip of water extending from a larger body of water into the land or between islands. **2** entrance.

in lo·co pa·ren·tis (in lō'kō pə ren'tis) *Latin.* in the place of a parent; as a parent.

in·ly (in'lē) *adv. Poetic.* **1** inwardly; within. **2** thoroughly; deeply. [OE *inlīce*]

in·mate (in'māt') *n.* a person who lives with others in the same building, especially one confined in a prison, asylum, hospital, etc. [< *in-³* + *mate¹*]

in me·di·as res (in me'dē as'rāz') *Latin.* into the midst of things.

in me·mo·ri·am (in'mə mô'rē əm) *Latin.* in memory of; to the memory of.

in·most (in'mōst') *adj.* **1** farthest in; deepest within: *We went to the inmost depths of the mine.* **2** most private or personal: *Her inmost desire was to be an astronaut.* [OE *innemest*, double superlative of *inne* within; influenced by *most*]

inn (in) *n.* **1** a public house for lodging and caring for travellers: *Many old inns in England are still flourishing.* **2** hotel. **3** tavern. [OE *inn* lodging]
☞ *Hom.* **in.**

in·nards (in'ərdz) *n.pl. Informal.* **1** the internal organs of the body; insides; viscera. **2** the internal workings or parts of any complex mechanism, structure, etc. [var. of *inwards*]

in·nate (i nāt' *or* in'āt) *adj.* natural; inborn: *an innate talent for drawing.* [< L *innatus* < *in-* + *nasci* be born] —**in·nate'ly,** *adv.* —**in·nate'ness,** *n.*

in·ner (in'ər) *adj.* **1** farther in; inside: *the inner bark of a tree, an inner room.* **2** intimate or private; close to the central or most important part: *the inner circle of government. She kept her inner thoughts to herself.* [OE *innera*, comparative of *inne* within]

inner city the older, central part of a large city, especially when it is densely populated and less affluent than the rest of the city. —**in'ner-cit'y,** *adj.*

inner ear the cavity behind the three bones of the middle ear. In human beings it contains the semicircular canals, the cochlea, and part of the auditory nerve. See **ear¹** for picture.

in·ner·most (in'ər mōst') *adj.* farthest in; inmost: *the innermost parts.*

inner tube a separate rubber tube that fits inside some tires and is inflated with air.

in·ning (in'ing) *n.* **1** *Baseball.* the period of play in which each team has a turn at bat. **2 innings,** *Cricket.* the period of a game when one team is batting (*used with a singular verb*). **3** Usually, **innings,** the time when a person or group has a chance for action or accomplishment (*usually used with a singular verb*): *The Tories are finally going to have their innings.* [OE *innung* a taking in]

inn·keep·er (in'kēp'ər) *n.* a person who owns, manages, or keeps an inn.

in·no·cence (in'ə səns) *n.* **1** the state or quality of being free from sin or moral guilt, or from legal guilt for a particular offence: *The trial established his innocence.* **2** the state or quality of being free from guile or cunning; simplicity: *the innocence of a child.* **3** lack of worldly experience; naïveté: *In his innocence, he believed everything the stranger told him.* **4** bluet.

in·no·cen·cy (in'ə sən sē) *n. Archaic.* innocence (def. 1).

in·no·cent (in'ə sənt) *adj., n.* —*adj.* **1** free from wrongdoing: *An innocent bystander was hit in the shootout between police and the bank robbers.* **2** not legally guilty of a particular offence: *The trial proved that the accused was innocent.* **3** not wrong or bad; harmless: *innocent amusements.* **4** without knowledge of evil, and therefore free from sin or wrong: *as innocent as a baby.* **5** free from cunning or guile; simple and open; artless: *an innocent question.* **6** naïve. **7** lacking (*used with* **of**): *a bare, bleak room, innocent of all adornment.*
—*n.* **1** a person who has no knowledge of evil or who is artless or naïve. **2** *Archaic.* a foolish or simple-minded person. [< L *innocens, -entis* < *in-* not + *nocere* harm] —**in'no·cent·ly,** *adv.*
☞ *Syn. adj.* **1. Innocent, blameless, guiltless** = free from fault or wrong. **Innocent** emphasizes having intended or consciously done no wrong, having broken no moral, social, or statute law: *The truck driver was proved innocent of manslaughter.* **Blameless** = not to blame, not to be held responsible or punished, whether or not wrong has actually been done: *He was held blameless, although the child was killed.* **Guiltless** = without guilt in thought, intention, or act: *The other driver was not guiltless.*

in·noc·u·ous (i nok'yü əs) *adj.* **1** harmless; not capable of causing damage or injury: *an innocuous medicine, an innocuous snake.* **2** not likely to arouse hostility or strong feelings; not offensive or stimulating: *innocuous remarks.* [< L *innocuus* < *in-* not + *nocuus* hurtful < *nocere* to harm] —**in·noc'u·ous·ly,** *adv.*

hat, āge, fär; let, ēqual, tèrm; it, īce
hot, ōpen, ôrder; oil, out; cup, pùt, rüle,
əbove, takən, pencəl, lemən, circəs

ch, child; ng, long; sh, ship
th, thin; ᴛʜ, then; zh, measure

in·no·vate (in'ə vāt') *v.* **-vat·ed, -vat·ing.** make changes; bring in something new or do something in a new way. [< L *innovare* < *in-* + *novus* new]

in·no·va·tion (in'ə vā'shən) *n.* **1** a change made in the established way of doing things. **2** the making of changes; bringing in new things or new ways of doing things: *He is strongly opposed to innovation of any kind.*

in·no·va·tive (in'ə vā'tiv) *adj.* characterized by or bringing in innovation.

in·no·va·tor (in'ə vā'tər) *n.* a person who makes changes or introduces new methods.

in·nu·en·do (in'yü en'dō) *n., pl.* **-does.** an indirect hint or reference, especially an indirect suggestion against someone's character or reputation; insinuation. [< L *innuendo*, literally, by giving a nod to, ablative gerund of *innuere* < *in-* + *-nuere* nod]

In·nu·it (in'ü it, in'yü it, *or* in'yə wit) See **Inuit.**

in·nu·mer·a·ble (i nyü'mər ə bəl *or* i nü'mər ə bəl) *adj.* too many to count; countless: *innumerable stars.* —**in·nu'mer·a·ble·ness,** *n.*
☞ *Syn.* See note at **many.**

in·nu·mer·a·bly (i nyü'mər ə blē *or* i nü'mər ə blē) *adv.* countlessly; in very great numbers.

in·oc·u·late (in ok'yə lāt') *v.* **-lat·ed, -lat·ing. 1** infect (a person or animal) with organisms that will cause a very mild form of a disease, thus reducing the individual's chances of contracting the disease thereafter. **2** use disease-producing organisms to prevent or cure diseases. **3** put bacteria, serums, etc. into. Farmers inoculate the soil with bacteria that will take nitrogen from the air and change it so that it can be used by plants. **4** fill (a person's mind) with ideas, opinions, etc. [< L *inoculare* engraft < *in-* + *oculus* bud, eye] —**in·oc'u·la'tor,** *n.*

in·oc·u·la·tion (in ok'yə lā'shən) *n.* the act or process of inoculating, especially in order to immunize against disease.

in·of·fen·sive (in'ə fen'siv) *adj.* not offensive; harmless; not arousing objections. —**in'of·fen'sive·ly,** *adv.* —**in'of·fen'sive·ness,** *n.*

in·op·er·a·ble (in op'ər ə bəl) *adj.* **1** unable to be cured by surgery: *an inoperable cancer.* **2** not practicable; unworkable: *an inoperable plan.*

in·op·er·a·tive (in op'rə tiv *or* in op'ər ə'tiv) *adj.* not operative; not working; without effect.

in·op·por·tune (in op'ər tyün' *or* in op'ər tün') *adj.* not opportune; coming at a bad time; inconvenient: *An inopportune call delayed us.* —**in·op'por·tune'ly,** *adv.* —**in·op'por·tune'ness,** *n.*

in·or·di·nate (in ôr'də nit) *adj.* much too great; excessive; immoderate: *He spends an inordinate amount of time tinkering with those old radios.* [< L *inordinatus* < *in-* not + *ordo, -dinis* order] —**in·or'di·nate·ly,** *adv.*
☞ *Syn.* See note at **excessive.**

in·or·gan·ic (in'ôr gan'ik) *adj.* **1** composed of or referring to matter that is not animal or vegetable; not having the organized structure of animals or plants: *Minerals are inorganic.* **2** of or referring to any chemical compound not classified as organic: *Most inorganic compounds are derived from minerals and do not contain carbon.* **3** of or referring to the branch of chemistry that deals with inorganic compounds and elements. **4** not resulting from natural growth; extraneous or artificial. —**in'or·gan'i·cal·ly,** *adv.*

inorganic chemistry the branch of chemistry dealing with inorganic compounds and elements, primarily compounds not containing carbon.

in·put (in'pùt') *n., v.* —*n.* **1** the act or process of putting in: *She felt there was too little opportunity for input as an ordinary member of the club.* **2** the amount of material, energy, resources, etc. put in: *hoping for an increased input of funds.* **3** energy, electric current, etc. supplied for the purpose of producing an output of some kind. **4** information fed into a computer or data processing system.
—*v.* feed (information) into a computer or data processing system.

in·quest (in'kwest) *n.* **1** a legal inquiry led by a coroner, usually with a jury to determine the cause of a sudden death when there is a possibility that the death was the result of a crime or of a situation that could be dangerous to others. **2** a jury appointed to hold such an inquiry: *The inquest was told that one of the witnesses had been delayed.* **3** any other investigation into the cause of an event,

situation, etc. [ME < OF *enqueste*, ult. < L *inquirere*. See INQUIRE.]

in·qui·e·tude (in kwī′ə tyüd′ *or* in kwī′ə tüd′) *n.* restlessness; uneasiness.

in·quire (in kwīr′) *v.* **-quired, -quir·ing. 1** try to find out by questions; ask. **2** make an investigation or examination, especially by asking questions; search into: *to inquire into someone's past.* [< L *inquirere* < *in-* into + *quaerere* ask] —**in·quir′er,** *n.*
☛ *Syn.* 1. See note at **ask.**

in·quir·y (in kwīr′ē *or* in′kwə rē) *n., pl.* **-quir·ies. 1** the act of inquiring. **2** a question. **3** an investigation or examination: *The authorities are conducting an inquiry into the cause of the explosion.* Also, **enquiry.**
☛ *Syn.* 3. See note at **investigation.**

in·qui·si·tion (in′kwə zish′ən) *n.* **1** an official investigation, a judicial inquiry. **2 the Inquisition, a** a court established by the Roman Catholic Church in 1229 to discover and suppress heresy and to punish heretics. During the 15th and 16th centuries, the powers of the Inquisition were tremendously enlarged, especially in Spain, Portugal, and parts of Italy. It was abolished in 1834. **b** the activities of this court. **3** any very severe or intensive questioning. [< L *inquisitio, -onis* < *inquirere.* See INQUIRE.]

in·quis·i·tive (in kwiz′ə tiv) *adj.* **1** curious; asking many questions. **2** too curious; prying into other people's affairs. —**in·quis′i·tive·ly,** *adv.* —**in·quis′i·tive·ness,** *n.*
☛ *Syn.* 1. See note at **curious.**

in·quis·i·tor (in kwiz′ə tər) *n.* **1** a person who makes an inquisition; official investigator; judicial inquirer. **2 Inquisitor,** a member of the Inquisition. **3** a person who conducts an inquiry in a very harsh or hostile manner.

in·quis·i·to·ri·al (in kwiz′ə tô′rē əl) *adj.* **1** of an inquisitor or inquisition. **2** making searching inquiry; thorough. **3** unduly curious.

in re (in rē′ *or* in rā′) *Latin.* concerning; in the matter of.

I.N.R.I. Jesus of Nazareth, King of the Jews (for L *Iesus Nazarenus Rex Iudaeorum*).

in·road (in′rōd′) *n.* **1** an attack or raid; entry by force. **2** Usually, **inroads,** *pl.* an advance or penetration that destroys, injures, or lessens something: *The unusual expenses made serious inroads on her savings.*

in·rush (in′rush′) *n.* a rushing in; inflow.

ins. 1 inches. **2** insurance. **3** insulated. **4** inspected.

in·sane (in sān′) *adj.* **1** not sane; mentally deranged; crazy. **2** *Law.* mentally unsound, temporarily or permanently, so as to be considered not competent or not responsible for one's actions. **3** (*noml.*) **the insane,** *pl.* those who are insane: *an institution for the criminally insane.* **4** characteristic of one who is insane: *an insane laugh.* **5** for insane people: *an insane asylum.* **6** extremely foolish; completely lacking in common sense: *an insane plot to overthrow the government.* —**in·sane′ly,** *adv.*
☛ *Syn.* 1. See note at **mad.**

in·san·i·tar·y (in san′ə ter′ē) *adj.* unhealthful. —**in·san′i·tar′i·ness,** *n.*

in·san·i·ty (in san′ə tē) *n., pl.* **-ties. 1** the state of being insane; mental illness; madness. **2** *Law.* any state of mental unsoundness, temporary or permanent, in which a person is not considered competent or held responsible for his actions. **3** extreme folly.

in·sa·tia·ble (in sā′shə bəl) *adj.* that cannot be satisfied; always wanting more: *an insatiable appetite for sweets.* —**in·sa′tia·bly,** *adv.*

in·sa·ti·ate (in sā′shē it) *adj.* insatiable. —**in·sa′ti·ate·ly,** *adv.* —**in·sa′ti·ate·ness,** *n.*

in·scribe (in skrīb′) *v.* **-scribed, -scrib·ing. 1** write or engrave on a surface: *Her initials were inscribed on the bracelet.* **2** write on or engrave with words, letters, etc.: *How shall we inscribe the ring?* **3** write a message in or informally dedicate (a book, etc.): *The book was inscribed, "To Paula, with love from Dad."* **4** impress deeply: *His father's words are inscribed on his memory.* **5** put in a list; enrol. **6** *Geometry.* draw a figure inside another figure so that their boundaries touch in as many places as possible. To inscribe a triangle in a circle, you must make all the points of the triangle touch the circle. [< L *inscribere* < *in-* on + *scribere* write] —**in·scrib′er,** *n.*

in·scrip·tion (in skrip′shən) *n.* **1** something inscribed; words, letters, etc. written or engraved on stone, metal, paper, etc. A monument or a coin has an inscription on it. **2** an informal dedication in a book, on a picture, etc. **3** the act of inscribing. [< L *inscriptio, -onis* < *inscribere.* See INSCRIBE.]

in·scru·ta·bil·i·ty (in skrü′tə bil′ə tē) *n.* **1** the quality of being inscrutable. **2** something inscrutable.

in·scru·ta·ble (in skrü′tə bəl) *adj.* that cannot be understood; so mysterious or obscure that one cannot make out its meaning; incomprehensible: *an inscrutable look.* [< LL *inscrutabilis* < L *in-* not + *scrutari* examine, ransack < *scruta* trash] —**in·scru′ta·ble·ness,** *n.* —**in·scru′ta·bly,** *adv.*
☛ *Syn.* See note at **mysterious.**

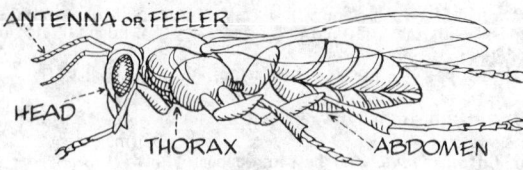

Insect (def. 1): a wasp

in·sect (in′sekt) *n.* **1** any of a large class (Insecta) of small invertebrate animals having the body divided into three well-defined parts (head, thorax, and abdomen), and having three pairs of legs and, usually, one or two pairs of wings. Flies, mosquitoes, grasshoppers, bees, and beetles are insects. **2** any similar small animal with its body divided into several parts, having several pairs of legs. Spiders, centipedes, mites, and ticks are often called insects. **3** an insignificant or contemptible person. [< L *insectum,* literally, divided, neut. pp. of *insecare* < *in-* into + *secare* cut]

in·sec·ti·cide (in sek′tə sīd′) *n.* a substance for killing insects. [< L *insectum* + E *-cide*[2]]

in·sec·ti·vore (in sek′tə vôr′) *n.* **1** any of an order (Insectivora) of mainly small mammals, most of which are active at night and feed largely on insects. Moles, hedgehogs, and shrews are insectivores. **2** any insect-eating animal or plant. [< F < NL *insectivorus.* See INSECTIVOROUS.]

in·sec·tiv·o·rous (in′sek tiv′ə rəs) *adj.* **1** insect-eating; feeding mainly on insects. **2** of or belonging to the insectivores. [< NL *insectivorus* < L *insectum* insect + *vorare* devour; formed on the pattern of L *carnivorus* meat-eating]

in·se·cure (in′si kyūr′) *adj.* **1** not properly guarded or maintained; not safe from danger, failure, etc.: *insecure investments, an insecure position, an insecure marriage.* **2** liable to give way; not firm: *an insecure lock.* **3** lacking confidence; not sure of oneself; filled with fear and anxiety: *an insecure person.* —**in·se·cure′ly,** *adv.*
☛ *Syn.* 1. See note at **uncertain.**

in·se·cu·ri·ty (in′si kyūr′ə tē) *n., pl.* **-ties. 1** a lack of security; being insecure. **2** something insecure.

in·sem·i·nate (in sem′ə nāt′) *v.* **-nat·ed, -nat·ing. 1** inject semen into; fertilize; impregnate. **2** sow; implant seeds into. **3** instil (ideas or opinions). [< L *inseminare* (with E *-ate*[1]) < *in-* not + *seminare* to sow < *semen, -inis* seed] —**in·sem′i·na′tion,** *n.*
—**in·sem′i·na′tor,** *n.*

in·sen·sate (in sen′sāt *or* in sen′sit) *adj.* **1** without sensation; inanimate: *the insensate stones.* **2** insensitive; unfeeling: *insensate cruelty.* **3** senseless; stupid: *insensate folly.* —**in·sen′sate·ly,** *adv.*

in·sen·si·bil·i·ty (in sen′sə bil′ə tē) *n., pl.* **-ties.** the quality or state of being insensible.

in·sen·si·ble (in sen′sə bəl) *adj.* **1** not having the power to perceive with the senses: *A blind person is insensible to colors.* **2** not able to respond emotionally: *We were thrilled by the view but Irene was insensible to it.* **3** not able to feel anything; unconscious: *The man hit by the truck was insensible for four hours.* **4** not easily felt or realized: *The room grew cold by insensible degrees.* —**in·sen′si·bly,** *adv.*

in·sen·si·tive (in sen′sə tiv) *adj.* **1** not responsive or susceptible to beauty, the thoughts or feelings of others, etc.; lacking feeling: *It was insensitive of her to laugh when he fell, because he had obviously hurt himself.* **2** not able to be affected by touch, light, etc.: *Dentists often give an injection to make a tooth insensitive so that the drilling does not hurt.* —**in·sen′si·tive·ly,** *adv.*

in·sen·si·tive·ness (in sen′sə tiv nəs) *n.* insensitivity.

in·sen·si·tiv·i·ty (in sen′sə tiv′ə tē) *n.* the quality or state of being insensitive.

in·sen·ti·ent (in sen′shē ənt *or* in sen′shənt) *adj.* unable to feel; lifeless.

in·sep·a·ra·bil·i·ty (in sep′ə rə bil′ə tē *or* in sep′rə bil′ə tē) *n.* the quality or state of being inseparable.

in·sep·a·ra·ble (in sep′ə rə bəl *or* in sep′rə bəl) *adj.* that cannot be separated or parted: *inseparable pals.* —*n.* **inseparables,** *pl.* inseparable persons or things. —**in·sep′a·ra·bly,** *adv.*

in·sert (*v.* in sėrt′; *n.* in′sėrt) *v., n.* —*v.* **1** thrust, fit, or set in,

into, between, etc.: *to insert elastic into the waistband of a skirt, to insert a lining. He inserted the key in the lock and turned it quietly.* 2 set or introduce something into written material, a newspaper, etc.: *to insert a missing letter into a word, to insert an advertisement in a newspaper.* —*n.* something set in or introduced: *Some magazines have a local insert for certain regions. The dress has lace inserts in the sleeves.* [< L *insertus,* pp. of *inserere* < *in-* in + *serere* entwine]

in·ser·tion (in sėr′shən) *n.* 1 the act or process of inserting. 2 a single appearance of an advertisement in a newspaper, etc. 3 a band of lace, embroidery, etc. set into a cloth article for decoration; an insert: *The dress had a lace insertion near the neckline.*

in–serv·ice (in′sėr′vis) *adj.* of or having to do with a program for the training of employees: *in-service courses for civil servants.*

in·set (*v.* in set′ *or* in′set′; *n.* in′set′) *n., v.* -**set,** -**set·ting.** —*n.* 1 a small map, photograph, etc. set within the border of a larger one, to show some part in detail or to give extra information, etc. 2 a piece of lace or other material set into a dress, etc. for decoration; insert. —*v.* set or put in as an inset.

in·shore (in′shôr′) *adj., adv.* —*adj.* 1 near the shore: *inshore shoals.* 2 done or working near the shore: *the inshore fishery of Newfoundland, inshore fishermen.* —*adv.* in toward the shore.

in·side (*n., adj.* in′sīd′; *adv., prep.* in′sīd′) *n., adj., adv., prep.* —*n.* 1 the side or surface that is within; inner part; contents: *the inside of a house.* 2 Often, **insides,** *pl. Informal.* the parts inside the body, especially the stomach and bowels. 3 *Informal.* those who are in a position to know about something or who are in a position of authority.
—*adj.* 1 being on the inside: *an inside seat.* 2 of or used for the inside: *an inside paint.* 3 *Informal.* done or known by those within an organization or group or inside a building (always precedes a noun): *inside information. The police suspected that the theft was an inside job.* 4 *Informal.* working within an organization or group, as an emissary or spy: *an inside man.* 5 indoor. 6 that is nearer the centre of a curve: *the inside skate.* 7 Baseball. **a** of a pitch, close to the batter and missing the strike zone. **b** of a part of the home plate, on the same side as the batter.
—*adv.* on, at, or to the inside of a place or thing; within: *Please go inside, into the living room. We had to clean the box inside before we could use it.*

inside out, a so that what should be inside is outside; with the inside showing: *He turned his pockets inside out.* **b** completely: *He learned his lessons inside out.*
—*prep.* on, at, or to the inside of: *We left the blankets inside the trunk. The nut is inside the shell.*

inside of, *Informal.* in a period of time less than; within the limits of: *We should be back inside of a week.*
☛ *Usage.* **Inside of** is a doubling of prepositions common in informal expressions of time: *He'll be back inside of an hour.* The more formal idiom is **within:** *He will return within an hour.*

in·sid·er (in′sīd′ər) *n.* a person who is recognized as being established within an organization, etc., especially someone who has power or access to important or confidential information: *an insider's report on the workings of Parliament.*

inside track 1 on a race track, the lane nearest the inside of the curve, and so the shortest way round. 2 *Informal.* an advantageous position or situation.

in·sid·i·ous (in sid′ē əs) *adj.* 1 wily; sly; crafty; tricky; treacherous: *an insidious plot.* 2 working secretly or subtly; developing gradually without attracting attention: *an insidious disease.* [< L *insidiosus* < *insidiae* ambush < *insidere* < *in-* in + *sedere* sit] —**in·sid′i·ous·ly,** *adv.* —**in·sid′i·ous·ness,** *n.*

in·sight (in′sīt′) *n.* 1 an understanding or awareness based on a seeing of the inside or inner nature of something. 2 wisdom and understanding in dealing with people or with facts. 3 *Psychology.* **a** the relatively sudden awareness of a solution to a problem. **b** understanding of oneself.
☛ *Syn.* **2. Insight, discernment, penetration** = ability to understand people or things. **Insight** suggests both the power to see deeply into the inner workings of things and of people's minds and feelings and the ability to understand them: *Good teachers have insight into the problems of their students.* **Discernment** = the ability to see below the surface clearly and sharply and to judge accurately: *In selecting employees he shows discernment.* **Penetration** emphasizes going deeply into things and seeing fine distinctions and relations: *Solving the mystery required penetration.*

in·sig·ni·a (in sig′nē ə) *n.pl.* 1 the emblems, badges, or other distinguishing marks of a high position, honor, military order, etc.: *The crown, orb, and sceptre are the insignia of monarchs.* 2 the distinguishing badges, crests, etc. of a unit or branch of the armed forces. [< L *insignia,* pl. of *insigne* badge < *in-* on + *signum* mark. Doublet of ENSIGN.]

in·sig·nif·i·cance (in′sig nif′ə kəns) *n.* 1 unimportance. 2 meaninglessness.

in·sig·nif·i·cant (in′sig nif′ə kənt) *adj.* 1 having little importance; trivial or trifling: *an insignificant error, insignificant losses.* 2 having little weight or influence: *The once thriving town*

hat, āge, fär; let, ēqual, tėrm; it, īce
hot, ōpen, ôrder; oil, out; cup, pùt, rüle,
əbove, takən, pencəl, lemən, circəs

ch, child; ng, long; sh, ship
th, thin; ᴛʜ, then; zh, measure

had become an insignificant backwater. He has an insignificant position in a large company. 3 having little or no meaning: *insignificant chatter.* —**in′sig·nif′i·cant·ly,** *adv.*

in·sin·cere (in′sin sēr′) *adj.* not sincere; not honest or candid; deceitful. —**in′sin·cere′ly,** *adv.*

in·sin·cer·i·ty (in′sin ser′ə tē) *n., pl.* -**ties.** a lack of sincerity; hypocrisy.

in·sin·u·ate (in sin′yü āt′) *v.* -**at·ed,** -**at·ing.** 1 suggest or hint indirectly, especially in an artful or scheming way: *He made no charge, but insinuated that the mayor had accepted bribes.* 2 get in or introduce by gradual, subtle, and stealthy means: *to insinuate doubt into a person's mind. The spy insinuated himself into the confidence of important army officers.* [< L *insinuare* < *in-* in + *sinus* a curve, winding] —**in·sin′u·a·tor,** *n.*
☛ *Syn.* **1.** See note at **hint.**

in·sin·u·a·tion (in sin′yü ā′shən) *n.* 1 the act or process of insinuating. 2 a hint or indirect suggestion, especially a sly, subtle, unpleasant one.

in·sip·id (in sip′id) *adj.* 1 without much taste: *A mixture of milk and water is an insipid drink.* 2 colorless and uninteresting; dull; lifeless: *insipid writing.* [< LL *insipidus* < L *in-* not + *sapidus* tasty] —**in·sip′id·ly,** *adv.* —**in·sip′id·ness,** *n.*

in·si·pid·i·ty (in′sə pid′ə tē) *n., pl.* -**ties.** 1 a lack of flavor; lack of interest. 2 something insipid.

in·sist (in sist′) *v.* keep firmly to some demand, statement, or position; take a stand and refuse to give in: *to insist that something should be done, to insist on one's innocence.* [< L *insistere* < *in-* on + *sistere* take a stand]

in·sist·ence (in sis′təns) *n.* 1 the act of insisting. 2 the quality of being insistent.

in·sist·en·cy (in sis′tən sē) *n.* insistence.

in·sist·ent (in sis′tənt) *adj.* 1 insisting; continuing to make a strong, firm demand or statement: *Although it was raining, he was insistent about going for a walk.* 2 compelling attention or notice; pressing; urgent: *an insistent knocking at the door.* —**in·sist′ent·ly,** *adv.*

in si·tu (in sī′tyü *or* sē′tü) *Latin.* in its original place; in position.

in·snare (in sner′) *v.* -**snared,** -**snar·ing.** ensnare.

in·so·bri·e·ty (in′sə brī′ə tē) *n.* intemperance; drunkenness.

in·so·far (in′sō fär′ *or* in′sə fär′) *adv.* to such a degree or extent (*usually used with* **as**): *He should be told the facts insofar as they concern him.*

in·sole (in′sōl′) *n.* 1 the inner sole of a shoe or boot. 2 a shaped piece of warm or waterproof material laid on the sole inside a shoe or boot.

in·so·lence (in′sə ləns) *n.* bold rudeness; insulting behavior or speech.

in·so·lent (in′sə lənt) *adj.* boldly rude; insulting. [< L *insolens, -entis* originally, unusual < *in-* not + *solere* be wont] —**in′so·lent·ly,** *adv.*

in·sol·u·bil·i·ty (in sol′yə bil′ə tē) *n.* being insoluble.

in·sol·u·ble (in sol′yə bəl) *adj.* 1 that cannot be dissolved: *Diamonds are insoluble.* 2 that cannot be solved or explained: *an insoluble mystery.* —**in·sol′u·bly,** *adv.*

in·solv·a·ble (in sol′və bəl) *adj.* that cannot be solved.

in·sol·ven·cy (in sol′vən sē) *n., pl.* -**cies.** the condition of not being able to pay one's debts; bankruptcy.

in·sol·vent (in sol′vənt) *adj., n.* —*adj.* 1 not able to pay one's debts; bankrupt. 2 of or having to do with bankrupt persons or bankruptcy. —*n.* an insolvent person.

in·som·ni·a (in som′nē ə) *n.* the inability to sleep, especially when chronic. [< L *insomnia* < *in-* not + *somnus* sleep]

in·som·ni·ac (in som′nē ak) *n., adj.* —*n.* a person who is unable to sleep, especially one who habitually has trouble getting enough sleep. —*adj.* of, having to do with, or affected with insomnia.

in·so·much (in′sō much′) *adv.* to such an extent or degree; so.

in·sou·ci·ance (in sü′sē əns) *n.* lack of concern; carelessness; indifference: *He seemed to go through the whole trial with a smiling insouciance.*

in·sou·ci·ant (in sü′sē ənt) *adj.* carefree; unconcerned: *an insouciant disposition.* [< F *insouciant* < *in-* not (< L *in-*) + *souciant,* ppr. of *soucier* care, ult. < L *sollicitus* solicitous]

insp. inspected; inspector.

in·spect (in spekt′) *v.* **1** look over carefully; examine: *A dentist inspects the children's teeth twice a year.* **2** examine officially: *The factory was inspected annually by a government official.* [< L *inspectus,* pp. of *inspicere* < *in-* upon + *specere* look]

in·spec·tion (in spek′shən) *n.* **1** inspecting: *An inspection of the roof showed no leaks.* **2** a formal or official examination: *The soldiers lined up for their daily inspection by their officers.*

in·spec·tor (in spek′tər) *n.* **1** a person who inspects. **2** an officer or official appointed to inspect. **3** a police officer, usually ranking next below a superintendent. [< L]

in·spi·ra·tion (in′spə rā′shən) *n.* **1** the influence of thought and strong feelings on actions, especially on good or creative actions: *Some people get inspiration from sermons; some from poetry.* **2** a person or thing that arouses effort to do well: *The captain was an inspiration to his men.* **3** an idea that is inspired. **4** a suggestion to another; the act of causing something to be told or written by another. **5** *Theology.* a divine influence directly and immediately exerted upon the mind or soul of man. **6** a breathing in; the drawing of air into the lungs.

in·spi·ra·tion·al (in′spə rā′shən əl *or* in′spə rāsh′nəl) *adj.* **1** inspiring. **2** inspired. **3** of or having to do with inspiration.

in·spire (in spīr′) *v.* **-spired, -spir·ing. 1** put thought, feeling, life, force, etc. into: *The speaker inspired the crowd.* **2** cause (thought or feeling): *The leader's courage inspired confidence in others.* **3** affect; influence; fill with a thought or feeling: *His sly ways inspire me with distrust.* **4** arouse or influence by a divine force. **5** suggest; cause to be told or written: *His enemies inspired false stories about him.* **6** breathe in; breathe in air. [< L *inspirare* < *in-* in + *spirare* breathe] —**in·spir′er,** *n.* —**in·spir′ing·ly,** *adv.*

in·spir·it (in spir′it) *v.* put spirit into; encourage; hearten.

in·spis·sate (in spis′āt) *v.* **-sat·ed, -sat·ing.** thicken, as by evaporation; condense. [< LL *inspissare* < L *in-* in + *spissus* thick] —**in·spis′sa·tion,** *n.*

inst. *Archaic.* instant. "The 10th inst." means "the tenth day of the present month."
☛ *Usage.* **inst.** Abbreviations such as **inst.** (of the current month) and **ult.** (of last month) are no longer considered good form in business correspondence.

Inst. **1** institute. **2** institution.

in·sta·bil·i·ty (in′stə bil′ə tē) *n.* the quality or state of being unstable: *the instability of the dollar. His emotional instability made him a poor risk as an employee.*

in·stall (in stol′ *or* in stôl′) *v.* **1** place formally in a position, office, etc.: *to install a new judge.* **2** put in a place or position; settle: *The cat installed itself in an easy chair.* **3** put in position for use: *to install a telephone.* [< Med.L *installare* < *in-* in (< L) + *stallum* stall¹ (< Gmc.)] —**in·stall′er,** *n.*

in·stal·la·tion (in′stə lā′shən) *n.* **1** an installing or being installed. **2** the thing installed; machinery placed in position for use: *They have requested new lighting installations.* **3** a military organization including personnel, equipment, buildings, etc.

in·stal·ment¹ or **in·stall·ment¹** (in stol′mənt *or* in stôl′-) *n.* **1** a part of a sum of money or of a debt to be paid at certain regular times: *The furniture cost $500; we paid for it in instalments of $50 a month for ten months.* **2** any of several parts furnished or issued at successive times as part of a series: *The magazine has a serial story in six instalments.* [alteration of earlier *(e)stallment* < *stall* agree to the payment of (a debt) by instalments < OF *estaler* fix, place < *estal* position < Gmc.]

in·stal·ment² or **in·stall·ment²** (in stol′mənt *or* in stôl′-) *n.* installing or being installed.

instalment plan or **installment plan** a system of paying for goods in instalments.

in·stance (in′stəns) *n., v.* **-stanced, -stanc·ing.** —*n.* **1** a person or thing serving as an example; case: *Her rude question was an instance of bad manners.* **2** a stage or step in an action; occasion: *He said he preferred, in this instance, to remain where he was.* **3** a request or suggestion; urging: *He came at instance.*
for instance, as an example: *Her many hobbies include, for instance, skating and stamp collecting.*
—*v.* **1** refer to as an example. **2** exemplify. [ME < OF < L *instantia* insistence < *instans* insistent. See INSTANT.]
☛ *Syn. n.* **1.** See note at **case¹.**

in·stant (in′stənt) *n., adj.* —*n.* **1** a particular moment: *Stop talking this instant!* **2** a moment of time: *He paused for an instant.*

the instant, just as soon as: *The instant he came in the door, everyone stopped talking.*
—*adj.* **1** immediate; without delay: *The medicine gave instant relief from pain.* **2** pressing; urgent: *When there is a fire, there is an instant need for action.* **3** prepared beforehand and requiring little or no cooking, mixing, or additional ingredients: *instant pudding, instant coffee.* **4** able, or seemingly able, to be done, acquired, or used immediately and effortlessly: *instant knowledge.* **5** of the present month; present: *The 10th instant means the tenth day of the present month.* [< L *instans, -antis,* ppr. of *instare* insist, stand near < *in-* in + *stare* stand]
☛ *Syn. n.* **2.** See note at **minute.**
☛ *Usage.* See note at **inst.**

in·stan·ta·ne·ous (in′stən tā′nē əs) *adj.* done, happening, or acting in an instant or without delay: *instantaneous applause. His reaction was instantaneous.* —**in′stan·ta′ne·ous·ly,** *adv.* —**in′stan·ta′ne·ous·ness,** *n.*

in·stan·ter (in stan′tər) *adv. Formal.* at once; immediately. [< L *instanter* insistently < *instans.* See INSTANT.]

in·stant·ly (in′stənt lē) *adv.* in an instant; at once; immediately.
☛ *Syn.* See note at **immediately.**

in·state (in stāt′) *v.* **-stat·ed, -stat·ing.** put into a certain state, position, or office; install.

in sta·tu quo (in stā′tyü kwō′ *or* in stach′ü kwō′) *Latin.* in the same situation, condition, or state.

in·stead (in sted′) *adv.* in place of someone or something; as a substitute or equivalent: *If you cannot go, let him go instead.*
instead of, rather than; in place of; as a substitute for: *Instead of studying, she read a story.*
[earlier *in stead* in place]

in·step (in′step) *n.* **1** the upper surface of the human foot between the toes and the ankle. See **leg** for picture. **2** the part of a shoe, stocking, etc. over the instep. **3** the front part of the hind leg of a horse between the hock and the pastern joint.

in·sti·gate (in′stə gāt′) *v.* **-gat·ed, -gat·ing.** stir up; set in motion, especially something undesirable: *Foreign agents instigated a rebellion.* [< L *instigare*]
☛ *Syn.* See note at **incite.**

in·sti·ga·tion (in′stə gā′shən) *n.* the act of instigating.
at the instigation of, instigated by.

in·sti·ga·tor (in′stə gā′tər) *n.* a person who instigates; person who stirs up evil or trouble.

in·stil or **in·still** (in stil′) *v.* **-stilled, -still·ing. 1** put in little by little; impart gradually: *Reading good books instils a love for really fine literature.* **2** put in drop by drop. [< L *instillare* < *in-* in + *stilla* a drop] —**in·still′er,** *n.*

in·stil·la·tion (in′stə lā′shən) *n.* **1** instilling. **2** something instilled.

in·stinct¹ (in′stingkt) *n.* **1** a natural feeling, knowledge, or power, such as guides animals; an inborn tendency to act in a certain way: *Birds do not learn to fly; they fly by instinct.* **2** a natural tendency or ability; talent: *Even as a child, the artist had an instinct for color.* [< L *instinctus,* n. < *instinctus,* pp. of *instinguere* impel]

in·stinct² (in stingkt′) *adj.* charged or filled with something: *The picture is instinct with life and beauty.* [< L *instinctus,* pp. of *instinguere* impel]

in·stinc·tive (in stingk′tiv) *adj.* **1** of or having to do with instinct. **2** caused or done by instinct; independent of thought, will, or training: *He felt an instinctive distrust of the stranger. Climbing is instinctive in monkeys.* —**in·stinc′tive·ly,** *adv.*

in·sti·tute (in′stə tyüt′ *or* in′stə tüt′) *n., v.* **-tut·ed, -tut·ing.** —*n.* **1** an organization or society for the support or promotion of a particular cause: *an art institute, the Canadian National Institute for the Blind.* **2** the building used by such an organization: *We spent the afternoon at the Art Institute.* **3** an educational institution; school: *a collegiate institute.* **4** an established principle, law, or custom. **5 institutes,** *pl. Esp.Law.* a collection or digest of established principles. **6** a short program of instruction for a particular group.
—*v.* originate or set going; establish or begin: *The police instituted an inquiry into the causes of the accident.* [< L *institutus,* pp. of *instituere* < *in-* in + *statuere* establish < *status* position]

in·sti·tu·tion (in′stə tyü′shən *or* in′stə tü′shən) *n.* **1** an organization or society established for some public or social purpose: *A church, school, college, hospital, or prison is an institution.* **2** a building used by such an organization or society. **3** an established law, custom, or system: *Giving presents on Christmas is an institution.* **4** a setting up; establishing; beginning: *Many people favor the institution of more clubs for young people.* **5** *Informal.* a familiar person or thing: *He's an institution around here.*

in·sti·tu·tion·al (in′stə tyü′shən əl *or* in′stə tü′shən əl) *adj.* **1** of, having to do with, like, or characteristic of institutions: *She*

hated the institutional life of the boarding school. Institutional food is sometimes bland and boring. **2** intended or designed for institutions: *Their main business is in institutional sales rather than retail trade.* **3** especially of advertising, designed to promote reputation and establish good will for a business rather than to help immediate sales. —**in′sti·tu′tion·al·ly**, *adv.*

in·sti·tu·tion·al·ism (in′stə tyü′ shən əl iz′əm *or* in′stə tü′shən əl iz′em) *n.* **1** belief in the importance of established organizations, especially religious institutions. **2** the care and maintenance in public institutions of people unable to care for themselves. **3** emphasis on the formal, impersonal aspects of the operation or maintenance of institutions: *She reacted against the institutionalism of education.*

in·sti·tu·tion·al·ize (in′stə tyü′shən əl īz′ *or* in′stə tü′shən əl īz′) *v.* **-ized, -iz·ing. 1** make into or treat as an acceptable and established principle or custom: *to institutionalize gambling in the form of lotteries.* **2** make impersonal and formal: *He argued that charity had become too institutionalized.* **3** commit to a public institution for care or detention: *They decided not to institutionalize their mentally retarded son.* —**in′sti·tu′tion·al·iz·a′tion**, *n.*

in·struct (in strukt′) *v.* **1** teach. **2** give directions or orders to; order: *The owner instructed his agent to sell the property.* **3** inform; tell: *My lawyer instructs me that your last payment is due March first.* **4** of a judge, give (the jury) a final explanation of the points of law in a case. **5** *Brit.* of a solicitor, engage the services of (a barrister) on behalf of his client. [< L *instructus,* pp. of *instruere* arrange, furnish, instruct < *in-* on + *struere* to pile]
☛ *Syn.* **1.** See note at **teach.**

in·struc·tion (in struk′shən) *n.* **1** teaching or lesson: *instruction in boat building.* **2** Usually, **instructions,** *pl.* orders: *Their instructions were to be there at 7 o'clock.* **3 instructions,** *pl.* an outline of procedure, etc.; directions: *The kit includes complete instructions for assembling the airplane.*

in·struc·tion·al (in struk′shən əl) *adj.* of or for instruction; educational. —**in·struc′tion·al·ly**, *adv.*

in·struc·tive (in struk′tiv) *adj.* useful for instruction; instructing; giving knowledge or information: *A trip around the world is an instructive experience.* —**in·struc′tive·ly**, *adv.* —**in·struc′tive·ness**, *n.*

in·struc·tor (in struk′tər) *n.* **1** teacher. **2** in some colleges and universities, a teacher ranking below an assistant professor. [< Med.L *instructor* teacher < L *instructor* preparer]

in·struc·tress (in struk′tris) *n.* a woman instructor or teacher.

in·stru·ment (in′strə mənt) *n., v.* —*n.* **1** a tool or mechanical device: *surgical instruments.* **2** a device for producing musical sounds: *wind instruments, stringed instruments.* **3** a device for measuring, recording, or controlling: *A thermometer is an instrument for measuring temperature.* **4** a person or thing by means of or through which something is done; agent or means. **5** a formal legal document, such as a contract, deed, or grant.
—*v.* **1** equip with instruments, especially with scientific recording devices: *a fully instrumented missile.* **2** score or arrange (music) for instruments; orchestrate. [< L *instrumentum* < *instruere* arrange, furnish, instruct < *in-* on + *struere* pile]

in·stru·men·tal (in′strə men′təl) *adj., n.* —*adj.* **1** acting or serving as a means; useful; helpful: *His uncle was instrumental in getting him a job.* **2** performed on or written for a musical instrument: *an instrumental arrangement. He prefers instrumental music to choral music.* **3** of, having to do with, or done by a device or tool.
—*n.* a piece of music composed for or played on a musical instrument. —**in′stru·men′tal·ly**, *adv.*

in·stru·men·tal·ist (in′strə men′təl ist) *n.* a person who plays on a musical instrument.

in·stru·men·tal·i·ty (in′strə mən tal′ə tē) *n., pl.* **-ties. 1** the quality or state of being instrumental; usefulness or helpfulness. **2** agency; means.

in·stru·men·ta·tion (in′strə men tā′shən) *n.* **1** the arrangement or composition of music for instruments. **2** the use of instruments; work done with instruments. **3** the mechanized use of instruments, especially for scientific or technical purposes.

instrument board instrument panel.

instrument flying the directing of an aircraft by instruments only, without being able to observe points or objects on the ground. Compare **contact flying.**

instrument panel on an aircraft, motor vehicle, or other machine, a panel displaying gauges, indicator lights, switches, etc., permitting the operator to check on and control specific functions of the machine.

in·sub·or·di·nate (in′sə bôr′də nit) *adj., n.* —*adj.* resisting authority; disobedient; unruly. —*n.* an insubordinate person. —**in′sub·or′di·nate·ly**, *adv.*

in·sub·or·di·na·tion (in′sə bôr′də nā′shən) *n.* resistance to

hat, āge, fär; let, ēqual, tėrm; it, īce
hot, ōpen, ôrder; oil, out; cup, pút, rüle,
əbove, takən, pencəl, lemən, circəs
ch, child; ng, long; sh, ship
th, thin; ᴛʜ, then; zh, measure

authority; active disobedience: *The private was charged with insubordination.*

in·sub·stan·tial (in′səb stan′shəl) *adj.* **1** frail; flimsy; weak: *A cobweb is very insubstantial.* **2** unreal; not actual; imaginary: *Dreams and ghosts are insubstantial.* —**in′sub·stan′tial·ly**, *adv.*

in·suf·fer·a·ble (in suf′ər ə bəl *or* in suf′rə bəl) *adj.* intolerable; unbearable: *insufferable insolence.* —**in·suf′fer·a·ble·ness**, *n.* —**in·suf′fer·a·bly**, *adv.*

in·suf·fi·cien·cy (in′sə fish′ən sē) *n.* too small an amount; lack; deficiency.

in·suf·fi·cient (in′sə fish′ənt) *adj.* not enough; less than is needed: *insufficient sleep.* —**in′suf·fi′cient·ly**, *adv.*

in·su·lar (in′sə lər) *adj.* **1** of or having to do with islands or islanders: *a moderate, insular climate.* **2** living or situated on an island: *an insular people.* **3** forming an island; standing alone like an island. **4** like or characteristic of people who live in isolation, especially when thought of as narrow-minded or ignorant: *an insular point of view, insular intolerance.* [< LL *insularis* < L *insula* island]

in·su·lar·i·ty (in′sə lar′ə tē *or* in′sə ler′ə tē) *n.* **1** the fact or condition of being an island or of living on an island. **2** narrow-mindedness or ignorance.

in·su·late (in′sə lāt′) *v.* **-lat·ed, -lat·ing. 1** keep from losing or transferring electricity, heat, sound, etc., especially by covering or surrounding with a non-conducting material: *Wires are often insulated by a covering of rubber. Our heating bills are lower now that our house is better insulated.* **2** pack with material that will not burn, so as to prevent the spread of fire. **3** set apart; separate from others; isolate. [< L *insula* island]

in·su·la·tion (in′sə lā′shən) *n.* **1** insulating or being insulated. **2** the material used in insulating.

in·su·la·tor (in′sə lā′tər) *n.* something that insulates, especially a material that prevents the passage of electricity or heat; a non-conductor: *Glass is an effective insulator.*

in·su·lin (in′sə lin) *n.* **1** a hormone secreted by the pancreas that enables the body to use sugar and other carbohydrates. **2** a preparation containing this hormone, used especially in the treatment of diabetes. Insulin is obtained from the pancreas of slaughtered animals. [< L *insula* island (i.e., of the pancreas)]

in·sult (*v.* in sult′; *n.* in′sult) *v., n.* —*v.* treat with scorn, abuse, or great rudeness: *The rebels insulted the flag by throwing mud on it.* —*n.* an insulting speech or action. [< L *insultare,* frequentative of *insilire* leap at or upon < *in-* on, at + *salire* leap] —**in·sult′ing·ly**, *adv.*
☛ *Syn. n.* **Insult, affront, indignity** = something said or done to offend by showing disrespect or contempt. **Insult** emphasizes insolence and abuse, and intention to hurt or shame: *Stamping on the flag is an insult.* **Affront** applies to a deliberate and open show of disrespect: *Leaving during her song was an affront to my sister.* **Indignity** applies to an act that hurts a person's dignity, suggests lack of respect, but emphasizes the feelings of the victim: *Spanking is an indignity to a teen-ager.*

in·su·per·a·ble (in sü′pər ə bəl) *adj.* that cannot be passed over or overcome: *an insuperable barrier.* —**in·su′per·a·ble·ness**, *n.* —**in·su′per·a·bly**, *adv.*

in·sup·port·a·ble (in′sə pôr′tə bəl) *adj.* **1** unbearable; unendurable; intolerable. **2** that cannot be upheld or justified: *insupportable rudeness.* —**in′sup·port′a·ble·ness**, *n.* —**in′sup·port′a·bly**, *adv.*

in·sur·a·ble (in shür′ə bəl) *adj.* capable of being insured; fit to be insured.

in·sur·ance (in shür′əns) *n.* **1** an insuring of property, person, or life: *fire insurance, burglary insurance, accident insurance, life insurance, health insurance.* **2** the business of insuring property, life, etc.: *My uncle works in insurance.* **3** the amount of money for which a person or thing is insured: *He has $100 000 insurance.* **4** the amount of money paid for insurance; premium: *She pays her insurance in two instalments.* **5** the contract made between insurer and insured; policy.

in·sure (in shür′) *v.* **-sured, -sur·ing. 1** arrange for money payment in case of loss of (property, profit, etc.) or in case of accident, sickness, or death; take out or give insurance on or for: *They do not have their house insured. She insured her art collection against theft, damage, and fire.* **2** give or buy insurance. **3** make

safe or certain; ensure. [ME; var. of *ensure* < AF *enseurer* < *en-* in + OF *seür* sure < L *securus*. Related to SURE.]
☛ *Usage.* See note at **ensure.**

in·sured (in shürd′) *n.* a person whose life or property is insured.

in·sur·er (in shür′ər) *n.* a person or company, etc. that insures; one that sells insurance.

in·sur·gence (in sėr′jəns) *n.* a rising in revolt; rebellion.

in·sur·gen·cy (in sėr′jən sē) *n.* insurgence.

in·sur·gent (in sėr′jənt) *n., adj.* —*n.* a person who rises in revolt; rebel. —*adj.* rising in revolt; rebellious. [< L *insurgens, -entis*, ppr. of *insurgere* < *in-* against + *surgere* rise]

in·sur·mount·a·ble (in′sər moun′tə bəl) *adj.* that cannot be overcome. —**in′sur·mount′a·bly**, *adv.*

in·sur·rec·tion (in′sə rek′shən) *n.* a rising against established authority; revolt. [ME < OF < LL *insurrectio, -onis* < L *insurgere*. See INSURGENT.]
☛ *Syn.* See note at **revolt.**

in·sur·rec·tion·ar·y (in′sə rek′shən er′ē) *adj.* 1 having a tendency to revolt. 2 having to do with revolt.

in·sur·rec·tion·ist (in′sə rek′shən ist) *n.* a person who takes part in or favors an insurrection; rebel.

in·sus·cep·ti·bil·i·ty (in′sə sep′tə bil′ə tē) *n.* the fact or quality of being insusceptible.

in·sus·cep·ti·ble (in′sə sep′tə bəl) *adj.* not susceptible; not easily influenced. —**in′sus·cep′ti·bly**, *adv.*

int. 1 interest. 2 international. 3 internal. 4 interior. 5 intransitive. 6 interval.

in·tact (in takt′) *adj.* with no part missing or damaged; whole: *I checked the dishes when we unpacked them and found that they were all intact.* [< L *intactus* < *in-* not + *tactus*, pp. of *tangere* touch]

in·tagl·io (in tal′yō *or* in täl′yō) *n., pl.* **in·tagl·ios.** 1 the process of engraving by making cuts in the surface. 2 ornamentation by designs sunk below the surface. 3 a design engraved in this way. 4 a gem ornamented in this way. 5 a method of printing in which paper is pressed into inked lines below the surface of the plate or cylinder. The ink is wiped off the surface but remains in the recesses, as in etching, photogravure, etc. [< Ital. *intaglio* < *intagliare* engrave < *in-* into + *tagliare* cut]

in·take (in′tāk′) *n.* 1 a place where water, air, gas, etc. enters a channel, pipe, or other narrow opening. 2 taking in. 3 the amount or thing taken in. 4 a narrowing or contraction in a tube, stocking, etc., or the point at which this begins.

in·tan·gi·bil·i·ty (in tan′jə bil′ə tē) *n.* the quality of being intangible.

in·tan·gi·ble (in tan′jə bəl) *adj., n.* —*adj.* 1 not capable of being touched or felt: *Sound and light are intangible.* 2 not easily grasped by the mind; vague: *She had that intangible quality called charm.* —*n.* something intangible. —**in·tan′gi·ble·ness**, *n.* —**in·tan′gi·bly**, *adv.*

in·te·ger (in′tə jər) *n.* 1 any positive or negative whole number or zero: *The numbers 4, –37, –8, 106, etc. are integers.* 2 a thing complete in itself; something whole. [< L *integer* whole. Doublet of ENTIRE.]

in·te·gral (in′tə grəl *or* in teg′rəl) *adj., n.* —*adj.* 1 necessary to the completeness of the whole; essential: *Steel is an integral part of a modern skyscraper.* 2 entire; complete. 3 *Mathematics.* having to do with whole numbers; not fractional.
—*n.* a whole; a whole number. [< LL *integralis* < L *integer* whole]

integral calculus the branch of mathematics dealing with the finding of integrals and their application to the finding of areas, lengths, volumes, etc. and to the solution of differential equations. Compare **differential calculus.**

in·te·grate (in′tə grāt′) *v.* **-grat·ed, -grat·ing.** 1 make more unified or harmonious: *The government should integrate its approach to unemployment.* 2 bring together (parts) into a whole. 3 bring in (individuals or groups) as part of a larger group: *to integrate immigrants into Canadian society.* 4 make (facilities, institutions, etc.) available to all people regardless of race, nationality, religion, etc.; desegregate: *to integrate a school.* 5 become unified, brought together, or desegregated: *The three neighboring cities have decided to integrate.* [< L *integrare* < *integer* whole] —**in′te·gra′tor**, *n.*

integrated circuit a miniature electronic circuit that is a complete system made up of many inseparable components incorporated into or on a single chip of semiconducting material, usually crystalline silicon.

in·te·gra·tion (in′tə grā′shən) *n.* the act or process of integrating.

in·te·gra·tion·ist (in′tə grā′shə nist) *n.* a person who believes in, or practises, integration.

in·te·gra·tive (in′tə grā′tiv) *adj.* directed toward or fostering integration: *an integrative approach to the study of Inuit art, involving persons trained in art and anthropology.*

in·teg·ri·ty (in teg′rə tē) *n.* 1 firm attachment to moral or artistic principle; honesty and sincerity; uprightness: *People realized that he was a victim of circumstances, and did not question his integrity. Her poetry is too slick and commercial to have integrity.* 2 wholeness; completeness. 3 the condition of being unmarred or uncorrupted; the original, perfect condition: *Several scholars have questioned the integrity of the text of this poem.* [< L *integritas* < *integer* whole]
☛ *Syn.* 1. See note at **honesty.**

in·teg·u·ment (in teg′yə mənt) *n.* a natural outer covering of an animal or plant or of one of its parts. The skin or shell of an animal and the husk of a seed or fruit are integuments. [< L *integumentum* < *integere* cover < *in-* on + *tegere* cover]

in·tel·lect (in′tə lekt′) *n.* 1 the power of knowing and understanding as distinguished from will and feeling. 2 great intelligence; high mental ability: *Isaac Newton was a man of intellect.* 3 a person having high mental ability: *Newton was one of the greatest intellects of all time.* [< L *intellectus* < *intelligere*. See INTELLIGENT.]
☛ *Syn.* 1. See note at **mind.**

in·tel·lec·tion (in′tə lek′shən) *n.* 1 the use of the intellect; reasoning or thought. 2 an idea or perception.

in·tel·lec·tu·al (in′tə lek′chü əl) *adj., n.* —*adj.* 1 of or having to do with the intellect: *Thinking is an intellectual process.* 2 needing or involving the intellect: *an intellectual puzzle. Mathematics is an intellectual discipline.* 3 inclined toward or favoring things that involve the intellect: *intellectual tastes, an intellectual person.* —*n.* a person who is interested in intellectual things; an intellectual person: *a magazine designed for intellectuals.*

in·tel·lec·tu·al·ism (in′tə lek′chü əl iz′əm) *n.* 1 the exercise of the intellect; a devotion to intellectual pursuits. 2 *Philosophy.* the doctrine that knowledge is wholly or chiefly derived from pure reason.

in·tel·lec·tu·al·i·ty (in′tə lek′chü al′ə tē) *n., pl.* **-ties.** being intellectual; intellectual nature or power.

in·tel·lec·tu·al·ize (in′tə lek′chü əl īz′) *v.* **-ized, -iz·ing.** interpret or express (feelings, attitudes, etc.) in intellectual or rational terms, especially in a narrow or formalized way: *The explanation is intellectual without being intellectualized.* —**in′tel·lec′tu·al·i·za′tion**, *n.* —**in′tel·lec′tu·al·iz′er**, *n.*

in·tel·lec·tu·al·ly (in′tə lek′chü əl ē) *adv.* 1 in an intellectual way. 2 so far as intellect is concerned.

in·tel·li·gence (in tel′ə jəns) *n.* 1 the ability to learn and know; the ability to use the reason or intellect in dealing with a new situation, solving a problem, etc. 2 knowledge or information: *The government received secret intelligence of the plans of the enemy.* 3 the getting or distributing of information, especially secret information: *She worked in intelligence during the war.* 4 a group or agency engaged in obtaining secret information: *Intelligence had informed them of the planned attack.* 5 Often, **Intelligence,** an intelligent being or spirit.

intelligence quotient a number used to describe a person's relative intelligence in terms of certain thinking skills. It is computed by dividing his apparent mental age, as shown by a standard test, by his actual age and multiplying by 100. *Abbrev.*: IQ or I.Q.

intelligence test a standardized test designed to measure a person's relative intelligence.

in·tel·li·gent (in tel′ə jənt) *adj.* 1 having intelligence; rational: *Is there intelligent life on other planets?* 2 having or showing a high degree of intelligence; clever, perceptive, or bright: *an intelligent student, an intelligent remark.* [< L *intelligens, -entis*, ppr. of *intelligere* understand < *inter-* between + *legere* choose]
—**in·tel′li·gent·ly**, *adv.*

in·tel·li·gent·si·a (in tel′ə jent′sē ə *or* in tel′ə gent′sē ə) *n. sing. or pl.* the persons representing, or claiming to represent, the superior intelligence or enlightened opinion of a country; the intellectuals. [< Russian *intelligentsiya* < L *intelligentia* < *intelligens*. See INTELLIGENT.]

in·tel·li·gi·bil·i·ty (in tel′ə jə bil′ə tē) *n.* the fact or quality of being intelligible.

in·tel·li·gi·ble (in tel′ə jə bəl) *adj.* capable of being understood; clear; comprehensible: *He was so upset that his account of the accident was hardly intelligible.* [< L *intelligibilis* < *intelligere*. See INTELLIGENT.] —**in·tel′li·gi·bly**, *adv.*

in·tem·per·ance (in tem′pər əns *or* in tem′prəns) *n.* **1** a lack of moderation or self-control; excess. **2** the excessive drinking of intoxicating liquor, especially habitually.

in·tem·per·ate (in tem′pər it *or* in tem′prit) *adj.* **1** not moderate; lacking in self-control; excessive: *an intemperate appetite, an intemperate anger.* **2** drinking too much intoxicating liquor. **3** not temperate; extreme in temperature; severe: *an intemperate climate.* —**in·tem′per·ate·ly,** *adv.*

in·tend (in tend′) *v.* **1** have in mind as a purpose; plan: *We intend to go home soon. He apologized and said he had intended no insult.* **2** mean for a particular purpose or use; design or destine: *That gift was intended for you.* **3** *Archaic.* direct: *to intend one's course.* [ME < OF < L *intendere* < *in-* toward + *tendere* stretch] —**in·tend′er,** *n.*

☛ *Syn.* **1. Intend, mean** = have in mind as a purpose. **Intend** = have some definite purpose or plan and to be determined to carry it out: *I intend to finish this work before I go to bed.* **Mean** is sometimes used interchangeably with **intend**, but puts greater emphasis on having something in mind to do or get and less emphasis on the determination to carry it out or gain it: *I meant to get up early, but forgot to set the alarm.*

in·tend·an·cy (in ten′dən sē) *n., pl.* **-cies. 1** the position or work of an intendant. **2** intendants. **3** a district under an intendant.

in·tend·ant (in ten′dənt) *n.* **1** a person in charge; superintendent; manager; director. **2** *Historical.* **a** the most important administrative office in New France, eventually responsible for the administration of finance, justice, and police in the colony. **b** an official who held this office: *Jean Talon was the first and greatest intendant of New France.* [< F, ult. < L *intendere* attend to. See INTEND.]

in·tend·ed (in ten′did) *adj., n.* —*adj.* **1** meant; planned. **2** prospective: *a woman's intended husband.* —*n. Informal.* a prospective husband or wife.

in·tense (in tens′) *adj.* **1** existing in or being of a very high degree; very strong; extreme: *intense pain, an intense color, an intense light.* **2** of action, activity, etc., strenuous, eager, or ardent: *intense thought. She lived an intense life.* **3** having or showing strong feeling, purpose, etc.: *an intense face. He is an intense person.* [< L *intensus,* pp. of *intendere* strain. See INTEND.] —**in·tense′ly,** *adv.* —**in·tense′ness,** *n.*

in·ten·si·fi·er (in ten′sə fī′ər) *n.* **1** *Photography.* a chemical used to increase contrast in a negative. **2** an intensive.

in·ten·si·fy (in ten′sə fī′) *v.* **-fied, -fy·ing. 1** make or become intense or more intense; strengthen; increase: *Blowing on a fire intensifies the heat. Her first failure only intensified her desire to succeed.* **2** *Photography.* make (parts of a negative) more dense or opaque by treating with chemicals. —**in·ten′si·fi·ca′tion,** *n.* —**in·ten′si·fi·er,** *n.*

in·ten·si·ty (in ten′sə tē) *n., pl.* **-ties. 1** the quality or state of being intense; very great strength, force, etc. **2** the strength of a color based on the degree of difference from the grey of the same brightness; saturation. **3** *Physics.* the amount or degree of strength of heat, light, sound, etc. per unit of area, volume, etc. **4** *Photography.* of parts of a negative, density; opaqueness.

in·ten·sive (in ten′siv) *adj., n.* —*adj.* **1** deep and thorough: *An intensive study of a few books is more valuable than a superficial reading of many.* **2** having to do with a system of farming in which more money and work is spent on a small area to produce larger crops. **3** *Grammar.* **a** serving as an intensive: *an intensive prefix.* **b** designating or belonging to a class of pronouns used to emphasize a noun or pronoun, such as *myself* in *I saw him myself.* —*n. Grammar.* a word element, word, phrase, etc. that adds force or emphasis but has little meaning of its own in the context. The prefix *super* in *superstar* is an intensive. —**in·ten′sive·ly,** *adv.*

in·tent¹ (in tent′) *n.* **1** the purpose; intention: *The thief shot with intent to kill.* **2** meaning; significance: *What is the intent of that sentence?*
to all intents and purposes, in almost every way; practically. [ME < OF *entent, entente* < L *intendere.* See INTEND.]

in·tent² (in tent′) *adj.* **1** very attentive; having the eyes or thoughts earnestly fixed on something; earnest: *an intent look.* **2** earnestly engaged; much interested; determined: *He is intent on making money.* [< L *intentus,* pp. of *intendere* strain. See INTEND.] —**in·tent′ly,** *adv.* —**in·tent′ness,** *n.*

in·ten·tion (in ten′shən) *n.* **1** the act or fact of having in mind as a purpose; determination to act in a certain way: *I'm sure he had no intention of hurting your feelings.* **2** what is intended; an object or purpose: *It wasn't my intention to start an argument.* **3 intentions,** *pl. Informal.* purpose with respect to marrying.

☛ *Syn.* **1. Intention, purpose, design** = what a person intends or plans to get or do. **Intention** = what one has in mind to do, but does not always suggest determination or definite planning: *My intention was to arrive early.* **Purpose** = a definite thing a person intends to do or get and toward which he strives with determination: *My purpose was to avoid the crowd.* **Design** suggests deliberate intention, with definite planning or preparations, often underhand, for carrying out one's purpose: *I arrived early by design. He had designs on her fortune.*

in·ten·tion·al (in ten′shən əl) *adj.* done on purpose; meant;

hat, āge, fär; let, ēqual, tèrm; it, īce
hot, ōpen, ôrder; oil, out; cup, pùt, rüle,
əbove, takən, pencəl, lemən, circəs

ch, child; ng, long; sh, ship
th, thin; ᴛʜ, then; zh, measure

planned; intended: *His insult was intentional; he wanted to hurt your feelings.* —**in·ten′tion·al·ly,** *adv.*
☛ *Syn.* See note at **deliberate.**

in·ter (in tėr′) *v.* **-terred, -ter·ring.** put (a dead body) into a grave or tomb; bury. [ME < OF *enterrer* + L *interrare* < *in-* in + *terra* earth]
☛ *Usage.* Do not confuse **inter** "bury" with **intern** "confine in a certain place". One **inters** a dead body; one **interns** a live person who might cause trouble.

inter- *prefix.* **1** together; one with the other: *intercommunicate* = communicate with each other. **2** between: *interpose* = put between. **3** between or among a group: *interscholastic* = between or among schools. [< L *inter-* < *inter,* prep. adv., among, between, during]

in·ter·act (in′tər akt′) *v.* act on each other.

in·ter·ac·tion (in′tər ak′shən) *n.* action on each other.

in·ter a·li·a (in′tər ā′lē ə) *Latin.* among other things.

in·ter–A·mer·i·can (in′tər ə mer′ə kən) *adj.* between or among countries of North, South, or Central America.

in·ter·bor·ough (in′tər bėr′ō) *adj.* between boroughs.

in·ter·breed (in′tər brēd′) *v.* **-bred, -breed·ing.** breed by the mating of different kinds; breed by using different varieties or species of animals or plants.

in·ter·ca·lar·y (in tėr′kə ler′ē) *adj.* **1** inserted in the calendar to make the calendar year agree with the solar year. February 29 is an intercalary day. **2** having an added day, month, etc. as a particular year. **3** put in between; interposed; intervening. [< L *intercalaris, intercalarius* < *intercalare.* See INTERCALATE.]

in·ter·ca·late (in tėr′kə lāt′) *v.* **-lat·ed, -lat·ing. 1** put into the calendar. **2** put between; interpolate. [< L *intercalare* < *inter-* between + *calare* proclaim]

in·ter·ca·la·tion (in tėr′kə lā′shən) *n.* **1** intercalating. **2** something intercalated.

in·ter·cede (in′tər sēd′) *v.* **-ced·ed, -ced·ing. 1** plead or ask a favor in another's behalf: *Friends of the condemned man interceded with the authorities for a pardon.* **2** intervene in order to bring about an agreement; mediate. [< L *intercedere* < *inter-* between + *cedere* go]

in·ter·cel·lu·lar (in′tər sel′yə lər) *adj.* situated between or among cells.

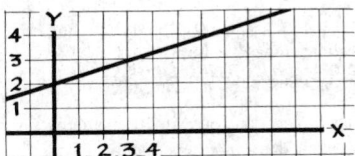

Intercept (def. 3).
In the diagram the
y-intercept is 2.

in·ter·cept (in′tər sept′) *v., n.* —*v.* **1** take, seize, or stop a person, vehicle, etc. on the way from one place to another: *to intercept a messenger or a letter, to intercept an enemy aircraft, to intercept a pass in football.* **2** interrupt or stop motion, passage, progress, etc.: *to intercept the flight of a criminal.* **3** intersect. —*n. Mathematics.* the distance from the origin to the point where a line crosses an axis on a graph. [< L *interceptus,* pp. of *intercipere* < *inter-* between + *capere* catch] —**in′ter·cep′tion,** *n.*

in·ter·cep·tor (in′tər sep′tər) *n.* a person or thing that intercepts, especially a fighter aircraft or missile designed to stop enemy aircraft or missiles.

in·ter·ces·sion (in′tər sesh′ən) *n.* **1** the act or fact of interceding. **2** a prayer or petition in behalf of another person or persons. [< L *intercessio, -onis* < *intercedere.* See INTERCEDE.]

in·ter·ces·sor (in′tər ses′ər *or* in′tər ses′ər) *n.* a person who intercedes.

in·ter·ces·so·ry (in′tər ses′ə rē) *adj.* making or relating to intercession; interceding.

in·ter·change (*v.* in′tər chānj′; *n.* in′tər chānj′) *v.* **-changed, -chang·ing;** *n.* —*v.* **1** put each of (two or more persons or things) in the other's place. **2** give and take; exchange: *to interchange gifts.* **3** cause to happen by turns; alternate: *to interchange severity with indulgence.*

—*n.* **1** the putting of each of two or more persons or things in the other's place: *The word* team *may be turned into* meat *by the interchange of the end letters.* **2** a road that permits traffic from one highway to change to another without crossing in front of other traffic; cloverleaf. **3** a giving and taking; exchanging. **4** an alternate succession; alternation: *an interchange of hard work with rest.* [ME *entrechange*(n) < OF *entrechangier* < *entre-* (< L *inter-*) + *changier* < L *cambiare* exchange; later influenced by *inter-*]
☞ *Syn. v.* **2.** See note at **exchange.**

in·ter·change·a·bil·i·ty (in'tər chān'jə bil'ə tē) *n.* the quality of being interchangeable.

in·ter·change·a·ble (in'tər chān'jə bəl) *adj.* capable of being used in place of each other: *This saw has several interchangeable blades.* —**in'ter·change'a·bly,** *adv.*

in·ter·class (in'tər klas') *adj.* between classes: *interclass swimming meets.*

in·ter·col·le·giate (in'tər kə lē'jit *or* -kə lē'jē it) *adj.* between colleges, universities, or high schools: *intercollegiate football games.*

in·ter·co·lo·ni·al (in'tər kə lō'nē əl) *adj.* between colonies; *intercolonial trade.*

in·ter·com (in'tər kom') *n. Informal.* a system of radio or telephone communication between rooms of a building, parts of a ship or aircraft, etc. [a shortened form of *intercommunication system*]

in·ter·com·mu·ni·cate (in'tər kə myü'nə kāt') *v.* **-cat·ed, -cat·ing.** communicate with each other. —**in'ter·com·mu'ni·ca'tion,** *n.*

in·ter·con·nect (in'tər kə nekt') *v.* connect with each other. —**in'ter·con·nec'tion,** *n.*

in·ter·con·ti·nen·tal (in'tər kon'tə nen'təl) *adj.* **1** extending or carried on between or among continents: *intercontinental travel.* **2** capable of travelling between continents: *intercontinental ballistic missiles.*

in·ter·cos·tal (in'tər kos'təl) *adj., n.* —*adj.* between the ribs. —*n. Anatomy.* a muscle or part situated between the ribs. [< NL *intercostalis* < L *inter-* between + *costa* rib]

in·ter·course (in'tər kôrs') *n.* **1** communication; dealings between people; exchange of thoughts, services, feelings, etc.: *Airplanes, good roads, and telephones make intercourse between different parts of the country far easier than it was fifty years ago.* **2** sexual intercourse. [ME *entercourse* < OF *entrecours* < L *intercursus* a running between, ult. < *inter-* between + *currere* run; later influenced by *inter-*]

in·ter·de·nom·i·na·tion·al (in'tər di nom'ə nā'shən əl *or* -di nom'ə näsh'nəl) *adj.* between or involving different religious denominations.

in·ter·de·part·men·tal (in'tər dē'pärt men'təl) *adj.* between departments. —**in'ter·de'part·men'tal·ly,** *adv.*

in·ter·de·pend·ence (in'tər di pen'dəns) *n.* dependence on each other; mutual dependence.

in·ter·de·pen·den·cy (in'tər di pen'dən sē) *n.* interdependence.

in·ter·de·pend·ent (in'tər di pen'dənt) *adj.* dependent each upon the other. —**in'ter·de·pend'ent·ly,** *adv.*

in·ter·dict (*v.* in'tər dikt'; *n.* in'tər dikt') *n., v.* —*n.* **1** an official prohibition; a formal, authoritative order forbidding something. **2** *Roman Catholic Church.* a censure excluding a place or person from certain sacraments and privileges. **3** *Cdn.* especially in British Columbia, a person forbidden to buy alcoholic liquor. —*v.* **1** place under an interdict: *to interdict a parish.* **2** prohibit or forbid by authority: *to interdict trade with other countries.* **3** restrain by authority: *interdicted from buying alcoholic liquor.* [ME < OF < L *interdictus,* pp. of *interdicere* prohibit < *inter-* between + *dicere* speak] —**in'ter·dic'tor,** *n.*

in·ter·dic·tion (in'tər dik'shən) *n.* inderdicting or being interdicted.

in·ter·est (in'trist *or* in'tər ist) *n., v.* —*n.* **1** a feeling of wanting to know, see, do, own, share in, or take part in: *He has no interest in sports.* **2** the power of arousing such a feeling: *A dull book lacks interest.* **3** something that stirs up such feelings. Any activity, pastime, or hobby can be an interest. **4** a share or part in property and actions: *He bought a half interest in the farm.* **5** something in which a person has a share or part. Any business, activity, or hobby can be an interest. **6** a group of people having the same business, activity, etc.: *mining interests.* **7** advantage; benefit: *Each person should look after his own interest.* **8** money paid for the use of money, usually a percentage of the amount invested, borrowed, or loaned: *The annual interest on the loan was 15 percent.*

9 something extra given in return: *She returned our favor with interest.*
in the interest of, for; to help.
—*v.* **1** make curious and hold the attention of: *An exciting story interests you.* **2** cause (a person) to take a share or part in something: *The agent tried to interest us in buying a car.* [ME < AF < L *interest* it is of importance, it makes a difference, 3rd person sing. present of *interesse* < *inter-* between + *esse* be]

in·ter·est·ed (in'tris təd, in'tər is təd, *or* in'tər es'təd) *adj.* **1** feeling or showing interest: *He gave a demonstration before a crowd of interested spectators. Are you interested in running for class president?* **2** involved or concerned; having an interest or share: *A meeting will be held tonight for all interested parties.* **3** influenced by personal considerations; prejudiced: *interested motives.* —**in'ter·est·ed·ly,** *adv.* —**in'ter·est·ed·ness,** *n.*
☞ *Usage.* **Interested.** The adjective **interested** has two opposites: **uninterested,** which is merely its negative, and **disinterested,** which means "free from selfish motives; impartial; fair": *He was uninterested in the outcome of the game. A disinterested spectator offered to referee.* See also **disinterested.**

in·ter·est·ing (in'tris ting, in'tər is ting, *or* in'tər es'ting) *adj.* arousing interest; holding one's attention. —**in'ter·est·ing·ly,** *adv.*

in·ter·face (in'tər fās') *n., v.* —*n.* **1** a surface that forms a common boundary between two regions, bodies, spaces, etc.: *the interface of air and water.* **2** an area or place where different systems, processes, etc. act on or influence each other: *Taxation is the most critical interface between government and business.* **3** the means by which different systems, processes, modes of thought, etc. interact: *serving as an interface between the two groups.* —*v.* **1** serve as or form an interface: *There are problems where the two groups interface.* **2** bring into contact or interaction: *Can one interface a kitchen stove with a computer?* **3** add interfacing to: *to interface a collar.*

in·ter·fac·ing (in'tər fā'sing) *n.* a relatively stiff material placed between two layers of fabric in a collar, cuff, etc. to give shape or body to it. The interfacing is sewn or fused between the outside layer and the facing.

in·ter·fere (in'tər fēr') *v.* **-fered, -fer·ing. 1** come into opposition; come between in a way that obstructs or hinders: *I will come on Saturday if nothing interferes. The weather interfered with our plans.* **2** disturb the affairs of others; meddle: *This has nothing to do with you, so don't interfere.* **3** intervene; take part for a purpose: *The police interfered to stop the riot.* **4** *Sports.* obstruct or hinder the action of an opposing player in an illegal way. **5** *Physics.* of waves, act upon one another in such a way as to increase, lessen, neutralize, etc. each other. [< OF *entreferir* strike each other < *entre-* between (< L *inter-*) + *ferir* strike < L *ferire*]
☞ *Syn.* **2.** See note at **meddle.**

in·ter·fer·ence (in'tər fēr'əns) *n.* **1** an interfering. **2** something that interferes; obstruction. **3** *Physics.* the effect that light or sound waves have on each other when their paths meet or cross, to intensify or neutralize each other, produce beats, etc. **4** *Radio and television.* **a** a confusion of radio signals, producing static, distortion of sound, etc. **b** something that produces such confusion. **5** *Football.* **a** the legal blocking of an opposing player to clear the way for the ball carrier. **b** the players protecting or blocking for the ball carrier. **6** *Sports.* the illegal obstructing or hindering of an opposing player.
run interference (for), a *Football.* clear the way for the ball carrier. **b** act as a go-between or screen: *She never has to deal directly with the public because her secretary runs interference for her.*

in·ter·fer·om·e·ter (in'tər fə rom'ət ər) *n.* an instrument for measuring wavelengths of light, testing the refraction of prisms and lenses, measuring very small distances, etc. by means of light interference patterns produced when parts of a ray of light that have travelled different distances overlap again.

in·ter·fer·on (in'tər fēr'on) *n. Biochemistry.* a substance produced in virus-infected cells to counteract the infection.

in·ter·fold (in'tər fōld') *v.* fold one with another; fold together.

in·ter·fuse (in'tər fyüz') *v.* **-fused, -fus·ing. 1** be diffused through; permeate. **2** fuse together; blend. [< L *interfusus,* pp. of *interfundere* < *inter-* between + *fundere* pour] —**in'ter·fu'sion,** *n.*

in·ter·ga·lac·tic (in'tər gə lak'tik) *adj.* occurring or situated between galaxies: *intergalactic travel.*

in·ter·gla·cial (in'tər glā'shəl) *adj., n.* —*adj. Geology.* of or occurring in the period between two glacial epochs. —*n.* the period between two glacial epochs.

in·ter·im (in'tər im) *n., adj.* —*n.* meantime; time between. —*adj.* for the meantime; temporary. [< L *interim* in the meantime < *inter* between]

in·te·ri·or (in tēr'ē ər) *n., adj.* —*n.* **1** the inside; inner surface or part: *The interior of the house was beautifully decorated.* **2** the part of a region or country away from the coast or border. **3** a picture or stage setting of the inside of a room, house, etc.
—*adj.* **1** on the inside; inner. **2** away from the coast or border.

3 having to do with affairs within a country; domestic. 4 private; secret. [< L *interior* inner]

in·te·ri·or angle 1 any of the four angles formed on the inner sides of two parallel lines by a straight line cutting through the parallel lines. 2 the angle formed on the inside of a polygon between two adjacent sides. Compare **exterior angle. See triangle** for picture.

interior decoration 1 the colors, materials, furnishings, etc. used in a room, house, etc. and their arrangement. 2 interior design.

interior decorator 1 a person whose work is painting or wallpapering the interiors of houses and other buildings. 2 interior designer.

interior design the art or practice of planning furnishings, decorations, etc. for the interiors of homes, offices, and other buildings.

interior designer a person trained in interior design, especially one whose work it is.

interj. interjection.

in·ter·ject (in′tər jekt′) v. throw in between other things; insert abruptly: *Every now and then the speaker interjected some witty remark.* [< L *interjectus*, pp. of *interjicere* < *inter-* between + *jacere* throw]

in·ter·jec·tion (in′tər jek′shən) n. 1 the act of interjecting. 2 something interjected, such as a word or remark. 3 *Grammar.* an exclamation of surprise, sorrow, delight, etc., that has no grammatical connection with what precedes or follows it. *Examples: Oh! Ah! Ouch! Whoops!*

in·ter·jec·tion·al (in′tər jek′shən əl) adj. 1 of an interjection; used as an interjection. 2 containing an interjection. 3 interjected. —**in′ter·jec′tion·al·ly,** adv.

in·ter·lace (in′tər lās′) v. **-laced, -lac·ing.** 1 arrange or cross (threads, strips, branches, etc.) so that they go over and under each other; weave together; intertwine: *Baskets are made by interlacing reeds or fibres.* 2 cross in an intricate manner: *interlacing highways.* 3 give variety to; intersperse: *a speech interlaced with silly jokes.*

in·ter·lard (in′tər lärd′) v. give variety to; mix so as to give variety to; intersperse: *The speaker interlarded his long speech with amusing stories.* [< F *entrelarder* < *entre-* between (< L *inter-*) + *larder* lard < L *lardum* fat]

in·ter·leaf (in′tər lēf′) n., pl. **-leaves.** a leaf of paper, usually blank, put between others, as in a book, for notes, to protect color plates, etc.

in·ter·leave (in′tər lēv′) v. **-leaved, -leav·ing.** insert a leaf or leaves of paper between the pages of (a book, album, etc.).

in·ter·line (in′tər līn′) v. **-lined, -lin·ing.** 1 insert (words etc.) between the lines of: *The document had been interlined in several places.* 2 write, print, or mark between the lines: *The teacher interlined corrections on the students' themes.* 3 provide with an interlining. [< Med.L *interlineare*]

in·ter·lin·e·ar (in′tər lin′ē ər) adj. 1 inserted between the lines: *an interlinear translation.* 2 containing two different languages or versions in alternate lines. —**in′ter·lin′e·ar·ly,** adv.

in·ter·lin·e·a·tion (in′tər lin′ē ā′shən) n. 1 interlining; the insertion of matter between the lines of writing or print. 2 the matter thus inserted.

in·ter·lin·ing (in′tər līn′ing) n. 1 an extra lining between the outer fabric of a garment and the lining: *The coat has a warm woollen interlining.* 2 a fabric used to interline.

in·ter·link (in′tər lingk′) v. link together.

in·ter·lock (in′tər lok′) v. join or fit tightly together; lock together: *The antlers of the two stags were interlocked.*

in·ter·loc·u·tor (in′tər lok′yə tər) n. 1 a person who takes part in a conversation or dialogue. 2 the man in a minstrel show, the man who asks the end man questions. [< L *interlocutus*, pp. of *interloqui* converse < *inter-* between + *loqui* speak]

in·ter·loc·u·to·ry (in′tər lok′yə tô′rē) adj. 1 of or in conversation or dialogue. 2 *Law.* **a** made during a lawsuit or other action; not final: *The judge granted an interlocutory degree after the hearing.* **b** of or having to do with a decision made in this way. 3 inserted into a conversation, speech, etc: *interlocutory anecdotes.*

in·ter·lop·er (in′tər lōp′ər) n. a person who intrudes on or meddles in others' affairs. [probably < Du. *enterlooper* < *entre-* between (< L *inter-*) + *looper* runner < *loopen* run]

in·ter·lude (in′tər lüd′) n. 1 anything thought of as filling the time between two things; interval: *There were only a few interludes of fair weather during the rainy season.* 2 *Music.* a composition played between the parts of a song, church service, play, etc. 3 an entertainment between the acts of a play. 4 in early English drama: **a** a short, humorous play, commonly introduced between the parts of the long mystery plays or given as part of other entertainment. **b** a stage play of a popular nature; comedy; farce. [< Med.L *interludium* < L *inter-* between + *ludus* play]

hat, āge, fär; let, ēqual, tèrm; it, īce
hot, ōpen, ôrder; oil, out; cup, put, rüle,
above, takən, pencəl, lemən, circəs

ch, child; ng, long; sh, ship
th, thin; ᴛʜ, then; zh, measure

in·ter·lu·nar (in′tər lü′nər) adj. between the old moon and the new moon.

in·ter·mar·riage (in′tər mar′ij or in′tər mer′ij) n. 1 marriage between members of different religious, social, or ethnic groups. 2 marriage between close blood relations.

in·ter·mar·ry (in′tər mar′ē or in′tər mer′ē) v. **-ried, -ry·ing.** 1 of families, tribes, etc., become connected by marriage. 2 marry within the family or with close relations.

in·ter·med·dle (in′tər med′əl) v. **-dled, -dling.** interfere; meddle.

in·ter·me·di·ar·y (in′tər mē′dē er′ē) n., adj. —n. 1 a person who deals with each side in settling a dispute, negotiating a business arangement, etc., go-between: *She acted as intermediary in the land deal between the city and the developer.* 2 a medium; means. 3 an intermediate form or stage. —adj. 1 acting between two persons or groups as an intermediary: *an intermediary agent.* 2 being between; intermediate: *A chrysalis is an intermediary stage between caterpillar and butterfly.* [< L *intermedius* intermediate < *inter-* between + *medius* in the middle]

in·ter·me·di·ate (in′tər mē′dē it) adj., n., v. —adj. being or occurring between extremes or in a middle stage, place, or degree: *Grey is intermediate between black and white. The language school offers only beginning and intermediate courses in French.* —n. 1 the second largest of the four basic sizes of automobile, generally larger than a compact and smaller than a standard. 2 anything intermediate. 3 intermediary; go-between. 4 a compound formed between the initial and final stages in a chemical process. —v. act as intermediary; mediate. [< Med.L *intermediatus* < L *intermedius* < *inter-* between + *medius* in the middle]

in·ter·ment (in tèr′mənt) n. the act of putting a dead body into a grave or tomb; burial.

in·ter·mez·zo (in′tər met′sō or -med′zō) n., pl. **-mez·zos, -mez·zi** (-met′sē or -med′zē). 1 a short dramatic, musical, or other entertainment of a light character between the acts of a drama or opera. 2 *Music.* **a** a short composition between the main divisions of an extended musical work. **b** an independent composition of similar character. [< Ital.]

in·ter·mi·na·ble (in tèr′mə nə bəl) adj. endless or so long as to seem endless; very long and tiring: *an interminable speech.* [ME < LL *interminabilis*, ult. < L *in-* not + *terminare* to end] —**in·ter′mi·na·ble·ness,** n. —**in·ter′mi·na·bly,** adv.

in·ter·min·gle (in′tər ming′gəl) v. **-gled, -gling.** mix together; mingle.

in·ter·mis·sion (in′tər mish′ən) n. 1 a time between periods of activity; a pause, especially between acts of a play, parts of a musical performance, etc.: *There were two fifteen-minute intermissions in the performance.* 2 a stopping for a time; interruption: *The rain continued all day without intermission.* [< L *intermissio, -onis* < *intermittere.* See INTERMIT.]

in·ter·mit (in′tər mit′) v. **-mit·ted, -mit·ting.** stop for a time. [< L *intermittere* < *inter-* between + *mittere* leave]

in·ter·mit·tent (in′tər mit′ənt) adj. stopping and beginning again; pausing at intervals. —**in′ter·mit′tent·ly,** adv.

in·ter·mix (in′tər miks′) v. mix or become mixed together; blend: *Oil and water do not intermix.*

in·ter·mix·ture (in′tər miks′chər) n. 1 a mixing together. 2 a mass of ingredients mixed together.

in·ter·mon·tane (in′tər mon tān′) adj. between or among mountains.

in·ter·mus·cu·lar (in′tər mus′kyə lər) adj. found or set between muscles or muscle fibres.

in·tern¹ (v. in tèrn′; n. in′tèrn) v., n. —v. confine within a country or place; force to stay in a certain place, especially during a war: *Aliens are sometimes interned in wartime.* —n. internee. [< F *interner* < *interne* inner, internal < L *internus* < *in* in] ☛ *Usage.* See note at **inter.**

in·tern² (in′tèrn) n., v. —n. 1 a medical doctor working as an assistant in a hospital. A doctor has to serve at least one year as an intern before he can practise medicine on his own. 2 a recent graduate, etc. in any of various other fields undergoing supervised practical training. —v. act as an intern. [< F *interne* < *interne*, adj. See INTERN¹.]

in·ter·nal (in tèr′nəl) adj. 1 inner; on the inside: *internal injuries.*

2 to be taken inside the body: *internal remedies*. **3** entirely inside; coming from within: *The date of the author's death is unknown, but events in the poem provide internal evidence that she was still alive in 1920*. **4** having to do with affairs within a country; domestic: *internal disturbances*. **5** of the mind; subjective: *Thoughts are internal*. [< Med.L *internalis* < L *internus* within < *in* in] —**in·ter′nal·ly,** *adv.*

internal–combustion engine 1 an engine in which the power comes from each piston being moved by explosions within its cylinder. **2** a gas-turbine engine that uses for its power the gas formed by burning or exploding fuel.

internal medicine the branch of medicine dealing with the diagnosis and nonsurgical treatment of diseases.

in·ter·na·tion·al (in′tər nash′ən əl *or* -nash′nəl) *adj.*, *n.* —*adj.* **1** between or among nations: *international trade*. **2** accepted by or agreed on by many or all nations: *an international driver's licence, an international unit of measure, international law*. **3** for the use of all nations: *international waters*. —*n.* **International,** any of several international socialist or communist organizations. —**in′ter·na′tion·al·ly,** *adv.*

International Date Line date line (def. 1).

In·ter·na·tio·nale (in′tər nash′ə näl *or* -nash′nəl; *French,* an ter nä syô näl′) *n.* the anthem of the international socialist and Communist organizations of the late 19th and early 20th centuries and the national anthem of the Soviet Union until 1944. [< F]

in·ter·na·tion·al·ism (in′tər nash′ən əl iz′əm *or* -nash′nə liz′əm) *n.* **1** the principle of international co-operation for the good of all nations. **2** international quality, character, interests, etc.

in·ter·na·tion·al·ist (in′tər nash′ən əl ist *or* -nash′nə list) *n.* a person who favors internationalism.

in·ter·na·tion·al·ize (in′tər nash′ən əl īz′ *or* -nash′nə līz′) *v.* **-ized, -iz·ing.** make international; bring (territory) under the control of several nations. —**in′ter·na′tion·al·i·za′tion,** *n.*

International Joint Commission a committee set up by Canada and the United States to settle possible disputes between the two countries concerning boundary waters.

in·terne (in′tèrn) See **intern²**.

in·ter·ne·cine (in′tər nē′sən, -nē′sīn *or* -nes′ēn) *adj.* **1** destructive to both sides. **2** deadly; destructive. [< L *internecinus* < *internecere* kill < *inter-* between + *nex, necis* slaughter]

in·tern·ee (in′tèr nē′) *n.* a person who is interned.

in·tern·ist (in′tər nist′ *or* in tèr′nist) *n.* a specialist in internal medicine, as distinguished from a surgeon, obstetrician, etc.

in·tern·ment (in tèrn′mənt) *n.* interning or being interned.

in·tern·ship (in′tèrn ship′) *n.* a position or period of service as an intern.

in·ter·o·ce·an·ic (in′tər ō′shē an′ik) *adj.* between oceans.

in·ter·pel·late (in′tər pel′āt *or* in tèr′pə lāt′) *v.* **-lat·ed, -lat·ing.** make an interpellation. [< L *interpellare* interrupt]

in·ter·pel·la·tion (in′tər pə lā′shən *or* in tèr′-) *n.* a formal request in a legislature for an explanation of official action or government policy.

in·ter·pen·e·trate (in′tər pen′ə trāt′) *v.* **-trat·ed, trat·ing.** penetrate thoroughly; permeate. —**in′ter·pen′e·tra′tion,** *n.*

in·ter·phone (in′tər fōn′) *n.* intercom.

in·ter·plan·e·tar·y (in′tər plan′ə ter′ē) *adj.* **1** existing or taking place between the planets; within the solar system, but outside the atmosphere of any of the planets or the sun: *interplanetary space*. **2** carried on between planets: *interplanetary travel*.

in·ter·play (in′tər plā′) *n.*, *v.* —*n.* the action or influence of things on each other; interaction: *the interplay of light and shadow*. —*v.* exert mutual influence; have reciprocal action.

In·ter·pol (in′tər pōl′ *or* in′tər pol′) *n.* an international organization of the criminal police forces of more than 100 countries, whose aim is to provide the greatest possible mutual assistance among the members, within the limits of the law in each country, for the prevention and suppression of crime. Its headquarters is in Paris. [*International poli*ce]

in·ter·po·late (in tèr′pə lāt′) *v.* **-lat·ed, -lat·ing. 1** alter (a book, passage, etc.) by putting in new words or groups of words. **2** put in (new words, passages, etc.). **3** *Mathematics*. insert (intermediate terms) in a series. **4** insert or introduce (something additional or different) between other things, or in a series; interpose. [< L *interpolare* freshen up]

in·ter·po·la·tion (in tèr′pə lā′shən) *n.* **1** the act of interpolating. **2** something interpolated.

in·ter·pose (in′tər pōz′) *v.* **-posed, -pos·ing. 1** put between; insert. **2** put forward; break in with; introduce as an interruption: *She interposed an objection.* **3** intervene in a dispute; mediate: *He quickly interposed between the angry children.* [< F *interposer* < *inter-* between (< L *inter-*) + *poser* place (see POSE¹)] —**in′ter·pos′er,** *n.*

in·ter·po·si·tion (in′tər pə zish′ən) *n.* **1** interposing. **2** the thing interposed.

in·ter·pret (in tèr′prit) *v.* **1** explain the meaning of: *to interpret a difficult passage in a book, to interpret a dream.* **2** bring out the meaning of dramatic part, a character, music, etc. **3** understand according to one's own judgment: *We interpreted your silence as consent.* **4** serve as an interpreter; translate orally for speakers of different languages. [< L *interpretari* < *interpres, -pretis* negotiator] ☞ *Syn.* **1.** See note at **explain.**

in·ter·pre·ta·tion (in tèr′prə tā′shən) *n.* **1** an interpreting; explanation: *different interpretations of the same facts.* **2** a bringing out of the meaning of a dramatic part, a piece of music, etc. **3** the explanation of the purpose and importance of national and provincial park systems and the influence of park visitors on the ecology of a park. **4** oral translation.

in·ter·pre·ta·tive (in tèr′prə tā′tiv *or* in tèr′prə tə tiv) *adj.* **1** used for interpreting; explanatory. **2** of, having to do with, or referring to the interpretation of parks and park systems. All Canada's national parks have interpretative programs. —**in′ter′pre·ta·tive·ly,** *adv.*

in·ter·pret·er (in tèr′prə tər) *n.* a person who interprets, especially one whose work is translating a language orally, as in a conversation between people who do not understand each other's language.

in·ter·pre·tive (in tèr′prə tiv) *adj.* interpretative. —**in·ter′pre·tive·ly,** *adv.*

in·ter·pro·vin·cial (in′tər prə vin′shəl) *adj.* **1** between or among provinces. **2** connecting two or more provinces: *an interprovincial highway.* —**in′ter·pro·vin′cial·ly,** *adv.*

in·ter·ra·cial (in′tər rā′shəl) *adj.* between or involving different races. —**in′ter·ra′cial·ly,** *adv.*

in·ter·reg·num (in′tər reg′nəm) *n.*, *pl.* **-nums, -na** (-nə). **1** the time between the end of one ruler's reign and the beginning of the next one. **2** any time during which a nation is without its usual ruler or government. **3** a period of inactivity; pause. [< L *interregnum* < *inter-* between + *regnum* reign]

in·ter·re·late (in′tər ri lāt′) *v.* **-lat·ed, -lat·ing.** relate to one another; connect: *The two proposals are interrelated.*

in·ter·ro·gate (in ter′ə gāt′) *v.* **-gat·ed, -gat·ing. 1** ask questions of, especially formally and systematically; examine by asking questions: *The lawyer took two hours to interrogate the witness.* **2** ask a series of questions. [< L *interrogare* < *inter-* between + *rogare* ask] ☞ *Syn.* **1, 2.** See note at **question.**

in·ter·ro·ga·tion (in ter′ə gā′shən) *n.* **1** a questioning. The formal examination of a witness by asking questions is an interrogation. **2** a question.

interrogation mark *or* **point** a question mark (?).

in·ter·rog·a·tive (in′tə rog′ə tiv) *adj.*, *n.* —*adj.* **1** of or having the form of a question: *an interrogative look or tone of voice.* **2** *Grammar.* used in asking questions: *an interrogative pronoun.* —*n. Grammar.* an interrogative word, especially a pronoun: *Who, why,* and *what* are interrogatives. —**in′ter·rog′a·tive·ly,** *adv.*

in·ter·ro·ga·tor (in ter′ə gā′tər) *n.* questioner.

in·ter·rog·a·to·ry (in′tə rog′ə tô′rē) *adj.*, *n.*, *pl.* **-to·ries.** —*adj.* questioning. —*n.* a formal question or set of questions.

in·ter·rupt (in′tə rupt′) *v.* **1** break in upon (talk, work, rest, a person speaking, etc.); hinder; stop. **2** break the continuity of; obstruct: *A building interrupts the view from our window.* **3** cause a break; break in: *It is not polite to interrupt when someone is talking.* [ME < L *interruptus,* pp. of *interrumpere* < *inter-* between + *rumpere* break] —**in′ter·rupt′er,** *n.*

in·ter·rup·tion (in′tə rup′shən) *n.* **1** interrupting or being interrupted. **2** something that interrupts. **3** an intermission.

in·ter·scho·las·tic (in′tər skə las′tik) *adj.* between schools: *interscholastic competition.* ☞ *Usage.* See note at **intramural.**

in·ter·sect (in′tər sekt′) *v.* **1** cut or divide by passing through or crossing: *Draw a line to intersect two parallel lines at an angle of 45°.* **2** cross each other: *Streets usually intersect at right angles.* [< L *intersectus,* pp. of *intersecare* < *inter-* between + *secare* cut]

in·ter·sec·tion (in′tər sek′shən *or* in′tər sek′shən) *n.* **1** the act or process of intersecting: *the intersection of two lines. Bridges and overpasses are used to avoid the intersection of a railway and a highway.* **2** a point, line, or place where two or more things cross each other: *The light changed just before we got to the intersection.*

3 *Mathematics.* the set of points or other elements common to two or more given sets.

in·ter·ses·sion (in′tər sesh′ən) *n.* a university session in late spring, similar to summer school, at which a student may take one full course in a five or six-week period.

in·ter·space (*n.* in′tər spās′; *v.* in′tər spās′) *n., v.* **-spaced, -spac·ing.** —*n.* a space between things; an interval. —*v.* **1** put a space between. **2** occupy or fill the space between.

in·ter·sperse (in′tər spèrs′) *v.* **-spersed, -spers·ing. 1** decorate or vary with other things put here and there: *The lawn was interspersed with beds of flowers. He interspersed his talk with amusing anecdotes.* **2** scatter or place here and there: *He interspersed amusing anecdotes throughout his talk.* [< L *interspersus* scattered < *inter-* between + *spargere* scatter]

in·ter·sper·sion (in′tər spèr′zhən *or* in′tər spèr′shən) *n.* an interspersing or being interspersed.

in·ter·state (in′tər stāt′) *adj.* between states: *an interstate highway.*

in·ter·stel·lar (in′tər stel′ər) *adj.* **1** existing between or among the stars: *interstellar space.* **2** carried on between stars or star systems: *dreams of interstellar travel.*

in·ter·stice (in tèr′stis) *n., pl.* **-sti·ces** (-stə sēz′). a small or narrow space between things or parts; chink. [< LL *interstitium* < L *inter-* between < *stare* to stand]

in·ter·sti·tial (in′tər stish′əl) *adj.* of, in, or forming interstices. —**in′ter·sti′tial·ly,** *adv.*

in·ter·tid·al (in′tər tī′dəl) *adj.* of, having to do with, or being the zone of a shore between the high-water and low-water marks.

in·ter·trib·al (in′tər trīb′əl) *adj.* between tribes. —**in′ter·trib′al·ly,** *adv.*

in·ter·twine (in′tər twīn′) *v.* **-twined, -twin·ing.** twine around each other; twist or become twisted together: *Two vines intertwined on the wall.*

in·ter·twist (in′tər twist′) *v.* twist one with another.

in·ter·ur·ban (in′tər èr′bən) *adj.* between cities or towns.

in·ter·val (in′tər vəl) *n.* **1** the time or space between: *an interval of a week, intervals of freedom from pain.* **2** *Music.* the difference in pitch between two tones. **3** intervale.
at intervals, a now and then: *Stir the pudding at intervals.* **b** here and there: *We saw many lakes at intervals along the way.* [< L *intervallum,* originally, space between palisades < *inter-* between + *vallum* wall]

in·ter·vale (in′tər vāl′) *n.* a low-lying area of rich land between hills or by a river. [< *interval,* influenced by *vale*[r]]

in·ter·vene (in′tər vēn′) *v.* **-vened, -ven·ing. 1** come or be between: *A week intervenes between Christmas and New Year's.* **2** come in to help settle a dispute: *The Prime Minister was asked to intervene in the railway strike.* [< L *intervenire* < *inter-* between + *venire* come] —**in′ter·ven′er,** *n.*

in·ter·ven·tion (in′tər ven′shən) *n.* **1** the act of intervening. **2** interference, especially by one nation in the affairs of another.

in·ter·ven·tion·ist (in′tər ven′shə nist) *n., adj.* —*n.* **1** a person who supports interference in the affairs of another country. **2** *Medicine.* a person who prefers medical action rather than letting a disease take its course. —*adj.* **1** of or having to do with intervention or interventionists. **2** approving intervention.

in·ter·view (in′tər vyü′) *n., v.* —*n.* **1** a meeting of people face to face, to talk over something special: *John applied for the job and had an interview with the manager.* **2** a meeting between a reporter, writer, radio or television commentator, etc. and a person from whom information is sought. **3** a printed report or broadcast of such a meeting. —*v.* meet and talk with, especially to obtain information: *Reporters interviewed the returning explorers.* [< F *entrevue* < *entrevoir* glimpse < L *inter-* between + *videre* see] —**in′ter·view′er,** *n.*

in·ter·weave (in′tər wēv′) *v.* **-wove** *or* **-weaved, -wo·ven** *or* **-wove** *or* **-weaved, -weav·ing. 1** weave together. **2** intermingle; blend; connect closely: *In his book he has interwoven the stories of two families.*

in·ter·wove (in′tər wōv′) *v.* a pt. and a pp. of **interweave.**

in·ter·wo·ven (in′tər wō′vən) *adj., v.* —*adj.* **1** woven together. **2** intermingled. —*v.* a pp. of **interweave.**

in·tes·ta·cy (in tes′tə sē) *n.* the condition of being intestate at death.

in·tes·tate (in tes′tāt *or* in tes′tit) *adj., n.* —*adj.* **1** having made no will. **2** not disposed of by a will. —*n.* a person who has died without making a will. [< L *intestatus* < *in-* not + *testari* make a will < *testis* witness]

in·tes·ti·nal (in tes′tə nəl) *adj.* of or in the intestines. —**in·tes′ti·nal·ly,** *adv.*

in·tes·tine (in tes′tən) *n., adj.* —*n.* **1** either of the two parts of

hat, āge, fär; let, ēqual, tèrm; it, īce
hot, ōpen, ôrder; oil, out; cup, pút, rüle,
above, takən, pencəl, lemən, circəs

ch, child; ng, long; sh, ship
th, thin; ₮H, then; zh, measure

the alimentary canal extending from the stomach to the anus. Partially digested food passes from the stomach into the small intestine for further digestion and for absorption of nutrients by the blood, and into the large intestine for elimination. In adults, the **small intestine** is about 640 cm long; the **large intestine** is about 165 cm long. See **alimentary canal** for picture. **2 intestines,** *pl.* the intestine; the bowels. —*adj.* within the country; internal: *Intestine strife is civil war.* [< L *intestina,* neut. pl., internal < *intus* within < *in* in]

in·thral (in throl′ *or* in thrôl′) *v.* enthral.

in·throne (in thrōn′) *v.* **-throned, -thron·ing.** enthrone.

in·ti·ma·cy (in′tə mə sē) *n., pl.* **-cies. 1** deep friendship; close association; being intimate. **2** a familiar or intimate act.

in·ti·mate[1] (in′tə mit) *adj., n.* —*adj.* **1** very familiar; known very well: *an intimate friend.* **2** resulting from close familiarity; close: *an intimate knowledge.* **3** personal; private: *A diary is a very intimate book.* **4** far within; inmost: *the intimate recesses of the heart.* —*n.* a close friend. [earlier *intime* < L *intimus* inmost (and, as a noun, close friend), superlative, to *in* in; later altered under the influence of L *intimatus,* pp. of *intimare.* See INTIMATE[2].] —**in′ti·mate·ly,** *adv.*
☛ *Syn.* **1.** See note at **familiar.**

in·ti·mate[2] (in′tə māt′) *v.* **-mat·ed, -mat·ing. 1** suggest indirectly; hint: *In his statement to the press, he intimated that an arrest would be made soon.* **2** announce; notify. [< L *intimare,* originally, press in < L *intimus* inmost. See INTIMATE[1].] —**in′ti·mat′er,** *n.*
☛ *Syn.* **1.** See note at **hint.**

in·ti·ma·tion (in′tə mā′shən) *n.* **1** an indirect suggestion; hint: *She said nothing, but her frown was an intimation of disapproval.* **2** an announcement; notice.

in·tim·i·date (in tim′ə dāt′) *v.* **-dat·ed, -dat·ing.** frighten, especially in order to influence or force: *The banker told police that the men had tried to intimidate him by telling him they were holding his wife as hostage.* [< Med.L *intimidare* < L *in-* + *timidus* fearful] —**in·tim′i·da′tion,** *n.* —**in·tim′i·da′tor,** *n.*

in·ti·tle (in tī′təl) *v.* **-tled, -tling.** entitle.

in·to (in′tü; *before consonants, often* in′tə) *prep.* **1** to the inside of; toward the inside; within: *to go into the house.* **2** to the condition of; to the form of: *to get into mischief, a house divided into ten rooms. Cold weather turns water into ice.* **3** to a further time in: *He worked on into the night.* **4** against: *He wasn't watching and ran into the wall.* **5** *Mathematics.* going into (implying or expressing division): *5 into 30 is 6.* **6** *Informal.* involved or concerned with: *He's really into philosophy these days.*
☛ *Usage.* See note at **in.**

in·tol·er·a·bil·i·ty (in tol′ər ə bil′ə tē) *n.* the quality of being intolerable.

in·tol·er·a·ble (in tol′ər ə bəl) *adj.* unbearable; too much, too painful, etc. to be endured. [< L *intolerabilis*] —**in·tol′er·a·ble·ness,** *n.*

in·tol·er·a·bly (in tol′ər ə blē) *adv.* unbearably; beyond endurance.

in·tol·er·ance (in tol′ər əns) *n.* **1** lack of tolerance; unwillingness to let others do and think as they choose, especially in matters of religion. **2** being unable or unwilling to endure: *intolerance to penicillin, intolerance of popular music.*

in·tol·er·ant (in tol′ər ənt) *adj.* **1** not tolerant; unwilling to let others do and think as they choose, especially in matters of religion. **2** unwilling to accept persons of different races, backgrounds, etc. as equals. **3** unable or unwilling to endure (*used with* **of**): *intolerant of certain drugs, intolerant of criticism.* —**in·tol′er·ant·ly,** *adv.*

in·tomb (in tüm′) *v.* entomb.

in·to·na·tion (in′tō nā′shən *or* in′tə nā′shən) *n.* **1** the act of intoning: *the intonation of a psalm.* **2** the opening phrase of a Gregorian chant. **3** the production of musical tones. **4** the manner of uttering or sounding words: *She has a monotonous intonation.* **5** *Linguistics.* the sound pattern of speech produced by differences in stress and pitch: *British intonation is different from standard Canadian intonation. The English sentence* she's gone *is a question if spoken with a rising intonation and a statement if spoken with a falling intonation.*

in·tone (in tōn′) *v.* **-toned, -ton·ing. 1** read or recite in a singing voice; chant. **2** utter with a particular tone. **3** make musical sounds,

especially in a slow, drawn-out manner. [ME < Med.L *intonare,* ult. < L *in-* in + *tonus* tone]

in to·to (in′ tō′tō) *Latin.* as a whole; completely.

in·tox·i·cant (in tok′sə kənt) *n., adj.* —*n.* something that intoxicates, especially alcoholic liquor. —*adj.* intoxicating: *an intoxicant drug.*

in·tox·i·cate (in tok′sə kāt′) *v.* **-cat·ed, -cat·ing. 1** make drunk: *Too much wine intoxicates people.* **2** excite greatly; exhilarate: *The early election returns intoxicated her supporters with thoughts of victory.* [< Med.L *intoxicare,* ult. < L *in-* in + *toxicum* poison < Gk. *toxicon (pharmakon)* (poison) for shooting arrows < *toxon* bow. Related to TOXIC.] —**in·tox′i·cat′ing·ly,** *adv.*

in·tox·i·cat·ed (in tok′sə kāt′id) *adj.* **1** drunk. **2** greatly excited. —**in·tox′i·cat′ed·ly,** *adv.*

in·tox·i·cat·ing (in tok′sə kā′ting) *adj.* that intoxicates: *intoxicating drinks, intoxicating beauty.* —**in·tox′i·cat′ing·ly,** *adv.*

in·tox·i·ca·tion (in tok′sə kā′shən) *n.* **1** drunkenness. **2** great excitement. **3** *Medicine.* poisoning.

intr. intransitive.

intra– *prefix.* within or inside, as in *intravenous.* [< L *intra-* < *intra,* prep., adv.]

in·trac·ta·bil·i·ty (in trak′tə bil′ə tē) *n.* the quality of being intractable; stubbornness.

in·trac·ta·ble (in trak′tə bəl) *adj.* hard to manage; stubborn. —**in·trac′ta·bly,** *adv.*

in·tra·dos (in trā′dos) *n. Architecture.* the interior curve or surface of an arch or vault. [< F < L *intra-* within + F *dos* back]

in·tra·mu·ral (in′trə myür′əl) *adj.* within the walls; inside. In intramural games, all the players belong to the same school.
☛ *Usage.* **Intramural** is written without a hyphen. It is applied specifically to school activities carried on by groups belonging to the same school, as contrasted with **intercollegiate,** which is applied to activities of groups belonging to different schools.

intrans. intransitive.

in·tran·si·gence (in tran′sə jəns) *n.* the quality of being intransigent; uncompromising hostility.

in·tran·si·gen·cy (in tran′sə jən sē) *n.* intransigence.

in·tran·si·gent (in tran′sə jənt) *adj., n.* —*adj.* unwilling to agree or compromise. —*n.* a person who is unwilling to agree or compromise. [< F < Sp. *los intransigentes,* name for various extreme political parties, ult. < L *in-* not + *transigere* come to an agreement < *trans-* through + *agere* drive] —**in·tran′si·gent·ly,** *adv.*

in·tran·si·tive (in tran′sə tiv) *adj., n.* —*adj. Grammar.* not taking a direct object. The verbs *belong, go,* and *seem* are intransitive. —*n.* an intransitive verb. *Abbrev.:* intr., intrans. —**in·tran′si·tive·ly,** *adv.*
☛ *Usage.* See note at **verb.**

in·tra·u·ter·ine (in′trə yü′tə rən *or* -yü′tə rīn′) *adj.* within the uterus.

intrauterine device a contraceptive device usually in the form of a metal or plastic loop, coil, or ring that is inserted and left in the uterus. *Abbrev.:* IUD

in·tra·ve·nous (in′trə vē′nəs) *adj.* **1** within a vein or the veins. **2** into a vein: *an intravenous injection.* [< *intra-* + L *vena* vein] —**in′tra·ve′nous·ly,** *adv.*

in·treat (in trēt′) *v.* entreat.

in·trench (in trench′) *v.* entrench.

in·trench·ment (in trench′mənt) *n.* entrenchment.

in·trep·id (in trep′id) *adj.* fearless; dauntless; courageous; very brave. [< L *intrepidus* < *in-* not + *trepidus* alarmed] —**in·trep′id·ly,** *adv.*

in·tre·pid·i·ty (in′trə pid′ə tē) *n.* fearlessness; dauntless courage; great bravery.

in·tri·ca·cy (in′trə kə sē) *n., pl.* **-cies. 1** the state or quality of being intricate; complexity: *They admired the delicacy and intricacy of the design.* **2** something intricate: *the intricacies of international diplomacy.*

in·tri·cate (in′trə kit) *adj.* **1** with many twists and turns; entangled or complicated: *an intricate knot, an intricate maze, an intricate plot.* **2** very hard to understand; obscure or puzzling: *an intricate problem.* [< L *intricatus* < *intricare* entangle, ult. < *in-* in + *tricae* hindrances] —**in′tri·cate·ly,** *adv.* —**in′tri·cate·ness,** *n.*

in·trigue (*n.* in trēg′ *or* in′trēg; *v.* in trēg′) *n., v.* **-trigued, -tri·guing.** —*n.* **1** underhand planning; secret scheming; plotting: *The royal palace was filled with intrigue.* **2** a crafty plot; a secret scheme. **3** a secret love affair. **4** the plot of a play, dramatic poem, etc., especially the development of a complex or involved situation. —*v.* **1** carry on an underhand plan; scheme secretly; plot. **2** excite the curiosity and interest of: *The book's unusual title intrigued me.*

3 have a secret love affair. **4** interest in a pleasing way: *That lady's hat intrigues me.* [< F < Ital. *intrigo* < *intrigare* < L *intricare* entangle. See INTRICATE.] —**in·tri′guer,** *n.* —**in·tri′guing·ly,** *adv.*

in·trin·sic (in trin′sik) *adj.* **1** belonging to a thing by its very nature; essential; inherent: *The intrinsic value of a dollar bill is only that of the paper it is printed on.* **2** *Anatomy.* originating or being inside the part on which it acts: *the intrinsic muscles of the larynx.* [< F < Med.L *intrinsecus* internal < L *intrinsecus* inwardly]

in·trin·si·cal (in trin′sə kəl) *adj.* intrinsic.

in·trin·si·cal·ly (in trin′sik lē) *adv.* by its very nature; essentially; inherently.

intro– *prefix.* **1** in or into, as in *introduce.* **2** inward or within, as in *introvert.* Compare **extro-.** [< L *intro-* < *intro,* adv.]

intro. *or* **introd.** introduction; introductory.

in·tro·duce (in′trə dyüs′ *or* in′trə düs′) *v.* **-duced, -duc·ing. 1** bring in: *to introduce a new subject into the conversation.* **2** put in; insert: *The doctor introduced a long tube into the man's throat.* **3** bring into use, notice, knowledge, etc.: *to introduce a reform, to introduce a new word.* **4** make known: *The chairman introduced the speaker to the audience.* **5** bring to acquaintance with something: *I introduced my country cousin to the city by showing him the sights.* **6** bring forward: *to introduce a question for debate.* **7** begin; start: *He introduced his speech with a joke.* [< L *introducere* < *intro-* in + *ducere* lead] —**in′tro·duc′er,** *n.*
☛ *Syn.* **4, 5. Introduce, present** = make someone known to another or others. **Introduce** = make a person known, in a more or less formal way, to another or to a group, or to make two people acquainted with each other: *Mrs. Brown, may I introduce Mr. Smith?* **Present,** always suggesting formality, means "introduce, with more or less ceremony, a person or group to one regarded or treated as superior": *The new ambassador was presented to the Governor General.*

in·tro·duc·tion (in′trə duk′shən) *n.* **1** introducing or being introduced: *The introduction of steel revolutionized the construction industry. They were waiting for an introduction to him.* **2** a preliminary part of a book, speech, musical composition, etc. that leads into the main part or gives information necessary for understanding the main part. **3** a first book for beginners in a given field of study: *an introduction to biology.* **4** something introduced; a thing brought into use: *Radios are a later introduction than telephones.* [ME < L *introductio, -onis* < *introducere.* See INTRODUCE.]
☛ *Syn.* **3. Introduction, preface, foreword** = a section at the beginning of a book, etc. **Introduction** applies to an actual part of the book, article, play, etc. that leads into or gives what is necessary for understanding the main part: *School editions of literary works usually have introductions.* **Preface** applies to a separate section coming before the actual book, explaining something, such as the purpose, method, importance, etc. **Foreword** may mean a short, simple preface but applies especially to an introductory note on the book or the author by a distinguished writer, scholar, or public figure: *A foreword by the President of the University came before the author's preface.*

in·tro·duc·to·ry (in′trə duk′tə rē *or* in′trə duk′trē) *adj.* used to introduce; serving as an introduction; preliminary.

in·tro·it (in trō′it) *n.* **1** *Roman Catholic Church.* a hymn or responsive anthem recited by the priest at the beginning of Mass or sung by the choir at High Mass. **2** *Anglican Church.* a psalm, hymn, etc. at the beginning of the communion service. [ME < L *introitus* entrance < *introire* enter < *intro-* in + *ire* go]

in·trorse (in trôrs′) *adj. Botany.* turned or facing inward. A violet has introrse stamens. [< L *introrsus,* ult. < *intro-* inward + *versus* turned]

in·tro·spec·tion (in′trə spek′shən) *n.* examination and analysis of one's own thoughts and feelings. [< L *introspectus,* pp. of *introspicere* < *intro-* into + *specere* look]

in·tro·spec·tive (in′trə spek′tiv) *adj.* inclined to examine one's own thoughts and feelings. —**in′tro·spec′tive·ly,** *adv.*

in·tro·ver·sion (in′trə vėr′zhən *or* -vėr′shən) *n.* **1** a tendency to be more interested in one's own thoughts and feelings than in other persons or in what is going on around one. Compare **extroversion.** **2** the act or fact of turning inward. [< *intro-* + *version,* as in *reversion,* etc.]

in·tro·vert (in′trə vėrt′) *n.* a person more interested in his own thoughts and feelings than in other persons or in what is going on around him; a person who is thoughtful rather than active or expressive. Compare **extrovert.** [< *intro-* within + L *vertere* turn]

in·trude (in trüd′) *v.* **-trud·ed, -trud·ing. 1** thrust oneself in; come unasked and unwanted: *If you are busy, I will not intrude.* **2** give when not wanted; force in: *Do not intrude your opinions upon others.* [< L *intrudere* < *in-* in + *trudere* thrust] —**in·trud′er,** *n.*
☛ *Syn.* **1. Intrude, trespass, encroach** = thrust oneself into or upon the presence, possessions, territory, or rights of others. **Intrude** = thrust in, without permission, where uninvited, unwanted, or having no right to go: *He intrudes upon their hospitality.* **Trespass** = intrude unlawfully or by overstepping the limits of what is proper or right: *Joe trespassed on another boy's paper route.* **Encroach** adds the idea of gradually or secretly taking the property or rights of another: *Our neighbor's irrigation system is encroaching on our land.*

in·tru·sion (in trü′zhən) *n.* **1** the act of intruding; coming unasked and unwanted. **2** an unlawful entry or seizure of land or rights belonging to another. **3** *Geology.* **a** the forcing of molten rock into fissures or between strata. **b** the molten rock forced in and solidified in place. [ME < Med.L *intrusio, -onis* < L *intrusus,* pp. of *intrudere.* See INTRUDE.]

in·tru·sive (in trü′siv) *adj.* **1** intruding; coming unasked and unwanted. **2** *Geology.* forced into fissures or between strata while molten. **3** *Phonetics.* inserted without any etymological or historical basis. The (r) often heard in *khaki* (kär′kē) is intrusive. —**in·tru′sive·ly,** *adv.*

in·trust (in trust′) *v.* entrust.

in·tu·it (in tyü′ət *or* in tü′ət) *v.* know or learn by intuition.

in·tu·i·tion (in′tyü ish′ən *or* in′tü ish′ən) *n.* **1** immediate perception or understanding of truths, facts, etc. without reasoning: *His intuition told him that the strangers were not what they appeared to be.* **2** something known or understood in this way. [< LL *intuitio, -onis* a gazing at < L *intueri* < *in-* at + *tueri* look]

in·tu·i·tion·al (in′tyü ish′ən əl *or* in′tü ish′ən əl) *adj.* of, having to do with, or characterized by, intuition; based on intuition. —**in·tu·i′tion·al·ly,** *adv.*

in·tu·i·tive (in tyü′ə tiv *or* in tü′ə tiv) *adj.* **1** perceiving by intuition: *intuitive power.* **2** acquired by intuition: *intuitive knowledge.* **3** of the nature of an intuition: *an intuitive guess.* —**in·tu′i·tive·ly,** *adv.*

I·nu·it (in′ü it, *or* in′yü it, *or* in′yə wit) *n., adj.* —*n.pl.* Cdn. a people living mainly in northern Canada, Greenland, Alaska, and eastern Siberia, who are the original inhabitants of the Arctic; the Eskimo people. —*adj.* of or having to do with the Inuit. [< Inuktitut (Eskimo) *inuit,* pl. of *inuk* man, person]
☛ *Usage.* In Canada, **Inuit** is now the preferred term, although many people still use the term **Eskimos.**

I·nuk (in′ùk) *n., pl.* **I·nu·it.** Cdn. a member of the Inuit.

i·nuk·shuk (i nùk′shùk) *n., pl.* **i·nuk·shuks** *or* **i·nuk·shu·it.** Cdn. a stone cairn having the rough outline of a human figure. Inukshuks were traditionally built by the Inuit to serve as landmarks or, in some parts of the Arctic, in long rows to drive caribou toward waiting hunters. Also, **inukshook.** [< Inuktitut (Eskimo) *inukshuk* something in the shape of a man]

I·nuk·ti·tuk (i nùk′tə tùk′) *n.* Cdn. Inuktitut.

I·nuk·ti·tut (i nùk′tə tùt′) *n.* Cdn. the language of the Inuit. There are many dialects of Inuktitut. [< Inuktitut (Eskimo) *inuk* man, person + *titut* speech]

in·un·date (in′ən dāt′ *or* in un′dāt) *v.* **-dat·ed, -dat·ing. 1** overflow; flood. **2** overwhelm, as if by a flood: *The radio station was inundated by requests for the pamphlet.* [< L *inundare* < *in-* onto + *undare* flow < *unda* wave]

in·un·da·tion (in′ən dā′shən) *n.* an overflowing; flood.
☛ *Syn.* See note at **flood.**

in·ure (in yür′) *v.* **-ured, -ur·ing. 1** toughen or harden; accustom; habituate: *Many years in the wilderness had inured them to hardships.* **2** especially of a law or agreement, take or have effect; become operative: *The agreement inures to the benefit of the employees.* [< *in* + obs. *ure* use, n. < AF *ure* < L *opera* work] —**in·ure′ment,** *n.*

inv. 1 invoice. **2** inventor; invented. **3** inventory. **4** investment.

in va·cu·o (in′vak′yü ō′) *Latin.* in a vacuum.

in·vade (in vād′) *v.* **-vad·ed, -vad·ing. 1** enter with force or as an enemy: *Soldiers invaded the country. Diseases invade the body.* **2** enter as if to take possession: *Tourists invaded the city. Night invades the sky.* **3** interfere with; break in on; violate: *The law punishes people who invade the rights of others.* [< L *invadere* < *in-* in + *vadere* go, walk] —**in·vad′er,** *n.*

in·va·lid¹ (in′və lid) *n., adj., v.* —*n.* a person who is weak because of sickness or injury: *An invalid cannot get about and do things.* —*adj.* **1** not well; disabled. **2** of or for an invalid or invalids. —*v.* **1** make weak or sick; disable. **2** release or retire from active service because of sickness or injury: *He was invalided out of the army.* [< L *invalidus* not strong; pronunciation influenced by F *invalide* (< L *invalidus*). 17c. See INVALID².]

in·val·id² (in val′id) *adj.* not valid; without force or effect; worthless: *If a will is not signed, it is invalid.* [< L *invalidus* < *in-* not + *validus* strong < *valere* be strong. 16c.] —**in·val′id·ly,** *adv.*

in·val·i·date (in val′ə dāt′) *v.* **-dat·ed, -dat·ing.** make valueless; deprive of force or effect: *A contract is invalidated if only one party signs it.* —**in·val′i·da′tion,** *n.* —**in′val′i·da′tor,** *n.*

in·va·lid·ism (in′və lid iz′əm) *n.* the condition of being an invalid; prolonged ill health.

in·va·lid·i·ty (in′və lid′ə tē) *n.* a lack of validity, force, or effect; worthlessness.

in·val·u·a·ble (in val′yə bəl *or* in val′yü ə bəl) *adj.*

hat, āge, fär; let, ēqual, tèrm; it, īce
hot, ōpen, ôrder; oil, out; cup, pùt, rüle,
əbove, takən, pencəl, lemən, circəs

ch, child; ng, long; sh, ship
th, thin; ҍн, then; zh, measure

priceless; very precious; valuable beyond measure. —**in·val′u·a·bly,** *adv.* —**in·val′u·a·ble·ness,** *n.*

in·var·i·a·bil·i·ty (in ver′ē ə bil′ə tē) *n.* unchangeableness; constancy; uniformity.

in·var·i·a·ble (in ver′ē ə bəl) *adj.* always the same; unchangeable; unchanging. —**in·var′i·a·bly,** *adv.*

in·va·sion (in vā′zhən) *n.* **1** the act of invading. **2** interference; encroachment; infringement: *She objected to the invasion of her privacy.* [< LL *invasio, -onis* < *invadere.* See INVADE.]

in·vec·tive (in vek′tiv) *n.* a violent attack in words; abusive language. [ME < LL *invectivus* abusive < L *invehi.* See INVEIGH.]

in·veigh (in vā′) *v.* make a violent attack in words; complain bitterly (*used with* **against**): *He inveighed against the poor working conditions in the factory.* [< L *invehi* launch an attack < *in-* against + *vehere* carry]

in·vei·gle (in vā′gəl *or* in vē′gəl) *v.* **-gled, -gling.** win over by trickery; entice; lure: *The saleswoman inveigled the poor girl into buying four hats.* [apparently alteration of earlier *avegle < F aveugler* make blind < *aveugle* blind < VL *aboculus* < L *ab-* without + *oculus* eye] —**in·vei′gler,** *n.*

in·vent (in vent′) *v.* **1** make for the first time; think out (something new): *Alexander Graham Bell invented the telephone.* **2** make up; think up; fabricate: *to invent an excuse.* [< L *inventus,* pp. of *invenire* < *in-* in + *venire* come]

in·ven·tion (in ven′shən) *n.* **1** the act or process of inventing: *The Chinese are credited with the invention of gunpowder.* **2** the thing invented: *Radio was a wonderful invention.* **3** the power of inventing; inventiveness: *To be a good novelist, a person needs invention.* **4** a made-up story, especially a falsehood: *His account of the robbery was pure invention.* **5** *Music.* a short instrumental composition consisting of one or two simple melodies developed in two- or three-part harmony.

in·ven·tive (in ven′tiv) *adj.* **1** good at inventing: *An inventive person thinks up ways to save time, money, and work.* **2** of invention. **3** showing power of inventing. —**in·ven′tive·ly,** *adv.* —**in·ven′tive·ness,** *n.*

in·ven·tor (in ven′tər) *n.* a person who invents: *Alexander Graham Bell was a great inventor.*

in·ven·to·ry (in′vən tô′rē) *n., pl.* **-to·ries;** *v.* **-to·ried, -to·ry·ing.** —*n.* **1** a detailed list of articles with their estimated value. **2** a collection of articles that are or may be so listed; stock: *A storekeeper had a sale to reduce his inventory.* —*v.* make a detailed list of; enter in a list: *Some stores inventory their stock once a month.* [< Med.L *inventorium* < LL < *inventus,* pp. of *invenire.* See INVENT.]

in·ver·ness (in′vər nes′) *n.* **1** a man's overcoat, often sleeveless, with a waist-length removable cape. **2** the cape itself. [< *Inverness,* Scotland]

in·verse (in vèrs′ *or* in′vèrs) *adj., n.* —*adj.* reversed in position, direction, or tendency; inverted: *DCBA is the inverse order of ABCD.* —*n.* **1** something reversed: *The inverse of 3/4 is 4/3.* **2** direct opposite: *Evil is the inverse of good.* [< L *inversus,* pp. of *invertere.* See INVERT.] —**in·verse′ly,** *adv.*

in·ver·sion (in vèr′zhən *or* in vèr′shən) *n.* **1** inverting or being inverted. **2** something inverted.

inversion layer *Meteorology.* a layer of air warmer than the air beneath it.

in·vert (in vèrt′) *v.* **1** turn upside down: *to invert a glass.* **2** turn the other way; reverse in position, direction, order, etc.: *If you invert I can, you have Can I?* **3** *Music.* change by making the lower or lowest octave higher or the higher or highest note an octave lower. [< L *invertere* < *in-* over, around + *vertere* turn] —**in·vert′er,** *n.*
☛ *Syn.* **1.** See note at **reverse.**

in·ver·te·brate (in vèr′tə brāt′ *or* in vèr′tə brit) *n., adj.* —*n.* any animal lacking a backbone; any animal that is not a vertebrate, including annelids, molluscs, arthropods, and echinoderms (starfishes, etc.). —*adj.* **1** of, having to do with, or designating the invertebrates. **2** lacking character, conviction, or purpose.

in·vest (in vest′) *v.* **1** use (money) to buy something that is expected to produce a profit, or income, or both: *He invested his money in stocks, bonds, and land.* **2** invest money: *Learn to invest wisely.* **3** spend or put in (time, energy, etc.) for later benefit: *The*

volunteer group invested its energies in developing new playgrounds. **4** clothe; cover; surround: *Darkness invests the earth by night.* **5** give power, authority, or right to: *He invested his lawyer with complete power to act for him.* **6** install in office with a ceremony: *A king is invested by crowning him.* **7** surround with soldiers or ships; besiege: *The enemy invested the city and cut it off from our army.* [< L *investire* < *in-* in + *vestis* clothing]

in·ves·ti·gate (in ves′tə gāt′) *v.* **-gat·ed, -gat·ing.** search into carefully; examine closely: *to investigate a complaint. Detectives investigate crimes.* [< L *investigare* < *in-* in + *vestigare* track, trace]

in·ves·ti·ga·tion (in ves′tə gā′shən) *n.* a careful search; detailed or careful examination.

☛ *Syn.* **Investigation, examination, inquiry** = a search for information or truth. **Investigation** emphasizes carefully tracking down everything that can be found out, in order to bring out hidden facts and learn the truth: *An investigation of the accident by the police put the blame on the drivers of both cars.* **Examination** emphasizes looking something or someone over closely or testing carefully in order to learn the facts about it, its condition, value, etc.: *The doctor gave him a physical examination.* **Inquiry** especially suggests a search made by asking questions: *Counsellors began an inquiry into the industrial needs of the region.*

in·ves·ti·ga·tive (in ves′tə gā′tiv) *adj.* of, having to do with, involving, or involved in investigation: *investigative news reporting, superior investigative powers.*

in·ves·ti·ga·tor (in ves′tə gā′tər) *n.* a person who investigates.

in·ves·ti·ga·to·ry (in ves′tə gā tôr′ē) *adj.* investigative.

in·ves·ti·ture (in ves′tə chůr′ *or in* ves′tə chər) *n.* **1** a formal investing of a person with an office, dignity, power, right, etc. **2** clothing; apparel; covering.

in·vest·ment (in vest′mənt) *n.* **1** an investing; a laying out of money: *Getting an education is a wise investment of time and money.* **2** the amount of money invested: *His investments amount to thousands of dollars.* **3** something that is expected to yield money as income or profit or both: *Canada Savings Bonds are a safe investment.* **4** the act of surrounding with soldiers or ships; siege. **5** investiture.

in·ves·tor (in ves′tər) *n.* a person who invests money.

in·vet·er·a·cy (in vet′ər ə sē) *n.* a settled, fixed condition; the nature of a fixed habit.

in·vet·er·ate (in vet′ər it) *adj.* **1** confirmed in a habit, practice, feeling, etc.; habitual: *an inveterate smoker.* **2** long and firmly established: *Cats have an inveterate dislike of dogs.* [< L *inveteratus,* pp. of *inveterascere* make old < *in-* in + *veterascere* grow old < *vetus, -teris* old] **—in·vet′er·ate·ly,** *adv.*

in·vid·i·ous (in vid′ē əs) *adj.* likely to arouse ill will or resentment; giving offence because unfair or unjust: *Such comparisons are invidious.* [< L *invidiosus* < *invidia* envy. Related to ENVY.] **—in·vid′i·ous·ly,** *adv.* **—in·vid′i·ous·ness,** *n.*

in·vig·i·late (in vij′ə lāt′) *v.* **-lat·ed, -lat·ing.** supervise students, etc. writing an examination.

in·vig·or·ate (in vig′ər āt′) *v.* **-at·ed, -at·ing.** give vigor to; fill with life and energy. [< *in-* in + *vigor*] **—in·vig′or·at′ing·ly,** *adv.*

in·vig·or·a·tion (in vig′ər ā′shən) *n.* invigorating or being invigorated.

in·vin·ci·bil·i·ty (in vin′sə bil′ə tē) *n.* the quality of being invincible.

in·vin·ci·ble (in vin′sə bəl) *adj.* impossible to overcome; unconquerable: *an invincible opponent.* [ME < OF < L *invincibilis* < *in-* not + *vincere* conquer] **—in·vin′ci·bly,** *adv.*

in vi·no ve·ri·tas (in vē′nō ver′ə tas) *Latin.* intoxication makes people reveal their true thoughts; literally, in wine (there is) truth.

in·vi·o·la·bil·i·ty (in vī′ə lə bil′ə tē) *n.* the quality of being inviolable.

in·vi·o·la·ble (in vī′ə lə bəl) *adj.* **1** that must not be violated or injured; sacred: *an inviolable vow, an inviolable sanctuary.* **2** that cannot be violated or injured: *The gods are inviolable.* **—in·vi′o·la·bly,** *adv.*

in·vi·o·late (in vī′ə lit *or in* vī′ə lāt′) *adj.* not violated; uninjured; unbroken; not profaned. **—in·vi′o·late·ly,** *adv.*

in·vis·i·bil·i·ty (in viz′ə bil′ə tē) *n.* the state or quality of being invisible.

in·vis·i·ble (in viz′ə bəl) *adj., n. —adj.* **1** not visible; not capable of being seen: *Thought is invisible.* **2** not in sight; hidden: *The queen kept herself invisible in her palace.* **3** too small to be seen: *Bacteria are invisible.* **4** not easily seen; inconspicuous: *invisible mending.* **5** *Business.* **a** not listed in the regular financial statements: *an invisible asset.* **b** not appearing in returns of exports and imports,

but from which payment is accepted or made to a foreign country. **—n. 1** an invisible being or thing. **2 invisibles,** *pl. Business.* invisible exports or imports: *Insurance, freight, royalties, investment earnings, etc. are invisibles.* **3 the Invisible,** God.

in·vis·i·bly (in viz′ə blē) *adv.* without being seen; so as not to be seen.

in·vi·ta·tion (in′və tā′shən) *n.* **1** a request to come to some place or to do something. Formal invitations are written or printed. **2** the act of inviting. **3** attraction; enticement.

in·vite (*v.* in vīt′; *n.* in′vīt) *v.* **-vit·ed, -vit·ing;** *n. —v.* **1** ask (someone) politely to come to some place or to do something: *We invited her to join our club.* **2** make a polite request for: *The author invited our opinion of his story.* **3** give a chance for; tend to cause: *The letter invites some questions.* **4** attract; tempt: *The calm water invited us to swim.* **—n.** *Slang.* invitation. [< L *invitare*] **—in·vit′er,** *n.* ☛ *Syn. v.* **1.** See note at **call.**

in·vit·ing (in vīt′ing) *adj.* attractive; tempting. **—in·vit′ing·ly,** *adv.*

in·vo·ca·tion (in′və kā′shən) *n.* **1** the act of calling upon in prayer; appeal for help or protection: *A church service often begins with an invocation to God.* **2** the form of words used in this. **3 a** a calling forth of spirits by magic. **b** a set of magic words used to call forth spirits; incantation. **4** a formal appeal at or near the beginning of a long poem, in which the poet asks a Muse to give him inspiration. **5** *Law.* a call for evidence, papers, etc. from another case.

in·voice (in′vois) *n., v.* **-voiced, -voic·ing. —n. 1** a list of goods sent to a purchaser showing prices, amounts, shipping charges, etc. **2** a shipment of invoiced goods. **3** the form used for listing such goods. **—v.** make an invoice of; enter on an invoice. [earlier *invoyes,* pl. of *invoy,* var. of *envoy* < OF *envoy* < *envoier* send < VL < L *in via* on the way]

in·voke (in vōk′) *v.* **-voked, -vok·ing. 1** call on in prayer; appeal to for help, protection, blessing, etc.: *The missionaries invoked God's help in their undertaking.* **2** appeal to for confirmation or judgment: *to invoke an authority.* **3** ask earnestly for; beg for: *The condemned criminal invoked the judge's mercy.* **4** call forth by magic: *Aladdin invoked the genie of the magic lamp.* [< L *invocare* < *in-* on + *vocare* call] **—in·vok′er,** *n.*

in·vo·lu·cre (in′və lü′kər) *n. Botany.* one or more circles of small leaves, called bracts, around the base of a flower, flower cluster, or fruit. See **composite** for picture. [< F < L *involucrum* a cover < *involvere.* See INVOLVE.]

in·vol·un·tar·y (in vol′ən ter′ē) *adj.* **1** not voluntary; not done of one's own free will; unwilling. **2** not done on purpose; not intended: *An accident is involuntary.* **3** not controlled by the will: *Breathing is mainly involuntary.* **—in·vol′un·tar′i·ly,** *adv.* **—in·vol′un·tar′i·ness,** *n.*

in·vo·lute (*adj., n.* in′və lüt′, *v.* in′və lüt′) *adj., n., v.* **-lut·ed, -lut·ing. —adj. 1** involved; intricate. **2** rolled up on itself; curved spirally. **3** *Botany.* of a leaf or petal, having the margins rolled inward toward the centre. **4** of a shell, having closely coiled whorls. **—n.** *Geometry.* the curve formed by a given point on a taut thread as it is unwound from another curve on the same plane. **—v.** become involute. [< L *involutus,* pp. of *involvere.* See INVOLVE.]

in·vo·lu·tion (in′və lü′shən) *n.* **1** involving. **2** being involved; entanglement; complexity. **3** something involved; a complication. **4** *Mathematics.* the raising of a quantity to any power. **5** *Biology.* degeneration; retrograde change. **6** *Botany.* **a** a rolling inward from the edge. **b** a part thus formed.

in·volve (in volv′) *v.* **-volved, -volv·ing. 1** have as a necessary part, condition, or result; take in; include: *Housekeeping involves cooking, washing dishes, sweeping, and cleaning.* **2** have an effect on; affect: *These changes in the business involve the interests of all the owners.* **3** cause to be unpleasantly concerned; bring (into difficulty, danger, etc.): *One foolish mistake can involve you in a good deal of trouble.* **4** entangle; complicate: *A sentence that is involved is generally hard to understand.* **5** take up the attention of; occupy: *She was involved in working out a puzzle.* **6** wrap; enfold; envelop: *The outcome of the war is involved in doubt.* **7** wind spirally; coil: *The serpent involved his scaly folds.* **8** *Mathematics.* raise to a given power. [ME < L *involvere* < *in-* in + *volvere* roll] **—in·volv′er,** *n.*

☛ *Syn.* **3. Involve, implicate** = draw someone or something into a situation hard to get out of. **Involve** = get someone or something caught in a situation that is unpleasantly embarrassing, mixed up, or complex and hard to solve or settle: *Buying an expensive car involved him in debt. Telling one lie usually involves you in many more.* **Implicate** = show that someone is involved in or closely connected with something, usually disgraceful or bad: *Having the stolen goods in his possession implicated him in the robbery.*

in·volve·ment (in volv′mənt) *n.* involving or being involved.

in·vul·ner·a·bil·i·ty (in vul′nər ə bil′ə tē) *n.* the quality of being invulnerable.

in·vul·ner·a·ble (in vul′nər ə bəl) *adj.* **1** that cannot be wounded or injured: *Achilles was invulnerable except for his heel.* **2** proof against attack; not easily assailable: *an invulnerable argument.* —**in·vul′ner·a·bly,** *adv.*

in·ward (in′wərd) *adv., adj.* —*adv.* **1** toward the inside: *a passage leading inward.* **2** into the mind or soul: *Turn your thoughts inward.*
—*adj.* **1** placed within; internal: *the inward parts of the body.* **2** directed toward the inside: *an inward slant of the eyes.* **3** in mind or soul: *inward peace.* **4** intrinsic; inherent; essential: *the inward nature of the thing.* [OE *inweard*]

in·ward·ly (in′wərd lē) *adv.* **1** on the inside; within. **2** toward the inside or centre. **3** in the mind or soul. **4** not openly; secretly: *He was inwardly pleased but said nothing.*

in·ward·ness (in′wərd nis) *n.* **1** inner nature or meaning. **2** spirituality. **3** earnestness.

in·wards (*adv.* in′wərdz; *n.* in′ərdz) *adv., n.pl.* —*adv.* inward. —*n. Slang.* parts inside the body; stomach and intestines; innards.

in·weave (in wēv′) *v.* -**wove** or -**weaved,** -**wo·ven** or -**wove** or -**weaved,** -**weav·ing.** weave in; weave together; interweave.

in·wove (in wōv′) *v.* a pt. and a pp. of **inweave.**

in·wo·ven (in wō′vən) *v.* a pp. of **inweave.**

in·wrap (in rap′) *v.* -**wrapped,** -**wrap·ping.** enwrap.

in·wreathe (in rēтн′) *v.* -**wreathed,** -**wreath·ing.** enwreathe.

in·wrought (in rot′ *or* -rôt′) *adj.* **1** having a decoration worked in. **2** worked in. **3** mixed together; closely blended.

I·o (ī′ō) *n.* **1** *Greek mythology.* a maiden loved by Zeus, who changed her into a white heifer to save her from the jealousy of Hera. Hera, however, sent a gadfly to torment Io and caused her to wander through many lands until she reached Egypt, where Zeus restored her to her natural form. **2** Io moth.

Io ionium.

IODE *or* **I.O.D.E.** Imperial Order Daughters of the Empire.

i·o·dide (ī′ə dīd′ *or* ī′ə did) *n.* a compound of iodine with another element or radical.

i·o·dine (ī′ə dīn′ *or* ī′ə din; *in chemistry,* ī′ə dēn′) *n.* **1** a chemical element of the halogen group usually obtained in the form of greyish-black crystals that give off a dense, violet-colored vapor with an irritating odor. Iodine is used in medicine, in making dyes, in photography, etc. *Symbol:* I; *at.no.* 53; *at.wt.* 126.9044. **2** a brown liquid, **tincture of iodine,** used as an antiseptic. [< F *iode* iodine < Gk. *ioeidēs* violet-colored < *ion* violet]

i·o·dize (ī′ə dīz′) *v.* -**dized,** -**diz·ing.** combine or impregnate with iodine or an iodide: *iodized salt.* —**i′o·diz′er,** *n.*

i·o·do·form (ī ō′də fôrm′ *or* ī od′ə fôrm′) *n.* a crystalline compound of iodine, used as an antiseptic. *Formula:* CHI₃ [< *iodo-* iodine (< NL *iodum*) + *form(yl)* (< *formic acid*)]

IOF *or* **I.O.F.** Independent Order of Foresters.

Io moth (ī′ō) a large North American moth (*Automeris io*) having yellow wings with a large, bluish, eyelike spot on each hind wing. [Named after *Io,* who was tormented by a gadfly, because of the larva's stinging spines; 19c.]

i·on (ī′ən *or* ī′on) *n.* **1** an atom or group of atoms having a negative or positive electric charge as a result of having lost or gained one or more electrons. **Positive ions** (cations) are formed in electrolysis by the loss of electrons. **Negative ions** (anions) are formed by the gain of electrons. **2** an electrically charged particle formed in a gas. [< Gk. *ion,* neut. ppr. of *ienai* go]

–ion *suffix.* **1** the act of —ing, as in *attraction, calculation.* **2** the condition or state of being —ed, as in *adoption, fascination.* **3** the result of —ing, as in *abbreviation, collection, connection.* [< F < L -*io, -ionis,* or directly < L]

I·o·ni·an (ī ō′nē ən) *n., adj.* —*n.* a member of an ancient Hellenic people that occupied Attica, the Ionian Islands, and the eastern coast of the Aegean Sea. —*adj.* of or having to do with the Ionians or Ionia, the region occupied by them.

i·on·ic (ī on′ik) *adj.* having to do with ions.

I·on·ic (ī on′ik) *n., adj.* —*n.* the dialect of ancient Greek spoken by the Ionians, including Homeric and Attic Greek. —*adj.* **1** of or having to do with Ionia, the Ionians, or their dialect. **2** *Architecture.* of, having to do with, or designating the second of the three orders of ancient Greek architecture. The characteristic Ionic column is nine diameters high, with an ornate base, a slender, deeply fluted shaft, and a capital with scrolls, called volutes, projecting on either side of its front and rear faces. See **order** for picture. [< L *Ionicus* < Gk. *Iōnikos*]

i·o·ni·um (ī ō′nē əm) *n.* a naturally occurring radio-active isotope of thorium having a mass number of 230. *Symbol:* Io; *half-life* 80 000 years. [< *ion* + *uranium;* for its ionizing action]

hat, āge, fär; let, ēqual, tèrm; it, īce
hot, ōpen, ôrder; oil, out; cup, pu̇t, rüle, ə above, takən, pencəl, lemən, circəs
ch, child; ng, long; sh, ship
th, thin; тн, then; zh, measure

i·on·i·za·tion (ī′ən ə zā′shən) *n.* a separation into ions; dissociation; formation of ions.

i·on·ize (ī′ən īz′) *v.* -**ized,** -**iz·ing.** separate into ions; produce ions in. Acids, bases, and salts ionize in solution. The gas in a neon light must be ionized before it can conduct an electric current. —**i′on·iz′er,** *n.*

i·on·o·sphere (ī on′ə sfēr′) *n.* a region of ionized layers of air above the stratosphere. Low pressure and solar radiation in the ionosphere help to reflect radio waves so that they travel over long distances.

IOOF *or* **I.O.O.F.** Independent Order of Odd Fellows.

i·o·ta (ī ō′tə) *n.* **1** the ninth letter of the Greek alphabet (I, ι). **2** a very small quantity: *There is not an iota of truth in the prisoner's story.* [< L < Gk. *iōta.* Doublet of JOT.]

IOU *or* **I.O.U.** (ī′ō′yü′) an informal note acknowledging a debt: *Write me an IOU for ten dollars.* [for the phrase *I owe you*]

IPA *or* **I.P.A.** **1** International Phonetic Alphabet. **2** International Phonetic Association.

ip·e·cac (ip′ə kak′) *n.* **1** a South American creeping plant (*Cephaelis ipecacuanha*) of the madder family. **2** the dried roots of this plant. **3** a medicine made from the dried roots, used as an emetic or purgative. [< Pg. < Tupi-Guarani *ipe-kaa-guéne* creeping plant causing nausea]

ip·e·cac·u·an·ha (ip′ə kak′yü an′ə) *n.* ipecac.

Iph·i·ge·ni·a (if′ə jə nī′ə) *n. Greek mythology.* the daughter of Agamemnon. He intended to sacrifice her to Artemis to obtain favorable winds for the Greek ships sailing to Troy, but Artemis put a hart in her place and carried Iphigenia off to Tauris to become her priestess.

ip·se dix·it (ip′sē dik′sit) a dogmatic assertion based merely on someone's authority. [< L *ipse dixit* he himself said (it)]
☛ *Usage.* **Ipse dixit.** The Latin phrase, when used in English as a noun, takes the regular plural ending: *His argument was merely a succession of ipse dixits.*

ip·so fac·to (ip′sō fak′tō) *Latin.* by that very fact; by the fact itself.

IQ *or* **I.Q.** *Psychology.* intelligence quotient.

ir–¹ *prefix.* the form of **in-¹** occurring before *r,* as in *irrational, irresolute.*

ir–² *prefix.* the form of **in-²** occurring before *r, r,* as in *irrigate, irradiate.*

Ir iridium.

Ir. Ireland; Irish.

I.R.A. *or* **IRA** Irish Republican Army.

I·ra·ni·an (i rā′nē ən *or* i rä′nē ən) *n., adj.* —*n.* **1** a native or inhabitant of Iran, a country in SW Asia. **2** a branch of the Indo-European family of languages that includes Persian and Kurdish. —*adj.* of or having to do with Iran or its people.

I·ra·qi (ē rä′kē) *n., adj.* —*n.* a native or inhabitant of Iraq, a country in SW Asia. —*adj.* of or having to do with Iraq or its people.

i·ras·ci·bil·i·ty (i ras′ə bil′ə tē) *n.* quickness of temper; irritability.

i·ras·ci·ble (i ras′ə bəl) *adj.* **1** easily made angry; irritable. **2** showing anger. [< LL *irascibilis* < L *irasci* grow angry < *ira* anger] —**i·ras′ci·bly,** *adv.* —**i·ras′ci·ble·ness,** *n.*
☛ *Syn.* **1.** See note at **irritable.**

i·rate (ī′rāt *or* ī rāt′) *adj.* angry. [< L *iratus* < *ira* anger] —**i′rate·ly,** *adv.*

IRBM intermediate range ballistic missile.

ire (īr) *n.* anger; wrath. [ME < OF < L *ira*]

Ire. Ireland.

ire·ful (īr′fəl) *adj.* angry; wrathful. —**ire′ful·ly,** *adv.*

ir·i·des·cence (ir′ə des′əns) *n.* a changing or play of colors, as in mother-of-pearl, opals, a peacock's feathers.

ir·i·des·cent (ir′ə des′ənt) *adj.* **1** displaying colors like those of the rainbow. **2** changing colors according to position. [< L *iris, iridis* rainbow < Gk.] —**ir′i·des′cent·ly,** *adv.*

i·rid·i·um (i rid′ē əm) *n.* a white rare metallic chemical element that resembles platinum and is twice as heavy as lead, used for the

points of pen nibs. *Symbol*: Ir; *at.no.* 77; *at.wt.* 192.2 [< NL < L *iris*, *-idis* rainbow; with reference to its iridescence in solution]

i·ris (ī′ris) *n*. **1** any of a large genus (*Iris*) of perennial plants found in temperate regions of the northern hemisphere, having sword-shaped leaves and large, showy flowers. There are many cultivated varieties of iris. **2** the flower of an iris. **3** (*adj.*) designating a family (Iridaceae) of plants found in tropical and temperate regions, growing from an underground stem or a bulb. Irises, crocuses, and gladiola belong to the iris family. **4** the colored part of the eye, having a round opening, called the pupil, in its centre. The iris is a kind of diaphragm that controls the amount of light entering the eye. See **eye** for picture. **5 Iris**, *Greek mythology*. the goddess of the rainbow and messenger of the gods. **6** rainbow. [< L *iris* rainbow < Gk.]

I·rish (ī′rish) *n*., *adj*. —*n*. **1 the Irish**, *pl*. the people of Ireland, a large island west of England. **2** the Celtic language spoken in parts of Ireland; Irish Gaelic. —*adj*. of or having to do with Ireland, its people, or their language. [ME *Irisc*, *Irish* < OE *Iras*, pl., the people of Ireland]

I·rish·man (ī′rish mən) *n*., *pl*. **-men. 1** a man who is a native or inhabitant of Ireland. **2** a man of Irish descent.

Irish moss carrageen.

Irish potato potato.

Irish setter a breed of large hunting dog having long, silky, reddish-brown hair.

Irish stew a stew made of meat, potatoes, and onions.

Irish terrier a breed of small dog having wiry brown or reddish hair.

Irish wolfhound a breed of very large, powerful dog, formerly used in hunting wolves.

I·rish·wom·an (ī′rish wùm′ən) *n*., *pl*. **-wom·en. 1** a woman who is a native or inhabitant of Ireland. **2** a woman of Irish descent.

irk (ėrk) *v*. weary; disgust; annoy; bore: *It irks us to wait for people who are always late*. [ME *irke*(n)]

irk·some (ėrk′səm) *adj*. tiresome; tedious. —**irk′some·ly**, *adv*. —**irk′some·ness**. *n*.

IRO or **I.R.O.** International Refugee Organization.

i·ron (ī′ərn) *n*., *adj*., *v*. —*n*. **1** a heavy, hard, strong, malleable silver-white metallic element. It is the commonest and most useful metal, used for tools, machinery, etc. *Symbol*: Fe; *at.no.* 26; *at.wt.* 55.847. **2** a tool, instrument, or weapon made from this metal. **3** great hardness and strength; firmness: *men of iron*. **4** a tool with a flat surface for smoothing cloth or pressing clothes. **5** a golf club with an iron or steel head. **6** *Slang*. a pistol; shooting iron. **7 a** a branding iron. **b** harpoon. **8** *Medicine*. a preparation of or containing iron, used as a tonic. **9 irons**, *pl*. chains or bands of iron; handcuffs; shackles.

have too many irons in the fire, try to do too many things at once.
strike while the iron is hot, act while conditions are favorable.
—*adj*. **1** made of iron; having to do with iron. **2** like iron; hard or strong; unyielding: *an iron will*. **3** harsh or cruel: *the iron hand of fate*.
—*v*. **1** smooth or press (cloth, etc.) with a heated iron. **2** furnish or cover with iron. **3** put in irons; fetter.
iron out, straighten out; smooth away: *A tactful person can iron out many problems between people*.
[OE *īren*, ? < Celtic] —**i′ron·er**, *n*.

Iron Age a period of human culture characterized by the use of tools, weapons, etc. made of iron. In Europe, the Iron Age began about 1000 B.C., following the Bronze Age.

i·ron·bark (ī′ərn bärk′) *n*. **1** any of the eucalyptus trees having hard, solid bark. **2** the wood of such a tree.

i·ron·bound (ī′ərn bound′) *adj*. **1** bound with iron. **2** hard; rigid; unyielding. **3** rocky.

i·ron·clad (ī′ərn klad′) *adj*., *n*. —*adj*. **1** protected with iron plates. **2** very hard to change or get out of: *an ironclad agreement*. —*n*. *Historical*. a warship protected with iron plates.

Iron Cross a German medal given for services in war.

Iron Curtain or **iron curtain** an imaginary wall or dividing line separating the Soviet Union and the nations under her control or influence from the rest of the world. [used by Sir Winston Churchill in a speech delivered in 1946]

i·ron·fist·ed (ī′ərn fis′tid) *adj*. unyielding; cruel; despotic.

i·ron–grey or **i·ron–gray** (ī′ərn grā′) *adj*. having the color of freshly broken cast iron.

iron hand a firm, strict manner.

i·ron–hand·ed (ī′ərn han′did) *adj*. exercising stern discipline or tight control.

i·ron·ic (ī ron′ik) *adj*. **1** expressing one thing and meaning the opposite: *"Speedy" would be an ironic name for a snail*. **2** contrary to what would naturally be expected: *It was ironic that the man was run over by his own car*. **3** using or having a habit of using irony: *an ironic person*. **4** showing irony: *an ironic statement*.

i·ron·i·cal (ī ron′ə kəl) *adj*. ironic. [< LL *ironicus* < Gk. *eirōnikos* dissembling < *eirōneia*. See IRONY.] —**i·ron′i·cal·ly**, *adv*.

ironing board a board covered with a smooth cloth, used for ironing clothes on.

i·ro·nist (ī′rə nist) *n*. a person who takes an ironical view of life and things, especially as a writer.

iron lung a device that gives artificial respiration by rhythmically alternating the air pressure in a chamber enclosing the patient's chest.

i·ron·mon·ger (ī′ərn mung′gər or -mong′gər) *n*. *Brit*. a dealer in ironware or hardware.

iron pyrites pyrite; fool's gold.

i·ron·sides (ī′ərn sīdz′) *n*. **1** a man of great strength or endurance. **2** an armor-plated warship. **3 Ironsides, a** the regiment led by Oliver Cromwell. **b** his army.

i·ron·stone (ī′ərn stōn′) *n*. any iron ore with clay or other impurities in it.

i·ron·ware (ī′ərn wer′) *n*. articles made of iron, such as pots, kettles, tools, etc.; hardware.

i·ron·weed (ī′ərn wēd′) *n*. any of several perennial plants (genus *Vernonia*) of the composite family found in many parts of the world, having lance-shaped, toothed leaves and clusters of tubular flowers, usually purple or red.

i·ron–willed (ī′ərn wild′) *adj*. having an exceptionally firm will.

i·ron·wood (ī′ərn wùd′) *n*. **1** any of various trees having very hard, heavy wood. **2** the wood itself.

i·ron·work (ī′ərn wėrk′) *n*. **1** works of iron. **2 ironworks,** a place where iron or steel is smelted or fashioned into heavy products (*often used with a singular verb*).

i·ron·work·er (ī′ərn wėr′kər) *n*. **1** a person who makes things of iron. **2** a person whose work is building the framework of bridges, skyscrapers, etc.

i·ro·ny (ī′rə nē) *n*., *pl*. **-nies. 1** a method of expression in which the intended meaning is the opposite of, or different from that expressed: *Calling their small bungalow a mansion is irony*. **2** an event or outcome contrary to what would naturally be expected: *It was an amusing irony when a fake diamond was stolen instead of the real one. It was the irony of fate that the great cancer doctor himself died of cancer*. [< L *ironia* < Gk. *eirōneia* dissimulation < *eirōn* dissembler]

☛ **Usage.** **Irony, sarcasm, satire** are often confused. **Irony,** applying to a kind of humor or way of expressing wit, emphasizes deliberately saying the opposite of what one means, depending on tone of voice or writing to show the real meaning: *the thrill of sitting still for two hours at a time*. **Sarcasm** applies only to cruel, biting, contemptuous remarks that may be stated ironically or directly but are always intended to hurt and ridicule: *When children call a boy "Four Eyes" because he wears glasses, they are using sarcasm*. **Satire** is the formal use of irony, sarcasm, and other kinds of humor to expose, criticize, or attack follies or vices.

Ir·o·quoi·an (ir′ə kwoi′ən) *n*., *adj*. —*n*. **1** a family of N American Indian languages, including Huron, Mohawk, Oneida, Onondaga, Cayuga, Seneca, Tuscarora, and Cherokee. **2** an Indian belonging to an Iroquoian tribe; an Iroquois. —*adj*. **1** of or having to do with Iroquoian languages. **2** of or having to do with Iroquois Indians or their languages.

Ir·o·quois (ir′ə kwo′) *n.sing.* or *pl*. **1** a powerful group of N American Indian tribes called the Five Nations (later, the Six Nations) living mostly in Quebec, Ontario, and New York State. **2** a member of any of the Iroquois tribes.

ir·ra·di·ance (i rā′dē əns) *n*. radiance; shine.

ir·ra·di·ant (i rā′dē ənt) *adj*. irradiating; radiant; shining.

ir·ra·di·ate (i rā′dē āt′) *v*. **-at·ed, -at·ing. 1** shine upon; make bright; illuminate. **2** shine. **3** radiate; give out. **4** treat with ultra-violet rays. [< L *irradiare* < *in-* + *radius* ray] —**ir·ra′di·a·tor**, *n*.

ir·ra·di·a·tion (i rā′dē ā′shən) *n*. **1** the act or process of irradiating. **2** the state or conditon of being irradiated. **3** a stream of light; ray. **4** enlightenment of the mind or spirit.

ir·ra·tion·al (i rash′ən əl or i rash′nəl) *adj*. **1** not rational; unreasonable: *It is irrational to be afraid of the number 13*. **2** unable to think and reason clearly. **3** *Mathematics*. **a** that cannot be expressed by a whole number or a common fraction. $\sqrt{3}$ is an irrational number. **b** of functions, that cannot be expressed as the ratio of two algebraic polynomials in its variables. [< L *irrationalis*] —**ir·ra′tion·al·ly**, *adv*.

ir·ra·tion·al·i·ty (i rash′ən al′ə tē) *n*., *pl*. **-ties. 1** being irrational. **2** something irrational; absurdity.

ir·re·claim·a·ble (ir′i klām′ə bəl) *adj.* that cannot be reclaimed. —**ir′re·claim′a·bly,** *adv.*

ir·rec·on·cil·a·ble (i rek′ən sīl′ə bəl *or* i rek′ən sīl′ə bəl) *adj., n.* —*adj.* that cannot be reconciled; that cannot be made to agree; opposed. —*n.* a person who refuses to compromise or collaborate: *The irreconcilables in the party made discussion of the proposal very difficult.* —**ir·rec′on·cil′a·bly,** *adv.*

ir·re·cov·er·a·ble (ir′i kuv′ər ə bel *or* ir′i kuv′rə bəl) *adj.* **1** that cannot be regained or got back: *Wasted time is irrecoverable.* **2** that cannot be remedied: *irrecoverable sorrow.* —**ir′re·cov′er·a·bly,** *adv.*

ir·re·deem·a·ble (ir′i dēm′ə bəl) *adj.* **1** that cannot be bought back. **2** that cannot be exchanged for coin: *irredeemable paper money.* **3** beyond remedy; hopeless. —**ir′re·deem′a·bly,** *adv.*

Ir·re·den·tist (ir′i den′tist) *n.* a member of an Italian political party that became important in 1878. The Irredentists advocated that Italy should gain control of neighboring regions with Italian populations that were under foreign rule. [< Ital, *irredentista* < (*Italia*) *irredenta* unredeemed (Italy), ult. < L *in-* not + *redemptus,* pp. of *redimere* redeem]

ir·re·duc·i·ble (ir′i dyüs′ə bəl *or* ir′i düs′ə bəl) *adj.* that cannot be reduced. —**ir′re·duc′i·bly,** *adv.*

ir·ref·ra·ga·ble (i ref′rə gə bəl) *adj.* that cannot be refuted; unanswerable; undeniable. [< LL *irrefragabilis* < L *in-* not + *refragari* oppose] —**ir·ref′ra·ga·bly,** *adv.*

ir·ref·u·ta·ble (i ref′yə tə bəl *or* ir′i fyüt′ə bəl) *adj.* that cannot be refuted or disproved. —**ir·ref′u·ta·bly,** *adv.*

ir·reg·u·lar (i reg′yə lər) *adj., n.* —*adj.* **1** not regular; not according to rule; out of the usual order or natural way: *irregular breathing.* **2** not even; not smooth; not straight; without symmetry: *irregular features, an irregular coastline.* **3** not according to law or morals: *irregular behavior.* **4** not in the regular army. **5** *Grammar.* not inflected in the usual way. *Be* is an irregular verb. —*n.* a soldier not in the regular army. —**ir·reg′u·lar·ly,** *adv.*

☛ *Syn. adj.* **1. Irregular, abnormal** = out of the usual or natural order or way. **Irregular** = not acording to rule or the accepted standard, pattern, way, etc. for the kind of thing or person described: *He has irregular habits.* **Abnormal** = departing from what is regarded as normal, average, or typical, and may describe people or things either above or below normal or showing little relation to the normal: *Two hundred centimeters is an abnormal height for a man.*

ir·reg·u·lar·i·ty (i reg′yə lar′ə tē *or* i reg′yə ler′ə tē) *n., pl.* **-ties. 1** a lack of regularity; being irregular. **2** something irregular.

ir·rel·e·vance (i rel′ə vəns) *n.* **1** the condition of being irrelevant. **2** something irrelevant.

ir·rel·e·van·cy (i rel′ə vən sē) *n.* irrelevance.

ir·rel·e·vant (i rel′ə vənt) *adj.* not to the point; off the subject: *A question about economics is irrelevant in a music lesson.* —**ir·rel′e·vant·ly,** *adv.*

ir·re·li·gion (ir′i lij′ən) *n.* **1** lack of religion. **2** hostility to or disregard of religion.

ir·re·li·gious (ir′i lij′əs) *adj.* **1** not religious; indifferent to religion. **2** contrary to religious principles; impious. [< L *irreligiosus*] —**ir′re·li′gious·ly,** *adv.* —**ir′re·li′gious·ness,** *n.*

ir·re·me·di·a·ble (ir′i mē′dē ə bəl) *adj.* that cannot be remedied; incurable. —**ir′re·me′di·a·bly,** *adv.*

ir·re·mov·a·ble (ir′i müv′ə bəl) *adj.* that cannot be removed. —**ir′re·mov′a·bly,** *adv.*

ir·rep·a·ra·ble (i rep′ə rə bəl) *adj.* that cannot be repaired or made good. —**ir·rep′a·ra·bly,** *adv.*

ir·re·place·a·ble (ir′i plās′ə bəl) *adj.* not replaceable; impossible to replace with another.

ir·re·press·i·bil·i·ty (ir′i pres′ə bil′ə tē) *n.* the condition of being irrepressible.

ir·re·press·i·ble (ir′i pres′ə bəl) *adj.* that cannot be repressed or restrained. —**ir′re·press′i·bly,** —*adv.*

ir·re·proach·a·ble (ir′i prōch′ə bəl) *adj.* free from blame; faultless: *He had led an irreproachable life.* —**ir′re·proach′a·bly,** *adv.*

ir·re·sist·i·ble (ir′i zis′tə bəl) *adj.* that cannot be resisted; too great to be withstood; overwhelming: *an irresistable desire to laugh.* —**ir′re·sist′i·bly,** *adv.*

ir·res·o·lute (i rez′ə lüt′) *adj.* **1** unable to make up one's mind; not sure of what one wants; hesitating: *He stood there irresolute, not knowing which path to try.* **2** lacking in resoluteness: *An irresolute person makes a poor leader.* —**ir·res′o·lute·ly,** *adv.* —**ir·res′o·lute·ness,** *n.*

ir·res·o·lu·tion (i rez′ə lü′shən) *n.* being irresolute; hesitation or a lack of resolution.

ir·re·spec·tive (ir′i spek′tiv) *adj.* regardless: *Any person, irrespective of age, may join the club.* —**ir′re·spec′tive·ly,** *adv.*

ir·re·spon·si·bil·i·ty (ir′i spon′sə bil′ə tē) *n.* lack of responsibility; being irresponsible.

ir·re·spon·si·ble (ir′i spon′sə bəl) *adj.* **1** not having or not showing a proper sense of responsibility: *It was irresponsible to leave the broken glass on the sidewalk.* **2** not responsible to any authority; that cannot be called to account: *A dictator is an irresponsible ruler.* —**ir′re·spon′si·bly,** *adv.*

ir·re·trace·a·ble (ir′i trās′ə bəl) *adj.* that cannot be retraced.

ir·re·triev·a·bil·i·ty (ir′i trēv′ə bil′ə tē) *n.* the quality or state of being irretrievable.

ir·re·triev·a·ble (ir′i trēv′ə bəl) *adj.* that cannot be retrieved or recovered; that cannot be recalled or restored to its former condition. —**ir·re·triev′a·bly,** *adv.*

ir·rev·er·ence (i rev′ər əns) *n.* **1** lack of reverence; disrespect. **2** an act showing irreverence.

ir·rev·er·ent (i rev′ər ənt) *adj.* not reverent; disrespectful. [< L *irreverens, -entis*] —**ir·rev′er·ent·ly,** *adv.*

ir·re·vers·i·bil·i·ty (ir′i ver′sə bil′ə tē) *n.* the quality or state of being irreversible.

ir·re·vers·i·ble (ir′i ver′sə bəl) *adj.* not capable of being reversed. —**ir′re·vers′i·bly,** *adv.*

ir·rev·o·ca·bil·i·ty (i rev′ə kə bil′ə tē) *n.* the state of being irrevocable.

ir·rev·o·ca·ble (i rev′ə kə bəl) *adj.* not to be recalled, withdrawn, or annulled: *an irrevocable decision.* —**ir·rev′o·ca·bly,** *adv.*

ir·ri·ga·ble (ir′ə gə bəl) *adj.* that can be irrigated.

ir·ri·gate (ir′ə gāt′) *v.* **-gat·ed, -gat·ing. 1** supply land with water by means of ditches, sprinklers, etc. **2** *Medicine.* wash out or flush a wound, cavity in the body, etc. with a flow of some liquid: *to irrigate the nose and throat with warm water.* [< L *irrigare* < *in-* + *rigare* wet] —**ir′ri·ga′tor,** *n.*

ir·ri·ga·tion (ir′ə gā′shən) *n.* irrigating or being irrigated: *Irrigation is needed to make crops grow in dry regions.*

ir·ri·ta·bil·i·ty (ir′ə tə bil′ə tē) *n., pl.* **-ties.** the quality or state of being irritable: *irritability of temper, irritability of skin.*

ir·ri·ta·ble (ir′ə tə bəl) *adj.* **1** easily made angry; impatient. **2** of an organ or part of the body, unnaturally sensitive or sore: *A baby's skin is often quite irritable.* **3** *Biology.* able to respond to stimuli. [< L *irritabilis*] —**ir′ri·ta·ble·ness,** *n.* —**ir′ri·ta·bly,** *adv.*

☛ *Syn.* **1. Irritable, irascible** = easily made angry. **Irritable** = easily annoyed or angered, especially by little things, and suggests having an impatient or excitable temperament or being in a nervous condition: *She has been so irritable lately that I think she must be ill.* **Irascible** = having a quick temper, being by nature or disposition liable to become angry at the slightest excuse: *Irascible people should not have positions which require them to meet the public.*

ir·ri·tant (ir′ə tənt) *n., adj.* —*n.* a thing that causes irritation: *A mustard plaster is an irritant.* —*adj.* causing irritation. [< L *irritans, -antis,* ppr. of *irritare* enrage, provoke]

ir·ri·tate (ir′ə tāt′) *v.* **-tat·ed, -tat·ing. 1** make impatient or angry; annoy; provoke; vex: *The boy's foolish questions irritated his father. Flies irritate horses.* **2** make unnaturally sensitive or sore: *Too much sun irritates the skin.* **3** bring (an organ or part) to an excessively sensitive condition. **4** *Biology.* stimulate (an organ, muscle, tissue, etc.) to perform some characteristic action or function: *A muscle contracts when it is irritated by an electric shock.* [< L *irritare* enrage, provoke] —**ir′ri·tat′ing·ly,** *adv.* —**ir′ri·ta′tor,** *n.*

☛ *Syn.* **1. Irritate, exasperate, provoke** = excite to impatience or anger. **Irritate** suggests annoying a person until he loses patience or flares up in anger: *Her untidiness irritates me.* **Exasperate** = make extremely annoyed or angry by irritating beyond endurance: *Her constant cheating exasperates me.* **Provoke** = do, or keep doing, something displeasing or disturbing to make a person lose patience and become very much annoyed, vexed, or angry: *Her constant interruptions provoke me.*

ir·ri·ta·tion (ir′ə tā′shən) *n.* **1** the act or process of irritating; annoyance; vexation. **2** an irritated condition.

ir·ri·ta·tive (ir′ə tā′tiv) *adj.* **1** producing or causing irritation; irritating. **2** accompanying or caused by irritation: *an irritative fever.*

ir·rupt (i rupt′) *v.* **1** rush in suddenly or violently. **2** of an animal population, increase suddenly in numbers, as when the natural ecological balance has been disturbed. [< L *irruptis,* pp. of *irrumpere* invade]

ir·rup·tion (i rup′shən) *n.* a breaking or bursting in; violent invasion. [< L *irruptio, -onis* < *irrumpere* < *in-* in + *rumpere* break]

ir·rup·tive (i rup′tiv) *adj.* bursting in; rushing in or upon anything. —**ir·rup′tive·ly,** *adv.*

is (iz) *v.* 3rd pers. sing., present indicative of **be.**
as is, as it is now; in its present condition. [OE]

Is. Island; Isle.

ISBN International Standard Book Number.

Is·car·i·ot (is kar′ē ət *or* is ker′ē ət) *n.* **1** the surname of Judas, the disciple who betrayed Jesus for thirty pieces of silver (Matthew 26:14-50). **2** any traitor.

is·chi·um (is′kē əm) *n.* **is·chi·a** (is′kē ə). the lower back and side portion of the hipbone. See **pelvis** for picture. [< NL < Gk. *ischion*]

–ise *suffix.* variant of **-ize.**
☛ *Usage.* See note at **ize.**

I·seult (i sült′) *n. Medieval legend.* **1** an Irish princess, wife of King Mark of Cornwall. She was loved by Tristram. **2** the daughter of the king of Brittany, whom Tristram married after his love for the Irish Iseult was discovered. Also, **Isolde, Isolt.**

–ish *suffix.* **1** somewhat, as in *oldish, sweetish.* **2** resembling; like, as in *a childish person.* **3** like that of; having the characteristics of, as in *a childish idea.* **4** of or having to do with; belonging to, as in *British, Spanish, Turkish.* **5** tending to; inclined to, as in *bookish, thievish.* **6** near, but usually somewhat past, as in *fortyish.* [OE *-isc*]

Ish·ma·el (ish′mē əl) *n.* **1** in the Bible, a son of Abraham. Because of Sarah's jealousy, he was driven out into the wilderness (Gen. 16:12). **2** any outcast; someone who is at odds with society.

Ish·ma·el·ite (ish′mē əl īt′) *n.* **1** a descendant of Ishmael. **2** an outcast.

i·sin·glass (ī′zing glas′) *n.* **1** a kind of gelatin obtained from air bladders of sturgeon, cod, and similar fishes, used for making glue, clarifying liquors, etc. **2** mica, especially when split into thin, semi-transparent sheets. [alteration of MDu. *huysenblas* sturgeon bladder; influenced by *glass*]

I·sis (ī′sis) *n. Egyptian mythology.* the goddess of fertility, represented as wearing on her head cow's horns enclosing a solar disk.

isl. island; Isle.

Is·lam (is′ləm *or* is läm′) *n.* **1** the religion of Moslems, including belief in Allah as the one God and following the teachings of Mohammed as the prophet of Allah. **2** Moslems as a group. **3** the civilization of Moslem peoples. **4** all the countries in which Islam is the main religion. [Arabic *islām* submission (to God) < *aslama* he surrendered himself]

Is·lam·ic (is lam′ik *or* is läm′ik) *adj.* of or having to do with Islam; Moslem.

Is·lam·ism (is′ləm iz′əm) *n.* the faith or cause of Islam.

Is·lam·ite (is′ləm īt′) *n. or adj.* Moslem.

is·land (ī′lənd) *n., v.* —*n.* **1** a body of land smaller than a continent and completely surrounded by water: *Cuba is a very large island.* **2** something resembling this. **3** a superstructure, especially of a battleship or aircraft carrier. **4 a** a piece of woodland surrounded by prairie. **b** an elevated piece of land surrounded by marshes, etc. **5** *Anatomy.* a group of cells different in structure or function from those around it.
—*v.* make into an island. [OE *īgland* < *īg* island + *land* land; spelling influenced by *isle*] —**is′land·like′,** *adj.*

is·land·er (ī′lən dər) *n.* a native or inhabitant of an island.

isle (īl) *n.* **1** a small island. **2** island. [ME < OF < L *insula*]
☛ *Hom.* **aisle, I'll.**

is·let (ī′lit) *n.* a little island. [< earlier F *islette,* dim of *isle* isle]
☛ *Hom.* **eyelet.**

ism (iz′əm) *n. Informal.* a distinctive doctrine, theory, system, or practice: *Capitalism, socialism, communism, and facism are well-known isms.* [see -ISM]

–ism *noun-forming suffix.* **1** an action; practice, as in *baptism, criticism.* **2** a doctrine; system; principle, as in *communism, socialism.* **3** a quality; characteristic; state; condition, as in *heroism, paganism.* **4** an illustration; case; instance, as in *colloquialism, witticism.* **5** an unhealthy condition caused by—, as in *alcoholism, morphinism.* [< Gk. *-ismos, -isma*]

I.S.M. Imperial Service Medal.

is·n't (iz′ənt) is not.

iso– *combining form.* equal; alike, as in *isosceles, isometric, isothermal, isotope.* [< Gk. *iso-* < *isos* equal]

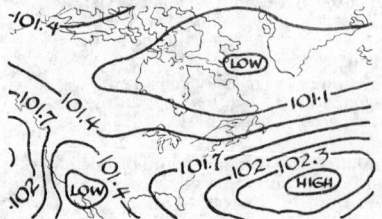

Isobars showing atmospheric pressures for an average July in North America and part of the North Atlantic Ocean. The pressures are given in kilopascals.

i·so·bar (ī′sə bär′) *n.* **1** a line on a weather map connecting places having the same average atmospheric pressure (after allowance for height above sea level). **2** *Physics and chemistry.* one of two or more kinds of atoms that have the same atomic weight, but in most cases different atomic numbers. [< Gk. *isobarēs* < *isos* equal + *baros* weight]

i·so·bar·ic (ī′sə bar′ik *or* ī′sə ber′ik) *adj.* **1** of or containing isobars. **2** having or indicating equal atmospheric pressure.

i·soch·ro·nal (ī sok′rə nəl) *adj.* **1** equal or uniform in time. **2** characterized by motions or vibrations of equal duration. [< Gk. *isochronos* < *isos* equal + *chronos* time] —**i·soch′ro·nal·ly,** *adv.*

i·soch·ro·nous (ī sok′rə nəs) *adj.* isochronal.
—**i·soch′ro·nous·ly,** *adv.*

i·so·gloss (ī′sə glos′) *n. Linguistic geography.* a line on a map to separate two adjacent areas in each of which different variants of a pronunciation, grammatical form, or word are current.

i·so·gon·ic (ī′sə gon′ik) *adj.* having equal angles; having to do with equal angles. [< Gk. *isogōnios* < *isos* equal + *gōnia* angle]

i·so·gram (ī′sə gram′) *n.* isoline.

i·so·hy·et (ī′sō hī′ət) *n.* a line on a map or chart connecting places having the same average precipitation.

i·so·hy·et·al (ī′sō hī′ət əl) *adj.* of, having to do with, or being an isohyet.

i·so·late (ī′sə lāt′ *or, esp.U.S.,* is′ə lāt′) *v.* **-lat·ed, -lat·ing;** *n.*
—*v.* **1** place apart; separate from others; keep alone: *People with contagious diseases should be isolated.* **2** *Chemistry.* obtain (a substance) in a pure or uncombined form: *A chemist can isolate the oxygen from the hydrogen in water.* —*n.* a person, thing, or group that is isolated or is the product of isolation. [< *isolated* < F *isolé* < Ital. *isolato,* pp. of *isolare* < L *insulare* < *insula* island]

i·so·la·tion (ī′sə lā′shən *or, esp.U.S.,* is′ə lā′shən) *n.* **1** the act or process of isolating. **2** the condition or state of being isolated: *living in isolation.*
☛ *Syn.* **2.** See note at **solitude.**

i·so·la·tion·ism (ī′sə lā′shən iz′əm *or, esp.U.S.,* is′ə lā′shən iz′əm) *n.* the principles or practice of isolationists.

i·so·la·tion·ist (ī′sə lā′shən ist *or, esp.U.S.,* is′ə lā′shən ist) *n.* **1** one who objects to his country's participation in international affairs. **2** in Canada and the United States, a person who favors keeping his country out of European affairs, wars, etc.

I·sol·de (i sōl′də, i sōld′, *or* i zôl′də) *n.* Iseult.

i·so·line (ī′sō līn′) *n.* a line on a map or chart connecting places sharing some geographical or meteorological feature or phenomenon, such as degree of atmospheric pressure, amount of precipitation, etc.

I·solt (i sōlt′) *n.* Iseult.

i·so·mer (ī′sə mər) *n.* an isomeric compound. [< Gk. *isomerēs* < *isos* equal + *meros* part]

i·so·mer·ic (ī′sə mer′ik) *adj.* **1** *Chemistry.* composed of the same elements in the same proportions by weight, and (in the usual, restricted sense of the term) having the same molecular weight, but differing in one or more properties because of the difference in arrangement of atoms. **2** of the nuclei of atoms, differing in energy and behavior, but having the same atomic number and mass number.

i·som·er·ous (ī som′ər əs) *adj.* **1** having an equal number of parts, markings, etc. **2** of a flower, having the same number of members in each whorl.

i·so·met·ric (ī′sə met′rik) *adj.* having to do with equality of measure; having equality of measure. A crystal is isometric if it has three equal axes at right angles to one another. Isometric exercises are done without perceptible movement of body parts. [< Gk. *isometros* < *isos* equal + *metron* measure] —**i·so·met′ri·cal·ly,** *adv.*

i·so·met·ri·cal (ī′sə met′rə kəl) *adj.* isometric.

i·so·morph (ī′sə môrf′) *n.* **1** an isomorphic organism or

substance. 2 *Linguistic geography.* an isogloss setting off different morphologial features.

i·so·mor·phic (ī′sə môr′fik) *adj.* 1 *Biology.* having similar appearance or structure, but different ancestry. 2 isomorphous. [< *iso-* + Gk. *morphē* form]

i·so·mor·phous (ī′sə môr′fəs) *adj. Chemistry.* crystallizing in the same form or related forms. Isomorphous is used especially of substances of analogous chemical composition.

i·so·ni·a·zid (ī′sō nī′ə zid) *n.* a drug chemically related to nicotinic acid, used in the treatment of tuberculosis. [< *isoni(cotinic acid hydr)azid(e)*. See iso-.]

i·so·pleth (ī′sə pleth′) *n.* isoline.

i·so·pod (ī′sə pod′) *n.* any of an order (Isopoda) of crustaceans having a long, somewhat flat, body made up of seven segments, each of which has a pair of legs. The sow bug is an isopod. [< NL *Isopoda*, pl. < Gk. *isos* equal + *pous, podos* foot]

i·so·prene (ī′sə prēn′) *n. Chemistry.* a volatile liquid hydrocarbon used in synthetic rubber and turpentine. *Formula:* C_3H_8 [< *iso-* + *propyl* + *-ene*, as in *benzene*, etc.]

i·sos·ce·les (ī sos′ə lēz′) *adj.* of a triangle, having two sides equal. See **triangle** for picture. [< LL < Gk. *isoskelēs* < *isos* equal + *skelos* leg]

i·so·therm (ī′sə thėrm′) *n.* a line on a weather map connecting places having the same average temperature. [< *iso-* + Gk. *thermē* heat]

i·so·ther·mal (ī′sə thėr′məl) *adj.* 1 indicating equality of temperatures. 2 having to do with isotherms.

i·so·ton·ic (ī′sə ton′ic) *adj.* 1 *Physiology and chemistry.* having the same osmotic pressure. 2 *Physiology.* having to do with muscle contractions caused by minor, but constant, tension. 3 *Music.* characterized by equal tones. [< Gk.]

i·so·tope (ī′sə tōp′) *n.* any of two or more kinds of atom of a chemical element having the same number of protons and almost the same chemical properties, but having a different number of neutrons and different physical properties. Most elements have naturally occurring isotopes; the known isotopes of hydrogen are ordinary hydrogen (sometimes called light hydrogen), deuterium, and tritium. [< *iso-* + Gk. *topos* place]

i·so·trop·ic (ī′sə trop′ik) *adj. Physics.* having the same properties, such as elasticity or conduction, in all directions. [< *iso-* + Gk. *tropos* turn, way]

i·sot·ro·pous (ī sot′rə pəs) *adj.* isotropic.

Is·ra·el (iz′rē əl *or* iz′rāl) *n.* 1 in the Bible, a name given to Jacob after he had wrestled with the angel (Gen. 32:28). 2 the name given to his descendants; the Jews; the Hebrews.

Is·rae·li (iz rā′lē) *n., pl.* **-lis;** *adj.* —*n.* a native or inhabitant of modern Israel, a country in SW Asia including a portion of Palestine. —*adj.* of or having to do with modern Israel or its people.

Israeli pound 1 a unit of money in Israel. See table at **money.** 2 a note or coin worth one Israeli pound.

Is·ra·el·ite (iz′rē əl īt′) *n., adj.* —*n.* a descendant of Jacob, especially a native or inhabitant of the ancient kingdom of Israel; a Jew; Hebrew. —*adj.* of or having to do with ancient Israel or the Israelites.

Is·ra·el·it·ish (iz′rē əl īt′ish) *adj.* Jewish.

Is·sei (ēs′sā′) *n., pl.* **-sei.** a first-generation Japanese living in Canada or the United States. A second-generation Japanese living in Canada or the United States is a Nisei. [< Japanese *is-sei* first generation < *ichi* one + *sei* generation]

ISSN International Standard Serial Number (*used for periodicals*).

is·su·ance (ish′ü əns) *n.* an issuing; issue.

is·sue (ish′ü) *v.* **-sued, -su·ing;** *n.* —*v.* 1 send out; put forth: *The government issues money and stamps.* 2 come out; go out; proceed: *Smoke issues from the chimney.* 3 be published. 4 put into public circulation; publish. 5 distribute; give out to a person or persons: *Heavy boots were issued to all the troops.* 6 send forth; discharge; emit: *The chimney issues smoke from the fireplace.* 7 emerge. 8 result or end (*in*): *The game issued in a tie.* 9 result (*from*). 10 be born; be descended; be derived. —*n.* 1 something sent out; quantity (of bonds, stamps, copies of a magazine, etc.) sent out at one time. 2 a sending out; putting forth: *The next issue of new stamps will be on June 11.* 3 a coming forth; a flowing out; a discharge: *A nosebleed is an issue of blood from the nose.* 4 a way out; outlet; exit. 5 that which comes out. 6 a profit; production. 7 the result; outcome: *The issue of the game remained uncertain until the last moment.* 8 a point to be debated; problem: *political issues.* 9 a child or children; offspring.
at issue, in question; to be considered or decided.
face the issue, admit the facts and do what must be done.
join issue, take opposite sides in an argument.
make an issue, cause to become a point of debate or argument: *He*

hat, āge, fär; let, ēqual, tėrm; it, īce
hot, ōpen, ôrder; oil, out; cup, put, rüle,
əbove, takən, pencəl, lemən, circəs

ch, child; ng, long; sh, ship
th, thin; ŦH, then; zh, measure

made an issue of every minor point of procedure at the meeting.
take issue, disagree: *I take issue with you on that point.*
[ME < OF *issue* < *eissir* go out < L *exire* < *ex-* out + *ire* go]
—**is′su·a·ble,** *adj.* —**is′su·er,** *n.*

☛ *Syn. v.* **2, 5. Issue, emerge, emanate** = come out. **Issue** = go or come out, usually through an opening, from a source or place where it has been confined, and often suggests flowing out in a moving mass like water: *Pus issued from the wound.* **Emerge** emphasizes coming into sight from a place where it has been hidden or covered up: *The train emerged from the tunnel.* **Emanate,** used only of things without physical body, means "flow out from a source": *Heat emanates from fire.*

–ist *suffix.* 1 a person who does or makes, as in *theorist, tourist.* 2 one who knows about or has skill with, as in *biologist, flutist.* 3 one engaged in or busy with, as in *horticulturist, machinist.* 4 one who believes in; an adherent of, as in *abolitionist, idealist.* [< Gk. *-istēs*]

isth·mi·an (is′mē ən) *adj.* 1 of or having to do with an isthmus. 2 **Isthmian, a** of or having to do with the Isthmus of Panama. **b** of or having to do with the Isthmus of Corinth in Greece. The **Isthmian games** were national festivals of ancient Greece.

isth·mus (is′məs) *n., pl.* **-mus·es.** 1 a narrow strip of land, having water on either side, connecting two large bodies of land: *The Isthmus of Panama joins North and South America.* 2 *Anatomy.* **a** a narrow structure connecting two larger structures. **b** a narrow cavity connecting two larger cavities. [< L < Gk. *isthmos*]

is·tle (is′tlē) *n.* a fibre of certain tropical American plants, used in making bags, carpets, cordage, nets, etc. [< Mexican *ixtli*]

it (it) *pron., subj. or obj.* **it,** *poss.* **its,** *pl. subj.* **they,** *pl. obj.* **them,** *pl. poss.* **theirs;** *n., pl.* **it's.** 1 this or that one; a thing, idea, part, animal, or person already mentioned: *The plan is basically sound, but it is too complicated. The dog was whimpering; I think it was hurt. There's somebody at the door, but I don't know who it is.* 2 the subject of an impersonal verb, that does not refer to an agent: *It is snowing.* 3 a subject of a clause that anticipates the real, or logical, subject that comes later (often used to shift emphasis from the logical subject to another part of a sentence): *It is hard to believe that he is dead. It was here that the fossils were found.* 4 a direct object without specific force of meaning: *He lorded it over us. She beat it back to town as soon as she heard.*
—*n.* 1 in certain children's games, the player who must catch, find, guess, etc. 2 something neither male nor female: *If it's not a he or a she, it must be an it.* [OE *hit*]

it. italic(s).

It. Italy; Italian.

ital. italic(s).

Ital. Italy; Italian.

I·tal·ian (i tal′yən) *n., adj.* —*n.* 1 a native or inhabitant of Italy, a country in S Europe. 2 a person of Italian descent. 3 the Romance language of Italy.
—*adj.* of or having to do with Italy, its people, or their language.

I·tal·ian·ate (*adj.* i tal′yə nāt′ *or* i tal′yə nit; *v.* i tal′yə nāt′) *adj., v.* **-at·ed, -at·ing.** —*adj.* of Italian style, manner, or form. —*v.* Italianize.

I·tal·ian·ize (i tal′yən īz′) *v.* **-ized, -iz·ing.** make Italian. —**I·tal′ian·i·za′tion,** *n.*

i·tal·ic (i tal′ik) *adj., n.* —*adj.* 1 of or designating a style of type in which the letters and numerals slant to the right. It is usually used in printing foreign words, book titles, etc., or to indicate emphasis: *This sentence is in italic.* Compare **roman.** 2 **Italic,** of ancient Italy, its people, or their languages.
—*n.* 1 an italic type, letter, or number. 2 Usually, **italics,** *pl.* italic type or print: *Example sentences in this dictionary are in italics.* 3 a branch of the Indo-European language family that includes French, Italian, Portuguese, Romanian, Spanish, Latin, etc. [< L *Italicus* < *Italia* Italy < Gk.]

☛ *Usage.* **Italics.** In manuscript, both longhand and typewritten, italics are shown by single underlining.

i·tal·i·ci·za·tion (i tal′ə sī zā′shən) *n.* the act or process of italicizing.

i·tal·i·cize (i tal′ə sīz′) *v.* **-cized, -ciz·ing.** 1 print in type in which the letters slant to the right: *This sentence is italicized.* 2 underline with a single line to indicate italics. 3 use italics.

Ital·o- *combining form.* 1 Italian, as in *Italo-Canadian.* 2 Italian and —: *the Italo-German alliance in World War II.*

itch (ich) *n., v.* —*n.* **1** a tickly, prickling feeling in the skin that makes one want to scratch. **2 the itch,** a contagious disease of the skin caused by a tiny mite, and accompanied by an itchy feeling. **3** a restless, uneasy feeling, longing, or desire for anything: *an itch to get away and explore.*
—*v.* **1** cause an itching feeling: *Mosquito bites itch.* **2** have an itching feeling. **3** have an uneasy desire: *He itched to know our secret.* [OE *gyccan*]

itch·y (ich′ē) *adj.* **itch·i·er, itch·i·est.** itching; like the itch. —**itch′i·ness,** *n.*

–ite¹ *suffix.* **1** a native or inhabitant of, as in *Israelite.* **2** a person associated with, as in *laborite.* **3** a mineral species, or a rock substance, as in *hematite.* **4** especially in the names of commercially manufactured products, resembling; derived from; having the property of, as in *dynamite, ebonite.* [< F -*ite* (< L -*ita, ites*) or < L (< Gk. -*itēs*) or directly < Gk. -*itēs*]

–ite² *suffix.* a salt of, as in *phosphite, sulphite, nitrite.* [< F -*ite,* arbitrarily created var. of -*ate²*]

i·tem (ī′təm) *n., adv.* —*n.* **1** a separate thing or article: *This list contains twelve items.* **2** a piece of news; a bit of information: *There were several interesting items in today's paper.* —*adv.* also; likewise (in introducing each item of an enumeration). [< L *item,* adv., likewise]
☛ *Syn. n.* **1. Item, detail, particular** = a separate thing that is part of a whole. **Item** applies to a separate thing included in a list, account, or total, or to an article listed: *An itemized account should list every item.* **Detail** applies to a separate thing that is part of something larger put together or done: *His report gave all the details.* **Particular** emphasizes the singleness or extreme smallness of a detail, item, point, circumstance, etc.: *Nobody wants to hear all the particulars of your troubles.*

i·tem·ize (ī′təm īz′) *v.* **-ized, -iz·ing.** give each item of; list by items: *to itemize the cost of a trip.* —**i′tem·i·za′tion,** *n.*

it·er·ate (it′ər āt′) *v.* **-at·ed, -at·ing.** repeat. [< L *iterare* < *iterum* again] —**it′er·a′tion,** *n.*

it·er·a·tive (it′ər ə tiv *or* it′ər ā′tiv) *adj.* repeating; full of repetitions.

i·tin·er·a·cy (ī tin′ər ə sē *or* i tin′ər ə sē) *n.* itinerancy.

i·tin·er·an·cy (ī tin′ər ən sē *or* i tin′ər ən sē) *n.* **1** a travelling from place to place. **2** a body of itinerant preachers or judges. **3** official work requiring much travel from place to place, or frequent changes of residence.

i·tin·er·ant (ī tin′ər ənt *or* i tin′ər ənt) *adj., n.* —*adj.* travelling from place to place, especially on a regular route: *an itinerant salesman.* —*n.* a person who travels from place to place. [< LL *itinerans, -antis,* ppr. of *itinerari* travel < L *iter, itineris* journey < *ire* go] —**i·tin′er·ant·ly,** *adv.*

i·tin·er·ar·y (ī tin′ər er′ē *or* i tin′ər er′ē) *n., pl.* **-ar·ies;** *adj.* —*n.* **1** the route or plan of a journey. **2** a travel diary. **3** a guidebook for travellers. —*adj.* of travelling or routes of travel.

i·tin·er·ate (ī tin′ər āt′ *or* i tin′ər āt′) *v.* **-at·ed, -at·ing.** travel from place to place. [< L *itinerari.* See ITINERANT.]

–itious *adjective-forming suffix.* of or having the nature of: *Fictitious means having the nature of fiction.*

–itis *noun-forming suffix.* inflammation of or inflammatory disease of, as in *appendicitis, tonsillitis.* [< Gk. -*itis,* fem. of -*itēs.* Cf. -ITE¹.]

it'll (it′əl) it will.

ITO International Trade Organization.

its (its) *adj., pron.* (possessive form of **it**). —*adj.* of, belonging to, or made or done by it or itself: *The dog hurt its paw. The report is important, and its delay now could cause problems.* —*pron.* that which belongs to it: *A dog's kennel is its and its alone.*

it's (its) **1** it is: *It's my turn.* **2** it has: *It's been a beautiful day.*

it·self (it self′) *pron.* **1** the emphatic form of **it:** *The land itself is worth more than the old house.* **2** the reflexive form of **it:** *The horse tripped and hurt itself.*

–ity *noun-forming suffix.* condition or quality, as in *absurdity, activity, hostility, sincerity,* or an instance of any of these, as in *a monstrosity, an activity.* [< F -*ité* < L *itas, -itatis*]

IU or **I.U.** international unit; international units.

IUD intrauterine device.

I've (īv) I have.

–ive *suffix.* **1** of or having to do with, as in *interrogative, inductive.* **2** tending to; likely to, as in *active, appreciative, imitative.* [< F -*ive* (fem. of -*if* < L -*ivus*) or directly < L -*ivus*]

i·vied (ī′vēd) *adj.* covered or overgrown with ivy.

i·vo·ry (īv′rē *or* ī′və rē) *n., pl.* **-ries;** *adj.* —*n.* **1** a hard, white substance, a form of dentine, composing the tusks of elephants, walruses, etc. Ivory is easy to carve and is used for many kinds of ornaments. **2** a substance like ivory. **3** a creamy white. **4 ivories,** *pl. Slang.* **a** piano keys. **b** dice. **c** billiard balls. **d** teeth. —*adj.* **1** made of ivory. **2** of or like ivory. **3** creamy white. [ME < AF *ivorie* < L *eboreus* of ivory < *ebur* ivory < Egyptian]

ivory black a fine-quality, deep-black pigment made from ivory that has been burned.

ivory nut the hard, white, nutlike seed of the ivory palm, formerly much used as a substitute for ivory.

ivory palm a short South American palm (*Phytelephas macrocarpa*) having featherlike leaves and fragrant flowers, whose seeds are called ivory nuts.

ivory tower a condition or attitude of withdrawal from the world of practical affairs into a world of ideas and dreams.

i·vy (ī′vē) *n., pl.* **i·vies. 1** any of a genus (*Hedera*) of Old World climbing or trailing plants of the ginseng family having woody stems and evergreen leaves, especially *H. helix,* a commonly grown climber. **2** any of various other climbing or creeping plants. [OE *ifig*]

iv·y–league (ī′vē lēg′) *adj.* characteristic of or having to do with the Ivy League, the colleges belonging to it, their faculties, or their students.

Ivy League 1 a group of eight old and prestigious universities of eastern U.S., including Harvard, Yale, and Princeton. **2** behavior, customs, etc. associated with the students of these colleges. [originally, an athletic association composed of the eight colleges]

i·wis (i wis′) *adv. Archaic.* certainly; indeed. [OE *gewis*]

Ix·i·on (iks ī′ən) *n. Greek legend.* the father of the Centaurs, who made love to Hera and was punished in Hades by being bound to a fiery wheel.

I·yar or **Iy·yar** (ē′yär) *n.* in the Hebrew calendar, the second month of the ecclesiastical year and the eighth month of the civil year.

–ize *verb-forming suffix.* **1** make, as in *legalize, centralize.* **2** become, as in *crystallize, materialize.* **3** engage in; be busy with; use, as in *apologize, theorize.* **4** treat or combine with, as in *macadamize, oxidize.* **5** other meanings, as in *alphabetize, colonize, criticize, memorize.* Also, **-ise.** [< F *iser* (< L -*izare*) or < L (< Gk. -*izein*) or directly < Gk. -*izein*]
☛ *Usage.* Many English verbs ending in the sound (īz) can be spelled with **-ize** or **-ise.** In Canadian usage **-ize** is preferred for words containing the Greek suffix, such as *apologize, civilize, visualize.* But **-ise** is usual in differently formed words derived from Old French, such as *advertise, exercise, supervise.* The spelling **-ize** is used in forming new words, such as *customize, slenderize.*

iz·zard (iz′ərd) *n. Archaic or dialect.* the letter Z.
from A to izzard, from beginning to end; completely.
[< *ezed,* variant of *zed,* ? < F *et zed* and Z]

Jj

j or **J** (jā) *n., pl.* **j's** or **J's. 1** the tenth letter of the English alphabet. **2** any speech sound represented by this letter. **3** a person or thing identified as *j*, especially the tenth in a series. **4** something shaped like the letter J. **5** (*adjl.*) of or being a J or j.

j *Physics.* joule.

J January.

J or **J. 1** judge. **2** justice. **3** journal.

Ja. January.

JA or **J.A.** judge advocate.

jab (jab) *v.* **jabbed, jab·bing;** *n.* —*v.* **1** thrust with something pointed; poke roughly: *He jabbed his fork into the potato.* **2** pierce; stab: *I just jabbed myself with a pin.* **3** punch with a short, straight blow; especially, in boxing, hit with the arm extended straight from the shoulder.
—*n.* **1** a thrust with a pointed thing, a fist, etc.: *She gave him a jab with her elbow.* **2** *Boxing.* a blow in which the arm is extended straight from the shoulder. [var. of *job.* v., ME *jobbe(n)*; probably imitative]

jab·ber (jab'ər) *v., n.* —*v.* talk very fast in a confused, senseless way; chatter. —*n.* very fast, confused, or senseless talk; chatter. [probably imitative] —**jab'ber·er,** *n.*

ja·bot (zha bō', zhab'ō, *or* jab'ō) *n.* a ruffle or frill of lace or cloth, worn at the throat or down the front of a blouse, shirt, etc. [< F *jabot*, originally, maw of a bird]

jac·a·ran·da (jak'ə ran'də) *n.* **1** any of a genus (*Jacaranda*) of tropical American trees of the bignonia family, having showy blue or violet flowers and compound leaves. **2** the hard, fragrant wood of any of these trees. **3** any of several similar trees or their wood, such as several trees (genus *Machaerium*) of the pea family. [< Pg.]

ja·cinth (jā'sinth *or* jas'inth) *n.* a reddish-orange gem, a kind of zircon. [ME < OF *jacinte* < L *hyacinthus* hyacinth < Gk. *hyakinthos*, a kind of flower. Doublet of HYACINTH.]

jack (jak) *n., v.* —*n.* **1** any of various mechanical devices for raising a heavy object a short distance. **2** a man or boy; fellow. **3** Also, **Jack,** a sailor. **4** a playing card with a picture of a court page on it; knave. **5 jacks,** a game in which stone or metal pieces are tossed up and caught or picked up in various groupings between bounces of a small rubber ball (*used with a singular verb*). **6** one of the pieces used in this game. **7** *Lawn bowling.* a small ball for players to aim at. **8** a small flag used on a ship to show nationality or to serve as a signal. **9** a device to turn roasting meat. **10** a male donkey. **11** jack-rabbit. **12** an electrical device to receive a plug. **13** jacklight. **14** jackfish. **15** *Slang.* money: *Have you got any jack?* **every man jack,** everyone.
—*v.* **1** raise by means of a jack (*often used with* **up**): *to jack up a car in order to change a tire.* **2** *Informal.* raise or increase the level or quality of (*usually used with* **up**): *to jack up prices.* **3** remind (someone) of his duty (*usually used with* **up**). **4** hunt or fish using a jacklight, especially when it is illegal. [ME *Jakke* < OF *Jaques*, a popular name for the French peasant < LL *Jacobus* Jacob]

jack·al (jak'əl, jak'ol, *or* jak'ôl) *n.* **1** any of several wild animals (genus *Canis*) of Asia, Africa and SW Europe, closely related to the dog. Jackals hunt in packs at night and feed on small animals and carrion left by large animals. **2** a person who does drudgery for another. [< Turkish *chakal* < Persian *shagal*]

jack·a·napes (jak'ə nāps') *n.* **1** an insolent, conceited fellow. **2** a saucy or mischievous child. [var. of ME *Jack Napes,* a name applied to William, Duke of Suffolk, whose badge was a clog and chain, such as was used for tame apes; probably originally the name for a tame ape]

jack·ass (jak'as') *n.* **1** a male donkey. **2** a very stupid person; fool. **3** See **laughing jackass.**

jack·boot (jak'büt') *n.* a heavy, leather, military boot reaching up to or above the knee.

jack·daw (jak'do' *or* -dô') *n.* a common black bird (*Corvus monedula*) of Europe and Asia closely related to the common crow, but smaller.

jack·et (jak'it) *n., v.* —*n.* **1** an outer garment for the upper part of the body, having a front opening, sleeves, and, usually, a collar with lapels. **2** any of various kinds of outer covering such as the skin of a potato or the casing around a steampipe. **3** dust jacket.

—*v.* put a jacket on; cover with a jacket. [ME < OF *jaquette,* dim. of *jaque* peasant's tunic < *Jaques.* See JACK.] —**jack'et·less,** *adj.*

jack·fish (jak'fish') *n., pl.* **-fish** *or* **-fish·es.** a common game fish (*Esox lucius*) of the pike family having a long, slender body and large head, found throughout most of Canada; northern pike.

Jack Frost frost or freezing cold weather personified.

jack·ham·mer (jak'ham'ər) *n.* a hand-held tool for drilling or breaking up rock, concrete, etc., driven by compressed air.

jack–in–a–box (jak'in ə boks') *n.* jack-in-the-box.

jack–in–the–box (jak'in THə boks') *n.* a toy figure that springs up from a box when the lid is unfastened.

jack–in–the–pul·pit (jak'in THə pùl'pit) *n.* any of several woodland plants (genus *Arisaema*) of the arum family, especially either of two North American species (*A. triphyllum* or *A. atrorubens*) found from Manitoba eastwards and south to the Gulf of Mexico, having a greenish, leaflike spathe arching over a clublike spadix.

Jack Ketch (kech) a public executioner; hangman. [< John *Ketch,* a British executioner, died 1686]

jack–knife or **jack·knife** (jak'nīf') *n., pl.* **-knives;** *v.* **-knifed, -knif·ing.** —*n.* **1** a large, strong pocketknife. **2** a kind of headfirst dive in which the diver touches his feet with his hands while keeping his legs straight, and then straightens out again before touching the water.
—*v.* **1** double up like a jack-knife. **2** perform a jack-knife dive. **3** of a tractor-trailer, a connected pair of railway cars, etc., double up at the connecting hitch when the brakes are applied suddenly or the vehicle is thrown off course.

jack·lad·der (jak'lad'ər) *n.* **1** *Nautical.* Jacob's ladder. **2** *Logging.* a slanting trough having an endless chain by means of which logs are moved from the water to the mill.

jack·light (jak'līt') *n., v.* —*n.* a light used for hunting or fishing at night. Fish or game are attracted by the jacklight so that they may be easily caught. —*v.* hunt or fish using a jacklight, especially when it is illegal; jack. —**jack'light·er,** *n.*

jack·light·ing (jak'līt'ing) *n.* the act or practice, often illegal, of hunting or fishing with a jacklight.

jack of all trades a person who can do many different kinds of work fairly well.

jack–o'–lan·tern (jak'ə lan'tərn) *n.* **1** a pumpkin hollowed out and cut to look like a face, used as a lantern at Halloween. **2** a will-o'-the-wisp (def. 1).

jack pine 1 a medium-tall pine (*Pinus banksiana*) found in central and E North America, having stiff, sharp, light-green needles and cones that are often curved. The wood of the jack pine is used in general construction and for pulp. **2** any of several other species of pine, such as the lodgepole or ponderosa pine.

jack·pot (jak'pot') *n.* **1** a large fund or pool of money that is competed for regularly and that increases as contestants fail to win it. **2** any large gain. **3** *Poker.* the stakes that accumulate until some player wins with a pair of jacks or something better.
hit the jackpot, a win a jackpot. **b** have a stroke of very good luck.

jack–rab·bit (jak'rab'it) *n.* any of several large hares (genus *Lepus*) of W North America, having very long ears and long back legs. [shortened from *jackass rabbit,* so called because of its long ears; 19c.]

jack·screw (jak'skrü') *n.* a kind of jack for lifting heavy masses short distances, operated by turning a screw.

jack·stone (jak'stōn') *n.* **1 jackstones,** the game of jacks (*used with a singular verb*). **2** one of the pieces used in this game.

jack·straw (jak'stro' *or* -strô') *n.* **1** a straw, strip of wood, bone, etc. used in a game. **2 jackstraws,** a game played with a set of these thrown down in a confused pile and picked up one at a time without moving any of the rest of the pile (*used with a singular verb*).

Jack Tar or **jack tar** a sailor.

Ja·cob (jā'kəb) *n.* in the Bible, the son of Isaac and younger twin brother of Esau. From Jacob's 12 sons the 12 tribes of Israel traced their descent (Gen. 25-50).

Jac·o·be·an (jak'ə bē'ən) *adj.* **1** of King James I of England (1566-1625). **2** of the early 17th century, especially the period of his

reign, from 1603 to 1625. Jacobean architecture is late English Gothic with a large admixture of Italian forms. [< NL *Jacobaeus* < LL *Jacobus* James]

Jac·o·bin (jak′ə bin) *n.* **1** in France, a member of a radical political organization formed at Versailles in 1789, later spreading throughout France, and abolished in 1796. **2** an extreme radical in politics. **3** a Dominican friar. [< F < Med.L *Jacobinus* of James < LL *Jacobus* James, from the Dominican convent near the Church of St. James of Compostella, where the Paris organization held its meetings]

Jac·o·bin·ism (jak′ə bin iz′əm) *n.* **1** the principles of the French Jacobins. **2** extreme radicalism in politics.

Jac·o·bite (jak′ə bīt′) *n.* in England, a supporter of James II (1633-1701) and his descendants in their claims to the throne after the Revolution in 1688. [< LL *Jacobus* James]

Jacob's ladder **1** any of a genus (*Polemonium*) of herbs of the phlox family found in most parts of the world, especially a widely cultivated European perennial (*P. caeruleum*) having blue or white flowers and pinnately compound leaves. **2** *Nautical.* a ladder with wooden or iron rungs supported by ropes or chains. [from the ladder to heaven, seen by Jacob in a dream (Gen. 28:12)]

jac·quard or **Jac·quard** (jə kärd′) *adj.* of or indicating a pattern or a fabric woven on a Jacquard loom.

Jacquard loom a loom that can produce more elaborate designs in woven fabrics than the limited patterns obtainable from a standard loom. [< Joseph *Jacquard* (1752-1834), a French weaver who invented it]

Jacque·rie (zhäk rē′) *n.* **1** a revolt of the peasants of N France against the nobles in 1358. **2** Also, **jacquerie.** any revolt of peasants. [< F *Jacquerie* peasants < *Jacques.* See JACK.]

jade¹ (jād) *n., adj.* —*n.* **1** either of two hard minerals, nephrite or jadeite, occurring in a wide variety of colors, especially green and white. **2** a gem or ornament made from this mineral. **3** a medium green.
—*adj.* **1** made of jade: *a jade bracelet.* **2** medium green. [< F < Sp. (*piedra de*) *ijada* (stone of) colic (jade being supposed to cure this), ult. < L *ilia* flanks]

jade² (jād) *n., v.* **jad·ed, jad·ing.** —*n.* **1** an inferior or worn-out horse. **2** *Derogatory or facetious.* woman. —*v.* **1** wear out; tire; weary. **2** dull by continual use; surfeit; satiate. [origin uncertain; cf. ON *jalda* mare]

jad·ed (jād′id) *adj.* **1** worn out; tired; weary: *a jaded horse, a jaded appearance.* **2** dulled from continual use; surfeited; satiated: *a jaded appetite.* —**jad′ed·ly,** *adv.* —**jad′ed·ness,** *n.*

jade·ite (jād′īt) *n.* a mineral, a silicate of sodium-aluminum that is harder and more valuable than nephrite, the other variety of jade.

jae·ger (yā′gər) *n.* any of three species of gull-like sea birds (genus *Stercorarius*) of northern seas having mainly dark-brown plumage and elongated central tail feathers, and noted for their aggressiveness against smaller birds, such as terns, which they frighten into dropping or disgorging their food. The jaegers and the skua make up the family Stercorariidae. [< G *Jäger,* literally, hunter]

Jaf·fa (jaf′ə) *n.* a type of orange from Jaffa, a seaport of Israel.

jag¹ (jag) *n., v.* **jagged, jag·ging.** —*n.* a sharp point sticking out; pointed projection. —*v.* **1** make notches or indentations in. **2** cut or tear unevenly. [origin uncertain]

jag² (jag) *n.* **1** *Dialect.* a small load: *a jag of fish.* **2** *Slang.* a state of intoxication. **3** *Slang.* a period of uncontrolled indulgence.

JAG or **J.A.G.** Judge Advocate General.

jag·ged (jag′id) *adj.* with sharp points sticking out; unevenly cut or torn: *jagged rocks.* —**jag′ged·ly,** *adv.* —**jag′ged·ness,** *n.*

jag·uar (jag′wär *or* jag′yü är′) *n.* a large wild animal (*Panthera onca*) of the cat family resembling the leopard but generally somewhat larger and having a typically tawny coat with black spots arranged in large rosettes with a spot in the centre. The jaguar was formerly common from Mexico south to central South America but is now greatly reduced in numbers and protected by law in most of the countries where it still exists. [< Tupi-Guarani *jaguara*]

Jah·veh or **Jah·ve** (yä′vä) *n.* See **Yahweh.**

jai a·lai (hī′lī′ *or* hī′ə lī′) a court game that is a variation of pelota, played by two or four players. [< Sp. < Basque < *jai* celebration, game + *alai* merry]

jail (jāl) *n., v.* —*n.* **1** a prison, especially one for people awaiting trial or being punished for minor offences. **2** imprisonment. **break jail,** escape from jail.
—*v.* put in jail; keep in jail. Also, *Brit.* **gaol.** [ME < OF *jaiole,* ult. < L *cavea* cage] —**jail′-like′,** *adj.*

jail·bird (jāl′bėrd′) *n. Slang.* **1** a prisoner in jail. **2** a person who has been in jail many times.

jail·break (jāl′brāk′) *n. Informal.* an escape from prison.

jail·er or **jail·or** (jāl′ər) *n.* **1** a keeper of a jail. **2** a person who keeps someone or something confined. Also, *Brit.* **gaoler.**

Jain (jān *or* jīn) *n., adj.* —*n.* a member or adherent of Jainism. —*adj.* of or having to do with the Jains or their religion. [< Hind. *Jaina* < *Jina* victorious]

Jain·ism (jā′niz əm *or* jī′niz əm) *n.* a religion of India founded about 500 B.C. and having Hindu and Buddhist elements. Its beliefs include non-violence, asceticism, and the transmigration of souls.

jal·ap (jal′əp) *n.* **1** a Mexican vine (*Exogonium purga*) of the morning-glory family having a turnip-shaped root that yields a resinous substance used as a laxative. **2** the dried root of this plant or the resinous powder prepared from it. **3** any of several similar or related plants or a resin obtained from them. [< Sp. *jalapa* < *Jalapa,* a city in Mexico]

ja·lop·y (jə lop′ē) *n., pl.* **-lop·ies.** *Informal.* an old automobile in a poor state of repair: *Is she still driving that old jalopy?* [origin uncertain]

jal·ou·sie (zhal′ü zē′) *n.* a window blind or shutter made of horizontal slats of wood, metal, or glass, that can be adjusted to regulate the light or air entering a room. [< F *jalousie,* literally, jealousy < *jaloux* jealous, from enabling one to see through the shutter without being seen]

jam¹ (jam) *v.* **jammed, jam·ming;** *n.* —*v.* **1** press; squeeze; hold; stick: *The ship was jammed between two rocks.* **2** crush; bruise: *Her fingers were jammed in the door.* **3** push or thrust (something) hard into a place; shove: *to jam one more book into the bookcase.* **4** fill up; block up: *The river was jammed with logs.* **5** stick fast or get caught so as not to work properly: *The window has jammed.* **6** make unworkable: *The key broke off and jammed the lock.* **7** make (radio signals, etc.) unintelligible by sending out others of approximately the same frequency.
—*n.* **1** a mass of people or things crowded together so that they cannot move freely: *a traffic jam.* **2** jamming or being jammed. **3** *Informal.* a difficult or tight spot. [? imitative]

jam² (jam) *n.* a preserve made by boiling fruit with sugar until thick. [? special use of *jam¹*] —**jam′like′,** *adj.*

Jam. Jamaica.

Jamaica mignonette henna.

Ja·mai·can (jə mā′kən) *n., adj.* —*n.* a native or inhabitant of Jamaica, an island country in the West Indies. —*adj.* of or having to do with Jamaica.

Ja·mai·ca rum (jə mā′kə) a dark, full-bodied rum made in Jamaica, an island country in the West Indies.

jamb (jam) *n.* the upright piece forming the side of a doorway, window, fireplace, etc. See **frame** for picture. [ME < OF *jambe,* originally, leg < LL *gamba* hock < Gk. *kampē* a bending]

jam·beau (jam′bō) *n.* a piece of armor for the leg below the knee; greave.

jam·bo·ree (jam′bə rē′) *n.* **1** *Slang.* a noisy party; lively entertainment. **2** a large rally or gathering of Boy Scouts. [coined from *jam¹* after *corroboree, shivaree*]

jam–packed (jam′pakt′) *adj. Informal.* filled to capacity; packed tightly.

jam session an informal gathering of jazz musicians at which they play improvisations.

Jan. January.

jan·gle (jang′gəl) *v.* **-gled, -gling;** *n.* —*v.* **1** sound harshly; make a loud, clashing noise. **2** cause to make a hard, clashing sound: *He jangled the bell.* **3** quarrel; dispute. **4** make tense or strained; upset: *Their continual complaints jangled her nerves.*
—*n.* **1** a harsh sound; clashing noise or ring: *The jangle of the telephone woke him up.* **2** quarrel; dispute. [ME < OF *jangler*] —**jan′gler,** *n.*

Jan·is·sar·y or **jan·is·sar·y** (jan′ə ser′ē) *n., pl.* **-sar·ies.** Janizary.

jan·i·tor (jan′ə tər) *n.* a person hired to take care of a building, offices, etc.; caretaker. [< L *janitor* doorkeeper < *janus* arched passageway]

jan·i·tress (jan′ə tris) *n.* a woman janitor.

Jan·i·zar·y or **jan·i·zar·y** (jan′ə zer′ē) *n., pl.* **-zar·ies. 1** in Turkey, a soldier in the Sultan's guard. Janizaries formed the crack fighting force of the Turkish army from the 14th century until 1826. **2** any Turkish soldier. Also, **Janissary** or **janissary.** [< F *janissaire* < Ital. *giannizzero* < Turkish *yeñicheri* < *yeñi* new + *cheri* soldiery]

Jan·sen·ism (jan′sə niz′əm) *n.* the doctrine of a Dutch theologian, Cornelius Jansen (1585-1638), who held that the human will is not free to do good and that salvation is limited to God's chosen few.

Jan·sen·ist (jan′sə nist) *n.* a believer in, or follower of, Jansenism.

Jan·u·ar·y (jan′yə wer′ē *or* jan′yü er′ē) *n., pl.* **-ar·ies.** the first month of the year. It has 31 days. [< L *Januarius* < *Janus* Janus]

Ja·nus (jā′nəs) *n. Roman mythology.* the god of gates and doors, and of beginnings and endings, represented as having two faces, one looking forward and the other looking backward.

Ja·nus–faced (jā′nəs fāst′) *adj.* two-faced; double-dealing; deceitful.

Jap (jap) *adj. or n. Derogatory.* Japanese.

Jap. Japan; Japanese.

ja·pan (jə pan′) *n., v.* **-panned, -pan·ning.** —*n.* **1** a hard, glossy varnish. Black japan is used on wood or metal. **2** articles varnished and decorated in the Japanese manner. **3** a liquid used to make paint dry faster.
—*v.* put japan on. [< *Japan*]

Japan current a current of warm water in the Pacific Ocean, flowing north from the Philippine Sea, past SE Japan, and then into the N Pacific Ocean.

Jap·a·nese (jap′ə nēz′) *n., pl.* **-nese;** *adj.* —*n.* **1** a native or inhabitant of Japan, an island country off the east coast of Asia. **2** a person of Japanese descent. **3** the language of the Japanese.
—*adj.* of or having to do with Japan, its people, or their language.

Japanese beetle a small, green-and-brown beetle (*Popillia japonica*) that eats fruits, leaves, and grasses. It was accidentally brought from Japan to North America, where it has done much damage to crops.

Japanese quince japonica.

jape (jāp) *n., v.* **japed, jap·ing.** —*n. or v.* joke or jest. [ME; origin uncertain] —**jap′er,** *n.*

ja·pon·i·ca (jə pon′ə kə) *n.* **1** any of several flowering quinces, especially *Chaenomeles japonica* or *C. speciosa.* Also called Japanese quince. **2** camellia. [< NL *japonica*, originally fem. adj., Japanese]

jar¹ (jär) *n.* **1** a deep container made of glass, earthenware, etc. with a wide mouth and a removable lid. **2** the amount that it holds. **3** a jar and its contents. [< F *jarre*, ult. < Arabic *jarrah*]

jar² (jär) *v.* **jarred, jar·ring;** *n.* —*v.* **1** cause to shake or rattle; vibrate: *The heavy footsteps jarred my desk so that I had trouble writing.* **2** make a harsh, discordant noise. **3** have a harsh, unpleasant effect on; shock: *The children's playful screams jarred his nerves.* **4** clash; quarrel: *Our opinions jar.*
—*n.* **1** a shake; rattle. **2** a harsh, discordant noise. **3** a harsh, unpleasant effect; shock. **4** a clash; quarrel. [probably imitative]

jar³ (jär) *n.* a turn; a turning.
on the jar, ajar; slightly open. [OE *cierr*]

jar·di·niere (jär′də nēr′) *n.* an ornamental pot or stand for flowers or plants. [< F *jardinière* < *jardin* garden]

jar·gon (jär′gən) *n.* **1** language that fails to communicate because it is full of long or fancy words, uses more words than necessary, and contains lengthy, awkward sentences. **2** a form of speech made up of features from two or more languages, used for communication between peoples whose native languages differ: *the Chinook jargon. Pidgin English is a jargon.* **3** the language of a particular group, profession, etc.: *the jargon of sailors.* **4** *Archaic.* any speech or language that is strange to one and therefore seems meaningless. **5** meaningless talk or chatter; gibberish. [ME < OF; probably ult. imitative]
➤ *Usage.* Definitions 2 and 3 carry no slur or criticism but are technical senses of **jargon** as used by linguists. They should not be confused with definition 1, which does suggest poor expression and muddled thinking.

jarl (yärl) *n.* in ancient Scandinavia, a chief or nobleman. [< ON. Related to EARL.]

jas·mine (jas′mən *or* jaz′mən) *n.* **1** any of a large genus (*Jasminum*) of tropical and subtropical shrubs and vines of the olive family, especially any of a number of species cultivated for their highly fragrant flowers, such as *J. officinalis*, whose usually white or yellow flowers are used in perfumery. **2** any of various other plants having fragrant flowers, such as the frangipani, often called **red jasmine,** or **yellow jasmine** (*Gelsemium sempervirens*). [< F *jasmin* < Arabic < Persian *yasmin*]

Ja·son (jā′sən) *n. Greek mythology.* the Greek hero who led the expedition of the Argonauts and won the Golden Fleece.

jas·per (jas′pər) *n.* **1** an opaque variety of quartz, usually red, yellow, or brown. **2** a gem made from this stone. [ME < OF *jaspre* < L < Gk. *iaspis* < Semitic]

ja·to (jā′tō) *n. Aeronautics.* a unit consisting of one or more jet engines, used to provide auxiliary propulsion for speeding up the take-off of an aircraft. [< *jet assisted take-off*]

jaun·dice (jon′dis *or* jôn′dis) *n., v.* **-diced, -dic·ing.** —*n.* **1** a disease of the liver, characterized by yellowness of the skin, eyes, and body fluids, and disturbed vision. **2** a disturbed or unnaturally sour mental outlook, due to envy, jealousy, etc. —*v.* **1** cause jaundice in. **2** prejudice the mind and judgment of by envy, discontent, etc.; sour the temper of. [ME < OF *jaunisse* < *jaune* yellow < L *galbinus* greenish yellow]

jaunt (jont *or* jônt) *n., v.* a short pleasure trip or excursion. —*v.* take a short pleasure trip or excursion. [origin uncertain]

jaunting car a light cart having two seats back to back, formerly used in Ireland.

jaun·ty (jon′tē *or* jôn′tē) *adj.* **-ti·er, -ti·est. 1** easy and lively; sprightly; carefree: *The happy boy walked with jaunty steps.* **2** smart; stylish: *She wore a jaunty little hat.* [formerly *janty* < F *gentil* noble, gentle < L *gentilis.* Doublet of GENTEEL, GENTILE, GENTLE.] —**jaun′ti·ly,** *adv.* —**jaun′ti·ness,** *n.*

Ja·va (jä′və *or* jav′ə) *n.* **1** a kind of coffee obtained from Java, a large island southeast of Asia, and nearby islands. **2** *Slang.* coffee.

Java man a very early form of man inferred from fossil remains found in Java.

Jav·a·nese (jav′ə nēz′) *n., pl.* **-nese;** *adj.* —*n.* **1** a native or inhabitant of Java, an island of Indonesia, in SE Asia. **2** the Austronesian language of the Javanese. —*adj.* of or having to do with Java, its people, or their language.

jave·lin (jav′lən *or* jav′ə lin) *n.* **1** a light spear thrown by hand. **2** a wooden or metal spear, thrown for distance in track and field contests. [< F *javeline*]

Ja·vel water (jə vel′) a solution of sodium or potassium hypochlorite, used as a bleach and disinfectant. [*Javel*, < F *Javelle,* a former town now included in Paris]

jaw (jo *or* jô) *n., v.* —*n.* **1** either of the two bones or sets of bones that hold the teeth and together form the framework of the mouth in most vertebrates. The lower jaw is usually movable; the upper jaw is usually fixed. **2** the lower part of the face, especially the lower jaw: *He has a square jaw.* **3 jaws,** *pl.* **a** the mouth with its jawbones and teeth. **b** a narrow entrance to a valley, mountain pass, channel, etc. **c** the parts in a tool or machine that grip and hold: *A vise has jaws.* **4** *Slang.* talk; gossip.
—*v. Slang.* **1** talk; gossip. **2** find fault; scold. [? related to CHEW; influenced by F *joue* cheek] —**jaw′less,** *adj.*

jaw·bone (jo′bōn′ *or* jô′-) *n.* **1** the bone of the lower jaw. **2** the bone of the upper jaw.

jaw·break·er (jo′brāk′ər *or* jô′-) *n. Slang.* **1** a big, hard piece of candy. **2** a word that is hard to pronounce. **3** a machine for crushing ore.

jay (jā) *n.* **1** any of various birds of the same family as the crows, noted for being noisy and aggressive, many species being brightly colored and having a crest. The bluejay and Canada jay are common Canadian birds. The common Eurasian jay (*Garrulus glandarius*) has mainly pinkish-brown plumage with mainly blue-and-black wings and a black-and-white crest. **2** *Informal.* an impertinent or foolish chatterer. **3** *Slang.* a silly, stupid person. [ME < OF < LL *gaius*]

Jay·cee (jā′sē′) *n.* a member of a Junior Chamber of Commerce. [from junior chamber]

jay·walk (jā′wok′ *or* -wôk′) *v. Informal.* walk across a street at a place other than a regular crossing or without paying attention to traffic. [< *jay* a stupid person + *walk*] —**jay′walk′er,** *n.*

jazz (jaz) *n., v.* —*n.* **1** a style of music characterized by strong, often complex rhythms, improvisation of a basic melody, and unusual features of musical tone, such as long-drawn wavering or wailing sounds. Jazz originated among black musicians in New Orleans in the rhythmic traditions of African music. **2** (*adj.*) of, having to do with, or playing jazz: *a jazz band.* **3** any popular dance music having a pronounced rhythm. **4** *Slang.* anything considered tiresome, affected, trite, etc.: *I'm tired of all that jazz about how hard he works.*
—*v.* **1** play or arrange (music) as jazz. **2** *Slang.* make more exciting, lively, or decorative (*usually used with* **up**): *to jazz up a dull color scheme.* [of American Negro origin] —**jazz′er,** *n.*

jaz·zy (jaz′ē) *adj.* **1** having the qualities of jazz. **2** *Informal.* loud, flashy, or unrestrained: *jazzy clothes.*

J.C. **1** Jesus Christ. **2** Julius Caesar.

J.C.C. Junior Chamber of Commerce.

J.C.D. **1** Doctor of Canon Law (for L *Juris Canonici Doctor*). **2** Doctor of Civil Law (for L *Juris Civilis Doctor*).

---

hat, āge, fär; let, ēqual, tèrm; it, īce
hot, ōpen, ôrder; oil, out; cup, pút, rüle,
əbove, takən, pencəl, lemən, circəs

ch, child; ng, long; sh, ship
th, thin; ᴛʜ, then; zh, measure

jct. or **jctn.** junction.

J.D. Doctor of Laws (for L *Jurum Doctor*).

Je. June.

jeal·ous (jel′əs) *adj.* **1** fearful that a person one loves may love or prefer someone else. One may be jealous of the person loved or of the rival. **2** full of envy; envious: *He is jealous of John or of John's marks.* **3** requiring complete loyalty or faithfulness: *"The Lord thy God is a jealous God."* **4** watchful in keeping or guarding something; careful: *A democracy is jealous of its freedom.* **5** close; watchful; suspicious: *The dog was a jealous guardian of the child.* [ME < OF *gelos* < LL *zelosus* < L *zelus* zeal < Gk. *zēlos.* Related to ZEAL.] —**jeal′ous·ly**, *adv.* —**jeal′ous·ness**, *n.*

jeal·ous·y (jel′əs ē) *n., pl.* **-ous·ies.** a jealous condition or feeling.

jean (jēn) *n.* **1** *pl.* pants made of denim, usually blue, or a similar strong cloth. **2** a strong, twilled cotton cloth used for work clothes, etc. [probably < F *Gênes* Genoa, Italy]
☛ *Hom.* **gene.**

Jean Baptiste (zhän bä tēst′) *Cdn. Slang.* a French-Canadian. [< Saint *Jean Baptiste* St. John the Baptist, regarded as a patron saint of French Canada]

jeep (jēp) *n.* a small, powerful, four-passenger motor vehicle in which power is transmitted to all four wheels, permitting the vehicle to be used on very rough or hilly terrain. Jeeps are used in the armed forces and by farmers, ranchers, builders, etc. [probably from *G.P.* general purpose. 20c.]

jeer (jēr) *v., n.* —*v.* make fun rudely or unkindly; mock; scoff. —*n.* a jeering remark; rude, sarcastic comment. [origin uncertain] —**jeer′er**, *n.*
☛ *Syn. v.* See note at **scoff.**

jeer·ing·ly (jēr′ing lē) *adv.* in a jeering manner; with derision.

Je·ho·vah (ji hō′və) *n.* God. [erroneous modern representation of Hebrew *Yahweh* (originally written without vowels as JHVH), interpreted as meaning "he that is," "the self-existent"]

Jehovah's Witnesses a Christian sect founded by Charles T. Russell in Pennsylvania in the 1870's. Some of their tenets are that organized religion is evil, that personal religious conviction is beyond civil authority, and that the end of the world is near.

je·hu (jē′hyü *or* jā′hyü) *n. Informal.* a fast driver. [< *Jehu* (842-815 B.C.), King of Israel (II Kings 9:20), with reference to his furious driving]

je·june (ji jün′) *adj.* **1** lacking nourishing qualities. **2** flat and uninteresting. **3** naïve; unsophisticated. [< L *jejunus*, originally, hungry] —**je·june′ly**, *adv.* —**je·june′ness**, *n.*

je·ju·num (ji jü′nəm) *n. Anatomy.* the middle portion of the small intestine, between the duodenum and the ileum. See **alimentary canal** for picture. [< NL < L *jejunum*, neut., empty]

Jek·yll (jek′əl *or* jē′kəl) *n.* **1 Dr. Jekyll,** the chief character in R. L. Stevenson's story *Dr. Jekyll and Mr. Hyde.* He discovered a drug that changed him into a brutal person (Mr. Hyde) and another that changed him back to himself. **2 Jekyll and Hyde,** a dual personality, part good or pleasant and part evil or unpleasant.

jell (jel) *v.* **1** set; become jelly. **2** *Informal.* take definite form; become fixed: *Our plans have jelled.* [< *jelly*]

jel·lied (jel′ēd) *adj.* **1** turned into jelly; having the consistency of jelly. **2** spread with jelly. **3** prepared in or covered with jelly: *jellied eels.*

jel·ly (jel′ē) *n., pl.* **-lies;** *v.* **-lied, -ly·ing.** —*n.* **1** a food that is liquid when hot but rather firm when cold. Jelly can be made by boiling fruit juice and sugar together, or by cooking bones and meat in water, or by using some stiffening preparation like gelatin. **2** a jellylike substance: *petroleum jelly.* —*v.* **1** become jelly; turn into jelly. **2** prepare in or cover with jelly. [ME < OF *gelee*, originally, frost < L *gelata*, originally fem. pp. of *gelare* congeal] —**jel′ly·like′**, *adj.*

jel·ly·bean (jel′ē bēn′) *n.* a small, bean-shaped candy, made of jellied sugar coated in different colors.

jel·ly·fish (jel′ē fish′) *n., pl.* **-fish** *or* **-fishes. 1** any of a class (Scyphozoa) of invertebrate marine animals having a jellylike, translucent, umbrella-shaped body with a tube-shaped mouth hanging from the bottom and tentacles around the margin of the body that are armed with stinging cells. **2** a free-swimming hydrozoan. **3** *Informal.* a person of weak will or character.

jel·ly·roll (jel′ē rōl′) *n.* a thin layer of sponge cake spread with jelly and rolled up while still warm.

je ne sais quoi (zhən sā kwä′) *French.* an indefinable something (literally, 'I don't know what).

jen·net (jen′it) *n.* **1** a breed of small Spanish horses. **2** a horse of this breed. **3** a female donkey. Also, **genet.** [< F *genet* < Sp. *jinete*

mounted soldier < Arabic *Zenāta,* a Berber tribe noted for its cavalry]

jen·ny (jen′ē) *n., pl.* **-nies. 1** a spinning jenny. **2** the female of certain animals and birds. [originally a proper name, dim. of *Jane,* fem. of *John*]

jeop·ard (jep′ərd) *v. Rare.* jeopardize.

jeop·ard·ize (jep′ər dīz′) *v.* **-ized, -iz·ing.** put in danger; risk; imperil: *Soldiers jeopardize their lives in war.*

jeop·ard·y (jep′ər dē) *n.* **1** risk; danger; peril: *The firefighters put their lives in jeopardy when they entered the burning building.* **2** *Law.* the peril of the defendant when put on trial for a crime. [ME < OF *jeu parti* an even or divided game, ult. < L *jocus* play + *pars, partis* part]

Jeph·thah (jef′thə) *n.* in the Bible, a judge of Israel who sacrificed his only daughter to fulfil a rash vow (Judges 11:30-40).

jer·bo·a (jər bō′ə) *n.* any of several small, nocturnal, mouselike, jumping rodents (family Dipodidae) of Asia and N Africa having very long hind legs, a long tail, and large ears. [< NL < Arabic *yarbū*]

jer·e·mi·ad (jer′ə mī′ad) *n.* a mournful complaint; lamentation. [< F *jérémiade* < *Jérémie* Jeremiah, the reputed author of *Lamentations* in the Bible]

Jer·e·mi·ah (jer′ə mī′ə) *n.* a Hebrew prophet of the 7th and 6th centuries B.C. who denounced and lamented the evils of his time, as recorded in the Book of Jeremiah in the Bible. **2** a pessimistic person who sees mainly evil around him and predicts a terrible future. Also called **Jeremias.**

Jer·i·cho (jer′ə kō′) *n., pl.* **-chos. 1** an ancient city in Palestine. According to the Bible, the walls of Jericho fell down at the noise made by the trumpets of Joshua's attacking army. **2** an out-of-the-way place.

jerk¹ (jėrk) *n., v.* —*n.* **1** a sudden, sharp pull, twist, or start. **2** a pull or twist of the muscles that one cannot control; twitch. **3** *Slang.* an unsophisticated or stupid person. —*v.* **1** pull or twist suddenly. **2** throw with a movement that stops suddenly. **3** move with a jerk: *The old wagon jerked along.* **4** speak or say abruptly. [probably imitative]
☛ *Syn. v.* **1.** See note at **pull.**

jerk² (jėrk) *v.* preserve (meat) by cutting it into long thin slices and drying it in the sun. The Indians taught the early settlers in North America how to jerk beef. [< Sp. *charquear* < *charquí* jerked meat < Quechua (Indian lang. of Peru)]

jer·kin (jėr′kən) *n.* a short, close-fitting coat or jacket without sleeves. Leather jerkins were worn by men in the 16th and 17th centuries. [origin uncertain]

jerk·wa·ter (jėrk′wot′ər *or* -wô′tər) *adj., n. Informal.* —*adj.* **1** remote and rustic: *a jerkwater town.* **2** trifling or insignificant. —*n. Historical.* a train on a branch railway. [from the fact that trains on branch lines had to get their water supply by "jerking" it in buckets from streams, etc. 19c.]

jerk·y¹ (jėr′kē) *adj.* **jerk·i·er, jerk·i·est.** with sudden starts and stops; with jerks. —**jerk′i·ly**, *adv.* —**jerk′i·ness**, *n.*

jerk·y² (jėr′kē) *n.* strips of dried beef. [< Sp. *charquí.* See JERK².]

jer·o·bo·am (jer′ə bō′əm) *n.* **1** a wine bottle holding one gallon. **2** this amount. **3** any large container or bottle for alcoholic beverages. **4** its contents. [< *Jeroboam,* a king of ancient Israel]

jer·ry or **Jer·ry** (jer′ē) *n. Slang.* **1** a German soldier. **2** a German. [probably dim. of *German*]

jer·ry-built (jer′ē bilt′) *adj.* built quickly and cheaply of poor materials; flimsy. [? alteration of an earlier *jury-built;* cf. *jury-rigged* rigged for temporary service. See JURY².]

jer·ry-can (je′rē kan′) *n. Slang.* a four-gallon gasoline container of rectangular shape. It was devised by the Germans during World War II. [< *jerry;* short for *jeroboam,* + *can²*]

jer·sey (jėr′zē) *n., pl.* **-seys. 1** a soft, somewhat elastic, machine-knitted fabric made with a plain stitch like that used in hand knitting. It may be of wool, cotton, silk, or synthetics and is used for undergarments and for dresses, blouses, etc. **2** a close-fitting knitted garment for the upper body. **3 Jersey,** a breed of small, fawn-colored dairy cattle that give very rich milk. [< *Jersey,* one of the Channel Islands. The knitted fabric and garments are named for the woollen sweaters traditionally worn by the fishermen of Jersey. Jersey cattle originally came from this island.]

Jerusalem artichoke (jə rü′sə ləm) **1** a perennial North American herb (*Helianthus tuberosus*) of the composite family closely related to the sunflower and widely cultivated for its edible tubers. **2** the tuber of this plant, which is cooked and eaten as a vegetable, especially in Europe. [< *Jerusalem,* as an alteration of Ital. *girasole* sunflower]

jess (jes) *n., v.* —*n.* a short strap fastened around a falcon's leg. A leash could be attached to it. —*v.* put the jesses on. [ME < OF *ges,* ult. < L *jacere* to throw]

jes·sa·mine (jes′ə min) *n.* jasmine.

Jes·se (jes′ē) *n.* in the Bible, the father of David, ancestor of Christ (1 Sam. 16). Jesse is often depicted as the root of a tree which bears as its fruit David and other royal ancestors of Christ, with the infant Jesus and His Mother on the highest branch.

jest (jest) *v., n.* —*v.* **1** act or speak playfully, teasingly, or amusingly; joke. **2** make fun of; laugh at.
—*n.* **1** joke. **2** the act of making fun of; mockery. **3** something intended to be mocked or laughed at.
in jest, in fun; not seriously. [< OF *geste,* originally, story, exploit < L *gesta,* neut. pl., exploits < *gestus,* pp. of *gerere* accomplish]
—**jest′ing·ly,** *adv.*
☛ *Syn. v.* **1.** See note at **joke.**

jest·er (jes′tər) *n.* a person who jests. In the Middle Ages kings often had jesters to amuse them.

Je·su (jē′zyü *or* jē′zü, jē′syü *or* jē′sü) *n. Archaic or poetic.* Jesus.

Jes·u·it (jez′yü it *or* jezh′ü it) *n.* **1** *Roman Catholic Church.* a member of a religious order called the Society of Jesus, founded by Saint Ignatius Loyola in 1534. Some of the first explorers of America were Jesuits. **2** *Derogatory.* a crafty or scheming person, especially in debate or argument. [< NL *Jesuita* < LL *Jesus* Jesus]

Jes·u·it·ic (jez′yü it′ik *or* jezh′ü it′ik) *adj.* **1** of or having to do with the Jesuits. **2 jesuitic,** *Derogatory.* scheming; using subtle reasoning.

Jes·u·it·ism (jez′yü ə tiz′əm *or* jezh′ü ə tiz′əm) *n.* **1** the religious order of the Jesuits, or their principles and practices. **2 jesuitism,** *Derogatory.* subtle distinctions; duplicity.

Je·sus (jē′zəs) *n.* Jesus of Nazareth (? 4 B.C. - A.D. ?29), who is regarded by Christians as the incarnate Son of God and the true Messiah. Brought up as a Jew and trained as a carpenter, he became a teacher of note, whose teachings incurred the wrath of the Roman and Jewish authorities and ultimately led to his death by crucifixion. His disciples' account of his birth, life, teachings, death, and resurrection constitute the four Gospels of the New Testament.

Jesus Christ Jesus.

jet¹ (jet) *n., v.* **-jet·ted, -jet·ting.** —*n.* **1** a stream of gas or liquid, sent with force, especially from a small opening: *A fountain sends up a jet of water.* **2** a spout or nozzle for sending out a jet. **3** a jet-propelled aircraft. **4** jet engine. **5** (*adj.*) of, having to do with, or involving the use of jet-propelled aircraft or jet propulsion: *the jet age, jet travel.*
—*v.* **1** gush out; shoot forth in a jet or forceful stream. **2** travel or carry by jet aircraft. [< F *jet* < *jeter* throw]

jet² (jet) *n.* a hard, black variety of lignite that can be carved and polished to a high sheen. Jet is used for making buttons, beads, etc. [ME < OF *jaiet* < L < Gk. *gagatēs* < *Gagas,* a town in Lycia, Asia Minor]

jet–black (jet′blak′) *adj.* deep black.

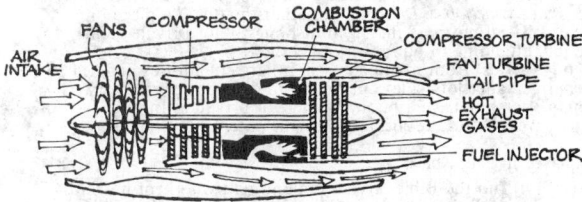

Jet engine: a turbofan

jet engine an engine that produces motion by jet propulsion, especially an aircraft engine that moves the aircraft forward by the reaction to the discharge of heated gases from the combustion chamber through one or more exhaust nozzles at the rear. Two types of jet engine are the turbojet and the ramjet.

jet lag a delayed effect of fatigue and sleepiness after a long flight in a jet aircraft, especially when several time zones have been crossed.

jet·lin·er (jet′līn′ər) *n.* a large jet aircraft used for carrying passengers on commercial flights.

jet plane an aircraft that is driven by one or more jet engines.

jet·port (jet′pôrt′) *n.* an airport for jet planes.

jet–prop (jet′prop′) *adj., n.* —*adj.* equipped with turboprop engines. —*n.* an aircraft thus equipped.

jet–pro·pelled (jet′prə peld′) *adj.* **1** driven by jet propulsion. **2** moving very fast and energetically.

hat, āge, fär; let, ēqual, tèrm; it, īce
hot, ōpen, ôrder; oil, out; cup, pùt, rüle,
əbove, takən, pencəl, lemən, circəs

ch, child; ng, long; sh, ship
th, thin; ŦH, then; zh, measure

jet propulsion propulsion in a given direction by a jet of air, gas, etc. forced in the opposite direction.

jet·sam (jet′səm) *n.* **1** goods thrown overboard to lighten a ship in distress. **2** such goods washed ashore. **3** anything tossed aside as useless. [var. of *jetson,* a var. of *jettison.* Doublet of JETTISON.]

jet set an international social set composed of wealthy people who frequent fashionable cities and resorts in various countries.

jet stream a current of air travelling at very high speed (often more than 350 km/h) from west to east at high altitudes (13 to 20 km). Jet streams are often used by airplane pilots to gain extra speed when travelling in an easterly direction.

jet·ti·son (jet′ə sən *or* jet′ə zən) *v., n.* —*v.* **1** throw (goods) overboard to lighten a ship, aircraft, etc. in distress. **2** throw away; discard. —*n.* **1** the act of throwing (goods) overboard to lighten a ship, aircraft, etc. in distress. **2** the goods thrown overboard; jetsam. [< OF *getaison* < L *jactatio, -onis* < *jactare* toss < *jacere* throw. Doublet of JETSAM.]

jet·ty (jet′ē) *n., pl.* **-ties. 1** a structure built out into the water to protect a harbor or to control the current or tide; breakwater. **2** a landing place; pier or dock. [< OF *jetee* (something) thrown out < *jeter* throw, ult. < L *jacere*]

Jew (jü) *n.* **1** a person descended from the ancient Israelites, who settled in Palestine and now live in Israel and many other countries; Hebrew. **2** a person whose religion is Judaism. **3** (*adj.*) Jewish. [ME < OF *giu, jueu* < L *Judaeus* < Gk. *Ioudaios* < Hebrew *y'hudi* belonging to the tribe of Judah]

jew·el (jü′əl) *n., v.* **-elled** *or* **-eled, -el·ling** *or* **-el·ing.** —*n.* **1** a precious stone; gem. **2** a valuable ornament to be worn, set with precious stones. **3** a person or thing that is very precious. **4** a gem or other piece of hard material used as a bearing in a watch. —*v.* set or adorn with jewels or with things like jewels: *a jewelled bracelet. The sky was jewelled with stars.* [ME < AF *juel* trinket, plaything < Med.L *jocalis* < L *jocus* joke, game] —**jew′el·like′,** *adj.*

jew·el·er (jü′əl ər *or* jü′lər) See **jeweller.**

jew·el·ler (jü′əl ər *or* jü′lər) *n.* a person who makes, sells, or repairs jewels, jewelled ornaments, watches, etc. Also, **jeweler.**

jew·el·er·y *or* **jew·el·ry** (jü′əl rē *or* jül′rē) *n.* jewels and ornaments set with gems.

jew·el·ry (jü′əl rē *or* jül′rē) See **jewellery.**

jew·el·weed (jü′əl wēd′) *n.* any of several species of wild impatiens having yellow or orange flowers; touch-me-not.

Jew·ess (jü′is) *n. Offensive.* a Jewish woman or girl.

jew·fish (jü′fish′) *n., pl.* **-fish** *or* **-fish·es.** any of various large, dark-colored fishes (family Serranidae) of warm seas, such as *Epinephelus itajara,* of the Atlantic coast of tropical America. [origin unknown]

Jew·ish (jü′ish) *adj., n.* —*adj.* **1** of, belonging to, or characteristic of the Jews: *Jewish customs.* **2** Yiddish. —*n.* Yiddish. —**Jew′ish·ness,** *n.*

Jewish calendar the Hebrew calendar, which dates the Creation at 3761 B.C. and divides the year into 12 months of 29 or 30 days each, allowing for an extra month of 29 days every second or third year. The ecclesiastical year begins in March or April, and the civil year in September or October.

Jew·ry (jü′rē) *n., pl.* **-ries. 1** Jews as a group; the Jewish people. **2** *Obsolete.* a district where Jews live; ghetto.

jews′-harp *or* **jew′s–harp** (jüz′härp′) *n.* a simple musical instrument, held between the teeth and played by striking with a finger the free end of a piece of metal.

Jez·e·bel (jez′ə bəl) *n.* **1** in the Bible, the depraved and wicked wife of Ahab, King of Israel (II Kings 9:7-10, 30-37). **2** any shameless, immoral woman.

J.H.S. junior high school.

jib¹ (jib) *n.* on a ship or boat, a triangular sail in front of the foremast. See **schooner** for picture.
cut of (one's) jib, *Informal.* one's outward appearance. [? < *jib²*]

jib² (jib) *v.* **jibbed, jib·bing.** jibe¹.

jib³ (jib) *n., v.* **jibbed, jib·bing.** —*v.* move sideways or backward instead of forward; refuse to go ahead. —*n.* a horse or other animal that jibs. [origin uncertain] —**jib′ber,** *n.*

jib⁴ (jib) *n.* the projecting arm of a crane or derrick. [probably < *gibbet*]

jib boom a spar extending out from a ship's bowsprit. See **bowsprit** for picture.

jibe¹ (jīb) v. **jibed, jib·ing. 1** shift (a sail) from one side of a ship to the other when sailing before the wind. **2** change the course of a ship so that the sails shift in this way. Also, **jib.** [< Du. *gijben*, var. of *gijpen*]

jibe² (jīb) See **gibe.**

jibe³ (jīb) v. **jibed, jib·ing.** *Informal.* be in harmony; agree. [origin uncertain]

jif·fy (jif′ē) n., pl. **jif·fies.** *Informal.* a very short time; moment. [origin unknown]

jig¹ (jig) n., v. **jigged, jig·ging. —n. 1** any of several lively dances, often in 3/4 time. **2** the music for a jig.
the jig is up, *Slang.* it's all over; there's no more chance.
in jig time, quickly; rapidly.
—v. 1 dance a jig. **2** move jerkily; jerk up and down or back and forth. **3** sing or play (music) as a jig or in the style of a jig. [< OF *giguer* dance < *gigue* fiddle < Gmc.]

jig² (jig) n., v. **jigged, jig·ging. —n. 1** a fishing lure made of one or more fish-hooks, weighted with a bright metal or having a spoon-shaped piece of bone attached, for bobbing up and down or drawing through the water. **2** any of various mechanical contrivances or devices; especially, a guide in using a drill, file, etc. **—v.** fish with a jig. [origin uncertain]

jig·ger¹ (jig′ər) n. **1** a small set of ropes and pulleys used on a ship. **2** a small sail. **3** a jigger mast. **4** any of various machines that operate with a jerky, up-and-down or back-and-forth motion. **5** *Informal.* some device, article, or part that one cannot name more precisely; gadget; contraption. **6** a jig used in fishing. **7** *Cdn.* a device used for setting a gill net under the ice on lakes and rivers. **8** a small glass used for measuring liquor in preparing drinks, usually holding about 43 mL. **9** the amount that a jigger can hold. **10** a jigger and its contents. **11** *Cdn.* a small, flat car used by work crews, etc. on a railway, driven by a handle that is pumped up and down or by a gas motor. [< *jig²*]

jig·ger² (jig′ər) n. **1** a small flea; chigoe. **2** chigger. [alteration of *chigoe*]

jigger mast a mast in the stern of a ship.

jig·ger·y-pok·er·y (jig′ər ē pōk′ər ē) n., pl. **-ies.** *Slang.* humbug; fraud; bunk.

jig·gle (jig′əl) v. **-gled, -gling;** n. **—v.** shake or jerk slightly. **—n.** a slight shake; light jerk. [< *jig²*]

jig·saw (jig′sò′ or -sô′) n. a saw with a narrow blade mounted in a frame and worked with an up-and-down motion, used to cut curves or irregular lines.

jigsaw puzzle a picture cut into irregular pieces that can be fitted together again.

jig time the lively tempo of a jig.
in jig time, *Informal.* in a hurry; fast.

jill or **Jill** (jil) n. *Archaic.* **1** a woman; girl. **2** a sweetheart; wife.

jilt (jilt) v., n. **—v.** cast off (a lover or sweetheart) after giving encouragement. **—n.** a woman who casts off a lover after encouraging him. **—jilt′er,** n.

Jim Crow (jim′ krō′) *Esp.U.S.* **1** segregation of or discrimination against blacks. **2** (*adj.*) of or having to do with such segregation or discrimination. **3** *Derogatory slang.* a black. Also, **jim crow.** [from the name of a song used in a minstrel show (c. 1835)]

jim–dan·dy (jim′dan′dē) adj., n. *Informal.* **—adj.** excellent; great: *Everything is jim-dandy.* **—n.** an excellent person or thing.

jim·jams (jim′jamz′) n. *Slang.* **1** delirium tremens. **2** jitters; a creepy, uneasy feeling. [coined word]

jim·my (jim′ē) n., pl. **-mies;** v. **-mied, -my·ing. —n.** a short crowbar used especially by burglars to force windows, doors, etc. open. **—v.** force open with or as if with a jimmy. [apparently a special use of *Jimmy,* familiar form of *James*]

jim·son·weed (jim′sən wēd′) n. a tall, coarse, poisonous annual plant (*Datura stramonium*) of the nightshade family having white or purplish, trumpet-shaped flowers and bad-smelling leaves. It is found throughout much of the northern hemisphere. [*jimson,* alteration of *Jamestown,* Va.]

jin·gle (jing′gəl) n., v. **-gled, -gling. —n. 1** a sound like that of little bells, or of coins or keys striking together. **2** a verse or song that repeats sounds or has a catchy rhythm: *She writes advertising jingles for radio and television.*
—v. 1 make a jingling sound: *The sleigh bells jingle as we ride.* **2** cause to jingle: *He jingled the coins in his pocket.* **3** contain many simple rhymes and repetitions: *jingling verses.* [imitative] **—jing′ler,** n.

jin·gly (jing′glē) adj. like a jingle.

jin·go (jing′gō) n., pl. **-goes. 1** a person who favors an aggressive foreign policy that might lead to war with other nations; chauvinist. **2** (*adj.*) of jingoes or like that of jingoes. [< *by Jingo,* a phrase in the refrain of a music-hall song, which became the "theme song" of Disraeli's supporters in 1878; *jingo,* a magician's term; origin uncertain]

jin·go·ism (jing′gō iz′əm) n. the attitude of mind, policy, or practices of jingoes; chauvinism.

jin·go·is·tic (jing′gō is′tik) adj. of jingoes or like that of jingoes.

jin·ker (jin′kər) n. *Cdn. Newfoundland.* **1** an imaginary creature to whom bad luck is attributed; gremlin. **2** a person blamed for bad luck; Jonah. [origin uncertain]

jinn (jin) n. pl. of **jinni** (*often used as a singular*). Also, **djinn.** [< Arabic *jinn,* pl. of *jinni*]

jin·ni or **jin·nee** (ji nē′) n., pl. **jinn.** *Moslem mythology.* a spirit that can appear in human or animal form and do good or harm to people. Also, **djinni.**

jin·rik·i·sha or **jin·rick·sha** (jin rik′shə *or* jin rik′sho) n. rickshaw. [< Japanese *jinrikisha* < *jin* man + *riki* power + *sha* vehicle]

jinx (jingks) n., v. *Slang.* **—n.** a person or thing that is believed to bring bad luck: *He must be a jinx; we've lost every game since he joined the team.* **—v.** bring bad luck to. [< L *iynx,* bird used in magic < Gk.]

jit·ney (jit′nē) n., pl. **-neys.** *Slang.* **1** an automobile that carries passengers for a small fare. It usually travels along a regular route. **2** *Rare.* a five-cent piece; nickel. [origin uncertain]

jit·ter (jit′ər) v. *Informal.* be nervous; act or speak nervously. [< ? var. of E dial. *chitter* shiver, tremble, var. of *chatter*]

jit·ter·bug (jit′ər bug′) n., v. **-bugged, -bug·ging.** *Informal.* **—n. 1** a person who is enthusiastic about swing music and excited by it to lively dance movements and gestures. **2** a frenzied dance with lively movement. **—v.** dance in such a way. [< *jitter,* v. (see JITTERS) + *bug*]

jit·ters (jit′ərz) n.pl. *Slang.* extreme nervousness.

jit·ter·y (jit′ər ē) adj. *Informal.* nervous. **—jit′ter·i·ness,** n.

jiu·jit·su or **jiu·jut·su** (jü jit′sü) See **jujitsu.**

jive (jīv) n., v. **jived, jiv·ing.** *Slang.* **—n. 1** a kind of lively jazz; swing music. **2** dancing to jive music. **3** the talk of swing enthusiasts. **4** the latest slang. **—v. 1** dance to this kind of music. **2** play jive music. [origin uncertain]
☛ *Hom.* **gyve.**

Jn John.

jo (jō) n., pl. **joes.** *Scottish.* sweetheart. Also, **joe.** [var. of *joy*]

job (job) n., v. **jobbed, job·bing. —n. 1** a piece of work: *Dick had the job of painting the boat.* **2** a definite piece of work undertaken for a fixed price: *If you want your house painted, Mr. Huebert will do the job for $2000.* **3** (*adj.*) done by the job; hired for a particular piece of work. **4** work; employment: *Mary's brother is hunting for a job.* **5** anything a person has to do: *I'm not going to wash the dishes; that's your job.* **6** *Informal.* an affair; matter. **7** a piece of public or official business managed dishonestly for private gain.
on the job, attending to one's work or duty.
—v. 1 buy (goods) from manufacturers in large quantities and sell to retailers in smaller lots. **2** let out (work) to different contractors, workmen, etc. **3** manage a public matter for private gain in a dishonest way. **4** work at odd jobs. [origin uncertain] **—job′less,** adj.
☛ *Syn.* **3.** See note at **position.**

Job (jōb) n. **1** in the Bible, a very patient man who kept his faith in God in spite of many troubles. His story forms the Book of Job. **2** any patient, enduring man.
Job's comforter, a person who increases the misery of the person he pretends to comfort (Job 16:2).
patience of Job, great self-control despite trouble or irritation.

job·ber (job′ər) n. **1** a person who buys goods from manufacturers in small quantities and sells to retailers in smaller quantities. **2** a person who manages public business dishonestly for private gain. **3** a person who works by the job; pieceworker.

job·hold·er (job′hōl′dər) n. a person regularly employed.

job·less (job′lis) adj. **1** not having regular work; unemployed. **2** (*noml.*) **the jobless,** pl. all the people who are unemployed. **—job′less·ness,** n.

job lot a quantity of goods bought or sold together, usually containing several different kinds of things.

jock¹ (jok) n. *Informal.* jockey.

jock² (jok) n. **1** *Slang.* a male athlete or sports enthusiast, or a person who adopts a lifestyle or values considered typical of athletes. **2** *Informal.* jockstrap.

jock·ey (jok′ē) *n., pl.* **-eys;** *v.* **-eyed, -ey·ing.** —*n.* a person whose occupation is riding horses in races.
—*v.* **1** ride (a horse) in a race. **2** trick; cheat: *Swindlers jockeyed Mr. Smith into buying some worthless land.* **3** manoeuvre to get advantage: *The crews were jockeying their boats to get into the best position for the race.* [originally a proper name, dim. of *Jock*, Scottish var. of *Jack*]

jock–strap (jok′strap′) *n.* athletic support. [< *jock* penis (*vulgar slang*) + *strap*]

jo·cose (jō kōs′) *adj.* jesting; humorous; playful: *He was fond of making jocose remarks about their old car.* [< L *jocosus* < *jocus* jest] —**jo·cose′ly,** *adv.* —**jo·cose′ness,** *n.*

jo·cos·i·ty (jō kos′ə tē) *n., pl.* **-ties. 1** the quality or state of being jocose. **2** a jocose remark, etc.

joc·u·lar (jok′yə lər) *adj.* **1** full of fun; jolly and fond of joking. **2** playful; jesting: *a jocular remark.* [< L *jocularis* < *joculus*, dim. of *jocus* jest] —**joc′u·lar·ly,** *adv.*

joc·u·lar·i·ty (jok′yə lar′ə tē *or* jok′yə ler′ə tē) *n., pl.* **-ties. 1** the quality of being jocular. **2** jocular talk, behavior, etc.

joc·und (jok′ənd *or* jō′kənd) *adj.* cheerful; merry; gay. [< L *jocundus*, var. (influenced by *jocus* jest) of *jucundus* pleasant < *juvare* please] —**joc′und·ly,** *adv.*

jo·cun·di·ty (jō kun′də tē) *n., pl.* **-ties. 1** cheerfulness; merriment; gaiety. **2** a jocund remark, act, etc.

jodh·purs (jod′pərz) *n.pl.* breeches for horseback riding, loose above the knees and fitting closely below. [< *Jodhpur*, India]

joe¹ (jō) See **jo.**

joe² or **Joe** *Slang. n.* fellow: *a good joe.*

joe–job (jō′job′) *n. Informal.* a dull, run-of-the mill job or task.

joe–pye weed (jō′pī′) any of several tall North American plants (genus *Eupatorium*) of the composite family having clusters of purplish flowers. [origin uncertain]

jog¹ (jog) *v.* **jogged, jog·ging;** *n.* —*v.* **1** shake with a push or jerk: *I jogged him to get his attention.* **2** stir up with a hint or reminder: *to jog one's memory.* **3** move up and down with a jerking or shaking motion: *The old horse jogged along, and jogged me up and down on his back.* **4** get along; carry on; go (on) in a steady or humdrum fashion: *He is not very enterprising but just jogs along.* **5** go forward heavily and slowly. **6** run at a slow, steady rate: *My father goes jogging every day for exercise.*
—*n.* **1** a shake, push, or nudge. **2** a hint or reminder: *Give your memory a jog.* **3** a slow walk or trot: *The riders went at a jog along the path.* [ME; origin uncertain] —**jog′ger,** *n.*

jog² (jog) *n., v.* —*n.* **1** a part that sticks out or in; the unevenness in a line or a surface: *a jog in a wall.* **2** an abrupt, temporary change in direction: *There's a jog in the road where it goes around the poplar bluff.* —*v.* make or form a jog: *The road jogs to the left just before you get to our place* [var. of *jag*]

jog·gle¹ (jog′əl) *v.* **-gled, -gling;** *n.* —*v.* shake or jolt slightly: *The milk spilled because you joggled my elbow.* —*n.* a slight shake or jolt. [< *jog¹*]

jog·gle² (jog′əl) *n., v.* **-gled, -gling.** —*n.* **1** a projection on one of two joining surfaces, or a notch on the other, to prevent slipping. **2** a joint made in this way. —*v.* join or fasten with a joggle. [? < *jog²*]

jog trot 1 a slow, regular trot. **2** a routine or humdrum way of doing things.

john (jon) *n. Informal.* toilet.

John (jon) *n.* the fourth book of the New Testament.

John Bar·ley·corn (bär′lē kôrn′) a personification of alcoholic beverages, especially malt liquor.

John Bull 1 a supposedly typical Englishman, often represented as stout and red-faced, in top hat and high boots. **2** a personification of England and its people. [named after the title character in *The History of John Bull* (1712) by John Arbuthnot, a Scottish writer]

John Doe a fictitious name used in legal forms, documents, proceedings, etc. to represent an unspecified person.

John Do·ry (dô′rē) *pl.* **John Dories** or (sometimes) **Dorys.** a European marine food fish (*Zeus faber*) having a very deep, almost oval, compressed body, spiny dorsal fins, and a large, yellow- ringed black spot on each side. [< *John* + *dory²*]

John Han·cock (han′kok) *Esp.U.S. Slang.* a person's signature. [< signature of *John Hancock*, first signer of the Declaration of Independence]

John Henry *Slang.* a person's signature: *Put your John Henry at the bottom of this form.*

john·ny·cake (jon′ē kāk′) *n.* corn bread in the form of a flat cake. [origin uncertain]

Johnny Canuck *Cdn.* **1** a Canadian, especially a member of the armed forces during the First or Second World War. **2** a

hat, āge, fär; let, ēqual, tèrm; it, īce
hot, ōpen, ôrder; oil, out; cup, pùt, rüle,
əbove, takən, pencəl, lemən, circəs

ch, child; ng, long; sh, ship
th, thin; ᴛʜ, then; zh, measure

personification of Canada: *Johnny Canuck can do a lot more than play hockey.*

John·ny–jump–up (jon′ē jump′up′) *n.* **1** wild pansy. **2** any of various North American violets.

John·son·ese (jon′sən ēz′) *n.* a learned, Latinate literary style, resembling that of Samuel Johnson (1709-1784), an English author, lexicographer, and literary leader.

John·so·ni·an (jon sō′nē ən) *adj.* of, having to do with, or characteristic of Samuel Johnson (1709-1784), his writings, or his literary style.

John the Baptist in the Bible, the man who foretold the coming of Christ and later baptized Him (Matt. 3).

joie de vi·vre (zhwä də vē′vʀ) *French.* joy of living; enjoyment of life.

join (join) *v., n.* —*v.* **1** bring or put together; connect; fasten: *to join hands.* **2** come together; meet: *The two roads join here.* **3** meet and unite with: *The brook joins the river.* **4** make or become one; combine; unite: *to join in marriage.* **5** take part (*in*) with others: *to join in song.* **6** become a member (of): *to join a church.* **7** come into the company of: *I'll join you later.* **8** return to or take one's place in: *After a few days on shore the sailor joined his ship.* **9** adjoin: *His farm joins mine.*
join battle, begin to fight.
join up, enlist in the armed forces.
—*n.* **1** a place or line of joining; seam. **2** a joining or being joined. [ME < OF *joindre* < L *jungere*]

☞ **Syn.** *v.* **4. Join, combine, unite** = put or come together so as to form one thing. **Join** emphasizes bringing or coming together, and does not suggest how firm or lasting the association may be: *The two clubs joined forces during the campaign.* **Combine** emphasizes mixing or blending into one, for a common purpose: *He combines business with pleasure.* **Unite** emphasizes the oneness of the result and the loss of separate or divided purposes, interests, etc.: *His family united to help him.*

join·er (join′ər) *n.* **1** a person or thing that joins. **2** a skilled woodworker and furniture maker. **3** *Informal.* a person who joins many clubs, societies, etc.

join·er·y (join′ər ē) *n.* **1** the skill or trade of a joiner. **2** woodwork or furniture made by a joiner.

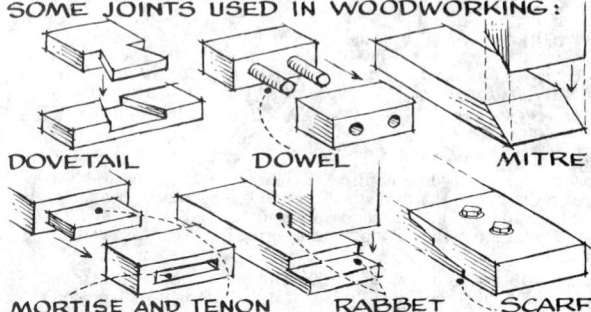

SOME JOINTS USED IN WOODWORKING:
DOVETAIL   DOWEL   MITRE
MORTISE AND TENON   RABBET   SCARF

joint (joint) *n., v., adj.* —*n.* **1** the place at which two things or parts are joined together. **2** the way parts are joined: *a perfect joint.* **3** *Anatomy.* the junction between two bones, usually formed of cartilage and connective tissue, and that allows movement. **4** one of the parts of which a jointed thing is made up: *the middle joint of the finger.* **5** *Botany.* the part of the stem from which a leaf or branch grows. **6** *Esp.Brit.* a large piece of meat for roasting. **7** *Slang.* **a** a low-class place for cheap eating, drinking, or entertainment, formerly for the illegal sale of liquor. **b** any place, building, etc. **8** *Slang.* a marijuana cigarette.
out of joint, a out of place at the joint. **b** out of order; in bad condition.
—*v.* **1** connect by a joint or joints. **2** divide at the joints: *Please joint this chicken before sending it.*
—*adj.* **1** shared or done by two or more persons: *By our joint efforts we managed to push the car back on the road.* **2** joined together; sharing: *My brother and I are joint owners of the house.* [ME < OF *joint* < *joindre*. See JOIN.] —**joint′er,** *n.*

joint·ly (joint′lē) *adv.* together; in common: *The two girls owned the boat jointly.*

joint–stock company a company or firm whose capital is owned in shares by stockholders, any of whom can sell some or all of his shares without the consent of the others.

join·ture (join′chər) *n. Law.* property given to a wife by her husband, for her support in the event of his death. [< F < L *junctura* a joining < *jungere* join. Doublet of JUNCTURE.]

joist (joist) *n.. v. —n.* one of the parallel horizontal pieces of timber extending from wall to wall across a building, to which the boards of a floor or ceiling are fastened. See **frame** for picture. *—v.* provide with or lay across joists. [ME < OF *giste*, ult. < L *jacere* lie]

joke (jōk) *n., v.* **joked, jok·ing. —n. 1** something said or done to make somebody laugh; remark that is clever and amusing; something amusing; jest: *This was a good joke on me.* **2** a person or thing laughed at. **3** something that is not in earnest or actually meant.
crack a joke, tell a joke; say something funny.
no joke, a serious matter.
—v. **1** make jokes; say or do something as a joke; jest. **2** laugh at; make fun of; tease. [< L *jocus*] **—jok′ing·ly,** *adv.*
☛ *Syn. n.* **1. Joke, jest** = something said or done to cause amusement or laughter. **Joke** applies to anything said or done in fun and intended to cause laughter. **Jest,** more formal, applies chiefly to language, and suggests playful and merry joking, teasing, or poking fun: *Many a truth has been spoken in jest.*

jok·er (jōk′ər) *n.* **1** a person who tells funny stories or plays tricks on others. **2** *Slang.* any person; a fellow: *Who does that joker think he is?* **3** *Card games.* an extra card added in some games as a wild card or the highest-ranking card. **4** a trick for getting the better of someone. **5** *Informal.* an obscure phrase or sentence in a law, contract, etc. inserted to defeat its original purpose.

jol·li·fi·ca·tion (jol′ə fə kā′shən) *n.* festivity; merrymaking.

jol·li·ty (jol′ə tē) *n., pl.* **-ties.** fun; merriment; festivity; gaiety.

jol·ly (jol′ē) *adj.* **-li·er, -li·est;** *adv., v.* **-lied, -ly·ing;** *n., pl.* **-lies.**
—adj. **1** full of fun; merry. **2** *Brit. Informal.* pleasant; agreeable; delightful.
—adv. Informal. **1** very: *You can jolly well wait like everyone else.* **2** *Esp.Brit.* extremely: *a jolly good film.*
—v. Informal. **1** flatter (a person) to make him feel good or agreeable. **2** tease playfully; banter.
—n. Usually, **jollies,** *pl. Slang.* good times, fun.
get (one's) jollies, *Slang.* obtain pleasure or excitement: *She gets her jollies by putting people down.*
[ME < OF *joli*, ? < Gmc.] **—jol′li·ly,** *adv.* **—jol′li·ness,** *n.*

jolly boat a small boat carried on a ship.

Jolly Rog·er (roj′ər) a traditional pirates' flag, with a white skull and crossbones on a black background.

jolt (jōlt) *v., n. —v.* **1** jar; shake up: *The wagon jolted us when the wheels went over a rock.* **2** move with a shock or jerk: *The car jolted across the rough ground. —n.* **1** a jar; jerk: *He put his brakes on suddenly and the car stopped with a jolt.* **2** a sudden surprise or shock: *The loss of so much money gave him a severe jolt.* [origin uncertain] **—jolt′er,** *n.*

jolt·y (jōl′tē) *adj.* jolting.

Jo·nah (jō′nə) *n.* **1** in the Bible, a Hebrew prophet who was thrown overboard during a storm, swallowed by a large fish, and later cast up on land. His story is told in the Book of Jonah. **2** any person whose presence is supposed to bring bad luck. Also called **Jonas.**

Jon·a·than (jon′ə thən) *n.* **1** in the Bible, David's devoted friend, the son of Saul (1 Sam. 19:1-10). See **David. 2** a bright-red apple that has a fine flavor and ripens in the late autumn.

jon·gleur (jong′glər; *French,* zhôn glœr′) *n.* a wandering minstrel or entertainer in medieval France. [< F < OF *jogleor* juggler; influenced by *jangleor* chatterer. Doublet of JUGGLER.]

jon·quil (jong′kwəl) *n.* a perennial bulbous plant (*Narcissus jonquilla*) of the amaryllis family, native to the Mediterranean but widely cultivated as a garden and greenhouse plant, having clusters of fragrant, yellow or white, short-tubed flowers and long, rushlike leaves. [< F < Sp. *junquillo,* dim. of *junco* reed < L *juncus*]

Jordan almond a large almond of high quality.

Jor·da·ni·an (jôr dā′nē ən) *n., adj. —n.* a native or inhabitant of Jordan, a kingdom in SW Asia. *—adj.* of or having to do with Jordan or its people.

jo·rum (jô′rəm) *n.* **1** a large drinking bowl. **2** the amount that a jorum can hold. **3** a jorum and its contents. [? < *Joram* (II Sam. 8:10), who brought David drinking vessels of silver]

josh (josh) *v., n. Slang. —v.* make good-natured fun of; tease playfully. *—n.* banter; raillery. [origin uncertain] **—josh′er,** *n.*

Josh·u·a (josh′ù ə *or* josh′yü ə) *n.* in the Bible, the successor of Moses, who led the children of Israel into the Promised Land. Also called **Josue.**

joss (jos) *n.* an image of a Chinese god; a Chinese idol. [pidgin English form of Pg. *deos* god < L *deus*]

joss house a Chinese temple.

joss stick a slender stick of dried, fragrant paste, burned by the Chinese as incense.

jos·tle (jos′əl) *v.* **-tled, -tling;** *n. —v.* crowd, shove, or push against; elbow roughly: *We were jostled by the impatient crowd at the entrance to the circus. —n.* a jostling; push; knock. [< *joust*] **—jos′tler,** *n.*

jot (jot) *n., v.* **jot·ted, jot·ting. —n.** a little bit; a very small amount: *I do not care a jot. —v.* write briefly or in haste: *The clerk jotted down the order.* [< L < Gk. *iōta* iota, the smallest letter in the Greek alphabet. Doublet of IOTA.] **—jot′ter,** *n.*

jot·ting (jot′ing) *n.* something jotted down; a short, informal note: *the published jottings of a noted wit.*

Jo·tun, Jo·tunn, or **Jö·tunn** (yô′tùn) *n. Norse mythology.* a giant.

Jo·tun·heim, Jo·tunn·heim, or **Jö·tunn·heim** (yô′tùn hām′) *n. Norse mythology.* the home of the giants.

joual (zhwäl) *n. Cdn.* uneducated or dialectal Canadian French. [< Cdn.F < dial. pronunciation of F *cheval* horse]

joule (joul *or* jül) *n.* an SI unit for measuring energy. One joule is the amount of work done, or energy used, in applying one newton of force to move a body one metre. *Symbol:* J [< James Prescott Joule (1818-1889), an English physicist]

jounce (jouns) *v.* **jounced, jounc·ing;** *n. —v. or n.* bounce; bump; jolt. [ME; origin uncertain]

jour·nal (jėr′nəl) *n.* **1** a daily record, such as a diary, a ship's log, or written records of the meetings of a society. **2** a book for keeping such a record. **3** a newspaper or magazine. **4** *Bookkeeping.* **a** a book in which every item of business is written down so that the item can be entered under the proper account. **b** a daybook. **5** the part of a shaft or axle that turns on a bearing. [ME < OF < LL *diurnalis.* Doublet of DIURNAL.]

jour·nal·ese (jėr′nəl ēz′) *n.* a careless or loose style of writing such as is sometimes used in newspapers, magazines, etc. Journalese is characterized by loose constructions, imprecise wording, and far-fetched or sensational expressions.

jour·nal·ism (jėr′nəl iz′əm) *n.* **1** the work of writing for, editing, managing, or publishing a newspaper or magazine. **2** newspapers and magazines as a group.

jour·nal·ist (jėr′nəl ist) *n.* a person engaged in journalism: *Editors and reporters are journalists.*

jour·nal·is·tic (jėr′nəl is′tik) *adj.* of or like journalism or journalists. **—jour′nal·is′tic·ally,** *adv.*

jour·ney (jėr′nē) *n., pl.* **-neys;** *v.* **-neyed, -ney·ing. —n. 1** a trip, especially a fairly long one: *a journey around the world.* **2** a passage or course from one stage to another: *one's journey through life. —v.* make a journey. [ME < OF *journee,* originally, a day, ult. < L *diurnus* of one day < *dies* day]
☛ *Syn. n.* See note at **trip.**

jour·ney·man (jėr′nē mən) *n., pl.* **-men. 1** a worker who has completed an apprenticeship or is otherwise qualified to practise his trade, but who is not a master or employer. Originally, journeymen were hired and paid by the day. **2** a person who is a competent worker or performer but is not outstanding or brilliant.

Two knights jousting

joust (joust, just, *or* jüst) *n., v. Historical. —n. 1** a combat, for sport or exercise, between two knights on horseback, in which they charged at each other, each trying to unseat the other with his lance. **2** Usually, **jousts,** *pl.* a tournament consisting of a series of such combats. Compare **tilt.** *—v.* engage in such a combat. [ME < OF *jouste* (n.), *jouster* (v.) < VL *juxtare* be next to < L *juxta* beside] **—joust′er,** *n.*

Jove (jōv) *n.* **1** *Roman mythology.* Jupiter. **2** *Poetic.* the planet Jupiter.

by Jove, an exclamation of surprise, pleasure, etc.

jo·vi·al (jō′vē əl) *adj.* good-hearted and full of fun; good-humored and merry. [< L *Jovialis* pertaining to Jupiter (those born under the planet's sign being supposedly cheerful)] —**jo′vi·al·ly,** *adv.* —**jo′vi·al·ness,** *n.*

jo·vi·al·i·ty (jō′vē al′ə tē) *n.* jollity; merriment.

Jo·vi·an (jō′vē ən) *adj.* **1** of or like the god Jove. **2** of the planet Jupiter.

jowl¹ (joul *or* jōl) *n.* **1** the part under the jaw; jaw. **2** cheek. [OE *ceafl,* influenced by F *joue* cheek]

jowl² (joul) *n.* a fold of flesh hanging from the jaw. [? related to OE *ceole* throat]

joy (joi) *n.* **1** a strong feeling of pleasure; gladness; happiness. **2** something that causes gladness or happiness: *"A thing of beauty is a joy forever."* **3** an expression of happiness; outward rejoicing. [ME < OF *joie* < L *gaudia,* pl. of *gaudium* joy < *gaudere* rejoice] ☛ *Syn. n.* **1.** See note at **pleasure.**

joy·ance (joi′əns) *n. Archaic.* joy; gladness; gaiety.

joy·ful (joi′fəl) *adj.* **1** glad; happy: *a joyful heart.* **2** causing joy: *joyful news.* **3** showing joy: *a joyful look.* —**joy′ful·ly,** *adv.* —**joy′ful·ness,** *n.*

joy·less (joi′lis) *adj.* **1** without joy; sad; dismal. **2** not causing joy: *a joyless prospect.* —**joy′less·ly,** *adv.* —**joy′less·ness,** *n.*

joy·ous (joi′əs) *adj.* joyful; glad: *a joyous song.* —**joy′ous·ly,** *adv.* —**joy′ous·ness,** *n.*

joy ride *Informal.* a ride in an automobile for pleasure, especially when the car is driven recklessly or is used without the owner's permission.

joy-ride (joi′rīd′) *v.* **-rode, -rid·den, -rid·ing.** *Informal.* take a joy ride. —**joy′-rid′er,** *n.*

J.P. Justice of the Peace.

Jr. or **jr.** Junior.

Ju·bal (jü′bəl) *n.* in the Bible, the inventor of musical instruments (Gen. 4:21).

ju·bi·lance (jü′bə ləns) *n.* a rejoicing; great joy.

ju·bi·lant (jü′bə lənt) *adj.* expressing or showing joy; rejoicing; exulting: *The people were jubilant when the war was over.* [< L *jubilans, -antis,* ppr. of *jubilare* shout with joy < *jubilum* wild shout] —**ju′bi·lant·ly,** *adv.*

Ju·bi·la·te (jü′bə lä′tē *or* jü′bə lä′tē) *n.* the 100th Psalm in the Protestant Bible or the 99th Psalm in the Roman Catholic Bible. [< L *jubilate* shout ye, the first word of the psalm < *jubilare* shout with joy. See JUBILANT.]

ju·bi·la·tion (jü′bə lā′shən) *n.* **1** rejoicing. **2** a joyful celebration.

ju·bi·lee (jü′bə lē′) *n.* **1** an anniversary thought of as a time of rejoicing: *a fiftieth wedding jubilee.* **2** a time of rejoicing or great joy: *to have a jubilee in celebration of a victory.* **3** rejoicing; great joy. **4** *Roman Catholic Church.* a year in which punishment for sin is remitted, after repentance and the performance of certain acts. [ME < OF *jubile* < LL *jubilaeus,* adj. < Gk. *iōbēlaios* < Hebrew *yobel* trumpet; originally, a ram's horn, ram]

Ju·dae·o-Chris·tian (jü dā′ō kris′chən *or* jü dē′ō-) *adj.* common to Christianity and Judaism; both Jewish and Christian: *the Judaeo-Christian heritage.* Also, **Judeo-Christian.** [< L *Judaeus* < Gk. *Ioudaios* Jew + E *Christian*]

Ju·dah (jü′də) *n.* **1** the son of Jacob and ancestor of the tribe of Judah (Gen. 29:35). **2** the most powerful of the twelve tribes of Israel.

Ju·da·ic (jü dā′ik) *adj.* of the Jews; Jewish.

Ju·da·ism (jü′dā iz′əm) *n.* **1** the religion of the Jews, based on the teaching of Moses and the prophets as found in the Bible and on the Talmud. **2** the following of Jewish rules and customs.

Ju·da·ist (jü′dē ist) *n.* **1** a follower of Judaism. **2** in the early Christian church, a Jewish convert who advocated retaining Jewish rites and customs.

Ju·da·ize (jü′dā īz′) *v.* **-ized, -iz·ing.** conform to Jewish usages or ideas.

Ju·das (jü′dəs) *n.* **1** in the Bible, the disciple who betrayed Jesus Christ for thirty pieces of silver; Judas Iscariot (Matthew 26:14-50). **2** any treacherous betrayer of friendship; traitor.

Judas tree redbud, especially a Eurasian species (*Cercis siliquastrum*), the tree on which, according to legend, Judas Iscariot hanged himself.

Ju·de·an (jü dē′ən) *n., adj.* —*n.* a native or inhabitant of Judea, the southern part of Palestine when it was a province of the Roman Empire. —*adj.* of or having to do with Judea. [< L *Judaeus.* See JEW.]

hat, āge, fär; let, ēqual, tėrm; it, īce
hot, ōpen, ôrder; oil, out; cup, pùt, rüle,
əbove, takən, pencəl, lemən, circəs

ch, child; ng, long; sh, ship
th, thin; ŦH, then; zh, measure

judge (juj) *n., v.* **judged, judg·ing.** —*n.* **1** a government official appointed or elected to hear and decide cases in a court of law. In Canada all judges are appointed. **2** a person chosen to settle a dispute or decide who wins. **3** a person who can decide how good a thing is: *a good judge of cattle; a poor judge of poetry.* **4** a ruler in ancient Israel before the time of the kings. —*v.* **1** hear and decide in a court of law. **2** settle (a dispute); decide who wins (a race, contest, etc.). **3** make up one's mind (about); form an opinion or estimate (of): *to judge the merits of a book.* **4** think; suppose; conclude: *I judged that you had forgotten to come.* **5** criticize; condemn: *You had little cause to judge him so harshly.* [ME < OF *juge* < L *judex* < *jus* law + root of *dicere* say] —**judg′er,** *n.*

judge advocate an officer appointed to superintend the proceedings of a court-martial, to advise the court on matters of law, and to elicit facts material to the defence.

Judge Advocate General the senior legal officer in the armed forces. *Abbrev:* JAG or J.A.G.

judge·ment (juj′mənt) See **judgment.**

judge·ship (juj′ship) *n.* the position, duties, or term of office of a judge.

judg·ment or **judge·ment** (juj′mənt) *n.* **1** the act of judging. **2** *Law.* **a** a decision, decree, or sentence given by a judge or court of law. **b** a debt arising from a judge's decision. **c** the official certificate recording such a decision. **3** an opinion or estimate: *It was a bad plan in my judgment.* **4** the ability to form opinions; good sense. **5** a decision made by anybody who judges. **6** criticism; condemnation. **7** a misfortune considered as a punishment from God: *The neighbors considered his broken leg a judgment on him for his evil deeds.* **8 the Judgment,** judgment day.

judg·men·tal (juj men′təl) *adj.* of, having to do with, or characterized by judgment.

Judgment Day the day of God's final judgment of mankind at the end of the world.

ju·di·ca·to·ry (jü′də kə tô′rē) *adj., n., pl.* **-to·ries.** —*adj.* of or having to do with the administration of justice. —*n.* **1** the administration of justice. **2** a court of law. [< LL *judicatorius* < L *judex, -dicis* judge]

ju·di·ca·ture (jü′də kə chər *or* jü′də kə chür′) *n.* **1** the administration of justice. **2** the position, duties, or authority of a judge. **3** the extent of jurisdiction of a judge or court of law. **4** a group of judges. **5** a court of law. [< Med.L *judicatura,* ult. < L *judex, -dicis* judge]

ju·di·cial (jü dish′əl) *adj.* **1** of or having to do with courts, judges, or the administration of justice. **2** ordered, permitted, or enforced by a judge or a court of law. **3** of or suitable for a judge; impartial; fair: *Before making a decision, a judicial mind considers fairly both sides of a dispute.* [ME < L *judicialis* < *judicium* judgment < *judex, -dicis* judge] —**ju·di′cial·ly,** *adv.*

ju·di·ci·ar·y (jü dish′ē er′ē) *n., pl.* **-ar·ies;** *adj.* —*n.* **1** the branch of government that administers justice; system of courts of law of a country. **2** judges as a group. —*adj.* of or having to do with courts, judges, or the administration of justice.

ju·di·cious (jü dish′əs) *adj.* having, using, or showing good judgment; wise; sensible: *A judicious historian selects and considers facts carefully and critically.* [< F *judicieux* < L *judicium* judgment < *judex, -dicis* judge] —**ju·di′cious·ly,** *adv.* —**ju·di′cious·ness,** *n.*

ju·do (jü′dō) *n.* jujitsu.

Ju·dy (jü′dē) *n.* the wife of Punch in the puppet show of *Punch and Judy.*

jug (jug) *n., v.* **jugged, jug·ging.** —*n.* **1** a container for liquids. A jug usually has a handle and either a spout or a narrow neck. **2** the amount that a jug can hold. **3** a jug and its contents. **4** *Slang.* jail. —*v. Slang.* jail. [probably originally proper name, alteration of *Joan,* fem. of *John*]

Jug·ger·naut (jug′ər not′ *or* jug′ər nôt′) *n.* **1** *Hinduism.* **a** Krishna. **b** an idol of Krishna in Puri, India, that is pulled through the streets on a huge chariot at an annual festival. Devotees are said to have formerly thrown themselves under the wheels to be crushed to death. **2** an idea, institution, etc. to which a person blindly devotes himself or is cruelly sacrificed. **3 juggernaut,** a huge, overpowering, inexorable force or object that destroys everything in

its path. [< Hind. *Jagannath* < Skt. *Jagannatha* < *jagat* world' + *natha* lord]

jug·gle (jug′əl) *v.* **-gled, -gling;** *n.* —*v.* **1** keep (several objects) in motion in the air at the same time by rapidly tossing them up in turn and catching them as they fall: *The acrobat juggled three plates while balancing on a wire.* **2** do tricks that require great dexterity. **3** manage to keep (several activities, etc.) going at the same time: *juggling two jobs and a night class.* **4** manipulate or change so as to deceive or cheat: *juggling accounts to hide a theft.* **5** deceive or cheat: *He juggled his brother out of his inheritance.* —*n.* **1** the act or an instance of juggling. **2** deception or fraud. [ME < OF *jogler* < L *joculari* joke < *joculus,* dim. of *jocus* jest]

jug·gler (jug′lər) *n.* **1** a person who can do juggling tricks. **2** a person who uses tricks, deception, or fraud. [ME < OF *jogleor* < L *joculator* joker, ult. < *jocus* jest. Doublet of JONGLEUR.]

jug·gler·y (jug′lər ē) *n., pl.* **-gler·ies. 1** the skill or tricks of a juggler; sleight of hand. **2** trickery; deception; fraud.

Ju·go·slav (yü′gō slav′ *or* -släv′) See **Yugoslav.**

Ju·go·slav·i·an (yü′gō slav′ē ən *or* -släv′ē ən) See **Yugoslavian.**

jug·u·lar (jug′yə lər *or* jü′gyə lər) *adj., n.* —*adj.* **1** of the neck or throat. **2** of the jugular vein. —*n.* the jugular vein. [< NL *jugularis* < L *jugulum* collarbone, dim. of *jugum* yoke]

jugular vein one of the two large veins on either side of the neck that return blood from the head to the heart.

juice (jüs) *n.* **1** the liquid in fruits, vegetables, and meats. **2** a natural liquid in the body. The gastric juices of the stomach help to digest food. **3** *Slang.* electricity. **4** *Slang.* gasoline. [ME < OF < L *jus* broth] —**juice′less,** *adj.*

juic·er (jü′sər) *n.* an apparatus for squeezing juice out of fruits or vegetables.

juic·i·ness (jüs′ē nis) *n.* the state or quality of being juicy.

juic·y (jüs′ē) *adj.* **juic·i·er, juic·i·est. 1** full of juice; having much juice. **2** full of interest; lively. —**juic′i·ly,** *adv.*

ju·jit·su (jü jit′sü) *n.* a traditional Japanese method of fighting without weapons, employing blows that can paralyse an opponent and holds and throws designed to use the opponent's own strength and weight against him. Also, **jujutsu, jiujitsu, jiujutsu.** [< Japanese *jūjutsu* < *jū* soft + *jutsu* art]

ju·jube (jü′jüb) *n.* **1** a chewy candy or lozenge made of fruit-flavored gelatine. **2** the edible, datelike fruit of any of several Old World trees (genus *Ziziphus*) of the buckthorn family, especially an Asian species (*Z. jujuba*). **3** a tree producing such fruit. [< F *jujube* or < Med.L *jujuba* < LL *zizyphum* < Gk. *zizyphon*]

ju·jut·su (jü jit′sü) See **jujitsu.**

juke box (jük) *Informal.* an automatic phonograph that plays a record when money is deposited in the slot. [< Gullah *juke* disorderly, wicked]

Jul. July.

ju·lep (jü′ləp) *n.* **1** a drink made with water, sugar or syrup, and, sometimes, flavoring. **2** mint julep, a drink made of whisky or brandy, sugar, crushed ice, and fresh mint. [< F < Arabic < Pers. *gulab,* originally, rose water]

Jul·ian (jül′yən) *adj.* of Julius Caesar.

Julian calendar a calendar in which the average length of a year was 365¼ days. It was introduced by Julius Caesar in 46 B.C.

ju·li·enne (jü′lē en′) *adj., n.* —*adj.* of vegetables, cut in thin strips or small pieces: *julienne potatoes.* —*n.* a clear soup containing vegetables cut into thin strips or small pieces. [< F]

Ju·li·et (jü′lē et′ *or* jü′lē ət) *n.* the heroine of Shakespeare's play *Romeo and Juliet.*

Ju·ly (jü lī′) *n., pl.* **-lies.** the seventh month of the year. It has 31 days. [OE *Julius* < L *Julius,* after *Julius* Caesar]

jum·ble (jum′bəl) *v.* **-bled, -bling;** *n.* —*v.* mix; confuse: *He jumbled up everything in the drawer when he was hunting for his socks.* —*n.* a confused mixture. [? imitative]

jum·bo (jum′bō) *n., pl.* **-bos;** *adj. Informal.* —*n.* a big, clumsy person, animal, or thing; something unusually large of its kind. —*adj.* very big: *a jumbo jet.* [< *Jumbo,* an elephant exhibited by P.T. Barnum (1810-1891), U.S. showman]

jump (jump) *v., n.* —*v.* **1** spring into the air by the muscular action of the legs and feet; leap; bound: *to jump high, to jump over a fence.* **2** leap over: *to jump a stream.* **3** cause to jump: *to jump a horse over a fence.* **4** give a sudden start or jerk: *You made me jump.* **5** rise suddenly: *Prices jumped.* **6** *Checkers.* pass over and capture (an opponent's piece). **7** pounce upon; attack: *The robbers jumped the shopkeeper.* **8** *Slang.* evade by running away: *to jump bail.* **9** *Slang.* get aboard (a train) by jumping.

jump a claim, seize a piece of land claimed by another.

jump at, accept eagerly and quickly.

jump on, *Slang.* blame; scold; criticize.

jump the track, of a train, leave the rails suddenly.
—*n.* **1** the act or an instance of jumping. **2** something to be jumped over. **3** the distance jumped. **4** a contest in jumping. **5** a sudden nervous start or jerk. **6** a sudden rise. **7** *Checkers.* a move made to capture an opponent's piece. **8** a sudden and abrupt transition from one thing to another. **9** jumps, *Informal.* a nervous condition characterized by sudden starts or jerks.

get or **have the jump on,** *Slang.* get or have an advantage over.

on the jump, *Informal.* rushing around; always busy.

[probably imitative]

☛ *Syn. v.* **1, 2. Jump, leap** = spring into or through the air. **Jump** emphasizes springing from the ground or other surface or point: *He jumped from the roof. He jumped across the puddle.* **Leap** emphasizes springing high into or through the air, or to a point and suggests more grace, lightness, or liveliness than **jump**: *I love to watch a dancer leap. He leaped lightly to the opposite bank of the stream.*

jump area the locality assigned for the landing of parachute troops, usually behind enemy lines.

jump·er¹ (jump′ər) *n.* **1** a person or thing that jumps. **2** a simply constructed sleigh on low wooden runners. **3** a short length of wire used to bypass part of an electric circuit or to make a temporary connection. [< *jump,* v.]

jump·er² (jump′ər) *n.* **1** a sleeveless dress, usually worn over a blouse. **2** a loose jacket. Jumpers are worn by workmen to protect their clothes and by sailors as part of their uniform. **3** a loose blouse reaching to the hips. **4** jumpers, *pl.* rompers. [< *jump* short coat, ? alteration of F *juppe,* ult. < Arabic *jubbah* long open coat]

jumper cables booster cables.

jump fire *Cdn.* a forest fire started by burning material that has been carried ahead by wind from another blaze.

jumping bean a seed of any of various Mexican shrubs (especially of genus *Sebastiana*) of the spurge family that contains a small moth caterpillar whose movements cause the seed to jump.

jumping jack a toy man or animal that can be made to jump by pulling a string.

jump·ing-off place or **point** (jump′ing of′) **1** *Cdn. Esp.North.* a place, usually a town, where one leaves the railway or other link with civilization to proceed into the wilderness. **2** *Cdn.* any starting place. **3** any place considered the ultimate in isolated, undeveloped wilderness.

jumping pound buffalo jump.

jump·master (jump′mas′tər) *n.* a person in charge of the dropping of parachutists from an aircraft.

jump-off (jump′of′) *n., adj.* —*n.* **1** the start of a race. **2** the beginning of an attack. **3** play-off. —*adj.* beginning; starting: *a jump-off place for northern exploration parties.*

jump seat 1 a collapsible extra seat in an automobile, hinged to the floor between the front and back seats. **2** any similar seat in an airplane, elevator, etc.

jump·suit (jump′süt′) *n.* a one-piece garment consisting of a usually close-fitting top and long or short pants. [< *jump* + *suit,* originally applied to a kind of suit worn by parachutists when jumping]

jump·y (jump′ē) *adj.* **jump·i·er, jump·i·est. 1** moving by jumps; making sudden, sharp jerks. **2** easily excited or frightened; nervous. —**jump′i·ly,** *adv.* —**jump′i·ness,** *n.*

jun (jun) *n., pl.* **jun.** a unit of money in North Korea, equal to ¹⁄₁₀₀ of a won. [< Korean]

Jun. 1 June. **2** Junior.

Junc. Junction.

jun·co (jung′kō) *n., pl.* **-cos.** any of a genus (*Junco*) of small North American finches having mainly grey plumage with white outer tail feathers and white underparts. Juncos are common winter birds in many parts of Canada. [< Sp. < L *juncus* reed]

junc·tion (jungk′shən) *n.* **1** a joining or being joined: *the junction of two rivers.* **2** a place where things join or meet. A railway junction is a place where railway lines meet or cross. [< L *junctio, -onis* < *jungere* join]

junc·ture (jungk′chər) *n.* **1** a point of time. **2** a state of affairs. **3** crisis. **4** joint. **5** a joining or being joined.

at this juncture, when affairs are (or were) in this state.

[< L *junctura* a joining < *jungere* join. Doublet of JOINTURE.]

June (jün) *n.* the sixth month of the year. It has 30 days. [< L *Junius,* originally a Roman gens name]

June beetle June bug.

June·berry (jün′ber′ē) *n.* serviceberry.

June bug any of various large, reddish-brown beetles (family Scarabaeidae) of the northern hemisphere that fly about especially in late spring, feeding on flowers and foliage at night. Their larvae

are white grubs that live in the soil, feeding mainly on plant roots.

Jung·i·an (yung′ē ən) *adj., n.* —*adj.* of, having to do with, or characteristic of Carl Jung (1875-1961), a Swiss psychologist, or his system of analytical psychology. —*n.* a follower of the theories of Jung.

jun·gle (jung′gəl) *n.* **1** wild land thickly overgrown with bushes, vines, trees, etc. **2** a tangled mass. **3** a place characterized by vicious competition or struggle for survival: *He says the city is a jungle.* **4** *Slang.* a hobos' camp. [< Hind. *jangal* < Skt. *jāngala* desert, forest]

jungle fowl any of several Asian wild birds (genus *Galus*), the males of which have a fleshy comb and wattles and a long, high-arched tail. The **red jungle fowl** (*Gallus gallus*) is believed to be the ancestor of the common domestic fowl.

jun·ior (jūn′yər) *adj., n.* —*adj.* **1 Junior,** the younger: *John Parker, Junior, is the son of John Parker, Senior.* **2** of lower position, rank, or standing; of more recent appointment: *a junior officer, a junior partner.* **3** of or having to do with students in grades 4 to 6. **4** of or for young people: *a junior tennis match, junior coats.* **5** of later date. —*n.* **1** a younger person. **2** a person of lower rank or shorter service. **3** *Esp.U.S.* in a high school or college, a student in the third year of a four-year course. [< L *junior,* comparative of *juvenis* young]

junior college a college giving only the first year or the first two years of a university-degree program.

junior high school a school consisting of grades 7, 8, and 9; any school intermediate between elementary school and high school.

ju·ni·per (jū′nə pər) *n.* **1** any of a genus (*Juniperus*) of evergreen shrubs and trees of the northern hemisphere, belonging to the cypress family, having tiny, scale-like, overlapping leaves, small, blue, berry-like cones and soft, fragrant wood that is used for lining closets and chests, etc. The four species of juniper native to Canada are the Rocky Mountain juniper, red juniper, dwarf or common juniper, and creeping juniper. **2** the wood of a juniper. [< L *juniperus*]

junk¹ (jungk) *n., v.* —*n.* **1** old metal, paper, rags, etc. **2** *Informal.* rubbish; trash. **3** a hard salted meat eaten by sailors. **4** old rope used for making mats, oakum, etc. **5** *Slang.* a narcotic drug, such as heroin or morphine; dope. —*v. Informal.* throw away or discard as junk: *We junked the old garden chairs last fall.* [origin uncertain]

junk² (jungk) *n.* a sailing ship traditionally used especially by the Chinese and Javanese, having a flat bottom, high stern, and two or three masts with lugsails stiffened by horizontal battens. [< Pg. *junco,* probably ult. < Javanese *jong*]

junk·er (jungk′ər) *n.* a worn-out automobile, usually one sold for scrap.

Jun·ker (yung′kər) *n.* a member of the aristocratic, formerly privileged class in Prussia. Also, **junker.** [< G]

jun·ket (jung′kit) *n., v.* —*n.* **1** curdled milk, sweetened and flavored. **2** a feast; picnic. **3** a pleasure trip. **4** *Informal.* an unnecessary trip taken by an official at the expense of his government or the firm he works for. —*v.* **1** feast; picnic. **2** go on a pleasure trip. [< dial. OF *jonquette* basket < *jonc* reed < L *juncus*] —**jun′ket·er,** *n.*

junk food food, especially prepackaged snack food, characterized by a high carbohydrate content and little nutritive value.

junk·ie (jung′kē) *n. Slang.* **1** a person who is addicted to narcotics. **2** a dealer in junk.

junk·man (jungk′man′) *n., pl.* **-men.** a man who buys and sells old metal, paper, rags, etc.

junk·y (jung′kē) *adj.* —**i·er,** —**i·est.** *Informal.* of or like junk; cheap or worthless: *junky magazines, junky furniture.*

Ju·no (jū′nō) *n., pl.* **-nos. 1** *Roman mythology.* the goddess of marriage and childbirth, wife of Jupiter and queen of the gods, corresponding to the Greek goddess Hera. **2** any stately, majestic woman.

Ju·no·esque (jū′nō esk′) *adj.* in the manner of Juno; stately and majestic.

jun·ta (hun′tə, jun′tə, or jun′tə; *Spanish,* ʜun′tä) *n.* **1** a group of persons forming a government, especially as the result of a revolution: *The country was ruled by a military junta.* **2** junto. **3** especially in Spanish or Latin-American countries, a legislative or administrative council. [< Sp. *junta,* ult. < L *jungere* join]

jun·to (jun′tō) *n., pl.* **-tos.** a political faction; a group of plotters or partisans. [alteration of junta]

Ju·pi·ter (jū′pə tər) *n.* **1** *Roman mythology.* the chief god, ruler of the gods and men, corresponding to the Greek god Zeus. **2** the largest planet.

hat, āge, fär; let, ēqual, tèrm; it, īce
hot, ōpen, ôrder; oil, out; cup, pùt, rüle,
əbove, takən, pencəl, lemən, circəs
ch, child; ng, long; sh, ship
th, thin; ʇʜ, then; zh, measure

ju·ral (jūr′əl) *adj.* **1** of law; legal. **2** having to do with rights and obligations. [< L *jus, juris* law]

Ju·ras·sic (jù ras′ik) *n., adj.* —*n. Geology.* **1** the middle period of the Mesozoic era, beginning approximately 170 million years ago, when birds first appeared. **2** the rocks formed during this period. See chart at **geology.** —*adj.* of or having to do with the period when birds first appeared or the rocks formed during it. [< F *jurassique,* after the Jura Mountains in France and Switzerland]

ju·rid·i·cal (jù rid′ə kəl) *adj.* **1** having to do with the administration of justice. **2** of law; legal. [< L *juridicus,* ult. < *jus, juris* law + *dicere* say] —**ju·rid′i·cal·ly,** *adv.*

ju·ris·con·sult (jùr′is kən sult′ or -kon′sult) *n.* jurist. [< L *jurisconsultus,* ult. < *jus, juris* law + *consulere* consult]

ju·ris·dic·tion (jùr′is dik′shən) *n.* **1** the right or power of administering law or justice. **2** authority; power; control. **3** the extent of authority: *The judge ruled that the case was not within his jurisdiction.* **4** the territory over which authority extends. [< L *jurisdictio, -onis,* ult. < *jus, juris* law + *dicere* say]

ju·ris·dic·tion·al (jùr′is dik′shə nəl) *adj.* of or having to do with jurisdiction.

ju·ris·pru·dence (jùr′is prü′dəns) *n.* **1** the science or philosophy of law. **2** a system of laws. **3** a branch of law. Medical jurisprudence deals with the application of medical knowledge to certain questions of law. [< L *jurisprudentia* < *jus, juris* law + *prudentia* prudence]

ju·rist (jùr′ist) *n.* **1** an expert in law. **2** a learned writer on law. **3** a civil lawyer. [< Med.L *jurista* < L *jus, juris* law]

ju·ris·tic (jù ris′tik) *adj.* of or having to do with jurists or jurisprudence; relating to law. —**ju·ris′ti·cal·ly,** *adv.*

ju·ror (jùr′ər) *n.* a member of a jury. [ME < AF *jurour* < L *jurator* a swearer < *jurare* swear]

ju·ry¹ (jùr′ē) *n., pl.* **ju·ries. 1** a group of persons selected to hear evidence in a court of law and sworn to give a true verdict on questions of fact based on the evidence presented to it. See also **trial jury, grand jury. 2** a group of persons chosen to give a judgment or to decide who is the winner in a contest. [ME < AF *jurie* < *jurer* swear < L *jurare*]

ju·ry² (jùr′ē) *adj.* for temporary use on a ship; makeshift. [probably ult. < OF *ajurie, adjutorie* help < L *adjutare* < *ad-* to + *juvare* aid]

ju·ry·man (jùr′ē mən) *n., pl.* **-men.** a member of a jury; juror.

just¹ (just) *adj., adv.* —*adj.* **1** right; fair: *a just price.* **2** righteous: *a just life.* **3** deserved; merited: *a just reward.* **4** having good grounds; well-founded: *just anger.* **5** lawful: *a just claim.* **6** in accordance with standards or requirements; proper: *just proportions.* **7** true; correct: *a just description.* **8** exact: *just weights.* —*adv.* **1** exactly: *just a metre.* **2** very close; immediately: *There was a picture just above the fireplace.* **3** a very short while ago: *He has just gone.* **4** barely: *I just managed to catch the train.* **5** only; merely: *He is just an ordinary man.* **6** *Informal.* quite; truly; positively: *The weather is just glorious.*
just now, a exactly at this moment; at present: *Just now we are trying to set a firm date for the meeting.* **b** only a very short time ago: *I saw him just now.*
[< L *justus* upright < *jus* right, law] —**just′ness,** *n.* —**just′ly,** *adv.*
☛ *Syn. adj.* **1.** See note at **fair.**

just² (just) *v. or n.* joust.

jus·tice (jus′tis) *n.* **1** just conduct; fair dealing: *have a sense of justice.* **2** a being just; fairness; rightness; correctness: *uphold the justice of our cause.* **3** rightfulness; lawfulness; well-founded reason: *He complained with justice of the bad treatment he had received.* **4** just treatment; deserved reward or punishment. **5** the exercise of power and authority to maintain what is just and right. **6** the administration of law; trial and judgment by process of law. **7** judge. **8** justice of the peace.
bring (someone) to justice, do what is necessary in order that a person shall be legally punished for his crime or crimes.
do justice to, a treat fairly. **b** see the good points of. **c** show proper appreciation for: *He did justice to the dinner.*
do (oneself) justice, do as well as one really can do: *He did not do himself justice on the test.*
[ME < OF < L *justitia* < *justus* just, upright. See JUST¹.]

justice of the peace a provincial judicial officer who tries

cases involving infractions of municipal by-laws, issues warrants for arrest, administers oaths, etc. *Abbrev.*: J.P.

jus·tice·ship (jus′tis ship′) *n.* the position, duties, or term of office of a justice.

jus·ti·fi·a·bil·i·ty (jus′tə fī′ə bil′ə tē) *n.* the state or quality of being justifiable.

jus·ti·fi·a·ble (jus′tə fī′ə bəl) *adj.* capable of being justified; that can be shown to be just and right; defensible. —**jus′ti·fi′a·bly,** *adv.*

jus·ti·fi·ca·tion (jus′tə fə kā′shən) *n.* **1** the act or process of justifying. **2** the state of being justified. **3** the fact or circumstance that justifies; a good reason or grounds for action, defence, complaint, etc.

jus·ti·fy (jus′tə fī′) *v.* **-fied, -fy·ing. 1** show to be just or right; give a good reason for: *The fine quality of the cloth justifies its high price.* **2** clear of blame or guilt. **3** *Printing.* adjust the space between the words of (a line of type) so that the line will conform to a given length. **4** *Law.* show a satisfactory reason or excuse for something done. [< MF *justifier* < LL *justificare* < L *justus* just + *facere* make] —**jus′ti·fi′er,** *n.*

jut (jut) *v.* **jut·ted, jut·ting;** *n.* —*v.* stick out; project: *The pier juts out from the shore into the water.* —*n.* the part that sticks out; projection. [var. of *jet¹*]

jute (jüt) *n.* **1** a strong fibre used for making coarse sacks, burlap, rope, etc. **2** either of two tropical Old World herbaceous plants (*Corchorus olitorius* and *C. capsularis*) of the linden family yielding such fibre. [< Bengali *jhoto* < Skt. *jata* mat of hair]

Jute (jüt) *n.* a member of an early Germanic tribe. Some of the Jutes invaded and settled in SE England in the fifth century A.D.

ju·ve·nes·cence (jü′və nes′əns) *n.* a renewal of youth; youthfulness.

ju·ve·nes·cent (jü′və nes′ənt) *adj.* growing young again; youthful. [< L *juvenescens, -entis,* ppr. of *juvenescere* grow young again < *juvenis* young]

ju·ve·nile (jü′və nīl′ *or* jü′və nəl) *adj., n.* —*adj.* **1** young; youthful. **2** of or for young people: *juvenile books, juvenile delinquency.*
—*n.* **1** a young person. **2** a book for young people. **3** an actor or actress who plays youthful parts. [< L *juvenilis* < *juvenis* young]
☞ *Syn. adj.* **1.** See note at **young.**

juvenile court a law court where cases involving boys and girls are heard. In Canada, the maximum age at which offenders are tried in juvenile courts varies in the different provinces but is usually either sixteen or eighteen.

ju·ve·nil·i·a (jü′və nil′ē ə) *n.pl.* early, immature works produced by an artist, author, or composer during childhood or adolescence.

ju·ve·nil·i·ty (jü′və nil′ə tē) *n.* a juvenile quality, condition, or manner.

jux·ta·pose (juks′tə pōz′ *or* juks′tə pōz′) *v.* **-posed, -posing.** put close together; place side by side. [< F *juxtaposer* < L *juxta* beside + F *poser* place. See POSE¹.]

jux·ta·po·si·tion (juks′tə pə zish′ən) *n.* **1** a putting close together; a placing side by side. **2** a position close together or side by side.

Kk

k or **K** (kā) *n., pl.* **k's** or **K's. 1** the eleventh letter of the English alphabet. **2** any speech sound represented by this letter. **3** a person or thing identified as *k*, especially the eleventh in a series. **4** something shaped like the letter K. **5** (*adj.*) of or being a K or k.

k 1 kilo- (an SI prefix). **2** karat.

k. 1 kopeck. **2** krona. **3** krone. **4** king. **5** knight.

K 1 potassium (for L *Kalium*). **2** kelvin(s). **3** karat. **4** one thousand (from *kilo-*).

K. 1 king. **2** knight.

Ka (kä) *n.* in the religion of ancient Egypt, the soul said to dwell in a man's body, and, after death, in his tomb or statue. [< Egyptian]

Kaa·ba (kä′bə) *n.* the most sacred Moslem shrine, a small structure within the Great Mosque at Mecca. It contains a black stone, supposedly given to Abraham by the angel Gabriel, toward which Moslems face when praying. Also, **Caaba.** [< Arabic *ka'bah,* literally, a square building]

Kab·loo·na or **kab·loo·na** (kab lü′nə) *n.* Cdn. a white man; European. Also, **Kadloona.** [< Eskimo *kabluna(k)* one having big eyebrows]

kad·dish (kä′dish) *n. Judaism.* a portion of the daily prayer said in the synagogue, also used as a public or official prayer of mourning for a dead relative. [< Aramaic *qaddish* holy]

Kad·loo·na (kad lü′nə) *n.* Kabloona.

Kaf·fir (kaf′ər) *n.* **1** Xhosa. **2** *South African. Offensive.* any black African. **3** kaffir, kaffir corn. [< Arabic *kāfir* unbeliever]

kaf·fir corn (kaf′ər) an E African variety of sorghum grown in dry regions for grain and fodder.

Kaf·ir (kaf′ər) See **Kaffir.**

kaf·ir corn (kaf′ər) See **kaffir corn.**

kaf·tan (kaf′tən or käf tän′) See **caftan.**

kai·ak (kī′ak) See **kayak.**

kail (kāl) See **kale.**

kai·ser[1] (kī′zər) *n.* **1** the title of the emperors of Germany, 1871-1918. **2** the title of the emperors of Austria, 1804-1918. **3** the title of the emperors of the Holy Roman Empire from A.D. 962 to 1806. **4** emperor. [< G < L *Caesar*]

kai·ser[2] (kī′zər) *n.* a large, round, crusty bun used especially for sliced meat sandwiches. Also called **kaiser bun.** [< G *kaisersemmel* kaiser bun, i.e. emperor's bun or roll. The kaisersemmel was invented by an anonymous Viennese baker for Emperor Frederick V in 1487.]

kale (kāl) *n.* **1** any of various kinds of cabbage that have loose leaves instead of a compact head. Kale resembles spinach in taste. **2** *Slang.* money; cash. [var. of *cole*]

ka·lei·do·scope (kə lī′də skōp′) *n.* **1** a tube containing bits of colored glass and two or more mirrors. As it is turned, it reflects continually changing patterns. **2** anything that changes continually; a continually changing pattern. [< Gk. *kalos* pretty + *eidos* shape + E *-scope*]

ka·lei·do·scop·ic (kə lī′də skop′ik) *adj.* of or like a kaleidoscope; continually changing.

kal·ends (kal′əndz) See **calends.**

Ka·le·va·la (kä′lä vä′lä) *n.* the national epic poem of Finland, a collection of heroic songs and poems compiled from oral tradition. [< Finnish *Kalevala,* literally, home of a hero]

kal·mi·a (kal′mē ə) *n.* the mountain laurel, or any similar evergreen shrub having clusters of cup-shaped flowers. [< NL, after Peter *Kalm* (1715-1779), a Swedish botanist]

Kal·muck or **Kal·muk** (kal′muk) *n.* **1** a member of a Mongol people of the U.S.S.R. **2** the Mongolic language spoken by the Kalmuck. —*adj.* of or having to do with the Kalmuck or their language. [< Turkic *kalmuk,* part of a Nomad Tartar tribe remaining at home]

kal·so·mine (kal′sə mīn′ or kal′sə min) See **calcimine.**

kame (kām) *n.* **1** *Geology.* a small hill or ridge deposited by retreating glaciers. **2** *Scottish.* comb. [northern E dial. var. of *combe*]

ka·mik (kä′mik) *n.* Cdn. a soft knee-length boot of sealskin or cariboo hide, worn in eastern arctic regions; mukluk. [< Eskimo]

ka·mi·ka·ze (kä′mi kä′zē) *n.* **1** a member of a Japanese air corps in World War II that carried out suicide missions in which an aircraft loaded with explosives was deliberately crashed on a target by the pilot. **2** an aircraft used in such a mission. **3** (*adj.*) of or having to do with such missions. **4** *Informal.* **a** a person who behaves in a self-destructive manner. **b** (*adj.*) of or like such a person; suicidal: *a kamikaze taxi driver.* [< Japanese *kamikaze,* literally, divine wind]

Kam·loops trout (kam′lüps) *Cdn.* a bright, silvery, medium-sized variety or stock of the rainbow trout found in British Columbia's small interior lakes, highly valued as a game and food fish. See also **rainbow trout** and **steelhead.** [< *Kamloops,* B.C.]

Kan. Kansas.

Ka·nak·a (kə nak′ə or kan′ə kə) *n.* **1** a native Hawaiian. **2** a native or inhabitant of any of the S Pacific islands. [< Hawaiian *kanaka* man]

kan·ga·roo (kang′gə rü′) *n., pl.* **-roos** or (*esp. collectively*) **-roo.** any of a family (Macropodidae) of marsupials of Australia, Tasmania, and New Guinea, typically having long, powerful hind legs adapted for leaping, a long, thick tail which is used for balancing, and small, short forelegs; especially, any of the genus *Macropus,* which includes the **red kangaroo** (*M. rufus*), the largest of all marsupials. See also **wallaby, wallaroo.** [probably < an Australian native language] —**kan′ga·roo′-like′,** *adj.*

kangaroo court *Informal.* an unauthorized or irregular court in which the law is deliberately disregarded or misinterpreted. A mock court held by convicts in prison is called a kangaroo court.

kangaroo rat any of a genus (*Dipodomys*) of small, mouselike, North American desert rodents having very long, strong hind legs adapted for leaping, a very long, tufted tail, and external fur-lined cheek pouches. Only one species (*D. ordii*) is found in Canada, in the sand hills of southern Saskatchewan and Alberta.

Kans. Kansas.

Kant·i·an (kan′tē ən) *adj., n.* —*adj.* of or having to do with Immanuel Kant (1724-1804), a German philosopher, or his system of philosophy. —*n.* a follower of Kant.

ka·o·lin or **ka·o·line** (kā′ə lin) *n.* a fine white clay, used in making porcelain. [< F < Chinese *Kao-ling,* a mountain in China]

ka·pok (kā′pok or kap′ək) *n.* the silky fibres around the seeds of a tropical tree, used for stuffing pillows, life preservers, mattresses, etc. [< Malay]

kap·pa (kap′ə) *n.* the tenth letter (κ) of the Greek alphabet.

ka·put (kä püt′ or kə püt′) *adj. Informal.* ruined, broken, useless, etc. (*never used before a noun*): *All our plans are kaput.*

kar·a·kul (kar′ə kəl or ker′ə kəl) *n.* **1** a variety of Russian or Asiatic sheep. **2** fur with flat, loose curls; caracul. **3** a coat or other garment made of this fur. [< *Kara Kul,* a lake in Turkestan]

kar·at (kar′ət or ker′ət) *n.* a unit used to specify the proportion of gold in an alloy; one of 24 equal parts. An 18-karat gold ring is 18 parts pure gold and 6 parts alloy. *Symbol:* K or k Compare **carat.** ☛ *Hom.* **carat, caret, carrot.**

ka·ra·te (kə rä′tē) *n.* a Japanese system of self-defence without weapons, using studied hand and foot strokes capable of crippling or killing. [< Japanese; literally, empty-handed]

kar·ma (kär′mə) *n.* **1** *Buddhism and Hinduism.* the totality of a person's thoughts, actions, etc. that are supposed to affect or determine his fate in his next incarnation. **2** destiny; fate. [< Skt. *karma* deed, action, fate]

kar·mic (kär′mik) *adj.* of, having to do with, or determined by karma.

karst (kärst) *n.* **1** an irregular limestone region marked by gullies, sinks, caverns, and underground streams. **2** (*adj.*) of or designating such a region. [< G *Karst,* from the name of a limestone plateau near Trieste]

kart (kärt) *n., v.* —*n.* go-kart. —*v.* take part in a go-kart race. —**kart′er,** *n.*

ka·tab·o·lism (kə tab′ə liz′əm) See **catabolism.**

ka·ty·did (kā′tē did′) *n.* any of various large, green, long-horned

grasshoppers. The male makes a shrill noise by rubbing its front wings together. [imitative of the insect's sound]

kau·ri (kou′rē) *n., pl.* **-ris. 1** a tall timber tree (*Agathis australis*) of the pine family found in New Zealand, having white, straight-grained wood. **2** the wood of this tree. **3** a resin that is obtained from it, used in varnish. [< Maori]

kau·ry (kou′rē) *n., pl.* **-ries.** See **kauri.**

A kayak

kay·ak (kī′ak) *n.* **1** a light, narrow boat with pointed ends, made of skins, etc. stretched over a frame of wood or bone leaving only a small opening in the middle for the user. A kayak is propelled by a double-bladed paddle. Kayaks were traditionally used by the Inuit for hunting. **2** any similar craft. [< Eskimo]

ka·zoo (kə zü′) *n.* a toy musical instrument made of a tube sealed off at one end with a membrane or paper that produces a buzzing sound when one hums into the tube. [imitative]

K.B. 1 Knight of the (Order of the) Bath. **2** Knight Bachelor. **3** King's Bench.

K.B.E. Knight Commander of the (Order of the) British Empire.

kc. kilocycle(s).

K.C. 1 Knight(s) of Columbus. **2** King's Counsel.

K.C.B. Knight Commander of the (Order of the) Bath.

K.C.M.G. Knight Commander of (the Order of) St. Michael and St. George.

Kčs. koruna(s).

K.C.V.O. Knight Commander of the (Royal) Victorian Order.

ke·a (kā′ə or kē′ə) *n.* a large, greenish parrot (*Nestor notabilis*) of New Zealand that normally feeds on insects, but sometimes kills sheep to feed upon their fat. [< Maori]

Kech·ua (kech′wä) See **Quechua.**

Kech·uan (kech′wən) See **Quechuan.**

kedge (kej) *v.* **kedged, kedg·ing;** *n.* —*v.* move (a ship, etc.) by pulling on a rope attached to an anchor that has been dropped some distance away. —*n.* a small anchor used in kedging a boat, etc. [origin uncertain]

kedg·er·ee (kej′ə rē′) *n.* **1** an Indian dish of rice, boiled with split peas, onions, eggs, butter, and spices. **2** a European dish made of fish, boiled rice, eggs, and spices, served hot. [< Hind. *khichri*]

keel (kēl) *n.* **1** the main timber or steel piece that extends the whole length of the bottom of a ship or boat. **2** *Poetic.* a ship. **3** a part, as on an aircraft, that is like a ship's keel.
on an even keel, a horizontal. **b** steady; properly balanced: *His business affairs are on an even keel again.*
—*v.* turn upside down; upset.
keel over, a turn over or upside down; upset: *The sailboat keeled over in the storm.* **b** fall over suddenly. **c** *Informal.* faint. [ME < ON *kjölr*]

keel·haul (kēl′hol′ or -hôl′) *v.* haul (a person) under the keel of a ship as a punishment. [< Du. *kielhalen* < *kiel* keel + *halen* haul]

keel·son (kel′sən or kēl′sən) *n.* a beam or line of timbers or iron plates fastened along the top of a ship's keel to strengthen it. Also, **kelson.** [ME ? < Scand.; cf. Swedish *kölsvin*]

keen[1] (kēn) *adj.* **1** sharp enough to cut well: *a keen blade.* **2** sharp; piercing; cutting: *a keen wind, keen hunger, keen wit, keen pain.* **3** strong; vivid: *keen competition.* **4** able to do its work quickly and accurately: *a keen mind, a keen sense of smell.* **5** *Informal.* full of enthusiasm; eager: *a keen player, keen about sailing.* [OE *cēne*] —**keen′ly,** *adv.*
☛ *Syn.* **4.** See note at **sharp. 5.** See note at **eager.**

keen[2] (kēn) *n., v.* —*n.* a wailing lament for the dead. —*v.* wail; lament. [< Irish *caoine*] —**keen′er,** *n.*

keen·ness (kēn′nis) *n.* **1** a keen or cutting quality; sharpness: *the keenness of an axe, the keenness of the cold wind, the keenness of a man's appetite.* **2** an interest in; enthusiasm for: *His keenness for sports was easy to see.*

keep (kēp) *v.* **kept, keep·ing;** *n.* —*v.* **1** have permanently or forever: *You may keep this book.* **2** have and not let go; hold; detain: *They were kept in prison. He was kept in hospital for ten*

days. **3** not reveal or divulge: *to keep a secret.* **4** have and take care of: *My uncle keeps chickens.* **5** take care of and protect: *May God keep you.* **6** have in one's service; employ: *to keep a servant.* **7** have; hold: *keep this in mind.* **8** hold back; prevent: *What is keeping her from accepting?* **9** restrain oneself (from); refrain: *The little boy couldn't keep from crying when he fell down.* **10** maintain in good or orderly condition: *to keep a garden. Mother keeps house.* **11** be preserved; stay in good condition: *Butter will keep in a refrigerator.* **12** stay the same; continue to be: *to keep awake. Keep going along this road for two kilometres.* **13** cause to continue in some stated place, condition, etc.; cause to stay the same: *to keep a light burning, to keep a student after school.* **14** make regular entries or records in: *to keep books, to keep a diary.* **15** record (transactions, events, etc.) regularly: *No record of this conversation was kept.* **16** observe; celebrate: *to keep Christmas as a holiday.* **17** be faithful to: *to keep a promise.* **18** provide for; support: *He is not able to keep himself, much less a family.* **19** have habitually for sale: *That store keeps canned goods.*
keep in with, *Informal.* keep acquaintance or friendship with.
keep on, continue; go on: *The boys kept on swimming in spite of the rain.*
keep time, go correctly; move at the proper rate.
keep up, a continue; prevent from ending. **b** maintain in good condition. **c** not fall behind; remain close or alongside.
keep up with, a not fall behind; go or move as fast as. **b** live or do as well as: *She tried hard to keep up with her wealthy neighbors.* **c** stay up to date with: *He keeps up with the news. Try to keep up with your reading.*
—*n.* **1** food and a place to sleep: *He earns his keep.* **2** the strongest part of a castle or fort. See **castle** for picture.
for keeps, a for the winner to keep his winnings. **b** *Informal.* forever.
[OE *cēpan* observe]
☛ *Syn. v.* **2. Keep, retain, withhold** = hold in one's possession. **Keep** is the general word meaning "have and not let go from one's possession, control, or care": *They were kept in prison.* **Retain,** more formal, emphasizes continuing to hold on to in spite of pressures or difficulties: *The invalid retained his sense of humor.* **Withhold** means keep or hold back and suggests some check or obstacle to letting go: *Fear made him withhold the truth.*

keep·er (kēp′ər) *n.* **1** a person or thing that keeps. **2** guard; watchman. **3** guardian; protector: *Am I my brother's keeper?* **4** *Brit.* gamekeeper. **5** a person who owns or carries on some establishment or business: *the keeper of an inn.* **6** any mechanical device for keeping something in its place, as a clasp, catch, or loop. **7** a link set across the poles of a magnet to preserve its magnetism when not in use. **8** a food or other produce that keeps (well or ill). **9** *Informal.* a fish large enough to be legally caught and kept. **10** goalkeeper.

keep·ing (kēp′ing) *n.* **1** care; charge; maintenance: *The keeping of the orphaned children was paid for by their uncle.* **2** celebration; observance: *the keeping of Thanksgiving Day.* **3** agreement; harmony: *Don't trust him; his actions are not in keeping with his promises.* **4** being kept for future use; preservation.

keep·sake (kēp′sāk′) *n.* something kept in memory of the giver: *My friend gave me his picture as a keepsake when he moved away.*

Kees·hond (kās′hond or kēs′hond) *n., pl.* **-hond·en** or **-honds.** a breed of small dog developed in the Netherlands, having a thick grey coat tipped with black. [< Du. *keeshond* < *kees* terrier + *hond* dog, hound]

Kee·wa·tin (kē wā′tən) *adj., n. Geology.* —*adj.* of or having to do with the earliest period of the Archeozoic era. —*n.* **1** the oldest period of the Archeozoic era. See chart at **geology. 2** the rocks or rock formations of this period. [< *Keewatin,* a district of the Northwest Territories]

keg (keg) *n.* **1** a small barrel or cask. **2** a keg and its contents. **3** as much as a keg can hold. [ME < ON *kaggi*]

kelp (kelp) *n.* **1** any of the large brown seaweeds, especially those of the order Laminariales, such as the giant Pacific kelps (genus *Macrocystis*) or the Atlantic kelps (genus *Laminaria*). **2** the ashes of such seaweeds, used especially as a source of iodine and potassium. [earlier also *kilpe,* ME *culp(e);* origin unknown]

kel·pie or **kel·py** (kel′pē) *n., pl.* **-pies.** in Scottish folklore, a water spirit, usually in the form of a horse, supposed to drown people or be an omen of death by drowning. [origin uncertain]

kel·son (kel′sən) *n.* keelson.

kelt (kelt) *n.* an Atlantic salmon or trout that has recently spawned. [origin unknown. 14c]

Kelt (kelt) *n.* Celt.

Kelt·ic (kel′tik) *adj.* or *n.* Celtic.

kel·vin (kel′vin) *n.* **1** (*adj.*) **Kelvin,** of, based on, or according to a scale of thermodynamic temperature used in science, on which 0 represents absolute zero, theoretically the coldest possible state. Zero on the Kelvin scale is equal to -273.16 degrees Celsius. **2** an SI unit of temperature on this scale. One kelvin is equal to one degree Celsius. The kelvin is one of the seven base units in the SI.

Symbol: K [after William Thomson *Kelvin* (1824-1907), a physicist and mathematician]

ken (ken) *n., v.* **kenned** or **kent** (kent), **ken·ning.** —*n.* **1** the range of sight. **2** the range of knowledge: *What happens on Mars is beyond our ken.* —*v. Scottish.* know. [OE *cennan* make declaration < *cann* know, can¹]

Ken. Kentucky.

Ken·dal green (ken′dəl) **1** a coarse, green woollen cloth. **2** the color of this cloth. [< *Kendal,* in Westmorland, England, where the cloth was originally made. 14c.]

ken·nel (ken′əl) *n., v.* **-nelled,** or **-neled, -nel·ling** or **-nel·ing.** —*n.* **1** a house for a dog or dogs. **2** Often, **kennels,** *pl.* **a** a place where dogs are bred. **b** a place where dogs may be lodged and cared for. **3** a pack of dogs. —*v.* **1** put or keep in a kennel. **2** take shelter or lodge in a kennel. [< AF, ult. < L *canis* dog]

ke·no (kē′nō) *n.* a gambling game resembling lotto and bingo in which the players cover numbers on their cards.

Kent·ish (ken′tish) *adj., n.* —*adj.* of Kent, a county in SE England, or its people. —*n.* an Old English dialect spoken in the early English kingdom of Kent.

kep·i (kep′ē) *n., pl.* **kep·is.** a cap with a round, flat top, worn by French soldiers. See **cap** for picture. [< F *képi,* ult. < G *Kappe* cap]

kept (kept) *v.* pt. and pp. of **keep.**

ker·a·tin (ker′ə tin) *n.* a complex protein, the chief constituent of horn, nails, hair, feathers, etc. [< Gk. *keras, -atos* horn]

kerb (kėrb) *n. Brit.* curb (of a pavement).

ker·chief (kėr′chif) *n.* **1** a square piece of cloth worn over the head or around the neck. **2** handkerchief. [ME < OF *couvrechief* < *couvrir* cover (< L *cooperire*) + *chief* head < L *caput*]

kerf (kėrf) *n.* **1** a cut made by an axe, saw, etc. **2** a piece cut off. [OE *cyrf* < *ceorfan* carve]

Ker·man (kėr män′) *n.* Kirman.

ker·mess (kėr′mis) See **kermis.**

ker·mis (kėr′mis) *n.* **1** in the Netherlands, Belgium, etc., a fair with games and merrymaking. **2** any fair or entertainment, usually to raise money for charity. Also, **kirmess.** [< Du. *kermis* < *kerk* church + *mis* Mass]

kern¹ or **kerne** (kėrn) *n.* **1** *Archaic.* **a** an Irish or Scottish foot soldier carrying light weapons. **b** a troop of such soldiers. **2** an Irish peasant. [< Irish *ceithern* troop of soldiers]

kern² (kėrn) *n. Printing.* the part of a letter that projects beyond the body of the piece of type. [< F *carne* edge < L *cardo, -dinis* hinge]

ker·nel (kėr′nəl) *n.* **1** the softer part inside the hard shell of a nut or inside the stone of a fruit. **2** a grain or seed like wheat or corn. **3** the central or most important part: *the kernel of an argument.* [OE *cyrnel* < *corn* seed, grain]
☞ *Hom.* **colonel.**

ker·o·sene (ker′ə sēn′ or ker′ə sēn′) *n. Cdn.* a thin oil, a mixture of hydrocarbons, usually produced by distilling petroleum; coal oil. It is used as a fuel in lamps, stoves, some types of engines, etc. [< Gk. *kēros* wax]

Ker·ry (ker′ē) *n.* **-ries.** a breed of small black dairy cattle. [< *Kerry,* a county in SW Irish Republic, where this breed originated]

ker·sey (kėr′zē) *n., pl.* **-seys. 1** a coarse, ribbed, woollen cloth with a cotton warp. **2 kerseys,** *pl.* trousers made of kersey. [probably < *Kersey,* a village in Suffolk, England]

kes·trel (kes′trəl) *n.* any of several small falcons noted for their habit of hovering against the wind while hunting, just before diving for their prey; especially, a common European species (*Falco tinnunculus*). The North American sparrow hawk is sometimes called the **American kestrel** because of its close relationship with the Old World kestrels. [probably < OF *cresserelle* < L *crista* crest]

ket·a (kit′ə or ket′ə) *n.* **ket·a.** a species of Pacific salmon, the chum. [origin uncertain]

ketch (kech) *n.* **1** a fore-and-aft-rigged sailing ship with a large mainmast toward the bow and a smaller mast toward the stern. **2** formerly, a sturdy sailing vessel with two masts. [? < *catch*]

ketch·up (kech′əp) *n.* a sauce for use with meat, fish, etc. Tomato ketchup is made of tomatoes, onions, salt, sugar, and spices. Also, **catchup, catsup.** [< Malay *kechap* sauce, probably < Chinese *kôe-chiap* brine of pickled fish]

ket·tle (ket′əl) *n.* **1** a metal container for boiling liquids, cooking fruit, etc. **2** teakettle.
kettle of fish, *Informal.* an awkward state of affairs; mess; muddle. [OE *cetel* < L *catillus,* dim. of *catinus* vessel]

ket·tle·drum (ket′əl drum′) *n.* a drum consisting of a hollow

hat, āge, fär; let, ēqual, tėrm; it, īce hot, ōpen, ôrder; oil, out; cup, pùt, rüle, əbove, takən, pencəl, lemən, circəs

ch, child; ng, long; sh, ship th, thin; ŦH, then; zh, measure

brass or copper hemisphere and a parchment top that can be tuned by adjusting the tension by means of the screws around the circumference. See **drum** for picture.

ke·tu·bah or **Ke·tu·bah** (kə tü′bə) *n. Judaism.* the marriage contract signed by a couple before the wedding, listing their obligations under Jewish law. [< Hebrew *kethubhah* a writing, written document]

Ke·wee·naw·an (kē′wə no′ən or kē′wə nô′ən) *adj., n.* —*adj.* of or having to do with the latest period of the Proterozoic era, between the Cambrian and the Huronian; Algonquian. —*n.* **1** the latest period of the Proterozoic era, between the Cambrian and the Huronian; Algonquian. **2** the copper-bearing rocks or rock formations of this period. See chart at **geology.** [< *Keweenaw,* a promontory on Lake Superior where these rocks are found]

kew·pie doll (kyü′pē) **1** a plastic or celluloid doll resembling a fat cherub with tiny wings and a curled topknot. **2 Kewpie Doll,** *Trademark.* a brand of such dolls. [? dim. of *Cupid*]

key¹ (kē) *n., pl.* **keys;** *adj., v.* **keyed, key·ing.** —*n.* **1** an instrument that locks and unlocks; something that turns the bolt in a lock: *I lost the key to the padlock on my bicycle.* **2** anything like this in shape or use: *a key to open a tin.* **3** something that explains or answers: *the key to a puzzle. The key to an arithmetic book gives the answers to all the problems.* **4** a place that commands or gives control of a sea, a district, etc. because of its position: *Gibraltar is the key to the Mediterranean.* **5** an important or essential person, thing, etc. **6** a pin, bolt, wedge, or other piece put in a hole or space to hold parts together. **7** a device to turn a bolt or nut, etc. Watches used to be wound with keys. **8** one of a set of parts pressed down by the fingers in playing a piano, in typewriting, and in operating other instruments. **9** *Music.* a scale or system of related tones based on a particular tone: *a song written in the key of B flat.* **10** a tone of voice; style of thought or expression: *The poet wrote in a melancholy key.* **11** *Botany.* a key fruit.
—*adj.* controlling; very important: *the key industries of a nation.*
—*v.* **1** lock. **2** fasten or adjust with a key. **3** provide with a key or keys. **4** *Music.* regulate the pitch of; tune: *to key a piano in preparation for a concert.* **5** adjust (a speech, etc.) as if to a particular key: *He wrote a letter keyed to a tone of defiance.*
key up, raise the courage or nerve of: *The coach keyed up the team for the big game.*
[OE *cǣg*] —**key′less,** *adj.*
☞ *Hom.* **cay** (kē), **quay.**

key² (kē) *n., pl.* **keys.** a low island; reef. There are keys south of Florida. [< Sp. *cayo* < Taino (an Arawakan language) *cayo,* or *caya* small island; influenced by *key¹*]
☞ *Hom.* **cay** (kē), **quay.**

key block a large conical block of snow, dropped into place at the centre of an igloo dome, serving to lock the structure firmly together.

key·board (kē′bôrd′) *n.* the set of keys on a piano, typewriter, calculator, etc.

keyed (kēd) *adj.* **1** having keys: *a keyed flute or trombone.* **2** set or pitched in a particular key. **3** fastened or strengthened with a key. **4** constructed with a keystone.

key fruit *Botany.* a dry, winged fruit. The seeds of elm, ash, maple, etc. are contained in key fruits.

key·hole (kē′hōl′) *n.* an opening in a lock through which a key is inserted to turn the lock.

key·note (kē′nōt′) *n., v.* **-not·ed, -not·ing.** —*n.* **1** *Music.* the note on which a scale or system of tones is based. **2** the main idea; guiding principle: *World peace was the keynote of his speech.* —*v.* give the keynote speech of (a conference, political campaign, etc.)

keynote speech a speech, as at a political gathering, that presents the principal issues in which those present are interested.

key signature *Music.* one or more sharps or flats placed after the clef at the beginning of each staff to indicate the key.

key·stone (kē′stōn′) *n.* **1** *Architecture.* the middle stone at the top of an arch, holding the other stones or pieces in place. See **arch** for picture. **2** the part on which other associated parts depend; essential principle: *Freedom is the keystone of our policy.*

kg kilogram(s).

K.G. Knight (of the Order) of the Garter.

KGB the secret police of the Soviet Union. [abbrev. of Russian

Komitet Gosudarstvennoi Bezopasnosti State Security Committee]

khak·i (kär′kē, kä′kē, or kak′ē) *n., pl.* **khak·is;** *adj.* —*n.* **1** a dull, yellowish brown. **2** a stout twilled cloth of this color, used for soldiers' uniforms. **3** a uniform or uniforms made of this cloth: *Khakis will be worn for drill.*
—*adj.* having the color khaki. [< Hind. *khaki*, originally, dust-colored < Persian *khak* dust]

kha·lif (kā′lif or kal′if) See **caliph.**

khan¹ (kän or kan) *n.* **1** the title of a ruler among Tartar or Mongol tribes, or of the emperor of China during the Middle Ages. **2** a title of dignity in Iran, Afghanistan, India, etc. [ME < MF < Turkish]

khan² (kän or kan) *n.* in Turkey and nearby countries, an inn without furnishings. [Arabic < Persian]

khan·ate (kän′āt or kan′āt) *n.* **1** the territory ruled by a khan. **2** the position or authority of a khan.

khe·dive (kə dēv′) *n.* the title of the Turkish viceroys who ruled Egypt between 1867 and 1914. [< F < Persian *khidiv* ruler]

kib·butz (ki bŭts′) *n., pl.* **kib·butz·im** (ki bŭ tsēm′). *Hebrew.* a communal settlement or farm co-operative in Israel.

kibe (kīb) *n.* a chapped or ulcerated sore, inflammation, or swelling on the heel caused by exposure to cold. [ME; cf. Welsh *cibwst* chilblains, kibes]

kib·itz (kib′its) *v. Slang.* look on as an outsider and offer unwanted advice. [< *kibitzer*]

kib·itz·er (kib′it sər) *n. Slang.* **1** a person watching a card game. **2** a person who watches a card game and insists on making suggestions to the players. **3** a person who gives unwanted advice; meddler. [< Yiddish]

ki·bosh (kī′bosh or ki bosh′) *n. Slang.* humbug; nonsense. **put the kibosh on,** finish off; squelch: *The boss put the kibosh on overlong coffee breaks.*
[origin uncertain; probably < Yiddish]

kick (kik) *v., n.* —*v.* **1** strike out with the foot: *That horse kicks when anyone comes near him.* **2** strike with the foot: *The horse kicked the boy.* **3** drive, force, or move by kicking: *to kick a ball.* **4** win by a kick: *to kick a goal in football.* **5** spring back when fired: *This shotgun kicks.* **6** *Informal.* complain; object; grumble. **7** *Slang.* overcome; break; make oneself free of (a habit, addiction, etc.).
kick about or **around,** *Informal.* **a** be in danger of being damaged; lie about. **b** go about aimlessly. **c** consider; toy with.
kick back, *Informal.* **a** spring back suddenly and unexpectedly. **b** *Informal.* return (a portion of money received) as a kickback.
kick in, *Slang.* **a** die. **b** pay what is due or expected.
kick off, **a** *Football.* put a ball in play with a kick. **b** *Slang.* begin. **c** *Slang.* die.
kick out, *Informal.* expel or turn out in a humiliating or disgraceful way: *She should be kicked out of our club.*
kick up, *Slang.* start; cause: *She kicks up a lot of trouble.*
—*n.* **1** the act of kicking. **2** the recoil of a gun when it is fired. **3** *Slang.* a complaint; cause for complaint; objection. **4** *Slang.* excitement; thrill: *He gets a kick out of gambling. He does it for kicks.* **5** *Slang.* the power of a drink, drug, etc. to intoxicate. **6** *Slang.* a period of intense interest or activity (in something): *She is on a classical music kick.* [origin uncertain]

kick·back (kik′bak′) *n.* **1** *Informal.* **a** payment, especially of part of a sum of money received, made by some illegal or otherwise secret agreement (such as for help in making profit) or by coercion. **b** money so paid. **2** a sudden violent or vigorous reaction, usually unexpected.

kick·er (kik′ər) *n.* **1** a person, animal, or thing that kicks. **2** *Informal.* an outboard motor. **3** *Slang.* a surprising or tricky twist, condition, etc.; a catch (def. 6): *The contract seemed generous; the kicker was that we would get no money until all the work was finished.*

kick·off (kik′ôf′) *n.* **1** *Football, soccer, etc.* the start of a game: *The kickoff is scheduled for 2:00 p.m.* **2** *Informal.* the start of any activity.

kick·shaw (kik′shô′ or kik′shô′) *n.* **1** a fancy article of food; delicacy. **2** trifle; trinket. [alteration of F *quelque chose* something]

kid¹ (kid) *n.* **1** a young goat. **2** its flesh, used as food. **3** its skin, used as fur. **4** the leather made from the skin of young goats, used for gloves, shoes, etc. **5 kids,** *pl.* gloves or shoes made of kid. **6** *Informal.* a child or young person: *The kids went to the circus.* [ME < ON *kith*]

kid² (kid) *v.* **kid·ded, kid·ding.** *Slang.* **1** tease playfully; talk jokingly; banter. **2** deceive; fool. [? < *kid¹* in sense of "treat as a child"] —**kid′der,** *n.*

kid–glove (kid′gluv′) *adj.* **1** wearing kid gloves. **2** *Informal.*

careful; considerate; gentle: *This job requires a kid-glove approach.* Also, **kid-gloved.**

kid gloves smooth gloves made of soft kidskin.
handle with kid gloves, treat with special care or consideration.

kid·nap (kid′nap) *v.* **-napped** or **-naped, -nap·ping** or **-nap·ing.** carry off and hold (a person) against his will by force or by fraud; abduct: *The banker's son was kidnapped and held for ransom.* [< *kid¹* child + *nap* snatch away] —**kid′nap·per** or **kid′nap·er,** *n.*

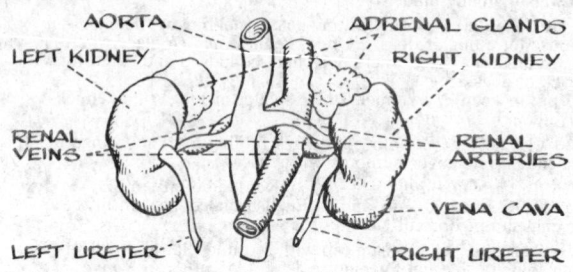

The kidneys of a human being, shown from the back

kid·ney (kid′nē) *n., pl.* **-neys. 1** in vertebrates, one of the pair of organs in the body that separate waste matter and water from the blood and pass them off through the bladder as urine. **2** the kidney or kidneys of an animal, cooked for food. **3** nature; kind; sort: *We must guard our leaders against terrorists, assassins, and people of that kidney.* [ME < *kidenei* < *kiden*-, of uncertain meaning and origin + *ey* egg] —**kid′ney-like′,** *adj.*

kidney bean 1 the kidney-shaped, usually dark-red seed of any of several cultivated varieties of bean, dried for use in soups, casseroles, etc. **2** a plant that bears such seeds.

kid·skin (kid′skin′) *n.* the leather made from the skin of young goats, used for gloves and shoes.

Ki·ku·yu (ki kü′ü) *n., pl.* **-yu** or **-yus;** *adj.* —*n.* **1** a member of a people living in the highlands of south central Kenya. **2** the Bantu language of the Kikuyu. —*adj.* of or having to do with the Kikuyu or their language.

kill (kil) *v., n.* —*v.* **1** put to death; cause the death of: *The blow from the axe killed him.* **2** cause death: *"Thou shalt not kill."* **3** put an end to; get rid of; destroy: *to kill odors, to kill rumors, to kill faith.* **4** cancel (a word, paragraph, item, etc.). **5** defeat or veto (a legislative bill). **6** destroy or neutralize the active qualities of: *to kill land in farming.* **7** spoil the effect of: *One color may kill another near it.* **8** use up (time): *We killed an hour at the zoo.* **9** *Hockey.* overcome the disadvantage of (a penalty) by thwarting the opposing team's attempts to score while the penalized player is off the ice: *Toronto managed to kill the penalty and were then able to score the winning goal.* **10** stop; cut off the fuel supply or electrical current of: *He killed the engine.* **11** *Informal.* overcome completely: *My sore foot is killing me. His jokes really kill me.* **12** *Tennis, etc.* hit (a ball) so hard that it cannot be returned.
kill off, exterminate; wipe out.
—*n.* **1** the act or an instance of killing. **2** an animal or animals killed, especially in a hunt. **3** an enemy aircraft, ship, etc. destroyed in battle. **4** *Tennis, etc.* a ball hit so hard as to be unreturnable. [ME *kyllen, cullen;* probably related to QUELL]
☛ *Hom.* **kiln.**
☛ *Syn. v.* **1. Kill, murder, slay** = cause death. **Kill** is the general word, meaning "put to death or in any way cause the death of a person, animal, or plant": *Overwork killed him. Lack of water kills flowers.* **Murder** emphasizes wicked and cold-blooded killing, and means "kill a person unlawfully, usually deliberately": *He murdered his rich uncle.* **Slay,** chiefly literary or journalistic, means "kill with violence, in battle or by murdering": *All the captives were slain.*

kill·deer (kil′dēr′) *n., pl.* **-deers** or (*esp. collectively*) **-deer.** a common plover (*Charadrius vociferus*) of open uplands from southern Canada west of the Maritimes south to Peru, having mostly brown-and- white plumage with two broad bands across its white breast and noted for its loud, penetrating call. [imitative of its call]

kill·er (kil′ər) *n.* **1** a person, animal, or thing that kills. **2** *Slang.* a criminal who recklessly or wantonly kills others. **3** *Slang.* anything that is very difficult: *That climb is a killer.* **4** killer whale.

killer whale a black-and-white, migratory whale (*Orcinus orca*), the largest member of the dolphin family, found in all seas. It is noted for its boldness and rapaciousness, preying on fish, seals, sea lions, sea otters, narwhals, etc., and even larger baleen whales.

kil·lick (kil′ək) *n.* an anchor made of wooden poles or sticks

bound around a rock or rocks, used especially in the Maritimes and New England. [origin unknown]

kill·ing (kil′ing) *adj., n.* —*adj.* **1** deadly; destructive; fatal: *a killing frost.* **2** overpowering; exhausting: *They rode at a killing pace.* **3** *Informal.* extremely funny.
—*n. Informal.* a sudden great financial success: *He made a killing in stocks.* —**kill′ing·ly,** *adv.*

kill–joy (kil′joi′) *n.* a person who spoils other people's fun.

kiln (kiln *or* kil) *n., v.* —*n.* **1** a furnace or oven for burning, baking, or drying something. Limestone is burned in a kiln to make lime. Bricks are baked in a kiln. **2** a building containing a furnace for drying grain, hops, etc. or for making malt. —*v.* burn, bake, or dry in a kiln. [OE *cyln, cylen* < L *culina* kitchen]
☛ *Hom.* **kill** (kil).

ki·lo (kē′lō *or* kil′ō) *n., pl.* **ki·los.** kilogram. [< F]

kilo– *SI prefix.* thousand. One kilowatt is one thousand watts. *Symbol:* k [< F < Gk. *chilioi*]

kil·o·cy·cle (kil′ə sī′kəl) *n.* 1000 cycles, especially 1000 cycles per second. Kilocycles have been replaced by kilohertz for expressing radio frequencies.

kil·o·gram (kil′ə gram′) *n.* an SI unit for measuring mass. The kilogram is one of the seven base units in the SI. *Symbol:* kg Also, **kilogramme.** [< F *kilogramme*]

kil·o·gram–me·tre (kil′ə gram′mē′tər) *n.* a unit formerly used for measuring work, equal to 9.81 newton metres. Also, **kilogram-meter.**

kil·o·hertz (kil′ə hėrts′) *n., pl.* **kil·o·hertz.** an SI unit for measuring frequency of waves and vibrations, equal to 1000 hertz. *Symbol:* kH

kil·o·joule (kil′ə jül′) *n.* an SI unit for measuring energy, equal to 1000 joules. *Symbol:* kJ

kil·o·li·tre (kil′ə lē′tər) *n.* a unit used with the SI for measuring volume or capacity, equal to 1000 litres. *Symbol:* kL Also, **kiloliter.** [< F *kilolitre*]

kil·o·me·tre (kil′ə mē′tər *or* kə lom′ə tər) *n.* an SI unit for measuring length or distance, equal to 1000 metres. It takes about 12 minutes to walk one kilometre. *Symbol:* km Also, **kilometer.** [< F *kilomètre*]

kil·o·met·ric (kil′ə met′rik) *adj.* **1** of a kilometre. **2** measured in kilometres.

kil·o·pas·cal (kil′ə pas′kəl) *n.* an SI unit for measuring pressure, equal to 1000 pascals. The kilopascal is used in recording air pressure; the standard pressure of the atmosphere is about 101 kPa. *Symbol:* kPa *n.*

kil·o·ton (kil′ə tun′) *n.* a unit for measuring explosive force, equal to 1000 tons of TNT (about 907 tonnes). [< *kilo-* + *ton* (of explosive energy of TNT)]

kil·o·watt (kil′ə wot′) *n.* an SI unit for measuring power, equal to 1000 watts. *Symbol:* kW

kil·o·watt hour a unit used with the SI for measuring electrical energy, defined as the number of kilowatts of electrical power used per hour. One kilowatt hour is equivalent to 3.6 megajoules. *Symbol:* kW·h

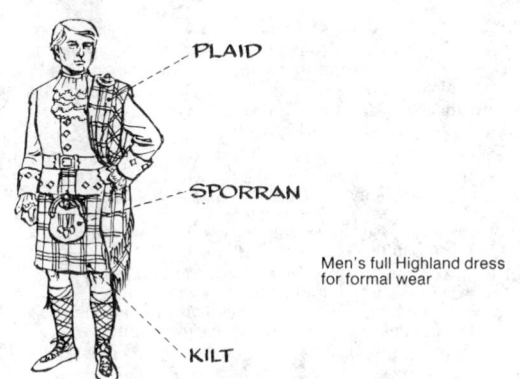

PLAID

SPORRAN

KILT

Men's full Highland dress for formal wear

kilt (kilt) *n., v.* —*n.* **1** a pleated, knee-length skirt worn by men in the Scottish Highlands and by soldiers in Scottish and Irish regiments, including those in Canada. **2** a similar garment worn by women and girls. —*v. Scottish.* tuck up; fasten up. [probably < Scand.; cf. Danish *kilte* tuck (up)] —**kilt′like′,** *adj.*

kil·ter (kil′tər) *n. Informal.* good condition; order: *Our radio is out of kilter.* [origin uncertain]

hat, āge, fär; let, ēqual, tėrm; it, īce
hot, ōpen, ôrder; oil, out; cup, pút, rüle,
əbove, takən, pencəl, lemən, circəs

ch, child; ng, long; sh, ship
th, thin; ŧн, then; zh, measure

A traditional Japanese kimono, worn with an obi

ki·mo·no (kə mō′nə *or* kə mō′nō) *n., pl.* **-nos.** **1** a loose outer garment held in place by a sash, worn by Japanese men and women. See **obi** for picture. **2** a loose dressing gown. [< Japanese]

kin (kin) *n., adj.* —*n.* **1** a person's family or relatives; kindred: *All our kin came to the family reunion.* **2** family relationship; connection by birth or marriage: *What kin is she to you?*
next of kin, nearest living relative: *His next of kin is his father.*
of kin, related.
—*adj.* related. [OE *cynn;* cf. *cennan* beget]

–kin *suffix.* little, as in *lambkin.* [ME; cf. MDu. *-kijn, -ken*]

ki·na (kē′nə) *n.* the basic unit of money in Papua New Guinea, divided into 100 toea. See table at **money.** [< a Papuan language]

ki·nase (kī′nās *or* kin′ās) *n.* an enzyme able to activate the inactive form of another enzyme. [< *kin*etic + diast*ase*]

kind¹ (kīnd) *adj.* **1** helpful, considerate, generous, etc.: *He is a kind person.* **2** gentle: *Be kind to animals.* **3** showing or characterized by helpfulness, gentleness, etc.: *a kind act, kind words.* [OE *(ge)cynde* natural < *(ge)cynd* nature, kind²]

kind² (kīnd) *n.* **1** class; sort; variety: *many kinds of candy. A kilt is a kind of skirt.* **2** a natural group; race.
after (one's) or (its) kind, *Archaic.* according to one's or its own nature.
in kind, **a** in goods or produce, not in money. **b** in something of the same sort. **c** in characteristic quality: *There is a difference in kind, not merely in degree, between a hound and a terrier.*
kind of, *Informal.* nearly; almost; somewhat; rather: *The room was kind of dark.*
of a kind, **a** of the same kind; alike: *The cakes were all of a kind—chocolate.* **b** of a poor or mediocre quality: *Two boxes and a plank make a table of a kind.*
[OE *(ge)cynd*]
☛ *Syn.* **1. Kind, sort** = a group of people or things alike in some way. **Kind** applies particularly to a group of the same nature or character, having enough closely similar essential qualities in their make-up to put them together as a class or division in some system of classification: *What kind of cake do you like best?* **Sort,** often interchangeable with **kind,** is usually vaguer, and sometimes carries a suggestion of contempt: *a girl of that sort. That sort of action disgusts me.*
☛ *Usage.* **Kind, sort. Kind** and **sort** can be singular or plural: *This kind of apple is likely to be wormy. These sorts of behavior are out of place here.* Avoid using a plural determiner with a singular noun, as in *these kind of books* or *those sort of ideas.*

kin·der·gar·ten (kin′dər gär′tən *or* kin′də gär′tən) *n.* **1** the year of school that comes before grade 1. **2** a school for younger children; nursery school. [< G *Kindergarten* < *Kinder* children + *Garten* garden]
☛ *Pronun.* The pronunciation (as in German) with *t* in the final syllable is standard, though a *d* is often heard.

kind–heart·ed (kīnd′här′tid) *adj.* having or showing a kind heart; kindly; sympathetic. —**kind′-heart′ed·ly,** *adv.* —**kind′-heart′ed·ness,** *n.*

kin·dle (kin′dəl) *v.* **-dled, -dling.** **1** set on fire; light. **2** catch fire; begin to burn: *This damp wood will never kindle.* **3** arouse; stir up: *His cruelty kindled our anger.* **4** become stirred up or aroused. **5** light up; brighten: *The boy's face kindled as he told about the circus.* [ME < ON *kynda* kindle] —**kin′dler,** *n.*
☛ *Syn.* **1. Kindle, ignite** = set on fire. **Kindle** emphasizes causing something like wood to burn by setting fire to it, and often suggests trouble in getting a fire going: *He kindled a fire in the fireplace.* **Ignite** emphasizes causing something inflammable (like dry wood and grass, cleaning fluids, gas, oil, etc.) to burst into flame by putting a spark, tiny flame, or great heat to or near it: *Firemen tried to keep flying sparks from igniting the shingles.*

kind·li·ness (kīnd′lē nis) *n.* **1** a kindly feeling or quality. **2** a kindly act.

kin·dling (kin′dling) *n.* material, such as small pieces of wood, for starting a fire.

kind·ly (kīnd′lē) *adj.* **-li·er, -li·est;** *adv.* —*adj.* **1** kind; friendly: *kindly faces.* **2** pleasant; agreeable: *a kindly shower.* —*adv.* **1** in a kind or friendly way. **2** pleasantly; agreeably: *He does not take kindly to criticism.* **3** please (*used in formal or impersonal requests or to express impatience, etc.*): *Kindly return this portion of the bill with your payment. Will you kindly get your feet off the chair!* [OE *(ge)cyndelīc*]

kind·ness (kīnd′nis) *n.* **1** a kind nature; being kind: *We admire his kindness.* **2** kind treatment. **3** a kind act: *He showed me many kindnesses.*

kin·dred (kin′drid) *n., adj.* —*n.* **1** family relationship; connection by birth or marriage. **2** one's family or relatives. —*adj.* **1** related: *kindred tribes.* **2** like; similar: *We are studying about dew, frost, and kindred facts of nature.* [ME < *kyn* family (ON *cynn*) + *rede*, OE *rǣden* condition]

kine (kīn) *n.pl. Archaic or dialect.* cows; cattle. [earlier *kyen*, double plural < OE *cȳ* pl. of *cū* cow + plural suffix *-en*]

kin·e·mat·ic (kin′ə mat′ik) *adj.* having to do with pure motion or with kinematics.

kin·e·mat·ics (kin′ə mat′iks) *n.* the branch of mechanics dealing with the different kinds of motion that are possible for a body or system of bodies, without reference to mass or to the force producing the motion. [< Gk. *kinēma, -atos* motion < *kineein* move]

kin·e·mat·o·graph (kin′ə mat′ə graf′) *n.* cinematograph.

kin·e·ma·tog·ra·phy (kin′ə mə tog′rə fē) *n.* cinematography.

kin·e·scope (kin′ə skōp′) *n.* **1** picture tube. **2** a record on film, which may be rebroadcast, made from images on a picture tube. [< *Kinescope*, a trademark for a picture tube]

ki·ne·sic (ki nē′sik *or* kī nē′sik) *adj.* of or having to do with kinesics.

ki·nes·ics (ki nē′siks *or* kī nē′siks) *n.* the study of communication by means of gestures, facial expressions, etc., especially as they accompany speech. [< Gk. *kinēsis* motion + E *-ics*]

ki·ne·sis (ki nē′sis *or* kī nē′sis) *n.* an involuntary reaction or movement, resulting from an external stimulus. [< Gk. *kinēsis* motion]

kin·es·the·sia (kin′əs thē′zhə) *n.* the sensation of movement in the muscles and joints. [< NL < Gk. *kineein* move + *-aisthesia* perception]

kin·es·thet·ic (kin′əs thet′ik) *adj.* having to do with sensations from the muscles and joints.

ki·net·ic (ki net′ik *or* kī net′ik) *adj.* **1** of motion. **2** caused by motion. [< Gk. *kinētikos* < *kineein* move]

ki·net·ics (ki net′iks *or* kī net′iks) *n.* the branch of mechanics dealing with the effects of forces in causing or changing the motion of bodies (*used with a singular verb*). Kinetics deals with the laws for predicting the motion that will occur in a particular situation.

kinetic theory the theory that the constituent particles of matter are in constant motion, and that the temperature of a substance is proportional to the velocity of the particles. Pressure, elasticity, diffusion, and other properties of gases are also explained in terms of molecular activity.

kin·folk (kin′fōk′) *n.pl.* kinsfolk.

king (king) *n.* **1** the male ruler of a nation; a male sovereign, with either absolute or limited power. **2** a person or animal or thing that is best or most important in a certain sphere or class: *The lion is called the king of the beasts. Babe Ruth was a king of baseball.* **3** *Chess.* the chief piece. **4** *Checkers.* a piece that has moved entirely across the board. **5** a playing card bearing a picture of a king. **6** king salmon (chinook salmon). [OE *cyning*] —**king′less,** *adj.*

king·bird (king′bėrd′) *n.* any of several New World flycatchers (genus *Tyrannus*), such as the **eastern king bird** (*T. tyrannus*), which is found throughout most of Canada.

king·bolt (king′bōlt′) *n.* a vertical bolt connecting the body of a wagon, etc. with the front axle, or the body of a railway car with a set of wheels.

King Charles spaniel a breed of black and tan toy spaniel.

king cobra a very large, poisonous snake (*Ophiophagus hannah*) of tropical Asia that feeds mainly on other snakes. The king cobra, often reaching a length of more than 3.5 metres, is the largest poisonous snake in the world.

king crab horseshoe crab.

king·craft (king′kraft′) *n.* the art of ruling; royal statesmanship.

king·dom (king′dəm) *n.* **1** a country that is governed by a king or a queen. **2** realm; domain; province: *The mind is the kingdom of thought.* **3** one of the three primary categories into which the natural world is commonly divided; the animal kingdom, the plant (or vegetable) kingdom, or the mineral kingdom. [OE *cyningdōm*]

king·fish (king′fish′) *n., pl.* **-fish** *or* **-fish·es.** any of various large marine food fishes of Atlantic or Pacific coastal waters, such as any of the genus *Menticirrhus* (family Sciaenidae) or any of certain mackerels.

king·fish·er (king′fish′ər) *n.* any of a family (Alcedinidae) of birds having a large head, large, sharp bill, and short tail, and most species having brightly colored plumage and a crest. The only Canadian species is the mainly blue-and-white **belted kingfisher** (*Megaceryle alcyon*), which has a tousled crest on its large head.

King James Version an English translation of the Bible published in 1611, during the reign of James I; Authorized Version.

king·let (king′lit) *n.* **1** a petty king; a ruler over a small country. **2** any of several very small songbirds (genus *Regulus*) of N North America having dull olive-brown plumage with a bright yellow, orange, or red patch on the top of the head.

king·ly (king′lē) *adj.* **-li·er, -li·est;** *adv.* —*adj.* **1** of a king or kings; of royal rank. **2** fit for a king: *a kingly crown.* **3** like a king; regal or noble: *a kingly bearing, kingly pride.* —*adv.* as a king does. —**king′li·ness,** *n.* ☛ **Syn.** *adj.* **1.** See note at **royal.**

king·mak·er (king′māk′ər) *n.* **1** a person who makes or establishes a king. **2** a person of consequence who can influence or dictate the choice of candidates for political office.

king-of-arms (king′əv ärms′) *n. Heraldry. Brit.* an official responsible for the investigation of rights and titles, the granting of coats of arms, etc.

king·pin (king′pin′) *n.* **1** *Bowling.* the pin in front or in the centre. **2** *Informal.* the most important person or thing. **3** kingbolt.

king post a vertical post between the apex of a triangular roof truss and a tie beam.

king salmon chinook salmon.

King's Counsel See Queen's Counsel. *Abbrev.:* K.C.

King's Domain *Cdn. Historical.* a vast tract of land lying north of the Lower St. Lawrence and originally belonging to the French kings. [< translation of F *Domaine du Roi*]

King's English See Queen's English.

King's evidence See Queen's evidence.

king's evil scrofula, a disease that was supposed to be cured by the touch of a king.

King's highway in Canada, a main road whose maintenance is the responsibility of the provincial government.

king·ship (king′ship) *n.* **1** the position, rank, or dignity of a king. **2** the rule of a king; government by a king.

king-size (king′sīz′) *adj.* **1** unusually large: *I made myself a king-size sandwich.* **2** longest or largest in a standard range of sizes: *king-size cigarettes. A king-size bed measures about 198 cm wide by 203 cm long.* **3** designed for use with a king-size bed: *king-size sheets.*

king-sized (king′sīzd′) *adj.* extra large.

King's Post *Cdn. Historical.* one of a number of fur-trading and fishing posts in Quebec, most of them in the region known as the King's Domain.

king's ransom a very large amount of money.

king truss a truss framed with a king post.

kink (kingk) *n., v.* —*n.* **1** a twist or curl in thread, rope, hair, etc. **2** a pain or stiffness in the muscles of the neck, back, etc.; crick. **3** a mental twist; eccentricity or quirk. **4** a hindrance or complication. —*v.* make or form a kink or kinks: *The rope kinked when he stretched it out.* [probably < Du. *kink* twist]

kin·ka·jou (king′kə jü′) *n.* a cat-sized, nocturnal mammal (*Potos flavus*) of the raccoon family found in the forests of Mexico and Central and South America, having soft, yellowish-brown fur and a very long, prehensile tail. [< F *quincajou* < Tupi-Guarani]

kink·y (kingk′ē) *adj.* **kink·i·er, kink·i·est. 1** full of kinks; twisted; curly. **2** *Slang.* eccentric or bizarre; very unconventional. —**kink′i·ly,** *adv.* —**kink′i·ness,** *n.*

kin·ni·kin·nick (kin′ə kə nik′) *n.* **1** a mixture of various ingredients, such as bearberry, sumac, or dogwood leaves, used by American Indians for smoking. **2** a plant, especially the bearberry, from which the mixture is made. Also, **kinnikinnic.** [< Algonquian *kinikinic* that which is mixed]

kins·folk (kinz′fōk′) *n.pl.* a person's family; relatives; kin.

kins·folks (kinz′fōks′) *n.pl.* kinsfolk.

kin·ship (kin′ship) *n.* **1** a family relationship. **2** relationship. **3** resemblance.

kins·man (kinz′mən) *n., pl.* **-men.** a male relative.

Kins·men (kins′mən) *n.pl. Cdn.* a national service-club organization of men in business and the professions, founded in 1920 at Hamilton, Ontario.

kins·wom·an (kinz′wům ən) *n., pl.* **-wom·en.** a female relative.

ki·osk (kē osk′ *or* kī′osk *for I;* kē osk′ *for 2*) *n.* **1** a small building, usually with one or more sides open, used as a newsstand, bus shelter, telephone booth, etc. **2** in Turkey, Persia, etc., a light, open summerhouse. [< F < Turkish *kiushk* pavilion]

kip[1] (kip) *n.* the hide of a young or undersized animal. [origin uncertain]

kip[2] (kip) *n., v.* **kipped, kip·ping.** *Slang.* —*n.* **1** a sleeping place; bed. **2** sleep. —*v.* go to bed. [cf. Danish *kippe* low alehouse]

kip[3] (kip) *n.* **1** the basic unit of money in Laos, divided into 100 at. See table at **money.** **2** a coin worth one kip. [< Thai]

kip·per (kip′ər) *n., v.* —*n.* **1** a herring, salmon, etc. that has been salted and dried or smoked. **2** the male salmon or sea trout during or after the spawning season. **3** *Slang.* **a** a person, especially a child. **b** an Englishman. —*v.* salt and dry or smoke (herring, salmon, etc.). [OE *cypera* male salmon]

Kir·ghiz (kir gēz′) *n., pl.* **-ghiz** *or* **-ghiz·es.** **1** a member of a Mongolian people widely scattered over the western part of central Asia. **2** the Turkic language of the Kirghiz.

kirk (kèrk) *n.* **1** *Scottish.* church. **2** **the Kirk,** the national church of Scotland; the Presbyterian Church of Scotland. [ME < ON *kirkja,* ult. < Gk. *kyriakon* (*doma*). See CHURCH.]

Kir·man (kèr män′) *n.* a type of Oriental rug having elaborate designs in soft, rich colors. Also, **Kerman.** [< *Kerman,* in Persia, where the rugs are made]

kir·mess (kèr′mis) See **kermis.**

kirsch (kirsh) *n.* a clear, sweet brandy made from fermented wild black cherries, originally from Germany and Alsace. [< F < G *Kirschwasser* cherry water]

kir·tle (kèr′təl) *n. Archaic.* **1** a skirt or dress. **2** a man's short coat. [OE *cyrtel,* probably < L *curtus* short]

Kis·lev *or* **Kis·lew** (kis′lef) *n.* in the Hebrew calendar, the ninth month of the ecclesiastical year, and the third month of the civil year.

kis·met (kiz′met *or* kis′met) *n.* fate; destiny. [< Turkish < Arabic *qisma*(*t*) < *qasama* divide]

kiss (kis) *v., n.* —*v.* **1** touch with the lips as a sign of love, greeting, or respect. **2** touch gently: *A soft wind kissed the treetops.* **3** put, bring, take, etc. by kissing: *He kissed away her tears.* —*n.* **1** a touch with the lips. **2** a gentle touch. **3** a piece of candy containing coconut, nuts, or the like and wrapped in a twist of paper. **4** a fancy cake made of white of egg and powdered sugar. [OE *cyssan*] —**kiss′a·ble,** *adj.*

kiss·er (kis′ər) *n.* **1** a person who kisses. **2** *Slang.* the face or mouth.

kit[1] (kit) *n.* **1** a set of materials, supplies, or tools required for a particular job or purpose: *a first-aid kit, a sewing kit, a shaving kit.* **2** a set of parts intended to be put together to make a particular thing: *a radio kit, a model airplane kit.* **3** a set of printed materials issued for instruction and information: *a selling kit, a visitor's kit.* **4** the uniform or other clothing and personal equipment required for a certain activity: *a soldier's kit, skiing kit.* **5** a bag, box, case, or other holder containing a set of materials or equipment. **6** such a container together with its contents.
the whole kit and caboodle, *Informal.* the complete group; the lot; everything or everybody: *They met the children and their friends at the theatre and took the whole kit and caboodle out to supper.* [probably < MDu. *kitte*]

kit[2] (kit) *n., v.* **kit·ted, kit·ting.** —*n.* **1** the young of certain fur-bearing wild animals. **2** kitten. —*v.* give birth to kits.

Kit·a·mat (kit′ə mat′) *n., pl.* **-mat** *or* **-mats.** See **Kitimat.**

kit·bag (kit′bag′) *n.* a tall, rounded bag, usually made of canvas and closed at the top by a drawstring, for carrying personal belongings.

kitch·en (kich′ən) *n.* **1** a room with facilities for cooking food and otherwise preparing it for eating. **2** (*adj.*) used in a kitchen: *a kitchen table.* **3** the people employed to cook and prepare food in a large household, restaurant, etc. [OE *cycene* < L *coquina* < *coquus* a cook]

kitch·en·ette (kich′ə net′) *n.* **1** a very small, compactly arranged kitchen. **2** a part of a room fitted up as a kitchen. Also, **kitchenet.**

kitchen garden a garden where vegetables and fruit for a household are grown.

hat, āge, fär; let, ēqual, tèrm; it, īce
hot, ōpen, ôrder; oil, out; cup, pùt, rüle,
above, takən, pencəl, lemən, circəs
ch, child; ng, long; sh, ship
th, thin; ŦH, then; zh, measure

kitch·en·maid (kich′ən mād′) *n.* a woman servant who helps in the kitchen.

kitchen midden a mound of shells, bones, and other refuse that accumulated at a site of prehistoric human habitation. [translation of Danish *kjökken-mödding* < *kjökken* kitchen + *mödding* dunghill]

kitchen police *Esp.U.S.* **1** an army duty of helping the cook prepare and serve the food, wash the dishes, and clean up the kitchen. **2** soldiers assigned to this duty, often as punishment for slight offences. *Abbrev:* K.P.

kitch·en·ware (kich′ən wer′) *n.* kitchen utensils. Pots, kettles, and pans are kitchenware.

kite (kīt) *n., v.* **kit·ed, kit·ing.** —*n.* **1** a light frame covered with paper, cloth, or plastic, designed to be flown in the air on the end of a long string. **2** a hawk having long pointed wings. **3** any of the very high and light sails of a ship. **4** a type of aircraft pulled by a towline and supported by the force of air currents. **5** a person who preys upon others; rapacious person; sharper. **6** a fictitious cheque, bill of exchange, etc. representing no actual transaction, used to raise money or to sustain credit. **7** *Slang.* any airplane that was used in World War II. —*v.* **1** *Informal.* fly like a kite; move rapidly and easily. **2** obtain money or credit by a kite. [OE *cȳta*]

kith (kith) *n.* friends.
kith and kin, friends and relatives.
[OE *cȳththe* acquaintance < *cunnan* know]

Kit·i·mat (kit′ə mat′) *n., pl.* **-mat** *or* **-mats.** a member of a Wakashan Indian people living near the Douglas Channel, B.C. Also, **Kitamat.**

kitsch (kitsh) *n.* **1** mass-produced decorative articles, especially when gaudy, trite, or pretentious. **2** trite, uninspired art or literature. [< G] —**kitsch·y,** *adj.*

kit·ten (kit′ən) *n.* **1** a young cat. **2** the young of certain other small animals, such as rabbits.
have a kitten *or* **kittens,** *Slang.* be emotionally upset about something.
[ME < AF var. of OF *cheton* < LL *cattus* cat]

kit·ten·ish (kit′ən ish) *adj.* **1** like a kitten. **2** coquettish.

kit·ti·wake (kit′ē wāk′) *n.* a medium-sized oceanic gull (*Rissa tridactyla*) of North Atlantic coasts having mainly white plumage with black-tipped grey wings. Kittiwakes come ashore only to breed, at which time they nest in colonies on narrow cliff ledges. [imitative of its call]

kit·ty[1] (kit′ē) *n., pl.* **-ties.** **1** kitten. **2** a pet name for a cat. [ult. < *kitten*]

kit·ty[2] (kit′ē) *n., pl.* **-ties.** **1** *Poker.* **a** the stakes. **b** a fund made up of contributions from each person's winnings, used to buy refreshments, etc. for the players. **2** a fund of money pooled by a group of people for a particular use: *a monthly contribution for the grocery kitty.* **3** *Card games.* a number of cards set aside that may be used by the player making the highest bid, etc. [origin uncertain]

kit·ty–cor·ner (kit′ē kôr′nər) *adj., adv.* —*adj.* diagonally opposite; on a diagonal line: *There is a small drugstore kitty-corner from the garage.* —*adv.* diagonally. Also, **kitty-cornered.** [< *catty-corner,* var. of *cater-corner* < F *quatre* four + E *corner*]

Ki·wa·ni·an (ki wä′nē ən) *n., adj.* —*n.* a member of a Kiwanis Club. —*adj.* of or having to do with Kiwanis Clubs.

Ki·wa·nis (ki wä′nis) *n.* an international group of clubs of business and professional men, organized for civic service and higher ideals in business and professional life. The first Kiwanis Club was founded at Detroit in 1915.

ki·wi (kē′wē) *n., pl.* **-wis.** **1** any of a small genus (*Apteryx,* constituting the order Apterygiformes) of flightless birds of New Zealand having shaggy, hairlike, greyish-brown plumage and a long, slender bill. **2** kiwi fruit or the vine that bears it. **3** *Informal.* a New Zealander. [< Maori]

kiwi fruit *or* **ki·wi·fruit** (kē′wē früt′) *n.* the plum-sized, oval, edible fruit of a subtropical Asian vine (*Actinidia chinensis*), having a hairy, brownish skin and sweet, bright-green pulp.

KKK Ku Klux Klan.

kL kilolitre(s).

Klan (klan) *n.* Ku Klux Klan.

Klans·man (klanz′mən) n., pl. **-men.** a member of the Ku Klux Klan.

klee·nex (klē′neks) n. **1** a small piece of very soft, absorbent paper, or tissue, used as a handkerchief, for removing cosmetics, etc.: *She put two kleenexes in her pocket.* **2** a box or supply of such tissues: *We need more kleenex.* **3 Kleenex,** *Trademark.* a brand of such tissues.

klep·to·ma·ni·a (klep′tə mā′nē ə) n. an uncontrollable impulse to steal. [< NL < Gk. *kleptēs* thief + *mania* madness]

klep·to·ma·ni·ac (klep′tə mā′nē ak′) n. a person who has uncontrollable impulses to steal.

klieg light (klēg) a bright, hot arc light used in taking motion pictures. [after Anton (1872-1927) *Kliegl* and his brother John (1869-1959), the inventors]

Klon·dike or **klon·dike** (klon′dīk) n. a variety of solitaire, or patience. [< *Klondike*, Y.T., where the game was first played]

Klon·di·ker (klon′dī kər) n. Cdn. a person who took part in the Klondike gold rush to the Yukon, 1897-1899.

klutz (kluts) n. Slang. a person who is physically clumsy or socially inept. **—klutz′y,** adj. [< Yiddish *klutz, klutz* < G. *klotz* wooden block, lout]

klys·tron (klis′tron) n. Electronics. a vacuum tube for generating an ultra-high-frequency current, using several resonators to bunch the electrons by advancing and retarding them. [? Gk. *klystēr* pipe syringe + *electron*]

km 1 kilometre(s). **2** kingdom.

kn knot (unit of speed).

knack (nak) n. **1** a special skill; power to do something easily. **2** a trick; habit. [origin uncertain]

knap·sack (nap′sak′) n. a cloth or leather bag for provisions, having straps for carrying on the back. [< LG *Knapsack* < *knappen* eat + *Sack* sack[1]]

knap·weed (nap′wēd′) n. any of several Eurasian perennial plants (genus *Centaurea*) of the composite family having purplish or white thistlelike flowers. Knapweeds have become naturalized as common weeds in many temperate regions, including North America. [OE *cnæp* knob + *weed*]

knave (nāv) n. **1** a dishonest person; rogue; rascal. **2** the jack, a playing card with a picture of a servant or soldier on it. **3** Archaic. a male servant; a man of humble birth or position. [OE *cnafa* boy]
☛ *Hom.* **nave.**

knav·er·y (nāv′ər ē or nāv′rē) n., pl. **-er·ies. 1** behavior characteristic of a knave. **2** a tricky, dishonest act.

knav·ish (nāv′ish) adj. tricky; dishonest. **—knav′ish·ly,** adv. **—knav′ish·ness,** n.

knead (nēd) v. **1** work (dough, clay, etc.) by pressing, stretching, and squeezing with the hands until it has the proper consistency: *Most dough for homemade bread has to be kneaded before it is ready for baking.* **2** press and squeeze with the hands; massage: *Stiffness in the muscles may be taken away by kneading.* **3** make or shape by kneading. [OE *cnedan*] **—knead′er,** n.
☛ *Hom.* **need.**

knee (nē) n., v. **kneed, knee·ing. —n. 1** the joint between the thigh and the lower leg. See **leg** for picture. **2** any joint corresponding to the human knee or elbow. **3** anything like a bent knee in shape or position. **4** the part of pants, stockings, etc. covering the knee. **bring to** (one's) **knees,** force to yield. **—v.** strike with the knee. [OE *cnēo*]

knee breeches breeches reaching to or just below the knees.

knee·cap (nē′kap′) n., v. **-capped, -cap·ping. —n. 1** the flat, movable bone at the front of the knee; patella. See **leg** for picture. **2** a covering to protect the knee. **—v.** shoot (a person) in the kneecaps, especially as an act of terrorism.

-kneed *combining form.* having a **—**knee or knees: *knock-kneed = having knock-knees.*

knee-deep (nē′dēp′) adj. so deep as to reach the knees.

knee-high (nē′hī′) adj. so high as to reach the knees.

kneel (nēl) v. **knelt** or **kneeled, kneel·ing. 1** go down on one's knee or knees: *She knelt down to pull a weed from the flower bed.* **2** remain in this position: *They knelt in prayer for several minutes.* [OE *cnēowlian* < *cnēo* knee]

kneel·er (nēl′ər) n. **1** one who kneels. **2** a stool, cushion, etc. to kneel on.

knee·pad (nē′pad′) n. a pad worn around the knee for protection.

knee·pan (nē′pan′) n. kneecap; patella.

knell (nel) n., v. **—n. 1** the sound of a bell rung slowly after a

death or at a funeral. **2** a sign or warning of death, failure, etc.: *Their refusal rang the knell of our hopes.* **3** a mournful sound. **—v. 1** ring slowly. **2** give a sign or warning of death, failure, etc. **3** make a mournful sound. [ME *knell, knyll* < OE *cnyll* (n.); ME *knelle(n), knylle(n)* < OE *cnyllan* (v.); possibly influenced by *bell*]

knelt (nelt) v. pt. and a pp. of **kneel.**

Knes·set (knes′ət) n. the legislature of Israel, consisting of one chamber, or house. [< Hebrew *Kneseth*, literally, assembly or gathering]

knew (nyü or nü) v. pt. of **know.**
☛ *Hom.* **gnu, new.**

Knick·er·bock·er (nik′ər bok′ər) n. U.S. **1** a person descended from the early Dutch settlers of New York. **2** a person living in New York. [< Diedrich *Knickerbocker*, fictitious author of Washington Irving's *Knickerbocker's History of New York*, 1809]

knick·er·bock·ers (nik′ər bok′ərz) n.pl. knickers.

knick·ers (nik′ərz) n.pl. short, loose-fitting trousers gathered in at, or just below, the knee. [short for *knickerbockers* < *Knickerbocker* (said to be due to the costume shown in illustrations in Washington Irving's *Knickerbocker's History of New York*)]

knick–knack (nik′nak′) n. a pleasing trifle; ornament; trinket. Also, **nick-nack.** [varied reduplication of *knack*]

knife (nīf) n., pl. **knives;** v. **knifed, knif·ing. —n. 1** a thin, flat blade, usually of metal, fastened in a handle so that it can be used to cut or spread. **2** any weapon having a short blade with a sharp edge and point, such as a dagger. **3** a cutting blade in a tool or machine: *The knives of a lawn mower cut grass.*
under the knife, *Informal.* undergoing a surgical operation.
—v. 1 cut or stab with a knife. **2** pierce or cut as with a knife: *The wind knifed through his thin jacket.* **3** Slang. try to defeat in an underhand way. [OE *cnīf*] **—knife′like′,** adj.

knife edge 1 the edge of a knife. **2** anything very sharp. **3** a wedge on the fine edge of which a scale, beam, pendulum, etc. is hung.

knight (nīt) n., v. **—n. 1** in the Middle Ages, a man raised to an honorable military rank and pledged to do good deeds. After serving as a page and a squire, a man was made a knight by the king or a lord. **2** in modern times, a man raised to an honorable rank because of personal achievement or because he has won distinction in some way. A knight has the title *Sir* before his name. **3** a man devoted to the service or protection of a lady. **4** Chess. a piece usually shaped like a horse's head. **5** a member or holder of a rank or degree in any order or society that bears the official title of *Knights: Knights of Columbus.*
—v. raise to the rank of knight. [OE *cniht* boy]
☛ *Hom.* **night.**

knight bachelor bachelor (def. 5).

knight banneret banneret.

knight–er·rant (nīt′er′ənt) n., pl. **knights-er·rant.** a knight travelling in search of adventure.

knight–er·rant·ry (nīt′er′ən trē) n., pl. **knight-er·rant·ries. 1** conduct or action characteristic of a knight-errant. **2** quixotic conduct or action.

knight·hood (nīt′hùd) n. **1** the rank or dignity of a knight. **2** the profession or occupation of a knight. **3** the character or qualities of a knight. **4** knights as a group or class: *All the knighthood of France came to the aid of the king.*

knight·ly (nīt′lē) adj., adv. **—adj.** of, like, or having to do with a knight; brave; generous; courteous; chivalrous. **—adv.** as a knight should do; bravely; generously; courteously. **—knight′li·ness,** n.

Knights Hospitallers or **Hospitalers** See Hospitaller.

Knights of Columbus a fraternal society of Roman Catholic men pledged to increase the religious and civic usefulness of its members and to encourage benevolence. It was founded in 1882.

Knight Templar pl. **Knights Templars** for 1; **Knights Templar** for 2. **1** Templar (def. 1). **2** a member of an order of Masons in the United States.

knit (nit) v. **knit·ted,** or **knit, knit·ting. 1** make by looping yarn or thread together by hand with long needles or by machinery which forms similar interlocking loops: *She is knitting a sweater.* **2** make an article or fabric by looping yarn or thread together with long needles or by machinery: *Jersey is knitted cloth.* **3** form (cloth or an article of clothing) by looping stitches, not by weaving: *Jersey is cloth knitted by machine.* **4** join closely and firmly together. **5** grow together; be joined closely and firmly: *A broken bone knits.* **6** draw (the brows) together in wrinkles. [OE *cnyttan* < *cnotta* knot[1]]
—knit′ter, n.
☛ *Hom.* **nit.**

knit·ting (nit′ing) n. knitted work.

knitting needle one of a pair of long needles used in knitting.

knives (nīvz) n. pl. of **knife.**

knob (nob) n. **1** a rounded lump. **2** the handle of a door, drawer,

etc. **3** a rounded hill or mountain. [cf. MLG *knobbe*] —**knob′like′,** *adj.*

knobbed (nobd) *adj.* having a knob or knobs.

knob·by (nob′ē) *adj.* **-bi·er, -bi·est. 1** covered with knobs. **2** rounded like a knob. —**knob′bi·ness,** *n.*

knock (nok) *v., n.* —*v.* **1** hit; strike a blow with the fist, knuckles or anything hard: *He knocked him on the head.* **2** hit and cause to fall: *Bill ran against another boy and knocked him down.* **3** make a noise by hitting: *to knock on a door.* **4** make a noise, especially a rattling or pounding noise: *The engine is knocking.* **5** *Slang.* criticize; find fault.
knock about, *Informal.* **a** wander from place to place. **b** hit repeatedly.
knock around, knock about.
knock down, a sell (an article) to the highest bidder at an auction. **b** take apart: *We knocked down the bookcase and packed it in the car.* **c** strike down.
knock off, *Informal.* **a** take off; deduct: *to knock off 10 cents from the price.* **b** stop work: *We knock off at noon for lunch.* **c** accomplish hastily; do quickly: *He knocked off a new poem in just a few minutes.* **d** *Slang.* defeat or kill.
knock out, a hit so hard as to make helpless or unconscious. **b** drive out of the contest; vanquish.
knock together, make or put together hastily.
knock up, a tire out; exhaust. **b** *Slang.* make pregnant. **c** *Esp.Brit.* get (someone) out of bed by knocking at the door.
—*n.* **1** a hit: *The hard knock made her cry.* **2** a hit with a noise. **3** the act of knocking. **4** the sound of knocking: *She did not hear the knock at the door.* **5** a pounding or rattling sound in an engine: *We learned that the knock was caused by loose parts.* **6** a severe criticism. [OE *cnocian*]

knock·a·bout (nok′ə bout′) *n., adj.* —*n.* **1** a small, easily handled sailboat equipped with one mast, a mainsail, and a jib, but no bowsprit. **2** *Brit.* slapstick; horseplay. —*adj.* **1** suitable for rough use. **2** noisy; boisterous: *a knockabout farce.*

knock·er (nok′ər) *n.* **1** a person or thing that knocks. **2** a knob, ring, etc. fastened on a door for use in knocking.

knock–knee (nok′nē′) *n.* **1** an inward curving of the legs, so that the knees tend to knock together in walking. **2** knock-knees, *pl.* knees that curve in this way.

knock–kneed (nok′nēd′) *adj.* having legs curved inward so that the knees tend to touch in walking.

knock·out (nok′out′) *n., adj.* —*n.* **1** the act of rendering unconscious or helpless by a punch: *The boxer won the fight by a knockout.* **2** the condition of being knocked out. **3** a blow that knocks out. **4** *Slang.* a person or thing considered outstanding; a success: *The party was a knockout.*
—*adj.* **1** *Slang.* that knocks out: *a knockout blow.* **2** that puts something out of operation or diminishes: *a knockout competition.*

knoll (nōl) *n.* a small, rounded hill; mound. [OE *cnoll*]

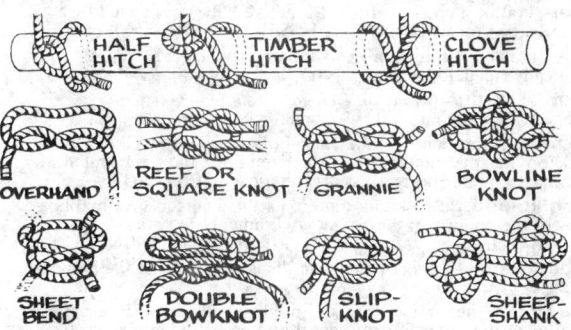

HALF HITCH; TIMBER HITCH; CLOVE HITCH; OVERHAND; REEF OR SQUARE KNOT; GRANNIE; BOWLINE KNOT; SHEET BEND; DOUBLE BOWKNOT; SLIP-KNOT; SHEEP-SHANK

knot¹ (not) *n., v.* **knot·ted, knot·ting.** —*n.* **1** a fastening made by tying or twining together pieces of rope, cord, string, etc. **2** an accidental tying or twisting of rope, cord, string, etc., usually drawn tight; tangle. **3** a bow of ribbon, etc. worn as an ornament. **4** a group; cluster: *A knot of people stood talking outside the door.* **5** a hard mass of wood formed where a branch grows out from a tree, which shows as a roundish, cross-grained piece in a board. **6** a hard lump. **7** *Botany.* a joint where leaves grow out on the stem of a plant. **8** a unit for measuring the speed of a ship or aircraft; one nautical mile per hour: *The ship averaged 12 knots.* **9** nautical mile. **10** a difficulty; problem. **11** something that unites closely or intricately.
—*v.* **1** tie or twine together in a knot. **2** tangle in knots. **3** make knots for (a fringe). **4** make (a fringe) by tying knots. **5** form into a

hat, āge, fär; let, ēqual, tèrm; it, īce
hot, ōpen, ôrder; oil, out; cup, put, rüle,
above, takən, pencəl, lemən, circəs
ch, child; ng, long; sh, ship
th, thin; ᴛH, then; zh, measure

hard lump. **6** unite closely or intricately; bind. [OE *cnotta*]
—**knot′ter,** *n.* —**knot′less,** *adj.*
☛ *Hom.* **Knot, naught, not,** and **nought** are pronounced the same (to rhyme with **got**) by most Canadians.

knot² (not) *n.* any of several small sandpipers (genus *Calidris*), especially *C. canutus,* which has a short, straight bill and greyish plumage except in the breeding season when it has a brownish-red throat and breast. Knots breed in the Arctic and winter in temperate or warm regions. [origin uncertain]
☛ *Hom.* See note at **knot¹.**

knot·grass (not′gras′) *n.* knotweed.

knot·hole (not′hōl′) *n.* a hole in a board where a knot has fallen out.

knot·ted (not′id) *adj.* having a knot or knots; knotty.

knot·ty (not′ē) *adj.* **-ti·er, -ti·est. 1** full of knots: *knotty wood.* **2** difficult; puzzling: *a knotty problem.* —**knot′ti·ly,** *adv.* —**knot′ti·ness,** *n.*

knot·weed (not′wēd′) *n.* any of several weedy plants (genus *Polygonum*) of the buckwheat family having jointed stems and very small flowers. Also called **knotgrass.**

knout (nout) *n., v.* —*n.* a whip formerly used in Russia to inflict punishment. —*v.* flog with a knout. [< F < Russian *knut* < Scand.]

know (nō) *v.* **knew, known, know·ing.** —*v.* **1** be sure of; have information about: *He knows the facts of the case.* **2** have firmly in the mind or memory: *to know a lesson.* **3** be aware of; have seen or heard; have information about: *to know a person's name.* **4** be sure or certain because of experience or knowledge: *He does not have to guess, he knows.* **5** be acquainted with; be familiar with: *I know her.* **6** have an understanding of; have experience with; be skilled in: *He knows Canadian literature.* **7** recognize; identify: *You would hardly know him since his illness.* **8** tell apart from others; distinguish: *You will know his house by the stone chimney.*
know what's what, *Informal.* be well informed. —*n.* **in the know,** *Informal.* having inside information.
[OE *cnāwan*] —**know′er,** *n.*
☛ *Hom.* **no.**
☛ *Syn. v.* **1. Know, understand** = be sure of the truth of something. **Know** emphasizes having a fact or idea firmly in mind or being well acquainted with a subject: *He knows more about Mexico than does anyone else in Canada.* **Understand** emphasizes having a thorough grasp of both facts and meaning, seeing clearly and fully not only the nature and all the implications of a fact or idea, but also its wider relationships: *He understands the workings of the stock market.*

know·a·ble (nō′ə bəl) *adj.* capable of being known.

know–all (nō′ol′ *or* -ôl′) *n. Slang.* know-it-all.

know–how (nō′hou′) *n. Informal.* the ability to do something; the knowledge required to get something done.

know·ing (nō′ing) *adj.* **1** having knowledge; well-informed. **2** clever; shrewd. **3** suggesting shrewd or secret understanding of matters: *His only answer was a knowing look.*

know·ing·ly (nō′ing lē) *adv.* **1** in a knowing way. **2** with knowledge; on purpose: *He would not knowingly hurt anyone.*

know–it–all (nō′it ol′ *or* -ôl′) *n. Slang.* a person having pretensions to knowing everything.

knowl·edge (nol′ij) *n.* **1** what one knows: *His knowledge of the subject is limited.* **2** all that is known or can be learned. **3** the act or fact of knowing: *a knowledge of the surrounding countryside. The knowledge of our victory caused great joy.* [ME *knawlechen* acknowledge, confess, ult. < OE *cnāwan* know]
☛ *Syn.* **1. Knowledge, information** = what a person knows. **Knowledge** applies to all that one knows and understands of facts and general truths and principles, whether gained from books and teachers or by personal experience and observation: *His knowledge of the subject is limited.* **Information** applies to things one has learned through having been told by people or books or through observation, and often suggests isolated or unrelated facts: *She has acquired much information about trips to Europe.*

knowl·edge·a·ble (nol′ij ə bəl) *adj. Informal.* well-informed, especially about a particular subject. —**knowl′edge·a·bly,** *adv.*

known (nōn) *adj., v.* —*adj.* in the knowledge of everyone; widely recognized: *a known fact, a known artist.* —*v.* pp. of **know.**

know–noth·ing (nō′nuth′ing) *n.* an ignorant person.

knuck·le (nuk′əl) *n., v.* **-led, -ling.** —*n.* **1** a finger joint; especially the joint between a finger and the rest of the hand. **2** the rounded protuberance formed when such a joint is bent. **3** the knee or hock

joint of an animal used as food: *boiled pigs' knuckles.* **4 knuckles,** *pl.* knuckle-duster.
—*v.* **1** press or rub with the knuckles. **2** put the knuckles on the ground in playing marbles.
knuckle down, *Informal.* **a** apply oneself earnestly; work hard: *Let's knuckle down and get the job done.* **b** knuckle under.
knuckle under, *Informal.* submit; yield: *He refused to knuckle under to his enemies.*
[ME < MDu., dim. of *knoke* bone]

knuckle ball *Baseball.* a slow pitch thrown from the knuckles and the heel of the palm.

knuck·le·bone (nuk′əl bōn′) *n.* **1** a bone forming part of a knuckle. **2** the rounded end of such a bone. **3 knuckles,** *pl.* the metacarpal and metatarsal bones of sheep, formerly used in games such as jacks.

knuck·le·dust·er (nuk′əl dus′tər) *n.* a piece of metal worn over the knuckles as a weapon.

knuck·le·head (nuk′əl hed′) *n. Slang.* a thoughtless or slow-witted person.

knurl (nèrl) *n.* **1** a knot; knob. **2** a small ridge, such as on the edge of a coin or round nut. [apparently dim. of *knur* knot, ME *knor(re);* cf. MDu. *knorre*]

knurl·y (nèr′lē) *adj.* **knurl·i·er, knurl·i·est.** gnarled.

KO or **K.O.** (kā′ō′) *v.* **KO'd** or **K.O.'d, KO'ing** or **K.O.'ing;** *n. Slang.* —*v.* knock out: *He was KO'd in the fourth round.* —*n.* knockout. [*knock* + *out*]

ko·a·la (kō ä′lə) *n.* a furry grey marsupial (*Phascolarctos cinereus*) of Australia that lives in eucalyptus trees and feeds on the leaves and shoots of these trees. [< native Australian]

ko·bo (kō′bō) *n.* **1** a unit of money in Nigeria, equal to ¹⁄₁₀₀ of a naira. **2** a coin worth one kobo.

ko·bold (kō′bold *or* kō′bōld) *n. German folklore.* **1** a sprite or goblin. **2** a gnome in mines or caves. [< G]

Ko·di·ak bear (kō′dē ak′) a subspecies of the brown bear, found on Kodiak Island and adjacent coastal areas. It is the largest living carnivorous animal, averaging 2.7 m in length.

K. of C. Knight(s) of Columbus.

Kog·mol·ik (kog mō′lik) *n., pl.* **-ik** or **-iks;** *adj. Cdn.* —*n.* **1** an Eskimo of a number of tribes living to the east of Mackenzie Delta in the Coronation Gulf area. **2** their language. —*adj.*
kogmolik, *Slang.* commonplace; inferior in style or quality: *a kogmolik knot.*

Koh·i·noor (kō′ə nür′) *n.* a very large and famous diamond from India that has been one of the British crown jewels since 1849. [< Persian *kohi nur,* literally, mountain of light]

kohl (kōl) *n.* a dark-grey or black powder, usually antimony sulphide, used for eye makeup, especially by women and girls in the Middle East and Asia. [< Arabic *kohl.* 18c. See ALCOHOL.]

kohl·ra·bi (kōl′rä′bē) *n., pl.* **-bies.** a cultivated variety of cabbage (*Brassica oleracea caulorapa*) having a thickened, turnip-shaped stem that is eaten as a vegetable and also used as fodder. [< G < Ital. *cavoli rape,* pl. See COLE, RAPE².]

Koi·ne (koi nā′) *n.* **1** the common literary language of the Greeks during the Hellenistic period, based on the dialect of Attica. It is the dialect used in the New Testament. **2** Often, **koine.** a dialect or language that has become the common tongue of several peoples over a wide area. [< Gk. *koinē (dialektos)* common (language)]

ko·ka·nee (kō′kə nē′) *n. Cdn.* a permanent freshwater form of the sockeye salmon, common in British Columbia lakes and rivers. [? < Kokanee Creek, B.C.]

ko·la (kō′lə) *n.* **1** either of two W African trees (*Cola acuminata* or *C. nitida*) of the same family as the cacao, cultivated extensively in tropical regions for their seeds, called kola nuts. Also called **kola tree. 2** kola nut. [< native African]

kola nut the caffeine-containing seed of the kola tree, chewed in tropical regions as a stimulant and exported to many parts of the world for use as a flavoring in soft drinks and medicines.

ko·lin·sky (kə lin′ski) *n., pl.* **-skies. 1** any of several Asian minks. **2** its tawny fur. **3** a coat or other garment made of this fur. [< Russian *kolinski,* adj. < *Kola,* a region of the Soviet Union]

ko·ma·tik (kō′mə tik′) *n. Cdn. North.* a large wooden dogsled made of closely-spaced crossbars lashed to two broad runners. [< eastern Inuktitut (Eskimo) *qamutik,* dual form of *qamut* sled runner]

Kom·so·mol (kom′sə mol′) *n.* **1** a Soviet youth organization for people between the ages of 14 and 23. **2** a member of this organization. [< Russian abbrev. of *Kommunisticheskij Sojuz Molodezhi* Communist League of Youth]

koo·doo (kü′dü) *n., pl.* **-doos.** kudu.

kook (kük) *n. Slang.* a peculiar or eccentric person; screwball. [? < *cuckoo*]

kook·a·bur·ra (kük′ə bèr′ə) *n.* a large Australian kingfisher (*Dacelo gigas*) noted for its cry that resembles loud, harsh laughter; laughing jackass. [< native Australian]

kook·y or **kook·ie** (kü′kē) *adj. Slang.* peculiar or eccentric: *a kooky person, kooky clothes.* —**kook′i·ness,** *n.*

koo·le·tah (kü′lə tä′) *n.* kuletuk.

koo·li·tak (kü′lə täk′) *n.* kuletuk.

Koo·ten·ay (kü′tə nā′) *n., pl.* **Koo·ten·ay** or **Koo·ten·ays. 1** a member of an Amerindian people living near Kootenay Lake in SE British Columbia. **2** the language of the Kootenay, constituting a separate language family.

ko·pek or **ko·peck** (kō′pek) *n.* **1** a unit of money in the Soviet Union, equal to ¹⁄₁₀₀ of a rouble. **2** a coin worth one kopek. [< Russian *kopejka,* orig. dim. of *kop'e* spear (kopecks minted from 1535-1719 bore a figure of Ivan IV with a lance)]

Ko·ran (kô rän′ *or* kô ran′) *n.* the sacred book of Islam, consisting of the revelations made to the prophet Mohammed by Allah through the angel Gabriel. [< Arabic *qurān* recitation < *qara'a* read]

Kor·a·tron (kôr′ə tron′) *n. Trademark.* a resin finish that is heat-cured into a fabric after cutting and imparts permanent crease and shape to a garment.

Ko·re·an (kə rē′ən *or* kô rē′ən) *n., adj.* —*n.* **1** a native or inhabitant of Korea, a small country in E Asia. **2** the language of the Koreans. —*adj.* of Korea, its people, or their language.

ko·ru·na (kô′rü nä′) *n.* **1** the basic unit of money in Czechoslovakia, divided into 100 halers. See table at **money. 2** a coin worth one koruna. [< Czech < L *corona* crown]

ko·sher (kō′shər) *adj., v., n.* —*adj.* **1** right or clean according to Jewish ritual law: *kosher meat.* **2** dealing in products that meet the requirements of Jewish ritual law: *a kosher butcher.* **3** *Slang.* all right; legitimate: *It's not kosher to change the rules once the game has started.*
—*v.* prepare (food) according to the Jewish law.
—*n. Informal.* **1** food thus prepared. **2** a shop selling such food. [< Hebrew *kasher* proper]

ko·tow (kō′tou′) *v.* kowtow.

kou·mis or **kou·miss** or **kou·myss** (kü′mis) See **kumiss.**

kow·tow (kou′tou′) *v., n.* —*v.* **1** kneel and touch the ground with the forehead to show deep respect, submission, or worship. **2** show slavish respect or obedience (*to*). —*n.* the act of kowtowing. [< Chinese *k'o-t'ou,* literally, knock (the) head] —**kow′tow′er,** *n.*

K.P. *Esp.U.S.* kitchen police. This abbreviation is sometimes used to mean menial work.

kPa kilopascal.

kr. 1 krona. **2** krone.

Kr krypton.

kraal (kräl) *n.* in South Africa: **1** a native village protected by a fence. **2** a pen for cattle or sheep. [< Afrikaans < Pg. *curral* corral]

kraft (kraft) *n.* a tough, brown wrapping paper made from chemically treated wood pulp. [< G *Kraft* strength]

kraut or **Kraut** (krout) *n. Derogatory slang.* a German. [< Sauer*kraut,* food commonly associated with Germans]

Krem·lin (krem′lən) *n.* **1** the citadel of Moscow. The chief offices of the Soviet government are in the Kremlin. **2** the government of the Soviet Union. [< F < Russian *kreml* citadel < Tartar]

Krem·lin·ol·o·gist (krem′lə nol′ə jist) *n.* a person who makes a study of the policies of the Soviet government.

Krem·lin·ol·o·gy (krem′lə nol′ə jē) *n.* the study and analysis of the domestic and foreign policies of the government of the Soviet Union.

krill (kril) *n.* the mass of tiny, shrimplike planktonic crustaceans (making up the order Euphausiacea) that occur in periodic swarms, especially in polar seas. Krill constitutes the chief food of baleen whales.

Krim·mer (krim′ər) *n.* a tightly curled grey fur similar to Persian lamb, made from the pelts of Crimean lambs. [< G *krimmer* < *Krim* Crimea. 20c.]

kris (krēs) *n.* a Malayan or Indonesian dagger with a wavy blade. [< Du. *kris* or Sp. or Pg. *cris* < Malay *kirīs,* krīs. 16c.]

Krish·na (krish′nə) *n.* an incarnation of the Hindu god Vishnu, occurring in many forms, but especially as the divine flute player, calling the human soul to God. [< Sanskrit]

Kriss Krin·gle (kris′ kring′gəl) Santa Claus. [< G dial. *Christkindl* Christ child, Christmas gift]

kro·na¹ (krō′nə) *n., pl.* **-nor** (-nôr). **1** the basic unit of money in

Sweden, divided into 100 öre. See table at **money. 2** a coin worth one krona. [< Swedish, ult. < L *corona* crown]

kro·na² (krō′nə) *n., pl.* **-nur** (-nər). **1** the basic unit of money in Iceland, divided into 100 aurar. **2** a coin worth one krona. [< Icelandic, ult. < L *corona* crown]

kro·ne¹ (krō′nə) *n., pl.* **-ner** (-nər). **1** the basic unit of money in Denmark and Norway, divided into 100 öre. See table at **money. 2** a coin worth one krone. [< Danish, ult. < L *corona* crown]

kro·ne² (krō′nə) *n., pl.* **-nen** (-nən). **1** the basic unit of money in Austria between 1892 and 1925. **2** a silver coin worth one krone. **3** a former German gold coin. [< G *Krone* < L *corona* crown]

krul·ler (krul′ər) See **cruller.**

kryp·ton (krip′ton) *n.* a rare, inert, gaseous chemical element. *Symbol:* Kr   *at.no.* 36; *at.wt.* 83.80. [< NL < Gk. *krypton*, neut. adj., hidden]

KS Kansas.

Kt. Knight.

K.T. 1 Knight Templar. **2** Knight of the (Order of the) Thistle.

kud·lik (küd′lik) *n. Cdn.* a dishlike soapstone lamp that burns caribou or seal oil, traditionally used by Inuit. [< Inuktitut (Eskimo) *gudlik*]

ku·dos (kyü′dos *or* kü′dos) *n. Informal.* prestige; glory; fame. [< Gk. *kydos*]

ku·du (kü′dü) *n.* either of two large antelopes of the bush country of Africa, the **greater kudu** (*Tragelaphus strepsiceros*) and the **lesser kudu** (*T. imberbis*), both having spirally curved horns. Also, **koodoo.** [< Hottentot]

Ku Klux Klan (kyü′kluks′klan′ *or* kü′-) *n. U.S.* **1** a secret society of white people formed in the S United States after the Civil War to regain and maintain their control. **2** a secret society founded in the U.S. in 1915, opposed to blacks, Jews, Catholics, and foreigners. *Abbrev.:* KKK. [probably < Gk. *kyklos* circle + E *clan*]

ku·lak (kü läk′) *n.* **1** in Russia, formerly, a well-to-do peasant, farmer, or trader who opposed collectivization. **2** a Russian peasant who owns and tills his land for his own profit. [< Russian *kulak*, literally, fist; hence, tight-fisted]

ku·le·tuk (kü′lə tuk′) *n. Cdn.* a hooded, close-fitting jacket made of skin, often trimmed with fur; parka. Also, **koolitah, koolitak.**

ku·mik (kü′mik) *n.* kamik.

ku·miss (kü′mis) *n.* **1** fermented mare's or camel's milk used as a drink by Asiatic nomads. **2** a drink made from cow's milk, used in special diets. **3** an intoxicating liquor distilled from Asian kumiss (def. 1). Also, **koumis, koumiss,** *or* **koumyss.** [< Russian *kumys* < Tatar *kumiz*]

küm·mel (kim′əl *or* kum′əl; *German,* kym′əl) *n.* a liqueur flavored with caraway seeds, anise, etc. [< G]

hat, āge, fär; let, ēqual, tèrm; it, īce
hot, ōpen, ôrder; oil, out; cup, put, rüle,
əbove, takən, pencəl, lemən, circəs
ch, child; ng, long; sh, ship
th, thin; ᴛʜ, then; zh, measure

kum·mer·bund (kum′ər bund′) See **cummerbund.**

kum·quat (kum′kwot) *n.* **1** an orange-yellow fruit resembling a small orange and having a sour pulp and a sweet rind, used especially for preserves and candy. **2** any of several trees or shrubs (genus *Fortunella*) of the rue family that produce this fruit. [< Chinese (Cantonese dial.)]

kung fu (kung′fü′) a Chinese art of fighting similar to karate, that dates back to ancient times.

Kuo·min·tang (kwō′min tang′ *or* kwō′min täng′) *n.* a Chinese nationalist party organized in 1912.

kur·cha·to·vi·um (kèr′chə tō′vē əm) *n.* proposed name for chemical element number 104. *Symbol:* Ku   See **rutherfordium.**

Kurd (kèrd *or* kürd) *n.* a member of a nomadic and warlike Moslem people living chiefly in Kurdistan, a region in SW Asia, divided between Turkey, Iran, and Iraq.

Kur·dish (kèr′dish *or* kür′dish) *adj., n.* —*adj.* of or having to do with the Kurds or their language. —*n.* the Iranian language of the Kurds.

ku·rus (kə rüsh′) *n., pl.* **kurus.** a unit of money in Turkey, equal to ¹⁄₁₀₀ of a lira. Also called **piastre.** [< Turkish]

kV kilovolt(s).

kW kilowatt(s).

kwa·cha (kwä′chä) *n., pl.* **kwacha. 1** the basic unit of money in Zambia, divided into 100 ngwee. **2** the basic unit of money in Malawi, divided into 100 tambala. See table at **money. 3** a note worth one kwacha. [native term; literally, dawn]

Kwa·ki·u·tl (kwä′kē ü′təl *or* kwä kyü′təl) *n.* **Kwa·ki·u·tl** *or* **Kwa·ki·u·tls. 1** a member of an Amerindian people living on the shores of Queen Charlotte Sound and on N Vancouver Island. **2** the Wakashan language of the Kwakiutl.

kwan·za (kwan′zə) *n.* the basic unit of money in Angola, divided into 100 lwei. See table at **money.** [< a Bantu language]

kW·h kilowatt hour(s).

Ky. Kentucky.

KY Kentucky.

kyat (kyät) *n.* **1** the basic unit of money in Burma, divided into 100 pyas. See table at **money. 2** a coin or note worth one kyat. [< Burmese]

Ll

l or **L** (el) *n., pl.* **l's** or **L's.** **1** the twelfth letter of the English alphabet. **2** any speech sound represented by this letter. **3** a person or thing identified as *l*, especially the twelfth in a series. **4** the Roman numeral for 50. **5** something shaped like the letter L, especially a wing of a building or a section of pipe; ell. **6** (*adj.*) of or being an L or l: *an L-shaped room.*

l or **l.** **1** line. **2** league. **3** length. **4** lira; lire. **5** leaf. **6** left. **7** book (for L *liber*).

L **1** Latin. **2** litre(s). **3** *Physics.* length. **4** longitude. **5** pound (sterling). **6** Libra. **7** large. **8** the land element of the Canadian Forces.

L. **1** Latin. **2** low. **3** licentiate. **4** lake. **5** law.

£ pound (or pounds) sterling.

la¹ (lä) *n. Music.* **1** the sixth tone of an eight-tone major scale. . See **do²** for picture. **2** the tone A. [see GAMUT]

la² (lä) *interj. Archaic.* an exclamation of surprise.

La lanthanum.

La. Louisiana.

LA Louisiana.

L.A. **1** Legislative Assembly. **2** Los Angeles.

lab (lab) *n. Informal.* laboratory.

Lab (lab) *n. Informal.* Labrador retriever.

Lab. **1** Labrador. **2** *Brit.* Labour (Party). **b** Labourite.

la·bel (lā′bəl) *n., v.* **-belled** or **-beled, -bel·ling** or **-bel·ing.** —*n.* **1** a slip of paper or other material attached to anything and marked to show what or whose it is, or where it is to go. **2** a short phrase used to describe some person, thing, or idea: *"Land of Opportunity" is a label often given to Canada.*
—*v.* **1** put or write a label on: *The bottle is labelled "Poison."* **2** describe as; call; name: *He labelled the boastful man a liar.* **3** infuse or treat (a substance) with a radio-active chemical or isotope so that its course or activity can be noted. [ME < OF < Gmc.] —**la′bel·ler** or **la′bel·er,** *n.*

la·bel·lum (lə bel′əm) *n., pl.* **-bel·la** (-bel′ə). *Botany.* the middle petal of an orchid, usually different in shape and color from the other two and suggestive of a lip. [< L *labellum,* dim. of *labium* lip]

la·bi·al (lā′bē əl) *adj., n.* —*adj.* **1** of or having to do with a lip or lips. **2** *Phonetics.* articulated mainly with the lips: *f, b, p,* and *m* are labial consonants. **3** *Music.* producing tones by the action of an air current across a narrow, liplike opening, as in a flue pipe of an organ.
—*n.* **1** *Phonetics.* a sound articulated with the lips. **2** a flue pipe on an organ, as distinguished from a reed pipe. [< Med.L *labialis* < L *labium* lip]

la·bi·ate (lā′bē āt′ or lā′bē it) *adj.* having one or more liplike parts. [< NL *labiatus* < L *labium* lip]

la·bile (lā′bīl or lā′bəl) *adj.* liable to change; unstable. [< L *labilis* < *labi* fall]

la·bil·i·ty (lə bil′ə tē) *n., pl.* **-ties.** the state of being labile.

labio– *combining form.* made with the lips and ——: *labiodental* = made with the lips and teeth.

la·bi·o·den·tal (lā′bē ō den′təl) *adj., n. Phonetics.* —*adj.* articulated with the lower lip and upper teeth. —*n.* a sound articulated in this way. The sounds *f* and *v* are labiodentals.

la·bi·um (lā′bē əm) *n., pl.* **-bi·a** (-bē ə). **1** a lip or liplike part. **2** *Botany.* a portion of the corolla of certain flowers, especially the lower part, shaped to suggest a lip. [< L]

la·bor or **la·bour** (lā′bər) *n., v.* —*n.* **1** the effort in doing or making something; work; toil: *He was well paid for his labor.* **2** a piece of work; task: *The king gave Hercules twelve labors to perform.* **3** physical work or toil done for wages. **4** *Economics.* the work of human beings that produces goods or services. *Land, labor,* and *capital* are the three principal factors of production. **5** skilled and unskilled workers as a group: *Labor favors safe working conditions.* **6** the process of childbirth or the time during which it takes place. **7** (*adj.*) of or having to do with this process: *labor pains.*
—*v.* **1** do work; work hard; toil: *He labored all day in the mill.* **2** elaborate with effort or in detail: *The speaker labored the point so much that we lost interest.* **3** move slowly and heavily: *The ship labored in the high waves.* **4** be burdened, troubled, or distressed: *labor under misapprehension.* **5** be in labor (def. 6). [ME < OF < L *labor*]
☞ *Syn. n.* **1.** See note at **work.**

lab·o·ra·to·ry (lab′rə tô′rē or lə bô′rə trē) *n., pl.* **-ries.** **1** a place where scientific work is done; a room or building fitted with apparatus for conducting scientific investigations, experiments, tests, etc. **2** a place fitted up for manufacturing chemicals, medicines, explosives, etc. **3** any place, not a classroom or library, equipped for systematic study: *a language laboratory.* [< Med.L *laboratorium* < L *laborare* to work < *labor* work]

Labor Day or **Labour Day** the first Monday in September, a legal holiday in Canada and the United States in honor of labor and laborers.

la·bored or **la·boured** (lā′bərd) *adj.* done with effort; forced; not easy or natural. —**lab′ored·ly** or **la′boured·ly,** *adv.*
☞ *Syn.* See note at **elaborate.**

la·bor·er or **la·bour·er** (lā′bər ər) *n.* **1** worker. **2** a person who does work requiring strength rather than skill or training.

la·bo·ri·ous (lə bô′rē əs) *adj.* **1** requiring much work; requiring hard work: *Climbing a mountain is laborious.* **2** willing to work hard; hard-working; industrious. **3** showing signs of effort; not easy. [< L *laboriosus* < *labor* labor] —**la·bo′ri·ous·ly,** *adv.* —**la·bo′ri·ous·ness,** *n.*

la·bor·ite or **la·bour·ite** (lā′bər īt′) *n.* a member of a labor party.

labor party or **labour party** **1** any political party organized to protect and promote the interests of workers. **2** See **labour party** (def. 2).

Labor Progressive party *Cdn. Historical.* the official name of the Communist Party of Canada from 1943-1959.

la·bor-sav·ing or **la·bour-sav·ing** (lā′bər sā′ving) *adj.* that takes the place of or lessens labor.

labor union or **labour union** an association of workers to protect and promote their common interests, and for dealing collectively with employers.

la·bour (lā′bər) See **labor.**

la·bour·ite (lā′bər īt′) *n.* **1** See **laborite.** **2** Labourite, in Great Britain, a member of the Labour Party.

labour party **1** See **labor party.** **2** Labour Party, in Great Britain, a political party that claims especially to protect and advance the interests of working people. It was founded by the trade unions.

Lab·ra·dor (lab′rə dôr′) *n. Cdn.* Labrador retriever.

Labrador Current the cold arctic current that flows southward past Labrador and Newfoundland, where it joins the Gulf Stream.

lab·ra·dor·ite (lab′rə dôr it′ or lab′rə dôr′īt) *n.* **1** a kind of feldspar that gleams with brilliant colors. **2** a piece of this stone, or a gem made from it. [< *Labrador,* where it is found + *-ite*]

Labrador retriever a breed of medium-sized retriever originating in Newfoundland but developed mainly in England, having a thick, short coat that is black, chocolate brown, or yellow. [< *Labrador,* where the breed was originated]

Labrador tea *Cdn.* **1** any of several small evergreen shrubs (genus *Ledum*) of the heath family, especially a common bog plant (*L. groenlandicum*) of Greenland and N North America, having white flowers and leathery, oblong leaves with rolled-under margins and brownish, woolly undersides. **2** an infusion made from the leaves of *L. groenlandicum,* traditionally used as a tea substitute in the North.

la·bret (lā′bret) *n.* an ornament of bone, shell, wood, etc. stuck into or through the lower lip to stretch it, worn by various primitive peoples. [< *labrum* + *-et*]

la·brum (lā′brəm or lab′rəm) *n., pl.* **la·bra** (lā′brə or lab′rə). **1** a lip or liplike part. **2** *Anatomy.* a ring of cartilage surrounding a bony socket.

la·bur·num (lə bėr′nəm) *n.* any of a genus (*Laburnum*) of Eurasian trees and shrubs of the pea family having hanging clusters of yellow flowers. Some laburnums are cultivated as ornamental trees; others are valued for their hard, durable wood. [< L]

lab·y·rinth (lab′ə rinth′ or lab′rinth) *n.* **1** a place through which

it is hard to find one's way; maze. 2 a confusing, complicated arrangement. 3 a confusing, complicated state of affairs. 4 **Labyrinth,** *Greek mythology.* the maze built by Daedalus for King Minos of Crete. The Minotaur was kept there. 5 *Anatomy.* the inner ear. [< L < Gk. *labyrinthos*]

lab·y·rin·thine (lab′ə rin′thən *or* lab′ə rin′thēn′) *adj.* 1 of a labyrinth; forming a labyrinth. 2 intricate; confusing; complicated.

lac (lak) *n.* a resinous substance secreted by certain homopterous insects of S Asia, especially *Laccifer lacca,* used especially for making shellac. [< Hind. *lakh* < Skt. *laksha*]

L.A.C. Leading Aircraftman.

lace (lās) *n., v.* **laced, lac·ing.** —*n.* 1 a delicate, openwork or netlike fabric made by connecting base threads with ornamental stitches or by twisting, braiding, or knotting threads together in an ornamental pattern. 2 a cord, string, leather strip, etc. for pulling or holding together. 3 gold or silver braid used for trimming uniforms, etc.
—*v.* 1 put laces through; pull or hold together with a lace or laces. 2 be fastened or admit of being fastened with a lace or laces: *These shoes lace.* 3 trim with or as if with lace: *a uniform laced with gold.* 4 interlace; intertwine. 5 mark with streaks; streak: *a white petunia laced with purple.* 6 *Informal.* lash; beat; thrash. 7 add a dash of brandy, whisky, etc. to (a beverage, especially coffee). 8 squeeze in the waist of (someone), by tightening the laces of a corset, etc. **lace into, a** attack. **b** criticize severely.
[ME < OF *laz* < L *laqueus* noose. Doublet of LASSO.] —**lace′like′,** *adj.*

Lace·dae·mo·ni·an (las′ə dē mō′nē ən) *adj. or n.* Spartan.

lac·er·ate (*v.* las′ər āt′; *adj.* las′ə rāt′ *or* las′ər it) *v.* **-at·ed, -at·ing;** *adj.* —*v.* 1 tear roughly; mangle: *The bear's claws lacerated his flesh.* 2 cause pain or suffering to; distress: *The coach's sharp words lacerated his feelings.* —*adj.* 1 deeply or irregularly indented as if torn: *lacerate leaves.* 2 torn; jagged. [< L *lacerare* < *lacer* mangled]

lac·er·a·tion (las′ər ā′shən) *n.* 1 the act of lacerating. 2 a rough or jagged tear or wound.

lace·wing (lās′wing′) *n.* any of numerous insects (order Neuroptera) having two pairs of large wings with a lacelike network of veins, long, delicate antennae, and a slender body; especially, any member of the **green lacewing** family (Chrysopidae) or **brown lacewing** family (Hemerobiidae).

lace·work (lās′wèrk′) *n.* 1 lace. 2 openwork like lace.

lach·es (lach′iz) *n. Law.* failure to do a thing at the right time; inexcusable negligence. [ME < OF *laschesse,* ult. < L *laxus* loose]

Lach·e·sis (lak′ə sis) *n. Greek mythology.* one of the three Fates. Lachesis measures off the thread of human life.

lach·ry·mal (lak′rə məl) *adj., n.* —*adj.* 1 of tears; producing tears. 2 for tears. 3 *Anatomy.* of, having to do with, or situated near the glands (lachrymal glands) that secrete tears, or the ducts leading from them.
—*n.* **lachrymals,** *pl. Anatomy.* the glands that produce tears. Also, **lacrimal.** [< Med.L *lachrymalis* < L *lacrima* tear]

lach·ry·ma·to·ry (lak′rə mə tô′rə) *adj., n.* **-ries.** —*adj.* 1 of tears; producing tears. 2 for tears. —*n.* a small vase with a narrow neck found in ancient Roman tombs and once believed to be used to hold the tears of mourning friends.

lach·ry·mose (lak′rə mōs′) *adj.* tearful; mournful. [< L *lacrimosus* < *lacrima* tear] —**lach′ry·mose·ly,** *adv.*

lac·ing (lās′ing) *n.* 1 a cord, string, etc. for pulling or holding something together. 2 gold or silver braid used for trimming. 3 *Informal.* a lashing; beating; thrashing.

lack (lak) *v., n.* —*v.* 1 have less than enough; need: *A desert lacks water.* 2 be without: *A homeless person lacks a home.* 3 be absent or missing.
—*n.* 1 a shortage; not having enough: *Lack of rest made her tired.* 2 the fact or condition of being without: *Lack of a fire made him cold.* 3 the thing needed: *The campers' main lack was fuel for a fire.* **supply the lack,** supply what is needed.
[cf. MDu. *lac,* MLG *lak*]

☛ *Syn. v.* **1, 2. Lack, want, need** = be without something. **Lack** = be completely without or without enough of something, good or bad: *A coward lacks courage.* **Want** = lack something worth having, desired, or, especially, necessary for completeness: *That dress wants a belt.* **Need** = lack something required for a purpose or that cannot be done without: *He does not have the tools he needs, does not have enough sleep.*

lack·a·dai·si·cal (lak′ə dā′zə kəl) *adj.* languid; listless; dreamy; weakly sentimental. [< *lackaday*] —**lack′a·dai′si·cal·ly,** *adv.* —**lack′a·dai′si·cal·ness,** *n.*

lack·a·day (lak′ə dā′) *interj. Archaic.* alas. [var. of *alack a day!*]

lack·ey (lak′ē) *n., pl.* **-eys;** *v.* **-eyed, -ey·ing.** —*n.* 1 a male servant; footman. 2 a slavish follower. —*v.* 1 wait on. 2 be slavish to. [< F *laquais* < Sp. *lacayo* foot soldier]

lack·ing (lak′ing) *adj., prep.* —*adj.* 1 not having enough; deficient: *A weak person is lacking in strength.* 2 absent; not present: *Water is lacking in a desert.* —*prep.* without; not having: *Lacking anything better, use what you have.*

lack·lus·tre (lak′lus′tər) *adj.* 1 not shining or bright; dull. 2 lacking vitality or interest: *a lacklustre production of a play.* Also, **lackluster.**

la·con·ic (lə kon′ik) *adj.* using few words; brief in speech or expression; concise. [< L < Gk. *lakōnikos* Spartan; Spartans were noted for the brevity, or terseness, of their speech]

la·con·i·cal·ly (lə kon′ik lē) *adv.* in few words; briefly; concisely.

lac·o·nism (lak′ə niz′əm) *n.* 1 laconic brevity. 2 a laconic speech or expression.

lac·quer (lak′ər) *n., v.* —*n.* 1 a varnish consisting of shellac dissolved in a solvent, used to give a protective coating or a shiny appearance to metals, wood, paper, etc. 2 a varnish made from the resin of a sumac tree of SE Asia. It gives a very high polish on wood. 3 wooden articles coated with such varnish. 4 a dressing for the hair, made from gum or resin.
—*v.* coat with lacquer. [< F < Pg. *laca* lac] —**lac′quer·er,** *n.*

lac·ri·mal (lak′rə məl) See **lachrymal.**

la·crosse (lə kros′) *n. Cdn.* a game played, either indoors (**box lacrosse**) or outdoors (**field lacrosse**) by two teams of players equipped with lacrosse sticks, by means of which an India rubber ball is carried and passed from player to player in an attempt to score a goal. [< Cdn.F *la crosse,* the racket used in the game]

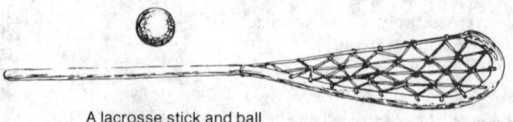

A lacrosse stick and ball

lacrosse stick an L-shaped stick strung with leather thongs that form a kind of pouch for carrying the ball in the game of lacrosse.

lac·tate[1] (lak′tāt) *n.* any salt of lactic acid. [< *lact(ic acid)* + *-ate*[2]]

lac·tate[2] (lak′tāt) *v.* **-tat·ed, -tat·ing.** 1 secrete milk. 2 give suck. 3 convert into milk; cause to resemble milk. [< L *lactare* suckle, with E *-ate*[1]]

lac·ta·tion (lak tā′shən) *n.* 1 the act of suckling a baby. 2 the time during which a mother gives milk. 3 the secretion or formation of milk.

lac·te·al (lak′tē əl) *adj., n.* —*adj.* 1 of or like milk; milky. 2 of lymphatic vessels, carrying chyle. —*n.* any of the lymphatic vessels in the wall of the intestine that carry chyle from the intestine to the thoracic duct, from which the chyle is taken into the bloodstream. [< L *lacteus* < *lac* milk]

lac·te·ous (lak′tē əs) *adj.* milky.

lac·tic (lak′tik) *adj.* of milk; from milk. [< L *lac, lactis* milk]

lactic acid a colorless, odorless organic acid occurring in several forms. One is produced by the action of bacteria on the lactose of milk in the process of souring; another form occurs in muscle tissue. Lactic acid is used in medicine and industry. *Formula:* $C_3H_6O_3$

lac·to·fla·vin (lak′tō flā′vən) *n.* riboflavin.

lac·tom·e·ter (lak tom′ə tər) *n.* an instrument for testing the purity or richness of milk. [< *lacto-* milk (< L *lac*) + *-meter*]

lac·tose (lak′tōs) *n.* a white, odorless crystalline sugar present in milk; milk sugar. *Formula:* $C_{12}H_{22}O_{11}$ [< L *lac, lactis* milk]

la·cu·na (lə kyü′nə) *n., pl.* **-nas, -nae** (-nē *or* -nī). 1 an empty space; gap; blank: *There were several lacunas in her letter where words had been erased.* 2 *Biology.* a tiny cavity in bones or tissues. [< L *lacuna* hole < *lacus* cistern, lake. Doublet of LAGOON.]

la·cus·trine (lə kus′trin) *adj.* 1 of lakes. 2 in or on lakes: *Some prehistoric peoples built lacustrine dwellings.* [< L *lacustris,* adj. of *lacus* lake + E *-ine*[1]]

lac·y (lās′ē) *adj.* **lac·i·er, lac·i·est.** 1 of lace. 2 like lace; having an open pattern: *the lacy leaves of a fern.* —**lac′i·ly,** *adv.* —**lac′i·ness,** *n.*

lad (lad) *n.* 1 a boy; young man. 2 *Informal.* man. [ME *ladde*]

lad·der (lad′ər) *n., v.* —*n.* 1 a set of rungs or steps fastened to two long sidepieces, for use in climbing. 2 a means of climbing higher. 3 an ascending series of little pools built to enable fish to swim upstream past a dam or falls; fishway. 4 anything resembling

or suggesting a ladder: *This company has an elaborate promotion ladder.* **5** a run in a knitted garment.
—*v.* of knitted garments, especially stockings, develop ladders as the result of the breaking of a thread. [OE *hlæder*] —**lad′der·like′**, *adj.*

lad·die (lad′ē) *n. Scottish.* **1** a young boy. **2** man.

lade (lād) *v.* **lad·ed, lad·en** or **lad·ed, lad·ing. 1** put a burden on; load. **2** dip; scoop; ladle. **3** take on cargo. [OE *hladan*]

lad·en (lā′dən) *adj., v.* —*adj.* loaded; burdened. —*v.* a pp. of **lade.**

lad·ing (lā′ding) *n.* **1** the act of loading. **2** load; freight; cargo.

la·dle (lā′dəl) *n., v.* **-dled, -dling.** —*n.* a large, cup-shaped spoon with a long handle, for dipping out liquids. —*v.* **1** dip out. **2** dip out and carry or serve in a ladle or other utensil: *The cook is ladling the soup.* [OE *hlædel* < *hladan* lade] —**la′dler,** *n.*

la·dy (lā′dē) *n., pl.* **-dies. 1** a woman of refinement and courtesy. **2** a woman of high social position. **3** any woman: *She's a courageous lady. The lady who waited on us is from my home town.* **4** a woman who has the rights or authority of a lord; a mistress of a household. **5** noblewoman; a woman who has the title of Lady. **6 Lady,** in Britain, a title given to women of certain ranks of nobility, such as a marchioness, countess, etc., a daughter of a duke, earl, etc., or the wife or widow of a knight or baronet. **7** a woman whom a man loves or is devoted to. **8** wife.
Our Lady, the Virgin Mary.
[OE *hlǽfdīge,* literally, loaf-kneader, < *hlāf* loaf + *-dīg-* to knead. Compare LORD.]
☛ *Syn.* See note at **female.**
☛ *Usage.* **Lady.** In formal English **lady** is used to mean a woman of refinement or high social position. Though **lady** is used in everyday speech to refer to any woman (*the lady selling tickets*), the term is often considered affected. **Woman** is the preferred general term.
☛ *Usage.* See note at **man.**

la·dy·bird (lā′dē bėrd′) *n.* ladybug.

la·dy·bug (lā′dē bug′) *n.* any of numerous small beetles (family Coccinellidae) having a rounded back, usually red or orange with black spots. Both as larvae and adults, ladybugs feed on insects and insect eggs.

Lady Day March 25, the day the angel told Mary that she would be the mother of Jesus; Annunciation Day.

la·dy·fin·ger (lā′dē fing′gər) *n.* a small sponge cake that resembles a finger in size and shape.

la·dy-in-wait·ing (lā′dē in wāt′ing) *n., pl.* **la·dies-in-wait·ing.** a lady who is an attendant of a queen or princess.

la·dy-kill·er (lā′dē kil′ər) *n. Slang.* a man supposed to be dangerously fascinating to women.

la·dy·like (lā′dē līk′) *adj.* **1** having or showing the manners or appearance of a lady; well-bred or refined: *a ladylike cough.* **2** suitable for a lady: *a ladylike costume.*

la·dy·love (lā′dē luv′) *n.* a woman who is loved by a man; sweetheart.

la·dy·ship (lā′dē ship′) *n.* **1** the rank or position of a lady. **2** Often, **Ladyship,** in Britain, a title used in speaking to or of a woman having the rank of Lady: *Your Ladyship, Her Ladyship.*

la·dy-slip·per (lā′dē slip′ər) *n.* lady's-slipper.

la·dy's-slip·per (lā′dēz slip′ər) *n.* any of several wild orchids (genus *Cypripedium*) found in temperate regions, having flowers whose shape suggests a slipper. The pink lady's-slipper (*C. acaule*) is the provincial flower of Prince Edward Island.

lag¹ (lag) *v.* **lagged, lag·ging. 1** move too slowly; fall behind in movement, development, etc. (*often used with* **behind**): *The child lagged because he was tired.* **2** slacken or weaken; fall behind in strength, intensity, etc.
—*n.* **1** the act or condition of lagging. **2** the amount by which a person or thing lags. **3** an interval of time, especially between related phenomena or events, such as an action and its effect. **4** the last or hindmost one (in a race, game, sequence of any kind). [origin unknown] —**lag′ger,** *n.*
☛ *Syn. v.* See note at **linger.**

lag² (lag) *n., v.* **lagged, lag·ging.** —*n.* **1** a strip of material used in encasing or insulating a drum, boiler, etc. **2** a barrel stave or slat. —*v.* cover with insulating material. [? < Scand.; cf. Old Icelandic *lögg* barrel rim. Related to Swedish *lagg* stave]

la·ger (lä′gər) *n.* a light beer which is slowly fermented at a low temperature and stored from six weeks to six months before being used. [short for *lager beer,* half translation of G *Lagerbier* < *Lager* bed, storehouse + *Bier* beer]

lag·gard (lag′ərd) *n., adj.* —*n.* a person who moves too slowly or falls behind; backward person. —*adj.* slow; falling behind; backward. —**lag′gard·ly,** *adv.* —**lag′gard·ness,** *n.*

lag·ging (lag′ing) *n.* **1** lag² (def. 1) or lags. **2** planking or framing

hat, āge, fär; let, ēqual, tėrm; it, īce
hot, ōpen, ôrder; oil, out; cup, pùt, rüle,
above, takən, pencəl, lemən, circəs
ch, child; ng, long; sh, ship
th, thin; ℸH, then; zh, measure

to prevent cave-ins of earthwork, or to support an arch in construction.

la·go·morph (lag′ə môrf′) *n.* any of an order (Lagomorpha) of mammals having two pairs of upper incisors, one behind the other, specialized for gnawing. The order comprises rabbits, hares, and pikas.

la·go·mor·phic (lag′ə môr′fik) *adj.* of, having to do with, or like the lagomorphs.

la·goon (lə gün′) *n.* **1** a pond or small lake connected with a larger body of water. **2** shallow water separated from the sea by low sandbanks. **3** the water within a ring-shaped coral island. [< Ital. *laguna* < L *lacuna* pond, hole. Doublet of LACUNA.]

lah (lä) See **la¹.**

la·ic (lā′ik) *adj., n.* —*adj.* lay; secular. —*n.* layman. [< LL *laicus* < Gk. *laikos* < *laos* people. Doublet of LAY².]

laid (lād) *v., adj.* —*v.* pt. and pp. of **lay¹.** —*adj.* marked with close parallel lines or watermarks: *laid paper.*
laid up, a stored up; put away for future use. **b** *Informal.* forced by illness or injury to stay indoors or in bed. **c** of ships, dismantled and put in dock.

laid-back (lād′bak′) *adj. Slang.* unexcited or unexcitable; relaxed and easygoing: *a laid-back entertainer. The whole evening was laid-back and low-key.*

lain (lān) *v.* pp. of **lie².**
☛ *Hom.* **lane.**

lair (ler) *n.* the den or resting place of a wild animal. [OE *leger* < *licgan* lie²]

laird (lerd) *n. Scottish.* an owner of land, especially of a landed estate. [Scottish var. of *lord*]

lais·sez faire or **lais·ser faire** (les′ā fer′) **1** the principle of letting people do as they please. **2** the absence of governmental regulation and interference in trade, business, industry, etc. [< F *laissez faire* allow to do]

lais·sez-faire (les′ā fer′) *adj.* of or based on laissez faire.

la·i·ty (lā′ə tē) *n., pl.* **-ties.** laymen; the people as distinguished from the clergy or from a professional class: *Doctors use many words that the laity do not understand.* [< *lay³* + *-ity*]

lake¹ (lāk) *n.* **1** a large body of water usually surrounded by land. **2** a wide place in a river. [< L *lacus*]

lake² (lāk) *n.* **1** a deep-red or purplish-red coloring matter. **2** an insoluble colored compound formed from animal, vegetable, or coal tar coloring matters and metallic oxides. **3** a pool of liquid, as of oil, tar, etc. [< F *laque,* ult. < Persian *lak*]

lake dweller a person who lived in a lake dwelling.

lake dwelling a prehistoric dwelling built on piles over a lake.

lake·front (lāk′frunt′) *n.* **1** land or land with buildings at the edge of a lake. **2** the part of a town or city next to a lake. **3** (*adj.*) of or on a lakefront: *We have a lakefront cottage.*

Lake·head (lāk′hed′) *n.* the city of Thunder Bay, Ontario, and the surrounding region, on the northwest shore of Lake Superior. Also, **lakehead.**

lake herring cisco.

lak·er (lā′kər) *n.* **1** a person living or working on a lake. **2** a lake boat, especially one operating on the Great Lakes. **3** *Cdn.* a lake fish, especially a lake trout.

lake trout a large char (*Salvelinus namaycush*), typically dark greenish or greyish with light spots, native to the lakes of N North America but now introduced to many other parts of the world. It is highly prized as a game and food fish.

lam (lam) *n. Slang.* **on the lam, a** escaping. **b** in hiding. [origin unknown]
☛ *Hom.* **lamb.**

lam. laminated.

la·ma (lä′mə *or* lam′ə) *n.* in Tibet and Mongolia, a Buddhist priest or monk. [< Tibetan *blama*]
☛ *Hom.* **llama.**

La·ma·ism (lä′mə iz′əm *or* lam′ə iz′əm) *n.* the religious system of the lamas in Tibet and Mongolia, a form of Buddhism.

La·marck·i·an (lə mär′kē ən) *adj., n.* —*adj.* of or having to do

with Jean de Lamarck or Lamarckism. —*n.* a person who supports Lamarckism.

La·marck·ism (lə mär′kiz əm) *n.* the evolutionary theory of Jean de Lamarck (1744-1829), a French naturalist, who held that characteristics acquired by parents tend to be inherited by their descendants.

la·ma·ser·y (lä′mə ser′ē *or* lam′ə ser′ē) *n., pl.* **-ser·ies.** in Tibet and Mongolia, a building, or group of buildings, where lamas live, work, and worship.

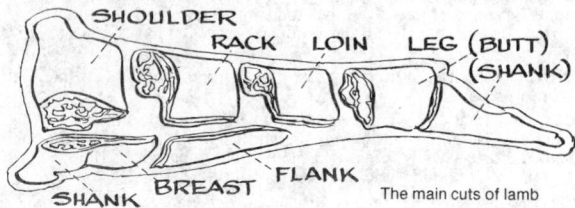

The main cuts of lamb

lamb (lam) *n., v.* —*n.* **1** a young sheep. **2** the meat from a lamb. **3** lambskin. **4 the Lamb,** Jesus Christ (John 1:29 and 36). **5** a young, dear, or innocent person. **6** *Slang.* a person who is easily cheated. **7** an inexperienced speculator. **8** *Informal.* Persian lamb. **like a lamb, a** meekly; timidly. **b** easily fooled. —*v.* give birth to a lamb or lambs. [OE] —**lamb′like′,** *adj.* ► *Hom.* lam.

lam·baste (lam bāst′) *v.* **-bast·ed, -bast·ing.** *Slang.* **1** beat; thrash. **2** scold roughly; denounce. [? < *lam* beat, thrash (cf. ON *lemja* and E *lame*) + *baste*³]

lamb·da (lam′də) *n.* the 11th letter of the Greek alphabet (λ).

lam·ben·cy (lam′bən sē) *n.* a lambent quality or condition.

lam·bent (lam′bənt) *adj.* **1** moving lightly over a surface: *a lambent flame.* **2** playing lightly and brilliantly over a subject: *a lambent wit.* **3** softly bright: *Moonlight is lambent.* [< L *lambens, -entis,* ppr. of *lambere* lick]

lamb·kin (lam′kin) *n.* **1** a little lamb. **2** a young or dear person.

Lamb of God Christ (John 1: 29 and 36).

lam·bre·quin (lam′brə kin *or* lam′bər kin) *n.* a drapery covering the top of a window or door, or hanging from a shelf. [< F]

lamb·skin (lam′skin′) *n.* **1** the skin of a lamb, especially with the wool on it. **2** leather made from the skin of a lamb. **3** parchment.

lambs·quar·ter (lamz′kwôr′tər) *n.* an edible weed of the same family as spinach, used in salad or as a potherb. Also, **lamb's quarter.**

lame (lām) *adj.* **lam·er, lam·est;** *v.* **lamed, lam·ing.** —*adj.* **1** not able to walk properly; having an injured leg or foot; crippled. **2** stiff and sore: *His arm is lame from playing ball.* **3** poor; weak; unsatisfactory: *Sleeping too long is a lame excuse for being late.* —*v.* **1** make lame; cripple: *The accident lamed him for life.* **2** become lame; go lame. [OE *lama*] —**lame′ly,** *adv.* —**lame′ness,** *n.*

la·mé (la mā′ *or* lä mā′) *n.* a rich fabric made, wholly or partly, of metal threads. [< F *lamé,* literally, laminated < *lame* metal leaf]

lame duck 1 *U.S.* an elected representative or group that has been defeated for re-election and is serving the last part of the current term. **2** *Informal.* a disabled or helpless person or thing.

la·mel·la (lə mel′ə) *n., pl.* **-mel·las, -mel·lae** (-mel′ē *or* -mel′ī). a thin plate, scale, or layer, especially of flesh or bone. [< L *lamella,* dim. of *lamina* thin plate]

la·mel·lar (lə mel′ər *or* lam′ə lər) *adj.* having, consisting of, or arranged in lamellas. —**la·mel′lar·ly,** *adv.*

lam·el·late (lam′ə lāt′, lam′ə lit, lə mel′āt, *or* lə mel′it) *adj.* lamellar.

la·ment (lə ment′) *v., n.* —*v.* **1** feel or show grief for; mourn for: *to lament the dead.* **2** feel or show grief; weep: *Why does she lament?* **3** regret: *We lamented his absence.* —*n.* **1** an expression of grief; wail. **2** a poem, song, or tune that expresses grief. **3** regret. [< L *lamentari* < *lamentum* a wailing] —**la·ment′er,** *n.* —**la·ment′ing·ly,** *adv.*

lam·en·ta·ble (lam′ən tə bəl) *adj.* **1** to be regretted or pitied; giving cause for sorrow: *a lamentable accident. It was a lamentable day when our dog died.* **2** not so good; inferior: *The singer gave a lamentable performance.* —**lam′en·ta·bly,** *adv.*

lam·en·ta·tion (lam′ən tā′shən) *n.* **1** the act or an instance of lamenting; grief or mourning. **2 Lamentations,** a poetic book of the Bible, said to have been written by Jeremiah, describing and lamenting the destruction of Jerusalem (*used with a singular verb*).

lam·i·na (lam′ə nə) *n., pl.* **-nae** (-nē′ *or* -nī′) **or -nas. 1** a thin plate, scale, or layer. **2** *Botany.* the flat, wide part of a leaf. [< L]

lam·i·nar (lam′ə nər) *adj.* having, consisting of, or arranged in thin layers, plates, or scales.

lam·i·nate (*v.* lam′ə nāt′; *adj. n.* lam′ə nāt′ *or* lam′ə nit) *v.* **-nat·ed, -nat·ing;** *adj., n.* —*v.* **1** split into thin layers. **2** make by putting layer on layer. **3** beat or roll (metal) into a thin plate. **4** cover with thin plates. —*adj.* laminated; laminar. —*n.* a laminated plastic.

lam·i·na·tion (lam′ə nā′shən) *n.* **1** the process of laminating. **2** the state of being laminated. **3** a laminated structure; an arrangement in thin layers. **4** a thin layer.

Lam·mas (lam′əs) *n.* **1** *Roman Catholic Church.* August 1, a religious feast commemorating the imprisonment and miraculous escape of Saint Peter (Acts 12:4-10). **2** August 1, the day of a harvest festival formerly held in England. Also, **Lammas Day.** [OE *hlāfmæsse* < *hlāf* bread, loaf + *mæsse* mass (because of the consecration of loaves made from the year's first grain)]

lamp (lamp) *n.* **1** a device that provides artificial light: *a gas lamp, a street lamp, a floor lamp. An oil lamp holds oil and a wick by which the oil is burned.* **2** a similar device that gives heat: *a spirit lamp.* **3** a device for providing healthful rays: *a sun lamp.* **4** an electric light bulb. **5** *Slang.* eye. [ME < OF < L < Gk. *lampas* < *lampein* shine]

lamp·black (lamp′blak′) *n.* a fine, black soot consisting of almost pure carbon that is deposited when oil, gas, etc. burn incompletely. Lampblack is used as a coloring agent in paint and ink.

lamp·light (lamp′līt′) *n.* the light from a lamp.

lamp·light·er (lamp′līt′ər) *n.* **1** a person who lights street lamps. **2** a torch, twisted paper, etc. used to light lamps.

lam·poon (lam pün′) *n., v.* —*n.* a piece of writing that attacks and ridicules a person in a malicious or abusive way. —*v.* attack in a lampoon. [< F *lampon* drinking song < *lampons* let us drink] —**lam·poon′er,** *n.*

lam·poon·ist (lam pün′ist) *n.* a person who writes lampoons.

lamp·post (lamp′pōst′) *n.* a post used to support a street lamp.

lam·prey (lam′prē *or* lam′prā) *n., pl.* **-preys.** any of a family (Petromyzonidae) of primitive fishes of fresh and saltwater, having an eel-like body and a round sucking mouth with horny teeth. Most adult lampreys live as parasites, attaching themselves to fish with their mouths and feeding on the blood and tissues of their host. [ME < OF *lampreie* < Med.L *lampreda* < LL *naupreda;* form influenced by L *lambere* lick. Doublet of LIMPET.]

Lan·cas·ter (lang′kəs tər) *n.* the English royal house from 1399 to 1461. Its emblem was a red rose.

Lan·cas·tri·an (lang kas′trē ən) *adj., n.* —*adj.* of the English royal house of Lancaster. —*n.* a supporter or member of the house of Lancaster.

lance (lans) *n., v.* **lanced, lanc·ing.** —*n.* **1** a long wooden spear with a sharp iron or steel head. In the Middle Ages knights were often armed with lances. **2** a soldier armed with a lance. **3** any instrument like a soldier's lance. **4** lancet. —*v.* **1** pierce with a lance. **2** cut open with a lancet: *The dentist lanced the gum so that the new tooth could come through.* [< F < L *lancea* light Spanish spear]

lance–bom·bar·dier (lans′bom′bə dēr′) *n.* a non-commissioned artillery officer of the lowest rank, junior to a bombardier. *Abbrev.:* L/Bdr.

lance–corporal (lans′kôr′pə rəl) *n.* a non-commissioned officer of the lowest rank in the armed forces of some countries.

Lan·ce·lot (lan′sə lot′) *n. Arthurian legend.* the bravest of the knights of the Round Table and the lover of Queen Guinevere.

lan·ce·o·late (lan′sē ə lāt′ *or* lan′sē ə lit) *adj.* shaped like the head of a lance: *a lanceolate leaf.* [< L *lanceolatus < lanceola,* dim. of *lancea* lance]

lanc·er (lan′sər) *n. Historical.* a mounted soldier armed with a lance.

lanc·ers (lan′sərz) *n.pl.* **1** a form of square dance. **2** the music for this dance.

lance–sergeant (lans′sär′jənt) *n.* a corporal appointed to act temporarily as sergeant. *Abbrev.:* L/Sgt.

lan·cet (lan′sit) *n.* **1** a small, sharp-pointed surgical knife, usually having two sharp edges. Doctors use lancets for opening boils, abscesses, etc. **2** a narrow, sharply pointed arch or window. [ME < OF *lancette,* dim. of *lance* lance < L *lancea*]

lance·wood (lans′wûd′) *n.* **1** a tough, straight-grained, springy wood, used for whip handles, fishing rods, cabinetwork, etc., and formerly much used for the shafts of carriages. **2** any of various tropical trees of the custard-apple family yielding this wood,

especially *Oxandra lanceolata* of the West Indies and NE South America.

land (land) *n., v.* —*n.* **1** the solid part of the earth's surface: *dry land.* **2** ground; soil: *This is good land for a garden.* **3** ground used as property: *The farmer invested in land and machinery.* **4** *Economics.* anything furnished by nature without the help of man, such as soil, mineral deposits, water, wildlife. *Land, labor,* and *capital* are the three principal factors of production. **5** country; region: *mountainous land.* **6** the people of a country; nation: *She collected folk songs from all the land.*

how the land lies, what the state of affairs is.

—*v.* **1** come to land; bring to land: *The ship landed at the pier. The pilot landed the airplane in a field.* **2** put on land; set ashore: *The ship landed its passengers.* **3** go ashore: *the passengers landed.* **4** *Cdn.* enter or be permitted to enter Canada as an immigrant. **5** come to a stop; arrive: *The thief landed in jail. The car landed in the ditch.* **6** cause to arrive: *This boat will land you in London.* **7** *Informal.* catch; get: *to land a job, to land a fish.* **8** *Slang.* get (a blow) home: *I landed one on his chin.* [OE] —**land′er,** *n.*

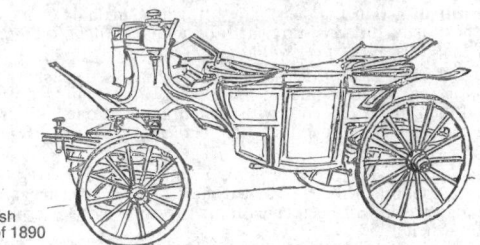

An English landau of 1890

lan·dau (land′o, lan′dô, *or* lan′dou) *n.* **1** a four-wheeled carriage with two seats that face each other and a top made in two parts that can be folded back. **2** an automobile with a similar top and seats. [< *Landau,* a town in West Germany, where this type of carriage was first made]

lan·dau·let *or* **lan·dau·lette** (lan′do let′ *or* lan′dô let′) *n.* **1** a small landau. **2** an automobile with a folding top.

land bank an area or areas of land bought up and held for future development: *The corporation owns one of the largest land banks in the country.*

land–banking (land′bang′king) *n.* the practice or business of setting up land banks.

land breeze a breeze blowing from the land toward the sea.

land·ed (lan′did) *adj.* **1** owning land: *landed gentry.* **2** consisting of land. Landed property is real estate. **3** *Cdn.* formally admitted into Canada as an immigrant: *to apply for landed status. The officer asked him if he was landed.*

landed immigrant *Cdn.* a person admitted to Canada as a settler and potential Canadian citizen.

land·fall (land′fol′ *or* -fôl′) *n.* **1** a sighting of land. **2** the land sighted or reached after a voyage or flight: *The explorer's landfall was near the mouth of the St. Lawrence.* **3** an approach to land from the sea or air; landing.

land·fill (land′fil′) *n.* **1** the disposal of waste by burying it under a shallow layer of ground. **2** a place where waste is disposed of in this way.

land·form (land′fôrm′) *n.* the natural physical features of the land.

land grant a grant of land; a gift of land by the government for universities, railways, etc.

land·grave (land′grāv′) *n.* **1** in the Middle Ages, a German count having authority over a considerable territory or over other counts. **2** in modern times, the title of certain German princes. [< G *Landgraf* < *Land* land + *Graf* count]

land·hold·er (land′hōl′dər) *n.* a person who owns or occupies land.

land·hold·ing (land′hōl′ding) *adj., n.* —*adj.* that owns or occupies land. —*n.* an owning or occupying of land.

land·ing (lan′ding) *n.* **1** coming to land; coming ashore: *The army made a landing in France.* **2** bringing to land. **3** *Cdn.* formal admission into Canada as an immigrant. **4** a place where persons or goods are landed from a ship, helicopter, etc.: *A wharf, dock, or pier is a landing for boats.* **5** a platform or floor area at the top of a flight of stairs. **6** *Logging.* a place where logs are gathered before being transported to a sawmill.

landing craft any of various kinds of boats or ships used for landing troops or equipment on a shore, especially during an assault.

hat, āge, fär; let, ēqual, tėrm; it, īce
hot, ōpen, ôrder; oil, out; cup, put, rüle,
above, taken, pencil, lemon, circus

ch, child; ng, long; sh, ship
th, thin; ŦH, then; zh, measure

landing field a field large enough and smooth enough for aircraft to land on and take off from safely.

landing gear the wheels, pontoons, etc. under an aircraft. When on land or water, an aircraft rests on its landing gear.

landing net a net attached to a handle, for taking fish from the water after they are caught.

landing stage a floating platform used for loading and unloading people and goods.

landing strip airstrip.

land·la·dy (land′lā′dē) *n., pl.* **-dies. 1** a woman who owns buildings or land that she rents to others. **2** a woman who keeps a boarding house, lodging house, or inn.

land·less (land′lis) *adj.* without land; owning no land. —**land′less·ness,** *n.*

land·line (land′līn′) *n.* a telegraph or similar cable running under ground or on the ground.

land·locked (land′lokt′) *adj.* **1** shut in, or nearly shut in, by land: *a landlocked harbor.* **2** living in waters shut off from the sea: *landlocked salmon.*

land·lord (land′lôrd′) *n.* **1** a person who owns buildings or land that he rents to others. **2** the keeper of a boarding house, lodging house, or inn.

land·lub·ber (land′lub′ər) *n.* a person not used to being on ships; a person clumsy on ships.

land·mark (land′märk′) *n.* **1** something familiar or easily seen, used as a guide. **2** an important fact or event; happening that stands out above others. The inventions of the printing press, telephone, telegraph, and radio are landmarks in the history of communications. **3** a stone or other object that marks the boundary of a piece of land.

land mine a container filled with explosives or chemicals, placed on the ground or lightly covered, and usually set off by the weight of vehicles or troops passing over it.

land office *U.S.* a government office that takes care of the business connected with public lands, and that records sales, transfers, etc.

Land of Promise in the Bible, the country promised by God to Abraham and his descendants; Canaan (Gen. 15:18; 17:8).

Land of the Little Sticks *Cdn.* a region of stunted trees at the southern limits of the Barren Ground in northern Canada.

land·own·er (land′ōn′ər) *n.* a person who owns lands.

land·own·er·ship (land′ōn′ər ship′) *n.* the state of being a landowner.

land–poor (land′pur′) *adj.* **1** owning much land but needing ready money. **2** poor because of taxes, etc. on one's land.

land·scape (land′skāp′ *or* lan′skāp′) *n., v.* **-scaped, -scap·ing.** —*n.* **1** a view of scenery on land. **2** a painting, etching, etc. showing such a view. —*v.* make (land) more pleasant to look at by arranging trees, shrubs, flowers, etc.: *The builder agreed to landscape the lot around the new house.* [< Du. *landschap* < *land* land + *-schap* -ship] —**land′scap·er,** *n.*

landscape gardener a person whose business is landscape gardening.

landscape gardening the arrangement of trees, shrubs, flowers, and lawns to give a pleasing appearance to grounds, parks, etc.

land·shark (land′shärk′) *n.* a person who buys up land illegally or unfairly to make large profits on its resale.

land·slide (land′slīd′) *n.* **1** a sliding down of a mass of soil or rock on a steep slope. **2** the mass that slides down. **3** an overwhelming majority of votes for one political party or candidate.

lands·man (landz′mən) *n., pl.* **-men. 1** a man who lives or works on land. **2** an inexperienced seaman.

land·ward (land′wərd) *adv. or adj.* toward the land.

land·wards (land′wərdz) *adv.* landward.

land wind a wind blowing from the land toward the sea.

lane (lān) *n.* **1** a narrow road or path, especially one between hedges, walls, or fences. **2** any narrow way. A highway is often marked off in lanes for separate lines of traffic. **3** an alley between buildings. **4** a course or route used by ships or aircraft going in the

same direction. **5** one of the narrow alleys on a track, marked by chalked lines, especially one in which a runner must stay during sprint or hurdle races. **6** bowling alley (def. 1). [OE *lanu*]
☛ *Hom.* **lain.**

lang. language.

lang syne (lang′ sīn′) *Scottish.* long since; long ago.

lan·guage (lang′gwij) *n.* **1** human speech, spoken or written. **2** the distinct form of speech common to a people nation, or group of peoples: *the French language.* **3** a form or style of verbal expression: *bad language, Shakespeare's language.* **4** the special vocabulary, etc. of a particular group, field, etc.: *the language of chemistry.* **5** the wording or words: *The lawyer explained the language of the contract to us.* **6** the expression of thoughts or feelings otherwise than by words: *sign language. A dog's language is made up of barks, looks, and actions.* **7** the study of language or languages; linguistics. **8** a set of assumptions or attitudes, often held by a group: *He just doesn't speak my language.* **9** *Computer technology.* a specific set of statements by which instructions are conveyed to a computer. [ME < OF *langage* < *langue* tongue < L *lingua*]
☛ *Syn.* **2. Language, dialect, idiolect, idiom** = the forms and patterns of speech of a particular group of people. **Language** applies to the body of words, forms, and patterns of sounds and structures making up the speech of a people, nation, or group of peoples: *French Canadians speak the French language.* **Dialect** applies to a socially or regionally restricted variety of a language: *The dialect of the English language spoken in Nova Scotia sounds strange to a westerner.* **Idiolect** applies to the sounds, usage, vocabulary, etc. used by an individual: *Her unusual idiolect is the result of her having lived in several different English-speaking countries.* **Idiom** applies to a particular language's characteristic manner of using words and putting them together in phrases and sentences: *Foreign students find the correct use of prepositions a difficult feature of English idiom.*

language arts the part of the school curriculum directly concerned with the study of language, especially that part devoted to reading, speaking, listening, and writing.

language laboratory in an educational institution, a room equipped with tape-recorders, record-players, etc. that enable students to practise hearing and speaking a language they are studying.

langue d'oc (läng dôk′) *French.* the group of dialects spoken in S France in the Middle Ages. One of these dialects developed into modern Provençal. [< OF; the two major OF dialect groups were named for the respective words for "yes": *oc* and *oïl* (see next entry)]

langue d'o·ïl (läng dô ēl′) *French.* the group of dialects spoken in N France in the Middle Ages. One of these dialects developed into modern standard French. [see LANGUE D'OC]

lan·guid (lang′gwid) *adj.* **1** drooping; weak; weary; without energy: *A hot, sticky day makes a person feel languid.* **2** without interest or enthusiasm; indifferent. **3** sluggish; dull; not brisk or lively. [< L *languidus* < *languere* be faint] —**lang′guid·ly,** *adv.* —**lan′guid·ness,** *n.*

lan·guish (lang′gwish) *v.* **1** become weak or weary; lose energy; droop: *The flowers languished from lack of water.* **2** suffer for a long period under unfavorable conditions: *to languish in poverty. Wild animals often languish in captivity.* **3** grow dull, slack, or less intense: *His vigilance never languished.* **4** long or pine (*for*): *She languished for home.* **5** assume a soft, tender look for effect. [< F *languiss-*, a stem of *languir* < L *languere*] —**lan′guish·er,** *n.*

lan·guish·ing (lang′gwish ing) *adj.* **1** drooping; pining; longing. **2** tender; sentimental; loving. **3** lasting; lingering. —**lan′guish·ing·ly,** *adv.*

lan·guish·ment (lang′gwish mənt) *n.* **1** languishing; drooping; pining condition. **2** a languishing look or manner.

lan·guor (lang′gər) *n.* **1** a lack of energy; weakness; weariness: *A long illness causes languor.* **2** a lack of interest or enthusiasm; indifference. **3** softness or tenderness of mood. **4** quietness; stillness: *the languor of a summer afternoon.* **5** lack of activity; sluggishness. [< L]

lan·guor·ous (lang′gər əs) *adj.* **1** languid. **2** causing languor. —**lan′guor·ous·ly,** *adv.*

lan·gur (lung gür′) *n.* any of various large, slender, long-tailed Old World monkeys (as of genera *Presbytis* and *Rhinopithecus*) of S and SE Asia. [< Hind.]

lan·iard (lan′yərd) *n.* See **lanyard.**

lank (langk) *adj.* **1** long and thin; slender; lean: *a lank boy.* **2** straight and flat; not curly or wavy: *lank hair.* [OE *hlanc*] —**lank′ly,** *adv.* —**lank′ness,** *n.*

lank·i·ly (langk′ə lē) *adv.* in a lanky condition or form.

lank·y (langk′ē) *adj.* **lank·i·er, lank·i·est.** awkwardly long and thin; tall and ungainly. —**lank′i·ness,** *n.*

lan·o·lin (lan′ə lin) *n.* fat or grease obtained from wool, used in cosmetics, ointments, etc. [< L *lana* wool + *oleum* oil]

lan·o·line (lan′ə lin *or* lan′ə lēn′) *n.* lanolin.

lan·tern (lan′tərn) *n.* **1** a case to protect a light from wind, rain, etc. It has sides of glass or some other material through which the light can shine. **2** the room at the top of a lighthouse where the light is. **3** an upright structure on a roof or dome, for letting in light and air or for decoration. **4** magic lantern. [ME < OF < L *lanterna*]

lan·tern–jawed (lan′tərn jod′ *or* -jôd′) *adj.* having hollow cheeks and long, thin jaws.

lantern slide a small, thin sheet of glass with a picture on it that is shown on a screen by a projector.

lan·tha·nide (lan′thə nīd′) *n.* **1** any of a group or series of metallic elements closely related in their chemical and physical properties, beginning with lanthanum (atomic number 57) or, sometimes, with cerium (at. no. 58) and ending with lutetium (at. no. 71); a rare-earth element. See table at **element.** **2** (*adj.*) designating this group of elements: *the lanthanide series.*

lan·than·um (lan′thə nəm) *n.* a soft, white, metallic element that tarnishes easily, found in rare-earth minerals. *Symbol:* La; *at.no.* 57; *at.wt.* 138.9l. [< NL < Gk. *lanthanein* escape notice]

lan·yard (lan′yərd) *n.* **1** a short rope or cord used on ships to fasten rigging. Sailors sometimes use a lanyard to hang a knife around their necks. **2** a cord with a small hook at one end, used in firing certain kinds of cannon. Also, **laniard.** [< *lanyer* (< F *lanière* thong) + *yard*²]

La·oc·o·ön (lā ok′ō on′ *or* lā ok′ə won′) *n. Greek mythology.* a priest of Apollo at Troy. He warned the Trojans against the wooden horse and was killed together with his two sons by two serpents sent by Athena.

La·od·i·ce·an (lā od′ə sē′ən) *n.* **1** a lukewarm or indifferent Christian. **2** a lukewarm or indifferent person. [with reference to the Christians of *Laodicea* in Asia Minor, mentioned in the Bible (Rev. 3:16)]

La·o·tian (lā ō′shən *or* lä ō′shən) *adj., n.* —*adj.* of or having to do with Laos, a country in SE Asia. —*n.* a native or inhabitant of Laos.

Lao·Tse *or* **Lao·Tze** (lou′tsē′) *n.* 604?-531? B.C., a Chinese philosopher and the founder of Taoism.

lap¹ (lap) *n.* **1** the front part from the waist to the knees of a person sitting down, with the clothing that covers it. **2** the place where anything rests or is cared for. **3** a loosely hanging edge of clothing; flap.
in the lap of luxury, in luxurious circumstances.
[OE *læppa*]
☛ *Hom.* **Lapp.**

lap² (lap) *v.* **lapped, lap·ping;** *n.* —*v.* **1** place or be placed together, one partly over or beside another; overlap: *We lapped shingles on the roof.* **2** extend beyond a limit: *The reign of Queen Elizabeth I lapped over into the seventeeth century.* **3** wind or wrap (*around*); fold (*over* or *about*): *He lapped the blanket around him.* **4** be wound or wrapped around something; be folded. **5** enwrap; wrap up (*in*): *He lapped himself in a warm blanket.* **6** surround; envelop. **7** in a race, get a lap or more ahead of (other racers). —*n.* **1** a lapping over. **2** the amount of lapping over. **3** the part that laps over. **4** one time around a race track. **5** a part of any course travelled: *The last lap of our all-day hike was the toughest.* [< *lap*¹]
☛ *Hom.* **Lapp.**

lap³ (lap) *v.* **lapped, lap·ping;** *n.* —*v.* **1** drink by lifting up with the tongue: *Cats and dogs lap water.* **2** move or beat gently with a lapping sound; splash gently: *Little waves lapped against the boat.*
lap up, **a** drink by lapping. **b** *Informal.* consume or absorb eagerly: *The advanced students lapped up the new math course.*
—*n.* **1** the act of lapping. **2** the sound of lapping: *the lap of the waves against my boat.* [OE *lapian*] —**lap′per,** *n.*
☛ *Hom.* **Lapp.**

lap·board (lap′bôrd′) *n.* a thin, flat board held on the lap and used as a table.

lap dog a small pet dog.

la·pel (lə pel′) *n.* the part of the front of a coat or jacket that is folded back just below the collar. [dim. form of *lap*¹ + dim. suffix *-el*]

lap·ful (lap′fül) *n., pl.* **-fuls.** as much as a lap can hold.

lap·i·dar·y (lap′ə der′ē) *n., pl.* **-dar·ies;** *adj.* —*n.* a person who cuts, polishes, or engraves precious stones.
—*adj.* **1** of or having to do with cutting or engraving precious stones. **2** engraved on stone. **3** characteristic of stone inscriptions; monumental; stately; grandiose: *lapidary language.* [< L *lapidarius* < *lapis, -idis* stone]

lap·in (lap′ən; *French,* lä paN′) *n.* **1** rabbit. **2** rabbit fur. **3** a coat or other garment of this fur. [< F]

lap·is laz·u·li (lap′is laz′yü li′ *or* laz′yü lē′) **1** a deep-blue,

opaque semiprecious stone containing sodium, aluminum, sulphur, and silicon in a mixture of minerals. **2** a piece of this stone or a gem made from it. **3** deep blue. [< Med.L < L *lapis* stone + Med.L *lazuli*, gen. of *lazulum* lapis lazuli < Arabic < Persian *lajward*. Cf. AZURE.]

Lap·land·er (lap′lan dər) *n.* Lapp (def. 1).

Lap·land long·spur (lap′land long′spėr′) a finch (*Calcarius lapponicus*) that breeds in the Arctic and winters in temperate and subtropical regions. It is a familiar summer bird in Canada's low Arctic.

Lapp (lap) *n.* **1** a member of a people living mainly in N Scandinavia and the NW Soviet Union. **2** the Finnic language of the Lapps, including several very different dialects. [< Swedish]
☞ *Hom.* lap.

lap·pet (lap′it) *n.* **1** a small flap or fold. **2** a loose fold of flesh or membrane. **3** the lobe of the ear. [< *lap¹*]

lap robe a blanket, fur robe, etc. used to keep the lap and legs warm when riding in an automobile, carriage, etc.

lapse (laps) *n., v.* **lapsed, laps·ing.** —*n.* **1** a slight mistake or error. A slip of the tongue, pen, or memory is a lapse. **2** a slipping or falling away from what is right: *a moral lapse.* **3** a slipping back; sinking down; slipping into a lower condition: *a lapse into savage ways.* **4** a slipping by; a passing away: *A minute is a short lapse of time.* **5** the ending of a right or privilege because it was not renewed, not used, or otherwise neglected: *the lapse of a lease.*
—*v.* **1** make a slight mistake or error. **2** slip or fall away from what is right. **3** slip back; sink down: *The house lapsed into ruin.* **4** slip by; pass away: *The boy's interest in the story soon lapsed.* **5** of a right or privilege, end because it was not renewed, not used, etc. If a legal claim is not enforced, it lapses after a certain number of years. [< L *lapsus* fall < *labi* to slip]

lap·strake (lap′strāk′) *adj., n.* —*adj.* of boats, made of boards or metal plates that overlap one another; clinker-built. —*n.* a boat that is clinker-built. Also, **lapstreak.**

lap·streak (lap′strēk′) *adj. or n.* lapstrake.

lap·sus lin·guae (lap′səs ling′gwē or ling′gwī) *Latin.* a slip of the tongue.

lap·wing (lap′wing′) *n.* a crested plover (*Vanellus vanellus*) of Europe, Asia, and N Africa that has a slow, irregular flight and a peculiar wailing cry. [OE *hlēapewince* < *hlēapan* leap + *-wince* (related to WINK)]

lar·board (lär′bərd or -bôrd) *n., adj.* —*n.* the side of a ship to the left of a person looking from the stern toward the bow; port. —*adj.* on this side of a ship. [ME *ladeborde*, originally, the loading side; influenced by *starboard*]

lar·ce·nous (lär′sə nəs) *adj.* **1** of or like larceny; characterized by larceny. **2** thievish; guilty of larceny.

lar·ce·ny (lär′sə nē) *n., pl.* **-nies.** theft. [< AF *larcin* < L *latrocinium* < *latro* bandit]

larch (lärch) *n.* **1** any of a small genus (*Larix*) of trees of the pine family found in the northern hemisphere, having small, upright cones and soft, flexible, needle-like leaves that are shed in the fall. The three species of larch native to Canada are the tamarack, alpine larch, and western larch. **2** The hard wood of any of these trees. [< G *Lärche*, ult. < L *larix, -icis*]

lard (lärd) *n., v.* —*n.* the fat of pigs melted down and made clear. It is used in cooking. —*v.* **1** insert strips of bacon or salt pork in (meat or poultry) before cooking. **2** put lard on; grease. **3** give variety to; enrich: *to lard a long speech with stories.* [ME < OF < L *lardum*] —**lard′like′,** *adj.*

lar·der (lär′dər) *n.* **1** a pantry; place where food is kept. **2** a supply of food. [ME < OF *lardier* < *lard* < L *lardum*]

lar·es (lär′ēz) *n.pl.* in ancient Rome, the guardian spirits of the house. [< L, pl. of *lar*]

lares and penates **1** in ancient Rome, the household gods, the lares protecting the home from outside damage, the penates protecting the interior. **2** the cherished possessions of a household. [< L]

large (lärj) *adj.* **larg·er, larg·est**; *n.* —*adj.* **1** of more than the usual size, amount, or number; big: *a large crowd, a large sum of money, a large animal. Canada is a large country.* **2** of great scope or range; extensive; broad: *a man of large experience.* **3** on a great scale: *a large employer of labor.*
—*n.*
at large, a at liberty; free: *Is the escaped prisoner still at large?* **b** fully; in detail. **c** as a whole; altogether: *The people at large want peace.* **d** representing a whole area, business, group, etc.: *the firm's representative at large.*
in large or **in the large,** on a big scale.
[ME < OF < L *largus* copious] —**large′ness,** *n.*
☞ *Syn. adj.* **1.** See note at **great.**

large–heart·ed (lärj′här′tid) *adj.* generous; liberal.

hat, āge, fär; let, ēqual, tėrm; it, īce
hot, ōpen, ôrder; oil, out; cup, pút, rüle,
ə above, takən, pencəl, lemən, circəs
ch, child; ng, long; sh, ship
th, thin; ᴛʜ, then; zh, measure

large intestine the lower part of the intestines, between the small intestine and the anus.

large·ly (lärj′lē) *adv.* **1** to a great extent; mainly; for the most part: *This region consists largely of desert.* **2** in great quantity; much.

large–scale (lärj′skāl′) *adj.* **1** wide; extensive; involving many persons or things: *a large-scale disaster.* **2** made or drawn to a large scale.

lar·gesse or **lar·gess** (lär′jis or lär jes′; *French,* lär zhes′) *n.* **1** generous giving. **2** a generous gift or gifts. [ME < OF *largesse* < *large* < L *largus* copious]

lar·ghet·to (lär get′ō) *adj., adv., n., pl.* **-ghet·tos.** *Music.* —*adj.* rather slow; not so slow as largo, but usually slower than andante. —*adv.* rather slowly. —*n.* a passage or composition in rather slow time. [< Ital. *larghetto,* dim. of *largo*]

larg·ish (lär′jish) *adj.* rather large.

lar·go (lär′gō) *adj., adv., n., pl.* **-gos.** *Music.* —*adj.* slow and dignified; stately. —*adv.* in largo tempo. —*n.* a slow, stately passage or piece of music. [< Ital. *largo* large, slow < L *largus* large]

lar·i·at (lar′ē ət or ler′ē ət) *n.* **1** a long rope with a running noose at one end; lasso. **2** a rope for fastening horses, mules, etc. to a stake while they are grazing. [< Sp. *la reata* the rope]

lark¹ (lärk) *n.* **1** any of a family (Alaudidae) of mostly Old World songbirds that live mainly on the ground, having plain or streaked brownish plumage and noted for their song. The most well-known European lark is the skylark. The only lark native to the New World is the horned lark. **2** any of various other, usually ground-living birds such as the meadowlark. [OE *lāwerce*]

lark² (lärk) *n., v. Informal.* —*n.* a merry adventure or time; frolic or prank. —*v.* have fun; sport, frolic, or play pranks: *They were larking about all afternoon.* [origin uncertain]

lark bunting a finch (*Calamospiza melanocorys*) of the central plains of North America, the adult male in summer having black plumage with white wing patches.

lark·spur (lärk′spėr) *n.* a delphinium, especially any of various wild species having blue or blue-and-white flowers. [< *lark¹* + *spur*]

lar·ri·gan (lar′ə gən or ler′ə gən) *n. Cdn.* an oiled leather moccasin, usually having a flexible sole. [origin unknown]

lar·rup (lar′əp) *v.* **-ruped, -rup·ing.** *Informal.* beat; thrash. [origin uncertain] —**lar′rup·er,** *n.*

lar·va (lär′və) *n., pl.* **-vae.** **1** the immature, wingless form of many insects from the time it leaves the egg until it becomes a pupa. A caterpillar is the larva of a butterfly or moth. A grub is the larva of a beetle. Maggots are the larvae of flies. **2** an immature form of certain animals that is different in structure from the adult form. A tadpole is the larva of a frog or toad. [< L *larva* ghost]

lar·vae (lär′vē, lär′vī, or lär′və) *n.* pl. of **larva.**

lar·val (lär′vəl) *adj.* **1** of or having to do with a larva or larvae. **2** characteristic of larvae. **3** in the form of a larva. **4** of a disease, latent; undeveloped.

la·ryn·ge·al (lə rin′jē əl) *adj., n.* —*adj.* **1** of or having to do with the larynx. **2** in or produced in the larynx. **3** used on the larynx. —*n.* a laryngeal sound. [< NL *laryngeus*]

lar·yn·gi·tis (lar′ən jī′tis or ler′ən jī′tis) *n.* inflammation of the larynx, often accompanied by a temporary loss of voice. [< NL *laryngitis* < *laryngo-* larynx < Gk. *larynx, -yngos*) + *-itis*]

la·ryn·go·scope (lə ring′gə skōp′) *n.* an instrument equipped with mirrors for examining the larynx. [< *laryngo-* larynx + *-scope*]

la·ryn·go·scop·ic (lə ring′gə skop′ik) *adj.* having to do with laryngoscopy or a laryngoscope.

lar·yn·gos·co·py (lar′ing gos′kə pē or ler′ing-) *n.* the examination of the larynx by means of a laryngoscope.

lar·ynx (lar′ingks or ler′ingks) *n., pl.* **la·ryn·ges** (lə rin′jēz) or **lar·ynx·es.** **1** the cavity at the upper end of the human windpipe, containing the vocal cords and acting as a speech organ. **2** *Zoology.* a similar organ or corresponding structure in other animals. [< Gk.]

la·sa·gna (lə zän′yə) *n.* **1** a dish consisting of broad, flat, pre-cooked noodles baked in layers with a sauce of tomatoes, cheese,

and meat (usually ground beef). **2** the noodles used for lasagna; lasagne. [< Ital.]

la·sa·gne (lə zän′yə *or* lə zän′yä) *n.* pasta in the form of broad, flat noodles, used especially for making lasagna.

las·car (las′kər) *n.* an East Indian sailor. [< Pg. *laschar,* probably < Persian *lashkar* army < Arabic *al′áskar*]

las·civ·i·ous (lə siv′ē əs) *adj.* **1** feeling lust. **2** showing lust. **3** causing lust. [ME < LL *lasciviosus* < L *lascivia* playfulness < *lascivus* playful] —**las·civ′i·ous·ly,** *adv.* —**las·civ′i·ous·ness,** *n.*

la·ser (lā′zər) *n.* **1** a device for amplifying and concentrating light waves, converting the different frequencies into a single intense, narrow beam of coherent light. Lasers are used for cutting through metal, performing delicate surgery, as on the eye, in communications, etc. **2** (*adj.*) of, having to do with, or utilizing such a device or the coherent light produced by such a device: *a laser knife.* [*l*ight *a*mplification by *s*timulated *e*mission of *r*adiation]

lash[1] (lash) *n., v.* —*n.* **1** a whip, especially the rope, thong, etc. that is attached to the handle. **2** a stroke or blow with a whip, etc. **3** a sudden, swift movement. **4** anything that hurts like a blow from a whip. **5** eyelash.
—*v.* **1** beat or drive with a whip, etc. **2** wave or beat back and forth: *The lion lashed its tail. The wind lashes the sails.* **3** rush violently; pour: *The rain lashed against the windows.* **4** strike violently; hit: *The horse lashed at him with its hoofs.* **5** attack severely with words; scold sharply: *The editorial lashed the government for its indifference.*
lash out, strike at or attack sharply, with or as if with a whip: *In his autobiography he lashes out at those he feels have wronged him.* [ME *lasche*; origin uncertain] —**lash′er,** *n.*

lash[2] (lash) *v.* tie or fasten with a rope, cord, etc. [? ult. < OF *lache* lace]

lash·ing[1] (lash′ing) *n.* **1** a whipping, especially as a punishment. **2** a severe attack in words; sharp scolding. **3 lashings,** *pl.* abundance; great plenty. [< *lash*[1]]

lash·ing[2] (lash′ing) *n.* rope, cord, etc. used in tying or fastening. [< *lash*[2]]

lass (las) *n.* **1** a girl or young woman. **2** sweetheart. [ME *lasse*; origin uncertain]

las·sie (las′ē) *n. Esp.Scottish.* **1** a young girl. **2** sweetheart.

las·si·tude (las′ə tyüd′ *or* las′ə tüd′) *n.* lack of energy; weakness; weariness. [< L *lassitudo* < *lassus* tired]

las·so (la sü′ *or, esp.U.S.,* las′ō) *n.* **-sos** *or* **-soes;** *v.* **-soed, -so·ing.** —*n.* a long rope with a running noose at one end; lariat. —*v.* catch with a lasso. [< Sp. *lazo* < L *laqueus* noose. Doublet of LACE.]

last[1] (last) *adj., adv., n.* —*adj.* **1** coming after all others; being at the end; final: *the last page of the book.* **2** next before a specified point of time: *last night, last week, last year.* **3** previous; the one before this one: *The last movie we saw was much better than this western.* **4** most unlikely; least suitable: *That is the last thing one would expect.* **5** very great; extreme: *a paper of last importance.* **6** that remains: *He spent his last dollar.*
—*adv.* **1** after all others; at the end; finally: *He arrived last.* **2** on the latest or most recent occasion: *When did you last see him?*
—*n.* **1** a person or thing that comes after all others: *She was the last in the line.* **2** the end: *You have not heard the last of this.*
at last, at the end; after a long time; finally: *So you have come home at last!*
breathe (one's) **last,** die.
see the last of, not see again.
[OE *latost, lætest,* superlative of *læt* late]
☛ *Syn. adj.* **1. Last, final, ultimate** = coming after all others. **Last** = coming after all others in a series or succession of things, events, or people. **Final** emphasizes the idea of bringing to a definite end or completing a series of events or a set of actions: *The last day of school each year is the final one for the graduating class.* **Ultimate** = the last possible that can ever be reached either by going forward or by tracing backward: *The ultimate cause of some diseases is unknown.*
☛ *Usage.* See note at **first.**

last[2] (last) *v.* **1** go on; hold out; continue to be; endure: *The storm lasted three days.* **2** continue in good condition, force, etc.: *I hope these shoes last a year.* **3** be enough or enough for: *while our money lasts.* [OE *læstan* < *læst* track. Related to LAST[3].]
☛ *Syn.* **1.** See note at **continue.**

last[3] (last) *n., v.* —*n.* a block shaped like a person's foot, on which shoes and boots are formed or repaired.
stick to (one's) **last,** pay attention to one's own work; mind one's own business.
—*v.* form (shoes and boots) on a last. [OE *læste* < *læst* track]

last-ditch (last′dich′) *adj.* **1** serving as a last resort or line of

defence: *a last-ditch move.* **2** resisting to the last extremity: *last-ditch survivors of the attack.*

last·ing (las′ting) *adj.* that lasts a long time; that lasts; that will last; permanent; durable. —**last′ing·ly,** *adv.*
☛ *Syn.* **Lasting, enduring, permanent** = existing or continuing for a long time or forever. **Lasting** emphasizes going on and on indefinitely, long past what would be normal or expected: *The experience had a lasting effect on him.* **Enduring** emphasizes the idea of being able to withstand the attacks of time and circumstance: *All the world hoped for enduring peace.* **Permanent** emphasizes staying in the same state or position, without changing or being likely to change: *At last he has a permanent job.*

Last Judgment God's final judgment of all mankind at the end of the world.

last·ly (last′lē) *adv.* finally; in the last place; in conclusion.

last name surname; family name.

last offices prayers for a dead person.

last post in the armed forces, the bugle call that gives the hour of retiring. It is blown also at military funerals, Remembrance Day ceremonies, etc.

last quarter the period between the second half moon and the new moon; the phase of the moon represented by the half moon after full moon.

last rites religious rites performed for a dying person or at a funeral.

last sleep death.

last straw the last of a series of troublesome things resulting in a collapse, outburst, etc.

Last Supper the supper of Jesus and His disciples on the evening before He was crucified.

last word **1** the last thing said; the last say on a subject. **2** *Informal.* the latest thing; most up-to-date style. **3** *Informal.* something that cannot be improved.

lat. latitude.

Lat. Latin.

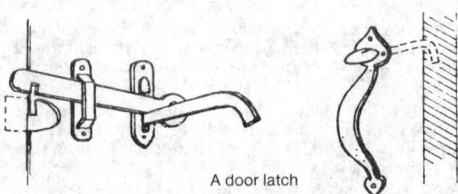

A door latch

latch (lach) *n., v.* —*n.* a catch for fastening a door, gate, or window. It consists of a movable piece of metal or wood that fits into a notch, opening, etc.
on the latch, not locked; fastened only with a latch.
—*v.* fasten with a latch. [OE *læccan* grasp]

latch·et (lach′it) *n. Archaic.* a strap or lace for fastening a shoe or sandal. [< dial. OF *lachet,* ult. < *laz* lace. See LACE.]

latch·key (lach′kē′) *n.* a key used to draw back or unfasten the latch of a door.

latch·string (lach′string′) *n.* a string used to unfasten the latch of a door.

late (lāt) *adj.* **lat·er** *or* **lat·ter, lat·est** *or* **last;** *adv.* **lat·er, lat·est** *or* **last.** —*adj.* **1** happening, coming, etc. after the usual or proper time: *We had a late dinner last night.* **2** happening, coming, etc. at an advanced time: *success late in life.* **3** recent: *The late storm did much damage.* **4** recently dead: *The late Harvey Todd was a fine man.* **5** gone out of or retired from office: *The late Prime Minister is still working actively.*
of late, lately; recently: *I haven't seen him of late.*
—*adv.* **1** after the usual or proper time: *He worked late.* **2** at an advanced time: *It rained late in the afternoon.* **3** recently. **4** recently but no longer: *John Smith, late of Victoria.* [OE *læt*] —**late′ness,** *n.*
☛ *Syn. adj.* **1. Late, tardy** = happening or coming after the usual or proper time. **Late,** describing people or things, emphasizes the idea of being after the usual, right, proper, expected time: *He was late for school this morning.* **Tardy** = not prompt, not on time, and emphasizes lateness and slowness in coming, getting somewhere, or doing something: *Please accept my tardy thanks.*
☛ *Usage.* **Latest.** See note at **first.**

late·com·er (lāt′kum′ər) *n.* a person or thing that arrives later than the expected or proper time: *Latecomers cannot be seated until the first intermission.*

la·teen (la tēn′) *adj.* having a lateen sail. [< F *voile latine* Latin sail]

la·teen-rigged (la tēn′rigd′) *adj.* having a lateen sail.

lateen sail a triangular sail held up by a long yard on a short mast.

Late Greek the Greek language from about A.D. 300 to 700.

Late Latin the Latin language from about A.D. 300 to 700.

late·ly (lāt′lē) *adv.* a short time ago; recently.

la·ten·cy (lā′tən sē) *n.* a latent condition or quality.

la·tent (lā′tənt) *adj.* present or existing and capable of development, but not manifest, visible, or active: *an latent talent, a latent infection, a latent bud or spore.* [< L *latens, -entis,* ppr. of *latere* lie hidden] —**la′tent·ly,** *adv.*

☛ *Syn.* **Latent, potential** = existing as a possibility or fact, but not now showing itself plainly. **Latent** = actually existing as a fact, but lying hidden, not active or plainly to be seen at the present time: *The power of a grain of wheat to grow into a plant remains latent if it is not planted.* **Potential** = existing as a possibility and capable of coming into actual existence or activity if nothing happens to stop development: *That boy has great potential ability in science.*

lat·er·al (lat′ər əl) *adj., n. —adj.* **1** of the side; at the side; from the side; toward the side. A lateral branch of a family is a branch not in the direct line of descent. **2** *Phonetics.* articulated so that the breath passes out on one or both sides of the tongue, as in pronouncing the English (l) in *law* or *all.*
—*n.* **1** a lateral part or outgrowth. **2** *Phonetics.* a lateral sound, such as *l* in *law* or *all.* **3** *Mining.* **a** a drift other than the main drift. **b** a connecting tunnel between main haulage ways. **4** *Football.* a lateral pass. [< L *lateralis < latus, -teris* side]

lat·er·al·ly (lat′ər əl ē) *adv.* **1** in a lateral direction; at the side; sideways. **2** from a lateral branch.

lateral pass *Football.* a throwing of a ball from one player to another in a direction almost parallel with the goal line.

la·tex (lā′teks) *n., pl.* **lat·i·ces** (lat′ə sēz′) or **la·tex·es** (lā′tək siz). **1** a milky liquid present in certain plants, such as milkweed, poppies, and rubber plants, that is the basis of rubber, balata, gutta-percha, and chicle. **2** an emulsion of synthetic rubber or plastic in water, used in paints, adhesives, etc. **3** (*adj.*) made with a base of synthetic latex: *latex paint.* [< L *latex* liquid]

lath (lath) *n., pl.* **laths** (laᴛʜz or laths); *v. —n.* **1** one of the thin, narrow strips of wood used to form a support for the plaster of a wall, ceiling, etc., or to make a lattice. **2** a wire cloth or sheet of metal with holes in it, used as a support for plaster. **3** a lining made of laths. The walls of a frame house are usually built with lath and plaster.
—*v.* cover or line with laths. [ME *laththe*]

lathe (lāᴛʜ) *n.* a machine for holding pieces of wood, metal, etc. and turning them against a cutting tool that shapes them. [cf. Danish (*dreje*)*lad* (turning) lathe]

lath·er¹ (laᴛʜ′ər) *n., v. —n.* **1** the foam made from soap or detergent mixed in water. **2** foam formed in sweating: *the lather on a horse after a race.* **3** *Informal.* an overwrought or greatly excited state: *to work oneself into a lather about nothing. He's in a big lather about that phone call.*
—*v.* **1** put lather on. **2** form a lather. **3** become covered with the foam formed in sweating. **4** *Informal.* beat; flog. [OE *lēathor*]

lath·er² (lath′ər) *n.* a workman who puts laths on walls, ceilings, etc. [< *lath*]

lath·ing (lath′ing) *n.* **1** laths collectively. **2** the work of putting laths on walls, etc.

lath·work (lath′wėrk′) *n.* lathing.

lat·i·go (lat′ə gō′) *n.* in the West, a tough leather strap on a saddle for tightening and the cinch. [< Sp.]

Lat·in (lat′ən) *n., adj. —n.* **1** the language of the ancient Romans, considered classical in the form it acquired during the 2nd and 1st centuries B.C. **2** a member of any of the peoples whose languages come from Latin. The Italians, French, Spanish, Portuguese, and Romanians are Latins. **3** a native or inhabitant of Latium, an ancient territory in W central Italy, or of ancient Rome. **4** Roman Catholic.
—*adj.* **1** of or in Latin: *a Latin grammar, a Latin passage in a book.* **2** of or having to do with the peoples speaking Romance languages, or the languages themselves. **3** of or having to do with Latium or its people; ancient Roman. **4** Roman Catholic. [< L *Latinus* of Latium]

Latin America South America, Central America, Mexico, and much of the West Indies.

Lat·in–A·mer·i·can (lat′ən ə mer′ə kən) *n., adj. —n.* a native or inhabitant of Latin America. —*adj.* of or having to do with Latin America.

Latin Church that part of the Roman Catholic Church which uses Latin in its worship.

Latin cross a cross in which the upright is longer than the crossbeam. See **cross** for picture.

Lat·in·ism (lat′ən iz′əm) *n.* **1** a Latin idiom or expression. **2** conformity to Latin models.

Lat·in·ist (lat′ən ist) *n.* a person with much knowledge of the Latin language; Latin scholar.

La·tin·i·ty (lə tin′ə tē) *n.* the use of Latin idioms or expressions.

hat, āge, fär; let, ēqual, tèrm; it, īce
hot, ōpen, ôrder; oil, out; cup, pút, rüle,
əbove, takən, pencəl, lemən, circəs

ch, child; ng, long; sh, ship
th, thin; ᴛʜ, then; zh, measure

Lat·in·ize (lat′ən īz′) *v.* **-ized, -iz·ing. 1** translate into Latin. **2** make like Latin. **3** cause to conform to the ideas, customs, etc. of the Latins or the Latin Church. —**Lat′in·i·za′tion,** *n.*

Latin Quarter a district in Paris, on the south bank of the Seine River, a traditional resort of artists. [translation of F *Quartier Latin*]

lat·ish (lāt′ish) *adj.* or *adv.* rather late.

lat·i·tude (lat′ə tyüd′ or lat′ə tüd′) *n.* **1** the distance north or south of the equator, measured in degrees. On maps, lines parallel to the equator represent latitudes. **2** a place or region having a certain latitude: *Polar bears live in the cold latitude.* **3** room to act or think; scope; freedom from narrow rules: *An artist is allowed more latitude than a physician.* **4** *Photography.* the range between the shortest and the longest exposures that produce good negatives on a given film. **5** *Archaic.* transverse dimension; width. [< L *latitudo < latus* wide]

lat·i·tu·di·nal (lat′ə tyü′də nəl or lat′ə tü′də nəl) *adj.* of or relating to latitude. —**lat·i·tu′di·nal·ly,** *adv.*

lat·i·tu·di·nar·i·an (lat′ə tyü′də ner′ē ən or lat′ə tü′də ner′ē ən) *adj., n. —adj.* allowing others their own beliefs; not insisting on strict adherence to established principles, especially in religious views. —*n.* a person who cares little about creeds, forms of worship, or methods of church government.

la·trine (lə trēn′) *n.* a toilet in a camp, factory, etc.; privy. [< F < L *latrina,* originally, washroom < *lavare* wash]

lat·ter (lat′ər) *adj.* **1** later; more recent; nearer the end: *Friday comes in the latter part of the week.* **2** (*noml.*) **the latter,** the second of two: *Canada and the United States are in North America; the former lies north of the latter.* [OE *lætra* later]

lat·ter–day (lat′ər dā′) *adj.* of recent or modern times: *latter-day religions.*

Latter–day Saint Mormon.

lat·ter·ly (lat′ər lē) *adv.* lately; recently.

lat·tice (lat′is) *n., v.* **-ticed, -tic·ing. —n. 1** a structure of crossed wooden or metal strips with open spaces between them. **2** a window, gate, etc. having a lattice. **3** any pattern or decoration resembling a lattice.
—*v.* **1** form into a lattice; make like a lattice. **2** furnish with a lattice. [ME < OF *lattis < latte* lath < Gmc.] —**lat′tice·like′,** *adj.*

lat·tice·work (lat′is wèrk′) *n.* a lattice or lattices.

Lat·vi·an (lat′vē ən) *adj., n. —adj.* of or having to do with Latvia, a republic in the NW Soviet Union, its people, or their language. —*n.* **1** a native or inhabitant of Latvia. **2** the Baltic language of Latvia; Lettish.

laud (lod or lôd) *v., n. —v.* extol; praise. —*n.* **1** a praise. **2** a song or hymn of praise. **3 lauds** or **Lauds,** *pl.* **a** a morning church service with psalms of praise to God. **b** *Roman Catholic Church.* a prescribed devotional service for priests and religious, forming, with matins, the first of the seven canonical hours. [ME < OF *laude* (*n.*) and L *laudare* (*v.*) < L *laus, laudis* praise] —**laud′er,** *n.*

laud·a·bil·i·ty (lod′ə bil′ə tē or lôd′-) *n.* praiseworthiness.

laud·a·ble (lod′ə bəl or lôd′-) *adj.* worthy of praise; commendable: *Selflessness is laudable.* —**laud′a·bly,** *adv.*

lau·da·num (lo′də nəm or lô′də nəm) *n.* a solution of opium in alcohol used, especially formerly, for the relief of pain. [< NL < Med.L *laudanum,* var. of L *ladanum* < Gk. *lādanon* mastic]

lau·da·tion (lo dā′shən or lô dā′shən) *n.* praise.

laud·a·to·ry (lod′ə tô′rē or lôd′-) *adj.* expressing praise.

laugh (laf) *v., n. —v.* **1** make the sounds and movements of the face and body that show amusement or pleasure at humor or nonsense, etc.: *We all laughed at the joke.* **2** express with laughter: *to laugh a reply.* **3** drive, put, bring, etc. by or with laughing: *to laugh one's tears away.* **4** suggest the feeling of joy; be lively.
laugh at, a make fun of; ridicule: *They laughed at me for believing in ghosts.* **b** disregard or make light of: *He laughed at danger.*
laugh off, pass off or dismiss with a laugh: *She laughed off my warning that the ice was not safe and walked to the middle of the pond.*
laugh on the other or **wrong side of** (one's) **face** or **mouth,** be made to change from amusement or joy to sorrow or anger.
laugh up (one's) **sleeve,** laugh secretly or to oneself.
—*n.* the act or sound of laughing. [OE *hliehhan*] —**laugh′er,** *n.*

laugh·a·ble (laf′ə bəl) *adj.* such as to cause laughter; amusing; ridiculous. —**laugh′a·ble·ness,** *n.* —**laugh′a·bly,** *adv.*
☛ *Syn.* See note at **funny.**

laugh·ing (laf′ing) *adj., n.* —*adj.* **1** that laughs or seems to laugh: *the laughing brook.* **2** accompanied by laughter.
no laughing matter, a matter that is serious.
—*n.* laughter. —**laugh′ing·ly,** *adv.*

laughing gas nitrous oxide, a colorless gas that makes one insensible to pain. This gas makes some people laugh and become excited. *Formula:* N₂O

laughing jackass kookaburra.

laugh·ing·stock (laf′ing stok′) *n.* an object of ridicule; a person or thing that is made fun of.

laugh·ter (laf′tər) *n.* **1** the action of laughing. **2** the sound of laughing: *Laughter filled the room.* [OE *hleahtor*]

launch[1] (lonch *or* lônch) *v., n.* —*v.* **1** cause to slide into the water; set afloat: *A new ship is launched from the supports on which it has been built.* **2** push out or put forth on the water or into the air: *to launch a plane from an aircraft carrier.* **3** start; set going; set out: *His friends launched him in business by lending him the necessary capital.* **4** throw or send out: *to launch a rocket or missile.*
launch out, begin; start.
—*n.* launching or being launched: *We watched the space launch on TV.* [ME < AF *launcher,* var. of *lancer* use a lance < *lance* lance < L *lancea*] —**launch′er,** *n.*

launch[2] (lonch *or* lônch) *n.* **1** a motorboat used for pleasure trips. **2** the largest boat carried by a warship. [< Sp., Pg. *lancha* < *lanchar* launch[2]]

launching pad a surface or platform on which a rocket or missile is prepared for launching and from which it is shot into the air.

laun·der (lon′dər *or* lôn′dər) *v.* **1** wash and iron (clothes, linens, etc.). **2** be able to be washed; stand washing: *Cotton fabrics usually launder well.* [ME *lander* one who washes linen < OF *lavandier* washer < VL *lavandarius* < L *lavanda* (things) to be washed < *lavare* wash] —**laun′der·er,** *n.*

laun·dress (lon′dris *or* lôn′dris) *n.* a woman whose work is washing and ironing clothes, linens, etc.

laun·dro·mat (lon′drə mat′ *or* lôn′drə-) *n.* a self-service laundry having automatic washing machines and dryers, especially one having coin-operated machines. [< *Laundromat,* a trademark]

laun·dry (lon′drē *or* lôn′drē) *n., pl.* -**dries. 1** a room or building where clothes, linens, etc. are washed and ironed. **2** clothes, etc. washed or to be washed. **3** the washing and ironing of clothes, etc.

laun·dry·man (lon′drē mən *or* lôn′drē-) *n.,* -**men. 1** a man who works in a laundry. **2** a man who collects and delivers laundry.

laun·dry·wom·an (lon′drē wům′ən *or* lôn′drē-) *n., pl.* -**wom·en.** laundress.

lau·re·ate (lô′rē it) *adj., n.* —*adj.* **1** crowned with a laurel wreath as a mark of honor. **2** honored; distinguished. —*n.* poet laureate. [< L *laureatus* < *laurea* laurel wreath < *laurus* laurel]

lau·re·ate·ship (lô′rē it ship′) *n.* **1** the position of poet laureate. **2** the time during which a poet is poet laureate.

lau·rel (lô′rəl) *n.* **1** any of a genus (*Laurus*) of evergreen trees or shrubs; especially, *L. nobilis* (also called *bay* and *sweet bay*), a large shrub or small tree native to S Europe and N Africa, having stiff, glossy, dark-green leaves, believed to be the leaves used by the ancient Greeks for wreaths to crown victors and heroes. **2** the foliage of the laurel: *wreaths of laurel.* **3** laurels, *pl.* **a** a wreath of laurel for a crown. **b** honor, fame, or victory: *The laurels went to a young athlete who had not competed before.* **4** (*adj.*) designating a family (Lauraceae) of evergreen shrubs and trees found mainly in tropical and subtropical regions, and including the laurel, cinnamon, avocado, etc. **5** any of various evergreen shrubs or trees not related to the true laurel. See **mountain laurel.**
look to (one's) **laurels,** guard one's reputation or record from rivals.
rest on (one's) **laurels,** be satisfied with honors already won.
[ME < OF *lorier, laurier* < *lor* < L *laurus*]

lau·relled *or* **lau·reled** (lô′rəld) *adj.* **1** crowned with a laurel wreath. **2** honored.

Lau·ren·tian (lôr ən′shən) *adj.* **1** of or having to do with the St. Lawrence River and adjoining lands. **2** *Geology.* of or having to do with intrusive granites found in the oldest pre-Cambrian rocks of the Canadian Shield. **3** of or having to do with the Laurentian Mountains; Laurentide. **4** of or having to do with Quebec. [< *Laurentius,* L form of *Lawrence* + *-ian*]

Laurentian Shield Canadian Shield.

Lau·ren·tide (lô′ren tīd′) *adj. Cdn.* of or having to do with the

Laurentians, the range of low mountains lying between Hudson Bay and the St. Lawrence River. [< Cdn.F]

la·va (lav′ə *or* lä′və) *n.* **1** the molten rock flowing from a volcano or fissure in the earth. **2** the rock formed by the cooling of this molten material. Some lavas are hard and glassy; others are light and porous. [< dial. Ital. *lava* stream, ult. < L *lavare* wash]

lava bed a layer or surface of lava.

la·va·bo (lə vä′ bō *or* lə vā′bō) *n.* **1** Also, **Lavabo.** *Roman Catholic Church.* **a** the ritual washing of the celebrant's hands during the Mass, before the consecration. **b** the portion of Psalm 25 said during this rite. **2** a washbasin and tank with a tap, hung on a wall. **3** an ornamental basin on a wall, used as a planter. [< L *lavabo* I will wash, the first word of Ps. 25:6 in the Douay version]

lava field a large area of cooled lava.

lav·a·liere, lav·a·lier, *or* **lav·al·lière** (lav′ə lēr′; *French,* lä vä lyer′) *n.* an ornament hanging from a small chain, worn around the neck by women. [< F *lavallière* < Louise, Duchesse de *La Vallière* (1644-1710), a mistress of Louis XIV of France]

lav·a·to·ry (lav′ə trē *or* lav′ə tô′rē) *n., pl.* -**ries. 1** washroom; toilet. **2** a room for washing one's hands and face. **3** washbasin. [ME < LL *lavatorium* < L *lavare* wash. Doublet of LAVER.]

lave (lāv) *v.* **laved, lav·ing.** *Poetic.* **1** wash; bathe. **2** wash or flow against: *The stream laves its banks.* [OE *lafian* < L *lavare*]

lav·en·der (lav′ən dər) *n., adj.* —*n.* **1** a pale purple. **2** any of a genus (*Lavandula*) of small aromatic shrubs or perennial herbs of the mint family, especially a small Mediterranean evergreen shrub (*L. officinalis,* also called *L. vera*) having greyish-green, hoary leaves and spikes of light-purple flowers which yield an essential oil used in perfumes. **3** the dried, fragrant flowers, leaves, and stalks of lavender, used in sachets.
—*adj.* having the color lavender. [ME < AF < Med.L *lavendula*]

la·ver (lā′vər) *n. Archaic.* a bowl or basin to wash in. [ME < OF *laveoir* < LL *lavatorium* a place for washing < L *lavare* wash. Doublet of LAVATORY.]

lav·ish (lav′ish) *adj., v.* —*adj.* **1** very free or too free in giving or spending; prodigal: *A rich person can afford to be lavish with his money.* **2** very abundant; more than enough; given or spent too freely: *many lavish gifts.* —*v.* give or spend very freely or too freely: *It is a mistake to lavish kindness on ungrateful people.* [ult. < OF *lavasse* flood < *laver* wash < L *lavare*] —**lav′ish·er,** *n.* —**lav′ish·ly,** *adv.* —**lav′ish·ness,** *n.*
☛ *Syn. adj.* **2.** See note at **profuse.**

law (lo *or* lô) *n.* **1** a body of rules recognized by a country, state, province, municipality, or community as binding on its members: *international law. English law is different from French law.* **2** one of these rules: *a law against slavery. Good citizens obey the laws.* **3** the controlling influence of these rules, or the condition of society brought about by their observance: *maintain law and order.* **4** law as a system: *courts of law.* **5** the department of knowledge or study concerned with these rules; jurisprudence: *study law.* **6** a body of such rules concerned with a particular subject or derived from a particular source: *commercial law, criminal law.* **7** the legal profession: *enter the law.* **8** legal action. **9** any statute passed by the legislative body of a province, state, or nation: *a Federal law.* **10** any rule or principle that must be obeyed: *the laws of hospitality, a law of grammar.* **11 a** legal authorities. **b** *Informal.* a policeman or detective. **12** a statement of a relation or sequence of phenomena invariable under the same conditions: *the law of gravitation, Mendel's law, Ohm's law.* **13** a divine rule or commandment. **14 the Law, a** the books of the Bible that contain the Mosaic law; Pentateuch. **b** the commandments or will of God as set forth in the Bible. **15** a mathematical rule on which the construction of a curve, a series, etc. depends.
go to law, appeal to law courts; take legal action.
lay down the law, a give orders that must be obeyed. **b** give a scolding.
read law, study to be a lawyer. **take the law into** (one's) **hands,** take steps to gain one's rights or avenge a wrong without going to court. [OE *lagu* < Scand.; cf. ON *lög*]
☛ *Syn.* **2. Law, statute** = a rule or regulation recognized by a community as governing the action or procedure of its members. **Law** is the general word applying to any such rule or regulation, written or unwritten, laid down by the highest authority, passed by action of a lawmaking body such as Parliament, a provincial legislature, or a city council, or recognized as custom and enforced by the courts. **Statute** applies to a formally written law passed by a legislative body.

L.A.W. Leading Aircraftwoman.

law–a·bid·ing (lo′ə bīd′ing *or* lô′-) *adj.* obedient to the law; peaceful and orderly.

law·break·er (lo′brāk′ər *or* lô′-) *n.* a person who breaks the law.

law·break·ing (lo′brāk′ing *or* lô′-) *n., adj.* —*n.* a breaking of the law. —*adj.* breaking the law.

law court a place where justice is administered; a court of law.

law·ful (lo′fəl *or* lô′-) *adj.* **1** according to law; done as the law directs: *lawful arrest.* **2** allowed by law; rightful: *lawful demands.* —**law′ful·ly,** *adv.*—**law′ful·ness,** *n.*

☛ *Syn.* **1, 2. Lawful, legal, legitimate** = according to law. **Lawful** = in agreement with or not against the laws of the community, the laws of a church, or moral law: *To some people gambling is not lawful.* **Legal** = authorized by or according to the actual terms of the laws of a community as enforced by the courts: *Lotteries are legal in most provinces.* **Legitimate** = rightful according to law, recognized authority, or established standards: *Sickness is a legitimate reason for a child's being absent from school.*

law·giv·er (lo′giv′ər *or* lô′-) *n.* a man who prepares and puts into effect a system of laws for a people; lawmaker.

law·less (lo′lis *or* lô′-) *adj.* **1** paying no attention to the law; breaking the law: *A thief leads a lawless life.* **2** hard to control; unruly: *a lawless mob.* **3** having no laws: *a lawless frontier town.* —**law′less·ly,** *adv.*—**law′less·ness,** *n.*

law·mak·er (lo′mākər *or* lô′-) *n.* a person who helps to make laws; a member of a parliament, legislature, or congress; legislator.

law·mak·ing (lo′māk′ing *or* lô′-) *adj., n.*—*adj.* having the duty and power of making laws; legislative.—*n.* the making of laws; legislation.

lawn¹ (lon *or* lôn) *n.* land covered with grass kept closely cut, especially near or around a house. [ME < OF *launde* wooded ground < Celtic]

lawn² (lon *or* lôn) *n.* a fine, sheer cotton or linen cloth. [? ult. < *Laon* a city in France]

lawn bowling a game played on a bowling green with a lopsided or unsymmetrically weighted wooden ball that is rolled toward a small, white target ball (the jack) that is stationary; bowls.

lawn mower a machine with revolving blades for cutting the grass on a lawn.

lawn tennis an outdoor game in which a ball is hit back and forth over a low net.

law of Moses the first five books of the Old Testament: Genesis, Exodus, Leviticus, Numbers, and Deuteronomy.

law of the Medes and Persians a law that cannot be changed. [so called because in ancient times these laws were thought to have come from the gods]

law·ren·ci·um (lô ren′sē əm) *n.* a short-lived artificial radio-active element produced from Californium. *Symbol:* Lr; *at.no.* 103; *at.wt.* (256); *half-life* 35 seconds. [after Ernest O. *Lawrence* (1901-1958), an American physicist]

law·suit (lo′süt′ *or* lô′-) *n.* a case in a court of law; application to a court for justice: *Injustices are often remedied by lawsuits.*

law·yer (loi′yər, *or* lô′yər, *or* lô′-) *n.* a person whose profession is giving advice about the laws or acting for others in a court of law.

lax (laks) *adj.* **1** not firm or tight; loose or slack. **2** not strict; careless: *lax behavior.* **3** loose in morals. **4** not exact; vague. [< L *laxus*]—**lax′ly,** *adv.*—**lax′ness,** *n.*

lax·a·tive (lak′sə tiv) *n., adj.*—*n.* a medicine that makes the bowels move.—*adj.* making the bowels move. [< L *laxativus* loosening, ult. < *laxus* loose]

lax·i·ty (lak′sə tē) *n.* the quality or state of being lax. [< F *laxité* < L *laxitas* < *laxus* loose]

lay¹ (lā) *v.* **laid, lay·ing;** *n.*—*v.* **1** bring down; beat down: *A storm laid the crops.* **2** put down; place in a certain position: *Lay your hat on the table.* **3** smooth down: *to lay the nap of cloth.* **4** place in a lying-down position or a position of rest: *Lay the baby down gently.* **5** place; put; set: *She lays great emphasis on good manners. The scene of the story is laid in Montreal. Lay aside the book for me. The horse laid its ears back.* **6** place in proper position or in orderly fashion: *to lay bricks.* **7** devise; arrange: *to lay plans.* **8** put down as a bet; wager: *I lay five dollars that he will not come.* **9** make quiet or make disappear: *to lay a ghost.* **10** impose a burden, penalty, etc.: *to lay a tax on property.* **11** present; bring forward: *to lay claim to an estate.* **12** impute; attribute: *The theft was laid to him.* **13** produce (an egg or eggs) from the body: *Birds, fish, and reptiles lay eggs.* **14** of hens, produce an egg or eggs: *All the hens are laying well.* **15** apply oneself vigorously: *The men laid to their oars.* **16** *Nautical.* take up a specified position: *to lay aft.*
lay about, hit out on all sides.
lay a course, *Nautical.* lie or sail in a certain direction without being obliged to tack.
lay aside, away, or **by, a** put away for future use; save: *I laid away ten dollars a week toward buying a bicycle.* **b** put away from one's person, from consideration, etc.; put on one side.
lay down, a declare; state. **b** give; sacrifice. **c** *Slang.* quit; resign. **d** store away for future use. **e** bet. **f** survey; draw in on a chart or map.
lay for, *Informal.* lie in wait for.
lay in, provide; save; put aside for future: *The trapper laid in enough supplies for the winter.*
lay into, a *Informal.* beat; thrash: *She laid into the vicious dog with*

hat, āge, fär; let, ēqual, tèrm; it, īce
hot, ōpen, ôrder; oil, out; cup, pùt, rüle,
əbove, takən, pencəl, lemən, circəs

ch, child; ng, long; sh, ship
th, thin; ŦH, then; zh, measure

a stick. **b** *Slang.* scold: *My parents laid into me for not doing my homework.*
lay low, humble; bring down.
lay off, a put aside. **b** *Slang.* stop for a time; take a rest. **c** stop teasing or interfering with; desist: *Let's lay off the new boy and give him a chance.* **d** put out of work: *Several men were laid off because of a shortage of steel.* **e** mark off: *He laid off the boundaries of the tennis court.*
lay on, a apply. **b** supply. **c** strike; inflict.
lay (oneself) **open,** expose oneself or another (*to*): *He lays himself open to ridicule by his many boasts.*
lay open, a make bare; expose. **b** make an opening in; wound.
lay (oneself) **out,** make a great effort; take pains (*to*): *He laid himself out to be agreeable.*
lay out, a spread out: *Supper was laid out on the table.* **b** prepare (a dead body) for burial. **c** arrange or plan: *to lay out a program.* **d** mark off: *They laid out a tennis court.* **e** *Slang.* spend: *They laid out two hundred dollars in repairs.* **f** *Slang.* knock unconscious; put out of the fight.
lay over, *Informal.* break a journey: *We'll lay over in Vancouver for a few days and then drive on to California.*
lay to, a blame on; accuse of. **b** of ships, head into the wind and stand still.
lay up, a put away for future use; save. **b** cause to stay in bed or indoors because of illness or injury: *He was laid up with flu for a week.* **c** put (a ship) in dock.
—*n.* **1** the way or position in which a thing is laid or lies: *the lay of the ground.* **2** the amount and direction of the twist given to the strands or other components of a rope. **3** a share of the profits or of the catch of a whaling or fishing vessel. **4** *Cdn. Historical.* a lease to work a gold claim for a share of the proceeds. **5** terms of employment or sharing. [OE *lecgan,* causative of *licgan* lie²]
☛ *Usage.* **Lay, lie.** Although the past tenses of **lay¹** and **lie²** are often confused, in standard English the two verbs are always kept distinct: **lie, lay, lain** and **lay, laid, laid. Lie** does not take an object: *He lay down for a rest. The village lies in a valley.* **Lay** always takes an object: *We laid a new floor in the kitchen. Lay the book on the table.*

lay² (lā) *v.* pt. of **lie².**

lay³ (lā) *adj.* **1** of ordinary people; not of the clergy. A lay sermon is one preached by a person who is not a clergyman. **2** of ordinary people; not of lawyers, doctors, or those learned in the profession in question: *The lay mind understands little of the cause of the disease.* [ME < OF *lai* < L *laicus.* Doublet of LAIC.]

lay⁴ (lā) *n.* **1** a short poem to be sung; poem. **2** a song; tune. [ME < OF *lai* origin uncertain]

lay·a·bout (lā′ə bout′) *n.* a lazy, shiftless person; a loafer or bum.

lay·er (lā′ər) *n., v.*—*n.* **1** one that lays. **2** one thickness or fold. A cake is often made of two or more layers put together. **3** a branch of a plant bent down and covered with earth so that it will take root and form a new plant.
—*v.* form (new plants) by layers; spread by layers.

lay·ette (lā et′) *n.* a set of clothes, bedding, etc. for a newborn baby. [< F *layette* < *laie* chest]

lay figure 1 a jointed model of a human body. Lay figures are used by artists and for window displays. **2** an unimportant person; puppet. [earlier *layman* < Du. *leeman* < *lee* limb + *man* man]

lay·man (lā′mən) *n., pl.* **-men. 1** a member of the church who is not a member of the clergy: *The priest and several laymen planned the church budget.* **2** a person who is not a member of a particular profession: *It is hard for most laymen to understand doctors' prescriptions.* [< *lay³* + *man*]

lay·off (lā′of′) *n.* **1** a temporary dismissal of workers: *Because of a shortage of steel, there was a layoff at the plant.* **2** the time during which such a dismissal lasts.

lay of the land 1 the nature of the place; the position of hills, water, woods, etc.: *Spies were sent out to find out the lay of the land.* **2** the existing situation; condition of things.

lay·out (lā′out′) *n.* **1** the act of laying out. **2** an arrangement; plan: *This map shows the layout of the camp.* **3** a plan or design for an advertisement, book, etc. **4** a thing laid or spread out; display. **5** outfit; supply; set.

lay·o·ver (lā′ō′vər) *n.* a stopping for a time in a place.

laz·ar (laz'ər *or* lā'zər) *n. Archaic.* **1** leper. **2** a poor, sick person. [ME < Med.L *lazarus* < *Lazarus*, the beggar]

laz·a·ret *or* **laz·a·rette** (laz'ə ret') *n.* lazaretto.

laz·a·ret·to (laz'ə ret'ō) *n., pl.* **-tos. 1** *Historical.* a hospital for people having contagious diseases, especially leprosy. **2** a building or ship used for quarantine purposes. **3** a place in some merchant ships, near the stern, in which supplies are kept. [< Ital. *lazzaretto*, blend of *lazzaro* lazar, and the name of a hospital, Santa Maria di *Nazaret*, Venice, Italy]

Laz·a·rus (laz'ə rəs) *n.* **1** in the Bible: **a** the brother of Mary and Martha, whom Jesus raised from the dead (John 11: 1-44). **b** a beggar who suffered on earth but went to heaven (Luke 16: 19-25). **2** any diseased beggar, especially a leper.

laze (lāz) *v.* **lazed, laz·ing. 1** be lazy or idle. **2** pass (time) lazily. [< *lazy*]

la·zi·ness (lā'zē nis) *n.* dislike of work; unwillingness to work or be active; the state of being lazy.

la·zy (lā'zē) *adj.* **la·zi·er, la·zi·est. 1** not willing to work or be active: *She was too lazy to get up and turn off the TV.* **2** characterized by, suggestive of, or conducive to idleness: *a lazy mood, a lazy summer day.* **3** moving slowly; not very active: *a lazy stream.* [? < MLG *lasich* weak, feeble] **—la'zi·ly,** *adv.*
☛ *Syn.* **1.** See note at **idle.**

la·zy·bones (lā'zē bōnz') *n.pl. or sing. Informal.* a lazy person.

lazy Susan a revolving tray for holding different kinds of food, condiments, etc., placed on a table or used for storage in a cupboard.

lb. pound(s) (for L *libra*).

LB Labrador (*used esp. in computerized address systems*).

L/Bdr. lance-bombardier.

lbs pounds.

l.c. lower case; in small letters, not capital letters.

L.C. 1 Lower Canada. **2** Library of Congress.

LCD, L.C.D., *or* **l.c.d.** least (or lowest) common denominator.

L.Cdr. *or* **LCdr** lieutenant-commander.

LCM, L.C.M., *or* **l.c.m.** least common multiple.

L.Col. *or* **LCol** lieutenant-colonel.

L/Cpl. Lance-Corporal.

Ld. 1 Lord. **2** Limited.

lea (lē) *n.* a grassy field; meadow; pasture. [OE *lēah*]
☛ *Hom.* **lee.**

leach (lēch) *v., n.* **—v. 1** run (water, etc.) through slowly; filter. **2** dissolve out by running water through slowly: *Potash is leached from wood ashes.* **3** dissolve out soluble parts from (ashes, etc.) by running water through slowly. **4** lose soluble parts when water passes through.
—n. a container for use in leaching. [OE *leccan* wet] **—leach'er,** *n.*
☛ *Hom.* **leech.**

lead¹ (lēd) *v.* **led, lead·ing;** *n.* **—v. 1** show the way by going along with or in front of; guide: *The star led the three Wise Men to Bethlehem.* **2** conduct by the hand, a rope, etc.: *to lead a horse.* **3** act as guide: *You lead, I will follow.* **4** be a means of proceeding to or effecting a certain result: *Hard work leads to success.* **5** conduct or bring (water, steam, a rope, etc.) in a particular channel or course. **6** pass or spend (life, time, etc.): *He leads a quiet life in the country.* **7** afford passage or way: *This road leads to the city.* **8** guide or direct in action, policy, opinion, etc.; influence; persuade: *Such actions led us to distrust him.* **9** be led; submit to being led: *This horse leads easily.* **10** *Archaic.* take or bring: *We led them away prisoners.* **11** go or be at the head of: *The elephants led the parade.* **12** go or be first; have first place: *In algebra he is low in the class, but in history he leads.* **13** be chief of; command; direct: *A general leads an army.* **14** be chief; direct; act as leader. **15** begin or open: *She led the dance.* **16** *Card games.* **a** begin with (the card or suit named). **b** make first play at cards. **17** *Boxing.* direct a blow at an opponent. **18** *Curling.* throw first on a team.
lead off, begin; start.
lead up to, prepare the way for.
—n. 1 guidance or direction; example: *to follow someone's lead.* **2** the first or foremost place; a position in advance: *take the lead.* **3** the distance, number of points, etc. that one is ahead: *He had a lead of three metres at the halfway mark.* **4** *Card games.* **a** the right of playing first. **b** the card or suit so played. **5** something that leads. **6** *Theatre or film.* **a** the principal role in a play, etc. **b** the person who plays such a part. **7** a string, strap, etc. for leading a dog or other animal. **8** a guiding indication; clue: *He was not sure where to look for the information, but the librarian gave him some good leads.* **9** *Mining.* lode. **10** an open channel through an ice field. **11** a

conductor conveying electricity. **12** *Boxing.* a blow directed at an opponent. **13** the opening paragraph in a newspaper article. **14** the main front-page story in a magazine, newspaper, etc. **15** *Curling.* the person on a team who throws first in each end, usually the least experienced player. [OE *lædan*]
☛ *Syn. v.* **1.** See note at **guide.**

lead² (led) *n., adj., v.* **—n. 1** a soft heavy, easily melted, bluish-grey, metallic chemical element. It is used to make pipes, in alloys, etc. *Symbol:* Pb; *at.no.* 82; *at.wt.* 207.19. **2** something made of this metal or one of its alloys. **3** a weight on a line used to find the depth of water; plummet. **4** bullets; shot. **5** a long, thin piece of graphite or other substance in or for a pencil. **6** *Printing.* a metal strip for widening the space between lines. **7 leads,** *pl.* **a** strips of lead used to cover roofs. **b** the frames of lead in which panes of glass are set.
—adj. made of lead: *lead pipe.*
—v. 1 *Printing.* insert leads between the lines of (print). **2** cover, frame, or weight with lead. **3** glaze (pottery) with glaze containing lead. [OE *lēad*]
☛ *Hom.* **led.**

lead·en (led'ən) *adj.* **1** made of lead: *a leaden coffin.* **2** heavy; hard to lift or move: *The tired runner's legs felt leaden.* **3** oppressive: *leaden air.* **4** dull; gloomy. **5** bluish grey: *leaden clouds.*

lead·er (lēd'ər) *n.* **1** a person or thing that leads: *a band leader.* **2** a person who is well fitted to lead. **3** the horse harnessed at the front of a team. **4** the dog that leads a dogsled team. **5** leading article. **6** a short length of nylon, wire, etc. used to attach the lure to a fishing line. **7** an article offered at a low price to attract customers. **8 leaders,** *pl.* a row of dots or dashes to guide the eye across a printed page. **—lead'er·less,** *adj.*

lead·er·ship (lēd'ər ship') *n.* **1** the state or position of being a leader. **2** the qualities of a leader. **3** the ability to lead: *Leadership is a great asset to a politician.*

lead-in (lēd'in') *n.* **1** a wire that runs from an antenna to a radio or television receiver or transmitter. **2** introduction: *a lengthy lead-in.*

lead·ing¹ (lēd'ing) *adj.* **1** guiding; directing. **2** most important; chief; principal: *the leading lady in a play.* [< *lead¹*]

lead·ing² (led'ing) *n.* **1** a covering or frame of lead. **2** the metal strips for widening the space between lines of type. [< *lead²*]

leading aircraftman an air-force serviceman ranking next above an aircraftman and below a corporal. *Abbrev.:* L.A.C.

leading aircraftwoman *or* **airwoman** an air-force servicewoman ranking next above an aircraftwoman and below a corporal. *Abbrev.:* L.A.W.

leading article (lēd'ing) an important editorial or article in a newspaper, magazine, etc.

leading question (lēd'ing) a question so worded that it suggests the answer desired or makes the desired answer unavoidable.

leading seaman 1 *Canadian Forces.* in Maritime Command, the equivalent of a corporal. See chart at **rank¹**. **2** a person of similar rank in the naval forces of other countries. *Abbrev.:* L.S. or LS

leading strings (lēd'ing) **1** strings for supporting a child when learning to walk. **2** a state of dependence or close guidance: *He was eighteen years old and still in leading strings.*

lead pencil (led) an ordinary pencil having a graphite core for writing.

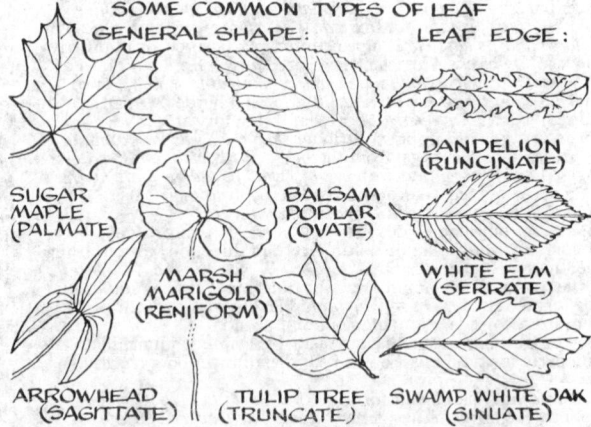

SOME COMMON TYPES OF LEAF
GENERAL SHAPE: LEAF EDGE:

SUGAR MAPLE (PALMATE)

BALSAM POPLAR (OVATE)

DANDELION (RUNCINATE)

MARSH MARIGOLD (RENIFORM)

WHITE ELM (SERRATE)

ARROWHEAD (SAGITTATE)

TULIP TREE (TRUNCATE)

SWAMP WHITE OAK (SINUATE)

leaf (lēf) *n., pl.* **leaves;** *v.* **—n. 1** one of the thin, flat green parts

that grow on the stem of a tree or other plant. **2** a petal of a flower: *a rose leaf.* **3** a sheet of paper. Each side of a leaf of a book is a page. **4** a very thin piece or sheet of metal, etc.: *gold leaf.* **5** a movable piece serving as an extension to a table. **6** the sliding, hinged, or movable part of a door, shutter, etc. **7** one of a number of curved metal strips that are clamped together to make up a spring.
in leaf, having completely developed foliage: *The trees were already in leaf when we came home.*
take a leaf from (someone's) **book,** *Informal.* follow someone's example; copy someone's conduct.
turn over a new leaf, start all over again; try to do or be better in the future: *I promised to turn over a new leaf and study harder.*
—*v.* **1** put forth leaves: *The trees along the river leaf earlier than those on the hill.* **2** turn the pages. [OE *lēaf*] —**leaf′like′,** *adj.*
☛ *Hom.* **lief.**

leaf·age (lēf′ij) *n.* leaves; foliage.

leaf bud a bud producing a stem having leaves only.

leaf·hop·per (lēf′hop′ər) *n.* any of a family (Cicadellidae) of small, often brightly colored homopterous insects, many of which are serious agricultural pests because they suck the juices of plants.

leaf·less (lēf′lis) *adj.* having no leaves. —**leaf′less·ness,** *n.*

leaf·let (lēf′lit) *n.* **1** a small, flat or folded sheet of printed matter: *advertising leaflets.* **2** a small or young leaf. **3** one of the separate blades or divisions of a compound leaf.

leaf·stalk (lēf′stok′ *or* -stôk′) *n.* the stalk by which a leaf is attached to a stem; petiole.

leaf·y (lēf′ē) *adj.* **leaf·i·er, leaf·i·est. 1** having many leaves; covered with leaves. **2** resembling a leaf: *We chose a fabric with a leafy design.* —**leaf′i·ness,** *n.*

league¹ (lēg) *n., v.* **leagued, lea·guing.** —*n.* **1** an association of persons, parties, or countries formed to help one another. **2** a group of teams that play a schedule of games against each other: *a hockey league, a bowling league.* **3** a class or level: *The two contractors are just not in the same league.*
in league, united; in association: *They were in league against us. The suspected spies were thought to be in league with the enemy.*
—*v.* associate in a league; form a league. [< F *ligue* < Ital. *liga,* var. of *lega* < *legare* bind]

league² (lēg) *n.* an old unit for measuring distance, usually equal to about 5 km. [ME < LL *leuga* < Celtic]

League of Nations an association of many countries, formed in 1919 to promote peace and co-operation among nations. It was dissolved in April, 1946.

lea·guer¹ (lē′gər) *v., n. Archaic.* —*v.* besiege. —*n.* **1** a siege. **2** the camp of a besieging army. [< Du. *leger* camp]

lea·guer² (lē′gər) *n.* a member of a league. [< *league¹*]

leak (lēk) *n., v.* —*n.* **1** a hole or crack, caused either by accident or by wear and tear, that lets something in or out: *a leak in a boat, a roof, a tire, etc.* **2** leakage. **3** a means of escape, loss, etc. **4** the escape or loss itself: *a news leak.* **5** *Electricity.* **a** an escape of current from a conductor, especially as a result of poor insulation. **b** the point where such escape occurs.
—*v.* **1** go in or out through a hole or crack. **2** let something in that should be kept out; let something out that should be kept in: *His boat leaks. Her teakettle leaks.* **3** let (something) pass in or out: *That pipe leaks gas.* **4** make or become known: *The secret leaked out.* **5** come in or go out in a secret or stealthy way: *Spies somehow leaked into the city.* **6** pass (away) by gradual waste: *The natural resources of our country are leaking away through misuse.* [< ON *leka*]
☛ *Hom.* **leek.**

leak·age (lēk′ij) *n.* **1** the act, process, or an instance of leaking: *a leakage in a pipeline, a leakage of news to the press.* **2** something that leaks in or out. **3** the amount of leaking: *The leakage was estimated at 40 litres an hour.*

leak·proof (lēk′prüf′) *adj.* that will not allow anything to leak in or out.

leak·y (lēk′ē) *adj.* **leak·i·er, leak·i·est.** leaking; having a leak or leaks. —**leak′i·ness,** *n.*

leal (lēl) *adj. Archaic or Scottish.* loyal. [ME < OF *leial* < L *legalis* legal < *lex* law. Doublet of LEGAL, LOYAL.]

lean¹ (lēn) *v.* **leaned** *or* **leant, lean·ing;** *n.* —*v.* **1** stand slanting, not upright; bend: *A small tree leans over in the wind.* **2** rest in a sloping or slanting position: *Lean against me.* **3** set or put in a leaning position: *Lean the picture against the wall till I am ready for it.* **4** depend; rely: *lean on a friend's advice.* **5** tend or incline; show a preference: *to lean toward mercy. Her favorite sport was tennis, but now she leans more to swimming.* **6** *Informal.* apply force or pressure to influence or persuade (*usually used with* **on**): *The school is starting to lean on students with poor attendance records.*
lean over backward, *Informal.* go to extremes in one direction so as

hat, āge, fär; let, ēqual, tèrm; it, īce
hot, ōpen, ôrder; oil, out; cup, pùt, rüle,
əbove, takən, pencəl, lemən, circəs

ch, child; ng, long; sh, ship
th, thin; ŦH, then; zh, measure

to more than balance a tendency in the opposite direction.
—*n.* the act or an instance of leaning; inclination: *The old barn has more of a lean this year.* [OE *hlinian*]

lean² (lēn) *adj., n.* —*adj.* **1** with little or no fat: *a lean horse.* **2** producing little; scant: *a lean harvest, a lean diet.* —*n.* meat having little fat. [OE *hlǣne*] —**lean′ness,** *n.* —**lean′ly,** *adv.*
☛ *Syn. adj.* **1.** See note at **thin.**

Le·an·der (lē an′dər) *n. Greek legend.* a lover who swam the Hellespont to visit his sweetheart, Hero, every night until he was finally drowned. See also **Hero.**

lean·ing (lēn′ing) *n.* a tendency; inclination.

Leaning Tower of Pisa a famous tower at Pisa, Italy, whose foundations have slipped so that it leans to one side.

leant (lent) *v.* a pt. and a pp. of **lean¹.**

lean-to (lēn′tü′) *n., pl.* **-tos. 1** a building attached to and partly supported by another, and having a sloping roof with its upper edge attached to the wall of the other building. **2** a crude shelter built or leaning against posts, trees, rock, etc.: *Hunters have a supply of wood in a lean-to here.* **3** (*adj.*) having supports pitched against or leaning on an adjoining wall or building: *a lean-to roof.*

leap (lēp) *n., v.* **leaped** *or* **leapt, leap·ing.** —*n.* **1** a jump or spring. **2** something to be jumped. **3** the distance covered by a jump.
by leaps and bounds, very fast and very much; swiftly and effectively.
leap in the dark, an action taken without knowing what its results will be.
—*v.* **1** jump: *A frog leaps.* **2** pass, come, rise, etc. as if with a leap or bound: *An idea leaped to her mind. A sudden breeze made the leaves leap.* **3** jump over: *leap a fence.* **4** cause to leap. [OE *hlȳp,* n., *hlēapan,* v.]
☛ *Syn. v.* **1.** See note at **jump.**

leap·frog (lēp′frog′) *n., v.* **-frogged, -frog·ging.** —*n.* a game in which one player jumps over the bent back of another. —*v.* **1** leap or jump as in the game of leapfrog. **2** skip over; side-step; avoid.

leapt (lept *or* lēpt) *v.* a pt. and a pp. of **leap.**

leap year a year having 366 days, the extra day being February 29. A year is a leap year if its number can be divided exactly by four except years at the end of a century, which must be exactly divisible by 400; thus 1960 and 2000 are leap years, whereas 1900 and 1961 are not.

learn (lèrn) *v.* **learned** *or* **learnt, learn·ing. 1** gain knowledge of (a subject) or skill in (an art, trade, etc.) by study, instruction, or experience: *learn French.* **2** acquire knowledge, skill, etc.: *He learns easily.* **3** memorize: *He learnt the poem in five minutes.* **4** find out; come to know: *He tried to learn the details of the train wreck.* **5** become informed; hear. **6** become able by study or practice: *to learn to fly an airplane.* [OE *leornian*] —**learn′a·ble,** *adj.*
☛ *Usage.* Do not confuse **learn** with **teach.** Standard English keeps these two verbs completely distinct: *I learned how to play chess. He taught me how to play chess.*

learn·ed (lèr′nid) *adj.* having, showing, or requiring much knowledge; scholarly: *a learned man, a learned book.* —**learn′ed·ly,** *adv.*

learned borrowing a word or expression borrowed from a language at the scholarly, technical, or scientific level. *Flora* and *fauna* are learned borrowings from Latin.

learn·er (lèr′nər) *n.* **1** a person who is learning. **2** beginner.

learn·ing (lèr′ning) *n.* **1** the gaining of knowledge or skill. **2** the possession of knowledge gained by study; scholarship. **3** knowledge.

learnt (lèrnt) *v.* a pt. and a pp. of **learn.**

lear·y (lēr′ē) See **leery.**

lease (lēs) *n., v.* **leased, leas·ing.** —*n.* **1** a contract, usually in the form of a written agreement, giving the right to use property for a certain length of time, usually by paying rent. **2** the length of time for which such an agreement is made: *They have a long lease on the property.* **3** the property held by a lease.
new lease on life, the chance to live a longer, better, or happier life.
—*v.* **1** give a lease on. **2** take a lease on. **3** be leased. [< AF *les* < *lesser* let, let go < L *laxare* loosen < *laxus* loose]

lease·hold (lēs′hōld′) *n.* **1** a holding by a lease. **2** real estate held by a lease. —**lease′hold′er,** *n.*

leash (lēsh) *n., v.* —*n.* **1** a strap, chain, etc. for restraining or leading a dog or other animal in check. **2** a group of three animals: *a leash of hounds.*
hold in leash, control; restrain.
—*v.* fasten or hold in with a leash; control. [ME < OF *laisse* < L *laxa*, fem., loose]

least (lēst) *adj., n., adv.* —*adj.* less than any other; smallest; slightest: *The least bit of dirt in a watch may make it stop.*
—*n.* the least amount or degree: *That is the least you can do.*
at least or **at the least, a** at the lowest estimate: *The temperature was at least 35°C.* **b** at any rate; in any case: *He may have been late but at least he came.*
not in the least, not at all.
—*adv.* to the least extent, amount, or degree: *He liked that book least of all.* [OE *lǣst*]

least common denominator the lowest common multiple of all the denominators of a group of fractions. 20 is the least common denominator of ½, ¾, ⁴/₅. *Abbrev.:* LCD, L.C.D. or l.c.d.

least common multiple the least quantity that contains two or more given quantities exactly. The least common multiple of 3 and 4 and 6 is 12. *Abbrev.:* LCM, L.C.M. or l.c.m.

least·ways (lēst′wāz′) *adv. Informal.* leastwise.

least·wise (lēst′wīz′) *adv. Informal.* at least; at any rate.

leath·er (leⁿH′ər) *n., v.* —*n.* **1** animal skin that has been prepared for use by removing all the flesh and hair from the skin and then tanning it. **2** (*adj.*) made of or covered with leather: *leather gloves, a leather chair.* **3** something made of leather.
—*v.* **1** furnish or cover with leather. **2** *Informal.* beat with a strap; thrash. [OE *lether*]

leath·er·ette (leⁿH′ər et′) *n.* imitation leather.

leath·ern (leⁿH′ərn) *adj.* **1** made of leather. **2** like leather.

leath·er·neck (leⁿH′ər nek′) *n. U.S. Slang.* a United States marine.

leath·er·y (leⁿH′ər ē) *adj.* like leather in appearance, texture, or toughness. —**leath′er·i·ness,** *n.*

leave¹ (lēv) *v.* **left, leav·ing. 1** go away: *We leave tonight.* **2** go away from: *He left the house.* **3** stop living in, belonging to, or working at or for: *leave the country, leave the club.* **4** go without taking: *I left a book on the table.* **5** go away and let remain in a particular condition: *leave a window open.* **6** let remain when one dies; bequeath: *He left a large fortune.* **7** give to be kept; deposit; give: *I left my suitcase in the station while I walked around the town.* **8** let (a person, etc.) alone to do something; let be: *Leave me to settle the matter.* **9** let remain for someone to do: *Leave the matter to me. I left the driving to my sister.* **10** let remain uneaten, unused, unremoved, etc.: *There is some coal left.*
leave off, stop: *Continue the story from where I left off.*
leave out, fail to do, say, or put in; omit: *She left out two words when she read the sentence.*
[OE lǣfan] —**leav′er,** *n.*
☞ *Hom.* **lieve.**
☞ *Syn.* **1, 2.** See note at **go.**
☞ *Usage.* See note at **let¹.**

leave² (lēv) *n.* **1** permission; consent: *They gave him leave to go.* **2** permission to be absent from duty. **3** the length of time that such permission lasts.
by your leave, with your consent; if you permit.
on leave, absent from duty with permission.
take leave (of), say goodbye (to): *We took leave of our hostess at the door.*
take (one's) leave, say goodbye and depart: *We took our leave soon after they did.*
[OE *lēaf*]
☞ *Hom.* **lieve.**

leave³ (lēv) *v.* **leaved, leav·ing.** put forth leaves: *Trees begin to leave in the spring.* [var. of *leaf*]
☞ *Hom.* **lieve.**

leav·en (lev′ən) *n., v.* —*n.* **1** any substance, such as yeast, that will cause fermentation and make dough rise. **2** a small amount of fermenting dough kept for this purpose. **3** an influence that, spreading silently and strongly, changes conditions or opinions: *A leaven of hope brightened our despair.* **4** a tempering or modifying element; a tinge or admixture: *The solemn speech had a leaven of humor.*
—*v.* **1** cause to rise by means of a leaven; make (dough) light or lighter. **2** spread through or blend with some modifying element: *Hope leavened our despair.* [ME < OF *levain* < L *levamen* a lifting < *levare* raise]

leav·en·ing (lev′ən ing) *n.* something that leavens.

leave of absence 1 permission to be absent from duty. 2 the

length of time that absence from duty is permitted.

leaves (lēvz) *n.* **1** pl. of **leaf. 2** pl. of **leave².**

leave–tak·ing (lēv′tāk′ing) *n.* the act of taking leave; saying goodbye.

leav·ings (lēv′ingz) *n.pl.* leftovers; remnants.

Leb·a·nese (leb′ə nēz′) *adj., n.* —*adj.* of or having to do with Lebanon, a country at the eastern end of the Mediterranean, or its people. —*n.* a native or inhabitant of Lebanon.

Le·bens·raum or **le·bens·raum** (lā′bəns roum′) *n. German.* **1** the territory that a nation supposedly must possess in order to be economically self-sufficient. **2** the space, freedom, etc. required for existence, activity, or expansion. [literally, living space]

lech·er (lech′ər) *n.* a man who indulges in lechery. [ME < OF *lecheor* licker < *lechier* lick < Gmc.]

lech·er·ous (lech′ər əs) *adj.* lewd; lustful.

lech·er·y (lech′ər ē) *n.* lewdness; gross indulgence of lust.

lec·tern (lek′tərn) *n.* **1** a reading desk in a church, especially the desk from which the lessons are read at daily prayer. **2** any reading desk or stand. [ME < OF *lettrun, leitrun* < Med.L. *lectrum* < L *legere* read]

lec·ture (lek′chər) *n., v.* **-tured, -tur·ing.** —*n.* **1 a** a speech or planned talk on a chosen subject, usually for the purpose of instruction. **b** such a speech or talk written down or printed. **2** a scolding.
—*v.* **1** give a lecture. **2** instruct or entertain by a lecture. **3** scold; reprove. [ME < LL *lectura* < L *legere* read]

lec·tur·er (lek′chər ər) *n.* **1** a person who gives a lecture or lectures. **2** a teacher of junior rank at some universities.

led (led) *v.* pt. and pp. of **lead¹.**
☞ *Hom.* **lead.**
☞ *Usage.* See note at **lead¹.**

LED or **L.E.D.** *Electronics.* light-emitting diode: *Many digital watches and clocks have an LED time display.*

Le·da (lē′də) *n. Greek mythology.* a queen of Sparta. Leda was visited by Zeus in the form of a swan and by him became the mother of Castor and Pollux and of Helen of Troy.

ledge (lej) *n.* **1** a narrow shelf: *a window ledge.* **2** a shelf or ridge of rock. **3** a layer or mass of metal-bearing rock. [ME < *legge(n)* lay¹]

ledg·er (lej′ər) *n.* a book of accounts in which a business keeps a record of all money transactions. [ME < *legge(n)* lay¹]

ledger line *Music.* a line added above or below the staff for notes that are too high or too low to be put on the staff.

lee (lē) *n., adj.* —*n.* **1** shelter. **2** the side or part sheltered or away from the wind: *the lee of the house.* **3** the direction toward which the wind is blowing.
—*adj.* **1** sheltered or away from the wind: *the lee side of a ship.* **2** on the side away from the wind. **3** in the direction toward which the wind is blowing. [OE *hlēo*]
☞ *Hom.* **lea.**

lee·board (lē′bôrd′) *n.* a large, flat board lowered into the water on the lee side of a sailboat to keep the boat from drifting sideways.

leech¹ (lēch) *n., v.* —*n.* **1** any of a class (Hirudinea) of mostly freshwater annelid worms having a segmented body with a sucker at either end. Many leeches live by sucking the blood of other animals; one large European species (*Hirudo medicinalis*) was formerly much used for medical bloodletting. **2** a person who persistently tries to get what he can out of others. **3** *Archaic.* physician.
—*v.* **1** use leeches on (a person) for bloodletting. **2** *Archaic.* cure or heal. [OE *lǣce*]
☞ *Hom.* **leach.**

leech² (lēch) *n.* the edge of a sail not fastened to a rope or spar. [origin uncertain]
☞ *Hom.* **leach.**

leek (lēk) *n.* a biennial plant (*Allium porrum*) of the lily family closely related to the onion but having a somewhat milder flavor. It resembles a very large green onion, with a slender bulb and thick stalk. [OE *lēac*]
☞ *Hom.* **leak.**

leer (lēr) *n., v.* —*n.* a sly, sidelong look; evil glance. —*v.* give a sly, sidelong look; glance evilly. [? OE *hlēor* cheek, from idea of looking over one's cheek, looking askance] —**leer′ing·ly,** *adv.*

leer·y (lēr′ē) *adj. Informal.* **1** wary; suspicious. **2** afraid. **3** sly; cunning and knowing. Also, **leary.** —**leer′i·ly,** *adv.* —**leer′i·ness,** *n.*

lees (lēz) *n.pl.* dregs; sediment. [< F *lie* < Celtic]

lee shore the shore toward which the wind is blowing.

lee·ward (lē′wərd or lü′ərd) *adj., adv., n.* —*adj. or adv.* **1** on the side away from the wind. **2** in the direction toward which the wind is blowing. —*n.* the side away from the wind.

lee·way (lē′wā′) *n.* **1** the side movement of a ship to leeward, out

of its course. **2** extra space at the side; more time, money, etc. than is needed; a margin of safety. **3** sufficient room or scope for action.

left¹ (left) *adj., adv., n.* —*adj.* **1** of the side that is toward the west when the main side faces north: *the left wing of an army. Make a left turn at the next light.* **2** when looking to the front, situated nearer the observer's or speaker's left hand than his right: *the left side of the room.* **3** Often, **Left,** *Politics.* of, having to do with, or belonging to the left.
—*adv.* on or to the left side: *turn left.*
—*n.* **1** the left side or hand. **2 the Left** or **the left, a** a group or party advocating or favoring social, political, and economic policies aimed at more or less equal distribution of rights, obligations, and wealth within the community or state; a progressive, liberal, radical, or revolutionary group or party. **b** especially in some European legislatures, the members occupying the seats to the left of the presiding officer by virtue of their more liberal or radical views. **3** *Boxing.* a blow struck with the left hand. [dial. OE *left* for *lyft* weak]

left² (left) *v.* pt. and pp. of **leave¹.**

left face a turn to the left.

left-hand (left′hand′) *adj.* **1** on or to the left. **2** of, for, or with the left hand.

left-hand·ed (left′han′did) *adj.* **1** using the left hand more easily and readily than the right. **2** done with the left hand. **3** made to be used with the left hand. **4** turning from right to left: *a left-handed screw.* **5** clumsy; awkward. **6** doubtful; insincere: *a left-handed compliment.* —**left′-hand′ed·ly,** *adv.*
—**left′-hand′ed·ness,** *n.*

left-hand·er (left′han′dər) *n.* **1** a left-handed person. **2** a stroke or blow with the left hand.

left·ist (lef′tist) *n., adj. Politics.* —*n.* a person who supports or favors the left. —*adj.* of, having to do with, or favoring or supporting the left: *leftist ideas.* —**left′ism,** *n.*

left·o·ver (left′ō′vər) *n., adj.* —*n.* anything that is left. Scraps of food from a meal are leftovers. —*adj.* that is left; remaining.

left wing 1 the more liberal or radical faction of an assembly, group, or party. **2** *Hockey, Lacrosse, etc.:* **a** the playing position to the left of centre of a forward line. **b** a left winger. —**left′—wing′,** *adj.* —**left′—wing′er,** *n.*

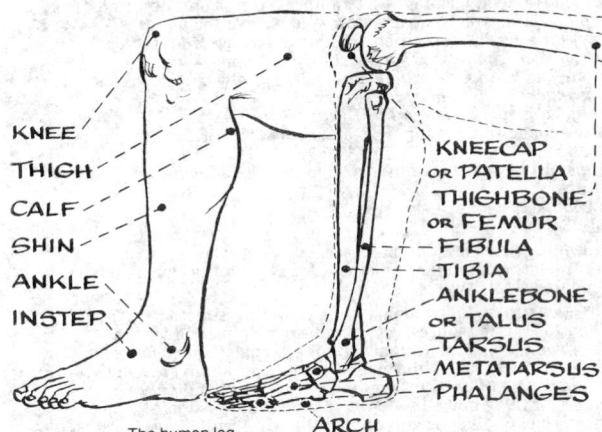

KNEE
THIGH
CALF
SHIN
ANKLE
INSTEP

KNEECAP
OR PATELLA
THIGHBONE
OR FEMUR
FIBULA
TIBIA
ANKLEBONE
OR TALUS
TARSUS
METATARSUS
PHALANGES
ARCH

The human leg

leg (leg) *n., v.* **legged, leg·ging.** —*n.* **1** one of the limbs on which human beings and animals support themselves and walk. **2** the part of a garment that covers a leg. **3** anything shaped or used like a leg: *a table leg.* **4** one of the distinct portions or stages of any course: *the last leg of a trip.* **5** the side of a triangle that is not the base or hypotenuse. **6** *Cricket.* **a** that part of the field to the left of and behind a right-handed batsman as he faces the bowler. **b** the fielder placed there.
give a leg up, *Informal.* help.
have not a leg to stand on, *Informal.* have no defence or reason.
on (one's) **last legs,** *Informal.* about to fall, collapse, die, etc.: *I feel as if I am on my last legs but a swim should revive me.*
pull (someone's) **leg,** *Informal.* fool, trick, or make fun of one: *I didn't know he was pulling my leg until I heard you laugh.*
shake a leg, *Slang.* **a** hurry up. **b** dance.
stretch (one's) **legs,** *Informal.* take a walk.
—*v. Informal.* walk; run: *We could not get a ride, so we had to leg it.* [ME < ON *leggr*] —**leg′less,** *adj.*

Leg. or **leg. 1** legislature; legislative. **2** legal. **3** legate. **4** legato.

leg·a·cy (leg′ə sē) *n., pl.* **-cies. 1** the money or other property left

---

hat, āge, fär; let, ēqual, tėrm; it, īce
hot, ōpen, ôrder; oil, out; cup, pút, rüle,
əbove, takən, pencəl, lemən, circəs

ch, child; ng, long; sh, ship
th, thin; ŦH, then; zh, measure

to a person by a will. **2** something that has been handed down from an ancestor or predecessor. [ME < OF *legacie* < Med.L. *legatia* < L *legatum* bequest, ult. < *lex, legis* covenant]

le·gal (lē′gəl) *adj.* **1** of law: *legal knowledge.* **2** of lawyers. **3** according to law; lawful. [< L *legalis* < *lex, legis* law. Doublet of LEAL, LOYAL.]
☛ *Syn.* **3.** See note at **lawful.**

le·gal·ese (lē′gə lēz′) *n.* the jargon of the legal profession commonly used in documents, legal submissions and forms, etc., especially when thought of as incomprehensible or excessively finicky.

le·gal·ism (lē′gəl iz′əm) *n.* strict adherence to law or prescription.

le·gal·ist (lē′gəl ist) *n.* a person who adheres strictly to laws or rules.

le·gal·is·tic (lē′gəl is′tik) *adj.* adhering strictly to law or prescription.

le·gal·i·ty (li gal′ə tē) *n., pl.* **-ties.** accordance with law; lawfulness.

le·gal·ize (lē′gəl īz′) *v.* **-ized, -iz·ing.** make legal; authorize by law; sanction. —**le′gal·i·za′tion,** *n.*

le·gal·ly (lē′gəl ē) *adv.* **1** in a legal manner. **2** according to law.

legal tender money that must, by law, be accepted in payment of debts.

leg·ate (leg′it) *n.* **1** a representative of the Pope. **2** an ambassador; representative; messenger. [< L *legatus,* originally, provided with a contract < *lex, legis* contract]

leg·a·tee (leg′ə tē′) *n.* a person to whom a legacy is left.

le·ga·tion (li gā′shən) *n.* **1** the diplomatic representative of a country and his staff of assistants. A legation ranks next below an embassy. **2** the official residence, offices, etc. of such a representative in a foreign country. **3** the office, position, or dignity of a legate. [ME < L *legatio, -onis,* ult. < *legare* dispatch < *legatus.* See LEGATE.]

le·ga·to (li gä′tō) *adj., adv., n. Music.* —*adj.* smooth and connected; without breaks between successive tones. *Legato* is the opposite of *staccato.*
—*adv.* in a legato manner.
—*n.* a legato passage, style, or performance. [< Ital. *legato* bound]

leg·end (lej′ənd) *n.* **1** a story coming down from the past, which has been widely accepted as true: *The stories about King Arthur and his Knights of the Round Table are legends, not history.* **2** such stories considered collectively. **3** the inscription on a coin or medal. **4** the words, etc. accompanying a picture, map, or diagram; caption. [ME < OF *legende* < Med.L. < L *legenda* (things) to be read < *legere* read]
☛ *Usage.* **Legend** and **myth** have somewhat different meanings. A **legend** is a story relating to a people's past and usually glorifies a hero, saint, great event, etc.; it may contain an element of fact, or it may be wholly untrue. A **myth** is a story relating to a people's religion and is usually about a god, gods, or other superhuman beings; its original aim was to explain a religious belief or some aspect of life or nature.

leg·end·ar·y (lej′ən der′ē) *adj.* of a legend or legends; like a legend; not historical. —**leg′end·ar′i·ly,** *adv.*

leg·er·de·main (lej′ər də mān′) *n.* **1** sleight of hand; conjuring tricks; jugglery. A common trick of legerdemain is to take rabbits from an apparently empty hat. **2** trickery. [< F *léger de main* quick of hand]

legged (legd *or* leg′id) **1** having a leg or legs. **2** having a leg or legs of a specified kind or number: *a three-legged stool, a long-legged bird.*

leg·gings (leg′ingz) *n.pl.* extra outer coverings of cloth or leather for the legs, for use out of doors; gaiters.

leg·gy (leg′ē) *adj.* **1** having long legs. **2** having awkwardly long legs. —**leg′gi·ness,** *n.*

leg·horn (leg′hôrn *or* leg′ərn) *n.* **1 Leghorn,** a breed of rather small chicken valued especially as a prolific egg layer. It produces white eggs. **2** a fine straw from an Italian wheat that is braided for making hats. **3** a hat made of this braided straw. [< *Leghorn* (*Livorno*), a seaport in W Italy]

leg·i·bil·i·ty (lej′ə bil′ə tē) *n.* a legible condition or quality; clearness of print or writing.

leg·i·ble (lej′ə bəl) *adj.* 1 that can be read. 2 easy to read; plain and clear: *legible handwriting.* [< LL *legibilis* < L *legere* read] —**leg′i·ble·ness,** *n.* —**leg′i·bly,** *adv.*

le·gion (lē′jən) *n.* 1 a large body of soldiers; army. 2 in the ancient Roman army, a body of soldiers consisting of 3000 to 6000 foot soldiers and 300 to 700 cavalrymen. 3 a great many; a very large number. 4 **Legion,** Royal Canadian Legion. [ME < OF < L *legio, -onis* < *legere* choose]

le·gion·ar·y (lē′jən er′ē) *adj., n., pl.* **-ar·ies.** —*adj.* of or belonging to a legion. —*n.* a soldier of a legion.

le·gion·naire (lē′jən er′) *n.* 1 a member of the Royal Canadian Legion. 2 *Historical.* a member of the French Foreign Legion. 3 a soldier of a legion. [< F]

Legion of Honor or **Honour** an honorary society founded by Napoleon in 1802, in which membership is given as a reward for great services to France.

leg·is·late (lej′is lāt′) *v.* **-lat·ed, -lat·ing.** 1 make laws: *Parliament legislates for Canada.* 2 force by legislation: *The council legislated him out of office.* [< *legislator*]

leg·is·la·tion (lej′is lā′shən) *n.* 1 the making of laws. 2 the laws made.

leg·is·la·tive (lej′is lā′tiv) *adj.* 1 having to do with making laws: *legislative reforms.* 2 having the duty and power of making laws: *Parliament is a legislative body.* 3 ordered by law. —**leg′is·la·tive·ly,** *adv.*

Legislative Assembly in Canada, the group of representatives elected to the legislature of any of certain provinces or the Yukon Territory.

Legislative Council *Historical. Cdn.* the upper chamber of the Quebec legislature, composed of 24 members appointed for life by the Lieutenant-Governor in Council. The Legislative Council in Quebec was abolished in 1968.

leg·is·la·tor (lej′is lā′tər) *n.* a lawmaker; a member of a legislative body. [< L *legis lator* proposer of a law]

leg·is·la·ture (lej′is lā′chər) *n.* 1 a group of persons having the duty and power to make laws for a country, province, or state. Each Canadian province has a legislature. 2 the place where the legislators meet.

le·git (lə jit′) *adj. Slang.* legitimate.

le·git·i·ma·cy (lə jit′ə mə sē) *n.* the quality or state or being legitimate or lawful.

le·git·i·mate (*adj.* lə jit′ə mit; *v.* lə jit′ə māt′) *adj., v.* **-mat·ed, -mat·ing.** —*adj.* 1 rightful; lawful: *The Prince of Wales is the legitimate heir to the throne of England.* 2 allowed; acceptable: *Sickness is a legitimate reason for absence from school or work.* 3 conforming to accepted standards: *a legitimate work of art.* 4 born of parents who are married. 5 resting on, or ruling by, the principle of hereditary right: *the legitimate title to a throne, a legitimate sovereign.* 6 logical: *a legitimate conclusion.* 7 of, having to do with, or designating drama acted on stage, as opposed to motion pictures and other stage entertainment such as vaudeville or burlesque: *the legitimate theatre.* —*v.* make or declare lawful. [< Med.L *legitimatus* < L *legitimus* lawful < *lex, legis* law] —**le·git′i·mate·ly,** *adv.* ☞ *Syn. adj.* 1. See note at **lawful.**

le·git·i·mist (lə jit′ə mist) *n.* a supporter of legitimate authority, especially of legitimacy to rule based on direct descent.

le·git·i·mize (lə jit′ə mīz′) *v.* **-mized, -miz·ing.** make or declare to be legitimate. —**le·git′i·mi·za′tion,** *n.*

leg·man (leg′man′) *n.* **-men.** 1 a reporter who collects information at the scene of an event. 2 anyone who collects information, delivers messages, or does similar work.

leg–of–mut·ton (leg′əv mut′ən) *adj.* having the shape of a leg of mutton; wide at one end and narrow at the other: *a leg-of-mutton sleeve.*

leg·ume (leg′yüm or li gyüm′) *n.* 1 the fruit or seed of any of various plants of the pea family used for food, especially beans or peas. 2 the plant bearing such fruit. 3 *Botany.* a long, dry, dehiscent fruit; pod. See **fruit** for picture. 4 any plant of the pea family: *Clover is a legume.* [< F < L *legumen*]

le·gu·mi·nous (li gyü′mə nəs) *adj.* 1 of or bearing legumes. 2 having to do with or belonging to the pea family of plants.

lei (lā) *n., pl.* **leis.** a wreath of flowers, leaves, etc. [< Hawaiian]

Lei·ces·ter (les′tər) *n.* a breed of sheep having long wool. [< *Leicester,* a county in England, where this breed originated]

leis·ter (lēs′tər or lis′tər) *n., v.* —*n.* a spear having two or more barbed prongs, used in fishing. —*v.* spear with a leister. [< ON *lióstr* < *liósta* strike]

lei·sure (lezh′ər or lē′zhər) *n.* 1 the time free from required work, in which a person may rest, amuse himself, and do the things he likes to do. 2 (*adj.*) free; not busy: *leisure hours.* 3 (*adj.*) having leisure.

at leisure, a free; not busy. **b** without hurry; taking plenty of time. **at (one's) leisure,** when one has free time; at one's convenience. [ME < OF *leisir* < L *licere* be allowed]

lei·sured (lezh′ərd or lē′zhərd) *adj.* 1 having leisure. 2 leisurely.

lei·sure·ly (lezh′ər lē or lē′zhər lē) *adj. or adv.* without hurry; taking plenty of time. —**leis′ure·li·ness,** *n.* ☞ *Syn. adj.* See note at **slow.**

leit·mo·tif or **leit·mo·tiv** (līt′mō tēf′) *n.* 1 *Music.* a short theme or passage in a composition, repeated throughout the work and associated with a certain person, situation, or idea. 2 any repeating theme or subject. [< G *Leitmotiv* leading motive]

lek (lek) *n.* 1 the basic unit of money in Albania, divided into 100 qintars. See table at **money.** 2 a coin worth one lek. [< Albanian]

lem·an (lem′ən or lē′mən) *n. Archaic.* 1 sweetheart or lover. 2 mistress. [ME *leofman* < OE *lēof* dear + *mann* man]

lem·ming (lem′ing) *n.* 1 any of various small, mouselike arctic rodents (genera *Lemmus* and *Dicrostonyx*) having greyish or brownish fur, a short tail and furry feet. [< Norwegian]

lem·on (lem′ən) *n., adj.* —*n.* 1 an acid-tasting, light-yellow citrus fruit growing in warm climates. 2 a thorny tree that bears this fruit. 3 a pale yellow. 4 *Slang.* a thing or person that is considered inferior or disagreeable: *The last car I bought was a lemon.* 5 a soft drink flavored with lemon juice. —*adj.* pale yellow. [ME < OF *limon* < Arabic *laimun* < Persian *limun*]

lem·on·ade (lem′ən ād′) *n.* a soft drink made of lemon juice, sugar, and water. [< F *limonade*]

lem·pi·ra (lem pē′rä) *n.* 1 the basic unit of money in Honduras, divided into 100 centavos. See table at **money.** 2 a coin worth one lempira. [< Am.Sp.]

le·mur (lē′mər) *n.* 1 any of a family (Lemuridae) of primates found mainly in the forests of Madagascar, having a foxlike face, large eyes, soft, woolly fur, and a long, bushy tail. 2 any of various similar or related animals, such as a loris. [< L *lemures,* pl., spectres, ghosts; with reference to their nocturnal habits]

lend (lend) *v.* **lent, lend·ing.** 1 let another have or use for a time: *Will you lend me your bicycle for an hour?* 2 give the use of (money) for a fixed or specified amount of payment: *Banks lend money and charge interest.* 3 make a loan or loans. 4 give; contribute; add: *A lace curtain lends charm to a window. The Red Cross lent aid to lend aid in time of disaster.*

lend a hand, help: *She lent a hand with the dishes.*
lend itself to, be suitable for: *The old engine lent itself to our purposes.*
lend (oneself) to, make oneself available for: *Don't lend yourself to foolish schemes.*
[OE *lænan* < *læn* loan] —**lend′er,** *n.* ☞ *Usage.* See note at **loan.**

lend–lease (lend′lēs′) *n., v.* **-leased, -leas·ing.** —*n.* a system of making a loan of equipment in return for some service or material. —*v.* lend under this system.

length (length) *n.* 1 how long a thing is; a thing's measurement from end to end; the longest way a thing can be measured: *the length of your arm.* 2 the distance a thing extends: *The length of a race is the distance run.* 3 the extent in time; duration: *the length of a visit, the length of an hour.* 4 a long stretch or extent: *Quite a length of hair hung down in a braid.* 5 a piece or portion of cloth, pipe, rope, etc. of given length often either cut from a larger piece, or meant to be joined to another piece: *a length of rope, three lengths of pipe.* 6 the distance from end to end of a boat, horse, etc., considered as a unit of measurement in racing: *The grey horse finished the race two lengths ahead of the brown one.*

at arm's length See **arm¹.**
at full length, with the body stretched out flat.
at length, a at last; finally: *At length, after many delays, the meeting started.* **b** with all the details; fully: *He told of his adventures at length.*
go to any length, do everything possible.
[OE *length* < *lang* long¹]

length·en (leng′thən) *v.* 1 make longer. 2 become or grow longer. ☞ *Syn.* 1, 2. **Lengthen, extend, prolong** = make or become longer. **Lengthen** = make or become longer in space or time: *There is no way to lengthen a day.* **Extend** suggests stretching out beyond the present point or limits: *We had to extend the time allowed for returning the questionnaires.* **Prolong** = lengthen in time beyond a normal, proper, or desirable limit: *She decided to prolong her visit.*

length·ways (length′wāz′) *adv. or adj.* lengthwise.

length·wise (length′wīz′) *adv. or adj.* in the direction of the length.

length·y (leng′thē) *adj.* **length·i·er, length·i·est.** long or too long:

len·ien·cy (lē′nē ən sē *or* lēn′yən sē) *n.* mildness; gentleness; mercy. Also, **lenience.**

len·ient (lē′nē ənt *or* lēn′yənt) *adj.* mild or gentle; merciful: *a lenient punishment.* [< L *leniens, -entis,* ppr. of *lenire* soften < *lenis* mild] **len′ient·ly,** *adv.*

len·i·tive (len′ə tiv) *adj., n.* —*adj.* **1** softening; soothing; mitigating. **2** mildly laxative. —*n.* **1** anything that soothes or softens; palliative. **2** a mild laxative. [< Med.L *lenitivus* < L *lenitus,* pp. of *lenire* soften]

len·i·ty (len′ə tē) *n., pl.* **-ties.** mildness; gentleness; mercifulness. [< L *lenitas* < *lenis* mild]

lens (lenz) *n., pl.* **lens·es. 1** a piece of glass or similar transparent substance having two curved surfaces or one plane and one curved surface, used singly or in combination to focus rays of light passing through it. Lenses are used in cameras to form images and in telescopes, etc. to make things look larger and nearer. See **concave** and **convex** for pictures. **2** a combination of two or more of these pieces, especially as used in a camera. **3** a clear, biconvex, lens-shaped, elastic structure in the eye directly behind the iris, that directs and focusses light rays upon the retina. The curvature of the lens changes to accomodate varying distances. See **eye** for picture. **4** a device that focusses sound waves, streams of electrons, etc. **5** something shaped like an optical lens such as a round, convex formation of ice in permafrost or bitumen in sand or rock. [< L *lens, lentis* lentil (which has a biconvex shape)]

lent (lent) *v.* pt. and pp. of *lend.*

Lent (lent) *n.* the forty weekdays before Easter, observed in many Christian churches as a time for fasting and repenting of sins. [OE *lencten* spring < W.Gmc. **lang* -long[1] (with reference to lengthening days)]

len·ta·men·te (len′tə men′tā) *adv. Music.* slowly. [< Ital.]

len·tan·do (len tän′dō) *adj. Music.* slowing down. [< Ital.]

Lent·en or **lent·en** (len′tən) *adj.* of Lent; during Lent; suitable for Lent. [originally noun; OE *lencten.* See LENT.]

len·ti·cel (len′tə səl) *n.* a ventilating pore in the bark of woody plants. [< F *lenticelle,* dim. of L *lens, lentis* lentil, because of its shape]

len·til (len′təl) *n.* **1** a plant (*Lens culinaris*) of the pea family, having seeds shaped like biconvex lenses, native to S Europe and Asia but widely cultivated elsewhere. **2** the edible seed of this plant. [< F *lentille* < L *lenticula,* dim. of *lens, lentis* lentil]

len·to (len′tō) *adj., adv., n. Music.* —*adj.* slow. —*adv.* slowly. —*n.* a slow movement or passage. [< Ital.]

l′en·voi or **l′en·voy** (len′voi *or* lon vwä′) *n.* **1** a short stanza ending a poem. **2** a postscript to a prose work, giving a moral, dedication, etc. [< F *l′envoi,* literally, the sending. Cf. ENVOY[2].]

Le·o (lē′ō) *n.* **1** *Astronomy.* a northern constellation thought of as having the shape of a lion. **2** *Astrology.* **a** the fifth sign of the zodiac. The sun enters Leo about July 22. See **zodiac** for picture. **b** a person born under this sign. [< L]

le·on·e (lē ō′nē) *n.* **1** the basic unit of money in Sierra Leone, divided into 100 cents. See table at **money. 2** a note worth one leone.

Le·o·nid (lē′ə nid) *n.* one of a shower of meteors occurring annually about November 14. The Leonids seem to come from the constellation Leo.

le·o·nine (lē′ə nīn′) *adj.* of or like a lion. [< L *leoninus* < *leo* lion]

leop·ard (lep′ərd) *n.* **1** a large animal (*Panthera pardus*) of the cat family native to Africa and southern Asia, having usually buff or tawny fur with small black spots arranged in rosettes. **2** any of several similar and related animals, such as the jaguar, cheetah, or ocelot. **3** the fur of the leopard. **4** *Heraldry.* a representation of a lion with the face turned towards the front and one leg raised, as in the arms of England. [ME < OF < L < Gk. *leopardos* < *leōn* lion + *pardos* leopard]

leop·ard·ess (lep′ər dis) *n.* a female leopard.

le·o·tard (lē′ə tärd′) *n.* **1** a one-piece, close-fitting knitted garment having long or short sleeves and usually extending just to the thighs, with holes for the legs. **2 leotards,** *pl.* tights. [< Jules *Léotard,* 19th-century French gymnast]

lep·er (lep′ər) *n.* a person who has leprosy. [ME < OF < L < Gk. *lepra* leprosy. See LEPROUS.]

lep·i·dop·ter·an (lep′ə dop′tə rən) *n.* any of a large order (Lepidoptera) of insects comprising the butterflies, moths, and skippers, all having four broad, membranous wings covered with very tiny, often brightly colored scales. The larvae of lepidopterans are called caterpillars and have chewing mouth parts for feeding on plants; the adults have sucking mouth parts. [< NL *Lepidoptera,* pl. < Gk. *lepis, -idos* scale + *pteron* wing]

lep·i·dop·ter·ous (lep′ə dop′tər əs) *adj.* of or having to do with the lepidopterans.

lep·re·chaun (lep′rə kon′ *or* lep′rə kôn′) *n. Irish folklore.* a sprite or goblin resembling a little old man. [< Irish *leipreachán, lupracán* < Old Irish *lúchorpán* < *lú* small + *corp* body < L *corpus* body; cf. *little people,* a term still used in Ireland for the fairies]

lep·ro·sy (lep′rə sē) *n.* a chronic, mildly infectious disease caused by the bacillus *Mycobacterium leprae,* which may attack the skin, flesh, or nerves, producing ulcers and white, scaly scabs, weakening and wasting of muscles, loss of sensation, and, in some forms of the disease, paralysis and gangrene, resulting in deformity and mutilation. [< *leprous*]

lep·rous (lep′rəs) *adj.* **1** having leprosy. **2** of or like leprosy. **3** scaly or scurfy. **4** causing leprosy. [< L *leprosus* < *lepra* leprosy < Gk. *lepra* < *lepein* to peel] —**lep′rous·ly,** *adv.*

lep·ta (lep′tə) *n.* pl. of **lepton**[1].

lep·ton[1] (lep′ton) *n., pl.* **-ta** (-tə). **1** a unit of money in Greece, equal to ¹⁄₁₀₀ of a drachma. Also called **lepto** (lep′tō). **2** a coin worth one lepton. [< Gk.]

lep·ton[2] (lep′ton) *n.* any of a class of elementary particles that take part in weak interactions, have a spin of ½, and have less mass than mesons or baryons. The leptons include the electron, the muon, and the neutrino, and their antiparticles.

les·bi·an (lez′bē ən) *n., adj.* —*n.* **1** a homosexual woman. **2 Lesbian,** a native or inhabitant of the Greek island of Lesbos. —*adj.* **1** of or having to do with lesbians or lesbianism. **2 Lesbian,** of or having to do with Lesbos or its people. [< *Lesbos,* the home of the supposedly homosexual Greek poetess *Sappho,* who lived about 600 B.C.]

les·bi·an·ism (lez′bē ə niz′əm) *n.* homosexuality in women.

lèse–ma·jes·té (lez′mä zhes tā′) *n. French.* lese-majesty.

lese–maj·es·ty (lēz′maj′is tē) *n.* a crime or offence against the sovereign power in a state; treason. [< F *lèse-majesté* < L *laesa majestas* injured majesty]

le·sion (lē′zhən) *n.* **1** an injury; hurt. **2** *Medicine.* a diseased condition often causing a change in the structure of an organ or tissue. [< L *laesio, -onis* injury < *laedere* to strike]

less (les) *adj., n., adv., prep.* —*adj.* **1** smaller; not so much: *of less width, to eat less meat.* **2** fewer: *Five is less than seven.* **3** lower in age, rank, or importance: *no less a person than the Prince of Wales.* **more or less, a** somewhat: *We are all more or less impatient.* **b** about, approximately: *The cost is fifty dollars, more or less.* —*n.* a smaller amount or quantity: *He refused to take less than five dollars.* —*adv.* to a smaller extent or degree: *less important.* —*prep.* lacking; without; minus: *a year less two days.* [OE *læs(sa)*]
☛ *Usage.* **Less, lesser.** Both are uses as comparative (of *little*), **less** more usually referring to size or quantity: *less time, less food; lesser,* a formal word, referring to value or importance: *a lesser writer.*
☛ *Usage.* See **fewer** for another note.

–less *adjective-forming suffix.* **1** without; that has no: *homeless = without a home.* **2** that does not: *ceaseless = that does not cease.* **3** that cannot be —*ed: countless = that cannot be counted.* [OE *-lēas,* suffixal use of *lēas* free from]
☛ *Usage.* **-less** is freely added to almost any noun and many verbs to form adjectives with the above meanings.

L. ès Sc. Licentiate in Sciences (for F *Licencié ès Sciences*).

les·see (les ē′) *n.* a person to whom a lease is granted.

less·en (les′ən) *v.* **1** grow less. **2** make less; decrease. **3** represent as less; minimize; belittle.
☛ *Hom.* **lesson.**

less·er (les′ər) *adj.* **1** less; smaller. **2** the less important of two.
☛ *Usage.* See note at **less.**

les·son (les′ən) *n., v.* —*n.* **1** something learned or studied. **2** a unit of learning or teaching; what is to be studied or practised at one time: *Our math text is divided into twenty lessons.* **3** a meeting of a student or class with a teacher to study a given subject: *She has gone for a piano lesson. There will be no lesson today.* **4** an instructive experience, serving to encourage or warn: *The accident was a lesson to me.* **5** a selection from the Bible or other sacred writings, read as part of a religious service. **6** a rebuke; lecture.

hat, āge, fär; let, ēqual, tèrm; it, īce
hot, ōpen, ôrder; oil, out; cup, pùt, rüle,
əbove, takən, pencəl, lemən, circəs

ch, child; ng, long; sh, ship
th, thin; ʈʜ, then; zh, measure

—v. **1** give a lesson to. **2** rebuke; lecture. [ME < OF *lecon* < L *lectio, -onis* reading < *legere* read]

☛ *Hom.* **lessen.**

les·sor (les′ôr *or* les ôr′) *n.* a person who grants a lease.

lest (lest) *conj.* **1** for fear that: *Be careful lest you fall from that tree.* **2** that: *They were afraid lest he should come too late to save them.* [ME *leste* < OE *thy̆ læs the* by so much the less that]

let¹ (let) *v.* **let, let·ting. 1** allow; permit: *Let the dog have a bone.* **2** allow to pass, go, or come: *Let all passengers board ship.* **3** allow to run out: *Doctors used to let blood from people to lessen a fever.* **4** rent; hire out: *to let a boat by the hour.* **5** be rented: *The house lets for $450 a month.* **6** *Let* is used in giving suggestions or giving commands. *Let's go home* means *I suggest that we go home.* **7** suppose; assume: *Let the two lines be parallel.*
let down, a lower. **b** slow up: *As her interest in the work wore off, she began to let down.* **c** disappoint: *Don't let us down today; we're counting on you to help us.* **d** humiliate.
let go, a allow to escape; set at liberty; release one's hold of: *to let go a rope or an anchor. Let me go.* **b** give up; abandon; cease to regard or consider: *He let go all thought of winning a prize.*
let in, admit; permit to enter.
let in for, open the way to; cause (trouble, unpleasantness, etc.): *He let his friends in for a lot of questioning when he left town so suddenly.*
let loose, allow to go free; liberate; release from restraint.
let off, a allow to go free; release: *let off steam.* **b** free from: *The teacher would not let us off homework.* **c** fire; explode: *to let off a detonation.* **d** discharge; allow to get off.
let on, *Informal.* **a** allow to be known; reveal one's knowledge of: *He didn't let on his surprise at the news.* **b** pretend; make believe: *She let on that she didn't see me.*
let (oneself) go, cease to restrain oneself.
let out, a permit to go out. **b** make (a garment) larger. **c** rent: *Has the room been let out yet?* **d** *Informal.* dismiss or be dismissed. **e** make known; disclose.
let up, *Informal.* stop; pause: *They refused to let up in the fight.* [OE *lætan*]

let² (let) *v.* **let·ted** *or* **let, let·ting;** *n.* —*v. Archaic.* prevent; hinder; obstruct. —*n.* **1** *Archaic.* a prevention; hindrance; obstruction. **2** *Tennis, etc.* interference with the ball. When this fault occurs, the ball or point must be played over again.
without let or hindrance, with nothing to prevent, hinder, or obstruct. [OE *lettan* < *læt* late]

–let *noun-forming suffix.* **1** little, as in *booklet, streamlet, wavelet.* **2** a thing worn as a band on, as an *anklet, armlet, wristlet.* **3** other meanings, as in *couplet, gauntlet, ringlet.* [< OF *-elet* < *-el* (< L *-ellus,* dim. suffix *or* < L *-ale,* neut.) + *-et* < VL *-ittus,* dim. suffix, ? < Celtic]

let·down (let′doun′) *n.* **1** a slowing up. **2** *Informal.* disappointment. **3** humiliation.

le·thal (lē′thəl) *adj.* causing death; deadly: *lethal weapons, a lethal dose.* [< L *let(h)alis* < *letum* death] —**le′thal·ly,** *adv.*
☛ *Syn.* See note at **fatal.**

le·thar·gic (lə thär′jik) *adj.* **1** unnaturally drowsy; sluggish; dull: *A hot, humid day often makes us feel lethargic.* **2** producing lethargy. —**le·thar′gi·cal·ly,** *adv.*

leth·ar·gy (leth′ər jē) *n., pl.* **-gies. 1** drowsy dullness; lack of energy; sluggish inactivity. **2** a condition of unnatural drowsiness or prolonged sleep. [< Gk. *lēthargia* < *lēthargos* forgetful < *lēthē* forgetfulness + *argos* lazy]

Le·the (lē′thē) *n.* **1** *Greek mythology.* a river in Hades. By drinking its water, the dead could forget the past. **2** forgetfulness; oblivion. [< L < Gk. *lēthē* oblivion]

Le·the·an (lē thē′ən) *adj.* **1** having to do with Lethe or its water. **2** causing forgetfulness.

let's (lets) let us.

Lett (let) *n.* **1** a member of a group of people living in Latvia, Lithuania, Estonia, and other Baltic regions. **2** their Baltic language; Lettish.

let·ter (let′ər) *n., v.* —*n.* **1** a symbol or sign, used alone or combined, that represents speech sounds; a character of an alphabet: *Both* must *and* mask *have four letters.* **2** a written or printed message. **3** an official document granting some right or privilege. **4** the exact wording; actual terms: *He kept the letter of the law but not the spirit.* **5** letters, *pl.* **a** literature. **b** a knowledge of literature; literary culture. **c** the profession of an author. **6** *Printing.* **a** a bit of metal type bearing a letter; type face. **b** a particular style of type. **7** a badge representing the initial letter of a school or college, given as an award for achievement, especially in athletics.

to the letter, very exactly; just as one has been told: *I carried out your order to the letter.*
—*v.* **1** mark with letters. **2** inscribe (something) in letters. **3** make letters. [ME < OF < L *littera*] —**let′ter·er,** *n.*
☛ *Syn. n.* **2. Letter, epistle** = a written message. **Letter** is the general word applying to a written, typed, or printed message, either personal, business, or official: *Put a stamp on that letter before you mail it.* **Epistle,** chiefly literary, applies to a long letter written in formal or elegant language, especially one intended to teach or advise: *the epistles of famous poets.*
☛ *Usage.* Sometimes a single sound is represented in spelling by a combination of letters. Thus, the two letters *sh,* as in *wish,* represent one sound; in *match,* three letters, *tch,* represent one sound. On the other hand, one combination of letters can stand for different sounds, as *ough* in *bough* and *though.*

letter carrier a person who collects or delivers mail; postman; mailman.

let·tered (let′ərd) *adj.* **1** marked with letters. **2** able to read and write; educated. **3** knowing literature; having literary culture.

let·ter·gram (let′ər gram′) *n.* a type of telegram in which up to 50 words are allowed at reduced rates, because it is transmitted outside regular business hours.

let·ter·head (let′ər hed′) *n.* **1** words printed at the top of a sheet of paper, usually a name and address. **2** a sheet of paper so printed.

let·ter·ing (let′ər ing) *n.* **1** letters drawn, painted, stamped, etc. **2** a marking with letters; making letters.

letter of credit a document issued by a bank, allowing the person named in it to draw money up to a certain amount from other specified banks.

let·ter·per·fect (let′ər pėr′fikt) *adj.* **1** knowing one's part or lesson perfectly. **2** correct in every detail.

let·ter·press (let′ər pres′) *n.* printed words, as distinguished from illustrations, etc.

letter press 1 a machine for making copies of letters. **2** printing from type, or from relief plates, as distinguished from offset, lithography, photogravure, etc.

letter rate the postage rate for first-class mail.

letters of marque *or* **letters of marque and reprisal** an official document giving a person permission from a government to capture the merchant ships of an enemy.

letters patent an official document giving a person or a corporation authority from a government to do some act or to have some right.

Let·tish (let′ish) *adj., n.* —*adj.* of or having to do with the Letts or their language. —*n.* the Baltic language of the Letts; Latvian.

let·tre de ca·chet (let′rə də kà shā′) *French. Historical.* a letter under the seal of the King of France, especially one ordering someone to be sent to prison or exile.

let·tuce (let′is) *n.* **1** any of a genus (*Lactuca*) of annual plants of the composite family, especially a common garden vegetable (*L. sativa*) grown in several varieties, all having large, crisp, green leaves that grow out from a very short central stalk. **2** the leaves of garden lettuce. Lettuce is usually eaten raw, in salads. [ME < OF *laitues,* pl. < L *lactuca* lettuce < *lac, lactis* milk; with reference to the milky juice of the plant]

let·up (let′up′) *n. Informal.* a lessening or stopping: *After a slight letup, the rain started again, harder than ever.*

leu (lē′ü) *n., pl.* **lei** (lā). **1** the basic unit of money in Romania, divided into 100 bani. See table at **money. 2** a coin or note worth one leu. [< Romanian]

leu·co·cyte *or* **leu·ko·cyte** (lü′kə sīt′) *n.* any of the white or colorless cells that occur in the blood and help the body fight infection; white blood cell. [< Gk. *leukos* white + E *-cyte*]

leu·ke·mi·a (lü kē′mē ə *or* lü kēm′yə) *n.* a type of cancer occurring in several forms, characterized by the abnormal growth of white blood cells (leucocytes) in the bone marrow, lymphatic tissue, or spleen, usually resulting in an excess of these cells in the blood. [< NL < Gk. *leukos* white + *-aimia* blood < *haima*]

lev (lef) *n., pl.* **leva** (lev′ə). **1** the basic unit of money in Bulgaria, divided into 100 stotinki. See table at **money. 2** a coin worth one lev. [< Bulgarian]

Lev. Leviticus.

Le·van·tine (lə van′tin, lev′ən tīn′, *or* lev′ən tēn′) *n., adj.* —*n.* **1** *Esp. Historical.* an inhabitant or a ship of the Levant, a region that includes the countries on the Mediterranean Sea east of Italy. **2** levantine, a strong, usually black, twilled silk cloth originally made in the Levant. —*adj.* of or having to do with the Levant.

lev·ee¹ (lev′ē) *n.* a bank built to keep a river from overflowing: *Many citizens manned the levees during the flood.* [< F *levée* < *lever* raise < L *levare*]

lev·ee² *or* **lev·ée** (lev′ē *or* le vē′) *n.* **1** a usually formal reception, especially one held during the day: *The regiment holds a levee on New Year's Day. He received an invitation to the Governor General's levee.* **2** *Historical.* a reception held by a person

of high rank on rising from bed. French kings used to hold levees in the morning while they were being dressed. [< F *levé, lever* a rising < *lever* raise. See LEVEE[1].]

A level. It has vertical and horizontal glass tubes containing a liquid with an air bubble inside. If the surface on or against which the level is placed is perfectly horizontal (or vertical) the bubble stays in the centre.

lev·el (lev′əl) *adj., n., v.* **-elled** or **-eled, -el·ling** or **-el·ing.** —*adj.*
1 having the same height everywhere; completely flat and even, like the surface of still water: *level ground.* **2** not sloping; horizontal: *The floor is not quite level.* **3** of equal height or in the same plane: *The table is level with the window sill.* **4** *Informal.* steady, calm, or sensible: *She's got a level head. He answered in a level voice.* **5** equal or balanced in rank, degree, quality, etc.: *The two friends remained level in rank, but not in salary.* **6** of, suited to, or involving a particular rank, degree, etc. (used only in compounds): *High-level talks have begun between the major powers.*
(one's) level best, *Informal.* one's very best; as well or as much as one can do: *He said he had tried his level best but couldn't pursuade her.*
—*n.* **1** an instrument for showing whether a surface is horizontal. **2** a measuring of differences in height or altitude between two points by means of such an instrument: *to take a level.* **3** a level position or condition. **4** a place or surface that is level: *The climbers stopped for breath when they reached the level.* **5** height: *We hung the picture at eye level. By evening the flood waters had risen to a level of three metres.* **6** degree, rate, or style: *The noise level in the library makes it hard to concentrate.* **7** a position or grade on a social, intellectual, or moral scale: *a professional level of work.*
find (one's) level, arrive at the most natural or most appropriate position, rank, etc.: *After failing as a painter, he found his level as a political cartoonist.*
on the level, *Informal.* **a** honest and straightforward: *Is that offer on the level?* **b** honestly and straightforwardly: *to work on the level.*
—*v.* **1** make level: *They used a bulldozer to level the ground.* **2** come to a level position or condition (usually used with **off** or **out**): *The path climbs for about 200 metres and then levels off.* **3** demolish or lay low; raze: *The tornado levelled every house in the village.* **4** raise and hold level for shooting; aim: *The soldier levelled his rifle.* **5** aim or direct (words, intentions, etc.): *She levelled a stinging rebuke at the speaker.* **6** *Slang.* be honest and frank; tell the truth (used with **with**): *You can level with me; what really happened?* **7** bring to a common level or plane; remove or reduce differences: *Death levels all human ranks.* [ME < OF *livel* < VL *libellum* < L *libella,* dim. of *libra* balance] —**lev′el·ler** or **lev′el·er,** *n.* —**lev′el·ly,** *adv.* —**lev′el·ness,** *n.*

level crossing a place where a railway track crosses a street or another railway track on the same level; railway crossing.

lev·el–head·ed (lev′əl hed′id) *adj.* having good common sense or good judgment; sensible. —**lev′el-head′ed·ly,** *adv.*

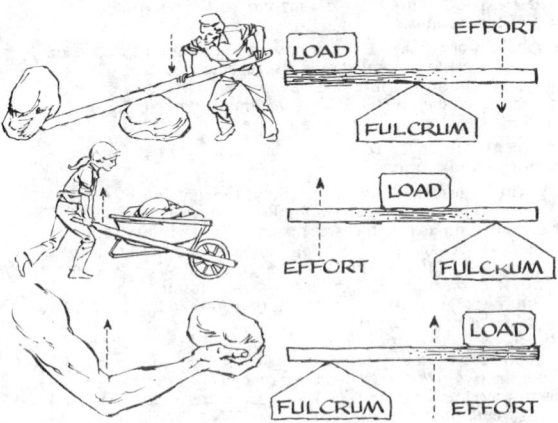

Lever (def. 3). The three classes of lever, with an example of each.

le·ver (lē′vər *or* lev′ər) *n., v.* —*n.* **1** a bar used for moving or

hat, āge, fär; let, ēqual, tėrm; it, īce
hot, ōpen, ôrder; oil, out; cup, pút, rüle,
above, takən, pencəl, lemən, circəs

ch, child; ng, long; sh, ship
th, thin; ᴛʜ, then; zh, measure

prying something: *A crowbar is a lever.* **2** anything used as a tool to influence or force: *He used his mother's name as a social lever.* **3** a simple machine consisting of a rigid bar supported and turning on a fixed point called the fulcrum, using force, or effort, at a second point to move or lift a mass situated at a third point: *A wheelbarrow is one kind of lever.*
—*v.* **1** pry, raise, or move with or as if with a lever: *She levered the rock out of the ground.* **2** use a lever or levers: *He levered for weeks and finally got the job.* [ME < OF *leveor* < *lever* raise < L *levare*]

lev·er·age (lē′vər ij *or* lev′ər ij) *n.* **1** the action of a lever. **2** the advantage or power gained by using a lever. **3** increased power of action.

lev·er·et (lev′ər it) *n.* a young hare. [< AF *leveret,* dim. of OF *lievre* < L *lepus, -poris* hare]

le·vi·a·than (lə vī′ə thən) *n.* **1** in the Bible, a huge sea animal. **2** a huge ship. **3** any great and powerful person or thing. [< LL < Hebrew *livyathan* dragon]

le·vis (lē′vīz) *n.pl.* **1** tight-fitting, heavy trousers of blue denim reinforced at strain points with copper rivets and extra stitching. **2 Levis,** *Trademark.* a brand of such trousers. [originally, *Levi's* < *Levi* Strauss and Company, an early manufacturer of overalls]

lev·i·tate (lev′ə tāt′) *v.* **-tat·ed, -tat·ing.** **1** rise or float in the air. **2** cause to rise or float in the air. [< L *levitas* lightness (See LEVITY), modelled after *gravitate*]

lev·i·ta·tion (lev′ə tā′shən) *n.* **1** a levitating. **2** the act or process of rising, or raising (a body), from the ground by spiritualistic means.

Le·vite (lē′vīt) *n.* a member of the tribe of Levi, from which assistants to the Jewish priests were chosen.

Le·vit·i·cal (lə vit′ə kəl) *adj.* **1** of the Levites. **2** of Leviticus or the law contained in it.

Le·vit·i·cus (lə vit′ə kəs) *n.* the third book of the Bible containing the laws for the priests and Levites and the ritual for Jewish rites and ceremonies. [< LL *Leviticus* (*liber*) (The Book) of the Levites < Gk. *Leuitikos* < *Leuitēs* Levite]

lev·i·ty (lev′ə tē) *n., pl.* **-ties.** lack of seriousness; lightness of spirit or mind, especially when excessive or not appropriate; frivolity: *The issue is a serious one and should not be treated with levity.* [< L *levitas* < *levis* light]

lev·u·lose (lev′yə lōs′) *n.* a form of sugar in honey, fruits, etc.; fruit sugar. Formula: $C_6H_{12}O_6$ [< L *laevus* left; under polarized light its plane of polarization is turned to the left]

lev·y (lev′ē) *v.* **lev·ied, lev·y·ing;** *n., pl.* **lev·ies.** —*v.* **1** order to be paid: *The government levies taxes to pay its expenses.* **2** draft or enlist for an army: *to levy troops in time of war.* **3** seize by law for unpaid debts.
levy war on, make war on; start a war against.
—*n.* **1** money collected by authority or force. **2** the troops drafted or enlisted for an army. **3** an act of levying. [< F *levée* < *lever* raise. See LEVEE[1].]

lewd (lüd) *adj.* **1** showing or designed to arouse sexual desire, especially in a coarse or offensive way; obscene: *a lewd glance, lewd pictures.* **2** *Archaic.* uneducated; ignorant. [OE *lǣwede* laic] —**lewd′ly,** *adv.* —**lewd′ness,** *n.*

lew·is·ite (lü′is īt′) *n.* a colorless or brown, oily liquid, developed for use in chemical warfare as a poison gas. It causes severe blistering of the skin and lungs. Formula: $C_2H_2AsCl_3$ [< *lewis* (W. Lee Lewis, 1878-1943, an American chemist) + *-ite*[1]]

lex (leks) *n., pl.* **le·ges** (leg′ās *or* lej′ās). *Latin.* law.

lex·i·cal (lek′sə kəl) *adj.* **1** of or having to do with words as separate units, rather than as elements of phrases, sentences, etc. **2** of or having to do with lexicography or a lexicon.

lex·i·cog·ra·pher (lek′sə kog′rə fər) *n.* a person who compiles dictionaries. [< Gk. *lexikographos* < *lexikon* wordbook + *graphein* write]

lex·i·co·graph·ic (lek′sə kə graf′ik) *adj.* lexicographical.

lex·i·co·graph·i·cal (lek′sə kə graf′ə kəl) *adj.* of or having to do with lexicography. —**lex·i·co·graph′i·cal·ly,** *adv.*

lex·i·cog·ra·phy (lek′sə kog′rə fē) *n.* the science or practice of compiling dictionaries.

lex·i·col·o·gist (lek′sə kol′ə jist) *n.* an expert in lexicology.

lex·i·col·o·gy (lek'sə kol'ə jē) *n.* the study of the history, form, and meaning of words. [< Gk. *lexikon* word + E *-logy*]

lex·i·con (lek'sə kən *or* lek'sə kon') *n.* **1** a dictionary, especially of Greek, Latin, or Hebrew. **2** the total vocabulary of a particular speaker or writer or of a particular subject. **3** the inventory, or total stock, of morphemes in a language. [< Gk. *lexikon* (*biblion*) wordbook < *lexis* word < *legein* say]

Ley·den jar (lī'dən) a device for collecting and storing an electric charge, consisting of a glass jar coated inside and outside with metal foil almost to the top, and having a conducting rod connected to the inner coating and passing up through an insulating stopper. [< *Leyden*, *Leiden*, Netherlands]

LF, L.F., *or* **l.f.** low frequency.

lg. *or* **lge.** large.

l.g. left guard.

LG Low German.

L.Gen. *or* **LGen** lieutenant-general.

LGk. Late Greek.

l.h. *or* **L.H.** left hand.

Lha·sa ap·so (lä'sə ap'sō) a Tibetan breed of small watchdog having a heavy, usually light brown, coat and much hair over the eyes. [< *Lhasa*, the capital of Tibet + Tibetan *apso* watchdog]

Li lithium.

L.I. Long Island.

li·a·bil·i·ty (lī'ə bil'ə tē) *n., pl.* **-ties. 1** the state of being susceptible: *liability to disease.* **2** the state of being under obligation: *liability for a debt.* **3** Usually, **liabilities,** *pl.* debts: *The monthly statement shows the company's assets and liabilities.* **4** a person or thing that acts as a disadvantage: *Her short temper is a liability in dealing with people.*

li·a·ble (lī'ə bəl *or, for def. 1,* lī'bəl) *adj.* **1** likely, especially unpleasantly likely: *Glass is liable to break. One is liable to slip on ice.* **2** in danger of having, doing, etc.: *We are all liable to diseases.* **3** legally responsible or answerable: *The Post Office is not liable for damage to an uninsured parcel. The defendant in a civil action may be found liable and ordered to pay damages.* **4** under obligation; subject: *Citizens are liable to jury duty.* [< F *lier* bind < L *ligare*]
➥ *Usage.* See note at **likely.**

li·aise (lē āz') *v.* **-aised, -ais·ing.** act as liaison officer or establish liaison (*with*): *An envoy liaises with a foreign government.* [back formation from *liaison*]
➥ *Usage.* Many people consider **liaise** to be jargon, unacceptable in good usage.

li·ai·son (lē ā'zon, lē'ā zon', *or* lē'ə zon') *n.* **1** communication in order to co-ordinate activities between parts of a whole, such as parts of a military unit, schools in a system, or departments within a government. **2** any close bond or connection. **3** an illicit love affair. **4** in speaking French, the pronouncing of a usually silent final consonant when it occurs before a word beginning with a vowel sound. The consonant is spoken as though it belonged to the second word. *Example: Comment allez-vous?* (ko mäN ta lä vü'). [< F < L *ligatio, -onis* < *ligare* bind]

liaison officer a person, especially an officer in the armed forces, who acts as a go-between to ensure proper co-operation between departments, units, etc.

li·a·na (lē ä'nə *or* lē an'ə) *n.* any of various woody vines found in tropical rain forests, that are rooted in the ground and twine around the trunks of trees, etc. for support. Some lianas may be 60 cm in diameter and reach a length of 100 metres, climbing from tree to tree. [< F *liane,* earlier *liorne*]

li·ane (lē än') *n.* liana.

li·ar (lī'ər) *n.* a person who tells lies; a person who says what is not true.

li·ard (lē'ärd, lē är', *or* lē ärd') *n.* Cdn. especially in the North, the balsam poplar; tacamahac. [< Cdn.F < OF *liard* gray]

lib (lib) *n. Informal.* liberation: *women's lib, kids' lib.*

lib. **1** librarian; library. **2** book (for L *liber*).

Lib. Liberal.

li·ba·tion (lī bā'shən) *n.* **1** a pouring out of wine, water, etc. as an offering to a god. **2** the wine, water, etc. offered in this way. [< L *libatio, -onis* < *libare* pour out]

li·bel (lī'bəl) *n., v.* **-belled** *or* **-beled, -bel·ling** *or* **-bel·ing.** —*n.* **1** *Law.* **a** a written or published statement, picture, etc. tending to damage a person's reputation. **b** the act or criminal offence of writing or publishing a libel. **2** any false or damaging statement about a person. —*v.* **1** write or publish a libel about. **2** make false or

damaging statements about. [< L *libellus,* dim. of *liber* book]
—**li'bel·ler** *or* **li'bel·er,** *n.*

li·bel·lous *or* **li·bel·ous** (lī'bəl əs) *adj.* **1** containing a libel. **2** spreading libels: *a libellous tongue.* —**li'bel·lous·ly,** *adv.*

lib·er·al (lib'ər əl *or* lib'rəl) *adj., n.* —*adj.* **1** generous: *a liberal donation.* **2** plentiful; abundant: *He put in a liberal supply of coal for the winter.* **3** broad-minded; not narrow in one's ideas: *a liberal thinker.* **4** designed to broaden the mind in a general way; not professional or technical: *a liberal education.* **5** favoring or following the principles of liberalism. **6 Liberal,** of, having to do with, or belonging to a political party advocating or associated with moderate progress and reform. **b** in Canada, of, having to do with, or belonging to the Liberal Party. **7** giving the general thought, not a word-for-word rendering: *a liberal interpretation of the speaker's ideas.*
—*n.* **1** a person who favors or follows principles of liberalism. **2 Liberal, a** a member or supporter of a political party advocating or associated with moderate progress and reform. **b** in Canada, of, having to do with, or belonging to the Liberal Party. [< L *liberalis* befitting free men < *liber* free] —**lib'er·al·ly,** *adv.* —**lib'er·al·ness,** *n.*

liberal arts subjects such as literature, languages, history, and philosophy as distinct from technical or professional subjects.

liberal education an education in the liberal arts, especially as distinct from a technical or professional education.

lib·er·al·ism (lib'ər əl iz'əm *or* lib'rəl iz'əm) *n.* **1** a political philosophy that emphasizes belief in progress, individual freedom, and a democratic form of government. **2** the quality or state of being liberal. **3 Liberalism.** the principles and practices of a Liberal political party.

lib·er·al·ist (lib'ər əl ist *or* lib'rəl ist) *n.* a person who holds liberal principles and ideas; a believer in progress and reforms.

lib·er·al·i·ty (lib'ər al'ə tē) *n., pl.* **-ties. 1** generosity; generous behavior. **2** gift. **3** broad-mindedness.

lib·er·al·ize (lib'ər əl īz' *or* lib'rəl īz') *v.* **-ized, -iz·ing.** make or become liberal. —**lib'er·al·i·za'tion,** *n.* —**lib'er·al·iz'er,** *n.*

liberal party 1 Liberal Party, one of the principal political parties of Canada. **2** a political party in certain other countries, usually one having moderately progressive policies.

lib·er·ate (lib'ər āt') *v.* **-at·ed, -at·ing. 1** set free. **2** *Chemistry.* set free from combination: *liberate a gas.* [< L *liberare* < *liber* free]
—**lib'er·a'tor,** *n.*

lib·er·a·tion (lib'ər ā'shən) *n.* **1** the act or process of liberating. **2** the state of being liberated. **3** the act or process of gaining equal social and economic status and rights: *women's liberation.*

Li·be·ri·an (lī bēr'ē ən) *n., adj.* —*n.* a native or inhabitant of Liberia, a country in W Africa. —*adj.* of or having to do with Liberia or its people.

lib·er·tar·i·an (lib'ər ter'ē ən) *n., adj.* —*n.* **1** one who advocates full civil liberty in thought and action. **2** one who advocates freedom of the will. **3 Libertarian,** a member or supporter of a Canadian political party advocating maximum individual freedom and minimum governmental control.
—*adj.* **1** of, having to do with, or being a libertarian. **2 Libertarian,** of or having to do with the Libertarians or their party.

lib·er·tar·i·an·ism (lib'ər ter'ē ə niz'əm) *n.* the doctrine or principles of libertarians.

lib·er·tine (lib'ər tēn') *n.* **1** a person who lives without regard to convention or accepted moral standards, especially a man who leads a dissolute, immoral life; rake. **2** (*adj.*) of, having to do with, or characteristic of such a person. **3** a freedman in ancient Rome. [< L *libertinus* freedman < *libertus* made free < *liber* free]

lib·er·tin·ism (lib'ər tēn iz'əm *or* lib'ər tin iz'əm) *n.* the behavior of a libertine.

lib·er·ty (lib'ər tē) *n., pl.* **-ties. 1** freedom; independence: *The prisoner yearned for liberty. The colony finally won its liberty.* **2** the right or power to do as one pleases; power or opportunity to do something: *liberty of speech or action.* **3** the leave granted to a sailor to go ashore. **4** the right of being in, using, etc.: *We give our dog the liberty of the yard.* **5** a privilege or right granted by a government. **6** too great freedom: *The author took liberties with the facts to make the story more interesting.*
at liberty, a free: *The escaped lion is still at liberty.* **b** allowed; permitted: *You are at liberty to make any choice you please.* **c** not busy: *The principal will see you as soon as he is at liberty.*
take liberties, be too familiar: *The soldiers soon gave up trying to take liberties with their new sergeant.*
[ME < OF < L *libertas* < *liber* free]
➥ *Syn.* **1.** See note at **freedom.**

Liberty Ship a cargo ship carrying about 10 000 gross tonnes, built in large numbers by the United States during the second World War.

li·bid·i·nous (lə bid′ə nəs) *adj.* lustful; lewd. [< L *libidinosus* < *libido*. See LIBIDO.] —**li·bid′i·nous·ly,** *adv.* —**li·bid′i·nous·ness,** *n.*

li·bi·do (lə bē′dō) *n.* **1** sexual desire or instinct. **2** emotional or mental drive or energy in general. [< L *libido* desire < *libere* be pleasing]

Li·bra (lī′brə) *n.* **1** *Astronomy.* a southern constellation thought of as having the shape of a pair of scales. **2** *Astrology.* **a** the seventh sign of the zodiac. The sun enters Libra about September 23. See **zodiac** for picture. **b** a person born under this sign. [< L *libra* a balance].

li·brar·i·an (lī brer′ē ən) *n.* **1** a person trained in library science, especially one whose work it is. **2** a person in charge of a library.

li·brar·y (lī′brer′ē *or* lī′brə rē) *n., pl.* **-brar·ies.** **1** a room or building where a collection of books, periodicals, phonograph records, tapes, etc. is kept to be used, rented, or borrowed, but not sold. **2** a collection of books, periodicals, etc., especially a large collection that is systematically arranged: *They have an extensive library of rare books.* [< L *librarium* bookcase < *liber* book]

library science the principles and practice of library organization and management.

li·bret·tist (lə bret′ist) *n.* the writer of a libretto.

li·bret·to (lə bret′ō) *n., pl.* **-tos. 1** the words of an opera, oratorio, operetta, etc. **2** a book containing these words. [< Ital. *libretto,* dim. of *libro* book]

Lib·y·an (lib′ē ən *or* lib′yən) *n., adj.* —*n.* **1** a native or inhabitant of Libya, a country in N Africa. **2** the Berber language of ancient Libya. —*adj.* **1** of or having to do with Libya or its people. **2** of or having to do with ancient Libya, which consisted of N Africa west of Egypt.

lice (līs) *n.* pl. of **louse.**

li·cence (lī′səns) *n.* **1** permission given by law to do something. **2** the paper, card, plate, etc. showing such permission: *The barber hung his licence on the wall.* **3** the fact or condition of being permitted to do something. **4** freedom of action, speech, thought, etc. that is permitted or conceded. Poetic licence is the freedom from rules that is permitted in poetry and art. **5** too much liberty; disregard of what is right and proper; abuse of liberty. Also, **license.** [ME < OF *licence* < L *licentia* < *licere* be allowed]

☛ *Spelling.* **Licence** is one of a few words that in Canadian English are usually spelled differently as nouns and verbs. The preferred spelling for the noun is **licence** and for the verb **license.** For this reason the noun and verb are entered separately in this dictionary.

li·cense *or* **li·cence** (lī′səns) *v.* **-censed** *or* **-cenced, -cens·ing** *or* **-cenc·ing. 1** give a licence to: *to license a new driver.* **2** permit or authorize, especially by law: *A doctor is licensed to practise medicine.* —**li′cens·er** *or* **li′cenc·er,** *n.*

☛ *Usage.* See note at **licence.**

li·censed *or* **li·cenced** (lī′sənst) *adj.* holding a government licence to sell alcoholic liquors for drinking on the premises: *a licensed restaurant. Beer parlors are licensed premises.*

li·cen·see (lī′sən sē′) *n.* a person to whom a licence is given.

li·cen·ti·ate (lī sen′shē it, lī sen′shē āt′, *or, esp. for def. 2,* lə sen′shē it) *n.* **1** a person who has a licence or permit to practise an art or profession. **2** in some European and French-Canadian universities, an academic degree ranking below the doctorate.

li·cen·tious (lī sen′shəs) *adj.* **1** disregarding commonly accepted moral principles, especially in sexual behavior; lewd. **2** *Archaic.* disregarding accepted rules or conventions; lawless. [< L *licentiosus* < *licentia.* See LICENSE.] —**li·cen′tious·ly,** *adv.* —**li·cen′tious·ness,** *n.*

li·chee (lē′chē) See **litchi.**

li·chen (lī′kən) *n.* any of a large group of complex plants made up of an alga and a fungus in a permanent symbiotic relationship, with alga cells interwoven with filaments of the fungus to form a plant body that may be crusty, scaly, or bushy, often resembling mosses. Lichens are classified mainly according to the type of fungus involved. [< L < Gk. *leichēn,* originally, what eats around itself < *leichein* lick]

☛ *Hom.* **liken.**

li·chen·ous (lī′kən əs) *adj.* of, like, or abounding in lichens.

lich–gate (lich′gāt′) *n.* a roofed gateway at the entrance to a churchyard where a coffin can be set down to await the clergyman's arrival. Also, **lych-gate.** [*lich,* OE *līc* body, corpse]

lic·it (lis′it) *adj.* lawful; permitted. [< L *licitus* < *licere* be allowed] —**lic′it·ly,** *adv.* —**lic′it·ness,** *n.*

lick (lik) *v., n.* —*v.* **1** pass the tongue over. **2** lap up with the tongue. **3** make or bring by using the tongue: *The cat licked the plate clean.* **4** pass about or play over as a tongue would: *The flames were licking the roof.* **5** *Informal.* beat; thrash. **6** *Informal.* defeat or overcome; conquer: *So far we've licked every problem without help. I could lick him with one hand tied behind my back.* **lick into shape,** *Informal.* make presentable or usable. —*n.* **1** a stroke of the tongue over something. **2** a place where

hat, āge, fär; let, ēqual, tėrm; it, īce
hot, ōpen, ôrder; oil, out; cup, pút, rüle,
əbove, takən, pencəl, lemən, circəs

ch, child; ng, long; sh, ship
th, thin; ŦH, then; zh, measure

natural salt is found and where animals go to lick it up. **3** *Informal.* a blow: *I lost the fight, but I got in a few good licks.* **4** a small quantity: *She didn't do a lick of work.* **5** *Informal.* a brief stroke of activity or effort: *a lick and a promise.* **6** *Informal.* **licks,** *pl.* opportunity; chance: *I'm sure you'll get your licks in later.* **7** *Informal.* speed; clip: *He came down the road at a great lick.* [OE *liccian*]

lick·er·ish (lik′ər ish) *adj. Archaic.* **1** fond of choice food. **2** greedy. **3** lecherous. [ME *lickerous* < an AF var. of OF *lecheros* lecherous < *lecheor.* See LECHER.]

☛ *Hom.* **licorice** (lik′ər ish).

lick·e·ty–split (lik′ət ē split′) *adv. Informal.* at a great speed; headlong: *She was off down the sidewalk lickety-split before they could stop her.*

lick·ing (lik′ing) *n. Informal.* **1** a thrashing or spanking. **2** a defeat or setback.

lick·spit·tle (lik′spit′əl) *n.* a contemptible flatterer; parasite.

lic·o·rice (lik′ə rish, lik′rish, *or* lik′ə ris) *n.* **1** a sweet, black, gummy substance obtained from the roots of a European plant (*Glycyrrhiza glabra*) of the pea family, used as a flavoring and as a laxative. **2** candy flavored with this substance. **3** the plant that yields this substance. **4** the dried root of this plant. Also, **liquorice.** [ME < AF *lycorys* < LL *liquiritia* < L *glycyrrhiza* < Gk. *glykyrrhiza* < *glykys* sweet + *rhiza* root]

☛ *Hom.* **lickerish** (lik′ar ish).

lic·tor (lik′tər) *n.* in ancient Rome, an attendant on a public official, who punished offenders at the official's orders. [< L *lictor,* related to *ligare* bind]

lid (lid) *n.* **1** a movable cover; top: *the lid of a box.* **2** the cover of skin that is moved in opening and shutting the eye; eyelid. **3** *Slang.* a hat; cap. **4** *Informal.* a restraint; check; curb: *put the lid on gambling.*
flip (one's) **lid,** *Slang.* get very excited.
[OE *hlid*]

L.I.D. Local Improvement District.

lid·less (lid′lis) *adj.* **1** having no lid. **2** having no eyelids. **3** *Poetic.* watchful.

lie¹ (lī) *n., v.* **lied, ly·ing.** —*n.* **1** a false statement, known to be false by the person who makes it. **2** something intended to give a false impression. **3** a false statement.
give the lie to, a call a liar; accuse of lying. **b** show to be false.
—*v.* **1** tell lies. **2** get, bring, put, etc. by lying: *lie oneself out of a difficulty.* **3** make a false statement. [OE *lyge,* n., *lēogan,* v.]
☛ *Hom.* **lye.**

☛ *Syn. n.* **1. Lie, falsehood, fib** = an untruthful statement. **Lie** applies to an untruthful statement deliberately made with the purpose of deceiving, sometimes of hurting, others: *Saying that his friend had stolen the money was a lie.* **Falsehood** refers to an untruthful statement made for a purpose, but can apply to one made when the truth would be undesirable or impossible: *Not wishing to hurt his sister's feelings, he told a falsehood and said he didn't know.* **Fib** means a lie or excusable falsehood about something unimportant: *Many children tell fibs.*

lie² (lī) *v.* **lay, lain, ly·ing;** *n.* —*v.* **1** have one's body in a flat position along the ground or on some other surface: *to lie on the grass.* **2** assume such a position: *to lie down on the couch.* **3** be in a horizontal or flat position: *The book was lying on the table.* **4** be kept or stay in a given position, state, etc.: *to lie idle.* **5** be; be placed: *The lake lies to the south of us.* **6** exist; be; have its place; belong: *The cure lies in education.* **7** be in the grave; be buried: *His body lies in Halifax.* **8** *Archaic.* spend the night; lodge.
lie in, be confined in childbirth.
lie off, of a ship, etc., stay not far from.
lie over, be left waiting until a later time.
lie to, of a ship, etc., come almost to a stop, facing the wind: *During the storm, the ship lay to.*
take (a thing) lying down, yield to (something); not to stand up to. —*n.* **1** the manner, position, or direction in which something lies. **2** the place where an animal is accustomed to lie or lurk. **3** *Golf.* the position of the ball after a drive, in regard to obstacles on the ground or accessibility to the green. [OE *licgan*]
☛ *Hom.* **lye.**
☛ *Usage.* See note at **lay¹.**

lie·der·kranz (lē′dər kränts′) *n.* **1** a smooth cheese with a strong odor. **2** **Liederkranz,** a trademark for this cheese. [< G *Liederkranz* garland or songs]

lief (lēf) *adv. Archaic.* willingly: *I'd as lief stay here.* Also, **lieve.** [OE *lēof* dear]
☞ *Hom.* leaf.

liege (lēj) *n., adj. Historical.* —*n.* in the Middle Ages: **1** a lord having a right to the homage and loyal service of his vassals. **2** a vassal obliged to give homage and loyal service to his lord. —*adj.* **1** having a right to the homage and loyal service of vassals. **2** obliged to give homage and loyal service to a lord. [ME < OF < LL *leticus* < *letus* freedman, ult. < Gmc.]

liege lord a feudal lord.

liege·man (lēj′mən) *n., pl.* **-men. 1** vassal. **2** a faithful follower.

lien (lēn *or* lē′ən) *n. Law.* a claim placed on the propery of another as a safeguard for payment of a debt in connection with that property. [< F < L *ligamen* bond < *ligare* bind]
☞ *Hom.* lean.

lie of the land 1 the natural features of a landscape. **2** the condition in which things are.

lieu (lū) *n. Archaic.* (except in **in lieu of**). place; stead.
in lieu of, in place of; instead of: *During the hard times they gave the landlord produce in lieu of money for rent.* [< F < L *locus*]

Lieut. lieutenant.

lieu·ten·an·cy (lef′ten′ən sē *or* lü ten′ən sē) *n., pl.* **-cies.** the rank, commission, or authority of a lieutenant.

lieu·ten·ant (lef ten′ənt; *esp.U.S.,* lü ten′ənt) *n.* **1** a person who acts for someone senior to him in authority: *He was one of the gang leader's lieutenants.* **2** *Canadian Forces.* **a** an officer ranking next above a second lieutenant and below a captain. *Abbrev.:* Lt. or Lt **b** in Maritime Command, the equivalent of a captain. *Abbrev.:* Lt.(N) or Lt(N) See chart at **rank**[1]. **3** an officer of similar rank in the armed forces of other countries. [< F *lieutenant* < *lieu* a place (< L *locus*) + *tenant,* ppr. of *tenir* hold < L *tenere.* 16c.]

lieutenant–colonel (lef ten′ənt kėr′nəl) *n.* an officer in the armed forces ranking next above a major and below a colonel. *Abbrev.:* L.Col., LCol, or Lt.Col. See chart at **rank**[1].

lieutenant commander 1 *Canadian Forces.* in Maritime Command, the equivalent of a major. See chart at **rank**[1]. **2** a naval officer of similar rank in other countries. *Abbrev.:* L.Cdr., LCdr, or Lt.Cdr.

lieutenant–general (lef ten′ənt jen′ər əl *or* -jen′rəl) *n.* an officer in the armed forces ranking next above a major general and below a general. *Abbrev.:* L.Gen., LGen, or Lt.Gen. See chart at **rank**[1].

lieutenant–governor (lef ten′ənt guv′ər nər; *Esp.U.S., for* 2, lü ten′ənt) *n.* **1** in Canada, the official head of a provincial government, appointed by the Governor General in Council, for a term of five years; representative of the Crown in a province. *Abbrev.:* Lt.Gov. **2** Often, **lieutenant governor,** a deputy governor.

lieve (lēv) *adv. Archaic.* lief.
☞ *Hom.* leave.

life (līf) *n., pl.* **lives. 1** living or being alive; the quality that people, animals, and plants have and that rocks, dirt, and metals lack. **2** the time of being alive: *a short life.* **3** the time of existence or action; a period of being in power, able to operate, etc.: *the short life of that government, the life of a battery, the life of a lease.* **4** a living being, especially a person: *Five lives were lost in the fire.* **5** living things considered together: *The desert island had almost no animal or vegetable life.* **6** a way of living: *a dull life.* **7** an account of a person's life; biography: *a life of Mackenzie King.* **8** spirit; vigor: *Put more life into your work.* **9** a source of activity or liveliness. **10** the living form or model, especially as represented in art: *The portrait was painted from life.*
as large or **as big as life, a** as big as the living person or thing. **b** in person.
for dear life, to save or as if to save one's life: *He ran for dear life.*
for life, a during the rest of one's life. **b** to save one's life.
for the life of me (or **him, her,** etc.), *Informal.* even if my (or his, her, etc.) life depended on it (*used only in negative expressions*): *I can't for the life of me remember where I put my keys.*
see life, *Informal.* get experience, especially of the exciting features of human activities.
take life, kill.
take (**one's**) **own life,** kill oneself.
to the life, like the model; exactly; perfectly.
true to life, true to reality; as in real life. [OE *līf*]

life and limb physical safety and survival: *The old bridge is a danger to life and limb.*

life belt a life preserver in the shape of a thick ring, worn around the chest and under the arms.

life·blood (līf′blud′) *n.* **1** blood necessary to life. **2** a source of strength and energy: *The young people became the lifeblood of the organization.*

life·boat (līf′bōt′) *n.* **1** a strong boat especially built for saving lives at sea or along the coast. **2** a boat carried on davits on a ship for use by passengers or crew in an emergency.

life buoy a life preserver (def. 1).

life·guard (līf′gärd′) *n.* a person who is trained in lifesaving and who is responsible for the safety of swimmers and bathers at a public pool or beach.

Life Guards two British cavalry regiments whose duty it is to guard the king and queen of England.

life insurance insurance that provides for the payment of a specified amount of money to a beneficiary or beneficiaries on the death of the insured, or, sometimes, to the insured when he reaches a certain age.

life jacket a life preserver in the form of a vest.

life·less (līf′lis) *adj.* **1** inanimate: *a lifeless statue.* **2** dead: *lifeless bodies on the battlefield.* **3** having no living things: *a lifeless planet.* **4** dull: *a lifeless performance.* —**life′less·ly,** *adv.* —**life′less·ness,** *n.*
☞ *Syn.* 2. See note at **dead.**

life·like (līf′līk′) *adj.* like life; looking as if alive; like the real thing: *a lifelike portrait.* —**life′like′ness,** *n.*

life line 1 a rope for saving life, such as one thrown to a ship from the shore. **2** a line across a deck or passageway of a ship to grab to prevent falling or being washed overboard. **3** a diver's signalling line. **4** anything that maintains or helps to maintain something that cannot exist by itself.

life·long (līf′long′) *adj.* lasting all one's life: *a lifelong friendship.*

life net a strong net or sheet of canvas, used especially to catch a person jumping from a burning building.

life peer *Brit.* a peer whose title is not hereditary.

life preserver 1 a device made of buoyant or inflatable material, designed to keep a person afloat in water to prevent drowning. It may be in the form of a vest, a wide belt, or a thick ring. **2** *Esp.Brit.* a short stick with a heavy head, used for self-defence.

lif·er (līf′ər) *n. Slang.* a convict in prison for life.

life raft an inflatable or wooden raft for saving lives in a shipwreck or from the wreck of an aircraft at sea.

life·sav·er (līf′sāv′ər) *n.* **1** a person or thing that saves people from drowning; especially, a lifeguard. **2** *Informal.* a person or thing that saves one from trouble, discomfort, embarrassment, etc.: *The interruption was a lifesaver, because I didn't know what to say to him any more.*

life·sav·ing (līf′sāv′ing) *n., adj.* —*n.* the skill, act, or practice of saving people's lives, especially by preventing drowning. —*adj.* designed for or having to do with saving people's lives: *lifesaving classes, lifesaving equipment.*

life–size (līf′sīz′) *adj.* having the same size as the living person, animal, etc.: *a life-size statue.*

life span the length of time that a person, animal, machine, institution, etc. continues or may be expected to continue to live or function.

life·style (līf′stīl′) *n.* a way of life; the typical habits, pastimes, attitudes, etc. of a person or group: *a casual lifestyle. Their downtown apartment suits their lifestyle.*

life·time (līf′tīm′) *n.* **1** the length of time that someone is alive or that something exists or functions: *In his whole lifetime he had never been in an airplane.* **2** (*adj.*) lasting for such a length of time: *a lifetime commitment.*

life·work (līf′wėrk′) *n.* work that takes or lasts a whole lifetime; main work in life.

lift (lift) *v., n.* —*v.* **1** raise; take up; raise into a higher position: *lift a chair.* **2** hold up; display on high. **3** raise in rank, condition, estimation, etc.; elevate; exalt. **4** rise and go; go away: *The fog lifted at dawn.* **5** go up; allow (itself, etc.) to be raised: *This window will not lift.* **6** pull or tug upward. **7** send up loudly: *lift a voice or cry.* **8** rise to view above the horizon. **9** tighten the skin and erase the wrinkles of (a person's face) through surgery. **10** take up out of the ground, as crops, treasure, etc. **11** *Informal.* pick or take up; steal: *lift things from a store.* **12** pay off: *lift a mortgage.*
—*n.* **1** an elevating influence. **2** the act of lifting. **3** the distance through which a thing is lifted. **4** a helping hand: *I gave him a lift with the heavy box.* **5** a ride in a vehicle given to a pedestrian or hiker; free ride: *He often gave the neighbor's boy a lift to school.* **6** *Esp.Brit.* elevator. **7** one of the layers of leather in the heel of a shoe. **8** a rise in ground. **9** elevated carriage (of the head, neck, eyes, etc.): *a haughty lift of the chin.* **10** an improvement in spirits: *The promotion gave him a lift.* **11** a cable or rope with seats or attachments for holding on to, to raise a skier to the top of a slope. **12** *Aeronautics.* **a** the force exerted on an airfoil by a flow of air over and around it acting perpendicular to the direction of flight.

b the upward tendency of an airship or balloon caused by the gas it contains. [ME < ON *lypta* to raise; akin to *lopt* air. See LOFT.] —**lift′er**, *n.*

☛ *Syn. v.* **1.** See note at **raise.**

lift lock a canal or river lock in which each water-filled compartment itself is hydraulically raised and lowered while the water level within the compartment remains the same.

lift-off (lift′ôf′) *n.* the vertical takeoff of an aircraft, rocket, etc.; the act or the moment of rising from the ground or launching pad.

lift pump a pump that lifts a liquid without forcing it out under pressure.

lig·a·ment (lig′ə mənt) *n.* **1** a band of strong tissue that connects bones or holds organs in place. **2** a tie; bond. [ME < L *ligamentum* < *ligare* bind]

li·gate (lī′gāt) *v.* **-gat·ed, -gat·ing.** bind; tie up: *ligate a bleeding artery.* [< L *ligare*] —**li·ga′tion,** *n.*

lig·a·ture (lig′ə chər *or* lig′ə chür′) *n., v.* **-tured, -tur·ing.** —*n.* **1** something used to bind or tie up, especially a thread or filament used in surgery to tie up a blood vessel, etc. **2** something that unites or connects; bond. **3** a binding or tying up. **4** *Music.* a slur or a group of notes connected by a slur. **5** *Printing.* two or three letters joined. Æ and *ffl* are ligatures.
—*v.* bind or tie up with a ligature. [ME < LL *ligatura* < L *ligare* bind]

light¹ (līt) *n., adj., v.* **light·ed** or **lit, light·ing.** —*n.* **1** that by which we see; the form of radiant energy that acts on the retina of the eye. **2** anything that gives light. The sun, a lamp, or a lighthouse is called a light. **3** a supply of light: *The tall building to the south of us cuts off our light.* **4** brightness; clearness; illumination: *a strong light, a dim light.* **5** a bright part: *light and shade.* **6** daytime. **7** dawn. **8** something by which to let light in, such as a window or a windowpane. **9** something with which to start something else burning. **10** knowledge; information; illumination of mind: *We need more light on this subject.* **11** public knowledge; open view. **12** the aspect in which a thing is viewed: *He put the matter in the right light.* **13** a shining figure; model; example: *The actor was a leading light in the theatre.* **14** favor; approval.
according to (one's) **lights,** following one's own ideas, intelligence, and conscience in the best way that one knows.
bring to light, reveal; expose: *Many facts were brought to light during the investigation.*
come to light, be revealed or exposed.
in the light of, a by considering. **b** from the standpoint of.
see the light, or **see the light of day, a** be born. **b** be made public. **c** get the right idea.
shed or **throw light on,** explain; make clear.
strike a light, make a light.
—*adj.* **1** having or much light: *a light room.* **2** bright; clear: *It is as light as day.* **3** pale in color; whitish: *light hair, light blue.*
—*v.* **1** cause to give light: *She lighted the lamp.* **2** give light to; provide with light: *The room is lighted by six windows.* **3** make or become bright: *Her face was lighted by a smile.* **4** become light: *The sky lights up at sunset.* **5** show the way by giving light: *His flashlight lighted us through the tunnel.* **6** set fire to: *She lighted the candles.* **7** take fire. [OE *lēoht*]
☛ *Usage.* **Lighted, lit.** Both forms are in good use as the past tense and past participle of *light. Lighted* is probably the form generally used as the adjective and past participle: *She carried a lighted lamp. He had lighted a fire. Lit* is perhaps more common as the past tense: *He lit a cigarette.*

light² (līt) *adj., adv.* —*adj.* **1** easy to carry; not heavy: *a light load.* **2** of little mass for its size: *a light metal.* **3** of less than usual mass: *light clothing.* **4** less than usual in amount, force, or strength: *a light meal, a light sleep, a light rain.* **5** easy to do or bear; not hard or severe: *light punishment, a light task.* **6** not looking heavy; graceful; delicate: *a light bridge, light carving.* **7** moving easily; nimble: *light on one's feet.* **8** cheerfully careless: *a light laugh, a light retort.* **9** not serious enough; fickle: *a light mind, light of purpose.* **10** aiming to entertain; not serious: *light reading.* **11** not important: *light losses.* **12** careless in morals. **13** not dense: *a light fog.* **14** porous; sandy: *a light soil.* **15** containing little alcohol: *a light wine.* **16** built small and without much weight; adapted for light loads and for swift movement: *a light truck.* **17** lightly armed or equipped: *light cavalry, in light marching order.*
light in the head, a dizzy. **b** silly; foolish. **c** crazy; out of one's head.
make light of, treat as of little importance.
—*adv.* **1** lightly. **2** with as little luggage as possible: *I like to travel light.* [OE *lēoht, līht*]

light³ (līt) *v.* **light·ed** or **lit, light·ing. 1** come down to the ground; alight: *He lighted from his horse.* **2** come down from flight: *A bird lighted on the branch.* **3** come by chance: *His eye lighted upon a familiar face in the crowd.* **4** fall suddenly: *The blow lit on his head.*
light into, *Slang.* **a** attack. **b** scold.
light out, *Slang.* leave suddenly; go away quickly.
[OE *līhtan < līht* light²]

light-armed (līt′ärmd′) *adj.* equipped with light weapons.

hat, āge, fär; let, ēqual, tèrm; it, īce
hot, ōpen, ôrder; oil, out; cup, pùt, rüle,
əbove, takən, pencəl, lemən, circəs
ch, child; ng, long; sh, ship
th, thin; ⫟н, then; zh, measure

light bulb a glass bulb containing a filament of very fine wire that becomes white hot and gives off light when an electric current flows through it.

light-e·mit·ting diode (līt′ē mit′ing) a semiconductor diode that emits light when voltage is applied, used especially for low-voltage displays of numerals, etc. in calculators and digital clocks and watches.

light·en¹ (līt′ən) *v.* **1** make or become bright or brighter: *Dawn lightens the sky. The sky gradually lightened.* **2** make or become pale or paler in color: *The summer sun lightened her hair.* **3** flash with lightning: *I just saw it lighten in the west.* [ME *lighten < light¹*]

light·en² (līt′ən) *v.* **1** reduce the load of (a ship, etc.); have the load reduced. **2** make or become less of a burden: *to lighten taxes.* **3** make or become more cheerful: *The good news lightened their hearts. His face lightened when he saw her.* [ME *lighten < light²*]

light·er¹ (līt′ər) *n.* a thing or person that starts something burning; especially, a device used to light a cigarette, cigar, or pipe. [ME *lighter < light¹, v.*]

light·er² (līt′ər) *n., v.* —*n.* a flat-bottomed barge used for loading and unloading ships. —*v.* carry (goods) in a flat-bottomed barge. [< *light²* or ? < Du. *lichter*]

light·er·age (līt′ər ij) *n.* **1** the loading, unloading, or carrying of goods in a lighter. **2** the charge for this.

light·face (līt′fās′) *n. Printing.* the type normally used in the body of a work; opposed to **boldface.** The definitions and illustrative phrases and sentences in this dictionary are printed in lightface.

light-fin·gered (līt′fing′gərd) *adj.* **1** thievish; skilful at picking pockets. **2** having nimble fingers.

light-foot (līt′fùt′) *adj. Poetic.* light-footed.

light-foot·ed (līt′fùt′id) *adj.* stepping lightly. —**light-foot′ed·ly,** *adv.* —**light′foot′ed·ness,** *n.*

light-head·ed (līt′hed′id) *adj.* **1** dizzy or giddy: *The fever was gone, but she still felt a little light-headed.* **2** not sensible; silly; frivolous. —**light′-head′ed·ly,** *adv.* —**light′-head′ed·ness,** *n.*

light-heart·ed (līt′här′tid) *adj.* carefree; cheerful; gay. —**light′-heart′ed·ly,** *adv.* —**light′-heart′ed·ness,** *n.*

light heavyweight a boxer who weighs between 76 and 81 kilograms.

light horse cavalry that carries light weapons and equipment.

light-horse·man (līt′hôrs′mən) *n., pl.* **-men.** a cavalryman who carries light weapons and equipment.

light·house (līt′hous′) *n.* a tower or framework with a bright light that shines far over the water. Lighthouses are usually located at dangerous places to warn and guide ships.

light infantry infantry that carries light arms and equipment.

light·ing (līt′ing) *n.* **1** the giving of light; providing with light. **2** the way in which lights are arranged. **3** a starting to burn.

light·ly (līt′lē) *adv.* **1** with little pressure, force, etc.; gently: *Her hand rested lightly on his arm. He held the bird lightly in his hand.* **2** to a small degree or extent: *lightly clad.* **3** quickly or easily: *She jumped lightly aside.* **4** cheerfully: *take bad news lightly.* **5** indifferently or carelessly: *The issue is too important to be passed over lightly.*

light meter a device for measuring the intensity of light, especially an exposure meter: *Some cameras have a built-in light meter.*

light-mind·ed (līt′mīn′did) *adj.* not serious; thoughtless and frivolous. —**light′-mind′ed·ly,** *adv.* —**light′-mind′ed·ness,** *n.*

light·ness¹ (līt′nis) *n.* **1** the quality or state of being bright or clear: *The lightness of the sky showed that the rain was over.* **2** the quality or state of being pale or light in color: *He has to be careful in the sun because of the lightness of his skin.* [OE *līhtnes < lēoht* light¹]

light·ness² (līt′nis) *n.* **1** the quality or state of having little mass; not being heavy: *The lightness of the second load was a relief after the first one he had carried.* **2** lack of severity; leniency: *The lightness of the sentence surprised the defendant.* **3** a lack of pressure or force; delicacy: *the lightness of a touch.* **4** cheerfulness or gaiety: *lightness of spirits.* **5** gracefulness or nimbleness: *the lightness of a step.* **6** a lack of proper seriousness: *Such lightness of conduct is not to be permitted in a courtroom.* [< *light²*]

light·ning (līt′ning) *n.* **1** a flash of light in the sky caused by a discharge of electricity between clouds, or between a cloud and the earth's surface. **2** (*adj.*) like lightning; very fast or sudden: *a lightning decision, a lightning change of mood.* [< *lighten*[1]]

lightning bug firefly.

lightning rod a metal rod fixed on a building or ship to conduct lightning into the earth or water to prevent fire.

light·proof (līt′prüf′) that will not let light in; sealed so that no light can enter: *A camera must be lightproof.*

lights (līts) *n.pl.* the lungs of sheep, pigs, etc. [so called because of their light weight]

light·ship (līt′ship′) *n.* a ship with a bright light that shines far over the water, anchored at a dangerous place to warn and guide ships.

light·some (līt′səm) *adj.* **1** nimble and lively: *lightsome feet.* **2** carefree; cheerful: *a lightsome heart.* **3** frivolous.

light·weight (līt′wāt′) *n., adj.* —*n.* **1** a person or thing of less than average mass. **2** a boxer weighing 58 and 60 kilograms. **3** a person of little importance or influence: *He is regarded as a lightweight in the literary world.*
—*adj.* **1** having less than the average or usual mass: *a lightweight portable sewing machine.* **2** of, having to do with, or characteristic of lightweights: *the lightweight boxing championship.*

light–year (līt′yēr′) *n. Astronomy.* a unit of distance equal to the distance that light travels in one year in a vacuum, about 9 460 500 000 000 km. The nearest star is more than four light-years away.

lig·ne·ous (lig′nē əs) *adj.* of or like wood; woody. [< L *ligneus* < *lignum* wood]

lig·nin (lig′nən) *n.* a complex polymer which, together with cellulose, makes up the woody tissues of plants.

lig·nite (lig′nīt) *n.* a very soft, brownish-black type of coal containing less carbon and more water than bituminous coal and often having a woody texture. Lignite is a poor quality, imperfectly formed coal, intermediate between peat and bituminous coal. [< F < L *lignum* wood]

lig·num vi·tae (lig′nəm vī′tē or vē′tī) **1** either of two tropical American trees (*Guaiacum officinale* or *G. sanctum*) having very heavy, hard, olive-brown wood. **2** the wood of either of these trees, highly valued for making pulleys, bearings, casters, etc. Lignum vitae is very resinous and so dense that it will not float in water. [< L *lignum vitae* wood of life; from its supposed medicinal value]

lig·ro·in (lig′rō ən) *n.* benzine.

Li·gu·ri·an (li gyü′rē ən) *n., adj.* —*n.* a native or inhabitant of Liguria, a district in NW Italy. —*adj.* of Liguria or its people.

lik·a·ble (līk′ə bəl) *adj.* having qualities that win good will or friendship; popular: *a likable person.* —**lik′a·ble·ness,** *n.* —**lik′a·bly,** *adv.*

like[1] (līk) *prep., adj.* **lik·er, lik·est;** *conj., n., adv., v.* **liked, lik·ing.** *Poetic.* —*prep.* **1** having the characteristics of; resembling; similar to: *Mary is like her sister. I never saw anything like it.* **2** in the same way as; in the manner of; similarly to: *She can run like a deer. He acted like a tyrant.* **3** such as one would expect; typical of: *Isn't that just like him?* **4** in the right state or frame of mind for doing or having: *He felt like working. I feel like a cup of coffee.* **5** indicative or giving promise of: *It looks like rain.* **6** such as; as for example: *They offer technical courses like mechanics, drafting, and plumbing.* **like crazy, mad,** etc. *Informal.* very much; to a great degree; with great speed, effort, or intensity: *She works like crazy.*
nothing like, not nearly: *It's nothing like as cold as it was yesterday.*
something like, about or almost like: *The tune goes something like this.*
—*adj.* **1** of the same or nearly the same form, kind, appearance, amount, etc.; similar: *Suzanne's uncle promised her $20 if she could earn a like sum.* **2** *Archaic.* likely: *The king is sick and like to die.*
—*conj. Informal.* **1** like as; as: *He reacted just like I did when I first saw it.* **2** as if: *It looks like we'll have to do it ourselves.*
—*n.* a person or thing like another; counterpart or equal; match: *We will not see his like again. They had never seen the like before.*
and the like, and similar things; and so forth: *He studied music, painting, and the like.*
—*adv.* **1** *Informal.* probably: *Like enough it will rain.* **2** *Archaic.* in the same manner or to the same extent or degree.
—*v.* **1** *Obsolete.* compare. **2** *Dialect.* come near: *I was so mad I like to walked out.* [OE *(ge)līc*]
☞ *Usage.* In standard written English, a distinction is made between the use of **like** and **as. As** and **as if** are used as conjunctions to introduce clauses of comparison: *He still writes as he used to when he was a child. Act as if you were familiar with the place.* **Like** is used as a preposition in phrases of comparison: *She swims like a fish. He writes like a child.* In informal English, however, **like** is often used in place of **as** to introduce clauses: *He writes like he used to when he was a child.*

like[2] (līk) *v.* **liked, lik·ing;** *n.* —*v.* **1** be pleased or satisfied with; enjoy: *Do you like milk? He likes the job but not the salary.* **2** have a friendly feeling toward; feel an attraction toward: *They like their new math teacher.* **3** wish for; want (used with **would**): *I would like a glass of milk, please. I'd like to get my hands on whoever took my bike.* **4** be inclined; choose: *Come whenever you like.*
—*n.* **likes,** *pl.* likings; preferences: *My mother knows most of my likes and dislikes.* [OE *līcian* to please]
☞ *Usage.* **Like, love** are not interchangeable. **Like** = find pleasure or satisfaction in something or someone, or have friendly feelings for a person, but does not suggest strong feelings or emotion: *I like books. Boys like to play.* **Love** emphasizes strong feelings and deep attachment, and is used to express the emotion of love: *She loves her mother. He loves music.* But *love* is often used informally instead of *like* in an intensified sense.

–like *adjective-forming suffix.* **1** like: *wolflike = like a wolf.* **2** like that of; characteristic of: *childlike = like that of a child.* **3** suited to; fit or proper for: *businesslike = suited to business.* [< *like*[1], adj.]
☞ *Usage.* **-like** is a living suffix that can be freely added to nouns to form adjectives.

like·a·ble (līk′ə bəl) *adj.* likable. —**like′a·ble·ness,** *n.* —**like′a·bly,** *adv.*

like·li·hood (līk′lē hüd′) *n.* probability: *Is there any likelihood of rain this afternoon?*

like·ly (līk′lē) *adj.* **-li·er, -li·est;** *adv.* —*adj.* **1** probable: *One likely result of the heavy rains is a flood.* **2** to be expected: *It is likely to be hot in August.* **3** suitable: *Is there a likely place to fish?* **4** promising: *a likely boy.*
—*adv.* probably: *I'll very likely be home all day.* [< ON *likligr*]
☞ *Usage.* **Likely, apt, liable.** The principal meanings of these words are—**likely:** expected, probable; **liable:** possible (of an unpleasant event), responsible (as for damages); **apt:** tending toward, naturally fit. **Likely** is the most commonly needed of the three, and informally both **apt** and (in some localities) **liable** are used in the ordinary sense of **likely:** *It's likely* (or *apt* or, locally, *liable*) *to rain when the wind is southwest.* In general, **liable** is best used when the reference is to something happening to someone or something: *He is liable to be blamed for the accident.*

lik·en (līk′ən) *v.* represent or describe as like; compare: *The poet likens life to a dream.*
☞ *Hom.* **lichen.**

like·ness (līk′nis) *n.* **1** a resemblance; being alike: *There is a strong likeness between the boy and his father.* **2** something that is like; a copy or representation, especially a painting, drawing, or photograph: *The portrait is a good likeness of her.* **3** the appearance or shape: *The wizard assumed the likeness of a very old man.*

like·wise (līk′wīz′) *adv.* **1** the same; in the same way: *See what I do. Now do likewise.* **2** also; moreover; too: *He was a painter, a sculptor, and likewise a writer.*

lik·ing (līk′ing) *n.* **1** a preference or taste: *He had a liking for apples.* **2** a fondness or kindly feeling: *She had a liking for children.* **3** taste; pleasure: *food to your liking.* [OE *līcung < līcian* to please]

li·ku·ta (lē kü′tä) *n., pl.* **ma·ku·ta** (mä kü′tä). **1** a unit of money in Zaire, equal to ¹⁄₁₀₀ of a zaire. **2** a coin worth one likuta.

li·lac (lī′lək or lī′lok) *n., adj.* —*n.* **1** any of various shrubs or small trees (genus *Syringa*) of the olive family, especially a European species (*S. vulgaris*) widely cultivated in temperate regions for its showy erect clusters of fragrant light to dark purple, pink, or white, spring-blooming flowers. **2** pale to medium purple.
—*adj.* having the color lilac. [< F < Sp. < Arabic < Persian *lilak* < *nil* indigo < Skt. *nila*]

Lil·ith (lil′ith or lī′lith) *n.* **1** in early Semitic legend, a female demon or vampire, believed to live in deserted places and to prey on children. **2** in medieval Jewish folklore, the first wife of Adam, ousted by Eve.

Lil·li·put (lil′ə put′) *n.* an imaginary island described in *Gulliver's Travels,* by Jonathan Swift. The island was inhabited by tiny people about 15 cm tall.

Lil·li·pu·tian (lil′ə pyü′shən) *adj., n.* —*adj.* **1** of or suitable for Lilliput. **2** very small; tiny; petty. —*n.* **1** an inhabitant of Lilliput. **2** a very small person; dwarf.

lilt (lilt) *v., n.* —*v.* sing or play (a tune) in a light, tripping manner. —*n.* **1** a lively song or tune with a swing. **2** a way of speaking in which the pitch of the voice varies in a pleasing manner: *He talks with an Irish lilt.* **3** a lively, springy movement. [ME *lulte,* ult. origin uncertain]

lil·y (lil′ē) *n., pl.* **lil·ies. 1** any of a genus (*Lilium*) of plants that grow from bulbs, having leafy stems and showy flowers. The prairie lily is the provincial flower of Saskatchewan. The Madonna lily is the provincial flower of Quebec. **2** any of various other plants of the same family having similar flowers: *The glacier lily is a common wildflower of the Rockies.* **3** (*adj.*) designating a family (Liliaceae) of plants that includes the lilies, as well as trilliums, hyacinths, tulips, onions, etc. **4** any of various other plants having showy flowers, such as the calla lily and water lily. **5** the flower of a lily. **6** the fleur-de-lis as a heraldic emblem. **7** (*adj.*) like a lily in being white or pale, fragile, pure, etc.: *her lily hands.*

gild the lily, try to improve on something that is already excellent or completely satisfactory.
[OE *lilie* < L *lilium* (akin to Gk. *leirion*)] —**lil′y-like′,** *adj.*

lil·y–liv·ered (lil′ē liv′ərd) *adj.* cowardly.

lily of the valley *pl.* **lilies of the valley.** a low-growing perennial plant (*Convallaria majalis*) of the lily family having small, bell-shaped, fragrant, white flowers growing on short stems along a main stem.

lily pad one of the large, round, floating leaves of a water lily.

li·ma bean (lī′mə) **1** any of several cultivated varieties of a tropical American bean (*Phaseolus lunatus*) having broad pods that contain broad, flat, light-green seeds. **2** the seed of this plant, used as food.

limb (lim) *n.* **1** a leg, arm, or wing. **2** a large branch of a tree; bough: *They sawed off the dead limb.* **3** the part that projects: *the four limbs of a cross.* **4** a person or thing thought of as a part, member, representative, etc.
out on a limb, in or into a dangerous or exposed position: *The producer of the play was left out on a limb when his backers suddenly withdrew their support.*
tear limb from limb, tear (a body) violently apart; dismember violently.
[OE *lim*] —**limb′less,** *adj.*
☛ *Syn.* n. **2.** See note at **branch.**

lim·ber¹ (lim′bər) *adj., v.* —*adj.* bending easily; flexible: *A pianist has to have limber fingers.* —*v.* make or become supple or more easily flexed (*used with* **up**): *We did some exercises to limber up before the game.* [? < *limp²* or *limb*] —**lim′ber·ness,** *n.*
☛ *Syn. adj.* See note at **flexible.**

lim·ber² (lim′bər) *n.* the detachable front part of the carriage of a field gun. [? < F *limonière* wagon with shafts < *limon* shaft]

lim·bo¹ (lim′bō) *n.* **1** Often, **Limbo.** *Roman Catholic theology.* a place for those who have not received the grace of Christ while living, and yet have not deserved the punishment of willful and impenitent sinners. **2** a condition or place of neglect or disregard: *The belief that the earth is flat belongs to the limbo of outworn ideas.* **3** an indefinite or intermediate condition or place: *He was left in limbo for some time before he was told he definitely had the job.* **4** prison or confinement. [< L (*in*) *limbo* on the edge]

lim·bo² (lim′bō) *n.* a dance that originated in the West Indies, in which dancers bend over backwards from the knees and pass under a low bar with only their feet touching the ground. The bar is brought lower for each pass a dancer makes.

Lim·burg·er (lim′bèr gər) *n.* a soft cheese made from whole milk and having a strong odor. [< *Limbourg*, a province of Belgium]

lime¹ (līm) *n., v.* **limed, lim·ing.** —*n.* **1** a white substance obtained by burning limestone, shells, bones, etc.; calcium oxide, quicklime. Lime is used to make mortar and on fields to improve soil. *Formula:* CaO **2** birdlime.
—*v.* **1** put lime on. **2** smear (branches, etc.) with birdlime. **3** catch (birds) with birdlime. [OE *līm*]

lime² (līm) *n.* **1** a tropical and subtropical citrus tree (*Citrus aurantifolia*) bearing small, round or oval fruit with a green rind and yellowish-green, fleshy, very acid pulp. **2** the fruit of this tree. Limes are used for flavoring food and drinks and as a source of vitamin C. **3** a soft drink flavored with the juice of limes or a substitute. [< F < Sp. < Arabic *lima*. Akin to LEMON.]

lime³ (līm) *n.* linden, especially the European linden. [var. of earlier *line* < OE *lind*]

lime·ade (līm′ād) *n.* a soft drink made of lime juice, sugar, and water.

lime·kiln (līm′kiln′ *or* -kil′) *n.* a furnace for making lime by burning limestone, shells, etc.

lime·light (līm′līt′) *n.* **1** an intense white light produced by heating lime, formerly used as a stage spotlight in theatres. **2** the centre of public attention and interest: *Some politicians try to avoid the limelight.*

lim·er·ick (lim′ər ik′ *or* lim′rik) *n.* a kind of humorous poem consisting of five lines, with the first two lines rhyming with the last, and the third and fourth rhyming with each other. *Example:*
There was a young lady from Lynn
Who was so exceedingly thin
That when she essayed
To drink lemonade
She slid down the straw and fell in.
[apparently from a song about *Limerick*, Irish Republic]

lime·stone (līm′stōn′) *n.* rock formed mainly from organic remains, such as shells or coral, and consisting mostly of calcium carbonate, used for building and for making lime. Marble is a kind of limestone.

lime·wa·ter (līm′wot′ər *or* -wô′tər) *n.* a solution of slaked lime (calcium hydroxide) in water, used to counteract an acid condition.

lim·ey *or* **Lim·ey** (lī′mē) *n., adj. Slang.* —*n.* **1** Englishman.

---

hat, āge, fär; let, ēqual, tèrm; it, īce
hot, ōpen, ôrder; oil, out; cup, pùt, rüle,
above, takən, pencəl, lemən, circəs

ch, child; ng, long; sh, ship
th, thin; ͭH, then; zh, measure

2 an English sailor or soldier. **3** an English ship.
—*adj.* English. [< *limejuicer*, from the former use of lime juice on British ships to prevent scurvy]

lim·it (lim′it) *n., v.* —*n.* **1** the farthest point or edge; where something ends or must end: *the limit of one's vision. I have reached the limit of my patience.* **2** *Mathematics.* a value toward which terms of a sequence, values of a function, etc. approach indefinitely near. **3** in betting games, the agreed maximum amount of any bet or raise. **4** *Logging. Cdn.* a concession; timber limit. **5** **limits,** *pl.* **a** boundary; bounds: *Keep within the limits of the school grounds.* **b** territories or regions. **6** the maximum quantity of fish or game that the law allows one to take in a specified period. **7** **the limit,** as much as, or more than, one can stand.
—*v.* set a limit to; restrict: *We must limit our expenditure to $60.* [ME < OF < L *limes, limitis* boundary] —**lim′it·a·ble,** *adj.* —**lim′it·er,** *n.*

lim·i·ta·tion (lim′ə tā′shən) *n.* **1** limiting. **2** a limited condition. **3** *Law.* a period of time after which a claim, suit, etc. cannot be brought in court. A **statute of limitations** is a statute that fixes such a period of time.

lim·i·ta·tive (lim′ə tā′tiv) *adj.* limiting; restrictive.

lim·it·ed (lim′ə tid) *adj., n.* —*adj.* **1** kept within limits; restricted: *a limited edition, a limited number of seats. He's having only limited success in his new business.* **2** of business organizations, restricted as to the amount of debt that any individual member is liable for. **3** travelling rapidly and making only a few stops: *a limited train or bus.*
—*n.* a train, bus, etc. that travels rapidly and makes only a few stops.

lim·it·ed–ac·cess (lim′ə tid ak′ses) *adj.* of highways, having access roads at relatively few points.

limited company a corporation in which the liability of stockholders is limited to a specified amount.

limited edition an edition of a book, etc. limited to a certain number of copies and often having a special format and binding.

limited monarchy a monarchy in which the ruler's powers are limited by law.

lim·it·less (lim′it lis) *adj.* without limits; boundless; infinite. —**lim′it·less·ly,** *adv.* —**lim′it·less·ness,** *n.*

limn (lim) *v.* **1** paint (a picture). **2** portray in words. [ME *lymne*(*n*), var. of *lumine*(*n*) < OF *luminer* < L *luminare* light up, make bright < *lumen* light] —**lim′ner,** *n.*

lim·no·log·i·cal (lim′nə loj′ə kəl) *adj.* of or having to do with limnology. —**lim′no·log′i·cal·ly,** *adv.*

lim·nol·o·gist (lim nol′ə jist′) *n.* a person trained in limnology, especially one whose work it is.

lim·nol·o·gy (lim nol′ə jē) *n.* the study of the physical and chemical properties of bodies of fresh water and the conditions of their plant and animal life. [< Gk. *limnē* lake + *-ology.* 20c.]

lim·o (lim′ō) *n., pl.* **lim·os.** *Informal.* limousine.

Li·moges (lì mōzh′; *French,* lē môzh′) *n.* a kind of fine porcelain made at Limoges, France.

li·mo·nite (lī′mə nīt′) *n.* a kind of iron ore, varying in color from dark brown to yellow. *Formula:* $2Fe_2O_3 \cdot 3H_2O$ [< Gk. *leimōn* meadow]

lim·ou·sine (lim′ə zēn′ *or* lim′ə zēn′) *n.* **1** a large, luxurious automobile, especially one driven by a chauffeur. A limousine sometimes has a glass partition separating the passenger compartment from the driver's seat. **2** a large automobile or small bus used to carry passengers to and from an airport, etc. [< F *limousine* < *Limousin,* former province of France]

limp¹ (limp) *n., v.* —*n.* a lame step or walk. —*v.* **1** walk with a limp: *After falling down the stairs, he limped for several days.* **2** proceed in a halting or labored manner: *The new project limped along, for no one seemed very interested in it.* [cf. OE *lemphealt* lame] —**limp′er,** *n.*

limp² (limp) *adj.* not stiff or firm; tending to bend or droop: *The lettuce had lost its crispness and was quite limp. I am so tired I feel as limp as a rag.* [origin uncertain; cf. ON *limpa* weakness] —**limp′ly,** *adv.* —**limp′ness,** *n.*
☛ *Syn.* **Limp, flabby** = lacking firmness, both literally and as used figuratively to describe character, principles, etc. **Limp** = lacking, or having lost, stiffness or firmness and strength, and suggests drooping or hanging loosely: *Hot weather always makes me feel limp. He has a limp handshake.* **Flabby** =

lacking firmness and hardness or lacking forcefulness, energy, or strength, and suggests being soft and weak, flapping or shaking easily: *She is so fat her flesh is flabby.*

lim·pet (lim′pit) *n.* any of various small, sea gastropod molluscs having a single shell shaped like a squat cone and having a broad, fleshy foot by which they cling to rocks, etc. [OE *lempedu* < Med.L *lampreda* lamprey. Doublet of LAMPREY.]

lim·pid (lim′pid) *adj.* clear; transparent: *limpid water, limpid eyes.* [< L *limpidus*] —**lim′pid·ly,** *adv.* —**lim′pid·ness,** *n.*

lim·pid·i·ty (lim pid′ə tē) *n.* a limpid quality or condition.

lim·y (līm′ē) *adj.* **lim·i·er, lim·i·est. 1** of, containing, or resembling lime. **2** smeared with birdlime.

lin·age (līn′ij) *n.* **1** the number of lines of printed or written matter on a page, or making up an article, advertisement, etc. **2** payment according to the number of lines.

linch·pin (linch′pin′) *n.* a locking pin inserted through a hole in the end of an axle to keep the wheel on. [< *linch-*, OE *lynis* linchpin + *pin*]

Lin·coln (ling′kən) *n.* a breed of English sheep having long wool. [< *Lincolnshire,* a county in E England, where this breed originated]

lin·dane (lin′dān) *n.* a benzene compound used as an insecticide. *Formula:* $C_6H_6Cl_6$

lin·den (lin′dən) *n.* **1** any of a genus (*Tilia*) of trees native to the temperate regions of the northern hemisphere, having heart-shaped leaves and fragrant flowers. Lindens are widely planted for ornament and shade. **2** the soft, fine-grained, white wood of a linden. **3** (*adj.*) designating a small family (Tiliaceae) of mainly tropical trees, shrubs, and a few herbs. The linden family includes the lindens and jutes. [OE *linden,* originally adj. < *lind* linden, lime[3]]

line[1] (līn) *n., v.* **lined, lin·ing.** —*n.* **1** a piece of rope, cord, or wire. **2** a cord for measuring, making level, etc. **3** a cord with a hook for catching fish. **4** a long, narrow mark: *Draw two lines along the margin.* **5** anything like such a mark: *the lines in your face.* **6** a wrinkle or crease: *the lines in his face. The fortune teller studied the lines on the palm of my hand.* **7** a straight line: *The lower edges of the two pictures are about on a line.* **8** *Geometry.* the straight or curved path that a point may be imagined to make as it moves; curve (def. 5). **9** the way in which lines are used in drawing: *clearness of line.* **10 lines,** *pl.* **a** outline; contour: *a ship of fine lines.* **b** the plan of construction: *The two books were written on the same lines.* **c** the words that an actor speaks in a play: *I forgot my lines and had to be prompted.* **d** reins. **e** one's fate or fortune: *His demotion was hard lines.* **f** *Informal.* a marriage certificate. **11** an edge; limit; boundary: *That hedge marks our property line.* **12** a row of persons or things: *a line of cars.* **13** a row of words on a page or in a column: *a column of 40 lines.* **14** a short letter; note: *Drop me a line.* **15** a connected series of persons or things following one another in time: *The Stuarts were a line of English kings.* **16** family or lineage: *of noble line.* **17** a course; track; direction: *the line of march of an army.* **18** a course of action, conduct, or thought: *a line of policy.* **19** *Military.* **a** the front. **b** lines, *pl.* a double row (front and rear rank) of soldiers. **c** troops or ships arranged abreast. **d** an arrangement of an army or fleet for battle. **20 the line, a** the equator. **b** the border between two countries, especially that between Canada and the United States: *south of the line.* **c** the regular armed forces; the soldiers, ships, or aircraft that do all the fighting. **21** in a telephone, telegraph, etc. system: **a** a wire or wires connecting points or stations. **b** the system itself. **22** any rope, wire, pipe, hose, etc. running from one point to another. **23** a single track of railway. **24 a** one branch of a system of transportation: *the main line of a railway.* **b** a whole system of transportation or conveyance: *the Cunard Line.* **25** a branch of business; kind of activity: *the dry-goods line.* **26** a kind or brand of goods: *a good line of hardware.* **27** *Slang.* an exaggerated story, intended to impress or deceive. **28** a single row of words in poetry. **29** *Music.* one of the horizontal lines that make a staff. **30** 1/12 of an inch. **31** *Cdn.* in Ontario, concession road.

all along the line, at every point; everywhere.
bring into line, cause to agree or conform: *She will bring the other members into line and the club will accept her plan.*
come into line, agree; conform.
get or **have a line on,** *Informal.* get or have information about.
in line, a in alignment. **b** in agreement. **c** ready. **d** in order; in succession: *next in line.*
on a line, even; level.
on the line, in between; neither one thing nor the other.
out of line, not in agreement; not suitable or proper: *Her last remark was out of line. He is always out of line with the rest of the club members.*

read between the lines, get more from the words than they say; find a hidden meaning.
—*v.* **1** mark with lines on paper, etc. **2** cover with lines: *a face lined by age.* **3** arrange in line. **4** form or arrange a line along: *Cars lined the road for a kilometre.* **5** form a line or form into a line (used with **up**): *People were lining up to get into the theatre.* **6** *baseball.* hit a liner. **7** *Cdn.* float a canoe downstream by guiding it from the shore with ropes attached to the bow and stern (*often used with* **down**): *We often lined down rapids instead of portaging.* [fusion of OE *line* line, rope and F *ligne* line, both < L *linea* line, linen thread < *linum* flax]

line[2] (līn) *v.* **lined, lin·ing. 1** put a layer inside (something). **2** fill: *to line one's pockets with money.* **3** serve as a lining for. [OE *lin* flax]

lin·e·age[1] (lin′ē ij) *n.* **1** one's descent in a direct line from an ancestor. **2** one's family or race. [ME < OF *lignage* < *ligne* line < L *linea*]

lin·e·age[2] (līn′ij) *n.* See **linage.**

lin·e·al (lin′ē əl) *adj.* **1** in the direct line of descent: *A granddaughter is a lineal descendant of her grandfather.* **2** having to do with or derived from ancestors; hereditary: *The lands were his by lineal right.* **3** linear. [ME < OF < LL *linealis* < L *linea* line[1]]

lin·e·al·ly (lin′ē əl ē) *adv.* in the direct line of descent.

lin·e·a·ment (lin′ē ə mənt) *n.* **1** a part or feature; distinctive characteristic. **2** a part or feature of a face with attention to its outline. [< L *lineamentum* < *linea* line[1]]

lin·e·ar (lin′ē ər) *adj.* **1** of or having to do with a line or lines: *linear symmetry.* **2** made of lines; making use of lines: *a linear drawing.* **3** *Mathematics and physics.* involving measurement in one dimension only: *linear measure.* **4** long, narrow, and even in width: *Grass has linear leaves.* [< L *linearis* < *linea* line[1]] —**lin′e·ar·ly,** *adv.*

linear accelerator an accelerator in which charged particles are speeded up in a straight line by a series of electrical impulses along their flight path.

linear algebra the algebra that deals primarily with number sets and variables arranged in rows or columns (matrices) and with line segments representing physical qualities such as force or velocity (vectors).

linear equation *Mathematics.* an equation whose graph is a straight line.

linear measure 1 measure of length. **2** a unit or system of units for measuring length.

line·back·er (līn′bak′ər) *n. Football.* a defensive player whose playing position is just behind the line of scrimmage.

line·man (līn′mən) *n., pl.* **-men. 1** a person who sets up or repairs telegraph, telephone, or electric wires. **2** *Football.* a centre, guard, tackle, or end. **3** *Hockey.* any person playing in the forward line. **4** a person who inspects railway tracks. **5** *Surveying.* the person who carries the line or chain.

lin·en (lin′ən) *n.* **1** thread or yarn spun from flax. **2** cloth made from flax thread or yarn: *Linen is very strong and is cool in summer.* **3** articles made of linen or of cotton, synthetics, or blends (*often used in the plural*). Tablecloths and serviettes are called table linen; sheets, pillow cases, etc. are called bed linen. **4** (*adj.*) made of linen. **5** (*adj.*) designed to hold or store linens: *a linen closet.*
wash (one's) **dirty linen in public,** See **dirty linen.**
[OE *līnen,* adj. < *līn* flax]

line of battle soldiers or ships in battle formation.

line of duty service or duty, especially military duty.
in the line of duty, in the course of doing one's duty, especially military duty.

line of fire 1 the path of a bullet, shell, etc. fired or about to be fired from a gun. **2** any very dangerous or vulnerable position.

line of force *Physics.* a line in a field of electrical or magnetic force, the line that indicates the direction in which the force is acting.

lin·er[1] (līn′ər) *n.* **1** a ship or airplane belonging to a transportation line or system. **2** a person or thing that makes lines. **3** *Baseball.* a ball hit so that it travels not far above the ground.

lin·er[2] (līn′ər) *n.* something that serves as a lining: *a diaper liner, a hat liner.*

lines·man (līnz′mən) *n., pl.* **-men. 1** lineman. **2** *Sports.* a person who watches the lines that mark out the field, rink, court, etc. and assists the umpire or referee.

line–up or **line-up** (līn′up′) *n.* **1** a number of persons arranged in a line; especially, a group including a suspected offender, lined up for identification by police or the victim of an offence. **2** *Sports.* **a** the list of players on a team arranged according to position of play, etc. **b** the players on such a list. **3** any arrangement of persons or things in a line or as if in a line.

ling (ling) *n., pl.* **ling** or **lings. 1** any of several edible fishes (genus

Molva) of the cod family found along the coasts of N Europe and Greenland, especially *M. molva*, having a long, slender body. 2 burbot. [ME *lenge* < OE *lang* long]

–ling *suffix.* **1** little, young, or unimportant, as in *duckling, princeling.* **2** one that is, as in *underling.* **3** one belonging to or concerned with, as in *earthling, hireling.* [OE]

ling. linguistics.

lin·ga (ling′gə) *n.* lingam.

lin·gam (ling′gəm) *n.* a phallus used as a symbol of the Hindu god Siva.

ling·cod (ling′cod′) *n.* an important food fish (*Ophiodon elongatus*) of the Pacific coast of North America, related to the greenlings.

lin·ger (ling′gər) *v.* **1** put off departure; stay on, especially because of reluctance to leave: *Several fans lingered at the stage door for some time after the actor had gone in.* **2** continue to stay or live, although gradually dying or becoming less: *Daylight lingers long in the summertime.* **3** go slowly; saunter; dally. **4** persist, especially in the mind: *The tune lingers in my mind.* [frequentative of earlier *leng* delay, OE *lengan* < *lang* long] **—lin′ger·er,** *n.* **—lin′ger·ing·ly,** *adv.*

☛ *Syn.* **Linger, loiter, lag** = delay in starting or along the way. **Linger** emphasizes delay in starting, and suggests slowness in going because unwilling to leave: *She lingered quite a while after the others had left.* **Loiter** emphasizes stopping along the way, and suggests moving slowly and aimlessly: *Mary loitered downtown, looking into all the shop windows.* **Lag** emphasizes falling behind others or in one's work, and suggests failing to keep up the necessary speed or pace: *The child lagged because he was tired.*

lin·ge·rie (lan′zhə rē′ *or* lon′zhə rā′) *n.* women's undergarments, nightgowns, etc. [< F *lingerie* < *linge* linen]

lin·go (ling′gō) *n., pl.* **-goes.** *Facetious or derogatory.* language, especially a dialect, jargon, etc. regarded as outlandish or incomprehensible: *the lingo of sports writers, the lingo of medical people.* [blend of Provençal *lengo* and Ital. *lingua,* both < L *lingua* tongue]

lin·gua fran·ca (ling′gwə frang′kə) **1** a language or dialect used as a common means of communication between peoples having different native languages: *Swahili is the lingua franca of central Africa.* **2** a hybrid language used for this purpose: *Chinook jargon was the lingua franca of Canada's Pacific Coast.* **3 Lingua Franca,** a hybrid language based on Italian and using elements of Spanish, French, Greek, Arabic, and Turkish, used in Mediterranean ports. **4** any code or system used as a common means of communication between people having different languages, backgrounds, etc.: *Pop music is the new lingua franca.* [< Ital. *lingua franca* Frankish language]

lin·gual (ling′gwəl) *adj., n.* **—adj. 1** of or having to do with the tongue: *a lingual defect.* **2** *Phonetics.* articulated with the aid of the tongue: *a lingual sound.* **3** of or having to do with speech or languages; linguistic. **—n.** *Phonetics.* a sound articulated with the aid of the tongue. The sounds generally represented by *d* and *t* are linguals. [< Med.L *lingualis* < L *lingua* tongue]

lin·guist (ling′gwist) *n.* **1** a person skilled in a number of languages besides his own; polyglot. **2** a person trained in linguistics, especially one whose work it is. **3** philologist. [< L *lingua* tongue + E *-ist*]

lin·guis·tic (ling gwis′tik) *adj.* of or having to do with language or the study of language or languages. **—lin·guis′ti·cal·ly,** *adv.*

lin·guis·tics (ling gwis′tiks) *n.* the study of human speech; the study of the structures, sounds, forms, functions, and varieties of language and languages (*used with a singular verb*). Compare **philology.**

lin·i·ment (lin′ə mənt) *n.* a liquid for rubbing on the skin to relieve soreness, sprains, bruises, etc. [< LL *linimentum* < *linere* anoint]

lin·ing (līn′ing) *n.* **1** a layer of material covering the inner surface of something: *the lining of a coat, a copper kettle with a tin lining.* **2** the material used for lining: *I bought satin lining for the coat.* [< *line²*]

link¹ (lingk) *n., v.* **—n. 1** one ring or loop of a chain. **2** anything that joins as a link joins: *a cuff link.* **3** a fact or thought that connects others: *a link in a chain of evidence.* **4** a unit of length used in surveying; one one-hundredth of a chain (about 20 cm). **5** *Chemistry.* a bond. **—v.** join as a link does; unite or connect. [ME < ON **hlenkr.* Akin to LANK.]

link² (lingk) *n.* a torch formerly used for lighting people's way through the streets. [origin uncertain]

link·age (lingk′ij) *n.* **1** linking or being linked. **2** an arrangement

or system of links. **3** *Biology.* the association of two or more genes on the same chromosome so that they are transmitted together.

linking verb a verb (such as **be, become,** or **seem**) that does not express action and is not followed by an object. It links a subject with an adjective that modifies the subject or with a noun that stands for the same person or thing as the subject; copula: *Examples: I am sleepy. He turned pale. She is a doctor. They became friends.*

☛ *Usage.* Many verbs with full meanings of their own (such as *taste, feel, act, look*) can also be used as linking verbs: *The butter tastes rancid. She felt sad. He acts old. This looks excellent.*

links (lingks) *n.pl. Esp.Brit.* golf course. [OE *hlinc* rising ground]

Lin·ne·an *or* **Lin·nae·an** (lə nē′ən) *adj.* of Carolus Linnaeus, 1707-1778, a Swedish botanist. The **Linnean system** of naming animals and plants uses two words, the first for the genus and the second for the species.

lin·net (lin′it) *n.* **1** a small, mainly brownish finch (*Acanthis cannabina;* also classified as *Carduelis cannabina*) found in dry, open regions of Europe and W Asia. The male has a red crown and breast and a beautiful song, which made it a popular cage bird in the 19th century. **2** any of various other finches of Europe or North America. [< OF *linette* < *lin* flax < L *linum;* it feeds on flaxseed]

li·no·le·um (lə nō′lē əm) *n.* **1** a durable, washable floor covering made by putting a hard surface of ground cork mixed with oxidized linseed oil on a canvas or burlap back. **2** any similar floor covering. [< *Linoleum,* a trademark, coined from L *linum* flax + *oleum* oil]

li·no·type (lī′nə tīp′) *n.* a typesetting machine that is operated like a typewriter and that casts each line of type in one piece. [originally *line o′ type* line of type]

lin·seed (lin′sēd′) *n.* the seed of flax. [OE *līnsǣd* flaxseed]

linseed oil a yellowish oil pressed from linseed, used especially in making paints, printing inks, and varnishes.

lin·sey (lin′zē) *n., pl.* **-seys.** linsey-woolsey.

lin·sey–wool·sey (lin′zē wúl′zē) *n., pl.* **-wool·seys.** a strong, coarse fabric made of linen and wool or of cotton and wool. [ME *linsey* a linen fabric (< *lin-,* OE *līn* linen) + E *wool,* with a rhyming ending]

lin·stock (lin′stok′) *n.* formerly, a stick used to hold a fuse or match in firing a cannon. [< Du. *lontstok* < *lont* match + *stok* stock]

lint (lint) *n.* **1** a soft down or fleecy material obtained by scraping linen. **2** fuzz or fluff consisting of tiny bits of fibre from yarn or cloth. [ME *linnet,* probably ult. < L *linum* or OE *līn* flax]

lin·tel (lin′təl) *n.* a horizontal beam or stone over a door, window, etc., that carries the weight of the wall above it. See **frame** for picture. [ME < OF *lintel,* ult. < L *limes, limitis* boundary]

li·on (lī′ən) *n.* **1** a large wild animal (*Panthera leo*) of the cat family, having a dull-yellow coat, a tufted tail, and, in the adult male, a heavy, shaggy, brown mane around the neck and shoulders. Lions are native to Africa and southwestern Asia. **2** a very brave or strong person. **3** a famous or important person: *a literary lion.* **4 a** the lion as the national emblem of the U.K. **b** the British nation itself. **5 Lion,** *Astronomy or astrology.* Leo.
beard the lion in his den, defy a person in his own home, office, etc.
put (one's) head in the lion's mouth, put oneself in a dangerous position.
twist the lion's tail, say or do something intended to excite the resentment of some government or other authority, especially the government or people of the U.K.
[ME < AF < L *leo* < Gk. *leōn*] **—li′on·like′,** *adj.*

li·on·ess (līən is) *n.* a female lion.

li·on–heart·ed (lī′ən här′tid) *adj.* brave.

li·on·ize (lī′ən īz′) *v.* **-ized, -iz·ing.** treat as very important: *The visiting artist was lionized by the press.* **—li′on·i·za′tion,** *n.* **—li′on·iz′er,** *n.*

lion's share the biggest or best part: *to get the lion's share of the publicity. She grabbed the lion's share of the dessert.*

lip (lip) *n., v.* **lipped, lip·ping. —n. 1** either of the two fleshy, movable edges of the mouth. **2 lips,** *pl.* the mouth. **3** a folding or bent-out edge of any opening: *the lip of a pitcher.* **4** *Music.* **a** the mouthpiece of a musical instrument. **b** the shaping of the lips in order to play a wind instrument. **5** *Slang.* impudent talk. **6** *Botany.* **a** either of the two parts of a labiate corolla or calyx, the upper lip

being closest to the axis of the inflorescence and the lower lip farthest away from the axis. **b** in an orchid, the labellum.
hang on the lips of, listen to with great attentiveness and admiration.
keep a stiff upper lip, be brave or firm; show no fear or discouragement.
—v. **1** touch with the lips. **2** use the lips in playing a musical wind instrument. **3** murmur. **4** hit a golf ball so that it touches the hole but does not drop in. [OE *lippa*] —**lip'like',** adj.

li·pase (lī'pās or lip'ās) n. an enzyme occurring in the pancreatic juice, certain seeds, etc., capable of changing fats into fatty acids and glycerin. [< Gk. *lipos* fat]

lip·id (lip'əd) n. any of a large group of natural organic compounds, including fats, oils, waxes, and steroids, that are insoluble in water but soluble in certain organic solvents such as alcohol. Lipids, proteins, and carbohydrates are the main structural components of living organisms. Also, **lipide.**

lip·ide (lip'īd or lip'əd) n. lipid.

lipped (lipt) adj. **1** having a lip or lips. **2** having a lip or lips of a specified kind (used in compounds): *thin-lipped, tight-lipped.*

lip·py (lip'ē) adj. Slang. insolent or impudent; talking back: *Don't get lippy with me.*

lip–read (lip'rēd') v. **-read, -read·ing.** understand speech by lip reading. —**lip'-read·er,** n.

lip reading the act or process of interpreting speech without hearing it by watching the lip movements and facial expression of the speaker.

lip–serv·ice (lip'sèr'vis) n. service expressed in words only; pretended loyalty or devotion; insincerity.

lip·stick (lip'stik') n. **1** a smooth cosmetic paste for the lips, usually colored and often in the form of a stick in a case. **2** a case containing this cosmetic.

liq. 1 liquid. **2** liquor.

liq·ue·fac·tion (lik'wə fak'shən) n. **1** the process of changing into a liquid. **2** the state of being a liquid.

liq·ue·fy (lik'wə fī') v. **-fied, -fy·ing.** change into a liquid; make or become liquid. [< L *liquefacere* < *liquere* be fluid + *facere* make] —**liq'ue·fi'a·ble,** adj. —**liq'ue·fi'er,** n.

li·ques·cence (li kwes'əns) n. a liquescent condition.

li·ques·cent (li kwes'ənt) adj. becoming liquid; melting. [< L *liquescens, -entis,* ppr. of *liquescere* become liquid]

li·queur (li kyür' or li kèr') n. a strong, sweet, highly flavored alcoholic drink. Doublet of LIQUOR.

liq·uid (lik'wid) n., adj. —n. **1** a substance that is neither a solid nor a gas; a substance that flows freely like water. **2** *Phonetics.* the sound of *l* or *r.*
—adj. **1** in the form of a liquid; melted: *liquid soap.* **2** clear and bright like water. **3** clear and smooth-flowing in sound: *the liquid notes of a bird.* **4** easily turned into cash: *Canada Savings Bonds are a liquid investment.* [ME < L *liquidus* < *liquere* be fluid]
☛ *Syn. n.* **1. Liquid, fluid** = a substance that flows. **Liquid** applies to a substance that is neither a solid nor a gas, but flows freely like water: *Milk and wine are liquids; oxygen is not.* **Fluid** applies to anything that flows in any way, either a liquid or a gas: *Milk, water, and oxygen are fluids.*

liquid air the intensely cold, transparent liquid formed when air is very greatly compressed and then cooled. Liquid air is used mainly as a refrigerant.

liq·ui·date (lik'wə dāt') v. **-dat·ed, -dat·ing. 1** pay (a debt). **2** settle or adjust accounts of (a business, etc.); clear up the affairs of (a bankrupt). **3** get rid of (an undesirable person or thing): *The Russian revolution liquidated the nobility.* **4** convert into cash. **5** *Law.* determine and apportion by agreement or litigation the amount of (indebtedness or damages). **6** kill ruthlessly; exterminate. [< Med.L *liquidare* < L *liquidus.* See LIQUID.] —**liq'ui·da'tion,** n. —**liq'ui·da'tor,** n.

liquid fire flaming oil or a flaming chemical usually hurled from flame throwers, used against fortified emplacements, tanks, etc.

li·quid·i·ty (li kwid'ə tē) n. **1** the state of being a liquid. **2** the state of having liquid assets.

liquid measure 1 the measurement of liquids. **2** a unit or system of units for measuring liquids.

liq·uor (lik'ər) n. **1** an alcoholic drink, such as brandy, gin, rum, or whisky. **2** any liquid, especially a liquid in which food is packaged, canned, or cooked: *Pickles are put up in salty liquor.* [< L. Doublet of LIQUEUR.]

liq·uo·rice (lik'ə rish, lik'rish, or lik'ə ris) See **licorice.**

li·ra (lēr'ə) n., pl. **li·re** (lēr'ā) or **li·ras. 1** the basic unit of money in Italy. **2** the basic unit of money in Turkey, divided into 100

kurus. Also called **pound.** See table at **money. 3** a coin worth one lira. [< Ital. < L *libra,* a unit of weight]

lisle (līl) n. **1** a fine, strong, linen or cotton thread, used for making stockings, gloves, etc. **2** (adj.) made of lisle. [< F *Lisle,* the former name of *Lille,* a town in N France]

lisp (lisp) v., n. —v. **1** produce a *th* sound or something like it instead of the sound of *s* or *z* in speaking: *A person who lisps might say "thing a thong" for "sing a song."* **2** speak imperfectly: *Babies are said to lisp.* —n. the act, habit, or sound of lisping: *He speaks with a lisp.* [ult. < OE *wlisp,* adj., lisping] —**lisp'er,** n.

lis·some or **lis·som** (lis'əm) adj. **1** lithe; limber; supple. **2** nimble; active. [var. of lithesome]

list¹ (list) n., v. —n. **1** a series of names, numbers, words, or other items: *a shopping list.* **2** list price. —v. **1** make a list of; enter in a list. **2** *Archaic.* enlist. [< F *liste* < Gmc.]
☛ *Syn. n.* **List, catalogue, roll** = a series of names or items. **List** is the general word applying to a series of names, figures, etc.: *This is the list of the people who are going to the picnic.* **Catalogue** applies to a complete list arranged alphabetically or according to some other system, often with short descriptions of the items: *Has the new mail-order catalogue come?* **Roll** applies to a list of the names of all members of a group: *His name is on the honor roll.*

list² (list) n., v. —n. **1** the woven edge of cloth, where the material is a little different; selvage. **2** a cheap fabric made out of such edges. —v. put a list around the edges of. [OE *līste*]

list³ (list) n., v. —n. a tipping to one side; tilt: *the list of a ship.* —v. tip to one side; tilt: *The sinking ship was listing so that water lapped her decks.* [extended use of *list* inclination, desire < *list⁴*]

list⁴ (list) v. Archaic. **1** be pleasing to; please: *It lists me not to speak.* **2** like; wish: *The wind bloweth where it listeth.* [OE *lystan* < *lust* pleasure]

list⁵ (list) v. Archaic and poetic. **1** listen. **2** listen to. [OE *hlystan* < *hlyst* hearing. Related to LISTEN.]

lis·ten (lis'ən) v. **1** try to hear; pay attention so as to hear: *She listened for the sound of the car. I like to listen to music.* **2** give heed (to advice, temptation, etc.); pay attention: *I don't know what he said because I wasn't listening.*
listen in, a listen to others talking on a telephone: *I listened in on the extension.* **b** listen to the radio: *Listen in next week for another drama.*
[OE *hlysna.* Related to LIST⁵.] —**lis'ten·er,** n.
☛ *Syn.* **1.** See note at **hear.**

list·er (lis'tər) n. a plough with a double mouldboard that throws the dirt to both sides of the furrow. [< *list²*]

list·less (list'lis) adj. seeming too tired to care about anything; not interested in things; not caring to be active: *a dull and listless mood.* [< *list* a desire < *list⁴*] —**list'less·ly,** adv. —**list'less·ness,** n.

list price the price given in a catalogue or list. Discounts are figured from it.

lists (lists) n.pl. **1** in the Middle Ages: **a** a place where knights fought in tournaments. **b** the barriers enclosing such a field. **2** any place or scene of combat.
enter the lists, join in a contest; take part in a fight, argument, etc. [blend of *list²* and OF *lice* place of combat < Gmc.]

lit (lit) v. a pt. and a pp. of **light¹** and **light³.**
☛ *Usage.* See note at **light.**

lit. 1 literature. **2** literally.

lit·a·ny (lit'ə nē) n., pl. **-nies. 1** a form of prayer for use in church services, consisting of a series of petitions recited by the clergy, alternating with fixed responses from the congregation. **2** any recital or account involving much repetition: *a litany of complaints.* [ME < OF < LL *litania* < Gk. *litaneia* litany, an entreating < *litesthai* entreat]

Lit.B. See **Litt.B.**

li·tchi (lē'chē) n., pl. **-tchis. 1** the small, round or oval fruit of a Chinese tree (*Litchi chinensis*) of the soapberry family having a brittle outer covering and white, very juicy pulp surrounding one seed. It is eaten fresh, canned, or dried. **2** the tree bearing this fruit. **3** See **litchi nut.** Also, **lichee.**

litchi nut the fruit of the litchi, especially when dried. [< Chinese]

Lit.D. See **Litt.D.**

–lite combining form. stone; stony: *Chrysolite = gold-colored stone.* [< F *-lite* < earlier *-lithe* < Gk. *lithos* stone]

li·ter (lē'tər) See **litre.**

lit·er·a·cy (lit'ər ə sē) n. the ability to read and write.

lit·er·al (lit'ər əl or lit'rəl) adj. **1** following the exact words of the original: *a literal translation.* **2** taking words in their usual or basic meaning; actual: *a literal interpretation. When we say He flew down the stairs to meet them, we do not mean fly in the literal sense of the word.* **3** concerned mainly with facts; matter-of-fact: *a literal type of mind.* **4** true to fact; not exaggerated: *a literal account. The literal truth of the matter is that he was terrified.* **5** of, having to do

with, or expressed by letters of the alphabet. [ME < LL *lit(t)eralis* < L *lit(t)era* letter] —**lit′er·al·ness,** *n.*
☛ *Hom.* **littoral** (lit′ər əl).

lit·er·al·ism (lit′ər əl iz′əm *or* lit′rəl iz′əm) *n.* keeping to the literal meaning in translation or interpretation.

lit·er·al·ist (lit′ər əl ist *or* lit′rəl ist) *n.* **1** a person who adheres to the exact literal meaning. **2** a person who represents or portrays without idealizing.

lit·er·al·ly (lit′ər əl ē *or* lit′rəl ē) *adv.* **1** word for word: *to translate literally.* **2** actually; without exaggeration: *I was literally penniless; I couldn't even make a phone call.*
☛ *Usage.* **Literally** is sometimes used informally as a general intensifier: *The desk was literally buried in papers.* This usage gives **literally** the exact opposite of its real meaning of 'actually; without exaggeration', and should, therefore, be avoided.

lit·er·ar·y (lit′ər er′ē) *adj.* **1** having to do with literature or the humanities: *a literary treatise.* **2** of or having to do with books: *a literary agent.* **3** of or having to do with writers, scholars, etc., or writing as a profession: *a literary journal.* **4** knowing much about and enjoying literature; fond of books and reading: *They are a very literary family.*

lit·er·ate (lit′ər it) *adj., n.* —*adj.* **1** able to read and write. **2** acquainted with literature; educated. —*n.* **1** a person who can read and write. **2** an educated person. [ME < L *lit(t)eratus* < *lit(t)era* letter] —**lit′er·ate·ly,** *adv.* —**lit′er·ate·ness,** *n.*

lit·e·ra·ti (lit′ə rä′tē *or* lit′ə rä′tī) *n.pl.* scholary or literary people. [< L *lit(t)erati,* pl., literally, lettered]

lit·e·ra·tim (lit′ə rä′tim) *adv.* letter for letter; exactly as written. [< Med.L. *lit(t)eratim* < L *lit(t)era* letter]

lit·er·a·ture (lit′ər ə chər, lit′rə chər, *or* lit′ər ə chür′) *n.* **1** the writings of a period or of a country, especially those kept alive by their excellence of style or thought: *Stephen Leacock is a famous name in Canadian literature.* **2** all the books and articles on a subject: *the literature of stamp collecting.* **3** the profession of a writer. **4** the study of literature: *I am going to take literature and mathematics this spring.* **5** *Informal.* printed matter of any kind: *Election campaign literature informs people about the candidates.* [ME < L *lit(t)eratura* writing < *lit(t)era* letter]

lith·arge (lith′ärj *or* li thärj′) *n.* a yellow oxide of lead, used in making glass, glazes for pottery, and dryers for paints and varnishes. *Formula:* PbO [ME < OF *litarge* < L < Gk. *lithargyros* < *lithos* stone + *argyros* silver]

lithe (līFH) *adj.* bending easily; supple: *lithe of body, a lithe willow.* [OE *līthe* mild] —**lithe′ly,** *adv.* —**lithe′ness,** *n.*

lithe·some (līFH′səm) *adj.* lithe.

lith·i·a (lith′ē ə) *n.* a white crystalline oxide of lithium. *Formula:* Li_2O [< NL < Gk. *lithos* stone]

lith·ic (lith′ik) *adj.* **1** consisting of stone or rock. **2** *Medicine.* of or having to do with stone or stony concretions formed within the body, especially in the bladder. [< Gk. *lithikos* < *lithos* stone]

lith·i·um (lith′ē əm) *n.* a soft, silver-white, metallic chemical element similar to sodium. Lithium is the lightest of all the metals. *Symbol:* Li; *at.no.* 3; *at.wt.* 6.939. [< NL < Gk. *lithos* stone]

litho- *combining form.* stone: *lithograph.* Also, **lith-** before vowels. [< L < Gk. *lithos* stone]

lith·o·graph (lith′ə graf′) *n., v.* —*n.* a picture, print, etc. made by lithography. —*v.* produce or print by lithography. [< *litho-* + *-graph*]

li·thog·ra·pher (li thog′rə fər) *n.* a person trained in lithography, especially one whose work it is.

lith·o·graph·ic (lith′ə graf′ik) *adj.* of, having to do with, or produced by lithography. —**lith′o·graph′i·cal·ly,** *adv.*

li·thog·ra·phy (li thog′rə fē) *n.* the art or process of transferring an image onto paper from a flat surface such as a metal plate, by preparing the surface so that certain parts receive ink while other parts repel it.

lith·o·pone (lith′ə pōn′) *n.* a white pigment that is a mixture of zinc sulphide, zinc oxide, and barium sulphate, used in paints as a nonpoisonous substitute for white lead. [< *litho-* + Gk. *ponos* work. 20c.]

lith·o·sphere (lith′ə sfēr′) *n.* the solid outer shell of the earth, including the crust and upper mantle, thought to be from about 70 to 150 kilometres thick. Many scientists believe the lithosphere to consist of separate rigid plates that move on the softer rock of the lower mantle. [< *litho-* + *sphere*]

Lith·u·a·ni·an (lith′ü ā′nē ən) *n., adj.* —*n.* **1** a native or inhabitant of Lithuania, a republic in the W Soviet Union. **2** the Baltic language of the Lithuanians. —*adj.* of or having to do with Lithuania, its people, or their language.

lit·i·ga·ble (lit′ə gə bəl) *adj.* capable of being made the subject of a suit in a law court.

hat, āge, fär; let, ēqual, tėrm; it, īce
hot, ōpen, ôrder; oil, out; cup, pút, rüle,
əbove, takən, pencəl, lemən, circəs

ch, child; ng, long; sh, ship
th, thin; ҬH, then; zh, measure

lit·i·gant (lit′ə gənt) *n., adj.* —*n.* a person engaged in a lawsuit. —*adj.* engaging in a lawsuit.

lit·i·gate (lit′ə gāt′) *v.* **-gat·ed, -gat·ing. 1** engage in a lawsuit. **2** contest in a lawsuit. [< L *litigare* < *lis, litis* lawsuit + *agere* drive] —**lit′i·ga′tor,** *n.*

lit·i·ga·tion (lit′ə gā′shən) *n.* **1** the act of carrying on a lawsuit. **2** going to law. **3** lawsuit.

li·ti·gious (lə tij′əs) *adj.* **1** having the habit of going to law. **2** offering material for a lawsuit; that can be disputed in a court of law. **3** of lawsuits. [< L *litigiosus* < *litigium* dispute < *litigare.* See LITIGATE.] —**li·ti′gious·ly,** *adv.* —**li·ti′gious·ness,** *n.*

lit·mus (lit′məs) *n.* a blue coloring matter obtained from lichens, that turns red in an acid solution and back to blue in an alkali solution. It is used to indicate whether a particular chemical solution is an acid or a base. [ME < ON *litmose* dyer's herb < *litr* color + *mosi* moss]

litmus paper paper treated with litmus, used to indicate whether a solution is an acid or a base.

li·to·tes (lī′tə tēz′ *or* lit′ə tēz′) *n.* a form of understatement in which something is said by denying its opposite. *Examples:* The palace was no small bungalow. He had plenty to eat and not a little to drink. [< Gk. *litotēs* < *litos* simple, plain]

li·tre (lē′tər) *n.* a unit used with the SI for measuring volume or capacity, equal to one cubic decimetre. One litre of water has a mass of one kilogram. The litre is used for measuring liquids and other products such as ice cream and fruit, and for measuring the capacity of containers such as gas tanks, cooking pots, jugs, and baskets. *Symbol:* L Also, **liter.** [< F *litre* < *litron,* an obs. French measure of capacity < Med.L. *litra* < Gk. *litra,* a unit of weight]
☛ *Usage.* The international symbol for **litre** is the upright lower-case letter 'l'. However, the capital letter 'L' has been adopted as the official symbol in Canada because the lower-case letter can be confused in printing with the numeral 'l'.

Litt.B. Bachelor of Letters or of Literature (for L *Litterarum Baccalaureus*).

Litt.D. Doctor of Letters or of Literature (for L *Litterarum Doctor*).

lit·ter (lit′ər) *n., v.* —*n.* **1** scattered rubbish; things scattered about or left in disorder. **2** disordered; untidiness. **3** the young animals born at the same time from one mother: *a litter of puppies.* **4** straw, hay, etc. used as bedding for animals. **5** a stretcher for carrying a sick or wounded person. **6** a framework to be carried on men's shoulders or by beasts of burden, with a couch usually enclosed by curtains.
—*v.* **1** leave (odds and ends) lying around; scatter (things) about. **2** make disordered or untidy: *He littered the yard with bottles and cans.* **3** give birth to (young animals). **4** make a bed for (an animal) with straw, hay, etc. [ME < AF *litere* < Med.L. *lectaria* < L *lectus* bed]

lit·té·ra·teur *or* **lit·te·ra·teur** (lit′ə rə tėr′) *n.* a literary man; a writer or critic of literature. [< F]

lit·ter·bug (lit′ər bug′) *n.* one who leaves litter lying about in public places.

lit·tle (lit′əl) *adj.* **less** or **less·er, least;** *or* **lit·tler, lit·tlest;** *adv.* **less, least;** *n.* —*adj.* **1** not great or big; small: *A grain of sand is little. The little dog barked loudly.* **2** not much; small in number, amount, degree, or importance: *little money, little hope, a little army.* **3** short, brief: *She took a little walk.* **4** mean and narrow in thought or feeling: *Only a little man would pinch a child. That little sneak stole my sweater.*
—*adv.* **1** in a small amount or degree; to a small extent; slightly: *They live in a little-known town. He travels little.* **2** hardly at all: *He little knows what will happen.*
—*n.* **1** a small amount, quantity, or degree: *add a little.* **2** a short time or distance: *move a little to the left.*
in little, on a small scale.
little by little, by a small amount at a time; slowly; gradually.
make little of, treat or represent as of little importance: *She made little of her troubles.*
not a little, much; very: *He was not a little upset by the accident.*
think little of, a not value much; consider as unimportant or worthless. **b** not hesitate about.
[OE *lȳtel*] —**lit′tle·ness,** *n.*
☛ *Syn. adj.* **1, 2. Little, small, diminutive** = not large or great. **Little** means not big or great in size, quantity, degree, importance, etc., and often suggests that a

person or thing is appealing in its lack of size: *He is a funny little boy.* **Small** suggests being below average in size, number, or measure: *He is small for his age.* **Diminutive** means very small in size: *Her feet are diminutive.*

Little Bear the northern constellation Ursa Minor.

Little Dipper the seven principal stars in the constellation Ursa Minor, arranged in a form that suggests a dipper. The star forming the end of the handle of the Little Dipper is the North Star. Compare **Big Dipper.**

Little Dog the constellation Canis Minor.

little finger the finger that is farthest from the thumb; the smallest finger: *She wears a ring on her little finger.*

little magazine or **review** a small magazine devoted to printing experimental writing, criticism, etc.

little people the fairies.

little theatre 1 a small, usually amateur, theatre group. Some little theatres present experimental plays. 2 such groups collectively, or the drama produced by them.

lit·to·ral (lit′ə rəl) *adj., n.* —*adj.* 1 of or having to do with a shore, especially of the sea. 2 found or growing on or near the shore. —*n.* the region along a shore, especially the zone between the marks of high and low tide. [ult. < L *litoralis* < *litus, litoris* shore]
☛ *Hom.* **literal.**

li·tur·gic (lə tėr′jik) *adj.* liturgical.

li·tur·gi·cal (lə tėr′jə kəl) *adj.* of or having to do with liturgy. —**li·tur′gi·cal·ly,** *adv.*

lit·ur·gy (lit′ər jē) *n., pl.* **-gies.** 1 a form or ritual for public worship: *Different churches use different liturgies.* 2 Often, **Liturgy,** the Eucharistic service, especially in the Eastern Orthodox Church. [< LL *liturgia* < Gk. *leitourgia* public worship, ult. < *leitos* public + *ergon* work]

liv·a·ble (liv′ə bəl) *adj.* 1 fit to live in. 2 easy to live with. 3 worth living; endurable.

live¹ (liv) *v.* **lived, liv·ing.** 1 have life; be alive; exist: *All creatures have an equal right to live.* 2 remain alive; last; endure: *He managed to live through the war.* 3 keep up life: *live on one's income.* 4 subsist: *They live on meat and potatoes. He lives on government grants.* 5 pass (life): *to live well, to live a life of ease.* 6 dwell: *My aunt lives in Victoria.* 7 carry out or show in life: *to live one's ideals.* 8 have a rich and full life: *Those people know how to live!*
live (something) **down,** live so worthily that (some fault or sin of the past) is overlooked or forgotten: *He is determined to live down that disgrace.*
live it up, *Slang.* enjoy life to the full.
live out, stay alive through; last through.
live up to, act according to; do (what is expected or promised): *The car has not lived up to the salesman's description.*
[OE *lifian, libban*]

live² (līv) *adj., adv.* —*adj.* 1 having life; alive: *a live dog.* 2 burning or glowing: *live coals.* 3 full of energy or activity: *She is a very live girl, always on the go.* 4 *Informal.* up-to-date: *live ideas.* 5 of present interest: *a live question.* 6 moving or imparting motion: *live wheels, a live axle.* 7 still in use or to be used: *live steam.* 8 carrying an electric current; charged electrically: *a live wire.* 9 of telephones, microphones, etc., not shut off; operating or functioning. 10 charged with explosive: *a live cartridge.* 11 in the native state; not mined or quarried: *live metal.* 12 *Radio and television.* broadcast as performed and not from tape or film made beforehand: *a live television show.*
—*adv.* of recordings or broadcasts, made as performed before an audience: *The concert was recorded live.* [var. of *alive*]

live·a·ble (liv′ə bəl) *adj.* See **livable.**

–lived (līvd *or* livd) *combining form.* having a—life or lives: *Short-lived = having a short life.*

live·li·hood (liv′lē hůd′) *n.* a means of living, that is, of obtaining the money necessary to buy food, clothing, and shelter; a means of supporting oneself; living (def. 2): *She writes for a livelihood. He earns his livelihood as a farmer.* [OE *līf(ge)lād* (see LIFE, LOAD), influenced by obs. *livelihood* liveliness]
☛ *Syn.* See note at **living.**

live load a variable weight that a structure carries in addition to its own weight, such as moving traffic on a bridge. Compare **dead load.**

live·long (liv′long′ *or* līv′-) *adj.* the whole length of; whole; entire: *She is busy the livelong day.*

live·ly (līv′lē) *adj.* **-li·er, -li·est;** *adv.* —*adj.* 1 full of life; active; vigorous; spirited. 2 exciting. 3 bright; vivid. 4 cheerful and spirited:

a lively conversation. 5 bouncing well and quickly: *a lively tennis ball.*
—*adv.* in a lively manner. [OE *līflīc* living] —**live′li·ness,** *n.*

liv·en (līv′ən) *v.* make or become more lively or interesting (*often used with* **up**): *The show isn't bad, but they could liven it up a little.*

live oak (līv) any of various North American evergreen oaks valued as ornamental or timber trees, especially *Quercus virginiana* of SE North America and Cuba, having very hard, heavy, strong wood formerly much used in shipbuilding.

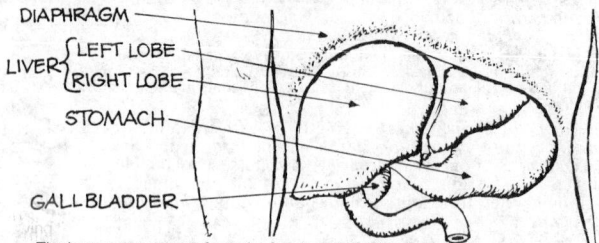

The human torso seen from the front, showing the liver, stomach, and gall bladder

liv·er¹ (liv′ər) *n.* 1 in vertebrates, a large, reddish-brown organ that secretes bile and helps in the absorption of food. The liver frees the blood of its waste matter and causes important changes in many of its substances. 2 an animal's liver used as food. [OE *lifer*]

liv·er² (liv′ər) *n.* a person who lives in a certain way: *He is a fast liver.* [< *live¹*]

liv·ere (liv′yər) See **liveyere.**

liv·er·ied (liv′ər ēd *or* liv′rēd) *adj.* clothed in a livery.

liv·er·ish (liv′ər ish) *adj. Informal.* having a sour or peevish disposition, one of the supposed symptoms of liver trouble; irritable.

liv·er·wort (liv′ər wėrt′) *n.* 1 any of a class (Hepaticae) of creeping, flowerless plants that grow in wet soil or on damp rocks, fallen logs, etc. Liverworts resemble mosses and together with them make up the plant division Bryophyta. 2 hepatica.

liv·er·wurst (liv′ər wėrst′ *or* -wůrst′) *n.* a sausage consisting largely of ground liver. [< G *Leberwurst* liver sausage]

liv·er·y (liv′ər ē *or* liv′rē) *n., pl.* **-er·ies.** 1 any special uniform provided for the servants of a household, or adopted by any group or profession. 2 any characteristic dress, garb, or outward appearance. 3 the feeding, stabling, and care of horses for pay. 4 the keeping of cars, boats, bicycles, etc. for hire. 5 livery stable. [ME < AF *livere* < *livrer* dispense < L *liberare* liberate; originally, provisions dispensed to servants]

liv·er·y·man (liv′ər ē mən *or* liv′rē-) *n., pl.* **-men.** 1 a person who owns or works in a livery stable. 2 a person who wears or is entitled to wear livery.

livery stable a place where horses and vehicles are kept for hire or where horses are fed and stabled for a fee.

lives (līvz) *n.* pl. of **life.**

live·stock (līv′stok′) *n.* farm animals. Cows, horses, sheep, and pigs are livestock.

live wire 1 a wire through which an electric current is flowing. 2 *Informal.* an energetic, wide-awake person.

live·yere (liv′yər) *n. Cdn.* 1 in Newfoundland, a permanent resident, as opposed to those who are on the island or in Labrador for the fishing or sealing season only. 2 a permanent resident of the north shore of the Gulf of St. Lawrence. Also, **livere, livier.** [< *livier,* formerly, a type of manorial worker having certain property rights < AF *livere.* Cf. LIVERY.]

liv·id (liv′id) *adj.* 1 having a dull-bluish or greyish color, as from a bruise: *livid marks on an arm.* 2 very pale: *livid with shock.* 3 flushed; reddish: *livid with anger.* 4 *Informal.* very angry: *The insults made him livid.* [< L *lividus* < *livere* be bluish] —**liv′id·ly,** *adv.* —**liv′id·ness,** *n.*

liv·ier (liv′yər) See **liveyere.**

liv·ing (liv′ing) *adj., n.* —*adj.* 1 having life; being alive: *a living plant.* 2 full of life; vigorous; strong; active: *a living faith.* 3 in actual existence: *a living language.* 4 true to life; vivid; lifelike: *a living picture.* 5 of life; for living in: *living conditions.* 6 sufficient to live on: *a living wage.*
—*n.* 1 the condition of being alive: *The old woman was filled with the joy of living.* 2 **the living,** *pl.* all the people who are alive. 3 a means of obtaining what is needed to support life; livelihood. 4 a manner of life: *healthful living.* 5 a position in the church, including the income attached to it; benefice.
☛ *Syn. n.* 2. **Living, livelihood, support** = a person's means of providing shelter, food, etc. for himself. **Living** is the general word and suggests nothing more: *He always had to work hard for his living.* **Livelihood** often applies to the

work a person does to earn enough to live on or to the pay he gets: *Mowing lawns is his only livelihood.* **Support** applies to the providing of a means of living: *They depend on his father for their support.*

living quarters a place to live.

living room a room in a house or apartment, used for the general leisure activities of the occupants, for entertaining guests, etc.

living wage a wage sufficient to enable a person or family to live in reasonable comfort and security.

li·vre (lē′vər) *n.* a former French silver coin. [< F < L *libra*, a unit of weight]

liz·ard (liz′ərd) *n.* **1** any of a suborder (Lacertilia, also called Sauria) of reptiles belonging to the same order as snakes, having external ears, eyes with movable lids, dry, scaly skin, and, in most species, a long, slender body with a long tail and four short legs. Geckos, chameleons, and iguanas are lizards. **2** any of various animals having a relatively long body, short legs, and a tail, such as salamanders, alligators, or dinosaurs. [ME < OF *lesard* < L *lacertus*] —**liz′ard·like′,** *adj.*

ll. lines.

LL Latin.

lla·ma (lä′mə *or* lam′ə) *n., pl.* **-mas** or (*esp. collectively*) **-ma.** a domesticated South American hoofed mammal (*Lama glama*) closely related to the guanaco (from which it may be descended) and the alpaca, having a long neck, a small head with large, erect ears, and thick, shaggy wool. Llamas have long been raised for their wool, milk, and meat and are also used as beasts of burden. [< Sp. < Quechua (Indian lang. of Peru)]
☞ *Hom.* **lama.**

lla·no (lä′nō *or* lan′ō) *n., pl.* **-nos.** a broad, treeless plain. [< Sp. < L *planus* level]

LL.B. Bachelor of Laws (for L *Legum Baccalaureus*).

LL.D. Doctor of Laws (for L *Legum Doctor*).

Lloyd's (loidz) *n.* in London, England, an association of businessmen dealing in many kinds of insurance, especially marine insurance.

LNG liquefied natural gas.

lo (lō) *interj.* look! see! behold! [OE *lā*]
☞ *Hom.* **low.**

loach (lōch) *n.* any of a family (Cobitidae) of small freshwater fishes of Asia and Europe having very small scales and having barbels around the mouth. [ME < OF *loche*, ? < Celtic]

load (lōd) *n., v.* —*n.* **1** whatever is being carried; a pack, cargo, burden, etc.: *The cart has a load of hay.* **2** the amount usually carried at one time; a more or less fixed quantity for a particular type of carrier (*often used in compounds*): *a planeload of tourists. Send us four loads of sand.* **3 loads,** *pl. Informal.* a great quantity or number: *Don't worry; we have loads of food.* **4** something that weighs down or oppresses: *That's a load off my mind!* **5** *Mechanics.* the weight supported by a structure or part. **6** the external resistance overcome by an engine, dynamo, or the like, under a given condition, measured by the power required. **7** one charge of powder and shot for a gun. **8** *Slang.* enough liquor to make one drunk.
—*v.* **1** place on or in a carrier of some kind: *The longshoremen are loading grain.* **2** put a load in or on: *to load a ship, to load a basket with groceries.* **3** take on a load: *The ship is still loading.* **4** oppress or burden (*often used with* **down**): *loaded down with debt. Don't load your mind with useless worry.* **5** supply amply or in excess: *They loaded him with compliments.* **6** add weight to: *load dice.* **7** put a charge in (a gun). [OE *lād* course, carrying; cf. *lode*] —**load′er,** *n.*
☞ *Hom.* **lode.**
☞ *Syn. n.* **1. Load, burden** = what one is carrying. **Load,** the general word, applies literally to whatever is carried by a person or animal or in a vehicle, boat, or plane: *That is a heavy load of groceries.* It is also used figuratively to apply to something that weighs heavily on the mind or spirit: *His many responsibilities give him a heavy load.* **Burden** applies to something borne and is now, except in a few phrases, used only figuratively, applying to sorrow, care, duty, or work: *She had too heavy a burden and became sick.*

load·ed (lōd′id) *adj.* **1** carrying a load. **2** with a charge in it: *a loaded gun.* **3** weighted, especially with lead: *a loaded stick or whip.* **4** *Slang.* drunk. **5** *Slang.* having plenty of money; rich. **6** *Informal.* full of half-hidden and unexpected meanings and suggestions: *Loaded questions are often intended to trap a person into saying more than he wants to say.*

load·star (lōd′stär′) See **lodestar.**

load·stone (lōd′stōn′) See **lodestone.** [< *load* + *stone*]

loaf[1] (lōf) *n., pl.* **loaves. 1** a quantity of bread baked as one piece in a more or less oblong or round shape: *Bread is usually sold by the loaf.* **2** any mass of food shaped like a loaf and baked: *a meat loaf, a salmon loaf.* **3** a cone-shaped mass of sugar. [OE *hlāf*]

loaf[2] (lōf) *v.* spend time idly; do nothing: *I can loaf all day Saturday.* [origin uncertain; cf. G dial. *lofen* run about, idle]

loaf·er (lōf′ər) *n.* **1** a person who loafs; idler. **2** Usually **loafers,** *pl.*

---

living quarters**675**lobelia

hat, āge, fär; let, ēqual, tèrm; it, īce
hot, ōpen, ôrder; oil, out; cup, pút, rüle,
ə above, takən, pencəl, lemən, circəs

ch, child; ng, long; sh, ship
th, thin; ŦH, then; zh, measure

a shoe resembling a moccasin, but with sole and heel stitched to the upper.

loam (lōm) *n., v.* —*n.* **1** rich, fertile earth in which decaying and decayed plant matter is mixed with clay and sand. **2** a mixture of clay, sand, and straw used to make moulds for large metal castings, and also to plaster walls, stop holes, etc. —*v.* cover or fill with loam. [OE *lām*]

loam·y (lōm′ē) *adj.* of or like loam.

loan (lōn) *n., v.* —*n.* **1** the act of lending; the granting of temporary use: *She asked for the loan of his pen.* **2** anything that is lent, especially money: *He asked his brother for a loan.* —*v.* make a loan; lend.
on loan, lent or granted for temporary use or service: *Our department manager is on loan to another department for a week. The book was out on loan so I had to wait.* [ME < ON *lán*] —**loan′er,** *n.*
☞ *Hom.* **lone.**
☞ *Usage.* **Loan, lend.** In formal usage *loan* is a noun and *lend* a verb. But in informal usage *loan* is both a verb and a noun: *I loaned* (or *lent*) *him my tuxedo. He asked me for a loan of five dollars.*

loan shark *Informal.* a person who lends money at an extremely high or unlawful rate of interest.

loan–shark·ing (lōn′shärk′ing) *n.* the practice of lending money at extremely high or unlawful rates of interest.

loan·word (lōn′wèrd′) *n.* a word taken into a language from another language and adopted as part of that language, often being slightly changed in the process. *Degree* is a very old loanword that came into English from French about 700 years ago. More recent loanwords are *khaki,* from Hindi, and *intelligentsia,* from Russian.

loath (lōth) *adj.* unwilling; reluctant: *The little girl was loath to leave her mother.*
nothing loath, willing;
willingly.
Also, **loth.** [OE *lāth* hostile]
☞ *Syn.* **1.** See note at **reluctant.**

loathe (lōŦH) *v.* **loathed, loath·ing.** feel strong dislike and disgust for; abhor; hate. [OE *lāthian* hate < *lāth* hostile]

loath·ing (lōŦH′ing) *n.* strong dislike and disgust; intense aversion.

loath·ly[1] (lōŦH′lē) *adj.* loathsome. [OE *lāthlīc* < *lāth* hostile, odious]

loath·ly[2] (lōth′lē; *older* lōŦH′lē) *adv. Rare.* unwillingly; reluctantly. [OE *lāthlīce* < *lāth* hostile]

loath·some (lōŦH′səm) *adj.* disgusting; sickening; *a loathsome odor.* —**loath′some·ly,** *adv.* —**loath′some·ness,** *n.*

loaves (lōvz) *n.* pl. of **loaf**[1].

lob (lob) *n., v.* **lobbed, lob·bing.** —*n.* **1** *Tennis.* a ball hit high to the back of the opponent's court. **2** a slow underarm throw. —*v.* **1** *Tennis.* hit (a ball) high to the back of an opponent's court. **2** throw (a ball) with a slow underarm movement. [ME *lobbe(n)* move clumsily]

lo·bar (lō′bər) *adj.* of or having to do with a lobe or lobes.

lo·bate (lō′bāt) *adj.* having a lobe or lobes; having the form of a lobe. The liver is lobate.

lo·ba·tion (lō bā′shən) *n.* **1** a lobate formation. **2** lobe.

lob·by (lob′ē) *n., pl.* **-bies;** *v.* **-bied, -by·ing.** —*n.* **1** a large entrance hall or vestibule in an apartment building, theatre, hotel, etc.: *A lobby often has chairs or couches to sit on.* **2** a room or hall outside a legislative chamber: *the lobby of the House of Commons.* **3** a person or group that tries to influence legislators.
—*v.* try to influence legislators: *The textile manufacturers are lobbying for a tax on imported fabrics.* [< Med.L *lobia* covered walk < Gmc. See LODGE.]

lob·by·ist (lob′ē ist) *n.* a person who tries to influence legislators.

lobe (lōb) *n.* a rounded projecting part. The lobe of the ear is the rounded lower end. The leaves of the white oak have deeply cut, narrow lobes. [< F < LL < Gk. *lobos*]

lobed (lōbd) *adj.* having a lobe or lobes.

lo·bel·ia (lō bēl′ē ə *or* lō bēl′yə) *n.* any of a genus (Lobelia) of plants having showy, usually blue, white, pink, or red, two-lipped

flowers. [< NL; after Matthias de *Lobel* (1538-1616), a Flemish botanist]

lo·bot·o·my (lō bot′ə mē) *n.* a surgical operation involving incision into a lobe of an organ; especially, the cutting of one or more nerve tracts in the frontal lobe of the brain, formerly used as a treatment for certain severe mental disorders thought to be otherwise incurable.

lob·ster (lob′stər) *n.* **1** any of a family (Homaridae) of edible sea crustaceans having eyes on stalks, a long body, and a pair of large pincers at the front with two pairs of much smaller pincers behind. Lobsters are found along the coasts on both sides of the Atlantic. **2** any of various similar crustaceans. **3** the flesh of a lobster used for food. [OE *loppestre* < L *locusta* locust; influenced by OE < *loppe* spider]

lob·ster·man (lob′stər mən) *n., pl.* **-men.** a man who catches lobsters.

lobster pot a trap for lobsters.

lob·stick (lob′stik′) *n. Cdn.* in the North, a tall, prominently situated spruce or pine trimmed of all but its topmost branches, originally used by the Indians as a talisman and landmark. The voyageurs often trimmed a lobstick as a memorial to an honored fellow traveller or a respected superior. Also, **lopstick.**

lob·ule (lob′yül) *n.* **1** a small lobe. **2** a part of a lobe.

lo·cal (lō′kəl) *adj., n.* —*adj.* **1** of or having to do with a certain place or places; limited to a certain place or places: *the local doctor, local politics, local news.* **2** restricted to one part of the body: *a local pain, local disease, local application of a remedy.* **3** making all, or almost all, stops: *a local train.* —*n.* **1** a train, bus, etc. that stops at all of the stations on its route. **2** a local inhabitant. **3** a branch or chapter of a labor union, fraternity, etc. **4** a newspaper item of interest to a particular place. **5** a person, team, etc. from a given locality. **6** a telephone extension. [< L *localis* < *locus* place] —**lo′cal·ly,** *adv.*

local color or **colour** the customs, peculiarities, etc. of a certain place or period, used in stories and plays to make them seem more real.

lo·cale (lō kal′) *n.* location, site, or place, especially with reference to events or circumstances connected with it. [< F *local* local]

local government **1** the system of administration of local affairs in a township, city, etc. by its own people through their elected representatives. **2** the group, or council, elected for this purpose.

local government district local improvement district.

local improvement district *Cdn.* in some provinces, a district administered by provincial officials because it is too thinly populated to have a municipal government of its own.

lo·cal·ism (lō′kəl iz′əm) *n.* **1** a local practice, custom, etc. **2** a word or expression, etc. peculiar to a certain area. *Outport,* meaning an outlying fishing village, is a Newfoundland localism. **3** provincialism. **4** attachment to a certain place.

lo·cal·i·ty (lō kal′ə tē) *n., pl.* **-ties. 1** a particular place, location, neighborhood, etc.: *Are there any stores in this locality?* **2** places and things considered as related to others in a region. A sense of locality enables one to find one's way.

lo·cal·ize (lō′kəl īz′) *v.* **-ized, -iz·ing.** make local; fix in, assign, or limit to a particular place or locality: *The infection seemed to be localized in the foot.* —**lo′cal·i·za′tion,** *n.* —**lo′cal·iz′er,** *n.*

local option the right of choice exercised by a minor political division, such as a county or city, especially as to whether the sale of liquor shall be permitted within its limits.

Lo·car·no Pact (lō kär′nō) a group of treaties and agreements made in 1925 to guarantee boundaries and maintain peace in western and central Europe between Germany and Britain, France, Belgium, Italy, Czechoslovakia and Poland.

lo·cate (lō′kāt *or* lō kāt′) *v.* **-cat·ed, -cat·ing. 1** establish in a place: *He located his new store in Yellowknife.* **2** establish oneself in a place: *Early settlers located where there was water.* **3** find out the exact position of: *The general tried to locate the enemy's camp.* **4** state or show the position of: *Locate Regina on the map.* **be located,** be situated. [< L *locare* < *locus* place] —**lo′ca·tor,** *n.*

lo·ca·tion (lō kā′shən) *n.* **1** locating or being located: *The scouts disputed about the location of the camp.* **2** a position or place: *The cottage was in a sheltered location.* **3** a plot of ground marked out by boundaries; lot: *a mining location.* **on location,** at a place outside the studio for the purpose of filming a motion picture: *All the outdoor scenes were shot on location.*

loc·a·tive (lok′ə tiv) *adj., n.* —*adj.* of, having to do with, or being the grammatical case, found in Latin and some other languages, that indicates place. —*n.* **1** the locative case. **2** a word or construction in the locative case. [< L *locatus,* pp. of *locate.* See LOCATE.]

loc. cit. in the place cited (for L *loco citato*).

loch (lok *or* loн) *n. Scottish.* **1** lake: *Loch Lomond.* **2** an arm of the sea partly shut in by land. [< Scots Gaelic]
➤ *Hom.* **lock** (lok).

Loch·in·var (lok′ən vär′) *n.* the hero of a poem by Scott, who boldly carries off his sweetheart just as she is about to be married to another man.

lo·ci (lō′sī *or* lō′sē, lō′kī *or* lō′kē) *n.* pl. of **locus.**

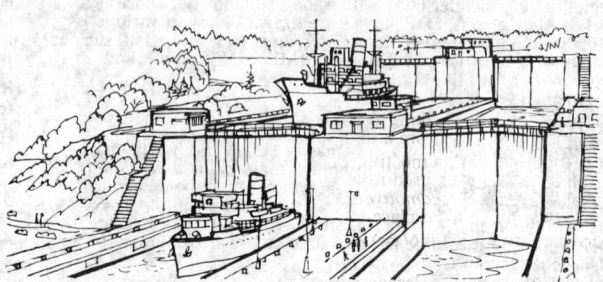

A set of locks in the Welland Canal, built to overcome the 99-metre difference in levels between Lake Ontario and Lake Erie. When a ship enters from above, the gates are closed and water is let out until the level is equal to that below the lock. Then the lower gates are opened. When a ship enters from below, the opposite process takes place.

lock¹ (lok) *n., v.* —*n.* **1** a means of fastening doors, boxes, etc., usually needing a key of special shape to open it. **2** an enclosed section in a canal, dock, etc. which permits vessels to be raised or lowered to different water levels outside this compartment, either by letting water in or out of the compartment or, in a lift lock, by raising or lowering the water-filled compartment itself. **3** the part of a gun by which the charge is fired; gunlock. **4** a device to keep a wheel from turning. A lock is used when a vehicle is going downhill. **5** an airtight chamber admitting to a compartment in which there is compressed air. **6** *Wrestling.* a kind of hold.
lock, stock, and barrel, *Informal.* completely; entirely.
under lock and key, locked up; in a place that is locked.
—*v.* **1** fasten with a lock: *I forgot to lock the door.* **2** fasten the door, lid, etc. of with a lock: *to lock a box. Is the garage locked?* **3** shut (a person or thing) in; make (a person or thing) secure or inaccessible by locking something: *to lock old letters away in a trunk, to lock up one's private papers. We always lock the cat in the basement for the night.* **4** keep (a person or thing) from entering or gaining access (used with **out**): *She was so angry she locked her sister out. They locked out of their minds all thought of returning.* **5** of an employer, try to coerce (employees) into accepting terms by refusing to let them work during an industrial dispute (used with **out**). **6** hold fast: *The ship was locked in ice. The secret was locked in her heart.* **7** join, fit, jam or link together: *The girls locked arms.* **8** become locked: *Two cars locked together in passing.* **9** fasten (a wheel) to keep from turning. **10** *Printing.* fasten (type, blocks, etc. in a chase) for printing or plating (often used with **up**). **11** make certain to accomplish or get (used with **up**): *We've got the championship locked up.* **12** go or pass by means of a lock; move (a ship) by means of a lock.
lock out, refuse to give work to workers until they accept the employer's terms.
[OE *loc*]
➤ *Hom.* **loch.**

lock² (lok) *n.* **1** a curl or ringlet of hair. **2 locks,** *pl.* the hair of the head: *The child has curly locks.* **3** a tuft of wool, cotton, etc. [OE *locc*]
➤ *Hom.* **loch.**

lock·age (lok′ij) *n.* **1** the construction, use or operation of locks in canals or streams. **2** the passing of ships through a lock. **3** the walls, gates, etc. forming a lock. **4** the amount of elevation and descent affected by a lock or locks. **5** the toll paid for passage through a lock.

lock·er (lok′ər) *n.* **1** a chest, drawer, closet, or cupboard that can be locked. **2** a large refrigerated compartment, as at a cold-storage plant, for storing frozen food for a long time. **3** any person or thing that locks or locks something.

lock·et (lok′it) *n.* a small ornamental case of gold, silver, etc. for holding a picture of someone or a lock of hair. It is usually worn

around the neck on a necklace. [< F *loquet* latch, dim. of OF *loc* < Gmc.]

lock·jaw (lok′jo′ or -jô′) *n.* tetanus. A characteristic symptom of the disease is a stiffness or spasm of the jaw muscles, which may become so severe that the jaws remain clamped shut.

lock·out (lok′out′) *n.* the closure of a factory, office, etc. or the refusal of work by an employer in order to make his employees agree to terms.

lock·smith (lok′smith′) *n.* a person who makes or repairs locks and keys.

lock step a way of marching in step very close together.

lock stitch a sewing-machine stitch in which two threads are fastened together at short intervals.

lock·up (lok′up′) *n. Informal.* jail.

lo·co (lō′kō) *n., pl.* **-cos;** *v.* **-coed, -co·ing;** *adj.* —*n.* 1 locoweed. 2 the disease caused by eating this weed.
—*v.* poison with this weed.
—*adj. Slang.* crazy. [< Sp. *loco* insane]

lo·co·mo·tion (lō′kə mō′shən) *n.* the act or power of moving from place to place. Walking and flying are common forms of locomotion. [< L *loco* from a place + E *motion*]

lo·co·mo·tive (lō′kə mō′tiv) *n., adj.* —*n.* an engine that runs on rails on its own power, used to move railway cars. —*adj.* 1 moving from place to place: *locomotive bacteria.* 2 of or having to do with the power to move from place to place.

lo·co·mo·tor (lō′kə mō′tər) *adj.* of or having to do with locomotion.

locomotor ataxia a degenerative disease of the spinal cord, marked by loss of control over walking and certain other movements.

lo·co·weed (lō′kō wēd′) *n.* any of various plants (genera *Astragalus* and *Oxytropis*) of the pea family found in arid regions of W North America, that are poisonous to livestock, producing frenzied behavior followed by impairment of vision, paralysis, and, sometimes, death.

lo·cum te·nens (lō′kəm tē′nənz) a person temporarily holding the place or office of another; deputy; substitute. [< Med.L < L *locum,* accus. of *locus* place < *tenens,* ppr. of *tenere* hold]

lo·cus (lō′kəs) *n., pl.* **lo·ci.** 1 place or locality. 2 the set or system of all points whose location satisfies given conditions. The locus of points equidistant from two parallel lines is a line halfway between the two lines and parallel to them. 3 the position of a particular gene on a chromosome. [< L]

lo·cust (lō′kəst) *n.* 1 any of a family (Acrididae) of grasshoppers having short antennae, especially any of several species that migrate in great swarms, often destroying all vegetation in the areas they pass through. 2 *Esp.U.S.* cicada. 3 any of various hardwood trees of the pea family, such as the **black locust** (*Robinia pseudoacacia*) or the **honey locust** (*Gleditsia triacantnos*), both tall North American trees often planted for ornament. 4 the hard, decay-resistant wood of a locust tree. 5 carob. [< L *locusta*]

lo·cu·tion (lō kyü′shən) *n.* 1 a particular form of expression or phrasing, especially a word or expression characteristic of a particular region, group of people, etc. 2 style of speech: *He has no sense of formal locution.* [< L *locutio, -onis* < *loqui* speak]

lode (lōd) *n.* a vein of metal ore: *The miners struck a rich lode of copper.* [OE *lād* course, carrying. Cf. LOAD.]
☛ *Hom.* **load.**

lode mining hardrock mining.

lode·star (lōd′stär′) *n.* 1 a star that shows the way, especially the North Star. 2 a guiding principle. Also, **loadstar.** [< *load* + *star*]

lode·stone (lōd′stōn′) *n.* 1 iron oxide (magnetite) that is naturally magnetic. 2 a person or thing that attracts strongly: *Gold was the lodestone that drew adventurers to the Yukon.* Also, **loadstone.** [< *load* + *stone*]

lodge (loj) *v.* **lodged, lodg·ing;** *n.* —*v.* 1 live in a place for a time. 2 provide with a place to live in or sleep in for a time: *Can you lodge us for the weekend?* 3 live in a rented room or rooms: *We are merely lodging at present.* 4 rent a room or rooms in. 5 get caught or stay in a place: *My kite lodged in the top of a tree.* 6 put or send into a place: *The hunter lodged a bullet in the lion's heart.* 7 put for safekeeping: *lodge money in a bank.* 8 put before some authority: *We lodged a complaint with the police.* 9 put (power, authority, etc.) in a person or thing. 10 of wind or rain, beat down (crops); lay flat.
—*n.* 1 an inn or resort hotel, etc. 2 a small or temporary house; house: *My uncle rents a lodge in the mountains every summer.* 3 a a branch of a club or society. b the place where such a group meets. 4 the den of an animal such as a beaver or otter. 5 a North American Indian dwelling. 6 a North American Indian household. [ME < OF *loge* arbor, covered walk < OHG **laubja.* Doublet of LOBBY, LOGE, LOGGIA.]

lodge·ment (loj′mənt) See **lodgment.**

hat, āge, fär; let, ēqual, tèrm; it, īce
hot, ōpen, ôrder; oil, out; cup, pùt, rüle,
əbove, takən, pencəl, lemən, circəs

ch, child; ng, long; sh, ship
th, thin; ŦH, then; zh, measure

lodge·pole pine (loj′pōl′) a pine (*Pinus contorta*) found throughout British Columbia and western Alberta, occurring in two quite distinct forms: a short, often crooked tree growing along the coast and a tall, straight, slender tree growing inland. The inland form is an important timber-producing tree. The coastal form is often called the shore pine.

lodg·er (loj′ər) *n.* a person who lives in a rented room or rooms.

lodg·ing (loj′ing) *n.* 1 a place to live in for a time. 2 **lodgings,** *pl.* a rented room or rooms in a house, not in a hotel.

lodging house a house in which rooms are rented.

lodg·ment or **lodge·ment** (loj′mənt) *n.* 1 lodging or being lodged: *the lodgment of a complaint.* 2 something lodged or deposited: *a lodgment of earth on a ledge or rock.* 3 *Military.* a position gained; foothold. b an entrenchment built temporarily on a position gained from the enemy.

lo·ess (lō′is or lœs) *n.* a deposit of fine, yellowish-brown loam found in river valleys in North America, Europe, and Asia, believed to have been deposited by the wind. Loess is very fertile when irrigated. [< G *Löss*]

loft (loft) *n., v.* —*n.* 1 attic. 2 a room under the roof of a barn or stable; hayloft. 3 a gallery in a church or hall: *a choir loft.* 4 *Golf.* a the backward slope of the face of a club to give elevation to a struck ball. b a stroke that drives a ball upward.
—*v.* 1 *Golf.* hit (a ball) high up into the air. 2 propel or lift high in the air. [OE < ON *lopt* air, sky, loft]

loft·y (lof′tē) *adj.* **loft·i·er, loft·i·est.** 1 very high: *lofty mountains.* 2 high in character or spirit; exalted; noble: *lofty aims, lofty ideals.* 3 proud; haughty: *He had a lofty contempt for others.* —**loft′i·ly,** *adv.* —**loft′i·ness,** *n.*
☛ *Syn.* 1. See note at **high.**

log¹ (log) *n., v.* **logged, log·ging.** —*n.* 1 a length of wood just as it comes from the tree. 2 the daily record of a ship's voyage. 3 the record of an airplane trip, performance of an engine, etc. 4 a float for measuring the speed of a ship.
—*v.* 1 cut down trees, cut them into logs, and get them out of the forest. 2 cut (trees) into logs. 3 cut down trees on (land). 4 enter in a logbook or log. 5 enter the name and offence of (a sailor) in a ship's log. 6 travel (a particular distance) or reach (a particular speed): *We logged 800 kilometres the first day.* [ME *logge;* origin uncertain] —**log′like′,** *adj.*

log² logarithm.

lo·gan (lō′gən) *n. Cdn.* pokelogan.

lo·gan·ber·ry (lō′gən ber′ē) *n., pl.* **-ries.** 1 a dark-red berry closely resembling a blackberry, that is the fruit of a trailing, prickly plant (*Rubus loganobaccus*) of the rose family thought to be a cross between the wild blackberry of the Pacific coast and the red raspberry. 2 the plant that bears these berries, cultivated along the Pacific coast of North America. [< J.H. *Logan* (1841-1928), an American jurist and horticulturist, its first grower]

log·a·rithm (log′ə riŦH′əm) *n.* 1 *Mathematics.* an exponent of the power to which a fixed number (usually 10) must be raised in order to produce a given number. If the fixed number is 10, the logarithm of 1000 is 3; the logarithm of 10 000 is 4; the logarithm of 100 000 is 5. 2 one of a system of such exponents used to shorten calculations in mathematics. [< NL *logarithmus* < Gk. *logos* proportion + *arithmos* number]

log·a·rith·mic (log′ə riŦH′mik) *adj.* of or having to do with a logarithm or logarithms.

log·a·rith·mi·cal (log′ə riŦH′mə kəl) *adj.* logarithmic.

log·book (log′bùk′) *n.* 1 a book containing a permanent record of all the details of the voyage of a ship or aircraft. 2 a traveller's diary. 3 any book containing a record of progress or performance over a period of time.

loge (loj or lōzh) *n.* 1 a box in a theatre or opera house. 2 a balcony or mezzanine in a theatre, especially the front part of such a balcony. [< F. See LODGE.]

log·ger (log′ər) *n.* 1 a person whose work is felling trees and getting the logs to the mill. 2 a machine for loading or hauling logs.

log·ger·head (log′ər hed′) *n.* 1 *Archaic or dialect.* a stupid person; blockhead. 2 any of various very large, large-headed marine turtles (genus *Caretta*) of the warmer waters of the western Atlantic, especially a carnivorous species (*C. caretta*). 3 an iron

instrument having a long handle with a ball at the end that is heated for melting pitch, etc.

at loggerheads, disputing; in disagreement: *The council members are still at loggerheads over the housing issue.*
[< *logger,* var. of *log* + *head*]

log·gia (loj′ə; Italian, lôd′jä) *n., pl.* **log·gias** (lôj′əz) or *(Italian)* **log·gie** (lôd′jā). a gallery or arcade open to the air on at least one side. [< Ital. < F *loge.* See LODGE.]

log·ging (log′ing) *n.* the work of cutting down trees, cutting them into logs, and removing them from the forest.

log·ic (loj′ik) *n.* 1 the science of getting new and valid information by reasoning from facts that one already knows. 2 a book on logic. 3 reasoning; the use of argument: *The lawyer won his case because his logic was sound.* 4 reason; sound sense: *There is much logic in what you say.* [ME < OF *logique* < LL < Gk. *logikē (technē)* reasoning (art) < *logos* word]

log·i·cal (loj′ə kəl) *adj.* 1 having to do with or according to the principles of logic: *logical reasoning.* 2 reasonable; reasonably expected. 3 reasoning correctly: *a clear and logical mind.* —**log′i·cal·ly,** *adv.* —**log′i·cal·ness,** *n.*

lo·gi·cian (lō jish′ən) *n.* a person trained or skilled in logic.

lo·gis·tic (lō jis′tik) *adj.* of or having to do with logistics.

lo·gis·ti·cal (lō jis′tə kəl) *adj.* logistic.

lo·gis·tics (lō jis′tiks) *n.* 1 the art of planning and carrying out military movement, evacuation, and supply. 2 the planning and handling of any complex operation. [< F *logistique,* ult. < *loger* lodge]

log·jam (log′jam′) *n., v.* **-jammed, -jam·ming.** —*n.* 1 an accumulation of floating logs jammed together in the water. 2 any deadlock or blockage. —*v.* delay, block, or obstruct.

lo·go (lō′gō or log′ō) *n.* an identifying symbol used as a trademark, in advertising, etc.

log·or·rhea (log′ə rē′ə) *n.* excessive, especially compulsive, wordiness or talkativeness.

log·o·type (log′ə tīp′) *n. Printing.* a word or several frequently used letters cast in one piece but not connected, such as *Ltd., Co.,* etc.

log·roll (log′rōl′) *v. Informal.* 1 take part in logrolling. 2 *Esp.U.S.* get (a bill) passed by logrolling. —**log′roll′er,** *n.*

log·roll·ing (log′rōl′ing) *n.* 1 the act of rolling logs, especially by treading on them. 2 the giving of political aid in return for a like favor.

log·wood (log′wùd′) *n.* 1 a tropical American tree (*Haematoxylon campechianum*) of the pea family. 2 its heavy, hard, brownish-red wood, from which a dye is obtained that is used especially in biological stains. 3 the dye.

lo·gy (lō′gē) *adj.* **-gi·er, -gi·est.** *Informal.* heavy; sluggish; dull. [cf. Du. *log*]

–logy *combining form.* 1 an account, doctrine, or science of, as in *biology, theology.* 2 speaking; discussion, as in *eulogy.* 3 special meanings, as in *analogy, anthology.* [< Gk. *-logia,* in a few cases < *logos* word, discourse, but usually < *-logos* treating of < *legein* speak (of), mention]

loin (loin) *n.* 1 Usually, **loins,** *pl.* the part of the body between the ribs and the hips. The loins are on both sides of the backbone. 2 a piece of meat from this part: *a loin of pork.* See **pork** for picture. **gird up** (one's) **loins,** get ready for action.
[ME < OF *loigne,* ult. < L *lumbus*]

loin·cloth (loin′kloth′) *n.* a piece of cloth fastened around the waist and covering the thighs. The loincloth is worn by people of warm countries.

loi·ter (loi′tər) *v.* 1 linger idly; stop and play along the way. 2 spend (time) idly: *to loiter the hours away.* [ME < MDu. *loteren* be loose] —**loi′ter·er,** *n.*
☞ *Syn.* 1. See note at **linger.**

Lo·ki (lō′kē) *n. Norse mythology.* the god who constantly created trouble and evil, especially among his fellow gods. He caused the death of Balder.

L.O.L. Loyal Orange Association (or Lodge).

loll (lol) *v., n.* —*v.* 1 recline or lean in a lazy manner: *to loll on a chesterfield.* 2 hang out loosely or droop: *A dog's tongue lolls out in hot weather.* 3 allow to hang out or droop: *A dog lolls out his tongue.*
—*n.* a lolling. [ME *lolle(n)*]

Lol·lard (lol′ərd) *n.* a follower of John Wycliffe, 1320?-1384, an English religious reformer. The Lollards advocated certain religious,

political, and economic reforms, and were persecuted as heretics.
[< MDu. *lollaerd* mumbler < *lollen* mumble]

Lol·lard·ism (lol′ər diz′əm) *n.* Lollardry.

Lol·lard·ry (lol′ər drē) *n.* 1 the principles and beliefs of the Lollards. 2 support for these principles and beliefs. Also, **Lollardy.**

Lol·lard·y (lol′ər dē) *n.* Lollardry.

lol·li·pop or **lol·ly·pop** (lol′ē pop′) *n.* a piece of hard candy, usually on the end of a small stick; sucker. [< dial. *lolly* tongue + *pop*]

Lom·bard (lom′bärd or lom′bərd, lum′bärd or lum′bərd) *n.* 1 a member of a Germanic tribe that in the sixth century A.D. conquered the part of N Italy since known as Lombardy. 2 a native or inhabitant of Lombardy. [< Ital. *Lombardo* < LL *Langobardus* < Gmc.; original meaning, long beard]

Lombard Street 1 a London street famous as a financial centre. 2 the London money market or financiers as a group.

Lom·bard·y poplar (lom′bər dē or lum′bər dē) a variety of European poplar (*Populus nigra italica*) having a narrow, spire-like crown and almost vertical branches, commonly grown in parts of Canada as an ornamental tree.

lon. longitude.

Lon·don·er (lun′dən ər) *n.* a native or inhabitant of London, England.

lone (lōn) *adj.* 1 having no company or companion; alone; solitary: *We met a lone traveller on our way.* 2 lonesome; lonely: *a lone life.* 3 standing apart; isolated: *a lone house on a hill.* 4 *Rare.* single or widowed. [var. of *alone*]
☞ *Hom.* **loan.**

lone·ly (lōn′lē) *adj.* **-li·er, -li·est.** 1 feeling oneself alone and longing for company of friends: *He was lonely while his brother was away.* 2 without many people: *a lonely road.* 3 alone: *a lonely tree.* —**lone′li·ness,** *n.*

lon·er (lōn′ər) *n. Informal.* a person who prefers to live or be alone.

lone·some (lōn′səm) *adj.* **-som·er, -som·est.** 1 feeling lonely. 2 making one feel lonely. 3 unfrequented; desolate: *a lonesome road.* 4 solitary: *One lonesome pine stood there.* —**lone′some·ly,** *adv.* —**lone′some·ness,** *n.*

lone wolf a person who prefers to work or live alone; loner.

long¹ (long) *adj.* **long·er** (long′gər), **long·est** (long′gist); *adv., n.* —*adj.* 1 measuring much, or more than usual, from end to end in space or time: *a long distance, a long speech.* 2 continuing too long; lengthy; tedious: *long hours of waiting.* 3 beyond the normal extension in space, duration, quantity, etc.: *a long dozen, a long ton.* 4 having a specified length in space or time: *five metres long, two hours long.* 5 thin and narrow: *a long pole.* 6 far-reaching; extending to a great distance in space or time: *a long memory, a long look into the future.* 7 of vowels or syllables, taking a relatively long time to pronounce. 8 involving considerable risk, liability to error, etc.: *a long chance.* 9 well supplied (with some commodity or stock). 10 depending on a rise in prices for profit.
a long face, a sad expression.
in the long run, over a long period of time; eventually: *The system will work out fairly well in the long run.*
—*adv.* 1 throughout the whole length of: *all night long.* 2 for a long time: *a reform long advocated.* 3 at a point of time far distant from the time indicated: *long before, long since.*
as long as or **so long as,** provided that.
—*n.* 1 a long time: *for long.* 2 a long sound.
before long, soon; in a short time.
the long and the short of it, the sum total (of something); substance; upshot.
[OE *lang*]

long² (long) *v.* wish very much; have a strong desire. [OE *langian* < *lang* long¹]

long. longitude.

long·boat (long′bōt′) *n.* the largest and strongest boat carried by a merchant sailing ship.

long·bow (long′bō′) *n.* a bow drawn by hand and shooting a long feathered arrow. A longbow is usually between 170 and 185 cm long.
draw the longbow, tell exaggerated stories.

long·cloth (long′kloth′) *n.* a kind of fine, soft cotton cloth.

long–dis·tance (long′dis′təns) *adj., n.* —*adj.* 1 of or having to do with telephone service to another town, city, etc. 2 for or over great distances: *a long-distance moving van.* —*n.* an operator or exchange that takes care of long-distance calls.

long division *Arithmetic.* division involving numbers containing usually two or more digits, and in which the steps of the process are written down in full.

long dozen thirteen.

long–drawn (long′dron′ or -drôn′) *adj.* lasting a long time; prolonged to great length: *the long-drawn howl of a coyote, a long-drawn speech.*

lon·gev·i·ty (lon jev′ə tē) *n.* long life. [< L *longaevitas* < *longaevus* long-lived < *longus* long + *aevum* age]

long·hair (long′her′) *n., adj. Informal.* —*n.* **1** a person who is interested in intellectual or artistic things, especially one who prefers classical music to popular music or jazz. **2** hippie. —*adj.* of, suitable for, or referring to longhairs: *longhair music.*

long·hand (long′hand′) *n.* ordinary writing, not shorthand or typewriting.

long–head·ed (long′hed′id) *adj.* **1** having foresight and good sense; shrewd. **2** having a long head.

long–horn (long′hôrn′) *n.* a breed of cattle having very long horns, formerly common in the SW United States.

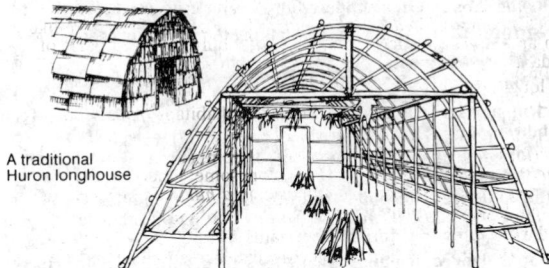
A traditional
Huron longhouse

long·house (long′hous′) *n.* a large dwelling of certain North American Indian peoples, especially the Iroquois, in which several families of a community lived together.

long·ing (long′ing) *n., adj.* —*n.* an earnest desire. —*adj.* having or showing earnest desire. —**long′ing·ly,** *adv.*
☛ *Syn. n.* See note at **desire.**

long·ish (long′ish) *adj.* rather long.

lon·gi·tude (lon′jə tyüd′ or lon′jə tüd′, long′gə tyüd′ or long′gə tüd′) *n.* **1** a distance east or west on the earth's surface, measured in degrees from a certain meridian. On maps, lines running between the North and South Poles represent longitudes. Usually the meridian through Greenwich, England, is used to measure longitude. See **equator** for picture. **2** *Archaic or facetious.* length. [ME < L *longitudo* length < *longus* long]

lon·gi·tu·di·nal (lon′jə tyü′də nəl or -tü′də nəl, long′gə tyü′də nəl or -tü′də nəl) *adj.* **1** of or having to do with length or the lengthwise dimension: *longitudinal measurements.* **2** running lengthwise: *longitudinal stripes.* **3** of or dealing with changes in an individual or group over an extended period of time: *a longitudinal study.* **4** of longitude. —**lon′gi·tu′di·nal·ly,** *adv.*

long·johns or **long–johns** (long′jonz′) *n.pl. Informal.* **1** underpants with long legs. **2** long underwear.

long jump 1 an athletic event or contest in which contestants try to jump over as much ground as possible. The long jump from a running start is one of the Olympic track and field events. **2** a jump of this kind. **3 standing long jump,** a long jump from a standing start. The standing long jump is often included in school field meets.

long·line (long′līn′) *n.* a fishing line, sometimes several kilometres long, that has many baited hooks, used for deep-sea fishing.

long·lin·er (long′līn′ər) *n.* a fishing vessel that uses longlines.

long–lived (long′livd′ or -līvd′) *adj.* living or lasting a long time.

long measure linear measure.

Long Parliament in England, the Parliament that assembled in 1640, was expelled by Cromwell in 1653, reassembled in 1659, and was dissolved in 1660.

long–play·ing (long′plā′ing) *adj.* designating or of a microgroove phonograph record designed to be played at 33⅓ revolutions per minute.

long–range (long′rānj′) *adj.* **1** looking ahead; future: *long-range plans.* **2** capable of covering a great distance: *long-range missiles.*

long·shore (long′shôr′) *adj.* **1** of or having to do with longshoremen or the waterfront. **2** employed or found along the shore.

long·shore·man (long′shôr′mən) *n.* **-men.** a person whose work is loading and unloading ships. [for *alongshoreman*]

long shot 1 *Informal.* a bet, or wager, against great odds, but which therefore carries great possible winnings. **2** *Informal.* any venture or undertaking involving great risk or only slight chance of

hat, āge, fär; let, ēqual, tèrm; it, īce
hot, ōpen, ôrder; oil, out; cup, pùt, rüle,
əbove, takən, pencəl, lemən, circəs
ch, child; ng, long; sh, ship
th, thin; ŦH, then; zh, measure

success, but offering great rewards if successful. **3** a motion picture or television scene photographed from a distance.

not by a long shot, not at all; certainly not.

long–sight·ed (long′sīt′id) *adj.* **1** far-sighted; focussing at more than the right distance. **2** having foresight; wise. —**long′–sight′ed·ly,** *adv.* —**long′–sight′ed·ness,** *n.*

long·spur (long′spėr′) *n.* any of various finches (genera *Rhyncophanes* and *Calcarius*) of the Arctic and the North American plains, having a long claw on the hind toe.

long–stand·ing (long′stan′ding) *adj.* having lasted for a long time: *a long-standing feud.*

long–suf·fer·ing (long′suf′ər ing or -suf′ring) *adj., n.* —*adj.* enduring trouble, pain, or injury long and patiently. —*n.* long and patient endurance of trouble, pain, or injury.

long suit 1 *Card games.* the suit in which one has most cards. **2** something in which a person excels; a strong point: *Patience is not her long suit.*

long–term (long′tėrm′) *adj.* **1** lasting or intended for a long time: *our long-term plans and ambitions.* **2** falling due in several years: *a long-term loan.*

long ton the British ton, 2240 pounds (about 1.02 tonnes).

long–tongued (long′tungd′) *adj.* **1** having a long tongue. **2** talking much or too much.

lon·gueur (lôn gœr′) *n.* a long and tedious period of time or a long or boring section in a book, motion picture, etc. [< F *longueur,* literally, length]

long underwear underwear consisting of ankle-length drawers and a top with long or short sleeves, the drawers and top often made in one piece.

long·ways (long′wāz′) *adv.* lengthwise; in the direction of the length.

long–wind·ed (long′win′did) *adj.* **1** capable of long effort without getting out of breath: *A long-distance runner must be long-winded.* **2** talking or writing at great lengths; tiresome: *a long-winded speaker.* —**long′–wind′ed·ly,** *adv.* —**long′–wind′ed·ness,** *n.*

long·wise (long′wīz′) *adv.* lengthwise.

loo¹ (lü) *n.* a kind of card game in which forfeits are paid into a pool. [short for *lanterloo* < F *lanturelu,* a meaningless word in the refrain of an old French song]

loo² (lü) *n. Esp.Brit. Informal.* toilet (defs. 1 and 2).

look (lùk) *v., n.* —*v.* **1** see; try to see; turn the eyes: *He looked this way.* **2** direct a look at: *to look one in the eye.* **3** examine; pay attention (*used with* **at**): *You must look at all the facts.* **4** search: *I looked everywhere for my socks: He looked through the drawer, trying to find his keys.* **5** appear equal to: *He doesn't look his age.* **6** seem; appear: *She looks pale.* **7** have a view; face: *Our house looks upon a garden.* **8** express or suggest by looks.

look after, attend to; take care of.

look alive, hurry.

look at, examine, pay attention.

look back, recollect; think about the past.

look daggers, look angrily.

look down on, despise; scorn.

look for, a seek or search for. **b** expect: *We'll look for you tonight.*

look forward to, expect: *We look forward to seeing you. When the crops failed, they knew they had to look forward to a bad winter.*

look in, make a short visit: *She said she'd look in on her way back.*

look into, investigate: *She promised to look into the matter.*

look on, a watch without taking part: *The teacher conducted the experiment while we looked on.* **b** regard; consider: *I look on her as a very able person.*

look (oneself), seem like oneself; look well: *She has been quite ill and still doesn't look herself.*

look out, be careful; watch out: *Look out for cars as you cross the street.*

look over, examine; inspect: *The police officer looked over his driver's licence.*

look through, direct the gaze through: *to look through a window, to look through a microscope.*

look to, a attend to; take care of. **b** turn to for help.

look up, a find; refer to: *She looked up the word in the dictionary.* **b** *Informal.* call on; visit: *Look me up when you come to town.* **c** *Informal.* get better; improve.

look up to, respect; admire.
—*n.* **1** a glance; seeing: *He took a quick look at the magazine.* **2** a search. **3** appearance; aspect. **4 looks,** *pl.* **a** personal appearance: *Good looks means a good appearance.* **b** *Informal.* general appearance: *the looks of a situation.* [OE *lōcian*]

look·er (lük′ər) *n.* **1** a person who looks. **2** *Slang.* a person who is good-looking; attractive person.

look·er-on (lük′ər on′) *n., pl.* **look·ers-on.** a person who watches without taking part; spectator.

looking glass mirror.

look·out (lük′out′) *n.* **1** a careful watch: *Be on the lookout for trouble.* **2** a person or group that keeps such a watch. **3** a place from which to watch, as for forest fires, ships, etc.: *A crow's-nest is a lookout.* **4** what is seen ahead; outlook. **5** *Informal.* something to be cared for or worried about: *That is his lookout.*

look-see (lük′sē) *n. Slang.* a quick search or survey. [< pidgin English]

loom¹ (lüm) *n., v.* —*n.* a machine for weaving cloth. —*v.* weave on a loom. [OE (*ge*)*lōma* implement]

loom² (lüm) *v.* appear dimly or vaguely as a large, often threatening, shape: *A large iceberg loomed through the thick, grey fog.* [origin uncertain]

loon¹ (lün) *n.* any of a small genus (*Gavia,* constituting the order Gaviiformes) of diving birds of northern regions having mainly black-and-white or grey-and- white plumage, a straight, pointed bill, and a long body with the legs set far back on it. The common loon (*G. immer*) is found throughout most of Canada, but generally in more or less remote areas. [earlier *loom* < ON *lómr*]
☛ *Hom.* **lune.**

loon² (lün) *n.* a crazy or stupid person. [cf. MDu. *loen* stupid fellow]
☛ *Hom.* **lune.**

loon·y (lü′nē) *adj.* **loon·i·er, loon·i·est;** *n., pl.* **loon·ies.** *Slang.*
—*adj.* crazy. —*n.* a crazy person; lunatic. [var. of *luny* < *lunatic*] —**loon′i·ness,** *n.*

loop (lüp) *n., v.* —*n.* **1** the shape of a curved string, ribbon, bent wire, etc. that crosses itself. In handwriting, *b* and *g* and *h* and *l* often have loops. **2** a thing, bend, course, or motion shaped somewhat like this: *The handwritten letter L usually has a loop. The road makes a wide loop around the lake.* **3** a fastening or ornament formed of cord, etc. bent and crossed. **4** a turn like the letter *l,* especially one made by an airplane.
—*v.* **1** make a loop or loops in. **2** fasten with a loop: *He looped the sail to the mast with rope.* **3** encircle with a loop. **4** form a loop or loops. **5** make a vertical turn or revolution in an airplane.
loop the loop, turn over and over; make a loop in the air. [ME *loupe,* ? < Celtic]

loop·hole (lüp′hōl′) *n.* **1** a small opening in a wall to shoot through, look through, or let in light and air. **2** a means of escape; especially, something in a law, contract, etc., that is ambiguous or unclear, which makes it possible to avoid the intent or consequences of the law, etc. [? < MDu. *lupen* peer]

loose (lüs) *adj.* **loos·er, loos·est;** *v.* **loosed, loos·ing;** *adv., n.* —*adj.*
1 not firmly set or fastened: *a loose tooth, a loose thread.* **2** not tight: *loose clothing.* **3** not bound together: *loose papers.* **4** not put up in a box, can, etc.: *loose coffee.* **5** free; not shut in or up: *We leave the dog loose at night.* **6** not close or solid; having spaces: *loose earth, cloth with a loose weave.* **7** not strict or exact: *a loose translation from another language, loose thinking.* **8** having or showing too little control or restraint: *loose conduct, a loose tongue.* **9** lewd or unchaste. **10** *Informal.* not tense; relaxed.
11 *Informal.* not employed; not appropriated: *loose hours, loose funds.* **12** of a chemical element, free; uncombined.
—*v.* **1** set free; let go: *They loosed the prisoners.* **2** shoot (an arrow, gun, etc.). **3** make loose; untie; unfasten. **4** relax.
—*adv.* in a loose manner.
—*n.*
break loose, a separate from anything; break a connection or relation. **b** run away; free oneself. **c** *Slang.* go on a spree.
cast loose, unfasten; separate.
cut loose, break loose.
let loose, set free; release; let go.
set or **turn loose,** set free; release; let go.
—*n.*
on the loose, *Informal.* **a** free; without restraint. **b** on a spree.
c absent without leave. [ME < ON *lauss*] —**loose′ly,** *adv.*
—**loose′ness,** *n.*

loose end 1 something left hanging loose: *There's a loose end hanging from the hem.* **2** an unfinished detail; a relatively minor thing that remains to be done: *We've finished the main job, but there are still a few loose ends to tie up.*
at loose ends, a in an unsettled or disorganized condition or

situation: *He has finished university, but is still at loose ends about what he wants to do.* **b** unemployed.

loose-joint·ed (lüs′join′tid) *adj.* **1** having loose joints; loosely built. **2** able to move very freely.

loose-leaf (lüs′lēf′) *adj.* of a notebook, etc., having pages or sheets that can be taken out and replaced.

loos·en (lü′sən) *v.* **1** make loose or looser; untie; unfasten: *The doctor loosened the stricken man's collar.* **2** become loose or looser. —**loos′en·er,** *n.*

loose·strife (lüs′strīf′) *n.* **1** any of a genus (*Lythrum*) of herbs, especially a common weed having long, showy spikes of purple flowers. **2** (*adj.*) designating a family (Lythraceae) of mainly tropical plants that includes the purple loosestrife and henna. **3** any of a genus (*Lysimachia*) of plants of the primrose family having leafy stems and spikes of yellow, white, or rose flowers. [literal translation of L *lysimachia* < Gk. *Lysimachos* (as if < *lyein* to loose + *machē* battle), the supposed discoverer]

loose-tongued (lüs′tungd′) *adj.* talking too much; irresponsible in speech.

loot (lüt) *n., v.* —*n.* **1** spoils; plunder; booty: *loot taken by soldiers from a captured town.* **2** *Slang.* money or other capital: *That's a lot of loot to spend for a record player.* —*v.* plunder; rob: *The jewellery store was looted by burglars.* [< Hind. *lūt*] —**loot′er,** *n.*
☛ *Hom.* **lute.**
☛ *Syn. n.* See note at **plunder.**

lop¹ (lop) *v.* **lopped, lop·ping. 1** cut (*usually used with* **off**): *We lopped off a big chunk of cheese.* **2** trim by cutting off branches, twigs, etc.: *to lop a tree.* [origin uncertain]

lop² (lop) *v.* **lopped, lop·ping. 1** hang loosely; droop. **2** flop. [origin uncertain]

lope (lōp) *v.* **loped, lop·ing;** *n.* —*v.* run with a long, easy stride: *The coyote loped along the trail.* —*n.* a long, easy stride. [ME < ON *hlaupa* leap] —**lop′er,** *n.*

lop-eared (lop′ērd′) *adj.* having ears that hang loosely or droop.

lop-sid·ed (lop′sīd′id) *adj.* larger or heavier on one side than the other; unevenly balanced; leaning to one side. —**lop′sid′ed·ly,** *adv.* —**lop′sid′ed·ness,** *n.*

lop·stick (lop′stik′) *n.* lobstick.

lo·qua·cious (lō kwā′shəs *or* lə kwā′ shəs) *adj.* talking much; fond of talking. —**lo·qua′cious·ly,** *adv.*
☛ *Syn.* See note at **talkative.**

lo·quac·i·ty (lō kwas′ə tē *or* lə kwas′ə tē) *n.* an inclination to talk a great deal; talkativeness. [< L *loquacitas* < *loquax* talkative < *loqui* talk]

lo·quat (lō′kwot *or* lō′kwat) *n.* **1** an evergreen tree (*Eriobotrya japonica*) of the rose family native to China and Japan, having small, yellow, edible, plumlike fruit. **2** the fruit of this tree.

lo·ran (lô′rən) *n.* a device by which a navigator can determine his geographical position by utilizing signals sent out from two or more radio stations. [*lo*ng *ra*nge *n*avigation]

lord (lôrd) *n., v.* —*n.* **1** a ruler, master, or chief; a person who has the power. **2** a feudal superior. **3 the Lord, a** God. **b** Christ. **4** in the United Kingdom, a man entitled by courtesy to the title of lord: *A baron is a lord.* **5 Lord, a** in the United Kingdom, a titled nobleman or peer of the realm belonging to the House of Lords. **b** a title used in writing or speaking to or of noblemen of certain ranks: *Lord Beaverbrook was born in Ontario.* **c** a title given by courtesy to men holding certain positions: *Lord Chief Justice.* **6 the Lords,** the House of Lords; the upper house of the British Parliament.
7 *Archaic.* a husband.
—*v.* **1** rule proudly or absolutely: *He lorded it over us.* **2** raise to the rank of lord.
lord it over, domineer over.
[OE *hlāford* < *hlāfweard* bread keeper < *hlāf* loaf + *weard* keeper, ward. Cf. LADY.]

Lord Chamberlain in Britain, a government officer and the official in charge of the royal household.

Lord Chancellor or **Lord High Chancellor** in the United Kingdom, the highest-ranking official of state, with the exception of the royal princes and the Archbishop of Canterbury. He is chairman of the House of Lords, keeper of the Great Seal, and a cabinet member by political appointment.

lord·ling (lôrd′ling) *n.* a little or unimportant lord.

lord·ly (lôrd′lē) *adj.* **-li·er, -li·est;** *adv.* —*adj.* **1** like or suitable for a lord; grand; magnificent. **2** haughty; insolent; scornful. —*adv.* in a lordly manner. —**lord′li·ness,** *n.*

Lord Mayor in Britain, the title of the mayors of London and of some other large cities.

lor·do·sis (lôr dō′sis) *n., pl.* **-ses** (-sēz). a curvature of the spine. [< Gk. *lordos* bent back + E *-osis*]

Lord's Day Sunday.

Lord's Day Alliance of Canada a national organization of Anglican, Baptist, Methodist, and Presbyterian churches founded in 1888 for preserving Sunday as a day of rest.

lord·ship (lôrd'ship) n. 1 the rank or position of a lord. 2 Often, **Lordship**, Brit. a title used in speaking to or of a lord: your Lordship, his Lordship. 3 rule; ownership.

Lord's Prayer in the Bible, a prayer given by Jesus to His disciples (Matt. 6:9-13).

Lord's Supper 1 Jesus' last supper with His disciples. 2 the Christian service in memory of this; Holy Communion.

lore (lôr) n. 1 the facts and stories about a certain subject. 2 learning; knowledge. [OE lār. Related to LEARN.]

Lor·e·lei (lôr'ə lī') n. German legend. a siren of the Rhine whose beauty and singing distracted sailors and caused them to wreck their ships. [< G]

lor·gnette (lôr nyet') n. 1 eyeglasses without sidepieces, mounted on a handle. 2 opera glasses mounted on a handle. [< F lorgnette < lorgner look sidelong at, eye < OF lorgne squinting]

lo·ris (lôr'is) n. any of several small, slow-moving, nocturnal primates (genera Loris and Nycticebus of the family Lorisidae) of the forests of S and SE Asia having soft, grey or brown fur, very large eyes, short index fingers, and no tail. [< F loris, ? < Du. loeris booby]

lorn (lôrn) adj. 1 forsaken; forlorn. 2 Archaic. lost; ruined. [OE -loren, pp. of -lēosan lose. Related to FORLORN.]

lor·ry (lôr'ē) n., pl. -ries. 1 a long, flat wagon without sides. 2 Brit. motor truck. [cf. dial. E lurry pull, lug]

lo·ry (lô'rē) n., pl. -ries. any of a number of small, brightly colored parrots native to Australia, New Guinea, and nearby islands, most of which have a fringed, brush-like tongue tip for feeding on nectar and soft fruits. [< Malay luri]

lose (lüz) v. lost, los·ing. 1 not have any longer; have taken away from one by accident, carelessness, gambling, parting, death, etc.: to lose one's life. 2 be unable to find: to lose one's way, to lose a book. 3 fail to keep or maintain; cease to have: to lose patience, to lose all fear. 4 miss; fail to get, catch, see, hear, or understand: to lose a train, to lose a few words of what was said, to lose a sale. 5 fail to win: to lose a bet. 6 be defeated: Our team lost. 7 bring to destruction; ruin: The ship and its crew were lost. 8 let pass without use or profit; waste: to lose an opportunity, lost time. The hint was not lost on him. 9 suffer loss: to lose on a contract. 10 cause the loss of: Delay lost the battle. 11 cause to lose: That one act lost him his job.

lose (oneself), **a** let oneself go astray; become bewildered. **b** become absorbed.

lose out, fail; be unsuccessful.

[OE losian be lost < los destruction] **—los'er,** n.

los·ing (lüz'ing) adj. that cannot win: His friends told him he was playing a losing game, but he wouldn't listen.

los·ings (lüz'ingz) n. pl. losses.

loss (los) n. 1 losing or being lost. 2 the person or thing lost: The fire was finally put out, but her house was a complete loss. 3 the amount lost. 4 the harm or damage caused by losing something. 5 a defeat: Our team had two losses and one tie out of ten games played. 6 Military. the losing of soldiers by death, capture, or wounding. 7 in insurance, the occurrence of death, property damage, or other contingency against which a person is insured under circumstances that make the insurer liable under the contract. 8 Electricity. the reduction in power, measured by the difference between the power input and power output, in an electric circuit, device, system, etc., corresponding to the transformation of electric energy into heat.

at a loss, puzzled; not sure; uncertain; in difficulty: He was at a loss for words.

at a loss to, unable to.

[OE los]

loss leader an article sold at a loss in order to attract customers.

lost (lost) v., adj. **—v.** pt. and pp. of lose. **—adj.** 1 no longer had or kept: lost friends. 2 no longer to be found; missing: lost articles. 3 no longer visible: He was soon lost in the crowd. 4 attended with defeat: a lost battle. 5 not used to good purpose; wasted: lost time. 6 having gone astray. 7 destroyed or ruined. 8 bewildered: She looked completely lost. 9 absorbed; rapt; engrossed (used with in): lost in thought.

get lost, Slang. go away: The older boys told him to get lost.

lost to, a no longer possible or open to: The chance of promotion was lost to him. **b** no longer belonging to: After that incident, her son was lost to her. **c** insensible to: He was lost to all sense of duty.

lost cause an undertaking already defeated or one certain to be defeated.

hat, āge, fär; let, ēqual, tèrm; it, īce
hot, ōpen, ôrder; oil, out; cup, pút, rüle,
above, takən, pencəl, lemən, circəs

ch, child; ng, long; sh, ship
th, thin; ᴛ H, then; zh, measure

lost sheep a person who has strayed from the right sort of conduct or religious belief.

lot (lot) n., adv., v. lot·ted, lot·ting. **—n.** 1 a large number or amount; a great many or a great deal: a lot of books, a lot of money. There is a lot of truth in what he said. 2 **lots,** Informal. a large number or amount: He has lots of money. There were lots of people. 3 a number of persons or things considered as a group; collection or set: This lot of ballots still has to be counted. 4 a plot of ground, especially one having fixed boundaries, as a subdivision of a block in a town or city: a vacant lot. Our house is on a corner lot. 5 a motion-picture studio together with the surrounding property. 6 an object used to decide something by chance: We drew lots to decide who should be captain. 7 such a method of deciding: divide property by lot. 8 a choice made in this way: The lot fell to me. 9 what one gets by lot; one's share. 10 one's fate; fortune: a happy lot.

cast or draw lots, use lots to decide something.

cast or throw in (one's) lot with, share the fate of; become a partner with.

—adv. lots, Informal. much: This table is lots nicer than that one. **—v.** divide into lots. [OE hlot]

▸ Usage. **Lots,** meaning 'a lot' is informal and is generally avoided in written English. In informal English, one might say, He tried lots of different shots, but lost the game anyway. In more formal English, one would say, He tried a lot of different (or many different) shots.

Lot (lot) n. in the Bible, a righteous man who was allowed to escape from Sodom before God destroyed it. His wife looked back and was changed into a pillar of salt (Gen. 19:1-26). [< Hebrew]

loth (lōth) See **loath.**

Lo·thar·i·o (lō ther'ē ō') n., pl. -thar·i·os. a man who makes love to many women; rake; libertine. [< Lothario, a character in Nicholas Rowe's The Fair Penitent]

lo·tion (lō'shən) n. a liquid medicine or cosmetic which is applied to the skin. Lotions are used to relieve pain, to heal, to cleanse, or to beautify the skin. [< L lotio, -onis, a washing, ult. < lavere wash]

lo·tos (lō'təs) See **lotus.**

lot·ter·y (lot'ər ē) n., pl. -ter·ies. 1 a scheme for distributing prizes by lot or chance. In a lottery a large number of tickets are sold, only some of which win prizes. 2 a distribution by chance of success, fortune, happiness, etc.: the lottery of life. [< Ital. lotteria < lotto lot. See LOTTO.]

lot·to (lot'ō) n. a game played by drawing numbered disks from a bag or box and covering the corresponding numbers on cards. [< Ital. lotto lot, ult. < Gmc. Akin to LOT.]

lo·tus (lō'təs) n. 1 any of various tropical Old World water lilies, especially the Egyptian white lotus (Nymphaea lotus) which was sacred to the ancient Egyptians and was often represented in art and architecture. 2 an Asian aquatic plant (Nelumbo nucifera) that is the sacred lotus of Hinduism and Buddhism. 3 the fruit eaten by the ancient Greek lotus-eaters that was supposed to cause a dreamy and contented forgetfulness. It is thought to have been the fruit of a tree of the buckthorn family. 4 any of a genus (Lotus) of plants of the pea family found in many parts of the world. Also, **lotos.** [< L < Gk. lōtos]

lo·tus-eat·er (lō'təs ēt'ər) n. a person who leads a life of dreamy, indolent ease.

loud (loud) adj., adv. **—adj.** 1 strong in sound; noisy: The music is too loud. 2 producing a loud sound; making a noise: He has a very loud voice. 3 clamorous; insistent: They were loud in their demands for higher pay. 4 Informal. showy, flashy, or vulgar: loud clothes. **—adv.** in a loud manner: He blew the bugle loud and long. Don't talk so loud.

out loud, loud enough to be heard; not to oneself or in a whisper; aloud: She repeated her lines out loud to herself. [OE hlūd] **—loud'ly,** adv. **—loud'ness,** n.

▸ Syn. adj. 1. **Loud, noisy** = making much or intense sound. **Loud** emphasizes the idea of being not quiet, low, or soft, and suggests strength or intensity of sound. The speaker's voice was quite vacant loud enough to be heard in the back of the room. **Noisy** means disagreeably loud or harsh, and emphasizes continued loudness or disturbances of sound: The people next door are noisy.

loud·hail·er (loud'hāl'ər) n. a megaphone with an electric amplifier; bullhorn.

loud·ish (loud'ish) adj. rather loud.

loud·mouth (loud'mouth') n. Slang. a loudmouthed person.

loud·mouthed (loud′mouᴛʜd′ or -moutht′) adj. offensively noisy; given to talking too loudly.

loud·speak·er (loud′spēk′ər) n. a device for amplifying the sound of a speaker's voice, music, etc.

lough (loh) n. Irish. 1 lake. 2 an arm of the sea; bay or inlet. [< Irish Gaelic loch]

lou·is d'or (lü′ē dôr′) 1 a French gold coin varying in value, first issued during the reign of Louis XIII and continued up to the Revolution. 2 a later French gold coin worth 20 francs. [< F louis d'or gold louis]

Lou·i·si·an·a Purchase (lù ē′zē an′ə) an extensive region that the United States bought from France in 1803. It extended from the Mississippi River to the Rocky Mountains and from Canada to the Gulf of Mexico.

Lou·is Qua·torze (lü′ē kä tôrz′) 1 a style in architecture, art, and decoration developed in France during the reign of King Louis XIV (1643-1715). 2 of or having to do with this style. 3 something, especially a piece of furniture, in this style. [< F Louis Quatorze Louis the Fourteenth]

Lou·is Quinze (lü′ē kaɴz′) 1 a style in architecture, art, and decoration developed in France during the reign of King Louis XV (1715-1774). 2 of or having to do with this style. 3 something, especially a piece of furniture, in this style. [< F Louis Quinze Louis the Fifteenth]

Lou·is Seize (lü′ē sez′) 1 a style in architecture, art, and decoration developed in France during the reign of King Louis XVI (1774-1792). 2 of or having to do with this style. [< F Louis Seize Louis the Sixteenth]

lounge (lounj) v. lounged, loung·ing; n. —v. 1 stand, stroll, sit, or lie at ease and lazily. 2 pass time indolently; idle at one's ease. —n. 1 the act or state of lounging. 2 a comfortable and informal room as in a theatre, ship, hotel, or club, in which one can lounge and be at ease. 3 a bar featuring comfortable chairs, etc. and, often, live music. [< 15th-century Scottish dial.; ? < lungis laggard] —loung′er, n.

loupe (lüp) n. an eyepiece fitted with a magnifying glass for use by jewellers, watchmakers, etc. [< F]

lour (lour) v. or n. lower².

louse (lous) n., pl. lice or (for def. 3) lous·es (lous′əz); v. loused, lous·ing. —n. 1 any of a large group of small, wingless insects constituting two orders (Anoplura and Mallophago, sometimes classified as suborders within the order Phthiraptera), that are parasites of mammals (including man) and birds. 2 any of various similar but unrelated insects or other arthropods. 3 Slang. a mean, contemptible person; heel. —v.
louse up, Slang. make a mess; spoil; botch: We loused up the filing so badly, we had to do it all over again. [OE lūs]

louse·wort (lous′wèrt′) n. any of a genus (Pedicularis) of plants of the figwort family found in north temperate regions, having spikes of white, yellow, or mauve flowers.

lous·y (lou′zē) adj. lous·i·er, lous·i·est. 1 Slang. inferior; bad; poor: The job isn't bad, but the pay is lousy. That was a lousy movie. 2 Slang. nasty; dirty; mean: a lousy swindler. 3 Slang. well-supplied (with): lousy with money. 4 infested with lice. —lous′i·ly, adv. —lous′i·ness, n.

lout (lout) n. an awkward, stupid fellow; boor. [< ON lútr bent down, stooping]

lout·ish (lout′ish) adj. awkward and stupid; boorish. —lout′ish·ly, adv. —lout′ish·ness, n.

lou·vre or **lou·ver** (lü′vər) n. 1 a window or other opening covered with louvre boards. 2 a ventilating slit. [ME < OF lover]

louvre boards or **louver boards** horizontal strips of wood, glass, etc. set slanting in a window or other opening, so as to keep out rain or light but provide ventilation.

lou·vred or **lou·vered** (lü′vərd) adj. 1 made or fitted with louvres. 2 arranged like louvres.

lov·a·ble (luv′ə bəl) adj. inspiring love; endearing. —lov′a·ble·ness, n. —lov′a·bly, adv.

love (luv) n., v. loved, lov·ing. —n. 1 a deep feeling of fondness and friendship; great affection or devotion: love of one's family, love for a sweetheart. 2 an instance of such feeling. 3 this feeling as a subject for books, or as a personified influence. 4 Love, a Venus. b Cupid. 5 a loved one; sweetheart. 6 a warm liking; fond or tender feeling. 7 a strong liking: a love of books. 8 Informal. something charming or delightful. 9 godly affection, devotion, and brotherhood. 10 Tennis, etc. no score.
fall in love, begin to love; come to feel love.

for love, a for nothing; without pay. b for pleasure; not for money.
for the love of, for the sake of; because of.
in love, feeling love.
make love, a have sexual intercourse. b Archaic. behave like lovers; woo.
not for love or money, not on any terms.
—v. 1 have a deep feeling of fondness and friendship for; have great affection for or devotion to: She loves her mother. I love my country. 2 be in love with. 3 be in love; fall in love. 4 make love to. 5 like very much; take great pleasure in: He loves music. Most people love ice cream. 6 be fond of; hold dear. [OE lufu, n., lufian, v.]
☛ Syn. n. 6. Love, affection = a feeling of warm liking and tender attachment. Love, an emotion, emphasizes strength, depth, sincerity, and warmth of feeling, suggesting also tenderness, devotion, loyalty, or passion: Every person needs to give and receive love. Affection applies to a less strong feeling, suggesting tenderness and warm fondness: I like my teacher, but feel no affection for her.
☛ Usage. See note at like.

love affair 1 a romantic relationship between two people who are not married to each other. 2 a lively or intense interest in or enthusiasm about something.

love apple Archaic. tomato.

love·bird (luv′bèrd′) n. 1 any of various small parrots, especially an African genus (Agapornis), often kept as cage birds, that appear to show great affection for their mates. 2 lovebirds, pl. two people very obviously in love with each other.

love child an illegitimate child.

love feast 1 a meal eaten together by the early Christians as a symbol of brotherly love. 2 a religous ceremony imitating this. 3 a banquet or other gathering to promote good feeling.

love–in–i·dle·ness (luv′in ī′dəl nis) n. wild pansy.

love knot an ornamental knot or bow of ribbon as a token of love.

love·less (luv′lis) adj. 1 not loving. 2 not loved.

love–lies–bleed·ing (luv′līz blēd′ing) n. an amaranth (Amaranthus caudatus) that is a popular garden plant, having long, drooping, tassel-like spikes of dark-red flowers.

love·li·ness (luv′lē nis) n. the quality or state of being lovely.

love·lock (luv′lok′) n. 1 a long lock of hair, often tied with a ribbon, worn by courtiers in the 17th and 18th centuries. 2 any separate lock of hair, such as one worn on the forehead.

love·lorn (luv′lôrn′) adj. suffering because of love; forsaken by the person whom one loves.

love·ly (luv′lē) adj. -li·er, -li·est. 1 having beauty, harmony, or grace; inspiring admiration or affection: a lovely woman. He is a lovely person. 2 Informal. very pleasing; delightful: a lovely holiday.
☛ Syn. 1. See note at beautiful.

love match a marriage for love, not for money or social position.

lov·er (luv′ər) n. 1 a person who is in love with another. 2 a man who is in love with a woman. 3 lovers, pl. a man and a woman who are in love with each other. 4 a person who loves illicitly; paramour. 5 a person having a strong liking for something: a lover of books. —lov′er·like′, adj.

love seat a small couch, or chesterfield, seating two persons.

love·sick (luv′sik′) adj. languishing because of love.

lov·ing (luv′ing) adj. feeling or showing love; affectionate; fond. —lov′ing·ly, adv.

loving cup a large cup having two or more handles, passed around for all to drink from.

lov·ing–kind·ness (luv′ing kīnd′nis) n. deep affection and tenderness.

low¹ (lō) adj., adv., n. —adj. 1 not high or tall: A low wall enclosed the garden. This stool is very low. 2 rising but slightly from a surface: low relief. 3 of less than average or ordinary height, depth, amount, or degree: The river is low this year. 4 near the ground, floor, or base: a low shelf. 5 lying or being below the general level: low ground. 6 almost used up; short: Supplies were low. Our furnace oil is low. 7 not loud; soft: We heard a low sound. 8 small in amount, degree, force, value, etc.: a low price. 9 not advanced in development, organization, complexity, etc.: Bacteria are low organisms. 10 lacking in dignity or elevation: low thoughts. 11 humble: She rose from a low position to president of the company. He is of low birth. 12 lacking health or strength; sick or weak: Her mother is very low. 13 unfavorable; poor: He had a low opinion of their abilities. 14 depressed or dejected: low spirits. 15 mean or base: a low trick. 16 coarse; vulgar: low language, low company. 17 near the horizon: a low sun. 18 near the equator: low latitudes. 19 of a dress or its neckline, cut so as to leave the neck and part of the breast exposed. 20 of a bow, made with the upper body deeply bent. 21 Music. not high in the scale; deep in pitch: a low note. 22 Phonetics. of a vowel, pronounced with the tongue

held low and relatively flat; open. *Examples*: (a), (ä), (o). **23** in the Anglican Church, maintaining Low-Church practices.
—*adv.* **1** at or to a low position, amount, rank, degree, pitch, etc.: *The lamp hangs too low. The sun sank low. Supplies are running low. He bowed low.* **2** in a low manner.
lay low, bring down; overthrow: *The first blow laid him low.*
lie low, *Informal.* stay hidden; keep still: *The robbers will lie low for a time.*
—*n.* **1** that which is low. **2** an arrangement of the gears in motor vehicles used for the lowest speed. **3** *Meteorology.* an area of low barometric pressure. [ME < ON *lágr*] —**low′ness,** *n.*
☛ *Hom.* **lo.**
☛ *Syn.* adj. **14.** See note at **base².**
low² (lō) *v., n.* —*v.* make the sound of a cow mooing; moo. —*n.* the sound a cow makes; mooing. [OE *hlōwan*]
☛ *Hom.* **lo.**
low·born (lō′bôrn′) *adj.* of humble birth; born into a family of low social rank.
low·boy (lō′boi′) *n.* a chest or side table with drawers, about the height of a table and having fairly short legs.
low·bred (lō′bred′) *adj.* coarse; rude; vulgar.
low·brow (lō′brou′) *n., adj. Informal.* —*n.* a person lacking in appreciation of intellectual or artistic things. —*adj.* **1** being a lowbrow; incapable of culture. **2** fit for lowbrows.
Low-Church (lō′chèrch′) *adj.* of a party in the Anglican Church, laying little stress on church authority and ceremonies; more like Protestant denominations, and less like the Roman Catholic Church.
low comedy broadly humorous comedy.
Low Countries the Netherlands, Belgium, and Luxemburg.
low-coun·try (lō′kun′trē) *adj.* of or having to do with the Low Countries (the Netherlands, Belgium, and Luxemburg).
low·down (lō′doun′) *n. Slang.* the actual facts or truth: *Can you give me the lowdown on what happened at the meeting?*
low-down (lō′doun′) *adj. Informal.* low; mean; nasty: *a low-down trick.*
low·er¹ (lō′ər) *v., adj., adv.* —*v.* **1** let down or haul down: *to lower the flag.* **2** make lower: *to lower the volume of a radio.* **3** sink; become lower: *The sun lowered slowly.* **4** *Music.* depress in pitch. **5** bring down in rank, station, or estimation; degrade; dishonor. —*adj. or adv.* the comparative of **low.** [< *low¹*]
low·er² (lou′ər) *v., n.* —*v.* **1** become or appear dark and threatening. **2** frown or scowl. —*n.* a frowning or threatening appearance or look. Also, **lour.** [ME *loure(n)*]
Lower Canada **1** a traditional name for the province of Quebec. **2** until 1841, the official name of the region between the Ottawa River and New Brunswick, now included in the province of Quebec. Lower Canada was lower down the St. Lawrence River than Upper Canada. *Abbrev.:* L.C.
lower case *Printing.* small letters, not capital.
low·er-case (lō′ər kās′) *adj. Printing.* in small letters, not capitals. *Abbrev.:* l.c.
Lower Chamber or **lower chamber** Lower House.
lower class Often, **lower classes,** *pl.* the people having the lowest social, political, and economic status, characterized especially by lower average incomes and a lower level of education than that of the middle class.
low·er-class (lō′ər klas′) *adj.* of, having to do with, or belonging to the lower class.
Lower House or **lower house** the more representative branch of a legislature that has two branches. The members of the Lower House of a legislature are usually elected.
low·er·ing (lou′ər ing) *adj.* **1** dark and threatening: *a lowering sky.* **2** frowning or scowling. —**low′er·ing·ly,** *adv.*
Lower Lakes the most southerly of the Great Lakes, Lakes Erie and Ontario.
low·er·most (lō′ər mōst′) *adj.* lowest.
lower regions hell; Hades.
lower world **1** hell; Hades. **2** earth.
lowest common denominator **1** *Mathematics.* the least common denominator. *Abbrev.:* LCD, L.C.D., or l.c.d. **2** the level of the feelings, tastes, or opinions supposedly common to the majority of people.
lowest terms fraction a fraction whose numerator and denominator have no factor in common.
low frequency the range of radio frequencies between 30 and 300 kilohertz. Low frequency is the range next above very low frequency. *Abbrev.:* LF, L.F., or l.f. —**low′-fre′quen·cy,** *adj.*
Low German **1** the Germanic speech of the Low Countries (Dutch, Flemish, etc.) and especially of N Germany. **2** the group of

hat, āge, fär; let, ēqual, tèrm; it, īce
hot, ōpen, ôrder; oil, out; cup, pút, rüle,
above, takən, pencəl, lemən, circəs

ch, child; ng, long; sh, ship
th, thin; ʞн, then; zh, measure

west Germanic dialects from which English, Flemish, Dutch, Frisian, etc. are derived.
low-key (lō′kē′) *adj.* played down; subdued or restrained: *a low-key attack on government policy.*
low·land (lō′lənd) *n.* **1** land that is lower and flatter than the neighboring country. **2** (*adjl.*) of or in the lowlands. **3 the Lowlands,** *pl.* a low, flat region in S and E Scotland.
Low·land·er (lō′lən dər) *n.* a native of the lowlands of Scotland.
Low Latin Latin as spoken in the Middle Ages.
low·life (lō′līf′) *n., adj. Slang.* —*n.* **1** a debased or vile person; a criminal. **2** immoral people or surroundings. —*adj.* **1** resembling a lowlife; debased; immoral. **2** crude; cheap.
low·lin·er (lō′līn′ər) *n.* **1** the boat in a Maritime fishing fleet making the smallest catch within a specified time. **2** the captain of such a boat.
low·ly (lō′lē) *adj.* **-li·er, -li·est;** *adv.* —*adj.* **1** low in rank, station, or position: *a lowly servant, a lowly occupation.* **2** modest in feeling, behavior, or condition; humble; meek: *He held a lowly opinion of himself.* —*adv.* humbly; meekly. —**low′li·ness,** *n.*
☛ *Syn.* adj. **2.** See note at **humble.**
Low Mass a Mass that is recited, not sung, and is simpler in form than a High Mass.
low-mind·ed (lō′mīn′did) *adj.* having or showing a low or vulgar mind.
low-necked (lō′nekt′) *adj.* of a dress, etc., cut low so as to show the neck, part of the bosom, and shoulders or back.
low-pitched (lō′picht′) *adj.* **1** having a deep tone: *a low-pitched musical instrument.* **2** having little slope; not steep: *a low-pitched roof.*
low-pres·sure (lō′presh′ər) *adj.* **1** having or using relatively little pressure: *a low-pressure laminate.* **2** having a low barometric pressure: *There is a low-pressure region to the south.* **3** not forceful; easy going: *a low-pressure sales pitch.*
low relief relief sculpture in which the modelled forms stand out only slightly from the background and no part of the forms is undercut; bas-relief. See **relief** for picture.
low-rise (lō′rīz′) *adj., n.* —*adj.* of a building, having only a few storeys: *Only low-rise apartments are permitted in this area of the city.* —*n.* a low-rise building.
low-spir·it·ed (lō′spir′i tid) *adj.* sad; depressed. —**low′-spir′it·ed·ly,** *adv.* —**low′-spir′it·ed·ness,** *n.*
low spirits sadness; depression.
low tide **1** the lowest level of the tide. **2** the time when the tide is lowest: *The boat must have left sometime after low tide.* **3** the lowest point of anything.
low water **1** the lowest level of water in a lake or river. **2** low tide.
low-water mark (lō′wo′tər *or* -wô′tər) **1** a mark showing low water. **2** the lowest point of anything.
lox¹ (loks) *n.* thinly sliced smoked salmon. [< Yiddish *laks* < MHG *lacs* salmon]
lox² (loks) *n.* liquid oxygen. [< *l*iquid *ox*ygen]
loy·al (loi′əl) *adj.* **1** faithful to love, promise, or duty. **2** faithful to one's sovereign, government, or country: *a loyal citizen.* [< F *loyal* < L *legalis* legal < *lex, legis* law. Doublet of LEAL, LEGAL.] —**loy′al·ly,** *adv.*
☛ *Syn.* **1, 2.** See note at **faithful.**
loy·al·ist (loi′əl ist) *n.* **1** a person who supports the existing government or sovereign, especially in time of revolt. **2 Loyalist,** a United Empire Loyalist. **b** any of the colonists who remained loyal to Great Britain during the American Revolution, or their descendants. **3 Loyalist,** in Spain, a person loyal to the Republic during the civil war (1936-1939).
Loyal Orange Association a Protestant organization, named after William, Prince of Orange, who became King William III of England.
loy·al·ty (loi′əl tē) *n., pl.* **-ties.** loyal feeling or behavior; faithfulness.
loz·enge (loz′inj) *n.* **1** a small tablet of medicine or a piece of candy: *Cough drops are sometimes called lozenges.* **2** a design or

figure shaped like this ◇; diamond. [ME < OF *losenge*, ult. < LL *lausa* slab < Celtic]

LP a long-playing phonograph record. [< a trademark]

L.P.P. Labour Progressive Party, the former name of the Communist Party in Canada.

Lr lawrencium.

LRC light, rapid, comfortable (designating a type of railway train).

LRT light rapid transit.

L.S. or **LS** leading seaman.

LSD lysergic acid diethylamide, a drug that can produce hallucinations and schizophrenic symptoms.

L.S.D. or **l.s.d.** pounds, shillings, and pence.

L/Sgt. lance-sergeant.

Lt. or **Lt** lieutenant.

Lt.Cdr. lieutenant-commander.

Lt.Col. lieutenant-colonel.

Ltd. limited.

Lt.Gen. lieutenant-general.

Lt.Gov. lieutenant-governor.

Lu lutecium.

lu·au (lü′ou) *n.* a Hawaiian feast, usually including entertainment. [< Hawaiian *lu′au*]

lub·ber (lub′ər) *n.* **1** a big, clumsy, stupid fellow. **2** a clumsy sailor. [ME *lober*]

lub·ber·ly (lub′ər lē) *adj., adv.* —*adj.* **1** loutish; clumsy; stupid. **2** awkward in the work of a sailor. —*adv.* in a lubberly manner.

lube (lüb) *n. Informal.* lubrication.

lu·bri·cant (lü′brə kənt) *n., adj.* —*n.* a substance such as oil, grease, or graphite for putting on surfaces that slide or move against one another, such as parts of machines, in order to reduce friction and make the surfaces move smoothly and easily. —*adj.* lubricating.

lu·bri·cate (lü′brə kāt′) *v.* **-cat·ed, -cat·ing. 1** put a lubricant on. **2** make slippery or smooth. [< L *lubricare* < *lubricus* slippery] —**lu′bri·ca′tion,** *n.*

lu·bri·ca·tion (lü′bri kā′shən) *n.* **1** lubricating or being lubricated. **2** oil, grease, etc. used for lubricating.

lu·bri·ca·tor (lü′brə kā′tər) *n.* a person or thing that lubricates, especially a lubricant or device for applying a lubricant to machinery.

lu·bric·i·ty (lü bris′ə tē) *n., pl.* **-ties. 1** oily smoothness; slipperiness. **2** shiftiness. **3** lewdness. [< LL *lubricitas* < L *lubricus* slippery, slimy]

lu·cent (lü′sənt) *adj. Archaic.* **1** shining; luminous. **2** letting the light through; clear. [< L *lucens, -entis,* ppr. of *lucere* shine] —**lu′cent·ly,** *adv.*

lu·cerne (lü sèrn′) *n.* alfalfa. [< F *luzerne* < Provençal *luzerno,* ult. < L *lux, lucis* light]

lu·cid (lü′sid) *adj.* **1** easy to understand: *a lucid explanation.* **2** shining; bright. **3** sane: *Insane persons sometimes have lucid intervals.* **4** clear; transparent: *a lucid stream.* [< L *lucidus < lux, lucis* light] —**lu′cid·ly,** *adv.* —**lu′cid·ness,** *n.*

lu·cid·i·ty (lü sid′ə tē) *n.* the quality or state of being lucid: *The critics admire the lucidity of her writing.*

Lu·ci·fer (lü′sə fər) *n.* **1** the chief rebel angel who was cast out of heaven; Satan, especially before his fall. **2** the planet Venus when it is the morning star. **3** a match that lights by friction. [< L *lucifer* the morning star, literally, bringing light < *lux, lucis* light + *ferre* bring]

Lu·cite (lü′sīt) *n. Trademark.* a clear plastic compound used for airplane windows, ornaments, etc. [< L *lux, lucis* light]

luck (luk) *n.* **1** that which seems to happen or come to one by chance; chance. **2** good fortune: *Lots of luck to you. He thinks a horseshoe brings luck.*

down on (one's) **luck,** *Informal.* having bad luck; unlucky.

in luck, having good luck; lucky: *I'm in luck today; I found a quarter.*

out of luck, having bad luck; unlucky.

try (one's) **luck,** see what one can do: *Try your luck with this puzzle.*

worse luck, unfortunately. [ME < MDu. *(ghe)luc,* MLG *(ge)lucke*]

luck·i·ly (luk′ə lē) *adv.* by good luck; fortunately.

luck·i·ness (luk′ə nəs *or* luk′ē nəs) *n.* the quality or state of being lucky.

luck·less (luk′lis) *adj.* having or bringing good luck. —**luck′less·ly,** *adv.* —**luck′less·ness,** *n.*

luck·y (luk′ē) *adj.* **luck·i·er, luck·i·est. 1** having good luck: *He was lucky to win the card game yesterday.* **2** bringing good luck: *a lucky day, a lucky charm.* **3** happening by good fortune; fortunate: *a lucky coincidence.*

☛ *Syn.* See note at **fortunate.**

lu·cra·tive (lü′krə tiv) *adj.* bringing in money; profitable. [ME < L *lucrativus < lucrari* to gain < *lucrum* gain] —**lu′cra·tive·ly,** *adv.* —**lu′cra·tive·ness,** *n.*

lu·cre (lü′kər) *n. Derogatory.* money: *filthy lucre.* [ME < L *lucrum*]

lu·cu·bra·tion (lü′kyə brā′shən) *n.* **1** study carried on late at night. **2** laborious study. **3** a learned or carefully written production, especially one that is labored and dull. [< L *lucubratio, -onis < lucubrare* work at night]

Lu·cul·li·an (lü kul′ē ən) *adj.* rich; luxurious; magnificent. [< *Lucullus* (110?-57? B.C.), a wealthy Roman famous for his luxurious banquets]

lu·di·crous (lü′də krəs) *adj.* amusingly absurd; ridiculous. [< L *ludicrus < ludus* sport] —**lu′di·crous·ly,** *adv.* —**lu′di·crous·ness,** *n.*

luff (luf) *v., n.* —*v.* turn the bow of a ship toward the wind.

luff the helm, move the helm so that the bow of the ship turns toward the wind.

—*n.* **1** the act of turning the bow of a ship toward the wind. **2** the forward edge of a fore-and-aft sail. [ME; cf. Du. *loef*]

Luft·waf·fe (lûft′väf′ə) *n. German.* the German air force, especially under the Nazis in World War II.

lug¹ (lug) *v.* **lugged, lug·ging. 1** pull along or carry with effort; drag. **2** of a ship, carry (sail) beyond the limit of safety in a strong wind. [ME; cf. Swedish *lugga* pull by the hair]

lug² (lug) *n.* **1** *Esp.Scottish.* ear. **2** a projecting part used to hold or grip something. **3** a flange or stud projecting from the outer surface of a wheel to increase traction on soft ground: *Tractors having lugs should stay off paved highways.* **4** *Slang.* a clumsy or stupid person. [origin uncertain; cf. Swedish *lugg* forelock]

lug³ (lug) *n.* lugsail. [? < *lug²*]

lug⁴ (lug) *n.* lugworm. [origin uncertain; cf. Du. *log* slow, heavy]

luge (lüzh) *n.* a small sled which a person rides lying on his back, used in downhill races over snow or ice, often on a specially designed course. [< Swiss dial.]

lu·ger or **Lu·ger** (lü′gər) *n.* an automatic pistol first made in Germany. [< George *Luger,* a 19th-century German engineer]

lug·gage (lug′ij) *n.* **1** suitcases, bags, etc. packed with belongings for a trip; baggage. **2** suitcases, bags, etc. for use on trips: *I bought a new set of luggage.* [< *lug¹*]

☛ *Syn.* See note at **baggage.**

lug·ger (lug′ər) *n.* a boat with lugsails.

lugs (lugz) *n.pl.* a cloth flap in certain kinds of caps, pulled down as protection for the ears in cold weather. [< *lug²*]

lug·sail (lug′sāl′ *or* lug′səl) *n.* a four-cornered sail held by a yard that slants across the mast.

lu·gu·bri·ous (lü gü′brē əs) *adj.* sad; mournful, especially in an exaggerated or affected way. [< L *lugubris < lugere* mourn] —**lu·gu′bri·ous·ly,** *adv.* —**lu·gu′bri·ous·ness,** *n.*

lug·worm (lug′wèrm′) *n.* any of a genus (*Arenicola*) of marine annelid worms that burrow in the sand along the seashore or on the sea bottom, having a row of tufted gills along each side of the body. Lugworms are often used for bait. [< *lug⁴*]

luke·warm (lük′wôrm′) *adj.* **1** of a liquid, neither hot nor cold; fairly warm. **2** showing little enthusiasm; half-hearted: *a lukewarm greeting.* [expansion of dial. *luke* lukewarm < dial. *lew*; cf. OE *hlēo* shelter (warm place)] —**luke′warm′ly,** *adv.* —**luke′warm′ness,** *n.*

lull (lul) *v., n.* —*v.* **1** hush to sleep: *The mother lulled the crying baby.* **2** make or become calm or more nearly calm: *The wind lulled.* —*n.* a temporary period of less noise or activity; brief calm: *a lull in a storm.* [ME *lulle(n)*]

lull·a·by (lul′ə bī′) *n., pl.* **-bies. 1** a song to lull a baby to sleep. **2** any soothing song or piece of music. [< *lull* + *by* as in *good-bye*]

lum·ba·go (lum bā′gō) *n.* an injury of the muscles in the lower back producing pain, sometimes intense. Lumbago can be caused by a sprain, lifting something that is too heavy, a sudden twisting movement, etc. [< LL < L *lumbus* loin]

lum·bar (lum′bər *or* lum′bär) *adj.* of, having to do with, or referring to the loins or a vertebra, artery, nerve, etc. in this part of the body. [< NL *lumbaris* < L *lumbus* loin]

☛ *Hom.* **lumber.**

lum·ber¹ (lum′bər) *n., v.* —*n.* **1** timber, logs, beams, boards, etc. roughly cut and prepared for use. **2** household articles no longer in use; old furniture, etc. that takes up room. —*v.* **1** cut and prepare lumber. **2** fill up or obstruct by taking space that is wanted for

something else. [original meaning "useless goods," ? < *lombard* pawnshop]
☛ *Hom.* **lumbar.**

lum·ber² (lum'bər) *v.* move along heavily and noisily. [ME *lomeren* < Scand.; cf. Swedish dial. *loma* walk heavily]
—**lum'ber·ing·ly**, *adv.*
☛ *Hom.* **lumbar.**

lum·ber·ing (lum'bər ing *or* lum'bring) *n.* the business of cutting and preparing timber for use.

lum·ber·jack (lum'bər jak') *n.* **1** a person whose work is cutting down trees and getting the logs to the mills; logger. **2** *Cdn.* Canada jay.

lum·ber·man (lum'bər mən) *n., pl.* **-men.** **1** lumberjack. **2** a man whose work is cutting and preparing timber for use. **3** a man whose business is buying and selling timber or lumber.

lum·ber·yard (lum'bər yärd') *n.* a place where lumber is stored and sold.

lu·men (lü'mən) *n.* **1** an SI unit for measuring the rate of emission or transmission of light rays from a given light source. One lumen is the rate of emission in a cone of one steradian of a light source having an intensity of one candela. *Symbol:* lm **2** the inner space or passage in a blood vessel or within a cell wall. [< L]

lu·mi·nar·y (lü'mə ner'ē) *n., pl.* **-nar·ies.** **1** the sun, moon, or other light-giving body. **2** a distinguished person, especially one who enlightens. [ME < Med.L *luminarium* < L *lumen*, *-minis* light]

lu·mi·nes·cence (lü'mə nes'əns) *n.* an emission of light by a process other than incandescence; any light produced at relatively low temperatures by chemical or electrical action, friction, etc. Luminescence includes phosphorescence, fluorescence and the light produced by fireflies. [< L *lumen, luminis* light + E *-escence* a beginning to be < L *-escentia*]

lu·mi·nes·cent (lü'mə nes'ənt) *adj.* **1** of or having to do with luminescence. **2** producing or capable of producing light by luminescence.

lu·mi·nif·er·ous (lü'mə nif'ər əs) *adj.* producing or transmitting light. [< L *lumen, luminis* light + E *-ferous*]

lu·mi·nos·i·ty (lü'mə nos'ə tē) *n., pl.* **-ties.** **1** the quality or state of being luminous. **2** something that is luminous.

lu·mi·nous (lü'mə nəs) *adj.* **1** shining by its own light: *The sun and stars are luminous.* **2** full of light; bright. **3** treated with some substance that glows in the dark: *The numbers on some watches are luminous.* **4** easily understood; clear; enlightening: *a luminous explanation.* [ME < L *luminosus* < *lumen* light] —**lu'mi·nous·ly**, *adv.* —**lu'mi·nous·ness**, *n.*

luminous flux the rate of flow of light, or luminous energy, measured in lumens.

lum·mox (lum'əks) *n. Informal.* an awkward, stupid person. [origin uncertain]

lump¹ (lump) *n., v.* —*n.* **1** a solid mass of no particular shape: *a lump of coal.* **2** a small cube or oblong piece of sugar. **3** a swelling; bump: *a lump on the head.* **4** a lot; mass. **5** (*adj.*) not divided or in parts; in a single lot or mass: *a lump payment.* **6** an awkward, dull, or stupid person. **7** **lumps,** *pl. Informal.* a beating or defeat; punishment or retribution; one's just desserts: *The outspoken mayor had to take her lumps from the press.*
—*v.* **1** make lumps of, on, or in. **2** form into a lump or lumps: *If you don't stir the pudding, it will lump.* **3** put together; deal with in a mass or as a whole: *We will lump all our expenses.* [ME < Scand.; cf. Danish *lump(e)*]

lump² (lump) *v. Informal.* put up with; endure: *If you don't like it, you can lump it.* [origin uncertain]

lump·ish (lump'ish) *adj.* **1** like a lump; heavy and clumsy. **2** stolid; stupid.

lump sugar small blocks of sugar shaped like cubes, dominoes, etc.

lump sum a relatively large sum of money given in payment at one time: *He paid off the last $500 of his loan in a lump sum.* —**lump'-sum'**, *adj.*

lump·y (lump'ē) *adj.* **lump·i·er, lump·i·est.** **1** full of lumps: *lumpy gravy.* **2** covered with lumps: *lumpy ground.* **3** heavy and clumsy: *a lumpy animal.* **4** of water in a lake, etc., rough; having choppy waves. —**lump'i·ly,** *adv.* —**lump'i·ness,** *n.*

Lu·na (lü'nə) *n.* **1** *Roman mythology.* the goddess of the moon. **2** the moon. [< L *luna* moon]

lu·na·cy (lü'nə sē) *n., pl.* **-cies.** **1** insanity. **2** extreme folly. [< *lunatic*]

luna moth a large North American saturniid moth (*Actias luna*) having light-green wings with crescent-shaped markings.

lu·nar (lü'nər) *adj.* **1** of or having to do with the moon: *a lunar eclipse.* **2** like the moon in shape. **3** measured by the revolutions of the moon: *a lunar month.* **4** designed for use on the moon: *a lunar vehicle.* [< L *lunaris* < *luna* moon]

---

hat, āge, fär; let, ēqual, tèrm; it, īce
hot, ōpen, ôrder; oil, out; cup, pút, rüle,
above, takən, pencəl, lemən, circəs

ch, child; ng, long; sh, ship
th, thin; ᴛʜ, then; zh, measure

lunar month the period of one complete revolution of the moon around the earth; the interval between one new moon and the next, about 29½ days.

lu·nate (lü'nāt) *adj.* crescent-shaped. [< L *lunatus* < *luna* moon]

lu·na·tic (lü'nə tik') *n., adj.* —*n.* **1** an insane person. **2** an extremely foolish person.
—*adj.* **1** insane. **2** for insane people. **3** extremely foolish; idiotic: *a lunatic search for buried treasure.* [ME < LL *lunaticus* < L *luna* moon]

lunatic fringe *Informal.* those whose zeal in some cause, movement, etc. goes beyond reasonable limits.

lunch (lunch) *n., v.* —*n.* **1** a light meal between breakfast and dinner, or breakfast and supper: *We usually have lunch at noon.* **2** a light meal eaten at any time: *We had a lunch at bedtime.* **3** food for lunch: *Leave your lunch in the locker.*
—*v.* eat lunch. [shortened form of *luncheon*] —**lunch'er,** *n.*

lunch·eon (lun'chən) *n., v.* —*n.* **1** a lunch. **2** a formal meal taken at noon. —*v.* eat luncheon. [< dial. *luncheon* hunk, large lump of food < dial. *lunch* lump, formed after obs. synonym *nuncheon*]

lunch·eon·ette (lun'chən et') *n.* a restaurant that serves lunches.

lunch·room (lunch'rüm' *or* -rûm') *n.* **1** a public dining room; restaurant. **2** a room in a plant, school, etc. where employees, teachers, or students may eat the lunches they have brought. Also, **lunch-room.**

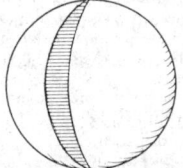

Lune (def. 2).
The shaded area
is a lune.

lune (lün) *n.* **1** anything shaped like a crescent or a half moon. **2** *Geometry.* a crescent-shaped figure formed on a sphere by two great semicircles intersecting at two points. [< F < L *luna* moon]
☛ *Hom.* **loon.**

lu·nette (lü net') *n.* **1** *Architecture.* **a** a crescent-shaped opening or space in a vaulted ceiling, dome, wall, etc. **b** a painting, piece of sculpture, etc. that fills this space. **c** an arched or rounded opening, window, etc. **2** a projecting part of a rampart, shaped like an arch. [< F *lunette*, dim. of *lune* moon < L *luna*]

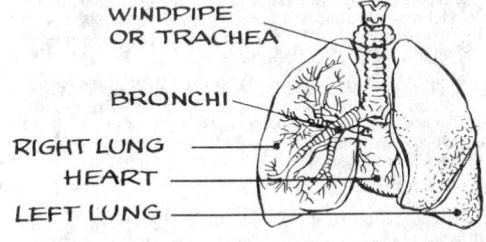

WINDPIPE
OR TRACHEA

BRONCHI

RIGHT LUNG

HEART

LEFT LUNG

Human lungs, seen from the front

lung (lung) *n.* **1** in vertebrates, one of the pair of breathing organs by means of which the blood receives oxygen and is relieved of carbon dioxide. **2** any of various similar organs in invertebrates. **3** a mechanical device for supplying respiration. [OE *lungen*]

lunge¹ (lunj) *n., v.* **lunged, lung·ing.** —*n.* any sudden forward movement; thrust: *The catcher made a lunge toward the ball.* —*v.* move suddenly forward; thrust. [ult. < F *allonger*, ult. < L *ad*-toward + *longus* long] —**lung'er,** *n.*

lunge² (lunj) *n., v.* **lunged, lung·ing.** —*n.* **1** a long rope used for training or exercising a horse. **2** the training of a horse with such a rope. **3** a ring or circular exercise track for training horses.
—*v.* train, exercise, or move (a horse tied with a lunge) around a circular track. [< F *longe* cord, halter < OF *loigne*]

lunge³ or **'lunge** (lunj) *n. Informal.* muskellunge.

lung·fish (lung'fish') *n., pl.* **-fish** or **fish·es.** any of six species of freshwater fishes, the only living members of the subclass Dipnoi, having an air-breathing lung as well as gills and found in the rivers of South America, Africa, and Australia.

lung·wort (lung'wèrt') *n.* any of several plants (genus *Pulmonaria*) of the borage family, especially a common European perennial (*P. officinalis*) having blue flowers and spotted leaves, and formerly used in medicine in the treatment of lung diseases.

lun·ker (lung'kər) *n. Informal.* anything considered large for its kind, especially a game fish. [origin uncertain]

Lu·per·ca·li·a (lü'pər kā'lē ə) *n.* in ancient Rome, a fertility festival celebrated on February 15. [< *Lupercus*, a rural god]

lu·pine¹ or **lu·pin** (lü'pən) *n.* any of a genus (*Lupinus*) of plants of the pea family found in the western hemisphere and the Mediterranean, having long spikes of brightly colored flowers, palmate compound leaves, and flat pods with bean-shaped seeds. [< L *lupinus, lupinum*. See LUPINE².]

lu·pine² (lü'pīn) *adj.* of or like a wolf or wolves. [ME < L *lupinus < lupus* wolf]

lu·pus (lü'pəs) *n.* a skin disease caused by the tubercle bacillus. [< L *lupus* wolf]

lurch¹ (lèrch) *n., v.* —*n.* a sudden leaning or roll to one side: *The car gave a lurch and overturned.* —*v.* lean or roll suddenly to one side. [origin uncertain]

lurch² (lèrch) *n. Archaic. Games.* a condition in which one player scores nothing or is badly beaten.
leave in the lurch, leave in a helpless condition or a difficult situation.
[< F *lourche*, the name of a game]

lurch·er (lèr'chər) *n.* **1** a prowler; petty thief; poacher. **2** *Brit.* a mongrel hunting dog much used by poachers.

lure (lür) *n., v.* **lured, lur·ing.** —*n.* **1** attraction: *the lure of the sea.* **2** a decoy; bait. —*v.* **1** lead away or into something by awakening desire; attract; tempt. **2** attract with a bait. [ME < OF *luerre* < Gmc.] —**lur'er,** *n.*
☛ *Syn. v.* **1. Lure, allure, entice** = attract or tempt. **Lure,** commonly in a bad sense, means tempt by arousing desire, usually to lead into something bad or not to one's advantage: *The hope of high profits lured him into questionable dealings.* **Allure,** seldom in a bad sense, means tempt by appealing to the senses and feelings and by offering pleasure or advantage: *The Caribbean allures many tourists.* **Entice,** in a good or bad sense, means tempt by appealing to hopes and desires and by using persuasion: *We enticed the kitten down from the tree.*

lu·rid (lür'id) *adj.* **1** lighted up with a red or fiery glare: *The sky was lurid with the flames of the burning city.* **2** causing horror; gruesome; terrible: *a lurid crime.* **3** sensational: *The newspaper carried a lurid account of the kidnapping.* **4** very pale and wan in appearance; livid. [< L *luridus*]

lurk (lèrk) *v.* **1** stay about without arousing attention; wait out of sight. **2** be hidden. [apparently < *lour* lower²] —**lurk'er,** *n.*
—**lurk'ing·ly,** *adv.*
☛ *Syn.* **1. Lurk, skulk** = keep out of sight or move in a secret or furtive way. **Lurk** means lie hidden and waiting or move about so as to keep from arousing attention, often but not always suggesting an evil purpose: *A tiger was lurking in the jungle.* **Skulk** suggests sneakiness and fear, cowardice, or shame: *The cattle thieves skulked in the woods until the posse had passed.*

lus·cious (lush'əs) *adj.* **1** delicious; richly sweet: *a luscious peach.* **2** very pleasing to the senses, especially those of taste and smell. [ME; ? var. of *delicious*] —**lus'cious·ly,** *adv.*
—**lus'cious·ness,** *n.*
☛ *Syn.* **1.** See note at **delicious.**

lush¹ (lush) *adj.* **1** tender and juicy; growing thick and green: *Lush grass grows along the river banks.* **2** characterized by abundant growth: *We passed many lush fields.* **3** abundant. **4** rich in ornament; flowery: *lush description.* [< OF *lasche* lax] —**lush'ly,** *adv.* —**lush'ness,** *n.*

lush² (lush) *n., v. Slang.* —*n.* **1** a person who habitually drinks excessive amounts of alcoholic liquor, especially an alcoholic. **2** alcoholic liquor. —*v.* drink alcoholic liquor. [? < *lush¹*]

lust (lust) *n., v.* —*n.* **1** sexual desire, especially when very intense. **2** any excessively strong desire; craving: *a lust for power, a lust for revenge.* —*v.* feel a very strong desire (*usually used with* **after** or **for**): *A miser lusts after gold.* [OE *lust* pleasure]

lus·ter (lus'tər) See **lustre.**

lus·ter·ware (lus'tər wer') See **lustreware.**

lust·ful (lust'fəl) *adj.* **1** full of lust. **2** *Archaic.* lusty. —**lust'ful·ly,** *adv.* —**lust'ful·ness,** *n.*

lus·tral (lus'trəl) *adj.* **1** of or used in ceremonial purification. **2** occurring every five years.

lus·trate (lus'trāt) *v.* **-trat·ed, -trat·ing.** purify by a ceremonial method, such as washing, sacrifice, etc. [< L *lustrare* brighten, clean < *lustrum* lustrum]

lus·tra·tion (lus trā'shən) *n.* a ceremonial purification.

lus·tre (lus'tər) *n., v.* —*n.* **1** a bright shine on the surface: *the lustre of pearls.* **2** brightness: *Her eyes lost their lustre.* **3** fame; glory; brilliance. **4** a kind of china or pottery that has a lustrous metallic, often iridescent surface. **5** a thin fabric of cotton and wool that has a lustrous surface.
—*v.* finish or shine with a lustre or gloss. Also, **luster.** [< F < Ital. *lustro < lustrare* < L *lustrare* illuminate]

lus·tre·ware (lus'tər wer') *n.* a kind of earthenware or china that has a lustrous, often iridescent glaze. Also, **lusterware.**

lus·trous (lus'trəs) *adj.* having lustre; shining; glossy: *lustrous satin.* —**lus'trous·ly,** *adv.*

lus·trum (lus'trəm) *n., pl.* **-trums, -tra** (-trə). **1** in ancient Rome, a ceremonial purification, performed every five years. **2** a period of five years. [< L]

lust·y (lus'tē) *adj.* **lust·i·er, lust·i·est.** strong and healthy; full of vigor. —**lust'i·ly,** *adv.* —**lust'i·ness,** *n.*

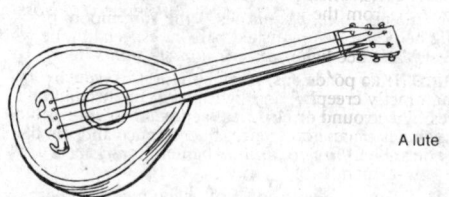
A lute

lute (lüt) *n.* a stringed musical instrument like a large mandolin, much used in the 1500's and 1600's. [ME < OF < Provençal *laut* < Arabic *al'ud* the lute]
☛ *Hom.* **loot.**

lu·te·ti·um (lü tē'shē əm) *n.* a rare metallic chemical element. Symbol: Lu; *at.no.* 71; *at.wt.* 174.97. Also, esp.formerly, **lutecium.** [< NL < L *Lutetia* Paris]

Lu·ther·an (lü'thər ən *or* lüth'rən) *n., adj.* —*n.* **1** a member of any of the churches that together constitute the largest Protestant denomination, originating in the 1520's as a result of the teachings of Martin Luther (1483-1546), and whose tenets include the belief that a person can be saved not by good works but only by faith, through the redemption of Christ, and that the individual can come to God on his own, with the Bible as a sufficient guide to truth. **2** a follower of Martin Luther. —*adj.* **1** of or having to do with Luther or his doctrines. **2** of or having to do with a Lutheran church.

Lu·ther·an·ism (lü'thər ən iz'əm *or* lüth'rən iz'əm) *n.* the doctrines or religious principles of Martin Luther and his followers or the Lutheran churches.

lux (luks) *n., pl.* **lux·es** or **lu·ces.** an SI unit for measuring illumination of a source of light per unit area on a surface. One lux is the illumination of one lumen over an area of one square metre. Symbol: lx [< L *lūx* light¹]

lux·ate (luk'sāt) *v.* **-at·ed, -at·ing.** dislocate; put out of joint. [< L *luxare* dislocate] —**lux·a'tion,** *n.*

luxe (lüks *or* luks; *French*, lүks) *n.* an elegant or luxurious quality. [< F < L *luxus* extravagance]

lux·u·ri·ance (lug zhür'ē əns *or* luk shür'ē əns) *n.* the quality or state of being luxuriant; rich abundance.

lux·u·ri·ant (lug zhür'ē ənt *or* luk shür'ē ənt) *adj.* **1** growing in a vigorous and healthy way; thick and lush: *In spring the grass on our lawn is luxuriant. She has a luxuriant head of hair.* **2** producing abundantly. **3** rich in ornament. [< L *luxurians, -antis,* ppr. of *luxuriare.* See LUXURIATE.] —**lux·u'ri·ant·ly,** *adv.*
☛ *Usage.* Do not confuse **luxuriant** and **luxurious**; they are related words with very different meanings.

lux·u·ri·ate (lug zhür'ē āt *or* luk shür'ē āt) *v.* **-at·ed, -at·ing.** **1** indulge oneself luxuriously; take great delight; revel (in): *luxuriating in a hot bath.* **2** grow very abundantly. [< L *luxuriare* < *luxuria* luxury < *luxus* excess]

lux·u·ri·ous (lug zhür'ē əs *or* luk shür'ē əs) *adj.* **1** fond of luxury; tending toward luxury; self-indulgent. **2** giving luxury; very comfortable and beautiful. —**lux·u'ri·ous·ly,** *adv.*
—**lux·u'ri·ous·ness,** *n.*
☛ *Usage.* See note at **luxuriant.**

lux·u·ry (luk'shə rē *or* lug'zhə rē) *n., pl.* **-ries. 1** an abundance of the comforts and beauties of life beyond what is really necessary. **2** the use of the best and most costly food, clothes, houses,

furniture, and amusements. **3** anything that one enjoys, usually something choice and costly. **4** something pleasant but not necessary. [< L *luxuria* < *luxus* excess]

LXX Septuagint.

–ly¹ *adverb-forming suffix*. **1** in a —— manner: *cheerfully* = *in a cheerful manner.* **2** in —— ways or respects: *financially* = *in financial respects.* **3** to a —— degree or extent: *greatly* = *to a great degree.* **4** in, to, or from a —— direction: *northwardly* = *to or from the north.* **5** in a —— place: *thirdly* = *in the third place.* **6** at a —— time: *recently* = *at a recent time.* [OE *-līce* < *-līc* -ly²]

–ly² *adjective-forming suffix*. **1** like a ——: *a ghostly form* = *a form like a ghost.* **2** like that of a ——; characteristic of a ——: *brotherly kiss* = *a kiss like that of a brother.* **3** suited to a ——; fit or proper for a ——: *womanly kindness* = *kindness suited to a woman.* **4** of each or every ——; occurring once per ——: *daily* = *of every day.* **5** being a ——; that is a ——: *a heavenly home* = *a home that is a heaven.* [OE *-līc*, representing *līc* body]

ly·cée (lē sā′) *n.* in France, a secondary school maintained by the government. [< F < L *Lyceum*. Doublet of LYCEUM.]

ly·ce·um (lī sē′əm *or* lī′sē əm) *n.* **1** a lecture hall; a place where lectures are given. **2** **Lyceum,** an ancient outdoor grove and gymnasium near Athens, where Aristotle taught. [< L *Lyceum* < Gk. *Lykeion* (def. 2), from the nearby temple of Apollo, *Lykeios*. Doublet of LYCÉE.]

lych–gate (lich′gāt′) See **lich-gate.**

ly·co·po·di·um (lī′kə pō′dē əm) *n.* **1** any of a large genus (*Lycopodium*) of chiefly creeping club mosses having needlelike evergreen leaves. The ground cedar (*L. complanatum*) and shining club moss (*L. lucidulum*) are two lycopodiums found in Canada. **2** a fine yellow powder made from the spores of certain lycopodiums, used in medicine and for making fireworks. [< NL < Gk. *lykos* wolf + *pous, podos* foot]

lydd·ite (lid′īt) *n.* a high explosive, consisting chiefly of picric acid. [< *Lydd*, a town in SE England]

Lyd·i·an (lid′ē ən) *n., adj.* —*n.* **1** a native or inhabitant of Lydia, an ancient kingdom in W Asia Minor. **2** the extinct Anatolian language of the Lydians. —*adj.* of or having to do with Lydia, its people, their language, or their music.

lye (lī) *n.* any strong alkaline substance, especially sodium hydroxide or potassium hydroxide. Lye is used in making soap and in cleaning. [OE *lēag*]
☛ *Hom.* **lie.**

ly·ing¹ (lī′ing) *n., adj., v.* —*n.* the telling of a lie; habit of telling lies. —*adj.* false; untruthful: *a lying report.*
—*v.* ppr. of **lie¹.**

ly·ing² (lī′ing) *v.* ppr. of **lie².**

ly·ing-in (lī′ing in′) *n.* confinement in childbirth.

lymph (limf) *n.* a nearly colorless liquid in the tissues of the body, resembling blood plasma and containing white blood cells but no red blood cells. [< L *lympha* clear water]

lym·phat·ic (lim fat′ik) *adj., n.* —*adj.* **1** of lymph; carrying lymph. **2** sluggish; lacking energy. —*n.* a vessel that contains or carries lymph.

lymph gland lymph node.

lymph node one of the rounded masses of tissue lying along the course of the lymphatic vessels, in which the lymph is purified and lymphocytes are formed.

lym·pho·cyte (lim′fə sīt′) *n.* one of the colorless cells of lymph produced in the lymph nodes, a variety of leucocyte. [< L *lympha* clear water + E *-cyte* hollow body (< Gk. *kytos*)]

lymph·oid (lim′foid) *adj.* **1** of, having to do with, or resembling lymph or lymphocytes. **2** of, having to do with, or resembling lymphoid tissue.

lynch (linch) *v.* kill, usually by hanging, through mob action and without a proper trial. [see LYNCH LAW] —**lynch′er,** *n.*

lynch law the punishment of an accused person without a lawful trial, usually by putting him to death. [originally *Lynch's law* < William *Lynch* (1742-1820), a Virginia magistrate]

lynx (lingks) *n., pl.* **lynx·es** *or* (*esp. collectively*) **lynx. 1** a medium-sized wildcat (*Felis lynx*) of Eurasia and N North America having long legs with large paws, tufted ears, and a short tail. See also **Canada lynx. 2** any of several other closely related wildcats, such as the bobcat or caracal. [< L < Gk.] —**lynx′like′,** *adj.*

lynx-eyed (lingks′īd′) *adj.* having sharp eyes; sharp-sighted.

ly·on·naise (lī′ə nāz′) *adj.* fried with pieces of onions: *lyonnaise*

hat, āge, fär; let, ēqual, tèrm; it, īce
hot, ōpen, ôrder; oil, out; cup, pùt, rüle,
əbove, takən, pencəl, lemən, circəs

ch, child; ng, long; sh, ship
th, thin; ŦH, then; zh, measure

potatoes. [< F *lyonnaise* < *Lyon* Lyons, a city in E France]

Ly·ra (lī′rə) *n.* a small northern constellation thought of as arranged in the shape of a lyre. It contains the star Vega.

ly·rate (lī′rāt) *adj.* shaped like a lyre.

A lyre

lyre (līr) *n.* an ancient stringed musical instrument resembling a small harp. [ME < L < Gk. *lyra*]

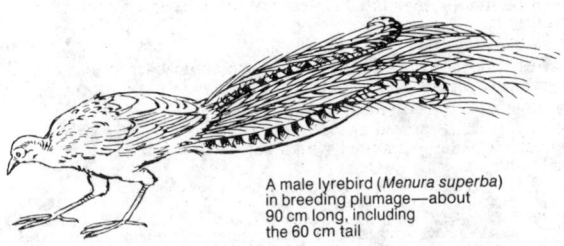

A male lyrebird (*Menura superba*) in breeding plumage—about 90 cm long, including the 60 cm tail

lyre·bird (līr′bèrd′) *n.* either of two Australian birds (*Menura superba* and *M. alberti*) that make up a separate family (Menuridae) of passerine birds. The adult males have a long tail that is lyre-shaped when spread.

lyr·ic (lir′ik) *n., adj.* —*n.* **1** a short poem expressing personal emotion. Love poems, patriotic songs, laments, and hymns are all lyrics. **2 lyrics,** *pl.* the words for a song.
—*adj.* **1** having to do with lyric poems: *a lyric poet.* **2** characterized by a spontaneous expression of feeling. **3** of or suitable for singing. **4** having a light, melodic singing voice: *a lyric soprano.* [< L *lyricus* < Gk. *lyrikos* of a lyre]

lyr·i·cal (lir′ə kəl) *adj.* **1** showing or expressing great enthusiasm and emotion: *She was lyrical in her praise of the new auditorium.* **2** lyric. —**lyr′i·cal·ly,** *adv.*

lyr·i·cism (lir′ə siz′əm) *n.* **1** a lyric style, quality, or form of expression: *Keats' lyricism.* **2** high-flown sentiments; exuberance.

lyr·i·cist (lir′ə sist) *n.* **1** a writer of lyrics or of popular songs. **2** a lyric poet.

ly·ser·gic acid (lī sèr′jik) *Chemistry.* a crystalline compound produced synthetically or as an extract from ergot. *Formula:* $C_{16}H_{16}N_2O_2$

lysergic acid di·eth·yl·am·ide (dī eth′ə lam′īd) a drug that can produce hallucinations and schizophrenic symptoms. *Formula:* $C_{20}H_{25}N_3O$ *Abbrev.:* LSD.

ly·sin (lī′sən) *n.* any of a class of substances that are developed in blood serum, and that are capable of causing the dissolution or destruction of bacteria, blood corpuscles, and other cellular elements. [< Gk. *lysis* a loosening]

Ly·sol (lī′sōl *or* lī′sol) *n. Trademark.* a brown, oily liquid containing cresols and soap, used as a disinfectant and antiseptic. [< Gk. *lysis* a loosening + L *oleum* oil]

Mm

m or **M** (em) *n., pl.* **m's** or **M's. 1** the thirteenth letter of the English alphabet. **2** any speech sound represented by this letter. **3** a person or thing identified as *m*, especially the thirteenth in a series. **4** the Roman numeral for 1000. **5** *Printing.* an em, a unit of measure. **6** something shaped like the letter M. **7** (*adj.*) of or being an M or m.

m 1 metre(s). **2** milli- (an SI prefix).

m mass.

m. 1 minute. **2** masculine. **3** mile. **4** married. **5** minim. **6** month. **7** manual. **8** *Currency.* mill.

M 1 mega- (an SI prefix). **2** *Currency.* mark.

M. 1 Monday. **2** Monsieur. **3** Master (in titles). **4** Mass. **5** minim. **6** *Currency.* mill. **7** Noon (for L *meridies*).

ma (mo, mä, *or* ma) *n. Informal.* mamma; mother.

MA 1 Massachusetts. **2** *Psychology.* mental age.

M.A. Master of Arts (for L *Magister Artium*).

ma'am (mam *or* mäm) *n. Informal.* madam.

Mac (mak) *n. Can. Informal.* a McIntosh apple.

ma·ca·bre (mə kä′brə *or* mə kä′bər) *adj.* gruesome; horrible; ghastly. [< F]

ma·ca·co (mə kä′kō) *n., pl.* **-cos.** any of several lemurs (genus *Lemur*), especially *L. macaco*, the male of which is black and the female brown. [< Pg. < native African]

mac·ad·am (mə kad′əm) *n.* **1** material for making roads, consisting of small, broken stones of nearly uniform size which are mixed with a binding agent such as tar or asphalt. Several layers of macadam are put down to make a road, each layer rolled until solid and smooth before the next layer is laid down. **2** a road made with layers of macadam. [after John L. *McAdam* (1756-1836), a Scottish engineer]

mac·ad·am·ize (mə kad′əm īz′) *v.* **-ized, -iz·ing.** surface a road with macadam. —**mac·ad′am·i·za′tion,** *n.*

ma·caque (mə käk′) *n.* any of a genus (*Macaca*) of short-tailed or tail-less Old World monkeys found mainly in Asia. The rhesus monkey and the Barbary ape are macaques. [< F < Pg. < native African]

mac·a·ro·ni (mak′ə rō′nē) *n., pl.* **-nis** or **-nies.** flour paste that has been dried, usually in the form of hollow tubes, to be cooked for food. [< earlier Ital. *maccaroni*, pl., ult. < LGk. *makaria* barley broth]

mac·a·roon (mak′ə rün′) *n.* a very sweet, chewy cookie, usually made of whites of eggs, sugar, and ground almonds or coconut. [< F < Ital. *maccarone*, sing. of *maccaroni*. See MACARONI.]

ma·caw (mə ko′ *or* mə kô′) *n.* any parrot belonging to either of two genera (*Ara* and *Anodorhynchus*) of large, brilliantly colored, tropical American parrots having a long, loose tail and a large, deep, hooked bill. [< Pg. *macao* < Brazilian]

Macc. Maccabees.

Mac·ca·bees (mak′ə bēz′) *n.pl.* **1** a family of Jewish patriots who led successful revolts against Syria in the second century B.C. **2** two books of the Old Testament Apocrypha telling about these revolts.

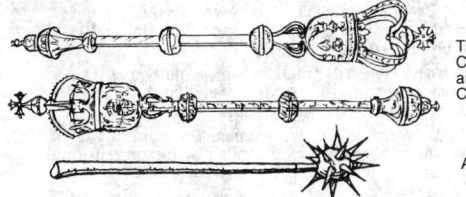

The maces of the Canadian Senate and the House of Commons

A medieval mace

mace¹ (mās) *n.* **1** a staff used as a symbol of authority. **2** the bearer of a mace. **3** in the Middle Ages, a war club having a heavy metal head. [ME < OF < VL *mattea* < L *matteola* kind of hammer]

mace² (mās) *n.* a spice made from the dried outer covering of nutmegs. [ME < OF *macis* < L *macir* reddish rind of an Indian root < Gk. *makir*]

Mace (mās) *n. Trademark.* a liquid chemical similar in effect to tear gas, producing tears and temporary blindness, dizziness, etc. when sprayed in a person's face. It has been used by some police forces, etc. for controlling riots.

mac·é·doine (mas′ə dwän′ *or* mas′ä dwän′) *n.* a mixture of vegetables or fruits, sometimes, in jelly. [< F *macédoine* Macedonian]

mac·er·ate (mas′ər āt′) *v.* **-at·ed, -at·ing. 1** soften by soaking for some time. **2** break up or soften (food) by the digestive process. **3** grow or cause to grow thin. [< L *macerare* soften] —**mac′er·a′tion,** *n.*

Mach (mäk *or* mak) *n.* Mach number.

ma·chet·e (mə shet′ *or* mə chet′ē; *Spanish,* mä chä′tā) *n.* a large, heavy knife, used as a tool and weapon in South America, Central America, and the West Indies. [< Sp., ult. < L *mactare* kill]

Mach·i·a·vel·li·an or **Mach·i·a·vel·i·an** (mak′ē ə vel′ē ən) *adj., n.* —*adj.* **1** of or having to do with Niccolo Machiavelli (1469-1527), an Italian statesman and writer who wrote *The Prince*, a detailed study of how force, deceit, and other unscrupulous methods were used to gain and hold power. **2** of or having to do with the crafty political methods described by Machiavelli. **3** characterized by subtle or unscrupulous cunning; crafty; wily; astute. —*n.* a person who uses such crafty political methods as were described by Machiavelli.

ma·chic·o·lat·ed (mə chik′ə lāt′id) *adj.* having machicolations.

ma·chic·o·la·tion (mə chik′ə lā′shən) *n.* **1** an opening in the floor of a projecting gallery or parapet, or in the roof of an entrance, through which missiles, hot liquids, etc. might be cast upon attackers. Machicolations were much used in medieval fortified structures. **2** a projecting gallery or parapet with such openings. [< Med.L *machicolatio, -onis* < OF < Provençal *machacol* projection, balcony < *macar* crush (< Gmc.) + *col* neck < L *collum*]

mach·i·nate (mak′ə nāt′ *or* mash′ə nāt′) *v.* **-nat·ed, -nat·ing.** contrive or devise artfully or with evil purpose; plot; intrigue. [< L *machinari* < *machina*. See MACHINE.] **mach′i·na′tor,** *n.*

mach·i·na·tion (mak′ə nā′shən *or* mash′ə nā′shən) *n.* **1** the act of machinating. **2** Usually, **machinations,** a secret or cunning scheme, especially one with an evil purpose: *He could not have been overthrown without the machinations of his enemies.*

ma·chine (mə shēn′) *n., v.* **-chined, -chin·ing.** —*n.* **1** a device consisting of an arrangement of interrelated fixed and moving parts powered mechanically, electrically, or electronically, designed to do a particular kind of work: *a sewing machine, a calculating machine.* **2** (*adj.*) of or having to do with a machine or machines: *the machine age, machine action.* **3** (*adj.*) produced by or with a machine, not by hand: *machine printing.* **4** a device for transmitting power, energy, or motion or changing its direction. Levers and pulleys are simple machines. **5** a coin-operated dispenser: *a cigarette machine.* **6** a motor vehicle, aircraft, bicycle, etc. **7** a person or group that acts mechanically, without thinking or feeling. **8** a highly organized group of people, especially a group controlling a political organization: *the Liberal machine.* —*v.* make or finish by machine. [< F < L *machina* < Gk. *machana,* dial. var. of *mēchanē* device, means] —**ma·chin′er,** *n.* —**ma·chine′like′,** *adj.*

machine gun a gun that uses small-arms ammunition automatically and can keep up a rapid fire of bullets.

ma·chine-gun (mə shēn′gun′) *v.* **-gunned, -gun·ning.** fire at with a machine gun.

machine language a system for expressing information or instructions in terms of numbers, symbols, etc. that can be used directly by a computer.

ma·chine-made (mə shēn′mād′) *adj.* made by machinery, not by hand.

ma·chin·er·y (mə shēn′ər ē *or* mə shēn′rē) *n., pl.* **-er·ies. 1** machines: *There is a lot of machinery in a shoe factory.* **2** the

parts or works of a machine: *He examined the machinery of his watch.* **3** any combination of persons or things by which something is kept going or something is done: *Police officers, judges, courts, prisons are the machinery of the law.*

machine shop a workshop where machines or parts of machines are made or repaired.

machine tool an electrically or mechanically driven tool, such as a lathe, drill, or punch press, used in manufacturing machinery.

ma·chin·ist (mə shēn′ist) *n.* **1** a person skilled in using machine tools. **2** a person who runs a machine. **3** a person who makes and repairs machinery.

ma·chis·mo (mä chēz′mō *or* mä chiz′mō) *n.* exaggerated or aggressive masculinity; a macho quality or condition.

Mach·me·ter (mäk′mē′tər *or* mak′-) *n.* an instrument for indicating the air speed of an aircraft as a Mach number.

Mach number a number representing the ratio of the speed of an object to the speed of sound in the same medium. Mach number 1 equals the speed of sound, Mach number 2 is twice the speed of sound, and Mach number 0.5 is half the speed of sound. [after Ernst *Mach* (1838-1916), an Austrian physicist]

ma·cho (mä′chō) *adj., n.* —*adj.* robust and virile in an exaggerated way; proudly or aggressively masculine: *a macho swagger, a macho image.* —*n.* **1** a man who is proudly or aggressively masculine. **2** manhood; virility.

mac·in·tosh (mak′ən tosh′) See **mackintosh.**

mack·er·el (mak′ər əl *or* mak′rəl) *n.* **-el** *or* **-els. 1** an important marine food fish (*Scomber scombrus*) of the N Atlantic coastal regions and the Mediterranean, having a rounded, torpedo-shaped, green-and-silver body and a deeply forked tail. **2** any of various other fishes of the same family (Scombridae), such as the **Spanish mackerels** (genus *Scomberomorus*) of warm seas or the **Pacific mackerel** (*Scomber japonicus*). [ME < AF *makerel*]

mackerel sky a sky spotted with small, white fleecy clouds.

mack·i·naw (mak′ə no′ *or* mak′ə nô′) *n.* **1** a kind of short coat made of heavy woollen cloth. **2** a kind of thick blanket that often has bars of color, used in the North and West by Indians, trappers, etc. **3** a large, heavy, flat-bottomed boat, formerly used in the region of the Upper Great Lakes. [< Cdn.F *Mackinac < Michilimackinac* Mackinac Island < Algonquian (Ojibwa) *mitchimackinak* large turtle]

mack·in·tosh (mak′ən tosh′) *n.* **1** raincoat. **2** waterproof cloth. Also, **macintosh.** [< Charles *Macintosh* (1766-1843), the inventor]

mac·ra·mé (mak′rə mä′) *n.* a coarse lace of fringe, made by knotting thread or cord in patterns. [apparently < Turkish *maqrama* napkin < Arabic]

mac·ro (mak′rō) *n.* a single instruction for a computer that will generate a sequence of computer code instructions to perform a specific task. Also called **macro instruction.**

macro– *combining form.* large, long, or large-scale, as in *macrocosm.*

mac·ro·cosm (mak′rə koz′əm) *n.* universe. [< F < Med.L *macrocosmus* < Gk. *makros* great + *kosmos* world]

ma·cron (mak′ron *or* mä′kron) *n.* a short, horizontal line (ˉ) placed over a vowel letter to identify a sound differing from that represented by the same letter without such a mark. *Example:* (mak′ron *or* māk′ron). [< Gk. *makron,* neut. adj., long]

mad (mad) *adj.* **mad·der, mad·dest. 1** out of one's mind; crazy; insane. **2** *Informal.* angry: *The article made him mad enough to write a letter to the editor.* **3** much excited; wild: *The dog made mad efforts to catch up with the automobile.* **4** foolish; unwise: *a mad undertaking.* **5** very lively: *a mad party.* **6** blindly and unreasonably fond: *mad about boats.* **7** *Informal.* very angry. **8** having rabies; rabid: *a mad dog.*
like mad, furiously; very hard or fast: *I ran like mad to catch the train.*
mad as a hatter, or **mad as a March hare,** completely crazy. [OE (*ge*)*mæded*]
☛ *Syn.* **Mad, crazy,** and **insane** have similar meanings. All three words have been commonly used at some time to describe someone who is mentally ill. This is still proper use in legal contexts for the word **insane:** *an institution for the criminally insane.* **Mad** is most often used to mean just very reckless or foolish: *Crossing the Pacific on a raft seems a mad thing to do.* **Crazy** usually suggests a more wild or disturbed state: *She was nearly crazy with fear.*

mad·am (mad′əm) *n., pl.* **mad·ams** *or* (for def. 1) **mes·dames** (mā dăm′). **1** a polite or formal title used in speaking to a woman (*used alone, not with a name*): *The line is busy, madam; would you care to hold?* **2** a formal title for a woman used before the name of her rank or office: *Madam Chairman, Madam Prime Minister.* **3** a woman who runs a brothel. [ME < OF *ma dame* my lady]

mad·ame (mad′əm; *French,* mä dăm′) *n., pl.* **mes·dames** (mā dăm′). **1** a French title for a married woman; Mrs. **2** a title often used by female singers, artists, etc. *Abbrev.:* Mme. [< F]

mad·cap (mad′kap) *adj., n.* —*adj.* impulsive, wild, or foolish: *a madcap escapade.* —*n.* a person who habitually does impulsive, wild, or foolish things.

mad·den (mad′ən) *v.* **1** make crazy. **2** make very angry or excited.

mad·der (mad′ər) *n.* **1** a perennial vine (*Rubia tinctorum*) native to Europe and Asia, having loose clusters of small, funnel-shaped, yellow flowers. **2** the root of this plant, formerly used for making a red dye. **3** the dye made from this root; alizarin. **4** bright red. **5** (*adj.*) designating the family (Rubiaceae) of mostly tropical and subtropical herbs, shrubs, and trees that includes the madder, gardenia, coffee tree, cinchona, etc. [OE *mædere*]

mad·ding (mad′ing) *adj.* **1** mad; acting as if mad: *the madding crowd.* **2** making mad.

made (mād) *v.* pt. and pp. of **make.**
—*adj.* **1** built; formed. **2** specially prepared. **3** artificially produced: *made land.* **4** invented. **5** *Informal.* certain of success; successful.
☛ *Hom.* **maid.**

Ma·dei·ra *or* **ma·dei·ra** (mə dēr′ə) *n.* a kind of wine made on the island of Madeira.

mad·e·moi·selle (mad′ə mə zel′; *French,* mäd mwä zel′) *n., pl.* **mes·de·moi·selles** (mād mwä zel′). a French title for an unmarried woman; Miss. *Abbrev.:* Mlle.

made-to-meas·ure (mād′tə mezh′ər) *adj.* of clothing, made to the buyer's own measurements.

made-to-or·der (mād′tə ôr′dər) *adj.* made according to the buyer's wishes.

made-up (mād′up′) *adj.* **1** put together. **2** invented; not real: *a made-up story.* **3** painted, powdered, etc. with cosmetics: *made-up lips.*

mad·house (mad′hous′) *n.* **1** *Historical.* an asylum for the insane. **2** a place of uproar and confusion: *The arena was a madhouse after the home team won the championship game.*

Mad·i·son Avenue (mad′ə sən) **1** in New York City, a street where most of the major U.S. advertising agencies have their offices. **2** the U.S. advertising industry, its techniques, language, influence, etc.

mad·ly (mad′lē) *adv.* **1** insanely. **2** furiously. **3** foolishly.

mad·man (mad′man′ *or* mad′mən) *n., pl.* **-men.** a man who is insane or behaves like someone who is insane.

mad money *Informal.* a small amount of money kept for minor emergencies; originally, money carried by a woman or girl on a date to enable her to get home on her own if necessary.

mad·ness (mad′nis) *n.* the state or condition of being mad; insanity, rage, or folly: *In his madness, he struck his best friend. It was madness to take a sailboat out in that storm.*

Ma·don·na (mə don′ə) *n.* **1** Usually, **the Madonna,** Mary, the mother of Jesus. **2** a picture or statue of her. [< Ital. *madonna* my lady]

Madonna lily a garden lily (*Lilium candidum*) having large, pure-white, bell-shaped flowers. It is the floral emblem of Quebec.

mad·ras (mad′rəs *or* mə dras′) *n.* **1** a medium or light weight cloth in a close, plain weave, usually of cotton, in white or with brightly colored woven stripes, checks, or plaids: *Madras is used for shirts, dresses, etc.* **2** a light, open-weave cloth with a heavier woven pattern, used for curtains, etc. [< *Madras,* a city and state in India]

mad·re·pore (mad′rə pôr′) *n.* any of various tropical stony corals (genus *Madrepora*) that form coral reefs. [< F < Ital. *madrepora < madre* mother (< L *mater*) + *poro,* ult. < Gk. *poros,* kind of stone]

mad·ri·gal (mad′rə gəl) *n.* **1** a short poem, often about love, that can be set to music. **2** a song with parts for several voices, sung without instrumental accompaniment. **3** any song. [< Ital. < LL *matricale* original, chief < *matrix* womb]

mad·ri·lene *or* **mad·ri·lène** (mad′rə lən *or* mad′rə len′) *n.* a consommé flavored with tomato, usually served cold. [< F *madrilène* of Madrid, Spain < Sp. *madrileño*]

mad·wom·an (mad′wùm′ən) *n., pl.* **-women. 1** a woman who is insane. **2** a woman whose behavior is so foolish or unconventional as to appear irrational.

Mae·ce·nas (mī sē′nəs *or* mi sē′nas) *n.* a generous patron of literature or art. [< *Maecenas* (74?-8 B.C.), a Roman statesman and patron of literature]

mael·strom (māl′strəm) *n.* **1** a great or turbulent whirlpool. **2** a violent confusion of feelings, ideas, or conditions. **3 Maelstrom,** a dangerous whirlpool off NW Norway. [< earlier Du. *maelstrom < malen* grind + *stroom* stream]

mae·nad (mē′nad) *n.* **1** *Greek and Roman mythology.* a female follower of Bacchus (or Dionysus), who participated in the wild, orgiastic rites that were characteristic of the worship of this god. **2** a frenzied woman. Also, **menad.** [< L *maenas, -adis* < Gk. *mainas, -adis*]

ma·es·to·so (mä′es tō′sō) *adj., adv., n. Music.* —*adj. or adv.* stately; with dignity. —*n.* a stately movement or passage; a composition to be played or sung in this way. [< Ital.]

maes·tro (mīs′trō; *Italian,* mä es′trō) *n., pl.* **-tros** or **(Italian) ma·es·tri** (mä es′tre). **1** a great composer, teacher, or conductor of music. **2** a master of any art. [< Ital. < L *magister* master]

Mae West (mā′ west′) an inflatable vest worn as a life preserver by an aviator in flying over water. [< *Mae West* (1892-1980), an American actress]

Ma·fi·a (mä′fē ə) *n.* **1** a world-wide secret organization of criminal elements engaged in illicit activities such as racketeering and gambling. **2 mafia,** any group that is thought to dominate in an underhanded way some segment or aspect of society: *an intellectual mafia.* [< Ital.]

ma·fi·o·so (mä′fē ō′sō) *n., pl.* **-si** (-sē). a member of the Mafia.

mag. 1 magazine. **2** magnet; magnetism. **3** *Astronomy.* magnitude.

mag·a·zine (mag′ə zēn′ *or* mag′ə zēn′) *n.* **1** a publication issued at regular intervals, especially weekly or monthly, which contains stories, articles, photographs, etc., by various contributors. **2** a room in a fort or warship for keeping gunpowder and other explosives. **3** a place for storing goods or supplies, such as a warehouse or military supply depot. **4** a holder in or on a repeating or automatic gun for the cartridges to be fed into the gun chamber. See **firearm** for picture. **5** a lightproof space in or container on a camera for holding film or plates. [< F < Ital. *magazzino,* ult. < Arabic *makhzan* storehouse]

Mag·da·lene (mag′də lēn′) *n.* **1** Mary Magdalene. **2 magdalene,** any woman who has reformed from a sinful life, especially a repentant prostitute.

mage (māj) *n. Archaic.* magician. [< OF < L *magus.* See MAGI.]

Ma·gen Da·vid (mog′ən dä′vid *or* mog′ən dov′id) Star of David. [< Hebrew *māghēn dāwīdh,* literally, shield of David]

ma·gen·ta (mə jen′tə) *n., adj.* —*n.* **1** a purplish-red dye. **2** a purplish red. —*adj.* purplish red. [< dye named after Battle of *Magenta,* Italy, 1859, because it was discovered in that year]

mag·got (mag′ət) *n.* a fly in the earliest, legless stage, just after leaving the egg. Maggots often live in decaying matter. [ME *magot;* origin uncertain]

Mag·i (mā′jī *or* maj′ī) *n.* pl. of **Magus. 1** in the Bible, the Three Wise Men who, according to the New Testament, brought gifts to the infant Jesus. Matt. 2:1 and 2: 7-12). **2** priests of ancient Persia. [< L *magi,* pl. of *magus* < Gk. *magos* < OPersian]

mag·ic (maj′ik) *n., adj.* —*n.* **1** the use of charms, spells, etc. to try to call up spirits or other occult powers and through them to control natural forces or change the normal course of events. **2** something that produces results as if by magic; mysterious influence; unexplained power; enchantment: *the magic of music.* —*adj.* **1** made or done by magic or as if by magic: *A magic palace stood in place of their hut.* **2** having supernatural powers: *a magic wand.* **3** producing a feeling of rapture or enchantment: *magic moments.* [ME < OF *magique,* ult. < Gk. *magikos* < *magos* astrologer < OPersian]

mag·i·cal (maj′ə kəl) *adj.* **1** of, used in or done by magic. **2** like magic; mysterious; unexplained. —**mag′i·cal·ly,** *adv.*

magic eye any of several electronic monitoring devices, used for checking the functioning of machinery for activating mechanisms, for operating traffic signals, etc.

ma·gi·cian (mə jish′ən) *n.* **1** a person skilled in the use of magic, especially a sorcerer. **2** a person skilled in the use of sleight of hand to entertain: *The magician pulled three rabbits out of his hat.* [ME < OF *magicien*]

magic lantern a device with a lamp and lenses for throwing a picture upon a screen, in magnified form, from a glass slide. A magic lantern is an early form of projector.

Ma·gi·not line (mazh′ə nō′) an elaborate system of defences built by France against Germany after the first World War. [after André *Maginot* (1877-1932), a French minister of war]

mag·is·te·ri·al (maj′is tēr′ē əl) *adj.* **1** of or suited to a magistrate: *A judge has magisterial rank.* **2** showing authority: *The captain spoke with a magisterial voice.* **3** imperious; domineering; overbearing. [< Med.L *magisterialis,* ult. < L *magister* master] —**mag′is·te′ri·al·ly,** *adv.*

mag·is·tra·cy (maj′is trə sē) *n., pl.* **-cies. 1** the position, rank, or duties of a magistrate. **2** magistrates as a group. **3** a district under a magistrate.

mag·is·trate (maj′is trāt′ *or* maj′is trit) *n.* a government official

hat, āge, fär; let, ēqual, tèrm; it, īce
hot, ōpen, ôrder; oil, out; cup, put, rüle,
əbove, takən, pencəl, lemən, circəs
ch, child; ng, long; sh, ship
th, thin; ⊦H, then; zh, measure

appointed to hear and decide cases in a magistrate's court or similar lower court. [< L *magistratus,* ult. < *magister* master]

magistrate's court a court that has limited jurisdiction, dealing with minor civil and criminal cases. In Canada, magistrate's courts are established by provincial legislation.

mag·ma (mag′mə) *n.* **1** any soft, pastelike mixture of mineral or organic substances. **2** *Geology.* the very hot, fluid substance that is found below the earth's crust and from which lava and igneous rocks are formed. **3** *Pharmacy.* a suspension of insoluble or almost insoluble material in a small volume of water. [< L *magma* dregs of an unguent < Gk. *magma* an unguent, ult. < *massein* knead, mould]

Mag·na Char·ta or **Car·ta** (mag′nə kär′tə) **1** the great charter, guaranteeing personal and political liberties, forcibly secured from King John of England by the barons at Runnymede on June 15, 1215. **2** any fundamental constitution guaranteeing civil and political rights. [< Med.L *magna charta* great charter]

mag·na cum lau·de (mag′nə küm′ lou′dā *or* kum lō′dā) with high honors. [< L *magna cum laude* with great praise]

mag·na·nim·i·ty (mag′nə nim′ə tē) *n., pl.* **-ties. 1** the quality of being magnanimous. **2** a magnanimous act.

mag·nan·i·mous (mag nan′ə məs) *adj.* **1** noble in soul or mind; generous in forgiving; free from mean or petty feelings or acts. **2** showing or arising from a generous spirit: *a magnanimous attitude toward a conquered enemy.* [< L *magnanimus* < *magnus* great + *animus* spirit] —**mag·nan′i·mous·ly,** *adv.* —**mag·nan′i·mous·ness,** *n.*

mag·nate (mag′nāt) *n.* an important or powerful person, especially in business or industry: *an oil magnate.* [< LL *magnas, -atis* < L *magnus* great]

mag·ne·sia (mag nē′zhə, mag nē′zē ə, *or* mag nē′shə) *n.* **1** magnesium oxide, a white, tasteless powder, used in medicine as a laxative, and in making fertilizers and some building materials. *Formula:* MgO **2** magnesium. [ME < Med.L < Gk. *hē Magnēsia lithos* the Magnesian stone (from *Magnesia,* in Thessaly)]

mag·ne·site (mag′nə sīt′) *n.* a mineral, carbonate of magnesium, occurring in white crystalline or granular masses, used industrially in making steel, etc. *Formula:* MgCO₃ [< *magnesi*um + *-ite*]

mag·ne·si·um (mag nē′zē əm, mag nē′zhē əm *or* mag nē′shē əm) *n.* a light, silver-white metallic chemical element that burns with a dazzling white light. Magnesium is used in metal alloys, fireworks, etc. *Symbol:* Mg; *at.no.* 12; *at.wt.* 24.312. [< NL < *magnesia.* See MAGNESIA.]

mag·net (mag′nit) *n.* **1** a mass or piece of iron, steel, etc. that has the property, or power, of attracting iron and some other metals to it. **2** an artificially magnetized piece of iron, steel, etc.: *a horseshoe magnet.* **3** anything that attracts: *The rabbits in our back yard were a magnet that attracted all the children in the neighborhood.* [ME < OF *magnete* < L < Gk. *hē Magnētis lithos* the magnet. Related to MAGNESIA.]

mag·net·ic (mag net′ik) *adj.* **1** having the properties of a magnet. **2** of or having to do with magnetism; producing magnetism. **3** of or having to do with the earth's magnetism: *the magnetic meridian.* **4** capable of being magnetized or of being attracted by a magnet. **5** attractive: *a magnetic personality.* —**mag·net′i·cal·ly,** *adv.*

magnetic field 1 the region of magnetic influence, or force, around a magnet, a magnetic body such as the earth, or a body carrying an electric current. **2** the magnetic forces present in such a region: *a strong magnetic field.*

magnetic mine an underwater mine that is exploded by the action of the metal parts of an approaching ship upon a magnetic needle.

magnetic needle a slender bar of magnetized steel that forms the basic part of a compass. When mounted horizontally so that it can turn freely, it will show the direction of the magnetic field of the earth, pointing toward the magnetic poles, approximately north and south.

magnetic pole 1 one of the two poles of a magnet. **2 Magnetic Pole,** one of the two points on the earth's surface toward which a magnetic needle points. The **North Magnetic Pole** is approximately in 71° North latitude and 95° West longitude. The **South Magnetic Pole** is approximately in 72° South latitude and 154° East longitude.

magnetic tape a plastic or paper ribbon coated on one side with

a substance that magnetizes easily, such as particles of iron oxide, used for recording sounds, pictures, and other kinds of information by electromagnetic means. Magnetic tape is used in computers, tape-recorders, and videotape recorders.

mag·net·ism (mag′nə tiz′əm) *n.* **1** the properties of a magnet; manifestation of magnetic properties. **2** the branch of physics dealing with magnets and magnetic properties. **3** the power to attract or charm: *His magnetism was shown by the number of his friends and admirers.*

mag·net·ite (mag′nə tīt′) *n.* an important iron ore that is strongly magnetic; black iron oxide. *Formula:* Fe_3O_4

mag·net·ize (mag′nə tīz′) *v.* **-ized, -iz·ing. 1** give the properties of a magnet to. An electric current in a coil around a bar of iron will magnetize the bar. **2** attract or influence like a magnet; charm: *Her beautiful voice magnetized the audience.* **—mag′net·iz′a·ble,** *adj.* **—mag′net·i·za′tion,** *n.* **—mag′net·iz′er,** *n.*

mag·ne·to (mag nē′tō) *n., pl.* **-tos.** a small machine which uses a magnetic field to produce an electric current. In some internal-combustion engines, a magneto supplies an electric spark to explode the gasoline vapor. [< *magneto* electric machine]

mag·ne·to·e·lec·tric (mag nē′tō i lek′trik) *adj.* of, designating, or using electricity produced by magnetic means.

mag·ne·tom·e·ter (mag′nə tom′ə tər) *n.* an instrument used to measure magnetic forces.

mag·ne·to·sphere (mag nē′tə sfēr′) *n.* **1** the region surrounding the earth in which ionized particles are controlled by the earth's magnetic field. **2** a similar region around any other celestial body, such as a planet.

mag·nif·ic (mag nif′ik) *adj. Archaic.* **1** magnificent. **2** pompous. [< L *magnificus* < *magnus* great + *facere* make]

mag·nif·i·cal (mag nif′ə kəl) *adj. Archaic.* magnific.

Mag·nif·i·cat (mag nif′ə kat′ *or* män yif′ə kät′) *n.* **1** a hymn of the Virgin Mary beginning "My soul doth magnify the Lord." (Luke 1:46-55). **2** the music for this hymn. [< L *magnificat* magnifies]

mag·ni·fi·ca·tion (mag′nə fə kā′shən) *n.* **1** the act of magnifying. **2** a magnified condition. **3** the power to magnify. **4** a magnified copy, model, or picture.

mag·nif·i·cence (mag nif′ə səns) *n.* the quality or state of being magnificent; grand beauty or splendor. [< OF < L *magnificentia* < *magnificus* noble. See MAGNIFIC.]

mag·nif·i·cent (mag nif′ə sənt) *adj.* **1** richly colored or decorated; splendid; grand; stately: *a magnificent royal palace, a magnificent ceremony.* **2** impressive; noble; exalted: *magnificent words, magnificent ideas.* **3** extraordinarily fine; superb: *a magnificent view of the mountains, a magnificent opportunity.* [< OF *magnificent* < *magnificence* < L *magnificentia.* See MAGNIFICENCE.] **—mag·nif′i·cent·ly,** *adv.*
☛ *Syn.* **Magnificent, splendid, superb** = impressive in dignity and beauty, brilliance, or excellence. **Magnificent** emphasizes impressive beauty and costly richness or stateliness of things like natural scenery, jewels, buildings, etc., and noble greatness of ideas: *Westminster Abbey is magnificent.* **Splendid** emphasizes impressive brilliance or shining brightness in appearance or character of things, people, or deeds: *He had a splendid record in the army.* **Superb** denotes the highest possible excellence, magnificence, splendor, richness, etc.: *We have a superb view of the ocean.*

mag·nif·i·co (mag nif′ə kō′) *n., pl.* **-coes. 1** a Venetian nobleman. **2** an important person. [< Ital.]

mag·ni·fi·er (mag′nə fī′ər) *n.* a person or thing that magnifies, especially a lens or combination of lenses that makes things appear larger than they really are.

mag·ni·fy (mag′nə fī′) *v.* **-fied, -fy·ing. 1** cause to look larger than the real size; increase the apparent size of an object. **2** make too much of; go beyond the truth in telling. **3** *Archaic.* praise highly. [< L *magnificare* esteem greatly, ult. < *magnus* great + *facere* make]

magnifying glass a lens or combination of lenses that makes things look larger than they really are.

mag·nil·o·quence (mag nil′ə kwəns) *n.* **1** a high-flown, lofty style of speaking or writing; the use of pompous and unusual words, elaborate phrases, etc. **2** boastfulness. [< L *magnus* great + *loquens,* ppr. of *loqui* speak]

mag·nil·o·quent (mag nil′ə kwənt) *adj.* **1** using big and unusual words; in high-flown language. **2** boastful. [< *magniloquence*] **—mag·nil′o·quent·ly,** *adv.*

mag·ni·tude (mag′nə tyüd′ *or* mag′nə tüd′) *n.* **1** greatness of size, extent, importance, effect, etc.: *a problem of magnitude. The magnitude of the crime called for a long sentence.* **2** relative size, extent, importance, etc.: *the magnitude of an angle or line, the magnitude of an earthquake.* **3** *Astronomy.* a measure of the

brightness of a heavenly body, expressed as a numerical value. Stars of the first magnitude are the brightest; stars barely visible to the naked eye are of about the sixth magnitude. **4** *Mathematics.* a number assigned to a quantity so that it may be used as a basis of comparison for measuring similar quantities.
of the first magnitude, of great importance or significance.
[< L *magnitudo* < *magnus* large]

mag·no·lia (mag nōl′ē ə *or* mag nōl′yə) *n.* **1** any of a genus (*Magnolia*) of shrubs and trees of North America and Asia having simple leaves and large, white, pink, or purple flowers that bloom in early spring. In some magnolias, the flowers appear before the leaves. **2** (*adj.*) designating a family (Magnoliaceae) of trees, shrubs, and a few vines that includes the magnolias and the tulip tree. [< NL < Pierre *Magnol* (1638-1715), a French botanist]

mag·num (mag′nəm) *n.* **1** a bottle that holds two quarts of alcoholic liquor. **2** the amount that it holds. [< L *magnum,* neut. adj., great]

mag·num o·pus (mag′nəm ō′pəs) *Latin.* a great work of literature, music, or art, especially the greatest work of a particular artist or writer. [< L]

mag·pie (mag′pī) *n.* **1** any of several mainly black-and-white, long-tailed birds (genus *Pica*) of the same family as crows and jays, having a chattering call. The **black-billed magpie** (*Pica pica*) is common in western Canada. **2** a person who chatters. [< *Mag,* for *Margaret* + *pie*[2]]

Ma·gus (mā′gəs) *n., pl.* **Ma·gi.** one of the Magi.

Mag·yar (mag′yär; *Hungarian,* mo′dyor) *n., adj.* **1** a member of a people that make up most of the population of Hungary. **2** the Hungarian language. **—adj.** of or having to do with the Magyars or their language. [< Hungarian]

Ma·ha·bha·ra·ta (mə hä′bä′rə tə) *n.* one of the two great Hindu epics, believed to have been written before 500 B.C. The other is the Ramayana. [< Skt.]

ma·ha·ra·jah (mä′hə rä′jə) *n.* any of certain ruling princes in India, especially a ruler of one of the former native states. Also, **maharaja.** [< Skt. *maharaja* < *maha-* great + *raja* rajah]

ma·ha·ra·nee (mä′hə rä′nē) *n.* **1** the wife of a maharajah. **2** a woman holding in her own right a rank equal to that of a maharajah. Also, **maharani.** [< Hind. *maharani* < Skt. *maha-* great + *rajni* queen]

ma·hat·ma (mə hat′mə *or* mə hät′mə) *n.* in India, a wise and holy person who has extraordinary powers. [< Skt. *mahatman* < *maha-* great + *atman* soul]

Mah·di (mä′dē) *n., pl.* **-dis. 1** *Islam.* a messianic leader expected to establish a reign of righteousness before the end of the world. **2** any of several Islamic revolutionary leaders who have claimed this title in the past. [< Arabic *mahdiy* one who is guided aright < *hada* lead aright]

mah–jong *or* **mah–jongg** (mä′jong′ *or* mä′zhong′) *n.* a western version of a Chinese game played with 136 or 144 domino-like pieces called tiles. Each player tries to form winning combinations by drawing or discarding. [< Trademark *Mah-Jongg,* coined by Joseph Babcock, U.S. resident in Shanghai, who introduced the game in the U.S. after World War I. The name is from a Chinese word meaning 'sparrow'; one of the tiles has a figure of a sparrow.]

ma·hog·a·ny (mə hog′ə nē) *n., pl.* **-nies. 1** any of various tropical American trees (genus *Swietenia*) having large compound leaves and hard yellowish-brown to reddish-brown wood, especially *S. mahagoni* or *S. macrophylla,* highly valued for timber. **2** any of various W African trees (genus *Khaya*) of the same family having similar wood. **3** any of various other trees of the same family, also used for timber. **4** (*adj.*) designating the family (Meliaceae) of trees and shrubs that includes the mahoganies. **5** the wood of a mahogany, used for fine furniture, etc. **6** (*adj.*) made of this wood: *a mahogany dresser.* **7** a medium reddish-brown color. [< obs. Sp. *mahogani,* probably of West Indian origin]

Ma·hom·et (mə hom′it) *n.* Mohammed.

Ma·hom·et·an (mə hom′ə tən) *adj. or n.* Mohammedan.

Ma·hom·et·an·ism (mə hom′ə tən iz′əm) *n.* Mohammedanism.

ma·hout (mə hout′) *n.* in India and the East Indies, the keeper and driver of an elephant. [< Hind. *mahaut*]

maid (mād) *n.* **1** a young unmarried woman; girl. **2** a woman servant: *a kitchen maid.* **3** a virgin. **4 the Maid,** Joan of Arc (1412-1431), a French heroine who led armies against the invading English and saved the city of Orléans. [shortened from *maiden*]
☛ *Hom.* **made.**

maid·en (mā′dən) *n., adj.* **—n. 1** a young unmarried woman; girl. **2** a virgin. **3** a racehorse that has never won a race.
—adj. 1 of, suited to, or characteristic of a maiden: *maiden grace, maiden blushes.* **2** unmarried: *a maiden aunt.* **3** first: *a ship's maiden voyage.* **4** new or untried; fresh: *maiden ground.* [OE *mægden*]

maid·en·hair (mā′dən her′) *n.* any of a genus (*Adiantum*) of ferns having very slender stalks and delicate, finely divided fronds. Also called **maidenhair fern.**

maidenhair tree ginkgo.

maid·en·head (mā′dən hed′) *n.* **1** hymen. **2** *Archaic.* maidenhood; virginity.

maid·en·hood (mā′dən húd′) *n.* **1** the condition of being a maiden. **2** the time when one is a maiden.

maid·en·ly (mā′dən lē) *adj.* **1** of a maiden or maidenhood. **2** like or suitable for a maiden; gentle; modest. —**maid′en·li·ness,** *n.*

maiden name the surname a married woman had before her marriage: *Mrs. Madsen's maiden name was Drury.*

maid-in-waiting (mād′in wāt′ing) *n., pl.* **maids-in-waiting.** an unmarried young woman who attends a queen or princess.

maid of all work a woman servant who does all kinds of housework.

maid of honor or **honour 1** an unmarried woman who is the chief attendant of the bride at a wedding. **2** an unmarried lady who attends a queen or princess.

Maid of Orléans Joan of Arc; the Maid.

maid·serv·ant (mād′ser′vənt) *n.* a female servant.

mail¹ (māl) *n., v.* —*n.* **1** letters, postcards, papers, parcels, etc. sent or to be sent by post. **2** the system by which such mail is sent, managed by the Post Office. **3** all that comes by one post or delivery. **4** a train, boat, etc. that carries mail. —*v.* post; send by mail; put in a mailbox: *He mailed the letter for his mother.* [ME < OF *male* wallet < Gmc.] ☛ *Hom.* **male.**

mail² (māl) *n., v.* —*n.* **1** flexible armor made of metal rings, loops of chain, or small plates linked together. See **armor** for picture. **2** the hard, protective covering of some animals, such as turtles. —*v.* cover or protect with mail. [ME < OF *maille* < L *macula* a mesh in network] ☛ *Hom.* **male.**

mail·box (māl′boks′) *n.* **1** a public box for depositing outgoing mail that is to be collected by the post office. **2** a private box outside a dwelling, where the occupant's mail is delivered.

mail coach *Historical.* a stagecoach that carried mail.

mailed (māld) *adj.* covered or protected with mail.

mailed fist military force; aggression, especially by one nation against another. —**mailed′-fist′,** *adj.*

mail·er (mā′lər) *n.* **1** a person who mails letters, etc. **2** a machine for stamping or addressing letters, etc. **3** a container in which to mail things. Cylindrical mailers are often used for maps, photographs, etc.

mail·lot (mä yō′) *n. French.* **1** a bathing suit, especially a one-piece bathing suit. **2** a one-piece, tightly fitting garment worn by dancers, gymnasts, etc.

mail·man (māl′man′) *n., pl.* **-men.** a person whose work is carrying or delivering mail; letter carrier.

mail order an order for goods sent by mail.

mail-or·der (māl′ôr′dər) *adj.* of or having to do with mail orders or a business establishment that does business by mail.

maim (mām) *v.* cause permanent damage to or loss of a part of the body; cripple; disable: *He lost two toes in the accident, but we were glad that he was not more seriously maimed.* [var. of *mayhem*] —**maim′er,** *n.*

main (mān) *adj., n.* —*adj.* most important; largest: *the main street of a town.*
by main force or **strength,** by using full strength.
—*n.* **1** a large pipe for water, gas, etc. **2** *Poetic.* the open sea; ocean. **3** *Archaic.* the mainland.
in the main, for the most part; chiefly; mostly: *Her grades were excellent in the main.*
with might and main, with all one's force: *They argued with might and main.*
[OE *mægen* power] ☛ *Hom.* **mane.**

main clause *Grammar.* a clause that can stand by itself as a sentence; independent clause.

main drag *Slang.* the chief thoroughfare of a town or city.

main·land (mān′land′ or mān′lənd) *n.* the principal part of a continent or land mass, apart from peninsulas and outlying islands.

main·land·er (mān′land′ər or mān′lənd ər) *n.* a person who lives on the mainland.

main·line (mān′līn′) *v.* **-lined, -lin·ing.** *Slang.* inject a drug, such as heroin, directly into a principal vein. —**main′lin′er,** *n.*

main·ly (mān′lē) *adv.* for the most part; chiefly; mostly.

main·mast (mān′mast′ or mān′məst) *n.* the principal mast of a

hat, āge, fär; let, ēqual, tèrm; it, īce
hot, ōpen, ôrder; oil, out; cup, pút, rüle,
əbove, takən, pencəl, lemən, circəs
ch, child; ng, long; sh, ship
th, thin; ŦH, then; zh, measure

sailing ship, usually the second one from the bow. See **mast¹** for picture.

main·sail (mān′sāl′ *or* mān′səl) *n.* the largest sail on the mainmast of a ship.

main·sheet (mān′shēt′) *n.* a rope that controls the angle at which the mainsail is set.

main·spring (mān′spring′) *n.* **1** the principal spring in a clock, watch, etc. **2** the main cause, motive, or influence.

main·stay (mān′stā′) *n.* **1** a supporting rope or wire extending from the maintop to the foot of the foremast. **2** the main support: *His friends were his mainstay through his time of trouble.*

main·stream (mān′strēm′) *n.* **1** the main current of a river, etc. **2** the main trend or direction of development of a fashion, body of opinion, activity, etc.: *She is not well known to the critics because her painting is outside the mainstream of modern art.* **3** (*adjl.*) of or in the mainstream: *mainstream culture.*

main·street·ing (mān′strē′ting) *n. Cdn.* the act or practice, by a politician, etc. of walking about the main streets of a town or city in order to meet and greet potential supporters. —**main′street′,** *v.*

main·tain (mān tān′) *v.* **1** keep; keep up; carry on: *to maintain a business, to maintain one's composure.* **2** keep from failing or declining; keep in good condition: *He employs a mechanic to maintain his fleet of trucks.* **3** pay the expenses of; provide for: *She maintains a family of four.* **4** uphold; argue for; keep to in argument or discussion: *to maintain an opinion.* **5** declare to be true: *He maintained that he was innocent.* [ME < OF *maintenir* < L *manu tenere* hold by the hand] —**main·tain′a·ble,** *adj.* —**main·tain′er,** *n.* ☛ *Syn.* **3.** See note at **support.**

main·te·nance (mān′tə nəns) *n.* **1** maintaining or being maintained; support: *A government collects taxes to pay for its maintenance.* **2** keeping in good repair; upkeep: *The army devotes much time to the maintenance of its equipment.* **3** enough to support life; means of living: *His small farm provides a maintenance, but not much more.* **4** *Law.* **a** the payment of money by a person after divorce to his or her former spouse for the support of the former spouse and any children: *Maintenance is awarded by court order and usually stops if the supported person remarries. Compare* **alimony.** **b** the payment of money by a person for the support of children living apart from him or her, after separation or divorce of the parents.

main·top (mān′top′) *n.* a platform at the head of the mainmast of a square-rigged ship. See **mast¹** for picture.

main·top·gal·lant (mān′top′gal′ənt *or* mān′tə gal′ənt) *n.* a mast, sail, or yard above the maintopmast.

main·top·mast (mān′top′mast′ *or* -top′məst) *n.* the second section of the mainmast above the lower mainmast. See **mast¹** for picture.

main-top·sail (mān′top′sāl′ *or* -top′səl) *n.* the sail above the mainsail.

main yard the yard from which a square mainsail is suspended.

mai·son·ette or **mai·son·nette** (mā′zə net′) *n.* an apartment, especially one that occupies more than one floor. [< F, dim. of *maison* house]

mai·tre d' (mā′tər dē′) *n., pl.* **mai·tre d's** (mā′tər dēz′). *Informal.* headwaiter.

maî·tre d'hô·tel (me′trə dō tel′) *n., pl.* **maîtres d'hôtel** (me′trə dō tel′). *French.* **1** a butler or steward; major-domo. **2** headwaiter. **3** (*adjl.*) of a sauce, etc., containing melted butter, chopped parsley, and lemon juice. [< F]

maize (māz) *n., adj.* —*n.* **1** corn¹ (defs. 1 and 2); Indian corn. **2** yellow. —*adj.* yellow. [< Sp. *maíz*, of West Indian origin] ☛ *Hom.* **maze.**

Maj. or **Maj** major.

ma·jes·tic (mə jes′tik) *adj.* grand; noble; dignified; stately.

ma·jes·ti·cal (mə jes′tə kəl) *adj.* majestic. —**ma·jes′ti·cal·ly,** *adv.*

maj·es·ty (maj′is tē) *n., pl.* **-ties. 1** grandeur; nobility; dignity; stateliness: *We were much impressed by the majesty of the coronation ceremony.* **2** the supreme power or authority: *the majesty of the law.* **3 Majesty,** a title used in speaking to or of a king, queen, emperor, empress, etc.: *Your Majesty, His Majesty, Her Majesty.* [ME < OF < L *majestas*]

Maj.Gen. major-general.

ma·jol·i·ca (mə jol′ə kə *or* mə yol′ə kə) *n.* **1** a kind of enamelled Italian pottery richly decorated in color. **2** something made of this pottery. [< Ital. < *Maiolica* Majorca]

ma·jor (mā′jər) *adj., n., v.* —*adj.* **1** larger; greater; more important: *Take the major share of the profits.* **2** of the first rank or order: *E.J. Pratt is a major poet.* **3** of legal age. **4** of, having to do with, or designating a student's principal subject or course of study. **5** *Music.* **a** of an interval, greater by a half step than the minor; having the difference of pitch which is found between the tonic and the second, third, sixth, or seventh tone (or step) of a major scale: *a major second, third, sixth, seventh.* **b** of a scale, key, or mode, in which the interval between the tonic and the third step is a major third (two whole steps): *C major scale or key.* **c** of a chord, especially a triad, containing a major third (two whole steps) between the root and the second tone or note. —*n.* **1** an officer in the armed forces ranking next above a captain and below a lieutenant-colonel. *Abbrev.*: Maj. or Maj See chart at **rank**[1]. **2** a person of the legal age of responsibility. **3** the subject or course of study to which a student gives most of his time and attention. **4** *Music.* a major interval, key, scale, chord, etc.: *The scale of C major has neither sharps nor flats.* **5** a major penalty. **6 the majors,** *pl.* the major leagues. —*v.* of a student, give most of one's time and attention (to a subject or course of study) (*used with* **in**): *to major in mathematics.* [< L *major,* comparative of *magnus* great. Doublet of MAYOR.]

ma·jor-do·mo (mā′jər dō′mō) *n., pl.* **-mos. 1** a man in charge of a royal or noble household. **2** a butler; steward. [< Sp. or Ital. < Med.L *major domus* chief of the household]

ma·jor·ette (mā′jə ret′) *n.* drum majorette.

ma·jor-gen·er·al (mā′jər jen′ə rəl *or* -jen′rəl) *n., pl.* **-als.** an officer in the armed forces ranking next above a brigadier-general and below a lieutenant-general. *Abbrev.*: M.Gen., MGen, or Maj.Gen. See chart at **rank**[1].

ma·jor·i·ty (mə jôr′ə tē) *n., pl.* **-ties. 1** the larger number; greater part; more than half. **2** in a contest involving two or more candidates, the number of votes cast for one candidate when that number is more than half the total number of votes for all candidates: *If Smith received 12 000 votes, Adams 7000, and White 3000, Smith had a majority of 2000.* **3** the legal age of responsibility. In some provinces a person reaches his majority at the age of 18. **4** the rank or position of major in the armed forces.

major league 1 *Baseball.* either of the two chief leagues of American professional teams. **2** *Hockey.* the National Hockey League.

major penalty *Hockey.* a five-minute penalty awarded for certain serious infractions of the rules, including fighting and instances of highsticking, slashing, etc. that draw blood.

major scale *Music.* a scale having eight tones, with half steps instead of whole steps after the third and seventh tones. Compare **minor scale.**

make (māk) *v.* **made, mak·ing;** *n.* —*v.* **1** bring into being; put together; build; form; shape: *to make a new dress, to make a poem, to make a boat, to make a medicine.* **2** have the qualities needed for: *Wood makes a good fire.* **3** cause; bring about: *to make trouble, to make a noise.* **4** cause to; force to: *He made me go.* **5** cause to be or become; cause oneself to be: *to make a room warm, to make a fool of oneself.* **6** turn out to be; become: *He will make a good legislator.* **7** get ready for use; arrange: *to make a bed.* **8** get; obtain; acquire, earn: *to make a fortune, to make one's living.* **9** do; perform: *to make an attempt, to make a mistake.* **10** amount to; add up to; count as: *Two and two make four.* **11** think of as; figure to be: *I make the distance across the room 5 metres.* **12** reach; arrive at: *The ship made port.* **13** go; travel: *Some airplanes can make 2000 kilometres per hour.* **14** cause the success of: *One big deal made the young businessman.* **15** *Informal.* get on; get a place on: *He made the football team.* **16** *Card games.* **a** win (a trick or hand). **b** state (the trump, or bid). **c** win a trick with (a card). **d** shuffle (the cards). **17** *Electricity.* close (a circuit). **18** *Sports and games.* score; have a score of.
make after, follow; chase; pursue.
make as if, pretend that; act as if.
make away with, a get rid of. **b** kill. **c** steal: *The treasurer made away with the club's funds.*
make believe, pretend: *The girl liked to make believe she was a queen.*
make fast, attach firmly.
make for, a go toward: *Make for the hills!* **b** rush at; attack. **c** help bring about: *Careful driving makes for fewer accidents.*
make fun of, mock; ridicule: *He refused to wear the jacket because his friends had made fun of it.*
make good, a succeed. **b** prove: *Can you make your claims good?*

make it, *Informal.* **a** succeed. **b** *Slang.* have sexual intercourse (with).
make like, *Informal.* **a** imitate; act the part of. **b** perform the services of: *to make like a cook.*
make off, run away.
make off with, steal; take without permission: *He made off with some apples.*
make or break, cause to succeed or fail.
make out, a write out: *He made out his application for camp.* **b** show to be; try to prove: *That makes me out most selfish.* **c** understand: *The boy had a hard time making out the problem.* **d** see with difficulty; distinguish: *I can barely make out three ships near the horizon.* **e** *Informal.* get along; manage: *We must try to make out with what we have.* **f** *Slang.* engage in extensive kissing and caressing, and, often, sexual intercourse.
make over, a alter; make different: *to make over a dress.* **b** hand over; transfer ownership of: *Grandfather made over his farm to my father.*
make time, go with speed.
make up, a put together: *to make up cloth into a dress.* **b** invent: *to make up a story.* **c** make satisfactory. **d** pay for; give or do in place of: *to make up for lost time.* **e** become friends again after a quarrel. **f** put paint, powder, etc. on the face. **g** arrange (type, pictures, etc.) in the pages of a book, paper, or magazine: *to make up a page of type, to make up an edition of a newspaper.* **h** complete; fill out: *We need two more eggs to make up a dozen.* **i** go to form or produce; constitute: *Girls make up most of that class.*
make up for, give or do in place of: *to make up for lost time.*
make up one's mind, decide.
make up to, try to get the friendship of; flatter.
—*n.* **1** the way in which a thing is made; a style, build, or character: *Do you like the make of that coat?* **2** a kind; brand: *What make of car is this?* **3** the nature; character. **4** the act of making. **5** the amount made.
on the make, *Informal.* trying for success, profit, etc.
[OE *macian*]
► *Syn. v.* **1. Make, construct, fashion** = put together or give form to something. **Make** is the general word, meaning "bring something into existence by forming or shaping it or putting it together": *She made a cake.* **Construct** means "put parts together in proper order, or build," and suggests a plan or design: *They constructed a bridge.* **Fashion** means "give a definite form, shape, or figure to something," and usually suggests that the maker is inventive or resourceful: *He fashions beautiful totems out of argillite.*

make-be·lieve (māk′bi lēv′) *n., adj.* —*n.* **1** pretence. **2** pretender. —*adj.* pretended.

mak·er (māk′ər) *n.* **1** a person or thing that makes. **2 Maker,** God. **meet (one's) Maker,** die: *He has gone to meet his Maker.*

make-read·y (māk′red′ē) *n. Printing.* the preparation of a form for the press by levelling and adjusting type, plates, etc. to ensure a clear and even impression.

make-shift (māk′shift′) *n., adj.* —*n.* something used for a time in the place of the proper thing; a temporary substitute: *When the power went off, we used candles as a makeshift.* —*adj.* **1** used for a time instead of the proper thing: *The boys made a makeshift tent out of a blanket.* **2** characterized by makeshifts: *makeshift endeavors.*

make-up *or* **make·up** (māk′up′) *n.* **1** the way of being put together; composition: *The make-up of a magazine is either the arrangement of type, illustrations, etc. or the kind of articles, stories, etc. used.* **2** one's nature or disposition; constitution: *a nervous make-up.* **3** the way in which an actor is dressed and painted to look his part. **4** the paint, powder, wigs, etc. used by actors taking part in a play: *His make-up was so effective that we didn't recognize him.* **5** face powder, lipstick, eye shadow, etc. used to beautify the face; cosmetics.

make-weight (māk′wāt′) *n.* anything added to make up for some lack.

make-work (māk′wèrk′) *n., adj.* —*n.* **1** the finding of unnecessary jobs; featherbedding. **2** the providing of work for unemployed people. —*adj.* **1** of or used for unnecessary work. **2** planned so as to provide work.

mak·ing (māk′ing) *n.* **1** the cause of a person's success; means of advancement: *Early hardships were the making of him.* **2** the material needed. **3** the qualities needed: *I see in him the making of a hero.* **4** something made. **5** the amount made at one time. **6 makings,** *pl. Informal.* **a** the tobacco and papers used in making one's own cigarettes. **b** a cigarette made with such materials.
in the making, in the process of being made; not yet fully developed.

ma·ku·ta (mä kü′tä) *n.* pl. of **likuta.**

mal- *combining form.* bad or badly; poor or poorly, as in *malnutrition, maltreat.* [< F *mal-* < L *male* badly < *malus* bad]

Mal. Malay; Malayan.

Malacca cane (mə lak′ə) a light walking stick made of rattan. [< *Malacca,* a state of Malaya]

mal·a·chite (mal′ə kīt′) *n.* a green mineral, copper carbonate, used as an ore of copper and as a stone for making ornamental objects. *Formula:* $Cu_2(OH)_2CO_3$ [< F < Gk. *malachē* mallow (from the similarity of color)]

mal·ad·just·ed (mal′ə jus′tid) *adj.* badly adjusted; especially, not in harmony with one's environment and conditions of life.

mal·ad·just·ment (mal′ə just′mənt) *n.* poor or unsatisfactory adjustment, especially to one's environment and conditions of life.

mal·ad·min·is·ter (mal′əd min′is tər) *v.* administer badly; manage inefficiently or dishonestly.

mal·ad·min·is·tra·tion (mal′əd min′is trā′shən) *n.* bad administration; inefficient or dishonest management.

mal·a·droit (mal′ə droit′) *adj.* unskilful; awkward; clumsy. [< F] —**mal′a·droit′ly,** *adv.* —**mal′a·droit′ness,** *n.*

mal·a·dy (mal′ə dē) *n.*, *pl.* **-dies. 1** a sickness or disease. **2** any unwholesome or disordered condition: *Poverty is a social malady.* [ME < OF *maladie* < *malade* ill < L *male habitus* doing poorly]

Mal·a·ga (mal′ə gə) *n.* **1** a kind of large, oval, white grape. **2** a kind of white wine. [< *Málaga*, a city and province in S Spain]

Mal·a·gas·y (mal′ə gas′ē) *n.*, *pl.* **-gas·y** or **-gas·ies**; *adj.* —*n.* **1** a native or inhabitant of Madagascar, an island country in the Indian Ocean. **2** the official language of Madagascar, belonging to the Malayo-Polynesian language family. —*adj.* of or having to do with Madagascar, its people, or their language.

ma·laise (ma lāz′) *n.* **1** a general but indefinite feeling of bodily discomfort and weakness, often the first signs of an illness. **2** a weakness or disorder tending toward disruption or decline: *Apathy is the malaise of democracy.* [< F *malaise* < *mal-* ill + *aise* ease]

mal·a·mute (mal′ə myūt′) *n.* a breed of large, powerful dog having a heavy grey or black-and-white coat, erect ears, and a tail that curls over the back. Malamutes have long been used as sled dogs in Alaska and the Canadian North. Also called **Alaskan malamute**. [< *Malemiut*, an Inuit people of W Alaska]

mal·a·pert (mal′ə pèrt′) *adj. Archaic.* too bold; impudent; saucy. [ME < OF *malapert* < *mal* badly + *apert* adroit, expert]

Mal·a·prop (mal′ə prop′) *n.* **Mrs.**, in Richard Brinsley Sheridan's play *The Rivals*, a woman noted for her ridiculous misuse of words. [< F *mal à propos.* See MALAPROPOS.]

mal·a·prop·ism (mal′ə prop iz′əm) *n.* **1** a ridiculous misuse of words, especially by confusing words that sound somewhat alike, as in the confusion of *immortality* with *immorality* in *They believe in the immorality of souls.* **2** a misused word. [after Mrs. *Malaprop*]
☛ *Usage.* **Malapropisms** are often unconscious, but are sometimes intentionally used for humorous effect.

mal·ap·ro·pos (mal′ap rə pō′) *adv.* or *adj.* at the wrong time or place. [< F *mal à propos*]

ma·lar·i·a (mə ler′ē ə) *n.* **1** a disease characterized by periodic chills followed by fever and sweating. Malaria is caused by microscopic parasitic animals in the red blood corpuscles, and is transmitted by the bite of anopheles mosquitoes that have bitten infected persons. **2** *Archaic.* unwholesome or poisonous air, especially that of marshes; miasma. [< Ital. *malaria* < *mala aria* bad air]

ma·lar·i·al (mə ler′ē əl) *adj.* **1** having or causing malaria. **2** of or like malaria.

ma·lar·key or **ma·lar·ky** (mə lär′kē) *n. Slang.* sheer nonsense. [origin uncertain]

ma·la·thi·on (mal′ə thī′ən) *n.* a very powerful insecticide recognizable by its pungent, unpleasant odor. *Formula:* $C_{10}H_{19}O_6PS_2$

Ma·lay (mə lā′ or mā′lā) *n.*, *adj.* —*n.* **1** a member of a people living in the Malay peninsula, Borneo, and nearby islands. **2** the language of the Malays, belonging to the Malayo-Polynesian family. —*adj.* of or having to do with the Malays or their language.

Mal·a·ya·lam (mal′ə yä′ləm) *n.* a Dravidian language, spoken in SW India.

Ma·lay·an (mə lā′ən) *n.* or *adj.* Malay.

Ma·lay·o-Pol·y·ne·sian (mə lā′ō pol′i nē′zhən) *n.*, *adj.* —*n.* a family of languages spoken throughout most of the islands of the Indian and Pacific oceans, including such languages as Fijian, Indonesian, Malagasy, Polynesian, and Tagalog.

Ma·lay·sian (mə lā′zhən or mə lā′shən) *n.*, *adj.* —*n.* a native or inhabitant of Malaysia. —*adj.* of or having to do with Malaysia, its people, or their languages.

mal·con·tent (mal′kən tent′) *adj.*, *n.* —*adj.* discontented or rebellious. —*n.* a discontented or rebellious person.

mal de mer (mäl də mer′) *French.* seasickness.

male (māl) *adj.*, *n.* —*adj.* **1** of, having to do with, or being the sex that produces the gametes, or sperm cells, that fertilize the eggs of a female to produce young: *the male organs.* **2** of, having to do with, or characteristic of men or boys: *a male voice.* **3** made up of men: *a*

hat, āge, fär; let, ēqual, tèrm; it, īce
hot, ōpen, ôrder; oil, out; cup, pût, rüle,
əbove, takən, pencəl, lemən, circəs
ch, child; ng, long; sh, ship
th, thin; ŦH, then; zh, measure

male choir. **4** designating a part of a machine or a connection, etc. that fits into a corresponding hollow part: *a male pipe fitting.* —*n.* an animal or plant that is male: *There were three puppies in the litter; two males and one female.* [ME < OF *male, masle* < L *masculus*, dim. of *mas* male] —**male′ness,** *n.*
☛ *Hom.* **mail.**
☛ *Syn. adj.* **1. Male, masculine, manly** = having to do with men or the sex to which they belong. **Male**, describing plants, animals, or human beings, suggests only sex: *We have a male avocado tree.* **Masculine** describes things and suggests qualities (especially strength, vigor, etc.) belonging to or characteristic of men and boys as distinguished from women and girls: *He is a big, masculine man.* **Manly** suggests the finer qualities of a man, such as courage and honor: *He is an upright, manly youth.*

Mal·e·cite (mal′ə sĕt′ or mal′ə sīt′) *n.*, *pl.* **-cite** or **-cites**; *adj.* —*n.* a member of an Amerindian people living in New Brunswick and eastern Quebec. The Malecite are an Algonquian people. —*adj.* of or having to do with the Malecite.

mal·e·dic·tion (mal′ə dik′shən) *n.* the uttering of a curse; the calling down of evil on a person. [ME < L *maledictio, -onis* < *maledicere* < *male* ill + *dicere* speak. Doublet of MALISON.]

mal·e·fac·tion (mal′ə fak′shən) *n.* a crime or evil deed.

mal·e·fac·tor (mal′ə fak′tər) *n.* a criminal or evildoer. [ME < L *malefactor* < *malefacere* < *male* badly + *facere* do]

ma·lef·i·cence (mə lef′ə səns) *n.* harm; evil. [< L *maleficentia* < *maleficus* wicked < *male* badly + *facere* do]

ma·lef·i·cent (mə lef′ə sənt) *adj.* harmful; evil. [< *maleficence*]

mal·e·mute (mal′ə myūt′) See **malamute.**

ma·lev·o·lence (mə lev′ə ləns) *n.* the wish that evil may happen to others; ill will; spite.

ma·lev·o·lent (mə lev′ə lənt) *adj.* having or showing vicious ill will; spiteful; malicious: *a malevolent smile.* [< L *malevolens, -entis*, ult. < *male* ill + *velle* wish] —**ma·lev′o·lent·ly,** *adv.*

mal·fea·sance (mal fē′zəns) *n.* misconduct by a public official; violation of a public trust or duty: *A judge is guilty of malfeasance if he accepts a bribe.* Compare **misfeasance, nonfeasance.** [< F *malfaisance*, ult. < *mal-* badly + *faire* do]

mal·for·ma·tion (mal′fôr mā′shən) *n.* an irregular, faulty, or abnormal shape or structure: *A hunchback is a malformation of the spine.*

mal·formed (mal fôrmd′) *adj.* badly shaped; having an abnormal or faulty structure.

mal·func·tion (mal′fungk′shən) *n.*, *v.* —*n.* an improper functioning; failure to work or perform: *a malfunction of an organ of the body, a malfunction in a machine.* —*v.* function badly; work or perform improperly.

mal·ic acid (mal′ik or mā′lik) an acid found in apples and numerous other fruits. *Formula:* $C_4H_6O_5$ [< F *malique* < L *malum* apple < Doric Gk. *malon*]

mal·ice (mal′is) *n.* **1** active ill will; a wish to hurt others; spite. **2** *Law.* intent to commit an act which will result in harm to another person without justification. [ME < OF < L *malitia* < *malus* evil]
☛ *Syn.* See note at **spite.**

ma·li·cious (mə lish′əs) *adj.* showing active ill will; wishing to hurt others; spiteful: *malicious gossip.* —**ma·li′cious·ly,** *adv.* —**ma·li′cious·ness,** *n.*

ma·lign (mə līn′) *v.*, *adj.* —*v.* speak evil of, often falsely; slander: *You malign him unjustly when you call him stingy, for he gives all he can afford to give.* —*adj.* **1** evil; injurious: *Gambling often has a malign influence.* **2** hateful; malicious. **3** very harmful; threatening to be fatal. [ME < OF *maligne, adj.* (v. < OF *malignier* < LL *malignare*) < L *malignus* < *malus* evil + *gen-* birth, nature] —**ma·lign′er,** *n.*

ma·lig·nance (mə lig′nəns) *n.* malignancy.

ma·lig·nan·cy (mə lig′nən sē) *n.* a malignant condition, quality, or tendency.

ma·lig·nant (mə lig′nənt) *adj.* **1** extremely evil, hateful, or malicious. **2** extremely harmful. **3** of a disease, very infectious and dangerous: *malignant cholera.* **4** of a tumor, cyst, etc., tending to grow and spread, causing harm to healthy tissues around it; cancerous. Compare **benign** (def. 3). [< LL *malignans, -antis* acting from malice < *malignus.* See MALIGN.] —**ma·lig′nant·ly,** *adv.*

ma·lig·ni·ty (mə lig′nə tē) *n.*, *pl.* **-ties. 1** great malice; extreme

hate. **2** great harmfulness; dangerous quality; deadliness. **3** a malignant act or feeling.

ma·lines or **ma·line** (mə lēn′) *n.* **1** Mechlin lace. **2** a thin, stiff, silk net used in dressmaking. [< F *malines*, after *Malines* (or *Mechlin*), a town in Belgium]

ma·lin·ger (mə ling′gər) *v.* pretend to be sick in order to escape work or duty; shirk. [< F *malingre* sickly < OF *mal-* badly (< L *male*) + *heingre* sick (< Gmc.)]

mal·i·son (mal′ə zən or mal′ə sən) *n. Archaic.* a malediction; curse. [ME < OF *maleison* < L *maledictio*. Doublet of MALEDICTION.]

mall (mol or môl) *n.* **1** a shaded walk; a public walk or promenade. **2** a walk lined with stores; a place to walk in a shopping centre. **3** shopping mall. [ME < OF *ma(i)l* mallet < L *malleus* hammer; originally, a mallet used in pall-mall (an old game); later, the game itself; then, a lane or alley in which the game was played]

mal·lard (mal′ərd) *n., pl.* **-lards** or (*esp. collectively*) **-lard.** a wild duck (*Anas platyrhynchos*) common throughout much of the northern hemisphere, having greyish-brown plumage with a conspicuous blue wing patch, the male in breeding plumage having a green head and neck, narrow white collar, and reddish-brown breast. The mallard is the ancestor of most domestic breeds of duck. [ME < OF *mallart*, probably < Gmc.]

mal·le·a·bil·i·ty (mal′ē ə bil′ə tē) *n.* the quality or state of being malleable.

mal·le·a·ble (mal′ē ə bəl) *adj.* **1** capable of being hammered or pressed into various shapes without being broken. Gold, silver, copper, and tin are malleable; they can be beaten into thin sheets. **2** adaptable; yielding: *A malleable person is easily persuaded to change his plans.* [ME < OF < L *malleare* to hammer < *malleus*, n.] —**mal′le·a·ble·ness,** *n.* —**mal′le·a·bly,** *adv.*

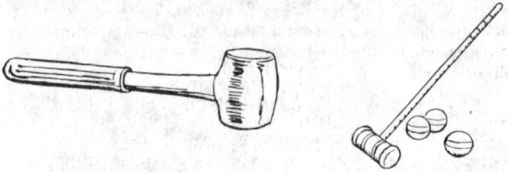

A rubber mallet (left) and a wooden croquet mallet

mal·let (mal′it) *n.* **1** a hammer having a head of wood, rubber, or other fairly soft material. **2** a long-handled wooden mallet used to play croquet or polo. [ME < OF *maillet*, dim. of *mail* < L *malleus* hammer]

mal·le·us (mal′ē əs) *n., pl.* **mal·le·i** (mal′ē ī). in mammals, the outermost of three small bones in the middle ear, shaped like a hammer. See **ear**[1] for picture. [< L *malleus* hammer]

mal·low (mal′ō) *n.* **1** any of a genus (*Malva*) of herbs native to Europe, Asia, and N Africa, having lobed leaves and usually large, showy flowers. Some mallows are cultivated as garden flowers, but others have become naturalized in North America as weeds. **2** any of several other related herbs and shrubs. **3** (*adj.*) designating a family (Malvaceae) of herbs, shrubs, and small trees found throughout the world, but especially in the tropics. The cotton plant, hollyhock, mallows, and hibiscus belong to the mallow family. [OE *mealwe* < L *malva*. Doublet of MAUVE.]

malm·sey (mom′zē or mäm′zē) *n.* a kind of strong, sweet wine. [ME < Med.L *malmasia*, from *Monembasia*, a town in Greece]

mal·nu·tri·tion (mal′nyü trish′ən or -nü trish′ən) *n.* poor nourishment; lack of nourishment. Malnutrition may come from eating the wrong kinds of food as well as from eating too little.

mal·oc·clu·sion (mal′ə klü′zhən) *n.* failure of the upper and lower teeth to meet or close properly.

mal·o·dor·ous (mal′ō′dər əs) *adj.* smelling bad. —**mal·o′dor·ous·ly,** *adv.* —**mal·o′dor·ous·ness,** *n.*

mal·peque (mal pēk′ or mal pek′) *n.* a variety of oyster, found in Malpeque Bay, Prince Edward Island.

mal·prac·tice (mal′prak′tis) *n.* **1** criminal neglect or unprofessional treatment of a patient by a doctor. **2** wrong practice or conduct in any official or professional position.

malt (molt or môlt) *n., v.* —*n.* **1** barley or other grain that is soaked in water until it sprouts and is then dried and aged. Malt has a sweet taste and is used in making beer and ale. **2** *Informal.* beer or ale. **3** malted milk. —*v.* **1** change or be changed into malt. **2** prepare with malt. [OE *mealt*]

malted milk a sweet, cold drink made from dried milk and powdered malted cereal mixed with milk and, usually, ice cream and flavoring.

Mal·tese (mol tēz′ or môl tēz′) *n., pl.* **-tese;** *adj.* —*n.* **1** a native or inhabitant of Malta, an island in the Mediterranean. **2** the language of the Maltese. It is a Semitic language with many Italian loan words. **3** a breed of toy dog usually weighing 2 to 3 kg, having long, silky, white hair, a black nose, and black eyes: *The Maltese is one of the oldest breeds of lap dog.* **4** Maltese cat. —*adj.* of or having to do with Malta, its people, or their language.

Maltese cat a bluish-grey variety of short-haired domestic cat.

Maltese cross a cross with arms that broaden out from the centre and are often indented at the ends. See **cross** for picture.

malt extract a sugary substance obtained by soaking malt in water.

Mal·thu·sian (mal thü′zhən or mal thü′zē ən) *adj., n.* —*adj.* of or having to do with Malthus or his theory that the world's population tends to increase faster than the food supply. —*n.* an advocate of Malthus' theory. [< Thomas Robert *Malthus* (1766-1834), an English economist]

malt·ose (mol′tōs or môl′tōs) *n.* a white, crystalline sugar made by the action of diastase on starch. Formula: $C_{12}H_{22}O_{11}·H_2O$

mal·treat (mal trēt′) *v.* treat roughly or cruelly; abuse: *Only vicious persons maltreat animals.*

mal·treat·ment (mal trēt′mənt) *n.* rough or cruel treatment; abuse.

malt·ster (molt′stər or môlt′stər) *n.* a person who makes or sells malt.

malt sugar maltose.

mal·ver·sa·tion (mal′vər sā′shən) *n.* corrupt conduct in a position of trust. [< F *malversation* < *malverser* peculate < L *maleversari* behave badly]

ma·ma or **mam·ma** (mo′mə or mä′mə; *esp.Brit.*, mə mä′) *n. Informal.* mother. [reduplication of an infantile sound]

mam·ba (mam′bə) *n.* any of a genus (*Dendroaspis*) of long, slender, very poisonous snakes of central and S Africa belonging to the same family (Elapidae) as the cobras and coral snakes.

mam·bo (mom′bō, mäm′bō, or mam′bō) *n.* **1** a ballroom dance of Caribbean origin. **2** the music for such a dance. [< Haitian Creole]

Mam·e·luke (mam′ə lük′) *n.* **1** a member of a military group that ruled Egypt from about 1250 to 1517 and had great power until 1811. The Mamelukes were originally slaves. **2** **mameluke,** in Moslem countries, a slave. [< Arabic *mamluk* slave]

mam·ma[1] (mo′mə or mä′mə; *esp.Brit.*, mə mä′) *n.* See **mama.**

mam·ma[2] (mä′mə) *n.* **mam·mae** (mam′ē or mam′ī). a milk-giving gland in female mammals. [< L *mamma* breast]

mam·mal (mam′əl) *n.* any of a class (Mammalia) of warm-blooded vertebrate animals, the females of which have glands (mammae) that produce milk for feeding their young. Human beings, horses, dogs, rats, and whales are all mammals. [< NL *mammalia*, pl., ult. < L *mamma* breast]

mam·ma·li·an (ma mā′lē ən or ma māl′yən) *adj., n.* —*adj.* of or having to do with mammals. —*n.* a mammal.

mam·mal·o·gist (ma mal′ə jist) *n.* a person trained in mammalogy, especially one whose work it is.

mam·mal·o·gy (ma mal′ə jē) *n.* the branch of zoology that deals with the study of mammals. [< *mammalia* + *-logy*]

mam·ma·ry (mam′ə rē) *adj.* of or designating the mammae. The mammary glands secrete milk.

mam·mog·ra·phy (ma mog′rə fē) *n.* examination of the breasts by X ray for the early detection of tumors. [< *mamma*[2] + *-graphy*. 20c.]

Mam·mon or **mam·mon** (mam′ən) *n.* **1** material wealth or possessions thought of as an object of worship. **2** material wealth or possessions thought of as an evil; greed for wealth. [< L *mammona* < Gk. *mammōnas* < Aramaic *mamon* riches]

mam·moth (mam′əth) *n., adj.* —*n.* any of an extinct genus (*Mammuthus*) of elephants of the Pleistocene epoch having a hairy skin and very long, curved tusks. —*adj.* huge; gigantic. [< earlier Russian *mammot*]

mam·my (mam′ē) *n., pl.* **-mies.** **1** *Informal.* mother. **2** *U.S. Historical.* a black woman who took care of white children, especially in the South.

man (man) *n., pl.* **men** *v.* **manned, man·ning,** *interj.* —*n.* **1** an adult male person. **2** a person; human being: *Death comes to all men.* **3** the human race; mankind: *Man has existed for thousands of years.* **4** men as a group; the average man: *The man of today likes to travel.* **5** a male follower, servant, or employee. **6** a member of the armed forces, especially one who is not an officer (*usually used*

in the plural). **7** a male member of a team, organization, etc. **8** a husband or lover. **9** one of the pieces used in chess, checkers, etc. **10** a man thought of as having all the best characteristics distinctive of manhood: *He was every inch a man.*

act the man, be courageous.

as a man, from a human point of view.

as one man, with complete agreement; unanimously.

be (one's) own man, a be free to do as one pleases. **b** have complete control of oneself.

man and boy, from boyhood on; as a youth and as an adult.

to a man, every one, without an exception; all: *We accepted his idea to a man.*

—*v.* **1** supply with a crew: *We can man ten ships.* **2** serve or operate; get ready to operate: *Man the guns.* **3** make (oneself) strong in anticipation; brace: *to man oneself for an ordeal.* —*interj. Informal.* an exclamation of surprise, joy, excitement, etc., or for effect: *Man, what a player!* [OE *mann*] —**man′less,** *adj.*

☛ *Usage.* **Man, gentleman. Man** is now generally preferred to **gentleman,** unless a note of special courtesy or respect is desired.

Man. Manitoba.

M.A.N. *Cdn. French.* Membre de l'Assemblée nationale (Member of the National Assembly of Quebec).

man about town a man who spends much of his time in fashionable clubs, theatres, etc.

man·a·cle (man′ə kəl) *n., v.* **-cled, -cling.** —*n.* **1** Usually, **manacles,** *pl.* a handcuff; fetter for the hands. **2** any restraint. —*v.* **1** put manacles on: *The pirates manacled their prisoners.* **2** restrain. [ME < OF < L *manicula,* dim. of *manicae* sleeves, manacles < *manus* hand]

man·age (man′ij) *v.* **-aged, -ag·ing. 1** control; conduct; handle; direct: *manage a business, manage a horse.* **2** conduct affairs. **3** succeed in accomplishing; contrive; arrange: *I finally managed to get the job done.* **4** get along: *manage on one's income.* **5** make use of. **6** get one's way with (a person) by craft or flattery. [< Ital. *maneggiare* < *mano* hand < L *manus*]

☛ *Syn. v.* **1. Manage, conduct, direct** = guide or handle with authority. **Manage** emphasizes the idea of skilful handling of people and details so as to get results: *He manages a large department store.* **Conduct** emphasizes the idea of supervising the action of a group working together for something: *The Scouts are conducting a safety drive.* **Direct** emphasizes the idea of guiding the affairs or actions of a group by giving advice and instructions to be followed: *A lawyer directed our anti-noise campaign.*

man·age·a·bil·i·ty (man′ij ə bil′ə tē) *n.* the condition or quality of being manageable.

man·age·a·ble (man′ij ə bəl) *adj.* that can be managed. —**man′age·a·ble·ness,** *n.* —**man′age·a·bly,** *adv.*

man·age·ment (man′ij mənt) *n.* **1** control; handling; direction: *The new store failed because of bad management.* **2** the persons that manage a business or an institution: *The management of the store decided to keep it open every evening.*

management consultant a specialist or expert who can be hired to examine the operations of a company and advise on planning, organization, and other management problems.

man·ag·er (man′ij ər) *n.* **1** a person who manages: *a bank manager, an advertising manager.* **2** a person skilled in managing (affairs, time, money, etc.): *Mrs. Jones is not much of a manager, but the family gets along somehow.*

man·a·ge·ri·al (man′ə jēr′ē əl) *adj.* of a manager; having to do with management. —**man′a·ge′ri·al·ly,** *adv.*

ma·ña·na (mä nyä′nä) *n. or adv.* tomorrow; some time. [< Sp.]

man-at-arms (man′ət ärmz′) *n., pl.* **men-at-arms.** *Historical.* a soldier, especially one who was heavily armed and mounted on horseback.

man·a·tee (man′ə tē′) *n.* any of a small genus (*Trichechus,* constituting the family Trichechidae) of sea mammals found in the coastal waters of tropical America and Africa, having a whalelike body with a broad, rounded tail flipper. [< Sp. *manati* < Carib lang.]

man·chet (man′chit) *n. Archaic.* **1** bread made of the finest white flour. **2** a small loaf or roll of such bread. [origin uncertain]

Man·chu (man′chü) *n.* **1** a member of an Asiatic people, the original inhabitants of Manchuria, who conquered China in 1644 and ruled it until 1912. **2** the Altaic language of the Manchus. —*adj.* of or having to do with the Manchus, their country, or their language.

Man·chu·ri·an (man chür′ē ən) *n., adj.* —*n.* a native or inhabitant of Manchuria, an E Asian region that includes several Chinese provinces. —*adj.* of or having to do with Manchuria.

man·ci·ple (man′sə pəl) *n.* a person who buys provisions for a college or other institution; steward. [ME < OF < L *manicipium* office of purchaser < *manceps* buyer, ult. < *manu capere* take in hand]

man·da·mus (man dā′məs) *n. Law.* a written order from a

hat, āge, fär; let, ēqual, tėrm; it, īce
hot, ōpen, ôrder; oil, out; cup, put, rüle,
əbove, takən, pencəl, lemən, circəs

ch, child; ng, long; sh, ship
th, thin; ŦH, then; zh, measure

higher court to a lower court, an official, a city, a corporation, etc. directing that a certain thing be done. [< L *mandamus* we order]

man·da·rin (man′də rin) *n.* **1** a kind of small, sweet orange having a thin, very loose, dark-orange peel. Also called **mandarin orange. 2** the small, spiny citrus tree (*Citrus reticulata;* sometimes classified as *C. nobilis*) bearing this fruit. The mandarin is native to China. **3 Mandarin, a** *Historical.* in the Chinese Empire, the language of the court, government officials, and other educated people: *Mandarin was a northern dialect.* **b** the main language of modern China, the standard form being the one used in Peking. **4** *Historical.* in the Chinese empire, an official of high rank. **5** a person of high position whose work is not publicized but who has, or is thought to have, considerable political or social influence: *the mandarins of Ottawa.* [< Chinese Pidgin English < Pg. *mandar* order (< L *mandare*), blended with Malay *mantri* < Hind. < Skt. *mantrin* adviser]

man·da·rin·ate (man′də rə nāt′) *n.* a group or establishment of mandarins.

man·da·tar·y (man′də ter′ē) *n., pl.* **-tar·ies. 1** a nation to which a mandate over another country has been given. **2** *Law.* a person to whom a mandate is given.

man·date (*n.* man′dāt *or* man′dit; *v.* man′dāt) *n., v.* **-dat·ed, -dat·ing.** —*n.* **1** a command or official order. **2** *Law.* an order from a higher court or official to a lower one. **3** a direction or authority given to a government by the votes of the people in an election: *The Prime Minister said he had a mandate to increase taxes.* **4** a commission given to one nation by a group of nations to administer the government and affairs of a territory, etc. **5** a territory, etc. under the administration of another nation. —*v.* **1** put (a territory, etc.) under the administration of another nation. **2** order (something) to be done or put into effect; make mandatory: *The new curriculum will be mandated next fall.* [< L *mandatum,* n. use of neut. pp. of *mandare*]

man·da·to·ry (man′də tô′rē) *adj., n., pl.* **-ries.** —*adj.* **1** of, like, or having to do with a mandate; giving a command or order. **2** required by a command or order. —*n.* mandatary.

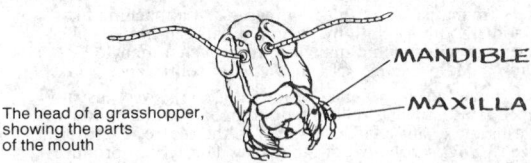

The head of a grasshopper, showing the parts of the mouth

man·di·ble (man′də bəl) *n.* **1** either member of the foremost pair of mouth parts of an insect, spider, lobster, etc., adapted for seizing and biting. **2** either the upper or lower part of the beak of a bird or of any other beaked animal, such as an octopus. **3** the jaw of a vertebrate, especially the lower jaw. [< LL *mandibula* < L *mandere* chew]

man·do·lin (man′də lin′ *or* man′də lin′) *n.* a musical instrument having a pear-shaped body, a neck with a fretted fingerboard, and four pairs of strings. It is usually played with a plectrum. [< F < Ital. *mandolino,* dim. of *mandola,* ult. < Gk. *pandoura* three-stringed instrument]

man·drag·o·ra (man drag′ə rə) *n.* mandrake. [ME < L < Gk. *mandragoras*]

man·drake (man′drāk) *n.* **1** a Eurasian plant (*Mandragora officinarum*) of the nightshade family having a short stalk, purplish flowers, and a thick, forked root formerly thought of as resembling the human form and therefore having magical powers. A drug used as a narcotic and sedative was also prepared from the root. **2** May apple. [by popular etymology < *mandragora*]

man·drel or **man·dril** (man′drəl) *n.* **1** on a lathe, the spindle or bar that is inserted into a hole in a piece of work to support it while it is being turned. **2** a rod or core around which metal is shaped. [< F *mandrin*]

man·drill (man′drəl) *n.* a large, terrestrial, Old World monkey (*Mandrillus sphinx*) of the forests of W Africa, having a stout body, short tail, and small, close-set eyes. The adult male has bare patches of red, blue, and pink skin on the face and buttocks. [< *man* + *drill* baboon (< native African)]

mane (mān) *n.* the long, heavy hair growing on the back or around the neck of a horse, lion, etc. [OE *manu*]
☛ *Hom.* main.

man–eater (man′ē′tər) *n.* **1** a tiger or other large member of the cat family that has acquired the habit of eating human flesh. **2** any of various sharks known to feed on human flesh, especially the white shark. **3** cannibal. **4** *Informal.* a sexually attractive and aggressive woman who preys on men.

ma·nège (mə nezh′ *or* mə nāzh′) *n.* **1** the art of training or riding horses; horsemanship. **2** the movements of a trained horse. **3** a riding school. [< F < Ital. *maneggio* < *maneggiare* manage]

ma·nes or **Ma·nes** (mā′nēz) *n.pl.* **1** in the ancient Roman religion, the deified souls of dead ancestors, together with the gods of the lower world. **2** the spirit or shade of a particular person. [< L]

ma·neu·ver (mə nü′vər) See **manoeuvre.** —**ma·neu′ver·a·ble,** *adj.* —**ma·neu′ver·a·bil′i·ty,** *n.*

man Friday a faithful servant. [< *Friday,* Robinson Crusoe's servant]

man·ful (man′fəl) *adj.* having or showing courage, resolution, etc.; manly. —**man′ful·ly,** *adv.* —**man′ful·ness,** *n.*

man·ga·nese (mang′gə nēz′ *or* mang′gə nēs′) *n.* a hard, brittle, greyish-white metallic element. Substances containing manganese are used in making steel, glass, paints, and medicines. *Symbol:* Mn; *at.no.* 25; *at.wt.* 54.9380. [< F < Ital. *manganese,* alteration of Med.L *magnesia.* See MAGNESIA.]

mange (mānj) *n.* an itchy skin disease of dogs, horses, cattle, etc., in which tiny skin sores form and the hair falls off in patches. [ME < OF *manjue* or *mangeue* the itch < *mangier* eat < L *manducare, mandere* chew]

mar·gel (mang′gəl) *n.* mangel-wurzel.

man·gel–wur·zel (mang′gəl wèr′zəl) *n.* a large, coarse, yellow variety of beet widely cultivated, especially in Europe, for cattle fodder. [< G *Mangelwurzel,* var. of *Mangoldwurzel* beet root]

man·ger (mān′jər) *n.* a box or trough in which hay can be placed for horses or cows to eat. [ME < OF *mangeoire,* ult. < L *manducare* eat]

man·gle[1] (mang′gəl) *v.* **-gled, -gling. 1** cut or tear roughly: *His arm was badly mangled in the accident.* **2** do or play badly; ruin: *The music was too difficult for her, and she mangled it.* [< AF *mangler,* ? < OF *mahaignier* < *mahaigne* injury. Cf. MAYHEM.]

man·gle[2] (mang′gəl) *n., v.* **-gled, -gling.** —*n.* **1** a machine for pressing and smoothing cloth by passing it between heated rollers. **2** a wringer. —*v.* press with a mangle; put through a mangle. [< Du. *mangel* < MDu. *mange* < LL *manganum* contrivance < Gk.]

man·go (mang′gō) *n., pl.* **-goes** or **-gos. 1** a juicy, sweet, usually oval-shaped fruit having a yellow, red, or greenish rind, yellow or orange flesh, and a single large, flat seed in the centre. **2** a tropical Asian tree (*Mangifera indica*) of the cashew family that produces this fruit. The tree is widely cultivated throughout the tropics. [< Pg. < Malay < Tamil *mankay*]

man·gold (mang′gold) *n.* mangel-wurzel.

man·go·nel (mang′gə nəl) *n. Historical.* a machine used in war for throwing large stones, etc. [ME < OF < VL *manganellum,* dim. of LL *manganum* deceive, contrivance < Gk. *manganon*]

man·go·steen (mang′gə stēn′) *n.* **1** a SE Asian tree (*Garcinia mangostana*) bearing edible fruit. **2** the fruit of this tree, having a hard, reddish skin and sweet, juicy, whitish pulp. [< Malay *mangustan*]

man·grove (mang′grōv) *n.* **1** any of a genus (*Rhizophora*) of tropical evergreen trees or shrubs that grow in salt marshes and along coasts, having prop roots that grow down from the branches, intertwining to form dense thickets. **2** any of various unrelated trees or shrubs with similar habits. [< Sp. *mangle* < Malay *manggi-manggi,* influenced by *grove*]

man·gy (mān′jē) *adj.* **-gi·er, -gi·est. 1** affected with or caused by the mange: *a mangy dog.* **2** shabby, dirty, scruffy, etc.: *a mangy old rug.* —**man′gi·ness,** *n.*

man·han·dle (man′han′dəl) *v.* **-dled, -dling. 1** treat roughly; pull or push about. **2** move by human strength without mechanical appliances.

Man·hat·tan (man hat′ən) *n.* a cocktail made of vermouth, rye whisky, and bitters.

man·hole (man′hōl′) *n.* a hole through which a workman may enter a sewer, steam boiler, etc.

man·hood (man′hùd) *n.* **1** the condition or time of being a man. **2** courage; manliness. **3** men as a group: *the manhood of Canada.*

man–hour (man′our′) *n.* an hour of work done by one person, used as a time unit in industry.

man·hunt (man′hunt′) *n.* an organized hunt for a criminal, escaped convict, etc.

ma·ni·a (mā′nē ə) *n.* **1** a form or phase of mental disorder characterized by extremes of joy or rage, uncontrolled and often violent activity, extravagant and irregular speech, etc., often followed by depression, as in manic-depressive psychosis. **2** an excessive fondness or enthusiasm; obsession or craze: *a mania for ice cream.* [< L < Gk. *mania* madness]

ma·ni·ac (mā′nē ak′) *n.* **1** a person who behaves in a wild, disorderly, or irresponsible way: *That driver is a maniac.* **2** a person who has an excessive fondness for something. **3** *Obsolete.* a person affected with mania (def. l).

ma·ni·a·cal (mə nī′ə kəl) *adj.* **1** having to do with, characteristic of, or affected with mania. **2** like or characteristic of a maniac; frenzied or frantic. —**ma·ni′a·cal·ly,** *adv.*

man·ic (man′ik *or* mā′nik) *adj., n.* —*adj.* of, designating, or affected with mania. —*n.* a person affected with mania.

man·ic–de·pres·sive (man′ik di pres′iv) *adj., n.* —*adj.* designating a psychosis characterized by periods of extreme confidence, excitement, activity, etc. alternating with deep depression. —*n.* a person affected with manic-depressive psychosis.

man·i·cure (man′ə kyür′) *v.* **-cured, -cur·ing;** *n.* —*v.* **1** care for (the fingernails and hands); especially, trim, clean, and polish (the fingernails). **2** trim closely and evenly: *a well-manicured lawn.* —*n.* a treatment for the hands and fingernails: *She made an appointment for a manicure at the salon.* [< F < L *manus* hand + *cura* care]

man·i·cur·ist (man′ə kyür′ist) *n.* a person whose work is manicuring.

man·i·fest (man′ə fest′) *adj., v., n.* —*adj.* clear to the eye or to mind; plain: *The thief left so many clues that his guilt was manifest.* —*v.* **1** show plainly; reveal; display. **2** prove; put beyond doubt. **3 a** record (an item) in a ship's manifest. **b** present the manifest of (a ship's cargo). —*n.* **1** a list of a ship's cargo. **2** a list of passengers, freight, etc. on an airplane flight. **3** a bill of lading. [< L *manifestus* palpable, near at hand; ult. < *manus* hand] —**man′i·fest′ly,** *adv.* —**man′i·fest·ness,** *n.*

man·i·fes·ta·tion (man′ə fes tā′shən) *n.* **1** manifesting or being manifested. **2** something that manifests: *A brave deed is a manifestation of courage.* **3** a public demonstration. **4** the occurrence or occasion of a spiritualistic materialization: *No manifestation occurred at the first séance.*

man·i·fes·to (man′ə fes′tō) *n., pl.* **-toes.** a public declaration of intentions, purposes, or motives by an important person or group; proclamation. [< Ital.]

man·i·fold (man′ə fōld′) *adj., n., v.* —*adj.* **1** of many kinds; many and various: *manifold duties.* **2** having many parts or forms: *The hero was praised for his manifold goodness.* **3** doing many things at the same time. —*n.* **1** a pipe or chamber having several openings for connection with other pipes. **2** a pipe in an internal-combustion engine, connecting the cylinders with a main inlet or outlet. **3** one of many copies. —*v.* **1** make many copies of. **2** make manifold; multiply. [OE *manigfeald*]

man·i·kin (man′ə kin) *n.* **1** a little man; dwarf. **2** mannequin. Also, **mannikin.** [< Du. *manneken,* dim. of *man* man]

ma·nil·a or **ma·nil·la** (mə nil′ə) *n.* **1** Manila hemp. **2** Manila paper. **3** Manila rope. **4** (*adj.*) made from manila paper or hemp: *a manila envelope.* [< *Manila,* the capital of Philippines]

Manila hemp a strong fibre made from the leafstalks of the abaca, used for making rope and fabrics.

Manila paper a strong, brown or brownish-yellow wrapping paper, made originally from Manila hemp.

Manila rope a strong rope made from Manila hemp.

man in the street the average person.

man·i·oc (man′ē ok′ *or* mā′nē ok′) *n.* cassava. [< Sp., Pg. < Tupi-Guarani *manioca*]

ma·nip·u·late (mə nip′yə lāt′) *v.* **-lat·ed, -lat·ing. 1** handle or treat skilfully; handle: *The driver of an automobile manipulates levers and pedals.* **2** manage by clever use of personal influence, especially unfair influence: *He so manipulated the ball team that he was elected captain.* **3** change for one's own purpose or advantage: *The bookkeeper manipulated the company's accounts to cover up his theft.* [back formation < *manipulation*] —**ma·nip′u·la·tor,** *n.*

ma·nip·u·la·tion (mə nip′yə lā′shən) *n.* **1** skilful handling or treatment. **2** clever use of influence. **3** a change made for one's own purpose or advantage. [< F, ult. < L *manipulus* handful < *manus* hand + root of *plere* to fill]

ma·nip·u·la·tive (mə nip′yə lə tiv *or* mə nip′yə lā′tiv) *adj.* **1** of

or having to do with manipulation. 2 done by manipulation.

man·i·to (man′ə tō′) n., pl. **-tos.** manitou.

Man·i·to·ba maple (man′ə tō′bə) a medium-sized maple (*Acer negundo*) common on the Prairies, the only Canadian maple normally having compound leaves; box elder.

Man·i·to·ban (man′ə tō′bən) n., adj. —n. a native or long-term resident of Manitoba. —adj. of or having to do with Manitoba.

man·i·tou or **man·i·tu** (man′ə tü′) n. in the traditional religion of the Algonquian peoples: **1** any of the spirits representing the power that dwells within all things in nature, both weak and strong, and having both good and evil influence. **2** Often, **Manitou,** the impersonal supreme being or supernatural force, author of life and all things; the chief of the manitous, called **gitche** (or **kitshi**) **manitou,** often translated as the Great Spirit. [< Algonquian]

man·kind (man′kīnd′ *for 1;* man′kīnd′ *for 2*) n. **1** the human race; all human beings. **2** men collectively, as opposed to women.

man·like (man′līk′) adj. **1** of an animal, having characteristics of a human being: *The chimpanzee is the most manlike of the apes.* **2** like or characteristic of a man or men. **3** suitable for a man; masculine.

man·ly (man′lē) adj. **-li·er, -li·est. 1** like a man; as a man should be; strong, frank, brave, noble, independent, and honorable. **2** suitable for a man; masculine. —**man′li·ness,** n.
☛ *Syn.* **1.** See note at **male.**

man-made (man′mād′) adj. made by man; not occurring naturally; artificial or synthetic: *Nylon is a man-made fibre.*

man·na (man′ə) n. **1** in the Bible, the food that miraculously fell from heaven to the Israelites when they were starving in the wilderness (Exod. 16:14-36). **2** food for the soul. **3** a much-needed thing that is unexpectedly supplied. [ME < LL < Gk. < Hebrew *man*]

man·ne·quin (man′ə kin) n. **1** a woman whose work is modelling clothes for designers, retail stores, etc. **2** a model of a human figure, used by artists, tailors, stores, etc.: *Many clothing stores use mannequins for their window displays.* [< F < Du. *manneken.* See MANIKIN.]

man·ner (man′ər) n. **1** the way something happens or is done: *The trouble arose in a curious manner.* **2** a way of acting or behaving: *She has a kind manner.* **3** kind or kinds: *We saw all manner of birds in the forest. What manner of person was he?* **4 manners,** pl. **a** ways or customs: *Books and movies show us the manners of other times and places.* **b** ways of behaving towards others: *bad manners.* **c** polite behavior: *It is nice to see a child with manners.*
by all manner of means, most certainly.
by no manner of means, not at all; under no circumstances.
in a manner of speaking, as one might say.
to the manner born, accustomed since birth to some way or condition.
[ME < AF *manere* < L *manuaria,* fem. of *manuarius* belonging to the hand, ult. < *manus* hand]
☛ *Hom.* **manor.**
☛ *Syn.* **1.** See note at **way.**

man·nered (man′ərd) adj. **1** having manners of a certain kind: *a well-mannered child.* **2** affected; artificial; having many mannerisms.

man·ner·ism (man′ər iz′əm) n. **1** too much use of some manner in speaking, writing, or behaving. **2** an odd little trick; a queer habit; a peculiar way of acting. **3 Mannerism,** a style in art and architecture developed in Europe during the late 16th century, marked by the use of distortion and exaggeration as a conscious revolt against the classical principles of the Renaissance.

man·ner·ist (man′ər ist) n. **1** an artist, musician, or anyone given to mannerisms. **2** Often, **Mannerist,** an artist whose work is characterized by Mannerism.

man·ner·less (man′ər lis) adj. having bad manners.

man·ner·ly (man′ər lē) adj., adv. **1** having or showing good manners; polite. —adv. politely. —**man′ner·li·ness,** n.

man·i·kin (man′ə kin) n. See **manikin.**

man·nish (man′ish) adj. **1** peculiar to a man: *a mannish way of holding a baby.* **2** generally associated with a man rather than a woman: *She has a mannish style of dress.* —**man′nish·ly,** adv. —**man′nish·ness,** n.

ma·noeu·vre (mə nü′vər) n., v. **-vred** or **-vring.** —n. **1** a planned movement of troops or warships: *The army practises warfare by holding manoeuvres.* **2** a skilful plan or movement; clever trick: *His superior manoeuvres won the game.*
—v. **1** perform manoeuvres. **2** cause to perform manoeuvres. **3** plan skilfully; use clever tricks; scheme: *He is always manoeuvring to gain some advantage over others.* **4** force by skilful plans; get by clever tricks: *She manoeuvred her mother into letting her have a party.* **5** move or manipulate skilfully: *He manoeuvred his car through the heavy traffic with ease.* Also, **maneuver.** [< F *manoeuvre,* ult. < L *manu operare* work by hand]

---

hat, āge, fär; let, ēqual, tėrm; it, īce
hot, ōpen, ôrder; oil, out; cup, pút, rüle,
əbove, takən, pencəl, lemən, circəs
ch, child; ng, long; sh, ship
th, thin; ŦH, then; zh, measure

—**ma·noeu′vra·ble,** adj. —**ma·noeu′vra·bil′i·ty,** n.

Man of Galilee Jesus.

man of God 1 a holy man; saint; prophet. **2** clergyman.

man of letters 1 writer. **2** a person who has a wide knowledge of literature.

man of straw straw man.

man of the world a man who has a wide experience of different kinds of people and customs; a sophisticated and worldly-wise or practical man.

man-of-war (man′əv wôr′) n., pl. **men-of-war.** warship.

ma·nom·e·ter (mə nom′ə tər) n. **1** an instrument for measuring the pressure of gases or vapors. **2** an instrument for measuring blood pressure. [< F < Gk. *manos* thin + *metron* measure]

man·o·met·ric (man′ə met′rik) adj. **1** having to do with a manometer. **2** having to do with the measurement of gas pressures.

man on horseback a military leader whose influence over the people threatens the government.

man·or (man′ər) n. **1** in the Middle ages, a feudal estate, part of which was set aside for the lord and the rest divided among his peasants. If the lord sold his manor, the peasants or serfs were sold with it. **2** a large holding of land. **3** a large house on an estate, especially a manor house. [ME < AF *maner* < L *manere* stay]
☛ *Hom.* **manner.**

manor house the house of the owner of a manor.

ma·no·ri·al (mə nô′rē əl) adj. of, having to do with, or forming a manor.

man·pow·er (man′pou′ər) n. **1** the power supplied by human physical work. **2** strength thought of in terms of the number of persons needed or available for service in a particular region, for a particular type of work, etc.

man·qué (män kā′) adj. French. frustrated or unfulfilled; that might have been (*used only after a noun*): *a novelist* manqué *teaching creative writing courses.*

man·sard (man′särd) n. a four-sided roof having two slopes on each side, with the lower slope much steeper than the upper one. See **roof** for picture. [after François *Mansard* (1598-1666), a French architect]

man·sard·ed (man′sär′dəd) adj. of a roof, built with two slopes on each of four sides.

manse (mans) n. a minister's house; parsonage. [ME < Med.L *mansa* dwelling, n. use of fem. pp. of L *manere* stay]

man·serv·ant (man′sèr′vənt) n., pl. **men·serv·ants.** a male servant.

man·sion (man′shən) n. a large stately house. [ME < OF < L *mansio, -onis* < *manere* stay]

man-sized (man′sīzd′) adj. **1** suited to a man; large: *a man-sized meal.* **2** *Informal.* requiring the strength, skill, judgment, etc. of a mature man: *a man-sized problem.*

man·slaugh·ter (man′slo′tər *or* -slô′tər) n. **1** *Law.* the unlawful killing of another human being accidentally or without malice or premeditation. The driver of a car that accidentally hits and kills a pedestrian while the pedestrian has the right of way may be charged with manslaughter. **2** the killing of a human being or human beings.

man·ta (man′tə) n. devilfish. Also called **manta ray.**

man·tel (man′təl) n. **1** a shelf above a fireplace. **2** (*adjl.*) designed to rest on a mantel or similar surface: *a mantel radio.* **3** a decorative facing above and around a fireplace: *a mantel of tile.* [var. of *mantle*]

man·tel·et (man′təl et′ *or* mant′lit) n. **1** a short mantle or cape. **2** *Historical.* a large movable shelter, shield, or screen, used in war to protect soldiers firing a gun.

man·tel·piece (man′təl pēs′) n. a shelf above a fireplace; mantel.

man·tid (man′tid) n. mantis.

man·til·la (man til′ə; *Spanish,* män tē′lyä) n. **1** a light scarf of lace, silk, etc. covering the hair and shoulders, worn especially by Spanish and Mexican women. **2** a short mantle or cape. [< Sp. < L *mantellum* mantle]

man·tis (man′tis) n., pl. **-tis·es** or **-tes** (-tēz). any of a large family

(Mantidae) of slow-moving, carnivorous, winged insects of tropical and warm temperate regions, having a long, slender, typically green body and having the habit of remaining still with their foremost pair of legs raised, suggesting a praying position. [< NL use of Gk. *mantis* prophet (from its praying posture)]

man·tis·sa (man tis'ə) *n. Mathematics.* the decimal part of a logarithm. In the logarithm 2.95424, the characteristic is 2 and the mantissa is .95424. [< L *mantissa* addition < Etruscan]

man·tle (man'təl) *n., v.* **-tled, -tling.** —*n.* **1** a loose cloak without sleeves. **2** anything that covers or conceals like a mantle: *The ground had a mantle of snow.* **3** the part of the earth's interior between the crust and the core, beginning at about 8 to 35 km from the surface and extending to a depth of about 2880 km and composed of very dense, solid rock believed to consist mainly of silicates of iron and magnesium. See **core** for picture. **4** a netlike sheath fixed around the flame of a gas lamp, made of a substance that glows with an intense white light when it becomes hot. **5** the plumage on the back and folded wings of a bird, especially when of a different color from the rest of the plumage.
—*v.* **1** clothe, cover, or conceal with or as if with a mantle: *mantled in a heavy fur coat, mountaintops mantled with snow, jealousy mantled in an outward friendliness.* **2** become covered with a coating or scum: *The pond was mantled.* **3** redden; blush: *His cheeks mantled.* [OE *mentel* < L *mantellum* and < OF *mantel* < L *mantellum*]

man-to-man (man'tə man') *adj., adv.* —*adj.* **1** honest; sincere; straightforward. **2** *Sports.* referring to a defence system in which players do not guard zones but cover individual opponents. —*adv.* honestly; sincerely.

man·tra (man'trə) *n.* **1** any of the metrical hymns of praise in the Veda. **2** *Hinduism or Buddhism.* a sacred word or formula used for incantation. [< Skt., literally, instrument of thought, ult. < *man* to think. 19c.]

man·tu·a (man'chü ə) *n.* **1** a loose gown or cloak formerly worn by women. **2** mantle. [< *Mantua*, a town in Italy]

man·u·al (man'yü əl) *adj., n.* —*adj.* **1** of, having to do with, or using the hands: *manual labor. He has great manual dexterity.* **2** done or operated by hand, not automatically: *The car has a manual choke.* —*n.* **1** a small book that helps its readers to understand or use something; handbook. **2** an organ keyboard played with the hands. [< L *manualis* < *manus* hand]
—**man'u·al·ly,** *adv.*

manual training training in work done with the hands, especially in making things out of wood, metal, or plastic.

man·u·fac·to·ry (man'yə fak'tə rē) *n., pl.* **-ries.** factory.

man·u·fac·ture (man'yə fak'chər) *v.* **-tured, -tur·ing;** *n.* —*v.* **1** make by hand or by machine: *This factory manufactures outboard motors.* **2** make into something useful: *Iron is manufactured into steel.* **3** invent; make up: *The dishonest lawyer manufactured evidence.*
—*n.* **1** the act of manufacturing. **2** the thing manufactured. [< F < Med.L *manufactura* < L *manu facere* make by hand]

man·u·fac·tur·er (man'yə fak'chər ər) *n.* a person whose business is manufacturing; owner of a factory.

man·u·mis·sion (man'yə mish'ən) *n.* freeing or being freed from slavery. [< L *manumissio, -onis*]

man·u·mit (man'yə mit') *v.* **-mit·ted, -mit·ting.** set free from slavery. [< L *manu mittere* release from control]

ma·nure (mə nyür' *or* mə nür') *n., v.* **-nured, -nur·ing.** —*n.* a substance, especially animal waste, put in or on the soil as fertilizer: *The dung from a stable is a kind of manure.* —*v.* put manure in or on. [ME < AF *maynoverer* work with the hands < OF *manuevre* hand-work (in F *manoeuvre*). See MANOEUVRE.]
—**ma·nur'er,** *n.*

man·u·script (man'yə skript') *n., adj.* —*n.* **1** a book or paper written by hand or with a typewriter. **2** especially of an unpublished book, article, etc., the condition of being handwritten or typewritten: *His last book was three years in manuscript.* **3** a book, document, etc. written by hand before the introduction of printing. **4** (*adj.*) of or being a manuscript: *a manuscript version. Abbrev.:* MS., MS, ms., or ms [< Med.L < L *manu scriptus* written by hand]

Manx (mangks) *adj.* of or having to do with the Isle of Man, its people, or their language. —*n.* **1** the Manx, *pl.* the people of the Isle of Man. **2** the Celtic language of the Manx, now extinct.
☛ *Usage.* **Manx,** meaning the people of the Isle of Man, is plural in use: *The Manx are hard-working people.* **Manx,** meaning the language of these people, is singular in use: *Manx is now extinct.*

Manx cat a breed of cat that is tail-less and has a thick undercoat and a longer-haired outer coat.

Manx·man (mangks'mən) *n., pl.* **-men.** a native of the Isle of Man.

man·y (men'ē) *adj.* **more, most;** *n.* —*adj.* in great number; numerous: *many people, many years ago.* —*n.* a large number of people or things: *There were many at the fair.*
a good many, a fairly large number.
a great many, a very large number.
one too many for, more than a match for.
the many, a most people. **b** the common people.
[OE *manig*]
☛ *Syn. adj.* **Many, innumerable** = consisting of a large number. **Many** is the general word: *Were many people there?* **Innumerable** means more than can be counted, or so many that counting would be very hard: *The sands of the desert are innumerable.*

man·y·plies (men'ē plīz') *n.* the third stomach of a cow or other ruminant; omasum. [< *many* + *plies,* pl. of *ply; n.*]

man·y-sid·ed (men'ē sīd'id) *adj.* **1** having many sides. **2** having many interests or abilities.

man·za·ni·ta (man'zə nē'tə) *n.* any of several evergreen shrubs and trees (genus *Arctostaphylos*) of the heath family that are native to the Pacific coastal areas of North America. [< Sp. *manzanita,* dim. of *manzana* apple]

Ma·o·ri (mou'rē *or* mä'ō rē) *n., pl.* **-ris;** *adj.* —*n.* **1** a member of a Polynesian people of New Zealand. **2** the Polynesian language of the Maoris. —*adj.* of or having to do with the Maoris or their language.

Mao·ism (mou'iz əm) *n.* Marxism-Leninism as interpreted and developed by Mao Tse-tung (1893-1976) and practised in the People's Republic of China during his leadership, from 1949 until his death.

Mao·ist (mou'ist) *n., adj.* —*n.* a follower of Mao Tse-tung. —*adj.* of or having to do with Maoism or Maoists.

map (map) *n., v.* **mapped, map·ping.** —*n.* **1** a drawing representing the earth's surface or part of it, usually showing countries, cities, rivers, seas, lakes, and mountains. **2** a drawing representing part of the sky, showing the position of the stars. **3** a maplike drawing of anything: *a highway map, a road map.*
off the map, *Informal.* of no importance; of no account.
put on the map, *Informal.* give prominence to; make well-known.
—*v.* **1** make a map of; show on a map. **2** plan; arrange in detail: *to map out the week's work.* [< Med.L *mappa mundi* map of the world (< L *mappa* napkin)]
☛ *Syn.* **Map, chart** = a drawing representing a surface or area. A **map** may refer especially to a plan of road or other routes on land, while **chart** is used especially for plans showing air or sea routes. An **atlas** is a book of maps covering a large area or the whole world.

ma·ple (mā'pəl) *n.* **1** any of a large genus (*Acer*) of trees and shrubs found throughout the north temperate regions of the world, having usually lobed leaves that grow in opposite pairs and dry fruits with normally two winglike extensions, each containing a seed. Two of the most common Canadian maples are the sugar maple and the Manitoba maple. **2** the light-colored, hard, close-grained wood of certain maples, valued for making furniture, flooring, etc. **3** (*adj.*) designating a family (Aceraceae) of trees and shrubs consisting of the maples and several trees of central and southern China. All the trees of the maple family have winged seeds. **4** (*adj.*) made of or flavored with maple sugar or syrup: *maple ice cream, maple candy.* [OE *mapeltrēow* maple tree]
—**ma'ple-like',** *adj.*

maple leaf 1 a leaf of the maple tree. **2** this leaf as a Canadian emblem. A red maple leaf on a white background is in the centre of the Canadian flag. The song "The Maple Leaf Forever" was written in 1867 by Alexander Muir.

maple sugar sugar made from the sap of the sugar maple.

maple syrup syrup made from the sap of the sugar maple.

ma·quette (ma ket') *n.* a sculptor's or architect's small model of a planned project.

Ma·quis (mä kē') *n., pl.* **maquis. 1 a** a scrubby bush consisting mainly of low-growing evergreens such as myrtle, heath, and ilex, found on islands and along the coast of the Mediterranean. **b** an area or region characterized by such vegetation. **2** Usually, **Maquis, a** the French underground resistance movement against the Germans in World War II. **b** a member of, or a guerilla fighter in, this movement. **c** (*adj.*) of or having to do with the Maquis or their tactics. [< F < *maquis* bushy land < Ital. *macchia* thicket; with reference to the cover bandits take in bushy regions]

mar (mär) *v.* **marred, mar·ring.** spoil the beauty of; damage; injure. [OE *merran* waste]

mar. 1 married. **2** marine. **3** maritime.

Mar. March.

mar·a·bou (mar'ə bü' *or* mer'ə bü') *n.* **1** a large, black-and-white stork (*Leptoptilos crumeniferus*) of Africa that feeds mainly on carrion and refuse. **2** a furlike trimming made from the soft, downy feathers of marabous or, sometimes, of other birds. [< F]

ma·ra·ca (mə rä'kə *or* mə rak'ə) *n.* a percussion instrument

resembling a rattle, consisting of a gourd or gourd-shaped body containing seeds or pebbles and attached to a handle, usually played in pairs. [< Pg.]

mar·a·schi·no (mar′ə shē′nō *or* mer′ə-, mar′ə skē′nō *or* mer′ə-) *n.* a strong, sweet liqueur made from a kind of small black cherry. [< Ital. *maraschino* < *marasca* shortened form of *amarasca* a sour cherry, ult. < L *amarus* sour]

maraschino cherries cherries preserved in a syrup flavored with or similar to maraschino.

mar·a·thon (mar′ə thon′ *or* mer′ə thon′) *n.* **1** a long-distance foot race, officially measured at 42.195 km. It is an Olympic event. **2** any long-distance race or endurance contest: *a marathon swim, a dance marathon.* [< *Marathon*, where the Greeks defeated the Persians in 490 B.C. A Greek messenger ran 37 km from Marathon to Athens to bring news of the victory. The official distance for the Olympic marathon is from a decision by the British Olympic Committee at the 1908 London Games to make the race the distance from Windsor Castle to the royal box at the London Stadium.]

ma·raud (mə rod′ *or* mə rôd′) *v.* go about in search of plunder; make raids for booty. [< F *marauder* < *maraud* rascal] —**ma·raud′er**, *n.*

mar·ble (mär′bəl) *n., v.* **-bled, -bling.** —*n.* **1** a hard, crystallized, metamorphic limestone that may be white, colored, or mottled or streaked, and that is capable of taking a high polish. It is extensively used for sculpture and building. **2** something made of marble, especially a sculpture. **3** (*adj.*) made of marble: *a marble statue.* **4** (*adj.*) resembling marble; white, hard, cold, or unfeeling: *a marble heart.* **5** a small ball of glass, clay, stone, etc. used in games. **6 marbles**, a game played with such little balls (used with a singular verb). **7 marbles**, *pl. Slang.* wits, common sense, or brains: *to lose one's marbles. He seems quite nice, but I don't think he's got all his marbles.* —*v.* color in imitation of the patterns in marble: *Binders marble the edges of some books.* [ME < OF *marbre* < L *marmor* < Gk. *marmaros* gleaming stone] —**mar′ble-like′**, *adj.*

mar·ca·site (mär′kə sit′) *n.* **1** a native iron disulphide, white iron pyrites, similar to and of the same composition as ordinary pyrites: *Marcasite is often used in jewellery. Formula:* FeS₂ **2** a piece of jewellery made from this material. [< Med.L *marcasita* < Arabic *marqashita* < Aramaic]

mar·cel (mär sel′) *n., v.* **-celled, -cel·ling.** —*n.* a series of regular waves put in the hair. —*v.* put a series of regular waves in (the hair). [after *Marcel*, a French hairdresser of the 19th century]

march¹ (märch) *v., n.* —*v.* **1** walk as soldiers do, in time and with steps of the same length. **2** walk or proceed steadily. **3** cause to march or go: *The policeman marched the thief off to jail.* **4** advance; progress. —*n.* **1** the movement of troops: *The army is prepared for the march.* **2** the act or fact of marching. **3** *Music.* **a** a composition to march to, having a regular, strongly accented metre, usually in 4/4 time. **b** any composition or part of a composition having similar characteristics: *He enjoyed listening to marches.* **4** the distance marched. **5** a long, hard walk. **6** advance; progress: *History records the march of events.* **on the march,** moving forward; advancing. **steal a march on,** gain an advantage over without being noticed. [< F *marcher*, earlier, to trample, ult. < LL *marcus* hammer < L *marculus* small hammer] —**march′er**, *n.*

march² (märch) *n.* **1** the land along the border of a country; frontier. **2 the Marches**, *pl.* the districts along the border between England and Scotland, or between England and Wales. [ME < OF *marche* < Gmc.]

March (märch) *n.* the third month of the year. It has 31 days. [ME < OF *marche* < L *Martius* (month) of Mars]

mar·chion·ess (mär′shən is *or* mär′shən es′) *n.* **1** the wife or widow of a marquis. **2** a woman with a rank equal to that of a marquis. [< Med.L *marchionissa* < *marchio* marquis < *marcha*, *marca* march² < Gmc.]

march·pane (märch′pān′) *n.* marzipan.

march·past (märch′past′) *n.* a display, especially a military parade, in which troops, etc. march past a reviewing stand.

Mar·di-gras (mär′dē grä′) the last day before Lent; Shrove Tuesday. [< F *mardi gras* fat (that is, meat-eating) Tuesday]

mare (mer) *n.* a female horse, donkey, etc. [OE *mere*]

mare's–nest (merz′nest′) *n.* **1** something supposed to be a great discovery that turns out to be a mistake or joke. **2** *Informal.* a situation that is disordered or confused.

mare's–tail (merz′tāl′) *n.* **1** a water plant (*Hippuris vulgaris*) having tiny flowers and many circles of narrow, hairlike leaves around the stems. **2** horsetail. **3** a long wisp of cirrus cloud.

mar·ga·rin (mär′jə rin) *n.* margarine.

mar·ga·rine (mär′jə rin *or* mär′jə rēn′) *n.* a compound of

vegetable oils, used for cooking or as a spread, often as a substitute for butter. [< F]

marge¹ (märj) *n. Poetic.* an edge; border. [< F]

marge² (märj) *n. Informal.* margarine.

mar·gin (mär′jən) *n., v.* —*n.* **1** an edge; border: *the margin of a lake.* **2** the blank space around the writing or printing on a page. **3** the space left at the left-hand side, or sometimes on both sides, by a person writing or typing. **4** an extra amount; amount beyond what is necessary; difference: *We allow a margin of 15 minutes when we want to catch a train.* **5** the difference between the cost and selling price of stocks, etc. **6** *Business.* **a** the money or security deposited with a broker to protect him from loss on contracts undertaken for the real buyer or seller. **b** the amount of such a deposit. **c** the transaction itself, financed by both the broker and his customer: *When you buy on margin, you put up only part of the total cost and the broker lends you the remainder.* **d** the customer's profit or loss in such a transaction. **7** the point at which an economic activity yields just enough return to cover its costs and below which the activity will result in a loss. **8** a condition beyond which something ceases to exist or be possible; limit: *the margin of subsistence, the margin of consciousness.* —*v.* **1** provide with a margin. **2** *Business.* **a** deposit a margin upon (stock, etc.). **b** secure by a margin. [ME < L *margo, -ginis* edge]

mar·gin·al (mär′jə nəl) *adj.* **1** written or printed in a margin. **2** of or being a margin, edge, or border: *marginal forests.* **3** at, on, or near a margin, border, or limit. **4** barely useful, acceptable, or profitable: *marginal knowledge, marginal land.* **5** of, having to do with, or obtained from goods produced and marketed so as to barely cover costs. —**mar′gin·al·ly**, *adv.*

mar·gi·na·li·a (mär′jə nā′lē ə *or* mär′jə nāl′yə) *n.pl.* notes written in the margin or margins of a manuscript, book, etc.

mar·gin·al·i·ty (mär′jə nal′ə tē) *n.* the quality or condition of being marginal.

mar·grave (mär′grāv) *n.* **1** a German nobleman whose rank corresponds to that of a British marquis. **2** *Historical.* the title of certain princes of the Holy Roman Empire. Originally, a margrave was a German military governor of a border province. [< MDu. *markgrave* count of the marches]

mar·gra·vine (mär′grə vēn′) *n.* the wife or widow of a margrave.

mar·gue·rite (mar′gə rēt′) *n.* **1** a garden plant (*Chrysanthemum frutescens*) of the composite family having daisylike flowers with white or pale-yellow rays around a yellow disk. **2** any of various other composite plants with daisylike flowers, such as the ox-eye daisy. [< F < L < Gk. *margarītēs* pearl]

mar·i·gold (mar′ə gōld′ *or* mer′ə gōld′) *n.* **1** any of various plants (genus *Tagetes*) of the composite family native to tropical and subtropical America that are widely cultivated for their showy yellow, orange, or red flowers. **2** any of various other yellow-flowered plants, such as the pot marigold or marsh marigold. [< (the Virgin) *Mary* + *gold*]

mar·i·jua·na *or* **mar·i·hua·na** (mar′ə wä′nə *or* mer′ə wä′nə) *n.* **1** hemp. **2** the dried leaves and flower clusters of the female hemp plant, especially when smoked as a cigarette for its intoxicating effect. [< Mexican Sp. *mariguana, marihuana*]

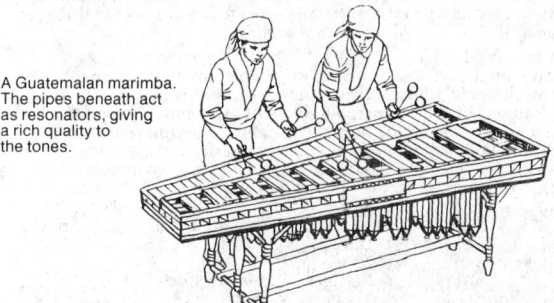

A Guatemalan marimba. The pipes beneath act as resonators, giving a rich quality to the tones.

ma·rim·ba (mə rim′bə) *n.* an African and Latin American

percussion instrument resembling a xylophone but having resonators below the bars. [< Bantu]

ma·ri·na (mə rē′nə) *n.* a place on a waterfront where boats may be moored and where fuel and equipment may be bought: *It is often possible to buy boats and motors at a marina.* [< Ital. *marina* shore, coast < L *marina.* See MARINE.]

mar·i·nade (*n.* mar′ə nād′ *or* mer′ə nād′; *v.* mar′ə nād′ *or* mer′ə nād′) *n., v.* **-nad·ed, -nad·ing.** —*n.* **1** a spiced vinegar or wine in which meat, fish, etc. are soaked before being cooked. Food may be marinaded both to give it flavor and to make it tender. **2** meat or fish soaked in such vinegar or wine. —*v.* marinate. [< F *marinade* < *mariner* marinate]

mar·i·nate (mar′ə nāt′ *or* mer′ə nāt′) *v.* **-nat·ed, -nat·ing. 1** soak in brine or marinade. **2** soak in oil and vinegar. [< F *mariner* < *marin* marine]

ma·rine (mə rēn′) *adj., n.* —*adj.* **1** of the sea; found in the sea; produced by the sea: *Whales are marine animals.* **2** of or having to do with shipping; maritime: *marine law.* **3** of or having to do with a navy; naval: *marine power.* **4** for use at sea, on a ship, etc.: *marine supplies, a marine engine.* **5** *Nautical.* **a** of or having to do with ships, sailors, etc.: *marine lore.* **b** of or having to do with navigation at sea: *a marine compass.* —*n.* **1** shipping; a fleet: *our merchant marine.* **2** a soldier formerly serving only at sea, now also participating in land and air action: *Canada has no marines.* **3** a picture showing a sea scene. [< F < L *marina,* fem. *mare* sea]

mar·i·ner (mar′ə nər *or* mer′ə nər) *n.* one who navigates or helps to navigate or run a ship; sailor; seaman. [ME < AF *mariner* < OF *marin* < L *marinus* < *mare* sea]

mar·i·o·nette (mar′ē ə net′ *or* mer′ē ə net′) *n.* a small doll or puppet made to imitate a person or an animal and moved by strings. A marionette show is often given on a miniature stage. [< F *marionette,* ult. < *Marie* Mary]

Mar·i·po·sa lily (mar′ə pō′sə *or* mer′-; mar′ə pō′zə *or* mer′-) any of a genus (*Calochortus*) of plants of the lily family found in W North America, having tuliplike flowers, usually white with yellow, purple, or lilac markings. [< Sp. *mariposa* butterfly]

mar·i·tal (mar′ə təl *or* mer′ə təl) *adj.* **1** of or having to do with marriage: *marital vows, a marital relationship.* **2** of or having to do with a husband: *a marital obligation.* [< L *maritalis* < *maritus* married man] —**mar′i·tal·ly,** *adv.*

mar·i·time (mar′ə tīm′ *or* mer′ə tīm′) *adj.* **1** on or near the sea: *Halifax is a maritime city.* **2** living near the sea: *Many maritime peoples live from fishing.* **3** of or having to do with the sea or with shipping and sailing: *Ships and sailors are governed by maritime law.* **4 Maritime,** of or having to do with the Maritime Provinces. [< L *maritimus* < *mare* sea]

Maritime Command *Cdn.* a major organizational element of the Canadian Forces, whose role is to provide operationally ready maritime forces to patrol and control Canadian territorial waters and adjacent ocean areas and to meet Canada's international defence commitments.

Maritime Provinces the provinces along the east coast of Canada, especially New Brunswick, Nova Scotia, and Prince Edward Island.

☛ *Usage.* The **Maritime Provinces** and **Maritimes** do not usually include Newfoundland; the **Atlantic Provinces** include the Maritime provinces and Newfoundland.

Mar·i·tim·er (mar′ə tīm′ər *or* mer′ə tīm′ər) *n.* a native or long-term resident of the Maritime Provinces.

Mar·i·times (mar′ə tīmz′ *or* mer′ə tīmz′) *n.* Maritime Provinces.

mar·jo·ram (mär′jə rəm) *n.* any of various plants (genera *Majorana* and *Origanum*) of the mint family, especially sweet marjoram, whose fragrant leaves are used for flavoring in cooking. [ME < OF *majorane* < Med.L. *majorana, majoraca,* ? < L *amaracus* < Gk.]

mark¹ (märk) *n., v.* —*n.* **1** a trace or impression made by some object on the surface of another. A line, dot, spot, stain, or scar is a mark. **2** an object, arrow, line, dot, etc. put as a guide or sign: *a mark for pilots, the starting mark in a race, a question mark.* **3** something that indicates quality or characteristic: *Courtesy is a mark of good breeding. She has the mark of a leader.* **4** a cross or other sign made by a person who cannot write, instead of signing his name: *Make your mark here.* **5** a letter or number to show how well one has done; grade or rating: *My mark in arithmetic was B.* **6** something to be aimed at; target; goal. **7** what is usual, proper, or expected; standard: *A tired person does not feel up to the mark.* **8** influence; impression: *A great man leaves his mark on whatever he does.* **9** *Informal.* a person who is an easy prey for pickpockets, tricksters, etc.; sucker; gull. **10** *Archaic.* a border or frontier. **11** in the Middle Ages, a tract of land held in common by a community.

beside the mark, a not hitting the thing aimed at. **b** not to the point; not relevant.
hit the mark, a succeed in doing what one tried to do. **b** be exactly right.
make (one's) mark, succeed; become famous.
miss the mark, a fail to do what one tried to do. **b** be not exactly right.
of mark, important or famous: *a man of mark.*
wide of the mark, a missing the thing aimed at by a considerable margin. **b** irrelevant.
—*v.* **1** make a mark on by stamping, cutting, writing, etc.: *Be careful not to mark the table.* **2** show by means of a sign: *Mark all the large cities on this map. This post marks the city limits.* **3** put a sign on an article, as a tag, label, brand, or seal, to show the price, quality, maker, or owner. **4** show clearly; make plain: *A tall pine marks the beginning of the trail. A frown marked her displeasure.* **5** set off; give interest or importance to: *Many important inventions mark the last 150 years.* **6** give grades to; rate. **7** give attention to; notice; observe; see: *Mark how carefully he moves. Mark well my words.* **8** keep (the score); record. **9** select as if by mark: *He was marked for promotion.*
mark down, a write down; note down. **b** mark for sale at a lower price.
mark off or **out,** make lines, etc. to show the position of or to separate.
mark out for, set aside for; select for.
mark time, a move the feet as in marching, but remaining in the same spot. **b** suspend progress temporarily. **c** go through the motions without accomplishing anything.
mark up, a spoil the look of by making marks on: *Don't mark up the desks.* **b** mark for sale at a higher price.
[OE *mearc*]

☛ *Syn. n.* **3. Mark, sign, token** can all refer to an indication of something not visible or readily apparent. **Mark** particularly suggests an indication of the character of the thing: *Generosity is often a mark of greatness.* **Sign** is the general word, applying to any indication, as of a quality, idea, mental or physical state, etc.: *We could see no sign of life.* **Token** applies especially to something that stands as a reminder or promise of something else, as of a feeling, event, etc.: *This gift is a token of my love.*

mark² (märk) *n.* **1** Deutsche Mark. **2** the basic unit of money in the German Democratic Republic (East Germany), equal to 100 pfennigs. **3** markka. **4** a coin worth one mark. [< G]

marked (märkt) *adj.* **1** having a mark or marks on it. **2** very noticeable; very clear; easily recognized: *There is a marked difference between a grape and an orange.*

mark·ed·ly (mär′kid lē) *adv.* in a marked manner or degree; conspicuously; noticeably; plainly.

marked man a person, such as a suspected criminal, who is picked out as someone to watch or take action against: *After he was reported as having been near the scene of the murder, John was a marked man.*

mark·er (mär′kər) *n.* **1** a person or thing that marks. **2** a person or thing that keeps the score in games. **3** bookmark.

mar·ket (mär′kit) *n., v.* —*n.* **1** a meeting of people for the purpose of buying and selling: *There is a fruit and vegetable market here every Saturday.* **2** the people so gathered. **3** a space or building in which provisions, cattle, etc. are shown for sale. **4** a store for the sale of provisions: *a meat market.* **5** trade, especially as regards a particular article: *the cotton market.* **6** the opportunity to buy or sell: *lose one's market.* **7** the demand (for goods): *There was not enough cheese to supply the market.* **8** a region where goods can be sold: *Africa is a new market for many products.* **9** (*adj.*) of or having to do with a market or markets: *market research, market variations.*
be in the market for, be a possible buyer of: *He is in the market for a new bike.*
play the market, speculate on the stock exchange.
price out of the market, lose business by setting a price above that of competitors or above what buyers will pay: *The firm priced itself out of the market.*
—*v.* **1** buy or sell in a market. **2** sell: *He cannot market the goods he makes.* **3** carry or send to market. [ME < ONF < L *mercatus* trade, ult. < *merx, mercis* merchandise] —**mar′ket·er,** *n.*

mar·ket·a·bil·i·ty (mär′kit ə bil′ə tē) *n.* the quality of being marketable.

mar·ket·a·ble (mär′kit ə bəl) *adj.* that can be sold.

market garden a farm where vegetables are raised for market. —**market gardener, n.** —**market gardening, n.**

mar·ket·ing (mär′ki ting) *n.* **1** the business or process of planning and implementing a strategy for the promotion, sale, and distribution of goods or services. **2** (*adj.*) of or having to do with marketing: *a marketing seminar.*

mar·ket·place (mär′kət plās′) *n.* **1** a place where a market is held. **2** the world of business and commerce.

market price the price that an article brings when sold; current price.

market value market price.

mark·ing (mär'king) n. 1 a mark or marks. 2 the arrangement of marks: *I like the marking on your cat's coat.*

mark·ka (märk'kä) n., pl. **-kaa** (-kä). 1 the basic unit of money in Finland, divided into 100 pennia. See table at **money.** 2 a coin worth one markka. [< Finnish]

marks·man (märks'mən) n., pl. **-men.** a person who shoots, especially one who shoots well: *He is a noted marksman.*

marks·man·ship (märks'mən ship') n. skill in shooting.

mark·up (märk'up') n. 1 an increase in the price of an article. 2 the amount of this increase. 3 the percentage or amount added to the cost to take care of profit and overhead when establishing the selling price of a commodity; the difference between the cost price and the selling price.

marl (märl) n. 1 soil containing clay and calcium carbonate, used in making cement and as a fertilizer. 2 *Poetic.* earth. [ME < OF *marle* < Med.L *margila* < L *marga*, probably < Celtic]

mar·lin (mär'lən) n. any of several large marine food and game fishes (genera *Makaira* and *Tetrapturus*) related to the sailfishes. [short for *marlinespike*]

mar·line (mär'lən) n. a small cord that sailors wind around the ends of a rope to keep it from fraying. [< Du. *marlijn* < *marren* tie + *lijn* line]

mar·line·spike or **mar·lin·spike** (mär'lən spīk') n. a pointed steel spike used, like a fid, for separating strands of rope or wire in splicing.

mar·ma·lade (mär'mə lād') n. a preserve resembling jam, made of oranges or other fruit. The peel is usually sliced and boiled with the fruit. [< F < Pg. *marmelada* < *marmelo* quince < L < Gk. *melimēlon* < *meli* honey + *mēlon* apple]

mar·mo·re·al (mär mô'rē əl) adj. 1 of marble. 2 like marble; cold; smooth; white. [< L *marmoreus* < *marmor* marble]

mar·mo·set (mär'mə set' or mär'mə zet') n. any of numerous small, squirrel-like monkeys (family Callithricidae, especially genus *Callithrix*) of South and Central America, having claws instead of nails, a long, furry tail, and, in many species, brightly colored fur and long tufts of hair around the head. The pygmy marmoset (*Cebuella pygmaea*) is the smallest monkey, measuring only about 20 cm long, including the tail. [< OF *marmouset* grotesque figurine < *merme* under age < L *minimus* very small, influenced by Gk. *mormotos* fearful]

mar·mot (mär'mət) n. any of a genus (*Marmota*) of burrowing rodents of the northern hemisphere belonging to the same family as squirrels and chipmunks, having a thickset body, broad, flat head, short, strong legs, and a relatively short, furry tail. [< F *marmotte* < *marmottaine* < Med.L. *mus* (*muris*) *montanus* mouse of the mountains]

mar·o·cain (mar'ə kān' or mer'-) n. a crepelike dress fabric of silk woven with cotton or wool. [< F *marocain* relating to Morocco < *Maroc* Morocco]

ma·roon[1] (mə rün') n. or adj. dark brownish red. [< Ital. *marrone* chestnut]

ma·roon[2] (mə rün') v., n. —v. 1 put (a person) ashore in a lonely place and leave him there: *Pirates used to maroon people on desert islands.* 2 leave in a lonely, helpless position.
—n. 1 a descendant of escaped Negro slaves living in the West Indies and Surinam. 2 an escaped Negro slave, an ancestor of these people. 3 a person who is marooned. [< F *marron*, ? < Sp. *cimarron* wild < *cimarra* bushes] —**ma·roon'er,** n.

mar·plot (mär'plot') n. a person who spoils some plan by meddling or blundering.

marque[1] (märk) See **letters of marque.** [< F < Provençal *marca* reprisal < *marcar* seize as a pledge, ult. < Gmc.]

marque[2] (märk) n. a make or brand of a product, especially an automobile.

mar·quee (mär kē') n. 1 a large tent, often one put up for some outdoor entertainment. 2 a rooflike shelter over an entrance. [< F *marquise* (misunderstood as plural) < OF (*tente*) *marquise* a large tent for officers, literally, for a marquis]

mar·quess (mär'kwis) n. *Esp.Brit.* marquis.

mar·que·try (mär'kə trē) n., pl. **-tries.** decoration made with thin pieces of wood, ivory, metal, etc. fitted together to form a design on furniture. [< F *marqueterie* < *marqueter* inlay < *marque* mark[1] < Gmc.]

mar·quis (mär'kwis or mär kē') n. a nobleman ranking below a duke and above an earl or count. [ME < OF *marquis, marchis* < *marche*[2] < Gmc.]

mar·quis·ate (mär'kwiz it) n. the position or rank of marquis.

mar·quise (mär kēz') n. 1 marchioness. 2 a gem of a pointed oval shape, or a ring set with such a stone. 3 marquee (def. 2). [< F *marquise*, fem. of *marquis*]

hat, āge, fär; let, ēqual, tèrm; it, īce
hot, ōpen, ôrder; oil, out; cup, pùt, rüle,
əbove, takən, pencəl, lemən, circəs
ch, child; ng, long; sh, ship
th, thin; ₮H, then; zh, measure

mar·qui·sette (mär'kə zet' or mär'kwə zet') n. a very thin fabric with square meshes, made of cotton, silk, rayon, nylon, etc. and often used for window draperies. [< F *marquisette*, dim. of *marquise* marquise]

mar·riage (mar'ij or mer'ij) n. 1 married life; living together as husband and wife: *We wished the bride and groom a happy marriage.* 2 the ceremony of being married; a marrying; a wedding. 3 a close union: *the marriage of words and melody.* [ME < OF *mariage* < *marier.* See MARRY.]
☛ *Syn.* 1, 2. **Marriage, matrimony, wedding** = the state of being married or the act of marrying. **Marriage** is the general and common word applying to the institution, the legal and spiritual relation, the state of being married, or, less often, the ceremony. **Matrimony** is the formal and religious word, and applies especially to the spiritual relation or the religious ceremony (sacrament). **Wedding** is the common word for the ceremony or celebration.

mar·riage·a·bil·i·ty (mar'ij ə bil'ə tē or mer'ij ə bil'ə tē) n. the state of being marriageable.

mar·riage·a·ble (mar'ij ə bəl or mer'ij ə bəl) adj. fit for marriage; old enough to marry.

marriage portion dowry.

mar·ried (mar'id or mer'ēd) adj., n. —adj. 1 living together as husband and wife. 2 having a husband or wife. 3 of marriage; of husbands and wives. 4 closely united: *The painter was married to his art.*
—n. a person who is married (*usually used in the plural*): *a roomful of young marrieds.*

married quarters housing provided for married members of the armed forces.

mar·row (mar'ō or mer'ō) n. 1 the soft tissue that fills the cavities of most bones. 2 the inmost or essential part: *He was chilled to the marrow.* 3 vegetable marrow. [OE *mearg*]

mar·row·bone (mar'ō bōn' or mer'ō bōn') n. 1 a bone containing marrow. 2 **marrowbones,** *pl.* **a** knees. **b** crossbones.

mar·row·fat (mar'ō fat' or mer'ō fat') n. a kind of pea that has a large seed.

mar·ry[1] (mar'ē or mer'ē) v. **-ried, -ry·ing.** 1 join as husband and wife: *The minister married them.* 2 take as husband or wife: *John planned to marry Grace.* 3 become married; take a husband or wife: *She married late in life.* 4 give in marriage (*often used with* **off**): *They married their daughter off to a young lawyer.* 5 unite closely. [ME < OF *marier* < L *maritare* < *maritus* husband, formed after *marita* woman with husband < *mas, mari-* a male]

mar·ry[2] (mar'ē or mer'ē) interj. *Archaic.* an exclamation showing surprise, indignation, etc. [< (the Virgin) *Mary*]

Mars (märz) n. 1 *Roman mythology.* the god of war, son of Jupiter and Juno, corresponding to the Greek god Ares. 2 the planet next beyond the earth and the fourth in order from the sun.

Mar·sa·la (mär sä'lə) n. a dark, sweet, fortified wine originally made in Marsala, Sicily.

Mar·seil·laise (mär'sə lāz') n. the national anthem of France, written in 1792 during the French Revolution. [< *Marseilles*, France; because first sung by a group of men from Marseilles]

mar·seilles (mär sälz') n. a thick cotton cloth woven in figures or stripes, used for bedspreads, etc. [< *Marseilles*]

marsh (märsh) n. an area of wet, muddy land sometimes partly covered with water and having plant life that consists mainly of grasses and sedges. [OE *mersc* < *mere* lake]

mar·shal (mär'shəl) n., v. **-shalled** or **-shaled, -shal·ling** or **-shal·ing.** —n. 1 any of various kinds of officer: *a fire marshal.* 2 in the armed forces of certain countries, an officer of a high, or the highest, rank: *a field marshal.* 3 a person who arranges the order of march in a parade: *a parade marshal.* 4 a person in charge of events or ceremonies.
—v. 1 arrange or order properly or effectively: *He spent a lot of time marshalling his arguments for the debate.* 2 conduct with ceremony: *We were marshalled before the king.* 3 arrange in military order; prepare for war. [ME < OF *mareschal* < LL *mariscalcus* groom < Gmc., literally, horse servant] —**mar'shal·ler** or **mar'shal·er,** n.
☛ *Hom.* martial.

marsh gas a gas formed by the decomposition of organic substances in marshes; methane.

marsh·land (märsh'land' or märsh'lənd) n. marshy land.

marsh·mal·low (märsh′mal′ō or märsh′mel′ō) n. 1 a soft, spongy confection originally made from the root of the marsh mallow, now made from corn syrup, sugar, gelatin, and flavoring. 2 a piece of this confection, covered with powdered sugar: a bag of marshmallows. [OE merscmealwe, originally made from the root of the marsh mallow]

marsh mallow a perennial herb (Althaea officinalis) of the mallow family native to Europe, Asia, and N Africa, found in marshy areas, having toothed leaves and pink flowers and a root that secretes a gummy substance originally used to make marshmallow. The marsh mallow has become naturalized in eastern North America.

marsh marigold a perennial marsh plant (Caltha palustris) of the buttercup family having roundish leaves and bright-yellow flowers.

marsh·y (mär′shē) adj. **marsh·i·er, marsh·i·est. 1** soft and wet like a marsh. **2** having many marshes. **3** of marshes. —**marsh′i·ness,** n.

mar·su·pi·al (mär süʹpē əl) n., adj. —n. any of an order (Marsupialia) of mammals typically lacking a placenta, and whose young are born at a very early stage of development, continuing their growth outside the womb while attached to the mother's nipples, usually inside a pouch, or marsupium. Kangaroos, bandicoots, wombats, and opossums are marsupials. —adj. **1** of, having to do with, or belonging to the order Marsupialia. **2** of, having to do with, or like a pouch.

mar·su·pi·um (mär süʹpē əm) n., pl. **-pi·a** (-pē ə). a pouch or fold of skin on the abdomen of a female marsupial for carrying the young. [< L < Gk. marsupion, dim. of marsipos pouch]

mart (märt) n. a market; a centre of trade. [< Du. markt market]

Mar·tel·lo tower (mär telʹō) a fort like a round tower, formerly built on coasts for defence against invasion. Also, **martello tower.** [< alteration (influenced by Ital. martello hammer) of Cape Mortella, Corsica, where such a tower was built]

mar·ten (märʹtən) n., pl. **-tens** or (esp. collectively) **-ten. 1** any of several small carnivorous mammals (genus Martes) related to the weasels, but larger, having a long, slender body and short legs. Martens spend most of their time in trees and are active mainly at night. **2** the valuable fur of marten. [ME < Du. martren < OF martrine, ult. < Gmc.]
☛ Hom. **martin.**

Mar·tha (märʹthə) n. **1** in the Bible, the sister of Lazarus and Mary (Luke 10: 38-42). **2** a practical woman who leads a busy, active life.

mar·tial (märʹshəl) adj. **1** of war; suitable for war: martial music. **2** fond of fighting; warlike; brave: a man of martial spirit. [ME < L Martialis < Mars, Martis Mars] —**mar′tial·ly,** adv.
☛ Syn. **1, 2.** See note at **military.**

martial law temporary rule by the army or militia with special military courts instead of by the usual civil authorities. Martial law is declared during a time of trouble or war.
☛ Usage. See note at **military law.**

Mar·tian (märʹshən) adj., n. —adj. of the planet Mars. —n. a supposed inhabitant of the planet Mars. [< L Martius of Mars]

mar·tin (märʹtən) n. any of various swallows, such as the black-and-white **house martin** (Delichon urbica) of Europe. See also **purple martin.** [< F Martin, the bird being supposed to migrate at Martinmas]
☛ Hom. **marten.**

mar·ti·net (märʹtə net′ or mär′tə net′) n. a person who enforces very strict discipline. [after Jean Martinet, a 17th-century French general]

mar·tin·gale (märʹtən gāl′) n. **1** the strap of a horse's harness that prevents the horse from rising on its hind legs or throwing back its head. **2** a rope or spar that steadies the jib boom on a ship. See **bowsprit** for picture. [< F martingale, ? ult. < Martigues, name of a town]

mar·ti·ni (mär tēʹnē) n. a cocktail made of gin and dry vermouth. [< Martini and Rossi, vermouth and wine makers]

Mar·tin·mas (märʹtən məs) n. November 11, a Christian church festival in honor of Saint Martin.

mar·tyr (märʹtər) n., v. —n. **1** a person who chooses to die or suffer rather than renounce his faith; a person who is put to death or made to suffer greatly for his religion or other beliefs. Many of the early Christians were martyrs. **2** a person who suffers great pain or anguish. **3** a person who puts on a false appearance of suffering in order to attract sympathy or attention.
—v. **1** put (a person) to death or torture because of his religion or other beliefs. **2** cause to suffer greatly; torture. [OE < L < Gk. martyr witness] —**mar′tyr·like′,** adj.

mar·tyr·dom (märʹtər dəm) n. **1** the death or suffering of a martyr. **2** great suffering; torment.

mar·vel (märʹvəl) n., v. **-velled** or **-veled, -vel·ling** or **-vel·ing.** —n. something wonderful; an astonishing thing: Television and the airplane are among the marvels of invention. —v. be filled with wonder; be astonished: She marvelled at the beautiful sunset. [ME < OF merveillier < VL < L mirabilia wonders, ult. < mirus strange]

mar·vel·lous or **mar·vel·ous** (märʹvəl əs) adj. **1** causing wonder; extraordinary. **2** improbable. **3** Informal. excellent; splendid; fine: a marvellous time. —**mar′vel·lous·ly** or **mar′vel·ous·ly,** adv. —**mar′vel·lous·ness** or **mar′vel·ous·ness,** n.
☛ Syn. **1.** See note at **wonderful.**

Marx·i·an (märkʹsē ən) adj., n. —adj. of or having to do with Karl Marx (1818-1883), a German writer on economics, or his theories. —n. Marxist.

Marx·ism (märkʹsiz əm) n. the political and economic theories of Karl Marx and Friedrich Engels, who interpreted history as a continuing economic class struggle and believed that the eventual result would be the establishment of a classless society and communal ownership of all natural and industrial resources.

Marx·ist (märkʹsist) n., adj. —n. a follower or disciple of Karl Marx or an advocate of his theories. —adj. of or having to do with Karl Marx or his theories; Marxian.

Mar·y (merʹē) n. in the Bible, the mother of Jesus (Matt. 1:18-25).

Mary Magdalene in the Bible, a woman from whom Jesus cast out seven devils (Luke 8:2).

mar·zi·pan (märʹzə pan′) n. a paste of ground almonds and sugar, often moulded into various forms. Also, **marchpane.** [< G < Ital. marzapane, a medieval coin < Arabic]

Ma·sai (mä sī′) n., pl. **Ma·sai** or **Ma·sais. 1** a tribe of tall hunting and cattle-raising natives of East Africa. **2** a member of this tribe.

masc. masculine.

M.A.Sc. Master of Applied Science.

mas·car·a (mas karʹə or mas kerʹə) n. a cosmetic preparation for darkening the eyelashes. [< Sp. máscara mask, Ital. maschera. See MASK.]

mas·cot (masʹkot) n. an animal, person, or thing supposed to bring good luck. [< F mascotte < Provençal mascotto, dim. of masco witch < Gmc.]

mas·cu·line (masʹkyə lin) adj., n. —adj. **1** of men; male. **2** like a man; manly; strong; vigorous. **3** having qualities suited to a man; mannish. **4** Grammar. of the gender to which male names normally belong. Actor, king, ram, and bull are masculine nouns.
—n. Grammar. **1** the masculine gender. **2** a word or form in the masculine gender. [< L masculinus, ult. < mas male] —**mas′cu·line·ly,** adv.
☛ Syn. adj. **1, 2.** See note at **male.**

masculine rhyme a rhyme in which the final syllables are stressed, as in disdain and complain.

mas·cu·lin·i·ty (masʹkyə lin′ə tē) n. a masculine quality or condition.

ma·ser (māʹzər) n. a device for amplifying microwaves to produce a very narrow, intense beam of radiation. [microwave amplification by stimulated emission of radiation]

mash (mash) n., v. —n. **1** a soft mixture; soft mass. **2** a warm mixture of bran or meal and water for horses and cattle. **3** any of various mixtures of ground grain, often supplemented with proteins, antibiotics, etc., used as feed for poultry, livestock, etc. **4** crushed malt or meal soaked in hot water for making beer. **5** a similar preparation of rye, corn, barley, etc., used to make whisky.
—v. **1** beat into a soft mass; crush to a uniform mass. **2** mix (crushed malt or meal) with hot water in brewing. [OE māsc-] —**mash′er,** n.

mask (mask) n., v. —n. **1** a covering for the face, worn for disguise or in fun: a Halloween mask. **2** anything that hides or disguises: He hid his evil plans under a mask of friendship. **3** Rare. a masked person. **4** a covering for the face, worn for protection from cold, etc.: a ski mask. **5** a covering for the nose and mouth, worn for protection against infection: a surgical mask. **6** a device covering the nose and mouth, designed to aid breathing, purify air before it is inhaled, etc.: a gas mask, an oxygen mask. **7** a clay, wax, or plaster likeness of a person's face. **8** the hollow figure of a human head worn by Greek and Roman actors to identify the character represented and increase the volume of the voice. **9** See **masque. 10** a carved or moulded face or head, usually grotesque, used as an architectural ornament.
—v. **1** cover (the face) with a mask. **2** hide; disguise: A smile masked his disappointment. [< F masque < Ital. maschera < Arabic maskhara′ buffoon < sakhira to ridicule] —**mask′er,** n.
☛ Hom. **masque.**

masked (maskt) adj. **1** wearing a mask; a masked gunman.

2 hidden or disguised; not apparent: *masked jealousy.*

masked ball a dance at which masks are worn.

mas·kin·onge (mas′kə nonj′) *n., pl.* **mas·kin·onge.** *Cdn.* muskellunge.

mas·och·ism (mas′ə kiz′əm *or* maz′ə kiz′əm) *n.* **1** a condition in which abnormal sexual pleasure results from being beaten, dominated, etc. Compare **sadism. 2** a tendency to experience pleasure from being mistreated, dominated, etc. [< Leopold Von Sacher-*Masoch* (1836–1895), an Austrian novelist who described the condition in his books]

mas·o·chist (mas′ə kist *or* maz′ə kist) *n.* a person who is characterized by masochism. —**mas′o·chis′tic,** *adj.*

ma·son (mā′sən) *n.* **1** a person whose work is building with stone, brick, or similar materials. **2** Usually, **Mason,** Freemason. [ME < OF *masson* < LL *machio, -onis,* probably < Gmc.]

Ma·son·ic (mə son′ik) *adj.* of or having to do with Freemasons or Freemasonry. Also, **masonic.**

Mason jar a wide-mouthed glass jar with a top that screws on, used especially for home canning and preserving. [after John L. *Mason,* an American inventor who patented such a jar. 19c.]

ma·son·ry (mā′sən rē) *n., pl.* **-ries. 1** the work done by a mason; stonework, brickwork, etc. **2** something constructed of stone, brick, etc., such as a chimney or wall. **3** the trade or skill of a mason. **4** Usually, **Masonry,** Freemasonry.

masque (mask) *n.* **1** an amateur dramatic entertainment in which fine costumes, scenery, music, and dancing are more important than the story. Masques were often given in England in the 16th and 17th centuries, at court and at the homes of nobles. **2** the play written for such an entertainment. **3** a masked ball; masquerade. [< F *masque.* See MASK.]
☞ *Hom.* **mask.**

mas·quer·ade (mas′kər ād′) *n., v.* **-ad·ed, -ad·ing.** —*n.* **1** a party or dance at which masks and fancy costumes are worn. **2** the costume and mask worn at such a party or dance. **3** a false pretence; disguise. **4** a going about or acting under false pretences. —*v.* **1** take part in a masquerade. **2** disguise oneself; go about under false pretences: *The king masqueraded as a beggar to find out if his people really liked him.* [< F < Ital. *mascherata* < *maschera.* See MASK.] —**mas′quer·ad′er,** *n.*

mass¹ (mas) *n., v.* —*n.* **1** a lump: *a mass of dough.* **2** a large quantity together: *a mass of flowers.* **3** the majority; greater part. **4** (*adj.*) done or occurring on a large scale: *mass buying, a mass protest.* **5** bulk; size. **6** *Physics.* a measure of the amount of matter a body contains. The bigger the mass of an object, the more force is needed to give it a particular acceleration. The mass of water is not changed by freezing it or changing it into steam, even though the volume changes. **7** a piece of metal having a specified mass, used to weigh something on a balance. **8** an expanse of color, light, shade, etc. in a painting. **9** *Pharmacy.* a thick, pasty preparation from which pills are made. **10 the masses,** the common people; the general population: *Most television programs are entertainment for the masses.* **11** (*adj.*) of, having to do with, or for the general population: *mass culture, a book designed for a mass market.*
in the mass, as a whole; without distinguishing parts or individuals. —*v.* form or collect into a mass; assemble. [ME < OF < L *massa* kneaded dough < Gk. *maza* barley bread < *massein* knead]

Mass or **mass²** (mas) *n.* **1** the central service of worship in the Roman Catholic Church and in some other Christian churches; Holy Eucharist as a sacrifice. The ritual of the Mass consists of various prayers and ceremonies. **2** a piece of music written for or suggested by certain parts of the Mass. [OE *mæsse* < LL *missa* < L *mittere* send away]

Mass. Massachusetts.

mas·sa·cre (mas′ə kər) *n., v.* **-cred, -cring.** —*n.* a wholesale, pitiless slaughter of people or animals. —*v.* kill (many people or animals) needlessly or cruelly; slaughter in large numbers. [< F *massacre,* in OF *macecle* shambles, ult. origin uncertain]

mas·sage (mə säzh′ *or* mə säj′) *n., v.* **-saged, -sag·ing.** —*n.* a rubbing and kneading of the body to stimulate the circulation of the blood and make the muscles and joints more supple: *A thorough massage relaxes tired muscles.* —*v.* give a massage to. [< F *massage,* ult. < *masse* mass]

mas·sa·sau·ga (mas′ə sô′gə *or* mas′ə sô′gə) *n.* a small rattlesnake (*Sistrurus catenatus*) found in southern Ontario and the E United States. [< *Mississauga* River, Ontario, < Algonquian (Ojibwa) < *misi* great + *sauk* river mouth]

mas·seur (ma sèr′; *French,* mä sœr′) *n.* a man whose work is massaging. [< F]

mas·seuse (ma sèz′; *French,* mä sœz′) *n.* a woman whose work is massaging.

mas·sif (mas′if; *French,* mä sēf′) *n. Geology.* **1** a main part or mass of a mountain range, surrounded by depressions. **2** a large

hat, āge, fär; let, ēqual, tèrm; it, īce
hot, ōpen, ôrder; oil, out; cup, pùt, rüle,
əbove, takən, pencəl, lemən, circəs
ch, child; ng, long; sh, ship
th, thin; ŦH, then; zh, measure

block of the earth's crust that has shifted as a unit and is bounded by faults. [< F]

mas·sive (mas′iv) *adj.* **1** big and heavy; large and solid; bulky: *a massive building, a massive wrestler.* **2** giving the impression of being large and broad: *a massive forehead.* **3** imposing; impressive. **4** in or by great numbers; broad in scope; extensive: *a massive assault, massive retaliation.* **5** of gold, silver, plate, etc., solid rather than hollow. **6 a** affecting a large area of bodily tissue: *a massive tumor.* **b** much larger or more than usual: *a massive dose.* **7** *Mineralogy.* not definitely crystalline. **8** *Geology.* without definite structural divisions. —**mas′sive·ly,** *adv.* —**mas′sive·ness,** *n.*

mass market the general population considered as a homogeneous market for goods or services. Goods produced for the mass market have to appeal to the average consumer. —**mass-market,** *adj.*

mass media the various modern means of communication that reach a vast audience, such as television, radio, motion pictures, and the press.

mass meeting a large public gathering of people to hear or discuss some matter of common interest.

mass number the whole number that most closely indicates the mass of an isotope, equal to the sum of the protons and neutrons in the nucleus.

mass–pro·duce (mas′prə dyüs′ *or* -prə düs′) *v.* **-duced, -duc·ing.** make or manufacture anything by mass production. —**mass′-pro·duc′er,** *n.*

mass production the making of goods in large quantities by machinery.

mass·y (mas′ē) *adj.* **mass·i·er, mass·i·est.** *Archaic or poetic.* massive. —**mass′i·ness,** *n.*

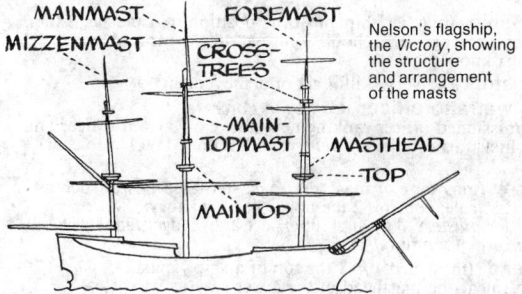

Nelson's flagship, the *Victory,* showing the structure and arrangement of the masts

MAINMAST
FOREMAST
MIZZENMAST
CROSS-TREES
MAIN-TOPMAST
MASTHEAD
TOP
MAINTOP

mast¹ (mast) *n.* **1** a long pole of wood or steel set upright to support the sails and rigging of a ship. **2** any upright pole: *a flag mast, a TV mast.*
before the mast, serving as an ordinary sailor. Sailors (not officers) used to sleep in the forward part of the ship.
[OE *mæst*] —**mast′less,** *adj.* —**mast′like′,** *adj.*

mast² (mast) *n.* acorns, chestnuts, beechnuts, etc. that have accumulated on the ground. Pigs eat mast. [OE *mæst*]

mas·ta·ba (mas′tə bə) *n.* an ancient Egyptian tomb, oblong in shape, with sloping sides and flat top, set over a mummy chamber or burial pit. [< Arabic *mastabah*]

mas·tec·to·my (ma stek′tə mē) *n.* the surgical removal of a breast.

mas·ter (mas′tər) *n., v.* **1** a person who has power or authority; one in control; employer; owner. **2** the man at the head of a household. **3** the captain of a merchant ship. **4** a male teacher, especially in private schools. **5** a great artist. **6** a picture or painting by a great artist: *an old master.* **7** a person who knows all about his work; expert. **8** a skilled workman, or craftsman, qualified to teach apprentices. **9 the Master,** Jesus. **10** a title of respect for a boy: *Master James Smith.* **11** (*adj.*) of or by a master. **12** (*adj.*) main; controlling: *a master switch, a master plan.*
13 See **master key. 14** victor. **15** a court officer appointed to assist the judge. **16** an initial recording, mould, stencil, etc. used for making duplications.
—*v.* **1** become master of; conquer; control. **2** become expert in;

become skilful at. [< OF *maistre*, OE *mægester* < L *magister*; cf. *magis* more]

mas·ter-at–arms (mas′tər ət ärmz′) *n., pl.* **mas·ters-at-arms.** a naval police officer who keeps order on a ship and takes charge of prisoners.

master builder 1 a person skilled in planning buildings; architect. 2 a person who directs the construction of buildings; contractor.

master corporal *Canadian Forces.* a non-commissioned officer ranking next above a corporal and below a sergeant. *Abbrev.*: M.Cpl. or MCpl See chart at **rank**[1].

mas·ter·ful (mas′tər fəl) *adj.* 1 fond of power or authority; domineering. 2 expert; skilful; masterly: *The actor gave a masterful performance.* —**mas′ter·ful·ly,** *adv.*

master key a key that opens all the different locks in a particular building, apartment block, etc.; passkey.

mas·ter·ly (mas′tər lē) *adj., adv.* —*adj.* expert; skilful: *Emily Carr was a masterly painter.* —*adv.* expertly; skilfully. —**mas′ter·li·ness,** *n.*

mas·ter·mind (mas′tər mīnd′) *n., v.* —*n.* a person who plans and directs a complex project. —*v.* plan and direct a complex project.

Master of Arts 1 a degree given by a college or university to a person who has completed an advanced course of study, or as an honor. *Abbrev.*: M.A. 2 a person who has this degree.

master of ceremonies a person in charge of a ceremony or entertainment who announces the successive events and makes sure that they take place in the proper order. *Abbrev.*: M.C.

Master of Science 1 a degree given by a college or university to a person who has completed an advanced course of study in science, or as an honor. *Abbrev.*: M.Sc. 2 a person who has this degree.

mas·ter·piece (mas′tər pēs′) *n.* 1 anything done or made with wonderful skill; a perfect piece of art or workmanship. 2 a person's greatest work.

master seaman *Canadian Forces.* in Maritime Command, the equivalent of a master corporal. *Abbrev.*: M.S. or MS See chart at **rank**[1].

mas·ter·ship (mas′tər ship′) *n.* 1 the position of a master. 2 the position of a teacher in a school. 3 power; rule; control. 4 great skill; expert knowledge.

master stroke a very skilful act or achievement.

master warrant officer *Canadian Forces.* a non-commissioned officer ranking next above a warrant officer and below a chief warrant officer. *Abbrev.*: M.W.O or MWO See chart at **rank**[1].

mas·ter·y (mas′tər ē *or* mas′trē) *n., pl.* **-ter·ies.** 1 power such as a master has; rule; control. 2 the upper hand; victory: *Two teams competed for mastery.* 3 great skill; expert knowledge: *Our teacher has a mastery of many subjects.*

mast·head (mast′hed′) *n.* 1 the top of a ship's mast. A crow's-nest near the masthead of the lower mast is used as a lookout. See **mast** for picture. 2 the part of a newspaper or magazine that gives the title, the names of the owners and editors and the publication address.

mas·tic (mas′tik) *n.* 1 a yellowish resin used in making varnish, chewing gum, and incense, and as an astringent. 2 any of various cements or mortars. [ME < OF < L < Gk. *mastichē*]

mas·ti·cate (mas′tə kāt′) *v.* **-cat·ed, -cat·ing.** 1 chew. 2 crush or knead (rubber, etc.) to a pulp. [< LL *masticare* < Gk. *mastichaein* gnash the teeth] —**mas′ti·ca′tion,** *n.*

mas·ti·ca·tor (mas′tə kā′tər) *n.* 1 an animal or organ that chews. 2 a machine for cutting things into small pieces.

mas·ti·ca·to·ry (mas′tə kə tô′rē) *adj., n., pl.* **-ries.** —*adj.* of chewing; used in chewing. —*n.* a substance chewed to increase the flow of saliva.

mas·tiff (mas′tif) *n.* a breed of large, strong dog having a short, thick coat, drooping ears, and hanging jowls. [ME < OF *mastin*, ult. < L *mansuetus* tame; influenced by OF *mestif* mongrel]

mas·ti·tis (ma stī′təs) *n.* inflammation of a breast or, in cows, sheep, etc., of the udder. [< Gk. *mastos* breast + E *-itis.* 19c.]

mas·to·don (mas′tə don′) *n.* any of several extinct elephant-like mammals (genus *Mammut*, also called *Mastodon*) that flourished from the Miocene to the Pleistocene epochs in the forests of Europe, Asia, and North America. [< NL < Gk. *mastos* breast + *odōn* tooth; from the nipple-like projections on its molars]

mas·toid (mas′toid) *n.* the projection of bone behind the ear. [< Gk. *mastoeidēs* < *mastos* breast + *eidos* form]

mas·toid·i·tis (mas′toid ī′tis) *n.* inflammation of the mastoid.

mas·tur·bate (mas′tər bāt′) *v.* **-bat·ed, -bat·ing.** engage in masturbation. [< L *masturbari*] —**mas′tur·ba′tor,** *n.*

mas·tur·ba·tion (mas′tər bā′shən) *n.* the manipulation of the genitals to induce sexual excitement.

mat[1] (mat) *n., v.* **mat·ted, mat·ting.** —*n.* 1 a piece of coarse fabric like a rug, made of woven grass, straw, rope, etc. 2 a piece of material to put under a dish, vase, lamp, etc. 3 a large, thick pad on the floor of a ring, etc. to protect wrestlers or gymnasts. 4 anything packed or tangled thickly together: *a mat of weeds, a mat of hair.* —*v.* 1 cover with mats. 2 pack or tangle together like a mat: *The swimmer's wet hair was matted. The fur collar mats when it gets wet.* [OE *matt* < LL *matta*]
☞ *Hom.* **matte.**

mat[2] (mat) *n., v.* **mat·ted, mat·ting.** —*n.* a border for a picture, usually between the picture and the frame. Also, **matte.** —*v.* put a mat around. [< F *mat*, originally adj., dull, dead. See MAT[3].]
☞ *Hom.* **matte.**

mat[3] (mat) *adj., n., v.* **mat·ted, mat·ting.** —*adj.* dull; not shiny. —*n.* a dull surface or finish. Also, **matte.** —*v.* give a dull finish to. [< F *mat* < *mater* subdue, checkmate]
☞ *Hom.* **matte.**

mat[4] (mat) *n.* matrix.
☞ *Hom.* **matte.**

mat. 1 matinee. 2 matins. 3 maturity.

mat·a·dor (mat′ə dôr′) *n.* the chief performer in a bullfight: *The matador kills the bull with his sword.* [< Sp. *matador* < *matar* kill < Arabic *mat*]

match[1] (mach) *n., v.* —*n.* 1 a short, slender piece of wood or pasteboard tipped with a mixture that takes fire when rubbed on a rough or specially prepared surface. 2 a cord prepared to burn at a uniform rate, for firing guns and cannon. [ME < OF *mesche*, probably ult. < Gk. *myxa* lamp wick, influenced by VL *muccare* snuff < L *muccus* mucus]

match[2] (mach) *n., v.* —*n.* 1 a person or thing equal to another. 2 a person or thing like another. 3 two persons or things that are alike and go well together: *Those two horses make a good match.* 4 a game; contest: *a boxing match, a tennis match.* 5 marriage. 6 a person considered as a possible husband or wife. —*v.* 1 be equal to; be a match for. 2 be alike; go well together. 3 be the same as. 4 find one like; get a match for. 5 make like; fit together. 6 put in opposition; oppose. 7 marry. [OE (ge)*mæcca* companion] —**match′er,** *n.*

match·book (mach′búk′) *n.* a small paper folder to hold safety matches, having a striking surface on the cover.

match·box (mach′boks′) *n.* a stiff cardboard box for matches, usually having a striking surface on one side.

match·less (mach′lis) *adj.* so great or wonderful that it cannot be equalled. —**match′less·ly,** *adv.* —**match′less·ness,** *n.*

match·lock (mach′lok′) *n.* an old type of gun fired by lighting the charge of powder with a wick or cord.

match·mak·er[1] (mach′māk′ər) *n.* 1 a person who arranges, or tries to arrange, marriages for others. 2 a person who arranges contests, prize fights, races, etc. [*match*[2] + *maker*]

match·mak·er[2] (mach′māk′ər) *n.* a person who makes matches for lighting. [*match*[1] + *maker*]

match·mak·ing[1] (mach′māk′ing) *n., adj.* —*n.* 1 the practice of trying to arrange marriages. 2 the business of arranging contests, prize fights, races, etc. —*adj.* having to do with matchmakers or matchmaking.

match·mak·ing[2] (mach′māk′ing) *n., adj.* —*n.* the business of making matches for lighting. —*adj.* of or having to do with matchmakers or matchmaking.

match play 1 *Golf.* a form of competition in which the game is won by the winner of the greatest number of holes rather than by the player or side taking the fewest strokes. 2 a play in any match, as in tennis or hardball.

match point *Tennis, etc.* the final point needed to win a game.

match·stick (mach′stik′) *n.* a small, thin stick of wood from which a match is made.

match·wood (mach′wúd′) *n.* 1 wood for making matches. 2 splinters; tiny pieces.

mate[1] (māt) *n., v.* **mat·ed, mat·ing.** —*n.* 1 one of a pair. 2 either of two animals or birds (male and female) who have come together as a pair: *The eagle mourned his dead mate.* 3 a husband or wife. 4 a ship's officer next below the captain. On large ships there is usually more than one mate: a first mate, a second mate, and sometimes, a third mate. 5 assistant. 6 a companion or fellow worker: *John and Bill were mates in the army.* —*v.* 1 put, bring, or come together as a pair: *Birds mate in the*

spring. 2 marry. [apparently < MLG *mate* messmate. Akin to
MEAT.]

mate² (māt) *n., v.* **mat·ed, mat·ing;** *interj. Chess.* —*n.*
a checkmate.
—*v.* checkmate; defeat.
—*interj.* checkmate. [ME < OF *mater* checkmate < *mat*
checkmated, defeated < Arabic]

ma·té or **ma·te³** (mä′tā or mat′ā) *n.* **1** a stimulating beverage
made from the dried aromatic leaves of a South American holly
(*Ilex paraguariensis*). Maté is a popular drink in many South
American countries. **2** the dried leaves, containing caffeine, from
which the drink is made. **3** the plant itself. [< Sp. < Quechua
(Indian lang. of Peru) *mati* calabash dish]

ma·ter (mā′tər) *n. Brit. Informal.* mother. [< L]

ma·te·ri·al (mə tēr′ē əl) *n., adj.* —*n.* **1** what a thing is made
from; substance of anything manufactured or built: *building
materials, raw materials.* **2** cloth: *I have enough material for a jacket
and pants.* **3** anything serving as crude or raw matter for working
upon or developing: *His files contain enough material for a score of
books.* **4** a person thought of in terms of his potential in a given field
or occupation: *Her coach is sure that she is Olympic material.*
—*adj.* **1** having to do with whatever occupies space; of matter;
physical. **2** of the body: *Food and shelter are material comforts.*
3 caring more for things of this world than for intellectual or
spiritual needs. **4** that matters; important: *Hard work is a material
factor in success.* [ME < OF < LL *materialis* < *materia* timber,
matter < *mater* trunk (of a tree). Doublet of MATÉRIEL.]
☞ *Syn. n.* See note at **substance.**

ma·te·ri·al·ism (mə tēr′ē əl iz′əm) *n.* **1** *Philosophy.* the doctrine
that matter is the fundamental reality and that all thought, feeling,
etc. can be explained in terms of physical laws. **2** a tendency to care
more for material possessions, physical wellbeing, etc. than for
intellectual or spiritual needs.

ma·te·ri·al·ist (mə tēr′ē əl ist) *n.* **1** a person who advocates
materialism. **2** a person who cares more for material possessions
and physical wellbeing than for intellectual or spiritual needs.

ma·te·ri·al·is·tic (mə tēr′ē əl is′tik) *adj.* of materialism; of
materialists. —**ma·te′ri·al·is′ti·cal·ly,** *adv.*

ma·te·ri·al·ize (mə tēr′ē əl īz′) *v.* **-ized, -iz·ing. 1** become an
actual fact; be realized: *Our plans for the party did not materialize.*
2 give material form to: *An inventor materializes his ideas by
building a model.* **3** appear or cause to appear in material or bodily
form: *A spirit materialized from the smoke of the magician's fire.*
4 cause to appear in bodily form. —**ma·te′ri·al·i·za′tion,** *n.*

ma·te·ri·al·ly (mə tēr′ē əl ē) *adv.* **1** with regard to material
things; physically: *He improved materially and morally.*
2 considerably; greatly. **3** in matter or substance; not in form.

ma·te·ri·a med·i·ca (mə tēr′ē ə med′ə kə) **1** drugs or other
substances used in medicine. **2** the branch of medical science
dealing with these drugs and substances. [< NL *materia medica*
medical matter]

ma·té·ri·el (mə tēr′ē el′) *n.* everything used by an army,
organization, undertaking, etc.; equipment. [< F *matériel* material
< L *materialis.* Doublet of MATERIAL.]

ma·ter·nal (mə tėr′nəl) *adj.* **1** of or like a mother; motherly.
2 related on the mother's side of the family: *maternal grandparents.*
3 received or inherited from a mother. [< F *maternel* < L *maternus*
< *mater* mother] —**ma·ter′nal·ly,** *adv.*

ma·ter·ni·ty (mə tėr′nə tē) *n., adj.* —*n.* **1** motherhood; being a
mother. **2** motherliness; qualities of a mother. —*adj.* for an
expectant mother: *a maternity dress.*

maternity hospital a hospital providing facilities for childbirth
and care for the mothers and their new-born babies.

math (math) *n. Informal.* mathematics.

math. mathematical; mathematician.

math·e·mat·i·cal (math′ə mat′ə kəl or math mat′ə kəl) *adj.* **1** of
or having to do with mathematics. **2** exact; accurate.
—**math′e·mat′i·cal·ly,** *adv.*

math·e·ma·ti·cian (math′ə mə tish′ən or math′mə tish′ən) *n.*
a person trained in mathematics, especially one whose work it is.

math·e·mat·ics (math′ə mat′iks or math mat′iks) *n.* (*used with
a singular verb*). the science dealing with the measurement,
properties, and relationships of quantities. Mathematics includes
arithmetic, algebra, geometry, calculus, etc. [pl. of *mathematic* < L
mathematicus < Gk. *mathēmatikos,* ult. < *manthanein* learn]

mat·i·née or **mat·i·nee** (mat′ə nā′ or mat′ə nā′) *n.*
a performance held in the afternoon, especially a dramatic or
musical one. [< F *matinée* < *matin* morning]

ma·tins (mat′ənz) *n. pl.* **1** *Roman Catholic Church.* the first of
the seven canonical hours in the breviary. **2** *Anglican Church.*
morning service; morning prayers. **3** Also, **matin.** *Poetic.* morning

mate   **707**   **matter**

hat, āge, fär; let, ēqual, tėrm; it, īce
hot, ōpen, ôrder; oil, out; cup, pût, rüle,
əbove, takən, pencəl, lemən, circəs
ch, child; ng, long; sh, ship
th, thin; ₮H, then; zh, measure

song. [ME < OF < LL *matutinus* of or in the morning < *Matuta*
dawn goddess]

ma·tri·arch (mā′trē ärk′) *n.* **1** a mother who is the ruler of a
family or tribe. **2** a venerable old woman. [< *matri-* (< L *mater,
matris* mother) + patri*arch*]

ma·tri·ar·chal (mā′trē är′kəl) *adj.* **1** of a matriarch or
matriarchy. **2** suitable for a matriarch.

ma·tri·ar·chy (mā′trē är′kē) *n., pl.* **-chies.** a form of social
organization in which the mother is the ruler of a family or tribe and
in which descent is traced through the mother.

matric. or **matric** matriculation.

ma·tri·ces (mā′trə sēz′ or mat′rə sēz′) *n.* pl. of **matrix.**

ma·tri·cid·al (mā′trə sīd′əl or mat′rə sīd′əl) *adj.* of, having to
do with, or involving matricide.

ma·tri·cide (mā′trə sīd′ or mat′rə sīd′) *n.* **1** the act of killing
one's own mother. **2** a person who kills his mother. [< L
matricidium the murder of one's mother < *mater* mother + *-cidium*
act of killing (for def. 1); < L *matricida* one who murders his
mother < *mater* + *-cida* killer (for def. 2). 16c.]

ma·tric·u·late (mə trik′yə lāt′) *v.* **-lat·ed, -lat·ing. 1** enrol as a
student in a college or university. **2** enrol as a candidate for a
degree. [< LL *matricula,* dim. of L. *matrix, -icis* register]
—**ma·tric′u·la·tor,** *n.*

ma·tric·u·la·tion (mə trik′yə lā′shən) *n.* **1** an examination held
at the end of secondary school or as a university entrance
requirement. **2** the necessary qualification for university entrance.
3 the act of matriculating or the state of being matriculated.

ma·tri·lin·e·al (ma′trə lin′ē əl or mā′trə lin′ē əl) *adj.* of, having
to do with, or designating descent or kinship through the maternal
line: *a matrilineal tradition.* —**ma′tri·lin′e·al·ly,** *adv.*

mat·ri·mo·ni·al (mat′rə mō′nē əl) *adj.* of marriage; having to do
with marriage.

mat·ri·mo·ni·al·ly (mat′rə mō′nē əl ē) *adv.* **1** according to the
custom or laws of matrimony. **2** with regard to matrimony. **3** by
matrimony.

mat·ri·mo·ny (mat′rə mō′nē) *n., pl.* **-nies. 1** married life. **2** the
act of marrying; the rite or ceremony of marriage. **3** the relation
between married persons. [< L *matrimonium* < *mater* mother]
☞ *Syn.* **2, 3.** See note at **marriage.**

ma·trix (mā′triks or mat′riks) *n., pl.* **ma·tri·ces** or **ma·trix·es.**
1 that which gives origin or form to something enclosed within it. A
mould for a casting or the rock in which gems are embedded is
called a matrix. **2** *Printing.* a mould for casting faces of type.
3 womb. [< L *matrix* womb]

ma·tron (mā′trən) *n.* **1** a married woman or widow, especially a
staid or dignified woman of middle age or older. **2** a woman who
manages the household affairs or supervises the inmates of a
school, hospital, or other institution. **3** a woman who is placed in
charge of female prisoners in a jail, penitentiary, etc. [ME < OF <
L *matrona* < *mater* mother]

ma·tron·ly (mā′trən lē) *adj.* like a matron; suitable for a matron;
dignified. —**ma′tron·li·ness,** *n.*

matron of honor or **honour** a married woman who is the
chief attendant of the bride at a wedding.

Matt. Matthew.

matte¹ (mat) *n.* an impure mixture of sulphides produced during
the smelting of a sulphide ore. [< F dial. *mate* lump]
☞ *Hom.* **mat.**

matte² (mat) *n.* See **mat²** and **mat³.**

mat·ted¹ (mat′id) *adj.* formed into a mat; entangled in a thick
mass: *a matted growth of shrubs.* [< *mat¹*]

mat·ted² (mat′id) *adj.* having a dull finish. [< *mat³*]

mat·ter (mat′ər) *n., v.* —*n.* **1** the material of which something is
made or composed; substance. **2** the substance of the material
world; the opposite of mind or spirit. Matter occupies space. **3** a
concern or occasion: *business matters, a matter of life and death.*
4 what is said or written, thought of apart from the way in which it
is said or written; content: *There was very little matter of interest in
his speech.* **5** grounds or cause; basis: *If a person is robbed, he has
matter for complaint to the police.* **6** an instance or case; a thing: *a
matter of fact, a matter of record, a matter of business.* **7** things

written or printed: *reading matter.* **8** an amount or quantity: *a matter of 20 kilometres.* **9** importance; significance. **10** mail: *Letters are first-class matter.* **11** a substance secreted by a living body, especially pus. **12** *Printing.* **a** something to be printed; copy. **b** type that has been composed.

as a matter of fact, actually; in reality.

for that matter, so far as that is concerned.

matter of course, something to be expected.

matter of opinion, a debatable assertion or belief.

no matter, a it is not important; let it go. **b** regardless of: *He wants a bicycle, no matter what it costs.*

what is the matter? what is wrong?

—*v.* **1** be important: *Nothing seems to matter when you are very sick.* **2** form or discharge pus. [ME < AF *matere* < L *materia,* originally, timber]

☛ *Syn. n.* See note at **substance.**

mat·ter–of–fact (mat′ər əv fakt′) *adj.* dealing with facts; not imaginative or fanciful: *a matter-of-fact report.*

mat·ting (mat′ing) *n.* fabric of grass, straw, hemp, or other fibre, for covering floors, for mats, for wrapping material, etc.

mat·tock (mat′ək) *n.* a tool like a pickaxe, but having a flat, adze-like blade on one or both sides. It is used for loosening soil and cutting roots. [OE *mattuc*]

mat·tress (mat′ris) *n.* a thick, more or less soft or resilient pad consisting of padded, coiled springs or material such as foam, rubber, cotton, or straw encased in a covering of strong cloth and used to form a bed or part of a bed. [ME < OF < Ital. *materasso* < Arabic *almatrah* cushion]

mat·u·rate (mach′ů rāt′) *v.* **-rat·ed, -rat·ing. 1** discharge pus; suppurate. **2** ripen; mature. [< L *maturare* < *maturus* ripe]

mat·u·ra·tion (mach′ů rā′shən) *n.* **1** a discharge of pus; suppuration. **2** a ripening; a maturing. **3** *Biology.* the final stages in the preparation of germ cells for fertilization.

ma·ture (mə chůr′ *or* mə tyůr′) *adj., v.* **-tured, -tur·ing.** —*adj.* **1** ripe or full-grown: *Grain is harvested when it is mature.* **2** having or showing full development of the body, mind, etc.: *a mature face, mature thinking.* **3** brought by time, treatment, etc. to the condition of full excellence: *mature wine, mature cheese.* **4** fully worked out; carefully and completely thought out: *By next year we will have a mature plan for the subway.* **5** due; payable: *a mature loan.*
—*v.* **1** come or bring to full growth; ripen: *The apples are maturing rapidly. We need more sun to mature the crops.* **2** of the body, mind, etc., come or bring to full development: *The experience has matured her understanding.* **3** make or become ready or complete: *to mature a plan.* **4** fall due; become payable: *The bonds will mature in ten years.* [< L *maturus* ripe] —**ma·ture′ly,** *adv.* —**ma·ture′ness,** *n.* —**ma·tur′er,** *n.*

ma·tu·ri·ty (mə chůr′ə tē *or* mə tyůr′ə tē) *n.* **1** a state of ripeness; full development. **2** a being completed or ready: *When their plans reached maturity, they were able to begin.* **3** a falling due; the time a debt is payable.

ma·tu·ti·nal (mə tyü′tə nəl *or* mə tü′tə nəl) *adj.* occurring in the morning; early in the day; having to do with the morning. [< LL *matutinalis* < *matutinus* of or in the morning. See MATINS.]

matz·o (mät′sō) *n., pl.* **matz·oth** (mät′sōth) **or matz·os** (mät′sōs). a thin piece of unleavened bread, eaten by Jews especially during the Passover. [< Hebrew *matstsōth,* pl. of *matstsāh,* a cake of unleavened bread]

maud·lin (mod′lən *or* môd′lən) *adj.* **1** sentimental in a weak, silly way: *maudlin sympathy.* **2** sentimental and tearful as a result of drinking too much alcoholic liquor. [alteration of Mary *Magdalene,* often painted as weeping]

mau·ger (mo′gər *or* mô′gər) See **maugre.**

mau·gre (mo′gər *or* mô′gər) *prep. Archaic.* in spite of; notwithstanding. [ME < OF *maugre,* originally n., ill will < L *malus* bad + *gratus* pleasing]

maul (mol *or* môl) *v., n.* —*v.* beat and pull about; handle roughly: *The lion mauled its keeper badly.* —*n.* a very heavy hammer or mallet. [var. of *mall*]

Mau Mau (mou′ mou′) a secret society consisting chiefly of Kikuyu tribesmen sworn to expel Europeans from Kenya by violent means, active approximately between 1952 and 1956.

maun·der (mon′dər *or* môn′dər) *v.* **1** talk in a rambling, foolish way: *People who maunder talk much but say little.* **2** move or act in an aimless, confused manner: *The injured man maundered about in a daze.* [origin uncertain] —**maun′der·er,** *n.*

Maun·dy Thursday (mon′dē *or* môn′di) the Thursday before Easter. [*Maundy,* ME < OF *mande* < L *mandatum* a command]

Mau·ser (mou′zər) *n. Trademark.* a kind of powerful repeating rifle or pistol. [after Paul *Mauser* (1838-1914), a German inventor]

mau·so·le·um (mo′sə lē′əm *or* mô-, mo′zə lē′əm *or* mô′-) *n., pl.* **-le·ums, -le·a** (-lē′ə). **1** Mausoleum, at Halicarnassus, the magnificent tomb of King Mausolos of Caria, in ancient times a kingdom in SW Asia Minor. The tomb was one of the seven wonders of the ancient world. **2** a large, magnificent tomb. [< L < Gk. *Mausōleion.*]

mauve (mōv, mov, *or* môv) *n. or adj.* delicate, pale purple. [< F < L *malva* mallow. Doublet of MALLOW.]

mav·er·ick (mav′ər ik) *n.* **1** a calf or other animal not marked with an owner's brand. **2** *Esp.U.S. Informal.* one who refuses to affiliate with a regular political party. **3** *Informal.* any person or organization that is unconventional or unwilling to conform; a rebel. [probably after Samuel *Maverick* (1803-1870), a Texan who did not brand his cattle]

ma·vis (mā′vis) *n.* the song thrush of Europe. [ME < OF *mauvis* < Celtic]

ma·vour·neen *or* **ma·vour·nin** (mə vür′nēn) *n. Irish.* my darling. [< Irish *mo mhuirnín*]

maw (mo *or* mô) *n.* **1** the mouth and throat of an animal, especially a carnivorous animal. **2** the stomach of an animal or bird. **3** anything thought of as resembling this in appetite: *Nations continue to pour wealth into the maw of war.* [OE *maga*]

mawk·ish (mok′ish *or* môk′ish) *adj.* **1** sickening. **2** sickly sentimental; weakly emotional. [originally, maggoty < *mawk* maggot < ON *mathkr*] —**mawk′ish·ly,** *adv.* —**mawk′ish·ness,** *n.*

max. maximum.

maxi– *combining form.* large; great; long: *a maxi-skirt.*

max·il·la (mak sil′ə) *n., pl.* **max·il·lae** (mak sil′ē *or* mak sil′ī). **1** in vertebrates, the jaw; jawbone; upper jawbone. **2** either of a pair of appendages just behind the mandibles of insects, crabs, etc. See **mandible** for picture. [< L *maxilla* jaw]

max·il·lar·y (mak′sə ler′ē) *adj., n., pl.* **-lar·ies.** —*adj.* of or having to do with the jaw or jawbone. —*n.* the maxilla.

max·im (mak′səm) *n.* a short rule of conduct; proverb; statement of a general truth: *"Look before you leap" is a maxim.* [ME < OF < LL *maxima (propositio)* axiom, literally, greatest proposition]

max·i·ma (mak′sə mə) *n.* a pl. of **maximum.**

max·i·mize (mak′sə mīz′) *v.* **-mized, -miz·ing.** increase or intensify as much as possible; make as great as possible. [< *maximum* + *-ize*] —**max′i·mi·za′tion,** *n.*

max·i·mum (mak′sə məm) *n., pl.* **-mums** *or* **-ma;** *adj.* —*n.* **1** the largest or highest amount; greatest possible amount: *He had decided that he would spend a maximum of $1000 at the auction.* **2** *Mathematics.* the greatest value of a function within a given interval of the domain of the function. —*adj.* largest; highest; greatest possible: *The maximum score on the test is 100.* [< L *maximum,* neut. adj., superlative of *magnus* great]

may (mā) *auxiliary v.* **might.** *May* is used to express: **1** possibility, opportunity, or permission: *You may enter.* **2** a wish or prayer: *May you be very happy.* **3** contingency, especially in clauses, expressing condition, concession, purpose, result, etc.: *I write that you may know my plans.* **4** ability or power (more commonly *can*). [OE *mæg*]
☛ *Usage.* See note at **can.**

May (mā) *n.* the fifth month of the year. It has 31 days. [< L *Maius*]

ma·ya (mä′yə) *n. Hinduism.* illusory nature of the sense world, often personified as a woman. [< Skt.]

Ma·ya (mä′yə) *n., pl.* **Ma·ya** *or* **Ma·yas. 1** a member of any of a large group of Amerindian peoples mainly of Yucatán, Belize, and Guatemala, who speak Mayan languages. **2** a member of the branch of the Maya living in Yucatán. The ancient Maya are famous for the remarkable civilization they developed, which flourished between about A.D. 250 and 900. **3** a Mayan language of the ancient Maya.

Ma·yan (mä′yən) *n., adj.* —*n.* **1** a language family of Mexico and Central America. **2** Maya (defs. 1 and 2). —*adj.* of or having to do with the Maya or their language.

may·ap·ple *or* **May apple** (mā′ap′əl) *n.* **1** a perennial herb (*Podophyllum peltatum*) of the barberry family found in E North America, having a single large, white flower and an edible, yellowish, oval fruit. **2** the fruit of this plant.

may·be (mā′bē) *adv.* possibly; perhaps; it may be so.
☛ *Usage.* **Maybe, may be. Maybe** is an adverb meaning "perhaps"; **may be** is a verb form: *Maybe you'll have better luck next time. He may be the next mayor.*

May·day (mā′dā′) *n.* an international signal of distress, used in emergencies by ships and aircraft. [< F *m'aider* help me]

May Day May 1, traditionally celebrated as a festival of spring, accompanied by the crowning of a May queen, and dancing around the Maypole. It is now celebrated as Labor Day in some countries.

May·fair (mā′fer′) *n.* **1** a fashionable section of London. **2** fashionable London society.

may·flow·er (mā′flou′ər) n. **1** trailing arbutus. **2** any of various other flowering plants that bloom in spring, such as the hawthorn. **3 Mayflower,** the ship on which the Pilgrims came to America in 1620.

may·fly (mā′flī′) n., pl. **-flies. 1** any of an order (Ephemeroptera) of insects, the larva of which is aquatic and the adult having large, membranous, triangular forewings, small hind wings, and a slender body. The mayfly lives as a larva for two or more years, but only a day or two as a winged adult. **2** an artificial fishing fly made in imitation of this insect.

may·hap (mā′hap′ or mā′hap′) adv. Archaic. perhaps. [for it may hap]

may·hem (mā′hem or mā′əm) n. **1** Law. the crime of maiming a person or injuring him so that he is less able to defend himself. **2** confusion and willful violence. [< AF mahaym maim; origin uncertain]

May·ing (mā′ing) n. the celebration of May Day; taking part in May festivities.

may·n't (mā′ənt or mānt) may not.

may·on·naise (mā′ə nāz′) n. a thick dressing for salads, made of egg yolks, vegetable oil, vinegar or lemon juice, and seasoning. [< F mayonnaise, ult. < Mahón, a seaport in Minorca, captured by the Duc de Richelieu, whose chef introduced the Mahonnaise after his master's victory]

may·or (mā′ər or mer) n. the person at the head of the government of a city, town, or village. [ME < OF maire, maor < L major. Doublet of MAJOR.]

may·or·al·ty (mā′ər əl tē or mer′əl tē) n., pl. **-ties. 1** the position of mayor. **2** a mayor's term of office.

May·pole or **may·pole** (mā′pōl′) n. a high pole decorated with flowers and ribbons, around which merrymakers dance on May Day.

May queen a girl crowned with flowers and honored as queen on May Day.

mayst (māst) v. Archaic. 2nd pers. sing. present tense of **may.** Thou mayst means you (sing.) may.

May·time (mā′tīm′) n. the month of May.

maze (māz) n. **1** a network of paths through which it is hard to find one's way. **2** any complicated arrangement, as of streets, buildings, etc. **3** a state of confusion; muddled condition. [var. of amaze]
► Hom. **maize.**

ma·zu·ma (mə zü′mə) n. Slang. money. [< Yiddish < Hebrew mazumon]

ma·zur·ka or **ma·zour·ka** (mə zèr′kə or mə zür′kə) n. **1** a lively Polish dance. **2** the music for this dance, in 3/4 or 3/8 time. [< Polish mazurka, a dance of Mazur (Mazovia), a province of Poland]

maz·y (māz′ē) adj. **maz·i·er, maz·i·est.** like a maze; intricate. —**maz′i·ly,** adv. —**maz′i·ness,** n.

MB 1 Cdn. Medal of Bravery. **2** Manitoba (used esp. in computerized address systems).

M.B.A. Master of Business Administration.

M.B.E. Member of (the Order of) the British Empire.

MC Cdn. Member of the Order of Canada.

M.C. 1 Military Cross. **2** Member of Congress. **3** master of ceremonies. **4** Medical Corps.

McCar·thy·ism (mə kär′thē iz′əm) n. **1** the act or practice of making sensational public accusations of political disloyalty or corruption, usually with little evidence. **2** the practice of holding public investigations, supposedly to reveal Communist sympathy or activity. [< Senator Joseph R. McCarthy (1909-1957), chairman of the U.S. Senate Permanent Investigations Committee]

Mc·Coy (mə koi′) n.
the real McCoy, a genuine person or thing. [origin uncertain]

Mc·In·tosh (mak′ən tosh′) n. a bright-red winter apple having crisp, white flesh. [< John McIntosh (1777-?), an Ontario farmer, who discovered the tree producing this apple in 1811]

McIntosh Red McIntosh apple.

MCpl. or **MCpl** master corporal.

Md mendelevium.

Md. Maryland.

MD Maryland.

M.D. 1 Doctor of Medicine (for L Medicinae Doctor). **2** Municipal District.

MDB or **M.D.B.** Maritime Development Board.

M.D.S. Master of Dental Surgery.

---

hat, āge, fär; let, ēqual, tèrm; it, īce
hot, ōpen, ôrder; oil, out; cup, put, rüle,
əbove, takən, pencəl, lemən, circəs

ch, child; ng, long; sh, ship
th, thin; ₮H, then; zh, measure

mdse. merchandise.

MDT, M.D.T., or **m.d.t.** Mountain Daylight Time.

M. du C. Médaille du Canada.

me (mē; unstressed, mi) pron. the objective form of I: The dog bit me. Give me a bandage. [OE mē]
► Usage. It is good English to say It is me (or It's me) in speech, though some people consider It is I to be correct in writing. Except in written conversation, It's me rarely occurs in writing.

Me methyl.

Me. Maine.

ME Maine.

ME or **M.E.** Middle English.

M.E. 1 Master of Engineering. **2** Mechanical Engineer. **3** Mining Engineer. **4** Methodist Episcopal.

mead¹ (mēd) n. Poetic. meadow. [OE mǣd]
► Hom. **meed, Mede.**

mead² (mēd) n. an alcoholic drink made from fermented honey. [OE medu]
► Hom. **meed, Mede.**

mead·ow (med′ō) n. **1** a piece of grassy land; a field where hay is grown. **2** low, wet, grassy land near a stream. [OE mǣdwe, oblique case of mǣd mead¹]

meadow·lark either of two North American songbirds (Sturnella neglecta and S. magna) of the same family as the blackbirds and orioles, both having mottled brown upper parts and yellow under parts, with a black crescent on the breast. The bubbling song of the western meadowlark (S. neglecta) is very different from the high whistle of the eastern meadowlark.

mead·ow·sweet (med′ō swēt′) n. **1** any of several North American plants (genus Spiraea) of the rose family having clusters of small, fragrant flowers. **2** a Eurasian plant (Filipendula ulmaria) of the rose family having dense clusters of small, fragrant, whitish flowers.

mead·ow·y (med′ō ē) adj. **1** like a meadow. **2** of meadows.

mea·gre (mē′gər) adj. **1** poor or scanty: a meagre meal. **2** thin or lean: a meagre face. **3** without fullness or richness; deficient in quality. Also, **meager.** [ME < OF maigre < L macer thin] —**mea′gre·ly,** adv. —**mea′gre·ness,** n.
► Syn. **1.** See note at **scanty.**

meal¹ (mēl) n. **1** breakfast, lunch, dinner, supper, or tea. **2** the food served or eaten at any one time. [OE mǣl]

meal² (mēl) n. **1** ground grain, especially corn meal. **2** anything ground to a powder. [OE melu]

meal ticket 1 a ticket authorizing a person to obtain a meal. **2** Slang. someone or something that provides a living for another or others.

meal·time (mēl′tīm′) n. the usual time for eating a meal.

meal·y (mēl′ē) adj. **meal·i·er, meal·i·est. 1** like meal; dry and powdery. **2** of meal. **3** covered with meal. **4** pale. **5** mealy-mouthed. —**meal′i·ness,** n.

meal·y–mouthed (mēl′ē mou₮Hd′ or -moutht′) adj. unwilling to tell the truth in plain words; using soft, insincere words.

mean¹ (mēn) v. **meant, mean·ing. 1** refer to; signify; denote: What does this word mean? **2** indicate or intend to express: Keep out; that means you. **3** convey; communicate: What is that look supposed to mean? **4** have as a purpose; have in mind; intend: I do not mean to go. **5** have intentions of some kind; be minded or disposed: She means well. **6** design for a definite purpose: This toy is meant for young children. **7** destine: Fate meant us for each other. He was meant for a soldier.
mean well by, have kindly feelings toward.
[OE mǣnan]
► Hom. **mien.**
► Syn. **4.** See note at **intend.**

mean² (mēn) adj. **1** low in quality or grade; poor. **2** low in social position or rank; humble: A peasant is of mean birth. **3** of little importance or value: the meanest flower. **4** of poor appearance; shabby: a mean house. **5** small-minded; ignoble: mean thoughts. **6** stingy; mean about money. **7** Informal. humiliated; ashamed; feel mean. **8** Informal. hard to manage; troublesome; bad-tempered: a mean horse. **9** selfish and ill-tempered; vicious; cruel. **10** Informal.

in poor physical condition; unwell: *I feel mean today.* **11** *Slang.* expert; effected with skill.

no mean, very good.

[OE (ge)mæne common] —**mean′ly,** *adv.*

☞ *Hom.* **mien.**

mean³ (mēn) *adj.* **1** halfway between the two extremes of a set of values; average: *The mean temperature for July in Yarmouth is 16.4°C.* **2** intermediate in kind, quality, or degree. **3** having a value intermediate between the values of other quantities: *a mean diameter.* —*n.* **1** the average; arithmetic mean: *The grades this year have been consistently above the mean for the course.* **2** a condition, quality, or course of action halfway between two extremes or opposites; a medium: *the golden mean.* **3** *Mathematics.* **a means,** *pl.* all the terms between the first and last terms of an arithmetic progression. **b** either of the two middle terms of a proportion of four terms: *The means in the proportion 8:4 = 4:2 are 4 and 4.* **4 means,** what a thing is done by; the method or methods or the agency by which something is brought about (*used with a singular or plural verb*): *by fair means. She thinks of her car as simply a means of transportation.* **5 means,** *pl.* a money resources: *to live within one's means.* **b** wealth; riches: *a woman of means.*

by all means, certainly; without fail.

by any means, in any possible way; at any cost.

by means of, by the use of; through; with: *I found my dog by means of a notice in the paper.*

by no means, certainly not; not at all; under no circumstances; in no way: *This work is by no means easy.*

means to an end, a way of getting or doing something.

[ME < OF *meien* < L *medianus* middle < *medius*]

☞ *Hom.* **mien.**

☞ *Usage.* **Means** meaning 'what a thing is done by' is plural in form and singular or plural in use: *A means of communication is lacking. The means of helping others are never lacking.* **Means** meaning 'wealth' is plural in form and in use: *His means permit him to live comfortably.*

me·an·der (mē an′dər) *v., n.* —*v.* **1** follow a winding course: *A brook meanders through the meadow.* **2** wander aimlessly: *We meandered through the park.* —*n.* **1** a winding course. **2** an aimless wandering. [< L < Gk. *Maiandros,* the name of a winding river in Asia Minor]

mean·ing (mēn′ing) *n., adj.* —*n.* what is meant or intended; significance. —*adj.* that means something; expressive: *a meaning look.* —**mean′ing·ly,** *adv.*

☞ *Syn. n.* **Meaning, sense, purport** = what is expressed or meant to be. **Meaning** is the general word applying to the idea expressed or intended by a word, statement, gesture, action, painting, etc.: *The meaning of the sentence is clear.* **Sense** applies to the meaning of something said, especially to a particular meaning of a word. In other senses this word is not a synonym of **meaning.** **Purport,** formal, means the main idea or general drift of a longer statement: *That was the purport of the president's address.*

mean·ing·ful (mēn′ing fəl) *adj.* full of meaning; having much meaning; significant. —**mean′ing·ful·ly,** *adv.* —**mean′ing·ful·ness,** *n.*

mean·ing·less (mēn′ing lis) *adj.* without meaning; not making sense; not significant. —**mean′ing·less·ly,** *adv.* —**mean′ing·less·ness,** *n.*

mean·ness (mēn′nis) *n.* **1** being selfish in small things; stinginess. **2** being mean in grade or quality; poorness. **3** a mean act.

meant (ment) *v.* pt. and pp. of **mean¹.**

mean·time (mēn′tīm′) *n., adv.* —*n.* the time between: *The carnival opens Friday; in the meantime we will make our costumes.* —*adv.* meantime.

mean·while (mēn′wīl′ or -hwīl′) *adv., n.* —*adv.* **1** in the time or period between: *Classes finish at 12 and start again at 2; meanwhile we can swim and have lunch.* **2** at the same time, especially in a different place. —*n.* meantime.

mea·sles (mē′zəlz) *n.* (*used with a singular verb*). **1** an infectious disease characterized by a bad cold, fever, and a breaking out of small, red spots on the skin. **2** a similar but much less severe disease, properly called **German measles. 3** a disease of pigs and cattle caused by the larvae of tapeworms. [ME *meseles,* pl. of *mesel* spot characteristic of measles; akin to MDu. *masel*]

mea·sly (mē′zlē) *adj.* **-sli·er, -sli·est. 1** of or like measles. **2** having measles. **3** *Slang.* scanty; meagre; worthless.

meas·ur·a·ble (mezh′ər ə bəl) *adj.* capable of being measured.

meas·ur·a·bly (mezh′ər ə blē) *adv.* to an amount or degree that can be measured; perceptibly.

meas·ure (mezh′ər) *v.* **-ured, -ur·ing;** *n.* —*v.* **1** find out the extent, size, quantity, capacity, etc. of (something); estimate by some standard: *to measure a room.* **2** be of specified measure: *This*

brick *measures 5 × 10 × 20 centimetres.* **3** get or take by measuring; mark off or out in metres, litres, etc.: *Measure off 2 metres of silk. Measure out a kilogram of potatoes.* **4** take measurements; find out sizes or amounts. **5** admit of measurement. **6** serve as a measure of. **7** assess; estimate: *One measures a man's character by his actions.* **8** adjust (*to*): *He measured his expenses to his income.* **9** *Poetic.* travel over; traverse.

measure (one's) **length,** fall, be thrown, or lie flat on the ground.

measure out, a distribute by measuring. **b** distribute carefully.

measure swords, a fight with swords. **b** take part in a duel, battle, debate, etc.

measure up, have the necessary features; meet a required standard: *The party did not measure up to her expectations.*

—*n.* **1** the act or process of finding extent, size, quantity, capacity, etc. of something, especially by comparison with a standard. **2** the size, dimensions, quantity, etc. thus ascertained: *His waist measure is 70 centimetres.* **3** an instrument for measuring: *A ruler is a linear measure.* **4** a system of measuring: *dry measure.* **5** a unit or standard of measuring. *Centimetre, kilogram, litre,* and *hour* are common measures. **6** any standard of comparison, estimation, or judgment. **7** a quantity or degree that should not be exceeded; reasonable limit: *angry beyond measure.* **8** quantity; extent; degree; proportion: *Accidents can in great measure be prevented. The measure of his courage was remarkable.* **9** rhythm, as in poetry or music: *the stately measures of blank verse.* **10** a metrical unit; foot of poetry. **11** *Music.* **a** a unit of rhythm, consisting of one strong beat and a number of weak beats. **b** the notes contained between two bar lines; bar. **12** a dance or dance movement. **13** a course of action; procedure: *take measures to relieve suffering.* **14** a legislative enactment. **15** *Mathematics.* a quantity contained in another a certain number of times without remainder. **16** a definite quantity measured out: *drink a measure.*

beyond measure, greatly; exceedingly.

for good measure, as something extra; as something not necessarily expected.

full measure, all it should be.

in a measure, to some degree; partly.

take measures, do something; act.

take (one's) **measure,** judge one's character or one's abilities.

tread a measure, *Archaic.* dance.

[ME < OF *mesure, mesurer* < L *mensura,* n., *mensurare,* v., < *mensus,* pp. of *metiri* to measure] —**meas′ur·er,** *n.*

meas·ured (mezh′ərd) *adj.* **1** regular; uniform. **2** rhythmical. **3** written in poetry, not in prose. **4** deliberate and restrained, not hasty or careless. —**meas′ured·ly,** *adv.*

meas·ure·less (mezh′ər lis) *adj.* too great to be measured; unlimited; vast. —**meas′ure·less·ly,** *adv.* —**meas′ure·less·ness,** *n.*

meas·ure·ment (mezh′ər mənt) *n.* **1** the act or process of measuring or finding the size, quantity, or amount: *The measurement of length by a metre-stick is easy.* **2** the size found by measuring: *The measurements of the room are 6 by 4.5 metres.* **3** a system of measuring or of measures.

measuring worm the larva of any geometrid moth. It moves by bringing the rear end of its body forward, forming a loop, and then advancing the front end. Also called **inchworm.**

meat (mēt) *n.* **1** animal flesh used as food. Fish and poultry are not usually called meat. **2** food of any kind: *meat and drink.* **3** the part of anything that can be eaten: *the meat of a nut.* **4** a meal: *Say grace before meat.* **5** the essential part or parts; substance; food for thought: *the meat of an argument, the meat of a book.* **6** *Slang.* something a person finds easy and pleasant: *Something to do with electronics would be more his meat than a job in commerce.* [OE *mete*] —**meat′less,** *adj.*

☞ *Hom.* **meet, mete.**

meat packing the business of slaughtering animals and preparing their meat for transportation and sale.

me·a·tus (mē ā′təs) *n.* **-tus·es** or **-tus.** *Anatomy.* a passage, duct, or opening. [< L *meatus* path < *meare* pass]

meat·y (mē′tē) *adj.* **meat·i·er, meat·i·est. 1** of meat; having the flavor of meat. **2** like meat. **3** full of meat. **4** full of substance; giving food for thought: *The speech was very meaty; it contained many valuable ideas.*

Mec·ca or **mec·ca** (mek′ə) *n.* **1** a place that many people visit: *a tourist Mecca.* **2** a place that many people long for as a goal. [< *Mecca* a capital of Saudi Arabia, the birthplace of Mohammed and holy city of the Moslems]

me·chan·ic (mə kan′ik) *n.* **1** a worker skilled with tools. **2** a worker who repairs machinery. [ME < L < Gk. *mēchanikos* < *mēchanē* machine]

me·chan·i·cal (mə kan′ə kəl) *adj.* **1** having to do with machinery or mechanisms. **2** made or worked by machinery. **3** like a machine; like that of a machine; automatic; without expression: *Her reading is very mechanical.* **4** of, having to do with, or in accordance with, the science of mechanics. —**me·chan′i·cal·ly,** *adv.*

TABLE OF MEASURES

The International System (SI) as Used in Canada

SI base units

name	symbol	quantity
metre	m	length
kilogram	kg	mass
second	s	time
ampere	A	electric current
kelvin	K	thermodynamic temperature
mole	mol	amount of substance
candela	cd	luminous intensity

SI prefixes

name	symbol	multiplying factor*
exa-	E	$\times 10^{18}$
peta-	P	$\times 10^{15}$
tera-	T	$\times 10^{12}$
giga-	G	$\times 10^{9}$
mega-	M	$\times 10^{6}$
kilo-	k	$\times 10^{3}$
hecto-	h	$\times 10^{2}$
deca-	da	$\times 10$
deci-	d	$\times 10^{-1}$
centi-	c	$\times 10^{-2}$
milli-	m	$\times 10^{-3}$
micro-	μ	$\times 10^{-6}$
nano-	n	$\times 10^{-9}$
pico-	p	$\times 10^{-12}$
femto-	f	$\times 10^{-15}$
atto-	a	$\times 10^{-18}$

$*10^2 = 100; 10^3 = 1000$
$10^{-1} = 0.1; 10^{-2} = 0.01$
Thus, 2 km = 2×1000 = 2000 m
3 cm = 3×0.01 = 0.03 m

Common SI derived units with special names

name	symbol	quantity
hertz	Hz	frequency
pascal	Pa	pressure, stress
watt	W	power, radiant flux
volt	V	electric potential, electromotive force
newton	N	force
joule	J	energy, work
coulomb	C	electric charge
ohm	Ω	electric resistance
farad	F	electric capacitance

Common units used with the SI

name	symbol	quantity
litre	L	volume or capacity ($= 1$ dm^3)
degree Celsius	°C	temperature ($= 1$ K; 0°C $= 273.2$ K)
hectare	ha	area ($= 10\ 000$ m^2)
tonne	t	mass ($= 1000$ kg)
electronvolt	eV	energy ($= 0.160$ aJ)
nautical mile	M	distance (navigation) ($= 1852$ m)
knot	kn	speed (navigation) ($= 1$ M/h)
standard atmosphere	atm	atmospheric pressure ($= 101.3$ kPa)

SI supplementary units

name	symbol	quantity
radian	rad	plane angle
steradian	sr	solid angle

Common Conversion Factors

1 centimetre	=	0.39 in.
1 metre	=	39.4 in.
1 kilometre	=	0.62 mi.
1 gram	=	0.04 oz.
1 kilogram	=	2.20 lb.
1 tonne	=	1.1 tons
1 square centimetre	=	0.16 sq.in.
1 square metre	=	1.20 sq.yd.
1 litre	=	0.88 qt.
1 cubic centimetre	=	0.06 cu.in.
1 cubic metre	=	1.31 cu.yd.

Conversion factors for common U.S. liquid measures.

U.S.	Cdn.	metric
1 fl.oz.	= 1.041 fl.oz.	(29.57 cm^3)
1 pt.	= 0.833 pt.	(0.473 dm^3)
1 qt.	= 0.833 qt.	(0.946 dm^3)
1 gal.	= 0.833 gal.	(3.785 dm^3)

Traditional Canadian Measures

name	abbrev. or symbol	equivalent in related units	metric equivalent
LENGTH			
inch	in. or "	—	2.54 cm
foot	ft. or '	12 in.	30.48 cm
yard	yd.	3 ft.; 36 in.	0.91 m
mile	mi.	1760 yd.; 5280 ft.	1.609 km
MASS (WEIGHT)			
grain	gr.	—	0.06 g
dram	dr.	27.343 gr.	1.77 g
ounce	oz.	16 dr.	28.35 g
pound	lb.	16 oz.	0.453 kg
hundredweight			
(short)	cwt.	100 lb.	45.36 kg
(long)	cwt.	112 lb.	50.80 kg
ton (short)	—	2000 lb.	0.907 t
ton (long)	—	2240 lb.	1.016 t
VOLUME AND CAPACITY			
fluid dram	fl.dr.	0.22 cu.in.	3.55 cm^3
fluid ounce	fl.oz.	8 fl.dr.; 1.7 cu.in.	28.41 cm^3
pint	pt.	20 fl.oz.; 34.7 cu.in.	568.3 cm^3
quart	qt.	2 pt.; 69.4 cu.in.	1.14 dm^3
gallon	gal.	4 qt.; 277 cu.in.	4.55 dm^3
peck	pk.	2 gal.; 555 cu.in.	9.09 dm^3
bushel	bu.	4 pk.; 2219 cu.in.	36.37 dm^3
barrel (oil)	—	35 gal.	0.159 dm^3
AREA			
acre	—	4840 sq.yd.	4047 m^2
square mile	sq.mi.	640 acres	2.590 km^2

mechanical drawing drawing done with the help of rulers, scales, compasses, etc.

mechanical engineering the branch of engineering that deals with the design, production, and use of machines and machinery.

mech·a·ni·cian (mek′ə nish′ən) *n.* a worker skilled in making and repairing machines.

me·chan·ics (mə kan′iks) *n.* **1** the branch of physics dealing with motion and the effect of forces on bodies to produce motion or a state of balance; it includes kinematics, kinetics, and statistics (*used with a singular verb*). **2** the application of the principles of mechanics to the design, construction, and operation of machinery (*used with a singular verb*). **3** the mechanical or technical part of something; technique (*used with a plural verb*): *the mechanics of playing the piano.*

mech·a·nism (mek′ə niz′əm) *n.* **1** a machine or its working parts: *Something must be wrong with the mechanism of our refrigerator.* **2** the system of parts working together as the parts of a machine do: *The bones and muscles are parts of the mechanism of the body.* **3** the means or way by which something is done; machinery: *Committees are a useful mechanism for getting things done.* **4** a mechanical part; technique. **5** *Psychology.* **a** the arrangements in the mind or brain that determine thought, feeling, or action in regular and predictable ways. **b** a response unconsciously selected to protect oneself or find satisfaction for an unfulfilled desire: *a defence mechanism.* **6** *Philosophy.* the theory that everything in the universe is produced by mechanical or material forces.

mech·a·nist (mek′ə nist) *n.* **1** a person who believes that all the changes in the universe are the effects of physical and chemical forces. **2** mechanician.

mech·a·nis·tic (mek′ə nis′tik) *adj.* of or having to do with mechanists, mechanism, mechanics, or mechanical theories. —**mech′a·nis′ti·cal·ly,** *adv.*

mech·a·ni·za·tion (mek′ə nə zā′shən *or* mek′ə nī zā′shən) *n.* mechanizing or being mechanized.

mech·a·nize (mek′ə nīz′) *v.* **-nized, -niz·ing. 1** make mechanical. **2** do by machinery, rather than by hand: *Much housework can be mechanized.* **3** replace men or animals by machinery (in a business, etc.). **4** equip (a military unit) with armored vehicles, tanks, and other machines.

Mech·lin (mek′lən) *n.* a fine lace with the pattern clearly outlined by a distinct thread. [< *Mechlin,* a city in N Belgium, where this lace is made]

med. **1** medical. **2** medieval. **3** medium.

Med. Medieval.

M.Ed. Master of Education.

Canadian and Commonwealth medals

med·al (med′əl) *n.* a small, flat piece of metal stamped with a figure and an inscription: *The captain won a medal for bravery. She won the gold medal for having the highest marks in the school. A medal was struck to commemorate the coronation.* [< F < Ital. *medaglia,* ult. < L *metallum* metal]
☛ *Hom.* **meddle.**

med·al·ist (med′əl ist) *n.* **1** a person who designs or makes medals. **2** a person who has won a medal. Also, **medallist.**

me·dal·lion (mə dal′yən) *n.* **1** a large medal. **2** a round or oval design or ornament, such as a design on a book or a pattern in lace. [< F < Ital. *medaglione* large medal]

med·al·list (med′əl ist) See **medalist.**

Medal of Bravery *Cdn.* a decoration awarded for an act of outstanding courage involving personal risk. It is one of a series of three Canadian bravery decorations, the other two being the Cross of Valour (the highest award) and the Star of Courage. *Abbrev.:* MB

med·dle (med′əl) *v.* **-dled, -dling.** busy oneself with other people's things or affairs without being asked or needed. [ME < OF *medler,* ult. < L *miscere* mix] —**med′dler,** *n.*
☛ *Hom.* **medal.**

☛ *Syn.* Meddle, tamper, interfere = concern oneself unnecessarily or unduly with someone or something. **Meddle** emphasizes busying oneself, without right or permission, with something not one's own affair or strictly the affair of another: *That old busybody is always meddling in someone's business.* **Tamper** emphasizes meddling in order to alter or experiment with a thing or improperly influence a person: *Don't tamper with electrical appliances.* **Interfere** suggests meddling in a way that disturbs or hinders: *She interferes when we scold the children.*

med·dle·some (med′əl səm) *adj.* fond of meddling in other people's affairs; meddling. —**med′dle·some·ly,** *adv.* —**med′dle·some·ness,** *n.*

Mede (mēd) *n.* a native or inhabitant of Media, an ancient country in SW Asia, south of the Caspian Sea.
☛ *Hom.* **mead, meed.**

Me·de·a (mə dē′ə) *n. Greek mythology.* a sorceress who helped Jason get the Golden Fleece. They were married but she was later deserted by him. Medea then killed their children as well as her rival, burned her palace, and fled to Athens.

Med.Gk. Medieval Greek.

me·di·a (mē′dē ə) *n.* pl. of **medium** (defs. 2-6). *Newspapers, magazines, billboards, television, and radio are important media for advertising.*
☛ *Usage.* See note at **medium.**

me·di·ae·val (mē′dē ē′vəl *or* med′ē ē′vəl) See **medieval.**

me·di·al (mē′dē əl) *adj.* **1** in the middle. **2** having to do with a mathematical mean or average. **3** average; ordinary. [< LL *medialis* < L *medius* middle] —**me′di·al·ly,** *adv.*

me·di·an (mē′dē ən) *adj., n.* —*adj.* **1** of, having to do with, or in the middle; middle. **2** having to do with or designating the plane that divides something into two equal parts. **3** of a median; having as many above as below a certain number: *The median age of the population was found to be 21 (that is, there were as many persons above 21 as below it), while the average age was found to be 25.* —*n.* **1** the middle number of a series: *The median of 1, 3, 4, 8, 9 is 4.* **2** a measurement so chosen that half the numbers in the series are above it and half are below it: *The median of 1, 3, 4, 8, 9, 10 is 6.* **3** a line or point in the middle. **4** on a highway, a central strip of grass or pavement separating the lanes used by traffic proceeding in opposite directions. [< L *medianus* < *medius* middle]

Me·di·an (mē′dē ən) *adj., n.* —*adj.* of Media, an ancient country in SW Asia, south of the Caspian Sea, or the Medes. —*n.* Mede.

me·di·ant (mē′dē ənt) *n. Music.* the third tone of a scale, half-way from the tonic or keynote to the dominant. [< Ital. *mediante* < LL *medians, -antis,* pres. part. of *mediari.* See MEDIATE.]

me·di·ate (*v.* mē′dē āt′; *adj.* mē′dē it) *v.* **-at·ed, -at·ing;** *adj.* —*v.* **1** be a go-between; act in order to bring about an agreement between persons or sides. **2** effect by intervening; settle by intervening. **3** be a connecting link between: *Canada is often said to mediate between the United States and Great Britain.* **4** be the medium for effecting (a result), for conveying (a gift), or for communicating (knowledge). —*adj.* **1** connected, but not directly; connected through some other person or thing. **2** intermediate. [< LL *mediari* be in the middle, intervene < L *medius* middle] —**me′di·a·tor,** *n.*

me·di·a·tion (mē′dē ā′shən) *n.* a mediating; effecting an agreement; friendly interference.

me·di·a·to·ry (mē′dē ə tô′rē) *adj.* mediating; having to do with mediation.

med·ic[1] (med′ik) *n. Informal.* **1** physician. **2** a medical student. **3** a member of the medical branch of any of the armed forces. [< L *medicus* physician]

med·ic[2] (med′ik) *n.* any of a genus (*Medicago*) of herbs of the pea family, such as alfalfa, having purple or yellow flowers. [< L *medica* < Gk. (*poa*) *Mēdikē* Median (herb)]

med·i·ca·ble (med′ə kə bəl) *adj.* capable of being cured or relieved by medical treatment.

med·i·cal (med′ə kəl) *adj., n.* —*adj.* of or having to do with healing or with the science and art of medicine: *medical advice, medical schools, medical treatment.* —*n. Informal.* medical examination. [< F < LL *medicalis* < L *medicus* doctor] —**med′i·cal·ly,** *adv.*

medical examination an examination of a person by a physician to determine state of health, physical fitness, etc.

me·dic·a·ment (mə dik′ə mənt *or* med′ə kə mənt) *n.* a substance used to cure or heal; medicine. [< L *medicamentum,* ult. < *medicus* healing]

med·i·care (med′ə ker′) *n.* a government-sponsored scheme of health insurance, usually covering hospital costs, doctors' fees, and other medical expenses. [< *medical + care*]

med·i·cate (med′ə kāt′) *v.* **-cat·ed, -cat·ing. 1** treat with medicine. **2** put medicine on or in. [< L *medicare* < *medicus* healing]

med·i·cat·ed (med′ə kāt′id) *adj.* containing medicine: *medicated gauze.*

med·i·ca·tion (med′ə kā′shən) *n.* 1 treatment with medicine. 2 putting medicine on or in: *The doctor was responsible for the medication of the wound.*

Med·i·ci (med′ə chē) *n.* a rich, famous, and powerful family of Florence, Italy, during the 15th and 16th centuries.

me·dic·i·nal (mə dis′ə nəl) *adj.* having value as medicine; healing; helping; relieving. —**me·dic′i·nal·ly,** *adv.*

med·i·cine (med′ə sən *or* med′sən) *n.* 1 any substance such as a drug, used to cure disease or improve health. 2 the science and art of treating or curing disease and sickness and improving or maintaining health. 3 the branch of this discipline that deals with the non-surgical treatment of disease. 4 among Amerindian peoples: **a** an object or ceremony traditionally believed to have power over natural or supernatural forces. **b** magical power.
take (one's) **medicine,** accept a punishment or other disagreeable result of one's own actions. [< L *medicina* < *medicus* doctor]

medicine ball a large, heavy leather ball tossed from one person to another for exercise.

medicine man a man believed by North American Indians and other primitive peoples to have magic power over diseases, evil spirits, and other things.

med·i·co (med′ə kō′) *n., pl.* **-cos.** *Informal.* 1 a doctor. 2 a medical student. [< Ital. *medico* or Sp. *médico* physician, learned borrowing from L *medicus.* See MEDIC.]

me·di·e·val (mē′dē ē′vəl *or* med′ē ē′vəl) *adj.* 1 belonging to or having to do with the Middle Ages, the period from about A.D. 500 to about 1450: *medieval customs.* 2 like that of the Middle Ages. Also, **mediaeval.** [< L *medium* middle + *aevum* age] —**me′di·e′val·ly,** *adv.*

me·di·e·val·ism (mē′dē ē′vəl iz′əm *or* med′ē ē′vəl iz′əm) *n.* 1 the spirit, ideals, and customs of the Middle Ages; medieval thought, religion, and art. 2 devotion to medieval ideals; adoption of medieval customs. 3 a medieval belief or custom. Also, **mediaevalism.**

me·di·e·val·ist (mē′dē ē′vəl ist *or* med′ē ē′vəl ist) *n.* 1 a person who knows much about the Middle Ages. 2 a person who is in sympathy with medieval ideals, customs, etc. Also, **mediaevalist.**

Medieval Latin the Latin language from about A.D. 700 to about 1500.

me·di·o·cre (mē′dē ō′kər *or* mē′dē ō′kər) *adj.* neither good nor bad; average; ordinary, but less than satisfactory: *a mediocre cake, a mediocre student.* [< F < L *mediocris,* originally, middling < *medius* middle]

me·di·oc·ri·ty (mē′dē ok′rə tē) *n., pl.* **-ties.** 1 mediocre quality. 2 mediocre ability or accomplishment. 3 a mediocre person. [< L *mediocritas*]

med·i·tate (med′ə tāt′) *v.* **-tat·ed, -tat·ing.** 1 think quietly and deeply; reflect: *Monks meditate on holy things.* 2 think about; consider; plan; intend. [< L *meditari*]
☛ *Syn.* 2. See note at **think.**

med·i·ta·tion (med′ə tā′shən) *n.* 1 continued thought; reflection. 2 contemplation on sacred or solemn subjects, especially as a devotional exercise. 3 a contemplative or devotional writing or talk.

med·i·ta·tive (med′ə tā′tiv) *adj.* 1 fond of meditating. 2 expressing meditation. —**med′i·ta′tive·ly,** *adv.* —**med′i·ta′tive·ness,** *n.*

Med·i·ter·ra·ne·an (med′ə tə rā′nē ən *or* med′ə tə rān′yən) *adj.* of or having to do with the Mediterranean Sea or the lands around it. [< L *mediterraneus* < *medius* middle + *terra* land]

me·di·um (mē′dē əm) *adj., n., pl.* **-di·ums** *or* **-di·a** (except for def. 7). *adj.* having a middle position; moderate.
—*n.* 1 that which is in the middle; neither one extreme nor the other; middle condition. 2 a substance or agent through which anything acts; a means: *Radio is a medium of communication.* 3 a means of artistic expression: *The sculptor did some carving in stone, but his favorite medium was wood.* 4 a substance in which something can live; environment: *Water is the medium in which fish live.* 5 **a** a nutritive substance, either liquid or solid, such as agar-agar or gelatin, in or upon which bacteria, fungi, and other micro-organisms are grown for study. **b** a substance used for displaying, preserving, etc. organic specimens. 6 a liquid with which paints are mixed. 7 a person through whom spirits of the dead can supposedly communicate with the living. [< L *medium* neut. adj., middle]
☛ *Usage.* **Mediums** is the only plural used when the reference is to persons (def. 7). **Media** is the only plural used for def. 3 and also is usual for defs. 4 and 5. Careful writers and speakers avoid using **media** as a singular or **medias** as a plural: *She gave up the medium of painting and took to other media instead.*

medium frequency the range of radio frequencies between 300 and 3000 kilohertz. Medium frequency is the range next above low frequency.

hat, āge, fär; let, ēqual, tèrm; it, īce
hot, ōpen, ôrder; oil, out; cup, pút, rüle,
əbove, takən, pencəl, lemən, circəs

ch, child; ng, long; sh, ship
th, thin; ᴛн, then; zh, measure

me·di·um–sized (mē′dē əm sīzd′) *adj.* neither large nor small of its kind.

Med.L. Medieval Latin.

med·lar (med′lər) *n.* 1 a small tree (*Mespilus germanica*) of the rose family native to Europe and Asia, bearing an edible brown fruit that resembles a crab apple. 2 the fruit of this tree, which is fit to eat only when it has become overripe. [ME < OF *meslier* (the tree) < *mesle* (its fruit), ult. < L < Gk. *mespilon*]

med·ley (med′lē) *n., pl.* **-leys;** *adj.* —*n.* 1 a mixture of things that ordinarily do not belong together. 2 *Music.* a vocal or instrumental composition made up of tunes, usually familiar, or excerpts from other pieces. —*adj.* made up of parts that are not alike; mixed. [ME < OF *meslee* < *mesler* mix, ult. < L *miscere.* Doublet of MELEE.]

Mé·doc *or* **Me·doc** (mā dok′) *n.* a red wine, a type of claret. [< *Médoc,* a district in SW France, where it is made]

me·dul·la (mə dul′ə) *n., pl.* **me·dul·lae** (-ē *or* -ī). 1 medulla oblongata. 2 bone marrow. 3 the innermost part of an organ or structure. The medulla of the adrenal gland produces the hormone adrenaline. 4 the pith of plants. [< L *medulla* marrow]

medulla ob·lon·ga·ta (ob′long gä′tə *or* ob′long gā′tə) *Anatomy.* the lowest part of the brain, at the top end of the spinal cord. See **brain** for picture. [< NL *medulla oblongata* prolonged medulla]

me·dul·lar·y (med′ə ler′ē *or* mə dul′ər ē) *adj.* of, having to do with, or like medulla or the medulla oblongata.

me·du·sa (mə dyü′sə *or* mə dü′sə, mə dyü′zə *or* mə dü′zə) *n., pl.* **-sas, -sae** (-sē *or* -sī, -zē *or* -zī). 1 one of two main body forms in which coelenterates exist; it is the gamete-producing form with a jelly-like, umbrella-shaped body, the typical form of the jellyfish. 2 jellyfish. [< *Medusa*]

Me·du·sa (mə dyü′sə *or* mə dü′sə, mə dyü′zə *or* mə dü′zə) *n., pl.* **-sas.** *Greek mythology.* a horrible monster, one of the three Gorgons. She had snakes for hair, and anyone who looked upon her was turned to stone. She was killed by Perseus. —**Me·du′sa-like′,** *adj.*

meed (mēd) *n. Poetic.* what one deserves; reward. [OE *mēd*]
☛ *Hom.* **mead, Mede.**

meek (mēk) *adj.* 1 patient; not easily angered; mild. 2 submitting tamely when ordered about or injured by others: *The boy was meek as a lamb when he was reproved.* [ME < ON *miukr* soft]
—**meek′ly,** *adv.* —**meek′ness,** *n.*
☛ *Syn.* 1. See note at **gentle.** 2. See note at **humble.**

meer·schaum (mēr′shəm, mēr′shom, *or* mēr′shôm) *n.* 1 a very soft, light magnesium silicate used to make tobacco pipes. *Formula:* $H_4Mg_2Si_3O_{10}$ 2 a tobacco pipe made of this material. [< G *Meerschaum* sea foam]

meet[1] (mēt) *v.* **met, meet·ing;** *n.* —*v.* 1 come face to face; come face to face with: *Their cars met on the narrow road.* 2 come together; come into contact or connection with: *Sword met sword in battle.* 3 join: *where two streets meet.* 4 be united; join in harmony: *His is a nature in which courage and caution meet.* 5 come into company with; be together: *The hosts met their guests at the restaurant.* 6 keep an appointment with: *Meet me at one o'clock.* 7 be introduced to; become acquainted with: *Have you met my sister?* 8 be present at the arrival of: *to meet a boat.* 9 satisfy; comply with: *to meet obligations, objections, etc.* 10 pay: *to meet bills, debts, etc.* 11 fight with; oppose; deal with. 12 fight. 13 face directly: *He met her glance with a smile.* 14 experience: *He met open scorn before he won fame.* 15 assemble: *Parliament will meet next month.*
meet the eye or the ear, be seen or heard.
meet up with, *Informal.* meet.
meet with, a come across; find. **b** have or get: *The plan met with approval.* **c** talk with.
—*n.* 1 a meeting or gathering; especially, a competition: *a racing meet, an athletic meet.* 2 the people at such a gathering, or the place where it is held. [OE *mētan*]
☛ *Hom.* **meat, mete.**

meet[2] (mēt) *adj. Archaic.* suitable; proper; fitting: *It is meet that you should help your friends.* [OE (ge)mǣte]
☛ *Hom.* **meat, mete.**

meet·ing (mēt′ing) *n.* 1 a coming together: *He looked forward to a meeting with his sister.* 2 a gathering or assembly for business discussion, social purposes, etc. 3 an assembly of people for

worship. **4** the place where things meet; junction: *a meeting of roads.*

☛ **Syn. 2.** Meeting, assembly, gathering = a coming together of a group of people. **Meeting** applies especially to the coming together of a body of people to discuss or arrange business or action: *The club held a meeting.* **Assembly,** more formal, emphasizes coming or calling together for a common purpose, such as social pleasure, religious worship, or, particularly, joining in deliberation or action: *The principal called an assembly.* **Gathering** suggests a less formal or less organized coming together: *There was a large gathering at her house.*

meeting house 1 a building used for worship by certain religious groups, such as Quakers. **2** any building used for meetings.

meet·ly (mēt′lē) *adv.* suitably; properly.

mega– *combining form.* **1** great; large, as in **megalith. 2** SI prefix. million: *A megavolt is one million volts. Symbol:* M [< Gk. *megas* great]

meg·a·ce·phal·ic (meg′ə sə fal′ik) *adj.* large-headed; having a skull with a cranial capacity above the average. [< *mega-* + Gk. *kephalē* head + E *-ic*]

meg·a·cy·cle (meg′ə sī′kəl) *n.* megahertz. [< *mega-* one million times (< Gk. *megas* great) + *cycle*]

meg·a·death (meg′ə deth′) *n.* the death of one million persons. [< *mega-* one million times (< Gk. *megas* great) + *death*]

meg·a·hertz (meg′ə herts′) *n., pl.* **meg·a·hertz.** an SI unit for measuring frequency, equal to 1 000 000 hertz. *Symbol:* MHz

meg·a·lith (meg′ə lith′) *n.* a stone of great size, especially in ancient construction work or in monuments left by people of prehistoric times. [< Gk. *megas* great + *lithos* stone]

meg·a·lith·ic (meg′ə lith′ik) *adj.* **1** of or having to do with megaliths. **2** like a megalith in size; gigantic.

megalo– *combining form.* great; large. [< Gk. *megas, -galou*]

meg·a·lo·ma·ni·a (meg′ə lō mā′nē ə) *n.* a mental illness characterized by delusions of greatness, wealth, etc. [< Gk. *megas, megalou* great + *mania* madness]

meg·a·lo·ma·ni·ac (meg′ə lō mā′nē ak′) *n.* a person who suffers from megalomania.

meg·a·lop·o·lis (meg′ə lop′ə lis) *n.* **1** a city of great or overpowering size, especially one thought of as a centre of the power, wealth, and influence of a country. **2** a heavily populated urban and industrial area made up of several cities. [< Gk. *mega, megalou* great + *polis* city]

meg·a·phone (meg′ə fōn′) *n.* a large, funnel-shaped horn used to increase the loudness of the voice or the distance at which it can be heard. [< Gk. *megas* great + *phōnē* sound]

meg·a·ton (meg′ə tun′) *n.* a measure of atomic power equivalent to the energy released by one million tons of high explosive, specifically TNT. [< *mega-* one million times (< Gk. *megas* great) + *(1000-kilo)ton*]

meg·ohm (meg′ōm′) *n.* an SI unit for measuring electric resistance, equal to one million ohms. *Symbol:* MΩ [< *mega-* one million times (< Gk. *megas* great) + *ohm*]

me·grim (mē′grim) *n. Archaic.* **1** migraine. **2** a whim; fancy. **3** megrims, *pl.* morbid low spirits. [var. of *migraine;* influenced by *grim*]

mei·o·sis (mī ō′sis) *n., pl.* **-ses** (-sēz). **1** the division of a living germ cell to produce gametes. Meiosis consists of two successive divisions of the nucleus of the parent cell, producing four haploid daughter cells (gametes); it also involves the interchange of genetic information between the maternal and paternal chromosome pairs, so that each daughter cell carries slightly different genes. Compare **mitosis. 2** *Rhetoric.* understatement; litotes. [< NL *meiosis* < Gk. *meiōsi* a lessening < *meioein* lessen < *meiōn* less]

mei·ot·ic (mī ot′ik) *adj.* of or having to do with meiosis.

Meis·sen (mī′sən) *n.* a kind of porcelain. [< *Meissen,* a city in East Germany, where it is made]

Meis·ter·sing·er (mīs′tər sing′ər; German, mīs′tər zing′ər) *n.* a member of one of the guilds, chiefly of workingmen, established in the principal German cities in the 14th, 15th, and 16th centuries for the cultivation of poetry and music.

mel·a·mine (mel′ə mēn′ or mel′ə min) *n.* **1** a white crystalline compound used to make a synthetic thermosetting resin. *Formula:* C₃H₆N₆ **2** the resin made from melamine or the hard, strong plastic made from the resin, used for making moulded articles, adhesives, and surface coatings. [< *mel*am, a chemical compound + *amine*]

mel·an·cho·li·a (mel′ən kō′lē ə) *n.* a mental disorder characterized by great depression of spirits and gloomy fears. [< LL < Gk. *melancholia* < *melas* black + *cholē* bile]

mel·an·chol·ic (mel′ən kol′ik) *adj.* **1** melancholy; gloomy. **2** suffering from melancholia.

mel·an·chol·y (mel′ən kol′ē) *n., pl.* **-chol·ies;** *adj.* **—n. 1** sadness; low spirits; a tendency to be sad. **2** sober thoughtfulness; pensiveness. **3** black bile, the one of the four humors of ancient physiology believed to cause low spirits.
—adj. 1 sad; gloomy. **2** causing sadness; depressing: *a melancholy scene.* **3** expressive of sadness: *a melancholy smile.* **4** lamentable; deplorable: *a melancholy fact.* **5** soberly thoughtful; pensive.

Mel·a·ne·sian (mel′ə nē′zhən or mel′ə nē′shən) *adj., n.* **—adj. 1** of or designating a major race of mankind that includes most of the peoples traditionally inhabiting Melanesia, a group of islands in the southwestern Pacific, especially New Guinea, New Britain, and the Solomon Islands. **2** of or having to do with Melanesia or the peoples, cultures, or languages of Melanesia.
—n. 1 a member of the Melanesian race. **2** a native or inhabitant of Melanesia. **3** a group of Austronesian languages widely spoken in Melanesia.

mé·lange (mā länzh′) *n.* a mixture; medley. [< F *mélange* < *mêler* mix]

me·lan·ic (mə lan′ik) *adj.* **1** of, having to do with, or characterized by melanism. **2** melanotic.

mel·a·nin (mel′ə nən) *n.* a dark-brown or black pigment present in the skin, hair, and eyes of man and animals.

mel·a·nism (mel′ə niz′əm) *n.* **1** the condition in an individual or type of organism of having a large amount of melanin, producing black or nearly black fur, feathers, skin, etc. **2** melanosis.

mel·a·no·ma (mel′ə nō′mə) *n.* a malignant tumor developed from cells that form melanin, usually occurring in the skin.

mel·a·no·sis (mel′ə nō′sis) *n.* abnormal, dark-brown or black pigmentation of tissues or organs caused by melanins or, sometimes, other substances resembling melanins. Melanosis of the skin can occur in pregnancy or as a result of sunburn.

mel·a·not·ic (mel′ə not′ik) *adj.* of, having to do with, or affected with melanosis.

Mel·ba toast (mel′bə) very thin, crisp toast.

meld (meld) *v., n.* **—v.** in canasta, pinochle, etc. announce and show (cards for a score). **—n. 1** the act of melding. **2** the cards that can be melded. [< G *melden* announce]

Mel·e·a·ger (mel′ē a′jər) *n. Greek mythology.* the hero who killed the Calydonian boar. He was one of the Argonauts.

me·lee or **mê·lée** (mel′ā, mā′lā, or mā lā′; French, me lā′) *n.* **1** a confused fight; hand-to-hand fight among a number of fighters. **2** any similar state of hectic confusion. [< F *mêlée* (in OF *meslee*). Doublet of MEDLEY.]

mel·i·nite (mel′ə nīt′) *n.* a powerful explosive containing picric acid. [< F < Gk. *mēlinos* quince-yellow < *mēlon* quince]

mel·io·rate (mēl′yə rāt′ or mē′lē ə rāt′) *v.* **-rat·ed, -rat·ing.** improve. [< LL *meliorare* < L *melior* better] **—mel′io·ra′tion,** *n.* **—mel′io·ra′tor,** *n.*

mel·io·ra·tive (mēl′yə rā′tiv or mē′lē ə rā′tiv) *adj.* tending to improve.

mel·lif·lu·ence (mə lif′lü əns) *n.* the quality or state of being mellifluous.

mel·lif·lu·ent (mə lif′lü ənt) *adj.* mellifluous. **—mel·lif′lu·ent·ly,** *adv.*

mel·lif·lu·ous (mə lif′lü əs) *adj.* sweetly or smoothly flowing: *a mellifluous speech.* [< LL *mellifluus* < L *mel* honey + *fluere* to flow] **—mel·lif′lu·ous·ly,** *adv.* **—mel·lif′lu·ous·ness,** *n.*

mel·low (mel′ō) *adj., v.* **—adj. 1** soft and full-flavored from ripeness; sweet and juicy: *a mellow apple.* **2** fully matured: *mellow wine.* **3** soft and rich: *a violin with a mellow tone, a mellow light in a picture, mellow color.* **4** rich; loamy: *mellow soil.* **5** softened and made wise by age and experience. **6** affected by liquor or drinking; slightly tipsy.
—v. make or become mellow. [var. of OE *mearu* soft, tender] **—mel′low·ly,** *adv.* **—mel′low·ness,** *n.*

me·lo·de·on (mə lō′dē ən) *n.* a small reed organ in which air is sucked inward by a bellows. [pseudo-Gk. form of earlier *melodium* < *melody*]

me·lod·ic (mə lod′ik) *adj.* **1** having to do with melody. **2** melodious. **—me·lod′i·cal·ly,** *adv.*

me·lo·di·ous (mə lō′dē əs) *adj.* **1** sweet-sounding; pleasing to the ear; musical: *a melodious voice.* **2** producing melody: *a melodious bird.* **—me·lo′di·ous·ly,** *adv.* **—me·lo′di·ous·ness,** *n.*

mel·o·dist (mel′ə dist) *n.* a composer or singer of melodies.

mel·o·dra·ma (mel′ə dram′ə or -drä′mə) *n.* **1** a sensational drama with exaggerated appeal to the emotions and, usually, a happy ending. **2** any sensational writing, speech, or action with exaggerated appeal to the emotions. [< F < Gk. *melos* song, music + *drama* drama]

mel·o·dra·mat·ic (mel′ə drə mat′ik) *adj.* of, like, or suitable for

melodrama; sensational and exaggerated. —**mel′o·dra·mat′i·cal·ly,** *adv.*

☛ *Syn.* See note at **dramatic.**

mel·o·dy (mel′ə dē) *n., pl.* **-dies. 1** any agreeable succession of sounds. **2** musical quality: *The melody of good speech.* **3** *Music.* **a** a succession of single tones, arranged in a rhythmical pattern; tune. **b** the main tune in a harmonized composition; air. **4** a poem to be sung to music. [ME < OF < LL < Gk. *melōidia,* ult. < *melos* song + *ōidē* song]

mel·on (mel′ən) *n.* **1** the large, thick-skinned, juicy fruit of any of various plants of the gourd family, such as the watermelon or muskmelon. **2** any plant producing such fruits. **3** a deep-pink color. **cut** or **split a melon,** *Slang.* divide extra profits among those considered to have a claim on them. [ME < OF < LL *melo, -onis,* short for L *melopepo* < Gk. *mēlopepōn* < *mēlon* apple + *pepōn* gourd] —**mel′on·like′,** *adj.*

Mel·pom·e·ne (mel pom′ə nē′) *n.* Greek mythology. the Muse of tragedy.

melt (melt) *v.* **melt·ed, melt·ed** or **mol·ten, melt·ing;** *n.* —*v.* **1** change or be changed from solid to liquid: *Great heat melts iron. The ice melted quickly.* **2** dissolve: *Sugar melts in water.* **3** disappear or cause to disappear gradually: *As the sun came out, the clouds melted away.* **4** blend or merge gradually: *In the rainbow, the green melts into blue, the blue into violet.* **5** waste away; dwindle: *His wealth melted away.* **6** make or become gentle, tender, etc.: *Pity for his wounded enemy melted his heart.* —*n.* **1** the act or process of melting. **2** the state of being melted. **3** a melted metal. **4** a quantity of metal melted at one operation or over a specified period, especially a single charge in smelting. [OE *meltan*] —**melt′er,** *n.*

☛ *Syn.* **1. Melt, dissolve, thaw** = change from a solid state. **Melt** suggests a gradual change caused by heat, by which a solid softens, loses shape, and finally becomes liquid: *The warm air melted the butter.* **Dissolve** emphasizes a breaking up of a solid into its smallest parts, caused by putting it in a liquid that reduces it and of which it becomes a part: *Dissolve some salt in a glass of water.* **Thaw,** used only of frozen things, means 'change to the unfrozen state': *She thawed the frozen fruit.*

melt·down (melt′doun′) *n.* a situation in a nuclear reactor resulting from a failure of the cooling system so that heat generated by the reaction is not removed, and the metal holder for the bundles of fuel melts. If this happened, the reaction could no longer be controlled and would speed up, producing more heat and ending in a violent reaction, possibly an explosion.

melting point the temperature at which a solid substance melts.

melting pot 1 a pot or other vessel to melt something in. **2** a country or city thought of as a place in which various races or sorts of people are assimilated. North America is often called a melting pot.

mel·ton (mel′tən) *n.* a smooth, heavy woollen cloth. Overcoats are often made of melton. [< *Melton* (Mowbray), a town in central England]

melt·wa·ter (melt′wo′tər or -wô′tər) *n.* water from melting glaciers or snows.

mem·ber (mem′bər) *n.* **1** a person belonging to a group: *a member of our club.* **2** a person elected to a legislative body: *a Member of Parliament, a Member of the Legislative Assembly.* **3** a constituent part of a whole: *a member of an equation.* **4** limb; a part of a human or animal body or of a plant, especially a leg, arm, wing, or branch. [ME < OF < L *membrum* limb, part]

Member of Parliament in Canada, a title given to each of the representatives elected to the Federal Parliament in Ottawa. *Abbrev.:* MP or M.P.

Member of Provincial Parliament in Ontario, a member of the Legislative Assembly. *Abbrev.:* MPP or M.P.P.

Member of the Legislative Assembly a title given to each of the representatives elected to the legislatures of most Canadian provinces. *Abbrev.:* MLA or M.L.A.

mem·ber·ship (mem′bər ship′) *n.* **1** the fact or state of being a member. **2** the members. **3** the number of members.

mem·brane (mem′brān) *n.* **1** a thin, soft sheet or layer of animal tissue, lining or covering some part of the body: *One kind of membrane lines the stomach and another covers the front of the eyeball.* **2** a similar layer of plant tissue. **3** a thin, pliable sheet of any of various materials, such as plastic, used to line or cover something or connect parts. [< L *membrana* < *membrum* member]

mem·bra·nous (mem′brə nəs or mem brā′nəs) *adj.* **1** of or like membrane. **2** characterized by the formation of a membrane. In **membranous croup,** a membrane forms in the throat and hinders breathing.

me·men·to (mə men′tō) *n., pl.* **-tos** or **-toes. 1** something serving as a reminder, warning, or remembrance: *These post cards are mementos of our trip abroad.* **2 Memento,** *Roman Catholic Church.* either of two prayers beginning *Memento* (Remember) in the canon

hat, āge, fär; let, ēqual, tėrm; it, īce
hot, ōpen, ôrder; oil, out; cup, pút, rüle,
above, takən, pencəl, lemən, circəs
ch, child; ng, long; sh, ship
th, thin; ŦH, then; zh, measure

of the Mass, in which the living and the dead respectively are commemorated. [< L *memento* remember!]

Mem·non (mem′non) *n.* **1** *Greek mythology.* an Ethiopian king killed by Achilles. **2** a huge statue of an Egyptian king at Thebes, Egypt.

mem·o (mem′ō) *n., pl.* **mem·os.** *Informal.* memorandum.

mem·oir (mem′wär or mem′wôr) *n.* **1** biography. **2** a report of a scientific or scholarly study. **3 memoirs,** *pl.* **a** a record of facts and events written from personal knowledge or special information. **b** a record of a person's own experiences; autobiography. [< F *mémoire* < L *memoria.* Doublet of MEMORY.]

mem·o·ra·bil·i·a (mem′ə rə bil′ē ə) *n.pl.* things or events worth remembering. [< L *memorabilia,* pl. of *memorabilis.* See MEMORABLE.]

mem·o·ra·ble (mem′ə rə bəl) *adj.* worth remembering; not to be forgotten; notable. [< L *memorabilis,* ult. < *memor* mindful] —**mem′o·ra·bly,** *adv.*

mem·o·ran·da (mem′ə ran′də) *n.* a pl. of **memorandum.**

mem·o·ran·dum (mem′ə ran′dəm) *n., pl.* **-dums** or **-da. 1** a short written statement for future use; a note to aid the memory. **2** an informal letter, note, or report. **3** a diplomatic communication consisting of a summary of facts and arguments on some issue or arrangement that concerns two or more governments. [< L *memorandum* (thing) to be remembered]

me·mo·ri·al (mə mô′rē əl) *n., adj.* —*n.* **1** something that is a reminder of some important event or person, such as a statue, an arch or column, a book, or a holiday. **2** a statement sent to a government or person in authority, usually giving facts and asking that some wrong be corrected. —*adj.* helping people to remember some person, thing, or event: *We have memorial services on Remembrance Day.* [ME < OF < L *memorialis* < *memoria.* See MEMORY.]

me·mo·ri·al·ize (mə mô′rē əl īz′) *v.* **-ized, -iz·ing. 1** preserve the memory of; commemorate. **2** submit a memorial to; petition. —**me·mo′ri·al·iz′er,** *n.*

me·mo·ri·am (mə môr′ē əm) *n. Latin.* See **in memoriam.**

mem·o·rize (mem′ə rīz′) *v.* **-rized, -riz·ing.** commit to memory; learn by heart. —**mem′o·ri·za′tion,** *n.* —**mem′o·riz′er,** *n.*

mem·o·ry (mem′ə rē or mem′rē) *n., pl.* **-ries. 1** the ability to remember. **2** the act of remembering; remembrance. **3** all that a person remembers. **4** a person, thing, or event that is remembered. **5** the length of time during which the past is remembered: *This has been the hottest summer within living memory.* **6** reputation after death.

in memory of, as a help in remembering; as a remembrance of: *On November 11 we observe a two-minute silence in memory of those who died fighting for their country.* [ME < OF < L *memoria* < *memor* mindful. Doublet of MEMOIR.]

☛ *Syn.* **2. Memory, recollection** = the act or fact of remembering. **Memory** emphasizes the ability to keep in the mind or call back something once learned, experienced, or otherwise known: *That vacation lives in her memory.* **Recollection,** applying to the act or to what is remembered, emphasizes calling back to mind, often with effort, something not thought of for a long time or forgotten: *I have little recollection of my childhood.*

mem·sa·hib (mem′sä′ib) *n. Historical.* a title of respect used in India when speaking to or of a married European lady, especially the wife of a British colonial official. [< Hind. *mem-sahib* < mem (< E *ma'am*) + *sahib* sir]

men (men) *n.* pl. of **man.**

men·ace (men′is) *n., v.* **-aced, -ac·ing.** —*n.* a threat: *In dry weather forest fires are a menace.* —*v.* threaten: *Floods menaced the valley towns with destruction.* [ME < OF < L *minaciae* (pl.), ult. < *minae* projecting points, threats] —**men′ac·ing·ly,** *adv.*

☛ *Syn. v.* See note at **threaten.**

me·nad (mē′nad) See **maenad.**

mé·nage or **me·nage** (mā näzh′) *n.* **1** a household; domestic establishment. **2** housekeeping; management of a household. [< F]

me·nag·er·ie (mə naj′ər ē or mə nazh′ər ē) *n.* **1** a collection of wild animals kept in cages for exhibition. **2** the place where such animals are kept. [< F *ménagerie,* literally, management of a household]

mend (mend) *v., n.* —*v.* **1** put in good condition again; make

whole; repair: *to mend a flat tire.* **2** set right; improve: *He should mend his manners.* **3** get back one's health.
—*n.* **1** a place that has been mended. **2** a mending; improvement. **on the mend, a** improving. **b** getting well.
[var. of *amend*] —**mend′er**, *n.*

☛ *Syn. v.* **1. Mend, repair, patch** = put in good or usable condition again. **Mend** = make whole again something that has been broken, torn, or worn, but is now seldom used of large things: *She mended the broken vase with cement.* **Repair** = make right again something damaged, run down, decayed, weakened, etc.: *He repaired the electric toaster.* **Patch** = mend by putting a piece (or amount) of material on or in a hole, tear, or worn place: *His mother patched his torn trousers.*

men·da·cious (men dā′shəs) *adj.* **1** lying; untruthful. **2** false; untrue. [< L *mendax, -acis* lying] —**men·da′cious·ly**, *adv.* —**men·da′cious·ness**, *n.*

men·dac·i·ty (men das′ə tē) *n., pl.* **-ties. 1** the habit of telling lies; untruthfulness. **2** lie.

men·de·le·vi·um (men′də lā′vē əm) *n.* a rare, radio-active, synthetic chemical element, produced as a by-product of nuclear fission. *Symbol:* Md; *at.no.* 101; *at.wt.* (258); *half-life* approx. 60 days. [after Dmitri Ivanovich *Mendeleev* (1834-1907), a Russian chemist]

Men·de·li·an (men dē′lē ən) *adj.* of or having to do with the laws of heredity formulated by Gregor Mendel (1822-1884), an Austrian monk and biologist, or with Mendelism.

Men·del·ism (men′dəl iz′əm) *n.* the science of heredity, based on Mendel's laws.

Mendel's laws (men′dəlz) the two basic principles of heredity formulated by Gregor Mendel, whose investigations laid the foundations for the science of genetics. The Law of Segregation states that each cell of an individual has a pair of factors (now called genes) for each inherited characteristic and that these pairs separate during meiosis so that each gamete carries only one unit of each pair. The **Law of Independent Assortment** states that the pairs of factors (genes) are segregated independently of each other, without influence from any other pair. This is now known not to be always true, since the genes on the same chromosome are affected by linkage (the tendency to be segregated together).

men·di·can·cy (men′də kən sē) *n.* the act of begging; the state of being a beggar.

men·di·cant (men′də kənt) *adj., n.* —*adj.* begging: *mendicant friars.* —*n.* **1** beggar. **2** a mendicant friar. [< L *mendicans, -antis* < *mendicus* beggar]

Men·e·la·us (men′ə lā′əs) *n. Greek mythology.* a king of Sparta, husband of Helen, and brother of Agamemnon.

men·folk (men′fōk′) *n.pl.* **1** men collectively. **2** a particular group of men, such as the male members of a family.

men·ha·den (men hā′dən) *n., pl.* **-den.** a marine fish (*Brevoortia tyrannus*) of the herring family found along the Atlantic coast of North and South America, valued as a source of fish meal, oil, and fertilizer. [< Algonquian]

me·ni·al (mē′nē əl *or* mēn′yəl) *adj., n.* —*adj.* suited to or belonging to a servant; low; mean. —*n.* **1** a servant who does the humblest and most unpleasant tasks. **2** a low, mean, or servile person; flunky. [ME < *meynie* household < OF *mesnie* < VL *mansionata* < L *mansio* habitation < *manere* remain] —**me′ni·al·ly**, *adv.*

me·nin·ges (mə nin′jēz) *n.* pl. of **me·ninx** (mē′ningks). *Anatomy.* the three membranes that surround the brain and spinal cord. [< NL (pl.) < Gk. *mēninx, -ingos*]

men·in·gi·tis (men′in jī′tis) *n.* a serious disease in which the meninges are inflamed. [< NL < Gk. *mēninx, -ingos* membrane + *-itis*]

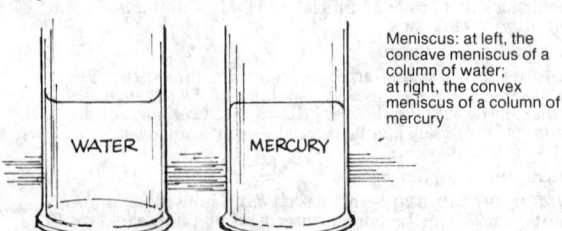

Meniscus: at left, the concave meniscus of a column of water; at right, the convex meniscus of a column of mercury

me·nis·cus (mə nis′kəs) *n., pl.* **-nis·cus·es, -nis·ci** (-nis′ī *or* -nis′ē). **1** the curved upper surface of a column of liquid, produced by surface tension. The meniscus is concave when the walls of the container are made wet by the liquid (i.e. if there is capillary

attraction) and convex when they are not (i.e. if there is capillary repulsion). **2** a lens that is concave on one side and convex on the other; a concavo-convex or convexo-concave lens. See **concave** and **convex** for pictures. **3** a crescent or crescent-shaped body. [< NL < Gk. *mēniskos*, dim. of *mēnē* moon]

Men·non·ite (men′ən īt′) *n.* **1** a member of any of several Christian churches having their roots within the radical left wing of the Reformation, whose tenets include pacifism and the rejection of infant baptism in favor of the baptism of adult believers. Most North American Mennonites stem from either of two traditional ethnic backgrounds: Swiss and Dutch/Prussian/Russian. **2** a member of a Mennonite ethnic group, especially a group characterized by adherence to a simple lifestyle and rejection of modern technology. [after *Menno* Simons (1492-1559), a Dutch leader of the Mennonites]

me·nom·i·nee (mə nom′ə nē) *n. Cdn.* wild rice. [< Cree]

men·o·paus·al (men′ə poz′əl *or* men′ə pôz əl) *adj.* having to do with, characteristic of, or undergoing the menopause.

men·o·pause (men′ə poz′ *or* -pôz′) *n.* the period in a woman's life during which menstruation ceases permanently, usually between the ages of 45 and 50; change of life. [< NL < Gk. *mēn* month + *pausis* pause]

men·o·rah *or* **Men·o·rah** (mə nôr′ə) *n.* a candelabrum used in Jewish worship. The seven-branched menorah is used in temple services; the nine-branched one is used during Hanukkah. [< Hebrew *manorah*]

men·ses (men′sēz) *n.pl.* menstruation. [< L *menses*, pl. of *mensis* month]

Men·she·vik *or* **men·she·vik** (men′shə vik′) *n., pl.* **-viks** *or* **-vi·ki** (-vē′kē); *adj.* —*n.* in Russia, a member of the conservative wing of the Social Democratic Party opposed to the more radical Bolsheviks from 1903 to 1917. —*adj.* of or having to do with the Mensheviks or Menshevism. [< Russian *Menshevik* < *menshe* less; because it was at one time the minority wing of the Party. Opposed to BOLSHEVIK.]

men·stru·al (men′strü əl) *adj.* of or having to do with menstruation.

men·stru·ate (men′strü āt′ *or* men′strat) *v.* **-at·ed, -at·ing.** have a period; undergo menstruation. [< LL *menstruare*, ult. < *mensis* month]

men·stru·a·tion (men′strü ā′shən *or* men strā′shən) *n.* the regular discharge of blood, secretions, and sloughed-off tissue from the uterus through the vagina, normally occurring about every four weeks in non-pregnant women from puberty to menopause.

men·stru·um (men′strü əm) *n., pl.* **-stru·ums, -stru·a** (-strü ə). *Archaic.* a liquid that dissolves solids; a solvent. [< Med.L *menstruum*, neut. of L *menstruus* monthly]

men·su·ra·bil·i·ty (men′shə rə bil′ə tē *or* men′sə rə bil′ə tē) *n.* the property of being mensurable.

men·su·ra·ble (men′shə rə bəl *or* men′sə rə bəl) *adj.* measurable. [< LL *mensurabilis* < L *mensurare*. See MEASURE, v.]

men·su·ra·tion (men′shə rā′shən *or* men′sə rā′shən) *n.* **1** the act, art, or process of measuring. **2** the branch of mathematics that deals with finding lengths, areas, and volumes. [< LL *mensuratio, -onis*, ult. < L *mensura*. See MEASURE.]

mens·wear (menz′wer′) *n., adj.* —*n.* **1** men's clothing. **2** cloth suitable for making men's clothing. —*adj.* of or made from this kind of cloth: *menswear terylene.*

–ment *noun-forming suffix.* **1** the act or state or fact of ——ing, as in *enjoyment, management.* **2** the state or condition or fact of being ——ed, as in *amazement, astonishment.* **3** the product or result of ——ing, as in *pavement.* **4** a means or instrument for ——ing, as in *inducement.* [< F < L *-mentum*]

men·tal (men′təl) *adj.* **1** of, having to do with, or involving the mind: *mental processes, mental alertness.* **2** done by or in the mind, without being spoken or written down: *a mental calculation. He accepted the invitation but with the mental reservation to leave early.* **3** of, having to do with, or suffering from a disorder of the mind that affects thoughts, feelings and behavior: *mental illness, a mental patient.* **4** designating a place for the care and treatment of people with mental illness: *a mental hospital.* [< LL *mentalis* < L *mens, mentis* mind] —**men′tal·ly**, *adv.*

mental age *Psychology.* an estimate of the level of mental development as measured against the chronological age at which this development is reached by the average person.

men·tal·ism (men′təl iz′əm) *n. Philosophy.* the doctrine that the fundamental reality is mind and the material world exists only as a perception of the mind.

men·tal·ist (men′təl ist) *n.* **1** a person who advocates mentalism. **2** mind reader.

men·tal·is·tic (men′təl is′tik) *adj.* of or having to do with mentalism or mentalists. —**men′tal·is′ti·cal·ly**, *adv.*

men·tal·i·ty (men tal′ə tē) *n., pl.* **-ties. 1** mental capacity; mind:

An idiot has a very low mentality. **2** attitude or outlook: *the Eastern mentality.*

mental reservation an unexpressed qualification of a statement.

mental telepathy extrasensory perception.

men·thol (men′thol) *n.* a white crystalline substance obtained from oil of peppermint, used in medicine. *Formula:* $C_{10}H_{20}O$ [< G < L *menta* mint + *oleum* oil]

men·tho·lat·ed (men′thə lāt′id) *adj.* containing menthol.

men·tion (men′shən) *v., n.* —*v.* speak about; refer to.
not to mention, not even considering; besides.
—*n.* a short statement (about); reference (to).
make mention of, speak of; refer to.
[ME < OF < L *mentio, -onis*] —**men′tion·a·ble,** *adj.*

men·tor (men′tər) *n.* a wise and trusted adviser. [< *Mentor,* a faithful friend of Odysseus. Disguised as Mentor, the goddess Athena acted as the teacher and adviser of Odysseus' son Telemachus.]

men·u (men′yü) *n.* **1** a list of the food served at a meal; bill of fare. **2** the food served. [< F *menu* small, detailed < L *minutus* made small. Doublet of MINUTE.]

me·ow (mē ou′) *n., v.* —*n.* the sound made by a cat. —*v.* make the sound of a cat. Also, **miaow, miaou.** [imitative]

Meph·i·stoph·e·les (mef′ə stof′ə lēz′) *n.* **1** in the Faust legend, the devil. **2** a powerful evil spirit; a crafty devil.

Meph·is·to·phe·li·an (mef′is tə fē′lē ən) *adj.* **1** like Mephistopheles; wicked and crafty; sardonic; scoffing. **2** of or having to do with Mephistopheles.

me·phit·ic (mi fit′ik) *adj.* **1** having a nasty smell. **2** noxious; poisonous; pestilential. [< LL *mephiticus* < *mephitis* stench]

me·phi·tis (mi fī′tis) *n.* **1** a foul or nasty smell. **2** a poisonous or nasty vapor arising from the earth. [< L < Gk.]

mer·can·tile (mèr′kən tīl′) *adj.* **1** of or having to do with merchants or trade; commercial: *a successful mercantile venture.* **2** engaged in trade or commerce: *a mercantile firm.* **3** of or having to do with mercantilism. [< F < Ital. *mercantile* < *mercante* merchant]

mercantile system mercantilism.

mer·can·til·ism (mèr′kən tīl iz′əm) *n.* a theory or system of political economy that stressed the holding of gold and other precious metals, a greater volume of exports than imports, and the exploitation of colonies. Mercantilism replaced feudalism.

mer·can·til·ist (mèr′kən tīl′ist) *n.* a person who favors mercantilism.

Mer·ca·tor projection (mèr kā′tər) a method of drawing maps with straight instead of curved lines for latitude and longitude. [after Gerhardus *Mercator* (1512-1594), a Flemish map maker]

mer·ce·nar·y (mèr′sə ne′rē) *adj., n., pl.* **-nar·ies.** —*adj.* **1** working for money only; acting with money as the sole motive. **2** done only for money or gain. —*n.* a soldier serving for pay in a foreign army. [ME < L *mercenarius* < *merces* wages] —**mer′ce·nar′i·ly,** *adv.* —**mer′ce·nar′i·ness,** *n.*

mer·cer (mèr′sər) *n. Brit.* a dealer in textile fabrics, especially fine silks, etc. [ME < AF < OF *mercier* merchant, ult. < L *merx, mercis* goods. See MARKET.]

mer·cer·ize (mèr′sər īz′) *v.* **-ized, -iz·ing.** treat (cotton thread or cloth) with a chemical solution that strengthens it, makes it hold dyes better, and gives it a silky lustre. [after John *Mercer* (1791-1866), a British calico printer, who patented the process in 1850]

mer·chan·dise (*n.* mèr′chən dīs′ *or* mèr′chən dīz′; *v.* mèr′chən dīz′) *n., v.* **-dised, -dis·ing.** —*n.* goods for sale; wares; articles bought and sold. —*v.* **1** buy and sell; trade. **2** strive for increased sales or greater acceptance of goods, services, etc. by attractive display, advertising, etc. [ME < OF *marchandise* < *marchand* merchant] —**mer′chan·dis′er,** *n.*

mer·chant (mèr′chənt) *n., adj.* —*n.* **1** a person who buys and sells commodities for profit. **2** storekeeper. —*adj.* trading; having to do with trade: *merchant ships.* [ME < OF *marchant,* ult. < L *merx, mercis* wares]

mer·chant·a·ble (mèr′chən tə bəl) *adj.* marketable. [ME < obs. *v. merchant* + *-able*]

mer·chant·man (mèr′chənt mən) *n., pl.* **-men.** a ship used in commerce.

merchant marine 1 ships used in commerce. **2** the sailors who work on such ships, thought of as a group: *John's brother is in the merchant marine.*

merchant vessel a ship used in commerce.

Mer·cian (mèr′sē ən, mèr′shē ən, *or* mèr′shən) *adj., n.* —*adj.* of Mercia, in ancient times an Anglo-Saxon kingdom in central England, its people, or their dialect. —*n.* **1** a native or inhabitant of

hat, āge, fär; let, ēqual, tèrm; it, īce
hot, ōpen, ôrder; oil, out; cup, pùt, rüle,
above, takən, pencəl, lemən, circəs

ch, child; ng, long; sh, ship
th, thin; ŦH, then; zh, measure

Mercia. **2** the dialect of Anglo-Saxon spoken in Mercia.

mer·ci·ful (mèr′si fəl) *adj.* having mercy; showing or feeling mercy; full of mercy. —**mer′ci·ful·ly,** *adv.* —**mer′ci·ful·ness,** *n.*

mer·ci·less (mèr′si lis) *adj.* without mercy; having or showing no mercy: *a merciless attack.* —**mer′ci·less·ly,** *adv.* —**mer′ci·less·ness,** *n.*

mer·cu·ri·al (mər kyür′ē əl) *adj., n.* —*adj.* **1** sprightly; quick. **2** changeable; fickle. **3** caused by the use of mercury: *mercurial poisoning.* **4** containing mercury: *a mercurial ointment.* —*n.* a drug containing mercury. —**mer·cu′ri·al·ly,** *adv.*

mer·cu·ric (mər kyür′ik) *adj.* of compounds, containing mercury with a valence of two.

mercuric chloride a poisonous crystalline compound used as a disinfectant, for engraving metals, etc. *Formula:* $HgCl_2$

Mer·cu·ro·chrome (mər kyür′ə krōm′) *n. Trademark.* a red liquid containing mercury, used as an antiseptic. *Formula:* $C_{20}H_8Br_2HgNa_2O_6$ [< *mercury* + *chrome*]

mer·cu·rous (mər kyür′əs *or* mèr′kyə rəs) *adj.* of compounds, containing mercury with a valence of one.

mer·cu·ry (mèr′kyə rē) *n., pl.* **-ries. 1** a heavy, silver-white metallic chemical element that is liquid at ordinary temperatures. *Symbol:* Hg; *at.no.* 80; *at.wt.* 200.59. **2** the column of mercury in a thermometer or barometer. **3 Mercury, a** *Roman mythology.* the messenger of the gods, the god of commerce, skill of hands, quickness of wit, and eloquence, corresponding to the Greek god Hermes. **b** *Astronomy.* the planet that is the smallest in the solar system and nearest to the sun. [< L *Mercurius* Mercury]

mer·cy (mèr′sē) *n., pl.* **-cies. 1** more kindness than justice requires; kindness beyond what can be claimed or expected: *The judge showed mercy to the young offender.* **2** kindly treatment; pity. **3** something to be thankful for; blessing: *It's a mercy that they arrived safely through the storm.*
at the mercy of, in the power of: *Without shelter we were at the mercy of the storm.*
[ME < OF *merci* < L *merces* reward]
➤ *Syn.* **1. Mercy, clemency** = kindness or mildness shown to an enemy, an offender, etc. **Mercy** = compassion shown by refraining from punishing severely those deserving severity or from treating harshly enemies and others in one's power: *The guard showed mercy to the prisoners.* **Clemency** suggests showing mercy because of mildness of disposition rather than from sympathy: *That judge's clemency is well-known.*

mercy flight *Cdn.* especially in the North, an aircraft flight to fetch a seriously ill or injured person to hospital for treatment.

mercy seat 1 in the Bible, the gold covering on the Ark of the Covenant, regarded as the resting place of God. **2** the throne of God.

mere¹ (mēr) *adj. superl.* **mer·est.** nothing else than; only; simple: *The cut was a mere scratch.* [< L *merus* pure]

mere² (mēr) *n. Poetic or dialect.* lake; pond. [OE]

mere·ly (mēr′lē) *adv.* simply; only; and nothing more; and that is all.

me·ren·gue (mə reng′gā′) *n.* **1** a fast, rhythmic Caribbean dance in duple time. **2** music for this dance. [< Sp.]

mer·e·tri·cious (mer′ə trish′əs) *adj.* attractive in a showy way; alluring by false charms: *A wooden building painted to look like marble is meretricious.* [< L *meretricius* < *meretrix, -tricis* prostitute < *mereri* earn] —**mer′e·tri′cious·ly,** *adv.* —**mer′e·tri′cious·ness,** *n.*

mer·gan·ser (mər gan′sər) *n., pl.* **-sers** *or* (*esp. collectively*) **-ser.** any of several large diving ducks (genera *Mergus* and *Lophodytes*) having a long, slender bill with a hooked top and sharp, toothlike projections along the edges which help to catch and hold fish. [< NL *merganser* < *mergus* diver + *anser* goose]

merge (mèrj) *v.* **merged, merg·ing. 1** combine or cause to combine into one: *The brothers decided to merge their two businesses.* **2** come or bring together gradually or smoothly; blend: *merging cultures, merging traffic. The distant walker merged with the darkness.* [< L *mergere* dip]

merg·er (mèr′jər) *n.* the act of merging; combination: *One big company was formed by the merger of four small ones.*

me·rid·i·an (mə rid′ē ən) *n., adj.* —*n.* **1** an imaginary circle

passing through any place on the earth's surface and through the North and South Poles. **2** the half of such a circle from pole to pole. All the places on the same meridian have the same longitude. See **equator** for picture. **3** the highest point that the sun or a star reaches in the sky. **4** the highest point; the time of greatest success and happiness: *The meridian of life is the prime of life.* **5** one of a series of north-south lines used as a basis of land surveys. See also **First Meridian.**
—*adj.* highest; greatest. [ME < OF < L *meridianus,* ult. < *medius* middle + *dies* day]

me·rid·i·o·nal (mə rid′ē ə nəl) *adj., n.* —*adj.* **1** southern; southerly; characteristic of the south or people living there, especially of southern France. **2** of, having to do with, or resembling a meridian. **3** along a meridian; in a north-south direction: *a meridional flow of air; a meridional chain of weather stations.*
—*n.* an inhabitant of the south, especially the south of France. [< LL *meridionalis* < L *meridies* noon, south < *medius* middle + *dies* day; patterned after *septentrionalis* northern] —**me·rid′i·o·nal·ly,** *adv.*

me·ringue (mə rang′) *n.* **1** a mixture of egg white and sugar, beaten until stiff: *Meringue is often spread on pies, puddings, etc. and lightly browned in the oven.* **2** a small cake, tart shell, etc. made of this mixture. [< F]

me·ri·no (mə rē′nō) *n., pl.* **-nos. 1** a breed of sheep, originating in Spain, having long, fine wool. **2** the wool of this sheep. **3** a soft yarn made from it. **4** a thin, soft cloth made from this yarn or some substitute. **5** (*adj.*) made of this wool, yarn, or cloth. [< Sp.]

mer·it (mer′it) *n., v.* —*n.* **1** goodness; worth or value. **2** anything that deserves praise or reward. **3** Usually, **merits,** *pl.* actual facts or qualities, whether good or bad: *The judge will consider the case on its merits.*
—*v.* deserve. [< F < L *meritum* earned]
☛ *Syn. n.* **1. Merit, worth** = the goodness or value of someone or something. **Merit** emphasizes the idea of something earned, and suggests an excellence in accomplishment or quality that deserves praise: *The merits of your plan outweigh the defects.* **Worth** emphasizes inherent excellence or value, apart from any connections or conditions affecting its usefulness, value, or importance: *The worth of the new drugs is certain, although all their uses are not yet known.*

mer·i·toc·ra·cy (mer′ə tok′rə sē) *n.* **1** an elite class of people distinguished for their high intellect or talent rather than for birth or wealth. **2** leadership or rule by such a group. **3** a social or educational system in which individuals achieve high status on the basis of intellect or talent.

mer·i·to·ri·ous (mer′ə tô′rē əs) *adj.* deserving reward or praise; having merit; worthy. —**mer′i·to′ri·ous·ly,** *adv.* —**mer′i·to′ri·ous·ness,** *n.*

merle or **merl** (mėrl) *n. Poetic.* the common European blackbird. [< F < L *merula*]

mer·lin (mėr′lən) *n.* the usual European name for pigeon hawk. Merlins are often trained for falconry. [ME < AF *merilun* < OF *esmerillon* < Gmc.]

Mer·lin (mėr′lən) *n. Arthurian legend.* the magician who was adviser to King Arthur.

mer·lon (mėr′lən) *n.* the solid part between two openings in a battlement. [< F < Ital. *merlone*]

mer·maid (mėr′mād′) *n.* an imaginary sea maiden having the form of a fish from the waist down. [< *mere*[2] + *maid*]

mer·man (mėr′man′ *or* mėr′mən) *n., pl.* **-men.** an imaginary man of the sea having the form of a fish from the waist down.

Mer·o·vin·gi·an (mer′ə vin′jē ən) *adj., n.* —*adj.* designating or having to do with the Frankish line of kings who reigned in France from about A.D. 500 to 751. —*n.* one of these kings.

mer·ri·ment (mer′ē mənt) *n.* laughter and gaiety; fun; mirth; merry enjoyment.

mer·ry (mer′ē) *adj.* **-ri·er, -ri·est. 1** full of fun; loving fun. **2** happy; joyful: *a merry holiday.* **3** *Archaic.* pleasant; delightful.
make merry, laugh and be happy; have fun.
[OE *myrge*] —**mer′ri·ly,** *adv.* —**mer′ri·ness,** *n.*
☛ *Syn.* **1.** See note at **gay.**

mer·ry–an·drew (mer′ē an′drü) *n.* a clown; buffoon.

mer·ry–go–round (mer′ē gō round′) *n.* **1** a set of animal figures and seats on a platform that is driven round and round by machinery and that people ride for fun. **2** any whirl or rapid round: *The holidays were a merry-go-round of parties.*

mer·ry·mak·er (mer′ē māk′ər) *n.* a person who is being merry; a person engaged in merrymaking.

mer·ry·mak·ing (mer′ē māk′ing) *n., adj.* —*n.* **1** laughter and

gaiety; fun. **2** a gay festival; merry entertainment. —*adj.* gay and full of fun; engaged in merrymaking.

mer·ry·thought (mer′ē thot′ *or* -thôt′) *n.* wishbone.

me·sa (mā′sə) *n. U.S.* an isolated, flat-topped hill or upland with steep sides, similar to a butte, but usually wider. [< Sp. < L *mensa* table]

més·al·li·ance (mā zal′ē əns; *French,* mā zä lyäns′) *n. French.* a misalliance; marriage with a person of lower social position.

mes·cal (mes kal′) *n.* **1** an alcoholic drink made from the fleshy leaves of any of various agaves. **2** any agave from which this drink is made. **3** a small, spineless cactus (*Lophophora williamsii*) of Mexico and the SW United States having buttonlike tubercles that yield mescaline and are used especially among Mexican Indian peoples for their stimulating and hallucinogenic effects. [< Sp. < Nahuatl *mexcalli* liquor]

mes·cal·in (mes′kə lin) *n.* mescaline.

mes·cal·ine (mes′kəl ēn′ *or* mes′kəl in) *n.* a narcotic drug that produces hallucinations and is chemically related to LSD, derived from mescal (def. 3). *Formula:* $C_{11}H_{17}NO_3$

mes·dames (me däm′) *n. pl.* of **madame.**

mes·de·moi·selles (med mwä zel′) *n. pl.* of **mademoiselle.**

me·seems (mi sēmz′) *v.* **-seemed.** *Archaic.* it seems to me.

mes·en·ter·y (mes′ən ter′ē) *n., pl.* **-ter·ies.** *Anatomy.* a membrane that enfolds and supports an internal organ, attaching it to the body wall or to another organ. [< Med.L < Gk. *mesenterion* < *mesos* middle + *enteron* intestine]

mesh (mesh) *n., v.* —*n.* **1** one of the open spaces of a net, sieve, or screen: *This net has one-centimetre meshes.* **2** a fabric of thread, cord, wire, etc. knitted, knotted, or woven in an open texture with small holes: *We found an old fly swatter made of wire mesh.* **3** the engagement of gear teeth.
in mesh, in gear; fitted together.
—*v.* **1** catch or be caught in a net. **2** engage or become engaged. The teeth of the small gear mesh with the teeth of a larger one. [cf. OE *mǣscre* net]

mes·mer·ic (mes mer′ik *or* mez mer′ik) *adj.* hypnotic. —**mes·mer′i·cal·ly,** *adv.*

mes·mer·ism (mes′mər iz′əm *or* mez′mər iz′əm) *n.* hypnotism. [after Franz Anton *Mesmer* (1734-1815), an Austrian physician who popularized it]

mes·mer·ist (mes′mər ist *or* mez′mər ist) *n.* hypnotist.

mes·mer·ize (mes′mər īz′ *or* mez′mər īz′) *v.* **-ized, -iz·ing.** hypnotize. —**mes′mer·iz′er,** *n.*

meso– *combining form.* mid, middle, as in *mesocarp, mesoderm, mesomorph.* Also, before vowels, **mes-.** [< Gk. *mesos* middle]

mes·o·carp (mes′ə kärp′) *n. Botany.* the middle layer of the pericarp, such as the fleshy part of a peach or plum. [< *meso-* + Gk. *karpos* fruit]

mes·o·derm (mes′ə dėrm′) *n. Biology.* the middle layer of cells in an embryo. [< *meso-* + Gk. *derma* skin]

mes·o·lith·ic or **Mes·o·lith·ic** (mes′ə lith′ik) *adj. Anthropology.* of or relating to the period in the Stone Age between the neolithic and the paleolithic periods. [< *meso-* + Gk. *lithos* stone + E *-ic*]

mes·o·morph (mes′ə môrf′) *n.* **1** a human body type characterized by a medium frame, medium height, and the capacity for good, even muscular development. It is one of three basic body types. Compare **ectomorph, endomorph. 2** a person having such a body structure. [< *meso-* + Gk. *morphē* form, shape]

mes·o·mor·phic (mes′ə môr′fik) *adj.* of, having to do with, or being a mesomorph.

mes·on (mes′on) *n.* a highly unstable particle found in the nucleus of an atom, having either a positive or negative charge and a very short lifetime (about a millionth of a second or less). Theoretically, mesons exert nuclear forces of attraction. [< Gk. *meson,* neut. of adj. *mesos* middle]

Mes·o·po·ta·mi·a (mes′ə pə tā′mē ə *or* mes′ə pə tam′yə) *n.* an ancient country in SW Asia, between the Tigris and Euphrates rivers. —**Mes′o·po·ta′mi·an,** *adj. or n.*

mes·o·sphere (mes′ə sfēr′) *n.* the layer of the earth's atmosphere lying above the stratosphere, extending from about 50 km to about 85 km above the earth's surface, and characterized by a decrease in temperature with increasing altitude, to about −90°C at the point where the thermosphere begins.

mes·o·tron (mes′ə tron′) *n.* meson. [< *meson* + *electron*]

Mes·o·zo·ic (mes′ə zō′ik *or* mes′ə zō′ik) *adj., n. Geology.* —*adj.* **1** of, having to do with, or designating the era before the present era, beginning about 200 million years ago. The Mesozoic era is the age of reptiles. **2** of, having to do with, or designating the

system of rocks formed during this era. —*n.* the Mesozoic era or its rocks. [< *meso-* + Gk. *zōē* life + E *-ic*]

mes·quite (mes kēt′ *or* mes′kēt) *n.* a spiny tree or shrub (*Prosopis juliflora*) of the pea family found in the southwestern United States and Mexico, bearing sugary pods of seeds used as fodder. [< Sp. *mezquite* < Nahuatl *mizquitl*]

mess (mes) *n., v.* —*n.* **1** a dirty or untidy mass or group of things; a dirty or untidy condition: *There was a mess of dirty dishes in the sink.* **2** confusion or difficulty: *His affairs are in a mess.* **3** an unpleasant or unsuccessful affair or state of affairs: *He made a mess of his final examinations.* **4** a group of people who eat together regularly, especially such a group in the armed forces. **5** a meal for such a group: *The officers are at mess now.* **6** in the armed forces: **a** an organization for social purposes: *He was secretary of the sergeants' mess.* **b** the dining-room, lounge, etc. used by members of such an organization. **7** a portion of food; portion of soft food: *a mess of porridge, a mess of fish.* **8** food that does not look or taste good. —*v.* **1** make dirty or untidy: *He messed up his book by scribbling on the pages.* **2** make a failure of; spoil: *He messed up his chances of winning the race.* **3** take one's meals (*with*).
mess about *or* **mess around,** busy oneself without seeming to accomplish anything.
[ME < OF *mes* < LL *missus* (course) put (i.e., on the dinner table), pp. of *mittere* send]

mes·sage (mes′ij) *n.* **1** information or instructions sent from one person to another. **2** an official speech or writing: *On Christmas Day we listened to the Queen's message to the Commonwealth.* **3** a lesson or moral implied in a work or works of fiction, a motion picture, play, etc. **4** inspired words: *the message of a prophet.* **5** the business entrusted to a messenger; mission; errand: *His message completed, he went on his way.* [ME < OF, ult. < L *missus*, pp. of *mittere* send]

mes·sa·line (mes′ə lēn′ *or* mes′ə lēn′) *n.* a thin, soft silk cloth with a surface like satin. [< F]

mes·sen·ger (mes′ən jər) *n.* **1** a person who carries a message or goes on an errand. **2** a sign that something is coming; forerunner: *Dawn is the messenger of day.* **3** a government official employed to carry dispatches; courier. [ME *messanger,* earlier *messager* < OF *messagier* < *message.* See MESSAGE.]

mess hall in the armed forces, a place where a group of people eat together regularly.

Mes·si·ah (mə sī′ə) *n.* **1** *Judaism.* according to some interpretations of the writings of the ancient Hebrew prophets, the deliverer promised to the Hebrews, who would establish a kingdom of righteousness on earth. **2** *Christianity.* Jesus Christ. **3 messiah,** a person thought of as a great savior or liberator of a people or country. [var. of LL *Messias* < Gk. < Hebrew *mashiah* anointed]

Mes·si·an·ic (mes′ē an′ik) *adj.* **1** of or having to do with the Messiah. **2 messianic,** of, having to do with, or characteristic of a messiah. —**mes′si·an′i·cal·ly,** *adv.*

mes·sieurs (mes′ərz; *French,* mā syœ′) *n.* pl. of **monsieur.** gentlemen. See note at **Messrs.**

mess·man (mes′mən) *n., pl.* **-men.** a waiter on a ship.

mess·mate (mes′māt′) *n.* especially in the armed services, one of a group of people who eat together regularly.

Messrs. (mes′ərz) *n.pl.* pl. of **Mr.** *Messrs. Trudeau* and *Clark.*
☛ *Usage.* **Messrs.** is also sometimes used in addressing firms (*Messrs. Elken, Marci, and Company*).

mess·y (mes′ē) *adj.* **mess·i·er, mess·i·est.** **1** in a mess; untidy; dirty. **2** badly done. —**mess′i·ness,** *n.*

mes·ti·zo (mes tē′zō) *n., pl.* **-zos** *or* **-zoes.** a person of mixed blood, especially the child of a Spaniard and an American Indian. [< Sp., ult. < L *mixtus* mixed]

met (met) *v.* pt. and pp. of **meet¹.**

met. 1 metaphor. **2** metaphysics. **3** meteorological. **4** metronome. **5** metropolitan.

meta– *prefix.* **1** behind, beyond, or after, as in *metaphysics.* **2** change of state or place, as in *metamorphosis.* **3** between or among, as in *metatarsal.* **4** transposed or reciprocal, as in *metathesis.* **5** similar in chemical composition, as in *metaphosphate.* [< Gk. *meta* with, after]

met·a·bol·ic (met′ə bol′ik) *adj.* having to do with metabolism. —**met′a·bol′i·cal·ly,** *adv.*

me·tab·o·lism (mə tab′ə liz′əm) *n.* the processes of building up food into living matter and using living matter so that it is broken down into simpler substances or waste matter, giving off energy. [< Gk. *metabolē* change < *meta-* into a different position + *bolē* a throwing]

me·tab·o·lize (mə tab′ə līz′) *v.* **-ized, -iz·ing. 1** subject to metabolism. **2** produce or perform metabolism.

hat, āge, fär; let, ēqual, tèrm; it, īce
hot, ōpen, ôrder; oil, out; cup, pùt, rüle,
ə above, takən, pencəl, lemən, circəs

ch, child; ng, long; sh, ship
th, thin; ᴛн, then; zh, measure

met·a·car·pal (met′ə kär′pəl) *Anatomy.* —*adj.* of or having to do with the metacarpus. —*n.* a metacarpal bone.

met·a·car·pus (met′ə kär′pəs) *n., pl.* **-pi** (-pī *or* -pē). **1** the part of the hand between the wrist (the carpus) and the fingers (the phalanges), containing five long bones. See **arm¹** for picture. **2** the corresponding part in the foreleg of an animal; the long bone or bones between the knee (the carpus) and the paw or hoof (the phalanges). [< NL, ult. < Gk. *meta-* after + *karpos* wrist]

met·a·gen·e·sis (met′ə jən′ə sis) *n.* alternation of generations.

met·al (met′əl) *n., v.* **-alled** *or* **-aled, -al·ing** *or* **-al·ing.** —*n.* **1** a substance that is usually shiny, a good conductor of heat and electricity, and can be made into wire, or hammered into sheets. Gold, silver, iron, copper, lead, tin, or aluminum are metals. **2** an alloy or mixture of these, such as steel and brass. **3** (*adj.*) made of metal or a mixture of metals: *a metal container, a metal coin.* **4** *Chemistry.* any element that can form a salt by replacing the hydrogen of an acid, or any mixture of such elements. **5** broken stone, cinders, etc. used for roads and roadbeds. **6** the melted material that becomes glass or pottery. **7** material; substance: *Cowards are not made of the same metal as heroes.* **8** *Printing.* **a** type metal. **b** the state of being set or composed in type. **9** the aggregate number, mass, or power of the guns of a warship. —*v.* furnish, cover, or fit with metal. [ME < OF < L < Gk. *metallon,* originally, mine]
☛ *Hom.* **mettle.**

metal fatigue the deterioration and breakdown of metal as a result of slight but constant stress, such as continual tapping, vibration, etc.

me·tal·lic (mə tal′ik) *adj.* **1** of, having to do with, or being a metal: *a metallic element.* **2** made of or containing a metal: *a metallic compound.* **3** that resembles or suggests metal; having a lustre, hardness, etc. like metal: *metallic blue, a metallic voice.* —**me·tal′li·cal·ly,** *adv.*

met·al·lif·er·ous (met′əl if′ər əs) *adj.* containing or yielding metal: *metalliferous rocks.* [< L *metallifer* < *metallum* metal + *ferre* to bear]

met·al·lize *or* **met·al·ize** (met′əl īz′) *v.* **-ized, -iz·ing. 1** treat or coat with metal. **2** make metallic. —**met′al·li·za′tion** *or* **met′al·i·za′tion,** *n.*

met·al·lur·gic (met′əl ėr′jik) *adj.* metallurgical.

met·al·lur·gi·cal (met′əl ėr′jə kəl) *adj.* of or having to do with metallurgy.

met·al·lur·gist (met′əl ėr′jist; *also, esp.Brit.,* mə tal′ər jist) *n.* a person who is trained in metallurgy.

met·al·lur·gy (met′əl ėr′jē; *also, esp.Brit.,* mə tal′ər jē) *n.* the science or art of working with metals. It includes the separation and refining of metals from their ores, the production of alloys, and the shaping and treatment of metals by heat, rolling, etc. [< NL *metallurgia,* ult. < Gk. *metallon* metal + *ergon* work]

met·al·work (met′əl wėrk′) *n.* **1** things made out of metal. **2** the act of making things out of metal.

met·al·work·er (met′əl wėr′kər) *n.* a person who makes things out of metal.

met·al·work·ing (met′əl wėr′king) *n.* the process of making things out of metal.

met·a·mor·phic (met′ə môr′fik) *adj.* **1** having to do with or characterized by change of form. **2** *Geology.* designating rock that has derived from either igneous or sedimentary rock that has undergone changes in composition, texture, or internal structure through the action of pressure, heat moisture, etc. Slate is a metamorphic rock formed from shale.

met·a·mor·phism (met′ə môr′fiz əm) *n.* **1** a change of form. **2** *Geology.* a change in the structure of a rock caused by pressure, heat, etc.

met·a·mor·phose (met′ə môr′fōz *or* met′ə môr′fōs) *v.* **-phosed, -phos·ing. 1** change in form; transform: *The witch metamorphosed people into animals.* **2** change the form or structure of by metamorphosis or metamorphism. **3** undergo metamorphosis or metamorphism.

met·a·mor·pho·sis (met′ə môr′fə sis *or* met′ə môr fō′sis) *n., pl.* **-ses** (-sēz′). **1** a change of form. Tadpoles become frogs by metamorphosis; they lose their tails and grow legs. **2** the changed

form. **3** a noticeable or complete change of character, appearance, or condition. **4** a marked change in the form, and usually the habits, of an animal in its development after the embryonic stage. **5** the structural or functional modification of a plant organ or structure during the course of its development. [< L < Gk. *metamorphōsis*, ult. < *meta-* over + *morphē* form]

met·a·phor (met′ə fər *or* met′ə fôr′) *n.* an implied comparison between two different things; a figure of speech in which a word or phrase that ordinarily means one thing is used of another thing in order to suggest a likeness between the two. *Examples: a copper sky, a heart of stone.* Compare **simile.**
mix metaphors, confuse two or more metaphors in the same expression.
[< F < L < Gk. *metaphora* transfer, ult. < *meta-* over + *pherein* carry]
☛ *Usage.* **Metaphor, simile.** Both are figures of speech that make comparisons. A **simile,** says explicitly that one thing is like another, using a word such as **like** or **as:** *This play reflects reality as a mirror does.* A **metaphor** compares implicitly by speaking of one thing as if it were another: *This play is a mirror of reality. This play uses a bent mirror to reflect a warped reality.*

met·a·phor·i·cal (met′ə fôr′ə kəl) *adj.* using metaphors; figurative. —**met′a·phor′i·cal·ly,** *adv.*
met·a·phys·i·cal (met′ə fiz′ə kəl) *adj.* **1** of metaphysics; about the real nature of things. **2** highly abstract; hard to understand. **3** concerned with abstract thought or subjects: *a metaphysical mind.* **4** of or having to do with a group of English poets of the 1600's whose verse is characterized by abstruse conceits and the use of unexpected or elaborate imagery. —**met′a·phys′i·cal·ly,** *adv.*
met·a·phy·si·cian (met′ə fə zish′ən) *n.* a person skilled in or familiar with metaphysics.
met·a·phys·ics (met′ə fiz′iks) *n.* **1** the branch of philosophy that tries to explain reality and knowledge; philosophical study of the real nature of the universe. **2** the more abstruse or speculative divisions of philosophy, thought of as a unit. **3** *Informal.* any process of reasoning thought of as abstruse or extremely subtle. [ME < Med.L. *metaphysica* < Med.Gk. (*ta*) *metaphysika* for Gk. *ta meta ta physika* those (works) after the Physics; with reference to the philosophical works of Aristotle]
me·tas·ta·sis (mə tas′tə sis) *n., pl.* **-ses** (-sēs′). **1** the spread or transfer of disease from one part of the body to another, especially the transfer of malignant cells of a tumor to another part of the body via the bloodstream or lymphatic system. **2** a change or transformation, such as a change of theme or subject in rhetoric. [< LL < Gk. *metastasis* removal, ult. < *meta-* + *histanai* place]
met·a·tar·sal (met′ə tär′səl) *adj., n.* —*adj.* of or having to do with the metatarsus. —*n.* a metatarsal bone: *The human foot has five metatarsals.*
met·a·tar·sus (met′ə tär′səs) *n., pl.* **-si** (-sī *or* -sē). **1** the part of the foot between the heel and ankle (the tarsus) and the toes (the phalanges), containing five long bones. The metatarsus includes the instep and arch of the foot. See **leg** for picture. **2** the corresponding part in the hind leg of an animal; the long bone or bones between the hock (the tarsus) and the paw or hoof (the phalanges). In a hoofed animal such as the horse, the metatarsus is called the cannon bone. [< NL < Gk. *meta-* after + *tarsos* flat of the foot]
me·tath·e·sis (mə tath′ə sis) *n., pl.* **-ses** (-sēz′). **1** the transposition of sounds, syllables, or letters in a word. **2** *Chemistry.* the interchange of atoms between two molecules. **3** a transposition; reversal. [< LL < Gk. *metathesis* transposition, ult. < *meta-* over + *tithenai* set]
met·a·zo·a (met′ə zō′ə) *n.* pl. of **metazoon.**
Met·a·zo·a (met′ə zō′ə) *n. Zoology.* a large division of animals comprising the metazoans. [< NL, ult. < Gk. *meta-* after + *zōion* animal]
met·a·zo·an (met′ə zō′ən) *n., adj.* —*n.* any animal belonging to a large zoological group (Metazoa) including all animals having a body composed of many cells arranged into different tissues and organs with specialized functions. This group includes most of the phyla in the animal kingdom. —*adj.* of, having to do with, or designating this group of animals. [< *Metazoa*]
met·a·zo·on (met′ə zō′on *or* -zō′ən) *n., pl.* **-zo·a** (-zō′ə). metazoan.
mete¹ (mēt) *v.* **met·ed, met·ing. 1** give to each a share of; distribute; allot. **2** *Poetic.* measure. [OE *metan*]
☛ *Hom.* **meat, meet.**
mete² (mēt) *n.* **1** boundary. **2** a boundary stone. [ME < OF < L *meta*]
☛ *Hom.* **meat, meet.**
met·em·psy·cho·sis (met′əm sī kō′sis *or* mə temp′sə kō′sis) *n., pl.* **-ses** (-sēz). the passing of the soul at death into a new body.

Some Oriental philosophies, such as Hinduism and Buddhism, teach that by metempsychosis a person's soul lives again in an animal's body. [< L < Gk. *metempsychōsis* < *meta-* over + *empsychoein* animate, ult. < *en* in + *psychē* soul]
me·te·or (mē′tē ər) *n.* a mass of stone or metal that comes toward the earth from outer space at enormous speed; shooting star. Meteors become so hot from hurtling through the air that they glow and usually burn up. [ME < Med.L. < Gk. *meteōron* (thing) in the air, ult. < *aeirein* lift]
me·te·or·ic (mē′tē ôr′ik) *adj.* **1** of meteors. **2** flashing like a meteor; brilliant and soon ended. **3** of the atmosphere: *Wind and rain are meteoric phenomena.*
me·te·or·ite (mē′tē ər īt′) *n.* a mass of stone or metal that has fallen to the earth from outer space; fallen meteor.
me·te·o·rit·ic (mē′tē ə rit′ik) *adj.* of or having to do with meteorites: *meteoritic craters.*
me·te·or·o·log·ic (mē′tē ər ə loj′ik) *adj.* meteorological.
me·te·or·o·log·i·cal (mē′tē ər ə loj′ə kəl) *adj.* **1** of or having to do with the atmosphere and weather. **2** of or having to do with meteorology.
me·te·or·o·log·i·cal·ly (mē′tē ər ə loj′ik lē) *adv.* in meteorological respects; by meteorology; according to meteorology.
me·te·or·ol·o·gist (mē′tē ər ol′ə jist) *n.* a person trained in meteorology, especially one whose work it is.
me·te·or·ol·o·gy (mē′tē ər ol′ə jē) *n.* the science of the atmosphere and atmospheric conditions, especially as they relate to the weather. [< Gk. *meteōrologia* < *meteōron* (thing) in the air + -*logos* treating of]
me·ter¹ (mē′tər) See **metre².**
me·ter² (mē′tər) *n., v.* —*n.* a device that measures, or that measures and records: *a parking meter, a water meter.* —*v.* measure with a meter. [< -*meter*]
☛ *Hom.* **metre.**
–meter *combining form.* **1** a device for measuring, as in *speedometer, thermometer.* **2** having a specified number of metrical feet, as in *pentameter, hexameter.* [< NL -*metrum* < Gk. *metron* measure]
Meth. Methodist.
meth·a·done (meth′ə dōn′) *n.* a synthetic narcotic drug similar to morphine but less habit-forming. It is used for the relief of pain and as a substitute narcotic in treatment of heroin addiction. *Formula:* $C_{21}H_{27}NO$ [< d*imethyl* + *amino* + d*iphenyl* + -*one.* 20c.]
meth·am·phet·a·mine (meth′am fet′ə mēn′ *or* -am fet′ə min) *n.* an amphetamine derivative used as a mood-elevating drug. *Formula:* $C_{10}H_{15}N$ [< *methyl* + *amphetamine.* 20c.]
meth·ane (meth′ān) *n.* a colorless, odorless, inflammable gas, the simplest of the hydrocarbons. Methane comes from marshes, petroleum wells, volcanoes, and coal mines. *Formula:* CH_4 [< *methyl*]
meth·a·nol (meth′ə nol′) *n.* a colorless, poisonous, volatile, flammable liquid obtained from the destructive distillation of wood or from the catalytic treatment of carbon monoxide and hydrogen. It is extensively used as a fuel, antifreeze, solvent, etc. *Formula:* CH_3OH [< *methane* + -*ol*]
me·theg·lin (mə theg′lin) *n.* an alcoholic drink made from fermented honey and water; a kind of mead. [< Welsh *meddyglyn*]
me·thinks (mi thingks′) *v.* **-thought.** *Archaic.* it seems to me. [OE *mē thyncth* it seems to me]
meth·od (meth′əd) *n.* **1** a way of doing something. **2** order or system in getting things done or in thinking: *If you used more method, you wouldn't waste so much time.*
method in (one's) **madness,** system and sense underlying apparent folly.
[< L < Gk. *methodos,* originally, pursuit < *meta-* after + *hodos* a travelling]
☛ *Syn.* **1.** See note at **way.**
me·thod·ic (mə thod′ik) *adj.* methodical.
me·thod·i·cal (mə thod′ə kəl) *adj.* **1** done or arranged according to a method or order: *a methodical procedure.* **2** tending to act according to a method: *a methodical thinker.* —**me·thod′i·cal·ly,** *adv.* —**me·thod′i·cal·ness,** *n.*
☛ *Syn.* See note at **orderly.**
Meth·od·ism (meth′əd iz′əm) *n.* the doctrines or religious principles of the Methodist churches.
Meth·od·ist (meth′əd ist) *n., adj.* —*n.* a member of any of the churches that grew out of a reform movement within the Church of England, led by John Wesley (1703-1791) and his brother Charles (1707-1788), both clergymen; these churches' tenets include acceptance of the Bible as the basic guide for faith and religious practice, with emphasis on faith through individual conversion, the

leading of a holy life in which good works are important, and the possibility of full salvation for all people. See also **United Church of Canada**. —*adj.* of or having to do with Methodists or Methodism.

meth·od·ize (meth′əd īz′) *v.* **-ized, -iz·ing.** reduce to a method; arrange with method. —**me′thod·iz′er,** *n.*

meth·od·ol·o·gist (meth′ə dol′ə jist′) *n.* a person knowledgable about or studying methodology.

meth·od·ol·o·gy (meth′ə dol′ə jē) *n.* **1** a system or body of procedures, methods, and rules used in a particular field or discipline. **2** the branch of logic that deals with the analysis of such procedures and methods. [< NL *methodologia* < Gk. *methodos* method + *-logia* science]

me·thought (mē thot′ *or* -thôt′) *v.* pt. of **methinks.** *Archaic.* it seemed to me.

Me·thu·se·lah (mə thü′zə lə) *n.* **1** in the Bible, a man said to have lived 969 years (Gen. 5:27). **2** a very old man.

meth·yl (meth′əl) *n.* a univalent, hydrocarbon radical that occurs in many organic compounds. *Formula:* CH_3 [< F *méthyle,* ult. < Gk. *methy* wine + *hylē* wood]

methyl alcohol a colorless, poisonous, inflammable liquid obtained from the distillation of wood or from the catalytic treatment of carbon monoxide and hydrogen. It is widely used as a fuel, as a solvent, etc. *Formula:* $CH_3ÖH$

methyl chloride a colorless gas used as a refrigerant and as a local anesthetic. *Formula:* CH_3Cl

meth·yl·ene (meth′ə lēn′) *n.* a bivalent organic radical derived from methane. *Formula:* CH_2

me·tic·u·lous (mə tik′yə ləs) *adj.* extremely or excessively careful about small details. [< L *meticulosus* < *metus* fear] —**me·tic′u·lous·ly,** *adv.*

mé·tier (mā tyā′) *n.* **1** a trade; profession. **2** the kind of work for which one has special ability. [< F < L *ministerium.* Doublet of MINISTRY.]

Mé·tis *or* **Me·tis** *n., pl.* **-tis;** *adj.* Cdn. *n.* a person of mixed blood, especially a person of French and North American Indian ancestry belonging to or descended from the people who established themselves in the Red, Assiniboine, and Saskatchewan river valleys during the nineteenth century, forming a cultural group distinct from both Europeans and Indians. —*adj.* of or having to do with the Métis. [< Cdn. F < F *métis* < LL *misticius, mixticius* of mixed blood]

Mé·tisse (mā tēs′) *n.* Cdn. *Rare.* a female Métis. [< Cdn.F.]

me·ton·y·my (mə ton′ə mē) *n.* the use of the name of one thing for that of another which it naturally suggests. *Example: The pen (power of literature) is mightier than the sword (military force).* [< LL < Gk. *metonymia,* literally, change of name < *meta-* over + dial. *onyma* name]

met·o·pe (met′ə pē′ *or* met′ōp) *n. Architecture.* one of the square spaces, often decorated, between triglyphs in a Doric frieze. See **order** for picture. [< L < Gk. *metopē* < *meta-* between + *opē* opening]

me·tre¹ (mē′tər) *n.* **1** *Prosody.* the rhythmical pattern resulting from the arrangement of stressed and unstressed syllables in regularly recurring groups (feet). **2** *Music. the combining of beats or notes into rhythmic groups, or the pattern formed in this way; time (def. 14).* Also, **meter.** [OE *meter* < L *metrum* poetic metre < Gk. *metron* measure, metre]
☛ *Hom.* **meter.**

me·tre² (mē′tər) *n.* an SI unit for measuring length. A twin bed is about one metre wide. The metre is one of the seven base units in the SI. *Symbol:* m Also, **meter.** [< F *mètre* < L < Gk. *metron* measure]

–metre *combining form.* metre, as in *kilometre, millimetre.*

metre–stick (mē′tər stik′) *n.* a measuring stick that is one metre long and is marked off in centimetres and millimetres.

met·ric (met′rik) *adj.* **1** of or having to do with the metre or the system of measurement based on it. **2** metrical. [(def. 1) < F *métrique* < *mètre* < L *metrum;* (def. 2) < L *metricus* < Gk. *metrikos* < *metron* measure, metre]

met·ri·cal (met′rə kəl) *adj.* **1** of or having to do with metre; having a regular arrangement of stresses; written in verse, not in prose: *a metrical translation of Homer.* **2** of, having to do with, or used in, measurement.

met·ri·cal·ly (met′rik lē) *adv.* in metre; according to metre.

met·ri·cate (met′rə kāt′) *v.* **-cat·ed, -cat·ing.** change into or express in a metric system or measurement.

met·ri·ca·tion (met′rə kā′shən) *n.* the act or process of converting from an existing system of measurement to a metric one.

metric system a decimal system of measurement, that is, one

---

hat, āge, fär; let, ēqual, tèrm; it, īce
hot, ōpen, ôrder; oil, out; cup, pùt, rüle,
əbove, takən, pencəl, lemən, circəs

ch, child; ng, long; sh, ship
th, thin; ŦH, then; zh, measure

based on tens, traditionally using the metre as the basic unit of length, the kilogram as the basic unit of mass, and the litre as the basic unit of volume or capacity. The metric system adopted by Canada is the new, simplified international version established in 1960, called the International System of Units (SI). It has a total of seven base units and two supplementary units from which all the other units are derived:

Quantity	Name	Symbol
length	metre	m
mass	kilogram	kg
time	second	s
electric current	ampere	A
thermodynamic temperature	kelvin	K
amount of substance	mole	mol
luminous intensity	candela	cd
plane angle	radian	rad
solid angle	steradian	sr

metric ton tonne.

met·ro (met′rō) *n. Informal.* **1** a metropolitan (adj., def. 3) government. **2** a metropolitan area.

me·trol·o·gy (mə trol′ə jē) *n.* **1** the science of weights and measures. **2** a system of weights and measures. [< Gk. *metron* measure + E *-logy*]

met·ro·nome (met′rə nōm′) *n.* a timing device having a pendulum that can be adjusted to tick at different speeds. A metronome is mainly used by persons practising musical instruments to help them keep time. [< Gk. *metron* measure + *-nomos* regulating < *nemein* regulate]

met·ro·nom·ic (met′rə nom′ik) *adj.* of, according to, or like a metronome.

me·trop·o·lis (mə trop′ə lis) *n.* **1** the most important city of a country or region: *London is the metropolis of England.* **2** a large city; important centre: *Montreal is a busy metropolis.* **3** the chief diocese of a church, or ecclesiastical province; the see of a metropolitan bishop. [< LL < Gk. *mētropolis* < *mētēr* mother + *polis* city]

met·ro·pol·i·tan (met′rə pol′ə tən) *adj., n.* —*adj.* **1** of, having to do with, or characteristic of a large city or large cities: *metropolitan newspapers.* **2** constituting a metropolis: *a metropolitan centre.* **3** designating a form of municipal government based on a federation of several adjacent municipalities that together form a large urban area. **4** of or having to do with the chief diocese of a church or province. **5** constituting the mother city or the mainland territory of the parent state: *metropolitan France.*
—*n.* **1** a person who lives in a large city and knows its ways. **2** *Orthodox Eastern Church.* the head of an ecclesiastical province, ranking next above an archbishop and below a patriarch. **3** *Roman Catholic Church, Anglican Church.* an archbishop having authority over the bishops of an ecclesiastical province.

metropolitan area the area or region including a large city and its suburbs.

–metry *combining form.* the process or art of measuring, as in *biometry.* [< Gk. *-metria* < *metron* measure]

met·tle (met′əl) *n.* **1** disposition or temperament. **2** spirit; courage.
on one's mettle, ready to do one's best.
[var. of *metal*]

met·tle·some (met′əl səm) *adj.* full of mettle; spirited; courageous.

me·tump (mə tump′) *n.* tumpline. [? < Abenaki]

Mev (mev) *n.* a million electron volts.

mew¹ (myü) *n., v.* —*n.* the sound made by a cat or kitten. —*v.* make such a sound. [imitative]

mew² (myü) *n.* a sea gull, especially *Larus canus.* Also called **mew gull.** [OE *mǣw*]

mew³ (myü) *n., v.* —*n.* **1** a cage in which hawks are kept, especially while moulting. **2** a place of retirement or concealment; secret place; den.
—*v.* **1** cage (a hawk), especially at moulting time. **2** shut up in a cage; conceal; confine. **3** *Archaic.* change (feathers, etc.); moult. [ME < OF *mue* < *muer* molt < L *mutare*]

mewl (myūl) *v.* cry like a baby; whimper. [imitative]
☛ *Hom.* mule.

mews (myūz) *n. Esp.Brit.* **1** stables built around a court or alley. **2** such stables converted into dwellings: *an apartment in a mews.* [originally pl. of *mew*³]
☛ *Hom.* muse.

Mex. **1** Mexico. **2** Mexican.

Mex·i·can (mek′sə kən) *n., adj.* —*n.* **1** a native or inhabitant of Mexico, a country in southern North America. **2** a person of Mexican descent. —*adj.* of or having to do with Mexico or its people.

me·zu·zah (me zü′zə) *n.* a piece of parchment inscribed with scriptural passages and kept in a small case or tube affixed to the doorpost of some Jewish homes as a sign and reminder of faith in God. [< Hebrew *mezûzāh* doorpost]

mez·za·nine (mez′ə nēn′) *n.* **1** a partial storey between two main floors of a building. It is usually just above the ground floor. **2** in a theatre, the lowest balcony, or its front section. [< F < Ital. *mezzanino* < *mezzano* middle < L *medianus.* See MEDIAN.]

mez·zo (met′sō *or* mez′ō) *adj., n.* —*adj.* **1** *Music.* middle; medium; half. **2** *Informal.* mezzo-soprano. —*n. Informal.* mezzo-soprano. [< Ital. < L *medius* middle]

mez·zo·for·te (met′sō fôr′tā *or* mez′ō-) *adj. or adv. Music.* moderately loud; half as loud as forte. [< Ital.]

mez·zo·so·pran·o (met′sō sə pran′ō *or* mez′ō-) *n., pl.* -pran·os; *adj.* —*n.* **1** an adult female singing voice having an intermediate range between soprano and alto. **2** a singer who has such a voice. —*adj.* having to do with, having the range of, or designed for a mezzo-soprano.

mez·zo·tint (met′sō tint′ *or* mez′ō-) *n., v.* —*n.* **1** an engraving on copper or steel made by polishing and scraping away parts of a roughened surface. **2** a print made from such an engraving. **3** this method of engraving. —*v.* engrave in mezzotint. [< Ital. *mezzotinto* half-tint]

mf. or **mf** *Music.* moderately loud (for Ital. *mezzo forte*).

M.F. Master of Forestry.

mfg. manufacturing.

mfr. manufacturer.

mg milligram(s).

Mg magnesium.

M.Gen. or **MGen** major-general.

Mgr. **1** manager. **2** Monsignor. **3** Monseigneur.

MHA or **M.H.A.** *Cdn.* Member of the House of Assembly (in Newfoundland).

MHG or **M.H.G.** Middle High German.

mho (mō) *n. Obsolete.* siemens. [*ohm* spelled backwards]

MHz megahertz.

mi (mē) *n. Music.* **1** the third tone of an eight-tone major scale. **2** the tone E. See **do**² for picture. [see GAMUT]

mi. **1** mile(s). **2** mill(s).

MI Michigan.

M.I.5 *Brit.* the branch of Military Intelligence dealing with security and counter-espionage in the United Kingdom.

mi·aow or **mi·aou** (mē ou′) See **meow.**

mi·as·ma (mī az′mə *or* mē az′mə) *n., pl.* -mas, -ma·ta (-mə tə). **1** a poisonous vapor rising from the earth and infecting the air. The miasma of swamps was formerly supposed to cause disease. **2** an atmosphere or influence that infects or corrupts: *a miasma of evil thoughts.* [< NL < Gk. *miasma* pollution < *miainein* pollute]

mi·ca (mī′kə) *n.* a mineral that divides into thin, partly transparent layers; isinglass. Mica withstands heat and is used for insulation. [< L *mica* grain, crumb]

mice (mīs) *n.* pl. of **mouse.**

Mich. **1** Michigan. **2** Michaelmas.

Mich·ael·mas (mik′əl məs) *n. Esp.Brit.* September 29, a Christian festival in honor of the archangel Michael.

mick·ey (mik′ē) *n. Slang.* **1** Mickey Finn. **2** *Cdn.* a half bottle of liquor or wine. **3** the detonator of a bomb.

Mickey Finn or **mickey finn** (mik′ē fin′) *Slang.* **1** a pill, etc. put into an alcoholic drink in order to drug it. **2** a drink so drugged.

Mickey Mouse not worthwhile or serious; insignificant or trivial: *a Mickey Mouse rehabilitation program, a school offering Mickey Mouse courses.*

mick·le (mik′əl) *adj., adv., n. Archaic or dialect.* much. [OE *micel*]

Mic·mac (mik′mak′) *n., pl.* -mac *or* -macs; *adj.* —*n.* **1** a member of an Amerindian people living in the Maritimes. **2** the Algonquian language of the Micmac. —*adj.* of or having to do with the Micmac or their language. [< Algonquian *migmac*, literally, allies]

micro– *combining form.* **1** very small, as in *micro-organism, microfilm.* **2** abnormally small, as in *microcephalic.* **3** done with or involving the use of a microscope, as in *microbiology.* **4** *SI prefix.* one-millionth: *A microsecond is one one-millionth of a second.* Symbol: *μ* [< Gk. *mikros* small]

mi·cro·bar·o·graph (mī′krō bar′ə graf′ *or* -ber′ə graf′) *n.* an instrument for recording very minor fluctuations in atmospheric pressure.

mi·crobe (mī′krōb) *n.* a micro-organism, especially a disease-producing bacterium. [< F < Gk. *mikros* small + *bios* life]

mi·cro·bi·ol·o·gy (mī′krō bī ol′ə jē) *n.* the biology of micro-organisms.

mi·cro·chem·is·try (mī′krō kem′əs trē) *n.* the branch of chemistry dealing with minute samples or quantities.

mi·cro·cir·cuit (mī′krō sèr′kit) *n.* an integrated circuit or other miniature electronic circuit.

mi·cro·coc·cus (mī′krō kok′əs) *n., pl.* -coc·ci (-kok′ī *or* -kok′sī). any of a genus (*Micrococcus*) of spherical bacteria, including species which cause the fermentation of milk. Micrococci are not generally disease-producing bacteria.

mi·cro·cop·y (mī′krō kop′ē) *n., pl.* -cop·ies; *v.* -cop·ied, cop·y·ing. —*n.* a copy made on microfilm. —*v.* make a copy of on microfilm.

mi·cro·cosm (mī′krō koz′əm) *n.* **1** a little world; universe in miniature. **2** man thought of as a miniature representation of the universe. [< F < LL *microcosmus* < LGk. *mikros kosmos* little world]

mi·cro·crys·tal·line (mī′krō kris′tə līn *or* -lən) *adj.* designating a solid composed of crystals of microscopic size: *Chalcedony is a microcrystalline variety of quartz.*

mi·cro·dot (mī′krō dot′) *n.* a photograph of a document, etc. reduced to the size of a tiny dot.

mi·cro–e·lec·tron·ic or **mi·cro·e·lec·tron·ic** (mī′krō i lek tron′ik) *adj.* of or having to do with micro-electronics.

mi·cro–e·lec·tron·ics or **mi·cro·e·lec·tron·ics** (mī′krō i lek tron′iks) *n. (used with a singular verb)* the branch of electronics that deals with the theory, manufacture, and use of electronic components of miniature size.

mi·cro·far·ad (mī′krō far′əd *or* -fer′əd) *n.* an SI unit for measuring electrical capacity, equal to one one-millionth of a farad. Symbol: *μF*

mi·cro·fiche (mī′krə fēsh′) *n., pl.* -fich·es (-fēsh′). a single sheet of microfilm, usually the same size as a filing card, carrying microcopies of numerous pages of printed matter. [< *micro-* + F *fiche* card]

mi·cro·film (mī′krō film′) *n., v.* —*n.* **1** a film for making very small photographs of pages of a book, newspapers, documents, etc. to preserve them in a very small space. **2** a photograph made on such film. —*v.* photograph on microfilm.

mi·cro·groove (mī′krō grüv′) *n.* a narrow groove used on long-playing phonograph records.

mi·crom·e·ter¹ (mī krom′ə tər) *n.* **1** an instrument for measuring very small distances, angles, objects, etc. Certain kinds are used with a microscope or telescope. **2** micrometer calliper. [< F *micromètre*]

mi·cro·me·ter² (mī′krō mē′tər) See **micrometre.**

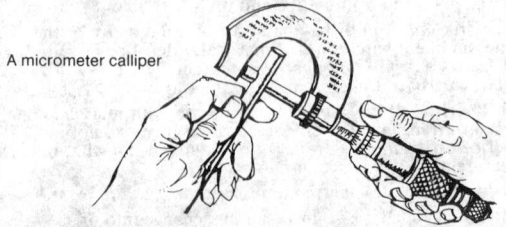

A micrometer calliper

micrometer calliper or **caliper** a calliper having an adjusting screw with a fine thread, and so capable of making very accurate measurements.

mi·cro·me·tre (mī′krō mē′tər) *n.* an SI unit for measuring length, equal to one one-millionth of a metre. The micrometre is used for measuring the size of bacteria and for other very precise

mi·cron (mī′kron) *n., pl.* **mi·crons** or **mi·cra** (mī′krə).
micrometre. [< NL < Gk. *micron,* neut. adj., small]

Mi·cro·ne·sian (mī′krō nē′zhən) *adj., n.* —*adj.* **1** of or
designating a major race of mankind that includes the traditional
inhabitants of Micronesia, a group of islands in the Pacific east of
the Philippines and north of Australia. This race, mostly closely
related to the Polynesian race, is distinguished by a combination of
biological characteristics, including dark skin and wavy or woolly
hair. **2** of or having to do with Micronesia or its peoples or their
languages.
—*n.* **1** a native or inhabitant of Micronesia. **2** a member of the
Micronesian race. Micronesians are most closely related to the
Polynesians, but are smaller, and have dark skin and wavy or
woolly hair. **3** a group of Austronesian languages spoken in
Micronesia.

mi·cro·or·gan·ism or **mi·cro·or·gan·ism** (mī′krō ôr′gən
iz′əm) *n.* any of a great number of one-celled organisms too small to
be seen with the naked eye, most of which contain no chlorophyl,
including the bacteria, viruses, yeasts, algae, fungi, and protozoans.
Because micro-organisms do not clearly show basic characteristics
identifying them as either plants or animals, some scientists group
them into a separate kingdom of living things.

mi·cro·phone (mī′krə fōn′) *n.* an instrument for increasing the
loudness of sounds or for transmitting sounds. Microphones change
sounds into variations of an electric current and are used in
recording and in radio and television broadcasting.

mi·cro·pho·to·graph (mī′krə fō′tə graf′) *n.* a very small
photograph, as on microfilm, that has to be magnified for viewing.

mi·cro·phy·sics (mī′krō fiz′iks) *n.* the branch of physics
dealing with the structure of molecules, atoms, electrons, and other
minute particles of matter.

mi·cro·pro·ces·sor (mī′krō prō′ses ər *or* -pros′es ər) *n.*
an integrated circuit consisting of usually a single chip of
semiconductor, that constitutes the central processing unit of a tiny
computer.

EYEPIECES

A binocular microscope. There
are magnifying lenses in the
eyepieces and objectives. Other
lenses, in the condenser, capture
the light rays diverging from the
light source, gathering them together
so they pass through the specimen
on the stage and on into the
objective, making the magnified
image visible.

OBJECTIVES

STAGE

CONDENSER

COARSE AND
FINE ADJUSTMENT

LIGHT
SOURCE

mi·cro·scope (mī′krə skōp′) *n.* an instrument with a lens or
combination of lenses for making small things look larger. [< NL
microscopium < Gk. *mikros* small + *-skopion* means of viewing <
skopeein look at]

mi·cro·scop·ic (mī′krə skop′ik) *adj.* **1** that cannot be seen
without using a microscope; tiny. **2** like a microscope; suggesting a
microscope: *a microscopic eye for mistakes.* **3** of or having to do
with a microscope; with a microscope.

mi·cro·scop·i·cal (mī′krə skop′ə kəl) *adj.* microscopic.

mi·cro·scop·i·cal·ly (mī′krə skop′ik lē) *adv.* **1** by the use of a
microscope. **2** as if with a microscope; in great detail.

mi·cros·co·pist (mī kros′kə pist *or* mī′krə skō′pist) *n.* a person
trained in the use of the microscope.

mi·cros·co·py (mī kros′kə pē *or* mī′krə skō′pē) *n.* the use of a
microscope; microscopic investigation.

mi·cro·sec·ond (mī′krō sek′ənd) *n.* an SI unit used for
measuring time, equal to one one-millionth of a second. *Symbol:* μs

mi·cro·spore (mī′krə spôr′) *n.* **1** *Botany.* a small spore from
which a male gametophyte develops. **2** in seed plants, a pollen
grain.

mi·cro·wave (mī′krō wāv′) *n.* **1** a very short electromagnetic
wave, especially one having a wavelength between one and one
hundred centimetres. **2** *Informal.* microwave oven.

microwave oven an oven in which food is cooked by means of
the heat produced by microwaves penetrating the food.

mid[1] (mid) *adj.* in the middle of; middle. [OE *midd*]

mid[2] or **'mid** (mid) *prep. Poetic.* amid. [var. of *amid*]

hat, āge, fär; let, ēqual, tèrm; it, īce
hot, ōpen, ôrder; oil, out; cup, put, rüle,
above, takən, pencəl, lemən, circəs

ch, child; ng, long; sh, ship
th, thin; ᴛʜ, then; zh, measure

mid– *combining form.* middle; mid; the middle point or part of:
midair = the middle part of the air.

mid. middle.

mid·air or **mid–air** (mid′er′) *n.* **1** the sky; air: *The parachute
floated in midair.* **2** uncertainty; doubt: *With the contract still in
midair, the board recessed.* **3** (*adjl.*) in midair: *a midair collision of
two jets.*

Mi·das (mī′dəs) *n.* **1** *Greek legend.* a king of Phrygia whose touch
turned everything to gold. Unable to eat or drink, he begged that his
gift be removed, and he was permitted to wash it away. **2** a man of
great moneymaking ability.
the Midas touch, the ability to make money
easily.
—**Mi′das·like′,** *adj.*

mid·brain (mid′brān′) *n.* the middle part of the brain.

mid·chan·nel (mid′chan′el) *n.* the middle part of the channel.

mid·con·ti·nent (mid′kon′tə nənt) *n.* the middle part of a
continent.

mid·day (mid′dā′) *n.* **1** the middle of the day; noon. **2** (*adjl.*) of
or like midday: *the midday meal.* [OE *middæg*]

mid·den (mid′ən) *n.* **1** a kitchen midden. **2** *Dialect.* a dunghill;
refuse heap. [apparently < Scand.; cf. Danish *mödding,* alteration
of *mög dynge* muck heap]

mid·dle (mid′əl) *adj., n.* —*adj.* **1** halfway between; in the centre;
at the same distance from either end or side; *the middle house in
the row.* **2** in between; medium: *a man of middle size.*
3 intermediate. **4** between old and modern: *Middle English.*
—*n.* **1** the point or part that is the same distance from each end or
side or other limit; central part. **2** the middle part of a person's
body; waist. [OE *middel*]
☛ *Syn. n.* **1. Middle, centre** = a point or part halfway between certain limits.
Middle most commonly applies to the part more or less the same distance from
each end, side, or other limit of a thing or between the beginning and end of a
period of action: *He came in the middle of the day.* **Centre** applies to the point
in the exact middle of something having a definite outline or shape, as of a
circle, sphere, square, or to something thought of as the point from, to, or
around which everything moves: *Ottawa is the centre of our government.*

middle age the time of life between youth and old age.

mid·dle-aged (mid′əl ājd′) *adj.* between youth and old age.

Middle Ages the period of European history between ancient
and modern times, from about A.D. 500 (or from A.D. 476, the date
of the Fall of Rome) to about A.D. 1450.

mid·dle·brow (mid′əl brou′) *n., adj.* —*n.* a person whose
intellectual and cultural interests are conventional and conservative;
one who is neither a highbrow nor a lowbrow. —*adj.* of, appealing
to, or suitable for middlebrows.

middle C *Music.* the note on the first added line below the treble
staff and the first above the bass staff.

middle class people between the aristocracy or the very
wealthy and the working class.

mid·dle-class (mid′əl klas′) *adj.* of or characteristic of the
middle class; bourgeois.

middle distance **1** the part of a landscape or scene between the
foreground and the background. **2** *Sports.* a category of footrace
between the sprints and the distance races, especially a race of 800
metres or 1500 metres. —**middle-distance,** *adjl.*

middle ear a cavity between the eardrum and the inner ear,
containing a chain of three tiny bones which transmit sound waves.
See **ear** for picture.

Middle East the region between the E Mediterranean and India,
including Egypt, the Sudan, Israel, Lebanon, Iran, Saudi Arabia,
and Turkey.

Middle English **1** the period in the development of the English
language between Old English and Modern English, lasting from
about 1100 to about 1500. **2** the language of this period. Chaucer
wrote in Middle English.

Middle French the French language from 1400 to 1600.

Middle High German the High German language from 1100 to
1450.

Middle Low German the Low German language from 1100 to
1450.

mid·dle·man (mid′əl man′) *n., pl.* **-men,** a trader or merchant

who buys goods from the producer and sells them to a retailer or directly to the consumer.

mid·dle·most (mid′əl mōst′) *adj.* in the exact middle; nearest the middle; midmost.

mid·dle-of-the-road (mid′əl əv тнə rōd′) *adj.* not extreme; moderate. —**mid′dle-of-the-road′er,** *n.*

middle term *Logic.* a term in the major and minor premises of a syllogism but not in the conclusion.

mid·dle·weight (mid′əl wāt′) *n.* **1** a boxer weighing between 71 and 75 kilograms. **2** any person or thing of average mass.

mid·dling (mid′ling) *adj., adv., n.* —*adj.* medium in size, quality, grade, etc.
—*adv. Informal or dialect.* moderately; fairly.
—*n.* **middlings,** *pl.* **a** products of medium size, quality, grade, or price. **b** coarse particles of ground wheat mixed with bran. [< *middle*]

mid·dy (mid′ē) *n., pl.* **-dies. 1** middy blouse. **2** *Informal.* a midshipman.

middy blouse a loose blouse like a sailor's, having a collar with a broad flap at the back.

Mid·gard (mid′gärd′) *n. Norse mythology.* the earth.

midge (mij) *n.* **1** any of a family (Chironomidae) of small, two-winged flies usually found in swarms around ponds and streams. Midges resemble mosquitoes, but do not bite. **2** any of various similar insects. **3** a very small person or animal. [OE *mycg*]

midg·et (mij′it) *n., adj.* —*n.* **1** a person very much smaller than normal. **2** anything much smaller than the usual size for its type or kind. —*adj.* **1** much smaller than the usual size for its type or kind: *a midget submarine.* **2** *Sports.* **a** of or for very young or very small players. **b** bantam. [< *midge*]
☞ *Syn.* See note at **dwarf.**

Mi·di (mē dē′) *n.* the south, especially the south of France.

Mid·i·an·ite (mid′ē ən īt′) *n.* in the Bible, a member of a wandering tribe of Arabs that fought against the Israelites.

mid·i·ron (mid′ī′ərn) *n. Golf.* a club with a steel or iron head having a face of medium slope.

mid·land (mid′lənd) *n., adj.* —*n.* the middle part of a country; the interior. —*adj.* in or of the midland.

mid·most (mid′mōst′) *adj.* in the exact middle; nearest the middle.

mid·night (mid′nīt′) *n.* **1** the middle of the night; especially 12 o'clock at night. **2** (*adj.*) of, at, or like midnight.
burn the midnight oil, work or study far into the night: *I'll have to burn the midnight oil again tonight if I want to get my project done.*

midnight sun the sun seen at midnight in the arctic and antarctic regions during the summer.

mid·point (mid′point′) *n.* a point at or near the centre or middle: *the midpoint of a line, the midpoint of a career.*

mid·rib (mid′rib′) *n.* the central vein of a leaf, running from the base to the tip.

mid·riff (mid′rif′) *n.* **1** the muscular wall separating the chest cavity from the abdomen; diaphragm. **2** the middle portion of the human body. [OE *midhrif* < *midd* mid + *hrif* belly]

mid·ship (mid′ship′) *adj.* in or of the middle of a ship.

mid·ship·man (mid′ship′mən) *n., pl.* **-men. 1** a person training for a naval commission; officer cadet. **2** *Historical.* a boy who assisted the officers of a ship.

mid·ships (mid′ships′) *adv.* amidships.

midst (midst) *n., prep.* —*n.* the middle.
in our (or your or their) midst, among us (or you or them): *a traitor in our midst.*
in the midst of, a in the middle of; among or surrounded by: *The bomb fell in the midst of the crowd.* **b** during: *The announcement was made in the midst of the program.*
—*prep.* amidst; amid. Also, **'midst** (for prep.). [OE *tō middes* in the middle; and < *mid* + *-est*]

mid·stream (mid′strēm′) *n.* the middle of a stream.

mid·sum·mer (mid′sum′ər) *n.* **1** the middle of summer. **2** the time around June 21, the summer solstice. **3** (*adj.*) of or in the middle of summer.

mid·town (mid′toun′) *n., adj.* —*n.* the most central location in a city or town. —*adj.* of or located in midtown.

mid·Vic·to·ri·an (mid′vik tô′rē ən) *adj., n.* —*adj.* **1** in Britain, of or having to do with the middle period of Queen Victoria's reign, from about 1850 to 1890. **2** like this period; old-fashioned; strict in morals. —*n.* **1** a person who lived during the middle period of

Queen Victoria's reign. **2** a person with old-fashioned ideas and tastes, and strict in morals.

mid·way (mid′wā′) *adv., adj., n.* —*adv. or adj.* halfway; in the middle: *midway between the two towns* (*adv.*), *a midway point on the chart* (*adj.*). —*n.* **1** a middle way or course. **2** at a fair or exhibition, the place for games, rides, and other amusements. [OE *midweg*]

mid·week (mid′wēk′) *n., adj.* —*n.* the middle of the week. —*adj.* in the middle of the week.

mid·wife (mid′wīf′) *n., pl.* **-wives** (-wīvz′). a woman who helps women in childbirth. [OE *mid* with + *wīf* woman]

mid·wife·ry (mid′wīf′ə rē *or* -wīf′rē, mid′wif′ə rē *or* -wif′rē) *n.* the helping of women in childbirth.

mid·win·ter (mid′win′tər) *n.* **1** the middle of winter. **2** the time around December 21, the winter solstice. **3** (*adj.*) of or in the middle of winter.

mid·year (mid′yēr′) *adj., n.* —*adj.* happening in the middle of the year. —*n.* **midyears,** *pl. Informal.* midyear examinations.

mien (mēn) *n.* one's manner of holding the head and body; a way of acting and looking: *The manager had the mien of a soldier.* [probably < *demean*; influenced by F *mine* expression < Celtic]
☞ *Hom.* **mean.**

miff (mif) *n., v. Informal.* —*n.* a peevish fit; petty quarrel. —*v.* be offended; have a petty quarrel. [origin uncertain]

MIG or **Mig** (mig) *n.* a Russian-designed jet fighter plane. [< Artem *M*ikoyan and Mikhail *G*urevish, Russian airplane designers of the 1900's]

might¹ (mīt) *v.* pt. of **may.** [OE *mihte*]
☞ *Hom.* **mite.**
☞ *Usage.* See note at **could.**

might² (mīt) *n.* great power; strength.
with might and main, with all one's strength.
[OE *miht*]
☞ *Hom.* **mite.**

might·i·ly (mī′tə lē) *adv.* **1** in a mighty manner; powerfully; vigorously. **2** very much; greatly.

might·i·ness (mī′tē nis) *n.* power; strength.

might·y (mī′tē) *adj.* **might·i·er, might·i·est;** *adv.* —*adj.* **1** having or showing strength or power; powerful: *a mighty ruler, a mighty blow.* **2** (*noml.*) **the mighty,** *pl.* all those who are mighty. **3** very great: *a mighty famine.*
—*adv. Informal.* very; extremely: *a mighty cold day.*
☞ *Syn. adj.* **1. Mighty, powerful** = having or showing great strength or force. **Mighty** in this sense is now used chiefly for effect, suggesting overwhelming strength or force or a power above all other: *The mighty battleship steamed into port.* **Powerful** = having the strength, energy, or authority to do great things or showing great force: *A heavy truck needs a powerful engine.*

mi·gnon (min′yon; *French,* mē nyoN′) *adj.* small and pretty; dainty. [< F]

mi·gnon·ette (min′yən et′) *n.* any of a genus (*Reseda*) of plants, especially an annual plant (*R. odorata*) widely grown for its pointed clusters of fragrant, greenish-yellow flowers. [< F]

mi·graine (mī′grān; *also, esp.Brit.,* mē′grān) *n.* a severe, recurring type of headache usually affecting only one side of the head and often accompanied by nausea and vomiting, dizziness, and sensitivity of the eyes to light. [< F < LL < Gk. *hemikrania* < *hemi-* half + *kranion* skull]

mi·grant (mī′grənt) *n., adj.* —*n.* a person, animal, bird, or plant that migrates. —*adj.* migrating: *Migrant workers were hired for the harvest.*

mi·grate (mī′grāt *or* mī grāt′) *v.* **-grat·ed, -grat·ing. 1** move from one place to settle in another. **2** go from one region to another with the change in the seasons. Many birds migrate to warmer countries in the winter. [< L *migrare*]

mi·gra·tion (mī grā′shən) *n.* **1** migrating. **2** a number of people or animals migrating together. **3 a** a movement of one or more atoms from one place to another within the molecule. **b** the movement of ions between the two electrodes during electrolysis.

mi·gra·to·ry (mī′grə tô′rē) *adj.* **1** migrating; that migrates. **2** of migration. **3** wandering.

mi·ka·do (mə kä′dō) *n., pl.* **-dos.** the ancient title of the emperor of Japan. [< Japanese *mikado* < *mi* august, honorable + *kado* door, gate]

mike (mīk) *n. Informal.* microphone.

mil¹ (mil) *n.* a unit for measuring length, equal to 0.001 inch (25.4 micrometres). The mil was used for measuring the diameter of wires. [< L *mille* thousand]

mil² (mil) *n.* **1** a unit of money in Cyprus and Malta, equal to 1/1000 of a pound. **2** a coin worth one mil. [< L *mille* thousand]

mil. **1** military. **2** militia. **3** mileage. **4** million.

mi·la·dy or **mi·la·di** (mi lā′dē) *n., pl.* **-dies. 1** my lady. **2** an English lady.

mil·age (mīl′ij) See **mileage.**

Mi·lan or **mi·lan** (mi lan′ *or* mil′ən) *n.* a finely woven straw used for hats. [< *Milan*, Italy, where it is made]

milch (milch) *adj.* giving milk; kept for the milk it gives: *a milch cow.* [OE -*milce* milking < *mioluc* milk]

mild (mīld) *adj.* **1** gentle; kind: *a mild old gentleman.* **2** warm; temperate; moderate; not harsh or severe: *a mild climate, a mild winter.* **3** soft or sweet to the senses; not sharp, sour, bitter, or strong in taste: *mild cheese, a mild cigar.* [OE *milde*] —**mild′ly,** *adv.* —**mild′ness,** *n.*
☛ *Syn.* **1.** See note at **gentle.**

mil·dew (mil′dyü *or* -dü) *n., v.* —*n.* **1** any of various fungi that attack plants or grow on food, paper, cloth, leather, etc., especially in damp conditions. **2** any of various plant diseases caused by such fungi. **3** a thin, furry coating or discoloration caused by the growth of such fungi, especially on cloth, paper, etc.
—*v.* affect or become affected with mildew. [OE *mildēaw* honeydew]

mile (mīl) *n.* **1** a unit for measuring distance or length on land, equal to about 1.609 kilometres; statute mile: *There are 5280 feet in a mile.* **2** nautical mile. **3** miles, *pl.* a relatively great distance: *The sun went down, but we were still miles from home. From here you can see for miles.* *Abbrev.:* mi. [OE *mīl* < L *milia* (*passuum*), pl. of *mille* (gen. pl. of *passus*) a thousand (paces)]

mile·age (mīl′ij) *n.* **1** the total number of miles travelled: *What's the mileage on your car?* **2** the length, extent, or distance of a road, journey, etc., expressed in miles. **3** the distance a motor vehicle can go on a given amount of fuel: *We get good mileage on our new car.* **4** an allowance for travelling expenses at a fixed rate per unit of distance: *She gets mileage on trips she makes for the company.* **5** the profit or benefit a person is getting or can get out of something: *He's getting a lot of mileage out of that one joke.*

mile·post (mīl′pōst′) *n.* a post set up to show the distance in miles to a certain place.

mile·stone (mīl′stōn′) *n.* **1** a stone set up to show the distance in miles to a certain place. **2** an important event: *The invention of printing was a milestone in the progress of education.*

mil·foil (mil′foil′) *n.* **1** yarrow. **2** water milfoil. [ME < OF < L *millefolium* < *mille* thousand + *folium* leaf]

mi·lieu (mē lyü′; *French,* mē lyœ′) *n.* surroundings; environment. [< F]

mil·i·tan·cy (mil′ə tən sē) *n.* warlike behavior or tendency; militant spirit or policy.

mil·i·tant (mil′ə tənt) *adj., n.* —*adj.* **1** aggressive; fighting; warlike. **2** aggressively active in serving a cause or in spreading a belief: *a militant churchman.* —*n.* a person aggressively active in serving a cause or in spreading a belief. [< L *militans, -antis* serving as a soldier, ult. < *miles* soldier] —**mil′i·tant·ly,** *adv.*

mil·i·tar·ism (mil′ə tə riz′əm) *n.* **1** the policy of making military organization and power very strong. **2** the political condition in which the military interest is predominant in government or administration. **3** military spirit and ideals.

mil·i·ta·rist (mil′ə tə rist) *n.* **1** a person who believes in a powerful military organization. **2** an expert in warfare and military matters.

mil·i·ta·ris·tic (mil′ə tə ris′tik) *adj.* of or having to do with militarists or militarism. —**mil′i·ta·ris′ti·cal·ly,** *adv.*

mil·i·ta·rize (mil′ə tə rīz′) *v.* **-rized, -riz·ing. 1** make the military organization of (a country) very powerful. **2** fill with military spirit and ideals. —**mil′i·ta·ri·za′tion,** *n.*

mil·i·tar·y (mil′ə ter′ē) *adj.* **1** of or having to do with soldiers or war. **2** done by soldiers. **3** fit for soldiers. **4** suitable for war; warlike: *military valor.* **5** belonging to the armed forces. **6** (*noml.*) **the military,** the armed forces; soldiers: *The military did rescue work during the flood.* [< L *militaris* < *miles* soldier] —**mil′i·tar′i·ly,** *adv.*
☛ *Syn. adj.* **1. Military, martial, warlike** = having to do with war. **Military** describes anything to do with affairs of war or the armed forces: *He studied military history.* **Martial** emphasizes the glory and pomp of war or the gallantry of fighting men: *Troops paraded in martial array.* **Warlike** suggests a fighting nature, and especially describes acts, feelings, words, etc. threatening or fit for war: *The Vikings were a warlike people.*

Military Cross an award for bravery for officers of the army up to the rank of captain. *Abbrev.:* M.C.

military law a system of regulations governing the armed forces and others in military service.
☛ *Usage.* **Military law** is not to be confused with *martial law*, which replaces *civil law* in times of emergency and applies to civilians as well as military personnel.

military police soldiers who act as police in an army. *Abbrev.:* MP or M.P.

hat, āge, fär; let, ēqual, tėrm; it, īce
hot, ōpen, ôrder; oil, out; cup, put, rüle,
above, takən, pencəl, lemən, circəs
ch, child; ng, long; sh, ship
th, thin; ŦH, then; zh, measure

Military Regime in Canada, the period of military rule between 1759 and 1764.

mil·i·tate (mil′ə tāt′) *v.* **-tat·ed, -tat·ing.** act; work; operate (*against* or *in favor of*): *Bad weather militated against the success of the picnic.* [< L *militare* serve as a soldier < *miles* soldier]

mi·li·tia (mə lish′ə) *n.* a part of an army made up of citizens who are not regular soldiers but who undergo training for emergency duty or national defence; the reserve army. [< L *militia* < *miles* soldier]

mi·li·tia·man (mə lish′ə mən) *n., pl.* **-men** a soldier in the militia.

Mil·i·um (mil′ē əm) *n. Trademark.* a fabric or material sprayed with a metal solution and used as insulation in clothing, draperies, etc.

milk (milk) *n., v.* —*n.* **1** the white liquid secreted by female mammals for the nourishment of their young. **2** any kind of liquid resembling this, such as the white juice of a plant, tree, or nut: *coconut milk.*
cry over spilt milk, waste sorrow or regret on what has happened and cannot be remedied.
—*v.* **1** draw milk from; strip of milk: *He used to milk twenty cows a day.* **2** yield or produce milk. **3** extract as if by milking; drain contents, strength, information, wealth, etc. from: *The dishonest treasurer milked the club treasury.* **4** draw juice, poison, etc. from: *milk a snake.* [OE *mioluc*]

milk bar a store or counter specializing in dairy products such as ice-cream, milk shakes, yogurt, etc.

milk·er (mil′kər) *n.* **1** a cow, goat, etc. that gives a specified quantity or quality of milk: *a good milker.* **2** a person or machine that milks.

milk·ing (mil′king) *n.* the amount of milk obtained at one time.

milk leg a painful swelling of the leg caused by clots in the veins.

milk·maid (milk′mād′) *n.* a woman or girl whose job it is to milk cows.

milk·man (milk′man′) *n., pl.* **-men.** a man who sells or delivers milk.

milk of human kindness natural sympathy and affection.

milk of magnesia a milky-white medicine in water, used as a laxative and antacid. *Formula:* $Mg(OH)_2$

milk shake a drink consisting of milk, flavoring, and often ice cream, shaken or beaten until frothy.

milk snake a small, harmless grey-and-brown snake (*Lampropeltis triangulum*, also called *L. doliata*) of North America. Milk snakes feed on small rodents, such as rats and mice.

milk·sop (milk′sop′) *n.* an unmanly fellow; coward.

milk sugar lactose.

milk tooth one of the first set of teeth; a temporary tooth of a young child or animal.

milk·weed (milk′wēd′) *n.* any of various weeds whose stem contains a white juice that looks like milk; especially, any of a genus (*Asclepias*) of mainly North American perennial plants with milky juice and pointed pods that burst open when ripe, releasing tufted seeds.

milk–white (milk′wīt′ *or* -hwīt′) *adj.* white as milk.

milk·y (mil′kē) *adj.* **milk·i·er, milk·i·est. 1** like milk; white as milk; whitish. **2** of milk; containing milk. **3** mild; weak; timid. —**milk′i·ness,** *n.*

Milky Way 1 a broad band of faint light that stretches across the sky at night. It is made up of countless stars, too far away to be seen separately without a telescope. **2** the galaxy in which these countless stars are found. The earth, sun, and all the planets around the sun are part of the Milky Way.

mill¹ (mil) *n., v.* —*n.* **1** a machine for grinding or crushing: *A flour mill grinds wheat into flour. A coffee mill grinds coffee beans.* **2** a building containing a machine for grinding grain. **3** a building where manufacturing is done: *A paper mill makes paper from wood pulp.* **4** *Slang.* a fight with the fists.
go through the mill, *Informal.* **a** get a thorough training or experience. **b** learn by hard or painful experience.
put through the mill, *Informal.* **a** test; examine; try out. **b** teach by hard or painful experience.
—*v.* **1** grind: *Some wheat will be milled before it is exported.*

2 manufacture. **3** cut a series of fine notches or ridges on the edge of (a coin): *A dime is milled.* **4** of people or animals in a group, move around in a confused or aimless way (*often used with* **about** *or* **around**): *There were many people milling around after the parade.* [OE *mylen* < LL *molinum* < L *mola* millstone]

mill² (mil) *n.* $.001, or $\frac{1}{10}$ of a cent. Mills are used in accounting, but not as coins. [short for L *millesimum* one thousandth < *mille* thousand]

mill·dam (mil'dam') *n.* **1** a dam built in a stream to supply water power for a mill. **2** a pond made by such a dam.

mil·leme (mə lēm') *n.* a unit of money in Libya, equal to $\frac{1}{1000}$ of a dinar.

mil·len·ni·al (mə len'ē əl) *adj.* **1** of a thousand years. **2** like that of the millennium; fit for the millennium.

mil·len·ni·um (mə len'ē əm) *n., pl.* **mil·len·ni·ums, mil·len·ni·a** (mə len'ē ə). **1** a period of a thousand years: *The world is many millenniums old.* **2** the period of a thousand years during which, according to the Bible, Christ is expected to reign on earth (Rev. 20:1-7). **3** a period of righteousness and happiness. [< NL < L *mille* thousand + *annus* year]

mil·le·pede (mil'ə pēd') See **millipede.**

mil·le·pore (mil'ə pôr') *n.* any of an order (Milleporina) of tropical hydrozoans having a calcareous skeleton and living in colonies which often form reefs. Millepores pass through a free-swimming medusa stage. [< NL *millepora* < L *mille* thousand + *porus* pore]

mill·er (mil'ər) *n.* **1** a person who owns or runs a mill, especially a flour mill. **2** a moth whose wings look as if they were powdered with flour.

mil·les·i·mal (mə les'ə məl) *adj., n.* —*adj.* **1** thousandth. **2** consisting of thousandth parts. —*n.* a thousandth part. [< L *millesimus* thousandth part < *mille* thousand]

mil·let (mil'it) *n.* **1** any of various annual grasses grown for grain or fodder, such as the East Indian grass (*Panicum miliaceum*), widely cultivated for grain in Europe, Asia, and Africa. **2** the small seed of any of these plants, used especially for cereals and unleavened breads. [< F, ult. < L *milium*]

milli– *SI prefix.* one thousandth: *A millilitre is one one-thousandth of a litre.* Symbol: m [< L *mille*]

mil·li·am·pere (mil'ē am' pēr) *n.* an SI unit for measuring electric current, equal to one one-thousandth of an ampere. *Symbol:* m

mil·liard (mil'yərd *or* mil'yärd) *n.* a thousand million; 1 000 000 000. [< F < L *mille* thousand]

mil·li·bar (mil'ə bär') *n.* a unit used with the SI for measuring pressure, equal to 0.1 kilopascals. Atmospheric pressure readings are sometimes given in millibars. *Symbol:* mbar

mil·lieme (mēl yem') *n.* **1** a unit of money in Egypt and Sudan, equal to $\frac{1}{100}$ of a piastre and $\frac{1}{1000}$ of a pound. **2** a coin worth one millieme. [< F]

mil·li·gram (mil'ə gram') *n.* an SI unit for measuring mass, equal to one one-thousandth of a gram. The milligram is used for very small masses, such as the amount of vitamins and minerals contained in a serving of food. *Symbol:* mg Also, **milligramme.**

mil·li·li·tre (mil'ə lē'tər) *n.* a unit used with the SI for measuring volume or capacity, equal to one-thousandth of a litre. Cooking measures are graduated in millilitres. *Symbol:* mL Also, **milliliter.**

mil·lime (mə lēm' *or* mil'ēm) *n.* **1** a unit of money in Tunisia, equal to $\frac{1}{1000}$ of a dinar. **2** a coin worth one millime.

mil·li·me·tre (mil'ə mē'tər) *n.* an SI unit for measuring length, equal to one one-thousandth of a metre: *A dime is about one millimetre thick.* *Symbol:* mm Also, **millimeter.**

mil·li·ner (mil'ə nər) *n.* a person who makes, trims, or sells women's hats. [var. of *Milaner,* a dealer in goods from Milan, Italy, famous for straw]

mil·li·ner·y (mil'ə ner'ē *or* mil'ə nər ē) *n.* **1** women's hats. **2** the business of making, trimming, or selling women's hats.

mill·ing (mil'ing) *n.* **1** the business or process of grinding grain in a mill. **2** manufacturing. **3** the business or process of cutting notches or ridges on the edge of a coin. **4** such notches or ridges.

mil·lion (mil'yən) *n. or adj.* **1** one thousand thousand; 1 000 000. **2** a very large number; very many. [ME < OF < Ital. *milione,* ult. < L *mille* thousand]

mil·lion·aire (mil'yən er') *n.* **1** a person whose wealth is equal to more than a million dollars, pounds, etc. **2** any very wealthy person. [< F]

mil·lion·fold (mil'yən fōld') *adv. or adj.* a million times as much or as many.

mil·lionth (mil'yənth) *adj. or n.* **1** last in a series of a million. **2** one of a million equal parts.

mil·li·pede (mil'ə pēd') *n.* any of a class (Diplopoda) of arthropod having a cylindrical, segmented body armored with hard plates, and with most segments bearing two pairs of legs each. [< *millepeda* < *mille* thousand + *pes, pedis* foot]

mil·li·sec·ond (mil'ə sek'ənd) *n.* an SI unit for measuring time, equal to one one-thousandth of a second. *Symbol:* ms

mill·pond (mil'pond') *n.* a pond supplying water to drive a mill wheel.

mill·race (mil'rās') *n.* **1** a current of water that drives a mill wheel. **2** the channel in which it flows to the mill.

mill rate a rate used for calculating municipal taxes. A mill rate of 45.6 means that a property owner pays a tax of 45.6 mills ($0.0456) for every dollar of the assessed value of his property.

mill·stone (mil'stōn') *n.* **1** either of a pair of round, flat stones used for grinding corn, wheat, etc. **2** a heavy burden. **3** anything that grinds or crushes.

mill·stream (mil'strēm') *n.* the stream in a millrace.

mill wheel a wheel that is turned by water and supplies power for a mill.

mill·work (mil'wèrk') *n.* **1** doors, windows, mouldings, etc. made in a planing mill. **2** the work done in a mill.

mill·wright (mil'rīt') *n.* **1** a person who designs, builds, or sets up mills or machinery for mills. **2** a mechanic who sets up and takes care of the machinery in a factory, etc.

mi·lord (mi lôrd') *n.* **1** my lord. **2** an English gentleman.

milque·toast (milk'tōst') *n.* an extremely timid person. [< Mr. Milquetoast, a comic-strip character]

milt (milt) *n.* **1** the sperm cells of male fishes together with the milky fluid containing them. **2** the reproductive gland in male fishes. [for older *milk;* influenced by *milt* spleen (OE *milte*), and perhaps by Du. *milt* milt of fish, spleen]

Mil·ton·ic (mil ton'ik) *adj.* **1** of or having to do with John Milton (1608-1674), an English poet. **2** resembling Milton's literary style; solemn and majestic.

mime (mīm) *n., v.* **mimed, mim·ing.** —*n.* **1** a form of drama in which the actors use movement and gestures but no words; pantomime. **2** communicating through gestures but without the use of words: *He told his story in mime.* **3** an actor communicating through gestures only. **4** in ancient Greece and Rome: **a** a coarse farce using funny actions and gestures. **b** an actor in such a farce. —*v.* communicate through gestures without the use of words. [< L < Gk. *mimos*] —**mim'er,** *n.*

mim·e·o·graph (mim'ē ə graf') *n., v.* —*n.* a machine for making copies of written or typewritten material, or of drawings, by means of stencils. —*v.* make (copies) on a mimeograph. [< *Mimeograph,* a trademark < Gk. *mimeesthai* imitate + E *-graph*]

mi·me·sis (mi mē'sis *or* mī mē'sis) *n.* **1** mimicry or imitation. **2** *Biology.* protective coloring or markings in plants, animals, etc., imitating the surroundings. **3** the imitation or representation of reality in art or literature. **4** the assuming of the symptoms of one disease by another disease. [< Gk. *mimēsis* < *mimeisthai* imitate < *mimos* mime]

mi·met·ic (mi met'ik *or* mī met'ik) *adj.* **1** imitative: *mimetic gestures.* **2** mimic or make-believe. **3** having to do with or exhibiting mimicry. [< Gk. *mimetikos* < *mimeesthai* imitate]

mim·ic (mim'ik) *v.* **-icked, -ick·ing;** *n., adj.* —*v.* **1** make fun of by imitating. **2** copy closely; imitate: *A parrot can mimic a person's voice.* **3** represent imitatively, as by drawing; simulate. **4** of things, be an imitation of. **5** resemble closely: *Some insects mimic leaves.* —*n.* a person or thing that imitates. —*adj.* **1** not real, but imitated or pretended for some purpose: *a mimic battle.* **2** imitative. [< L *mimicus* < Gk. *mimikos* < *mimos* mime]

mim·ic·ry (mim'ik rē) *n., pl.* **-ries.** mimicking.

mi·mo·sa (mi mō'sə *or* mi mō'zə) *n.* any of a genus (Mimosa) of shrubs, trees, and herbs found in tropical and warm regions, having compound, fernlike leaves that in some species are sensitive to touch or to changes in light or temperature. See also **sensitive plant.** [< NL *mimosa* < L *mimus* mime < Gk. *mimos;* from mimicry of animal reactions]

min minute(s).

min. minimum.

mi·na (mī'nə) *n., pl.* **mi·nae** (mī'nē *or* mī'nī) *or* **mi·nas.** a unit of weight and value used by the ancient Greeks, Egyptians, and others. [< L < Gk. *mna* < Semitic; cf. Babylonian *manū*]

mi·na·cious (mi nā'shəs) *adj.* menacing; threatening. [< L

minax, minacis, ult. < *minae* projecting points, threats]
—**mi·na′cious·ly,** *adv.* —**mi·na′cious·ness,** *n.*

Min·a·ma·ta disease (min′ə mä′tə) a disease caused by methyl mercury poisoning as a result of eating contaminated fish, and characterized by slurred speech, numbness, and progressive paralysis. [< *Minamata,* a fishing settlement in Japan, where the disease first appeared in the 1950's]

min·a·ret (min′ə ret′ *or* min′ə ret′) *n.* a slender, high tower of a Moslem mosque, having one or more projecting balconies, from which a muezzin or crier calls the people to prayer. [< F or Sp. < Arabic *manāret* lighthouse]

min·a·to·ry (min′ə tô′rē) *adj.* menacing; threatening. [< LL *minatorius* < L *minari* threaten, ult. < *minae* projecting points, threats]

mince (mins) *v.* **minced, minc·ing;** *n.* —*v.* **1** chop or grind into very small pieces. **2** speak or move in a prim, affected way. **3** soften or moderate (words, etc.), as when stating unpleasant facts: *The judge addressed the jury bluntly, without mincing words.*
not to mince matters, to speak plainly and frankly.
—*n.* **1** meat cut or ground up into very small pieces. **2** mincemeat. **3** (*adj.*) made with mincemeat: *mince pie.* [ME < OF *mincier,* ult. < L *minutus* small]

mince·meat (mins′mēt′) *n.* **1** a mixture of chopped apples, raisins, currants, etc., flavored with spices, used as a filling for pies. **2** minced meat.
make mincemeat of, reduce as if into little pieces; cut down; defeat overwhelmingly: *Our team made mincemeat of the rest of the league.*

mince pie a pie filled with mincemeat.

minc·ing (min′sing) *adj.* too polite or nice; affectedly elegant or dainty: *a mincing courtier.* —**minc′ing·ly,** *adv.*

mind (mīnd) *n., v.* —*n.* **1** that which knows, thinks, remembers, feels, and wills. **2** intellect. **3** a person who has intelligence. **4** the intellectual powers or capacities of a body of persons: *the popular mind.* **5** reason; sanity: *be out of one's mind.* **6** mental or physical activity in general, as opposed to matter. **7** a conscious or intelligent agency or being: *the doctrine of a mind creating the universe.* **8** a way of thinking and feeling: *change one's mind.* **9** one's desire, purpose, intention, or will. **10** remembrance or recollection; memory: *Keep the rules in mind.*
bear in mind, keep one's attention on; remember.
be in (or of) two (many etc.**) minds,** vacillate between two (many, etc.) intentions.
be of one mind, agree.
call to mind, a recall. **b** remember.
give (someone) a piece of (one's) mind, speak to angrily or without holding back.
have a mind of (one's) own, have definite or decided opinions, inclinations, or purposes.
have a mind to, intend to; think of favorably: *I have a mind to watch hockey tonight.*
have half a mind, be somewhat inclined.
have in mind, a remember. **b** think of; consider. **c** intend; plan.
keep in mind, remember.
know (one's) mind, know what one really thinks, wishes, or intends.
make up (one's) mind, decide; resolve.
on (one's) mind, in one's thoughts; troubling one.
pass out of mind, be forgotten.
put in mind, remind.
set (one's) mind on, want very much.
speak (one's) mind, give one's frank opinion.
take (one's) mind off, distract one's attention from; divert from (something unpleasant).
to (one's) mind, in one's opinion; to one's way of thinking.
—*v.* **1** bear in mind; give heed to: *Mind my words!* **2** take notice; observe. **3** be careful concerning: *Mind the step.* **4** be careful. **5** look after; take care of: tend: *Mind the baby.* **6** obey: *Mind your father and mother.* **7** feel concern about; object to: *We mind parting from a friend.* **8** feel concern; object: *Do you mind?* **9** *Archaic or dialect.* remember. **9** *Archaic or dialect.* remind.
mind the store See store.
[OE (ge)*mynd*] —**mind′er,** *n.*
☛ *Syn. n.* **1, 2. Mind, intellect** = the part of a human being that enables him to know, think, and act effectively. **Mind** in general usage is the inclusive word, meaning the part that knows, thinks, feels, wills, remembers, etc., thought of as distinct from the body: *To develop properly, the mind needs training and exercise.* **Intellect** applies to the knowing and thinking powers of the mind, as distinct from the powers of feeling and will: *Many motion pictures appeal to the feelings rather than the intellect.*

mind·ed (mīn′did) *adj.* **1** having a certain kind of mind: *high-minded, strong-minded.* **2** inclined; disposed: *I am minded to stay home today.*

mind·ful (mīnd′fəl) *adj.* having in mind: *Mindful of your advice, I went slowly.* —**mind′ful·ly,** *adv.* —**mind′ful·ness,** *n.*

mind·less (mīnd′lis) *adj.* **1** without intelligence; stupid. **2** not taking thought; careless. —**mind′less·ly,** *adv.* —**mind′less·ness,** *n.*

hat, āge, fär; let, ēqual, tėrm; it, īce
hot, ōpen, ôrder; oil, out; cup, pùt, rüle,
əbove, takən, pencəl, lemən, circəs
ch, child; ng, long; sh, ship
th, thin; ᴛʜ, then; zh, measure

mind reader a person who can perceive another's thoughts directly.

mind's eye imagination.

mine¹ (mīn) *pron., adj.* —*pron.* a possessive form of I; that which belongs to or is associated with me: *The dog is mine. These are his records; mine are over there.*
of mine, belonging to or associated with me: *She's a friend of mine. My mother found some old essays of mine.*
—*adj.* my (used only before a vowel or h, or after a noun): *mine eyes, mine heart, sister mine.* [OE *mīn*]
☛ *Usage.* See note at **my.**

mine² (mīn) *n., v.* **mined, min·ing.** —*n.* **1** a large hole or space dug in the earth to get out valuable minerals: *a coal mine, a gold mine.* **2** a rich or plentiful source: *a mine of information.* **3** an underground passage in which an explosive is placed to blow up the enemy's forts, etc. **4** a container holding an explosive charge that is put under water and exploded by propeller vibrations (**acoustic** or **sonic mine**), or by magnetic attraction (**magnetic mine**), or laid on the ground or shallowly buried and exploded by contact with a vehicle, etc. (**land mine**).
—*v.* **1** dig a mine; make a hole, space, passage, etc. below the earth. **2** dig into (the earth, a hill, etc.) for coal, ore, etc. **3** get (metal etc.) from a mine. **4** dig in; make (passages, etc.) by digging. **5** put explosive mines in or under; lay explosive mines. **6** destroy secretly; ruin slowly; undermine. [< F < Celtic]

mine field **1** an area throughout which explosive mines have been laid. **2** the pattern of mines in such an area.

min·er (mī′nər) *n.* **1** a person who works in a mine: *a coal miner.* **2** a soldier who lays explosive mines.
☛ *Hom.* **minor.**

min·er·al (min′ər əl *or* min′rəl) *n.* **1** any inorganic, naturally occurring, solid chemical element or compound having a crystalline structure. **2** any natural substance that is neither plant nor animal. **3** a substance obtained by mining, especially an ore. **4** (*adj.*) of, having to do with, or containing minerals: *mineral water. There are mineral deposits at the mouth of the river.* [ME < OF *mineral,* ult. < *mine* mine² < Celtic]

min·er·al·ize (min′ər əl īz′ *or* min′rəl īz′) *v.* **-ized, -iz·ing.**
1 convert into mineral substance; transform (metal) into an ore. **2** impregnate or supply with mineral substances. **3** search for minerals. —**min′er·al·i·za′tion,** *n.*

mineral kingdom one of the three basic groups into which all things found in nature are divided. The mineral kingdom includes all non-living, or inorganic, things. Compare **animal kingdom** and **plant kingdom.**

min·er·a·log·i·cal (min′ər ə loj′ə kəl) *adj.* of or having to do with mineralogy. —**min′er·a·log·i·cal·ly,** *adv.*

min·er·al·o·gist (min′ər ol′ə jist *or* min′ər al′ə jist) *n.* a person trained in mineralogy, especially one whose work it is.

min·er·al·o·gy (min′ər ol′ə jē *or* min′ər al′ə jē) *n.* the science that deals with the physical and chemical properties of minerals, their classification, and the form and structure of their crystals.

mineral oil any oil derived from a mineral substance, especially a colorless, odorless, tasteless oil obtained from petroleum, used as a laxative and as a base for cold creams, etc.

mineral right a right both to the mineral deposits in a given piece of land and to the royalties accruing from their extraction.

mineral water water containing mineral salts or gases. People drink mineral water for its healthful properties.

Mi·ner·va (mə nėr′və) *n. Roman mythology.* the goddess of wisdom, the arts, and defensive war, corresponding to the Greek goddess Athena.

min·e·stro·ne (min′ə strō′nē) *n.* a soup containing vegetables, vermicelli, etc. [< Ital.]

mine sweeper a warship equipped for dragging a harbor or the sea in order to remove enemy mines or make them harmless.

Ming (ming) *n.* **1** a kind of fine porcelain. **2** something made of this porcelain. [< *Ming,* a dynasty that ruled China 1368-1644, when this porcelain was made]

min·gle (ming′gəl) *v.* **-gled, -gling.** **1** mix or blend: *The Fraser and Thompson rivers join and mingle their waters near Lytton, B.C.*

2 associate: *to mingle with important people.* [ME *mengele(n)* < OE *mengan* mix] —**min′gler,** *n.*

min·i (min′ē) *n. Informal.* something small, short, etc. for its kind, such as a miniskirt, minicar, or minibus: *She was wearing a mini.* [< *miniature*]

mini– *combining form.* small for its kind; very small, very short, etc., as in *miniskirt, minicar.*

min·i·a·ture (min′ə chər *or* min′ē ə chər) *n.* **1** a small model or copy: *In the museum there is a miniature of the ship* Victory. **2** (*adjl.*) done or made on a very small scale: *She had miniature furniture for her doll house.* **3** a very small painting, usually a portrait.
in miniature, on a small scale; reduced in size.
[< Ital. *miniatura* < Med.L *miniare* illuminate (a manuscript) < L *miniare* paint red < *minium* red lead; confused with L *minutus* small]

miniature camera a camera using narrow film (35 mm or smaller).

min·i·a·tur·ize (min′ə chə rīz′ *or* min′ē ə chə rīz′) *v.* **-ized, -iz·ing.** reduce to a very small size: *miniaturized electronic devices.* —**min′i·a·tur·i·za′tion,** *n.*

min·i·bike (min′ē bīk′) *n.* a small motorcycle.

min·i·bus (min′ē bus′) *n.* a small bus used for short runs, as between an airport and a hotel, etc.

min·i·car (min′ē kär′) *n.* a very small automobile, such as a small subcompact.

min·i·fy (min′ə fī′) *v.* **-fied, -fy·ing.** make small or less important. [< L *minor,* neuter of *minus* less + E *-fy*]

min·im (min′əm) *n.* **1** a unit for measuring liquids, equal to one sixtieth of a fluid dram (about 0.06 cm³). The minim is the smallest unit in the imperial system of liquid measure. **2** a very small amount. **3** something very small or insignificant. **4** *Music.* a half note. [< L *minimus* smallest]

min·i·ma (min′ə mə) *n.* a pl. of **minimum.**

min·i·mal (min′ə məl) *adj.* least possible; very small; having to do with a minimum: *The article claimed that the side effects of the drug were minimal.* —**min′i·mal·ly,** *adv.*

min·i·mize (min′ə mīz′) *v.* **-mized, -miz·ing.** **1** reduce to the least possible amount or degree: *The polar explorers took every precaution to minimize the dangers of their trip.* **2** state at the lowest possible estimate; make the least of: *An ungrateful person minimizes the help others have given him.* —**min′i·miz′er,** *n.*

min·i·mum (min′ə məm) *n., pl.* **-mums** *or* **-ma. 1** the least amount or smallest quantity possible or permitted: *I need a minimum of eight hours sleep a night.* **2** *Mathematics.* the least value of a function within a given interval of the domain of the function. **3** (*adjl.*) least possible; lowest: *a minimum rate. Eighteen is the minimum age for voting in federal elections.* [< L *minimum* smallest (thing)]
☛ *Usage.* **Minimum** has two plurals: *minimums* and *minima.* The first is more common in informal English.

minimum wage the lowest wage paid or allowed, especially the wage fixed by law as the lowest that can be paid to any employed person or to certain categories of employed persons.

min·ing (mīn′ing) *n.* **1** the act, process, or business of digging coal, ore, etc. from mines. **2** (*adjl.*) of or having to do with this process or business: *a mining camp, a mining school.* **3** the act or process of laying explosive mines.

min·ion (min′yən) *n.* **1** a person willing to do whatever he is ordered, especially a servile or obsequious follower. **2** *Derogatory.* a darling; favorite. **3** *Printing.* a size of type, 7-point. [< F *mignon* dainty]

min·is·cule (min′ə skyül′) *adj.* minuscule.

min·i·skirt (min′ē skėrt′) *n.* a very short skirt ending well above the knees.

min·is·ter (min′is tər) *n., v.* —*n.* **1** a clergyman serving a church; spiritual guide; pastor. **2** a member of the cabinet who is in charge of a government department: *the Minister of Labor.* **3** a person sent to a foreign country to represent his own government; a diplomat ranking below an ambassador: *the British Minister to France.* **4** a person or thing employed in carrying out (purpose, will, etc.): *The storm which killed the murderer seemed the minister of God's vengeance.* **5** *Archaic.* a servant.
—*v.* **1** act as a servant or nurse; be of service: *She ministers to the sick.* **2** be helpful; give aid; contribute. **3** *Archaic.* furnish; supply. [< L *minister* servant < *minus* less; patterned after *magister* master]

min·is·te·ri·al (min′is tēr′ē əl) *adj.* **1** of, having to do with, or suitable for a minister of religion or the ministry. **2** of or having to do with a government minister or ministry. **3** having to do with or characteristic of administrative functions of government; executive. **4** acting as an agent; instrumental. —**min′is·te′ri·al·ly,** *adv.*

minister plenipotentiary *pl.* **ministers plenipotentiary.** a plenipotentiary.

minister without portfolio a cabinet minister who is not connected with any particular cabinet post or department.

min·is·trant (min′is trənt) *adj., n.* —*adj.* ministering. —*n.* one who ministers. [< L *ministrans, -antis,* ppr. of *ministrare* < *minister* servant]

min·is·tra·tion (min′is trā′shən) *n.* the act or process of ministering: *ministration to the sick.*

min·is·try (min′is trē) *n., pl.* **-tries. 1** the office, duties, or time of service of a minister. **2** the ministers of a church. **3** the ministers of a government. **4** in the United Kingdom, Europe, Canada, etc.: **a** a government department under a minister. **b** the offices of such a department. **5** a ministering or serving. [< L *ministerium* office, service < *minister.* See MINISTER. Doublet of METIER.]

min·i·ver (min′ə vər) *n.* a white or spotted white fur formerly much used for lining and trimming garments. Miniver was originally worn by members of the medieval nobility and is still sometimes used on ceremonial robes. [ME < OF *menu vair* small vair (a type of fur used in the 14th century and the animal from which it was obtained); *menu* < L *minutus* made small (see MINUTE²); *vair* < L *varius* variegated]

mink (mingk) *n., pl.* **mink** *or* **minks. 1** any of several semiaquatic mammals (genus *Mustela*) closely related to and resembling the weasels, having thick, soft, lustrous fur generally ranging in color from brown to almost black. The common North American mink is *M. vison.* **2** the fur of a mink, one of the most valuable commercial furs. **3** a coat or other garment made of this fur. [apparently < Scand.; cf. Swedish *mänk*] —**mink′like′,** *adj.*

Minn. Minnesota.

min·ne·sing·er *or* **Min·ne·sing·er** (min′ə sing′ər) *n.* a German lyrical poet and singer in the 12th, 13th, and 14th centuries. [< G *Minnesinger* love singer]

min·now (min′ō) *n.* **1** any of various small, freshwater cyprinid fishes, such as a common, small-scaled Eurasian species (*Phoxinus phoxinus*). **2** (*adjl.*) designating the family (Cyprinidae) of chiefly freshwater, mostly very small fishes that includes the minnows, goldfish, chubs, daces, shiners, breams, and carp. **3** any of various other small fishes or the young of larger fishes, especially when used as live bait. [ME *minwe*; cf. OE *myne*]

Mi·no·an (mi nō′ən) *adj.* —*n.* —*adj.* of, having to do with, or designating a Bronze Age culture of Crete that flourished between about 2500 and 1100 B.C. —*n.* a native or inhabitant of Crete during this period. [< *Minos*]

mi·nor (mī′nər) *adj., n., v.* —*adj.* **1** smaller; lesser; less important: *a minor fault, a minor poet.* **2** under legal age. **3** *Music.* **a** of an interval, less by a half step than the corresponding major interval. **b** of or designating a scale, mode, or key whose third tone is minor in relation to the fundamental tone.
—*n.* **1** a person who is legally considered not an adult. In various provinces, minors are under 18, 19, and 21 years of age. A minor cannot make legal contracts and needs the consent of a parent or guardian to marry. **2** *Music.* a minor interval, key, scale, chord, etc.: *the scale of A minor.* **3** a subject or course of study to which a student gives much time and attention, but less than to his major subject. **4** a minor penalty. **5 the minors,** *pl.* the minor leagues.
—*v.* have or take as a minor subject of study (*used with* **in**). [< L *minor* lesser]
☛ *Hom.* miner.

Mi·nor·ca (mə nôr′kə) *n.* a breed of large chicken originally developed in Spain. [< *Minorca,* one of the Balearic Islands]

mi·nor·i·ty (mə nôr′ə tē *or* mī nôr′ə tē) *n., pl.* **-ties. 1** a smaller number or part; less than half: *The minority must often accept what the majority decides to do.* **2** a group within a country, state, etc. that differs in race, religion, or national origin from the larger part of the population. **3** (*adjl.*) of or constituting a minority: *a minority vote group, etc.* **4** (*adjl.*) belonging to a minority: *a minority opinion.* **5** the condition or time of being under the legal age of responsibility.

minor league any professional sports league or association, as in baseball or hockey, other than the major leagues.

mi·nor–league (mī′nər lēg′) *adj.* **1** of or having to do with minor leagues. **2** *Informal.* inferior; second rate; not top quality.

minor penalty *Hockey.* a two-minute penalty awarded for certain infractions of the rules, such as highsticking, hooking, slashing, tripping, etc. The referee may award a major penalty for many such infractions, especially when injury results.

minor scale *Music.* a scale having eight tones with half steps

instead of whole steps after the 2nd and 5th tones. Compare **major scale.**

Mi·nos (mī′nəs *or* mī′nos) *n. Greek mythology.* a son of Zeus and Europa who was a king and lawgiver of Crete. After his death, Minos became a judge in Hades.
☛ *Hom.* minus.

Min·o·taur (min′ə tôr′) *n. Greek mythology.* a monster with a bull's head and a man's body, kept in the Labyrinth of Crete and fed with human flesh. The Minotaur was killed by Theseus. [< L < Gk. *Minotauros* < *Minos* Minos + *tauros* bull]

min·ster (min′stər) *n. Esp.Brit.* **1** the church of a monastery. **2** a large or important church; cathedral. [OE *mynster* < LL *monasterium.* Doublet of MONASTERY.]

min·strel (min′strəl) *n.* **1** any of a class of medieval entertainers, especially a singer or musician who sang or recited poetry, often composed by himself, and accompanied himself on a harp or lute. **2** *Poetic.* any musician or poet. **3** a performer in a minstrel show. [ME < OF < LL *ministerialis* < L *ministerium.* See MINISTRY.]

minstrel show a comic variety show featuring performers, usually with blackened faces and hands in imitation of Negroes, who entertain with songs, music, and jokes supposedly reflecting Negro life. Minstrel shows were popular in the United States until the end of the 1800's.

min·strel·sy (min′strəl sē) *n., pl.* **-sies. 1** the art or practice of a minstrel. **2** a collection of songs and ballads. **3** a company of minstrels.

mint¹ (mint) *n.* **1** any of a genus (*Mentha*) of strongly scented herbs, especially any of several species used for seasoning or flavoring food, such as peppermint or spearmint. **2** any of several other plants of the same family. **3** (*adj.*) designating a family (Labiatae) of plants found especially in the Old World, having square stems and aromatic leaves that have been used in cooking and medicine since ancient times. The mint family includes lavender, peppermint, sage, rosemary, savory and thyme. **4** a piece of candy flavored with mint, especially peppermint or spearmint. [OE *minte* < L *menta* < Gk. *minthē*]

mint² (mint) *n., v.* —*n.* **1** a place where money is made by government authority. Mints also often make special commemorative coins and medals. **2** (*adj.*) of a stamp or coin, in perfect condition, as issued. **3** *Informal.* a large sum or amount, especially of money: *She made a mint when she sold her house.* **4** a place where anything is made or fabricated.
in mint condition, without a blemish; as good as new: *an old car in mint condition.*
—*v.* **1** make (coins, medals, etc.): *This quarter was minted in 1938.* **2** make or fabricate; originate. [OE *mynet* coin < L *moneta* mint, money. Doublet of MONEY.] —**mint′er,** *n.*

mint·age (min′tij) *n.* **1** a minting; coinage. **2** the product of minting; output of a mint. **3** a charge for coining; cost of coining. **4** a stamp or character impressed.

min·u·end (min′yü end′) *n.* a number or quantity from which another is to be subtracted. In 100−23 = 77, the minuend is 100. [< L *minuendus* be made smaller < *minus* less]

min·u·et (min′yü et′) *n.* **1** a slow, stately dance, popular in the 1700's. **2** the music for it. [< F *menuet,* dim. of *menu* small]

mi·nus (mī′nəs) *prep., n., adj.* —*prep.* **1** decreased by; reduced by; less: *Five minus two is three.* **2** *Informal.* without or lacking: *a book minus its cover.*
—*n.* the sign (−) meaning that the quantity following it is to be subtracted.
—*adj.* **1** showing subtraction: *The minus sign is −.* **2** less than (*never used before a noun*): *A mark of B minus is not as high as B.* **3** *Mathematics, etc.* less than zero; negative: *a minus quantity: The temperature this morning was minus thirteen degrees.* [< L *minus* less]
☛ *Hom.* Minos.

mi·nus·cule (mi nus′kyül *or* min′ə skyül′) *adj., n.* —*adj.* **1** Also, **miniscule.** minute; very small. **2** *Paleography.* of or written in small letters, or in minuscules. —*n.* **1** a lower case letter. **2** *Paleography.* **a** the small, cursive script developed from the uncial, about A.D. 600-800. **b** a small letter, neither capital nor uncial. [< F *minuscule,* learned borrowing from L *minuscula* (*littera*) slightly smaller (letter) < *minus* less]

min·ute¹ (min′it) *n.* **1** a unit used with the SI for measuring time, equal to sixty seconds or one sixtieth of an hour. *Symbol:* min **2** any short period of time; moment: *It will only take me a minute to put the dishes away. He paused for a minute to listen.* **3** a point in time: *Come here this minute.* **4** a unit used with the SI for measuring plane angles, equal to sixty seconds or one sixtieth of a degree. The minute and second are used mainly by geographers. *Symbol:* ′ **5** a memorandum or written record. **6 minutes,** *pl.* the official record of the proceedings of a society, board, committee, etc.
up to the minute, up-to-date.

hat, āge, fär; let, ēqual, tèrm; it, īce
hot, ōpen, ôrder; oil, out; cup, pùt, rüle,
əbove, takən, pencəl, lemən, circəs

ch, child; ng, long; sh, ship
th, thin; ᴛʜ, then; zh, measure

[ME < OF < LL *minuta* small part < L *minuta,* fem. of *minutus,* adj. See MINUTE².]
☛ *Syn.* **2, 3. Minute, moment, instant** = a point or extremely short period of time. **Minute** usually suggests a measurable, although very short, amount of time: *May I rest a minute?* **Moment** is more vague, suggesting a very brief period that is noticeable but not measurable or definite: *I'll be with you in a moment.* **Instant,** often used interchangeably with *moment,* is more definite and particularly suggests a point of time, a period too brief to be noticed: *Come this instant!*

mi·nute² (mī nyüt′ *or* mī nüt′) *adj.* **1** very small; tiny: *a minute speck of dust.* **2** going into or concerned with very small details: *a minute observer, minute instructions.* **3** unimportant, petty. [ME < L *minutus* made small < *minus* less. Doublet of MENU.]

minute hand (min′it) on a watch or clock, the longer of the two hands, indicating the minutes. It moves around the dial once every hour.

mi·nute·ly (mī nyüt′lē *or* mī nüt′lē) *adv.* in minute manner, form, degree, or detail.

mi·nute·ness (mī nyüt′nis *or* mī nüt′nis) *n.* **1** extreme smallness. **2** attention to very small details.

mi·nu·ti·ae (mi nyü′shē ē′ *or* mi nü′shē ē′, mi nyü′shē ī′ *or* mi nü′shē ī′) *n.pl.* very small matters; trifling details. [< L *minutiae* trifles, pl. of *minutia* smallness < *minutus.* See MINUTE².]

minx (mingks) *n.* a bold or impudent girl. [? < LG *minsk,* impudent woman; cf. G *Mensch* person]

Mi·o·cene (mī′ə sēn′) *n., adj. Geology:* —*n.* **1** a period of the Cenozoic era, beginning approximately 30 million years ago. **2** the rocks formed in this period. See chart at **geology.** —*adj.* of or having to do with this period or the rocks formed during it. [< Gk. *meiōn* less + *kainos* new]

mir (mēr) *n.* a peasant village community in Imperial Russia. [< Russian]

Mi·ra (mī′rə) *n.* a first magnitude star in the constellation Cetus, the first variable star discovered. [< NL *Mira* < L *mira* wonderful]

mir·a·cle (mir′ə kəl) *n.* **1** a wonderful happening that is contrary to or independent of the known laws of nature: *It would be a miracle if the sun stood still in the heavens for an hour.* **2** something marvellous; a wonder. **3** a remarkable example: *a miracle of patience.* **4** a miracle play. [ME < OF < L *miraculum,* ult. < *mirus* wonderful]

miracle play a class of medieval religious dramas dealing with the lives of the saints.

mi·rac·u·lous (mə rak′yə ləs) *adj.* **1** contrary to or independent of the known laws of nature; suggesting a miracle; supernatural. **2** wonderful; marvellous: *Meeting you here is miraculous good fortune.* **3** having the power to produce a miracle. [Med.L *miraculosus* < L *miraculum.* See MIRACLE.] —**mi·rac′u·lous·ly,** *adv.* —**mi·rac′u·lous·ness,** *n.*

mi·rage (mə räzh′) *n.* **1** a misleading appearance in which some distant scene is viewed as being close and, often, upside down. In a mirage, the actual scene is reflected by layers of air of different temperatures. **2** an illusion; thing that does not exist. [< F *mirage* < *mirer* look at carefully, se *mirer* look at oneself in a mirror, see reflected < L *mirare,* var. of *mirari* wonder (at), admire]

mire (mīr) *n., v.* **mired, mir·ing.** —*n.* **1** soft, deep mud; slush. **2** a bog; swamp.
—*v.* **1** stick or cause to stick in mire: *He mired his car and had to go for help.* **2** soil with mud or mire. **3** hamper or hold back, as if in a mire; involve in difficulties: *He got mired in a traffic jam.* [ME < ON *mýrr*]

mirk (mèrk) See **murk.**

mir·ror (mir′ər) *n., v.* —*n.* **1** a looking glass; a surface that reflects light. **2** whatever reflects or gives a true description: *This book is a mirror of Laurier's life.* **3** a model; example; pattern: *That knight was a mirror of chivalry.*
—*v.* **1** reflect as a mirror does: *The still water mirrored the trees along the bank.* **2** give a true description or picture of: *The book mirrored colonial life in Canada.* [ME < OF *mirour,* ult. < L *mirari* wonder, admire] —**mir′ror·like′,** *adj.*

mirth (mèrth) *n.* merriment or gaiety accompanied by laughter: *His sides shook with mirth.* [OE *myrgth* < *myrge* merry]

mirth·ful (mèrth′fəl) *adj.* laughing and merry. —**mirth′ful·ly,** *adv.* —**mirth′ful·ness,** *n.*

mirth·less (mèrth′lis) *adj.* without mirth; joyless; gloomy.
—**mirth′less·ly**, *adv.* —**mirth′less·ness**, *n.*

mir·y (mīr′ē) *adj.* **mir·i·er**, **mir·i·est**. **1** muddy; swampy. **2** dirty;
filthy. —**mir′i·ness**, *n.*

mis– *prefix.* **1** bad, as in *misformation, misgovernment.* **2** badly,
as in *misbehave, mismanage.* **3** wrong, as in *mispronunciation.*
4 wrongly, as in *misunderstand, mislabel.* [OE *mis(s)-*, or in
borrowed words < OF *mes-* < OHG *missi-, missa-*]

mis·ad·ven·ture (mis′ad ven′chər) *n.* **1** an unfortunate accident;
an instance of bad luck. **2** bad luck; misfortune. *By some
misadventure, the letter got lost.*

mis·al·li·ance (mis′ə lī′əns) *n.* an unsuitable alliance or
association, especially in marriage.

mis·an·thrope (mis′ən thrōp′ or miz′ən thrōp′) *n.* a hater of
mankind; person who dislikes or distrusts human beings. [< Gk.
misanthrōpos < *miseein* hate + *anthrōpos* < man]

mis·an·throp·ic (mis′ən throp′ik) *adj.* of or like a misanthrope.
—**mis·an·throp′i·cal·ly**, *adv.*

mis·an·throp·ist (mis an′thrə pist) *n.* misanthrope.

mis·an·thro·py (mis an′thrə pē) *n.* a hatred, dislike, or distrust
of human beings.

mis·ap·pli·ca·tion (mis′ap lə kā′shən) *n.* a wrong application;
misapplying or being misapplied.

mis·ap·ply (mis′ə plī′) *v.* **-plied, -ply·ing.** apply wrongly; make a
wrong application or use of.

mis·ap·pre·hend (mis′ap ri hend′) *v.* misunderstand.

mis·ap·pre·hen·sion (mis′ap ri hen′shən) *n.*
a misunderstanding; wrong idea.

mis·ap·pro·pri·ate (mis′ə prō′prē āt′) *v.* **-at·ed, -at·ing.**
make use of for oneself without authority or right: *The treasurer
had misappropriated the club funds.*

mis·ap·pro·pri·a·tion (mis′ə prō′prē ā′shən) *n.* **1** a dishonest
use of something as one's own. **2** any act of putting something to a
wrong use.

mis·be·came (mis′bi kām′) *v.* pt. of **misbecome.**

mis·be·come (mis′bi kum′) *v.* **-came, -come, -com·ing.**
be unbecoming to; be unfit for.

mis·be·got·ten (mis′bi got′ən) *adj.* **1** begotten unlawfully;
illegitimate: *a misbegotten child.* **2** poorly done or conceived;
pitiable: *He was ready to throw out the whole misbegotten plan.*

mis·be·have (mis′bi hāv′) *v.* **-haved, -hav·ing.** behave oneself
badly: *The child was punished for misbehaving at the party.*

mis·be·hav·ior or **mis·be·hav·iour** (mis′bi hāv′yər) *n.*
bad behavior.

mis·be·lief (mis′bi lēf′) *n.* a false or erroneous belief, especially
in religion.

mis·be·liev·er (mis′bi lēv′ər) *n.* **1** one who holds a wrong or
erroneous belief. **2** a person who believes in a religion that is not
the regularly accepted one.

mis·brand (mis brand′) *v.* brand or mark incorrectly.

misc. **1** miscellaneous. **2** miscellany.

mis·cal·cu·late (mis kal′kyə lāt′) *v.* **-lated, -lat·ing.**
calculate wrongly; judge or count wrongly: *His arrow fell short
because he had miscalculated the distance.* —**mis′cal·cu·la′tion**, *n.*
—**mis·cal′cu·la′tor**, *n.*

mis·call (mis kol′ or -kôl′) *v.* call by a wrong name.

mis·car·riage (mis kar′ij or mis ker′ij) *n.* **1** a failure: *The jury
was biassed, and the trial resulted in a miscarriage of justice.* **2** the
involuntary expulsion of a fetus from the womb before it has
developed enough to survive. A pregnant woman might have a
miscarriage because of an accident or illness. **3** a failure to arrive:
the miscarriage of a letter.

mis·car·ry (mis kar′ē or mis ker′ē) *v.* **-ried, -ry·ing.** **1** go wrong:
John's plans miscarried, and he could not come. **2** have a
miscarriage (def. 2). **3** fail to arrive.

mis·cast (mis kast′) *v.* cast in an unsuitable role: *The young
actress was badly miscast as a bank manager.*

mis·ce·ge·na·tion (mis′ə jə nā′shən) *n.* marriage or sexual
relations between a man and woman of different races, especially
between a white person and one of another race. [< L *miscere* mix
+ *genus* race]

mis·cel·la·ne·ous (mis ə lā′nē əs) *adj.* **1** formed or consisting of
different things or parts, not arranged in a particular pattern or
system: *a miscellaneous collection of stamps. He writes a
newspaper column of miscellaneous comments.* **2** having or showing
various qualities, interests, etc.; many-sided: *a miscellaneous*

writer. [< L *miscellaneus* < *miscellus* mixed, ult. < *miscere* mix]
—**mis′cel·la′ne·ous·ly**, *adv.* —**mis′cel·la′ne·ous·ness**, *n.*

☛ **Syn. 1. Miscellaneous, indiscriminate** = including various things or kinds,
without plan or order in selection. **Miscellaneous**, describing a group or mass,
emphasizes the idea of mixing, and means 'of varied nature, usually gathered
together without special order, plan, or care in selection': *A person's
miscellaneous expenses include stamps and haircuts.* **Indiscriminate**, applying
chiefly to actions, feelings, methods, purposes, etc., emphasizes lack of
selection or judgment in selection, and means 'including all, good and bad,
deserving and undeserving, etc. without distinction': *Indiscriminate buying is
wasteful.*

mis·cel·la·ny (mis′ə lā′nē or mi sel′ə nē) *n.*, pl. **-nies. 1** a
miscellaneous collection; a mixture of various things. **2 miscellanies,**
pl. a collection of separate articles, etc. in one book. [< L
miscellania, neut. pl. of *miscellaneus.* See **MISCELLANEOUS**.]

mis·chance (mis chans′) *n.* misfortune; bad luck.

mis·chief (mis′chif) *n.* **1** action or conduct that causes trouble or
harm, often not intentionally: *A child's mischief with matches may
cause a serious fire. She's always getting into mischief.* **2** merry
teasing; playful mocking or fooling: *Her eyes were full of mischief.*
3 harm or injury, especially when done by a person: *He'll try to do
you a mischief if you meddle.* **4** a person who causes annoyance,
irritation, or harm: *He's a little mischief.* [ME < OF *meschief*, ult.
< *mes-* bad (see **MIS-**) + *chever* come to an end < *chief* head < L
caput]

mis·chief–mak·er (mis′chif māk′ər) *n.* a person who makes
mischief by tale-bearing, inciting quarrels, gossiping, etc.

mis·chief–mak·ing (mis′chif māk′ing) *adj., n.* —*adj.*
stirring up trouble. —*n.* the act or practice of stirring up trouble.

mis·chie·vous (mis′chə vəs) *adj.* **1** causing or tending to cause
harm or annoyance: *mischievous gossip, mischievous behavior.*
2 full of pranks and teasing fun: *mischievous children, a
mischievous look.* —**mis′chie·vous·ly**, *adv.* —**mis′chie·vous·ness**, *n.*

mis·ci·ble (mis′ə bəl) *adj.* especially of liquids, capable of being
mixed to form a substance having the same composition throughout.
Water and alcohol are miscible; water and oil are not. [< L *miscere*
mix]

mis·con·ceive (mis′kən sēv′) *v.* **-ceived, -ceiv·ing.** have a wrong
idea about; misunderstand.

mis·con·cep·tion (mis′kən sep′shən) *n.* a mistaken idea or
notion; incorrect conception.

mis·con·duct (*n.* mis kon′dukt; *v.* mis′kən dukt′) *n.* **1** bad or
dishonest management, especially by a public or government official
or a member of the military: *The ambassador was censured by the
government for misconduct of diplomatic affairs.* **2** bad behavior;
improper conduct. **3** *Hockey.* a ten-minute penalty awarded for
improper behavior, such as insulting the referee or using foul or
abusive language. **4** *Law.* **a** adultery. **b** malfeasance.
—*v.* **1** manage badly. **2** behave badly.

mis·con·struc·tion (mis′kən struk′shən) *n.* the act or process
of misconstruing or an instance of this; a taking in the wrong sense;
misinterpretation: *Such vague and ambiguous statements are open
to misconstruction.*

mis·con·strue (mis′kən strü′) *v.* **-strued, -stru·ing.** take in a
wrong sense; misinterpret: *Shyness is sometimes misconstrued as
rudeness.*

mis·count (*v.* mis kount′; *n.* mis′kount) *v., n.* —*v.*
count incorrectly. —*n.* an incorrect count.

mis·cre·ant (mis′krē ənt) *adj., n.* —*adj.* **1** morally base;
depraved. **2** *Archaic.* unbelieving; heretical. —*n.* **1** villain.
2 *Archaic.* an unbeliever; heretic. [ME < OF *mescreant* < *mes-*
wrongly (see **MIS-**) + *creant*, ppr. of *creire* believe < L *credere*]

mis·cue (mis kyü′) *n.* **-cued, -cu·ing.** —*n.* **1** *Billiards.* a bad
stroke in which the cue slips and does not hit the ball squarely.
2 *Informal.* mistake; slip-up. —*v.* **1** *Billiards.* make a miscue.
2 *Theatre.* miss one's cue; respond to a wrong cue.

mis·date (mis dāt′) *v.* **-dat·ed, -dat·ing.** date wrongly; put a
wrong date on or assign to a wrong date: *to misdate a document, to
misdate an event.*

mis·deal (*v.* mis dēl′; *n.* mis′dēl′) *v.* **-dealt, -deal·ing;** *n.*
Card games. —*v.* deal incorrectly. —*n.* an incorrect deal.

mis·dealt (mis delt′) *v.* pt. and pp. of **misdeal.**

mis·deed (mis dēd′ or mis′dēd′) *n.* a bad or wicked act;
offence.

mis·de·mean (mis′di mēn′) *v.* behave badly.

mis·de·mean·or or **mis·de·mean·our** (mis′di mēn′ər) *n.*
1 an offence or wrong deed, especially a minor one. **2** *Law.*
Esp.U.S. a minor criminal offence, less serious than a felony. A
misdemeanor is similar to a summary conviction offence in Canada.

mis·did (mis did′) *v.* pt. of **misdo.**

mis·di·rect (mis′də rekt′ or -dī rekt′) *v.* direct incorrectly.

mis·di·rec·tion (mis′də rek′shən or -dī rek′shən) *n.*

1 misdirecting or being misdirected. **2** a wrong direction.

mis·do (mis dü′) v. **-did, -done, -do·ing.** do wrongly or improperly. [OE *misdōn*] **—mis·do′er,** n.

mis·do·ing (mis dü′ing) n. wrongdoing; misdeed.

mis·done (mis dun′) v. pp. of **misdo.**

mis·doubt (mis dout′) v., n. *Archaic.* **—**v. **1** have doubts about; distrust. **2** suspect; fear. **—**n. suspicion; distrust; doubt.

mis·em·ploy (mis′əm ploi′) v. use wrongly or improperly. **—mis′em·ploy′ment,** n.

mi·ser (mī′zər) n. a person who loves money for its own sake, especially one who lives poorly in order to save money and keep it. A miser dislikes spending money, except to gain more money. [< L *miser* wretched]

mis·er·a·ble (miz′ər ə bəl *or* miz′rə bəl) adj. **1** unhappy; wretched: *A sick child is often miserable.* **2** causing trouble or unhappiness: *a miserable cold.* **3** poor; pitiful: *They live in a miserable, cold house.* **4** pitiable; deplorable; sorry: *a miserable failure, miserable sinners.* [< L *miserabilis,* ult. < *miser* wretched] **—mis′er·a·ble·ness,** n. **—mis′er·a·bly,** adv.
☛ *Syn.* **1.** See note at **wretched.**

Mis·e·re·re (miz′ə rer′ē *or* miz′ə rēr′ē) n. **1** the 51st Psalm in the Revised and Authorized versions of the Bible (the 50th Psalm in the Douay version). **2** a musical setting for it. **3** miserere, a speech, prayer, etc. for mercy. [< L *miserere* have pity, the first word of this psalm in the Vulgate]

mi·ser·ly (mī′zər lē) adj. of or like a miser; stingy. **—mi′ser·li·ness,** n.

mis·er·y (miz′ər ē *or* miz′rē) n., pl. **-er·ies. 1** a miserable, extremely unhappy state of mind. **2** poor, mean, or miserable conditions: *Some very poor people live in misery, without beauty or comfort around them.* **3** *Informal.* a wretched or miserable person: *He's an old misery.* [< L *miseria* < *miser* wretched]

mis·fea·sance (mis fē′zəns) n. *Law.* the wrongful performance of a lawful act; wrongful and injurious exercise of lawful authority. Compare **malfeasance** and **nonfeasance.** [ME < OF *mesfaisance* < *mes-* wrong (see MIS-) + *faire* do < L *facere*]

mis·fire (mis fīr′) v. **-fired, -fir·ing. —**v. **1** of a firearm, missile, etc., fail to discharge or go off. **2** of an internal combustion engine, fail to ignite properly or at the right moment. **3** fail to have an intended effect; go wrong: *The robber's scheme misfired.* **—**n. a failure to discharge or explode properly.

mis·fit (n. mis′fit′; v. mis fit′) n., v. **-fit·ted, -fit·ting. —**n. **1** a bad fit. **2** a person who is not suited to his environment or does not get along well with other people. **—**v. fit badly.

mis·for·tune (mis fôr′chən) n. **1** bad luck. **2** a piece of bad luck; unlucky accident.
☛ *Syn.* **1, 2. Misfortune, adversity, mishap** = bad luck. **Misfortune** applies to either an unfortunate condition, ordinarily not one's own fault, or a particular turning of affairs against one, or an unlucky happening: *She had the misfortune to break her arm.* **Adversity** applies chiefly to a condition of great and continued misfortune, marked by serious accidents, hardships, and distress: *Displaced persons have experienced adversity.* **Mishap** applies to a minor accident or unlucky accident: *Breaking a dish is a mishap.*

mis·give (mis giv′) v. **-gave, -giv·en, -giv·ing.** cause to feel doubt, suspicion, or anxiety.

mis·giv·en (mis giv′ən) v. pp. of **misgive.**

mis·giv·ing (mis giv′ing) n. a feeling of doubt, suspicion, or anxiety: *We started off through the storm with some misgivings.*

mis·gov·ern (mis guv′ərn) v. govern or manage badly. **—mis·gov′ern·ment,** n. **—mis·gov′ern·or,** n.

mis·guid·ance (mis gīd′əns) n. bad or wrong guidance.

mis·guide (mis gīd′) v. **-guid·ed, -guid·ing.** lead into mistakes or wrongdoing; mislead.

mis·guid·ed (mis gīd′id) adj. erring or misled in thought or action: *He mixed everything up in a well-meaning but misguided attempt to help.*

mis·han·dle (mis han′dəl) v. **-dled, -dling. 1** handle roughly or harshly; maltreat: *to mishandle a horse.* **2** manage badly or ignorantly; mismanage: *to mishandle a business deal.*

mis·hap (mis′hap *or* mis hap′) n. an unlucky accident.
☛ *Syn.* See note at **misfortune.**

mish·mash (mish′mash′) n. jumble; hodgepodge: *a mishmash of styles.*

Mish·nah *or* **Mish·na** (mish′nə) n. the collection of the interpretations and discussions of the law of Moses by the Jewish rabbis, completed about A.D. 200; the oral law of the Hebrews. The Mishna is the first part of the Talmud. [< post-Biblical Hebrew *mishnah* instruction < *shanah* teach, learn < Hebrew *shanah* repeat]

mis·in·form (mis′in fôrm′) v. give incorrect or misleading information to. **—mis·in·form′er,** n.

hat, āge, fär; let, ēqual, tèrm; it, īce
hot, ōpen, ôrder; oil, out; cup, pùt, rüle,
əbove, takən, pencəl, lemən, circəs

ch, child; ng, long; sh, ship
th, thin; ⟦ᴛʜ⟧, then; zh, measure

mis·in·for·ma·tion (mis′in fər mā′shən) n. incorrect, inaccurate, or misleading information.

mis·in·ter·pret (mis′in tèr′prit) v. interpret wrongly; give a wrong meaning to: *to misinterpret a signal.*

mis·in·ter·pre·ta·tion (mis′in tèr′prə tā′shən) n. an incorrect interpretation; an incorrect explanation; misunderstanding.

mis·judge (mis juj′) v. **-judged, -judg·ing. 1** judge or estimate wrongly: *The archer misjudged the distance to the target and his arrow fell short.* **2** judge unfairly; have an unjust opinion: *The teacher soon discovered that she had misjudged the girl's capabilities.*

mis·judg·ment *or* **mis·judge·ment** (mis juj′mənt) n. a wrong or unjust judgment.

mis·laid (mis lād′) v. pt. and pp. of **mislay.**

mis·lay (mis lā′) v. **-laid, -lay·ing.** put (something) in a place and then forget where it is: *Mother is always mislaying her glasses.*

mis·lead (mis lēd′) v. **-led, -lead·ing.** cause to go in a wrong direction or to do or believe in something that is wrong: *Her cheerfulness misled us into believing that everything was all right. He was accused of misleading his followers.* **—mis·lead′er,** n.

mis·lead·ing (mis lēd′ing) adj. tending to mislead; deceptive or deceiving: *misleading advertising. The calmness of the sea was misleading.* **—mis·lead′ing·ly,** adv.

mis·led (mis led′) v. pt. and pp. of **mislead.**

mis·like (mis līk′) v. **-liked, -lik·ing. 1** dislike. **2** *Archaic.* displease.

mis·man·age (mis man′ij) v. **-aged, -ag·ing.** manage badly. **—mis·man′a·ger,** n.

mis·man·age·ment (mis man′ij mənt) n. bad management.

mis·match (v. mis mach′; n. mis′mach) v. match incorrectly or unsuitably, or fail to match: *He was wearing a mismatched pair of socks.* **—**n. a poor or unsuitable match: *That marriage is definitely a mismatch.*

mis·mate (mis māt′) v. **-mat·ed, -mat·ing.** mate unsuitably.

mis·name (mis nām′) v. **-named, -nam·ing.** call by a wrong or unsuitable name: *The horse was misnamed 'Lightning'.*

mis·no·mer (mis nō′mər) n. **1** a wrong or unsuitable name or term: *'Lightning' is a misnomer for that old horse.* **2** an error in naming a person in a legal document. [ME < AF < OF *mesnommer* < *mes-* wrongly (see MIS-) + *nommer* to name < L *nominare*]

mi·sog·a·mist (mi sog′ə mist) n. a person who hates marriage.

mi·sog·a·my (mi sog′ə mē) n. a hatred of marriage. [< Gk. *misos* hatred + *gamos* marriage; formed on the pattern of *misogyny, misanthrope,* etc.]

mi·sog·y·nist (mi soj′ə nist) n. a hater of women.

mi·sog·y·nous (mi soj′ə nəs) adj. hating women.

mi·sog·y·ny (mi soj′ə nē) n. a hatred of women. [< Gk. *misogynia* < *misogynēs* woman-hater < *misos* hatred + *gynē* woman]

mis·place (mis plās′) v. **-placed, -plac·ing. 1** put in the wrong place: *a misplaced adjective.* **2** put (something) in a place and then forget where it is; mislay. **3** place (one's affections, trust, etc.) on an unworthy or unsuitable object. **—mis·place′ment,** n.

mis·play (n. mis plā′ *or* mis′plā; v. mis plā′) n. a wrong or unskilful play, as in a game: *A misplay in the last quarter almost cost us the game.* **—**v. play wrongly or unskilfully.

mis·print (n. mis′print′; v. mis print′) n., v. **—**n. a mistake in printing. **—**v. print incorrectly.

mis·pri·sion (mis prizh′ən) n. **1** a wrongful action or omission, especially by a public official. **2** *Law.* the failure of an individual to give to the proper authorities information which he knows may lead to the apprehension of a felon: *misprision of treason.* [ME < AF < OF *mesprision* < *mesprendre* mistake, act wrongly < *mes-* wrongly (see MIS-) + *prendre* take < L *prehendere*]

mis·prize (mis prīz′) v. **-prized, -priz·ing.** despise; undervalue; slight. [ME < OF *mesprisier* < *mes-* wrongly (see MIS-) + *prisier,* var. of *preisier* praise, ult. < L *pretium* price]

mis·pro·nounce (mis′prə nouns′) v. **-nounced, -nounc·ing.** pronounce in a way considered incorrect.

mis·pro·nun·ci·a·tion (mis′prə nun′sē ā′shən) *n.* an incorrect pronunciation.

mis·quo·ta·tion (mis′kwō tā′shən) *n.* an incorrect quotation.

mis·quote (mis kwōt′) *v.* **-quot·ed, -quot·ing.** quote incorrectly.

mis·read (mis rēd′) *v.* **-read** (-red′), **-read·ing. 1** read wrongly: *I misread tapering as papering and got the whole sentence wrong.* **2** misinterpret; misunderstand: *She misread his silence as agreement.*

mis·rep·re·sent (mis′rep ri zent′) *v.* **1** represent falsely; give a wrong or untrue idea of, especially in order to deceive: *He misrepresented the car when he said it was in good running order.* **2** be a bad or inadequate representative of: *His new novel misrepresents his status as a writer.*

mis·rep·re·sen·ta·tion (mis′rep ri zen tā′shən) *n.* the action or an instance of misrepresenting: *She obtained the part by misrepresentation. The report contains a serious misrepresentation of the facts.*

mis·rule (mis rül′) *n., v.* **-ruled, -rul·ing. —n. 1** bad or unwise rule. **2** disorder. **—v.** rule badly; misgovern.

miss¹ (mis) *v., n.* **—v. 1** fail to hit: *He fired twice, but both shots missed.* **2** fail to find, get, meet, attend, use, catch, hear, read, do, solve, etc.: *miss a train.* **3** let slip by; not seize: *I missed my chance.* **4** escape or avoid: *barely miss being hit.* **5** notice the absence of: *I did not miss my purse till I got home.* **6** feel keenly the absence of: *He missed his mother when she went away.* **7** fail to work properly; misfire: *The car was missing on two cylinders.* **—n.** a failure to hit, attain, etc.
a miss is as good as a mile, a close or narrow miss is in effect no better or worse than a wide miss. [OE *missan*]

miss² (mis) *n., pl.* **miss·es. 1** a girl or young woman. **2 Miss,** a title put before a girl's or unmarried woman's name: *Miss Brown, the Misses Brown, the Miss Browns.* [short for *mistress*]

Miss. Mississippi.

mis·sal (mis′əl) *n.* **1** *Roman Catholic Church.* a book containing the prayers, etc. for celebrating the Mass throughout the year. **2** any book of devotions, prayers, etc. [< Med.L *missale* < LL *missa* Mass]
☛ *Hom.* **missile.**

mis·say (mis sā′) *v.* **-said, -say·ing.** *Archaic.* **1** speak ill of; slander. **2** say wrongly. **3** speak wrongly.

mis·shape (mis shāp′) *v.* **-shaped, -shaped** or **-shap·en, -shap·ing.** shape badly; deform; make in the wrong shape.

mis·shap·en (mis shāp′ən) *adj., v.* **—adj.** badly shaped; deformed. **—v.** a pp. of **misshape.**

mis·sile (mis′il *or* mis′əl) *n.* **1** an object that is thrown or shot at a target, such as a stone, arrow, bullet, etc. **2** a self-propelled rocket containing explosives: *Missiles can be launched from land, air, or water.* [< L *missilis,* ult. < *mittere* send]
☛ *Hom.* **missal** (mis′əl).

mis·sile·man (mis′əl mən) *n., pl.* **-men.** *Esp.U.S.* a person whose work is designing, building, or operating guided missiles.

miss·ing (mis′ing) *adj.* **1** out of the usual or a known place; lost or gone: *The missing ring was found under the dresser.* **2** absent: *Only two students were missing from class today.* **3** lacking or wanting: *It was quite a good dinner, but there was something missing.*

mis·sion (mish′ən) *n.* **1** a sending or being sent on some special work; errand. An operation by one or more aircraft against the enemy is called a mission. **2** a group of persons sent on some special business: *He was one of a mission sent by our government to France.* **3** the business on which a person or group is sent: *Their mission was to blow up the bridge.* **4** the station or headquarters of a religious mission. **5** a program or course of religious services for converting unbelievers or stimulating faith and zeal. **6 missions,** *pl.* organized missionary work, especially of Christian churches. **7** a district or local church served by a priest or pastor from a nearby parish. **8** a place where persons may go for aid, such as food, clothing, shelter, or counsel. **9** a particular purpose in life; calling: *He felt that his mission was to take care of his brother's children.* [< L *missio, -onis* < *mittere* send]

mis·sion·ar·y (mish′ən er′ē) *n., pl.* **-ar·ies. 1** a person sent by a church, etc. on a religious mission: *Many Christian churches have missionaries in non-Christian countries or areas.* **2** a person who works to advance some cause or idea: *a missionary for science.* **3** *(adj.)* of, having to do with, or characteristic of missions or missionaries: *He spoke with missionary zeal of a new social order.*

mission furniture heavy, plain, dark furniture.

mis·sis (mis′əz) *n.* See **missus.**

miss·ish (mis′ish) *adj.* prim; prudish; affected.

Mis·sis·sip·pi·an (mis′ə sip′ē ən) *adj., n.* **—adj. 1** of or having to do with Mississippi or the Mississippi River. **2** *Geology.* having to do with or designating the early Carboniferous period of the Paleozoic era in North America. See chart at **geology. —n. 1** a native or inhabitant of Mississippi. **2** *Geology.* the Mississippian period or rock system.

mis·sive (mis′iv) *n.* a written message; letter. [< Med.L *missivus,* ult. < L *mittere* send]

mis·spell (mis spel′) *v.* **-spelled** or **spelt, -spell·ing.** spell incorrectly.

mis·spell·ing (mis spel′ing) *n.* an incorrect spelling.

mis·spelt (mis spelt′) *v.* a pt. and a pp. of **misspell.**

mis·spend (mis spend′) *v.* **-spent, -spend·ing.** spend foolishly or wrongly; waste: *an old man regretting a misspent youth.*

mis·spent (mis spent′) *v.* pt. and pp. of **misspend.**

mis·spoke (mis spōk′) *v.* pt. of **misspeak.**

mis·spo·ken (mis spō′kən) *v.* pp. of **misspeak.**

mis·state (mis stāt′) *v.* **-stat·ed, -stat·ing.** make incorrect or misleading statements about.

mis·state·ment (mis stāt′mənt) *n.* a wrong or erroneous statement.

mis·step (mis step′ *or* mis′step′) *n.* **1** a wrong step: *A single misstep would have plunged her into the abyss.* **2** an error in judgment; blunder: *A misstep now could ruin his career.*

mis·sus or **mis·sis** (mis′əz) *n.* Often, **the missus,** *Informal.* wife: *You'll have to ask the missus about that. Are you going to bring your missus along?*
☛ *Usage.* See note at **Mrs.**

miss·y (mis′ē) *n., pl.* **missies.** *Informal.* little miss; miss.

mist (mist) *n., v.* **—n. 1** a cloud of very fine drops of water in the air; fog. **2** anything that dims, blurs, or obscures: *The ideas were lost in a mist of long words.* **3** a haze before the eyes due to illness or tears.
—v. 1 come down in mist; rain in very fine drops. **2** become covered with or as if with mist *(often used with* **over** *or* **up**): *The bathroom window has misted.* **3** cover with or as if with mist: *Tears misted her eyes.* [OE]

mis·tak·a·ble (mis tāk′ə bəl) *adj.* that may be mistaken or misunderstood.

mis·take (mis tāk′) *n., v.* **-took, -tak·en, -tak·ing. —n.** an error; blunder; misunderstanding of the meaning or use of something: *I used your towel by mistake.*
and no mistake, without a doubt; surely.
—v. 1 make a mistake; misunderstand what is seen or heard: *I was mistaken when I said she would not come.* **2** take wrongly; take to be some other person or thing: *I mistook that stick for a snake.* [ME < ON *mistaka*]
☛ *Syn. n.* **1.** See note at **error.**

mis·tak·en (mis tāk′ən) *adj.* **1** wrong in opinion; having made a mistake: *A mistaken person should admit his error.* **2** wrong; wrongly judged; misplaced: *It was a mistaken kindness to give that boy more candy.* **—v.** pp. of **mistake. —mis·tak′en·ly,** *adv.*

mis·ter (mis′tər) *n.* **1 Mister,** the spoken form of **Mr.,** a title for a man, used before his last name or the name of his rank or office: *He always called his teacher 'Mister'.* **2** *Informal.* a title used in speaking to a man (used alone, not with a name): *Hey, mister! You dropped your wallet.* **3** *Informal.* husband: *How's your mister these days?*
☛ *Usage.* When used as a title before a name or office, the word **mister** is generally written in its abbreviated form. Compare with the note at **Mrs.** [var. of *master*]

mis·time (mis tīm′) *v.* **-timed, -tim·ing. 1** say or do at the wrong time. **2** misstate the time of.

mis·tle·toe (mis′əl tō′) *n.* **1** any of various evergreen plants genera *Viscum* and *Phoradendron* that grow as parasites on certain trees; especially, a European shrub *V. album* often growing on apple trees, having yellow flowers and small, waxy, white berries, traditionally used as a Christmas decoration. **2** *(adj.)* designating the family (Loranthaceae) of parasitic plants that includes the mistletoes. **3** a sprig of mistletoe used as a Christmas decoration. [OE *misteltān* < *mistel* mistletoe + *tān* twig]

mis·took (mis tŭk′) *v.* pt. of **mistake.**

mis·tral (mis′trəl *or* mis trål′) *n.* a cold, dry, northerly wind common in S France and neighboring regions. [< F < Provençal *mistral,* originally, dominant < L *magistralis < magister* master]

mis·trans·late (mis′trans lāt′ *or* mis trans′lāt, mis′tranz lāt′ *or* mis tranz′lāt) *v.* **-lat·ed, -lat·ing.** translate incorrectly.

mis·trans·la·tion (mis′trans lā′shən *or* -tranz lā′shən) *n.* an incorrect translation.

mis·treat (mis trēt′) v. treat badly; abuse.

mis·treat·ment (mis trēt′mənt) n. ill treatment.

mis·tress (mis′tris) n. 1 a woman who has power or authority, such as the female head of a household or institution. 2 a woman or girl as owner or possessor: *The dog was sitting outside the door, waiting for its mistress.* 3 a woman having a thorough knowledge or mastery: *mistress of the difficult art of fencing. She is mistress of the situation.* 4 a state or country that is in control or can rule: *Britain was mistress of the seas.* 5 a woman who has a continuing sexual relationship with a man without being legally married to him. 6 *Archaic or poetic.* a woman loved and courted by a man; sweetheart: *"My mistress' eyes are nothing like the sun."* 7 *Esp.Brit.* a female teacher: *the dancing mistress.* 8 **Mistress,** *Archaic or dialect.* a title for a woman, used before the name. It is replaced in modern use by **Mrs.** (pronounced mis′əz), **Miss,** or **Ms.** (pronounced miz). [ME < OF *maistresse < maistre.* See MASTER.]

mis·tri·al (mis trī′əl) n. 1 a trial declared void in law because of some error or serious misconduct in the proceedings. 2 a trial that is inconclusive because the jury has failed to reach a verdict.

mis·trust (mis trust′) v., n. —v. have no confidence or trust in; doubt: *She mistrusted her ability to learn to swim.* —n. a lack of trust or confidence; distrust. —**mis·trust′er,** n.

mis·trust·ful (mis trust′fəl) adj. lacking confidence; distrustful; doubting; suspicious. —**mis·trust′ful·ly,** adv.

mist·y (mis′tē) adj. **mist·i·er, mist·i·est.** 1 full of or covered with mist: *misty hills, misty air.* 2 not clearly seen or outlined: *a misty shape in the distance.* 3 as if seen through a mist; vague; indistinct: *a misty idea.* [OE *mistig*] —**mist′i·ly,** adv. —**mist′i·ness,** n.

mis·un·der·stand (mis′un dər stand′) v. **-stood, -stand·ing.** 1 understand wrongly. 2 take in a wrong sense; give the wrong meaning to.

mis·un·der·stand·ing (mis′un dər stan′ding) n. 1 a failure to understand; a mistake as to meaning; wrong understanding. 2 a disagreement: *After their misunderstanding, they scarcely spoke to each other for months.*

mis·un·der·stood (mis′un dər stůd′) v., adj. —v. pt. and pp. of **misunderstand.** —adj. not understood or properly appreciated: *As a child, he had always felt misunderstood.*

mis·us·age (mis yüs′ij or -yüz′ij) n. 1 a wrong or improper usage, especially of words. 2 ill usage; harsh treatment.

mis·use (v. mis yüz′; n. mis yüs′) v. **-used, -us·ing;** n. —v. 1 use for the wrong purpose: *He misuses his knife at the table by lifting food with it.* 2 abuse; ill-treat: *He misuses his sled dogs by driving them too hard.* —n. wrong, improper, or harsh usage: *the misuse of public funds, a misuse of words.*

mite (mīt) n., adv. —n. 1 any of a large number of tiny arachnids (order Acarina) that are often parasites on plants or animals, and some of which carry diseases. Some species are so small they cannot be seen with the naked eye. 2 any very small object or creature: *I'm not really hungry, but I'll have just a mite of toast.* 3 a tiny bit; very little: *I think she's a mite tired.* 4 a small coin or a small sum of money: *Though poor herself, she gave her mite to charity.*
—adv. *Informal.* somewhat; little: *She's a mite greedy.* [OE, defs. 2-4 and adv. influenced by MDu. *mite*]
☛ *Hom.* **might.**

mi·ter (mī′tər) See **mitre.**

mi·tered (mī′tərd) See **mitred.**

Mith·ra·ic (mith rā′ik) adj. of or having to do with Mithras or his cult.

Mith·ras (mith′ras) n. *Persian mythology.* the god of light, truth, and justice, often taken as representing the sun. He became the subject of an extensive cult during the late Roman Empire.

mit·i·gate (mit′ə gāt′) v. **-gat·ed, -gat·ing.** make or become less severe, painful, or harsh; make or become mild or milder; soften or moderate: *to mitigate a person's anger, to mitigate pain, to mitigate the effects of war.* [< L *mitigare < mitis* gentle] —**mit′i·ga′tor,** n.

mit·i·ga·tion (mit′ə gā′shən) n. the action of mitigating or the fact or state of being mitigated.

mit·i·ga·tive (mit′ə gā′tiv) adj., n. —adj. tending to mitigate. —n. something that mitigates.

mi·to·sis (mi tō′sis or mī tō′sis) n. the division of the nucleus of a living animal or plant cell to produce two daughter nuclei that are identical to the parent. In mitosis, each chromosome is exactly duplicated, forming two chromatids which separate and move apart, after which a new nuclear membrane forms around each group of daughter chromosomes and these daughter nuclei are then in most cases separated into two individual, identical daughter cells. Compare **meiosis.** [< NL < Gk. *mitos* thread]

mi·tot·ic (mi tot′ik or mī tot′ik) adj. of mitosis.

mi·tre (mī′tər) n., v. **mi·tred, mi·tring.** —n. 1 a tall, pointed,

---

hat, āge, fär; let, ēqual, tėrm; it, īce
hot, ōpen, ôrder; oil, out; cup, pút, rüle,
əbove, takən, pencəl, lemən, circəs

ch, child; ng, long; sh, ship
th, thin; ₮H, then; zh, measure

folded cap worn by bishops and abbots during certain ceremonies as a symbol of office. See **cope**[2] for picture. 2 the official headdress of the ancient Jewish high priests. 3 mitre joint. 4 the bevel on either of the pieces in a mitre joint. 5 a finished or hemmed corner on a garment, tablecloth, etc. made by joining the seam allowances of the sides in a diagonal seam.
—v. 1 bestow a mitre on; make a bishop. 2 join or prepare (ends of wood) for joining in a mitre joint. 3 finish (a corner of a hem) in a mitre. [ME < OF < L < Gk. *mitra* headband]

mi·tred (mī′tərd) adj. 1 having a mitre joint. 2 wearing a bishop's mitre.

mitre joint a right-angled joint made by cutting the ends of two pieces of wood, etc. on equal slants and fitting them together. Picture frames usually have mitre joints at the corners. See **joint** for picture.

mitt (mit) n. 1 mitten. 2 a padded, oversized mitten used for catching the ball in baseball, etc.: *a catcher's mitt.* 3 a knitted or lace hand covering that resembles a glove but does not cover the fingers. 4 a covering or pad worn over the hand, designed for a particular use: *a bath mitt, oven mitts.* 5 *Slang.* a hand. [short for *mitten*]

mit·ten (mit′ən) n. 1 a kind of winter glove covering the four fingers together and the thumb separately. 2 mitt (def. 3). [< F *mitaine* half glove, ult. < L *medius* middle]

mix (miks) v. **mixed** or **mixt, mix·ing;** n. —v. 1 put together; stir well together: *mix ingredients to make a cake.* 2 prepare by blending different things: *to mix a cake.* 3 join: *mix business and pleasure.* 4 be mixed: *Milk and water mix.* 5 get along together; make friends easily: *She found it difficult to mix with strangers. He doesn't mix very well.* 6 confuse or muddle (*usually used with* up): *Don't mix me up; I'm trying to count. He got his facts mixed.*
—n. 1 mixture. 2 *Informal.* a mixed condition; mess. 3 an already mixed preparation: *a cake mix.* 4 ginger ale, soda water, etc. to mix with alcoholic drinks. [< *mixt* mixed < F < L *mixtus,* pp. of *miscere* mix]
☛ *Syn.* v. **1. Mix, blend** = put two or more things together. **Mix** emphasizes forming a mass or compound in which the parts or ingredients are well scattered or spread into one another: *Mix the dry ingredients before adding a liquid.* **Blend** = mix thoroughly and smoothly together, or one thing little by little into the other, so that each part loses its separate and distinct existence and the whole has the qualities of both (or all): *Blend the flour into the melted butter.*

mixed (mikst) adj. 1 put together or formed by mixing; composed of different parts or elements; of different kinds combined: *mixed candies, mixed emotions.* 2 of different classes, kinds, etc.; not exclusive: *mixed company.* 3 of or for persons of both sexes: *She sings in the mixed chorus.*

mixed up, involved; concerned, especially in something dishonest or disreputable (*used with* in *or* with): *He was mixed up in a plot to overthrow the king.*

mixed bag *Informal.* a collection of different people or things; assortment: *The people at the party were really a mixed bag.*

mixed farm a farm on which both crops and livestock are raised.

mixed farming raising crops and livestock.

mixed metaphor a metaphor in which two or more different images or ideas get confused. *Example: The horse sailed down the course at full throttle.*

mixed number a number consisting of a whole number and a fraction, such as $1\frac{1}{2}$, $16\frac{2}{3}$.

mixed train a train composed of both freight and passenger cars.

mix·er (mik′sər) n. 1 an apparatus or appliance for mixing foods, etc. 2 a person whose work is mixing ingredients. 3 a person who gets along well with others, making friends easily: *She is a good mixer.* 4 mix (def. 4).

mix·ture (miks′chər) n. 1 mixing or being mixed. 2 something made by mixing: *The mixture is put into a greased dish and baked. Green is a mixture of blue and yellow.* 3 *Chemistry.* a substance consisting of two or more ingredients that keep their individual chemical properties and can be separated by non-chemical means: *A sugar-and-water mixture can be separated by boiling off the water.* Compare **compound**[1] (def. 2). [< L *mistura < miscere* mix]

mix·up (miks′up′) n. *Informal.* 1 confusion; mess. 2 a confused fight.

miz·zen (miz′ən) *n.* **1** a fore-and-aft sail on the mizzenmast. See **yawl** for picture. **2** mizzenmast. [< F < Ital. *mezzana* < L *medianus* in the middle < *medius* middle]

miz·zen·mast (miz′ən mast′ *or* miz′ən məst) *n.* the mast next behind the mainmast on a sailing ship or sailboat. See **mast** for picture.

mk. mark.

mkt. market.

mL millilitre(s).

MLA or **M.L.A.** *Cdn.* Member of the Legislative Assembly (in most provinces).

MLG or **M.L.G.** Middle Low German.

Mlle or **Mlle.** *pl.* **Mlles or Mlles.** Mademoiselle.

M.L.S. Master of Library Science.

mm millimetre(s).

MM. or **MM** Messieurs.

M.M. Military Medal.

Mme or **Mme.** *pl.* **Mmes or Mmes.** Madame.

MMM *Cdn.* Member of the Order of Military Merit.

Mn manganese.

MN Minnesota.

MNA or **M.N.A.** *Cdn.* Member of the National Assembly (in Quebec).

mne·mon·ic (ni mon′ik) *adj., n.* —*adj.* **1** aiding or intended to aid memory: *a set of mnemonic symbols.* **2** of or having to do with memory: *great mnemonic power.* —*n.* a device to aid the memory. —**mne·mon′i·cal·ly,** *adv.* [< Gk. *mnēmonikos* < *mnamnasthai* remember]

Mne·mos·y·ne (ni mos′ə nē′) *n. Greek mythology.* the goddess of memory and mother of the Muses.

mo. month(s).

Mo molybdenum.

Mo. Missouri.

MO Missouri.

M.O. **1** Money Order. **2** Medical Officer.

mo·a (mō′ə) *n.* any of several extinct, flightless birds of New Zealand (family Dinornithidae), most of them very large, and including one species that stood about 3.5 metres tall. The moas looked something like the modern kiwi or the ostrich. [< Maori]

Mo·ab·ite (mō′əb īt′) *n., adj.* —*n.* an inhabitant of Moab, an ancient kingdom in Syria. The Moabites were related to the Hebrews. —*adj.* of or having to do with Moab or its people.

moan (mōn) *n., v.* —*n.* **1** a long, low sound of suffering. **2** any similar sound: *the moan of the wind.* **3** complaint or lamentation. —*v.* **1** make moans. **2** utter with a moan. **3** complain or bewail: *He was always moaning about his luck.* **4** grieve or lament: *He moaned the loss of his friends.* [ME *man*; cf. OE *mǣnan* complain] —**moan′ing·ly,** *adv.*
☛ Hom. **mown.**
☛ Syn. *v.* **1.** See note at **groan.**

moat (mōt) *n., v.* —*n.* **1** a deep, wide ditch dug around a castle or town as a protection against enemies. Moats were usually kept filled with water. See **castle** for picture. **2** a similar ditch used to separate areas in a zoo. —*v.* surround with a moat. [ME < OF *mote* mound]
☛ Hom. **mote.**

mob (mob) *n., v.* **mobbed, mob·bing.** —*n.* **1** a large number of people; crowd: *There was a great mob at the gate, waiting to get in.* **2** an uncontrollable crowd, easily moved to destructive or riotous action: *The crowd had turned into an ugly mob.* **3** *Slang.* a gang of criminals. **4 the mob, a** the common mass of people, thought of as lacking taste, culture, judgment, etc.; the masses; rabble.
—*v.* **1** attack with violence, as a mob does. **2** crowd around too closely in excessive eagerness, curiosity, etc.: *Autograph hunters mobbed the singer outside her hotel.* [shortened form of L *mobile vulgus* fickle common people]

mob·cap (mob′kap′) *n.* a large, loose cap, fitting down over the ears, formerly worn indoors by women. [< obs. *mob* muffle the head]

mo·bile¹ (mō′bīl, mō′bəl, *or* mō′bēl) *adj.* **1** capable of being moved easily; moving easily: *A car is a mobile machine.* **2** easily changed; quick to change from one position to another: *mobile features, a mobile mind.* [< L *mobilis* movable < *movere* move]

mo·bile² (mō′bīl *or* mō′bēl) *n.* a decorative construction of small metal, plastic, wood, or paper shapes suspended from a balanced arrangement of more or less horizontal bars or wires, etc. so that the shapes will move in a current of air. [< *mobile¹*]

Mobile Command *Cdn.* a major organizational element of the Canadian Forces, whose role is to maintain combat-ready land forces to meet Canada's national and international defence commitments.

mobile home a large trailer used as a more or less permanent home.

mo·bil·i·ty (mō bil′ə tē) *n., pl.* **-ties.** a being mobile; ability or readiness to move or be moved.

mo·bi·li·za·tion (mō′bə lə zā′shən *or* mō′bə lī zā′shən) *n.* **1** mobilizing; calling troops, ships, etc. into active military service. **2** being mobilized.

mo·bi·lize (mō′bə līz′) *v.* **-lized, -liz·ing. 1** call (troops, warships, etc.) into active military service; organize for war. **2** assemble and prepare for war: *The troops mobilized quickly.* **3** put into action or active use: *mobilize the wealth of a country.* [< F *mobiliser* < *mobile* mobile] —**mo′bi·liz′a·ble,** *adj.* —**mo′bi·liz′er,** *n.*

Mö·bi·us strip or **Moe·bi·us strip** (mō′bē əs *or* mē′bəs; *German,* moe′bē ŭs) a one-sided, continuous surface, bounded by a continuous curve, made by twisting one end of a long, narrow, rectangular strip through 180° and joining it to the other end.

mob·ster (mob′stər) *n. Slang.* a member of a gang of criminals.

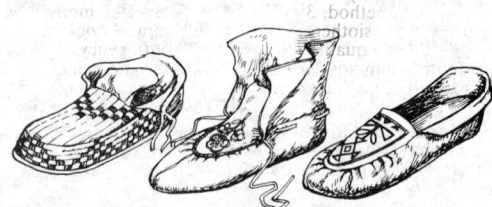

Three traditional styles of North American Indian moccasin

moc·ca·sin (mok′ə sən) *n.* **1** a soft, heel-less leather shoe or boot having the bottom and sides made of a single piece of leather which is joined in a puckered seam to the rounded piece forming the top. Moccasins were the traditional footwear of many North American Indian peoples. **2** a shoe or slipper similar in construction or appearance. [< Algonquian]

moccasin dance *Slang.* a dance, often held outdoors or in a rink, for which moccasins are worn.

moccasin flower any of several lady's-slippers, especially one (*Cypripedium acaule*) having pink or, sometimes, white flowers, found from Newfoundland to Alberta and south to Georgia and Alabama.

moccasin telegraph *Cdn. Informal.* **1** grapevine (def. 2). **2** *Historical.* the sending of messages by Indian runner.

mo·cha (mō′kə) *n.* **1** a choice variety of coffee originally coming from the Arabian peninsula. **2** a flavoring made from strong coffee or a mixture of coffee and cocoa or chocolate. **3** (*adj.*) flavored with mocha. **4** a soft suede leather made from sheepskin, used especially for gloves. **5** a dark brown; chocolate brown. [< *Mocha,* a port in SW Yemen]

mock (mok) *v., n.* —*v.* **1** laugh at; make fun of. **2** make fun of by copying or imitating. **3** imitate; copy. **4** scoff. **5** make light of; pay no attention to. **6** deceive or disappoint. **7** (*adj.*) not real; sham or imitation (*used only before a noun*): *a mock battle.*
—*n.* **1** an action or speech that mocks. **2** a person or thing scorned or deserving scorn.
make mock of, ridicule.
[ME < OF *mocquer*] —**mock′er,** *n.*
☛ Syn. *v.* **1.** See note at **ridicule.**

mock·er·y (mok′ər ē) *n., pl.* **-er·ies. 1** a making fun; ridicule. **2** a person or thing to be made fun of: *He had become a mockery in the village.* **3** a poor copy or imitation. **4** a disregarding; a setting at naught: *The trial was a mockery of justice.*
make mockery of, ridicule.

mock–he·ro·ic (mok′hi rō′ik) *adj., n.* —*adj.* imitating or burlesquing what is heroic. Pope's *Rape of the Lock* is a mock-heroic poem. —*n.* an imitation or burlesque of what is heroic.

mock·ing (mok′ing) *adj.* that mocks; ridiculing or mimicking: *mocking laughter.* —**mock′ing·ly,** *adv.*

mock·ing·bird (mok′ing bèrd′) *n.* a North American songbird (*Minus polyglottos*) related to the thrashers, famous for being able to imitate the songs of other birds. It is especially common in the southern United States.

mock orange or **mock–orange** any of a genus

(*Philadelphus*) of shrubs of the saxifrage family having showy white, sometimes fragrant flowers. Several species of mock orange are widely grown in temperate regions as ornamental shrubs.

mock sun parhelion.

mock turtle soup a soup made in imitation of green turtle soup.

mock–up (mok′up′) *n.* a full-sized model of an aircraft, machine, piece of landscape, etc., built accurately to scale and used for display or for teaching or experimental purposes.

mod·a·cryl·ic (mod′ə kril′ik) *adj.* designating any of various synthetic fibres made by copolymerization of acrylonitrile with modifying materials such as vinyl chloride. Modacrylic fibres contain between 35% and 85% of acronitrile. [abbrev. of *modified acrylic*]

mo·dal (mō′dəl) *adj., n.* —*adj.* 1 *Grammar.* of, having to do with, or being a verb form or auxiliary verb that characteristically expresses action, state, or quality in terms of possibility, probability, power, etc. rather than simple fact. *Can, may, will, should, ought,* etc. are modal verbs. 2 of or having to do with mode, manner, or form. —*n. Grammar.* a modal auxiliary. [< Med.L *modalis* < L *modus* measure]

modal auxiliary an auxiliary verb, such as *may, can, must, would,* and *should,* used with a verb expressing action, state, or quality to indicate possibility, probability, obligation, etc.

mo·dal·i·ty (mō dal′ə tē) *n.* 1 the fact, state, or quality of being modal; form. 2 mode; method. 3 *Medicine.* a therapeutic method or apparatus, especially physiotherapy or electrotherapy. 4 *Logic.* a proposition having some qualification, such as contingency, necessity, possibility, or impossibility.

mode¹ (mōd) *n.* 1 the manner or way in which a thing is done. 2 *Grammar.* mood². 3 *Music.* a any of various arrangements of the tones of an octave. b either of the two main scale systems in modern music: *major and minor modes.* c any of various Greek or medieval scales, each having a different pattern of intervals: *The keyboard of the modern piano represents the Dorian mode.* 4 *Logic.* a the form of a proposition with reference to the necessity, contingency, possibility, or impossibility of its content. b any of the various forms of valid syllogisms, depending on the quantity and quality of their constituent propositions. 5 the actual mineral composition of a sample of igneous rock, stated quantitatively in percentages by mass. [< L *modus* measure]

mode² (mōd) *n.* the style, fashion, or custom that prevails; the way most people are behaving, talking, dressing, etc. [< F < L *modus* mode¹]

Mod.E. Modern English.

mod·el (mod′əl) *n., v.* **-elled** or **-eled, -el·ling** or **-el·ing**; *adj.* —*n.* 1 a small copy: *a model of a ship.* 2 a figure, object, etc. in clay, wax, etc. that is to be copied in marble, bronze, etc.: *a model for a statue.* 3 a particular style or design of a thing: *Some car makers produce a new model every year. I want a dress like yours, for that model would suit me.* 4 a thing or person to be imitated: *The boy wrote so well that the teacher used his composition as a model for the class.* 5 a person, especially a woman, who poses for artists, photographers, etc. 6 a person employed to help sell clothing by wearing it for customers to see. —*v.* 1 make; shape; fashion; design; plan: *model a bird's nest in clay.* 2 in drawing or painting, show the effects of light and shade on objects or figures to make them appear three-dimensional. 3 make models; design: *model in clay.* 4 follow as a model; form (something) after a particular model: *He modelled himself on his father.* 5 be a model. 6 display clothes by wearing them: *That girl usually models evening gowns.* —*adj.* 1 used or serving as a model. 2 just right or perfect, especially in conduct: *a model child.* [< F < Ital. *modello,* dim. of *modo* mode¹]

☛ *Syn. n.* **4. Model, example, pattern** = someone or something to be copied or followed. **Model** applies to a person or thing thought especially worth copying or imitating: *This famous surgeon is John's model.* **Example** applies to a person, to his conduct, or to actions of his that are likely for some reason to be imitated: *He follows his father's example.* **Pattern** applies particularly to a fine example or model set up worth imitating or following closely: *Her book gives a pattern for behavior.*

mod·el·ling or **mod·el·ing** (mod′əl ing) *n.* 1 the act or occupation of a person who models clothes: *She is interested in modelling.* 2 the making of solid forms or figures in clay, wax, etc., especially by pressing and shaping with the hands. 3 in drawing or painting, the showing of the effects of light and shade on objects or figures to give a three-dimensional appearance.

mod·er·ate (*adj., n.* mod′ər it; *v.* mod′ər āt′) *adj., n., v.* **-at·ed, -at·ing.** —*adj.* 1 kept or keeping within proper bounds; not extreme: *moderate expenses, moderate styles.* 2 not violent; calm or gentle: *moderate winds.* 3 fair; medium; not very large or good: *a moderate profit.* —*n.* a person who holds moderate opinions. —*v.* 1 make or become less extreme or violent: *The wind is*

moderating. 2 act as moderator; preside (over). [< L *moderatus,* pp. of *moderare* regulate < *modus* measure] —**mod′er·ate·ly,** *adv.*

☛ *Syn. adj.* **1, 2. Moderate, temperate** mean 'not extreme in any way,' and are often interchangeable. But **moderate** emphasizes freedom from excess, not going beyond or above the proper, right, or reasonable limit: *He is a moderate eater.* **Temperate** emphasizes restraint, holding back within limits, especially with regard to the feelings or appetites: *He feels things deeply, but is always temperate in speech.*

mod·er·a·tion (mod′ər ā′shən) *n.* 1 freedom from excess; proper restraint; temperance. 2 a moderating or moving away from an extreme: *The rain brought moderation to the uncomfortably hot weather.* 3 calmness; lack of violence.

in moderation, within limits; not going to extremes: *She eats sweets in moderation.*

mod·e·ra·to (mod′ə rä′tō) *adj., adv., n. Music.* —*adj. or adv.* in moderate time. —*n.* a moderate movement or passage; a composition to be played or sung at this tempo. [< Ital.]

mod·er·a·tor (mod′ər ā′tər) *n.* 1 a presiding officer; chairman. 2 an arbitrator; mediator. 3 the chief elected officer of certain churches. 4 material used in a reactor to slow down nuclear fission.

mod·ern (mod′ərn) *adj., n.* —*adj.* 1 of the present time or times not long past: *Television is a modern invention.* 2 using or involving recent techniques, ideas, etc.; up-to-date; not old-fashioned. —*n.* 1 a person of the present time or of times not long past: *He is studying English dramatists, specializing in the moderns.* 2 a person who has modern ideas and tastes. [< LL *modernus* < L *modo* just now (originally, with measure, ablative of *modus* measure)] —**mod′ern·ly,** *adv.* —**mod′ern·ness,** *n.*

☛ *Syn. adj.* **1.** See note at **new.**

Modern English the English language from about 1500 to the present.

mod·ern·ism (mod′ər niz′əm) *n.* 1 modern attitudes, methods, etc. or sympathy with what is modern. 2 Usually, **Modernism,** the tendency to interpret the teachings of the Bible or the Christian church in accordance with modern scientific theories. 3 a modern word or phrase.

mod·ern·ist (mod′ər nist) *n.* 1 a person who holds modern views or follows modern techniques or ideas. 2 Usually, **Modernist,** a person who advocates or adheres to theological Modernism.

mod·ern·is·tic (mod′ər nis′tik) *adj.* 1 of or having to do with modernism or modernists. 2 following modern styles, methods, etc., especially in art or music.

mo·der·ni·ty (mə dèr′nə tē or mō dèr′nə tē) *n., pl.* **-ties.** 1 being modern. 2 something modern.

mod·ern·i·za·tion (mod′ər nə zā′shən or mod′ər nī zā′shən) *n.* 1 modernizing or being modernized. 2 something modernized; a modernized version.

mod·ern·ize (mod′ər nīz′) *v.* **-ized, -iz·ing.** 1 make modern; bring up to present ways or standards. 2 adopt modern ideas, techniques, etc. —**mod′ern·iz′er,** *n.*

mod·est (mod′ist) *adj.* 1 having or showing a moderate estimate of one's own abilities or merits: *a modest reply. She is very modest about her accomplishments.* 2 unassertive or diffident: *modest behavior.* 3 proper and respectable in dress and conduct. 4 not extreme or excessive: *a modest request.* 5 not pretentious, gaudy, etc.: *a modest living room.* [< L *modestus* in due measure < *modus* measure] —**mod′est·ly,** *adv.*

☛ *Syn.* **Modest, demure** = not bold or pushing oneself forward in the presence of others. **Modest** emphasizes a sense of fit and proper behavior and a lack of conceit that hold a person back from calling attention to himself: *I like a modest girl, one who is neither shy nor bold.* **Demure** now chiefly suggests an unnatural modesty or pretended shyness thought to be attractive and put on for effect: *She sipped her soda and looked demure.*

mod·es·ty (mod′is tē) *n., pl.* **-ties.** the quality or condition of being modest.

mod·i·cum (mod′ə kəm) *n.* a small or moderate quantity. [< L *modicum,* neut., moderate < *modus* measure]

mod·i·fi·ca·tion (mod′ə fə kā′shən) *n.* 1 a slight or partial change in form: *a modification in plans.* 2 a reduction; making less; moderation. 3 a limitation or qualification of a statement. 4 a modified form or variety: *The most recent modification of the long-range missile performs flawlessly.* 5 *Biology.* a change in an animal or plant caused by environment and not inheritable.

mod·i·fi·er (mod′ə fī′ər) n. 1 Grammar. a word or group of words that limits the meaning of another word or group of words. In a very tight coat, the adjective tight is a modifier of coat, and the adverb very is a modifier of tight. 2 a person or thing that modifies.

mod·i·fy (mod′ə fī′) v. -fied, -fy·ing. 1 change somewhat: to modify the terms of a lease. 2 make less; reduce or moderate: to modify one's demands. 3 Grammar. limit the meaning of; qualify. Adverbs modify verbs, adjectives, and other adverbs. 4 Biology. bring about or make important structural changes in (a part), usually resulting in a different function or orientation of the part. The tusk of a narwal is a modified tooth. In birds, the front limbs have become modified for flight. [< L modificare limit < modus measure + facere make] —**mod′i·fi′a·ble**, adj.

mod·ish (mōd′ish) adj. fashionable; stylish. —**mod′ish·ly**, adv. —**mod′ish·ness**, n.

mo·diste (mō dēst′) n. a maker of or dealer in women's clothes, hats, etc.; dressmaker or milliner. [< F]

Mo·dred (mō′dred) n. Arthurian legend. King Arthur's treacherous nephew, who led the rebellion against Arthur.

mod·u·lar (moj′ə lər) adj. 1 of, having to do with, or based on a module or modulus. 2 designed or constructed in standardized sizes or units that can be interchanged and fitted together in a variety of ways: modular storage units, modular furniture.

mod·u·late (moj′ə lāt′) v. -lat·ed, -lat·ing. 1 regulate; adjust; vary; soften; tone down. 2 alter (the voice) for expression. 3 Music. change from one key or note to another. 4 vary the frequency of (electrical waves). 5 change (a radio current) by adding sound waves to it. [< L modulari, ult. < modus measure]

mod·u·la·tion (moj′ə lā′shən) n. 1 a modulating or being modulated. 2 Music. a change from one key to another. 3 Electronics. a varying of high-frequency waves.

mod·u·la·tor (moj′ə lā′tər) n. a person or thing that modulates, especially a device for varying the range of frequency of a signal or wave in radio, television, etc.

mod·ule (moj′ül) n. 1 a standard or unit for measuring. 2 the size of some part taken as a unit of measure. 3 a standardized piece or component. 4 an independent unit that forms part of a larger, complex structure, program, etc. The command module of a spacecraft can function independently. [< L modulus, dim. of modus measure. Doublet of MOULD¹.]

mod·u·lus (moj′ə ləs) n., pl. -li (-lī′ or -lē′). Mathematics. a quantity expressing the measure of some function, property, or the like, especially under conditions where the measure is unity.

mo·dus o·pe·ran·di (mō′dəs op′ə ran′dī or op′ə ran′dē) Latin. a method or manner of working.

mo·dus vi·ven·di (mō′dəs vi ven′dī or vi ven′dē) Latin. a mode of living; a way of getting along; a temporary arrangement while waiting for a final settlement.

mo·gul¹ (mō′gul or mō gul′) n. 1 **Mogul**, a Mongolian, especially one of the Mongol conquerors of India in the 16th century or one of their descendants. 2 an important of influential person; magnate. [< Arabic and Persian Mugul < the native name Mongol]

mo·gul² (mō′gəl) n. a mound or bump of hard snow on a ski run. [origin uncertain]

M.O.H. Medical Officer of Health.

mo·hair (mō′her) n. 1 cloth or yarn made from the long, silky hair of the Angora goat, sometimes blended with other fibres, such as wool or cotton. 2 the hair of the Angora goat. 3 (adj.) made of mohair: mohair yarn, a mohair coat. [ult. < Arabic mukhayyar; conformed to hair]

Mo·ham·med (mō ham′id) n. A.D. 570?-632, a prophet and the founder of Islam, one of the world's great religions. His words are preserved in the Koran.

Mo·ham·med·an (mō ham′ə dən) adj., n. —adj. of or having to do with Mohammed or Islam. —n. Moslem.

Mo·ham·med·an·ism (mō ham′ə dən iz′əm) n. Islam.

Mo·hawk (mō′hok or mō′hôk) n., pl. -hawk or -hawks; adj. —n. 1 a member of an Amerindian people now living mainly in southern Ontario and Quebec. The Mohawk belonged to the Iroquois Confederacy. 2 the Iroquoian language of the Mohawk. —adj. of or having to do with the Mohawk or their language.

Mo·hi·can (mō hē′kən) n., adj. —n. a member of either of two closely related Amerindian peoples of the eastern United States, the **Mahican** of the upper Hudson River valley and the **Mohegan** of southeastern Connecticut. —adj. of or having to do with either of these peoples. [< Algonquian word for "wolf"]

Mo·hole (mō′hōl′) n. a drilling project for geological study of the

earth's crust down to the Mohorovicic discontinuity. [< Mohorovicic + hole. See MOHOROVICIC DISCONTINUITY.]

Mo·hor·o·vic·ic discontinuity (mə hôr′ə vis′ik or mə hôr′ə vich′ik) Geology. a rock layer separating the earth's crust and its mantle at a depth of about 6 miles under ocean beds and 20 miles on land. [after Andrija Mohorovicic, a Yugoslavian geologist who discovered it in 1909]

moi·dore (moi′dôr) n. a former gold coin of Portugal, worth about $6.50. [< Pg. moeda d'ouro coin of gold]

moi·e·ty (moi′ə tē) n., pl. -ties. 1 half. 2 an indefinite part: Only a moiety of high-school graduates go to college. [ME < OF < LL medietas half < L medietas the middle < medius middle]

moil (moil) v., n. —v. work hard; drudge. —n. 1 hard work; drudgery. 2 trouble; confusion. [ME < OF moillier moisten < L mollis soft]

moi·ré or **moire** (mwä rā′, mwär, or mô rā′) n., adj. —n. cloth having an irregular wavy finish; watered fabric. —adj. having such a finish; watered: moiré taffeta. [< F moire, alteration of E mohair]

moist (moist) adj. 1 slightly wet; damp. 2 humid. 3 filled with tears: His eyes were moist, but he did not cry. [ME < OF moiste < LL muccidus mouldy, musty < L mucus mucus] —**moist′ly**, adv. —**moist′ness**, n.
☞ **Syn.** 1. See note at **damp**.

moist·en (moi′sən) v. make or become moist: He moistened his dry lips. Her eyes moistened with tears.

mois·ture (mois′chər) n. a slight wetness; water or other liquid spread in very small drops in the air or on a surface.

mol mole⁴.

mo·lar¹ (mō′lər) n., adj. —n. a tooth with a broad surface for grinding. A person's back teeth are molars. See **teeth** for picture. —adj. 1 pulverizing by friction; grinding or capable of grinding. 2 of or having to do with the molar teeth. [< L molaris < mola mill]

mo·lar² (mō′lər) adj. Physics. of mass, acting on or by means of large masses of matter. [< L moles mass]

mo·las·ses (mə las′iz) n. a sweet syrup obtained in making sugar from sugar cane. [< Pg. < LL mellaceum must < mel honey]

mold (mōld) See **mould**.

mold·board (mōld′bôrd′) See **mouldboard**.

mold·er (mōl′dər) See **moulder**.

mold·ing (mōl′ding) See **moulding**.

mold·y (mōl′dē) See **mouldy**. —**mold′i·ness**, n.

mole¹ (mōl) n. a small, permanent spot on the skin, usually brown and slightly raised. [OE māl]

mole² (mōl) n. 1 any of a family (Talpidae) of small, burrowing, insect-eating mammals having a thick body covered with soft fur, short legs with the front feet modified for digging, small, weak eyes, and a long, pointed snout. 2 Cdn. especially in the Prairie Provinces, pocket gopher. [ME molle] —**mole′like′**, adj.

mole³ (mōl) n. 1 a barrier built of stone to break the force of the waves; breakwater. 2 a harbor formed by a mole. [< L moles mass]

mole⁴ (mōl) n. an SI unit for measuring amounts of substances that take part in chemical reactions. One mole of an element, compound, etc. is the amount that contains as many elementary units (atoms, molecules, ions, etc.) as there are atoms in 0.012 kg of carbon-12. The mole is one of the seven base units in the SI. Symbol: mol

mo·lec·u·lar (mə lek′yə lər) adj. of, having to do with, produced by, or consisting of molecules.

mol·e·cule (mol′ə kyül′) n. 1 the smallest part, or unit, into which a substance can be divided without chemical change. A molecule of an element consists of one or more atoms. A molecule of a compound consists of two or more atoms. 2 any very small bit or particle. [< NL molecula, dim. of L moles mass]

mole·hill (mōl′hil′) n. a small mound or ridge of earth raised up by moles burrowing under the ground.
make a mountain (out) of a molehill, give great importance to something which is really insignificant, especially a hindrance or obstacle.

mole·skin (mōl′skin′) n. 1 the skin of the mole used as fur. 2 a strong cotton fabric used for sportsmen's and laborers' clothing. 3 **moleskins**, pl. trousers made of this fabric.

mo·lest (mə lest′) v. 1 annoy, meddle with, or persecute, especially so as to injure: It is cruel to molest animals. 2 make improper sexual advances to. [< OF < L molestare < molestus troublesome < moles burden] —**mo·lest′er**, n.

mo·les·ta·tion (mō′les tā′shən or mol′es tā′shən) n. a molesting or being molested.

moll (mol) n. Slang. 1 a female companion of a criminal or vagrant. 2 a prostitute. [short for Molly, familiar var. of Mary]

mol·li·fy (mol′ə fī′) v. **-fied, -fy·ing. 1** soothe; appease: *The angry child refused all our attempts to mollify him.* **2** soften or mitigate: *His anger was finally mollified.* [< F < LL *mollificare* < *mollis* soft + *facere* make] —**mol′li·fi·ca′tion,** n. —**mol′li·fi′er,** n.

mol·lusc or **mol·lusk** (mol′əsk) n. any of a phylum (Mollusca) of invertebrate animals having soft, unsegmented bodies covered with a mantle that in most species produces a hard shell. Abalones, chitons, clams, cockles, limpets, mussels, nautiluses, octopuses, oysters, scallops, slugs, snails, and whelks are molluscs. [< F < L *molluscus* soft (of a nutshell)]

mol·ly·cod·dle (mol′ə kod′əl) n., v. **-dled, -dling. —**n. a person, especially a boy or man, accustomed to being fussed over and pampered; milksop. —v. coddle; pamper. [< *Molly* (familiar var. of *Mary*) + *coddle*] —**mol′ly·cod′dler,** n.

Mo·loch (mō′lok) n. **1** an ancient Canaanite god to whom children were sacrificed by their parents. **2** anything thought of as requiring frightful sacrifice: *War is a Moloch.*

Mol·o·tov cocktail (mol′ə tof) a simple incendiary hand grenade consisting usually of a gasoline-filled bottle with a short fuse or wick that is ignited just before being thrown.

molt (mōlt) See **moult.**

mol·ten (mōl′tən) adj. **1** of metal, rock, etc., made liquid by heat; melted: *molten steel, molten lava.* **2** *Archaic.* made by melting and casting: *a molten image.* —v. *Archaic.* a pp. of **melt.**

mo·ly (mō′lē) n., pl. **mo·lies. 1** a mythical herb with a milk-white flower and a black root, having magic properties. Hermes gave Odysseus moly to counteract the spells of Circe. **2** a European wild garlic (*Allium moly*). [< L < Gk.]

mo·lyb·de·nite (mə lib′də nīt′ or mol′ib dē′nīt′) n. a sulphide mineral of molybdenum that occurs in soft, bluish-silver flakes resembling graphite. It is the chief ore of molybdenum. *Formula:* MoS₂

mo·lyb·de·nous (mə lib′də nəs or mol′ib dē′nəs) adj. **1** of molybdenum. **2** containing molybdenum that has a valence of two.

mo·lyb·de·num (mə lib′də nəm or mol′ib dē′nəm) n. a heavy, silver-white, metallic chemical element of the chromium group. Molybdenum occurs only in combination and is used to harden steel. Symbol: Mo; at.no. 42, at.wt. 95.94. [< NL < L *molybdaena* < Gk. *molybdaina* < *molybdos* lead]

mom (mom or mum) n. *Informal.* mother; mum.

mo·ment (mō′mənt) n. **1** a very short, indefinite space of time: *In a moment, all was changed.* **2** a particular point of time: *We both arrived at the same moment.* **3 the moment,** the present point of time; right now: *He's busy at the moment.* **4** a definite state, period, or turning point in a course of events. **5** a period of temporary excellence or distinction: *He has his moments.* **6** importance or significance: *a matter of moment.* **7** *Physics.* **a** a tendency to cause motion, especially rotation around an axis or point. **b** the product of a given quantity (such as force) and its distance from an axis or point. Moment of force is measured in newton metres. [< L *momentum* < *movere* move. Doublet of MOMENTUM.]
☛ *Syn.* 1. See note at **minute.**

mo·men·ta (mō men′tə) n. a pl. of **momentum.**

mo·men·tar·i·ly (mō′mən ter′ə lē or mō′mən ter′ə lē) adv. **1** for a moment: *hesitate momentarily.* **2** at every moment; from moment to moment: *The danger was momentarily increasing.* **3** at any moment: *We expect him to arrive momentarily.*

mo·men·tar·y (mō′mən ter′ē) adj. lasting only a moment —**mo′men·tar′i·ness,** n.

mo·ment·ly (mō′mənt lē) adv. **1** every moment; from moment to moment. **2** at any moment. **3** for a moment.

moment of truth 1 the moment when an important decision must be made or action taken: *The guard turned and saw him and he knew that this was the moment of truth.* **2** the moment in a bullfight when the matador faces the bull to kill it.

mo·men·tous (mō men′təs) adj. very important: *a momentous decision. His graduation was a momentous occasion.* —**mo·men′tous·ly,** adv. —**mo·men′tous·ness,** n.

mo·men·tum (mō men′təm) n., pl. **-tum** or **-ta** (-tə). **1** the force with which a body moves, the product of its mass and its velocity. A falling object gains momentum as it falls. **2** the impetus resulting from movement: *The runner's momentum carried him beyond the finish line.* [< L *momentum* moving power. Doublet of MOMENT.]

mom·ism (mom′iz əm) n. an excessively sentimental worship of motherhood. [< *mom* + *-ism* (coined by Philip Wylie, a U.S. author, born 1902)]

Mo·mus (mō′məs) n. **1** *Greek mythology.* the god of mockery, who was banished from heaven for his ridicule and criticism of the gods. **2** any critical person; fault-finder.

mon. 1 monetary. **2** monastery.

Mon. Monday.

---

hat, āge, fär; let, ēqual, tėrm; it, īce
hot, ōpen, ôrder; oil, out; cup, pút, rüle,
əbove, takən, pencəl, lemən, circəs
ch, child; ng, long; sh, ship
th, thin; ℱH, then; zh, measure

mon·ad (mon′ad or mō′nad) n. **1** *Philosophy.* a fundamental metaphysical unit or entity. **2** a one-celled organism, especially a flagellate protozoan. **3** *Chemistry.* an atom, element, or radical having a valence of one. **4** unit; one. [< LL < Gk. *monas, -ados* unit < *monos* alone]

mo·nad·nock (mə nad′nok) n. an isolated hill or mass of rock left by erosion in a peneplain. [after Mount *Monadnock* in New Hampshire]

mo·nan·drous (mə nan′drəs) adj. **1** having only one husband at a time. **2** of a flower, having only one stamen. **3** of a plant, having monandrous flowers. [< Gk. *monandros* < *monos* single + *anēr, andros* husband]

mon·arch (mon′ərk) n. **1** a ruler or sovereign head of state with the title of king or queen, or emperor or empress. **2** a person or thing having supreme power or pre-eminence. **3** a large, migratory butterfly (*Danaus plexippus*) having orange wings with black veins and a black border. [< LL < Gk. *monarchēs* < *monos* alone + *archein* rule]

mo·nar·chal (mə när′kəl) adj. of, having to do with, characteristic of, or suitable for a monarch; royal; regal. —**mo·nar′chal·ly,** adv.

mo·nar·chi·al (mə när′kē əl) adj. monarchal.

mo·nar·chic (mə när′kik) adj. monarchical.

mo·nar·chi·cal (mə när′kə kəl) adj. of, having to do with, or characteristic of a monarch or monarchy. —**mo·nar′chi·cal·ly,** adv.

mo·nar·chism (mon′ər kiz′əm) n. **1** the principles of monarchy. **2** attachment to monarchy.

mon·ar·chist (mon′ər kist) n. a person who supports or favors government by a monarch.

mon·ar·chy (mon′ər kē) n., pl. **-chies. 1** government by or under a monarch. **2** a nation governed or headed by a monarch. [ME < LL < Gk. *monarchia* < *monos* alone + *archein* rule]

mon·as·te·ri·al (mon′əs tēr′ē əl) adj. of, having to do with, or characteristic of a monastery or monastic life.

mon·as·ter·y (mon′es ter′ē) n., pl. **-ter·ies. 1** a building or buildings where monks or nuns live and work according to religious rules. **2** the monks or nuns who live in such a building. [ME < LL *monasterium* < Gk. *monastērion*, ult. < *monos* alone. Doublet of MINSTER.]

mo·nas·tic (mə nas′tik) adj., n. —adj. **1** of or having to do with monks or nuns: *monastic vows.* **2** of or having to do with monasteries. **3** like that of monks or nuns: *He lives an almost monastic life.* —n. monk. [< LL *monasticus* < LGk. *monastikos*, ult. < *monos* alone] —**mo·nas′ti·cal·ly,** adv.

mo·nas·ti·cal (mə nas′tə kəl) adj. monastic.

mo·nas·ti·cism (mə nas′tə siz′əm) n. the system or condition of living according to fixed rules and under religious vows, usually in a monastery or convent.

mon·au·ral (mon ô′rəl) adj. monophonic (def. I).

Mon·day (mun′dē or -dā) n. the second day of the week, following Sunday. [OE *mōn(an)dæg* day of the moon, a translation of LL *lunae dies* (whence F *lundi*)]

Mo·nel metal (mō nel′) *Trademark.* a silver-colored alloy containing 67 percent nickel and 28 percent copper, made from ore having the metals in this proportion. [< Ambrose *Monel*, an American manufacturer]

mon·e·tar·ism (mon′ə tə riz′əm or mun′-) n. the theory that economic growth, the control of inflation, and the creation of jobs depend primarily on the regulation of the money supply (monetary policy), especially through the control of interest rates.

mon·e·tar·ist (mon′ə tə rist′ or mun′-) n. a person who advocates or practises monetarism.

mon·e·tar·y (mon′ə ter′ē or mun′ə ter′ē) adj. **1** of or having to do with the currency of a country: *The monetary unit in Canada is the dollar.* **2** of money: *a monetary reward.* [< LL *monetarius* < *moneta*. See MONEY.] —**mon′e·tar′i·ly,** adv.
☛ *Syn.* 2. See note at **financial.**

mon·e·tize (mon′ə tīz′ or mun′ə tīz′) v. **-tized, -tiz·ing. 1** legalize as money. **2** coin into money. —**mon′e·ti·za′tion,** n.

mon·ey (mun′ē) *n., pl.* **-eys** or **-ies. 1** officially issued coins and paper notes used as a standard medium of exchange: *I have five dollars left in American money.* **2** a particular form or denomination of money. **3** a sum of money used for a particular purpose or belonging to a particular person. **4** wealth: *She has a lot of money.* **5 money** or **monies, a** sums of money: *The treasurer was responsible for the moneys entrusted to him.* **b** more than one kind of money: *He had a collection of the moneys issued by different countries.* **6** any object or material serving as a medium of exchange and a measure of value, as cheques drawn on a bank, or nuggets or the dust of a precious metal.
for my money, *Informal.* for my choice; in my opinion; as I see it.
make money, a earn or receive money. **b** become rich.
[ME < OF *moneie* < L *moneta* mint, money < *Juno Moneta*, in whose temple money was coined. Doublet of MINT².] —**mon′ey·less,** *adj.*
☛ *Usage.* **Money.** Exact sums of money that are not round amounts are usually written in figures: *72 cents; $4.98; $5; $168.75; $42 810.* Round or approximate amounts are more likely to be written in words: *two hundred dollars, a million and a half dollars.* In factual books or articles involving frequent references to sums of money, however, figures are often used throughout.

mon·ey·bags (mun′ē bagz′) *n. Slang.* a wealthy person.

mon·ey·chang·er (mun′ē chān′jər) *n.* a person whose business is to exchange money, usually that of one country for that of another.

mon·eyed (mun′ēd) *adj.* **1** having money; wealthy: *a moneyed family.* **2** consisting of or representing money or people having money: *moneyed resources, moneyed interests.* Also, **monied.**

mon·ey·lend·er (mun′ē len′dər) *n.* a person whose business is lending money at interest.

mon·ey–mak·er (mun′ē māk′ər) *n.* **1** a person who is clever at making money; one who is paid well. **2** a product that yields large profits.

mon·ey–mak·ing (mun′ē māk′ing) *n., adj.* —*n.* the gaining or accumulating of wealth. —*adj.* **1** engaged in gaining wealth. **2** yielding large profits; lucrative.

money of account a monetary denomination used in reckoning, especially one not issued as a coin. In Canada, the mill is a money of account but not a coin. The nickel is a coin, but not a money of account.

money order an order issued by a post office or bank for the payment of a particular amount of money by a post office or bank in another place. You can buy a money order in one town and mail it to a person in another town, where that person can cash it.

–monger (mung′gər or mong′gər) *combining form.* **1** a dealer in—; a person who sells—: *Fishmonger = a dealer in fish.* **2** a person who exploits—; a person who spreads or busies himself with—: *Scandalmonger = a person who spreads scandal.* [OE *mangere,* ult. < L *mango* trader < Gk.]

mon·go (mong′gō) *n., pl.* **-gos** or **-go.** a unit of money in Mongolia, equal to ¹⁄₁₀₀ of a tugrik. [< Mongolian]

Mon·gol (mong′gəl, mong′gol, or mong′gōl) *n., adj.* —*n.* **1** a member of an Asiatic people now inhabiting Mongolia. **2** the language of the Mongols; Mongolian. **3** Asiatic.
—*adj.* **1** of or having to do with the Mongols or their language. **2** Asiatic.

Mon·go·li·an (mong gō′lē ən) *n., adj.* —*n.* **1** a native or inhabitant of the Mongolian People's Republic, a country in central Asia, or of Mongolia, a vast region in Asia including the Mongolian People's Republic and part of China and Siberia. **2** the Altaic language of the Mongols. **3** Mongoloid.
—*adj.* **1** of, having to do with, or designating the Mongolian People's Republic, Mongolia, the Mongols, or the language of the Mongols. **2** Mongoloid.

Mon·gol·ic (mong gol′ik) *n.* **1** a branch of the Altaic family of languages, including Mongolian and Kalmuck. **2** Mongoloid.

mon·gol·ism (mong′gəl iz′əm) *n.* a condition of mental retardation accompanied by certain abnormal physical characteristics, such as a broad, short skull, skin folds on the upper eyelids, a thick tongue, and broad hands with short fingers; Down's syndrome. Mongolism is not inherited, but exists from birth because it is caused by an abnormal development of one of the 46 chromosomes in some or all cells.

Mon·gol·oid (mong′gəl oid′) *adj., n.* —*adj.* **1** designating the Asiatic race. **2** *Obsolete.* of or designating a racial grouping that includes the traditional or aboriginal inhabitants of Asia, Greenland, and the western hemisphere. The human species was formerly classified into three main racial groups: Caucasoid, Mongoloid, and Negroid. **3 mongoloid,** of, having to do with, or affected with mongolism.
—*n.* **1** a member of the Asiatic race. **2** *Obsolete.* a member of a racial group including the traditional or aboriginal inhabitants of Asia, Greenland, and the western hemisphere. **3 mongoloid,** a person affected with mongolism.

mon·goose (mong′gūs) *n., pl.* **-goos·es. 1** any of a genus (*Herpestes*) of small, carnivorous mammals of tropical Africa and Asia, especially a slender, ferretlike species (*H. nyula*) of India, used for destroying rats, and noted for its ability to kill certain poisonous snakes without being harmed. **2** any of various other related mammals of Asia and Africa. [< Marathi (lang. of W. India) *mangus*]

mon·grel (mong′grəl or mung′grəl) *n., adj.* —*n.* an animal or plant of mixed breed, especially a dog. —*adj.* of mixed breed, race, origin, nature, etc.: *He habitually used a mongrel speech that was half English and half French.* [cf. OE *gemang* mixture]

mon·ies (mun′ēz) *n.* a pl. of **money.**

mon·i·ker or **mon·ick·er** (mon′ə kər) *n. Informal.* **1** a person's name, nickname, or signature. **2** any identifying mark or sign, such as initials, used by a tramp. [origin uncertain]

mon·ism (mon′iz əm or mō′niz əm) *n. Philosophy.* **1** the doctrine that the universe can be explained by one substance or principle. **2** the doctrine that reality is an indivisible, universal organism. [< NL < Gk. *monos* single]

mon·ist (mon′ist or mō′nist) *n.* a person who adheres to monism.

mo·nis·tic (mō nis′tik) *adj.* of or having to do with monism.

mo·ni·tion (mō nish′ən) *n.* **1** a warning or sign of danger. **2** a formal warning from a bishop or religious court to correct an offence. [< L *monitio, -onis,* < *monere* warn]

mon·i·tor (mon′ə tər) *n., v.* —*n.* **1** a person, piece of equipment, etc. that checks, reminds, or gives warning. **2** in schools, a pupil with special duties, such as helping to keep order and taking attendance. **3** a device used for checking and listening to radio and television transmissions, telephone messages, etc., as they are being recorded or broadcast. **4** any of a genus (*Varanus*) constituting the family Varanidae) of large, tropical lizards of Africa, S Asia, and Australia.
—*v.* **1** check the quality, etc. of (a radio or television broadcast, etc.) by means of a receiver. **2** *Physics.* test the intensity of radiation, especially of that produced by radio-activity. **3** act as a monitor of. [< L *monitor* < *monere* admonish]

mon·i·to·ri·al (mon′ə tô′rē əl) *adj.* **1** of, having to do with, or using a monitor or monitors. **2** monitory. —**mon′i·to′ri·al·ly,** *adv.*

mon·i·tor·ship (mon′ə tər ship′) *n.* the office, work, or period of service of a monitor.

mon·i·to·ry (mon′ə tô′rē) *adj., n., pl.* **-ries.** —*adj.* admonishing; warning. —*n.* a letter containing admonition.

monk (mungk) *n.* a man who has taken certain vows to live his life in a way prescribed by a religious brotherhood. Monks usually live in monasteries. [OE *munuc* < LL < LGk. < Gk. *monachos* individual < *monos* alone]

mon·key (mung′kē) *n., pl.* **-keys;** *v.* **-keyed, -key·ing.** —*n.* **1** any of the smaller, usually long-tailed and tree-living primates, as distinguished from man, apes, lemurs, etc. There are two main groups: the **Old World monkeys,** comprising a single family (Cercopithecidae) that includes langurs and baboons and some tailless species, such as the macaques; and the **New World monkeys,** comprising the family Cebidae, which includes many arboreal species with prehensile tails, and the family Callithricidae, which includes the marmosets. **2** any primate, excluding the lemurs and man. **3** a person, especially a child, who is full of mischief.
—*v. Informal.* play; fool; trifle: *Don't monkey with the TV set.* [probably < MLG *Moneke,* son of Martin the Ape in the story of Reynard] —**mon′key·like,** *adj.*

monkey bars 1 an open structure of vertical and horizontal pipes or bars, designed for children to climb and play on: *Many playgrounds have monkey bars.* **2** a structure of horizontal bars built against a wall, as in a gymnasium, used for climbing exercises.

monkey business *Informal.* **1** silly or mischievous acts: *Those kids are always full of monkey business.* **2** deceitful or treacherous acts: *There must have been some monkey business, because a few of the files were missing.*

monkey jacket a short, close-fitting jacket, formerly worn by sailors, now worn only as part of a military dress uniform.

mon·key·shines (mung′kē shīnz′) *n.pl. Informal.* mischievous tricks and jokes; pranks: *Those kids have been up to their monkeyshines again.*

monkey wrench an adjustable wrench, similar to a pipe wrench, but having smooth jaws.

monk·ish (mungk′ish) *adj.* **1** of or having to do with monks. **2** like or characteristic of monks or their way of life. —**monk′ish·ly,** *adv.* —**monk′ish·ness,** *n.*

MONEY: MAJOR CURRENCIES OF THE WORLD

Country	Currency Unit	Lesser Unit	Country	Currency Unit	Lesser Unit
Afghanistan	afghani	100 puls	Laos	kip	100 at
Albania	lek	100 qintars	Lebanon	pound	100 piastres
Algeria	dinar	100 centimes	Liberia	dollar	100 cents
Angola	kwanza	100 lwei	Libya	dinar	1000 millemes
Argentina	peso	100 centavos	Liechtenstein	Swiss franc	100 centimes
Australia	dollar	100 cents	Luxembourg	franc	100 centimes
Austria	schilling	100 groschen	Madagascar	franc	100 centimes
Bahamas	dollar	100 cents	Malawi	kwacha	100 tambala
Bahrain	dinar	1000 fils	Malaysia	ringgit	100 sen
Bangladesh	taka	100 paisa	Mali	franc	100 centimes
Barbados	dollar	100 cents	Malta	pound	100 cents
Belgium	franc	100 centimes	Mauritania	ouguiya	5 khoums
Belize	dollar	100 cents	Mauritius	rupee	100 cents
Benin	franc CFA	100 centimes	Mexico	peso	100 centavos
Bermuda	dollar	100 cents	Monaco	French franc	100 centimes
Bolivia	peso	100 centavos	Mongolia	tugrik	100 mongo
Brazil	cruzeiro	100 centavos	Morocco	dirham	100 centimes
Bulgaria	lev	100 stotinki	Mozambique	escudo	100 centavos
Burma	kyat	100 pyas	Nepal	rupee	100 pice
Burundi	franc	100 centimes	The Netherlands	gulden	100 cents
Cameroon	franc CFA	100 centimes	New Zealand	dollar	100 cents
Canada	dollar	100 cents	Nicaragua	cordoba	100 centavos
Central African			Niger	franc CFA	100 centimes
Republic	franc CFA	100 centimes	Nigeria	naira	100 kobo
Chile	peso	1000 escudos	Norway	krone	100 öre
People's Republic			Oman	rial	1000 baiza
of China	yuan	100 fen	Pakistan	rupee	100 paisas
Colombia	peso	100 centavos	Panama	balboa	100 cents
Congo	franc CFA	100 centimes	Papua New Guinea	kina	100 toea
Costa Rica	colon	100 centimos	Paraguay	guarani	100 centimos
Cuba	peso	100 centavos	Peru	sol	100 centavos
Cyprus	pound	1000 mils	Philippines	peso	100 centavos
Czechoslovakia	koruna	100 haler	Poland	zloty	100 groszy
Denmark	krone	100 öre	Portugal	escudo	100 centavos
Dominican Republic	peso oro	100 centavos	Romania	leu	100 bani
Ecuador	sucre	100 centavos	Rwanda	franc	100 centimes
Arab Republic of Egypt	pound	100 piastres	Saudi Arabia	rial	100 halalas
El Salvador	colon	100 centavos	Senegal	franc CFA	100 centimes
Equatorial Guinea	ekpwele	—	Sierra Leone	leone	100 cents
Ethiopia	birr	100 cents	Singapore	dollar	100 cents
Finland	markka	100 pennia	Somalia	shilling	100 cents
France	franc	100 centimes	South Africa	rand	100 cents
Fiji	dollar	100 cents	Spain	peseta	100 centimos
Gabon	franc CFA	100 centimes	Sri Lanka	rupee	100 cents
The Gambia	dalasi	100 butut	Sudan	pound	100 piastres
German Democratic			Suriname	guilder	100 cents
Republic (East)	mark	100 pfennige	Sweden	krona	100 öre
Federal Republic of			Switzerland	franc	100 centimes
Germany (West)	Deutsche Mark	100 pfennige	Syria	pound	100 piastres
Ghana	cedi	100 pesewas	Tanzania	shilling	100 cents
Greece	drachma	100 lepta	Thailand	baht	100 satang
Guatemala	quetzal	100 centavos	Togo	franc CFA	100 centimes
Guinea	syli	100 cauris	Trinidad and Tobago	dollar	100 cents
Guyana	dollar	100 cents	Tunisia	dinar	100 millimes
Haiti	gourde	100 centimes	Turkey	lira (pound)	100 kurus (piastres)
Honduras	lempira	100 centavos	Uganda	shilling	100 cents
Hong Kong	dollar	100 cents	United Arab Emirates	dirham	10 dinar, 1000 fils
Hungary	forint	100 filler	United Kingdom	pound sterling	100 new pence
Iceland	krona	100 aurar	United States	dollar	100 cents
India	rupee	100 paise	Upper Volta	franc CFA	100 centimes
Indonesia	rupia	100 sen	Uruguay	nuevo peso	100 centesimos
Iran	rial	100 dinars	U.S.S.R.	rouble	100 kopeks
Iraq	dinar	1000 fils	Venezuela	bolivar	100 centimos
Irish Republic	pound	100 new pence	Vietnam	dong	100 hao
Israel	shekel	10 pounds	West Indies		
Italy	lira	—	(Leeward Islands,		
Ivory Coast	franc CFA	100 centimes	Windward Islands)	dollar	100 cents
Jamaica	dollar	100 cents	People's Republic		
Japan	yen	100 sen	of Yemen	dinar	1000 fils
Jordan	dinar	1000 fils	Yemen Arab Republic	riyal	100 rial
Kenya	shilling	100 cents	Yugoslavia	dinar	100 paras
Korea	won	100 chon	Zaire	zaire	100 makuta
North Korea	won	100 jun	Zambia	kwacha	100 ngwee
Kuwait	dinar	1000 fils	Zimbabwe	dollar	100 cents

monks·hood (mungks′hud′) *n.* any of several aconites, having flowers shaped somewhat like the hoods worn by monks.

mon·o¹ (mon′ō) *n. Informal.* mononucleosis.

mon·o² (mon′ō) *adj. Informal.* monophonic (def. 1).

mono– *combining form.* one; single, as in *monogamy, monosyllable, monotone.* [< Gk. *monos* single]

mon·o·ba·sic (mon′ō bā′sik) *adj.* of an acid, having but one atom of hydrogen replaceable by an atom or radical of a base in forming salts.

mon·o·chord (mon′ə kôrd′) *n.* **1** a sounding board with a single string, used for measuring musical intervals. **2** a harmonious combination of sounds. **3** harmony; agreement.

mon·o·chro·mat·ic (mon′ə krō mat′ik) *adj.* **1** of one color only: *a monochromatic color scheme in blue and white.* **2** consisting of only one wave length of light or other radiation.

mon·o·chrome (mon′ə krōm′) *n.* a painting, drawing, etc. in a single color or shades of a single color. [< Gk. *monochrōmos < monos* single + *chrōma* color]

A monocle. It rests on the cheekbone and is held in place by the eyebrow muscle.

mon·o·cle (mon′ə kəl) *n.* an eyeglass for one eye. [< F < LL *monoculus* one-eyed < Gk. *monos* single + L *oculus* eye]

mon·o·cled (mon′ə kəld) *adj.* wearing a monocle.

mon·o·cot (mon′ə kot′) *n.* monocotyledon.

mon·o·cot·y·le·don (mon′ə kot′ə lē′dən) *n.* any flowering plant having a single seed leaf (cotyledon) in the embryo, including grasses, lilies, orchids, and palms. See also **dicotyledon.**

mo·noc·u·lar (mə nok′yə lər) *adj.* **1** of, involving, or affecting only one eye: *monocular vision.* **2** suitable for or adapted to only one eye: *a microscope with a monocular eyepiece.*

mon·o·cul·ture (mon′ə kul′chər) *n.* the use of land for the cultivation of a single product to the exclusion of any other.

mon·o·dy (mon′ə dē) *n., pl.* **-dies. 1** a mournful song. **2** a plaintive poem in which one person laments another's death. **3** *Music.* **a** a style of composition that has only one predominating melody or part. **b** a composition written in such a style. [< LL < Gk. *monōidia,* ult. < *monos* single + *aeidein* sing]

mo·noe·cious or **mo·ne·cious** (mə nē′shəs) *adj.* **1** *Botany.* having the stamens and the pistils in separate flowers on the same plant. **2** *Zoology.* having both male and female organs in the same individual; hermaphroditic. [< NL *Monoecia,* pl., class name < Gk. *monos* single + *oikos* house]

mo·nog·a·mist (mə nog′ə mist) *n.* a person who practises or believes in monogamy.

mo·nog·a·mous (mə nog′ə məs) *adj.* **1** practising or advocating monogamy. **2** of or having to do with monogamy.

mo·nog·a·my (mə nog′ə mē) *n.* **1** the practice or condition of being married to only one person at a time. **2** *Zoology.* the habit of having only one mate. [< L < Gk. *monogamia < monos* single + *gamos* marriage]

mon·o·gram (mon′ə gram′) *n.* a design made by combining letters, usually the initials of a person's name. Monograms are often used on notepaper, table linen, clothing, jewellery, etc. [< L *monograma* < L.Gk. *monogrammon,* neut., consisting of a single letter < Gk. *monos* single + *gramma* letter]

mon·o·graph (mon′ə graf′) *n., v.* —*n.* a scholarly book or article on one aspect of a subject. —*v.* write a monograph on; treat in a monograph.

mon·o·graph·ic (mon′ə graf′ik) *adj.* **1** having to do with or like a monograph. **2** of or having to do with a monogram. —**mon′o·graph′i·cal·ly,** *adv.*

mo·nog·y·nous (mə noj′ə nəs) *adj.* **1** having one wife at a time. **2** *Botany.* **a** of a flower, having one pistil. **b** of a plant, having such flowers.

mo·nog·y·ny (mə noj′ə nē) *n.* the practice or state of having one wife at a time. [< *mono-* + Gk. *gynē* woman + E *-y³*]

mon·o·lin·gual (mon′ə ling′gwal or mon′ə ling′gyə wəl) *adj.* knowing or using only one language: *a monolingual person, a monolingual conversation.*

mon·o·lith (mon′ə lith′) *n.* **1** a single large block of stone. **2** a

monument, column, statue, etc. formed of a single large block of stone. **3** an organization that is massive, uniform, and therefore rigid and unyielding in its attitudes and policy. [< L < Gk. *monolithos < monos* single + *lithos* stone]

mon·o·lith·ic (mon′ə lith′ik) *adj.* **1** of or being a monolith. **2** massively uniform: *a monolithic society, a monolithic state.*

mon·o·logue (mon′ə log′) *n.* **1** a long speech by one person in a group. **2** an entertainment by a single speaker. **3** a scene or short play for one actor, often written to tell a story, to show character, or to describe a humorous or dramatic situation. **4** a part of a play in which a single actor speaks alone. [< F < LGk. *monologos < monos* single + *logos* speech, discourse]

mon·o·logu·ist (mon′ə log′ist) *n.* one who talks or acts in monologue, or delivers monologues.

mon·o·ma·ni·a (mon′ə mā′nē ə) *n.* an excessive concern with or interest in one thing or idea.

mon·o·ma·ni·ac (mon′ə mā′nē ak′) *n.* a person having an excessive interest in one thing or idea.

mon·o·ma·ni·a·cal (mon′ə mə nī′ə kəl) *adj.* of or having to do with a monomania.

mon·o·mer (mon′ə mər) *n.* a chemical compound consisting of single molecules that can join together to form a polymer or copolymer. [< *mon-* + *-mer* (as in *polymer*). 20c.]

mon·o·mer·ic (mon′ə mer′ik) *adj.* of or having to do with monomers.

mon·o·me·tal·lic (mon′ō mə tal′ik) *adj.* **1** using one metal only. **2** having to do with monometallism.

mon·o·met·al·lism (mon′ō met′əl iz′əm) *n.* the use of one metal only as the standard of money values.

mo·no·mi·al (mō nō′mē əl) *adj., n.* —*adj.* consisting of a single word or term. —*n.* **1** a name consisting of a single word. **2** *Mathematics.* an expression consisting of a single term. z, a^3b^4, and $\frac{m_1m_2}{d^2}$ are monomials. [< *mono-* + *-nomial,* modelled after *binomial*]

mon·o·nu·cle·o·sis (mon′ə nyü′klē ō′sis *or* -nü′klē ō′sis) *n.* an infectious disease characterized by an abnormal increase of leucocytes. Also called **infectious mononucleosis.**

mon·o·pho·nic (mon′ə fon′ik) *adj.* **1** in sound reproduction or recording, having only one channel for transmission of sound: *a monophonic record.* **2** *Music.* having a single melody, with little or no accompaniment or harmonization.

mon·oph·thong (mon′əf thong′ *or* mon′ə thong′) *n.* **1** a single vowel sound. **2** a letter representing a single vowel sound.

mon·o·plane (mon′ə plān′) *n.* an airplane having one set of wings. Most modern planes are monoplanes.

mo·nop·o·list (mə nop′ə list) *n.* **1** a person who has a monopoly. **2** a person who favors monopoly.

mo·nop·o·lis·tic (mə nop′ə lis′tik) *adj.* **1** that monopolizes. **2** of or having to do with monopolies or monopolists. —**mo·nop′o·lis′ti·cal·ly,** *adv.*

mo·nop·o·lize (mə nop′ə līz′) *v.* **-lized, -liz·ing. 1** have or get exclusive possession or control of. **2** occupy wholly; keep entirely to oneself. —**mo·nop′o·liz′er,** *n.*

mo·nop·o·ly (mə nop′ə lē) *n., pl.* **-lies. 1** control of a commodity or service for a particular market, with little or no competition: *The new dairy bought out the other two dairies in town and now has a monopoly on milk.* **2** such control granted by a government: *An inventor has a monopoly on the manufacture and sale of his invention for a certain number of years.* **3** a commodity or service that one company, etc. has a monopoly on: *In some provinces, the telephone service is a government monopoly.* **4** a company having a monopoly. **5** the exclusive possession or control of something: *No one person has a monopoly on virtue.* [< L < Gk. *monopōlion < monos* single + *pōleein* sell]

mon·o·rail (mon′ə rāl′) *n.* **1** a single rail serving as a complete track for a wheeled vehicle. **2** a railway in which cars run on a single rail.

mon·o·so·di·um glu·ta·mate (mon′ə sō′dē əm glü′tə māt′) a white, crystalline powder made from various vegetable proteins and used for seasoning foods. *Formula:* $C_5H_8NNaO_4$

mon·o·syl·lab·ic (mon′ə sə lab′ik) *adj.* **1** having only one syllable. **2** consisting of a word or words of one syllable each.

mon·o·syl·la·ble (mon′ə sil′ə bəl) *n.* a word of one syllable. *Yes* and *no* are monosyllables.

mon·o·the·ism (mon′ə thē′iz əm) *n.* the doctrine or belief that there is only one God. [< *mono-* + Gk. *theos* god]

mon·o·the·ist (mon′ə thē′ist) *n.* a believer in only one God.

mon·o·the·is·tic (mon′ə thē′is′tik) *adj.* **1** believing in only one God. **2** having to do with the belief in only one God.

mon·o·tone (mon′ə tōn′) *n.* **1** sameness of tone, of style of writing, of color, etc. **2** a person who cannot produce the correct musical intervals in singing and so cannot follow a melody. **3** (*adjl.*) continuing on one tone; of one tone, style, or color.

mo·not·o·nous (mə not′ə nəs) *adj.* **1** continuing in the same tone: *She spoke in a monotonous voice.* **2** tedious or wearying because of lack of variety: *monotonous food, monotonous work.* —**mo·not′o·nous·ly,** *adv.*

mo·not·o·ny (mə not′ə nē) *n.* **1** sameness of tone or pitch. **2** a wearisome sameness. [< Gk. *monotonia,* ult. < *monos* single + *tonos* tone]

mon·o·treme (mon′ə trēm′) *n.* any of an order (Monotremata) of lower mammals comprising the platypus and echidna. [< *mono-* + Gk. *trēma* hole]

mon·o·type (mon′ə tīp′) *n., v.* **-typed, -typ·ing.** —*n.* **1** Monotype, *Trademark.* a set of two machines (keyboard machine and casting machine) for setting and making type in separate letters. **2** the sole type of its group. A single species constituting a genus is a monotype. **3 a** a print from a metal plate on which a picture has been painted in color with oil or printing ink, which is transferred to paper by a rubbing process. **b** the method of producing such a print. —*v.* set with a Monotype machine.

mon·o·va·lent (mon′ə vā′lənt) *adj. Chemistry.* having a valence of one.

mon·ox·ide (mon ok′sīd *or* -ok′sid) *n.* an oxide containing one oxygen atom in each molecule.

Monroe Doctrine the doctrine that European nations should not interfere with American nations or try to acquire more territory in America. [< James *Monroe* (1758-1831), President of the United States from 1817 to 1825]

Mon·sei·gneur *or* **mon·sei·gneur** (môN se nyœr′) *n., pl.* **Mes·sei·gneurs** *or* **mes·sei·gneurs** (mā se nyœr′). *French.* **1** a title of honor given to princes, bishops, and other persons of importance, usually used in front of a title of office. **2** a person having this title. [< F < *mon* my + *seigneur* lord]

mon·sieur (mə syœr′) *n., pl.* **mes·sieurs** (mā syœ′). *French.* Mr.; sir. [< F *monsieur,* earlier *mon sieur* my lord]

Mon·si·gnor *or* **mon·si·gnor** (mon sēn′yər; *Italian,* môn′sē nyôr′) *n., pl.* **Mon·si·gnors** *or* **mon·si·gnors;** *Italian,* **Mon·si·gno·ri** *or* **mon·si·gno·ri** (môn′sē nyō′rē) *Roman Catholic Church.* **1** a title given to certain dignitaries. **2** a person having this title. [< Ital. *monsignor,* half-translation of F *monseigneur* monseigneur]

mon·soon (mon sün′) *n.* **1** a large wind system that reverses its direction with the seasons, especially a wind of the Indian Ocean and SE Asia that blows from the southwest from April to October and from the northeast during the rest of the year. **2** in India and adjacent regions, the season when the monsoon blows from the southwest, characterized by heavy rains. [< Du. < Pg. < Arabic *mausim* season]

mon·ster (mon′stər) *n., adj.* —*n.* **1** any animal or plant that is out of the usual course of nature: *A two-headed calf is a monster.* **2** an imaginary creature of strange appearance: *Mermaids and centaurs are monsters.* **3** a huge creature or thing. **4** a person who is extremely evil or cruel: *The man in charge of the slaves was a monster.* —*adj.* huge. [ME < OF *monstre* < L *monstrum* divine warning < *monstrare* show] —**mon′ster·like′,** *adj.*

mon·strance (mon′strəns) *n. Roman Catholic Church.* a receptacle in which the consecrated Host is shown for adoration or is carried in procession. [< Med.L *monstrantia* < L *monstrare* show]

mon·stros·i·ty (mon stros′ə tē) *n., pl.* **-ties. 1** monster. **2** the state or character of being monstrous.

mon·strous (mon′strəs) *adj., adv.* —*adj.* **1** huge; enormous. **2** unnaturally formed or shaped; like a monster. **3** shocking; horrible; dreadful. —*adv. Informal.* very; extremely. —**mon′strous·ly,** *adv.* —**mon′strous·ness,** *n.*

Mont. Montana.

mon·tage (mon täzh′) *n.* **1** the combination of several distinct pictures to make a composite picture. **2** a composite picture so made. **3** in motion pictures or television, the use of a sequence of rapidly changing pictures to suggest an emotional reaction, a state of mind, etc. **4** any combining or blending of different elements: *His latest novel is a montage of biography, history, and fiction.* [< F *montage* < *monter* mount]

Mon·ta·gnais (mon′tə nyā′) *n., pl.* **-gnais** (-nyā′ *or* -nyāz′) *or* **-gnaises** (-nyāz′). **1** an Indian tribe of N Quebec. **2** a member of this tribe. **3** the Cree dialect spoken by this tribe. **4** Chipewyan. [< F < *montagne* mountain]

mon·te (mon′tē) *n.* a Spanish gambling game played with cards. [< Sp. *monte* mountain, i.e., of cards]

---

hat, āge, fär; let, ēqual, tèrm; it, īce
hot, ōpen, ôrder; oil, out; cup, put, rüle,
above, takən, pencəl, lemən, circəs

ch, child; ng, long; sh, ship
th, thin; ᴛʜ, then; zh, measure

Mon·te·ne·grin (mon′tə nē′grin) *adj., n.* —*adj.* of or having to do with Montenegro, a former kingdom in S Europe (now part of Yugoslavia) or its people. —*n.* a native or inhabitant of Montenegro.

month (munth) *n.* **1** one of the 12 parts into which the year is divided. **2** the period of time from any day of one month to the corresponding day of the next month: *It will take us about a month to finish the project.* **3** *Astronomy.* **a** the time it takes the moon to make one complete revolution around the earth; lunar month. **b** the time from one new moon to the next, about 29.53 days; synodical month. **c** one twelfth of a solar year, about 30.41 days; solar month. **d** a sidereal month. [OE *mōnath.* Related to MOON.]

☛ *Usage.* **Months.** In reference matter and informal writing, the names of months with more than four letters are abbreviated in dates: *Jan. 21, 1951,* but *June 30, 1950.* When only the month or month and year are given, abbreviations are rare: *January 1950. Every January he tries again.* In formal writing, the names of the months are not abbreviated.

month·ly (munth′lē) *adj., adv., n., pl.* **-lies.** —*adj.* **1** of a month; for a month. **2** done, happening, payable, etc. once a month. —*adv.* once a month; every month. —*n.* a magazine published once a month.

Mont·re·al canoe (mont′rē ol′ *or* mun′trē ol′) *Cdn. Historical.* the largest canoe of the fur trade, used especially on the Great Lakes and the St. Lawrence River. It was up to 40 ft. long and could carry a cargo of four or five tons. Also, **canot du maître.**

mon·u·ment (mon′yə mənt) *n.* **1** something set up to preserve the memory of a person or an event. A monument may be a building, pillar, arch, statue, tomb, or stone. **2** anything that keeps alive the memory of a person or an event. **3** an enduring or prominent instance or example: *The professor's publications were monuments of learning.* **4** something set up to mark a boundary. [< L *monumentum* < *monere* remind]

mon·u·men·tal (mon′yə men′təl) *adj.* **1** of or serving as a monument. **2** like a monument; weighty, lasting and important: *The B.N.A. Act is a monumental document.* **3** very great: *monumental ignorance, a monumental achievement.* —**mon′u·men′tal·ly,** *adv.*

moo (mü) *n., pl.* **moos;** *v.* **mooed, moo·ing.** —*n.* the sound made by a cow. —*v.* make the sound of a cow.

mooch (müch) *v. Slang.* **1** sneak; skulk; rove about. **2** steal. **3** beg; get (something) at another person's expense. **4** *Cdn.* fish by drifting with light tackle for big fish. [origin uncertain] —**mooch′er,** *n.*

mood¹ (müd) *n.* **1** a state of mind or feeling. **2** moods, *pl.* fits of depression or bad temper. [OE *mōd* spirit]

mood² (müd) *n. Grammar.* the form of a verb that shows whether the act or state expressed is thought of as fact, or as something else, such as command, possibility, or wish. The indicative mood is used for statements of facts; the imperative mood is used for commands. [alteration of *mode*; influenced by *mood¹*]

mood·y (mü′dē) *adj.* **mood·i·er, mood·i·est. 1** likely to have changes of mood; temperamental: *He's a very moody person so it's hard to say how he'll react.* **2** often having gloomy moods. **3** sullen or gloomy: *He sat there in moody silence.* —**mood′i·ly,** *adv.* —**mood′i·ness,** *n.*

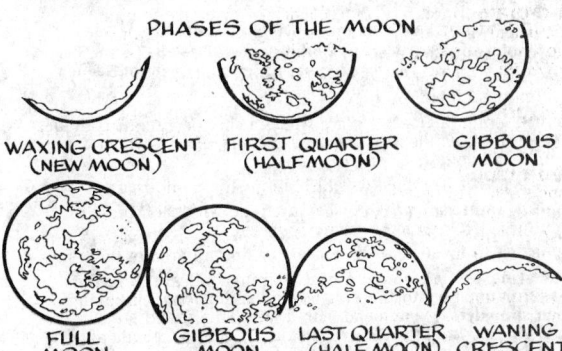

PHASES OF THE MOON

WAXING CRESCENT (NEW MOON)   FIRST QUARTER (HALF MOON)   GIBBOUS MOON

FULL MOON   GIBBOUS MOON   LAST QUARTER (HALF MOON)   WANING CRESCENT

moon (mün) *n., v.* —*n.* **1** a heavenly body that revolves around

the earth from west to east once in approximately 29½ days with reference to the sun or 27⅓ days with reference to the stars. It shines by the sun's reflected light. **2** the moon at a certain period of time: **new moon** (visible as a slender crescent), **half moon** (visible as a half circle), **full moon** (visible as a circle), **old moon** (waning). **3** a lunar month; about a month or 29 days. **4** moonlight. **5** something shaped like the moon. **6** a natural or artificial satellite: *the moons of Jupiter.*
—*v.* wander about or gaze idly or listlessly. [OE *mōna*]
—**moon′less,** *adj.* —**moon′like′,** *adj.*

moon·beam (mün′bēm′) *n.* a ray of moonlight.

moon·calf (mün′kaf′) *n.* a foolish or absent-minded person.

moon·eye (mün′ī′) *n., pl.* **-eye** or **-eyes. 1** a medium-sized, olive-and-silver freshwater fish (*Hiodon tergisus*) of northern North America having a deep, laterally compressed body, a deeply forked tail, and large, golden eyes set far forward on the head. **2** (*adjl.*) designating the family Hiodontidae, whose only living members are the mooneye and the closely related goldeye.

moon·less (mün′less) *adj.* **1** lacking the light of the moon: *a moonless night.* **2** having no satellite: *a moonless planet,*

moon·light (mün′līt′) *n., v.* —*n.* **1** the light of the moon. **2** (*adjl.*) having the light of the moon: *a moonlight night.* **3** (*adjl.*) while the moon is shining; by night: *a moonlight swim.*
—*v. Informal.* work at a second job, usually at night, in order to supplement the wages earned at a regular job. —**moon′light′er,** *n.*

moon·lit (mün′lit′) *adj.* lighted by the moon.

moon·quake (mün′kwāk′) *n.* an agitation of the surface of the moon, of the same kind as an earthquake.

moon·rise (mün′rīz′) *n.* **1** the rising of the moon above the horizon. **2** the time when the moon rises above the horizon.

moon·scape (mün′skāp′) *n.* **1** a view of the details of the surface of the moon. **2** a barren and desolate area on earth thought of as resembling the surface of the moon.

moon·shine (mün′shīn′) *n.* **1** moonlight. **2** empty talk; empty show; nonsense. **3** *Informal.* intoxicating liquor made unlawfully, or smuggled.

moon·shin·er (mün′shīn′ər) *n. Informal.* **1** a person who makes intoxicating liquor contrary to law. **2** a person who follows an unlawful trade at night.

moon·shot (mün′shot′) *n.* the action or an instance of launching a spacecraft to the moon.

moon·stone (mün′stōn′) *n.* **1** a translucent, whitish variety of feldspar having a pearly lustre. **2** a gem made from this stone.

moon·struck (mün′struk′) *adj.* dazed; crazed.

moon·y (mü′nē) *adj.* **moon·i·er, moon·i·est. 1** of the moon. **2** like the moon; crescent-shaped. **3** dreamy; listless.

moor¹ (mür) *v.* **1** put or keep (a ship, etc.) in place by means of ropes or chains fastened to the shore or to anchors. **2** moor a ship. **3** be made secure by ropes, anchors, etc. [ME *more(n);* cf. OE *mærels* mooring rope]

moor² (mür) *n. Brit.* open wasteland, usually hilly or high up and having low plant growth. [OE *mōr*]

Moor (mür) *n.* a member of a people of mixed Arab and Berber descent who conquered Spain in the eighth century A.D. The present-day Moors are a nomadic people of Mauritania and nearby areas. [ME < OF *More, Maure* < L < Gk. *Mauros*]

moor·age (mür′ij) *n.* **1** mooring or being moored. **2** a place for mooring. **3** the charge for its use.

moor·cock (mür′kok′) the male of the red grouse.

moor·fowl (mür′foul′) *n. Archaic.* red grouse.

moor hen (mür′hen′) **1** the female of the red grouse. **2** *Esp.Brit.* the common gallinule.

moor·ing (mür′ing) *n.* **1** a place where a ship or aircraft is made fast. **2** **moorings,** *pl.* the ropes, cables, anchors, etc. by which a ship, etc. is made fast.

mooring mast the mast to which an airship is moored.

Moor·ish (mür′ish) *adj.* of or having to do with the Moors or their culture: *Moorish architecture.*

moor·land (mür′land′ or mür′lənd) *n. Brit.* an area of moors.

moose (müs) *n., pl.* **moose.** a large mammal (*Alces alces*), the largest living member of the deer family having long legs, high humped shoulders, a long head with a large snout, and large, palmate antlers. In North America it occurs across Canada and south to parts of the N United States. In Europe, this animal is called an elk. [< Algonquian]

moose·bird (müs′bėrd′) *n. Cdn.* Canada jay.

moose·milk (müs′milk′) *n. Cdn. Slang.* **1** a drink made of rum or other liquor and milk. **2** in the North, home-distilled liquor.

moose pasture *Cdn. Slang.* mining claims that are considered worthless.

moose–yard (müs′yärd′) *n. Cdn.* a space in the woods where moose in winter tread down the snow, remaining there for protection and warmth, feeding on tender shoots and saplings.

moot (müt) *adj., v., n.* —*adj.* debatable; doubtful: *a moot point.*
—*v.* **1** argue. **2** bring forward (a point, subject, case, etc.) for discussion.
—*n.* an assembly. [OE (ge)*mōt* meeting]

moot court a mock court held in a law school to give students practice.

mop¹ (mop) *n., v.* **mopped, mop·ping.** —*n.* **1** a bundle of coarse yarn, rags, etc. fastened at the end of a stick, for cleaning floors, dishes, etc. **2** something like a mop: *He is going to have his mop of hair cut before he goes for his interview.* —*v.* **1** wash or wipe up; clean with a mop. **2** wipe.
mop up, a finish. **b** *Military.* clear out or rid (an area, town, etc.) of scattered or remaining enemy troops.
[probably < OF *mappe* < L *mappa* napkin] —**mop′per,** *n.*

mop² (mop) *v.* **mopped, mop·ping;** *n.* —*v. Archaic or poetic.* grimace.
mop and mow, make faces.
—*n. Archaic or poetic.* a grimace. [cf. Du. *moppen* to pout]

mope (mōp) *v.* **moped, mop·ing;** *n.* —*v.* be dull, silent, and sad.
—*n.* a person who mopes. [? related to MOP²] —**mop′er,** *n.*

mo·ped (mō′ped) *n.* a motorized bicycle.

mop·ish (mōp′ish) *adj.* inclined to mope; sad and listless.

mop·pet (mop′it) *n. Informal.* child. [< obs. *mop* doll]

mop–up (mop′up′) *n. Informal.* **1** a finishing off or a wiping out; a clean-up. **2** in battle, the finishing off of an action in an area by the killing or capture of enemy troops.

mo·quette (mō ket′) *n.* a thick, velvety carpet. [< F]

mo·raine (mə rān′) *n.* a mass or ridge of rocks, dirt, etc. deposited at the sides or end of a glacier after being carried down or pushed aside by the pressure of the ice. [< F]

mor·al (môr′əl) *adj., n.* —*adj.* **1** good in character or conduct; virtuous according to civilised standards of right and wrong; right; just: *a moral act, a moral man.* **2** capable of understanding right and wrong: *A little baby is not a moral being.* **3** having to do with character or with the difference between right and wrong: *a moral question.* **4** based on the principles of right conduct rather than on law or custom. **5** teaching a good lesson; having a good influence: *a moral book.* **6** that encourages and gives confidence: *We gave moral support to the team by cheering loudly.* **7** depending upon considerations of what generally occurs; resting upon grounds of probability: *moral evidence, moral arguments.*
—*n.* **1 morals,** *pl.* **a** character or behavior in matters of right and wrong: *The boy's morals were excellent.* **b** one's principles in regard to conduct. **2** the lesson, inner meaning, or teaching of a fable, a story, or an event: *The moral of the story was "Look before you leap."* [ME < L *moralis* < *mos, moris* custom (pl., manners)]
—**mor′al·ly,** *adv.*

☛ *Syn. adj.* **1. Moral, ethical** = in agreement with a standard of what is right and good in character or conduct. **Moral** means right and good according to the customary rules and accepted standards of society: *He leads a moral life.* **Ethical** particularly suggests agreement with principles of right conduct or good living expressed in a system or code, especially of the branch of philosophy dealing with moral conduct or of a profession or business: *It is not considered ethical for doctors to advertise.*

☛ *Usage.* **Moral, morale.** Do not confuse **moral** (a lesson) with **morale** (mental condition as regards courage, confidence, enthusiasm, etc.): *He understood the moral of the story. The general was pleased with the morale of his soldiers.*

moral certainty a probability so great that it might just as well be a certainty.

mo·rale (mə ral′ *or* mə räl′) *n.* the mental condition or attitude as regards courage, confidence, enthusiasm, etc.: *The morale of the team was low after its defeat.* [< F *moral,* mistakenly spelt *morale* in English to keep the pronunciation]
☛ *Usage.* See note at **moral.**

mor·al·ist (môr′əl ist) *n.* **1** a person who thinks much about moral duties, sees the moral side of things, and leads a moral life. **2** a person who teaches, studies, or writes about morals. **3** a person concerned with regulating or improving the morals of others.

mor·al·is·tic (môr′əl is′tik) *adj.* **1** moralizing; teaching the difference between right and wrong. **2** of or having to do with a moralist or moral teaching. —**mor′al·is′ti·cal·ly,** *adv.*

mo·ral·i·ty (mə ral′ə tē) *n., pl.* **-ties. 1** the right or wrong of an action. **2** the doing of right; virtue. **3** a system of morals; a set of rules or principles of conduct. **4** moral instruction; a moral lesson or precept. **5** morality play. **6** (*adjl.*) of or belonging to a morality squad: *a morality officer.*

morality play a form of drama popular during the 15th and 16th centuries, in which vices and virtues are personified.

morality squad a police division that deals with the enforcement of laws concerning gaming and prostitution.

mor·al·ize (môr′əl īz′) v. -ized, -iz·ing. 1 think, talk, or write about questions of right and wrong. 2 point out the lesson or inner meaning of. 3 improve the morals of. —**mor′al·i·za′tion,** n. —**mor′al·iz′er,** n.

moral philosophy ethics.

Moral Rearmament a twentieth-century religious movement to reform the world through the improvement of personal morals and character; Buchmanism.

moral support approval but not active or tangible help.

moral victory a defeat that has the effect on the mind that a victory would have.

mo·rass (mə ras′) n. 1 a piece of low, marshy ground; swamp. 2 a difficult situation; a puzzling mess. [< Du. *moeras* < OF *marais* < Gmc.]

mor·a·to·ri·um (môr′ə tô′rē əm) n., pl. -ri·ums, -ri·a (-rē ə). 1 a legal authorization to delay payments of money due. 2 the period during which such authorization is in effect. 3 a temporary pause in action, negotiation, etc. on any issue. [< NL < L *morari* delay < *mora* a delay]

Mo·ra·vi·an (mô rā′vē ən) n., adj. —n. 1 a native or inhabitant of Moravia, a region in central Czechoslovakia. 2 the Czech dialect spoken by Moravians. 3 a member of the Moravian church. —adj. 1 of or having to do with Moravia, its people, or their dialect. 2 of, having to do with, or designating the Protestant church which developed from a 15th century reform movement in Moravia and Bohemia.

mo·ray (mô′rā or mô rā′) n. any of numerous eels (family Muraenidae) found in warm seas, having a heavy, often brilliantly colored body and a large mouth with strong, sharp teeth. [< Pg. *moreia* < L *murena*, var. of *muraena* < Gk. *muraina*]

mor·bid (môr′bid) adj. 1 unhealthy; not wholesome: *His mother thinks his liking of horror movies is morbid.* 2 caused by disease; characteristic of disease; diseased: *Cancer is a morbid growth.* 3 horrible; frightful: *the morbid details of a murder.* [< L *morbidus* < *morbus* disease] —**mor′bid·ly,** adv. —**mor′bid·ness,** n.

mor·bid·i·ty (môr bid′ə tē) n. 1 a morbid state or quality. 2 the proportion of sickness in a certain group or locality: *Morbidity statistics show that tuberculosis is on the decline in Canada.*

mor·dan·cy (môr′dən sē) n. a mordant quality.

mor·dant (môr′dənt) adj., n. —adj. 1 biting; cutting; sarcastic: *Their mordant criticisms hurt his feelings.* 2 in dyeing, that fixes colors. —n. 1 a substance that fixes colors. 2 an acid that eats into metal. [< OF *mordant,* ppr. of *mordre* bite < L *mordere*]

Mor·dred (môr′dred) n. Modred.

more (môr) adj. (used as comparative of **much** and **many,** with the superlative **most**), n., adv. —adj. 1 greater in number, quantity, amount, degree, or importance: *more men, more help.* 2 further; additional: *Take more time.* —n. 1 a greater number, quantity, amount, or degree: *The more they have, the more they want.* 2 an additional amount: *Tell me more.* —adv. 1 in or to a greater extent or degree: *It hurts more to beg than to borrow.* 2 in addition; further; longer; again: *Sing once more.*

be no more, be dead.

more or less, a rather; somewhat: *Most people are more or less selfish.* **b** nearly; approximately: *The distance is five kilometres, more or less.* [OE *māra*]

☛ *Usage.* **More** and **most** are often used before adjectives and adverbs to form comparatives and superlatives. **More** and **most** are put before all adjectives and adverbs of three syllables or more, and before some adjectives and most adverbs of two syllables. Other adjectives and adverbs, apart from a few irregular ones, use **-er** and **est** to form the comparative and superlative.

mo·reen (mə rēn′) n. a strong, heavy, woven fabric used for curtains and upholstery, made of wool, cotton, or a mixture of wool and cotton, and usually having a watered finish. [? related to MOIRÉ]

mo·rel (mə rel′) n. any of a genus (Morchella) of edible fungus having a fleshy, pitted head on a stalk. [< F *morille* < Gmc.]

more·o·ver (môr ō′vər) adv. also; besides: in addition to that: *His power is absolute and, moreover, hereditary.*

mores (mô′rēz or mô′rāz) n.pl. customs prevailing among a people or a social group that are accepted as right and obligatory; traditional rules; ways; manners. [< L *mores* manners]

Mo·resque (mə resk′) adj. Moorish; in the Moorish style.

mor·ga·nat·ic (môr′gə nat′ik) adj. designating or having to do with a form of marriage in which a man of high rank marries a woman of lower rank with an agreement that neither she nor her children shall have any claim to his title or property. [< NL

morality play 743 Morpheus

hat, āge, fär; let, ēqual, tėrm; it, īce hot, ōpen, ôrder; oil, out; cup, pùt, rüle, above, takən, pencəl, lemən, circəs

ch, child; ng, long; sh, ship th, thin; ŧH, then; zh, measure

morganaticus < Med.L. (*matrimonium ad*) *morganaticam* (marriage with) morning gift, ult. < OHG *morgangeba* < *morgan* morning + *geban* give; the "morning gift" to the bride on the day after the wedding was her only share in her husband's goods and rights]

Mor·gan le Fay (môr′gən lə fā′) Arthurian legend. a fairy and King Arthur's half sister, usually represented as trying to harm him at every opportunity.

morgue (môrg) n. 1 a place, usually in a police station or hospital, in which unclaimed bodies of dead persons are kept until they can be identified. 2 that part of a hospital where autopsies are performed. 3 in a newspaper office, the reference library. [< F]

mor·i·bund (môr′ə bund′) adj. dying. [< L *moribundus,* ult. < *mori* die]

mo·ri·on (mô′rē on′) n. a helmet without a visor, shaped somewhat like a hat with a high crest, worn especially by Spanish foot soldiers in the 1500's and 1600's. [< F < Sp. *morrion* < *morra* crown of head]

Mor·mon (môr′mən) n., adj. —n. 1 a member of The Church of Jesus Christ of Latter-day Saints, founded in the United States in 1830 by Joseph Smith. 2 **The Book of Mormon,** a sacred book of The Church of Jesus Christ of Latter-day Saints. —adj. of or having to do with the Mormons or their religion. [< the name of the narrator of "The Book of Mormon"]

Mor·mon·ism (môr′mən iz′əm) n. the religious system of the Mormons.

morn (môrn) n. Poetic. dawn or morning. [OE *morgen*]

morn·ing (môr′ning) n., adj. —n. 1 the early part of the day, ending at noon. 2 the first or early part of anything: *the morning of life.* —adj. of or in the morning. [ME *morwening* < *morwen* morn (OE *morgen*) = -*ing;* patterned on *evening*]
☛ Hom. **mourning.**

morning coat a man's coat used for formal daytime wear, cut away diagonally from the waist in front, tapering down to the knees at the back; cutaway; tailcoat; swallow-tailed coat.

morn·ing–glo·ry (môr′ning glô′rē) n., pl. -ries. 1 any of numerous twining plants (genus Ipomoea) having showy, trumpet-shaped, blue, mauve, pink, or white flowers and heart-shaped leaves. 2 (adjl.) designating a family (Convolvulaceae) of herbs, shrubs, and trees that includes the morning-glories.

morning sickness a feeling of nausea, often accompanied by vomiting, that occurs in the morning, especially during the early months of pregnancy.

morning star a planet, especially Venus, seen in the eastern sky before sunrise.

Mo·ro (mô′rō) n., pl. **Mo·ros.** 1 a member of any of various tribes of Moslem Malays in the S Philippine Islands. 2 the language of these people. [< Sp. *Moro* a Moor]

Mo·roc·can (mə rok′ən) n., adj. —n. a native or inhabitant of Morocco, a country in NW Africa. —adj. of or having to do with Morocco or its people.

mo·roc·co (mə rok′ō) n., pl. -cos. 1 a fine leather made from goatskins, using in binding books. 2 a leather imitating this. [< *Morocco,* a country in NW Africa, where it was first made]

mo·ron (mô′ron) n. 1 a person who is unable to develop mentally to the normal level of an adult. Moron was formerly used as a grade in a classification system for mentally retarded people. 2 Informal. a stupid or annoyingly ignorant person; dullard; dunce. [< Gk. *mōron,* neut. of *mōros* foolish, dull]

mo·ron·ic (mô ron′ik) adj. of or having to do with morons or being a moron.

mo·rose (mə rōs′) adj. gloomy, sullen; ill-humored: *He has a morose expression.* [< L *morosus,* originally, set in one's ways < *mos, moris* habit] —**mo·rose′ly,** adv. —**mo·rose′ness,** n.

mor·pheme (môr′fēm′) n. Linguistics. the smallest meaningful element of a language or dialect, such as *un-, -ing, do, make,* or *snow.* Simple words, bases, and affixes are morphemes.

Mor·phe·us (môr′fē əs or môr′fyüs) n. Greek mythology. the god of dreams; popularly thought of as the god of sleep. [ME < L *Morpheus* fashioner or moulder < Gk. *morphē* form, shape, in allusion to the forms seen in dreams]

mor·phi·a (môr′fē ə) *n.* morphine.

mor·phine (môr′fēn) *n.* a bitter, crystalline addictive drug made from opium, used to dull pain and to cause sleep. *Formula:* $C_{17}H_{19}NO_3$ [< F < G *Morphin* < *Morpheus* Morpheus]

mor·phin·ism (môr′fin iz′əm) *n.* 1 a morbid condition caused by habitual use of morphine. 2 the morphine habit.

mor·pho·log·ic (môr′fə loj′ik) *adj.* morphological.

mor·pho·log·i·cal (môr′fə loj′ə kəl) *adj.* of or having to do with morphology; relating to form; structural. **—mor′pho·log′i·cal·ly,** *adv.*

mor·phol·o·gy (môr fol′ə jē) *n.* 1 the branch of biology that deals with the forms and structure of animals and plants. 2 the form and structure of an organism or of one of its parts. 3 the branch of linguistics that deals with the forms of words. 4 the system of word-forming elements and processes of a language. The morphology of English is very different from that of French. 5 the study of forms in any science, as in physical geography or geology. [< Gk. *morphē* form + E *-logy*]

mor·ris (môr′is) *n.* morris dance.

Morris chair or **morris chair** an armchair with an adjustable back. [after William *Morris* (1834-1896), an English poet and painter, who invented it]

morris dance 1 an old English dance performed by people in fancy costumes. 2 the music for such a dance. [*morris*, earlier *morys* Moorish]

mor·row (môr′ō) *n. Archaic or poetic.* the following day or time: *We expected her on the morrow.*

good morrow, *Archaic.* good morning. [ME *morwe*, var. of *morwen* morn, OE *morgen*]

Morse (môrs) *adj., n.* **—adj.** having to do with or designating the Morse code, or a telegraph system using it. **—n.** the Morse code. [< Samuel F.B. *Morse* (1791-1872), American inventor of the telegraph]

Morse code a signalling system by which letters, numbers, etc. are represented by dots, dashes, and spaces or by long and short sounds or flashes of light.

mor·sel (môr′səl) *n.* 1 a small bite; mouthful. 2 a piece; fragment. 3 a dish of food; tidbit: *a dainty morsel.* 4 something to be enjoyed, disposed of, or endured: *to find a person a tough morsel. This decision was a bitter morsel.* [ME < OF *morsel*, dim. of *mors* a bite, ult. < L *morsum*, pp. of *mordere* bite]

mort (môrt) *n. Hunting.* a note sounded on a horn at the death of a deer. [< F *mort* death < L *mors, mortis*]

mor·tal (môr′təl) *adj., n.* **—adj.** 1 sure to die sometime. 2 of man; of mortals. 3 of death. 4 causing death of the soul: *mortal sin.* 5 causing death: *a mortal wound, a mortal illness.* 6 lasting until death: *a mortal enemy, a mortal battle.* 7 very great deadly: *mortal terror.*
—n. 1 a being that is sure to die sometime. All living creatures are mortals. 2 a man; human being. [< L *mortalis* < *mors, mortis* death]
☛ *Syn. adj.* See note at **fatal.**

mor·tal·i·ty (môr tal′ə tē) *n.* 1 mortal nature; the state of being sure to die sometime. 2 a loss of life on a large scale: *The mortality from automobile accidents is very serious.* 3 the death rate; number of deaths per thousand cases of a disease, or per thousand persons in the population.

mor·tal·ly (môr′təl ē) *adv.* 1 fatally; so as to cause death: *mortally wounded.* 2 very greatly; bitterly; grievously: *mortally offended.*

mortal sin *Theology.* a sin so serious that it can cause the death of the soul. Compare **venial sin.**

mor·tar¹ (môr′tər) *n., v.* **—n.** a mixture of lime, cement, sand, and water, used for holding bricks or stones together. **—v.** plaster or fix with mortar. [ME < OF *mortier* < L *mortarium*]

mor·tar² (môr′tər) *n.* 1 a bowl of very hard material, in which substances may be pounded to a powder. See **pestle** for picture. 2 a very short artillery piece for shooting shells at high angles. [ME < OF *mortier* < L *mortarium*]

mor·tar·board (môr′tər bôrd′) *n.* 1 a flat, square board used by masons to hold mortar. 2 an academic cap with a close-fitting crown topped by a stiff, flat, cloth-covered square piece, worn by faculty and students in some schools and universities on certain occasions.

mort·gage (môr′gij) *n., v.* **-gaged, -gag·ing.** **—n.** 1 a claim on property, given to a person, bank, or firm that has loaned money in case the money is not repaid when due. 2 a document that gives such a claim. **—v.** 1 give a lender a claim to (one's property) in case a debt is not paid when due. 2 put under some obligation; pledge:

Faust mortgaged his soul to the devil. [ME < OF *mortgage* < *mort* dead (< L *mortuus*) + *gage* pledge, gage¹ < Gmc.]

mort·ga·gee (môr′gi jē′) *n.* the person, bank, or company to whom property is mortgaged; the creditor in a mortgage.

mort·gag·er or **mort·ga·gor** (môr′gi jər) *n.* a person or company whose property is mortgaged; the debtor in a mortgage.

mor·tice (môr′tis) *n., v.* **-ticed, -tic·ing.** See **mortise.**

mor·ti·cian (môr tish′ən) *n. Esp.U.S.* undertaker. [< *mortu*ary + *-ician*, probably an analogy with *physician*]

mor·ti·fi·ca·tion (môr′tə fə kā′shən) *n.* 1 extreme embarrassment; shame: *The boy was overcome with mortification when he spilled milk on his host's suit.* 2 the cause of such feelings. 3 gangrene. 4 the control and subjection of one's physical desires and feelings through self-denial or endurance of pain.

mor·ti·fy (môr′tə fī′) *v.* **-fied, -fy·ing.** 1 make ashamed or embarrassed; humiliate: *They were mortified by their cousin's rudeness to their friend.* 2 control or overcome one's physical desires and feelings through self-denial or the endurance of pain. 3 become affected with or cause gangrene. [ME < OF *mortifier* < L *mortificare* kill < *mors, mortis* death + *facere* make] **—mor′ti·fi′er,** *n.*
☛ *Syn.* 1. See note at **ashamed.**

mor·tise (môr′tis) *n., v.* **-tised, -tis·ing.** **—n.** a hole in one piece of wood cut to receive a projection on another piece, called the tenon, so as to form a joint (**mortise and tenon joint**). See **joint** for picture. **—v.** fasten by a mortise: *Good furniture is mortised together, not nailed.* [ME < OF *morteise* < Arabic *murtazz* fastened]

mort·main (môrt′mān) *n. Law.* an inalienable possession; the condition of lands or tenements held without right to sell them or give them away. [ME < OF *mortemain*, translation of Med.L. *mortua manus* dead hand; with reference to corporations as not being persons]

mor·tu·a·ry (môr′chü er′ē) *n., pl.* **-ries;** *adj.* **—n.** 1 that part of a funeral parlor or of a cemetery where bodies of dead people await burial. 2 a morgue. **—adj.** of death or burial. [ME < AF < Med.L *mortuarium*, ult. < L *mors, mortis* death]

mos. months.

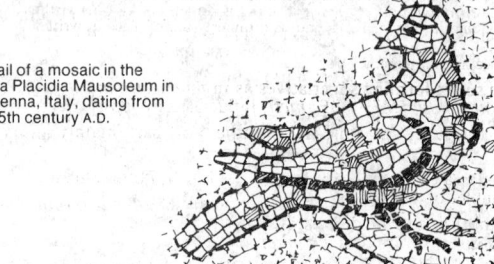

Detail of a mosaic in the Galla Placidia Mausoleum in Ravenna, Italy, dating from the 5th century A.D.

mo·sa·ic (mō zā′ik) *n.* 1 a picture or design made of small pieces of stone, glass, wood, etc. of different colors, set together or inlaid: *Mosaics are used in floors, walls, ceilings, etc.* 2 the art or process of making such pictures or designs. 3 something made up of varied parts or elements, like a mosaic: *Canada is often called a cultural mosaic.* 4 (*adj.*) of, having to do with, or used for mosaic or mosaics. 5 any of several virus diseases of plants that cause the leaves to become mottled, with small, yellow or brownish spots. Mosaic occurs especially in tobacco, corn, and sugar cane. [< F *mosaique* < Italian < Med.L *mosaicus*, var. of *musaicus* of the Muses, artistic]

Mo·sa·ic (mō zā′ik) *adj.* of Moses or of writings ascribed to him.

Mosaic law 1 the ancient law of the Hebrews, ascribed to Moses. 2 the part of the Bible where these laws are stated.

Mo·selle (mō zel′) *n.* 1 a dry white wine produced near the Moselle River in Germany. 2 a similar wine produced elsewhere.

Mo·ses (mō′ziz or mō′zis) *n.* in the Bible, the great leader and lawgiver who led the Israelites out of captivity in Egypt toward the Promised Land, and who received the Ten Commandments from God on Mount Sinai.

mo·sey (mō′zē) *v.* **-seyed, -sey·ing.** *Slang.* move in an aimless or leisurely manner; amble. [origin uncertain]

Mos·lem (moz′ləm or mos′ləm) *n., adj.* **—n.** a believer in Islam. **—adj.** of or having to do with Islam or its doctrines or the Islamic culture. Also, **Muslim.** [< Arabic *muslim* one who submits < *aslama* submit. Related to SALAAM.]

mosque (mosk) *n.* a Moslem place of worship. [< F < Ital. < Arabic *masjid* < *sajada* prostrate oneself]

mos·qui·to (məs kē′tō) *n., pl.* **-toes** or **-tos.** any of a large family (Culicidae) of two-winged insects, the females of which have mouthparts adapted for piercing the skin of human beings and animals and sucking their blood. Some species transmit serious diseases, such as malaria, yellow fever, one type of sleeping sickness, etc. [< Sp. *mosquito,* dim. of *mosca* < L *musca* fly]

moss (mos) *n.* **1** any of a class (Musci) of flowerless and rootless plants usually growing as low, dense, carpetlike masses on tree trunks, rocks, moist ground, etc. See also **peat moss. 2** a mass of these plants growing together. **3** any of various other plants resembling mosses, such as reindeer moss, club moss, or Spanish moss. [OE *mos* bog] —**moss′like′,** *adj.*

moss agate a variety of agate that has brown, black, or green mosslike markings.

moss·back (mos′bak′) *n. Slang.* a person whose ideas are out of date; fogey.

moss–bag (mos′bag′) *n. Cdn.* a kind of bag of leather or cloth used by certain North American Indian peoples to carry a baby. Packed with dry moss, which serves as a diaper, it is laced up in front and usually carried strapped to a cradle-board. See **cradle-board** for picture.

moss rose a cultivated variety of cabbage rose having very fragrant, usually pink flowers and having a mosslike growth on the calyx and stem.

moss·y (mos′ē) *adj.* **moss·i·er, moss·i·est. 1** covered with moss: *a mossy bank.* **2** like moss; *mossy green.* —**moss′i·ness,** *n.*

most (mōst) *adj.* (superlative of **many** and **much**), *n., adv.* (superlative of **much**). —*adj.* **1** greatest in quantity, amount, measure, degree, or number: *The winner gets the most money.* **2** the majority of; almost all: *Most children like candy.*
for the most part, mainly or usually.
—*n.* the greatest quantity, amount, degree, or number: *He did most of the work.*
at (the) most, not more than.
make the most of, make the best use of.
—*adv.* **1** in or to the greatest extent or degree: *Which movie did you like most?* **2** to a very great degree: *a most persuasive argument.* **3** *Informal.* almost; nearly: *We go there most every week.* [OE *māst*]
☛ *Usage.* **Most, almost. Most** is the common informal shortening of **almost:** *A drop in prices will appeal to most everybody.* It is sometimes used in writing conversation and in informal style, but is ordinarily out of place in written English.
☛ *Usage.* See note at **more.**

–most a suffix forming superlatives as in *foremost, inmost, topmost, uttermost.* [ME < OE *-mest;* influenced by *most*]

most·ly (mōst′lē) *adv.* almost all; for the most part; mainly; chiefly.

mot (mō) *n.* a clever or witty remark. [< F < L *muttum* grunt, word. Doublet of MOTTO.]

mote¹ (mōt) *n.* a speck of dust. [OE *mot*]
☛ *Hom.* **moat.**

mote² (mōt) *v. Archaic.* may; might. [OE *mōtan.* Related to MUST¹.]
☛ *Hom.* **moat.**

mo·tel (mō tel′) *n.* a kind of hotel consisting of a building or group of buildings having rooms that can be reached directly from an outdoor parking area. [< *mo*tor + ho*tel*]

mo·tet (mō tet′) *n. Music.* a polyphonic composition having a sacred theme, usually sung unaccompanied. [ME < OF *motet,* dim. of *mot* word]

moth (moth) *n., pl.* **moths** (moᴛʜz *or* moths). any of a large number of mostly nocturnal insects (order Lepidoptera) having broad wings that in most species are held flat on the back when at rest, feathery or threadlike antennae, usually a fairly stout body, and whose larvae are caterpillars that in most species feed on plants. Compare **butterfly.** [OE *moththe*]

moth·ball (moth′bol′ *or* moth′bôl′) *n., v.* —*n.* a small ball made of naphthalene, or some other strong-smelling substance, used for putting in garments or in clothes closets to keep moths away.
in mothballs, a in protective storage. **b** in an inactive state or condition: *The plans for expansion have been put in mothballs.* —*v.* **1** put in protective storage: *to mothball a ship.* **2** set aside or postpone for an indefinite period: *to mothball a project.*

moth–eat·en (moth′ēt′ən) *adj.* **1** eaten by moths; having holes made by moths. **2** worn-out; out-of-date.

moth·er¹ (muᴛʜ′ər) *n., v.* —*n.* **1** a female parent. **2** (*adjl.*) of, like, or being a mother: *mother love. We saw a mother squirrel with three babies.* **3** the cause; source: *Necessity is the mother of invention.* **4** the head of a community of nuns. **5** a woman exercising control and responsibility like that of a mother. **6** *Informal.* an old or elderly woman (*used especially as a title or form of address*).

hat, āge, fär; let, ēqual, tèrm; it, īce
hot, ōpen, ôrder; oil, out; cup, pút, rüle,
əbove, takən, pencəl, lemən, circəs

ch, child; ng, long; sh, ship
th, thin; ᴛʜ, then; zh, measure

7 (*adjl.*) native or innate: *mother courage. Scotland is my mother country and English is my mother tongue.*
—*v.* **1** be mother of; give birth to or produce. **2** act as mother to; care for and protect as a mother does: *mothering a tearful child.* **3** acknowledge oneself the mother or originator of. [OE *mōdor*] —**moth′er·less,** *adj.*

moth·er² (muᴛʜ′ər) *n.* a stringy, sticky substance, consisting of bacteria that is formed in vinegar or on the surface of liquids that are turning to vinegar. [special use of *mother¹*]

Mother Car·ey's chicken (ker′ēz) **1** the stormy petrel. **2** any of various petrels.

mother church a church from which or by which others have been formed.

mother country 1 the country where a person was born. **2** a country in relation to its colonies.

Mother Goose 1 the imaginary author of a book of fairy tales by Charles Perrault (1628-1703), a French author, published in 1697. **2** the imaginary author of English nursery rhymes, actually of folk origin and first published in book form by John Newbury (1713-1767). Mother Goose is a traditional character of nursery tales in Europe.

moth·er·hood (muᴛʜ′ər hùd′) *n.* **1** the state of being a mother. **2** mothers: *The motherhood of our city want more day nurseries.*

Mother Hub·bard (hub′ərd) **1** the subject of a well-known Mother Goose nursery rhyme beginning "Old Mother Hubbard went to the cupboard." **2** a woman's full, loose gown.

moth·er–in–law (muᴛʜ′ər in lo′ *or* -lô′) *n., pl.* **moth·ers–in–law.** the mother of one's husband or wife.

moth·er·land (muᴛʜ′ər land′) *n.* **1** one's native country. **2** the land of one's ancestors.

mother lode the main vein of ore in an area or mine.

moth·er·ly (muᴛʜ′ər lē) *adj.* **1** of, suitable for, or characteristic of a mother: *motherly advice.* **2** like a mother; kindly: *She's a warm, motherly person.* —**moth′er·li·ness,** *n.*

moth·er–of–pearl (muᴛʜ′ər əv pèrl′) *n.* the hard, smooth, pearly lining of certain marine shells, such as that of the pearl oyster and abalone. Mother-of-pearl is used to make buttons and ornaments.

Mother's Day the second Sunday of May, set apart in Canada and the United States in honor of mothers.

mother ship a whaling ship, fishing vessel, spacecraft, etc. that acts as a base or supply point for one or more smaller craft.

mother superior a woman who is in charge of a convent of nuns.

mother tongue 1 one's native language. **2** a language to which other languages owe their origin.

mother wit natural intelligence; common sense.

moth·proof (moth′prüf′) *adj., v.* —*adj.* treated chemically so as to keep clothes moths away: *The carpet is mothproof.* —*v.* make mothproof: *a mothproofed fibre.*

moth·y (moth′ē) *adj.* **moth·i·er, moth·i·est.** containing moths or having holes made by moths.

mo·tif (mō tēf′) *n.* **1** *Art or literature.* a subject for development or treatment; dominant, usually recurring idea or feature; theme: *The Cinderella motif is found in the literature of many countries.* **2** a distinctive, often repeated figure in a decorative design. **3** *Music.* **a** a recurring melodic or rhythmic fragment of a theme or subject. **b** a subject. **c** a leitmotif. [< F < Med.L *motivus* moving. Doublet of MOTIVE.]

mo·tile (mō′tīl *or* mō′təl) *adj. Biology.* able to move about; capable of motion. [< L *motus* moved + E *-ile,* capable of (< L *-ilis*)]

mo·til·i·ty (mō til′ə tē) *n.* the quality of being motile.

mo·tion (mō′shən) *n., v.* —*n.* **1** the condition or state of moving; a movement or a change of position or place: *He swayed with the motion of the moving train. Everything is either in motion or at rest.* **2** a formal proposal for action made in a meeting, etc. **3** *Law.* an application made to a court or judge for an order, ruling, etc. **4** *Music.* **a** the melodic progression of a single part or voice from

one pitch to another. **b** the progression of two or more parts or voices with relation to each other.
in motion, moving; going.
—*v.* **1** make a movement, as of the hand or head, to show one's meaning. **2** show (a person) what to do by such a motion: *He motioned me out.* [< L *motio, -onis* < *movere* move]

mo·tion·less (mō′shən lis) *adj.* not moving. —**mo′tion·less·ly,** *adv.* —**mo′tion·less·ness,** *n.*

motion picture **1** a series of pictures on a continuous strip of film, projected on a screen in such rapid succession that the viewer gets the impression that the persons and things pictured are moving. **2** a story or drama told by this means; moving picture or movie.

motion sickness nausea and dizziness caused by motion, such as the pitching and rolling of a ship or boat, the swaying, etc. of a train or car, or the swinging of a hammock.

mo·ti·vate (mō′tə vāt′) *v.* -**vat·ed,** -**vat·ing.** make someone want to act; provide with a motive: *His offer to help was motivated by a desire to please.*

mo·ti·va·tion (mō′tə vā′shən) *n.* the act or process of furnishing with an incentive or inducement to action.

mo·ti·va·tion·al (mō′tə vā′shə nəl) *adj.* **1** of or having to do with motivation: *Advertisers use the techniques of motivational research to find out why people buy or do not buy a product.* **2** motivating.

mo·tive (mō′tiv) *n., adj.* —*n.* **1** the thought or feeling that makes one act: *His motive in going away was a wish to travel.* **2** motif. —*adj.* that makes something move. [< Med.L *motivus* moving, impelling < L *motus,* pp. of *movere* move. Doublet of MOTIF.]
☞ **Syn.** *n.* **1.** See note at **reason.**

motive power **1** power used to impart motion to machinery; any source of mechanical energy: *The motive power of trains is usually steam or electricity.* **2** all the locomotives of a railway collectively.

mot juste (mō zhyst′) *French.* a word or phrase that exactly fits the situation.

mot·ley (mot′lē) *adj., n., pl.* -**leys.** —*adj.* made up of different colors and of different things; varied: *a motley collection of old books and toys.* —*n.* a suit of more than one color worn by clowns: *At the party he wore motley.* [ME *motteley,* apparently < AF *motelé* < OE *mot* mote[1]]

mo·tor (mō′tər) *n., v.* —*n.* **1** a machine that converts electrical energy into mechanical energy, used to operate another machine: *the motor of a pump.* **2** an internal-combustion engine. **3** (*adj.*) powered by a motor: *a motor car.* **4** (*adj.*) of, by, or by means of automobiles: *a motor tour.* **5** (*adj.*) causing or having to do with motion or action; functioning like a motor: *Motor nerves arouse muscles to action.* **6** something that causes or imparts motion. —*v.* travel or transport by automobile. [< L *motor* mover < *movere* move] —**mo′tor·less,** *adj.*

motor area the part of the brain that is believed to control muscular movement.

mo·tor·bike (mō′tər bīk′) *n. Informal.* a motorcycle, especially a small, lightweight one.

mo·tor·boat (mō′tər bōt′) *n.* a boat that is propelled by a motor.

mo·tor·bus (mō′tər bus′) *n.* bus.

mo·tor·cade (mō′tər kād′) *n.* a procession or long line of automobiles.

motor car automobile.

motor coach bus.

mo·tor·cy·cle (mō′tər sī′kəl) *n., v.* -**cy·cled,** -**cy·cling.** —*n.* a two-wheeled motor vehicle, sometimes having a sidecar with a third supporting wheel. —*v.* travel by motorcycle.

mo·tor·cy·clist (mō′tər sī′klist) *n.* a person who rides a motorcycle.

motor generator an apparatus consisting of a combination of motor and generator, used to reduce voltage, etc.

motor home a large motor vehicle built on a truck chassis, having a completely enclosed body that is equipped for use as a travelling home. Compare **mobile home.**

motor hotel or **inn** a hotel for accommodating motorists, somewhat more elaborate than a motel and usually consisting of several floors of rooms and suites.

mo·tor·ist (mō′tər ist) *n.* a person who drives or travels by automobile.

mo·tor·ize (mō′tər īz′) *v.* -**ized,** -**iz·ing.** **1** furnish with a motor. **2** supply with motor-driven vehicles in place of horses and horse-drawn vehicles. **3** equip (infantry) with motor-driven transport vehicles, especially trucks. —**mo′tor·i·za′tion,** *n.*

motor lodge motel.

mo·tor·man (mō′tər mən) *n., pl.* -**men.** the driver of a streetcar or subway train.

motor scooter a light, two-wheeled motor vehicle steered by handlebars attached to the front wheel and having a seat for the rider with a broad footboard in front of it.

motor truck a truck with an engine and chassis made for carrying heavy loads.

motor vehicle a vehicle that travels under its own power, having rubber-tired wheels and designed for use on roads and highways rather than on rails; especially, an automobile, bus, or truck.

mo·tor·way (mō′tər wā′) *n. Brit.* expressway.

mot·tle (mot′əl) *v.* -**tled,** -**tling;** *n.* —*v.* mark with spots or streaks of different colors. —*n.* a mottled coloring or pattern. [apparently < AF **moteler* speckle < OE *mot* speck, mote[1]. Related to MOTLEY.]

mot·to (mot′ō) *n., pl.* -**toes** or -**tos.** **1** a brief sentence adopted as a rule or conduct: *"Think before you speak" is a good motto.* **2** a sentence, word, or phrase written or engraved on some object. [< Ital. < L *muttum* grunt, word. Doublet of MOT.]

moue (mü) *n.* a grimace; pout. [< F]

mou·fle (mü′fəl) *n. Cdn.* the thick, edible upper part of the snout of the moose. Also, **muffle.** [< Cdn.F < F *mufle* flabby face]

mouf·lon or **mouf·flon** (müf′lon) *n.* a wild sheep (*Ovis musimon*) of the mountainous regions of Sardinia and Corsica, having a dark reddish-brown coat used as fur. The adult male has large, curved horns. [< F < Corsican Ital. < LL *mufro*]

mou·jik (mü zhik′ *or* mü′zhik) See **muzhik.**

mou·lage (mü läzh′) *n.* **1** the making of a cast or mould of a footprint or other evidence connected with criminal investigation. **2** the mould itself. **3** a rubber or wax model of a body injury used in physiotherapy. [< F]

mould[1] or **mold** (mōld) *n., v.* —*n.* **1** a hollow shape in which anything is formed or cast: *Molten metal is poured into a mould to harden into shape.* **2** the shape or form which is given by a mould. **3** the model according to which anything is shaped. **4** something shaped in a mould: *a mould of pudding.* **5** the nature or character of anything. **6** the shape or frame on or about which something is made.
—*v.* **1** form; shape: *We mould statues out of clay.* **2** make or form into shape: *We are moulding clay to make model animals. Her character was moulded by suffering.* [ME < OF *modle* < L *modulus.* Doublet of MODULE.]

mould[2] or **mold** (mōld) *n., v.* —*n.* **1** a woolly or furry growth of fungus that appears on food and other animal or vegetable substances when they are left too long in a warm, moist place. **2** any fungus that produces mould. —*v.* make or become covered with mould: *The boots moulded in the cellar.* [ME *mould,* earlier *muwle(n),* probably influenced by *mould[3]*]

mould[3] or **mold** (mōld) *n.* **1** soft, rich, crumbly soil; earth mixed with decaying leaves, manure, etc.: *Many wild flowers grow in the forest mould.* **2** *Archaic.* ground; earth. [OE *molde*]

mould·board or **mold·board** (mōld′bôrd′) *n.* a curved metal plate on a plough, that turns over the earth from the furrow.

mould·er[1] or **mold·er** (mōl′dər) *v.* turn into dust by natural decay; crumble; waste away. [probably < *mould[3]*]

mould·er[2] or **mold·er** (mōl′dər) *n.* a person or thing that moulds, especially a person who shapes something or one who makes moulds for casting. [< *mould[1]*]

mould·ing or **mold·ing** (mōl′ding) *n.* **1** something produced by shaping or casting. **2** *Architecture.* a decorative shaping or contour given to a cornice along the top of a wall, to the jamb of a door or window, etc. **3** a shaped strip of wood or plaster, such as that often used around the upper walls of a room. Mouldings may be simply ornamental, or they may be used to support pictures, to cover electric wires, etc.

moulding board or **molding board** a board used for kneading bread, rolling cookies, etc.

mould·y or **mold·y** (mōl′dē) *adj.* **mould·i·er** or **mold·i·er, mould·i·est** or **mold·i·est.** **1** covered with mould. **2** musty; stale: *a mouldy smell.* —**mould′i·ness** or **mold′i·ness,** *n.*

mou·lin (mü lan′) *n. Geology.* a nearly vertical cavity in a glacier, worn by water falling through a crevice. [< F *moulin,* literally, mill; from the noise sometimes made by the rushing water]

moult or **molt** (mōlt) *v., n.* —*v.* **1** shed the feathers, skin, shells, or horns periodically before a new growth. Birds and snakes moult. **2** shed (feathers, etc.): *We saw the snake moult its skin.* —*n.* the act or process of moulting. [ME *mout* < OE *mūtian* (as in *bemūtian* exchange for) < L *mutare* change]

mound (mound) *n., v.* —*n.* **1** a bank or heap of earth or stones. **2** a small hill. **3** *Baseball.* the slightly elevated ground from which a pitcher pitches.

—*v.* **1** enclose with a mound. **2** heap up. [OE *mund* protection; meaning influenced by *mount²*]

Mound Builders people who lived in North America long ago, from the Great Lakes region to Florida. They built mounds of earth to bury their dead or for defence.

mount¹ (mount) *v., n.* —*v.* **1** go up; ascend: *mount stairs.* **2** move or proceed upwards: *A flush mounted to her brow.* **3** raise; increase; rise in amount: *The cost of living mounts steadily.* **4** get up on: *mount a platform.* **5** get on a horse; get up on something: *mount and ride away.* **6** put on a horse; furnish with a horse: *The police who patrol this park are mounted.* **7** put in proper position or order for use: *The scientist mounted the sample on a slide for his microscope.* **8** fix in a proper setting, backing, support, etc.: *to mount a picture on cardboard.* **9** have or carry (guns) as a fortress or ship does. **10** provide (a play) with scenery and costumes. **11** go on (guard) as a sentry or watch does. **12** set or place upon an elevation: *a small house mounted on poles.*
—*n.* **1** a horse provided for riding. **2** an act or occasion of riding a horse, especially in a race. **3** the act or manner of mounting. **4** that on which anything is mounted, fixed, supported, or placed: *the mount for a picture.* [ME < OF *monter* < L *mons, montis* mountain] —**mount′a·ble,** *adj.*
☞ *Syn. v.* **1.** See note at **climb.**

mount² (mount) *n.* Poetic (except before a proper name). a mountain or high hill: *Mount Robson.* [OE *munt* < L *mons, montis*]

moun·tain (moun′tən) *n.* **1** a very high hill: *Mount Robson is Canada's highest mountain.* **2 mountains,** *pl.* a series of such hills: *You can sometimes see the mountains from here. They stayed at a lodge in the mountains.* **3** (*adj.*) of, having to do with, or resembling a mountain or mountains: *mountain air.* **4** (*adj.*) living, growing, or found on mountains: *mountain plants.* **5** a large heap or pile of anything: *a mountain of rubbish.* **6** a huge amount: *a mountain of difficulties.*
make a mountain (out) of a molehill, See **molehill.**
[ME < OF *montaigne* < *mont* < L *mons, montis*]

mountain ash any of several trees (genus *Sorbus*) of the rose family having pinnate leaves, white flowers, and bright-red berries.

mountain avens (av′ənz) any of a small genus (*Dryas*) of woody, evergreen plants of the rose family found especially in northern and mountainous regions, having horizontal branches, small, leathery leaves, and white or yellow, roselike flowers. The white mountain avens (*D. octopetala*) is the flower of the Northwest Territories.

mountain badger hoary marmot.

mountain cat **1** cougar. **2** bobcat.

mountain chain a connected series of mountains.

mountain cranberry a low-growing, creeping, evergreen shrub (*Vaccinium vitis-idaea*) found in dry and mountainous north temperate regions, bearing edible red berries. The North American mountain cranberry is a subspecies (*V. vitis-idaea minus*), generally smaller than the typical European shrub.

moun·tain·eer (moun′tə nēr′) *n., v.* —*n.* **1** a person who lives in the mountains. **2** a person skilled in mountain climbing. **3 Mountaineer,** a Montagnais.
—*v.* climb mountains.

mountain goat a shaggy, white mountain antelope (*Oreamnos americanus*) of the Cordilleran region of NW North America, having a stocky body with high shoulders, a long, low-slung head, relatively short, black, backward-curving horns, and hooves with thick, spongy pads.

mountain laurel an evergreen shrub (*Kalmia latifolia*) of the heath family found in E North America, having glossy leaves and clusters of pink or white flowers.

mountain lion cougar.

moun·tain·ous (moun′tə nəs) *adj.* **1** covered with mountain ranges: *mountainous country.* **2** huge; *a mountainous wave.*

mountain range a row of connected mountains; series of mountains.

mountain sickness sickness caused by the rarefied air at high altitudes. The common symptoms are difficulty in breathing, headache, and nausea.

moun·tain·side (moun′tən sīd′) *n.* the side or face of a mountain: *The whole mountainside was covered with trees.*

moun·tain·top (moun′tən top′) *n.* the top or summit of a mountain.

moun·te·bank (moun′tə bangk′) *n.* **1** a person who sells quack medicines in public, appealing to his audience by tricks, stories, jokes, etc. **2** anybody who tries to deceive people by tricks, stories, and jokes. [< Ital. *montambanco* for *monta in banco* mount-on-bench]

mount·ed (moun′tid) *adj.* **1** on horseback. **2** in a position for use:

hat, āge, fär; let, ēqual, tèrm; it, īce
hot, ōpen, ôrder; oil, out; cup, pùt, rüle,
əbove, takən, pencəl, lemən, circəs

ch, child; ng, long; sh, ship
th, thin; ŦH, then; zh, measure

a mounted gun. **3** having a proper support or setting: *a mounted photograph.*

Mount·ie or **mount·ie** (moun′tē) *n., pl.* **-ies.** Cdn. Informal. a member of the Royal Canadian Mounted Police, maintained by the government of Canada.

mount·ing (moun′ting) *n.* a support, setting, or the like. The mounting of a photograph is the paper or cardboard on which it is pasted.

mourn (môrn) *v.* **1** grieve. **2** feel or show sorrow over: *Sherri mourned her lost turtle.* [OE *murnan*] —**mourn′er,** *n.*
☞ *Hom.* **morn.**

mourners′ bench a front seat reserved for repenting sinners at a religious revival meeting.

mourn·ful (môrn′fəl) *adj.* **1** sad; sorrowful. **2** gloomy; dreary. —**mourn′ful·ly,** *adv.* —**mourn′ful·ness,** *n.*

mourn·ing (môr′ning) *n., adj.* —*n.* **1** the act of sorrowing; lamentation. **2** the wearing of black or some other color (white in the Orient), or the draping of buildings, the flying of flags at half-mast, etc. as outward signs of sorrow for a person's death. **3** clothes, decorations, draperies, etc. worn or displayed to show such sorrow: *The widow was dressed in mourning.* **4** the period during which such signs of sorrow are shown.
—*adj.* of or used in mourning. —**mourn′ing·ly,** *adv.*
☞ *Hom.* **morning.**

mourning dove a North American wild dove (*Zenaidura macroura*) having brown plumage and a long, pointed tail. It has a slow and mournful-sounding call.

mouse (*n.* mous; *v. usually,* mouz) *n.* mice; *v.* **moused, mous·ing.**
—*n.* **1** a small rodent (*Mus musculus*) native to the Old World but now common throughout North America, having a pointed snout, large ears, and a long, scaly tail. Mice live mainly in or near buildings. Also called **house mouse. 2** any of various other small Old World rodents of the same family (Muridae). **3** any of numerous small New World rodents (family Cricetidae) resembling the house mouse but usually having a long tail more or less covered with hair, such as the deer mouse. **4** a shy, timid person.
—*v.* **1** of a cat, owl, etc., hunt for or catch mice. **2** search or move carefully or stealthily, as a cat does. [OE *mūs*] —**mouse′like,** *adj.*

mous·er (mou′sər *or* mou′zər) *n.* an animal that catches mice: *Our cat is a good mouser.*

mouse·trap (mous′trap′) *n.* a trap for catching mice.

mous·ey (mou′sē) *adj.* **mous·i·er, mous·i·est.** See **mousy.**

mous·ing (mou′zing) *n.* Nautical. a lashing of small line joining the shank of a hook to the point to keep the hook from jumping or slipping out of a ringbolt or eye.

mousse (müs) *n.* **1** a chilled or frozen dessert made with sweetened whipped cream or gelatin: *chocolate mousse.* **2** finely ground cooked meat or fish mixed with cream and other ingredients and poached, steamed, or set with gelatin. [< F *mousse* moss < Gmc.]

mousse·line (müs lēn′) *n.* a fine, sheer, somewhat crisp fabric resembling muslin, originally of silk, but now usually made of rayon. It is used especially for evening dresses.

mousse·line de laine (müs lēn də len′) French. a fine, light, woollen fabric used for dresses.

mousse·line de soie (müs lēn′də swä′) French. a fine, sheer silk fabric with a crisp finish.

mous·tache (mus′tash *or* məs tash′) See **mustache.**

mous·y (mou′sē) *adj.* **mous·i·er, mous·i·est. 1** resembling or suggesting a mouse in being timid, drab in color, quiet, etc.: *mousy hair.* **2** infested with mice. Also, **mousey.**

mouth (*n.* mouth; *v.* mouŦH) *n., pl.* **mouths** (mouŦHz); *v.* —*n.*
1 the opening through which a person or an animal takes in food; space in the head containing the tongue and teeth. **2** the part of the face around the mouth; the lips. **3** an opening suggesting a mouth: *the mouth of a cave.* **4** a part of a river, creek, etc. where its waters are emptied into some other body of water: *the mouth of the St. Lawrence River.* **5** a grimace. **6** a person or an animal requiring food or support: *He has seven mouths to feed in his family.* **7 a** the mouth as the source of spoken words. **b** utterance of words; speech: *get news by mouth, give mouth to one's thoughts.*
down in the mouth, Informal. in low spirits; discouraged.

have a big mouth, *Informal.* have a tendency to talk indiscreetly or excessively.
laugh on the other side or **wrong side of** (one's) **mouth.** See **laugh.**
open (one's) **big mouth,** *Informal.* talk indiscreetly or out of turn.
shoot off (one's) **mouth,** *Slang.* talk freely and indiscreetly.
the horse's mouth, the original source; the person who knows: *The news came straight from the horse's mouth.*
—*v.* 1 utter (words) in an affected or pompous way. 2 speak oratorically. 3 make grimaces. 4 accustom (a horse) to the bit and bridle. [OE *mūth*] —**mouth'like'** *adj.*

mouthed (mouᴛHd *or* moutht) *adj.* having a mouth, especially of a specified kind (*usually used in compounds*): big-mouthed, close-mouthed.

–mouthed *combining form.* having a ——mouth: *small-mouthed = having a small mouth.*

mouth·er (mou'ᴛHər) *n. Informal.* a long-winded talker.

mouth·ful (mouth'fŭl) *n., pl.* **-fuls.** 1 the amount that the mouth can easily hold. 2 what is taken into the mouth at one time. 3 a small amount. 4 *Slang.* an important or significant statement: *You said a mouthful.*

mouth·less (mouth'lis) *adj.* having no mouth or opening.

mouth organ 1 harmonica. 2 Panpipe.

mouth·part (mouth'pärt') *n.* (*usually used in the plural*) a structure or appendage near or around the mouth of arthropods, variously adapted for piercing, sucking, biting, grasping, etc.

mouth·piece (mouth'pēs') *n.* 1 the part of a musical instrument that is placed against or in the mouth of the player. 2 the part of a bit that goes in a horse's mouth. 3 a piece placed at or forming the mouth of something: *the mouthpiece of a telephone, the mouthpiece of a pipe.* 4 a person, newspaper, etc. used by other persons or groups to express their views: *That newspaper is just a mouthpiece for the government.*

mouth–to–mouth (mouth'tə mouth') *adj.* of, having to do with, or designating a method of artificial resuscitation in which the rescuer places his mouth closely over the mouth of a person who has stopped breathing and forces his breath into the person's lungs.

mouth·wash (mouth'wosh') *n.* an antiseptic liquid for rinsing the inside of the mouth or gargling.

mouth–wa·ter·ing (mouth'wo'tər ing *or* -wô'tər ing) *adj.* very appealing, especially to the appetite; very appetizing: *a mouth-watering menu, a mouth-watering bowl of fruit.*

mouth·y (mou'ᴛHē *or* mou'thē) *adj.* **mouth·i·er, mouth·i·est.** loud-mouthed; ranting; bombastic. —**mouth'i·ly,** *adv.* —**mouth'i·ness,** *n.*

mou·ton (mü'ton) *n.* 1 fur made from sheepskin that is pressed and dyed to look like beaver or seal. 2 (*adj.*) made of mouton: *mouton coats.* [< F]

mov·a·bil·i·ty (mü'və bil'ə tē) *n.* the state or quality of being movable. Also, **moveability.**

mov·a·ble (mü'və bəl) *adj., n.* —*adj.* 1 that can be moved. 2 that can be carried from place to place as personal possessions can. 3 changing from one date to another in different years: *Easter is a movable holy day.*
—*n.* 1 a piece of furniture that is not a fixture but can be moved to another house. 2 a thing that can be moved, removed, or set in motion. 3 Usually, **movables,** *pl.* in law, personal property. —**mov'a·ble·ness,** *n.* —**mov'a·bly,** *adv.*

move (müv) *v.* **moved, mov·ing;** *n.* —*v.* 1 change the place or position of: *Do not move your hand. The chess player moved a pawn.* 2 change place or position: *The child moved in his sleep. We moved out to the veranda for coffee.* 3 change one's place of living or working: *We move to the country next week.* 4 put or keep in motion: *The wind moves the leaves.* 5 of the bowels, empty or cause to be emptied. 6 act: *God moves in a mysterious way.* 7 impel; rouse; excite: *What moved you to do this?* 8 effect with emotion; excite to tender feeling: *The sad story moved her to tears.* 9 make a formal request, application, or proposal; propose: *Mr. Chairman, I move that we adjourn.* 10 sell or be sold: *These pink dresses are moving slowly.* 11 make progress: *The train moved slowly.* 12 exist; be active: *She moved in the best society.* 13 turn; swing; operate: *Most doors move on a hinge.* 14 carry oneself: *move with dignity and grace.* 15 *Informal.* start off; depart: *It's time to be moving.*
move heaven and earth, do everything possible.
move in, move oneself, one's family, one's belongings, etc. into a new place to live or work.
move out, move oneself, one's family, one's belongings, etc. out of a place where one has lived or worked.
—*n.* 1 *Games.* **a** the moving of a piece: *That was a good move.* **b** a player's turn to move: *It's your move now.* 2 the act of moving; movement. 3 an action taken to bring about some result.

get a move on, *Slang.* **a** make haste; hurry up. **b** begin to move.
on the move, moving about: *They are restless and always on the move.*
[ME < AF < L *movere*]
☛ *Syn. v.* 8. **Move, actuate** = rouse a person to action or to act in a certain way. **Move,** the general word, does not suggest whether the thing that rouses is an outside force or influence or an inner urge or personal motive: *Praise moved him to work harder.* **Actuate,** a formal word, always implies a powerful inner force, like a strong feeling, desire, principle, etc.: *He was actuated by desire for praise.*

move·a·ble (müv'ə bəl) *adj.* movable.

move·ment (müv'mənt) *n.* 1 the act or fact of moving. 2 the moving parts of a machine; a special group of parts that move on each other. The movement of a watch consists of many little wheels. 3 *Music.* **a** the kind of rhythm of a composition: *a waltz movement.* **b** its speed. **c** one section of a long composition: *the second movement of a symphony.* 4 the suggestion of action or progress in a novel, painting, etc. 5 a program by a group of people to bring about some one thing: *the movement for peace.* 6 a change in the market price, as of stocks or commodities. 7 **a** an emptying of the bowels. **b** the matter discharged by it.
☛ *Syn.* 1. See note at **motion.**

mov·er (müv'ər) *n.* a person or thing that moves, especially a person whose work is moving furniture, etc. from one residence or place of work to another: *The movers will be here tomorrow.*

mov·ie (müv'ē) *n. Informal.* a motion picture.

mov·ie·go·er (mü'vē gō'ər) *n. Informal.* a person who goes to movies.

mov·ing (müv'ing) *adj.* 1 capable of or characterized by movement. 2 of or having to do with changing a place of residence or work: *a moving company, moving expenses.* 3 causing a strong emotional response; touching: *a moving story.* —**mov'ing·ly,** *adv.*

moving picture motion picture.

mow¹ (mō) *v.* **mowed, mowed** or **mown, mow·ing.** 1 cut down with a machine or scythe. 2 cut down the grass or grain from. 3 cut down grass, etc.: *The men are mowing today.* 4 destroy at a sweep or in large numbers, as if by mowing: *The machine guns mowed down our men like grass.* [OE *māwan*] —**mow'er,** *n.*

mow² (mou *or* mō) *n.* 1 the place in a barn where hay, alfalfa, grain, or straw is piled or stored. 2 a pile of hay, grain, etc. in a barn. [OE *mūga*]

mow³ (mō *or* mou) *v. or n. Archaic.* grimace. [ME < OF *moue*]

mow·ing (mō'ing) *n.* 1 the act or process of cutting grass with a scythe or machine. 2 meadowland. 3 the hay mowed at one time.

mown (mōn) *v.* a pp. of **mow¹.**
☛ *Hom.* **moan.**

mox·ie (mok'sē) *n. Slang.* 1 courage; bravery; nerve. 2 know-how; skill; experience. [< earlier *Moxie,* a trademark for a soft drink (because the drink supposedly gave courage)]

Moz·za·rel·la or **moz·za·rel·la** (moz'ə rel'ə *or* mot'sə rel'ə) *n.* a soft Italian cheese, used especially in the making of pizza. [< Ital.]

MP or **M.P.** 1 Member of Parliament. 2 Military Police. 3 Mounted Police. 4 Metropolitan Police.

mph or **m.p.h.** miles per hour.

MPP or **M.P.P.** *Cdn.* Member of the Provincial Parliament (in Ontario).

Mr. or **Mr** (mis'tər) *pl.* **Messrs.** Mister. a title for a man, used before his last name or the name of his rank or office: *Mr. Einola, Mr. Speaker, Mr. Chief Justice.* [abbrev. of **mister.** See MISTER.]
☛ *Usage.* See note at **mister. Mr.** is written out only when it represents informal usage and when it is used without a name: *"They're only five cents for two, mister."*

Mrs. or **Mrs** (mis'iz) *pl.* **Mrs.** or **Mesdames** (mā däm') a title for a married woman, used before her last name: *Mrs. Perlman.* [< abbrev. of **mistress,** female equivalent of **master,** when used as a title before a name. The pronunciation became weakened to (mis'əz) in this usage.]
☛ *Usage.* Even when used in writing to represent conversation or to talk about the word itself, it is rarely written out in full: *"Did you say Miss Jarvis?" "No. Mrs."* I think **Mrs.** sounds so formal. The form **missus** is used only for writing the word with its informal meaning of 'wife': *That's my missus over there.*

Ms. or **Ms** (miz) a title used in front of the name of a woman or girl: *Ms. Jackson.*
☛ *Usage.* **Ms.** is a form made up in the early 1950's to parallel **Mr.** and **Mrs.** Unlike them, it is not an abbreviation, but it imitates them in being followed by a period. Like **Mr.,** but unlike **Mrs.** or **Miss, Ms.** does not identify a person as being married or unmarried.

MS 1 multiple sclerosis. 2 Mississippi.

MS., MS, ms., or **ms** manuscript.

M.S. 1 Master of Surgery. 2 Master of Science.

M.S. or **MS** master seaman.

M.Sc. Master of Science.

Msgr. 1 Monsignor. 2 Monseigneur.

m'sieur (mə syœ′) *n. French.* monsieur.

M.S.M. Meritorious Service Medal.

MSS., MSS, mss., or **mss** manuscripts.

MST or **M.S.T.** Mountain Standard Time.

M.S.W. Master of Social Work.

Mt. *pl.* **Mts.** Mount; Mountain.

MT Montana.

mtg. 1 meeting. 2 mortgage.

mtge. mortgage.

Mtl. Montreal.

Mtn. *pl.* **Mtns.** Mountain.

Mt.Rev. Most Reverend.

mu (myü *or* mü) *n.* the 12th letter of the Greek alphabet (M, μ).

much (much) *adj., adv.* **more, most;** *n.* —*adj.* in great quantity, amount, or degree: *much money, much time.*
—*adv.* 1 to a great extent or degree: *much pleased.* 2 nearly; about: *This is much the same as the others.*
—*n.* 1 a great deal: *Much of this is not true.* 2 a great, important, or notable thing or matter: *The rain did not amount to much.*
make much of, treat, represent, or consider as of great importance.
much of a size, height, etc., nearly the same size, height, etc.
not much of a, not a very good: *This is not much of a game.*
too much for, more than a match for; more than one can cope with, stand, or bear: *The work is too much for him. Their team was too much for ours.*
[var. of OE *micel*]

much·ness (much′nis) *n.* greatness; magnitude.
much of a muchness, much alike; nearly equivalent.

mu·ci·lage (myü′sə lij) *n.* 1 a gummy substance used to make things stick together. 2 a substance in plants that resembles glue or gelatin. [< F < LL *mucilago* musty juice < L *mucus* mucus]

mu·ci·lag·i·nous (myü′sə laj′ə nəs) *adj.* 1 sticky; gummy. 2 containing mucilage.

mu·cin (myü′sin) *n.* any of a group of proteins that are the main constituent of mucus.

muck (muk) *n., v.* —*n.* 1 dirt; filth. 2 anything filthy, dirty, or disgusting. 3 moist farmyard manure. 4 a well-decomposed peat, used as manure. b a heavy soil containing a high percentage of this. 5 *Mining.* unwanted earth, rock, etc. that is dug out or otherwise removed. 6 *Informal.* mess; untidy condition.
—*v.* 1 soil or make dirty. 2 put muck on. 3 *Mining.* remove unwanted earth, rock, etc.
muck about or **around,** waste time; putter or go about aimlessly: *She's mucking about in the basement.*
muck out, clean out (a stable, mine, etc.).
muck up, *Informal.* mess up; ruin or spoil.
[ME < ON *myki* cow dung]

muck·er (muk′ər) *n.* 1 *Slang.* a vulgar, ill-bred person. 2 *Mining, etc.* one who removes muck.

muck·rake (muk′rāk′) *v.* **-raked, -rak·ing.** hunt out and expose real or imagined corruption or misconduct of prominent people, public officials, etc. —**muck′rak′er,** *n.*

muck·y (muk′ē) *adj.* **muck·i·er, muck·i·est.** 1 of muck; like muck. 2 filthy; dirty.

mu·cous (myü′kəs) *adj.* 1 of or like mucus. 2 containing or secreting mucus. [< L *mucosus* < *mucus* mucus]

mucous membrane the tissue that lines the nose, throat, and other cavities of the body that are open to the air.

mu·cus (myü′kəs) *n.* a slimy substance that is secreted by and moistens the mucous membranes. A cold in the head causes a discharge of mucus. [< F]

mud (mud) *n., v.* **mud·ded, mud·ding.** —*n.* 1 soft, sticky, wet earth. 2 slander; libel; defamation. 3 any place, situation, etc. that is mean or degrading.
clear as mud, incomprehensible; obscure.
—*v.* cover with mud; put mud on: *The log house was mudded on the outside.* [ME *mudde*]

mud dauber any of various solitary (i.e. nonsocial) wasps (family Sphecidae, especially genus *Sceliphron*) that construct their nests of mud, usually in the form of several long, narrow, adjacent cells. Mud daubers are black and yellow, with the abdomen connected to the thorax by a long, thin "waist".

mud·dle (mud′əl) *v.* **-dled, -dling;** *n.* —*v.* 1 mix or mess up; cause confusion or disorder in; bungle (*often used with* **up**): *to muddle a piece of work. She was trying to help, but she only muddled it up.* 2 make confused or stupid; befog. 3 make (water, etc.) muddy. 4 think or act in a confused, blundering way.

hat, āge, fär; let, ēqual, tèrm; it, īce
hot, ōpen, ôrder; oil, out; cup, pút, rüle,
əbove, takən, pencəl, lemən, circəs
ch, child; ng, long; sh, ship
th, thin; ŦH, then; zh, measure

muddle through, manage somehow; succeed in one's object in spite of lack of skill or foresight: *Don't worry, I'll muddle through.*
—*n.* a mess; disorder; confusion.
make a muddle of, bungle.
[< *mud*] —**mud′dle·ment,** *n.*

mud·dle–head·ed (mud′əl hed′id) *adj.* confused or scatterbrained: *You're awfully muddle-headed today.*

mud·dler (mud′lər) *n.* 1 one who muddles or muddles through. 2 a thin plastic or metal stick for stirring drinks or other liquids.

mud·dy (mud′ē) *adj.* **-di·er, -di·est;** *v.* **-died, -dy·ing.** —*adj.* 1 full of or covered with mud: *a muddy sidewalk, muddy water.* 2 suggesting or resembling mud; dull, impure, etc.: *a muddy color, a muddy flavor.* 3 confused; not clear: *muddy thinking.*
—*v.* make or become muddy: *Don't muddy the water.* —**mud′di·ly,** *adv.* —**mud′di·ness,** *n.*

mud·fish (mud′fish′) *n.* bowfin.

mud·guard (mud′gärd′) *n.* a guard or shield so placed as to protect riders or passengers from the mud thrown up by the moving wheels of a vehicle.

mud hen coot, especially a North American species, *Fulica americanus.*

mud puppy any of a genus (*Necturus*) of North American aquatic salamanders, especially one species (*N. maculosus*) having fluffy, red external gills on either side of the head.

mud room in a school or other building, a room near the entrance in which overshoes, rubbers, etc. are deposited before entering.

mud·sill (mud′sil′) *n.* the lowest sill of a structure, usually one placed in or on the ground.

mud·sling·ing (mud′sling′ing) *n.* the use of offensive charges, misleading or slanderous accusations, etc. against an opponent in a political campaign, public meeting, or the like.

mud trout brook trout.

mud turtle any of a genus (*Kinosternon*) of freshwater turtles of North America.

mu·ez·zin (myü ez′ən) *n.* a crier who, at certain hours, calls Moslems to prayer. [< Arabic *mu'adhdhin* < *adhana* proclaim]

muff (muf) *n., v.* —*n.* 1 a cylindrical covering of fur or other material into which the hands are thrust from both ends to keep them warm. 2 a clumsy failure to catch and hold a ball that comes into one's hands. 3 awkward handling; bungling.
—*v.* 1 fail to catch and hold (a ball) when it comes into one's hands. 2 handle awkwardly; bungle: *My brother muffed his chance to get that job.* [< Du. *mof* < F *moufle* mitten < OF *moufle* thick glove (cf. Med.L *muffula*), probably < Gmc. Related to MUFFLE.]

muf·fin (muf′ən) *n.* 1 a small, round kind of quick bread made of wheat flour, corn meal, and egg, often eaten with butter. 2 *Esp.Brit.* a round, flat, spongy cake, usually eaten toasted and with butter. [origin uncertain]

muf·fle¹ (muf′əl) *v.* **-fled, -fling;** *n.* —*v.* 1 wrap or cover up in order to keep warm and dry. 2 wrap oneself in garments, etc. 3 wrap or cover in order to soften or stop the sound: *A bell can be muffled with cloth.* 4 keep (a person, organization, etc. from expressing (something); stifle; suppress: *All opposition had been muffled.* 5 dull or deaden (a sound): *a muffled cry for help.*
—*n.* 1 a muffled sound. 2 something that muffles. [ME < OF *mofler* stuff (cf. OF *enmouflé,* pp., wrapped up) < *moufle* thick glove. Related to MUFF.]

muf·fle² (muf′əl) See **moufle.**

muf·fler (muf′lər) *n.* 1 a wrap or scarf worn around the neck for warmth. 2 a device attached to an automobile or similar engine in order to reduce the noise of the exhaust. 3 anything used to deaden sound.

muf·ti (muf′tē) *n.* 1 ordinary clothes, not a uniform: *The retired general appeared in mufti.* 2 a Moslem official who assists a judge by formal exposition of the religious law. 3 in Turkey, the official head of the state religion, or one of his deputies. [< Arabic *mufti* judge (apparently because of the informal costume traditional for the stage role of a *mufti*)]

mug (mug) *n., v.* **mugged, mug·ging.** —*n.* 1 a usually large and heavy earthenware or metal drinking cup with a handle, used without a saucer. 2 the amount a mug holds. 3 *Slang.* the face.

4 *Slang.* the mouth. **5** *Slang.* a ruffian; hoodlum; petty criminal. —*v.* **1** attack and rob a person. **2** make a photograph of (a person's face) for police purposes. **3** *Slang.* make faces, especially before an audience or camera: *He loves to mug for the camera.* [cf. Norwegian *mugge;* defs. 3 and 4 derive from the common shape of mugs in earlier times]

mug·gy (mug′ē) *adj.* **-gi·er, -gi·est.** warm and humid; damp and close. [< dial. *mug.* drizzle < Scand.; cf. ON *mugga* fine rain] —**mug′gi·ness,** *n.*

mug–up (mug′up′) *n.* a light meal, especially one taken at a break in a journey.

mug·wump (mug′wump′) *n. U.S.* an independent in politics. [< Algonquian *mukquomp* great man]

Mu·ham·mad (mŭ ham′əd) *n.* Mohammed.

mu·jik (mü zhik′ *or* mü′zhik) *n.* See **muzhik.**

muk·luk (muk′luk′) *n. Cdn.* **1** a high, waterproof boot, often made of sealskin, worn by Inuit and others in the North. **2** *Informal.* any boot. [< Eskimo *muklok* bearded seal, a large seal]

muk·tuk (muk′tuk′) *n. Cdn.* the thin outer skin of the beluga, used as food (often eaten raw) in the Arctic. [< Eskimo]

mu·lat·to (mə lat′ō *or* myü lat′ō) *n., pl.* **-toes. 1** a person having one white and one black parent. **2** a person having both European and African ancestors. [< Sp. and Pg. *mulato* < *mulo* mule < L; from the mule's hybrid origin]

mul·ber·ry (mul′ber′ē *or* mul′bər ē) *n., pl.* **-ries;** *adj.* —*n.* **1** any of a genus (*Morus*) of trees and shrubs having edible, usually purple, berrylike fruit. The leaves of the white mulberry of Europe and Asia are used for feeding silkworms. **2** the fruit of a mulberry. **3** (*adj.*) designating a family (Moraceae) of mainly tropical trees, shrubs, and herbs that includes the mulberry, fig and breadfruit trees, as well as the hop vine and hemp. **4** a dark reddish-purple. —*adj.* dark reddish-purple. [OE *mōrberie* < L *morum* mulberry + OE *berie* berry]

mulch (mulch) *n., v.* —*n.* straw, leaves, loose earth, etc. spread on the ground around trees or plants. Mulch is used to protect roots from cold or heat, to prevent evaporation of moisture from the soil, to control weeds, or to enrich the soil. —*v.* cover with straw, leaves, etc. [OE *mylsc* mellow]

mulct (mulkt) *v., n.* —*v.* **1** deprive of something by fraud or deceit; swindle: *He was mulcted of his money by a shrewd trick.* **2** punish by a fine. —*n.* a fine; penalty. [< L *mulctare,* erroneous var. of *multare* < *multa* a fine]

mule¹ (myül) *n.* **1** the sterile, hybrid offspring of a donkey and a horse, especially of a male donkey and a mare, used as a beast of burden. It has the form and size of a horse, but the large ears, small hoofs, and tufted tail of a donkey. Compare **hinny. 2** *Informal.* a stupid or stubborn person. **3** a kind of spinning machine. [ME < OF < L *mulus*]
☛ *Hom.* **mewl.**

mule² (myül) *n.* a loose slipper, worn by women, covering only the toes and part of the instep, and leaving the rest of the foot and the heel uncovered. [< F < Du. *muil* < L *mulleus* shoe of red leather]
☛ *Hom.* **mewl.**

mule deer a deer (*Odocoileus hemionus*) of Western North America that has very long ears and a white tail with a black tip. The mule deer is larger than the white-tailed deer.

mule–skin·ner (myül′skin′ər) *n. Informal.* muleteer. [*mule¹* + *skinner,* so called because the driver figuratively skins his horses, mules, etc. with his whip]

mu·le·teer (myü′lə tēr′) *n.* a driver of mules. [< F *muletier* < *mulet,* dim. of OF *mul* mule < L *mulus*]

mul·ish (myü′lish) *adj.* like a mule; stubborn; obstinate. —**mul′ish·ly,** *adv.* —**mul′ish·ness,** *n.*

mull¹ (mul) *v. Informal.* think (about) without making much progress: *He mulled over his problems.* [origin uncertain]

mull² (mul) *v.* make (wine, beer, or cider) into a hot drink, with sugar, spices, etc. [origin uncertain]

mull³ (mul) *n.* a thin, soft muslin. [for *mulmul* < Hind., Persian *malmal*]

mul·lah (mul′ə *or* mŭl′ə) *n.* a title of respect for a Moslem who is learned in Islamic theology and the sacred law. [< Turkish, Persian, Hind. *mulla* < Arabic *maula*]

mul·lein (mul′ən) *n.* any of a genus (*Verbascum*) of plants of the figwort family having coarse, woolly leaves and spikes of yellow, pink, or white flowers. Some mulleins are common weeds; others are grown as garden flowers. Also, **mullen.** [ME < AF *moleine*]

mul·let (mul′it) *n., pl.* **-let** *or* **-lets. 1** any of a family (Mugilidae) of important food fishes of small or medium size, having soft fins and a streamlined, rounded body. Mullet are found in fresh and salt water. Also called **grey mullet. 2** any of a family (Mullidae) of bright-colored, medium-sized saltwater fishes having barbels on the lower jaw. Some species are valued as food fish. Also called **red mullet.** [ME < OF *mulet* < L *mullus* red mullet < Gk. *myllos*]

mul·li·gan (mul′ə gən) *n. Slang.* a stew of meat or, sometimes, fish and vegetables. [origin uncertain]

mul·li·ga·taw·ny (mul′ə gə to′nē *or* mul′ə gə tô′nē) *n.* a soup made of chicken or meat stock and flavored with curry. [< Tamil *milagu-tanni* pepper water]

mul·lion (mul′yən) *n.* a vertical bar between the panes of a window, the panels in the wall of a room, or the like. [alteration of ME *muniall, monial* < OF *moi(e)nel,* earlier *meienel* in the middle < *meien* in the middle < L *medianus* < *medius*]

mul·lioned (mul′yənd) *adj.* having mullions.

multi– *combining form.* **1** having or consisting of several or many as in *multicolored, multiform.* **2** involving or affecting many as in *multinational.* **3** several or many times more than; several or many times over as in *multimillionaire.* [< L *multi-* < *multus* much, many]
☛ *Pronun.* See note at **anti-**.

mul·ti·cel·lu·lar (mul′tē sel′yə lər) *adj.* having more than one cell.

mul·ti·col·ored *or* **mul·ti·col·oured** (mul′tē kul′ərd) *adj.* having many colors.

mul·ti·cul·tur·al (mul′tē kul′chər əl) *adj.* **1** of or having a number of distinct cultures existing side by side in the same country, province, etc.: *Canada is a multicultural country.* **2** designed for a country, province, etc. having a number of distinct cultures existing side by side: *multicultural programs.*

mul·ti·cul·tur·al·ism (mul′tē kul′chər ə liz′əm) *n.* **1** the fact or condition of being multicultural: *She wrote a report on multiculturalism in the schools.* **2** a policy supporting or promoting the existence of a number of distinct cultural groups side by side within a country, province, etc.: *Canada has a federal minister responsible for multiculturalism.* **3** the practice or support of such a policy: *Our city council's multiculturalism is too half-hearted.*

mul·ti·far·i·ous (mul′tə fer′ē əs) *adj.* having many different kinds; extremely varied: *multifarious talents.* [< L *multifarius*] —**mul′ti·far′i·ous·ly,** *adv.* —**mul′ti·far′i·ous·ness,** *n.*

mul·ti·fold (mul′tə fōld′) *adj.* manifold.

mul·ti·form (mul′tə fôrm′) *adj.* having many different shapes, forms, or kinds.

mul·ti·lat·er·al (mul′tē lat′ər əl) *adj.* **1** having many sides; many-sided. **2** involving two or more nations, parties, etc.: *a multilateral trade agreement.* —**mul′ti·lat′er·al·ly,** *adv.*

mul·ti·lin·gual (mul′tē ling′gwəl *or* mul′tē ling′gyə wəl) *adj.* **1** able to speak several languages well: *The company needs several multilingual sales representatives.* **2** expressed in or containing several languages: *a multilingual conversation, a multilingual dictionary.* —**mul′ti·lin′gual·ly,** *adv.*

mul·ti·lin·gual·ism (mul′tē ling′gwə liz′əm *or* mul′tē ling′gyə wə liz′əm) *n.* the ability to speak several languages: *Multilingualism is common in some ethnic groups.*

mul·ti·me·di·a (mul′tē mē′dē ə) *adj.* using, involving, or including several media together: *a multimedia sales presentation, a multimedia art exhibition.*

mul·ti·mil·lion·aire (mul′tē mil′yen er′) *n.* a person whose wealth amounts to many millions of dollars, pounds, etc.

mul·ti·na·tion·al (mul′tē nash′nəl *or* mul′tē nash′ən əl) *adj., n.* —*adj.* **1** of, having to do with, or involving several nations: *a multinational empire, a multinational agreement.* **2** of a business organization, having divisions in several nations: *a multinational food corporation.* **3** of or having to do with a multinational business organization. —*n.* a multinational company: *Several large multinationals have already located in this area.*

mul·tip·a·rous (mul tip′ə rəs) *adj., n.* —*adj. Biology.* producing more than one offspring at a birth. [< NL *multiparus* < L *multus* much, many + *parere* bring forth]

mul·ti·ple (mul′tə pəl) *adj., n.* —*adj.* of, having, or involving many parts, elements, relations, etc.: *a man of multiple interests.* —*n.* **1** a number or quantity that contains another number or quantity a certain number of times without a remainder: *Twelve is a multiple of three. The kilometre is a multiple of the metre.* **2** submultiple: *Ten is a multiple of one hundred.* [< F < LL *multiplus* manifold]

multiple sclerosis a disease of the brain and spinal cord, that usually eventually results in permanent paralysis. The cause of multiple sclerosis is unknown. *Abbrev.:* MS

mul·ti·plex (mul′tə pleks′) *adj.* manifold; multiple. **Multiplex telegraphy** is a system by which it is possible to send more than two

messages in opposite directions over the same wire at the same time. [< L *multiplex* < *multus* much + *-plex* -fold]

mul·ti·pli·cand (mul′tə plə kand′) *n. Mathematics.* the number or quantity to be multiplied by another. In 5 times 497, the multiplicand is 497. [< L *multiplicandus*, gerundive of *multiplicare*. See MULTIPLY.]

mul·ti·pli·ca·tion (mul′tə plə kā′shən) *n.* 1 multiplying or being multiplied. 2 *Mathematics.* the operation of multiplying one number by another.

mul·ti·plic·i·ty (mul′tə plis′ə tē) *n., pl.* **-ties.** 1 a manifold variety. 2 a great many: *a multiplicity of interests.* [< LL *multiplicitas* < L *multiplex*. See MULTIPLEX.]

mul·ti·pli·er (mul′tə plī′ər) *n.* 1 the number by which another number is to be multiplied. In 5 times 83, the multiplier is 5. 2 a person or thing that multiplies.

mul·ti·ply (mul′tə plī′) *v.* **-plied, -ply·ing.** 1 increase in number or amount: *As we climbed up the mountain, the dangers and difficulties multiplied.* 2 take (a number or quantity) a given number of times. To multiply 16 by 3 means to take 16 three times, making a total of 48. 3 increase by procreation. 4 produce (animals or plants) by propagation. [ME < OF *multiplier* < L *multiplicare* < *multiplex*. See MULTIPLEX.]

mul·ti·ra·cial (mul′tē rā′shəl) *adj.* having to do with, comprising or representing many different races: *a multiracial society.*

mul·ti·stage (mul′tē stāj′) *adj.* 1 of a rocket or missile, having several sections, each of which lifts it to a greater height before burning out and dropping off. 2 having a number of stages for the completion of a process: *a multistage investigation.*

mul·ti·tude (mul′tə tyüd′ *or* mul′tə tüd′) *n.* 1 a great many; crowd. 2 **the multitude,** the common people. [< L *multitudo* < *multus* much]

mul·ti·tu·di·nous (mul′tə tyü′də nəs *or* mul′tə tü′də nəs) *adj.* 1 forming a multitude; very numerous. 2 including many parts, elements, items, or features. **—mul′ti·tu′di·nous·ly,** *adv.* **—mul′ti·tu′di·nous·ness,** *n.*

mul·ti·va·lence (mul′tə vā′ləns *or* mul tiv′ə ləns) *n.* polyvalence.

mul·ti·va·lent (mul′tə vā′lənt *or* mul tiv′ə lənt) *adj.* polyvalent.

mum[1] (mum) *adj., interj.* **—***adj.* silent; saying nothing. **—***interj.* be silent! say nothing!
mum's the word, keep silent. [ME; ? imitative]

mum[2] (mum) *n. Informal.* mother.

mum[3] (mum) *v.* **mummed, mum·ming.** 1 be a mummer; act or play in a mask or disguise. 2 masquerade. 3 *Archaic.* act in a dumb show. [perhaps back formation < *mommyng* mummer's play. See MUMMER.]

mum[4] (mum) *n. Informal.* chrysanthemum.

mum·ble (mum′bəl) *v.* **-bled, -bling;** *n.* **—***v.* 1 speak indistinctly, as a person does when he moves his lips only slightly. 2 chew as a person does who has no teeth. **—***n.* a mumbling. [ME *momele(n)*, ? < *mum*[1]—**mum′bler,** *n.* **—mum′bling·ly,** *adv.*
➧ *Syn. v.* **1.** See note at **murmur.**

mum·bo jum·bo (mum′bō jum′bō) 1 a foolish or meaningless ritual; ceremonial nonsense. 2 meaningless or unintelligible language; gibberish. 3 an object foolishly worshipped or feared. [? < a West African language]

mum·mer (mum′ər) *n.* 1 a person who wears a mask, fancy costume, or disguise for fun. 2 actor. 3 an actor in one of the rural plays traditionally performed in England and elsewhere at Christmas. [ME < OF *momeur* < *momer* mask oneself]

mum·mer·y (mum′ər ē) *n., pl.* **-mer·ies.** 1 a performance of mummers. 2 any useless or silly show or ceremony. [< OF *mommerie*]

mum·mi·fy (mum′ə fī′) *v.* **-fied, -fy·ing.** 1 make (a dead body) into a mummy; make like a mummy. 2 dry or shrivel up. **—mum′mi·fi·ca′tion,** *n.*

mum·my[1] (mum′ē) *n., pl.* **-mies.** 1 a dead body preserved from decay by the ancient Egyptian method. Egyptian mummies have lasted more than 3000 years. 2 a dead human or animal body dried and preserved by nature. 3 a withered or shrunken living being. [< F *momie* < Med.L *mumia* < Arabic *mumiya* mummy < *mum* wax]

mum·my[2] (mum′ē) *n., pl.* **-mies.** *Informal.* mother.

mumps (mumps) *n.* (*used with a singular verb*) a contagious disease caused by a virus, characterized especially by inflammation and swelling of the saliva glands below the ears and by difficulty in swallowing. It is generally a childhood disease. [pl. of obs. *mump* grimace]
➧ *Usage.* **Mumps** is plural in form and singular in use: *Mumps is dangerous when caught by adults.*

munch (munch) *v.* chew vigorously and steadily; chew noisily: *A horse munches its oats.* [apparently imitative]

hat, āge, fär; let, ēqual, tèrm; it, īce
hot, ōpen, ôrder; oil, out; cup, pùt, rüle,
əbove, takən, pencəl, lemən, circəs
ch, child; ng, long; sh, ship
th, thin; ᴛʜ, then; zh, measure

mun·dane (mun′dān *or* mun dān′) *adj.* 1 ordinary; everyday; humdrum: *mundane matters of business.* 2 of this world, not of heaven; earthly. [< F < L *mundanus* < *mundus* world]

Mu·nich (myü′nik) *n.* an instance of appeasement which ultimately or immediately involves yielding to an aggressor at the expense of a principle or ally, and hence brings shame to the appeaser. [< *Munich* Pact, an agreement signed September 29, 1938, by Germany, France, Great Britain, and Italy]

mu·nic·i·pal (myü nis′ə pəl) *adj.* 1 of or having to do with the affairs of a city, town, or other municipality. 2 run by a municipality: *municipal affairs.* 3 having local self-government: *a municipal district.* [< L *municipalis*, ult. < *munia* official duties + *capere* take on]

mu·nic·i·pal·i·ty (myü nis′ə pal′ə tē) *n., pl.* **-ties.** a city, town, county, district, township, or other area having local self-government.

mu·nic·i·pal·ly (myü nis′ip lē) *adv.* by a city or town; with regard to a city or town or to municipal affairs.

mu·nif·i·cence (myü nif′ə səns) *n.* 1 very great generosity. 2 ample measure; bountiful quality: *the munificence of a gift.* [< L *munificentia* < *munificus* generous, ult. < *munus* gift + *facere* make]

mu·nif·i·cent (myü nif′ə sənt) *adj.* 1 extremely generous. 2 characterized by great generosity: *a munificent reward.* [< *munificence*] **—mu·nif′i·cent·ly,** *adv.*

mu·ni·ment (myü′nə mənt) *n.* 1 **muniments,** *pl. Law.* a document or documents kept as evidence of inheritance, title to property, etc. 2 *Archaic.* a defence; protection. [< Med.L *munimentum* document, title deed < L *munimentum* defence, fortification < *munire* fortify < *moenia* walls]

mu·ni·tion (myü nish′ən) *n., v.* **—***n.* 1 Usually, **munitions,** *pl.* material used in war: *Munitions are military supplies, such as guns, powder, or bombs.* 2 (*adj.*) having to do with military supplies. A munition plant is a factory for making munitions. **—***v.* provide with military supplies: *to munition a fort.* [< L *munitio, -onis* < *munire* fortify < *moenia* walls]

mu·on (myü′on) *n.* a highly unstable elementary particle of the lepton group having a positive or negative charge and a mass equal to about 207 times the mass of an electron. Cosmic-ray showers detected on earth are composed mainly of muons. [short for *mu meson*; it was formerly classified as a meson. 20c.]

mu·ral (myür′əl) *adj., n.* **—***adj.* 1 on, in, or for a wall. A mural painting is painted on a wall of a building. 2 of, having to do with, or like a wall. **—***n.* a painting done directly on a wall or a large photograph, etc. attached directly to a wall. [< F < L *muralis* < *murus* wall]

mu·ral·ist (myür′ə list) *n.* a designer or painter of murals.

mur·der (mèr′dər) *n.* 1 the unlawful killing of a human being by another. In Canada, **first-degree murder** is the intentional and unlawful killing of a person or the accidental killing of a person by someone committing any of certain crimes (such as kidnapping, hijacking of an aircraft, or rape). 2 an instance of such a crime: *There has never been a murder in this town.* 3 *Informal.* something very hard, disagreeable, or dangerous: *The traffic was murder last night. The last part of the climb is murder.*
murder will out, a murder cannot be hidden. **b** any great wrong will be found out.
—*v.* 1 commit the crime of murder: *Cain murdered his brother.* 2 do something very badly; spoil or ruin: *She really murders that song.* [var. of *murther*]
➧ *Syn. v.* **1.** See note at **kill.**

mur·der·er (mèr′dər ər) *n.* a person who is guilty of murder.

mur·der·ess (mèr′dər is) *n.* a woman guilty of murder.

mur·der·ous (mèr′dər əs) *adj.* 1 able or likely to kill: *a murderous blow.* 2 ready or intending to murder: *a murderous villain.* 3 causing or characterized by murder or bloodshed: *a murderous plot.* 4 *Informal.* very dangerous, unpleasant, or difficult. **—mur′der·ous·ly,** *adv.*

mu·ri·ate (myür′ē āt′) *n.* a chloride, especially potassium chloride, used for fertilizer. [< F *muriate* < L *muria* brine]

mu·ri·at·ic acid (myür′ē at′ik) hydrochloric acid. [< L *muriaticus* < *muria* brine]

murk (mèrk) *n., adj.* —*n.* darkness; gloom. —*adj. Poetic.* dark; gloomy. Also, **mirk**. [OE *mirce*]

murk·y (mèr′kē) *adj.* **murk·i·er, murk·i·est. 1** dark or gloomy. **2** very thick and obscure; misty; hazy: *murky smoke.* **3** obscure in meaning: *murky prose.* —**murk′i·ly,** *adv.* —**murk′i·ness,** *n.*

mur·mur (mèr′mər) *n., v.* —*n.* **1** a soft, low, indistinct sound that rises and falls a little but goes on without breaks: *the murmur of a stream, of little waves, or of voices in another room.* **2** a sound in the heart or lungs, especially an abnormal sound due to a leaky valve in the heart. **3** a softly spoken word or speech. **4** a complaint made under the breath, not aloud.
—*v.* **1** make a soft, low, indistinct sound. **2** utter in a murmur. **3** complain under the breath; grumble. [< L] —**mur′mur·er,** *n.* —**mur′mur·ing·ly,** *adv.*
☛ *Syn. v.* **2. Murmur, mumble, mutter** = speak indistinctly. **Murmur** = speak too softly to be clearly heard or plainly understood: *He murmured his thanks.* **Mumble** = speak with the lips partly closed, so that the sounds are not properly formed or articulated: *This boy mumbles half the time.* **Mutter** = mumble in a low voice, as if not wanting to be heard, and especially suggests complaint or anger: *He muttered some rude remarks.*

Murphy bed a bed that may be folded or swung up into a wall cabinet when not in use.

mur·rain (mèr′ən) *n.* **1** an infectious disease of cattle. **2** *Archaic.* a pestilence; plague. [ME < OF *morine,* ult. < L *mori die*]

murre (mèr) *n.* **1** any of a small genus (*Uria*) of black-and-white sea birds belonging to the auk family. **2** *Rare.* razorbill. [origin uncertain]

mur·ther (mèr′ᴛнər) *n. or v. Dialect.* murder. [OE *morthor*] —**mur′ther·er,** *n.*

mus. 1 music. **2** museum.

Mus.B. or **Mus. Bac.** Bachelor of Music (for L *Musicae Baccalaureus*).

mus·cat (mus′kat or mus′kət) *n.* **1** any of several varieties of grapevine that produce sweet, highly-scented, white grapes used especially for wine or raisins but also as table grapes. **2** muscatel. [< F < Provençal *muscat* having the fragrance of musk < *musc* musk < LL *muscus.* See MUSK.]

mus·ca·tel (mus′kə tel′) *n.* **1** a rich, sweet dessert wine made from muscat grapes. **2** the raisin from muscat grapes. [< MF, dim. of *muscat* < Provençal. See MUSCAT.]

mus·cle (mus′əl) *n., v.* **-cled, -cling.** —*n.* **1 a** a kind of animal tissue consisting of long cells that contract and relax to produce movement. **b** an organ made up of a bundle of muscle tissue, attached at each end to a particular bone or joint, which moves or stops the movement of a part of the body. **2** strength: *It takes muscle to move a piano.* **3** *Informal.* power or influence, especially when based on force or the threat of force: *The organization has enough muscle to get its way with the city council.*
not move a muscle, keep perfectly still.
—*v. Informal.* move or gain by using force or the threat of force: *He muscled his way past the doorman.*
muscle in, *Slang.* force oneself into a situation when one is not wanted: *Why should he muscle in on our meeting?*
[< F < L *musculus,* dim. of *mus* mouse; from the way in which certain muscles move when they are tensed and relaxed]
☛ *Hom.* **mussel.**

mus·cle–bound (mus′əl bound′) *adj.* having some of the muscles stiff or tight, usually as a result of too much or too little exercise.

mus·cle·man (mus′əl man′) *n., pl.* **-men. 1** *Informal.* a brawny, muscular man. **2** *Slang.* a ruffian; strong-arm man.

Mus·co·vite (mus′kə vīt′) *n., adj.* —*n.* **1** a native or inhabitant of Muscovy or of Moscow. **2** Russian. **3 muscovite,** the common, light-colored variety of mica.
—*adj.* of or having to do with Muscovy, Moscow, or Russia, or its inhabitants.

Mus·co·vy (mus′kə vē) *n.* **1** *Historical.* a grand duchy of the 13th to 16th centuries, that had Moscow as its capital. **2** *Archaic.* Russia.

Muscovy duck a large, crested, greenish-black duck (*Cairina moschata*) native to tropical America, but now widely domesticated. [for *musk duck*]

mus·cu·lar (mus′kyə lər) *adj.* **1** of or having to do with muscle or the muscles: *a muscular strain, muscular activity.* **2** having well-developed muscles; strong: *a muscular arm.* **3** consisting of muscle. —**mus′cu·lar·ly,** *adv.*

muscular dystrophy a disease characterized by progressive wasting away of muscle fibres.

mus·cu·lar·i·ty (mus′kyə lar′ə tē or mus′kyə ler′ə tē) *n.* muscular development or strength.

mus·cu·la·ture (mus′kyə· lə chər or mus′kyə lə chür′) *n.* a system or arrangement of muscles. [< F]

muse (myüz) *v.* **mused, mus·ing. 1** think in a dreamy way; think; meditate. **2** look thoughtfully. **3** say thoughtfully. [ME < OF *muser* loiter] —**mus′er,** *n.*
☛ *Hom.* **mews.**

Muse (myüz) *n.* **1** *Greek mythology.* one of the nine goddesses of the fine arts and sciences, daughters of Zeus and Mnemosyne. Their names are Calliope, Clio, Erato, Euterpe, Melpomene, Polyhymnia, Terpsichore, Thalia, and Urania. **2 muse,** a spirit that inspires a poet or composer. [ME < OF < L *Musa* < Gk. *Mousa*]
☛ *Hom.* **mews.**

mu·sette (myü zet′) *n.* **1 a** a gentle pastoral air written for a bagpipe, or imitating the effect of a bagpipe. **b** a dance for this air. **2** a kind of bagpipe. **3** a musette bag. [< F < OF *musette* < *muse* bagpipe < *muser* play the musette]

musette bag a small bag carried by means of a shoulder strap, used by soldiers and hikers to carry food, belongings, etc.

mu·se·um (myü zē′əm) *n.* the building or rooms where a collection of objects illustrating science, history, art, or other subjects is kept and displayed. [< L < Gk. *mouseion* seat of the Muses < *Mousa* Muse]

mush[1] (mush) *n.* **1** *Esp.U.S.* corn meal boiled in water. **2** any soft, thick mass. **3** *Informal.* weak sentiment; sentimentality; silly talk. [var. of *mash*; cf. Du. *moes*]

mush[2] (mush) *n., v. Cdn.* —*n.* **1** a command to advance given to sled dogs. **2** a journey made by dogsled, especially while driving the team from behind the sled. —*v.* **1** urge sled dogs onward by shouting commands: *He mushed his dog team through the blinding storm.* **2** follow a dogsled on foot: *For six days he mushed across the barren lands.* [< F *marche (donc),* a command to horses, etc. < *marcher* go, walk] —**mush′er,** *n.*

mush·mel·on (mush′mel′ən) *n. Dialect.* muskmelon.

mush·room (mush′rüm or -rüm) *n., v.* —*n.* **1** the large, often umbrella-shaped fruiting body of any of various fungi (class Basidiomycetes, especially of order Agaricales). Many mushrooms are edible. Compare **toadstool. 2** anything shaped or growing like a mushroom. **3** (*adj.*) of or like a mushroom in shape or rapid growth: *a mushroom town, growing out of control.*
—*v.* **1** grow very fast: *His business mushroomed when he opened the new store.* **2** of a bullet, flatten at the end on impact against something very hard. [ME < OF *mousseron* < LL *mussirio, -onis*]

mushroom cloud a rapidly rising mushroom-shaped cloud of radio-active matter that follows a nuclear explosion.

mush·y (mush′ē) *adj.* **mush·i·er, mush·i·est. 1** like mush; pulpy. **2** *Informal.* weakly sentimental. —**mush′i·ly,** *adv.* —**mush′i·ness,** *n.*

mu·sic (myü′zik) *n.* **1** the art and science of organizing sounds of varying pitch and volume into rhythmical, harmonic, and melodic patterns to produce a composition having structure and unity. **2** such an organization of sounds; a musical composition or compositions. **3** written or printed music; a score or composition set down on paper using special signs and symbols to indicate tone, rhythm, etc.: *a songbook with words and music.* **4** a specific category or kind of music: *baroque music, folk music, Indian music.* **5** a pleasant sound or succession of sounds: *the music of the wind.* **6** responsiveness to, or appreciation of, music.
face the music, *Informal.* meet difficulties or punishment resulting from one's actions.
set to music, compose a melody to accompany (a poem, etc.)
[ME < OF *musique* < L *musica* < Gk. *mousikē (technē)* art of the Muse < *Mousa* Muse]

mu·si·cal (myü′zə kəl) *adj., n.* —*adj.* **1** of or having to do with music: *musical knowledge, musical instruments.* **2** like music; melodious and pleasant. **3** set to music or accompanied by music. **4** fond of music. **5** skilled in music; talented as a musician.
—*n.* **1** a stage entertainment or motion picture in which a story is told through music, singing, and dancing as well as dialogue. **2** *Archaic.* musicale. —**mu′si·cal·ly,** *adv.*

musical chairs an elimination game in which players march to music around chairs numbering always one fewer than the players. When the music stops, everyone rushes to sit down and the person left standing is eliminated.

musical comedy a gay and amusing play in which plot and characterization are less important than singing, dancing, and costumes.

mu·si·cale (myü′zə kal′) *n.* a social gathering to enjoy music. [< F *musicale,* short for *soirée musicale* musical evening]

musical instrument 1 any stringed, wind, or percussion instrument, as a violin, trumpet, or drum, employed, or designed to be employed, in producing music or musical sounds. **2** an electronic instrument used to produce, not reproduce, musical sounds.

mu·si·cal·i·ty (myü′zə kal′ə tē) *n.* **1** ability or skill in playing, conducting, or composing music. **2** musical quality.

music box a box or case containing apparatus for producing music mechanically, usually a revolving cylinder set with pins that strike the tuned teeth of a comblike strip, or bar, of steel.

music drama 1 a type of opera in which words and music are intimately linked, the music's prime purpose being to indicate dramatic development, character, mood, etc.: *Wagner's "Lohengrin" is a music drama.* 2 any opera.

music hall *Esp.Brit.* 1 a theatre for singing, dancing, variety shows, etc.; vaudeville theatre. 2 vaudeville entertainment.

mu·si·cian (myü zish′ən) *n.* a person trained in music, especially one who earns a living by playing, conducting, composing, or singing music; *An orchestra is made up of many musicians.*

mu·si·co·log·i·cal (myü′zə kə loj′ə kəl) *adj.* of or having to do with musicology.

mu·si·col·o·gist (myü′zə kol′ə jist) *n.* a person knowledgable about or studying musicology.

mu·si·col·o·gy (myü′zə kol′ə jē) *n.* the study of the forms, principles, literature, and history of music.

mus·ing (myüz′ing) *adj.* dreamy; meditative; absorbed in thought.

musk (musk) *n.* 1 a substance with a strong and lasting odor, used as a perfume base and fixative. It is obtained from a special gland in the abdomen of the male musk deer. 2 a similar substance produced by any of various other animals, such as the mink, civet, or muskrat. 3 a synthetic substance with similar characteristics. 4 the odor of musk or something like it in heaviness or persistence. 5 any plant whose leaves or flowers smell like musk, such as the musk rose. [ME < OF < LL *muscus* < LGk. *moschos* < Persian *mushk* < Skt. *mushka* testicle]

musk deer a small, hornless deer (*Moschus moschiferus*) of central Asia, the male of which has a gland containing musk.

mus·keg (mus′keg) *n. Cdn.* 1 a swamp or marsh. 2 an area of bog composed of decaying plant life, especially moss. There are vast regions of muskeg in northern Alberta. [< Algonquian; cf. Cree *muskak* swamp]

mus·kel·lunge (mus′kə lunj′) *n., pl.* **-lunge. Cdn.** a very large freshwater fish (*Esox masquinongy*) of the pike family: *The muskellunge is highly valued as a food and game fish.* [< Algonquian (Objibwa) *mashkinonge* great pike]

mus·ket (mus′kit) *n.* an old type of long-barrelled gun used by soldiers before rifles were invented. [< F *mousquet* < Ital. *moschetto*, originally a kind of hawk < *mosca* fly < L *musca*]

mus·ket·eer (mus′kə tēr′) *n.* a soldier armed with a musket.

mus·ket·ry (mus′kit rē) *n.* 1 muskets. 2 the act of shooting with muskets or rifles. 3 soldiers armed with muskets.

mus·kie (mus′kē) *n. Cdn. Informal.* muskellunge.

musk·mel·on (musk′mel′ən) *n.* 1 any of several varieties of melon with a musky odor, the fruits of varieties of an annual trailing vine (*Cucumis melo*) of the gourd family, having a hard, rough or smooth, rind and sweet, juicy, pale-orange, green, or yellowish flesh. 2 any of the vines that bear such fruits.

musk–ox or **musk·ox** (musk′oks′) *n., pl.* **-ox** or **-ox·en.** *Cdn.* a large, heavy-set bovid mammal (*Ovibos moschatus*) native to northern Canada, Alaska, and NW Greenland, having a brown, shaggy coat, large, downward-curving horns, and a musky odor.

musk·rat (musk′rat′) *n., pl.* **-rats** or (*esp. collectively*) **-rat.** 1 a water rodent (*Ondatra zibethica*) native to North America, related to and resembling the voles, but larger, having webbed hind feet, a scaly, laterally compressed tail, and dark-brown, glossy fur. 2 the fur of a muskrat. 3 (*adj.*) made of this fur: *a muskrat coat.*

musk rose a rose (*Rosa moschata*) native to the Mediterranean region, having white flowers with a musky scent.

musk·y (mus′kē) *adj.* **musk·i·er, musk·i·est.** of, like, or having an odor of musk: *a musky perfume.*

Mus·lim (muz′ləm or mus′ləm) *n. or adj.* Moslem.

mus·lin (muz′lən) *n.* 1 a cotton cloth in a plain weave, made in a wide variety of weights ranging from sheer to heavy or coarse, and used for dresses, sheets, curtains, etc. 2 (*adj.*) made of muslin. [< F < Ital. *mussolina* < *Mussolo* Mosul, a city in Iraq]

Mus.M. Master of Music (for L *Musicae Magister*).

mus·pike (mus′pīk′) *n. Cdn.* a hybrid game fish crossbred from muskellunge and pike.

mus·quash (mus′kwosh) *n., pl.* **-quash.** muskrat.

muss (mus) *v., n. Informal.* —*v.* put into disorder; rumple; rumple or disarrange: *The child's clothes were mussed. Don't muss up my hair.* —*n.* disorder; a mess. [var. of *mess*]

mus·sel (mus′əl) *n.* 1 any of a family (Mytilidae) of marine bivalve molluscs having a dark, elongated shell. The common edible mussel is *Mytilus edulis.* 2 any of a superfamily (Unionacea) of freshwater bivalve molluscs having a flattened, green, blue, or

hat, āge, fär; let, ēqual, tèrm; it, īce
hot, ōpen, ôrder; oil, out; cup, pùt, rüle,
əbove, takən, pencəl, lemən, circəs

ch, child; ng, long; sh, ship
th, thin; ₮H, then; zh, measure

brown shell which in many species has a pearly lining used for making buttons, etc. [OE *muscle, musle* < L *musculus* mussel, muscle. See MUSCLE.]
☛ *Hom.* muscle.

Mus·sul·man (mus′əl mən) *n., pl.* **-mans.** *Archaic.* Moslem. [< Persian *musulmān*, adj., Mohammedan < *muslim* a Moslem < Arabic *muslim*. See MOSLEM.]

muss·y (mus′ē) *adj.* **muss·i·er, muss·i·est.** *Informal.* untidy; messy; rumpled. —**muss′i·ly,** *adv.*

must¹ (must; *unstressed,* məst) *auxiliary verb* **must,** *n., adj.* —*aux.v.* 1 be obliged to; be forced to: *We must eat to live.* 2 ought to; should: *I must go home soon.* 3 be certain to: *I must seem very rude.* 4 be supposed or expected to: *You must have that book.* 5 *Must* is sometimes, when motion is implied, used with its verb omitted: *We must to horse. We must away.* —*n.* something necessary; obligation: *This rule is a must.* —*adj. Informal.* demanding attention or doing; necessary: *a must item, must legislation.* [OE *mōste,* pt. of *mōtan* mote²]

must² (must) *n.* the unfermented juice of the grape; new wine. [OE < L (*vinum*) *mustum* fresh (wine)]

must³ (must) *n., v.* —*n.* a musty condition; mould. —*v.* make musty; become musty. [< *musty*]

mus·tache (mus′tash *or* məs tash′) *n.* 1 the hair that grows on a man's upper lip, especially when groomed and not shaved smooth. 2 the hair growing on any person's upper lip. 3 the hairs or bristles growing near the mouth of an animal. Sometimes, **moustache.** [< F < Ital. < Med.L *mustacia* < Gk. *mystax* upper lip, mustache]

mus·ta·chio (məs tä′shō *or* məs tä′shē ō′) *n., pl.* **-chios.** mustache.

mus·tang (mus′tang) *n.* the small, wild or half-wild horse of the North American plains. [< Sp. *mestengo* untamed]

mus·tard (mus′tərd) *n.* 1 a yellow powder or paste used as seasoning to give food a pungent taste. 2 any of several plants (genus *Brassica*) of the mustard family, whose seeds are ground for this seasoning. 3 a dark-yellow color. 4 designating a family (Cruciferae) of plants having cross-shaped flowers and pointed pods. Some plants of the mustard family are the mustards, cabbage, horseradish, radish, turnip, and broccoli. [ME < OF *moustarde,* ult. < L *mustum* must²]

mustard gas a poison gas that causes burns, blindness, and death. *Formula:* (ClCH₂CH₂)₂S

mustard plaster a poultice made of mustard and water, or of mustard, flour, and water, used as a counter-irritant in the treatment of chest colds, bronchitis, etc.

mustard seed the seed of the mustard plant.

mus·ter (mus′tər) *v., n.* —*v.* 1 assemble; gather together; collect: *muster soldiers.* 2 summon: *muster up courage.*

muster in, enlist.

muster out, discharge.
—*n.* 1 an assembly; collection. 2 a bringing together of men or troops for review or service. 3 the list of those mustered. 4 the number mustered.

pass muster, be inspected and approved; come up to the required standards.
[ME < OF *mostrer* < L *monstrare* show < *monstrum* portent]

must·n't (mus′ənt) must not.

mus·ty (mus′tē) *adj.* **-ti·er, -ti·est.** 1 having a smell or taste suggesting mould or damp; mouldy: *a musty room, musty crackers.* 2 stale; out-of-date: *musty laws.* 3 lacking vigor; dull: *a musty old fellow.* [? < *moisty* < *moist* + *-y¹*] —**mus′ti·ly,** *adv.* —**mus′ti·ness,** *n.*

mu·ta·bil·i·ty (myü′tə bil′ə tē) *n.* the quality of being mutable: *the mutability of species.*

mu·ta·ble (myü′tə bəl) *adj.* 1 liable to change: *mutable customs.* 2 capable of or liable to undergo mutation. 3 fickle: *a mutable person.* [< L *mutabilis* < *mutare* change]

mu·tant (myü′tənt) *adj., n.* —*adj.* of, having to do with, or produced by mutation. —*n.* a new variety of plant or animal resulting from mutation.

mu·tate (myü′tāt *or* myü tāt′) *v.* **-tat·ed, -tat·ing.** 1 change. 2 produce mutations. 3 change by umlaut.

mu·ta·tion (myü tā′shən) *n.* 1 a change; alteration. 2 a sudden

change in the genetic structure of an animal or plant that produces a new feature or characteristic. **3** a new variety of animal or plant resulting from such a change. **4** umlaut. [< L *mutatio, -onis* < *mutare* change]

mu·ta·tis mu·tan·dis (myü tä′tis myü tan′dis) *Latin.* with the necessary changes.

mute (myüt) *adj., n., v.* **mut·ed, mut·ing.** —*adj.* **1** not making any sound; silent. **2** unable to speak; dumb. **3** of alphabetical letters, not pronounced. The *e* in *mute* is mute.
—*n.* **1** a person who cannot speak. **2** a clip or some other device put on a musical instrument to soften the sound. **3** a silent letter.
—*v.* soften or deaden the sound of (a musical instrument): *He muted the strings of his violin.* [< L *mutus*] —**mute′ly,** *adv.*
—**mute′ness,** *n.*
☛ *Syn. adj.* **1, 2.** See note at **dumb.**

mu·ti·late (myü′tə lāt′) *v.* **-lat·ed, -lat·ing. 1** cut or tear off or destroy a part of a living body: *Many of the victims of the accident had been badly mutilated.* **2** tear, break, cut off or remove some part of something as to damage or ruin it: *The book had been mutilated by someone who had torn some pages and written on others. The story had been mutilated by an editor.* [< L *mutilare* < *mutilus* maimed] —**mu′ti·la′tor,** *n.*

mu·ti·la·tion (myü′tə lā′shən) *n.* mutilating or being mutilated.

mu·ti·neer (myü′tə nēr′) *n.* a person who takes part in a mutiny. [< MF *mutinier*]

mu·ti·nous (myü′tə nəs) *adj.* **1** rebelling against authority, especially the authority of a superior officer or officers on a ship or in the armed forces: *a mutinous crew.* **2** of or having to do with mutiny: *mutinous talk.* **3** unruly. —**mu′ti·nous·ly,** *adv.*

mu·ti·ny (myü′tə nē) *n., pl.* **-nies;** *v.* **-nied, -ny·ing.** —*n.* an open rebellion against lawful authority, especially by sailors or soldiers against their officers. —*v.* take part in a mutiny; rebel. [< obs. *mutine* revolt < OF *mutiner* < *mutin* rebellious, ult. < L *movere* move]

mutt (mut) *n. Slang.* **1** a dog, especially a mongrel. **2** a stupid person. [origin uncertain]

mut·ter (mut′ər) *v., n.* —*v.* **1** speak softly and indistinctly with lips partly closed: *He was muttering the numbers to himself as he counted.* **2** complain; grumble **3** say in low and indistinct tones, especially when expressing secret anger or discontent: *"I'll get even with him," he muttered.* ·
—*n.* **1** the act of muttering. **2** muttered words. [ME *mutere(n)*; probably imitative] —**mut′ter·er,** *n.*
☛ *Syn. v.* **1.** See note at **murmur.**

mut·ton (mut′ən) *n.* the meat from a mature sheep. [ME < OF *moton* < Med.L *multo, -onis*, ram < Celtic]

mutton chop 1 a small piece of mutton, usually from the ribs or loin, for broiling or frying. **2 mutton chops,** *pl.* side whiskers shaped somewhat like mutton chops, narrow at the top, in front of the ears, and broad at the bottom, along the sides of the lower jaw.

mu·tu·al (myü′chü əl) *adj., n.* —*adj.* **1** done, said, felt, etc. by each toward the other; given and received: *mutual promises, mutual dislike.* **2** each to the other: *mutual enemies.* **3** *Informal.* belonging to each of several: *our mutual friend.* **4** of or having to do with mutual insurance: *a mutual company.*
—*n.* **1** a mutual insurance company. **2** a mutual fund. [< L *mutuus* reciprocal] —**mu′tu·al·ly,** *adv.*
☛ *Usage.* See note at **common.**

mutual fund a financial organization that invests the pooled capital of its members in diversified securities.

mutual insurance or **plan** a system of insurance by which the policyholders own the company and share the gains and losses of a common fund.

mu·tu·al·i·ty (myü′chü al′ə tē) *n.* the state or quality of being mutual.

mu·u·mu·u (mü′mü′; *Hawaiian,* mü′ü mü′ü) *n.* a woman's long, loose, flowing gown that is gathered at the neckline. [< Hawaiian]

Mu·zak (myü′zak) *n. Trademark.* music that is transmitted by telephone or FM radio, used by restaurants, offices, public areas, etc.

mu·zhik (mü zhik′ *or* mü′zhik) *n.* a Russian peasant. Also, **moujik, mujik.** [< Russian]

muz·zle (muz′əl) *n., v.* **-zled, -zling.** —*n.* **1** the nose, mouth, and jaws of a four-footed animal. **2** a cover of straps or wires for putting over an animal's head to keep it from biting or eating. **3** the open front end of a firearm.

put a muzzle on, prevent persons, newspapers, etc. from expressing free opinions.
—*v.* **1** put a muzzle (def.2) on. **2** compel to keep silent about something; prevent from expressing views: *The government muzzled the newspapers during the recent rebellion.* [ME < OF *musel* < *muse* muzzle] —**muz′zler,** *n.*

muz·zle·load·er (muz′əl lōd′ər) *n.* a muzzleloading gun.

muz·zle·load·ing (muz′əl lōd′ing) *adj.* of firearms, loaded by putting gunpowder in through the open front end of the barrel and ramming it down.

MVD the Ministry of Internal Affairs of the Soviet Union; the secret police, formerly called OGPU and, later, NKVD.

M.V.O. Member of the (Royal) Victorian Order.

M.W.O. or **MWO** master warrant officer.

my (mī) *adj., interj.* —*adj.* **1** a possessive form of **I**; of, belonging to, or made or done by me or myself: *I hurt my arm. Please hand me my coat. I'm getting a new watch for my graduation.* **2** a word used as part of any of certain formal titles when using the title to address the person holding it: *The horses are ready, my lord.*
3 *Informal:* a word used before certain other words in addressing a person: *my boy, my dear fellow.*
—*interj. Informal.* **1** a word used as an exclamation of surprise, often together with another word: *My! what a big cat! My, oh my! My word!* **2** a word used together with the name of some part of the body as an exclamation of disbelief or doubt: *Accident, my eye! It was plain carelessness.* [OE *mīn*]
☛ *Usage.* **My, mine** are the possessive forms of **I. My** is a determiner and is always followed by a noun: *This is my hat.* **Mine** stands alone: *This hat is mine.* **Theirs** is a pronoun and stands alone.

my·ce·li·um (mī sē′lē əm) *n., pl.* **-li·a** (-lē ə). the vegetative body of a fungus, consisting of a mass of white threadlike fibres spread through a nutritive body or substance, such as soil or organic matter. [< NL < Gk. *mykēs* mushroom]

My·ce·nae·an (mī′sə nē′ən) *n., adj.* —*n.* a native or inhabitant of Mycenae, a city in ancient Greece. —*adj.* of or having to do with Mycenae its people or the civilization that flourished there.

my·col·o·gy (mī kol′ə jē) *n.* the branch of botany that deals with fungi. [< Gk. *mykēs* fungus + E -*logy*]

my·e·lin (mī′ə lən) *n.* a soft, white substance consisting of lipids and protein that forms a sheath around the axon of certain nerve fibres.

my·na or **my·nah** (mī′nə) *n.* any of various tropical Asian starlings (especially genera *Acridotheres* and *Gracula*), some of which can be trained to mimic human speech and are kept as cage birds. [< Hind. *maina*]

my·o·car·di·al (mī′ə kär′dē əl) *adj.* of or having to do with the myocardium.

myocardial infarction the destruction of an area of the heart muscle as a result of a stoppage or insufficiency of blood supply to that area, usually caused by blockage of a coronary artery. Compare **coronary thrombosis.**

my·o·car·di·um (mī′ə kär′dē əm) *n.* the muscular middle layer of the wall of the heart.

my·o·pi·a (mī ō′pē ə) *n.* **1** near-sightedness. **2** shortsightedness: *intellectual myopia.* [< NL < Gk. *myōps*, ult. < *myein* shut + *ōps* eye]

my·op·ic (mī op′ik) *adj.* near-sighted.

myr·i·ad (mir′ē əd) *n., adj.* —*n.* **1** a very large, indefinite number: *myriads of stars.* **2** *Archaic.* ten thousand. —*adj.*
1 countless: *We saw myriad stars that summer night.* **2** highly varied; having many aspects or elements. [< LL < Gk. *myrias, -ados* ten thousand, myriad]

myr·i·a·pod (mir′ē ə pod′) *n.* any of a group (formerly the toxonomic class Myriapoda) of arthropods having a wormlike body with many segments and many legs. Centipedes and millipedes are myriapods. [< Gk. *myrias* myriad + *pous, podos* foot]

Myr·mi·don (mèr′mə don′) *n.* **1** *Greek mythology.* a member of a warlike people of ancient Thessaly who accompanied Achilles, their king, to the Trojan War. **2 myrmidon,** an obedient and unquestioning follower.

myrrh (mèr) *n.* a fragrant, gummy substance with a bitter taste, used in medicines, perfumes, and incense. It is obtained from a shrub that grows in Arabia and E Africa. [OE *myrre* < L *myrrha* < Gk. *myrra*, ult. < Semitic]

myr·tle (mèr′təl) *n.* **1** any of a genus (*Myrtus*) of evergreen shrubs, especially the common myrtle (*M. communis*) of southern Europe having shiny leaves, fragrant white flowers, and black berries. **2** designating a family (Myrtaceae) of evergreen trees and shrubs. The myrtle family includes the myrtle, pimento or allspice, clove, and eucalyptus. **3** a low, creeping evergreen vine having blue flowers; periwinkle. [ME < OF *mirtile*, dim. of L *myrtus* < Gk. *myrtos*]

my·self (mī self′) *pron., pl.* **ourselves. 1** a reflexive pronoun, the form used instead of **I** or **me** when referring back to the subject of the sentence: *I hurt myself. I told myself that it didn't really matter.* **2** a form of **I** or **me** used to make a statement stronger: *I will go myself.* **3** my usual self: *I'm sorry I shouted; I'm not myself today.*

My·si·a (mish′ə ə) *n.* in ancient times, a country in Asia Minor.

mys·te·ri·ous (mis tēr′ē əs) *adj.* **1** full of mystery; hard to explain or understand; secret; hidden. **2** suggesting mystery. —**mys·te′ri·ous·ly,** *adv.* —**mys·te′ri·ous·ness,** *n.*
☛ *Syn.* **1. Mysterious, inscrutable** = hard to explain or understand. **Mysterious** describes a person, thing, or situation about which there is something secret, hidden, or unknown that arouses curiosity, conjecture, or wonder: *She had a mysterious telephone call.* **Inscrutable** describes a thing that is so mysterious or such a riddle that it is impossible to make out its meaning, or a person who keeps his feelings, thoughts, and intentions completely hidden: *His mother began to cry, but his father's face was inscrutable.*

mys·ter·y¹ (mis′tər ē *or* mis′trē) *n.* **-ter·ies. 1** a secret; something that is hidden or unknown. **2** secrecy; obscurity. **3** a story, play, etc. of suspense, telling of the development and solution of a crime or crimes: *a writer of mysteries.* **4** something that is not explained or understood: *the mystery of the migration of birds.* **5** a religious idea or doctrine that human reason cannot understand. **6** a secret religious rite to which only initiated persons are admitted. **7** mystery play. **8 a** a sacramental rite of the Christian religion. **b** the Eucharist; Communion; Mass. [ME < L < Gk. *mystērion* < *mystēs* an initiate < *myein* close (i.e., the lips or eyes)]

mys·ter·y² (mis′tər ē *or* mis′trē) *n., pl.* **-ter·ies.** *Archaic.* **1** a craft; trade. **2** an association of craftsmen or merchants; guild. [< Med.L *misterium* for L *ministerium* ministry; form influenced by *mystery¹*]

mystery play a medieval religious play based on the Bible, centring mainly on the life, death, and resurrection of Christ. These plays were called mystery plays because they were performed by members of a "mystery" or medieval workers' union or guild.

mys·tic (mis′tik) *adj., n.* —*adj.* **1** mystical. **2** having to do with the ancient religious mysteries or other occult rites: *mystic arts.* **3** of or having to do with mystics or mysticism. **4** of hidden meaning or nature; enigmatical; mysterious.
—*n.* a person who believes that truth or God can be known through spiritual insight. [< L < Gk. *mystikos* < *mystēs* an initiate. See MYSTERY¹.]

mys·ti·cal (mis′tə kəl) *adj.* **1** having a spiritual meaning that is beyond human understanding: *the mystical food of the sacrament.* **2** spiritually symbolic: *The lamb and the dove are mystical symbols of the Christian religion.* **3** of or concerned with mystics or mysticism: *a mystical experience.* **4** of or having to do with secret rites open only to the initiated; cryptic. —**mys′ti·cal·ly,** *adv.* —**mys′ti·cal·ness,** *n.*

mys·ti·cism (mis′tə siz′əm) *n.* **1** the beliefs or mode of thought

hat, āge, fär; let, ēqual, tèrm; it, īce
hot, ōpen, ôrder; oil, out; cup, pùt, rüle,
əbove, takən, pencəl, lemən, circəs

ch, child; ng, long; sh, ship
th, thin; ŦH, then; zh, measure

of mystics. **2** the doctrine that truth or God may be known through spiritual insight, independent of the mind.

mys·ti·fi·ca·tion (mis′tə fə kā′shən) *n.* **1** a mystifying or being mystified; bewilderment; perplexity. **2** something that mystifies or is designed to mystify.

mys·ti·fy (mis′tə fī′) *v.* **-fied, -fy·ing. 1** bewilder purposely; puzzle; perplex: *The magician's tricks mystified the audience.* **2** make mysterious; involve in mystery. [< F *mystifier* < *mystique* mystic (< L *mysticus*; see MYSTIC) + *-fier* < L *-ficare* make < *-ficus* making < *facere* make] —**mys′ti·fi′er,** *n.*

mys·tique (mis tēk′) *n.* **1** a mystical or peculiar way of interpreting reality. **2** an aura of mystery and awe associated with a particular person, profession, skill, institution, etc.

myth (mith) *n.* **1** a traditional story about superhuman beings, such as gods, goddesses, heroes, and monsters, usually explaining the origin of natural events and forces, cultural practices, etc. **2** mythology (def. 1 or 2). **3** an invented story. **4** an imaginary person or thing: *Her wealthy uncle was a myth invented to impress her friends.* [< NL < LL < Gk. *mythos* word, story]
☛ *Usage.* See note at **legend.**

myth. mythology.

myth·ic (mith′ik) *adj.* mythical.

myth·i·cal (mith′ə kəl) *adj.* **1** of, like, or in myths: *a mythical interpretation of nature, mythical monsters.* **2** not real; made-up; imaginary. —**myth′i·cal·ly,** *adv.*

myth·o·log·i·cal (mith′ə loj′ə kəl) *adj.* of or having to do with mythology. —**myth·o·log′i·cal·ly,** *adv.*

my·thol·o·gist (mi thol′ə jist) *n.* **1** a writer of myths. **2** a person knowledgeable about or studying mythology.

my·thol·o·gy (mi thol′ə jē) *n., pl.* **-gies. 1** a body of myths relating to a particular culture or person: *Greek mythology.* **2** myths collectively: *Mythology is an aspect of religion.* **3** the study of myths. [< LL < Gk. *mythologia* < *mythos* word, story + *logos* word, discourse]

myx·o·ma·to·sis (mik′sō mə tō′sis) *n.* a highly infectious and usually fatal disease of rabbits, characterized by the growth of many skin tumors. [< Gk. *myxa* mucus + E *-oma* + *-osis*]

Nn

n or **N** (en) *n., pl.* **n's** or **N's. 1** the fourteenth letter of the English alphabet. **2** any speech sound represented by this letter. **3** a person or thing identified as n, especially the 14th in a series. **4** *Printing.* an en. **5** *Mathematics.* an indefinite number. See **nth. 6** something shaped like the letter N. **7** (*adj.*) of or being an N or n.

n nano- (an SI prefix).

n. 1 born (for L *natus*). **2** name. **3** noun. **4** neuter. **5** nominative. **6** new. **7** number. **8** *Chemistry.* normal. **9** *Business.* net. **10** noon.

N 1 nitrogen. **2** north; northern. **3** noun. **4** newton(s).

N. 1 north; northern. **2** new. **3** noon. **4** November. **5** National; Nationalist. **6** Norse. **7** Navy.

Na sodium (for L *natrium*).

N.A. 1 North America. **2** not applicable.

NAACP *U.S.* National Association for the Advancement of Colored People.

nab (nab) *v.* **nabbed, nab·bing.** *Slang.* **1** catch or seize suddenly; grab. **2** arrest: *The police soon nabbed the thief.* [earlier *nap*, probably < Scand.; cf. Swedish *nappa* catch, snatch]

na·bob (nā′bob) *n.* **1** a provincial governor under the Mogul empire in India. **2** a wealthy man, originally one who had returned to Europe after making a fortune in India. **3** any important or powerful person. [< Hind. *nabab*, colloquial var. of *nav(v)ab*. See NAWAB.]

na·celle (nə sel′) *n.* an enclosed part on an aircraft for an engine or for passengers or crew. [< F < L *navicella*, double dim. of *navis* ship]

na·cre (nā′kər) *n.* mother-of-pearl. [< F < OItal. naccara < Arabic < *naggārah* shell, drum]

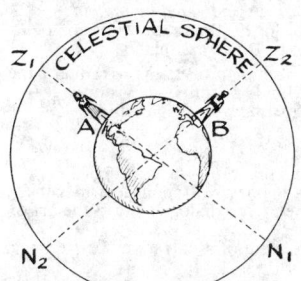

The zenith and nadir for observer A are Z₁ and N₁. For observer B, the zenith and nadir are Z₂ and N₂.

na·dir (nā′dər) *n.* **1** the point in the heavens directly beneath the place where one stands; point opposite the zenith. **2** the lowest point. [ME < OF < Arabic *nadir* opposite (i.e., to the zenith)]

nae (nā) *adj.* or *adv.* Scottish. no.

nag¹ (nag) *v.* **nagged, nag·ging. 1** find fault or annoy by peevish complaints: *He's always nagging at me to walk faster. If you nag her too much she won't do anything.* **2** continue to cause annoyance, irritation, or pain: *a nagging headache. The thought kept nagging at the back of my mind that I had left the door unlocked.* [< Scand.; cf. Icelandic *nagga* grumble. Akin to GNAW.] —**nag′ger,** *n.*

nag² (nag) *n.* **1** *Informal.* a horse, especially one that is old and worn out. **2** a small riding horse; pony. [ME; cf. Du. *negge*]

Na·hua·tl (nä′wä təl) *n., adj.* —*n.* any of a group of languages spoken by the Aztecs, Toltecs, and other Amerindian peoples of central Mexico and parts of Central America. —*adj.* of or having to do with this group of languages.

nai·ad (nī′ad or nā′ad) *n., pl.* **-ads, -a·des** (-ə dēz′). *Greek and Roman mythology.* a nymph guarding a stream or spring. [< L < Gk. *Naias, -ados* (related to *naein* flow)]

nail (nāl) *n., v.* —*n.* **1** a slender piece of metal to be hammered into or through pieces of wood or other material to hold them together. **2** the hard, horny substance covering the upper side of the end of a finger or toe.

hard as nails, **a** tough; physically fit. **b** without pity; merciless.

hit the nail on the head, *Informal.* guess or understand correctly; say or do something just right.

on the nail, especially of making a payment, at once; immediately. —*v.* **1** fasten with a nail or nails. **2** *Informal.* hold or keep fixed. **3** *Informal.* catch; seize. **4** *Informal.* secure by prompt action; catch; seize. **5** *Informal.* detect and expose (a lie, etc.).

nail down, **a** fix with nails: *The shingles were nailed down with a hammer.* **b** *Informal.* win, settle, or get with certainty: *He nailed down first place in the singing competition.* [OE *nægel*] —**nail′er,** *n.*

nail·set (nāl′set′) *n.* a tool for driving nails beneath the surface.

nain·sook (nān′sùk or nan′sùk) *n.* a very soft, fine, mercerized cotton cloth in a plain weave. [< Hind. *nainsukh* < *nain* eye + *sukh* pleasure]

nai·ra (nī′rə or nä er′ə) *n.* **1** the basic unit of money in Nigeria, divided into 100 kobo. **2** a note worth one naira.

na·ïve or **na·ive** (nī ēv′; *French,* nä ēv′) *adj.* **1** simple in nature; like a child; artless. **2** not sophisticated; inexperienced; showing a lack of informed judgment: *She was naïve to believe their promises.* [< F *naïve*, fem. of *naif* < L *nativus.* Doublet of NATIVE.] —**na·ïve′ly** or **na·ive′ly,** *adv.*

na·ïve·te or **na·ive·te** (nī ēv′tā or nī ēv′ə tā′; *French,* nä ēv tä′) *n.* **1** the quality of being naïve; unspoiled freshness. **2** a naïve action, remark, etc. [< F]

na·ïve·ty or **na·ive·ty** (nī ēv′tē) *n.* naïvete.

na·ked (nā′kid) *adj.* **1** with no clothes on: *The boys enjoyed swimming naked.* **2** bare; not covered; stripped of usual cover: *The trees stood naked in the snow.* **3** not protected; exposed: *a naked sword.* **4** without addition of anything else; plain: *the naked truth.*

naked eye, the eye alone, not helped by any glass, telescope, or microscope: *too small to be seen with the naked eye.* [OE *nacod*] —**na′ked·ly,** *adv.* —**na′ked·ness,** *n.*

☛ *Syn.* **1.** See note at **bare.**

N.Am. North America.

nam·a·ble (nām′ə bəl) *adj.* that can be named.

nam·ay·cush (nam′ā kúsh′) *n., pl.* **-cush.** *Cdn. Rare.* lake trout. [< Algonquian]

nam·by–pam·by (nam′bē pam′bē) *adj., n., pl.* **-bies.** —*adj.* weakly simple or sentimental; insipid: *That valentine is too namby-pamby.* —*n.* **1** namby-pamby talk or writing. **2** a namby-pamby person. [alteration of *Nam,* short for *Ambrose Philips,* (1674-1749), a British poet ridiculed by Alexander Pope]

name (nām) *n., v.* **named, nam·ing.** —*n.* **1** the word or words by which an individual person, group, animal, place, or, sometimes, a thing is known and spoken to or about: *Our dog's name is Sparky. Did they mention him by name? The name of the town is Aurora.* **2** a word or words used to identify a type or class of animal, plant, thing, etc.: *What's the name of that plant?* **3** a word or words applied descriptively; an appellation, title, or epithet: *to give someone the name of friend.* **4** the persons grouped under one name; family or clan. **5** reputation: *He made a name for himself as a writer.* **6** (*adj.*) having a reputation that is known by a name: *The plumber buys all his supplies from name manufacturers.* **7** a famous person or thing: *She's a name in the industry.*

call names, insult by using bad names; swear at.

in name only, supposed to be but not really so.

in the name of, **a** on the authority of; acting for: *He bought the car in the name of his father.* **b** for the sake of: *We did it in the name of charity.*

know (only) by name, know only by hearing about: *I know her by name but I've never met her.*

to (one's) name, belonging to one: *I've got only about $10 to my name.* —*v.* **1** give a name to: *They named the baby Mary.* **2** call by name; mention by name: *Three persons were named in the report.* **3** give the right name for; identify: *Can you name these flowers?* **4** mention or speak of; state: *She named several reasons for her decision.* **5** specify or fix: *to name a price.* **6** nominate; appoint: *Jim was named captain of the team.* **7** choose; settle on: *They named the day for their wedding.* [OE *nama*] —**nam′er,** *n.*

☛ *Syn. n.* **3. Name, title** = a word or words that describe or characterize. **Name** is used for a descriptive or characterizing word or phrase applied to a person or thing because of certain qualities or acts or to express an attitude toward him

(or it): *"Gastown" was an old name for Vancouver.* **Title** is used of a descriptive or characterizing name given to a book, song, play, etc. or to a person as a sign of honor, rank, office, occupation: *His title is Secretary.*

name brand a product or brand of product identified and backed by the name and reputation of the manufacturer or distributor: *He usually buys name brands.* —**name′-brand′**, *adj.*

name–call·ing (nām′kol′ing *or* -kôl′ing) *n.* the act or fact of giving a bad name to a person; slandering; defamation.

name day **1** the feast day of the saint whose name one bears. **2** the day on which a child is named; baptismal day.

name–drop·ping (nām′drop′ing) *n.* the act or habit of mentioning the names of famous people frequently in familiar or casual conversation, so as to convey the impression that one has met them or is familiar with them. —**name′-drop′per**, *n.*

name·less (nām′lis) *adj.* **1** having no name: *a nameless baby.* **2** not marked with a name: *a nameless grave.* **3** not named; unknown: *a book by a nameless writer.* **4** that cannot be named or described: *a strange, nameless longing.* **5** not fit to be mentioned: *nameless crimes.* **6** unknown to fame; obscure. —**name′less·ly**, *adv.* —**name′less·ness**, *n.*

name·ly (nām′lē) *adv.* that is to say: *Only two students got a perfect mark, namely, Fred and Jean.*

name·plate (nām′plāt′) *n.* a strip of metal, wood, plastic, etc. mounted on a door, wall, etc. or set on a desk or table and imprinted with the name of the occupant.

name·sake (nām′sāk′) *n.* a person having the same name as another; especially, one named after another. [for *name's sake*]

nan·keen (nan kēn′) *n.* **1** a firm, yellow or buff cotton cloth originally woven in China from a native cotton having a yellowish color. **2 nankeens,** *pl.* trousers made of nankeen. [alteration of *Nanking*, China]

nan·ny (nan′ē) *n., pl.* **-nies. 1** *Informal.* a woman hired to look after the children of a family. **2** nanny goat.

nan·ny goat a female goat.

nano– *SI prefix.* one billionth: *A nanometre is one one-billionth of a metre.* Symbol: **n** [< Gk. *nanos* dwarf]

na·nook (na′nük) *n. Cdn.* polar bear. [< Inuktitut (Eskimo) *nanuq*]

Na·o·mi (nā′ō′mē *or* nā′ō mē) *n.* in the Bible, Ruth's mother-in-law, from whom Ruth refused to part.

nap¹ (nap) *n., v.* **napped, nap·ping.** —*n.* a short sleep. —*v.* take a short sleep.
catch napping, find off guard; take unprepared: *The test caught me napping.* [OE *hnappian* sleep lightly]

nap² (nap) *n., v.* **napped, nap·ping.** —*n.* **1** a fuzzy or furry surface on cloth, consisting of fibres that have been raised by brushing, as on flannel, or sheared threads or loops, as on velvet. **2** the direction in which these fibres lie on the surface, when smoothed down. —*v.* raise the nap on. [ME *noppe* < MDu. or MLG] —**nap′less**, *adj.*

na·palm (nā′pom′, nā′päm′, *or* nap′om) *n., v.* —*n.* **1** a chemical substance used to thicken gasoline for use in certain military weapons, especially incendiary bombs. **2** the thickened gasoline. —*v.* attack or destroy with napalm. [< *naphthenic* and *palmitic* acids, used in its manufacture]

nape (nāp) *n.* the back of the neck. [ME; origin uncertain]

na·per·y (nā′pər ē *or* nāp′rē) *n.* tablecloths, serviettes, and doilies; table linen. [ME < OF *naperie* < *nape* < L *mappa* napkin]

naph·tha (nap′thə *or* naf′thə) *n.* any of various colorless, often highly flammable liquids distilled from petroleum, coal tar, etc. used as a solvent, paint thinner, etc. [< L < Gk. *naphtha*, originally, an inflammable liquid issuing from the earth < Iranian]

naph·tha·lene (naf′thə len′ *or* nap′thə len′) *n.* a white crystalline hydrocarbon, usually prepared from coal tar, used in mothballs and in the manufacture of organic compounds such as dyes. *Formula:* $C_{10}H_8$ Also, **naphthaline.** [< *naphtha*]

naph·thol (naf′thol *or* naf′thôl, nap′thol *or* nap′thôl) *n.* a colorless crystalline substance obtained from naphthalene, used in making dyes, as an antiseptic, etc. [< *naphtha*]

nap·kin (nap′kin) *n.* **1** a piece of cloth or paper used at meals for protecting the clothing or for wiping the lips or fingers; serviette. **2** a baby's diaper. **3** sanitary napkin. [ME *napekyn*, dim. of OF *nape* cloth. See NAPERY.]

na·po·le·on (nə pō′lē ən *or* nə pōl′yən) *n.* **1** a former French gold coin worth 20 francs. **2** a kind of pastry with a cream or jam filling. [< *Napoleon* Bonaparte (1769-1821), Emperor of the French]

Na·po·le·on·ic (nə pō′lē on′ik) *adj.* of, having to do with, or resembling, Napoleon Bonaparte (1769-1821), Emperor of the French.

nap·pie *or* **nap·py** (nap′ē) *n., pl.* **-pies. 1** a small dish used for serving fruit; a fruit dish. **2** *Esp.Brit.* a baby's diaper, or napkin.

nar·cis·sism (när sis′iz əm) *n.* excessive absorption in one's own personal comfort, importance, etc.; self-love.

nar·cis·sist (när sis′ist) *n.* a person who indulges in narcissism.

nar·cis·sis·tic (när′si sis′tik) *adj.* of or having to do with narcissism.

nar·cis·sus (när sis′əs) *n., pl.* **-cis·sus·es, -cis·si** (-sis′ī *or* -sis′ē). **1** any of a genus (*Narcissus*) of plants of the amaryllis family having yellow, white, or pink, spring-blooming flowers with a central trumpet-shaped or cup-shaped corona, especially any of several species having mainly white flowers with a relatively short corona. See also **daffodil, jonquil. 2 Narcissus,** *Greek mythology.* a beautiful youth who was caused to fall in love with his own reflection in the water of a spring. He pined away and was changed into the flower called narcissus. [< L < Gk. *narkissos*; associated (from the sedative effect of the plant) with *narkē* numbness]

nar·co·sis (när kō′sis) *n.* a stupor or state of insensibility, brought about by narcotics or other chemicals. [< NL < Gk. *narkōsis* < *narkoein* benumb. See NARCOTIC.]

nar·cot·ic (när kot′ik) *n., adj.* —*n.* **1** any of a group of drugs, including opium and its derivatives and similar compounds, that have a strong pain-killing effect and produce drowsiness, dullness, or sleep, and that have the potential for physiological dependence with prolonged use. **2** any drug subject to legal restrictions because of its narcotic or mood-altering effects or its potential for psychological or physiological dependence. **3** something that numbs, soothes, or dulls.
—*adj.* **1** of, having to do with, or being a narcotic: *narcotic drugs.* **2** induced by a narcotic: *a narcotic stupor.* **3** producing mental lethargy or dullness; soporific. **4** of, involving, or intended for the treatment of drug addicts. [ME < Med.L < Gk. *narkōtikos* < *narkoein* benumb < *narkē* numbness]

nard (närd) *n.* spikenard. [ME < L < Gk. *nardos* < Phoenician < Skt.]

nar·es (ner′ēz) *n.* pl. of **nar·is** (ner′is). the nostrils; nasal passages. [< L *nares,* pl.]

nar·ghi·le *or* **nar·gi·le** (när′gə lē′) *n.* hookah. [ult. < Persian *nargileh* < *nargil* coconut, the original material used in making the pipe]

nar·rate (na rāt′, nar′āt, *or* ner′āt) *v.* **-rat·ed, -rat·ing. 1** tell (a story or the story) of: *A strange tale was narrated by the old fisherman.* **2** provide the narration for (a film, etc.): *The travelogue was narrated by a local journalist.* [< L *narrare* relate]

nar·ra·tion (na rā′shən) *n.* **1** the act or process of narrating. **2** the verbal accompaniment to certain kinds of films, television programs, etc.: *the narration for a travelogue.* **3** something narrated; narrative.
☛ *Syn.* **3.** See note at **narrative.**

nar·ra·tive (nar′ə tiv *or* ner′ə tiv) *n., adj.* —*n.* **1** a report, account, story, etc. **2** the part of a literary work that describes the sequence of events, as distinguished from dialogue, etc. **3** the art or technique of narrating; storytelling.
—*adj.* having to do with or in the form of a narrative: *Earl Birney's "David" is a narrative poem.*
☛ *Syn. n.* **1. Narrative, narration** = something told as a story. **Narrative** chiefly applies to what is told, a story or an account of real events or experiences told like a story in connected and interesting form: *The account of his trip through the Near East made an interesting narrative.* **Narration** chiefly applies to the act of telling a story or relating an experience or a series of events, and emphasizes the way in which the narrative is put together and presented: *His narration of their trip was interesting.*

nar·ra·tor (na rā′tər, nar′ā tər, *or* ner′ā tər) *n.* a person who narrates.

nar·row (nar′ō *or* ner′ō) *adj., n., v.* —*adj.* **1** not wide; having little width; of less than the specified, understood, or usual width: *narrow ribbon. A path 30 centimetres wide is narrow.* **2** limited in extent, space, amount, range, scope, opportunity, etc.: *He had only a narrow circle of friends.* **3** close; with a small margin: *a narrow escape.* **4** lacking sympathy; not tolerant; prejudiced: *A person who says that all modern art is rubbish has a narrow mind about art.* **5** close; careful; minute: *a narrow scrutiny.* **6** with barely enough to live on: *to live in narrow circumstances.* **7** *Phonetics.* **a** pronounced with tense articulation; tense. **b** indicating minute details of pronunciation: *a narrow transcription.*
—*n.* **narrows** *pl.* the narrow part of a river, strait, sound, valley, pass, etc.
—*v.* make or become narrow; decrease in width: *The road narrows here.* [OE *nearu*] —**nar′row·ly**, *adv.* —**nar′row·ness**, *n.*

nar·row–gauge (nar′ō gāj′ *or* ner′ō-) *adj.* having railway tracks less than 56½ inches (about 130 cm) apart.

nar·row–mind·ed (nar′ō mīn′did *or* ner′ō-) *adj.* lacking understanding; blind to other points of view; prejudiced.
—**nar′row·mind′ed·ly**, *adv.* —**nar′row·mind′ed·ness**, *n.*

narrow squeak *Informal.* a narrow escape.

nar·thex (när′theks) *n.* **1** a portico or vestibule in ancient churches. **2** a vestibule leading into the nave of a church. [< Gk.]

nar·whal (när′wəl *or* när′hwəl) *n.* a small toothed whale (*Monodon monoceros*) of the arctic seas. The male has a long tusk extending forward from a tooth in the upper jaw. [< Danish or Swedish *narval* < ON *nár* corpse + *hval* whale]

nar·y (ner′ē) *adj. Dialect.* not any; none: *There was nary a thing to eat.*

NASA in the United States, National Aeronautics and Space Administration.

na·sal (nā′zəl) *adj., n.* —*adj.* **1** of, in, or from the nose: *nasal bones, nasal discharge, nasal passages.* **2** spoken through the nose with the mouth passage closed: M, n, *and* ng *represent nasal sounds.* **3** of a voice, characterized by resonance produced through the nose: *a nasal voice.* —*n. Phonetics.* a speech sound produced by expelling air through the nose. The sounds of (m), (n), and (ng) are nasals. [< L *nasus* nose] —**na′sal·ly,** *adv.*

na·sal·i·ty (nā zal′ə tē) *n.* of a voice or utterance, the quality of being nasal.

na·sal·ize (nā′zəl īz′) *v.* **-ized, -iz·ing.** utter or speak with a nasal sound: *Many vowels in French and Portuguese are nasalized.* —**na′sal·i·za′tion,** *n.*

nas·cent (nas′ənt *or* nā′sənt) *adj.* **1** in the process of coming into existence; just beginning to exist, grow, or develop. **2** *Chemistry.* **a** having to do with the state or condition of an element at the instant it is set free from a combination. **b** of an element, being in a free or uncombined state: *nascent chlorine.* [< L *nascens, -entis,* ppr. of *nasci* be born]

Nas·ka·pi (nas′kə pē′) *n., pl.* **Nas·ka·pi** or **Nas·ka·pis. 1** a member of an Algonquian people of northern Quebec and the interior of Labrador. **2** the Cree dialect spoken by the Naskapi. —*adj.* of or having to do with the Naskapi or their dialect.

na·stur·tium (nə stèr′shəm) *n.* **1** any of a genus (*Tropaeolum*) of plants having showy yellow, orange, or red flowers, and sharp-tasting seeds and leaves. **2** the flower. [< L *nasturtium* < *nasus* nose + *torquere* twist; from its pungent odor]

nas·ty (nas′tē) *adj.* **-ti·er, -ti·est. 1** disgustingly dirty, etc.; physically repugnant: *a nasty smell. There was a nasty, slimy mess at the bottom of the pit.* **2** sordid, vile, or obscene: *a nasty mind, a nasty story of betrayal.* **3** very unpleasant or disagreeable: *nasty weather. She has a nasty temper.* **4** rather serious or dangerous: *a nasty wound, a nasty accident.* **5** difficult or frustrating: *a nasty problem.* [ME; cf. Du. *nestig*] —**nas′ti·ly,** *adv.* —**nas′ti·ness,** *n.*

nat. 1 national. **2** native. **3** natural; naturalist.

na·tal (nā′təl) *adj.* **1** of, having to do with, or present at birth: *a natal star. Your natal day is your birthday.* **2** *Poetic.* native. [ME < L *natalis,* ult. < *nasci* be born. Doublet of NOËL.]

na·tal·i·ty (nā tal′ə tē) *n.* birth rate.

na·tant (nā′tənt) *adj.* swimming; floating; represented as swimming. [< L *natans, -antis,* ppr. of *natare* float, swim, ult. < *nare* float]

na·ta·to·ri·al (nā′tə tô′rē əl) *adj.* having to do with, adapted for, or characterized by swimming: *Ducks are natatorial birds.* [< LL *natatorialis,* ult. < L *natare* swim. See NATANT.]

na·ta·to·ri·um (nā′tə tô′rē əm) *n., pl.* **-ri·ums, -ri·a** (-rē ə). a swimming pool, especially an indoor one. [< LL]

na·ta·to·ry (nā′tə tô′rē) *adj.* natatorial.

nathe·less (nāth′lis *or* nath′lis) *adv., prep. Archaic.* —*adv.* nevertheless. —*prep.* notwithstanding. [OE *nā thȳ lǣs* never the less]

nath·less (nath′lis) *adv. or prep. Archaic.* natheless.

na·tion (nā′shən) *n.* **1** a community of people occupying and possessing a defined territory and united under one government; especially, such a community that is politically independent; country; state. **2 the nation, a** the people of such a community: *The prime minister appealed to the nation to support the government's policy of restraint.* **b** the territory of such a community: *The entire nation experienced unusually cold weather over the weekend.* **3** a people having the same descent and social and political history and, usually, sharing a common language; race or tribe: *the Scottish nation, the French-Canadian nation.* **4** a confederacy of North American Indian peoples: *The Iroquois Nation included the Seneca, Mohawk, Oneida, Onondaga, and Cayuga tribes, and later the Tuscarora.* **5** one of the peoples or tribes making up such a confederacy. [< L *natio, -onis* stock, race, ult. < *nasci* be born]

☞ *Syn.* **1.** See note at **people.**

☞ *Usage.* Def. I, referring to people under an independent government, is the primary meaning of **nation** in English. But def. 3, referring to people with common ties of birth, language, and culture, has in recent years become more

hat, āge, fär; let, ēqual, tèrm; it, īce
hot, ōpen, ôrder; oil, out; cup, pùt, rüle,
əbove, takən, pencəl, lemən, circəs
ch, child; ng, long; sh, ship
th, thin; ᴛʜ, then; zh, measure

widely established. In Canada this use of the word has been reinforced by similar uses of the word **nation** in Canadian French.

na·tion·al (nash′nəl *or* nash′ən əl) *adj., n.* —*adj.* **1** of a nation; affecting or belonging to a whole nation: *national laws, a national disaster.* **2** strongly upholding one's own nation; patriotic. **3** extending throughout the nation; having chapters, branches, or members in every part of the nation. —*n.* a citizen of a nation: *Each year many nationals of Canada visit the United States.*

National Assembly in Quebec, the group of representatives elected to the legislature; legislative assembly.

na·tion·al·ism (nash′nəl iz′əm *or* nash′ən əl iz′əm) *n.* **1** patriotic feelings or efforts. **2** the desire and plans for national independence. **3** the desire of a people to preserve its own language, religion, traditions, etc.

na·tion·al·ist (nash′nəl ist *or* nash′ən əl ist) *n., adj.* —*n.* **1** an upholder of nationalism; a person who believes in nationalism. **2 Nationalist,** a member of a political party supporting national independence or a strong national government. —*adj.* **1** nationalistic. **2 Nationalist,** of, having to do with, or being a political party supporting national independence or a strong national government: *the Nationalist platform.*

na·tion·al·is·tic (nash′nəl is′tik *or* nash′ən əl is′tik) *adj.* **1** of or having to do with nationalism or nationalists. **2** supporting nationalism: *a very nationalistic speech.* —**na′tion·al·is′ti·cal·ly,** *adv.*

na·tion·al·i·ty (nash nal′ə tē *or* nash′ən al′ə tē) *n., pl.* **-ties. 1** the fact of belonging to a nation: *His passport showed that his nationality was Canadian.* **2** the condition of being an independent nation; nationhood.

na·tion·al·ize (nash′nəl īz′ *or* nash′ən əl īz′) *v.* **-ized, -iz·ing. 1** make national. **2** bring (land, industries, railways, etc.) under the control or ownership of a nation. **3** make into a nation. —**na′tion·al·i·za′tion,** *n.*

na·tion·al·ly (nash′nəl ē *or* nash′ən əl ē) *adv.* **1** in a national manner; as a nation. **2** throughout the nation: *The opposition leader's speech was broadcast nationally.*

national park land kept by the government of a country for people to enjoy because of its beautiful scenery, historical interest, etc.

National Socialist Party the political party, led by Adolf Hitler, that controlled Germany from 1933 to 1945.

na·tion·hood (nā′shən hùd′) *n.* the condition or state of being a nation; the fact of having national existence: *A country's nationhood is sometimes threatened by civil wars.*

na·tion–wide (nā′shən wīd′) *adj.* extending throughout the nation: *a nation-wide election.*

na·tive (nā′tiv) *n., adj.* —*n.* **1** a person born in a certain place or country: *He is a native of Montreal.* **2** a member of a people who are the traditional or original inhabitants of a region or country, as contrasted with conquerors, settlers, visitors, etc. **3** an indigenous animal or plant. —*adj.* **1** born in a certain place or country: *He is a native son of Winnipeg.* **2** belonging to or associated with one by birth: *one's native land.* **3** belonging to one because of his country or the nation to which he belongs: *one's native language.* **4** born in a person; natural: *native ability, native courtesy.* **5** of, having to do with, or designating people who are the traditional or original inhabitants of a region or country: *the native peoples of Canada, native customs, native rights.* **6** originating, grown, or produced in a certain place: *The Manitoba maple is native to Canada.* **7** found pure in nature: *native copper.* **8** found in nature; not produced: *Native salt is refined for use.*

go native, of a conqueror, settler, visitor, etc., give up one's own culture and live as the natives do.

[*adj.* < L *nativus* innate, ult. < *nasci* be born, 14c; *n.* < Med.L *nativus* a native < L *nativus adj.*; 15c. Doublet of NAÏVE.] —**na′tive·ly,** *adv.* —**na′tive·ness,** *n.*

☞ *Syn. adj.* **4. Native, natural** = belonging to someone or something by birth or nature. **Native** emphasizes the idea of being born in a person, as contrasted with being acquired: *He has native artistic talent.* **Natural** emphasizes being part of the nature of a person, animal, or thing, belonging by birth or because of essential character: *Sugar has natural sweetness.*

na·tive–born (nā′tiv bôrn′) *adj.* born in a particular town,

country, etc.: *My father is a native-born Canadian, but my mother was born in Iceland.*

na·tiv·ism (nā′təv iz′əm) *n.* **1** the protection and perpetuation of a native culture, especially in opposition to assimilation by another culture. **2** a policy of favoring the native inhabitants of a country over immigrants.

na·tiv·ist (nā′təv ist) *n., adj.* —*n.* a person who advocates or supports nativism. —*adj.* of or having to do with nativism or nativists.

na·tiv·i·ty (nə tiv′ə tē *or* nā tiv′ə tē) *n., pl.* **-ties. 1 Nativity, a** the birth of Christ. **b** a picture showing the new-born infant Jesus, usually with Mary and Joseph and often with animals, shepherds, and the three Wise Men grouped around them. **c** Christmas. **2** birth. **3** horoscope. [ME < OF *nativite* < LL *nativitas*]

natl. national.

NATO (nā′tō) *n.* North Atlantic Treaty Organization.

na·tron (nā′tron) *n.* native sodium carbonate. *Formula:* $Na_2CO_3 \cdot 10H_2O$ [< F < Sp. < Arabic *natrun* < Gk. *nitron* < Semitic. Doublet of NITRE.]

nat·ter (nat′ər) *v.* **1** talk on at length; chatter. **2** mutter discontentedly; fret. [< earlier *gnatter*; origin uncertain]

nat·ty (nat′ē) *adj.* **-ti·er, -ti·est.** trim and tidy; neatly smart in dress or appearance: *a natty uniform, a natty young officer.* [origin uncertain] —**nat′ti·ly,** *adv.* —**nat′ti·ness,** *n.*

nat·u·ral (nach′rəl *or* nach′ə rəl) *adj., n.* —*adj.* **1** produced by nature; based on some state of things in nature: *Scenery has natural beauty.* **2** not artificial: *Coal and oil are natural products.* **3** instinctive; inborn: *natural ability.* **4** coming or occurring in the ordinary course of events; normal: *a natural death.* **5** in accordance with the nature of things or the circumstances of the case: *a natural response.* **6** instinctively felt to be right and fair: *natural law, natural rights.* **7** like nature; true to nature: *The picture looked natural.* **8** free from affectation or restraint: *a natural manner.* **9** of or having to do with nature: *the natural sciences.* **10** concerned with natural science. **11** based on what is learned from nature: *natural religion.* **12** *Music.* **a** neither sharp nor flat; without sharps and flats. **b** neither sharped nor flatted: *C natural.* **c** having the pitch affected by the natural sign. **d** produced without the aid of valves or keys, as in brass instruments. **13** by birth; not legally recognized; illegitimate: *a natural son.* **14** *Mathematics.* having 1 as the base of the system (applied to a function or number belonging or referred to such a system).
—*n.* **1** that which is natural. **2** *Music.* **a** a natural tone or note. **b** a sign (♮) used to cancel the effect of a preceding sharp or flat. **c** a white key on keyboard instruments. **3** *Archaic.* a half-witted person. **4** *Informal.* a person who seems especially suited for something: *He's a natural for the football team.* **5** *Informal.* a sure success. [ME < L *naturalis* < *natura.* See NATURE.] —**nat′u·ral·ness,** *n.*
☛ *Syn. adj.* **3.** See note at **native.**

natural childbirth childbirth with a minimum use of anesthetic and with the conscious participation of the mother, who has learned techniques for relaxation and has done exercises designed to facilitate the process of labor and delivery.

natural gas a combustible gas commonly used as a fuel, that occurs dissolved in petroleum and is also found in separate natural deposits in the earth. Natural gas consists of methane and other hydrocarbons.

natural history **1** the study of animals, plants, minerals, and other things in nature. **2** a book or article on some aspect of nature.

nat·u·ral·ism (nach′rəl iz′əm *or* nach′ə rəl iz′əm) *n.* **1** a style in art and literature characterized by a realistic and objective portrayal of nature, life, etc. **2** the principles of certain 19th-century writers, especially in France, who strove for a type of realism that stressed the unpleasant and sordid aspects of life. **3** action based on natural instincts. **4** *Philosophy.* a view of the world which takes account only of natural elements and forces, excluding the supernatural or spiritual. **5** the doctrine that all religious truth is derived from the study of nature.

nat·u·ral·ist (nach′rəl ist *or* nach′ə rəl ist) *n., adj.* —*n.* **1** a person who studies animals and plants; a field biologist. **2** a person who supports or practises naturalism. —*adj.* naturalistic.

nat·u·ral·is·tic (nach′rəl is′tik *or* nach′ə rəl is′tik) *adj.* **1** of, having to do with, or characterized by naturalism: *a naturalistic painting.* **2** of natural history or naturalists.

nat·u·ral·ize (nach′rəl īz′ *or* nach′ə rəl īz′) *v.* **-ized, -iz·ing.** **1** grant the rights of citizenship to persons native to other countries; admit (a foreigner) to citizenship: *My father is a naturalized Canadian but my mother was born here.* **2** adopt (a foreign word or custom): *The French word* chauffeur *has been naturalized in English.* **3** introduce and make at home in another country: *The*

English sparrow has become naturalized in parts of Canada. **4** make natural; free from conventional characteristics. **5** regard or explain as natural rather than supernatural. **6** become like a native. —**nat′u·ral·i·za′tion,** *n.*

natural law **1** a law, or the laws, of nature. **2** a rule of conduct supposedly based on reason inherent in nature.

nat·u·ral·ly (nach′rəl ē *or* nach′ə rəl ē) *adv.* **1** in a natural way: *speak naturally.* **2** by nature: *a naturally obedient child.* **3** as might be expected; of course.

natural magnet a piece of magnetite; lodestone.

natural number any positive whole number: *The numbers* 1 *and* 2 *are natural numbers;* -1 *and* -2 *are not.*

natural philosophy physics.

natural resource a kind of material that is supplied by nature and is useful or necessary to man: *Minerals and water power are natural resources.*

natural science any of the sciences that deal with nature and the physical world, including biology, chemistry, physics, and geology.

natural selection the process by which animals and plants best adapted to their environment tend to survive.

natural sign natural (n. def. 2b).

na·ture (nā′chər) *n.* **1** the world; all things except those made by man. **2** the sum total of the forces at work throughout the universe: *the laws of nature.* **3 Nature,** the personification of all natural facts and forces. **4** the instincts or inherent tendencies directing conduct. *It is against nature for a mother to kill her child.* **5** reality: *true to nature.* **6** a primitive, wild condition; condition of human beings before social organization. **7** the qualities or abilities with which a person or animal is born; character; way or manner: *It is the nature of birds to fly. She has a kind nature.* **8** sort; kind. **9** physical being; vital powers: *food sufficient to sustain nature.* **10** moral nature unaffected by grace.
by nature, because of the essential character of the person or thing.
of or **in the nature of,** having the nature of; being a kind of.
[ME < OF < L *natura* birth, character, ult. < *nasci* be born]

–natured *combining form.* having the nature of: *bad-natured = having a bad nature.*

nature study the study of animals, plants, and other things and events in nature.

nature trail a trail through a conservation area, park, or game sanctuary providing opportunities for the enjoyment and study of nature. Nature trails often have signs, information boards, and displays at intervals along the way.

na·tur·o·path (nā′chə rə path′) *n.* a person who practises the treatment of disease by means of naturopathy.

na·tur·o·path·ic (nā′chə rə path′ik) *adj.* of, having to do with, or using naturopathy.

na·tur·op·a·thy (nā′chə rop′ə thē) *n.* a system or method of treating diseases and disorders without the use of surgery or synthetic drugs, relying instead on natural forces such as good nutrition, and on the use of natural herbal medicines.

naught (not *or* nôt) *n.* nothing: *All his work went for naught.* [OE *nāwiht* < *nā* no + *wiht* wight]
☛ *Hom.* **knot, not** (not), and **nought** (not *or* nôt).

naugh·ty (not′ē *or* nô′tē) *adj.* **-ti·er, -ti·est.** **1** bad; not obedient. **2** improper. [< *naught* wickedness] —**naugh′ti·ly,** *adv.* —**naugh′ti·ness,** *n.*

nau·se·a (no′zē ə *or* nô′zē ə, no′shə *or* nô′shə) *n.* **1** the feeling that one has when about to vomit. **2** extreme disgust; loathing. [< L < Gk. *nausia* < *naus* ship. Doublet of NOISE.]

nau·se·ate (no′zē āt′ *or* nô′zē āt′, no′sē āt′ *or* nô′sē āt′) *v.* **-at·ed, -at·ing.** **1** cause nausea in; make sick. **2** feel nausea; become sick. **3** cause to feel loathing. [< L *nauseare*] —**nau′se·at′ing·ly,** *adv.*

nau·se·ous (no′zē əs *or* nô′zē əs, no′shəs *or* nô′shəs) *adj.* **1** causing nausea; sickening. **2** affected with nausea or disgust. [< L *nauseosus*] —**nau′seous·ly,** *adv.*

naut. nautical.

nautch (noch *or* nôch) *n.* in India, an entertainment consisting of dancing by professional dancing girls. [< Hind. *nach* dance]

nau·ti·cal (no′tə kəl *or* nô′tə kəl) *adj.* of or having to do with ships, sailors, or navigation. [< L < Gk. *nautikos*, ult. < *naus* ship] —**nau′ti·cal·ly,** *adv.*

nautical mile a unit for measuring distance in air and sea navigation, equal to 1852 metres. *Abbrev.:* n.mi.

nau·ti·lus (no′tə ləs *or* nô′tə ləs) *n., pl.* **-lus·es, -li** (-lī′ *or* -lē′). **1** any of a genus (*Nautilus*) of cephalopod molluscs comprising six species found in the S Pacific and Indian oceans, which are the only living representatives of a subclass of cephalopods that flourished

millions of years ago. The nautilus has a pearly-lined, chambered shell coiled in a flat spiral; the animal lives in the outermost chamber. Also called **pearly nautilus**. 2 paper nautilus. [< L < Gk. *nautilos*, originally, sailor, ult. < *naus* ship]

nav. 1 naval. 2 navigation.

Nav·a·ho or **Nav·a·jo** (nav′ə hō′) *n., pl.* **-ho** or **-hos, -jo** or **-jos. 1** a member of an Amerindian people of New Mexico, Arizona, and Utah. **2** the Athapascan language of the Navaho. —*adj.* of or having to do with the Navaho or their language.

na·val (nā′vəl) *adj.* **1** of, having to do with, or for warships or the navy: *a naval officer, naval supplies*. **2** having a navy: *the naval powers*. [< L *navalis* < *navis* ship] —**na′val·ly,** *adv.*
☞ *Hom.* **navel**.

naval stores materials, such as tar, resin, turpentine, etc. that are used for building and repairing wooden ships.

nave[1] (nāv) *n.* the main part of a church between the side aisles. The nave extends from the main entrance to the transepts. See **basilica** and **transept** for pictures. [< Med.L < L *navis* ship]
☞ *Hom.* **knave**.

nave[2] (nāv) *n.* the central part of a wheel; hub. [OE *nafu*]
☞ *Hom.* **knave**.

na·vel (nā′vəl) *n.* the small scar, usually a hollow, in the middle of the abdomen, marking the place where the umbilical cord was attached before and at birth. [OE *nafela*. Related to NAVE[2].]
☞ *Hom.* **naval**.

navel orange a seedless orange having a small growth that resembles a navel in shape and contains a small secondary fruit.

nav·i·ga·bil·i·ty (nav′ə gə bil′ə tē) *n.* the fact or quality of being navigable.

nav·i·ga·ble (nav′ə gə bəl) *adj.* **1** that ships can travel on: *The St. Lawrence River is deep enough to be navigable*. **2** seaworthy. **3** that can be steered.

nav·i·gate (nav′ə gāt′) *v.* **-gat·ed, -gat·ing. 1** sail, manage, or steer (a ship, aircraft, etc.). **2** sail on or over (a sea, river, etc.): *Many ships navigate the St. Lawrence Seaway each year.* **3** travel by water; sail. **4** convey (goods) by water. **5** sail through (the air) in an aircraft, etc. **6** plot the position and course of a ship, aircraft, vehicle, etc. **7** move; find one's way: *The old man could hardly navigate along the icy streets.* [< L *navigare* < *navis* ship + *agere* drive]

nav·i·ga·tion (nav′ə gā′shən) *n.* **1** the act or process of navigating. **2** the science of determining the position, course, and distance travelled of a ship, aircraft, or spacecraft. **3** traffic by ship, especially commercial shipping.

nav·i·ga·tion·al (nav′ə gā′shə nəl) *adj.* of, having to do with, or used in navigation.

nav·i·ga·tor (nav′ə gā′tər) *n.* **1** a person who is qualified to navigate, especially one whose work is navigating ships or aircraft: *They took on a special navigator to guide the ship through the dangerous waters. He served as a navigator in the air force.* **2** a person who sails the seas as an explorer: *a story of one of the early navigators.* [< L]

nav·vy (nav′ē) *n., pl.* **-vies.** *Brit.* an unskilled laborer who works on canals, railways, roads, etc. [< *navigator*]

na·vy (nā′vē) *n., pl.* **-vies;** *adj.* **1** all the ships of war of a country, together with their personnel. **2** Often, **Navy,** the branch of the armed forces of a nation comprising warships and personnel, as well as all the organization for their maintenance. In Canada, the function of a navy is served by Maritime Command of the Canadian Forces. **3** *Archaic or poetic.* a fleet of ships. **4** a dark blue. —*adj.* having the color navy. [ME < OF *navie*, ult. < L *navis* ship]

navy bean the small white seed of a variety of kidney bean commonly used in baked bean dishes, soups, etc. [from its former extensive use in the U.S. navy]

navy blue a dark blue.

na·wab (nə wob′) *n.* **1** *Historical.* in India, a title of a governor or nobleman. **2** in Pakistan, a title of a distinguished Moslem. [< Hind. *nav(v)ab* < Arabic *nuwwab*, pl. of *nā'ib* deputy]

nay (nā) *adv., n.* —*adv.* **1** *Archaic.* no. not only that, but also: *We are willing, nay, eager to go.* —*n.* **1** no; a denial or refusal. **2** a negative vote or voter. [ME < ON *nei* < *ne* not + *ei* ever]
☞ *Hom.* **neigh**.

Naz·a·rene (naz′ə rēn′ or naz′ə rēn′) *n., adj.* —*n.* **1** a native or inhabitant of Nazareth, the boyhood home of Jesus. **2 the Nazarene,** Jesus. **3** an early Christian. —*adj.* of or having to do with the Nazarenes or with Nazareth.

Naz·a·rite (naz′ə rīt′) *n.* **1** among the ancient Hebrews, a Jew who had taken certain strict religious vows (Num. 6). **2** a native of Nazareth. Also, **Nazirite.**

Na·zi (nat′sē or nä′tsē) *n., pl.* **Na·zis. 1** a member or supporter of the National Socialist German Workers' Party which controlled Germany from 1933 to 1945, under the leadership of Adolf Hitler.

hat, āge, fär; let, ēqual, tèrm; it, īce
hot, ōpen, ôrder; oil, out; cup, pùt, rüle,
əbove, takən, pencəl, lemən, circəs

ch, child; ng, long; sh, ship
th, thin; ᴛʜ, then; zh, measure

2 (*adj.*) of or having to do with the Nazis. **3** Often, **nazi,** an advocate of similar doctrines in any country; fascist. [< G *Nazi*, short for *Nationalsozialist* National Socialist]
☞ *Usage.* **Nazi** was a political nickname for the National Socialist Party in Germany and is capitalized like **Conservative** or **Liberal.** The type of party represented by the Nazis is usually referred to as fascist or totalitarian.

Na·zi·fy or **na·zi·fy** (nat′sə fī′ or nä′tsə fī′) *v.* **-fied, -fy·ing. 1** place under control of the Nazis. **2** indoctrinate with Nazi views. —**Na′zi·fi·ca′tion, na′zi·fi·ca′tion,** *n.*

Na·zi·ism (nat′sē iz′əm or nä′tsē iz′əm) *n.* Nazism.

Na·zism (nat′siz əm or nä′tsiz əm) *n.* the doctrines and policies of the Nazi party, based on the idea of the innate superiority of the "Aryan" race, especially the Nordic type of that race, and its destiny and responsibility to rule the world. Nazism also glorified strength and discipline within an authoritarian hierarchy having at its apex an infallible leader, or Führer.

Nb niobium.

NB New Brunswick (*used esp. in computerized address systems*).

N.B. New Brunswick.

N.B. or **n.b.** nota bene.
☞ *Usage.* **N.B.,** the abbreviation of the Latin **nota bene** meaning "note well," is occasionally found in formal announcements: *N.B. Members are to pay their dues not later than Monday, May 5.*

NBC in the United States, National Broadcasting Company.

N.C. North Carolina.

NCO or **N.C.O.** non-commissioned officer.

n.d. **1** no date. **2** not dated.

Nd neodymium.

ND North Dakota.

N.Dak. or **N.D.** North Dakota.

NDP or **N.D.P.** New Democratic Party.

NDT or **N.D.T.** Newfoundland Daylight Time.

Ne neon.

NE Nebraska.

NE or **N.E.** northeast; northeastern.

N.E., NE, or **n.e. 1** northeast. **2** northeastern.

Ne·an·der·thal (nē an′dər täl′, nē an′dər thol′, *or* nē an′dər thôl′) *adj.* of or having to do with Neanderthal man.

Neanderthal man an extinct people widespread in Europe, N Africa, and parts of Asia in the early Stone Age. [< *Neanderthal*, a valley in W Germany, where evidence of this people was found]

neap (nēp) *adj., n.* —*adj.* of, having to do with, or designating a neap tide. —*n.* neap tide. [OE *nēp*]

Ne·a·pol·i·tan (nē′ə pol′ə tən) *n., adj.* —*n.* a native or inhabitant of Naples, a city in Italy. —*adj.* of or having to do with Naples. [< L *Neapolitanus* < *Neapolis* Naples < Gk.]

Neapolitan ice cream ice cream consisting of several flavors in layers, usually chocolate, strawberry, and vanilla.

neap tide the tide that occurs when the difference in height between high and low tide is least; lowest level of high tide. Neap tide occurs at the first and last quarters of the moon; that is, about twice a month.

near (nēr) *adv., adj., prep., v.* —*adv.* **1** at or to a place or time not far away; close by: *The train drew near.* **2** closely: *tribes near allied.* **3** *Informal.* all but; almost: *near crazy with fright.*
come near (doing), almost do: *I came near forgetting my glasses again.*
near at hand, a within easy reach: *My pen is always near at hand.* **b** not far in the future.
—*adj.* **1** close by; not distant (*never used before a noun*): *The post office is quite near.* **2** intimate; familiar: *a near friend.* **3** closely related: *a near relative.* **4** approximating or resembling closely: *near silk, near beer.* **5** on the left-hand side (*used of a horse, team of horses, vehicle, etc.*): *the near foreleg. The near horse is a bit stronger than the off horse.* Compare **off** (def. 10). **6** short; direct: *Go by the nearest route.* **7** stingy. **8** by a close margin: *a near escape.*
—*prep.* at or to a place, time, or condition not far away; close to: *Our house is near the river. They were both near tears.*
—*v.* come or draw near; approach: *The ship neared the land.* [OE *nēar,* comparative of *nēah* nigh] —**near′ness,** *n.*

near·by (*adv.* nēr'bī'; *adj.* nēr'bī') *adj. or adv.* near; close at hand: *They live in a nearby house. They live nearby.*

Near East 1 the countries of SW Asia (including Saudi Arabia, Israel, Lebanon, Iran, etc.) and Egypt. 2 Middle East.
☛ *Usage.* The term **Middle East,** which often refers to a broader area, is now more commonly used than **Near East.**

near·ly (nēr'lē) *adv.* 1 almost: *I nearly missed the train.* 2 closely: *a matter that concerns you very nearly.*

near–miss (nēr'mis') *n.* 1 a narrow escape from danger. 2 anything approaching, but not quite fulfilling, excellence or perfection.

near–sight·ed (nēr'sīt'id) *adj.* having a condition of the eyes in which the visual images of distant objects come to a focus before they reach the retina, so that they are not clear. A near-sighted person has better vision for nearby objects than for distant objects. Compare **far-sighted. —near'-sight'ed·ly,** *adv.*
—near'-sight'ed·ness, *n.*

neat[1] (nēt) *adj.* 1 clean and in order: *a neat desk, a neat room, a neat dress.* 2 able and willing to keep things in order: *He's a very neat person.* 3 well-formed; in proportion: *a neat design.* 4 skilful; clever: *a neat trick.* 5 especially of alcoholic liquor, not having anything mixed in it; undiluted; straight: *He prefers his whisky neat.* 6 *Slang.* very pleasing; fine: *a neat party.* [< F *net* < L *nitidus* gleaming < *nitere* shine] **—neat'ly,** *adv.* **—neat'ness,** *n.*
☛ *Syn.* 1. **Neat, tidy, trim** = in good order. **Neat** emphasizes cleanness and absence of disorder or litter: *Her clothes are always neat.* **Tidy** emphasizes orderliness and showing painstaking care in having a place for everything and everything in its place: *She keeps her room tidy.* **Trim** adds the idea of being pleasing in appearance, sometimes suggesting smartness, sometimes good proportion, clean lines, and compactness: *That is a trim sailing boat.*

neat[2] (nēt) *n.pl. or sing. Archaic.* cattle; oxen. [OE *nēat*]

neat·en (nēt'ən) *v.* make neat; tidy up.

neath or **'neath** (nēth) *prep. Poetic.* beneath.

neat·herd (nēt'hėrd') *n. Archaic.* cowherd.

neat's–foot oil (nēts'fut') an oil obtained from the feet and shinbones of cattle by boiling. Neat's-foot oil is used to soften leather.

neb (neb) *n. Scottish.* 1 a bill; beak. 2 a person's mouth or nose. 3 an animal's snout. 4 the tip of anything; nib. [OE *nebb*]

Nebr. or **Neb.** Nebraska.

neb·u·la (neb'yə lə) *n., pl.* **-lae** (-lē' *or* -lī') **or -las.** 1 a cloudlike cluster of stars or a mass of dust particles visible in the sky at night. 2 a cloudlike spot on the cornea of the eye. [< L *nebula* mist]

neb·u·lar (neb'yə lər) *adj.* of or concerning a nebula or nebulae.

nebular hypothesis the hypothesis that the solar system developed from a luminous mass of gas.

neb·u·los·i·ty (neb'yə los'ə tē) *n., pl.* **-ties.** 1 the quality or state of being nebulous. 2 cloudlike matter; nebula.

neb·u·lous (neb'yə ləs) *adj.* 1 hazy; vague; indistinct: *Our holiday plans are still somewhat nebulous.* 2 of, having to do with, or resembling a nebula; nebular. [< L *nebulosus* < *nebula* mist] **—neb'u·lous·ly,** *adv.* **—neb'u·lous·ness,** *n.*

nec·es·sar·i·ly (nes'ə ser'ə lē *or* nes'ə ser'ə lē) *adv.* because of necessity; because it must be; invariably or inevitably: *Leaves are not necessarily green. War necessarily causes misery and waste.*

nec·es·sar·y (nes'ə ser'ē) *adj., n., pl.* **-sar·ies. —adj.** that must be, be had, or be done; inevitable; required; indispensable: *Death is a necessary end.*
—n. 1 something essential; something that cannot be done without: *Food, clothing, and shelter are necessaries of life.* 2 **necessaries,** *pl. Law.* the things, as food, shelter, clothing, etc., required to support a dependent or similar person in a way suitable to his station in life. 3 **the necessary,** money: *Have you the necessary?* [< L *necessarius* < *necesse* unavoidable, ult. < *ne-* not + *cedere* withdraw]
☛ *Syn. adj.* **Necessary, indispensable, essential** = needed or required. **Necessary** applies to whatever is needed but not absolutely required: *Work is a necessary part of life.* **Indispensable** implies that, without the thing referred to, the intended result or purpose cannot be achieved: *Determination is indispensable for success.* **Essential** implies that the existence or proper functioning of something depends upon the thing referred to: *Good health is essential to happiness.*

ne·ces·si·tar·i·an (nə ses'ə ter'ē ən) *adj., n. —adj.* of or having to do with necessitarianism. **—n.** an advocate of necessitarianism.

ne·ces·si·tar·i·an·ism (nə ses'ə ter'ē ən iz'əm) *n. Philosophy.* the theory that every event in the universe is causally determined and cannot occur by chance. The theory of necessitarianism applied to the human will is identical with determinism.

ne·ces·si·tate (nə ses'ə tāt') *v.* **-tat·ed, -tat·ing.** 1 make

necessary: *His broken leg necessitated an operation.* 2 *Archaic.* compel; force.

ne·ces·si·tous (nə ses'ə təs) *adj.* very poor; needy.
—ne·ces'si·tous·ly, *adv.* **—ne·ces'si·tous·ness,** *n.*

ne·ces·si·ty (nə ses'ə tē) *n., pl.* **-ties.** 1 the fact of being necessary; extreme need: *We understand the necessity of eating.* 2 the quality of being necessary. 3 anything that cannot be done without: *Water is a necessity.* 4 that which forces one to act in a certain way: *Necessity often drives people to do disagreeable things.* 5 that which is inevitable: *Night follows day as a necessity.* 6 need; poverty: *This poor family is in great necessity.*
of necessity, because it must be: *We left early of necessity; there is no bus service at night.*
[< L *necessitas* < *necesse.* See NECESSARY.]

neck (nek) *n., v. —n.* 1 the part of the body that connects the head with the shoulders. 2 the part of a garment that fits the neck. 3 any narrow part like a neck: *a neck of land, the neck of a vase.* 4 a narrow strip of land. 5 the slender part of a bottle, flask, retort, or other container. 6 *Architecture.* the lowest part of the capital of a column. 7 the long slender part of a violin or similar instrument, extending from the body to the head; finger board. 8 the part of a tooth between the crown and the root. 9 a slender or constricted part of a bone or organ. 10 *Racing.* the length of the neck of a horse or other animal to a measure.
get it in the neck, *Slang.* receive a severe scolding, defeat, etc.
neck and neck, **a** abreast. **b** being equal or even in a race or contest: *The two horses ran neck and neck for a kilometre.*
neck of the woods, *Informal.* locality or region: *There are few good roads in this neck of the woods.*
neck or nothing, venturing all.
risking (one's) neck, put oneself in a dangerous position; risk one's life.
stick (one's) neck out, *Informal.* put oneself in a dangerous and vulnerable position by foolish or zealous action.
win by a neck, **a** win a horse race by the length of a head and neck. **b** win by a close margin.
—v. *Slang.* embrace; hug; kiss and caress. [OE *hnecca*]

neck·band (nek'band') *n.* 1 a band worn around the neck. 2 the part of a shirt, blouse, etc. to which the collar is attached. 3 the part of a garment that fits the neck.

neck·cloth (nek'kloth') *n.* a cloth worn round the neck; cravat.

neck·er·chief (nek'ər chif) *n.* a cloth worn round the neck.

neck·lace (nek'lis) *n.* a string of jewels, gold, silver, beads, etc. worn around the neck as an ornament.

neck·line (nek'līn') *n.* the line formed by the neck opening of a garment: *a plain neckline, a low neckline.*

neck·piece (nek'pēs') *n.* a separate article of clothing, such as a scarf, worn around the neck: *a fur neckpiece.*

neck·tie (nek'tī') *n.* a tie (def. 2).

neck·wear (nek'wer') *n.* collars, ties, and other articles that are worn around the neck.

nec·ro– *combining form.* death, dead body, dead tissue. [< Gk. *nekr-, nekro-* < *nekros* corpse]

ne·crol·o·gy (ne krol'ə jē) *n., pl.* **-gies.** 1 a list of persons who have recently died. 2 a notice of a person's death; obituary. [< Med.L *necrologia* < Gk. *nekros* dead body + *logos* count, reckoning]

nec·ro·man·cer (nek'rə man'sər) *n.* 1 a person who is supposed to foretell the future by communicating with the dead. 2 a magician; sorcerer; wizard.

nec·ro·man·cy (nek'rə man'sē) *n.* 1 a supposed foretelling of the future by communicating with the dead. 2 magic; enchantment; sorcery. [ME < OF < Med.L *nigromantia* < L *necromantia* < Gk. *nekromanteia* < *nekros* dead body + *manteia* divination; confusion with L *niger* "black" led to interpretation as "black art"]

ne·crop·o·lis (ne krop'ə lis) *n., pl.* **-lis·es.** cemetery. [< NL < Gk. *nekropolis* < *nekros* dead body + *polis* city]

ne·cro·sis (ne krō'sis) *n., pl.* **-ses** (-sēz). 1 the death of body cells of of a portion of tissue or an organ, resulting from irreversible damage caused by an outside agent. 2 any of various bacterial diseases of plants characterized by spots of decayed tissue. [< NL < Gk. *necrosis,* ult. < *nekros* dead body]

nec·tar (nek'tər) *n.* 1 *Greek mythology.* **a** the drink of the gods. **b** the food of the gods. 2 any delicious drink. 3 a sweet liquid found in many flowers. Bees gather nectar and make it into honey. [< L < Gk. *nektar*] **—nec'tar·like',** *adj.*

nec·tar·ine (nek'tər ēn' *or* nek'tər ēn') *n.* a kind of peach having no down on its skin. [< *nectar*]

nec·ta·ry (nek'tə rē) *n., pl.* **-ries.** the part of a flower that secretes nectar.

née or **nee** (nā) *adj.* born. [< F *née,* fem. pp. of *naître* be born < L *nasci*]

☛ *Usage.* **Née** may be placed after the name of a married woman to show her maiden name: *Mrs. Smith, née Adams.*

need (nēd) *n., v.* —*n.* **1** want; lack of a useful or desired thing: *The loss by our team showed the need of practice.* **2** a useful or desired thing that is lacking: *In the desert their need was water.* **3** necessity; something that has to be; requirement: *There is no need to hurry.* **4** a situation or time of difficulty: *a friend in need.* **5** extreme poverty.
have need to, be required to; should or must.
if need be, if it has to be.
—*v.* **1** have need of; want; require: *to need money.* **2** be necessary. **3** must; should; have to; ought to: *He need not go. Need she go?* **4** be in want: *Give to those that need.* [OE *nēd*] —**need′er,** *n.*
☛ *Hom.* **knead.**
☛ *Syn. v.* **1.** See note at **lack.**

need·ful (nēd′fəl) *adj.* needed; necessary. —**need′ful·ly,** *adv.*

nee·dle (nē′dəl) *n., v.* **-dled, -dling.** —*n.* **1** a slender tool, pointed at one end and having a hole, or eye, at the other to pass a thread through, used in sewing. **2** a slender rod used in knitting. **3** a rod with a hook at one end used in crocheting, etc. **4** a thin steel pointer on a compass or on electrical machinery. **5** a slender, hollow tube with a sharp point, used for injecting or extracting something: *The doctor jabbed the needle into my arm.* **6** injection: *The doctor gave him a needle.* **7** an instrument resembling a needle, used in etching and engraving. **8** a phonograph needle; stylus. **9** any of various small objects resembling a needle in sharpness: *needles of broken glass, ice, etc.* **10** a slender, needle-shaped rod that controls the opening of a valve. **11** the needle-shaped leaf of the fir, pine, spruce, or larch. **12** a pillar; obelisk: *Cleopatra's needle.* **13** *Mineralogy and chemistry.* a crystal or spicule like a needle in shape. **14** *Geology.* a pinnacle of rock tapering to a point.
—*v. Informal.* tease; goad or incite: *The boys needled him into losing his temper.* [OE *nēdl*]

nee·dle·fish (nē′dəl fish′) *n.* any of a family (Belonidae) of sea fishes having a long, pipelike body, a long snout, and many sharp teeth.

nee·dle·point (nē′dəl point′) *n.* **1** embroidery done on canvas, using straight, even stitches to cover the entire surface, giving a tapestry-like effect. **2** (*adj.*) of, designating, or made or decorated with such embroidery. **3** point lace.

need·ler (nēd′lər) *n. Informal.* a person who nags or irritates others; heckler.

need·less (nēd′lis) *adj.* not needed; unnecessary. —**need′less·ly,** *adv.* —**need′less·ness,** *n.*

needle valve a valve whose very small opening is controlled by a slender, needle-shaped rod.

nee·dle·wom·an (nē′dəl wùm′ən) *n., pl.* **-wom·en.** a woman who does needlework, especially one who earns her living by sewing.

nee·dle·work (nē′dəl wėrk′) *n.* work done with a needle, especially handwork such as embroidery, needlepoint, or fine hand sewing.

need·n't (nē′dənt) need not.

needs (nēdz) *adv.* because of necessity; necessarily: *A soldier needs must go where duty calls.* [OE *nēdes,* originally gen. of *nēd* need]

need·y (nē′dē) *adj.* **need·i·er, need·i·est.** very poor; not having enough to live on. —**need′i·ness,** *n.*

ne'er (ner) *adv. Poetic.* never.

ne'er-do-well (ner′dü wel′) *n., adj.* —*n.* a worthless fellow; good-for-nothing person. —*adj.* worthless; good-for-nothing.

ne·far·i·ous (ni fer′ē əs) *adj.* very wicked; villainous. [< L *nefarius,* ult. < *ne-* not + *fas* right, originally, (divine) decree < *fari* speak] —**ne·far′i·ous·ly,** *adv.* —**ne·far′i·ous·ness,** *n.*

ne·gate (ni gāt′) *v.* **-gat·ed, -gat·ing.** deny; nullify. [< L *negare* say no]

ne·ga·tion (ni gā′shən) *n.* **1** a denying; denial: *Shaking the head is a sign of negation.* **2** the absence or opposite of some positive thing or quality: *Darkness is the negation of light.* [< L *negatio, -onis* < *negare* say no]

neg·a·tive (neg′ə tiv) *adj., n., v.* **-tived, -tiv·ing.** —*adj.* **1** saying no: *His answer was negative.* **2** not positive or helpful: *Not being unkind is only negative kindness.* **3** *Mathematics and physics.* **a** counting down from zero; minus: *Three below zero is a negative quantity.* **b** measured or proceeding in the opposite direction to that considered positive. **4** having more electrons than protons: *a negative particle.* **5 a** of or having to do with the kind of electricity produced on resin when it is rubbed with silk. **b** characterized by the presence or production of such electricity. **6** *Photography.* showing the lights and shadows reversed: *the negative image on a photographic plate.* **7** *Chemistry.* having a tendency to gain electrons, and thus to become charged with negative electricity, as an element or radical. **8** showing an absence of the germs,

hat, āge, fär; let, ēqual, tėrm; it, īce
hot, ōpen, ôrder; oil, out; cup, pùt, rüle,
ə above, takən, pencəl, lemən, circəs
ch, child; ng, long; sh, ship
th, thin; ᴛʜ, then; zh, measure

symptoms, etc. of an illness. **9** *Psychology.* resisting suggestions; very unco-operative. —*n.* **1** an affix, word, or statement that says no or denies. **2** the side that says no or argues against a question being debated; side opposing the affirmative. **3** a negative quality or characteristic. **4** a minus quantity, sign, etc. **5** the negative element in an electric cell. **6** *Photography.* an image in which the lights and shadows are reversed and from which prints can be made. **7** the right of veto.
in the negative, a in favor of denying (a request, suggestion, etc.). **b** expressing disagreement by saying no; denying: *Most of the replies were in the negative.*
—*v.* **1** say no to; deny; vote against. **2** disprove. **3** make useless; counteract; neutralize. [< L *negativus* < *negare* say no] —**neg′a·tive·ly,** *adv.*
☛ *Usage.* **Double negatives.** Two negatives should not be used in a sentence where only one is required. *She won't tell us nothing* should be corrected to *She won't tell us anything.* Double negatives were used in and before Shakespeare's time, but they are no longer accepted in standard English. See also note at **hardly.**

neg·a·tiv·ism (neg′ə tiv iz′əm) *n.* **1** a tendency to say or do the opposite of what is suggested. **2** *Psychology.* a type of behavior marked by resistance to suggestion.

neg·lect (ni glekt′) *v., n.* —*v.* **1** give too little care, respect, or attention to: *to neglect one's health. He neglected his lawyer's advice.* **2** leave undone; not attend to: *The maid neglected her work.* **3** omit; fail: *Don't neglect to water the plants.*
—*n.* **1** the act or fact of neglecting; disregard: *His neglect of the truth was astonishing.* **2** a want of attention to what should be done. **3** being neglected. [< L *neglectus,* pp. of *negligere, neglegere,* var. of *neclegere* < *nec* not (< *ne-* not + *que* and) + *legere* pick up] —**neg·lect′er,** *n.*
☛ *Syn. v.* **1.** See note at **slight.** —*n.* **1. Neglect, negligence** = lack of proper care or attention. **Neglect** applies especially to the act or fact of giving too little care or attention to one's duty or work or leaving it undone: *That car has been ruined by neglect.* **Negligence** applies especially to the quality of being inclined to neglect, possessed by a person or group or shown by inattentiveness to work or duty or carelessness in doing it: *Many accidents in industry are caused by the negligence of workers.*

neg·lect·ful (ni glekt′fəl) *adj.* careless; negligent. —**neg·lect′ful·ly,** *adv.*

né·gli·gé (nā glē zhā′) *n. French.* negligee.

neg·li·gee (neg′lə zhā′ *or* neg′lə zhā′) *n.* **1** a woman's loose, often sheer, dressing gown. **2** easy, informal dress or attire. [< F *négligée,* fem. pp. of *négliger* neglect]

neg·li·gence (neg′lə jəns) *n.* **1** a lack of proper care or attention; neglect: *Because of the owner's negligence the house was in great need of repair.* **2** carelessness; indifference. **3** *Law.* failure to take due care, as required by law, resulting in damage to property or injury to a person or persons. [< L *negligentia* < *negligere.* See NEGLECT.]
☛ *Syn.* **1.** See note at **neglect.**

neg·li·gent (neg′lə jənt) *adj.* **1** neglectful; given to neglect; showing neglect. **2** careless; indifferent: *His negligent behavior resulted in an accident.* [< L *negligens, -entis,* ppr. of *negligere.* See NEGLECT.] —**neg′li·gent·ly,** *adv.*

neg·li·gi·ble (neg′lə jə bəl) *adj.* that can be disregarded; of little importance; trifling: *a negligible difference in price.*

ne·go·tia·bil·i·ty (ni gō′shə bil′ə tē *or* ni gō′shē ə bil′ə tē) *n.* being negotiable.

ne·go·tia·ble (ni gō′shə bəl *or* ni gō′shē ə bəl) *adj.* **1** capable of being negotiated or sold; whose ownership can be transferred. **2** that can be got past or over.

ne·go·ti·ate (ni gō′shē āt′) *v.* **-at·ed, -at·ing. 1** talk over and arrange terms; parley; confer; consult: *The rebels negotiated for peace with the government.* **2** arrange for: *They finally negotiated a peace treaty.* **3** sell. **4** *Informal.* get past or over: *The car negotiated the sharp curve by slowing down.* [< L *negotiare* < *negotium* business < *neg-* not + *otium* ease] —**ne·go′ti·a′tor,** *n.*

ne·go·ti·a·tion (ni gō′shē ā′shən) *n.* talking over and arranging; arrangement: *Negotiations for the new school are finished.*

Ne·gress (nē′gris′) *n. Offensive.* a black girl or woman.

Ne·gri·to (ni grē′tō) *n., pl.* **-tos** *or* **-toes.** a member of any of several dark-skinned peoples living in the Philippines and other islands in SE Asia. The Negritos are very small people, averaging less than 150 cm tall. [< Sp. *negrito,* dim. of *negro* Negro]

neg·ri·tude (neg′rə tyüd *or* -tüd, nē′grə tyüd *or* -tüd) *n.* **1** the condition of being a black, or Negro. **2** awareness of and pride in black or African culture and heritage.

Ne·gro (nē′grō) *n., pl.* **-groes;** *adj.* —*n.* **1** a member of the African race; a black. **2** a person having some African ancestors. —*adj.* of or having to do with Negroes. [< Sp. < L *niger* black]

Ne·groid (nē′groid) *adj., n.* —*adj.* **1** African (def. 2). **2** *Obsolete.* of or having to do with a racial grouping that includes the traditional inhabitants of Africa south of the Sahara, Melanesia, New Guinea and nearby islands, and the original inhabitants of Australia. The human species was formerly classified into three racial groups: the Caucasoid, Mongoloid, and Negroid. —*n.* **1** African (def. 3). **2** *Obsolete.* a member of the African, Australoid, or Melanesian race.

ne·gus (nē′gəs) *n.* a drink made of wine, hot water, sugar, lemon, and nutmeg. [after Colonel Francis *Negus* (died 1732), its inventor]

Ne·gus (nē′gəs) *n.* the ruler of Ethiopia. [< Amharic]

neigh (nā) *n., v.* —*n.* the sound that a horse makes. —*v.* make the sound that a horse makes or one like it. [OE *hnǣgan*]
☛ *Hom.* nay.

neigh·bor or **neigh·bour** (nā′bər) *n., v.* —*n.* **1** a person who lives near another: *We asked our next-door neighbors to take in our mail while we were away. Their nearest neighbors are 20 kilometres away.* **2** a person or thing that is near another: *The big tree brought down several of its smaller neighbors as it fell.* **3** (*adj.*) living or situated near or next to another; neighboring. **4** a fellow human being.
—*v.* **1** be near or next to; adjoin. **2** be friendly with. [OE *nēahgebūr* < *nēah* nigh + *gebūr* dweller, countryman] —**neigh′bor·less** or **neigh′bour·less,** *adj.*

neigh·bor·hood or **neigh·bour·hood** (nā′bər hůd′) *n., adj.* —*n.* **1** the region near some place or thing. **2** a place; district: *Is your new house in an attractive neighborhood?* **3** the people of a place or district: *The whole neighborhood came to the big party.* **4** neighborly feeling or conduct. **5** (*adj.*) of or having to do with a neighborhood: *a neighborhood newspaper.* **6** nearness.
in the neighborhood of, *Informal.* somewhere near; about: *The car cost in the neighborhood of $9000.*
—*adj.* of or having to do with a neighborhood: *a neighborhood newspaper.*

neigh·bor·ing or **neigh·bour·ing** (nā′bər ing *or* nā′bring) *adj.* living or being near; bordering; adjoining; near.

neigh·bor·ly or **neigh·bour·ly** (nā′bər lē) *adj.* of, having to do with, or characteristic of neighbors who get along with each other; especially, sociable or kindly: *a neighborly chat, a neighborly atmosphere.* —**neigh′bor·li·ness** or **neigh′bour·li·ness,** *n.*

neigh·bour (nā′bər) See **neighbor.**

nei·ther (nē′ᵺər *or* nī′ᵺər) *conj., adj., pron.* —*conj.* **1** not either: *Neither you nor I will go.* **2** nor yet: *"They toil not, neither do they spin."*
—*adj.* not either: *Neither statement is true.*
—*pron.* not either: *Neither of the statements is true.* [ME *neither* < *ne* not + *either*]

nel·son (nel′sən) *n.* either of two holds in wrestling. See **half nelson** and **full nelson.** [origin uncertain]

nem·a·to·cyst (nem′ə tə sist′ *or* nə mat′ə sist′) *n.* one of the tiny stinging organs of jellyfish, and other coelenterates. Each nematocyst contains a coiled thread that can be projected as a sting.

nem·a·tode (nem′ə tōd′) *n.* any of a class (Nematoda) of worms having a long, unsegmented, round body. Some nematodes, such as hookworms, pinworms, and trichinae, are parasites in human beings and animals. [< NL *Nematoda*, pl., ult. < Gk. *nēma, -atos* thread < *neein* spin]

Ne·me·an games (ni mē′ən *or* nē′mē ən) in ancient Greece, a Panhellenic festival held every two years in Nemea.

Nemean lion the lion killed by Hercules as one of his twelve tasks.

ne·mer·te·an (ni mėr′tē ən) *n., adj.* —*n.* ribbon worm. —*adj.* of or having to do with the nemerteans or ribbon worms. [< NL *Nemertea*, the class name < Gk. *Nēmertēs*, a sea nymph + E *-an, -ian*]

nem·er·tine (nem′ər tīn′) *n., adj.* —*n.* ribbon worm; nemertean. —*adj.* of or having to do with the nemertines, or ribbon worms.

nem·e·sis (nem′ə sis) *n., pl.* **-ses** (-sēz′). **1** Nemesis, *Greek mythology.* the goddess of vengeance and retribution; the punisher of excessive pride. **2** just punishment for evil deeds. **3** a person who punishes another for evil deeds; the agent of just punishment. **4** any person or thing that seems to have the power to defeat: *When he saw his opponent, he knew he had met his nemesis.* [< Gk. *Nemesis* < *nemein* give what is due]

neo- *combining form.* new or recent, as in *Neozoic.* [< Gk. *neos*]

Ne·o·cene (nē′ə sēn′) *n., adj. Geology.* —*n.* **1** the later division of the Tertiary system, comprising the Miocene and Pliocene periods. **2** the rocks formed during this division. —*adj.* of or having to do with this division or the rocks formed during it. [*neo-* + Gk. *kainos* recent]

ne·o·clas·sic (nē′ō klas′ik) *adj.* of or having to do with neoclassicism.

ne·o·clas·si·cal (nē′ō klas′ə kəl) *adj.* neoclassic.

ne·o·clas·si·cism (nē′ō klas′ə siz′əm) *n.* **1** *Arts.* the revival of classical ideals of form, proportion, and restraint. **2** *Literature.* a similar style or movement, especially that which prevailed in 18th-century England. **3** *Music.* a 20th-century movement marked by a return to the style of classical composers such as Johann Sebastian Bach.

ne·o·clas·si·cist (nē′ō klas′ə sist) *n.* a follower of neoclassicism.

ne·o·dym·i·um (nē′ō dim′ē əm) *n.* a rare-earth metallic chemical element found in certain rare minerals. Symbol: Nd; at.no. 60; at.wt. 144.24. [< *neo-* + *didymium*]

ne·o·fas·cism (nē′ō fash′iz əm) *n.* any movement to restore the former beliefs or principles of fascism.

ne·o·fas·cist (nē′ō fash′ist) *n., adj.* —*n.* **1** a member of a political party favoring neofascism. **2** a person who supports or favors neofascism. —*adj.* of or having to do with neofascists.

ne·o·lith·ic (nē′ə lith′ik) *adj.* of the later Stone Age, when polished stone weapons and tools were first made and used, marked also by the appearance of settled agriculture and of accompanying social development: *neolithic man.* [< *neo-* + Gk. *lithos* stone]

ne·ol·o·gism (ni ol′ə jiz′əm) *n.* **1** the use of new words or new meanings for old words. **2** a new word; new meaning for an old word. [< F < Gk. *neos* new + *logos* word]

ne·o·my·cin (nē′ō mī′sən) *n.* an antibiotic or mixture of antibiotics produced by a bacterium (*Streptomyces fradiae*) found in the soil. [< *neo-* + Gk. *mykēs* fungus]

ne·on (nē′on) *n.* an inert chemical element that is a colorless, odorless gas found in very small quantities in the atmosphere. Neon is used in electric lights and signs because it gives off a glow when electricity is passed through it in a low-pressure tube. Symbol: Ne; at.no. 10; at.wt. 20.183. [< NL < Gk. *neon*, neut., new]

ne·o·na·tal (nē′ə nā′təl) *adj.* of, having to do with, or affecting the newborn child, especially a child less than a month old: *neonatal distress, a neonatal hospital unit.* —**ne′o·na′tal·ly,** *adv.*

ne·o·nate (nē′ə nāt′) *n.* a newborn child, especially one less than a month old.

ne·o·Na·zi (nē′ō nat′sē *or* -nä′tsē) *n., adj.* —*n.* **1** a member of a political party favoring neo-Naziism. **2** a person who supports or favors neo-Naziism. —*adj.* of or having to do with neo-Naziism or neo-Nazis.

ne·o·Na·zi·ism (nē′ō nat′sē iz′əm *or* -nä′tsē iz′əm) *n.* a movement to restore the principles and beliefs of Naziism.

ne·o·Na·zism (nē′ō nat′siz əm *or* -nä′tsiz əm) *n.* neo-Naziism.

ne·o·phyte (nē′ə fīt′) *n.* **1** a new convert; one recently admitted to a religious body. **2** a beginner; novice. [< L < Gk. *neophytos* < *neos* new + *phyein* to plant]

ne·o·plasm (nē′ə plaz′əm) *n.* an abnormal growth of tissue; tumor.

ne·o·prene (nē′ə prēn′) *n.* a synthetic rubber made from chloroprene.

Ne·o·zo·ic (nē′ə zō′ik) *adj. Geology.* noting or having to do with the period from the end of the Mesozoic to the present; Cenozoic. [< *neo-* + Gk. *zōē* life]

Nep·al·ese (nep′ə lēz′) *n., adj.* —*n.* a native or inhabitant of Nepal, a country lying between India and China. —*adj.* of or having to do with Nepal or its people.

ne·pen·the (ni pen′thē) *n.* **1** a drug or potion used by the ancients to bring forgetfulness of trouble or sorrow. **2** anything that brings forgetfulness. [< L < Gk. *nēpenthēs* < *nē-* not + *penthos* grief]

neph·ew (nef′yü; *esp.Brit.* nev′yü) *n.* **1** the son of one's brother or sister. **2** the son of one's brother-in-law or sister-in-law. [ME < OF *neveu* < L *nepos*]

neph·rite (nef′rīt) *n.* a silicate of calcium and either magnesium or iron, one of the two varieties of jade. It is not as hard or as valuable as jadeite, the other variety of jade. [< G *Nephrit* < Gk. *nephros* kidney (from its supposed value in curing kidney disease)]

ne·phrit·ic (ni frit′ik) *adj.* **1** of, having to do with, or located

near the kidneys; renal. 2 of, having to do with, or affected with nephritis, a kidney disease.

ne·phri·tis (ni frī′tis) *n.* acute or chronic inflammation of the kidney, caused by infection, degeneration of tissue, or disease of the blood vessels. [< LL < Gk. *nephritis* < *nephros* kidney]

ne plus ul·tra (nē′plus′ul′trə *or* nā′-) *Latin.* the highest or furthest point or state attainable; the height of excellence or achievement. [literally, 'not more beyond', said to have been inscribed on the Pillars of Hercules, the two rocks forming the western exit from the Mediterranean]

nep·o·tism (nep′ə tiz′əm) *n.* the showing of too much favor by one in power to his relatives, especially by giving them desirable appointments. [< F < Ital. *nepotismo* < *nepote* nephew]

Nep·tune (nep′tyün *or* nep′tün) *n.* **1** *Roman mythology.* the god of the sea, corresponding to the Greek god Poseidon. **2** the ocean. **3** the fourth largest planet in the solar system and the eighth in distance from the sun. It is too far from the earth to be seen with the naked eye.

nep·tu·ni·um (nep tyü′nē əm *or* nep tü′nē əm) *n.* a radio-active chemical element similar to uranium, obtained as a by-product in the production of plutonium. *Symbol:* Np; *at.no.* 93; *at.wt.* (237); *half-life* about 2.1 million years. [< *Neptune*]

Ne·re·id *or* **ne·re·id** (nēr′ē id) *n. Greek mythology.* any of the fifty daughters of Nereus. The Nereids were sea nymphs who attended Poseidon.

Ne·reus (nēr′üs *or* nēr′ē əs) *n. Greek mythology.* a sea god, father of the Nereids.

ner·ka (nēr′kə) *n.* sockeye. [? a native name]

ner·va·tion (nēr vā′shən) *n.* the arrangement of veins or ribs in a leaf or an insect's wing; venation.

nerve (nērv) *n., v.* **nerved, nerv·ing.** —*n.* **1** *Physiology.* a fibre or bundle of fibres connecting the brain or spinal cord with the eyes, ears, muscles, glands, etc. **2** mental strength; courage: *The diver lost his nerve and wouldn't go off the high board.* **3** strength; vigor; energy. **4** *Informal.* rude boldness; impudence. **5** a vein of a leaf or an insect's wing. **6 nerves,** *pl.* **a** nervousness. **b** an attack of nervousness.
get on (someone's) **nerves,** annoy or irritate one.
strain every nerve, exert oneself to the utmost.
—*v.* put strength or courage in: *The soldiers nerved themselves for the battle.* [< L *nervus* sinew, tendon]

nerve cell 1 the basic functional unit of nerve tissue, that conducts nervous impulses; neuron. **2** the cell body of a neuron, excluding its fibres.

nerve centre 1 a group of nerve cells closely connected with one another and having a common function. **2** a source of leadership or energy; a control centre or headquarters: *the economic nerve centre of the nation.*

nerve fibre one of the long, threadlike fibres of a nerve cell that conduct impulses toward or away from the body of the nerve cell.

nerve gas a gas containing invisible particles that penetrate the skin and attack the central nervous system, causing extreme weakness or death. Nerve gas is used in warfare.

nerve·less (nērv′lis) *adj.* **1** without strength or vigor; feeble; weak. **2** without courage or firmness. **3** without nerves. —**nerve′less·ly,** *adv.*

nerve–wrack·ing *or* **nerve–rack·ing** (nērv′rak′ing) *adj.* trying to the limit of endurance; exasperating.

ner·vous (nēr′vəs) *adj.* **1** of the nerves: *The brain is a part of the nervous system of the body.* **2** having delicate or easily excited nerves. **3** having or proceeding from nerves that are out of order: *a nervous patient, a nervous tapping of the fingers.* **4** deriving from a tense or quickened condition of the nerves: *nervous energy.* **5** restless; uneasy; timid. **6** having nerves. **7** strong; vigorous. [< L *nervosus* sinewy < *nervus* sinew, tendon] —**nerv′ous·ly,** *adv.* —**nerv′ous·ness,** *n.*

nervous breakdown a psychiatric disorder characterized by extreme physical and mental fatigue, irritability, chronic aches and pains of a general nature, local digestive and circulatory disturbances of uncertain origin, etc.

nervous system the system in the body of an animal or human being that receives and interprets different stimuli and conducts impulses to the glands, muscles, etc. concerned. In vertebrates, the nervous system includes the brain, spinal cord, ganglia nerves, and the parts of the sense organs that receive the stimuli.

ner·vure (nēr′vyür) *n. Biology.* **1** a vein of a leaf. **2** a rib of an insect's wing. [< F]

nerv·y (nēr′vē) *adj.* **nerv·i·er, nerv·iest. 1** *Slang.* rude and bold. **2** showing courage or firmness. **3** *Archaic or poetic.* strong; vigorous. **4** nervous.

NES or **N.E.S.** National Employment Service.

---

hat, āge, fär; let, ēqual, tèrm; it, īce
hot, ōpen, ôrder; oil, out; cup, pút, rüle,
above, takən, pencəl, lemən, circəs
ch, child; ng, long; sh, ship
th, thin; ᴛʜ, then; zh, measure

nes·cience (nesh′əns *or* nesh′ē əns) *n.* ignorance. [< LL *nescientia,* ult. < L *ne-* not + *scire* know]

ness (nes) *n.* a cape or promontory. [ME *nasse* < OE *næs,* akin to OE *nosu* nose]

–ness *noun-forming suffix.* **1** the quality, state, or condition of being—: *preparedness = the state of being prepared.* **2**—action;—behavior: *carefulness (in some uses) = careful action; careful behavior.* [OE *-nes(s)*]
☞ *Usage.* -ness is a living suffix and can be freely used to form new words.

Nes·sus (nes′əs) *n. Greek mythology.* a centaur shot by Hercules with a poisoned arrow. Hercules was himself fatally poisoned by a shirt steeped in the blood of Nessus.

nest (nest) *n., v.* —*n.* **1** a structure or place used by birds for laying eggs and rearing young. **2** a place used by insects, fish, turtles, rabbits, etc. for depositing eggs or young. **3** a snug abode, retreat, or resting place. **4** a place where evil or harmful persons gather; a den: *a nest of thieves.* **5** the birds, animals, or insects living in a nest. **6** a set or series (often from large to small) such that each fits within another: *a nest of drinking cups.* **7** *Informal.* a base for guided missiles.
—*v.* **1** build or have a nest. **2** place or fit together in a nest: *The chairs were nested and placed along the wall.* [OE]

nest egg 1 a natural or artificial egg left in a nest to induce a hen to continue laying eggs there. **2** something, usually a sum of money, as the beginning of a fund or as a reserve: *When he got married, he had already saved quite a nest egg.*

nes·tle (nes′əl) *v.* **-tled, -tling. 1** settle oneself or be settled comfortably and cosily: *to nestle down in a big chair, a house nestling among trees.* **2** press close in love or for comfort: *The mother nestled her baby in her arms.* **3** make or have a nest; settle in a nest. [OE *nestlian* < *nest* nest] —**nes′tler,** *n.*

nest·ling (nest′ling) *n.* **1** a bird too young to leave the nest. **2** a young child.

Nes·tor (nes′tər) *n.* **1** *Greek mythology.* a king who in his old age served as counsellor for the Greeks at the siege of Troy. **2** Sometimes, **nestor,** a wise old man; a patriarch or leader.

net¹ (net) *n., v.* **net·ted, net·ting.** —*n.* **1** an open fabric made of string, cord, thread, or wire, knotted together in such a way as to leave holes regularly arranged: *Veils are made of very fine net.* **2** a piece of such a fabric used for some special purpose: *a fish net, a hair net, a tennis net.* **3** anything like a net; a set of things that cross each other; network. **4** a lacelike cloth. **5** a trap or snare. **6** *Tennis, badminton, etc.* a ball that hits the net.
—*v.* **1** catch in or as if in a net: *net a fish.* **2** cover, confine, or protect with or as if with a net. **3** make into a net. **4** make with net. **5** *Tennis, badminton, etc.* hit (a ball) into the net. [OE *nett*] —**net′like′,** *adj.*

net² (net) *adj., n., v.* **net·ted, net·ting.** —*adj.* **1** real or actual; clear and free from deductions or additions. A net gain or profit is the actual gain after all working expenses have been paid. The net weight of a glass jar of candy is the weight of the candy itself. **2** final: *the net result.*
—*n.* the net weight, profit, price, etc.
—*v.* gain: *The sale netted me a good profit.* [< F. See NEAT¹.]

neth·er (neᴛʜ′ər) *adj.* lower: *nether garments, nether regions.* [OE *neothera*]

Neth·er·land·er (neᴛʜ′ər lan′dər) *n.* a native or inhabitant of the Netherlands, a small country in NW Europe, on the North Sea.

neth·er·most (neᴛʜ′ər mōst′) *adj.* lowest.

net·ting (net′ing) *n.* **1** a netted or meshed material: *mosquito netting, wire netting for window screens.* **2** the process of making a net.

net·tle (net′əl) *n., v.* **-tled, -tling.** —*n.* **1** any of a genus (*Urtica*) of plants of the nettle family having sharp hairs on the leaves and stems that sting the skin when touched. **2** any of various other prickly or stinging plants. **3** (*adj.*) designating the family (Urticaceae) of mainly tropical plants that includes the nettles. Most plants of the nettle family have stinging hairs. —*v.* sting the mind of; irritate; make angry: *She was nettled by the boy's frequent interruptions.* [OE *netele*] —**net′tle-like′,** *adj.*

net·work (net′wèrk′) *n.* **1** a netting; net. **2** any netlike combination or system of lines or channels: *a network of vines, a network of highways.* **3** a group of radio or television stations so

connected that the same program may be broadcast by all: *the French network of CBC radio.*

neu·ral (nyur′əl *or* nur′əl) *adj.* of or having to do with, or affecting a nerve or the nervous system. [< Gk. *neuron* nerve]

neu·ral·gia (nyü ral′jə *or* nü ral′jə) *n.* pain, usually sharp, along the course of a nerve. [< NL < Gk. *neuron* nerve + *algos* pain]

neu·ral·gic (nyü ral′jik *or* nü ral′jik) *adj.* of or having to do with neuralgia.

neu·ras·the·ni·a (nyür′əs thē′nē ə *or* nür′əs thē′nē ə) *n.* nervous breakdown. [< NL < Gk. *neuron* nerve + *astheneia* weakness]

neu·ras·then·ic (nyür′əs then′ik *or* nür′əs then′ik) *adj., n.* —*adj.* having to do with or suffering from neurasthenia. —*n.* a person suffering from neurasthenia.

neu·ri·tis (nyü rī′tis *or* nü rī′tis) *n.* inflammation of a nerve or nerves. [< NL < Gk. *neuron* nerve + *-itis*]

neu·rol·o·gist (nyü rol′ə jist *or* nü rol′ə jist) *n.* a person trained in neurology, especially a physician who specializes in the diagnosis and treatment of diseases of the nervous system.

neu·rol·o·gy (nyü rol′ə jē *or* nü rol′ə jē) *n.* the study of the nervous system and its diseases. [< Gk. *neuron* nerve + E *-logy*]

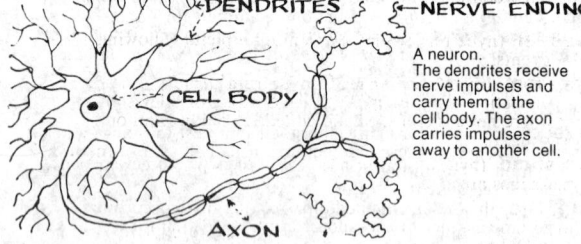

DENDRITES — NERVE ENDING

CELL BODY

AXON

A neuron. The dendrites receive nerve impulses and carry them to the cell body. The axon carries impulses away to another cell.

neu·ron (nyür′on *or* nür′on) *n.* one of the conducting cells of which the brain, spinal cord, and nerves are composed. The neuron is the basic functional unit of nervous tissue. It consists of a cell body, containing the nucleus, and its outgrowths, some of which may be very long.

neu·rone (nyür′ōn *or* nür′ōn) *n.* neuron. [< Gk. *neuron* nerve]

neu·ro·phys·i·ol·o·gy (nyür′ō fiz ē ol′ə jē *or* nür′ō-) *n.* the branch of physiology dealing with the nervous system.

neu·ro·psy·chi·a·try (nyür′ō sī kī′ə trē *or* nür′ō-) *n.* the branch of medicine dealing with neurology and psychiatry.

neu·ro·sis (nyü rō′sis *or* nü rō′sis) *n., pl.* **-ses** (-sēz) any of various usually comparatively mild mental disorders having no demonstrable physical basis and characterized chiefly by anxiety and obsessive behavior. [< NL < Gk. *neuron* nerve]

neu·ro·sur·ge·ry (nyür′ō sèr′jə rē *or* nür′ō-) *n.* surgery of the nervous system, especially of the brain.

neu·rot·ic (nyü rot′ik *or* nü rot′ik) *adj., n.* —*adj.* **1** of, having to do with, or suffering from a neurosis. **2** *Informal.* having or showing a tendency toward erratic behavior or obsession with certain unrealistic ideas. —*n.* a neurotic person. —**neu·rot′i·cal·ly,** *adv.* —**neu·rot′i·cism** (-ə siz′əm), *n.*

neut. neuter.

neu·ter (nyü′tər *or* nü′tər) *adj., n., v.* —*adj.* **1** *Grammar.* belonging to or designating the grammatical gender that includes words for a great many inanimate things and also some words for persons or animals of which the sex is not specified. In German, the words *Kind* (child), *Haus* (house), and *Licht* (light) are neuter. French has no neuter gender. Compare **feminine, masculine. 2** of insects, etc., having no sex organs or having nonfunctional or underdeveloped sex organs: *Worker bees are neuter.* **3** of flowers, having neither stamens nor pistils; sterile. **4** taking no sides; neutral. —*n.* **1** *Grammar.* **a** the neuter gender. **b** a word or form in the neuter gender. **2** a neuter insect, etc. **3** a castrated domestic animal. **4** a flower having neither stamens nor pistils. —*v.* castrate or spay (an animal). [< L *neuter* < *ne-* not + *uter* either]

neu·tral (nyü′trəl *or* nü′trəl) *adj., n.* —*adj.* **1** not taking part in a quarrel, contest, or war: *Switzerland was neutral during the last two wars in Europe.* **2** of or belonging to a neutral country or neutral zone: *a neutral port.* **3** being neither one thing nor the other; indefinite. **4** having little or no color; greyish. **5** *Chemistry.* neither acid not alkaline. **6** *Electricity.* neither positive nor negative. **7** *Biology.* not developed in sex. —*n.* **1** a neutral person or country; one not taking part in a quarrel

or war. **2** the position of gears when they do not transmit motion from the engine to the wheels or other working parts. [< L *neutralis* < *neuter.* See NEUTER.] —**neu′tral·ly,** *adv.*

neu·tral·ism (nyü′trəl iz′əm *or* nütrəl iz′əm) *n.* a policy, or the support of a policy, of remaining neutral, especially in international conflicts.

neu·tral·ist (nyü′trəl ist *or* nü′trəl ist) *n.* **1** a person who practises or advocates neutralism. **2** (*adj.*) practising or advocating neutralism: *a neutralist country.*

neu·tral·i·ty (nyü tral′ə tē *or* nü tral′ə tē) *n.* **1** the quality or state of being neutral. **2** the policy of not taking part in a quarrel, contest, or war.

neu·tral·ize (nyü′trəl īz′ *or* nü′trəl īz′) *v.* **-ized, -iz·ing. 1** make neutral; keep from taking part in war. **2** take away the power or effect or (something) by using an opposite power or force. Bases neutralize acids. —**neu′tral·i·za′tion,** *n.* —**neu′tral·iz′er,** *n.*

neutral vowel schwa.

neu·tri·no (nyü trē′nō *or* nü trē′nō) *n., pl.* **-nos.** *Physics.* an elementary particle that has no electric charge and is believed by scientists to have no mass, and that interacts only weakly with matter. Neutrinos are produced in the process of particle decay.

neu·tron (nyü′tron *or* nü′tron) *n.* a nuclear particle having almost the same mass as a proton but having no electric charge, found in the nucleus of every kind of atom except that of hydrogen. [< *neutral* neither positively nor negatively charged + *-on* (after *electron, proton*)]

neu·tron bomb a nuclear bomb designed to explode with relatively little force but to produce intense radiation over a wide area, thus causing great loss of life but relatively little destruction of property.

Nev. Nevada.

né·vé (nā′vā′) *n.* **1** granular snow that is compacted and partly converted into ice, found at the surface on the upper part of a glacier. **2** a field of this snow. [< F, ult. < L *nix, nivis* snow]

nev·er (nev′ər) *adv.* **1** not ever; at no time: *He never had to work for a living.* **2** in no case; not at all; to no extent or degree: *He was never the better for his experience. If we're careful, she'll never be the wiser.*

never mind, a pay no attention to; forget about: *Never mind the noise. Never mind your coats.* **b** it doesn't matter; forget it: *Never mind; I'll do it myself.*

never so, no matter to what extent: *He won't be able to do it, though he try never so hard.*
[OE *nǣfre* < *ne* not + *ǣfre* ever]

nev·er·more (nev′ər môr′) *adv.* never again.

nev·er-nev·er (nev′ər nev′ər) *adj., n.* —*adj. Informal.* **1** illusory; imaginary. **2** ideal; not easily visualized; implausible. —*n.* Also, **never never.** *Brit. Slang.* instalment buying.

nev·er·the·less (nev′ər Ŧнə les′) *adv.* however; none the less; for all that; in spite of it: *She was very tired; nevertheless, she kept on working.*

new (nyü *or* nü) *adj., adv.* —*adj.* **1** not existing before; having been made, grown, thought of, or produced only a short time ago: *a new invention, a new idea, a new house.* **2** now first used; not worn or used up: *a new path.* **3** beginning again: *The new moon is the moon when seen as a thin crescent.* **4** as if new; fresh: *go on with new courage. After taking a shower he felt a new man.* **5** different; changed: *He is a new man now.* **6** not familiar: *a new country to me.* **7** not yet accustomed: *new to the work.* **8** later; modern; recent: *new dances.* **9** just come; having just reached the position: *a new arrival, a new president.* **10** being the later or latest of two or more things of the same kind: *New France, New Testament.* **11** further; additional; more: *He sought new information on the subject.* —*adv.* **1** newly; recently or lately; freshly: *new-mown hay.* **2** again; anew. [OE *nīwe*] —**new′ness,** *n.*

☞ *Hom.* **gnu, knew.**

☞ *Syn. adj.* **1. New, novel, modern** = having only now or recently come into existence or knowledge. **New** describes something now existing, made, seen, or known for the first time: *They own a new house.* **Novel** adds and emphasizes the idea of being unusual, strikingly different, or strange, not of the ordinary kind: *Their house has a novel dining room.* **Modern** describes people and things belonging to or characteristic of the present time, or recent times, and sometimes suggests being up-to-date, not old-fashioned: *The architecture is modern.*

new·born (nyü′bôrn′ *or* nü′-) *adj.* **1** recently or only just born: *a newborn baby.* **2** ready to start a new life; born again.

New Bruns·wick·er (brunz′wik ər) a native or long-term resident of New Brunswick.

New Caledonia an early name for that part of British Columbia lying between the Rocky Mountains and the Coast Range.

New Canadian 1 a person who has recently arrived in Canada from another country and plans to become a Canadian citizen. **2** a person originally from another country who has recently become a Canadian citizen.

New·cas·tle (nyü′kas′əl *or* nü′-) *n.*
carry coals to Newcastle, a waste one's time, effort, etc. **b** bring something to a place where it is not needed (as coal to Newcastle, England, where it is plentiful).

new·com·er (nyü′kum′ər *or* nü′-) *n.* a person who has just come or who came not long ago.

New Deal in the United States, the policies and measures advocated in the 1930's by President Franklin D. Roosevelt as a means of improving economic and social welfare.

New Democratic Party a Canadian political party. It was formed in 1961 from the old CCF party with the assistance and support of the Canadian Labour Congress.

new·el (nyü′əl *or* nü′əl) *n.* **1** the post at the top or bottom of a stairway that supports the railing. **2** the central post of a winding stairway. [ME < OF *nouel,* ult. < L *nux* nut; influenced by OF *noel* bud, ult. < L *nodus* knot]

New Englander a native or inhabitant of New England, the NE part of the United States.

new·fan·gled (nyü′fang′gəld *or* nü′-) *adj. Facetious or derogatory.* lately come into fashion; new; novel: *He's always coming up with newfangled ideas.* [ME *newefangle* < *newe* new + *fange(n)* take]

new–fash·ioned (nyü′fash′ənd *or* nü′-) *adj.* of a new fashion; lately come into style.

New·fie (nyü′fē *or* nü′fē) *n., adj. Cdn. Informal.* —*n.*
1 Newfoundlander. **2** Newfoundland. **3** Newfoundland dog.
—*adj.* of or having to do with Newfoundland or Newfoundlanders. Also, **Newfy.**
☛ *Usage.* This term is considered offensive by many Newfoundlanders.

New·found·land (nyü′found′lənd *or* nü′-) *n.* a breed of very large, intelligent dog resembling a Saint Bernard, having a shaggy, usually black, coat. Also, **Newfoundland dog.** [< *Newfoundland,* where this powerful swimming dog was originally trained to rescue people from drowning]

New·found·land·er (nyü′fənd land′ər *or* nü′fənd land′ər, nyü′fənd land′ər *or* nü′fənd land′ər, nyü′found′lənd ər *or* nü′found′lənd ər) *n.* a native or long-term resident of Newfoundland.

New France the name of the territory in North America belonging to France from 1609 to 1763. Among other regions, it included Quebec, Acadia, and the Louisiana Territory.

New·fy (nyü′fē *or* nü′fē) See **Newfie.**

New·gate (nyü′gāt *or* nü′-) *n.* a famous prison in London. It was demolished in 1902.

New Jerusalem heaven.

New Latin the Latin language after 1500, especially as used for scientific terms. *Abbrev.:* NL or N.L.

new·ly (nyü′lē *or* nü′-) *adv.* **1** lately; recently: *newly discovered.* **2** once again; anew: *newly painted walls.* **3** in a new way: *newly arranged furniture.*

new·ly·wed (nyü′lē wed′ *or* nü′lē-) *n.* a newly married person.

new moon 1 the phase of the moon when it is between the earth and the sun, so that its dark side is toward the earth and its face is invisible. **2** the thin crescent that appears at sunset two or three days after this phase, with the hollow side on the left. See **moon** for picture. **3** the time of the new moon.

new penny *n., pl.* **new pence.** *Brit.* penny (def. 2).

news (nyüz *or* nüz) *n.* (*used with a singular verb*). **1** something told as having just happened; information about something that has just happened or will soon happen: *The news that he had been fired was a tremendous shock to his friends.* **2** a report of a current happening or happenings in a newspaper, on television, radio, etc.
break the news, make something known; tell something. [ME *newes,* pl. of *newe* that which is new, adj. used as n.]

news·a·gent (nyüz′ā′jənt *or* nüz′-) *n.* a person who owns or manages a shop selling newspapers, magazines, etc.

news·boy (nyüz′boi′ *or* nüz′-) *n.* a boy who sells newspapers.

news·cast (nyüz′kast′ *or* nüz′-) *n., v.* —*n.* a radio or television program devoted to current events, news bulletins, etc. —*v.* broadcast (news). —**news′cast′er,** *n.*

news·hound (nyüz′hound′ *or* nüz′-) *n. Informal.* a news reporter.

news·let·ter (nyüz′let′ər *or* nüz′-) *n.* a written or printed letter presenting an informal or confidential coverage of the news.

news magazine (nyüz′mag′ə zēn′ *or* nüz′-) a magazine, usually one published weekly, that reports, comments on, and interprets the news and current events.

news·man (nyüz′man′ *or* nüz′-) *n., pl.* **-men. 1** a man who sells or delivers newspapers. **2** a newspaperman or newscaster.

hat, āge, fär; let, ēqual, tėrm; it, īce
hot, ōpen, ôrder; oil, out; cup, pút, rüle,
əbove, takən, pencəl, lemən, circəs
ch, child; ng, long; sh, ship
th, thin; ᴛн, then; zh, measure

news·mon·ger (nyüz′mung′gər *or* nüz′-, nyüz′mong′gər *or* nüz′-) *n.* a person who gathers and spreads news.

news·pa·per (nyüz′pā′pər *or* nüz′-) *n.* **1** a publication consisting of folded sheets of paper usually printed daily or weekly and containing news stories and pictures, advertisements, and other reading matter of general interest. **2** the company or organization that publishes a newspaper: *She used to work for a newspaper.* **3** the printed sheets making up a newspaper: *The plants were wrapped in newspaper.*

news·pa·per·man (nyüz′pā′pər man′ *or* nüz′-) *n., pl.* **-men,** a newspaper reporter, editor, etc.

new·speak (nyü′spēk′ *or* nü′spēk′) *n.* ambiguous or contradictory language deliberately intended to mislead or confuse. [coined by George Orwell in the novel *1984,* pub. 1949]

news·print (nyüz′print′ *or* nüz′-) *n.* a soft, cheap, coarse paper made from wood pulp, the kind on which newspapers are usually printed.

news·reel (nyüz′rēl′ *or* nüz′-) *n.* a motion picture showing current events.

news·room (nyüz′rüm′ *or* nüz′-, nyüz′rùm′ *or* nüz′-) *n.* a room or section of a newspaper office or radio or television station where news is collected and edited for publication or broadcasting.

news·stand (nyüz′stand′ *or* nüz′-) *n.* a place where newspapers and magazines are sold.

New Style the present method of reckoning time, according to the Gregorian calendar. It was adopted in Great Britain in 1752. Compare **Old Style.**

news·wor·thy (nyüz′wėr′ᴛнē *or* nüz′-) *adj.* having the qualities of news; interesting or important enough to the general public to be included in a newspaper or newscast: *The reporter tried to think of an angle that would make the basically ordinary story newsworthy.*

news·y (nyüz′zē *or* nüz′zē) *adj.* **news·i·er, news·i·est;** *n., pl.*
news·ies. *Informal.* —*adj.* full of news. —*n.* a newsboy or newsman.

newt (nyüt *or* nüt) *n.* any of various small salamanders (family Salamandridae, especially genera *Triturus* and *Diemectylus*), the males of which develop an enlarged crest, or fin, on the back and tail during the breeding season. Most adult newts are aquatic only during the breeding season; some like the **red-spotted newt** (*Diemectylus viridescens*) of E North America, become permanently aquatic after a terrestrial stage lasting two or three years. [OE *efete;* ME *an ewt* taken as *a newt*]

New Testament the second part of the Christian Bible, containing the life and teachings of Jesus, as recorded by his disciples, and the teachings of the Apostle Paul.

new·ton (nyü′tən *or* nü′tən) *n.* an SI unit for measuring force. One newton is the force required to give an acceleration of one metre per second squared to a mass of one kilogram. *Symbol:* N [after Sir Isaac *Newton.* See NEWTONIAN.]

newton metre an SI unit for measuring torque or moment of force. *Symbol:* N·m

New·to·ni·an (nyü tō′nē ən *or* nü tō′nē ən) *adj.* of, having to do with, or according to Sir Isaac Newton (1642-1727), the English scientist and mathematician, or his discoveries: *Newtonian physics.*

new–world (nyü′wėrld′ *or* nü′-) *adj.* of or having to do with the Western Hemisphere.

New World 1 the western hemisphere. **2** (*adj.*) of, having to do with, or found in the New World: *New World monkeys have tails adapted for grasping and holding on.*

new year 1 the year approaching or newly begun. **2 New Year** or **New Year's,** the first day or days of the year.

New Year's Day January 1, observed as a legal holiday in many countries, including Canada.

New Zea·land·er (zē′lən dər) a native or inhabitant of New Zealand, a country of islands in the S Pacific Ocean.

next (nekst) *adj., prep., adv.* —*adj.* **1** following at once; nearest: *We'll catch the next train.* **2** the first time after this: *When you next come, bring your guitar.*
—*prep.* nearest to: *We live in the house next the church.*
next to, a immediately following or adjacent to: *Who was the girl*

next to you? **b** almost, nearly: *Chairs like these cost next to nothing. It was next to impossible to move in the crowd.* —*adv.* in the place, time, or position that is nearest: *I am going to do my arithmetic problems next.* [OE *nēhst,* superlative of *nēah* nigh]

next door 1 in or at the next house: *He lives next door to us. The woman next door owns two Saint Bernards.*
next door to, almost; very close to: *His silence was next door to an admission of guilt.*
—**next-door,** *adj.*

next of kin the nearest blood relative or relatives.

nex·us (nek′səs) *n., pl.* **nex·us.** 1 a connection; link. 2 a connected series. [< L *nexus,* ult. < *nectere* bind]

Nez Per·cé (nez′pèrs′; *French,* nā per sā′) *n., pl.* **Nez Per·cés** (nez′ pèr′siz; *French,* nā per sā′). 1 a member of an Amerindian people living in Idaho, Oregon, and Washington. 2 the language of the Nez Percés. [< F *nez percé,* literally, pierced nose]

Nez Percé horse appaloosa.

NF Newfoundland (*used esp. in computerized address systems*).

N.F. 1 Norman French. 2 New France. 3 Newfoundland.

NFB or **N.F.B.** National Film Board.

Nfld. Newfoundland.

N.G. or **n.g.** no good.

ngwee (əng gwā′ *or* əng gwē′) *n., pl.* **ngwee.** a unit of money in Zambia, equal to ¹⁄₁₀₀ of a kwacha.

NH New Hampshire.

N.H. New Hampshire.

NHL or **N.H.L.** National Hockey League.

Ni nickel.

N.I. Northern Ireland.

ni·a·cin (nī′ə sin) *n.* nicotinic acid. [< trademark < *ni*(*cotinic*) *ac*(*id*)]

nib (nib) *n.* 1 the point of a pen. 2 point or tip of anything. 3 a bird's bill. [var. of *neb*]

nib·ble (nib′əl) *v.* **-bled, -bling;** *n.* —*v.* 1 eat away with quick, small bites, as a rabbit or a mouse does. 2 bite gently or lightly: *A fish nibbles at the bait.* 3 eat little or lightly. 4 take apart or attack, as if by taking small bites: *critics nibbling at a new play.* —*n.* 1 an act of nibbling: *We've been fishing all morning and haven't had a nibble.* 2 a small piece, especially of food: *I just want a nibble of the cake.* [cf. LG *nibbelen*] —**nib′bler,** *n.*

Ni·be·lung (nē′bə lŭng′) *n., pl.* **-lungs** or **-lung·en** (-lŭng′ən). 1 *Germanic mythology.* any of a race of northern dwarfs: *Siegfried and his followers captured the treasure of the Nibelungs.* 2 one of Siegfried's followers. 3 one of the Burgundian kings in the Nibelungenlied.

Ni·be·lung·en·lied (nē′bə lŭng′ən lēd′; *German,* nē′bə lŭng′ən lēt′) *n.* a German epic poem based on Germanic legends, written in the 13th century in S Germany by an unknown author. [< G, literally, Lay of the Nibelungs]

nibs (nibz) *n.* **his** (or **her,** etc.) **nibs,** *Facetious.* a title of pretended respect for someone who is, or supposes himself to be, of importance: *How is his nibs today?* [origin uncertain]

Nic·a·ra·guan (nik′ə rä′gwən *or* nik′ə rag′wən) *n., adj.* —*n.* a native or inhabitant of Nicaragua, a republic of Central America. —*adj.* of or having to do with Nicaragua or its people.

nice (nīs) *adj.* **nic·er, nic·est.** 1 pleasing; agreeable; satisfactory: *a nice day, a nice ride, a nice child.* 2 thoughtful; kind: *He was nice to us.* 3 fine; subtle; precise: *a nice distinction, a nice shade of meaning.* 4 delicately skilful; requiring care, skill, or tact: *a nice problem.* 5 exacting; particular; hard to please; fastidious; dainty: *nice in his eating.* 6 proper; suitable. 7 scrupulous: *too nice to be a crook.* 8 *Archaic.* modest; reserved. 9 refined; cultured: *nice manners.* [ME < OF *nice* silly < L *nescius* ignorant < *ne-* not + *scire* know] —**nice′ly,** *adv.* —**nice′ness,** *n.*

Ni·cene (nī sēn′ *or* nī′sēn) *adj.* of or having to do with Nicaea, an ancient town in Asia Minor.

Nicene Council either of two general ecclesiastical councils that met at Nicaea, the first in A.D. 325 to deal with the Arian heresy, the second in A.D. 787 to consider the question of images.

Nicene Creed a formal statement of the chief tenets of Christian belief, based on that adopted by the first Nicene Council, and generally accepted throughout western Christendom.

ni·ce·ty (nī′sə tē) *n., pl.* **-ties.** 1 exactness; accuracy; delicacy: *Television sets require nicety of adjustment.* 2 a fine point; small

distinction; detail. 3 the quality of being very particular; daintiness; refinement. 4 something dainty or refined.
to a nicety, just right: *cakes browned to a nicety.*
[ME < OF *nicete* < *nice.* See NICE.]

niche (nich) *n.* 1 a recess or hollow in a wall for a statue, vase, etc. 2 a suitable place or position; place for which a person is suited: *John will find his niche in the world.* [< F *niche,* ult. < L *nidus* nest]

Nich·o·las (nik′ə ləs or nik′ləs) See **Saint Nicholas.**

nick (nik) *n., v.* —*n.* a place where a small bit has been cut or broken out; notch; groove: *He cut nicks in a stick to keep count of his score.*
in the nick of time, just in time; barely in time.
—*v.* 1 make a nick or nicks in: *I nicked the edge of the plate while washing it.* 2 cut into or wound slightly: *The bullet just nicked his arm.* 3 hit, guess, catch, etc. exactly. [origin uncertain]

nick·el (nik′əl) *n., v.* **-elled** or **-eled, -el·ling** or **-el·ing.** —*n.* 1 a hard, malleable, silvery-white metallic element that is resistant to rust, used mainly in alloys. *Symbol:* Ni; *at.no.* 28; *at.wt.* 58.71. 2 a five-cent piece. 3 five cents: *The paper costs a nickel a sheet.* —*v.* cover or coat with nickel. [< Swedish < G *Kupfernickel,* literally, copper devil; the ore resembles copper but yields none]

nick·el·o·de·on (nik′əl ō′dē ən) *n.* 1 in the early days of motion pictures, a place of amusement with motion-picture exhibitions, etc., to which the price of admission was five cents. 2 juke box. [< *nickel* + *odeon,* var. of *odeum* < L < Gk. *oideion* music hall < *ōidē* song]

nickel plate a thin coating of nickel deposited on a metal object to prevent rust, improve the appearance, etc.

nick·el–plate (nik′əl plāt′) *v.* **-plat·ed, -plat·ing.** coat with nickel.

nickel silver a hard, tough, silver-white alloy of copper, zinc, and nickel used to make utensils, wire, etc.

nick–nack (nik′nak′) *n.* knick-knack.

nick·name (nik′nām′) *n., v.* **-named, -nam·ing.** —*n.* 1 a short or familiar form of a proper name: *"The Alex" is a nickname for the Royal Alexandra Theatre. Elizabeth's nickname is "Betty."* 2 a name used instead of a proper name: *Roy's nickname was "Buzz."* —*v.* give a nickname to: *They nicknamed the short boy "Shorty."* [ME *ekename* < *eke* an addition, OE *ēaca* + *name* name, OE *nama; an ekename* taken as *a nekename*]

nic·o·tine (nik′ə tēn′) *n.* a poisonous alkaloid contained in the leaves of tobacco. *Formula:* $C_{10}H_{14}N_2$ [< F < NL *herba nicotiana* Nicot's plant, after Jacques *Nicot* (1530-1600), a French ambassador to Portugal, who introduced tobacco into France about 1560]

nic·o·tin·ic acid (nik′ə tin′ik) an acid of the vitamin B complex found in meat, eggs, wheat germ, etc.; niacin. A deficiency of nicotinic acid can cause pellagra. *Formula:* $C_6H_5NO_2$

nic·ti·tate (nik′tə tāt′) *v.* **-at·ed, -at·ing.** wink. [< Med.L *nictitare* blink repeatedly < *nictare* blink]

nictitating membrane in reptiles, birds, and some other animals, a thin membrane inside the lower eyelid or at the inside corner of the eye, that can be extended across the eye. Also called **third eyelid.**

niece (nēs) *n.* 1 the daughter of one's brother or sister. 2 a daughter of a brother or sister of one's spouse. [ME < OF *niece,* ult. < L *neptis* granddaughter]

nif·ty (nif′tē) *adj.* **-ti·er, -ti·est.** *Slang.* attractive; stylish. [origin uncertain]

Ni·ger–Con·go (nī′gər kong′gō) *n.* a family of languages of Africa that includes the Bantu languages and most of the languages of the coastal regions of W Africa.

Ni·ge·ri·an (nī jēr′ē ən) *n., adj.* —*n.* a native or inhabitant of Nigeria, a country in W Africa. —*adj.* of or having to do with Nigeria or its people.

nig·gard (nig′ərd) *n., adj.* —*n.* a stingy person. —*adj.* stingy. [ME < earlier *nig* < Scand. + E pejorative suffix *-ard,* as in *drunkard;* cf. ON *hnöggr* stingy]

nig·gard·ly (nig′ərd lē) *adj., adv.* —*adj.* 1 stingy. 2 meanly small or scanty: *a niggardly gift.* —*adv.* stingily. —**nig′gard·li·ness,** *n.*

nig·ger (nig′ər) *n.* 1 *Offensive.* a member of a dark-skinned race, especially a Negro. 2 *Slang.* any person discriminated against or treated as a second-class citizen. [< *neger* < *nègre* < Sp. *negro.* See NEGRO.]

nig·gle (nig′əl) *v.* **-gled, -gling.** be concerned with petty or trifling things or details. [apparently < Scand.; cf. dial. Norwegian *nigla*] —**nig′gler,** *n.*

nigh (nī) *adv., adj.* **nigh·er, nigh·est** or **next;** *prep. Archaic, poetic, or dialect.* —*adv.* 1 near: *Dawn was nigh.* 2 nearly: *He was nigh dead with fright.* —*adj.* or *prep.* near. [OE *nēah*]

night (nīt) *n.* 1 the period of darkness between evening and morning; the time between sunset and sunrise. 2 the darkness of

night; the dark: *She went out into the night.* **3** the darkness of ignorance, sin, sorrow, old age, death, etc.: *the night of despair.* **4** nightfall: *We expect to get back before night.* **5** (*adj.*) of or having to do with night: *cold night winds.* **6** (*adj.*) working or for use at night: *a night light.* **7** (*advl.*) **nights,** regularly or habitually in the nighttime: *He works nights.*

make a night of it, celebrate until very late at night. [OE *niht*]
☞ *Hom.* knight.

night blindness the inability to see well in dim light, as at night.

night·cap (nīt′kap′) *n.* **1** a cap for wearing in bed: *Nightcaps are not much worn these days.* **2** a drink taken just before going to bed. **3** *Informal.* the last event in a sports program, especially the second baseball game of a double-header.

night·club (nīt′klub′) *n.* a place for dancing, eating, and entertainment, open only at night.

night·crawl·er (nīt′krol′ər *or* -krôl′ər) *n. Esp.U.S.* dew-worm.

night·dress (nīt′dres′) *n.* nightgown.

night·fall (nīt′fol′ *or* -fôl′) *n.* the coming of night.

night·gown (nīt′goun′) *n.* **1** a loose women's or girls' garment for wearing in bed. **2** nightshirt.

night·hawk (nīt′hok′ *or* -hôk′) *n.* **1** any of a genus (*Chordeiles*) of North American goatsuckers having dark, mottled plumage. The **common nighthawk** (*C. minor*) is a familiar bird throughout most of Canada. **2** *Informal.* night owl.

night·ie (nīt′ē) *n. Informal.* nightgown.

night·in·gale (nīt′ən gāl′ *or* nīt′ing gāl′) *n.* **1** any of several thrushes (genus *Luscinia*) of Europe and Asia noted for the sweet song of the male; especially, a small, reddish-brown bird (*L. megarhynchos*) having a varied song with loud and soft notes which it sings by night or day. **2** any of various other birds noted for their song. [for *nightgale*, OE *nihtegale* < *niht* night + *galan* sing]

night·jar (nīt′jär′) *n.* **1** a common European goatsucker (*Caprimulgus europaeus*) having greyish-brown mottled and barred plumage and noted for its chirring call. **2** *Esp.Brit.* any goatsucker.

night latch a door lock opened by a key from the outside or by a knob from the inside.

night letter a reduced-rate telegram that is delivered the day after it is accepted by the telegraph office. A night letter is accepted at any time during the day or night up to 2:00 a.m. for delivery after 8:00 a.m. the next day.

night light a small lamp that provides a dim light, used especially by the bed of a child or of a sick person at night.

night·light·ing (nīt′līt′ing) *n.* jacklighting. —**night′light′er,** *n.*

night·long (nīt′long′) *adj., adv.* —*adj.* lasting all night. —*adv.* through the whole night.

night·ly (nīt′lē) *adj., adv.* —*adj.* **1** done, happening, or appearing every night. **2** done, happening, or appearing at night. —*adv.* **1** every night: *Performances are given nightly except on Sunday.* **2** at night; by night.
☞ *Hom.* knightly.

night·mare (nīt′mer′) *n.* **1** a frightening dream. **2** a very unpleasant or frightening experience: *The dust storm was a nightmare.* **3** a sight, object, or person such as might be seen in a nightmare. [ME < OE *niht* night + *mare* monster oppressing men during sleep]

night·mar·ish (nīt′mer′ish) *adj.* like a nightmare; strange and horrifying; causing fear. —**night′mar′ish·ly,** *adv.*

night owl *Informal.* a person who often stays up late.

night school a school held in the evening for persons who work during the day.

night·shade (nīt′shād′) *n.* **1** any of various plants of the nightshade family having berries that are often poisonous. The common nightshade, also called bittersweet, and the deadly nightshade, also called belladonna, both have poisonous berries. **2** (*adj.*) designating a family (Solanaceae) of mainly tropical herbs, shrubs, and trees having flowers in clusters and fruit in the form of a capsule or berry. The tomato, potato, eggplant, peppers, and hemp belong to the nightshade family. [OE *nihtscada*]

night·shirt (nīt′shėrt′) *n.* a man's or boy's loose garment for wearing in bed.

night·spot (nīt′spot′) *n. Informal.* nightclub.

night·stick (nīt′stick′) *n.* a police officer's stick or club; billy; truncheon.

night·time (nīt′tīm′) *n.* the time between evening and morning.

night watch **1** a watch or guard kept during the night. **2** the person or persons keeping such a watch. **3** a period or division of the night.

night watchman a person who guards a store, factory, etc. at night.

hat, āge, fär; let, ēqual, tėrm; it, īce
hot, ōpen, ôrder; oil, out; cup, pùt, rüle,
əbove, takən, pencəl, lemən, circəs
ch, child; ng, long; sh, ship
th, thin; ŦH, then; zh, measure

ni·hil (nī′hil) *n. Latin.* nothing.

ni·hil·ism (nī′ə liz′əm) *n.* **1** the entire rejection of the usual beliefs in religion, morals, government, laws, etc. **2** *Philosophy.* the denial of all existence. **3** in Russia, the beliefs of a revolutionary party, which found nothing good in the old order of things and wished to clear it away to make place for a better state of society. **4** the use of violent methods against a ruler. [< L *nihil* nothing]

Ni·hil·ism (nī′ə liz′əm) *n.* the beliefs of a 19th-century Russian revolutionary party, that advocated the removal of the old society by violence and terror.

ni·hil·ist (nī′ə list) *n.* **1** a person who believes in some form of nihilism. **2** terrorist.

Ni·hil·ist (nī′ə list) *n.* a member of the Russian revolutionary party that advocated Nihilism.

ni·hil·is·tic (nī′ə lis′tik) *adj.* of nihilists or nihilism.

Ni·ke (nī′kē *or* nē′kā) *n. Greek mythology.* the goddess of victory, usually represented with outspread wings.

nil (nil) *n.* nothing. [< L *nil*, a shortened form of *nihil*]

nim·ble (nim′bəl) *adj.* **-bler, -blest. 1** able to move lightly and quickly; agile: *Her nimble fingers flew over the piano keys.* **2** quick to understand; clever: *a nimble mind.* [ME *nymel* < OE *niman* take] —**nim′ble·ness,** *n.* —**nim′bly,** *adv.*

nim·bo·stra·tus (nim′bō strā′təs *or* -strat′əs) *n., pl.* **-ti** (-tī *or* -tē). a low, dark-grey cloud layer that brings rain or snow. [< L *nimbus* + E *stratus*]

nim·bus (nim′bəs) *n., pl.* **-bus·es, -bi** (-bī *or* -bē). **1** a light disk or other radiance about the head of a divine or sacred person in a picture. **2** a bright cloud surrounding a god, person, or thing. **3** a rain cloud. [< L *nimbus* cloud]

Nim·rod (nim′rod) *n.* **1** in the Bible, a king who was a great builder and a mighty hunter (Gen. 10: 8-9). **2** any enthusiastic hunter.

nin·com·poop (nin′kəm püp′ *or* ning′kəm püp′) *n.* a fool; simpleton. [origin uncertain]

nine (nīn) *n., adj.* —*n.* **1** one more than eight; 9. **2** the numeral 9: *The 9 is bigger than the other numerals.* **3** the ninth in a set or series; especially a playing card having nine spots: *the nine of clubs.* **4** *Baseball.* a team of nine players. **5** *Golf.* the first or last nine holes of an 18-hole course. **6** any set or series of nine persons or things. **7 the Nine,** the Muses.

dressed (up) to the nines, *Informal.* very formally or elaborately dressed: *I showed up in my jeans and found that everyone else was dressed to the nines.*

—*adj.* **1** being one more than eight. **2** being ninth in a set or series (*used mainly after the noun*): *Chapter Nine was very exciting.* [OE *nigon*]

nine days' wonder anything that causes a short period of excitement and great interest.

nine–eight (nīn′āt′) *adj. Music.* indicating or having nine eighth notes in a bar or measure.

nine·fold (nīn′fōld′) *adj., adv.* —*adj.* **1** nine times as much or as many. **2** having nine parts. —*adv.* nine times as much or as many.

nine·pins (nīn′pinz′) *n.* **1** a game in which nine large wooden pins are set up to be bowled down with a ball (*used with a singular verb*): *Ninepins resembles tenpins.* **2** the pins used in this game.

nine·teen (nīn′tēn′) *n., adj.* —*n.* **1** nine more than ten; 19. **2** the numeral 19: *The nineteen is bigger than the other numbers.* **3** the nineteenth in a set or series. **4** a set or series of nineteen persons or things.

—*adj.* **1** being nine more than ten; 19: *He lived there for nineteen years.* **2** being nineteenth in a set or series (*used after the noun*): *Chapter Nineteen.* [OE *nigontēne*]

nine·teenth (nīn′tēnth′) *adj., n.* —*adj.* next after the 18th; last in a series of 19; 19th. —*n.* **1** the next after the 18th; last in a series of 19. **2** one of 19 equal parts.

nine·ti·eth (nīn′tē ith) *adj., n.* —*adj.* next after the 89th; last in a series of 90; 90th. —*n.* **1** the next after the 89th; last in a series of 90. **2** one of 90 equal parts.

nine·ty (nīn′tē) *n., pl.* **-ties;** *adj.* —*n.* **1** nine times ten; 90. **2 nineties,** *pl.* the years from ninety through ninety-nine, especially of a century or of a person's life: *He was in his nineties when he died.* —*adj.* being nine times ten; 90. [OE *nigontig*]

Nin·e·veh (nin'ə və) *n.* an ancient city of Assyria. Its ruins are on the Tigris River, opposite Mosul in N Iraq.

nin·ny (nin'ē) *n., pl.* **-nies.** fool. [? < *an innocent naïve*, simple person; 16c.]

ninth (nīnth) *adj., n.* —*adj.* next after the eighth; last in a series of nine; 9th. —*n.* **1** the next after the eighth; last in a series of nine. **2** one of nine equal parts.

Ni·o·be (nī'ō bē *or* nī'ə bē) *n. Greek mythology.* a mother whose fourteen beautiful children were slain because she boasted about them. Turned by Zeus into a stone fountain, she weeps forever for her children.

ni·o·bi·um (nī ō'bē əm) *n.* a rare, steel-grey, metallic chemical element that resembles tantalum in chemical properties. *Symbol*: Nb; *at.no.* 41; *at.wt.* 92.906. [< NL; after *Niobe*]

nip¹ (nip) *v.* **nipped, nip·ping;** *n.* —*v.* **1** squeeze tight and suddenly; pinch; bite: *The crab nipped my toe.* **2** take off by biting, pinching, or snipping. **3** stop or spoil the growth, progress, or fulfilment of: *a new government policy designed to nip inflation.* **4** injure or make numb with cold: *The cold wind nipped our ears. The flowers were all nipped by frost.*
nip in the bud, stop or spoil at the very beginning: *All his plans were nipped in the bud by the sudden death of his benefactor.*
—*n.* **1** a tight squeeze or pinch; sudden bite. **2** stinging cold; chill: *There was a nip in the air.* **3** a strong, sharp flavor; tang: *cheese with a nip.* **4** a small bit.
nip and tuck, *Informal.* in a race or contest, so evenly matched that the issue remains in doubt till the end.
[ME *nyppen*; cf. Du. *nijpen*]

nip² (nip) *n., v.* **nipped, nip·ping.** —*n.* a small drink: *a nip of brandy.* —*v.* drink nips. [for *nipperkin* a small vessel; origin uncertain]

nip·per (nip'ər) *n.* **1** a person or thing that nips, especially a big claw of a lobster or crab. **2** *Informal.* a small boy. **3 nippers,** *pl.* pincers, forceps, pliers, or any tool that nips.

nip·ple (nip'əl) *n.* **1** the round projection in the centre of the mammary gland which, in females, contains the outlet of the milk ducts. **2** the mouthpiece of a baby's bottle. **3** something shaped or used like a nipple. [earlier *neble*, probably dim. of *neb* peak, tip]

Nip·pon·ese (nip'ə nēz') *adj. or n.* **-ese.** Japanese.

nip·py (nip'ē) *adj.* **-pi·er, -pi·est. 1** chilly; biting: *nippy weather.* **2** sharp; pungent: *nippy cheese.*

nir·va·na *or* **Nir·va·na** (nèr vä'nə *or* nèr van'ə) *n.*
1 *Buddhism.* the enlightened level of being a person who has overcome the desires and the pain or worldly existence; a peaceful, pure, and deathless state which becomes complete and perfect when the body dies. The desires of life are thought of as a fever and Nirvana is the extinguishing or cooling of this fever. **2** *Hinduism.* freedom of the soul; reunion with the universal soul reached by the suppression of individual existence. **3** blessed oblivion. [< Skt. *nirvāna* extinction < *nis-* out + *vā-* blow]

Ni·san (nē sän' *or* nis'ən) *n.* in the Hebrew calendar, the first month of the ecclesiastical year, and the seventh month of the civil year.

Ni·sei (nē'sā') *n., pl.* **-sei.** a native-born Canadian or United States citizen whose parents were Japanese immigrants. [< Japanese *nisei* second generation < *ni* two + *sei* generation]

Nis·sen hut (nis'ən) a prefabricated shelter for soldiers, semicylindrical in shape, made of corrugated iron, with a concrete floor. [after Lt.Col. Peter N. *Nissen* (1871-1930), who designed it]

nit¹ (nit) *n.* the egg or the young of a louse or similar insect. [OE *hnitu*]
☛ *Hom.* **knit.**

nit² (nit) *n. Esp.Brit. Informal.* nitwit.

nitch·ie (nich'ē) *n. Cdn.* **1** in Indian use, a friend (especially of another Indian). **2** *Derogatory slang.* an Indian. **3** *Rare.* a small Indian pony; cayuse. [< Algonquian]

ni·ter (nī'tər) See **nitre.**

nit–pick (nit'pik') *v.* engage in nit-picking. —**nit'–pick'er,** *n.*

nit–pick·ing (nit'pik'ing) *n. or adj.* criticizing and complaining in a petty manner; criticizing unimportant details; faultfinding: *You're being a little nit-picking in your criticism.*

ni·trate (nī'trāt) *n., v.* **-trat·ed, -trat·ing.** —*n.* **1** a salt or ester of nitric acid. **2** potassium nitrate or sodium nitrate, used as a fertilizer. —*v.* treat with nitric acid or a nitrate. —**ni·tra'tion,** *n.*

ni·tre (nī'tər) *n.* **1** potassium nitrate, obtained from potash, used in making gunpowder; saltpetre. *Formula*: KNO_3 **2** sodium nitrate or Chile saltpetre, used as a fertilizer. *Formula*: $NaNO_3$ Also, **niter.** [< F < L *nitrum* < Gk. *nitron.* < Semitic. Doublet of NATRON.]

ni·tric (nī'trik) *adj.* of or containing nitrogen, especially with a higher valence than in corresponding nitrous compounds. [< F *nitrique*]

nitric acid a clear, colorless liquid that eats into flesh, clothing, metal, and other substances. Nitric acid is used as an oxidizing agent and in making dyes, fertilizers, and explosives. *Formula*: HNO_3

ni·tride (nī'trīd *or* nī'trid) *n.* a compound of nitrogen with a more electropositive element or radical, such as phosphorus, boron, or a metal.

ni·tri·fy (nī'trə fī') *v.* **-fied, -fy·ing. 1** oxidize (ammonia compounds, etc.) to nitrites or nitrates, especially by bacterial action. **2** impregnate (soil, etc.) with nitrates. [< F *nitrifier*]
—**ni'tri·fi·ca'tion,** *n.*

ni·trite (nī'trīt) *n.* a salt or ester of nitrous acid.

ni·tro·ben·zene (nī'trō ben'zēn *or* -ben zēn') *n.* a poisonous, yellowish liquid obtained from benzene by the action of nitric acid, used as a solvent, etc. *Formula*: $C_6H_5NO_2$

ni·tro·gen (nī'trə jən) *n.* a colorless, odorless, tasteless gaseous chemical element that forms about four fifths of the earth's atmosphere by volume. *Symbol*: N; *at.no.* 7; *at.wt.* 14.0067. [< F *nitrogène* < Gk. *nitron* native sodium carbonate + *-genēs* born, produced]

ni·trog·e·nous (nī troj'ə nəs) *adj.* of or containing nitrogen or a compound of nitrogen.

ni·tro·glyc·er·in *or* **ni·tro·glyc·er·ine** (nī trə glis'ər in) *n.* a heavy, oily, explosive liquid made by treating glycerin with nitric and sulphuric acids. Nitroglycerin is used in dynamite. *Formula*: $C_3H_5(NO_3)_3$

ni·trous (nī'trəs) *adj.* **1** of or containing nitrogen, especially with a lower valence than in corresponding nitric compounds. **2** of or containing nitre. [< L *nitrosus* < *nitrum.* See NITRE.]

nitrous oxide a colorless, nonflammable gas having a sweet taste and smell, used as an anesthetic, especially in dentistry. Also called **laughing gas.** *Formula*: N_2O

nit·ty–grit·ty (nit'ē grit'ē) *n. Informal.* basic reality; actual fact or essence: *Let's get down to the nitty-gritty of who is going to pay for the broken window.*

nit·wit (nit'wit') *n. Slang.* a stupid or scatterbrained person. [< *nit* + *wit*]

nix¹ (niks) *n., interj., v. Slang.* —*n. or interj.* **1** no. **2** nothing. —*v.* reject or veto: *The city council nixed the proposal.* [< G *nix*, dial. var. of *nichts* nothing]

nix² (niks) *n., pl.* **nix·es.** *Germanic mythology.* a water sprite. [< colloquial Du. *or* G]

nix·ie (nik'sē) *n. German mythology.* a female nix. [< G *Nixe*]

Ni·zam (ni zäm' *or* ni zam', nī zäm' *or* nī zam') *n. Historical.* the title of the ruler of Hyderabad, India. [< Urdu and Turkish *nizām* < Arabic *nizām* order, arrangement]

NJ New Jersey.

N.J. New Jersey.

NKVD *Historical.* the secret police of the Soviet Union, now the MVD.

NL *or* **N.L.** New Latin.

NM New Mexico.

N.Mex. New Mexico.

NNE *or* **N.N.E.** north-northeast.

NNW *or* **N.N.W.** north-northwest.

no (nō) *n., pl.* **noes;** *adj., adv.* —*n.* **1** a word used to deny, refuse, or disagree. **2** a denial; refusal. **3** a negative vote or voter: *The noes have it.*
—*adj.* not any; not a: *He has no friends.* [var. of *none*]
—*adv.* **1** a word used to deny, refuse, or disagree: *Will you come with us? No.* **2** not in any degree; not at all: *He is no better.* **3** not, chiefly in phrases like *whether or no.* [OE *nā* < *ne* not + *ā* ever]
☛ *Hom.* **know.**
☛ *Usage.* See note at **yes.**

No nobelium.

No. 1 north; northern. **2** Also, **no.,** number (for L *numero,* ablative of *numerus* number).
☛ *Usage.* **No.** The abbreviation **No.** for **number** (from the Latin *numero* by number) is usually written with a capital. It is appropriate chiefly in business and technical English, although nowadays it is usually replaced by the symbol #.

no–ac·count (nō'ə kount') *adj., n. Informal.* —*adj.* no good; worthless. —*n.* a good-for-nothing person; a person of no importance at all.

No·ah (nō'ə) *n.* in the Bible, a man who was told by God to build an ark to save himself, his family, and a pair of each kind of animal from the Flood (Gen. 5:28-9:29).

Noah's Ark the ark built by Noah.

nob (nob) *n. Slang.* **1** head. **2** a person of wealth or social importance. [? var. of *knob*]
☛ *Hom.* **knob.**

nob·by (nob′ē) *adj.* **-bi·er, -bi·est.** *Slang.* **1** smart; fashionable; elegant. **2** first-rate.

no·be·li·um (nō bē′lē əm) *n.* an artificial radio-active element. *Symbol:* No; *at.no.* 102; *at.wt.* (255); *half-life* approx. 180 seconds. [< Alfred B. *Nobel*, who established the Nobel prizes]

No·bel prize (nō bel′) any of a group of prizes for physics, chemistry, physiology or medicine, literature, economic sciences, and the promotion of peace, established by Alfred B. Nobel (1833-1896), a Swedish chemist, engineer, and philanthropist, to be given annually to the person or persons who have contributed most in each of these fields. The prizes were first awarded in 1901.

no·bil·i·ty (nō bil′ə tē) *n., pl.* **-ties. 1** people of noble rank. Earls, marquises, and counts belong to the nobility. **2** noble birth; noble rank. **3** noble character or quality: *the nobility of an act.* [ME < OF < L *nobilitas*]

no·ble (nō′bəl) *adj.* **-bler, -blest;** *n.* —*adj.* **1** high and great by birth, rank, or title. **2** high and great in character; showing greatness of mind; illustrious; outstanding: *a noble person, a noble deed.* **3** excellent; fine; splendid; magnificent: *Niagara Falls is a noble sight.* **4** of metals, resisting oxidation or corrosion: *Gold is a noble metal.* **5** of certain gaseous elements, chemically inert: *Helium, neon, etc. are noble gases.*
—*n.* **1** a person high and great by birth, rank, or title: *A duke is a noble.* **2** a former British gold coin worth one third of a pound. [< F < L *nobilis* renowned] —**no′ble·ness, n.**
☛ *Syn. adj.* 3. See note at **grand.**

no·ble·man (nō′bəl mən) *n., pl.* **-men.** a man who belongs to nobility; a man of noble rank or birth.

no·blesse o·blige (nô bles′ ô blēzh′) *French.* persons of noble rank should behave nobly.

no·ble·wom·an (nō′bəl wùm′ən) *n., pl.* **-wom·en.** a woman who belongs to nobility; a woman of noble birth or rank.

no·bly (nō′blē) *adv.* in a noble manner; splendidly; as a noble person would do.

no·bod·y (nō′bud′ē, nō′bod′ē *or* nō′bə dē) *pron., n., pl.* **-bod·ies.** —*pron.* no one; no person. —*n.* a person of no importance.
☛ *Usage.* **Nobody, nothing, nowhere** are written as single words. **Nobody** and **nothing** are singular, although informally **nobody** is sometimes followed by a plural pronoun: *Nothing is further from the truth. Nobody thinks that his own dog is a nuisance.* Informal: *Nobody thinks their own dog is a nuisance.* See also the note at **everybody.**

nock (nok) *n., v.* —*n.* a notch on a bow or arrow for the bowstring. —*v.* **1** make such a notch. **2** fit (an arrow) to the bowstring for shooting. [ME *nocke*]
☛ *Hom.* **knock.**

noc·tur·nal (nok tėr′nəl) *adj.* **1** of, belonging to, or occurring at night: *a nocturnal journey. The stars are a nocturnal sight.* **2** of animals, active during the night instead of the day: *The owl is a nocturnal bird.* **3** of plants, having flowers that open only at night: *One species of cereus cactus is nocturnal.* [< LL *nocturnalis,* ult. < L *nox, noctis* night]

noc·tur·nal·ly (nok tėr′nəl ē) *adv.* **1** at night. **2** every night.

noc·turne (nok′tėrn) *n.* **1** *Music.* a dreamy or pensive composition. **2** a painting of a night scene. [< F]

nod (nod) *v.* **nod·ded, nod·ding;** *n.* —*v.* **1** bow (the head) slightly and raise it again quickly. **2** show agreement by nodding: *I asked him if the baby was asleep and he nodded.* **3** express by bowing the head: *nod consent.* **4** let the head fall forward and bob about when sleepy or falling asleep. **5** be sleepy; become careless and dull: *She was beginning to nod before the meeting was halfway through.* **6** droop, bend, or sway back and forth: *Trees nod in the wind.*
—*n.* a nodding of the head.
get or **give the nod,** *Informal.* **a** receive or give approval. **b** receive or give a victory or decision to.
[ME *nodden*; origin uncertain]

nod·al (nō′dəl) *adj.* having to do with, located near, or being a node: *the nodal joints of a stem.*

nod·ding (nod′ing) *adj.* casual; slight: *a nodding acquaintance.*

nod·dle (nod′əl) *n. Informal.* the head. [ME *nodel, nodul;* origin uncertain]

nod·dy (nod′ē) *n., pl.* **-dies.** a fool. [origin uncertain]

node (nōd) *n.* **1** a knot; knob; swelling. **2** a joint in a stem; the part of a stem from which leaves grow. See **stem**[1] for picture. **3** *Physics.* a point, line, or plane in a vibrating body at which there is comparatively no vibration. **4** a knotlike swelling or mass of specialized tissue on the body or an organ: *a lymph node.* **5** *Geometry.* a point at which a curve intersects itself so that each of

the branches has a distinct tangent. **6** a central point in a system; point of concentration. **7** a complication or predicament in the plot or character development of a story, play, etc. [< L *nodus* knot]

nod·u·lar (noj′əl ər) *adj.* having nodules.

nod·ule (noj′ül) *n.* **1** a small knot, knob, or swelling. **2** a small, rounded mass or lump: *nodules of pure gold.* **3** *Botany.* a small tuber. [< L *nodulus,* dim. of *nodus* knot]

no·ël (nō əl′) *n.* **1** a Christmas song; carol. **2 Noël,** Christmas. [< F < L *natalis* natal (i.e. the natal day of Christ) < *nasci* be born. Doublet of NATAL.]

no-fault (nō′folt′ *or* -fôlt′) *adj.* of, having to do with, or designating a type of automobile insurance under which a person is compensated by his own insurance company for injury or damage due to an accident, regardless of who is to blame for the accident.

nog·gin (nog′ən) *n.* **1** a small mug. **2** a small measure of liquor, usually one gill (about 0.142L). **3** *Informal.* a person's head. [origin uncertain]

no-hit·ter (nō′hit′ər) *n. Baseball.* a game in which the pitcher prevents the opposing team from gaining any base hits.

no-holds-barred (nō′hōldz′bärd′) *adj. Informal.* **1** without rules or restrictions; unrestrainedly violent: *a no-holds-barred fight.* **2** complete; utmost: *a no-holds-barred effort.*

no-how (nō′hou′) *adv. Informal.* in no way; not at all.

noil (noil) *n.* **1** a short fibre combed out during the preparation of wool, cotton, or silk yarn. **2** the waste material composed of these fibres. [origin unknown]

noise (noiz) *n., v.* **noised, nois·ing.** —*n.* **1** a sound that is not musical or pleasant; loud or harsh sound: *The noise kept me awake.* **2** any sound: *the noise of rain on the roof.* **3** a din of voices and movements; loud shouting; outcry; clamor. **4** *Physics.* a group of sound waves which are not periodic and which are produced by irregular vibrations; sound of no single fundamental frequency but many nonharmonic frequency components of varying amplitudes randomly placed. **5** any undesired or unintended disturbance in a radio or television signal.
—*v. Archaic.* spread the news of; tell: *It was noised abroad that the king was dying.* [ME < OF *noise* < L *nausea.* Doublet of NAUSEA.]
☛ *Syn. n.* 1. Noise, din, uproar = disagreeably loud, confused, or harsh and clashing sound. **Noise** applies to any disagreeably unmusical or loud sound made by one or more people or things: *The noise kept me awake.* **Din** applies to a prolonged and deafening confusion of clanging or piercing noises: *The din of machines and factory whistles hurt my ears.* **Uproar** applies especially to the tumult, shouting, and loud noises of a crowd: *You should have heard the uproar when officials called back the touchdown.*

noise·less (noiz′lis) *adj.* making little or no noise: *a noiseless electric fan.* —**noise′less·ly,** *adv.* —**noise′less·ness,** *n.*

noise·mak·er (noiz′māk′ər) *n.* a person or thing that makes noise, especially, a horn, rattle, etc. used to make noise at a party, sports event, etc.

noi·some (noi′səm) *adj.* **1** offensive; disgusting; smelling bad: *a noisome slum.* **2** harmful; injurious: *a noisome pestilence.* [< *noy* (var. of *annoy*) + *-some*] —**noi′some·ly,** *adv.* —**noi′some·ness,** *n.*

nois·y (noi′zē) *adj.* **nois·i·er, nois·i·est. 1** making much noise: *a noisy boy.* **2** full of noise: *a noisy street.* **3** characterized by noise; accompanied by much noise: *a noisy quarrel, a noisy game.*
—**nois′i·ly,** *adv.* —**nois′i·ness,** *n.*
☛ *Syn.* 1. See note at **loud.**

nom. nominative.

no·mad (nō′mad) *n.* **1** a member of a people that moves from place to place so as to have pasture for its cattle or to be near its own food or water supply: *The Inuit have traditionally been nomads.* **2** (*adj.*) nomadic: *nomad peoples, a nomad way of life.* **3** wanderer. [< L < Gk. *nomas, -ados,* ult. < *nemein* to pasture]

no·mad·ic (nō mad′ik) *adj.* of, having to do with, or designating nomads or their way of life: *Many North American Indian peoples were traditionally nomadic.* —**no·mad′i·cal·ly,** *adv.*

no·mad·ism (nō′mad iz′əm) *n.* the way that nomads live.

no-man's-land or **no man's land** (nō′manz′land′) *n.* **1** in war, the land or area between opposing armies. **2** a tract of land to which no one has a recognized or established claim. **3** any area of involvement or operation that is not clearly defined or is ambiguous or inconsistent: *a legal no-man's-land.*

nom de guerre (nom′də ger′; *French,* nôɴ də ger′) *French.* an

hat, āge, fär; let, ēqual, tėrm; it, īce
hot, ōpen, ôrder; oil, out; cup, pùt, rüle,
əbove, takən, pencəl, lemən, circəs

ch, child; ng, long; sh, ship
th, thin; ᴛʜ, then; zh, measure

assumed name under which to pursue a profession, undertaking, or the like.

nom de plume (nom′də plüm′) a pen name; name used by a writer instead of his real name. [formed in E from F words: *nom* name, *de* of, *plume* pen]

no·men·cla·ture (nō′mən klā′chər *or* nō men′klə chər) *n.* a system of names or terms used in a particular field of science, art, etc.: *the nomenclature of music, the international Latin nomenclature for animals and plants.* [< L *nomenclatura* < *nomen* name + *calare* to call]

nom·i·nal (nom′ə nəl) *adj., n.* —*adj.* **1** being so in name only; not real: *The president is the nominal head of the club, but the secretary really runs its affairs.* **2** so small that it is not worth considering; unimportant compared with the real value: *We paid a nominal rent for the cottage—$25 a month.* **3 a** giving the name or names: *a nominal roll of the pupils in our room.* **b** mentioning specifically by name: *a nominal appeal.* **c** assigned to a person by name: *a nominal share of stock.* **4** of, having to do with, or being a name. **5** *Grammar.* of, having to do with, being, or used as a noun. *Day* is the nominal root of *daily, daybreak,* and *Sunday.* —*n.* a word or group of words used as a noun. *Rich* and *poor* in the phrase *the rich and the poor* are nominals. [< L *nominalis* < *nomen, -inis* name]

nom·i·nal·ly (nom′ə nəl ē) *adv.* **1** in name; as a matter of form; in a nominal way only. **2** by name.

nom·i·nate (nom′ə nāt′) *v.* -nat·ed, -nat·ing. **1** name as candidate for an office; propose for an office: *Mrs. Conroy has been nominated as Liberal candidate in our riding.* **2** appoint to an office or duty: *The Prime Minister nominated him Secretary of State.* [< L *nominare,* ult. < *nomen* name] —**nom′i·na′tor,** *n.*

nom·i·na·tion (nom′ə nā′shən) *n.* **1** the naming of someone as a candidate for an office. **2** a selection for office or duty; appointment to office or duty. **3** being nominated.

nom·i·na·tive (nom′ə nə tiv *or* nom′nə tiv) *adj., n.* —*adj.* of, having to do with, or being the grammatical case, found in many languages, that shows that a noun, pronoun, or adjective is part of the subject of a sentence. The English personal pronouns *I, he, she, we,* and *they* correspond to the nominative case in languages such as German and Latin because they are special forms used only as subjects in a sentence. —*n.* **1** the nominative case. **2** a word or construction in the nominative case. *Abbrev.:* nom. [< L *nominativus*]

nom·i·nee (nom′ə nē′) *n.* a person who is nominated.

noml. *Grammar.* nominal.

non- *prefix.* not; opposite of; lack of, as in *nonconformity, nonflammable, nonsmoking.* [< L *non* not < OL *ne-* not + *oinom* one]

non-ac·cept·ance (non′ak sep′təns) *n.* a failure or refusal to accept.

non·age (non′ij *or* nō′nij) *n.* **1** being under the legal age of responsibility; minority. **2** an early stage; period before maturity. [ME < AF *nonnage* < *non-* not (< L) + *age* age < VL *aetaticum* < L *aetas*]

non·a·ge·nar·i·an (non′ə jə ner′ē ən *or* nō′nə-) *n., adj.* —*n.* a person who is 90 years old or between 90 and 100 years old. —*adj.* 90 years old or between 90 and 100 years old. [< L *nonagenarius* of ninety]

non-ag·gres·sion (non′ə gresh′ən) *n.* absence of aggression: *a pact of non-aggression.*

non·a·gon (non′ə gon′) *n.* a polygon having nine sides. [< L *nonus* ninth + Gk. *gōnia* angle]

non-ap·pear·ance (non′ə pēr′əns) *n.* the fact of not appearing; failure to appear.

non-at·tend·ance (non′ə ten′dəns) *n.* failure to be present.

non-capital murder formerly, in Canada, murder not punishable by death.

nonce (nons) *n., adj.* —*n.* the one or particular occasion or purpose.
for the nonce, for the present time or occasion.
—*adj.* serving a single occasion: *a nonce word, nonce use.* [ME (*for then*) ones (for the) once, taken as (*for the*) *nones*]

nonce word a word formed and used for a single occasion.

non·cha·lance (non′shə lons′ *or* non′shə ləns) *n.* cool unconcern or indifference: *Eleanor received the prize with pretended nonchalance.*

non·cha·lant (non′shə lont′ *or* non′shə lənt) *adj.* coolly unconcerned or indifferent: *She remained quite nonchalant during all the excitement.* [< F *nonchalant* < *non-* not (< L) + *chaloir* be warm < L *calere*] —**non′cha·lant·ly,** *adv.*

non–com (non′kom′) *n. Informal.* a non-commissioned officer.

non–com·bat·ant (non′kəm bat′ənt *or* non kom′bə tənt) *n., adj.* —*n.* a person in the armed forces who is not a fighter. Military surgeons, nurses, chaplains, etc. are non-combatants. **2** a civilian in wartime. —*adj.* **1** not fighting. **2** having civilian status in wartime.

non–com·mis·sioned (non′kə mish′ənd) *adj.* without a commission; not commissioned. Corporals and sergeants are non-commissioned officers.

non·com·mit·tal (non′kə mit′əl) *adj.* without committing oneself; not saying yes or no. *I will think it over* is a noncommittal answer. —**non′com·mit′tal·ly,** *adv.*

non–com·pli·ance (non′kəm plī′əns) *n.* the fact of not complying; failure to comply.

non com·pos men·tis (non′kom′pəs men′tis) *Law.* mentally unable to manage one's own affairs; legally insane.

non–con·duct·ing (non′kən duk′ting) *adj.* not conducting; that is a non-conductor. Asbestos is a non-conducting material used in heat insulation.

non–con·duc·tor (non′kən duk′tər) *n.* a substance that does not readily allow heat, electricity, or sound to pass through it. Rubber is a non-conductor of electricity.

non·con·form·ist (non′kən fôr′mist) *n.* **1** Often, **Nonconformist,** a person who does not conform to an established church, especially a Protestant in Britain who does not belong to the Church of England. **2** a person who does not conform to accepted practices, conventions, etc.

non·con·form·i·ty (non′kən fôr′mə tē) *n.* **1** a lack of conformity; failure or refusal to conform. **2** a failure or refusal to conform to an established church. **3** Usually, **Nonconformity,** in England, the principles or practices of Protestants who do not belong to the Church of England.

non–co·op·er·a·tion (non′kō op′ər ā′shən) *n.* **1** a failure or refusal to co-operate. **2** a refusal to co-operate with a government for political reasons.

non–dair·y (non′der′ē) *adj.* designating a synthetic product used as a substitute for cream or milk or whipped cream, etc.: *a non-dairy whipped topping, a non-dairy creamer for coffee.*

non′-a·bra′sive	non′-be·liev′ing	non′-col·laps′i·ble	non′-con·fi·den′tial	non′-con·vert′i·ble
non′-ab·sor′bent	non′-bel·lig′er·ent	non′-col·lect′a·ble	non′-con·flict′ing	non′-co-op′er·a·tive
non′-ac·a·dem′ic	non-break′a·ble	non′-col·lect′i·ble	non′-con·form′ing	non′-cor·rob′o·ra·tive
non′-ad·dic′tive	non′-Ca·na′di·an	non′-col·le′gi·ate	non′-con·gen′i·tal	non′-cor·rod′ing
non′-ad·ja′cent	non-car′bon·at′ed	non-com′bat	non′-con·nec′tive	non′-cor·ro′sive
non′-ad·min·is·tra·tive	non′-car·niv′o·rous	non′-com·bin′ing	non′-con·sec′u·tive	non′-cre·a′tive
non′-ag·gres′sive	non-Cath′o·lic	non′-com·bust′i·ble	non′-con·sent′	non′-crim′i·nal
non′-ag·ri·cul′tur·al	non′-Cau·ca′sian	non-com·mer′cial	non′-con·serv′a·tive	non-crys′tal·line′
non′-al·co·hol′ic	non-cel′lu·lar	non′-com·mu′ni·ca·ble	non′-con·sti·tu′tion·al	non-cul′ti·vat′ed
non′-al·ler·gen′ic	non-cen′tral	non′-com·mun′i·cant	non′-con·strain′ing	non-cul′mu·la·tive
non′-a·quat′ic	non′-ce·re′bral	non′-com·mu′ni·ca·tive	non′-con·ta′gious	non-cur′rent
non′-as·sess′a·ble	non′-charge′a·ble	non-com′mu·nist	non′-con·tem′po·rar·y	non′-de·cep′tive
non′-as·sim′i·la′tion	non′-chem′i·cal	non′-com·pet′ing	non′-con·tin′u·ance	non′-de·cid′u·ous
non′-ath·let′ic	non-Chris′tian	non′-com·pet′i·tive	non′-con·tin′u·ous	non′-de·duct′i·ble
non′-at·trib′u·tive	non-civ′i·lized	non′-com·pul′sion	non-con′tra·band	non′-de·liv′er·y
non′-au·thor′i·ta′tive	non-clas′sic	non′-com·pul′so·ry	non′-con·tra·dic′to·ry	non′-de·mo·crat′ic
non-au·to·mat′ed	non-clas′si·cal	non′-con·cil′i·a·to′ry	non′-con·trib′u·ting	non′-de·mon′stra·ble
non′-au·to·mat′ic	non-clas′si·fied′	non′-con·clu′sive	non′-con·tro·ver′sial	non′-de·nom′i·na′tion·al
non-bas′ic	non-cler′i·cal	non′-con·cur′rent	non′-con·ven′tion·al	non′-de·part′men′tal
non′-be·liev′er	non-clin′i·cal	non′-con·duc′tive	non′-con·ver′gent	non′-de·pen′dence
	non′-co·ag′u·lat′ing		non′-con·ver′sant	

non·de·script (non′də skript′) *adj., n.* —*adj.* not easily classified; not of any one particular kind: *eyes of nondescript shade, neither brown, blue, nor grey.* —*n.* a nondescript person or thing. [< *non-* + L *descriptus* described]

none¹ (nun) *pron., adv.* —*pron.* **1** not any: *We have none of that paper left.* **2** no one; not one: *None of these is a typical case.* **3** no persons or things: *None have arrived.* **4** no part; nothing: *She has none of her mother's beauty.* —*adv.* to no extent; in no way; not at all: *Our supply is none too great.* [OE *nān* < *ne* not + *ān* one]
☛ *Hom.* **nun.**
☛ *Usage.* **None, no one. None** is a single word, but **not one** or **no one** is often used instead of **none** for emphasis. **None** may be either singular or plural, and now is more common with the plural: *As only ten jurors have been chosen so far, none of the witnesses were called (or was called.) She tried on ten hats, but none of them were attractive. I read three books on the subject, no one of which was helpful.*

none² (nōn) *n.* sing. of **nones²**.
☛ *Hom.* **nun.**

non·en·ti·ty (non en′tə tē) *n., pl.* **-ties. 1** a person or thing of little or no importance. **2** something that does not exist.

nones¹ (nōnz) *n.pl.* in the ancient Roman calendar, the ninth day before the ides, counting both days, this being the 7th of March, May, July, and October, and the 5th of the other months. [< L *nonae*, originally fem. pl. of *nonus* ninth]

nones² (nōnz) *n.pl.* **1** the first of the seven canonical hours. **2** the service or services for it. [pl. of *none²*, OE *nōn* < L *nona*. Doublet of NOON.]

non·es·sen·tial (non′ə sen′shəl) *adj., n.* —*adj.* not essential; not necessary. —*n.* a person or thing not essential.

none·such (nun′such′) *n.* a person or thing without equal or parallel; paragon. Also, **nonsuch.**

none·the·less (nun′THə les′) *adv.* nevertheless.

non·fea·sance (non fē′zəns) *n. Law.* the failure to perform some act that duty requires to be done. Compare **malfeasance** and **misfeasance.**

non·fic·tion (non fik′shən) *n.* prose literature that is not a novel, short story, or other form of writing based on imaginary people and events. Biographies and histories are non-fiction.

non·fig·ur·a·tive (non′fig′ər ə tiv *or* -fig′yər ə tiv) *adj.* **1** *Painting, sculpture, etc.* non-objective; having abstract as opposed to traditional or recognizable forms. **2** not figurative; literal: *a non-figurative use of a word.*

non·flam·ma·ble (non′flam′ə bəl) *adj.* not easily set on fire and not fast-burning if set on fire; not flammable.
☛ *Usage.* See note at **flammable.**

non·ful·fil·ment *or* **non·ful·fill·ment** (non′fŭl fil′mənt) *n.* a failure to fulfil; failure to be fulfilled.

non·in·ter·ven·tion (non′in tər ven′shən) *n.* **1** a failure or refusal to intervene. **2** the systematic avoidance of any interference

hat, āge, fär; let, ēqual, tèrm; it, īce
hot, ōpen, ôrder; oil, out; cup, pút, rüle,
above, takən, pencəl, lemən, circəs
ch, child; ng, long; sh, ship
th, thin; ᴛʜ, then; zh, measure

by a nation in the affairs of other nations or of its own states, etc.

non·ju·ror (non jür′ər) *n.* **1** one who refuses to take a required oath. **2 Non-juror,** in England, one of those clergymen of the Church of England who in 1689 refused to swear allegiance to William and Mary.

non·liv·ing (non′liv′ing) *adj.* not living.

non·met·al (non′met′əl) *n.* any chemical element not having the character of a metal. Carbon and nitrogen are non-metals.

non·me·tal·lic (non′mə tal′ik) *adj.* not like a metal. Carbon, oxygen, sulphur, and nitrogen are non-metallic chemical elements.

non·mor·al (non môr′əl) *adj.* having no relation to morality; neither moral nor immoral.

no-no (nō′nō′) *n. Informal.* an action, form of behavior, etc. that is ill-advised or forbidden.

non·pa·reil (non′pə rel′) *adj., n.* —*adj.* having no equal. —*n.* **1** a person or thing having no equal. **2** a kind of apple. **3** *Printing.* a size of type; 6-point. This sentence is in nonpareil. [< F *nonpareil* < *non-* not (< L) + *pareil* equal, ult. < L *par*]

non·par·ti·san (non pär′tə zən *or* -par′tə zan′) *adj.* not partisan; especially, not controlled by or supporting any single faction or political party.

non·pay·ment (non pā′mənt) *n.* a failure to pay; condition of not being paid.

non·per·form·ance (non′pər fôr′məns) *n.* the fact of not performing; failure to perform.

non·per·son (non′pèr′sən) *n.* someone who is ignored, especially by a government or organization, or treated as if non-existent.

non·plus (non plus′ *or* non′plus) *v.* **-plussed** *or* **-plused, -plus·sing** *or* **-plus·ing;** *n.* —*v.* puzzle completely; make unable to say or do anything: *We were nonplussed to see two roads leading off to the left where we had expected only one.* —*n.* a state of being nonplussed. [< L *non plus* no further]

non·pro·duc·tive (non′prə duk′tiv) *adj.* **1** failing to produce; unproductive. **2** not directly connected with production. —**non′·pro·duc′tive·ness,** *n.*

non′-de·struc′tive	non′-ex·clu′sive	non′-id·i·o·mat′ic	non-li·tur′gi·cal	non-o′dor·ous
non′-de·tach′a·ble	non′-ex·ist′ence	non′-im·mu′ni·ty	non-lo′cal	non′-of·fi′cial
non′-det′o·nat′ing	non′-ex·ist′ent	non′-im·por·ta′tion	non-log′i·cal	non′-op′er·at′ing
non′-dic·ta′to·ri·al	non′-ex·ist′ing	non′-im·preg′nat·ed	non-lu′mi·nous	non′-op·e·ra′tion·al
non′-di·rec′tion·al	non′-ex·plo′sive	non′-in·clu′sion	non′-mag·net′ic	non′-or·gan′ic
non′-dir′i·gi·ble	non′-ex·port′a·ble	non′-in·clu′sive	non′-ma·lig′nant	non′-or′tho·dox
non-dis·ci′pli·nar′y	non′-ex·tend′ed	non′-in·de·pen′dent	non-mar′i·time′	non-par′al·lel
non′-dis·crim′i·nat′ing	non′-ex·tra·dit′a·ble	non′-in·dict′a·ble	non-mar′ry·ing	non′-par′a·sit′ic
non′-dis·crim′i·na′tion	non-fac′tu·al	non′-in·dict′ment	non-mar′tial	non′-par·en′tal
non′-dis·crim′i·na·to·ry	non-fad′ing	non′-in·dus′tri·al	non′-ma·te′ri·al·is′tic	non′-par·lia·men′tar·y
non′-dis·pos′al	non-fa′tal	non′-in·fec′tious	non′-ma·ter′nal	non′-pa·ro′chi·al
non′-dis·tinc′tive	non-fat′ten·ing	non′-in·flam′ma·ble	non′-math·e·mat′i·cal	non′-par·tic′i·pa′tion
non′-di·ver′gent	non-fed′er·al	non′-in·flect′ed	non′-me·chan′i·cal	non′-pa·ter′nal
non′-di·vis′i·ble	non-fed′e·rat′ed	non′-in·form′a·tive	non-med′i·cal	non-pay′ing
non′-dog·mat′ic	non-fer′rous	non′-in·her′ent	non′-me·dic′i·nal	non-per′ma·nent
non′-do·mes′ti·cat·ed	non-fes′tive	non′-in·her′it·a·ble	non′-me·lo′dic	non′-per·me·a·ble
non′-dra·mat′ic	non-fic′tion·al	non′-in·ju′ri·ous	non′-me·lo′di·ous	non′-per·pen·dic′u·lar
non′-drink′er	non′-fic·ti′tious	non′-in·stinc′tive	non-melt′ing	non′-per·sist′ence
non′-driv′er	non-fi′nite	non′-in·sti·tu′tion·al	non-mem′ber	non′-phil·o·soph′i·cal
non-dry′ing	non-fis′cal	non-in′te·grat′ed	non-mem′ber·ship	non′-po·et′ic
non-earn′ing	non-fis′sion·a·ble	non-in′tel·lec′tu·al	non′-mi·gra·to′ry	non′-poi·son·ous
non′-e·co·nom′ic	non-flex′i·ble	non′-in·ter·change′a·ble	non′-mil′i·tant	non′-po·lit′i·cal
non-ed′i·ble	non-flow′er·ing	non′-in·ter·fer′ence	non′-mil′i·tar′y	non-po′rous
non-ed′u·ca·ble	non-flu′id	non′-in·ter·sect′ing	non-min′er·al	non′-pos·ses′sion
non′-ed·u·ca′tion·al	non-freez′ing	non′-in·tox′i·cant	non′-min·is·te′ri·al	non-prac′ti·cal
non′-e·las′tic	non-func′tion·al	non′-in·tox′i·cat·ing	non-moun′tain·ous	non-pre′cious
non′-e·lec′tive	non-fus′i·ble	non′-in·tu′i·tive	non-mys′ti·cal	non-pred′a·to′ry
non′-el′i·gi·ble	non-gas′e·ous	non-ir′ri·ga·ble	non-myth′i·cal	non′-pre·dict′a·ble
non′-e·mo′tion·al	non′-gov·ern·men′tal	non′-ir′ri·tant	non-na′tion·al	non-preg′nant
non′-en·force′ment	non-hab′it·a·ble	non′-ir′ri·tat′ing	non-na′tive	non′-pre·hen′sile
non-Eng′lish	non-haz′ard·ous	non-Jew′ish	non-nat′u·ral	non′-pre·ju′di·cial
non-e′qual	non′-he·red′i·tar′y	non-ko′sher	non-nav′i·ga·ble	non′-pre·scrip′tive
non′-e·quiv′a·lent	non′-her′it·a·ble	non-lam′i·nat′ed	non′-ne·go′ti·a·ble	non′-pre·serv′a·tive
non′-es·tab′lish·ment	non′-his·tor′i·cal	non-le′gal	non-neu′tral	non′-pres·er·va′tion
non-eth′i·cal	non-hu′man	non-le′thal	non′-o·be′di·ence	non′-pro·duc′ing
non′-Eu·clid′e·an	non-hu′mor·ous	non-lin′e·ar	non′-ob·lig′a·to′ry	non′-pro·fes′sion·al
non′-ex·change′a·ble	non′-i·den′ti·cal	non-lit′er·ar′y	non′-ob·serv′ance	
	non′-i·den′ti·ty	non-lit′er·ate	non′-oc·cur′rence	

non-prof·it (non prof'it) *adj.* not conducted for the purpose of making a profit: *a non-profit organization.*

non-rep·re·sen·ta·tion·al (non'rep ri zen tā'shə nəl) *adj.* not intended to represent or resemble natural objects; abstract: *non-representational art.*

non-res·i·dence (non rez'ə dəns) *n.* a being non-resident.

non-res·i·dent (non rez'ə dənt) *adj., n.* —*adj.* 1 not residing in a particular place. 2 not residing where official duties require one to reside. —*n.* a non-resident person.

non-re·sist·ance (non'ri zis'təns) *n.* 1 the state or condition of being non-resistant. 2 the principles or practice of not resisting established authority, even when it is unjust or tyrannical.

non-re·sist·ant (non'ri zis'tənt) *adj., n.* —*adj.* 1 not resistant to the bad effects of something, such as an insecticide or a disease-producing organism. 2 not resisting; practising non-resistance. —*n.* a person who practises non-resistance.

non-re·stric·tive (non'ri strik'tiv) *adj.* 1 *Grammar.* adding descriptive detail. Modifiers which do not limit the meaning of a noun but add a descriptive detail are non-restrictive modifiers. 2 that does not restrict.

non-sched·uled (non'skej'üld of -shej'üld) *adj.* not according to a set plan, program, or schedule: *a non-scheduled flight, a non-scheduled stop.*

non-sec·tar·i·an (non'sek ter'ē ən) *adj.* not connected with any religious denomination.

non·sense (non'sens *or* non'səns) *n.* 1 words, ideas, or acts without meaning: *The magician talks nonsense as he is doing the tricks.* 2 foolish talk or doings; a plan or suggestion that is foolish: *It is nonsense to say that we can walk that far in an hour.* 3 impudent or silly behavior or conduct: *She doesn't take any nonsense from her employees.* [< *non-* + *sense*]

non·sen·si·cal (non sen'sə kəl) *adj.* foolish; absurd. —**non·sen'si·cal·ly,** *adv.*

non-sep·a·ra·tist (non'sep'rə tist) *n.* in Quebec, a person who is against the separation of the province from Confederation.

non seq. non sequitur.

non se·qui·tur (non sek'wə tər) 1 a statement or reply that has no direct relationship with what has just been said. 2 *Logic.* an inference or conclusion that does not follow from the premises. [< L *non sequitur* it does not follow]

non-skid (non'skid') *adj.* made so as to prevent skidding: *non-skid tires.*

non-slip (non'slip') *adj.* non-skid.

non-stand·ard (non'stan'dərd) *adj.* 1 not conforming to regulations, accepted specifications, etc. 2 outside the generally accepted pattern; different from what is held to be normal. ☛ *Usage.* For non-standard English, see note at **standard.**

non-stop (*adj.* non'stop'; *adv.* non'stop') *adj. or adv.* without stopping: *We took a non-stop flight from Toronto to Rome. We worked non-stop from noon till supper time.*

non·such (nun'such') See **nonesuch.**

non-suit (non'süt') *n., v.* —*n. Law.* a judgment given against a person beginning a lawsuit who neglects to prosecute, or who fails to show a legal case, or who fails to bring sufficient evidence. —*v.* stop by a nonsuit.

non-sup·port (non'sə pôrt') *n.* failure to support, especially the failure to provide for someone for whom one is legally responsible.

non-treat·y (non'trē'tē) *adj. Cdn.* of Indians, not under the terms of a treaty with the Canadian government but living, usually, on a reserve.

non trop·po (nōn trō'pō) *Music.* not too much. [< Ital.]

non-U (non yü') *adj. Esp.Brit. Informal.* not belonging to or characteristic of the upper class.

non-un·ion (non yün'yən) *adj.* 1 not belonging to a trade union. 2 made by other than union labor. 3 not recognizing or favoring trade unions.

non-un·ion·ism (non yün'yən iz'əm) *n.* the theories or practices of those opposed to trade unions.

non-un·ion·ist (non yün'yən ist) *n.* 1 a person who is opposed to trade unions. 2 a person who does not belong to a trade union.

non-vi·o·lence (non'vī'ə ləns) *n.* 1 the absence of violence. 2 passive non-co-operation with authority, as opposed to violence, used as a means of gaining political ends.

non-vi·o·lent (non'vī'ə lənt) *adj.* 1 free from violence: *a non-violent demonstration.* 2 supporting or practising non-violence.

non-vot·er (non vōt'ər) *n.* a person who does not vote or does not have the right to vote.

non-white (non'wīt' *or* -hwīt') *n., adj.* —*n.* 1 a person who is not Caucasian. 2 in South Africa, a person who is not of European origin. —*adj.* 1 not Caucasian. 2 of or having to do with non-whites.

noo·dle (nü'dəl) *n.* 1 a very stupid person; fool. 2 *Slang.* the head. [origin uncertain]

noo·dles (nü'dəlz) *n.pl.* 1 a food made of flour and water, or flour and eggs, a kind of pasta resembling macaroni, but made in flat strips. 2 **noodle, a** a single strip of this pasta. **b** (*adj.*) made of or with noodles: *noodle soup.* [< G *Nudel*]

nook (nůk) *n.* 1 a cosy little corner. 2 a hidden spot; sheltered place. [ME *noke*]

noon (nün) *n.* 1 twelve o'clock in the daytime; the middle of the day. 2 (*adj.*) of noon. [OE *nōn* < L *nona* (*hora*) ninth (hour), 3 p.m.; the meaning shifted with a change in time of church service. Doublet of NONE[2] (see NONES[2]).]

noon·day (nün'dā') *n.* 1 noon; midday. 2 (*adj.*) of noon: *the noonday meal.*

no one *or* **no-one** (nō'wun') no person; nobody. ☛ *Usage.* See note at **none.**

noon hour noon; the time around noon. —**noon'-hour',** *adj.*

noon·ing (nü'ning) *n.* 1 a rest or time for rest at noon. 2 a meal at noon. 3 noon.

noon·tide (nün'tīd') *n.* noon.

noon·time (nün'tīm') *n.* noon.

noose (nüs) *n., v.* **noosed, noos·ing.** —*n.* 1 a loop with a slip-knot that tightens as the string or rope is pulled. Nooses are used especially in lassos and snares. 2 anything that restricts or snares like a noose. 3 **the noose,** death by hanging. —*v.* 1 catch in a noose or as if in a noose; snare. 2 make a noose with or in. [probably < OF *nos* < Provençal *nous* < L *nodus* knot]

Noot·ka (nüt'kə) *n.* **Noot·ka** or **-kas;** *adj.* —*n.* 1 a member of an Amerindian people living mainly on Vancouver Island. 2 the Wakashan language of the Nootka. —*adj.* of or having to do with the Nootka or their language.

Nootka cypress *Cdn.* yellow cypress. [< *Nootka* Sound, Vancouver Island, B.C.]

nope (nōp) *adv. Informal.* no.

---

non'-prof·i·teer'ing	non'-rep·re·sent'a·tive	non-sink'a·ble	non'-suc·ces'sive	non'-us'age
non'-pro·gres'sive	non'-res·i·den'tial	non-skilled'	non'-sup·por'ter	non'-use'
non'-pro·por'tion·al	non'-re·strict'ed	non'smok'er	non'-sup·port'ing	non'-us'er
non'-pro·tec'tive	non'-re·turn'a·ble	non'smok'ing	non'-sur'gi·cal	non-ven'om·ous
non-Prot'es·tant	non'-re·vers'i·ble	non-so'cial	non'-sus·tain'ing	non-ver'bal
non-ra'cial	non'rhym'ing	non-so·lu'ble	non'swim'mer	non'-ver·i·fi'a·ble
non-rad'i·cal	non-rhyth'mic	non-speak'ing	non'-sym·bol'ic	non-ver'ti·cal
non-ra'di·o·ac'tive	non-rig'id	non-spe'cial·ist	non'-sym·met'ri·cal	non-vet'er·an
non-ra'tion·al	non-ru'ral	non-spe'cial·ized	non-sym'pa·thiz'er	non'-vi·o·la'tion
non-read'er	non-Rus'sian	non'-spe·cif'ic	non'-sys·tem·at'ic	non-vis'u·al
non're·al·is'tic	non-sal'a·ble	non-sport'ing	non-tax'a·ble	non-vo'cal
non're·al'i·ty	non-sal'a·ried	non-spot'ted	non-teach'a·ble	non'-vo·cal'ic
non'-re·cip'ro·cal	non'-sci·en·tif'ic	non-stain'a·ble	non-tech'ni·cal	non'-vo·ca'tion·al
non-rec·og·ni'tion	non-sea'son·al	non-stain'ing	non-tem'po·ral	non-vol'a·tile
non'-re·cov'er·a·ble	non-sec'tion·al	non'-stand·ard'ized	non'-ter·ri·to'ri·al	non-vol'un·tar·y
non'-re·cur'rent	non-sec'u·lar	non'-sta·tis'ti·cal	non'-the·at'ri·cal	non-vot'ing
non'-re·fill'a·ble	non-seg're·gat'ed	non-stra·te'gic	non-tox'ic	non-wood'y
non're·flec'tive	non'-se·lec'tive	non-strik'er	non'-tra·di'tion·al	non-work'er
non-reg'i·ment'ed	non-sen'si·tive	non-strik'ing	non'-trans·fer'a·ble	non-work'ing
non'reg'is·tered	non-sex'u·al	non'-struc'tur·al	non-trop'i·cal	non-wo'ven
non're·li'gious	non-shar'ing	non'-sub·mis'sive	non-typ'i·cal	non-yield'ing
non'-re·mu'ner·a·tive	non-shrink'a·ble	non'-sub·scrib'er	non-u'ni·form	
non're·new'a·ble	non'-sig·nif'i·cant		non-ur'ban	

nor (nôr; *unstressed*, nər) *conj.* and not; or not; neither; and not either. *Nor* is used: **1** with a preceding *neither* or negative: *Not a boy nor a girl stirred.* **2** *Poetic.* with preceding *neither* or *not* left out: *"Great brother, thou nor I have made the world."* **3** *Poetic.* instead of *neither* as correlative to a following *nor*: *"Drake nor Devil nor Spaniard feared."* [OE (unstressed) *nā(hwæ)ther < ne* not + *ā(hwæ)ther* either]

Nor. **1** Norway; Norwegian. **2** Norman. **3** North.

NORAD (nôr′ad) North American Air Defence (Command).

Nor·dic (nôr′dik) *adj., n.* —*adj.* **1** of, having to do with, or designating the Germanic peoples of northern Europe, especially of Scandinavia. **2** of, having to do with, or designating a type of people characterized by tall stature, blond hair, blue eyes, and long heads. **3** of or designating cross-country as opposed to downhill skiing. —*n.* a person who is Nordic. [< F *nordique < nord* north < Gmc.]

Nor·folk jacket (nôr′fək) a loose-fitting, belted jacket having pleats at the front and back.

norm (nôrm) *n.* the standard for a certain group; type; model; pattern: *In mathematics this class is above the norm for the senior year.* [< L *norma* a rule, pattern]

nor·mal (nôr′məl) *adj., n.* —*adj.* **1** of the usual standard or type; regular; usual: *The normal temperature of the human body is 37°C. It's normal for children to be energetic.* **2** *Geometry.* being at right angles; perpendicular. **3** *Chemistry.* **a** of an acidic or basic solution, containing the equivalent of one gram of hydrogen ion per litre. **b** of or denoting an aliphatic hydrocarbon or hydrocarbon derivative. **c** not found in association, as molecules. **4** *Medicine, psychology.* of average intelligence, mental or physical health, etc.; not diseased, defective, or disturbed. —*n.* **1** the usual state or level: *two kilograms above normal.* **2** *Geometry.* a line or plane that is at right angles to another. [< L *normalis < norma* a rule, pattern]

nor·mal·cy (nôr′məl sē) *n.* a normal condition.

nor·mal·i·ty (nôr mal′ə tē) *n.* a normal condition.

nor·mal·ize (nôr′məl īz′) *v.* -ized, -iz·ing. make normal. —**nor′mal·i·za′tion**, *n.* —**nor′mal·iz′er**, *n.*

nor·mal·ly (nôr′məl ē) *adv.* in the normal way; regularly; if things are normal.

normal school a school where people are trained to be elementary-school teachers. [after F *école normale*]

Nor·man (nôr′mən) *n., adj.* —*n.* **1** a native or inhabitant of Normandy in France. **2** a member of the Scandinavian people who conquered Normandy in the 10th century A.D. **3** a member of the Norman-French people who conquered England in 1066. **4** Norman French. —*adj.* of or having to do with the Normans or Normandy: *The rounded arch is characteristic of Norman architecture.* [< OF *Normans*, pl. of *Normant* < Gmc.]

Norman Conquest the conquest of England by the Normans in 1066, under the leadership of William the Conqueror.

Norman French 1 the dialect of French spoken by the medieval Normans, especially as spoken by the Norman conquerors of England. **2** a form of this dialect used as the language of law in England until the late 17th century. **3** the dialect of the modern-day inhabitants of Normandy.

nor·ma·tive (nôr′mə tiv) *adj.* of, following, or establishing a norm or standard: *normative grammar, a normative statement.*

Norn (nôrn) *n. Norse mythology.* one of the three goddesses of fate, who rule over gods and men.

Norse (nôrs) *n., adj.* —*n.* **1 the Norse**, *pl.* **a** the people of ancient Scandinavia; Norsemen. **b** the people of Norway, a country in N Europe. **2** the language of the ancient Scandinavians, often called Old Norse. —*adj.* **1** of or having to do with ancient Scandinavia, its people, or their language. **2** of or having to do with Norway or its people. [< Du. *Noorsch* Norwegian]

Norse·man (nôrs′mən) *n.* -men. a member of a people that lived in ancient Scandinavia. The Vikings were Norsemen.

north (nôrth) *n., adj., adv.* —*n.* **1** the direction to which a compass needle points; direction to the right as one faces the setting sun. **2** Also, **North**, the part of any country toward the north. **3 the North**, in Canada, the northern parts of the provinces from Quebec westward and the territory lying north of these provinces. —*adj.* **1** toward the north: *We walked north.* **2** from the north: *a north wind.* **3** in the north; northern: *north China.* —*adv.* toward the north: *Their trip north was long but uneventful.* [OE]

North American 1 a native or inhabitant of North America. **2** of or having to do with North America or its people.

north·bound (nôrth′bound′) *adj.* going toward the north.

North canoe *Cdn. Historical.* a canoe used by the fur brigades on the rivers of the north and northwest. It was about 7.5 m long and carried three or four passengers and about a tonne of cargo.

hat, āge, fär; let, ēqual, tėrm; it, īce
hot, ōpen, ôrder; oil, out; cup, put, rüle,
above, takən, pencəl, lemən, circəs
ch, child; ng, long; sh, ship
th, thin; ғH, then; zh, measure

North Country 1 the northern parts of North America. **2** northern England.

north·east (nôrth′ēst′) *adj., n., adv.* —*adj.* **1** halfway between north and east. **2** lying toward or situated in the northeast. **3** of, at, in, toward, or from the northeast: *a northeast wind.* **4** directed toward the northeast. —*n.* **1** a northeast direction. **2** a place that is in the northeast part or direction. —*adv.* **1** toward the northeast. **2** from the northeast. **3** in the northeast.

north·east·er (nôrth′ēs′tər) *n.* a wind or storm from the northeast.

north·east·er·ly (nôrth′ēs′tər lē) *adj. or adv.* **1** toward the northeast. **2** from the northeast.

north·east·ern (nôrth′ēs′tərn) *adj.* of, at, in, to, toward, or from the northeast.

north·east·ward (nôrth′ēst′wərd) *adv., adj., n.* —*adv. or adj.* **1** toward the northeast. **2** northeast. —*n.* the northeast.

north·east·ward·ly (nôrth′ēst′wərd lē) *adj., adv.* —*adj.* **1** toward the northeast. **2** of winds, from the northeast. —*adv.* toward the northeast.

north·east·wards (nôrth′ēst′wərdz) *adv.* northeastward.

north·er (nôr′ғHər) *n.* a wind or storm from the north.

north·er·ly (nôr′ғHər lē) *adj., adv.* —*adj.* **1** toward the north. **2** from the north: *a northerly wind.* **3** of the north. —*adv.* **1** toward the north. **2** from the north.

north·ern (nôr′ғHərn) *adj.* **1** toward the north. **2** from the north: *a northern breeze.* **3** of or in the north: *He has travelled in northern countries.* **4** of or in the Canadian North: *Churchill is a northern port.* [OE *northerne*]

north·ern·er (nôr′ғHər nər) *n.* **1** a native or inhabitant of the north. **2 Northerner**, *Cdn.* a native or inhabitant of the Far North.

northern lights the streamers and bands of light that appear in the northern sky at night; aurora borealis.

north·ern·most (nôr′ғHərn mōst′) *adj.* farthest north.

northern pike a common game fish (*Esox lucius*) of the pike family having a long, slender body and large head, found throughout most of Canada.

northern service officer *Cdn.* a federal government officer in charge of a district in the Far North.

North Germanic a subdivision of the Germanic languages that comprises Danish, Norwegian, Swedish, and Icelandic, along with their related dialects.

north·ing (nôr′thing *or* nôr′ғHing) *n.* the distance measured in a northerly direction.

north·land (nôrth′land′) *n.* **1** Usually, **Northland**, *Cdn.* the northern regions of Canada; the Far North. **2** a northern region or country. [OE]

north·land·er (nôrth′lən dər) *n.* an inhabitant of the northland.

North·man (nôrth′mən) *n., pl.* -men. **1** Norseman. **2** a native or inhabitant of northern Europe, especially Norway.

North Pole the northern end of the earth's axis. See **equator** for picture.

North Star the bright star almost directly above the North Pole.

North·um·bri·an (nôr thum′brē ən) *n., adj.* —*n.* **1** a native or inhabitant of Northumbria, an ancient kingdom in N England. **2** a dialect of Old English spoken in Northumbria. **3** a native or inhabitant of Northumberland. **4** the Northumberland dialect. —*adj.* **1** of or having to do with Northumbria, its people, or their dialect. **2** of or having to do with Northumberland, its people, or their dialect.

north·ward (nôrth′wərd) *adv., adj., n.* —*adv.* toward the north; north: *Rocks lay northward of the ship's course.* —*adj.* toward the north; north: *the northward slope of a hill.* —*n.* a northward part, direction, or point.

north·ward·ly (nôrth′wərd lē) *adj., adv.* —*adj.* **1** toward the north. **2** of winds, from the north. —*adv.* toward the north.

north·wards (nôrth′wərdz) *adv.* northward.

north·west (nôrth′west′) *adj., n., adv.* —*adj.* **1** halfway between

north and west. 2 lying toward or situated in the northwest. 3 of, at, in, to, toward, or from the northwest: *a northwest wind.* 4 directed toward the northwest.
—*n.* 1 a northwest direction. 2 a place that is in the northwest part or direction. 3 **Northwest,** the general region of Canada north and west of the Great Lakes.
—*adv.* 1 toward the northwest. 2 from the northwest. 3 in the northwest.

North West Company a loosely organized group of companies and individuals formed in Montreal during the late eighteenth century to promote the fur trade in Canada. It was absorbed by the Hudson's Bay Company in 1821.

north·west·er (nôrth′wes′tər) *n.* 1 a wind or storm from the northwest. 2 **Northwester,** *Cdn. Historical.* a wintering partner or employee of the North West Company.

north·west·er·ly (nôrth′wes′tər lē) *adj. or adv.* 1 toward the northwest. 2 of winds, from the northwest.

north·west·ern (nôrth′wes′tərn) *adj.* of, at, in, to, toward, or from the northwest.

North West Mounted Police a former name of the Royal Canadian Mounted Police. *Abbrev.:* NWMP or N.W.M.P.

Northwest Passage a route for ships from the Atlantic to the Pacific along the northern coast of North America.

Northwest Rebellion an armed uprising of Métis and Indians in Saskatchewan in 1885, springing from grievances similar to those that had led to the Red River Rebellion.

north·west·ward (nôrth′west′wərd) *adj., adv., n.* —*adj. or adv.* 1 toward the northwest. 2 northwest.
—*n.* the northwest.

north·west·ward·ly (nôrth′west′wərd lē) *adj., adv.* —*adj.* 1 toward the northwest. 2 of winds, from the northwest. —*adv.* toward the northwest.

north·west·wards (nôrth′west′wərdz) *adv.* northwestward.

Nor·way pine (nôr′wā) red pine.

Nor·we·gian (nôr wē′jən) *n., adj.* —*n.* 1 a native or inhabitant of Norway, a country in N Europe. 2 the language of the Norwegians. —*adj.* of or having to do with Norway, its people, or their language.

Norwegian elkhound a breed of medium-sized hunting dog having a thick grey coat, pointed ears, and a curled tail. Also called **elkhound.**

nor'west·er (nôr wes′tər) *n.* a heavy, waterproof oilskin coat worn by seamen.

Nor'West·er (nôr′west′ər) *n. Cdn.* Northwester.

Nos. or **nos.** numbers.

nose (nōz) *n., v.* **nosed, nos·ing.** —*n.* 1 the part of the face or head just above the mouth, serving as the opening for breathing and as the organ of smell. 2 the sense of smell: *a dog with a good nose.* 3 a faculty for perceiving or detecting: *A reporter must have a nose for news.* 4 a part that stands out. The bow of a ship or airplane is often called the nose.
count noses, find out how many people are present.
follow (one's) nose, a go straight ahead. **b** be guided by one's instinct. **c** be guided by one's sense of smell.
lead by the nose, have complete control over.
look down (one's) nose at, *Informal.* feel contempt for.
on the nose, a exactly. **b** solidly.
pay through the nose, pay a great deal too much.
poke (one's) nose into, pry into; meddle in.
put (someone's) nose out of joint, *Informal.* **a** take one's place in another's favor. **b** destroy one's hopes, plans, etc.
thumb (one's) nose, put one's thumb to one's nose in scorn.
turn up (one's) nose at, treat with contempt or scorn.
under (one's) nose, in plain sight; very easy to notice.
—*v.* 1 discover by smelling; smell out. 2 smell; sniff. 3 rub with the nose. 4 push with the nose or forward end. 5 push (one's) way: *The little boat nosed carefully between the rocks.* 6 search (for); pry (into).
nose out, find out by looking around quietly or secretly. [OE *nosu*]

nose bag a bag containing food, to be hung on a horse's head.

nose·band (nōz′band′) *n.* the part of a bridle that goes over the animal's nose.

nose·bleed (nōz′blēd′) *n.* a bleeding from the nose.

nose cone a protective, cone-shaped cap at the forward end of a spacecraft, designed to streamline the craft and to provide

protection against the intense heat encountered especially on re-entry into the earth's atmosphere.

nosed (nōzd) *adj.* having a nose of a specified kind (*used in compounds*): *long-nosed.*

nose-dive (nōz′dīv′) *n., v.* **-dived, -div·ing.** —*n.* 1 a swift plunge straight downward by an aircraft. 2 a sudden, sharp drop. —*v.* 1 of an aircraft, plunge swiftly downward. 2 take a sharp, sudden drop: *The price of gasoline nose-dived overnight.*

no-see-em or **no-see-um** (nō sē′əm) *n.* any of various tiny, two-winged insects (genus *Culicoides*) that have a nasty bite.

nose·gay (nōz′gā′) *n.* a bunch of flowers; a small bouquet. [< *nose* + *gay*, obs. n., something gay or pretty]

nose·guard (nōz′gärd′) *n.* a part on a helmet, such as a football helmet, that covers and protects the nose.

nose·piece (nōz′pēs′) *n.* 1 the part of a helmet that covers and protects the nose. 2 a noseband for an animal. 3 the bridge of a pair of eyeglasses.

nos·ey (nō′zē) *adj.* **nos·i·er, nos·i·est.** *Informal.* too curious about other people's business; prying; inquisitive. Also, **nosy.**

Nosey Park·er (pär′kər) a person showing a persistent and offensive curiosity about things which do not concern him.

nosh (nosh) *n., v. Slang.* —*n.* a snack or tidbit. —*v.* eat or chew: *noshing on a cookie.*

nos·tal·gia (nos tal′jə or nos tal′jē ə) *n.* 1 homesickness. 2 a yearning for something in the past; sentimental longing for the return of a past period or of some former condition or circumstance: *He thought with nostalgia of how they used to go hiking in the hills.* [< NL < Gk. *nostos* homecoming + *algos* pain]

nos·tal·gic (nos tal′jik) *adj.* of, having to do with, or characterized by nostalgia: *A nostalgic film about the sixties.* —**nos·tal′gi·cal·ly,** *adv.*

nos·tril (nos′trəl) *n.* either of the two external openings in the nose. Air is breathed into the lungs through the nostrils. [OE *nosthyrl* < *nosu* nose + *thyrel* hole]

nos·trum (nos′trəm) *n.* 1 a medicine of secret ingredients prepared and recommended by the same person, usually without scientific evidence of its effectiveness; patent medicine. 2 a pet scheme for producing wonderful results; cure-all. [< L *nostrum* ours; because usually prepared by the person recommending it]

nos·y (nō′zē) *adj.* **nos·i·er, nos·i·est.** See **nosey.**

Nosy Parker See **Nosey Parker.**

not (not) *adv.* a word used to make a negative statement: *That is not true.* [unstressed var. of *nought*]
➤ *Hom.* **knot, naught, nought.**

no·ta· be·ne (nō′tə bē′nē or ben′ē) *Latin.* note well; observe what follows; take notice. *Abbrev.:* N.B. or n.b.

no·ta·bil·i·ty (nō′tə bil′ə tē) *n., pl.* **-ties.** 1 the quality of being notable; distinction. 2 a prominent person: *There were several notabilities at the reception.*

no·ta·ble (nō′tə bəl) *adj., n.* —*adj.* 1 worthy of notice; striking; remarkable; important: *a notable event, a notable man, a notable book, a notable painter.* 2 that can be noted or perceived; perceptible; appreciable: *a notable quantity.* —*n.* an important or famous person: *Many notables attended the Governor General's levee.* [ME < OF < L *notabilis* < *notare* note < *nota* a mark] —**no′ta·ble·ness,** *n.* —**no′ta·bly,** *adv.*

no·tar·i·al (nō ter′ē əl) *adj.* 1 of or having to do with a notary public. 2 made or done by a notary public.

no·ta·rize (nō′tə rīz′) *v.* **-rized, -riz·ing.** certify (a contract, deed, will, etc.).

no·ta·ry (nō′tə rē) *n., pl.* **-ries.** 1 notary public. 2 in Quebec, a lawyer who has the same training as a barrister but who is not permitted to plead in court. [< L *notarius* clerk, ult. < *nota* note]

notary public a person authorized to certify deeds and contracts, take oaths, and attend to certain other legal matters. *Abbrev.:* N.P.

no·ta·tion (nō tā′shən) *n.* 1 a set of signs or symbols used to represent numbers, quantities, or other values: *In arithmetic we use the Arabic notation (1, 2, 3, 4, etc.).* 2 the representing of numbers, quantities, or other values by symbols or signs: *Music and chemistry have special systems of notation.* 3 a note to assist memory; record; jotting. 4 the act of noting. [< L *notatio, -onis* < *notare* to mark]

notch (noch) *n., v.* —*n.* 1 a V-shaped nick or cut made in an edge or on a curving surface: *The Indians cut notches on a stick to keep count of numbers.* 2 a deep, narrow pass or gap between mountains. 3 in Newfoundland, an entrance to a harbor. 4 a grade; step; degree.
—*v.* 1 make a notch or notches in. 2 record by notches; score; tally. [< MF *oche* < OF *oschier* notch; *an och* taken as *a noch*]

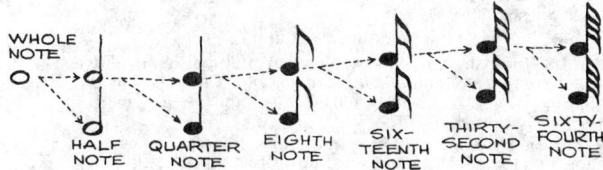

WHOLE NOTE · HALF NOTE · QUARTER NOTE · EIGHTH NOTE · SIXTEENTH NOTE · THIRTY-SECOND NOTE · SIXTY-FOURTH NOTE

Musical notes (def. 7)

hat, āge, fär; let, ēqual, tėrm; it, īce
hot, ōpen, ôrder; oil, out; cup, pút, rüle,
əbove, takən, pencəl, lemən, circəs
ch, child; ng, long; sh, ship
th, thin; ŦH, then; zh, measure

note (nōt) *n., v.* **not·ed, not·ing.** —*n.* **1** a short sentence, phrase, or single word written down to remind one of something; memorandum: *Her notes helped her remember what the speaker said.* **2** notice; heed; observation. **3** a comment or piece of information in a book, often added to help students. **4** a brief letter. **5** a formal letter from one government to another; diplomatic or official communication in writing: *England sent a note of protest to France.* **6** a single sound of definite pitch made by a musical instrument or voice. **7** *Music.* **a** a written sign to show the pitch and length of a sound. **b** any one of the keys of a piano: *to strike the wrong note.* **8** a bird's song or call. **9** a song; melody; tune. **10** a tone of voice or way of expression: *There was a note of anxiety in her voice.* **11** a sign, token, or proof of genuineness; characteristic or distinguishing feature. **12** distinction, importance, or consequence. **13** *Business.* a written promise to pay a certain sum of money at a certain time. **14** a certificate of a government or bank that may be used as money.
compare notes, exchange ideas or opinions.
make a note of, write down as something to be remembered.
of note, a that is important, great, or notable: *a writer of note.* **b** of being noticed: *worthy of note.*
strike the right note, say or do something suitable.
take note of, give attention to or notice: *Take note of the time, please; we must not be late.*
take notes, write down things to be remembered.
—*v.* **1** write down as a thing to be remembered. **2** observe carefully; give attention to; take notice of: *Now note what I do next.* **3** mention specially. **4** indicate, signify, or denote. [ME < OF < L *nota* mark] —**note′less,** *adj.* —**not′er,** *n.*

note·book (nōt′búk′) *n.* a book in which to write notes of things to be learned or remembered.

not·ed (nō′tid) *adj.* conspicuous or well-known; celebrated; famous: *Samson was noted for his strength. Shakespeare is a noted English author.*
☛ *Syn.* See note at **famous.**

note·paper (nōt′pā′pər) *n.* paper used for writing letters.

note·wor·thy (nōt′wėr′ŦHē) *adj.* worthy of notice; remarkable: *noteworthy achievement.* —**note′wor′thi·ness,** *n.*

noth·ing (nuth′ing) *n., adv.* —*n.* **1** not anything; no thing: *Nothing arrived by mail.* **2** something that does not exist: *create a world out of nothing.* **3** a thing of no importance or value; person of no importance: *People regard him as a nothing.* **4** zero; nought.
make nothing of, a be unable to understand. **b** fail to use or do. **c** treat as unimportant or worthless.
nothing less than, just the same as.
think nothing of, a consider as easy to do. **b** treat as unimportant or worthless.
—*adv.* not at all: *She is nothing like her sister in looks.* [< *no* + *thing*]
☛ *Usage.* See note at **nobody.**

noth·ing·ness (nuth′ing nis) *n.* **1** being nothing; non-existence. **2** being of no value; worthlessness. **3** an unimportant or worthless thing. **4** unconsciousness.

no·tice (nō′tis) *n., v.* **-ticed, -tic·ing.** —*n.* **1** observation; heed; attention: *escape one's notice.* **2** advance information; warning: *The whistle blew to give notice that the boat was about to leave.* **3** a written or printed sign; paper posted in a public place. **4** a warning or announcement that one will end an agreement with another at a certain time: *The servant gave notice.* **5** a paragraph or article about something: *The new book got a favorable notice.* **6 serve notice,** give warning; inform; announce. **7 take notice,** give attention; observe; see.
—*v.* **1** take notice of; give attention to; perceive: *I noticed a big difference at once.* **2** mention; refer to. [< F < L *notitia* < *notus* known]

no·tice·a·ble (nō′tis ə bəl) *adj.* **1** easily seen or noticed: *The class has made noticeable improvement.* **2** *Archaic.* worth noticing; noteworthy.

no·tice·a·bly (nō′tis ə blē) *adv.* to a noticeable degree: *It is noticeably cooler in the shade.*

no·ti·fi·ca·tion (nō′tə fə kā′shən) *n.* **1** a notifying. **2** a notice: *Have you received a notification of the meeting?*

no·ti·fy (nō′tə fī′) *v.* **-fied, -fy·ing.** give notice to; let know; inform; announce to: *Our teacher notified us that there would be a test on Monday.* [ME < OF < L *notificare* < *notus* known + *facere* make] —**no′ti·fi′er,** *n.*
☛ *Syn.* See note at **inform.**

no·tion (nō′shən) *n.* **1** an idea; understanding: *He has no notion of what I mean.* **2** an opinion; view; belief: *It is a common notion that red hair means a quick temper.* **3** intention: *He has no notion of risking his money.* **4** an inclination; whim: *She had a notion to visit her grandmother.* **5 notions,** *pl.* small useful articles, such as pins, needles, thread, tape, etc. [< L *notio, -onis,* ult. < *noscere* know]
☛ *Syn.* **1.** See note at **idea.**

no·tion·al (nō′shən əl) *adj.* **1** having to do with ideas or opinions. **2** in one's imagination or thought only; not real.

no·to·chord (nō′tə kôrd′) *n.* **1** a rodlike structure that is the primitive cartilaginous backbone of the lowest vertebrates. **2** a similar structure in the embryos of higher vertebrates. [< Gk. *nōton* back + E *chord*²]

no·to·ri·e·ty (nō′tə rī′ə tē) *n., pl.* **-ties. 1** a being famous for something bad; ill fame: *A crime or scandal brings much notoriety to those involved in it.* **2** the state of being widely known. **3** a well-known person.

no·to·ri·ous (nō tô′rē əs) *adj.* **1** widely known because of some unfavorable or bad quality, action, etc.: *a notorious criminal, a notorious gossip. He is notorious for being late.* **2** widely known. [< Med.L *notorius* < L *notus* known] —**no·to′ri·ous·ly,** *adv.* —**no·to′ri·ous·ness,** *n.*

No·tre Dame (nō′trə däm′) **1** *French.* Our Lady, the Virgin Mary. **2** in Paris, France, a famous cathedral.

no–trump (nō′trump′) *adj., n. Bridge, etc.* —*adj.* of a contract, hand, etc., played or suitable for playing without trumps. —*n.* **1** a declaration or bid to play with no suit as trumps. **2** a hand that is so played.

not·with·stand·ing (not′with stan′ding *or* -wiŦH-) *prep., conj., adv.* —*prep.* in spite of: *He bought it notwithstanding the high price.*
—*conj.* in spite of the fact that: *Notwithstanding there was a need for haste, he still delayed.*
—*adv.* in spite of it; nevertheless: *It is raining; but I shall go, notwithstanding.*

nou·gat (nü′gət *or* nü′gä) *n.* a kind of soft candy made from sugar paste, containing nuts and sometimes, fruit. [< F < Provençal *noga,* ult. < L *nux, nucis* nut]

nought (not *or* nôt) *n., adv.* —*n.* **1** zero; 0. **2** naught; nothing. —*adv. Archaic.* in no way; not at all. [see NAUGHT]
☛ *Hom.* **knot,** not (not), and **naught** (not or nôt).

noughts and crosses *Esp. Brit.* tick-tack-toe.

noun (noun) *n., adj.* —*n.* a word used as the name of a person, place, thing, quality, event, etc. Words like *John, table, school, kindness, skill,* and *party* are nouns. —*adj.* used as a noun. [ME < AF *nom* < L *nomen* name]
☛ *Usage.* **Forms of nouns.** Nouns may be single words or compound words written solid or as two words or hyphenated: *ceremony, bookcase, high school, go-getter.* Most nouns change their form to make the plural, most of them adding -s or -es: *boys, kindnesses, manufacturers.* Nouns change their form for case only in the genitive or possessive, typically by adding 's or s': *boy's, Harriet's, Dickens'.*

nour·ish (nėr′ish) *v.* **1** make grow, or keep alive and well, with food; feed: *Milk nourishes a baby.* **2** maintain; foster: *nourish a hope.* [ME < OF *noriss-,* a stem of *norir* < L *nutrire* feed] —**nour′ish·er,** *n.*

nour·ish·ment (nėr′ish mənt) *n.* **1** food. **2** the act of nourishing or the condition of being nourished.

nou·veau riche (nü vō rēsh′) *pl.* **nou·veaux riches** (nü vō rēsh′). *French.* one who has recently become rich; often, one who makes a vulgar display of his wealth.

Nov. November.

no·va (nō′və) *n., pl.* **no·vae** (nō′vē *or* nō′vī), **no·vas.** *Astronomy.* a star that suddenly becomes brighter and then gradually fades away. [< L *nova (stella)* new (star)]

No·va Sco·tia duck tolling retriever (nō′və skō′shə)
Cdn. a breed of retriever developed in Nova Scotia in the early 19th
century, having a fairly long, sleek, reddish coat. These dogs are
trained to lure and retrieve waterfowl; they run and play along the
water's edge, arousing the curiosity of the birds so that they
approach within shooting range.

No·va Sco·tian (nō′və skō′shən) *n., adj.* —*n.* a native or
long-term resident of Nova Scotia. —*adj.* of or having to do with
Nova Scotia.

nov·el[1] (nov′əl) *adj.* **1** of a new kind or nature: *a novel
experience.* **2** strikingly new; original: *Red snow is a novel idea to
us.* [ME < OF L *novellus,* dim. of *novus* new]
☛ *Syn.* See note at **new.**

nov·el[2] (nov′əl) *n.* **1** a fictional story with characters and a plot,
long enough to fill one or more volumes. **2 the novel,** the branch of
literature having to do with such works: *He is studying the novel.*
[< Ital. *novella* < L *novella* new things, neut. pl. of *novellus* (see
NOVEL[1]); intermediate meaning probably "a composition showing
originality"]

nov·el·ette (nov′əl et′) *n.* a short novel.

nov·el·ist (nov′əl ist) *n.* a writer of novels.

nov·el·is·tic (nov′əl is′tik) *adj.* of or like novels.

nov·el·ize (nov′ə līz′) *v.* **-ized, iz·ing.** convert (a play,
motion-picture script, etc.) into the form of a novel.
—**nov′el·i·za′tion,** *n.*

no·vel·la (nō vel′ə; *Italian,* nō vel′lä) *n.* **no·vel·las, no·vel·le**
(*Italian,* nō vel′lä). **1** a short novel or an extended short story.
2 originally, a short prose narrative, often satirical or moralistic. [<
Ital.]

nov·el·ty (nov′əl tē) *n., pl.* **-ties. 1** newness; novel character:
After the novelty of washing dishes wore off, Mary lost interest. **2** a
new or unusual thing: *Staying up late was a novelty to the children.*
3 novelties, *pl.* small, unusual articles; toys, cheap jewellery, etc.
[ME < OF *novelte* < L *novellitas* < *novellus.* See NOVEL[1].]

No·vem·ber (nō vem′bər) *n.* the 11th month of the year. It has
30 days. [< L *November* < *novem* nine; from the order of the early
Roman calendar]

no·ve·na (nō vē′nə) *n., pl.* **-nas, -nae** (-nē *or* -nī).
Roman Catholic Church. a religious exercise consisting of prayers
or services on nine days, or nine corresponding days in consecutive
months, usually as a petition or supplication for some special
purpose: *a novena of nine first Fridays.* [< Med.L. *novena,* ult. <
L *novem* nine]

nov·ice (nov′is) *n.* **1** one who is new to what he is doing;
beginner. **2** a person who has been received into a religious order or
community but has not yet taken final vows. Before becoming a
monk or a nun, a person is a novice. [ME < OF < L *novicius* <
novus new]

no·vi·ti·ate or **no·vi·ci·ate** (nō vish′ē it *or* nō vish′ē āt′) *n.*
1 a period of probation and preparation before taking final vows in a
religious order or community. **2** novice. **3** a house or rooms
occupied by religious novices. **4** the state or period of being a
beginner in anything. [< Med.L *novitiatus,* ult. < *novus* new]

no·vo·caine or **no·vo·cain** (nō′və kān′) *n.* **1** an alkaloid
compound, used as a local anesthetic; procaine. **2 Novocain,**
Trademark. a brand of product containing this compound. [< L
novus new + E (*co*)*caine*]

now (nou) *adv., n., conj., interj.* —*adv.* **1** at the present time: *He
is here now.* **2** at once: *Do it now!* **3** then; next: *Now you see it;
now you don't. We have signed the petition and it now goes to the
school principal.* **4** at the time referred to: *The clock now strikes
three.* **5** under the present circumstances; as things are; as it is: *I
would believe almost anything now.* **6 Now** is also used to
introduce, emphasize, lessen the severity of a sentence, or
sometimes just to fill in: *Now what do you mean? Oh, come now!*
just now See **just.**
now and again, from time to time; once in a while.
now and then, from time to time; once in a while.
—*n.* the present; this time.
—*conj.* since; inasmuch as: *Now I am older, I have changed my
mind.*
—*interj.* be careful! please! [OE *nū*]

now·a·days (nou′ə dāz′) *adv., n.* —*adv.* at the present day; in
these times. —*n.* the present day; these times.

no·way (nō′wā′) *adv.* nowise.

no way *Slang.* in no way; definitely not or definitely no: *No way
could he pass an exam like that!*

no·ways (nō′wāz′) *adv.* noway.

no·where (nō′wer′ *or* nō′hwer′) *adv., n.* —*adv.* in no place; at
no place; to no place. —*n.* a nonexistent place. [OE *nāhwēr*]
☛ *Usage.* See note at **nobody.**

no·wise (nō′wīz′) *adv.* in no way; not at all.

nox·ious (nok′shəs) *adj.* **1** extremely harmful; poisonous: *Fumes
from the exhaust of an automobile are noxious.* **2** morally hurtful;
corrupting. [< L *noxius* < *noxa* hurt < *nocere* hurt] —**nox′ious·ly,**
adv. —**nox′ious·ness,** *n.*

noz·zle (noz′əl) *n.* **1** a tip or spout put on a hose, pipe, can, etc.
to allow one to control the outward flow of liquid or gas, often
made so that the user can adjust the force and shape of that flow:
He adjusted the nozzle so that the water came out in a fine spray.
2 *Slang.* nose. [dim. of *nose*]

Np neptunium.

NP noun phrase.

N.P. Notary Public.

n.p.t. normal pressure and temperature.

nr. near.

NRC or **N.R.C.** National Research Council.

Ns *Meteorology.* nimbo-stratus.

NS Nova Scotia (*used esp. in computerized address systems*).

N.S. 1 Nova Scotia. **2** New Style.

NSF or **nsf** not sufficient funds.

N.S.O. or **NSO** northern service officer.

NST or **N.S.T.** Newfoundland Standard Time.

N.S.W. New South Wales.

NT Northwest Territories (*used esp. in computerized address
systems*).

N.T. New Testament.

nth (enth) *adj. Mathematics.* being of the indefinitely large or
small value or amount denoted by *n*: *the nth power.*
to the nth degree or **power, a** to any degree or power. **b** *Informal.*
to the utmost: *He was dressed to the nth degree for the occasion.*

nt.wt. net weight.

nu (nyü *or* nü) *n.* the 13th letter (N, *ν*) of the Greek alphabet,
pronounced like English *n.*

nu·ance (nyü äns′ *or* nü äns′, nyü′äns *or* nü′äns) *n.* **1** a shade
of expression, meaning, feeling, etc. **2** a shade of color or tone. [<
F]

nub (nub) *n.* **1** a knob; protuberance. **2** a lump or small piece.
3 *Informal.* the point or gist of anything. [apparently var. of *knob*]

nub·bin (nub′ən) *n.* **1** a small lump or piece. **2** a small or
imperfect ear of corn. **3** an undeveloped fruit. [dim. of *nub*]

Nu·bi·an (nyü′bē ən *or* nü′bē ən) *n., adj.* —*n.* **1** a native or
inhabitant of Nubia, an ancient region of NE Africa. **2** any of
several languages spoken in this region. —*adj.* of or having to do
with Nubia, its people, or the languages spoken there.

nu·bile (nyü′bīl *or* nü′bīl, nyü′bəl *or* nü′bəl) *adj.* of a girl or
young woman: **1** old or mature enough to be married. **2** sexually
developed and attractive. [< L *nubilis* marriageable < *nubere* take a
husband]

nu·cle·ar (nyü′klē ər *or* nü′klē ər) *adj.* **1** of, having to do with,
or contained within the nucleus of a cell: *nuclear membranes.* **2** of
or having to do with the nuclei of atoms: *nuclear physics, nuclear
energy.* **3** of, having to do with, or using nuclear energy: *a nuclear
submarine, the nuclear age.* **4** of, having to do with, involving or
possessing nuclear weapons: *nuclear disarmament, nuclear nations.*
5 of, having to do with, or forming any kind of nucleus: *the nuclear
family.*

nuclear fission fission (def. 3).

nuclear fuel a fissile substance that will sustain a chain reaction.

nuclear fusion fusion (def. 4).

nuclear physics the branch of physics that is concerned with
atoms and their nuclear structure.

nuclear power electrical or motive power from nuclear energy
produced in a reactor.

nuclear reactor an apparatus for producing controlled nuclear
energy instead of an explosion as in a bomb. Energy and neutrons
are released when an atom splits on being struck by a neutron. A
chain reaction starts as these additional neutrons hit more atoms. In
a reactor this chain reaction is slowed down, by means of control
rods which absorb many of the neutrons. (In a bomb the reaction is
uncontrolled and happens very fast, producing an explosion.)

nu·cle·ate (*v.* nyü′klē āt′ *or* nü′klē āt′; *adj.* nyü′klē it *or*
nü′klē it, nyü′klē āt′ *or* nü′klē āt′) *v.* **-at·ed, -at·ing;** *adj.* —*v.*
form into a nucleus or around a nucleus. —*adj.* having a nucleus.

[< LL *nucleare* become full of kernels < L *nucleus* kernel]
—**nu′cle·a′tion,** *n.*

nu·cle·i (nyü′klē ī′ *or* nü′klē ī′) *n.* pl. of **nucleus.**

nu·cle·ic acid (nyü klē′ik *or* nyü klā′ik, nü klē′ik *or* nü klā′ik) any of a group of complex acids, including DNA and RNA, found especially in the nuclei of cells. All nucleic acids are composed of phosphoric acid, a carbohydrate, and a base and are essential to life.

nu·cle·o·lus (nyü klē′ə ləs *or* nü klē′ə ləs) *n., pl.* -**li** (-lī′ *or* -lē′). *Biology.* a small structure, usually round, found within the nucleus in most cells. [< LL *nucleolus,* dim. of L *nucleus* kernel]

nu·cle·on (nyü′klē on′ *or* nü′klē on′) *n.* one of the atomic particles that make up the nucleus of an atom, such as a neutron or proton.

nu·cle·on·ics (nyü′klē on′iks *or* nü′klē on′iks) *n.pl.* the study and science of the behavior and characteristics of nucleons.

nu·cle·us (nyü′klē əs *or* nü′klē əs) *n., pl.* -**cle·i** *or* -**cle·us·es.** **1** a beginning to which additions are to be made. **2** a central part or thing around which other parts or things are collected: *The family is the nucleus of our society.* **3** *Physics.* the group of particles forming the central part of an atom and carrying a positive electric charge, consisting of protons and neutrons (except for the hydrogen atom, which contains only a proton) and sometimes, other particles. The nucleus makes up most of the mass of an atom but only a tiny fraction of its size. **4** *Chemistry.* a basic, stable group of atoms in a compound: *the benzene nucleus.* **5** *Biology.* a mass of protoplasm found in most plant and animal cells, without which a cell cannot grow and divide. See **cell** for picture. **6** *Anatomy.* a group of nerve cells in the central nervous system. **7** *Astronomy.* the dense, central part of a comet's head. **8** *Meteorology.* a particle of dust, etc., upon which water vapor condenses so as to form a drop. [< L *nucleus* < *nux, nucis* nut]

nude (nyüd *or* nüd) *adj., n.* —*adj.* **1** uncovered or naked; especially, with the clothing removed. **2** being the color of light-colored, or fair, skin. —*n.* **1** a representation of a naked person in painting, sculpture, photography, etc. **2** a naked person. **in the nude,** without clothes on; naked: *The boys went swimming in the nude.* [< L *nudus*] —**nude′ness,** *n.*
☛ *Syn. adj.* See note at **bare.**

nudge (nuj) *v.* **nudged, nudg·ing;** *n.* —*v.* **1** push slightly; jog with the elbow to attract attention. **2** prod; stimulate: *to nudge one's memory, to nudge a person into action.* **3** approach closely: *She is nudging forty.* —*n.* a slight push or jog. [origin uncertain]

nud·ism (nyü′diz əm *or* nü′diz əm) *n.* the cult or practice of going naked, especially for the sake of one's health.

nud·ist (nyü′dist *or* nü′dist) *n., adj.* —*n.* a person who practises nudism. —*adj.* of nudism or nudists.

nu·di·ty (nyü′də tē *or* nü′də tē) *n., pl.* -**ties.** **1** nakedness. **2** something naked.

nu·ga·to·ry (nyü′gə tô′rē *or* nü′gə tô′rē) *adj.* **1** trifling; worthless. **2** of no force; invalid. **3** ineffective; useless. [< L *nugatorius* < *nugari* trifle < *nugae* trifles]

nug·get (nug′it) *n.* **1** a lump, especially a small lump of gold in its natural state. **2** anything small but valuable: *a few nuggets of truth.* [? < *nug* lump]

nui·sance (nyü′səns *or* nü′səns) *n.* a thing or person that annoys, troubles, offends, or is disagreeable: *Flies are a nuisance.* [ME < OF *nuisance* < *nuire* harm < L *nocere*]

nuisance ground *Cdn.* in the West, a garbage dump; a place where worn-out and useless material is thrown.

nuisance tax a tax that is annoying because it is collected in very small amounts from the consumer.

nuke (nyük *or* nük) *n. Slang.* **1** a nuclear weapon. **2** nuclear reactor.

null (nul) *adj.* **1** not binding; of no effect; as if not existing: *A promise obtained by force is legally null.* **2** unimportant; useless; meaningless; valueless. **3** not any; zero. **null and void,** without legal force or effect; worthless. [< L *nullus* < *ne-* not + *ullus* any]

nul·li·fy (nul′ə fī′) *v.* -**fied, -fy·ing.** **1** make not binding; render void; *nullify a law.* **2** make unimportant, useless, or meaningless; destroy; cancel: *The difficulties of the plan nullify its advantages.* [< L *nullificare* < *nullus* not any + *facere* make] —**nul′li·fi·ca′tion,** *n.* —**nul′li·fi′er,** *n.*

nul·li·ty (nul′ə tē) *n., pl.* -**ties.** **1** futility; nothingness. **2** a mere nothing. **3** something that is null, such as a nullified law or agreement. [< Med.L *nullitas* < L *nullus* not any]

Num. Numbers.

numb (num) *adj., v.* —*adj.* having lost the power of feeling or

hat, āge, fär; let, ēqual, tėrm; it, īce
hot, ōpen, ôrder; oil, out; cup, pút, rüle,
əbove, takən, pencəl, lemən, circəs
ch, child; ng, long; sh, ship
th, thin; ᵮн, then; zh, measure

moving: *My fingers are numb with cold.* —*v.* **1** make numb. **2** dull the feelings of: *The old lady was numbed with grief when her grandchild died.* [ult. < OE *numen* taken, seized] —**numb′ly,** *adv.* —**numb′ness,** *n.*

num·ber (num′bər) *n., v.* —*n.* **1** a word or symbol used in counting. Two, fourteen, twenty-six, second, fourteenth, twenty-sixth, 2, 14, and 26 are all numbers. **2** the amount of units; sum; total: *The number of your fingers is ten.* **3** a quantity: *a number of reasons.* **4** a collection or company: *the number of saints.* **5** the particular number that indicates the place of a person or object in a series, and is a means of identifying it: *an apartment number, a licence number.* **6** one of a numbered series, often a particular numeral or set of numerals identifying a person or thing: *a telephone number, a house number.* Symbol: # **7** a single item on a program, etc.: *The program consisted of four musical numbers.* **8** a song or other piece of music: *She sings many old numbers.* **9** a single issue of a periodical. **10** *Informal.* any thing or person thought of as standing apart from a collection or company: *That dress is the most fashionable number in the store.* **11** *Grammar.* **a** a system for varying the form of nouns, pronouns, and adjectives to indicate reference to one or more than one person or thing. English distinguishes only singular and plural number. Some languages also distinguish dual number. **b** a form or group of forms indicating this. **12** numbers, *pl.* **a** arithmetic. **b** many: *Numbers were turned away.* **c** numerical preponderance; a being more: *win a battle by force of numbers.* **d** *Archaic.* poetry; a group of musical notes or measures. **13** Numbers, the fourth book of the Bible, which tells about the counting of the Israelites after they left Egypt.
a number of, several; many.
beyond number, too many to count.
(someone's) number is up, *Informal.* someone is doomed.
without number, too many to be counted.
—*v.* **1** mark with a number; assign a number to; distinguish with a number: *The pages of this book are numbered.* **2** be able to show; have: *This city numbers a million inhabitants.* **3** amount to: *a crew numbering 20 men.* **4** include as one of a class or collection: *I number you among my best friends.* **5** fix the number of; limit: *His days in office are numbered.* **6** count. [ME < OF *nombre* < L *numerus*] —**num′ber·er,** *n.*
☛ *Syn. n.* **2. Number, sum** = the total of two or more persons, things, or units taken together. **Number** applies to the total reached by counting the persons or things in a group or collection: *Only twelve came, a smaller number than usual.* **Sum** applies to the total reached by adding figures or things: *The sum of two and two is four.*
☛ *Usage.* **Number** is a collective noun, requiring a singular or plural verb according as the total or the individual units are meant: *A number of tickets have already been sold. The number of tickets sold is astonishing.* See also the note at **amount.**
☛ *Usage.* **Numbers.** Usage varies in writing numbers that are parts of consecutive sentences. In general, newspapers and informal writing have figures for numbers over ten, words for smaller numbers; a more formal style is to spell out all numbers that can be written in one or two words. Informal: *four, ten, 15, 92, 114.* Formal: *four, ten, fifteen, ninety-two, 114.* Practice within a piece of writing should be consistent.

num·ber·less (num′bər lis) *adj.* **1** very numerous; too many to count: *There are numberless fish in the sea.* **2** without a number.

number one 1 *Informal.* oneself: *He worries too much about number one.* **2** the first or best in a series.

numb·skull (num′skul′) *n.* numskull.

nu·mer·a·ble (nyü′mər ə bəl *or* nü′mər ə bəl) *adj.* that can be counted.

nu·mer·al (nyü′mər əl *or* nü′mər əl) *n.* a word, figure, or a group of figures standing for a number. 2, 15 and 100 are Arabic numerals. II, XV, and C are Roman numerals for 2, 15, and 100. [< LL *numeralis* < L *numerus* number]

nu·mer·ate (nyü′mər āt′ *or* nü′mər āt′) *v.* -**at·ed, -at·ing.** **1** enumerate. **2** read (a numerical expression). [< L *numerare* < *numerus* number]

nu·mer·a·tion (nyü′mər ā′shən *or* nü′mər ā′shən) *n.* **1** the process or a method of numbering, counting, or calculating. **2** the expression in words of a written numeral.

nu·mer·a·tor (nyü′mər ā′tər *or* nü′mər ā′tər) *n.* **1** in a fraction, the number above the line: *In ³/₈, 3 is the numerator and 8 is the denominator.* **2** a person or thing that makes a count, takes a census, etc. [< LL *numerator* (def. 2)]

nu·mer·ic (nyü mer′ik *or* nü mer′ik) *adj.* numerical.

nu·mer·i·cal (nyü mer′ə kəl or nü mer′ə kəl) adj. 1 of or having to do with number or numbers; in numbers; by numbers. 2 shown by numbers, not by letters: 10 is a numerical quantity; bx is a literal or algebraic quantity. 3 of a mathematical quantity, designating the value in figures without considering the sign: The numerical value of +4 is less than that of −7, though its algebraic value is more. —**nu·mer′i·cal·ly**, adv.

nu·mer·ol·o·gist (nyü′mə rol′ə jist or nü′mə rol′ə jist) n. a person who practises numerology.

nu·mer·ol·o·gy (nyü mə rol′ə jē or nü mə rol′ə jē) n. a system of foretelling the future, based on the supposedly mystic influence of numbers.

nu·mer·ous (nyü′mər əs or nü′mər əs) adj. 1 very many: He has numerous acquaintances. 2 consisting of great numbers: He has a numerous circle of acquaintances. [< L numerosus] —**nu′mer·ous·ly**, adv. —**nu′mer·ous·ness**, n.

Nu·mid·i·an (nyü mid′ē ən) n., adj. —n. 1 a native or inhabitant of Numidia, an ancient country in N Africa. 2 the Hamitic language of Numidia. —adj. of or having to do with Numidia, its people, or their language.

nu·mis·mat·ic (nyü′miz mat′ik or nü′miz mat′ik) adj. 1 of numismatics or numismatists. 2 of coins and medals.

nu·mis·mat·ics (nyü′miz mat′iks or nü′miz mat′iks) n. the study of coins and medals. [< F < L numisma coin < Gk. nomisma < nomizein have in use]

nu·mis·ma·tist (nyü miz′mə tist or nü miz′mə tist) n. a person knowledgable about or studying numismatics.

num·skull (num′skul′) n. Informal. a stupid person; blockhead. [for numb skull]

nun (nun) n. a woman who is a member of a religious order and lives a life of service, prayer, and worship. Some nuns teach; some nurse the sick. [OE nunne < LL nonna, fem. of nonnus monk] ☞ Hom. none.

nu·na·tak (nü′nə tak′) n. an isolated mountain peak or hill rising above the surrounding glacial ice. [< Inuktitut (Eskimo)]

Nunc Di·mit·tis (nungk′dē mit′is) the canticle of Simeon, beginning "Lord, now lettest thou thy servant depart in peace." (Luke 2:29-32). [< L Nunc dimittis now dost thou dismiss, the first words as given in the Vulgate]

nun·ci·o (nun′shē ō′) n., pl. -ci·os. an ambassador from the Pope to a government. [< Ital. < L nuntius messenger]

nun·ner·y (nun′ər ē) n., pl. -ner·ies. a building or buildings where nuns live; convent.

nun·ny bag (nun′ē) Cdn. in Newfoundland, a kind of haversack, often made of sealskin.

nun's veiling a thin, plain-woven, woollen fabric, used mainly for women's dresses.

nup·tial (nup′shəl or nup′chəl) adj., n. —adj. of marriage or weddings. —n. **nuptials**, pl. a wedding; the wedding ceremony. [< L nuptialis, ult. < nubere take a husband]

nurse (nėrs) n., v. **nursed, nurs·ing.** —n. 1 a person who takes care of the sick, the injured, or the old, or is trained to do this. 2 a woman who cares for and brings up the young children or babies of another person. 3 one who feeds and protects. —v. 1 be a nurse; act as a nurse; work as a nurse. 2 act as a nurse for; wait on or try to cure (the sick); take care of (sick, injured, or old people). 3 cure or try to cure by care: She nursed a bad cold by going to bed. 4 take care of and bring up (another's baby or young child). 5 make grow; nourish and protect: to nurse a plant, to nurse a hatred in the heart. 6 use or treat with special care: He nursed his sore arm by using it very little. 7 hold closely; clasp fondly. 8 feed milk to (a baby) at the breast. 9 suck milk from the breast. [ME < OF nurrice < L nutricia < nutrire feed, nourish]

nurse·ling (nėrs′ling) See **nursling.**

nurse·maid (nėrs′mād′) n. a maid employed to care for children.

nurs·er·y (nėr′sər ē or nėrs′rē) n., pl. -er·ies. 1 a room set apart for the use of babies and children. 2 a day-care centre. 3 nursery school. 4 a piece of ground or place where young plants are grown for transplanting or sale. 5 a place or condition that helps something to grow and develop: Slums are often nurseries of disease.

nurs·er·y·maid (nėr′sər ē mād′ or nėrs′rē-) n. nursemaid.

nurs·er·y·man (nėr′sər ē mən or nėrs′rē-) n., pl. -men. a man who grows or sells young trees and plants.

nursery rhyme a short poem for young children: "Humpty Dumpty sat on a wall" is the beginning of a famous nursery rhyme.

nursery school a school for young children, usually for those under five.

nursing home 1 a residence providing personal or nursing care for old, chronically ill, or disabled persons. 2 Brit. a private hospital.

nursing station 1 in a hospital, a location serving as a base and office area for the nurses on duty on a floor or part of a floor. 2 Cdn. in the North, a small hospital for emergency cases, served by nurses and visited periodically by a doctor.

nurs·ling (nėrs′ling) n. 1 a baby that is being nursed. 2 any person or thing that is having tender care.

nur·ture (nėr′chər) v. -tured, -tur·ing; n. —v. 1 bring up; care for; rear: She nurtured the child as if he had been her own. 2 nourish: Minerals in the soil nurture the plants. —n. 1 the act or process of raising or rearing; a bringing up; training; education. 2 food; nourishment. [ME < OF nourture < LL nutritura a nursing, suckling < L nutrire nurse] —**nur′tur·er,** n.

nut (nut) n., v. **nut·ted, nut·ting;** adj. —n. 1 a dry fruit or seed with a hard, woody, or leathery shell and a kernel inside. Some nuts, including walnuts, almonds, and pecans, are good to eat. See fruit for picture. 2 the kernel of a nut. 3 a small square or six-sided block, usually metal, having a threaded hole in the centre, by means of which it is screwed on to a bolt to hold the bolt in place. 4 a piece at the upper end of a violin, cello, etc. over which the strings pass. 5 Slang. the head. 6 Slang. an eccentric or crazy person. 7 Slang. an enthusiast: a car nut.
hard nut to crack, Informal. a difficult question, problem, or undertaking.
—v. gather nuts.
—adj. **nuts,** Slang. eccentric or crazy. [OE hnutu] —**nut′like′,** adj.

nut·crack·er (nut′krak′ər) n. 1 an instrument for cracking the shells of nuts. 2 any of several birds of the same family as the crow, that feed on nuts.

nut·gall (nut′gol′ or -gôl′) n. a lump or ball that swells up on an oak tree where it has been injured by an insect; gall.

nut·hatch (nut′hach′) n. any of a family (Sittidae) of small songbirds having a strong, straight, pointed bill, long, pointed wings, and a short tail, and typically having plumage that is greyish-blue above and white or reddish on the under parts. [ME notehache, literally nut hacker; from the birds' habit of opening nuts by hammering them with the bill until the shell is broken]

nut·house (nut′hous′) n. Slang. a mental hospital.

nut·let (nut′lit) n. 1 a small nut. 2 the stone of a peach, plum, cherry, etc.

nut·meat (nut′mēt′) n. the kernel of a nut.

nut·meg (nut′meg) n. 1 a hard, spicy seed about as big as a marble, obtained from the fruit of an East Indian tree. Nutmeg is grated and used for flavoring food. 2 the tree. [ME; half-translation of OF *nois mugue, var. of nois muguete, originally nut smelling like musk (nois < L nux; mugue, ult. < LL muscus)]

nu·tri·a (nyü′trē ə or nü′trē ə) n. 1 the durable, valuable, beaverlike fur of the coypu. 2 (adjl.) made of this fur: a nutria coat. 3 coypu. [< Sp. < L lutra]

nu·tri·ent (nyü′trē ənt or nü′trē ənt) n., adj. —n. a nutritive substance. —adj. nourishing. [< L nutriens, -entis, ppr. of nutrire nourish]

nu·tri·ment (nyü′trə mənt or nü′trə mənt) n. nourishment; food. [< L nutrimentum < nutrire nourish]

nu·tri·tion (nyü trish′ən or nü trish′ən) n. 1 food; nourishment: A balanced diet gives good nutrition. 2 the series of processes by which food is changed to living tissues.

nu·tri·tion·al (nyü trish′ən əl or nü trish′ən əl) adj. having to do with nutrition. —**nu·tri′tion·al·ly,** adv.

nu·tri·tion·ist (nyü trish′ə nist or nü trish′ə nist) n. an expert in the processes of nutrition.

nu·tri·tious (nyü trish′əs or nü trish′əs) adj. valuable as food; nourishing. [< L nutritius, nutricius < nutrix nurse < nutrire nourish] —**nu·tri′tious·ly,** adv. —**nu·tri′tious·ness,** n.

nu·tri·tive (nyü′trə tiv or nü′trə tiv) adj. 1 having to do with foods and the use of foods. Digestion is part of the nutritive process. 2 nutritious. —**nu′tri·tive·ness,** n.

nut·shell (nut′shel′) n. 1 the shell of a nut. 2 something extremely small in size or scanty in amount.
in a nutshell, in very brief form; in a few words.

nut·ting (nut′ing) n. the act of looking for nuts; gathering nuts.

nut·ty (nut′ē) adj. -ti·er, -ti·est. 1 containing many nuts: nutty cake. 2 like nuts; tasting like nuts. 3 Slang. eccentric; crazy. 4 Slang. very interested or enthusiastic. —**nut′ti·ly,** adv. —**nut′ti·ness,** n.

nux vom·i·ca (nuks′vom′ə kə) 1 the poisonous seed of an Asian tree (Strychnos nux-vomica), containing strychnine and other poisonous alkaloids. 2 a drug prepared from these seeds, formerly

used in medicine. **3** the tree itself. [< Med.L *nux vomica* vomiting nut < L *nux* nut + *vomere* vomit]

nuz·zle (nuz′əl) *v.* **-zled, -zling. 1** poke or rub with the nose; press the nose against: *The calf nuzzles its mother.* **2** nestle; snuggle; cuddle. **3** burrow or dig with the nose. [< *nose*; influenced by *nestle*]

NV Nevada.

NW or **N.W.** northwest; northwestern.

NWMP or **N.W.M.P.** North West Mounted Police.

N.W.T. Northwest Territories.

NY New York State.

N.Y. New York State.

ny·lon (nī′lon) *n.* **1** an extremely strong and durable, plastic substance, used to make textiles, utensils, bristles, etc. **2 nylons,** *pl.* stockings made of nylon. **3** (*adj.*) made of nylon: *Many toothbrushes have nylon bristles.* [< *Nylon,* a trademark; 20c.]

nymph (nimf) *n.* **1** *Greek and Roman mythology.* one of a group of minor goddesses of nature, beautiful maidens living in seas, rivers, springs, hills, woods or trees. **2** *Poetic.* a beautiful or graceful young woman. **3** any of certain insects in the stage of

hat, āge, fär; let, ēqual, tėrm; it, īce
hot, ōpen, ôrder; oil, out; cup, put, rüle,
above, takən, pencəl, lemən, circəs
ch, child; ng, long; sh, ship
th, thin; ŦH, then; zh, measure

development between larva and adult. It resembles the adult but has no wings. [ME < OF < L < Gk. *nymphē*] —**nymph′like′,** *adj.*

nymph·et (nim′fət *or* nim fet′) *n.* an attractive young girl who is at or close to the age of puberty and shows herself to be aware of her sexuality.

nym·pho·ma·ni·a (nim′fə mā′nē ə) *n. Psychiatry.* excessive, uncontrollable sexual desire in a woman. [< Gk. *nymphē* nymph, bride + E *mania*]

nym·pho·ma·ni·ac (nim′fə mā′nē ak′) *adj., n.* —*adj.* **1** of or characterized by nymphomania. **2** suffering from nymphomania. —*n.* a woman who suffers from nymphomania.

N.Z. New Zealand.

Oo

o or **O¹** (ō) *n., pl.* **o's** or **O's.** **1** the fifteenth letter of the English alphabet. **2** any speech sound represented by this letter. **3** a person or thing identified as *o*, especially the 15th in a series. **4** zero. **5** O, the type of human blood not containing either of the antigens A or B. It is one of the four blood types in the ABO system. **6** something shaped like the letter O. **7** (*adj.*) of or being an O or o.
☛ *Hom.* **oh, owe.**

O² (ō) See **oh.**
☛ *Hom.* **owe.**

☛ *Usage.* **O** is usually used only before a name or something treated as a name: *O Canada. O Happy Day!* In other cases, the spelling generally used is **Oh.**

o' (ə *or* ō) *prep.* **1** of: *man-o'-war.* **2** on.

o– *prefix.* the form of *ob-* occurring before *m*, as in *omit.*

o ohm.

o. **1** octavo. **2** *Baseball.* out.

O oxygen.

O. **1** Ohio. **2** Ocean. **3** October. **4** Octavo.

oaf (ōf) *n., pl.* **oafs.** a clumsy and usually stupid or boorish person. [orig. = elf's child, or changeling < dial. *aufe, aulfe,* ult. < ON *álfr* elf. 17c.]

oaf·ish (ō'fish) *adj.* clumsy and stupid. —**oaf'ish·ly,** *adv.* —**oaf'ish·ness,** *n.*

oak (ōk) *n.* **1** any of a genus (*Quercus*) of deciduous or evergreen trees or shrubs of the beech family, having usually lobed or toothed leaves and bearing single-seeded nuts called acorns. **2** the hard, durable wood of an oak, valued for the construction of buildings, furniture, etc. **3** (*adj.*) made of oak: *an oak desk.* **4** any of various trees or shrubs resembling oaks in some way, such as poison oak. **5** the leaves of an oak, used as decoration. **6** something made of oak. [OE *āc*] —**oak'like',** *adj.*

oak apple a lump or ball on an oak leaf or stem resulting from injury by an insect.

oak·en (ō'kən) *adj. Archaic or poetic.* made of oak wood: *the old oaken bucket.*

oak gall oak apple.

oa·kum (ō'kəm) *n.* a loose fibre obtained by untwisting and picking apart old ropes, used for stopping up the seams or cracks in ships. [OE *ācumba* offcombings]

oar (ôr) *n., v.* —*n.* **1** a long pole with a broad, flat blade at one end, used for rowing or steering a boat. See **rowboat** for picture. **2** a person who rows: *He's the best oar in our crew.*
put (one's) **oar in,** meddle; interfere.
rest on (one's) **oars,** stop working or trying and take a rest.
—*v.* row. [OE *ār*]

oar·lock (ôr'lok') *n.* a support for an oar; rowlock. [OE *ārloc*]

oars·man (ôrz'mən) *n., pl.* **-men.** **1** a man who rows. **2** a man who rows well.

OAS or **O.A.S.** Organization of American States.

o·a·ses (ō ā'sēz *or* ō'ə sēz') *n.* pl. of **oasis.**

o·a·sis (ō ā'sis *or* ō'ə sis) *n., pl.* **-ses.** **1** a fertile spot in the desert: *Water is always available at an oasis.* **2** any fertile spot in a barren land; any pleasant place in a desolate region. [< L < Gk. *oasis,* apparently < Egyptian]

oat (ōt) *n.* **1** Usually, **oats,** *pl.* a tall cereal grass (*Avena sativa*), widely cultivated for its edible seeds. **2** oats, *pl.* the seeds of the oat plant. **3** any of various other grasses of the same genus. **4** *Poetic.* a musical pipe made of an oat straw.
feel (one's) **oats,** *Slang.* **a** be lively or frisky. **b** feel pleased or important and show it.
sow (one's) **wild oats,** do the things that wild young people do before settling down.
[OE *āte*]

oat·cake (ōt'kāk') *n.* a thin cake made of oatmeal.

oat·en (ō'tən) *adj.* made of oats, oat straw, or oatmeal.

oath (ōth) *n., pl.* **oaths** (ōŦHZ *or* ōths). **1** a solemn promise or statement that something is true, especially such a promise made to a judge, coroner, etc. If a person tells lies after taking an oath he can be punished by the law. **2** the name of God or some holy person or thing used as an exclamation to add force or to express anger. **3** a curse; swear word.
take oaths or **take** (someone's) **oath,** certify or attest an oath: *A notary public is authorized to take oaths.*
take oath or **take an oath,** make an oath; promise or state solemnly.
under oath, bound by an oath: *He gave his evidence under oath.*
[OE *āth*]

oat·meal (ōt'mēl') *n.* **1** oats made into meal; ground oats. **2** rolled oats. **3** porridge made from rolled oats or oatmeal.

ob- *prefix.* **1** against; in the way; opposing; hindering, as in *obstruct.* **2** inversely; contrary to the usual position, as in *oblate.* **3** toward; to, as in *obvert.* **4** on; over, as in *obscure.* Also: **o-,** before *m*; **oc-,** before *c*; **of-,** before *f*; **op-,** before *p*; **os-,** in some cases before *c* and *t.* [< L]

ob. **1** died (for L *obiit;* used on tombstones, etc.). **2** oboe.

ob·bli·ga·to (ob'lə gä'tō) *adj., n., pl.* **-tos.** *Music.* —*adj.* accompanying a solo, but having a distinct character and independent importance. —*n.* an obbligato part or accompaniment. Also, **obligato.** [< Ital. *obbligato,* literally, obliged]

ob·du·ra·cy (ob'dyə rə sē) *n.* being obdurate.

ob·du·rate (ob'dyə rit) *adj.* **1** stubborn; unyielding: *an obdurate refusal.* **2** hardened in feelings or heart; not repentant: *an obdurate criminal.* [< L *obduratus,* pp. of *obdurare* < *ob-* against + *durare* harden] —**ob'du·rate·ly,** *adv.* —**ob'du·rate·ness,** *n.*

O.B.E. Officer (of the Order) of the British Empire.

o·be·di·ence (ō bē'dē əns *or* ō bē'dyəns) *n.* the act or habit of doing what one is told; submission to authority or law: *Our puppy is already learning obedience. Soldiers act in obedience to the orders.*

o·be·di·ent (ō bē'dē ənt) *adj.* doing what one is told; willing to obey. [< F < L *oboediens, -entis,* ppr. of *oboedire* obey] —**o·be'di·ent·ly,** *adv.*

☛ *Syn.* **Obedient, compliant, docile** = acting as another asks or commands. **Obedient** emphasizes being willing to follow instructions and carry out orders of someone whose authority one acknowledges: *an obedient servant.* **Compliant** emphasizes bending easily, sometimes too easily, to another's will: *Compliant people are not good leaders.* **Docile** emphasizes having a submissive disposition, especially a willingness to be taught: *a docile horse.*

o·bei·sance (ō bā'səns *or* ō bē'səns) *n.* **1** a movement of the body expressing deep respect; deep bow: *The men made obeisance to the king.* **2** deference; homage. [ME < OF *obeisance* obedience < *obeir* obey < L *oboedire.* See OBEY.]

ob·e·lisk (ob'ə lisk') *n.* **1** a tapering, four-sided shaft of stone with a top shaped like a pyramid. Obelisks were often used as monuments in ancient Egypt. **2** *Printing.* dagger (†). [< L *obeliscus* < Gk. *obeliskos,* dim. of *obelos* a spit]

O·ber·on (ō'bər on') *n. Medieval folklore.* the king of the fairies and husband of Titania. He is one of the chief characters in Shakespeare's *A Midsummer Night's Dream.*

o·bese (ō bēs') *adj.* extremely fat. [< L *obesus* < *ob-* in addition + *edere* eat] —**o·bese'ly,** *adv.* —**o·bese'ness,** *n.*

o·bes·i·ty (ō bēs'ə tē *or* ō bēs'ə tē) *n.* extreme fatness.

o·bey (ō bā') *v.* **1** do what one is told: *The dog obeyed immediately, when told to sit.* **2** follow the orders of: *They obeyed their father.* **3** act in accordance with; comply with: *to obey the laws.* **4** yield to the control of: *A car obeys the driver.* [< F *obeir* < L *oboedire* < *ob-* to + *audire* give ear] —**o·bey'er,** *n.*

ob·fus·cate (ob'fus kāt' *or* ob fus'kāt) *v.* **-cat·ed, -cat·ing.** **1** confuse; stupefy: *A man's mind may be obfuscated by liquor.* **2** darken; obscure. [< L *obfuscare* < *ob-* + *fuscus* dark] —**ob'fus·ca'tion,** *n.* —**ob·fus'ca·tor,** *n.*

o·bi (ō'bē) *n.* a long, broad sash worn around the waist of a kimono by Japanese women and children. See **kimono** for picture. [< Japanese]

ob·i·ter dic·tum (ob'ə tər *or* ō'bə tər dik'təm) *pl.* **ob·i·ter dic·ta** (dik'tə). **1** an incidental remark. **2** *Law.* an incidental opinion given by a judge. [< L *obiter dictum* said by the way]

o·bit·u·ar·y (ō bich'ü er'ē) *n., pl.* **-ar·ies;** *adj.* —*n.* a notice of death, often with a brief account of the person's life. —*adj.* of a death; recording a death. [< Med.L *obituarius,* ult. < L *obire* (*mortem*) meet (death) < *ob-* up to + *ire* go]

obj. object; objective; objection.

ob·ject (*n.* ob′jikt *or* ob′jekt; *v.* əb jekt′) *n., v.* —*n.* **1** anything that can be seen or touched; thing; article. **2** a person or thing toward which feeling, thought, or action is directed: *an object of charity.* **3** something aimed at; end; purpose. **4** *Grammar.* a word or group of words toward which the action of the verb is directed or to which a preposition expresses some relation. In *He threw the ball to his brother, ball* is the object of *threw,* and *brother* is the object of *to.* **5 a** anything that can be presented to the mind: *objects of thought.* **b** a thing with reference to the impression it makes on the mind: *an object of pity.*
—*v.* **1** make objection; be opposed; feel dislike: *I made my suggestion, but John objected. Many people object to loud noise.* **2** give a reason against; bring forward in opposition; oppose: *Mother objected that the weather was too wet to play outdoors.* [< Med.L *objectum* thing presented to the mind or thought, neut. of L *objectus,* pp. of *obicere* throw before, put in the way of < *ob*- against + *jacere* throw] —**ob·ject′ing·ly,** *adv.* —**ob·jec′tor,** *n.*

object glass in a telescope, microscope, etc., the lens or combination of lenses that first receives light rays from the object and forms the image viewed through the eyepiece.

ob·jec·ti·fy (əb jek′tə fī′) *v.* **-fied, -fy·ing.** make objective; externalize: *Experiments in chemistry objectify the teaching. Kind acts objectify kindness.* —**ob·jek′ti·fi·ca′tion,** *n.*

ob·jec·tion (əb jek′shən) *n.* **1** something said in objecting; reason or argument against something: *One of his objections to the plan was that it would cost too much.* **2** a feeling of disapproval or dislike: *A lazy person has strong objections to working.* **3** the act of objecting: *What is the basis for your objection?* **4** a ground or cause of objecting.

ob·jec·tion·a·ble (əb jek′shən ə bəl) *adj.* **1** likely to be objected to. **2** unpleasant; disagreeable. —**ob·jec′tion·a·bly,** *adv.*

ob·jec·tive (əb jek′tiv) *n., adj.* —*n.* **1** something aimed at: *My objective this summer will be learning to play tennis better.* **2** something real and observable. **3** *Grammar.* **a** the grammatical form of an English pronoun that shows that it is an object of a verb or preposition, corresponding to the dative and accusative cases in German and Latin. **b** a word or construction in this form. **4** the lens or set of lenses in a microscope or telescope that is nearest to the object being viewed and that forms the image of the object.
—*adj.* **1** existing outside the mind as an actual object and not merely in the mind as an idea; real. Buildings and landscapes are objective; ideas and feelings are subjective. **2** dealing with facts or objects, not with the thoughts and feelings of the speaker, writer, painter, etc.; impersonal: *A scientist must be objective in his experiments. The report was not objective, but was biased in favor of the one firm.* Compare **subjective** (def. 1). **3** *Grammar.* of, having to do with, or being the objective. The six English pronouns with special objective forms are *me, us, him, her, them,* and *whom.* Compare **subjective** (def. 4). **4 a** of a work of art, representing or resembling natural objects; not abstract. **b** in perspective, that is, or belongs to, the object of which the delineation is required: *an objective point.* **5** being the object of endeavor. —**ob·jec′tive·ly,** *adv.* —**ob·jec′tive·ness,** *n.*

ob·jec·tiv·i·ty (ob′jek tiv′ə tē) *n.* the state or quality of being objective.

object lesson 1 instruction conveyed by means of material objects. **2** a practical illustration of a principle: *Most street accidents are object lessons in the dangers of carelessness.*

ob·jet d'art (ôb zhe där′) *pl.* **ob·jets d'art** (ôb zhe där′). *French.* a small picture, vase, etc. of some artistic value.

ob·jur·gate (ob′jər gāt′ *or* əb jėr′gāt) *v.* **-gat·ed, -gat·ing.** reproach vehemently; upbraid violently; berate. [< L *objurgare < ob*- against + *jurgare* scold] —**ob′jur·ga′tion,** *n.* —**ob′jur·ga′tor,** *n.*

ob·jur·ga·to·ry (əb jėr′gə tô′rē) *adj.* vehemently reproachful; upbraiding; berating.

ob·late[1] (ob′lāt *or* ob lāt′) *adj.* flattened at the poles; having an equatorial diameter greater than the polar diameter. The earth is an oblate spheroid. Compare **prolate.** [< NL *oblatus* < L *ob*- inversely + (*pro*)*latus* prolate] —**ob′late·ly,** *adv.* —**ob′late·ness,** *n.*

ob·late[2] (ob′lāt *or* ô′blāt′) *n., adj.* —*n. Roman Catholic Church.* a member of any of various secular institutes devoted to religious work. —*adj.* dedicated to religious work. [< Med.L *oblatus,* noun use of pp. of L *offerre* offer]

ob·la·tion (ob lā′shən) *n.* **1** an offering to God or a god. **2** the offering of bread and wine in the Communion service. [< LL *oblatio, -onis < ob*- up to + *latus,* pp. of *ferre* bring]

ob·li·gate (ob′lə gāt′) *v.* **-gat·ed, -gat·ing.** bind morally or legally; pledge: *A witness in court is obligated to tell the truth.* [< L *obligare < ob*- to + *ligare* bind. Doublet of OBLIGE.]

ob·li·ga·tion (ob′lə gā′shən) *n.* **1** a duty under the law or due to a promise or contract, social relationship, etc.: *a person's obligation to his family. It is her obligation to pay for the damage. He is under obligation to paint our house first.* **2** a binding legal agreement; bond; contract: *The firm was not able to meet its obligations.* **3** being in debt for a favor, service, or the like. **4** a service; favor; benefit: *An independent person likes to repay all obligations.*
☛ *Syn.* **1.** See note at **duty.**

ob·li·ga·to (ob′lə gä′tō) See **obbligato.**

ob·lig·a·to·ry (əb lig′ə tô′rē *or* ob′lə gə tô′rē) *adj.* binding morally or legally; required: *Attendance at school is obligatory.* [< LL *obligatorius*]

o·blige (ə blīj′) *v.* **o·bliged, o·blig·ing. 1** bind by a promise, contract, duty, etc.; compel; force: *The law obliges parents to send their children to school.* **2** put under bonds of thanks for a favor or service: *She obliged us with a song.* **3** do a favor to: *Kindly oblige me by closing the door.* [ME < OF *obliger* < L *obligare.* Doublet of OBLIGATE.] —**o·blig′er,** *n.*

ob·li·gee (ob′lə jē′) *n.* **1** *Law.* one to whom another is bound by contract; creditor. **2** one under obligation to another.

o·blig·ing (ə blī′jing) *adj.* willing to do favors; helpful. —**o·blig′ing·ly,** *adv.* —**o·blig′ing·ness,** *n.*

ob·lique (ə blēk′) *adj., n., v.* **-liqued, -liqu·ing.** —*adj.* **1** not vertical or horizontal; not perpendicular or parallel; slanting. **2** *Geometry.* **a** containing no right angle: *an oblique triangle.* **b** having the axis not perpendicular to the base: *an oblique cone.* **3** not straightforward; indirect: *an oblique glance, an oblique movement.* **4** underhanded or evasive: *oblique dealings.* **5** *Grammar.* of or designating any case other than nominative or vocative. **6** *Botany.* having unequal sides: *an oblique leaf.*
—*n.* something oblique, especially a stroke or line.
—*v.* have or advance in an oblique direction; angle or slant. [< L *obliquus*]

oblique angle any angle that is not a right angle. See **angle**[1] for picture.

ob·liq·ui·ty (əb lik′wə tē) *n., pl.* **-ties. 1** indirectness or crookedness of thought or behavior, especially conduct that is not upright and moral. **2** being oblique.

ob·lit·er·ate (əb lit′ər āt′) *v.* **-at·ed, -at·ing.** remove all traces of; blot out; destroy: *Heavy rain obliterated the footprints.* [< L *oblit(t)erare < ob literas (scribere)* (draw) across the letters] —**ob·lit′er·a′tion,** *n.* —**ob·lit′er·a′tor,** *n.*

ob·liv·i·on (əb liv′ē ən) *n.* **1** the condition of being entirely forgotten: *Many ancient cities have long since passed into oblivion.* **2** the condition of being unaware of what is going on; forgetfulness. [< L *oblivio, -onis < oblivisci* forget, originally, even off, smooth out + *ob*- + *levis* smooth]

ob·liv·i·ous (əb liv′ē əs) *adj.* **1** forgetful; not mindful; unaware: *The book was so interesting that I was oblivious of my surroundings.* **2** bringing or causing forgetfulness. [< L *obliviosus*] —**ob·liv′i·ous·ly,** *adv.* —**ob·liv′i·ous·ness,** *n.*

ob·long (ob′lông) *adj., n.* —*adj.* **1** longer than broad or round: *an oblong loaf of bread, an oblong tablecloth.* **2** of a plane figure, having four sides and four right angles, but not square; rectangular with adjacent sides unequal. —*n.* a rectangle that is not square. See **quadrilateral** for picture. [< L *oblongus < ob*- + *longus* long]

ob·lo·quy (ob′lə kwē) *n., pl.* **-quies. 1** public reproach; abuse; blame. **2** disgrace; shame. [< LL *obloquium,* ult. < L *ob*- against + *loqui* speak]

ob·nox·ious (əb nok′shəs) *adj.* very disagreeable; offensive; hateful: *His disgusting table manners made him obnoxious to us.* [< L *obnoxiosus,* ult. < *ob*- + *noxa* injury] —**ob·nox′ious·ly,** *adv.* —**ob·nox′ious·ness,** *n.*
☛ *Syn.* See note at **hateful.**

An oboe

o·boe (ō′bō) *n.* **1** a wooden musical wind instrument in which a

thin, poignant tone is produced by a double reed. **2** a reed stop in an organ that produces a tone like that of the oboe. [< Ital. < F *hautbois* hautboy]

o·bo·ist (ō′bō ist) *n.* a player of the oboe.

obs. 1 obsolete. **2** observation; observatory.

ob·scene (əb sēn′ *or* ob sēn′) *adj.* **1** grossly indecent or lewd: *an obscene dance, an obscene remark.* **2** *Law.* of written or printed material, etc., tending to deprave or corrupt. **3** repugnant; highly offensive: *an obscene display of wealth.* [< L *obscenus*] —**ob·scene′ly,** *adv.*

ob·scen·i·ty (əb sen′ə tē *or* əb sēn′ə tē) *n., pl.* **-ties. 1** the quality or state of being obscene. **2** something that is obscene, such as an utterance or an act.

ob·scur·ant·ism (əb skyür′ən tiz′əm *or* ob′skyə ran′tiz əm) *n.* **1** opposition to progress and the spread of knowledge and enlightenment. **2** an artistic or literary style characterized by deliberate complexity and obscurity. [< L *obscurans, -antis,* ppr. of *obscurare* to obscure < *obscurus* obscure]

ob·scur·ant·ist (əb skyür′ən tist) *n., adj.* —*n.* a person who is opposed to progress and the spread of knowledge. —*adj.* of obscurantists or obscurantism.

ob·scu·ra·tion (ob′skyə rā′shən) *n.* obscuring or being obscured.

ob·scure (əb skyür′) *adj.* **-scur·er, -scur·est;** *v.* **-scured, -scur·ing.** —*adj.* **1** not clearly expressed: *an obscure passage in a book.* **2** not expressing meaning clearly: *an obscure style of writing.* **3** not well known; attracting no notice: *an obscure little village, an obscure poet, an obscure position in the government.* **4** not easily discovered; hidden: *an obscure path, an obscure meaning.* **5** not distinct; not clear: *an obscure form, obscure sounds, an obscure view.* **6** dark; dim: *an obscure corner.* **7** indefinite: *an obscure brown, an obscure vowel.*
—*v.* hide from view; make obscure; dim; darken: *Clouds obscure the sun.* [ME < OF < L *obscurus* < *ob-* over + *scur-* cover] —**ob·scure′ly,** *adv.* —**ob·scure′ness,** *n.* —**ob·scur′er,** *n.*
☛ *Syn. adj.* **1. Obscure, vague, ambiguous** = not clearly expressed or understood. **Obscure** suggests that the meaning of something is hidden from the understanding, because it is not plainly expressed or the reader lacks the knowledge necessary for understanding: *Much legal language is obscure.* **Vague** suggests not definite, too general in meaning or statement or not clearly and completely thought out: *No one can be sure what a vague statement means.* **Ambiguous means** so expressed that either of two meanings is possible: *She kissed her when she left is an ambiguous statement.*

ob·scu·ri·ty (əb skyür′ə tē) *n., pl.* **-ties. 1** a lack of clearness; difficulty in being understood: *The obscurity of the passage makes several interpretations possible.* **2** something obscure; something hard to understand; doubtful or vague meaning: *The movie had so many obscurities that we didn't enjoy it.* **3** the state or condition of being unknown: *The Premier rose from obscurity to fame.* **4** a little-known person or place. **5** a lack of light; dimness.

ob·se·quies (ob′sə kwēz) *n.pl.* funeral rites or ceremonies; stately funeral. [ME < OF < Med.L *obsequiae,* pl., for L *exsequiae* < *ex-* out + *sequi* follow]

ob·se·qui·ous (əb sē′kwē əs) *adj.* polite or obedient from hope of gain or from fear; servile; fawning: *Obsequious courtiers greeted the king.* [< L *obsequiosus,* ult. < *ob-* after + *sequi* follow] —**ob·se′qui·ous·ly,** *adv.* —**ob·se′qui·ous·ness,** *n.*

ob·serv·a·ble (əb zėr′və bəl) *adj.* **1** that can be or is noticed; noticeable; easily seen. **2** that can be or is observed: *Lent is observable by most churches.*

ob·serv·a·bly (əb zėr′və blē) *adv.* so as to be observed; to an observable degree.

ob·serv·ance (əb zėr′vəns) *n.* **1** the act of observing or keeping laws or customs: *the observance of the Sabbath.* **2** an act performed as a sign of worship or respect; a religious ceremony. **3** a rule or custom to be observed. **4** *Archaic.* respectful attention or service. **5** an observation.
☛ *Usage.* See note at **observation.**

ob·serv·ant (əb zėr′vənt) *adj.* **1** quick to notice; watchful; observing: *If you are observant in the fields and woods, you will find many flowers that others fail to notice.* **2** careful in observing (a law, rule, custom, etc.): *observant of the traffic rules.* [< L *observans, -antis,* ppr. of *observare.* See OBSERVE.] —**ob·serv′ant·ly,** *adv.*

ob·ser·va·tion (ob′zər vā′shən) *n.* **1** the act, habit, or power of seeing and noting: *His keen observation helped him to become a good scientist.* **2** the fact of being seen; being seen; notice: *The tramp escaped observation.* **3** something seen and noted. **4** the act of watching for some special purpose; study: *The observation of nature is important in science.* **5** a remark; comment. **6** *Obsolete or rare.* an observance.
☛ *Usage.* **Observation, observance** are sometimes confused because both are related to the verb **observe. Observation,** connected with the meaning "watch closely," applies especially to the act or power of noticing things or watching closely, or to being watched or noticed: *An observatory is a building designed*

---

hat, āge, fär; let, ēqual, tėrm; it, īce
hot, ōpen, ôrder; oil, out; cup, pu̇t, rüle,
ǝbove, takǝn, pencǝl, lemǝn, circǝs

ch, child; ng, long; sh, ship
th, thin; ᴛʜ, then; zh, measure

for the observation of the stars. **Observance,** connected with the meaning "keep," applies to the act of keeping and following duties or customs, or to a rule, rite, etc. kept or celebrated: *You go to church for the observance of religious duties.* **Observation** sometimes means "observance," but this meaning is obsolete or rare.

ob·ser·va·tion·al (ob′zǝr vā′shǝn ǝl) *adj.* of, having to do with, or founded on observation, rather than on experiment.

observation car a railway passenger car having large windows, a glass dome, or an open platform at one end, to enable passengers to view the scenery easily.

ob·serv·a·to·ry (ǝb zėr′vǝ tô′rē) *n., pl.* **-ries. 1** a place or building equipped with a telescope, etc. for observing the stars and other heavenly bodies. **2** a place or building for observing facts or happenings of nature. **3** a high place or building giving a wide view.

ob·serve (ǝb zėrv′) *v.* see and note; notice: *I observed nothing queer in his behavior.* **2** examine for some special purpose; study: *An astronomer observes the stars.* **3** remark; comment: *"Foul weather," the captain observed.* **4** keep; follow in practice: *to observe silence, to observe a rule.* **5** show regard for; celebrate: *to observe the Sabbath.* [ME < OF < L *observare* < *ob-* over + *servare* watch, keep]
☛ *Syn.* **1.** See note at **see.**

ob·serv·er (ǝb zer′vǝr) *n.* **1** one who watches or examines. **2** one who follows or celebrates a rule, custom, etc.: *an observer of the Sabbath.* **3** one who attends a meeting as a guest but can take no official part in it.

ob·serv·ing (ǝb zėr′ving) *adj.* observant.

ob·sess (ǝb ses′) *v.* fill the mind of; keep the attention of; haunt: *The fear that someone might steal his money obsesses him.* [< L *obsessus,* pp. of *obsidere* < *ob-* by + *sedere* sit]

ob·ses·sion (ǝb sesh′ǝn) *n.* **1** obsessing or being obsessed; the influence of a feeling, idea, or impulse that a person cannot escape. **2** the feeling, idea, or impulse itself. **3** *Psychiatry.* a compelling or fixed idea or feeling, usually irrational, over which a person has little conscious control; compulsion.

ob·ses·sion·al (ǝb sesh′ǝn ǝl) *adj.* of or having to do with obsession: *an obsessional neurosis.* —**ob·ses′sion·al·ly,** *adv.*

ob·ses·sive (ǝb ses′iv) *adj.* of, having to do with, or causing obsession. —**ob·ses′sive·ly,** *adv.*

ob·sid·i·an (ob sid′ē ǝn) *n.* a hard, dark, glassy rock that is formed when lava cools; volcanic glass. [< L *obsidianus,* mistaken reading for *obsianus;* after *Obsius,* its discoverer]

ob·so·les·cence (ob′sǝ les′ǝns) *n.* the condition or state of passing out of use; getting out of date; a becoming obsolete.

ob·so·les·cent (ob′sǝ les′ǝnt) *adj.* **1** passing out of use; tending to become out-of-date: *Fountain pens are obsolescent.* **2** *Biology.* gradually disappearing; imperfectly or slightly developed: *obsolescent organs.* [< L *obsolescens, -entis,* ppr. of *obsolescere* fall into disuse, ult. < *ob-* + *solere* be usual, be customary]

ob·so·lete (ob′sǝ lēt′) *adj.* **1** no longer in use. *Eft,* meaning *again,* is an obsolete word. **2** out-of-date: *We still use this machine although it is obsolete.* [< L *obsoletus,* pp. of *obsolescere.* See OBSOLESCENT.] —**ob′so·lete·ly,** *adv.* —**ob′so·lete·ness,** *n.*

ob·sta·cle (ob′stǝ kǝl) *n.* something that stands in the way or stops progress: *Blindness is an obstacle in most occupations.* [ME < OF < L *obstaculum* < *ob-* in the way of + *stare* stand]
☛ *Syn.* **Obstacle, obstruction, hindrance** = something that gets in the way of action or progress. **Obstacle** suggests an object, condition, etc. that stands in the way and must be moved or overcome before someone or something can continue toward a goal: *A tree fallen across the road was an obstacle to our car.* **Obstruction** applies especially to something that blocks a passage: *The enemy built obstructions in the road.* **Hindrance** applies to a person or thing that holds back or makes progress difficult: *Noise is a hindrance to studying.*

ob·stet·ric (ob stet′rik) *adj.* having to do with the care of women in childbirth.

ob·stet·ri·cal (ob stet′rǝ kǝl) *adj.* obstetric; of or having to do with obstetrics. —**ob·stet′ri·cal·ly,** *adv.*

ob·ste·tri·cian (ob′stǝ trish′ǝn) *n.* a physician who specializes in obstetrics.

ob·stet·rics (ob stet′riks) *n.* the branch of medicine and surgery concerned with caring for and treating women before, during, and after childbirth. [< L *obstetrica,* fem. *obstetrix, -tricis* midwife < *ob-* by + *stare* stand]

ob·sti·na·cy (ob′stə nə sē) *n., pl.* **-cies.** 1 stubbornness; being obstinate. 2 an obstinate act.

ob·sti·nate (ob′stə nit) *adj.* 1 not giving in; stubborn: *The obstinate girl would go her own way, in spite of all warnings.* 2 hard to control or treat: *an obstinate cough.* [ME < L *obstinatus,* pp. of *obstinare,* ult. < *ob-* by + *stare* stand] —**ob′sti·nate·ly,** *adv.*
☛ *Syn.* **1. Obstinate, stubborn** = fixed in purpose or opinion. **Obstinate** suggests a persistent holding to a purpose, opinion, or way of doing something, sometimes unreasonably or contrarily: *The obstinate man refused to obey orders.* **Stubborn,** often interchangeable with **obstinate,** especially suggests a quality of character that makes a person resist attempts to change his mind: *He is stubborn as a mule.* **Stubborn** is used more often than **obstinate** to describe animals or things.

ob·strep·er·ous (əb strep′ər əs) *adj.* 1 noisy; boisterous. 2 unruly; disorderly. [< L *obstreperus* < *ob-* against + *strepere* make a noise] —**ob·strep′er·ous·ly,** *adv.* —**ob·strep′er·ous·ness,** *n.*

ob·struct (əb strukt′) *v.* 1 make hard to pass through; block up: *Fallen trees obstruct the road.* 2 be in the way of; hinder: *Trees obstruct our view of the ocean.* [< L *obstructus,* pp. of *obstruere* < *ob-* in the way of + *struere* pile] —**ob·struct′er,** *n.*

ob·struc·tion (əb struk′shən) *n.* 1 anything that obstructs; something in the way; obstacle: *The soldiers had to get over such obstructions as ditches and barbed wire. Anger is an obstruction to clear thinking.* 2 the act of obstructing or the state of being obstructed.
☛ *Syn.* **1.** See note at **obstacle.**

ob·struc·tion·ism (əb struk′shən iz′əm) *n.* the hindering of the progress of business in a meeting, legislature, etc.

ob·struc·tion·ist (əb struk′shən ist) *n.* one who hinders (progress, legislation, reform, etc.).

ob·struc·tive (əb struk′tiv) *adj.* tending or serving to obstruct; blocking; hindering. —**ob·struct′ive·ly,** *adv.* —**ob·struct′ive·ness,** *n.*

ob·tain (əb tān′) *v.* 1 get or procure through diligence or effort; come to have: *He worked hard to obtain the prize. We study to obtain knowledge.* 2 be in use; be customary: *Different rules obtain in different schools.* [ME < OF < L *obtinere* < *ob-* to + *tenere* hold] —**ob·tain′a·ble,** *adj.* —**ob·tain′er,** *n.*
☛ *Syn.* **1.** See note at **get.**

ob·trude (əb trüd′) *v.* **-trud·ed, -trud·ing.** 1 put forward unasked and unwanted; force: *Don't obtrude your opinions on others.* 2 come unasked and unwanted; force oneself; intrude. 3 push out; thrust forward: *A turtle obtrudes its head from its shell.* [< L *obtrudere* < *ob-* toward + *trudere* thrust] —**ob·trud′er,** *n.*

ob·tru·sion (əb trü′zhən) *n.* 1 obtruding. 2 something obtruded. [< LL *obtrusio, -onis* < L *obtrudere.* See OBTRUDE.]

ob·tru·sive (əb trü′siv) *adj.* 1 too noticeable; not blending or fitting in: *obtrusive colors.* 2 protruding. 3 intrusive or pushy. —**ob·tru′sive·ly,** *adv.* —**ob·tru′sive·ness,** *n.*

ob·tuse (əb tyüs′ *or* əb tüs′) *adj.* 1 not sharp or acute; blunt. 2 having more than 90° of angle but less than 180°. See **angle** for picture. 3 slow in understanding; stupid: *He was too obtuse to take the hint.* 4 not sensitive; dull: *One's hearing often becomes obtuse in old age.* [< L *obtusus,* pp. of *obtundere* < *ob-* on + *tundere* beat] —**ob·tuse′ly,** *adv.* —**ob·tuse′ness,** *n.*

obtuse angle an angle greater than 90 degrees but less than 180 degrees; an angle greater than a right angle. See **angle** for picture.

ob·verse (*n.* ob′vėrs; *adj.* ob vėrs′ *or* ob′vėrs) *n., adj.* —*n.* 1 the side of a coin, medal, etc. that has the principal design (opposed to **reverse**). 2 the face of anything that is meant to be turned toward the observer; front. 3 a counterpart. 4 *Logic.* a proposition derived through obversion; the negative (or affirmative) counterpart of a given affirmative (or negative) proposition. —*adj.* 1 turned toward the observer. 2 being a counterpart to something else. 3 having the base narrower than the top or tip: *an obverse leaf.* [< L *obversus,* pp. of *obvertere* < *ob-* toward + *vertere* to turn] —**ob·verse′ly,** *adv.*

ob·vert (ob vėrt′) *v.* 1 turn (something) toward an object. 2 *Logic.* change (a proposition) to the denial of its opposite. [< L *obvertere.* See OBSERVE.]

ob·vi·ate (ob′vē āt′) *v.* **-at·ed, -at·ing.** meet and dispose of; clear out of the way; remove: *to obviate a difficulty, to obviate danger, to obviate objections.* [< LL *obviare* < *obvius* in the way. See OBVIOUS.] —**ob′vi·a′tion,** *n.* —**ob′vi·a′tor,** *n.*

ob·vi·ous (ob′vē əs) *adj.* easily seen or understood; clear to the eye or mind; not to be doubted; plain: *It is obvious that two and two make four.* [< L *obvius* < *obviam* in the way < *ob* across + *via* way] —**ob′vi·ous·ly,** *adv.* —**ob′vi·ous·ness,** *n.*
☛ *Syn.* **Obvious, apparent, evident** = plain to see, easy to understand. **Obvious** suggests standing out so prominently that the eye or mind cannot miss it: *His exhaustion was obvious when he fell asleep standing up.* **Apparent** means

plainly to be seen as soon as one looks (with eye or mind) toward it: *A change in government policy is now apparent.* **Evident** means plainly to be seen because all the apparent facts point to it: *When he did not drive the car home, it was evident that he had had an accident.*

oc– a form of **ob-** before *c,* as in *occasion.*

OC *Cdn.* Officer of the Order of Canada.

O.C. Officer in Charge; Officer Commanding.

oc·a·ri·na (ok′ə rē′nə) *n.* a simple wind instrument having an oval body with six to eight finger holes and a protruding, whistlelike mouthpiece on one side. [probably dim. of Ital. *oca* goose; with reference to the shape]

oc·ca·sion (ə kā′zhən *or* ō kā′zhən) *n., v.* —*n.* 1 a particular time: *We have met Mr. Smith on several occasions.* 2 a special event: *The jewels were worn only on great occasions.* 3 a good chance; opportunity. 4 a cause; reason: *The dog that was the occasion of the quarrel had run away.*
improve the occasion, take advantage of an opportunity.
on occasion, now and then; once in a while.
—*v.* cause; bring about: *His queer behavior occasioned talk.* [< L *occasio, -onis,* ult. < *ob-* in the way of + *cadere* fall]

oc·ca·sion·al (ə kā′zhən əl *or* ə kāzh′nəl) *adj.* 1 happening or coming now and then, or once in a while: *We had fine weather except for an occasional thunderstorm.* 2 caused by or used for some special time or event: *He composed a piece of occasional music to be played at the opening concert in the new auditorium.* 3 for use as called for, not forming part of a set: *occasional chairs.*

oc·ca·sion·al·ly (ə kā′zhən əl ē *or* ə kāzh′nəl ē) *adv.* now and then; once in a while; at times.

Oc·ci·dent (ok′sə dənt) *n.* 1 the countries in Europe and America; the West. Compare **Orient.** 2 **occident,** the west. [< L *occidens, -entis,* ppr. of *occidere* fall towards, go down < *ob-* towards + *cadere* fall; with reference to the setting sun]

Oc·ci·den·tal (ok′sə den′təl) *adj., n.* —*adj.* 1 Western; of the Occident. 2 **occidental,** western. —*n.* a native of the West. Europeans are Occidentals.

oc·cip·i·tal (ok sip′ə təl) *adj., n.* —*adj.* of or having to do with the back part of the head or skull. —*n.* the occipital bone. [< Med.L *occipitalis* < L *occiput.* See OCCIPUT.]

occipital bone *Anatomy.* the compound bone forming the lower back part of the skull.

oc·ci·put (ok′sə pət) *n., pl.* **oc·cip·i·ta** (ok sip′ə tə). *Anatomy.* the back part of the head or skull. [< L *occiput* < *occipitium* < *ob-* behind + *caput* head]

oc·clude (o klüd′) *v.* **-clud·ed, -clud·ing.** 1 stop up (a passage, pores, etc.); close. 2 shut in, out, or off. 3 *Chemistry.* absorb and retain (gases). Platinum occludes hydrogen. 4 *Dentistry.* meet closely. The teeth in the upper jaw and those in the lower jaw should occlude. [< L *occludere* < *ob-* up + *claudere* close]

oc·clu·sion (o klü′zhən) *n.* occluding or being occluded. [< L *occlusus,* pp. of *occludere.* See OCCLUDE.]

oc·cult (o kult′ *or* ok′ult) *adj., n. occult.* —*adj.* 1 beyond the bounds of ordinary knowledge; mysterious. 2 outside the laws of the natural world; magical: *Astrology and alchemy are occult sciences.* —*n.*
the occult, the occult sciences. [< L *occultus* hidden, pp. of *occulere* < *ob-* up + *celare* cover]

oc·cul·ta·tion (ok′ul tā′shən) *n.* 1 a hiding of one heavenly body by another passing between it and the observer: *the occultation of a star by the moon.* 2 a disappearance from view or notice.

oc·cult·ism (o kul′tiz əm *or* ok′ul tiz′əm) *n.* 1 a belief in occult powers. 2 the study or use of occult sciences.

oc·cult·ist (o kul′tist *or* ok′əl tist′) *n., adj.* —*n.* a person who believes in or practises occultism. —*adj.* of or having to do with occultism.

oc·cu·pan·cy (ok′yə pən sē) *n.* the act or fact of occupying; holding (land, houses, a pew, etc.) by being in possession.

oc·cu·pant (ok′yə pənt) *n.* 1 a person who occupies: *the occupant of a chair.* 2 the person in actual possession of a house, office, etc. [< L *occupans, -antis,* ppr. of *occupare.* See OCCUPY.]

oc·cu·pa·tion (ok′yə pā′shən) *n.* 1 one's business or employment; trade: *Teaching is a teacher's occupation.* 2 occupying or being occupied; possession: *the occupation of a town by the enemy.* [< L *occupatio, -onis* < *occupare.* See OCCUPY.]
☛ *Syn.* **1. Occupation, business, employment** = work a person does regularly or to earn his living. **Occupation** = work of any kind one does regularly or for which one is trained: *By occupation she is a housewife.* **Business** = work done for profit, often for oneself, especially in commerce, banking, merchandising, etc.: *My business is real estate.* **Employment** = work done for another, for which one is paid: *He has no employment.*

oc·cu·pa·tion·al (ok′yə pā′shən əl *or* ok′yə pāsh′nəl) *adj.* of or having to do with occupation, especially of or having to do with trades, callings, etc.: *occupational diseases.*

occupational therapy the treatment of persons having physical

disabilities through specific types of exercises, work, etc. to promote rehabilitation.

oc·cu·py (ok′yə pī′) *v.* **-pied, -py·ing. 1** take up; fill: *The building occupies an entire block.* **2** keep busy; engage; employ: *Sports often occupy a boy's attention.* **3** take possession of: *The enemy occupied our fort.* **4** keep possession of; have; hold: *The judge occupies an important position.* **5** live in: *The owner and his family occupy the house.* [ME < OF < L *occupare* seize < *ob-* onto + *cap-* grasp] **—oc·cu·pi′er,** *n.*

oc·cur (ə kėr′) *v.* **-curred, -cur·ring. 1** take place; happen: *Storms often occur in winter.* **2** be found; exist: *E occurs in English more than any other letter.* **3** come to mind; suggest itself: *Did it occur to you to close the window?* [< L *occurrere* < *ob-* in the way of + *currere* run]

oc·cur·rence (ə kėr′əns) *n.* **1** occurring: *The occurrence of storms delayed our trip.* **2** event: *an unexpected occurrence.*
☛ *Syn.* **2.** See note at **event.**

O.Cdt. or **OCdt** officer cadet.

o·cean (ō′shən) *n.* **1** the great body of salt water that covers almost three fourths of the earth's surface. **2** any of its four main divisions—the Atlantic, Pacific, Indian, and Arctic oceans. **3** a vast expanse or quantity: *oceans of trouble.* [< L *oceanus* < Gk. *ōkeanos*]

o·cean·ar·i·um (ō′shə ner′ē əm) *n., pl.* **i·ums** or **i·a** (-ē ə). a large saltwater aquarium for ocean fish and other animals.

ocean bed the bottom of the ocean.

o·cean·go·ing (ō′shən gō′ing) *adj.* of, having to do with, or designed for travel on the ocean: *an ocean-going ship.*

ocean greyhound a swift ship, especially an ocean liner.

o·ce·an·ic (ō′shē an′ik) *adj.* **1** of the ocean. **2** living in the ocean. **3** like the ocean; wide; vast.

O·ce·a·nid (ō sē′ə nid) *n. Greek mythology.* a sea nymph; daughter of Oceanus, the ocean god.

o·cean·og·ra·pher (ō′shə nog′grə fər) *n.* a person skilled in oceanography, especially one whose work it is.

o·cean·o·graph·ic (ō′shə nə graf′ik) *adj.* of or having to do with oceanography.

o·cean·og·ra·phy (ō′shə nog′rə fē) *n.* the branch of physical geography dealing with oceans and ocean life.

O·ce·a·nus (ō sē′ə nəs) *n. Greek mythology.* **1** the god of the sea before Poseidon. Oceanus was a Titan and the father of the Oceanids. **2** the river that was believed to encircle the earth.

oc·el·late (os′ə lāt′) *adj.* ocellated.

o·cel·lat·ed (os′ə lā′təd) *adj.* having or marked with ocelli.

o·cel·lus (ō sel′əs *or* o sel′əs) *n., pl.* **o·cel·li** (ō sel′ī *or* o-, ō sel′ē *or* o-). **1** a small, simple eye of insects and some other invertebrates. **2** an eyelike spot or marking, such as the spot on any of the tail feathers of a peacock. [< L *ocellus,* dim. of *oculus* eye]

o·ce·lot (ō′sə lot′ *or* os′ə lot′) *n.* a medium-sized New World mammal (*Felis pardalis*) of the cat family found from Texas south to central South America, having a buff coat spotted and striped with black. [< F < Mexican *ocelotl*]

o·chre (ō′kər) *n., adj.* —*n.* **1** any of various clays ranging in coloring from pale yellow to orange, brown, and red, used as pigments. **2** a pale brownish yellow. —*adj.* pale brownish-yellow. Also, **ocher.** [ME < OF *ocre* < L < Gk. *ōchra* < *ōchros* pale yellow]

o'clock (ə klok′) according to a time shown on the clock: *It is one o'clock.* [contraction of *of the clock*]

OCR optical character recognition.

oct– *combining form.* the form of *octo-* or *octa-* before vowels, as in *octet.*

Oct. October.

octa– *combining form.* a variant of *octo-,* as in *octagon.*

oc·ta·gon (ok′tə gon′ *or* ok′tə gən) *n.* a polygon having eight sides. See **polygon** for picture. [< Gk. *oktagōnos* < *oktō* eight + *gōnia* angle]

oc·tag·o·nal (ok tag′ə nəl) *adj.* having eight angles and eight sides.

oc·ta·he·dral (ok′tə hē′drəl) *adj.* having eight plane faces.

oc·ta·he·dron (ok′tə hē′drən) *n., pl.* **-drons, -dra** (-drə). a polyhedron having eight faces. [< Gk. *oktaedron,* neut. of *oktaedros* < *oktōs* eight + *hedra* seat, base]

oc·tane (ok′tān) *n.* any of a group of colorless, liquid hydrocarbons obtained from petroleum. *Formula:* C_8H_{18} [< *oct-* eight (< Gk. *oktō*) + *-ane,* chemical suffix < L *-anus,* adj. suffix]

octane number the number indicating the quality of a motor fuel, based on its antiknock properties.

oc·tave (ok′tiv *or* ok′tāv) *n.* **1** *Music.* **a** the interval between a

hat, āge, fär; let, ēqual, tėrm; it, īce
hot, ōpen, ôrder; oil, out; cup, pút, rüle,
əbove, takən, pencəl, lemən, circəs
ch, child; ng, long; sh, ship
th, thin; ŦH, then; zh, measure

tone and another tone having twice or half as many vibrations. From middle C on a piano or organ to the C above it is an octave. **b** the eighth tone above or below a given tone, having twice or half as many vibrations per second. **c** the series of tones or of keys of an instrument, filling the interval between a tone and its octave. **d** the combination of a tone and its octave. **2** a group of eight. **3** *Prosody.* **a** an eight-line stanza. **b** the first eight lines of a sonnet; octet. **4** a church festival and the week after it or the last day of such a week. [< L *octavus* eighth < *octo* eight]

oc·ta·vo (ok tā′vō *or* ok tav′ō) *n., pl.* **-vos. 1** the page size of a book in which each leaf is one eighth of a whole sheet of paper. **2** a book having this size, usually about 15 by 24 cm. [< Med.L *in octavo* in an eighth]

oc·tet or **oc·tette** (ok tet′) *n.* **1** a musical composition for eight voices or instruments. **2** eight singers or players. **3** *Prosody.* **a** the first eight lines of a sonnet. **b** an eight-line stanza; octave. **4** any group of eight. [< *oct-* eight + *-et,* patterned on *duet,* etc.]

oc·til·lion (ok til′yən) *n.* **1** in Canada, the United States, and France, 1 followed by 27 zeros. **2** in Great Britain and Germany, 1 followed by 48 zeros. [< F < L *octo* eight + F *million* million]

octo– or **oct–** or **octa–** *combining form.* eight, as in *octopus* and *octagon.* [< Gk. *oktō*]

Oc·to·ber (ok tō′bər) *n.* the tenth month of the year. October has 31 days. [< L *October* < *octo* eight; from the order of the early Roman calendar]

oc·to·ge·nar·i·an (ok′tə jə nėr′ē ən) *n., adj.* —*n.* a person who is 80 years old or between 80 and 90 years old. —*adj.* 80 years old or between 80 and 90 years old. [< L *octogenarius* containing eighty]

oc·to·pod (ok′tə pod′) *n.* any of an order (Octopoda) of cephalopods, including octopuses and the paper nautilus, having eight armlike tentacles with suckers and lacking an internal shell.

oc·to·pus (ok′tə pəs) *n., pl.* **-pus·es. 1** any of a genus (*Octopus*) of marine cephalopods having a soft, rounded body, large, highly developed eyes, a beaklike mouth, and eight muscular arms, or tentacles, bearing rows of suckers. **2** something that resembles an octopus in being able to reach out and grasp, especially a large organization with many far-reaching branches: *The octopus of organized crime threatens the business life of every major city.* [< NL < Gk. *oktopous* < *oktō* eight + *pous* foot]

oc·to·roon (ok′tə rün′) *n.* a person having one eighth African ancestry. [< *octo-* eight + quad*roon*]

oc·u·lar (ok′yə lər) *adj., n.* —*adj.* **1** of or having to do with the eye: *an ocular muscle.* **2** like an eye. **3** received by actual sight; seen. —*n.* the eyepiece of a telescope, microscope, etc. [< LL *ocularis* of the eyes < L *oculus* eye]

oc·u·lar·ist (ok′yə lər ist) *n.* a person who makes and fits artificial eyes.

oc·u·list (ok′yə list) *n.* a physician who specializes in the treatment of the eyes; ophthalmologist. [< F *oculiste*]
☛ *Usage.* See note at **ophthalmologist.**

OD (ō′dē′) *n., pl.* **OD's;** *v.* **OD'd, OD'ing.** *Slang.* —*n.* an overdose of a narcotic. —*v.* take an overdose.

O.D. Officer of the Day.

o·da·lisque or **o·da·lisk** (ō′də lisk′) *n.* a female slave in an Oriental harem. [< F < Turkish *odaliq* < *odah* room in a harem; influenced by suffix *-isque* -ish]

odd (od) *adj.* **1** not divisible by two; being an odd number. **2** of or having an odd number: *The odd pages are always on the right in an open book.* **3** being one of a matched pair or set when the other or others are missing: *an odd glove in the drawer, some odd volumes of an encyclopedia.* **4** being a small, leftover or additional quantity or amount: *odd bits of lace, a few odd dollars in her purse.* **5** occasional, extra, or random: *He earns a living doing odd jobs around town.* **6** somewhat more than a quantity, distance, etc. specified in round numbers (*used in compounds*): *The whole job should cost 300-odd dollars. We still had 20-odd kilometres to go.* **7** peculiar or strange: *It's odd that she's not back yet. He had an odd expression on his face.* **8** remote or secluded. [ME < ON *odda-*] **—odd′ness,** *n.*
☛ *Syn.* See note at **strange.**

odd·ball (od′bol′ *or* -bôl′) *n., adj. Slang.* —*n.* a person whose

behavior is eccentric or unconventional. —*adj.* eccentric; unconventional.

odd·i·ty (od′ə tē) *n., pl.* **-ties. 1** strangeness; queerness; peculiarity. **2** a strange, queer, or peculiar person or thing.

odd·ly (od′lē) *adv.* queerly; strangely.

odd–man–out (od′man′out′) *n.* **1** one who does not fit into a group. **2** one who is left out of a group. **3 a** a person chosen by lot to do something special. **b** a method of selection used to choose such a person.

odd·ment (od′mənt) *n.* a thing left over; an extra bit.

odd number a number that has a remainder of 1 when divided by 2: *Three, five, and seven are odd numbers.*

odds (odz) *n.pl. or sing.* **1** a difference in favor of one as against another; advantage. In betting, odds of 3 to 1 mean that 3 will be paid if the bet is lost for every 1 that is received if the bet is won. **2** *Games.* an extra allowance given to the weaker side. **3** things that are odd, uneven, or unequal. **4** difference: *It makes no odds when he goes.*
at odds, quarrelling or disagreeing: *The two boys had been at odds for months.*
odds and ends, things left over; extra bits; odd pieces; scraps; remnants.
the odds are, the chances are; the probability is: *The odds are we'll win since they will be without their best player.*

odds–on (odz′on′) *adj.* having the odds in one's favor; having a good chance to win in a contest.

ode (ōd) *n.* a lyric poem full of noble feeling expressed with dignity, often addressed to some person or thing: *Ode to a Nightingale.* [< F < LL *ode* < Gk. *ōidē,* ult. < *aeidein* sing]

O·din (ō′dən) *n. Norse mythology.* the chief deity and god of wisdom, culture, war, and the dead, corresponding to the Anglo-Saxon god *Woden.*

o·di·ous (ō′dē əs) *adj.* very displeasing; hateful; offensive: *odious behavior.* [ME < OF < L *odiosus* < *odium* hate]
—**o′di·ous·ly,** *adv.* —**o′di·ous·ness,** *n.*
☛ *Syn.* See note at **hateful.**

o·di·um (ō′dē əm) *n.* **1** hatred; dislike. **2** reproach; blame. [< L *odium* < *odisse* hate]

o·dom·e·ter (ō dom′ə tər) *n.* an instrument for measuring the distance a vehicle travels by counting the number of wheel revolutions. [< F *odomètre* < Gk. *hodometron* < *hodos* way + *metron* a measure]

o·don·tol·o·gy (ō′don tol′ə jē) *n.* the branch of anatomy dealing with the structure, development, and diseases of the teeth; dentistry. [< Gk. *odous, -ontos* tooth + E *-logy*]

o·dor or **o·dour** (ō′dər) *n.* **1** a smell or scent: *the odor of roses, the odor of garbage.* **2** repute: *They were in bad odor because of a suspected theft.* **3** a taste or quality characteristic or suggestive of something: *There is no odor of impropriety about the case.* **4** *Archaic.* a fragrance or perfume. [ME < AF < L] —**o′dor·less** or **o′dour·less,** *adj.*
☛ *Syn.* **1.** See note at **smell.**

o·dor·if·er·ous (ō′dər if′ər əs) *adj.* giving forth an odor; fragrant. [ME < L *odorifer* < *odor* + *ferre* bear] —**o′dor·if′er·ous·ly,** *adv.* —**o′dor·if′er·ous·ness,** *n.*

o·dor·ous (ō′dər əs) *adj.* giving forth an odor; having an odor; sweet-smelling; fragrant: *Spices are odorous.* [< L *odorous*] —**o′dor·ous·ly,** *adv.* —**o′dor·ous·ness,** *n.*

o·dour (ō′dər) See **odor.**

O·dys·se·us (ō dis′ē əs) *n. Greek mythology.* a king of Ithaca, the shrewdest of the Greek leaders in the Trojan war, who spent ten years in adventurous wanderings before returning home. Latin name: **Ulysses.**

Od·ys·sey (od′ə sē) *n., pl.* **-seys. 1** a long Greek epic poem by Homer, describing the ten years of wandering of Odysseus after the Trojan War and his final return home. **2** Also, **odyssey,** any long series of wanderings and adventures.

OE or **O.E.** Old English (Anglo-Saxon).

OECD or **O.E.C.D.** Organization for Economic Co-operation and Development (an international association to promote trade).

oec·u·men·i·cal (ek′yə men′ə kəl) See **ecumenical.**

Oed·i·pus (ē′də pəs or ed′ə pəs) *n. Greek mythology.* a king of Thebes who killed his father and married his mother, unaware of their identity. When he learned what he had done, he blinded himself and passed the rest of his life wandering miserably.

o'er (ôr) *prep. or adv. Poetic.* over.

oe·soph·a·gus (ē sof′ə gəs) *n., pl.* **-gi** (-jī′ or -jē′). See **esophagus.**

of (uv or ov; *unstressed,* əv) *prep.* **1** belonging to; associated with; forming a part of: *the children of a family.* **2** made from: *a house of bricks.* **3** that has; containing; with: *a house of six rooms.* **4** that has as a quality: *a look of pity.* **5** that is; named: *the city of Vancouver.* **6** away from; from: *north of Brandon.* **7** in regard to; concerning; about: *to think well of someone.* **8** that has as a purpose: *the hour of prayer.* **9** by: *the writings of Shakespeare.* **10** as a result of; through: *to die of grief.* **11** out of: *She came of a noble family.* **12** among: *a mind of the finest.* **13** during: *of late years.* **14** in telling time, before: *ten minutes of six.* **15** in; as to: *She is sixteen years of age.* **16** *Of* connects nouns and adjectives having the meaning of a verb with what would be the object of the verb: *The eating of fruit, a hall smelling of onions.* [OE (unstressed) *of.* Cf. **off.**]
☛ *Usage.* In informal English **of** is sometimes used unnecessarily to make such double prepositions as *inside of, outside of.* This usage is usually avoided in formal writing. Using **of** after **off** is not normally acceptable in standard English: *She stepped off the sidewalk* (not *off of*).

of– *prefix.* the form of **ob-** occurring before *f,* as in *offer.*

OF or **O.F.** Old French.

off (of) *prep., adv., adj., interj., n.* —*prep.* **1** not in the usual or correct position on; not in the usual or correct condition of; not on: *A button is off his coat.* **2** from; away from; far from: *You are off the road.* **3** of ships at sea, just away from: *The ship anchored off Victoria.* **4** supported by; using the resources of: *He lived off his relatives.*
—*adv.* **1** from the usual or correct position, condition, etc.: *He took off his hat.* **2** away; at a distance; to a distance: *to go off on a journey.* **3** distant in time: *Christmas is only five weeks off.* **4** so as to stop or lessen: *Turn the water off. The game was called off.* **5** without work: *an afternoon off.* **6** in full; wholly: *Pay off the debt.* **7** on one's way: *The train started and we were off on our trip.*
be off, go away; leave quickly.
off and on, at some times and not at others; now and then.
—*adj.* **1** no longer due to take place: *Our trip to Europe is off.* **2** not connected; stopped: *The electricity is off.* **3** without work: *He pursues his hobby during off hours.* **4** in a specified condition in regard to money, property, etc.: *How well off are the Smiths?* **5** not very good; not up to average: *Bad weather made last summer an off season for fruit.* **6** deteriorated in quality, etc.: *The milk seems to be off.* **7** possible but not likely: *I came on the off chance that I would find you.* **8** in error; wrong: *Your figures are way off.* **9** more distant; farther: *the off side of a wall.* **10** on the right-hand side (used of a horse, team of horses, vehicle, etc.): *the off wheel. The off horse doesn't pull as well as the near horse.* Compare **near** (def. 5). **11** seaward.
—*interj.* go away! stay away!
off with, a take off. **b** cut off: *Off with his head!* **c** away with!
—*n. Cricket.* the side opposite to the batsman. [OE (stressed) *of.* Cf. **off.**]
☛ *Usage.* Avoid using the double preposition **off of.** See note at **of.**

off. office; officer; official.

of·fal (of′əl) *n.* **1** the waste parts of an animal killed for food. **2** garbage; refuse. [< *off* + *fall*]

off–and–on (of′ən on′) *adj., adv. Informal.* —*adj.* intermittent; uncertain. —*adv.* intermittently.

off·bal·ance (of′bal′əns) *adj., adv.* —*adj.* unsteady; unprepared. —*adv.* unsteadily; by surprise.

off·beat (of′bēt′) *n., adj.* —*n. Music.* a beat that has relatively little stress. —*adj. Music.* of or having to do with offbeats. **2** *Informal.* unconventional; not usual; odd.

off·cast (of′kast′) *adj., n.* —*adj.* rejected; cast off. —*n.* a person or thing that is cast off or rejected.

off–col·or or **off–col·our** (of′kul′ər) *adj.* **1** defective in color. **2** somewhat improper: *an off-color joke.* **3** not well: *She was feeling off-color yesterday.*

of·fence (ə fens′, ō fens′, or, *for defs.* 5, 6, ō′fens) *n.* **1** a breaking of the law; sin. Offences against the law are punished by fines or imprisonment. **2** something that offends or causes displeasure: *Rudeness is always an offence.* **3** the condition of being offended; hurt feelings; anger: *He tried not to cause offence.* **4** the act of offending or hurting someone's feelings: *No offence was intended.* **5** the act of attacking: *The army proved weak in offence.* **6** an attacking team or force.
give offence, offend.
take offence, be offended. Also, **offense.**
[ME *offens* < OF < L *offensum* offence, annoyance; and ME *offense* < OF < L *offensa* hurt, injury, wrong; both L nouns < L *offendere.* See **OFFEND.**]
☛ *Syn.* **1.** See note at **crime.**

of·fence·less (ə fens′lis) *adj.* **1** without offence; incapable of offence or attack. **2** not offending; inoffensive. Also, **offenseless.**

of·fend (ə fend′) *v.* **1** hurt the feelings of; make angry; displease. **2** give offence; cause displeasure. **3** sin; do wrong. [ME < OF < L *offendere* < *ob-* against + *-fendere* strike]

of·fend·er (ə fen′dər) *n.* **1** a person who offends. **2** a person who does wrong or breaks a law.

of·fense (ə fens′ *or* ō fens′) See **offence**.

of·fen·sive (ə fen′siv) *adj., n.* —*adj.* **1** giving offence; irritating; annoying: *"Shut up" is an offensive retort.* **2** unpleasant; disagreeable; disgusting: *Bad eggs have an offensive odor.* **3** ready to attack; attacking: *an offensive army.* **4** used for attack; having to do with attack: *offensive weapons, an offensive war for conquest.* —*n.* **1** the position or attitude of attack: *The army took the offensive.* **2** an attack: *An offensive against polio was begun when the proper vaccine was developed.* —**of·fen′sive·ly,** *adv.* —**of·fen′sive·ness,** *n.*

of·fer (of′ər) *v., n.* —*v.* **1** hold out to be taken or refused; present: *He offered us his help.* **2** present for sale: *to offer suits at reduced prices.* **3** be willing; volunteer: *He offered to help us.* **4** bring forth for consideration; propose: *She offered a few ideas to improve the plan.* **5** present in worship: *to offer prayers.* **6** give; show: *The enemy offered resistance to our soldiers' attack.* **7** present itself; occur: *I will come if the opportunity offers.* **8** show intention; attempt; try: *The thieves offered no resistance to the policemen.* **9** present to sight or notice. **10** bid as a price: *He offered twenty dollars for our old stove.* —*n.* **1** the act of offering: *an offer of money, an offer to sing, an offer of marriage, an offer of $60 000 for a house.* **2** a thing that is offered. **3** *Law.* a proposal from one person to another which, if accepted, will become a contract. **4** an attempt or show of intention. [OE *offrian* < L *offerre* < *ob-* to + *ferre* bring]
➤ *Syn.* —*v.* **1. Offer, proffer, tender** = hold out something to someone to be accepted. **Offer** is the common word meaning "hold out" something to be taken or refused as one chooses or pleases: *She offered him coffee.* **Proffer** is the literary word, usually suggesting volunteering or offering with warmth, courtesy, or earnest sincerity: *He refused the proffered hospitality.* **Tender** is a formal word meaning "offer formally" something like services, not objects: *He tendered his apologies.*

of·fer·ing (of′ər ing *or* of′ring) *n.* **1** the act of one who offers. **2** a contribution or gift, as for the support of a church. **3** a sacrifice of an animal, etc. made to a deity.

of·fer·to·ry (of′ər tô′rē) *n., pl.* **-ries. 1** a collection, usually of money, at a religious service. **2** the verses said or the music sung or played while the offering is received. **3 a** *Roman Catholic Church.* the part of the Mass at which bread and wine are offered to God. **b** *Anglican Church.* a similar offering of bread and wine to God. **c** the prayers said or sung at this time. [< LL *offertorium* place to which offerings were brought]

off·hand (*adv.* of′hand′; *adj.* of′hand′) *adv., adj.* —*adv.* without previous thought or preparation: *The carpenter could not tell offhand how much the work would cost.* —*adj.* **1** done or made on the spur of the moment without previous thought or planning: *His offhand remarks were often very funny.* **2** casual; informal. **3** impolite; without due courtesy: *The boy's offhand ways angered his father.*

off·hand·ed (of′han′did) *adj.* offhand. —**off′hand′ed·ly,** *adv.* —**off′hand′ed·ness,** *n.*

of·fice (of′is) *n.* **1** the place in which the work of a business or profession is done; a room or rooms in which to do such work: *The executive offices were on the second floor.* **2** a position, especially in the public service: *The MP was appointed to the office of Minister of Defence.* **3** the duty of one's position; one's job or work: *A teacher's office is teaching.* **4** the staff or persons carrying on work in an office: *Half the office is on vacation.* **5** an administrative department of a governmental organization. **6** an act of kindness or unkindness; attention; service; injury: *Through the good offices of a friend, he was able to get a job.* **7** a religious ceremony or prayer: *the Communion office, last offices.* **8 offices,** *pl. Esp.Brit.* the parts of a house devoted to household work, such as kitchen, pantry, laundry, etc., often also stables and buildings. [ME < OF < L *officium* service < *opus* work + *facere* do]

office boy a boy whose work is doing odd jobs in an office.

of·fice·hold·er (of′is hōl′dər) *n.* a person who holds a public office; governmental official.

of·fi·cer (of′ə sər) *n., v.* —*n.* **1** a person who commands others in the armed forces such as a colonel, a lieutenant, or a captain. **2** the captain of a ship or any of his chief assistants. **3** a person who holds an office in the government, the church, the public service, etc.: *a health officer, a police officer.* **4** a person appointed or elected to an administrative position in a company, club, society, etc. **5** in some societies, any member above the lowest rank. —*v.* **1** provide with officers. **2** direct; conduct; manage. [ME < AF *officer,* OF *officier* < Med.L *officiarius* < L *officium* service] —**of·fi′cer·less,** *adj.*

officer cadet a person training for a commission in the armed forces; cadet (def. 1). *Abbrev.:* O.Cdt. or OCdt

officer of the day *Military.* an officer who has charge, for the time being, of the guards, prisoners, barracks, etc. *Abbrev.:* O.D.

office seeker a person who tries to obtain a public office.

hat, āge, fär; let, ēqual, tèrm; it, īce
hot, ōpen, ôrder; oil, out; cup, pùt, rüle,
ə above, takən, pencəl, lemən, circəs

ch, child; ng, long; sh, ship
th, thin; ᴛʜ, then; zh, measure

of·fi·cial (ə fish′əl *or* ō fish′əl) *n., adj.* —*n.* **1** a person who holds a public position or who is in charge of some public work or duty: *Postmasters are government officials.* **2** a person holding office; officer: *bank officials.* —*adj.* **1** of or having to do with an office or officers: *Policemen wear an official uniform.* **2** having authority: *An official record is kept of the proceedings of Parliament.* **3** being an official: *Each province has its own official representatives in Parliament.* **4** suitable for a person in office: *the official dignity of a judge.* **5** holding office. [< LL *officialis* < *officium* service] —**of·fi′cial·ly,** *adv.*

of·fi·cial·dom (ə fish′əl dəm *or* ō fish′əl-) *n.* **1** the position or domain of officials. **2** officials collectively.

of·fi·cial·ese (ə fish′ə lēz′) *n.* pompous, involved, or obscure language thought of as characteristic of official statements, reports, etc.

of·fi·cial·ism (ə fish′əl iz′əm *or* ō fish′əl-) *n.* **1** official methods or systems. **2** an excessive attention to official routine.

of·fi·ci·ate (ə fish′ē āt′ *or* ō fish′ē āt′) *v.* **-at·ed, -at·ing. 1** perform the duties of any office or position: *The president officiates as chairman at all club meetings.* **2** perform the duties of a priest, minister, or rabbi: *The bishop officiated at the cathedral.* **3** do anything as a ritual or ceremony: *to officiate in carving the Thanksgiving turkey.* [< Med.L *officiare* < L *officium* service]

of·fic·i·nal (ə fis′ə nəl *or* ō fis′ə nəl) *adj., n.* —*adj.* **1** kept in stock by druggists. **2** recognized by the pharmacopoeia. —*n.* a drug that is kept in stock. [< Med.L *officinalis* < L *officina* shop, storeroom, ult. < *opus* work + *facere* do]

of·fi·cious (ə fish′əs *or* ō fish′əs) *adj.* too ready to offer services or advice; minding other people's business; fond of meddling. [< L *officiosus* dutiful < *officium* service] —**of·fi′cious·ly,** *adv.* —**of·fi′cious·ness,** *n.*

off·ing (of′ing) *n.* **1** the more distant part of the sea as seen from the shore. **2** a position at a distance from the shore.
in the offing, a just visible from the shore. **b** within sight. **c** not far off. **d** due to come, happen, etc. soon but at a time as yet unspecified: *There is a general election in the offing.*

off·ish (of′ish) *adj. Informal.* inclined to keep aloof; distant and reserved in manner. —**off′ish·ness,** *n.*

off–key (of′kē′) *adj.* **1** *Music.* not in the correct musical key; inharmonious. **2** *Informal.* improper; ill-timed.

off–line (of′līn′) *adj.* of, involving, or designating a piece of equipment that is not directly connected to or controlled by the main unit of a computer.

off·load (of lōd′) *v.* unload.

off·print (*n.* of′print′; *v.* of′print′) *n., v.* —*n.* a separate reprint or reproduction of a story, article, etc. from a journal, book, etc.; printed excerpt. —*v.* reprint separately as an excerpt.

off·scour·ings (of′skour′ingz) *n.pl.* **1** filth; refuse. **2** low, worthless people.

off–screen (of′skrēn′) *adj., adv.* —*adj.* **1** not seen on a movie or television screen: *an off-screen commentary.* **2** not engaged in acting for movies or television. —*adv.* so as not to be seen on a movie or television screen.

off–sea·son (of′sē′zən) *n., adj.* —*n.* the slack of slow season of a business, sport, etc. —*adj.* in or for the off-season: *Off-season hotel rates are usually low.*

off·set (*v.* of′set′; *n.* of′set′) *v.* **-set, -set·ing;** *n.* —*v.* **1** make up for; counterbalance; compensate for: *The better roads offset the greater distance.* **2** balance (one thing) by another as an equivalent: *We offset the greater distance by the better roads.* **3** set off or balance: *We offset the better roads against the greater distance.* **4** form an offset. **5** *Printing.* make an offset. —*n.* **1** something that makes up for something else; compensation. **2** *Botany.* a short side shoot from a main stem or root that starts a new plant. **3** any offshoot. **4** *Printing.* a process in which an inked impression is first made on a rubber roller and then on the paper, instead of directly on the paper. **b** an impression made by such a process. **5** *Surveying.* a short distance measured perpendicularly from a main line. **6** *Architecture.* a ledge formed on a wall by lessening its thickness above. **7** an abrupt bend in a pipe or bar to carry it past some obstruction.

off·shoot (of′shüt′) *n.* **1** *Botany.* a shoot or branch growing out

from the main stem of a plant, tree, etc. **2** anything coming, or thought of as coming, from a main part, stock, race, etc.

off·shore (ôf'shôr') *adj., adv.* —*adj.* **1** off or away from the shore: *an offshore wind.* **2** done or working away from the shore: *offshore fisheries.* —*adv.* toward the water; from the shore: *The wind was blowing offshore.*

off·side or **off-side** (ôf'sīd') *adj.* away from one's own or the proper side; being on the wrong side.

off·spring (ôf'spring') *n.* **1** the young of a person, animal, or plant; descendant: *Every one of Mr. Kelly's offspring had red hair.* **2** a result; effect. [OE *ofspring*]

off-stage (ôf'stāj') *adj.* away from the part of the stage that the audience can see.

off-street (ôf'strēt') *adj.* away from the street: *More off-street parking will ease downtown traffic congestion.*

off-the-cuff (ôf'тнə kuf') *adj., adv. Informal.* —*adj.* not prepared beforehand; impromptu: *The minister's speech was off-the-cuff, not a formal statement.* —*adv.* extemporaneously; on the spur of the moment.

off-the-rec·ord (ôf'тнə rek'ərd) *adj., adv.* —*adj.* **1** not to be written in the minutes or proceedings (of a meeting, conference, etc.). **2** not for publication or release as news. —*adv.* so as to be off-the-record.

off-track (ôf'trak') *adj.* **1** not conducted at a race track: *off-track betting.* **2** out of the way; off the beaten track.

off-white (ôf'wīt' *or* -hwīt') *n., adj.* —*n.* a very pale beige or light grey, almost white. —*adj.* almost white.

off-year (ôf'yēr') *n.* a year of lower returns or of poor conditions in business, farming, etc.

oft (oft) *adv. Archaic.* often. [OE]

of·ten (ôf'ən *or* ôf'tən) *adv.* in many cases; many times; frequently: *Blame is often misdirected. He comes here often.* [ME *often* oft, the form of *ofte* before a vowel]

☛ *Syn.* **Often, frequently** = many times or in many instances, and are mostly interchangeable. But **often** suggests only that something happens or occurs a number of times or in a considerable proportion of the total number of instances: *We often see him.* **Frequently** emphasizes happening or occurring again and again, regularly or at short intervals: *We saw him frequently last week.*

of·ten·times (ôf'ən tīmz' *or* ôf'tən-) *adv.* often.

oft·times (oft'tīmz') *adv. Poetic.* often.

o·gee (ō jē' *or* ō'jē) *n.* **1** an S-shaped curve or line. **2** *Architecture.* a moulding with such a curve. **3** an ogee arch. [< F *ogive*]

ogee arch a form of pointed arch, each side of which has the curve of an ogee.

og·ham or **og·am** (og'əm *or* ō'əm) *n.* an alphabetical writing system used on monuments by the ancient Celts in Ireland and Britain from about the 4th or 5th century A.D. to the early 7th century. [< Old Irish *ogam*, associated with *Ogma*, legendary inventor of this writing system. 17c.]

o·give (ō'jīv *or* ō jīv') *n.* **1** *Architecture.* **a** a pointed arch. **b** a diagonal rib across a vault. **2** *Statistics.* a distribution graph or curve showing cumulative frequencies. [< MF; origin uncertain]

o·gle (ō'gəl) *v.* **o·gled, o·gling;** *n.* —*v.* **1** look at with desire; make eyes at. **2** look with desire; make eyes: *He is always ogling.* —*n.* an ogling look. [< Du. *oogelen* < *oog* eye] —**o'gler,** *n.*

Og·pu (og'pü) *n.* in the Soviet Union, the official organization of secret police from 1922 to 1935. [Abbrev. of Russian for "Unified State Political Administration"]

o·gre (ō'gər) *n.* **1** *Folklore.* a giant or monster that supposedly eats people. **2** a brutal or terrifying person. [< F]

o·gre·ish (ō'gər ish) *adj.* like an ogre.

o·gress (ō'gris) *n.* a female ogre.

oh or **Oh** (ō) *interj.* **1** a word used before names in addressing persons: *Oh Mary, look!* **2** an expression of surprise, joy, grief, pain, and other feelings. Also, **O.**

☛ *Hom.* **o, owe.**

☛ *Usage.* **Oh** is preferred to **o,** except before names: *Oh, what a lovely day!*

OH Ohio.

OHG or **O.H.G.** Old High German.

ohm (ōm) *n.* an SI unit for measuring the resistance of a conductor to an electric current sent through it. A conductor has a resistance of one ohm if it takes one volt of pressure to send a current of one ampere through it. *Symbol:* Ω *n.* [after Georg Simon Ohm (1787-1854), a German physicist]

ohm·ic (ōm'ik) *adj.* of or having to do with the ohm.

OHMS or **O.H.M.S.** On Her (or His) Majesty's Service.

o·ho or **O·ho** (ō hō') *interj.* an exclamation expressing a taunt, surprise, or exultation.

-oid *suffix.* **1** like; like that of, as in *Mongoloid, amoeboid.* **2** thing like a, as in *spheroid, alkaloid.* [< Gk. *-oeidēs < eidos* form]

oil (oil) *n., v.* —*n.* **1** any of several kinds of thick, fatty, or greasy liquids that are lighter than water, that burn easily, and that dissolve in alcohol, but not in water. Mineral oils are used for fuel; animal and vegetable oils are used in cooking, medicine, and in many other ways. Essential or volatile oils, such as oil of peppermint, are distilled from plants, leaves, flowers, etc. and are thin and evaporate very quickly. **2** petroleum. **3** any substance that resembles oil in some respect. Sulphuric acid is sometimes called oil of vitriol. **4** Often, **oils** *pl.* oil paint. **5** an oil painting.

pour oil on troubled waters, make things calm and peaceful.

strike oil, a find oil by boring a hole in the earth. **b** find something very profitable.

—*v.* **1** become oil: *Butter oils when heated.* **2** put oil on or in. **3** make smooth or oily. **4** seek to persuade by bribery, flattery, etc. [ME < ONF *olie* < L *oleum* < Gk. *elaion*]

oil burner 1 a furnace, ship, etc. that uses oil for fuel. **2** the part of such a furnace in which the fuel oil is atomized, mixed with air, and burned.

oil cake a mass of linseed, cottonseed, etc. from which the oil has been pressed. Oil cakes are used as a food for cattle and sheep or as a fertilizer.

oil·can (oil'kan') *n.* a can for oil, especially one with a narrow spout or a nozzle, for oiling machinery, etc.

oil·cloth (oil'kloth') *n.* **1** a cloth made waterproof and glossy on one side by coating it with a mixture of oil, clay, and coloring. Oilcloth is used to cover shelves, tables, etc. **2** oilskin.

oil color or **colour 1** oil paint. **2** a painting done in oil colors.

oil·er (oil'ər) *n.* **1** a person or thing that oils. **2** a can with a long spout used in oiling machinery. **3** an oil tanker. **4 oilers,** *pl.* oilskins or other waterproof clothing.

oil field an area where petroleum has been found (*usually used in the plural*).

oil of turpentine a colorless, inflammable, volatile oil made from turpentine, used in mixing paints.

oil of vitriol sulphuric acid.

oil paint paint made by mixing pigment with an oil, such as linseed oil.

oil painting 1 a picture painted with oil paints. **2** the art of painting with oil paints.

oil·pa·per (oil'pā'pər) *n.* paper treated with oil to make it transparent and waterproof.

oil sand any area of sand or rock, especially sandstone, that contains large deposits of oil.

oil·skin (oil'skin') *n.* **1** cloth treated with oil to make it waterproof. **2 oilskins,** *pl.* a coat and trousers made of this cloth.

oil·stone (oil'stōn') *n.* a fine-grained stone used for sharpening tools, the rubbing surface of which is oiled.

oil tanker a ship having special tanks to transport oil.

oil well a well drilled in the earth to get oil.

oil·y (oil'ē) *adj.* **oil·i·er, oil·i·est. 1** of oil: *an oily smell.* **2** containing oil: *oily salad dressing.* **3** covered or soaked with oil. **4** like oil; smooth; slippery. **5** too smooth; suspiciously or disagreeably smooth: *an oily smile, an oily manner.* —**oil'i·ness,** *n.*

oint·ment (oint'mənt) *n.* a substance made from oil or fat, often containing medicine, used on the skin to heal or to make it soft and white. Cold cream and salve are ointments. [ME < OF *oignement*, ult. < L *unguere* anoint; form influenced by *anoint*]

O·jib·wa or **O·jib·way** (ō jib'wä) *n., pl.* **-wa** or **-was, -way or -ways;** *adj.* —*n.* **1** a member of an Amerindian people living in the region around Lake Superior and westward. The Ojibwa traditionally occupied an area stretching from the Ottawa Valley to the prairies. **2** an Algonquian language spoken by the Ojibwa, Algonquins, Ottawas and Salteaux. —*adj.* of or having to do with the Ojibwa or their language.

OK Oklahoma.

O.K. or **OK** (ō'kā') *adj., adv., v.* **O.K.'d** or **OK'd, O.K.'ing or OK'ing;** *n., pl.* **O.K.'s** or **OK's.** *Informal.* —*adj.* or *adv.* all right; correct; approved: *The new schedule is O.K.* —*v.* endorse; approve. —*n.* approval: *The supervisor has given us his O.K.* [probably from the "O.K. Club," a Democratic club of New York City formed in 1840 by supporters of Martin Van Buren; so called in allusion to "Old Kinderhook," Van Buren having been born at Kinderhook, N.Y.]

O·ka (ō'kə) *n. Cdn.* a cheese, cured with brine, made by Trappist monks in Oka, Quebec.

o·ka·pi (ō kä′pē) *n., pl.* **-pis** or **-pi.** an African mammal (*Okapia johnstoni*) related to and resembling the giraffe, but smaller and having a much shorter neck. [< an African lang.]

o·kay (ō′kā′) See **O.K.**

O·kie (ō′kē) *n. U.S. Informal.* a migratory farm worker, originally one of many from Oklahoma who wandered in search of work during the depression of the 1930's.

Okla. Oklahoma.

o·kra (ō′krə) *n.* **1** a tall annual herb (*Hibiscus esculentus*) of the mallow family having heart-shaped lobed leaves and long, tapering seed pods. The okra is native to Africa but is commonly cultivated in the United States and other countries. **2** the unripe, tender pods of this plant, used as a vegetable and for thickening soups; gumbo. [< West African lang.]

-ol *combining form.* containing, derived from, or like an alcohol or phenol. [< alcoh*ol*]

old (ōld) *adj.* **old·er** or **eld·er, old·est** or **eld·est;** *n.* —*adj.* **1** having existed long; dating from a relatively long time ago: *an old house, an old debt. They are old friends.* **2** of (a specified) age: *She is one year old today.* **3** advanced in age: *an old woman. He doesn't look at all old.* **4** (*noml.*) **the old,** people who are old: *the young and the old.* **5** Often, **Old,** designating the earlier or earliest of two or more periods, types, etc.: *Old English, the Old Testament. They're still using the old edition.* **6** showing the effects of age or use: *Are you still wearing that old coat?* **7** former: *an old student of hers. Infantile paralysis is an old name for polio.* **8** familiar: *an old excuse, good old Tony.* **9** experienced: *an old hand, old in wrongdoing.* **10** *Informal.* a word used as an intensifier: *any old day. We had a high old time at the party.* —*n.* **1** time long ago: *the heroes of old.* **2** a person of a specified age (used in compounds): *a six-year-old.* [OE *ald*] —**old′ness,** *n.*

➤ *Syn. adj.* **1. Old, elderly, ancient** = having existed a long time. **Old,** describing people, animals, or things, means not young or new but having been alive, in existence, or in a particular state for a long or relatively long time: *We are old friends.* **Elderly,** describing people, means past middle age and getting old: *He is an elderly man, about seventy.* **Ancient** suggests having come into existence or use, or having existed or happened, in the distant past: *Jerusalem is an ancient city.*

➤ *Usage.* See note at **elder.**

old age the last part of life, when a person is old; the years of life from about 70 on.

Old Bai·ley (bā′lē) in London, England, the chief court for trying criminal cases.

Old Country the native land of persons living elsewhere: *To many New Canadians Britain is the Old Country.*

old·en (ōl′dən) *adj. Poetic.* of old; old; ancient.

Old English 1 the language of the English people up to about 1100 A.D.; Anglo-Saxon. **2** *Printing.* gothic, or black-letter, type, especially a style of this type used in England up to about the 18th century.

Old English sheepdog a breed of English work dog, having a long, shaggy, blue or grizzly grey coat and docked tail.

old fashioned a cocktail made of whisky, sugar, and bitters with a slice of orange and a cherry, mixed with soda and served cold.

old–fash·ioned (ōld′fash′ənd) *adj.* **1** of an old fashion; out of date in style, construction, etc.: *an old-fashioned dress.* **2** keeping to old ways, ideas, etc.: *an old-fashioned housekeeper.*

old–fo·gey or **old–fo·gy** (ōld′fō′gē) *adj.* out-of-date; behind the times.

old–fo·gey·ish or **old–fo·gy·ish** (ōld′fō′gē ish) *adj.* old-fogey.

Old French the French language from about A.D. 800 to about 1400.

Old Guard 1 the imperial guard of Napoleon I. It made the last French charge at Waterloo. **2** Usually, **old guard,** the conservative members of a country, community, organization, etc.

old hand an expert; a very skilled or experienced person.

Old Har·ry (har′ē *or* her′ē) the Devil.

old hat 1 *Informal.* well-known; familiar. **2** old-fashioned; out-of-date.

Old High German the form of the German language that was spoken in S Germany from about A.D. 800 to 1100. Modern standard German is descended from Old High German.

Old Icelandic Old Norse (def. 2).

old·ie (ōl′dē) *n. Informal.* an old thing or person: *They asked the band to play some oldies.*

old·ish (ōld′ish) *adj.* somewhat old.

Old Latin the Latin language before the second century B.C.

old–line (ōld′līn′) *adj.* **1** keeping to old ideas and ways; conservative. **2** having a long history; established.

hat, āge, fär; let, ēqual, tėrm; it, īce
hot, ōpen, ôrder; oil, out; cup, pùt, rüle,
əbove, takən, pencəl, lemən, circəs
ch, child; ng, long; sh, ship
th, thin; ᵺH, then; zh, measure

old maid 1 a woman who has not married and seems unlikely to do so. **2** a prim, fussy person: *What an old maid he is!* **3** a very simple card game.

old–maid·ish (ōld′mād′ish) *adj.* like, suggesting, or befitting an old maid; prim; fussy.

Old Man of the Sea 1 in *the Arabian Nights,* a horrible old man who clung to the back of Sinbad. **2** any person or thing that is hard to get rid of.

old master 1 any great painter who lived before 1700. **2** a painting by such a painter.

old moon the moon when seen as a thin crescent with the hollow side on the right. See **moon** for picture.

Old Nick (nik) the Devil.

Old Norse 1 Scandinavian speech from the Viking period to about 1300. **2** the Icelandic language from about 900 to about 1600.

Old Prussian a language of the Baltic branch of the Indo-European language family, spoken in East Prussia until about 1700.

Old Saxon the form of Low German spoken by the Saxons in NW Germany from about A.D. 800 to about 1100.

old school any group of people who have old-fashioned or conservative ideas.

old–squaw (ōld′skwo′) *n.* a common marine duck (*Clangula hyemalis*) of the northern hemisphere, the male having distinctive plumage, with a large white patch on each side of the dark-brown head and neck in summer and a brown-and-grey patch on each side of the white head and neck in winter.

old·ster (ōld′stər) *n. Informal.* an old or older person.

Old Style 1 the method of reckoning time according to the Julian calendar, used before the adoption of the Gregorian calendar. Compare **New Style. 2** old style, *Printing.* a style of type characterized by slanting serifs and only slight distinction between light and heavy strokes. *Example*: old style

Old Testament the sacred Scriptures of the Hebrews, as constituting the first part of the Christian Bible. It contains the religious and social laws of the Hebrews, a record of their history, their important literature, and writings of their prophets.

old–time (ōld′tīm′) *adj.* of or like former times.

old–tim·er (ōld′tīm′ər) *n. Informal.* **1** a person who has long been a resident, member, or worker in a place, group, or community. **2** a person who favors old ideas and ways.

old wives' tale a foolish story; silly belief.

old–wom·an·ish (ōld′wùm′ən ish) *adj.* like, suggesting, or befitting an old woman; fussy.

old–world (ōld′wèrld′) *adj.* **1** of or having to do with the ancient world: *an old-world mammoth.* **2** belonging to or characteristic of a former period: *old-world courtesy.* **3** of, having to do with, or characteristic of the Old World; especially, having a picturesque or charming quality associated with Europe, N Africa, etc.: *an old-world market.*

Old World 1 Europe, Asia, and Africa. **2** (*adj.*) of, having to do with, or found in the Old World: *Pythons are the Old World equivalent of the New World boas.*

o·le·ag·i·nous (ō′lē aj′ə nəs) *adj.* oily. [< L *oleaginus* of the olive < *olea* olive, alteration of *oliva.* See OLIVE.]

o·le·an·der (ō′lē an′dər) *n.* a poisonous evergreen shrub (*Nerium oleander*) of the dogbane family native to the Mediterranean but widely cultivated in warm regions for its fragrant red, pink, or white flowers. [< Med.L]

o·le·as·ter (ō′lē as′tər *or* ō′lē as′tər) *n.* **1** any of several shrubs (genus *Elaeagnus*) cultivated for their attractive silvery foliage and also often planted as hardy windbreaks. The Russian olive and silverberry are oleasters. **2** (*adj.*) designating the family of shrubs and trees that includes the oleaster, buffalo berry, etc.

o·le·ate (ō′lē āt′) *n.* a salt of oleic acid.

o·le·ic acid (ō lē′ik *or* ō′lē ik) an oily liquid obtained by hydrolyzing various animal and vegetable oils and fats. *Formula*: $C_{17}H_{33}COOH$ [*oleic* < L *oleum* oil]

o·le·in (ō′lē in) *n.* an ester of oleic acid and glycerin. Lard, olive oil, and cottonseed oil are mostly olein. [< L *oleum* oil]

o·le·o (ō′lē ō) *n. Archaic.* margarine.

o·le·o·mar·ga·rine (ō′lē ō mär′jə rin *or* ō′lē ō mär′jə rēn′) *n.* *Archaic.* margarine. Also, **oleomargarin.** [< L *oleum* oil + E *margarine*]

o·le·o·res·in (ō′lē ō rez′ən) *n.* a natural or prepared solution of resin in oil. [< L *oleum* oil + E *resin*]

ol·fac·tion (ol fak′shən) *n.* **1** the act of smelling. **2** the sense of smell. [< L *olfactus,* pp. of *olfacere* smell at < *olere* emit a smell + *facere* make]

ol·fac·to·ry (ol fak′tə rē) *adj., n., pl.* **-ries.** —*adj.* having to do with smelling; of smell. The nose is an olfactory organ. —*n.* an olfactory organ.

ol·i·garch (ol′ə gärk′) *n.* one of a small number of persons holding the ruling power in a state.

ol·i·gar·chic (ol′ə gär′kik) *adj.* of an oligarchy or oligarchs; having to do with rule by a few.

ol·i·gar·chi·cal (ol′ə gär′kə kəl) *adj.* oligarchic.

ol·i·gar·chy (ol′ə gär′kē) *n., pl.* **-chies. 1** a form of government in which a few people have the power. **2** a country or state having such a government. Ancient Sparta was really an oligarchy, though it had two kings. **3** the ruling few. [< Gk. *oligarchia,* ult. < *oligos* few + *archos* leader]

Ol·i·go·cene (ol′ə gō sēn′) *n., adj.* *Geology.* —*n.* **1** an early period of the Cenozoic era, beginning approximately 40 million years ago. **2** the rocks formed in this period. See chart at **geology.** —*adj.* of or having to do with this period or rocks formed during it. [< Gk. *oligos* small, little + *kainos* new, recent]

ol·i·gop·o·lis·tic (ol′ə gop′ə lis′tik) *adj.* of or having to do with an oligopoly or oligopolies.

ol·i·gop·o·ly (ol′ə gop′ə lē) *n.* a market situation in which a few large producers control an industry so that there is limited competition and each producer is able to calculate the direct effect on the other firms of its own decisions with respect to pricing, etc. Compare **monopoly.** [< Gk. *oligos* few + E monopoly]

ol·i·go·troph·ic (ol′ə gō trof′ik *or* -trō′fik) *adj.* of a lake or river, deficient in plant nutrients and plant life and rich in oxygen throughout its depth, thus able to support a large fish population. Compare **eutrophic.** [< Gk. *oligos* little, few + *trophikos* nourishing < *trophē* food, nourishment. 20c.]

ol·i·got·roph·y (ol′ə got′rə fē) *n.* the condition of being oligotrophic.

ol·ive (ol′iv) *n., adj.* —*n.* **1** a subtropical evergreen tree (*Olea europaea*) having narrow, leathery, greyish-green leaves, fragrant white flowers, and edible fruits that are bluish black when ripe. **2** the fruit of this tree, which is also the source of olive oil. **3** the wood of this tree, used for ornamental carving, etc. **4** (*adj.*) designating the family of trees and shrubs of tropical and warm temperate regions that includes the olive and many species cultivated as ornamentals, such as lilac, forsythia, and jasmine. **5** a branch or wreath of olive leaves, used as a symbol of peace. **6** a medium to dark yellowish-green color. **7** a yellowish-brown color (*used to describe complexions*). —*adj.* having the color olive: *olive skin.* [ME < OF < L *oliva* < Gk. **elaiwa,* dial. var. of *elaia*]

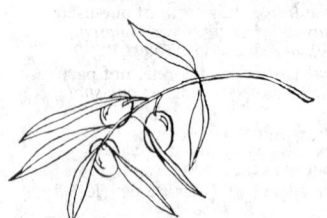
An olive branch with olives

The emblem of the United Nations, using olive branches as a symbol of peace

olive branch 1 a branch of the olive tree as an emblem of peace. **2** anything offered as a sign of peace. **3** child.

olive drab a dark greenish-yellow.

olive oil oil pressed from olives, used in cooking, in medicine, etc.

Ol·i·ver (ol′ə vər) *n.* one of Charlemagne's heroic followers and the close friend of Roland, with whom he engaged in a fight which neither of them could win. See also **Roland.**

ol·i·vine (ol′ə vēn′ *or* ol′ə vēn′) *n.* chrysolite, especially when greenish. [< *olive;* from the color]

ol·o·gy (ol′ə jē) *n., pl.* **-gies.** any science or branch of knowledge. [< connective *-o-* + *-logy*]

O·lym·pi·a (ō lim′pē ə) *n.* in ancient Greece, a plain where games were held every four years in honor of Zeus.

O·lym·pi·ad *or* **o·lym·pi·ad** (ō lim′pē ad′) *n.* **1** in ancient Greece, a period of four years reckoned from one celebration of the Olympic games to the next, by which Greeks computed time from 776 b.c. **2** the celebration of the modern Olympic games. [< L < Gk. *Olympias, -ados,* ult. < *Olympus,* a mountain in NE Greece]

O·lym·pi·an (ō lim′pē ən) *adj.* **1** having to do with Olympia or with Mount Olympus. **2** like a god; heavenly. **3** rather too gracious; magnificent; superior: *Olympian calm, Olympian manners.* —*n.* **1** any of the major Greek gods. **2** a contender in the Olympic games.

Olympian games Olympic games.

O·lym·pic (ō lim′pik) *adj., n.* —*adj.* **1** of or having to do with Olympia in ancient Greece: *the Olympic games.* **2** of or having to do with Mount Olympus. —*n.* **Olympics,** *pl.* the Olympic games.

Olympic games 1 in ancient Greece, contests in athletics, poetry, and music, held every four years by the Greeks in honor of Zeus. **2** a modern event imitating the athletic contests of these games. They were revived in 1896 and are held once every four years in a different country, and athletes from many nations compete in them.

O·lym·pus (ō lim′pəs) *n.* heaven. [< Mount *Olympus,* in Greece, regarded as the home of the ancient Greek deities]

O.M. Order of Merit.

-oma *combining form.* a tumor or growth, as in *carcinoma.* [< Gk. noun suffix *-ōma, -ōmatos*]

o·ma·sum (ō mā′səm) *n., pl.* **-sa** (-sə). the third stomach of a cow or other ruminant. The omasum receives the food when it is swallowed the second time. [< L]

om·buds·man (om budz′mən *or* om′bədz mən) *n., pl.* **-men.** a government official appointed to receive and investigate citizens' grievances against the government. The office of ombudsman originated in the Scandinavian countries. [< Swedish]

o·meg·a (ō meg′ə, ō mē′gə, *or* ō′mig ə) *n.* **1** the last of any series; end. **2** the last letter of the Greek alphabet. (Ω or ω). [< LGk. *o mega* big *o*]

om·e·lette *or* **om·e·let** (om′ə lit *or* om′lit) *n.* a food dish of eggs beaten with milk or water, cooked, and folded over. Omelettes are sometimes filled with chopped meat, mushrooms, or some other filling.

o·men (ō′mən) *n., v.* —*n.* **1** a sign of what is to happen; object or event that is believed to mean good or bad fortune: *Spilling salt is said to be an omen of misfortune.* **2** prophetic meaning: *Some people consider a black cat a creature of ill omen.* —*v.* be a sign of; presage. [< L]

☛ *Syn. n.* **1.** See note at **sign.**

O.M.I. Oblates of Mary Immaculate.

om·i·cron (ō′mə kron′ *or* om′ə kron′) *n.* the 15th letter of the Greek alphabet (O or *o*). [< Gk. *o micron* small *o*]

om·i·nous (om′ə nəs) *adj.* of bad omen; unfavorable; threatening: *The watchdog gave an ominous growl.* [< L *ominosus* < *omen* omen] —**om′i·nous·ly,** *adv.* —**om′i·nous·ness,** *n.*

o·mis·sion (ō mish′ən) *n.* **1** an omitting or being omitted. **2** anything omitted: *His song was the only omission from the program.* [< LL *omissio, -onis* < L *omittere.* See OMIT.]

o·mit (ō mit′) *v.* **o·mit·ted, o·mit·ting. 1** leave out: *You have omitted a letter in this word.* **2** fail to do; neglect: *Mary omitted to make her bed.* [< L *omittere* < *ob-* by + *mittere* let go]

OMM *Cdn.* Officer of the Order of Military Merit.

om·ni·bus (om′nə bəs′ *or* om′nə bəs) *n., pl.* **-bus·es;** *adj.* —*n.* **1** a large passenger vehicle having seats inside and sometimes also on the roof; bus. **2** a volume of works by a single author, or of similar works by several authors: *a Hemingway omnibus, a science-fiction omnibus.* —*adj.* covering many things at once: *an omnibus law.* [< L *omnibus* for all]

om·ni·far·i·ous (om′nə fer′ē əs) *adj.* of all forms, varieties, or kinds. [< LL *omnifarius* < L *omnis* all + *fas, faris,* originally, pronouncement < *fari* speak]

om·nip·o·tence (om nip′ə təns) *n.* complete power; unlimited power: *the omnipotence of God.*

om·nip·o·tent (om nip′ə tənt) *adj.* —*adj.* having all power; almighty: *an omnipotent ruler.* —*n.* **the Omnipotent,** God. [< L *omnipotens, -entis* < *omnis* all + *potens* being able] —**om·nip′o·tent·ly,** *adv.*

om·ni·pres·ence (om'nə prez'əns) *n.* presence everywhere at the same time: *God's omnipresence.*

om·ni·pres·ent (om'nə prez'ənt) *adj.* present everywhere at the same time. [< Med.L *omnipraesens, -entis* < L *omnis* all + *praesens* present]

om·nis·cience (om nis'ē əns *or* om nish'əns) *n.* knowledge of everything; complete or infinite knowledge. [< Med.L *omniscientia* < L *omnis* all + *scientia* knowledge]

om·nis·cient (om nis'ē ənt *or* om nish'ənt) *adj.* knowing everything; having complete or infinite knowledge. —**om·nis'cient·ly,** *adv.*

om·ni·um–gath·er·um (om'nē əm gaᴛʜ'ər əm) *n.* a miscellaneous collection; a confused mixture. [< L *omnium* of all + *gatherum,* pseudo-Latin form from E *gather*]

om·niv·o·rous (om niv'ə rəs) *adj.* 1 eating every kind of food. 2 eating both animal and vegetable food: *Man is an omnivorous animal.* 3 taking in everything; fond of all kinds: *An omnivorous reader reads all kinds of books.* [< L *omnivorus* < *omnis* all + *vorare* eat greedily] —**om·niv'o·rous·ly,** *adv.* —**om·niv'o·rous·ness,** *n.*

on (on) *prep., adv., adj.* —*prep.* 1 above and supported by: *The book is on the table.* 2 touching so as to cover, be around, etc.: *There's new paint on the ceiling. Put the ring on her finger.* 3 close to; along the edge of: *a house on the shore. He lives on the next street.* 4 in the direction of; toward: *The workers marched on the capital.* 5 against; upon: *the picture on the wall.* 6 by means of; by the use of: *This news is on good authority.* 7 in the condition of; in the process of; in the way of: *on half pay, on purpose, on duty.* 8 at the time of; during: *They greeted us on our arrival.* 9 in relation to; in connection with; concerning: *a book on animals.* 10 for the purpose of: *He went on an errand.* 11 in addition to: *Defeat on defeat discouraged them.* 12 among: *I am on the committee.* —*adv.* 1 on something: *The walls are up, and the roof is on.* 2 to something: *Hold on, or you may fall.* 3 toward something: *Some played; the others looked on.* 4 farther: *March on.* 5 in or into a condition, process, manner, action, etc.: *Turn the gas on.* 6 from a time; forward: *later on, from that day on.*
and so on, and more of the same.
on and off, at some times and not others; now and then.
on and on, without stopping.
—*adj.* taking place: *The race is on.* [OE]
☞ *Usage.* **on to, onto.** See note at **onto.**

ON¹ Ontario (*used esp. in computerized address systems*).

ON² *or* **O.N.** Old Norse.

once (wuns) *adv., n., conj., adj.* —*adv.* 1 one time: *He comes once a day.* 2 at some one time in the past; formerly: *a once powerful nation.* 3 even a single time; ever: *If the facts once become known everybody would laugh at her.*
once and again, repeatedly.
once and for all, *or* **once for all,** finally.
once in a while, now and then; at one time or another.
once or twice, a few times.
once over, a single time over.
once upon a time, long ago.
—*n.* a single occasion: *Once is enough.*
at once *or* **all at once, a** immediately: *Come at once.* **b** at the same time: *Everyone shouted at once.*
for once, for one time at least.
—*conj.* whenever or if ever; after: *Once you cross the river, you are safe.*
—*adj.* former: *a once friend.* [OE *ānes* < *ān* one]

once–o·ver (wuns'ō'vər) *n. Informal.* a short, quick look.

on·co·log·i·cal (ong kə loj'ə kəl) *adj.* of or having to do with oncology.

on·col·o·gist (ong kol'ə jist) *n.* a specialist in oncology.

on·col·o·gy (ong kol'ə jē) *n.* the branch of medicine dealing with the study and treatment of tumors. [< Gk. *onkos* swelling, tumor + E *-logy.* 19c.]

on·com·ing (on'kum'ing) *adj., n.* —*adj.* approaching: *oncoming winter.* —*n.* approach: *the oncoming of the storm.*

one (wun) *n., adj., pron.* —*n.* 1 the first and lowest whole number; 1. 2 the numeral 1: *What does the 1 in the margin mean?* 3 a single person or thing: *I gave him the one he wanted.* 4 the first in a set or series; especially, a playing card or side of a die having one spot; ace. 5 a one-dollar bill: *I got a five and three ones in change.*
at one, in agreement: *The two judges were at one about the winner.*
make one, a form or be the one of a number, assembly, or party. **b** join together; unite in marriage.
one and all, everyone.
one by one, one after another.
one up on, *Informal.* an advantage over.
—*adj.* 1 being a single unit or individual: *one apple.* 2 some: *One day he will be sorry. I saw him one day last week.* 3 the same: *They*

*hat, āge, fär; let, ēqual, tèrm; it, īce
hot, ōpen, ôrder; oil, out; cup, pút, rüle,
above, takən, pencəl, lemən, circəs*

*ch, child; ng, long; sh, ship
th, thin; ᴛʜ, then; zh, measure*

held one opinion. 4 joined together; united: *They replied in one voice.* 5 being the first in a set or series (*used mainly after the noun*): *We'll start with Chapter One.* 6 a certain: *One John Smith was elected.*
all one, a exactly the same: *They are all one in their love of hockey.* **b** making no difference: *It is all one to me whether you stay or go.*
one or two, a few.
—*pron.* 1 some person or thing: *One of the poems was selected for the book.* 2 any person or thing: *One must work hard to achieve success.* 3 the same person or thing: *Dr. Jekyll and Mr. Hyde were one and the same.*
one or two, a few.
[OE (*stressed*) *ān.* Cf. A¹, AN¹.]
☞ *Hom.* **won.**
☞ *Usage.* The use of the impersonal pronoun **one** is characteristically formal, especially if it must be repeated. Informal: *You can't be too careful, can you?* Formal: *One can't be too careful, can one?*

one another each of several in an action or relation that is common to all: *They struck at one another. They were in one another's way.*
☞ *Usage.* **One another, each other.** As a reciprocal pronoun, **one another** is usually used with reference to more than two, **each other** with reference to two: *The members of the team support one another. The two hate each other.*

one–celled (wun'seld') *adj.* having only one cell.

one–horse (wun'hôrs') *adj.* 1 drawn or worked by a single horse: *a one-horse sleigh.* 2 using or having only a single horse: *a one-horse farmer.* 3 *Informal.* of little scope, capacity, or importance; minor: *a one-horse town.*

O·nei·da (ō nī'də) *n., pl.* **-da** *or* **-das;** *adj.* —*n.* 1 a member of an Amerindian people belonging to the Five Nations confederacy, originally of New York State and later living in SW Ontario and Wisconsin. 2 the Iroquoian language of the Oneida. —*adj.* of or having to do with the Oneida or their language.

one–man (wun'man') *adj.* 1 of or by only one person: *one-man rule, a one-man art show.* 2 made for or to be used by one man: *a one-man space ship.* 3 showing loyalty to or affection for one person only: *one-man dog.*

one·ness (wun'nis) *n.* 1 the quality of being one in number or the only one of its kind; singleness. 2 the quality of being the same in kind; sameness. 3 the fact of forming one whole; unity. 4 agreement in mind, feeling, or purpose; harmony.

one–night stand (wun'nīt') 1 a single performance at a particular place, such as a play presented by a travelling theatre group. 2 *Informal.* a single sexual encounter, especially between people who do not know each other and do not see each other again.

on·er·ous (on'ər əs *or* ō'nər əs) *adj.* burdensome; oppressive: *an onerous task.* [< L *onerosus* < *onus* burden] —**on'er·ous·ly,** *adv.* —**on'er·ous·ness,** *n.*

one·self (wun self') *pron.* 1 a reflexive pronoun, the form used instead of **one** when referring back to the subject of the sentence: *One might ask oneself if it is worth the trouble.* 2 a form used to make a statement stronger: *One has to do the real work oneself.* 3 one's usual self: *It's nice to be oneself again after an illness.*

one–shot (wun'shot') *adj. Informal.* being the only one, not part of a series; being or involving a single act, attempt, etc.: *a one-shot effort.*

one–sid·ed (wun'sīd'id) *adj.* 1 seeing only one side of a question; partial; unfair; prejudiced. 2 uneven; unequal: *If one team is much better than the other, a game is one-sided.* 3 having but one side. 4 on only one side. 5 having one side larger or more developed than the other.

one's self oneself.

one·step (wun'step') *n., v.* **-stepped, -step·ping.** —*n.* 1 a ballroom dance in 2/4 time much like a quick walk. 2 the music for such a dance. —*v.* dance the onestep.

one–time (wun'tīm') *adj.* of the past; former.

one–track (wun'trak') *adj.* 1 having only one track. 2 *Informal.* understanding or preoccupied with only one thing at a time: *one-track mind.*

one–up·man·ship (wun'up'mən ship') *n. Informal.* the art or practice of getting the better of someone else in business, social life, etc.

one–way (wun′wā′) *adj.* moving or allowing movement in only one direction: *one-way traffic.*

on·go·ing (on′gō′ing) *adj.* actually going on; in process; continuing: *This is not an isolated crime, but part of an ongoing social problem.*

on·ion (un′yən) *n.* **1** a commonly cultivated herb (*Allium cepa*) of the lily family having an edible bulb with a very sharp, strong taste and smell. The many varieties of onion include the Spanish onion, Bermuda onion, and green onion. **2** the bulb of this plant, used as a vegetable or seasoning: *Fried onions do not have the sharp taste of raw onions.* [< F *oignon* < L *unio, -onis* onion, kind of pearl] —**on′ion·like′,** *adj.*

on·ion·skin (un′yən skin′) *n.* **1** the thin, papery outer skin of an onion: *Onionskins can be used to make a yellow dye.* **2** a thin, glossy, translucent paper.

on–line (on′līn′) *adj.* of, involving, or designating a piece of equipment that is directly connected to the main unit of a computer.

on·look·er (on′lŭk′ər) *n.* a person who watches without taking part; spectator.

on·look·ing (on′lŭk′ing) *adj. or n.* watching; seeing; noticing.

on·ly (ōn′lē) *adj., adv., conj.* —*adj.* **1** by itself or themselves; one and no more; these and no more; sole, single, or few of the kind or class: *an only son. Those were the only clothes he owned. This is the only road along the shore.* **2** best; finest: *As far as she is concerned, he is the only writer.* —*adv.* **1** merely; just: *He sold only two.* **2** and no one or nothing more; and that is all: *Only he remained. I did it only through friendship.*
if only, I wish: *If only wars would cease!*
only too, very: *She was only too glad to help us.* —*conj.* **1** except that; but: *I would have gone only I didn't have the money.* **2** it must be added that; however: *We camped right beside a stream, only the water was not fit to drink.* [OE *ānlīc*]
☛ *Syn. adj.* **1.** See note at **single.**
☛ *Usage.* To avoid uncertainty, **only** as an adverb should be placed immediately before the word or words it modifies. The following three sentences all have different meanings: *He only wrote to his parents last week* (He didn't telephone). *He wrote only to his parents last week* (not to anyone else). *He wrote to his parents only last week* (just last week).

on·o·mat·o·poe·ia (on′ə mat′ə pē′ə) *n.* **1** the naming of a thing or action by imitating the sound associated with it, as in *buzz, hum, cuckoo, slap, splash.* **2** the adaptation of the sound to the sense for rhetorical effect, as in "the murmurous haunt of flies on summer eves." [< L < Gk. *onomatopoiia* < *onoma, -matos* word, name + *-potos* making]

on·o·mat·o·poe·ic (on′ə mat′ə pē′ik) *adj.* having to do with or like onomatopoeia; imitative in sound; echoic.

on·o·mat·o·po·et·ic (on′ə mat′ə pō et′ik) *adj.* onomatopoeic.

On·on·da·ga (on′ən do′gə *or* on′ən dä′gə) *n., pl.* **-ga** *or* **-gas;** *adj.* —*n.* **1** a member of an Amerindian people belonging to the Five Nations confederacy, living mainly in New York State. **2** the Iroquoian language of the Onondaga. —*adj.* of or having to do with the Onondaga or their language. [< Iroquois *Ononta′ gé,* a place name meaning "on top of the hill"]

on·rush (on′rush′) *n.* a violent forward movement: *He was knocked down by the onrush of water.*

on·set (on′set′) *n.* **1** an attack: *The onset of the enemy took us by surprise.* **2** the beginning: *the onset of a disease, the onset of winter.*

on·shore (on′shôr′) *adv. or adj.* **1** toward the land: *an onshore wind.* **2** on the land: *an onshore patrol.*

on·side (on′sīd′) *adj. or adv.* in a position allowed by the rules of a game.

on·site (on′sīt′) *adj.* on the spot; at the actual location: *an on-site inspection.*

on·slaught (on′slot′ *or* on′slôt′) *n.* a vigorous attack: *The attackers were driven back by a sudden onslaught from within the city.*

Ont. Ontario.

On·tar·i·an (on ter′ē ən) *n., adj.* —*n.* a native or long-term resident of Ontario. —*adj.* of or having to do with Ontario.

On·tar·i·o·an (on ter′ē ō′ən) *n.* Ontarian.

on·to (on′tü; *before consonants often* on′tə) *prep.* **1** on to; to a position on: *throw a ball onto the roof, get onto a horse, a boat driven onto the rocks.* **2** *Informal.* familiar with or aware of: *Are you onto your new job yet? We're onto his tricks.*
☛ *Usage.* **Onto, on to.** When **on** is an adverb and **to** is a preposition, they should be written as two words: *The rest of us drove on to the city.* When the two words are combined to make a compound preposition, they are usually written solid: *The team trotted onto the floor. They looked out onto the park.*

onto– *combining form.* being, existence, as in *ontogenesis.* [< Gk. *ōn, ontos* ppr. of *einai* to be]

on·to·gen·e·sis (on′tə jen′ə sis) *n.* the growth processes of an organism, ontogeny. [< *onto-* + Gk. *-geneia* origin < *-genēs* born, produced]

on·to·ge·net·ic (on′tō jə net′ik) *adj.* of or having to do with ontogenesis.

on·tog·e·ny (on toj′ə nē) *n. Biology.* the development of an individual organism. [< Gk. *ōn, ontos* being + *-geneia* origin < *-genēs* born, produced]

on·to·log·i·cal (on′tə loj′ə kəl) *adj.* of or having to do with ontology.

on·tol·o·gy (on tol′ə jē) *n.* the part of philosophy that deals with the nature of reality. [< NL *ontologia* < Gk. *ōn, ontos* being + *-logos* treating of]

o·nus (ō′nəs) *n.* a burden; responsibility: *Since he made the accusation, the onus is on him to prove it.* [< L]

on·ward (on′wərd) *adv. or adj.* toward the front; on or further on; forward: *The army marched onward. She continued her onward course.*

on·wards (on′wərdz) *adv.* onward.

on·yx (on′iks) *n.* a translucent variety of quartz in layers of different colors. Onyx is used as a semiprecious stone, especially for making cameos. [< L < Gk. *onyx* nail, claw]

oo·dles (ü′dəlz) *n.pl. Informal.* large or unlimited quantities; heaps; loads: *oodles of money.*

An ookpik

Ook·pik (ük′pik) *n. Cdn. Trademark.* a doll resembling an owl, invented by an unnamed Inuit artist in 1963, and soon adopted as a symbol of Canadian handicraft exhibits abroad. [< Eskimo *ukpik* snowy owl]

oo·li·chan (ü′lə kən) *n., pl.* **oo·li·chan** *or* **oo·li·chans.** *Cdn.* a small, highly valued food fish (*Thaleichthys pacificus*) of the smelt family found along the Pacific coast of North America, having a slender body and very oily, rich flesh. Oolichan spend most of their lives in the sea, but swim into freshwater rivers to spawn, after which they die. Also, **eulachon.** [< Chinook jargon]

o·o·lite *or* **o·ö·lite** (ō′ə līt′) *n.* rock, usually limestone, consisting of small rounded grains cemented together. [< F *oölithe* < Gk. *ōon* egg + *lithos* stone]

oo·long (ü′long) *n.* tea made from leaves that have been partially fermented before being dried in ovens. Oolong is greenish brown in color. [< Chinese *wu-lung* black dragon]

oo·loo (ü′lü) *Cdn.* See **ulu.**

oo·mi·ak (ü′mē ak) *Cdn.* See **umiak.**

ooze¹ (üz) *v.* **oozed, ooz·ing;** *n.* —*v.* **1** pass slowly through small openings; leak slowly and quietly: *Blood oozed from his scraped knee. The mud oozed into his boots.* **2** disappear or drain away: *His courage oozed away as he waited.* **3** give out slowly: *The cut oozed blood.* —*n.* **1** a slow flow. **2** something that oozes. [OE *wōs* juice]

ooze² (üz) *n.* a soft mud or slime, especially that at the bottom of a pond, lake, river, or ocean. [OE *wāse* mud]

oo·zy¹ (ü′zē) *adj.* oozing. [< *ooze¹*] —**oo′zi·ly,** *adv.*

oo·zy² (ü′zē) *adj.* containing ooze; muddy and soft; slimy. [< *ooze²*] —**oo′zi·ly,** *adv.*

op (op) *n.* **1** op art. **2** (*adj.*) of or designating op art: *an op artist.*

op– the form of **ob-** before *p,* as in *oppress.*

op. **1** opus; opera. **2** opposite. **3** operation.

OP, O.P., *or* **o.p.** out of print.

O.P. **1** Order of Preachers (Dominican). **2** observation post.

o·pac·i·ty (ō pas′ə tē) *n., pl.* **-ties. 1** the quality or state of being opaque: *Onionskin has less opacity than bond paper.* **2** something opaque: *A cataract is an opacity on the lens of the eye.* [< L *opacitas* < *opacus* dark]

o·pal (ō′pəl) *n.* a mineral, an amorphous form of silica that is softer and less dense than quartz, found in many varieties and colors, certain of which have a peculiar rainbow play of colors and are valued for gems. **Black opals** are green and blue with brilliant

colored lights; some are so dark as to seem almost black. **Milk opals** are milky white with rather pale lights. **Fire opals** are similar with more red and yellow lights. [< L *opalus* < Gk. *opallios* < Skt. *upala* precious stone]

o·pal·esce (ō′pəl es′) *v.* **-esced, -esc·ing.** exhibit a play of colors like that of the opal. [< *opal* + *-esce* begin to be, become (< L *-escere*)]

o·pal·es·cence (ō′pəl es′əns) *n.* the exhibition of a play of colors like an opal's.

o·pal·es·cent (ō′pəl es′ənt) *adj.* showing opalescence.

o·pal·ine (ō′pəl īn′ *or* ō′pəl in) *adj.* of or like opal.

o·paque (ō pāk′) *adj., n.* —*adj.* **1** not letting light through; not transparent: *Muddy water is opaque.* **2** not shining; dark; dull. **3** obscure; hard to understand. **4** stupid. —*n.* something opaque. [< L *opacus* dark, shady] —**o·paque′ly,** *adv.* —**o·paque′ness,** *n.*

opaque projector an apparatus for projecting written, drawn, or printed material onto a screen or wall. An opaque projector projects images directly from paper or books rather than from transparencies.

op art (op) a style of drawing and painting that creates optical illusions of motion and depth by means of complex geometrical designs. [shortened from *optical art*, on analogy with *pop art*]

op.cit. in the book, passage, etc. previously referred to. [for L *opere citato* in the work cited]

ope (ōp) *v.* **oped, op·ing.** *Poetic.* open.

OPEC Organization of Petroleum Exporting Countries.

o·pen (ō′pən) *adj., n., v.* —*adj.* **1** not shut; not closed; letting (anyone or anything) in or out: *an open drawer. Open windows let in the fresh air.* **2** not having its lid, cover, gate, etc. closed: *an open box, an open cage.* **3** not closed in: *an open field.* **4** unfilled; not taken up: *have an hour open. The position is still open.* **5** that may be entered, used, shared, competed for, etc. by all: *an open meeting, an open market.* **6** accessible or available: *the only course still open.* **7** ready for business or for admission of the public: *The exhibition is now open. This store stays open till 9:30 p.m.* **8** without restriction or prohibition: *open season for hunting.* **9** *Informal.* allowing liquor, gambling, etc.: *an open town.* **10** undecided; not settled: *an open question.* **11** having no cover, roof, etc.; letting in air freely: *an open car.* **12** not covered or protected; exposed: *open to temptation.* **13** not obstructed: *an open view.* **14** unprejudiced; ready to consider new ideas: *an open mind.* **15** exposed to general view, knowledge, etc.; not secret: *open disregard of rules.* **16** having spaces or holes: *open ranks, cloth of open texture.* **17** *Music.* **a** of an organ pipe, not closed at the upper end. **b** of a string on a violin, cello, etc., not stopped by the finger. **c** of a note, produced by such a pipe or string, or without aid of slide, key, etc. **18** *Phonetics.* **a** designating a vowel uttered with relatively wide opening between the tongue and the roof of the mouth. **b** designating a syllable that ends with a vowel sound as in *to.* **19** unreserved, candid, or frank: *an open face.* **20** that is spread out; expanded: *an open flower, an open newspaper.* **21** generous; liberal: *Give with an open hand.* **22** free from frost: *an open winter.* **23** free from hindrance, especially from ice: *open water on the lake, a river or harbor now open.* **24** of an electric circuit, not complete or closed. **25** of a city, town, etc., unfortified; protected from enemy attack under international law: *In World War II Rome was declared an open city.*
open to, a ready to take; willing to consider. **b** liable to. **c** to be had or used by.
—*n.* **1 the open, a** the open country, air, sea, etc.: *I spent the afternoon out in the open and got badly sunburned.* **b** public view or knowledge: *It would be better to bring the problem out into the open.* **2** a competition, tournament, etc. open to anyone who wishes to enter. **3** opening.
—*v.* **1** cause to become open; move or remove so as to allow entry or exit: *Open the door. I can't open the vent. We opened the lid and looked in the box.* **2** open the lid, cover, etc. of: *to open a parcel, to open a cage.* **3** establish or set going: *He has opened a new store.* **4** begin; start: *School opens today.* **5** begin the proceedings of; initiate formally: *to open negotiations. The Queen opened Parliament.* **6** have or make entrance; allow entry: *This hall opens into the bedrooms.* **7** become open or more open; become accessible: *The valley opens wide lower down.* **8** cause to be open or more open; make accessible: *Open a path through the woods.* **9** clear of obstructions; make (a passage, etc.) clear. **10** make or become accessible to knowledge, sympathy, etc.; enlighten or become enlightened: *to open a person's eyes.* **11** uncover; lay bare; expose to view; disclose. **12** come to view. **13** expand, extend, or spread out; make or become less compact: *The ranks opened.* **14** cut into: *open a wound.* **15** come apart, especially so as to allow passage or show the contents: *The wound opened. The clouds opened and the sun shone through.* **16** *Law.* make the first statement of (a case) to the court or jury.
open up, a make or become open. **b** unfold; spread out. **c** open a

hat, āge, fär; let, ēqual, tèrm; it, īce
hot, ōpen, ôrder; oil, out; cup, pùt, rüle,
əbove, takən, pencəl, lemən, circəs

ch, child; ng, long; sh, ship
th, thin; ᵺ, then; zh, measure

way to and develop: *The early settlers opened up the West.* [OE. Related to UP.] —**o′pen·er,** *n.* —**o′pen·ly,** *adv.*

open air the out-of-doors.

o·pen–air (ō′pən er′) *adj.* outdoor.

o·pen–and–shut (ō′pən ən shut′) *adj. Informal.* simple and direct; obvious; straight-forward: *The Crown attorney was sure they had an open-and-shut case against the defendant.*

open door 1 freedom of access; unrestricted admission. **2** a policy of a country giving all other countries an equal chance to trade with it.

o·pen–end (ō′pən end′) *adj.* **1** allowing for change or revision: *an open-end mortgage.* **2** of or having to do with investment groups that issue or recall shares on demand, since the capital is open, not fixed.

o·pen–end·ed (ō′pən end′id) *adj.* **1** having no set boundary or limit; not rigidly defined or controlled; adaptable to a changing situation or need: *an open-ended agreement. The audience participated in an open-ended discussion after the speech.* **2** not closed at either end: *an open-ended container.*

o·pen·er (ō′pə nər *or* ōp′nər) *n.* **1** a person or thing that opens, especially a device for opening bottles, cans, letters, etc. **2** *Informal.* the first game of a scheduled series. **3 openers,** *Card games.* cards of high enough value to allow the player holding them to open the bidding.
for openers, *Slang.* as a beginning.

o·pen–eyed (ō′pən īd′) *adj.* **1** having eyes wide open as in wonder. **2** having the eyes open; watchful or vigilant; observant. **3** done or experienced with the eyes open.

o·pen–face (ō′pən fās′) *adj.* of a sandwich, made without the top slice of bread.

o·pen–faced (ō′pən fāst′) *adj.* **1** open-face. **2** not having the face or surface covered. **3** of a watch, having no cover over the dial. **4** having a frank and honest face. **5** honest; ingenuous.

o·pen–hand·ed (ō′pən han′did) *adj.* generous; liberal. —**o′pen–hand′ed·ly,** *adv.* —**o′pen–hand′ed·ness,** *n.*

o·pen–heart·ed (ō′pən här′tid) *adj.* **1** candid; frank; unreserved. **2** kindly; generous. —**o′pen–heart′ed·ly,** *adv.* —**o′pen–heart′ed·ness,** *n.*

o·pen–hearth (ō′pən härth′) *adj.* having an open hearth; using a furnace with an open hearth.

open–hearth process a process of making steel in a furnace in which the flame is directed onto the raw material, the impurities becoming oxidized.

open house 1 an informal social event that is open to all who wish to come: *They dropped in at their neighbor's open house before leaving for Christmas.* **2** an occasion when a school, university, factory, etc. is opened for inspection by the public: *The art college has an open house every spring to display student work and demonstrate the facilities of the college.*
keep open house, offer food, or food and lodging, to all visitors.

o·pen·ing (ō′pən ing *or* ōp′ning) *n.* **1** an open or clear space; gap; hole: *an opening in a wall, an opening in the forest.* **2** the first part; beginning: *the opening of a lecture.* **3** an official ceremony to mark the beginning of a new business, institution, etc.: *The opening of the new city hall was last week. Were you there for the opening?* **4** a job, place, or position that is open or vacant. **5** a favorable chance or opportunity: *He waited for an opening to ask to borrow the car.* **6** *Law.* the statement of the case made by the lawyer to the court or jury before adducing evidence.

open letter a letter addressed to a particular person but published in a newspaper, magazine, etc.

o·pen–line (ō′pən lin′) *adj.* hot-line: *an open-line radio show.*

open mind a mind ready to consider new arguments or ideas: *A politician ought to keep an open mind.*

o·pen–mind·ed (ō′pən mīn′did) *adj.* having or showing a mind open to new arguments or ideas. —**o′pen–mind′ed·ly,** *adv.* —**o′pen–mind′ed·ness,** *n.*

o·pen–mouthed (ō′pən mouᵺd′ *or* -moutht′) *adj.* **1** having the mouth open. **2** gaping with surprise or astonishment. **3** greedy; ravenous, or rapacious. **4** vociferous or clamorous: *open-mouthed hounds.* **5** having a wide mouth: *an open-mouthed pitcher.*

o·pen·ness (ō′pən nis) *n.* the quality or state of being open:

They like the new location because of its openness to the sea. Her openness to different opinions and ideas makes her a very popular politician.

o·pen–pit (ō′pən pit′) *adj.* worked on from the exposed surface, or slightly below the surface; not underground: *open-pit mining.*

open question a matter that has not been decided and on which differences of opinion are accepted.

open season a period during which it is legal to hunt and kill fish or game that is protected by law at other times.

open secret a matter that is supposed to be secret but that everyone knows about: *It's an open secret that he has applied for another job.*

open ses·a·me (ses′ə mē) **1** in the *Arabian Nights*, the magic words that opened the door of the robbers' den in the story of Ali Baba. **2** any password at which doors or barriers fly open.

open shop a factory, shop, or other establishment that will employ both union and non-union workers.

open syllable a syllable that ends with a vowel sound. *Examples*: *free-* in *freedom, o-* in *open*. Compare **closed syllable**.

open water **1** water free of obstructions. **2** *Cdn.* especially in the North: **a** the time when rivers and lakes become free of ice; break up: *At open water he got twenty beaver and two otter.* **b** the period during which rivers and lakes are free of ice; the time between break-up and freeze-up: *We have good hunting here during open water.*

o·pen·work (ō′pən wėrk′) *n.* ornamental work in cloth, metal, etc. that has openings in the material.

op·er·a¹ (op′ər ə *or* op′rə) *n.* **1** a kind of drama set to music, performed by a group of singers usually to an orchestral accompaniment. In an opera, the words are usually sung, rather than spoken. **2** the art of creating or performing operas: *the history of opera.* **3** a performance of an opera. **4** the music of an opera. **5** a company that performs opera. **6** a theatre where operas are performed. [< Ital. *opera*, for *opera in musica* a (dramatic) work to music; *opera* < L *opera* effort (related to OPUS a work)]

op·er·a² (op′ər ə) *n.* pl. of **opus.**

op·er·a·ble (op′ər ə bəl *or* op′rə bəl) *adj.* **1** fit for, or admitting of, a surgical operation. **2** fit or able to be operated.

o·pé·ra bouffe (op′ər ə büf′ *or* op′rə büf′; *French*, ô pā rä büf′) **1** comic opera; light opera. **2** an absurd situation; ridiculous arrangement. [< F *opéra bouffe* comic opera]

opera glasses small, low-powered binoculars for use at the opera, in theatres, etc.

opera hat a man's tall, collapsible hat worn with formal clothes.

opera house 1 a theatre where operas are performed. **2** any theatre.

op·er·and (op′ə rand′) *n. Mathematics.* any symbol or quantity that is subject to an operation. [< L *operandum*, gerundive of *operari*. See OPERATE.]

op·er·ate (op′ər āt′) *v.* **-at·ed, -at·ing. 1** be at work; run: *The machinery operates night and day.* **2** keep at work; drive: *Who operates this elevator?* **3** direct the working of as owner or manager; manage: *That company operates factories in seven countries.* **4** take effect; produce an effect; work; act: *Several causes operated to bring on the war.* **5** go into action; become effective: *The medicine operated quickly.* **6** *Medicine.* perform a surgical operation: *Will they have to operate? The doctor operated on the injured man immediately.* **7** carry on military movements. **8** buy and sell stocks and bonds: *to operate in stocks or grain futures.* [< L *operare* < *opus* a work, or *opera* effort]

op·er·at·ic (op′ər at′ik) *adj.* of, like, or having to do with the opera: *operatic music.* —**op′er·at′i·cal·ly,** *adv.*

op·er·a·tion (op′ər ā′shən) *n.* **1** working: *The operation of a railway requires many men.* **2** the way a thing works: *the operation of a machine.* **3** an action; activity: *the operation of brushing one's teeth.* **4** *Medicine.* a treatment for injury or disease, in which instruments are used to cut into the body in order to remove, replace, or repair an injured or diseased part: *She had her operation yesterday and is doing well.* **5** movements of soldiers, ships, supplies, etc. for military purposes. **6** *Mathematics.* something done to a number or quantity. Addition, subtraction, multiplication, and division are the four commonest operations in arithmetic. **7** a commercial transaction, especially one that is speculative and on a large scale: *operations in stocks or wheat.*

in operation, a running; working; in action. **b** in use or effect.

op·er·a·tion·al (op′ə rā′shə nəl *or* op′ər rāsh′nəl) *adj.* **1** of or having to do with any kind of operation. **2** of equipment, in working order. **3** of a military operation, ready or equipped to perform a certain mission. —**op′er·a′tion·al·ly,** *adv.*

op·er·a·tive (op′ər ə tiv, op′ər ā′tiv, *or* op′rə tiv) *adj., n.* —*adj.* **1** operating; effective: *the laws operative in a community.* **2** having to do with work or productiveness: *operative departments of a manufacturing establishment.* **3** of, concerned with, or resulting from a surgical operation.
—*n.* **1** a person who operates a machine. **2** a private detective or secret agent.

op·er·a·tor (op′ər ā′tər) *n.* **1** a person who operates something, especially: **a** a skilled worker who runs a machine, telephone exchange, telegraph, etc. **b** the owner or manager of a business, factory, etc. **2** *Informal.* a person who is skilled in avoiding problems or restrictions or manipulating people for his own needs. **3** a person who speculates in stocks or a commodity. **4** *Mathematics.* a symbol denoting a specific operation.

o·per·cu·lum (ō pėr′kyə ləm) *n., pl.* **-la** (-lə) *or* **-lums.** *Biology.* any lidlike part or organ; any flap covering an opening. [< L *operculum* < *operire* cover]

op·er·et·ta (op′ər et′ə) *n., pl.* **-tas.** a short, amusing opera with some words spoken rather than sung. [< Ital. *operetta*, dim. of *opera* opera]

o·phid·i·an (ō fid′ē ən) *n., adj.* —*n.* snake. —*adj.* of, having to do with, or like snakes. [< NL *Ophidia* an order of reptiles < Gk. *ophidion*, dim. of *ophis* serpent]

O·phir (ō′fər) *n.* in the Bible, a place from which Solomon obtained gold (I Kings 9:28).

oph·thal·mi·a (of thal′mē ə) *n.* an acute infection of the eyeball or the membrane covering the front of the eyeball. [< LL < Gk. *ophthalmia* < *ophthalmos* eye; cf. *ōps* eye, *thalamos* chamber]

oph·thal·mic (of thal′mik) *adj.* **1** of or having to do with the eye. **2** having to do with or affected with ophthalmia.

oph·thal·mol·o·gist (of′thal mol′ə jist) *n.* a physician who specializes in ophthalmology.
☛ *Usage.* An **ophthalmologist** (or **oculist**), an **optometrist** and an **optician** all have to do with the health of the eyes. An **ophthalmologist** is a doctor who can treat diseases of the eye as well as recommending corrective lenses. An **optometrist** is not a doctor but is trained to examine eyes and recommend corrective lenses. An **optician** prepares, fits, and sells glasses and contact lenses.

oph·thal·mol·o·gy (of′thal mol′ə jē) *n.* the branch of medicine that deals with the structure, functions, and diseases of the eye. [< Gk. *ophthalmos* eye + E *-logy*]

oph·thal·mo·scope (of thal′mə skōp′) *n.* an instrument for examining the interior of the eye or the retina. [< Gk. *ophthalmos* eye + E *-scope*]

o·pi·ate (ō′pē it *or* ō′pē āt′) *n., adj.* —*n.* **1** any powerful drug containing opium or a derivative of opium (such as morphine) and used especially to dull pain or to bring sleep. **2** anything that quiets. —*adj.* **1** containing opium or a derivative. **2** bringing sleep or ease. [< Med.L *opiatus* < L *opium* opium]

o·pine (ō pīn′) *v.* **o·pined, o·pin·ing.** *Esp. facetious.* express or have an opinion; suppose: *He opined that the weather would improve by evening.* [< F < L *opinari*] —**o·pin′er,** *n.*

o·pin·ion (ə pin′yən *or* ō pin′yən) *n.* **1** an appraisal or judgment formed in the mind about the truth or probability of something: *I prefer to learn the facts and form my own opinion.* **2** a view or impression: *She has a poor opinion of such shoddy workmanship.* **3** a formal judgment made by an expert; professional advice. **4** *Law.* a statement by a judge or jury of the reasons for the decision of the court. [< L *opinio, -onis*]
☛ **Syn. 1. Opinion, view** = what a person thinks about something. **Opinion** is the general word and particularly suggests a carefully thought-out conclusion based on facts, but without the certainty of knowledge: *I try to learn the facts and form my own opinions.* **View** applies to a particular way of looking at something, and especially suggests a personal opinion affected by personal leanings or feelings: *His views are conservative.*

o·pin·ion·at·ed (ə pin′yən āt′id) *adj.* obstinate or conceited with regard to one's opinions; dogmatic.

o·pin·ion·a·tive (ə pin′yən ā′tiv) *adj.* opinionated. —**o·pin′ion·a·tive·ly,** *adv.* —**o·pin′ion·a′tive·ness,** *n.*

o·pi·um (ō′pē əm) *n.* **1** a powerful, addictive drug that causes sleep and eases pain, made from the dried juice extracted from the unripe seed capsules of the opium poppy. **2** anything that has a dulling or tranquillizing effect. [ME < L < Gk. *opion*, dim. of *opos* vegetable juice]

o·pos·sum (ə pos′əm) *n.* any of a family (Didelphidae) of New World marsupials, especially an arboreal species (*Didelphis marsupialis*) found in wooded regions near water from southern Ontario south to Argentina, having light-grey to black fur, a pointed snout, and a hairless prehensile tail. Also called **possum.** [< Algonquian word meaning "white animal"]

op·po·nent (ə pō′nənt) *n., adj.* —*n.* a person who is on the other side in a fight, game, or argument; a person fighting, struggling, or speaking against another. —*adj.* opposing. [< L *opponens, -entis* < *ob-* against + *ponere* place]

☛ *Syn. n.* **Opponent, antagonist, adversary** = someone against a person or thing. **Opponent** applies to someone on the other side in an argument, game, or other contest, or against a proposed plan, law, etc., but does not suggest personal ill will: *He defeated his opponent in the election.* **Antagonist,** more formal, suggests active, personal, and unfriendly opposition, often in a fight for power or control: *Hamlet and his uncle were antagonists.* **Adversary** now usually means a definitely hostile antagonist actively blocking or openly fighting another: *Gamblers found a formidable adversary in the new chief of police.*

op·por·tune (op'ər tyün' *or* op'ər tün') *adj.* fortunate; well-chosen; suitable; favorable: *You have come at a most opportune moment.* [< L *opportunus* favorable (of wind) < *ob portum* (*ferens*) (bringing) to port] **—op'por·tune'ly,** *adv.* **—op'por·tune'ness,** *n.*
☛ *Syn.* See note at **timely.**

op·por·tun·ism (op'ər tyün'iz əm *or* op'ər tün'iz əm) *n.* the policy or practice of taking advantage of opportunities and particular circumstances, especially with little regard for principles.

op·por·tun·ist (op'ər tyün'ist *or* op'ər tün'ist) *n.* a person who practises opportunism: *She's just an opportunist, using the organization as a stepping-stone to political power.*

op·por·tu·ni·ty (op'ər tyü'nə tē *or* op'ər tü'nə tē) *n., pl.* **-ties.** a good chance; favorable time; convenient occasion.

op·pos·a·ble (ə pōz'ə bəl) *adj.* **1** capable of being opposed or resisted. **2** capable of being placed opposite something else. The human thumb is opposable to the fingers.

op·pose (ə pōz') *v.* **-posed, -pos·ing. 1** act, fight, or struggle against; try to hinder or stop; resist: *The residents opposed the widening of the street. The army's advance was fiercely opposed.* **2** put against as a defence, reply, or contrast: *Let us oppose good nature to anger.* **3** put in contrast: *to oppose European and North American culture.* **4** put in front of; cause to face: *to oppose one's finger to one's thumb.* [ME < OF *opposer* < *op-* (< L *ob-*) against + *poser* put (see POSE¹)] **—op·pos'er,** *n.*
☛ *Syn.* **Oppose, resist, withstand** = act or stand against someone or something. **Oppose** means set oneself against a person or thing, especially an idea, plan, etc., but does not suggest the nature, purpose, form, or effectiveness of the action or stand taken: *We opposed the plan because of the cost.* **Resist** suggests making a stand and actively striving against an attack or force of some kind: *The bank messenger resisted the attempt to rob him.* **Withstand** emphasizes holding firm against attack: *The bridge withstood the flood.*

op·posed (ə pōzd') *adj.* placed in opposition; contrary or contrasted: *We talked of the merits of train travel as opposed to bus travel. The two brothers had strongly opposed characters.*

op·po·site (op'ə zit *or* op'sit) *adj., n., prep.* **—adj. 1** place face to face, back to back, or at the other end or side: *the opposite side of the street. The map is opposite page 37. The printing on the opposite side of the page shows through to this side.* **2** as different as can be; just contrary: *Sour is opposite to sweet.* **3** *Botany.* of leaves, flowers, etc. growing singly and directly opposite each other along either side of a stem. Compare **alternate.**
—n. a thing or person that is opposite: *Black is the opposite of white.*
—prep. 1 opposite to: *opposite the church.* **2** in a motion picture or play, acting as the leading lady or man of: *She played opposite a famous actor in her first starring role.* [< L *oppositus,* pp. of *opponere* < *ob-* against + *ponere* place] **—op'po·site·ly,** *adv.* **—op'po·site·ness,** *n.*
☛ *Syn. adj.* **2. Opposite, contrary** = completely different (from each other). **Opposite** particularly suggests two things thought of as standing one at each end of a line, so far apart in position, nature, meaning, etc. that they can never be brought together: *True and false have opposite meanings.* **Contrary** particularly suggests two things going in opposite directions, or set against each other, often in strong disagreement or conflict: *Your statement is contrary to the facts.*

op·po·si·tion (op'ə zish'ən) *n.* **1** action against; resistance: *The mob offered opposition to the police.* **2** contrast: *His views were in opposition to mine.* **3** the political party or parties not in power: *In parliament, the party having the second largest number of elected members is called the official opposition.* **4** any opponent or group of opponents: *Our team easily defeated the opposition.* **5** the act of placing opposite: *the opposition of the thumb to the fingers.* **6** an opposite direction or position. **7** *Astrology and astronomy.* the position of two heavenly bodies when their longitude differs by 180 degrees. [< L *oppositio, -onis* < *opponere.* See OPPOSITE.]

op·press (ə pres' *or* ō pres') *v.* **1** govern harshly; keep down unjustly or by cruelty: *A good government will not oppress the poor.* **2** weigh down; lie heavily on; burden: *A fear of trouble ahead oppressed my spirits.* [< Med.L *oppressare,* ult. < L *ob-* against + *premere* press]

op·pres·sion (ə presh'ən *or* ō presh'ən) *n.* **1** cruel or unjust treatment; tyranny; persecution; despotism: *The oppression of the people by the dictator caused the war. They fought against oppression.* **2** a heavy, weary feeling.

op·pres·sive (ə pres'iv *or* ō pres'iv) *adj.* **1** harsh; severe; unjust. **2** hard to bear; burdensome. **—op·pres'sive·ly,** *adv.* **—op·pres'sive·ness,** *n.*

op·pres·sor (ə pres'ər *or* ō pres'ər) *n.* a person who is cruel or unjust to people over whom he has authority or power.

hat, āge, fär; let, ēqual, tèrm; it, īce
hot, ōpen, ôrder; oil, out; cup, pút, rüle,
əbove, takən, pencəl, lemən, circəs
ch, child; ng, long; sh, ship
th, thin; ⟨ᴛʜ⟩, then; zh, measure

op·pro·bri·ous (ə prō'brē əs) *adj.* expressing scorn, reproach, or abuse: *Coward, liar, and thief are opprobrious names.* [< LL *opprobriosus*] **—op·pro'bri·ous·ly,** *adv.*

op·pro·bri·um (ə prō'brē əm) *n.* disgrace or reproach caused by conduct considered shameful or vicious; infamy; scorn; abuse. [< L *opprobrium,* ult. + *ob-* at + *probrum* infamy, reproach]

op·so·nin (op'sə nin) *n.* a substance in the blood serum that weakens bacteria and other foreign cells so that the white blood cells can destroy them more easily. [< L *opsonium* relish (meat, fish) < Gk. *opsonion* pay, originally, relish-money < *opson* relish + *ōnos* price]

opt (opt) *v.* make a choice, especially in favor of something; decide (*usually used with* for): *The class opted for a field trip.*
opt out (of), decide to leave; choose to drop out of some activity or organization: *Several nations wanted to opt out of the alliance.* [< L *optare* choose, desire]

opt. 1 optative. **2** optical; optics. **3** optional.

op·ta·tive (op'tə tiv) *adj., n. Grammar.* **—adj. 1** expressing a wish: *"Oh! that I had wings to fly!" is an optative expression.* **2 a** in Greek and certain other languages, having to do with the verbal mood that expresses desire, wish, etc. **b** having to do with distinctive verb forms with such meaning or function. **—n. 1** the optative mood. **2** a verb in the optative mood. [< LL *optativus* < L *optare* wish]

op·tic (op'tik) *adj., n.* **—adj.** of the eye or the sense of sight. **—n.** *Informal.* the eye. [< Med.L *opticus* < Gk. *optikos* < *op-* see]

op·ti·cal (op'tə kəl) *adj.* **1** of or having to do with the eye or the sense of sight; visual: *an optical illusion. Being near-sighted is an optical defect.* **2** made to assist sight or according to the principles of optics: *A microscope is an optical instrument. An optical telescope uses light waves, but a radio telescope uses radio waves.* **3** of or having to do with optics. **—op'ti·cal·ly,** *adv.*

op·ti·cian (op tish'ən) *n.* a person who prepares, fits, and sells glasses and contact lenses that have been prescribed by an optometrist or an opthalmologist. [< F *opticien*]
☛ *Usage.* See note at **ophthalmologist.**

optic nerve the cranial nerve that conducts visual stimuli from the eye to the brain. See **eye** for picture.

op·tics (op'tiks) *n.* (*used with a singular verb*) the science that deals with light and vision.

op·ti·mal (op'tə məl) *adj.* most favorable or desirable; optimum. **—op'ti·mal·ly,** *adv.*

op·ti·mism (op'tə miz'əm) *n.* **1** a tendency to look on the bright side of things and make the best of any situation or event as it comes about. **2** a belief that everything will turn out for the best. **3** *Philosophy.* the doctrine that the existing world is the best of all possible worlds. [< NL *optimismus* < L *optimus* best]

op·ti·mist (op'tə mist) *n.* **1** a person who tends to look on the bright side of things, making the best of any situation or event as it comes about. **2** a person who believes that everything in life will turn out for the best. **3** a person who believes in the doctrine of optimism.

op·ti·mis·tic (op'tə mis'tik) *adj.* **1** inclined to look on the bright side of things. **2** hoping for the best. **3** having to do with optimism. **—op'ti·mis'ti·cal·ly,** *adv.*

op·ti·mize (op'tə mīz') *v.* **-mized, -miz·ing.** make the most of; make as satisfactory or effective as possible: *She checked every detail of design to optimize the effect of the advertisement.*

op·ti·mum (op'tə məm) *n., pl.* **-mums** *or* **-ma** (-mə); *adj.* **—n.** the best or most favorable point, degree, amount, etc. for a particular purpose. **—adj.** most favorable, desirable, or satisfactory; best: *an optimum temperature for growth.* [< L]

op·tion (op'shən) *n., v.* **—n. 1** the right or power to choose: *We have the option of rejecting this offer and waiting for a better one.* **2** the act of choosing: *to make an option.* **3** something chosen or that may be chosen: *One of the options opened to her was to accept a grant to study abroad. One of the options offered with this car model is air conditioning.* **4** a right to buy something at a certain price within a certain time: *to hold an option on land.*
—v. obtain or grant an option in reference to (something). [< L *optio, -onis*]

op·tion·al (op'shən əl) *adj.* involving an option; not required or standard: *optional equipment on a car.* **—op'tion·al·ly,** *adv.*

op·tom·e·trist (op tom′ə trist) *n.* a person who is qualified to practise optometry. An optometrist does not prescribe drugs or surgery.
☛ *Usage.* See note at **ophthalmologist.**

op·tom·e·try (op tom′ə trē) *n.* the art or profession of examining the eyes for defects in vision and prescribing lenses or exercises to correct such defects. [< Gk. *optos* seen + E *-metry*]

op·u·lence (op′yə ləns) *n.* **1** wealth; affluence. **2** luxuriant abundance; lavishness.

op·u·lent (op′yə lənt) *adj.* **1** wealthy; affluent. **2** abundant and luxuriant; lavish. [< L *opulens, -entis* < *ops* power, resources]

o·pus (ō′pəs) *n., pl.* **op·er·a** or **o·pus·es.** a literary work or musical composition: *The violinist played his own opus, No. 16.* [< L]
☛ *Usage.* **Opera, opuses.** Because the Latin plural is identical with **opera,** "musical drama," it is now generally replaced, except in learned use, by **opuses.**

or¹ (ôr; *unstressed,* ər) *conj.* **1** a word used to indicate: **a** a choice, alternative, or difference: *Do you prefer coffee or tea? We intend to go, whether or not they do. Either the blue or the brown would be suitable.* **b** equivalence of two words: *This is the termination, or end.* **c** approximate quantity, etc.: *They'll be gone for three or four days.* **2** if not, then; otherwise: *Hurry, or you'll be late.* [OE (unstressed) ā(hwæ)ther < ā ever + hwæther either, whether]
☛ *Hom.* **oar, ore.**

or² (ôr) *prep. or conj. Archaic.* before; ere. [OE *ār* early, confused with OE *ǣr* ere]
☛ *Hom.* **oar, ore.**

or³ (ôr) *n. Heraldry.* gold or yellow. [< F < L *aurum* gold]
☛ *Hom.* **oar, ore.**

-or *suffix.* **1** a person or thing that —s, as in *actor, accelerator, orator, survivor, sailor.* **2** an act, state, condition, quality, characteristic, etc., especially in words from Latin, as in *error, horror, labor, terror.* [< L]
☛ *Spelling.* **-or, -our.** In Canada usage varies in such words as **color/colour, honor/honour, labor/labour.** Both spellings are accepted, though **-or** is more common in printed materials. Exceptions are **glamour** (usually), **Honourable** (as a title), and **Saviour** (as a name for Jesus Christ). In British usage, which prefers **-our** spellings, derivatives ending in **-ation, -ary, -ific,** and **-ous** are spelled with **-or-.** Thus, *honorific,* **honorary, humorous,** *odoriferous* are so spelled on both sides of the Atlantic.

o.r. owner's risk.

OR¹ Oregon.

OR² or **O.R.** **1** operating room. **2** orderly room.

or·a·cle (ôr′ə kəl) *n.* **1** in ancient times: **a** an answer given by a god through a priest or priestess to some question. **b** the place where the god gave answers. A famous oracle was at Delphi. **c** the priest, priestess, or other means by which the god's answer was given. **2** a person who gives wise advice. **3** something regarded as a reliable and sure guide. [ME < OF < L *oraculum* < *orare,* originally, recite solemnly]

o·rac·u·lar (ô rak′yə lər) *adj.* **1** of or like an oracle. **2** with a hidden meaning that is difficult to make out. **3** very wise.
—**o·rac′u·lar·ly,** *adv.*

o·ral (ô′rəl) *adj.* **1** spoken; using speech. **2** of the mouth. **3** taken by mouth: *oral medicine.* [< L *os, oris* mouth] —**o′ral·ly,** *adv.*
☛ *Hom.* **aural.**
☛ *Usage.* **Oral, verbal.** Strictly, **oral** means "spoken," and **verbal,** used as an adjective, means "in words"; but **verbal** has been used so long with the same sense as **oral** that there is no longer a distinction between the two: *He gave an oral report. They had only a verbal agreement.*

or·ange (ôr′inj) *n., adj.* —*n.* **1** a round, reddish-yellow, edible citrus fruit having a bitter rind and a sweet or tangy, juicy pulp. **2** any of several citrus trees that produce such fruit. The **sweet orange** (*Citrus sinensis*), cultivated in many varieties, is one of the most important commercial species. See also **mandarin. 3** any fruit or tree that suggests an orange. **4** a color made by mixing red and yellow. **5** a soft drink flavored with orange juice or a synthetic substitute.
—*adj.* **1** of or like an orange. **2** of or having the color orange. [ME < OF *orenge* < Sp. *naranja* < Arabic < Persian *narang;* in OF blended with the word *or* meaning "gold"] —**or′ange·like′,** *adj.* —**or′ang·y** or **or′ange·y,** *adj.*

Or·ange (ôr′inj) *n.* a princely family of Europe that ruled the former principality of Orange in W Europe, now a part of SE France. William III of England was of this family, and so is the present royal family of the Netherlands.

or·ange·ade (ôr′inj ād′) *n.* a drink made of orange juice, sugar, and water.

Orange Association the Loyal Orange Association.

Or·ange·ism (ôr′inj iz′əm) *n.* the principles and practices of the Loyal Orange Association.

Or·ange·man (ôr′inj mən) *n., pl.* **-men. 1** a member of a secret society, formed in the north of Ireland in 1795, to uphold the Protestant religion and Protestant control in Ireland. **2** a member of the Loyal Orange Association.

Orange Order the Loyal Orange Association.

orange pekoe a black tea that comes from Sri Lanka or India.

o·rang·ou·tang or **o·rang–ou·tang** (ô rang′ü tang′) *n.* orangutan.

o·rang·u·tan or **o·rang–u·tan** (ô rang′ü tan′ *or* ô rang′ə tan′) *n.* a large anthropoid ape (*Pongo pygmaeus*) of the forests of Borneo and Sumatra, having very long arms and long, reddish-brown hair. Orangutans live much of the time in trees and eat fruits and leaves. [< Malay *orangutan* < *orang* man + *utan* wild]

o·rate (ô rāt′ *or* ô′rāt) *v.* **o·rat·ed, o·rat·ing.** *Informal.* make an oration; talk in a grand manner. [< *oration*]

o·ra·tion (ô rā′shən) *n.* **1** a formal public speech delivered on a special occasion. **2** a speech given in an overly formal or affected style. [< L *oratio, -onis* < *orare* speak formally. Doublet of ORISON.]
☛ *Syn.* See note at **speech.**

or·a·tor (ôr′ə tər) *n.* **1** a person who makes an oration. **2** a person who can speak very well in public.

or·a·tor·i·cal (ôr′ə tôr′ə kəl) *adj.* **1** of oratory; having to do with orators or oratory: *an oratorical contest.* **2** characteristic of orators or oratory: *an oratorical manner.* —**or′a·tor′i·cal·ly,** *adv.*

or·a·to·ri·o (ôr′ə tô′rē ō′) *n., pl.* **-ri·os. 1** a musical drama performed without action, costumes, or scenery, for solo voices, chorus, and orchestra. Oratorios are usually based on Biblical or historical themes. **2** the art of creating or performing oratorios. **3** a performance of an oratorio. **4** the music of an oratorio. [< Ital. *oratorio,* originally, place of prayer < LL *oratorium.* Doublet of ORATORY².]

or·a·to·ry¹ (ôr′ə tô′rē) *n.* **1** the art of public speaking. **2** skill in public speaking; fine speaking. **3** language used in public speaking; words appropriate to fine speaking. [< L (*ars*) *oratoria* oratorical (art), ult. < *orare* plead, speak formally]

or·a·to·ry² (ôr′ə tô′rē) *n., pl.* **-ries.** a small chapel; a room set apart for prayer. [< LL *oratorium* < *orare* pray. Doublet of ORATORIO.]

orb (ôrb) *n., v.* —*n.* **1** a sphere, especially a heavenly body such as the sun, moon, or a star. **2** a jewelled sphere, especially a symbol of royal power. **3** *Esp.poetic.* the eyeball or eye.
—*v.* **1** form into a circle or sphere. **2** *Archaic or poetic.* encircle; enclose. [< L *orbis* circle]

or·bic·u·lar (ôr bik′yə lər) *adj.* **1** spherical; globular. **2** circular; disk-shaped: *an orbicular leaf.* [< LL *orbicularis* < L *orbiculus,* dim. of *orbis* circle]

or·bic·u·late (ôr bik′yə lit *or* ôr bik′yə lāt′) *adj.* orbicular. [< L *orbiculatus* < *orbiculus.* See ORBICULAR.]

or·bit (ôr′bit) *n., v.* —*n.* **1** the path of a heavenly body, planet, or satellite around another body in space: *the earth's orbit around the sun, the moon's orbit around the earth, the orbit of a weather satellite around the earth.* **2** the regular course of life or experience. **3** the bony cavity or socket in which the eyeball is set.
—*v.* **1** travel in an orbit: *Many artificial satellites are orbiting the earth.* **2** put into an orbit: *They plan to orbit a new weather satellite.* [< L *orbita* wheel track < *orbis* wheel, circle] —**or′bit·er,** *n.*

or·bit·al (ôr′bə təl) *adj.* of an orbit.

or·chard (ôr′chərd) *n.* **1** a piece of ground on which fruit trees are grown. **2** the trees in an orchard. [OE *ortgeard* < *ort-* (apparently < L *hortus* garden) + *geard* yard¹]

orchard grass a European bunch grass (*Dactylis glomerata*) widely cultivated as a pasture grass and also for hay.

or·ches·tra (ôr′kis trə) *n.* **1** a relatively large group of musicians, including especially players of violins and other stringed instruments, organized to perform music together. Compare **band. 2** all the instruments played together by the musicians in such a group. **3** the part in a theatre just in front of the stage, where the musicians sit to play. **4** the main floor of a theatre, especially the part near the front. [< L < Gk. *orchēstra* the space where the chorus of dancers performed, ult. < *orcheesthai* dance]

or·ches·tral (ôr kes′trəl) *adj.* of, composed for, or performed by an orchestra. —**or·ches′tral·ly,** *adv.*

or·ches·trate (ôr′kis trāt′) *v.* **-trat·ed, -trat·ing. 1** compose or arrange (music) for performance by an orchestra. **2** arrange or control all the various stages or elements of something to achieve a particular end or effect.

or·ches·tra·tion (ôr′kis trā′shən) *n.* **1** an arrangement of music for an orchestra. **2** the art of creating such an arrangement.

or·chid (ôr′kid) *n., adj.* —*n.* **1** any of a large family (Orchidaceae) of perennial plants, some of which grow on other plants, obtaining their food and moisture from the air. Most orchids have showy, often brilliantly colored flowers with three petals, one of which is much larger and shaped somewhat like a lip. **2** the flower of an orchid: *Cultivated varieties of tropical orchids are much valued for corsages.* **3** a light purple.
—*adj.* light purple. [< NL *orchideae*, ult. < L < Gk. *orchis* testicle; from shape of root]

or·dain (ôr dān′) *v.* **1** order or establish by law or by decree: *The law ordains that convicted murderers shall be imprisoned.* **2** officially appoint or consecrate as a member of the clergy. [ME < OF < L *ordinare* < *ordo, -inis* order] —**or·dain′er,** *n.*

or·deal (ôr dēl′ *or* ôr′dēl) *n.* **1** a severe test or experience. **2** an ancient method of establishing the guilt or innocence of an accused person by making him do something dangerous such as putting his hand in a fire or taking poison. It was supposed that an innocent person would be given divine protection and so would escape harm. [OE *ordǣl* judgment]

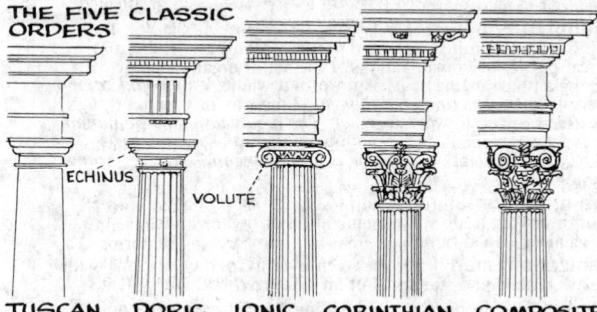

THE FIVE CLASSIC ORDERS

ECHINUS   VOLUTE

TUSCAN   DORIC   IONIC   CORINTHIAN   COMPOSITE

Order (def. 21): columns and entablatures illustrating the five orders of classical Greek and Roman architecture

or·der (ôr′dər) *n.* **1** the way one thing follows another: *in order of size, in alphabetical order.* **2** a condition in which every part or piece is in its right place: *to put a room in order.* **3** a condition; state: *My affairs are in good order.* **4** the way the world works; way things happen: *the order of nature.* **5** the state or condition of things in which the law is obeyed and there is no trouble: *The police officer tried hard to keep order.* **6** the principles and rules by which a meeting is run. **7** a telling what to do; command: *The orders of the captain must be obeyed.* **8** a spoken or written request for goods that one wants to buy or receive: *a grocery order.* **9** the goods so requested: *Mother asked when they would deliver our order.* **10** the direction of a court or judge made in writing and not included in a judgment. **11** a paper saying that money is to be given or paid, or something handed over: *a money order.* **12** a kind or sort: *to have ability of a high order.* **13** *Biology.* a major category in the classification of plants and animals, more specific than a class and more general than a family. Butterflies, moths, and skippers belong to the insect order Lepidoptera. See chart at **classification. 14** a social rank, grade, or class: *all orders of society.* **15** a rank or position in the church: *the order of bishops.* **16** Usually, **orders,** holy orders. **17** a group of people banded together for some purpose or united by something they share in common: *the Franciscan order, the Imperial Order Daughters of the Empire.* **18** a society to which one is admitted as an honor: *the Order of the Golden Fleece.* **19** a modern fraternal organization: *the Order of Freemasons.* **20** a badge worn by those belonging to an honorary order. **21** any of five types of column and entablature forming the basis of the five classical styles of architecture. The five orders are Doric, Ionic, and Corinthian of ancient Greek origin, and Tuscan and Composite of ancient Roman origin. **22** the regular form of worship for a given occasion. **23** a portion or serving of food served in a restaurant, etc.: *I'd like one order of toast, please.*

by order, according to an order given by the proper person: *by order of the Premier.*
call to order, ask to be quiet and start work: *She called the meeting to order.*
in order, a in the right arrangement or condition: *Are all the pages in order?* **b** working properly. **c** allowed by the rules of a meeting, etc.
in order that, so that; with the purpose that.
in order to, as a means to; with a view to; for the purpose of: *She worked hard in order to win the prize.*
in short order, quickly: *They got the broken window replaced in short order.*
made to order, made to fit a certain person or place.

hat, āge, fär; let, ēqual, tėrm; it, īce
hot, ōpen, ôrder; oil, out; cup, pút, rüle,
above, takən, pencəl, lemən, circəs

ch, child; ng, long; sh, ship
th, thin; ᴛʜ, then; zh, measure

on order, having been ordered but not yet received.
on the order of, resembling; similar to: *a house on the order of ours.*
out of order, a in a wrong arrangement or condition: *These pages are out of order.* **b** not working properly: *The radio is out of order.* **c** against the rules of a meeting, etc.: *Your motion is out of order.*
to order, according to the buyer's wishes: *They had the chesterfield made to order.*
—*v.* **1** put in order; arrange: *to order one's affairs.* **2** tell what to do; command; bid: *The judge ordered the people in the courtroom to be quiet.* **3** give a request or directions (for): *Please order dinner for me. Are you ready to order?* **4** give (a store, etc.) an order for: *He ordered a new car from the dealer.* **5** decide; will; determine: *The authorities ordered it otherwise.* **6** invest with clerical rank or authority.
order about or **around,** send here and there; tell to do this and that: *Stop ordering me around.*
[ME < OF *ordre* < L *ordo, -inis* row, rank]

or·dered (ôr′dərd) *adj.* **1** characterized by regular arrangement or order; systematic, harmonious, etc.: *They led a quiet, ordered existence. The window gave a wide view of ordered lawns and gardens.* **2** *Mathematics, etc.* having elements arranged in a specific order: *an ordered set of rules. A point on a line can be identified by an ordered pair of numbers.*

or·der-in-coun·cil (ôr′dər in koun′səl) *n., pl.* **or·ders-in-coun·cil.** a regulation made by the federal cabinet under the authority of the Governor General or by a provincial cabinet under the authority of the lieutenant-governor of that province.

or·der·ly (ôr′dər lē) *adj., n., pl.* **-lies.** —*adj.* **1** in order; with regular arrangements, method, or system: *an orderly arrangement of dishes on shelves, an orderly mind.* **2** keeping order; well-behaved or regulated: *an orderly class.* **3** concerned with carrying out orders; being on duty.
—*n.* **1** *Military.* a person who attends a superior officer to carry messages, etc. **2** a hospital attendant who keeps things clean and in order. —**or′der·li·ness,** *n.*
► *Syn. adj.* **1. Orderly, methodical, systematic** = following a plan of arrangement or action. **Orderly** suggests lack of confusion and arrangement of details or things in proper relation to each other according to some rule or scheme: *The chairs are in orderly rows.* **Methodical** suggests an orderly way of doing something, following step by step a plan carefully worked out in advance or regularly followed: *Police made a methodical search for the weapon.* **Systematic** adds to **methodical** and emphasizes the idea of thoroughness and completeness: *The committee began a systematic investigation of crime.*

orderly officer officer of the day.

Order of Canada *Cdn.* an order established in 1967 to honor Canadians for outstanding achievement and service to their country or to humanity at large. Memberships are awarded by the Governor General, in three categories: companion (CC), officer (OC), and member (CM).

Order of Military Merit *Cdn.* an order established in 1972 to recognize conspicuous merit and exceptional service by members of the Canadian Forces, both regular and reserve. Memberships are awarded by the Governor General, in three levels: commander (CMM), officer (OMM), and member (MMM).

Order of the Garter the oldest and highest order of British knighthood, established about 1344. It includes the sovereign.

or·di·nal (ôr′də nəl) *adj., n.* —*adj.* **1** showing order or position in a series. **2** *Biology.* of or having to do with an order of animals or plants. —*n.* **1** ordinal number. **2** a book of special forms for certain church ceremonies. [ME < LL *ordinalis* < L *ordo, -inis* order]

ordinal number a number, such as first, second, twentieth, that shows the place an item has in an ordered sequence. Compare **cardinal number.**

or·di·nance (ôr′də nəns) *n.* **1** a rule or law made by authority; decree or regulation, especially a municipal regulation: *Many cities have ordinances against burning leaves or garbage.* **2** an established religious ceremony. [ME < OF *ordenance,* ult. < L *ordinare* arrange, regulate. See ORDAIN.]

or·di·nar·i·ly (ôr′də ner′ə lē *or* ôr′də ner′ə lē) *adv.* **1** usually; regularly. **2** to the usual extent.

or·di·nar·y (ôr′də ner′ē) *adj., n., pl.* **-nar·ies.** —*adj.* **1** usual; customary; normal: *She ate her ordinary breakfast of cereal, toast, and coffee.* **2** not special; common; everyday; average: *an ordinary person, an ordinary situation.* **3** somewhat below the average: *The speech was ordinary and tiresome.*
—*n.* **1** *Archaic.* **a** a meal served at a fixed price. **b** an inn or the

dining room of an inn. **2** a person who has authority in his own right, especially a bishop or a judge. **3** a form for saying Mass. **4** *Heraldry*. a bearing of the earliest, simplest, and commonest kind, usually bound by straight lines.

in ordinary, in regular service: *physician in ordinary to the king.*
out of the ordinary, unusual; not regular or customary: *It wasn't anything out of the ordinary for her to jog 15 kilometres.*
[< L *ordinarius* < *ordo, -onis* row, rank] —**or′di·nar′i·ness,** *n.*
☛ *Syn. adj.* **1.** See note at **common.**

ordinary seaman 1 *Canadian Forces.* in Maritime Command, a person of the lowest rank, equivalent to a private. See chart at **rank¹. 2** a person of similar rank in the naval forces of other countries. *Abbrev.:* O.S. or OS

or·di·nate (ôr′də nit *or* ôr′də nāt′) *n. Mathematics.* the second number in an ordered pair; the vertical co-ordinate, or *y*-value, in a system of Cartesian co-ordinates. Compare **abscissa.** [< L *ordinatus,* pp. of *ordinare.* See ORDAIN.]

or·di·na·tion (ôr′də nā′shən) *n.* **1** the act or ceremony of admitting a person to the ministry of the church. **2** the state of being admitted as a minister in a church. [< L *ordinatio, -onis* < *ordinare.* See ORDAIN.]

ord·nance (ôrd′nəns) *n.* **1** artillery; big guns or cannon. **2** military weapons and equipment of all kinds. [var. of *ordinance*]

Or·do·vi·cian (ôr′də vish′ən) *n., adj. Geology.* —*n.* **1** an early period of the Paleozoic era, beginning approximately 445 million years ago. **2** the rocks formed in this period. See chart at **geology.** —*adj.* of or having to do with an early Paleozoic period or the rocks formed during it. [< L *Ordovices* an ancient Celtic tribe in Wales where this rock abounds]

or·dure (ôr′jər *or* ôr′dyər) *n.* **1** filth; dung. **2** vile language. [ME < OF *ordure* < *ord* filthy < L *horridus* horrid]

ore (ôr) *n.* a naturally occurring mineral containing a valuable substance such as metal: *Iron ore is mined and worked to extract the iron it contains.* [OE *ār* brass]
☛ *Hom.* oar, or.

ö·re (œ′rə) *n.* **1** a unit of money in Norway and Denmark, equal to ¹⁄₁₀₀ of a krone. **2** a unit of money in Sweden, equal to ¹⁄₁₀₀ of a krona. [< Danish, Norwegian, Swedish, ult. < L *aureus* a gold coin]

Ore. Oregon.

O·re·ad *or* **o·re·ad** (ô′rē ad′) *n. Greek mythology.* a mountain nymph. [< L *Oreas, -adis,* < Gk. *Oreias* < *oros* mountain]

ore·bod·y (ôr′bod′ē) *n., pl.* **-bod·ies.** a vein or bed of ore.

Oreg. Oregon.

o·reg·a·no (ə reg′ə nō′ *or* ôr′ə gä′nō) *n.* the dried leaves and flowering tops of any of several perennial herbs (genus *Origanum*) of the mint family, especially *O. vulgare,* used as a seasoning. Oregano has a flavor like sweet marjoram, but more pungent; it is used especially in Latin and Mediterranean dishes. [< Sp. *orégano* < L < Gk. *origanon* wild marjoram]

O·res·tes (ô res′tēz) *n. Greek mythology.* the son of Agamemnon and Clytemnestra, who killed his mother because she had murdered his father. He was pursued by the Furies for his crime.

or·gan (ôr′gən) *n.* **1** a large musical wind instrument consisting of sets of pipes of different diameters and lengths which are sounded by forcing air through them by means of keys and pedals; pipe organ. **2** an instrument in which a similar sound is produced by electronic means. **3** any of various other instruments such as a mouth organ or harmonium. **4** any structure in an animal or plant, such as an eye, lung, stamen, or pistil, that is composed of different cells and tissues organized to perform some particular function. **5** a group or organization that performs a particular function within a larger group or organization: *A court is an organ of government.* **6** a means of giving information or expressing opinions; a newspaper or magazine that speaks for and gives the views of a political party or some other group or organization. [ME < OF < L < Gk. *organon* instrument < *ergon* work]

or·gan·dy *or* **or·gan·die** (ôr′gən dē) *n., pl.* **-dies.** a very fine, thin, sheer cotton cloth with a crisp finish, woven in a plain weave with tightly twisted yarns. Organdy is used for dresses, curtains, blouses, trimming, etc. [< F *organdi*]

organ grinder a person who plays a hand organ by turning a crank.

or·gan·ic (ôr gan′ik) *adj.* **1** of, having to do with, or affecting a bodily organ: *an organic disease.* **2** of, having to do with, or characteristic of beings having organs or an organized physical structure; of, having to do with, or characteristic of animals and plants: *organic substances, organic nature.* **3** made up of related and co-ordinated parts; organized: *Every part of an organic whole depends on every other part.* **4** forming part of the basic structure of

something fundamental: *The music is not just background but an organic part of the film.* **5** of, designating, or containing compounds of carbon: *Organic compounds exist naturally as constituents of animals and plants.* **6** designating the branch of chemistry dealing with such compounds. **7** obtained from animals or plants: *organic fertilizer.* **8** designating a method of raising plants or animals without using chemical fertilizers, pesticides, or drugs: *organic gardening.* **9** of vegetables, meat, etc. produced in this way: *organic beef.* [< L *organicus* < Gk. *organikos* < *organon* instrument]
—**or·gan′i·cal·ly,** *adv.*

organic chemistry the branch of chemistry that deals with compounds of carbon. Organic chemistry teaches us about foods and fuels.

or·gan·ism (ôr′gən iz′əm) *n.* **1** a living body having organs or an organized structure in which each part has a particular function but all depend on each other; an individual animal or plant. **2** a very tiny animal or plant. **3** a complex structure made of related parts that work together and are dependent on each other and on the whole structure. A community may be spoken of as a social organism.

or·gan·ist (ôr′gən ist) *n.* a person who plays the organ, especially a skilled player.

or·gan·i·za·tion (ôr′gən ə zā′shən *or* ôr′gən ī zā′shən) *n.* **1** a group of persons united for some purpose. Churches, clubs, and political parties are organizations. **2** the act of organizing; the grouping and arranging of parts to form a whole: *The organization of a big picnic takes time and thought.* **3** the way in which a thing's parts are arranged to work together: *The organization of the human body is very complicated.* **4** something made up of related parts, each having a special duty: *A tree is an organization of roots, trunk, branches, leaves, and fruit.*

or·ga·ni·za·tion·al (ôr′gə nə zā′shən əl *or* ôr′gə nī zā′shən əl) *adj.* of or having to do with organization or organizations.
—**or′ga·ni·za′tion·al·ly,** *adv.*

organization man a person given over to total conformity with the expectations and standards of an organized body or system.

or·gan·ize (ôr′gən īz′) *v.* **-ized, -iz·ing. 1** arrange to work or come together as a whole: *The general organized his soldiers into a powerful fighting force.* **2** plan and lead, get started, or carry out: *The explorer organized an expedition to the North Pole.* **3** arrange in a system: *She organized her thoughts. He organized his stamp collection.* **4** *Informal.* make oneself ready to do what is required: *Please wait—I'm not organized yet.* **5** bring or form into a labor union; unionize: *to organize the workers in a plant, to organize the garment industry.* [ME < LL *organizare* < L *organum* < Gk. *organon.* See ORGAN.] —**or′gan·iz′a·ble,** *adj.* —**or′gan·iz′er,** *n.*

organized labor *or* **labour** workers who belong to labor unions.

or·gan·za (ôr gan′zə) *n.* a silky cloth of silk, rayon, nylon, etc. that is more crisp and sheer than organdy. [probably < *Lorganza,* a trade name]

or·gasm (ôr′gaz əm) *n.* **1** the climax or culmination of sexual excitement. **2** an instance of frenzied excitement or behavior. [NL *orgasmus* < Gk. *orgasmos* < *orgaein* swell]

or·gi·as·tic (ôr′jē as′tik) *adj.* of, having to do with, or of the nature of orgies; wild; frenzied. [< Gk. *orgiastikos,* ult. < *orgia* secret rites] —**or′gi·as′ti·cal·ly,** *adv.*

or·gy (ôr′jē) *n., pl.* **-gies. 1** wild, drunken or licentious revelry. **2** something resembling an orgy in lack of control; excessive indulgence in something: *an orgy of destruction, an orgy of bloodshed.* **3** Usually, **orgies,** *pl.* secret rites or ceremonies in the worship of certain Greek and Roman gods, especially Dionysus, the god of wine, celebrated with drinking, wild dancing, and singing. [< L < Gk. *orgia* secret rites]

o·ri·el (ô′rē əl) *n.* a bay window projecting from a wall, usually in an upper storey, and supported by a bracket. [ME < OF *oriol* porch]

o·ri·ent (*n., adj.* ô′rē ənt; *v.* ô′ri ent′) *n., adj., v.* —*n.* **1 the Orient, a** the Far East. China, Japan, Korea, and Vietnam are in the Orient. **b** *Archaic.* the regions lying to the east of Europe and the Mediterranean Sea, including Asia Minor and the Indian subcontinent as well as the Far East. **2 the orient,** *Poetic.* the east. **3** the lustre of a pearl. **4** a pearl of great value.
—*adj.* **1** *Poetic.* eastern or Oriental. **2** lustrous; shining: *an orient pearl.* **3** *Archaic.* rising in the east.
—*v.* **1** put or build facing east. **2** place in a certain position or face or tend in a certain direction: *The building is oriented north and south. She is oriented toward a career in business.* **3** find the direction or position of. **4** bring into the right relationship with one's surroundings; adjust to a new situation (*usually used with a reflexive pronoun*): *It takes a while to orient yourself in a strange city.* [< L *oriens, -entis,* ppr. of *oriri* rise with reference to the rising sun]

O·ri·en·tal (ô′rē en′təl) *adj., n.* —*adj.* Sometimes, **oriental,** of,

having to do with, or characteristic of the Orient or its inhabitants: *Oriental music.* —*n.* a native or inhabitant of the Orient.

O·ri·en·tal·ism or **o·ri·en·tal·ism** (ô′rē en′təl iz′əm) *n.* **1** a custom, habit, etc. that is characteristic of Oriental peoples. **2** a knowledge of Oriental languages, literature, etc.

O·ri·en·tal·ist or **o·ri·en·tal·ist** (ô′rē en′təl ist) *n.* a person who specializes in the study of Oriental languages, literature, cultures, history, etc.

o·ri·en·tate (ô′rē en tāt′) *v.* **-tat·ed, -tat·ing.** orient.

o·ri·en·ta·tion (ô′rē en tā′shən) *n.* **1** the act or process of orienting or the state of being oriented. **2** a change in position of an organism or part of an organism in response to an external stimulus, such as light. **3** the homing instinct of certain animals. **4** a general tendency or direction of interest or thought: *Her orientation toward the dramatic shows clearly in her dress designs.*

or·i·en·teer (ôr′ē ən tēr′) *v., n.* —*v.* find one's way through unfamiliar territory by means of a map or compass or both. —*n.* a person who participates in the sport of orienteering.

or·i·en·teer·ing (ôr′ē ən tēr′ing) *n.* the sport or practice of finding one's way through unfamiliar territory by means of a map or compass or both, usually involving a given starting and finishing point with a series of check points in between.

or·i·fice (ôr′ə fis) *n.* an opening, such as a mouth, hole, or vent through which something may pass. [< F < L *orificium* < *os, oris* mouth + *facere* make]

or·i·flamme (ôr′ə flam′) *n.* **1** the red banner carried as a military ensign by the early kings of France. **2** any banner used as an ensign or standard. **3** anything that is bright, colorful, or showy. [ME < OF *orieflambe*; ult. < L *aurum* gold + *flamma* flame]

orig. **1** origin. **2** originally.

or·i·ga·mi (ôr′i gä′mē) *n.* a kind of paper sculpture developed by the Japanese in which paper is folded in a great variety of simple or intricate ways to make birds, flowers, etc. [< Japanese]

or·i·gin (ôr′ə jin) *n.* **1** the thing from which anything comes; source; beginning: *the origin of a quarrel, the origin of a disease.* **2** parentage or ancestry: *a man of humble origin. The word beef is of French origin.* **3** *Mathematics.* the intersection of co-ordinate axes or planes. **4** *Anatomy.* the firmer or larger of the two points of attachment of a muscle. [< L *origo, -ginis* < *oriri* rise]

o·rig·i·nal (ə rij′ə nəl) *adj., n.* —*adj.* **1** belonging to the beginning; first; earliest: *the original settlers.* **2** fresh and unusual; novel: *She has written a very original story. They thought up several original games for the party.* **3** able to do, make, or think something new; inventive. **4** not copied, imitated, or translated from something else: *This is the original manuscript.*
—*n.* **1** the first version or actual thing from which something is copied, imitated, or translated: *This sculpture is a plaster copy; the original is in Rome.* **2** the language in which a book was first written: *She has read* War and Peace *in the original.* **3** an unusual or eccentric person. **4** *Archaic.* originator.

o·rig·i·nal·i·ty (ə rij′ə nal′ə tē) *n.* **1** the quality or state of being original: *Several experts questioned the originality of the manuscript.* **2** freshness or novelty of style, etc.: *The furniture has a striking originality of design.* **3** the ability to do, make, or think up something new: *He is known for his originality in thinking up plots.*

o·rig·i·nal·ly (ə rij′ə nəl ē) *adv.* **1** by origin: *The family was originally Irish.* **2** at first; in the first place: *a house originally small.* **3** in an original manner.

original sin *Theology.* the state of sin in which, according to Christian theology, all human beings exist because of Adam's disobedience to the word of God.

o·rig·i·nate (ə rij′ə nāt′) *v.* **-nat·ed, -nat·ing. 1** cause to be; invent. **2** come into being; begin; arise. —**o·rig′i·na′tor,** *n.*

o·rig·i·na·tion (ə rij′ə nā′shən) *n.* the act or fact of originating.

o·rig·i·na·tive (ə rij′ə nə tiv *or* ə rij′ə nā′tiv) *adj.* inventive; creative.

o·ri·ole (ô′rē əl *or* ô′rē ōl′) *n.* **1** any of a genus (Icterus) of New World songbirds belonging to the same family (Icteridae) as the bobolink, meadowlark, and blackbirds, the adult males having black and orange, yellow, or reddish-brown plumage, the females mainly yellowish. **2** any of a family (Oriolidae) of Old World songbirds, especially any of a genus (*Oriolus*) that includes the yellow-and-black **golden oriole** of Europe and Asia. The orioles of North America were given their name by early settlers from Britain because of their resemblance to the golden oriole. [< NL *oriolus* < OF, ult. < L *aurum* gold]

O·ri·on (ô rī′ən) *n.* **1** *Greek and Roman mythology.* a hunter loved by the goddess Diana, who was accidentally killed by her and placed among the stars after his death. **2** a constellation near the equator of the heavens, suggesting a man with a belt around his waist and a sword by his side.

o·ri·son (ôr′ə zən) *n. Archaic or poetic.* prayer. [ME < OF < LL

hat, āge, fär; let, ēqual, tèrm; it, īce
hot, ōpen, ôrder; oil, out; cup, pút, rüle,
əbove, takən, pencəl, lemən, circəs
ch, child; ng, long; sh, ship
th, thin; ŦH, then; zh, measure

oratio, -onis prayer < L *oratio* speech < *orare* pray. Doublet of ORATION.]

Or·lon (ôr′lon) *n. Trademark.* any of several kinds of strong, elastic acrylic fibres that resist sun, water, and chemicals, and combine well with other fibres. Orlon is used for knitted clothing, rugs, draperies, etc.

or·mo·lu (ôr′mə lü′) *n.* an alloy of copper and zinc, used to imitate gold. Ormolu is used in decorating furniture, clocks, etc. [< F *or moulu* ground gold]

or·na·ment (*n.* ôr′nə mənt; *v.* ôr′nə ment′) *n., v.* —*n.* **1** something used to add beauty, especially a beautiful object or part that has no particular function in itself: *Jewellery and vases are ornaments.* **2** the use of ornaments; ornamentation: *Ornament played an important part in rococo architecture.* **3** a person or an act, quality, etc. that adds beauty, grace, or honor: *He was an ornament to his time.* **4** Usually, **ornaments,** *pl.* things used in church services, such as the organ, bells, silver plate, etc. **5** *Music.* an additional note or notes introduced as an embellishment but not essential to the harmony or melody.
—*v.* add beauty to; make more pleasing or attractive; decorate: *A single brooch ornamented her dress.* [ME < OF < L *ornamentum* < *ornare* adorn]
☛ *Syn. v.* See note at **decorate.**

or·na·men·tal (ôr′nə men′təl) *adj.* **1** of or having to do with ornament: *ornamental purposes.* **2** used for ornament; decorative: *an ornamental staircase, ornamental plants.* —**or′na·men′tal·ly,** *adv.*

or·na·men·ta·tion (ôr′nə men tā′shən) *n.* **1** the act of ornamenting or the condition of being ornamented. **2** decorations; ornaments.

or·nate (ôr nāt′) *adj.* **1** much adorned; much ornamented: *She liked ornate furniture.* **2** characterized by the use of elaborate figures of speech, flowery language, etc.: *an ornate style of writing.* [< L *ornatus,* pp. of *ornare* adorn] —**or·nate′ly,** *adv.* —**or·nate′ness,** *n.*

or·ner·y (ôr′nər ē) *adj. Informal or dialect.* having an irritable or mean disposition; tending to be hard to get along with: *an ornery horse. He was born ornery.* [contraction of *ordinary*] —**or′ner·i·ness,** *n.*

or·ni·tho·log·i·cal (ôr′nə thə loj′ə kəl) *adj.* dealing with birds.

or·ni·thol·o·gist (ôr′nə thol′ə jist) *n.* a person trained in ornithology, especially one whose work it is.

or·ni·thol·o·gy (ôr′nə thol′ə jē) *n.* **1** a branch of zoology dealing with birds. **2** an article or book on this subject. [< NL *ornithologia* < Gk. *ornis, -nithos* bird + *-logos* treating of]

o·ro·tund (ô′rə tund′) *adj.* **1** strong, full, rich, and clear in voice or speech; sonorous. **2** pompous; bombastic. [alteration of L *ore rotundo,* literally, with round mouth]

or·phan (ôr′fən) *n., v.* —*n.* **1** a child whose parents are dead or, sometimes, a child who has lost one parent. **2** (*adj.*) of or for such children: *an orphan home.* **3** (*adj.*) without a father or mother or both.
—*v.* make an orphan of. [< LL < Gk. *orphanos* bereaved]

or·phan·age (ôr′fən ij) *n.* **1** a home for orphans. **2** the condition of being an orphan.

Or·phe·an (ôr fē′ən) *adj.* **1** of or having to do with Orpheus. **2** like the music of Orpheus.

Or·phe·us (ôr′fē əs *or* ôr′fyəs) *n. Greek mythology.* the son of Calliope and Apollo, who played his lyre so sweetly that animals and even trees and rocks followed him. With his music he charmed Pluto into releasing his wife Eurydice from Hades, but he lost her again when he disobeyed Pluto's order not to look back at her before reaching Earth.

Or·phic (ôr′fik) *adj.* **1** of or having to do with Orpheus or the religious or philosophical cults associated with his name. **2** Often, **orphic, a** mystic; oracular. **b** melodious or entrancing.

Or·ping·ton (ôr′ping tən) *n.* a breed of large buff, white, or black chickens. [< *Orpington,* a town in Kent, England]

or·rer·y (ôr′ər ē) *n., pl.* **-rer·ies.** a device with balls representing various planets, that are moved by clockwork to illustrate motions of the solar system. [after Charles Boyle, Earl of *Orrery* (1676-1731), who first had such a device made]

or·ris (ôr′is) *n.* **1** any of several European irises, especially *Iris florentina*, having fragrant rootstocks which are used in making perfumes, etc. **2** orrisroot. [apparently an alteration of *iris*]

or·ris·root (ôr′is rüt′) *n.* the fragrant rootstock of an orris, used especially in making perfumes, sachets, cosmetics, etc.

ortho- *combining form.* **1** straight, as in *orthopterous.* **2** correct; accepted, as in *orthodox.* **3** correcting irregularities in; corrective, as in *orthodontics.* [< Gk. *orthos* straight]

or·tho·don·tia (ôr′thə don′shə *or* ôr′thə don′shē ə) *n.* orthodontics.

or·tho·don·tics (ôr′thə don′tiks) *n.* (*used with a singular verb*). the branch of dentistry that deals with the straightening and adjusting of irregular or crooked teeth. [< NL < Gk. *orthos* straight + *odōn, odontos* tooth]

or·tho·don·tist (ôr′thə don′tist) *n.* a dentist who specializes in orthodontics.

or·tho·dox (ôr′thə doks′) *adj.* **1** conforming to established doctrine, especially in religion: *orthodox views, an orthodox Anglican.* **2** conforming to custom; conventional: *The orthodox Christmas dinner is turkey and plum pudding.* **3 Orthodox, a** of, having to do with or designating the Orthodox Eastern Church or any of its member churches. **b** of, having to do with, or designating the branch of Judaism following most closely the ancient laws, customs and traditions. [< LL < Gk. *orthodoxos* < *orthos* correct + *doxa* opinion < *dokeein* think]

Orthodox Church Orthodox Eastern Church.

Orthodox Eastern Church the common name for a Federation of independent Christian churches, mainly in E Europe and the Near East, that recognize the Patriarch of Constantinople as their head.

or·tho·dox·y (ôr′thə dok′sē) *n., pl.* **-dox·ies.** the holding of correct or generally accepted beliefs; orthodox practice, especially in religion; being orthodox.

or·tho·ep·ic (ôr thō ep′ik) *adj.* **1** relating to correct pronunciation. **2** describing the relationship between spelling and pronunciation: *orthoepic rules.*

or·tho·e·pist (ôr thō′ə pist *or* ôr′thō ə pist) *n.* a person skilled in orthoepy.

or·tho·e·py (ôr thō′ə pē *or* ôr′thō ə pē) *n.* **1** the standard pronunciation of a language. **2** the part of grammar that deals with pronunciation; phonology. [< Gk. *orthoepeia* < *orthos* correct + *epos* utterance]

or·tho·gen·e·sis (ôr′thō jen′ə sis) *n.* **1** the theory that the evolutionary development of one species into another takes place in a fixed direction that is determined solely by internal factors and influenced by external, or environmental, factors. **2** the theory that all human cultures pass through the same stages of development in the same order.

or·thog·o·nal (ôr thog′ə nəl) *adj.* rectangular; having to do with or involving right angles. [< obs. *orthogon* a right-angled triangle < L < Gk. *orthogōnios* < *orthos* right + *gōnia* angle]

or·thog·ra·pher (ôr thog′rə fər) *n.* a person skilled in orthography.

or·tho·graph·ic (ôr′thə graf′ik) *adj.* **1** having to do with orthography. **2** correct in spelling.

or·tho·graph·i·cal (ôr′thə graf′ə kəl) *adj.* orthographic. **—or′tho·graph′i·cal·ly,** *adv.*

or·thog·ra·phy (ôr thog′rə fē) *n., pl.* **-phies. 1** the spelling of a language; the representation of the sounds of a language by written symbols. **2** the art of using the correct, or standard, spelling. **3** the study of letters and spelling. **4** orthographic projection. [< L < Gk. *orthographia* < *orthos* correct + *graphien* write]

or·tho·pae·dic (ôr′thə pē′dik) See **orthopedic.**

or·tho·pe·dic (ôr′thə pē′dik) *adj.* of, having to do with, or used in orthopedics: *Orthopedic shoes are worn to help correct deformities of the feet.*

or·tho·pe·dics (ôr′thə pē′diks) *n.* (*used with a singular verb*) the branch of surgery that deals with deformities, diseases, and injuries of bones and joints. [< Gk. *orthos* correct + *paideia* rearing of children < *pais, paidos* child]

or·tho·pe·dist (ôr′thə pē′dist) *n.* a surgeon who specializes in orthopedics.

or·thop·ter·an (ôr thop′tər ən) *n., adj.* —*n.* any of a large order (Orthoptera) of mostly plant-eating insects having two pairs of wings, the membranous hind wings covered by hard, narrow front wings or, in some species, having no wings at all. Crickets, grasshoppers and cockroaches are orthopterans. —*adj.* of or designating this order of insects. [< NL < Gk. *orthos* straight + *pteron* wing]

or·thop·ter·ous (ôr thop′tər əs) *adj.* of or having to do with the orthopterans or the order they belong to.

or·to·lan (ôr′tə lən) *n.* **1** a European bunting (*Emberiza hortulana*) considered a table delicacy in the autumn, when it grows fat. **2** any of several other small birds considered delicacies, such as the bobolink. [< F < Provençal < L *hortulanus* of gardens < *hortus* garden]

–ory *suffix.* **1** —ing, as in *compensatory, contradictory.* **2** of or having to do with —; of or having to do with —ion, as in *advisory, auditory.* **3** characterized by —ion, as in *adulatory.* **4** serving to —, as in *expiatory.* **5** tending to —; inclined to —, as in *conciliatory.* **6** a place for —ing; establishment for —ing, as in *depository.* **7** other meanings, as in *conservatory, desultory.* [< L *-orius, -orium*]

o·ryx (ô′riks) *n., pl.* **o·ryx·es** (ô′rik siz) *or* (*esp. collectively*) **o·ryx.** any of a genus (*Oryx*) of large African antelope having long, nearly straight horns. [ME < L < Gk. *oryx* antelope, pickaxe; with reference to pointed horns]

os[1] (os) *n., pl.* **os·sa** (os′ə). *Latin.* bone.

os[2] (os) *n., pl.* **o·ra** (ô′rə). *Latin.* a mouth; opening.

os- *prefix* the form of **ob-** (from the form *obs-*) occurring in some cases before *c* and *t*, as in *oscine, ostensible.*

Os osmium.

O.S. Old Style.

O.S. *or* **OS** ordinary seaman.

O.S.A. Order of St. Augustine.

Osage orange (ō′sāj) **1** a small, thorny, North American tree (*Maclura pomifera*) of the mulberry family having small, glossy, oval leaves and hard, orange wood. The osage orange is often planted as an ornamental tree. **2** the inedible yellow fruit of this tree.

os·car (os′kər) *n.* a small statuette awarded annually by the American Academy of Motion Picture Arts and Sciences for the best performances, production, photography, etc. during the year. [supposedly from the remark, "He reminds me of my Uncle Oscar," made by the secretary of the Academy upon seeing one of the statuettes]

os·cil·late (os′ə lāt′) *v.* **-lat·ed, -lat·ing. 1** swing to and fro like a pendulum. **2** move or travel to and fro between two points. **3** vary between opposing opinions, purposes, theories, etc. **4** *Physics.* vary regularly above and below a mean value, as an electric current. **5** cause to oscillate. [< L *oscillare*]

os·cil·la·tion (os′ə lā′shən) *n.* **1** the fact or process of oscillating. **2** a single swing of an oscillating body. **3** *Physics.* **a** a single forward and backward surge of a charge of electricity. **b** a rapid change in electromotive force. **c** a single complete cycle of an electric wave.

os·cil·la·tor (os′ə lā′tər) *n.* a person or thing that oscillates, especially a device for producing the oscillations that give rise to an alternating electrical current.

os·cil·la·to·ry (os′ə lə tô′rē) *adj.* oscillating.

os·cil·lo·graph (os′ə lə graf′ *or* sil′ə graf′) *n.* an instrument for recording oscillations.

os·cil·lo·scope (ə sil′ə skōp′) *n.* an electronic instrument for representing wave oscillations on the screen of a cathode-ray tube. Tuning pianos and checking motors can be done with very great accuracy by means of oscilloscopes.

os·cine (os′in *or* os′īn) *adj. —n.* any of a suborder (Passeres also called Oscines) of songbirds that includes the larks, swallows, and finches. Oscines have well-developed, specialized vocal organs and most species sing. —*adj.* of or designating this order of birds. [< L *oscines,* pl., < *ob-* to + *canere* sing]

os·cu·late (os′kyə lāt′) *v.* **-lat·ed, -lat·ing. 1** kiss. **2** come into close contact. **3** *Geometry.* **a** have three or more points coincident with: *A plane or a circle is said to osculate when it has three coincident points in common with the curve.* **b** of two curves, surfaces, etc., osculate each other. [< L *osculari* < *osculum* little mouth, kiss, dim. of *os* mouth]

os·cu·la·tion (os′kyə lā′shən) *n.* **1** the act of kissing. **2** a kiss. **3** *Geometry.* a contact between two curves, surfaces, etc. at three or more common points.

os·cu·la·to·ry (os′kyə lə tô′rē) *adj.* **1** kissing. **2** coming into close contact.

–ose[1] *suffix.* **1** full of; having much or many, as in *verbose.* **2** inclined to; fond of, as in *jocose.* **3** like, as in *schistose.* [< L *-osus*]

–ose[2] *suffix.* used to form chemical terms, especially names of sugars and other carbohydrates, as in *fructose, lactose,* and of protein derivations, as in *proteose.* [< F *-ose* in *glucose*]

o·sier (ō′zhər) *n.* **1** any of various willows, especially a common willow (*Salix viminalis*) of Europe and Asia having long, slender,

straight branches used in making baskets, furniture, etc. **2** a branch or twig of an osier. **3** (*adj.*) made of osier. **4** red-osier dogwood. [< F]

O·si·ris (ō sī′ris) *n.* one of the most important gods of ancient Egypt, a god of fertility and also ruler of the lower world and the dead.

–osis *combining form.* **1** denoting an act, process, state, or condition, as in *osmosis*. **2** *Medicine.* denoting an abnormal or diseased condition, as in *neurosis*. [< L < Gk.]

Os·man·li (oz man′lē *or* os man′lē) *n., pl.* **-lis;** *adj.* —*n.* **1** an Ottoman. **2** the language of the Ottoman Turks. —*adj.* Ottoman. [< Turkish *Osmanli* belonging to *Osman,* Arabic *Othman.* See OTTOMAN.]

os·mi·um (oz′mē əm) *n.* a hard, heavy, greyish metallic element of the platinum group, used for electric light filaments, as a catalyst, and in hard alloys. Osmium is the heaviest metal known. *Symbol:* Os; *at.no.* 76; *at.wt.* 190.2. [< NL < Gk. *osmē* smell, odor; from the odor of one of the osmium oxides]

os·mo·sis (oz mō′sis *or* os mō′sis) *n.* **1** the tendency of a fluid separated from a more concentrated solution by a porous partition to pass through the partition until the concentration on each side is the same. Nutrients dissolved in fluids pass in and out of plant and animal cells by osmosis. **2** a process of gradual, often unconscious absorption that suggests osmosis: *He thought he could learn German by osmosis, without taking a course.* [Latinized var. of *osmose* < Gk. *ōsmos* a thrust]

os·mot·ic (oz mot′ik *or* os mot′ik) *adj.* of or having to do with osmosis.

os·prey (os′prē *or* os′prā) *n., pl.* **-preys. 1** a large, long-winged, brown-and-white hawk (*Pandion haliaetus*) that feeds on fish. **2** an ornamental feather, used for trimming hats, etc. [ult. < L *ossifraga* < *os* bone + *frangere* break]

Os·sa (os′ə) *n.* **Mount,** a mountain in NE Greece. In Greek legend, when the giants made war on the gods, they piled Mount Ossa on Mount Olympus and Mount Pelion upon Mount Ossa in an attempt to reach heaven.

os·se·ous (os′ē əs) *adj.* consisting of or resembling bone; bony. [< L *osseus* < *os, ossis* bone]

Os·si·an (os′ē ən *or* ō shēn′) *n. Irish legend.* a Gaelic warrior and poet of about the 3rd century A.D.

os·si·fi·ca·tion (os′ə fə kā′shən) *n.* **1** the process of developing or changing into bone. **2** a mass of tissue that has been ossified; a part that is ossified. **3** a tendency to settle into a conventional, rigid, or unimaginative condition.

os·si·fy (os′ə fī′) *v.* **-fied, -fy·ing. 1** change into bone; become bone: *The soft parts of a baby's skull ossify as the baby grows older.* **2** harden; make or become fixed and rigid, or very conservative: *The once free and spontaneous exchange of ideas among the group members had ossified into mere ritual.* [< L *os, ossis* bone + E -(*i*)*fy*]

os·su·ary (os′yü er′ē *or* osh′ü er′ē) *n., pl.* **-ar·ies.** an urn, vault, or other place to hold the bones of the dead. [< LL *ossuarium,* neuter of *ossuarius* of bones]

os·ten·si·ble (os ten′sə bəl) *adj.* apparent; pretended; professed: *They were sure that the ostensible reason for her resignation was not the true one.* —**os·ten′si·bly,** *adv.* [< F < L *ostendere* show < *os-* obs- toward + *tendere* stretch]

os·ten·sive (os ten′siv) *adj.* **1** ostensible. **2** directly or manifestly demonstrative.

os·ten·ta·tion (os′tən tā′shən *or* os′ten tā′shən) *n.* a showing off; display intended to impress others. [L *ostentatio, -onis,* ult. < *ob-* toward + *tendere* stretch]

os·ten·ta·tious (os′tən tā′shəs *or* os′ten tā′shəs) *adj.* having or showing a desire to attract notice and arouse admiration or envy, etc.: *an ostentatious display of wealth.* —**os′ten·ta′tious·ly,** *adv.*

osteo- *combining form.* bone, as in *osteoarthritis.* [< Gk. *osteon* bone]

os·te·o·ar·thri·tis (os′tē ō är thrī′tis) *n.* arthritis caused by joint and cartilage degeneration.

os·te·ol·o·gy (os′tē ol′ə jē) *n.* **1** the branch of anatomy that deals with bones. **2** the bony structure or system of bones of an animal or major part of an animal, as the head, trunk, etc. [< Gk. *osteon* bone + E -*logy*]

os·te·o·my·e·li·tis (os′tē ō mī′ə lī′tis) *n.* inflammation of the bone, or bone marrow. [< *osteo-* + Gk. *myelos* marrow + E -*itis*]

os·te·o·path (os′tē ə path′) *n.* a person who practises osteopathy. [< *osteopathy*]

os·te·o·path·ic (os′tē ə path′ik) *adj.* of osteopathy or osteopaths.

os·te·op·a·thist (os′tē op′ə thist) *n.* osteopath.

os·te·op·a·thy (os′tē op′ə thē) *n.* a system of medical practice

hat, āge, fär; let, ēqual, tėrm; it, īce
hot, ōpen, ôrder; oil, out; cup, pùt, rüle,
əbove, takən, pencəl, lemən, circəs

ch, child; ng, long; sh, ship
th, thin; ŦH, then; zh, measure

based on the theory that the muscles and bones of the body are closely interrelated with all other parts of the body and that many diseases can be treated by manipulating the bones and muscles. [< Gk. *osteon* bone + E -*pathy*]

os·ti·na·to (os′tə nä′tō) *n., pl.* **-tos.** *Music.* a phrase repeated over and over in the same voice or pitch. [< Ital. *ostinato,* literally, obstinate < L *obstinatus*]

ost·ler (os′lər) *n.* hostler.

ost·mark (ost′märk) *n.* mark[2] (def. 2); the East German mark.

os·tra·cism (os′trə siz′əm) *n.* **1** an ancient Greek method of banishing an unpopular or dangerous citizen for a number of years by popular vote, without a trial or formal accusation. **2** the act or state of being shut out from society, from favor, from privileges, or from association with one's fellows.

os·tra·cize (os′trə sīz′) *v.* **-cized, -ciz·ing. 1** banish by the ancient Greek method of ostracism. **2** shut out from society, from favor, from privileges, etc. [< Gk. *ostrakizein* < *ostrakon* tile, potsherd, originally used in balloting]

os·tra·cod (os′trə cod′) *n.* any of a subclass (Ostracoda) of tiny, mainly freshwater crustaceans having a two-valved shell.

os·trich (os′trich) *n.* **1** a very large, two-toed, flightless bird (*Struthio camelus*) of Africa, the largest living bird, having dark plumage on the body, with the head, neck, thighs, and legs bare, and strong legs which enable it to run very fast. Ostriches have large, showy tail plumes valued for ornamentation. **2** a person who avoids facing reality or an approaching danger (from the ostrich's supposed habit of burying its head in the sand to avoid oncoming danger). [ME < OF < LL *avis struthio* < L *avis* bird, LL *struthio* < Gk. *strouthiōn* < *strouthos* ostrich]

ostrich fern a tall fern (*Matteuccia struthiopteris*) having long, soft, bright-green sterile fronds and short fertile fronds. The fiddleheads of this fern are a popular delicacy, especially in Nova Scotia and New Brunswick.

Os·tro·goth (os′trə goth′) *n.* a member of the eastern division of Goths that overran the Roman Empire and controlled Italy from A.D. 493 to 555. [< LL *Ostrogothi,* earlier *Austrogothi* < Gmc.; probably originally "the splendid Goths," but later taken as "the eastern Goths"]

O.T. Old Testament.

oth·er (uŦH′ər) *adj., pron., adv.* —*adj.* **1** remaining: *John is here, but the other boys are at school.* **2** additional or further: *I have no other books with me.* **3** not the same as one or more already mentioned: *Come some other day.* **4** different: *I would not have him other than he is.*
every other, every second; alternate: *She buys cream every other day.*
none other than, no one else but: *The presentation was made by none other than the Prime Minister.*
the other day (night, etc.), recently.
—*pron.* **1** the other one; not the same ones: *Each praises the other.* **2** another person or thing: *There are others to be considered.*
of all others, more than all others.
—*adv.* otherwise; differently: *I can't do other than to go.* [OE ōther]

oth·er·ness (uŦH′ər nəs) *n.* the quality or state of being separate, distinct, or special in nature, character, etc.

oth·er·wise (uŦH′ər wīz′) *adv., adj., conj.* —*adv.* **1** in a different way; differently: *I could not do otherwise.* **2** in other ways: *He is noisy, but otherwise a very nice boy.* **3** under other circumstances; in a different condition: *He reminded me of what I should otherwise have forgotten.*
—*adj.* different: *It might have been otherwise.*
—*conj.* or else; if not: *Come at once; otherwise you will be too late.* [< *other* + *wise*[2]]

other world the world to come; life after death.

oth·er·world·ly (uŦH′ər wèrld′lē) *adj.* **1** of or devoted to another world, such as the world of mind or imagination, or the world to come. **2** supernatural; weird. —**oth′er·world′li·ness,** *n.*

o·ti·ose (ō′shē ōs′ *or* ō′tē ōs′) *adj.* **1** at leisure; lazy or idle: *an otiose individual sunning himself in the park.* **2** ineffective; futile: *otiose excuses.* **3** having no real function; superfluous: *The article was wordy and full of otiose comments and digressions.* [< L *otiosus* < *otium* leisure]

o·to·log·i·cal (ō′tə loj′ə kəl) *adj.* of or having to do with otology.

o·tol·o·gist (ō tol′ə jist) *n.* a physician who specializes in otology.

o·tol·o·gy (ō tol′ə jē) *n.* the branch of medicine dealing with the ear and its diseases, including their diagnosis and treatment. [< Gk. *ous, ōtos* ear + E *-logy*]

ot·ta·va ri·ma (ō tä′və rē′mə) *pl.* **rimas.** a stanza of eight lines with the lines according to the rhyme scheme *a b a b a b c c*. In Italian each line normally has eleven syllables; in English, ten. [< Ital. *ottava rima* octave rhyme]

Ot·ta·wa (ot′ə wo′ *or* ot′ə wə) *n., pl.* **-was** *or* **-wa;** *adj.* —*n.* **1** a member of an Amerindian people living in southern Ontario and Michigan. **2** the dialect of Ojibwa spoken by the Ottawas. —*adj.* of or having to do with the Ottawas or their language.

ot·ter (ot′ər) *n., pl.* **-ters** *or* (*esp. collectively*) **-ter. 1** any of several fish-eating water mammals of the weasel family having a long, lithe body, long neck, small ears, and webbed feet with claws. The common North American river otter is *Lutra canadensis*. The large sea otter of the N Pacific coasts is *Enhydra lutris*. **2** the short, thick, glossy brown fur of an otter. [OE *oter*]

ot·to·man (ot′ə mən) *n., pl.* **-mans;** *adj.* —*n.* **1** a low, cushioned seat without back or arms. **2** a cushioned footstool. **3** a heavy, corded fabric of silk or rayon, often with cotton or wool. **4 Ottoman,** Turk. —*adj.* **Ottoman, 1** Turkish. **2** of or having to do with the Turkish dynasty founded by Osman I about 1300 or the Ottoman Empire. [< F < Ital. *Ottomano* < Arabic *Othmani* belonging to *Othman*, the name of the founder of the empire]

Ottoman Empire a former empire of the Turks in SE Europe, SW Asia, and N Africa; Turkish Empire.

oua·na·niche (wä′nə nish′) *n., pl.* **-niche.** *Cdn.* a landlocked Atlantic salmon native to Lake St. John and some other freshwater lakes in Quebec and Ontario. The ouananiche was formerly thought to be a subspecies of the Atlantic salmon, or even a separate species. [< Cdn.F < Algonquian (Montagnais *wananish* little salmon)]

ou·bli·ette (ü′blē et′) *n.* a secret dungeon having a trapdoor in the ceiling as its only entrance. [< F *oubliette* < *oublier* forget]

ouch (ouch) *interj.* an exclamation expressing sudden pain.

ought¹ (ot *or* ôt) *auxiliary verb.* **1** have a duty; be obliged: *You ought to obey your parents.* **2** be right or suitable: *The theatre ought to allow children in free.* **3** be wise: *I ought to go before it rains.* **4** be expected: *At your age you ought to know better.* **5** be very likely: *The fastest one ought to win the race.* [OE *āhte* (infinitive, *āgan* owe)]
☛ *Hom.* **aught.**
☛ *Usage.* **Ought. Had ought** and **hadn't ought** are not used in careful English: *He ought* (not *had ought*) *to dress more carefully.*

ought² (ot *or* ôt) *n. or adv.* aught; anything.
☛ *Hom.* **aught.**

ought³ (ot *or* ôt) *n. Informal.* nought; zero; the cipher 0. [var. of *nought*, a *nought* taken as an *ought*]
☛ *Hom.* **aught.**

Oui·ja (wē′jə) *n. Trademark.* a device consisting of a small board on legs that rests on a larger board marked with words, letters of the alphabet, or other characters. The person wishing an answer to questions rests his fingers lightly on the small board which may then move and touch letters or words. Ouijas are used at spiritualistic meetings and as games. [< F *oui* yes + G *ja* yes]

ounce¹ (ouns) *n.* **1** a unit for measuring mass, one sixteenth of a pound (about 28g) in avoirdupois and one twelfth of a pound (about 31g) in troy weight. **2** a unit for measuring liquids, equal to one twentieth of a pint; fluid ounce (about 28 cm³). **3** a little bit; very small amount: *an ounce of prevention. He hadn't an ounce of strength left.* [ME < OF *unce* < L *uncia* twelfth part. Doublet of INCH.]

ounce² (ouns) *n.* snow leopard. [ME < OF *once* for *lonce* < L *lynx* lynx < Gk.]

our (our *or* är) *adj.* a possessive form of **we:** of, belonging to, or made or done by us or ourselves: *Would you like to see our garden? We went to get our coats.* [OE *ūre*]
☛ *Hom.* **hour** (our).
☛ *Usage.* **Our, ours** are the possessive forms of **we. Our** is a determiner and is always followed by a noun: *This is our car.* **Ours** is a pronoun and stands alone: *This car is ours.*

Our Lady the Virgin Mary.

ours (ourz *or* ärz) *pron.* a possessive form of **we:** that which belongs to us: *That car is ours.* They got their tickets yesterday, but ours haven't come yet.*
☛ *Usage.* See note at **our.**

our·self (our self′ *or* är self′) *pron.* myself (*used when* **we** *is used as the subject instead of* **I,** *as by a sovereign, writer, or judge*): "*We shall ourself reward the victor,*" *said the queen.*

our·selves (our selvz′ *or* är selvz′) *pron.pl.* **1** a reflexive pronoun used instead of **we** or **us** when referring back to the subject of the sentence: *We cook for ourselves. We cannot see ourselves as others see us.* **2** a form of **we** or **us** used to make a statement stronger: *We ourselves are responsible for what happened.* **3** our usual or true selves: *We weren't ourselves when we let them get away with that.*

-ous *adjective-forming suffix.* **1** having; having much; full of, as in *joyous, perilous.* **2** characterized by, as in *blasphemous, parsimonious, zealous.* **3** having the nature of, as in *murderous, idolatrous.* **4** of or having to do with, as in *monogamous.* **5** like, as in *thunderous.* **6** committing or practising, as in *bigamous.* **7** inclined to, as in *amorous.* **8** *Chemistry.* implying a larger proportion of the element indicated by the word than *-ic* implies. *Stannous* means containing tin in larger proportions than a corresponding *stannic* compound. [ME < OF < L *-osus*; often used to represent L *-us*, adj. (e.g., *omnivorus* omnivorous) or Gk. *-os,* adj. (e.g., *anonymos* anonymous)]

ou·sel (ü′zəl) See **ouzel.**

oust (oust) *v.* force out; drive out. [< AF *ouster* (cf. F *ôter*) < L *obstare* block, hinder < *ob-* in the way of + *stare* stand. Related to OBSTACLE.]

oust·er (ous′tər) *n.* the act of ousting, especially an illegal eviction or dispossession.

out (out) *adv., adj., n., prep., v., interj.* —*adv.* **1** away; forth: *to rush out.* **2** not in or at a place, position, state, etc.: *That dress is out of fashion. The miners are going out on strike.* **3** into the open air: *He went out at noon.* **4** to or at an end: *to fight it out.* **5** from the usual place, condition, position, etc.: *Put the light out. The boy turned his pockets out.* **6** completely; effectively: *to fit out.* **7** so as to project or extend: *to stand out.* **8** into or in existence, activity, or outward manifestation: *Fever broke out. Flowers are out.* **9** aloud; loudly: *Speak out.* **10** to others: *Give out the books.* **11** from a number, stock, store, source, cause, material, etc.; from among others: *Pick out an apple for me. She picked out a new coat.* **12** in the wrong: *to be out in one's calculations.* **13** from a state of composure, satisfaction, or harmony: *to feel put out.* **14** at a money loss: *to be out ten dollars.* **15** *Baseball, etc.* not in play; no longer at bat or on base.

out and away, by far: *She is out and away the best player.*

out and out, thoroughly: *out and out discouraged.*

out of, a from within: *He came out of the house.* **b** not within; away from; outside of; beyond: *out of town, sixty kilometres out of Calgary. The boat has gone out of sight.* **c** without; not having: *We are out of coffee.* **d** so as to take away: *She was cheated out of her money.* **e** from: *My dress is made out of silk.* **f** from among: *We picked our puppy out of that litter.* **g** because of: *I went only out of curiosity.*

out of hand, out of control: *The excited crowd soon got out of hand.* —*adj.* **1** not in possession or control: *The Liberals are out, the Conservatives in.* **2** not in use, action, fashion, etc.: *The fire is out. Full skirts are out this season.* **3** without money, supplies, etc.: *Have you any cigarettes left? No, I'm right out.* **4** *Baseball, cricket, etc.* of a player or side, not allowed to continue in play. **5** external; exterior; outer; outlying: *an out island.* **6** not usual: *an out size.*

out for, looking for; trying to get: *We have a holiday and are out for a good time.*

out to, eagerly or earnestly trying to: *Their team is out to make the finals.* —*n.* **1** one who is out. **2** something wrong. **3** that which is omitted. **4** a defence or excuse: *to have an out for stealing.* **5** *Baseball.* an instance of putting out or being put out.

at outs or **on the outs,** quarrelling; disagreeing: *to be on the outs with a friend.* —*prep.* **1** from out; forth from: *He went out the door.* **2** *Informal.* out along: *Drive out Main Street.* —*v.* **1** go or come out: *Murder will out.* **2** put out: *Please out the fire.* —*interj. Archaic.* an exclamation of indignation, reproach, etc.: *Out upon you!* [OE *ūt*]

out- *prefix.* **1** outward; forth; away, as in *outburst, outgoing.* **2** outside; at a distance, as in *outbuilding, outfield, outlying.* **3** more than; longer than, as in *outbid, outlive, outnumber.* **4** better than, as in *outdo, outrun.*

out·age (ou′tij) *n.* **1** a time of interrupted service, especially a suspension of gas, electric, or water power. **2** an interruption or failure in service, function, or use.

out-and-out (out′ən out′) *adj.* thorough.

out·back (out′bak′) *n.* **1** in Australia, the unsettled part of the

interior; back country. **2** any similarly unsettled area.

out·bal·ance (out'bal'əns) *v.* **-anced, -anc·ing.** outweigh.

out·bid (out bid') *v.* **-bid, -bid** or **-bid·den, -bid·ding.** bid higher than (someone else).

out·board (out'bôrd') *adj., adv., n.* —*adj.* or *adv.* **1** outside the hull of a ship or boat. **2** away from the middle of a ship or boat. —*n.* **1** a boat equipped with an outboard motor. **2** the motor itself.

outboard motor a portable internal-combustion engine with an attached propeller, that is mounted on the outside of the stern of a small boat or canoe.

out·bound (out'bound') *adj.* outward bound.

out·brave (out brāv') *v.* **-braved, -brav·ing. 1** face bravely. **2** be braver than.

out·break (out'brāk') *n.* **1** breaking out; a sudden occurrence or increase: *outbreaks of anger, an outbreak of flu.* **2** a riot; public disturbance.

out·build·ing (out'bil'ding) *n.* a shed or building built near a main building: *Barns are outbuildings on a farm.*

out·burst (out'bėrst') *n.* a bursting forth: *an outburst of laughter, anger, smoke, etc.*

out·cast (out'kast') *n., adj.* —*n.* a person or animal cast out from home and friends: *Criminals are outcasts of society.* —*adj.* being an outcast; homeless; friendless.

out·class (out klas') *v.* be of higher class than; be much better than: *He is a good runner, but his younger brother definitely outclasses him.*

out·come (out'kum') *n.* a result or consequence: *The outcome of the election was in doubt until the very end.*

out·crop (*n.* out'krop'; *v.* out krop') *n., v.* **-cropped, -crop·ping.** —*n.* **1** a coming to the surface of the earth: *the outcrop of a vein of coal.* **2** the part that comes to the surface: *The outcrop that we found proved to be very rich in gold.* —*v.* come to the surface; appear.

out·cry (out'krī') *n., pl.* **-cries. 1** crying out; a sudden cry or clamor. **2** a strong protest: *There was a public outcry against the proposal to widen the street into a four-lane highway.*

out·dat·ed (out dāt'id) *adj.* out-of-date; old-fashioned; obsolete: *The coal-oil lamp is outdated.*

out·did (out did') *v.* pt. of **outdo.**

out·dis·tance (out dis'təns) *v.* **-tanced, -tanc·ing.** leave behind; outstrip: *She outdistanced all the other runners and won the race.*

out·do (out dü') *v.* **-did, -done, -do·ing.** do more or better than; surpass.
☛ *Syn.* See note at **excel.**

out·done (out dun') *v.* pp. of **outdo.**

out·door (out'dôr') *adj.* done, used, or living outdoors: *outdoor games.*

out·doors (out'dôrz') *adv., n.* —*adv.* out in the open air; not indoors: *The minute it stopped raining, they all went outdoors.* —*n.* **the outdoors,** the world outside of buildings; the open air (*used with a singular verb*): *We spend most of the summer in the outdoors.*

out·doors·man (out'dôrz'mən) *n., pl.* **-men.** a person who enjoys the outdoors and spends much time in outdoor activities or sports.

out·door·sy (out'dôr'zē) *adj. Informal.* of, having to do with, or fond of the outdoors or outdoor activities: *She's an outdoorsy person, always going off on hikes.*

out·er (ou'tər) *adj.* **1** of or on the outside: *The outer door is locked.* **2** farther out; farther from the centre: *The outer suburbs of the city.*

outer ear the outer, visible part of the ear that serves to direct sound waves toward the eardrum.

out·er·most (ou'tər mōst') *adj.* farthest out.

outer space 1 space immediately beyond the earth's atmosphere: *The moon is in outer space.* **2** space between the planets or between the stars. —**out'er·space',** *adj.*

out·face (out fās') *v.* **-faced, -fac·ing. 1** face boldly; defy. **2** stare at (a person) until he stops staring back; browbeat; abash.

out·fall (out'fol' *or* -fôl') *n.* the mouth or outlet of a stream, sewer, etc. where it discharges into a lake or the sea.

out·field (out'fēld') *n. Baseball.* **1** the part of the field beyond the diamond or infield. **2** the three players in the outfield.

out·field·er (out'fēl'dər) *n. Baseball.* a player stationed in the outfield.

out·fit (out'fit') *n., v.* **-fit·ted, -fit·ting.** —*n.* **1** all the articles or equipment necessary for any undertaking or purpose: *a sailor's outfit, the outfit for a camping trip.* **2** a group or organization thought of as a single unit; a military company, business firm, ranch, etc.: *They were in the same outfit during the war. He worked*

hat, āge, fär; let, ēqual, tėrm; it, īce
hot, ōpen, ôrder; oil, out; cup, pút, rüle,
əbove, takən, pencəl, lemən, circəs
ch, child; ng, long; sh, ship
th, thin; ŦH, then; zh, measure

for the same outfit for five years. **3** a set of clothes to be worn together; ensemble: *a bride's outfit, a summer outfit.* **4** *Cdn.* a vehicle and its team, such as a sled and dogs. **5** *Cdn. Historical.* **a** the annual shipment of trading goods and supplies sent by a fur company to its trading posts; also, any part of this shipment dispatched to or received by any particular post. **b** the trading goods and supplies taken into the interior by fur-company employees.
—*v.* **1** furnish with everything necessary for any purpose; equip: *John outfitted himself for camp.* **2** supply: *The whole family was outfitted with new coats last winter.*

out·fit·ter (out'fit'ər) *n.* **1** a person or company that provides outfits, such as a dealer in camping supplies, a shop selling men's clothing, etc. **2** *Cdn.* a guide and manager of an expedition, such as a hunting or exploring party in the wilderness.

out·flank (out flangk') *v.* **1** go or extend beyond the flank of (an opposing army, etc.); turn the flank of. **2** get the better of; circumvent: *They outflanked us and won the debate.*

out·flow (out'flō') *n.* **1** a flowing out: *the outflow from a waterpipe, an outflow of sympathy.* **2** that which flows out.

out·fox (out'fox') *v.* get the better of; outsmart: *The escaped convict outfoxed his pursuers.*

out·gen·er·al (out jen'ər əl *or* -jen'rəl) *v.* **-alled** or **-aled, -al·ling** or **-al·ing.** be a better general than; get the better of by superior strategy.

out·go (out'gō') *n., pl.* **-goes.** what goes out; what is paid out; an amount that is spent.

out·go·ing (out'gō'ing) *adj.* **1** departing; outward bound: *outgoing ships, the outgoing mail.* **2** retiring or withdrawing from office: *A dinner was held for the outgoing president.* **3** friendly; sociable: *She is very outgoing and enjoys giving parties.*

out·grow (out grō') *v.* **-grew, -grown, -grow·ing. 1** grow too large for. **2** grow beyond or away from; get rid of by growing older: *outgrow early friends, outgrow a babyish habit.* **3** grow or increase faster than: *She outgrew her twin sister. The population was rapidly outgrowing the food supply.*

out·growth (out'grōth') *n.* **1** a natural development, product, or result: *This big store is an outgrowth of the little shop started ten years ago.* **2** an offshoot; something that has grown out of something else: *A corn is an outgrowth on a toe.* **3** a growing out or forth: *the outgrowth of new leaves in the spring.*

out·guess (out ges') *v.* get the better of by anticipating a person's actions: *She outguessed her competitor and got her proposal accepted.*

out·house (out'hous') *n.* **1** an outdoor toilet. **2** a separate building used in connection with a main building.

out·ing (ou'ting) *n.* a short pleasure trip; walk or airing; holiday spent outdoors away from home.

outing flannel a cotton cloth woven to look like flannel.

out·land (out'land) *adj., n.* —*adj.* **1** *Archaic.* foreign. **2** outlying: *outland districts.* —*n.* **1** *Archaic.* a foreign land. **2** outlying land: *the outland of an estate.*

out·land·er (out'lan'dər) *n.* **1** a foreigner; alien. **2** *Informal.* an outsider; stranger.

out·land·ish (out lan'dish) *adj.* **1** not familiar; queer; strange or ridiculous. **2** looking or sounding foreign. —**out·land'ish·ly,** *adv.* —**out·land'ish·ness,** *n.*

out·last (out last') *v.* last longer than.

out·law (out'lo' *or* -lô') *n., v.* —*n.* **1** a person outside the protection of the law; exile; outcast. **2** a lawless person; criminal. **3** an unbroken horse.
—*v.* **1** make or declare (a person) an outlaw. **2** make or declare illegal: *A group of nations agreed to outlaw war.* **3** deprive of legal force: *An outlawed debt is one that cannot be collected because it has been due too long.* [OE *ūtlaga* < ON *útlagi*]

out·law·ry (out'lo'rē) *n., pl.* **-ries. 1** the condition of being outlawed. In the early Middle Ages outlawry was used as a punishment in England. **2** the condition of being an outlaw.

out·lay (*n.* out'lā'; *v.* out lā') *n., v.* **-laid, -lay·ing.** —*n.* **1** spending; laying out of money, energy, etc.: *a large outlay for clothing.* **2** the amount spent. —*v.* expend: *outlay money in improvements.*

out·let (out'let' *or* out'lət) *n.* **1** a means or place of letting out or

getting out; way out: *the outlet of a lake, an outlet for one's energies.* **2** a market for a product. **3** a store selling the products of a particular manufacturer: *The shoe manufacturer had several retail outlets.* **4** a place in a wall, etc. for inserting an electric plug to make connection with an electric circuit.

out·li·er (out′lī′ər) *n.* **1** a person, place, or thing that is detached from the main body or system. **2** *Geology.* a formation surrounded by older strata and exposed because of erosion, denudation, etc.

out·line (out′līn′) *n., v.* **-lined, -lin·ing.** —*n.* **1** the line that shows the shape of an object; line that bounds a figure: *We saw the outlines of the mountains against the evening sky.* **2** a drawing or style of drawing that gives only outer lines. **3** a general plan; rough draft: *Make an outline before trying to write a composition.* **in outline, a** with only the outline shown. **b** with only the main features. —*v.* **1** draw the outer line of. **2** indicate or define the outline of: *hills outlined against the sky.* **3** give a plan of; sketch: *She outlined their trip abroad.* —**out′lin·er,** *n.*

☞ *Syn. n.* **1. Outline, contour, profile** = the line or lines showing the shape of something. **Outline** applies to the line marking the outer limits or edge of an object, figure, or shape: *We could see the outline of a man.* **Contour** emphasizes the shape shown by the outline: *The contours of his face are rugged.* **Profile** applies to the side view of something seen in outline, especially against a background: *You would stand up straight if you could see your profile when you slouch.*

out·live (out liv′) *v.* **-lived, -liv·ing.** live or last longer than: *The idea was good once, but it has outlived its usefulness.*

out·look (out′lŭk′) *n.* **1** what one sees on looking out; view: *The room has a pleasant outlook.* **2** what seems likely to happen; prospect: *Because of the black clouds, the outlook for our picnic is not very good.* **3** a way of thinking about things; attitude of mind; point of view: *a gloomy outlook on life.* **4** a lookout; tower or other high place to watch from.

out·ly·ing (out′lī′ing) *adj.* lying outside the boundary; far from the centre; remote: *the outlying houses in the settlement.*

out·ma·noeu·vre (out′mə nü′vər) *v.* **-vred, -vring. 1** get the better of by skilful manoeuvring; outwit: *They were outmanoeuvred in the negotiations and lost the contract.* **2** surpass in being manoeuvrable: *This car can outmanoeuvre any other car of its size on the market. Also,* **outmaneuver.**

out·mode (out′mōd′) *v.* **-mod·ed, -mod·ing.** make out of date or out of fashion.

out·mod·ed (out′mōd′id) *adj.* out-of-date.

out·most (out′mōst′) *adj.* outermost.

out·num·ber (out′num′bər) *v.* be more than; exceed in number: *They outnumbered us three to one.*

out-of-bounds (out′əv boundz′) *adj. or adv.* **1** *Sports.* outside the boundary line. **2** outside the established limits of use or entry.

out-of-date (out′əv dāt′) *adj.* old-fashioned; not in present use.

out-of-door (out′əv dôr′) *adj.* outdoor.

out-of-doors (out′əv dôrz′) *adj., n., adv.* —*adj.* outdoor. —*n. or adv.* outdoors.

out-of-the-way (out′əv ᴛнə wā′) *adj.* **1** remote; unfrequented; secluded: *an out-of-the-way cottage.* **2** seldom met with; unusual: *out-of-the-way bits of information.*

out-of-town (out′əv toun′) *adj.* of, having to do with, or situated on land outside a city or town.

out·pace (out′pās′) *v.* **-paced, -pac·ing. 1** run faster than. **2** outdo; excel.

out·pa·tient (out′pā′shənt) *n.* a patient receiving treatment at a hospital but not staying there.

out·play (out′plā′) *v.* play better than.

out·point (out′point′) *v.* **1** score more points than. **2** sail closer to the wind than.

out·port (out′pôrt′) *n.* *Cdn.* a small harbor, especially one of the isolated fishing villages along the coasts of Newfoundland.

out·post (out′pōst′) *n.* **1** a guard, or small number of soldiers, placed at some distance from an army or camp to prevent surprise attack. **2** the place where they are stationed. **3** a settlement or village in an outlying place: *an outpost in the North, a distant outpost of civilization.* **4** anything thought of as an outpost or advance guard.

out·pour (*n.* out′pôr′; *v.* out′pôr′) *n., v.* —*n.* **1** a pouring out. **2** an uncontrolled expression of thoughts or feelings. —*v.* pour out.

out·pour·ing (out′pôr′ing) *n.* **1** anything that is poured out. **2** an uncontrolled expression of thoughts or feelings.

out·put (out′pŭt′) *n.* **1** the amount produced; product or yield: *the daily output of automobiles.* **2** a putting forth: *a sudden output*

of effort. **3** information produced from the storage unit of a computer.

out·rage (out′rāj′; *sometimes, v.* out′rāj′) *n., v.* **-raged, -rag·ing.** —*n.* **1** an act showing no regard for the rights or feelings of others. **2** an overturning of the rights of others by force; act of violence; offence; insult. **3** the hurt angry feeling aroused by such treatment. —*v.* **1** insult; offend greatly or arouse great anger in. **2** break (the law, a rule of morality, etc.) openly; treat as nothing at all. [ME < OF *outrage,* ult. < L *ultra* beyond]

out·ra·geous (out rā′jəs) *adj.* shocking; very offensive or insulting. —**out·ra′geous·ly,** *adv.* —**out·ra′geous·ness,** *n.*

out·ran (out′ran′) *v.* pt of. **outrun.**

out·rank (out′rangk′) *v.* rank higher than.

ou·tré (ü trā′) *adj.* passing the bounds of what is usual and considered proper; eccentric; bizarre. [< F *outré,* pp. of *outrer* exaggerate, ult. < L *ultra* beyond]

out·reach (*v.* out rēch′; *n.* out′rēch′) *v., n.* —*v.* **1** exceed or reach beyond: *Her accomplishments far outreached those of her predecessors.* **2** *Esp.Poetic.* reach or stretch out; extend: *He outreached his arms.* —*n.* **1** the act or fact of reaching out: *The social aid program has too little outreach into the community.* **2** the extent or limit of reach: *the outreach of the flood.*

out·ride (out′rīd′) *v.* **-rode, -rid·den, -rid·ing. 1** ride faster or better than. **2** of ships, last through (a storm).

out·rid·er (out′rīd′ər) *n.* a servant or attendant riding on a horse before or beside a carriage or wagon, etc.: *A chuckwagon team consists of a driver and his outriders.*

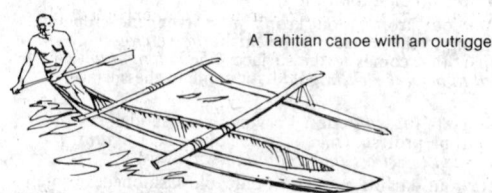
A Tahitian canoe with an outrigger

out·rig·ger (out′rig′ər) *n.* **1** a framework ending in a float, extending outward from the side of a light boat or canoe to prevent upsetting. **2** a boat or canoe with an outrigger. **3** a bracket extending outward from either side of a boat to hold a rowlock. **4** a boat equipped with such brackets. **5** a projecting spar, framework, or part: *an outrigger from a ship's mast to extend a sail, an outrigger from an airplane to support the rudder.*

out·right (out′rīt′) *adv., adj.* —*adv.* **1** altogether; entirely; not gradually: *sell a thing outright.* **2** openly; without restraint: *I laughed outright.* **3** at once; on the spot: *She fainted outright.* —*adj.* **1** complete; thorough: *an outright loss.* **2** downright; straightforward; direct: *an outright refusal.* **3** entire; total.

out·run (out′run′) *v.* **-ran, -run, -run·ning. 1** run faster than. **2** leave behind; go beyond; pass the limits of: *I am afraid your story outruns the facts.*

out·sell (out′sel′) *v.* **-sold, -sell·ing. 1** outdo in selling or salesmanship: *She can easily outsell any of the other sales reps.* **2** sell in greater amounts than; exceed in the number of items sold: *His second novel outsold his first by a wide margin.*

out·set (out′set′) *n.* a start; a beginning: *At the outset, it looked like a nice day.*

out·shine (out′shīn′) *v.* **-shone, -shin·ing. 1** shine more brightly than. **2** be more brilliant or excellent than; surpass.

out·shoot (*v.* out′shüt′; *n.* out′shüt′) *v.* **-shot, -shoot·ing;** *n.* —*v.* **1** shoot better or farther than. **2** shoot forth. —*n.* **1** projection. **2** offshoot.

out·side (out′sīd′; *prep. also,* out′sīd′) *n., adj., adv., prep.* —*n.* **1** the side or surface away from the centre or inside: *the outside of a circle or a balloon. The cupboards were blue on the outside and white on the inside.* **2** the external appearance. **3** a space or position on the outer side or beyond a boundary or limit: *She opened the window from the outside.* **4** *Cdn.* the settled parts of Canada: *In the North, people refer to the rest of Canada as the outside.* **at the outside,** at the most; at the limit: *It will take me a week, at the outside.* **outside in,** so that what should be outside is inside; inside out. —*adj.* **1** of, having to do with, on, or toward the outer part or surface: *The outside leaves are turning brown.* **2** not belonging to a certain group, set, district, etc.: *Outside people tried to get control of the business.* **3** being, acting, done, or originating without or beyond a wall, boundary, etc.: *Outside noises disturbed the class.* **4** maximum or extreme: *What is your outside estimate on costs?* **5** of a chance or possibility, slight; remote: *He had only an outside chance of winning the race.*

—*adv.* **1** on or to the outside. **2** outdoors.
—*prep.* out of; beyond the limits of: *Stay outside the house.*
out·side of, *Informal.* with the exception of: *Outside of John, none of us liked the play.*

out·sid·er (out′sīd′ər) *n.* **1** a person who does not belong to a particular group, company, party, etc. **2** *Cdn.* a person who does not live in the North: *The people of Whitehorse, Y.T., call the people of Edmonton outsiders.* **3** a person, horse, etc. believed to have no chance of winning a competition.

out·size (out′sīz′) *adj., n.* —*adj.* larger than the usual size. —*n.* an article of clothing, etc. larger than the usual size.

out·skirts (out′skėrts′) *n.pl.* the outer parts or edges of a town, district, etc.; outlying parts.

out·smart (out′smärt′) *v. Informal.* outdo in cleverness.

out·spo·ken (out′spō′kən) *adj.* frank; not reserved: *an outspoken person, outspoken criticism.* —**out′spo′ken·ly,** *adv.* —**out′spo′ken·ness,** *n.*
☛ *Syn.* See note at **frank.**

out·spread (*adj.* out′spred′; *v.* out′spred′) *adj., v.* **-spread, -spreading.** —*adj.* spread out; extended: *an eagle with outspread wings.* —*v.* spread out; extend.

out·stand·ing (out stan′ding) *adj.* **1** standing out from others; well-known; important: *an outstanding basketball player, an outstanding performance.* **2** unpaid: *outstanding debts.* **3** needing attention; *outstanding letters.* **4** projecting. —**out·stand′ing·ly,** *adv.*

out·stay (out′stā′) *v.* **1** stay beyond the limit of; overstay: *He outstayed his welcome.* **2** stay longer than; have more staying power than: *She outstayed all the other buyers. He outstayed the other guests.*

out·stretched (out′strecht′) *adj.* stretched out; extended: *He welcomed his old friend with outstretched arms.*

out·strip (out′strip′) *v.* **-stripped, -strip·ping. 1** go faster than; leave behind in a race. **2** do better than; excel.

out·talk (out′tok′ *or* -tôk′) *v.* talk better, faster, longer, or louder than; get the better of by talking.

out·vote (out′vōt′) *v.* **-vot·ed, -vot·ing.** defeat in voting; cast more votes than.

out·ward (out′wərd) *adj., adv.* —*adj.* **1** going toward the outside; turned toward the outside: *an outward motion, an outward glance.* **2** outer: *to all outward appearances.* **3** on the surface; external: *an outward transformation.*
—*adv.* **1** toward the outside; away. **2** away from the dock, station, etc.: *That ship is outward bound.* **3** on the outside: *He folded the coat with the lining outward.* [OE *ūtweard*]

out·ward·ly (out′wərd lē) *adv.* **1** on the outside or outer surface. **2** toward the outside. **3** as regards appearance or outward manifestation.

out·wards (out′wərdz) *adv.* outward.

out·wash (out′wash′) *n. Geology.* rock fragments or other glacial debris carried beyond the glacier by meltwater.

out·wear (out′wer′) *v.* **-wore, -worn, -wear·ing. 1** wear longer than. **2** wear out. **3** outgrow.

out·weigh (out′wā′) *v.* **1** weigh more than. **2** exceed in value, importance, influence, etc.: *The advantages of the plan outweigh its disadvantages.*

out·wit (out′wit′) *v.* **-wit·ted, -wit·ting.** get the better of by being more intelligent; be too clever for: *The prisoner outwitted his guards and escaped.*

out·work (*n.* out′wėrk′; *v.* out′wėrk′) *n., v.* —*n.* a part of the fortifications of a place lying outside the main ones; a less important defence: *the outworks of a castle.* —*v.* surpass in working; work harder or faster than.

out·worn (*adj.* out′wôrn′; *v.* out′wôrn′) *adj., v.* —*adj.* **1** worn out. **2** out-of-date. —*v.* pp. of **outwear.**

ou·zel (ü′zəl) *n.* **1** ring ouzel. **2** water ouzel; dipper (def. 2). Also, **ousel.** [OE *ōsle*]

ou·zo (ü′zō) *n.* a strong, colorless Greek alcoholic liquor flavored with aniseed. [Mod.Gk. *ouzon*]

o·va (ō′və) *n.* pl. of **ovum.**

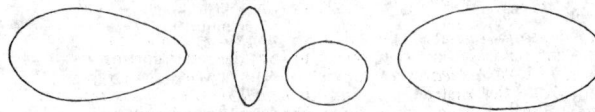

Ovals: the three on the right are ellipses.

o·val (ō′vəl) *adj., n.* —*adj.* **1** egg-shaped. **2** shaped like an ellipse.

hat, āge, fär; let, ēqual, tėrm; it, īce
hot, ōpen, ôrder; oil, out; cup, put, rüle,
əbove, takən, pencəl, lemən, circəs
ch, child; ng, long; sh, ship
th, thin; ᴛн, then; zh, measure

—*n.* something having an oval shape. [ME < NL *ovalis* < L *ovum* egg]

o·val·ly (ō′vəl ē) *adv.* in an oval form.

o·var·i·an (ō ver′ē ən) *adj.* of or having to do with an ovary.

o·va·ry (ō′və rē) *n., pl.* **-ries. 1** in female animals, the reproductive organ that produces the egg cells and, in vertebrates, female sex hormones. 1 one ovary on each side of the abdomen. **2** in a seed-bearing plant, the part of the pistil that contains the young seeds, called ovules. See **flower** for picture. [< NL *ovarium* < L *ovum* egg]

o·vate (ō′vāt) *adj.* egg-shaped: *an ovate leaf.* See **leaf** for picture. [< L *ovatus* < *ovum* egg]

o·va·tion (ō vā′shən) *n.* an enthusiastic public welcome; burst of applause. [< L *ovatio, -onis* < *ovare* rejoice]

ov·en (uv′ən) *n.* **1** a space in a stove or near a fireplace, for baking food. **2** a small furnace for heating or drying. [OE *ofen*]

ov·en·bird (uv′ən bėrd′) *n.* **1** any of several small brown songbirds (genus *Furnarius*) of South America that build a dome-shaped nest of clay and leaves or twigs, etc. The nest of an ovenbird has a side entrance and is often quite elaborate, with more than one chamber. **2** a North American songbird (*Seiurus aurocapillus*), a large wood warbler that builds a dome-shaped nest of leaves and plant fibres on the forest floor. This ovenbird's nest also has a side entrance.

ov·en·proof (uv′ən prüf′) *adj.* able to stand the heat of an oven without cracking.

ov·en·ware (uv′ən wer′) *n.* dishes made to be ovenproof.

o·ver (ō′vər) *prep., adv., adj., n.* —*prep.* **1** above in place or position: *the roof over one's head.* **2** above in authority, power, etc.: *We have a captain over us.* **3** on; upon: *a blanket lying over a bed.* **4** at all or various places on: *A blush came over her face. Farms were scattered over the valley.* **5** above and to the other side of; across: *to leap over a wall.* **6** on the other side of: *lands over the sea.* **7** out and down from: *He fell over the edge of the cliff.* **8** more than; beyond: *It costs over ten dollars.* **9** here and there on or in; round about; all through: *We will be travelling over Europe.* **10** from end to end of; along: *We drove over the new highway.* **11** during; in the course of: *over many years.* **12** in reference to; concerning; about: *He is troubled over his health.* **13** while engaged on or concerned with: *to fall asleep over one's work.* **14** by means of: *They spoke over the telephone.* **15** until the end of: *to stay over the weekend.*
—*adv.* **1** above: *The cliff hung over.* **2** so as to cover the surface, or affect the whole surface: *Cover the tar over with sand until it has hardened.* **3** from side to side; to the other side; across any intervening space: *Go over to the store for me.* **4** from one to another: *Hand the money over.* **5** on the other side; at some distance: *over in Europe, over by the hill.* **6** down; out and down: *The ball went too near the edge and rolled over. When he lost his balance, he fell over.* **7** so as to bring the upper side or end down or under: *to turn over a page.* **8** again; in repetition: *ten times over. I'll have to do that assignment over.* **9** too (used chiefly in compounds), as in *overnice.* **10** through a region, area, etc.: *to travel all over.* **11** from beginning to end: *to read a newspaper over.* **12** throughout or beyond a period of time: *Please stay over till Monday.* **13** more; besides; in excess or addition: *He spent seventy cents and had thirty cents over.*
over again, once more: *Let's do that over again.*
over against, a opposite to; in front of. **b** so as to bring out a difference.
over and above, besides; in addition to.
over and over, again and again: *He keeps telling the same story over and over.*
over with or **over and done with,** *Informal.* finished; completed: *I have to get this homework over with today.*
—*adj.* **1** upper; higher up: *the over crust of a pie.* **2** higher in authority, station, etc. (used chiefly in compounds), as in *overlord.* **3** surplus; extra (used chiefly in compounds), as in *to pay for overtime.* **4** too much; too great (used chiefly in compounds), as in *overuse of drugs.* **5** at an end: *The play is over.*
—*n.* **1** the amount in excess. **2** *Cricket.* **a** the number of balls (usually six) delivered between successive changes of bowlers. **b** the part of the game between such changes. [OE *ofer*]
☛ *Syn. prep.* **1, 2. Over, above** express a relation in which one thing is thought of as being higher than the other. **Over,** the opposite of **under,** suggests being

directly higher or in the position or space immediately higher up: *Carry the umbrella over your head. A sergeant is over a corporal. Above*, opposed to **below** and **beneath**, suggests being on or at or rising to a higher level, but seldom suggests being straight up or a direct connection: *The plane flew above the clouds. A general is above a sergeant.*

☛ *Usage.* **Over with.** Used in informal speech and writing to mean "over" or "finished." Spoken: *I'd like to get this over with today.* More formal: *I'd like to get this finished today.*

over– *prefix.* **1** too; too much; too long, etc., as in *overcrowded, overfull, overburden, overpay, oversleep.* **2** extra, as in *oversize, overtime.* **3** over, as in *overflow, overlord, overseas, overthrow.*

o·ver·act (ōv′vər akt′) *v.* act to excess; overdo in acting; act (a part) in an exaggerated manner.

o·ver·ac·tive (ō′vər ak′tiv) *adj.* too active; active to excess. —**o′ver·ac′tive·ly,** *adv.*

o·ver·age[1] (ō′vər āj′) *adj.* over a specified age, especially too old to be of use, etc.

o·ver·age[2] (ō′vər ij) *n.* a surplus or extra amount, as of goods.

o·ver·all (ō′vər ol′ *or* -ôl′) *adj., adv., n.* —*adj.* **1** from one end to the other: *The overall length of the house is ten metres.* **2** including everything: *an overall estimate.* —*adv.* as a whole; generally: *Overall, it was a successful meeting.* —*n.* **1 overalls,** *pl.* loose trousers of strong, usually cotton, cloth worn over clothes to keep them clean: *Overalls usually have a part that covers the chest.* **2** *Esp.Brit.* a loose-fitting smock, etc. worn over other clothes to protect them.

o·ver·arch (ō′vər ärch′) *v.* **1** arch over; span with or like an arch: *The street was overarched by elm trees.* **2** curve like an arch.

o·ver·arm (ō′vər ärm′) *adj. or adv.* with the arm raised above the shoulder; overhand: *an overarm stroke, to throw overarm.*

o·ver·awe (ō′vər o′ *or* -ô′) *v.* **-awed, -aw·ing.** overcome or restrain with awe: *He was overawed by the grandeur of the estate.*

o·ver·bal·ance (ō′vər bal′əns) *v.* **-anced, -anc·ing. 1** be greater than in weight, importance, value, etc.: *The gains overbalanced the losses.* **2** cause to lose balance. **3** lose balance: *He overbalanced and fell from the wall.*

o·ver·bear (ō′vər ber′) *v.* **-bore, -borne, -bear·ing. 1** overcome by weight or force; oppress; master: *His father overbore his objections.* **2** bear down by weight or force; overthrow; upset.

o·ver·bear·ing (ō′vər ber′ing) *adj.* inclined to dictate; forcing others to one's own will; domineering. —**o′ver·bear′ing·ly,** *adv.*
☛ *Syn.* See note at **proud.**

o·ver·bid (ō′vər bid′) *v.* **-bid, -bid** or **-bid·den, -bid·ding. 1** bid more than the value of (a thing). **2** bid higher than (a person).

o·ver·blouse (ō′vər blouz′ *or* ō′vər blous′) *n.* a blouse for women, designed to be worn outside a skirt or pants instead of tucked in. An overblouse is usually slightly longer than a regular blouse.

o·ver·blown (ō′vər blōn′) *adj.* **1** of a flower, past its peak of beauty; too fully open. **2** inflated or pompous; pretentious: *His acceptance speech was filled with flowery, overblown sentiments.*

o·ver·board (ō′vər bôrd′) *adv.* from a ship or boat into the water: *He fell overboard.*
go overboard, go too far in an effort because of extreme enthusiasm: *She went overboard and bought more than she needed.*
throw overboard, *Informal.* get rid of; abandon or discard: *We had to throw all our plans overboard and start again from scratch.*

o·ver·book (ō′vər buk′) *v.* issue tickets or reservations to more people than there is room for: *The airline had overbooked the flight and we had to wait for the next one.*

o·ver·bore (ō′vər bôr′) *v.* pt. of **overbear.**

o·ver·borne (ō′vər bôrn′) *v.* pp. of **overbear.**

o·ver·bur·den (*v.* ō′vər bėr′dən; *n.* ō′vər bėr′dən) *v., n.* —*v.* overload. —*n.* **1** too great a burden; something that overloads. **2** *Geology.* **a** rock, clay, etc. that overlays and hides a deposit of ore. **b** soil, gravel, or other material that overlays bedrock.

o·ver·came (ō′vər kām′) *v.* pt. of **overcome.**

o·ver·cap·i·tal·ize (ō′vər kap′ə təl īz′) *v.* **-ized, -iz·ing.** fix or estimate the capital of (a company, enterprise, etc.) at too high an amount. —**o′ver·cap′i·tal·i·za′tion,** *n.*

o·ver·cast (ō′vər kast′) *adj. v.* **-cast, -cast·ing.** —*adj.* **1** cloudy; dark; gloomy: *The sky was overcast before the storm.* **2** sad; gloomy: *His face was overcast.* **3** sewn with overcast stitches. —*v.* **1** cover or be covered with clouds or darkness. **2** sew over and through (the raw edges of a seam) with long stitches to prevent ravelling.

o·ver·charge (*v.* ō′vər chärj′; *n.* ō′vər chärj′) *v.* **-charged, -charg·ing;** *n.* —*v.* **1** charge too high a price: *The grocer overcharged you for the eggs.* **2** load too heavily; fill too full: *The overcharged musket burst.* —*n.* **1** a charge that is too great. **2** too heavy or too full a load.

o·ver·cloud (ō′vər kloud′) *v.* **1** cloud over; become clouded over; darken. **2** make or become gloomy.

o·ver·coat (ō′vər kōt′) *n.* a coat worn for warmth over regular clothing.

o·ver·come (ō′vər kum′) *v.* **-came, -come, -com·ing. 1** get the better of; win the victory over; conquer; defeat: *to overcome an enemy, one's faults, all difficulties.* **2** make weak or helpless: *to overcome by weariness.* **3** confuse or overwhelm: *The girl was so overcome by the noise and the lights that she couldn't speak.* [OE *ofercuman*]
☛ *Syn.* **1.** See note at **defeat.**

o·ver·com·pen·sate (ō′vər kom′pən sāt′) *v.* go too far in trying, consciously or unconsciously, to make up for or get rid of a feeling of not being good enough or worthy enough: *She overcompensated for her shyness at the party by insulting half the guests.*

o·ver·com·pen·sa·tion (ō′vər kom′pən sā′shən) *n.* the act or an instance of overcompensating.

o·ver·de·vel·op (ō′vər di vel′əp) *v.* develop too much or too long. If a photograph is overdeveloped, it will be too dark.

o·ver·do (ō′vər dü′) *v.* **-did, -done, -do·ing. 1** do or attempt too much: *She overdoes exercise. He overdid and became tired.* **2** exaggerate: *The funny scenes in the play were overdone.* **3** cook too much. **4** exhaust; tire. [OE *oferdōn*]

o·ver·dose (*n.* ō′vər dōs′; *v.* ō′vər dōs′) *n., v.* **-dosed, -dos·ing.** —*n.* too big a dose. —*v.* give too large a dose to.

o·ver·draft (ō′vər draft′) *n.* **1** an overdrawing of a bank account. **2** the amount of the excess.

o·ver·draw (ō′vər drô′) *v.* **-drew, -drawn, -draw·ing. 1** draw from (a bank account) more money than one has there. **2** exaggerate: *The characters in the book were greatly overdrawn.*

o·ver·dress (*v.* ō′vər dres′; *n.* ō′vər dres′) *v., n.* —*v.* dress or decorate too formally or elaborately: *He decided not to wear his tuxedo because he did not want to risk being overdressed.* —*n.* a dress worn over another dress: *a sheer overdress.*

o·ver·drive (ō′vər drīv′) *n.* an arrangement of gears whereby less power produces more speed in high gear.

o·ver·due (ō′vər dyü′ *or* -dü′) *adj.* **1** late coming or arriving: *The plane is overdue.* **2** due but not yet paid: *This bill is overdue.*

o·ver·es·ti·mate (*v.* ō′vər es′tə māt′; *n.* ō′vər es′tə mit) *v.* **-mat·ed, -mat·ing;** *n.* —*v.* estimate at too high a value, amount, rate, etc. —*n.* an estimate that is too high. —**o′ver·es′ti·ma′tion,** *n.*

o·ver·ex·ert (ō′vər ek zėrt′) v. put forth too much effort; exert too much (usually used with a reflexive pronoun): He hurt his back when he overexerted himself in gymnastics.

o·ver·ex·er·tion (ō′vər ek zėr′shən) n. the act or an instance of overexerting: The injury was the result of overexertion.

o·ver·ex·pose (ō′vər ek spōz′) v. -posed, -pos·ing. expose to too much light or radiation: to overexpose a film.

o·ver·ex·po·sure (ō′vər eks pō′zhər) n. the quality or state of being overexposed: an overexposure in photography, overexposure to the sun.

o·ver·ex·tend (ō′vər ek stend′) v. extend too far; especially, commit oneself financially beyond what one can pay.

o·ver·fill (ō′vər fil′) v. fill too full; fill so as to cause overflowing.

o·ver·flight (ō′vər flīt′) n. the act or fact of flying over an area, especially the territory of another country.

o·ver·flow (v. ō′vər flō′; n. ō′vər flō′) v. -flowed, -flown, -flow·ing; n. —v. 1 flow over the bounds: Rivers often overflow in the spring. 2 cover; flood: The river overflowed my garden. 3 have the contents flowing over: The bathtub is overflowing. 4 flow over the top of: The milk is overflowing the cup. 5 extend out beyond; be too many for: The crowd overflowed the little parlor and filled the hall. 6 be very abundant: an overflowing harvest, overflowing kindness.
—n. 1 an overflowing: The sink has an extra drain near the top to prevent an overflow. 2 an excess: We caught the overflow in a pail. 3 an outlet or container for overflowing liquid. [OE oferflōwan]

o·ver·gar·ment (ō′vər gär′mənt) n. an outer garment.

o·ver·grow (ō′vər grō′) v. -grew, -grown, -grow·ing. 1 grow over: The wall is overgrown with vines. 2 grow too fast; become too big. 3 outgrow.

o·ver·grown (ō′vər grōn′) adj., v. —adj. grown too big: an overgrown tree. —v. pp. of overgrow.

o·ver·growth (ō′vər grōth′) n. 1 too great or too rapid growth. 2 growth overspreading or covering something.

o·ver·hand (ō′vər hand′) adj., adv., n., v. —adj. 1 done or made with the hand brought forward and down from above the shoulder: an overhand throw. 2 with the back of the hand upward or outward. 3 of or designating a method of sewing two edges together, with the stitches passing successively over the line formed by the two edges. —adv. in an overhand manner: to pitch overhand. —n. Sports. an overhand stroke or throw: He's practising his overhand. —v. sew overhand.

overhand knot a knot made by forming a loop in a cord, etc. and passing the end of the cord through it. See knot for picture.

o·ver·hang (v. ō′vər hang′; n. ō′vər hang′) v. -hung, -hang·ing; n. —v. 1 project over: Trees overhang the street to form an arch of branches. 2 threaten or menace; impend: The threat of an invasion overhung the city. —n. 1 something that projects: The overhang of the roof shaded the flower bed beneath. 2 the extent of projecting.

o·ver·haul (v. ō′vər hol′ or -hôl′; n. ō′vər hol′ or -hôl′) v., n. —v. 1 examine thoroughly so as to make any repairs or changes that are needed. 2 gain upon; overtake. —n. a thorough examination to find problems, weaknesses, etc. and make necessary repairs or changes.

o·ver·head (adv. ō′vər hed′; adj. or n. ō′vər hed′) adv., adj., n. —adv. over or above one's head; aloft or on high: the stars overhead, the family overhead, the flag overhead. —adj. 1 being, working, or passing overhead: overhead wires. 2 applying to one and all; general. —n. general expenses of running a business, such as rent, lighting, heating, taxes, repairs.

overhead projector a projecting device in which transparencies are placed on a glass surface that is lit from below, the image being focussed and reflected onto a wall or screen by means of an overhead lens and mirror.

o·ver·hear (ō′vər hėr′) v. -heard, -hear·ing. hear when one is not supposed to hear: They spoke so loudly that I could not help overhearing what they said. [OE oferhīeran]

o·ver·hung (adj. ō′vər hung′; v. ō′vər hung′) adj., v. —adj. 1 hung from above: an overhung door. 2 of the upper jaw, projecting beyond the lower jaw. —v. pt. and pp. of overhang.

hat, āge, fär; let, ēqual, tèrm; it, īce
hot, ōpen, ôrder; oil, out; cup, pùt, rüle,
above, takən, pencəl, lemən, circəs
ch, child; ng, long; sh, ship
th, thin; ᴛʜ, then; zh, measure

o·ver·joyed (ō′vər joid′) adj. filled with great joy: He was overjoyed at finding them safe and sound.

o·ver·kill (ō′vər kil′) n. a capacity for destruction in excess of that required to destroy a target or enemy.

o·ver·lad·en (ō′vər lā′dən) adj. overloaded.

o·ver·laid (ō′vər lād′) v. pt. and pp. of overlay[1].

o·ver·lain (ō′vər lān′) v. pp. of overlie.

o·ver·land (ō′vər land′ or ō′vər lənd) adv. or adj. on land; by land: We travelled overland from Halifax to Montreal.

O·ver·land·er (ō′vər land′ər) n. Cdn. a person who went from eastern Canada to the Cariboo gold rush in 1862; Argonaut (def. 3).

o·ver·lap (v. ō′vər lap′; n. ō′vər lap′) v. -lapped, -lap·ping; n. —v. lap over; place or be placed so that one piece covers part of the next: Shingles are laid to overlap each other. —n. 1 a lapping over. 2 the part or amount that overlaps: Allow for an overlap of ten centimetres.

o·ver·lay[1] (v. ō′vər lā′; n. ō′vər lā′) v. -laid, -lay·ing; n. —v. 1 lay or place (one thing) over or upon another. 2 cover, overspread, or surmount with something; especially, finish with an ornamental layer of something: The dome is overlaid with gold. —n. 1 something laid over something else; a covering. 2 an ornamental layer: The lid of the box had a gold overlay. 3 a sheet of transparent material having marks on it, that is keyed to a design, chart, or map over which it is placed to give additional information.

o·ver·lay[2] (ō′vər lā′) v. pt. of overlie.

o·ver·leap (ō′vər lēp′) v. leap over; pass beyond.

o·ver·lie (ō′vər lī′) v. -lay, -lain, -ly·ing. 1 lie over or upon. 2 smother (an infant or other newborn creature) by lying on.

o·ver·load (v. ō′vər lōd′; n. ō′vər lōd′) v., n. —v. load too heavily. —n. too great a load.

o·ver·look (ō′vər lùk′) v. 1 fail to see: Here are the letters you overlooked. 2 pay no attention to; excuse: His boss said he would overlook the mistake. 3 have a view of from above; be higher than: This high window overlooks half the city. 4 manage; look after and direct. —o′ver·look′er, n.
☛ Syn. 1. See note at slight.

o·ver·lord (ō′vər lôrd′) n. 1 a person who is lord over another lord or other lords: The duke was the overlord of barons and knights who held land from him. 2 a ruler with absolute or dictatorial powers; despot.

o·ver·ly (ō′vər lē) adv. overmuch; excessively; too: overly sensitive to criticism.

o·ver·mas·ter (ō′vər mas′tər) v. overcome; overpower.

o·ver·match (ō′vər mach′) v. be more than a match for; surpass.

o·ver·much (ō′vər much′) adj., adv. —adj. or adv. too much. —n. too great an amount.

o·ver·nice (ō′vər nīs′) adj. too fastidious.

o·ver·night (adv. ō′vər nīt′; adj., n. ō′vər nīt′) adv., adj., n. —adv. 1 for one night: to stay overnight. 2 at once; immediately; in a very short time: Change will not come overnight. 3 on the night before: Preparations were made overnight for an early start. —adj. 1 done, occurring, etc. from one day to the next: an overnight stop. 2 for use for one night: An overnight bag contains articles needed for one night's stay. 3 of or having to do with the night before. —n. the previous evening.

overnight bag a bag used to carry articles needed for a night's stay.

o·ver·pass (n. ō′vər pas′; v. ō′vər pas′) n., v. -passed or -past,

-pass·ing. —*n.* a bridge over a road, railway, canal, etc. —*v.* **1** pass over, across, or beyond. **2** overlook; disregard.

o·ver·play (ō′vər plā′) *v.* **1** play (a part, etc.) in an exaggerated manner. **2** overestimate or rely too much on the strength of (one's position, etc.): *He overplayed his price advantage, failed to guarantee quick delivery, and lost the contract.* **3** *Golf.* hit (the ball) past the green.

o·ver·plus (ō′vər plus′) *n.* a surplus; too great an amount.

o·ver·pop·u·late (ō′vər pop′yə lāt′) *v.* **-at·ed, -at·ing.** permit or cause (a city, region, etc.) to become too densely populated, resulting in deterioration of the environment, reduced standard of living, shortage of food, etc. —**o′ver·pop′u·la′tion,** *n.*

o·ver·pow·er (ō′vər pou′ər) *v.* **1** overcome; master; overwhelm: *overpower one's enemies.* **2** be so much greater than, that nothing else is felt: *Sudden anger overpowered every other feeling.* —**o′ver·pow′er·ing·ly,** *adv.*

o·ver·price (ō′vər prīs′) *v.* **-priced, -pric·ing.** set too high a price on: *His paintings aren't selling well because they're overpriced.*

o·ver·print (*v.* ō′vər print′; *n.* ō′vər print′) *v., n.* —*v.* **1** print additional matter, revisions, etc. on sheets already printed. **2** *Photography.* print a positive darker than desired. —*n.* **1** anything overprinted. **2** any design or mark printed across a stamp to change its use, value, etc. **3** a postage stamp printed in this way.

o·ver·pro·duce (ō′vər prə dyüs′ *or* -prə düs′) *v.* **-duced, -duc·ing.** **1** produce more than necessary. **2** produce more than can be sold profitably.

o·ver·pro·duc·tion (ō′vər prə duk′shən) *n.* **1** production of more than is needed. **2** production of more than can be sold at a profit.

o·ver·proof (ō′vər prüf′) *adj.* higher than 100 proof; containing more alcohol than proof spirit contains.

o·ver·pro·tect (ō′vər prə tekt′) *v.* protect too much; exercise more control over than is necessary or desirable in trying to shield from hurt, disappointment, etc.: *He had a hard time when he first left home because he had been overprotected as a child.*

o·ver·pro·tec·tive (ō′vər prə tek′tiv) *adj.* having or showing a tendency to protect: *an overprotective parent.*

o·ver·qual·i·fied (ō′vər kwo′li fīd′) *adj.* having more education, training, or experience than a job calls for.

o·ver·rate (ō′vər rāt′) *v.* **-rat·ed, -rat·ing.** rate or estimate too highly: *The movie was overrated; it really wasn't very good.*

o·ver·reach (ō′vər rēch′) *v.* **1** reach over or beyond. **2** reach too far. **3** get the better of by cunning: *to overreach a man in a bargain.* **4** cheat. **overreach oneself, a** fail or miss by trying for too much. **b** fail by being too crafty or tricky.

o·ver·re·act (ō′vər rē akt′) *v.* react too strongly and unreasonably. —**o′ver·re·ac′tion,** *n.*

o·ver·ride (ō′vər rīd′) *v.* **-rode, -rid·den, -rid·ing.** **1** act in spite of: *to override advice or objections.* **2** prevail over: *The new rule overrides all previous ones.* **3** ride over; trample on. **4** ride over (a region, place, etc.). **5** tire out by riding; ride too much. [OE *oferrīdan*]

o·ver·rule (ō′vər rül′) *v.* **-ruled, -rul·ing.** **1** decide against (an argument, objection, etc.); set aside: *The president overruled my plan.* **2** be stronger than; prevail over: *The majority overruled me.* —**o′ver·rul′ing·ly,** *adv.*

o·ver·run (*v.* ō′vər run′; *n.* ō′vər run′) *v.* **-ran, -run, -run·ing;** *n.* —*v.* **1** spread over rapidly or in great numbers: *Weeds had overrun the old garden. The barn was overrun with rats.* **2** invade and conquer, occupy, or destroy: *Enemy troops overran most of the country.* **3** run or go beyond; exceed: *The speaker overran the time set for him.* **4** *Printing.* **a** carry over (words or lines of type) into another line or page to provide for addition or removal of other matter. **b** remake (columns, pages, etc.) by carrying over words, lines, etc. —*n.* **1** overrunning. **2** the amount overrunning or carried over, as a balance or surplus; an excess.

o·ver·saw (ō′vər so′ *or* -sô′) *v.* pt. of **oversee.**

o·ver·sea (*adv.* ō′vər sē′; *adj.* ō′vər sē′) *adv. or adj.* overseas.

o·ver·seas (*adv.* ō′vər sēz′; *adj.* ō′vər sēz′) *adv., adj.* —*adv.* **1** across the sea; beyond the sea; abroad: *to travel overseas.* **2** *Military.* serving across the sea: *My grandfather was overseas during the war.* —*adj.* **1** done, used, or serving overseas: *overseas service.* **2** of countries across the sea; foreign: *overseas trade.*

o·ver·see (ō′vər sē′) *v.* **-saw, -seen, -see·ing.** look after and direct (work or workers); superintend; manage. [OE *ofersēon*]

o·ver·se·er (ō′vər sē′ər) *n.* **1** a person who oversees the work of others. **2** *Cdn.* in certain provinces, the head of a township council; reeve.

o·ver·sell (ō′vər sel′) *v.* **-sold, -sell·ing.** **1** sell to excess; sell more of than can be delivered. **2** *Informal.* urge (a person) to buy something too aggressively or too long, often at the risk of losing a sale.

o·ver·sew (ō′vər sō′ *or* ō′vər sō′) *v.* **-sewed** *or* **-sewn, -sew·ing.** sew overhand with close stitches.

o·ver·sexed (ō′vər sekst′) *adj.* having excessive sexual desire or capacity.

o·ver·shad·ow (ō′vər shad′ō) *v.* **1** be or appear more important than: *The boy overshadowed his older brother as a hockey player.* **2** cast a shadow over.

o·ver·shoe (ō′vər shü′) *n.* a waterproof shoe or boot, often made of rubber, worn over another shoe to keep the foot dry and warm.

o·ver·shoot (ō′vər shüt′) *v.* **-shot, -shoot·ing.** **1** of an aircraft, pass beyond the limit of the runway or landing field when trying to land. **2** shoot or go beyond the target, mark, limit, etc.

o·ver·shot (*adj.* ō′vər shot′; *v.* ō′vər shot′) *adj., v.* —*adj.* **1** of a water wheel, driven by water flowing over it from above. See **water wheel** for picture. **2** of the upper jaw, projecting beyond the lower. —*v.* pt. and pp. of **overshoot.**

o·ver·sight (ō′vər sīt′) *n.* **1** a failure to notice or think of something; an unintentional mistake or omission: *Through an oversight, the kitten had no supper last night.* **2** watchful care.

o·ver·sim·pli·fi·ca·tion (ō′vər sim′plə fə kā′shən) *n.* the act or fact of oversimplifying: *It is an oversimplification to say that his success is due to hard work.*

o·ver·sim·pli·fy (ō′vər sim′plə fī′) *v.* **-fied, -fying.** simplify too much; simplify to the point of distortion: *She has oversimplified the problem; there are several important factors she did not even consider.*

o·ver·size (ō′vər sīz′) *adj., n.* —*adj.* **1** larger than the usual size; outsize. **2** too big. —*n.* something that is oversize.

o·ver·skirt (ō′vər skèrt′) *n.* **1** an outer skirt. **2** a separate skirt over the main skirt.

o·ver·sleep (ō′vər slēp′) *v.* **-slept, -sleep·ing.** sleep beyond the time set for waking; sleep too long; sleep in: *I was late for work this morning because I overslept.*

o·ver·spread (ō′vər spred′) *v.* **-spread, -spread·ing.** spread over: *A smile overspread his broad face.*

o·ver·state (ō′vər stāt′) *v.* **-stat·ed, -stat·ing.** state too strongly; exaggerate. —**o′ver·state′ment,** *n.*

o·ver·stay (ō′vər stā′) *v.* stay beyond the time or limits of: *to overstay one's welcome.*

o·ver·step (ō′vər step′) *v.* **-stepped, -step·ping.** go beyond; exceed: *He overstepped the limits of politeness by asking such personal questions.*

o·ver·stock (*v.* ō′vər stok′; *n.* ō′vər stok′) *v., n.* —*v.* stock or supply with more than is needed or can readily be used: *Stores often have sales when they're overstocked.* —*n.* too great a stock or supply.

o·ver·strung (ō′vər strung′) *adj.* too nervous or sensitive.

o·ver·stuff (ō′vər stuf′) *v.* **1** stuff more than is necessary; stuff too much. **2** of furniture, upholster with very thick stuffing.

o·ver·stuffed (ō′vər stuft′) *adj.* of furniture, having very thick stuffing: *a large, comfortable, overstuffed armchair.*

o·ver·sub·scribe (ō′vər səb skrīb′) *v.* **-scribed, -scrib·ing.** subscribe or subscribe for in excess of what is available or required.

o·ver·sub·scrip·tion (ō′vər səb skrip′shən) *n.* oversubscribing.

o′ver·plump′	o′ver·prompt′	o′ver·right′eous·ness	o′ver·se·vere′	o′ver·stim′u·late′
o′ver·pop′u·lous	o′ver·pro·vide′	o′ver·ripe′	o′ver·sharp′	o′ver·strain′
o′ver·pow′er·ful	o′ver·proud′	o′ver·roman′ti·cize′	o′ver·so·lic′i·tous	o′ver·stretch′
o′ver·praise′	o′ver·pub′li·cize′	o′ver·scep′ti·cal	o′ver·so·phis′ti·cat′ed	o′ver·strict′
o′ver·pre·cise′	o′ver·scru′pu·lous	o′ver·spar′ing	o′ver·stu′dious	
o′ver·prize′	o′ver·re·li′gious	o′ver·sen′si·tive	o′ver·spe′cial·i·za′tion	o′ver·stud′y
o′ver·prom′i·nent	o′ver·right′eous	o′ver·se′rious	o′ver·spe′cial·ize′	o′ver·sub′tle

o·ver·sup·ply (*v.* ō′vər sə plī′; *n.* ō′vər sə plī′) *v.* **-plied,** **-ply·ing;** *n., pl.* **-plies.** —*v.* supply more than is needed or wanted. —*n.* an excessive supply.

o·vert (ō′vèrt *or* ō vèrt′) *adj.* open; evident; not hidden; public: *Hitting someone is an overt act.* [ME < OF *overt*, pp. of *ovrir* open < L *aperire*] —**o′vert·ly,** *adv.*

o·ver·take (ō′vər tāk′) *v.* **-took, -tak·en, -tak·ing. 1** come up with; catch up to: *If you hurry, you might be able to overtake him before he reaches his car.* **2** catch up with and pass: *They overtook us and arrived before we did.* **3** come upon suddenly: *A storm overtook the children.*

o·ver·task (ō′vər task′) *v.* give too long or too hard tasks to.

o·ver·tax (ō′vər taks′) *v.* **1** tax too heavily. **2** put too heavy a burden on. —**o′ver·tax·a′tion,** *n.*

o·ver·threw (ō′vər thrü′) *v.* pp. of **overthrow.**

o·ver·throw (*v.* ō′vər thrō′; *n.* ō′vər thrō′) *v.* **-threw, -thrown, -throw·ing.** —*v.* **1** take away the power of; defeat: *to overthrow a government.* **2** put an end to; destroy: *to overthrow slavery.* **3** overturn; upset; knock down. **4** throw a ball over or past (the player or place aimed for). —*n.* **1** a defeat; upset: *the overthrow of one's plans.* **2** a ball thrown over or past the player or place aimed for.

o·ver·thrown (ō′vər thrōn′) *v.* pp. of **overthrow.**

o·ver·thrust (ō′vər thrust′) *n. Geology.* a fault in which rocks of an older, lower stratum are pushed on top of those of a newer, originally higher stratum.

o·ver·time (*n., adv., adj.* ō′vər tīm′; *v.* ō′vər tīm′) *n., adv., adj., v.* **-timed, -tim·ing.** —*n.* **1** extra time; time beyond the regular hours. **2** wages for this period: *They don't pay overtime.* **3** *Sports.* a period or periods beyond the normal game time. —*adv.* **1** beyond the regular hours: *He worked overtime.* **2** beyond the allotted or permitted time. —*adj.* **1** of or for overtime: *overtime work.* **2** being beyond the allotted or permitted time: *overtime parking.* —*v.* give too much time to: *to overtime a camera exposure.*

o·ver·tone (ō′vər tōn′) *n.* **1** *Music.* a tone heard along with the main or fundamental tone and whose rate of vibration is an integral multiple of the main tone; harmonic. **2** a hint or suggestion of something felt, believed, etc.: *an overtone of anger.*

o·ver·took (ō′vər tůk′) *v.* pt. of **overtake.**

o·ver·top (ō′vər top′) *v.* **-topped, -top·ping. 1** rise above; be higher than. **2** surpass; excel.

o·ver·train (ō′vər trān′) *v.* subject to or undergo excessive athletic training; train too hard or too much, with a resulting loss of proficiency.

o·ver·trump (ō′vər trump′) *v.* play a higher trump; play a higher trump than.

o·ver·ture (ō′vər chür′ *or* ō′vər chər) *n.* **1** a formal proposal or offer; the beginning of negotiations with another (*usually used in the plural*): *overtures for peace.* **2** *Music.* **a** a composition played by the orchestra as an introduction to an opera, oratorio, etc. **b** an independent orchestral composition having one movement. [ME < OF < L *apertura* opening. Doublet of APERTURE.]

o·ver·turn (*v.* ō′vər tèrn′; *n.* ō′vər tèrn′) *v., n.* —*v.* **1** turn upside down. **2** upset; fall down; fall over: *The boat overturned.* **3** make fall down; overthrow; destroy the power of: *The rebels overturned the government.* —*n.* an overturning. ☛ *Syn. v.* **2.** See note at **upset.**

o·ver·view (ō′vər vyü′) *n.* a brief, general survey.

o·ver·watch (ō′vər woch′) *v.* **1** watch over. **2** *Archaic.* make weary by watching.

o·ver·ween·ing (ō′vər wēn′ing) *adj.* thinking too much of oneself; conceited; self-confident; presumptuous. [ppr. of *overween* < over- + *ween* expect (OE *wēnan*)] —**o′ver·ween′ing·ly,** *adv.*

o·ver·weigh (ō′vər wā′) *v.* **1** be greater than in weight, importance, etc.; outweigh. **2** oppress; burden.

o·ver·weight (*adj. n.* ō′vər wāt′; *v.* ō′vər wāt′) *adj., n., v.* —*adj.* **1** of a person or animal, having a mass that is too great in proportion to height and build. **2** totalling a greater mass than allowed by regulations: *overweight baggage.* —*n.* more mass than is needed, desired, or specified; extra or excessive mass: *The butcher gave us overweight on this roast.* —*v.* overweigh.

o·ver·whelm (ō′vər welm′ *or* -hwelm′) *v.* **1** overcome completely; crush: *to overwhelm with grief.* **2** cover completely as a

hat, āge, fär; let, ēqual, tèrm; it, īce
hot, ōpen, ôrder; oil, out; cup, půt, rüle,
əbove, takən, pencəl, lemən, circəs
ch, child; ng, long; sh, ship
th, thin; ₮H, then; zh, measure

flood would: *A great wave overwhelmed the boat.* [< over- + ME *whelmen* turn upside down < Gmc.; cf. ON *hvelfa* overturn]

o·ver·whelm·ing (ō′vər wel′ming *or* -hwel′ming) *adj.* too many, too great, or too much to be resisted; overpowering: *an overwhelming majority of votes.* —**o′ver·whelm′ing·ly,** *adv.*

o·ver·work (*n.* ō′vər wèrk′; *v.* ō′vər wèrk′) *n., v.* —*n.* **1** too much or too hard work. **2** extra work. —*v.* **1** work or cause to work too hard or too long. **2** *Informal.* use to excess: *to overwork a pose of childlike innocence.* **3** work too much upon (a book, speech, etc.); elaborate too much. **4** figure or decorate the surface of.

o·ver·wrap (ō′vər rap′) *n.* a second, outside wrapper of transparent paper, cellophane, etc.

o·ver·wrought (ō′vər rot′ *or* -rôt′) *adj.* **1** wearied or exhausted by too much excitement; overly excited: *overwrought nerves.* **2** decorated all over: *an overwrought platter.* **3** too elaborate.

o·vi·duct (ō′və dukt′) *n.* the tube through which the ovum, or egg, passes from the ovary. [< NL *oviductus* < L *ovum* egg + *ductus* duct]

o·vi·form (ō′və fôrm′) *adj.* egg-shaped. [< L *ovum* egg + E *-form*]

o·vine (ō′vīn *or* ō′vin) *adj.* of, like, or having to do with sheep. [< LL *ovinus* < *ovis* sheep]

o·vip·a·rous (ō vip′ə rəs) *adj.* producing eggs that are hatched after leaving the body. Birds are oviparous. Compare **viviparous.** [< L *oviparus* < *ovum* egg + *parere* bring forth]

o·vi·pos·i·tor (ō′və poz′ə tər) *n.* an organ at the end of the abdomen of certain insects, by which eggs are deposited. [< L *ovum* egg + *positor* placer < *ponere* place]

o·void (ō′void) *adj., n.* —*adj.* egg-shaped. —*n.* an egg-shaped object. [< L *ovum* egg]

o·vu·lar (ō′vyə lər) *adj.* of or being an ovule.

o·vu·la·tion (ō′vyə lā′shən) *n.* **1** the period when an ovum or female germ cell is produced or formed. **2** the discharge of ova from the ovary. [ult. < NL *ovulum*, dim. of *ovum* egg]

o·vule (ō′vyül) *n.* **1** a small ovum, especially one in an early stage of growth. **2** the part of a plant that develops into a seed. [< NL *ovulum*, dim. of L *ovum* egg]

o·vum (ō′vəm) *n., pl.* **o·va.** the mature female reproductive cell produced by the ovary of a plant or animal; a female gamete. A new plant or animal develops from a fertilized ovum. [< L *ovum* egg]

owe (ō) *v.* **owed, ow·ing. 1** have to pay; be in debt for: *I owe the grocer $10.* **2** be in debt: *He is always owing for something.* **3** be obliged or indebted for. **4** have or cherish toward another: *to owe a grudge.* **5** be obliged to give or offer: *We owe friends our trust.* [OE *āgan*] ☛ *Hom.* **o, oh.**

ow·ing (ō′ing) *adj.* due; owed: *to pay what is owing.*

owing to, on account of; because of; due to; as a result of: *The ball game was called off owing to rain.*

owl (oul) *n.* any of an order (Strigiformes) of birds of prey found throughout the world, having a very big head in proportion to the body, big eyes set in the front of the head, and a flexible neck which allows the head to be turned almost completely around to the back: *Most owls are active at night.* [OE *ūle*] —**owl′·like′,** *adj.*

owl·et (ou′lit) *n.* **1** a young owl. **2** a small owl.

owl·ish (ou′lish) *adj.* like or characteristic of an owl, especially in having large, unblinking eyes or a seemingly wise expression: *He gave me an owlish look.* —**owl′ish·ly,** *adv.*

own (ōn) *adj., v.* —*adj.* **1** of oneself or itself; belonging to oneself or itself: *We have our own troubles. The house is her own.* **2** in closest relationship: *Own brothers have the same parents.* —*n.* the one or ones belonging to oneself or itself.

come into (one's) **own, a** get what belongs to one. **b** get the success or credit that one deserves.

hold (one's) **own,** keep one's position; not be forced back.

of (one's) **own,** belonging to oneself.

on (one's) own, *Informal.* on one's own account, responsibility, resources, etc.
—*v.* **1** possess: *He owns much land.* **2** acknowledge; admit, confess: *He owned his guilt. She owns to many faults.* **3** acknowledge as one's own: *His father will not own him.*
own up (to), confess; admit: *The prisoner owned up to the crime.* [OE *āgen*, originally pp. of *āgan* owe]
☛ *Syn. v.* **1.** See note at **have.**

own·er (ōn′ər) *n.* one who owns: *the owner of the dog.*
—**own′er·less,** *adj.*

own·er·ship (ōn′ər ship′) *n.* the state of being an owner; the possessing (of something); right of possession.

ox (oks) *n., pl.* **ox·en. 1** a full-grown, castrated male of cattle, usually at least three or four years old. Oxen are used as draft animals or for beef. Compare **steer. 2** any of a tribe (Bovini) of bovid mammals that includes cattle, the yak, and buffalo; bovine. [OE *oxa*] —**ox′like′,** *adj.*

ox·a·late (ok′sə lāt′) *n.* a salt of oxalic acid.

ox·al·ic acid (oks al′ik) a poisonous organic acid that occurs in wood sorrel and various other plants. It is used for bleaching, removing stains, making dyes, etc. *Formula:* $C_2H_2O_4$ [< F < L *oxalis* sorrel² < Gk. *oxalis* < *oxys* sour]

ox·a·lis (ok′sə lis) *n.* wood sorrel. [< L < Gk. *oxalis* < *oxys* sour]

ox·blood (oks′blud′) *n.* a deep red.

ox·bow (oks′bō′) *n.* **1** a U-shaped frame of wood or iron that forms the lower part of a yoke for an ox. The oxbow fits under and around the neck of the ox, with the upper ends inserted in the bar of the yoke. See **yoke** for picture. **2** a U-shaped bend in a river. **3** the land contained within such a bend.

oxbow lake a small pond or lake which originally formed an oxbow but which became a separated body of water when the river straightened its course.

ox·cart (oks′kärt′) *n.* a cart drawn by an ox or oxen.

ox·en (ok′sən) *n.* pl. of **ox.**

ox·eyed (oks′īd′) *adj.* having large full eyes like those of an ox.

ox–eye daisy (ok′sī′) the common North American daisy (*Chrysanthemum leucanthemum*), having large flower heads composed of tiny yellow disk flowers surrounded by white ray flowers. The ox-eye daisy was introduced to North America from Europe and has become a common weed.

ox·ford (oks′fərd) *n.* a kind of low shoe, laced over the instep. See **shoe** for picture. [< *Oxford*, a city in S England]

Ox·ford blue dark, sometimes purplish, blue.

oxford cloth a cotton cloth with a soft finish, in a plain or basket weave, used especially for shirts.

Oxford grey a very dark grey.

Oxford Movement 1 a movement in the Church of England, favoring High-Church principles, which originated at Oxford University about 1833. **2** a modern religious movement that stresses public confession of one's faults and direct guidance by God.

ox·heart (oks′härt′) *n.* a large, heart-shaped variety of sweet cherry.

ox·i·da·tion (ok′sə dā′shən) *n.* **1** the act or process of oxidizing; the combining of oxygen with another element to form one or more new substances. Burning is one kind of oxidation. **2** the state or result of being oxidized.

ox·ide (ok′sīd *or* ok′sid) *n.* a compound of oxygen with another element or a radical. [< F *oxide* (now *oxyde*) < *ox*(*ygène*) oxygen + (*ac*)*ide* acid]

ox·i·dize (ok′sə dīz′) *v.* **-dized, -diz·ing. 1** combine with oxygen. When a substance burns or rusts, it is oxidized. **2** rust. **3** lose or cause to lose hydrogen. **4** change to a higher positive valence.
—**ox′i·diz′er,** *n.*

ox·lip (oks′lip′) *n.* a primrose (*Primula elatior*) of Europe and Asia having clusters of pale-yellow flowers. [OE *oxanslyppe* < *oxan* ox's + *slyppe* slime]

Oxon. 1 Oxford. **2** Oxonian. **3** Oxfordshire.

Ox·o·ni·an (oks ō′nē ən) *adj., n.* —*adj.* of or having to do with Oxford University or Oxford, England. —*n.* **1** a member or graduate of Oxford University. **2** a native or inhabitant of Oxford, England. [< Med.L *Oxonia* Oxford]

ox·tail (oks′tāl′) *n.* the tail of a cow, ox, or steer, skinned and cut up to make soup.

oxy–¹ *combining form.* **1** pointed, as in *oxymoron.* **2** acid, as in *oxygen.* [< Gk. *oxys* sharp, acid]

oxy–² *combining form.* **1** oxygen, or containing oxygen or one of its compounds, as in *oxygenated.* **2** a product of oxidation, as in *oxysulphide.* [< *oxygen*]

ox·y·a·cet·y·lene (ok′sē ə set′ə lēn′) *adj.* of, having to do with, or using a mixture of oxygen and acetylene.

oxyacetylene torch a tool with a very hot flame for welding or cutting metals. It uses a mixture of oxygen and acetylene.

ox·y·gen (ok′sə jən) *n.* a colorless, odorless, tasteless gas that forms one fifth of the air and is also combined in water and most mineral and organic substances. Oxygen is the most abundant of all elements and is essential to plant and animal life. *Symbol:* O; *at.no.* 8; *at.wt.* 16.00. [< F *oxygène,* intended as "acidifying (principle)" < Gk. *oxys* sharp + *-genēs* born]

ox·y·gen·ate (ok′sə jən āt′) *v.* **-at·ed, -at·ing.** treat, combine, or supply with oxygen: *to oxygenate the blood.* —**ox′y·gen·a′tion,** *n.*

ox·y·gen·ize (ok′sə jən īz′) *v.* **-ized, -iz·ing.** oxygenate. —**ox′y·gen·iz′a·ble,** *adj.*

oxygen mask a device worn over the nose and mouth through which oxygen is supplied from a storage tank. Oxygen masks are worn in unpressurized aircraft at high altitudes.

oxygen tent a small, clear plastic tent or canopy that can be placed over the head of a patient lying in bed and provided with a measured flow of oxygen.

ox·y·hy·dro·gen (ok′sē hī′drə jən) *adj.* of, having to do with, or using a mixture of oxygen and hydrogen.

oxyhydrogen torch a tool with a very hot flame for welding or cutting metals. It uses a mixture of oxygen and hydrogen.

ox·y·mor·on (ok′sē môr′on) *n., pl.* **-mor′a** (-môr′ə). a figure of speech in which contradictory words or connotations are placed together. *Example: Avoid accidents by making haste slowly.* [< Gk. *oxymōron,* neuter of *oxymōros* pointedly stupid, foolish < *oxys* sharp + *mōros* stupid]

ox·y·to·cin (ok′sə tō′son) *n.* a peptide hormone secreted by the pituitary gland, which in females causes the muscles of the uterus to contract during labor and also stimulates the release of milk from the breast of a nursing mother. *Formula:* $C_{43}H_{66}N_{12}O_{12}S_2$

O·yez *or* **O·yes** (ō′yes *or* ō′yez) *interj. or n.* Hear! Attend! A cry uttered, usually three times, by a public or court crier to command silence and attention before a proclamation, etc. is made. [ME < AF *oyez* hear ye! < *oyer* hear, var. of *oïr* < L *audire*]

oys·ter (ois′tər) *n.* **1** any of a family (Ostreidae) of bivalve molluscs having a rough, irregular shell; especially, any edible species of the genus *Ostrea.* **2** any of various other similar bivalve molluscs, such as the **pearl oysters** (family Aviculidae). **3** an oyster-shaped bit of dark meat in the hollow of the pelvic bone of a fowl. **4** *Informal.* a very uncommunicative person. **5** something from which to take or derive advantage. [ME < OF *oistre* < L < Gk. *ostreon*]

oyster bed a place where oysters breed or are cultivated.

oyster catcher any of a small genus (*Haematopus,* constituting the family Haematopodidae) of shore birds resembling plovers, having a long, stout, wedge-shaped, red bill, long, pointed wings, and black or black-and-white plumage.

oyster crab a small crab (*Pinnotheres ostreum*) that lives within the shell of a live oyster, but without harm to its host.

oyster cracker a small, round or hexagonal, salted cracker eaten with oysters, soups, etc.

oyster farm a place where oysters are raised for the market.

oyster plant salsify, a plant.

oz. ounce(s).

o·zone (ō′zōn) *n.* **1** a form of oxygen consisting of molecules composed of three atoms instead of the usual two, produced by electricity and present in the air, especially after a thunderstorm. *Formula:* O_3 **2** *Informal.* pure air that is refreshing. [< F *ozone* < Gk. *ozein* smell + F *-one,* chemical suffix]

o·zo·nic (ō zō′nik *or* ō zon′ik) *adj.* ozoniferous.

o·zo·nif·er·ous (ō′zə nif′ər əs) *adj.* of, having to do with, or containing ozone.

o·zo·no·sphere (ō zō′nə sfēr′) *n.* a region of the upper stratosphere containing a relatively high concentration of ozone that protects earth from excessive ultraviolet radiation from the sun.

P p

p or **P** (pē) *n., pl.* **p's** or **P's. 1** the sixteenth letter of the English alphabet. **2** any speech sound represented by this letter. **3** a person or thing identified as *p*, especially the sixteenth in a series. **4** something shaped like the letter P. **5** (*adj.*) of or being a P or p.
mind (one's) p's and q's, be careful about what one says or does.

p 1 *Music.* piano. **2** *Baseball.* pitcher. **3** *Brit.* penny; pence. **4** *p*, pressure. **5** pico- (an SI prefix).

p. 1 page. **2** participle. **3** part. **4** past. **5** *Baseball.* pitcher. **6** peso. **7** peseta. **8** pint. **9** population. **10** *Brit.* penny; pence.

P 1 phosphorus. **2** *Chess.* pawn. **3** *P,* power.

P. 1 pastor. **2** president. **3** priest. **4** prince. **5** Father (for F *père*; L *pater*).

P1 petty officer 1st class.

P2 petty officer 2nd class.

pa (po *or* pä) *n. Informal.* papa; father.

p.a. 1 participial adjective. **2** per annum.

Pa protactinium.

Pa. Pennsylvania.

PA Pennsylvania.

P.A. 1 public address (system). **2** press agent. **3** power of attorney. **4** private account. **5** purchasing agent.

PABA para-aminobenzoic acid.

pab·u·lum (pab'yə ləm) *n.* **1** food. **2** intellectual or spiritual nourishment; food for the mind. [< L *pabulum* fodder]

Pac. Pacific.

pace¹ (pās) *n., v.* **paced, pac·ing.** —*n.* **1** rate of movement; speed: *a fast pace in walking.* **2** a step. **3** the length of a step in walking, used as a unit for measuring length or distance; about 76 cm. **4** a way of stepping. The walk, trot, and canter are some of the paces of a horse. **5** a particular pace of some horses in which both legs on one side are raised at the same time.
keep pace with, keep up with; go as fast as.
put (someone) through (his) paces, try one out; find out what one can do.
set the pace, a set speed for others to keep up with. **b** be an example or model for others to follow.
—*v.* **1** set the pace for: *A motorboat will pace the boys training for the rowing match.* **2** walk over with regular steps: *to pace the floor.* **3** walk with regular steps. **4** measure by paces: *We paced off the distance.* **5** train (a horse) to a certain step, especially to lift and put down the feet on the same side together. **6** of a horse, move at a pace. [ME < OF < L *passus* step]

pa·ce² (pā'sē *or* pä'che) *prep.* with due respect to (used to refer politely to someone with whom the speaker or writer disagrees). [< L *pax* peace. 19c.]

pace·mak·er (pās'māk'ər) *n.* **1** a person or thing that sets the pace for another, as in a race. **2** a node of specialized tissue near the top of the wall of the right auricle of the heart where the impulse that results in the heartbeat begins. **3** an electrical device for steadying or stimulating the heartbeat in cases where the natural pacemaker does not function properly.

pac·er (pās'ər) *n.* **1** a person or thing that paces, especially a horse that normally runs by raising both legs on the same side at the same time. **2** pacemaker.

pace·set·ter (pās'set'ər) *n.* a person who leads the way or serves as a model for others in fashion, ideas, etc.

pa·cha (pə shä', pash'ə, *or* pä'shə) *n.* pasha.

pa·chi·si (pə chē'zē) *n.* parcheesi.

pach·y·derm (pak'ə dèrm') *n.* **1** any of several large, thick-skinned, hoofed mammals, such as the elephant, hippopotamus, or rhinoceros, that were formerly classified together. **2** a thick-skinned person; one who is not sensitive to criticism or ridicule. [< F < Gk. *pachydermos* < *pachys* thick + *derma* skin]

pa·cif·ic (pə sif'ik) *adj.* **1** tending to make peace; making peace. **2** loving peace; not warlike: *a pacific nation.* **3** peaceful; calm; quiet: *a pacific nature.* **4 Pacific, a** of or having to do with the Pacific Ocean, the great ocean west of North and South America. **b** on, in, over, or near the Pacific Ocean: *a Pacific storm.* [< L

pacificus, ult. < *pax, pacis* peace + *facere* make] —**pa·cif'i·cal·ly,** *adv.*

pac·i·fi·ca·tion (pas'ə fə kā'shən) *n.* pacifying or being pacified.

pa·cif·i·ca·to·ry (pə sif'ə kə tô'rē) *adj.* tending to make peace; conciliatory.

Pacific salmon any of a small genus (*Oncorhynchus*) of important food and game fishes of the salmon and trout family, found in the Pacific Ocean. The five species of Pacific salmon found along the North American coast are sockeye, chum, coho, pink, and spring.

pac·i·fi·er (pas'ə fī'ər) *n.* **1** a person or thing that pacifies. **2** a rubber nipple or ring given to a baby to suck.

pac·i·fism (pas'ə fiz'əm) *n.* the principle or policy of opposing war or violence as a means of settling disputes; the refusal to take up arms or to resist violence by force.

pac·i·fist (pas'ə fist) *adj., n.* —*adj.* of or having to do with pacifism or pacifists. —*n.* a person who is strongly opposed to conflict, especially war.

pac·i·fis·tic (pas'ə fis'tik) *adj.* pacifist.

pac·i·fy (pas'ə fī') *v.* **-fied, -fy·ing. 1** make calm; quiet down: *Can't you pacify that screaming baby?* **2** bring order to; make submissive: *Soldiers were sent to pacify the country.* [< L *pacificare* < *pax, pacis* peace + *facere* make]
➤ *Syn.* **1.** See note at **appease.**

pack¹ (pak) *n., v.* —*n.* **1** a bundle of things wrapped up or tied together for carrying. **2** the amount packed: *This year's pack of fish is larger than last year's.* **3** a set; lot; a number of things together: *a pack of thieves, a pack of nonsense, a pack of lies.* **4** a group of dogs, etc. trained to run and hunt together. **5** a number of wild animals running or hunting together: *a pack of wolves.* **6** a complete set of playing cards, usually 52. **7** a large area of floating pieces of ice pushed together; ice pack: *A ship forced its way through the pack.* **8** something put on the body or skin as a treatment. A cloth soaked in hot or cold water is often used as a pack. **9** a company or troop of Wolf Cubs or Brownies.
—*v.* **1** put together in a bundle, box, bale, etc.: *Pack your clothes in this bag.* **2** put things together in a bundle, box, bale, etc.: *Are you ready to pack?* **3** fill with things; put one's things into: *Pack your trunk.* **4** fit together closely; admit of storing and shipping: *These goods pack well.* **5** press or crowd closely together: *A hundred men were packed into one small room.* **6** press together; make firm: *The heavy trucks packed the snow on the highway.* **7** fill (a space) with all that it will hold: *to pack a small theatre with a large audience.* **8** become packed; crowd together. **9** become relatively compact: *Some mud will pack easily to make bricks.* **10** put into a container to be sold or stored: *Meat, fish, and vegetables are often packed in cans.* **11** make tight with something that water, steam, air, etc. cannot leak through. **12** load (an animal) with a pack; burden. **13** *Informal.* carry: *to pack a gun.* **14** carry in a pack: *He packed his supplies into the bush.* **15** cover, surround, or protect with closely applied materials: *The fish was packed in ice.* **16** treat with a therapeutic pack: *to pack the gum after a tooth extraction.* **17** *Informal.* have as a power or capacity: *That guy packs quite a punch.*
pack off, send away: *The child was packed off to bed.*
pack up, *Informal.* **a** stop working; cease operating; fail: *One of the aircraft's engines packed up.* **b** die.
send packing, send away abruptly.
[ME < MLG *packe*]

pack² (pak) *v.* arrange unfairly. To pack a jury or a convention is to fill it unfairly with those who will favor one side. [? akin to PACT; partly associated with *pack¹*]

pack·age (pak'ij) *n., v.* **-aged, -ag·ing.** —*n.* **1** a bundle of things packed or wrapped together; a box with things packed in it; parcel. **2 a** a box, can, bottle, jar, case, or other receptacle for packing goods, especially one designed for a particular commodity and printed with matter intended both to identify it and to attract buyers. **b** such a package with its contents, as offered for sale. **3** a group of related items or elements, such as goods, services, laws, articles of agreement in a negotiation, etc., offered, provided, sold, accepted, or rejected as a unit, often as an indivisible unit: *Our Montreal package includes transportation, hotel, and meals for a week.*

—v. **1** put in a package. **2** make a package or packages out of: *to wrap and package Christmas presents.* —**pack′ag·er,** n.

package deal a bargain, sale, or business deal in which a number of items are presented as a single offer.

pack·ag·ing (pak′əj ing) n. **1** the design and manufacture of packages. **2** the process of putting goods into such packages. **3** such packages collectively.

pack animal an animal used for carrying loads or packs.

pack–board (pak′bôrd′) n. a light wooden or metal frame, covered usually with canvas and strapped to the back for carrying heavy loads.

pack·er (pak′ər) n. a person or thing that packs, especially: **a** a person or company whose business is packing meat, fruit, vegetables, etc. to be sold at wholesale: *a meat packer.* **b** a person or machine that puts things in containers for storage, preservation, or sale.

pack·et (pak′it) n. **1** a small package; parcel. **2** packet boat. [< AF *pacquet,* dim. of ME *pakke* back]

packet boat a boat that carries mail, passengers, and goods regularly on a fixed route, usually along a river or the coast.

pack horse a horse used to carry packs of goods.

pack ice ice pushed by wind or current into a solid mass.

pack·ing (pak′ing) n. **1** material used to pack or to make watertight, steamtight, etc.: *the packing around the valves of a radiator.* **2** the business of preparing and packing meat, fish, fruit, vegetables, etc. to be sold.

packing house a place where meat, fruit, vegetables, etc. are prepared and packed to be sold.

pack mule a mule used for carrying loads.

pack rat 1 wood rat; especially, a large, bushy-tailed species (*Neotoma cinerea*) found especially in the Rocky Mountains, well known for picking up and hoarding objects of various kinds. **2** a person who has a tendency to hoard objects, especially useless ones.

pack·sack (pak′sak′) n. a bag of canvas or leather for carrying gear, clothing, etc. when travelling on foot, usually worn strapped to the back; knapsack.

pack·sad·dle (pak′sad′əl) n. a saddle specially adapted for supporting the load on a pack animal.

Pack Scouter an adult responsible for the operation of a pack of Wolf Cubs or Brownies.

pack strap tumpline.

pack·thread (pak′thred′) n. a strong thread or twine for sewing or tying up packages.

pack train a line or group of animals carrying loads.

pack·y (pak′ē) adj. of snow, of such consistency that it packs and binds together easily.

pact (pakt) n. an agreement; compact: *The two nations signed a peace pact.* [< L *pactum,* originally, pp. of *pacisci* covenant]

pad¹ (pad) n., v. **pad·ded, pad·ding.** —n. **1** something soft used for comfort, protection, or stuffing; cushion. **2** a soft, stuffed saddle. **3** one of the cushionlike parts on the bottom side of the feet of dogs, foxes, and some other animals. **4** the foot of such animals. **5** a large floating leaf of a water lily or similar water plant. **6** a number of sheets of paper fastened along an edge or edges; tablet: *a writing pad.* **7** a cloth soaked with ink to use with a rubber stamp; stamp pad. **8** the launching platform for a rocket or missile; launching pad: *The man-made satellite rose from the pad at midnight.* **9** *Slang.* a place where a person sleeps, such as a bed, a room, an apartment, etc.
—v. **1** fill with something soft; stuff. **2** make (a written paper or speech) longer by using unnecessary words just to fill space: *Don't pad your compositions.* **3** increase the amount of (a bill, expense account, etc.) by false entries. [origin uncertain]

pad² (pad) v. **pad·ded, -pad·ding;** n. —v. **1** walk; tramp; trudge. **2** walk or trot softly, with a muffled sound: *a wolf padding through the bush.* —n. **1** a dull or muffled sound, as of footsteps on the ground: *We heard the pad of hoofs on the path.* **2** a slow horse for riding on a road. [< Du. or LG. Akin to PATH.]

pad·ded cell (pad′id) in a mental institution, a room having padded walls to prevent a violent patient from injuring himself.

pad·ding (pad′ing) n. **1** material to pad with, such as foam rubber, cotton or synthetic fibre, or straw. **2** unnecessary words used to make a speech or a written paper longer.

pad·dle¹ (pad′əl) n., v. **-dled, -dling.** —n. **1** a short oar with a broad blade at one end or both ends, used without resting it against the boat. **2** the act of paddling; a turn at the paddle. **3** one of the

broad boards fixed around a water wheel or a paddle wheel to push, or be pushed by, the water. **4** a paddle-shaped piece of wood used for stirring, for mixing, for beating clothes, etc.
—v. **1** move (a boat or canoe) with a paddle or paddles. **2** use a paddle to move a canoe, etc. **3** row gently. **4** *Informal.* beat with a paddle or something similar; spank. [origin uncertain] —**pad′dler,** n.

pad·dle² (pad′əl) v. **-dled, -dling. 1** move the hands or feet about in water. **2** wade barefoot in water: *Children love to paddle at the beach.* [apparently < *pad²*] —**pad′dler,** n.

pad·dle·fish (pad′əl fish′) n., pl. **-fish** or **-fish·es.** either of two large freshwater fishes, *Polyodon spathula* of the Mississippi River valley and *Psephurus gladius* of the Yangtze River valley, comprising the family Polyodontidae. Both species have a smooth, scaleless body and a very long, flat snout resembling a spatula.

paddle wheel a wheel having an arrangement of paddles around its rim, used for propelling a boat.

pad·dle·wheel·er (pad′əl wēl′ər or -hwēl′ər) n. a boat propelled by means of one or more paddle wheels.

pad·dock (pad′ək) n. **1** a small field near a stable or house, used for exercising animals or as a pasture. **2** an enclosure at a race track for saddling and displaying horses before they race. [var. of *parrock,* OE *pearroc* enclosed space, fence < Med.L *parricus* enclosure. Doublet of PARK.]

pad·dy (pad′ē) n., pl. **-dies. 1** rice, especially before threshing or in the husk. **2** a field of rice. [< Malay *padi*]

Pad·dy (pad′ē) n., pl. **-dies.** a nickname for an Irishman.

paddy wagon *Slang.* patrol wagon.

A hasp with a padlock

pad·lock (pad′lok′) n., v. —n. a removable lock having a hinged bar that is passed through a loop or eye in the door, box, etc. to be locked and snapped shut. —v. fasten with such a lock.

pa·dre (pä′drā) n. **1** father. It is used as a name for a priest. **2** a chaplain in the armed forces. **3** a chaplain at certain universities. [< Ital., Sp., Pg. < L *pater* father]

pae·an (pē′ən) n. a song of praise, joy, or triumph. Also, **pean.** [< L < Gk. *paian* hymn to Apollo (called *Paian*)]

paed·er·ast (ped′ər ast′) See pederast.

paed·er·as·ty (ped′ər as′tē) See pederasty.

pae·do·log·y (pə dol′ə jē) See pedology¹.

pa·gan (pā′gən) n., adj. —n. **1** a person who is not a Christian, Jew, or Moslem; heathen. The ancient Greeks and Romans were pagans. **2** a person who has no religion. —adj. **1** of or having to do with the pagans: *pagan customs.* **2** not religious. [< L *paganus* rustic (at a time when Christianity was accepted by the urban population), in LL, heathen < *pagus* village]
☛ *Syn.* n. **1.** See note at **heathen.**
☛ *Usage.* See note at **heathen.**

pa·gan·dom (pā′gən dəm) n. the pagan world; pagans collectively.

pa·gan·ism (pā′gən iz′əm) n. **1** pagan beliefs and practices. **2** a pagan religion. **3** the quality or state of being a pagan.

page¹ (pāj) n., v. **paged, pag·ing.** —n. **1** one side of a leaf or sheet of paper: *The book has 350 pages.* **2** a leaf or sheet of paper, especially in a book, magazine, etc.: *The page was torn. Write on only one side of the page.* **3** what is printed, written, or pictured on one side of a leaf: *This page is hard to read.* **4** a written record: *the pages of history.* **5** an event or period worth recording: *a glorious page in the history of the country.*
—v. number the pages of: *Make sure you page your essay.* [< F < L *pagina* < *pangere* fasten]

page² (pāj) n., v. **paged, pag·ing.** —n. **1** a servant, often a boy, who runs errands, carries hand luggage, etc. for guests at hotels, etc. **2** a young person employed to carry messages, books, etc. for members of the House of Commons, the Senate, or a legislative assembly. **3** a young man who attends a person of rank. **4** *Historical.* a young man preparing to be a knight.
—v. **1** try to get a message to a person by means of an announcement, either by a page or on a public-address system. **2** act as a page to. [ME < OF < Ital. *paggio,* ult. < Gk. *paidion* lad, dim. of *pais, paidos* child]

pag·eant (paj′ənt) n. **1** an elaborate spectacle; procession in costume; pomp; display: *The coronation of the new king was a*

splendid pageant. **2** a public entertainment that represents scenes from history, legend, or the like. **3** empty show, not reality. [ME *pagent, pagen* < Med.L *pagina* movable scaffold fixed with planks, serving as a stage < L *pangere* fix]

pag·eant·ry (paj′ənt rē) *n., pl.* **-ries. 1** a splendid show; gorgeous display; pomp. **2** mere show; empty display.

page-boy (pāj′boi′) *n.* a hairstyle in which the hair, usually about shoulder length, is curled smoothly under at the ends.

page-boy (pāj′boi′) *n.* a boy serving as a page.

pag·i·na·tion (paj′ə nā′shən) *n.* **1** the act of numbering the pages of books, etc. **2** the figures with which pages are numbered. **3** the number of pages in a book, etc.

A pagoda in the Chinese style of architecture

pa·go·da (pə gō′də) *n.* a temple having many storeys, with a roof curving upward from each storey. Pagodas are found especially in India and the Far East. [< Pg. *pagode* < Tamil *pagavadi* < Skt. *bhagavati* of a goddess < *bhagavat* a deity]

paid (pād) *adj., v.* —*adj.* **1** receiving money; hired. **2** no longer owed; settled. **3** cashed.
—*v.* pt. and pp. of **pay**[1].
☞ *Usage.* **Paid, payed. Paid** is the spelling of the past tense and past participle of *pay*[1] (He *paid* his bills) in all senses except "let out" (They *payed* out the rope), and occasionally in that sense also.

pail (pāl) *n.* **1** a fairly large, usually round container for carrying liquids, having a wide top and a handle that is attached at each side and arches over the top. **2** the amount a pail holds. **3** a pail and its contents. [OE *pægel* < OF *paielle*, both < Med.L *pagella* a measure, dim. of L *pagina*, originally, something fixed]
☞ *Hom.* **pale.**

pail·ful (pāl′ful) *n., pl.* **-fuls.** the amount that fills a pail.

pail·lasse (pal′ē as′ *or* pal′yas) *n.* a mattress filled with straw. [< F *paillasse* < *paille* straw < L *palea*]

pain (pān) *n., v.* —*n.* **1** an unpleasant sensation in the body or a particular part of it, due to some stimulus of the nerve endings from injury, disorder, or disease: *A cut usually causes pain. He felt a sharp pain in his back.* **2** mental suffering; grief: *The memory still gave her pain.* **3 pains,** *pl.* **a** care; effort; trouble to do something: *He said he would not interfere, because he would get nothing but trouble for his pains.* **b** the throes of childbirth; spasms of labor: *The pains had started.* **4** *Obsolete* (*except in* **on** *or* **under pain of**). punishment; penalty.
be at pains, make a conscientious effort: *She was at great pains to make them understand.*
on *or* **under pain of,** subject to the penalty of (if a given command is not fulfilled): *He was ordered never to return on pain of death.*
pain in the neck, *Slang.* a very troublesome or irritating thing or person.
take pains, be careful: *She took pains to do a good job.*
—*v.* cause to suffer; give rise to pain; ache: *His tooth was paining him a great deal.* [ME < OF *peine* < L *poena* penalty < Gk. *poinē*]
☞ *Hom.* **pane.**
☞ *Syn. n.* **Pain, ache** = a feeling of being hurt, bodily or mentally. **Pain** particularly suggests a sharp hurt of any degree from a sudden jab in one spot to a very severe and sometimes long-lasting hurt of the whole body, or, figuratively, a sorrow that causes severe mental suffering: *I have a pain in my side.* **Ache** means a steady, usually dull hurt, and, when used figuratively, suggests longing for something: *I have an earache.*

pained (pānd) *adj.* **1** distressed, grieved, mentally hurt, etc. **2** showing pain: *a pained face.*

pain·ful (pān′fəl) *adj.* **1** causing pain; unpleasant; hurting: *a painful illness, a painful duty.* **2** difficult. —**pain′ful·ly,** *adv.* —**pain′ful·ness,** *n.*

pain·kill·er (pān′kil′ər) *n.* anything, especially a drug, that relieves pain.

pain·less (pān′lis) *adj.* causing or producing no pain: *The treatment is painless.* —**pain′less·ly,** *adv.* —**pain′less·ness,** *n.*

pains·tak·ing (pānz′tāk′ing) *adj.* very careful.
—**pains′tak·ing·ly,** *adv.*

paint (pānt) *n., v.* —*n.* **1 a** a mixture of a solid coloring matter and

hat, āge, fär; let, ēqual, tèrm; it, īce
hot, ōpen, ôrder; oil, out; cup, pút, rüle,
above, takən, pencəl, lemən, circəs

ch, child; ng, long; sh, ship
th, thin; ŦH, then; zh, measure

liquid that can be put on a surface to dry as a colored coating. **b** the solid coloring matter alone; pigment: *a box of paints.* **2** any cosmetic that colors or tints.
—*v.* **1** cover or decorate with paint: *to paint a house.* **2** use paint. **3** represent (an object, etc.) in colors. **4** make pictures: *She spends her weekends painting.* **5** picture vividly in words. **6** put on like paint: *The doctor painted iodine on the cut.* **7** use cosmetics to color or tint.
paint black, represent as evil or wicked: *not so black as he is painted.*
[ME < OF *peint,* pp. of *peindre* paint < L *pingere*]

paint·brush (pānt′brush′) *n.* **1** a brush for applying paint. **2** Indian paintbrush.

paint·er[1] (pān′tər) *n.* **1** a person who paints pictures; artist. **2** a person who paints houses, woodwork, etc. [< OF *peintour,* ult. < L *pictor* < *pingere* to paint]

paint·er[2] (pān′tər) *n.* a rope, usually fastened to the bow of a boat, for tying it to a ship, pier, etc. [probably < OF *pentoir* hanging cordage, ult. < L *pendere* hang]

paint·er·ly (pān′tər lē) *adj.* **1** of, having to do with, or characteristic of a painter. **2** of or designating a style of painting that emphasizes the qualities peculiar to the medium of paint, such as texture or masses of color, as opposed to linear elements.

paint·ing (pān′ting) *n.* **1** the art or occupation of using paints to create pictures or other artistic compositions. **2** a work produced by the art of painting. **3** the act or process of applying paint to a surface.

pair (per) *n., pl.* **pairs** or (*sometimes after a numeral*) **pair;** *v.* —*n.* **1** a set of two; two that go together: *a pair of shoes, a pair of horses.* **2** a single thing consisting of two parts that cannot be used separately: *a pair of scissors, a pair of trousers.* **3** two people who are married or are engaged to be married. **4** two partners in a dance. **5** two animals that are mated. **6** *Card games.* **a** two cards of the same value in different suits, viewed as a unit in one's hand: *a pair of sixes, jacks, etc.* **b** in games using a multiple deck, two identical cards. **7** in a legislative body: **a** two members on opposite sides who arrange not to vote on a certain question. **b** the arrangement thus made.
—*v.* **1** arrange or be arranged in pairs. **2** join in marriage. **3** of animals, mate. **4** in a legislative body, form or cause to form a voting pair.
pair off or **up,** arrange or form into pairs: *The guests paired off for the first dance.*
[< F *paire* < L *paria,* neut. pl., equals]
☞ *Hom.* **pare, pear.**
☞ *Syn. n.* **1. Pair, couple** = two of the same kind. **Pair** applies to two things that belong together—because they go together to make a set, because they are used together and each is needed to make the other useful, or because they are so well matched they seem to belong together: *I bought a new pair of gloves.* **Couple** applies to any two of the same kind: *I bought a couple of shirts.*
☞ *Usage.* **Pair.** In informal usage the plural of **pair** is sometimes **pair** when it comes after a number: *six pair of socks.* Some people now consider this usage substandard.
☞ *Usage.* When a **pair** is thought of as a unit, it takes a singular verb: *This pair of shoes is getting old.* When a **pair** is thought of as referring to two individual items, it takes a plural verb: *The pair of vases were both chipped.*

pai·sa (pī′sä) *n., pl.* **pai·se.** (pī′sä′) in India, **pai·sas** in Pakistan. **1** a unit of money in India and Pakistan, equal to ¹⁄₁₀₀ of a rupee. **2** a coin worth one paisa. [< Hind.]

pais·ley (pāz′lē) *n., pl.* **-leys;** *adj.* —*n.* **1** an elaborate, colorful fabric design of curving lines and figures: *silk paisley.* **2** something made of this fabric having such a design. —*adj.* made of fabric having a paisley design; having a design like paisley. [< *Paisley,* a city in Scotland, where woollen shawls having this design were first made]

pa·ja·mas (pə jam′əz *or* pə jä′məz) See **pyjamas.**

Pak·i·stan·i (pak′i stan′ē) *n., adj.* —*n.* a native or inhabitant of Pakistan, a country in S Asia. —*adj.* of or having to do with Pakistan or its people.

pal (pal) *n., v.* **palled, pal·ling.** *Informal.* —*n.* a comrade; mate; partner; chum; accomplice. —*v.* associate as pals. [< Romany *pal* brother, var. of *phral* or *plal,* ult. < Skt. *bhratr* brother]

pal·ace (pal′is) *n.* **1** the official home of a king, queen, bishop, or some other important person. **2** a very fine house or building. **3** a gaudy or pretentious place of entertainment: *an old movie palace.*

[ME < OF *palais* < L *Palatium* Palatine Hill, the site of the Roman emperor's palace]
☛ *Hom.* **Pallas.**

pal·a·din (pal′ə din) *n.* **1** one of the twelve knights in attendance on Charlemagne. **2** a knightly defender. [< F < Ital. *paladino*]

palaeo– See **paleo–**.

pa·laes·tra (pə les′trə) *n.* **1** in ancient Greece, a public place for physical exercise and training. **2** a wrestling school. [< L < Gk. *palaistra* < *palaiein* wrestle]

pal·an·quin or **pal·an·keen** (pal′ən kēn′) *n.* a covered couch, or litter, for one person, carried by means of poles resting on the shoulders of four or six men. They were formerly used in E Asia. [< Pg. *palanquim*; cf. Skt. *palyanka* couch]

pal·at·a·ble (pal′ə tə bəl) *adj.* agreeable to the taste; pleasing. —**pal′at·a·bly,** *adv.*

pal·a·tal (pal′ə təl) *adj., n.* —*adj.* **1** of or having to do with the palate. **2** *Phonetics.* designating a sound made with the tongue near or in contact with the hard palate. The (y) in *yet* is palatal. —*n.* *Phonetics.* a palatal sound. [< F < L *palatum* palate]

pal·a·tal·ize (pal′ə təl īz′) *v.* **-ized,** **-iz·ing.** change into or pronounce as a palatal sound. —**pal′a·tal·i·za′tion,** *n.*

pal·ate (pal′it) *n.* **1** the roof of the mouth. The bony part in front is the **hard palate;** the fleshy part at the back is the **soft palate. 2** the sense of taste: *The new flavor pleased his palate.* **3** a liking. [< L *palatum*]
☛ *Hom.* **palette, pallet.**

pa·la·tial (pə lā′shəl) *adj.* like or fit for a palace; magnificent: *a palatial apartment.* [< L *palatium* palace] —**pa·la′tial·ly,** *adv.*

pa·lat·i·nate (pə lat′ə nāt′ or pə lat′ə nit) *n.* a territory under the rule of a count palatine. See **palatine** (def. 1).

pal·a·tine (pal′ə tīn′ or pal′ə tin) *adj., n.* —*adj.* **1** having royal rights in his own territory. A count palatine was subject only to the emperor or king. **2** of a lord who has royal rights in his own territory. **3** palatial. **4 Palatine,** of the Palatinate, a region in West Germany, west of the Rhine.
—*n.* **1** a lord having royal rights in his own territory. **2 Palatine,** a native or inhabitant of the Palatinate. **3 Palatine,** the Palatine Hill. [< L *palatinus,* adj., < *palatium* palace]

Palatine Hill one of the seven hills on which the city of Rome was built.

pa·lav·er (pə lav′ər or pə lä′vər) *n., v.* —*n.* **1** a parley or conference, especially (in historical use) between European travellers or explorers and African natives. **2** empty or idle talk. **3** smooth, persuading talk; fluent talk; flattery.
—*v.* **1** talk. **2** talk fluently or flatteringly. [< Pg. *palavra* < *parabola* story, parable. Doublet of PARABLE, PAROLE.]

pa·laz·zo (pä lät′sō) *n., pl.* **pa·laz·zi** (-sē). *Italian.* a palace or mansion.

pale¹ (pāl) *adj.* **pal·er, pal·est;** *v.* **paled, pal·ing.** —*adj.* **1** without much color; whitish: *His face is still pale after his illness.* **2** not intense or bright; faint or dim: *pale blue. The streetlight gave a pale light in the fog.* **3** lacking vigor; feeble: *a pale foreign policy.*
—*v.* turn or cause to turn pale: *Helen's face paled at the bad news.* [ME < OF < L *pallidus* < *pallere* be pale. Doublet of PALLID.] —**pale′ly,** *adv.* —**pale′ness,** *n.*
☛ *Hom.* **pail.**

☛ *Syn. adj.* **1. Pale, pallid, wan** = with little or no color. **Pale,** describing the face of a person, means "without much natural or healthy color," and describing things, "without much brilliance or depth": *She is pale and tired-looking. The walls are pale green.* **Pallid,** chiefly describing the face, suggests having all color drained away as by sickness or weakness: *Her pallid face shows her suffering.* **Wan** emphasizes the idea of a faintness and whiteness coming from a weakened or unhealthy condition: *The starved refugees looked wan.*

pale² *n., v.* **paled, pal·ing.** —*n.* **1** a long, narrow board pointed at the top, used for fences; picket. **2** enclosure. **3** a territory with fixed bounds, under a particular jurisdiction or subject to particular restrictions. **4** a boundary; the limits within which one has a right to protection: *Murder is an act outside the pale of society.* **5** *Heraldry.* a broad vertical stripe in the middle of an escutcheon.
—*v.* enclose with pales. [ME < OF *pal* < L *palus.* Doublet of POLE¹.]
☛ *Hom.* **pail.**

pale– *combining form.* the form of **paleo–** usually used before vowels, as in *paleontology.*
☛ *Hom.* **pail.**

pale·face (pāl′fās′) *n.* a white person. The North American Indians are said to have called white people palefaces.

paleo– *combining form.* **1** old; ancient: *paleography = ancient writing.* **2** of a relatively early time division: *Paleocene = the*

earliest epoch of the Tertiary period. [< Gk. *palaio-* < *palaios* ancient]

Pa·le·o·cene (pā′lē ə sēn′ or pal′ē ə-) *n., adj.* *Geology.* —*n.* the oldest epoch of the Tertiary period, before the Eocene. See chart at **geology.** —*adj.* of or having to do with this epoch, its strata, etc. [< *paleo-* + Gk. *kainos* new]

pa·le·og·ra·pher (pā′lē og′rə fər or pal′ē og′rə fər) *n.* a person trained in paleography, especially one whose work it is.

pa·le·o·graph·ic (pā′lē ə graf′ik or pal′ē ə-) *adj.* of or having to do with paleography.

pa·le·og·ra·phy (pā′lē og′rə fē or pal′ē og′rə fē) *n.* **1** ancient writing or ancient forms of writing. **2** the study of ancient writings to determine their dates, origins, meaning, etc. [< Gk. *palaios* ancient + E *-graphy*]

pa·le·o·lith·ic (pā′lē ə lith′ik or pal′ē ə-) *adj.* of or having to do with the earlier part of the Stone Age. [< Gk. *palaios* ancient + *lithos* stone]

pa·le·on·tol·o·gist (pā′lē on tol′ə jist or pal′ē on tol′ə jist) *n.* a person trained in paleontology, especially one whose work it is.

pa·le·on·tol·o·gy (pā′lē on tol′ə jē or pal′ē on tol′ə jē) *n.* the science that deals with the forms of life existing long ago in other geological periods, as known from fossil remains of animals and plants. [< Gk. *palaios* ancient + *ōn, ontos* being + E *-logy*]

Pa·le·o·zo·ic (pā′lē ə zō′ik or pal′ē ə-) *adj., n.* *Geology.* —*adj.* **1** of, having to do with, or designating the era before the Mesozoic era, beginning about 600 million years ago. The Paleozoic era is the age of fishes. **2** of, having to do with, or designating the system of rocks formed during this era. —*n.* the Paleozoic era or its rock system. [< Gk. *palaios* ancient + *zōē* life]

pal·ette (pal′it) *n.* **1** a thin board, usually oval or oblong, with a thumb hole at one end, used by painters to lay and mix colors on. **2** a set of colors on this board. **3** the range or quality of color used by an artist: *He uses a bright palette.* [< F *palette* < L *pala* spade]
☛ *Hom.* **palate, pallet.**

palette knife a tool used by artists for mixing colors on a palette, etc. and, often, instead of a brush for applying paint, consisting of a thin, flexible, more or less blunt-tipped steel blade set into a handle.

pal·frey (pol′frē or pôl′frē) *n., pl.* **-freys.** *Archaic or poetic.* a gentle riding horse, especially one used by ladies. [ME < OF *palefrey* < LL *paraveredus* < Gk. *para-* beside + L *veredus* light horse < Celtic]

pal·imp·sest (pal′imp sest′) *n.* a piece of parchment or other writing material from which one writing has been erased to make room for another; a manuscript with one text written over another. [< L < Gk. *palimpsestos* scraped again, ult. < *palin* again + *psaein* rub smooth]

pal·in·drome (pal′in drōm′) *n.* a word, phrase, or sentence which reads the same backward as forward. The sentence *Madam, I'm Adam* is a palindrome. [< Gk. *palindromos* a running back < *palin* again, back + *dromos* a running, related to *dramein* run]

pal·ing (pāl′ing) *n.* **1** a fence of pales. **2** pales collectively, as fencing material. **3** a pale in a fence.

pal·i·sade (pal′ə sād′) *n., v.* **-sad·ed, -sad·ing.** —*n.* **1** a high fence of heavy, pointed wooden stakes set firmly in the ground, built especially for defence. **2** one of the stakes used in such a fence. **3** Usually, **palisades,** *pl.* a line of high, steep cliffs.
—*v.* furnish or surround with a palisade. [< F *palissade* < Provençal *palissada* < L *palus* stake]

pal·ish (pā′lish) *adj.* somewhat pale.

pall¹ (pol or pôl) *n.* **1** a heavy cloth, often made of velvet, spread over a coffin, a hearse, or a tomb. **2** a dark, gloomy covering: *A pall of smoke shut out the sun from the city.* [OE *pæll* < L *pallium* cloak]

pall² (pol or pôl) *v.* **1** become distasteful or very tiresome because there has been too much of it. **2** cloy. [var. of *appall*]

Pal·la·di·an (pə lā′dē ən) *adj.* of, having to do with, or based on the classical Roman style of architecture as modified by the Italian architect Andrea Palladio (1518-1580).

pal·la·di·um¹ (pə lā′dē əm) *n.* a rare, silver-white metallic chemical element, harder than platinum. *Symbol:* Pd; *at.no.* 46; *at.wt.* 106.40. [< NL; after the asteroid *Pallas*]

pal·la·di·um² (pə lā′dē əm) *n., pl.* **-di·a** (-dē ə). **1** anything regarded as an important safeguard. **2 Palladium,** in Troy, the statue of Pallas Athena, on which the safety of the city was supposed to depend. [< L < Gk. *palladion,* dim. of *Pallas*]

Pal·las (pal′əs) *n.* a title of the Greek goddess Athena.
☛ *Hom.* **palace.**

pall·bear·er (pol′ber′ər or pôl′-) *n.* a person who accompanies or helps to carry the coffin at a funeral.

pal·let¹ (pal′it) *n.* **1** a straw bed. **2** a small, hard, or inferior bed. [ME < OF *paillet* < *paille* straw < L *palea*]
☞ *Hom.* palate, palette.

pal·let² (pal′it) *n.* **1** an instrument with a flat wooden blade, used by potters, etc. **2** *Mechanics.* a projection on a pawl. **3** a portable platform on which goods can be stacked and transported from place to place in a factory, warehouse, etc. **4 palette** (def. 1). [var. of *palette*]
☞ *Hom.* palate, palette.

pal·liasse (pal yas′ *or* pal′yas) *n.* a straw-filled mattress. [< F *paillasse* < Ital. *pagliaccio*, ult. < L *palea* straw. 18c.]

pal·li·ate (pal′ē āt′) *v.* **-at·ed, -at·ing. 1** lessen without curing; mitigate: *to palliate a disease.* **2** make appear less serious; excuse: *to palliate a fault.* [< L *palliare* cover with a cloak < *pallium* cloak] —**pal′li·a′tion,** *n.*

pal·li·a·tive (pal′ē ə tiv *or* pal′ē ā′tiv) *adj., n.* —*adj.* useful to lessen or soften; mitigating; excusing. —*n.* something that lessens, softens, mitigates, or excuses.

pal·lid (pal′id) *adj.* lacking color; having less color than normal or usual; pale: *a pallid face.* [< L *pallidus.* Doublet of PALE¹.]
☞ *Syn.* See note at **pale¹.**

pal·lor (pal′ər) *n.* a lack of color from fear, illness, death, etc.; paleness. [< L]

pal·ly (pal′ē) *adj. Informal. Often derogatory.* on familiar or intimate terms: *trying to be pally with the press.*

palm¹ (pom *or* päm) *n., v.* —*n.* **1** the inside of the hand between the wrist and the fingers. **2** the part of a glove or mitten covering the palm. **3** a broad, flat part resembling a palm, such as the blade of an oar or paddle or the flattened part of an antler of a moose, etc. **4** the width of the hand as a unit for measuring length; about 10 cm.
grease the palm of, bribe.
have an itching palm, be greedy for money.
—*v.* **1** conceal in the hand: *The magician palmed a nickel.* **2** touch or stroke with the palm or hand; handle.
palm off, pass off or get accepted by fraud or deceit: *The book he palmed off on me turned out to have some pages missing.* [ME < OF < L *palma*]

palm² (pom *or* päm) *n.* **1** any of a family (Palmae) of mainly tropical and subtropical trees, shrubs, and vines, most species having a tall, pillar-like trunk crowned by very large, fan-shaped or feather-shaped leaves. **2** a leaf of a palm tree used as a symbol of victory or triumph. **3** a victory; triumph.
bear or **carry off the palm,** be the victor; win: *He bore off the palm both in tennis and swimming.*
yield the palm to, admit defeat by.
[OE < L *palma* palm tree, from the spreading shape of the leaves. See PALM¹.]

pal·mate (pal′māt) *adj.* **1** shaped like a hand with the fingers spread out; having lobes radiating from a central point: *a palmate leaf, palmate antlers.* See **leaf** for picture. **2** of the feet of many water birds, having the front toes joined by a web; webbed. [< L *palmatus* < *palma* palm (of the hand)] —**pal·ma·tion** (pal mā′shən) *n.* a palmate formation or structure; one division of a palmate structure.

palm·er¹ (pom′ər *or* päm′ər) *n.* **1** *Historical.* a pilgrim returning from the Holy Land bringing a palm branch as a token. **2** pilgrim. [ME < AF < Med.L *palmarius* < L *palma* palm²]

palm·er² (pom′ər *or* päm′ər) *n.* a person who palms or conceals something. [< palm¹]

palm·er–worm (pom′ər wèrm′ *or* päm′ər-) *n.* any of various caterpillars that injure or destroy fruit trees by eating the leaves, especially a small green caterpillar that is the larva of a North American moth (*Dichomeris ligulella*). [< *palmer¹*; so named from its wandering habits]

pal·met·to (pal met′ō) *n., pl.* **-tos** *or* **-toes.** any of a genus (*Sabal*) of mainly small palms found in the Caribbean, Central America, and the SE United States, having fan-shaped leaves. [< Sp. *palmito,* dim. of *palma* palm]

palm·ist (pom′ist *or* päm′ist) *n.* a person who practises palmistry.

palm·is·try (pom′is trē *or* päm′is trē) *n.* the art or practice of telling a person's future or reading his character from the lines and marks in the palm of his hand. [ME *pawmestry, palmestrie < paume, palme* palm (of the hand) + a word element of uncertain origin]

palm leaf a leaf of a palm tree, used for making hats, baskets, fans, etc.

palm oil an edible yellow fat obtained from the fruit of any of several palms, used especially to make soap and candles.

Palm Sunday the Sunday before Easter Sunday.

palm·y (pom′ē *or* päm′ē) *adj.* **palm·i·er, palm·i·est. 1** abounding in palm trees. **2** flourishing; prosperous.

hat, āge, fär; let, ēqual, tèrm; it, īce
hot, ōpen, ôrder; oil, out; cup, pùt, rüle,
əbove, takən, pencəl, lemən, circəs

ch, child; ng, long; sh, ship
th, thin; ᴛн, then; zh, measure

pal·o·mi·no (pal′ə mē′nō) *n., pl.* **-nos.** a horse of mainly Arabian stock, having a cream, golden, or tan coat and a white or ivory mane and tail. [< Sp.]

pa·loo·ka (pə lü′kə) *n. Slang.* **1** a poor or inferior boxer. **2** a stupid lout, especially a muscular one. [coined word]

palp (palp) *n.* palpus. [< F *palpe*]

pal·pa·bil·i·ty (pal′pə bil′ə tē) *n.* the state or quality of being palpable.

pal·pa·ble (pal′pə bəl) *adj.* **1** readily seen or heard and recognized; obvious: *a palpable error.* **2** that can be touched or felt: *a palpable hit.* [ME < LL *palpabilis* < L *palpare* feel]

pal·pa·bly (pal′pə blē) *adv.* **1** plainly; obviously. **2** to the touch.

pal·pate¹ (pal′pāt) *v.* **-pat·ed, -pat·ing.** examine or feel with the hands, especially for purposes of medical diagnosis. [< L *palpatus,* pp. of *palpare* feel, pat] —**pal·pa·tion,** *n.*

pal·pate² (pal′pāt) *adj.* having a palpus or palpi.

pal·pi (pal′pī *or* pal′pē) *n. pl.* of **palpus.**

pal·pi·tate (pal′pə tāt′) *v.* **-tat·ed, -tat·ing. 1** beat very rapidly; throb: *Your heart palpitates when you are excited.* **2** quiver; tremble: *His body palpitated with terror.* [< L *palpitare* throb < *palpare* pat]

pal·pi·ta·tion (pal′pə tā′shən) *n.* **1** very rapid beating of the heart. **2** a quivering; trembling.

pal·pus (pal′pəs) *n., pl.* **pal·pi.** a jointed feeler that is an organ of touch or taste, attached to one of the mouthparts of insects, crustaceans, etc. [< L]

pal·sied (pol′zēd *or* pôl′zēd) *adj.* suffering from palsy.

pal·sy (pol′zē *or* pôl′zē) *n., pl.* **-sies;** *v.* **-sied, -sy·ing.** —*n.* paralysis, especially when accompanied by uncontrollable tremors of the body or a part of the body. —*v.* paralyse. [ME *palesie* < OF *paralysie* < L < Gk. *paralysis.* Doublet of PARALYSIS.]

pal·ter (pol′tər *or* pôl′tər) *v.* **1** talk or act insincerely; trifle deceitfully. **2** act carelessly; trifle: *Do not palter with a decision involving life and death.* **3** deal crookedly; use tricks and dodges in bargaining. [origin uncertain]

pal·try (pol′trē *or* pôl′trē) *adj.* **-tri·er, -tri·est. 1** almost worthless; trifling. **2** petty; mean. [? < dial. *palt* trash] —**pal′tri·ly,** *adv.* —**pal′tri·ness,** *n.*

pal·y·no·log·i·cal (pal′ə nə loj′ə kəl) *adj.* of or having to do with palynology. —**pal′y·no·log′i·cal·ly,** *adv.*

pal·y·nol·o·gist (pal′ə nol′ə jist) *n.* a person trained in palynology, especially one whose work it is.

pal·y·nol·o·gy (pal′ə nol′ə jē) *n.* the branch of science dealing with living and fossil plant spores and pollen.

pam·pas (pam′pəz *or* pam′pəs; *Spanish,* päm′päs) *n.pl.* **1** the vast, almost treeless plains of South America south of the Amazon and east of the Andes, especially in central Argentina. **2** (*adj.*) of or found on the pampas: *pampas dwellers, pampas grass.* [< Sp. *pampas,* pl., < Peruvian *pampa* a plain]

pam·pas grass (pam′pəs) any of various very tall, reedlike grasses (especially genus *Cortaderia*) of S South America having silvery plumes.

pam·per (pam′pər) *v.* indulge too much; allow too many privileges to: *to pamper a child, to pamper one's appetite.* [ME *pampere(n)*] —**pam′per·er,** *n.*

pam·phlet (pam′flit) *n.* a short printed work, usually with no binding or having a stapled paper cover: *an advertising pamphlet, a pamphlet on the care of hamsters.* [ME < Anglo-L *panfletus,* for *Pamphilet,* the popular name for the 12th-century poem, "Pamphilus, seu de Amore" (Pamphilus, or About Love)]

pam·phlet·eer (pam′flit ēr′) *n., v.* —*n.* a writer of pamphlets. —*v.* write and issue pamphlets.

pan¹ (pan) *n., v.* **panned, pan·ning.** —*n.* **1** a dish for cooking and other household uses, usually broad, shallow, and having no cover. **2** anything like this. Gold and other metals are sometimes obtained by washing ore in pans. The dishes on a pair of scales are called pans. **3** in old-fashioned guns, the hollow part of the lock that held a little gunpowder to set the gun off. **4** hard subsoil. **5** ice-pan. **6** *Slang.* the human face. **7** *Slang. Baseball.* the home plate. **8** *Slang.* a severely critical review of a play, motion picture, etc. —*v.* **1** cook in a pan. **2** wash in a pan: *to pan gold.* **3** wash (gravel,

sand, etc.) in a pan to get gold. **4** yield gold. **5** *Informal.* criticize severely.
pan out, *Informal.* turn out.
[OE *panne*]

pan² (pan) *v.* **panned, pan·ning.** move a motion picture or television camera so as to take in a whole scene, follow a moving character or object, etc. [< *panorama*]

Pan (pan) *n. Greek mythology.* the god of forests, pastures, flocks, and shepherds, represented as a man having the horns, ears, and legs of a goat and playing upon a reed pipe, or panpipe.

pan– *combining form.* all, as in *Pan-American, Pan-Christian, pandemonium.* [< Gk. *pan,* neut. of *pas* all]

pan·a·ce·a (pan′ə sē′ə) *n.* a remedy for all diseases or ills; cure-all. [< L < Gk. *panakeia,* ult. < *pan-* all + *akos* cure]

pa·nache (pə nash′ or pə näsh′) *n.* **1** an ornamental plume or bunch of feathers, especially on a helmet. **2** swagger; verve. [< F *panache* < MF *penache* < Ital. *pennaccio,* var. of *pennachio* < *penna* feather < L]

Pan–Af·ri·can (pan af′rə kən) *adj.* of or for all African peoples: *Pan-African freedom.*

Pan–Af·ri·can·ism (pan af′rə kə niz′əm) *n.* **1** the theory of or movement towards a political union of all African peoples. **2** belief in or support of such a theory or movement.

pan·a·ma (pan′ə mä′) *n.* **1** a fine hat woven from the young leaves of a palmlike plant of Central and South America. **2** the leaves from which the hat is made.

Pan·a·ma·ni·an (pan′ə mä′nē ən or pan′ə mä′nē ən) *n., adj.* —*n.* a native or inhabitant of Panama, a country on the Isthmus of Panama. —*adj.* of or having to do with Panama or its people.

Pan–A·mer·i·can (pan′ə mer′ə kən) *adj.* **1** of all Americans. **2** including all the countries of North, Central, and South America.

Pan–A·mer·i·can·ism (pan′ə mer′ə kən iz′əm) *n.* the principle or policy that all the countries in South America, Central America, and North America should co-operate for the improvement of their welfare.

Pan American Union a permanent body and the central office of the Organization of American States.

pan·a·tel·la or **pan·a·tel·a** (pan′ə tel′ə) *n.* a long, slender cigar with a rounded end.

pan·broil (pan′broil′) *v.* cook with little or no fat in a heavy frying pan over high heat.

pan·cake (pan′kāk′) *n., v.* **-caked, -cak·ing.** —*n.* **1** a thin, flat cake of batter, fried in a pan or on a griddle. **2** pancake landing. —*v.* of an aircraft, make a pancake landing.

Pancake Day Shrove Tuesday.

pancake landing a quick landing in which an aircraft is levelled off at a higher altitude than for a normal landing, a manoeuvre that causes it to stall and drop almost straight down while remaining in a horizontal position.

pan·chro·mat·ic (pan′krō mat′ik) *adj.* sensitive to light of all colors: *a panchromatic photographic film.*

pan·cre·as (pan′krē əs) *n.* a large gland near the stomach that secretes digestive enzymes into the small intestine and the hormone insulin into the blood. The pancreas of animals, when used for food, is called sweetbread. [< NL < Gk. *pankreas* < *pan-* all + *kreas* flesh]

pan·cre·at·ic (pan′krē at′ik) *adj.* of the pancreas. The pancreatic juice aids digestion.

pan·da (pan′də) *n.* **1** a large, black-and-white, bearlike mammal (*Ailuropoda melanoleuca*) found in the bamboo forests of Tibet; giant panda. Zoologists differ on whether the panda is more closely related to the bears or the raccoons. **2** a small, mainly reddish-brown mammal (*Ailurus fulgens*) found in the Himalayas, having a bushy tail, white face with a reddish stripe on each side, and soft, thick fur. This panda, also called the lesser, or common, panda, belongs to the same family as the raccoon. [origin uncertain]

pan·dect (pan′dekt) *n.* **1** a complete body of laws. **2** a comprehensive digest. **3 Pandects,** *pl.* a digest of Roman civil law in 50 books, made by order of Justinian in the sixth century A.D. [< L < Gk. *pandektēs* < *pan-* all + *dechesthai* receive]

pan·dem·ic (pan dem′ik) *adj., n.* of a disease, affecting a large proportion of the population over an extensive geographical area: *a pandemic outbreak of influenza.* —*n.* a disease that has become pandemic.

pan·de·mo·ni·um (pan′də mō′nē əm) *n.* **1** a scene or place of wild disorder and confusion. **2** wild disorder and confusion; tumult. [< NL < Gk. *pan-* all + *daimōn* demon; coined by Milton]

pan·der (pan′dər) *n., v.* —*n.* a person who caters to or exploits the weaknesses of others; one who helps people indulge evil designs or base passions. —*v.* act as a pander; supply material or opportunity for vices: *The newspaper pandered to people's liking for sensational stories.* [< *Pandarus* (Ital. *Pandoro*) a character in a story told by Boccaccio and Chaucer]

Pan·do·ra (pan dô′rə) *n. Greek mythology.* the first woman, created by the gods to punish mankind for having learned the use of fire. Curiosity led her to open a box (**Pandora's box**) and thus let out all sorts of ills into the world; only Hope remained at the bottom.

pan·dow·dy (pan dou′dē) *n., pl.* **-dies.** *Esp.U.S.* a deep apple pie with top crust only; brown betty. [origin uncertain]

pane (pān) *n.* a single sheet of glass in a window, a door, or a sash. [ME < OF *pan* < L *pannus* piece of cloth]
☛ *Hom.* **pain.**

pan·e·gyr·ic (pan′ə jir′ik or pan′ə jīr′ik) *n.* **1** something written or spoken in praise of a person or thing; eulogy. **2** enthusiastic or extravagant praise. [< L < Gk. *panēgyrikos* < *pan-* all + *agyris* assembly]

pan·e·gyr·ist (pan′ə jir′ist or pan′ə jīr′ist) *n.* a person who praises enthusiastically or extravagantly.

pan·el (pan′əl) *n., v.* **-elled** or **-eled, -el·ling** or **-el·ing.** —*n.* **1** a separate strip or surface that is usually set off in some way from what is around it. A panel is often sunk below or raised above the rest, and used for a decoration. Panels may be in a door or other woodwork, on large pieces of furniture, or made as parts of a dress. **2** a long, narrow picture, hanging, or design. **3** a list of persons called as jurors; the members of a jury. **4** a small group of persons selected for a special purpose, such as holding a discussion, judging a contest, or participating in a quiz: *The panel gave its opinion on the recent election.* **5 a** one section of a switchboard. **b** a board containing the instruments, controls, or indicators used in operating an automobile, aircraft, computer, or other mechanism. **6** a panel truck.
—*v.* arrange in panels; furnish or decorate with panels. [ME < OF *panel* piece < VL *pannellus* < L *pannus* piece of cloth]

panel discussion the discussion of a particular issue by a selected group of people, usually experts.

pan·el·ing (pan′əl ing) See **panelling.**

pan·el·ist or **pan·el·list** (pan′əl ist) *n.* one of a group of persons making up a panel.

pan·el·ling or **pan·el·ing** (pan′əl ing) *n.* panels joined together to make a single surface, especially wooden panels forming a decorative wall surface: *We have pine panelling in the study.*

panel truck a small, light motor truck with a completely enclosed body.

pan·fish (pan′fish′) *n.* any small food fish suitable for frying whole in a pan.

pan–fry (pan′frī′) *v.* **-fried, -fry·ing.** fry in a frying pan or skillet: *pan-fried fish.*

pang (pang) *n.* **1** a sudden, short, sharp pain or feeling: *the pangs of a toothache.* **2** a sudden feeling of distress or anguish: *a pang of remorse.* [origin uncertain]

pan·go·lin (pang gō′lən) *n.* any of an order (Pholidota, usually considered to consist of a single genus, *Manis*) of tropical Asian and African mammals having a body covered with an armor of overlapping horny scales, a long, toothless snout, and a long, wormlike tongue used for catching termites, ants, and other insects for food. Pangolins curl up into a ball when they feel threatened. Also called **scaly anteater.** [< Malay *peng-goling* roller]

pan·han·dle¹ (pan′han′dəl) *n.* **1** the handle of a pan. **2** a narrow strip of land projecting like a handle: *the Alaska Panhandle.*

pan·han·dle² (pan′han′dəl) *v.* **-dled, -dling.** *Informal.* beg, especially in the streets. [? < *panhandle* < *pan* receptacle used for collecting money + *handler*] —**pan′han′dler,** *n.*

Pan·hel·len·ic or **pan·hel·len·ic** (pan′hə len′ik) *adj.* **1** of or having to do with all Greece or all Greek people. **2** *Esp.U.S.* of or having to do with all college fraternities and sororities with names made up of Greek letters.

pan·ic (pan′ik) *n., adj., v.* **-icked, -ick·ing.** —*n.* **1** a sudden fear that causes an individual or entire group to lose self-control; unreasoning fear: *When the theatre caught fire, there was a panic.* **2** *Slang.* a very amusing person or thing: *His costume is a panic.* —*adj.* **1** of, showing, or caused by unreasoning fear: *panic terror, panic haste, panic selling of stocks.* **2** Often, **Panic,** of or having to do with the god Pan or the mental state considered to be induced by him.
push (or **press** or **hit**) **the panic button,** *Informal.* react with panic in the face of a supposed emergency.
—*v.* **1** lose control of oneself through fear. **2** cause panic in. **3** *Slang.* amuse greatly. [< F < L *panicus* < Gk. *panikos* of god Pan (who caused fear)]

pan·ick·y (pan′ik ē) *adj.* **1** affected with panic; panic-stricken. *He began to get panicky as the deadline approached.* **2** liable to panic.

pan·i·cle (pan′ə kəl) *n.* a loose, diversely branching flower cluster; compound raceme: *a panicle of oats.* See **inflorescence** for picture. [< L *panicula*, dim. of *panus* a swelling, thread wound on a bobbin, ear of millet; cf. Gk. *pēnos* web]

pan·ic–strick·en (pan′ik strik′ən) *adj.* frightened out of one's wits; demoralized by fear.

pa·nic·u·late (pə nik′yə lāt′) *adj. Botany.* growing in a panicle; arranged in panicles.

Pan·ja·bi (pun jä′bē) *n.* an Indo-European language spoken in the Punjab, derived from Sanskrit. Also, **Punjabi.**

pan·jan·drum (pan jan′drəm) *n.* a mock title for an official of imaginary or exaggerated importance or power. [coined by Samuel Foote (1720-1777), an English dramatist]

pan·ni·er (pan′ē ər) *n.* **1** a basket, especially one of a pair of considerable size to be slung across the shoulders or across the back of a beast of burden. **2** *Historical.* a frame to stretch out the skirt of a woman's dress at the hips. **3** puffed drapery about the hips. [ME < OF < L *panarium* bread basket < *panis* bread]

pan·ni·kin (pan′ə kin) *n.* **1** a small pan. **2** a metal cup or mug.

pa·no·cha (pə nō′chə) *n.* **1** a coarse dark-brown sugar from Mexico. **2** penuche. [< Mexican Sp.]

pan·o·plied (pan′ə plēd) *adj.* covered with or dressed or arrayed in a panoply.

pan·o·ply (pan′ə plē) *n., pl.* **-plies. 1** a complete suit of armor. **2** complete equipment or covering: *the panoply of war.* [< Gk. *panoplia* < *pan-* all + *hopla* arms]

pan·o·ram·a (pan′ə ram′ə) *n.* **1** a wide, unbroken view of a surrounding region. **2** a complete survey of some subject: *a panorama of the development of the snowmobile.* **3** a presentation of a landscape or other scene surrounding the spectator on all sides or gradually unrolled to pass continuously before the spectator's eyes. **4** a continuously passing or changing scene: *the panorama of city life.* [< *pan-* + Gk. *horama* view]

pan·o·ram·ic (pan′ə ram′ik) *adj.* of or like a panorama: *a panoramic view.* **—pan′o·ram′i·cal·ly,** *adv.*

pan·pipe (pan′pīp′) *n.* Sometimes, **Panpipe,** an early instrument made of reeds or tubes of different lengths, fastened together in the order of their length. The reeds or tubes were closed at one end; the player blew across their tops.

Pan's pipes panpipe.

pan·sy (pan′zē) *n., pl.* **-sies. 1** a common flowering garden plant (*Viola tricolor hortensis*) of the violet family having large, showy flowers with velvety petals of several colors, usually combinations of blue, yellow, and white. The pansy is a hybrid derived mainly from the wild pansy of Europe. **2** the flower of this plant. **3** *Slang.* **a** a homosexual man or boy. **b** an effeminate man or boy. [< F *pensée* thought < *penser* think. Related to PENSIVE.]

pant (pant) *v., n.* —*v.* **1** breathe hard and quickly. **2** speak with short, quick breaths: *"Come quickly! Come quickly!" panted Joe.* **3** long eagerly. **4** throb; pulsate. —*n.* **1** a short, quick breath. **2** a throbbing or puffing sound: *the pant of an engine.* [ME < OF *pantoisier* < VL *phantasiare* be oppressed with nightmare, ult. < L < Gk. *phantasia* appearance, image]

pan·ta·lets or **pan·ta·lettes** (pan′tə lets′) *n.pl.* **1** long drawers extending to the ankles and having a ruffle at the bottom of each leg that showed beneath the skirt, worn by women and girls in the early 19th century. **2** detachable ruffles for pantalets. [dim. < *pantaloon*]

pan·ta·loon (pan′tə lün′) *n.* **1** a clown. **2 Pantaloon,** in traditional Italian comedy and in pantomime, a thin, foolish old man wearing pantaloons and slippers with attached stockings. **3 pantaloons,** *pl. Archaic.* close-fitting trousers. [< F < Ital. *Pantalone*, a comic character in early Italian comedies; originally a Venetian < *Pantaleone* the patron saint of Venice]

pan·the·ism (pan′thē iz′əm) *n.* **1** the belief that God and the universe are identical. **2** the worship of the gods of all cultures together.

pan·the·ist (pan′thē ist) *n.* a person who believes in pantheism.

pan·the·is·tic (pan′thē is′tik) *adj.* of or having to do with pantheism or pantheists.

pan·the·is·ti·cal·ly (pan′thē is′tik lē) *adv.* according to pantheism; from a pantheist's point of view.

pan·the·on (pan′thē on′ or pan thē′ən) *n.* **1 Pantheon,** in Rome, a temple for all the gods, built about 27 B.C. and later used as a Christian church. **2** a temple dedicated to all the gods. **3** all the gods of a people, especially those that are officially recognized. **4** a

hat, āge, fär; let, ēqual, tėrm; it, īce
hot, ōpen, ôrder; oil, out; cup, put, rüle,
əbove, takən, pencəl, lemən, circəs

ch, child; ng, long; sh, ship
th, thin; ᴛн, then; zh, measure

public building containing tombs or memorials of the illustrious dead of a nation. **5** a group of illustrious people. [ME < L < Gk. *pantheion* < *pan-* all + *theos* god]

pan·ther (pan′thər) *n., pl.* **-thers** or (*esp. collectively*) **-ther. 1** a leopard, especially one of the black color phase. **2** cougar. **3** jaguar. [ME < OF < L *panthera* < Gk. *panthēr*]

pan·tie (pan′tē) *n.* **1** panties. **2** pantie-girdle. Also, **panty.**

pan·tie–girdle (pan′tē gėr′dəl) *n.* a light girdle, or corset, made like panties, with or without garters.

pan·ties (pan′tēz) *n.pl.* **1** an undergarment worn by women and girls, covering the lower part of the torso and having separate leg holes or short legs. **2** a similar undergarment for babies and young children. [dim. of **pants**]

pan·ti·hose (pan′tē hōz′) See **pantyhose.**

pant leg the leg of a pair of pants.

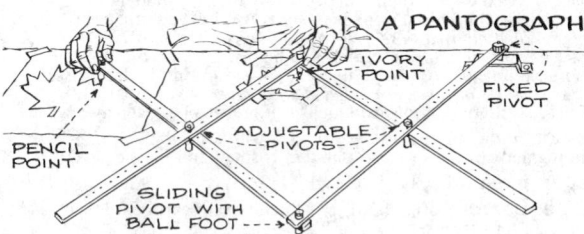

pan·to·graph (pan′tə graf′) *n.* an instrument for copying plans, drawings, etc. on any scale desired. [< Gk. *pas, pantos* all + E *-graph*]

pan·to·mime (pan′tə mīm′) *n., v.* **-mimed, -mim·ing.** —*n.* **1** a play without words, in which the actors express themselves by gestures. **2** gestures without words. **3** *Esp.Brit.* a lavish stage entertainment, usually presented at Christmas and based on a fairy story or other traditional tale, featuring singing, dancing, and clowning. —*v.* express by gestures. [< L < Gk. *pantomimos* < *pas, pantos* all + *mimos* mimic]

pan·to·mim·ic (pan′tə mim′ik) *adj.* of, in, or like pantomime.

pan·to·mim·ist (pan′tə mīm′ist) *n.* an actor in a pantomime.

pan·to·then·ic acid (pan′tə then′ik) an oily acid belonging to the vitamin B complex and found in all living tissues. *Formula:* $C_9H_{17}NO_5$

pan·try (pan′trē) *n., pl.* **-tries.** a small room in which food, dishes, silverware, table linen, etc. are kept. [ME < OF *paneterie,* ult. < L *panis* bread]

pants (pants) *n.pl.* **1** an outer garment for the lower body, reaching from the waist to the ankles or, sometimes, to the knees, and covering each leg separately; trousers. **2** the lower part of a pair of pyjamas. **3** panties. [short for *pantaloons*]

pant·suit (pant′süt′) *n.* a suit for women, consisting of a jacket and long pants.

pan·ty (pan′tē) See **pantie.**

pan·ty·hose (pan′tē hōz′) *n.pl.* a garment for women, consisting of sheer stockings knitted in one piece with a pantie-like top of the same or slightly heavier material. Also, **panty-hose, pantihose.**

pan·ty·waist (pan′tē wāst′) *n.* **1** a child's garment consisting of short pants and shirt buttoned together. **2** *Slang.* sissy (def. 2).

pan·zer (pan′zər) *adj.* armored; mechanized and armored. A panzer division consists largely of tanks. [< G *Panzer* armor]

pap (pap) *n.* **1** soft food for infants or invalids. **2** ideas or facts watered down to a characterless consistency, considered as innocuous and as unsuitable for adults as baby food. [cf. LG *pappe*]

pa·pa (po′pə *or* pä′pə) *n.* father; daddy. [< F]

pa·pa·cy (pā′pə sē) *n., pl.* **-cies. 1** the position, rank, or authority of the Pope. **2** the time during which a pope rules. **3** all the popes. **4** government by the Pope. [< Med.L *papatia* < LL *papa* pope. See POPE.]

pa·pal (pā′pəl) *adj.* **1** of or having to do with the Pope: *a papal*

letter. **2** of or having to do with the papacy. **3** of or having to do with the Roman Catholic Church: *papal ritual.* [< Med.L *papalis* < LL *papa* pope. See POPE.]

pa·paw (po′po or pô′pô) *n.* See **pawpaw**. [< Sp. *papaya.* See PAPAYA.]

pa·pa·ya (pə pä′yə) *n.* **1** a treelike plant (*Carica papaya*) native to tropical America but widely cultivated in warm regions, having a straight, unbranched, palmlike trunk, large palmately lobed leaves, and large, round or oval, edible fruit. **2** the fruit of this tree, having juicy, orange or dark-yellow flesh. [< Sp. *papaya* < Carib. 15c.]

pa·per (pā′pər) *n., adj., v.* —*n.* **1** a material in the form of thin sheets made from wood pulp, rags, etc. and used for writing, printing, wrapping packages, etc. **2** a piece or sheet of paper. **3** a piece or sheet of paper with writing or printing on it; document: *Important papers were stolen.* **4** a wrapper, container, or sheet of paper containing something. **5** newspaper. **6** an article; essay: *Professor Smith read a paper on the teaching of English.* **7** a written examination. **8** a written promise to pay money; note. **9** paper money. **10 papers,** *pl.* documents telling who or what one is. **11** wallpaper.
on paper, a in writing or in print. **b** in theory: *The plan looks all right on paper but it may not work.*
—*adj.* **1** made of paper: *paper dolls.* **2** having to do with or used with paper: *a paper clip.* **3** like paper; thin: *almonds with paper shells.* **4** of, consisting of, or carried on by means of letters to newspapers, pamphlets, or books: *paper warfare.* **5** existing only on paper: *When he tried to sell, his paper profits disappeared.*
—*v.* **1** cover with paper, especially wallpaper. **2** *Slang.* fill (a place of entertainment) with an audience admitted mostly by free passes: *To get a crowd at the concert they had to paper the house.* [ME < AF *papir* < L < Gk. *papyros.* Doublet of PAPYRUS.] —**pa′per·er,** *n.*

pa·per·back (pā′pər bak′) *n.* a book with a flexible paper binding and cover, especially one that is small and inexpensive.

paper birch white birch (def. 1).

pa·per·board (pā′pər bôrd′) *n.* a thick type of cardboard, such as that used for cartons, etc.

pa·per·boy (pā′pər boi′) *n.* a boy who delivers or sells newspapers.

paper clip a flat clip of flexible, bent wire, used to slip over the edge of a small bundle of loose sheets to hold them together.

pa·per·girl (pā′pər gėrl′) *n.* a girl who delivers or sells newspapers.

pa·per·hang·er (pā′pər hang′ər) *n.* a person whose work is applying wallpaper.

paper knife a knife with a blade of metal, wood, ivory, etc. used to slit open letters or uncut pages of books.

pa·per·mak·er (pā′pər māk′er) *n.* a person who makes or manufactures paper.

pa·per·mak·ing (pā′pər māk′ing) *n.* the science, process, or business of making paper.

paper money money made of paper, not metal. A dollar bill is paper money.

paper nautilus any of a genus (*Argonauta*) of marine cephalopod molluscs belonging to the same order as the octopus, especially *A. argo,* found in warm seas, the female of which produces a very thin, paperlike shell in which the young are hatched and which the animal casts off afterwards.

paper profits profits existing on paper but not yet realized.

pa·per·weight (pā′pər wāt′) *n.* a small, heavy object put on papers to keep them from being scattered.

pa·per·work (pā′pər wėrk′) *n.* work done on or with paper, such as writing, filing, or other clerical work: *She hates all the paperwork involved in her job.*

pa·per·y (pā′pər ē) *adj.* thin like paper.

pap·e·te·rie (pap′ə trē; *French,* päp trē′) *n.* a set of stationery, such as note paper and envelopes, in a box or other package. [< F]

pa·pier–mâ·ché (pā′pər ma shā′; *French,* pä pyä mä shā′) *n.* **1** a paper pulp mixed with some stiffener and used for modelling. It becomes hard and strong when dry. **2** (*adj.*) made of papier-mâché. [< F *papier mâché* chewed paper]

pa·pil·la (pə pil′ə) *n., pl.* **-pil·lae. 1** a small, nipple-like projection. **2** a small vascular process at the root of a hair or feather. **3** one of certain small protuberances concerned with the senses of touch, taste, or smell: *the papillae on the tongue.* [< L *papilla* nipple]

pa·pil·lae (pə pil′ē or pə pil′ī) *n.* pl. of **papilla.**

pap·il·lar·y (pap′ə ler′ē) *adj.* of, like, or having papillae.

pap·il·lo·ma (pap′ə lō′mə) *n.* a benign tumor, such as a wart or polyp, on mucous membranes or the skin. [< *papilla* + *-oma.* 19c.]

pap·il·lose (pap′ə lōs′) *adj.* having many papillae.

pa·pist (pā′pist) *n. or adj. Usually derogatory.* Roman Catholic. [< NL < LL *papa* pope. See POPE.]

pa·poose (pa püs′) *n.* a North American Indian baby. Also, **pappoose.** [< Algonquian *papeisses* < *peisses* child]

pap·pus (pap′əs) *n., pl.* **pap·pi** (pap′ī or pap′ē). *Botany.* an appendage to a seed, often made of down or bristles. Dandelion and thistle seeds have pappi. [< NL < Gk. *pappos*]

pap·py (pap′ē) *adj.* like pap; soft; mushy.

pap·ri·ka (pa prē′kə or pap′rə kə) *n.* **1** a kind of mild, red-colored pepper made of the dried, ground-up pods of any of various sweet-pepper plants. **2** a pod of pepper used for making paprika. [< Hungarian]

Pap smear or **test** (pap) a test for early stages of cancer of the uterus or cervix, consisting of a microscopic examination of castoff cells found in vaginal fluid, using a special staining technique that separates abnormal cells from normal ones. [named after George Papanicolaou (1883-1962), a U.S. scientist, who devised it. 20c.]

Pap·u·an (pap′yü ən) *n., adj.* —*n.* **1** any of a group of very different languages spoken in New Guinea, New Britain, and the Solomon Islands in the SW Pacific. **2** a member of any of the Papuan-speaking peoples who live in this area. —*adj.* of or having to do with Papua, the peoples living there, or their languages.

pa·py·rus (pə pī′rəs) *n., pl.* **-ri** (-rī or -rē). **1** a tall water plant (*Cyperus papyrus*) of the Nile valley from which the ancient Egyptians, Greeks, and Romans made a kind of paper to write on. **2** a writing material made from the pith of the papyrus plant. **3** an ancient record written on papyrus. [< L < Gk. *papyrus.* Doublet of PAPER.]

par (pär) *n., adj.* —*n.* **1** equality; an equal level: *The gains and losses are about on a par. He is quite on a par with his brother in intelligence.* **2** an average or normal amount, degree, or condition: *A sick person feels below par.* **3** the value of a bond, a note, a share of stock, etc. that is printed on it; face value: *That stock is selling above par.* **4** the established normal value of the money of one country in terms of the money of another country. **5** *Golf.* the number of strokes set as an expert score for any one hole. The sum of the par scores for each hole is par for the course.
—*adj.* **1** average; normal. **2** of or at par. [< L *par* equal. Doublet of PEER[1].]

par– *prefix.* the form of **para–** before vowels and *h,* as in *parenthesis, parhelion.*

par. 1 paragraph. **2** parallel. **3** parenthesis. **4** parish.

pa·ra (pä rä′) *n.* a unit of money in Yugoslavia, equal to ¹/₁₀₀ of a dinar. [< Turkish]

para–[1] *prefix.* **1** beside, near, or beyond, as in *parathyroid, parapsychology.* **2** functionally disordered, as in *paranoia.* Also, **par–** before vowels and *h.* [< Gk. *para–* < *para,* prep.]

para–[2] *combining form.* **1** a defence or protection against, as in *parachute* (protection against a fall), *parasol* (protection against the sun). **2** that uses a parachute, as in *paratrooper.* [< F < Ital. < *para,* imperative of *parare* ward off, defend against < L *parare* prepare against]

para. paragraph.

Para. Paraguay.

par·a–a·mi·no·ben·zo·ic (par′ə ə mē′nō ben zō′ik or per′ə–) a yellowish, crystalline acid belonging to the vitamin B complex, found especially in yeast and liver. *Formula:* $C_7H_7NO_2$

par·a·bi·o·sis (par′ə bī ō′sis or per′ə–) *n.* the anatomical union of two individuals, in which they share a common blood circulation, occurring naturally as in Siamese twins, or produced for experimental purposes in animals.

par·a·bi·ot·ic (par′ə bī ot′ik or per′ə–) *adj.* of or having to do with parabiosis. —**par′a·bi·ot′i·cal·ly,** *adv.*

par·a·ble (par′ə bəl or per′ə bəl) *n.* a short, simple story used to teach some truth or moral lesson: *Jesus often taught in parables.* [< L *parabola* < Gk. *parabolē* comparison < *para–* alongside + *bolē* a throwing. Doublet of PALAVER, PAROLE.]
☞ *Syn.* See note at **allegory.**

pa·rab·o·la (pə rab′ə lə) *n., pl.* **-las.** *Geometry.* a plane curve formed by the intersection of a cone with a plane parallel to a side of the cone. See **cone** for picture. [< NL < Gk. *parabolē* juxtaposition. See PARABLE.]

par·a·bol·ic[1] (par′ə bol′ik or per′ə–) *adj.* having to do with or resembling a parabola.

par·a·bol·ic[2] (par′ə bol′ik or per′ə–) *adj.* of, having to do with, or expressed in a parable.

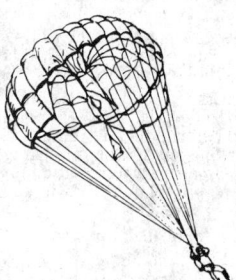

A man descending by parachute. The parachute is fastened to a harness worn by the jumper. When not in use it is folded into a pack that is usually worn on the back or chest.

par·a·chute (par′ə shüt′ *or* per′ə shüt′) *n., v.* **-chut·ed, -chut·ing.** —*n.* an apparatus made to give a slow, gradual fall to a person or thing that jumps or is dropped from an aircraft. The top of a parachute resembles that of an umbrella and is made from nylon or silk. —*v.* **1** come or send down by, or as if by, a parachute. **2** *Cdn.* **a** *Politics.* introduce (a non-resident candidate) into a riding, usually a well-known figure, in an attempt to win the seat. **b** bring in (an outsider) to do a specific job or act in a specific capacity, especially at a senior level. [< F *parachute* < *para-* (< Ital. *para* guard against, ult. < L *parare* prepare) + *chute* a fall]

par·a·chut·ist (par′ə shüt′ist *or* per′ə-) *n.* a person who uses a parachute; person skilled in making descents with a parachute.

pa·rade (pə rād′) *n., v.* **-rad·ed, -rad·ing.** —*n.* **1** a march for display; procession: *The circus had a parade.* **2** a group of people walking for display or pleasure. **3** a place where people walk for display or pleasure. **4** a great show or display: *A modest man will not make a parade of his wealth.* **5** a military display or review of troops. **6** a parade ground or parade square.
—*v.* **1** march through with display: *The performers and animals paraded the streets.* **2** march in procession; walk proudly as if in a parade. **3** make a great show of. **4** come together in military order for review or inspection. **5** assemble (troops) for review. [< F < Sp. *parada,* ult. < L *parare* prepare] —**pa·rad′er,** *n.*

parade ground *Esp.U.S.* parade square.

parade square the area where troops parade, drill, etc.

par·a·digm (par′ə dīm′ *or* per′ə-, par′ə dim′ *or* per′ə-) *n.* **1** a pattern; example. **2** *Grammar.* an example of a noun, verb, pronoun, etc. in all its inflections. [< L < Gk. *paradeigma* pattern, ult. < *para-* side by side + *deiknunai* to show]

par·a·di·sa·ic·al (par′ə də sā′ə kəl *or* per′ə-) *adj.* paradisiacal. [alt. of *paradisiacal* on the pattern of Judaic, Mosaic, etc.]

par·a·dise (par′ə dīs′ *or* per′ə dīs′) *n.* **1** heaven. **2** a place or condition of great happiness. **3** a place of great beauty. **4** Also, **Paradise,** the Garden of Eden. [ME < OF < L *paradisus* < Gk. *paradeisos* < OPersian *pairidaeza* park < *pairi* around + *daeza* wall]

par·a·di·si·ac·al (par′ə də sī′ə kəl *or* per′ə-) *adj.* of, having to do with, or resembling paradise.

par·a·dox (par′ə doks′ *or* per′ə doks′) *n.* **1** a statement that may be true but seems to say two opposite things. *More haste, less speed* and *The child is father to the man* are paradoxes. **2** a statement that is false because it says two opposite things. **3** a person or thing that seems to be full of contradictions. **4** any inconsistent or contradictory fact, action, or condition. [< L < Gk. *paradoxos* < *para-* contrary to + *doxa* opinion]
☞ *Usage.* See note at **epigram.**

par·a·dox·i·cal (par′ə dok′sə kəl *or* per′ə-) *adj.* **1** of or involving a paradox. **2** having the habit of using paradoxes. —**par′a·dox′i·cal·ly,** *adv.*

par·af·fin (par′ə fin *or* per′ə fin) *n., v.* —*n.* **1 a** a flammable, white, waxy substance that is a mixture of hydrocarbons obtained especially from petroleum or shale, used for making candles and for coating or sealing. **b** any of various other mixtures of hydrocarbons. **2** *Chemistry.* any hydrocarbon of the methane series. **3** *Esp.Brit.* kerosene.
—*v.* treat with paraffin. [< G < L *parum* not very < *affinis* related; from its small affinity for other substances]

par·af·fine (par′ə fin *or* per′ə fin) *n., v.* **-fined, -fin·ing.** See **paraffin.**

par·a·gon (par′ə gon′ *or* per′ə gon′) *n.* **1** a model of excellence or perfection. **2** a flawless diamond weighing 100 carats or more. [< OF < Ital. *paragone* touchstone < Med.Gk. *parakonē* whetstone]

par·a·graph (par′ə graf′ *or* per′ə graf′) *n., v.* —*n.* **1** a group of sentences relating to the same idea or topic and forming a distinct part of a chapter, letter, or other piece of writing. Paragraphs usually begin on a new line and are indented. **2** a separate note or item of news in a newspaper. **3** a sign (¶) used to show where a

paragraph begins or should begin. It is used mostly in correcting written work.
—*v.* **1** divide into paragraphs. **2** write paragraphs about. [< LL < Gk. *paragraphos* line (in the margin) marking a break in sense < *para-* beside + *graphein* write] —**par′a·graph′er,** *n.*

Par·a·guay·an (par′ə gwā′ən *or* per′ə-, par′ə gwī′ən *or* per′ə-) *n., adj.* —*n.* a native or inhabitant of Paraguay, a country in central South America. —*adj.* of or having to do with Paraguay or its people.

par·a·keet (par′ə kēt′ *or* per′ə kēt′) *n.* any of various small parrots, most of which have slender bodies and long tails. Also, **parrakeet.** [< OF *paroquet,* apparently alteration of *perrot* parrot < *Perrot,* dim. of *Pierre* Peter]

par·al·lac·tic (par′ə lak′tik *or* per′ə-) *adj.* of or having to do with a parallax.

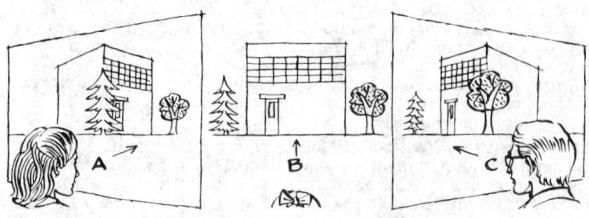

Parallax. The trees appear to be in different positions in relation to the building when viewed from different points.

par·al·lax (par′ə laks′ *or* per′ə laks′) *n.* the apparent change or amount of change in the direction or position of an object as seen from two different points. [< Gk. *parallaxis* deviation, ult. < *para-* + *allassein* to change]

par·al·lel (par′ə lel′ *or* per′ə lel′) *adj., n., v.* **-lelled** or **-leled, -lel·ling** or **-lel·ing.** —*adj.* **1** at or being the same distance apart everywhere, like the two rails of a railway track. See **parallelogram** for picture. **2** similar; corresponding: *parallel points in the characters of different men.*
—*n.* **1** a parallel line or surface. **2** *Geography.* **a** any of the imaginary circles around the earth parallel to the equator, marking degrees of latitude: *The 49th parallel marks much of the boundary between Canada and the United States.* **b** the markings on a map that represent these circles. **3** something like or similar to another: *Her experience was an interesting parallel to ours.* **4** a comparison to show likeness: *Draw a parallel between this winter and last winter.* **5** *Electricity.* an arrangement of the wiring of batteries, lights, etc. in which all the positive poles or terminals are joined to one conductor, and all the negative to the other. —
—*v.* **1** be at the same distance from throughout the length: *The street parallels the railway.* **2** cause to be or run parallel to. **3** be like; be similar to: *Your story closely parallels what he told me.* **4** find a case which is similar or parallel to: *Can you parallel that for friendliness?* **5** compare in order to show likeness. [< L < Gk. *parallēlos* < *para allēlōn* beside one another]

parallel bars a gymnastic apparatus consisting of two parallel wooden bars mounted horizontally on upright posts, used for various exercises.

par·al·lel·e·pi·ped (par′ə lel′ə pī′pid *or* per′ə-) *n.* a geometric solid whose faces are all parallelograms. A parallelepiped is a six-sided prism. [< Gk. *parallēlepipedon* body with parallel surfaces < *parallēlos* parallel + *epipedon* a plane surface]

par·al·lel·ism (par′ə lel iz′əm *or* per′ə lel iz′əm) *n.* **1** the quality or state of being parallel. **2** a likeness; correspondence; agreement.

par·al·lel·o·gram (par′ə lel′ə gram′ *or* per′ə-) *n.* a four-sided plane figure having opposite sides parallel and equal. Squares, oblongs, rhombuses, and rhomboids are parallelograms. See **quadrilateral** for picture. [< Gk. *parallēlogrammon,* neut. < *parallēlos* parallel + *grammē* line]

par·a·lyse *or* **par·a·lyze** (par′ə līz′ *or* per′ə līz′) *v.* **-lysed** or **-lyzed, -lys·ing** or **-lyz·ing.** **1** affect with a lessening or loss of the power of motion or feeling in a part of the body: *His left arm was paralysed after the accident.* **2** make powerless or ineffective;

cripple: *The whole project was paralysed when the funds were cut off.* **3** stun or deaden: *paralysed with fear.*

pa·ral·y·sis (pə ral'ə sis) *n., pl.* **-ses** (-sēz'). **1** a lessening or loss of the power of motion or sensation in any part of the body. **2** a condition of powerlessness or helpless inactivity; crippling: *The war caused a paralysis of trade.* [< L < Gk. *paralysis*, ult. < *para-* from beside + *lyein* to loosen, disable. Doublet of PALSY.]

par·a·lyt·ic (par'ə lit'ik *or* per'ə lit'ik) *adj., n.* —*adj.* **1** of, having to do with, or like paralysis. **2** having paralysis: *a paralytic limb.* —*n.* a person affected with paralysis.

par·a·lyze (par'ə līz' *or* per'ə līz') *v.* See **paralyse.**

par·a·me·ci·um (par'ə mē'sē əm *or* per'ə-; par'ə mē'shē əm *or* per'ə-) *n., pl.* **-ci·a** (-sē ə *or* -shē ə). any of a genus (*Paramecium*) of free-swimming protozoans shaped somewhat like the sole of a slipper, completely covered with cilia and having a groove along one side leading into the mouth cavity. [< NL < Gk. *paramēkēs* oblong < *para-* on one side + *mēkos* length]

par·a·med·ic (par'ə med'ik *or* per'ə med'ik) *n.* a person trained in paramedical work.

par·a·med·i·cal (par'ə med'ə kal *or* per'ə-) *adj.* of, having to do with, or designating auxiliary medical personnel such as medical technicians, X-ray technicians, or midwives, or the work they do.

pa·ram·e·ter (pə ram'ə tər) *n.* **1** *Mathematics.* a quantity that is constant in a particular calculation or case but varies in other cases. **2** any of a set of measurable features or properties that determine the characteristics or behavior of something: *parameters of space and time.* **3** any limiting or defining element or feature: *He found the parameters of his life too restricting.* [< NL *parametrum* < Gk. *para-* beside + *métron* meter]

par·a·mil·i·tar·y (par'ə mil'ə ter'ē *or* per'ə-) *adj.* **1** of or designating a group, unit, etc. organized along military lines and functioning as a civil force or an auxiliary military force: *a paramilitary police force.* **2** of or for such a force: *paramilitary training.*

par·a·mount (par'ə mount' *or* per'ə mount') *adj., n.* —*adj.* chief in importance; above others; supreme: *Truth is of paramount importance.* —*n.* an overlord; supreme ruler. [< AF *paramont* above < *par* by (< L *per*) + *amont* up < L *ad montem* to the mountain]
☛ *Syn.* See note at **dominant.**

par·amour (par'ə mür' *or* per'ə mür') *n.* **1** a person who takes the place of a husband or wife illegally. **2** *Archaic.* lover. [ME < OF *paramour* < *par amour* by love < L *per amorem*]

par·a·noi·a (par'ə noi'ə *or* per'ə noi'ə) *n.* a serious mental illness characterized by the firm belief that one is being persecuted or by delusions of grandeur. [< NL < Gk. *paranoia*, ult. < *para-* amiss + *nous* mind]

par·a·noi·ac (par'ə noi'ak *or* per'ə noi'ak) *adj. or n.* paranoid.

par·a·noid (par'ə noid' *or* per'ə noid') *adj., n.* —*adj.* **1** of, like, or showing paranoia. **2** having an extreme tendency to mistrust people and suspect them of ill will or bad intentions. —*n.* a person suffering from paranoia.

par·a·nor·mal (par'ə nôr'məl *or* per'ə-) *adj.* that cannot be explained in normal scientific terms: *paranormal phenomena, a paranormal experience.* —**par'a·nor'mal·ly,** *adv.*

par·a·pet (par'ə pet' *or* per'ə pet) *n.* **1** a low wall or mound of stone, earth, etc. to protect soldiers. **2** a low wall at the edge of a balcony, roof, bridge, etc. [< Ital. *parapetto* < *para* defend (< L *parare* prepare) + *petto* breast < L *pectus*]

par·a·pet·ed (par'ə pet'əd *or* per'ə-) *adj.* having a parapet or parapets.

par·a·pher·nal·ia (par'ə fə nā'lē ə *or* per'ə-, par'ə fər nāl'yə *or* per'ə-) *n.pl.* (*often used with a singular verb*) **1** personal belongings. **2** equipment; outfit. [< Med.L *paraphernalia*, ult. < Gk. *parapherna* < *para*, besides + *phernē* dowry]
☛ *Usage.* **Paraphernalia,** meaning "personal belongings," is plural in form and use: *My paraphernalia are ready to be shipped.* When the meaning is "equipment" *paraphernalia* is sometimes singular in use: *Military paraphernalia includes guns, rifles, ammunition, etc.*

par·a·phrase (par'ə frāz' *or* per'ə frāz') *v.* **-phrased, -phras·ing;** *n.* —*v.* state the meaning of (a passage) in other and different words. —*n.* an expression of the meaning of a passage in other words. [< F < L < Gk. *paraphrasis* < *para-* alongside of + *phrazein* say]

par·a·ple·gi·a (par'ə plē'jē ə *or* per'ə-) *n.* paralysis of the legs and the lower part of the trunk. [< NL < Gk. *paraplēgia* paralysis of one side of the body]

par·a·ple·gic (par'ə plē'jik *or* per'ə-, par'ə plej'ik *or* per'ə-) *n.,*

adj. —*n.* a person afflicted with paraplegia. —*adj.* having to do with, or afflicted with, paraplegia.

par·a·psy·chol·o·gy (par'ə sī kol'ə jē *or* per'ə-) *n.* the study of mental phenomena not explainable in terms of known physical laws, such as clairvoyance, telepathy, and psychokinesis.

par·a·site (par'ə sīt' *or* per'ə sīt') *n.* **1** an animal or plant that lives on, with, or in another, from which it gets its food. Lice and tapeworms are parasites. Mistletoe is a parasite on oak trees. **2** a person who lives on others without making any useful and fitting return. **3** in ancient Greece and Rome, a person who ate at the table or at the expense of another, earning meals by flattery or wit. [< L < Gk. *parasitos* < *para-* alongside of + *sitos* food]

par·a·sit·ic (par'ə sit'ik *or* per'ə-) *adj.* of or like a parasite; living on others. —**par'a·sit'i·cal·ly,** *adv.*

par·a·sit·i·cal (par'ə sit'ə kal *or* per'ə-) *adj.* parasitic.

par·a·sol (par'ə sol' *or* per'ə sol', par'ə sôl' *or* per'ə sôl') *n.* a light umbrella used as a protection from the sun. [< F < Ital. *parasole* < *para* ward off + *sole* sun]

par·a·thy·roid (par'ə thī'roid *or* per'ə-) *adj., n.* —*adj.* **1** near the thyroid gland. **2** of, having to do with, or caused by the parathyroid glands. —*n.* parathyroid gland. [< *para-¹* + *thyroid*]

parathyroid gland any of usually four small glands situated near or imbedded in the thyroid gland and producing a hormone that regulates the level of calcium in the body. The hormone of the parathyroid gland is necessary for life.

par·a·troop·er (par'ə trüp'ər *or* per'ə-) *n.* a soldier trained to use a parachute for descent from an aircraft into a battle area. [< *parachute* + *trooper*]

par·a·troops (par'ə trüps' *or* per'ə trüps') *n.pl.* troops moved by air and landed by parachutes in a battle area.

par·a·ty·phoid (par'ə tī'foid *or* per'ə-) *n.* a type of infectious disease having symptoms resembling those of typhoid fever. [< *para¹-* + *typhoid*]

par·boil (pär'boil') *v.* **1** boil till partly cooked. **2** overheat. [< F < LL *perbullire* < *per-* thoroughly + *bullire* boil; *par-* confused with *part*]

Par·cae (pär'sē *or* pär'kī) *n.pl. Roman mythology.* the Fates.

par·cel (pär'səl) *n., v.* **-celled** *or* **-celed, -cel·ling** *or* **-cel·ing.** —*n.* **1** a bundle of things wrapped or packed together; package. **2** a container with things packed in it. **3** a piece: *a parcel of land.* **4** a group; lot; pack.
—*v.* make a parcel of.
parcel out, divide into or distribute in portions.
[ME < OF *parcelle*, ult. < L *particula*, dim. of *pars, partis* part]
☛ *Syn. n.* **1.** See note at **bundle.**

parcel post **1** a class of postal service for sending heavy or large parcels. **2** mail handled by this service.

parch (pärch) *v.* **1** make hot and dry or thirsty: *The fever parched her.* **2** become dry, hot, or thirsty: *He was parched with the heat.* **3** dry by heating; roast slightly: *Corn is sometimes parched.* [ME *parchen, perchen*; origin uncertain]

par·chee·si *or* **par·che·si** (pär chē'zē *or* pär chē'zə) *n.* a game resembling backgammon, played by moving pieces according to throws of dice. [< Hind. *pachisi* < *pachis* twenty-five (highest throw)]

parch·ment (pärch'mənt) *n.* **1** the skin of sheep, goats, etc. prepared for use as a writing material. **2** a manuscript or document written on parchment. **3** a kind of paper that looks like parchment. [ME < OF *parchemin* < VL *particaminum*, blending of *parthica* (*pellis*) Parthian (leather) and *pergamina* of Pergamum, a city in Greece, whence it came]

pard¹ (pärd) *n. Archaic.* leopard; panther. [ME < OF < L < Gk. *pardos*]

pard² (pärd) *n. Slang.* a partner; friend; companion. [for *partner*]

par·don (pär'dən) *n., v.* —*n.* **1** forgiveness; excuse: *I beg your pardon but I'm afraid I am late.* **2** a setting free from punishment. **3** a legal document setting a person free from punishment. **4** a papal indulgence.
—*v.* **1** forgive; excuse: *to pardon someone's bad manners.* **2** set free from punishment: *to pardon a criminal.* [ME < OF *pardon* < *pardonner* to pardon < LL *perdonare* < L *per-* thoroughly + *donare* give < *donum* gift. DONATE.]
☛ *Syn. v.* **1.** See note at **excuse.**
☛ *Usage.* See note at **excuse.**

par·don·a·ble (pär'dən ə bəl *or* pärd'nə bəl) *adj.* that can be pardoned; excusable. —**par'don·a·bly,** *adv.*

par·don·er (pär'dən ər *or* pärd'nər) *n.* **1** in the Middle Ages, a person authorized by the church to sell papal pardons, called indulgences. **2** a person who pardons.

pare (per) *v.* **pared, par·ing.** **1** trim by cutting away irregular bits: *to pare a corn.* **2** cut or shave off the outer skin or layer of; peel: *to*

pare an apple. **3** cut away or lessen little by little: *We're trying to pare expenses.* [ME < OF < L *parare* make ready. Doublet of PARRY.]

☞ Hom. **pair, pear.**

par·e·gor·ic (par′ə gôr′ik *or* per′ə-) *n., adj.* —*n.* a soothing medicine containing camphor and a little opium. —*adj.* soothing. [< LL < Gk. *parēgorikos* soothing, ult. < *para-* at the side of + *-agoros* speaking]

paren. parenthesis.

pa·ren·chy·ma (pə reng′kə mə) *n.* **1** a soft tissue of higher plants composed of thin-walled; unspecialized, living cells that make up much of the substance of the softer parts of leaves, the pulp of fruits, the pith of stems, etc. **2** the essential, functional tissue of an animal organ, as distinguished from its connective or supporting tissue. [< Gk. *parenchyma* < *para-* beside + *en-* in + *chyma* what is poured]

par·ent (per′ənt) *n.* **1** a father or mother. **2** any animal or plant that produces offspring or seed. **3** a source; cause: *Danger is often the parent of fear.* [ME < OF < L *parens, -entis,* originally active pp. of *parere* bring forth]

par·ent·age (per′ən tij) *n.* **1** descent from parents; family line; ancestry. **2** the state of being a parent.

pa·ren·tal (pə ren′təl) *adj.* of or having to do with a parent or parents; like a parent's: *parental advice.* —**pa·ren′tal·ly,** *adv.*

par·en·ter·al (pə ren′tə rəl) *adj.* **1** of a drug, food, etc., taken into the body otherwise than by way of the digestive tract, especially by injection. **2** situated or occurring outside of the intestines. [< *para-′* + *enter-* (< Gk. *entera* intestines) + *-al′.* 20c.]

pa·ren·the·ses (pə ren′thə sēz′) *n.* pl. of **parenthesis.**

pa·ren·the·sis (pə ren′thə sis) *n., pl.* **-ses. 1** a word, phrase, or sentence, inserted within a sentence to explain or qualify something, and usually set off by brackets, commas, or dashes. A parenthesis is not grammatically essential to the sentence it is in. **2** either or both of two curved lines ( ) used to set off such an expression; bracket. [< L < Gk. *parenthesis,* ult. < *para-* beside + *en-* in + *thesis* a placing]

pa·ren·the·size (pə ren′thə sīz′) *v.* **-sized, -siz·ing.** insert as or in a parenthesis; put between the marks of parenthesis; put many parentheses in.

par·en·thet·ic (par′ən thet′ik *or* per′ən thet′ik) *adj.* **1** qualifying; explanatory. **2** put in parentheses. **3** using parentheses. —**par′en·thet′i·cal·ly,** *adv.*

par·en·thet·i·cal (par′ən thet′ə kəl *or* per′ən thet′ə kəl) *adj.* parenthetic.

par·ent·hood (per′ənt hùd′) *n.* the state of being a parent.

pa·re·sis (pə rē′sis, par′ə sis, *or* per′ə sis) *n.* **1** an incomplete paralysis resulting from spinal cord disease, muscular dystrophy, etc., affecting the ability to move but not the ability to feel. **2** a psychosis due to extensive destruction of brain tissue that is a late manifestation of syphilis, generally characterized by mental deterioration, seizures, speech defects, and progressive paralysis. Also called **general paresis** or **general paralysis of the insane.** [< NL < Gk. *paresis* a letting go, ult. < *para-* by + *hienai* let go]

pa·ret·ic (pə ret′ik *or* pə rē′tik) *adj.* of, having to do with, or caused by paresis. —*n.* a person suffering from paresis.

par ex·cel·lence (pär ek sə läns′: *French,* pä rek se läns′) *French.* beyond comparison; above all others of the same sort.

par·fait (pär fā′; *French,* pär fe′) *n.* **1** ice cream with syrup or crushed fruit and whipped cream, served in a tall glass. **2** a rich ice cream, containing eggs and whipped cream, frozen unstirred. [< F *parfait* perfect]

par·fleche (pär′flesh *or* pär flesh′) *n. Cdn.* **1** rawhide made from buffalo skin that has been soaked in lye to remove the hair and then dried in the sun. **2** an article, such as a shield or bag, made from this rawhide. [< Cdn.F *parflèche,* apparently < F *parer* to parry, ward off + *flèche* arrow]

par·he·lic (pär hē′lik) *adj.* of, having to do with, or resembling a parhelion.

parhelic circle a luminous ring in the sky parallel to the horizon and at the same altitude as the sun, caused by the reflection of light by ice crystals in the atmosphere. Compare **halo** (def. l).

par·he·li·on (pär hē lē ən *or* pär hēl′yən) *n., pl.* **-he·li·a** (-hē′lē ə *or* -hēl′yə). a bright, often colored, spot that sometimes appears to either side of the sun on the parhelic circle. Also called **mock sun.** [< L < Gk. *parēlion < para-* beside + *hēlios* sun]

pa·ri·ah (pə rī′ə) *n.* **1** an outcast. **2** a member of a low caste in S India and Burma. [< Tamil *paraiyar,* pl. of *paraiyan* drummer; because this caste provided the drummers at festivals]

pa·ri·e·tal (pə rī′ə təl) *adj., n.* —*adj.* of, having to do with, or forming the walls of a body cavity: *Two parietal bones form part of*

hat, āge, fär; let, ēqual, tèrm; it, īce
hot, ōpen, ôrder; oil, out; cup, pùt, rüle,
əbove, takən, pencəl, lemən, circəs
ch, child; ng, long; sh, ship
th, thin; ŦH, then; zh, measure

the sides and top of the skull. —*n.* a parietal bone or plate. [< LL *parietalis* < L *paries, -etis* wall]

pa·ri·mu·tu·el (par′ē myü′chü əl *or* per′ē-) *n.* **1** a system of betting on horse races in which those who have bet on the winning horses divide all the money bet. **2** a machine for recording such bets. [< F *pari-mutuel* mutual wager; *pari < parier* bet < L *pariare* make equal < *par* equal]

par·ing (per′ing) *n.* a part pared off; skin; rind.

par·i pas·su (par′ē pas′ü *or* per′ē-, par′ī pas′yü *or* per′ī-) *Latin.* at an equal rate of progress; side by side; equally.

Par·is (par′is *or* per′is) *n. Greek legend.* a son of Priam, king of Troy. His abduction of Helen, the wife of King Menelaus of Sparta, caused the Trojan war.

Paris green a very poisonous, emerald-green powder used as an insecticide and pigment. It is a compound of copper, arsenic, and acetic acid.

par·ish (par′ish *or* per′ish) *n.* **1** a district that has its own church and clergyman. **2** the people of a parish. **3** the members of the congregation of a particular church. **4** in New Brunswick, a political unit similar to a township. **5** in Quebec, a civil district, a municipality similar to a township and related to a religious parish. **6** in Great Britain, a civil district. [ME < OF *paroisse* < LL *parochia* < Gk. *paroikia,* ult. < *para-* near + *oikos* dwelling]

☞ Hom. **perish** (per′ish).

pa·rish·ion·er (pə rish′ən ər *or* pə rish′nər) *n.* a member of a parish. [earlier *parishion* < OF *paroissien*]

Pa·ri·sian (pə rizh′ən *or* pə rē′zyən) *n., adj.* —*n.* a native or inhabitant of Paris, the capital of France. —*adj.* of or having to do with Paris, or its people.

par·i·ty (par′ə tē *or* per′ə tē) *n.* **1** equality; similarity or close correspondence with regard to state, position, condition, value, quality, degree, etc. **2** an equality between the market prices received by a farmer for his commodities and the prices that he has to pay for labor, taxes, etc. [< L *paritas < par* equal]

park (pärk) *n., v.* —*n.* **1** a piece of land in or near a city, town, etc. set apart for public recreation: *Let's have a picnic in the park.* **2** a large area of land kept as a recreation area (for camping, picnicking, hiking, canoeing, etc.) and as a refuge for wildlife: *Canada has fine national and provincial parks.* **3** the grounds around a fine house. **4** parking lot. **5** a space where army vehicles, supplies, and artillery are put when an army camps. **6** a commercially operated recreation area with facilities for picnicking, swimming, etc.
—*v.* **1** leave (an automobile, etc.) for a time in a certain place. **2** arrange (army vehicles, artillery, etc.) in a park. **3** *Informal.* place, put, or leave: *Just park your books on the table.* [ME < OF *parc* < Med.L *parricus* enclosure. Doublet of PADDOCK.]

A traditional Inuit parka

A style of parka commonly worn in most parts of Canada in winter

par·ka (pär′kə) *n.* **1** a fur jacket with a hood, worn in the North. **2** a long, warm jacket with a hood, worn in winter. [< Innuktitut (Aleutian Eskimo) *purka* skin, outer coat < Russian 'hide, pelt' < Samoyed]

par·kade (pär kād′) *n.* a multi-storeyed structure for parking a large number of automobiles. [blend of *park* and *arcade*]

parking lot an area used for parking motor vehicles.

parking meter a device containing a coin-operated clock mechanism for indicating the amount of parking time that has been bought for a vehicle and the passing of that time.

Par·kin·son's disease (pär′kən sənz) a progressive disorder of the central nervous system occurring especially in men over the age of fifty and characterized by tremors, muscular rigidity, and impaired muscular co-ordination. [named after James *Parkinson* (1755-1824), an English surgeon, who first described it. 19c.]

park·land (pärk′land′) *n*. **1** *Cdn.* the region between the foothills of the Rockies and the prairie. **2** *Cdn.* the wooded region between the Barrens and the prairie. **3** land kept free from buildings, factories, etc. and maintained as a public park: *Parklands are intended to preserve the scenic beauty of the countryside.*

park ranger an official who patrols and helps maintain a national or provincial park.

park·way (pärk′wā′) *n*. a broad road through an area kept up as a park, made attractive by grass, trees, flowers, etc.: *There is a beautiful parkway running through Ottawa.*

par·lance (pär′ləns) *n*. a way of speaking; idiom: *The will was written in legal parlance.* [< OF *parlance* < *parler* speak. See PARLEY.]

par·lay (pär′lā or pär′lē) *v., n.* —*v.* **1** risk (an original bet and its winnings) on another bet. **2** build up by taking risks: *He parlayed a few hundred dollars into a fortune.* —*n.* a series of bets made by parlaying. [alteration of *paroli* < F < Ital. *paroli* grand cast at dice] ☛ *Hom.* **parley** (pär′lē).

par·ley (pär′lē) *n., pl.* **-leys**; *v.* **-leyed, -ley·ing.** —*n.* a conference or informal talk, especially one with an enemy to discuss terms of surrender, exchange of prisoners, etc. —*v.* discuss terms, especially with an enemy. [< F *parlée* < a pp. of *parler* speak, ult. < L *parabola* parable] ☛ *Hom.* **parlay.**

par·lia·ment (pär′lə mənt) *n*. **1** the highest lawmaking body in certain countries. **2** **Parliament**, **a** the national lawmaking body of Canada, consisting of the Senate and the House of Commons. **b** the national lawmaking body of the United Kingdom, consisting of the House of Lords and the House of Commons. **c** the lawmaking body of a country or colony having the British system of government. [ME < OF *parlement* < *parler* speak. See PARLEY.] p0809b

par·lia·men·tar·i·an (pär′lə men ter′ē ən) *n*. **1** a person skilled in parliamentary procedure or debate. **2** **Parliamentarian**, a person who supported Parliament against Charles I of England.

par·lia·men·ta·ry (pär′lə men′tə rē or pär′lə men′trē) *adj*. **1** of a parliament: *parliamentary authority.* **2** according to the rules and customs of a parliament or other lawmaking body: *Our debating society is run by the rules of parliamentary procedure.* **3** done by a parliament. **4** having a parliament: *a parliamentary democracy.*

parliamentary secretary a member of the House of Commons appointed to assist a Cabinet Minister in his parliamentary work.

par·lor or **par·lour** (pär′lər) *n*. **1** a room for receiving or entertaining guests; sitting room or living room. **2** a room or rooms specially furnished or equipped for a certain kind of business; shop: *a beauty parlor, a funeral parlor.* **3** a place where refreshments of various kinds are sold: *an ice-cream parlor, a beer parlor.* [ME < AF *parlour* < *parler* speak. See PARLEY.]

parlor car or **parlour car** *Archaic.* club car.

par·lour (pär′lər) *n*. parlor.

par·lous (pär′ləs) *adj., adv. Archaic* or *dialect.* —*adj.* **1** perilous. **2** very clever; shrewd. —*adv.* extremely. [var. of *perilous*]

Par·me·san (pär′mə zan′) *n*. a very hard, dry Italian cheese with a sharp flavor, usually used in grated form. [< *Parma*, Italy]

Par·nas·sus (pär nas′əs) *n*. **1** the fabled mountain of poets of which the summit is supposed to be their goal. **2** a collection of poems or belles lettres.
try to climb Parnassus, try to write poetry.
[< Mount *Parnassus*, in S Greece, in ancient times sacred to Apollo and the Muses]

pa·ro·chi·al (pə rō′kē əl) *adj*. **1** of or in a parish: *a parochial school.* **2** narrow; limited: *a parochial viewpoint.* [ME < OF < LL *parochialis* < *parochia* parish. See PARISH.] —**pa·ro′chi·al·ly,** *adv.*

pa·ro·chi·al·ism (pə rō′kē əl iz′əm) *n*. a parochial character or tendency; narrowness of interests or views.

parochial school a local school maintained by a church.

par·o·dist (par′ə dist or per′ə dist) *n*. a writer of parodies.

par·o·dy (par′ə dē or per′ə dē) *n., pl.* **-dies**; *v.* **-died, -dy·ing.** —*n.* **1** a humorous imitation of a serious writing. A parody follows the form of the original, but changes its sense to nonsense, thus making fun of the characteristics of the original. **2** any work of art that makes fun of another. **3** a poor imitation.

—*v.* **1** make fun of by imitating; make a parody on. **2** imitate poorly. [< L < Gk. *parōidia* < *para-* beside + *ōidē* song]

pa·role (pə rōl′) *n., v.* **-roled, -rol·ing.** —*n.* **1** a conditional release from prison or jail before the full term is served: *The prisoner was released on parole.* **2** conditional freedom allowed in place of imprisonment. **3** word of honor: *The prisoner of war gave his parole not to try to escape.*
—*v.* give a parole: *The boys were paroled on condition that they report to the judge every three months.* [< F *parole* word < L *parabola* parable. Doublet of PARABLE, PALAVER.]

pa·rot·id (pə rot′id) *adj., n.* —*adj.* near the ear. The **parotid glands,** one in front of each ear, supply saliva to the mouth through the **parotid ducts.** —*n.* a parotid gland. [< L < Gk. *parōtis, -idos* < *para-* beside + *ous, ōtos* ear]

par·ox·ysm (par′ək siz′əm or per′ək-) *n*. **1** a sudden attack or increase of symptoms of a disease; convulsion: *a paroxysm of coughing.* **2** a sudden violent emotion, etc.: *a paroxysm of rage.* [< Med.L < Gk. *paroxysmos,* ult. < *para-* + *oxynein* render acute]

par·ox·ys·mal (par′ək siz′məl or per′ək-) *adj*. of, like, or having paroxysms. —**par′ox·ys′mal·ly,** *adv.*

par·quet (pär kā′ or pär′kā) *n., v.* **-queted** (-kād′), **-quet·ing** (-kā′ing). —*n.* **1** a flooring made of inlaid pieces of wood, often of different kinds, fitted together to form a pattern. **2** the main floor of a theatre, especially from the orchestra pit to the part under the balconies; orchestra. —*v.* furnish with a parquet floor: *to parquet a room.* [< F *parquet,* dim. of *parc* park]

parquet circle the part of the main floor of a theatre that is under the balcony.

par·quet·ry (pär′kit rē) *n., pl.* **-ries.** woodwork of small pieces of wood, often in different shapes and of different kinds, arranged in a geometric pattern. Parquetry is used especially for floors.

parr (pär) *n., pl.* **parr** or **parrs.** a young salmon before it leaves fresh water and enters the sea. Parr have dark vertical markings on the sides. [< Scottish dial.]

par·ra·keet (par′ə kēt or per′ə kēt) *n*. See **parakeet.**

par·ri·cid·al (par′ə sīd′əl or per′ə-) *adj*. of or having to do with parricide.

par·ri·cide (par′ə sīd′ or per′ə sīd′) *n*. **1** the crime of killing one's parent or a close relative. **2** a person who commits parricide. [< F < L *parricidium* the murder of a kinsman < **parus* kinsman + *-cidium* the act of killing (for def. 1); < F < L *parricida* one who murders a kinsman < **parus* + *-cida* killer (for def. 2)]

par·rot (par′ət or per′ət) *n., v.* —*n.* **1** any of a family (Psittacidae, constituting the order Psittaciformes) of birds of the tropics and southern temperate regions, having a stout, hooked bill and, usually, brightly colored plumage. Parrots are excellent mimics. **2** a person who repeats words or acts without understanding them. —*v.* repeat without understanding. [< F *Perrot,* dim. of *Pierre* Peter] —**par′rot·like′,** *adj.*

par·ry (par′ē or per′ē) *v.* **-ried, -ry·ing;** *n., pl.* **-ries.** —*v.* **1** ward off; turn aside; evade (a thrust, stroke, weapon, question, etc.): *He parried the sword with his dagger.* **2** dodge; counter: *She parried our question by asking us one.* —*n.* the act of parrying; avoiding. [< F *parez,* imperative of *parer* < Ital. *parare* ward off < L *parare* prepare. Doublet of PARE.]

parse (pärs or pärz) *v.* **parsed, pars·ing.** **1** analyse (a sentence) grammatically, describing the function of each part. **2** describe (a word) grammatically, telling what part of speech it is, its form, and its use in a sentence. [< L *pars (orationis)* part (of speech)]

par·sec (pär′sek) *n*. a unit used with the SI for measuring distance in interstellar space, equal to about 30.857 petametres. *Symbol:* pc

Par·see or **Par·si** (pär′sē or pär sē′) *n*. in India, a member of a Zoroastrian sect, descended from Persians who first settled there early in the eighth century A.D. [< Persian and Hind. *Parsi* a Persian]

Par·si·fal (pär′sə fəl or pär′sə fäl′) *n*. Parzifal.

par·si·mo·ni·ous (pär′sə mō′nē əs) *adj*. too economical; stingy. —**par′si·mo′ni·ous·ly,** *adv.* —**par′si·mo′ni·ous·ness,** *n.*

par·si·mo·ny (pär′sə mō′nē) *n*. **1** carefulness in using money; thrift. **2** extreme carefulness in using money; stinginess. [< L *parsimonia* < *parcere* spare]

pars·ley (pärs′lē) *n., pl.* **-leys.** **1** a Mediterranean plant (*Petroselinum crispum*) widely cultivated for its aromatic leaves, which are used for flavoring and also for garnishing meats, etc. **2** (*adj.*) designating the family (Umbelliferae, also called Apiaceae) of plants mainly of north temperate regions that includes parsley and other plants used as herbs and spices, such as dill, caraway, and cumin, as well as a number of common vegetables such as the carrot, celery, and parsnip. [OE *petersilie,* also < OF *peresil*; both <

VL *petrosilium* < L < Gk. *petroselinon* < *petros* rock + *selinon* parsley]

pars·nip (pärs′nip) *n.* **1** a plant (*Pastinaca sativa*) of the parsley family native to Europe and Asia but widely cultivated for its long, tapering, fleshy, whitish root. **2** the root of this plant, usually eaten as a cooked vegetable. [ME < OF *pasnaie* < L *pastinaca* (cf. *pastinare* dig); form influenced by ME *nep* turnip]

par·son (pär′sən) *n.* **1** a minister in charge of a parish; rector. **2** any member of the clergy; minister. [< Med.L *persona* parson < L *persona* person, character. Doublet of PERSON.]

par·son·age (pär′sən ij) *n.* the house provided for a minister by his church.

part (pärt) *n., v., adj., adv.* —*n.* **1** something less than the whole: *What part of the chicken do you like best?* **2** each of several equal quantities into which a whole may be divided: *A dime is a tenth part of a dollar.* **3** a thing that helps to make up a whole: *spare parts. A radio has many parts.* **4** a share: *Everyone must do his part.* **5** a side in a dispute or contest: *He always takes his brother's part.* **6** a character in a play, motion picture, etc.; role: *She played the part of Juliet.* **7** the words spoken by a character: *An actor has to learn his part quickly.* **8** a role played by a person in real life. **9** a dividing line left in combing one's hair. **10** *Music.* **a** one of the voices or instruments. The four parts in singing are soprano, alto, tenor, and bass. **b** the music for one voice or instrument. **11** ability; talent: *a man of parts.* **12** a region; district; place: *He has travelled much in foreign parts.*

for (someone's) **part,** as far as one is concerned: *For my part, I'd rather just forget it.*

for the most part, mostly: *The attempts were for the most part unsuccessful.*

in good part, in a friendly or gracious way: *He took the teasing in good part.*

in part, in some measure or degree; to some extent; partly.

on (someone's) **part** or **on the part of** (someone), done by or proceeding from someone: *We had never heard of any improprieties on his part.*

part and parcel, a necessary or essential part: *Practising is part and parcel of learning to play the piano.*

take part, take or have a share.

—*v.* **1** divide into two or more pieces. **2** force apart; divide: *The policeman on horseback parted the crowd.* **3** go apart; separate: *The friends parted in anger.* **4** comb (the hair) away from a dividing line.

part from, go away from; leave.

part with, give up; let go.

—*adj.* less than the whole: *part-time.*

—*adv.* in some measure or degree; partly. [OE < L *pars, partis*; ME < OF *part*, n., and *partir* (< L *partire*), v., < L *pars, partis*]

☛ *Syn. n.* **1. Part, portion, piece** = something less than the whole. **Part** is the general word and means an element, fraction, or member of a whole, considered apart from the rest: *Save part of the roast for tomorrow night.* **Portion** means a part thought of not so much in relation to the whole from which it is taken as an amount or quantity making up a section or share: *Give a portion of each day to recreation.* **Piece** means a separate part, often thought of as complete in itself: *He ate a big piece of cake.*

☛ *Usage.* **On the part of** is often a rather clumsy substitute for **by, among, for,** and the like: *In recent years there has been a noticeable feeling on the part of (among) students that education is all-important.*

part. **1** participle. **2** particular.

par·take (pär tāk′) *v.* **-took, -tak·en, -tak·ing.** *Formal or jocular.* **1** eat or drink some: *We are eating lunch. Will you partake?* **2** take or have a share or part (*used with* **of**): *Would you care to partake of dessert?* **3** have to some extent the nature or character (*of*): *Her graciousness partakes of condescension.* [< *partaker*, for *part-taker*] —**par·tak′er,** *n.*

☛ *Syn.* **2.** See note at **share.**

par·tak·en (pär tāk′ən) *v.* pp. of **partake.**

par·terre (pär ter′) *n.* **1** the part of the main floor of a theatre under the balcony. **2** an ornamental arrangement of flower beds. [< F *parterre* < *par terre* on the ground]

par·the·no·gen·e·sis (pär′thə nō jen′ə sis) *n.* reproduction by the development of an unfertilized ovum, occurring especially among the lower plants and invertebrate animals.

par·the·no·ge·net·ic (pär′the nō jə net′ik) *adj.* of, having to do with, or produced by parthenogenesis. —**par′the·no·ge·net′i·cal·ly,** *adv.* [< Gk. *parthenos* virgin + E *genesis*]

Par·the·non (pär′thə non′ *or* pär′thə nən) *n.* in Athens, the temple of Athena on the Acropolis, regarded as the finest example of Doric architecture. [< L < Gk. *Parthenon* < *hē parthenos* the Virgin, i.e., Athena]

Par·thi·an (pär′thē ən) *n., adj.* —*n.* a native or inhabitant of Parthia, an ancient Asian kingdom that is now part of Iran. —*adj.* of or having to do with Parthia or its people.

Par·thi·an shot (pär′thē ən) a sharp parting remark or action. Parthian archers used to aim at their enemies while fleeing or pretending to flee.

hat, āge, fär; let, ēqual, tėrm; it, īce
hot, ōpen, ôrder; oil, out; cup, pút, rüle,
əbove, takən, pencəl, lemən, circəs

ch, child; ng, long; sh, ship
th, thin; ŦH, then; zh, measure

par·tial (pär′shəl) *adj.* **1** not complete; not total: *a partial loss.* **2** inclined to favor one side more than another; favoring unfairly; biassed: *A father should not be partial to any one of his children.* **3** having a liking; favorably inclined (*used with* **to**): *He is partial to sports.* [< LL *partialis* < L *pars, partis* part]

par·ti·al·i·ty (pär′shē al′ə tē *or* pär shal′ə tē) *n., pl.* **-ties. 1** a favoring of one more than another or others; the quality or state of being partial. **2** a particular liking; fondness: *Children often have a partiality for candy.*

par·tial·ly (pär′shəl ē) *adv.* **1** in part; not generally or totally; partly. **2** in a partial manner; with undue bias.

☛ *Syn.* **1.** See note at **partly.**

Par·tic·i·pac·tion (pär tis′ə pak′shən) *n. Cdn.* a private, non-profit organization whose purpose is to encourage and motivate the general public to become physically fit through participation in regular exercise. It is partly funded by the federal government.

par·tic·i·pant (pär tis′ə pənt) *n., adj.* —*n.* a person who shares or participates. —*adj.* participating.

par·tic·i·pate (pär tis′ə pāt′) *v.* **-pat·ed, -pat·ing.** have a share; take part: *The teacher participated in the children's games.* [< L *participare*, ult. < *pars, partis* part + *capere* take] —**par·tic′i·pa′tor,** *n.* —**par·tic′i·pa·to′ry,** *adj.*

☛ *Syn.* See note at **share.**

par·tic·i·pa·tion (pär tis′ə pā′shən) *n.* a participating; a taking part.

par·ti·cip·i·al (pär′tə sip′ē əl) *adj. Grammar.* of, having to do with, or formed from a participle; as, a **participial adjective** (a *masked* man, a *becoming* dress), a **participial noun** (in *cutting* ice, the fatigue of *marching*). —**par′ti·cip′i·al·ly,** *adv.*

par·ti·ci·ple (pär′tə sip′əl) *n.* a form of a verb used as an adjective. [ME < OF *participle*, var. of *participe* < L *participium* a sharing. Related to PARTICIPATE.]

par·ti·cle (pär′tə kəl) *n.* **1** a very small bit: *I had a particle of dust in my eye.* **2** a prefix or suffix. **3** *Physics.* **a** a minute mass of matter that while still having inertia and attraction is treated as a point without length, breadth, or thickness. **b** one of the fundamental units of matter, as the electron, neutron, photon, or proton; elementary particle. **4** a preposition, conjunction, article, or interjection. *In, if, an,* and *ah* are particles. [< L *particula*, dim. of *pars, partis* part]

particle board a kind of board used in building, furniture-making, etc., made of sawdust or small pieces of wood pressed together with a synthetic resin or similar binding agent.

par·ti-col·ored or **par·ti-col·oured** (pär′tē kul′ərd) *adj.* colored differently in different parts; partly of one color or tint, partly of another or others. [*parti-* < F *parti* divided, pp. of *partir* < L *partire* < *pars, partis* a part]

par·tic·u·lar (pər tik′yə lər) *adj., n.* —*adj.* **1** apart from others; considered separately; single: *That particular chair is already sold.* **2** belonging to some one person, thing, group, occasion, etc.: *A particular characteristic of a skunk is his smell.* **3** different from others; unusual; special: *a particular friend.* **4** hard to please; wanting everything to be just right; very careful: *She is very particular; nothing but the best will do.* **5** giving details; full of details: *a particular account of the game.* —*n.* an individual part; item; point: *The work is complete in every particular.*

in particular, especially.

[ME < OF < L *particularis* < *particula.* See PARTICLE.]

☛ *Syn. adj.* **1.** See note at **special.** —*n.* See note at **item.**

par·tic·u·lar·i·ty (pər tik′yə lar′ə tē *or* -ler′ə tē) *n., pl.* **-ties. 1** a detailed quality; minuteness. **2** special carefulness. **3** attentiveness to details. **4** a particular feature or trait. **5** the quality of being hard to please. **6** the quality or fact of being particular.

par·tic·u·lar·ize (pər tik′yə lər īz′) *v.* **-ized, -iz·ing. 1** mention particularly or individually; treat in detail; specify. **2** mention individuals; give details. —**par·tic′u·lar·iz′er,** *n.* —**par·tic′u·lar·i·za′tion,** *n.*

par·tic·u·lar·ly (pər tik′yə lər lē) *adv.* **1** in a high degree; especially. **2** in a particular manner. **3** in detail; minutely.

☛ *Syn.* **1.** See note at **especially.**

part·ing (pär′ting) *n., adj.* —*n.* **1** a departure; going away; taking

leave. **2** a division; separation. **3** a place of division or separation: *Her hair is arranged with a side parting.*
—*adj.* **1** given, taken, spoken, done, etc. on going away: *a parting request, a parting shot.* **2** departing. **3** dividing; separating. [< *part*, v.]

Parti Québécois (pär tē′ kā bek wä′) *Cdn.* a major political party in Quebec, formed as a separatist party in 1968.

Par·ti rouge (pär′tē rüzh′) *Cdn. French.* the name of a radical French-Canadian political party of the mid-nineteenth century, inspired by Louis Joseph Papineau, that supported universal suffrage, called for the abolition of the seigniorial system, and opposed political action by the Church.

par·ti·san (pär′tə zan′ *or* pär′tə zən) *n., adj.* —*n.* **1** a strong supporter of a person, party, or cause, especially one whose support is based on feeling rather than on reasoning. **2** a member of light, irregular troops; guerrilla. —*adj.* of or like a partisan. [< F < Ital. *partigiano* < *parte* part]

par·ti·san·ship (pär′tə zən ship′) *n.* **1** strong loyalty to a party or cause. **2** the act of taking sides.

par·ti·tion (pär tish′ən) *n., v.* —*n.* **1** a division into parts: *the partition of a man's wealth when he dies.* **2** one of the parts of a whole. **3** something that separates, especially a thin inside dividing wall or membrane.
—*v.* **1** divide into parts: *The empire was partitioned after the emperor's death.* **2** separate by a partition (*often used with* off): *A corner of the basement was partitioned off for a washroom.* [< L *partitio, -onis* < *partire*. See PART, v.]

par·ti·tive (pär′tə tiv) *n., adj.* —*n. Grammar.* a word or phrase referring to a part of a collective whole. *Some, few,* and *any* are partitives. —*adj.* expressing a part of a collective whole: *a partitive adjective.* —**par′ti·tive·ly,** *adv.*

par·ti·zan (pär′tə zan′ *or* pär′tə zən) See **partisan.**

part·ly (pärt′lē) *adv.* in part; in some measure or degree.
☞ *Syn.* **Partly, partially** = in part or to a certain extent, not wholly or totally. **Partly** = not wholly or entirely but only in part or in some measure or degree: *He is partly to blame.* **Partially** = not totally or generally but affecting only one part or to only a limited extent: *He is partially paralyzed.*

part·ner (pärt′nər) *n., v.* —*n.* **1** a member of a partnership. **2** associate or colleague: *The thief climbed through the window while his partner watched the street.* **3** spouse. **4** either person of a couple dancing together. **5** *Sports and games.* either of two players playing together against another pair. **6** one who shares: *My sister was the partner of my walks.*
—*v.* be a partner of. [var. of *parcener* < AF *parconier* < *parçon* partition < L *partitio, -onis*; influenced by *part.* See PARTITION.]

part·ner·ship (pärt′nər ship′) *n.* **1** a legal association of two or more persons in a business enterprise. The members of a partnership share the risks and profits of their business. **2** the people associated in a partnership. **3** the state of being a partner; association: *the partnership of marriage.*

part of speech any of several classes into which words are grouped according to their use or function in sentences. The main parts of speech in English are noun, pronoun, adjective, verb, adverb, preposition, conjunction, and interjection.
☞ *Usage.* **Parts of speech.** One of the fundamental facts of English grammar is that a word may function as more than one part of speech: In *spell the word,* we use **word** as a noun; *How will I word the message?,* **word** is the verb.

par·took (pär tůk′) *v.* pt. of **partake.**

par·tridge (pär′trij) *n.* **-tridg·es** or (*esp. collectively*) **-tridge.**
1 any of numerous medium-sized game birds (family Phasianidae) native to the Old World. The Hungarian partridge was introduced to Canada from Europe early in this century. **2** any of various North American game birds resembling the partridges, such as the ruffed grouse or the quail. [ME < OF *perdriz* < L < Gk. *perdix*]

par·tridge·ber·ry (pär′trij ber′ē) *n., pl.* **-ries. 1** a North American trailing evergreen plant (*Mitchella repens*) of the madder family having fragrant white flowers and scarlet berries. **2** the edible but almost tasteless berry of this plant.

part song a song consisting of parts for two or more voices in harmony, with one voice carrying the melody. Part songs are usually sung without accompaniment.

part time part of the time.

part–time (pärt′tīm′) *adj., adv.* —*adj.* using or working only part of the standard or usual number of hours: *a part-time job, part-time employees.* —*adv.* for only part of the usual number of hours: *He's working part-time this year.*

par·tu·ri·ent (pär tyür′ē ənt *or* pär tür′ē ənt) *adj.* **1** bringing forth young; about to give birth to young. **2** of or having to do with parturition. **3** about to produce an idea, literary work, etc.

par·tu·ri·tion (pär′tyə rish′ən, pär′tə-, *or* pär′chə-) *n.* the act or process of giving birth to young. [< L *parturitio, -onis* < *parturire* be in labor, ult. < *parere* bear]

par·ty (pär′tē) *n., pl.* **-ties; v. -tied, -ty·ing.** —*n.* **1** a group of people doing something together: *a sewing party, a dinner party, a scouting party of three soldiers.* **2** a gathering for pleasure: *On her birthday she had a party and invited her friends.* **3** a group of people having similar political aims and opinions, organized together to gain influence and control: *the Liberal, Conservative, or New Democratic Party.* **4** (*adj.*) of or having to do with a party. **5** one who takes part in, aids, or knows about: *He was a party to our plot.* **6** each of the persons or sides in a contract, lawsuit, etc. **7** *Informal.* person. **8** any one of two or more persons or families using the same telephone line.
—*v.* hold, attend, or take part in a party or parties: *partying till dawn.* [ME < OF *partie* < a pp. of *partir* divide < L *partire* < *pars, partis* part]
☞ *Usage.* See note at **person.**

party line 1 a telephone line by which two or more subscribers are connected with the exchange by one circuit. **2** the official policy or policies of a political party: *The members of parliament were not expected to vote along party lines on the issue.*

par·ty–lin·er (pär′tē lī′nər) *n.* a person who follows closely the officially adopted policies of his political party.

party wall *Law.* a wall dividing adjoining properties. Each owner has certain rights in it.

par value the value of a stock, bond, note, etc. printed on it; face value.

par·ve·nu (pär′və nyü′ *or* pär′və nü′) *n., adj.* —*n.* a person who has risen quickly to a position of wealth or power, but is not yet socially accepted in this new position; upstart. —*adj.* like or characteristic of a parvenu. [< F *parvenu,* pp. of *parvenir* arrive < L *pervenire* < *per-* through + *venire* come]

Par·zi·fal (pär′tsi fäl′) *n. German legend.* a knight who successfully sought the Holy Grail. As **Parsifal,** he is the hero of a music drama by Wagner. Compare **Perceval.**

pas (pä) *n. French.* **1** *Dancing.* a step or movement. **2** a kind of dance.

pas·cal (pas kal′) *n.* an SI unit for measuring pressure or stress, equal to the pressure produced by the force of one newton applied to an area of one square metre. *Symbol:* Pa [after Blaise *Pascal* (1623-62), a French mathematician]

pas·chal (pas′kəl) *adj.* **1** of or having to do with the Passover. **2** of or having to do with Easter; used in Easter celebrations. [ME < OF < LL *paschalis* < L *pascha* < Gk. < Aramaic *paskhā,* related to Hebrew *pesakh* Passover]

pa·sha (pash′ə, po shä′, *or* pä′shə) *n. Historical.* in Turkey, a title of honor or rank, placed after the name. Also, **pacha.** [< Turkish *pasha,* var. of *basha* < *bash* head]

pasque–flow·er (pask′flou′ər) *n.* any of various anemones, especially a Eurasian species, *Anemone pulsatilla,* widely cultivated as a garden flower. The prairie crocus is also sometimes called a pasque-flower. [< F *passefleur* < *passer* excel + *fleur* flower, altered to *pasque-flower* Easter flower (< OF *pasque* Easter, related to PASCHAL) because it blooms at Easter time; 16c.]

pas·quin·ade (pas′kwə nād′) *n., v.* **-ad·ed, -ad·ing.** —*n.* a publicly posted satirical writing; lampoon. —*v.* attack by lampoons. [< F < Ital. *pasquinata* < *Pasquino,* the name of a statue on which lampoons were posted]

pass (pas) *v.* **passed, passed, pass·ing;** *n.* —*v.* **1** go by; move past: *The parade passed. We passed the big truck.* **2** move on; go: *The salesman passed from house to house.* **3** go from one to another: *His estate passed to his children.* **4** cause to go from one to another; hand around: *The old coin was passed around for everyone to see.* **5** get through or by: *We passed the dangerous section of the road successfully.* **6** go across or over: *The horse passed the stream.* **7** put or direct (a rope, string, etc.): *He passed a rope around his waist for support.* **8** go away; depart: *The pain will soon pass.* **9** cause to go, move onward, or proceed: *to pass troops in review.* **10** discharge from the body. **11** be successful in (an examination, a course, etc.): *Jim passed Latin.* **12** cause or allow to go through something; sanction or approve: *to pass accounts as correct.* **13** ratify or enact: *to pass a bill or law.* **14** be approved by (a law-making body, etc.): *The new law passed the city council.* **15** go beyond; exceed; surpass: *His strange story passes belief.* **16** come to an end; die: *King Arthur passed in peace.* **17** use; spend: *We passed the days pleasantly.* **18** change: *Water passes from a liquid to a solid state when it freezes.* **19** take place; happen: *Tell me all that passed.* **20** go about; circulate: *Money passes from person to person.* **21** be accepted (*used with* **for** *or* **as**): *Use silk or a material that will pass as silk. She could pass for twenty.* **22** give approval to: *The inspector passed the item after examining it.* **23** express; pronounce: *A judge passes sentence on guilty persons.* **24** give a judgment or opinion: *The judges passed on each contestant.* **25** go

without notice: *He was rude, but let that pass.* **26** let go without action. **27** leave out; omit. **28** *Football, hockey, etc.* transfer (the ball, etc.). **29** *Card games.* give up a chance to play a hand, refuse to play a hand, or refuse to bid. **30** *Fencing.* make a thrust.
bring to pass, accomplish; cause to be.
come to pass, take place; happen.
pass away, a come to an end. **b** die.
pass by, fail to notice; overlook; disregard.
pass off, a go away. **b** take place; be done. **c** get accepted; pretend to be.
pass on, a pass from one person to another. **b** die.
pass out, a *Informal.* faint; lose consciousness. **b** hand out or circulate: *The teacher passed out the report cards.*
pass over, a fail to notice; overlook; disregard: *The teacher passed over my mistake.* **b** ignore the claims of (a person) to promotion, a post, honor, etc.
pass up, a give up; renounce: *to pass up a chance to go to college.* **b** fail to take advantage of.
—*n.* **1** the act of passing; passage: *The invading army made a swift pass through the country.* **2** success in an examination, etc.; passing an examination but without honors. **3** a note, licence, etc. allowing one to do something: *He needed a pass to enter the fort.* **4** free ticket: *a pass to the circus.* **5** state; condition: *Things have come to a strange pass when children give orders to their parents.* **6** a motion of the hands. **7** a sleight-of-hand motion; manipulation; trick. **8** a narrow road, path, way, channel, etc.; a narrow passage through mountains. **9** *Football, hockey, etc.* a transference of a ball, puck, etc. **10** *Fencing.* a thrust. **11** *Card games.* a decision not to bet, raise, double, etc. **12** *Informal.* a sexual approach; an attempt to kiss, etc.: *He made a pass at her as soon as they were alone.* [ME < OF *passer,* ult. < L *passus* step] —**pass′er,** *n.*

pass. 1 passive. **2** passenger.

pass·a·ble (pas′ə bəl) *adj.* **1** fairly good; tolerable; mediocre: *a passable performance. Her French is passable, but not good.* **2** that can be crossed or travelled on: *the roads are just barely passable.* **3** that can be freely circulated; current; valid: *passable coin.* **4** of a proposed law, able to be passed. [< F *passable* < *passer* to pass]

pass·a·bly (pas′ə blē) *adv.* fairly; moderately.

pas·sage (pas′ij) *n.* **1** a hall or way through a building; passageway. **2** a means of passing; way through: *to ask for passage through a crowd.* **3** right, liberty, or leave to pass: *The guard refused us passage.* **4** a passing: *the passage of time.* **5** a piece from a speech, writing, or musical composition: *a passage from the Bible.* **6** a journey, especially by sea: *We had a stormy passage across the Atlantic.* **7** a ticket that entitles the holder to transportation, especially by boat: *to secure a passage for Europe.* **8** a making into law by a favoring vote of a legislature: *the passage of a bill.* **9** what passes between persons. **10** an exchange of blows. **11** *Music.* a phrase or other division of a composition. [ME < OF *passage* < *passer* pass. See PASS.]

passage of arms an exchange of blows; quarrel.

pas·sage·way (pas′ij wā′) *n.* a way along which one can pass; passage. Halls and alleys are passageways.

pas·sant (pas′ənt) *adj. Heraldry.* walking and looking towards the right side: *a lion passant.* [ME < OF *passant* walking, ppr. of *passer.* See PASS.]

pass·book (pas′búk′) *n.* bankbook.

pas·sé (pa sā′; *French,* pä sā′) *adj.* **1** past one's prime. **2** no longer useful or fashionable; out of date: *That expression is very passé.* [< F *passé* passed]

pas·sen·ger (pas′ən jər) *n.* a traveller in a train, motor vehicle, boat, or aircraft who has nothing to do with its operation. [ME < OF *passagier* < *passage.* See PASSAGE.]

passenger pigeon a migratory wild pigeon (*Ectopistes migratorius*) of North America that was hunted to extinction by man. Passenger pigeons were abundant in E North America in the early 1800's, but by the early 1900's the species was extinct.

passe par·tout (pas′ pär tü′) **1** a frame for a picture, consisting of strips of gummed paper that fasten the glass to the backing. **2** paper prepared for this purpose. **3** something that passes or allows one to pass everywhere. [< F *passe partout* pass everywhere]

pass·er–by (pas′ər bī′) *n., pl.* **pass·ers·by.** a person who passes by: *The robbery was seen by a passer-by who called the police.*

pas·ser·ine (pas′ər īn′ or pas′ər in) *adj.* —*adj.* of, having to do with, or designating an order (Passeriformes) of birds, including more than half of all the existing species in the world. Passerine birds are perching birds and, because most of them sing, they are also called songbirds. —*n.* a bird belonging to this order. [< L *passerinus* < *passer* sparrow]

pas·sim (pas′im) *adv. Latin.* here and there; in various places.
☛ *Usage.* Passim is used in footnotes in referring to material found in several places in a book, article, series, etc.

pass·ing (pas′ing) *adj., n.* —*adj.* **1** going past or by: *A passing motorist drove them to a service station.* **2** not lasting; fleeting: *a*

passing idea; *a passing fashion.* **3** superficial or incidental: *a passing remark.* **4** that is now happening: *the passing scene.* **5** designating satisfactory completion of a course of study or examination: *The passing grade for the course is B–.* **6** of or designating a track, lane, etc. for passing another vehicle, etc. —*n.* **1** the act of one that passes: *the passing of summer. They mourned the passing of their father.* **2** a means or place of passing.
in passing, incidentally; by the way: *She mentioned in passing that she was planning a trip to the Far East.*

pas·sion (pash′ən) *n.* **1** very strong feeling: *Love and hate are passions.* **2** a violent anger; rage: *He flew into a passion.* **3** intense love or sexual desire. **4** a very strong liking or devotion: *a passion for music.* **5** the object of a passion: *Music is her passion.* **6** *Archaic.* suffering. **7** Usually, **the Passion, a** the sufferings of Jesus on the cross or after the Last Supper. **b** the story of these sufferings in the Bible. **c** a musical setting or a series of paintings, etc. of this. [ME < OF < L *passio, -onis,* ult. < *pati* suffer]
☛ *Syn.* **1.** See note at **feeling.**

pas·sion·ate (pash′ən it) *adj.* **1** affected with or easily moved to strong emotion, especially anger or indignation: *a passionate believer in freedom, a passionate person.* **2** caused by or showing strong emotion: *a passionate defence of the accused man.* **3** affected with or influenced by sexual desire. [< Med.L *passionatus* < L *passio, -onis.* See PASSION.] —**pas′sion·ate·ly,** *adv.* —**pas′sion·ate·ness,** *n.*

pas·sion·flow·er (pash′ən flou′ər) *n.* any of a genus (*Passiflora*) of mainly tropical vines having showy red, purple, white, or yellow flowers and, in some species, edible fruit.

pas·sion·less (pash′ən lis) *adj.* without passion; calm.

Passion Play or **passion play** a play representing the sufferings and death of Christ. A Passion Play is given every ten years at Oberammergau, West Germany.

Passion Sunday the second Sunday before Easter Sunday. It is the fifth Sunday in Lent.

Passion Week the second week before Easter; the fifth week in Lent, between Passion Sunday and Palm Sunday.

pas·sive (pas′iv) *adj., n.* —*adj.* **1** not acting in return; being acted on without itself acting: *a passive disposition.* **2** not resisting: *The passive obedience of a slave.* **3** *Grammar.* of or designating a form (called the voice) of a verb that shows the grammatical subject of a clause as the recipient of the action expressed in the verb. In *The window was broken by John, was broken* is passive; the subject *the window* receives the action represented by the verb *was broken.* Compare **active** (def. 8). **4** produced or induced by an outside agency: *passive exercise.* **5** not readily entering into chemical combination; inert; inactive.
—*n. Grammar.* **1** the passive voice. **2** a verb in the passive voice, consisting of a form of the verb **be** followed by a past participle. [< L *passivus,* ult. < *pati* suffer] —**pas′sive·ness,** *n.*

pas·sive·ly (pas′iv lē) *adv.* **1** in a passive manner. **2** as a passive verb. **3** in the passive voice.

passive resistance resistance to a government or other authority, especially by non-violent refusal to co-operate.

pas·siv·i·ty (pa siv′ə tē) *n.* the quality or state of being passive; lack of action; non-resistance.

pass·key (pas′kē′) *n., pl.* **-keys. 1** a key for opening several locks; master key. **2** a private key.

Pass·o·ver (pas′ō′vər) *n.* an annual Jewish holiday in memory of the escape of the Hebrews from Egypt, where they had been slaves. It is so called because, according to the Bible, a destroying angel "passed over" the houses of the Hebrews when it killed the first-born child in every Egyptian home. [from the *passing over* of the destroying angel]

pass·port (pas′pôrt) *n.* **1** an official document identifying and giving the citizenship of the holder, and giving the holder permission to leave and return to the country issuing the document, and to travel abroad under the protection of its government. **2** anything that gives one admission or acceptance: *An interest in gardening was a passport to my aunt's favor.* [< F *passeport* < *passer* pass + *port* harbor]

pass·word (pas′wėrd′) *n.* a secret word or phrase that identifies a person speaking it and allows him to pass.

past (past) *adj., n., prep., adv., v.* —*adj.* **1** gone by; ended: *Our*

---

hat, āge, fär; let, ēqual, tèrm; it, īce
hot, ōpen, ôrder; oil, out; cup, pút, rüle,
əbove, takən, pencəl, lemən, circəs
ch, child; ng, long; sh, ship
th, thin; ᴛʜ, then; zh, measure

troubles are past. **2** just gone by: *The past year was full of trouble.* **3** having served a term in office: *a past president.* **4** *Grammar.* of or designating a verb form expressing actions, happenings, or states that have ended or been completed at the time of utterance of a statement, etc.: *the past tense, a past participle.*
—*n.* **1** time gone by; time before: *Life began far back in the past.* **2** a past life or history: *Our country has a glorious past.* **3** a person's past life, especially if hidden or unknown: *He was a man with a past; no one knew that he had been in prison.* **4** the past tense or a verb form in it.
—*prep.* **1** beyond; farther on than: *The arrow went past the mark.* **2** after; later than: *ten past two. It is past noon.* **3** beyond in number, amount, or degree. **4** beyond the ability, range, scope, etc. of: *absurd fancies that are past belief.*
—*adv.* so as to pass by or beyond: *The cars go past once an hour.*
—*v. Archaic.* a pp. of **pass.**
☛ *Usage.* **Past** should never be used as a verb. The past tense of the verb **pass** should always be spelled **passed.**

pas·ta (pas′tə *or* päs′tə) *n.* **1** a type of flour paste used to make foods such as spaghetti, macaroni, ravioli, or noodles. **2** food or foods made of this paste. [< Ital.]

past absolute the past tense; preterite.

paste (pāst) *n., v.* **past·ed, past·ing.** —*n.* **1** a mixture, such as flour and water, that will stick paper together, stick it to a wall, etc. **2** dough for pastry. **3** a soft, dough-like mixture. Fish paste is pounded fish, highly seasoned. Pottery is made from a paste of clay and water. **4 a** a hard, glassy material used in making imitations of precious stones. **b** an artificial gem made of this. **5** a soft, jellylike candy. **6** a mixture of meal, fish, etc. used for spreading on sandwiches: *liver paste, chicken paste.*
—*v.* **1** stick with paste: *to paste a label on a box.* **2** cover by pasting: *to paste a door over with notices.* **3** *Slang.* hit with a hard, sharp blow. [ME < OF *paste* < Gk. *pasta* porridge < *passein* sprinkle] —**past′er,** *n.*

paste·board (pāst′bôrd′) *n.* **1** a stiff material made of sheets of paper pasted together or of paper pulp pressed and dried. **2** (*adj.*) made of pasteboard. **3** (*adj.*) flimsy; sham. **4** *Slang.* a ticket or card.

pas·tel (pas tel′ *or* pas′tel) *n., adj.* —*n.* **1** a kind of crayon made of ground coloring matter and gum, used in drawing. **2** a drawing made with such crayons. **3** the art of drawing with pastels. **4** a soft, pale shade of some color. **5** a short and slight prose sketch.
—*adj.* of a color, soft and pale: *pastel blue.* [< F < Ital. *pastello* < LL < Gk. *pasta.* See PASTE.]

pas·tern (pas′tərn) *n.* **1** the part of a horse's foot between the fetlock and the hoof. See **horse** for picture. **2** a corresponding part in other animals. [ME < OF *pasturon,* dim. of *pasture* tether for a horse, ult. < L *pastor* shepherd. See PASTOR.]

pas·teur·i·za·tion (pas′chər ə zā′shən *or* -ī zā′shən, pas′tər ə zā′shən *or* -ī zā′shən) *n.* **1** the process of pasteurizing. **2** the fact or state of being pasteurized.

pas·teur·ize (pas′chər īz′ *or* pas′tər īz′) *v.* **-ized, -iz·ing.** heat (milk, beer, etc.) to a high temperature and chill it quickly to destroy harmful bacteria without causing a major chemical change to the substance itself. [after Louis *Pasteur* (1822-1895), a French chemist]

pas·til (pas′təl) *n.* pastille.

pas·tille (pas tēl′) *n.* **1** a flavored or medicated lozenge. **2** a small roll or cone of aromatic paste, burnt as a disinfectant, incense, etc. **3** pastel (defs. 1, 2). [< F < L *pastillus* roll, aromatic lozenge, dim. of *panis* bread]

pas·time (pas′tīm′) *n.* something that causes the time to pass pleasantly; a form of amusement or recreation. Games and sports are pastimes. [< *pass* + *time*]

past master 1 one who has filled the office of master in a society, lodge, etc. **2** a person who has much experience in any profession, art, etc.

pas·tor (pas′tər) *n.* a minister in charge of a church; spiritual guide. [< L *pastor* shepherd, ult. < *pascere* feed]

pas·tor·al (pas′tər əl) *adj., n.* —*adj.* **1** of or having to do with shepherds or country life. **2** simple or naturally beautiful like the country: *a pastoral scene.* **3** of a pastor or his duties.
—*n.* **1** a pastoral play, poem, or picture. **2** a letter from a bishop to his clergy or to the people of his church district. [< L *pastoralis* < *pastor.* See PASTOR.] —**pas′tor·al·ly,** *adv.*
☛ *Syn. adj.* **1.** See note at **rural.**

pas·tor·ate (pas′tər it) *n.* **1** the position or duties of a pastor. **2** the term of service of a pastor. **3** pastors as a group.

past participle a participle that indicates time gone by, or a former action or state. *Played* and *thrown* are past participles in *She has played all day. The ball should have been thrown to me.*

past perfect *Grammar.* **1** a verb form employing the preterite of the verb *have* with a past participle and showing that an event was completed before a given past time. In *He had learned to read before he went to school, had learned* is the past perfect of *learn. Past perfect* and *pluperfect* mean the same. **2** the past perfect tense or a verb form in this tense.

pas·tra·mi (pəs trä′mē) *n.* smoked and highly seasoned beef, especially from a shoulder cut. [< Yiddish]

pas·try (pās′trē) *n., pl.* **-tries. 1** a paste, or dough, of flour and lard, butter, or shortening, used to make pie crusts, tarts, and certain other sweet foods: *Pastry has a flaky texture when it is baked.* **2** food made wholly or partly of this paste: *He eats too much pastry.* **3** a piece of pastry; a tart, turnover, etc. [< *paste* + *-ry*]

past tense 1 a tense expressing time gone by, or a former action or state. **2** a verb form in the past tense.

pas·tur·age (pas′chər ij) *n.* **1** the growing grass and other plants for cattle, sheep, or horses to feed on. **2** pasture land. **3** the pasturing of cattle, etc. **4** the right to pasture cattle, etc. on certain land. [< OF *pasturage,* ult. < *pasture.* See PASTURE.]

pas·ture (pas′chər) *n., v.* **-tured, -tur·ing.** —*n.* **1** a grassy field or hillside; grasslands on which cattle, sheep, or horses can feed. **2** grass and other growing plants. —*v.* **1** put (cattle, sheep, etc.) out to pasture. **2** of cattle, sheep, etc., feed on (growing grass, etc.). [ME < OF *pasture* < LL *pastura,* ult. < L *pascere* feed]

past·y¹ (pās′tē) *adj.* **past·i·er, past·i·est.** of or like paste in appearance or texture; especially, pale and flabby. [< *paste*] —**past′i·ness,** *n.*

pas·ty² (pas′tē) *n., pl.* **-ties.** pie filled with game, fish, etc.: *a venison pasty.* [ME < OF *pastee* < *paste* paste < LL *pasta.* See PASTE. Doublet of PATTY.]

pat¹ (pat) *v.* **pat·ted, pat·ting;** *n.* —*v.* **1** strike or tap lightly with something flat: *She patted the dough into a flat cake.* **2** tap lightly with the hand as a sign of sympathy, approval, or affection: *to pat a dog.* **3** walk or run with a patting sound.
pat on the back, praise; compliment.
—*n.* **1** a light stroke or tap with the hand or with something flat. **2** the sound made by patting. **3** a small mass, especially of butter.
pat on the back, a compliment.
[? imitative]

pat² (pat) *adj., adv.* —*adj.* apt; suitable; to the point: *a pat reply.* —*adv.* aptly; exactly; suitably.
have pat or **know pat,** *Informal.* have perfectly; know thoroughly: *John has the history lesson pat.*
stand pat, *Informal.* keep the same position; hold to things as they are and refuse to change: *Many people were angry with the government but the Prime Minister stood pat.*
[probably special use of *pat¹*]

Pat·a·go·ni·an (pat′ə gō′nē ən *or* pat′ə gōn′yən) *n., adj.* —*n.* a native or inhabitant of Patagonia, a region in S South America, including territory in Argentina and Chile. —*adj.* of or having to do with Patagonia or its people.

patch (pach) *n., v.* —*n.* **1** a piece of some material put on to mend a hole or a tear, or to strengthen a weak place. **2** a protective pad for placing over an injured eye: *The doctor ordered him to wear a patch over his right eye.* **3** a small piece of cloth, especially one used for patchwork. **4** a tiny bit of black cloth that women used to wear on their faces to hide a blemish or to set off their fair skin. **5** a small area different from that around it: *a patch of brown on the skin.* **6** a piece of ground: *a garden patch.*
—*v.* **1** put on a patch; mend, protect, or cover with a patch or patches: *to patch a torn sleeve, to patch a leaky pipe.* **2** put together or mend hastily or poorly (*usually used with* **up** *or* **together**): *to patch up a costume for Halloween.* **3** form or make with patches: *to patch a quilt.* **4** put an end to; settle (*usually used with* **up**): *to patch up a quarrel.* [ME *pacche,* ? var. of *pece* piece. See PIECE.]
—**patch′er,** *n.*
☛ *Syn. v.* **1.** See note at **mend.**

patch logging a system of logging by which only patches of trees in a stand are cut down, the surrounding trees being left intact to ensure natural reseeding of the cutover patch.

patch·ou·li or **patch·ou·ly** (pach′ù lē *or* pə chü′lē) *n.* **1** any of several Asian trees (genus *Pogostemon*) of the mint family having leaves that yield an essential oil used for perfumes. **2** a perfume with a heavy fragrance, made from this oil. [< Tamil]

patch·work (pach′wėrk′) *n.* **1** pieces of cloth of various colors or shapes sewed together. **2** sewing things in this way: *She enjoys patchwork.* **3** (*adj.*) made in this way: *a patchwork quilt.* **4** anything like this: *From the airplane, we saw a patchwork of fields and woods.*

patch·y (pach′ē) *adj.* **patch·i·er, patch·i·est. 1** abounding in or characterized by patches: *a patchy lawn.* **2** occurring in, forming or resembling patches. **3** not consistent or regular; not uniform in quality, etc.: *a patchy performance.* —**patch′i·ly,** *adv.* —**patch′i·ness,** *n.*

pate (pāt) *n.* **1** the top of the head; head: *a bald pate.* **2** brains. [ME; origin uncertain]

pâ·té (pä tā′) *n. French.* **1** a pastry case filled with chicken, sweetbreads, oysters, etc.; patty. **2** a meat paste, usually highly seasoned.

pâté de foie gras (pä tä də fwä grä′) *French.* a rich paste made with livers of specially fattened geese.

pa·tel·la (pə tel′ə) *n., pl.* **-tel·las, -tel·lae** (-tel′ē *or* -tel′ī). **1** kneecap. **2** an ancient Roman small pan or shallow vessel. **3** *Biology.* a panlike or cuplike formation or structure. [< L *patella,* dim. of *patina* pan. See PATEN.]

pa·tel·lar (pə tel′ər) *adj.* of or having to do with the kneecap.

pat·en (pat′ən) *n.* **1** the plate on which the bread is placed at the celebration of the Eucharist or Mass. **2** a plate or flat piece of metal. [ME < OF < L *patena* or *patina* pan, dish < Gk. *patanē*]

pa·ten·cy (pā′tən sē *or* pat′ən sē) *n.* being patent; obviousness.

pat·ent (*n., adj. 1, v.* pat′ənt *or* pā′tənt; *adj. 2* pā′tənt) *n., adj., v.* —*n.* **1** a right given by a government to a person by which he is the only one allowed to make, use, or sell a new invention for a certain number of years. **2** an invention that is protected by a patent. **3** an official document from a government giving a right or privilege. —*adj.* **1** protected by a patent: *a patent lock.* **2** evident; plain: *She smiled at the patent ineptness of their scheme.* —*v.* get a patent for. [< L *patens, -entis,* ppr. of *patere* lie open] —**pat′ent·a·ble,** *adj.*

pat·ent·ee (pat′ən tē′) *n.* **1** a person to whom a patent is granted. **2** a person licensed to use another's patent.

patent leather leather with a very glossy, smooth surface, usually black, made by a process formerly patented.

pa·tent·ly (pā′tənt lē *or* pat′ənt lē) *adv.* **1** plainly; clearly; obviously. **2** openly.

patent medicine a product advertised and sold as a remedy for certain ailments or illnesses, though its ingredients are not listed for the consumer.

Patent Office a government office that issues patents.

pa·ter (pā′tər) *n. Brit. Informal.* father. [< L]

pa·ter·fa·mil·i·as (pat′ər fə mil′ē əs *or* pā′tər-) *n.* a father or head of a family. [< L *paterfamilias* < *pater* father + OL *familias,* gen., of a family]

pa·ter·nal (pə tėr′nəl) *adj.* **1** of, having to do with, or like a father; fatherly. **2** related on the father's side of the family: *a paternal aunt.* **3** received or inherited from one's father: *Mary's blue eyes were a paternal inheritance.* [< LL *paternalis,* ult. < L *pater* father] —**pa·ter′nal·ly,** *adv.*

pa·ter·nal·ism (pə tėr′nəl iz′əm) *n.* the principle or practice of managing the affairs of a country or group of people as a father manages the affairs of his children.

pa·ter·nal·is·tic (pə tėr′nəl is′tik) *adj.* having to do with or characterized by paternalism.

pa·ter·ni·ty (pə tėr′nə tē) *n.* **1** the fact or state of being a father; fatherhood. **2** paternal origin. [< LL *paternitas* < L *paternus* fatherly < *pater* father]

pat·er·nos·ter (pat′ər nos′tər *or* pā′tər-) *n.* **1** the Lord's Prayer, especially in Latin. **2** one of the beads of a rosary on which the Lord's Prayer is said. [< L *pater noster* our father]

path (path) *n., pl.* **paths** (paᴛHz). **1** a track made by people or animals walking. It is usually too narrow for automobiles or wagons. **2** a way made to walk upon or to ride horses, bicycles, etc. upon: *He laid stone for a garden path.* **3** a line along which a person or thing moves; route; track: *The moon has a regular path through the sky.* **4** a way of acting or behaving; way of life: *"Some choose paths of glory, some choose paths of ease."* [OE *pæth*] —**path′less,** *n.*

pa·thet·ic (pə thet′ik) *adj.* **1** arousing pity and compassion; pitiful: *A lost child is a pathetic sight.* **2** arousing contempt; pitifully inadequate or unsuccessful: *a pathetic attempt to be funny.* [< LL < Gk. *pathētikos,* ult. < *pathein* suffer] —**pa·thet′i·cal·ly,** *adv.*

pa·thet·i·cal (pə thet′ə kəl) *adj.* pathetic.

pathetic fallacy the attribution of human emotions and characteristics to nature or inanimate things, especially as a figure of speech.

path·find·er (path′fīn′dər) *n.* **1** a person who finds a path or way, especially through a wilderness. **2** **Pathfinder,** a member, aged 12 to 15, of the Girl Guides.

patho– *combining form.* disease, as in *pathology.* [< Gk. *pathos* disease, suffering]

path·o·gen (path′ə jən) *n.* a disease-causing agent.

path·o·gen·ic (path′ə jen′ik) *adj.* having to do with pathogeny; producing disease. [< Gk. *pathos* disease + *gen-* produce]

hat, āge, fär; let, ēqual, tėrm; it, īce
hot, ōpen, ôrder; oil, out; cup, pùt, rüle,
ə above, takən, pencəl, lemən, circəs

ch, child; ng, long; sh, ship
th, thin; ᴛH, then; zh, measure

pa·thog·e·ny (pa thoj′ə nē) *n.* the production of disease.

path·o·log·ic (path′ə loj′ik) *adj.* pathological.

path·o·log·i·cal (path′ə loj′ə kəl) *adj.* **1** of pathology; dealing with diseases or concerned with diseases: *pathological studies.* **2** due to disease or accompanying disease: *a pathological condition of the blood cells.* **3** caused or controlled by an obsession; compulsive: *a pathological hatred of cats. He's a pathological liar.* —**path′o·log′i·cal·ly,** *adv.*

pa·thol·o·gist (pa thol′ə jist) *n.* a physician who is a specialist in pathology.

pa·thol·o·gy (pa thol′ə jē) *n., pl.* **-gies. 1** the study of the nature and causes of disease and of the changes in the body caused by them. **2** unhealthy conditions and processes caused by a disease.

pa·thos (pā′thos) *n.* the quality in experience or events, or in literature, art, or music that arouses a feeling of pity or sadness. [< Gk. *pathos* suffering, feeling]

path·way (path′wā′) *n.* path.

–pathy *combining form.* **1** a feeling, as in *telepathy.* **2** a disorder or disease, as in *neuropathy.* **3** the treatment of disease, as in *osteopathy.* [< Gk. *-patheia*]

pa·tience (pā′shəns) *n.* **1** the ability to accept calmly things that trouble or annoy, or that require long waiting or effort. **2** long, hard work; steady effort. **3** a card game played by one person; solitaire. [ME < OF < L *patientia < patiens, -entis.* See PATIENT.]

➤ *Syn.* **1. Patience, forbearance, fortitude** = power to endure, without complaining, something unpleasant or painful. **Patience** suggests calmness and self-control in enduring suffering or trouble, in waiting, or in doing something requiring steady effort: *Teachers need patience.* **Forbearance** suggests uncommon patience and self-control in keeping oneself from doing or saying something when greatly tried or provoked: *I admire their forbearance.* **Fortitude** sometimes suggests patience but emphasizes strength and firmness of character and indicates calm courage in facing danger or enduring hardship: *With fortitude the disabled veteran learned a new trade.*

pa·tient (pā′shənt) *adj., n.* —*adj.* **1** having or showing patience: *patient suffering.* **2** with steady effort or long, hard work: *patient research.* —*n.* a person who is being treated by a doctor, dentist, etc. [ME < OF < L *patiens, -entis* suffering] —**pa′tient·ly,** *adv.*

pat·i·na (pat′ə nə) *n.* **1** a film or incrustation, usually green, formed naturally over time on the surface of copper or bronze. **2** a smooth surface appearance produced by age and exposure on substances such as wood or stone: *The old table had a beautiful glossy patina.* **3** an appearance or aura assumed by something as a result of association, etc.: *the patina of success.* [< Ital. *patina,* ? < L *patina* dish, pan]

pat·i·o (pat′ē ō) *n., pl.* **-i·os. 1** an inner court or yard open to the sky. **2** a terrace for outdoor meals, lounging, etc. [< Sp.]

pat·ois (pat′wä; *French,* pä twä′) *n., pl.* **pat·ois** (pat′wäz; *French,* pä twä′). **1** a dialect different from the standard language of a country or district, especially one spoken in rural areas. **2** the special language characteristic of a particular group; jargon. [< F *patois* < OF *patoier* handle clumsily < *pate* paw < Gmc.]

pa·tri·arch (pā′trē ärk′) *n.* **1** the father and ruler of a family or tribe. In the Bible, Abraham, Isaac, and Jacob are patriarchs. **2** a person thought of as the father or founder of something. **3** a venerable old man. **4** in the early Christian church, a bishop of the highest rank. **5** a high-ranking bishop in certain churches, especially the Roman Catholic Church and the Eastern Orthodox Church. [< L < Gk. *patriarchēs < patria* family + *archos* leader]

pa·tri·ar·chal (pā′trē är′kəl) *adj.* **1** having to do with or suitable for a patriarch. **2** under the rule of a patriarch: *patriarchal life, a partriarchal church.*

pa·tri·ar·chate (pā′trē är′kit) *n.* **1** the position, dignity, or authority of a church patriarch. **2** a church district under a patriarch's authority. **3** patriarchy.

pa·tri·ar·chy (pā′trē är′kē) *n., pl.* **-chies. 1** a form of social organization in which the father is head of the family and in which descent is reckoned in the male line, the children belonging to the father's clan. **2** a family community, or tribe governed by a patriarch or the eldest male.

pa·tri·ate (pā′trē āt′ *or* pat′rē āt′) *v.* **at·ed, -at·ing.** *Cdn.* bring (government, decision-making powers, etc.) under the direct control of the people of a given region, nation, etc.: *The British parliament voted in 1982 to patriate the Canadian constitution.* [back formation from *repatriate*] —**pa′tri·a′tion,** *n.*

pa·tri·cian (pə trish′ən) n., adj. —n. **1** in ancient Rome, a member of the nobility. Compare **plebeian** (def. 1). **2** a person of noble birth or high social rank; aristocrat. —adj. **1** of or having to do with patricians. **2** noble; aristocratic. [< L *patricius*, adj. < *patres* senators (literally, fathers) of Rome]

pat·ri·cide¹ (pat′rə sīd′) n. the crime of killing one's father. [< LL *patricidium* < L *pater* father + *-cidium* act of killing]

pat·ri·cide² (pat′rə sīd′) n. one who kills his father. [< Med.L *patricida* < L *pater* father + *-cida* killer]

pat·ri·mo·ni·al (pat′rə mō′nē əl) adj. having to do with a patrimony; inherited from one's father or ancestors.

pat·ri·mo·ny (pat′rə mō′nē) n., pl. **-nies. 1** property inherited from one's father or ancestors. **2** property belonging to a church, monastery, or convent. **3** any heritage. [ME < OF < L *patrimonium* < *pater* father]

pat·ri·ot (pā′trē ət or pat′rē ət) n. a person who loves and loyally supports the interests and rights of his country. [< LL < Gk. *patriōtēs*, ult. < *patris* fatherland]

pat·ri·ot·ic (pā′trē ot′ik or pat′rē ot′ik) adj. inspired by love and loyal support for one's country: *a patriotic speech. She is very patriotic.* —**pa′tri·ot′i·cal·ly,** adv.

pat·ri·ot·ism (pā′trē ət iz′əm or pat′rē ət iz′əm) n. love and loyal support for the interests and rights of one's country.

pa·tris·tic (pə tris′tik) adj. having to do with the early leaders, or fathers, of the Christian church or with their writings.

pa·trol (pə trōl′) v. **-trolled, -trol·ling;** n. —v. **1** go the rounds as a watchman or a police officer does. **2** go around (a town, camp, etc.) to watch or guard.
—n. **1** the persons who patrol: *The patrol was changed at midnight.* **2** a going of the rounds to watch or guard: *He was on patrol last night.* **3** a group of soldiers, ships, or aircraft, sent out to find out all they can about the enemy. **4** one of the subdivisions of a troop of Boy Scouts or a company of Girl Guides. There are eight people in a patrol, including a patrol leader and a second. [< F *patrouiller* paddle in mud]

patrol leader **1** the person in charge of a military patrol. **2** the person in charge of a patrol of Boy Scouts or Girl Guides.

pa·trol·man (pə trōl′mən) n., pl. **-men** (-mən). a person who patrols, especially a police officer who patrols a certain district.

patrol wagon a closed van or truck used by the police for carrying prisoners.

pa·tron (pā′trən) n., adj. —n. **1** one who buys regularly at a given store or goes regularly to a given restaurant, hotel, etc. **2** a person, especially one having social or political influence, who sponsors or supports another person or a cause, institution, etc.: *a patron of the arts.* **3** a guardian saint or god; protector. **4** in ancient Rome, an influential man who took certain persons under his protection. —adj. guarding; protecting: *a patron saint.* [ME < OF < L *patronus* < *pater* father. Doublet of PADRONE, PATROON.]

pa·tron·age (pā′trən ij or pat′rə nij) n. **1** the regular business given to a store, hotel, etc. by customers. **2** the favor, encouragement, or support given by a patron. **3** favor, kindness, etc. given in a haughty, condescending way: *an air of patronage.* **4** the power to give jobs or favors: *the patronage of a premier, mayor, or reeve.* **5** jobs or favors given in return for political support.

pa·tron·ess (pā′trən is or pat′rən is) n. **1** a woman, especially one having social or political influence, who sponsors or supports another person or a cause, institution, etc. **2** a woman who is a guardian saint or a goddess.

pa·tron·ize (pā′trən īz′ or pat′rən īz′) v. **-ized, -iz·ing. 1** be a regular customer of; give regular business to. **2** act as a patron toward; support or protect: *to patronize the ballet.* **3** treat in a haughty, condescending way: *Children do not like being patronized by adults.* —**pa′tron·iz′er,** n. —**pa′tron·iz′ing·ly,** adv.

patron saint a saint regarded as the special guardian of a person, church, city, etc.

pat·ro·nym·ic (pat′rə nim′ik) n. a name derived from the name of a father or ancestor: *Williamson, meaning "son of William," is a patronymic.* [< LL < Gk. *patrōnymikos* < *patēr* father + dial. *onyma* name]

pa·troon (pə trün′) n. U.S. a landowner who had certain privileges under the former Dutch governments of New York and New Jersey. A patroon usually owned a large amount of land. [< Du. < L *patronus.* Doublet of PADRONE, PATRON.]

pat·ten (pat′ən) n. **1** a wooden overshoe with a thick sole. **2** a kind of wooden sandal or overshoe, mounted on an iron ring, to raise the foot above wet ground. [ME < OF *patin* < *pate* paw < Gmc.]

pat·ter¹ (pat′ər) v., n. —v. **1** make rapid taps: *bare feet pattering along the floor. The rain pattered against the window.* **2** move or run with light, rapid steps: *She pattered down the stairs.* —n. a series of quick taps or the sound they make: *the patter of hail on the roof.* [< pat¹]

pat·ter² (pat′ər) n., v. —n. **1** rapid and easy talk, such as that of a magician, comedian, or circus barker. **2** the specialized vocabulary of a certain group, especially thieves, etc.; cant. **3** rapid speech, usually for comic effect, introduced into a song.
—v. talk or say rapidly and easily, without much thought: *to patter a prayer.* [var. of *pater* in paternoster]

pat·tern (pat′ərn) n., v. —n. **1** an arrangement of shapes, lines, colors, etc.; design: *wallpaper with a floral pattern, frost patterns on the windows, a checkered pattern of sunlight and shade on the lawn.* **2** a model or guide for making something: *a paper dressmaking pattern.* **3** a fine example; model to be followed. **4** a configuration suggesting a design: *the pattern of events, traffic patterns.* **5** a standard group of traits, qualities, movements, acts, etc. that characterize a type or individual: *a behavior pattern, speech patterns.* **6** form and style in a work of literature or music: *the pattern of a Haydn symphony.* **7** a wooden or metal form used in a foundry to make a mould.
—v. **1** make or do according to a pattern; model (often used with **after** or **on**): *She patterned herself after her mother.* **2** form into or decorate with a pattern. [ME < OF *patron* pattern, patron < L *patronus* (see PATRON; with reference to a client's copying his patron]
☛ Syn. n. **2.** See note at **model.**

pat·ty (pat′ē) n., pl. **-ties. 1** a small pie or filled pastry. **2** a small, flat, usually round cake of chopped food: *hamburger or chicken patties.* **3** a small, round, flat piece of candy: *a peppermint patty.* [< F *pâté* < OF *pastee.* Doublet of PASTY².]

patty pan a small pan for baking little cakes, patties, etc.

pau·ci·ty (po′sə tē or pô′sə tē) n. **1** a small number; fewness. **2** a small amount; scarcity; lack. [< L *paucitas* < *paucus* few]

Paul Bunyan *North American folklore.* a giant lumberjack who did many incredible deeds, often assisted by his giant blue ox, Babe.

Pau·line (pol′īn or pôl′īn) adj. **1** of, having to do with, or written by the Apostle Paul. **2** of his doctrines or writings, especially the epistles attributed to him in the New Testament.

paunch (ponch or pônch) n. **1** the belly; abdomen. **2** a large, protruding belly; pot belly. **3** the first stomach of a cud-chewing animal; rumen. [ME < ONF *panche* < L *pantex, -ticis*]

paunch·y (pon′chē or pôn′chē) adj. having a big paunch. —**paunch′i·ness,** n.

pau·per (po′pər or pô′pər) n. **1** a very poor person. **2** a person supported by charity or by public welfare. [< L *pauper* poor. Doublet of POOR.]

pau·per·ism (po′pər iz′əm or pô′pər iz′əm) n. poverty.

pau·per·ize (po′pər īz′ or pô′pər īz′) v. **-ized, -iz·ing.** make a pauper of. —**pau′per·i·za′tion,** n. —**pau′per·iz·er,** n.

pause (poz or pôz) v. **paused, paus·ing;** n. —v. **1** stop for a time; wait. **2** dwell; linger: *to pause upon a word.*
—n. **1** a moment of silence; stop; rest. **2** a brief stop in speaking or reading. **3** any punctuation mark indicating such a stop. **4** *Music.* **a** the holding of a note, chord, or rest beyond its written time value. The length of a pause is at the discretion of the performer. **b** the symbol for this ⌣ or ⌢, written above or below the note or rest. [ME < OF < L *pausa* < Gk. *pausis* < *pauein* to stop] —**paus′er,** n.
☛ Syn. v. **1.** See note at **stop.**

pa·vane or **pavan** (pə vän′, pə van′, or pav′ən) n. **1** a slow, stately dance, usually in 4/4 time, popular in the 16th and 17th centuries. **2** music for this dance. [< MF < Sp. *pavana* < OItal. *padovana* Paduan (dance) < *Padova* Padua]

pave (pāv) v. **paved, pav·ing.** cover (a street, sidewalk, etc.) with pavement.
pave the way, prepare a smooth or easy way; facilitate progress or development: *The maps made by the earliest explorers paved the way for those who followed.*
[ME < OF *paver*, ult. < L *pavire* beat, tread down] —**pav′er,** n.

pave·ment (pāv′mənt) n. **1** a covering, or surface, for streets, sidewalks, etc. made of stones, gravel, concrete, asphalt, etc. **2** the material used for paving. **3** a paved road, etc. [ME < OF *pavement*, ult. < L *pavimentum* a beaten-down floor < *pavire* beat, tread down]

pa·vil·ion (pə vil′yən) n., v. —n. **1** a building, usually open-sided, used for shelter, pleasure, etc.: *a bathing pavilion.* **2** a large tent, often luxurious, for entertainment or shelter. **3** any building that houses an exhibition at a fair. **4** a part of a building higher and more decorated than the rest. **5** any of the group of detached or semi-detached buildings forming an institution, such as a hospital.

—v. furnish with a pavilion; enclose or shelter in a pavilion. [ME < OF < L *papilio, -onis* tent, butterfly]

pav·ing (pāv′ing) *n.* **1** the material for pavement. **2** pavement.

paw (po *or* pô) *n., v.* —*n.* **1** the foot of an animal having claws. Cats and dogs have paws. **2** *Informal.* a hand, especially when large or clumsy.
—*v.* **1** strike at or touch with a paw: *The kitten pawed the ball of yarn.* **2** scrape or strike with or as if with a hoof: *The horse was pawing the ground, eager to go.* **3** handle or touch awkwardly, rudely, or too intimately. **4** grab at or for wildly: *He pawed the air in an effort to keep himself from falling.* [ME < OF *powe* < Gmc.]

pawl (pol *or* pôl) *n.* a pivoted bar arranged to catch in the teeth of a ratchet wheel or the like so as to allow rotation in only one direction. See **ratchet wheel** for picture. [origin uncertain]

pawn¹ (pon *or* pôn) *v., n.* —*v.* give (something) as security that borrowed money will be repaid: *He pawned his watch to buy food until he could get work.* —*n.* **1** something left as security. **2** a pledge.
in pawn, in another's possession as security: *His watch is in pawn to the man who lent him money.*
[ME < OF *pan*]

pawn² (pon *or* pôn) *n.* **1** *Chess.* one of the 16 pieces of lowest value. **2** a person or thing used by someone to further his own purposes: *She used her friends and colleagues as pawns in her race for political power.* [ME < AF *paon*, var. of OF *peon* < LL *pedo, pedonis* foot soldier < L *pes, pedis* foot. Doublet of PEON. Related to PIONEER.]

pawn·bro·ker (pon′brō′kər *or* pôn′-) *n.* a person who lends money at interest on articles that are left with him as security for the loan.

pawn·shop (pon′shop′ *or* pôn′-) *n.* a pawnbroker's shop.

paw·paw (po′po *or* pô′pô) *n.* **1** a small North American tree (*Asimina triloba*) of the custard-apple family bearing oblong, yellowish, edible fruit with many beanlike seeds. **2** the fruit of this tree. **3** papaya. Also, **papaw**.

pax vo·bis·cum (paks′ vō bis′kəm) *Latin.* peace be with you.

pay¹ (pā) *v.* **paid** *or* (*obsolete except for def. 12*) **payed, pay·ing; n., adj.* —*v.* **1** give (a person) what is due for goods, services, work, etc. **2** give (money, etc.) that is due. **3** give money; give what is owed. **4** give money for: *Pay your way.* **5** hand over (money owed); hand over the amount of: *pay a debt.* **6** give; make; offer: *to pay attention, to pay compliments, to pay a visit.* **7** be profitable to; be worth while to: *It pays me to keep that stock. It wouldn't pay me to take that job.* **8** yield as a return: *That stock pays me four percent* **9** be profitable: *It paid her to be patient.* **10** reward or punish: *He paid them for their insults by causing them trouble.* **11** suffer; undergo: *The one who does wrong must pay the penalty.* **12** let out (a rope, etc.). **13** *Nautical.* fall off to leeward.
pay as you go, pay or discharge obligations as they are incurred.
pay back, a give the same treatment as received: *I'll pay her back for her hospitality by inviting her for dinner.* **c** take revenge on: *I'll pay you back yet!*
pay off, a give all the money that is owned; pay in full. **b** get even with; get revenge on. **c** *Informal.* pay money for so-called protection, but actually as a tribute to racketeers, etc.
pay up, pay; especially pay in full.
—*n.* **1** money or equivalent given for goods, services, or work; wages; salary. **2** a reward; punishment: *Dislike is the pay for being mean.* **3** a return for favors or hurts: *Dislike is the pay for being mean.* **4** the act of paying; payment, especially of wages: *rate of pay.* **5** the condition of being paid, or receiving wages: *workers in a person's pay or employment.* **6** (*adj.*) requiring a cash payment or the insertion of coins or tokens: *a pay telephone.*
in the pay of, paid by and working for.
—*adj.* containing enough metal, oil, etc. to be worth mining, drilling, etc.: *a pay lode.* [ME < OF *paier* < L *pacare* pacify < *pax, pacis* peace]

☛ *Syn. v.* **1. Pay, compensate, remunerate** = give someone money or its equivalent in return for something. **Pay** is the common word and means 'give someone money due for goods, work, or services': *He paid the doctor.* **Compensate** suggests making up for time spent, things lost, service given, etc.: *The railway compensated the farmer for his cow.* **Remunerate** suggests giving a reward in return for services, trouble, etc. and, like **compensate,** is used especially as being more polite than **pay** and as not suggesting crudely that money is expected or due: *The club remunerated the lecturer.*

☛ *Usage.* See note at **paid.**

pay² (pā) *v.* **payed, pay·ing.** cover (a ship's bottom, seams, rope, etc.) with tar, pitch, or another waterproof substance. [ME < OF *peier* < L *picare* < *pix, picis* pitch]

pay·a·ble (pā′ə bəl) *adj.* **1** required to be paid; due: *accounts payable.* **2** that may or can be paid. **3** of a mine or other business, profitable.

pay·day (pā′dā′) *n.* a day on which wages are paid.

pay dirt **1** earth, ore, etc. containing enough metal to be worth

hat, āge, fär; let, ēqual, tėrm; it, īce
hot, ōpen, ôrder; oil, out; cup, pút, rüle,
əbove, takən, pencəl, lemən, circəs
ch, child; ng, long; sh, ship
th, thin; ŦH, then; zh, measure

mining. **2** *Informal.* something that yields a profit or beneficial result.

pay·ee (pā ē′) *n.* a person to whom money is paid or is to be paid.

pay·er (pā′ər) *n.* one who pays; one who is to pay.

pay·load (pā′lōd′) *n.* **1** the part of a vehicle's load that produces revenue. **2** the warhead, instruments, etc. carried by a missile or rocket.

pay·mas·ter (pā′mas′tər) *n.* a person whose job is to pay wages.

pay·ment (pā′mənt) *n.* **1** the act or fact of paying. **2** the amount paid: *a monthly payment of $30.* **3** reward or punishment: *He said his child's good health was payment enough.*

pay·nim (pā′nim) *n. or adj. Archaic.* **1** pagan; heathen. **2** Moslem; Saracen. [ME < OF *paienisme* < LL *paganismus* < L *paganus* rustic. See PAGAN.]

pay·off (pā′of′) *n.* **1** a paying of wages. **2** the time of such payment. **3 a** returns from an enterprise, specific action, etc. **b** *Informal.* a dividing of the returns from some undertaking among those having an interest in it. **4** *Slang.* the climax of a story, situation, etc.

pay phone a coin-operated telephone.

pay·roll (pā′rōl′) *n.* **1** an employer's list of persons to be paid, together with the amount that each is to receive. **2** the total amount to be distributed among these persons.

payt. payment.

Pb lead (for L *plumbum*).

PBX Private Branch (Telephone) Exchange.

pc. **1** piece. **2** price.

p.c. **1** percent. **2** postcard. **3** petty cash.

P.C. **1** Police Constable. **2** Progressive Conservative. **3** Privy Council; Privy Councillor. **4** Past Commander.

PCB *pl.* **PCB's.** polychlorinated biphenyl, any of a group of poisonous organic compounds formerly widely used in industrial processes and as a heat-transfer and insulating fluid in cooling systems and electrical equipment, but since found to be dangerous environmental pollutants that tend to accumulate in animal tissues. PCB's are produced by replacing hydrogen atoms in biphenyl with chlorine atoms.

pct. percent.

pd. paid.

p.d. **1** per diem. **2** potential difference.

Pd palladium.

P.D. **1** per diem. **2** Postal District. **3** Esp.U.S. Police Department.

PDT or **P.D.T.** Pacific Daylight Time.

PE Prince Edward Island (*used esp. in computerized address systems*).

P.E. **1** Protestant Episcopal. **2** Petroleum Engineer.

pea (pē) *n.* **1** an annual vine (*Pisum sativum*) grown in many varieties for its smooth, round, protein-rich seeds borne in pods. **2** the seed of this plant, used as a vegetable when green or for soups, etc. when ripened and dried. **3** any of various plants that are related to or resemble the garden pea (*usually used in compounds*): *chick-pea, sweet pea.* **4** (*adj.*) designating a very large family (Leguminosae, also called Fabaceae) of herbs, climbing plants, shrubs, and trees found throughout the world, having usually compound leaves and bearing fruit in the form of oblong pods that split open evenly along the middle when ripe and in which the seeds are arranged in rows: *The bean, pea, clover, alfalfa, wisteria, and rosewood are some members of the pea family.* **5** especially in the West Indies, the fresh or dried seed of a legume, especially any of various beans or peas: *Rice and peas is a common West Indian dish.* **6** something resembling a pea.
like as two peas, exactly alike. [< *pease*, originally sing., later taken as a pl.]

peace (pēs) *n., interj.* —*n.* **1** freedom from war or strife of any kind. **2** public quiet, order, and security. **3** an agreement between contending parties to end a war: *to sign the peace, the Peace of Paris.* **4** quiet; calm; stillness: *peace of mind.*
at peace, a not in a state of war. **b** not quarrelling. **c** in a state of quietness; quiet; peaceful.

hold or keep (one's) **peace,** be silent.

keep the peace, refrain, or prevent others, from disturbing the (public) peace; maintain public order.

make peace, a effect a reconciliation between persons or parties at variance. **b** conclude peace with a nation at the close of a war.

—*interj.* **1** keep still! be silent! **2** a call of greeting or farewell. [ME < OF *pais* < L *pax, pacis*]

peace·a·ble (pēs'ə bəl) *adj.* **1** liking peace; keeping peace. **2** peaceful. —**peace'a·ble·ness,** *n.* —**peace'a·bly,** *adv.*

peace·ful (pēs'fəl) *adj.* **1** free of turmoil, commotion, or conflict; quiet; calm: *a peaceful day, a peaceful scene.* **2** keeping peace: *peaceful neighbors.* **3** of or having to do with peace or a time of peace: *peaceful uses for nuclear energy.* **4** without violence or force: *to settle a dispute by peaceful means.* —**peace'ful·ly,** *adv.* —**peace'ful·ness,** *n.*

☛ *Syn.* **1. Peaceful, placid, serene** = quiet and calm. **Peaceful** suggests a state of deep inner quiet, coming from release or freedom from everything that disturbs or excites: *It was peaceful in the mountains.* **Placid** suggests contentment and absence of excitement, especially associated with a disposition or nature that stays even and calm in the midst of excitement: *Placid cows grazed beside the highway.* **Serene** suggests a state of peacefulness and calmness that is above all disturbance: *She is always cool, gracious, and serene.*

peace·keep·ing (pēs'kē'ping) *n.* the preserving of peace, especially the enforcement of peace between hostile nations by means of an international body. —**peace'keep'er,** *n.*

peace·mak·er (pēs'māk'ər) *n.* a person who makes peace, especially by reconciling conflicts or quarrels between individuals or groups.

peace offering **1** an offering made to obtain peace. **2** in old Jewish custom, an offering of thanksgiving to God.

peace officer a person responsible for preserving public peace, such as a mayor, justice of the peace, or police officer, or officer of a prison.

peace pipe calumet.

Peace River Block a settled region in northern British Columbia and Alberta, lying in the fertile valley of the Peace River. It is often called the Peace River Country.

peace·time (pēs'tīm') *n.* **1** a time of peace. **2** (*adj.*) of or having to do with a time of peace.

peach¹ (pēch) *n., adj.* —*n.* **1** a juicy, roundish fruit having a soft, pinkish-yellow, fuzzy skin and a rough stone, or pit. **2** the small tree (*Prunus persica*) of the rose family that bears peaches. It is cultivated in temperate regions. See also **nectarine. 3** a yellowish pink color. **4** *Informal.* a person or thing especially admired or liked.

—*adj.* having the color peach. [ME < OF *pesche,* ult. < L *Persicum* (*malum*) Persian apple < Gk.]

peach² (pēch) *v. Slang.* give secret information; turn informer. [ME, var. of *appeach* < AF var. of OF *empechier* hinder < LL *impedicare* < L *in-* on + *pedica* shackle. Cf. IMPEACH.]

peach·y (pēch'ē) *adj.* **peach·i·er, peach·i·est. 1** like a peach, as in color or texture. **2** *Slang.* fine; wonderful. —**peach'i·ness,** *n.*

pea·cock (pē'kok') *n., pl.* **-cocks** or (*esp. collectively*) **-cock;** *v.* —*n.* **1** the male of a peafowl, a large bird having iridescent green, blue, and gold plumage, with a very large tail that can be erected and spread out like a fan. Most of the upper tail feathers have an eyelike spot at the tip. **2** peafowl. **3** a person who is vain and fond of showing off.

—*v.* strut like a peacock. [ult. < OE *pēa* (< L *pavo* peafowl) + *cock¹*]

peacock blue greenish blue.

pea·fowl (pē'foul') *n.* any of several large, brightly colored birds of the same family as pheasants, found in S Asia and Africa. The males of the **blue peafowl** (*Pavo cristatus*) of India and Sri Lanka and the **green peafowl** (*P. muticus*) of Burma and Java have the characteristic iridescent plumage. Both sexes of the rare **Congo peafowl** (*Afropavo congensis*) of Africa have bright plumage.

pea green light green.

pea·hen (pē'hen') *n.* an adult female peafowl.

pea jacket a short, double-breasted coat of thick woollen cloth, worn especially by sailors. [< Du. *pij-jekker* < *pij* a coarse woollen cloth + *jekker* jacket]

peak (pēk) *n., v.* —*n.* **1** the pointed top of a mountain or hill. **2** a mountain that stands alone. **3** the highest level or degree; maximum or high point: *the peak of a career, the peak of an election campaign.* **4** (*adj.*) of or being a peak, or maximum: *peak output.* **5** any pointed end or top: *the peak of a beard, the peak of a roof.* **6** a projecting brim at the front of a cap; visor. **7** the narrow part of a ship's hold at the bow or the stern. **8** the upper rear corner of a four-sided fore-and-aft sail. **9** promontory; headland. **10** a downward

point formed by the hairline in the middle of the forehead; widow's peak.

—*v.* **1** *Nautical.* tilt up: *to peak a gaff.* **2** come or cause to come to a maximum or high point: *The unemployment rate peaked in February. Their election campaign peaked too early.* [var. of *pick²*]

☛ *Hom.* **peek, pique.**

peaked¹ (pēkt *or* pēk'id) *adj.* having a peak; pointed: *a peaked hat.*

peak·ed² (pēk'id) *adj.* sickly in appearance; wan; thin. [< *peak,* v., look sick; origin uncertain]

peal (pēl) *n., v.* —*n.* **1** the loud, prolonged ringing of bells. **2** any loud, long, usually reverberating sound: *a peal of thunder, peals of laughter.* **3** a set of tuned bells, usually hung in a tower. **4** a complete series of changes rung on a given number of bells: *to ring a peal.*

—*v.* **1** sound out in a peal; ring: *The bells pealed.* **2** cause (bells) to ring in peals. **3** give forth loudly. [ME *pele*]

☛ *Hom.* **peel.**

pe·an (pē'ən) See **paean.**

pea·nut (pē'nut') *n.* **1** an annual plant (*Arachis hypogaea*) of the pea family having yellow flowers whose stalks later grow down into the ground where the ovary ripens and the pods are formed. **2** one of these pods, containing from one to three seeds that are roasted and eaten as nuts, and also yield an oil used in cooking, etc. **3** one of the seeds. **4 peanuts,** *Slang.* something of little value, especially a small amount of money: *It costs peanuts to run this car.* **5** a small or unimportant person.

peanut butter a spread made from roasted, ground peanuts, used as a filling for sandwiches, etc.

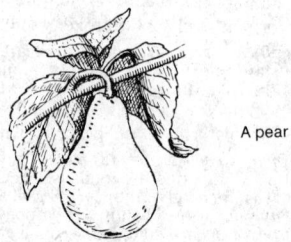

A pear

pear (per) *n.* **1** a sweet, juicy, edible fruit rounded at one end and smaller toward the stem end. **2** the widely cultivated tree (*Pyrus communis*) of the rose family that bears this fruit. **3** *Informal.* especially in the West Indies, avocado. [OE *pere* < LL *pira* < L *pirum*]

☛ *Hom.* **pair, pare.**

pearl (pèrl) *n., adj., v.* —*n.* **1** a white or nearly white gem that has a soft shine like satin. Pearls are formed inside the shell of a kind of oyster, and in other similar shellfish. **2** a similar gem made artificially. **3** anything that looks like a pearl, such as a dewdrop or a tear. **4** a very fine one of its kind. **5** a very pale bluish-grey. **6** mother-of-pearl. **7** *Printing.* a size of type; 5 point.

cast pearls before swine, offer or display something very fine to a person who cannot appreciate it.

—*adj.* **1** very pale bluish-grey. **2** formed into small, round pieces: *pearl tapioca.*

—*v.* **1** hunt or dive for pearls. **2** adorn or set with or as with pearls, or with mother-of-pearl. **3** make pearly in color or lustre. **4** convert or reduce to small, round pieces. [ME < OF *perle* < VL *perla*]

☛ *Hom.* **purl.**

pearl·ash (pèrl'ash') *n.* potassium carbonate, usually made by refining potash.

pearl grey a soft, pale, bluish-grey.

pearl·y (pèr'lē) *adj.* **pearl·i·er, pearl·i·est. 1** like a pearl; having the color or lustre of pearls: *pearly teeth.* **2** like mother-of-pearl. **3** adorned with or containing many pearls. —**pearl'i·ness,** *n.*

pearly nautilus nautilus (def. 1).

peas·ant (pez'ənt) *n., adj.* —*n.* a person who lives in the country and works on the land, especially a farm laborer or tenant farmer. —*adj.* of peasants: *peasant labor.* [ME < AF var. of OF *paysant* < *pays* country, ult. < L *pagus* district]

peas·ant·ry (pez'ənt rē) *n.* peasants collectively.

peas·cod (pēz'kod') See **peasecod.**

pease (pēz) *n. Archaic.* pea (*sometimes treated as a plural*). [OE *pise* < LL *pisa* < L *pisum* < Gk. *pison*]

pease·cod (pēz'kod') *n.* the pod of a pea.

pea·shoot·er (pē'shü'tər) *n.* a toy blowgun for shooting dried peas or other small objects.

pea soup **1** a thick soup made from dried peas, meat, and other

vegetables and, in Canada, associated especially with Quebec. 2 peasouper.

pea·soup·er (pē'süp'ər) n. 1 Cdn. Slang. a French Canadian. 2 Informal. a thick, heavy fog. Also, **peasoup.**

peat (pēt) n. vegetable matter consisting of mosses and other plants that have decomposed in water and become partly carbonized, used as fertilizer and as a fuel when dried. [ME pete < Anglo-L peta; origin uncertain] —**peat'y,** adj.

peat bog a bog composed of peat.

peat moss any of a genus (Sphagnum) of mosses that grow only in wet, acid areas; sphagnum. Peat moss forms peat when it dies and decomposes together with other plants.

A logger using a peavey to move a log

pea·vey (pē'vē) n., pl. **-veys.** a strong pole fitted with a movable hook like a canthook but having a sharp iron or steel spike at the end, used by loggers for handling logs in a drive, etc. [origin uncertain; poss. from a Joseph Peavey, who has been claimed as inventor]

pea·vy (pē'vē) n., pl. **-vies.** See **peavey.**

peb·ble (peb'əl) n., v. **-bled, -bling.** —n. 1 a small stone, usually worn smooth and round by being rolled about by water. 2 a rough, uneven surface on leather, paper, etc. —v. 1 prepare (leather) so that it has a grained surface. 2 pelt with pebbles. [OE pæbbel (in place names)] —**peb'ble·like,** adj.

peb·bly (peb'lē) adj. having many pebbles; covered with pebbles.

pe·can (pē'kan or pi kan') n. 1 a large hickory tree (Carya pecan, also called C. illinoensis) of the S United States and Mexico having deeply furrowed bark and hard wood and bearing olive-shaped, edible nuts. 2 the nut of this tree, having a thin, smooth shell and a sweet, oily kernel. 3 the wood of the pecan tree. [< Algonquian pakan hard-shelled nut]

pec·ca·dil·lo (pek'ə dil'ō) n., pl. **-loes** or **-los.** a slight sin or fault. [< Sp. pecadillo, dim. of pecado sin < L peccatum]

pec·ca·ry (pek'ə rē) n., pl. **-ries** or (esp. collectively) **-ry.** either of two small, piglike animals (Tayassu tajacu or T. albirostris) of North and South America having sharp tusks, small, erect ears, and a very short tail. The peccaries constitute the family Tayassuidae, and are distantly related to pigs. [< Carib pakira]

peck[1] (pek) n. 1 a unit for measuring volume of grain, fruit, etc. equal to eight quarts or one fourth of a bushel (about 9.1 dm³). 2 a container, for measuring, holding just a peck. 3 a great deal: a peck of trouble. [ME pec; origin uncertain]

peck[2] (pek) v., n. —v. 1 strike and pick with the beak or with something pointed like a beak. 2 make by striking with the beak or with something pointed: Woodpeckers peck holes in trees. 3 aim with a beak; make a pecking motion. 4 strike at and pick up with the beak: A hen pecks corn. 5 Informal. eat only a little, bit by bit. 6 Informal. kiss lightly and hurriedly. 7 find fault. **peck at, a** try to peck. **b** Informal. eat only a little, bit by bit: She just pecked at her food. **c** keep criticizing. —n. 1 a stroke made with the beak. 2 a hole or mark made by pecking. 3 Informal. a hurried or casual kiss: She gave him a peck on the cheek as she hurried out the door. [akin to pick[1]]

peck·er (pek'ər) n. 1 a person or thing that pecks, especially a bird such as a woodpecker. 2 Esp.Brit. Slang. courage: Keep your pecker up!

pecking order 1 an order of superiority established in flocks of chickens, etc., each bird enjoying the right of dominating those weaker than itself. 2 any similar hierarchy or order of precedence in human society.

peck·ish (pek'ish) adj. Esp.Brit. Informal. somewhat hungry.

pec·ten (pek'tən) n. a comblike part; especially, a membrane in the eyes of birds and reptiles that has parallel folds suggesting the teeth of a comb. [< L pecten < pectere to comb]
☞ Hom. pectin.

pec·tin (pek'tən) n. a substance that occurs in ripe fruits and is

hat, āge, fär; let, ēqual, tèrm; it, īce
hot, ōpen, ôrder; oil, out; cup, pút, rüle,
əbove, takən, pencəl, lemən, circəs

ch, child; ng, long; sh, ship
th, thin; ŦH, then; zh, measure

used to stiffen fruit jelly. [< Gk. pēktos congealing, curdling < pēgnynai make stiff]
☞ Hom. pecten.

pec·to·ral (pek'tə rəl) adj., n. —adj. 1 of, in, or on the breast or chest. 2 good for diseases of the lungs. —n. a medicine for the lungs. [< L pectoralis < pectus, pectoris chest]

pec·u·late (pek'yə lāt') v. **-lat·ed, -lat·ing.** steal (money or goods entrusted to one); embezzle. [< L peculari embezzle < peculium property < pecu money, cattle] —**pec'u·la'tion,** n. —**pec'u·la'tor,** n.

pe·cul·iar (pi kyül'yər) adj. 1 strange; odd; unusual. 2 belonging to one person or thing and not to any other; special; particular: This old Bible has a peculiar value. Some minerals are peculiar to the Canadian Shield. [< L peculiaris of one's own < peculium property. See PECULATE.] —**pe·cul'iar·ly,** adv.
☞ Syn. 1. See note at strange.

pe·cu·li·ar·i·ty (pi kyü'lē ar'ə tē or -er'ə tē) n., pl. **-ties.** 1 the quality or state of being peculiar. 2 a peculiar feature, characteristic, thing, etc.: They had grown used to his behavioral peculiarities.

pe·cu·ni·ar·y (pi kyü'nē er'ē) adj. of or having to do with money; in the form of money. [< L pecuniarius < pecunia money < pecu money, cattle]

ped·a·gog (ped'ə gog') See **pedagogue.**

ped·a·gog·ic (ped'ə goj'ik or ped'ə gō'jik) adj. of teachers or teaching; of pedagogy. —**ped'a·gog'i·cal·ly,** adv.

ped·a·gog·i·cal (ped'ə goj'ə kəl or ped'ə gō'jə kəl) adj. pedagogic.

ped·a·gogue (ped'ə gog') n. 1 Archaic. teacher; schoolmaster. 2 a narrow-minded or pedantic teacher. [ME < OF < L < Gk. paidagōgos < pais, paidos boy + agōgos leader]

ped·a·go·gy (ped'ə gō'jē or ped'ə gō'jē) n. 1 the profession of teaching. 2 the science or art of teaching.

ped·al (n. v. ped'əl; adj. ped'əl or pē'dəl) n., v. **-alled** or **-aled, -al·ling** or **-al·ing;** adj. —n. a lever worked by the foot; the part on which the foot is placed to move any kind of machinery. Organs and pianos have pedals for changing the tone. The two pedals of a bicycle, pushed down one after the other, make it go. —v. 1 work or use the pedals of; move by pedals: to pedal a bicycle up a hill. 2 work pedals. —adj. Zoology. of or having to do with the foot or feet, as of a mollusc. [< F < Ital. < L pedale (thing) of the foot < pes, pedis foot]
☞ Hom. peddle.

ped·ant (ped'ənt) n. 1 a person who displays his knowledge in an unnecessary or tiresome way. 2 a teacher or scholar who places too much emphasis on detail and precision in the use or presentation of knowledge. [< Ital. pedante, ult. < Gk. paideuein educate < pais, paidos boy]

pe·dan·tic (pi dan'tik) adj. 1 displaying one's knowledge more than is necessary. 2 tediously learned; scholarly in a dull and narrow way. —**pe·dan'ti·cal·ly,** adv.

ped·ant·ry (ped'ənt rē) n., pl. **-ries.** 1 a pedantic way of presenting or applying knowledge. 2 an example or instance of pedantry: The author's many pedantries make the book difficult to read.

ped·ate (ped'āt) adj. 1 having feet. 2 footlike. 3 having divisions like toes: a pedate leaf. [< L pedatus < pes, pedis foot]

ped·dle (ped'əl) v. **-dled, -dling.** 1 carry from place to place and sell. 2 sell or deal out in small quantities: to peddle candy, to peddle gossip. 3 travel about with things to sell. [apparently < peddler]
☞ Hom. pedal.

ped·dler (ped'lər) n. a person who travels about selling things that he carries in a pack, in a cart, or on a truck. Also, **pedlar.** [ME pedlere < pedder < ped basket]

ped·er·ast (ped'ər ast') n. a man who practises pederasty.

ped·er·as·ty (ped'ər as'tē) n. the practice of homosexual relations, especially by a man with a boy. [< NL paederastia < Gk. < pais, paidos boy + erastēs lover. 17c.]

ped·es·tal (ped'is təl) n. 1 the base supporting a column or pillar. See **column** for picture. 2 the base or foot of a statue or a large vase, lamp, etc. 3 any foundation or support.

put or **set on a pedestal,** regard as extremely admirable or important; idolize.
[< F < Ital. *piedestallo* < *pie* foot (< L *pes, pedis*) + *di* of + *stallo* stall[1] (< Gmc.)]

pe·des·tri·an (pə des'trē ən) *n., adj.* —*n.* a person who goes on foot; walker. —*adj.* **1** going on foot; walking. **2** without imagination; dull; slow: *a pedestrian style in writing.* [< L *pedester, -tris* on foot < *pes, pedis* foot]

pe·des·tri·an·ism (pə des'trē ən iz'əm) *n.* walking.

pe·di·at·ric (pē'dē at'rik) *adj.* of or having to do with pediatrics.

pe·di·a·tri·cian (pē'dē ə trish'ən *or* ped'ē ə trish'ən) *n.* a physician who is a specialist in pediatrics.

pe·di·at·rics (pē'dē at'riks *or* ped'ē at'riks) *n.* (*used with a singular verb*) the branch of medicine dealing with children's diseases and the care and development of babies and children. [pl. of *pediatric* < Gk. *pais, paidos* child + *iatreia* medical treatment < *iaesthai* heal]

ped·i·cab (ped'ə kab') *n.* a three-wheeled, pedal-operated vehicle having a seat over the rear wheels for one or two passengers and a seat in front for the driver. Pedicabs are available for hire in some countries in the Far East.

ped·i·cel (ped'ə səl) *n.* **1** a plant stalk that supports a single flower or spore-bearing organ. See **peduncle** for picture. **2** a short, narrow structure joining organs or parts; stalk. [< NL *pedicellus,* ult. < L *pes, pedis* foot]

ped·i·cure (ped'ə kyür') *n.* **1** a treatment for the feet, toes, and toenails, especially a cosmetic treatment including trimming and polishing of the toenails. **2** the care of the feet, toes, and toenails.

ped·i·cur·ist (ped'ə kyür'ist) *n.* a person whose work is giving pedicures.

ped·i·gree (ped'ə grē') *n.* **1** the list of ancestors of a person or animal; family tree. **2** ancestry; line of descent. **3** derivation, as from a source: *the pedigree of a word.* **4** the recorded line of descent of a purebred animal. **5** (*adj.*) of an animal, purebred: *a pedigree cat.* [apparently < F *pied de grue* foot of a crane; from appearance of 3-branched mark used in genealogies]

ped·i·greed (ped'ə grēd') *adj.* having a known pedigree.

ped·i·ment (ped'ə mənt) *n.* **1** *Classical architecture.* a low, triangular, gable-like part forming the front of a building with a two-pitched roof, especially over a portico. **2** a similar form used as a decoration on any building, piece of furniture, etc. See **portico** for picture. [earlier *periment, peremint,* probably alteration of *pyramid*]

ped·lar (ped'lər) *n.* peddler.

ped·o·log·i·cal[1] (ped'ə loj'ə kəl) *adj.* of or having to do with the study of children.

ped·o·log·i·cal[2] (ped'ə loj'ə kəl) *adj.* of or having to do with the study of soils.

pe·dol·o·gist[1] (pə dol'ə jist) *n.* a person trained in the study of children, especially one whose work it is.

pe·dol·o·gist[2] (pə dol'ə jist) *n.* a person trained in the study of soils, especially one whose work it is.

pe·dol·o·gy[1] (pə dol'ə jē) *n.* the study of the growth and development of children. [< Gk. *pais, paidos* boy, child + *-ology*]

pe·dol·o·gy[2] (pə dol'ə jē) *n.* the study of soils, including their formation and characteristics. [< Russian *pedologiya* < Gk. *pedan* ground + *-ologeia*]

pe·dom·e·ter (pi dom'ə tər) *n.* an instrument for recording the number of steps taken and thus measuring the distance travelled. [< F *pédomètre* < L *pes, pedis* foot + Gk. *metron* measure]

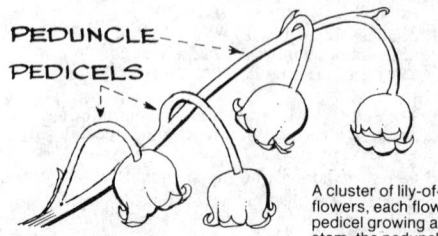

PEDUNCLE
PEDICELS

A cluster of lily-of-the-valley flowers, each flower on a pedicel growing along the main stem, the peduncle

pe·dun·cle (pi dung'kəl) *n.* **1** a plant stalk that supports a solitary flower or a flower cluster. **2** a narrow structure connecting an organ or part to a larger part or the whole body; pedicel (def. 2). [< NL *pedunculus,* dim. of L *pes, pedis* foot]

pe·dun·cu·lar (pi dung'kyə lər) *adj.* of or having to do with a peduncle.

pe·dun·cu·late (pi dung'kyə lit *or* pi dung'kyə lāt') *adj.* having a peduncle; growing on a peduncle.

pee (pē) *v.* **peed, pee·ing;** *n. Slang.* —*v.* urinate. —*n.* **1** urine. **2** the act of urinating.

peek (pēk) *v.* look quickly or secretly: *He pretended to have his eyes covered, but I could see he was peeking between his fingers. She peeked around the corner.* —*n.* a quick or secret look: *We took a peek through the crack in the door.* [ME *piken;* origin uncertain]
☞ Hom. **peak, pique.**

peel[1] (pēl) *n., v.* —*n.* the rind or outer covering of certain fruit or vegetables. —*v.* **1** strip skin, rind, or bark from. **2** strip: *The Indians peeled the bark from trees to make canoes.* **3** come off: *When I was sunburnt, my skin peeled.* **4** *Informal.* remove clothing, entirely or in part; strip.
keep (one's) eyes peeled, *Informal.* be on the alert: *Keep your eyes peeled for cars turning off the highway here.* [var. of obs. *pill;* ME *pele(n)* < OE *pilian* and OF *peler,* both < L *pilare* strip of hair < *pilus* body hair] —**peel'er,** *n.*
☞ Hom. **peal.**

peel[2] (pēl) *n.* a long-handled shovel used to put bread, pies, etc. into an oven or take them out. [ME < OF *pele* < L *pala* spade]
☞ Hom. **peal.**

peel·ing (pēl'ing) *n.* a piece or strip, as of rind or skin, peeled or pared off: *potato peelings.*

peen (pēn) *n., v.* —*n.* a usually rounded or wedge-shaped end opposite the striking face of the head of a hammer. —*v.* strike with a peen in order to flatten, shape, or bend.

peep[1] (pēp) *v., n.* —*v.* **1** look through a small or narrow hole or crack. **2** look quickly or secretly; peek. **3** emerge or show slightly, as if peeping: *violets peeping through the leaves. Her toe peeped through a hole in her sock.*
—*n.* **1** a look through a hole or crack. **2** a small hole or crack to look through. **3** a quick or secret look; peek: *to take a peep into the pantry.* **4** the first glimpse or coming out: *at the peep of day.* [? var. of *peek*]

peep[2] (pēp) *n., v.* —*n.* **1** a short, high sound such as that made by a baby bird; cheep: *the peeps of newly hatched chicks.* **2** a slight, feeble utterance, especially of protest: *I don't want to hear another peep out of you.* —*v.* **1** make a short, high sound like a baby bird. **2** speak in a small, weak voice. [imitative]

peep·er (pēp'ər) *n.* **1** a person or thing that peeps. **2** any of certain frogs that make peeping noises. **3** *Informal.* an eye.

peep·hole (pēp'hōl') *n.* a hole through which one may peep.

Peeping Tom a man who derives pleasure or satisfaction from secretly watching women undressing, etc. [from the name of the Coventry tailor who, according to legend, peeped at Lady Godiva as she rode naked through the streets]

peep show an exhibition of objects or pictures viewed through a small opening, usually fitted with a magnifying glass.

peer[1] (pēr) *n.* **1** a person of the same rank, ability, etc. as another; equal: *a jury of one's peers. He is so fine a man that it would be hard to find his peer.* **2** a member of the peerage; a noble. Dukes, marquises, earls, counts, viscounts, and barons are British peers. [ME < OF *per* < L *par* equal. Doublet of PAR.]
☞ Hom. **pier.**

peer[2] (pēr) *v.* **1** look closely to see clearly, as a near-sighted person does: *She peered at the tag to read the price.* **2** come out slightly; peep out: *The sun was peering from behind a cloud.* **3** *Poetic.* appear. [apparently a var. of *appear*]
☞ Hom. **pier.**

peer·age (pēr'ij) *n.* **1** all the titled persons of a country; the body of peers. **2** the rank or dignity of a peer. **3** a book giving a list of the peers of a country with their genealogy, titles, etc.

peer·ess (pēr'is) *n.* **1** a woman who is a member of the peerage; noblewoman. **2** the wife or widow of a peer.

peer group the people of approximately the same age, social status, etc. within a culture or community: *peer-group pressure. As a boy, he was heavily influenced by his peer group at school.*

peer·less (pēr'lis) *adj.* without an equal; matchless: *He was a peerless leader.* —**peer'less·ly,** *adv.* —**peer'less·ness,** *n.*

peeve (pēv) *v.* **peeved, peev·ing;** *n. Informal.* —*v.* make cross; annoy. —*n.* an annoyance.

pee·vish (pē'vish) *adj.* cross; fretful; complaining. [ME *pevysh;* origin uncertain] —**pee'vish·ly,** *adv.* —**pee'vish·ness,** *n.*

pee·wee (pē'wē) *n.* **1** a very small person or thing. **2** *Juvenile sports.* a player aged between 8 and 12. Also, **pewee.**

peg (peg) *n., v.* **pegged, peg·ging.** —*n.* **1** a pin or small bolt of wood, metal, etc. used to fasten parts together, to hang things on, to stop a hole, to make fast a rope or string, to mark the score in a game, etc. **2** a step; degree. **3** a small drink of alcoholic liquor. **take (someone) down a peg**, lower the pride of; humble. —*v.* **1** fasten or hold with pegs. **2** mark with pegs. **3** work hard and steadily (*usually used with* **away**): *pegging away at one's studies.* **4** keep the price of (a stock, bond, etc.) from going up or down. **5** *Informal.* aim; throw. [apparently < MDu. *pegge*]

Peg·a·sus (peg′ə səs) *n.* **1** *Greek mythology.* a winged horse that by stamping his hoof caused the Hippocrene, the fountain of the Muses, to flow on Mount Helicon. **2** poetic genius or inspiration. **3** *Astronomy.* a northern constellation.

peg·board (peg′bôrd′) *n.* a board with evenly spaced holes in which pegs or hooks are inserted to hold tools, displays, etc.

peg leg **1** a wooden leg. **2** *Informal.* a person who has a wooden leg.

peg top a wooden top spinning on a metal peg.

P.E.I. Prince Edward Island.

peign·oir (pān wär′ *or* pān′wär) *n.* **1** a woman's dressing gown. **2** negligee. [< F *peignoir* < *peigner* < L *pectinare* comb < *pecten* a comb]

pe·jo·ra·tive (pi jôr′ə tiv *or* pē′jə rā′tiv) *adj., n.* —*adj.* tending to make worse; disparaging; depreciatory. —*n.* a pejorative word, suffix, or phrase. [< L *pejoratus* < *pejor* worse] —**pe·jo′ra·tive·ly**, *adv.*

Pe·kin (pē kin′) *n.* a breed of large white ducks, originally from China, raised primarily for their meat. [< F *Pékin* Peiping, the capital of China]

Pe·kin·ese (pē′kən ēz′) *n., pl.* **-ese;** *adj.* —*n. or adj.* Pekingese.

Pe·king·ese (pē′king ēz′) *n., adj.* —*n.* **1** a breed of small dog with long, soft hair and a broad, flat nose, originally developed in China. **2** a native or inhabitant of Peking, the capital of the People's Republic of China. **3** the Chinese dialect spoken in Peking. —*adj.* of or having to do with Peking, its people, or their dialect. [< *Peking* Peiping, the capital of China]

pe·koe (pē′kō) *n.* a kind of black tea. [< Chinese *pek-ho* white down; because the leaves are picked young with the "down" still on them]

pel·age (pel′ij) *n.* the hair, fur, wool, or other soft covering of a mammal. [< F < OF *peil* hair < L *pilus*]

pe·lag·ic (pə laj′ik) *adj.* of, having to do with, or living in the ocean or the open sea. [< L < Gk. *pelagikos* < *pelagos* sea]

pelf (pelf) *n.* money or riches, thought of as bad or degrading. [ME < OF *pelfre* spoils]

pel·i·can (pel′ə kən) *n.* any of a small genus (*Pelacanus*, constituting the family Pelecanidae) of large, fish-eating, web-footed aquatic birds having a very long bill with a distensible pouch on the underside for scooping up and holding food. The largest species are among the largest flying birds. [< LL < Gk. *pelekan*, ? ult. < *pelekys* axe]

pe·lisse (pə lēs′) *n.* **1** a coat lined or trimmed with fur. **2** a woman's long cloak. [< F *pelisse*, ult. < LL *pelliceus* of fur < *pellis* skin]

pel·lag·ra (pə lag′rə *or* pə lā′grə) *n.* a disease associated chiefly with a deficiency of niacin, characterized by burning and itching skin, diarrhea and vomiting, and, in severe cases, nervous and mental disorders. [< Ital. < *pelle* skin; apparently patterned after *podagra* gout in the feet (< Gk.)]

pel·let (pel′it) *n.* **1** a little ball of paper, mud, medicine, compressed food for animals, etc. **2** bullet. **3** a piece of small shot. [ME < OF *pelote* < L *pila* ball]

pel·let·ize (pel′ə tīz′) *v.* **-ized, iz·ing.** form into pellets: *pelletized iron ore.* —**pel′let·i·za′tion,** *n.* —**pel′let·iz′er,** *n.*

pel·li·cle (pel′ə kəl) *n.* a very thin skin; membrane. [< L *pellicula*, dim. of *pellis* skin]

pell–mell *or* **pell·mell** (pel′mel′) *adv., adj., n.* —*adv.* **1** in a rushing, tumbling mass or crowd. **2** in headlong haste. —*adj.* headlong; tumultuous. —*n.* violent disorder or confusion. [< F *pêle-mêle*, latter element apparently < *mêler* mix]

pel·lu·cid (pə lü′sid) *adj.* **1** transparent; clear: *a pellucid stream.* **2** clearly expressed; easy to understand: *pellucid language.* [< L *pellucidus*, ult. < *per-* through + *lucere* to shine] —**pel·lu′cid·ly,** *adv.* —**pel·lu′cid·ness,** *n.*

Pel·o·pon·ne·sian (pel′ə pə nē′shən *or* -nē′zhən) *n., adj.* —*n.* a native or inhabitant of Peloponnesus, a peninsula in S Greece. —*adj.* of or having to do with the Peloponnesus or its people.

Pel·o·pon·ne·sus (pel′ə pə nē′səs) *n.* a peninsula that constitutes the southern part of Greece.

pe·lo·ta (pe lō′tə) *n.* a game of Basque or Spanish origin played

hat, āge, fär; let, ēqual, tėrm; it, īce
hot, ōpen, ôrder; oil, out; cup, pút, rüle,
əbove, takən, pencəl, lemən, circəs
ch, child; ng, long; sh, ship
th, thin; ᴛʜ, then; zh, measure

on a walled court with a hard ball that is struck with a curved wicker racket fastened to a glove on the hand. [< Sp. *pelota* < *pella* ball < L *pila*]

pelt¹ (pelt) *v., n.* —*v.* **1** throw things at; attack; assail: *The boys were pelting the dog with stones.* **2** beat heavily: *The rain came pelting down.* **3** throw: *The clouds pelted rain upon us.* **4** hurry. —*n.* **1** the act of pelting. **2** speed: *The horse is coming at full pelt.* [ME *pelten*, ? var. of *pulten* hasten, thrust < L *pultare* strike]

pelt² (pelt) *n.* **1** the skin of a fur-bearing animal before it has been dressed or tanned. **2** *Facetious.* human skin. [probably < *peltry*]
☛ *Syn.* **1.** See note at **skin.**

pel·try (pel′trē) *n., pl.* **-ries. 1** pelts; skins; furs. **2** a pelt. [< AF var. of OF *peleterie* < *pel* skin < L *pellis*]

pel·vic (pel′vik) *adj.* of, having to do with, or located in or near the pelvis.

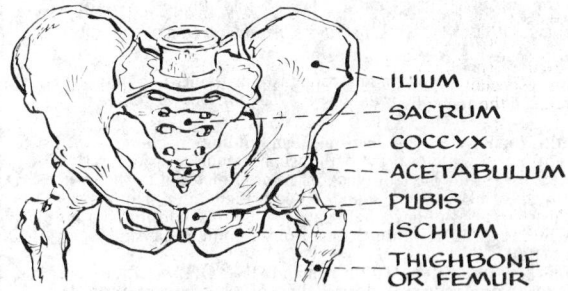

The pelvis of a man, seen from the front

pel·vis (pel′vis) *n., pl.* **-ves** (-vēz). **1** the basin-shaped structure in many vertebrates formed by the hipbones and the end of the backbone. **2** the cavity of the pelvis. [< L *pelvis* basin]

pem·bi·na (pem′bə nə *or* pem bē′nə) *n.* *Cdn.* highbush cranberry. [< Cdn.F *pimbina* < ? Cree]

pembina cart *Cdn. Historical.* a simple two-wheeled cart used by the early settlers of the Canadian West. [? < *Pembina* (now Cavalier), a town in North Dakota, probably after *pembina* growing in its valleys]

pem·mi·can (pem′ə kən) *n.* *Cdn.* dried, lean meat pounded into a paste with melted fat. Pemmican was the usual food of the voyageurs because it would keep for a long time under almost any conditions. [< Algonquian (Cree) *pimikan* < *pimikew* he makes grease]

pen¹ (pen) *n., v.* **penned, pen·ning.** —*n.* **1** a small metal instrument with a split point used with a holder, for writing with ink. **2** such an instrument together with its holder. **3** a writing instrument supplying a continuous flow of ink, such as a fountain pen, ball-point, or felt-tip pen. **4** writing or a style of writing: *She makes her living with her pen.* —*v.* write: *He penned a few lines to his father.* [ME < OF < L *penna* feather] —**pen′like′,** *adj.*

pen² (pen) *n., v.* **penned** *or* **pent, pen·ning.** —*n.* **1** a small, closed yard for cows, sheep, pigs, chickens, etc. **2** the animals in a pen. **3** any small place of confinement. **4** a dock or slip, often protected by a concrete superstructure, for docking and reconditioning submarines. —*v.* **1** shut in a pen. **2** confine closely: *I kept the dog penned in a corner while they hunted for the leash.* [OE *penn*] —**pen′like′,** *adj.*

pen³ (pen) *n.* *Slang.* penitentiary.

pen⁴ (pen) *n.* a female swan.

Pen. *or* **pen.** peninsula.

pe·nal (pē′nəl) *adj.* **1** of, having to do with, or given as punishment: *penal laws, penal labor.* **2** liable to be punished: *Robbery is a penal offence.* **3** used as a prison or place of punishment: *a penal colony.* [ME < L *poenalis* < *poena* punishment < Gk. *poinē* penalty]

pe·nal·ize (pē′nəl īz′ *or* pen′əl īz′) *v.* **-ized, -iz·ing. 1** declare punishable by law or by rule; set a penalty for: *Speeding on city*

streets is penalized. Fouls are penalized in many games. **2** inflict a penalty on; punish: *Our team was penalized five yards.*

pen·al·ty (pen′əl tē) *n., pl.* **-ties. 1** a punishment for breaking a law or rule: *His penalty for speeding was a fine of fifty dollars.* **2** a disadvantage imposed on a side or player for breaking the rules of a sport or game. **3** a disadvantage attached to some act or condition: *the penalties of old age.* **4** a handicap.

penalty box *Hockey or lacrosse. Cdn.* a special bench where penalized players serve their penalties.

pen·al·ty-kill·er (pen′əl tē kil′ər) *n. Hockey.* a player put on the ice when his team is shorthanded, to check the opposing forwards closely and to control the puck as much as possible in order to prevent any scoring by the opposite side.

pen·al·ty-kill·ing (pen′əl tē kil′ing) *n. Hockey.* the preventing of the opposite side from scoring while one's own team is shorthanded.

pen·ance (pen′əns) *n.* **1** a punishment borne to show sorrow for sin, to make up for a wrong done, and to obtain pardon from the church for sin. **2** *Roman Catholic Church.* the sacrament that includes contrition, confession, satisfaction, and absolution. **do penance,** perform some act, or undergo some penalty, in repentance for sin. [ME < OF *pen(e)ance* < L *paenitentia* penitence. Doublet of PENITENCE.]

pe·na·tes or **Pe·na·tes** (pə nä′tēz) *n.pl.* in ancient Rome, the gods of the household. [< L *penates* < *penus* interior of the house]

pence (pens) *n. Brit.* a pl. of **penny.**

pen·chant (pen′chənt) *n.* a strong taste or liking; inclination: *a penchant for taking long walks.* [< F *penchant,* ppr. of *pencher* incline, ult. < L *pendere* hang]

pen·cil (pen′səl) *n., v.* **-cilled** or **-ciled, -cil·ling** or **-cil·ing. —n. 1** a pointed tool to write or draw with, usually made of wood and having a long, thin piece of black or colored material in the centre. **2** an object of like shape. **3** a stick of coloring matter. **4** an artist's paintbrush. **5** a set of lines, light rays, or the like, coming to a point or extending in different directions from a point. **6** the skill or style of an artist. **—v.** mark, write or draw with a pencil. [ME < OF *pincel,* ult. < L *penicillus* (painter's brush), double dim. of *penis,* originally, tail]

pend (pend) *v.* remain undecided or unsettled. [< L *pendere* hang]

pend·ant (pen′dənt) *n., adj.* **—n. 1** a hanging ornament, especially one attached to an earring, necklace, or bracelet. **2** an ornament hanging down from a ceiling or roof. Pendants were common in later Gothic architecture. **3** an attachment by which something is suspended. **—adj.** pendent. [ME < OF *pendant,* ppr. of *pendre* hang, ult. < L *pendere*]

pend·ent (pen′dənt) *adj., n.* **—adj. 1** hanging: *the pendent branches of a willow.* **2** overhanging. **3** pending. **—n.** a pendant. [ME < L *pendens, -entis,* ppr. of *pendere* hang]

pend·ing (pen′ding) *adj., prep.* **—adj.** waiting to be decided or settled: *The agreement was pending.* **—prep. 1** while waiting for; until: *Pending his return, let us get everything ready.* **2** during: *pending the investigation.*

pen·drag·on or **Pen·drag·on** (pen drag′ən) *n.* the chief leader, a title of ancient British chiefs. [< Welsh *pendragon* < *pen* chief + *dragon* war leader, dragon]

pen·du·lous (pen′jə ləs or pen′dyə ləs) *adj.* **1** hanging downward: *pendulous jowls.* **2** suspended so as to swing freely. [< L *pendulus* < *pendere* hang] **—pen′du·lous·ly,** *adv.* **—pen′du·lous·ness,** *n.*

pen·du·lum (pen′jə ləm or pen′dyə ləm) *n.* a body or mass hung from a fixed point so as to swing freely to and fro under the forces of gravity and momentum. The movement of the works of a tall clock is often timed by a pendulum. [< NL *pendulum,* neut. < L *pendulus.* See PENDULOUS.]

Pe·nel·o·pe (pə nel′ə pē) *n. Greek legend.* the faithful wife of Odysseus. She waited twenty years for his return from the Trojan War in spite of the entreaties of her many suitors. She told them she would remarry when she had finished the weaving on which she was working, but each night she undid the work she had done during the day.

pe·ne·plain (pē′nə plān′) *n.* a formerly mountainous or hilly area reduced nearly to a plain by erosion. [< L *paene* almost + E *plain*]

pen·e·tra·bil·i·ty (pen′ə trə bil′ə tē) *n.* the capability of being penetrated.

pen·e·tra·ble (pen′ə trə bəl) *adj.* that can be penetrated. [< L *penetrabilis*]

pen·e·trate (pen′ə trāt′) *v.* **-trat·ed, -trat·ing. 1** pass into or through: *The bullet penetrated five centimetres into the wall.*

2 pierce through: *Our eyes could not penetrate the darkness.* **3** make a way: *Even where the trees were thickest, the sunshine penetrated.* **4** soak through; spread through: *The smell penetrated the whole house.* **5** see into; understand: *I could not penetrate the mystery.* **6** affect or impress very much. [< L *penetrare,* ult. < *penitus* inmost]

☛ *Syn.* **1. Penetrate, pierce** = go into or through something. **Penetrate** means go deeply into something, or into it and out the other side, and suggests the driving force or keenness of what goes in: *The bullet penetrated the board.* **Pierce** means stab through the surface, or pass right through, with a sharp-pointed object or something sharp and cutting, as a knife: *The dagger pierced his side.*

pen·e·trat·ing (pen′ə trāt′ing) *adj.* **1** sharp; piercing: *a penetrating scream.* **2** acute or keen: *a penetrating insight.* **3** that can penetrate: *a penetrating medication.* **—pen′e·trat′ing·ly,** *adv.*

pen·e·tra·tion (pen′ə trā′shən) *n.* **1** the act or power of penetrating. **2** the act of entering a country and gaining influence there. **3** the depth to which something penetrates. **4** the ability to understand deeply: *a mind of great acuteness and penetration.*

☛ *Syn.* **3.** See note at **insight.**

pen·e·tra·tive (pen′ə trā′tiv) *adj.* penetrating; piercing, acute, or keen. **—pen′e·tra′tive·ly,** *adv.* **—pen′e·tra′tive·ness,** *n.*

P.Eng. Professional Engineer.

pen·guin (pen′gwin or peng′gwin) *n.* any of a family (Spheniscidae, constituting the order Sphenisciformes) of flightless sea birds native to the cold regions of the southern hemisphere, having webbed feet, legs set far back on the body so that they walk erect, and wings modified into flippers for diving and swimming. [? < Breton *penguin* white head; cf. Welsh *pen* head + *gwyn* white]

pen·hold·er (pen′hōl′dər) *n.* **1** the handle or holder for a pen nib. **2** a stand or rack for a pen or pens.

pen·i·cil·lin (pen′ə sil′ən) *n.* a very powerful antibiotic drug made from a penicillium mould and used to destroy or check certain kinds of bacteria. [< *penicillium*]

pen·i·cil·li·um (pen′ə sil′ē əm) *n., pl.* **-cil·li·ums** or **-cil·li·a** (-sil′ē ə). any of a genus (*Penicillium*) of fungi typically occurring as green or blue mould on stale food or on damp natural fabrics or leather. Some species are used in making cheese; others are a source of penicillin. [< L *penicillus* small brush or tail, double dim. of *penis* tail]

pen·in·su·la (pən in′sə lə or pən in′syə lə) *n.* a piece of land almost surrounded by water, or extending far out into the water. Nova Scotia is a peninsula. [< L *paeninsula* < *paene* almost + *insula* island]

pen·in·su·lar (pən in′sə lər or pən in′syə lər) *adj.* of, in, or like a peninsula.

pe·nis (pē′nis) *n., pl.* **-nis·es** (-nis iz) or **-nes** (-nēz). the male sexual organ, which, in mammals, is also the organ through which urine is excreted. [< L *penis* penis, originally, tail]

pen·i·tence (pen′ə təns) *n.* sorrow for sinning or doing wrong; repentance. [ME < OF *penitence* < L *paenitentia* < *paenitere* repent. Doublet of PENANCE.]

pen·i·tent (pen′ə tənt) *adj., n.* **—adj.** sorry for sinning or doing wrong; repenting. **—n. 1** a person who is sorry for sin or wrongdoing. **2** a person who confesses and does penance for his sins under the direction of a church. **—pen′i·tent·ly,** *adv.*

pen·i·ten·tial (pen′ə ten′shəl) *adj., n.* **—adj. 1** of, showing, or having to do with penitence: *The penitential psalms express remorse for sin.* **2** of or having to do with penance. **—n. 1** a person performing or undergoing penance; penitent. **2** a book or code of the church canons on penance, its imposition, etc.

pen·i·ten·tia·ry (pen′ə ten′shə rē) *n., pl.* **-ries;** *adj.* **—n.** a prison, especially a federal prison for persons convicted of serious crimes. **—adj. 1** making one liable to punishment in a prison: *a penitentiary offence.* **2** used for punishment, discipline, and reformation: *penitentiary measures.* **3** of penance; penitential.

pen·knife (pen′nīf′) *n., pl.* **-knives.** a small pocketknife.

pen·man (pen′mən) *n., pl.* **-men** (-mən). **1** a person whose handwriting is good. **2** a person who writes; author.

pen·man·ship (pen′mən ship′) *n.* **1** skill in writing with pen, pencil, etc. **2** a style of handwriting.

Penn. or **Penna.** Pennsylvania.

pen name a name used by a writer instead of his real name.

pen·nant (pen′ənt) *n.* **1** a flag, usually long and narrow and tapering to a point or swallowtail, used on ships for signalling, as a school banner, etc. **2** a flag or other trophy competed for in an athletic contest: *Our team won the baseball pennant.* [blend of *pendant* and *pennon*]

pen·nate (pen′āt) *adj.* having wings; having feathers. [< L *pennatus* < *penna* feather, wing]

pen·ni (pen′ē) *n., pl.* **-ni·a** (-ē ə) or **-nis. 1** a unit of money in

Finland, worth ¹⁄₁₀₀ of a markka. **2** a coin worth one penni. [< Finnish < G *Pfennig* penny]

pen·ni·less (pen′i lis) *adj.* having no money; very poor.
☞ *Syn.* See note at **poor.**

pen·non (pen′ən) *n.* **1** a long, triangular or swallow-tailed flag, originally carried on the lance of a knight. **2** any flag or banner. [ME < OF *penon*, ult. < L *penna* feather]

Penn·syl·va·ni·a Dutch (pen′səl vā′nē ə) **1** the descendants of 17th- and 18th-century immigrants to SE Pennsylvania from S Germany and Switzerland. **2** people of this stock who settled in Upper Canada after the American Revolution. **3** the German dialect spoken by the Pennsylvania Dutch.

Penn·syl·va·ni·an (pen′səl vā′nē ən) *n., adj.* —*n.* **1** a native or inhabitant of Pennsylvania. **2** *Geology.* the Pennsylvanian period or rock system. —*adj.* **1** of or having to do with the state of Pennsylvania. **2** *Geology.* of or having to do with the later Carboniferous period of the Paleozoic era in North America. See chart at **geology.**

pen·ny (pen′ē) *n., pl.* **pen·nies** or *Esp.Brit.* (collectively for defs 2, 3) **pence. 1** in Canada and the United States, cent. **2** a unit of money in the United Kingdom equal to one one-hundredth of a pound. *Abbrev.:* p. **3** *Historical.* a unit of money in the United Kingdom and other Commonwealth countries equal to one twelfth of a shilling. *Symbol:* d. **4** a coin worth one penny. **5** a piece or sum of money: *I wouldn't give him a penny.*
a pretty penny, *Informal.* a large sum of money.
turn an honest penny, earn money honestly.
[OE *pen(d)ing, penig*; cf. ON *penning* and G *Pfennig* < OHG *pfenning*]

pen·ny–pinch·ing (pen′ē pinch′ing) *adj., n.* —*adj.* excessively thrifty; too careful about spending money. —*n.* excessive thrift. —**pen′ny-pinch′er,** *n.*

pen·ny·roy·al (pen′ē roi′əl) *n.* **1** a European mint (*Mentha pulegium*) having small, aromatic leaves and mauve flowers. **2** a strongly aromatic North American plant (*Hedcoma pulegioides*) of the same family. **3** an oil obtained from either of these plants, traditionally used in medicine. [apparently alteration of earlier *puliall royal; puliall* < OF *pouliol* < VL dim. of L *puleium* pennyroyal]

pen·ny·weight (pen′ē wāt′) *n.* a unit for measuring mass, equal to 24 grains or one twentieth of an ounce in troy weight (about 1.56 g).

pen·ny–wise (pen′ē wīz′) *adj.* thrifty in regard to small sums.
penny-wise and pound-foolish, thrifty in small expenses and wasteful in big ones.

pen·ny·worth (pen′ē wèrth′) *n.* **1** as much as can be bought for a penny. **2** a small amount.

pe·nol·o·gy (pē nol′ə jē) *n.* the study of the treatment of criminals and the management of prisons. Penology is a branch of criminology. [< Gk. *poinē* punishment + E *-logy*]

pen pal a person with whom one develops a friendship through correspondence, without ever having met the person.

pen·sile (pen′sīl *or* pen′səl) *adj.* **1** hanging; pendent. **2** of birds, building a hanging nest. [< L *pensilis* < *pendere* hang]

pen·sion¹ (pen′shən) *n., v.* —*n.* money other than wages paid regularly to a person under certain conditions. Pensions are paid to people who have retired from regular work because of old age, sickness, or injury, or for long service or special merit. —*v.* give a pension to.
pension off, cause to retire from service with a pension.
[ME < OF < L *pensio, -onis* < *pendere* weight, pay]

pen·sion² (päN syôN′) *n. French.* **1** boarding house. **2** accommodation; board and lodging. [< OF *pension* rent, payment. See PENSION¹.]

pen·sion·er (pen′shən ər) *n.* a person who receives or lives on a pension, especially an old-age pension.

pen·sive (pen′siv) *adj.* **1** thoughtful in a serious or sad way. **2** melancholy. [ME < OF *pensif < penser* think < L *pensare* weight; ponder < *pendere* weigh] —**pen′sive·ly,** *adv.* —**pen′sive·ness,** *n.*

pen·stock (pen′stok′) *n.* **1** a channel for carrying water to a water wheel. **2** a gate for controlling the flow of water, etc. [< *pen²* + *stock*, in the sense of "trough"]

pent (pent) *adj., v.* —*adj.* closely confined; shut (*used with* **in** *or* **up**): *He was pent up in the house most of the winter because of illness.* —*v.* a pt. and a pp. of **pen².**

penta– *combining form.* five: *A pentagon is a plane figure with five angles.* Also, **pent–** before vowels. [< Gk. *penta- < pente* five]

pen·ta·gon (pen′tə gon′) *n.* **1** a polygon having five sides. See **polygon** for picture. **2 the Pentagon,** in the United States: **a** a building that is the headquarters of the Department of Defense, just

hat, āge, fär; let, ēqual, tèrm; it, īce
hot, ōpen, ôrder; oil, out; cup, pút, rüle,
əbove, takən, pencəl, lemən, circəs
ch, child; ng, long; sh, ship
th, thin; ᴛн, then; zh, measure

outside Washington, D.C. **b** the Department of Defense, its policies, etc. [< LL < Gk. *pentagōnon < pente* five + *gōnia* angle]

pen·tag·o·nal (pen tag′ə nəl) *adj.* having five sides and five angles.

pen·ta·he·dron (pen′tə hē′drən) *n., pl.* **-drons, -dra** (-drə). a polyhedron having four faces. [< Gk. *pente* five + *hedra* base]

pen·tam·e·ter (pen tam′ə tər) *n.* **1** a line of verse consisting of five metrical feet. *Example:*
A lĭt | tle lĕarn | ĭng ĭs | a dăn | g′rŏus thĭng.
2 (*adj.*) designating such a line of verse or verse consisting of such lines. [< L < Gk. *pentametros < pente* five + *metron* meter]

pen·tane (pen′tān) *n.* any of three hydrocarbons of the methane series. *Formula:* C_5H_{12} [< Gk. *pente* five]

Pen·ta·teuch (pen′tə tyük′ *or* pen′tə tük′) *n.* the first five books of the Bible. Genesis, Exodus, Leviticus, Numbers, and Deuteronomy make up the Pentateuch. [< L < Gk. *pentateuchos < pente* five + *teuchos* vessel, book]

pen·tath·lon (pen tath′lən) *n.* an athletic contest consisting of five different events, in which the person having the highest total score wins. [< Gk. *pentathlon < pente* five + *athlon* contest]

pen·ta·ton·ic (pen′tə ton′ik) *adj. Music.* having five tones in the scale: *pentatonic scale.*

Pen·te·cost (pen′tə kost′) *n.* **1** the seventh Sunday after Easter, a Christian festival in memory of the descent of the Holy Ghost upon the Apostles (Acts 2). Also called **Whitsunday. 2** a Jewish religious holiday, observed about seven weeks after the Passover, celebrating the harvest and also the giving of the law to Moses. [OE < LL *pentecoste* < Gk. *pentēkostē (hēmera)* fiftieth (day)]

Pen·te·cos·tal or **pen·te·cos·tal** (pen′tə kos′təl) *adj.* of or having to do with Pentecost.

pent·house (pent′hous′) *n.* **1** an apartment or house built on the top of a building. **2** a sloping roof projecting from a building. **3** a shed with a sloping roof attached to a building. [ME *pentis* < OF *apentis*, ult. < L *appendere* append < *ad-* on + *pendere* hang]

pent–up (pent′up′) *adj.* shut up; closely confined: *pent-up feelings.*

pe·nu·che or **pe·nu·chi** (pə nü′chē) *n.* a candy or fudge made of brown sugar, butter, milk, and nuts. [< Mexican Sp. *panocha* brown or raw sugar]

pe·nult (pi nult′ *or* pē′nult) *n.* the next to the last syllable in a word. [< L *paenultima (syllaba)* next-to-last (syllable) < *paene* almost + *ultimus* last]

pe·nul·ti·mate (pi nul′tə mit) *adj., n.* —*adj.* **1** next to the last. **2** of or having to do with the penult. —*n.* the penult.

pe·num·bra (pi num′brə) *n., pl.* **-brae** (-brē *or* -brī) or **-bras. 1** the partial shadow outside of the complete shadow formed by the sun, moon, etc. during an eclipse. See **eclipse** for picture. **2** the greyish outer part of a sunspot. [< NL *penumbra* < L *paene* almost + *umbra* shadow]

pe·nu·ri·ous (pi nyür′ē əs *or* pi nür′ē əs) *adj.* **1** characteristic of or suffering from penury; poor: *penurious surroundings, penurious times.* **2** mean about spending or giving money; stingy. —**pe·nu′ri·ous·ly,** *adv.* —**pe·nu′ri·ous·ness,** *n.*

pen·u·ry (pen′yə rē) *n.* great poverty. [< L *penuria*]

pe·on (pē′on *or* pē′ən) *n.* **1** in Latin America, a person doing work that requires little skill. **2** any of various workers, etc. in India or Sri Lanka, such as a foot soldier, attendant, or unskilled laborer. [< Sp. < LL *pedo, -onis* foot soldier. Doublet of PAWN². Related to PIONEER.]

pe·on·age (pē′ən ij) *n.* the condition or service of a peon.

pe·o·ny (pē′ə nē) *n., pl.* **-nies. 1** any of a genus (*Paeonia*) of perennial herbaceous or shrubby plants, many of which are cultivated for their large, showy, pink, red, or white flowers. **2** the flower of any of these plants. [ult. < Gk. *paiōnia < Paiōn* physician of the gods; from the plant's use in medicine]

peo·ple (pē′pəl) *n., pl.* **-ple** or (for def. 2) **-ples;** *v.* **-pled, -pling.** —*n.* **1** men, women, and children; persons. **2** a race; nation. **3** the body of citizens of a state; the public. **4** the persons of a place, class, or group: *city people, Prairie people.* **5** the common people; the lower classes. **6** persons in relation to a superior: *A king rules over his people.* **7** *Informal.* family; relatives.

—v. fill or supply with inhabitants; populate or stock: *Canada was very largely peopled by Europeans.* [ME < AF < L *populus*]

☞ *Syn.* n. **2. People, race, nation** = a group of persons thought of as a unit larger than a family or community. **People** emphasizes cultural and social unity, applying to a group united by a common culture, common ideas, and a feeling of unity arising from common responsibilities and interests: *The Letts are a people, not a nation.* **Race** emphasizes biological unity, having common descent and common physical characteristics: *The Japanese belong to the Asiatic race.* **Nation** emphasizes political unity, applying to a group united under one government: *Norwegians are a people and a nation, not a race.*

pep (pep) *n., v.* **pepped, pep·ping.** *Informal.* —*n.* spirit; energy; vim or enthusiasm. —*v.* fill or inspire with energy, etc.: put new life into (*used with* **up**): *to pep up a party.* [short for *pepper*]

pep·lum (pep′ləm) *n., pl.* **-lums. 1** a short flared, gathered, or pleated piece of material attached to the waistline of a jacket, blouse, or dress and extending to the hips. **2** in ancient Greece, a full garment worn by women. [< L < Gk. *peplos*]

pep·lumed (pep′ləmd) *adj.* furnished with a peplum.

pep·per (pep′ər) *n., v.* —*n.* **1** a seasoning with a hot taste, made from the ground-up berries of a tropical woody vine. See **black pepper** and **white pepper. 2** any of a genus (*Piper*) of tropical climbing shrubs having fragrant leaves; especially, *Piper nigrum*, which bears the red berries from which white and black pepper are made. **3** (*adj.*) designating the family (Piperaceae) of plants that includes pepper and cubeb. **4** any of various capsicums, especially one species (*Capsicum frutescens*) cultivated in numerous varieties for its mild or hot-tasting fruit. **5** the fruit of any of these capsicums. See **red pepper, sweet pepper.**
—*v.* **1** season or sprinkle with black, white, or red pepper. **2** sprinkle thickly: *His face is peppered with freckles.* **3** hit with small objects sent thick and fast: *We peppered the enemy with shot.* [OE *pipor* < L *piper* < Gk. *peperi*]

pep·per-and-salt (pep′ər ən solt′ *or* -sôlt′) *adj.* black and white finely mixed: *a pepper-and-salt coat.*

pep·per·box (pep′ər boks′) *n.* a container with holes in the top for sprinkling pepper on food.

pep·per·corn (pep′ər kôrn′) *n.* a dried berry of the pepper plant (*Piper nigrum*). [OE *piporcorn*]

pep·per·grass (pep′ər gras′) *n.* any of a genus (*Lepidium*) of plants of the mustard family, especially garden cress.

pep·per·mint (pep′ər mint′) *n.* **1** a common herb (*Mentha piperita*), a species of mint yielding a sweet-smelling oil used in medicine and as a flavoring for candy. **2** the oil of this herb. **3** candy flavored with peppermint oil.

pep·per·y (pep′ər ē) *adj.* **1** of, like, or full of pepper: *a peppery stew.* **2** sharp; pungent. **3** having a hot temper; easily made angry. —**pep′per·i·ness,** *n.*

pep pill *Informal.* any of various stimulant drugs, such as amphetamine, in pill form.

pep·py (pep′ē) *adj.* **-pi·er, -pi·est.** *Slang.* full of pep; energetic; lively. —**pep′pi·ness,** *n.*

pep rally *Informal.* a meeting organized to stimulate support and enthusiasm for a team, cause, campaign, etc.

pep·sin (pep′sən) *n.* **1** an enzyme in the gastric juice of the stomach that helps to digest meat, eggs, cheese, and other proteins. **2** a medicine containing this enzyme, used to help digestion. [< Gk. *pepsis* digestion]

pep talk a short, emotional talk intended to encourage a person or group in some activity: *The coach gave us a pep talk before the game.*

pep·tic (pep′tik) *adj.* **1** promoting digestion; digestive. **2** of or having to do with pepsin. **3** having to do with or caused by the action of digestive juices: *a peptic ulcer.* [< L < Gk. *peptikos* < *peptos* cooked, digested]

pep·tide (pep′tīd) *n.* any of a group of compounds consisting of two or more amino acids chemically bonded, or linked, together. [< G *peptid.* See PEPTONE.]

pep·tone (pep′tōn) *n.* any of a class of diffusible, soluble substances into which meat, eggs, cheese, and other proteins are changed by the action of pepsin in digestion. [< G *Pepton* < Gk. *pepton,* neut. of *peptos* cooked, digested]

Pé·quiste (pā kēst′) *n. Cdn.* a member or supporter of the Parti Québécois. Also, **péquiste.**

per (pər; *stressed,* pèr) *prep.* **1** for each: *We need 125 grams of ground beef per person.* **2** by; through; by means of: *The letter was sent per messenger.* **3** according to: *a payment calculated per number of children in the family. The order was sent out as per instructions.* [< L]

☞ *Usage.* **Per,** the Latin for **through, by, by the, among,** is found chiefly in business or technical English: *$28 per week, 45 revolutions per minute.* The

English equivalent is usually more appropriate in general English: *$28 a week, eight hours a day.*

per- *prefix.* **1** through or throughout, as in *perforate, pervade.* **2** thoroughly or utterly, as in *perceive, perfect.* **3** *Chemistry.* the maximum or a large amount of, as in *peroxide.* [< L]

per. 1 person. **2** period.

per·ad·ven·ture (pèr′əd ven′chər) *adv., n.* —*adv. Archaic.* perhaps: *Peradventure he will come today.* —*n.* chance; doubt. [ME < OF *par aventure* < *par* by (< L *per*) + *aventure* adventure < L *adventura (res)* (thing) about to happen + *advenire* arrive]

per·am·bu·late (pər am′byə lāt′) *v.* **-lat·ed, -lat·ing. 1** walk through, over, etc.: *perambulating the street.* **2** walk about from place to place. **3** walk through and inspect. [< L *perambulare* < *per-* through + *ambulare* walk] —**per·am′bu·la′tion,** *n.*

per·am·bu·la·tor (pər am′byə lā′tər) *n.* **1** a small carriage in which a baby is pushed about; pram. **2** a person who perambulates.

per an·num (per an′əm) yearly; for each year: *Her salary was $19 000 per annum.* [< L]

per·cale (pər kāl′ *or* pər kal′) *n.* a smooth, firm cotton cloth in a plain weave made in different grades. High-grade percale with a very close weave and a lustrous finish is used for bed linen. [< F < Persian]

per cap·i·ta (pər kap′ə tə) for each person: *$40 for eight people amounts to $5 per capita.* [< L *per capita* by heads]

per·ceive (pər sēv′) *v.* **-ceived, -ceiv·ing. 1** be aware of through the senses; see, hear, taste, smell, or feel. **2** take in with the mind; observe: *I perceived that I could not make him change his mind.* [ME < OF *perceivre* < L *percipere* < *per-* fully + *capere* grasp] —**per·ceiv′er,** *n.*

☞ *Syn.* **1, 2.** See note at SEE.

per·cent or **per cent** (pər sent′) *n.* **1** hundredths; parts in each hundred. Five percent (5%) is 5 out of each 100, or ⁵⁄₁₀₀ of the whole. Five percent of 40 is 2. *Symbol:* % **2** for each hundred; in each hundred: *Seven percent of the students failed.* **3** *Informal.* percentage: *A large percent of the apple crop was ruined.* [for Ital. *per cento* or LL *per centum*]

☞ *Usage.* **Percent,** whether written as one word or two, is not followed by a period. The one-word form is more common, possibly through the influence of **percentage** and **percentile.**

per·cent·age (pər sen′tij) *n.* **1** the rate or proportion of each hundred; part of each hundred: *What percentage of children were absent?* **2** a part; proportion: *A large percentage of schoolbooks now have pictures.* **3** an allowance, commission, discount, rate of interest, etc. figured by percent. **4** *Slang.* advantage or profit.

per·cen·tile (pər sen′tīl *or* pər sen′təl) *n.* any value in a series of points on a scale arrived at by dividing a group into a hundred equal parts in order of magnitude: *A student at the fiftieth percentile is at a point halfway between the top and the bottom of his group.*

per centum *Latin.* percent.

per·cept (pèr′sept) *n.* **1** that which is perceived. **2** understanding that is the result of perceiving. [< L *perceptum,* pp. neut. of *percipere* perceive. See PERCEIVE.]

per·cep·ti·bil·i·ty (pər sep′tə bil′ə tē) *n.* the fact, quality, or state of being perceptible.

per·cep·ti·ble (pər sep′tə bəl) *adj.* that can be perceived.

per·cep·ti·bly (pər sep′tə blē) *adv.* in a perceptible way or amount; to a perceptible degree.

per·cep·tion (pər sep′shən) *n.* **1** the act of perceiving: *His perception of the change came in a flash.* **2** the power of perceiving: *a keen perception.* **3** percept. [< L *perceptio, -onis* < *percipere* perceive. See PERCEIVE.]

per·cep·tive (pər sep′tiv) *adj.* **1** having to do with perception. **2** having the power of perceiving. —**per·cep′tive·ly,** *adv.* —**per·cep′tive·ness,** *n.*

per·cep·tu·al (pər sep′chü əl) *adj.* of or having to do with perception.

Per·ce·val (pèr′sə vəl) *n. Arthurian legend.* one of only three Knights of the Round Table who see the Holy Grail. In the earliest legends about the Quest for the Holy Grail, Perceval (in German, Parzifal) is the main hero.

perch[1] (pèrch) *n., v.* —*n.* **1** a bar, branch, or anything else on which a bird can come to rest. **2** a rather high place or position. **3** a unit for measuring length; rod (about 5.03 m). **4** a unit for measuring area; square rod (about 25.3 m²).
—*v.* **1** alight and rest: *A robin perched on our porch railing.* **2** sit, especially on something rather high: *He perched on a stool.* **3** place or situate high up: *The village was perched on a high hill.* [ME < OF *perche* < L *pertica* pole] —**perch′er,** *n.*

perch[2] (pèrch) *n., pl.* **perch** or **perch·es. 1** any of a genus (*Perca*) of small freshwater food fishes, especially the **yellow perch** (*P. flavescens*) of North America or a similar European species.

2 (adj.) designating a family (Percidae) of freshwater fishes including the perches, darters, and the walleye. Fishes of the perch family have two dorsal fins, the first having spiny rays and the second having soft rays. **3** any of various similar freshwater or saltwater fishes, especially of families Centrarchidae and Serranidae. [ME < OF *perche* < L < Gk. *perkē*]

per·chance (pər chans′) *adv. Archaic or poetic.* perhaps. [ME < AF *par chance* < *par* by (< L *per*) + *chance* < L *cadentia* a falling < *cadere* fall]

Per·che·ron (pèr′chə ron′ *or* pèr′shə ron′) *n.* a breed of large, strong draft horse originally developed in France. [< F *Percheron* < *Le Perche*, a district in France]

per·chlo·ro·eth·yl·ene (pèr′klôr ō eth′ə lēn′) *n.* a chlorinated hydrocarbon, the most common solvent used in dry cleaning. *Formula:* C_2Cl_4

per·cip·i·ence (pər sip′ē əns) *n.* perception.

per·cip·i·ent (pər sip′ē ənt) *adj., n.* —*adj.* capable of perceiving, especially quickly or keenly; discerning. —*n.* a person who perceives. [< L *percipiens, -entis*, ppr. of *percipere.* See PERCEIVE.]

per·co·late (pèr′kə lāt′) *v.* -**lat·ed**, -**lat·ing**. **1** drip or drain through small holes or spaces. **2** filter through; permeate: *Water percolates sand.* **3** make coffee in a percolator. **4** of coffee, bubble up and drip through in a percolator. [< L *percolare*, ult. < *per*- through + *colum* strainer] —**per′co·la′tion,** *n.*

per·co·la·tor (pèr′kə lā′tər) *n.* **1** a kind of coffee pot in which boiling water continually bubbles up through a tube and drips down through ground coffee. **2** anything that percolates.

per·cus·sion (pər kush′ən) *n.* **1** the striking of one body against another with force; stroke; blow. **2** the shock made by the striking of one object against another with force. **3** the striking of sound upon the ear. **4** *Medicine.* the technique of tapping a part of the body to find out the condition of the parts underneath by the resulting sound. **5** *Music.* the section of an orchestra or band composed of percussion instruments. [< L *percussio, -onis* < *per*- (intensive) + *quatere* strike, beat]

percussion cap a small cap containing powder that explodes when struck by the hammer of a gun.

percussion instrument a musical instrument played by striking it, such as a drum or cymbal.

per di·em (pər dē′əm *or* dī′əm) *Latin.* **1** per day; for each day. **2** an allowance of so much every day. [< L *per diem* per day]

per·di·tion (pər dish′ən) *n.* **1** the loss of one's soul and the joys of heaven; eternal death. **2** hell. **3** *Archaic.* utter loss. [< L *perditio, -onis* < *perdere* destroy < *per*- (intensive) + *dare* give]

per·e·grin (per′ə grin) *n. or adj.* peregrine.

per·e·gri·nate (per′ə grə nāt′) *v.* -**nat·ed**, -**nat·ing**. travel; journey. [< L *peregrinari* < *peregrinus.* See PEREGRINE.] —**per′e·gri·na′tion,** *n.* —**per′e·gri·na′tor,** *n.*

per·e·grine (per′ə grin *or* per′ə grēn′) *adj., n.* —*adj.* **1** wandering or migratory. **2** *Archaic.* foreign; coming from abroad. —*n.* peregrine falcon. [< L *peregrinus* from foreign parts, ult. < *per*- outside + *ager* (*Romanus*) the (Roman) territory. Doublet of PILGRIM.]

peregrine falcon a large falcon (*Falco peregrinus*) formerly much used in falconry.

per·emp·to·ry (pər emp′tə rē *or* per′əmp tô′rē) *adj.* **1** imperious; positive: *a peremptory teacher.* **2** allowing no denial or refusal: *a peremptory command.* **3** leaving no choice; decisive; final; absolute: *a peremptory decree.* [< L *peremptorius* deadly, that puts an end to, ult. < *per*- (intensive) + *emere*, originally, take] —**per·emp′to·ri·ly,** *adv.* —**per·emp′to·ri·ness,** *n.*

per·en·ni·al (pər en′ē əl) *adj., n.* —*adj.* **1** lasting through the whole year: *a perennial stream.* **2** lasting for a very long time; enduring: *the perennial beauty of the hills.* **3** having underground parts that live more than two years: *perennial garden plants.* —*n.* a perennial plant. Roses are perennials. Compare **annual** and **biennial.** [< L *perennis* lasting < *per*- through + *annus* year] —**per·en′ni·al·ly,** *adv.*

perf. **1** perfect. **2** perforated.

per·fect (*adj.* -*n.* pèr′fikt; *v.* pər fekt′) *adj., v., n.* —*adj.* **1** without defect; faultless: *Perfect work is the result when attention is given to detail.* **2** completely skilled; expert: *a perfect golfer.* **3** having all its parts; complete: *The set was perfect; nothing was missing or broken.* **4** entire; utter: *He was a perfect stranger to us.* **5** *Grammar.* showing an action or state thought of as being completed. There are three perfect tenses: **perfect, past perfect,** and **future perfect. 6** *Botany.* having both stamens and pistils. **7** *Music.* having to do with the intervals or original consonances of unison, a fourth, fifth, and octave, as contrasted with the major intervals of a third and sixth.
—*v.* **1** remove all faults from; make perfect; improve; add the

hat, āge, fär; let, ēqual, tèrm; it, īce
hot, ōpen, ôrder; oil, out; cup, pút, rüle,
above, takən, pencəl, lemən, circəs
ch, child; ng, long; sh, ship
th, thin; ŦH, then; zh, measure

finishing touches to: *The artist was perfecting his picture. We will perfect our plan as it is tried out.* **2** complete.
—*n. Grammar.* **1** the perfect tense. **2** a verb form in this tense. *Have eaten* is the perfect of *eat.* [ME < OF < L *perfectus* completed, pp. of *perficere* < *per*- thoroughly + *facere* make, do] —**per·fect′er,** *n.* —**per′fect·ness,** *n.*

per·fect·i·bil·i·ty (pər fek′tə bil′ə tē) *n.* the capability of becoming, or being made, perfect.

per·fect·i·ble (pər fek′tə bəl) *adj.* capable of becoming, or being made, perfect.

per·fec·tion (pər fek′shən) *n.* **1** a perfect condition; faultlessness; highest excellence. **2** a perfect person or thing. **3** a making complete or perfect: *The perfection of our plans will take another week.* **to perfection,** perfectly: *He played the violin concerto to perfection.*

per·fec·tion·ism (pər fek′shən iz′əm) **1** a striving for absolute perfection in what one does. **2** a doctrine that a state of freedom from sin can and should be achieved on earth.

per·fec·tion·ist (pər fek′shən ist) *n.* **1** a person who is not content with anything that is not perfect or nearly perfect. **2** a person who believes it possible to lead a sinless life.

per·fect·ly (pèr′fikt lē) *adv.* **1** in a perfect manner or degree; completely and faultlessly: *a perfectly drawn circle.* **2** to an adequate extent: *This skirt is still perfectly good.*

perfect number a number that is equal to the sum of its factors. Six is a perfect number because its factors, 1, 2, and 3, add up to six.

per·fec·to (pər fek′tō) *n., pl.* -**tos.** a thick cigar that tapers at both ends. [< Sp. *perfecto* perfect]

perfect participle a participle, preceded by a form of the verb *have*, expressing action completed before the time of speaking or acting. In *Having written the letter, she mailed it, having written* is a perfect participle.
☛ *Usage.* See note at **participle.**

per·fer·vid (pèr fèr′vid) *adj.* very fervid.

per·fid·i·ous (pər fid′ē əs) *adj.* deliberately faithless; treacherous. [< L *perfidiosus* < *perfidia.* See PERFIDY.] —**per·fid′i·ous·ly,** *adv.* —**per·fid′i·ous·ness,** *n.*

per·fi·dy (pèr′fə dē) *n., pl.* -**dies.** a breaking faith; base treachery; being false to a trust. [< L *perfidia*, ult. < *per*- away + *fides* faith]

per·fo·li·ate (pər fō′lē it *or* -fō′lē āt′) *adj. Botany.* having the stem apparently passing through the leaf: *a perfoliate leaf.* [< NL *perfoliatus* < L *per*- through + *folium* leaf]

per·fo·rate (*v.* pèr′fə rāt′; *adj.* pèr′fə rit *or* pèr′fə rāt′) *v.* -**rat·ed**, -**rat·ing**; *adj.* —*v.* **1** make a hole or holes through: *His bullets perforated the target.* **2** make a series of small holes through in order to make separation easier: *Sheets of postage stamps are perforated.* —*adj.* pierced. [< L *perforare* < *per*- through + *forare* bore]

per·fo·ra·tion (pèr′fə rā′shən) *n.* **1** a hole or series of holes bored or punched through something: *He removed the coupon by tearing along the perforation.* **2** perforating or being perforated.

per·fo·ra·tor (pèr′fə rā′tər) *n.* **1** one that perforates. **2** an instrument or machine for perforating.

per·force (pər fôrs′) *adv.* by necessity; necessarily. [< F *par* by + *force*]

per·form (pər fôrm′) *v.* **1** do; carry out: *Perform your duties well.* **2** put into effect; fulfil: *Perform your promise.* **3** go through; render: *to perform a piece of music.* **4** act, play, sing, or do tricks in public. [< AF *performer*, var. of OF *parfournir* < *par*- completely + *-fournir* furnish, finish; influenced by *forme* form]
☛ *Syn.* 2. Perform, execute, discharge = carry out or put into effect. **Perform** = carry out a process, usually one that is long or that requires effort, attention, or skill: *The surgeon performed an operation.* **Execute** = put into effect a plan or proposal or carry out an order: *The nurse executed the doctor's orders.* **Discharge** = carry out an obligation or duty, by performing or executing the acts or steps necessary to relieve oneself of the responsibility: *She gave a large party to discharge all her social obligations.*

per·form·ance (pər fôr′məns) *n.* **1** a performing: *in the performance of one's regular duties.* **2** the thing performed; act; deed. **3** the giving of a play, concert, circus, or other show: *The evening performance is at eight o'clock.*

per·form·er (pər fôr′mər) *n.* a person who performs, especially one who performs for the entertainment of others; player.

per·fume (*n.* pèr′fyüm *or* pər fyüm′; *v.* pər fyüm′) *n., v.* **-fumed, -fum·ing.** —*n.* **1** the scent of something that smells sweet: *the perfume of flowers.* **2** a substance having a sweet smell, especially a liquid prepared from essences of flowers or from synthetic substances and applied to the skin or clothes to produce a pleasant scent. [< F *parfum* < *parfumer* scent. See v.] —*v.* **1** fill with a sweet odor: *Flowers perfumed the air.* **2** put a sweet-smelling liquid on. [< F *parfum,* n., and *parfumer,* v., < OItal. < L *per-* through + *fumare* smoke; 16c.]

per·fum·er (pər fyüm′ər) *n.* **1** a maker or seller of perfumes. **2** a person or thing that perfumes.

per·fum·er·y (pər fyüm′ər ē *or* pər fyüm′rē) *n., pl.* **-er·ies. 1** the products made by a perfumer; perfumes. **2** the art or process of making perfumes. **3** a place where perfumes are made or sold.

per·func·to·ry (pər fungk′tə rē) *adj.* **1** done merely for the sake of getting rid of the duty; mechanical; indifferent: *The little boy gave his face a perfunctory washing.* **2** acting in a perfunctory way: *The new nurse was perfunctory; she did not really care about her work.* [< LL *perfunctorius,* ult. < L *perfungi* perform < *per-* to the end + *fungi* execute] —**per·func′to·ri·ly,** *adv.* —**per·func′to·ri·ness,** *n.*

per·fuse (pər fyüz′) *v.* **-fused, -fus·ing. 1** overspread (something) with a vapor, fluid, color, etc.; permeate; suffuse. **2** cause (something) to flow through or spread over. [< L *perfusus,* pp. of *perfundere* pour out < *per-* (intensive) + *fundere* pour out] —**per·fu′sion,** *n.*

per·go·la (pèr′gə lə) *n.* an arbor formed by vines, etc. growing over an open roof of latticework or rafters supported by posts. [< Ital. < L *pergula,* probably dim. of **perga* timber work]

per·haps (pər haps′ *or* pər aps′) *adv.* maybe; possibly. [ME *per happes* by chances (pl. of *hap* chance)]

pe·ri (pēr′ē) *n., pl.* **pe·ris.** *Persian mythology.* a beautiful fairy shut out from paradise until forgiven. [< Persian]

peri- *prefix.* **1** around; surrounding, as in *periscope, periphery.* **2** near, as in *perigee, perihelion.* [< Gk.]

per·i·anth (per′ē anth′) *n. Botany.* the envelope of a flower, including the calyx and the corolla. [< NL < Gk. *peri-* around + *anthos* flower]

per·i·car·di·ac (per′ə kär′dē ak′) *adj.* pericardial.

per·i·car·di·al (per′ə kär′dē əl) *adj.* **1** of, having to do with, or affecting the pericardium. **2** around the heart.

per·i·car·di·tis (per′ə kär dī′tis) *n. Medicine.* an inflammation of the pericardium.

per·i·car·di·um (per′ə kär′dē əm) *n., pl.* **-di·a** (-dē ə). the membranous sac enclosing the heart and the roots of the great blood vessels. [< Gk. *pericardion* < *peri-* around + *kardia* heart]

per·i·carp (per′ə kärp′) *n. Botany.* the walls of a ripened ovary or fruit, sometimes consisting of three layers, the epicarp, mesocarp, and endocarp; seed vessel. [< NL < Gk. *perikarpion* < *peri-* around + *karpos* fruit]

Per·i·cle·an (per′ə klē′ən) *adj.* of or having to do with Pericles, an Athenian statesman (died 429 B.C.), or with the period of his leadership.

per·i·cra·ni·um (per′ə krā′nē əm) *n., pl.* **-ni·a** (-nē ə). *Anatomy.* the membrane covering the bones of the skull. [< Gk. *perikranion* < *peri-* around + *kranion* skull]

per·i·cyn·thi·on (per′ə sin′thē ən) *n.* the point in the lunar orbit of an earth-launched spacecraft where it is nearest to the moon. Compare **apocynthion, perilune.** [< *peri-* + *-cynthion* < *Cynthia* (goddess of the moon)]

per·i·gee (per′ə jē′) *n.* the point in the orbit of a satellite of the earth or an orbiting vehicle where it comes closest to the earth. Compare **apogee.** [< F < NL < Gk. *perigeion* < *peri-* near + *gē* earth]

per·i·he·li·on (per′ə hē′lē ən *or* per′ə hēl′yən) *n., pl.* **-he·li·a** (-hē′lē ə *or* -hēl′yə). the point in the orbit of a planet or other heavenly body where it is closest to the sun. Compare **aphelion.** [< NL < Gk. *peri-* near + *hēlios* sun]

per·il (per′əl) *n., v.* **-illed** *or* **-iled, -il·ling** *or* **-il·ing.** —*n.* a chance of harm; exposure to danger or the risk of being injured or destroyed. —*v.* put in danger; expose to risk. [ME < OF < L *periculum*]

☛ *Syn. n.* See note at **danger.**

per·il·ous (per′ə ləs) *adj.* dangerous; full of peril: *a perilous journey.* [< AF *perillous* < L *periculosus*] —**per′il·ous·ly,** *adv.* —**per′il·ous·ness,** *n.*

per·i·lune (per′ə lün′) *n.* the point in the lunar orbit of a

moon-launched spacecraft where it is nearest to the moon. Compare **apolune, pericynthion.** [< *peri-* + *-lune* < L *luna* moon]

pe·rim·e·ter (pə rim′ə tər) *n.* **1** the outer boundary of a plane figure or an area: *the perimeter of a circle. A fence marks the perimeter of a field.* **2** the distance around such a boundary. The perimeter of a square equals four times the length of one side. [< L < Gk. *perimetros* < *peri-* around + *metron* measure]

per·i·ne·al (per′ə nē′əl) *adj.* of or having to do with the perineum.

per·i·ne·um (per′ə nē′əm) *n., pl.* **-ne·a** (-nē′ə). *Anatomy.* **1** the region of the body between the thighs. **2** the region included in the opening of the pelvis. [< LL < Gk. *perinaion*]

pe·ri·od (pēr′ē əd) *n., interj.* —*n.* **1** a span of time, especially one having certain features or conditions: *He visited us for a short period.* **2** (*adj.*) characteristic of a certain period of time: *period furniture.* **3** a portion of time marked off by events that happen again and again; time after which the same things begin to happen again. A month, from new moon to new moon, is a period. **4** *Geology.* a subdivision of an era. **5** the portion of a game during which there is actual play: *There are three twenty-minute periods in a hockey game.* **6** one of the portions of time into which a school day is divided. **7** the time needed for a disease to run its course. **8** an occurrence of menstruation. **9** a mark (.) of punctuation, marking the end of most sentences or showing an abbreviation. *Examples: Mr., Dec.* **10** the pause at the end of a sentence. **11** a complete sentence: *The orator spoke in stately periods.* **12** an end; termination; final stage. **13** *Physics.* the interval of time between the recurrence of like phases in a vibration or other periodic motion or phenomenon.
—*interj. Informal.* that's it! that's final! *The discussion is over, period!* [< L < Gk. *periodos* a going around, cycle < *peri-* around + *hodos* a going]

☛ *Usage.* **Period.** A period coming at the end of a quotation is generally placed inside the quotation marks: *"The longer you put it off," he said, "the harder it's going to be."*

pe·ri·od·ic (pēr′ē od′ik) *adj.* **1** occurring, appearing, or done again and again at regular intervals: *periodic attacks of malaria.* **2** happening every now and then: *a periodic fit of clearing up one's desk.* **3** having to do with a period. **4** expressed in formal sentences whose meanings are not complete without the final words.

pe·ri·od·i·cal (pēr′ē od′ə kəl) *n., adj.* —*n.* a magazine that appears regularly.
—*adj.* **1** of or having to do with periodicals. **2** published at regular intervals, less often than daily. **3** periodic.

pe·ri·od·i·cal·ly (pēr′ē od′ik lē) *adv.* **1** at regular intervals. **2** every now and then.

pe·ri·o·dic·i·ty (pēr′ē ə dis′ə tē) *n., pl.* **-ties.** a periodic character; tendency to happen at regular intervals.

periodic law *Chemistry.* the law stating that, when the chemical elements are arranged in the order of their atomic numbers, the elements with similar chemical properties appear at regular intervals.

periodic table *Chemistry.* a table in which the elements, arranged in the order of their atomic weights, are shown in related groups.

per·i·o·don·tal (per′ē ə don′təl) *adj.* **1** of or affecting the tissues or structures around the teeth: *periodontal disease.* **2** situated around a tooth.

per·i·o·don·tia (per′ē ə don′shə) *n.* periodontics.

per·i·o·don·tic (per′ē ə don′tik) *adj.* of or having to do with periodontics. —**per′i·o·don′ti·cal·ly,** *adv.*

per·i·o·don·tics (per′ē ə don′tiks) *n.* (*used with a singular verb*) the branch of dentistry dealing with diseases of the tissues and structures around the teeth.

per·i·o·don·tist (per′ē ə don′tist) *n.* a dentist who is a specialist in periodontics.

per·i·os·te·um (per′ē os′tē əm) *n., pl.* **-te·a** (-tē ə). the dense fibrous membrane closely covering the surface of bones except at the joints. [< NL < LL < Gk. *periosteon* < *peri-* around + *osteon* bone]

per·i·pa·tet·ic (per′ə pə tet′ik) *adj., n.* —*adj.* **1** walking about; travelling from place to place; itinerant. **2** **Peripatetic,** having to do with the philosophy of Aristotle, who taught while walking. —*n.* **1** a person who wanders or travels about from place to place. **2** **Peripatetic,** a disciple of Aristotle. [< L < Gk. *peripatētikos* < *peri-* around + *pateein* walk; with reference to Aristotle's manner of teaching]

pe·riph·er·al (pə rif′ər əl) *adj.* **1** of, having to do with, or forming a periphery. **2** incidental or minor: *peripheral issues.* **3** of, having to do with, or situated on or near the surface of the body: *peripheral nerves.* **4** auxiliary or supplementary: *a peripheral computer unit.* —**pe·riph′er·al·ly,** *adv.*

peripheral vision the area of vision outside the line of direct sight; the outer part of the field of vision.

pe·riph·er·y (pə rif′ər ē) *n., pl.* **-er·ies. 1** an outside boundary; perimeter. The periphery of a circle is called the circumference. **2** an area outside the centre or main area; outer parts: *the periphery of a city.* **3** *Anatomy.* the area surrounding a nerve ending, such as a sense organ or muscle. [< LL < Gk. *periphereia* < *peri-* around + *pherein* carry]

pe·riph·ra·sis (pə rif′rə sis) *n., pl.* **-ses** (-sēz′). a roundabout way of speaking or writing; circumlocution. *The wife of your father's brother* is a periphrasis for *your aunt.* [< L < Gk. *periphrasis*, ult. < *peri* around + *phrazein* speak]

per·i·phras·tic (per′ə fras′tik) *adj.* **1** expressed in a roundabout way. **2** *Grammar.* formed by using auxiliaries or particles rather than inflection. *Examples*: *of John* rather than *John's* (periphrastic genitive); *did run* rather than *ran* (periphrastic conjugation). —**per′i·phras′ti·cal·ly**, *adv.*

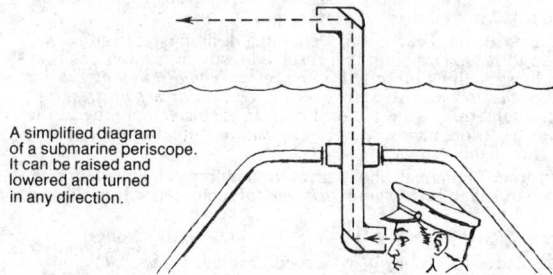

A simplified diagram of a submarine periscope. It can be raised and lowered and turned in any direction.

per·i·scope (per′ə skōp′) *n.* an instrument consisting of a tube with an arrangement of mirrors or prisms that permits a person to see things that are otherwise out of sight. Periscopes are used to get a view of the surface from a trench or a submerged submarine, to see around a corner or over the heads of people in a crowd, etc. [< Gk. *peri-* around + E *-scope*]

per·i·scop·ic (per′ə skop′ik) *adj.* **1** giving distinct vision obliquely as well as in a direct line. **2** of or having to do with periscopes.

per·ish (per′ish) *v.* **1** die or be destroyed: *Many soldiers perished in the battle. The building perished in the flames.* **2** decay; become spoiled: *Fruit perishes quickly in hot weather.* [ME < OF *periss-*, a stem of *perir* < L *perire* < *per-* (intensive) + *ire* go]
☞ *Syn.* See note at **die.**

per·ish·a·ble (per′ish ə bəl) *adj., n.* —*adj.* liable to spoil or decay: *Fresh fruit is perishable.* —*n.* Usually, **perishables,** *pl.* things that are liable to spoil or decay, especially fresh food. —**per′ish·a·bil′i·ty, per′ish·a·ble·ness,** *n.*

per·i·stal·sis (per′ə stal′sis) *n., pl.* **-ses** (-sēz′). the successive wavelike contractions of the alimentary canal or other hollow muscular organ by which its contents are propelled onward. [< NL < Gk. *peristalsis*, ult. < *peri-* around + *stellein* wrap]

per·i·stal·tic (per′ə stal′tik) *adj.* of or having to do with peristalsis.

per·i·style (per′ə stīl′) *n.* **1** a row of columns surrounding a building, court, etc. **2** a space or court so enclosed. [< F < L < Gk. *peristylon* < *peri* around + *stylos* pillar]

per·i·to·ne·al (per′ə tə nē′əl) *adj.* of or having to do with the peritoneum.

per·i·to·ne·um or **per·i·to·nae·um** (per′ə tə nē′əm) *n., pl.* **-ne·a** or **-nae·a** (-nē′ə). the smooth, transparent membrane that lines the walls of the abdomen of a mammal and covers the abdominal organs. [< LL < Gk. *peritonaion*, neut. adj., stretched over, ult. < *peri-* around + *teinein* stretch]

per·i·to·ni·tis (per′ə tə nī′tis) *n.* inflammation of the peritoneum. [< NL < LL *peritonaeum* peritoneum + Gk. *-itis*]

per·i·wig (per′ə wig′) *n.* wig. [earlier *perewyke* < F *perruque.* Cf. PERUKE.]

per·i·win·kle¹ (per′ə wing′kəl) *n.* any of several evergreen plants (genus *Vinca*) of the dogbane family having trailing stems and blue or white flowers. [< L *pervinca*; influenced by *periwinkle²*]

per·i·win·kle² (per′ə wing′kəl) *n.* any of various edible marine snails (family Littorinidae), especially the common periwinkle (*Littorina littorea*) native to N Europe, having a thick, cone-shaped, spiral shell. [OE *pīnewincle* < L *pina* mussel < Gk. *pinē*]

per·jure (per′jər) *v.* **-jured, -jur·ing.** make (oneself) guilty of perjury; swear falsely; lie when under oath (*used with a reflexive pronoun*): *The witness perjured himself at the trial.* —**per′jur·er,** *n.* [ME < AF < L *perjurare* < *per-* to destruction + *jurare* swear < *jus, juris* right (n.)]

hat, āge, fär; let, ēqual, tėrm; it, īce
hot, ōpen, ôrder; oil, out; cup, pút, rüle,
ə bove, takən, pencəl, lemən, circəs

ch, child; ng, long; sh, ship
th, thin; ₮H, then; zh, measure

per·jured (pėr′jərd) *adj.* **1** guilty of perjury: *a perjured witness.* **2** characterized by or involving perjury: *perjured evidence.*

per·ju·ry (pėr′jər ē) *n., pl.* **-ries.** *Law.* the deliberate violation of an oath or affirmation, either by saying that something is true which one knows to be false or by omitting to tell something that one has promised to tell. [ME < AF *perjurie* < L *perjurium* < *perjurare.* See PERJURE.]

perk¹ (pėrk) *v.* **1** move, lift the head, or act briskly or saucily. **2** raise smartly or briskly: *The sparrow perked up his tail.* **3** make trim or smart: *She is all perked out in her Sunday clothes.* **4** put oneself forward briskly or assertively.
perk up, brighten up; become lively and vigorous.
[ME *perke(n)* ? < OF *perquer* perch]

perk² (pėrk) *v. Informal.* **1** percolate: *to perk a pot of coffee. We could hear the coffee perking.* **2** be in a state of activity; go well: *a tax measure to keep the economy perking.* [short for *percolate*]

perk³ (pėrk) *n. Informal.* perquisite: *enjoying perks such as free theatre tickets.*

perk·y (pėr′kē) *adj.* **perk·i·er, perk·i·est.** smart; brisk; saucy; pert. —**perk′i·ly,** *adv.* —**perk′i·ness,** *n.*

perm (pėrm) *n. Informal.* a permanent wave.

per·ma·frost (pėr′mə frost′) *n. Cdn.* ground or subsoil that is permanently frozen.

per·ma·nence (pėr′mə nəns) *n.* the state or condition of being permanent; lasting quality or condition.

per·ma·nen·cy (pėr′mə nən sē) *n., pl.* **-cies. 1** permanence. **2** something that is permanent.

per·ma·nent (pėr′mə nənt) *adj., n.* —*adj.* lasting; intended to last; not for a short time only: *a permanent filling in a tooth. After doing odd jobs for a week, he got a permanent position as office boy.* —*n. Informal.* a permanent wave. [< L *permanens, -entis* staying to the end, ppr. of *permanere* < *per-* through + *manere* stay] —**per′ma·nent·ly,** *adv.*
☞ *Syn. adj.* See note at **lasting.**

permanent married quarters government housing for married members of the armed forces and their immediate families.

permanent press 1 a chemical treatment given to a fabric to make it resistant to creases and, often, to provide a garment with permanent pleats, etc. **2** (*adj.*) **permanent-press,** designating fabric or a garment that has been treated in this way.

permanent tooth one of the second set of teeth in a mammal that follow the baby teeth, or milk teeth.

permanent wave a wave produced in the hair by chemicals or heat, that lasts even after the hair is washed many times.

per·man·ga·nate (pər mang′gə nāt′) *n.* a salt of an acid containing manganese. A solution of potassium permanganate is used as an antiseptic.

per·me·a·bil·i·ty (pėr′mē ə bil′ə tē) *n.* the quality or state of being permeable.

per·me·a·ble (pėr′mē ə bəl) *adj.* that can be permeated: *A sponge is permeable by water.* [< LL *permeabilis* < L *permeare.* See PERMEATE.]

per·me·ate (pėr′mē āt′) *v.* **-at·ed, -at·ing. 1** spread through the whole of; penetrate throughout; pass into or through and affect all of: *Smoke permeated the house. Water will not permeate this fabric.* **2** spread or diffuse itself: *Anger permeated through the crowd.* [< L *permeare* < *per-* through + *meare* pass]

per·me·a·tion (pėr′mē ā′shən) *n.* permeating or being permeated.

Per·mi·an (pėr′mē ən) *n., adj. Geology.* —*n.* **1** a late period of the Paleozoic era, beginning approximately 235 million years ago. **2** the rocks formed in this period. See chart at **geology.** —*adj.* of or having to do with this period or the rocks formed during it. [< *Perm,* a former province in E Russia where such rocks are found]

per·mis·si·ble (pər mis′ə bəl) *adj.* that may be permitted; allowable. —**per·mis′si·bly,** *adv.*

per·mis·sion (pər mish′ən) *n.* consent; leave; permitting: *He asked the teacher's permission to go early.* [< L *permissio, -onis* < *permittere.* See PERMIT.]

per·mis·sive (pər mis′iv) *adj.* **1** not strict in discipline; allowing a great deal of freedom; lenient; indulgent: *a permissive society.*

permissive parents. **2** permitting; giving permission: *a permissive statute.* **3** *Archaic.* permitted; allowed. **—per·mis′sive·ly,** *adv.* **—per·mis′sive·ness,** *n.*

per·mit (*v.* pər mit′; *n.* pėr′mit *or* pər mit′) *v.* **-mit·ted, -mit·ting;** *n.* *—v.* **1** allow (a person, etc.) to do something: *Permit me to explain.* **2** let (something) be done or occur: *The law does not permit smoking in this store.* *—n.* **1** a formal written order giving permission to do something: *a permit to fish or hunt.* **2** permission. [< L *permittere* < *per-* through + *mittere* let go]
☛ *Syn. v.* **1. Permit, allow** = let someone or something do something. **Permit** emphasizes the idea of expressing willingness or giving consent: *His parents permitted him to have a car when he was eighteen.* **Allow** often means not to forbid or prevent, without necessarily giving permission or approval: *That teacher allows too much noise in the room.*

per·mu·ta·tion (pėr′myə tā′shən) *n.* **1** alteration. **2** *Mathematics.* **a** a changing of the order of a set of things; arranging in different orders. **b** such an arrangement or group. The permutations of *a*, *b*, and *c* are *abc, acb, bac, cab, cba.* [< L *permutatio, -onis* < *permutare* < *per-* across + *mutare* change]

per·mute (pər myüt′) *v.* **-mut·ed, -mut·ing.** alter the order or arrangement of; especially, alter in all possible ways. [< L *permutare.* See PERMUTATION.]

per·ni·cious (pər nish′əs) *adj.* **1** that will destroy or ruin; causing harm or damage; injurious: *pernicious habits.* **2** fatal. [< L *perniciosus,* ult. < *per-* thoroughly + *nex, necis* death] **—per·ni′cious·ly,** *adv.* **—per·ni′cious·ness,** *n.*

pernicious anemia a severe disease characterized by a continued decrease in the number of red blood cells and, often, white cells and platelets in the blood. It is unrelated to iron deficiency and is caused by deficiency of vitamin B_{12}, usually due to the body's inability to absorb the vitamin from food.

per·nick·e·ty (pər nik′ə tē) *adj. Informal.* **1** fastidious; fussy. **2** requiring precise and careful handling. [origin uncertain]

Per·nod (per nō′ *or* per′nō) *n. Trademark.* a French alcoholic liquor flavored with aniseed.

per·o·gy (pə rog′ē) *n.pl.* pastries with a meat, cheese, or other filling; pyrohy. [< Ukrainian < Old Slavic *pir* feast + *og*]
☛ *Usage.* Though **perogy** is originally plural, it is sometimes taken as a singular having an Anglicized plural **perogies.**

per·o·rate (per′ə rāt′) *v.* **-rat·ed, -rat·ing. 1** make a formal conclusion to a speech. **2** speak at length; make a long and majestic speech. [< L *perorare.* See PERORATION.]

per·o·ra·tion (per′ə rā′shən) *n.* the last part of an oration or discussion, summing up what has been said. [< L *peroratio, -onis* < *perorare* < *per-* to a finish + *orare* speak formally]

per·ox·ide (pər ok′sīd) *n., v.* **-id·ed, -id·ing.** *—n.* **1** *Chemistry.* an oxide of a given element or radical that contains the greatest, or an unusual, amount of oxygen. **2** hydrogen peroxide. *—v.* bleach (hair) by applying hydrogen peroxide.

per·pen·dic·u·lar (pėr′pən dik′yə lər) *adj., n.* *—adj.* **1** at right angles to the plane of the horizon; vertical; upright. **2** very steep: *a perpendicular cliff.* **3** at right angles to a given line, plane, or surface. One line is perpendicular to another when it makes a square corner with the other. **4** Often, **Perpendicular,** of or designating a late stage of medieval English Gothic architecture characterized by a marked emphasis on vertical lines. *—n.* **1** a perpendicular line, plane, or surface. **2** a perpendicular position. [< L *perpendicularis* < *perpendiculum* plumb line, ult. < *per-* + *pendere* hang] **—per′pen·dic′u·lar·ly,** *adv.*

per·pe·trate (pėr′pə trāt′) *v.* **-trat·ed, -trat·ing.** do or commit (crime, fraud, or anything bad or foolish). [< L *perpetrare* < *per-* (intensive) + *patrare* perform] **—per′pe·tra′tion,** *n.* **—per′pe·tra′tor,** *n.*

per·pet·u·al (pər pech′ü əl) *adj.* **1** lasting forever; eternal: *the perpetual hills.* **2** lasting throughout life: *a perpetual income.* **3** continuous; never ceasing: *a perpetual stream of visitors; perpetual motion.* **4** *Horticulture.* being in bloom more or less continuously throughout the year or the season. [< L *perpetualis* < *perpetuus* < *perpes, -etis* continuous < *per-* to the end + *petere* seek]

perpetual calendar a calendar or table that allows one to find out the day of the week for any given date over a wide range of years.

per·pet·u·al·ly (pər pech′ü əl ē) *adv.* forever.

per·pet·u·ate (pər pech′ü āt′) *v.* **-at·ed, -at·ing.** make perpetual; cause to last indefinitely: *attempts to perpetuate a species. The Brock Monument was built to perpetuate the memory of a great man.* [< L *perpetuare* < *perpetuus.* See PERPETUAL.] **—per·pet′u·a′tion,** *n.* **—per·pet′u·a′tor,** *n.*

per·pe·tu·i·ty (pėr′pə tyü′ə tē *or* pėr′pə tü′ə tē) *n., pl.* **-ties.**
1 the state of being perpetual; endless time. **2** a perpetual possession, tenure, or position. **3** *Law.* **a** of an estate, the quality or condition of being inalienable perpetually or longer than the legal time limit. **b** the estate so restricted. **4** a perpetual annuity. **in perpetuity,** forever.
[< F < L *perpetuitas* < *perpetuus.* See PERPETUAL.]

per·plex (pər pleks′) *v.* **1** trouble with doubt; make unable to think about clearly or logically; puzzle: *a perplexing attitude. The problem is hard enough to perplex even the instructor.* **2** complicate (something). [originally adj., < L *perplexus* confused, ult. < *per-* completely + *plectere* intertwine] **—per·plex′ing·ly,** *adv.*
☛ *Syn.* **1.** See note at **puzzle.**

per·plexed (pėr plekst′) *adj.* not knowing what to do or how to act; puzzled and confused: *She was greatly perplexed by her friend's strange manner.*

per·plex·ed·ly (pėr plek′səd lē) *adv.* in a perplexed manner.

per·plex·i·ty (pər plek′sə tē) *n., pl.* **-ties. 1** a perplexed condition; confusion; the state of being puzzled or not knowing what to do or how to act. **2** something that perplexes.

per·qui·site (pėr′kwə zit) *n.* **1** anything desirable received in addition to regular pay and that results directly from one's position, especially something promised or expected: *Included among the maid's perquisites were expensive dresses cast off by her mistress.* **2** a tip. **3** something expected or due as an exclusive right, by virtue of status, position, etc. [< Med.L *perquisitum* (thing) gained, ult. < L *per-* thoroughly + *quaerere* seek]

per·ry (per′ē) *n.* an alcoholic drink resembling cider, made from the juice of pears. [ME *pereye, perrye* < OF *peré,* ult. < L *pirum* pear]

per se (pėr sē′ *or* pėr sā′) by, of, or in itself; intrinsically. [< L]

per·se·cute (pėr′sə kyüt′) *v.* **-cut·ed, -cut·ing. 1** treat badly; do harm to again and again; oppress, especially for religious, racial, or political reasons: *Christians were persecuted in ancient Rome. The child was persecuted by other children in the neighborhood because he seemed different.* **2** annoy: *persecuted with endless questions.* [< *persecution*] **—per′se·cu′tor,** *n.*
☛ *Usage.* Both **persecute** and **prosecute** come from the same Latin word *sequi,* meaning "follow" or "pursue." But **persecute** means to pursue or harass a person (or other creature) with the idea of doing him harm, while **prosecute** means to bring someone before a court of law or to pursue a plan, a job, or idea in the sense of carrying it out or bringing it to completion.

per·se·cu·tion (pėr′sə kyü′shən) *n.* **1** the act or practice of persecuting. **2** the condition or state of being persecuted. [< L *persecutio, -onis,* ult. < *per-* perseveringly + *sequi* follow]

Per·seph·o·ne (pər sef′ə nē′) *n. Greek mythology.* a daughter of Zeus and Demeter, who was carried off by Pluto to become his wife and queen of the underworld. Persephone corresponds to the Roman goddess Proserpina.

Per·se·us (pėr′sē əs *or* pėr′syüs) *n.* **1** *Greek mythology.* a Greek hero who slew Medusa and rescued Andromeda from a sea monster. **2** *Astronomy.* a constellation in the northern sky between Taurus and Cassiopeia.

per·se·ver·ance (pėr′sə vēr′əns) *n.* a sticking to a purpose or an aim; never giving up what one has set out to do; persistence.
☛ *Syn.* See note at **persistence.**

per·se·vere (pėr′sə vēr′) *v.* **-vered, -ver·ing.** continue steadily in doing something hard; persist. [< F < L *perseverare* < *per-* very + *severus* strict] **—per′se·ver′ing·ly,** *adv.*

Per·sian (pėr′zhən) *n., adj.* *—n.* **1** a native or inhabitant of Persia (or Iran), a country in SW Asia. **2** the language of Persia (or Iran). *—adj.* of or having to do with Persia (or Iran), its people, or their language.

Persian cat a breed of cat having a chunky build and long, glossy hair.

Persian lamb **1** a very curly fur from karakul lambs raised in Iran and some parts of central Asia. **2** a coat or other garment made from this fur.

per·si·flage (pėr′sə fläzh′) *n.* light, joking talk; banter. [< F *persiflage* < *persifler* banter, apparently < *per-* (< L) + *siffler* whistle, hiss < L *sibilare*]

per·sim·mon (pər sim′ən) *n.* **1** any of several tropical trees (genus *Diospyrus*) of the ebony family bearing edible, round fruit. **2** the fruit of any of these trees, typically orange-red in color and sweet-tasting when ripe. [< Algonquian]

per·sist (pər sist′ *or* pər zist′) *v.* **1** continue firmly; refuse to stop or be changed: *He persists in eating with his fingers. She persisted till she had solved the difficult problem.* **2** last; stay; endure, especially past a usual, normal, or expected time: *The cold weather will persist for some time.* **3** say again and again; maintain. [< *persistere* < *per-* to the end + *sistere* stand]

per·sist·ence (pər sis′təns *or* pər zis′təns) *n.* **1** the quality or state of being persistent. **2** the continuing existence: *the persistence of a cough.*

☛ *Syn.* **1. Persistence, perseverance** = a holding fast to a purpose or course of action. **Persistence**, having a good or bad sense according to one's attitude toward what is done, emphasizes holding stubbornly or obstinately to one's purpose and continuing firmly and often annoyingly against disapproval, opposition, advice, etc.: *By persistence many people won religious freedom.* **Perseverance**, always in a good sense, emphasizes refusing to be discouraged by obstacles or difficulties and continuing steadily with courage and patience: *Perseverance leads to success.*

per·sist·en·cy (pər sis′tən sē *or* pər zis′tən sē) *n.* persistence.

per·sist·ent (pər sis′tənt *or* pər zis′tənt) *adj.* **1** persisting; having lasting qualities, especially in the face of dislike, disapproval, or difficulties: *a persistent worker, a persistent beggar.* **2** lasting; going on; continuing: *a persistent headache that lasted for three days.* **3** *Botany.* continuing without withering, as a calyx which remains after the corolla has withered; permanent. **4** *Zoology.* permanent; not lost or altered during development: *persistent horns.* —**per·sist′ent·ly**, *adv.*

per·son (pèr′sən) *n.* **1** a man, woman or child; human being: *Any person who wishes may come to the fair.* **2** a human body: *The person of the king was well guarded.* **3** bodily appearance: *He kept his person neat and trim.* **4** *Grammar.* **a** reference in discourse to the speaker, the person spoken to, or another person or thing, indicated by a distinction of form in pronouns and, in many languages, verbs. **b** any of the three groups of pronoun or verb forms indicating distinction of person: **first person** (speaker), **second person** (person spoken to), or **third person** (person or thing spoken about). In *I asked her where she met you,* the pronoun *I* is the singular form for the first person, *her* and *she* are singular forms for the third person, and *you* is the singular or plural form for the second person. **5** *Christianity.* any of the three modes of being in the Trinity (Father, Son, and Holy Ghost). **6** *Law.* a human being, or an entity such as a corporation, a partnership, or occasionally a collection of property, as the estate of a dead person, recognized by the law as capable of having legal rights and duties.
in person, by or with one's own action or presence; personally: *You may phone in your order or shop in person. The artist was there in person.*
[ME < OF < L *persona* character, mask worn by actor. Doublet of PARSON.]
☛ *Syn.* **Person, individual, party. Person** is the ordinary word for a human being of either sex: *A well-known person came into the room.* **Individual** emphasizes the person's uniqueness: *A strange individual came into the room.* Unlike **person, individual** can also be applied to animals and objects: *Our cat is a fascinating individual.* The phrase **a person** is often used instead of the impersonal pronoun **one**: *Exercise makes a person hungry.* It is, as a rule, awkward and pretentious to use **individual** in this way. **Party** is used especially in legal documents to refer to one of the people involved in a contract, agreement, etc.

per·so·na (pər sō′nə) *n., pl.* **-nae** (-nē *or* nī) **1** a character or personality that a person adopts and presents to the public: *In private life the premier drops his public persona. Some novelists display a different persona in each of their books.* **2** *Jungian psychology.* the technique or system by which a person adapts to his environment in life in accordance with his own inner needs, or ego. **3** Usually, **personae**, *pl.* the characters in a novel, play, etc.

per·son·a·ble (pèr′sən ə bəl) *adj.* having a pleasing appearance and personality; attractive: *a personable young man.*

per·son·age (pèr′sən ij) *n.* **1** a person of importance. **2** person. **3** a character in a book, play, etc. [< OF]

per·so·na gra·ta (pər sō′nə grä′tə, grat′ə, *or* grā′tə) *Latin.* an acceptable person.

per·son·al (pèr′sən əl *or* pèrs′nəl) *adj., n.* —*adj.* **1** individual; private: *a personal letter.* **2** done in person; directly by oneself, not through others or by letter: *a personal visit.* **3** of the body or bodily appearance: *personal beauty.* **4** about or against a person or persons: *personal abuse.* **5** inclined to make remarks or to ask questions of others: *Don't be too personal.* **6** *Grammar.* showing person. *I, we, thou, you, he, she, it,* and *they* are **personal pronouns. 7** *Law.* of or having to do with possessions that can be moved, not land or buildings.
—*n.* a short paragraph in a newspaper about a particular person or persons. [< LL *personalis*]
☛ *Usage.* Do not confuse **personal** and **personnel. Personal** is usually an adjective and is stressed on the first syllable. **Personnel** is a noun and is stressed on the last syllable.

personal effects personal belongings normally worn or carried, such as clothing, cosmetics, etc.

personal equation individual tendencies for which allowance should be made.

per·son·al·i·ty (pèr′sə nal′ə tē) *n., pl.* **-ties. 1** the personal or individual quality that makes one person be different or act differently from another: *A baby two weeks old does not have much personality.* **2** the pleasing or attractive qualities of a person: *He is popular because he has a lot of personality.* **3** a remark made about or against some person: *Tactful people avoid personalities.* **4** a person of importance or renown; personage: *personalities of the stage and screen.* **5** a person who regularly faces the public in his or

her work, such as television announcer. **6** the quality or state of being a person, not a thing.
☛ *Syn.* **1.** See note at **character.**

per·son·al·ize (pèr′sən əl īz′) *v.* **-ized, -iz·ing. 1** make personal or individual; especially, mark with one's name, etc.: *Personalized stationery has the owner's monogram, name, or name and address stamped on it.* **2** personify. —**per′son·al·i·za′tion,** *n.*

per·son·al·ly (pèr′sən əl ē *or* pèrs′nəl ē) *adv.* **1** in person; not by the aid of others: *The hostess personally saw to the comforts of her guests.* **2** as far as oneself is concerned. **3** as a person: *We like him personally, but dislike his way of living.* **4** as being meant for oneself: *He intended no insult to you; do not take what he said personally.*

personal property property that is not land, buildings, mines, or forests; movable possessions.

per·son·al·ty (pèr′sən əl tē) *n., pl.* **-ties.** *Law.* personal property.

per·so·na non gra·ta (pər sō′nə non grät′ə, grat′ə, *or* grä′tə) *Latin.* a person who is not acceptable.

per·son·ate (pèr′sən āt′) *v.* **-at·ed, -at·ing. 1** act the part of (a character in a play, etc.). **2** give a personality or personal characteristics to; personify. **3** *Law.* pretend to be (someone else), especially for purposes of fraud; impersonate. [< obs. *personate,* adj., feigned < L *personatus,* < *persona* a mask] —**per′son·a′tor,** *n.*

per·son·a·tion (pèr′sən ā′shən) *n.* **1** personating. **2** personifying.

per·son·i·fi·ca·tion (pər son′ə fə kā′shən) *n.* **1** representation of a thing or idea as a person or as having human qualities: *Personification is a common figure of speech. The expression* Duty *calls us involves a personification of the idea of duty.* **2** a person, creature, or divinity imagined as representing a thing or idea: *Satan is the personification of evil.* **3** a person or thing seen as a striking example of embodiment of a quality, etc.: *A miser is the personification of greed.*

per·son·i·fy (pər son′ə fī′) *v.* **-fied, -fy·ing. 1** regard or represent as a person or as having human qualities: *The sea is often personified in poetry.* **2** be a type of; embody: *She personifies kindness.*

per·son·nel (pèr′sə nəl′) *n.* persons employed in any work, business, or service. [< F *personnel* personal; adj. used as n.]
☛ *Usage.* See note at **personnel.**

per·spec·tive (pər spek′tiv) *n.* **1 a** the art of picturing objects on a flat surface so as to give the appearance of distance. **b** a drawing or picture in perspective. **2** (*adj.*) drawn so as to show the proper perspective. **3** the effect of distance on the appearance of objects: *Railway tracks seem to meet at the horizon because of perspective.* **4** the effect that the distance of events has on the mind: *Many happenings of last year seem less important when viewed in perspective.* **5** a view of things or facts in which they are in the right relations: *This editorial puts the crisis in perspective.* **6** a view in front; distant view. [< Med.L *perspectiva (ars)* (science) of optics, ult. < L *per-* through + *specere* look]

per·spi·ca·cious (pèr′spə kā′shəs) *adj.* keen in observing and understanding; discerning: *a perspicacious judgment.* [< L *perspicax, -acis* sharp-sighted, ult. < *per-* through + *specere* to look] —**per′spi·ca′cious·ly,** *adv.*

per·spi·cac·i·ty (pèr′spə kas′ə tē) *n.* keen perception; discernment; wisdom and understanding in dealing with people or with facts.

per·spi·cu·i·ty (pèr′spə kyü′ə tē) *n.* clearness in expression; ease in being understood: *The premier was noted for the perspicuity of his speeches.*

per·spic·u·ous (pər spik′yü əs) *adj.* clear; easily understood: *a perspicuous style.* [< L *perspicuus,* ult. < *per-* through + *specere* look] —**per·spic′u·ous·ly,** *adv.* —**per·spic′u·ous·ness,** *n.*

per·spi·ra·tion (pèr′spə rā′shən) *n.* **1** sweat. **2** a sweating or perspiring.
☛ *Syn.* **1.** See note at **sweat.**

per·spire (pər spīr′) *v.* **-spired, -spir·ing.** sweat. [< L *perspirare* < *per-* through + *spirare* breathe]

per·suade (pər swād′) *v.* **-suad·ed, -suad·ing. 1** cause (a person) to do something by urging, arguing, etc.; prevail upon: *I knew I should study but he persuaded me to go to the movies.* **2** cause (a person) to believe something by urging, arguing, etc.; convince:

hat, āge, fär; let, ēqual, tèrm; it, īce
hot, ōpen, ôrder; oil, out; cup, pùt, rüle,
əbove, takən, pencəl, lemən, circəs
ch, child; ng, long; sh, ship
th, thin; ŦH, then; zh, measure

They finally persuaded him of the truth of the rumor. We tried to persuade her that we had known all along what she was up to. [< L *persuadere* < *per-* strongly + *suadere* urge] —**per·suad´er,** *n.*

☛ *Syn.* **1. Persuade, convince** = get someone to do or believe something. **Persuade** emphasizes winning a person over to a desired belief or action by appealing to his feelings as well as to his mind. **Convince** emphasizes overcoming a person's objections or disbelief by proof or arguments appealing to his reason and cannot persuade her to take one.

per·sua·si·ble (pər swā´sə bəl) *adj.* that can be persuaded; open to persuasion.

per·sua·sion (pər swā´zhən) *n.* 1 a persuading: *All our persuasion was of no use; she would not come.* 2 the power of persuading. 3 a firm belief: *He and his brother were of different political persuasions.* 4 a a religious belief; creed: *All Christians are not of the same persuasion.* b a body of persons holding a particular religious belief; sect; denomination. 5 *Facetious.* kind; sort. [ME < L *persuasio, -onis* < *persuadere.* See PERSUADE.]

per·sua·sive (pər swā´siv *or* pər swā´ziv) *adj.* able to persuade; effective in persuading: *The salesman had a very persuasive way of talking.* —**per·sua´sive·ly,** *adv.* —**per·sua´sive·ness,** *n.*

pert (pèrt) *adj.* 1 too forward or free in speech or action; saucy; bold. 2 *Informal.* lively; in good health or spirits. [for *apert,* ME < OF *apert* open < L *apertus;* influenced by OF *aspert* expert] —**pert´ly,** *adv.* —**pert´ness,** *n.*

per·tain (pər tān´) *v.* 1 belong or be connected as a part, possession, etc.: *We own the house and the land pertaining to it.* 2 refer; be related (*to*): *an editorial pertaining to the coming election.* 3 be appropriate: *We had turkey and everything else that pertains to Thanksgiving Day.* [ME < OF < L *pertinere* < *per-* across + *tenere* reach]

per·thite (pèr´thīt) *n.* a type of feldspar. [< *Perth,* Ontario, where it occurs]

per·ti·na·cious (pèr´tə nā´shəs) *adj.* 1 holding firmly to a purpose, action, or opinion; very persistent: *A bulldog is a pertinacious fighter.* 2 stubborn to excess; obstinate or perverse. 3 obstinately or persistently continuing; not yielding to treatment: *a pertinacious cough.* [< L *pertinacia* firmness < *per-* very + *tenax, -acis* tenacious] —**per´ti·na´cious·ly,** *adv.* —**per´ti·na´cious·ness,** *n.*

per·ti·nac·i·ty (pèr´tə nas´ə tē) *n.* great persistence; holding firmly to a purpose, action, or opinion.

per·ti·nence (pèr´tə nəns) *n.* being to the point; fitness; relevance: *The pertinence of the boy's replies showed that he was not stupid.*

per·ti·nen·cy (pèr´tə nən sē) *n.* pertinence.

per·ti·nent (pèr´tə nənt) *adj.* having to do with what is being considered; relating to the matter in hand; to the point. [< L *pertinens, -entis,* ppr. of *pertinere* pertain. See PERTAIN.] —**per´ti·nent·ly,** *adv.*

☛ *Syn.* **Pertinent, relevant** = relating to the matter in hand. **Pertinent** means directly to the point of the matter, belonging properly and fittingly to what is being considered and helping to explain or solve it: *He asked for all the pertinent information about the events leading up to this situation.* **Relevant** means having some bearing on the problem or enough connection with it to have some significance: *Even incidents seeming unimportant in themselves might be relevant.*

per·turb (pər tèrb´) *v.* disturb greatly; make uneasy or troubled: *The management was perturbed at the possibility of another strike.* [< L *perturbare* < *per-* thoroughly + *turbare* confuse] —**per·turb´er,** *n.*

per·tur·ba·tion (pèr´tər bā´shən) *n.* 1 perturbing or being perturbed. 2 something that perturbs.

pe·ruke (pə rük´) *n.* a wig, especially a style of wig commonly worn by European men in the 17th and 18th centuries. [< F *perruque*]

pe·rus·al (pə rüz´əl) *n.* a perusing; reading: *the perusal of a letter.*

pe·ruse (pə rüz´) *v.* **-rused, -rus·ing.** 1 read thoroughly and carefully. 2 read. 3 examine, inspect, or consider in detail. [originally, use up, < L *per-* to the end + E *use*]

Pe·ru·vi·an (pə rü´vē ən) *n., adj.* —*n.* a native or inhabitant of Peru, a country on the western coast of South America. —*adj.* of or having to do with Peru, or its people.

Peruvian bark a bark from which quinine is obtained; cinchona.

per·vade (pər vād´) *v.* **-vad·ed, -vad·ing.** 1 go or spread throughout; be throughout: *The odor of pines pervades the air.* 2 be found throughout (the body of a work, etc.), so as to characterize, flavor unmistakably, etc.: *The author's anger at injustice pervades the whole novel.* [< L *pervadere* < *per-* through + *vadere* go] —**per·vad´er,** *n.*

per·va·sion (pər vā´zhən) *n.* pervading or being pervaded; permeation.

per·va·sive (pər vā´siv *or* pər vā´siv) *adj.* tending to pervade. —**per·va´sive·ly,** *adv.* —**per·va´sive·ness,** *n.*

per·verse (pər vèrs´) *adj.* 1 contrary and willful; stubborn: *The perverse child did just what we told him not to do.* 2 persistent in wrong. 3 wicked. 4 not correct; wrong: *perverse reasoning.* [< L *perversus* turned away, pp. of *pervertere.* See PERVERT.] —**per·verse´ly,** *adv.* —**per·verse´ness,** *n.*

per·ver·sion (pər vèr´zhən *or* pər vèr´shən) *n.* 1 a turning or being turned to what is wrong; change to what is unnatural, abnormal, or wrong: *A tendency to eat sand is a perversion of appetite.* 2 a perverted form.

per·ver·si·ty (pər vèr´sə tē) *n., pl.* **-ties.** 1 the quality of being perverse. 2 a perverse character or conduct.

per·vert (*v.* pər vèrt´; *n.* pèr´vèrt) *v., n.* —*v.* 1 lead or turn from the right way or from the truth: *Reading comic books often perverts our taste for good books.* 2 give a wrong meaning to: *His enemies perverted his friendly remark and made it into an insult.* 3 use for wrong purposes or in a wrong way: *A clever criminal perverts his talents.* 4 change from what is natural or normal, now especially what is generally accepted or defined by law as natural or normal in sexual behavior. —*n.* a perverted person, now especially one who practises sexual perversion. [< L *pervertere* < *per-* (intensive) + *vertere* turn] —**per·vert´er,** *n.*

per·vi·ous (pèr´vē əs) *adj.* 1 giving passage or entrance; permeable: *Sand is easily pervious to water.* 2 open to influence, argument, etc.; accessible; pervious to reason. [< L *pervius* < *per-* through + *via* way] —**per·vi·ous·ness,** *n.*

pe·se·ta (pə sā´tə) *n.* 1 the basic unit of money in Spain, divided into 100 centimos. See table at **money.** 2 a coin or note worth one peseta. [< Sp., dim. of *peso*]

pe·se·wa (pə sā´wä) *n.* 1 a unit of money in Ghana, equal to ¹⁄₁₀₀ of a cedi. 2 a coin worth one pesewa.

pes·ky (pes´kē) *adj.* **-ki·er, -ki·est.** *Informal.* troublesome; annoying. [? alteration of *pesty* < *pest*]

pe·so (pā´sō) *n., pl.* **-sos.** 1 the basic unit of money in Argentina, Bolivia, Colombia, Cuba, Dominican Republic, Mexico, and the Philippines, divided into 100 centavos. 2 the basic unit of money in Uruguay divided into 100 centesimos. 3 the basic unit of money in Chile, divided into 1000 escudos. See table at **money.** 4 a coin or note worth one peso. [< Sp. < L *pensum,* pp. of *pendere* weigh]

pes·si·mism (pes´ə miz´əm) *n.* 1 a tendency to look on the dark side of things or to see difficulties and disadvantages. 2 a belief that things naturally tend to evil, or that life is not worth while. [< L *pessimus* worst + *-ism*]

pes·si·mist (pes´ə mist) *n.* 1 a person inclined to see all the difficulties and disadvantages or to look on the dark side of things. 2 a person who thinks that life holds more evil than good, and so is not worth living.

pes·si·mis·tic (pes´ə mis´tik) *adj.* of, having to do with, or characterized by pessimism: *a pessimistic outlook on life.* —**pes·si·mis´ti·cal·ly,** *adv.*

☛ *Syn.* **1.** See note at **cynical.**

pest (pest) *n.* 1 any thing or person that causes trouble, injuries, or destruction; nuisance: *Mosquitoes are pests.* 2 *Archaic.* pestilence. [< L *pestis* plague]

pes·ter (pes´tər) *v.* 1 annoy; trouble; vex: *If we sit outside we'll be pestered by flies.* 2 bother with repeated requests or demands; keep after: *He kept pestering his older sister till she gave in and took him along.* [apparently < OF *empestrer* hobble (an animal); influenced by *pest*] —**pes´ter·er,** *n.*

☛ *Syn.* See note at **tease.**

pest·house (pest´hous´) *n. Archaic.* a hospital for persons ill with highly infectious and dangerous diseases.

pes·ti·cide (pes´tə sīd´) *n.* any chemical agent or other substance used to destroy plant or animal pests. [< L *pestis* plague, pest + E *-cide;* probably patterned on *insecticide*]

pes·tif·er·ous (pes tif´ər əs) *adj.* 1 bringing disease or infection. 2 bringing moral evil: *the pestiferous influence of a bad example.* 3 *Informal.* troublesome; annoying. [< L *pestiferus* < *pestis* plague + *ferre* bring]

pes·ti·lence (pes´tə ləns) *n.* 1 a deadly epidemic infectious disease, especially bubonic plague. 2 anything that is extremely destructive or deadly in its effect.

pes·ti·lent (pes´tə lənt) *adj.* 1 often causing death: *a pestilent disease.* 2 harmful to morals; destroying peace: *a pestilent den of vice, the pestilent effects of war.* 3 troublesome; annoying. [< L *pestilens, -entis* < *pestis* pest] —**pes´ti·lent·ly,** *adv.*

pes·ti·len·tial (pes´tə len´shəl) *adj.* 1 of, having to do with, or causing pestilence. 2 morally or socially harmful. 3 irritating. —**pes´ti·len´tial·ly,** *adv.*

A neolithic mortar and pestle, made of stone

hat, āge, fär; let, ēqual, tèrm; it, īce
hot, ōpen, ôrder; oil, out; cup, pút, rüle,
əbove, takən, pencəl, lemən, circəs

ch, child; ng, long; sh, ship
th, thin; ŦH, then; zh, measure

pes·tle (pes′əl) *n., v.* **-tled, -tling.** —*n.* **1** a tool for pounding or crushing substances into a powder in a mortar. **2** any of various mechanical appliances for pounding, stamping, pressing, etc., as a vertically moving or pounding part in a machine. —*v.* pound or crush with a pestle. [ME < OF *pestel* < L *pistillum,* ult. < *pinsere* pound. Doublet of PISTIL.]

pet¹ (pet) *n., adj., v.* **pet·ted, pet·ting.** —*n.* **1** an animal kept as a favorite and treated with affection. **2** a darling; a favorite.
—*adj.* **1** treated as a pet. **2** showing affection: *a pet name.* **3** darling; favorite. **4** *Informal.* particular; special: *a pet aversion, a pet theory, a pet phrase.*
—*v.* **1** treat as a pet. **2** stroke; pat; touch lovingly and gently. **3** yield to the wishes of; indulge. [< Scots Gaelic *peata*]

pet² (pet) *n.* a fit of peevishness; fretful discontent. [origin uncertain]

peta– (pet′ə) *SI prefix.* one quadrillion; 10¹⁵: *petametre. Symbol:* P

pet·al (pet′əl) *n.* one of the parts of a flower that are usually colored; one of the leaves of a corolla. A daisy has many petals. See **flower** for picture. [< NL < Gk. *petalon* leaf, originally neut. adj., outspread] —**pet′al·like** *adj.*

–pet·alled or **–pet·aled** (pet′əld) *combining form.* having—petals: *six-petalled = having six petals.*

pe·tard (pi tärd′) *n.* an explosive device formerly used in warfare to break down a door or gate or to breach a wall. It was fastened to the gate, etc. and ignited.
hoist with (one's) own petard, injured or destroyed by one's own scheme or device for the ruin of others. [< F *pétard* < *péter* break wind, ult. < L *pedere*]

pet·cock (pet′kok′) *n.* a small tap or valve for draining a pipe or cylinder, releasing pressure, etc. [< obs. *pet* < F *péter* break wind + *cock¹*]

pe·ter (pē′tər) *v. Informal.* gradually fail or come to an end; give out or become exhausted (*used with* **out**): *We were forced to ration our food as supplies began to peter out.* [origin unknown]

Pe·ter·bor·ough or **Pe·ter·bor·o** (pē′tər bėr′ə) *n. Cdn.* a type of canoe made from wood or birchbark, formerly manufactured at Peterborough, Ontario.

Pe·ter·head or **pe·ter·head** (pē′tər hed′) *n. Cdn.* a decked launch or large whaleboat equipped with a sail and a small motor, much used by Eskimos and others in the E Arctic. Also, **Peterhead boat.** [< *Peterhead,* Scotland, where early boats of this type were made]

pet·i·o·late (pet′ē ə lāt′) *adj.* having a petiole.

pet·i·ole (pet′ē ōl′) *n.* **1** *Botany.* the slender stalk by which a leaf is attached to the stem. See **stem** for picture. **2** *Zoology.* a stalklike part. A petiole connects the thorax and abdomen of a wasp. [< L *petiolus,* dim. of *pes, pedis* foot]

pet·it (pet′ē) *adj.* petty (*now used only in legal phrases*): *petit larceny.* [< F *petit* < VL stem *pit-* little. Doublet of PETTY.]

petit bourgeois (pə tē bür zhwä′) *pl.* **petits bourgeois** (pə tē bür zhwä′). *French.* **1** a member of the lower middle class. **2** the lower middle class.

pe·tite (pə tēt′) *adj.* little; of small size; tiny, especially with reference to a woman or girl. [< F *petite,* fem. of *petit* little]

pet·it four (pet′ē fôr′) *pl.* **pet·its fours** (pet′ē fôrz′). a small fancy cake with decorative frosting. [< F *petit four* little oven]

pe·ti·tion (pə tish′ən) *n., v.* —*n.* **1** a formal request to a superior or to one in authority for some privilege, right, benefit, etc.: *The people signed a petition asking the city council for a new sidewalk.* **2** *Law.* a written application for an order of court for some action by a judge. **3** prayer. **4** that which is requested or prayed for. **5** the act of formally asking or humbly requesting.
—*v.* **1** ask earnestly; make a petition to: *They petitioned the mayor to use his influence with the city council.* **2** pray. [< L *petitio, -onis* < *petere* seek] —**pe·ti′tion·er,** *n.*

pe·ti·tion·ar·y (pə tish′ən er′ē) *adj.* of a petition.

petit jury trial jury.

petit larceny *U.S.* in some states, a theft in which the value of the property stolen is less than a certain amount fixed by law. Compare **grand larceny.**

pe·tit mal (pə tē mal′ *or* -mäl′) a mild type of epilepsy. [< F]

pet·it point (pet′ē point′) **1** a small, diagonal needlepoint stitch used for fine, allover embroidery. **2** embroidery done with such stitches: *Petit point is usually done with embroidery floss.* [< F *petit* small + *point* stitch]

pet·rel (pet′rəl) *n.* any of various small, web-footed sea birds (order Procellariiformes) having thick, usually black-and-white plumage, long, pointed wings, and a hooked bill. Petrels roam far out at sea between breeding seasons. See also **stormy petrel.** [apparently dim. of St. *Peter,* who walked on the sea]
☛ *Hom.* **petrol.**

Petri dish or **petri dish** (pä′trē *or* pē′trē) a round, shallow, glass container with a loose cover, used in laboratories to hold bacteria cultures. [< Julius *Petri* (1852-1922), a German bacteriologist, who invented it]

pet·ri·fac·tion (pet′rə fak′shən) *n.* **1** the process of petrifying. **2** the condition or quality of being petrified. **3** something petrified.

pet·ri·fi·ca·tion (pet′rə fə kā′shən) *n.* petrifaction.

Petrified Forest an ancient forest in Arizona whose trees have turned to stone.

pet·ri·fy (pet′rə fī′) *v.* **-fied, -fy·ing. 1** replace animal or vegetable cells with mineral deposits; turn into stone (*usually used in the passive*): *petrified wood.* **2** make or become stiff, dull, etc.; deaden. **3** paralyse with fear, horror, or surprise: *They heard a footstep upstairs and stopped, petrified.* [< F *pétrifier,* ult. < L *petra* stone < Gk.]

petro– *combining form.* **1** rock: *petroglyph = a rock carving.* **2** petroleum: *petrochemical = a chemical made of or from petroleum.* [< Gk. *petra* rock]

pet·ro·chem·i·cal (pet′rō kem′ə kəl) *n., adj.* —*n.* any of various important chemicals made from petroleum or natural gas, used in the manufacture of plastics, synthetic fibres, paints, etc. —*adj.* of or having to do with petrochemicals or petrochemistry.

pet·ro·chem·is·try (pet′rō kem′is trē) *n.* **1** the branch of chemistry dealing with petroleum and petrochemicals. **2** the chemistry of rocks.

pet·ro·dol·lar (pet′rō dol′ər) *n.* Usually, **petrodollars,** *pl.* money earned from the sale of petroleum and available as dollars, especially when thought of as a source of economic or political power.

pet·ro·glyph (pet′rə glif′) *n.* a carving or inscription on rock. [< F *petroglyphe* < Gk. *petra* rock + *glyphē* a carving]

pet·ro·graph (pet′rə graf′) *n.* a painting or inscription on rock.

pe·trog·ra·phy (pi trog′rə fē) *n.* a branch of petrology dealing mainly with the detailed description and classification of rocks. [< Gk. *petra* rock, *petros* stone + E *-graphy*]

pet·rol (pet′rəl) *n. Esp.Brit.* gasoline. [< F < Med.L *petroleum.* Doublet of PETROLEUM.]
☛ *Hom.* **petrel.**

pet·ro·la·tum (pet′rə lā′təm) *n.* **1** a salve or ointment made from petroleum. **2** mineral oil. [< NL < E *petrol*]

pe·tro·le·um (pə trō′lē əm) *n.* a combustible, usually dark-colored liquid, a kind of oil that occurs in deposits within the rock strata of many parts of the world and consists of a complex mixture of hydrocarbons and small amounts of many other substances. Petroleum is processed to produce gasoline, fuel oils, kerosene, paraffin, lubricants, etc. [< Med.L < Gk. *petra* rock, *petros* stone + L *oleum* oil. Doublet of PETROL.]

petroleum jelly a smooth, greasy, odorless, and tasteless substance obtained from petroleum, used as an ointment and as a lubricant.

pet·ro·log·i·cal (pet′rə loj′ə kəl) *adj.* of or having to do with petrology. —**pet′ro·log′i·cal·ly,** *adv.*

pe·trol·o·gist (pi trol′ə jist) *n.* a person trained in petrology, especially one whose work it is.

pe·trol·o·gy (pi trol′ə jē) *n.* the branch of geology that deals with rocks, including their origin, history, structure, chemical composition, classification, etc. [< Gk. *petra* rock, *petros* stone + E *-logy*]

pet·ti·coat (pet′ē kōt′) *n.* **1** a skirt worn beneath a dress or outer skirt by women or girls. **2** a skirt. **3** *Slang.* a woman or girl. **4** (*adj.*)

female; feminine: *petticoat government.* [originally, *petty coat* little coat]

pet·ti·fog (pet′ē fog′) *v.* **-fogged, -fog·ging. 1** use petty, underhanded, or dishonest methods: *a pettifogging lawyer.* **2** quibble over small details. [back formation from *pettifogger*]

pet·ti·fog·ger (pet′ē fog′ər) *n.* **1** a lawyer who uses petty, underhanded, or dishonest methods; shyster. **2** any person who uses petty, underhanded, or dishonest methods. **3** a person who quibbles over small details. [apparently < *petty* + *fogger* (origin unknown)]

pet·tish (pet′ish) *adj.* peevish; cross: *a pettish reply, a pettish child.* [< *pet²*] —**pet′tish·ly,** *adv.* —**pet′tish·ness,** *n.*

pet·ty (pet′ē) *adj.* **-ti·er, -ti·est. 1** having little importance or value; small: *She insisted on telling me all her petty troubles.* **2** mean; narrow-minded. **3** lower in rank or importance; subordinate: *a petty official.* [ME < OF *petit* < VL stem *pit-* little. Doublet of PETIT.] —**pet′ti·ly,** *adv.* —**pet′ti·ness,** *n.*

petty cash 1 small sums of money spent or received. **2** a sum of money kept on hand to pay small expenses.

petty jury petit jury.

petty larceny petit larceny.

petty officer 1 *Canadian Forces.* in Maritime Command, either of two ranks: petty officer 2nd class (*abbrev.:* P2), equivalent to a sergeant; and petty officer 1st class (*abbrev.:* P1), equivalent to a warrant officer. See chart at **rank¹. 2** a naval non-commissioned officer of similar rank in other countries. *Abbrev.:* P.O. or PO

pet·u·lance (pech′ū ləns) *n.* the quality or state of being irritated by trifles; peevishness; bad humor.

pet·u·lan·cy (pech′ū lən sē) *n.* petulance.

pet·u·lant (pech′ū lənt) *adj.* peevish; subject to little fits of bad temper; irritable over trifles. [< L *petulans, -antis,* ult. < *petere* seek, aim at] —**pet′u·lant·ly,** *adv.*

Pe·tun (pə tün′) *n.* **1** an extinct North American Indian people who lived between Lakes Huron and Ontario, noted for their tobacco cultivation and trade. **2** a member of this people. **3** the Iroquoian dialect of this people. [< Cdn.F < MF *petun* tobacco]

pe·tu·ni·a (pə tyü′nē ə, pə tyün′yə *or* pə tü′nē ə) *n.* any of a genus (*Petunia*) of tropical American plants of the nightshade family cultivated for their large, white, red, purple, or blue, funnel-shaped flowers. [< NL < F *petun* tobacco < South Am.Ind.]

pew (pyü) *n.* in a church, a bench for people to sit on, having a back and often fastened to the floor. In some churches the pews are separated by partitions. [ME < OF *puie* < L *podia,* pl. of *podium* elevated place, balcony. See PODIUM.]

pe·wee (pē′wē) *n.* any of several small North American flycatchers (genus *Contopus*) having greyish-olive plumage. [imitative]

pe·wit (pē′wit *or* pyü′it) *n.* lapwing. [imitative]

pew·ter (pyü′tər) *n.* **1** any of various alloys composed mainly of tin; especially, a dull alloy containing lead, formerly used for eating and cooking utensils. **2** dishes or other utensils made of pewter. **3** (*adj.*) made of pewter. [ME < OF *peutre*]

pey·o·te (pā ō′tē; *Spanish,* pā yō′tā) *n.* **1** any of several New World cactuses (genus *Logophora*), especially mescal. **2** mescaline. [< Mexican Sp. *peyote* < Nahuatl *peyotl,* literally, a caterpillar; from the mescal's soft, furry centre]

pf. 1 pfennig. **2** preferred.

Pfc. *U.S.* private first class.

pfd. preferred.

pfen·nig (pfen′ig) *n., pl.* **pfen·nigs, pfen·ni·ge** (pfen′i gə). **1** a unit of money in the Federal Republic of Germany and the German Democratic Republic, equal to ¹⁄₁₀₀ of a mark. **2** a coin worth one pfennig. [< G]

pfg. pfennig.

PFRA *Cdn.* Prairie Farm Rehabilitation Administration.

pg. page.

Pg. Portugal; Portuguese.

pH *Chemistry.* a symbol used to express acid or alkaline content, used in testing water and soils, for various applications in industry, etc. A pH of 14 denotes high alkaline content, and a pH of 0 indicates high acidity; pH 7 is taken as neutral. [< *potential* of *H*ydrogen]

Ph phenyl.

Phae·dra (fē′drə) *n. Greek mythology.* the wife of Theseus, who falls in love with her stepson Hippolytus and, when he rejects her advances, falsely accuses him of attacking her.

Pha·ë·thon (fā′ə thon′ *or* fā′ə tən) *n. Greek mythology.* the son of Helios, who tried for one day to drive the sun, his father's chariot. He so nearly set the earth on fire that Zeus had to strike him dead with a thunderbolt.

pha·e·ton (fā′ə tən) *n.* **1** a light, four-wheeled carriage with or without a top. **2** an open automobile of the touring-car type. [< F *phaéton,* after *Phaëthon,* son of Helios]

–phage *combining form.* eating; devouring, as in *bacteriophage.* [< Gk. *phagein* eat]

phag·o·cyte (fag′ə sīt′) *n. Physiology.* a white blood corpuscle, or leucocyte, capable of absorbing and destroying waste or harmful material, such as disease microbes. [< Gk. *-phagos* -eating + E *-cyte* cell (< Gk *kytos* hollow container)]

pha·lan·ger (fə lan′jər) *n.* any of various Australasian tree-climbing marsupials (family Phalangeridae) having thick, woolly fur and a long tail which in many species is prehensile. [< NL < Gk. *phalangion* spiderweb < *phalanx, -angos* spider; with reference to webbed toes]

pha·lan·ges (fə lan′jēz) *n.* a plural of **phalanx.** The bones of the fingers and toes are called the phalanges. See **arm** and **leg** for pictures.

pha·lanx (fal′angks *or* fā′langks) *n., pl.* **pha·lanx·es** *or* **pha·lan·ges** (fə lan′jēz) (for def. 1), **pha·lanx·es** (defs. 2, 3), **pha·lan·ges** (def. 4). **1** in ancient Greece, a special battle formation of infantry fighting in close ranks with their shields joined and long spears overlapping each other. **2** a compact or closely massed body of persons, animals, or things: *a phalanx of trees. The speaker could not get past the phalanx of angry residents.* **3** a number of persons united for a common purpose: *They were opposed in the debate by a phalanx of Conservative MP's.* **4** any one of the bones of the fingers or toes. [< L < Gk.]

phal·a·rope (fal′ə rōp′) *n., pl.* **phal·a·rope.** any three species, constituting a family (Phalaropodidae) of shore birds resembling sandpipers, having a long, slender bill and lobed toes adapted for swimming. Phalaropes are noted for the reversal of the typical male and female roles: the female is larger and more brightly colored than the male; the male rears the young. [< F < NL, ult. < Gk. *phalaros* white-crested + *pous, podos* foot]

phal·lic (fal′ik) *adj.* of or having to do with a phallus; symbolic of male generative power. [< Gk. *phallikós* < *phallós* penis, phallus]

phal·lus (fal′əs) *n., pl.* **phal·li** (fal′ī). **1** an image or model of the penis, symbolizing the generative power of nature. **2** penis. [< L *phallus* < Gk. *phallós* penis, phallus]

phan·tasm (fan′taz əm) *n.* **1** a thing seen only in one's imagination; unreal fancy: *the phantasms of a dream.* **2** a supposed appearance of an absent person, living or dead. **3** a deceiving likeness (of something). [< L < Gk. *phantasma* image, ult. < *phainein* show. Doublet of PHANTOM.]

phan·tas·ma·go·ri·a (fan taz′mə gô′rē ə) *n.* **1** a shifting scene of real things, illusions, imaginary fancies, deceptions, and the like: *the phantasmagoria of a dream.* **2** a display of optical illusions in which figures increase or decrease in size, fade away, and pass into each other. [< Gk. *phantasma* image + ? *agora* assembly]

phan·tas·mal (fan taz′məl) *adj.* of, having to do with, or being a phantasm; unreal; imaginary.

phan·ta·sy (fan′tə sē *or* fan′tə zē) *n., pl.* **-sies.** See **fantasy.**

phan·tom (fan′təm) *n.* **1** an image of the mind: *phantoms of a dream.* **2** a vague, dim, or shadowy appearance; ghost. **3** (*adj.*) like a ghost; unreal: *a phantom ship.* **4** a mere show; appearance without material substance: *a phantom of a government.* [ME < OF *fantosme* < VL < Gk. *phantasma* image. Doublet of PHANTASM.]

Phar·aoh (fer′ō) *n.* a title given to the kings of ancient Egypt.

Phar·i·sa·ic (far′ə sā′ik *or* fer′ə sā′ik) *adj.* **1** of or having to do with the Pharisees. **2 pharisaic, a** making an outward show of religion or morals without the real spirit. **b** thinking oneself more moral than others; hypocritical.

phar·i·sa·i·cal (far′ə sā′ə kəl *or* fer′ə-) *adj.* pharisaic. —**phar′i·sa·i·cal·ly,** *adv.*

Phar·i·sa·ism (far′ə sā iz′əm *or* fer′ə-) *n.* **1** the doctrine and practice of the Pharisees. **2 pharisaism, a** rigid observance of the external forms of religion without genuine piety. **b** self-righteousness; hypocrisy.

Phar·i·see (far′ə sē′ *or* fer′ə sē′) *n.* **1** in ancient times, a member of a Jewish sect that was very strict in keeping to tradition and the laws of its religion. **2 pharisee, a** a person who makes a show of religion rather than following its spirit. **b** a person who considers himself much better than other men. [OE *farisē* < L *pharisaeus* < Gk. *pharisaios* < Aramaic *perishaiya* separated]

phar·i·see·ism (far′ə sē iz′əm *or* fer′ə-) *n.* pharisaism.

phar·ma·ceu·tic (fär′mə sü′tik) *adj.* pharmaceutical. [< LL < Gk. *pharmakeutikos,* ult. < *pharmakon* drug, poison]

phar·ma·ceu·ti·cal (fär′mə sü′tə kəl) *adj., n.* —*adj.* of or

having to do with pharmacy or pharmacists. —n. a medicinal drug.

phar·ma·ceu·tics (fär′mə sü′tiks) n. (used with a singular verb) pharmacy (def. 1).

phar·ma·cist (fär′mə sist) n. a person who is qualified to prepare and dispense medicinal drugs; druggist.

phar·ma·co·log·i·cal (fär′mə kə loj′ə kəl) adj. of or having to do with pharmacology. —**phar′ma·co·log′i·cal·ly**, adv.

phar·ma·col·o·gist (fär′mə kol′ə jist) n. a person trained in pharmacology, especially one whose work it is.

phar·ma·col·o·gy (fär′mə kol′ə jē) n. the science of drugs, including their sources and properties, and their preparation, uses, and effects. [< Gk. pharmakon drug + E -logy]

phar·ma·co·poe·ia (fär′mə kə pē′ə) n. 1 a book containing an official list and description of drugs and medicines. 2 a stock or collection of drugs. [< Gk. pharmakopoiia < pharmakon drug + poieein make]

phar·ma·cy (fär′mə sē) n., pl. -cies. 1 the art and practice of preparing and dispensing drugs and medicines. 2 drugstore. 3 the department of a hospital where drugs, medicines, etc. are prepared. [< LL < Gk. pharmakeia, ult. < pharmakon drug]

pha·ryn·gal (fə ring′gəl) adj. pharyngeal.

pha·ryn·ge·al (fə rin′jē əl, far′in jē′əl, or fer′in-) adj., n. —adj. 1 of or having to do with the pharynx. 2 located or produced in the region of the pharynx. —n. Phonetics. a pharyngeal speech sound. Also, **pharyngal**.

phar·yn·gi·tis (far′in jī′tis or fer′in jī′tis) n. an inflammation of the mucous membrane of the pharynx. [< NL < Gk. pharynx, -yngos pharynx + -itis]

phar·ynx (far′ingks or fer′ingks) n., pl. **phar·ynx·es** or **pha·ryn·ges** (fə rin′jēs). in vertebrates, the muscular tube connecting the mouth cavity with the esophagus. The pharynx is part of the alimentary canal. See **windpipe** for picture. [< NL < Gk.]

phase (fāz) n., v. —n. 1 one of the changing states or stages of development of a person or thing: The pupa is a phase in the life cycle of the moth. 2 one side, part, or view (of a subject): What phase of mathematics are you studying now? 3 Astronomy. the shape of the moon or of a planet as it is seen at a given time. The last quarter is a phase of the moon. 4 Physics. a particular stage or point in a recurring sequence of movements or changes, considered in relation to a starting point of normal position: The current in all parts of a series circuit is in the same phase. 5 Zoology. a a marked variation, especially in color of fur, plumage, etc. in an individual animal or a subgroup of animals that distinguishes it from typical members of the group to which it belongs: A leopard of the black color phase is usually called a panther. b an individual or subgroup distinguishable in this way: The blue goose is a color phase of the snow goose. 6 Biology. one of the distinct states in meiosis or mitosis. —v. plan an enterprise or project in orderly stages: a phased withdrawal of troops.

phase in, bring about an innovation or reform of existing conditions in orderly stages.

phase out, eliminate an old system, order, etc. gradually, in planned stages. [< NL < Gk. phasis appearance < phainein show]
☛ Hom. **faze**.

Ph.B. Bachelor of Philosophy (for L Philosophiae Baccalaureus).

Ph.D. Doctor of Philosophy (for L Philosophiae Doctor).

pheas·ant (fez′ənt) n., pl. -ants or (esp. collectively) -ant. 1 any of various large, long-tailed game birds (family Phasianidae), native to the Old World, the male of which has brightly colored plumage, especially the **ring-necked pheasant** (Phasianus colchicus). 2 any of various other Old or New World birds of the same order (Galliformes), such as various partridges or grouse. [ME < AF < Provençal faisan < L < Gk. phasianos, literally, Phasian; with reference to the river Phasis in Colchis]

phe·nac·e·tin (fə nas′ə tin) n. a white crystalline powder used to relieve fever and pain. Formula: $C_{10}H_{13}NO_2$ [< Gk. phainein show + E acet(ic)]

phe·no·bar·bi·tal (fē′nō bär′bə tol′ or -bär′bə tôl′) n. a white crystalline barbiturate drug used as a hypnotic or sedative. Formula: $C_{12}H_{12}N_2O_3$

phe·nol (fē′nol or fē′nōl) n. carbolic acid. [< Gk. phainein show + E -ol, chemical suffix (shortened form of alcohol)]

phe·nol·ic (fə nol′ik) adj., n. —adj. of, like, or pertaining to phenol. —n. Chemistry. any of a group of synthetic plastics or resins, used in varnishes, coatings, etc.

phe·nol·phthal·ein (fē′nōl thal′ēn or fē′nōl fthal′ēn) n. a white or yellowish crystalline compound used in testing acidity, making dyes, and as a laxative. Its solution is red when basic, colorless when acid. Formula: $C_{20}H_{14}O_4$

hat, āge, fär; let, ēqual, tėrm; it, īce
hot, ōpen, ôrder; oil, out; cup, put, rüle,
above, takən, pencəl, lemən, circəs
ch, child; ng, long; sh, ship
th, thin; ᴛʜ, then; zh, measure

phe·nom·e·na (fə nom′ə nə) n. pl. of **phenomenon**.

phe·nom·e·nal (fə nom′ə nəl) adj. 1 of or having to do with a phenomenon or phenomena. 2 having the nature of or being a phenomenon. 3 extraordinary: a phenomenal memory. —**phe·nom′e·nal·ly**, adv.

phe·nom·e·nal·ism (fə nom′ə nəl iz′əm) n. the theory that knowledge is limited to physical and mental phenomena (things as they are experienced) and either that there is no reality behind the phenomena or that there is a reality, but it is unknowable.

phe·nom·e·no·log·i·cal (fə nom′ə nəl oj′ə kəl) 1 of or having to do with phenomenology or phenomenalism. 2 of or having to do with a phenomenon or phenomena; phenomenal. —**phe·nom′e·no·log′i·cal·ly**, adv.

phe·nom·e·nol·o·gy (fə nom′ə nol′ə jē) n. Philosophy. the purely descriptive study of consciousness and the objects of consciousness (phenomena), without any attempt to explain causes, origins, etc.

phe·nom·e·non (fə nom′ə non′ or fə nom′ə nən) n. -na or (esp. for def. 2) -nons. 1 a fact, event, or circumstance that can be observed: Lightning is an electrical phenomenon. Fever and inflammation are phenomena of disease. 2 something or someone extraordinary or remarkable. 3 Philosophy. a something known through the senses rather than through thought. b something as it is observed through the senses and understood, as distinct from the thing itself. [< L < Gk. phainomenon, neut. ppr. of phainesthai appear]

phe·no·type (fē′nə tīp′) n. 1 the physical, especially visible, characteristics or properties of an organism as determined by the interaction of its genetic inheritance (genotype) and its environment. 2 a group of organisms sharing such characteristics or properties. [< Gk. phaino- < phainein show + E type]

phen·yl (fen′əl or fē′nəl) n. Chemistry. a univalent radical derived from benzene, that forms the basis of phenol, aniline, and other aromatic compounds. Formula: C_6H_5 Abbrev.: Ph

pher·o·mone (fer′ə mōn′) n. a chemical substance exuded by certain organisms, such as insects, that serves as a means of communication with others of the same species, affecting their behavior, etc.

phew (fyü) interj. an exclamation of disgust, impatience, surprise, relief, etc.

phi (fī or fē) n. the 21st letter of the Greek alphabet (Φ, φ).

phi·al (fī′əl) n. a small bottle; vial. [ME < OF < LL < L phiala < Gk. phialē a broad flat vessel]

Phi Be·ta Kap·pa (fī′bā′tə kap′ə or bē′tə) an honorary society composed of college students and graduates who are ranked high in scholarship.

Phil. 1 Philip. 2 Philippine.

phi·lan·der (fə lan′dər) v. of a man, make love without serious intentions; flirt. [originally n., < Gk. philandros < philos loving + anēr, andros man; apparently taken as "lover"] —**phi·lan′der·er**, n.

phil·an·throp·ic (fil′ən throp′ik) adj. of, having to do with, or characterized by philanthropy; charitable; benevolent.

phil·an·throp·i·cal (fil′ən throp′ə kəl) adj. philanthropic. —**phil′an·throp′i·cal·ly**, adv.

phi·lan·thro·pist (fə lan′thrə pist) n. a person who practises philanthropy, especially a wealthy person who supports charitable organizations, etc.

phi·lan·thro·py (fə lan′thrə pē) n., pl. -pies. 1 love of mankind, especially as shown by practical kindness and active efforts to help humanity: Charitable institutions appeal to one's philanthropy. 2 a philanthropic act, institution, etc. [< LL < Gk. philanthrōpia, ult. < philos loving + anthrōpos man]

phil·a·tel·ic (fil′ə tel′ik) adj. of or having to do with philately.

phi·lat·e·list (fə lat′ə list) n. a person who makes a hobby of philately; stamp collector.

phi·lat·e·ly (fə lat′ə lē) n. the collecting and studying of postage stamps and, often, envelopes or postcards with postmarked stamps on them; stamp collecting. [< F philatélie, ult. < Gk. philos loving + ateleia exemption from tax; the stamp indicated the tax was paid]

–phile combining form. a lover of —; a person who is fond of —: discophile = a person who is fond of records, or disks. Also, **phil-**. [< F -phile, ult. < Gk. philos loving]

phil·har·mon·ic (fil′här mon′ik *or* fil′ər mon′ik) *adj., n.* —*adj.*
1 devoted to music; loving music. A musical club is often called a
philharmonic society. 2 given by a philharmonic society: *a
philharmonic concert.* —*n.* 1 a philharmonic society or concert.
2 **Philharmonic,** a symphony orchestra: *the London Philharmonic.*
[< F *philharmonique,* ult. < Gk. *philos* loving + *harmonia* music]

Phi·lip·pic (fə lip′ik) *n.* 1 any of several orations by
Demosthenes denouncing King Philip II of Macedonia and arousing
the Athenians to resist Philip's growing power. 2 any of several
orations by the Roman statesman, Cicero, denouncing Mark
Antony. 3 **philippic,** a bitter attack in words. [< L < Gk.
Philippikos having to do with *Phillipos* Philip]

Phil·ip·pine (fil′ə pēn′) *adj.* of or having to do with the
Philippines, a country consisting of about 7000 islands in the W
Pacific Ocean, or its inhabitants. Also, **Filipine, Filipino.**

Phi·lis·ti·a (fə lis′tē ə) *n.* 1 the land of the ancient Philistines. 2 a
place inhabited or frequented by people with uncultured tastes.

Phi·lis·tine (fə lis′tən, fil′əs tīn′ *or* fil′əs tēn′) *n., adj.* —*n.* 1 a
member of the non-Semitic people who inhabited ancient Philistia.
2 Sometimes, **philistine,** a person having commonplace ideas and
tastes and indifferent to or contemptuous of artistic or intellectual
values. —*adj.* 1 of the Philistines. 2 Usually, **philistine,** smugly
commonplace and uncultured. [< LL *Philistini,* pl, < Gk.
Philistinoi < Hebrew]

phil·lis·tin·ism (fə lis′tən iz′əm *or* fil′əs tin iz′əm) *n.*
the character, habits, or views of persons indifferent to artistic or
intellectual values. Also, **Philistinism.**

phil·o·den·dron (fil′ə den′drən) *n., pl.* -**drons** *or* -**dra** (drə).
any of a genus (*Philodendron*) of tropical plants of the arum family
that are cultivated for their thick, glossy leaves. Philodendrons are
popular house plants because they thrive with little care. [< NL
Philodendron the genus name < Gk. *philodendron,* neut. of
philodendros < *philos* fond of + *dendron* tree, because it clings to
trees]

phil·o·log·i·cal (fil′ə loj′ə kəl) *adj.* of or having to do with
philology.

phi·lol·o·gist (fə lol′ə jist) *n.* a person trained in philology.

phi·lol·o·gy (fə lol′ə jē) *n.* the historical and comparative study
of languages, especially through literature and written documents.
Compare **linguistics.** [< L < Gk. *philologia,* ult. < *philos* loving +
logos word, speech, story]

Phil·o·mel (fil′ə mel′) *n. Poetic.* nightingale. Also, **philomel.** [<
L < Gk. *philomēlā* nightingale]

Phil·o·me·la (fil′ə mē′lə) *n.* 1 *Greek mythology.* an Athenian
princess who was turned into a nightingale and, as a bird, continued
to lament the tragedy of her life. 2 *Poetic.* nightingale.

phi·los·o·pher (fə los′ə fər) *n.* 1 a person who studies
philosophy. 2 a person who has a system of philosophy. 3 a person
who shows the calmness of philosophy under hard conditions,
accepting life and making the best of it. [ME < AF < L < Gk.
philosophos lover of wisdom < *philos* loving + *sophos* wise]

philosophers′ stone an imaginary stone, substance, or
chemical preparation sought for by alchemists in the belief that it
had the power to change base metals into gold or silver.

phil·o·soph·ic (fil′ə sof′ik) *adj.* 1 of or having to do with
philosophers or philosophy. 2 devoted to or skilled in philosophy: *a
philosophic society.* 3 like a philosopher, especially in being wise or
in taking a calm, patient attitude in the face of trouble;
philosophical: *a philosophic person.*

phil·o·soph·i·cal (fil′ə sof′ə kəl) *adj.* philosophic; like a
philosopher. —**phil·o·soph′i·cal·ly,** *adv.*

phi·los·o·phize (fə los′ə fīz′) *v.* -**phized,** -**phiz·ing.** think or
reason as a philosopher does; try to understand and explain things:
philosophizing about life and death. —**phi·los′o·phiz′er,** *n.*

phi·los·o·phy (fə los′ə fē) *n., pl.* -**phies.** 1 the study of the truth
or principles underlying all knowledge; study of the most general
causes and principles of the universe. 2 an explanation or theory of
the universe: *Hegelian philosophy.* 3 a system for guiding life, such
as a body of principles of conduct, religious beliefs, or traditions.
4 the broad general principles of a particular subject: *the philosophy
of history, the philosophy of science.* 5 a calm and reasonable
attitude; the practice of accepting things as they are and making the
best of them. [< L < Gk. *philosophia* love of wisdom, ult. < *philos*
loving + *sophos* wise]

phil·tre (fil′tər) *n.* 1 a potion, drug, or charm supposed to arouse
sexual love, especially toward a particular person. 2 any magic
drink. Also, **philter.** < F < L Gk. *philtron* love charm, ult. < *philos*
loving]

phle·bi·tis (fli bī′tis) *n.* inflammation of the wall of a vein. [<
NL < Gk. *phleps, phlebos* vein + -*itis*]

phle·bot·o·mist (fli bot′ə mist) *n.* a person who treats patients
by phlebotomy.

phle·bot·o·my (fli bot′ə mē) *n.* the opening of a vein to let
blood; bleeding. [ME < OF < LL < Gk. *phlebotomia,* ult. <
phleps, phlebos vein + -*tomos* cutting]

phlegm (flem) *n.* 1 the thick discharge from the nose and throat
during a cold or other respiratory disease. 2 the one of the four
humors of ancient physiology believed to cause sluggishness.
3 sluggishness or indifference. 4 coolness or calmness. [ME < OF
< LL < Gk. *phlegma* clammy humor (resulting from heat) <
phlegein burn]

phleg·mat·ic (fleg mat′ik) *adj.* 1 sluggish or indifferent. 2 cool or
calm: *John is phlegmatic; he never seems to get excited about
anything.* [< LL < Gk. *phlegmatikos* < *phlegma.* See PHLEGM.]

phleg·mat·i·cal (fleg mat′ə kəl) *adj.* phlegmatic.
—**phleg·mat′i·cal·ly,** *adv.*

phlo·em *or* **phlo·ëm** (flō′əm) *n.* the soft tissue in the vascular
system of plants or trees, consisting mainly of sieve tubes and
parenchyma cells, that serves to transport and store food materials
and help support the plant. Compare **xylem.** [< G < Gk. *phloos*
bark]

phlo·gis·ton (flō jis′tən) *n.* a supposed element causing
flammability, once thought to exist in all things that burn. [< NL <
Gk. *phlogiston,* neut. adj., flammable, ult. < *phlox, phlogos* flame]

phlox (floks) *n.* 1 any of a genus (*Phlox*) of annual or perennial
plants cultivated for their showy clusters of red, white, or purple
flowers. 2 (*adjl.*) designating the family (Polemoniaceae) of plants
that includes phlox and Jacob's-ladder. [< L < Gk. *phlox,* a kind of
plant, literally, flame]

Phm.B. Bachelor of Pharmacy.

-**phobe** *combining form.* a person who has irrational hatred or
fear toward —: *Anglophobe = a person who hates or fears the
English or England.* [< L < F *phobe,* learned borrowing < L
phobus < Gk. *phobos* panic, fear]

pho·bi·a (fō′bē ə) *n.* an irrational, exaggerated fear of or aversion
to a particular thing or situation.

-**phobia** *combining form.* extreme or irrational hatred or fear
of—: *Claustrophobia means fear of being in an enclosed or confined
space.* [< Gk. *phobia* < *phobos.* See -PHOBE.]

pho·bic (fō′bik) *adj.* of, having to do with, or being a phobia.

phoe·be (fē′bē) *n.* any of several North American flycatchers
(genus *Sayornis*), such as the **eastern phoebe** (*S. phoebe*), having a
greyish-brown back, yellowish-white under parts, and a small crest.
[imitative, but spelling adapted to that of *Phoebe*]

Phoe·be (fē′bē) *n.* 1 *Greek mythology.* Artemis, goddess of the
moon. 2 *Poetic.* the moon.

Phoe·bus (fē′bəs) *n.* 1 *Greek mythology.* Apollo, god of the sun.
2 *Poetic.* the sun.

Phoe·ni·cian (fə nish′ən) *n., adj.* —*n.* 1 a native or inhabitant of
Phoenicia, an ancient country on the Mediterranean Sea, in the
region of modern Syria and Lebanon. 2 the Semitic language of
ancient Phoenicia. —*adj.* of or having to do with Phoenicia, its
people, or their language.

phoe·nix (fē′niks) *n.* a mythical bird, the only one of its kind,
said to live 500 or 600 years, to burn itself to ashes on a funeral
pyre, and to rise again from the ashes, fresh and beautiful, for
another long life. [ME < OF < L < Gk. *phoinix,* probably <
Egyptian *bonū, bennu* heron]

phone[1] (fōn) *n., v.* **phoned, phon·ing.** *Informal.* telephone. [short
for *telephone*]

phone[2] (fōn) *n. Phonetics.* a speech sound considered as a
physical thing without reference to its function in the sound system
of any language. [< Gk.]

-**phone** *combining form.* sound: *telephone = sound from far.* [<
Gk. *phōnē* sound]

pho·neme (fō′nēm) *n. Linguistics.* one of a set of sounds used to
distinguish the words of a language one from another. The words
cat and *bat* are distinguished by their initial phonemes /k/ and /b/.
A phoneme comprises several slightly different sounds (allophones),
the differences between which cannot be used to distinguish one
word from another. The *p* in *pin* and the *p* in *spin,* though differing
slightly in pronunciation, belong to the one phoneme /p/. [< Gk.
phōnēma a sound]

pho·net·ic (fə net′ik) *adj.* 1 of or having to do with speech
sounds: *phonetic laws.* 2 **a** representing the sounds of speech. In
this dictionary the phonetic symbol (ə) stands for the vowel sound
in the second syllable of *taken, pencil, lemon, circus.* **b** of a system
of spelling, having each sound represented by one letter and each

letter representing one sound: *a phonetic alphabet*. [< NL < Gk. *phōnētikos*, ult. < *phōnē* sound]

pho·net·i·cal·ly (fə net′ik lē) *adv.* in a phonetic manner; as regards the sound and not the spelling of words.

pho·ne·ti·cian (fō′nə tish′ən) *n.* a person trained in phonetics, especially one whose work it is.

pho·net·ics (fə net′iks) *n.* (*used with a singular verb*) **1** the scientific study and classification of sounds made in speech. **2** the system of speech sounds of a language or group of languages: *The phonetics of English is very different from that of French.*

phon·ic (fon′ik *or* fō′nik) *adj.* **1** of or having to do with sound; acoustic. **2** of sounds made in speech; phonetic. **3** of or having to do with phonics. [< Gk. *phōnē* sound]

phon·ics (fon′iks *or* fō′niks) *n.* (*used with a singular verb*) **1** a method of teaching people to read or pronounce words by learning the relationship between the sounds of the language and the letters or groups of letters used to represent them. **2** the science of sound; acoustics.

phono– *combining form.* sound or sounds: *Phonology means the study of sounds used in speech.* [< Gk. *phōnē* sound]

pho·no·gram (fō′nə gram′) *n.* a character or symbol representing a single speech sound, syllable, or word.

pho·no·graph (fō′nə graf′) *n.* record player.

pho·no·graph·ic (fō′nə graf′ik) *adj.* **1** for, having to do with, or produced by a phonograph. **2** of or having to do with phonography. —**pho′no·graph′i·cal·ly,** *adv.*

pho·nog·ra·phy (fō′nog′rə fē) *n.* **1** the art of writing according to sound; phonetic spelling. **2** phonetic shorthand.

pho·nol·o·gist (fō nol′ə jist) *n.* a person trained in phonology, especially one whose work it is.

pho·nol·o·gy (fō nol′ə jē) *n.* **1** the study of human speech sounds, especially of their systems and historical changes in particular languages. **2** the sounds and sound system of a given language at a particular time.

pho·non (fō′non) *n.* one unit, or quantum, of vibrational energy, usually associated with transfer of heat energy among atoms in crystalline materials.

pho·ny (fō′nē) *adj.* **-ni·er, -ni·est;** *n.,* pl. **-nies.** *Slang.* —*adj.* not genuine; counterfeit; fake. —*n.* a fake; pretender. [< *fawney,* a gilt brass ring used by swindlers < Irish Gaelic *fáinne* ring] —**pho′ni·ness,** *n.*

phoo·ey (fü′ē) *interj. Slang.* an exclamation of contempt or distaste; bah. [< Yiddish < G *pfui*]

–phore *combining form.* a thing that carries: *semaphore = a device that carries signals.* [< Gk. *-phoros* < *pherein* to bear, carry]

phos·gene (fos′jēn) *n.* a colorless, poisonous gas, a compound of carbon monoxide and chlorine; carbonyl chloride. *Formula*: $COCl_2$ [< Gk. *phōs* light + *-genēs* born, produced]

phos·phate (fos′fāt) *n.* **1** a salt or ester of an acid containing phosphorus. Bread contains phosphates. **2** a fertilizer containing such salts. **3** a drink made of carbonated water flavored with fruit syrup, and containing a little phosphoric acid. [< F *phosphate* < *phosphore* phosphorus]

phos·phat·ic (fos fat′ik) *adj.* of, having to do with, or containing phosphates or phosphoric acid: *a phosphatic fertilizer.*

phos·phide (fos′fīd *or* fos′fid) *n.* a compound of phosphorus with another element or a radical.

phos·phite (fos′fīt) *n.* a salt or ester of phosphorous acid.

phos·phor (fos′fər) *n.* **1** a phosphorescent substance, especially one that emits light when subjected to radiation. **2 Phosphor,** *Poetic.* the morning star; Venus when appearing before sunrise. [< G *or* F < L *phosphorus.* See PHOSPHORUS.]

phos·pho·rate (fos′fə rāt′) *v.* **-rat·ed, -rat·ing.** combine or impregnate with phosphorus.

phos·pho·resce (fos′fə res′) *v.* **-resced, -resc·ing.** be luminous without noticeable heat.

phos·pho·res·cence (fos′fə res′əns) *n.* **1** a giving out light without burning or by very slow burning that seems not to give out heat. **2** such light. **3** the property of a substance that causes this. **4** *Physics.* light given off by a substance as a result of the absorption of certain rays, as X rays or ultraviolet rays, and continuing for a period of time after the substance has ceased to be exposed to these rays.

phos·pho·res·cent (fos′fə res′ənt) *adj.* showing phosphorescence.

phos·phor·ic (fos fôr′ik) *adj.* of, having to do with, or containing phosphorus, especially with a higher valence than in phosphorous compounds.

phosphoric acid a colorless, odorless acid containing phosphorus, used especially in preparing phosphates for fertilizers,

hat, āge, fär; let, ēqual, tèrm; it, īce
hot, ōpen, ôrder; oil, out; cup, put, rüle,
above, takən, pencəl, lemən, circəs
ch, child; ng, long; sh, ship
th, thin; ᴛн, then; zh, measure

in rust-proofing metals, and in flavoring soft drinks. *Formula*: H_3PO_4

phos·pho·rous (fos′fə rəs) *adj.* of, having to do with, or containing phosphorus, especially with a lower valence than in phosphoric compounds.

phosphorous acid a colorless, unstable, crystalline acid used especially in making compounds and as a chemical reducing agent. *Formula*: H_3PO_3

phos·pho·rus (fos′fə rəs) *n.* a common, non-metallic chemical element occurring especially in phosphate rocks. It has three main allotropic forms: white phosphorus is poisonous, extremely flammable, and luminous in the dark; red phosphorus is nonpoisonous and less flammable; black phosphorus is the most stable form. *Symbol*: P; *at.no.* 15; *at.wt.* 30.9738. [< L *phosphoros* morning star < Gk. *phōsphoros* light-bringing < *phōs* light + *pherein* bring]

phos·phu·ret·ted *or* **phos·phu·ret·ed** (fos′fyə ret′id) *adj.* combined with phosphorus.

phot. photograph; photographic; photography.

pho·to (fō′tō) *n.,* pl. **-tos.** *Informal.* photograph.

photo– *combining form.* **1** light, as in *photometry.* **2** photographic or photograph, as in *photo-engraving.* [< Gk. *phōs, phōtos* light]

pho·to·chem·i·cal (fō′tə kem′ə kəl) *adj.* **1** of, having to do with, or resulting from the chemical action of light or other radiant energy. **2** of or having to do with photochemistry: *photochemical studies.* —**pho′to·chem′i·cal·ly,** *adv.*

pho·to·chem·is·try (fō′tə kem′is trē) *n.* the branch of chemistry dealing with the chemical changes produced by light and other electromagnetic radiation.

pho·to·cop·i·er (fō′tə kop′ē ər) *n.* a machine or instrument for making photocopies.

pho·to·cop·y (fō′tə kop′ē) *n.,* pl. **-cop·ies;** *v.* **-cop·ied, -cop·y·ing.** —*n.* a photographic reproduction of a document or other printed matter. —*v.* make a photocopy.

pho·to·e·lec·tric (fō′tō i lek′trik) *adj.* of or having to do with the electrical effects produced by light or other electromagnetic radiation.

photo–electric cell a cell in which variations in electric current are produced by variations in the light falling upon it; electric eye: *Photo-electric cells can be used to open doors automatically, set off alarms, etc.*

pho·to·en·grave (fō′tō en grāv′) *v.* **-graved, -grav·ing.** produce by photo-engraving. —**pho′to·en·grav′er,** *n.*

pho·to·en·grav·ing (fō′tō en grāv′ing) *n.* **1** a process by which plates to print from are produced with the aid of photography. **2** a plate so produced. **3** a picture printed from it.

photo finish **1** *Racing.* a finish so close that a photograph is required to decide the winner. **2** any contest decided by a narrow margin of victory.

pho·to·flash lamp (fō′tə flash′) *Photography.* a flash bulb.

pho·to·flood lamp (fō′tə flud′) an electric lamp that gives very bright, sustained light for taking pictures.

pho·to·gen·ic (fō′tə jen′ik) *adj.* **1** looking or likely to look attractive in photographs or motion pictures: *a photogenic face. He's very photogenic.* **2** *Biology.* phosphorescent; luminescent. *Certain bacteria are photogenic.* [< *photo-* + Gk. *gen-* producing, produced (by)] —**pho′to·gen′i·cal·ly,** *adv.*

pho·to·gram·me·trist (fō′tə gram′ə trist) *n.* a person trained in photogrammetry, especially one whose work it is.

pho·to·gram·me·try (fō′tə gram′ə trē) *n.* the technique of making maps or surveys with the help of photographs, especially of aerial photographs. [< *photogram,* obs. var. of *photograph* + *-metry;* probably influenced by G *Photogrammetrie*]

pho·to·graph (fō′tə graf′) *n., v.* —*n.* a picture made with a camera. A photograph is made by the action of the light rays from the thing pictured coming through the lens of the camera onto a film spread over the surface of glass, paper, celluloid, or metal. —*v.* **1** take a photograph of. **2** take photographs. **3** look (clear, natural, etc.) in a photograph: *She does not photograph well.*

pho·tog·ra·pher (fə tog′rə fər) *n.* **1** a person who takes photographs. **2** a person whose business is taking photographs.

pho·to·graph·ic (fō'tə graf'ik) *adj.* 1 of or like photography: *photographic accuracy.* 2 used in or produced by photography: *photographic plates, a photographic record of a trip.* —**pho'to·graph'i·cal·ly,** *adv.*

pho·tog·ra·phy (fə tog'rə fē) *n.* the art or process of making photographs.

pho·to·gra·vure (fō'tə grə vyür' *or* -grā'vyür) *n.* 1 photo-engraving. 2 a picture printed from a metal plate on which a photograph has been engraved.

pho·to·me·chan·i·cal (fō'tə mə kan'ə kəl) *adj.* relating to or designating any of various methods, such as photo-engraving or phototype, of making printing plates with the aid of photography.

pho·tom·e·ter (fō tom'ə tər) *n.* an instrument for measuring the intensity of light or the relative illuminating power of different lights.

pho·to·met·ric (fō'tə met'rik) *adj.* having to do with photometry or a photometer. —**pho'to·met'ri·cal·ly,** *adv.*

pho·tom·e·try (fō tom'ə trē) *n.* 1 the branch of physics dealing with the measurement of the intensity of light. 2 the measurement of the intensity of light, especially by means of a photometer.

pho·to·mi·cro·graph (fō'tə mī'krə graf) *n.* a photograph of an object as seen through a microscope.

pho·ton (fō'ton) *n. Physics.* a quantum or unit particle of light, having a momentum equal to its energy and moving with the velocity of light. [< *photo* electron]

pho·to·play (fō'tə plā') *n.* motion picture (def. 2).

pho·to·re·con·nais·sance (fō'tə rə kon'ə səns) *n.* reconnaissance made by aerial photographs.

pho·to·sen·si·tive (fō'tə sen'sə tiv) *adj.* sensitive to light; easily stimulated by light or other radiant energy.

pho·to·sphere (fō'tə sfēr') *n.* 1 the dazzling surface of the sun as seen from the earth. 2 a sphere of light or radiance.

pho·to·stat (fō'tə stat) *n., v.* —*n.* 1 **Photostat,** *Trademark.* a special camera for making copies of maps, drawings, pages of books, etc. directly on specially prepared paper. 2 a photograph made with it. —*v.* make a photostat of. [< *photo*- light + Gk. *-states* that brings to a stop]

pho·to·syn·the·sis (fō'tə sin'thə sis) *n.* the process by which plant cells make sugar from carbon dioxide and water in the presence of chlorophyl and light. [< NL]

pho·to·te·leg·ra·phy (fō'tə tə leg'rə fē) *n.* 1 telegraphy by means of light, as with a heliograph. 2 the electric transmission of facsimiles of photographs.

pho·tot·rop·ism (fō tot'rə piz'əm) *n. Botany.* a tendency to turn in response to light. [< *photo*- + Gk. *-tropos* turning]

pho·to·type (fō'tə tīp') *n.* 1 a block on which a photograph is reproduced so that it can be printed. 2 the process used in making such a block. 3 a picture printed from such a block.

pho·to·vol·ta·ic (fō'tō vol tā'ik) *adj.* 1 of or having to do with the production of voltage or electric current by means of light and other electromagnetic radiation. 2 producing or utilizing such voltage or electric current. In a **photovoltaic cell** an electric current is produced when a junction between two dissimilar materials, such as a metal and a semiconductor, is exposed to electromagnetic radiation.

phras·al (frā'səl) *adj.* of, having to do with, or consisting of a phrase: *a phrasal verb.* —**phras'al·ly,** *adv.*

phrase (frāz) *n., v.* **phrased, phras·ing.** —*n.* 1 a combination of words: *He spoke in simple phrases so that the children understood him.* 2 a short, often used expression. *Call up* is the common phrase for *making a telephone call to.* 3 a short, striking expression. *Examples: From sea to sea. Atoms for peace. A war to end wars.* 4 *Grammar.* a group of words not containing a subject and predicate and used as a unit in a clause or sentence. In *He went to the house,* the words *to the house* form a prepositional phrase. 5 *Music.* a short part of a composition, usually containing four measures. —*v.* 1 express in a particular way: *She phrased her excuse politely.* 2 *Music.* mark off or bring out the phrases of (a composition). [< L < Gk. *phrasis* < *phrazein* express]

phrase·book (frāz'bůk') *n.* a collection of idioms and everyday phrases used in a language, with their translations.

phras·e·o·log·i·cal (frā'zē ə loj'ə kəl) *adj.* 1 of or having to do with phraseology. 2 characterized by a special phraseology, or by the choice of particular words, expressions, etc.

phra·se·ol·o·gy (frā'zē ol'ə jē) *n., pl.* **-gies.** the selection and arrangement of words; the particular way in which a person expresses himself in language.

☞ *Syn.* See note at **diction.**

phras·ing (frāz'ing) *n.* 1 a the style of wording or verbal expression; phraseology. b the grouping of spoken words by pauses. 2 *Music.* a a grouping or dividing into phrases. b the playing of phrases. c the style in which the composition is phrased.

phra·try (frā'trē) *n., pl.* **-tries.** 1 in ancient Athens, each of the subdivisions of a tribe. 2 a similar tribal division among primitive races. [ME < Gk. *phratria* < *phratēr* clansman, brother]

phre·net·ic (fri net'ik) *adj.* See **frenetic.** [ME < OF < L < Gk. *phrenetikos* < *phrenitis* disease of the mind < *phrēn* mind. Doublet of FRANTIC.] —**phre·net'i·cal·ly,** *adv.*

phren·o·log·i·cal (fren'ə loj'ə kəl) *adj.* of or having to do with phrenology.

phre·nol·o·gist (fri nol'ə jist) *n.* a person who professes to tell a person's character from the shape of his skull.

phre·nol·o·gy (fri nol'ə jē) *n.* a theory that the shape of the skull shows what sort of mind and character a person has; practice of reading character from the shape of the skull. [< Gk. *phrēn* mind + E *-logy*]

Phryg·i·an (frij'ē ən) *n., adj.* —*n.* 1 a native or inhabitant of Phrygia, an ancient country in west central Asia Minor. 2 the Indo-European language of the ancient Phrygians. —*adj.* of or having to do with Phrygia, its people, or their language.

phthis·ic (tiz'ik) *n. Archaic.* phthisis.

phthis·i·cal (tiz'ə kəl) *adj.* having to do with, having the nature of, or affected by phthisis.

phthi·sis (thī'sis) *n.* tuberculosis of the lungs; consumption. [< L < Gk. *phthisis* < *phthinein* waste away]

phy·lac·ter·y (fə lak'tər ē) *n., pl.* **-ter·ies.** 1 either of two small leather cases containing texts from the Jewish law, worn by orthodox Jews during prayer to remind them to keep the law. 2 reminder. 3 a charm worn as a protection. [ME < LL < Gk. *phylaktērion* safeguard, ult. < *phylax, phylakos* watchman]

phy·le (fī'lē) *n., pl.* **-lae** (-lē *or* -lī). in ancient Greece: 1 a clan or tribe. 2 in Athens, a large political sub-division. [< Gk.]

phyl·lox·e·ra (fil'ək sēr'ə *or* fə lok'sə rə) *n.* any of a genus (*Phylloxera*) of small insects, especially *P. vitifolia,* which destroys grapevines by feeding on the plant juices. [< NL < Gk. *phyllon* leaf + *xēros* dry]

phy·lo·gen·e·sis (fī'lō jen'ə sis) *n.* phylogeny.

phy·lo·ge·net·ic (fī'lō jə net'ik) *adj.* of or having to do with phylogeny. —**phy'lo·ge·net'i·cal·ly,** *adv.*

phy·lo·gen·ic (fī'lō jen'ik) *adj.* of or having to do with phylogeny.

phy·log·e·ny (fī loj'ə nē) *n., pl.* **-nies.** 1 racial history. 2 the origin and development of anything, especially of an animal or plant. [< G < Gk. *phylon* race + *-geneia* origin]

phy·lum (fī'ləm) *n., pl.* **-la** (-lə). *Biology.* a major category in the classification of animals, more general than a class. It corresponds to a division in the classification of plants. See chart at **classification.** [< NL < Gk. *phylon* race, stock]

phys·ic (fiz'ik) *n., v.* **-icked, -ick·ing.** *Archaic.* —*n.* 1 medicine, especially one that moves the bowels. 2 the art of healing; science and practice of medicine. —*v.* 1 move the bowels of. 2 give medicine to. 3 act like a medicine on; cure. [ME < OF *fisique* < L < Gk. *physikē* (*epistēmē*) (knowledge) of nature, ult. < *phyein* produce]

phys·i·cal (fiz'ə kəl) *adj.* 1 of the body: *physical exercise.* 2 of matter; material: *The tide is a physical force.* 3 according to the laws of nature: *It is a physical impossibility to stop the earth's movement around the sun.* 4 of the science of physics. —**phys'i·cal·ly,** *adv.*

physical chemistry the branch of chemistry that deals with the physical properties of substances and their relations to chemical composition and changes.

physical education instruction in how to exercise and take care of the body, especially as a course at school or university.

physical geography the study of land forms, climate, winds, and all other features of the earth.

physical science 1 physics. 2 physics, chemistry, geology, astronomy, and other sciences dealing with inanimate matter.

physical training the practice of doing exercises of various kinds so as to keep the body in good condition.

phy·si·cian (fə zish'ən) *n.* a doctor of medicine. [ME < OF *fisicien* < L *physica.* See PHYSIC.]

phys·i·cist (fiz'ə sist) *n.* a person trained in physics, especially one whose work it is.

phys·i·co·chem·i·cal (fiz'ə kō kem'ə kəl) *adj.* 1 of or having to do with both physics and chemistry. 2 of or having to do with physical chemistry.

phys·ics (fiz'iks) *n.* (*used with a singular verb*) the science that

deals with matter and energy and their relationships, excluding chemical and biological change. Physics deals with mechanics, heat, light, sound, electricity, etc. [pl. of *physic* (= Gk. *ta physika* the natural things)]

physio– *combining form.* of or having to do with physical form or function, as in *physiography.* Also, **physi-** before vowels. [< Gk. *physis* nature]

phys·i·og·no·my (fiz´ē og´nə mē *or* fiz´ē on´ə mē) *n., pl.* **-mies.** **1** the kind of features or type of face one has; one's face. **2** the art of estimating character from the features of the face or the form of the body. **3** the general aspect or looks of a countryside, a situation, etc. [ME < OF < LL < Gk. *physiognōmonia* < *physis* nature + *gnōmōn* judge < *gnōnai* recognize]

phys·i·og·ra·pher (fiz´ē og´rə fər) *n.* a person trained in physiography, especially one whose work it is.

phys·i·o·graph·ic (fiz´ē ə graf´ik) *adj.* of or having to do with physiography.

phys·i·og·ra·phy (fiz´ē og´rə fē) *n.* physical geography.

phys·i·o·log·i·cal (fiz´ē ə loj´ə kəl) *adj.* **1** having to do with physiology: *Digestion is a physiological process.* **2** having to do with the normal or healthy functioning of an organism: *Food and sleep are physiological needs.* **—phys´i·o·log´i·cal·ly,** *adv.*

phys·i·ol·o·gist (fiz´ē ol´ə jist) *n.* a person trained in physiology.

phys·i·ol·o·gy (fiz´ē ol´ə jē) *n.* **1** the science dealing with the normal functions of living things or their parts: *animal physiology, plant physiology.* **2** all the functions and activities of a living thing or of one of its parts. [< L < Gk. *physiologia* < *physis* nature + *-logos* treating of]

phys·i·o·ther·a·pist (fiz´ē ō ther´ə pist) *n.* a person trained in physiotherapy, especially one whose work it is.

phys·i·o·ther·a·py (fiz´ē ō ther´ə pē) *n.* the treatment of diseases and defects by physical remedies, such as massage or electricity (rather than by drugs).

phy·sique (fə zēk´) *n.* the body; bodily structure, organization, or development: *a man of strong physique.* [< F *physique* physical]

–phyte *combining form.* a growth; plant, as in *epiphyte.* [< Gk. *phyton*]

phyto– *combining form.* a plant; plants: *phytology = the science of plants.* Also, **phyt-** before vowels. [< Gk. *phyton* plant]

phy·to·bi·ol·o·gy (fī´tō bī ol´ə jē) *n.* the branch of biology that deals with plants.

phy·to·chem·is·try (fī´tō kem´is trē) *n.* the chemistry of plants.

phy·to·gen·e·sis (fī´tō jen´ə sis) *n.* the science of the evolution and development of plants.

phy·to·ge·net·ic (fī´tō jə net´ik) *adj.* **1** of or having to do with phytogenesis. **2** of plant or vegetable origin.

phy·tog·e·ny (fī toj´ə nē) *n.* phytogenesis.

phy·to·ge·og·ra·phy (fī´tō jē og´rə fē) *n.* the science that deals with the geographical distribution of plant life.

phy·to·pa·tho·log·i·cal (fī´tō path´ə loj´ə kəl) *adj.* of or having to do with phytopathology.

phy·to·pa·thol·o·gist (fī´tō pə thol´ə jist) *n.* a person trained in phytopathology, especially one whose work it is.

phy·to·pa·thol·o·gy (fī´tō pə thol´ə jē) *n.* the science that deals with diseases of plants.

phy·to·plank·ton (fī´tə plangk´tən) *n.* microscopic plants, mainly one-celled algae, that are a constituent of plankton.

pi¹ (pī) *n., pl.* **pis.** **1** the ratio of the circumference of any circle to its diameter, equal to about 3.141 592. The circumference of a circle equals pi times the diameter of the circle (*C* = π*d*). Symbol: π **2** the 16th letter of the Greek alphabet (Π, π). [def. 1, use of Gk. letter to mean Gk. *periphereia* periphery. See PERIPHERY.]

pi² (pī) *n., v.* **-pied, -pi·ing.** *—n.* **1** printing types all mixed up. **2** any confused mixture. *—v.* mix up (type). Also, **pie.** [extended use of *pie¹*]

P.I. Philippine Islands.

pi·a ma·ter (pī´ə mā´tər) *Anatomy.* the innermost of three membranes enveloping the brain and spinal cord. [< Med.L *pia mater* pious mother, a wrong translation of Arabic *al 'umm al raqīqah* thin or tender mother]

pi·a·nis·si·mo (pē´ə nis´ə mō´) *adj., adv., n. Music. —adj.* very soft. *—adv.* very softly. *—n.* a very soft movement or passage; composition to be played or sung very softly. *Abbrev.:* pp. [< Ital. *pianissimo,* superlative of *piano* soft. See PIANO².]

pi·an·ist (pē an´ist *or* pē´ə nist) *n.* a person who plays the piano, especially a skilled player.

pi·an·o¹ (pē an´ō) *n., pl.* **-an·os.** a large musical instrument having strings that sound when struck by hammers operated by the keys on a keyboard. [for *pianoforte*]

pi·a·no² (pē ä´nō) *adj., adv., n. Music. —adj.* soft. *—adv.* softly. *—n.* a soft movement or passage; composition to be played or sung softly. *Abbrev.:* p. [< Ital. *piano* < L *planus* plain, flat. Doublet of PLAIN¹ and PLAN.]

piano accordion an accordion having a keyboard for the right hand and buttons on the other side for producing chords with the left hand.

pi·a·no·for·te (pē an´ə fôr´tē *or* pē an´ə fôrt´) *n.* piano¹. [< Ital. *pianoforte* < *piano* soft + *forte* loud]

pi·as·tre (pē as´tər) *n.* **1** a unit of money in Egypt, Lebanon, Sudan, and Syria, equal to ¹/₁₀₀ of a pound. **2** kurus. **3** a coin worth one piastre. Also, **piaster.** [< Ital. *piastra* metal plate < L]

pi·az·za (pē at´sə *for 1,* pē az´ə *for 2*) *n.* **1** in Italy, an open public square in a town. **2** a large porch or veranda along one or more sides of a house. [< Ital. *piazza* < L < Gk. *plateia (hodos)* broad (way). Doublet of PLACE and PLAZA.]

pi·broch (pē´brok) *n.* music, usually warlike or sad, played on the bagpipe. [< Scots Gaelic *piobaireachd* pipe music, ult. < *piob* pipe]

pi·ca (pī´kə) *n.* **1** *Printing.* a size of type, 12 point.

This sentence is in pica.

2 this size of type used as a measure; about 4 mm. **3** a size of typewriter type, larger than elite, corresponding to 12-point printing type. There are 10 pica characters to the inch. [< Anglo-L *pica,* the name of a book of rules concerning holy days, supposed (? erroneously) to be printed in pica]

pic·a·dor (pik´ə dôr´) *n.* one of the horsemen who begin a bullfight by irritating the bull with pricks of their lances. [< Sp. *picador* < *picar* pierce]

pic·a·resque (pik´ə resk´) *adj.* dealing with wandering rogues and their adventures: *a picaresque novel.* [< Sp. *picaresco* < *picaro* rogue]

pic·a·roon (pik´ə rün´) *n., v. —n.* **1** a rogue; thief; brigand. **2** a pirate. **3** a piratical or privateering ship. *—v.* act or cruise as a brigand or pirate. [< Sp. *picarón* < *picaro* rogue]

pic·a·yune (pik´ə yün´) *adj.* small; petty; mean. [< Louisiana F *picaillon* coin worth 5 cents < Provençal *picaioun* coin]

pic·ca·lil·li (pik´ə lil´ē) *n.* a relish made of chopped pickles, onions, tomatoes, etc. and hot spices. [origin uncertain; ? < *pickle*]

pic·co·lo (pik´ə lō´) *n., pl.* **-los.** a small flute, pitched an octave higher than the ordinary flute. [< Ital. *piccolo* small]

pice (pīs) *n., pl.* **pice.** a unit of money in Nepal, equal to ¹/₁₀₀ of a rupee.

pick¹ (pik) *v., n. —v.* **1** choose; select: *I picked a winning horse at the races.* **2** pull away with the fingers; gather: *We pick fruit and flowers.* **3** pierce, dig into, or break up with something pointed: *to pick ground, rocks, etc.* **4** use something pointed to remove things from: *to pick one's teeth, to pick a bone.* **5** open or unlock with a wire or other pointed instrument rather than a key: *to pick a lock.* **6** steal the contents of: *to pick someone's pocket.* **7** prepare for use by removing feathers, waste parts, etc.: *to pick a chicken.* **8** pull apart: *The stuffing in the pillow has matted and needs to be picked.* **9** use the fingers on with a plucking motion: *to play the banjo by picking its strings.* **10** seek and find occasion for: *to look for and hope to find: to pick a quarrel, to pick flaws.* **11** take up (seeds, small pieces of food, etc.) with the bill or teeth, as a bird or squirrel does. **12** eat (food) in small pieces, slowly, or without appetite.

pick a lock, open a lock with a pointed instrument, wire, etc.

pick (someone's) brains, find out and turn to one's own advantage, or use as one's own, the ideas, skills, etc. of another.

pick at, a pull on with the fingers: *The sick man picked at the blankets.* **b** eat only a little at a time. **c** *Informal.* find fault with; nag.

pick off, a shoot one at a time. **b** *Baseball.* catch (a runner) off base and throw him out.

pick on, a *Informal.* find fault with: *The teacher picked on him for always being late.* **b** *Informal.* annoy; tease: *The big boys picked on*

the new boy during recess. **c** bully; take advantage of. **d** select: *Why did he pick on you first?*

pick (one's) **way** or **pick** (one's) **steps,** move with great care and caution over treacherous ground, a difficult situation, etc.

pick out, a choose; select: *Pick out a dress you will like to wear.* **b** distinguish a thing from surroundings: *Can you pick me out in this group picture?* **c** make out the sense or meaning. **d** select the notes of (a tune) one by one, especially laboriously, on a keyboard, etc., and so play it. **e** embellish, especially by lines or spots of contrasting color following outlines, etc. **f** remove or extract by picking.

pick over, a look over carefully. **b** prepare for use.

pick up, a take up: *The boy picked up a stone. She picked up the chance to make some money by baby-sitting.* **b** summon courage; etc. **c** get by chance: *to pick up a bargain.* **d** give (a person) fresh energy, courage, etc.: *A good dinner will pick you up.* **e** acquire (a particular skill); become skilful at; master: *He picked up the trumpet after just a few lessons.* **f** learn without being taught: *He picks up games easily.* **g** take up into a vehicle or ship: *The bus picked up passengers at every other corner.* **h** get and take along with one: *to pick up a coat at the cleaners.* **i** *Informal.* improve; recover: *He seemed to pick up quickly after his fever.* **j** regain; find again. **k** succeed in seeing, hearing, etc.: *to pick up a radio program from Paris.* **l** go faster; increase in speed. **m** become acquainted with without being introduced. **n** tidy up; put in order. —*n.* **1** a choice or selection. **2** the best or most desirable part. **3** the amount of a crop gathered at one time. **4** something held in the fingers and used to pluck the strings of a musical instrument; plectrum. [ME *picke(n)*; cf. OE *pīcung* pricking]

pick² (pik) *n.* **1** pickaxe. **2** a sharp-pointed tool. Ice is broken into pieces with a pick. [ME *picke,* var. of *pike* pike², OE *pīc*]

pick·a·back (pik'ə bak') *adv.* on the back or shoulders; piggyback.

pick·a·nin·ny (pik'ə nin'ē) *n., pl.* **-nies.** *U.S. Usually, derogatory.* **1** a small Negro child. **2** any small child. [< Pg. *pequenino* very small]

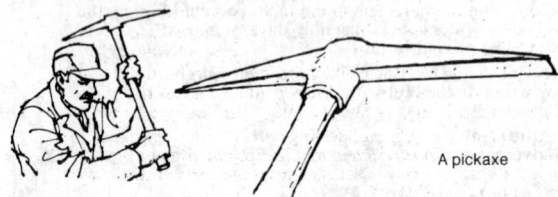

A pickaxe

pick·axe (pik'aks') *n.* a heavy metal tool that is pointed at one or both ends and has a long wooden handle, used for breaking up dirt, rocks, etc.; pick. Sometimes, **pickax.** [alteration of ME *picois* < OF *picois* (cf. OF *pic* pike¹)]

picked (pikt) *adj.* **1** with waste parts removed and ready for use. **2** specially chosen or selected for merit: *a crew of picked men.*

pick·er (pik'ər) *n.* **1** a person who gathers, picks, or collects. **2** a tool for picking anything. **3 a** a machine for separating and cleaning the fibres of cotton, wool, etc. **b** a person who runs such a machine.

pick·er·el (pik'ər əl or pik'rəl) *n., pl.* **-el** or **-els. 1** any of three small fishes of the pike family (*Esox niger, E. americanus americanus,* and *E. americanus vermiculatus*). **2** walleye (def. 7). [dim. of *pike²*]

pick·er·el·weed (pik'ər əl wēd' or pik'rəl-) *n.* any of various aquatic plants (family Pontederiaceae, especially genus *Pontederia*) having arrow-shaped leaves and blue or purple flowers.

pick·et (pik'it) *n., v.* —*n.* **1** a pointed stake or peg placed upright to make a fence, to tie a horse to, etc. **2** a small body of troops, or a single man, posted at some place to watch for the enemy and guard against surprise attack. **3** a person stationed by a labor union near a place of work where there is a strike. Pickets try to prevent employees from working or customers from buying. —*v.* **1** enclose with pickets; fence. **2** tie to a picket. **3** station as pickets. **4** station pickets at or near: *to picket a factory during a strike.* **5** act as a picket. [< F *piquet,* dim. of *pic* a pike. See PIKE¹.] —**pick'et·er,** *n.*

picket fence a fence made of pickets.

picket line a group or line of people picketing a business, etc.

picket ship a ship using radar for ocean patrol.

pick·ings (pik'ingz) *n.pl.* **1** the amount picked. **2** things left over; scraps. **3** things stolen or received dishonestly.

pick·le (pik'əl) *n., v.* **-led, -ling.** —*n.* **1** a cucumber or other vegetable preserved in salt water, vinegar, or some other liquid. **2** the liquid in which foods can be preserved. **3** *Informal.* trouble;

difficulty. **4** a chemical bath for removing surface scale from metal castings, etc. —*v.* **1** preserve in pickle: *to pickle beets.* **2** clean (metal, etc.) with a chemical, such as acid. [< MDu. *pekel*]

pick·pock·et (pik'pok'it) *n.* a person who steals from people's pockets.

pick·up (pik'up') *n.* **1** a picking up: *the daily pickup of mail.* **2** *Informal.* improvement: *a pickup in business.* **3** a going faster; increase in speed; acceleration. **4** *Informal.* an acquaintance made without an introduction, especially an acquaintance of the opposite sex. **5** something obtained or secured without planning and as chance offers, such as a bargain or a hurried meal. **6** (*adj.*) using or made up of available material, personnel, etc., without planning or organizing beforehand: *a pickup meal, a pickup team.* **7** a catching or hitting of a ball very soon after it has bounced on the ground. **8** *Radio.* **a** the reception of sound waves and their conversion into electrical waves for broadcasting. **b** an apparatus for such reception. **c** the place where it occurs. **d** the electrical system for connecting to the broadcasting station or studio a program originating outside. **9** *Television.* **a** the reception of images and their conversion into electric waves for broadcasting. **b** an apparatus that does this. **10** a motion picture. **11** a small truck for collecting and delivering light loads. **12** anything that is picked up. **13** (*adj.*) of or for collecting and delivering: *a pickup schooner plying along the coast.*

Pick·wick·i·an (pik wik'ē ən) *adj.* **1** of, having to do with, or characteristic of Samuel Pickwick, the kindly, genial hero of Dickens' *Pickwick Papers,* or his club. **2** given a special meaning for the occasion: *words used in a Pickwickian sense.*

pick·y (pik'ē) *adj.* **pick·i·er, pick·i·est.** *Informal.* too fussy or particular; inclined to find fault with trifles.

pic·nic (pik'nik) *n., v.* **-nicked, -nick·ing.** —*n.* **1** a pleasure trip with a meal in the open air. **2** *Slang.* a pleasant time or experience; very easy job. —*v.* **1** go on a picnic. **2** eat in picnic style. [< F *piquenique*]

pic·nick·er (pik'nik ər) *n.* a person who picnics.

picnic shoulder or **ham** a smoked shoulder of pork, cut to resemble a ham. See **pork** for picture.

pico– (pē'kə or pi'kə) *SI prefix.* one one-trillionth; 10^{-12}, as in *picofarad. Symbol:* p [< Sp. *pico* small quantity]

pi·cot (pē'kō) *n., v.* —*n.* one of a number of fancy loops in embroidery, tatting, etc. or along the edge of lace, ribbon, etc. —*v.* trim with picots. [< F *picot,* dim. of *pic* a pick. See PICK¹.]

pic·ric acid (pik'rik) a yellow, intensely bitter acid used as a dye and in explosives. *Formula:* $C_6H_3N_3O_7$ [< Gk. *pikros* bitter]

Pict (pikt) *n.* a member of a people of disputed origin, formerly living in Scotland, especially N Scotland. [< LL *Picti,* pl.]

Pict·ish (pik'tish) *adj.* of or having to do with the Picts.

VULTURE MOTION FLINT KNIFE RAIN FLOWER

Pictographs from the Aztec calendar stone

pic·to·graph (pik'tə graf') *n.* a picture used as a sign or symbol. [< L *pictus* painted + E *-graph*]

pic·to·graph·ic (pik'tə graf'ik) *adj.* of pictographs. —**pic'to·graph'ical·ly,** *adv.*

pic·to·ri·al (pik tô'rē əl) *adj., n.* —*adj.* **1** having to do with pictures; expressed in pictures. **2** making a picture for the mind; vivid. **3** illustrated by pictures: *a pictorial history.* **4** having to do with painters or painting. —*n.* a magazine in which pictures are an important feature. [< L *pictorius* < *pictor* painter] —**pic·to'ri·al·ly,** *adv.*

pic·ture (pik'chər) *n., v.* **-tured, -tur·ing.** —*n.* **1** a drawing, painting, portrait, or photograph; a print of any of these. **2** a scene. **3** a mental image; a visualized conception; idea: *to have a clear picture of the problem.* **4** something beautiful: *She was a picture in her new dress.* **5** image; likeness: *He is the picture of his father.* **6** an example; embodiment: *She was a picture of despair.* **7** a vivid description. **8** motion picture. **9** an image on a television screen. **10** *Informal.* state of affairs; condition; situation: *the employment picture.* —*v.* **1** draw, paint, etc.; make into a picture. **2** form a picture of in the mind; imagine: *It is hard to picture life a hundred years ago.* **3** show by words; describe vividly: *The speaker pictured the suffering of the poor.* [ME < L *pictura,* ult. < *pingere* to paint]

picture hat a woman's hat having a very wide brim, originally often trimmed with ostrich feathers.

pic·tur·esque (pik′chər esk′) *adj.* **1** quaint or interesting enough to be used as the subject of a picture: *a picturesque old mill.* **2** making a picture for the mind; vivid. [< F *pittoresque* < Ital. *pittoresco* in the style of a painter < *pittore* painter < L *pictor;* influenced by *picture*] —**pic′tur·esque′ly,** *adv.* —**pic′tur·esque′ness,** *n.*

picture tube a cathode ray tube that produces a transmitted picture on a television screen.

picture writing **1** the recording of events or expressing of ideas by pictures. **2** pictures used to record events or express ideas.

pid·dle (pid′əl) *v.* **-dled, -dling;** *n.* —*v.* **1** do anything in a trifling or ineffective way. **2** urinate. —*n. Informal.* urine. [origin uncertain] —**pid′dler,** *n.*

pid·dling (pid′ling) *adj.* trifling; petty.

pid·gin (pij′ən) *n.* a mixed jargon, combining simplified grammatical forms and vocabulary from two different languages, used for trade or communication between different peoples or groups. [< *pidgin English*]

pidgin English one of several forms of English, with simplified grammatical structure and vocabulary, used in W Africa, Australia, Melanesia, and formerly in China, as a trade or communication jargon. [*pidgin*, Chinese alteration of *business*]

pie¹ (pī) *n.* **1** a food consisting of fruit, meat, etc. set in a shell of pastry, fine crumbs, etc. and sometimes covered with pastry, and baked or chilled. **2** a layer cake with a filling of whipped cream, jelly, etc.: *Boston cream pie.* **3** something that may be divided into portions. **4** *Slang.* something that is desirable: *as easy as pie.* [ME *pye;* origin uncertain]

pie² (pī) *n.* magpie. [ME < OF < L *pica*]

pie³ (pī) *n. v.* **pied, pie·ing.** See **pi².** [? extended use of *pie¹*]

pie·bald (pī′bôld′ *or* -bōld′) *adj., n.* —*adj.* spotted in two colors, especially black and white. —*n.* a spotted animal, especially a horse. [apparently < *pie²* + *bald;* with reference to dark color of magpie]

piece (pēs) *n., v.* **pieced, piec·ing.** —*n.* **1** one of the parts into which a thing is divided or broken; bit: *a piece of wood. The cup broke in pieces.* **2** a portion; part; small quantity: *a piece of land, a piece of bread.* **3** a single thing of a set or class: *a piece of luggage. This set of china has 144 pieces.* **4** a coin: *A nickel is a five-cent piece.* **5** an example; instance: *Sleeping with the light on is a piece of nonsense.* **6** a single work of art: *a piece of music, a piece of poetry.* **7** a gun; cannon. **8** the quantity in which goods are made: *She bought the whole piece of muslin.* **9** *Checkers, chess, etc.* a figure, disk, block, etc. used in playing. **10** a snack between meals. **11** *Cdn. Historical.* a package of goods or furs weighing about 90 pounds (about 40 kg), the standard load carried by the fur brigades.
go to pieces, a fall apart; break up: *Another ship had gone to pieces on the rocks.* **b** break down; collapse: *When his business failed, he went completely to pieces.*
of a piece, of the same kind; in keeping: *That plan is of a piece with the rest of his silly suggestions.*
piece of (one's) mind, *Informal.* **a** candid opinion. **b** a scolding: *He gave the boy a piece of his mind for coming late.*
speak (one's) piece, voice one's opinions.
—*v.* **1** make or repair by adding or joining pieces. **2** join the pieces of. **3** eat between meals: *The child was always piecing.* [ME *pece* < OF < Med.L *petia* fragment < Celtic] —**piec′er,** *n.*
☛ *Hom.* **peace.**
☛ *Syn. n.* **2.** See note at **part.**

pièce de ré·sis·tance (pyes′də rā zis toNs′; *French,* pyez də Rā zēs täNs′) *French.* **1** the chief dish of a meal. **2** the most important or outstanding item in any collection or series.

piece·meal (pēs′mēl′) *adv., adj.* —*adv.* **1** piece by piece; a little at a time: *work done piecemeal.* **2** piece from piece; to pieces; into fragments. —*adj.* done piece by piece. [ME *pecemele* < *pece* piece + *-mele* < OE *mæl* part, measure]

piece of eight a former Spanish coin equal to eight reals.

piece·work (pēs′wėrk′) *n.* work paid for the amount done, not by the time it takes.

piece·work·er (pēs′wèr′kər) *n.* a person who does piecework.

pie·crust (pī′krust′) *adj.* having a fluted edge like that of a pie crust: *a piecrust table.*

pie crust pastry used for the bottom or top of a pie.

pied (pīd) *adj.* **1** having patches of two or more colors; many-colored. **2** spotted. **3** wearing a costume of two or more colors. [< *pie²;* with reference to magpie's plumage]

pied–à–terre (pyā tä ter′) *n., pl.* **pieds–à–terre.** *French.* a house or apartment kept for occasional use: *They live on a ranch but have a pied-à-terre in Vancouver.* [literally, foot on (the) ground]

Pie·gan (pē′gan) *n., pl.* **-gan** *or* **-gans.** a member of an

---

hat, āge, fär; let, ēqual, tėrm; it, īce
hot, ōpen, ôrder; oil, out; cup, pút, rüle,
above, takən, pencəl, lemən, circəs
ch, child; ng, long; sh, ship
th, thin; ᴛʜ, then; zh, measure

Amerindian people of the Plains, one of the three Algonquian tribes of the Blackfoot confederacy.

pie in the sky *Slang.* something pleasant but unattainable; an impractical ideal.

pier (pēr) *n.* **1** a structure supported on columns extending into the water, used as a walk or a landing place for ships. **2** breakwater. **3** one of the solid supports on which the arches of a bridge rest; any solid support of masonry. **4** the solid part of a wall between windows, doors, etc. [< Med.L *pera*]
☛ *Hom.* **peer.**

pierce (pērs) *v.* **pierced, pierc·ing.** **1** make a hole in; bore into or through: *A nail pierced the tire of our car.* **2** go into; go through: *A tunnel pierces the mountain.* **3** force a way; force a way through or into: *A sharp cry pierced the air.* **4** make a way through with the eye or mind: *to pierce a disguise, to pierce a mystery.* **5** affect sharply with some feeling: *a heart pierced with grief.* [< OF *percier,* ult. < L *pertusus* pierced, pp. of *pertundere* < *per-* through + *tundere* beat]
☛ *Syn.* **1.** See note at **penetrate.**

pierc·ing (pēr′sing) *adj.* that pierces; penetrating; sharp; keen: *piercing cold, a piercing look.* —**pierc′ing·ly,** *adv.* —**pierc′ing·ness,** *n.*

pier glass a tall mirror, as originally used to fill the space, or pier, between two windows.

Pi·er·i·an (pī ēr′ē ən) *adj.* of or having to do with the Muses. [< *Pieria,* in ancient Thessaly, supposed home of the Muses]

Pierian spring the supposed fountain of knowledge and poetic inspiration.

Pi·er·rot (pē′ər ō′; *French,* pye rō′) *n.* a clown who is a traditional character in French pantomime. He has his face whitened and wears white pantaloons and, usually, a white jacket with big buttons. [< F *Pierrot,* dim. of *Pierre* Peter]

pie·tà *or* **Pie·tà** (pyā tä′) *n. Art.* a representation of the Virgin holding the dead Christ in her arms. [< Ital. *pietà* piety, pity < L *pietas*]

pi·e·tism (pī′ə tiz′əm) *n.* **1** deep piety. **2** pretended piety. **3 Pietism,** a 17th-century movement for reviving piety in the Lutheran Church. [< G *Pietismus* (def. 3)]

pi·e·tist (pī′ə tist) *n.* **1** one conspicuous for pietism. **2 Pietist,** an adherent of Pietism.

pi·e·tis·tic (pī′ə tis′tik) *adj.* conspicuous for pietism; very pious.

pi·e·ty (pī′ə tē) *n., pl.* **-ties.** **1** the condition of being pious or of having reverence for God; devotion to religion; holiness. **2** a dutiful regard for one's parents. **3** a pious act, remark, belief, etc. [ME < OF *piete* < L *pietas* < *pius* pious. Doublet of PITY.]

pif·fle (pif′əl) *n. Informal.* silly talk; nonsense. [? related to OE *pyffan* puff]

pif·fling (pif′ling) *adj. Informal.* insignificant; trifling, piddling.

pig (pig) *n., v.* —*n.* **1** a cloven-hoofed domestic mammal (*Sus scrofa*) having a long snout, a stout, heavy body, and short legs; swine. Pigs are raised for their meat. **2** any other mammal of the same family (Suidae). **3** a young swine. **4** pork. **5** *Informal.* a greedy, dirty, disagreeable person. **6** metal, such as iron, cast in an oblong shape for storage or transportation.
buy a pig in a poke, buy something without seeing or knowing its real nature or value.
make a pig of (oneself), *Informal.* overindulge oneself, especially in eating.
—*v.* **1** of a sow, give birth; farrow. **2** *Informal.* Also, **pig it,** live in poor or crowded conditions. [OE *picg* (in *picg-bred* mast², literally, pig-bread); origin uncertain]

pi·geon (pij′ən) *n.* **1** any of a family (Columbidae) of birds having a stout body and small head. There are many domesticated varieties of pigeon bred from the wild rock pigeon. **2** clay pigeon. **3** *Slang.* a person who is easily tricked. [ME < OF *pijon* < VL < LL *pipio, -onis* squab; named from the sound (cf. L *pipiare* cheep)]

pigeon hawk a pigeon-sized falcon (*Falco columbarius*) which breeds in N North America, related to the merlin.

pi·geon·hole (pij′ən hōl′) *n., v.* **-holed, -hol·ing.** —*n.* **1** a small place built, usually as one of a series, for a pigeon to nest in. **2** one of a set of boxlike compartments for holding papers and other articles in a desk, a cabinet, etc.

—*v.* **1** put in a pigeonhole; put away. **2** classify and lay aside in memory where one can refer to it. **3** put aside with the idea of dismissing, forgetting, or neglecting: *The city council pigeonholed the request for a new park.*

pi·geon–toed (pij′ən tōd′) *adj.* having the toes or feet turned inward.

pig·ger·y (pig′ər ē) *n., pl.* **-ger·ies.** *Esp.Brit.* a place where pigs are kept.

pig·gish (pig′ish) *adj.* like a pig; greedy; filthy. —**pig′gish·ly,** *adv.* —**pig′gish·ness,** *n.*

pig·gy (pig′ē) *n., pl.* **-gies.** a little pig.

pig·gy·back (pig′ē bak′) *n., adv., v.* —*n.* **1** a carrying or being carried on the back or shoulders: *He gave the child a piggyback.* **2** the act or process of transporting loaded truck trailers on flatcars. —*adv.* **1** on the back or shoulders. **2** by piggyback. —*v.* carry by piggyback.

piggy bank 1 a small container in the shape of a pig, with a slot in the top for coins. **2** any coin bank.

pig–head·ed (pig′hed′id) *adj.* stupidly obstinate or stubborn. —**pig′-head·ed·ness,** *n.*

pig iron crude iron as it first comes from the blast furnace or smelter, usually cast into oblong masses called pigs.

pig latin a children's jargon in which the syllable *-ay* (ā) is added to the end of a word, any initial consonant being placed immediately before this ending. *Examples*: oodgay = good, offay = off, ordway = word. Also, **pig Latin.**

pig·let (pig′lit) *n.* a little pig; baby pig.

pig·ment (pig′mənt) *n.* **1** a coloring matter, especially a powder or some easily pulverized dry substance, that, when mixed with oil, water, or other liquid vehicle, constitutes a paint. **2** *Biology.* the natural coloring matter of a cell or tissue. [ME < L *pigmentum,* ult. < *pingere* paint. Doublet of PIMENTO.]

pig·men·tar·y (pig′mən ter′ē) *adj.* of or containing pigment.

pig·men·ta·tion (pig′mən tā′shən) *n.* **1** a deposit of pigment in the tissue of a living animal or plant, causing coloration or discoloration. **2** the coloring of an animal or plant resulting from pigment in the tissues.

pig·my (pig′mē) See **pygmy.**

pig·nut (pig′nut′) *n.* **1** the bitter nut of any of several North American hickory trees, such as *Carya glabra.* **2** a tree bearing such nuts. **3** earthnut.

pig·pen (pig′pen′) *n.* **1** a pen where pigs are kept. **2** a filthy place.

pig·skin (pig′skin′) *n.* **1** the skin of a pig. **2** leather made from it. **3** *Informal.* football.

pig·sty (pig′stī′) *n., pl.* **-sties.** pigpen.

pig·tail (pig′tāl′) *n.* **1** a braid of hair hanging from the back of the head. **2** a twist of tobacco.

pig·weed (pig′wēd′) *n.* **1** any of several North American amaranths that are troublesome weeds, especially **red-root pigweed** (*A. retroflexus*), having hairy leaves and stems and small green flowers. **2** a tall, annual plant (*Axyris amaranthoides*) of the goosefoot family native to Asia but now a common Canadian weed, especially in the Prairies. Also called **Russian pigweed.**

pi·ka (pī′kə) *n.* any of a family (Ochotonidae) of small, short-eared, short-legged, tail-less mammals resembling guinea pigs but belonging to the same order as rabbits and hares. All 14 living species, found in the mountainous regions of W North America and Asia, belong to the genus *Ochotona.* [< Tungus (Siberia) *piika,* probably imitative of its cry]

pike¹ (pīk) *n.* a weapon having a long wooden handle and a pointed metal head, once carried by foot soldiers; spear. [< F *pique* < *piquer* pierce < *pic* < pack < Gmc.]

pike² (pīk) *n.* a sharp point; spike. [OE *pīc* pick]

pike³ (pīk) *n.* **1** a large, long freshwater food and game fish (*Esox lucius*) having a long, narrow, pointed head with many sharp teeth. Also called **northern pike. 2** (*adj.*) designating a family (Esocidae) of freshwater food and game fishes found in North America, Europe, and Asia. The pike family is made up of one genus (*Esox*), which includes the pike, muskellunge, and pickerels. **3** pickerel. [apparently < *pike²* + *fish* (because of the shape of its snout)]

pike⁴ (pīk) *n.* turnpike.

pike·man (pīk′mən) *n., pl.* **-men** (-mən). a soldier armed with a pike.

pike·perch or **pike–perch** (pīk′pėrch′) *n.* walleye (def. 7); doré.

pike–pole or **pike·pole** (pīk′pōl′) *n.* a long pole with a pike or spike, at one end, especially one used by lumbermen to direct floating logs.

pik·er (pīk′ər) *n. Slang.* a person who does things in a small or cheap way. [origin uncertain]

pike·staff (pīk′staf′) *n., pl.* **-staves.** (-stāvz′). **1** the staff or shaft of a pike or spear. **2** a staff with a metal point or spike, used by travellers.

pi·laf or **pi·laff** (pi läf′) *n.* pilau.

pi·las·ter (pə las′tər) *n.* a rectangular pillar, especially when it forms part of a wall from which it projects slightly. [< F < Ital. *pilastro* < L *pila* pillar]

pi·lau or **pi·law** (pi lo′, pi lau′, *or* pi lō′) *n.* a dish consisting of steamed or boiled rice flavored with spices and often including chopped meat, poultry, or fish. [< Turkish < Persian *pilāw.* 17c.] [< Persian *pilaw*]

pil·chard (pil′chərd) *n.* **1** an important European food fish (*Sardina pilchardus*) of the herring family. **2** any of various other fishes of the herring family, such as *Sardinops sagax* of Pacific coastal waters from Alaska to Baja California and from Peru to Chile. [origin uncertain]

pile¹ (pīl) *n., v.* **piled, pil·ing.** —*n.* **1** many things lying one upon another in a more or less orderly way: *a pile of wood.* **2** a heap; mass like a hill or mound: *a pile of dirt.* **3** pyre. **4** a large structure or mass of buildings. **5** Often, **piles,** *pl. Informal.* a large amount or number: *a pile of dishes to wash, a pile of work to do.* **6** *Informal.* a large amount of money: *He made a pile on that deal.* **7** nuclear reactor. **8** *Electricity.* **a** a series of plates of different metals, arranged alternately with cloth or paper wet with acid between them, for producing an electric current. **b** any similar arrangement for producing an electric current; battery. —*v.* **1** make into or as if into a pile; heap (*often used with* **up**): *We piled the blankets in a corner.* **2** accumulate or become heaped in or as if in a pile (*usually used with* **up**): *Snow had piled up against the door. A lot of work had piled up while he was away.* **3** move or press forward in a group, especially in a rushed or confused way (*used with* **in, into, out, off,** *etc.*): *to pile out into the street. Two more players piled into the scrimmage.* **pile (something) on,** *Informal.* employ (description, flattery, humor, etc.) in great amounts or to excess: *Some authors like to pile on the sex and violence. It's nice to be complimented, but she really piles it on.* [ME < OF < L *pila* pillar] —**pil′er,** *n.*

pile² (pīl) *n., v.* **piled, pil·ing.** —*n.* a heavy beam driven upright into the earth, often under water, to help support a bridge, wharf, building, etc. —*v.* furnish with piles; drive piles into. [OE *pīl* stake < L *pilum* javelin]

pile³ (pīl) *n.* **1** the surface of certain fabrics woven with loops of yarn which may be uncut, as in towelling, or cut, as in velvet, carpeting, etc. **2** the cut or uncut loops that form the surface. **3** a soft, fine hair or down. [< L *pilus* hair]

pi·le·ate (pī′lē ət *or* pil′-; pī′lē āt′ *or* pil′-) *adj.* having a pileus.

pi·le·at·ed (pī′lē ā′təd *or* pil′ē ā′təd) *adj.* **1** of a bird, having a crest: *a pileated woodpecker.* **2** pileate.

piled (pīld) *adj.* having a soft, thick nap.

pile driver a machine for driving down piles or stakes, usually a tall framework in which a heavy weight is raised to a height and then allowed to fall upon the pile.

piles (pīlz) *n.pl.* a swelling of blood vessels at the anus; often painful; hemorrhoids. [ME *pyle,* sing., ? < L *pila* ball]

pi·le·um (pī′lē əm *or* pil′ē əm) *n., pl.* **-le·a** (-lē ə). the top of a bird's head, from the base of the bill to the nape.

pile–up (pīl′up′) *n. Informal.* **1** a collision involving several or many vehicles: *Five people were killed in the pile-up on the parkway yesterday.* **2** a great mass or jumble of people or things: *a pile-up on the football field.*

pi·le·us (pī′lē əs *or* pil′ē əs) *n., pl.* **-le·i** (-lē ī′). the umbrella-shaped fruiting body of a mushroom or similar fungus.

pil·fer (pil′fər) *v.* steal in small quantities; steal. [ME < OF *pelfrer* rob] —**pil′fer·er,** *n.*
☛ *Syn.* See note at **steal.**

pil·grim (pil′grəm) *n.* **1** a person who goes on a journey to a sacred or holy place as an act of religious devotion. **2** a traveller; wanderer. **3 Pilgrim,** one of the English Puritan settlers who found Plymouth Colony (in what is now Massachusetts) in 1620. [ME < AF *pelegrim,* var. of OF *pelerin* < Med.L *peregrinus* pilgrim < L *peregrinus* foreigner. Doublet of PEREGRINE.]

pil·grim·age (pil′grə mij) *n.* **1** a pilgrim's journey; journey to some sacred place as an act of religious devotion. **2** a long journey, especially one to see or visit a special place, etc. **3** life thought of as a journey. [ME < OF *pelerinage* < *peleriner* go as a pilgrim]

pil·ing (pīl′ing) *n.* **1** piles or heavy beams driven into the ground, etc. **2** a structure made of piles.

pill (pil) *n.*, *v.* —*n.* **1** medicine in a small, solid, usually rounded mass to be swallowed whole. **2 the pill** or **the Pill,** any of various pills for contraception; an oral contraceptive. **3** *Slang.* a baseball or golf ball. **4** something unpleasant that has to be endured: *Our defeat was a bitter pill.* **5** *Slang.* an unpleasant or boring person. —*v.* of knitted or brushed woven fabric, become matted into small balls: *This sweater is pilling badly.* [< MDu. or MLG < L *pilula,* dim. of *pila* ball]

pil·lage (pil′ij) *v.* **-laged, -lag·ing;** *n.* —*v.* rob with violence; plunder: *Pirates pillaged the towns along the coast.* —*n.* plunder; robbery. [ME < OF *pillage* < *piller* plunder < VL *pileare* flay] —**pil′lag·er,** *n.*

pil·lar (pil′ər) *n.* **1** a slender, upright structure; column. Pillars are usually made of stone, wood, or metal and used as supports or ornaments for a building. **2** anything slender and upright like a pillar. **3** an important support or supporter: *He is a pillar of the church.*
from pillar to post, from one thing or place to another without any definite purpose.
pillar of society, an influential and dependable member of the community.
[ME < OF *piler,* ult. < L *pila* pillar, pile¹]

pil·lared (pil′ərd) *adj.* **1** having pillars. **2** formed into pillars.

Pillars of Hercules two high points of land at the eastern end of the Strait of Gibraltar, one on either side of the strait. The point on the European side is the Rock of Gibraltar and the one on the African side is Jebel Musa.

pill·box (pil′boks′) *n.* **1** a box, usually shallow and often round, for holding pills. **2** a small, low fortress with very thick walls and roof, having machine guns, anti-tank weapons, etc. **3** a small, round, brimless hat with a low, flat crown: *Royal Military College cadets wear pillboxes.*

pil·lion (pil′yən) *n.* a pad attached behind a saddle on a horse or motorcycle for a person to sit on. [< Scots Gaelic *pillin* or *pillean,* dim. of *pell* cushion < L *pellis* skin]

A pillory

pil·lo·ry (pil′ə rē) *n.*, *pl.* **-ries;** *v.* **-ried, -ry·ing.** —*n.* **1** *Historical.* a device used for the public punishment of an offender, consisting of a wooden frame with holes through which the person's head and hands were put and which was then locked in place. **2** exposure to public ridicule, scorn, or abuse. —*v.* **1** *Historical.* put in a pillory as punishment. **2** expose to public ridicule, scorn, or abuse. [< OF *pelori* < Provençal *espilori;* origin uncertain]

pil·low (pil′ō) *n.*, *v.* —*n.* **1** a bag or case filled with feathers, down, or some other soft material, usually used to support the head when resting or sleeping. **2** anything used for a similar purpose. **3** a pad on which a kind of lace is made. **4** a supporting piece or part, such as the block on which the inner end of a bowsprit rests. —*v.* **1** rest on or as if on a pillow: *He pillowed his head on a pile of leaves.* **2** be a pillow for. [OE *pyle, pylu,* ult. < L *pulvinus*] —**pil′low·like′,** *adj.*

pil·low·case (pil′ō kās′) *n.* a removable cotton or linen cover for a pillow.

pil·low·slip (pil′ō slip′) *n.* pillowcase.

pi·lose (pī′lōs) *adj.* covered with soft hair; hairy. [< L *p...sus* < *pilus* hair]

pi·lot (pī′lət) *n.*, *v.* —*n.* **1** a person trained to operate the controls of an aircraft or spacecraft in flight. **2** a person who steers a ship; helmsman. **3** one whose business is steering ships in or out of a harbor or through dangerous waters. A ship takes on a pilot before coming into a strange harbor. **4** (*adj.*) of or having to do with a pilot: *The crash was the result of a pilot error.* **5** a guide or leader. **6** a device that controls the action of one part of a machine, motor, etc. **7** a television show produced to serve as a sample of a projected series. **8** (*adj.*) serving as an advance or experimental version or sample of some action, operation, device, etc.: *a pilot project, a pilot film.* **9** (*adj.*) that serves to activate, guide, or control: *a pilot star for navigation.* **10** pilot light.

—*v.* **1** act as the pilot of; steer. **2** guide or lead: *The manager piloted us through the big factory.* [< F < Ital. *pilota*]

pi·lot·age (pī′lət ij) *n.* **1** piloting. **2** a pilot's art or duties. **3** the fee paid for a pilot's service.

pilot biscuit or **bread** a ship biscuit; large, flat cracker.

pilot fish a tropical or subtropical marine fish (*Naucrates ductor*) of the same family as the pompano, that often accompanies a shark.

pilot house an enclosed place on the deck of a ship, sheltering the steering wheel and helmsman.

pilot light a small flame kept burning all the time and used to light a main burner whenever desired. Gas stoves and gas water heaters have pilot lights.

pilot officer an air-force officer of the lowest commissioned rank, junior to a flying officer. *Abbrev.*: P.O.

pilot whale any of a genus (*Globicephala*) of small, mostly black, toothed whales found in most seas. Some authorities recognize only one species in the genus; others recognize two or three different species.

Pil·sen·er (pil′sə nər *or* pil′snər) *n.* a pale lager beer. [< G *Pilsener* < *Pilsen,* a city in Czechoslovakia]

Pilt·down man (pilt′doun′) a supposed type of prehistoric man of which fossil remains found at Piltdown, Sussex, were thought to be the most ancient yet discovered in England; they are now generally considered to have been a hoax.

pi·men·to (pə men′tō) *n.*, *pl.* **-tos. 1** any of various sweet red peppers, the fruit of a capsicum, especially *C. annuum,* used especially as a relish and, as stuffing for green olives. Pimentos are also dried and ground up to make paprika. **2** a small evergreen tree (*Pimenta officinalis*) of the myrtle family native to the West Indies. **3** a spice made from the dried berries of the West Indian pimento; allspice. [< Sp. *pimienta* pepper, *pimiento* capsicum < Med.L *pigmentum* spice < LL *pigmentum* vegetable juice < L *pigmentum* pigment. Doublet of PIGMENT.]

pi·mien·to (pi myen′tō) *n.*, *pl.* **-tos.** pimento (def. 1). [< Sp. *pimiento.* See PIMENTO.]

pim·o·la (pim ō′lə) *n.* an olive stuffed with red sweet pepper. [? < *pimento*]

pimp (pimp) *n.*, *v.* —*n.* **1** a man who solicits for or manages one or more prostitutes and takes part of their earnings. **2** a man who procures sexual entertainment for others; pander. —*v.* be or act as a pimp. [origin unknown]

pim·per·nel (pim′pər nel′) *n.* any of a genus (*Anagallis*) of plants of the primrose family, especially the **scarlet pimpernel** (*A. arvensis*), having scarlet, purple, or white, star-shaped flowers that close in cloudy or rainy weather. [ME < OF *pimprenele,* ult. < VL *piperinus* of peppercorns < L *piper* pepper]

pim·ple (pim′pəl) *n.* a small, inflamed swelling in the skin, containing pus. A pimple is a small abscess. [cf. OE *piplian* grow pimply]

pim·pled (pim′pəld) *adj.* having pimples.

pim·ply (pim′plē) *adj.* **-pli·er, -pli·est.** having pimples.

pin (pin) *n.*, *v.* **pinned, pin·ning.** —*n.* **1** a short, slender piece of wire with a point at one end and a head at the other, used for fastening things together. **2** a kind of badge with a pin or clasp to fasten it to the clothing. **3** a brooch. **4** any of various fastenings consisting essentially or in part of a slender, often pointed, bar or wire: *a safety pin, a hatpin, a bobby pin.* **5** a peg made of wood, metal, or plastic used to fasten things together, hold something, hang things on, etc.: *a clothes pin.* **6** a belaying pin. **7** a peg that holds an oar in place. **8** in a stringed musical instrument, a peg to which a string is fastened. **9** *Bowling.* any of the bottle-shaped pieces of wood used as targets. **10 pins,** *Informal.* legs: *He's getting better, but is still a little shaky on his pins.* **11** *Wrestling.* a position in which a person controls his opponent completely, especially by holding both the opponent's shoulders to the ground. **12** *Golf.* a stick for the flag marking a hole on a course. **13** something small or worthless.
on pins and needles, very anxious or uneasy.
—*v.* **1** fasten with a pin or pins; put a pin through. **2** fasten or attach firmly to or on; tack; fasten as if with pins. **3** hold fast in one position: *When the tree fell, it pinned his shoulder to the ground.* **4** *Wrestling.* gain control over (an opponent) by holding his shoulders to the ground.

pin down, a hold or bind to an undertaking or pledge. **b** fix firmly; determine with accuracy; establish.
pin on, *Informal.* fix blame, responsibility, etc. on: *The police could not pin the crime on him.*
[OE *pinn* peg] —**pin′like′,** *adj.*

pin·a·fore (pin′ə fôr′) *n.* **1** a garment like a full apron worn by children or women to protect other clothes. **2** *Esp.Brit.* a sleeveless dress usually worn over a blouse or sweater; jumper. [< *pin.* v. + *afore*]

pin·ball (pin′bol′ *or* -bôl′) *n.* a game in which a ball rolls down a board, which is studded with pins or pegs, into numbered compartments.

pinball machine a gambling device used for playing pinball.

pince-nez (pans′nā′ *or* pins′nā′; *French,* paNs nā′) *n.* eyeglasses kept in place by a spring that pinches the nose. [< F *pince-nez* pinch-nose]

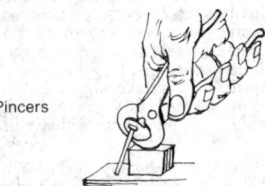
Pincers

pin·cer (pin′sər) *n.* **1** a claw of a crab, lobster, etc., resembling a pair of pincers; chela. **2 pincers,** *pl.* a tool for gripping and holding tight, made like scissors but with jaws instead of blades. **3 pincers,** *pl. Military.* a manoeuvre in which two parts of a military force converge on the enemy from opposite sides. Also called **pincer movement** or **pincers movement.** —**pin′cer·like′,** *adj.* [ME < AF < OF *pynceour* < *pincier* to pinch]

pinch (pinch) *v., n.* —*v.* **1** squeeze between two hard edges; squeeze with thumb and forefinger. **2** squeeze or press so as to hurt; get squeezed. **3** cause sharp discomfort or distress to. **4** cause to shrink or become thin: *a face pinched by hunger.* **5** limit closely; stint: *to be pinched for space.* **6** be stingy. **7** be stingy with: *The miser knew how to pinch pennies.* **8** *Slang.* arrest. **9** *Slang.* steal; pilfer.
—*n.* **1** a squeeze between two hard edges; squeeze with thumb and forefinger. **2** sharp pressure that hurts; squeeze. **3** as much as can be taken up with the tips of finger and thumb: *a pinch of salt.* **4** sharp discomfort or distress: *the pinch of hunger.* **5** a time of special need; emergency. **6** *Slang.* an arrest. **7** *Slang.* a stealing. [ME < ONF < OF *pinchier* < *pincer* to pinch] —**pinch′er,** *n.*

pinch·beck (pinch′bek′) *n., adj.* —*n.* **1** an alloy of zinc and copper, used in imitation of gold. **2** something not genuine; an imitation. —*adj.* **1** made of pinchbeck. **2** not genuine; sham. [after Christopher *Pinchbeck* (1670?-1732), the inventor]

pin cherry a North American wild cherry (*Prunus pensylvanica*) having shiny, bright-green leaves, small, five-petalled, white flowers, and small, bright-red, sour fruit used for jellies and preserves.

pinch·ers (pin′chərz) *n.pl.* pincers.

pinch-hit (pinch′hit′) *v.* -**hit, -hit·ting. 1** *Baseball.* bat for another player, especially when a hit is badly needed. **2** take another's place in an emergency. —**pinch′hit′ter,** *n.*

pinch-pen·ny (pinch′pen′ē) *adj., n., pl.* -**nies.** *Informal.* —*adj.* too thrifty; overfrugal; mean with money. —*n.* a niggardly or miserly person.

pin curl a curl kept in place by a hairpin or clip.

pin·cush·ion (pin′kush′ən) *n.* a small cushion to stick pins in for use as needed.

Pin·dar·ic (pin dar′ik *or* pin der′ik) *adj.* of, having to do with, or in the style of Pindar (522?-443? B.C.), a Greek lyric poet.

pin·dling (pin′dling) *adj. Informal.* puny; sickly. [? euphemistic var. of *piddling*]

pine[1] (pīn) *n.* **1** any of a large genus (*Pinus*) of evergreen trees found in many parts of the northern hemisphere, having long, needle-like leaves growing in tufts from the stems. The **soft pines** include the white pines; the **hard pines** include the ponderosa, red, and jack pines. **2** the wood of any of these trees. **3** (*adj.*) made of pine: *a pine floor.* **4** (*adj.*) designating a family (Pinaceae) of evergreen trees, including pines, larches, spruces, firs, and true cedars. [OE *pīn* < L *pinus*] —**pine′like′,** *adj.*

pine[2] (pīn) *v.* **pined, pin·ing. 1** long eagerly; yearn. **2** waste away

with pain, hunger, grief, or desire. [OE *pīnian* < *pīn,* n., torture < L *poena* penalty < Gk. *poinē*]

pin·e·al (pin′ē əl) *adj.* **1** resembling a pine cone in shape. **2** of or having to do with the pineal body. [< F < L *pinea* pine cone < *pinus* pine]

pineal body or **pineal gland** a small body present in the brain of vertebrates, whose function has not been definitely established.

pine·ap·ple (pīn′ap′əl) *n.* **1** a perennial plant (*Ananas comosus*) native to tropical and subtropical America but widely cultivated in other warm regions as well, for its large, edible fruit. **2** the fruit of this plant, resembling a large pine-cone and having juicy, sweet, yellow flesh. **3** (*adj.*) designating the tropical and subtropical American family (Bromeliaceae) of plants that includes the pineapple and Spanish moss. **4** *Slang.* a hand grenade or bomb.

pine-cone (pīn′kōn′) *n.* a cone of a pine tree or of any of various other members of the pine family, such as spruce or fir.

pine·drops (pīn′drops′) *n.sing. or pl.* a purplish, leafless plant (*Pterospora andromedea*) of North America that has clusters of white or red flowers and is a parasite on the roots of pine trees.

pine needle the very slender, needle-like leaf of a pine tree or of other members of the pine family, such as spruce or fir.

pin·er·y (pīn′ər ē) *n., pl.* -**er·ies. 1** a forest or plantation of pine trees. **2** a place where pineapples are grown.

pine siskin a small North American finch (*Spinus pinus*) having streaky, greyish-brown and yellowish plumage. It is found in coniferous and mixed forests from S Alaska, across Canada, and south to Mexico.

pine tar a brownish-black, semisolid tar obtained by distilling pine wood and used especially in roofing materials, paints, and varnishes, and as an antiseptic.

pine·y (pī′nē) *adj.* **pin·i·er, pin·i·est.** See **piny.**

pin·feath·er (pin′feᴛH′ər) *n.* an undeveloped feather just emerging through the skin. A pinfeather looks like a small stub.

pin·fold (pin′fōld′) *n., v.* —*n.* a place where stray animals, especially cattle, are kept; pound. —*v.* confine in a pinfold. [OE *pundfald* < *pund-* pound[3] + *fald* fold[2]; later influenced by ME *pind* enclose < OE *pyndan*]

ping (ping) *n., v.* —*n.* a sound like that of a rifle bullet whistling through the air or striking an object. —*v.* produce a ping. [imitative]

pin·go (ping′gō) *n., pl.* **ping·os** or **ping·oes.** *Cdn.* a cone-shaped or dome-shaped mound or hill of peat or soil, usually with a core of ice, found in tundra regions and produced by the pressure of water or ice accumulating underground and pushing upward. [< Eskimo]

ping-pong (ping′pong′) *n.* table tennis. [< *Ping-pong,* a trademark]

pin·head (pin′hed′) *n.* **1** the head of a pin. **2** something very small or unimportant. **3** *Informal.* a very stupid person.

pin·head·ed (pin′hed′əd) *adj. Informal.* very stupid or silly: *That was a pinheaded thing to do.*

pin·hole (pin′hōl′) *n.* **1** a tiny hole made by or as if by a pin. **2** a hole made for a pin or peg to go into.

pin·ion[1] (pin′yən) *n., v.* —*n.* **1** the outermost segment of a bird's wing. **2** *Poetic.* a bird's wing. **3** any one of the stiff flying feathers of a bird's wing.
—*v.* **1** cut off or tie the pinions of (a bird) to prevent its flying. **2** bind: *His arms were pinioned behind his back.* **3** bind the arms of or bind (to something): *The thieves pinioned him securely. He was pinioned to the chair.* [ME < OF *pignon,* ult. < L *pinna* feather]

pin·ion[2] (pin′yən) *n.* a small gear with teeth that fit into those of a larger gear or rack. See **differential** and **gear** for pictures. [< F *pignon* < OF *pignon* battlement, ult. < L *pinna* pinnacle]

pink[1] (pingk) *n., adj.* —*n.* **1** a color made by mixing red and white. Pink may vary from a very pale, light color to a vivid, almost red color. **2** any of a genus (*Dianthus*) of plants native to Europe, Asia, and Africa, having long, slender leaves, stems with swollen joints, and sepals joined together to form a tube below the petals. Many pinks are cultivated for their showy, often fragrant flowers. **3** the highest degree or condition of excellence: *An athlete needs to be in the pink of health.* **4** *Informal.* a person who is somewhat sympathetic to communist doctrine.
—*adj.* **1** of or having the color pink: *a pink rose.* **2** designating a family (Caryophyllaceae) of annual or perennial herbs having flowers with four or five petals, simple leaves, and stems with swollen joints. Pinks, chickweeds, and baby's-breath belong to the pink family. **3** *Informal.* somewhat sympathetic to communist doctrine. **4** *Informal.* over-refined; exquisite; smart: *a pink tea.* [origin uncertain]

pink[2] (pingk) *v.* **1** prick or pierce with a sword, spear, or dagger. **2** cut the edge of (cloth) in small notches or scallops. **3** ornament with small, round holes. **4** adorn. [ME *pynke(n)* < OE *pynca* point]

pink[3] (pingk) *n.* a flat-bottomed, narrow-sterned sailing vessel with

bulging sides. Also, **pinkie**. [apparently < MDu. *pincke* small ship, fishing boat]

pink·eye (pingk′ī′) *n.* an acute, highly contagious type of conjunctivitis of man and some domestic animals.

pink·ie[1] (pingk′ē) *n. Informal.* the smallest finger.

pink·ie[2] (pingk′ē) *n.* pink[3].

pinking shears shears for pinking cloth.

pink·ish (pingk′ish) *adj.* somewhat pink.

pink·o (ping′kō) *n., pl.* **-os**; *adj. Slang, usually derogatory.* —*n.* a pink (def. 4). —*adj.* of or being a pink.

pink salmon the smallest Pacific salmon (*Onchorhynchus gorbuscha*), found along the coast especially from the Columbia River north to Alaska. The pink salmon is blue and silver in color and has pink flesh.

pin money 1 money set aside for buying extra or minor things. 2 *Archaic.* an allowance of money given to a wife for her own use.

pin·na (pin′ə) *n., pl.* **pin·nae** (pin′ē *or* pin′ī) *or* **pin·nas.** 1 *Zoology.* a projecting body part such as a feather, wing, or fin. 2 the upper part of the external ear. 3 one of the main divisions of a pinnate leaf; leaflet. [< L]

pin·nace (pin′is) *n.* 1 a ship's boat. 2 a very small schooner. [< F < Ital. *pinaccia* or Sp. *pinaza*, ult. < L *pinus* pine]

pin·na·cle (pin′ə kəl) *n., v.* **-cled, -cling.** —*n.* 1 *Architecture.* a slender turret or spire, used especially in Gothic buildings at the top of a buttress. 2 a high peak or point of rock. 3 the highest point of development or achievement: *At the pinnacle of her fame.* —*v.* 1 put on a pinnacle. 2 furnish with pinnacles. [ME < OF < L *pinnaculum*, dim. of *pinna* wing, point]

pin·nate (pin′āt *or* pin′it) *adj.* 1 like a feather, especially in having parts arranged on opposite sides of an axis. 2 of a leaf, consisting of leaflets arranged on opposite sides of the leaf stalk. The Manitoba maple has pinnate leaves. See **leaf** for picture. [< L *pinnatus* < *pinna* feather] —**pin′nate·ly,** *adv.*

pin·nat·ed grouse (pin′ā təd) prairie chicken.

pin·ni·ped (pin′ə pəd′) *n., adj.* —*n.* any of an order (Pinnepedia) of aquatic mammals having a streamlined body and limbs modified into flippers, and including seals, sea lions, and the walrus. —*adj.* of, having to do with, or belonging to this order.

pi·noch·le *or* **pi·noc·le** (pē′nuk′əl *or* pē′nok′əl) *n.* 1 a game played with 48 cards, in which points are scored according to the value of certain combinations of cards. 2 a combination of the jack of diamonds and the queen of spades in this game. [origin uncertain]

pi·ñon (pin′yən *or* pēn′yōn) *n.* 1 any of several small pines, such as *Pinus cembroides* or *P. monophylla*, of the Rocky Mountains in the SW United States and N Mexico, producing large, edible, nutlike seeds. 2 the seed of this tree. [< Sp. *piñón* < *piña* pine cone]

pin·point (pin′point′) *n., v.* —*n.* 1 the point of a pin. 2 something very small or sharp: *We could see a pinpoint of light through a hole in the blind.* 3 (*adj.*) extremely fine or precise: *pinpoint bombing, pinpoint accuracy.* 4 (*adj.*) very small; minute. —*v.* aim at or locate precisely: *to pinpoint the heart of the problem.*

pin·prick (pin′prik′) *n., v.* —*n.* 1 a tiny puncture or prick from a pin or something like a pin. 2 a minor irritation. —*v.* puncture or prick with or as if with a pin.

pin·scher (pin′shər) *n.* Doberman pinscher.

pin·stripe (pin′strīp′) *n.* 1 a fine stripe. 2 cloth having fine stripes. 3 a garment made of such cloth.

pint (pīnt) *n.* 1 a unit for measuring liquids, equal to half a quart (about 0.57 dm³). *Abbrev.*: p., pt. 2 a container holding a pint. 3 this amount of liquid: *He drank a whole pint.* [< F < MDu. *pinte* plug]

pin·tail (pin′tāl′) *n.* 1 a slender North American duck (*Anas acuta*) having grey, white, and brown plumage, the adult male having a white stripe running up each side of the neck just behind the head and two long, black feathers in the centre of the tail. 2 a common grouse of the Prairies, having a pointed tail.

pin·tle (pin′təl) *n.* a pin or bolt, especially an upright one which something turns, as in a hinge. [OE *pintel* penis]

pin·to (pin′tō) *adj., n., pl.* **-tos.** —*adj.* spotted in two colors or more colors; pied. —*n.* a pinto horse. [< Sp. *pinto* painted]

pint-sized (pīnt′sīzd′) *adj. Informal.* small.

pin-up (pin′up′) *n.* 1 a picture of a sexually attractive person put up on a wall, especially by admirers who have not met the person. 2 a person who has posed for such pictures or is considered a suitable subject for them. 3 (*adj.*) of or having to do with pin-ups: *a pin-up calendar.*

pin·wheel (pin′wēl′ *or* -hwēl′) *n.* 1 a toy made of a wheel fastened to a stick by a pin so that it revolves in the wind. 2 a kind of firework that revolves when lighted.

pin·worm (pin′wėrm′) *n.* any of various small, threadlike worms

hat, āge, fär; let, ēqual, tèrm; it, īce
hot, ōpen, ôrder; oil, out; cup, pùt, rūle,
əbove, takən, pencəl, lemən, circəs
ch, child; ng, long; sh, ship
th, thin; ᴛʜ, then; zh, measure

(family Oxyuridae) that are intestinal parasites in vertebrates, especially one (*Enterobius vermicularis*) that infests the rectum and large intestine of human beings, most commonly children.

pin·y (pīn′ē) *adj.* **pin·i·er, pin·i·est.** 1 abounding in or covered with pine trees; *piny mountains.* 2 having to do with or suggesting pine trees: *a piny fragrance.* Also, **piney.**

pi·on (pī′on) *n.* a meson having no electric charge and a mass about 264 times that of an electron or a positive or negative charge and a mass 273 times that of an electron.

pi·o·neer (pī′ə nēr′) *n., v.* —*n.* 1 a person who settles in a region that has not been settled before. 2 a person who goes first or does something first and so prepares a way for others. 3 *Military.* a member of an engineering unit whose job it is to go in advance of other troops, preparing camps, roads, trenches, etc. —*v.* prepare or open up for others; take the lead: *Astronauts are pioneering in exploring outer space.* [< F *pionnier* < OF *peon* foot soldier < LL *pedo, pedonis,* < L *pes, pedis* foot. Related to PAWN[2], PEON.]

pi·ous (pī′əs) *adj.* 1 having or showing reverence for God; religious: *a pious person, a pious act.* 2 showing religious scruples in a smug or ostentatious way, especially when not sincere: *pious platitudes about work and duty.* 3 *Archaic.* dutiful to parents. [< L *pius*] —**pi′ous·ly,** *adv.* —**pi′ous·ness,** *n.*
☛ *Syn.* 1. Pious, devout = religious. **Pious** emphasizes showing religion or reverence for God by carefully observing religious duties and practices, such as going to church, and sometimes suggests that more religion is shown than felt: *She is pious enough to go to church in the morning but she gossips all afternoon.* **Devout** emphasizes feeling true reverence that usually is expressed in prayer or devotion to religious observances, but may not be outwardly shown at all: *He is a devout Christian and a good man.*

pip[1] (pip) *n.* 1 the seed of an apple, orange, etc. 2 *Slang.* a person or thing that is very attractive, admirable, or extraordinary: *Wait till you meet her——she's really a pip!* [short for *pippin*]

pip[2] (pip) *n.* 1 a contagious disease of poultry, etc. characterized by thick mucus in the mouth and throat and, often, a scale or crust on the tongue. 2 *Informal.* any slight, unspecified illness of human beings.
give (someone) **the pip,** *Informal.* cause irritation or disgust: *His superior attitude gives me the pip.*
[ME < MDu. < VL *pippita* < L *pituita* phlegm]

pip[3] (pip) *n.* 1 one of the spots on playing cards, dominoes, or dice. 2 in the British army, etc., one of the stars of rank worn on the shoulders of certain officers: *A captain wears three pips, a lieutenant two.* [earlier *peep*; origin uncertain]

pip[4] (pip) *v.* **pipped, pip·ping.** 1 peep; chirp. 2 of a young bird, break through (the shell). [? var. of *peep*]

pipe (pīp) *n., v.* **piped, pip·ing.** —*n.* 1 a tube through which a liquid or gas flows. 2 a bowl of clay, wood, etc. at one end, for smoking. 3 a quantity of tobacco a pipe will hold. 4 a musical wind instrument with a single tube into which the player blows. 5 pipes, *pl.* **a** a set of musical tubes: *the pipes of Pan.* **b** bagpipe. 6 any one of the tubes in an organ. 7 a shrill sound, voice, or song. 8 a boatswain's whistle. 9 a cask for wine. 10 anything shaped like a tube. 11 *Cdn. Historical.* in the fur trade: **a** a rest period on a journey, originally one in which to smoke a pipe. **b** a spell of travelling between rest periods. —*v.* 1 carry by means of a pipe or pipes. 2 supply with pipes. 3 transmit (music, speech, etc.) by electric or electronic means, especially from one room or part of a building to another (*used with in*): *The background music for the reception will be piped in.* 4 play on a pipe. 5 make a shrill noise; sing or speak in a shrill voice. 6 sing; utter. 7 give orders, signals, etc. with a boatswain's whistle. 8 summon by a pipe: *All hands were piped on deck.* 9 trim (a dress, etc.) with piping (def. 5).
pipe down, *Slang.* be quiet; stop talking, crying, etc.
pipe up, **a** begin to play (music). **b** *Slang.* speak.
[OE *pīpe*, n., *pīpian*, v., < Gmc. < VL < L *pipare* chirp; certain meanings reinforced by or, as n. 9 and 11, borrowed direct from F] —**pipe′like′,** *adj.*

pipe clay a fine white clay used for making tobacco pipes, whitening shoes, etc.

pipe dream *Informal.* an impractical idea.

pipefish (pīp′fish′) *n.* any of various small fishes of the same family (Syngnathidae) as the seahorses, having a long, slender body and a long, tubular snout with a small mouth.

pipe·ful (pīp′fŭl) *n., pl.* **-fuls.** the quantity sufficient to fill the bowl of a pipe.

pipe·line (pīp′līn′) *n., v.* **-lined, -lin·ing.** —*n.* **1** a line of pipes for carrying gas, oil, or other liquids. **2** a direct channel for supplying information, etc.: *He's got a pipeline into the manager's office and always knows what's going on.* **3** a flow of materials through a series of productive processes.
—*v.* **1** carry by a pipeline. **2** provide with a pipeline.

pipe·lin·er (pīp′lī′nər) *n.* a person working on a pipeline (def. 1).

pipe organ a large musical wind instrument consisting of sets of pipes of different diameters and lengths which are sounded by forcing air through them by means of keys and pedals. Pipe organs usually have two or more keyboards for producing many different varieties of sound.

pip·er (pīp′ər) *n.* a person who plays on a pipe or bagpipe.
pay the piper, pay for one's pleasure; bear the consequences (from the proverb *He who pays the piper calls the tune,* meaning "the one who pays has the right to be in control").

pi·pette (pi pet′ *or* pī pet′) *n.* a slender pipe or tube for transferring or measuring liquids. [< F *pipette,* dim. of *pipe* pipe]

pipe wrench a wrench with adjustable, toothed jaws set at right angles to the handle, used especially for turning pipes, rods, and similar curved surfaces.

pip·ing (pīp′ing) *n., adj.* —*n.* **1** a quantity or system of pipes. **2** material that can be used for pipes. **3** the music of a pipe. **4** a shrill sound or call: *the piping of frogs in the spring.* **5** a narrow band of material, sometimes containing a cord, used for trimming along edges and seams of clothing, cushions, etc. **6** ornamental lines of icing, meringue, etc.
—*adj.* shrill.
piping hot, very hot.

pip·it (pip′it) *n.* any of a genus (*Anthus*) of songbirds found in open country, having streaked brownish or greyish plumage, a slender bill, very long hind toenails, and a fairly long tail that the birds habitually wag up and down when perching. Pipits resemble larks. [imitative]

pip·kin (pip′kin) *n.* a small earthen pot. [? dim. of *pipe* (def. 9)]

pip·pin (pip′ən) *n.* any of several varieties of apple having a yellowish-green skin. [ME < OF *pepin*]

pip·sis·se·wa (pip sis′ə wə) *n.* any of a genus (*Chimaphila*) of small evergreen plants of the wintergreen family, whose jagged, leathery leaves were formerly used in medicine as a tonic, diuretic, etc. Some authorities classify the pipsissewas in the heath family. [< Algonquian]

pip·squeak (pip′skwēk) *n. Slang.* a small or insignificant person or thing. [name given to a small German high-speed shell of World War I, so named because of its sound in flight]

pi·quan·cy (pē′kən sē) *n.* the quality or state of being piquant.

pi·quant (pē′kənt) *adj.* **1** sharp or pungent in an agreeable way; pleasantly stimulating to the taste: *a piquant sauce.* **2** pleasantly stimulating to the mind, etc.; intriguing: *a piquant bit of news.* [< F *piquant* pricking, stinging] —**pi′quant·ly,** *adv.*

pique (pēk) *n., v.* **piqued, pi·quing.** —*n.* a feeling of anger at being slighted; wounded pride: *She left the party in a pique.* —*v.* **1** cause a feeling of anger or resentment in; wound the pride of: *It piqued him that they had gone ahead with their plans without consulting him.* **2** arouse; stir up: *The curiosity of the boys was piqued by the locked trunk.*
pique (oneself) on *or* **upon,** feel proud about.
[< F *pique,* n., and *piquer,* v., prick, sting < *pic* a pick (< Gmc.)]
☛ *Hom.* **peak, peek.**

pi·qué (pē kā′) *n.* a cloth, usually cotton or cotton blend, woven with raised, narrow lengthwise ribs or cords, sometimes also having a honeycomb, waffle, or bird's eye pattern. [< F *piqué* quilted, pp. of *piquer* stitch, prick]

pi·quet (pi ket′) *n.* a complicated card game for two people, played with a deck of 32 cards. [< F]

pi·ra·cy (pī′rə sē) *n., pl.* **-cies.** **1** robbery on the high seas. **2** the act of publishing, reproducing, or using a book, play, musical composition, etc. without permission. **3** *Informal.* the charging of excessively high prices: *the price of the dress was sheer piracy.* [ME < Med.L < Gk. *peirateia*]

pi·ra·gua (pə rä′gwə *or* pə rag′wə) *n.* pirogue.

pi·ra·nha (pi rän′yə) *n., pl.* **-nha** *or* **-nhas.** any of various small carnivorous freshwater fishes (genus *Serrasalmus*) of tropical America noted for their voracity. Schools of piranhas will attack and devour human beings or large animals. [< Portuguese *piranha* < Tupi (Brazil) *pira nya,* toothed fish]

pi·rate (pī′rit) *n., v.* **-rat·ed, -rat·ing.** —*n.* **1** one who attacks and robs ships; a robber on the high seas. **2** a ship used by pirates. **3** a person who publishes, reproduces, or uses a book, play, musical composition, etc. without permission. **4** a person or group that operates an illegal radio or television station.
—*v.* **1** be a pirate; plunder; rob. **2** publish, reproduce, use, or broadcast illegally or without permission. [ME < L < Gk. *peiratēs* < *peirain* attack] —**pi′rate·like′,** *adj.*

pi·rat·i·cal (pī rat′ə kəl) *adj.* of or like pirates or piracy.
—**pi·rat′i·cal·ly,** *adv.*

pi·ro·gi (pi rō′gē) *n.pl.* pyrohy. [< Russian, sing. *pirog* < Old Slavic *pir* feast + *og*]

pi·rogue (pə rōg′) *n.* **1** a canoe hollowed from the trunk of a tree; dugout. **2** any canoe. **3** a two-masted, flat-bottomed sailing barge. [< F; probably < Carib. dial.]

pi·rosh·ki *or* **pi·rozh·ki** (pir′əsh kē′) *n.pl.* small pastry turnovers filled usually with a ground beef mixture. [< Russian, sing. *pirozhok,* dim. of *pirog.* See PYROHY.]

pir·ou·ette (pir′ü et′) *n., v.* **-et·ted, -et·ting.** —*n.* a whirling about on one foot or on the toes, as in dancing. —*v.* whirl in this way. [< F *pirouette* spinning top]

pis·ca·to·ri·al (pis′kə tô′rē əl) *adj.* of or having to do with fishermen or fishing. [< L *piscatorius,* ult. < *piscis* fish]

pis·ca·to·ry (pis′kə tô′rē) *adj.* piscatorial.

Pis·ces (pī′sēz, pis′ēz, *or* pis′kēz) *n.* (*used with a singular verb*) **1** *Astronomy.* a northern constellation thought of as having the shape of two fishes with a ribbon connecting their tails. **2** *Astrology.* **a** the twelfth sign of the zodiac. The sun enters Pisces about February 21. See **zodiac** for picture. **b** a person born under this sign. **3** a taxonomic group that includes all fishes. [< L *pisces,* pl. of *piscis* fish]

pis·cine (pis′īn *or* pis′in) *adj.* of, having to do with, or characteristic of a fish or fishes. [< L *piscis* fish + E *-ine*[1]]

pish (pish *or* psh) *interj., n., v.* —*interj.* *or n.* a sound made to express contempt or impatience. —*v.* make such a sound.

pis·mire (pis′mīr) *n. Archaic.* ant. [ME *pissemire* < *pisse* urine (with reference to the formic acid discharged by ants, popularly regarded as urine) + *mire* ant < Scand.; cf. Norwegian *myre*]

piss (pis) *v., n. Vulgar slang.* —*v.* urinate.
piss off, a go away; leave. **b** irritate; annoy.
—*n.* **1** urine. **2** the act or an instance of urinating. [ME < OF *pisser,* prob. < Med. L and originally echoic]

pissed (pist) *adj. Vulgar slang.* drunk.

pis·ta·chi·o (pis tash′ē ō′ *or* pis tä′shē ō) *n., pl.* **-chi·os;** *adj.*
—*n.* **1** a small tree (*Pistacia vera*) of the cashew family that grows in warm climates. **2** the greenish, edible seed of this tree. Pistachios have a flavor similar to almonds. **3** the flavor of the pistachio nut. **4** light, yellowish green.
—*adj.* having the color pistachio. [< Ital. < L *pistachium* < Gk. *pistakion* < *pistakē* the tree < OPersian]

pis·ta·reen (pis′tə rēn′) *n., adj.* —*n.* a former Spanish silver coin used as currency in the West Indies, the United States, and Canada during the eighteenth century. —*adj.* petty; trifling. [apparently < modification of Sp. *peseta* peseta]

pis·til (pis′təl) *n.* the part of a flower that produces seeds, consisting of a base section called the ovary, a thinner middle section, the style, and, at the top, the stigma. A simple pistil, like that of the pea, consists of one carpel; a compound pistil, like that of the iris, consists of several carpels fused together. See **flower** for picture. [< NL *pistillum* < L *pistillum* pestle. Doublet of PESTLE.]
☛ *Hom.* **pistol.**

pis·til·late (pis′tə lit *or* pis′tə lāt′) *adj.* **1** having a pistil or pistils. **2** having a pistil or pistils but no stamens.

pis·tol (pis′təl) *n.* a small, short gun capable of being held and fired with one hand: *A revolver is a kind of pistol.* See **firearm** for picture. [< F *pistole* < G < Czech *pišt′ala*]
☛ *Hom.* **pistil.**

pis·tole (pis tōl′) *n.* **1** a former gold coin of Spain. **2** any of various other old European gold coins of about the same value. [< F *pistole* coin, pistol. See PISTOL.]

pis·ton (pis′tən) *n.* **1** in an engine, pump, etc., a short cylinder, or a flat, round piece of wood or metal, fitting closely inside a tube or hollow cylinder in which it is moved back and forth by the force of exploding vapor or steam. A piston receives or transmits motion by means of the piston rod that is attached to it. See **cylinder** for picture. **2** in a wind instrument, a sliding valve that, when pressed by the fingers, lowers the pitch. [< F < Ital. *pistone* < *pistare* pound, ult. < L *pistus,* pp. of *pinsere* pound]

piston ring a metal ring, split so it can expand, put around a piston to insure a tight fit.

piston rod a rod that moves, or is moved by, a piston.

pit¹ (pit) *n., v.* **pit·ted, pit·ting.** —*n.* **1** a hole or cavity in the ground: *Deep pits are used to trap wild animals. A mine or the shaft of a mine is a pit.* **2** a hollow on the surface of the body: *the armpit.* **3** a little hole or scar in the skin, such as is left by smallpox; pockmark. **4** the bottom of a body cavity: *the pit of the stomach.* **5** an unsuspected danger; a trap or snare. **6** *Brit.* **a** the rear part of the main floor of a theatre, where the seats are cheap. **b** the people who sit there. **7** a usually sunken area in front of the stage of a theatre where the orchestra sits. **8** the part of the floor of an exchange where a particular kind of trading is done: *the wheat pit.* **9** an enclosed place where animals or birds are made to fight each other. **10** an area in a garage, often below floor level, for repairing and servicing automobiles. **11** an area alongside an automobile race track where cars are serviced or repaired during a race. **12 the pit,** hell. —*v.* **1** mark with small pits or scars. **2** set to fight or compete; match: *The man pitted his brains against the strength of the bear.* [OE *pytt*, ult. < L *puteus* well]

pit² (pit) *n., v.* **pit·ted, pit·ting.** —*n.* the hard seed of a cherry, peach, plum, date, etc.; stone. —*v.* remove pits from (fruit). [< Du. *pit* kernel]

pit·a·pat (pit′ə pat′) *adv., n.* —*adv.* with a quick succession of beats or taps. —*n.* the movement or sound of something going pitapat.

pitch¹ (pich) *v., n.* —*v.* **1** throw; fling; hurl; toss: *The men were pitching horseshoes.* **2** pick up and fling (hay, straw, etc.) in a mass with a pitchfork onto a vehicle, into a barn, etc. **3 a** *Baseball.* throw the ball for the batter to hit. **b** *Golf.* loft (a ball) so that it alights with little roll. **4** *Slang.* sell or try to sell (a product, service, etc.) often by high-pressure means. **5** erect or set up: *to pitch a tent, to pitch camp.* **6** take up a position; settle. **7** fix firmly, in or as if in the ground. **8** fall or plunge forward: *The man lost his balance and pitched over the cliff.* **9** of a boat or ship, plunge with the bow rising and then falling: *The ship pitched about in the storm.* **10** set at a certain point, degree, or level. **11** *Music.* determine the key of (a tune, instrument, etc.). **12** slope. **13** *Card games.* **a** indicate one's choice of trump by an opening lead of (a card of the suit chosen). **b** settle (the trump suit) thus.
pitch in, *Informal.* work or begin to work vigorously: *All the boys pitched in to get the job done.*
pitch into, *Informal.* attack.
pitch on or **upon,** choose; select.
—*n.* **1** a throw; fling; hurl; toss. **2** a point; position; degree: *The poor man has reached the lowest pitch of bad fortune.* **3** the highness or lowness of a sound. The pitch of a sound is determined by the frequency of the waves producing the sound; a sound with a low pitch has a lower frequency than one with a high pitch. **4** *Music.* **a** the exact number of vibrations producing a particular tone. **b** a particular standard of pitch: *concert pitch.* **5** height. **6** the act or manner of pitching. **7** that which is pitched. **8** *Slang.* **a** a talk, argument, plan, etc. used to persuade, as in selling, or to promote an idea, product, etc. **b** a television or radio commercial. **9 a** a place of pitching or encamping or taking up a position. **b** a spot in a street or market place where a peddler, street performer, etc. regularly stations himself; stand. **10** the amount of slope. **11** the distance between the successive teeth of a cogwheel. **12** the distance between two things in a machine. **13** the piece of ground on which certain games are played: *a cricket pitch, a horseshoe pitch.* **14** the movement of the longitudinal axis of an aircraft up or down from the horizontal plane. **15** a plunge forward or headlong; lurch. **16** a downward plunging of the fore part of a ship in a rough sea.
make a pitch for, *Informal.* make a persuasive request for; make a bid for.
[ME *picche(n)*]

pitch² (pich) *n., v.* —*n.* **1** a black, sticky substance obtained from the distillation of tar, petroleum, etc., used to waterproof the seams of ships, cover roofs, make pavements, etc. **2** bitumen. **3** resin obtained from various evergreens, often used as medicine. **4** any of various artificial mixtures resembling pitch. —*v.* cover or smear with pitch. [OE *pic* < L *pix, picis*]

pitch–black (pich′blak′) *adj.* very dark or black.

pitch·blende (pich′blend′) *n.* a mineral consisting largely of uranium oxide, occurring in black, pitchlike masses. It is a source of radium, uranium, and actinium. [half-translation of G *Pechblende*]

pitch–dark (pich′därk′) *adj.* very dark; with no light at all: *It was pitch-dark in the room.*

pitched battle **1** a planned battle with lines of troops, etc. arranged beforehand. **2** an intense battle involving close combat.

pitch·er¹ (pich′ər) *n.* **1** a container for holding and pouring liquids, with a lip on one side and a handle on the other; jug. **2** the amount that a pitcher holds. [ME < OF *pichier*]

pitch·er² (pich′ər) *n. Baseball.* the player who throws the ball to the batter. [< *pitch¹*]

hat, āge, fär; let, ēqual, tėrm; it, īce
hot, ōpen, ôrder; oil, out; cup, put, rüle,
above, takən, pencəl, lemən, circəs

ch, child; ng, long; sh, ship
th, thin; ᴛʜ, then; zh, measure

pitch·er·ful (pich′ər ful) *n., pl.* **-fuls.** the quantity sufficient to fill a pitcher.

pitcher plant **1** any of a genus (*Sarracenia*) of plants found in the bogs and peat barrens of northern and eastern Canada and the United States, having leaves modified into pitchers in which insects are trapped, to be digested by the plant by means of an enzyme secreted by the leaves. The species *S. purpurea* is the provincial flower of Newfoundland. **2** designating a family (Sarraceniaceae) of insect-eating plants of North and South America that includes the pitcher plants. **3** any of various other plants, especially of the Old World family Nepentheceae.

pitch·fork (pich′fôrk′) *n., v.* —*n.* a large fork with a long handle and two or three slightly curved prongs, used for lifting and throwing hay or straw. —*v.* lift and throw with a pitchfork.

pitch·man (pich′man′) *n., pl.* **-men. 1** *Informal.* a man who sells articles such as small toys on the street or at carnivals. **2** *Slang.* a high-pressure promoter or salesman: *a television pitchman.*

pitch pine any of various pines from which pitch or turpentine is obtained, especially a North American species (*Pinus rigida*) having yellowish-green needles, reddish-brown bark, and relatively hard, heavy, resinous wood.

pitch pipe a small musical pipe having one or more fixed tones, used to give the desired musical pitch for singing or for tuning an instrument.

pitch·y (pich′ē) *adj.* **pitch·i·er, pitch·i·est. 1** full of pitch. **2** like pitch; sticky. **3** black.

pit·e·ous (pit′ē əs) *adj.* to be pitied; moving the heart; deserving pity. [ME < OF *pitos* < Med.L *pietosus* pitiful < L *pietas* pity; influenced in form by ME *pite* pity] —**pit′e·ous·ly,** *adv.* —**pit′e·ous·ness,** *n.*
☛ *Syn.* See note at **pitiful.**

pit·fall (pit′fol′ *or* -fôl′) *n.* **1** a hidden pit to catch animals in. **2** any trap or hidden danger.

pith (pith) *n.* **1** the central, spongy tissue in the stems of certain plants. **2** a similar tissue occurring in other parts of plants, as that lining the skin of an orange. **3** the soft inner substance of a bone, feather, etc. **4** an important or essential part: *the pith of a speech.* **5** strength; energy. [OE *pitha*]

pit·head (pit′hed′) *n.* **1** the top of a mine shaft. **2** the area surrounding this, with its buildings, etc.

Pith·e·can·thro·pus (pith′ə kan thrō′pəs *or* pith′ə kan′thrə pəs) *n., pl.* **-pi** (-pī *or* -pē). a type of extinct, prehistoric ape man, whose existence is assumed from remains found in Java in 1891 and 1892. [< NL < Gk. *pithēkos* ape + *anthrōpos* man]

pith helmet a sun hat shaped like a helmet, originally made from the dried pith of Bengal spongewood.

pith·y (pith′ē) *adj.* **pith·i·er, pith·i·est. 1** full of substance, meaning, force, or vigor: *pithy phrases, a pithy speaker.* **2** of or like pith. **3** having much pith: *a pithy orange.* —**pith′i·ly,** *adv.* —**pith′i·ness,** *n.*

pit·i·a·ble (pit′ē ə bəl) *adj.* **1** to be pitied; moving the heart; deserving pity. **2** deserving contempt; mean; to be scorned. —**pit′i·a·ble·ness,** *n.* —**pit′i·a·bly,** *adv.*
☛ *Syn.* **1.** See note at **pitiful.**

pit·i·ful (pit′ē fəl) *adj.* **1** to be pitied; arousing pity: *The deserted children were a pitiful sight.* **2** deserving contempt; mean; to be scorned: *a pitiful performance.* **3** *Archaic.* feeling or showing pity; compassionate. —**pit′i·ful·ly,** *adv.*
☛ *Syn.* **1. Pitiful, piteous, pitiable** = arousing pity or to be pitied. **Pitiful** emphasizes the effect on others, that of arousing pity, made by someone or something felt to be touching or pathetic: *The deserted children were pitiful.* **Piteous** emphasizes the quality in the thing itself that makes it appeal for pity and move the heart: *Their sad faces were piteous.* **Pitiable** emphasizes the arousing of sorrow or regret for what deserves or needs to be pitied: *Their bodies and clothes were in a pitiable condition.*

pit·i·less (pit′ē lis) *adj.* showing no pity or mercy: *a pitiless tyrant, a pitiless act.* —**pit′i·less·ly,** *adv.* —**pit′i·less·ness,** *n.*
☛ *Syn.* See note at **cruel.**

pi·ton (pē′ton *or* pi ton′; *French*, pē tôɴ′) *n.* **1** an iron spike with a ring at one end, used in mountain climbing. It can be driven into a crack in rock or ice and used to secure a rope or as a step. **2** a sharply pointed mountain or rock peak. [< F *piton* point, peak]

pit·tance (pit′əns) *n.* **1** a small allowance or wage. **2** a small amount or share. [ME < OF *pitance*, ult. < L *pietas* piety]

pit·ter–pat·ter (pit′ər pat′ər) *n., adv.* —*n.* a rapid succession of light beats or taps, as of rain. —*adv.* with a rapid succession of beats or taps.

pi·tu·i·tar·y (pə tyü′ə ter′ē *or* pə tü′ə ter′ē) *adj., n.* —*adj.* of or having to do with the pituitary gland. —*n.* **1** the pituitary gland. **2** medicine made from an extract of this gland. [< L *pituitarius* < *pituita* phlegm]

pituitary body pituitary gland.

pituitary gland a small, oval endocrine gland situated at the base of the brain. It secretes hormones that promote growth, stimulate other glands, and regulate many other basic bodily functions. See **brain** for picture.

pit viper any of a family (Crotalidae) of New World poisonous snakes that includes the rattlesnakes and the water moccasin, similar to the Old World vipers but having a heat-sensitive pit on each side of the head, by means of which they can sense the presence of warm-blooded animals. Some authorities classify pit vipers and vipers as constituting subfamilies within the single family Viperidae.

pit·y (pit′ē) *n., pl.* **pit·ies**; *v.* **pit·ied, pit·y·ing.** —*n.* **1** sympathy; sorrow for another's suffering or distress; a feeling for the sorrows of others. **2** a cause for pity or regret; something to be sorry for: *It is a pity to be kept in the house in good weather.*
have or take pity on, show pity for.
—*v.* feel pity for. [ME < OF *pite* < L *pietas.* Doublet of PIETY.]
—**pit′y·ing·ly,** *adv.*
☛ *Syn. n.* **1. Pity, compassion, sympathy** = a feeling for the sorrows or suffering of others. **Pity** suggests a feeling of sorrow for someone who is suffering or in sorrow or distress, and who is, often, felt to be weak or unfortunate: *Nobody wants pity from his friends.* **Compassion** adds the idea of tenderness, a sharing and understanding of feelings, and a strong desire to help or protect: *He had compassion for the sobbing child.* **Sympathy** emphasizes feeling with another in his sorrow: *He expects sympathy from his brother.*

piv·ot (piv′ət) *n., v.* —*n.* **1** a shaft, pin, or point on which something turns. **2** a person, thing, etc. serving as a central point or having a central role or function. **3** *Hockey.* the centre player of a forward line.
—*v.* **1** mount on, attach by, or provide with a pivot. **2** turn on a pivot or something like a pivot: *to pivot on one's heel.* [< F]

piv·ot·al (piv′ə təl) *adj.* of, having to do with, or serving as a pivot; being that on which something turns, hinges, or depends; very important.

pix·ie or **pix·y** (pik′sē) *n., pl.* **pix·ies.** a fairy or elf. [origin uncertain]

pix·i·lat·ed (pik′sə lā′təd) *adj.* whimsical, eccentric, or crazy. [< *pixie-led* + *-ated.* 20c.] —**pix′i·la′tion,** *n.*

pizza (pēt′sə) *n.* an open pie, usually made of a layer of dough covered with a savory mixture of tomatoes, cheese, olives, etc. and baked. [< Ital.]

pizza pie pizza.

piz·zazz (pə zaz′) *n. Slang.* glamorous vitality or sparkle; dash and style: *a political leader with pizzazz, accessories to add pizzazz to a basic suit.*

piz·ze·ri·a (pēt′sə rē′ə) *n.* a place where pizzas are made and sold, for taking out or eating on the premises.

piz·zi·ca·to (pit′sə kä′tō) *adj., adv., n., pl.* **-ti** (-tē). *Music.* —*adj.* played by plucking the strings of a musical instrument with the finger instead of using the bow.
—*adv.* in a pizzicato manner.
—*n.* a note or passage so played. [< Ital. *pizzicato* picked]

pk. **1** peck. **2** peak. **3** park. **4** pack.

PK psychokinesis.

pkg. package.

pl. **1** plural. **2** place. **3** plate.

pla·ca·ble (plak′ə bəl *or* plā′kə bəl) *adj.* forgiving; easily quieted; mild. [ME < OF < L *placabilis* < *placare* placate]
—**pla′ca·ble·ness,** *n.* —**pla′ca·bly,** *adv.*

plac·ard (*n.* plak′ärd; *v.* plə kärd′ *or* plak′ärd) *n., v.* —*n.* a notice to be posted in a public place; poster.
—*v.* **1** put placards on or in: *The circus placarded the city with advertisements.* **2** give notice of with placards. **3** post as a placard. [< F *placard* < *plaque* plaque]

pla·cate (plak′āt, plā′kāt, *or* plə kāt′) *v.* **-cat·ed, -cat·ing.** soothe or satisfy the anger of; make peaceful: *to placate a person one has offended.* [< L *placare*] —**pla′cat·er,** *n.* —**pla′cat·ing·ly,** *adv.*

place (plās) *n., v.* **placed, plac·ing.** —*n.* **1** a particular part of space, of a definite or indefinite size: *This would be a good place for a picnic.* **2** a city, town, village, district, etc. **3** a building or spot used for a certain purpose. A church is a place of worship. A store or office is a place of business. **4** a house or dwelling: *We all went to my place for supper after skating. They have a beautiful place in the country.* **5** a part or spot in something: *There's a sore place on my leg where I bumped the table.* **6** a particular page or other point in a book or other writing: *to mark one's place.* **7** reasonable ground or occasion: *There was no place for such behavior.* **8** the proper, original, or usual position or location: *The book is back in its place on the shelf.* **9** a proper, suitable, or designated rank or position: *He has found his place in teaching. Somebody should put her in her place.* **10** a position in time: *The performance went too slowly in several places.* **11** a space or seat for a person: *Keep a place for me if you get there first.* **12** a post or office: *In his place as corresponding secretary he is responsible for sending out the notices.* **13** duty; business: *It is not my place to find fault.* **14** a step or point in order of proceeding: *In the first place, the room is too small; in the second place, it was too dirty.* **15** *Mathematics.* the position of a figure in a number or series: *in the third decimal place.* **16** a position among the leaders at the finish of a race or competition: *John won first place.* **17** the second position at the end of a horse race. **18** a short street or court. **19** an open space or square in a city, town, etc.
give place, a make room. **b** yield; give in: *His anger gave place to remorse.*
go places, *Slang.* advance rapidly toward success; achieve success.
in place, a on or in the proper, original, or usual place: *dishes in place on the shelf, members of the chorus in place on the stage.* **b** fitting, appropriate, or timely.
in place of, instead of: *You can use water in place of milk in this recipe.*
know (one's) **place,** act according to one's position in life.
out of place, a not in the proper or usual place. **b** inappropriate or ill-timed.
take place, happen; occur.
—*v.* **1** put (in a spot, position, condition, or relation). **2** put in the proper order or position; arrange; dispose. **3** give the place, position, or condition of; identify: *I remember his name, but I cannot place him.* **4** determine the date of; assign to an age, etc. **5** appoint (a person) to a post or office; find a situation, etc. for. **6** attribute or ascribe. **7** entrust to an appropriate person, firm, etc. for action, treatment, disposal, etc. **8** *Sports.* **a** be among the leaders at the finish of a race or competition: *He failed to place in the first race and was eliminated.* **b** finish second in a race or competition, especially in a horse race. Compare **win** (def. 1) and **show** (def. 13b). **9** produce (sounds of song or speech) with emphasis upon resonance assisted by the body organs involved. [ME < OF < VL *plattia* < L < Gk. *plateia* (*hodos*) broad (way) < *platys* broad. Doublet of PLAZA and PIAZZA.]
☛ *Hom.* **plaice.**
☛ *Syn. v.* **1.** See note at **put.**

pla·ce·bo (plə sē′bō) *n., pl.* **-bos** or **-boes. 1** a pill, etc. containing no active substance given to humor or satisfy a patient, or to serve as a control in an experiment to test a new drug. **2** something said only to flatter or mollify. **3** *Roman Catholic Church.* the vespers of the office for the dead. [< L *placebo* I shall please, the opening word of the church service]

place card a small card with a person's name on it, to indicate where he is to sit at the table.

place holder *Mathematics.* the symbol zero when used to indicate the place value of another digit. In the number 40, the 0 is a place holder indicating that the 4 is in the tens place.

place in the sun a favorable position; as favorable a position as any occupied by others.

place mat a small, usually oblong, or oval mat of cloth, paper, plastic, etc. that serves as an individual table cover for a person at a meal.

place·ment (plās′mənt) *n.* **1** placing or being placed; location; arrangement. **2** the finding of work or a job for a person. **3** *Football.* **a** a placing of the ball on the ground for a placement kick. **b** a placement kick.

placement kick *Football.* a kick given to a ball after it has been placed on the ground.

place name a name of a place, city, area, country, etc.; any geographical name. Athens, Asia, Niagara Falls, Arctic Ocean are place names.

pla·cen·ta (plə sen′tə) *n., pl.* **-tae** (-tē *or* -tī) or **-tas. 1** the organ by which the fetus is attached to the wall of the womb and nourished. **2** the part of the ovary of flowering plants that bears the ovules. [< NL < L *placenta* flat cake < Gk. *plakounta,* accus. < *plax, plakos* flat surface]

pla·cen·tal (plə sen′təl) *adj.* **1** of or having to do with the placenta. **2** having a placenta.

plac·er¹ (plās′ər) *n.* a person or thing that places.

plac·er² (plas′ər) *n.* a deposit of sand or gravel containing gold or other valuable minerals in particles that can be washed out. [< Am.Sp. *placer* sandbank. Akin to PLAZA.]

placer mining the process of washing loose sand or gravel for gold or other minerals: *Placer mining was a common practice in the Klondike.*

place setting the dishes and cutlery required to set one person's place at a table.

plac·id (plas′id) *adj.* calm; peaceful; quiet: *a placid lake.* [< L *placidus* < *placere* please] —**plac′id·ly,** *adv.* —**plac′id·ness,** *n.*
☛ *Syn.* See note at **peaceful.**

pla·cid·i·ty (plə sid′ə tē) *n.* calmness; peace.

plack·et (plak′it) *n.* an opening or slit at the top of a skirt, the side or back of a dress, etc. to make it easy to put on and take off. [? var. of *placard*]

pla·gia·rism (plā′jə riz′əm) *n.* **1** the act of plagiarizing. **2** an idea, expression, plot, etc. taken from another and used as one's own. [< L *plagiarius* kidnapper, ult. < *plaga* net]

pla·gia·rist (plā′jə rist) *n.* a person who plagiarizes.

pla·gia·rize (plā′jə rīz′) *v.* **-rized, -riz·ing.** take and use as one's own (the thoughts, writings, inventions, etc. of another); especially, to take and use a passage, plot, etc. from the work of another writer. —**pla′gia·riz′er,** *n.*

plague (plāg) *n., v.* **plagued, pla·guing.** —*n.* **1** a very dangerous disease that spreads rapidly and often causes death. It occurs in several forms, one of which is bubonic plague. The plague is common in Asia and has several times swept through Europe. **2** any epidemic disease; pestilence. **3** a punishment thought to be sent from God. **4** anything or anyone that torments, vexes, annoys, troubles, offends, or is disagreeable: *My hay fever is a plague this year.*
—*v.* **1** cause to suffer from a disease or calamity. **2** vex; annoy; bother: *Stop plaguing me for money.* [ME < L *plaga* blow, pestilence < dial. Gk. *plaga* blow]
☛ *Syn. v.* **2.** See note at **tease.**

pla·guey (plā′gē) See **plaguy.**

pla·guy (plā′gē) *adj. Informal.* troublesome; annoying.

plaice (plās) *n., pl.* **plaice** or **plaic·es. 1** a red and brown European flounder (*Pleuronectes platessa*) that is a commercially important food fish. **2** a reddish or brownish flat fish (*Hippoglossoides platessoides*) of the same family (Pleuronectidae), found in the western North Atlantic. [ME < OF < LL *platessa* flatfish < Gk. *platys* flat]
☛ *Hom.* **place.**

plaid (plad) *n.* **1** a pattern consisting of a repeated design of broad and narrow unevenly spaced stripes crossing each other at right angles. **2** such a pattern as the distinctive identification of a Scottish clan or other group; tartan. **3** cloth woven or printed with a plaid. **4** (*adj.*) having such a pattern: *a plaid dress.* **5** an oblong length of woollen cloth, usually woven with a tartan design, worn over the left shoulder as part of the traditional dress of the Scottish Highlanders. See **kilt** for picture. [< Scots Gaelic *plaide*]

plaid·ed (plad′id) *adj.* **1** made of plaid; having a plaid pattern. **2** wearing a plaid.

plain¹ (plān) *adj., adv., n.* —*adj.* **1** easy to see, hear, or understand; clear: *The meaning is plain.* **2** that is clearly what the name expresses; unmistakable; downright; absolute: *plain foolishness.* **3** not intricate; uncomplicated: *plain sewing.* **4** frank and honest; straightforward: *plain speech. She believes in plain dealing.* **5** without ornament or decoration; simple: *a plain dress.* **6** without figured pattern, varied weave, or variegated color: *a plain-blue fabric.* **7** not rich or highly seasoned: *plain food.* **8** simple or ordinary in manner: *They're plain people.* **9** not good-looking: *a plain face.* **10** *Archaic.* level; plane.
—*adv.* in a plain manner, clearly: *Speak it plain.*
—*n.* Often, **plains,** *pl.* a large, more or less flat and treeless stretch of land: *Buffalo used to roam the North American plains.* [ME < OF < L *planus* flat. Doublet of PIANO², PLAN.] —**plain′ly,** *adv.* —**plain′ness,** *n.*
☛ *Hom.* **plane.**

plain² (plān) *v. Archaic or dialect.* complain. [ME < OF, ult. < L *plangere* lament]
☛ *Hom.* **plane.**

plain–clothes (plān′klōz′ or -klōᵗʜz′) *adj.* wearing ordinary clothes, not a uniform, when on duty, as some police detectives.

plain sailing 1 sailing in a straightforward course. **2** a clear, simple course of action; easy, unobstructed progress: *We had some problems at first but after that it was plain sailing.*

Plains Cree one of the two main groups of the Cree tribe of North American Indians. The Plains Cree migrated to the prairies from the eastern woodlands.

plains·man (plānz′mən) *n., pl.* **-men.** an inhabitant of the plains.

hat, āge, fär; let, ēqual, tėrm; it, īce
hot, ōpen, ôrder; oil, out; cup, put, rüle,
əbove, takən, pencəl, lemən, circəs
ch, child; ng, long; sh, ship
th, thin; ᴛʜ, then; zh, measure

Plains of A·bra·ham (ā′brə ham′) a plain outside and just west of Quebec City, the site of the battle of 1759 that gave the British supremacy in North America.

plain·song (plān′song′) *n.* vocal music used in the Christian church from very early times, sung in unison and unaccompanied, employing a limited musical scale and free rhythm.

plain–spo·ken (plān′spō′kən) *adj.* plain or frank in speech.

plaint (plānt) *n.* **1** *Archaic or poetic.* lamentation. **2** *Law.* accusation or complaint. [ME < OF < L *planctus* lamentation < *plangere* lament]

plain·tiff (plān′tif) *n.* a person who begins a lawsuit. [ME < OF *plaintif* complaining. See PLAINTIVE.]

plain·tive (plān′tiv) *adj.* mournful; sad. [ME < OF *plaintif*, ult. < L *planctus* complaint] —**plain′tive·ly,** *adv.* —**plain′tive·ness,** *n.*

plais·ter (plās′tər) *n. or v. Obs.* plaster.

plait (plāt *or* plat) *n. or v.* **1** braid. **2** *Rare.* pleat. [ME < OF *pleit*, ult. < L *plicare* fold]

plan (plan) *n., v.* **planned, plan·ning.** —*n.* **1** a way of making or doing something that has been worked out beforehand; a scheme or method for achieving an end: *a plan for attracting more tourists to the city.* **2** goal; aim: *Her plan was to have the business firmly established by the end of the year.* **3** a drawing or diagram made on a flat surface, especially one showing how a floor of a building is arranged and the relative size of all its rooms, etc. **4** a large-scale, detailed map of a small area such as a town or district.
—*v.* **1** think out beforehand how (something) is to be made or done; design, scheme, or devise: *to plan a program.* **2** make plans. **3** have in mind as a purpose; intend: *We are planning to take a long vacation this year.* **4** make a drawing or diagram of. [< F *plan,* literally, a plane < L *planus;* with reference to a sketch on a flat surface. Doublet of PLAIN¹, PIANO².]
☛ *Syn. n.* **1. Plan, design, project** = a proposed way of doing or making something. **Plan** is the general word meaning "an arrangement of parts or a method of procedure worked out beforehand": *He has a plan for increasing production.* **Design** emphasizes careful arrangement of details according to the purpose, intention, or end in view: *They have a design for a rich, full life.* **Project** applies to a plan proposed for trial or experiment, often worked out on a grand scale and sometimes impracticable: *He introduced a project for slum clearance.*

pla·nar·i·an (plə ner′ē ən) *n.* any of an order (Tricladida) of free-living, mainly aquatic flatworms having three-branching intestines, a soft, flat body, and the power of growing again when cut apart. [< NL *Planaria* < L *planus* level + E *-an*]

plan·chette (plan shet′) *n.* **1** a small triangular or heart-shaped board supported on casters at two points and having a vertical pencil at the third. It is believed to produce automatic writing when a person rests his fingers lightly on the board. **2** a similar board without a pencil, such as that used with a Ouija board. [< F *planchette,* dim. of *planche* plank]

plane¹ (plān) *n., adj., v.* **planed, plan·ing.** —*n.* **1** any flat or level surface. **2** a level of development, thought, conduct, achievement, etc.: *the intellectual plane. He keeps his work on a high plane.* **3** a thin, flat or curved supporting surface of an airplane. **4** airplane. **5** *Geometry.* a surface such that if any two points on it are joined by a straight line, the line will be contained wholly in the surface.
—*adj.* **1** flat; level. **2** being wholly in a plane: *Rectangles and circles are plane figures.* **3** of or having to do with such figures: *plane geometry.*
—*v.* **1** glide as an airplane does. **2** of a speedboat, etc., rise slightly out of the water while moving; skim over the water. **3** travel by airplane. [< L *planum* level place]

A carpenter's plane. The blade is set crosswise, projecting at a set angle through a slot in the bottom plate. The blade can be raised or lowered to shave more or less wood at each stroke.

plane² (plān) *n., v.* **planed, plan·ing.** —*n.* carpenter's tool with a blade for smoothing or shaping wood. —*v.* **1** make smooth or level by means of a plane; use a plane on. **2** remove with a plane. [< F *plane,* ult. < LL *plana*]

plane³ (plān) *n.* plane tree.

plane angle an angle formed by two straight lines lying on the same plane.

plane geometry a branch of geometry dealing with plane figures.

plane·load (plān′lōd′) *n.* a load that fills an airplane: *a planeload of supplies.*

plan·er (plān′ər) *n.* a person or thing that planes, especially a machine for planing wood or for finishing flat surfaces on metal.

plan·et (plan′it) *n.* 1 one of the heavenly bodies (except comets and meteors) that move around the sun in regular paths. Mercury, Venus, the Earth, Mars, Jupiter, Saturn, Uranus, Neptune, and Pluto are planets. 2 *Astrology.* a heavenly body, including the sun and the moon, thought to influence people's lives. [< LL < Gk. *planētēs* < *planaesthai* wander]

plan·e·tar·i·um (plan′ə ter′ē əm) *n., pl.* **-i·a** (-ē ə) **or -i·ums.** 1 an apparatus that shows the movements of the sun, moon, planets, and stars by projecting lights on the inside of a dome. 2 a room or building with such an apparatus. [< NL]

plan·e·tar·y (plan′ə ter′ē) *adj.* 1 of, having to do with, or being a planet: *planetary influence, planetary motion.* 2 wandering; erratic. 3 of, having to do with, or belonging to the earth; terrestrial. 4 of or designating a type of gear train used for automobile transmissions.

plan·e·tes·i·mal (plan′ə tes′ə məl) *adj.* of or having to do with minute bodies in space that, according to a certain hypothesis, move in planetary orbits and gradually unite to form the planets of a given planetary system. [< *planet*, modelled on *infinitesimal*]

plan·et·oid (plan′ə toid′) *n.* a minor planet; asteroid.

plane–tree or **plane tree** (plān′trē′) *n.* any of a genus (*Platanus*) making up a family (Platanaceae) of trees native to North America, Europe, and Asia, having large, broad, lobed leaves, spreading branches, and small fruits hanging in ball-shaped clusters from long stems; sycamore. [ME < OF < L < Gk. *platanos* < *platys* broad]

plank (plangk) *n., v.* —*n.* 1 a long, flat piece of sawed timber thicker than a board. 2 an item or feature of the platform of a political party, etc. 3 a flat timber forming part of the outer side of a ship's hull. 4 anything that supports or saves in time of need (with allusion to the use of a plank to save a ship-wrecked man from drowning).
walk the plank, be forced to walk off a plank extending from a ship's side over the water. Pirates used to make their prisoners do this.
—*v.* 1 cover or furnish with planks. 2 cook and serve on a board. Steak is sometimes planked. 3 *Informal.* put or set with force (*used with* **down**): *He planked down the package.* 4 *Informal.* pay at once; pay on the spot (*used with* **down** *or* **out**): *She planked her money down.* [ME < ONF < L *planca*]

plank·ing (plangk′ing) *n.* 1 the act of laying or covering with planks. 2 a quantity of planks together: *They bought planking for the floor of the shed.*

plank·ter (plangk′tər) *n.* an individual planktonic organism.

plank·ton (plangk′tən) *n.* the mass of very small or microscopic animal or plant life that floats or drifts near the surface of bodies of salt and fresh water, providing food for fish and other water animals. Plankton contains algea, protozoans, fish in a larval stage, etc. —**plank·ton′ic**, *adj.* [< F < Gk. *plankton*, neut., wandering, verbal adj. to *plazesthai* wander]

plan·ner (plan′ər) *n.* a person who plans, especially one whose job is planning things. Most cities have a city planner who looks after the arrangement of parks, residential and business areas, etc. of the city.

pla·no–con·cave (plā′nō kon′kāv) *adj.* flat on one side and concave on the other. See **concave** for picture. [< L *planus* flat + E *concave*]

pla·no–con·vex (plā′nō kon′veks) *adj.* flat on one side and convex on the other. See **convex** for picture. [< L *planus* flat + E *convex*]

plant (plant) *n., v.* —*n.* 1 any living thing that is not an animal. Trees, shrubs, herbs, fungi, algae, etc. are plants. 2 a living thing that has leaves, roots, and a soft stem, and is small in contrast with a tree or shrub. 3 a young tree, plant, vine, or herb ready to be planted: *The farmer set out 100 cabbage plants.* 4 the buildings, machinery, etc. used in manufacturing: *There is an aluminum plant in Kingston.* 5 the workmen employed at a plant: *The whole plant is on strike.* 6 the complete apparatus used for a specific mechanical operation or process: *the heating plant on a ship.* 7 buildings, equipment, etc. for any purpose: *a college plant.* 8 *Slang.* a scheme

to trap, trick, mislead, or deceive. 9 *Informal.* a person or thing placed or devised so as to trap, lure, or deceive: *She claimed that the money found in her room was a plant.*
—*v.* 1 put or set in the ground to grow. 2 provide with seed or plants; stock; put seed in: *We planted our garden last weekend.* 3 deposit (young fish, spawn, oysters) in a river, lake, etc. 4 set firmly; put; place: *He planted his feet firmly apart and pulled hard.* 5 post; station: *to plant guards at an entrance.* 6 establish or set up (a colony, city, etc.). 7 implant (principles, doctrines, etc.). 8 *Slang.* deliver (a blow, etc.) with a definite aim. 9 *Informal.* place (a person or thing) so as to trap, lure, or deceive: *The evidence was planted.* 10 *Slang.* conceal. [OE *plante* < L *planta* sprout]

Plan·tag·e·net (plan taj′ə net) *n.* a member of the royal family that ruled England from 1154 to 1485. The English kings from Henry II through Richard III were Plantagenets.

plan·tain¹ (plan′tən) *n.* 1 a tree-like plant (*Musa paradisiaca*) closely related to the banana, yielding an edible fruit similar to the common banana. 2 the fruit of this plant, larger and starchier than a banana. Plantains are not eaten raw; they are boiled or fried and also dried and ground up into meal or flour. [< Sp. *plántano*]

plan·tain² (plan′tən) *n.* any of a genus (*Plantago*) of plants having spikes of tiny, greenish flowers and usually broad leaves that spread out from the base of the stem. Several species of plantain are common Canadian weeds. [ME < OF < L *plantago, -ginis* < *planta* sole of the foot; from its flat leaves]

plantain lily any of several plants (genus *Hosta*) of the lily family native to Asia but widely cultivated as garden plants, having large, often wavy and variegated leaves and spikes of white, lilac, or blue flowers.

plan·tar (plan′tər) *adj.* of, having to do with, or on the sole of the foot: *plantar warts.*

plan·ta·tion (plan tā′shən) *n.* 1 a large farm or estate, especially in a tropical or semitropical country, on which cotton, tobacco, sugar, etc. are grown. The work on a plantation is done by laborers who live there. 2 a large group of trees or other plants that have been planted. 3 a colony; settlement: *Plantations were established in Newfoundland in the early 1600's.* [< L *plantatio, -onis* a planting < *planta* sprout]

plant·er (plan′tər) *n.* 1 a person who owns or runs a plantation: *a cotton planter.* 2 a machine for planting. 3 a person who plants. 4 an enclosure in which flowers are planted alongside of a building. 5 a box, stand, or pot used for growing plants indoors, on a patio or balcony, etc. 6 *Cdn.* in Newfoundland, a small trader; a person who hires others to fish for him, advancing their supplies and taking a share of the catch. 7 an early settler; colonist.

plan·ti·grade (plan′tə grād′) *adj.* walking on the whole sole of the foot. A bear is a plantigrade animal. [< L *planta* sole + *gradi* walk]

plant kingdom one of the three basic groups into which all things found in nature are divided. The plant kingdom includes all living and extinct plants, from the tiniest algae to the biggest trees. Compare **animal kingdom** and **mineral kingdom.**

plant louse aphid.

plaque (plak) *n.* 1 an ornamental, inscribed tablet of metal, porcelain, etc. 2 a flat, thin ornament or badge. 3 a thin film of saliva, mucus, etc., together with bacteria, that forms on the teeth. Plaque hardens into calculus, or tartar, if not removed. 4 an abnormal patch on the body, such as a spot of psoriasis. 5 a clear space in a bacterial culture, resulting from the localized destruction of cells by a virus. 6 an area marked by destruction or loss of the myelin sheath normally enveloping the nerve fibres, characteristic of multiple sclerosis. [< F < Du. *plak* flat board]

plash (plash) *v. or n.* splash.

plasm (plaz′əm) *n.* plasma.

plas·ma (plaz′mə) *n.* 1 the liquid part of blood or lymph, as distinguished from the corpuscles. 2 the watery part of milk, as distinguished from the globules of fat. 3 *Physics.* a highly ionized gas, consisting of almost equal numbers of free electrons and positive ions. 4 protoplasm. 5 a green, faintly translucent variety of quartz. [< LL < Gk. *plasma* something formed or moulded < *plassein* mould]

plas·ter (plas′tər) *n., v.* —*n.* 1 a soft mixture of lime, sand, and water that hardens in drying, used for covering walls or ceilings. 2 plaster of Paris. 3 a medicated or protective dressing consisting of a pastelike substance spread on cloth, etc., that will stick to the body and protect cuts, relieve pain, etc.
—*v.* 1 cover (walls, ceilings, etc.) with plaster. 2 spread with anything thickly: *My shoes were plastered with mud.* 3 make smooth and flat: *He plastered his wet hair down.* 4 apply a plaster on. 5 apply like a plaster. [OE < Med.L *plastrum* < L *emplastrum* < Gk. *emplastron* < *en-* on + *plassein* mould] —**plas′ter·like′**, *adj.*

plas·ter·board (plas′tər bôrd′) *n.* a relatively thin board consisting of a layer of plaster between layers of pressed felt

hat, āge, fär; let, ēqual, tėrm; it, īce
hot, ōpen, ôrder; oil, out; cup, pu̇t, rüle,
əbove, takən, pencəl, lemən, circəs
ch, child; ng, long; sh, ship
th, thin; ᴛʜ, then; zh, measure

covered with paper, made in large sheets and used for walls and partitions.

plaster cast 1 a rigid casing made of layers of gauze soaked in wet plaster of Paris and formed around an arm or other part of the body to keep a broken bone in place. 2 a sculptor's model of a statue made of plaster of Paris.

plas·tered (plas′tərd) *adj. Slang.* drunk; intoxicated.

plas·ter·er (plas′tər ər) *n.* a person who plasters walls, etc.

plas·ter·ing (plas′tər ing) *n.* a covering of plaster on walls, etc.

plaster of Paris (par′is *or* per′is) a mixture of powdered gypsum and water, which hardens quickly and is used for making moulds, cheap statuary, casts, etc.

plas·tic (plas′tik) *n., adj.* —*n.* **1** any of various materials that harden and retain their shape after being moulded or shaped when subjected to heat, pressure, etc. Glass, celluloid, Bakelite, vulcanite, and nylon are all plastics. **2** such a substance produced in a laboratory from raw materials such as petroleum, urea, phenol, or glycerin; a synthetic plastic. Plastics may be rigid or soft and are often used in place of natural substances such as leather, wood, or metal. Some of the most widely used plastics are polyethylene, vinyl, styrene, and polyester. **3 plastics,** the branch of chemistry that deals with the production and use of plastics (*used with a singular verb*): *John is studying plastics.*
—*adj.* **1** made of synthetic plastic: *plastic cups.* **2** moulding or giving shape to material. **3** concerned with moulding or modelling: *Sculpture is a plastic art.* **4** easily moulded or shaped: *Clay, wax, and plaster are plastic substances.* **5** easily influenced; impressionable. **6** artificial or phoney; not natural or real: *a plastic hero, plastic food.* [< L *plasticus* < Gk. *plastikos,* ult. < *plassein* form, shape]

Plas·ti·cine (plas′ti sēn′) *n. Trademark.* an oil-base modelling paste made in several different colors, that remains soft and malleable. Plasticine is used especially by children.

plas·tic·i·ty (plas tis′ə tē) *n.* the quality or state of being plastic; especially, the capacity for being moulded.

plas·ti·cize (plas′tə sīz′) *v.* **1** make or become plastic. **2** treat with a plastic: *a plasticized fabric for raincoats.*

plastic surgeon a medical doctor who is a specialist in plastic surgery.

plastic surgery a branch of surgery concerned with repairing or restoring parts of the body that are deformed or have been lost or injured, or with improving the outward appearance, especially of the face.

plas·tron (plas′trən) *n.* **1** a metal breastplate worn under a coat of mail. **2** a leather guard worn over the chest of a fencer. **3** an ornamental, detachable front of a woman's bodice. **4** the ventral part of the shell of a turtle or tortoise. [< F < Ital. *piastrone* < *piastra* plate of metal < Med.L *plastrum* plaster. See PLASTER.]

plat[1] (plat) *n., v.* **plat·ted, plat·ting.** —*n.* **1** a map; chart; plan. **2** a small piece of ground; plot. —*v.* map; chart; plan. [ME < OF < VL < Gk. *platys* broad, flat; meaning of def. 2 from *plot*]
☛ *Hom.* **plait** (plat).

plat[2] (plat) *n., v.* **plat·ted, plat·ting.** braid; plait. [var. of *plait*]
☛ *Hom.* **plait** (plat).

plate (plāt) *n., v.* **plat·ed, plat·ing.** —*n.* **1** a dish, usually round, that is almost flat: *a dinner plate.* **2** plateful: *a plate of meat and potatoes.* **3** a part of a meal, served on or in a separate dish; course: *I ordered the cold plate.* **4** the dishes and food served to one person at a meal: *The dinner will cost $10 a plate.* **5** a tray or other container similar to a plate: *A plate is passed in church to receive the collection.* **6** dishes or containers made of or covered with a thin layer of silver or gold: *The family plate included an antique silver pitcher.* **7** a thin, flat sheet or piece of metal: *The warship was covered with steel plates.* **8** armor made of such pieces of metal. **9** a platelike part, organ, or structure. Some animals and fishes have a covering of horny or bony plates. **10** a thin, flat piece of metal, plastic, etc. on which something is engraved. Plates are used for printing pictures. **11** something printed from such a piece of metal. **12** a metal copy of a page of type. **13** any full-page inserted illustration forming part of a book. **14** a thin sheet of glass coated with chemicals that are sensitive to light. Plates are sometimes used in taking photographs. **15** *Geology.* one of the enormous segments of which the crust of the earth appears to be composed, that float and move on the softer mantle below. **16** *Baseball.* **a** the place where the batter stands to hit a pitched ball; home base. **b** the place where the pitcher stands; slab. **17** *Dentistry.* the part of a set of false teeth that fits to the gums, and in which the teeth are fixed: *a partial plate, an upper plate.* **18** a thin cut of beef from the lower end of the ribs. See **beef** for picture. **19** the anode of an electron tube, especially when flat. **20** a piece of timber laid horizontally to support rafters or studs. **21** a gold or silver cup or other prize given to the winner of a race, especially a horse race. **22** a horse race, etc. in which the prize is (or was originally) such an object.
—*v.* **1** cover with a thin layer of silver, gold, or other metal. **2** cover with metal plates for protection. **3** make a plate from (type) for printing. [ME < OF *plate,* ult. < VL *plattus* flat < Gk. *platys*]
☛ *Hom.* **plait** (plāt).

pla·teau (pla tō′) *n., pl.* **-teaus** or **-teaux** (-tōz′). **1** a large level or mainly level area of land in the mountains or rising sharply from the sea or a lowland area. Many plateaus have a very dry climate. **2** a period or level at which something is stabilized for a time, represented on a graph as a horizontal line; a period or state of levelling off: *Our volleyball team improved rapidly at first, but then we reached a plateau.* [< F < OF *platel,* dim. of *plat* flat < VL *plattus.* See PLATE.]

plate·ful (plāt′fu̇l) *n., pl.* **-fuls.** the contents of a plate or as much or as many as a plate will hold: *a plateful of cookies.*

plate glass thick sheet glass that has been ground and polished to make it very smooth and clear. Plate glass is used for mirrors, large windows, etc.

plate·let (plāt′lit) *n.* one of the very tiny, colorless disks found in the blood of vertebrates, that assist in blood clotting.

plat·en (plat′ən) *n.* **1** a flat metal plate in a printing press that presses the paper against the inked type. **2** the roller in a typewriter against which the paper rests. [< F *platine* < *plat* flat < VL *plattus.* See PLATE.]

plate tectonics the study of the structure of the earth's crust on the basis of the theory that the crust is made up of huge segments, called plates, that float on the mantle below, and whose individual movement is responsible for continental drift, mountain building, etc.

plat·form (plat′fôrm) *n.* **1** a raised, level surface. There usually is a platform beside the track at a railway station. A hall usually has a platform for speakers. **2** a plan of action or statement of principles of a group. A political party is said to have a platform. **3** an extra layer in a sole of a shoe, to give additional thickness. [< F *plateforme* flat form]

platform rocker a rocking chair that rocks on a stable platform.

plat·ing (plāt′ing) *n.* **1** a thin layer of silver, gold, or other metal. **2** a covering of metal plates.

plat·i·num (plat′ə nəm) *n.* **1** a heavy, precious, metallic chemical element that looks like silver or white gold and does not tarnish or melt easily. It is used as a catalyst, in jewellery, etc. *Symbol:* Pt; *at.no.* 78; *at.wt.* 195.09. **2** a light-grey color, less bright than silver and having a faint bluish tinge. [< NL *platinum,* ult. < Sp. *plata* silver]

platinum blond **1** the color of whitish silver. **2** having this color. **3** a person having hair of this color.
☛ *Usage.* See note at **blond.**

platinum blonde a woman or girl having hair the color of whitish silver.
☛ *Usage.* See note at **blond.**

plat·i·tude (plat′ə tyüd′ *or* plat′ə tüd′) *n.* **1** a dull or commonplace remark, especially one given out solemnly as if it were fresh and important: *"Better late than never" is a platitude.* **2** flatness; triteness; dullness. [< F *platitude* < *plat* flat]

plat·i·tu·di·nous (plat′ə tyü′də nəs *or* plat′ə tü′də nəs) *adj.* characterized by, using, or being a platitude. —**plat′i·tu′di·nous·ly,** *adv.* —**plat′i·tu′di·nous·ness,** *n.*

Pla·ton·ic (plə ton′ik) *adj.* **1** of or having to do with Plato (427?-347? B.C.), a Greek philosopher, or his philosophy. **2** Usually, **platonic, a** having to do with or designating love or affection between a man and woman that has a purely spiritual or intellectual character, free from sexual desire or activity. **b** feeling or declaring such love. **3** idealistic or impractical: *a Platonic scheme for international disarmament.* —**pla·ton′i·cal·ly,** *adv.*

Pla·to·nism (plā′tə niz′əm) *n.* **1** the philosophy or doctrines of Plato or his followers. **2** any philosophy or doctrine based on that of Plato. **3** the doctrine or practice of platonic love.

Pla·to·nist (plā′tə nist) *n.* a follower of Plato; person who believes in Plato's philosophy.

pla·toon (plə tün′) *n.* **1** one of the formations of soldiers making up a company. A platoon is smaller than a company and larger than a section. **2** a small group of people sharing an activity or interest. **3** *Football, etc.* a group of players specially trained for a particular kind of play: *The coach sent in the punt-return platoon.* [< F

peloton group, little ball, dim. of *pelote* ball. Related to PELLET.]

plat·ter (plat′ər) *n.* a large, often oval or oblong plate, used especially for holding or serving a main dish such as meat or fish. **on a platter,** *Informal.* involving no effort: *The position was practically handed to him on a platter.* [ME < AF *plater* < OF *plat* plate < VL *plattus* flat. See PLATE.]

plat·y·pus (plat′ə pəs) *n., pl.* **-pus·es, -pi** (-pī′). a small, egg-laying water mammal (*Ornithorhynchus anatinus*) of Australia and Tasmania having a broad, flat, rubbery snout resembling a duck's bill, thick fur, four webbed feet, and a broad, flat tail. The platypus makes up a separate mammal family. [< NL < Gk. *platypous* < *platys* flat + *pous* foot]

plau·dit (plo′dit *or* plô′dit) *n.* **1** a round of applause. **2** Usually, **plaudits,** *pl.* enthusiastic expression of approval or praise: *He basked in the plaudits of the critics.* [alteration of L *plaudite* applaud!]

plau·si·bil·i·ty (plo′zə bil′ə tē *or* plô′zə bil′ə tē) *n.* **1** the quality or state of being plausible. **2** something plausible.

plau·si·ble (plo′zə bəl *or* plô′zə bəl) *adj.* **1** appearing true, reasonable, or fair. **2** apparently worthy of confidence but often not really so: *a plausible liar.* [< L *plausibilis* deserving applause, pleasing < *plaudere* applaud] —**plau′si·bly,** *adv.*

play (plā) *n., v.* —*n.* **1** something done to amuse oneself; fun; sport; recreation. **2** a turn, move, or act in a game: *It is your play next. The centre made a brilliant play.* **3** the act of carrying on a game: *Play was slow in the first half of the game.* **4** a way of carrying on a game. **5 a** a story written for or presented as a dramatic performance; drama. **b** a stage, radio, television, etc. performance of such a story. **6** action: *foul play.* **7** a light, quick movement or change: *the play of sunlight on leaves, the play of color in an opal.* **8** freedom for action, movement, etc. **9** operation; working. **10** gambling. **11** the act of lightly or briskly wielding or plying (*used in compounds*): *sword play.* **in play,** *Sports.* of a ball, in a position or condition to be legally played. **out of play,** *Sports.* of a ball, not in a position to be legally played. —*v.* **1** have fun; do something in sport; take part in a game or active pastime: *children playing on the lawn, a kitten playing with its tail.* **2** do or perform for amusement or to deceive, make fun of, etc.: *to play a joke on someone. He played a mean trick.* **3** take part in (a game): *to play tag.* **4** take part in a game against. **5** put in the game; cause to play in a game: *Each coach played his best goalie.* **6** act on or as if on a stage; act a part: *to play in a tragedy.* **7** act the part of (a character in a play, etc.). **8** give theatrical performances in: *to play the larger cities.* **9** act in a specified way: *to play sick.* **10** make believe; play in fun: *to play cowboys.* **11** make music: *The pianist played beautifully.* **12** produce (music) on an instrument: *to play a tune.* **13** perform on (a musical instrument): *to play a piano.* **14** of a musical instrument, radio, etc., produce sound: *We could hear the piano playing in the next apartment.* **15** move lightly or quickly: *A breeze played on the water.* **16** cause to act, move, or work; direct (on, over, along): *to play a hose on a burning building.* **17** put into action in a game: *Play your ten of hearts.* **18** operate with continued or repeated action: *A fountain played in the garden.* **19** allow (a hooked fish) to exhaust itself by pulling on the line. **20** do something foolishly or pointlessly; trifle: *Do not play with your food. Don't play with matches.* **21** gamble; bet. **22** bet on: *He plays the horses.*
play down, make unimportant or less important; avoid or reduce emphasis on: *The government tried to play down the unfavorable results of the opinion poll.*
played out, a exhausted. **b** finished; done with.
play into (someone's) **hands,** act so as to give a person an advantage over oneself.
play off, a hold a competition in which players or teams are pitted against each other to decide the championship. **b** play an extra game or round to settle a tie.
play on or **upon,** take advantage of; make use of: *She played on her mother's good nature.*
play out, play (drama, etc.) to the end.
play up, make the most of; exploit: *The singer's agent played up her extensive background in classical music.*
play up to, *Slang.* try to get the favor of; flatter: *to play up to a famous person.*
[OE *plegan,* v., *plega,* n., exercise]
☛ *Syn. n.* **1. Play, sport, game** = activity or exercise of mind or body engaged in for recreation or fun. **Play** is the general word: *Play is as necessary as work.* **Sport** applies to any form of athletics or an outdoor pastime, whether it requires much or little activity or is merely watched for pleasure: *Fencing, swimming, fishing, and horse racing are his favorite sports.* **Game** applies especially to an activity in the form of a contest, mental or physical, played by certain rules: *Tennis and chess are games.*

play·a·ble (plā′ə bəl) *adj.* **1** that can be played. **2** fit to be played on.

play–act (plā′akt′) *v.* **1** pretend; make believe. **2** perform in a play.

play–back (plā′bak′) *n.* a replaying of a tape recording or videotape, especially when it has just been made.

play–bill (plā′bil′) *n.* **1** a handbill or placard announcing a play. **2** the program of a play.

play–boy (plā′boi′) *n.* a man, usually rich, who devotes his time to the pursuit of pleasure.

play–by–play (plā′bī plā′) *adj.* giving each event or action as it happens or happened: *a play-by-play broadcast of a hockey game. He gave us a play-by-play account of the whole silly misunderstanding.*

play·down (plā′doun′) *n.* playoff.

play·er (plā′ər) *n.* **1** a person who plays a game: *a baseball player.* **2** an actor in a theatre. **3** a person who plays a musical instrument; musician. **4** a device that plays: *a record player.*

player piano a piano that has machinery for playing pieces automatically.

play·fel·low (plā′fel′ō) *n.* playmate.

play·ful (plā′fəl) *adj.* **1** full of fun; fond of playing. **2** joking; not serious. —**play′ful·ly,** *adv.* —**play′ful·ness,** *n.*

play·go·er (plā′gō′ər) *n.* a person who goes often to the theatre.

play·ground (plā′ground′) *n.* **1** a place for outdoor play, especially an area equipped with swings, slides, etc. for children. **2** a popular or, sometimes, notorious place for leisure activity, such as a resort area: *The Riviera is a playground of the wealthy.*

play·house (plā′hous′) *n.* **1** a small house for children to play in. **2** a theatre for live dramatic performances. [OE *pleghūs*]

playing card one of a set of small, oblong plastic or paper cards used in games, having one side marked with numbers and symbols for rank and group, or suit. Most sets, or decks, of playing cards consist of 52 cards with 13 cards in each of 4 suits.

play·mate (plā′māt′) *n.* a person who plays with another; a playing companion.

play·off (plā′of′) *n.* **1** an extra game or round played off to settle a tie. **2** one of a series of games played by the top teams in a league to determine the winner of the championship, of a special trophy, etc.

play on words pun.

play·pen (plā′pen′) *n.* a small, portable enclosure for very young children to play in.

play·room (plā′rüm′ *or* plā′rùm′) *n.* a room for children to play in.

play·thing (plā′thing′) *n.* a thing to play with; toy.

play·time (plā′tīm′) *n.* time for playing.

play·wright (plā′rīt′) *n.* a writer of plays; dramatist.

pla·za (plaz′ə *or* plä′zə) *n.* **1** a shopping centre. **2** a public square in a city or town. [< Sp. *plaza* < L < Gk. *plateia* (*hodos*) broad (way). Doublet of PLACE and PIAZZA.]

plea (plē) *n.* **1** a request or appeal; asking: *a plea for pity.* **2** an excuse: *The man's plea was that he had not seen the signal.* **3** *Law.* **a** the answer made by a defendant to a charge against him in a court. **b** an argument or allegation of fact made in support of one side in a lawsuit. **c** a plea which alleges some new fact on the basis of which the suit should be dismissed, delayed, or barred, but does not answer the charge; special plea. [ME < OF *plaid* < L *placitum* (that) which pleases]

pleach (plēch) *v.* interweave (growing branches, vines, etc.); entwine. [ME < OF *plechier,* ult. < L *plectere* weave]

plead (plēd) *v.* **plead·ed** *or* **pled** (pled), **plead·ing. 1** offer reasons for or against; argue. **2** ask earnestly; make an earnest appeal: *He pleaded for more time to finish his paper.* **3** offer as an excuse: *The woman who stole pleaded poverty.* **4** *Law.* **a** act as counsel for; speak for: *She had a good lawyer to plead her case.* **b** conduct a case in court: *Who is pleading for the defence?* **c** answer to a charge in court: *Do you plead guilty or not guilty?* [ME < OF *plaidier* < VL *placitare,* ult. < L *placere* please] —**plead′ing·ly,** *adv.*

plead·er (plēd′ər) *n.* a person who pleads, especially in a court of law.

plead·ings (plēd′ingz) *n.pl. Law.* the claim made by the plaintiff and the defendant's answer to it in a court.

pleas·ance (plez′əns) *n. Archaic.* **1** a pleasant place, usually an area with trees, fountains, and flowers, attached to a mansion. **2** pleasure; enjoyment. [ME < OF *plaisance* < *plaisant* pleasing. See PLEASANT.]

pleas·ant (plez′ənt) *adj.* **1** pleasing; agreeable; giving pleasure. **2** easy to get along with; friendly. **3** fair; not stormy. [ME < OF *plaisant,* ppr. of *plaisir* please < L *placere*] —**pleas′ant·ly,** *adv.* —**pleas′ant·ness,** *n.*

Syn. 1. Pleasant, pleasing, agreeable = giving pleasure or satisfaction to the mind, feelings, or senses. **Pleasant** emphasizes that the person or thing described has certain qualities that give pleasure: *We spent a pleasant evening.* **Pleasing** emphasizes the effect on the one knowing or experiencing what is described: *It was pleasing to me because I wanted to see them.* **Agreeable** means pleasing because to a person's own taste or liking: *I think this cough medicine has an agreeable flavor.*

pleas·ant·ry (plez'ənt rē) *n., pl.* **-ries. 1** a good-natured joke; a witty remark: *His speech was full of pleasantries.* **2** lively, good-humored talk; banter.

please (plēz) *v.* **pleased, pleas·ing. 1** be agreeable to: *Toys please children.* **2** be agreeable: *Such a fine meal cannot fail to please.* **3** wish; think fit: *Do what you please.* **4** be the will of: *It pleased her to remain anonymous.* **5** may it please you (now used merely as a polite addition to requests or commands): *Come here, please. Could you please tell me the time? Two orders of fish and chips, please. Please come in.*
be pleased, a be moved to pleasure: *He was pleased at the good news.* **b** be disposed; like; choose: *I will be pleased to go.*
if you please, if you like; with your permission.
please God, if it is God's will.
[ME < OF *plaisir* < L *placere*]

pleas·ing (plēz'ing) *adj.* giving pleasure; pleasant: *a pleasing manner.* —**pleas'ing·ly,** *adv.*
Syn. See note at **pleasant.**

pleas·ur·a·ble (plezh'ər ə bəl) *adj.* pleasant; agreeable. —**pleas'ur·a·bly,** *adv.*

pleas·ure (plezh'ər) *n.* **1** a feeling of being pleased; enjoyment; delight. **2** something that pleases; cause of joy or delight. **3** wordly or frivolous enjoyment. **4** one's will, desire, or choice: *What is your pleasure in this matter?*
at (one's) pleasure, as or when one pleases; at will; at discretion.
during (one's) pleasure, while one pleases.
take pleasure, be pleased; delight: *He takes his pleasure in hunting and fishing.*
[ME < OF *plaisir*, nominal use of infinitive. See PLEASE.]
Syn. 1. Pleasure, delight, joy = a feeling of satisfaction and happiness coming from having, experiencing, or expecting something good or to one's liking. **Pleasure** is the general word applying to this feeling whether or not it is shown in any way: *The compliment gave her pleasure.* **Delight** suggests great pleasure, usually shown or expressed in a lively way: *The child clapped her hands in delight.* **Joy** applies to a strong emotion of intense delight and shining happiness, expressing itself in gladness or rejoicing: *Success brought him joy.*

pleat (plēt) *n., v.* —*n.* a flat, relatively narrow fold made by doubling material on itself. Pleats made in cloth, as in a skirt, are usually pressed in place. —*v.* fold or arrange in pleats. [var. of *plait*] —**pleat'er,** *n.*

ple·be·ian (pli bē'ən) *n., adj.* —*n.* **1** a member of the lower class, or common people, of ancient Rome. Compare **patrician** (def. 1). **2** one of the common people of any country. **3** a vulgar, coarse, or unrefined person.
—*adj.* **1** of or having to do with the common people of ancient Rome or any country. **2** vulgar or crude in manner or style. [< L *plebeius* < *plebs* the common people]

ple·be·ian·ism (pli bē'ən iz'əm) *n.* plebeian character or ways.

pleb·i·scite (pleb'ə sīt' *or* pleb'ə sit') *n.* a direct vote by the qualified voters of a country, province, municipality, etc. on some question. [< L *plebiscitum* < *plebs* the common people + *scitum* decree]

plebs (plebz) *n., pl.* **ple·bes** (plē'bēz). in ancient Rome, the common people. [< L]

plec·trum (plek'trəm) *n., pl.* **-trums, -tra** (-trə). a small piece of ivory, horn, metal, etc. used for plucking the strings of a guitar, mandolin, lyre, zither, etc. [< L *plectrum* < Gk. *plēktron* < *plēssein* strike]

pled (pled) *v.* a pt. and a pp. of **plead.**

pledge (plej) *n., v.* **pledged, pledg·ing.** —*n.* **1** a solemn promise. **2** something that secures or makes safe; security: *The knight left a jewel as pledge for the borrowed horse.* **3** the condition of being held as security. **4** a person who has promised to join an organization but is serving a probationary period before being granted membership. **5** something given to show favor or love or as a promise of something to come; sign; token. **6** the drinking of a health or toast.
take the pledge, *Informal.* promise not to drink alcoholic liquor.
—*v.* **1** promise solemnly. **2** cause to promise solemnly; bind by a promise. **3** give as security. **4** drink a health to; drink in honor of (someone) and wish (him) well. [ME < OF *plege* < Med.L *plebium* < Gmc. Akin to PLIGHT².] —**pledg'er,** *n.*

pledg·ee (plej ē') *n.* a person with whom something is deposited as a pledge.

Plei·ad (plē'ad *or* plī'ad) *n.* any of the Pleiades.

Ple·ia·des (plē'ə dēz' *or* plī'ə dēz') *n.pl.* **1** a group of hundreds of stars in the constellation Taurus, of which only six can normally be seen with the naked eye. **2** *Greek mythology.* the seven

hat, āge, fär; let, ēqual, tėrm; it, īce
hot, ōpen, ôrder; oil, out; cup, put, rüle,
above, takən, pencəl, lemən, circəs
ch, child; ng, long; sh, ship
th, thin; ŦH, then; zh, measure

daughters of Atlas who were turned into a group of stars. [< L *Pleiades,* pl. of *Pleias* < Gk.]

Plei·o·cene (plī'ə sēn') *n. or adj.* Pliocene.

Pleis·to·cene (plīs'tə sēn') *n., adj. Geology.* —*n.* **1** the period before the present period, beginning approximately one million years ago; ice age. **2** the deposits of gravel, etc. made in this period. See chart at **geology.** —*adj.* of or having to do with this period or these deposits. [< Gk. *pleistos* most + *kainos* recent]

ple·na·ry (plē'nə rē *or* plen'ə rē) *adj.* **1** complete; entire; absolute. **2** attended or to be attended by all qualified members: *a plenary session.* [< LL *plenarius* < L *plenus* full] —**ple'na·ri·ly,** *adv.*

plen·i·po·ten·ti·ar·y (plen'ə pə ten'shē er'ē *or* -pə ten'shə rē) *n., pl.* **-ar·ies;** *adj.* —*n.* a diplomatic agent having full power or authority. —*adj.* having or giving full power and authority. [< Med.L, ult. < L *plenus* full + *potens, -entis* powerful]

plen·i·tude (plen'ə tyüd' *or* plen'ə tüd') *n.* **1** fullness; completeness: *in the plenitude of health and vigor.* **2** abundance: *a plenitude of food.* [ME < OF < *plenitudo* < *plenus* full]

plen·te·ous (plen'tē əs) *adj.* plentiful. —**plen'te·ous·ly,** *adv.* —**plen'te·ous·ness,** *n.*

plen·ti·ful (plen'tē fəl) *adj.* more than enough; abundant: *a plentiful supply of gasoline for the trip, a plentiful harvest.* —**plen'ti·ful·ly,** *adv.* —**plen'ti·ful·ness,** *n.*

plen·ty (plen'tē) *n., pl.* **-ties;** *adj., adv.* —*n.* **1** a full supply; all that one needs; large enough number or quantity: *There is plenty of time.* **2** the quality or condition of being plentiful; abundance: *years of peace and plenty.*
—*adj.* enough; plentiful; abundant: *Six potatoes will be plenty.*
—*adv. Informal.* quite; fully: *plenty good enough.* [ME < OF < L *plenitas* fullness < *plenus* full]

ple·num (plē'nəm *or* plen'əm) *n.* **1** an enclosed space containing a gas at a pressure higher than that of the surrounding atmosphere. **2** an assembly of all members, especially of a legislative body. **3** space completely filled by matter. **4** the quality or condition of being full. [< NL < L *plenus* full]

ple·o·nasm (plē'ə naz'əm) *n.* **1** the use of more words than are necessary to express an idea; redundancy; tautology. *Examples: The two twins arrived together. The realization of his dream came true.* **2** an instance of pleonasm. [< LL < Gk. *pleonasmos,* ult. < *pleon* more]

ple·o·nas·tic (plē'ə nas'tik) *adj.* characterized by or using pleonasm; redundant. —**ple·o·nas'ti·cal·ly,** *adv.*

ple·si·o·saur (plē'sē ə sôr') *n.* any of a suborder (Plesiosauria) of sea reptiles, now extinct, having a small head, long neck, and four flippers instead of legs. The plesiosaurs lived during the age of the dinosaurs. [< NL *plesiosaurus* < Gk. *plēsios* near + *sauros* lizard]

pleth·o·ra (pleth'ə rə) *n.* **1** excessive abundance or fullness; too much. **2** a condition of the body caused by an excess of red blood cells or an overall increase in the quantity of blood, characterized by swelling and a florid complexion. [< NL < Gk. *plēthorē* < *plēthein* be full]

ple·thor·ic (ple thôr'ik *or* pleth'ə rik) *adj.* having to do with or characterized by plethora; especially, swollen, overfull, or overstocked.

pleu·ra (plur'ə) *n., pl.* **pleu·rae** (plur'ē *or* plur'ī). in mammals, either of the thin membranes lining the two halves of the thorax and folded back over the surface of the lung on the same side. [< NL < Gk. *pleura* rib]

pleu·ral (plur'əl) *adj.* of or having to do with the pleura.
Hom. plural.

pleu·ri·sy (plur'ə sē) *n.* inflammation of the pleura, in which varying amounts of fluid from the inflamed membrane enter the chest cavity. Pleurisy is usually accompanied by severe pain in breathing. [ME < OF *pleurisie* < LL *pleurisis,* for L *pleuritis* < Gk. *pleuritis* < *pleura* rib]

pleu·rit·ic (plü rit'ik) *adj.* of, causing, or having pleurisy.

Plex·i·glas (plek'sə glas') *n. Trademark.* a light, transparent, acrylic plastic, often used in place of glass. [*plastic* + *flexible* + *glass*]

plex·us (plek'səs) *n., pl.* **-us·es** *or* **-us. 1** a network of nerves,

blood vessels, etc. The **solar plexus** is a collection of nerves behind the stomach. **2** an interwoven combination of parts in a system; network. [< L *plexus* < *plectere* twine, braid]

pli·a·bil·i·ty (plī′ə bil′ə tē) *n.* the state or quality of being pliable.

pli·a·ble (plī′ə bəl) *adj.* **1** easily bent; flexible; supple: *Willow twigs are pliable.* **2** easily influenced; yielding: *He is too pliable to be a good leader.* [< F *pliable* < *plier* bend]

pli·an·cy (plī′ən sē) *n.* the state or quality of being easily bent or influenced.

pli·ant (plī′ənt) *adj.* **1** bending easily; flexible; supple. **2** easily influenced; yielding. [ME < OF *pliant* bending, ppr. of *plier*. See PLY².] —**pli′ant·ly**, *adv.*
☛ *Syn.* **1.** See note at **flexible.**

pli·cate (plī′kāt) *adj.* folded like a fan. [< L *plicatus* folded]

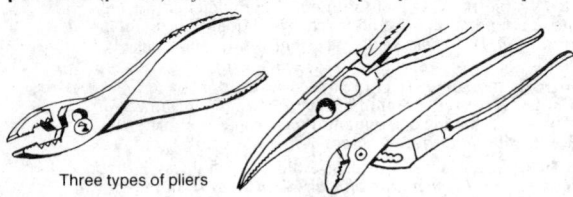

Three types of pliers

pli·ers (plī′ərz) *n.* (*used with a plural or singular verb*) small pincers with long jaws, used for bending wire, holding small objects, etc. [< *ply¹*]

plight¹ (plīt) *n.* a condition or state, especially a bad one. [ME < AF *plit*, originally, manner of folding, ult. < L *plicare* fold; confused with *plight²*]
☛ *Syn.* See note at **predicament.**

plight² (plīt) *v., n.* —*v.* pledge; promise.
plight (one's) **troth, a** *Archaic.* pledge one's word. **b** promise to marry.
—*n.* a solemn promise; pledge. [OE *pliht* danger]

Plimsoll mark or **line** (plim′səl) a mark or line painted on a ship's hull to show how heavily it may be loaded. This mark is required by law on British merchant ships and also on most other merchant ships. [< Samuel *Plimsoll* (1824-1898), a member of Parliament, who had the law on overloading passed]

plink (plingk) *v., n.* —*v.* **1** play on a musical or other instrument so as to produce a tinkling sound. **2** aim or throw at a target casually. —*n.* a tinkling sound.

plinth (plinth) *n.* **1** *Architecture.* the lower, square part of the base of a column. See **column** for picture. **2** any square base, as of a pedestal, etc. [< L < Gk. *plinthos*]

Pli·o·cene (plī′ə sēn′) *n., adj. Geology.* —*n.* **1** a period beginning approximately 12 million years ago. **2** the rocks formed in this period. See chart at **geology.** —*adj.* of or having to do with this period or the rocks formed during it. Also, **Pleiocene.** [< Gk. *pleiōn* more + *kainos* recent]

PLO or **P.L.O.** Palestine Liberation Organization.

plod (plod) *v.* **plod·ded, plod·ding. 1** walk heavily; trudge. **2** walk slowly or heavily along: *We plodded the mountain path.* **3** proceed in a slow or dull way; work patiently with effort: *He plods away at his lessons until he learns them.* [? imitative] —**plod·der,** *n.*
☛ *Syn.* **1.** See note at **walk.**

plonk¹ (plongk) *v.* put down or drop heavily or suddenly; plunk.

plonk² (plongk) *n. Esp.Brit. Informal.* wine, especially cheap or inferior wine. [origin uncertain]

plop (plop) *n., v.* **plopped, plop·ping;** *adv.* —*n.* **1** a sound like that of a flat object striking water without a splash. **2** a fall that makes such a sound.
—*v.* **1** fall or drop with a sound like that of a flat object striking water without a splash: *The stone plopped into the water.* **2** allow oneself to fall heavily: *She plopped into the first soft chair she came to.*
—*adv.* with a plop. [imitative]

plo·sive (plō′siv or plō′ziv) *adj. or n. Phonetics.* explosive.

plot (plot) *n., v.* **plot·ted, plot·ting.** —*n.* **1** a secret plan, especially to do something wrong: *Two men formed a plot to rob the bank.* **2** the plan or main story of a play, novel, poem, etc. **3** a small piece of ground: *a garden plot.* **4** a map; diagram.
—*v.* **1** plan secretly with others; plan. **2** divide (land) into plots. **3** make a map or diagram of. **4** mark (something) on a map or diagram: *The nurse plotted the patient's temperature over several days.* **5** *Mathematics.* **a** determine the location of a point by means of its co-ordinates; mark a point on graph paper. **b** make a curve by

connecting points marked out on a graph. **c** represent (an equation, etc.) by means of a curve drawn through points on a graph. [OE *plot* patch of ground; meaning influenced by *complot* a joint plot (< F)] —**plot′less,** *adj.* —**plot′ter,** *n.*
☛ *Syn.* **v. 1. Plot, conspire, scheme** = plan secretly. **Plot** means to form secretly alone or together with others, a carefully designed plan, usually harmful or treacherous, against a person, group, or country: *Enemy agents plotted to blow up the plant.* **Conspire** emphasizes the combining of one person or group with another, usually secretly, to carry out an illegal act, especially treachery or treason: *They conspired to overthrow the government.* **Scheme** suggests careful planning, often in a crafty or underhand way, to gain one's own ends: *He schemed to become president.*

plough or **plow** (plou) *n., v.* —*n.* **1** a farm implement used for cutting the soil and turning it over. **2** a machine for removing snow; snowplough.
—*v.* **1** turn over (soil) with a plough. **2** use a plough. **3** move as a plough does; advance slowly and with effort: *The ship ploughed through the waves. The girl ploughed through two books to get material for her essay.* **4** remove with a plough or as if with a plough: *to plough up old roots.* **5** furrow: *to plough a field, wrinkles ploughed in one's face by time.* **6** cut the surface of (water). **7** *Esp.Brit. Informal.* reject (a candidate) or be rejected in an examination.
plough back, reinvest (profits) in the same business.
plough into, a hit hard or at speed and travel into: *The car went out of control and ploughed into the building.* **b** undertake (a job, project, etc.) with energy and determination.
plough under, a plough into the ground to enrich the soil. **b** defeat; destroy; overwhelm.
[OE *plōg*] —**plough′er** or **plow′er,** *n.*

plough·boy or **plow·boy** (plou′boi′) *n.* **1** boy who guides the horses drawing a plough. **2** a country boy.

plough·man or **plow·man** (plou′mən) *n., pl.* **-men. 1** a man who guides a plough. **2** a farm worker.

plough·share or **plow·share** (plou′sher′) *n.* the part of a plough that cuts the soil.

plov·er (pluv′ər or plō′vər) *n.* any of numerous shore birds (family Charadriidae) having a plump, compact body with brownish or greyish plumage, a fairly short bill and tail, long wings, and, usually, no hind toes. The killdeer is a plover. **2** upland plover. [ME < AF *plover*, ult. < L *pluvia* rain]

plow (plou) See **plough.**

plow·boy (plou′boi′) See **ploughboy.**

plow·man (plou′mən) *n., pl.* **-men.** See **ploughman.**

plow·share (plou′sher′) See **ploughshare.**

ploy (ploi) *n.* **1** *Informal.* an action or words by which advantage over another may be gained: *He won the game by a clever ploy.* **2** *Brit. Informal.* a sporting or amusing action or proceeding. [? < *employ*; n., in obs. meaning of "use"]

pluck (pluk) *v., n.* —*v.* **1** pull off; pick: *to pluck flowers. She plucked a bit of lint from the blanket.* **2** pick or pull (at); tug or grasp: *to pluck the strings of a violin for a pizzicato passage. The little boy plucked at her sleeve.* **3** play (a musical instrument) by picking at the strings: *to pluck a banjo.* **4** pull off the feathers or hair from: *to pluck a chicken, to pluck one's eyebrows.* **5** *Slang.* rob; swindle.
pluck up (one's) **spirits** (or **courage** etc.), take courage: *He plucked up his spirits and carried on.*
—*n.* **1** the act of picking or pulling. **2** courage; boldness and spirit: *It took pluck to stand up to that bully.* **3** the heart, liver, and lungs of an animal as food. [OE *pluccian*]

pluck·y (pluk′ē) *adj.* **pluck·i·er, pluck·i·est.** having or showing courage. —**pluck′i·ly,** *adv.* —**pluck′i·ness,** *n.*

plug (plug) *n., v.* **plugged, plug·ging.** —*n.* **1** a piece of wood or some other substance used to stop up a hole. **2** a disk of rubber or metal for stopping the drain of a sink, basin, bathtub, etc. **3** a device to make an electrical connection. **4** a place where a hose can be attached; hydrant. **5** spark plug. **6** *Informal.* an advertisement or recommendation: *The interview was mainly a plug for his latest book. I'll put in a plug for you when I talk to her.* **7** a cake of pressed tobacco or a piece of this cut off for chewing. **8** *Informal.* a worn-out or inferior horse. **9** a lure for catching fish. **10** *Geology.* a cylindrical mass of igneous rock formed in the crater of an extinct volcano.
—*v.* **1** stop up or fill with a plug. **2** insert the plug of (an electrical appliance or device) into an outlet (*used with* **in** or **into**): *Where can I plug in the hair dryer?* **3** of an electrical appliance or device, able to be connected to (a certain type of outlet) (*used with* **into**): *They got a coffee maker that plugs into the cigarette lighter of the car.* **4** *Slang.* hit or shoot. **5** *Informal.* work steadily; plod. **6** *Informal.* recommend or advertise, especially on a radio or television program: *to plug a new product.* [< MDu. *plugge*] —**plug′ger,** *n.*

plug hat *Informal.* a man's tall silk hat.

plug-in (plug′in′) *n., adj.* —*n.* a receptacle in a wall, etc. designed to receive a plug attached to an electrical appliance in

order to complete the circuit and operate the appliance; electrical outlet: *There are only two plug-ins in the bedroom.* —*adj.* designed to operate by being plugged into an electrical outlet: *a plug-in light fixture.*

plug-ug·ly (plug′ug′lē) *n., pl.* **-lies.** *Slang.* ruffian.

plum (plum) *n., adj.* —*n.* **1** any of various trees and shrubs (of genus *Prunus* of the rose family) producing roundish or oval, edible fruit with a smooth skin, juicy flesh, and a somewhat flat, oblong stone or pit. **2** the fruit of any of these trees or shrubs. Plums may be purple, red, green, or yellow when ripe. **3** any of various other trees bearing edible fruit resembling plums. **4** the fruit of any of these trees. **5** a raisin when used in a pudding, cake, etc.: *plum pudding.* **6** something very good or desirable: *His new job is quite a plum.* **7** a dark, reddish purple. —*adj.* having the color plum. [OE *plūme* < VL *pruna* < L *prunum* < Gk. *proumnon.* Doublet of PRUNE.] —**plum′like′,** *adj.*
☞ *Hom.* **plumb.**

plum·age (plüm′ij) *n.* the feathers covering the body of a bird: *Many parrots have bright plumage.* [ME < OF *plumage* < *plume* plume. See PLUME.]

plumb (plum) *n., adj., adv., v.* —*n.* a small weight used on the end of a line to find the depth of water or to see if a wall is vertical. **out of plumb** or **off plumb,** not vertical. —*adj.* **1** vertical. **2** *Informal.* complete; thorough. —*adv.* **1** vertically. **2** *Informal.* completely; thoroughly. —*v.* **1** test or adjust by a plumb line; test; sound: *Our line was not long enough to plumb the depths of the lake.* **2** get to the bottom of: *No one could plumb the mystery.* [ME < OF *plomb* < L *plumbum* lead]
☞ *Hom.* **plum.**

plum·ba·go (plum bā′gō) *n.* graphite. [< L *plumbago* lead ore < *plumbum* lead]

plumb bob weight at the end of a plumb line.

plumb·er (plum′ər) *n.* a person whose work is putting in, maintaining, and repairing water pipes and fixtures in buildings. [ME < OF *plummier* < L *plumbarius,* ult. < L *plumbum* lead]

plumb·ing (plum′ing) *n.* **1** the work or trade of a plumber. **2** the water pipes and fixtures in a building or part of a building: *the bathroom plumbing.*

plumb line the line with a plumb at the end, used to find the depth of water or to test the straightness of a wall.

plume (plüm) *n., v.* **plumed, plum·ing.** —*n.* **1** a large, long feather; feather. **2** a feather, bunch of feathers, or tuft of hair worn as an ornament on a hat, helmet, etc. **3** something resembling a plume, as on a plant or animal. **4** a moving column of something such as smoke or snow: *Snow rose in a plume from the snowblower.* —*v.* **1** furnish with plumes. **2** smooth or arrange the feathers of: *The eagle plumed its wing.* **plume (oneself) on,** be proud of; show pride concerning: *She plumed herself on her skill in dancing.* [ME < OF < L *pluma*]

plum·met (plum′it) *v., n.* —*v.* plunge; drop. —*n.* a weight fastened to a line; plumb. [ME < OF *plommet* < *plomb* lead. See PLUMB.]

plum·my (plum′ē) *adj.* **1** like or full of plums: *a plummy flavor, a plummy cake.* **2** *Informal.* good; desirable: *She got herself a plummy part in the new play.* **3** of a voice, rich and full in tone.

plu·mose (plü′mōs) *adj.* **1** having feathers or plumes; feathered. **2** feathery; like a plume. [< L *plumosus* < *pluma* feather]

plump¹ (plump) *adj., v.* —*adj.* rounded out; full; attractively fat. —*v.* make or become plump: *He plumped the pillows on the bed.* [cf. MDu. *plomp,* MLG *plump* blunt, thick] —**plump′ness,** *n.*

plump² (plump) *v., n., adv., adj.* —*v.* **1** fall or drop heavily or suddenly: *All out of breath, she plumped down on a chair.* **2 a** drop, let fall, etc.: *to plump down one's bags at the station.* **b** pay at once and in one lot: *to plump down $10.* **3** *Informal.* burst or plunge: *to plump out of a room, to plump into the water.* **plump for,** give one's complete support to; champion vigorously: *to plump for lower taxes.* —*n.* **1** *Informal.* a sudden plunge; heavy fall. **2** *Informal.* the sound made by a plunge or fall. —*adv.* **1** heavily or suddenly: *He ran plump into me.* **2** directly; bluntly. —*adj.* direct; downright; blunt. [cf. Du. *plompen,* LG *plumpen,* and *plump¹*]

plum pudding a rich, cooked pudding containing raisins, currants, spices, etc.

plu·mule (plü′myül) *n.* **1** the bud of a plant embryo that becomes the growing stem tip. See **embryo** for picture. **2** a small, soft feather; a down feather. [< L *plumula,* dim. of *pluma* feather]

plum·y (plüm′ē) *adj.* **1** having plumes or feathers. **2** adorned with a plume or plumes. **3** like a plume.

hat, āge, fär; let, ēqual, tèrm; it, īce
hot, ōpen, ôrder; oil, out; cup, put, rüle,
əbove, takən, pencəl, lemən, circəs

ch, child; ng, long; sh, ship
th, thin; ŦH, then; zh, measure

plun·der (plun′dər) *v., n.* —*v.* rob by force; rob. —*n.* **1** things taken in plundering; booty; loot: *They carried off the plunder in their ships.* **2** the act of plundering; pillaging or robbing by force. [< G *plündern* < *Plunder* household goods] —**plun′der·er,** *n.*
☞ *Syn. n.* **1.** Plunder, booty, loot = things taken by force. **Plunder** applies to things carried off by invading soldiers during a war or by bandits and other robbers: *The soldiers returned home with their plunder.* **Booty** applies particularly to things carried off and shared later by a band of robbers: *The bandits fought over their booty.* **Loot** applies particularly to things carried off from bodies and buildings in a city destroyed in war or at the scene of a fire, wreck, etc., but is used also of anything taken by robbery or some other crime: *Much loot was sold after the great earthquake.*

plunge (plunj) *v.* **plunged, plung·ing;** *n.* —*v.* **1** throw or thrust with force into something, especially a liquid: *He plunged his hand into the water.* **2** throw suddenly or violently into a certain condition: *to plunge the world into war, to plunge the room into darkness.* **3** throw oneself (into water, danger, a fight, etc.). **4** move or act recklessly or in great haste: *She plunged into the crowd.* **5** pitch or lurch suddenly and violently: *The ship plunged about in the storm.* **6** *Slang.* gamble heavily. —*n.* **1** the act or an instance of plunging. **2** a place for diving. **3** a swim. [ME < OF *plungier,* ult. < L *plumbum* lead]
☞ *Syn. v.* **1.** See note at **dip.**

plung·er (plun′jər) *n.* **1** a part of a machine that acts with a plunging motion. **2** a rubber suction cup on a long stick, used for unplugging stopped-up drains, toilets, etc. **3** *Informal.* a reckless gambler or speculator. **4** any person or thing that plunges.

plunk (plungk) *v., n., adv.* —*v.* **1** hit or pluck so as to produce a short hollow or metallic sound: *to plunk a banjo string.* **2** put down or drop heavily or suddenly: *She plunked her books on the table.* **plunk down,** hand over payment: *He plunked down eight thousand dollars for the car.* **plunk for,** *Informal.* plump for. —*n.* the act or sound of plunking. —*adv.* with a thud or twang: *He sat down plunk on the ground.* [imitative]

plu·per·fect (plü′pèr′fikt) *n. or adj.* *Grammar.* past perfect. [short for L *plus quam perfectum* more than perfect]

plupf. pluperfect.

plur. **1** plural. **2** plurality.

plu·ral (plür′əl) *adj., n.* —*adj.* **1** more than one: *plural citizenship.* **2** *Grammar.* signifying or denoting reference to more than one. Almost all English nouns and pronouns have a distinct form to indicate **plural number.** In language having dual number (see **dual**), the plural number refers to more than two. —*n.* *Grammar.* **1** the plural number. **2** a word or construction in the plural number. [ME < L *pluralis* < *plus* more]
☞ *Hom.* **pleural.**

plu·ral·ism (plür′ə liz′əm) *n.* **1** the quality or state of being plural. **2** *Philosophy.* the theory that ultimate being or reality consists of several essential principles or entities. **3** a condition of society in which a number of diverse cultural, religious, or racial groups maintain their diversity within a single nation or civilization. **4** the practice or system in some churches of having two or more ecclesiastical offices held by one person.

plu·ral·is·tic (plür′ə lis′tik) *adj.* of, having to do with, or characterized by pluralism: *a pluralistic society.* —**plu′ral·is′ti·cal·ly,** *adv.*

plu·ral·i·ty (plü ral′ə tē) *n., pl.* **-ties. 1** in a contest involving more than two candidates, the number of votes cast for one candidate when that number is more than for any other one, but not more than half the total number of votes for all candidates: *He won by only a plurality, not a majority.* **2** a greater number of votes cast for a candidate than for an opposing candidate. **3** a number that is greater than another. **4** a large number; multitude. **5** the state or fact of being plural or numerous.

plu·ral·ize (plür′ə līz′) *v.* **-ized, -iz·ing.** make plural or express in the plural form.

plu·ral·ly (plür′əl ē) *adv.* in the plural number; so as to express or imply more than one.

plus (plus) *prep., adj., n., conj.* —*prep.* **1** added to: *Three plus two equals five.* **2** and also: *The work of an engineer requires intelligence plus experience.* —*adj.* **1** and more: *His mark was B plus.* **2** showing addition: *the plus sign.* **3** greater than zero; positive: *a plus quantity.* **4** *Informal.*

additional; extra: *a plus value.* **5** electrically positive.
—*n.* **1** the plus sign (+). **2** an added quantity; something extra; a gain. **3** a positive quantity.
—*conj. Informal.* in addition: *We had to buy a new water heater; plus we had to get the furnace fixed.* [< L *plus* more]

plus fours loose-fitting baggy trousers gathered below the knee.

plush (plush) *n., adj.* —*n.* cloth of silk, wool, cotton, etc. having a softer and longer pile than velvet. —*adj.* **1** of, resembling, or made of plush: *plush toys, plush upholstery.* **2** luxurious and showy: *plush surroundings.*

plush·y (plush′ē) *adj.* **1** like or covered with plush. **2** luxurious; rich-looking: *a plushy apartment.* [< MF *pluche*, ult. < L *pilus* hair]

Plu·to (plü′tō) *n.* **1** *Greek mythology.* the god of the lower world, also called Hades, corresponding to the Roman god Dis. **2** the planet that is farthest from the sun.

plu·toc·ra·cy (plü tok′rə sē) *n., pl.* **-cies. 1** a system of government in which the rich rule. **2** a ruling class of wealthy people. [< Gk. *ploutokratia* < *ploutos* wealth + *kratos* power]

plu·to·crat (plü′tə krat′) *n.* **1** a person who has power or influence because of his wealth. **2** any wealthy person.

plu·to·crat·ic (plü′tə krat′ik) *adj.* **1** having power and influence because of wealth. **2** of or having to do with plutocrats or plutocracy. —**plu′to·crat′i·cal·ly,** *adv.*

Plu·to·ni·an (plü tō′nē ən) *adj.* of or having to do with Pluto or the lower world.

Plu·ton·ic (plü ton′ik) *adj.* **1** Plutonian; infernal. **2** of or having to do with the theory that the present condition of the earth's crust is mainly due to igneous action. **3** *plutonic,* of or having to do with a class of igneous rocks that have solidified far below the earth's surface.

plu·to·ni·um (plü tō′nē əm) *n.* an extremely toxic, radio-active metallic element found naturally in trace amounts in uranium ores and produced in great amounts from uranium in nuclear reactors. The most important isotope of plutonium is plutonium-239 (half-life 24 360 years), used as a fuel in nuclear fission. *Symbol*: Pu; *at.no.* 94; *at.wt.* (244); *half-life* 80 million years. [< L *plutonium*, neut. < *Pluto, -onis* Pluto]

plu·vi·al (plü′vē əl) *adj.* **1** of or having to do with rain. **2** characterized by much rain. **3** *Geology.* caused or formed by the action of rain. [< L *pluvialis* < *pluvia* rain]

plu·vi·om·e·ter (plü′vē om′ə tər) *n.* an instrument for measuring the amount of rainfall. [< L *pluvia* rain + E *-meter*]

plu·vi·ous (plü′vē əs) *adj.* rainy; of rain.

ply¹ (plī) *v.* **plied, ply·ing. 1** work with; use: *The dressmaker plies her needle.* **2** work steadily or busily at or on something: *a carpenter plying his trade. For three hours we plied the water with our paddles.* **3** set upon forcefully: *The messenger was plied with questions.* **4** supply with in a pressing manner: *to ply a person with food or drink.* **5** travel regularly along (a course or route) or between (specified places): *Boats ply the river. A bus plies between the airport and the hotel.* [ult. var. of *apply*]

ply² (plī) *n., pl.* **plies. 1** a thickness or layer, as of laminated wood or cloth: *three-ply plywood.* **2** a strand or twist, as of rope or yarn. [< F *pli* < OF *plier* < L *plicare* fold]

Ply·mouth Brethren (plim′əth) a Protestant religious sect that recognizes no formal creed or ministerial orders. It originated about 1830 in Plymouth, England.

Plymouth Rock a breed of medium-sized, white, grey, or grey-and-black chicken. [< the rock at Plymouth, Massachusetts, on which the Pilgrims are said to have landed in 1620]

ply·wood (plī′wůd′) *n.* a kind of board made of several thin layers of wood glued together, with the grain in adjacent layers running at right angles to each other. Plywood is made in large sheets and is used for furniture, floors, walls, etc.

p.m. 1 post meridiem; after noon. **2** post mortem.

Pm promethium.

P.M. 1 Prime Minister. **2** post meridiem; after noon. **3** Postmaster. **4** Provost Marshal. **5** Police Magistrate. **6** Paymaster.

PMQ's permanent married quarters.

P/N or **p/n** promissory note.

pneu·mat·ic (nyü mat′ik *or* nü mat′ik) *adj.* **1** worked by air pressure: *a pneumatic drill.* **2** holding or inflated with compressed air: *a pneumatic tire.* **3** of or having to do with compressed air: *pneumatic pressure.* **4** of or having to do with pneumatics. [< L < Gk. *pneumatikos* < *pneuma, -atos* wind] —**pneu·mat′i·cal·ly,** *adv.*

pneu·mat·ics (nyü mat′iks *or* nü mat′iks) *n.* (*used with a* singular verb) the branch of physics that deals with the pressure, elasticity, mass, etc. of air and other gases.

pneu·mo·ni·a (nyü mōn′yə *or* nü-, nyü mō′nē ə *or* nü-) *n.* a disease in which the lungs are inflamed. [< NL < Gk. *pneumonia* < *pneumōn* lung]

Po polonium.

P.O. 1 Post Office. **2** petty officer. **3** pilot officer. **4** personnel officer. **5** postal order.

poach¹ (pōch) *v.* **1** trespass on (another's land), especially to hunt or fish. **2** take (game or fish) illegally. **3** trample (soft ground) into muddy holes. **4** of land, become soft, miry, and full of holes by being trampled. **5** sink into wet, heavy ground in walking. **6 a** mix with water and reduce to a uniform consistency. **b** mix thoroughly (paper pulp) with the bleach liquor. [< MF *pocher* poke out < Gmc. Akin to POKE¹.] —**poach′er,** *n.*

poach² (pōch) *v.* **1** cook (eggs) by breaking them into boiling water or into a very small pan over boiling water. **2** cook (fish, etc.) by simmering in milk, water, or stock. [ME < OF *pochier* < *poche* cooking spoon < Celtic] —**poach′er,** *n.*

pock (pok) *n., v.* —*n.* **1** a pustule caused by a disease such as smallpox. **2** any mark or spot suggesting such a pustule. **3** pockmark.
—*v.* **1** mark or pit with pocks. **2** scatter over (an area) like pocks. [OE *pocc*]

pock·et (pok′it) *n., v.* —*n.* **1** a small, flat bag or pouch sewn into or onto clothing for carrying small articles such as a handkerchief, pocket watch, comb or money. **2** (*adj.*) small enough to go in a pocket: *a pocket calculator.* **3** a pouch attached to the inside of a suitcase, car door, etc. **4** one of the bags at each corner and on each side of a pool or billiard table. **5** a hollow place: *She hid in a pocket in the side of the hill.* **6** *Geology.* a cavity in the earth containing ore, oil, water, etc. **7** a small deposit of ore: *The miner struck a pocket of silver.* **8** any current or condition in the air that causes an aircraft to drop suddenly.
be out of pocket, a spend or lose money. **b** be a loser.
in pocket, having or gaining money.
—*v.* **1** put in one's pocket: *He pocketed his change.* **2** shut in or hem in. **3** hold back; suppress; hide: *He pocketed his pride and said nothing.* **4** take and endure; put up with: *He pocketed the insult.* **5** take secretly or dishonestly: *Tom pocketed all the profits.* **6** *Billiards, etc.* drive into a pocket. [ME < AF *pokete,* dim. of *poke* poke²]

pock·et·book (pok′it bůk′) *n.* **1** Often, **pocket book,** a small, inexpensive, paper-covered edition of a book; paperback. **2** a small case for carrying money, papers, etc. in a pocket. **3** financial resources: *The dress was just too expensive for her pocketbook.* **4** *Esp.U.S.* a woman's handbag.

pock·et·ful (pok′it fůl) *n., pl.* **-fuls.** as much as a pocket will hold.

pocket gopher any of various rat-sized rodents (of family Geomyidae) found on the North American plains, having fur-lined, external cheek pouches, a heavy body, a broad, flat head, short legs, and a short tail.

pock·et·knife (pok′it nīf′) *n., pl.* **-knives.** a small knife with one or more blades that fold into the handle.

pocket money money for occasional or minor personal expenses.

pocket mouse any of a genus (*Perognathus*) of small, mouselike, North American rodents of the same family as the kangaroo rats, having large hind feet, small forefeet, and external cheek pouches. The **olive-backed pocket mouse** (*P. fasciatus*) of the southern Prairies is probably the smallest rodent found in Canada.

pock·et·size (pok′it sīz′) *adj.* **1** small enough to go in a pocket: *a pocket-size radio, camera, etc.* **2** *Informal.* small for its kind: *a pocket-size country.*

pock·mark (pok′märk′) *n., v.* —*n.* **1** a scar or pit in the skin such as those left by smallpox. **2** any small hollow suggesting such a scar. —*v.* cover or scar with pockmarks.

pock·marked (pok′märkt′) *adj.* having pockmarks.

po·co (pō′kō) *adv. Music.* slightly; little. [< Ital. *poco* < L *paucus* little, few]

po·co a po·co (pō′kō ä pō′kō) *Music.* little by little; gradually. [< Ital.]

pod¹ (pod) *n., v.* **pod·ded, pod·ding.** —*n.* **1** the fruit of a leguminous plant, such as beans or peas, consisting of a long, bivalve case that contains several seeds in a row and that splits along both sides when ripe, releasing the seeds. See **fruit** for picture. **2** the case itself, as distinct from the seeds. **3** any similar fruit or seedcase. **4** a streamlined cover over anything carried externally, especially on the wings or fuselage of an aircraft: *a gun pod or missile pod.* **5** a part of a spacecraft that can be detached from the main part.

—v. **1** produce pods. **2** fill out into a pod. [origin uncertain]
—**pod′like′,** adj.

pod² (pod) n. **1** a small flock of birds. **2** a small herd of whales, seals, etc. [origin unknown]

podg·y (poj′ē) adj. **podg·i·er, podg·i·est.** short and fat; pudgy. —**podg′i·ness,** n.

po·di·a·trist (pō dī′ə trist) n. a person trained and licensed to practise podiatry.

po·di·a·try (pə dī′ə trē) n. **1** chiropody. **2** U.S. the branch of medicine dealing with the treatment of major foot disorders by means of surgery, drugs, or corrective devices. [< Gk. pous, podos foot + iatreia a healing]

po·di·um (pō′dē əm) n., pl. **-di·a** (-dē ə). **1** a small raised platform, especially one used by an orchestra conductor. **2** a low wall around the arena of an ancient amphitheatre, serving as a base for the tiers of seats. **3** a projecting base or plinth supporting a wall, etc. [< L < Gk. podion, dim. of pous, podos foot]

pod·zol (pod′zol) n. a type of leached, whitish grey soil usually found in moist, sub-polar climates. Also, **podsol.** [< Russian podzol < pod under + zola ashes]

pod·zol·ic (pod zol′ik) adj. of or pertaining to podzol soil. Also, **podsolic.**

po·em (pō′əm) n. **1** a piece of writing that uses language that is more concentrated than in prose or ordinary speech, in which the words and phrases have a controlled rhythm and are usually arranged in lines to produce pattern, with or without rhyme. **2** a composition showing great beauty or nobility of language or thought. **3** something very beautiful: The runner was a poem in motion. [< L < Gk. poēma, var. of poiēma < poiein make, compose]

po·e·sy (pō′ə sē or pō′ə zē) n., pl. **-sies.** Archaic. poetry. [ME < OF poesie < L poesis < Gk. poēsis, var. of poiēsis composition]

po·et (pō′it) n. **1** a person who writes poetry. **2** a person, especially a creative artist, who has great ability to feel and express beauty, emotion, etc.: He is a poet with his paintbrush. [ME < OF < L poeta < Gk. poētēs composer, maker]

po·et·as·ter (pō′it as′tər) n. a writer of rather poor poetry. [< NL poetaster < L poeta + -aster, denoting inferiority]

po·et·ess (pō′it is) n. a woman who writes poetry.

po·et·ic (pō et′ik) adj. **1** of, having to do with, or characteristic of poets or poetry: poetic imagery. Alas, o'er, plenteous, and blithe are poetic words. **2** written in verse: Her poetic compositions are all very short. **3** showing beautiful or noble language, imagery, or thought: a poetic description of a scene. —**po·et′i·cal·ly,** adv.

po·et·i·cal (pō et′ə kəl) adj. poetic.

poetic justice ideal justice, thought of as being characteristic of drama and dramatic poetry, with the proper distribution of rewards and punishments.

poetic licence a freedom traditionally granted to poets to violate certain grammatical rules or to alter fact or history for effect within a poetic work. Also, **poetic license.**

po·et·ics (pō et′iks) n. (used with a singular verb). the theory or study of poetry.

poet laureate pl. **poets laureate. 1** Brit. a poet appointed by the monarch to write poems in celebration of court and national events. The first poet laureate was Ben Jonson. **2** the official poet of any country, state, etc.

po·et·ry (pō′it rē) n. **1** poetical works; poems: a book of poetry. **2** the art or theory of writing poems. Poetry uses many effects of sound, imagery, and vocabulary to achieve a heightened, intensive form of expression. **3** a poetic quality; poetic spirit or feeling: Her skating is pure poetry. [ME < OF < LL poetria < L poeta poet. See POET.]

po·gey or **po·gy** (pō′gē) n., adj. —n. Cdn. Slang. **1** money or forms of relief given by the government to unemployed persons, especially in times of extreme economic depression; dole. **2** the office providing such relief. **3** a hostel supervised by the local relief agency. **4** unemployment insurance.
on the pogey, drawing such relief.
—adj. obtained from the relief office: pogey boots. [originally, hobo slang for "workhouse"]

po·go stick (pō′gō) a stick used in playing to hop from place to place by jumping up and down on the spring-supported footrests near the bottom of the stick, while holding the handle at the top.

po·grom (pō grom′ or pō′grəm) n. an organized, often officially sanctioned, massacre, especially of Jews. [< Russian pogrom devastation]

poign·an·cy (poin′yən sē or poin′ən sē) n. **1** the quality or state of being poignant: They were moved by the poignancy of his appeal for help. **2** an instance of poignancy.

poign·ant (poin′yənt or poin′ənt) adj. **1** deeply affecting; causing

hat, āge, fär; let, ēqual, tèrm; it, īce
hot, ōpen, ôrder; oil, out; cup, pút, rüle, əbove, takən, pencəl, lemən, circəs
ch, child; ng, long; sh, ship
th, thin; ᴛʜ, then; zh, measure

sympathy; touching: a poignant cry, a poignant story. **2** painfully sharp to the feelings; piercing: poignant suffering. **3** stimulating; keen or intense: a subject of poignant interest. **4** sharp in taste or smell. [ME < OF poignant, ppr. of poindre prick < L pungere]
—**poign′ant·ly,** adv.

poi·lu (pwä′lü) n. a nickname for a French soldier. [< F poilu, originally, hairy, ult. < L pilus hair]

poin·ci·a·na (poin′sē an′ə or -sē ä′nə) n. **1** any of a genus (Poinciana) of tropical trees or shrubs of the pea family having showy red or orange flowers. **2** royal poinciana. [< NL Poinciana, the genus name < de Poinci, a governor of the Antilles in the 1600's, who wrote a natural history of the islands]

poin·set·ti·a (poin set′ē ə) n. a shrub (Euphorbia pulcherrima), a kind of spurge native to Mexico and Central America, having clusters of small flowers surrounded by large, petal-like, scarlet bracts. [< NL; after Joel R. Poinsett (1779-1851), its discoverer]

point (point) n., v. —n. **1** a sharp end; something having a sharp end: the point of a needle. **2** a tiny, round mark; dot: A period is a point. Use a point to set off decimals. **3** Mathematics. something that has position but not extension: Two lines meet or cross at a point. **4** a particular place or spot: This is the point where we turned around and went back. **5** a particular time or moment: At this point he lost interest in the game. **6** a particular or definite position, state, condition, or degree; stage: boiling point. **7** an item; detail: He answered my questions point by point. **8** a distinguishing mark or quality: one's good points. **9** a physical characteristic or feature of an animal. **10** the main idea; the important or essential thing: I missed the point of his talk. **11** force; effectiveness. **12** a particular aim, end, or purpose. **13 a** each of the 32 positions indicating direction marked at the circumference of the card of a compass. **b** the interval between any two adjacent points of a compass; 11 degrees 15 minutes. **14** a piece of land with a sharp end sticking out into the water; cape. **15** a unit of credit, scoring, or measuring; unit of price quotations: We're three points ahead. The stock has gone up half a point. **16** Printing. a unit for measuring type; ¹⁄₁₂ of a pica (about 0.33 mm). **17** Informal. a hint; suggestion. **18** lace made with a needle. **19** Brit. a railway switch. **20** Hockey. a position at the opponents' blueline, taken by an offensive player when the puck is within their defensive zone, especially during a power play. **21** Lacrosse. one of the defencemen playing out in front of the goalie. **22** Hunting. the attitude, usually with muzzle pointing and one foreleg raised, assumed by a pointer or setter on finding game. **23 a** a tungsten or platinum piece, especially in the distributor of an automobile engine, for making or breaking the flow of current. **b** Esp.Brit. an outlet; socket.
at the point of, very near to; on the verge of: at the point of death.
beside the point, having little or nothing to do with the subject; not appropriate.
in point, apt or relevant: the case in point.
in point of, as regards.
in point of fact, as a matter of fact: In point of fact, he never left the house at all.
make a point, convince a person that an idea or argument is reasonable or correct: He is not a very good speaker, but he made his point.
make a point of, be particular about: He always makes a point of being on time.
on the point of, just about; on the verge of: She was on the point of going out when a neighbor came in.
strain or **stretch a point, a** exceed the reasonable limit. **b** make a special exception.
to the point, apt; appropriate: His speech was brief and to the point.
—v. **1** mark with dots; punctuate. **2** give force to (speech, action, etc.). **3** aim; tend. **4** indicate position or direction, or direct attention with, or as if with, the finger. **5** show with the finger; call attention to. **6** direct a finger, weapon, etc. **7** have or face a specified direction: The signboard points north. **8** of a dog, show the presence of game by standing rigid and looking toward it. **9** fill joints of (brickwork) with mortar or cement. **10** of an abscess, come to a head. **11** sharpen: to point a pencil.
point off, mark off with points or dots.
point out, show or call attention to: Please point out my mistakes.
point up, put emphasis on; call or give special attention to.
[ME < OF point mark, moment and pointe sharp point, both ult. < L pungere prick]

point–blank (adj. point′blangk′; adv. point′blangk′) adj., adv.

adj. **1** aimed straight at the mark, without allowing for the bullet, shell, etc. dropping from the original line of flight. **2** close enough for aim to be taken in this way: *He fired the gun from point-blank range.* **3** plain and blunt; direct: *a point-blank question.* —*adv.* **1** straight at the mark. **2** from close range. **3** plainly and bluntly; directly: *One boy gave excuses, but the other refused point-blank.* [apparently < *point,* v. + *blank* the white mark in the centre of a target]

point blanket *Cdn.* a Hudson's Bay Company blanket.

pointe (pwANT *or* point; *French,* pwANT) *n. Ballet.* **1** the toe or the tip of the toe. **2** the reinforced toe of a ballet slipper. **3** a ballet position in which the dancer stands and moves on the tips of the toes. **4** (*adj.*) of, in, or indicating this position: *pointe work.* [< F]

point·ed (poin'tid) *adj.* **1** sharpened to or having a point or points: *a pointed pencil, a pointed roof.* **2** sharp; piercing: *a pointed wit.* **3** directed; aimed: *a pointed remark.* **4** emphasized; conspicuous: *a pointed refusal.* —**point'ed·ly,** *adv.* —**point'ed·ness,** *n.*

point·er (poin'tər) *n.* **1** a person or thing that points. **2** a long, tapering stick used in pointing things out on a map, blackboard, etc. **3** a hand of a clock, meter, etc. **4** any of several breeds of hunting dog, having short, smooth hair, and trained to show where game is by standing rigid and looking toward it. **5** *Informal.* a useful hint or suggestion: *She gave him some pointers on improving his tennis.* **6** *Cdn.* a river boat that is pointed at both bow and stern and is of shallow draft, designed for use in logging drives.

poin·til·lism (pwan'tə liz'əm) *n.* a painting technique that developed from impressionism, using tiny dots, or points, of unmixed color placed close together on a white background so that they blend together when seen from a distance. It was developed by the French painter Georges Seurat (1859-1891). [< F *pointillisme < pointiller* mark with little dots or points]

poin·til·list (pwan'tə list') *n., adj.* —*n.* an artist who practises pointillism. —*adj.* of or having to do with pointillism.

point lace lace made with a needle, using buttonhole stitch on a paper pattern.

point·less (point'lis) *adj.* **1** without a point; blunt. **2** without force or meaning. **3** in a game, not having scored a point. —**point'less·ly,** *adv.* —**point'less·ness,** *n.*

point man *Hockey.* a player assigned to play the point.

point of honor or **honour** a matter that seriously affects a person's honor or principles: *It was a point of honor with her to give every applicant equal time.*

point of no return a stage in an action or event after which there is no turning back, so that one is obliged to continue.

point of order a question raised as to whether proceedings are according to the rules.

point-of-pur·chase (point'əv pėr'chəs) *adj.* relating to a type of advertising aimed at a buyer when he is in a store.

point of view **1** a position from which objects are considered. **2** an attitude of mind.

point-to-point (point'tə point') *n., adj.* —*n.* a steeplechase or cross-country race over a course marked by flags at the main points. —*adj.* made in a direct line from one point or place to another.

poise (poiz) *n., v.* **poised, pois·ing.** —*n.* **1** mental balance, composure, or self-possession: *She has perfect poise and never seems embarrassed.* **2** the way in which the body, head, etc. are held; carriage: *He admired the actor's poise.* —*v.* **1** balance: *Poise yourself on your toes.* **2** hold or carry evenly or steadily: *The athlete poised the weight in the air before throwing it.* [ME, n. < OF *pois, peis < L pensum* weight; v. < OF *poise, peise < peser* weigh < L *pensare,* intensive of *pendere* weigh]

poi·son (poi'zən) *n., v., adj.* —*n.* **1** a drug or other substance that is very dangerous to health and capable of causing death. Strychnine and opium are poisons. **2** anything dangerous or deadly: *Hate becomes a poison in the mind.* —*v.* **1** kill or harm by poison. **2** put poison in or on. **3** have or exert a dangerous or harmful effect on: *Lies poison the mind. He poisoned his friend's mind against the girl.* —*adj.* poisonous or poisoned: *a poison plant, a poison arrow.* [ME < OF *poison < L potio, -onis* potion. Doublet of POTION.] —**poi'son·er,** *n.*

poison ivy **1** a North American woody vine or shrub (*Rhus radicans*) of the cashew family having greenish flowers, white berries, and leaves composed of three leaflets, and producing a toxic oil in its leaves, flowers, fruit, and bark that causes a severe rash on contact with the skin. **2** any of several other plants of the genus *Rhus.*

poison oak **1** a plant (*Rhus diversiloba*) of the cashew family found along the Pacific coast of North America. The poison oak has leaflets shaped like oak leaves. **2** poison sumac.

poi·son·ous (poi'zən əs) *adj.* **1** containing poison; very harmful to health and capable of causing death. **2** having a dangerous or harmful effect: *a poisonous lie.* —**poi'son·ous·ly,** *adv.* —**poi'son·ous·ness,** *n.*

poi·son–pen (poi'sən pen') designating an abusive, insulting, or threatening letter, etc. written out of malice and usually anonymously.

poison sumac a shrub (*Rhus vernix*) of the cashew family found in swamps in E North America, having pinnate leaves with seven to thirteen leaflets, greenish flowers, and greenish-white berries. Most people will get an itchy skin rash if they touch this plant.

poke¹ (pōk) *v.* **poked, pok·ing;** *n.* —*v.* **1** push against with something pointed; jab: *He poked me in the ribs with his elbow.* **2** thrust; push: *He poked his head in the kitchen window.* **3** stir a fire with a poker. **4** *Informal.* punch: *He threatened to poke his brother in the nose.* **5** pry: *She's always poking into other people's business.* **6** make by poking: *to poke a hole in something.* **7** go lazily; loiter: *poking along at 40 kilometres per hour.* **8** search or putter (usually used with **around** or **about**): *poking around in the attic.* —*n.* **1** a poking; thrust; push. **2** *Informal.* a punch. **3** a slow, lazy person. **4** a projecting brim on the front of a poke bonnet, or the bonnet itself. [ME; cf. MDu., MLG *poken*]

poke² (pōk) *n. Dialect (except in* **buy a pig in a poke**). a bag or sack. **buy a pig in a poke,** buy something without seeing it first. [ME; akin to OE *pocca* bag, pocket]

poke³ (pōk) *n.* a bonnet or hat with a large brim in front. [? n. use of *poke¹*]

poke⁴ (pōk) *n.* pokeweed. [< Algonquian]

poke·ber·ry (pōk'ber'ē) *n., pl.* **-ries. 1** a berry of the pokeweed. **2** pokeweed.

poke bonnet a bonnet with a projecting brim at the front.

poke check *Hockey.* a quick thrust or jab with one's stick at the puck in order to get it away from an opponent.

poke–check (pōk'chek') *v.* **1** carry out a poke check. **2** administer a poke check to (an opposing player).

poke·lo·gan (pōk'lō'gən) *n. Cdn.* a small stagnant backwater in a stream; logan. [< Algonquian]

pok·er¹ (pōk'ər) *n.* a person or thing that pokes, especially a metal rod for stirring a fire. [< *poke¹*]

pok·er² (pōk'ər) *n.* any of several card games in which a player bets that the value of the cards he holds in his hand is greater than that of the cards held by the other players. [origin uncertain]

poker face *Informal.* **1** a face or facial expression that does not show one's thoughts or feelings. **2** a person having such a face or facial expression.

poke·weed (pōk'wēd') *n.* a tall North American perennial plant (*Phytolacca americana*) having juicy purple berries and a large, poisonous root. The red juice of the berries has been used as ink and to color wine, candies, cloth, etc., but is considered poisonous. [*poke⁴* + *weed*]

pok·ey¹ or **pok·y¹** (pōk'ē) *n., pl.* **-eys** or **-ies.** *Slang.* jail.

pok·ey² or **pok·y²** (pōk'ē) *adj.* **pok·i·er, pok·i·est. 1** annoyingly slow or unenergetic: *a pokey old horse.* **2** small and mean or cramped: *a pokey room.* **3** shabby or dowdy. [< *poke¹*] —**pok'i·ly,** *adv.*

pol (pol) *n. Slang.* a politician, especially one with experience and expertise.

pol. **1** political. **2** politics.

Pol. Polish.

Po·lack (pō'lok *for* 1; pō'lak *for* 2) *n.* **1** *Derogatory slang.* a person of Polish descent. **2** *Obsolete.* **a** a native or inhabitant of Poland. **b** the king of Poland. [< Polish *Polak*]

po·lar (pō'lər) *adj.* **1** of, having to do with, or coming from the North or South Pole or the region around it: *the polar wastes, a polar wind.* **2** passing over the North or South Pole: *a satellite in polar orbit. We flew the polar route to Europe last year.* **3** of or having to do with the poles of a magnet, battery, etc. **4** directly opposite in character, like the poles of a magnet: *Good and evil are polar elements.* **5** *Chemistry.* ionizing when dissolved or fused. [< Med.L *polaris < L polus* pole. See POLE².]

polar bear a large, white, semi-aquatic bear (*Thalarctos maritimus*) found in arctic regions.

polar front the line or region where cold air from the polar regions meets warm air from the tropics, usually producing strong winds and storms.

Po·lar·is (pō ler′is) *n.* the North Star; polestar.

po·lar·i·scope (pō lar′ə skōp′ *or* -ler′ə skōp′) *n.* an instrument for showing the polarization of light, or for examining substances in polarized light.

po·lar·i·ty (pō lar′ə tē *or* -ler′ə tē) *n.* 1 the possession of two opposed poles. A magnet or battery has polarity. 2 a positive or negative polar condition, as in electricity. 3 the possession or exhibition of two opposite or contrasted principles or tendencies.

po·lar·i·za·tion (pō′lər ə zā′shən *or* pō′lər ī-) *n.* 1 the production or acquisition of polarity. 2 a process by which gases produced during electrolysis are deposited on one or both electrodes of a cell, giving rise to a reverse electromotive force. 3 a state, or the production of a state, in which rays of light exhibit different properties in different directions.

po·lar·ize (pō′lər īz′) *v.* **-ized, -iz·ing.** give polarity to; cause polarization in. [< F *polariser*]

pol·der (pol′dər) *n.* an area of low, marshy land reclaimed from the sea or some other body of water and protected by dikes. [< Du.]

pole¹ (pōl) *n., v.* **poled, pol·ing.** —*n.* 1 a long, slender, usually round piece of wood, metal, etc.: *a telephone pole, a flagpole, a ski pole.* 2 a unit for measuring length, equal to a rod, or perch (about 5.03 m). 3 a unit for measuring area, equal to a square rod (about 25.3 m²). —*v.* push or make something go with a pole: *to pole a raft. We poled down the river.* [OE *pāl* < L *palus* stake. Doublet of PALE².]
☛ *Hom.* Pole, poll.

pole² (pōl) *n.* 1 either end of the earth's axis. The North Pole and the South Pole are opposite each other. 2 either of two parts or points where opposite forces are strongest. A magnet or battery has both a positive pole and a negative pole. 3 either end of the axis of any sphere. 4 either of two opinions, forces, etc. considered as being opposite extremes.
poles apart, very much different; in strong disagreement: *The two bargaining parties are still poles apart and there is no sign of a settlement.*
[ME < L *polus* < Gk. *polos*]
☛ *Hom.* pole, poll.

Pole (pōl) *n.* 1 a native or inhabitant of Poland, a country in central Europe. 2 a person of Polish descent.
☛ *Hom.* pole, poll.

pole·axe (pōl′aks′) *n., v.* **-axed, -ax·ing.** —*n.* an axe with a long handle and a hook or spike opposite the blade. —*v.* fell with or as if with a poleaxe. Sometimes, **poleax.** [ME *pollax* < *pol(le)* poll, head + *ax* axe]

pole·cat (pōl′kat′) *n.* 1 a small, dark-brown carnivorous European mammal (*Mustela putorius*) of the weasel family. 2 *Esp.U.S.* the North American skunk. 3 *Esp.U.S. Informal.* a mean or contemptible person. [ME *polcat* < OF *poule* fowl, hen (< VL *pulla,* fem. to L *pullus* young fowl) + ME *cat* cat; so called because it preys on poultry]

po·lem·ic (pə lem′ik) *n., adj.* —*n.* 1 a strong argument against or attack on an idea, belief, or opinion: *The book is nothing but a long polemic against communism.* 2 Usually, **polemics,** the art or practice of argument or controversy (*used with a singular or plural verb*): *This is not the time to indulge in polemics.* —*adj.* of, having to do with, or actively engaged in controversy or disagreement: *a polemic writer.* [< Gk. *polemikos* belligerent < *polemos* war]

po·lem·i·cal (pə lem′ə kəl) *adj.* polemic. —**po·lem′i·cal·ly,** *adv.*

po·lem·i·cist (pə lem′ə sist′) *n.* a person given to or skilful in polemics.

pole·star (pōl′stär′) *n.* 1 the North Star, formerly much used as a guide by sailors. 2 a guiding principle; guide. 3 a centre of attraction, interest, or attention.

pole vault 1 an athletic event or contest in which contestants jump, or vault, over a high, horizontal bar, with the aid of a long, flexible pole. The pole vault is one of the Olympic track and field events. 2 a vault of this kind.

pole–vault (pōl′volt *or* -vôlt) *v.* make a vault with the aid of a pole. —**pole′-vault′er,** *n.*

po·lice (pə lēs′) *n., v.* **-liced, -lic·ing.** —*n.* 1 the organized civil force of a community, province, or state whose duty is to guard people's lives and property, to preserve peace and order, and to arrest those who commit crimes. 2 the people who carry out this duty for a community: *The police arrived within 10 minutes.* —*v.* guard or keep order in: *to police the streets, to police an army camp.* [< F *police* < L < Gk. *politeia* polity. Doublet of POLICY¹, POLITY.]

police court a court of limited jurisdiction, such as a magistrate's court.

police dog 1 a dog trained for use in police work. German

hat, āge, fär; let, ēqual, tèrm; it, īce
hot, ōpen, ôrder; oil, out; cup, pút, rüle,
əbove, takən, pencəl, lemən, circəs
ch, child; ng, long; sh, ship
th, thin; ŦH, then; zh, measure

shepherds, Doberman pinschers, and Airedales are often used as police dogs. 2 German shepherd.

police force the law-enforcing body of a community.

po·lice·man (pə lēs′mən) *n., pl.* **-men.** 1 a member of a police force. 2 *Hockey.* a rugged player responsible for keeping opposing players from treating his team-mates roughly.

police state a country strictly controlled by governmental authority, especially with the aid of a secret police organization.

police station the headquarters of the police of a particular area or district in a city, or of the local police force of a small community.

police village *Cdn.* in Ontario, an unincorporated village administered by a board of trustees.

po·lice·wom·an (pə lēs′wúm′ən) *n., pl.* **-wom·en.** a woman who is a member of a police force.

pol·i·cy¹ (pol′ə sē) *n., pl.* **-cies.** 1 a plan of action; a course or method of action that has been deliberately chosen and that guides or influences future decisions: *It is poor policy to promise more than you can give. The candidate explained his party's policy.* 2 practical wisdom; prudence, shrewdness, or sagacity. [ME < OF *policie* < L < Gk. *politeia* polity. Doublet of POLICE, POLITY.]

pol·i·cy² (pol′ə sē) *n., pl.* **-cies.** a written contract about insurance. [< F < Ital. *polizza* < Med.L < Gk. *apodeixis* declaration]

pol·i·cy·hold·er (pol′ə sē hōl′dər) *n.* the owner of an insurance policy.

po·li·o (pō′lē ō′) *n.* poliomyelitis.

po·li·o·my·e·li·tis (pō′lē ō mī′ə lī′tis *or* pol′ē ō-) *n.* 1 an acute infectious disease caused by a virus, characterized by symptoms ranging from fever, headaches, vomiting, etc. to extensive permanent paralysis of muscles. 2 any inflammation of the grey matter of the spinal cord. [< NL < Gk. *polios* grey + *myelos* marrow + *-itis*]

pol·ish (pol′ish) *v., n.* —*v.* 1 make smooth and shiny: *to polish shoes.* 2 become smooth and shiny: *This leather polishes well.* 3 remove by smoothing (*used with off or away*). 4 put into a better condition; improve (*often used with up*): *to polish a manuscript, to polish up one's French.* 5 make elegant; refine: *to polish one's manners.*
polish off, *Informal.* get done with; finish.
—*n.* 1 a substance used to give smoothness or shine or to remove dirt, tarnish, etc.: *silver polish.* 2 shininess; smoothness: *The table has a high polish.* 3 culture; elegance; refinement: *a woman of breeding and polish.* 4 the act or process of polishing: *I gave the table a quick polish.* [ME < OF *poliss-,* a stem of *polir* < L *polire*] —**pol′ish·er,** *n.*

Pol·ish (pōl′ish) *n., adj.* —*n.* the language of Poland, a country in central Europe. —*adj.* of or having to do with Poland, its people, or their language.

Po·lit·bu·ro (pə lit′byúr ō *or* pol′it byúr′ō) *n.* an executive committee of the Communist Party that controls policy and matters of state in the Soviet Union, Bulgaria, and some other Communist countries.

po·lite (pə līt′) *adj.* 1 having or showing good manners; behaving properly. 2 refined; elegant. [< L *politus* polished] —**po·lite′ly,** *adv.* —**po·lite′ness,** *n.*
☛ *Syn.* 1. Polite, civil, courteous = having the manners appropriate to good social relations. **Polite** suggests having and showing good manners at all times, and emphasizes following the rules for behaving properly: *That polite boy gave me his seat.* **Civil** means being just polite enough not to be rude: *All I expect is a civil answer.* **Courteous** adds to *polite* the idea of showing thoughtful attention to the feelings and wishes of others: *I go to that store because the clerks are courteous.*

pol·i·tic (pol′ə tik′) *adj.* 1 characterized by prudence and practical wisdom; sensible and expedient: *It was not politic to arouse his irritation.* 2 scheming; crafty. 3 *Archaic.* political: *The state is a body politic.* [ME < OF < L < Gk. *politikos,* ult. < *polis* city-state] —**pol′i·tic·ly,** *adv.*

po·lit·i·cal (pə lit′ə kəl) *adj.* 1 of or concerned with politics. 2 having to do with public affairs or government: *Treason is a political offence.* 3 of politicians or their methods. 4 having a definite system of government. —**po·lit′i·cal·ly,** *adv.*

political economy 1 a social science dealing with the ways in which political and economic processes are related to each other;

the study of the economic problems of government. **2** *Archaic.* economics.

political science a social science dealing with political institutions and processes, especially with the principles and conduct of government.

pol·i·ti·cian (pol'ə tish'ən) *n.* **1** a person holding a political office. **2** a person active in politics, especially one seeking political office.
☛ *Syn.* **1. Politician, statesman** = someone active or skilled in public or governmental affairs. **Politician** especially suggests ability to deal with people and accomplish things for the good of the people and the country, but often is used slightly or contemptuously to suggest an unprincipled person scheming for his own or his party's good: *All office-holders are politicians.* **Statesman,** always in a good sense, emphasizes sound judgment, shrewdness, far-sightedness, and skill in dealing with public problems and managing national affairs: *Churchill was a great statesman.*

po·lit·i·cize (pə lit'ə sīz') *v.* **-ized, -iz·ing. 1** make politically aware: *a politicized electorate.* **2** give a political character or tone to: *to politicize a social issue.* **3** talk about or take part in politics. —**po·lit'i·ci·za'tion,** *n.*

pol·i·tick (pol'ə tik') *v.* take part in political activity, especially in order to directly or indirectly solicit votes: *He's politicking in the Maritimes this week.* —**pol'i·tick'er,** *n.*

po·lit·i·co (pə lit'ə kō') *n., pl.* **-cos.** *Often derogatory.* politician.

pol·i·tics (pol'ə tiks') *n.* **1** the science and art of government; political science (*used with a singular verb*). **2** the management and conduct of government as a business or profession (*used with a singular verb*): *She was in politics for many years.* **3** political activities, practices, or policies (*used with a plural or singular verb*): *party politics.* **4** political methods or manoeuvres, especially for gaining or keeping power, often suggesting scheming or dishonesty (*used with a singular or plural verb*): *He played politics to win the contract.* **5** political principles or opinions (*used with a plural verb*): *His politics are very conservative.* **6** the complex of relationships between people, especially as they involve authority or power (*used with a singular verb*): *We are studying the politics of volunteer organizations.*

pol·i·ty (pol'ə tē) *n., pl.* **-ties. 1** political organization; government. **2** a particular form or system of government. **3** a community with a government; state. [< obs. F *politie* < L < Gk. *politeia,* ult. < *polis* city-state. Doublet of POLICE, POLICY¹.]

pol·ka (pōl'kə or pō'kə) *n., v.* **-kaed, -ka·ing.** —*n.* **1** a kind of lively dance. **2** the music for this dance. —*v.* dance a polka. [< F *polka* or G *Polka* < Czech *pulka* half-step < *pul* half]

pol·ka dot 1 a dot or round spot repeated to form a regular pattern on cloth. **2** a pattern or fabric with such dots. —**polka-dot** or **polka-dotted,** *adj.*

poll (pōl) *n., v.* —*n.* **1** a voting; collection of votes: *The class took a vote to decide where the picnic would be held.* **2** the number of votes cast: *If it rains on election day, there may be a light poll.* **3** the results of these votes. **4** a list of persons, especially a list of voters. **5** the place where votes are cast and counted: *The polls will be open till 8 o'clock tonight.* **6** a survey of public opinion concerning a particular subject. **7** the head, especially the part of it on which the hair grows.
—*v.* **1** receive (as votes): *The mayor polled a record vote.* **2** vote; cast (a vote). **3** take or register the votes of. **4** question or canvass in a public-opinion poll. **5** cut off or cut short the hair, wool, horns, branches, etc. of. [cf. MDu. *pol(le)* top, MLG *pol* head]
☛ *Hom.* **pole, Pole.**

pol·lack (pol'ək) See **pollock.**

pol·len (pol'ən) *n.* a fine, yellowish powder formed in the anthers of flowers, consisting of tiny grains that are male sex cells which fertilize the ovules. [< L *pollen* mill dust]

pollen basket an area surrounded by stiff hairs on each hind leg of a honeybee, in which the bee collects pollen to carry back to the hive.

pol·li·nate (pol'ə nāt') *v.* **-nat·ed, -nat·ing.** carry pollen from stamens to pistils of; shed pollen on. Many flowers are pollinated by bees. —**pol'li·na'tion,** *n.*

polling booth a screened or otherwise enclosed space in a polling station where a voter marks his ballot in privacy.

polling station a room or building set up during an election as a place where the people living nearby may vote.

pol·li·wog (pol'ē wog') *n.* tadpole. [cf. ME *polwigle* < *pol(le)* poll, head + *wigle* wiggle]

pol·lock (pol'ək) *n., pl.* **-lock** or **-locks. 1** an important food fish (*Pollachius virens*) of the cod family found in the N Atlantic Ocean, having a long body with a deep-green back and pale belly and having a small barbel under the jaw. **2** a closely related species

(*Pollachius pollachius*) found in European coastal waters, having a brownish or olive back and lacking a barbel. It is a popular game fish but has no commercial value.

poll·ster (pōl'stər) *n.* one who takes a public-opinion poll.

poll tax a tax on every person, or on every person of a specified class, especially as a prerequisite to the right to vote.

pol·lu·tant (pə lü'tənt) *n.* something that pollutes: *Automobile exhaust is a major air pollutant.*

pol·lute (pə lüt') *v.* **-lut·ed, -lut·ing. 1** make physically impure or unclean; especially, contaminate (the air, water, soil, etc.) with man-made waste materials: *the polluted air of cities. The lake has been polluted with waste from a large factory.* **2** make morally impure; defile. [< L *pollutus,* pp. of *polluere*] —**pol·lut·er,** *n.*

pol·lu·tion (pə lü'shən) *n.* **1** the action of polluting or the condition of being polluted. **2** something that pollutes; pollutant: *That's not fog, that's pollution.*

Pol·lux (pol'əks) *n.* **1** *Greek and Roman mythology.* one of the twin sons of Zeus and Leda. Pollux was immortal; his brother Castor was mortal. **2** one of the two brightest stars in the constellation Gemini. [< L < Gk. *Polydeukēs*]

Pol·ly·an·na (pol'ē an'ə) *n.* one who is always cheerful, or overly cheerful, and always sees good in everything, even in the face of disaster. [after *Pollyanna,* the heroine of stories by Eleanor H. Porter (1868-1920)]

pol·ly·wog (pol'ē wog') See **polliwog.**

po·lo (pō'lō) *n.* **1** a game played by two teams of players on horseback, who use long-handled mallets to drive a wooden ball through the opposing team's goal. **2** water polo. [? ult. < Tibetan *pulu*]

pol·o·naise (pol'ə nāz' or pō'lə nāz') *n.* **1** a slow, stately dance in 3/4 time. **2** the music for such a dance. **3** a woman's overdress consisting of a bodice and a draped, cutaway overskirt. < F *polonaise,* fem. adj., literally, Polish]

po·lo·ni·um (pə lō'nē əm) *n.* a radio-active element that occurs naturally in trace amounts in uranium ores and is also produced artificially in nuclear reactors. The most commonly produced isotope is polonium-210 (half-life approximately 138 days), a highly radio-active and toxic material used as a heat and power source. *Symbol:* Po; *at.no.* 84; *at.wt.* (209); *half-life* approx. 103 years. [< NL < Med.L *Polonia* Poland, the homeland of Marie Curie (1867-1934), who, with her husband, discovered it]

Po·lo·ni·us (pə lō'nē əs) *n.* a pompous old man who is the father of Ophelia in Shakespeare's *Hamlet.*

pol·ter·geist (pol'tər gīst') *n.* a ghost or spirit that is essentially harmless but mischievous, supposedly responsible for unexplained happenings and noises such as door slamming, chain rattling, or rapping sounds on walls or tables. [< G *Poltergeist* noisy ghost]

pol·troon (pol trün') *n.* a wretched coward. [< F *poltron* < Ital. *poltrone* < *poltro* colt, ult. < L *pullus* young animal]

poly– *combining form.* **1** more than one; many; extensive, as in *polyangular.* **2** polymeric; polymerized, as in *polyethylene, polystyrene.* [< Gk. *poly-* < *polys* much, many]

pol·y·am·ide (pol'ē am'īd) *n.* any of a group of synthetic polymers containing two or more amide groups (-CONH-). The most common polyamides are the various forms of nylon.

pol·y·an·drous (pol'ē an'drəs) *adj.* **1** having to do with or practising polyandry. **2** *Botany.* having many stamens.

pol·y·an·dry (pol'ē an'drē) *n.* the practice or condition of having more than one husband or male mate at one time. Compare **polygamy** and **polygyny.** [< Gk. *polyandria* < *polys* many + *anēr, andros* man, husband]

pol·y·an·thus (pol'ē an'thəs) *n.* **1** a hybrid primrose (*Primula polyantha*) cultivated in several varieties for its large, brightly colored flowers. **2** a narcissus (*Narcissus tazetta*) having clusters of small yellow or white flowers. [< NL < Gk. *polyanthos* < *polys* many + *anthos* flower]

pol·y·car·pous (pol'i kär'pəs) *adj. Botany.* consisting of many or several carpels. [< *poly-* + Gk. *karpos* fruit]

pol·y·chlo·rin·at·ed biphenyl (pol'ē klôr'ə nā'təd) PCB.

pol·y·chro·mat·ic (pol'i krō mat'ik) **1** having a variety of colors. **2** of or designating light or other electromagnetic radiation composed of more than one wavelength.

pol·y·chrome (pol'i krōm') *adj., n.* —*adj.* having to do with or made or decorated with several colors. —*n.* **1** a work of art in several colors, especially a painted statue. **2** a combination of many colors. [< Gk. *polychrōmos* < *polys* many + *chrōma* color]

pol·y·clin·ic (pol'i klin'ik) *n.* a clinic or hospital for treating many different diseases.

pol·y·es·ter (pol'ē es'tər) *n.* **1** any of a group of synthetic organic polymers usually formed from glycols and certain acids,

prepared in the form of plastics, fibres, etc. **2** thread, yarn or fabric made of a polyester.

pol·y·eth·y·lene (pol′ē eth′ə lēn′) *n.* any of various very strong, lightweight synthetic polymers of ethylene that are good insulators and are resistant to chemicals and moisture. Polyethylenes are used for insulation and a wide variety of moulded containers and also in the form of thin films or sheets for packaging, etc. *Formula:* $(C_2H_4)_n$

po·lyg·a·mist (pə lig′ə mist) *n.* a person who practises or favors polygamy.

po·lyg·a·mous (pə lig′ə məs) *adj.* **1** having to do with or practising polygamy. **2** *Botany.* bearing both unisexual and hermaphrodite flowers on the same plant or on different plants of the same species. **3** *Zoology.* having more than one mate at one time: *Baboons are polygamous.* —**po·lyg′a·mous·ly,** *adv.*

po·lyg·a·my (pə lig′ə mē) *n.* **1** the practice or condition of having more than one spouse at one time. Compare **polygyny** and **polyandry. 2** *Zoology.* the practice of mating with several individuals of the opposite sex during one breeding season, usually one male with several females. [< Gk. *polygamia* < *polys* many + *gamos* marriage]

pol·y·glot (pol′i glot′) *adj., n.* —*adj.* **1** knowing several languages; multilingual. **2** written in several languages. —*n.* **1** a person who knows several languages. **2** a book written in several languages. **3** a mixture or confusion of several languages. [< Gk. *polyglōttos* < *polys* many + *glōtta* tongue]

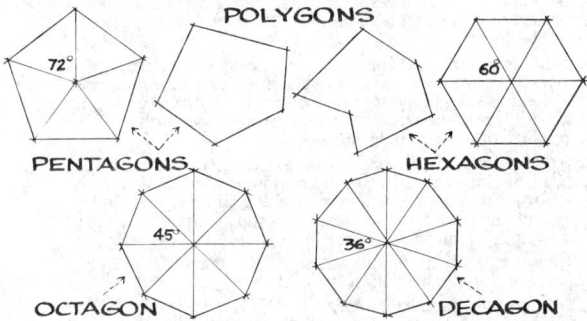

POLYGONS

72° PENTAGONS

60° HEXAGONS

45° OCTAGON

36° DECAGON

pol·y·gon (pol′i gon′) *n. Geometry.* a closed plane figure having straight sides, especially one with more than four sides. [< LL < Gk. < *polys* many + *gōnia* angle]

po·lyg·o·nal (pə lig′ə nəl) *adj. Geometry.* having three or more angles and sides.

pol·y·graph (pol′i graf′) *n.* **1** an instrument for recording various physiological responses (such as changes in blood pressure, respiration, etc.) to verbal stimuli. Polygraphs are often used as lie detectors; the physiological evidence is interpreted as indicating the probable truth or falsehood of specific statements made by the person being tested. **2** a device resembling a pantograph, for drawing or writing two or more copies of the same thing at the same time. **3** a versatile or prolific writer.

pol·y·graph·ic (pol′i graf′ik) *adj.* of or having to do with polygraphs. —**pol′y·graph′i·cal·ly,** *adv.*

po·lyg·y·nous (pə lij′ə nəs) *adj.* **1** having to do with or practising polygyny. **2** *Botany.* having many pistils.

po·lyg·y·ny (pə lij′ə nē) *n.* the practice or condition of having more than one wife or female mate at one time. Compare **polygamy** and **polyandry.**

pol·y·he·dral (pol′i hē′drəl) *adj.* **1** of or having to do with a polyhedron. **2** having many faces.

pol·y·he·dron (pol′i hē′drən) *n., pl.* **-drons, -dra** (-drə). a solid figure having four or more plane faces, all of which are polygons. The faces of a **regular polyhedron** are all identical polygons. A cube is a regular polyhedron with six square faces. [< NL < Gk. *polyedros* < *polys* many + *hedra* seat, side]

pol·y·math (pol′i math′) *n.* a person of great and encyclopedic learning. [< Gk. *polumathēs* very learned, ult. < *polu-* poly- + *manthanein* to learn. 17c. See MATHEMATICS.]

pol·y·mer (pol′i mər) *n.* any of a large number of natural or synthetic, organic or inorganic compounds composed of very large molecules that are made up of many light, simple molecules chemically linked together. Cellulose and proteins are naturally occurring polymers; concrete, plastics, and glass are synthetic polymers.

pol·y·mer·ic (pol′i mer′ik) *adj.* of, having to do with, or being a

hat, āge, fär; let, ēqual, tėrm; it, īce
hot, ōpen, ôrder; oil, out; cup, put, rüle,
əbove, takən, pencəl, lemən, circəs
ch, child; ng, long; sh, ship
th, thin; ŧH, then; zh, measure

polymer: *a polymeric compound.* [< Gk. *polymerēs* < *polys* many + *meros* part]

pol·y·mer·i·za·tion (pol′i mər ə zā′shən *or* pol′i mər ī zā′shən) *n.* the chemical union of many small, simple molecules into very large molecules to form a polymer. The molecules produced in polymerization contain repeating structural units of the simple molecules in the form of a chain or network.

pol·y·mer·ize (pol′i mə rīz′ *or* pə lim′ə rīz′) *v.* **-rized, -riz·ing. 1** form a polymer; make polymeric. **2** undergo polymerization.

pol·y·morph (pol′i môrf′) *n.* a polymorphic organism.

pol·y·mor·phic (pol′i môr′fik) *adj.* having, assuming, or passing through many or various forms, stages, etc.

pol·y·mor·phism (pol′i môr′fiz əm) *n.* **1** *Biology.* the occurrence of different forms or color types in an individual organism or in different individuals of one species. **2** *Chemistry.* the property of a compound of crystallizing in at least two distinct forms.

pol·y·mor·phous (pol′i môr′fəs) *adj.* polymorphic. [< Gk. *polymorphos* < *polys* many + *morphē* form]

Pol·y·ne·sian (pol′i nē′zhən) *adj., n.* —*adj.* **1** of or designating a major race of mankind that includes most of the peoples traditionally inhabiting Polynesia, a large group of islands in the E Pacific, extending from Hawaii south to New Zealand and east to Easter Island. The Polynesian race includes the Hawaiians, Maoris, Samoans, and Tahitians. **2** of or having to do with Polynesia, its peoples, or their languages. —*n.* **1** a member of the Polynesian race. **2** a branch of the Malayo-Polynesian family of languages, including Hawaiian, Maori, etc.

pol·y·no·mi·al (pol′i nō′mē əl) *n., adj.* —*n.* **1** *Algebra.* an expression consisting of two or more terms. *ab, x^2y* and *3npq* are monomials; *$ab + x^2y$* and *$pq - p^2 + q$* are polynomials. **2** *Biology.* a taxonomic name consisting of more than two terms, as for designating a subspecies. —*adj.* consisting of two or more terms: *polynomial equations.* [< *poly-* + *-nomial,* as in *binomial*]

po·lyn·ya *or* **po·lyn·ia** (pə lin′yə) *n.* a fairly large area of open water surrounded by pack ice. [< Russian]

pol·yp (pol′ip) *n.* **1** any of various small, simple water animals (of phylum Coelenterata) having a tubelike body that is closed at one end and has at the other end a mouthlike opening surrounded by tentacles for gathering in food. Polyps often grow in colonies, with their bases connected. Corals and sea anemones are polyps. **2** a smooth, projecting growth arising from the surface of a mucous membrane. [< F < L < Gk. *polypous* < *polys* many + *pous* foot]

pol·y·phon·ic (pol′i fon′ik) *adj.* **1** *Music.* of, having to do with, or characterized by polyphony: *polyphonic music.* **2** producing many sounds; many-voiced. **3** *Phonetics.* representing more than one sound, as English *oo* in *food, good.*

po·lyph·o·ny (pə lif′ə nē) *n.* **1** *Music.* the combination of two or more independent melodies or musical parts so that they relate harmonically to each other; counterpoint. **2** a multiplicity of sounds. **3** *Phonetics.* the representation of more than one sound by the same letter or symbol. [< Gk. *polyphōnia* < *polys* many + *phōnē* voice]

pol·y·pro·py·lene (pol′i prō′pə lēn′) *n.* a lightweight thermoplastic, similar to, but harder than, polyethylene, used for a wide variety of moulded articles, insulating materials, etc. It is a polymer of propylene. *Formula:* $(C_3H_6)_n$

pol·y·pus (pol′i pəs) *n., pl.* **-pi** (-pī′ *or* -pē′). polyp (def. 2).

pol·y·sac·cha·ride (pol′i sak′ə rīd′) *n.* any of a large group of natural carbohydrates, including starch, cellulose, and glycogen, whose molecules consist of two or more molecules of simple sugars linked together.

pol·y·sty·rene (pol′i stī′rēn *or* -stir′ən) *n.* a synthetic organic polymer formed from styrene. It is a rigid, colorless, thermoplastic resin, resistant to acids, alkalis, and many solvents and having excellent insulating properties. Polystyrene is used as an insulator and for many moulded products such as dishes, toys, etc.

pol·y·syl·lab·ic (pol′i sə lab′ik) *adj.* **1** having more than three syllables. **2** of a style of writing or speaking, characterized by polysyllabic words. —**pol′y·syl·lab′i·cal·ly,** *adv.*

pol·y·syl·la·ble (pol′i sil′ə bəl) *n.* a word of more than three syllables.

pol·y·syn·the·sis (pol′i sin′thə sis) *n., pl.* **-ses** (-sēz′). **1** the

synthesis of several elements. **2** *Linguistics.* the combination of the subject, object, verb, and modifiers into one unit or expression of which the elements have no separate existence as words, as in Eskimo or certain Amerindian languages.

pol·y·syn·thet·ic (pol'i sin thet'ik) *adj.* of or having to do with polysynthesis.

pol·y·tech·nic (pol'i tek'nik) *adj., n.* —*adj.* having to do with or giving instruction in many technical arts or applied sciences. —*n.* a polytechnic school. [< F < Gk. *polytechnos* < *polys* many + *technē* art]

pol·y·the·ism (pol'i thē'iz əm) *n.* belief in more than one god. The religion of the ancient Greeks was polytheism. [< F *polythéisme,* ult. < Gk. *polys* many + *theos* god]

pol·y·the·ist (pol'i thē'ist) *n.* a person who believes in more than one god.

pol·y·the·is·tic (pol'i thē is'tik) *adj.* having to do with or characterized by belief in many gods. —**pol'y·the·is'ti·cal·ly,** *adv.*

pol·y·thene (pol'i thēn') *n.* polyethylene.

pol·y·ton·al (pol'i tōn'əl) *adj. Music.* using or having polytonality. —**pol·y·ton'al·ly,** *adv.*

pol·y·ton·al·i·ty (pol'i tō nal'ə tē) *n. Music.* **1** the use of several keys at the same time. **2** the sounds thus produced.

pol·y·un·sat·u·rat·ed (pol'i un sach'ə rā'təd) *adj.* having to do with or designating a class of vegetable and animal fats whose molecules consist of long carbon chains with many double bonds.

pol·y·ur·e·thane (pol'ē yür'ə thān') *n.* any of a group of synthetic organic polymers that may be rubbery, resinous, or fibrous. Polyurethanes are most often made in the form of flexible foams used for mattresses, cushions, etc. and rigid foams used for insulation, lightweight cores for aircraft wings, etc.

pol·y·va·lence (pol'i va'ləns) *n.* the condition or quality of being polyvalent.

pol·y·va·lent (pol'i va'lənt) *adj. Chemistry.* **1** having more than one valence. **2** having a valence of more than one. **3** of a vaccine, effective against more than one micro-organism, toxin, etc.

pol·y·vi·nyl (pol'i vī'nəl) *adj.* of or having to do with a group of thermoplastic resins formed by the polymerization of vinyl.

polyvinyl chloride a colorless, synthetic thermoplastic material produced by the polymerization of vinyl chloride. It is widely used in a rigid form for moulded articles and in a flexible form for tubing, electrical insulation, clothing, etc. *Abbrev.:* PVC

pom·ace (pum'is) *n.* **1** apple pulp or similar fruit pulp before or after the juice has been pressed out. **2** the crushed matter that is left after oil has been pressed out of fish, seeds, etc. [ult. < Med.L *pomacium* cider < L *pomum* apple]

po·ma·ceous (pə mā'shəs) *adj.* of, having to do with, or resembling apples or similar fruits. [< NL *pomaceus* < L *pomum* apple]

po·made (pom ād' *or* pomäd') *n.* a perfumed ointment for the scalp and hair. [< F < Ital. *pomata* < L *pomum* fruit]

po·man·der (pə man'dər *or* pō'man dər) *n.* a ball of mixed aromatic substances formerly carried for perfume or as a guard against infection. [var. of earlier *pomeamber* < *pome* + *amber*]

pome (pōm) *n.* an apple or any fruit like it; a fruit consisting of firm, juicy flesh surrounding a core that contains several seeds. Apples, pears, and quinces are pomes. See **fruit** for picture. [ME < OF *pome,* ult. < L *pomum* apple]

pome·gran·ate (pom'gran'it *or* pom'ə gran'it) *n.* **1** a fruit with a thick, leathery, red or brownish-yellow skin, juicy red pulp, and many seeds. The pulp of a pomegranate has a pleasant tart taste. **2** the small tropical tree or bush (*Punica granatum*) that bears this fruit. [ME < OF *pome grenate* < *pome* fruit (ult. < L *pomum*) + *grenate* having grains < L *granata,* fem. < *granum* grain]

Pom·er·a·ni·an (pom'ər ā'nē ən) *n., adj.* —*n.* **1** a native or inhabitant of Pomerania, a region in central Europe on the Baltic Sea. **2** a breed of small dog having a sharp nose, pointed ears, and long, thick, silky hair. —*adj.* of or having to do with Pomerania or its people.

pom·mel (*n.* pom'əl *or* pum'əl; *v.* pum'əl) *n., v.* **-melled or -meled, -mel·ling** *or* **-mel·ing.** —*n.* **1** the part of a saddle that sticks up at the front. See **saddle** for picture. **2** a rounded knob on the hilt of a sword, dagger, etc. —*v.* pummel. [ME < OF *pomel,* ult. < L *pomum* apple] —**pom'mel·ler** *or* **pom'mel·er,** *n.*

po·mol·o·gist (pō mol'ə jist) *n.* a person who is skilled in pomology. [< NL *pomologia* < L *pomum* fruit, apple + *-logia* -logy]

po·mol·o·gy (pə mol'ə jē) *n.* the science or practice of fruit growing. [< NL < L *pomum* fruit + Gk. *-logos* treating of]

pomp (pomp) *n.* **1** a stately display; splendor; magnificence: *The king was crowned with great pomp.* **2** an excessively showy display. [ME < OF < Gk. *pompē* parade]

pom·pa·dour (pom'pə dôr') *n.* **1** a woman's hairstyle in which the hair is puffed high over the forehead and turned under in a roll. **2** a man's hairstyle in which the hair is brushed straight up and back from the forehead. [after Jeanne Antoinette Poisson, Marquise de *Pompadour* (1721-1764), a mistress of Louis XV of France]

pom·pa·no (pom'pə nō') *n., pl.* **-nos. 1** a saltwater food fish (*Trachinotus carolinus*) of the West Indies and neighboring coasts of North America having a deep body, no teeth, and a forked tail. **2** any of several related fishes. [< Sp.]

Pom·pei·an (pom pā'ən) *n., adj.* —*n.* a native or inhabitant of Pompeii, a city in ancient Italy. —*adj.* of or having to do with Pompeii or its people.

Pom·pe·ii (pom pā'ē *or* pom pā') *n.* a city in ancient Italy, which was buried by an eruption of Mount Vesuvius in A.D. 79. Its ruins have been partly laid bare by excavation.

pom·pom (pom'pom) *n.* **1** an ornamental ball or tuft of yarn, feathers, etc. used especially on clothing, hats, shoes, etc. **2** any of several varieties of chrysanthemum or dahlia having small, rounded flower heads. [< F *pompon* < *pompe* pomp]

pom–pom (pom'pom) *n.* an automatic anti-aircraft gun, used especially on shipboard. [imitative]

pom·pon (pom'pon) *n.* pompom.

pom·pos·i·ty (pom pos'ə tē) *n., pl.* **-ties. 1** the quality of being pompous; pompous behavior, speech, etc.: *He is a good speaker, except for his tendency toward pomposity.* **2** a pompous act, gesture, remark, etc.

pom·pous (pom'pəs) *adj.* **1** having or showing a tendency to display oneself in an overly grand or self-important way: *a pompous speech. The band leader bowed in a pompous way.* **2** marked by pomp; splendid; magnificent. [< F *pompeux* < LL *pomposus*] —**pom'pous·ly,** *adv.* —**pom'pous·ness,** *n.*

pon·cho (pon'chō) *n., pl.* **-chos. 1** a cloak consisting basically of a large piece of cloth with a slit in the middle for the head to go through, worn especially in Latin America. **2** a similar garment, especially one that is waterproof, worn by cyclists, hikers, etc. as a raincoat. [< Sp. < Araucanian (S.Am.Ind.) *pontho*]

pond (pond) *n.* **1** a body of still water, smaller than a lake. **2** *Cdn., esp.Nfld.* a lake. [originally, var. of *pound³*]

pon·der (pon'dər) *v.* consider carefully; think over. [ME < OF < L *ponderare* weigh < *pondus, -deris* weight] —**pon'der·er,** *n.* —**pon'der·ing·ly,** *adv.*

pon·der·a·ble (pon'dər ə bəl) *adj.* **1** capable of being weighed; having perceptible mass. **2** capable of being appraised, or mentally weighed.

pon·de·ro·sa pine (pon'də rō'sə) **1** a large pine (*Pinus ponderosa*) found from southern British Columbia to California, usually 25 to 30 metres tall but sometimes reaching a height of about 50 metres, having very long needles and large cones with prickles; yellow pine. The ponderosa pine is one of the main timber-producing trees of W North America. **2** its yellowish wood. [< L *ponderosus* heavy. See PONDEROUS.]

pon·der·os·i·ty (pon'dər os'ə tē) *n.* the quality of being ponderous; ponderousness.

pon·der·ous (pon'dər əs) *adj.* **1** very heavy. **2** heavy and clumsy: *Slowly he lifted his ponderous bulk from the chair.* **3** overly serious and labored: *a ponderous way of speaking.* [ME < OF < L *ponderosus* < *pondus, -deris* weight] —**pon'der·ous·ly,** *adv.*

pon·der·ous·ness (pon'dər əs nəs) *n.* the quality of being ponderous.

pond hockey *Cdn.* **1** unorganized hockey played on frozen ponds, streams, etc. **2** *Slang.* poorly played hockey; hockey of a low standard.

pond lily water lily.

pond·weed (pond'wēd') *n.* any of a genus (*Potamogeton*) of aquatic plants found in ponds and slow streams, with some species occurring in brackish water, having jointed stems and, in many species, broad floating leaves and grasslike submerged leaves. Some species are entirely submerged.

pone (pōn) *n. Southern U.S.* corn pone. [< Algonquian]

pon·gee (pon jē') *n.* a kind of soft, plain-woven silk, usually left in natural brownish-yellow color. [? < dial. Chinese *punchi* home-woven]

pon·iard (pon'yərd) *n.* dagger. [< F *poignard,* ult. < L *pugnus* fist]

pon·ti·fex (pon'tə feks') *n., pl.* **pon·tif·i·ces. 1** in ancient Rome, a member of the principal college of priests. **2** pontiff. [< L *pontifex* a high priest of Rome, probably < *pons, pontis* bridge + *facere* make. Doublet of PONTIFF.]

pon·tiff (pon′tif) n. 1 the Pope. 2 bishop. 3 a high priest; chief priest. [< F *pontife* < L *pontifex* a high priest of Rome. Doublet of PONTIFEX.]

pon·tif·i·cal (pon tif′ə kəl) adj., n. —adj. 1 of or having to do with the Pope; papal. 2 of or having to do with a bishop. 3 pompous. —n. Usually, **pontificals,** pl. the vestments and marks of dignity used by cardinals and bishops at certain ecclesiastical functions or ceremonies. —**pon·tif′i·cal·ly,** adv.

Pontifical Zouave a member of a force of volunteers from various countries, including Canada, recruited to fight for the Holy See in the 19th century when the independence of the Vatican was threatened by Piedmont.

pon·tif·i·cate (n. pon tif′ə kit or -kāt′; v. pon tif′ə kāt′) n., v. -cat·ed, -cat·ing. —n. the office or term of office of a pontiff. —v. 1 officiate as a pontiff, especially at Mass. 2 speak dogmatically and pompously: *He loved to pontificate on the virtues of thrift.*

pon·tif·i·ces (pon tif′ə sēz′) n. pl. of **pontifex.**

pon·til (pon′təl) n. a steel or iron rod used as a glass blower's tool. Also called **pontil rod.** [< F *pontil* < Ital. *pontello,* diminutive < *punto* < L *punctum*]

pon·toon (pon tün′) n. 1 a low, flat-bottomed boat. 2 such a boat, or some other floating structure, used as one of the supports of a temporary bridge. 3 a boat-shaped float on an aircraft, used for coming down on or taking off from water. [< F *ponton* < L *ponto, -onis* < *pons, pontis* bridge]

pontoon bridge a temporary bridge supported by low, flat-bottomed boats or other floating structures.

Pon·tus (pon′təs) n. 1 an ancient name of the Black Sea. 2 an ancient country in NE Asia Minor, just south of the Black Sea. It became a Roman province.

pon·y (pō′nē) n., pl. -nies. 1 a very small horse, especially any of several breeds of very small, stocky, gentle horse, usually less than 130 cm high. 2 *Informal.* something that is small for its kind, especially a small liqueur glass or the amount it will hold. 3 *Slang.* racehorse. 4 a literal translation of a text, especially such a translation of a Latin or other text used dishonestly by students in preparing or reciting lessons. [< obs. F *poulenet,* ult. < L *pullus* foal]

pony express *U.S. Historical.* a system of carrying mail, etc. by men on fast ponies or horses.

pooch (püch) n. *Slang.* dog. [origin uncertain]

pood (püd) n. a Russian unit for measuring mass, equal to about 16.4 kg. [< Russian, ult. < L *pondus* weight]

poo·dle (pü′dəl) n. a breed of intelligent, active dog having thick, wool-like hair that is not shed and that is often clipped in any of several standard patterns. [< G *Pudel,* short for *Pudelhund* < dial. *pudeln* splash-water] —**poo′dle-like′,** adj.

poof (püf) n., interj. —n. a sound resembling the puff of breath in blowing out a candle. —interj. an expression of rejection or contempt. Also, **pouf.** [imitative]

pooh (pü) interj. or n. an exclamation of contempt.

Pooh-Bah (pü′bä′) n. 1 a self-important, pompous person. 2 a person holding many insignificant offices. [< *Pooh-Bah,* a character in Gilbert and Sullivan's *The Mikado*]

pooh-pooh (pü′pü′) v., interj. —v. express contempt for; make light of. —interj. an exclamation of contempt.

pool¹ (pül) n. 1 a small body of still water; a small pond. 2 a still, deep place in a stream: *Trout are often found in the pools of a brook.* 3 a puddle of water or any other liquid: *There was a pool of grease under the car. The water stood in pools in the garden after the rain.* 4 a large tank made of concrete, plastic, etc. for swimming or bathing in; swimming pool. [OE *pōl*]

pool² (pül) n., v. —n. 1 a game played on a special table with six pockets. The players try to drive balls into the pockets with cues. 2 the things or money put together by different persons for common advantage. 3 *Cdn.* in the West, a co-operative grain-marketing organization among farmers. 4 a group of people, usually having the same skills, who are drawn upon as needed: *a secretarial pool.* 5 an arrangement between business firms to create a monopoly in order to control prices. 6 car pool. 7 a fund raised by a group of persons for purposes of speculation, as in the stock market, commodities, etc. 8 the persons who form a pool. 9 the stake played for in some games. —v. 1 put (things or money) together for common advantage: *The three boys pooled their savings for a year to buy a boat.* 2 form a pool. [< F *poule* booty, originally hen < LL *pulla* chick; meaning influenced by *pool¹*]

pool·room (pül′rüm′ or -rüm′) n. a room or place in which the game of pool is played.

pool train *Historical. Cdn.* a train that is operated over a line of

track by more than one railway company. A pool train used to run between Toronto and Montreal.

poop¹ (püp) n., v. —n. 1 a deck at the stern of a ship above the ordinary deck, often forming the roof of a cabin. 2 *Archaic.* the stern of a ship. —v. of a wave, break over the stern of (a ship). [ME < OF < Ital. *poppa* < L *puppis* stern]

poop² (püp) v. *Slang.* make or become exhausted (*often used with out*): *All of us were pooped after the climb. That last dance pooped me out.* [origin unknown]

poor (pür) adj., n. —adj. 1 not having enough income to maintain a standard of living regarded as normal in the community in which one lives: *They were poor, but never destitute.* 2 not good in quality; lacking something needed: *poor soil, a poor crop, a poor cook, poor health.* 3 scanty. 4 needing pity; unfortunate: *This poor child has hurt himself.* 5 not favorable: *a poor chance for recovery.* —n. **the poor,** pl. persons who are needy. [ME < OF *povre* < L *pauper.* Doublet of PAUPER.] —**poor′ness,** n.

☛ *Syn. adj.* 1. **Poor, penniless, impoverished** = with little or no money or property. **Poor** has a rather wide range of meaning, from "having no money or property at all and being dependent on charity for the necessities of life," to "having no money to buy comforts or luxuries": *She is a poor widow.* **Penniless** suggests being without any money at all, but sometimes only temporarily: *She found herself penniless in a strange city.* **Impoverished** emphasizes being reduced to poverty from comfortable circumstances, even wealth: *The deposed king died alone and impoverished.*

poor·house (pür′hous′) n. *Historical.* a place in which paupers live at public expense.

poor law *Historical.* a law providing for or regulating the relief or support of the poor through public funds.

poor·ly (pür′lē) adv., adj. —adv. in a poor manner; badly or inadequately. —adj. *Informal.* in bad health; somewhat ill: *I feel poorly today.*

poor-spir·it·ed (pür′spir′ə tid) adj. having or showing a poor, cowardly, or abject spirit.

poor white in the S United States, a member of a group or class of white people characterized by poverty, lack of education, opportunity, etc.

poor·will (pür′wil) n. a small goatsucker (*Phalaenoptilus nuttalli*) of W North America having a short, rounded tail, mottled grey plumage, and bristles on the sides of its mouth. [imitative]

pop¹ (pop) v. **popped, pop·ping;** n., adv. —v. 1 make a short, quick, explosive sound. 2 move, go, or come suddenly or unexpectedly. 3 thrust or put suddenly: *He popped a candy into his mouth.* 4 put (a question) suddenly. 5 *Informal.* shoot. 6 burst open with a pop. 7 heat or roast (popcorn) until it bursts with a pop. 8 of the eyes, bulge or open very wide: *The surprise made her eyes pop.* 9 *Baseball.* hit a short, high ball over the infield. 10 *Slang.* take (a drug or drugs) habitually, especially in pill form: *He used to pop a lot of pills.*

pop off, *Slang.* a fall asleep. b die. c state loudly as a complaint.
pop the question, *Informal.* propose marriage.

—n. 1 a short, quick, explosive sound. 2 a shot from a gun, etc. 3 a non-alcoholic carbonated drink. 4 *Baseball.* a fly ball that can be easily caught.

—adv. with a pop; suddenly. [imitative]

pop² (pop) adj., n. *Slang.* —adj. popular. —n. 1 a piece of popular music. 2 pop art.

pop³ (pop) n. *Informal.* papa; father.

pop. 1 population. 2 popular.

pop art an art style, especially in painting and sculpture, that is based on the style of advertising art, comic strips, etc., and uses commonplace objects such as hamburgers or soup cans as subject matter.

pop·corn (pop′kôrn′) n. 1 a variety of corn whose kernels burst open and puff out in a white mass when heated. 2 the white, puffed-out kernels, usually eaten salted and buttered.

Pope or **pope** (pōp) n. the supreme head of the Roman Catholic Church; the Pope, the last three popes. [OE *pāpa* < LL *papa* pope < L *papa* tutor, bishop < Gk. *pap(p)as* father]

pop·er·y (pōp′ər ē) n. *Derogatory.* the doctrines, customs, and ceremonies of the Roman Catholic Church.

pop·eye (pop′ī′) n. a prominent or bulging eye. —**pop′eyed′,** adj.

---

hat, āge, fär; let, ēqual, tèrm; it, īce
hot, ōpen, ôrder; oil, out; cup, pút, rüle,
əbove, takən, pencəl, lemən, circəs
ch, child; ng, long; sh, ship
th, thin; ᴛн, then; zh, measure

pop·gun (pop′gun′) *n.* a toy gun that shoots with a popping sound.

pop·in·jay (pop′in jā′) *n.* **1** a vain, overtalkative person; conceited, silly person. **2** *Obsolete.* parrot. [ME < OF *papingay* parrot < Sp.; cf. Arabic *babaghā*]

pop·ish (pōp′ish) *adj. Derogatory.* of or having to do with the Roman Catholic Church. —**pop′ish·ly,** *adv.* —**pop′ish·ness,** *n.*

pop·lar (pop′lər) *n.* **1** any of a genus (*Populus*) of slender, fast-growing trees found mainly in north temperate regions, having oval or heart-shaped leaves, flowers in drooping catkins, and light, soft wood. **2** the wood of a poplar. Poplar is used for veneer, boxes, barrels, etc. [ME < OF *poplier* < L *populus*]

poplar bluff *Cdn.* in the Prairies, a grove of poplar trees: *The farmhouse nestled in the shady poplar bluff.*

pop·lin (pop′lən) *n.* a strong, plain-woven fabric with a crosswise rib, used for sportswear, raincoats, etc. [< F < Ital. *papalina,* fem., papal, perhaps from the one-time papal capital Avignon, France, where the fabric was first made]

pop·o·ver (pop′ō′vər) *n.* a very light and hollow muffin.

pop·per (pop′ər) *n.* a person or thing that pops, especially a wire basket or metal pan used for popping popcorn.

pop·pet (pop′it) *n.* **1** a valve that controls the flow of water, gas, etc. by moving straight up and down instead of being hinged. **2 a** one of the small pieces of wood on the gunwhale of a boat forming the rowlocks. **b** a timber placed beneath a ship's hull to support the ship in launching. **3** a bead that can be attached to other beads by a snap coupling to form a chain. Poppets are used especially to make necklaces, bracelets, etc. adjustable in length. **4** a small or dainty person, especially a pretty child, girl, etc.; pet. [var. of *puppet*]

pop·py (pop′ē) *n., pl.* **-pies;** *adj.* —*n.* **1** any of a genus (*Papaver*) of annual, perennial, or biennial plants having lobed leaves, a milky sap, showy flowers, and seeds in a capsule. Opium is made from the juice in the seed capsule of one species of poppy. Other species are cultivated as garden plants. **2** the flower of a poppy. **3** a bright orange-red.
—*adj.* **1** bright orange-red. **2** designating a family (Papaveraceae) of plants having lobed, showy flowers, that includes the poppies and celandine. [OE *popæg, papig,* ult. < L *papaver*]

pop·py·cock (pop′ē kok′) *n. or interj. Informal.* nonsense; bosh.

pop·si·cle (pop′sə kəl) *n.* fruit-flavored ice on a small stick. [< trademark]

pop·u·lace (pop′yə lis) *n.* the people in general; the masses. [< F < Ital. *popolaccio,* ult. < L *populus* people]
☛ *Hom.* **populous.**

pop·u·lar (pop′yə lər) *adj.* **1** liked by most acquaintances or associates: *He was always popular with his co-workers.* **2** liked by a great many people: *The song quickly became popular.* **3** intended to appeal to the current tastes of the general public: *popular music, popular science.* **4** within the means of the average person: *popular prices.* **5** of or by the people; representing the people: *Canada has a popular government.* **6** widespread among many people; of people in general: *It is a popular belief that black cats bring bad luck.* [< L *popularis* < *populus* people]
☛ *Syn.* **3.** See note at **general.**

popular front or **Popular Front** a coalition of communist, socialist, and moderate political parties against fascism, especially in France.

pop·u·lar·i·ty (pop′yə lar′ə tē *or* -ler′ə tē) *n.* the quality or state of being liked by most people.

pop·u·lar·ize (pop′yə lər īz′) *v.* **-ized, -iz·ing. 1** change, especially by simplifying and presenting in an interesting form, so as to appeal to a great number of people instead of a special group: *history in a popularized form.* **2** cause to be generally liked: *to popularize a tune.* —**pop′u·lar·i·za′tion,** *n.* —**pop′u·lar·iz′er,** *n.*

pop·u·lar·ly (pop′yə lər lē) *adv.* **1** by the people as a whole; in general: *The defendant was popularly believed to have been guilty, though she was acquitted.* **2** in a popular manner.

popular vote the vote of the entire electorate thought of as including all the people.

pop·u·late (pop′yə lāt′) *v.* **-lat·ed, -lat·ing. 1** inhabit: *This city is densely populated.* **2** furnish with inhabitants: *Europeans populated much of the Canadian West.* [< Med.L *populare,* ult. < L *populus* people]

pop·u·la·tion (pop′yə lā′shən) *n.* **1** the people of a city or a country: *The population was up in arms.* **2** the total number of such people. **3** a part of the inhabitants distinguished in any way from the rest: *the urban population, the Inuit population.* **4** the act or process of furnishing with inhabitants. **5** the total number of organisms of a specific kind in a given area: *the caribou population of the North.* **6** the total number of individuals or things from which samples are taken for statistical measurement.

population explosion a great and rapid increase in a population.

pop·u·lism (pop′yə liz′əm) *n.* a political movement supporting or appealing to the interests of ordinary people, or that section of society having little or no personal power or influence. [< L *populus* people + E *-ism*]

pop·u·list (pop′yə list′) *n., adj.* —*n.* a person who advocates populism or belongs to a populist party. —*adj.* of, having to do with, or supporting populism: *a populist crusade.*

pop·u·lous (pop′yə ləs) *adj.* heavily populated; inhabited by many people: *a populous region.* [ME < L *populosus* < *populus* people] —**pop′u·lous·ly,** *adv.* —**pop′u·lous·ness,** *n.*
☛ *Hom.* **populace.**

por·ce·lain (pôr′sə lin *or* pôrs′lən) *n.* **1** a hard, white, translucent pottery fired at very high temperatures, consisting basically of kaolin, a fine, white clay that melts only at a very high temperature, quartz, and feldspar. Compare **earthenware, stoneware. 2** articles made of porcelain: *We packed all the porcelain ourselves.* **3** (*adj.*) made of porcelain. [< F < Ital. *porcellana,* a kind of shell, ult. < L *porcus* hog; from the shell being shaped like a pig's back]

porch (pôrch) *n.* **1** a covered, sometimes enclosed, entrance to a building. **2** veranda. **3** a platform at the entrance to a house; stoop. **4** a sun porch. [ME < OF *porche* < L *porticus.* Doublet of PORTICO.]

por·cine (pôr′sīn *or* pôr′sən) *adj.* of, having to do with, or like pigs. [< L *porcinus* < *porcus* pig]

por·cu·pine (pôr′kyə pīn′) *n.* any of a number of large, heavy-set, short-legged rodents having long, sharp, barbed spines mixed in with the coarse hair of the back and tail. Porcupines make up two families: the New World family (Erethizontidae) of tree-dwelling porcupines and the Old World family (Hystricidae) of ground-dwelling porcupines. [ME < OF *porc-espin,* ult. < L *porcus* pig + *spina* thorn]

porcupine fish any of various marine fishes (family Diodontidae, especially genus *Diodon*) having a spine-covered body that the fishes can inflate into a ball as a means of defence when disturbed. Porcupine fishes belong to the same order as the puffers.

pore[1] (pôr) *v.* **pored, por·ing. 1** study long and steadily (used with *over*): *He pored over the magnificent old book for hours.* **2** meditate or ponder intently (used with *over*): *to pore over a problem.* **3** *Archaic.* gaze earnestly or steadily. [origin uncertain] —**por′er,** *n.*
☛ *Hom.* **pour.**

pore[2] (pôr) *n.* a very tiny opening through which fluids may pass; especially, one of the openings in the skin of people or animals or in the leaves of plants through which fluids are absorbed or excreted. Sweat comes through the pores of our skin. See **epidermis** for picture. [ME < OF < L < Gk. *poros,* literally, passage]
☛ *Hom.* **pour.**

por·gy (pôr′gē) *n., pl.* **-gies** *or* (esp. collectively) **-gy.** any of various marine fishes (family Sparidae) found mainly in tropical and subtropical coastal waters, having a deep, compressed body with a single, long dorsal fin and a small mouth with strong teeth.

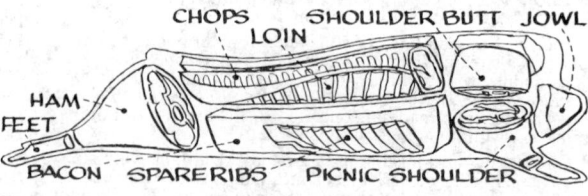

CHOPS SHOULDER BUTT JOWL
LOIN
HAM
FEET
BACON SPARERIBS PICNIC SHOULDER

The main cuts of pork

pork (pôrk) *n.* **1** the flesh of a pig used for food. **2** *U.S. Slang.* money from Federal or State appropriations, taxes, licences, etc. spent to confer local benefits for political reasons. [ME < OF < L *porcus* pig]

pork barrel *Slang. Esp. U.S.* a term used to describe government appropriations for projects that may not be needed but are likely to appeal to certain constituents. —**pork′-bar′rel,** *adj.*

pork·eat·er (pôrk′et′ər) *n. Cdn. Historical. Derogatory.* a voyageur, especially one in the employ of the North West Company, plying between Montreal and the Grande Portage, so called because pork was the staple of the diet of such men, as opposed to the pemmican and coarser foods endured by winterers and others who ventured into the interior.

pork·er (pôr′kər) *n.* a pig, especially one fattened to eat.

pork·pie (pôrk′pī′) *n.* 1 a deep, crusted pie filled with minced pork. 2 a hat having a low, flat crown resembling a porkpie. Also, **pork pie**.

pork·y (pôr′kē) *adj.* 1 of or like pork. 2 fat.

porn (pôrn) *n. Slang.* pornography. Also, **porno**.

por·nog·ra·pher (pôr nog′rə fər) *n.* a person who produces pornography.

por·no·graph·ic (pôr′nə graf′ik) *adj.* of, having to do with, or being pornography.

por·nog·ra·phy (pôr nog′rə fē) *n.* writings, pictures, films, etc. depicting sexual activity with the intention of arousing sexual desire. [ult. < Gk. *pornē* harlot + *-graphos* writing about]

po·ros·i·ty (pô ros′ə tē) *n.* the quality or state of being porous.

po·rous (pô′rəs) *adj.* full of pores or tiny holes; permeable by water, air, etc.: *Cloth, blotting paper, and ordinary clay flowerpots are porous.* —**po′rous·ness,** *n.*

por·phy·ry (pôr′fə rē) *n., pl.* **-ries.** 1 a hard rock quarried in ancient Egypt, consisting of white or red feldspar crystals embedded in a fine-grained, dark red or purplish base. 2 any igneous rock in which crystals are scattered through a mass of fine-grained minerals. [< F *porfire,* ult. < Gk. *porphyra* purple dye of shellfish]

por·poise (pôr′pəs) *n., pl.* **-pois·es** or (esp. collectively) **-poise.** 1 any of several small toothed whales (constituting genera *Phocaena, Phocaenoides,* and *Neomeris*) allied to the dolphins but smaller and having a blunt snout and flattened, spade-shaped teeth. Many authorities classify porpoises as forming a separate family (Phocaenidae), but others classify them in the same family (Delphinidae) as the dolphins, killer whale, etc. 2 dolphin. [ME < OF *porpeis,* ult. < L *porcus* hog + *piscis* fish]

por·ridge (pôr′ij) *n.* a food made of oatmeal or other cereal boiled in water or milk until it thickens. [var. of *pottage*]

por·rin·ger (pôr′ən jər) *n.* a small dish, often having a handle, used for soup, porridge, etc. [earlier *pottanger,* alteration of *potager* < OF *potager* < *potage.* See POTTAGE.]

port¹ (pôrt) *n.* 1 a harbor; a place where ships and boats can take shelter from storms. 2 a city or town with a harbor where ships and boats may take on or unload cargo. 3 See **port of entry.** 4 any place where one can find shelter. [OE < L *portus*]
☛ *Syn.* 1, 2. See note at **harbor.**

port² (pôrt) *n.* 1 an opening in the side of a ship for letting in light and air; porthole. 2 an opening in a wall, ship's side, etc. through which guns may be fired. 3 the cover for such an opening. 4 an opening in machinery for steam, air, water, etc. to pass through. 5 *Curling and lawn bowling.* an opening between stones or woods, large enough for another stone or wood to pass through. [< L *porta* gate]

port³ (pôrt) *n., adj., v.* —*n.* the left side of a ship or aircraft when facing forward. See **aft** for picture. —*adj.* on the left side of a ship. —*v.* turn or shift to the left side (*used mainly as a command*). [origin uncertain]

port⁴ (pôrt) *n., v.* —*n.* 1 a way of holding one's head and body; bearing. 2 the position of a weapon when ported. —*v.* bring, hold, or carry (a rifle or sword) across and close to the body with the barrel or blade near the left shoulder. [< F *port* < *porter* carry < L *portare*]

port⁵ (pôrt) *n.* a strong, sweet wine that is dark red or tawny. [< *Oporto,* a city in Portugal]

Port. Portugal; Portuguese.

port·a·bil·i·ty (pôr′tə bil′ə tē) *n.* the quality or state of being portable.

port·a·ble (pôr′tə bəl) *adj., n.* —*adj.* 1 capable of being carried by hand or readily moved about: *a portable typewriter, a portable TV set.* 2 capable of being transferred: *a portable pension.* —*n.* 1 a portable radio, phonograph, etc. 2 a temporary building on the grounds of an overcrowded school, used as an extra classroom. [< LL *portabilis* < L *portare* carry]

portable pension a pension plan under which, if a person changes his job, his pension contributions and entitlements continue unchanged.

por·tage (pôr tázh′ *or* pôr′tij) *n., v.* **-taged, -tag·ing.** —*n.* 1 a carrying of boats, canoes, provisions, etc. overland from one stretch of water to another. 2 a place where such a carrying takes place. 3 the act of carrying. 4 the cost of carrying. 5 an instance of such a carrying: *He made the trip without a single portage.* —*v.* 1 carry canoe, etc. from one stretch of water to another. 2 make a portage. [ME < OF *portage* < *porter* carry]

por·tal (pôr′təl) *n.* a door, gate, or entrance, especially an imposing one. [< Med.L *portale* < L *porta* gate]

hat, āge, fär; let, ēqual, tėrm; it, īce
hot, ōpen, ôrder; oil, out; cup, pút, rüle,
above, takən, pencəl, lemən, circəs
ch, child; ng, long; sh, ship
th, thin; ᴛʜ, then; zh, measure

portal-to-portal pay wages paid to an employee for the time he spends moving to and from his actual place of work while on the grounds or premises of the employer.

por·ta·men·to (pôr′tə men′tō; *Italian,* pôr′tä men′tō) *n., pl.* **-ti** (-tē). *Music.* a smooth, legato movement gliding from one note or pitch to another without a break. [< Ital. *portamento* < L *portare* carry]

port authority a commission appointed to manage a port.

port·cul·lis (pôrt kul′is) *n.* a strong gate or grating of iron sliding up and down in grooves, used to close the gateway of a castle or fortress. [ME < OF *porte coleice* sliding gate, ult. < L *porta* gate + *colare* filter through]

porte-co·chere *or* **porte-co·chère** (pôrt′kō sher′) *n.* 1 a porch at the door of a building under which carriages and automobiles stop so that persons getting in or out are sheltered. 2 an entrance for carriages, leading into a courtyard. [< F *porte-cochère* coachgate]

porte-mon·naie (pôrt′mun′ē; *French,* pôrt mô ne′) *n.* a purse; pocketbook. [< F *porte-monnaie* < *porter* carry + *monnaie* (small) change]

por·tend (pôr tend′) *v.* indicate beforehand; be a portent of: *Black clouds portend a storm.* [ME < L *portendere* < *por-* before + *tendere* extend]

por·tent (pôr′tent) *n.* 1 a significant sign of something to come; omen: *The scandal was regarded as a portent of worse things to come.* 2 prophetic significance: *happenings of dire portent.* [< L *portentum,* originally neut. pp. of *portendere.* See PORTEND.]

por·ten·tous (pôr ten′təs) *adj.* 1 of, having to do with, or being a portent: *an event of portentous significance.* 2 amazing; extraordinary: *a portentous effort of will.* 3 self-important; pompous: *With a portentous clearing of the throat, he began to speak.* —**por·ten′tous·ly,** *adv.* —**por·ten′tous·ness,** *n.*

por·ter¹ (pôr′tər) *n.* 1 a person employed to carry things, especially one who carries luggage for patrons at a hotel, airport, etc. 2 an attendant in a sleeping car or club car of a railway train. [ME < OF *porteour,* ult. < L *portare* carry]

por·ter² (pôr′tər) *n.* 1 a person who guards a door or entrance; doorkeeper. 2 janitor. [ME < OF *portier* < LL *portarius* < L *porta* gate]

por·ter³ (pôr′tər) *n.* a heavy, dark-brown beer made from browned or charred malt. [short for *porter's ale* (i.e., ale for a *porter¹*)]

por·ter·house (pôr′tər hous′) *n.* a choice beefsteak containing the tenderloin. [possibly because made popular about 1814 by the keeper of a New York porterhouse (a place where porter and other liquors were sold)]

porterhouse steak porterhouse.

port·fo·li·o (pôrt fō′lē ō′) *n., pl.* **-li·os.** 1 a brief case; portable case for loose papers, drawings, etc. 2 the position and duties of the office of a cabinet minister or a minister of state: *The Minister of Defence resigned his portfolio.* 3 holdings in the form of stocks, bonds, etc. [< Ital. *portafoglio,* ult. < L *portare* carry + *folium* sheet, leaf]

port·hole (pôrt′hōl′) *n.* 1 an opening in a ship's side to let in light and air. 2 an opening in a wall, ship's side, etc. through which guns may be fired.

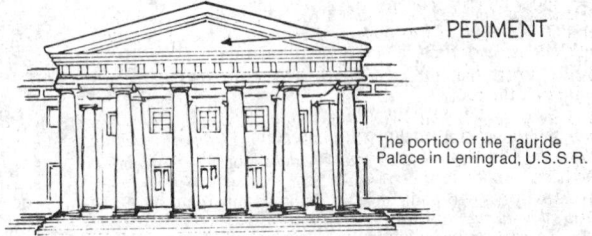

— PEDIMENT

The portico of the Tauride Palace in Leningrad, U.S.S.R.

por·ti·co (pôr′tə kō) *n., pl.* **-coes** or **-cos.** a porch or a covered

walk having the roof supported by columns. [< Ital. *portico* < L *porticus*. Doublet of PORCH.]

por·tiere or **por·tière** (pôr tyer′) *n.* a curtain hung at a doorway. [< F *portière* < *porte* door]

por·tion (pôr′shən) *n., v.* —*n.* 1 a part or share. 2 the quantity of food served for one person. 3 the part of an estate that goes to an heir; property inherited. 4 dowry. 5 one's lot; fate. —*v.* 1 divide into parts or shares. 2 give (a thing to a person) as share; give a portion, inheritance, dowry, etc. to. [ME < OF < L *portio, -onis*] —**por′tion·less**, *adj.*
☛ *Syn. n.* 1. See note at **part**.

Port·land cement (pôrt′lənd) a kind of cement made by burning limestone and clay in a kiln. [< Isle of *Portland*, a peninsula of S England]

port·ly (pôrt′lē) *adj.* **-li·er, -li·est. 1** stout; corpulent. 2 stately; dignified. [< *port*⁴] —**port′li·ness**, *n.*
☛ *Syn.* 1. See note at **fat**.

port·man·teau (pôrt man′tō) *n., pl.* **-teaus** or **-teaux** (-tōz). *Esp.Brit.* a travelling bag, especially a stiff, oblong one with two compartments opening like a book. [< F *portmanteau* < *porter* carry + *manteau* mantle]

portmanteau word *Linguistics.* a word that is made by combining parts of two other words; blend. *Smog* is a portmanteau word from *smoke* and *fog*.

port of entry any harbor, airport, etc. in a country that has customs facilities where goods and persons are cleared for entry into or exit from the country.

por·trait (pôr′trit *or* pôr′trāt) *n.* 1 a picture, especially a painting, of a person. 2 a picture in words; description. [< F *portrait*, originally pp. of *portraire* portray]

por·trait·ist (pôr′trā tist) *n.* a person who paints portraits.

por·trai·ture (pôr′trə chər *or* pôr′trə chür′) *n.* 1 the act of portraying. 2 the art of making portraits. 3 a portrait or portraits. [ME < OF *portraiture* < *portrait* portrait < *portraire*. See PORTRAY.]

por·tray (pôr trā′) *v.* 1 describe or picture in words: *The book portrays life long ago.* 2 make a picture of. 3 represent on the stage. [ME < OF *portraire* < L *protrahere* < *pro-* forth + *trahere* draw] —**por·tray′er**, *n.*

por·tray·al (pôr trā′əl) *n.* 1 a portraying by pictures or in words. 2 a picture or description.

Por·tu·guese (pôr′chü gēz′ *or* pôr′chü gēz′) *n., pl.* **-guese**; *adj.* —*n.* 1 a native or inhabitant of Portugal, a country in SW Europe. 2 a person of Portuguese descent. 3 the Romance language of Portugal and Brazil. —*adj.* of or having to do with Portugal, its people, or Portuguese.

por·tu·lac·a (pôr′chü lak′ə) *n.* any of a genus (*Portulaca*) of succulent herbs of the purslane family, mainly of tropical and subtropical regions, especially a trailing annual plant (*P. grandiflora*) cultivated in gardens for its showy, yellow, pink, red, purple, or white flowers. See also purslane. [< L *portulaca* purslane]

pose¹ (pōz) *n., v.* **posed, pos·ing.** —*n.* 1 a position of the body; a way of holding the body. 2 an attitude assumed for effect; pretence; affectation: *She takes the pose of being an invalid when really she is well and strong.* —*v.* 1 hold a position: *He posed for an hour for his portrait.* 2 put in a certain position: *The artist posed him before painting his picture.* 3 pretend; make a pretence, especially for effect: *He posed as a rich man though he owed more than he owned.* 4 put forward; state: *to pose a question.* [< F *poser* < LL *pausare* pause < L *pausa* a pause; in Romance languages influenced by stem *pos-* of L *ponere* place (from meaning "cause to pause, set down"); this influence spread to many compounds, e.g., *compose, dispose, oppose*]

pose² (pōz) *v.* **posed, pos·ing.** puzzle completely. [var. of *appose*, var. of *oppose*]

Po·sei·don (pə sī′dən) *n. Greek mythology.* the god of the sea and of horses, corresponding to the Roman god Neptune. He is usually represented carrying a trident.

po·ser¹ (pōz′ər) *n.* a person who poses. [< *pose¹*]

pos·er² (pōz′ər) *n.* a very puzzling problem. [< *pose²*]

po·seur (pō′zèr; *French,* pō zœr′) *n.* an affected person, one who poses to impress others. [< F *poseur* < *poser* pose]

posh (posh) *adj. Informal.* well-appointed; stylish; elegant. [origin uncertain]

pos·it (poz′it) *v.* lay down or assume as a fact or principle; affirm. [< L *positus*, pp. of *ponere* set, place]

po·si·tion (pə zish′ən) *n., v.* —*n.* 1 a place where a thing or person is: *The house is in a sheltered position. Your careless remark put me in an awkward position.* 2 a way of being placed: *Sit in a more comfortable position.* 3 the proper place. 4 a condition with reference to place or circumstances: *The army manoeuvered for position before attacking.* 5 job. 6 a rank; standing, especially high standing: *He was raised to the position of captain.* 7 a way of thinking; set of opinions: *What is your position on this question?* 8 the place held by a player on the team: *My position on the hockey team was defence.* —*v.* put in position; place: *The general positioned his soldiers behind the line of trees.* [< L *positio, -onis* < *ponere* set]
☛ *Syn.* 5. **Position, job, situation** = employment. **Position** is the formal word, but usually suggests white-collar work, in business or a profession: *He has a position in a bank.* **Job** is the informal and colloquial word applying to any kind of employment, but emphasizes the idea of having work to do: *He has a job on a ranch this summer.* **Situation** emphasizes the idea of a place to work, and now chiefly means a position or job wanted or applied for: *She desires a situation as housekeeper.*

po·si·tion·al (pə zish′ə nəl) *adj.* of, having to do with, or dependent on position or context.

pos·i·tive (poz′ə tiv) *adj., n.* —*adj.* 1 admitting of no question; without doubt; sure. 2 too sure; too confident: *Her positive manner annoys people.* 3 definite; emphatic: *a positive refusal.* 4 affirmative or approving: *Do you think we can expect a positive answer? You should take a more positive attitude.* 5 that can be thought of as real and present: *Light is a positive thing; darkness is only the absence of light.* 6 showing that a particular disease, condition, germ, etc. is present. 7 that definitely does something or adds something; practical: *Don't just make criticisms; give us some positive help.* 8 tending in the direction thought of as that of increase or progress: *Motion in the direction in which the hands of a clock move is positive.* 9 greater than zero; plus: *Positive numbers are used to count things. Five above zero is a positive quantity.* 10 of the kind of electrical charge produced on glass by rubbing it with silk; lacking or losing electrons. 11 *Photography.* showing light and shadow or color as in the subject photographed. 12 *Grammar.* of the simple form of an adjective or adverb. 13 *Biology.* moving or turning toward light, the earth, or any other stimulus. 14 having a tendency to lose electrons and thus become charged with positive electricity, as a chemical element or radical. 15 *Philosophy.* concerned with or based on matters of experience; not speculative or theoretical; empirical. 16 having no relation to or comparison with other things; absolute; unconditional. —*n.* 1 a positive degree or quantity. 2 *Electricity.* the positive terminal or plate in a battery, etc. 3 *Photography.* a positive photograph or a print made from a negative. 4 *Grammar.* the simple form of an adjective or adverb, as distinct from the comparative and superlative. *Fast* is the positive; *faster* is the comparative; *fastest* is the superlative. [ME < OF < L *positivus*, ult. < *ponere* to set] —**pos′i·tive·ly**, *adv.* —**pos′i·tive·ness**, *n.*

pos·i·tiv·ism (poz′ə tiv iz′əm) *n.* 1 a philosophical system founded by Auguste Comte (1798-1857), a French philosopher and sociologist, which deals only with positive facts and phenomena, rejecting abstract speculation. 2 the state or quality of being positive; definiteness; assurance; dogmatism.

pos·i·tron (poz′ə tron′) *n.* the antiparticle of the electron, having the same mass, etc. as the electron and an equal but opposite electric charge. [< *positive* + *electron*]

pos·i·tro·ni·um (poz′ə trō′nē əm) *n.* a very short-lived entity like an atom, composed of a positron and an electron bound together, differing from hydrogen in that both particles have the same mass. The two particles annihilate each other to produce two or three photons.

poss. 1 possessive; possession. 2 possibly; possible.

pos·se (pos′ē) *n.* 1 a group of persons summoned to help a law officer, especially in an emergency. Posses were often formed to capture criminals during frontier days in the American West. 2 *Cdn.* in western Canada, a troop of horses and riders trained for special exercises and drills, often giving exhibitions at stampedes and rodeos. [<Med.L *posse* power < L *posse* be able]

pos·sess (pə zes′) *v.* 1 own; have: *The general possessed great wisdom.* 2 hold as property; hold; occupy. 3 control; influence strongly. 4 control by an evil spirit: *He fought like one possessed.* 5 maintain; keep: *Possess your soul in patience.* 6 *Archaic.* take; win. [ME < OF *possessier* < *possession* possession < L *possessio* < *possidere* possess]

pos·sessed (pə zest′) *adj.* 1 dominated by passion, or as by an evil spirit; lunatic; demoniac. 2 owning or having as one's own: *He is possessed of great courage.* 3 maintaining poise and calm; unruffled.

pos·ses·sion (pə zesh′ən) *n.* 1 a possessing; holding. 2 ownership. 3 something possessed; property. 4 a territory under the rule of a country: *Ascension Island is a possession of the United Kingdom.* 5 domination by a particular feeling, idea, etc. 6 self-control.

pos·ses·sive (pə zes′iv) adj., n. —adj. **1** of or having to do with possession: *the possessive instinct.* **2** having or showing a strong desire to own or dominate: *a possessive manner. That boy has a possessive nature. She is very possessive.* **3** *Grammar.* of, having to do with, or being the form of an English noun or pronoun that shows that it refers to the possessor or source of something or to a part of a larger whole. *My* is the possessive form of *I* in *my books; bird's* is the possessive form of *bird* in *a bird's wing.* —n. *Grammar.* **1** the possessive form. The English possessive corresponds roughly to the genitive case in German and Latin. **2** a word or construction in the possessive form. *Their* and *man's* are possessives. —**pos·ses′sive·ly,** adv. —**pos·ses′sive·ness,** n.

possessive adjective the form of a possessive pronoun used with a noun. In *My friend was late, my* is a possessive adjective.
➤ *Usage.* See note at **possessive pronoun.**

possessive pronoun **1** a pronoun representing the possessive form. In *the book is hers, hers* is a possessive pronoun. **2** possessive adjective.
➤ *Usage.* Many grammarians use the term **possessive pronoun** to include possessive adjectives as well. That is, they will call both **my** and **mine** possessive pronouns.

pos·ses·sor (pə zes′ər) n. one that occupies, owns, or controls: *the possessor of a lease. She is the proud possessor of a grand piano.*

pos·set (pos′it) n. a hot drink made of milk with ale, wine, etc., and spices. [ME *possot*]

pos·si·bil·i·ty (pos′ə bil′ə tē) n., pl. **-ties. 1** the condition or fact of being possible: *There is a possibility that the train may be late.* **2** any thing or event that is possible; a person considered as a possible choice: *He would be a good possibility for captain.*

pos·si·ble (pos′ə bəl) adj., n. —adj. **1** that can happen or be done: *If it's at all possible, they'll come. It is possible to cure tuberculosis.* **2** that may be true or a fact: *It is possible that he left by the rear exit.* **3** that can be done, chosen, etc. properly: *the only possible candidate.* —n. **1** a possible candidate, winner, etc. **2** a perfect score: *The marksman scored a possible on one target.* [ME < L *possibilis* < *posse* be able]
➤ *Syn.* **1. Possible, practicable, feasible** = capable of happening or being done. **Possible** means that with suitable conditions and methods something may exist, happen, or be done: *It is possible to cure tuberculosis.* **Practicable** suggests that under present circumstances or by available means something (a plan, method, invention) can easily or effectively be carried out, done, or used: *The X-ray is a practicable way of discovering unsuspected diseases.* **Feasible** especially suggests something that is not yet tried but seems likely to be practicable: *Would compulsory X-rays be feasible?*

pos·si·bly (pos′ə blē) adv. **1** by any possibility; no matter what happens: *I cannot possibly go.* **2** perhaps: *Possibly you are right.*

pos·sum (pos′əm) n. **1** opossum. **2** *Australian.* phalanger, especially *Trichosurus vulpecula.*
play possum, pretend to be dead or asleep. [var. of *opossum*]

post¹ (pōst) n., v. —n. **1** a length of timber, metal, etc. set upright, usually as a support or marker: *the posts of a door or bed, a hitching post.* **2** the post, line, etc. where a race starts or ends. —v. **1** fasten (a notice) up in a place where it can easily be seen. **2** make known by, or as if by, a posted notice; offer publicly: *to post a reward.* **3** announce in a posted notice. **4** cover (a wall, etc.) with notices or bills. **5** put up notices warning people to keep out of. [OE < L *postis*]

post² (pōst) n. **1** a place where a soldier, police officer, etc. is stationed; a place where one is supposed to be when on duty. **2** a place where soldiers are stationed; a military station, fort, etc. **3** the soldiers occupying a military station. **4** a job or position: *She has a new post as district manager.* **5** a trading station, especially in an uncivilized or unsettled country: *a Hudson's Bay Company post.* **6** either of two bugle calls (first post and last post) calling soldiers to their quarters for the night. **7** *Esp.U.S.* a local branch of a veterans' organization. —v. **1** send to a station or post: *We posted guards at the door.* **2** in the armed forces, appoint to a post, unit, etc. [< F < Ital. < L *positus,* pp. of *ponere* station, place]

post³ (pōst) n., v., adv. —n. **1** an established system for carrying letters, papers, packages, etc.; the mail: *to send by post.* **2** *Esp.Brit.* a single mail; the letters, etc. thus delivered: *this morning's post.* **3** *Archaic* or *dialect.* postman. **4** *Archaic.* a person, vehicle, or ship that carries mail. **5** post office. **6** a letter box. **7** one of a series of fixed stations along a route for furnishing relays of men and horses for carrying letters, etc. and supplying service to travellers by post horse, post chaise, etc. **8** a size of paper, about 40 x 50 cm. —v. **1** send by post; mail: *to post a letter.* **2** travel with post horses or by post chaise. **3** travel with haste; hurry. **4** rise and fall in the saddle in rhythm with the horse's trot. **5** supply with up-to-date information; inform: *She keeps posted on current events.* **6** *Bookkeeping.* **a** transfer (an entry) from journal to ledger. **b** enter

hat, āge, fär; let, ēqual, tèrm; it, īce
hot, ōpen, ôrder; oil, out; cup, pùt, rüle,
əbove, takən, pencəl, lemən, circəs

ch, child; ng, long; sh, ship
th, thin; ғн, then; zh, measure

(an item) in due place and form. **c** make all requisite entries in (a ledger, etc.).
—adv. by post; speedily. [< F < Ital. < L *posita,* fem. ppf. of *ponere* place]

post- *prefix.* after, as in *postgraduate, post-mortem, postscript.* [< L *post-* < *post,* prep. adv., after, behind]

post·age (pōs′tij) n. the amount paid on anything sent by mail.

postage meter a machine that prints marks on mail to indicate that postage has been paid, and that keeps a record of the cost of postage and the number of pieces processed.

postage stamp an official stamp for use on mail to show that postage has been paid.

post·al (pōs′təl) adj. of or having to do with the mail or the post office.

postal card postcard.

postal code *Cdn.* a part of an address that uses a system of letters and numerals to identify a particular postal delivery route or point. The system is designed to speed the processing of machine-sorted mail: *The postal code of Ladysmith, B.C. is V0R 2E0.*

postal station one of several branch post offices (def. 2) in a large community.

post–and–lin·tel (pōst′ ən lin′təl) adj. *Architecture.* of or having to do with a type of construction based on the use of vertical supports and horizontal beams rather than vaults and arches.

post bel·lum (pōst bel′əm) *Latin.* after the war.

post box a box into which letters, parcels, etc. are put for collection and delivery by the Post Office; mailbox.

post·boy (pōst′boi′) n. **1** a boy or man who carries mail. **2** a man who rides one of the horses drawing a carriage or coach; postilion.

post·card (pōst′kärd′) n. a card used without an envelope for sending a short message by mail. Most postcards have a picture on one side.

post chaise a hired carriage that was used for travelling before there were railways.

post·date (pōst′dāt′) v. **-dat·ed, -dat·ing. 1** give (to a letter, cheque, etc.) a later date than the actual date of writing. **2** follow in time.

post·ed (pōs′tid) adj. **1** having posts. **2** informed.

pos·ter (pōs′tər) n. **1** a large printed advertisement, or notice, often illustrated, put up in some public place; placard. **2** a large printed picture or message, used for room decoration. **3** a person who posts notices, etc.

pos·te·ri·or (post tēr′ē ər) adj., n. —adj. **1** situated behind; back; rear; hind. **2** later; coming after. —n. *Informal.* the buttocks; rump. [< L *posterior,* comparative of *posterus* subsequent < *post* after]

pos·ter·i·ty (pos ter′ə tē) n. **1** the generations of the future: *Posterity may travel to distant planets.* **2** all of a person's descendants. [ME < OF < L *posteritas < posterus.* See POSTERIOR.]

pos·tern (pōs′tərn or pos′tərn) n., adj. —n. **1** a back door or gate. **2** any small door or gate. —adj. **1** of or like a postern. **2** rear; lesser: *The castle had a postern door.* [ME < OF *posterne,* ult. < L *posterus* behind. See POSTERIOR.]

post exchange *Esp.U.S.* a general store at a military post or station that sells food and other goods to members of the armed forces and authorized civilians. *Abbrev.:* PX or P.X.

post·grad·u·ate (pōst′graj′ü it) n., adj. —n. a student who continues university studies at a level beyond that of a bachelor's degree. —adj. **1** taking a course of study at such a level. **2** of or for postgraduates.
➤ *Usage.* In the United States, **postgraduate** can refer to studies following a high-school diploma, as well as to studies following a bachelor's degree. In Canada and the United Kingdom it refers only to studies following a bachelor's degree. On the other hand, in both Canada and the U.S., the term **graduate,** used as a noun, can refer to anyone who has completed high school, community college, or university. As an adjectival, however, it means the same thing in Canada as **postgraduate:** e.g. *a graduate student.*

post·haste (pōst′hāst′) adv. very speedily; in great haste. [< *post³* + *haste*]

post horse *Historical.* a horse hired for use in travelling by

relay, each horse being changed for a fresh one after a certain distance.

post·hu·mous (pos′chŭ məs) *adj.* **1** born after the death of the father: *a posthumous son.* **2** published after the death of the author. **3** happening after death: *posthumous fame.* [< LL *posthumus,* var. of L *postumus* last, originally superlative of *post* after; *h* added by confusion with *humus* earth, in sense of "burial"]

post·hu·mous·ly (pos′chŭ məs lē) *adv.* after death.

post·ie (pōs′tē) *n. Informal.* a postal worker, especially a letter carrier.

pos·til·ion or **pos·til·lion** (pōs til′yən or pos til′yən) *n.* a person who rides one of the horses drawing a carriage or coach. [< F *postillon*]

post–im·pres·sion·ism (pōst′im presh′ən iz′əm) *n.* a movement in painting in late 19th-century France which developed out of and went beyond impressionism to eliminate the illusion of depth by treating areas of shadow as color shapes in their own right.

post–im·pres·sion·ist (pōst′im presh′ən ist) *n., adj.* —*n.* an adherent or follower of post-impressionism. —*adj.* of or having to do with post-impressionism or post-impressionists.

post–im·pres·sion·is·tic (pōst′im presh′ən is′tik) *adj.* post-impressionist.

post·lude (pōst′lüd) *n.* **1** a closing piece of music, especially a composition played at the end of a church service. **2** a final or concluding phase: *the postlude of an era.* [< *post-* + pre*lude*]

post·man (pōst′mən) *n., pl.* **-men.** letter carrier; mailman.

post·mark (pōst′märk′) *n., v.* —*n.* an official mark stamped on mail to cancel the postage stamp and record the place and date of mailing. —*v.* stamp with a postmark.

post·mas·ter (pōst′mas′tər) *n.* the person in charge of a post office.

Postmaster General *pl.* **Postmasters General.** the federal cabinet minister responsible for the Post Office.

post·me·rid·i·an (pōst′mə rid′ē ən) *adj.* occuring after noon; of or having to do with the afternoon.

post me·rid·i·em (pōst′ mə rid′ē əm) after noon. *Abbrev.:* P.M. or p.m. [< L *post meridiem* after midday]

post·mis·tress (pōst′mis′tris) *n.* a woman in charge of a post office.

post–mor·tem (pōst′môr′təm) *adj., n.* —*adj.* after death. —*n.* an examination of a dead body; autopsy. [< L *post mortem* after death]

post·na·tal (pōst nā′təl) *adj.* having to do with or for the mother of a newborn baby: *postnatal care, postnatal depression.*

post–o·bit (pōst′ō′bit or -ob′it) *n., adj.* —*n.* a written agreement signed by a borrower promising to pay a certain sum of money to the lender on the death of a person whose heir the borrower expects to be. —*adj.* effective after a person's death. [< L *post obitum* after death]

post office **1** Usually, **Post Office,** a government agency or department responsible for handling, transporting, and delivering mail. **2** a local office where mail is received and sorted for delivery or placement in individual boxes, and where stamps and money orders are sold, mail is registered or insured, etc. **3** a small office, located in a drug store, etc., where stamps and money orders are sold and mail can be registered or insured, etc., but that does not function as a distribution centre for mail. *Abbrev.:* P.O.

post–op·er·a·tive (post op′ər ə tiv or -op′ə rā′tiv) *adj.* of or occurring in the period immediately following a surgical operation: *a post-operative infection.*

post·paid (pōst′pād′) *adj.* with the postage paid for.

post·pone (pōs pōn′ or pōst pōn′) *v.* **-poned, -pon·ing.** put off till later; put off to a later time; delay. [< L *postponere* < *post-* after + *ponere* put]
☛ *Syn.* See note at **delay.**

post·pone·ment (pōs pōn′mənt or pōst pōn′mənt) *n.* a putting off till later; delay: *the postponement of a game.*

post·pos·i·tive (pōst′pos′ə tiv) *adj., n.* —*adj.* of a modifier, coming after the word it modifies. An adjective coming immediately after its noun is a postpositive adjective. —*n.* a postpositive modifier. —**post′pos′i·tive·ly,** *adv.*
☛ *Usage.* See note at **attributive.**

post·pran·di·al (pōst′pran′dē əl) *adj.* after-dinner: *postprandial speeches.* [< *post-* + L *prandium* lunch] —**post′pran′di·al·ly,** *adv.*

post·rid·er (pōst′rīd′ər) *n. Historical.* a person who travelled by means of relays of horses, especially one who carried mail. See also **post horse.**

post road **1** a road or route over which mail is or was carried. **2** *Historical.* a road with stations providing post horses.

post·script (pōst′skript) *n.* **1** an addition to a letter, written after the writer's name has been signed. **2** a supplementary part appended to any composition or literary work. [< L *postscriptum,* originally neut. pp., < *post-* after + *scribere* write]

pos·tu·lant (pos′chə lənt) *n.* **1** a candidate, especially for admission to a religious order. **2** a person who asks or applies for something; petitioner. [< L *postulans, -antis,* ppr. of *postulare* demand]

pos·tu·late (*n.* pos′chə lit; *v.* pos′chə lāt′) *n., v.* **-lat·ed, -lat·ing.** —*n.* something taken for granted or assumed as a basis for reasoning; a fundamental principle; necessary principle: *One postulate of geometry is that a straight line may be drawn between any two points.* —*v.* **1** take for granted; assume without proof as a basis of reasoning; require as a fundamental principle or necessary condition. **2** require; demand; claim. [< L *postulatum,* originally pp. neut. of *postulare* demand] —**pos′tu·la′tion,** *n.* —**pos′tu·la′tor,** *n.*

pos·tur·al (pos′chər əl) *adj.* of or having to do with posture.

pos·ture (pos′chər) *n., v.* **-tured, -tur·ing.** —*n.* **1** a position of the body; way of holding the body: *Good posture is important for health.* **2** a condition; situation; state: *In the present posture of public affairs it is difficult to invest money safely.* **3** a mental or spiritual attitude.
—*v.* **1** take a certain posture: *The dancer postured before the mirror, bending and twisting her body.* **2** put in a certain posture. **3** pose for effect. [< F < L *positura* < *ponere* place]

post·war (pōst′wôr′) *adj.* of, having to do with, or happening during the period immediately following a war: *a postwar construction boom.*

po·sy (pō′zē) *n., pl.* **-sies.** **1** a flower. **2** a bunch of flowers; bouquet. **3** *Archaic.* a motto or line of poetry engraved within a ring. [var. of *poesy.* 16c.]

pot (pot) *n., v.* **pot·ted, pot·ting.** —*n.* **1** a deep, usually round, container made of metal, earthenware, glass, etc.: *a cooking pot, a flower pot, a coffee pot.* **2** a pot and what is in it; the amount a pot can hold. **3** a basket used to catch fish, lobsters, etc. **4** *Informal.* a large sum of money. **5** *Informal.* all the money bet at one time. **6** *Slang.* marijuana. **7** *Slang.* potbelly.
go to pot, go to ruin: *After losing his job he took to drinking and went to pot.*
keep the pot boiling, *Informal.* **a** make a living. **b** keep things going in a lively way.
—*v.* **1** put into a pot: *to pot young tomato plants.* **2** cook and preserve in a pot. **3** take a pot shot at; shoot. [OE *pott* < VL *pottus* < LL *potus* cup < L *potus* a drinking] —**pot′like′,** *adj.*

pot. potential.

po·ta·ble (pō′tə bəl) *adj., n.* —*adj.* fit for drinking. —*n.* Usually, **potables,** *pl.* anything drinkable. [< LL *potabilis* < L *potare* to drink]

pot·ash (pot′ash′) *n.* **1** any of several substances, such as sodium carbonate, made from wood ashes and used in soap, fertilizers, etc. **2** any of several potassium salts, such as potassium chloride, mined and processed for use in agriculture and industry. **3** potassium, or a potassium oxide, especially K_2O. **4** potassium hydroxide. [< Du. *potasch,* literally, pot ash]

po·tas·si·um (pə tas′ē əm) *n.* a soft, silver-white metallic chemical element, occurring in nature only in compounds. *Symbol:* K; *at.no.* 19; *at.wt.* 39.102. [< NL < E *potash*]

potassium bromide a white crystalline compound with a salty taste, used in medicine, photography, etc. *Formula:* KBr

potassium carbonate a white crystalline compound that forms a strongly alkaline solution and is used especially in making glass and soap. *Formula:* K_2CO_3

potassium chlorate a colorless crystalline compound used as an oxidizing agent in explosives, matches, etc. *Formula:* $KClO_3$

potassium chloride a crystalline compound that occurs naturally as a mineral, used in fertilizers. *Formula:* KCl

potassium cyanide a very poisonous white crystalline compound used for removing gold from ore, electroplating, etc. *Formula:* KCN

potassium hydroxide a very strong alkali used especially in making soap and as a reagent; caustic potash. *Formula:* KOH

potassium nitrate a colorless crystalline compound used as an oxidizing agent, in gunpowder, in explosives, etc.; nitre; saltpetre. *Formula:* KNO_3

potassium permanganate a nearly black crystalline compound used as an oxidizing agent, disinfectant, etc. *Formula:* $KMnO_4$

po·ta·tion (pō tā′shən) *n.* **1** the act of drinking. **2** a drink,

especially of alcoholic liquor. [ME < OF < L *potatio, -onis* < *potare* to drink]

po·ta·to (pə tā′tō) *n., pl.* **-toes. 1** a starchy tuber having crisp, whitish flesh and a thin brown or red skin, widely eaten as a cooked vegetable. It is the traditional basic vegetable of North America and much of Europe. **2** the plant (*Solanum tuberosum*), a New World member of the nightshade family that produces these tubers. **3** sweet potato. [< Sp. *patata* < Haitian]

potato beetle a yellow-and-black striped beetle (*Leptinotarsa decemlineata*) that is a serious pest of potato plants. Also called **potato bug, Colorado potato beetle.**

potato bug potato beetle.

potato chip 1 a crisp, thin, dry slice of potato that has been fried in deep fat and is eaten cold as a snack. **2** French fry; chip (def. 5).

pot·bel·lied (pot′bel′ēd) *adj.* **1** having a potbelly. **2** shaped like a potbelly: *a potbellied stove.*

pot·bel·ly (pot′bel′ē) *n.* a large, protruding belly; paunch.

potbelly stove or **potbellied stove** a squat, bulging stove that burns wood or coal.

pot·boil·er (pot′boil′ər) *n. Informal.* a work of literature, art, or music produced merely to make a living.

pot·bound (pot′bound′) *adj.* of plants, having roots that have outgrown the size of the pot and so cannot continue growing without being replanted.

pot·boy (pot′boi′) *n.* a man or boy who works in a tavern, serving customers, washing glasses, etc.

po·ten·cy (pō′tən sē) *n., pl.* **-cies. 1** the quality or state of being potent; power; strength: *the potency of an argument, the potency of a drug.* **2** the power or capacity to develop; potentiality. **3** sexual capability. [< L *potentia* < *potens*. See POTENT.]

po·tent (pō′tənt) *adj.* **1** having power or effectiveness in action; effective: *a potent remedy for a disease.* **2** of a drink, etc., strong: *potent tea.* **3** powerful or mighty: *a potent leader.* **4** of males, capable of having sexual intercourse. [< L *potens, -entis,* ppr. of OL **potere* be powerful] **—po′tent·ly,** *adv.*

po·ten·tate (pō′tən tāt′) *n.* a ruler having great power. The Roman emperors were potentates. [ME < LL < L *potentatus* power, dominion < *potens, -entis.* See POTENT.]

po·ten·tial (pə ten′shəl) *adj., n.* **—adj. 1** possible as opposed to actual; capable of coming into being or action: *a potential danger.* **2** *Grammar.* expressing possibility by the use of *may, might, can, could,* etc.: *the potential mood of a verb.* **—n. 1** something potential; possibility. **2** *Grammar.* the potential mood. **3** the amount of electrification of a point with reference to some standard. A current of high potential is used in transmitting electric power over long distances. [< LL *potentialis,* ult. < L *potens, -entis* potent]

☛ *Syn. adj.* **1.** See note at **latent.**

potential energy the energy that something has that is due to its structure, not to motion. A tightly coiled spring or a raised weight has potential energy.

po·ten·ti·al·i·ty (pə ten′shē al′ə tē) *n., pl.* **-ties. 1** a potential state or quality; possibility as opposed to actuality; latent power or capacity. **2** something potential; a possibility.

po·ten·tial·ly (pə ten′shəl ē) *adv.* possibly, but not yet actually.

po·ten·ti·ate (pə ten′shē āt′) *v.* **-ated, -ating.** make more active or potent. **—po·ten′ti·a′tion,** *n.*

po·ten·ti·om·e·ter (pə ten′shē om′ə tər) *n.* an instrument for measuring electromotive force. [< *potential* + *-meter*]

pot·ful (pot′fūl′) *adj., n.* **—adj.** as much or as many as a pot will hold: *a potful of potatoes.* **—n.** a large amount: *She made a potful of money on that deal.*

pot·head (pot′hed′) *n.* **1** *Cdn., esp.Nfld.* pilot whale. **2** *Slang.* a person who habitually smokes marijuana.

poth·er (poTH′ər) *n., v.* **—n.** confusion; disturbance; fuss. **—v.** bother; fuss. [origin uncertain]

pot·herb (pot′ėrb′ *or* -hėrb′) *n.* **1** any plant whose leaves and stems are boiled as a vegetable, such as spinach. **2** any plant used as seasoning in cooking. Sage and parsley are potherbs.

pot·hold·er (pot′hōl′dər) *n.* a small pad used for protecting one's hands when handling hot pots, etc.

pot·hole (pot′hōl′) *n.* **1** a deep, round hole, especially one made in the rocky bed of a river by stones and gravel being spun around in the current. **2** a hole in the surface of a road. **3** *Cdn.* slough. **4** *Cdn.* dugout (def. 4).

pothole trout *Cdn.* on the Prairies, trout planted in sloughs or dugouts.

pot·hook (pot′hūk′) *n.* **1** an S-shaped hook for hanging a pot or kettle over an open fire. **2** a rod with a hook for lifting hot pots, etc.

hat, āge, fär; let, ēqual, tėrm; it, īce
hot, ōpen, ôrder; oil, out; cup, pūt, rüle,
əbove, takən, pencəl, lemən, circəs
ch, child; ng, long; sh, ship
th, thin; ŦH, then; zh, measure

3 an S-shaped stroke, especially one made by children in learning to write.

pot·hunt·er (pot′hun′tər) *n.* **1** a person who shoots anything he comes upon regardless of rules of sport. **2** a person who takes part in contests merely to win prizes. **3** a person who hunts for food or for profit.

po·tion (pō′shən) *n.* a drink, especially one used as a medicine or poison, or in magic. [< L *potio, -onis.* Doublet of POISON.]

pot·latch (pot′lach) *n., v. Cdn., esp.West Coast.* **—n. 1** *Historical.* among Indian peoples of the West Coast, a large gathering to celebrate some event, at which the host would present costly gifts to his guests. Because potlatches were thought to have become too extravagant, they were outlawed in 1884. **2** a present-day festival and ceremony that is a modified version of the historical one, involving races, dancing, games, etc. **3** *Informal.* a party or celebration. **—v. 1** hold or take part in a potlatch. **2** give with the expectation of a gift in return. **3** give freely. [< Chinook Jargon < Nootka *patshatl* gift]

pot·luck (pot′luk′) *n.* whatever food happens to be ready or on hand for a meal.

take potluck, **a** be a guest and eat whatever food is ready or on hand. **b** accept whatever is available.

pot marigold a popular garden flower (*Calendula officinalis*) having huge, double yellow or orange flowers. The flowers of the pot marigold were once used for flavoring in cakes, soups, etc.

pot·pie (pot′pī′) *n.* **1** a baked meat pie. **2** a stew with dumplings.

pot·pour·ri (pō′pü rē′ *or* pot pür′ē) *n.* **1** a musical or literary medley. **2** a fragrant mixture of dried flower petals and spices. [< F *potpourri,* translation of Sp. *olla podrida* rotten pot < L *olla* pot and VL *putrita,* fem. pp. of *putrire* rot < L *puter* soft, rotten]

pot roast a large piece of meat, usually beef, cooked slowly with a little water in a deep, heavy, tightly covered dish.

pot·sherd (pot′shėrd′) *n.* a broken piece of earthenware. [< *pot* + *sherd,* var. of *shard*]

pot shot 1 a shot taken at game just to provide a meal, with little regard to the rules of sport. **2** a quick shot at something from close range without careful aim.

pot·tage (pot′ij) *n.* a thick soup. [ME < OF *potage* < *pot* pot < VL *pottus.* See POT.]

pot·ted (pot′id) *adj.* **1** put into a pot. **2** cooked and preserved in pots or cans. **3** *Slang.* drunk; intoxicated.

pot·ter[1] (pot′ər) *n.* a person who makes pottery. [OE *pottere* < *pott.* See POT.]

pot·ter[2] (pot′ər) *v.* putter[1]. [< earlier *pote* poke, OE *potian* push. Related to PUT.] **—pot′ter·er,** *n.*

potter's field a burial ground for paupers, unknown persons, etc. [with reference to the story of Judas (Matt. 27:7)]

potter's wheel a horizontal disk that revolves by means of a treadle or motor and on which clay is moulded by hand into round objects such as vases or pots.

pot·ter·y (pot′ər ē) *n., pl.* **-ter·ies. 1** pots, dishes, vases, or other earthenware, especially as distinct from porcelain or stoneware. Pottery is not as strong as stoneware and not as fine as porcelain. **2** the art or craft of making pottery. **3** a place where pottery is made. [< OF *poterie* < *potier* potter < *pot* pot < VL *pottus.* See POT.]

pot·tle (pot′əl) *n.* **1** *Archaic.* a unit for measuring liquids equal to two quarts (about 2.2 L). **2** a pot or tankard holding a pottle. [ME < OF *potel,* dim. of *pot* pot < VL *pottus* pot. See POT.]

pouch (pouch) *n., v.* **—n. 1** a bag or sack: *a letter carrier's pouch.* **2** a baglike receptacle or cavity in any of various animals, such as that on the abdomen of a kangaroo, in which the young are carried. **3** a loose fold of skin: *pouches under the eyes.* **4** a large bag that can be locked, used for transporting mail or government dispatches: *a diplomatic pouch.* **—v.** form a pouch or form into a pouch. [ME < ONF *pouche* < Gmc. Akin to POKE[2].] **—pouch′like′,** *adj.*

pouch·y (pouch′ē) *adj.* like a pouch, or having pouches; baggy.

pouf (püf) *n.* **1** a woman's hairstyle popular in the 18th century and consisting of high rolls or puffs of hair. **2** a loose roll of hair.

3 a puffed or gathered part of a dress. **4** a soft hassock or ottoman. Also, **pouff** or **pouffe**. [< F *pouf* a puff]

pou·lard (pü lärd′) *n.* a pullet that has been spayed to improve its eating qualities; a fattened hen. [< MF *poularde* < *poule* hen + *-arde*, a noun suffix]

poult (pōlt) *n.* a young chicken, turkey, pheasant, etc. [ME *poult*, short for *poullet* pullet]

poul·ter·er (pōl′tər ər) *n.* a dealer in poultry. [< obs. *poulter*, of the same meaning < OF *pouletier* < *poulet*. See POULTRY.]

poul·tice (pōl′tis) *n., v.* **-ticed, -tic·ing.** —*n.* a soft, moist mass of mustard, herbs, etc. applied to the body as a medicine. —*v.* put a poultice on. [ult. < L *pultes*, pl. of *puls* mush]

poul·try (pōl′trē) *n.* domesticated birds, such as chickens, turkeys, ducks, and geese, raised for meat, eggs, or feathers. [ME < OF *pouleterie* < *poulet*, dim. of *poule* hen < VL *pulla*, fem. to L *pullus* young fowl. Related to PULLET.]

pounce¹ (pouns) *v.* **pounced, pounc·ing;** *n.* —*v.* **1** come down with a rush and seize. **2** dash, come, or jump suddenly. —*n.* **1** a sudden swoop or pouncing. **2** a claw or talon of a bird of prey. [ME < *ponson, pounson*, dagger, pointed instrument < MF *poinçon*, ult. < L *punctus*, pp. of *pungere* prick. Related to PUNCHEON, POINT.]

pounce² (pouns) *n., v.* —*n.* **1** a fine powder formerly used to prevent ink from spreading in writing, or to prepare parchment for writing. **2** a fine powder used for transferring a design through a stencil. —*v.* **1** trace (a design) with pounce rubbed through perforations. **2** dust, smooth, or finish with pounce. [< F *ponce* < L *pumex, -micis* pumice. Doublet of PUMICE.]

pound¹ (pound) *n., pl.* **pounds** or (esp. collectively) **pound. 1** a unit for measuring mass. In the avoirdupois system, formerly in general use in English-speaking countries, one pound equals 16 ounces (about 454 g). In the troy system, used for precious metals and gems, one pound equals 12 troy ounces (about 373 g). **2** the basic unit of money of the United Kingdom, divided into 100 pence; pound sterling. A pound was formerly divided into 20 shillings and 240 pence. *Symbol:* £ See table at **money. 3** the basic unit of money in certain other countries: in the Irish Republic, divided into 100 pence; in Egypt, Lebanon, Sudan, and Syria, divided into 100 piastres; in Cyprus, divided into 1000 mils; in Malta, divided into 100 cents. See table at **money. 4** the Turkish lira. **5** a unit of money in Israel equal to ¹⁄₁₀ of a shekel. **6** *Historical.* a monetary unit of Scotland originally worth an English pound, but which later declined to one shilling eight pence. Also called **pound Scots. 7** a note worth one pound. [OE *pund* < L *pondo*, originally, *libra pondo* a pound by weight, ult. < *pendere* to weigh]

pound² (pound) *v., n.* —*v.* **1** hit hard again and again; hit heavily: *He pounded the door with his fist.* **2** beat hard; throb: *After running fast, you can feel your heart pound.* **3** crush to powder or pulp by beating. **4** move heavily: *John pounded down the hill to catch the bus.* **5** produce (sound) by pounding or as if by pounding: *We could hear drums pounding in the distance.* —*n.* **1** the act of pounding. **2** a heavy or forcible blow. **3** the sound of a blow. [OE *pūnian*]
☛ *Syn. v.* **1.** See note at **beat.**

pound³ (pound) *n.* **1** an enclosed place for keeping stray or unlicensed animals, especially dogs, cats, etc. until claimed by the owners. Most cities and towns have a pound. **2** a place for keeping automobiles or other personal property until redeemed by the owners. **3** an enclosure for keeping or trapping animals. **4** any place of confinement. [OE *pund-*]

pound·age¹ (poun′dij) *n.* **1** a tax, commission, rate, etc. of so much per pound sterling or per pound of mass. **2** mass expressed in pounds.

pound·age² (poun′dij) *n.* **1** confinement in a pound. **2** the fee required for the release of an impounded animal.

pound·al (poun′dəl) *n.* a unit for measuring force, equal to about 0.138 newtons. [< *pound¹*]

pound cake a rich butter cake containing equal amounts of the principal ingredients. The original recipe for pound cake required one pound each of sugar, flour, and butter.

pound·er¹ (poun′dər) *n.* a person or thing that pounds, especially an instrument such as a pestle for pounding or crushing. [< *pound²*]

pound·er² (poun′dər) *n.* a person or thing weighing, having, or associated with a specified number of pounds (*used in compounds*): *We caught a ten-pounder in the lake yesterday.* [< *pound¹*]

pound–fool·ish (pound′fül′ish) *adj.* foolish or careless in regard to large sums of money.

penny-wise and pound-foolish See **penny-wise.**

pound sterling the basic unit of money in the United Kingdom; pound¹ (def. 2).

pour (pôr) *v., n.* —*v.* **1** cause to flow in a steady stream: *I poured the milk from the bottle.* **2** flow in a steady stream: *The crowd poured out of the church. The rain poured down.* **3** pour tea or coffee at a formal reception. **4** make known freely or without reserve: *The melancholy poet poured forth his sorrow in a song.*
it never rains but it pours, events of a kind, especially misfortunes, come all together or not at all.
pour it on, *Informal.* **a** to do or express something with great vigor and enthusiasm, especially in advancing one's interest, using persuasion, etc. **b** keep increasing one's score or advantage in a game, even when victory is no longer at issue.
—*n.* **1** the act of pouring. **2** a heavy rain. [ME *poure(n)*; origin uncertain] —**pour′er,** *n.*
☛ *Hom.* pore.

pour·boire (pür bwär′) *n. French.* a small present of money; tip; literally, (money) for drinking.

pout¹ (pout) *v., n.* —*v.* **1** thrust or push out the lips, as a displeased or sulky child does. **2** show displeasure. **3** swell out; protrude.
—*n.* **1** a pushing out of the lips when displeased or sulky. **2** a fit of sullenness. [ME *poute(n)*]

pout² (pout) *n., pl.* **pout** or **pouts.** a kind of freshwater catfish. [OE *-pūte*, as in *ælepūte* eelpout]

pout·er (pout′ər) *n.* **1** a person who pouts. **2** a breed of domestic pigeon that has the ability to inflate its crop, producing a puffed-up breast.

pout·y (pout′ē) *adj. Informal.* inclined to pout.

pov·er·ty (pov′ər tē) *n.* **1** the condition of being poor or needy; the condition of not having enough income to maintain a standard of living regarded as normal in a community: *He died in poverty.* **2** the renunciation of the right to own property as an individual: *A person joining any of certain religious orders takes a vow of poverty.* **3** a lack of what is needed; inadequacy: *The poverty of the soil in this region makes farming difficult.* **4** scarcity; dearth: *a poverty of ideas.* [ME < OF < L *paupertas* < *pauper* poor]
☛ *Syn.* **1.** Poverty, want, destitution = the condition of being in need. **Poverty** emphasizes being in actual need, owning nothing at all or having not enough for all the necessities of life: *Their tattered clothes and broken furniture indicated their poverty.* **Want** emphasizes extreme need, having too little to live on: *Welfare agencies help those in want.* **Destitution** emphasizes complete lack even of food and shelter, and often suggests having been deprived of possessions once had: *The Red Cross relieved the destitution following the floods.*

pov·er·ty–strick·en (pov′ər tē strik′ən) *adj.* extremely poor.

P.O.W. or **POW** prisoner of war.

pow·der (pou′dər) *n., v.* —*n.* **1** a solid reduced to dust by pounding, crushing, or grinding. **2** something made or prepared as powder: *face powder, powders taken as medicine.* **3** gunpowder.
keep (one's) powder dry, *Informal.* stay ready for action (from the use of gunpowder in old muskets, cannon, etc.).
take a powder, *Slang.* leave; run off: *He took a powder as soon as things got rough.*
—*v.* **1** make into powder. **2** become powder. **3** sprinkle or cover with powder. **4** apply powder to (the face, etc.). **5** sprinkle. [ME < OF *poudre* < L *pulvis, -veris* dust] —**pow′der·er,** *n.*

powder blue pale blue.

powder burn a burn on the skin resulting from the explosion of gunpowder at close range.

powder flask *Historical.* a flask or case of horn, metal, or leather for carrying gunpowder.

powder horn a powder flask made of an animal's horn.

powder keg 1 a small cask for holding gunpowder or blasting powder. **2** something that is liable to explode: *The whole country was a powder keg after the death of the dictator.*

powder magazine a place where gunpowder is stored.

powder puff a soft puff or pad for applying cosmetic powder to the skin.

powder room a small rest room or lavatory, especially one having a dressing table for make-up, etc.

pow·der·y (pou′dər ē) *adj.* **1** of, like, or in the form of powder. **2** easily made into powder; crumbling: *powdery topsoil.* **3** covered with or as if with powder.

pow·er (pou′ər) *n., v., adj.* —*n.* **1** strength; might; force. **2** the ability to do or act: *I will give you all the help in my power.* **3** a particular ability: *He has great powers of concentration.* **4** control; authority; influence; right: *Parliament has power to declare war.* **5** any person, thing, body, or nation having authority or influence: *Five powers held a peace conference.* **6** *Mechanics.* energy or force that can do work: *Running water produces power to run mills.* **7** a simple machine. **8** the capacity for exerting mechanical force, as measured by the rate at which it is exerted or at which the work is done. In the SI, all power is expressed in watts or in multiples or sub-multiples of the watt. **9** *Mathematics.* the product of a number multiplied by itself: *16 is the 4th power of 2.* **10** the capacity of an

instrument to magnify. The higher the power of a telescope or microscope the more details you can see. **11** Often, **powers,** *pl.* deity; divinity. **12** an order of angels.

in power, having control or authority: *the government in power.*
the powers that be, those who have control or authority.
—*v.* provide with power or energy: *a boat powered by an outboard motor.*
—*adj.* operated by a motor; equipped with its own motor: *power tools, power steering.* [ME < *poer,* n. < AF *poër,* var. of OF *poeir,* n. use of infinitive < VL *potere* for L *posse* be able]
☞ *Syn. n.* **1. Power, strength, force** = ability to do something or capacity for something. **Power** is the general word applying to any physical, mental or moral ability or capacity, whether used or not: *Every normal, healthy person has power to think.* **Strength** suggests a power within the person or thing, belonging to it, as a quality, to do, bear, or resist much: *He has strength of character.* **Force** emphasizes the active use of power or strength to get something done or bring something about: *We had to use force to get into the house.*

pow·er·boat (pou′ər bōt′) *n.* a motorboat, especially a boat propelled by an engine on board.

power brakes in a motor vehicle, a braking system that uses power produced by the engine to increase the effect of pressure on the brake pedal. It takes very little pressure to stop a car that has power brakes.

power dive *Aeronautics.* a dive of an aircraft speeded up by the power of the engine.

po·wer–dive (pou′ər dīv′) *v.* **-dived** or **-dove, -dived, -div·ing.** make a power dive.

power drill a drill worked by a motor, not by hand.

pow·er·ful (pou′ər fəl) *adj.* having great power or force; mighty; strong.
☞ *Syn.* See note at **mighty.**

pow·er·ful·ly (pou′ər fəl ē *or* pou′ər flē) *adv.* strongly; with power.

pow·er·house (pou′ər hous′) *n.* **1** a building containing boilers, engines, generators, etc. for generating electric power. **2** *Informal.* a person or group having great power, energy, drive, etc.: *That new teacher is a real powerhouse.*

pow·er·less (pou′ər lis) *adj.* without power; helpless.
—**pow′er·less·ly,** *adv.* —**pow′er·less·ness,** *n.*

power loom a loom worked by steam, electricity, water power, etc., not by hand.

power mower a lawn mower powered by a motor.

power of attorney a written statement giving one person legal power to act for another. *Abbrev.:* P.A.

power plant 1 a building with machinery for generating power. **2** a motor; engine.

power play *Cdn. Hockey.* a special combination of players put on the ice when the opposition is shorthanded.

power politics international political strategy that uses the threat of superior military or economic power to advance national interests (*used with a singular or plural verb*).

power saw a saw powered by a motor.

power squadron an association of owners and operators of powerboats, yachts, etc. to promote safe boating, good seamanship, etc.

power station powerhouse (def. l).

power steering in a motor vehicle, a steering mechanism that uses power from the engine to increase the effect of the force used in turning the steering wheel. It requires little effort to turn the steering wheel of a car with power steering.

pow·wow (pou′wou′) *n., v.* —*n.* **1** among North American Indian peoples, a celebration or ceremony, usually featuring feasting and dancing and certain rites, held before an expedition, hunt, council, or conference. **2** the hubbub and noise accompanying such a celebration. **3** a council or conference of or with a North American Indian people. **4** *Informal.* any conference or meeting. **5** among some North American Indian peoples, a medicine man.
—*v.* hold a powwow. [< Algonquian]

pox (poks) *n.* **1** any of several diseases that are characterized by pustules, or pocks (*used especially in compounds*): *chicken pox, smallpox.* **2** syphilis.
a pox on (someone or something), *Archaic.* an exclamation of anger or impatience.
[var. of *pocks,* pl. of *pock.* See POCK.]

poz·zo·lan (pot′sə lən) *n.* pozzuolana.

poz·zo·la·na (pot′sə lä′nə) *n.* pozzuolana.

poz·zuo·la·na (pot′sù ə lä′nə) *n.* **1** volcanic ash, etc. used by the ancient Romans in making mortar. **2** a cement additive, usually made from shale and containing silica, alumina, etc. [< Ital. *pozzuolana,* n. use of fem. adj. < *Pozzuoli,* a seaport in S Italy, where it was first found]

hat, āge, fär; let, ēqual, tèrm; it, īce
hot, ōpen, ôrder; oil, out; cup, pùt, rüle,
əbove, takən, pencəl, lemən, circəs
ch, child; ng, long; sh, ship
th, thin; ŦH, then; zh, measure

pp. 1 pages. **2** past participle. **3** *Music.* pianissimo. **4** privately printed.

P.P. 1 Parcel Post. **2** Parish Priest.

ppd. 1 postpaid. **2** prepaid.

ppm or **p.p.m.** parts per million.

ppr. or **p.pr.** present participle.

P.P.S. or **p.p.s. 1** a second postcript (for L *post postscriptum*). **2** in Britain, Parliamentary Private Secretary.

PQ 1 Parti Québécois. **2** Province of Quebec. (*used esp. in computerized address systems*).

P.Q. Province of Quebec.

pr. 1 pair. **2** price. **3** present. **4** prince. **5** printing. **6** pronoun.

Pr praseodymium.

PR Puerto Rico.

P.R. 1 Puerto Rico. **2** proportional representation.

P.R. or **PR** public relations.

praam (präm) *n.* pram².

prac·ti·ca·bil·i·ty (prak′tə kə bil′ə tē) *n.* the quality of being practicable; feasibility.

prac·ti·ca·ble (prak′tə kə bəl) *adj.* **1** that can be done; capable of being put into practice; feasible: *a practicable idea.* **2** that can be used: *a practicable road.* [< F *practicable* < *pratiquer* practise; influenced in English by obs. *practic.* See PRACTICAL.]
—**prac′ti·ca·bly,** *adv.*
☞ *Syn.* **1.** See note at **possible. Practicable, practical** = able to be done or put into practice. **Practicable,** often used with **not,** emphasizes that it is possible (or not possible) for something to be done: *Building an apartment tower on soft marshland is not practicable.* **Practical** suggests that what can be done is (or is not) also reasonable or worthwhile: *Building on this drained swamp would cost too much for the project to be practical.* See also the note at **impracticable.**

prac·ti·cal (prak′tə kəl) *adj.* **1** having to do with action or practice rather than thought or theory: *Earning a living is a practical matter.* **2** able to be put into practice: *a practical plan.* **3** useful in practice: *His legal knowledge was not very practical when he became a chemist.* **4** having good sense. **5** engaged in actual practice or work: *A practical farmer runs a farm.* **6** being such in effect; virtual: *So many of our soldiers were killed that our victory was a practical defeat.* [< earlier *practic* < LL *practicus* < Gk. *praktikos* < *prassein* do] —**prac′ti·cal·ness,** *n.*
☞ *Syn.* **1.** See note at **sensible. 2.** See note at **practicable.**

prac·ti·cal·i·ty (prak′tə kal′ə tē) *n., pl.* **-ties. 1** the quality of being practical; practical usefulness; a practical habit of mind. **2** a practical matter.

practical joke a kind of trick that depends for its effect or humor on a person being put at a disadvantage or embarrassed or abused in some way.

practical joker a person who plays practical jokes on others.

prac·ti·cal·ly (prak′tik lē) *adv.* **1** almost; nearly: *We're practically home.* **2** in effect; virtually: *They practically ran the show.* **3** in a practical way: *reacting very practically to the emergency.*

practical nurse a nurse whose occupation is to care for the sick, but who has not the theoretical training required of a registered nurse.

prac·tice (prak′tis) *n.* **1** an action done many times over in order to gain skill: *Practice makes perfect.* **2** the skill gained by experience or exercise: *He was out of practice at batting.* **3** the action or process of doing or being something: *His plan is good in theory, but not in actual practice.* **4** the usual way; custom: *It is the practice at the factory to blow a whistle at noon.* **5** the working at or following of a profession or occupation: *engaged in the practice of law.* **6** the business of a doctor, dentist, or lawyer: *Dr. Adams sold his practice.* **7** *Archaic.* a scheme; plot. **8** *Law.* the established method of conducting legal proceedings. **9** a period set aside for practising: *He went to the hockey practice last night.* Sometimes **practise.** [ME < *practise,* v. < OF *practiser,* ult. < LL *practicus.* See PRACTICAL.]
☞ *Syn.* See note at **custom.**
☞ *Usage.* **Practice** is one of a few words that in Canadian English are usually spelled differently as nouns and verbs. The preferred spelling for the noun is **practice** and for the verb **practise.** For this reason the noun and verb are entered separately in this dictionary.

prac·ti·cum (prak'tə kəm) n., pl. **-cums** or **-ca** (-kə). in schools and colleges: **1** a course in independent research or in practical work. **2** a practical part of a course, such as laboratory or field work. [< NL (collegium) practicum practical course < Med.L practicare to practise]

prac·tise or **prac·tice** (prak'tis) v. **-tised** or **-ticed, -tis·ing** or **-tic·ing. 1** do something again and again so as to learn to do it well: practise playing the piano. **2** do as a rule; make a custom of; follow, observe, or use day after day: to practise moderation. Practise what you preach. **3** work at or follow as a profession, art, or occupation: to practise medicine, to practise architecture. **4** practise a profession, especially law, medicine, or dentistry: My uncle practises in Thunder Bay. **5** give training to; drill. **6** Archaic. scheme; plot. **7** take advantage of. [see PRACTICE] —**prac'tis·er** or **prac'tic·er,** n.
☛ Syn. 1. See note at **exercise.**
☛ Usage. See note at **practice.**

prac·tised or **prac·ticed** (prak'tist) adj. **1** experienced; skilled; expert; proficient. **2** acquired or perfected through practice.

prac·tis·ing or **prac·tic·ing** (prak'tə sing) adj. actively engaged in a particular profession or career: a practising lawyer.

prac·ti·tion·er (prak tish'ən ər or prak tish'nər) n. a person engaged in the practice of an art or profession: He was a medical practitioner for ten years; later he taught medicine.

prae·fect (prē'fekt) See **prefect.**

prae·no·men (prē nō'mən) n., pl. **-nom·i·na** (-nom'ə nə). in ancient Rome, the first or personal name of a citizen. [< L praenomen < prae- before + nomen name]

prae·tor (prē'tər or prē'tôr) n. in ancient Rome, a magistrate or judge, ranking next below a consul. Also, **pretor.** [< L praetor, ult. < prae- before + ire go]

prae·to·ri·an (prē tô'rē ən) adj., n. —adj. in ancient Rome: **1** of or having to do with a praetor. **2** having to do with or being the bodyguard of a commander or emperor. —n. **1** a man having the rank of a praetor. **2** a soldier of the bodyguard of a commander or emperor.

prag·mat·ic (prag mat'ik) adj. **1** of or concerned with practical results or values, not with theories or ideals: He is a very pragmatic person. **2** of or having to do with the philosophy of pragmatism. **3** having to do with the affairs of a state or community. **4** treating the facts of history systematically, with special reference to their causes and effects. [< L pragmaticus < Gk. pragmatikos efficient, ult. < prassein do]

prag·mat·i·cal (prag mat'ə kəl) adj. pragmatic. —**prag·mat'i·cal·ly,** adv.

pragmatic sanction any of various imperial decrees issued as fundamental law.

prag·ma·tism (prag'mə tiz'əm) n. **1** the quality or condition of being pragmatic, or practical and matter-of-fact. **2** a philosophy that tests the value and truth of ideas by their practical consequences.

prag·ma·tist (prag'mə tist) n. a person who believes in pragmatism.

prai·rie (prer'ē) n., adj. —n. **1** a large area of level or rolling land with grass but very few or no trees. **2 the Prairies,** pl. **a** the great, almost treeless, plain that covers much of central North America. **b** the part of this plain that covers much of central and southern Manitoba, Saskatchewan, and Alberta. —adj. Often, **Prairie,** of or having to do with the Prairies. [< F prairie, ult. < L pratum meadow]

prairie chicken 1 either of two grouse having brown-and-white, barred plumage: the **greater prairie chicken** (Tympanuchus cupido) of the central North American plains, formerly common in the Canadian Prairies but now rare; or the smaller, paler **lesser prairie chicken** (T. pallidicinctus) of the plains of the SW United States. **2** sharp-tailed grouse.

prairie crocus crocus (def. 2).

prairie dog any of several North American burrowing rodents (genus Cynomys) found especially on the central plains, related to and resembling ground squirrels, but somewhat larger and stouter and having a shorter tail. Prairie dogs live in colonies often called "towns"; in Canada, they occur only in extreme southern Saskatchewan.

prairie lily a North American wild lily (Lilium philadelphicum) found in dry or wet places on the prairies and in open woods from Quebec to British Columbia and south to New Mexico. The prairie lily is the provincial flower of Saskatchewan.

prairie oyster 1 a raw egg swallowed whole or drunk in vinegar, brandy, etc. **2** Cdn. a testicle of a bull calf prepared for eating.

Prairie Provinces Manitoba, Saskatchewan, and Alberta.

prairie schooner a large covered wagon used by pioneers in crossing the plains before the railways were built, especially in the United States.

prairie wolf coyote.

praise (prāz) n., v. **praised, prais·ing.** —n. **1** the act of saying that a thing or person is good; words that tell the worth or value of a thing or person. **2** words or song setting forth the glory and goodness of God.
damn with faint praise, praise with so little enthusiasm as to condemn.
sing the praise or **praises of,** praise with enthusiasm.
—v. **1** express approval or admiration of. **2** worship in words or song: to praise God. [ME < OF preisier, ult. < L pretium price] —**prais'er,** n.
☛ Syn. v. 1. Praise, approve, commend = think or speak well of. **Praise** means to express in a hearty or enthusiastic way one's high opinion or admiration of someone or something: The coach praised the team for its fine playing. **Approve** means to think or express a favorable opinion or admiration: Everyone approved his idea. **Commend** means to suggest a more formal expression of favorable opinion: The mayor commended the boys for their quick thinking at the disaster.

praise·wor·thy (prāz'wėr'ᴛᴴē) adj. worthy of praise; deserving approval. —**praise'wor'thi·ly,** adv. —**praise'wor'thi·ness,** n.

Pra·krit (prä'krit) n. any of the Indo-European vernacular languages or dialects of northern and central India, especially those of the ancient and medieval periods. [< Skt. prakrta natural, common, vulgar. Cf. SANSKRIT.]

pra·line (prä'lēn) n. a small cake of brown candy made of sugar and nuts, usually pecans or almonds. [< F; invented by the cook of Marshal Duplessis-Praslin (1598-1675)]

pram[1] (pram) n. Esp.Brit. a perambulator; baby carriage.

pram[2] (pram) n. a small flat-bottomed boat having a blunt, square bow. Also, **praam.** [< Du. praam]

prance (prans) v. **pranced, pranc·ing;** n. —v. **1** spring about on the hind legs. Horses prance when they feel lively. **2** ride on a horse doing this. **3** move gaily or proudly; swagger. **4** caper; dance. —n. the act of prancing. [ME prance(n), praunce(n); origin uncertain] —**pranc'er,** n. —**pranc'ing·ly,** adv.

prank[1] (prangk) n. a piece of mischief; playful trick: On April Fool's Day people play pranks on each other. [origin uncertain]

prank[2] (prangk) v. **1** dress in a showy way; adorn. **2** make a show or display. [cf. MLG prank showiness]

prank·ish (prangk'ish) adj. **1** full of pranks; fond of pranks. **2** like a prank. —**prank'ish·ly,** adv. —**prank'ish·ness,** n.

prank·ster (prangk'stər) n. a person who plays pranks.

pra·se·o·dym·i·um (prā'zē ō dim'ē əm) n. a rare metallic chemical element of the same group as cerium. Symbol: Pr; at.no. 59; at.wt. 140.907. [< NL praseodymium, ult. < Gk. prasios bluish-green + E (di)dymium, a rare element < Gk. didymos twin]

prat (prat) n. Slang. the rump or backside; buttocks. [origin unknown. 16c.]

prate (prāt) v. **prat·ed, prat·ing;** n. —v. talk a great deal in a foolish way; prattle; chatter. —n. empty or foolish talk. [cf. MDu., MLG praten] —**prat'er,** n. —**prat'ing·ly,** adv.

prat·fall (prat'fol or -fôl) n. Slang. **1** a fall on the rump or backside, as part of a slapstick performance. **2** any laughable or disconcerting blunder.

prat·tle (prat'əl) v. **-tled, -tling;** n. —v. **1** talk as a child does; tell freely and carelessly. **2** talk or tell in a foolish way; prate. **3** sound like baby talk; babble. —n. **1** foolish or childish talk. **2** a sound like baby talk; babble: the prattle of a brook. [< prate] —**prat'tler,** n.

prawn (pron or prôn) n., v. —n. **1** any of various long-bodied, marine decapod crustaceans (suborder Natantia, especially genera Palaemon, Penaeus, etc.). Compare **shrimp. 2** any large, edible shrimp. Prawns may be up to 20 centimetres long. —v. fish for or catch prawns. [ME prane; origin uncertain] —**prawn'er,** n.

prax·is (prak'səs) n., pl. **prax·is·es** or **prax·es** (-sēz). **1** the practice of an art, science, etc. as opposed to the theory or study of it. **2** an established practice; custom. [< Med.L < Gk. prâxis action, doing < prassein to do, practise. 16c.]

pray (prā) v. **1** speak to God in worship; enter into spiritual communion with God; offer worship. **2** make earnest request to God or to any other object of worship: to pray for help, to pray for one's family. **3** ask earnestly: They prayed the kidnappers to let them go. **4** ask earnestly for: to pray someone's forgiveness. **5** bring or get by praying. **6** please: Pray come with me. [ME < OF preier < L precari < prex, precis prayer] —**pray'er,** n.
☛ Hom. prey.

prayer (prer) n. **1** an earnest request, especially one made to God. **2** the act of praying: She was at prayer. **3** the thing prayed for: Our prayers were granted. **4** the form of words to be used in praying. **5** a

form of worship; religious service consisting mainly of prayers. [ME < OF *preiere*, ult. < L *prex, precis* prayer]

prayer book 1 a book of prayers. **2 Prayer Book,** the Book of Common Prayer.

prayer·ful (prer′fəl) *adj.* **1** having the custom of praying often; devout. **2** like a prayer; earnest. —**prayer′ful·ly,** *adv.* —**prayer′ful·ness,** *n.*

prayer meeting a meeting for prayer and worship.

prayer rug a small rug used by Moslems to kneel on when praying.

prayer shawl a shawl with a fringe traditionally worn over the head and shoulders by Jewish men for morning prayers.

prayer wheel a wheel or cylinder inscribed with prayers, each turn of the wheel counting as an uttered prayer, used by the Buddhists of Tibet.

praying mantis mantis.

pre– *prefix.* before in place, time, order, or rank, as in *prepay, preheat, prewar, premolar.* [< L *prae-* before]

preach (prēch) *v.* **1** speak publicly on a religious subject. **2** deliver (a sermon). **3** make known by preaching; proclaim: *to preach the Gospel.* **4** advise or recommend strongly; urge: *The coach was always preaching exercise and fresh air.* **5** give earnest advice, usually in a meddling or tiresome way: *He is forever preaching about good table manners.* [ME < OF *prechier* < L *praedicare* declare, preach. Doublet of PREDICATE.]

preach·er (prēch′ər) *n.* a person who preaches; clergyman; minister.

preach·i·fy (prēch′ə fī′) *v.* **-fied, -fy·ing.** *Informal.* preach or moralize too much.

preach·ing (prēch′ing) *n.* what is preached; sermon.

preach·ment (prēch′mənt) *n.* **1** the act of preaching. **2** a long, tiresome sermon or speech.

preach·y (prēch′ē) *adj.* **preach·i·er, preach·i·est.** *Informal.* having or showing too great an inclination to preach or moralize.

pre·am·ble (prē′am′bəl *or* prē am′bəl) *n.* **1** a preliminary statement; introduction to a speech or a writing. The reasons for a law and its general purpose are often stated in a preamble. **2** a preliminary or introductory fact or circumstance. [< F < Med.L *praeambulum,* originally neut. adj., walking before, ult. < L *prae-* before + *ambulare* walk]

pre·am·pli·fi·er (prē am′plə fī′ər) *n.* a unit that amplifies very weak signals enabling them to be sent into the main amplifier.

pre·ar·range (prē′ə rānj′) *v.* **-ranged, -rang·ing.** arrange beforehand: *a prearranged meeting place, a prearranged signal.* —**pre′ar·range′ment,** *n.*

pre·as·signed (prē′ə sīnd′) *adj.* assigned beforehand: *The seats at the conference table were preassigned.*

preb·end (preb′ənd) *n.* **1** the salary given to a clergyman connected with a cathedral or a collegiate church. **2** the particular property or church tax from which the money comes for this salary. **3** prebendary. [ME < OF < LL *praebenda* allowance < L *praebenda* (things) to be furnished < *praebere* furnish < *prae-* before + *habere* have]

preb·en·dar·y (preb′ən der′ē) *n., pl.* **-dar·ies.** a clergyman who has a prebend.

prec. preceding.

Pre·cam·bri·an *or* **Pre–Cam·bri·an** (prē′kam′brē ən) *adj., n. Geology.* —*adj.* of, having to do with, or referring to the earliest era of geological time, including all the time before the Paleozoic era, or the rocks formed during this time. The Canadian Shield consists of Precambrian rock. —*n.* **the Precambrian,** the Precambrian era or its rock system.

pre·can·cel (prē kan′səl) *v.* **-celled, -celed, -cel·ling** *or* **-cel·ing;** *n.* —*v.* cancel (a postage stamp) before sale. —*n.* a precancelled postage stamp.

pre·car·i·ous (pri ker′ē əs) *adj.* **1** not safe or secure; uncertain; risky, or dangerous: *a precarious hold on a branch. An active soldier leads a precarious life.* **2** poorly founded; doubtful; assumed: *a precarious opinion or conclusion.* **3** *Archaic.* dependent on the will or pleasure of another: *precarious tenure.* [< L *precarius,* originally, obtainable by entreaty, ult. < *prex, precis* prayer] —**pre·car′i·ous·ly,** *adv.* —**pre·car′i·ous·ness,** *n.*

pre·cau·tion (pri ko′shən *or* -kô′shən) *n.* **1** something done beforehand to prevent harm or to secure good results: *Locking the door of a house is a precaution against theft.* **2** taking care beforehand; foresight: *Proper precaution is necessary when taking a trip by car in winter.* [< LL *praecautio, -onis* < L *praecavere* guard against beforehand < *prae-* before + *cavere* be on one's guard]

pre·cau·tion·ar·y (pri ko′shən er′ē *or* -kô′shən er′ē) *adj.* of or using precaution.

hat, āge, fär; let, ēqual, tėrm; it, īce
hot, ōpen, ôrder; oil, out; cup, pùt, rüle,
above, takən, pencəl, lemən, circəs

ch, child; ng, long; sh, ship
th, thin; ŦH, then; zh, measure

pre·cede (prē sēd′) *v.* **-ced·ed, -ced·ing. 1** go or come before: *The rain was preceded by a violent windstorm. A band preceded the first float in the parade.* **2** be higher than in rank or importance: *A major precedes a captain.* [< L *praecedere* < *prae-* before + *cedere* go] ☛ *Usage.* Do not confuse **precede** 'go or come before' with **proceed** 'move forward': *January precedes February. The year proceeds slowly.*

prec·e·dence (pres′ə dəns *or* prē sēd′əns) *n.* **1** the act or fact of preceding. **2** a higher position or rank; greater importance: *to take precedence over all others.* **3** the right to precede others in ceremonies or social affairs; social superiority: *A major takes precedence over a captain.*

prec·e·den·cy (pres′ə dən sē *or* prē sēd′ən sē) *n., pl.* **-cies.** precedence.

prec·e·dent (*n.* pres′ə dənt *or* prē′sə dənt; *adj.* prē- sēd′ənt *or* pres′ə dənt) *n., adj.* —*n.* **1** a case that may serve as an example or reason for a later case. **2** *Law.* a judicial decision, case, proceeding, etc. that serves as a guide or pattern in future similar or analogous situations. —*adj.* preceding. [< L *praecedens, -entis,* ppr. of *praecedere.* See PRECEDE.]

pre·ced·ing (prē sēd′ing) *adj.* going or coming before; previous: *the preceding page, the preceding year.* ☛ *Syn.* See note at **previous.**

pre·cen·tor (pri sen′tər) *n.* a person who leads and directs the singing of a church choir or congregation. [< LL *praecentor,* ult. < L *prae-* before + *canere* sing]

pre·cept (prē′sept) *n.* a general rule of action or behavior; maxim: *"If at first you don't succeed, try, try, try again" is a familiar precept.* [< L *praeceptum,* originally neut. pp. of *praecipere* enjoin, anticipate < *prae-* before + *capere* take]

pre·cep·tor (pri sep′tər) *n.* an instructor; teacher. [< L *praeceptor* < *praecipere.* See PRECEPT.]

pre·cep·to·ri·al (prē′sep tô′rē əl) *adj.* **1** of a preceptor; like that of a preceptor. **2** using preceptors.

pre·cep·tress (pri sep′tris) *n.* a woman preceptor.

pre·ces·sion (prē sesh′ən) *n.* the act, fact, or condition of going first; precedence. [< LL *praecessio, -onis* < L *praecedere.* See PRECEDE.]

pre·cinct (prē′singkt) *n.* **1** Usually, **precincts,** *pl.* a space enclosed by walls, a fence, etc.: *the school precincts.* **2** Often, **precincts,** *pl.* a boundary; limit. **3** *U.S.* a district within certain boundaries, for administration or other purposes: *a police precinct.* [< Med.L *praecinctum,* originally neut. pp. of *praecingere* enclose < *prae-* before + *cingere* gird]

pre·ci·os·i·ty (presh′ē os′ə tē) *n., pl.* **-ties.** too much refinement; affectation. [< F *préciosité* < *précieux* precious]

pre·cious (presh′əs) *adj., adv.* —*adj.* **1** worth much; valuable. Gold, platinum, and silver are often called the precious metals. **2** much loved; dear. **3** too nice; overrefined; affected. **4** *Informal.* very great; thoroughgoing: *a precious mess.* **5** of great moral or spiritual worth: *the precious blood of Christ* (I Peter 1:19). —*adv. Informal.* very: *precious little money.* [ME < OF *precios* < L *pretiosus* < *pretium* value] —**pre′cious·ness,** *n.* ☛ *Syn. adj.* **1.** See note at **valuable.**

pre·cious·ly (presh′əs lē) *adv.* **1** at great cost. **2** in a valuable manner or degree. **3** extremely. **4** with extreme care in matters of detail.

precious metal a valuable metal such as gold, silver, or platinum.

precious stone a jewel; gem. Diamonds, rubies, and sapphires are precious stones.

prec·i·pice (pres′ə pis) *n.* **1** a very steep cliff; almost vertical slope; the face of a cliff. **2** a very dangerous situation; the brink of disaster. [< F < L *praecipitium* < *praeceps, -cipitis* steep, literally, headlong < *prae-* first + *caput* head]

pre·cip·i·tance (pri sip′ə təns) *n.* headlong haste; rashness.

pre·cip·i·tan·cy (pri sip′ə tən sē) *n.* precipitance.

pre·cip·i·tant (pri sip′ə tənt) *n., adj.* —*n.* a substance that causes another substance in solution in a liquid to be deposited in solid form; a precipitating agent. —*adj.* precipitate. [< L *praecipitans, -antis,* ppr. of *praecipitare.* See PRECIPITATE.] —**pre·cip′i·tant·ly,** *adv.*

pre·cip·i·tate (*v.* pri sip′ə tāt′; *adj.* pri sip′ə tāt′ *or* -tit) *v.*

-tat·ed, -tat·ing; *adj., n.* —*v.* **1** hasten the beginning of; bring about suddenly: *to precipitate a war.* **2** throw headlong; hurl: *to precipitate a rock down a cliff.* **3** separate (a substance) out from a solution as a solid. **4 a** condense from vapor in the form of rain, dew, etc. **b** be condensed in this way. —*adj.* **1** very hurried; sudden: *A cool breeze caused a precipitate drop in the temperature.* **2** with great haste and force; plunging or rushing; hasty; rash: *precipitate actions.* —*n.* a substance, usually crystalline, separated out from a solution as a solid. [< L *praecipitare* < *praeceps* headlong. See PRECIPICE.] —**pre·cip′i·tate·ly,** *adv.* —**pre·cip′i·ta′tor,** *n.*

pre·cip·i·ta·tion (pri sip′ə tā′shən) *n.* **1** the act or state of precipitating; a throwing down or falling headlong. **2** hastening or hurrying. **3** a sudden bringing on: *the precipitation of a war without warning.* **4** unwise or rash speed; sudden haste. **5 a** the separating out of a substance from a solution as a solid. **b** substance separated out from a solution as a solid. **6 a** the depositing of moisture in the form of rain, dew, or snow. **b** something that is precipitated, such as rain, dew, or snow. **c** the amount that is precipitated.

pre·cip·i·tous (pri sip′ə təs) *adj.* **1** like a precipice; very steep: *precipitous cliffs.* **2** hasty; rash. —**pre·cip′i·tous·ly,** *adv.* —**pre·cip′i·tous·ness,** *n.*
☛ *Syn.* **1.** See note at **steep.**

pré·cis (prā′sē *or* prā sē′) *n., pl.* **-cis.** a summary of an essay, speech, book, etc.; abstract. [< F *précis,* originally adj. < L *praecisus.* See PRECISE.]

pre·cise (pri sīs′) *adj.* **1** exact; accurate; definite: *The precise sum was $31.28.* **2** careful: *precise handwriting.* **3** strict; scrupulous. [< L *praecisus* abridged, pp. of *praecidere* < *prae-* in front + *caedere* cut] —**pre·cise′ly,** *adv.* —**pre·cise′ness,** *n.*

pre·ci·sion (pri sizh′ən) *n.* **1** the quality or state of being precise; exactness: *the precision of a machine. The precision of his calculations was amazing.* **2** the degree of refinement or exactness obtained. **3** (*adj.*) designed for or marked by precision: *precision instruments, precision bombing.*

pre·clude (pri klüd′) *v.* **-clud·ed, -clud·ing.** shut out; make impossible; prevent: *Buying a house now would preclude any possibility of a holiday trip for the next few years.* [< L *praecludere* < *prae-* before + *claudere* shut]

pre·clu·sion (pri klü′zhən) *n.* the act of precluding or the state of being precluded. [< L *praeclusus,* pp. of *praecludere.* See PRECLUDE.]

pre·clu·sive (pri klü′siv) *adj.* tending or serving to preclude. —**pre·clu′sive·ly,** *adv.*

pre·co·cious (pri kō′shəs) *adj.* **1** developed much earlier than normal in knowledge, skill, etc.: *She was so precocious as a child that she was composing music at the age of six.* **2** of a plant, developing or maturing very early. [< L *praecox, -ocis,* ult. < *prae-* before (its time) + *coquere* ripen] —**pre·co′cious·ly,** *adv.* —**pre·co′cious·ness,** *n.*

pre·coc·i·ty (pri kos′ə tē) *n.* precocious development; early maturity.

pre·cog·ni·tion (prē′kog nish′ən) *n.* **1** prior knowledge or cognition; foreknowledge. **2** *Scottish law.* **a** a preliminary examination of witnesses, etc. **b** the evidence taken at this examination.

pre·con·ceive (prē′kən sēv′) *v.* **-ceived, -ceiv·ing.** form an idea or opinion of before having any actual experience or knowledge: *Her first sea voyage didn't fit any of her preconceived notions of what it would be like.*

pre·con·cep·tion (prē′kən sep′shən) *n.* an idea or opinion formed beforehand.

pre·con·cert (prē′kən sèrt′) *v.* arrange beforehand.

pre·con·di·tion (prē′kən dish′ən) *n., v.* —*n.* something that must be fulfilled before something else can come about; prerequisite. —*v.* prepare or condition in advance.

pre·cook (prē kùk′) *v.* cook (food) partially or completely ahead of time in order to shorten or simplify its final preparation.

pre·cur·sor (pri kèr′sər) *n.* a forerunner: *A severe cold may be the precursor of pneumonia.* [< L *praecursor,* ult. < *prae-* before + *currere* run]

pre·cur·so·ry (pri kèr′sə rē) *adj.* indicative of something to follow; introductory.

pred. predicate.

pre·da·cious (pri dā′shəs) *adj.* living by preying; predatory. [< L *praedari* rob < *praeda* prey]

pre·date (prē′dāt′) *v.* **-dat·ed, -dat·ing.** **1** to come before in time: *His teaching career predated his entry into politics.* **2** assign

something to a date before its actual date: *She predated her letter to make it look as if she had written it a week earlier.*

pre·da·tion (prē dā′shən) *n.* **1** the act or fact of preying on other animals. **2** *Obsolete.* the act of pillaging; depredation.

pred·a·tor (pred′ə tər) *n.* **1** an animal that lives by killing and eating animals. **2** a person who lives by exploiting or preying on others.

pred·a·to·ry (pred′ə tô′rē) *adj.* **1** of or inclined to plundering or robbery: *Predatory tramps infested the highways.* **2** living by preying upon other animals. Hawks and owls are predatory birds. **3** inclined to injure or exploit others for the sake of one's own interests, profit, etc. [< L *praedatorius,* ult. < *praeda* prey]

pred·e·ces·sor (prē′də ses′ər *or* pred′ə ses′ər) *n.* **1** a person holding a position or office before another: *Edward VII was the predecessor of George V.* **2** something that came before another. **3** *Archaic.* ancestor; forefather. [< LL *praedecessor,* ult. < *prae-* before + *decedere* retire < *de-* from + *cedere* withdraw]

pre·des·ti·nate (prē des′tə nāt′) *v.* **-nat·ed, -nat·ing.** **1** decree or ordain by divine purpose. **2** foreordain by divine purpose. [< L *praedestinare* appoint beforehand < *prae-* before + *destinare* make fast, ult. < *de-* + *stare* stand]

pre·des·ti·na·tion (prē′des tə nā′shən) *n.* **1** an ordaining beforehand; destiny; fate. **2** an action of God in deciding beforehand what shall happen. **3** a doctrine that by God's decree certain souls will be saved and others lost.

pre·des·tine (prē des′tən) *v.* **-tined, -tin·ing.** determine or settle beforehand, especially by predestination; foreordain: *predestined to failure and disappointment, predestined to rule.*

pre·de·ter·mine (prē′di tèr′mən) *v.* **-mined, -min·ing.** **1** determine or decide beforehand: *The time for the meeting was predetermined.* **2** direct or impel beforehand (to something). —**pre′de·ter′mi·na′tion,** *n.*

pred·i·ca·ble (pred′ə kə bəl) *adj.* that can be predicated or affirmed. —**pred′i·ca·bly,** *adv.*

pre·dic·a·ment (pri dik′ə mənt) *n.* **1** an unpleasant, difficult, or dangerous situation. **2** *Archaic.* a specific condition, state, or situation. [< LL *praedicamentum* quality, category < L *praedicare.* See PREDICATE.]
☛ *Syn.* **1.** **Predicament, plight, dilemma** = a difficult situation. **Predicament** suggests a position or situation that is hard to get out of or presents a problem difficult to solve: *The world is in a dangerous predicament.* **Plight** applies to an unfortunate state or condition, usually unhappy or miserable, often hopeless: *He is worried by the plight of his relatives in enemy-conquered territory.* **Dilemma** applies to a predicament forcing a choice between two things, both disagreeable: *He is faced with the dilemma of telling a lie or betraying his friend.*

pred·i·cate (*n., adj.* pred′ə kit; *v.* pred′ə kāt′) *n., adj., v.* **-cat·ed, -cat·ing.** —*n.* **1** *Grammar.* a word or words expressing what is said about the subject; that part of a sentence or clause that contains a verb. *Examples:* We **work.** The committee **has organized a fund-raising drive.** She **is a journalist.** **2** *Logic.* that which is said of the subject in a proposition. —*adj. Grammar.* belonging to the predicate. In *Horses are strong,* **strong** is a **predicate adjective.** —*v.* **1** found or base (a statement, action, etc.) on something. **2** declare, assert, or affirm to be real or true: *Most religions predicate life after death.* **3** connote; imply. **4** declare to be an attribute or quality of some person or thing: *We predicate determination of those we admire and obstinacy of those we dislike.* **5** *Logic.* assert (something) about the subject of a proposition. [< L *praedicatus,* pp. of *praedicare* < *prae-* before + *dicare* make known. Doublet of PREACH.]
☛ *Usage.* **Predicate.** A predicate of a clause or sentence is the verb with its modifiers, object, complement, etc. It may be a simple verb of complete meaning (The big bell *tolled*), a verb and adverbial modifier (The sun *went behind the cloud*), a transitive verb and its modifiers and object (He *finally landed the big fish*), or a linking verb and its complement (My sister is an excellent skier.)

pred·i·ca·tion (pred′ə kā′shən) *n.* **1** the act of predicating; affirming; assertion. **2** *Logic.* the assertion of something about the subject of a proposition.

pred·i·ca·tive (pred′ə kā′tiv *or* pri dik′ə tiv) *adj.* **1** predicating; expressing predication. **2** acting as a predicate. —**pred′i·ca·tive·ly,** *adv.*

pre·dict (pri dikt′) *v.* tell beforehand; prophesy: *The weather office predicts rain for tomorrow. He predicted that the novel would be a bestseller.* [< L *praedictus,* pp. of *praedicere* < *prae-* before + *dicere* say] —**pre·dic′tor,** *n.*

pre·dict·a·bil·i·ty (pri dik′tə bil′ə tē) *n.* the quality or condition of being predictable.

pre·dict·a·ble (pri dik′tə bəl) *adj.* that can be predicted. —**pre·dict′a·bly,** *adv.*

pre·dic·tion (pri dik′shən) *n.* **1** the act of predicting. **2** something predicted; prophecy: *The weather prediction was for a storm.*

pre·dic·tive (prik dik′tiv) *adj.* foretelling; prophetic.

pre·di·gest (prē′dī jest′ or -di jest′) v. **1** cause food to be partly digested beforehand by a natural or artificial process: *Predigested food is sometimes used for persons who are ill or whose digestion is impaired.* **2** simplify to make easier to use: *a predigested edition of Gulliver's Travels for children.*

pre·di·ges·tion (prē′dī jes′chən or prē′di jes′chən) n. partial digestion beforehand.

pre·di·lec·tion (prē′də lek′shən or pred′ə lek′shən) n. a liking; preference. [< F *prédilection,* ult. < L *prae-* before + *diligere* choose]

pre·dis·pose (prē′dis pōz′) v. **-posed, -pos·ing. 1** give an inclination or tendency to; make liable or susceptible (*used with* to): *A cold predisposes a person to other diseases.* **2** put into a favorable or suitable frame of mind, emotional condition, etc.: *He is predisposed to be generous to his friends.* **3** dispose of, give away, or bequeath before the usual or specified time.

pre·dis·po·si·tion (prē′dis pə zish′ən) n. a previous inclination or tendency; susceptibility or liability: *a predisposition to look on the dark side of things.*

pre·dom·i·nance (pri dom′ə nəns) n. the quality or state of being predominant.

pre·dom·i·nant (pri dom′ə nənt) adj. **1** having more power, authority, or influence than others; superior. **2** prevailing; most noticeable or frequent. **—pre·dom′i·nant·ly,** adv.
☛ *Syn.* **1.** See note at **dominant.**

pre·dom·i·nate (pri dom′ə nāt′) v. **-nat·ed, -nat·ing.** be greater in power, strength, influence, or numbers. **—pre·dom′i·nat′ing·ly,** adv. **—pre·dom′i·na′tor,** n.

pre·dom·i·na·tion (pri dom′ə nā′shən) n. predominance.

pre-Dor·set (prē dôr′sit) n. an Inuit culture of northeastern Canada and N Greenland, earlier than the Dorset and dating from about 2000 B.C.

pree·mie (prē′mē) n. *Informal.* a baby born prematurely.

pre-em·i·nence (prē em′ə nəns) n. the quality or state of being pre-eminent; superiority: *the pre-eminence of Edison among the inventors of his day.*

pre-em·i·nent (prē em′ə nənt) adj. standing out above all others; superior to others in some quality: *a pre-eminent scientist.* [< L *praeeminens, -entis,* ppr. of *praeeminere* < *prae-* before + *eminere* stand out] **—pre-em′i·nent·ly,** adv.

pre-empt (prē empt′) v. **1** secure before someone else can; acquire or take possession of beforehand: *The cat pre-empted the comfortable chair.* **2** take the place of: *The regular programs were pre-empted by the Grey Cup telecast.* **3** U.S. settle in (land) with the right to buy it before others. [< *pre-emption*] **—pre-emp′tor,** n.

pre-emp·tion (prē emp′shən) n. a pre-empting or being pre-empted. [< *pre-* + L *emptio, -onis* buying < *emere* to buy]

pre-emp·tive (prē emp′tiv) adj. having to do with pre-emption; having pre-emption.

preen (prēn) v. **1** of birds, smooth or arrange (the feathers) with the beak. **2** arrange or dress up (one's hair, clothing, etc.) in a fussy, self-satisfied way: *She preened in front of the mirror for fifteen minutes. He's always preening himself.* **3** show pride and self-satisfaction in an achievement or skill (*used with a reflexive pronoun*): *He preens himself on his dancing skill.* [? var. of *prune* preen, dress carefully, influenced by ME *preonen* prick with a pin < OF *prēon* pin]

pre-ex·ist (prē′eg zist′) v. exist beforehand, or before something else.

pre-ex·ist·ence (prē′eg zis′təns) n. a previous existence.

pre-ex·ist·ent (prē′eg zis′tənt) adj. existing previously.

pref. **1** preface. **2** prefix. **3** preferred.

pre·fab (prē fab′) n. *Informal.* a prefabricated structure, especially a building.

pre·fab·ri·cate (prē fab′rə kāt′) v. **-cat·ed, -cat·ing. 1** make all standardized parts of at a factory, so that construction at the site consists mainly of assembling the various sections: *a prefabricated house.* **2** put together or prepare in advance, especially in an artificial way: *a prefabricated excuse.* **—pre·fab·ri·ca′tion,** n.

pref·ace (pref′is) n., v. **-aced, -ac·ing.** —n. an explanatory introduction to a written work or speech describing its scope, subject, purpose, etc. or giving background information. —v. **1** introduce by written or spoken remarks; give a preface to. **2** be a preface to; begin. [ME < OF *preface,* ult. < L *praefatio* < *prae-* before + *fari* speak]
☛ *Syn.* n. See note at **introduction.**

pref·a·to·ry (pref′ə tô′rē) adj. of, like, or given as a preface; given as a preface; introductory; preliminary.

pre·fect (prē′fekt) n. **1** in ancient Rome, etc., a title of various military and civil officers. **2** in France, the chief administrative official of a department. **3** in some schools, a senior student who

hat, āge, fär; let, ēqual, tèrm; it, īce
hot, ōpen, ôrder; oil, out; cup, pùt, rüle,
əbove, takən, pencəl, lemən, circəs
ch, child; ng, long; sh, ship
th, thin; ₮H, then; zh, measure

has some authority over other students; monitor. Also, (for def. 1), **praefect.** [< L *praefectus,* originally pp. of *praeficere* put in charge < *prae-* in front + *facere* make]

pre·fec·ture (prē′fek chər) n. the office, jurisdiction, territory, or official residence of a prefect. [< L *praefectura*]

pre·fer (pri fèr′) v. **-ferred, -fer·ring. 1** like better; choose rather: *I will come later, if you prefer.* **2** put forward; present: *to prefer a claim to property. The constable preferred charges of speeding against the driver.* **3** promote; advance. [ME < OF < L *praeferre* < *prae-* before + *ferre* carry] **—pre·fer′rer,** n.
☛ *Usage.* **Prefer** (def. 1). The idiom is with **to:** *I prefer chemistry to physics. She preferred dressing formally to wearing sports clothes.*

pref·er·a·ble (pref′ər ə bəl or pref′rə bəl) adj. to be preferred; more desirable: *He decided that going along was preferable to staying home alone.* **—pref′er·a·bly,** adv.

pref·er·ence (pref′ər əns or pref′rəns) n. **1** liking better; the favoring of one above another: *A teacher should not show preference for any one student.* **2** something preferred; first choice: *Her preference in reading is historical novels.* **3** in international trade, a granting of certain concessions, especially lower import tariffs, to another country or countries.
☛ *Syn.* **1.** See note at **choice.**

pref·er·en·tial (pref′ər en′shəl) adj. of, having to do with, or showing preference: *preferential treatment, preferential tariffs.* **—pref′er·en′tial·ly,** adv.

preferential shop a shop giving preference to union members in hiring, promotion, etc.

preferential voting a system of voting whereby the voter can indicate an order in the choice of candidates, as first, second, third, etc. so that in case no one candidate gets a clear majority, the election may be determined by totalling the points for first choice, second choice, etc.

pre·fer·ment (pri fèr′mənt) n. **1** advancement; promotion: *Captain White seeks preferment in the army.* **2** a position, office, or honor to which a person is advanced: *a sought-after preferment.* **3** the act of putting forward a charge or claim.

preferred stock stock that entitles the holder to a fixed rate of return on his investment, with guaranteed priority over common stock in the payment of dividends and, usually, in the distribution of assets in the event of liquidation of the company.

pre·fig·u·ra·tion (prē′fig ər ā′shən or -fig yər ā′shən) n. **1** prefiguring or being prefigured. **2** that in which something is prefigured; prototype.

pre·fig·u·ra·tive (prē′fig′ər ə tiv or prē′fig′yər ə tiv) adj. of, having to do with, or showing by prefiguration.

pre·fig·ure (prē fig′ər or -fig′yər) v. **-ured, -ur·ing. 1** show or suggest beforehand by a figure or type: *In one painting of Christ, His shadow resembles that of a cross, prefiguring the Crucifixion.* **2** imagine to oneself beforehand; foresee. [ME < LL *praefigurare* < L *prae-* before + *figurare* form, shape < *figura* a form] **—pre·fig′ure·ment,** n.

pre·fix (n. prē′fiks; v. prē′fiks or prē fiks′) n., v. —n. *Grammar.* a syllable, syllables, or word put at the beginning of a word to change its meaning or to form a new word, as in *pre*paid, *under*line, *dis*appear, *un*like. —v. put before: *We prefix "Mr." to a man's name.* [< L *praefixum,* neut. of *praefixus,* pp. of *praefigere* < *prae-* in front + *figere* fix]

preg·na·ble (preg′nə bəl) adj. open to attack; assailable. [ME < OF *prenable* < *prendre* < L *prendere,* shortened form of *prehendere* seize, take]

preg·nan·cy (preg′nən sē) n., pl. **-cies. 1** the state or condition of being pregnant. **2** the time this condition lasts. **3** the quality of being pregnant: *the pregnancy of his remarks.*

preg·nant (preg′nənt) adj. **1** having an embryo or embryos developing in the uterus; being with child or young. **2** filled; teeming; abounding: *a mind pregnant with ideas, a scheme pregnant with possibilities.* **3** filled with meaning; very significant: *a pregnant remark, a pregnant pause.* [ME < L *praegnans, -antis* < *prae-* before + *gen-* bear] **—preg′nant·ly,** adv.

pre·heat (prē hēt′) v. heat beforehand; especially, of an oven, heat to a particular temperature before placing something in it to cook.

pre·hen·sile (pri hens′īl or pri hen′səl) adj. adapted for seizing,

grasping, or holding on: *New World monkeys have prehensile tails; Old World monkeys do not.* [< F *préhensile*, ult. < L *prehendere* grasp]

pre·his·tor·ic (prē′his tôr′ik) *adj.* of, having to do with, or existing in periods before recorded history: *Fossils and artifacts provide us with information about prehistoric people and animals.*

pre·his·tor·i·cal (prē′his tôr′ə kəl) *adj.* prehistoric. —**pre′his·tor′i·cal·ly,** *adv.*

pre·his·to·ry or **pre–his·to·ry** (prē his′tə rē or -his′trē) *n.* 1 the history of mankind before the period of written history, learned from anthropology, archaeology, geology, paleontology, etc. 2 a history or account of the background of a situation or event.

pre·judge (prē juj′) *v.* -judged, -judg·ing. judge beforehand; judge without knowing all the facts. —**pre·judg′ment or pre·judge′ment,** *n.*

prej·u·dice (prej′ə dis) *n., v.* -diced, -dic·ing. —*n.* 1 an opinion or judgment based on irrelevant considerations or inadequate knowledge, especially an unfavorable opinion or judgment: *a prejudice against doctors.* 2 unreasonable hostility toward a particular person, group, race, nation, etc.: *The battle against prejudice. She was accused of prejudice.* 3 injury or disadvantage resulting from another's action or judgment that ignores one's rights: *They feel that the new bylaw works to the prejudice of apartment dwellers.* —*v.* 1 cause prejudice in: *The unpleasant experience prejudiced her against lawyers.* 2 injure or damage: *He was careful to say nothing that might prejudice their interests.* [ME < OF < L *praejudicium* < **prae-** before + *judicium* judgment]

prej·u·diced (prej′ə dist) *adj.* having or showing a prejudice for or, more often, against a person, group, idea, or thing: *a prejudiced report. She is very prejudiced.*

prej·u·di·cial (prej′ə dish′əl) *adj.* causing prejudice or disadvantage; hurtful.

prej·u·di·cial·ly (prej′ə dish′əl ē) *adv.* in a prejudiced manner; with prejudice.

prel·a·cy (prel′ə sē) *n., pl.* -cies. 1 the position or rank of a prelate. 2 prelates as a group. 3 church government by prelates.

prel·ate (prel′it) *n.* a high-ranking member of the clergy, such as a bishop or abbot. [< Med.L *praelatus* one preferred, originally pp. to L *praeferre* prefer. See PREFER.]

prelim. preliminary.

pre·lim·i·nar·y (pri lim′ə ner′ē) *adj., n., pl.* -nar·ies. —*adj.* coming before the main business; leading to something more important: *After preliminary remarks by the principal, the school play began.* —*n.* a preliminary step; something preparatory: *A physical examination is a preliminary to joining the armed forces.* [< NL *praeliminaris,* ult. < L *prae-* before + *limen, -minis* threshold] —**pre·lim′i·nar′i·ly,** *adv.*

pre·lit·er·ate (prē lit′ər it) *adj.* having to do with or designating a society or culture that has not developed a written language.

prel·ude (prel′yüd or prē′lüd) *n., v.* -ud·ed, -ud·ing. —*n.* 1 anything serving as an introduction. 2 *Music.* **a** a composition, or part of it, that introduces another composition or part. **b** an independent instrumental composition, usually short. **c** a composition played at the beginning of a church service. —*v.* 1 be a prelude or introduction to. 2 introduce with a prelude. [< F < Med.L *praeludium,* ult. < L *prae-* before + *ludere* play]

pre·mar·i·tal (prē mar′i təl or prē mer′i təl) *adj.* existing or happening before marriage: *premarital counselling.*

pre·ma·ture (prē′mə chür′ or prem′ə chür′, prē′mə chür′ or prem′ə chür′) *adj.* before the proper time; too soon. [< L *praematurus* < *prae-* before + *maturus* ripe] —**pre′ma·ture′ly,** *adv.*

pre·med·i·cal (prē med′ə kəl) *adj.* preparing for the study of medicine: *a premedical student.*

pre·med·i·tate (prē med′ə tāt′) *v.* -tat·ed, -tat·ing. consider or plan beforehand: *to premeditate a murder.* [< L *praemeditari* < *prae-* before + *meditari* meditate]

pre·med·i·tat·ed (prē med′ə tā′təd) *adj.* thought out or planned beforehand; characterized by conscious forethought and intent: *It looked more like accidental death than premeditated murder.* —**pre·med′i·tat′ed·ly,** *adv.*

pre·med·i·ta·tion (prē′med ə tā′shən) *n.* a previous deliberation or planning.

pre·mier (prē′mēr, prē′myər, or pri mēr′) *n., adj.* —*n.* 1 in Canada, the chief executive officer of a provincial government; the head of a provincial cabinet: *The ten premiers are attending a conference with the Prime Minister in Ottawa.* 2 the chief officer of any government; prime minister. The term *premier* is sometimes

used in Great Britain to refer to the prime minister. —*adj.* 1 first in rank or quality: *a novel of premier importance.* 2 first in time; earliest. [< F *premier* first < L *primarius* primary < *primus* first]

premier danseur (prə myä′ dän sœr′) French. the principal male dancer in a ballet or ballet company.

pre·mière or **pre·miere** (pri mēr′ or prə myer′; French, prə myer′) *n., v.* -mièred or -miered, -mièr·ing or -mier·ing. —*n.* 1 the first public performance or showing: *the première of a play.* 2 the leading actress in a theatrical cast or company. —*v.* 1 give a first public performance or showing of: *The theatre group is premièring a new play by a Winnipeg playwright.* 2 have a first public performance: *The film is premièring at the festival tonight.* 3 appear for the first time as a star: *He premièred last year in a musical comedy.* [< F *première,* originally fem. of *premier.* See PREMIER.]

pre·mière dan·seuse (prə myer′ dän sœz′) French. the principal female dancer in a ballet or ballet company.

pre·mier·ship (prē′myər ship′ or pri mēr′ship) *n.* 1 the rank or office of a prime minister or premier. 2 the state of being first in any rank.

prem·ise (*n.* prem′əs; *v.* pri mīz′ or prem′əs) *n., v.* **pre·mised, pre·mis·ing.** —*n.* 1 *Logic.* a statement assumed to be true and used to draw a conclusion. *Example:* Major premise: *Children should go to school.* Minor premise: *He is a child.* Conclusion: *He should go to school.* 2 **premises,** *pl.* **a** a house or building with its grounds. **b** *Law.* things mentioned previously, such as the names of the parties concerned, a description of the property, the price, etc. **c** *Law.* the property forming the subject of a document. —*v.* set forth as an introduction or explanation; mention beforehand. [< Med.L *praemissa,* originally fem. pp., put before, ult. < L *prae-* before + *mittere* send]

pre·mi·um (prē′mē əm) *n., adj.* —*n.* 1 a reward; prize: *Some magazines give premiums to sales representatives who obtain new subscriptions.* 2 something more than the ordinary price or wages; an extra payment or charge: *They had to pay a considerable premium to get first-quality goods.* 3 money paid regularly for an insurance policy. 4 something given away or offered at a reduced price to purchasers of a product, service, etc. 5 the excess value of one form of money over another of the same nominal value. 6 an unusually high value: *The company puts a premium on accuracy of work.*
at a premium, much valued and in demand: *Good housing is at a premium these days.*
—*adj.* of a higher grade or quality. [< L *praemium* reward < *prae-* before + *emere,* originally, take]

pre·mo·lar (prē mō′lər) *n., adj.* —*n.* one of the permanent teeth in front of the molars; bicuspid. —*adj.* having to do with or being the premolars.

pre·mo·ni·tion (prē′mə nish′ən or prem′ə nish′ən) *n.* 1 a feeling that something bad is about to happen; foreboding. 2 a forewarning. [< obs. F < L *praemonitio, -onis,* ult. < *prae-* before + *monere* warn]

pre·mon·i·to·ry (pri mon′ə tô′rē) *adj.* giving warning beforehand.

pre·na·tal (prē nā′təl) *adj.* 1 having to do with or for a woman who is expecting a child: *prenatal classes, prenatal care.* 2 before birth: *a prenatal diagnosis of defects.*

pren·tice (pren′tis) *n., adj.* Archaic. —*n.* apprentice. —*adj.* of or like an apprentice; inexperienced; unskilled.

pre·oc·cu·pa·tion (prē ok′yə pā′shən) *n.* preoccupying or being preoccupied; especially, complete absorption of the mind in something.

pre·oc·cu·pied (prē ok′yə pīd′) *adj.* lost in thought; with thoughts elsewhere: *He stood in the middle of the room, looking about him with a preoccupied air.*

pre·oc·cu·py (prē ok′yə pī′) *v.* -pied, -py·ing. 1 take up all the attention of; engross the mind of: *The question of getting to Vancouver preoccupied her mind.* 2 occupy or take possession of beforehand or before others: *Our favorite seats had been preoccupied.*

pre·or·dain (prē′ôr dān′) *v.* decide or settle beforehand; foreordain.

pre·or·di·na·tion (prē′ôr də nā′shən) *n.* the act of preordaining or the state of being preordained.

prep (prep) *adj.* Informal. preparatory.

prep. 1 preposition. 2 preparatory.

pre·pack·age (prē pak′ij) *v.* -aged, -ag·ing. package before sale according to certain weights, grades, prices, etc.

pre·paid (prē pād′) *v.* pt. and pp. of **prepay.**

prep·a·ra·tion (prep′ə rā′shən) *n.* 1 the act of preparing. 2 the state of being prepared; readiness. 3 anything done to prepare for something: *He made careful preparations for his holidays.* 4 a

medicine, food, or other substance made by a special process: *The preparation included camphor.*

pre·par·a·tive (pri par'ə tiv *or* -per'ə tiv) *adj., n.* —*adj.* preparatory. —*n.* something that helps to prepare.

pre·par·a·to·ry (pri par'ə tô'rē *or* -per'ə tô'rē) *adj.* **1** of or for preparation; preparing: *Preparatory schools fit students for college.* **2** as an introduction; preliminary.

pre·pare (pri per') *v.* **-pared, -par·ing. 1** put together or make from ingredients or parts: *They prepared a delicious meal for us. The witch prepared a magic brew.* **2** make or get ready for some purpose: *to prepare for school, to prepare someone for bad news.* **3** work out the details of; plan: *to prepare an adequate defence.* [< L *praeparare* < *prae-* before + *parare* make ready] —**pre·par'er**, *n.*

pre·par·ed·ness (pri per'id nis *or* -perd'nis) *n.* **1** the state or quality of being prepared; readiness. **2** the possession of adequate military forces and defences to meet threats or outbreaks of war.

pre·pay (prē pā') *v.* **-paid, -pay·ing.** pay or pay for in advance: *prepaid charges, a prepaid shipment.* —**pre·pay'ment**, *n.*

pre·pense (prə pens') *adj. Law.* planned beforehand; premeditated; deliberate (*usually placed after the noun*): *malice prepense.* [ME, ult. < OF *purpenser* meditate (with prefix *pre-* substituted) < *pur-* (< L *pro-* before) + *penser* think. See PENSIVE.]

pre·pon·der·ance (pri pon'dər əns) *n.* **1** a greater power, importance, or influence: *the preponderance of good over evil.* **2** a greater number or quantity: *a preponderance of oaks in the woods.*

pre·pon·der·ant (pri pon'dər ənt) *adj.* **1** having greater power, importance, or influence: *Greed is a miser's preponderant characteristic.* **2** having greater number or quantity; being prevalent: *Mixed farms are preponderant in the region.* —**pre·pon'der·ant·ly**, *adv.*

pre·pon·der·ate (pri pon'dər āt') *v.* **-at·ed, -at·ing. 1** be the chief or most important, influential, or numerous element or item; predominate (*often used with* **over**): *Oaks and maples preponderate in our eastern woods.* **2** be weighed down, as one end of a balance. **3** *Archaic.* be heavier; weigh more. [< L *praeponderare* outweigh, ult. < *prae-* before + *pondus, -deris* weight]

prep·o·si·tion (prep'ə zish'ən) *n. Grammar.* a word that shows relationships of time, direction, position, etc. between other words. *With, for, by,* and *in* are prepositions in the following sentence: *A man with rugs for sale walked by our house in the morning.* [< L *praepositio, -onis,* ult. < *prae-* before + *ponere* place]

☛ *Usage.* **Preposition at end of sentence.** Under certain conditions, it is normal English structure for a preposition to stand at the end of the clause or sentence it belongs to, as in *What did you do it for?* Efforts to avoid this in favor of a more formal style often result in awkwardness: *This is the sort of writing up with which I will not put.*

prep·o·si·tion·al (prep'ə zish'ən əl) *adj.* having to do with, containing, or having the nature or function of a preposition: *prepositional usage, a prepositional phrase.* —**prep'o·si'tion·al·ly**, *adv.*

pre·pos·sess (prē'pə zes') *v.* **1** fill with a favorable feeling or opinion: *We were prepossessed by the boy's modest behavior.* **2** fill with a feeling or opinion.

pre·pos·sess·ing (prē'pə zes'ing) *adj.* making a favorable first impression; attractive; pleasing.

pre·pos·ses·sion (prē'pə zesh'ən) *n.* bias; prejudice; a favorable feeling or opinion formed beforehand.

pre·pos·ter·ous (pri pos'tər əs *or* pri pos'trəs) *adj.* contrary to nature, reason, or common sense; absurd; senseless: *It would be preposterous to shovel snow with a teaspoon.* [< L *praeposterus* in reverse order, ult. < *prae-* before + *post* after] —**pre·pos'ter·ous·ly**, *adv.* —**pre·pos'ter·ous·ness**, *n.*

☛ *Syn.* See note at **ridiculous.**

pre·puce (prē'pyüs) *n.* foreskin. [< F < L *praeputium*]

Pre–Raph·a·el·ite (prē'raf'ē əl īt' *or* -rā'fē əl īt) *n.* **1** any Italian painter preceding Raphael (1483-1520), a famous Italian painter. **2** one of a group of English artists and poets formed in 1848, including Millais and Dante Gabriel Rossetti, who aimed to work in the spirit that prevailed before the time of Raphael. **3** any modern artist having similar aims or methods.

pre·req·ui·site (prē rek'wə zit) *n., adj.* —*n.* something that is necessary to achieve an end; something required as a condition before something else can be considered: *A high-school course is the usual prerequisite to university studies.* —*adj.* required beforehand.

pre·rog·a·tive (pri rog'ə tiv) *n., adj.* —*n.* a right or privilege that nobody else has: *The government has the prerogative of coining money.* —*adj.* having or exercising a prerogative. [< L *praerogativa,* originally fem. adj., asked to vote first, ult. < *prae-* before + *rogare* ask]

☛ *Syn. n.* See note at **privilege.**

pres. present.

hat, āge, fär; let, ēqual, tèrm; it, īce
hot, ōpen, ôrder; oil, out; cup, pút, rüle,
əbove, takən, pencəl, lemən, circəs

ch, child; ng, long; sh, ship
th, thin; ŦH, then; zh, measure

Pres. 1 president. **2** Presbyterian.

pres·age (*n.* pres'ij; *v.* pri sāj') *n., v.* **pre·saged, pre·sag·ing.** —*n.* **1** something that foreshadows a future event; portent; omen: *a sure presage of evil.* **2** a feeling that something is about to happen; presentiment. —*v.* **1** give warning of; foreshadow: *Some people think that a circle around the moon presages a storm.* **2** have or express a presentiment of: *He presaged a disaster from the experiment.* [ME < OF < L *praesagium,* ult. < *prae-* before + *sagus* prophetic] —**pre·sag'er**, *n.*

Presb. Presbyterian.

pres·by·ter (prez'bə tər *or* pres'bə tər) *n.* **1** an elder in the early Christian church. **2** *Presbyterian Church, United Church of Canada.* a member of a presbytery. **3** a priest or minister in a church having an episcopal heirarchy. [L *presbyter* elder < Gk. *presbyteros,* comparative of *presbys* old. Doublet of PRIEST.]

Pres·by·te·ri·an (prez'bə tēr'ē ən *or* pres'bə tēr'ē ən) *n., adj.* —*n.* a member of any of several Christian churches that constitute the main branch of the Reformed churches, whose government is by presbyters (elders) and whose doctrines emphasize the sovereignty of God and acceptance of the Bible as the only infallible rule of faith and life. The doctrines of these churches are more or less modified forms of Calvinism. —*adj.* of or having to do with Presbyterians or Presbyterianism. See also **United Church of Canada.**

Pres·by·te·ri·an·ism (prez'bə tēr'ē ən iz'əm *or* pres'bə tēr'ē ən iz'əm) *n.* **1** the doctrines or religious principles of the Presbyterian churches. **2** a system of church government by presbyters, all of equal rank.

pres·by·ter·y (prez'bə ter'ē *or* pres'bə ter'ē) *n., pl.* **-ter·ies. 1** *Presbyterian Church, United Church of Canada.* **a** a local governing body composed of the ministers and representative lay members of the congregations of a given area. **b** the congregations or area under the jurisdiction of such a body. **2** the part of a church set aside for the clergy. **3** *Roman Catholic Church.* the residence of a parish priest.

pre·school (prē'skül') *adj.* **1** of, for, or being the period in a child's life after infancy and before the child begins elementary school: *the preschool years, preschool activities.* **2** of, for, or designating a child of this age.

pre·school·er (prē'skü'lər) *n.* a child who is too young to go to elementary school; especially, one between the ages of two and five: *This game is designed for preschoolers.*

pre·sci·ence (prē'shē əns *or* presh'ē əns) *n.* a knowledge of things before they exist or happen; foreknowledge; foresight. [< LL *praescientia* < L *praesciens,* ppr. of *praescire* foreknow < *prae-* before + *scire* know]

pre·sci·ent (prē'shē ənt *or* presh'ē ənt) *adj.* knowing beforehand; foreseeing. —**pre'sci·ent·ly**, *adv.*

pre·scribe (pri skrīb') *v.* **-scribed, -scrib·ing. 1** lay down as a rule or guide; order; direct: *to do what the law prescribes. There are two prescribed texts for this course.* **2** order as a remedy or treatment: *The doctor prescribed quinine.* **3** give medical advice. **4** *Law.* **a** make or become invalid or outlawed because of the passage of time. **b** claim a right or title to something by virtue of long use and enjoyment of it. [< L *praescribere* < *prae-* before + *scribere* write]

pre·script (*n.* prē'skript; *adj.* pri skript' *or* prē'skript) *n., adj.* —*n.* rule; order; direction. —*adj.* prescribed. [< L *praescriptum,* neut. of *praescriptus,* ppr. of *praescribere.* See PRESCRIBE.]

pre·scrip·tion (pri skrip'shən) *n.* **1** an order; direction. **2** a written direction or order for preparing and using a medicine: *a prescription for a cough. Symbol:* ℞ **3** medicine that has been prescribed: *Did you use up the whole prescription?* **4** *Law.* **a** the possession or use of a thing long enough to give one a right or title to it. **b** the right or title thus established.

pre·scrip·tive (pri skrip'tiv) *adj.* **1** that prescribes. **2** depending or based on legal prescription. **3** established by long use or custom. —**pre·scrip'tive·ly**, *adv.* —**pre·scrip'tive·ness**, *n.*

pres·ence (prez'əns) *n.* **1** the fact or condition of being present in a place: *I knew of his presence in the other room.* **2** the place within immediate proximity and view of a person or thing: *She signed the statement in the presence of two witnesses. The messenger was admitted to the leader's presence.* **3** personal appearance and bearing, especially when impressive or imposing: *a*

man of noble presence. He has no stage presence. **4** a person who is present, especially one of high rank or great dignity. **5** a spirit or supernatural being felt to be near. [ME < OF < L *praesentia* < *praesens* present. See PRESENT¹.]

presence chamber the room in which a king or some very important person receives guests.

presence of mind the ability to think calmly and quickly when taken by surprise.

pres·ent¹ (prez′ənt) *adj., n.* —*adj.* **1** being in a proper or expected place; at hand; not absent: *Every member of the class was present.* **2** at this time; being or occurring now: *present prices.* **3** *Grammar.* designating the verb tense that expresses action or a state of the present time or the time of speaking. —*n.* **1** the present time: *At present people need courage.* **2** *Grammar.* the present tense or a verb form in that tense. **by these presents,** *Formal.* by these words; by this document. [ME < OF < L *praesens, -entis* < *prae-* before + *esse* be]
☛ *Syn. adj.* **2.** See note at **current.**

pres·ent² (*v.* pri zent′; *n.* prez′ənt) *v., n.* —*v.* **1** being in a proper or expected place; at hand; not absent: *Every member of the class was present.* **2** at this time; being or occurring now: *the present ruler, present prices.* **3** bring before the mind; offer for consideration: *He presented reasons for his action.* **4** offer to view or notice: *The new City Hall presents a fine appearance.* **5** bring before the public: *The school presented a play.* **6** set forth in words. **7** hand in or send in: *The grocer presented his bill.* **8** introduce socially: *Ms. Janzen, may I present Mr. Bindon?* **9** bring before a person of high rank: *He was presented to the Governor General.* **10** direct, point, or turn in a particular direction: *The handsome actor presented his profile to the camera.*
present arms, salute by bringing a rifle, etc. to a vertical position in front of one's body.
—*n.* something given; gift: *I got the record player as a birthday present.* [ME < OF < L *praesentare* < *praesens, -entis* present. See PRESENT¹.]
☛ *Syn. v.* **1.** See note at **give. 8.** See note at **introduce.**

pre·sent·a·ble (pri zen′tə bəl) *adj.* **1** fit to be introduced or go into company; suitable in appearance, dress, manners, etc.: *It took him an hour to make himself presentable again after cleaning the basement.* **2** suitable to be offered or given: *That is a very presentable gift. Make the essay more presentable before you hand it in.* —**pre·sent′a·bly,** *adv.*

pres·en·ta·tion (prez′ən tā′shən) *n.* **1** a giving: *the presentation of a gift.* **2** gift. **3** a proposal for consideration. **4** an offering to be seen; showing: *the presentation of a play.* **5** a formal introduction, especially to somebody of high rank: *the presentation of a person to the Queen.* **6** a function at which a gift is presented: *A presentation was held when the manager retired.*

pres·ent-day (prez′ənt dā′) *adj.* of the present time.

pre·sen·ti·ment (pri zen′tə mənt) *n.* a feeling or impression that something is about to happen; premonition. [< MF *presentiment,* ult. < L *prae-* before + *sentire* sense]
☛ *Usage.* Do not confuse **presentiment** with **presentment.**

pres·ent·ly (prez′ənt lē) *adv.* **1** before long; soon: *The clock will strike presently.* **2** at present; now: *The Prime Minister is presently in Ottawa.* **3** *Archaic.* at once.
☛ *Syn.* **1.** See note at **immediately.**

pre·sent·ment (pri zent′mənt) *n.* **1** a bringing forward; offering to be considered. **2** a showing; offering to be seen. **3** a representation on the stage or by a portrait. **4** a statement by a grand jury of an offence from their own knowledge. [ME < OF *presentement* < *presenter* < L *praesentare.* See PRESENT².]
☛ *Usage.* Do not confuse **presentment** with **presentiment.**

present participle a participle that expresses the same time as that expressed by the finite verb of the clause. In the sentence *Saying good night, they started for home, saying* is a present participle expressing the same time as the verb *started.* In *We are leaving now, leaving* is a present participle expressing the same time as *are. Abbrev.:* ppr. or p.pr.
☛ *Usage.* In modern English the present participle always ends in -*ing.*

present perfect 1 a tense that expresses action or a state that is completed at the time of speaking. It is formed in English with the present tense of *have* plus a past participle, as in *They have gone.* **2** a verb form in the present perfect.

pre·serv·a·ble (pri zėr′və bəl) *adj.* that can be preserved.

pres·er·va·tion (prez′ər vā′shən) *n.* preserving or being preserved: *the preservation of one's health. The artifacts were in an excellent state of preservation.*

pre·serv·a·tive (pri zėr′və tiv) *n., adj.* —*n.* any substance that will prevent decay or injury. *Paint is a preservative for wood*

surfaces. *Salt is a preservative for meat.* —*adj.* that preserves.

pre·serve (pri zėrv′) *v.* -**served,** -**serv·ing;** *n.* —*v.* **1** keep from harm or change; keep safe; protect. **2** keep up; maintain. **3** keep from spoiling: *Ice helps to preserve food.* **4** prepare (food) to keep it from spoiling. Boiling with sugar, salting, smoking, and pickling are different ways of preserving food.
—*n.* **1** an area or region where wild animals, fish, or trees and plants are protected. **2** Usually, **preserves,** *pl.* fruit cooked with sugar and sealed from the air: *plum preserves.* [ME < OF < LL *praeservare* < L *prae-* before + *servare* keep] —**pre·serv′a·ble,** *adj.*

pre·serv·er (pri zėr′vər) *n.* a person or thing that preserves or protects from danger: *a life preserver.*

pre·set (prē set′) *v.* -**set,** -**set·ting.** set beforehand.

pre·side (pri zīd′) *v.* -**sid·ed,** -**sid·ing. 1** hold the place of authority; have charge of a meeting. **2** have authority; have control: *The manager presides over the business of the store.* [< L *praesidere* < *prae-* before + *sedere* sit] —**pre·sid′er,** *n.*

pres·i·den·cy (prez′ə dən sē) *n., pl.* -**cies. 1** the office of president. **2** the time during which a president is in office. **3 Presidency,** the office or time of office of a President of the United States.

pres·i·dent (prez′ə dənt) *n.* **1** Often, **President,** the highest executive officer of a republic. **2** the chief officer of a company, university, society, club, etc. [< L *praesidens, -entis* presiding, ppr. of *praesidere.* See PRESIDE.]

pres·i·dent-e·lect (prez′ə dənt i lekt′) *n.* a president who has been elected but has not yet taken office.

pres·i·den·tial (prez′ə den′shəl) *adj.* of, having to do with, or belonging to a president or presidency. —**pres′i·den′tial·ly,** *adv.*

pre·sid·i·um (pri sid′ē əm) *n.* in the Soviet Union and other communist countries, a permanent executive committee set up at a high level of government to act for a larger body, such as a legislature, between sessions. [< L *praesidium* a presiding over < *praesidere.* See PRESIDE.]

press¹ (pres) *v., n.* —*v.* **1** use force or weight steadily against; push with steady force: *Press the button to ring the bell.* **2** squeeze; squeeze out. **3** use force steadily. **4** clasp; hug. **5** make smooth; flatten: *Press clothes with an iron.* **6** put a crease in: *My mother pressed my trousers.* **7** push forward; keep pushing: *The boy pressed on in spite of the wind.* **8** move by pushing steadily (up, down, against, etc.). **9** urge onward; cause to hurry. **10** crowd; throng. **11** urge (a person); keep asking; entreat: *Because it was so stormy, we pressed our guest to stay all night.* **12** lay stress upon; insist on. **13** constrain; compel; force. **14** urge for acceptance. **15** harass; oppress; trouble. **16** weigh heavily upon (the mind, a person, etc.) **17** demand prompt action; be urgent.
—*n.* **1** a pressing; presssure; push: *the press of ambition. She was kept busy by the press of many duties.* **2** a pressed condition. **3** any of various instruments or machines for exerting pressure. **4** a machine for printing; printing press. **5** an establishment for printing books, etc. **6** the process or art of printing. **7** newspapers, magazines, and the people who work for them: *The concert was reported by the press.* **8** a notice given in newspapers or magazines: *The star actress got a good press for her performance.* **9** a crowd; throng. **10** a pressing forward or together; crowding. **11** urgency; hurry. **12** a cupboard for clothes, books, etc. **13** a crease.
go to press, begin to be printed: *The newspaper goes to press at midnight.* [ME < OF < L *pressare,* ult. < *premere* press] —**press′er,** *n.*

press² (pres) *v., n.* —*v.* **1** force into service, usually naval or military. **2** seize and use. —*n.* **1** an impressment into service, usually naval or military. **2** an order for such impressment. [obs. *prest* < OF *prester* furnish, ult. < L *praesto* ready]

press agent an agent in charge of publicity for a person, organization, etc.

press box at a sports stadium, arena, race track, etc. an enclosed space set aside for reporters.

press conference a meeting for the giving of information to reporters by a person or group. Some press conferences are called to announce specific items of news, others to provide opportunities for reporters to question particular individuals.

press gallery 1 an area reserved for the news media, especially in a legislative assembly. **2** the group of reporters covering the sessions of a legislative assembly: *The Prime Minister's speech puzzled the press gallery.*

press gang in former times, a group of men whose job it was to obtain men, often by force, for service in the navy or army.

press·ing (pres′ing) *adj., n.* —*adj.* requiring immediate action or attention; urgent. —*n.* the act of pressing or creasing with an iron: *That dress needs a good pressing.* —**press′ing·ly,** *adv.*

press·man (pres′mən) *n., pl.* **-men.** a man who operates or has charge of a press, especially a printing press.

pres·sure (presh′ər) *n., v.* —*n.* **1** the continued action of a weight or force: *The pressure of the wind filled the sails of the boat.* **2** the force per unit of area: *The tires of a 3-speed bicycle need a pressure of about 300 kPa.* **3** a state of trouble or strain: *the pressure of poverty.* **4** a compelling force or influence: *He changed his mind under pressure from others.* **5** the need for prompt or decisive action; urgency: *the pressure of business.* **6** electromotive force.
—*v.* force or urge by exerting pressure: *The opposition pressured the government into debating the matter.* [ME < OF < L *pressura*, ult. < *premere* press]

pressure cooker an airtight apparatus for cooking with steam under pressure.

pressure group any business, professional, or labor group that attempts to further its interests in the federal or provincial legislatures or elsewhere.

pressure ice ridges of ice formed by vast areas of sea ice pressing against each other.

pressure ridge a ridge of pressure ice.

pres·sur·ize (presh′ər īz′) *v.* **-ized, -iz·ing. 1** keep the atmospheric pressure inside of (the cabin of an aircraft) at a normal level in spite of the altitude. **2** place under high pressure.

press·work (pres′wėrk′) *n.* **1** the working or management of a printing press. **2** the work done by a printing press.

Pres·ter John (pres′tər) a legendary Christian priest and king of the Middle Ages, said to have ruled a kingdom somewhere in Asia or Africa.

pres·ti·dig·i·ta·tion (pres′tə dij′ə tā′shən) *n.* sleight of hand. [< F]

pres·ti·dig·i·ta·tor (pres′tə dij′ə tā′tər) *n.* a man skilled in sleight of hand. [< F < L *praestigiator* juggler; form influenced by F *preste* quick and L *digitus* finger]

pres·tige (pres tēzh′ *or* pres tēj′) *n.* **1** good reputation, influence, or social status derived from achievements, associations, wealth, etc. **2** (*adj.*) having or giving prestige: *prestige accessories for your desk.* [< F *prestige* magic spell, ult. < L *praestigiae* tricks]

pres·ti·gious (pres tij′əs) *adj.* having or conferring prestige. —**pres·ti′gious·ly,** *adv.*

pres·tis·si·mo (pres tis′ə mō′) *adv., adj., n. Music.* —*adv.* very quickly.
—*adj.* very quick.
—*n.* a very quick movement or passage; composition to be played or sung at this tempo. [< Ital. *prestissimo,* superlative of *presto* quick, quickly]

pres·to (pres′tō) *adv., adj., n., pl.* **-tos.** —*adv.* quickly.
—*adj.* quick.
—*n.* a quick movement or passage; composition to be played or sung at this tempo. [< Ital. *presto,* ult. < L *praesto,* adv., ready]

pre-stressed concrete (prē′strest′) concrete that has been cast around steel cables which are under tension. The tension of the cables compresses the concrete, thus increasing its strength. The cables can also be bent to exert force in any direction in order to counteract the effect of the pressure of a load on the concrete.

pre·sum·a·ble (pri züm′ə bəl *or* -zyüm′ə bəl) *adj.* that can be presumed or taken for granted; probable; likely. —**pre·sum′a·bly,** *adv.*

pre·sume (pri züm′ *or* pri zyüm′) *v.* **-sumed, -sum·ing. 1** take for granted without proving; suppose: *The law presumes innocence until guilt is proved.* **2** take upon oneself; venture; dare: *May I presume to tell you what to do?* **3** take an unfair advantage (*used with* **on** *or* **upon**): *Don't presume on his good nature by taking favours from him every week.* [ME < OF < L *praesumere* take for granted < *prae-* before + *sumere* take] —**pre·sum′er,** *n.* —**pre·sum′ing·ly,** *adv.*

pre·sum·ed·ly (pri züm′id lē *or* pri zyüm′id lē) *adv.* as is or may be supposed.

pre·sump·tion (pri zump′shən) *n.* **1** the act of presuming. **2** something taken for granted; a conclusion based on good evidence: *Since he had the stolen jewels, the presumption was that he was the thief.* **3** a cause or reason for presuming; probability. **4** unpleasant boldness: *It is presumption to ask for a four-day week.* [ME < OF < L *praesumptio, -onis* < *praesumere.* See PRESUME.]

pre·sump·tive (pri zump′tiv) *adj.* **1** based on likelihood; presumed: *heir presumptive.* **2** giving ground for presumption or belief: *The man's running away was regarded as presumptive evidence of his guilt.*

pre·sump·tive·ly (pri zump′tiv lē) *adv.* by presumption; presumably.

pre·sump·tu·ous (pri zump′chü əs) *adj.* acting without permission or right; too bold; forward. [ME < OF < LL

hat, āge, fär; let, ēqual, tėrm; it, īce
hot, ōpen, ôrder; oil, out; cup, put, rüle,
əbove, takən, pencəl, lemən, circəs

ch, child; ng, long; sh, ship
th, thin; ᵺH, then; zh, measure

praesumptuosus < L *praesumptio* audacity (< *praesumere.* See PRESUME.), but modelled on *sumptuosus* expensive < *sumptus* expense] —**pre·sump′tu·ous·ly,** *adv.* —**pre·sump′tu·ous·ness,** *n.*

pre·sup·pose (prē′sə pōz′) *v.* **-posed, -pos·ing. 1** take for granted in advance; assume beforehand: *Let us presuppose that he wants more money.* **2** require as a necessary condition; imply: *A fight presupposes fighters.*

pre·sup·po·si·tion (prē′sup ə zish′ən) *n.* **1** the act of presupposing. **2** a thing presupposed.

pret. preterite.

pre·tence (pri tens′ *or* prē′tens) *n.* **1** a false appearance: *Under pretence of picking up the handkerchief, she took the money.* **2** a false claim: *The girls made a pretence of knowing the answer.* **3** a claim. **4** a pretending; make-believe: *His anger was all pretence.* **5** a showing off; display: *Her manner is free from pretence.* **6** anything done to show off. Also, **pretense.** [ME < AF *pretense,* ult. < L *praetendere.* See PRETEND.]

pre·tend (pri tend′) *v.* **1** make believe. **2** claim falsely: *She pretended to like the meal so she wouldn't offend the hostess.* **3** claim falsely to have: *She pretended illness.* **4** claim: *I don't pretend to be a musician.* **5** lay claim: *James Stuart pretended to the English throne.* **6** venture; attempt; presume: *I cannot pretend to judge between them.* [ME < OF < L *praetendere* < *prae-* before + *tendere* stretch]
☛ **Syn. 2, 3. Pretend, affect, assume** = claim falsely to have or be something. **Pretend** means speak or act as if one has or feels something: *She pretended ignorance of the whole affair.* **Affect** emphasizes putting on some characteristic or feeling, for some intended effect: *When she applied for a job, she affected simplicity.* **Assume** suggests putting on the appearance of feeling something, to cover up one's real feelings: *She assumed a look of sorrow.*

pre·tend·ed (pri ten′did) *adj.* claimed falsely; asserted falsely. —**pre·tend′ed·ly,** *adv.*

pre·tend·er (pri ten′dər) *n.* **1** a person who pretends. **2** a person who makes claims to a throne without just right.

pre·tense (pri tens′ *or* prē′tens) See **pretence.**

pre·ten·sion (pri ten′shən) *n.* **1** a claim: *The young prince has pretensions to the throne.* **2** a putting forward of a claim. **3** a pretentious display.

pre·ten·tious (pri ten′shəs) *adj.* **1** making claims to excellence or importance: *a pretentious person, book, or speech.* **2** doing things for show or to make a fine appearance; showy: *a pretentious style of entertaining guests.* [< F *prétentieux,* ult. < L *praetendere.* See PRETEND.] —**pre·ten′tious·ly,** *adv.* —**pre·ten′tious·ness,** *n.*

pret·er·ite *or* **pret·er·it** (pret′ər it) *n., adj.* —*n.* a verb form that expresses occurrence in the past; the past tense. *Obeyed* is the preterite of *obey, spoke,* of *speak;* and *saw,* of *see.* —*adj.* expressing past time. [ME < OF < L *praeteritus,* ult. < *praeter-* past + *ire* go]

pre·ter·mit (prē′tər mit′) *v.* **-mit·ted, -mit·ting. 1** leave out; omit. **2** let pass without notice. [< L *praetermittere* < *praeter-* past + *mittere* let go]

pre·ter·nat·u·ral (prē′tər nach′ə rəl *or* -nach′rəl) *adj.* **1** out of the ordinary course of nature; abnormal. **2** due to something above or beyond nature; supernatural. [< Med.L *praeternaturalis,* ult. < L *praeter-* beyond + *natura* nature] —**pre·ter·nat′u·ral·ly,** *adv.*

pre-test (*n.* prē′test′; *v.* prē′test′) *n., v.* —*n.* a preliminary test. Pre-tests are sometimes given at the beginning of a course of study to determine the students' level of knowledge or comprehension. —*v.* give a pre-test to.

pre·text (prē′tekst) *n.* a false reason concealing the real reason; pretence; excuse: *He used his sore finger as a pretext for not going to school.* [< L *praetextus,* ult. < *prae-* in front + *texere* weave]

pre·tor (prē′tər *or* prē′tôr) See **praetor.**

pret·ti·fy (prit′ə fī′) *v.* **-fied, -fy·ing.** decorate, especially in an artificial or overly cute way.

pret·ty (prit′ē) *adj.* **-ti·er, -ti·est; n., pl.* **-ties;** *adv., v.* —*adj.* **1** attractive or pleasing. **2** not at all pleasing: *a pretty mess.* **3** too dainty or delicate. **4** *Archaic.* brave; bold; fine. **5** *Informal.* considerable in amount or extent.
sitting pretty, *Slang.* well off; in a good position.
—*n.* a pretty person or thing.
—*adv.* fairly; rather: *It is pretty late.*
—*v.*

pretty up, *Informal.* make pretty.
[OE *prættig* cunning < *prætt* trick]—**pret′ti·ly,** *adv.*—**pret′ti·ness,** *n.*

pretty penny *Informal.* a large sum of money.

pret·zel (pret′səl) *n.* a hard biscuit, usually made in the shape of a loose knot and salted on the outside. [< G *Brezel* < Med.L *bracellus* bracelet, ult. < Gk. *brachion* arm]

pre·vail (pri vāl′) *v.* 1 exist in many places; be in general use: *That custom still prevails.* 2 be the most usual or strongest: *Sadness prevailed in our minds.* 3 be the stronger; win the victory; succeed: *The knights prevailed against their foe.* 4 be effective.
prevail on, upon, or **with,** persuade.
[< L *praevalere* < *prae-* before + *valere* have power]

pre·vail·ing (pri vāl′ing) *adj.* 1 that prevails; having superior force or influence; victorious. 2 in general use; most common.
—**pre·vail′ing·ly,** *adv.*
☞ *Syn.* 2. See note at **current.**

prev·a·lence (prev′ə ləns) *n.* widespread occurrence; general use: *the prevalence of complaints about the weather.*

prev·a·lent (prev′ə lənt) *adj.* 1 widespread; general; common: *Colds are prevalent in the winter.* 2 predominant; victorious. [< L *praevalens, -entis,* ppr. of *praevalere* prevail. See PREVAIL.]

pre·var·i·cate (pri ver′ə kāt′ or -var′ə kāt′) *v.* -cat·ed, -cat·ing. turn aside from the truth in speech or act; lie. [< L *praevaricari* make a sham accusation, ult. < *prae-* before + *varicus* straddling < *varus* crooked]—**pre·var′i·ca′tor,** *n.*

pre·var·i·ca·tion (pri ver′ə kā′shən or -var′ə kā′shən) *n.* the act of prevaricating; departure from the truth.

pre·vent (pri vent′) *v.* 1 keep (*from*): *Illness prevented him from doing his work.* 2 keep from happening: *Rain prevented the game.* 3 hinder. [< L *praeventus,* pp. of *praevenire* < *prae-* before + *venire* come]—**pre·vent′er,** *n.*
☞ *Syn.* **Prevent, hinder, impede** = get in the way of action or progress. **Prevent** = keep a person or thing from doing something or making progress by acting or setting up an obstacle to stop him or it: *Business prevented his going.* **Hinder** = hold back, so that making, starting, going ahead, or finishing is late, difficult, or impossible: *An unbalanced diet hinders growth.* **Impede** = slow up movement and progress by putting something binding, fouling, etc. on or in the way: *Mud impedes the advance of troops.*

pre·vent·a·ble (pri ven′tə bəl) *adj.* that can be prevented.

pre·vent·a·tive (pri ven′tə tiv) *adj. or n.* preventive.

pre·vent·i·ble (pri ven′tə bəl) *adj.* preventable.

pre·ven·tion (pri ven′shən) *n.* 1 a preventing: *the prevention of fire.* 2 something that prevents.

pre·ven·tive (pri ven′tiv) *adj., n.*—*adj.* that prevents: *preventive measures against disease.*—*n.* something that prevents: *Vaccination is a preventive against smallpox.*—**pre·ven′tive·ly,** *adv.*—**pre·ven′tive·ness,** *n.*

preventive war an aggressive war waged against another nation, supposedly started in anticipation of attack by that nation.

pre·view (prē′vyü) *n., v.*—*n.* 1 a previous view, inspection, survey, etc. 2 an advance showing of scenes from a motion picture, play, television program, etc.—*v.* view beforehand.

pre·vi·ous (prē′vē əs) *adj.* 1 coming or going before; that came before; earlier. 2 *Informal.* quick; hasty; premature: *Don't be too previous about refusing.*
previous to, before: *Previous to her departure she gave a party.*
[< L *praevius* leading the way < *prae-* before + *via* road]
☞ *Syn.* 1. **Previous, preceding, prior** = coming before something. **Previous** suggests earlier in time, made or done sometime earlier or being the last one before the present: *I cannot go, for I have a previous engagement* (made before). **Preceding** means coming immediately before in order of time or in place: *Check the preceding statement.* **Prior** adds to **previous** the idea of coming first in order of importance: *I have a prior engagement* (one that has first call).

pre·vi·ous·ly (prē′vē əs lē) *adv.* at a previous time: *I had not met him previously.*

previous question the question whether a vote shall be taken on the main question without further debate.

pre·vi·sion (prē vizh′ən) *n.* 1 foresight; foreknowledge. 2 a prophetic vision or perception: *prevision of trouble.*

pre·vi·sion·al (prē vizh′ən əl) *adj.* foreseeing; forecasting; of or having to do with prevision.

pre·war (prē′wôr′) *adj.* before the war.

prex·y (prek′sē) *n. Slang.* president, especially of a college or university.

prey (prā) *n., v.*—*n.* 1 an animal hunted or seized for food, especially by another animal: *Mice and birds are the prey of cats.* 2 a person or thing injured; victim: *to be a prey to fear or disease.*
—*v.*

prey on or **upon, a** hunt or kill for food: *Cats prey on mice.* **b** be a strain upon; injure; irritate. **c** rob; plunder. **d** hunt.
[ME < OF < L *praeda*]
☞ *Hom.* **pray.**

pri·ap·ic (prī ap′ik) *adj.* phallic. [< L *Priapus* < Gk. *Priapos,* a god, the son of Dionysus and Aphrodite, who symbolizes male generative power]

price (prīs) *n., v.* **priced, pric·ing.**—*n.* 1 the amount for which a thing is sold or can be bought; cost to the buyer. 2 a reward offered for the capture of a person alive or dead: *Every member of the gang has a price on his head.* 3 what must be given, done, undergone, etc. to obtain a thing: *We paid a heavy price for the victory, for we lost ten thousand soldiers.* 4 value; worth.
at any price, at any cost, no matter how great: *He wanted to win at any price.*
beyond or **without price,** so valuable that it cannot be bought or be given a value in money.
—*v.* 1 put a price on; set the price of. 2 *Informal.* ask the price of; find out the price of: *price a rug.* [ME < OF < L *pretium*]
☞ *Syn. n.* 1. **Price, charge, cost** = the amount asked or paid for something. **Price** means the amount of money for which something is sold, but especially suggests what the seller asks for things: *The price of meat is high now.* **Charge** is the amount asked, especially for services: *There is no charge for delivery.* **Cost** suggests the amount paid for goods or services or whatever is given or spent, such as effort, to get anything: *The cost of the house was high.*

price·less (prīs′lis) *adj.* beyond price; extremely valuable: *a priceless painting.*—**price′less·ness,** *n.*

price support a system by which the government guarantees a given price to the farmer for his produce.

price tag 1 a ticket or tag on merchandise showing its price. **2** *Informal.* an estimated value, price, or cost.

price war a system in which sellers try to capture the market by repeatedly undercutting the prices of competitors.

pric·ey (prī′sē) *adj. Informal.* expensive: *It's a nice restaurant, but a bit too pricey for me.* Also, **pricy.**

prick (prik) *n., v.*—*n.* 1 a sharp point. 2 a little hole or mark made by a sharp point. 3 the act or an instance of pricking. 4 a sharp pain. 5 *Slang.* a stupid or ineffectual person.
kick against the pricks, make useless resistance that only hurts oneself.
—*v.* 1 make a little hole in with a sharp point. 2 mark with a sharp point. 3 cause sharp pain to. 4 cause or feel a sharp pain. 5 raise or erect: *The dog pricked his ears at the sound of footsteps.* 6 *Archaic.* spur; urge on. 7 *Archaic.* ride fast.
prick up, point upward.
prick up (one's) ears, a point the ears upward. **b** give sudden attention; listen carefully: *The boy pricked up his ears when the teacher started talking about a trip.*
[OE *prica* point]—**prick′er,** *n.*

prick·le (prik′əl) *n., v.* **-led, -ling.**—*n.* 1 a small, sharp point; thorn; spine. 2 a prickly or smarting sensation.—*v.* 1 feel a prickly or smarting sensation. 2 cause such a sensation in. [OE *pricel* < *prica* point]

prick·ly (prik′lē) *adj.* **-li·er, -li·est.** 1 having many sharp points like thorns: *a prickly rosebush, the prickly porcupine.* 2 sharp and stinging; itching: *Heat sometimes causes a prickly rash on the skin.* 3 hard to deal with; likely to raise problems, controversy, etc.: *a prickly question.* 4 quick to take offence; easily angered: *He is a prickly individual.*—**prick′li·ness,** *n.*

prickly heat a red, itching rash on the skin caused by inflammation of the sweat glands.

prickly pear 1 any of a genus (*Opuntia*) of cactuses having spiny, flat or cylindrical joints, usually yellow flowers, and oval or pear-shaped fruit. 2 the pulpy, edible fruit of several of these cactuses.

prickly rose a common North American wild rose (*Rosa acicularis*) found along roadsides, on grassy slopes, and in clearings from Quebec to Alaska and south to Colorado, having large pink flowers and leaves usually consisting of five leaflets. The prickly rose is the provincial flower of Alberta.

pric·y (prī′sē) *adj.* See **pricey.**

pride (prīd) *n., v.* **prid·ed, prid·ing.**—*n.* 1 a high opinion of one's own worth or possessions. 2 pleasure or satisfaction in something concerned with oneself: *to take pride in a hard job well done.* 3 something that one is proud of. 4 too high an opinion of oneself. 5 an acting as if better than others; scorn of others. 6 the best part; most flourishing period: *in the pride of manhood.* 7 a group or company of lions.
—*v.* be proud; indulge in pride (*used with a reflexive pronoun*): *He prides himself on his mathematical ability.* [OE *prýde* < *prúd* proud]
☞ *Syn. n.* 1. **Pride, conceit** = a high opinion of oneself. **Pride** applies to a feeling of pleased satisfaction with what one is, has, or has done, and suggests either proper self-respect and personal dignity because of real worth or excessive self-love and arrogance because of imagined superiority: *A man*

without pride deserves contempt. **Conceit** suggests much too high an opinion of one's own abilities and accomplishments, and often implies an unpleasantly assertive manner: *Conceit makes the criminal think he is too clever to be caught.*

pride·ful (prīd′fəl) *adj.* proud. —**prid′ful·ly,** *adv.*

prie–dieu (prē dyœ′) *n. French.* a small desk for a prayer book, etc. with a piece on which to kneel. [< F *prie-dieu,* literally, pray God]

pries (prīz) *n.* pl. of **pry**².

priest (prēst) *n.* **1** a special servant of a god: *a priest of Apollo.* **2** a clergyman or minister of certain Christian churches. **3** a clergyman authorized to administer the sacraments and pronounce absolution. **4** a minister of any religion: *a Buddhist priest.* [OE *prēost,* ult. < L *presbyter.* Doublet of PRESBYTER.]

priest·ess (prēs′tis) *n.* a woman who serves at an altar or in sacred rites: *a priestess of the goddess Diana.*

priest·hood (prēst′hùd) *n.* **1** the position or rank of priest. **2** priests as a group.

priest·ly (prēst′lē) *adj.* **-li·er, -li·est. 1** of or having to do with a priest: *priestly duties.* **2** like a priest; suitable to a priest. —**priest′li·ness,** *n.*

prig (prig) *n.* someone who is smug and affected, and thinks he is a better person than others. [origin uncertain]

prig·ger·y (prig′ər ē) *n., pl.* **-ger·ies.** the conduct or character of a prig.

prig·gish (prig′ish) *adj.* too particular about doing right in things that show outwardly; priding oneself on being better than others. —**prig′gish·ly,** *adv.* —**prig′gish·ness,** *n.*

prim (prim) *adj.* **prim·mer, prim·mest.** stiffly precise, neat, proper, or formal. [< MF *prim* fine, delicate < L *primus* first. Doublet of PRIME¹, adj.] —**prim′ly,** *adv.* —**prim′ness,** *n.*

prim. 1 primitive. **2** primary.

prima ballerina the principal female dancer in a ballet or a ballet company.

pri·ma·cy (prī′mə sē) *n., pl.* **-cies. 1** the condition of being first in order, rank, importance, etc. **2** the position or rank of a primate (def. 1). **3** *Roman Catholic Church.* the supreme power of the Pope. [ME < OF < Med.L *primatia* < L *primas, -atis* of first rank. See PRIMATE.]

pri·ma don·na (prē′mə don′ə) *pl.* **pri·ma don·nas. 1** the principal woman singer in an opera. **2** a temperamental person. [< Ital. *prima donna* first lady]

pri·ma fa·ci·e (prī′mə fā′shē ē *or* fā′shē; *Latin,* prē′mä fä′kē ā) at first view; before investigation. [< L *prima facie,* abl. of *prima facies* first appearance]

prima facie case or **evidence** an argument or evidence sufficiently convincing in itself to establish a fact or presumption of a fact unless subsequently refuted.

pri·mal (prī′məl) *adj.* **1** of early times; first; primeval. **2** chief; fundamental. [< Med.L *primalis* < L *primus* first] —**pri′mal·ly,** *adv.*

pri·ma·ri·ly (prī′mer′ə lē, prī′mə rə lē, *or* prī mer′ə lē) *adv.* **1** chiefly; principally: *Napoleon was primarily a general.* **2** at first; originally.

pri·ma·ry (prī′mer′ē *or* prī′mə rē) *adj., n., pl.* **-ries.** —*adj.* **1** first in time; first in order. **2** from which others have come; original; fundamental. **3** first in importance; chief. **4** *Electricity.* of or having to do with the inducing circuit, coil, or current in an induction coil or the like. **5** of or having to do with one of the large flight feathers growing on the distal section of a bird's wing. **6** utilizing the crude products of nature as raw materials: *a primary industry.* **7** *Education.* of or having to do with grades 1, 2, and 3: *primary teachers.* —*n.* **1** anything that is first in order, rank, or importance. **2** a primary color. **3** a primary coil or circuit. **4** *U.S.* primary election. **5** a primary feather. [ME < L *primarius* first in rank < *primus* first] ☛ *Syn. adj.* **1.** See note at **elementary.**

primary accent primary stress.

primary color or **colour** one of three colors that can be mixed together to make any other color. Red, yellow, and blue are the primary colors in pigments; in light, they are red, green, and blue.

primary election *U.S.* an election to choose candidates for office from a certain political party.

primary school the first grades of elementary school, usually grades 1, 2, and 3.

primary stress **1** the strongest stress or accent in the pronunciation of a word. **2** a mark, such as (′) used to show where this stress falls.

pri·mate (prī′mit *or* prī′māt) *n.* **1** an archbishop or bishop ranking above all other bishops in a country or church province. **2** any of an order (Primates) of placental mammals that includes

hat, āge, fär; let, ēqual, tèrm; it, īce
hot, ōpen, ôrder; oil, out; cup, pùt, rüle,
above, takən, pencəl, lemən, circəs

ch, child; ng, long; sh, ship
th, thin; ᴛʜ, then; zh, measure

man together with apes, monkeys, lemurs, lorises, etc. [ME < OF < L *primas, -atis* of first rank < *primus* first]

prime¹ (prīm) *adj., n.* —*adj.* **1** first in rank; chief: *His prime object was to lower the tax rate.* **2** first in time or order; fundamental. **3** first in quality; first-rate; excellent: *prime ribs of beef.* **4** *Mathematics.* **a** of or designating a prime number. **b** having no common divisor but 1. 2 is prime to 9. —*n.* **1** the best time; condition: *A man of forty is in the prime of life.* **2** the best part. **3** the first part; beginning. **4** springtime. **5** early manhood or womanhood; youth. **6** the second of the seven canonical hours, or the service for it, originally fixed for the first hour of the day (beginning at 6 a.m.). **7** prime number. **8 a** one of the sixty minutes in a degree. **b** the mark (′) indicating such a part. **9** *Music.* **a** the tonic, or keynote. **b** the interval between two tones of the same or different quality but identical pitch; unison. **c** a tone sung or played in unison with another. [ME < L *primus* first (def. 6 < OE *prīm* < L *prima hora* first hour). Doublet of PRIM.] —**prime′ness,** *n.*

prime² (prīm) *v.* **primed, prim·ing. 1** prepare by putting something in or on. **2** supply a gun with powder. **3** cover (a surface) with a first coat of paint or oil so that the finishing coat of paint will not soak in. **4** equip (a person) with information, words, etc. **5** pour water into (a pump) to start action. [probably < *prime¹*]

prime meridian the meridian from which the longitude east and west is measured. It passes through Greenwich, England, and its longitude is 0°.

prime minister the chief minister in certain governments, usually the leader of the majority party in parliament; head of the cabinet: *The Prime Minister of Canada is the first minister of the federal government.* *Abbrev.:* P.M.

prime number an integer not exactly divisible by any whole number other than itself and 1; prime. The integers 2, 3, 5, 7, and 11 are prime numbers. Compare **composite number.**

prim·er¹ (prim′ər) *n.* **1** a first book in reading. **2** a beginner's book. [ME < Med.L *primarius* < L *primarius* first in rank. See PRIMARY.]

prim·er² (prīm′ər) *n.* **1** a person or thing that primes. **2** a cap or cylinder containing a little gunpowder, used for firing a charge of dynamite, etc. **3** a first coat of paint, etc. [< *prime²*]

prime time *Radio and television.* the period of the day when the largest audience can be expected, usually the early evening hours.

pri·me·val (prī mē′vəl) *adj.* **1** of or having to do with the earliest time: *In its primeval state the earth was without any form of life.* **2** ancient: *primeval forests untouched by the axe.* [< L *primaevus* early in life < *primus* first + *aevum* age] —**pri·me′val·ly,** *adv.*

prim·ing (prīm′ing) *n.* **1** powder or other material used to set fire to an explosive. **2** a first coat of paint, sizing, etc.

prim·i·tive (prim′ə tiv) *adj., n.* —*adj.* **1** of early times; of long ago: *Primitive people often lived in caves.* **2** first of the kind: *primitive Christians.* **3** very simple; such as people had early in human history; crude: *A primitive way of making fire is by rubbing two sticks together.* **4** original; primary. **5** *Biology.* **a** primordial. **b** representing or related to an ancient group or species. **6** old-fashioned: *The farmer drove a primitive buggy.* —*n.* **1** an artist belonging to an early period, especially before the Renaissance. **2** an artist who imitates early painters, or who paints with directness and simplicity. **3** a picture by such an artist. **4** a person living in a primitive society or in primitive times. **5** an algebraic or geometrical expression from which another is derived. **6** a word from which another is derived. [ME < OF < L *primitivus,* ult. < *primus* first] —**prim′i·tive·ly,** *adv.* —**prim′i·tive·ness,** *n.*

prim·i·tiv·ism (prim′ə təv iz′əm) *n.* **1** the condition of being primitive. **2** the theory or notion that primitive cultures are superior to technologically advanced cultures. **3** the principles, qualities, etc. of the art of primitive peoples or primitive artists.

prim·i·tiv·ist (prim′ə tə vist′) *n., adj.* —*n.* a person who advocates or practises primitivism. —*adj.* of or having to do with primitivists or primitivism. —**prim′i·tiv·is′tic,** *adj.*

pri·mo·gen·i·tor (prī′mə jen′ə tər) *n.* **1** an ancestor; forefather. **2** the earliest ancestor. [< LL *primogenitor* < L *primus* first + *genitor* begetter]

pri·mo·gen·i·ture (prī′mə jen′ə chər *or* -chür′) *n.* **1** the state, condition, or fact of being the first-born of the children of the same

parents. 2 the right or principle of inheritance or succession by the first-born, especially the inheritance of a family estate by the eldest son. [< Med.L *primogenitura*, ult. < L *primus* first + *gignere* beget]

pri·mor·di·al (prī môr′dē əl) *adj.* 1 existing at the very beginning; primitive. 2 *Biology.* formed first in the course of development: *primordial leaves.* 3 original; elementary: *primordial laws.* [ME < LL *primordialis* < L *primordium* beginning]

pri·mor·di·al·ly (prī môr′dē əl ē) *adv.* under original conditions; at the beginning.

primp (primp) *v.* dress oneself or arrange one's hair or clothing in a fussy or careful way, to make oneself look smart or showy: *primping in front of a mirror.* [apparently var. of *prim*, v. < *prim*, adj.]

prim·rose (prim′rōz′) *n., adj.* —*n.* 1 any of a genus (*Primula*) of perennial garden plants having large leaves and showy flowers of many different colors. Primroses are very popular garden plants. 2 the flower of any of these plants. 3 a pale yellow, the color of the common European primrose.
—*adj.* 1 designating a family (Primulaceae) of plants found mainly in the northern hemisphere, having leaves that grow from the base of the plant and flowers growing in clusters. The primrose family includes the primroses, cyclamens, and loosestrife. 2 pale yellow. 3 of or like a primrose; pleasant. [< Med.L *prima rosa* first rose]

primrose path a pleasant way; path of pleasure.

pri·mus (prī′məs) *n.* a portable stove that burns vaporized oil. [< trademark]

prin. 1 principally. 2 principle.

prince (prins) *n.* 1 a male member of a royal family; especially, in the United Kingdom, a son or grandson of a king or queen. 2 sovereign. 3 a ruler of a small state subordinate to a king or emperor. 4 in certain countries, a high-ranking member of the nobility. 5 the greatest or best of a group; chief: *a merchant prince, a prince of artists.* [ME < OF < L *princeps* chief < *primus* first + *capere* take]

Prince Albert a man's long, double-breasted coat.

prince consort a prince who is the husband of a queen or empress ruling in her own right.

prince·dom (prins′dəm) *n.* 1 the territory ruled by a prince. 2 the position, rank, or dignity of a prince.

Prince Edward Islander a native or long-term resident of Prince Edward Island.

prince·ling (prins′ling) *n.* a young, subordinate, or insignificant prince.

prince·ly (prins′lē) *adj.* **-li·er, -li·est.** 1 of a prince or his rank; royal. 2 like a prince; noble. 3 fit for a prince; magnificent: *He earns a princely salary.* —**prince′li·ness,** *n.*

Prince of Darkness the Devil; Satan.

prince of the blood a prince of a royal family.

Prince of Wales in the United Kingdom, a title conferred on the eldest son, or heir apparent, of the sovereign. Prince Charles was named Prince of Wales in 1956.

prince royal the eldest son of a king or queen.

prin·cess (prin′sis *or* prin′ses) *n.* 1 a daughter of a king or queen or of a king's son or queen's son. 2 the wife or widow of a prince. 3 a woman having the same rank as a prince. [< F *princesse*, fem. of *prince* prince]

prin·cesse *or* **prin·cess** (prin ses′, prin′ses, *or* prin′sis) *adj.* of women's one-piece dresses, having an unbroken line from the shoulder to the hem, a fitted top, and a gently flaring skirt. [< F *princesse* princess]

princess royal the eldest daughter of a king or queen.

prin·ci·pal (prin′sə pəl) *adj., n.* —*adj.* most important; main; chief: *St. John's is the principal city in Newfoundland.* —*n.* 1 a chief person; one who gives orders. 2 the head, or one of the heads, of a school, college, etc. 3 a sum of money that has been borrowed, as opposed to the interest payable on it. 4 the main body, or capital, of an investment or property, as opposed to the income received from it. 5 a person who hires another person to act for him. 6 a person directly responsible for a crime. 7 a person responsible for the payment of a debt that another person has endorsed or guaranteed. 8 a person who employs an agent. [< L *principalis* < *princeps* chief. See PRINCE.]
☛ *Hom.* **principle.**
☛ *Usage.* **Principal, principle.** Do not confuse these two words of entirely different meaning. **Principal** as an adjective means "chief," and as a noun, "chief person" or "main sum of money". **Principle** is used only as a noun, meaning a basic truth (*the principles of democracy*), or a rule of conduct (*Good character depends upon high principles*).

prin·ci·pal·i·ty (prin′sə pal′ə tē) *n., pl.* **-ties.** 1 a small state or country ruled by a prince. 2 a country from which a prince gets his title. 3 a supreme power.

prin·ci·pal·ly (prin′sə plē *or* prin′sə pəl ē) *adv.* for the most part; above all; chiefly.
☛ *Syn.* See note at **especially.**

Principal Meridian *Cdn.* See **First Meridian.**

principal parts the main parts of a verb, from which the rest can be derived. In English the principal parts are the present infinitive, past tense or preterite, and past participle. *Examples: go, went, gone; do, did, done; drive, drove, driven; push, pushed, pushed.*

prin·ci·pal·ship (prin′sə pəl ship′) *n.* the position or office of a principal.

prin·ci·pate (prin′sə pāt′) *n.* 1 a chief place or authority. 2 principality. [ME < L *principatus* < *princeps* chief. See PRINCE.]

prin·ci·ple (prin′sə pəl) *n.* 1 a fact or belief on which other ideas are based: *Science is based on the principle that things can be explained.* 2 a rule of action or conduct: *I make it a principle to save some money each week.* 3 uprightness; honor: *Joseph Howe was a man of principle.* 4 a rule of science explaining how things act: *the principle of the lever.* 5 the method of operation. 6 a source; origin; first cause or force. 7 one of the elements that compose a substance, especially one that gives some special quality or effect: *the bitter principle in a drug.*
in principle, as regards the general truth or rule: *to approve something in principle.*
on principle, **a** according to a certain principle. **b** for reasons of right conduct.
[ME < OF < L *principium* < *princeps* chief. See PRINCE.]
☛ *Hom.* **principal.**
☛ *Usage.* See note at **principal.**

prin·ci·pled (prin′sə pəld) *adj.* showing, characterized by, or based on high moral principle: *a principled act of protest, a principled person.*

prink (pringk) *v.* primp. [origin uncertain] —**prink′er,** *n.*

print (print) *v., n.* —*v.* 1 use type, blocks, plates, etc. and ink or dye to reproduce (words, pictures, or designs) on paper or some other surface. 2 reproduce letters, words, or designs on with type, etc. 3 cause to be printed; publish. 4 produce books, newspapers, etc. by printing press. 5 make (words or letters) the way they look in print instead of in writing. 6 make with such letters: *Print your name clearly.* 7 stamp with designs, patterns, pictures, etc.: *Machines print wallpaper, cloth, etc.* 8 stamp; produce (marks or figures) by pressure; impress. 9 fix: *The scene is printed on my memory.* 10 take an impression from type, etc. 11 produce a photograph by transmission of light through (a negative).
—*n.* 1 printed words, letters, etc.: *This book has clear print.* 2 a printed condition. 3 a printed publication; newspaper or magazine. 4 an edition or impression of a book, etc. made at one time. 5 a picture or design printed from an engraved block, plate, etc. 6 cloth with a pattern printed on it. 7 a mark made by pressing or stamping: *the print of a foot.* 8 something that prints; stamps; die. 9 something that has been marked or shaped by pressing or stamping. 10 a photograph produced from a negative.
in print, **a** in printed or published form. **b** of books, etc., still available for purchase from the publisher.
out of print, no longer sold by the publisher.
[ME < OF *priente*, ult. < L *premere* press]

print·a·ble (prin′tə bəl) *adj.* 1 capable of being printed. 2 capable of being printed from. 3 fit to be printed.

print·er (prin′tər) *n.* 1 a person whose business or work is printing or setting type. 2 a machine or device used for printing, such as the part of a computer that produces printouts.

printer's devil *Historical.* an errand boy or apprentice in a printing office.

print·ing (prin′ting) *n.* 1 the art, process, or business of producing printed matter. 2 printed words, letters, etc. 3 all the copies printed at one time. 4 letters made like those in print.

printing press a machine for printing from types, plates, etc.

print·out (print′out′) *n.* a typewritten or printed record of the output of a computer, produced automatically.

pri·or[1] (prī′ər) *adj.* coming before; earlier: *I can't go with you because I have a prior engagement.*
prior to, coming before in time, order, or importance; earlier than; before.
[< L]
☛ *Syn.* 1. See note at **previous.**

pri·or[2] (prī′ər) *n.* the head of a priory or monastery for men. Priors usually rank below abbots. [OE < Med.L *prior*, n. use of L *prior* prior[1]]

pri·or·ess (prī′ər is) *n.* the head of a convent or priory for women. Prioresses usually rank below abbesses.

pri·or·i·ty (prī ôr′ə tē) *n., pl.* **-ties. 1** the fact of being earlier in time. **2** a coming before in order or importance: *Fire engines and ambulances have priority over other traffic.* **3** governmental rating giving right of way to persons or things important in national defence, essential affairs of state, etc. in order of importance. **4** a preferential position allotted to any project, research, development, etc., giving it first claim to the necessary resources.

pri·o·ry (prī′ə rē) *n., pl.* **-ries.** a monastery, convent, etc. governed by a prior or prioress. A priory is often, but not necessarily, dependent on an abbey. [ME < AF < Med.L *prioria* < *prior.* See PRIOR².]

prise (prīz) *v.* **prised, pris·ing.** See **prize⁴.**

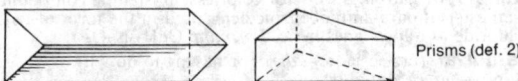

Prisms (def. 2)

prism (priz′əm) *n.* **1** *Geometry.* a polyhedron (geometric solid) whose bases, or ends, are parallel and of the same size and shape, and whose other faces are parallelograms. **2** a transparent prism having triangular bases and rectangular sides, used for separating white light into the colors of the spectrum. [< LL < Gk. *prisma* < *priein* to saw]

pris·mat·ic (priz mat′ik) *adj.* **1** of or like a prism. **2** formed by a transparent prism. **3** varied in color.

pris·mat·i·cal·ly (priz mat′ik lē) *adv.* by, or as if by, a prism.

prismatic colors colors formed when white light is passed through a prism; red, orange, yellow, green, blue, indigo, and violet; the colors of the rainbow.

pris·on (priz′ən) *n., v.* **—n. 1** a public building in which criminals are confined. **2** any place where a person is shut up against his will. **3** a place that confines or restricts: *The small apartment was a prison to the big farm dog.* **—v.** imprison. [ME < OF < L *pre-* hensio, -onis arrest < *prehendere* seize] **—pris′on·like′,** *adj.*

pris·on·er (priz′ən ər *or* priz′nər) *n.* **1** a person who is under arrest or held in a jail or prison. **2** a person who is confined against his will or who is not free to move.

prisoner of war, a person taken by the enemy in war.

pris·sy (pris′ē) *adj.* **-si·er, -si·est. 1** too precise and fussy. **2** too easily shocked; overnice. [blend of *prim* and *sissy*]

pris·tine (pris′tēn, pris′tən, *or* pris′tīn) *adj.* as it was in its earliest time or state; original; primitive: *The colors of the paintings inside the pyramid had kept their pristine freshness.* [< L *pristinus*]

prith·ee (priᴛн′ē) *interj. Archaic.* I pray thee: *Prithee, come hither.*

pri·va·cy (prī′və sē) *n., pl.* **-cies. 1** the condition of being private; the state of being away from others: *in the privacy of one's home.* **2** an absence of publicity; secrecy: *He told me his reasons in strict privacy.*

pri·vate (prī′vit) *adj., n.* **—adj. 1** not for the public; for just a few special people or for one: *a private car, a private house, a private letter.* **2** not public; individual; personal: *the private life of a king, my private opinion.* **3** secret; confidential: *a private drawer.* **4** secluded: *some private corner.* **5** having no public office: *a private citizen.*
—n. 1 a person holding the lowest rank in the armed forces. *Abbrev.:* Pte. or Pte See chart at **rank¹. 2 privates,** *pl.* private parts; genitals.

in private, a not publicly or openly: *privately: They met in private to discuss the salary increases.*
[ME < L *privare* apart from the state, originally pp. of *privare* set apart, deprive < *privus* one's own. Doublet of PRIVY.] **—pri′vate·ly,** *adv.* **—pri′vate·ness,** *n.*

private enterprise 1 the production and sale of goods, etc. by industries under private control and ownership rather than under government control or ownership. **2** a business operating under this system.

pri·va·teer (prī′və tēr′) *n., v.* **—n. 1** an armed ship owned by private persons and holding a government commission to attack and capture enemy ships. **2** the commander or one of the crew of a privateer. **—v.** cruise as a privateer.

pri·va·teers·man (prī′və tērz′mən) *n., pl.* **-men.** an officer or sailor of a privateer.

private eye *Slang.* a person who is not a member of a public police force but engages in detective work on behalf of private individuals or corporations.

private member backbencher: *to table a private member's bill in Parliament.*

private parts genitals.

private school a school that is under private or corporate

hat, āge, fär; let, ēqual, tèrm; it, īce
hot, ōpen, ôrder; oil, out; cup, pùt, rüle,
əbove, takən, pencəl, lemən, circəs
ch, child; ng, long; sh, ship
th, thin; ᴛн, then; zh, measure

management and is not part of the government-supported system of a province, state, or country.

pri·va·tion (prī vā′shən) *n.* **1** the lack of the usual comforts or some of the necessities of life: *the privations of a life as an explorer. Privation led him to begin stealing.* **2** the state of being deprived; loss; absence. [ME < L *privatio, -onis* < *privare* deprive. See PRIVATE.]

priv·a·tive (priv′ə tiv) *adj., n. Grammar.* **—adj.** expressing deprivation or denial of something. *Un-* is a privative prefix. *Unwise* means *not wise.* **—n.** a privative prefix or suffix. [< L *privativus* < *privare* deprive. See PRIVATE.]

priv·et (priv′it) *n.* any of a genus (*Ligustrum*) of Old World shrubs and small trees of the olive family having small, oval, dark-green leaves, especially the common privet (*L. vulgare*), widely cultivated for hedges. [origin uncertain]

priv·i·lege (priv′ə lij *or* priv′lij) *n., v.* **-leged, -leg·ing. —n.** a special right, advantage, or favor. **—v.** give a privilege to. [ME < L *privilegium* law applying to one individual < *privus* individual + *lex* law]

☛ **Syn. n. Privilege, prerogative** = a special right. **Privilege** suggests a special right given to a person as a favor or due him because of his position, age, sex, citizenship, etc. that often gives him an advantage over others: *Alumni have the privilege of buying football tickets at special rates.* **Prerogative** suggests a privilege or legal right belonging to a person by birth, office, position, etc., which always places him before or above others: *Changing her mind is often jokingly called a woman's prerogative.*

priv·i·leged (priv′ə lijd) *adj.* **1** having a privilege or privileges: *the privileged classes of society.* **2** not having to be revealed in a court of law: *Communication between a lawyer and client is privileged.*

priv·i·ly (priv′ə lē) *adv.* in a private manner; secretly.

priv·y (priv′ē) *adj., n., pl.* **priv·ies. —adj. 1** private. **2** *Archaic.* secret; hidden.

privy to, having secret or private knowledge of.
—n. a small outhouse used as a toilet. [ME < OF *prive* < L *privatus.* Doublet of PRIVATE.]

privy council 1 a group of personal advisers to a ruler. **2 Privy Council, a** in Canada, the body of advisers to the Governor General, made up of the ministers of the federal cabinet and all former cabinet ministers. **b** in the United Kingdom, a body of advisers to the Queen, including members of the cabinet and certain commonwealth leaders. *Abbrev.:* P.C.

privy councillor 1 a member of a privy council. **2 Privy Councillor,** a member of the Privy Council. Privy Councillors in Canada hold office for life, but can advise the Governor General only while they are cabinet ministers.

privy seal in the United Kingdom, the seal affixed to grants, etc. that are afterwards to receive the great seal, and to documents that do not require the great seal.

prize¹ (prīz) *n., adj.* **—n. 1** a reward won or offered in a contest or competition: *Prizes will be given for the three best stories.* **2** a reward worth working for.
—adj. 1 given as a prize. **2** that has won a prize. **3** worthy of a prize. [alteration of ME *pris* < OF *pris* (see PRICE) under the influence of *prise.* See PRIZE².]

prize² (prīz) *n.* a thing or person taken or captured in war, especially an enemy's ship and its cargo taken at sea. [ME *prise* < OF *prise* seizure, alteration (under the influence of pp. *pris* seized) VL *presa* < stem of L *prensus,* pp. of *pre(he)ndere* seize]

prize³ (prīz) *v.* **prized, priz·ing. 1** value highly: *She prizes her best china.* **2** estimate the value of. [ME < OF *prisier,* var. of *preisier* praise. See PRAISE.]

prize⁴ (prīz) *v.* **prized, priz·ing.** raise or move by force; pry. Also, **prise.** [< obs. *prize* lever < OF *prise* a taking hold, grasp. See PRIZE².]

prize court an international court that makes decisions concerning ships and other property captured at sea during a war.

prize fight a boxing match fought for money.

prize fighter a person who fights boxing matches for money.

prize fighting the fighting of boxing matches for money.

prize money 1 money obtained by the sale of ships and other property captured at sea in the course of a war, sometimes divided

among those who made the capture. **2** in a race, contest, etc., the money offered as a prize.

prize ring **1** a square space enclosed by ropes, used for prize fights. **2** prize fighting.

pro¹ (prō) *adv., n., pl.* **pros.** —*adv.* in favor of; for. —*n.* **1** reason in favor. The pros and cons of a question are the arguments for and against it. **2** a person who votes for or favors something. **3** a vote in favor of something. [abstracted from *pro and con,* or independent use of *pro-¹*]

pro² (prō) *n., pl.* **pros;** *adj. Informal.* **1** a professional. **2** prostitute.

pro-¹ *prefix.* **1** forward, as in *proceed, project.* **2** forth; out, as in *prolong, proclaim.* **3** on the side of; in favor of; in behalf of, as in *pro-British.* **4** in place of; acting as, as in *pronoun, proconsul.* [< L *pro,* prep.]

pro-² *prefix.* before; in front of, as in *prologue, proscenium.* [< Gk. *pro,* prep.]

pro·a (prō′ə) *n.* a swift Malay sailing boat built with one side flat and balanced by an outrigger. [< Malay *prau*]

pro·am (prō′am′) *adj.* of or designating a sports tournament involving both professional and amateur players.

prob·a·bil·i·ty (prob′ə bil′ə tē) *n., pl.* **-ties.** **1** the quality or fact of being likely or probable; a good chance: *There is a probability that the field trip will be cancelled because of the weather.* **2** something likely to happen: *A storm is one of the probabilities for tomorrow.* **3** the ratio $\frac{p}{p+q}$, where *p* is the probable number of occurrences and *q* is the probable number of non-occurrences. **in all probability,** probably.

prob·a·ble (prob′ə bəl) *adj.* **1** likely to happen: *Cooler weather is probable after this shower.* **2** likely to be true: *Something he ate is the probable cause of his pain.* [ME < OF < L *probabilis* < *probare.* See PROVE.]

prob·a·bly (prob′ə blē) *adv.* more likely than not.

pro·bate (prō′bāt) *n., adj., v.* **-bat·ed, -bat·ing.** *Law.* —*n.* **1** the official proving of a will as genuine. **2** a true copy of a will with a certificate that it has been proved genuine. —*adj.* of or concerned with the probating of wills: *a probate court.* —*v.* prove by legal process the genuineness of (a will). [ME < L *probatum,* originally neut. pp. of *probare* make good < *probus* good]

pro·ba·tion (prō bā′shən) *n.* **1** a trial or testing of conduct, character, qualifications, etc.: *After a period of probation the novice became a nun.* **2** the time of trial or testing. **3** the system of letting convicted persons, especially young or first offenders, go free under the supervision of a probation officer. **4** the length of time that such a person is kept under supervision by a probation officer.

pro·ba·tion·al (prō bā′shən əl) *adj.* probationary.

pro·ba·tion·ar·y (prō bā′shən er′ē) *adj.* **1** of or having to do with probation. **2** on probation.

pro·ba·tion·er (prō bā′shən ər) *n.* a person who is on probation.

probation officer an officer appointed to supervise offenders who have been placed on probation.

pro·ba·tive (prō′bə tiv) *adj.* **1** giving proof or evidence. **2** for a trial or test.

probe (prōb) *v.* **probed, prob·ing;** *n.* —*v.* **1** search into; examine thoroughly; investigate: *to probe one's thoughts or feelings to find out why one acted as one did.* **2** search; penetrate: *to probe into the causes of crime.* **3** examine with a probe. —*n.* **1** a thorough examination; investigation. **2** an investigation, usually by a legislative body, in an effort to discover evidences of law violation. **3** a slender instrument with a rounded end for exploring the depth or direction of a wound, cavity in the body, etc. **4** an instrument, often electronic, used to test or explore. **5** an artificial satellite, etc. equipped to obtain scientific information about other planets, conditions in outer space, etc. and radio this information back to earth. [< LL *proba,* n., < L *probare* prove. Doublet of PROOF.] —**prob′er,** *n.* —**prob′ing·ly,** *adv.*

pro·bie (prō′bē) *n. Informal.* a nursing student who is on probation; a probationer.

pro·bi·ty (prō′bə tē) *n.* uprightness; honesty; high principle. [< L *probitas* < *probus* righteous]

prob·lem (prob′ləm) *n.* **1** a question, especially a difficult question. **2** a matter of doubt or difficulty. **3** something to be worked out: *a problem in algebra.* **4** (*adj.*) that causes difficulty: *a problem child.* [ME < OF < L < Gk. *problēma < proballein* propose < *pro-* forward + *ballein* throw]

prob·lem·at·ic (prob′ləm at′ik) *adj.* having the nature of a problem; doubtful; uncertain; questionable.

prob·lem·at·i·cal (prob′ləm at′ə kəl) *adj.* problematic. —**prob′lem·at′i·cal·ly,** *adv.*

pro bo·no pu·bli·co (prō′ bō′nō pub′lə kō) *Latin.* for the public welfare.

pro·bos·cis (prō bos′is) *n., pl.* **-bos·cis·es. 1** an elephant's trunk. **2** any long, flexible snout such as that of an aardvark or tapir. **3** a tubular organ of some insects, such as flies or mosquitoes, adapted for piercing or sucking. **4** *Facetious.* a person's nose, especially when prominent. [< L < Gk. *proboskis*]

proc. 1 proceedings. **2** procedure. **3** process.

pro·caine (prō′kān) *n.* a white or colorless crystalline compound that is an ester of para-aminobenzoic acid, used in the form of its hydrochloride as a local anesthetic. *Formula:* $C_{13}H_{20}N_2O_2$

pro·ce·dur·al (prə sē′jər əl) *adj.* of or having to do with procedure. —**pro·ce′dur·al·ly,** *adv.*

pro·ce·dure (prə sē′jər) *n.* **1** a way of proceeding; a method of doing things. **2** the customary manners or ways of conducting business: *parliamentary procedure, legal procedure.* [< F *procédure < procéder* proceed]

pro·ceed (*v.* prə sēd′ *or* prō sēd′; *n.* prō′sēd) *v., n.* —*v.* **1** go on after having stopped; move forward: *Please proceed with your story.* **2** be carried on; take place: *The trial may proceed.* **3** carry on any activity: *He proceeded to light his pipe.* **4** come forth; issue; go out: *Heat proceeds from fire.* **5** advance to a higher status: *He proceeded to office manager.* **6** begin and carry on an action at law. —*n.* Usually, **proceeds,** *pl.* money obtained from a sale, etc.: *The proceeds from the school play will be used to buy a new curtain for the stage.* [ME < OF < L *procedere < pro-* forward + *cedere* move] —**pro·ceed′er,** *n.*
☞ *Syn. v.* **1.** See note at **advance.**
☞ *Usage.* See note at **precede.**

pro·ceed·ing (prə sēd′ing) *n.* **1** action; conduct; what is done. **2 proceedings,** *pl.* **a** the action in a case in a law court. **b** a record of what was done at the meetings of a society, club, etc.; minutes.

pro·cess (prō′ses *or* pros′es) *n., v., adj.* —*n.* **1** a set of actions or changes in a special order: *By what process or processes is cloth made from wool?* **2** a part that grows out or sticks out: *the process of a bone.* **3** a written command or summons to appear in a court of law. **4** the proceedings in a legal case or action.
in process, a in the course of or condition: *In process of time the house will be finished.* **b** in the course or condition of being done: *The author has just finished one book and has another in process.* —*v.* **1** treat or prepare by some special method. **2** start legal action against. —*adj.* treated or prepared by some special method. [ME < OF < L *processus* progress < *procedere.* See PROCEED.]

process cheese or **processed cheese** a blend of cheddar or other natural cheeses and flavorings, powdered milk, emulsifier, etc.

pro·ces·sion (prə sesh′ən) *n.* **1** something that moves forward; persons marching or riding: *A funeral procession filled the street.* **2** an orderly moving forward: *We formed lines to march in procession onto the platform.*

pro·ces·sion·al (prə sesh′ən əl) *adj., n.* —*adj.* **1** of a procession. **2** used or sung in a procession. —*n.* **1** processional music: *The choir and clergy marched in to the church singing the processional.* **2** a book containing hymns, etc., for use in religious processions.

pro·ces·sor (prō′ses ər *or* pros′es ər) *n.* **1** a computer or the part of a computer that processes data. **2** food processor. **3** any person or thing that processes.

pro·claim (prə klām′) *v.* **1** make known publicly and officially; declare publicly: *War was proclaimed. The people proclaimed him king.* **2 a** declare (a person) an outlaw; denounce. **b** subject (a place) to legal restrictions. [ME < L *proclamare < pro-* forth + *clamare* shout]
☞ *Syn.* **1.** See note at **announce.**

proc·la·ma·tion (prok′lə mā′shən) *n.* an official announcement; a public declaration: *A proclamation was issued to announce the forthcoming election.*
☞ *Syn.* **Proclamation, edict** = a notice or order issued by authority. **Proclamation** = an official public announcement by an executive or administrative officer, such as a president, premier, mayor: *The Prime Minister issued a proclamation declaring martial law in the disaster area.* **Edict** = a public order or law proclaimed by the highest authority, usually a decree of a ruler or court with supreme or absolute authority: *The dictator issued an edict seizing the mines.*

pro·cliv·i·ty (prō kliv′ə tē) *n., pl.* **-ties.** a tendency; inclination. [< L *proclivitas,* ult. < *pro-* forward + *clivus* slope]

pro·con·sul (prō kon′səl) *n.* **1** in ancient Rome, the governor or military commander of a province, with duties and powers like those of a consul. **2** the governor of a British or French colony. **3 Proconsul,** a manlike ape of the Miocene period, that lived in

Africa approximately 25 000 000 years ago and is considered by some anthropologists to be an ancestor of man. [ME < L *proconsul*, from the phrase *pro consule* in place of consul]

pro·con·su·lar (prō kon′sə lər) *adj.* of, having to do with, or governed by a proconsul.

pro·con·su·late (prō kon′sə lit) *n.* the position or term of a proconsul.

pro·con·sul·ship (prō kon′səl ship′) *n.* proconsulate.

pro·cras·ti·nate (prō kras′tə nāt′) *v.* **-nat·ed, -nat·ing.** put things off until later; delay; delay repeatedly. [< L *procrastinare*, ult. < *pro-* forward + *cras* tomorrow] —**pro·cras′ti·na′tor,** *n.*

pro·cras·ti·na·tion (prō kras′tə nā′shen) *n.* the act or habit of putting things off till later; delay.

pro·cre·ate (prō′krē āt′) *v.* **-at·ed, -at·ing. 1** become father to; beget. **2** produce offspring. **3** bring into being; produce. [< L *procreare* < *pro-* forth + *creare* create] —**pro′cre·a′tor,** *n.*

pro·cre·a·tion (prō′krē ā′shen) *n.* **1** begetting; becoming a father. **2** production.

pro·cre·a·tive (prō′krē ā′tiv) *adj.* **1** begetting; bringing into being. **2** concerned with or having to do with procreation. —**pro′cre·a′tive·ness,** *n.*

Pro·crus·te·an (prō krus′tē ən) *adj.* **1** of or having to do with Procrustes or his bed. **2** tending to produce conformity by violent or arbitrary means.

Pro·crus·tes (prō krus′tēz) *n. Greek legend.* a robber who attacked travellers and either stretched them or cut off their legs to make them fit the length of his bed.

proc·tor (prok′tər) *n., v.* —*n.* **1** in a university or school: **a** an official who keeps order. **b** a person who supervises students during an examination. **c** a prefect or monitor. **2** a person employed to manage another's case in a court of law. —*v.* serve as a proctor at an examination. [short for *procurator*]

proc·to·ri·al (prok tô′rē əl) *adj.* of or having to do with a proctor.

proc·tor·ship (prok′tər ship′) *n.* the position of a proctor.

pro·cum·bent (prō kum′bənt) *adj.* **1** lying face down; prone; prostrate. **2** of a plant or stem, lying along the ground but not sending down roots. [< L *procumbens, -entis,* ppr. of *procumbere* lean forward]

proc·u·ra·tor (prok′yə rā′tər) *n.* **1** a person employed to manage the affairs of another; a person authorized to act for another; agent. **2** in ancient Rome, a financial agent or administrator of a province. [< L *procurator* < *procurare.* See PROCURE.]

pro·cure (prə kyūr′) *v.* **-cured, -cur·ing. 1** obtain by care or effort; get: *A friend procured a position in the bank for her son.* **2** bring about; cause: *to procure a person's death.* **3** obtain women or girls for prostitution. [ME < OF < L *procurare* manage, ult. < *pro-* before + *cura* care] —**pro·cur′a·ble,** *adj.*

pro·cure·ment (prə kyūr′mənt) *n.* the act of procuring.

pro·cur·er (prə kyūr′ər) *n.* a person who procures, especially a man who obtains women or girls for prostitution.

pro·cur·ess (prə kyūr′is) *n.* a female keeper of a brothel; bawd.

Pro·cy·on (prō′sē on) *n.* a star of the first magnitude in the constellation Canis Minor. [< L < Gk. *Prokyon* < *pro-* before + *kyon* dog; because it rises before the Dog Star, Sirius]

prod (prod) *v.* **prod·ded, prod·ding;** *n.* —*v.* **1** poke or jab with something pointed: *to prod an animal with a stick.* **2** stir up; urge on: *to prod a lazy boy to action by threats and entreaties.* —*n.* **1** poke or thrust. **2** a sharp-pointed stick; goad. **3** something that prods; reminder. [OE *prod-,* as in *prodbor* borer] —**prod′der,** *n.*

prod. product; produced.

prod·i·gal (prod′ə gəl) *adj., n.* —*adj.* **1** spending too much; wasting money or other resources; wasteful: *Canada has been prodigal of its forests.* **2** abundant; lavish. **3** returning, especially after a long absence or after leading a reckless and wasteful life. —*n.* **1** a person who is wasteful or extravagant; spendthrift. **2** a returning wanderer, wastrel, etc.; prodigal son. [< MF, back-formation from *prodigalite* < LL *prodigalitas.* See PRODIGALITY.] —**prod′i·gal·ly,** *adv.*

prod·i·gal·i·ty (prod′ə gal′ə tē) *n., pl.* **-ties. 1** wasteful or reckless extravagance. **2** rich abundance; profuseness. [< LL *prodigalitas* (modelled on L *liberalitas* < *liber*) < L *prodigus* wasteful < *prodigere* drive forth, squander < *prod-* (var. of *pro-*) forth + *agere* drive]

prodigal son a person who is welcomed back into a family or group after having been away, especially one who has been gone for a long time or who returns repentant of having done wrong. See also **prodigal.** [< the story in the Bible of the wastrel son whose father welcomes him back (Luke 15:11-33)]

hat, āge, fär; let, ēqual, tèrm; it, īce
hot, ōpen, ôrder; oil, out; cup, pút, rüle,
əbove, takən, pencəl, lemən, circəs
ch, child; ng, long; sh, ship
th, thin; ŦH, then; zh, measure

pro·di·gious (prə dij′əs) *adj.* **1** very great; huge; vast: *The ocean contains a prodigious amount of water.* **2** wonderful; marvellous: *a prodigious achievement.* [< L *prodigiosus* < *prodigium* prodigy, omen] —**pro·di′gious·ly,** *adv.* —**pro·di′gious·ness,** *n.*

prod·i·gy (prod′ə jē) *n., pl.* **-gies. 1** a marvel; wonder. An infant prodigy is a child remarkably brilliant in some respect. **2** a marvellous example: *The warriors performed prodigies of valor.* **3** *Rare.* a wonderful sign or omen. [< L *prodigium* omen]

pro·duce (*v.* prə dyüs′ or prə düs′; *n., adj.* prod′yüs or prō′düs) *v.* **-duced, -duc·ing;** *n., adj.* —*v.* **1** make; bring into existence: *The factory produces stoves.* **2** bring about; cause: *Hard work produces success.* **3** bring forth or yield offspring, crops, products, dividends, interest, etc. **4** bring forth; supply; create: *Hens produce eggs.* **5** bring forward; show; present: *Produce your proof.* **6** bring (a play, etc.) before the public. **7** extend; continue (a line or plane).
—*n.* **1** what is produced; yield: *Vegetables are a garden's produce.* **2** fruit and vegetables.
—*adj.* of fruit and vegetables: *He owns a produce market.* [ME < L *producere* < *pro-* forth + *ducere* bring]

pro·duc·er (prə dyü′sər or prə dü′sər) *n.* **1** one who produces. **2** a person who grows or makes things that are to be used or consumed by others. **3** a person in charge of presenting a play, motion picture, television program, etc.
☛ *Usage.* For def. 3, see note at **director.**

pro·duc·i·ble (prə dyü′sə bəl or -dü′sə bəl) *adj.* capable of being produced. —**pro·duc′i·bil′i·ty,** *n.*

prod·uct (prod′əkt) *n.* **1** that which is produced; result of work or of growth: *factory products, farm products.* **2** a number or quantity resulting from multiplying: *The product of 5 and 8 is 40.* **3** *Chemistry.* a substance obtained from another substance through chemical change. [ME < L *productus,* pp. of *producere.* See PRODUCE.]

pro·duc·tion (prə duk′shən) *n.* **1** the act of producing; creation; manufacture: *His business is the production of automobiles.* **2** something that is produced: *The school play was a fine production.* **3** the total amount produced.

production line a row of machines and equipment in a factory, along which workers oversee the various stages of production; assembly line.

production model an article in regular production; a standard or standardized product.

production number a part of a musical play, motion picture, television show, etc. that is given spectacular presentation with elaborate scenery, costumes, dances, etc.: *The first act ended with a colorful production number.*

pro·duc·tive (prə duk′tiv) *adj.* **1** capable of producing or bringing forth: *fields now productive only of weeds, hasty words that are productive of quarrels.* **2** producing food or other articles of commerce: *Farming is productive labor.* **3** producing abundantly; fertile: *a productive farm, writer, etc.* —**pro·duc′tive·ly,** *adv.* —**pro·duc′tive·ness,** *n.*
☛ *Syn.* **3.** See note at **fertile.**

pro·duc·tiv·i·ty (prō′duk tiv′ə tē or prod′ək-) *n.* the power to produce; productiveness.

pro·em (prō′em) *n.* an introduction; preface. [ME < OF < L < Gk. *prooimion* < *pro-* before + *oimē* song]

prof (prof) *n. Informal.* professor.

Prof. professor.

prof·a·na·tion (prof′ə nā′shən) *n.* the act of showing contempt or disregard toward something holy; mistreatment of something sacred.

pro·fan·a·to·ry (prə fan′ə tô′rē) *adj.* profaning.

pro·fane (prə fān′ or prō fān′) *adj., v.* **-faned, -fan·ing.** —*adj.* **1** not sacred; worldly: *Mozart wrote both religious and profane music.* **2** with contempt or disregard for God or holy things: *profane language.* —*v.* **1** treat (holy things) with contempt or disregard: *Soldiers profaned the church by stabling horses there.* **2** put to wrong or unworthy use. [ME < OF < L *profanus* not sacred < *pro-* in front (outside) of + *fanum* shrine] —**pro·fane′ly,** *adv.* —**pro·fane′ness,** *n.*

pro·fan·i·ty (prə fan′ə tē) *n., pl.* **-ties. 1** the use of profane

language; swearing. 2 the quality of being profane; lack of reverence.

pro·fess (prə fes′) v. 1 lay claim to; claim: *He professed the greatest respect for the law. I don't profess to be an expert.* 2 declare openly: *He professed his loyalty to his country.* 3 declare one's belief in: *Christians profess Christ and the Christian religion.* 4 have as one's profession or business: *to profess law.* 5 receive or admit into a religious order. [< *professed*]

pro·fessed (prə fest′) adj. 1 alleged; pretended. 2 avowed or acknowledged; openly declared. 3 having taken the vows of, or been received into, a religious order. [ME < L *professus,* ppr. of *profiteri* < *pro-* forth + *fateri* confess]

pro·fess·ed·ly (prə fes′id lē) adv. 1 avowedly. 2 ostensibly.

pro·fes·sion (prə fesh′ən) n. 1 an occupation requiring special education and training, especially law, medicine, teaching, or the ministry. 2 the people engaged in such an occupation. 3 the act of professing; open declaration: *I welcomed her profession of friendship.* 4 a declaration of belief in a religion. 5 the religion or faith professed. 6 the act of taking vows and entering a religious order.

pro·fes·sion·al (prə fesh′ən əl *or* -fesh′nəl) adj., n. —adj. 1 of or having to do with a profession; appropriate to a profession: *professional skill, a professional manner.* 2 engaged in a profession: *A lawyer or a doctor is a professional man.* 3 making a business or trade of something that others do for pleasure: *a professional ballplayer.* 4 undertaken or engaged in by professionals rather than amateurs: *a professional ball game.* 5 making a business of something not properly to be regarded as a business: *a professional politician.* —n. a person who makes a business or trade of something that others do for pleasure.

pro·fes·sion·al·ism (prə fesh′ən əl iz′əm *or* prə fesh′nəl-) n. 1 professional character, spirit, or methods. 2 the standing, practice, or methods of a professional, as distinguished from those of an amateur.

pro·fes·sion·al·ize (prə fesh′ən əl īz′ *or* -fesh′nəl īz′) v. -ized, -iz·ing. make or become professional.

pro·fes·sion·al·ly (prə fesh′ən əl ē *or* -fesh′nəl ē) adv. in a professional manner; in professional matters; because of one's profession.

pro·fes·sor (prə fes′ər) n. 1 a teacher of the highest rank in a university or college. 2 *Informal.* any teacher at a university or college. 3 a person who professes. 4 a person who declares his belief in a religion. [ME < L *professor* < *profiteri* profess. See PROFESSED.]

pro·fes·sor·ate (prə fes′ər it) n. professoriate.

pro·fes·so·ri·al (prof′ə sô′rē əl *or* prō′fə-) adj. of, having to do with, or characteristic of a professor. —**pro′fes·so′ri·al·ly,** adv.

pro·fes·sor·i·ate (prof′ə sô′rē it) n. 1 the office or term of service of a professor. 2 a group of professors.

pro·fes·sor·ship (prə fes′ər ship′) n. the position or rank of a professor.

prof·fer (prof′ər) v., n. —v. offer for acceptance; present: *We proffered regrets at having to leave so early.* —n. an offer made: *His proffer of advice was accepted.* [ME < AF < *pro-* forth (< L *pro-*) + *offrir* offer < L *offerre*]
☛ *Syn. v.* See note at **offer.**

pro·fi·cien·cy (prə fish′ən sē) n., pl. -cies. the quality or condition of being proficient; knowledge; skill; expertness.

pro·fi·cient (prə fish′ənt) adj., n. —adj. advanced in any art, science, or subject; skilled; expert: *She was very proficient in music.* —n. an expert. [< L *proficiens, -entis* making progress, ppr. of *proficere* < *pro-* forward + *facere* make] —**pro·fi′cient·ly,** adv.
☛ *Syn. adj.* See note at **expert.**

pro·file (prō′fīl) n., v. -filed, -fil·ing. —n. 1 a side view, especially of the human face. 2 an outline. 3 a drawing of a transverse vertical section of a building, bridge, etc. 4 a concise description of a person's abilities, character, or career. —v. draw a profile of. [< Ital. *profilo* < *profilare* draw in outline < L *pro-* forth + *filum* thread]
☛ *Syn. n.* 2. See note at **outline.**

prof·it (prof′it) n., v. —n. 1 Often, **profits,** pl. the gain from a business; what is left when the cost of goods and of carrying on the business is subtracted from the amount of money taken in. 2 advantage; benefit: *What profit is there in worrying?* —v. 1 make a gain from a business; make a profit. 2 get advantage; gain; benefit: *A wise person profits by his mistakes.* 3 be an advantage or benefit (to). [ME < OF < L *profectus* advance <

proficere. See PROFICIENT.] —**prof′it·er,** n. —**prof′it·less,** adj.
☛ *Hom.* prophet.
☛ *Syn. n.* 2. See note at **advantage.**

prof·it·a·bil·i·ty (prof′ə tə bil′ə tē) n. the quality of being profitable.

prof·it·a·ble (prof′ə tə bəl) adj. 1 yielding a financial profit: *a profitable deal.* 2 giving a gain or benefit; useful: *We spent a profitable afternoon in the library.* —**prof′it·a·bly,** adv.

prof·it·a·ble·ness (prof′ət ə bəl nəs) n. profitability.

prof·it·eer (prof′ə tēr′) n., v. —n. a person who makes an unfair profit by taking advantage of public necessity. —v. seek or make excessive profits by taking advantage of public necessity.

profit sharing the sharing of profits between employer and employees. —**prof′it-shar′ing,** adj.

prof·li·ga·cy (prof′lə gə sē) n. 1 great wickedness; vice. 2 reckless extravagance.

prof·li·gate (prof′lə git) adj., n. —adj. 1 very wicked; shamelessly bad. 2 recklessly extravagant. —n. a person who is very wicked or extravagant. [< L *profligatus,* pp. of *profligare,* intensive of *profligere* ruin < *pro-* down + *fligere* strike, dash] —**prof′li·gate·ly,** adv.

pro for·ma (prō′fôr′mə) 1 done in a set or perfunctory manner or for the sake of form. 2 providing or prescribing a set form or method: *a pro forma invoice, a pro forma balance sheet.* [< L]

pro·found (prə found′) adj. 1 very deep: *a profound sigh, a profound sleep.* 2 deeply felt; very great: *profound despair, profound sympathy.* 3 having or showing great depth of knowledge or understanding: *a profound book, a profound thinker.* 4 low; carried far down; going far down: *a profound bow.* [ME < OF < L *profundus* < *pro-* towards + *fundus* bottom] —**pro·found′ly,** adv. —**pro·found′ness,** n.

pro·fun·di·ty (prə fun′də tē) n., pl. -ties. 1 the state or quality of being profound; great depth. 2 a very deep thing or place. [< LL *profunditas* < L *profundus.* See PROFOUND.]

pro·fuse (prə fyūs′) adj. 1 very abundant: *profuse thanks.* 2 spending or giving freely; lavish; extravagant: *He was so profuse with his money that he is now poor.* [ME < L *profusus* poured forth, pp. of *profundere* < *pro-* forth + *fundere* pour] —**pro·fuse′ly,** adv. —**pro·fuse′ness,** n.
☛ *Syn.* 1, 2. Profuse, lavish = occurring, spending, or given freely. **Profuse** suggests a quantity that is more than enough, poured out in streams, sometimes too freely: *They were profuse in their praise.* **Lavish** suggests pouring out in a flood, showing no attempt to limit the amount or to save, but implies generosity or liberality more than extravagance: *It was a lavish display of gifts.*

pro·fu·sion (prə fyū′zhən) n. 1 a great abundance: *There was a profusion of gulls on the breakwater.* 2 extravagance; lavishness.

Prog. Progressive.

pro·gen·i·tor (prō jen′ə tər) n. an ancestor in the direct line; forefather. [< L *progenitor* < *pro-* forth + *gignere* beget]

pro·gen·i·ture (prō jen′ə chər) n. 1 begetting; birth. 2 offspring.

prog·e·ny (proj′ə nē) n., pl. -nies. children; offspring; descendants. [ME < OF < L *progenies,* ult. < *pro-* forth + *gignere* beget]

prog·na·thous (prog′nə thəs *or* prog nā′thəs) adj. of a skull or a person, having the jaws protruding beyond the upper part of the face. [< *pro-²* forward + Gk. *gnathos* jaw]

prog·no·sis (prog nō′sis) n., pl. -ses (-sēz). 1 a forecast of the probable course of a disease. 2 an estimate of what will probably happen. [< LL < Gk. *prognōsis,* ult. < *pro-* before + *gignōskein* recognize]

prog·nos·tic (prog nos′tik) adj., n. —adj. indicating something in the future. —n. 1 an indication; sign. 2 a forecast; prediction. [< Med.L < Gk. *prognōstikos* foretelling, ult. < *pro-* before + *gignōskein* recognize]

prog·nos·ti·cate (prog nos′tə kāt′) v. -cat·ed, -cat·ing. predict from facts; forecast. —**prog·nos′ti·ca′tion,** n. —**prog·nos′ti·ca′tor,** n.

pro·gram *or* **pro·gramme** (prō′gram *or* prō′grəm) n., v. -grammed, -gram·ming. —n. 1 a list of items or events; list of performers, players, etc.: *a theatre program.* 2 the items composing an entertainment: *The entire program was delightful.* 3 a plan of what is to be done: *a school program, a business program, a government program.* 4 a set of instructions fed into a computer outlining the steps to be performed by the machine in a specific operation. 5 a set of instructions arranged for any automatic machine to follow. 6 a unit of subject matter arranged in a series of small steps for programmed learning. —v. 1 arrange or enter in a program. 2 draw up a program or plan for. 3 prepare a set of instructions for (a computer or other automatic machine). 4 arrange in a series of small steps for programmed learning. [< LL < Gk. *programma* proclamation, ult. < *pro-* forth + *graphein* write]

pro·gram·mat·ic (prō′grə mat′ik) *adj.* **1** of or having to do with a program. **2** of or having to do with program music.

programmed learning a method of study by which a person works step by step through a series of problems, checking the correctness of his response to each step before proceeding to the next.

pro·gram·mer (prō′gram ər) *n.* a person who prepares a program or programs, especially for a computer or other automatic machine.

program music or **programme music** music that portrays or suggests a particular event, story, atmosphere, etc.

prog·ress (*n.* prō′gres or prog′res; *v.* prə gres′) *n., v.* —*n.* **1** an advance; growth; development: *the progress of science.* **2** a moving forward; going ahead: *make rapid progress on a journey.* —*v.* **1** get better; advance; develop: *We progress in learning step by step.* **2** move forward; go ahead: *The building of the city hall has progressed a great deal this week.* [< L *progressus,* ult. < *pro-* forward + *gradi* walk]

pro·gres·sion (prə gresh′ən) *n.* **1** a moving forward; going ahead: *Creeping is a slow method of progression.* **2** *Mathematics.* a succession of quantities in which there is always the same relation between each quantity and the one succeeding it. 2, 4, 6, 8, 10 are in **arithmetical progression.** 2, 4, 8, 16 are in **geometrical progression.** **3** *Music.* **a** a moving from one tone or chord to another. **b** a sequence of tones, chords, etc.

pro·gres·sive (prə gres′iv) *adj., n.* —*adj.* **1** of, having to do with, or characterized by progress; interested in or using new ideas, etc. in order to advance to something better: *a progressive nation.* **2** Often, **Progressive,** favoring moderate social or political reform through government action. **3** moving forward; developing: *a progressive disease.* **4** having to do with, based on, or designating an educational theory or system which places emphasis on the individual interests and capabilities of the child, encouraging self-expression in an informal classroom atmosphere. **5** involving regular shifts of players or guests, as in card games, dances, etc. **6** *Grammar.* having to do with or designating a verb form that expresses action in progress at the time of speaking or at the time spoken of. *Is reading, was reading,* and *has been reading* are progressive forms of *read.* **7** increasing in proportion to the increase of something else: *A progressive income tax increases as a person's earnings increase.* —*n.* **1** a person who favors or follows a progressive policy, as in politics or education. **2** *Grammar.* **a** the progressive form of a verb. **b** a verb in this form. —**pro·gres′sive·ly,** *adv.* —**pro·gres′sive·ness,** *n.*

Progressive Conservative **1** a member of the Progressive Conservative Party. **2** a person who supports the policies of this party.

Progressive Conservative Party one of the principal political parties of Canada.

progressive jazz a style of jazz that evolved in the late 1940's and early 1950's, characterized by very complex and subtle harmonies and rhythms.

pro·gres·siv·ism (prə gres′iv iz′əm) *n.* the principles, doctrines, or beliefs of progressives.

pro·gres·siv·ist (prə gres′iv ist′) *n., adj.* —*n.* a person who favors or follows progressive policies; a progressive. —*adj.* of or having to do with progressivists or progressivism.

pro·hib·it (prō hib′it) *v.* **1** forbid by law or authority: *Picking flowers in this park is prohibited.* **2** prevent: *The high price prohibits my buying the bicycle.* [ME < L *prohibitus,* pp. of *prohibere* < *pro-* away + *habere* keep] —**pro·hib′i·tor,** *n.*
☛ *Syn.* **1.** See note at **forbid.**
☛ *Usage.* **Prohibited** is followed by **from,** not **against: We are prohibited from smoking on school grounds.** The noun **prohibition** is followed by **against:** *The prohibition against smoking in laboratories is strictly enforced.*

pro·hi·bi·tion (prō′ə bish′ən) *n.* **1** the act of prohibiting or forbidding. **2** a law or order that prohibits. **3** a law or laws against making or selling alcoholic liquors. **4** the time during which such a law, or laws, is enforced.
☛ *Usage.* See note at **prohibit.**

pro·hi·bi·tion·ist (prō′ə bish′ən ist) *n.* one who favors laws against the manufacture and sale of alcoholic liquors.

pro·hib·i·tive (prō hib′ə tiv) *adj.* **1** prohibiting; preventing. **2** preventing or discouraging purchase: *The cost of the house was prohibitive.*

pro·hib·i·to·ry (prō hib′ə tô′rē) *adj.* prohibitive.

proj·ect (*n.* prō′jekt or proj′ekt; *v.* prə jekt′) *n., v.* —*n.* **1** a plan; scheme: *Flying in a heavy machine was once thought an impossible project.* **2** an undertaking; enterprise.
—*v.* **1** plan; scheme. **2** stick out: *The rocky point projects far into the water.* **3** cause to stick out or protrude. **4** throw or cast forward: *A catapult projects stones.* **5** cause to fall on a surface: *Motion*

hat, āge, fär; let, ēqual, tėrm; it, īce
hot, ōpen, ôrder; oil, out; cup, pùt, rüle,
above, takən, pencəl, lemən, circəs
ch, child; ng, long; sh, ship
th, thin; ∓H, then; zh, measure

pictures are projected on the screen. The tree projects a shadow on the grass. **6** draw lines through (a point, line, figure, etc.) and reproduce it on a surface. **7** *Psychology.* treat as objective and external (what is essentially subjective). [< L *projectus,* pp. of *proicere, projicere* < *pro-* forward + *jacere* to throw]
☛ *Syn. n.* **1.** See note at **plan.**

pro·jec·tile (prə jek′til or prə jek′təl) *n., adj.* —*n.* any object that is thrown, hurled, or shot, as a rocket, stone, or bullet. —*adj.* **1** capable of being thrown, hurled, or shot. **2** forcing forward; impelling: *a projectile force.* **3** that can be thrust forward: *the projectile jaws of a fish.*

pro·jec·tion (prə jek′shən) *n.* **1** a part that projects or sticks out: *rocky projections on the face of a cliff.* **2** a sticking out. **3** a throwing or casting forward: *the projection of a shell from a field gun.* **4** *Geometry.* the projecting of a figure, etc. upon a surface. **5** a representation, upon a flat surface, of all or part of the surface of the earth. **6** a forming of projects or plans. **7** *Psychology and psychiatry.* the treating of what is essentially subjective as objective and external.

pro·jec·tion·ist (prə jek′shən ist) *n.* a person who operates a motion-picture projector or a television camera.

pro·jec·tor (prə jek′tər) *n.* **1** an apparatus for projecting a picture on a screen. **2** a person who forms projects; schemer.

prol. prologue.

pro·lac·tin (prō lak′tən) *n.* a protein hormone produced by the front lobe of the pituitary gland, that stimulates the secretion of milk.

pro·late (prō′lāt) *adj.* elongated in the direction of the polar diameter; having a polar diameter greater than the equatorial diameter. A prolate spheroid is generated by the revolution of an ellipse about its longer axis. Compare **oblate**[1]. [< L *prolatus,* pp. to *proferre* extend, bring forward < *pro-* forth + *ferre* bring]

prole (prōl) *n. Slang.* proletarian.

pro·le·tar·i·an (prō′lə ter′ē ən) *adj., n.* —*adj.* of or belonging to the proletariat. —*n.* a person belonging to the proletariat. [< L *proletarius* furnishing the state only with children < *proles* offspring < *pro-* forth + *alescere* grow]

pro·le·tar·i·at (prō′lə ter′ē ət) *n.* **1** the lowest class in economic and social status. The proletariat includes unskilled laborers, casual laborers, and tramps. **2** the laboring class. [< F *prolétariat*]

pro·lif·er·ate (prə lif′ə rāt′) *v.* **-at·ed, -at·ing. 1** grow, reproduce, or propagate rapidly and abundantly, as in cell division, budding, etc. **2** spread; multiply: *Housing projects proliferate in the suburbs.*

pro·lif·er·a·tion (prə lif′ə rā′shən) *n.* **1** rapid reproduction or propagation. **2** spreading; multiplication.

pro·lif·er·ous (prə lif′ər əs) *adj.* growing or spreading rapidly.

pro·lif·ic (prə lif′ik) *adj.* **1** producing offspring abundantly: *prolific animals.* **2** producing much: *a prolific garden, imagination, or writer.* [< Med.L *prolificus* < L *proles* offspring + *facere* make] —**pro·lif′i·cal·ly,** *adv.*

pro·lif·i·ca·cy (prə lif′ə kə sē) *n.* the quality or state of being prolific.

pro·lix (prō liks′ or prō′liks) *adj.* using too many words; too long; tedious. [ME < L *prolixus* stretched out < *pro-* forth + *lixus,* a pp. of *liquere* flow, be liquid] —**pro·lix′ness,** *n.*

pro·lix·i·ty (prō lik′sə tē) *n.* too great length; tedious length of speech or writing.

pro·logue (prō′log) *n.* **1** a speech or poem addressed to the audience by one of the actors at the beginning of a play, opera, etc. **2** an introduction to a novel, poem, or other literary work. **3** any introductory act or event. [ME < OF < L < Gk. *prologos* < *pro-* before + *logos* speech]

pro·long (prə long′) *v.* make longer; draw out. [ME < LL *prolongare* < *pro-* forth + *longus* long] —**pro·long′er,** *n.*
☛ *Syn.* See note at **lengthen.**

pro·lon·ga·tion (prō′long gā′shən) *n.* **1** an extension; lengthening in time or space: *the prolongation of one's school days by graduate study.* **2** an added part.

prom (prom) *n. Informal.* a dance or ball given by a college or high-school class. [short for *promenade*]

prom·e·nade (prom′ə nād′ or prom′ə näd′) *n., v.* **-nad·ed,**

-nad·ing. —*n.* **1** walk for pleasure or display: *The Easter promenade is well known as a fashion show.* **2** a public place for such a walk. **3** a dance; ball. **4** a march of all the guests at the opening of a formal dance. **5** a square-dancing figure in which a couple or, usually, all the couples of a set march once around the square, circle, etc.
—*v.* **1** walk about or up and down for pleasure or for display: *He promenaded back and forth on the ship's deck.* **2** walk through. **3** take on a promenade. [< F *promenade* < *promener* take for a walk] —**prom′e·nad′er,** *n.*

promenade deck an enclosed upper deck on a ship, where passengers can walk.

Pro·me·the·an (prə mē′thē ən) *adj.* of, having to do with, or suggestive of Prometheus.

Pro·me·the·us (prə mē′thē əs *or* prə mē′thyüs) *n.* *Greek mythology.* one of the Titans. He stole fire from heaven and taught men its use. Zeus punished him by chaining him to a rock.

pro·me·thi·um (prə mē′thē əm) *n.* an artificially produced, radio-active metallic element. *Symbol:* Pm; *at.no.* 61; *at.wt.* (145); *half-life* 17.7 years. [< *Prometheus*]

prom·i·nence (prom′ə nəns) *n.* **1** the quality or fact of being prominent, distinguished, or conspicuous: *the prominence of athletics in some schools.* **2** something that juts out or projects, especially upward. A hill is a prominence.

prom·i·nent (prom′ə nənt) *adj.* **1** well-known; important: *a prominent citizen.* **2** easy to see: *A single tree in a field is prominent.* **3** standing out; projecting: *Some insects have prominent eyes.* [< L *prominens, -entis,* ppr. of *prominere* project < *pro-* forward + *men-* jut] —**prom′i·nent·ly,** *adv.*
☛ *Syn.* **1.** See note at **eminent. 2. Prominent, conspicuous** = attracting attention and easily seen. **Prominent** describes something that so stands out above its surroundings or from its background that it attracts attention and is easy to see: *He put her picture in a prominent position on his desk.* **Conspicuous** describes something so plain that it is impossible not to see, or so unusual, odd, loud, colorful, etc. that it attracts attention: *There was a conspicuous lack of warmth in his greeting.*

prom·is·cu·i·ty (prom′is kyü′ə tē) *n.* the fact, state, or condition of being promiscuous.

pro·mis·cu·ous (prə mis′kyü əs) *adj.* **1** mixed and in disorder: *a promiscuous heap of clothing on your closet floor.* **2** making no distinctions; lacking discrimination, especially in sexual relations: *promiscuous behavior.* [< L *promiscuus* < *pro* for + *miscere* mix] —**pro·mis′cu·ous·ly,** *adv.* —**pro·mis′cu·ous·ness,** *n.*

prom·ise (prom′is) *n., v.* **-ised, -is·ing.** —*n.* **1** the words that bind a person to do or not to do something. **2** an indication of what may be expected: *The clouds give promise of rain.* **3** an indication of future excellence; something that gives hope of success: *a young scholar who shows promise.*
—*v.* **1** make a promise of (something) to (a person, etc.). **2** give one's word; make a promise. **3** give indication of; give hope of; give ground for expectation: *The rainbow promises fair weather tomorrow.* [< L *promissum,* originally neut. pp. of *promittere* promise < *pro-* before + *mittere* put] —**prom′is·er,** *n.*

Promised Land 1 in the Bible, the country promised by God to Abraham and his descendants; Canaan (Gen. 15:18; 17:1-8). **2** heaven. **3 promised land,** a place or condition of expected happiness: *Canada is a promised land for many immigrants.*

prom·is·ing (prom′is ing) *adj.* likely to turn out well: *a promising student.* —**prom′is·ing·ly,** *adv.*

prom·is·so·ry (prom′ə sô′rē) *adj.* containing a promise.

promissory note a written promise to pay a stated sum of money to a certain person at a certain time. *Abbrev:* P/N or p/n

pro·mo (prō′mō) *n. Informal.* a promotion piece, especially a brief television announcement advertising a forthcoming program.

prom·on·to·ry (prom′ən tô′rē) *n., pl.* **-ries. 1** a high point of land jutting into a body of water; headland. **2** *Anatomy.* a prominent or projecting structure or part. [< Med.L *promontorium,* var. of L *promunturium* < *pro-* forward + *mons, montis* mountain]

pro·mote (prə mōt′) *v.* **-mot·ed, -mot·ing. 1** raise in rank, condition, or importance: *Those who pass the test will be promoted to the next higher grade.* **2** help to grow or develop; help to success: *The United Nations has done much to promote peace.* **3** help to organize; start: *Several bankers promoted the new company.* **4** further the sale of (an article) by advertising. [< L *promotus,* pp. of *promovere* < *pro-* forward + *movere* move]
☛ *Syn.* **2. Promote, further** = help something move toward a desired end. **Promote** emphasizes causing a movement, cause, scheme, undertaking to move forward by giving open and active support and encouragement and helping it grow and develop: *The scholarships promote better understanding of the West Indies.* **Further** emphasizes helping a cause, project, etc. to keep going ahead: *Getting the scholarship will allow him to further his education.*

pro·mot·er (prə mōt′ər) *n.* **1** a person or thing that promotes. **2** one who organizes new companies and secures capital for them.

pro·mo·tion (prə mō′shən) *n.* **1** advancement or an advance in rank or importance: *The clerk was given a promotion and an increase in salary.* **2** the act or process of furthering the development, growth, or acceptance of something: *the promotion of peace, the promotion of a health campaign.* **3** publicity; advertising: *We are increasing our budget for promotion.*

pro·mo·tion·al (prə mō′shə nəl) *adj.* of, having to do with, or used in the promotion of a product, enterprise, etc.; pertaining to publicity. —**pro·mo·tion·al·ly,** *adv.*

prompt (prompt) *adj., v., n.* —*adj.* **1** on time; quick: *Be prompt to obey.* **2** done at once; made without delay: *I expect a prompt answer.* **3** of a prompter; used in prompting: *a prompt box on a stage.*
—*v.* **1** cause (someone) to do something: *His curiosity prompted him to ask questions.* **2** give rise to; suggest; inspire: *A kind thought prompted the gift.* **3** remind (a learner, speaker, actor, etc.) of the words or actions needed.
—*n.* **1** an act of prompting. **2** something that prompts. **3** *Business.* **a** a limit of time allowed for payment of goods purchased. **b** the contract determining this limit of time. [ME < L *promptus,* originally pp. of *promere* bring forth < *pro-* forward + *emere,* originally, take. Doublet of PRONTO.] —**prompt′ly,** *adv.* —**prompt′ness,** *n.*
☛ *Syn. adj.* **1.** See note at **ready.**

prompt·er (promp′tər) *n.* a person who supplies actors, speakers, etc. with their lines from off the stage when they forget them.

promp·ti·tude (promp′tə tyüd′ *or* -tüd′) *n.* promptness; readiness in acting or deciding.

pro·mul·gate (prom′əl gāt′ *or* prō mul′gāt) *v.* **-gat·ed, -gat·ing. 1** proclaim formally; announce officially: *The king promulgated a decree.* **2** spread far and wide: *Schools try to promulgate knowledge and good habits.* [< L *promulgare* < *pro-* forth + **mulgare,* intensive of *mulgere,* originally, press]

pro·mul·ga·tion (prō′mul gā′shən *or* prom′əl-) *n.* **1** the act of promulgating. **2** the state of being promulgated.

pro·mul·ga·tor (prō mul′gā tər *or* prom′əl gā′tər) *n.* one that promulgates.

pron. 1 pronoun. **2** pronunciation.

prone (prōn) *adj.* **1** inclined; liable (*to*): *prone to evil. He was prone to believe the worst of everyone.* **2** very likely to have (*used in compounds*): *She is accident-prone.* **3** lying face downwards. Compare **supine. 4** lying flat. [ME < L *pronus* < *pro-* forward]

prone·ness (prōn′nis) *n.* **1** an inclination; tendency; preference. **2** a prone position.

prong (prong) *n., v.* —*n.* **1** one of the pointed ends of a fork, antler, etc. **2** a branch or fork of a small stream. —*v.* pierce or stab with a prong. [ME *prange;* origin uncertain]

pronged (prongd) *adj.* having prongs.

prong·horn antelope (prong′hôrn′) *n., pl.* **-horns** or (*esp. collectively*) **-horn.** antelope (def. 2); the North American antelope. Also called **pronghorn.**

pro·nom·i·nal (prō nom′ə nəl) *adj.* of or having to do with pronouns; having the nature of a pronoun. [< LL *pronominalis* < L *pronomen.* See PRONOUN.]

pro·nom·i·nal·ly (prō nom′ə nəl ē) *adv.* like a pronoun.

pro·noun (prō′noun) *n.* a word used to indicate without naming; word used instead of a noun. *Examples: I, we, you, he, it, they, who, whose, which, this, mine, whatever.* [< F *pronom* < L *pronomen* < *pro-* in place of + *nomen* noun]

pro·nounce (prə nouns′) *v.* **-nounced, -nounc·ing. 1** make the sounds of; speak: *Pronounce your words clearly.* **2** pronounce words. **3** give an opinion or decision: *Only an expert should pronounce on this case.* **4** declare (a person or thing) to be: *The doctor pronounced her cured.* **5** declare formally or solemnly: *The judge pronounced sentence on the criminal.* [ME < OF < L *pronuntiare,* ult. < *pro-* forth + *nuntius* messenger] —**pro·nounce′a·ble,** *adj.* —**pro·nounc′er,** *n.*

pro·nounced (prə nounst′) *adj.* strongly marked; decided: *She held pronounced opinions on gambling.*

pro·nounc·ed·ly (prə noun′sid lē) *adv.* in a pronounced manner; to a pronounced degree.

pro·nounce·ment (prə nouns′mənt) *n.* **1** a formal statement; declaration. **2** an opinion; decision.

pron·to (pron′tō) *adv. Informal.* promptly; quickly; right away. [< Sp. *pronto* < L *promptus* prompt. Doublet of PROMPT.]

pronun. pronunciation.

pro·nun·ci·a·men·to (prə nun′sē ə men′tō) *n., pl.* **-tos.** a formal announcement; proclamation. [< Sp. *pronunciamiento* < *pronunciar* pronounce]

pro·nun·ci·a·tion (prə nun′sē ā′shən) *n.* **1** the way of pronouncing. Most dictionaries give the pronunciation of each entry word. **2** the act or an instance of pronouncing. [< L *pronuntiatio, -onis* < *pronuntiare*. See PRONOUNCE.]

proof (prüf) *n., adj.* —*n.* **1** a way or means of showing beyond doubt the truth of something. **2** the establishment of the truth of anything. **3** the act of testing; trial. **4** the condition of having been tested and approved. **5** *Printing.* a trial impression from type. A book is first printed in proof so that errors can be corrected. **6** a trial print of an etching, photographic negative, etc. **7 a** the standard strength of alcoholic liquors, considered as 100; in Canada, 57.1% by volume of alcohol at 15.6° C. **b** strength with reference to this standard: *What proof is this brandy?* —*adj.* **1** of tested value against something: *Now we know that we are proof against being taken by surprise.* **2** of an alcoholic liquor, of standard strength: *proof spirit.* [ME < OF *prueve* < LL *proba* < L *probare* prove. Doublet of PROBE.]
☛ *Syn. n.* **1.** See note at **evidence.**

-proof *adjective-forming suffix.* protected against; safe from, as in *fireproof, waterproof, bombproof.*

proof·read (prüf′rēd′) *v.* **-read** (-red′), **-read·ing.** read (printers' proofs, etc.) and mark errors to be corrected.

prop¹ (prop) *v.* **propped, prop·ping;** *n.* —*v.* **1** hold up by placing a support under or against (*often used with* **up**): *Prop the clothesline with a stick.* **2** support; sustain (*often used with* **up**): *to prop a failing cause.* —*n.* a support; a thing or person used to support another: *Many branches are heavy with apples and need a prop.* [cf. MDu. *proppe*]

prop² (prop) *n. Informal.* any article, such as a table or a weapon, used in staging a play. [short for (*stage*) *property*]

prop³ (prop) *n. Informal.* a propeller (def. 1). [short for *propeller*]

prop. 1 proprietor. **2** properly. **3** proposition.

prop·a·gan·da (prop′ə gan′də) *n.* **1** systematic efforts to spread opinions or beliefs, especially by distortion and deception: *The Nazis were experts in propaganda.* **2** any plan or method for spreading opinions or beliefs. **3** the opinions or beliefs thus spread. [< NL *congregatio de propaganda fide* congregation for propagating the faith]

prop·a·gan·dism (prop′ə gan′diz əm) *n.* the use of propaganda.

prop·a·gan·dist (prop′ə gan′dist) *n.* **1** a person who gives time or effort to the spreading of some opinion, belief, or principle. **2** (*adj.*) of propaganda or propagandists. —**prop′a·gan·dis′tic,** *adj.*

prop·a·gan·dize (prop′ə gan′dīz) *v.* **-dized, -diz·ing. 1** propagate or spread (doctrines, etc.) by propaganda. **2** carry on propaganda.

prop·a·gate (prop′ə gāt′) *v.* **-gat·ed, -gat·ing. 1** produce offspring; reproduce. **2** increase in number; multiply: *Trees propagate themselves by seeds.* **3** cause to increase in number by the production of young. **4** spread (news, knowledge, etc.): *Don't propagate unkind reports.* **5** pass on; send further: *Sound is propagated by vibrations.* [< L *propagare,* originally, plant slips < *pro-* widely + *pagare,* frequentative of *pangere* make fast] —**prop′a·ga′tor,** *n.*

prop·a·ga·tion (prop′ə gā′shən) *n.* **1** the breeding of plants or animals: *Our propagation of poppies is by seed, and of roses by cuttings.* **2** the spreading of something, such as a belief; making more widely known; dissemination: *the propagation of the principles of science.* **3** a passing on; sending further; spreading or extending: *the propagation of the shock of an earthquake.*

pro·pane (prō′pān) *n.* a heavy, colorless hydrocarbon gas of the methane series, found in petroleum and used for fuel, refrigeration, etc. Formula: C_3H_6 [*propyl* + *methane*]

pro pat·ri·a (prō′pat′rē ə *or* pā′trē ə) *Latin.* for one's country or native land.

pro·pel (prə pel′) *v.* **-pelled, -pel·ling.** drive forward; force ahead: *to propel a boat by oars, a person propelled by ambition.* [ME < L *propellere* < *pro-* forward + *pellere* push] —**pro·pel′la·ble,** *adj.*

pro·pel·lant (prə pel′ənt) *n.* **1** something that propels, such as the fuel of a missile or the explosive charge of a shell. **2** a person who propels.

pro·pel·lent (prə pel′ənt) *adj., n.* —*adj.* propelling; driving forward. —*n.* a propellant.

pro·pel·ler (prə pel′ər) *n.* **1** a device consisting of a revolving hub with blades, for propelling boats and aircraft. See **airplane** for picture. **2** a person or thing that propels.

pro·pen·si·ty (prə pen′sə tē) *n., pl.* **-ties.** a natural inclination or bent; inclination: *Most boys have a propensity for playing with machinery.* [< L *propensus* inclined, ult. < *pro-* forward + *pendere* hang]

prop·er (prop′ər) *adj.* **1** correct; right; fitting: *Night is the proper time to sleep, and bed the proper place.* **2** strictly so called; in the strict sense of the word: *The population of Vancouver proper does not include that of the suburbs.* **3** decent; respectable: *proper*

hat, āge, fär; let, ēqual, tèrm; it, īce
hot, ōpen, ôrder; oil, out; cup, pút, rüle,
ə·bove, tak·en, pen·cil, lem·on, circ·us

ch, child; ng, long; sh, ship
th, thin; ᴛʜ, then; zh, measure

conduct. **4** *Informal.* complete; thorough; fine; excellent. **5** *Archaic.* good-looking; handsome. **6** belonging exclusively or distinctively: *qualities proper to a substance.* **7** *Heraldry.* represented in its natural colors: *an eagle proper.* [ME < OF < L *proprius*]
☛ *Usage.* **Proper adjectives.** Proper nouns used as adjectives, and adjectives directly derived from proper names and still referring to the place or person, are capitalized: *the French language, Roman ruins.* If proper adjectives lose the reference to their origins, they become simple adjectives and are not capitalized: *roman type.*

proper fraction a fraction less than 1. $^2/_3$, $^1/_8$ and $^{199}/_{200}$ are proper fractions.

prop·er·ly (prop′ər lē) *adv.* **1** in a proper, correct, or fitting manner: *This job must be done properly.* **2** rightly; justly: *to be properly indignant at the offer of a bribe.* **3** strictly: *Properly speaking, a whale is not a fish.*

proper noun *or* **name** *Grammar.* a noun that identifies one particular person, place, organization, period of time, etc.; a name used to identify an individual. *Sarah, Calgary,* and *Renaissance* are proper nouns. Compare **common noun.**
☛ *Spelling.* Proper nouns are always capitalized.

prop·er·tied (prop′ər tēd) *adj.* owning property.

prop·er·ty (prop′ər tē) *n., pl.* **-ties. 1** any thing or things owned; possession or possessions. **2** a piece of land or real estate: *He owns some property out West.* **3** the right to possess, use, and dispose of anything; ownership. **4** a quality or power belonging specially to something: *Soap has the property of removing dirt.* **5 properties,** *pl.* the furniture, weapons, etc. used in staging a play, motion picture, or television scene. [ME < OF *propriete* < L *proprietas* < *proprius* one's own]
☛ *Syn.* **1. Property, goods, effects** = what someone owns. **Property** suggests whatever someone legally owns, including land, buildings, animals, money, stocks, documents, objects, and rights: *Landed property is taxable.* **Goods** suggests movable personal property, as distinguished from land, buildings, etc. and applies chiefly to things of use in the house or on the land, such as furniture, furnishings, and implements, but never to money or papers, etc.: *Professional movers packed our goods.* **Effects** applies to personal possessions, including goods, clothing, jewellery, personal belongings, and papers: *I packed our other effects.*

proph·e·cy (prof′ə sē) *n., pl.* **-cies. 1** a telling of what will happen; the foretelling of future events. **2** something told about the future. **3** a divinely inspired utterance, revelation, writing, etc. [ME < OF < L < Gk. *propheteia* < *prophetes.* See PROPHET.]

proph·e·sy (prof′ə sī′) *v.* **-sied, -sy·ing. 1** tell what will happen. **2** foretell; predict: *The sailor prophesied a severe storm.* **3** speak when or as if divinely inspired: *Daniel prophesied the destruction of Babylon.* **4** utter in prophecy. —**proph′e·si′er,** *n.*

proph·et (prof′it) *n.* **1** a person who tells what will happen. **2** a person who believes his preaching to be inspired by God: *Every religion has its prophets.* **3 the Prophet, a** Mohammed. **b** Joseph Smith, the founder of the Mormon religion. **4 the Prophets,** *pl.* **a** the twenty-one books that constitute the second main division of the Hebrew Bible, following the Pentateuch (the Law). **b** in Christian use, the sixteen books of the Old Testament that are named after prophets. [ME < OF < L < Gk. *prophetes,* ult. < *pro-* before + *phanai* speak]
☛ *Hom.* **profit.**

proph·et·ess (prof′it is) *n.* a woman prophet.

pro·phet·ic (prə fet′ik) *adj.* **1** belonging to a prophet; such as a prophet has: *prophetic power.* **2** containing prophecy: *a prophetic saying.* **3** giving warning of what is to happen; foretelling. —**pro·phet′i·cal·ly,** *adv.*

pro·phy·lac·tic (prō′fə lak′tik *or* prof′ə lak′tik) *adj., n.* —*adj.* **1** protecting from disease. **2** protective; preservative; precautionary. —*n.* **1** a medicine or treatment that protects against disease. **2** precaution. [< Gk. *prophylaktikos,* ult. < *pro-* before + *phylassein* guard < *phylax, -akos* a guard] —**pro′phy·lac′ti·cal·ly,** *adv.*

pro·phy·lax·is (prō′fə lak′sis *or* prof′ə lak′sis) *n.* **1** protection from disease. **2** treatment to prevent disease. [< NL < Gk. *pro-* before + *phylaxis* protection]

pro·pin·qui·ty (prō ping′kwə tē) *n.* **1** nearness in place, especially personal nearness. **2** nearness of blood; kinship. [< L *propinquitas,* ult. < *prope* near]

pro·pi·ti·ate (prə pish′ē āt′) *v.* **-at·ed, -at·ing.** prevent or reduce the anger of; win the favor of; appease or conciliate. [< L

propitiare, ult. < *propitius* propitious. See PROPITIOUS.]
—**pro·pi′ti·a·tor**, *n.*

pro·pi·ti·a·tion (prə pish′ē ā′shən) *n.* 1 the act of propitiating.
2 something that propitiates.

pro·pi·ti·a·to·ry (prə pish′ē ə tô′rē) *adj.* intended to propitiate;
making propitiation; conciliatory: *a propitiatory offering.*

pro·pi·tious (prə pish′əs) *adj.* 1 favorable: *It seemed propitious
weather for our trip.* 2 favorably inclined; gracious. [< L *propitius,*
originally, falling forward < *pro-* forward + *petere* go toward]
—**pro·pi′tious·ly**, *adv.* —**pro·pi′tious·ness**, *n.*

pro·po·nent (prə pō′nənt) *n.* 1 one who makes a proposal or
proposition. 2 a favorer; supporter. [< L *proponens, -entis,* ppr. of
proponere set forth. See PROPOUND.]

pro·por·tion (prə pôr′shən) *n., v.* —*n.* 1 the relation in size,
number, amount, or degree of one thing compared to another: *Each
man's pay will be in proportion to his work.* 2 a proper relation
between parts: *His short legs were out of proportion with his long
body.* 3 **proportions,** *pl.* **a** size; extent: *Canada has forests of huge
proportions.* **b** dimensions: *The proportions of the furniture are
wrong for this small room.* 4 a part; share: *A large proportion of
British Columbia is mountainous.* 5 *Mathematics.* **a** an equality of
ratios: *Examples:* 4 *is to* 2 *as* 10 *is to* 5. **b** a method of finding the
fourth term of such a proportion when three are known.
—*v.* 1 fit one thing to another so that they go together: *The designs
in that rug are well proportioned.* 2 adjust in proper proportion or
relation. [< L *proportio, -onis* < phrase *pro portione* in relation to
the part] —**pro·por′tion·er**, *n.* —**pro·por′tion·ment**, *n.*

pro·por·tion·a·ble (prə pôr′shən ə bəl) *adj.* being in due
proportion; proportional.

pro·por·tion·al (prə pôr′shən əl) *adj., n.* —*adj.* in the proper
proportion; corresponding: *The increase in price is proportional to
the improvement in the car.* —*n. Mathematics.* one of the terms of
a proportion.

pro·por·tion·al·ly (prə pôr′shən əl ē) *adv.* in proportion.

proportional representation an electoral system in which the
number of seats that each party or group is given is proportional to
its share of the total number of votes cast.

pro·por·tion·ate (prə pôr′shən it) *adj.* in the proper proportion;
proportioned; proportional: *The money obtained by the bazaar was
really not proportionate to the effort we put into it.*

pro·por·tion·ate·ly (prə pôr′shən it lē) *adv.* in proportion.

pro·por·tioned (prə pôr′shənd) *adj.* adjusted in proportion.

pro·pos·al (prə pōz′əl) *n.* 1 something proposed; a suggestion,
offer, plan, etc.: *a proposal to adjourn for lunch. Her proposal for a
new bridge will be presented to the city council tomorrow.* 2 an
offer of marriage. 3 the act of proposing: *Proposal is easier than
performance.*
▰ *Syn.* 1. Proposal, proposition = something put forward for consideration.
Proposal indicates a suggestion, offer, plan, or terms put forward for
consideration and acceptance or action, but emphasizes the idea of offering for
acceptance or refusal or suggesting for consideration: *The young people made a
proposal to the City Council.* **Proposition,** sometimes confused with *proposal*
but interchangeable with it only in business use, emphasizes what is put
forward as a proposal and how it is set forth, the statement of the terms, plan,
scheme: *The Council approved the idea, but not the proposition set forth.*

pro·pose (prə pōz′) *v.* -**posed,** -**pos·ing.** 1 put forward for
consideration, discussion, acceptance, etc.; suggest. 2 present (the
name of someone) for office; membership, etc. 3 present as a toast
to be drunk. 4 intend; plan: *She proposes to save half of all she
earns.* 5 make an offer of marriage. [< F *proposer* < *pro-* forth (<
L) + *poser* (see POSE[1])] —**pro·pos′er,** *n.*

prop·o·si·tion (prop′ə zish′ən) *n., v.* —*n.* 1 something presented
or offered for consideration; proposal. 2 assertion; statement.
3 *Logic.* a statement affirming or denying something, that is to be
proved true or false. 4 *Mathematics.* a problem or theorem, usually
together with its proof. 5 *Informal.* a person or thing to be dealt
with: *He can be a difficult proposition if you don't approach him in
the right way.* 6 *Informal.* a suggestion or invitation to engage in
sexual intercourse.
—*v. Informal.* make a proposition to (someone), especially to
engage in sexual intercourse. [< L *propositio, -onis* a setting forth
< *proponere* < *pro-* forth + *ponere* put, place]
▰ *Syn.* 1. See note at **proposal.**

pro·pound (prə pound′) *v.* put forward; propose: *to propound a
theory, a question, or a riddle.* [earlier *propone* < L *proponere* <
pro- before + *ponere* set]

pro·prae·tor or **pro·pre·tor** (prō prē′tər or -tôr′) *n.* in ancient
Rome, an officer who, after having served as praetor, was sent to
govern a province. [< L]

pro·pri·e·tar·y (prə prī′ə ter′ē) *adj., n., pl.* -**tar·ies.** —*adj.*
1 belonging to a proprietor. 2 holding property. 3 owned by a

private person or company; belonging to or controlled by a private
person as property. A proprietary medicine is a patent medicine,
that is, one which can be made and sold only by some one person
or certain persons.
—*n.* 1 an owner. 2 a group of owners. 3 ownership; the holding of
property. 4 *Historical.* the holder or group of holders of a grant
from a king of England. 5 a proprietary medicine. [< LL
proprietarius < L *proprietas* ownership. See PROPRIETY.]

pro·pri·e·tor (prə prī′ə tər) *n.* an owner, especially of a business;
manager. [alteration of *proprietary*]

pro·pri·e·tor·ship (prə prī′ə tər ship′) *n.* ownership.

pro·pri·e·tress (prə prī′ə tris) *n.* a woman owner or manager.

pro·pri·e·ty (prə prī′ə tē) *n., pl.* -**ties.** 1 the quality of being
proper; fitness. 2 proper behavior: *She acted with propriety.*
3 **proprieties,** *pl.* the conventional standards or requirements of
proper behavior: *Most of the proprieties are matters of common
politeness.* [< L *proprietas* appropriateness, peculiar nature
(translation by Cicero of Gk. *idiotēs*) < *proprius* one's own, proper
(= Gk. *idios*)]

pro·pul·sion (prə pul′shən) *n.* 1 the act or process of driving
forward or onward. 2 a propelling force or impulse: *the propulsion
of jet engines.* [< F]

pro·pul·sive (prə pul′siv) *adj.* propelling; driving forward or
onward.

prop·y·lae·um (prop′ə lē′əm) *n.* an elaborate or imposing
gateway, entrance, or vestibule to a temple or other building. [< L
propylaeum < Gk. *propylaion* entrance]

pro·py·lene (prō′pə lēn′) *n.* a colorless hydrocarbon gas
obtained from propane, similar in type and structure to ethylene.
Formula: C_3H_6

pro ra·ta (prō′rä′tə or rā′tə) in proportion; according to the
share, interest, etc. of each. [< L *pro rata* (*parte*) according to the
portion figured (for each); *rata* < *ratus,* pp. of *reri* count, figure]

pro·rate (prō rāt′ or prō′rāt′) *v.* -**rat·ed, -rat·ing.** distribute or
access proportionally: *We prorated the money according to the
number of days each had worked.* [< pro rata]

pro·ro·ga·tion (prō′rə gā′shən) *n.* the discontinuance of the
meetings of a lawmaking body without dissolving it.

pro·rogue (prō rōg′) *v.* -**rogued, -rogu·ing.** discontinue the
regular meetings of (a lawmaking body) for a time. [< F < L
prorogare defer < *pro-* forward + *rogare* ask for]

pro·sa·ic (prō zā′ik) *adj.* like prose; matter-of-fact; ordinary; not
exciting. [< Med.L *prosaicus* < L *prosa.* See PROSE.]
—**pro·sa′i·cal·ly,** *adv.*

pro·sce·ni·um (prō sē′nē əm) *n., pl.* -**ni·a** (-nē ə). 1 the part of
the stage in front of the curtain. 2 the curtain and the framework
that holds it. 3 the stage of an ancient theatre, or of a modern
theatre having no curtain. [< L *proscaenium* < Gk. *proskēnion* <
pro- in front of + *skēnē* stage, originally, tent]

pro·scribe (prō skrīb′) *v.* -**scribed, -scrib·ing.** 1 prohibit as wrong
or dangerous; condemn: *In earlier days, the church proscribed
dancing and cardplaying.* 2 put outside of the protection of the law;
outlaw. 3 forbid to come into a certain place; banish. [< L
proscribere < *pro-* openly, publicly + *scribere* write]
—**pro·scrib′er,** *n.*

pro·scrip·tion (prō skrip′shən) *n.* 1 the act of proscribing. 2 the
state of being proscribed. [< L *proscriptio, -onis* < *proscribere.* See
PROSCRIBE.]

pro·scrip·tive (prō skrip′tiv) *adj.* proscribing; tending to
proscribe. —**pro·scrip′tive·ly,** *adv.*

prose (prōz) *n., v.* -**prosed, pros·ing.** —*n.* 1 the ordinary form of
spoken or written language. 2 language not arranged in poetic
metre: *This writer's prose is better than his poetry. Milton and
Samuel Johnson are masters of the Latin style of prose.* 3 (*adj.*) of
or in prose. 4 dull, ordinary talk. 5 (*adj.*) lacking imagination;
matter-of-fact; commonplace.
—*v.* talk or write in a dull, commonplace way. [< F < L *prosa
(oratio)* straight (speech), ult. < *pro-* forward + *vertere* turn]

pros·e·cute (pros′ə kyūt′) *v.* -**cut·ed, -cut·ing.** 1 *Law.* **a** bring
before a court: *Reckless drivers will be prosecuted.* **b** bring a case
before a court; follow up: *He prosecuted an inquiry
into reasons for the company's failure.* 3 carry on (a business or
occupation). [ME < L *prosecutus,* pp. of *prosequi* pursue < *pro-*
forth + *sequi* follow. Related to PURSUE.]
▰ *Usage.* See note at **persecute.**

pros·e·cu·tion (pros′ə kyū′shən) *n.* 1 *Civil Law.* **a** the carrying
on of a lawsuit: *He abandoned his prosecution of the case for
damages.* **b** *Criminal Law.* the side that institutes criminal
proceedings against another. The prosecution makes charges against
the defence. 2 a carrying out; following up: *In prosecution of his
plan, he stored away a supply of food.*

pros·e·cu·tor (pros′ə kyū′tər) *n.* 1 *Criminal Law.* a lawyer who

represents the state in the conducting of proceedings in a court of law against persons accused of crime. In Canada, such a person is a **Crown prosecutor,** who is a full-time or part-time officer of the court. **2** *Civil Law.* any person who carries on legal proceedings against another or others. **3** a person who carries out or follows up something.

pros·e·lyte (pros′ə līt′) *n., v.* **-lyt·ed, -lyt·ing.** —*n.* a person who has been converted from one opinion, religious belief, etc. to another. —*v.* convert from one opinion, religious belief, etc. to another. [ME < LL < Gk. *prosēlytos* having arrived < pros- over + *ely-* come] —**pros′e·lyt′er,** *n.*

pros·e·lyt·ism (pros′ə līt iz′əm *or* -lə tiz′əm) *n.* the act or fact of proselyting.

pros·e·lyt·ize (pros′ə lə tīz′ *or* pros′ə lī tīz′) *v.* **-ized, -iz·ing.** make converts; proselyte.

Pro·ser·pi·na (prō sėr′pə nə) *n.* Roman mythology. the daughter of Jupiter and Ceres and queen of the underworld, corresponding to the Greek goddess Persephone. Also, **Proserpine.**

Pro·ser·pi·ne (pros′ər pīn′ *or* prō sėr′pə nē′) *n.* Proserpina.

pro·sit (prō′sit) *interj.* to your health! [< L *prosit* may it benefit]

pros·o·dist (pros′ə dist) *n.* a person skilled in the technique of versification.

pros·o·dy (pros′ə dē) *n.* the science of poetic metres and versification. [< L < Gk. *prosōidia* all the features (accent, modulation, etc.) that characterize speech < *pros* in addition to + *ōidē* song, poem]

pros·pect (pros′pekt) *n., v.* —*n.* **1** anything expected or looked forward to. **2** the act of looking forward; expectation: *The prospect of a vacation is pleasant.* **3** the outlook for the future. **4** a person who may be a customer, candidate, etc.; prospective customer: *The salesman had several prospects in mind.* **5** a view; scene: *The prospect from the mountain was grand.*
in prospect, expected; looked forward to.
—*v.* search: *to prospect for gold, to prospect a region for silver.* [< L *prospectus,* ult. < *pro-* forward + *specere* look]

pro·spec·tive (prə spek′tiv) *adj.* **1** probable; expected: *a prospective client.* **2** looking forward to the future: *a prospective suggestion.* —**pro·spec′tive·ly,** *adv.*

pros·pec·tor (pros′pek tər *or* prə spek′tər) *n.* a person who explores or examines a region for gold, silver, oil, etc.

pro·spec·tus (prə spek′təs) *n.* a printed statement describing and advertising something. [< L *prospectus.* See PROSPECT.]

pros·per (pros′pər) *v.* **1** be successful; have good fortune; flourish. **2** make successful. [ME < OF < L *prosperare* < *prosperus* prosperous]

pros·per·i·ty (pros per′ə tē) *n., pl.* **-ties.** a prosperous condition; good fortune; success.

pros·per·ous (pros′pər əs) *adj.* **1** successful; thriving; doing well; fortunate. **2** favorable; helpful: *prosperous weather for growing wheat.* [< L *prosperus* < *pro-* according to + *spes* hope] —**pros′per·ous·ly,** *adv.* —**pros′per·ous·ness,** *n.*

pros·tate (pros′tāt) *n., adj.* Anatomy. —*n.* a large gland surrounding the male urethra in front of the bladder. —*adj.* designating or having to do with this gland. [< Med.L < Gk. *prostatēs* one standing in front, ult. < *pro-* before + *stenai* stand]

pros·the·sis (pros′thə sis *or* pros thē′sis) *n., pl.* **-ses** (-sēz) **1** the addition of a false tooth, artificial leg, etc. to the body. **2** the part itself. [< LL < Gk. *prosthesis* addition, ult. < *pros* to + *tithenai* put]

pros·thet·ics (pros thet′iks) *n.* (*used with a singular verb*) the branch of dentistry or surgery pertaining to prosthesis.

pros·ti·tute (pros′tə tyüt′ *or* pros′tə tüt′) *n., v.* **-tut·ed, -tut·ing.** —*n.* **1** a girl or woman who accepts money to engage in sexual acts with men. **2** any person who accepts payment for sexual acts: *a male prostitute.* **3** a person who gives up himself or his talents to an unworthy cause. —*v.* **1** offer oneself or another person for hire to commit sexual acts. **2** give up oneself or one's talents to an unworthy cause: *He has prostituted his art by selling paintings that he knows are not well done.* [< L *prostitutus,* pp. of *prostituere* prostitute < *pro-* publicly + *statuere* cause to stand]

pros·ti·tu·tion (pros′tə tyü′shən *or* -tü′shən) *n.* **1** the act or business of offering oneself or another person for hire to engage in sexual acts. **2** the act of giving up oneself or one's talents to an unworthy cause: *Churning out those cheap romances is a prostitution of her talents as a writer.*

pros·trate (pros′trāt) *v.* **-trat·ed, -trat·ing;** *adj.* —*v.* **1** lay down flat; cast down: *The captives prostrated themselves before the conqueror.* **2** make very weak or helpless; exhaust: *Sickness often prostrates people.*
—*adj.* **1** lying flat, with the face downward. **2** lying flat. **3** helpless;

hat, āge, fär; let, ēqual, tėrm; it, īce
hot, ōpen, ôrder; oil, out; cup, pút, rüle,
əbove, takən, pencəl, lemən, circəs
ch, child; ng, long; sh, ship
th, thin; ᴛʜ, then; zh, measure

overcome: *a prostrate enemy.* [< L *prostratus,* pp. of *prosternere* < *pro-* forth + *sternere* strew]

pros·tra·tion (pros trā′shən) *n.* **1** the act of prostrating; bowing down low or lying face down in submission, respect, or worship. **2** the state or condition of being very much worn out in body or mind; exhaustion; dejection.

pros·y (prō′zē) *adj.* **pros·i·er, pros·i·est.** like prose; commonplace; dull; tiresome. —**pros′i·ly,** *adv.* —**pros′i·ness,** *n.*

Prot. Protestant.

prot·ac·tin·i·um (prōt′ak tin′ē əm) *n.* a silver-grey, radio-active metallic element found in uranium ores. *Symbol:* Pa; *at.no.* 91; *at.wt.* (231); *half-life* 32 500 years. [< *proto-* (< Gk. *protos* first) + *actinium*]

pro·tag·o·nist (prō tag′ə nist) *n.* **1** the main character in a play, story, or novel. **2** a person who takes a leading part; an active supporter. [< Gk. *prōtagōnistēs* < *prōtos* first + *agōnistēs* actor < *agōn* contest < *agein* do]

pro·te·an (prō′tē ən *or* prō tē′ən) *adj.* readily assuming different forms or characters; exceedingly variable. [< *Proteus*]

pro·tect (prə tekt′) *v.* **1** shield from harm or danger; shelter; defend; guard. **2** guard (home industry) by taxing competing foreign goods that are imported into the country. [< L *protectus,* pp. of *protegere* < *pro-* in front + *tegere* to cover]
☛ *Syn.* **1.** See note at **guard.**

pro·tect·ing·ly (prə tek′ting lē) *adv.* so as to protect.

pro·tec·tion (prə tek′shən) *n.* **1** the act of protecting; condition of being kept from harm; defence: *We have policemen for our protection.* **2** a thing or person that prevents damage: *This apron is my protection against paint splatters.* **3** the system of taxing imported foreign goods so that people are more likely to buy goods made in their own country; the opposite of free trade. **4** something that assures safe passage through a region; a passport. **5** *Informal.* the payment of money to racketeers or gangsters as a form of tribute in order not to be molested.

pro·tec·tion·ism (prə tek′shən iz′əm) *n.* Economics. the system or theory of protection.

pro·tec·tion·ist (prə tek′shən ist) *n.* **1** a person who favors protectionism. **2** (*adj.*) of or having to do with protectionism or protectionists.

pro·tec·tive (prə tek′tiv) *adj.* **1** being a defence; protecting: *the hard protective covering of a turtle.* **2** preventing injury to those around: *a protective device on a machine.* **3** guarding against the competition of foreign-made goods by putting a high tax or duty on them: *a protective tariff.* —**pro·tec′tive·ly,** *adv.* —**pro·tec′tive·ness,** *n.*

protective coloring or **colouring** a coloring some animals have that makes them hard to distinguish from their surroundings, and so hides them from their enemies.

protective mimicry a close resemblance of an animal to its surroundings or to some different animal, that prevents its enemies from attacking it.

pro·tec·tor (prə tek′tər) *n.* **1** a person or thing that protects; defender. **2** the head of a kingdom when the king or queen cannot rule.

pro·tec·tor·ate (prə tek′tər it) *n.* **1** a weak or underdeveloped country or territory under the partial control of a strong country. **2** such protection and control. **3** the position or term of a protector. **4** government by a protector. **5 Protectorate,** the period (1653-1659) during which Oliver and Richard Cromwell were Lord Protectors of England.

pro·tec·tress (prə tek′tris) *n.* a woman protector.

pro·té·gé (prō′tə zhā′) *n.* a person under the patronage or protection of another. [< F *protégé,* pp. of *protéger* < L *protegere.* See PROTECT.]

pro·té·gée (prō′tə zhā′) *n.* a woman protégé.

pro·te·id (prō′tē id) *n. or adj.* protein.

pro·te·in (prō′tēn *or* prō′tē in) *n.* a complex compound containing nitrogen that is a necessary part of the cells of animals and plants. Meat, milk, cheese, eggs, and beans contain protein. [< L < Gk. *prōteios* of the first quality]

pro tem. pro tempore.

pro tem·po·re (prō′tem′pə rē) *Latin.* for the time being; temporarily.

Prot·er·o·zo·ic (prot′ər ə zō′ik) *n., adj. Geology.* —*n.* **1** a very early era, beginning approximately 1200 million years ago. **2** the rocks formed in this era. See chart at **geology**. —*adj.* of or having to do with this era or the rocks formed during it. [< Gk. *proteros* prior + *zōē* life]

pro·test (*n.* prō′test; *v.* prə test′, prō test′, or prō′test) *n., v.* —*n.* **1** a statement that denies or objects strongly: *They yielded only after protest.* **2** a solemn declaration: *The accused man was judged guilty in spite of his protest of innocence.* **3** under protest, unwillingly; though objecting. **4** a written statement by a notary public that a bill, note, cheque, etc. has been presented to someone who has refused to pay it or accept it. **5** *Sports.* an objection to a player or a play as illegal.
—*v.* **1** make objections; object: *The boys protested against having girls in the game.* **2** object to: *to protest a decision.* **3** declare solemnly; assert: *The accused man protested his innocence.* **4** state that (a cheque, note, bill, etc.) has not been paid. [ME < OF *protest* < *protester* protest < L *protestari,* ult. < *pro-* forth + *testis* witness] —**pro·test′er,** *n.* —**pro·test′ing·ly,** *adv.*

Prot·es·tant (prot′is tənt) *n., adj.* —*n.* **1** a member or adherent of certain Christian churches that have developed after the break with the Roman Catholic Church in the sixteenth century. Baptists, Presbyterians, Anglicans, United Church members, and many others are Protestants. **2 protestant,** a person who protests. —*adj.* **1** of Protestants or their religion. **2 protestant,** protesting. [< L *protestans, -antis* ppr. of *protestari.* See PROTEST.]

Protestant Episcopal Church in the United States, a Protestant church having principles and beliefs similar to those of the Anglican Church of Canada.

Prot·es·tant·ism (prot′is tənt iz′əm) *n.* **1** the religion of Protestants. **2** their principles and beliefs. **3** Protestants or Protestant churches as a group.

prot·es·ta·tion (prot′is tā′shən) *n.* **1** a solemn declaration; protesting: *to make a protestation of one's innocence.* **2** a protest.

Pro·te·us (prō′tē əs or prō′tyüs) *n. Greek mythology.* a sea god who had the power of assuming many different forms.

pro·thal·li·um (prō thal′ē əm) *n., pl.* **-thal·li·a** (-thal′ē ə). prothallus.

pro·thal·lus (prō thal′əs) *n., pl.* **-li** (-lī). a tiny, flat, free-living plant body that is the gametophyte of a fern or other pteridophyte. It develops from a spore. [< NL < Gk *pro-* before + *thallos* sprout]

pro·tho·rax (prō thôr′aks) *n., pl.* **-tho·rax·es** or **-tho·rac·es** (-thôr′ə sēz′). the anterior segment of an insect's thorax, bearing the first pair of legs. [< F *prothorax* < NL < Gk. *pro-* + *thorax* chest, throat]

proto- *combining form.* **1** first in time, as in *prototype.* **2** first in importance, order, or rank. **3** Proto- designating the earliest reconstructed stage of a language, as in *Proto-Germanic.*

pro·to·ac·tin·i·um (prō′tō ak tin′ē əm) *n.* the former name of protactinium.

pro·to·col (prō′tə kol) *n.* **1** a first draft or record from which a document, especially a treaty, is prepared. **2** the rules of etiquette of the diplomatic corps. **3** the rules for any procedure. [< OF < Med.L *protocollum* < Gk. *prōtokollon* a first leaf (with date and contents) glued onto a papyrus roll < *prōtos* first + *kolla* glue]

pro·ton (prō′ton) *n.* a nuclear particle carrying one unit of positive electric charge, found in the nucleus of every kind of atom. An element is identified and classified according to the number of protons in the nucleus of each of its atoms; the number of protons gives the element its atomic number. [< Gk. *prōton,* neut. adj., first]

pro·to·plasm (prō′tə plaz′əm) *n.* living matter; a colorless substance somewhat like soft jelly or white of egg that is the living substance of all plant and animal cells. [< G *Protoplasma* < Gk. *prōtos* first + *plasma* something moulded < *plassein* mould]

pro·to·plas·mic (prō′tə plaz′mik) *adj.* of or having to do with protoplasm.

pro·to·typ·al (prō′tə tīp′əl) *adj.* of, having to do with, or being a prototype.

pro·to·type (prō′tə tīp′) *n.* the first or primary type of anything; the original or model: *A modern ship has its prototype in the hollowed log used by primitive peoples.* [< NL < Gk. *prōtotypon,* originally neut. of *prōtotypos* original, primitive < *prōtos* first + *typos* type, model]

pro·to·typ·i·cal (prō′tō tīp′ə kəl) *adj.* prototypal.

pro·to·zo·an (prō′tə zō′ən) *n., pl.* **-zo·ans** or **-zo·a** (-zō′ə); *adj.* —*n.* any of a phylum (Protozoa) of minute, mostly microscopic,

single-celled organisms found throughout the world in fresh water, in the oceans at all depths, and in the soil. Protozoans have traditionally been classified as simple animals, some of which have plantlike characteristics, but some authorities place them in a separate kingdom (Protista), along with algae and fungi. —*adj.* of, having to do with, or belonging to the Protozoa.

pro·tract (prō trakt′) *v.* **1** draw out; lengthen in time: *to protract a visit.* **2** slide out; thrust out; extend. **3** draw by means of a scale and protractor. [< L *protractus,* pp. of *protrahere* < *pro-* forward + *trahere* drag]

pro·trac·tile (prō trak′tĭl or -trak′təl) *adj.* capable of being lengthened out, or of being thrust forth. The turtle has a protractile head.

pro·trac·tion (prō trak′shən) *n.* **1** the act of drawing out; extension. **2** a drawing that has exactly the same proportions as the thing it represents.

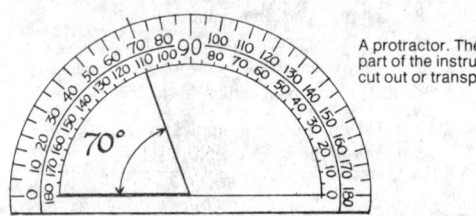

A protractor. The middle part of the instrument is cut out or transparent

pro·trac·tor (prō trak′tər) *n.* **1** an instrument for drawing or measuring angles. **2** a person or thing that protracts.

pro·trude (prō trüd′ or prə trüd′) *v.* **-trud·ed, -trud·ing. 1** thrust forth; stick out: *The saucy child protruded her tongue.* **2** be thrust forth; project: *Her teeth protrude too far.* [< L *protrudere* < *pro-* forward + *trudere* thrust]

pro·trud·ent (prō trüd′ənt) *adj.* protruding.

pro·tru·sion (prō trü′zhən) *n.* **1** the act of protruding or the state of being protruded. **2** something that sticks out; projection. [< L *protrusus,* pp. of *protrudere.* See PROTRUDE.]

pro·tru·sive (prō trü′siv) *adj.* sticking out; projecting. —**pro·tru′sive·ly,** *adv.*

pro·tu·ber·ance (prō tyü′bər əns or -tü′bər əns) *n.* a part that sticks out; bulge; swelling.

pro·tu·ber·ant (prō tyü′bər ənt or -tü′bər ənt) *adj.* bulging out; sticking out; prominent. [< LL *protuberans, -antis* bulging, ppr. of *protuberare,* ult. < *pro-* forward + *tuber* lump] —**pro·tu′ber·ant·ly,** *adv.*

proud (proud) *adj.* **1** thinking well of oneself. **2** feeling or showing pleasure or satisfaction: *I am proud to call him my friend.* **3** having a becoming sense of what is due to oneself, one's position, or character. **4** thinking too well of oneself; haughty; arrogant: *He was too proud to share a taxi with a stranger.* **5** such as to make a person proud; highly honorable, creditable, or gratifying: *a proud moment.* **6** proceeding from pride; due to pride: *a proud smile.* **7** imposing; stately; majestic; magnificent: *proud cities.* **8** of persons, of exalted rank or station: *proud nobles.* **9** full of spirit or mettle: *a proud war horse.*

do (someone or oneself) **proud,** honor or distinguish: *Her generosity did her proud.*

proud of, thinking well of; being well satisfied with; proud because of: *to be proud of oneself, to be proud of one's family.*

[OE *prūd* < OF *prod, prud* valiant < LL *prode* of use < L *prodesse* be useful] —**proud′ly,** *adv.* —**proud′ness,** *n.*

☛ *Syn.* **1. Proud, overbearing, supercilious** = having or showing a high opinion of oneself. **Proud** may mean either holding oneself above anything low, mean, or contemptible or thinking oneself better than others, but usually also suggests a haughty or conceited manner or appearance: *He has a strong, proud face.* **Overbearing** suggests being rudely dictatorial or haughtily insulting in behavior and speech: *Promoted too quickly, the conceited youth became overbearing.* **Supercilious** suggests conceit, but emphasizes a coolly scornful attitude: *With a supercilious smile he refused our invitation.*

proud flesh the formation of too many grainlike particles of flesh during the healing of a wound or sore.

prov. 1 province; provincial. **2** provisional. **3** provost.

Prov. 1 Proverbs. **2** Provence. **3** Province. **4** Provost.

prove (prüv) *v.* **proved, proved** or **prov·en, prov·ing. 1** establish as true; make certain. **2** establish the genuineness or validity of, especially of a will. **3** be found to be: *This book proved interesting.* **4** show (oneself) to be: *He proved himself honest.* **5** try out; test; subject to some testing process: *The test pilot spent months proving the new plane.* [ME < OF *prover* < L *probare* < *probus* worthy] —**prov′a·ble,** *adj.*

prov·en (prüv′ən) *v.* a pp. of **prove.**

prov·e·nance (prov′ə nəns) *n.* origin or source: *the provenance of a painting.*

Pro·ven·çal (prov′ən sal′; *French,* prô vän säl′) *n., adj.* —*n.* **1** a native or inhabitant of Provence, a region in SE France. **2** the language of Provence. —*adj.* of or having to do with Provence, its people, or their language.

prov·en·der (prov′ən dər) *n.* **1** dry food for animals, such as hay or corn. **2** *Informal.* food. [ME < OF *provendre* < VL *probenda* < L *praebenda.* See PREBEND.]

pro·ve·ni·ence (prō vē′nē əns) *n.* provenance.

prov·erb (prov′èrb) *n.* **1** a short saying expressing a general truth, accepted and used for a long time. **2** an enigmatic statement. **3** a well-known example: *He is a proverb for carelessness.* **4 Proverbs,** a book of the Old Testament made up of sayings of the wise men of Israel, including Solomon. [ME < OF < L *proverbium* < *pro-* forth + *verbum* word, originally, a speaking]
☛ *Usage.* See note at **epigram.**

pro·ver·bi·al (prə vèr′bē əl) *adj.* **1** of proverbs; expressed in a proverb; like a proverb: *proverbial brevity, proverbial wisdom, a proverbial saying.* **2** that has become a proverb: *the proverbial stitch in time.* **3** well-known: *the proverbial loyalty of dogs.* —**pro·ver′bi·al·ly,** *adv.*

pro·vide (prə vīd′) *v.* **-vid·ed, -vid·ing. 1** supply; furnish: *Sheep provide us with wool.* **2** supply means of support; arrange to supply means of support: *Parents provide for their children.* **3** take care for the future: *to provide against accident, to provide for old age.* **4** state as a condition beforehand: *Our club's rules provide that dues must be paid monthly.* **5** get ready; prepare. [< L *providere* < *pro-* ahead + *videre* see. Doublet of PURVEY.] —**pro·vid′er,** *n.*

pro·vid·ed (prə vīd′id) *conj.* on the condition that; if: *She will go provided her friends can go also.*

prov·i·dence (prov′ə dəns) *n.* **1** God's care and help. **2** an instance of God's care and help. **3** care for the future; good management. **4 Providence,** God.

prov·i·dent (prov′ə dənt) *adj.* **1** having or showing foresight; careful in providing for the future: *Provident men lay aside money for their families.* **2** economical; frugal. [ME < L *providens, -entis,* ppr. of *providere.* See PROVIDE.] —**prov′i·dent·ly,** *adv.*

prov·i·den·tial (prov′ə den′shəl) *adj.* **1** fortunate: *Our delay seemed providential, for the train we had planned to take was wrecked.* **2** of or proceeding from divine power or influence. —**prov′i·den′tial·ly,** *adv.*

pro·vid·ing (prə vīd′ing) *conj.* on the condition that: *I shall go providing it doesn't rain.*

prov·ince (prov′əns) *n.* **1** one of the ten main political units, or divisions, which, together with the two Territories, make up Canada. **2** a similar political or administrative division in other countries. **3 the provinces,** *pl.* the parts of a country at a distance from the capital or the largest cities: *He was accustomed to city life and did not like living in the provinces.* **4** proper extent or scope of function or activity; sphere: *It was not within the province of the committee to make such decisions.* **5** an area or division of learning, art, government, etc.: *the province of science, the province of literature.* **6** in ancient Rome, a territory outside Italy, ruled by a Roman governor. **7** a large church district governed by an archbishop. [ME < OF < L *provincia*]

pro·vin·cial (prə vin′shəl) *adj., n.* —*adj.* **1** of a province. **2** belonging or peculiar to some particular province or provinces rather than to the whole country; local: *provincial English, provincial customs.* **3** having the manners, speech, dress, point of view, etc. of people living in the provinces. **4** lacking refinement or polish; narrow: *a provincial point of view.* —*n.* **1** a person born or living in the provinces. **2** a person who lacks refinement or polish. **3** *Cdn.* a member of the provincial police. —**pro·vin′cial·ly,** *adv.*

pro·vin·cial·ise (prə vin′shə līz′) *v.* **-ised, -is·ing.** provincialize.

pro·vin·cial·ism (prə vin′shəl iz′əm) *n.* **1** provincial manners, habits of thought, etc. **2** narrow-mindedness. **3** a word, expression, or way of pronunciation peculiar to a district of a country; localism.

pro·vin·ci·al·i·ty (prə vin′shē al′ə tē) *n., pl.* **-ties. 1** a provincial quality or character. **2** a provincial characteristic or trait.

pro·vin·cial·ize (prə vin′shə līz′) *v.* **-ized, -iz·ing. 1** bring under the authority of a province. **2** give a provincial status or name to; make provincial. Also, **provincialise.**

provincial judge magistrate.

provincial park *Cdn.* a tract of land established by a provincial government as a preserve for wild life and as a holiday area: *Algonquin Park in Ontario is a well-known provincial park.*

provincial parliament *Cdn.* the legislative assembly of a province.

provincial police in Ontario and Quebec, a police force maintained by the provincial government.

pro·vi·sion (prə vizh′ən) *n., v.* —*n.* **1** a statement making a condition: *A provision of the lease is that the rent must be paid promptly.* **2** a taking care for the future. **3** care taken for the future; an arrangement made beforehand: *There is a provision for making the building larger if necessary.* **4** that which is made ready; supply; stock, especially of food; food. **5 provisions,** *pl.* a supply of food and drinks.
make provision, take care for the future; make arrangement beforehand.
—*v.* supply with provisions. [ME < OF < *provisio, -onis* < *providere.* See PROVIDE.]
☛ *Syn. n.* **6.** See note at **food.**

pro·vi·sion·al (prə vizh′ən əl) *adj., n.* —*adj.* for the time being; temporary or conditional: *a provisional agreement, a provisional government.* —*n.* a postage stamp issued for use until the regular issue is available.

pro·vi·sion·al·ly (prə vizh′ə nəl ē) *adv.* **1** for the time being; temporarily. **2** conditionally.

pro·vi·so (prə vī′zō) *n., pl.* **-sos** or **-soes.** a sentence or part of a sentence in a contract, or other agreement, that states a condition; condition: *He was admitted to the advanced course with the proviso that he was to be put back if he failed.* [< L *proviso* it being provided < *providere.* See PROVIDE.]

pro·vi·so·ry (prə vī′zə rē) *adj.* **1** containing a proviso; conditional. **2** provisional.

pro·vo·ca·teur (prô vô kä tœr′) *n. French.* one who stirs up trouble or provokes violence.

prov·o·ca·tion (prov′ə kā′shən) *n.* **1** the act of provoking. **2** something that stirs one up; a cause of anger: *Their insulting remarks were a provocation.* [ME < OF < L *provocatio, -onis* < *provocare.* See PROVOKE.]

pro·voc·a·tive (prə vok′ə tiv) *adj., n.* —*adj.* **1** irritating; vexing. **2** tending or serving to call forth action, thought, laughter, anger, etc.: *a remark provocative of mirth.* —*n.* something that rouses or irritates. —**pro·voc′a·tive·ly,** *adv.* —**pro·voc′a·tive·ness,** *n.*

pro·voke (prə vōk′) *v.* **-voked, -vok·ing. 1** make angry; vex. **2** stir up; excite: *An insult provokes a person to anger.* **3** call forth; bring about; start into action; cause. [< L *provocare* < *pro-* forth + *vocare* call] —**pro·vok′er,** *n.*
☛ *Syn.* **1.** See note at **irritate.**

pro·vok·ing (prə vōk′ing) *adj.* that provokes; irritating. —**pro·vok′ing·ly,** *adv.*

pro·vo·lo·ne (prō′və lō′nā) *n. Italian.* a hard, sharp cheese having a smoky flavor.

prov·ost (prov′əst) *n.* **1** a person appointed to superintend, maintain discipline, or preside, such as the head of certain colleges or churches. **2** in Scotland, the chief magistrate of a town. [partly OE *profost,* partly < OF *provost,* both < Med.L *propositus,* used for L *praepositus* placed in charge of, originally pp. of *praeponere* place before < *prae-* at the head of + *ponere* to place]

pro·vost marshal (prō′vō) an officer in charge of the military police in a camp or region. *Abbrev.:* P.M.

prow (prou) *n.* **1** the pointed front part of a ship or boat; bow. **2** the projecting front part of anything: *the prow of an aircraft.* [< F *proue* < Ital. < L < Gk. *prōira*]

prow·ess (prou′is) *n.* **1** bravery; daring. **2** brave or daring acts. **3** unusual skill or ability. [ME < OF *proece* < *prod* valiant. See PROUD.]

prowl (proul) *v., n.* —*v.* **1** go about slowly and secretly hunting for something to eat or steal: *Many wild animals prowl at night.* **2** wander or cruise about (a place): *prowling the streets.* —*n.* the act of prowling.
on the prowl, prowling about.
[ME *prolle(n)*; origin uncertain] —**prowl′er,** *n.*

prowl car scout car.

prox·i·mal (prok′sə məl) *adj.* situated toward the point of origin or attachment. *Proximal* is opposed to *distal.* [< L *proximus* nearest]

prox·i·mate (prok′sə mit) *adj.* **1** next; nearest. **2** near the exact amount; approximate. [< pp. of Med.L *proximare* bring near < L *proximare* come near < *proximus* nearest]

prox·i·mate·ly (prok′sə mit lē) *adv.* next; very nearly; approximately.

prox·im·i·ty (proks im′ə tē) *n.* nearness; closeness. [< L *proximitas* < *proximus* nearest]

proximity fuse a tiny electronic device set in the nose of a projectile to make the shell explode at a certain distance from the target.

prox·i·mo (prok′sə mō′) *adv.* in or of the coming month: *on the 1st proximo.* [short for L *proximo mense* during next month]

prox·y (prok′sē) *n., pl.* **-prox·ies.** 1 the action of a deputy or substitute. In marriage by proxy, someone is substituted for the absent bridegroom at the marriage service. 2 a person authorized to act for another: *John acted as a proxy for the child's godfather at the christening.* 3 a written statement authorizing a proxy to act or vote for a person. 4 the vote so given. [ME *prokecye*, alteration of *procuracy* the office of proctor < Med.L *procuratia*, ult. < L *procurare*. See PROCURE.]

prude (prūd) *n.* a person who shows excessive propriety or modesty, especially with regard to sexual matters. [< F *prude* < *prudefemme* excellent woman < OF *prou, prod* excellent + *femme* woman]

pru·dence (prū′dəns) *n.* 1 the exercising of careful thought before taking action; good judgment or discretion. 2 good management; economy.
☛ *Syn.* 1. Prudence, foresight = thought in acting and planning. **Prudence** emphasizes common sense in directing oneself and one's affairs, giving thought to one's actions and their consequences, and usually suggests caution, watchfulness, and saving: *Prudence is wisdom in everyday life.* **Foresight** emphasizes ability to see what is likely to happen, and giving thought to being prepared: *He had the foresight to carry fire insurance.*

pru·dent (prū′dənt) *adj.* 1 planning carefully ahead of time; taking no chances; sensible; discreet: *A prudent man saves part of his wages.* 2 characterized by good judgment or good management: *a prudent policy.* [ME < L *prudens, -entis*, var. of *providens.* See PROVIDENT.] —**pru′dent·ly,** *adv.*

pru·den·tial (prü den′shəl) *adj.* of, marked by, or showing prudence. —**pru·den′tial·ly,** *adv.*

prud·er·y (prü′dər ē) *n., pl.* **-er·ies.** 1 extreme modesty or propriety, especially when not genuine. 2 a prudish act or remark.

prud·ish (prü′dish) *adj.* like a prude; extremely proper or modest; too modest. —**prud′ish·ly,** *adv.* —**prud′ish·ness,** *n.*

prune¹ (prün) *n.* 1 a kind of dried sweet plum. 2 a plum suitable for drying. 3 *Slang.* a person thought to be unattractive, stupid, or unpleasant. [ME < OF < VL *pruna* < L *prunum* < Gk. *proumnon.* Doublet of PLUM.]

prune² (prün) *v.* **pruned, prun·ing.** 1 cut out useless or undesirable parts from: *to prune a wordy manuscript.* 2 cut superfluous or undesirable twigs or branches from (a bush, tree, etc.). 3 cut off or out. [ME < OF *prooignier* < *por-* (< L *pro-*) + *rooignier* clip, originally, round off < L *rotundus* round] —**prun′er,** *n.*

pruning hook an implement with a hooked blade, used for pruning vines, etc.

pru·ri·ence (prür′ē əns) *n.* the state or quality of being prurient.

pru·ri·en·cy (prür′ē ən sē) *n.* prurience.

pru·ri·ent (prür′ē ənt) *adj.* having lustful thoughts or wishes. [< L *pruriens, -entis,* ppr. of *prurire* itch, be wanton] —**pru′ri·ent·ly,** *adv.*

Prus·sian (prush′ən) *n., adj.* —*n.* 1 a native or inhabitant of Prussia, a former state on the Baltic Sea and later a part of Germany. 2 a member of a Baltic people formerly inhabiting East Prussia. 3 See **Old Prussian.** —*adj.* of or having to do with Prussia or Prussians.

Prussian blue a deep-blue pigment, essentially a cyanogen compound of iron. [so called from its discovery in Berlin, the capital of Prussia, in 1704]

prus·sic acid (prus′ik) a deadly poison that smells like bitter almonds; hydrocyanic acid. [*prussic* < F *prussique* < *Prusse* Prussia]

pry¹ (prī) *v.* **pried, pry·ing;** *n., pl.* **pries.** —*v.* look or inquire into with curiosity, especially so as to give offence: *They accused him of prying into their affairs.* —*n.* an inquisitive person. [ME *prie(n);* origin uncertain]

pry² (prī) *v.* **pried, pry·ing;** *n., pl.* **pries.** —*v.* 1 raise or move by force. 2 get with much effort: *We finally pried the secret out of him.* —*n.* a lever for prying. [< obs. *prize* a lever, taken as a pl. See PRIZE⁴.]

pry·ing (prī′ing) *adj.* looking or searching curiously; inquisitive.
☛ *Syn.* See note at **curious.**

Ps. Psalm(s).

P.S. 1 postscript (for L *post scriptum*). 2 privy seal. 3 public school. 4 public sale. 5 passenger steamer.

psalm (som *or* säm) *n.* 1 a sacred song or poem. 2 **Psalm,** any of the 150 sacred songs or hymns that together form a book of the Old Testament. 3 **Psalms,** a book of the old Testament consisting of 150 psalms. [OE *psalm, sealm* < LL < Gk. *psalmos,* originally, performance on a stringed instrument < *psallein* pluck]

psalm·book (som′bůk′ *or* säm′-) *n.* a collection of metrical translations of the Psalms prepared for public worship.

psalm·ist (som′ist *or* säm′ist) *n.* 1 the author of a psalm or psalms. 2 **the Psalmist,** King David.

psalm·o·dy (som′ə dē *or* säm′ə dē) *n., pl.* **-dies.** 1 the act, practice, or art of singing psalms or hymns. 2 psalms or hymns. [ME < LL < Gk. *psalmōidia* < *psalmos* psalm + *ōidē* song]

Psal·ter (sol′tər *or* sôl′tər) *n.* 1 the Book of Psalms. 2 a version of the Psalms for liturgical or devotional use. 3 Usually, **psalter,** a prayer book containing such a version. [ME < OF < L < Gk. *psaltērion.* See PSALTERY.]

psal·ter·y (sol′tər ē *or* sôl′tər ē) *n., pl.* **-ter·ies.** an ancient musical instrument played by plucking the strings. [OE *saltere* < L < Gk. *psaltērion,* originally, stringed instrument < *psallein* pluck]

pse·phol·o·gist (se fol′ə jist′) *n.* a person trained in psephology, especially one whose work it is.

pse·phol·o·gy (se fol′ə jē) *n.* the study of election trends, based on the evaluation of statistical evidence.

pseud. pseudonym.

pseu·do (sü′dō) *adj.* 1 false; sham; pretended. 2 having only the appearance of. [< Gk. *pseudēs* false]

pseudo– *combining form.* false; spurious. Also, sometimes before a vowel, **pseud-.**

pseu·do·nym (sü′də nim′) *n.* a name used by an author instead of his real name. Ralph Connor is a pseudonym for Charles William Gordon. [< Gk. *pseudonymon* < *pseudēs* false + dial. *onyma* name]

pseu·don·y·mous (sü don′ə məs) *adj.* done or written under, done, or using a pseudonym: *a pseudonymous novel.* —**pseu·don′y·mous·ly,** *adv.*

p.s.f. pounds per square foot.

pshaw (sho *or* shô) *interj. or n.* an exclamation expressing impatience, contempt, etc.

psi¹ (sī *or* psē) *n.* the 23rd letter of the Greek alphabet (Ψ, ψ).

psi² (sī *or* sē) *n.* psychic or psychological processes or phenomena, such as extrasensory perception, telepathy, clairvoyance, etc. [< Gk. *psi,* the first letter of *psychē* soul, life]

psit·ta·co·sis (sit′ə kō′sis) *n.* a contagious disease of parrots and other birds, communicable to people. [< NL < Gk. *psittakos* parrot + *-osis* diseased condition]

PST *or* **P.S.T.** Pacific Standard Time.

psych *or* **psyche** (sīk) *v.* **psyched, psych·ing.** *Informal.* 1 psychoanalyse. 2 intimidate by indirect psychological means (*often used with* **out**): *He was psyched out by his opponent's extremely cool attitude before the match even started.* 3 prepare mentally or emotionally for a task, performance, etc. (*usually used with* **up**): *to psych oneself up for the opening-night performance.* 4 figure out or analyse mentally or intuitively (*often used with* **out**): *She managed to psych it out for herself.* [shortened form of *psychoanalyse*]

psych. psychology; psychological.

psy·che (sī′kē) *n.* 1 the human soul or spirit. 2 the mind. [< L < Gk. *psychē* breath, life < *psychein* breathe, blow]

Psy·che (sī′kē) *n. Greek and Roman mythology.* the human soul or spirit pictured as a beautiful young girl, usually with butterfly wings. Psyche was loved by Cupid, and was made immortal by Jupiter.

psy·che·de·li·a (sī′kə dē′lē ə) *n.* the way of life, ideas, objects, etc. associated with the use of psychedelic drugs: *a film dealing with psychedelia.*

psy·che·del·ic (sī kə del′ik) *adj., n.* —*adj.* 1 of, having to do with, or designating drugs that can produce abnormal changes in the mind, including intensified awareness of light, sound, color, etc., often accompanied by hallucinations or delusions: *LSD is a psychedelic drug.* 2 produced by such a drug: *a psychedelic experience.* 3 suggesting or imitating the intensified or bizarre colors, sounds, etc. associated with the mental effects of psychedelic drugs: *a psychedelic pink miniskirt, psychedelic music.* —*n.* 1 a psychedelic drug. 2 a person who uses psychedelic drugs. [coined word; lit. "mind-revealing," < Gk. *psychē* + *dēlein* to show + E *-ic*]

psy·chi·at·ric (sī′kē at′rik) *adj.* of or having to do with psychiatry. —**psy·chi·at′ri·cal·ly,** *adv.*

psy·chi·a·trist (sī kī′ə trist *or* si kī′ə trist) *n.* a physician who specializes in psychiatry.

psy·chi·a·try (sī kī′ə trē *or* si kī′ə trē) *n.* the branch of medicine dealing with the diagnosis and treatment of mental disorders. [< *psycho-* + Gk. *iatreia* cure, ult. < *iaesthai* heal]

psy·chic (sī′kik) *adj., n.* —*adj.* **1** of the soul or mind; mental: *illness due to psychic causes.* **2** outside the known laws of physics; supernatural. A psychic force or influence is believed by spiritualists to explain second sight, telepathy, table moving, tappings, etc. **3** especially susceptible to psychic influences. —*n.* **1** a person supposed to be specially sensitive or responsive to psychic force or spiritual influences; medium. **2** things that are psychic. [< Gk. *psychikos* < *psyche* soul, mind]

psy·chi·cal (sī′kə kəl) *adj.* psychic. —**psy′chi·cal·ly**, *adv.*

psy·cho (sī′kō) *n., pl.* -chos; *adj. Slang.* —*n.* psychopath. —*adj.* psychopathic.

psycho– *combining form.* mind, as in *psychoanalysis.* Also, **psych–** before some vowels. [< Gk. *psyche* soul, mind]

psy·cho·an·a·lyse or **psy·cho·an·a·lyze** (sī′ko an′ə līz′) *v.* -lysed or -lyzed, -lys·ing or -lyz·ing. examine or treat by psychoanalysis. —**psy′cho·an′a·lys′er** or **psy′cho·an′a·lyz′er,** *n.*

psy·cho·a·nal·y·sis (sī′kō ə nal′ə sis) *n.* **1** a method of studying human thought patterns, especially with a view to treating mental disorders, by which unconscious or subconscious forces that have impaired a person's ability to function satisfactorily in life are brought to the person's consciousness and their role in the person's life interpreted in order to enable him to deal with them. **2** the body of knowledge and theory that originated with the work of Sigmund Freud (1856-1939), an Austrian physician.

psy·cho·an·a·lyst (sī′kō an′ə list) *n.* a person trained in psychoanalysis, especially one whose work it is.

psy·cho·an·a·lyt·ic (sī′kō an′ə lit′ik) *adj.* having to do with or of the nature of psychoanalysis.

psy·cho·an·a·lyt·i·cal (sī′kō an′ə lit′ə kəl) *adj.* psychoanalytic. —**psy′cho·an′a·lyt′i·cal·ly,** *adv.*

psy·cho·an·a·lyze (sī′kō an′ə līz′) *v.* See **psychoanalyse.**

psy·cho·chem·i·cal (sī′kō kem′ə kəl) *adj., n.* —*adj.* of chemical compounds, capable of modifying people's behavior, attitudes, etc. —*n.* any chemical compound of this nature.

psy·cho·ki·ne·sis (sī′kō ki nē′sis *or* -kī nē′sis) *n.* the control of the movement of physical objects by the force of the mind alone, without the use of any known physical energy.

psy·cho·log·ic (sī′kə loj′ik) *adj.* psychological.

psy·cho·log·i·cal (sī′kə loj′ə kəl) *adj.* **1** of the mind. **2** of or having to do with psychology or psychologists. —**psy′cho·log′i·cal·ly,** *adv.*

psychological moment **1** the moment psychologically most appropriate to achieve a desired end. **2** the critical moment.

psychological warfare systematic efforts to affect morale, loyalty, etc., especially of large national groups.

psy·chol·o·gist (sī kol′ə jist) *n.* a person trained in psychology, especially one whose work it is.

psy·chol·o·gy (sī kol′ə jē) *n., pl.* -gies. **1** the study of the mind and the ways of thought. Psychology tries to explain why people act, think, and feel as they do. **2** a textbook or handbook of psychology. **3** the mental states and processes of a person or persons; mental nature and behavior: *Mrs. Jones knew her husband's psychology.* [< NL *psychologia* < Gk. *psyche* soul, mind + *-logos* treating of]

psy·cho·met·ric (sī′kə met′rik) *adj.* of or having to do with psychometrics or psychometry. —**psy′cho·met′ri·cal·ly,** *adv.*

psy·cho·me·tri·cian (sī′kə mə trish′ən) *n.* psychometrist.

psy·cho·met·rics (sī′kō met′riks) *n.* (*used with a singular verb*)**1** the branch of psychology dealing with psychological testing and measurement. **2** the technique of making such tests or measurements, using statistical and mathematical formulae and methods.

psy·cho·met·rist (sī kom′ə trist′) *n.* a person trained in psychometrics.

psy·chom·e·try (sī kom′ə trē) *n.* **1** the ability to deduce facts about the history of an object or about its owner by touching or being near the object. **2** psychometrics.

psy·cho·mo·tor (sī′kō mō′tər) *adj.* of or having to do with muscular activity resulting from mental processes.

psy·cho·neu·ro·sis (sī′kō nyü rō′sis *or* -nü rō′sis) *n.* -ses (-sēz). a mental disorder with physical symptoms but without apparent organic disease.

psy·cho·path (sī′kə path′) *n.* one who is suffering from mental illness.

psy·cho·path·ic (sī′kə path′ik) *adj.* **1** of or having to do with

hat, āge, fär; let, ēqual, tèrm; it, īce
hot, ōpen, ôrder; oil, out; cup, pút, rüle,
əbove, takən, pencəl, lemən, circəs
ch, child; ng, long; sh, ship
th, thin; ₮H, then; zh, measure

mental disorders. **2** having a mental disorder. —**psy′cho·path′i·cal·ly,** *adv.*

psy·cho·path·o·log·i·cal (sī kə path′ə loj′ə kəl) *adj.* of or having to do with psychopathology.

psy·cho·pa·thol·o·gy (sī′kə pə thol′ə jē) *n.* the science dealing with mental and behavioral disorders, including abnormal psychology and psychiatry.

psy·chop·a·thy (sī kop′ə thē) *n.* **1** mental disorder. **2** mental eccentricity or instability so extreme as to border on mental illness.

psy·cho·ses (sī kō′sēz) *n. pl.* of **psychosis.**

psy·cho·sis (sī kō′sis) *n., pl.* -ses. any severe form of mental disturbance or disease. [< NL < Gk. *psychosis* < *psyche* soul, mind]

psy·cho·so·mat·ic (sī′kō sə mat′ik) *adj.* **1** of or having to do with both mind and body. **2** of or having to do with physical disorders caused by mental or emotional disturbances. —**psy′cho·so·mat′i·cal·ly,** *adv.*

psychosomatic medicine the branch of medicine that deals with the inter-relationships between physical disorders and mental or emotional disturbances.

psy·cho·ther·a·pist (sī′kō ther′ə pist) *n.* a person trained in psychotherapy, especially one whose work it is.

psy·cho·ther·a·py (sī′kō ther′ə pē) *n.* the treatment of mental or physical disorders by psychological methods.

psy·chot·ic (sī kot′ik) *adj., n.* —*adj.* of, having to do with, or affected with psychosis; unstable or mentally ill. —*n.* an unstable or mentally ill person.

psy·cho·trop·ic (sī′kō trop′ik) *adj.* of a drug, capable of acting on the mind. Tranquillizers and hallucinogens are psychotropic drugs.

psy·chrom·e·ter (sī krom′ə tər) *n.* a type of hygrometer having dry-bulb and wet-bulb thermometers, for measuring humidity. [< Gk. *psychros* cold + E *-meter*]

pt. **1** pint. **2** part. **3** point. **4** past tense. **5** preterite. **6** port.

Pt platinum.

P.T. physical training.

PTA or **P.T.A.** Parent-Teacher Association.

ptar·mi·gan (tär′mə gən) *n., pl.* -gans or (*esp. collectively*) -gan. any of several species of arctic and alpine grouse (genus *Lagopus*) having feathered feet and plumage that is mainly white in winter and mainly brown and grey in summer. [< Scots Gaelic *tarmachan,* p added by mistaken analogy with Gk. word]

PT boat *U.S.* a small, fast motorboat that carries torpedoes, depth bombs, etc. [< Patrol Torpedo *boat*]

Pte. private (military rank).

pter·i·do·phyte (ter′ə dō fīt′) *n.* any of a major group of flowerless plants that have vascular tissue and reproduce by spores, including ferns, club mosses, and horsetails. In some classifications, these plants constitute the division Pteridophyta, but most authorities now classify them together with the flowering plants in the division Tracheophyta. See **tracheophyte.** [< Gk. *pteris, pteridos* fern + E *-phyte*]

pter·o·dac·tyl (ter′ə dak′təl) *n.* any of an order (Pterosauria) of extinct flying reptiles that lived during the Jurassic and Cretaceous periods, having membranous wings resembling those of a bat. [< Gk. *pteron* wing + *daktylos* finger, toe]

pter·o·pod (ter′ə pod′) *n.* sea butterfly.

pter·o·saur (ter′ə sôr′) *n.* pterodactyl.

P.T.O. or **p.t.o.** please turn (the page) over.

Ptol·e·ma·ic (tol′ə mā′ik) *adj.* **1** of or having to do with Claudius Ptolemy, a Greek mathematician, astronomer, and geographer, who lived in the second century A.D. The Ptolemaic **system** of astronomy taught that the earth was the fixed centre of the universe, around which the heavenly bodies moved. **2** of or having to do with the Ptolemies, who were rulers of Egypt from 323 to 30 B.C.

Ptol·e·my (tol′ə mē) *n., pl.* -mies. any of a certain family of Egyptian rulers who ruled from 323 to 30 B.C.

pto·maine or **pto·main** (tō′mān *or* tō mān′) *n.* any of several chemical compounds produced in decaying matter. Food poisoning

is caused not by ptomaines, as formerly believed, but by bacteria or other sources of infection. [< Ital. *ptomaina* < Gk. *ptōma* corpse]

ptomaine poisoning poisoning caused by ptomaines.

pty·a·lin (tī′ə lin) *n.* an enzyme contained in the saliva of man and of certain other animals that converts starch into dextrin and maltose, thus aiding digestion. [< Gk. *ptyalon* saliva < *ptyein* spit]

Pu plutonium.

pub (pub) *n., v.* **pubbed, pub·bing.** *Informal.* —*n.* a beer parlor or tavern. —*v.* visit or drink in a pub or pubs: *We went pubbing last night.* [short for *public house*]

pu·ber·ty (pyü′bər tē) *n.* the physical beginning of manhood and womanhood. Puberty usually comes at about 14 in boys and at about 12 in girls. [< L *pubertas* < *pubes* adult]

pu·bes·cence (pyü bes′əns) *n.* 1 arrival at puberty. 2 a soft, downy growth on plants and some insects. 3 the fact of having such a growth.

pu·bes·cent (pyü bes′ənt) *adj.* 1 arriving or arrived at puberty. 2 covered with down or fine, short hair: *a pubescent stem or leaf.* [< L *pubescens, -entis* reaching puberty < *pubes* adult]

pu·bic (pyü′bik) *adj.* having to do with the pubis.

pu·bis (pyü′bis) *n., pl.* **-bes** (-bēz). the lower, front portion of the hipbone. See **pelvis** for picture. [< NL *os pubis* bone of the groin]

pub·lic (pub′lik) *adj., n.* —*adj.* 1 of, belonging to, or concerning the people as a whole: *public affairs.* 2 done, made, acting, etc. for the people as a whole: *public relief.* 3 open to all the people; serving all the people: *a public park.* 4 of or engaged in the affairs or service of the people: *a public official.* 5 known to many or all; not private: *The fact became public.* 6 international: *public law.* —*n.* 1 **the public, a** the people in general; all the people: *The public is not likely to accept more restraints.* **b** a particular group of people sharing an interest, etc.: *the reading public.* 2 a particular section of the people: *A popular actor has a large public.*
in public, not in private or secretly; publicly; openly.
[< L *publicus,* ult. < *populus* the people; form influenced by *pubes* adult male population]

public address system an arrangement of loudspeakers used to carry speeches, messages, music, etc. to an audience in a large room, in different rooms of one building, or in the open air. *Abbrev.:* P.A. system.

pub·li·can (pub′lə kən) *n.* 1 *Brit.* a keeper of a public house. 2 in ancient Rome, a tax collector. [< L *publicanus* (def. 2) < *publicum* public revenue, originally neut. of *publicus.* See PUBLIC.]

pub·li·ca·tion (pub′lə kā′shən) *n.* 1 a book, newspaper, or magazine; anything that is published. 2 the printing and selling of books, newspapers, magazines, etc. 3 the act of making known; the fact or state of being made known. [< L *publicatio, -onis,* ult. < *publicus.* See PUBLIC.]

public domain lands belonging to the government.
in the public domain, of works, material, etc., available for unrestricted use because unprotected by copyright or patent.

public enemy a person who is a menace to the public.

public funds money provided by the government: *Public funds are used to pay for defence.*

public house 1 *Brit.* a place where alcoholic liquor is sold to be drunk; saloon. 2 an inn; hotel.

pub·li·cist (pub′lə sist) *n.* 1 a person skilled or trained in law or in public affairs. 2 a writer on law, politics, or public affairs.

pub·lic·i·ty (pub lis′ə tē) *n.* 1 the fact of being brought to public notice by special effort, through newspapers, signs, radios, etc. 2 public notice: *the publicity that actors desire.* 3 measures used for getting, or the process of getting, public notice: *a campaign of publicity for a new automobile.* 4 the state of being public; being seen by or known to everybody: *in the publicity of the street.*

pub·li·cize (pub′lə sīz′) *v.* **-cized, -ciz·ing.** give publicity to.

pub·lic·ly (pub′lik lē) *adv.* 1 in a public manner; openly. 2 by the public.

public opinion the opinion of the people in a country, community, etc.

public relations the relations of an organization, institution, etc. with the public and the activities it undertakes to create and keep up a favorable public image of itself. *Abbrev.:* P.R. or PR.

public school 1 in Canada and the United States, a free school maintained by taxes. 2 in the United Kingdom, an endowed private boarding school.

public servant a member of the public service (def. 1 or 2).

public service 1 civil service. 2 employment by any level of government: *School teachers are in the public service.* 3 the business of supplying a service or commodity to a community, especially one subsidized by public funds or administered by public servants: *Bus service is a public service in most cities.* 4 a service given for the benefit of the community: *That church runs a drop-in centre as a public service.* 5 (*adj.*) **public-service,** of or being a public service: *a public-service announcement.*

pub·lic–spir·it·ed (pub′lik spir′ə tid) *adj.* having or showing an unselfish desire for the public good.

public utility a company formed or chartered to render services to the public, such as a company furnishing electricity or gas, a railway, a streetcar or bus line, etc.

public works things built by the government at public expense and for public use, such as roads, docks, canals, and waterworks.

pub·lish (pub′lish) *v.* 1 prepare and offer a book, paper, map, piece of music, etc. for sale or distribution. 2 bring out the book or books of: *Some Canadian writers are published abroad before being published in Canada.* 3 come into circulation; be published: *The newspapers here publish every weekday.* 4 make publicly or generally known: *Don't publish the faults of your friends.* [ME < OF *publier,* ult. < L *publicus* (see PUBLIC); modelled after *punish,* etc.] —**pub′lish·a·ble,** *adj.*

pub·lish·er (pub′lish ər) *n.* a person or company whose business is to publish books, newspapers, magazines, etc.

PUC or **P.U.C.** Public Utilities Commission.

puce (pyüs) *n.* or *adj.* purplish or dark brown. [< F *puce* a flea < OF *pulce* < L *pulex, -licis*]

puck¹ (puk) *n.* 1 a mischievous spirit; goblin. 2 **Puck,** in English folklore, a mischievous fairy who appears in Shakespeare's play *A Midsummer Night's Dream.* [OE *pūca* goblin]

puck² (puk) *n.* a hard, black rubber disk used in hockey. [E dial. var. of *poke*¹]

puck·a (puk′ə) See **pukka.**

puck–car·ri·er (puk′kar′ē ər *or* -′ker′ē ər) *n. Hockey.* the player in possession of the puck.

puck·er (puk′ər) *v., n.* —*v.* draw into wrinkles or irregular folds: *to pucker one's brow, to pucker cloth in sewing. The baby's lips puckered just before he began to cry.* —*n.* an irregular fold; wrinkle: *There are puckers at the shoulders of this ill-fitting coat.* [apparently < *poke*¹]

puck·ish (puk′ish) *adv.* mischievous; impish. —**puck′ish·ly,** *adv.* —**puck′ish·ness,** *n.*

pud·ding (pùd′ing) *n.* 1 a soft dessert food, often having a milk base, and flavored and sweetened: *rice pudding.* 2 a cakelike dessert, usually steamed or baked: *plum pudding.* 3 a kind of sausage. 4 anything soft like a pudding. [cf. F *boudin* stuffed sausage, ult. < L *botulus* sausage; cf. also OE *puduc* wart]

pud·dle (pud′əl) *n., v.* **-dled, -dling.** —*n.* 1 a small pool of water, especially dirty water. 2 a small pool of any liquid. 3 wet clay and sand stirred into a paste.
—*v.* 1 make wet or mudddy. 2 mix up (wet clay and sand) into a thick paste. 3 use a mixture of wet clay and sand to stop water from running through: *Puddle up that hole.* 4 stir (melted iron) with an oxidizing agent to make wrought iron. [ME *puddel,* dim. of OE *pudd* ditch] —**pud′dler,** *n.*

pud·dling (pud′ling) *n.* the act or process of converting pig iron into wrought iron by stirring the molten metal with an oxidizing agent.

pud·dly (pud′lē) *adj.* 1 full of puddles. 2 like a puddle.

pudg·y (puj′ē) *adj.* **pudg·i·er, pudg·i·est.** short and fat or thick. [Scots dial.] —**pudg′i·ly,** *adv.* —**pudg′i·ness,** *n.*

pueb·lo (pweb′lō) *n., pl.* **-los** (defs. 1 and 2), **-lo** or **los** (def. 3). 1 a communal dwelling of certain Amerindian peoples of the SW United States, consisting of contiguous, flat-roofed houses of adobe or stone. 2 an Indian village or town in the SW United States. 3 **Pueblo,** a member of any of several Amerindian peoples of the SW United States, who live or lived in pueblos. [< Sp. *pueblo* people < L *populus*]

pu·er·ile (pyü′ər īl′ *or* pyü′ər əl) *adj.* foolish for a grown person to say or do; childish. [< L *puerilis* < *puer* boy] —**pu′er·ile′ly,** *adv.* —**pu′er·ile′ness,** *n.*

pu·er·il·i·ty (pyü′ər il′ə tē) *n., pl.* **-ties.** 1 childishness; foolishness. 2 a foolish act, idea, or statement.

pu·er·per·al (pyü ėr′pər əl) *adj.* of or having to do with childbirth. [< NL *puerperalis,* ult. < L *puer* child + *parere* bear]

Puer·to Ri·can (pwer′tə rē′kən) *n., adj.* —*n.* a native or inhabitant of Puerto Rico, a country in the West Indies. —*adj.* of or having to do with Puerto Rico or its inhabitants.

puff (puf) *v., n.* —*v.* 1 blow with short, quick blasts. 2 breathe quickly and with difficulty. 3 give out puffs; move with puffs: *The engine puffed out of the station.* 4 move or come in puffs: *Smoke*

puffed out of the chimney. **5** smoke: *to puff a cigar.* **6** swell with air or pride: *He puffed out his cheeks.* **7** arrange in soft, round masses. **8** praise in exaggerated language: *They puffed him to the skies.* —*n.* **1** a short, quick blast: *a puff of wind.* **2** a small quantity of air, smoke, etc. blown out in short, quick blasts. **3** a quick, hard breath. **4** the act or process of swelling. **5** a soft, round mass: *a puff of hair.* **6** a small pad for putting powder on the skin, etc. **7** a light pastry filled with whipped cream, jam, etc. **8** extravagant praise. **9** a portion of material gathered and held down at the edges but left full in the middle, as in a sleeve of a dress. [cf. OE *pyffan*]

puff adder a large, very poisonous viper (*Bitis arietans*) of the semi-arid regions of Africa that gives warning by hissing loudly and inflating its body.

puff·ball (puf′bôl′ *or* -bôl′) *n.* any of various fungi (order Lycoperdales, especially genera *Calvatia* and *Lycoperdon*) having a ball-shaped fruiting body which, when ripe, will give off a cloud of powdery spores if disturbed. Some puffballs are edible when immature.

puffed-up (puft′up′) *adj.* **1** bloated; swollen. **2** conceited; vain. **3** inflated with air.

puff·er (puf′ər) *n.* **1** a person or thing that puffs. **2** any of various marine fishes (family Tetraodontidae) mainly of tropical and subtropical seas, having a beaklike snout and a prickly or spiny body. Puffers are noted for their ability, when disturbed, to inflate their body with air or water into a globelike shape.

puf·fer·y (puf′ər ē) *n.* exaggerated praise or publicity. [< *puff*, v. + -*ery.* 18c.]

puf·fin (puf′ən) *n.* any of several northern diving birds of the auk family having a thickset body with the legs set far back on it, a short neck, and a high, laterally compressed bill which in breeding season becomes even larger and brighter, with yellow, red, and blue stripes. [ME *poffin*; ? ult. < L *puff* (from its puffed-up appearance)]

puff pastry a very light, flaky, rich pastry used in making pies, tarts, sausage rolls, etc.

puff·y (puf′ē) *adj.* **puff·i·er, puff·i·est. 1** puffed out; swollen: *Her eyes are puffy from crying.* **2** puffed up; vain. **3** blowing or breathing in puffs. —**puff′i·ness,** *n.*

pug (pug) *n.* **1** a breed of small, tan dog having a curly tail and turned-up nose. **2** pug nose. [probably a variant of *puck*¹]

pu·gi·lism (pyü′jə liz′əm) *n.* the art of fighting with the fists; boxing. [< L *pugil* boxer]

pu·gi·list (pyü′jə list) *n.* a person who fights with the fists; boxer.

pu·gi·lis·tic (pyü′jə lis′tik) *adj.* of or having to do with pugilism or pugilists. —**pu·gi·lis′ti·cal·ly,** *adv.*

pug·na·cious (pug nā′shəs) *adj.* having the habit of fighting; fond of fighting; quarrelsome. [< L *pugnax, -acis,* ult. < *pugnus* fist] —**pug·na′cious·ly,** *adv.* —**pug·na′cious·ness,** *n.*

pug·nac·i·ty (pug nas′ə tē) *n.* a fondness for fighting; quarrelsomeness.

pug nose a short, turned-up nose.

pug-nosed (pug′nōzd′) *adj.* having a pug nose.

puis·ne (pyü′nē) *adj., n.* —*adj.* **1** designating a superior court judge of subordinate rank. The Supreme Court of Canada is composed of a chief justice and eight puisne judges. **2** *Law. Esp.Brit.* subsequent; later: *puisne mortgages.* —*n.* a puisne judge. [< AF < OF *puisné* born later. 16c. See PUNY.]

pu·is·sance (pyü′ə səns *or* pwis′əns) *n.* power; might; force; strength.

pu·is·sant (pyü′ə sənt *or* pwis′ənt) *adj.* powerful; mighty; strong. [ME < OF *puissant* being powerful, ult. < var. of L *posse* be able] —**pu′is·sant·ly,** *adv.*

puke (pyük) *n. or v.* **puked, puk·ing.** *Vulgar slang.* vomit. [origin uncertain]

puk·ka (puk′ə) *adj. Anglo-Indian.* **1** reliable; good. **2** solid; substantial. **3** permanent. Also, **pucka.** [< Hind. *pakka* cooked, ripe]

pul (pül) *n.* a unit of money in Afghanistan, equal to ¹⁄₁₀₀ of an afghani. [< Persian]

pul·chri·tude (pul′krə tyüd′ *or* pul′krə tüd′) *n.* beauty. [ME < L *pulchritudo* < *pulcher* beautiful]

pule (pyül) *v.* **puled, pul·ing.** *Archaic.* cry in a thin voice, as a sick child does; whimper or whine. [? imitative]

Pu·lit·zer Prize (pyü′lit sər *or* pul′it sər) in the United States, any one of various prizes given each year for the best American drama, novel, biography, history, book of verse, editorial, and cartoon. They were established by Joseph Pulitzer (1847-1911), an American journalist, and first awarded in 1917.

pull (pùl) *v., n.* —*v.* **1** move (something) by grasping it and drawing toward oneself: *to pull a trigger. Pull the door open; don't push it.* **2** take hold of and tug: *He pulled at his tie.* **3** move, usually

hat, āge, fär; let, ēqual, tėrm; it, īce
hot, ōpen, ôrder; oil, out; cup, pùt, rüle,
above, takən, pencəl, lemən, circəs
ch, child; ng, long; sh, ship
th, thin; ᴛʜ, then; zh, measure

with effort or force: *to pull a sleigh up hill. I pulled ahead of the others in the race.* **4** pick; pluck: *to pull flowers.* **5** tear; rip: *The baby pulled the toy to pieces.* **6** stretch too far; strain: *The football player pulled a ligament in his leg.* **7** row: *Pull for the shore.* **8** be provided or rowed with: *The boat pulls eight oars.* **9** drink. **10** suck: *to pull at a cigar.* **11** hold back, especially to keep from winning: *to pull one's punches in a fight.* **12** *Informal.* perform; carry through: *Don't pull any tricks.* **13** *Golf.* hit (a ball) so that, in the case of a right-handed player, it curves to the left. **14** *Printing.* take (an impression or proof).

pull apart, a separate into pieces by pulling. **b** be severely critical of: *to pull apart a term paper.*

pull for, *Informal.* give help to: *to pull for the underdog.*

pull in, a stop; check. **b** *Informal.* arrest: *He was pulled in for speeding.* **c** arrive: *He pulled in this morning.*

pull off, *Slang.* do successfully.

pull (oneself) **together,** gather one's faculties, energy, etc.

pull out, a withdraw from a venture, undertaking, etc. **b** leave: *The train pulled out of the station.*

pull through, get through a difficult or dangerous situation.

pull together, work in harmony; get on together.

pull up, a tear up; uproot. **b** remove utterly. **c** bring or come to a halt; stop. **d** move ahead.

—*n.* **1** the act or effort of pulling. **2** a difficult climb, journey, or other effort: *It was a hard pull to get up the hill.* **3** handle, rope, ring, or other thing to pull by: *a curtain pull.* **4** a drink. **5** a suck: *a pull at a cigar.* **6** a force that attracts: *magnetic pull.* **7** *Golf.* a pulling of the ball. **8** *Informal.* influence; advantage. **9** *Printing.* an impression or proof. [OE *pullian*] —**pull′er,** *n.*

☞ *Syn. v.* **1.** Pull, tug, jerk = draw toward oneself. **Pull** = draw (or try to draw) toward or after oneself or in a particular stated or implied direction: *Pull the curtains across.* **Tug** = pull hard and, often, long, but does not always mean causing the thing or person to move: *The dog tugged at the tablecloth.* **Jerk** = pull, push, or twist quickly and suddenly: *She jerked her hand away. He jerked his hat off.*

pul·let (pùl′it) *n.* a young hen, usually less than a year old. [ME < OF *poulette,* dim. of *poule* hen < VL *pulla,* fem. of L *pullus* young fowl]

pul·ley (pùl′ē) *n., pl.* **-leys. 1** a wheel with a grooved rim in which a rope, belt, or wire can run, making it possible to change the direction of the pull. See **block and tackle** for picture. **2** a set of such wheels used to increase the power applied. **3** a wheel used to transfer power by driving a belt that moves some other part of the machine. [ME < OF *poulie,* ult. < Gk. *polos* axle]

Pull·man (pùl′mən) *n.* Pullman car.

Pullman car 1 a railway car with berths or small rooms for passengers to sleep in. **2** a railway car with specially comfortable seats. [after George M. *Pullman* (1831-1897), an American inventor]

pull·o·ver (pùl′ō′vər) *n.* a sweater put on by pulling it over the head.

pul·lu·late (pul′yə lāt′) *v.* **-lat·ed, -lat·ing. 1** of seeds or shoots, sprout or bud. **2** breed rapidly or profusely. **3** teem; swarm. [< L *pullulare* to sprout < *pollulus,* dim. of *pullus* young animal or bird. 17c. See PULLET.]

pul·mo·nar·y (pul′mə ner′ē) *adj.* **1** of or having to do with the lungs. Tuberculosis and pneumonia are pulmonary diseases. **2** having lungs. [< L *pulmonarius* < *pulmo* lung]

Pul·mo·tor (pul′mō′tər *or* pul mō′tər) *n. Trademark.* a device used to restore natural breathing in persons rescued from suffocation. [< L *pulmo* lung + E *motor*]

pulp (pulp) *n., v.* —*n.* **1** the soft part of any fruit or vegetable. **2** of a tooth, the soft inner part containing blood vessels and nerves. **3** a soft, moist mixture of ground-up wood, rags, or other material, from which paper is made. **4** any soft, wet mass. **5** (*adj.*) designating a type of magazine or book printed usually on rough, cheap paper and often containing sensational stories or articles. —*v.* **1** reduce to pulp. **2** remove pulp from. [< L *pulpa*] —**pulp′less,** *adj.*

pul·pit (pùl′pit) *n.* **1** a platform or raised structure in a church from which the minister preaches. **2** members of the clergy as a group, or their sermons. [ME < LL *pulpitum* < L *pulpitum* scaffold, platform]

pulp·wood (pulp′wùd′) *n.* **1** wood reduced to pulp for making paper. **2** any soft wood suitable for making paper.

pulp·y (pul′pē) *adj.* **pulp·i·er, pulp·i·est.** of pulp; like pulp; soft. —**pulp′i·ness,** *n.*

pul·sar (pul′sär) *n.* a body or mass of energy in space that emits regular, rapid, pulsating radio waves. [< *pulse* + *ar,* as in *quasar*]

pul·sate (pul′sāt) *v.* **-sat·ed, -sat·ing. 1** beat; throb: *The patient's heart was pulsating rapidly.* **2** vibrate; quiver. [< L *pulsare,* frequentative of *pellere* beat. Doublet of PUSH.]

pul·sa·tion (pul sā′shən) *n.* **1** the action of beating or vibrating. **2** a beat or vibration.

pulse¹ (puls) *n., v.* **pulsed, puls·ing.** —*n.* **1** the beating of the arteries caused by the rush of blood into them after each contraction of the heart. **2** the rate of this beating. **3** any series of regular, measured beats, waves, or vibrations: *the pulse in music, the pulse of an engine.* **4** one of the beats, waves, etc. in such a series. **5** *Physics, Electronics.* **a** a sudden, brief increase in the magnitude of a physical quantity, such as voltage or current, whose value is usually constant. **b** one of a series of such brief changes occurring at regular intervals and having a characteristic geometric shape when plotted on a graph. **c** (*adj.*) of or designating a pulse: *pulse modulation, a pulse generator.* **6** feeling; sentiment: *the pulse of the nation.* —*v.* beat, throb, or vibrate: *a heart pulsing with excitement, the pulsing of an engine.* [< L *pulsus* < *pellere* beat]

pulse² (puls) *n.* the edible seeds of peas, beans, lentils, etc. [ME < OF < L *puls* porridge]

pulse·jet (puls′jet′) *n.* a type of jet engine into which the air necessary for the burning of the fuel is admitted in spurts by valves.

pul·ver·ize (pul′vər īz′) *v.* **-ized, -iz·ing. 1** grind to powder or dust. **2** become dust. **3** break to pieces; demolish. [< LL *pulverizare* < L *pulvis, -veris* dust] —**pul′ver·i·za′tion,** *n.* —**pul′ver·iz′er,** *n.*

pu·ma (pyü′mə) *n.* cougar. [< S. < Quechua (S. Am. Ind.)]

pum·ice (pum′is) *n., v.* **-iced, -ic·ing.** —*n.* a light, spongy stone thrown up from volcanoes, used for cleaning, smoothing, and polishing. —*v.* clean, smooth, or polish with pumice. [ME < OF < L *pumex, -micis.* Doublet of POUNCE².]

pumice stone pumice.

pum·mel (pum′əl) *v.* **-melled** or **-meled, -mell·ing** or **-mel·ing.** beat; beat with the fists. Also, **pommel.**

pump¹ (pump) *n., v.* —*n.* an apparatus or machine for forcing liquids or gases into or out of things. —*v.* **1** move (liquids, air, etc.) by a pump. **2** blow air into. **3** remove water, etc. from by a pump. **4** work a pump. **5** work as a pump does. **6** move up and down like a pump handle. **7** move by, or as if by, a pump handle: *He pumped my hand.* **8** draw, force, etc. as if from a pump. **9** *Informal.* get information out of; try to get information out of: *Don't let him pump you.* [< F *pompe,* ? < Gmc.] —**pump′er,** *n.*

pump² (pump) *n.* a low-cut shoe with no laces, straps, or other fastenings. See **shoe** for picture. [origin uncertain]

pum·per·nick·el (pum′pər nik′əl) *n.* a heavy, dark, slightly sour bread made of unsifted rye flour. [< G]

pump·kin (pump′kin) *n.* **1** the edible fruit of any of certain trailing varieties of two plants (*Cucurbita pepo* and *C. moschata*) of the gourd family, usually very large and round or oblong in shape, with a smooth, orange or yellowish rind and golden flesh that is used as a vegetable and for pies, etc. **2** a vine that produces such fruits. [alteration (with substitution of -*kin*) of earlier *pumpion* < MF *pompon* < L < Gk. *pepōn*]

pump·kin·seed (pump′kin sēd′) *n.* a common North American freshwater sunfish (*Lepomis gibbosus*) having a golden brown to olive back and sides and a bronze to red-orange belly, with sides marked with blue, green, red, and orange spots and lines.

pun (pun) *n., v.* **punned, pun·ning.** —*n.* a humorous use of a word in which it can be taken as having two or more different meanings; a play on words. *Example:* "*We must all hang together, or we shall all hang separately.*" —*v.* make puns. [? < first syllable of Ital. *puntiglio* verbal quibble] —**pun′ner,** *n.*

punch¹ (punch) *v., n.* —*v.* **1** hit with the fist: *They punched each other like boxers.* **2** *Informal.* deliver with force or effectiveness. **3** herd or drive (cattle). —*n.* **1** a quick thrust or blow. **2** *Informal.* vigorous force or effectiveness: *This story lacks punch.* [? var. of *pounce¹*] —**punch′er,** *n.*

punch² (punch) *n., v.* —*n.* **1** a tool for making holes. **2** a tool or apparatus for piercing, perforating, or stamping materials, impressing a design, forcing nails beneath a surface, driving bolts out of holes, etc. —*v.* **1** make (a hole) with a punch or any pointed instrument. **2** pierce, cut, stamp, force, or drive with a punch: *The*

train conductor punched our tickets. [short for *puncheon¹*] —**punch′er,** *n.*

punch³ (punch) *n.* a drink made of different liquids mixed together. [probably < Hind. *panc* five (< Skt. *pañca*), from the number of ingredients in the drink]

Punch (punch) *n.* a hook-nosed, hump-backed doll in the puppet show *Punch and Judy.*
pleased as Punch, very much pleased.
[shortened form of *punchinello*]

Punch–and–Ju·dy show (punch′ən jü′dē) a puppet show in which Punch quarrels violently with his wife Judy.

punch card a card on which information is recorded by means of holes punched according to a code, for use in processing data by machine, electronic computer, etc.

punch–drunk (punch′drunk′) *adj.* **1** suffering from slight brain damage as a result of repeated blows to the head received in boxing. **2** *Informal.* behaving as if punch-drunk; appearing bewildered or dazed.

pun·cheon¹ (pun′chən) *n.* **1** a slab of timber, or a piece of a split log, with the face roughly smoothed. **2** a short, upright piece of wood in the frame of a building. **3** a punching or stamping tool used by goldsmiths, etc. [ME < OF *poinchon, ponson,* ult. < L *pungere* pierce]

pun·cheon² (pun′chən) *n.* **1** a large cask for liquor. **2** the amount that it holds. [ME < OF *poinchon;* origin uncertain]

pun·chi·nel·lo (pun′chə nel′ō) *n., pl.* **-los** or **-loes.** clown. [< dial. Ital. *Pulcinella,* prob. ult. < L *pullus* chick]

punching bag a leather bag filled with air or stuffed, and hung up to be punched with the fists for exercise.

punch line a telling phrase, sentence, etc. that makes the point of a joke, story, or other narrative.

punch·y (pun′chē) *adj.* **punch·i·er, punch·i·est.** *Informal.* **1** forceful or incisive: *punchy talk.* **2** punch-drunk.

punc·til·i·o (pungk til′ē ō′) *n., pl.* **-i·os. 1** a detail of honor, conduct, ceremony, etc. **2** care in attending to such details. [< Ital. < Sp. *puntillo,* ult. < L *punctum* point]

punc·til·i·ous (pungk til′ē əs) *adj.* **1** very careful and exact: *A nurse should be punctilious in obeying the doctor's orders.* **2** paying strict attention to details of conduct and ceremony.
—**punc′til′i·ous·ly,** *adv.* —**punc·til′i·ous·ness,** *n.*
➤ *Syn.* **1.** See note at **scrupulous.**

punc·tu·al (pungk′chü əl) *adj.* **1** prompt; on time: *He is punctual to the minute.* **2** being a point; resembling a point. [< Med.L *punctualis* < L *punctus* point] —**punc′tu·al·ly,** *adv.*

punc·tu·al·i·ty (pungk′chü al′ə tē) *n.* promptness; being on time.

punc·tu·ate (pungk′chü āt′) *v.* **-at·ed, -at·ing. 1** use periods, commas, and other marks in writing or printing to help make the meaning clear. **2** put punctuation marks in. **3** interrupt now and then. **4** give point or emphasis to. [< Med.L *punctuare* < L *punctus* point]

punc·tu·a·tion (pungk′chü ā′shən) *n.* **1** the use of periods, commas, and other marks in writing or printing to help make the meaning clear. Punctuation does for writing and printing what pauses and changes in the pitch of voice do for speech. **2** punctuation marks.

punctuation marks marks used in writing or printing to help make the meaning of a sentence clear. Periods, commas, question marks, colons, and exclamation marks are punctuation marks.

punc·ture (pungk′chər) *n., v.* **-tured, tur·ing.** —*n.* **1** a hole made by something pointed. **2** the act or process of puncturing. —*v.* **1** make a hole in with something pointed. **2** have or get a puncture. **3** reduce, spoil, or destroy as if by a puncture. [ME < L *punctura* < *pungere* prick]

pun·dit (pun′dit) *n.* a learned person; expert; authority. [< Hind. < Skt. *pandita* learned]

pung (pung) *n. Maritimes and New England. Historical.* a low, horse-drawn sleigh with a boxlike body. [shortened form of earlier *tom pung* < *tow-pung,* ult. < Algonquian and related to *toboggan.* See TOBOGGAN.]

pun·gen·cy (pun′jən sē) *n.* a pungent quality.

pun·gent (pun′jənt) *adj.* **1** sharply affecting the organs of taste and smell: *a pungent pickle, the pungent smell of burning leaves.* **2** sharp; biting: *pungent criticism.* **3** stimulating to the mind; keen; lively: *a pungent wit.* [< L *pungens, -entis,* ppr. of *pungere* prick] —**pun′gent·ly,** *adv.*

Pu·nic (pyü′nik) *adj.* **1** of or having to do with ancient Carthage or its inhabitants. **2** treacherous; faithless. [< L *Punicus* < *Poenus* Carthaginian (cf. Gk. *Phoinix*)]

pun·ish (pun′ish) *v.* **1** cause pain, loss, or discomfort to (a person) because of some fault or offence: *The government punishes*

criminals. **2** cause pain, loss, or discomfort for: *The law punishes crimes.* **3** *Informal.* deal with severely, roughly, or greedily. [ME < OF *puniss-*, a stem of *punir* < L *punire* < *poena* penalty] —**pun′ish·er,** *n.*

pun·ish·a·ble (pun′ish ə bəl) *adj.* **1** liable to punishment: *First-degree murder is punishable by life imprisonment.* **2** deserving punishment: *a punishable offence.*

pun·ish·ment (pun′ish mənt) *n.* **1** a punishing; being punished. **2** pain, suffering, or loss. **3** *Informal.* severe or rough treatment.

pu·ni·tive (pyü′nə tiv) *adj.* **1** concerned with punishment. **2** inflicting punishment. —**pu′ni·tive·ly,** *adv.* —**pu′ni·tive·ness,** *n.*

pu·ni·to·ry (pyü′nə tô′rē) *adj.* punitive.

Pun·ja·bi (pun jä′bē) *n., adj.* —*n.* **1** a native or inhabitant of the Punjab. **2** Panjabi. —*adj.* of or having to do with the Punjab or its people.

punk¹ (pungk) *n.* **1** decayed wood that smoulders when ignited, used as tinder. **2** a preparation that burns very slowly, especially one used to light fireworks. [< Am.Ind.]

punk² (pungk) *n., adj.* —*n.* **1** *Slang.* a young, inexperienced person, especially one regarded as presumptuous, ill-mannered, etc. **2** *Slang.* a hoodlum or petty gangster. **3** punk rock. **4** a person who follows or performs punk rock. **5** *Obsolete.* prostitute. —*adj.* **1** *Slang.* inferior in quality, condition, etc. **2** *Slang.* somewhat unwell: *I was feeling punk all day yesterday.* **3** of or designating punk rock. [origin uncertain]

pun·kah or **pun·ka** (pung′kə) *n.* in India and the East Indies, a fan, especially a large swinging fan hung from the ceiling and kept in motion by a servant or by machinery. [< Hind. *pankha*]

pun·ster (pun′stər) *n.* a person fond of making puns.

punt¹ (punt) *v., n.* —*v.* *Football.* kick (a ball) before it touches the ground after being dropped from the hands. —*n.* *Football.* such a kick: *The punt went over the goal line.* [origin uncertain]

punt² (punt) *n., v.* —*n.* a shallow, flat-bottomed boat having square ends, usually moved by pushing with a pole against the bottom of a river, etc. —*v.* **1** propel (a boat) by pushing with a pole against the bottom of a river, etc. **2** use a punt; travel by punt: *We loved to punt on the river.* [< L *ponto* punt (a kind of ship), pontoon]

punt³ (punt) *v.* **1** *Card games.* bet against the banker. **2** gamble. [< F *ponter* < Sp. *puntar,* ult. < L *punctum* point]

punt·er¹ (pun′tər) *n.* a person who punts a football.

punt·er² (pun′tər) *n.* a person who punts a boat.

punt·er³ (pun′tər) *n.* a person who bets; gambler.

pun·ty (pun′tē) *n.* a steel or iron rod used as a glass blower's tool. [var. of PONTIL.]

pu·ny (pyü′nē) *adj.* **-ni·er, -ni·est. 1** of less than usual size and strength; weak. **2** petty; not important. [< OF *puisne* later-born < *puis* (ult. < L *postea*) afterwards + *ne* born < L *natus*] —**pu′ni·ly,** *adv.* —**pu′ni·ness,** *n.*

pup (pup) *n., v.* **pupped, pup·ping.** —*n.* **1** a young dog; puppy. **2** a young fox, wolf, seal, etc. **3** a silly, conceited young man. —*v.* give birth to a pup or pups. [var. of *puppy*]

pu·pa (pyü′pə) *n., pl.* **-pae** (-pē, -pī, *or* -pā) **or -pas. 1** a stage between the larva and the adult in the development of many insects. **2** the form of an insect in this stage. Most pupae are inactive and some, such as those of many moths, are enclosed in a tough case or cocoon. [special NL use of L *pupa* girl, doll]

pu·pal (pyü′pəl) *adj.* of, having to do with, or in the form of the pupa.
☛ *Hom.* **pupil.**

pu·pate (pyü′pāt) *v.* **-pat·ed, -pat·ing.** pass through the pupal stage: *Some moths pupate in shallow chambers they have constructed in the ground.*

pu·pil¹ (pyü′pəl) *n.* a person who is learning in school or being taught by someone. [< MF < L *pupillus, pupilla* ward < *pupus* boy, *pupa* girl]
☛ *Hom.* **pupal.**
☛ *Syn.* See note at **student.**

pu·pil² (pyü′pəl) *n.* the opening in the centre of the iris of the eye which looks like a black spot. The pupil, which is the only place where light can enter the eye, expands and contracts, thus controlling the amount of light that strikes the retina. [< L *pupilla,* originally, little doll, dim. of *pupa* girl, doll]
☛ *Hom.* **pupal.**

pup·pet (pup′it) *n.* **1** a small doll. **2** a figure made to look like a person or animal and moved by wires, strings, rods, or the hands. **3** anybody who is not independent, who waits to be told how to act, or who does what somebody else says. [earlier *poppet* < OF *poupette* < L *pupa* girl, doll] —**pup′pet·like′,** *adj.*

pup·pe·teer (pup′ə tēr′) *n.* a person who designs or makes puppets or who manipulates puppets in puppet shows.

hat, āge, fär; let, ēqual, tèrm; it, īce
hot, ōpen, ôrder; oil, out; cup, put, rüle,
əbove, tākən, pencəl, lemən, circəs
ch, child; ng, long; sh, ship
th, thin; ₮н, then; zh, measure

pup·pet·ry (pup′it rē) *n.* the act of making and manipulating puppets.

pup·py (pup′ē) *n., pl.* **-pies. 1** a young dog. **2** a young fox, wolf, etc. **3** a silly, conceited young man. [probably < F *poupée* doll, ult. < L *pupa*] —**pup′py·like′,** *adj.*

puppy love sentimental love that often exists briefly between adolescent girls and boys.

pur (pèr) *n. or v.* **purred, pur·ring.** See **purr.**

pur·blind (pèr′blīnd) *adj.* **1** nearly blind. **2** slow to discern or understand. [earlier *pur blind* pure blind] —**pur′blind′ness,** *n.*

pur·chase (pèr′chəs) *v.* **-chased, -chas·ing;** *n.* —*v.* **1** get by paying a price; buy. **2** get in return for something: *to purchase safety at the cost of happiness.* —*n.* **1** the act of buying. **2** the thing bought. **3** a firm hold to help move something or to keep from slipping: *Wind the rope twice around the tree to get a better purchase.* **4** a device for obtaining such a hold. [ME < AF *purchacer* pursue < *pur-* forth (< L *pro-*) + *chacer* chase¹ < LL *captiare* < L *captare* take] —**pur′chas·er,** *n.*

pur·dah (pèr′də) *n.* in India: **1** a curtain serving to screen women from the sight of men or strangers. **2** a veil worn by women to hide the face. **3** the condition of being kept hidden from men or strangers. [< Hind. < Persian *pardah* veil, curtain]

pure (pyür) *adj.* **pur·er, pur·est;** *n.* —*adj.* **1** not mixed with anything else; unadulterated; genuine: *pure gold.* **2** perfectly clean; spotless: *pure hands.* **3** perfect; correct; without defects: *Does anyone speak pure French?* **4** nothing else than; mere; sheer: *pure accident.* **5** with no evil; without sin; chaste: *a pure mind.* **6** abstract or theoretical (opposed to *applied*): *pure mathematics.* **7** keeping the same qualities, characteristics, etc. from generation to generation; of unmixed descent: *a pure Indian family.* —*n.* that which is pure. [ME < OF < L *purus*] —**pure′ness,** *n.*

pure–bred (pyür′bred′) *adj., n.* —*adj.* designating an animal or plant whose ancestors are known to have all belonged to one breed and that will itself breed true to type: *purebred Holstein cows.* —*n.* an animal or plant of this type.

pu·rée (pyü rā′ *or* pyür′ā) *n., v.* **-réed, -ré·ing.** —*n.* **1** food boiled soft and put through a sieve or blender. **2** a thick soup. —*v.* make into a purée. [< F *purée* < *purer* strain]

pure·ly (pyür′lē) *adv.* **1** in a pure manner. **2** exclusively; entirely. **3** merely: *He scored the goal purely by chance.* **4** innocently; chastely.

pur·ga·tion (pèr gā′shən) *n.* a purging; cleansing.

pur·ga·tive (pèr′gə tiv) *n., adj.* —*n.* a medicine that empties the bowels. Castor oil is a purgative. —*adj.* purging. [ME < L *purgativus* < *purgare.* See PURGE.]

pur·ga·to·ri·al (pèr′gə tô′rē əl) *adj.* of, like, or having to do with purgatory.

pur·ga·to·ry (pèr′gə tô′rē) *n., pl.* **-ries. 1** *Roman Catholic Church.* a temporary condition or place in which the souls of those who have died penitent are purified from sin or the effects of sin by punishment. **2** any condition or place of temporary suffering or punishment. [< Med.L *purgatorium,* originally neut. adj., purging < L *purgare.* See PURGE.]

purge (pèrj) *v.* **purged, purg·ing;** *n.* —*v.* **1** wash away all that is not clean from; make clean. **2** become clean. **3** clear of any undesired thing or person, such as air in a water pipe or opponents in a nation. **4** empty (the bowels). **5** clear of defilement or imputed guilt. —*n.* **1** the act of purging. **2** a medicine that purges. **3** the elimination of undesired persons from a nation or party. [ME < OF < L *purgare* cleanse, ult. < *purus* pure + *agere* drive]

pu·ri·fi·ca·tion (pyür′ə fə kā′shən) *n.* purifying; being purified.

pu·ri·fy (pyür′ə fī′) *v.* **-fied, -fy·ing. 1** make free from impurities, contamination, etc.: *to purify water. The blood is purified in the lungs before it returns to the heart.* **2** make free from sin or guilt: *to purify the heart.* **3** make ceremonially clean: *to purify the altar.* **4** make free from blemish or corruption: *a country purified of sedition.* **5** become pure. [ME < OF < L *purificare* < *purus* pure + *facere* make] —**pu′ri·fi′er,** *n.*

Pu·rim (pyür′im *or* pür′im; *Hebrew,* pü rēm′) *n.* a Jewish religious festival, celebrated each year in February or March, commemorating Esther's deliverance of the Jews from being

massacred by Haman (Esther 9:20-32). [< Hebrew *purim*, pl. of *pur* lot]

pur·ism (pyür′iz əm) *n.* an insistence on purity and correctness, especially in language or art.

pur·ist (pyür′ist) *n.* 1 a person who is very careful or too careful about purity and correctness, especially in language. A purist dislikes slang and all expressions that are not formally correct. 2 anyone overcareful about principles of purity in art.

pu·ris·tic (pyü ris′tik) *adj.* very careful or too careful about purity and correctness, especially in language.

Pu·ri·tan (pyür′ə tən) *n., adj.* —*n.* 1 during the 16th and 17th centuries, a member of a group in the Church of England who wanted simple forms of worship and stricter morals. 2 **puritan**, a person who is very strict in morals and religion. —*adj.* 1 of the Puritans. 2 **puritan**, very strict in morals and religion. [< LL *puritas* purity + E *-an*]

pu·ri·tan·ic (pyür′ə tan′ik) *adj.* puritanical.

pu·ri·tan·i·cal (pyür′ə tan′ə kəl) *adj.* of or like a puritan; very strict or too strict in morals or religion. —**pur′i·tan′i·cal·ly,** *adv.*

Pu·ri·tan·ism (pyür′ə ten iz′əm) *n.* the principles and practices of the Puritans.

pu·ri·ty (pyür′ə tē) *n.* 1 freedom from dirt or mixture; clearness; cleanness. 2 freedom from evil; innocence. 3 freedom from foreign or inappropriate elements; correctness: *purity of style.* [< LL *puritas* < *purus* pure]

purl[1] (pėrl) *v., n.* —*v.* flow with rippling motions and a murmuring sound: *A shallow brook purls.* —*n.* a purling motion or sound. [? < Scand.; cf. Norwegian *purla*]
☞ *Hom.* **pearl.**

purl[2] (pėrl) *v., n.* —*v.* 1 knit with inverted stitches. 2 border (material) with small loops. 3 *Archaic.* embroider with gold or silver thread. —*n.* 1 an inversion of stitches in knitting, producing a ribbed appearance. 2 a loop or chain of small loops along the edge of lace, braid, ribbon, etc. 3 a thread of twisted gold or silver wire. [< *pirl* twist; origin uncertain]
☞ *Hom.* **pearl.**

pur·lieu (pėr′lü) *n.* 1 a piece of land on the border of a forest. 2 one's haunt or resort; one's bounds. 3 any bordering, neighboring, or outlying region or district. [alteration of earlier *puraley* (influenced by F *lieu* place) < AF *puralee* < *poraler* go through < *por-* forth (< L *pro-*) + *aler* go]

pur·lin or **pur·line** (pėr′lən) *n.* a horizontal beam running the length of a roof and supporting the top rafters of the roof. [ME; ? < OF]

pur·loin (pėr loin′) *v.* steal. [ME < AF *purloigner* remove < *pur-* forth (< L *pro-*) + *loin* afar < L *longe*] —**pur·loin′er,** *n.*

pur·ple (pėr′pəl) *n., adj., v.* **-pled, -pling.** —*n.* 1 a color made by mixing red and blue. 2 Tyrian purple. 3 a dye or pigment that produces purple. 4 cloth or clothing of this color, especially as worn to symbolize noble or royal rank. 5 Usually, **the purple,** noble or royal rank. 6 the rank, position, or authority of a cardinal. —*adj.* 1 of the color purple. 2 noble or royal. 3 of rhetorical style, excessively elaborate and showy: *purple prose.*
turn purple, become very angry or furious.
—*v.* make or become purple. [OE *purple*, var. of *purpure* < L *purpura* < Gk. *porphyra* a shellfish, or the purple dye from it]

purple martin a large New World swallow (*Progne subis*) having a stout bill and forked tail, the adult male having dark, glossy, purplish-blue plumage.

pur·plish (pėr′plish) *adj.* somewhat purple.

pur·port (*v.* pər pôrt′ or pėr′pôrt; *n.* pėr′pôrt) *v., n.* —*v.* 1 claim; profess: *The document purported to be official.* 2 have as its main idea; mean. —*n.* the meaning; main idea. [ME < AF *purporter* < *pur-* forth (< L *pro-*) + *porter* carry < L *portare*]
☞ *Syn. n.* See note at **meaning.**

pur·pose (pėr′pəs) *n., v.* **-posed, -pos·ing.** —*n.* 1 something one intends to get or do; plan; aim; intention: *His purpose was to pass his exams.* 2 an object or end for which a thing is made, done, used, etc.: *What is the purpose of this machine?*
on purpose, with a purpose; not by accident: *He tripped me on purpose.*
to good purpose, with good results.
to little (or **no**) **purpose,** with few (or no) results.
—*v.* plan; aim; intend. [ME < OF *pourpos* < *pourposer* propose < *pour-* (< L *pro-*) + *poser* (see POSE[1])]
☞ *Syn. n.* **1.** See note at **intention.**

pur·pose·ful (pėr′pəs fəl) *adj.* having or showing conscious

intention: *He walked with a purposeful stride.* —**pur′pose·ful·ly,** *adv.* —**pur′pose·ful·ness,** *n.*

pur·pose·less (pėr′pəs lis) *adj.* lacking a purpose. —**pur′pose·less·ly,** *adv.* —**pur′pose·less·ness,** *n.*

pur·pose·ly (pėr′pəs lē) *adv.* on purpose; intentionally.

pur·pos·ive (pėr′pə siv) *adj.* 1 having a function or use; useful: *purposive accuracy and precision.* 2 having or showing conscious intention; purposeful: *a purposive steadfastness.*

purr (pėr) *n., v.* —*n.* a low, murmuring sound such as a cat makes when pleased. —*v.* make a low, murmuring sound. Also, **pur.** [imitative]

purse (pėrs) *n., v.* **pursed, purs·ing.** —*n.* 1 a bag or case for carrying money, usually carried in a handbag or pocket. 2 handbag: *She put her keys and gloves in her purse.* 3 money; resources; treasury: *The family purse affords a vacation.* 4 a sum of money offered as a prize or gift: *A purse was made up for the victims of the fire.*
—*v.* draw together; press into folds or wrinkles. [OE *purs* < LL *bursa* < Gk. *byrsa* hide, skin. Doublet of BOURSE, BURSA.]

purse–proud (pėrs′proud′) *adj.* proud of being rich.

purs·er (pėr′sər) *n.* an officer who keeps the accounts of a ship or airplane, pays wages, and attends to other matters of business.

purse seine a large fishing net held by two boats, one on each side of a school of fish, so arranged that the ends can be pulled like a purse to enclose the fish.

purse strings strings pulled to close a purse.
control or **hold the purse strings,** control the expenditure of money.
tighten (or **loosen**) **the purse strings,** be sparing (or generous) in spending money.

purs·lane (pėrs′lān or pėrs′lən) *n.* 1 any of various low-growing plants (genus *Portulaca*), especially a common, troublesome weed (*P. oleracea*) having prostrate reddish stems, fleshy leaves, and small yellow flowers. 2 (*adj.*) designating the family (Portulacaceae) of herbs and a few small shrubs that includes purslane, portulaca, spring beauty, etc. [ME < OF *porcelaine*, alteration of L *porcilaca*, var. of *portulaca*]

pur·su·ance (pər sü′əns) *n.* a following; carrying out; pursuit: *to risk one's life in pursuance of one's duty.*

pur·su·ant (pər sü′ənt) *adj.* following; carrying out; according.
pursuant to, following; carrying out; according.

pur·sue (pər sü′) *v.* **-sued, -su·ing.** 1 follow to catch or kill; chase. 2 proceed along; follow in action; follow: *He pursued a wise course, taking no chances.* 3 strive for; try to get; seek: *to pursue pleasure.* 4 carry on; keep on with: *She pursued the study of French for four years.* 5 continue to annoy or trouble: *to pursue a person with questions.* [ME < AF *pursuer*, ult. < L *prosequi.* See PROSECUTE.] —**pur·su′a·ble,** *adj.* —**pur·su′er,** *n.*

pur·suit (pər süt′) *n.* 1 the act of pursuing; chase. 2 an occupation or pastime.

pursuit plane a fighter aircraft that has high speed and a high rate of climb, and that can be manoeuvred with ease.

pur·sui·vant (pėr′swə vənt) *n.* 1 an assistant to a herald; officer below a herald in rank. 2 a follower; attendant. [ME < OF *poursuivant*, originally ppr. of *poursuivre* purse, ult. < L *prosequi.* See PURSUE.]

pur·sy (pėr′sē) *adj.* **-si·er, -si·est.** 1 shortwinded or puffy. 2 fat. [ME < AF *pursif*, var. of OF *polsif* < *polser* pant] —**pur′si·ness,** *n.*

pu·ru·lence (pyür′ə ləns or pyür′yə ləns) *n.* the formation or discharge of pus; suppuration.

pu·ru·len·cy (pyür′ə lən sē or pyür′yə lən sē) *n.* purulence.

pu·ru·lent (pyür′ə lənt or pyür′yə lənt) *adj.* 1 full of pus; discharging pus; like pus: *a purulent sore.* 2 corrupt; rotten cheap. [< L *purulentus* < *pus* pus] —**pu′ru·lent·ly,** *adv.*

pur·vey (pėr vā′) *v.* supply (food or provisions); provide; furnish: *to purvey meat for an army, to purvey for a royal household.* [ME < AF *porveier* < L *providere.* Doublet of PROVIDE.]

pur·vey·ance (pėr vā′əns) *n.* 1 the act of purveying. 2 provisions; supplies. 3 *Historical.* in England, the right of the king or queen to supplies, use of horses, and personal service.

pur·vey·or (pėr vā′ər) *n.* 1 a person who supplies provisions. 2 a person who supplies anything. 3 *Historical.* in England, an officer who provided or exacted food, etc. in accordance with the right of purveyance.

pur·view (pėr′vyü) *n.* a range of operation, activity, concern, etc.; scope; extent. [ME < AF *purveu*, originally pp. of *proveier* purvey. See PURVEY.]

pus (pus) *n.* a liquid formed by inflammation of infected tissue in the body, consisting of white blood cells, bacteria, serum, etc. [< L]

push (push) *v., n.* —*v.* 1 move (something) away by pressing against it: *Push the door; don't pull it.* 2 move up, down, back,

forward, etc. by pressing: *Push him outdoors.* **3** thrust: *Trees push their roots down into the ground.* **4** press hard: *to push with all one's might.* **5** go forward by force: *to push on at a rapid pace.* **6** force (one's way): *We had to push our way through the crowd.* **7** make go forward; urge: *He pushed his plans cleverly.* **8** continue with; follow up: *to push a claim.* **9** extend: *Alexander pushed his conquests still farther east.* **10** *Informal.* urge the use, sale, etc. of.
push around, *Informal.* treat roughly or with contempt; bully.
push off, a move from shore: *We pushed off in the boat.* **b** *Informal.* go away; depart.
—*n.* **1** *Informal.* force; energy. **2** the act of pushing. **3** a hard effort; determined advance. [ME < OF < L *pulsare* beat. Doublet of PULSATE.]
☛ *Syn. v.* **1. Push, shove** = move someone or something by pressing against it. **Push** emphasizes pressing against the person or thing in order to move it ahead, aside, etc. away from oneself or something else: *She pushed the drawer shut.* **Shove** emphasizes moving someone or something out of the way by pushing roughly, or something hard to move or heavy by pushing it along with force and effort: *He shoved his way through the crowd. He shoved the piano across the room.*

push·ball (pùsh'bol' *or* -bôl') *n.* **1** a game played with a large, heavy ball, usually about 180 cm in diameter. Two sides of players try to push the ball toward opposite goals. **2** the ball used in this game.

push button a small button or knob that is pushed to close or open an electric circuit.

push–but·ton (pùsh'but'ən) *adj.* operated by means of a push button or buttons: *a push-button telephone.*

push·cart (pùsh'kärt') *n.* a light cart pushed by hand.

push·er (pùsh'ər) *n.* **1** a person or thing that pushes. **2** an airplane with propeller behind instead of in front. **3** *Slang.* a person who sells drugs illegally.

push–o·ver (pùsh'ō'vər) *n. Slang.* **1** something very easy to do. **2** a person very easy to beat in a contest. **3** a person easily influenced or swayed or unable to resist a particular appeal.

push–up *or* **push·up** (pùsh'up') *n.* **1** an exercise performed in a prone position, in which the person alternately raises and lowers his body by straightening and bending the arms while keeping the body and legs straight. **2** *Cdn.* a structure of grass and other vegetation pushed by a muskrat into a breathing-hole in the ice to keep it from freezing up; used also by the muskrat as a home or shelter.

push·y (pùsh'ē) *adj.* offensively forceful and aggressive.

pu·sil·la·nim·i·ty (pyü'sə lə nim'ə tē) *n.* cowardliness; timidity.

pu·sil·lan·i·mous (pyü'sə lan'ə məs) *adj.* cowardly; mean-spirited; faint-hearted. [< L *pusillanimus* < *pusillus* little + *animus* courage] —**pu'sil·lan'i·mous·ly,** *adv.*

puss¹ (pùs) *n.* **1** cat. **2** girl. [cf. Du. *poes,* LG *puus, puss-katte*]

puss² (pùs) *n. Slang.* the face; mouth. [< Irish Gaelic *pus* mouth, lips]

puss·y¹ (pùs'ē) *n., pl.* **puss·ies. 1** cat. **2** catkin. [dim. of *puss*]

puss·y² (pùs'ē) *adj.* **-si·er, -si·est.** full of pus. [< *pus* + *-y¹*]

puss·y·foot (pùs'ē fùt') *v., n., pl.* **-foots.** *Informal.* —*v.* **1** move softly and cautiously to avoid being noticed. **2** be cautious and timid about revealing one's opinions or committing oneself. —*n.* a person who pussyfoots.

pussy willow a North American willow (*Salix discolor*) having soft, furry, silvery grey catkins that appear before the leaves and are looked for as a harbinger of spring. Pussy willow branches with young catkins are often dried and kept for ornament.

pus·tu·lar (pus'chə lər) *adj.* of, like, or having to do with pustules; characterized by pustules.

pus·tu·late (*v.* pus'chə lāt'; *adj.* pus'chə lit) *v.* **-lat·ed, -lat·ing;** *adj.* —*v.* form or cover with pustules. —*adj.* having pustules. [< L *pustulare* < *pustula* + E *-ate¹*]

pus·tu·la·tion (pus'chə lā'shən) *n.* the formation of pustules.

pus·tule (pus'chül) *n.* **1** a pimple containing pus. **2** any swelling like a pimple or blister, such as the pustules of chicken pox. [< L *pustula* < *pus* pus]

put (pùt) *v.* **put, put·ting;** *n.* —*v.* **1** cause to be in some place or position; place; lay: *I put sugar in my tea. Put away your toys.* **2** cause to be in some state, condition, position, relation, etc.: *The murderer was put to death. Put your room in order.* **3** express: *The teacher puts things clearly.* **4** propose or submit for answer, consideration, deliberation, etc.: *He put several questions before me. Put one's course.* **5** take one's course; go; turn; proceed: *The ship put out to sea.* **6** throw or cast with an overhand motion from the shoulder: *to put the shot.* **7** set at a particular place, point, amount, etc. in a scale of estimation; appraise: *He puts the distance at five kilometres.* **8** apply: *A doctor puts his skill to good use.* **9** impose: *to put a tax on gasoline.* **10** assign; attribute: *He put a wrong construction on my action.*

hat, āge, fär; let, ēqual, tèrm; it, īce
hot, ōpen, ôrder; oil, out; cup, pút, rüle,
above, takən, pencəl, lemən, circəs

ch, child; ng, long; sh, ship
th, thin; ⱦH, then; zh, measure

put about, a put (a ship) on the opposite tack. **b** change direction.
put across, *Informal.* **a** carry out successfully. **b** get accepted.
put aside *or* **by, a** save for future use. **b** set aside; turn away.
put away, a lay aside for future use: *I've already put my winter clothes away for the summer.* **b** *Slang.* consume (food, drink, etc.) **c** *Informal.* kill (a pet or other domestic animal) to prevent suffering, etc.: *We had to put our dog away after she was hit by a car.* **d** *Slang.* commit to a prison, mental hospital, etc.: *The judge put him away for ten years.* **e** *Slang.* pawn. **f** *Archaic.* divorce.
put down, a put an end to; suppress. **b** write down. **c** pay as a down payment. **d** preserve. **e** snub; belittle. **f** *Esp.Brit.* put (an animal) to death humanely; put to sleep.
put forth, a stretch. **b** grow; sprout; issue: *to put forth buds.* **c** use fully; exert: *to put forth effort.* **d** start, especially to sea.
put in, a *Informal.* spend time doing; do; accomplish: *He always puts in a good day's work.* **b** enter port. **c** enter a place for safety, supplies, etc. **d** make a claim, plea, or offer: *She put in for a loan.*
put off, a lay aside; postpone: *Don't put off going to the dentist.* **b** go away; start out: *The ship put off for England.* **c** bid or cause to wait. **d** get rid of.
put on, a clothe or adorn oneself with; don: *She put on her new hat.* **b** assume or take on, especially as a pretence: *She put on an air of innocence.* **c** add to; increase: *The driver put on speed.* **d** apply or exert: *to put on pressure.* **e** advance; move ahead: *to put on the clock.* **f** present on a stage; produce: *The class put on a play.*
put out, a extinguish. **b** confuse; embarrass. **c** distract, disturb, or interrupt. **d** destroy (an eye, etc.). **e** cause to be out in a game. **f** dislocate: *I put out my knee when I fell.* **g** publish. **h** offend; provoke.
put over, *Informal.* **a** carry out successfully. **b** impose (something false or deceptive) on a person.
put through, carry out successfully.
put to it, force to a course; put in difficulty.
put up, a offer; give; show: *to put up a house for sale.* **b** make. **c** build: *to put up a monument.* **d** lay aside. **e** put in its usual place. **f** prepare or pack up (food) for later use. **g** preserve (fruit, etc.). **h** give lodging or food to. **i** *Informal.* incite: *Who put you up to this?* **j** make available: *He put up the money for the car.* **k** *Informal.* plan beforehand craftily.
put upon, impose upon; take advantage of; victimize.
put up with, bear with patience; tolerate.
—*n.* a throw or cast. [cf. OE *putung* impulse]
☛ *Syn. v.* **1, 2. Put, place, set** = cause someone or something to be in some place, position, condition, relation, etc. **Put** emphasizes the action of moving something into or out of a place or position or bringing it into some condition, state, or relation: *Put your hand in mine.* **Place** emphasizes the idea of a definite spot, condition, etc. more than action: *Place your hands behind your head.* **Set** emphasizes causing to be in a stated or certain position, etc.: *Set the box down over there.*

pu·ta·tive (pyü'tə tiv) *adj.* supposed; reputed: *the putative author of a book.* [< L *putativus* < *putare* think] —**pu'ta·tive·ly,** *adv.*

put·down (pùt'doun') *n. Informal.* **1** a slighting or belittling of a person or thing. **2** a comment, reply, etc. intended to snub or belittle.

put–on (pùt'on') *adj., n.* —*adj.* assumed; affected; pretended. —*n.* **1** a pretension or affectation. **2** *Slang.* a mischievous joke or trick played for fun; practical joke; hoax.

put–put (put'put') *n., v.* **-put·ted, -put·ting.** —*n.* **1** the series of short, explosive sounds made by a small motor. **2** a small boat or other vehicle run by such a motor. **3** the motor itself. —*v.* move or travel by means of this type of motor.

pu·tre·fac·tion (pyü'trə fak'shən) *n.* decay; rotting.

pu·tre·fac·tive (pyü'trə fak'tiv) *adj.* **1** causing putrefaction. **2** characterized by or having to do with putrefaction.

pu·tre·fy (pyü'trə fī') *v.* **-fied, -fy·ing.** rot; decay. [ME < OF < L *putrifieri,* ult. < *puter* rotten + *fieri* become]

pu·tres·cence (pyü tres'əns) *n.* a putrescent condition.

pu·tres·cent (pyü tres'ənt) *adj.* **1** becoming putrid; rotting. **2** having to do with putrefaction. [< L *putrescens, -entis,* ppr. of *putrescere* grow rotten, ult. < *puter* rotten]

pu·trid (pyü'trid) *adj.* **1** rotten; foul. **2** thoroughly corrupt or depraved; extremely bad. **3** gangrenous: *putrid flesh.* [< L *putridus,* ult. < *puter* rotten] —**pu'trid·ly,** *adv.* —**pu'trid·ness,** *n.*

pu·trid·i·ty (pyü trid′ə tē) n. 1 a putrid condition. 2 putrid matter.

putt (put) v., n. Golf. —v. strike (a ball) gently and carefully in an effort to make it roll into the hole. —n. the stroke itself. [var. of put]

put·tee (put′ē or pu tē′) n. 1 a long, narrow strip of cloth wound round the leg from ankle to knee, formerly worn by soldiers, sportsmen, etc. 2 a legging of leather or cloth reaching from ankle to knee, worn by soldiers, riders, etc. [< Hind. patti bandage, strip] ☛ Hom. putty (put′ē).

put·ter¹ (put′ər) v. keep busy in a rather useless way. Also, **potter.** [var. of potter²] —**put′ter·er,** n.

putt·er² (put′ər) n. 1 a person who putts. 2 Golf. a club with an upright face and a short, rigid shaft, used in putting. [< putt]

put·ter³ (pŭt′ər) n. one that puts. [< put]

putt·ing green (put′ing) that part of a golf course within about 18 metres of a hole, except the hazards; the smooth turf or sand around a golf hole.

put·ty (put′ē) n., pl. -ties; v. -tied, -ty·ing. —n. 1 a soft mixture of whiting and linseed oil, used mainly for fastening panes of glass into window frames. 2 a pipe-joint compound. 3 the color of putty, a kind of light grey. —v. fix, cement, stop up, or cover with putty: to putty holes in woodwork. [< F potée, originally, potful < pot pot] —**put′ti·er,** n. ☛ Hom. **puttee.**

put–up (pŭt′up′) adj. Informal. planned beforehand, or deliberately, in a secret or crafty manner: a put-up job.

puz·zle (puz′əl) n., v. -zled, -zling. —n. 1 a difficult problem. 2 a problem or task to be done for fun. 3 a puzzled condition. —v. 1 make unable to answer, solve, or understand something; perplex. 2 exercise one's mind on something hard.
puzzle out, find out by thinking or trying hard: to puzzle out the meaning of a sentence.
puzzle over, think hard about; try hard to do or work out: They puzzled over their arithmetic.
[origin uncertain] —**puz′zler,** n.
☛ Syn. v. 1. Puzzle, perplex, bewilder = make a person uncertain what to think, say, or do. Puzzle suggests a problem having so many parts or sides and being so mixed up or involved that it is hard to understand or solve: My friend's behavior puzzles me. Perplex adds the idea of troubling with doubt about how to decide or act: The boy's obstinacy perplexes his parents. Bewilder adds to and emphasizes the idea of confusing and causing one to feel lost among all the various possibilities: City traffic bewilders him.

puz·zled (puz′əld) adj. not understanding; unable to find an answer or solve a problem: We could see by the frown on his face that he was puzzled. —**puz′zled·ly,** adv.

puz·zle·ment (puz′əl mənt) n. a puzzled condition.

PVC polyvinyl chloride.

pwt. pennyweight.

PX or **P.X.** Esp.U.S. post exchange.

pya (pyä or pē yä′) n. 1 a unit of money in Burma, equal to 1/100 of a kyat. 2 a coin worth one pya. [< Burmese]

py·e·mi·a or **py·ae·mi·a** (pī ē′mē ə) n. a form of blood poisoning caused by bacteria that produce pus. [< NL < Gk. pyon pus + haima blood]

Pyg·ma·li·on (pig mā′lē ən or -māl′yən) n. Greek mythology. a sculptor who made a statue of a woman and then fell in love with it. Aphrodite gave the statue life, and it became Galatea.

pyg·my (pig′mē) n., pl. -mies; adj. —n. 1 Pygmy, a a member of a small people of equatorial Africa, usually less than 150 cm tall. b a member of a race of dwarfs described by ancient authors as living in Ethiopia or India. 2 a very short or insignificant person. 3 anything that is unusually small for its kind; dwarf.
—adj. unusually or abnormally small or insignificant. Also, **pigmy.**
[< L < Gk. pygmaioi, originally pl. adj., dwarfish < pygmē cubit, fist]
☛ Syn. See note at **dwarf.**

py·ja·mas or **pa·ja·mas** (pə jam′əz or pə jä′məz) n.pl., adj. —n. 1 garments for sleeping or lounging in, consisting of a loose jacket or top and a pair of loose pants usually having an elastic or drawstring waist. 2 loose trousers worn by men and women in various Middle Eastern and Eastern countries. —adj. **pyjama** or **pajama,** of or forming a part of pyjamas: pyjama pants. [< Hind. < Persian paejamah < pae leg + jamah garment]

py·lon (pī′lon) n. 1 a post or tower for guiding aircraft pilots. 2 a tall steel framework used to carry high-tension wires across country. 3 either of a pair of high supporting structures marking an entrance at either end of a bridge. 4 a gateway, particularly of an ancient Egyptian temple. [< Gk. pylōn gateway < pylē gate]

py·lor·ic (pī lôr′ik) adj. of or having to do with the pylorus.

py·lo·rus (pī lô′rəs) n., pl. -ri (rī or -rē). Anatomy. the opening that leads from the stomach into the intestine. [< LL < Gk. pylōros, originally, gatekeeper < pylē gate + -horos watching (cf. horaein see)]

py·or·rhe·a or **py·or·rhoe·a** (pī′ə rē′ə) n. a disease of the gums in which pockets of pus form about the teeth, the gums shrink, and the teeth become loose. [< NL < Gk. pyon pus + rhoia a flow < rheein flow]

pyr·a·mid (pir′ə mid′) n., v. —n. 1 Geometry. a solid having a polygon for its base and having triangular sides meeting in a point. See **solid** for picture. 2 any structure or object having a form similar to this. 3 any of the huge, massive stone pyramids, having four triangular sides, built by the ancient Egyptians to serve as royal tombs.
—v. 1 be or put in the form of a pyramid. 2 raise or increase (costs, wages, etc.) gradually. 3 increase (one's operations) in buying or selling stock on margin by using the profit to buy or sell more. [< L < Gk. pyramis, -idos < Egyptian]

py·ram·i·dal (pə ram′ə dəl) adj. shaped like a pyramid.

pyre (pīr) n. 1 a pile of wood on which a dead body is burned as a funeral rite. 2 any large pile or heap of burnable material. [< L < Gk. pyra < pyr fire]

Pyr·e·ne·an (pir′ə nē′ən) adj. of the Pyrenees, a mountain range between France and Spain.

py·re·thrum (pī rē′thrəm) n., pl. -thrums. 1 any of several Eurasian chrysanthemums cultivated for their showy red, white, or lilac flowers or as a source of insecticide. 2 an insecticide prepared from the dried flower heads of some of these plants. [< L pyrethrum feverfew < Gk. pyrethron, probably < pyr fire]

py·ret·ic (pī ret′ik) adj. 1 of or having to do with fever. 2 producing fever. 3 feverish. [< NL < Gk. pyretos fever < pyr fire]

Py·rex (pī′reks) n. Trademark. a kind of glassware that is highly resistant to heat.

pyr·i·dox·ine (pir′ə dok′sēn or pir′ə dok′sən) n. vitamin B₆, essential to human nutrition, found in wheat germ, fish, liver, etc. Formula: $C_8H_{11}O_3N$

py·rite (pī′rīt) n. a common mineral consisting of iron sulphide, having a yellow color and a metallic glitter that suggests gold; fool's gold. Formula: FeS_2 [< L < Gk. pyritēs flint < pyr fire]

py·ri·tes (pī rī′tēz or pī′rīts) n.pl. any of various compounds of sulphur and a metal: Pyrite is the commonest pyrites.

pyro– combining form. fire, as in pyrography. [< Gk. pyr, pyros]

py·rog·ra·phy (pī rog′rə fē) n. the art of burning designs on wood, leather, etc.

py·ro·hy (per′ō hā′ or pir′ō hē′) n.pl. 1 pastry turnovers filled with meat, cheese, vegetables, etc. 2 varenyky. [< W Ukrainian (Ukrainian perogy, Russian pirogi) < Old Slavic pir feast + og]

py·ro·ma·ni·a (pī′rə mā′nē ə) n. an obsessive desire to set things on fire.

py·ro·ma·ni·ac (pī′rə mā′nē ak′) n. a person affected with pyromania.

py·ro·ma·ni·a·cal (pī′rō mə nī′ə kəl) adj. 1 caused by a pyromaniac. 2 of or having a tendency toward pyromania.

py·ro·met·al·lur·gi·cal (pī′rō met′əl ėr′jə kəl) adj. of or having to do with pyrometallurgy.

py·ro·met·al·lur·gy (pī rō met′əl ėr′jē; also, esp.Brit., pī′rō mə tal′ər jē) n. the branch of metallurgy involving processes that depend on high temperatures, such as smelting, sintering, and casting.

py·ro·tech·nic (pī′rə tek′nik) adj. 1 of or having to do with fireworks. 2 resembling fireworks; brilliant; sensational: pyrotechnic eloquence.

py·ro·tech·ni·cal (pī′rə tek′nə kəl) adj. pyrotechnic.

py·ro·tech·nics (pī′rə tek′niks) n. 1 the making of fireworks. 2 use of fireworks. 3 a display of fireworks. 4 a brilliant or sensational display.

py·rox·y·lin (pī rok′sə lin) n. any of various substances made by nitrating certain forms of cellulose. Guncotton and the soluble cellulose nitrates used in making celluloid, collodion, etc. are pyroxylins. [< pyro– + Gk. xylon wood]

Pyr·rhic (pir′ik) adj. of or having to do with Pyrrhus, King of Epirus.

Pyrrhic victory a victory won at too great a cost, so named after Pyrrhus, who won a battle with an enormous loss of life. [< Pyrrhus, king of Epirus in Greece, 300-272 B.C.]

pyr·rho·tite (pir′ə tīt′) n. a bronze-colored, slightly magnetic iron sulphide, sometimes containing nickel. Formula: FeS [< Gk.

pyrrhotēs redness < *pyrrhos* fiery red < *pyr*
fire (because of its color) + E -*ite*[1]]

Py·thag·o·re·an (pə thag′ə rē′ən) *adj., n.* —*adj.* of or having to
do with Pythagoras (582?-500? B.C.), a Greek philosopher and
mathematician, his teachings, or his followers. —*n.* a follower of
Pythagoras.

Pyth·i·a (pith′ē ə) *n.* the priestess of Apollo at Delphi, who
delivered the divine responses to questions asked of the oracle.

Pyth·i·an (pith′ē ən) *adj.* of or having to do with Apollo or the
oracle at Delphi. [< L < Gk. *Pythios* of Delphi (earlier called
Pytho), or the Delphic Apollo]

Pythian games in ancient Greece, one of the great Panhellenic
festivals, held every four years at Delphi in honor of Apollo.

Pyth·i·as (pith′ē əs) *n. Roman legend.* a man famous for his
devoted friendship with Damon, who pledged his life for him. See
Damon.

py·thon (pī′thon *or* pī′thən) *n.* **1** any of a subfamily (Pythoninae)
of large, nonvenomous, Old World snakes of the same family as the
boas, that kill their prey by constriction but, unlike the boas, lay
eggs rather than bearing live young. The **reticulated python** (*Python
reticulatus*), which may reach a length of over nine metres, is one of
the largest snakes in the world. **2** any large constricting snake. [< L
< Gk.]

hat, āge, fàr; let, ēqual, tèrm; it, īce
hot, ōpen, ôrder; oil, out; cup, pút, rüle,
əbove, takən, pencəl, leman, circəs

ch, child; ng, long; sh, ship
th, thin; ᴛʜ, then; zh, measure

py·tho·ness (pī′thə nis) *n.* **1** the priestess of Apollo at Delphi,
who gave out the answers of the oracle. **2** any prophetess. [earlier
phytoness < OF < LL *pythonissa* < Gk. *pythōn* familiar spirit <
Pythō, seat of the Delphic oracle]

pyx (piks) *n.* **1** *Ecclesiastical.* a box in which the bread of the
Eucharist is kept or carried. **2** a box at the British mint in which
specimen coins are kept to be tested for weight and purity. [< L <
Gk. *pyxis* < *pyxos* boxwood]

pyx·id·i·um (piks id′ē əm) *n., pl.* **-i·a** (-ē ə). the fruit of certain
plants such as the plantain or portulaca, consisting of a dry seed
capsule having a caplike upper part that falls off when the capsule is
mature, releasing the seeds. [< NL < Gk. *pyxidion*, dim. of *pyxis*
box. See PYX.]

pyx·is (pik′sis) *n.* pyxidium.

Q q

q or **Q** (kyü) *n., pl.* **q's** or **Q's.** 1 the seventeenth letter of the English alphabet. 2 any speech sound represented by this letter. 3 a person or thing identified as *q*, especially the seventeenth in a series. 4 (*adjl.*) of or being a Q or q.

q. 1 quart(s). 2 quarterly.

Q. 1 Queen. 2 question; query. 3 quarto. 4 quire. 5 quarterly.

Q.B. Queen's Bench.

Q.C. or **QC** Queen's Counsel.

Q.E.D. which was to be demonstrated or proved (for L *quod erat demonstrandum*).

qin·tar (kin tär') *n.* a unit of money in Albania, equal to 1/100 of a lek. [< Albanian, akin to *quintal*]

qiv·i·ut (kiv'ē ùt') *n.* the soft, silky underfur of the arctic muskox, used as a textile fibre. [< Inuktitut (Eskimo)]

Q.M. or **QM** quartermaster.

Q.M.G. or **QMG** quartermaster-general.

qr. 1 quarter; quarterly. 2 quire.

Q.R. Queen's Regulations.

qt. 1 quart(s). 2 quantity.

q.t. or **Q.T.** *Slang.* quiet.
on the q.t., very secretly; quietly.

qto. quarto.

qu. 1 quart. 2 quarterly. 3 question.

qua (kwā *or* kwä) *adv.* as; in the capacity of: *Qua father, he pitied the boy; qua judge, he condemned him.* [< L *qua*, abl. fem. sing. of rel. pron, *qui* who]

quack¹ (kwak) *n., v.* —*n.* 1 the sound a duck makes. 2 any similar sound. —*v.* make the sound of a duck or one like it. [imitative]

quack² (kwak) *n., adj.* —*n.* 1 a person who practises as a doctor but lacks professional training. 2 an ignorant pretender to knowledge or skill of any sort. —*adj.* 1 used by quacks. 2 not genuine: *quack medicine.* [short for *quacksalver*]

quack·er·y (kwak'ər ē) *n., pl.* **-er·ies.** the practices or methods of a quack.

quack grass couch grass, a common, very troublesome weed.

quack·sal·ver (kwak'sal'vər) *n. Archaic.* a quack doctor. [< earlier Du. *quacksalver < quacken* boast of + *salf* salve]

quad¹ (kwod) *n. Esp.Brit. Informal.* a quadrangle of a college.

quad² (kwod) *n. Informal.* quadruplet.

quad³ (kwod) *n.* quadrat.

quad⁴ (kwod) *adj., n. Informal.* —*adj.* quadraphonic. —*n.* quadraphonics.

Quad·ra·ges·i·ma (kwod'rə jes'ə mə) *n.* 1 the first Sunday in Lent. 2 the forty days of Lent. [< L *quadragesima*, fem. adj., fortieth]

quad·ran·gle (kwod'rang'gəl) *n.* 1 a four-sided space or court wholly or nearly surrounded by buildings. 2 the buildings around a quadrangle. 3 a quadrilateral. [< LL *quadrangulum < L quadri-* four + *angulus* angle]

quad·ran·gu·lar (kwod rang'gyù lər) *adj.* like a quadrangle; having four corners or angles.

quad·rant (kwod'rənt) *n.* 1 a quarter of a circle or of its circumference. 2 an instrument used in astronomy and navigation for measuring altitudes. [< L *quadrans, -antis* a fourth]

quad·ra·phon·ic (kwod'rə fon'ik) *adj.* of, having to do with, or produced by quadraphonics.

quad·ra·phon·ics (kwod'rə fon'iks) *n.* (*used with a singular verb*) a system for the recording or reproduction of sound using four transmission channels that feed four separate loudspeakers.

qua·draph·o·ny (kwo draf'ə nē) *n.* quadraphonics.

quad·rat (kwod'rət) *n. Printing.* a piece of metal used for wide spaces in setting type. [var. of *quadrate*, n.]

quad·rate (*adj., n.* kwod'rit *or* kwod'rāt; *v.* kwod'rāt) *adj., n., v.* **-rat·ed, -rat·ing.** —*adj.* square; rectangular. —*n.* something square or rectangular.

—*v.* agree or conform (*often used with* with). [< L *quadratus < quadrus* square, ult. < *quattuor* four]

quad·rat·ic (kwod rat'ik) *adj., n. Algebra.* —*adj.* involving a square or squares, but no higher powers. —*n.* a quadratic equation.

quadratic equation an equation involving a square or squares, but no higher powers, of the unknown quantity or quantities. *Example:* $x^2 + 3x + 2 = 12$

quad·rat·ics (kwod rat'iks) *n.* the branch of algebra that deals with quadratic equations.

quad·ra·ture (kwod'rə chür' *or* kwod'rə chər) *n.* 1 the act of squaring. 2 the finding of a square equal in area to a given surface bounded by a curve. 3 *Astronomy.* the position of any planet or star that is 90 degrees away from another. [< L *quadratura < quadratus.* See QUADRATE.]

quad·ren·ni·al (kwod ren'ē əl *or* kwod ren'yəl) *adj.* 1 occurring every four years: *a quadrennial election.* 2 of or for four years. [< L *quadriennium* period of four years < *quadri-* four + *annus* year] —**quad·ren'ni·al·ly,** *adv.*

quad·ri·ceps (kwod'rə seps') *n.* the large, four-part, extensor muscle of the front of the thigh.

QUADRILATERALS

TRAPEZIUM (NO SIDES PARALLEL)	TRAPEZOID (TWO SIDES PARALLEL)

PARALLELOGRAMS (OPPOSITE SIDES PARALLEL)

RECTANGLES

SQUARE	OBLONG	RHOMBUS	RHOMBOID

quad·ri·lat·er·al (kwod'rə lat'ər əl) *adj., n.* —*adj.* having four sides and four angles. —*n.* 1 a plane figure having four sides and four angles. 2 something having this form. [< L *quadrilaterus < quadri-* four + *latus, -teris* side]

qua·drille (kwə dril') *n.* 1 a square dance for four couples that has five parts or movements. 2 the music for such a dance. [< F < Sp. *cuadrilla* troop < *cuadro* battle square < L *quadrus* square]

quad·ril·lion (kwod ril'yən) *n. adj.* 1 in Canada, the United States, and France, 1 followed by 15 zeros. 2 in Britain and Germany, 1 followed by 24 zeros. [< F *quadrillon < quadri-* four (< L) + *million*]

quad·ri·no·mi·al (kwod'rə nō'mē əl) *adj., n.* —*adj.* consisting of four terms. —*n.* an expression having four terms. *Example:* $a^2 - ab + 4a - b^2$. [< *quadri-* four (< L) + *-nomial*; modelled after *binomial*]

quad·ri·va·lence (kwod'rə vā'ləns *or* kwod riv'ə lens) *n.* a quadrivalent quality or condition.

quad·ri·va·len·cy (kwod'rə vā'lən sē *or* kwod riv'ə lən sē) *n.* quadrivalence.

quad·ri·va·lent (kwod'rə vā'lənt *or* kwod riv'ə lənt) *adj., n. Chemistry.* —*adj.* 1 having a valence of four. 2 having four separate valences. —*n.* a quadrivalent atom or element. —**quad'ri·va'lent·ly,** *adv.*

quad·riv·i·um (kwod riv'ē əm) *n.* in the Middle Ages, arithmetic, geometry, astronomy, and music, the more advanced group of the seven liberal arts; opposed to *trivium.* [< LL < L *quadrivium* crossroads < *quadri-*four + *via* way]

quad·roon (kwod rün') *n.* a person having one-fourth African ancestry. [< Sp. *cuarterón < cuarto* fourth < L *quartus*]

quad·ru·ped (kwod'rə ped') *n., adj.* —*n.* an animal, especially a mammal, that has four feet. —*adj.* having four feet. [< L *quadrupes, -pedis < quadru-* four + *pes, pedis* foot]

quad·ru·ple (kwod'rə pəl *or* kwod rü'pəl) *adj., adv., n., v.* **-pled, -pling.** —*adj.* 1 fourfold; consisting of four parts; including four

parts or parties. 2 four times; four times as great. 3 *Music.* having four beats to each measure, with the first and third beats accented. —*adv.* four times; four times as great.
—*n.* a number, amount, etc., four times as great as another: *80 is the quadruple of 20.*
—*v.* make or become four times as great. [< L *quadruplus* < *quadru-* four + *-plus* fold]

quad·ru·plet (kwod rü′plit *or* kwod′rə plit) *n.* 1 one of four children born at the same time from the same mother. 2 a group of four. [< *quadruple*, adj., modelled on *triplet*]

quad·ru·plex (kwod′rə pleks′) *adj.* 1 fourfold. 2 *Telegraphy.* of or having to do with a former system in which four messages, two in each direction, may be sent over one wire simultaneously. [< L *quadruplex* fourfold < *quadru-* four + *-plex* fold]

quad·ru·pli·cate (*adj. n.* kwod rü′plə kit; *v.* kwod rü′plə kāt′) *adj., v.* **-cat·ed, -cat·ing;** *n.* —*adj.* fourfold; quadruple.
—*v.* make fourfold; quadruple.
—*n.* one of four things, especially four copies of a document, exactly alike. [< L *quadruplicatus*, ult. < *quadru-* four + *plicare* to fold]

quad·ru·pli·ca·tion (kwod rü′plə kā′shən) *n.* 1 quadruplicating. 2 something quadruplicated.

quaes·tor (kwes′tər *or* kwēs′tər) *n.* in ancient Rome: 1 an official in charge of the public funds; treasurer. 2 a public prosecutor in certain criminal cases. [< L *quaestor* var. of *quaesitor* < *quaerere* inquire]

quaes·tor·ship (kwes′tər ship′ *or* kwēs′tər-) *n.* the position or term of office of a quaestor.

quaff (kwof *or* kwaf) *v., n.* —*v.* drink in large drafts; drink deeply and freely. —*n.* an act of quaffing. [origin uncertain]

quag (kwag *or* kwog) *n.* a bog; quagmire.

quag·gy (kwag′ē *or* kwog′ē) *adj.* **-gier, -gi·est.** 1 boggy; soft and marshy; swampy. 2 flabby; soft and wobbly: *quaggy flesh.* [probably < *quag* bog]

quag·mire (kwag′mīr′) *n.* 1 soft, muddy ground; a boggy or miry place. 2 a difficult situation. [< obs. *quag* to shake + *mire*]

qua·hog (kwo′hog *or* kwə hog′) *n.* an edible clam (*Venus mercenaria,* also called *Mercenaria mercenaria*) of the Atlantic coast of North America, having a hard, thick, rounded shell. Also, **quahaug.** [< Algonquian]

quail¹ (kwāl) *n., pl.* **quails** *or* (esp. collectively) **quail.** 1 any of various plump-bodied, small to medium-sized, Old World game birds (subfamily Perdicinae, especially genus *Cortunix*) belonging to the same family as partridges and pheasants. 2 any of various New World birds (subfamily Odontophorinae) belonging to the same family and resembling Old World quail, but generally larger and more colorful and having no leg spurs. The commonest and best-known species is the bobwhite. [ME < OF *quaille* < Gmc.]

quail² (kwāl) *v.* be afraid; lose courage; shrink back in fear: *The slave quailed at his master's look.* [ME; origin uncertain]

quaint (kwānt) *adj.* strange or odd in an interesting, pleasing, or amusing way: *Old photographs seem quaint to us today.* [ME < OF *cointe* pretty < L *cognitus* known] —**quaint′ly,** *adv.* —**quaint′ness,** *n.*

quake (kwāk) *v.* **quaked, quak·ing;** *n.* —*v.* shake; tremble: *She quaked with fear.* —*n.* 1 a shaking; trembling. 2 earthquake. [OE *cwacian*]
☛ *Syn. v.* See note at **shiver.**

Quak·er (kwā′kər) *n.* a member of a Christian group called the Society of Friends. Quakers favor simple religious services and refuse to fight in a war or to take oaths. [< *quake,* v.; said to refer to the fact that George Fox, the founder, bade his followers "tremble at the word of the Lord"]

Quak·er·ess (kwā′kər is) *n.* a Quaker woman or girl.

Quak·er·ism (kwā′kər iz′əm) *n.* the principles and customs of the Quakers.

qual·i·fi·ca·tion (kwol′ə fə kā′shən) *n.* 1 that which makes a person fit for a job, task, office, etc.: *Good eyesight is a necessary qualification for a marksman.* 2 a modification; limitation; restriction: *The statement was made without any qualification. His pleasure had one qualification; his friends could not enjoy it, too.*

qual·i·fied (kwol′ə fīd′) *adj.* 1 having the desirable or required qualifications; fitted; adapted: *He is fully qualified for his job.* 2 modified; limited; restricted: *His qualified answer was, "I will go, but only if you will come with me."*

qual·i·fi·er (kwol′ə fī′ər) *n.* 1 a person or thing that qualifies. 2 a word that qualifies another word: *Adjectives and adverbs are qualifiers.*

qual·i·fy (kwol′ə fī′) *v.* **-fied, -fy·ing.** 1 make fit or competent: *to qualify oneself for a job.* 2 furnish with legal power; make legally capable. 3 become fit; show oneself fit: *Can you qualify for the Boy Scouts?* 4 *Sports.* gain the right to compete in a race, contest, or tournament. 5 make less strong; change somewhat; limit; modify: *Qualify your statement that dogs are loyal by adding "usually."* 6 *Grammar.* limit or modify the meaning of: *Adverbs qualify verbs.* [< Med.L *qualificare* < L *qualis* of what sort + *facere* make]

qual·i·ta·tive (kwol′ə tā′tiv) *adj.* concerned with quality or qualities. —**qual′i·ta′tive·ly,** *adv.*

qualitative analysis the process of determining the chemical components of a substance.

qual·i·ty (kwol′ə tē) *n., pl.* **-ties.** 1 something special about an object that makes it what it is: *One quality of iron is hardness; one quality of sugar is sweetness.* 2 a characteristic; attribute: *She has many fine qualities.* 3 grade of excellence; degree of worth: *That is a poor quality of cloth.* 4 nature; disposition; temper: *Trials often test a man's quality.* 5 character; position; relation: *Dr. Smith was present, but in the quality of a friend, not of a physician.* 6 fineness; merit; excellence: *Look for quality rather than quantity.* 7 an accomplishment; attainment. 8 high rank; good or high social position. 9 people of high rank. 10 the character of a sound aside from pitch and volume or intensity. [ME < OF < L *qualitas* < *qualis* of what sort]

qualm (kwom *or* kwäm) *n.* 1 a sudden disturbing feeling in the mind; uneasiness; misgiving; doubt: *I tried the test with some qualms.* 2 a disturbance or scruple of conscience: *She felt some qualms at staying away from church.* 3 a momentary feeling of faintness or sickness, especially of nausea. [OE *cwealm* pain]

qualm·ish (kwom′ish *or* kwäm′ish) *adj.* 1 inclined to have qualms. 2 having qualms.

quan·da·ry (kwon′də rē *or* kwon′drē) *n., pl.* **-ries.** a state of perplexity or uncertainty; dilemma. [origin uncertain]

quan·ta (kwon′tə) *n.* pl. of **quantum.**

quan·ti·fy (kwon′tə fī′) *v.* **-fied, -fy·ing.** 1 determine the quantity of; count or measure. 2 *Prosody.* express the quantity of: *to quantify a syllable of verse.* 3 *Logic.* express explicitly the quantity or extent of, by using such words as *all, some,* or *most.* [< Med.L *quantificare* < L *quantus* how much + *facere* make]
—**quan′ti·fi′a·ble,** *adj.* —**quan′ti·fi′a·bly,** *adv.*
—**quan′ti·fi·ca′tion,** *n.*

quan·ti·ta·tive (kwon′tə tā′tiv) *adj.* 1 concerned with quantity. 2 that can be measured. —**quan′ti·ta′tive·ly,** *adv.*

quantitative analysis the process of determining the amount or proportion of each chemical component of a substance.

quan·ti·ty (kwon′tə tē) *n., pl.* **-ties.** 1 amount: *Equal quantities of nuts and raisins were used in the cake.* 2 a large amount; a large number: *The baker buys flour in quantity. She owns quantities of books.* 3 something that is measurable. 4 *Music.* the length of a note. 5 *Prosody.* the length of a vowel sound or syllable. 6 *Mathematics.* **a** something having magnitude, or size, extent, amount, etc. **b** a figure or symbol representing this. [< L *quantitas* < *quantus* how much]

quan·tum (kwon′təm) *n., pl.* **-ta** (-tə). *Physics.* **a** the smallest amount of energy capable of existing independently. **b** such a discrete amount of energy regarded as a unit. [< L *quantum,* neut. adj., how much]

quantum leap *or* **jump** 1 *Physics.* a sudden change of an atom, electron, etc. from one discrete energy level or state to another. 2 any sudden major change or advance: *a quantum leap in electronic technology.*

quantum mechanics the branch of physics dealing with the interpretation of the behavior of atoms and elementary particles, such as electrons, on the basis of the quantum theory.

quantum theory the theory that whenever radiant energy is transferred, the transfer occurs in pulsations or stages rather than continuously, and that the amount of energy transferred during each stage is of a definite quantity.

quar·an·tine (kwôr′ən tēn′) *v.* **-tined, -tin·ing;** *n.* —*v.* isolate from others for a time, especially in order to prevent the spread of an infectious disease: *People with smallpox are quarantined.*
—*n.* 1 the state of being quarantined: *The house was in quarantine when the child had scarlet fever.* 2 detention, isolation, and other measures taken to prevent the spread of an infectious disease. 3 a place where people, animals, plants, ships, etc. are held until it is sure that they have no infectious diseases, insect pests, etc. 4 a period of detention or isolation imposed on ships, persons, etc. when liable or suspected to be bringing some infectious disease. 5 isolation, exclusion, and similar measures taken against an undesirable person, group, etc. [< Ital. *quarantina* < *quaranta* forty < L *quadraginta*; with reference to 40 days as the original period of isolation]

quark (kwôrk *or, sometimes,* kwärk) *n. Physics.* any of the fundamental particles from which the composite particles called hadrons (including protons and neutrons) are formed, and which, together with leptons, are believed to be the basic constituents of all matter. Quarks differ from leptons in that they do not occur as free particles and in having fractional charges, either $+\frac{2}{3}$ or $-\frac{1}{3}$ the charge of an electron. There is strong experimental evidence for the existence of fifteen quarks, with an additional three predicted but not yet seen. [< a nonsense word coined by James Joyce in *Finnigan's Wake* and applied to these particles in 1963 by American physicist Murray Gell-Mann (b. 1929), who first postulated their existence]

quar·rel[1] (kwôr′əl) *n., v.* **-relled** or **-reled, -rel·ling** or **-rel·ing.** —*n.* **1** an angry dispute or disagreement; a breaking off of friendly relations. **2** a cause for a dispute or disagreement; reason for breaking off friendly relations: *A bully likes to pick quarrels.* **3** one's cause or side in a dispute or contest: *The knight took up the poor man's quarrel and fought his oppressor.* —*v.* **1** dispute or disagree angrily; break off friendly relations. **2** find fault: *It is useless to quarrel with undeniable facts.* [ME < OF < L *querella,* var. of *querela* complaint < *queri* complain] —**quar′rel·ler** or **quar′rel·er,** *n.*

☞ *Syn. n.* **1. Quarrel, feud** = an angry disagreement or unfriendly relation between two people or groups. **Quarrel** particularly applies to a fight in words, an angry disagreement or dispute, spoken over or ending in a fist fight or in severed relations: *The children had a quarrel over the division of the candy.* **Feud** suggests a long-lasting quarrel, marked by violent and sometimes murderous attacks and revenge when between two groups, by bitter hatred and unfriendly acts and verbal attacks when between individuals: *The senator and the columnist carried on a feud.*

quar·rel[2] (kwôr′əl) *n.* **1** a bolt or arrow used with a crossbow. **2** a small, square, or diamond-shaped pane of glass, used in latticed windows. **3** a stonemason's chisel. [ME < OF < Med.L *quadrellus,* dim. of L *quadrus* square]

quar·rel·some (kwôr′əl səm) *adj.* too ready to quarrel; fond of fighting and disputing. —**quar′rel·some·ly,** *adv.* —**quar′rel·some·ness,** *n.*

quar·ry[1] (kwôr′ē) *n., pl.* **-ries;** *v.* **-ried, -ry·ing.** —*n.* a place where stone is dug, cut, or blasted out for use in building. —*v.* **1** obtain from a quarry. **2** dig out by hard work, as if from a quarry. [ME < Med.L *quareia,* ult. < L *quadrus* square] —**quar′ri·er,** *n.*

quar·ry[2] (kwôr′ē) *n., pl.* **-ries. 1** an animal chased in a hunt; prey or game. **2** anything hunted or eagerly pursued. [ME < OF *cuiree* < *cuir* hide < L *corium*]

quart (kwôrt) *n.* **1** a unit for measuring volume or capacity, equal to one fourth of a gallon or one eighth of a peck (about 1.14 dm³). **2** a container having a capacity of one quart. **3** such a container and its contents: *a quart of milk. Abbrev.:* qt. or qu. [ME < OF < L *quarta,* fem. adj., fourth]

quar·tan (kwôr′tən) *adj., n.* —*adj.* recurring every fourth day, by inclusive counting. —*n.* a fever or ague with two days between attacks. [< F < L (*febris*) *quartana* quartan (fever) < *quartus* fourth]

quar·ter (kwôr′tər) *n., v.* —*n.* **1** one fourth; half of a half; one of four equal or corresponding parts. **2** in Canada, the United States, etc.: **a** one fourth of a dollar; 25 cents. **b** a coin worth 25 cents. **3** fifteen minutes; especially, the moment marking fifteen minutes before or after a specified hour: *They left at a quarter to three.* **4** one fourth of a year; three months: *Sales increased in the first quarter.* **5** one of the four phases of the moon. The quarters of the moon are four periods of about seven days each. **6** one fourth of any of various units of measure: *a quarter of a hectare of land.* **7** (*adj.*) being or consisting of one of four equal or more or less equal parts: *a quarter package of peanuts.* **8** a region or district: *They live in the Latin quarter of the city.* **9** a section of a community, group, etc.: *The bankers' theory was not accepted in other quarters.* **10** a point of the compass; direction: *In what quarter is the wind?* **11** mercy or indulgence, as shown to a defeated opponent or enemy: *He asked no quarter and was given none.* **12** one of four parts into which an animal's carcass is divided. **13** the leg and its adjoining parts. **14** the part of a ship's side near the stern. **15** *Heraldry.* **a** one of four more or less equal parts into which a shield may be divided by two lines crossing at right angl **b** a charge, or emblem, occupying the upper right fourth of a shield (from the bearer's point of view). **16** the part of a boot or shoe above the heel and below the top of either side of the foot from the middle of back to vamp. **17** *Music.* a quarter note: *That note is held for two quarters.* **18** *Football, basketball, etc.* one of the four equal periods of play into which a game is divided. **19 quarters,** *pl.* **a** a place to live or stay: *officers' quarters.* **b** proper position or station. **at close quarters,** fighting or struggling close together: *The two armies were at close quarters for several days.* —*v.* **1** divide into quarters. **2** give a place to live in: *Soldiers were quartered in houses of the town.* **3** live or stay in a place. **4** cut the body of (a person or animal) into quarters. **5** of the wind, blow on a ship's quarter. **6** place or bear (coats of arms) in quarters of a shield. [ME < OF < L *quartarius* a fourth < *quartus* fourth]

hat, āge, fär; let, ēqual, tèrm; it, īce
hot, ōpen, ôrder; oil, out; cup, pùt, rüle,
əbove, takən, pencəl, lemən, circəs

ch, child; ng, long; sh, ship
th, thin; ᴛн, then; zh, measure

quar·ter·back (kwôr′tər bak′) *n., v.* —*n.* **1** *Football.* the player whose position is immediately behind the centre of the line of scrimmage: *The quarterback usually directs his team's play in the field.* **2** a person who directs any group or activity. —*v.* play in this position; act as quarterback.

quarter day the day beginning or ending a quarter of the year.

quar·ter·deck (kwôr′tər dek′) *n.* **1** on a sailing vessel, the part of the upper deck between the mainmast and the stern, used especially by the officers of a ship. **2** on a steam naval vessel, a deck area designated as the ceremonial post of the commanding officer.

quar·tered (kwôr′tərd) *adj.* **1** divided into quarters. **2** furnished with rooms or lodging. **3** *Heraldry.* divided or arranged in quarters. **4** quartersawn.

quarter horse a breed of horse orginally bred from thoroughbred stock for racing on quarter-mile tracks, now much used in Canada and the United States for working with cattle, playing polo, etc.

quar·ter–hour (kwôr′tər our′) *n.* **1** fifteen minutes. **2** the point one fourth or three fourths of the way through an hour.

quar·ter·ing (kwôr′tər ing) *n., adj.* —*n.* **1** the act of dividing into fourths. **2** the act of assigning quarters, especially for soldiers. **3** *Heraldry.* **a** the division of a shield into quarters or parts. **b** one of such parts. **c** the coat of arms on a quartering. —*adj.* of a wind, blowing on a ship's side near the stern.

quar·ter·ly (kwôr′tər lē) *adj., adv., n., pl.* **-lies.** —*adj.* happening, done, etc., four times a year. —*adv.* once each quarter of a year. —*n.* a magazine published four times a year: *The Society publishes a quarterly.*

quar·ter·mas·ter (kwôr′tər mas′tər) *n. Military.* **1** an officer who has charge of providing quarters, clothing, fuel, transportation, etc. for troops. **2** an officer on a ship who has charge of the steering, the compasses, signals, etc. *Abbrev.:* Q.M. or QM

quar·tern (kwôr′tərn) *n.* **1** a quarter; fourth part. **2** one fourth of a pint; gill. [ME < OF *quarteron < quart* fourth < L *quartus*]

quarter note *Music.* a note equal to one fourth of a whole note. See **note** for picture.

quarter rest *Music.* a rest lasting as long as a quarter note.

quar·ter·saw (kwôr′tər sô′ *or* -sô′) *v.* **-sawed, -sawed** or **-sawn, -saw·ing.** saw (a log) lengthwise into quarters and then into boards.

quarter section a piece of land, usually square, containing 160 acres (about 65 hectares).

quarter sessions 1 *Historical.* an English court held quarterly before a recorder or two justices of the peace, having limited criminal and civil jurisdiction and empowered to hear appeals; replaced in 1972 by the crown court. **2** any of various courts held quarterly.

quar·ter·staff (kwôr′tər staf′) *n., pl.* **-staves.** a weapon consisting of a stout pole about two metres long and tipped with iron, formerly used by English peasants.

quar·ter·staves (kwôr′tər stāvz′) *n.* pl. of **quarterstaff.**

quar·tet or **quar·tette** (kwôr tet′) *n.* **1** a group of four musicians (singers or players). **2** a piece of music for four voices or instruments. **3** any group of four. [< F < Ital. *quartetto < quarto* fourth < L *quartus*]

quar·tile (kwôr′tīl) *n. Statistics.* any of the three values of a variable that divide the items of a population into four equal groups with respect to the value of the variable.

quar·to (kwôr′tō) *n., pl.* **-tos. 1** the page size of a book in which each leaf is one fourth of a whole sheet of paper. **2** (*adj.*) having this size. **3** a book having this size. [< Med.L *in quarto* in the fourth (of a sheet)]

quartz (kwôrts) *n.* a very common, very hard, crystalline mineral consisting of silica, that is present in many rocks and solids in a variety of forms, many of which are used as gemstones. It occurs in the form of pure, colorless crystals (rock-crystal) and impure, colored crystals, such as amethyst, and also in microcrystalline forms, such as jasper, carnelian, and flint. *Formula:* SiO_2 [< G *Quarz*]

quartz·ite (kwôrts′īt) *n.* a granular rock consisting mostly of quartz.

qua·sar (kwā′sär or kwä′zär) n. any of various starlike bodies that are very distant from the earth and give off strong light and radio waves. [< quas(i)-(stell)ar]

quash¹ (kwosh) v. put down completely; crush: to quash a revolt. [ME < OF quasser < L quassare shatter, intensive of quatere to shake]

quash² (kwosh) v. make void; annul: The judge quashed the charges against the prisoner. [ME < OF quasser < LL cassare < cassus null; influenced in OF by quasser quash¹]

qua·si (kwā′sē or kwä′zē, kwo′sē or kwo′zē) adj., adv. —adj. seeming; not real; halfway: quasi humor. —adv. seemingly; not really; partly; almost. [< L]

quasi– combining form. in some sense or to a certain extent: a quasi-historical account, quasi-official.

quas·sia (kwosh′ə) n. 1 a bitter drug obtained from the wood or bark of any of various tropical trees (genera Quassia and Picrasma) of the same family as the ailanthus, used as a tonic and medicine and also as an insecticide. 2 any of the trees whose wood or bark yields this drug. 3 the bark or wood of any of these trees. [< NL; after Quassi, a Surinam slave who first used the bark as a fever remedy]

Qua·ter·na·ry (kwə tėr′nə rē) n., adj. Geology. —n. 1 the period that includes the Pleistocene and Recent. See chart at geology. 2 the deposits made in this period. —adj. of or having to do with this period or the deposits made during it. [< L quaternarius, ult. < quater four times]

quat·rain (kwot′rān) n. a stanza or poem of four lines. [< F quatrain < quatre four < L quattuor]

quat·re·foil (kat′ər foil′ or kat′rə foil′) n. 1 a leaf or flower composed of four leaflets or petals. The four-leaf clover is a quatrefoil. 2 Architecture. an ornament having four lobes. [ME < OF quatre four (< L quattuor) + feuil leaf < L folium]

qua·ver (kwā′vər) v., n. —v. 1 shake tremulously; tremble: The old man's voice quavered. 2 sing or say in trembling tones. 3 trill in singing or in playing on an instrument.
—n. 1 a shaking or trembling, especially of the voice. 2 a trill in singing or in playing on an instrument. 3 Music. an eighth note. [frequentative of quave shake, ME cwavie(n)] —**qua′ver·ing·ly**, adv.

qua·ver·y (kwā′vər ē) adj. quavering.

quay (kē) n. a solid landing place where ships load and unload, often built of stone. [ME < OF kay < Celtic]
☛ Hom. cay, key.

Que. Quebec.

quean (kwēn) n. 1 Archaic. a bold, impudent girl or woman; hussy. 2 prostitute. 3 Scottish. a girl or young woman. 4 Slang. queen (def. 8). [OE cwene]

quea·sy (kwē′zē) adj. -si·er, -si·est. 1 inclined to nausea; easily upset. 2 tending to unsettle the stomach. 3 uneasy; uncomfortable. 4 squeamish; fastidious. [origin uncertain] —**quea′si·ly**, adv. —**quea′si·ness**, n.

Quebec heater (kwi bek′ or kā bek′) a type of heating stove that burns wood or coal in a tall, cylindrical firebox.

Quebec highlander Cdn. Slang. a French-Canadian Roman Catholic cleric.

Que·beck·er or **Que·bec·er** (kwi bek′ər or kā bek′ər) n. a native or long-term resident of the province of Quebec.

Qué·béc·ois (kā bek wä′) n., pl. **Qué·béc·ois**. French. a Quebecker, especially a Francophone.

que·bra·cho (kā brä′chō) n. 1 any of several South American hardwood trees (genus Schinopsis) of the cashew family, especially S. lorentzii and S. balansae, whose wood is valued as a source of tannin, and several other species that are important timber trees. 2 a South American hardwood tree (Aspidosperma quebracho) of the dogbane family whose bark is valued as a source of alkaloids used in medicine and tanning. 3 the wood or bark of any of these trees. [< Sp. quebracho, literally, break-axe < quebrar break < L crepare]

Quech·ua (kech′wä) n., pl. **Quech·ua** or **Quech·uas**. 1 the principle language of the Inca empire, still surviving as a dialect spoken in S Peru. 2 any of several related dialects and languages. 3 Quechuan. 4 a member of any of a group of Amerindian peoples of the Andes, including the peoples who constituted the dominant element in the Inca empire. Also, **Kechua**.

Quech·uan (kech′wən) adj., n. —adj. of or having to do with Quechua or the Quechua peoples. —n. a family or subfamily of languages of the Andes in South America, including Quechua. Also, **Kechuan**.

queen (kwēn) n., v. —n. 1 the wife of a king. 2 a female ruler. 3 a woman judged to be first in importance or best in beauty or some other quality: the queen of society, the queen of the May. 4 a fully developed egg-laying female in a colony of bees, ants, etc. There is usually only one queen in a hive of bees. 5 a playing card bearing a picture of a queen. 6 Chess. a piece that can move in any straight or diagonal row. 7 the chief, best, finest, etc.: the rose, queen of flowers. 8 Slang. a male homosexual, especially one who appears very effeminate.
—v. 1 be a queen or act like a queen. 2 make a queen of. [OE cwēn] —**queen′like′**, adj.

Queen Anne 1 a style of English architecture of the early 18th century, characterized by simple design and the use of red brick. 2 a style of upholstered furniture designed in England in the early 18th century.

Queen Anne's lace a common biennial plant (Daucus carota) of the parsley family native to Europe and Asia but naturalized in North America and elsewhere, having lacy-looking, flat-topped clusters of small white flowers. The cultivated carrot is probably derived from this plant. Also called **wild carrot**.

Queen City 1 Toronto. 2 Regina.

queen consort the wife of a reigning king.

queen·dom (kwēn′dəm) n. 1 the realm of a queen. 2 the position or dignity of a queen.

queen dowager the widow of a king.

queen·ly (kwēn′lē) adj. -li·er, -li·est; adv. —adj. 1 of a queen; fit for a queen. 2 like a queen; like a queen's. —adv. in a queenly manner; as a queen does. —**queen′li·ness**, n.

queen mother the widow of a former king and mother of a reigning king or queen.

queen post one of a pair of timbers extending vertically upward from the tie beam of a roof truss or the like, one on each side of its centre.

queen regent 1 a queen ruling in place of an absent or unfit monarch. 2 a queen ruling in her own right.

Queen's Counsel a lawyer who has been appointed counsel to the Crown and is entitled to wear a silk gown. In Britain the title is awarded to barristers on the basis of superior learning and talent, but in Canada it has been merely a formal appointment since the early 1900's. Abbrev.: Q.C. or QC. Also, during the reign of a king, **King's Counsel**.

Queen's English the English that is recognized as correct and standard in Britain. Also, during the reign of a king, **King's English**.

Queen's evidence testimony given in court by an accomplice in a crime against his associate or associates.
turn Queen's evidence, testify in court against one's associates in a crime.

Queen's Highway in Canada, a main road, usually surfaced, that is the responsibility of the provincial government for maintenance, etc.

Queen's Proctor in British law, an officer of the crown having the right to intervene in certain divorce and nullity cases.

queer (kwēr) adj., v., n. —adj. 1 different from what is normal or usual; strange; odd; peculiar: a queer remark, a queer noise, a queer reaction. 2 Informal. eccentric or mildly crazy: She's a little bit queer. 3 Informal. not as it should be; causing doubt or suspicion: There's something queer going on here. 4 Slang. counterfeit; worthless: queer money. 5 not well; faint or giddy: I started to feel queer and had to sit down. 6 Slang. especially of a man, homosexual.
—v. Slang. spoil; ruin: to queer a deal.
—n. 1 Informal. a person who is strange or peculiar. 2 Slang. a homosexual, especially a male. [< G quer oblique] —**queer′ly**, adv.

queer·ness (kwēr′nis) n. 1 queer nature or behavior. 2 something strange or odd; a peculiarity.

quell (kwel) v. 1 put down (disorder, rebellion, etc.): to quell a riot. 2 put an end to; overcome: to quell one's fears. [OE cwellan kill]

quench (kwench) v. 1 put an end to; stop: to quench a thirst. 2 drown out; put out: Water quenched the fire. 3 cool suddenly by plunging into water or other liquid. Hot steel is quenched to harden it. [OE cwencan as in ācwencan]

quench·less (kwench′lis) adj. that cannot be quenched; inextinguishable.

que·nelle (kə nel′) n. a small ball of seasoned, finely minced meat or fish cooked in water or stock or fried as a croquette and often served with a sauce. [< F < G Knödel dumpling < MHG knode knot. 19c. Akin to KNOT¹.]

quern (kwėrn) n. 1 a primitive handmill for grinding grain, consisting commonly of two circular stones, the upper one being

turned by hand. **2** a small hand mill used to grind pepper or other spices. [OE *cweorn*]

quer·u·lous (kwer′ə ləs *or* kwer′yə ləs) *adj.* **1** complaining; faultfinding. **2** fretful; peevish. [< L *querulus* < *queri* complain] —**quer′u·lous·ly,** *adv.* —**quer′u·lous·ness,** *n.*

que·ry (kwēr′ē) *n., pl.* **-ries;** *v.* **-ried, -ry·ing.** —*n.* **1** a question; inquiry. **2** a doubt: *There was a query in his mind about the whole procedure.* **3** question mark.
—*v.* **1** put as a question; ask: *"How long will that be?" she queried.* **2** ask questions of: *They queried him about his future plans.* **3** ask questions about, enquire into, especially to express doubt: *She queried the wisdom of accepting the first offer.* [< Med.L *quere* < L *quaere* ask!]
☛ *Syn. n.* **1.** See note at **question.**

quest (kwest) *n., v.* —*n.* **1** the act or an instance of seeking or searching: *a quest for treasure. He descended to the cellar in quest of the sherry.* **2** an expedition or journey in search of something noble, ideal, or holy: *There are many stories about the quest for the Holy Grail.* **3** the object or goal of a search.
—*v.* seek or hunt: *questing for gold in faraway places.* [ME < OF < VL *quaesita* < L *quaerere* seek]

ques·tion (kwes′chən) *n., v.* —*n.* **1** something asked; a sentence in interrogative form, addressed to someone to get information; inquiry. **2** a judicial examination or trial; interrogation. **3** a matter of doubt or dispute; controversy: *A question arose about the ownership of the property.* **4** a matter to be talked over, investigated, considered, etc.; problem: *the question of automation.* **5** a proposal to be voted on. **6** the taking of a vote on a proposal.
beside the question, off the subject.
beyond question, without doubt; not to be disputed: *The statements in that book are true beyond question.*
call in question, dispute; challenge.
in question, a under consideration or discussion. **b** in dispute.
out of the question, not to be considered; impossible.
without question, without a doubt; not to be disputed: *He is without question the brightest student in the school.*
—*v.* **1** ask in order to find out; seek information from. **2** ask; inquire. **3** doubt; dispute: *I question the truth of his story.* [ME < OF < L *quaestio, -onis,* ult. < *quaerere* ask] —**ques′tion·er,** *n.* —**ques′tion·ing·ly,** *adv.*
☛ *Syn. n.* **1. Question, query** = something asked. **Question** applies to any request for information: *I have some questions about today's lesson.* **Query** applies particularly to a question raised as a matter of doubt or objection and seeking a specific or authoritative answer: *He put several queries concerning items in the budget.* —*v.* **1. Question, ask, interrogate** = seek information from someone. **Ask** is the general word, and suggests nothing more: *I asked him why he did it.* **Question** often means ask a series of questions, sometimes formally and according to some plan: *I questioned the boy until he told all he knew.* **Interrogate** is a formal word meaning "to question formally and methodically": *The intelligence officer interrogated the prisoners.*

ques·tion·a·ble (kwes′chən ə bəl) *adj.* **1** open to question or dispute; doubtful; uncertain. **2** of doubtful propriety, honesty, morality, respectability, or the like. —**ques′tion·a·bly,** *adv.*

question mark a mark (?) put after a question or used to express doubt about something written or printed.

ques·tion·naire (kwes′chən er′ *or, esp.Brit.,* kes′chən er′) *n.* **1** a set of questions designed for obtaining statistical information: *The questionnaire was quite straightforward.* **2** a form containing such questions, usually having spaces for answers: *to fill out a questionnaire.* [< F]

question time 1 in the House of Commons, a short period several times a week in which ministers answer questions submitted in advance by Members of Parliament. **2** a similar period in any assembly.

quet·zal (ket säl′) *n.* **1** a Central American bird (*Pharomachrus mocinno*) having brilliant golden-green and scarlet plumage. The male has long, flowing tail feathers. **2** the basic unit of money in Guatemala, divided into 100 centavos. See table at **money. 3** a note worth one quetzal. [< Mexican Sp. < Nahuatl]

queue (kyü) *n., v.* **queued, queu·ing.** —*n.* **1** a long line of people, automobiles, etc.; line-up. **2** a braid of hair hanging down the back.
—*v.* form or stand in a line while waiting to be served, etc. (*usually used with* **up**): *We had to queue up to get tickets.* [< F < L *coda,* var. of *cauda* tail]
☛ *Hom.* **cue.**

quib·ble (kwib′əl) *n., v.* **-bled, -bling.** —*n.* **1** an evasion of the main point, especially a petty one or one that depends on words that are vague or have a double meaning: *a legal quibble.* **2** a minor criticism or objection: *The meeting was delayed for several minutes because of a quibble about procedure.* —*v.* use quibbles; resort to petty objections or evasions. [apparently dim. of obs. *quib* quip < L *quibus* (dat. and abl. pl. of *qui* who, which), used in legal jargon] —**quib′bler,** *n.*

quiche (kēsh) *n.* a kind of pie usually served as a main dish, consisting of a pastry shell filled with an egg and cream custard

hat, āge, fär; let, ēqual, tèrm; it, īce
hot, ōpen, ôrder; oil, out; cup, pút, rüle,
əbove, takən, pencəl, lemən, circəs
ch, child; ng, long; sh, ship
th, thin; ŦH, then; zh, measure

together with any of various other ingredients, such as ham, bacon, cheese, or seafood.

quiche Lor·raine (kēsh′lôr ān′) a quiche containing bacon and, usually, cheese.

quick (kwik) *adj., n., adv.* —*adj.* **1** fast and sudden; swift: *a quick turn.* **2** begun and ended in a very short time: *a quick visit.* **3** coming soon; prompt: *a quick reply.* **4** not patient; hasty: *a quick temper.* **5** brisk: *a quick fire.* **6** acting quickly; ready; lively: *a quick wit.* **7** understanding or learning quickly: *a child who is quick in school.* **8** *Archaic.* alive; living.
quick with child, *Archaic.* pregnant.
—*n.* **1** tender, sensitive flesh, especially the flesh under a fingernail or toenail: *The child bit his nails down to the quick.* **2** the tender, sensitive part of one's feelings: *Their insults cut him to the quick.* **3** *Archaic.* **the quick,** *pl.* living persons: *the quick and the dead.* —*adv.* quickly: *Come quick!* [OE *cwic* alive] —**quick′ness,** *n.*
☛ *Syn. adj.* **1. Quick, fast, rapid** = done, happening, moving, or acting with speed. **Quick** especially describes something done or made or happening with speed or without delay: *You made a quick trip.* **Fast** especially describes something moving or acting, and emphasizes the swiftness with which it acts or moves: *I took a fast plane.* **Rapid** emphasizes the speed, the swiftness of the action or movement, or series of movements, performed: *I had to do some rapid planning.*

quick bread bread, biscuits, etc. made with a leavening agent that does not require the dough to be left to rise before baking.

quick·en (kwik′ən) *v.* **1** make or become more rapid; accelerate: *He quickened his pace. His pulse quickened.* **2** make or become stimulated or animated: *Her interest quickened when the discussion turned to travel.* **3** of a child in the womb, show life by movements. **4** *Archaic.* cause to burn brighter: *to quicken hot ashes into flames.*

quick–freeze (kwik′frēz′) *v.* **-froze, -fro·zen, -freez·ing.** freeze (food) quickly in preparation for storage, so that the ice crystals formed during the freezing process are too small to rupture the cells, thus preserving the natural juices and flavor of the food.

quick–hatch (kwik′hach′) *n. Cdn.* wolverine.

quick·ie (kwik′ē) *n. Informal.* **1** something made or done very quickly or superficially: *His last film was just a quickie. Let's stop for coffee; we've got time for at least a quickie.* **2** an alcoholic drink consumed in a hurry. **3** (*adj.*) done, made, etc. hastily or quickly.

quick kick *Football.* a punt kicked from a running play formation during a down other than the third, the objective being to catch the opposing players out of position and thus to gain ground.

quick·lime (kwik′līm′) *n.* a white, caustic, alkaline substance usually obtained by burning limestone and used for making calcium hydroxide, mortar, and cement; calcium oxide.

quick·ly (kwik′lē) *adv.* with haste or speed: *They walked quickly. The wound healed quickly.*

quick march in the armed forces, an order to begin marching in quick time.

quick·sand (kwik′sand′) *n.* **1** soft, wet sand that will not support a heavy weight: *The horse was swallowed by the quicksand.* **2** a deep expanse of such sand.

quick·set (kwik′set′) *n.* **1** *Esp.Brit.* a plant or cutting, especially of hawthorn, set to grow in a hedge. **2** such plants collectively. **3** a hedge of such plants.

quick·sil·ver (kwik′sil′vər) *n., adj.* —*n.* mercury. —*adj.* unpredictable or quick-changing: *a quicksilver temperament.* [OE *cwicseolfor,* after L *argentum vivum* living silver]

quick·step (kwik′step′) *n.* **1** a lively dance step. **2** music in a brisk march rhythm, such as that used to accompany marching in quick time. **3** a step used in marching in quick time.

quick–tem·pered (kwik′tem′pərd) *adj.* easily angered.

quick time a marching rate of 120 paces per minute, or about 5.5 kilometres per hour.

quick·wa·ter (kwik′wo′tər *or* -wô′tər) *n.* a stretch of a stream with a strong current but no rapids.

quick–wit·ted (kwik′wit′id) *adj.* having a quick mind; mentally alert.

quid[1] (kwid) *n.* **1** a piece to be chewed. **2** a bite of chewing tobacco. [OE *cwidu* cud]

quid[2] (kwid) *n., pl.* **quid.** *Brit. Slang.* one pound sterling: *She gets 80 quid a week.* [origin uncertain]

quid·nunc (kwid′nungk′) *n.* a newsmonger; gossip; inquisitive person. [< L *quid nunc* what now]

quid pro quo (kwid′prō kwō′) *Latin.* one thing in return for another; compensation. [*literally,* which for what]

qui·es·cence (kwī es′əns *or* kwē′es əns) *n.* an absence of activity; quietness; stillness; motionlessness.

qui·es·cent (kwī es′ənt *or* kwē′es ənt) *adj.* inactive; quiet; still; motionless. [< L *quiescens, -entis,* ppr. of *quiescere* rest < *quies,* n., rest] **—qui·es′cent·ly,** *adv.*

qui·et (kwī′ət) *adj., v., n., adv.* **—adj. 1** moving very little; still: *a quiet river.* **2** with no or little noise: *quiet footsteps, a quiet room.* **3** saying little. **4** peaceful; gentle; unobtrusive: *a quiet mind, quiet manners.* **5** not showy or bright: *Grey is a quiet color.* **6** not active: *a quiet life in the country.*
—v. 1 make quiet: *The mother quieted her frightened child.* **2** become quiet: *The wind quieted down.*
—n. a state of rest or stillness; freedom from disturbance; peace: *to read in quiet, the quiet of early morning.*
—adv. in a quiet manner. [< L *quietus* resting, pp. of *quiescere* rest < *quies* quiet. Doublet of COY and QUIT, adj.] **—qui′et·er,** *n.*
—qui′et·ly, *adv.* **—qui′et·ness,** *n.*
☛ *Syn. adj.* **1.** See note at **still.**

qui·et·en (kwī′ə tən) *v.* **1** cause to become quiet; make still or peaceful: *The mother quietened her excited child.* **2** become quiet (*usually used with* **down**): *The wind finally quietened down.*

qui·e·tude (kwī′ə tyüd′ *or* kwī′ə tüd′) *n.* quietness; stillness; calmness. [< LL *quietudo* < L *quietus* quiet]

qui·e·tus (kwī ē′təs) *n.* **1** final extinction, riddance, or end: *to give an ugly rumor its quietus. The government's refusal of funds has given the quietus to the project.* **2** release from life; death. **3** settlement or discharge of a debt, obligation, etc. [< Med.L *quietus est* he is discharged < L *quietus est* he is at rest. See QUIET.]

quill (kwil) *n.* **1** a large, stiff feather. **2** the hollow stem of a feather. **3** anything made from the stem of a feather, such as a pen or toothpick. **4** one of the stiff sharp spines of a porcupine or hedgehog. [ME *quil*]

quill·back (kwil′bak′) *n.* a North American freshwater fish (*Carpiodes cyprinus*), a kind of sucker having a very deep, laterally compressed, buff-and-white body and a dorsal fin with the first rays much elongated.

quilt (kwilt) *n., v.* **—n. 1** a bed covering made of two layers of cloth with a filling between them that is held in place by lines of stitching, often in decorative patterns. Quilts are filled with down or feathers or a batting of wool, cotton, or a synthetic fibre such as terylene. **2** any thick bed covering.
—v. 1 fill or pad like a quilt: *to quilt a jacket.* **2** stitch with lines or patterns through layers of cloth: *to quilt a traditional design.* **3** stitch in layers with a padding between: *I bought some quilted material for a vest.* **4** make quilts: *They enjoy quilting.* [ME < OF *cuilte* < L *culcita* cushion] **—quilt′er,** *n.*

quilt·ing (kwil′ting) *n.* **1** quilted work. **2** material that is quilted or used for making quilts.

quilting bee a social gathering of women to work on a quilt.

quince (kwins) *n.* **1** a hard, yellowish, acid fruit, used for preserves and jelly. **2** the Asiatic tree (*Cydonia oblonga*) it grows on, a member of the rose family. **3** japonica. [originally pl. of ME *quyne* < OF *cooin* < L *cotoneum*]

quin·cun·cial (kwin kun′shəl) *adj.* of, having to do with, or being a quincunx.

quin·cunx (kwin′kungks) *n.* an arrangement or group of five objects with four forming the corners of a square or rectangle and the fifth in the centre, such as the five on a die or playing card.

quin·el·la (kwi nel′ə) *n.* a system of betting that two horses in a particular race will occupy the first two places, though either horse may come first.

qui·nine (kwī′nīn *or* kwi nēn′) *n.* **1** a bitter, colorless crystalline drug made from cinchona bark, used in medicine. **2** any of various compounds of quinine that are used as medicine. [< Sp. *quina* < Quechua (S. Am.Ind.) *kina* bark]

quinine water tonic (def. 3).

Quin·qua·ges·i·ma (kwing′kwə jes′ə mə) *n.* the Sunday before the beginning of Lent; Shrove Sunday. [< L *quinquagesima,* fem. adj. fiftieth]

quin·quen·ni·al (kwing kwen′ē əl) *adj., n.* **—adj. 1** occurring every five years. **2** of or for five years. **—n. 1** something that occurs every five years. **2** something lasting five years. [< L *quinquennium* < *quinque* five + *annus* year] **—quin·quen′ni·al·ly,** *adv.*

quin·que·reme (kwing′kwə rēm′) *n.* an ancient Roman galley with five tiers of oars. [< L *quinqueremis* < *quinque* five + *remus* oar]

quin·sy (kwin′zē) *n.* an abscess behind the tonsils, usually caused by a severe case of tonsillitis. [ME < Med.L *quinancia* < Gk. *kynanchē,* originally, dog's collar < *kyon, kynos* dog + *anchein* choke]

quint (kwint) *n. Informal.* quintuplet.

quin·tal (kan′təl *for 1,* kwin′təl *or* kan′təl *for 2, 3*) *n.* **1** *Cdn. Newfoundland.* **a** a unit used for weighing fish, especially cod, equal to 112 pounds (about 50.8 kg). **b** a quantity of fish weighing one quintal: *The first day they got 50 quintals of cod.* **c** a container holding one quintal, used for packing and shipping dried, salted cod. **2** a unit for measuring mass, equal to 100 pounds (about 45.4 kg). **3** a unit for measuring mass, equal to 100 kilograms. [ME < Med.L *quintale* < Arabic *qintar* weight of a hundred pounds, probably ult. < L *centenarius* < *centum* hundred]

quin·tes·sence (kwin tes′əns) *n.* **1** the essence of a thing in its purest form. **2** the best example or representative of something: *He was the quintessence of goodness.* [ME < Med.L *quinta essentia* fifth essence]

quin·tes·sen·tial (kwin′tə sen′shəl) *adj.* having the nature of a quintessence; of the purest or most perfect kind: *the quintessential detective of modern fiction.* **—quin′tes·sen′tial·ly,** *adv.*

quin·tet *or* **quin·tette** (kwin tet′) *n.* **1** a group of five musicians who perform together. **2** a piece of music for five voices or instruments. **3** any group of five. [< F < Ital. *quintetto* < *quinto* fifth < L *quintus*]

quin·til·lion (kwin til′yən) *n.* **1** in Canada and the United States, a cardinal number represented by 1 followed by 18 zeros. **2** in Britain, France, and Germany, 1 followed by 30 zeros. [< L *quintus* fifth + E *million*]

quin·tu·ple (kwin tyü′pəl, kwin tü′pəl, *or* kwin′tə pəl) *adj., v.,* -pled, -pling; *n.* **—adj. 1** fivefold; consisting of five parts. **2** five times as great or as many.
—v. make or become five times as great or as many: *He quintupled his investment.*
—n. a number, amount, etc. five times as great as another. [< F *quintuple* < L *quintus* fifth; patterned on *quadruple*]

quin·tu·plet (kwin tyü′plit, kwin tü′plit, *or* kwin′tə plit) *n.* **1** one of five offspring born at one birth. **2** any group or combination of five. [< *quintuple,* adj., modelled on *triplet*]

quip (kwip) *n., v.,* quipped, quip·ping. **—n. 1** a clever or witty saying, especially one made on the spur of the moment. **2** a sharp, cutting remark. **3** a quibble. **4** something odd or strange.
—v. make quips. [for earlier *quippy* < L *quippe* indeed, I dare say]

quire[1] (kwīr) *n.* **1** 24 or, sometimes, 25 sheets of paper of the same size and quality; one twentieth of a ream. **2** four sheets of paper folded to form a section of eight leaves, or 16 pages, as often done in medieval manuscripts. [ME < OF *quaier,* ult. < L *quaterni* four each]

quire[2] (kwīr) *n. Archaic.* choir.

Quir·i·nal (kwir′ə nəl) *n.* **1** one of the seven hills upon which Rome was built. **2** a palace built on this hill. **3** *Historical.* the Italian royal court or government, as distinguished from the Vatican (representing the papacy). [< L *Quirinalis* < *Quirinus,* an ancient Roman god of war]

quirk (kwėrk) *n.* **1** a peculiar trait; an odd mannerism or way of behaving: *She has some irritating quirks.* **2** an unexpected or sudden happening, action, etc.: *a quirk of fate.* **3** a sudden turn or curve, such as a flourish in writing. [origin uncertain]

quirk·y (kwėr′kē) *adj.* characterized by a quirk or quirks; especially, odd, peculiar, or unexpected: *a quirky viewpoint.* **—quirk′i·ly,** *adv.* **—quirk′i·ness,** *n.*

quirt (kwėrt) *n., v.* **—n.** a riding whip with a short, stout handle and a lash of braided leather. **—v.** strike with a quirt. [< Sp. *cuarta,* originally, a long whip]

quis·ling (kwiz′ling) *n.* a person who collaborates with an enemy occupying his country, especially by serving in a puppet government. [< Vidkun *Quisling* (1887-1945), a Norwegian army officer and politician, who co-operated with the Germans when they invaded Norway during World War II]

quit (kwit) *v.* quit *or* quit·ted, quit·ting; *adj.* **—v. 1** stop: *The men quit work when the whistle blew.* **2** stop working: *It's almost time to quit.* **3** leave: *He quit his room in anger.* **4** give up; let go. **5** pay back; pay off (a debt). **6** free; clear; rid. **7** *Archaic.* behave or conduct (oneself).
—adj. free; clear; rid: *I gave him money to be quit of him.* [(v.) ME < OF *quiter* < Med.L *quietare* discharge < L *quietus.* See QUIET; (adj.) ME < OF *quite* < L *quietus.* Doublet of QUIET and COY.]

quitch *or* **quitch grass** (kwich) *n.* couch grass; quack grass. [OE *cwice.* Related to QUICK.]

quit·claim (kwit′klām′) *n., v.* **—n. 1** the giving up of a claim. **2** a

document stating that somebody gives up a claim. —v. give up claim to (a right or claim). [ME < AF *quiteclamer* < OF *quite* + *clamer*. See QUIT, CLAIM.]

quite (kwīt) adv. **1** completely; wholly; entirely: *That's not quite true. I'm afraid it's quite impossible for me to go.* **2** really; positively: *It's quite the thing these days.* **3** to a considerable extent or degree: *This dress is quite nice but I like the other one better. He plays the piano quite well.*
quite a, a a considerable number, amount, size, etc.: *There are quite a few left. It cost quite a lot. We waited quite a while.* **b** *Informal.* impressive or unusual: *That's quite a ring you have. He's quite a guy.*
[originally adj., var. of *quit* in sense of "clear"]
☛ *Usage.* **Quite.** The formal meaning of **quite** is "entirely, wholly." In informal English, it is generally used with the reduced meaning of "to a considerable extent or degree." Formal: *The fox was quite exhausted when we reached it.* Informal: *He is quite worried. I hiked quite a distance.* A number of convenient phrases with **quite** are good informal usage: *quite a few people, quite a little time,* and so on.

quit·rent (kwit′rent′) n. under the feudal system, the rent paid in money, instead of services rendered. [< *quit,* adj. + *rent*]

quits (kwits) adj. on even terms by repayment or retaliation (*never used before a noun*): *After the book was returned undamaged, the boys were quits.*
call it quits, stop doing something: *The mosquitoes got so bad that we finally had to call it quits and go home.*
cry quits, admit that things are now even; agree to stop quarrelling, etc.
[< *quit,* adj.]

quit·tance (kwit′əns) n. *Archaic.* **1** a release from debt or obligation. **2** the paper certifying a release from debt; a receipt. **3** repayment. [ME < OF *quitance* < *quiter* quit. See QUIT, v.]

quit·ter (kwit′ər) n. *Informal.* a person who gives up too easily.

quiv·er[1] (kwiv′ər) v., n. —v. shake; shiver; tremble: *His voice quivered. The dog quivered with excitement.* —n. shaking or trembling: *A quiver of his mouth showed that he was about to cry.* [cf. OE *cwiferlīce* actively]
☛ *Syn. v.* See note at **shake.**

quiv·er[2] (kwiv′ər) n. **1** a tubelike case for holding and carrying arrows. **2** the arrows in a quiver. [ME < AF *quiveir,* probably < Gmc.]

qui vive? (kē′vēv′) who goes there?
on the qui vive, watchful; alert.
[< F *qui vive?,* literally, (long) live who?; expecting such a reply as *Vive le roi!* Long live the king!]

Qui·xo·te (kē hō′tē *or* kwik′sət; *Spanish,* kē HŌ′tā) n. See **Don Quixote.**

quix·ot·ic (kwiks ot′ik) adj. characterized by very high but impractical ideals or extravagant chivalry. —**quix·ot′i·cal·ly,** adv.

quix·ot·ism (kwik′sət iz′əm) n. a quixotic character or behavior.

quiz (kwiz) n., pl. **quiz·zes;** v. **quizzed, quiz·zing.** —n. **1** a short or informal test: *a quiz in geography.* **2** *Archaic.* a person who makes fun of others.
—v. **1** give such a test to: *to quiz a class in history.* **2** question; interrogate: *The lawyer quizzed the witness.* **3** *Archaic.* make fun of. [origin uncertain] —**quiz′zer,** n.

quiz·mas·ter (kwiz′mas′tər) n. the person who asks questions of the contestants in a quiz show.

quiz show a radio or television program in which contestants are given prizes for answering questions correctly.

quiz·zi·cal (kwiz′ə kəl) adj. **1** odd; queer; comical. **2** that suggests making fun of others; teasing: *a quizzical smile.* —**quiz′zi·cal·ly,** adv.

quoin (koin *or* kwoin) n. **1** an external angle of a wall or building. **2** the stone forming an outside angle of a wall; a cornerstone. **3** a wedge-shaped piece of wood, metal, etc. [var. of *coin*]

quoit (kwoit) n. **1** a heavy, flattish ring of iron or circle of rope, rubber, etc., used in a game in which it is thrown at a peg stuck in the ground to encircle it or come as close to it as possible. **2** **quoits,** the game in which quoits are thrown at a peg (*used with a singular verb*): *Quoits is similar to horseshoes.* [ME < OF *coite* cushion]
☛ *Usage.* **Quoits,** meaning the game, is plural in form and singular in use: *Quoits is often played with horseshoes.*

quon·dam (kwon′dəm) adj. that once was; former. [< L *quondam* at one time]

Quon·set hut (kwon′sit) a prefabricated, largely metal building with a semicircular roof. [< *Quonset,* Rhode Island, where such a building was first used at the naval air base]

quo·rum (kwô′rəm) n. the number of members of any society or assembly that must be present if the business done is to be legal or binding. [< L *quorum* of whom]

quot. quotation.

hat, āge, fär; let, ēqual, tėrm; it, īce
hot, ōpen, ôrder; oil, out; cup, pút, rüle,
əbove, takən, pencəl, lemən, circəs
ch, child; ng, long; sh, ship
th, thin; ᴛʜ, then; zh, measure

quo·ta (kwō′tə) n. **1** a share or proportion that is required of or due to a person or group: *Each club member was given his quota of tickets to sell for the banquet.* **2** a quantity or proportion that is allowed: *a government quota on imports.* [< Med.L < L *quota pars* how large a part]

quot·a·ble (kwōt′ə bəl) adj. suitable for or worth quoting: *a quotable comment.*

quo·ta·tion (kwō tā′shən) n. **1** somebody's words repeated exactly by another person; a passage quoted from a book, speech, etc.: *From what author does this quotation come?* **2** the act or habit of quoting: *Quotation is a habit of some preachers.* **3** the stating of the current price of a stock, commodity, etc. **4** the price so stated: *today's quotation on wheat.*

quotation mark one of a pair of marks used to indicate the beginning and end of a quotation. The usual marks are (" ") for a single quotation and (' ') for a quotation within a quotation.
☛ *Usage.* **Punctuation with quotation marks.** A period or comma at the end of a quotation is normally placed before the closing quotation mark: *"The longer you put it off,"* he said, *"the harder it's going to be."* Other marks of punctuation are placed inside or outside the quotation marks, depending on the meaning: *His abrupt reply was "What do you think?" Have you heard him sing "If you could read my mind"?*

quote (kwōt) v. **quot·ed, quot·ing;** n. —v. **1** repeat the exact words of; give words or passages from: *to quote Shakespeare. He often quotes his grandchildren's sayings.* **2** repeat exactly the words of another or a passage from a book: *She quoted from the Bible.* **3** bring forward as an example or authority; cite: *The judge quoted various cases in support of his opinion.* **4** give (a price): *to quote a price on a home.* **5** enclose within quotation marks: *The dialogue in old books is not quoted.*
—n. **1** quotation. **2** quotation mark. [< Med.L *quotare* to number chapters < L *quotus* which (in sequence)] —**quot′er,** n.
☛ *Syn. v.* **3. Quote, cite** = bring forward as authority or evidence. Although the distinction is not always kept, **quote** means to bring forward the words of another, either repeated exactly or given in a summary, identifying the speaker: *The Commissioner was quoted as saying action will be taken.* **Cite** means to name as evidence or authority, but not to quote, a passage, author, or book, with exact title, page, etc.: *To support his argument he cited Article 68, Chapter 10, of the Charter of the United Nations.*

quoth (kwōth) v. *Archaic.* said. [pt. of *queathe* (OE *cwethan*). Related to BEQUEATH.]

quoth·a (kwōth′ə) interj. *Archaic.* quoth he (*used ironically or contemptuously in repeating the words of another*).

quo·tid·i·an (kwō tid′ē ən) adj., n. —adj. reappearing daily; daily. —n. a fever or ague that occurs daily. [< L *quotidianus,* var. of *cotidianus* < *cotidie* daily < *quotus* which (in sequence) + *dies* day]

quo·tient (kwō′shənt) n. the number obtained by dividing one number by another. In $26 \div 2 = 13$, 13 is the quotient. [< L *quotiens* how many times]

quo war·ran·to (kwō wə ran′tō) *Latin.* **1** a writ commanding a person to show by what authority he holds a public office, privilege, franchise, etc. **2** the legal proceedings taken against such a person as distinct from a private citizen. [< Med.L *quo warranto* by what warrant]

Qur·an (kù rän′ *or* kə rän′) n. Koran. Also, **Qu'ran.** [< Arabic < *qurān* recitation < *qara'a* read]

qursh *or* **qurush** (kùrsh *or* kür′əsh) n. **1** a unit of money in Saudi Arabia, worth ¹⁄₂₀ of a riyal. **2** a coin worth one qursh. [< Arabic *qirsh*]

q.v. see this word (for L *quod vide* which see).
☛ *Usage.* The abbreviation **q.v.** is used as an instruction to refer to another book, article, etc. already mentioned. It is now often replaced in reference works by the English word **see.**

Rr

r or **R** (är) *n., pl.* **r's** or **R's.** **1** the eighteenth letter of the English alphabet. **2** any speech sound represented by this letter. **3** a person or thing identified as *r*, especially the eighteenth in a series. **4** (*adj.*) of or being an R or r.

the three R's, the basic elements of an education; reading, writing, and arithmetic.

r **1** ratio. **2** radius. **3** in church usage, respond or response. **4** *Physics.* resistance in ohms.

r. **1** railway. **2** rod. **3** ruble. **4** rupee. **5** road. **6** rare. **7** residence; resides. **8** retired. **9** ratio.

R. **1** River. **2** Republican. **3** Railway; Railroad. **4** King (for L *rex*). **5** Queen (for L *regina*). **6** Royal. **7** Rabbi. **8** Radical. **9** Réaumur. **10** Rector.

Ra (rä) *n.* the Egyptian sun god and supreme deity, typically represented as a hawk-headed man bearing the sun on his head. [< Egyptian *Rā* the sun]

Ra radium.

R.A. **1** rear-admiral. **2** Royal Academy; Royal Academician. **3** Royal Artillery.

rab·bet (rab′it) *n., v.* **-bet·ed, -bet·ing.** —*n.* **1** a groove, slot, or recess made on the edge or surface of a board, etc. to receive the end or edge of another piece of wood shaped to fit it. **2** a joint so made, also called a **rabbet joint.** See **joint** for picture. —*v.* **1** cut or form a rabbet in. **2** join with a rabbet. [ME < OF *rabat* a beating down < *rabbatre.* See REBATE.]
☞ *Hom.* **rabbit.**

rab·bi (rab′ī) *n., pl.* **-bis.** **1** a teacher or scholar of the Jewish law. **2** a Jewish religious leader, especially the spiritual head of a congregation. [< L < Hebrew *rabbī* my master]

rab·bin·ate (rab′ə nit *or* rab′ə nāt′) *n.* **1** the position or office of rabbi. **2** rabbis collectively.

rab·bin·ic (rə bin′ik) *adj.* **1** rabbinical. **2 Rabbinic,** Rabbinic Hebrew.

Rabbinic Hebrew the Hebrew language as used by rabbis of the Middle Ages in their writings.

rab·bin·i·cal (rə bin′ə kəl) *adj.* of or having to do with rabbis, their learning, writings, etc. —**rab·bin′i·cal·ly,** *adv.*

rab·bit (rab′it) *n., v.* —*n.* **1** any of various gregarious burrowing mammals (family Leporidae, especially genera *Oryctolagus* and *Sylvilagus*) related to and resembling hares but generally smaller, with shorter ears, and bearing naked young whose eyes are closed at birth. The common European rabbit (*Oryctolagus cuniculus*) has been introduced into many parts of the world; the various domestic breeds have also been developed from this species. The common North American rabbits are the cottontails. **2** the fur of a rabbit. **3** the flesh of a rabbit, used as food. **4** Welsh rabbit.
—*v.* hunt or catch rabbits. [ME *rabet*; cf. MDu. *robbe*]
—**rab′bit·like′,** *adj.*
☞ *Hom.* **rabbet.**

rabbit ears *Informal.* a small indoor television antenna consisting of two rods of adjustable length attached to a small base in such a way that they can be swivelled apart to form a wide or narrow V.

rab·ble (rab′əl) *n.* **1** a disorderly crowd; mob. **2 the rabble,** *Derogatory.* the lowest class of people. [cf. Du. *rabbelen* prattle]

rab·ble–rous·er (rab′əl rouz′ər) *n.* a person who tries to stir up groups of people to violence, as a form of social or political protest; demagogue.

rab·ble–rous·ing (rab′əl rouz′ing) *adj., n.* —*adj.* acting like a rabble-rouser; demagogic. —*n.* the methods or actions of a rabble-rouser; demagoguery.

Rab·e·lai·si·an (rab′ə lā′zē ən *or* rab′ə lā′zhən) *adj.* of, having to do with, or suggesting François Rabelais (1495?-1553), a French writer of satire and humor; characterized by broad, coarse humor.

rab·id (rab′id) *adj.* **1** unreasonably extreme; fanatical; violent: *a rabid idealist.* **2** furious; raging. **3** of or affected with rabies: *a rabid dog.* [< L *rabidus* < *rabere* be mad] —**rab′id·ly,** *adv.* —**rab′id·ness,** *n.*

ra·bies (rā′bēz) *n.* an acute, usually fatal, infectious virus disease of the central nervous system that can be transmitted to any warm-blooded animal, including man, by the bite of an animal that has the disease. The usual symptoms of rabies are wild excitement and aggressiveness, followed by paralysis and death. [< L *rabies* madness < *rabere* be mad]

rac·coon (ra kün′) *n.* **1** any of a genus (*Procyon*) of small, greyish-brown, carnivorous mammals having a thickset body, a long, bushy, ringed tail, a dark patch around the eyes, and a pointed snout, especially the common raccoon (*P. lotor*) of North and Central America and the West Indies. Raccoons live mainly in trees and are active at night. **2** the fur of a raccoon. **3** (*adj.*) designating the family (Procyonidae) of mammals that includes the raccoons, the kinkajou, etc. Also **racoon.** [< Algonquian]

race[1] (rās) *n., v.* **raced, rac·ing.** —*n.* **1** a contest of speed, as in running, driving, riding, sailing, etc. **2** Often, **races,** *pl.* a series of horse races run at a set time over a regular course. **3** any contest that suggests a race: *a political race.* **4** onward movement: *the race of life.* **5** a strong or fast current of water: *a mill race.* **6** the channel of a stream. **7** a channel leading water to or from a place where its energy is utilized. **8** a track, groove, etc. for a sliding or rolling part of a machine.
—*v.* **1** engage in a contest of speed. **2** try to beat in a contest of speed; run a race with. **3** cause to run in a race. **4** run, move, or go swiftly. **5** cause to run, move, or go swiftly. **6** of a motor, wheel, etc., run too fast when load or resistance is lessened without corresponding lessening of power. [ME < ON *rás*]

race[2] (rās) *n.* **1** *Anthropology.* a major grouping of human beings, distinguished biologically mainly by such hereditary traits as dominant blood types and resistance to particular diseases and also by skin color, body proportions, etc. The nine major races now generally recognized are the African, Amerindian, Asiatic, Australoid, European, Indic, Melanesian, Micronesian, and Polynesian. **2** one of the major divisions of living things: *the human race, the race of birds.* **3** a group, class, or kind of people having some feature or quality in common: *the Scottish race, the Nordic race, the brave race of seamen.* **4** subspecies; variety. **5** the state or condition of belonging to a particular race: *Intelligence does not depend on race.* [< F < Ital. *razza*]
☞ *Syn.* **1, 2.** See note at **people.**

race·course (rās′kôrs′) *n.* a course or track for racing; racetrack.

race·horse (rās′hôrs′) *n.* a horse bred or kept for racing.

ra·ceme (rā sēm′ *or* rə sēm′) *n.* a type of inflorescence consisting of a simple flower cluster having the flowers on short stalks along a stem, the lower flowers blooming first. The lily of the valley, the currant, and the chokecherry have racemes. See **inflorescence** for picture. [< L *racemus* cluster. Doublet of RAISIN.]

rac·er (rās′ər) *n.* **1** a person who races or an animal, vehicle, boat, or aircraft that is used for racing. **2** any of several harmless North American snakes (genera *Coluber* and *Mastigophis*) that can move very fast, especially the blacksnake.

race riot an outbreak of violence resulting from hostility or hatred between races.

race suicide the extinction of a people that tends to result when by deliberate limitation of the number of children, the birth rate falls below the death rate.

race–track (rās′trak′) *n.* **1** a track or course, usually oval in shape, on which races with horses or vehicles are run. **2** a place where races are held, including the track, viewing stands, etc.

ra·chis (rā′kis) *n., pl.* **ra·chis·es, rach·i·des.** (rak′ə dēz′ *or* rā′kə dēz′) **1** the stem from which the individual flowers of a flower cluster or the leaflets of a compound leaf grow. **2** the shaft of a feather. **3** spinal column. [< NL < Gk. *rhachis* backbone]

ra·chit·ic (rə kit′ik) *adj.* having to do with or affected with rickets; rickety.

ra·chi·tis (rə kī′tis) *n.* rickets. [< NL < Gk. *rhachis* backbone + -itis]

ra·cial (rā′shəl) *adj.* **1** of, having to do with, or characteristic of a human race: *racial traits.* **2** occurring between or involving two or more races: *racial tensions, racial harmony.*

ra·cial·ism (rā′shə liz′əm) *n.* racism.

ra·cial·ly (rā′shəl ē) *adv.* in respect to race.

rac·i·ness (rās′ē nis) *n.* the quality or condition of being racy.

rac·ism (rās′iz əm) *n.* **1** prejudice or discrimination against a person or group because of a difference of race. **2** prejudice or discrimination against a person or group because of a difference of cultural or ethnic background. **3** belief in the superiority of a particular race, based on the theory that human abilities, character, etc. are determined by race.

rac·ist (rās′ist) *n., adj.* —*n.* one who favors or practises racism. —*adj.* of or having to do with racism: *racist policies.*

rack¹ (rak) *n., v.* —*n.* **1** a frame with bars, shelves, or pegs to hold, arrange, or keep things on: *a towel rack, a hat rack, a baggage rack.* **2** a frame of bars to hold hay and other food for cattle, etc. **3** a framework set on a wagon for carrying hay, straw, etc. **4** a pair, or set, of antlers. **5** an instrument of torture that stretched the body of the victim. **6** a cause or condition of great suffering in body or mind. **7** a stretch; strain. **8** a bar with pegs or teeth on one edge, into which teeth on the rim of a wheel can fit. See **gear** for picture. **9** *Billiards.* a triangular frame used for arranging the balls.
on the rack, in great pain; suffering very much.
—*v.* **1** hurt very much: *racked with grief. A toothache racked his jaw.* **2** stretch; strain. **3** torture on the rack.
rack (one's) brains, think as hard as one can.
rack up, *Informal.* accumulate.
[probably < MDu. or MLG *recke*]
☞ *Hom.* wrack.

rack² (rak) *n.* wreck; destruction: *a vacant house going to rack and ruin.* [var. of *wrack¹*]
☞ *Hom.* wrack.

rack³ (rak) *n., v.* —*n.* **1** a horse's gait in which the forefeet move as in a slow gallop, while the hind feet move as in a trot or pace; single-foot. **2** a pace. —*v.* **1** go at a rack. **2** pace. [origin uncertain]
☞ *Hom.* wrack.

rack⁴ (rak) *n.* flying, broken clouds driven by the wind. [ME < Scand.; cf. Swedish dial. *rak* wreckage]
☞ *Hom.* wrack.

rack⁵ (rak) *n.* the neck portion of a forequarter of pork, veal, or mutton, sometimes made into a roast. See **lamb** for picture. [origin uncertain]
☞ *Hom.* wrack.

rack·et¹ (rak′it) *n., v.* —*n.* **1** loud noise or talking; uproar; din: *Who's making all the racket?* **2** a dishonest scheme for getting money from people, especially by threatening violence. **3** *Informal.* any dishonest or fraudulent scheme or activity. **4** *Slang.* an easy, very profitable means of livelihood: *He has quite a racket going, with the edible wrapping paper he invented.* **5** *Slang.* any business or occupation: *What's your racket?*
stand the racket, hold out against strain or wear and tear.
—*v.* **1** make a racket; move about in a noisy way. **2** take part in an exciting social life. [formerly British slang (from early 19th century); ? imitative]

rack·et² or **rac·quet** (rak′it) *n.* **1** a light, wide bat used in games like tennis, badminton, and squash, consisting of a network of nylon, gut, etc. stretched in an open oval or round frame attached to a handle. **2** Usually, **racquets,** a game for two or four players with a ball and rackets, played in a walled court (*used with a singular verb*). **3** raquette. [< F *raquette* < Ital. < Arabic *rāha* palm of the hand]

rack·et·eer (rak′ə tēr′) *n., v.* —*n.* a person who operates a racket, especially one who extorts money by threatening violence or by blackmail. —*v.* obtain money, etc. by such means.

rack·et·eer·ing (rak′ə tēr′ing) *n.* the business of a racketeer.

rack·et·y (rak′ə tē) *adj.* **1** making a racket; noisy. **2** characterized by revelry or dissipation.

rac·on·teur (rak′on tėr′) *n.* a person who is skilful at telling stories, anecdotes, etc. [< F]

ra·coon (ra kün′) *n.* raccoon.

rac·quet (rak′it) *n.* racket².

rac·quet·ball (rak′t bol′ or rak′it bôl′) *n.* an indoor game similar to handball, played by two or four players in a walled court, using a short racket and a hollow rubber ball about the size of a tennis ball.

rac·y (rās′ē) *adj.* **rac·i·er, rac·i·est. 1** vigorous; lively. **2** having the distinctive quality characteristic of something in its best or original form: *racy flavor.* **3** risqué; suggestive; slightly indecent: *a racy novel.* [< *race²*, in the sense of particular class or special flavor] —**rac′i·ly,** *adv.*

rad¹ (rad) *n.* a unit of nuclear radiation equal to 100 ergs of energy per gram, for measuring absorbed doses of radiation. [< *radiation*]

rad² (rad) *n. Informal.* radiator.

rad. radical.

ra·dar (rā′där) *n.* **1** a system for determining the distance, direction, speed, etc. of unseen objects by the reflection of high-frequency radio waves. **2** an instrument used for this. [short for *radio detecting and ranging*]

radar trap an apparatus, usually located in a hidden or unexpected place, that uses radar to detect road vehicles travelling faster than the speed limit.

ra·di·al (rā′dē əl) *adj., n.* —*adj.* **1** arranged like or in radii or rays from a centre: *radial symmetry. The petals of a daisy and the spokes of a wagon wheel have a radial form.* **2** of, having to do with, or near the bone called the radius. —*n.* radial tire. —**ra′di·al·ly,** *adv.*

radial engine an internal-combustion engine for an airplane, having radially arranged cylinders.

radial tire an automobile tire in which the plies of cord extending to the edges of the tire are at right angles to the centre line of the tread.

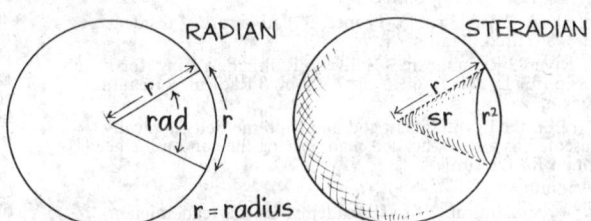

RADIAN   STERADIAN

r = radius

ra·di·an (rā′dē ən) *n.* an SI unit for measuring plane angles, equal to the angle formed between two radii of a circle that cuts off an arc on the circumference equal in length to the radius. There are two pi (2 π) radians in a circle. The radian, which is used especially in mathematics, is one of the two supplementary units in the SI. *Symbol:* rad [< *radius*]

ra·di·ance (rā′dē əns) *n.* the quality or state of being radiant; vivid brightness: *the radiance of the sun, the radiance of a smile.*

ra·di·an·cy (rā′dē ən sē) *n.* radiance.

ra·di·ant (rā′dē ənt) *adj., n.* —*adj.* **1** shining; bright; beaming: *a radiant smile.* **2** sending out rays of light or heat: *The sun is a radiant body.* **3** bright with light. **4** sent off in rays from some source; radiated: *We get radiant energy from the sun.* **5** strikingly fine or splendid, as looks, beauty, etc. or the person. —*n. Physics.* a point or object from which light or heat radiates. [< L *radians, -antis,* ppr. of *radiare* beam < *radius* ray] —**ra′di·ant·ly,** *adv.*
☞ *Syn. adj.* **1.** See note at **bright.**

radiant energy a form of energy that is transmitted by electromagnetic waves and is perceived as heat, light, X rays, etc. The sun is our main source of radiant energy.

radiant heating a method of heating a room, building, etc. by means of heating units let into pipes or wires concealed in walls, baseboards, or floors.

ra·di·ate (rā′dē āt′) *v.* **-at·ed, -at·ing;** *adj.* —*v.* **1** give out rays of: *The sun radiates light and heat.* **2** give out rays; shine. **3** issue in rays: *Heat radiates from those hot steam pipes.* **4** give out; send forth: *Her face radiates joy.* **5** spread out from or as if from a centre: *Roads radiate from the city in every direction.* —*adj.* **1** having rays: *A daisy is a radiate flower.* **2** radiating from a centre. [ME < L *radiare.* See RADIANT.]

ra·di·a·tion (rā′dē ā′shən) *n.* **1** the act or process of giving out light, heat, or other radiant energy. **2** the energy radiated. **3** a radio-active ray or rays. Radiation is harmful to living tissues. **4** the process of treating disease by radiation from a radio-active material such as radium. **5** *Informal.* the radiators of a central heating system referred to collectively, or their capacity: *The plumbing contractor will figure out how much radiation you need.*

radiation counter any device, such as a Geiger counter, for detecting and counting radiation rays.

radiation sickness a disease resulting from an overdose of radiation from radio-active materials. It is usually characterized by internal bleeding and changes in tissue structure.

ra·di·a·tor (rā′dē ā′tər) *n.* **1** a heating device consisting of a set of pipes through which steam or hot water passes. **2** a device for circulating water. The radiator of an automobile gives off heat very quickly and so cools the water inside it. **3** any person or thing that radiates, or transmits something.

rad·i·cal (rad′ə kəl) *adj., n.* —*adj.* **1** going to the root; fundamental: *Cruelty is a radical fault. If she wants to reduce, she must make a radical change in her diet.* **2** *Politics.* **a** advocating or

favoring fundamental changes in the social or economic structure; leftist. **b** *Radical*, of or having to do with certain 20th-century parties, especially in Europe, whose programs range from somewhat leftist to conservative. **3** of or from the root or roots. **4** *Botany*. arising from the root or the base of the stem; basal. **5** *Mathematics*. having to do with or forming the root of a number or quantity.
—*n.* **1** *Politics.* a person who has radical views. **2** *Radical*, a member of a Radical party. **3** *Chemistry.* an atom or group of atoms acting as a unit in reactions. Ammonium (NH_4) is a radical in NH_4OH and NH_4Cl. **4** *Mathematics*. the sign ($\sqrt{}$) put before an expression to show that some root of it is to be extracted.
5 *Grammar.* a root. **6** anything fundamental or basic. [ME < LL *radicalis* < L *radix, -icis* root] —**rad′i·cal·ly,** *adv.* —**rad′i·cal·ness,** *n.*
☛ *Hom.* **radicle.**

rad·i·cal·ism (rad′ə kəl iz′əm) *n.* **1** the condition or quality of being radical. **2** *Politics.* the principles or practices of radicals; extreme views.

rad·i·cal·ize (rad′ə kəl īz′) *v.* **-ized, iz·ing.** make politically radical.

rad·i·ces (rad′i sēz′) *n.* a plural of **radix.**

rad·i·cle (rad′ə kəl) *n.* **1** the lower end of the stem (hypocotyl) of a plant embryo, that develops into the main root. See **embryo** for picture. **2** a small root; rootlet. [< L *radicula,* dim. of *radix, -icis* root]
☛ *Hom.* **radical.**

ra·di·i (rā′dē ī′) *n.* a pl. of **radius.**

ra·di·o (rā′dē ō′) *n., pl.* **-di·os;** *adj., v.* **-di·oed, -di·o·ing.** —*n.*
1 the sending and receiving of sound in the form of electric signals by means of electromagnetic waves without connecting wires. **2** an apparatus for receiving and making audible the sounds so sent.
3 *Informal.* a message sent by radio. **4** the business of radio broadcasting: *He left the movies and got a job in radio.* **5** the branch of physics dealing with electromagnetic waves as used in communication.
—*adj.* **1** of, having to do with, used in, or sent by radio. **2** of or having to do with electric frequencies higher than 15 000 per second.
—*v.* transmit or send out by radio. [independent use of *radio-,* abstracted from *radiotelegraphy,* etc.]

radio– *combining form.* **1** having to do with radio: *Radiotelegraphy means telegraphing by radio. Radio-controlled means controlled from a distance by radio.* **2** having to do with rays or radiation: *A radiograph is a picture produced by X rays.* **3** having to do with radio-activity: *A radio-isotope is a radio-active isotope.*
4 of or having to do with a radius: *Radio-symmetrical means radially symmetrical; that is, symmetrical around a central point.* [< *radius*]
☛ *Usage.* Practice varies as to using a hyphen in combination with **radio-**. In this dictionary a hyphen is used when **radio-** is followed immediately by another vowel, as *radio-active,* but *radiotelegraphy.*

ra·di·o·ac·tive or **ra·di·o·ac·tive** (rā′dē ō ak′tiv) *adj.* giving off radiant energy in the form of alpha, beta, or gamma rays as a result of the breaking up of atoms. Radium, uranium, and thorium are radio-active metallic elements.

ra·di·o·ac·tiv·i·ty (rā′dē ō ak tiv′ə tē) *n.* **1** the property of being radio-active. **2** the radiation given off.

radio astronomy the branch of astronomy that studies objects in space by analysing radio waves given off by or reflected from them.

radio beacon a radio transmitter that sends out special radio signals to help ships, aircraft, etc. determine their position or come in safely when visibility is poor.

ra·di·o·bi·o·log·i·cal (rā′dē ō bī′ə loj′ə kəl) *adj.* **1** of or having to do with radiobiology. **2** caused by radiation.

ra·di·o·bi·ol·o·gist (rā′dē ō bī ol′ə jist) *n.* a person trained in radiobiology, especially one whose work it is.

ra·di·o·bi·ol·o·gy (rā′dē ō bī ol′ə jē) *n.* the branch of biology that deals with the effects of radiation on living bodies.

ra·di·o·car·bon (rā′dē ō kär′bən) *adj.* radio-active carbon, especially carbon 14, used in finding out the age of ancient organic materials. The amount of radiocarbon in a piece of bone, fabric, etc. is an indication of how old it is.

ra·di·o·chem·i·cal (rā′dē ō kem′ə kəl) *adj.* of or having to do with radiochemistry.

ra·di·o·chem·ist (rā′dē ō kem′ist) *n.* one who is an expert in radiochemistry.

ra·di·o·chem·is·try (rā′dē ō kem′is trē) *n.* the branch of chemistry dealing with radio-active phenomena and substances.

radio control control by means of radio signals: *Our garage door is operated by radio control.*

ra·di·o–con·trolled (rā′dē ō kən trōld′) *adj.* controlled from a

hat, āge, fär; let, ēqual, tèrm; it, īce
hot, ōpen, ôrder; oil, out; cup, pùt, rüle,
əbove, takən, pencəl, lemən, circəs

ch, child; ng, long; sh, ship
th, thin; ŦH, then; zh, measure

distance by means of radio signals: *a radio-controlled model airplane.*

ra·di·o–el·e·ment (rā′dē ō el′ə mənt) *n.* a radio-active element.

radio frequency any frequency of electromagnetic waves between about 10kHz and 300 000 MHz, used especially in transmitting radio and television signals. *Abbrev.:* RF

ra·di·o·gram (rā′dē ō gram′) *n.* **1** a message transmitted by radiotelegraphy. **2** radiograph.

ra·di·o·graph (rā′dē ō graf′) *n., v.* —*n.* a picture produced by X rays or other rays on a photographic plate, commonly called an X-ray picture. —*v.* make a radiograph of.

ra·di·og·ra·phy (rā′dē og′rə fē) *n.* the production of photographs by means of X rays.

ra·di·o·i·so·tope (rā′dē ō ī′sə tōp′) *n.* a radio-active isotope, especially one produced artificially.

ra·di·o·log·i·cal (rā′dē ə loj′ə kəl) *adj.* **1** of or having to do with radiology. **2** of or having to do with the rays from radio-active substances. —**ra·di·o·log′i·cal·ly,** *adv.*

ra·di·ol·o·gist (rā′dē ol′ə jist) *n.* a physician who specializes in radiology.

ra·di·ol·o·gy (rā′dē ol′ə jē) *n.* the branch of medicine dealing with the use of radio-active substances and X rays in the diagnosis and treatment of disease.

ra·di·o·man (rā′dē ō man′) *n., pl.* **-men. 1** a radio operator or technician on an airplane, ship, etc. **2** one who works in radio broadcasting.

ra·di·om·e·ter (rā′dē om′ə tər) *n.* an instrument for indicating the conversion of radiant energy into mechanical force, often consisting of a glass vessel containing vanes that are in a vacuum and rotate when exposed to light.

ra·di·o·met·ric (rā′dē ō met′rik) *adj.* of, having to do with, or using a radiometer.

ra·di·om·e·try (rā′dē om′ə trē) *n.* the measurement of radiant energy by means of a radiometer.

ra·di·o·phone (rā′dē ō fōn′) *n.* radiotelephone.

ra·di·o·sonde (rā′dē ō sond′) *n.* a miniature radio transmitter carried up in a balloon to broadcast information about atmospheric humidity, temperature, pressure, etc. at various altitudes. [< *radio* + F *sonde* depth, sounding]

ra·di·o·sym·met·ri·cal (rā′dē ō sə met′ri kəl) *adj.* radially symmetrical; symmetrical about a central point.

ra·di·o·tel·e·graph (rā′dē ō tel′ə graf′) *n., v.* —*n.* a telegraph worked by radio. —*v.* telegraph by radio.

ra·di·o·te·leg·ra·phy (rā′dē ō tə leg′rə fē) *n.* the system of telegraphing by radio.

ra·di·o·tel·e·phone (rā′dē ō tel′ə fōn′) *n., v.* **-phoned, -phon·ing.** —*n.* **1** a radio transmitter using voice communication. —*v.* telephone by radio.

ra·di·o·te·leph·o·ny (rā′dē ō tə lef′ə nē) *n.* radio communication by means of voice signals.

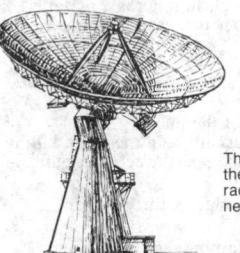

The main radio telescope at the National Research Council's radio astrophysical observatory near Penticton, B.C.

radio telescope an apparatus consisting of a radio receiver and an antenna, for the study of phenomena or bodies in outer space through observation of radio waves emanating from them.

ra·di·o·ther·a·py (rā′dē ō ther′ə pē) *n.* the treatment of disease by means of radiation.

radio wave an electromagnetic wave of radio frequency (between about 10 kHz and 300 000 MHz).

rad·ish (rad′ish) *n.* **1** an annual or biennial herb (*Raphanus sativus*) of the mustard family widely cultivated for its thick, edible root. **2** the root of this plant, having red or white skin and crisp, more or less hot-tasting, white flesh, and which is eaten raw, in salads, etc. [OE *rædic* < L *radix radicis* root. Doublet of RADIX.]

ra·di·um (rā′dē əm) *n.* a rare, silvery-white, radio-active metallic element found in uranium ores, used in radiotherapy, in the manufacture of luminous paints, etc. *Symbol*: Ra; *at.no.* 88; *at.wt.* (226); *half-life* 1620 years. [< NL < L *radius* ray]

ra·di·us (rā′dē əs) *n., pl.* **-di·i** or **-di·us·es. 1** any line going straight from the centre to the outside of a circle or a sphere. See **circle** for picture. **2** a circular area measured by the length of its radius: *The explosion could be heard within a radius of ten kilometres.* **3** that one of the two bones of the forearm that is on the thumb side. See **arm**[1] for picture. **4** a corresponding bone in the forelimb of vertebrates other than man. [< L *radius* ray, spoke of a wheel. Doublet of RAY[1].]

ra·dix (rā′diks) *n., pl.* **rad·i·ces** (rad′ə sēz′ *or* rā′də sēz′) **or ra·dix·es. 1** a root; radical; source or origin. **2** *Mathematics.* a number taken as the base of a system of numbers, logarithms, or the like. The radix of the decimal system is ten. [< L *radis, radicis* root. Doublet of RADISH.]

R.Adm. or **RAdm** rear-admiral.

ra·don (rā′don) *n.* a rare, highly radio-active gaseous chemical element, the densest gas known, used as a source of alpha particles in radiotherapy. *Symbol*: Rn; *at.no.* 86; *at.wt.* (222); *half-life* 3.82 days. [< *radium*]

RAF or **R.A.F.** Royal Air Force (United Kingdom).

raf·fi·a (raf′ē ə) *n.* **1** a fibre from the leafstalks of a palm (*Raphia ruffia*) native to Madagascar, used in making baskets, mats, etc. **2** the tree itself, also called **raffia palm.** [< Malagasy *rafia*]

raf·fish (raf′ish) *adj.* **1** crude; rowdy; vulgar. **2** disreputable; unconventional. —**raf′fish·ly,** *adv.* —**raf′fish·ness,** *n.*

raf·fle (raf′əl) *n., v.* **-fled, -fling.** —*n.* a lottery, often held for charity, in which many people each pay a small sum for a chance to win a prize. —*v.* sell an article by a raffle (*usually used with* **off**): *to raffle off a quilt.* [ME *rafle* a dice game < OF *rafle* plundering, stripping, ult. < Du. *rafelen* ravel, pluck]

raft[1] (raft) *n., v.* —*n.* **1** a platform made of logs, boards, etc. fastened together and used for transportation or support on water. **2** *Cdn. Logging.* **a** pieces of timber lashed together for floating downstream, as to a mill. **b** *Historical.* a larger formation of square timber, composed of smaller units called drams, as used on the Great Lakes and the streams of the St. Lawrence River system. **3** a floating ice formation resulting from the piling up of cakes of ice in layers. —*v.* **1** send by or carry on a raft. **2** make into a raft. **3** of ice, be piled high, layer upon layer, as a result of pressure. [ME < ON *raptr* log]

raft[2] (raft) *n. Informal.* a large number; abundance. [var. of *raff* heap < *riffraff*]

raft·er[1] (raf′tər) *n.* a supporting beam, often slanting, of a roof. See **frame** for picture. [OE *ræfter*]

raft·er[2] (raf′tər) *n.* a person who rafts timber.

rag[1] (rag) *n.* **1** a torn or waste piece of cloth. **2** (*adj.*) made from rags: *a rag doll, a rag rug.* **3** any small cloth used for cleaning, washing, etc. **4** anything like a rag, such as a fragment or scrap of something. **5** *Derogatory or facetious.* an article of cloth, such as a piece of clothing, a flag, or a theatre curtain. **6 rags,** *pl.* tattered or worn-out clothes. **7** *Informal.* a newspaper, especially one considered as inferior. [ME < OE *ragg < ON *rögg* shaggy tuft] —**rag′like′,** *adj.*

rag[2] (rag) *v.* **ragged, rag·ging;** *n.* —*v. Slang.* **1** scold. **2** tease, torment, or play jokes on.

rag the puck, *Hockey.* keep control of the puck by skilful stick-handling and elusive skating, usually as a means of killing time when one's own team is shorthanded. —*n.* the act of ragging. [origin uncertain]

rag·a·muf·fin (rag′ə muf′ən) *n.* a ragged, dirty person, especially a child. [probably < *rag*[1]]

rag·bag (rag′bag′) *n.* **1** a bag containing rags, scraps, etc. **2** a miscellaneous or motley collection.

rage (rāj) *n., v.* **raged, rag·ing.** —*n.* **1** violent anger: *a voice quivering with rage.* **2** a fit of violent anger: *be in a rage.* **3** violence: *the rage of a savage tiger.* **4** a movement, idea, or fashion that is popular for a short time. **5** great enthusiasm. —*v.* **1** be furious with anger. **2** speak or move with furious anger.

3 act violently; move, proceed, or continue with great violence: *A storm is raging.* [ME < OF < VL *rabia* < L *rabies*]

☛ *Syn. n.* **1. Rage, fury** = violent anger. **Rage** suggests anger so violent that it causes either complete loss of self-control or a bitter desire to get revenge: *In his rage the child broke his mother's favorite vase.* **Fury** suggests rage so wild and fierce that it destroys common sense and makes a person like an enraged wild animal, wanting to harm and destroy: *In their fury the hoodlums went through the streets wrecking cars.*

rag·ged (rag′id) *adj.* **1** worn or torn into rags. **2** wearing torn or badly worn-out clothing: *a ragged beggar.* **3** not straight and tidy; rough: *an Airedale's ragged coat, a ragged garden.* **4** having loose shreds or bits: *a ragged wound.* **5** having rough or sharp points; uneven; jagged: *ragged rocks.* **6** harsh: *a ragged voice.* **7** faulty; imperfect; irregular: *ragged rhyme.* —**rag′ged·ly,** *adv.* —**rag′ged·ness,** *n.*

rag·gle–tag·gle (rag′əl tag′əl) *adj. Informal.* ragged; slovenly; down-at-heel.

A coat with raglan sleeves

rag·lan (rag′lən) *n.* **1** an overcoat having sleeves that continue up to the neckline so that there is no seam at the top of the arm. **2** (*adj.*) having such sleeves. [after Fitzroy James Somerset, Baron Raglan (1788-1855), a British field marshal]

raglan sleeve a sleeve that is cut to continue up to the neckline instead of ending at the shoulder.

rag·man (rag′man′) *n., pl.* **-men.** a man who gathers, buys, or sells rags.

ra·gout (ra gü′) *n.* a highly seasoned stew of meat and vegetables. [< F *ragoût* < *ragoûter* restore the appetite]

rag·pick·er (rag′pik′ər) *n.* a person who picks up rags and junk, usually to sell them.

rag·time (rag′tīm′) *n.* an early style of jazz performed especially on the piano, characterized by a strong, regular rhythm base and a highly syncopated melody. [origin uncertain]

rag·weed (rag′wēd′) *n.* **1** any of a genus (*Ambrosia*) of North American plants of the composite family, especially **common ragweed** (*A. artemesiifolia*), whose greenish flowers produce large amounts of pollen that is one of the most important causes of hay fever in eastern North America. **2** an annual plant (*Iva xanthifolia*) of the composite family native to the North American plains, whose pollen is also an important cause of hay fever. Also called **false ragweed.**

rag·wort (rag′wert′) *n.* any of several weedy plants (genus *Senecio*) of the composite family, especially **tansy ragwort** (*S. jacobaea*), having daisylike yellow flowers and tall stems. It is native to Europe and Asia but has become a troublesome weed along the eastern and western coasts of North America.

rah (rä) *interj. or n.* hurrah.

raid (rād) *n., v.* —*n.* **1** an attack, especially a sudden attack. **2** a sudden attack by a small force having no intention of holding the territory invaded. **3** an entering and seizing what is inside. **4** a deliberate attempt by speculators to force down prices on stock exchanges. —*v.* **1** attack suddenly. **2** force a way into; enter and seize what is in: *The police raided the gambling house.* **3** engage in a raid. [northern form of OE *rād* a ride, riding. Cf. ROAD.] —**raid′er,** *n.*

rail[1] (rāl) *n., v.* —*n.* **1** a horizontal or slanting bar of wood or metal extending between posts, brackets, etc. and used as a barrier, guard, or support: *a stair rail. She leaned against the top rail of the fence.* **2** a steel bar or series of bars forming a continuous track for a train, etc. **3** railway: *They shipped their car by rail.* **4** the upper part of the bulwarks of a ship. —*v.* supply or furnish with rails or a railing. **rail in,** enclose within a fence. **rail off,** separate by a fence. [ME < OF *reille* < L *regula* straight rod. Doublet of RULE.]

rail[2] (rāl) *v.* complain bitterly; use violent and abusive language: *He railed at his hard luck.* [< F *railler*, ult. < LL *ragere* to scream. Doublet of RALLY[2].] —**rail′er,** *n.*

rail[3] (rāl) *n., pl.* **rails** or (*esp. collectively*) **rail. 1** any of numerous small or medium-sized wading birds (family Rallidae) having short wings and tail, a narrow body, and strong legs with very long toes that allow them to run over the mud of marshes and swamps. Rails

have a harsh cry. **2** (*adj.*) designating the family of birds that includes the rails and gallinules. [< F *râle* < VL *rascla*; probably imitative]

rail·head (rāl′hed′) *n.* **1** the end or terminus of a railway. **2** the farthest point to which the tracks of a railway under construction have been laid; end of steel. **3** a point on a railway that serves as a depot for military supplies, etc.

rail·ing (rāl′ing) *n.* **1** a barrier made of rails, especially along the side of a staircase, the edge of a balcony, etc. **2** material for making rails. **3** rails collectively: *A pile of railing lay by the barn.*

rail·ler·y (rāl′ər ē) *n., pl.* **-ler·ies. 1** good-humored ridicule; joking; teasing. **2** a bantering remark. [< F *raillerie* < *railler.* See RAIL².]

rail·road (rāl′rōd′) *n., v.* —*n.* railway. *Abbrev.*: R.R. —*v.* **1** send or carry on a railway. **2** work on a railway: *He has been railroading all his life.* **3** *Informal.* rush through or into hastily, especially so as to prevent fair and careful consideration: *to railroad a bill through a committee.* **4** *Slang.* send to prison on insufficient or false evidence. —**rail′road′er,** *n.*

rail·road·ing (rāl′rōd′ing) *n.* **1** the construction or operation of railways. **2** the act or process of hurrying (a thing or person) along.

rail·way (rāl′wā′) *n.* **1** a road or track for trains, consisting of parallel steel rails along which the wheels of the locomotives and cars go. The rails of a railway are supported on heavy wooden crosswise beams called ties. **2** tracks, stations, trains, and other property of a system of transportation that uses rails: *One of Canada's railways is owned by the government.* **3** the company or corporation which owns and operates such a system. *Abbrev.*: Ry.

railway crossing a place where a railway track crosses a street or highway on the same level; level crossing.

rai·ment (rā′mənt) *n.* clothing; garments. [short for *arraiment* < *array*]

rain (rān) *n., v.* —*n.* **1** water falling in the form of drops from clouds, produced by the rapid condensation of water vapor in low-lying clouds. **2** the fall of such drops: *The rain lasted all morning.* **3** a thick, fast fall of anything: *a rain of bullets.* **4** the **rains,** *pl.* the rainy season, as in tropical climates. —*v.* **1** be the case that rain is falling (*used with the subject* it): *It was raining when we left.* **2** pour down like rain: *Tears rained down his cheeks. She rained furious blows on the door.*

rain cats and dogs, *Informal.* rain very hard.

rained out, of an outdoor sports event, etc., cancelled because of rain: *The first game of the season was rained out.* [OE *regn*]

☛ *Hom.* **reign, rein.**

rain·bow (rān′bō′) *n.* **1** an arch of colored light, showing the different colors of the spectrum, that is seen in the sky when the sun's rays are seen through rain, mist, or spray. The colors of the rainbow are violet, indigo, blue, green, yellow, orange, and red. **2** rainbow trout. [OE *regnboga*]

rainbow trout a trout (*Salmo gairdneri*) of the rivers and streams of W North America, having a greenish back and whitish belly, with many black spots and a pinkish or reddish band along each side. This trout is so variable in appearance that it has several common names, depending on its habitat, etc. See also **Kamloops trout** and **steelhead.**

rain check 1 a ticket for future use, given to the spectators at a baseball game or other outdoor performance stopped by rain. **2** any similar ticket, such as that given by a supermarket to guarantee to a customer for a limited time the advertised price on a sale item that is out of stock. **3** *Informal.* an understanding that an invitation which cannot presently be accepted will be renewed on a future occasion: *May I take a rain check on your invitation to dinner?*

rain cloud a low, dark-grey cloud that brings rain.

rain·coat (rān′kōt′) *n.* a waterproof or water-repellant coat worn for protection from rain.

rain·drop (rān′drop′) *n.* a drop of rain.

rain·fall (rān′fol′ *or* -fôl′) *n.* **1** a shower of rain: *There was a light rainfall during the night.* **2** the amount of water in the form of rain that falls in a particular area over a certain period of time: *Rainfall is measured in millimetres.*

rain forest a region of dense evergreen forest characterized by very tall trees and much undergrowth, where rainfall is very heavy throughout the year. The **tropical rain forests** of South America, Africa, and SE Asia are made up of broad-leaved evergreen trees, which form a continuous canopy over the undergrowth, and have many lianas and air plants.

rain gauge an instrument for measuring rainfall.

rain·mak·er (rān′māk′ər) *n.* a person who tries to produce rain.

rain·mak·ing (rān′māk′ing) *n.* the making of rain artificially, or by supernatural means. One method is to seed a cloud with crystals of silver iodide, which expand with heat, collecting particles of moisture that are released from the cloud as rain.

hat, āge, fär; let, ēqual, tèrm; it, īce

hot, ōpen, ôrder; oil, out; cup, put, rüle, əbove, takən, pencəl, lemən, circəs

ch, child; ng, long; sh, ship

th, thin; ᴛʜ, then; zh, measure

rain·proof (rān′prüf′) *adj.* that will not let rain through; impervious to rain: *The roof of our cottage isn't rainproof any more.*

rain·storm (rān′stôrm′) *n.* a storm with much rain.

rain·wa·ter (rān′wo′tər *or* rān′wô′tər) *n.* water that has been collected from rain, not taken from a well, etc. Rainwater is soft water.

rain·wear (rān′wer′) *n.* clothing made to be worn in the rain, such as rubbers, raincoats, etc.

rain·y (rān′ē) *adj.* **rain·i·er, rain·i·est. 1** having rain, especially much rain: *rainy weather, the rainy season.* **2** wet with rain: *rainy streets.* **3** of clouds or winds, bringing rain. —**rain′i·ly,** *adv.* —**rain′i·ness,** *n.*

rainy day a time of need in the future: *to save for a rainy day.*

raise (rāz) *v.* **raised, rais·ing;** *n.* —*v.* **1** lift up: *to raise one's hand.* **2** set upright: *to raise a statue.* **3** cause to rise: *to raise a cloud of dust.* **4** put or take into a higher position; make higher or nobler; elevate: *to raise a salesman to manager.* **5** increase in degree, amount, price, pay, etc.: *to raise the rent.* **6** make louder or of higher pitch: *I cannot hear you; please raise your voice.* **7** *Games.* bid or bet more than an opponent. **8** gather together; collect; manage to get: *The leader raised an army.* **9** breed; grow: *The farmer raises crops and cattle.* **10** cause to appear: *to raise the ghost of Napoleon.* **11** cause; bring about: *A funny remark raises a laugh.* **12** bring forward; mention: *The speaker raised an interesting point.* **13** build; create; produce; start; set up: *to raise a monument, to raise a fund.* **14** rouse; stir up: *The dog raised a rabbit from the underbrush.* **15** bring up; rear: *Parents raise their children.* **16** cause to become light: *Yeast raises bread.* **17** bring back to life: *to raise the dead.* **18 a** put an end to: *Our soldiers raised the siege of the fort by driving away the enemy.* **b** break up and remove. **19** come in sight of: *After a long voyage the ship raised land.* **20** falsify the value of (a cheque, note, etc.) by making the sum larger.

raise Cain, the devil, mischief, or **the roof,** *Slang.* make a disturbance; create an uproar or confusion.

—*n.* **1** a raised place. **2** an increase in amount, price, pay, etc. **3** the amount of such an increase. [ME < ON *reisa* < Gmc. causative of *rīsan* rise]

☛ *Syn. v.* **1. Raise, lift, elevate** = move to a higher position. **Raise** means to bring something to a high or, especially, vertical position or to move it up from a lower to a higher level: *Raise your right hand.* **Lift** means to take something, usually heavy, up from the ground or some other low level: *Please lift the table.* **Elevate** chiefly means "to raise to a higher rank or nobler state": *Good reading elevates the mind.*

rais·er (rāz′ər) *n.* a person who grows or raises things: *a cattle raiser.*

rai·sin (rā′zən) *n.* a sweet dried grape. [ME < OF < L *racemus* grape cluster. Doublet of RACEME.]

rai·son d'être (re zôɴ detr′) *French.* reason for being; justification.

raj (räj) *n. Historical.* in India, sovereignty; dominion: *the British raj.* [< Hind. *rāj*]

ra·jah (rä′jə) *n.* a member of a hereditary class of noblemen and rulers in countries of southern Asia, including Malaysia and, formerly, India. Also, **raja.** [< Hind. *rājā* < Skt.]

Raj·put (räj′put) *n.* a member of a Hindu military, land-owning, and ruling caste. [< Hind. *rājput* < Skt. *rājaputra* king's son]

rake¹ (rāk) *n., v.* **raked, rak·ing.** —*n.* a long-handled tool having a bar at one end with teeth in it. A rake is used for smoothing the soil or gathering together loose leaves, hay, or straw. —*v.* **1** move with a rake: *Rake the leaves off the grass.* **2** use a rake. **3** gather or bring together: *He raked up enough money to rent a canoe.* **4** search carefully: *He raked the newspapers for descriptions of the accident.* **5** fire guns along the length of (a ship, line of soldiers, etc.). [OE *raca*]

rake² (rāk) *n.* a dissolute or debauched man, especially one who belongs to fashionable society. [short for *rakehell*]

rake³ (rāk) *n. or v.* **raked, rak·ing.** slant; slope. A ship's smokestacks have a slight backward rake. [origin uncertain]

rake·hell (rāk′hel′) *n. Archaic.* a libertine; roué. [< *rake¹* + *hell*; replacing ME *rakel* rash]

rake·off (rāk′of′) *n. Slang.* a commission or share of profits, especially when part of an illicit transaction.

rak·ish[1] (rāk′ish) *adj.* **1** smart; jaunty; dashing: *a hat set at a rakish angle.* **2** suggesting dash and speed: *He owns a rakish boat.* [< *rake*[3]; influenced in def. 1 by association with *rakish*[2]]

rak·ish[2] (rāk′ish) *adj.* of, having to do with, or like a rake; immoral; dissolute; licentious. [< *rake*[2]]

rall. rallentando.

ral·len·tan·do (räl′en tän′dō) *adj., adv., n. Music.* —*adj.* slackening; becoming slower. —*adv.* gradually more slowly. —*n.* **1** a gradual decrease in tempo. **2** a passage to be played or sung in this manner. [< Ital. *rallentando* slowing down < *lento* slow]

ral·ly[1] (ral′ē) *v.* **-lied, -ly·ing;** *n., pl.* **-lies.** —*v.* **1** bring together; bring together again; get in order again: *The commander was able to rally the fleeing troops.* **2** pull together; revive: *He rallied all his energy for one last effort.* **3** come together in a body for a common purpose or action. **4** come to help a person, party, or cause: *He rallied to the side of his injured friend.* **5** recover health and strength: *The sick man may rally now.* **6** *Tennis, etc.* hit the ball back and forth several times. —*n.* **1** the act of rallying; recovery. **2** a meeting or assembly of many people for a common purpose or action: *a political rally, a sports-car rally.* **3** *Tennis, etc.* a series of strokes between players before one player wins a point. [< F *rallier* < *re-* again + *allier* ally]

ral·ly[2] (ral′ē) *v.* **-lied, -ly·ing.** make fun of or tease in a good-natured way. [< F *railler* rail[2]. Doublet of RAIL[2].]

ram (ram) *n., v.* **rammed, ram·ming.** —*n.* **1** a male sheep. **2** a machine or part of a machine that strikes heavy blows. The ram on a pile driver is the weight that drives the piles into the ground. **3** battering ram. **4** the beak at the bow of a warship, used to break the sides of enemy ships. **5** a ship with such a beak. **6** the plunger of a force pump. **7** a pump in which the force of a descending column of water raises some of the water above its original level. **8** Ram, *Astronomy or astrology.* Aries. —*v.* **1** butt against; strike head on; strike violently: *One ship rammed the other ship.* **2** push hard; drive down or in by heavy force or effort: *He rammed the bolt into the wall.* **3** force acceptance or passage of: *trying to ram an unpopular bill through Parliament.* [OE *ramm*]

Ra·ma (rä′mə) *n. Hinduism.* an incarnation of the god Vishnu, depicted as the ideal ruler, representing grace and justice toward mankind.

Ram·a·dan (ram′ə dän′) *n.* **1** the ninth month of the Moslem year; during which fasting is rigidly practised daily from dawn until sunset. **2** the fasting itself. [< Arabic *Ramadān*, originally, the hot month]

Ra·ma·ya·na (rä mä′yə nə) *n.* one of the two great epics of India, that tells the story of Rama, written in Sanskrit early in the Christian era. The other Sanskrit epic is the **Mahabharata.**

ram·ble (ram′bəl) *v.* **-bled, -bling;** *n.* —*v.* **1** wander about for pleasure: *We rambled here and there through the woods.* **2** talk or write about first one thing and then another with no clear connections. **3** grow or spread irregularly in various directions: *Vines rambled over the wall.* —*n.* a walk for pleasure, with or without any definite route. [var. of ME *romblen,* a frequentative of *romen* roam]
☛ *Syn. v.* **1.** See note at **roam.**

ram·bler (ram′blər) *n.* **1** a person or thing that rambles. **2** any of various climbing roses.

ram·bunc·tious (ram bungk′shəs) *adj.* uncontrollably exuberant; boisterous and unruly: *The kids were very rambunctious after travelling all day.* [? a mock word formed from *ram* knock around + a var. of *bumptious*]

ram·e·kin or **ram·e·quin** (ram′ə kin) *n.* **1** a small, separately cooked portion of some food, especially one topped with cheese and bread crumbs. **2** a small baking dish holding enough for one portion. [< F *ramequin* < Du.]

ram·ie (ram′ē) *n.* **1** a tall perennial plant (*Boehmeria nivea*) of the nettle family native to E Asia, having stalks that yield a strong, lustrous fibre. **2** the fibre from this plant, used for fabrics and cordage. [< Malay *rami* plant]

ram·i·fi·ca·tion (ram′ə fə kā′shən) *n.* **1** a dividing or spreading out into branches or parts. **2** a branch; part. **3** something that springs out like a branch. **4** a result, consequence, extension, etc.: *the ramifications of an idea.*

ram·i·fy (ram′ə fī′) *v.* **-fied, -fy·ing.** divide or spread out into branchlike parts. [< F < Med.L *ramificare* < L *ramus* branch + *facere* make]

ram·jet (ram′jet′) *n.* the simplest type of jet engine, in which the fuel is fed into air that is compressed by the forward speed of the aircraft, missile, etc., instead of by means of a mechanical compressor.

ram·mer (ram′ər) *n.* a person or thing that rams, especially a device for driving or compacting something.

ra·mose (rā′mōs *or* rə mōs′) *adj.* consisting of or having many branches; branching. [< L *ramosus* < *ramus* branch]

ra·mous (rā′məs) *adj.* **1** ramose. **2** of or like a branch.

ramp[1] (ramp) *n.* **1** a sloping walk or roadway connecting two different levels of a building, road, etc. **2** a stairway for going into or out of aircraft. [< F *rampe* < *ramper.* See RAMP[2].]

ramp[2] (ramp) *v.* **1** rush wildly about; behave violently. **2** jump or rush with fury. **3** *Heraldry.* of beasts, rear on their hind feet. [< F *ramper* creep < Gmc.]

ram·page (*n.* ram′pāj; *v.* ram pāj′ *or* ram′pāj) *n., v.* **-paged, -pag·ing.** —*n.* a spell of violent behavior often accompanied by rushing about wildly; wild outbreak: *The mad elephant went on a rampage and killed its keeper.* —*v.* rush wildly about; behave violently; rage. [? < *ramp*[2]]

ram·pa·geous (ram pā′jəs) *adj.* wild; unruly; boisterous. —**ram·pa′geous·ly,** *adv.* —**ram·pa′geous·ness,** *n.*

ramp·an·cy (ram′pən sē) *n.* the state of being rampant.

ramp·ant (ram′pənt) *adj.* **1** growing without any check: *The vines ran rampant over the fence.* **2** passing beyond restraint or usual limits; unchecked: *Anarchy was rampant after the dictator died.* **3** angry; excited; violent. **4** *Heraldry.* of beasts, standing up on the left hind leg, with the forelegs raised, the right above the left, and the head and body in profile. **5** of animals, rearing. [ME < OF *rampant* ramping] —**ramp′ant·ly,** *adv.*

ram·part (ram′pärt) *n.* **1** a wide bank of earth, usually with a parapet on top, built around a fort to help defend it. See **fort** for picture. **2** anything that defends; defence; protection. **3** *Cdn.* in the Northwest, a steep, high bank of a river or stream flowing through a gorge or canyon. [< F *rempart* < *remparer* fortify, ult. < L *re-* back + *ante* before + *parare* prepare]

ram·pike (ram′pīk′) *n. Cdn.* a tall, dead tree, especially one that has been blackened and stripped of its branches by fire.

ram·rod (ram′rod′) *n.* **1** a rod for ramming down the charge in a gun that is loaded from the muzzle. **2** a rod for cleaning the barrel of a gun.

ram·shack·le (ram′shak′əl) *adj.* loose and shaky; likely to come apart: *ramshackle old buildings.* [? ult. < *ransack*]

ran (ran) *v.* pt. of **run.**

ranch (ranch) *n., v.* —*n.* **1** a large farm with grazing land, for raising cattle, sheep, or horses in large numbers. **2** any farm, especially one used to raise one kind of animal or crop: *a mink ranch, a fruit ranch.* **3** the persons working or living on a ranch: *The entire ranch was at the party.* **4** rancherie. **5** on the West coast, an Indian house or dwelling. —*v.* work on or operate a ranch. [< Sp. *rancho* camp, mess]

ranch·er (ran′chər) *n.* a person who owns or operates a ranch.

ranch·er·ie (ranch′ər ē) *n.* in British Columbia, a camp or settlement of Indians. [< Sp. *ranchería*]

ranch hand a person employed on a ranch, especially a cattle ranch.

ranch house **1** the main building on a ranch. **2** on the West coast, a large communal dwelling or house of the Indians. **3** a long, low, spacious, one-storey house.

ranch·man (ranch′mən) *n., pl.* **-men.** rancher.

ran·cid (ran′sid) *adj.* **1** stale; spoiled: *rancid butter.* **2** tasting or smelling like stale fat or butter: *a rancid odor.* [< L *rancidus* < *rancere* be rank] —**ran′cid·ly,** *adv.* —**ran′cid·ness,** *n.*

ran·cid·i·ty (ran sid′ə tē) *n.* the quality or state of being rancid.

ran·cor or **rancour** (rang′kər) *n.* a deep-seated, bitter resentment or ill will; extreme hatred or spite. [ME < OF < LL *rancor* rankness < L *rancere* be rank]

ran·cor·ous (rang′kər əs) *adj.* spiteful; bitterly malicious. —**ran′cor·ous·ly,** *adv.*

ran·cour (rang′kər) See **rancor.**

rand (rand) *n.* **1** the basic unit of money in South Africa, divided into 100 cents. See table at **money.** **2** a coin worth one rand. [< Afrikaans < the *Rand,* the gold-mining district in the Transvaal]

R & B rhythm and blues.

R and D or **R & D** *Informal.* research and development: *They're spending millions on R and D in the energy field.*

ran·dom (ran′dəm) *adj., n.* —*adj.* by chance; with no plan. —*n.* **at random,** by chance; with no plan or purpose: *She took a book at random from the shelf.* [ME < OF *randon* rapid rush] —**ran′dom·ly,** *adv.*
☛ *Syn. adj.* **Random, haphazard** = made, done, happening, or coming by chance, not plan. **Random** emphasizes being without definite aim, direction,

purpose, or plan. **Haphazard** emphasizes being determined by chance, not by plan or fitness for a purpose or aim: *Because of her haphazard way of choosing clothes, she never looks well dressed.*

random access the capability of a computer memory to store data so that the location is independent of the content, giving the user immediate and direct access to any part of it, without working through the body of data from the beginning. —**ran′dom-ac′cess,** *adj.*

ran·dy (ran′dē) *adj. Scottish.* **1** coarse and boisterous in behavior. **2** lustful; lecherous. [origin uncertain]

ra·nee (rä′nē) *n.* **1** in India, a queen or princess. **2** the wife or widow of a rajah. Also, **rani.** [< Hind. *rani* < Skt. *rajni*]

rang (rang) *v.* pt. of **ring²**.

range (rānj) *n., v.* **ranged, rang·ing;** *adj.* —*n.* **1** the distance between certain limits; extent: *a range of prices from 5 cents to 25 dollars.* **2** the distance a gun, etc. can shoot. **3** the distance from a gun, etc. of an object aimed at. **4** a place to practise shooting. **5** land for grazing. **6** the act of wandering or moving about. **7** a row or line of mountains. **8** a row; line. **9** a line of direction: *The two barns are in direct range with the house.* **10** a rank, class, or order. **11** a district in which certain plants or animals live. **12** a stove for cooking. **13** a row of lots, concessions, or townships. —*v.* **1** vary within certain limits: *prices ranging from $5 to $10.* **2** wander; rove; roam: *Her eyes ranged over the crowd.* **3** wander over: *Buffalo once ranged these plains.* **4** put in a row or rows: *We ranged the chairs across the stage.* **5** put in groups or classes: *The swimming classes are ranged by age and ability.* **6** put or group on someone's side: *Loyal citizens ranged themselves with the king.* **7** run in a line; extend: *a boundary ranging east and west.* **8** be found; occur: *a plant ranging from Canada to Mexico.* —*adj.* of or on land for grazing. [ME < OF *ranger* array, ult. < *renc* line. See RANK¹.]

☛ *Syn. n.* **1. Range, scope, compass** = the extent of what something can do or take in. **Range** emphasizes the extent (and variety) that can be covered or taken in by something in operation or action, such as the mind, eye, a machine, force, etc.: *The car was out of his range of vision.* **Scope** emphasizes the idea of limits beyond which the understanding, view, application, etc. cannot extend: *Some technical terms are beyond the scope of this dictionary.* **Compass** emphasizes the limits within which something can act or operate: *Geographical names are within its compass.*

range finder an instrument for determining the distance between an object or target and an observer, camera, gun, etc.

rang·er (rān′jər) *n.* **1** a person or thing that ranges; rover. **2** a person employed to guard a tract of forest. **3** a soldier of certain regiments originally organized for fighting in the North American forests: *the Queen's Rangers.* **4 Ranger, a** a member, aged 15 or over, of the Girl Guides. **b** *Cdn.* in the North, an Indian or Inuk who acts as a volunteer military scout or observer.

rang·ette (rän jet′) *n.* a cooking stove smaller than a range.

rang·y (rān′jē) *adj.* **rang·i·er, rang·i·est. 1** fitted for ranging or moving about. **2** slender and long-limbed: *a rangy horse.* —**rang′i·ness,** *n.*

hat, āge, fär; let, ēqual, tèrm; it, īce hot, ōpen, ôrder; oil, out; cup, pùt, rüle, əbove, takən, pencəl, lemən, circəs

ch, child; ng, long; sh, ship th, thin; ŦH, then; zh, measure

ra·ni (rä′nē) See ranee.

rank¹ (rangk) *n., v.* —*n.* **1** a row or line, especially of soldiers, placed side by side. **2 ranks,** *pl.* a private soldiers. and junior non-commissioned officers. **b** rank and file. **3** a position; grade; class: *the rank of colonel.* **4** a high position: *A duke is a man of rank.* **5** an orderly arrangement or array. —*v.* **1** arrange in a row or line. **2** have a certain place or position in relation to other persons or things: *Bill ranked low in the test.* **3** put in some special order in a list: *Rank the continents in order of size.* **4** be more important than; outrank: *A major ranks a captain.* [ult. < OF *renc* < Gmc.] —**rank′er,** *n.*

rank² (rangk) *adj.* **1** large and coarse: *rank grass.* **2** growing richly. **3** producing a dense but coarse growth: *rank swamp land.* **4** having a strong, unpleasant smell or taste: *rank meat, rank tobacco.* **5** strongly marked; extreme: *rank ingratitude, rank nonsense.* **6** coarse; not decent. [OE *ranc* proud] —**rank′ly,** *adv.* —**rank′ness,** *n.*

rank and file 1 an armed force excluding its officers. **2** the members of an organization, society, or other group, excluding the leaders: *The union leaders were in favor of the offer but it was rejected by the rank and file.*

rank·ing (rang′king) *adj.* **1** having the highest rank: *the ranking poet of the age, the ranking officer on a military base.* **2** recognized as being of high calibre or merit: *Most of the association members are ranking artists.*

ran·kle (rang′kəl) *v.* **-kled, -kling.** cause anger, bitterness, or irritation: *Even after all those years, the memory of the insult still rankled.* [ME < OF *rancler,* var. of *draoncler* < Med.L *dracunculus* sore, dim. of L *draco* serpent < Gk. *drakōn*]

ran·sack (ran′sak) *v.* **1** search thoroughly through: *I ransacked the whole closet, but couldn't find the belt.* **2** plunder or rob: *Burglars had ransacked the house.* [ME < ON *rannsaka,* literally, search a house < *rann* house + *-saka* search] —**ran′sack·er,** *n.*

ran·som (ran′səm) *n., v.* —*n.* **1** the price paid or demanded before a captive is set free: *The robber chief held the travellers as prisoners for ransom.* **2** the act of ransoming. —*v.* **1** obtain the release (of a captive) by paying a price. **2** redeem. **3** release upon payment. [ME < OF *ranson* < L *redemptio, -onis.* Doublet of REDEMPTION.]

CANADIAN MILITARY RANKS

Ranks in the Canadian Forces

COMMISSIONED RANKS

General [Admiral]*
Lieutenant-General   [Vice Admiral]
Major-General   [Rear-Admiral]
Brigadier-General   [Commodore]
Colonel   [Captain (N)]
Lieutenant-Colonel   [Commander]
Major   [Lieutenant Commander]
Captain   [Lieutenant (N)]
Lieutenant   [Sub Lieutenant]
2nd Lieutenant   [Acting Sub Lieutenant]
   Officer Cadet   [Officer Cadet or Midshipman]

*The titles in square brackets are the traditional naval ranks, used especially in Maritime Command.

NON-COMMISSIONED RANKS

Chief Warrant Officer   [Chief Petty Officer 1st Class]
Master Warrant Officer   [Chief Petty Officer 2nd Class]
Warrant Officer   [Petty Officer 1st Class]
Sergeant   [Petty Officer 2nd Class]
Master Corporal   [Master Seaman]
Corporal   [Leading Seaman]
Private { [Able Seaman]
         { [Ordinary Seaman]

Ranks in the Royal Canadian Air Force
(now obsolete)

COMMISSIONED RANKS

Air Chief Marshal
Air Marshal
Air Vice-Marshal
Air Commodore
Group Captain
Wing Commander
Squadron Leader
Flight Lieutenant
Flying Officer
Pilot Officer
   Flight Cadet

NON-COMMISSIONED RANKS

Warrant Officer, Class 1
Warrant Officer, Class 2
Flight Sergeant
Sergeant
Corporal
Leading Aircraftman/woman
Aircraftman/woman, 1st class
Aircraftman/woman, 2nd class

rant (rant) v., n. —v. speak wildly, extravagantly, violently, or noisily.

rant and rave, scold violently. —n. an extravagant, violent, or noisy speech. [< MDu. *ranten*] —**rant′er**, n.

rap¹ (rap) n., v. **rapped, rap·ping.** —n. **1** a quick, light blow; a light, sharp knock. **2** *Slang.* **a** blame; rebuke. **b** conviction; prison sentence. **3** *Slang.* a chat; informal discussion.
beat the rap, *Slang.* escape conviction or prison sentence.
take the rap, *Slang.* pay the penalty; take the blame. —v. **1** knock sharply; tap. **2** say sharply; *rap out an answer.* **3** *Slang.* rebuke; criticize; condemn. **4** *Slang.* talk; chat. [imitative] —**rap′per**, n.
☛ *Hom.* **wrap.**

rap² (rap) n. *Informal.* the least bit: *I don't care a rap.* [originally, a counterfeit Irish half-penny]
☛ *Hom.* **wrap.**

rap³ (rap) v. **rapped, rap·ping;** n. *Slang.* —v. talk freely and informally; chat: *rapping till 2 in the morning.* —n. a free, informal talk. [origin uncertain]
☛ *Hom.* **wrap.**

ra·pa·cious (rə pā′shəs) adj. **1** seizing by force; plundering. **2** grasping; greedy; voracious. **3** of animals, living by the capture of prey. [< L *rapax, -acis* grasping < *rapere* seize] —**ra·pa′cious·ly**, adv. —**ra·pa′cious·ness**, n.

ra·pac·i·ty (rə pas′ə tē) n. the quality of being rapacious.

rape¹ (rāp) n., v. **raped, rap·ing.** —n. **1** the crime of a man or boy having sexual intercourse with a woman or girl forcibly and without her consent. **2** any forcible or outrageous interference or violation: *the rape of a country's natural resources.* **3** *Archaic or poetic.* the act or an instance of seizing and carrying off by force: *the rape of the Sabine women.*
—v. **1** force (a woman or girl) to have sexual intercourse; commit rape on. **2** violate, destroy; or despoil. **3** *Archaic or poetic.* seize and carry off by force. [< L *rapere* seize]

rape² (rāp) n. a plant (*Brassica napus*) of the mustard family, native to Europe and Asia but widely cultivated for its seeds (rapeseed), which yield rapeseed oil, and as a forage crop for sheep and hogs. [ME < L *rapa, rapum*]

rape oil rapeseed oil.

rape·seed (rāp′sēd′) n. the seed of the rape plant.

rapeseed oil an oil made from rapeseed and used as a cooking oil, fuel, or lubricant, and in making soap and synthetic rubber.

rap·id (rap′id) adj., n. —adj. **1** quick; swift; moving; acting; or doing with speed: *a rapid worker.* **2** going on or forward at a fast rate: *rapid growth.* **3** arranged for brief exposures to light: *rapid film.*
—n. Usually, **rapids**, pl. a part of a river's course where the water rushes quickly, often over rocks near the surface. [< L *rapidus* < *rapere* hurry away] —**rap′id·ly**, adv. —**rap′id·ness**, n.
☛ *Syn. adj.* **1.** See note at **quick.**

rapid eye movement a rapid movement of the eyes under the closed lids that is characteristic of a particular stage of sleep during which a person dreams. *Abbrev.:* REM

rap·id–fire (rap′id fīr′) adj. **1** firing or adapted for firing shots in quick succession. **2** rapid and lively; done or carried on quickly or sharply: *a rapid-fire style of speaking.*

ra·pid·i·ty (rə pid′ə tē) n. quickness; swiftness; speed.

rapid transit a system of fast public transportation by railway in urban areas, often underground.

ra·pi·er (rā′pē ər) n. a light, straight, two-edged sword used for thrusting. See **sword** for picture. [< MF *rapière* < *râpe* grater, rasp; with reference to the perforated guard] —**ra′pi·er·like′**, adj.

rap·ine (rap′ēn) n. a seizing by force and carrying off; plundering. [< L *rapina*]

rap·ist (rā′pist) n. a person who commits the crime of rape.

rap·pel (ra pel′ or rə pel′) n., v. **-pelled** or **-peled, -pel·ling** or **-pel·ing.** —n. a technique for descending a cliff, etc. by means of a double rope that is secured above and passed around the climber's body in such a way that he can control the rate of descent. —v. descend a cliff, etc. by this means.

rap·port (ra pôrt′; *French,* rä pôr′) n. a connection or relationship, especially a harmonious or agreeable one: *He has no rapport with his students. There was good rapport among the leaders throughout the negotiations.*
en rapport (äN rä pôr′), *French.* in close relation, accord, or harmony. [< F *rapport* < *rapporter* bring back]

rap·proche·ment (ra prosh′mоN; *French,* rä prôsh mäN′) n. the establishment or renewal of friendly relations. [< F *rapprochement* < *rapprocher* bring near]

rap·scal·lion (rap skal′yən) n. a rascal; rogue; scamp. [earlier *rascallion* < *rascal*]

rapt (rapt) adj. **1** entranced or completely engrossed; lost in delight. **2** caused by or showing rapture or delight: *a rapt smile.* [< L *raptus*, pp. of *rapere* seize] —**rapt′ly**, adv. —**rapt′ness**, n.
☛ *Hom.* **wrapped.**

rap·tor (rap′tər) n. bird of prey. [< L *raptor* plunderer, robber < *rapere* seize]

rap·to·ri·al (rap tô′rē əl) adj. **1** of, having to do with, or designating birds of prey. **2** adapted for seizing prey: *raptorial claws.* **3** predatory.

rap·ture (rap′chər) n. **1** a strong feeling that absorbs the mind; very great joy. **2** Often, **raptures**, pl. an expression of great joy. [< *rapt*]

rap·tur·ous (rap′chər əs) adj. full of rapture; expressing or feeling rapture. —**rap′tur·ous·ly**, adv.

ra·quet (rā ket′) n. raquette.

ra·quette (rā ket′) n. *Cdn.* snowshoe. Also **racket** and **raquet.** [< Cdn.F]

rare¹ (rer) adj. **rar·er, rar·est. 1** seldom seen or found; uncommon: *The whooping crane has become very rare.* **2** not happening often; unusual: *a rare event.* **3** unusually good or great: *Shakespeare had rare powers as a dramatist.* **4** thin; not dense: *The higher you go, the rarer the air becomes.* [< L *rarus*] —**rare′ness**, n.
☛ *Syn.* **1. Rare, scarce** = not often or easily found. **Rare** describes something uncommon or unusual at any time because it seldom occurs or only a few specimens exist; it often suggests excellence or value above the ordinary: *The Gutenberg Bible is a rare book.* **Scarce** describes something usually or formerly common or plentiful, but not existing or produced in large enough numbers or quantities at the present time: *Water is becoming scarce in some parts of the country.*

rare² (rer) adj. **rar·er, rar·est.** of meat, not cooked much; cooked so that the inside is still red: *She prefers her steak rare.* [OE *hrēr*] —**rare′ness**, n.

rare·bit (rer′bit) n. Welsh rabbit. [altered < (*Welsh*) *rabbit*]

rare earth any of the oxides of rare-earth elements.

rare–earth (rer′ėrth′) adj. of or having to do with rare earths.

rare–earth or **metal** any of the rare metallic elements that have atomic numbers from 57 to 71.

rar·e·fac·tion (rer′ə fak′shən) n. the act or process of rarefying or the state of being rarefied.

rar·e·fy (rer′ə fī′) v. **-fied, -fy·ing. 1** make less dense: *The air in the mountains is rarefied.* **2** become less dense. **3** refine; purify. [< L *rarefacere* < *rarus* rare + *facere* make]

rare·ly (rer′lē) adv. **1** seldom; not often. **2** unusually; unusually well: *a rarely carved panel.*

rar·ing (rer′ing) adj. *Informal.* very eager: *raring to go, raring for a fight.*

rar·i·ty (rer′ə tē) n., pl. **-ties. 1** something rare: *A thirty-year-old car is a rarity.* **2** the quality or state of being rare or scarce; scarcity. **3** a lack of density; thinness: *The rarity of mountain air is bad for people with weak hearts.*

ras·cal (ras′kəl) n. **1** a dishonest person; rogue. **2** a mischievous person or animal. [ME < OF *rascaille* < *rasque* filth, ult. < L *radere* scratch]

ras·cal·i·ty (ras kal′ə tē) n., pl. **-ties. 1** the character or actions of a rascal. **2** a rascally act.

ras·cal·ly (ras′kəl ē) adj. of or characteristic of a rascal; mean, dishonest, mischievous, etc.

rase (rāz) v. **rased, ras·ing.** *Esp.Brit.* See **raze.**

rash¹ (rash) adj. too hasty or too bold; reckless; impetuous; taking too much risk. [ME *rasch* quick] —**rash′ly**, adv.
☛ *Syn.* **Rash, reckless** = acting or speaking without due care or thought. **Rash** emphasizes being in too great a rush, speaking hastily or plunging into action without stopping to think: *You should never make rash promises.* **Reckless** emphasizes being without caution, acting carelessly without paying attention to possible consequences: *The dog was killed by a reckless driver.*

rash² (rash) n. **1** an eruption of small red spots on the skin, as a symptom of a disease, an allergic reaction, etc.: *Perfumed soaps give me a rash.* **2** a sudden appearance of a large number of instances or cases of something unpleasant or unhappy: *There was a rash of angry letters following the publication of the article.* [< OF *rasche* scurf, ult. < L *radere* scratch]

rash·er (rash′ər) n. a thin slice of bacon or ham for frying or broiling. [origin uncertain]

rash·ness (rash′nis) n. unwise boldness; recklessness.

rasp (rasp) n., v. —v. **1** make a harsh, grating sound: *The file rasped on the scythe.* **2** utter with a grating sound: *to rasp out a command.* **3** have a harsh or irritating effect (*on*); grate. **4** scrape with a rough instrument.
—n. **1** a harsh, grating sound: *the rasp of crickets, a rasp in a person's voice.* **2** a coarse file with pointlike teeth. [ME < OF *rasper* < Gmc.] —**rasp′er**, n. —**rasp′ing·ly**, adv.

rasp·ber·ry (raz′ber′ē) *n., pl.* **-ries;** *adj.* —*n.* **1** any of several prickly shrubs (genus *Rubus*) of the rose family having pale-pink flowers and red, purple, black, or yellow edible berries. **2** the juicy berry of any of these shrubs, which is an aggregate fruit consisting of small drupes crowded together around a fleshy receptacle. Red raspberries are the most common. **3** a dark purplish-red color. **4** *Slang.* a sound of disapproval or derision made with the tongue and lips.
—*adj.* **1** made of or flavored with raspberries. **2** having the color raspberry. [< earlier *raspis* raspberry (origin uncertain) + *berry*] —**rasp′ber′ry·like′,** *adj.*

rasp·y (ras′pē) *adj.* **rasp′i·er, rasp′i·est. 1** harsh; rasping: *a raspy voice.* **2** irritable; short-tempered.

Ras·ta·far·i·an (ras′tə far′ē ən *or* -fer′ē ən) *n., adj.* —*n.* **1** a person who believes in Rastafarianism. **2** a person who identifies with Rastafarianism as a social and political movement. —*adj.* of or having to do with Rastafarians or Rastafarianism.

Ras·ta·far·i·an·ism (ras′tə far′ē ən iz′əm *or* -fer′ē ən-) *n.* a Jamaican religion or cult based on the divinity of Haile Selassie (1892-1975), emperor of Ethiopia (1930-36; 1941-74), that stresses Africa as the home to which black people must return some day. [< *Ras Tafari* Prince Tafari, the name and title of Haile Selassie before he became emperor]

rat (rat) *n., v.* **rat·ted, rat·ting;** *interj.* —*n.* **1** any of numerous long-tailed Old World rodents (especially genus *Rattus*) related to and resembling the Old World mouse, but larger. Rats are now common disease-carrying pests in communities throughout the western hemisphere. **2** any of various other rodents, such as the wood rat of North America. **3** *Slang.* a low, mean, disloyal person. **4** *Cdn.* muskrat. **5** a small pad over which a woman's hair is arranged to make it look thicker.
smell a rat, *Informal.* suspect a trick or scheme.
—*v.* **1** hunt for or catch rats. **2** betray, inform on, or desert one's friends or associates (*usually used with* **on**).
—*interj.*
rats, *Slang.* an exclamation of frustration, disappointment, disgust, etc. [OE *rætt*]

rat·a·ble (rāt′ə bəl) *adj.* **1** capable of being rated. **2** taxable. Also, **rateable.**

ra·tan (ra tan′) See **rattan.**

ratch (rach) *n.* ratchet.

ratch·et (rach′it) *n.* **1** a wheel or bar with teeth that strike against a catch fixed so that motion is permitted in one direction but not in the other. **2** the catch. **3** the entire device, wheel and catch or bar and catch. [< F < Ital. *rocchetto*, ult. < Gmc.]

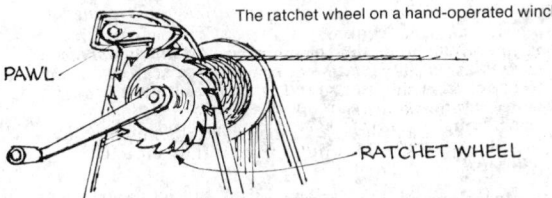

The ratchet wheel on a hand-operated winch

PAWL

RATCHET WHEEL

ratchet wheel a wheel with teeth and a catch that permits motion in only one direction.

rate¹ (rāt) *n., v.* **rat·ed, rat·ing.** —*n.* **1** a quantity, amount, or degree measured in proportion to something else: *The rate of interest is 6 cents on the dollar. The car was going at the rate of 85 kilometres an hour.* **2** a price: *We pay the regular rate.* **3** a class; grade; rating. **4** a local tax, often on property.
at any rate, in any case; under any circumstances.
at that or **this rate,** in that or this case; under such circumstances.
—*v.* **1** put a value on: *We rated the house as worth $75 000.* **2** consider; regard: *He was rated as one of the richest men in town.* **3** subject to a certain tax. **4** fix at a certain rate. **5** put in a certain class or grade. **6** be regarded; be classed; rank. **7** *Informal.* have value; be worthy of: *He doesn't rate. She rates the best seat in the house.* [ME < OF < Med.L *rata* (*pars*) fixed (amount), pp. of L *reri* reckon] —**rat′er,** *n.*

rate² (rāt) *v.* **rat·ed, rat·ing.** scold. [ME *rate(n)*; ? < OF *rater, areter* scold < L *ad* + *reputare* count. See REPUTE.]

rate·a·ble (rāt′ə bəl) See **ratable.**

rate·pay·er (rāt′pā′ər) *n.* a person who pays municipal taxes.

rathe (rāТН) *adj.* or *adv. Archaic* or *poetic.* early; growing or blooming early. [OE *hrathe* quickly]

rath·er (rаТН′ər) *adv., interj.* —*adv.* **1** more readily; more willingly: *I would rather go today than tomorrow.* **2** more properly or justly; with better reason: *This is rather for your parents to decide than for you.* **3** more precisely; more truly: *It was late Monday night or, rather, early Tuesday morning.* **4** (with verbs) in

hat, āge, fär; let, ēqual, tėrm; it, īce
hot, ōpen, ôrder; oil, out; cup, pút, rüle,
above, takən, pencəl, lemən, circəs

ch, child; ng, long; sh, ship
th, thin; ŦH, then; zh, measure

some degree: *He rather felt that this was unwise.* **5** to some extent; somewhat; more than a little: *rather good.* **6** on the contrary: *The sick man is no better today; rather he is worse.*
had rather, would more willingly; prefer to.
—*interj. Informal.* yes, indeed! certainly! very much so! [OE *hrathor,* comparative of *hrathe* quickly]
☛ *Usage.* See note at **had.**

raths·kel·ler (räts′kel′ər) *n.* a restaurant, usually below street level, selling alcoholic drinks. [< G *Ratskeller, Rathskeller* < *Rat(haus)* town hall + *Keller* cellar]

rat·i·fi·ca·tion (rat′ə fə kā′shən) *n.* formal approval and sanction: *the ratification of a treaty by Parliament.*

rat·i·fy (rat′ə fī′) *v.* **-fied, -fy·ing.** approve formally; confirm; authorize: *The two countries will ratify the agreement made by their representatives.* [ME < OF < Med.L *ratificare,* ult. < L *ratus* fixed + *facere* make] —**rat′i·fi′er,** *n.*
☛ *Syn.* See note at **approve.**

rat·ing (rāt′ing) *n.* **1** a class; grade. **2** a position in a class or grade: *the rating of a seaman, the rating of a ship according to tonnage.* **3** in some navies, a sailor of the lowest rank; an ordinary seaman. **4** an amount fixed as a rate or grade: *a rating of 80% in English.* **5** any survey of public taste, especially one taken to establish the popularity of one or more television programs. **6** a level of merit or popularity established by survey. **7** a credit rating.

ra·ti·o (rā′shē ō′ *or* rā′shō) *n., pl.* **-ti·os. 1** the relative magnitude. *He has sheep and cows in the ratio of 10 to 3 means that he has ten sheep for every three cows, or 3⅓ times as many sheep as cows.* **2** a quotient. The ratio between two quantities is the number of times one contains the other. The ratio of 6 to 10 is 6/10. The ratio of 10 to 6 is 10/6. [< L *ratio* reckoning < *reri* reckon. Doublet of RATION, REASON.]

ra·ti·oc·i·nate (rash′ē os′ə nāt′ *or* rat′ē os′ə nāt′) *v.* **-nat·ed, -nat·ing.** carry on a process of reasoning; reason. [< L *ratiocinari* < *ratio.* See RATIO.] —**ra′ti·oc′i·na′tion,** *n.* —**ra′ti·oc′i·na·tor,** *n.*

ra·ti·oc·i·na·tive (rash′ē os ə nā′tiv *or* rat′ē os ə nā′tiv) *adj.* of, having to do with, or involving ratiocination.

ra·tion (rash′ən *or* rā′shən) *n., v.* —*n.* **1** a fixed allowance of food; daily allowance of food for a person or animal. **2** a portion of anything dealt out: *rations of sugar, of coal, etc.*
—*v.* **1** supply with rations: *to ration an army.* **2** allow only certain amounts to: *to ration citizens when supplies are scarce.* **3** distribute in limited amounts: *to ration food to the public in wartime.* [< F < Med.L *ratio, -onis* < L *ratio* reckoning. Doublet of RATIO, REASON.]
☛ *Syn. n.* **1.** See note at **food.**

ra·tion·al (rash′ən əl *or* rash′nəl) *adj.* **1** sensible; reasonable; reasoned out: *Angry people seldom act in a rational way.* **2** able to think and reason clearly: *As children grow older, they become more rational.* **3** of reason; based on reasoning: *There is a rational explanation for thunder and lightning.* **4** *Mathematics.* **a** expressible as a whole number or a fraction composed of whole numbers. **b** involving no root that cannot be extracted. [< L *rationalis* < *ratio.* See RATIO.] —**ra′tion·al·ly,** *adv.*
☛ *Syn.* **3.** See note at **reasonable.**

ra·tion·ale (rash′ən al′) *n.* the whys and wherefores; the fundamental reason or logical basis. [< L *rationale,* neut. of *rationalis.* See RATIONAL.]

ra·tion·al·ism (rash′ən əl iz′əm *or* rash′nəl iz′əm) *n.* **1** the principle or habit of accepting reason as the supreme authority in matters of opinion, belief, or conduct. **2** the philosophical doctrine that reason is in itself a source of knowledge, independent of the senses.

ra·tion·al·ist (rash′ən əl ist *or* rash′nəl ist) *n.* a person who accepts reason as the supreme authority in matters of opinion, belief, or conduct.

ra·tion·al·is·tic (rash′ən əl is′tik *or* rash′nəl is′tik) *adj.* of or having to do with rationalism or rationalists.
—**ra′tion·al·is′ti·cal·ly,** *adv.*

ra·tion·al·i·ty (rash′ən al′ə tē *or* rash′nal′ə tē) *n.* **1** the quality or state of being rational. **2** the possession of reason; reasonableness: *Mr. Wallace is eccentric, but no one doubts his rationality.*

ra·tion·al·ize (rash′ən əl īz′ *or* rash′nəl īz′) *v.* **-ized, -iz·ing. 1** make rational or conformable to reason. **2** treat or explain in a

rational manner. **3** find (often unconsciously) an explanation or excuse for: *She rationalizes her gluttony by thinking, "I must eat enough to keep up my strength."* **4** find excuses for one's desires. —**ra′tion·al·i·za′tion**, *n.* —**ra′tion·al·iz′er**, *n.*

rational number *Mathematics.* any number that can be expressed as an integer or as a ratio between two integers, excluding zero as a denominator. 2, 5, and ½ are rational numbers.

rat·line or **rat·lin** (rat′lən) *n.* one of the small ropes that cross the shrouds of a ship, used as steps for going aloft. See **shroud** for picture. [origin uncertain]

RA·TO or **ra·to** (rā′tō) *n.* a unit of one or more rockets, providing extra power to speed up an aircraft during take-off. [< rocket assisted *take-off*]

ra·toon (ra tün′) *n.*, *v.* —*n.* a new shoot or sprout that grows from the root of a plant already cropped: *ratoons of banana trees.* —*v.* sprout after being cut. Also, **rattoon.** [< Sp. *retoño* < *retoñar* to sprout]

rat race *Slang.* a fierce, frantic scramble or struggle, especially with reference to competing and keeping one's place in the business world.

rats·bane (rats′bān′) *n.* any poison for rats. [< *rat* + *bane*]

rat·tan (ra tan′) *n.* **1** any of several climbing palms (especially of genera *Calamus* and *Daemonorops*) having very long, jointed, pliable stems. **2** the stem of any of these palms, used for wickerwork, canes, etc. **3** a cane or switch made from a piece of such a stem. [ult. < Malay *rotan*]

rat·ter (rat′ər) *n.* **1** an animal, or sometimes, a person that catches rats: *Our terrier is a good ratter.* **2** *Slang.* a person who deserts his associates.

rat·tle (rat′əl) *v.* **-tled, -tling;** *n.* —*v.* **1** make a number of short, sharp sounds. **2** cause to rattle. **3** move with short, sharp sounds: *The cart rattled down the street.* **4** talk quickly, on and on. **5** say quickly. **6** *Informal.* confuse; upset: *She was so rattled that she forgot her speech.*
—*n.* **1** a number of short, sharp sounds: *the rattle of empty bottles.* **2** a sound in the throat, occurring in some diseases of the lungs and also often just before death. **3** a racket; uproar. **4** a toy, instrument, etc. that makes a noise when it is shaken. **5** a series of horny pieces at the end of a rattlesnake's tail. [ME *ratele(n)*; probably imitative]

rat·tle·brain (rat′əl brān′) *n.* a giddy, foolish, unthinking person.

rat·tler (rat′lər) *n.* *Informal.* rattlesnake.

rat·tle·snake (rat′əl snāk′) *n.* any of the snakes constituting two genera (*Crotalus* and *Sistrurus*) of pit vipers that produce a whirring sound of warning by vibrating the end of the tail, which consists of a series of loosely connected horny segments.

rat·tle·trap (rat′əl trap′) *n.* **1** something shaky, rickety or rattling, especially an old, worn-out car. **2** (*adj.*) rickety or rattling.

rat·tling (rat′ling) *adj.* **1** that rattles. **2** lively; very fast: *a rattling pace.* **3** *Informal.* great; very good. **4** (*advl.*) *Informal.* extremely; especially: *a rattling good time.*

rat·toon (ra tün′) See **ratoon.**

rat–trap (rat′trap′) *n.* **1** a trap to catch rats. **2** a dirty, run-down building. **3** a desperate situation.

rat·ty (rat′ē) *adj.* **-ti·er, -ti·est. 1** of or like rats. **2** full of rats. **3** *Slang.* poor; shabby: *a ratty old jacket.* **4** *Slang.* angry or irritable.

rau·cous (ro′kəs or rô′kəs) *adj.* hoarse; harsh-sounding: *the raucous caw of a crow.* [< L *raucus*] —**rau′cous·ly,** *adv.*

raun·chy (ron′chē or rôn′chē) *adj.* **-chi·er, -chi·est.** *Slang.* **1** lewd; indecent: *The entertainer's raunchy songs bordered on the obscene.* **2** smelly or disreputable: *He insists on wearing those raunchy sneakers.* **3** boisterously and vulgarly exuberant: *Some of the Grey Cup fans got pretty raunchy at the game.* —**raun′chi·ly,** *adv.* —**raun′chi·ness,** *n.*

rav·age¹ (rav′ij) *v.* **-aged, -ag·ing;** *n.* —*v.* lay waste; damage greatly; destroy: *The forest fire ravaged huge areas of country.* —*n.* violence; destruction; great damage: *War causes ravage.* [< F *ravager* < *ravir* ravish] —**rav′ag·er,** *n.*

rav·age² (rav′ij) *n. Cdn.* a place where a group of moose, deer, or other animals stay for a time feeding on the surrounding vegetation before moving on. [< Cdn.F]

rave (rāv) *v.* **raved, rav·ing;** *n.* —*v.* **1** talk wildly and incoherently, as when extremely excited, delirious, etc. **2** talk with too much enthusiasm: *She raved about the food.* **3** howl; roar; rage: *The wind raved about the lighthouse.*
—*n.* **1** the act or an instance of raving. **2** *Informal.* unrestrained praise, especially a highly enthusiastic review of a play, film, etc.: *The play got raves in the local press.* **3** (*adj.*) unrestrained enthusiastic: *rave notices.* [ME ? < OF *raver*, var. of *rêver* dream]

rav·el (rav′əl) *v.* **-elled** or **-eled, -el·ling** or **-el·ing;** *n.* —*v.*

1 separate the threads of; fray. **2** fray out; separate into threads: *The sweater was ravelled at the wrist.* **3** make plain or clear; unravel. **4** become tangled, involved, or confused. **5** tangle; involve; confuse.
—*n.* an unravelled thread or fibre. [probably < MDu. *ravelen*]

rav·el·ling or **rav·el·ing** (rav′əl ing or rav′ling) *n.* something ravelled out; a thread drawn from a woven or knitted fabric.

ra·ven¹ (rā′vən) *n.*, *adj.* —*n.* **1** a very large passerine bird (*Corvus corax*) closely related to the crows, found throughout much of the northern hemisphere, having a large, straight bill and glossy black plumage. **2** any of various other large members of the same family. —*adj.* having the glossy black color of a raven: *raven hair.* [OE *hræfn*]

rav·en² (rav′ən) *v.*, —*v.* **1** devour greedily. **2** prey on; plunder. —*n.* plunder; rapine. Also, **ravin.** [< OF *raviner* < *ravine* violent rush, robbery. Doublet of RAVINE.]

rav·en·ing (rav′ən ing) *adj.* **1** seeking eagerly for prey: *ravening wolves.* **2** greedy and hungry; voracious.

rav·en·ous (rav′ən əs) *adj.* **1** very hungry; famished: *The hikers were all ravenous by the time they stopped to eat.* **2** very eager or greedy: *ravenous hunger. He was ravenous for praise.* **3** rapacious. [ME < OF *ravineus* rapacious, violent < *ravine.* See RAVIN.] —**rav′en·ous·ly,** *adv.* —**rav′en·ous·ness,** *n.*

rav·in¹ (rav′ən) *n.* rapine. [ME < OF *ravine* robbery < L *rapina* < *rapere* snatch. Doublet of RAVINE.]

rav·in² (rav′ən) See **raven².**

ra·vine (rə vēn′) *n.* a long, deep, narrow gorge worn by running water or by the action of glaciers. [< F *ravine* < OF *ravine* violent rush, robbery. Doublet of RAVIN.]

rav·ing (rāv′ing) *adj.*, *n.* —*adj.* **1** that raves; delirious; frenzied; raging. **2** *Informal.* remarkable; extraordinary. —*n.* delirious, incoherent talk. —**rav′ing·ly,** *adv.*

rav·i·o·li (rav′ē ō′lē) *n.* small, thin cases of pasta filled with chopped meat, cheese, etc., cooked in water and usually served with a highly seasoned tomato sauce. [< Ital. *ravioli*, ult. < L *rapum* beet]

rav·ish (rav′ish) *v.* **1** fill with delight; charm; enrapture: *ravished by the beauty of the scene.* **2** commit rape on. **3** *Archaic.* carry off by force. [ME < OF *raviss-*, a stem of *ravir* < L *rapere* seize] —**rav′ish·er,** *n.*

rav·ish·ing (rav′ish ing) *adj.* very delightful; enchanting: *jewels of ravishing beauty.* —**rav′ish·ing·ly,** *adv.*

rav·ish·ment (rav′ish mənt) *n.* **1** the act of ravishing. **2** rapture; ecstasy.

raw (ro or rô) *adj.* **1** not cooked: *raw oysters.* **2** in the natural state; not manufactured, treated, or prepared: *raw materials, raw hides. Raw milk is milk that has not been pasteurized.* **3** not experienced; not trained: *a raw recruit.* **4** unpleasantly damp or cold: *raw weather.* **5** with the skin off; sore: *a raw spot.* **6** uncivilized; brutal: *the raw frontier.* **7** having a crude quality; not refined in taste: *a raw piece of work, a raw story.* **8** *Slang.* harsh; unfair: *a raw deal.*
—*n.*
the raw, a raw or sore place or condition.
in the raw, **a** naked: *to sleep in the raw.* **b** in an unrefined or crude state: *experiencing life in the raw.*
[OE *hrēaw*] —**raw′ly,** *adv.* —**raw′ness,** *n.*

☛ *Syn. adj.* **2. Raw, crude** = not processed or prepared for use. **Raw** applies to a material or natural product that has not yet been processed for use or shaped or made into something by treating, tanning, finishing, manufacturing, etc.: *Raw milk is pasteurized to make it ready to drink.* **Crude** applies to a product in a natural state, not freed from impurities or prepared for use or greater usefulness and value by refining, tempering, or treating with chemicals and heat: *Crude rubber is treated with sulphur and heat to make it more elastic and durable.*

raw–boned (ro′bōnd′ or rô′-) *adj.* **1** having little flesh on the bones; gaunt. **2** having a heavy, large, somewhat bony frame: *He was tall and raw-boned.*

raw·hide (ro′hīd′ or rô′-) *n.*, *v.* **-hid·ed, -hid·ing.** —*n.* **1** the untanned skin of cattle. **2** a rope or whip made of this skin. **3** *Cdn. Historical.* the dressed but untanned hide of an animal, usually buffalo, used to pack goods in and lashed to rope tugs for hauling over ice and snow. —*v.* whip or drive with a rawhide. —**raw′hid′er,** *n.*

raw material 1 material that can or will be treated, prepared, or manufactured into something else: *Petroleum is one of the basic raw materials of industry.* **2** a person or thing thought of as having potential for development, elaboration, training, etc.: *There is some good raw material for the football team among the new students.*

raw milk unpasteurized milk.

ray¹ (rā) *n.*, *v.* —*n.* **1** a line or beam of light. **2** a line or stream of radiant energy in the form of heat, electricity, light, etc.: *x rays.* **3** a

thin line like a ray, coming out from a centre. **4** any part like a ray. The petals of a daisy and the arms of a starfish are rays. **5** a slight trace; faint gleam: *Not a ray of hope pierced our gloom.*
—*v.* **1** send forth in rays; radiate. **2** treat with rays. [ME < OF *rai* < L *radius.* Doublet of RADIUS.]
☛ *Syn. n.* **1.** See note at **beam.**

ray² (rā) *n.* any of an order (Batoidea, also called Rajiformes) of fishes having a flattened body with the eyes and spiracles on the top of the head and the mouth and gill slits on the underside and having broad, winglike pectoral fins and a tapering tail often bearing one or more poisonous spines. See also **electric ray, devilfish, sting-ray.** [ME < OF < L *raia*]

ray flower one of the petal-like flowers forming the outside of the flower head of a composite plant. The flower head of a daisy consists of central disk flowers surrounded by ray flowers. See **composite** for picture.

ray·on (rā′on) *n.* **1** any of a group of textile fibres made from cellulose. The cellulose in solution is extruded through minute holes and solidified in the form of filaments. **2** a yarn or fabric made from any of these fibres. [< *ray* beam, light]

raze (rāz) *v.* **razed, raz·ing.** tear down; destroy completely; demolish: *The old school was razed and a new one was built in the same place.* Also, *esp.Brit.,* **rase.** [< F *raser* scrape, ult. < L *radere*]

ra·zor (rā′zər) *n.* a cutting instrument used for shaving or cutting hair: *an electric razor, a safety razor.* [ME < OF *rasor* < *raser* scrape, ult. < L *radere.* Related to RAZE.]

ra·zor·back (rā′zər bak′) *n.* **1** a kind of thin, half-wild, mongrel hog with a ridged back. Razorbacks are common in the southern United States. **2** a finback whale; rorqual. **3** a sharp ridge on a hill, mountain, etc.

ra·zor·bill (rā′zər bil′) *n.* a common North Atlantic auk (*Alca torda*) having a deep, curved, laterally compressed bill with a white line down the sides and black-and-white plumage.

ra·zor–billed auk (rā′zər bild′) razorbill.

razor clam any of various marine bivalve molluscs (family Solenidae) having a narrow, elongated shell resembling a straight razor, and a large, muscular foot adapted for burrowing deep in the sand in coastal waters.

razor shell razor clam.

razz (raz) *v., n. Slang.* —*v.* tease, ridicule, or heckle; make fun of: *Several people in the crowd were razzing the speaker. We razz her about the old car she drives.* —*n.* a sound of disapproval or contempt; raspberry. [< *raspberry*]

raz·zle–daz·zle (raz′əl daz′əl) *n., adj., v.* **-zled, -zling.** *Slang.* —*n.* **1** confusing or bewildering activity, especially of a colorful and spectacular nature. **2** *Sports.* a deceptive play involving fast movement, crisscrossing, etc. by several players, intended to bewilder the opposing team.
—*adj.* bewildering; flashy.
—*v.* bewilder; confuse. [varied reduplication of *dazzle*]

razz·ma·tazz (raz′mə taz′) *n. Slang.* **1** razzle-dazzle; excitement and fanfare: *political razzmatazz.* **2** (*adj.*) characterized by razzmatazz: *the razzmatazz heyday of journalism.*

Rb rubidium.

RBI (är′bē ī′) *n., pl.* **RBI's, RBIs,** or **RBI.** *Baseball.* a run batted in.

R.C. **1** Roman Catholic. **2** Red Cross.

RCA or **R.C.A.** Royal Canadian Artillery.

RCAF or **R.C.A.F.** Royal Canadian Air Force.

rcd. received.

RCMP or **R.C.M.P.** Royal Canadian Mounted Police.

RCN or **R.C.N.** Royal Canadian Navy.

RCR or **R.C.R.** Royal Canadian Regiment.

RCSC or **R.C.S.C.** Royal Canadian Service Corps.

rd. **1** road. **2** rod(s).

Rd. Road.

R.D. *U.S.* Rural Delivery.

re¹ (rā *or* rē) *n. Music.* **1** the second tone of an eight-tone major scale. **2** the tone D. See **do²** for picture. [see GAMUT.]

re² (rē) *prep.* with reference to; in the matter or case of; about; concerning. [for L *in re* in the matter of]

re– *prefix.* **1** again; anew; once more, as in *reappear,* rebuild, *reheat, reopen, re-enter.* **2** back, as in *recall, repay, replace.* [< L]
☛ *Usage.* Most words beginning with **re-** are not hyphenated:

hat, āge, fär; let, ēqual, tėrm; it, īce
hot, ōpen, ôrder; oil, out; cup, půt, rüle,
əbove, takən, pencəl, lemən, circəs

ch, child; ng, long; sh, ship
th, thin; ŦH, then; zh, measure

rearm, refine, remit. However, a hyphen is often used if the letter following the **re-** is also *e*: *re-entry, re-establish.* In addition, a hyphen is always used to distinguish a word in which **re-** means 'again' from another word that would otherwise have the same spelling: *recover* 'get back, get better', *re-cover* 'cover again'; *reform* 'make better, improve', *re-form* 'make or shape again'.

Re rhenium.

reach (rēch) *v., n.* —*v.* **1** get to; come to; arrive at: *to reach the top of a hill, the end of a book, an agreement, etc.* **2** stretch; stretch out: *to reach toward a book.* **3** extend in space, time, operation, effect, influence, etc. (to): *The power of Rome reached to the ends of the known world.* **4** extend to: *Radio reaches millions.* **5** get or come; function: *farther than the eye can reach.* **6** get in touch with by anything extended, cast, etc.; touch: *The anchor reached bottom.* **7** make a stretch of certain length with the hand, etc.: *I cannot reach to the top of the wall.* **8** make a stretch in a certain direction: *The man reached for his gun.* **9** get at; influence: *Men are reached by flattery.* **10** amount to; be equal to: *The cost of the war reached billions.* **11** *Informal.* take or pass with the hand: *Please reach me the sugar.* **12** sail on a course with the wind forward of the beam. **13** deliver (a blow, kick, etc.).
—*n.* **1** a stretching out; reaching: *By a long reach, the drowning man grasped the rope.* **2** the extent or distance of reaching: *out of one's reach.* **3** range; power; capacity: *the reach of the mind.* **4** a continuous stretch or extent: *a reach of woodland.* **5** a part of a river between bends. **6** a part of a canal between locks. **7** the distance sailed on one tack. [OE *rǣcan*] —**reach′er,** *n.*

re·act (rē akt′) *v.* **1** act back; have an effect on the one that is acting: *Unkindness often reacts on the unkind person.* **2** act in response: *Dogs react to kindness by showing affection.* **3** act unfavorably or in opposition to something or somebody (used with **against**): *Some people react against fads.* **4** act chemically; undergo a reaction. *Acids react on metals.* **5** return to a previous state, level, etc.

re–act (rē akt′) *v.* act over again.

re·act·ance (rē ak′təns) *n. Electricity.* that part of the impedance of an alternating-current circuit which is due to inductance or capacitance or both. It is expressed in ohms.

re·ac·tion (rē ak′shən) *n.* **1** a response to some influence or force: *Our reaction to a joke is to laugh. The announcement of the new government budget brought an immediate reaction in the stock market.* **2** a response to an idea, plan, action, etc., indicating attitude or feeling: *What was her reaction to the idea?* **3** the occurrence of a condition directly opposed to a previous one: *We lived in a state of euphoria for several days before the reaction set in.* **4** the equal but opposite force exerted by a body when it is subjected to any force from another body. **5** a tendency toward a previous political or economic policy or system. **6** the interaction of two or more chemical elements or compounds involving the formation of different chemical bonds to produce different substances. The reaction between nitrogen and hydrogen produces ammonia. **7** a process in which the nucleus of an atom is transformed by interaction with another nucleus or a particle. **8** the response of the body to a drug or other substance, especially an adverse response.

re·ac·tion·ar·y (rē ak′shən er′ē) *adj., n., pl.* **-ar·ies.** —*adj.* having to do with, marked by, or favoring reaction. —*n.* a person who favors reaction, especially in politics, economics, etc.

re·ac·tor (rē ak′tər) *n.* **1** a device, such as a coil, having low resistance and high inductance, used to introduce reactance into an alternating-current circuit. **2** a person or animal that reacts, especially one that reacts positively to a medical test for a disease, allergy, etc. **3** nuclear reactor.

read¹ (rēd) *v.* read (red), read·ing; *n.* —*v.* **1** distinguish and understand the meaning of symbols such as those used in writing or printing: *to read a book. The blind read Braille with their fingers.* **2** learn from writing or printing: *We read of heroes of other days.* **3** speak (printed or written words); say aloud the words one sees, or touches: *Read this story to me.* **4** show by letters, figures, signs, etc.: *The thermometer reads 70 degrees.* **5** give as the word or words in a particular passage: *For "fail," a misprint, read "fall."*

re′ab·sorb′	re′ac·cept′	re′ac·com′mo·date′	re′ac·cus′tom	re′ac·quire′
re′ab·sorp′tion	re′ac·cep′tance	re′ac·com′mo·da′tion	re′ac·quaint′	re′ac·qui·si′tion
re′ac·cent′	re′ac·claim′	re′ac·cred′it	re′ac·quaint′ance	

6 study: *to read law.* **7** get the meaning of; understand: *to read a person's mind. He read her angry look and hurriedly left the room.* **8** give the meaning of; interpret: *A prophet reads the future.* **9** introduce (something not expressed or directly indicated) by one's manner of understanding or interpreting: *to read a hostile intent in a friendly letter.* **10** produce a certain impression when read; mean; be in effect when read: *This does not read like a child's composition.* **11** be worded in a certain way: *This line reads differently in the first edition.* **12** admit of being read or interpreted: *A rule that reads two different ways.* **13** bring or put by reading: *He reads himself to sleep.* **14** give (a lecture or a lesson) as a reprimand. **15** of an electronic device, absorb information directly from (written or printed matter) by means of a photo-electric cell.

read between the lines, discover a meaning or implication not stated outright in something.

read into, interpret in a certain way, often attributing more than intended: *He read into the statement a deep insult.*

read out, a read aloud: *She read out her answer to the class.* **b** produce a readout of.

read out of, expel from (a political party, etc.).

read the water, *Cdn.* scan the water from one's boat or canoe for signs of danger such as shoals, rapids, and snags.

—*n.* **1** a spell of reading. **2** a piece of reading matter considered in terms of the pleasure it gives: *That novel is a good read.* [OE *rǣdan* guess, read, counsel]

☛ *Hom.* **reed.**

read² (red) *adj., v.* —*adj.* having knowledge gained by reading; informed: *a well-read man.* —*v.* pt. and pp. of **read.** [originally pp. of *read¹*]

☛ *Hom.* **red.**

read·a·bil·i·ty (rēd′ə bil′ə tē) *n.* the quality or condition of being readable.

read·a·ble (rēd′ə bəl) *adj.* **1** interesting or enjoyable to read: *His novels are very readable.* **2** easy to read; legible: *readable handwriting.* —**read′a·ble·ness,** *n.* —**read′a·bly,** *adv.*

re·ad·dress (rē′ə dres′) *v.* **1** put a new address on: *to readdress a letter.* **2** speak to again: *to readdress a question.* **3** apply (oneself) anew.

read·er (rēd′ər) *n.* **1** a person who reads: *She is an avid reader. They are both poor readers.* **2** a book for learning and practising reading. **3** a person employed to read manuscripts and estimate their fitness for publication. **4** proofreader. **5 a** *Esp.Brit.* a senior instructor in certain universities. **b** an assistant who grades and corrects examinations, reads papers, etc. for a professor. **6** a person who reads or recites to entertain an audience. **7** an electronic device that absorbs information directly from written or printed matter through a photo-electric cell or scanner.

read·er·ship (rēd′dər ship′) *n.* **1** the reading public or audience of a particular publication or author. **2** *Esp.Brit.* the position of a reader (def. 5).

read·i·ly (red′ə lē) *adv.* **1** without reluctance; willingly: *She answered our questions readily. He doesn't readily accept advice.* **2** without difficulty; easily: *the parts fitted together readily.*

read·i·ness (red′ē nis) *n.* **1** the state of being ready; preparedness. **2** quickness; promptness. **3** ease; facility. **4** willingness.

read·ing (rēd′ing) *n.* **1** the act or process of getting the meaning of written or printed words. **2** a speaking out loud of written or printed words; a public recital. **3** the study of books, etc. **4** written or printed matter read or to be read: *There's good reading in this magazine.* **5** (adj.) that reads: *the reading public.* **6** (adj.) used in or for reading: *reading glasses, a reading room.* **7** the information shown by some letters, figures, or signs on a gauge or the scale of an instrument: *The reading on the thermometer was 38 degrees.* **8** the interpreting of symbols, designs, plans, etc. **9** the form of a given word or passage in a particular edition of a book: *No two editions have the same reading for that passage.* **10** an interpretation: *Each actor gave the lines a different reading.* **11** the extent to which one has read; literary knowledge. **12** one of the three stages in the passage of a bill by a legislative assembly. The bill must be presented and voted on at each assembly.

reading room a special room for reading in a library, club, etc.

read·out (rēd′out′) *n.* **1** the process of retrieving information from a computer storage or memory device and displaying it in understandable form, such as words or numerals. **2** the information so displayed.

read·y (red′ē) *adj.* **read·i·er, read·i·est;** *n., v.* **read·ied, read·y·ing.**
—*adj.* **1** prepared for immediate action or use; prepared: *Dinner is ready. The soldiers are ready for battle.* **2** willing: *The knights were ready to die for their lords.* **3** quick; prompt: *a ready welcome.* **4** quick in thought or action; dexterous: *a ready wit.* **5** apt; likely; liable: *She is too ready to find fault.* **6** immediately available: *ready money.*

make ready, prepare.

—*n.* **the ready,** the condition of being ready for action: *The soldiers walked down the road with their guns at the ready.*

—*v.* make ready; prepare. [OE *rǣde* ready]

☛ *Syn. adj.* **3, 4. Ready, prompt** = quick to understand, observe, or act in response. **Ready,** chiefly describing a person, his mind, hands, instrument, etc., suggests being prepared to act or respond without delay or hesitation and with skill or ease in doing: *With ready fingers the surgeons explored the wound.* **Prompt,** more often referring specifically to what is done, emphasizes being quick to act when the occasion demands or a request is made: *He is prompt to help students.*

read·y-made (red′ē mād′) *adj.* **1** of clothes, made beforehand in standard sizes; not made to order. **2** not original; commonplace: *a magazine article filled with ready-made ideas.* **3** already established and available: *The postal strike provided him with a ready-made excuse for not writing.*

read·y-mix (red′ē miks′) *adj.* ready to cook or use after adding liquid and, sometimes, other ingredients: *ready-mix muffins, ready-mix concrete.*

read·y-to-wear (red′ē tə wer′) *adj.* ready-made.

re·a·gent (rē ā′jənt) *n.* **1** a person, force, etc. that reacts. **2** *Chemistry.* **a** a substance that takes part in a reaction. Reagents are widely used in medicine, photography, and industry. **b** something that, when added to a substance, causes a reaction that aids in determining the composition of the substance.

re·al¹ (rē′əl *or* rēl) *adj., adv.* —*adj.* **1** existing as a fact; not imagined or made up; actual; true: *a real experience, the real reason.* **2** genuine: *a real diamond.* **3** *Law.* of or having to do with immovable property. Lands and houses are called real property. **4** *Mathematics.* either rational or irrational, not imaginary. **5** of or having to do with an optical image formed by actual convergence of light rays, as by a lens or mirror. **6** *Economics.* measured by reference to useful goods rather than money: *In a period of rising prices, real incomes fall if money incomes remain steady.*
—*adv. Informal.* really; very: *He talked real loud.* [LL *realis* < L *res* matter] —**re′al·ness,** *n.*

☛ *Hom.* **reel** (rēl).

☛ *Syn.* **1. Real, actual, true** = existing as a fact. **Real** means that what is described is in fact what it seems, is thought, or is said to be, not pretended, imaginary, or made up: *Give your real name.* **Actual** means that what it describes has in reality happened or come into existence, and is not merely capable of happening or existing only in theory: *Name an actual case of bravery.* **True** means "in agreement with what is real or actual, not false": *Tell the true story.*

☛ *Usage.* **Real.** In formal and most written English, **real** is used only as an adjective: *The excursion was a real pleasure for all of us.* In non-standard and some informal use, it is also an adverb meaning "really" or "very": *It was real kind of you to come.*

re·al² (rē′əl; *Spanish,* rā äl′) *n., pl.* **re·als** *or* **(Spanish) re·a·les** (rā ä′lās.) **1** a former unit of money of Spain and its possessions. **2** a silver coin worth one real. [< Sp. < L *regalis* regal. Doublet of REGAL, ROYAL, RIAL.]

re·al³ (rā äl′) *n., pl.* **reis. 1** a former unit of money of Portugal or Brazil. **2** a coin worth one real.

real estate a piece of land, together with the buildings, fences, trees, water, and minerals that belong with it.

re·al·ise (rē′əl īz′) *Esp.Brit.* See **realize.**

re·al·ism (rē′əl iz′əm) *n.* **1** practical tendency: *His realism caused him to dislike fanciful schemes.* **2** a style in literature and art characterized by picturing nature, life, people, etc. objectively and factually. **3** *Philosophy.* **a** the doctrine that material objects have a real existence independent of our consciousness of them. **b** the doctrine that general ideas have a real existence independent of the mind.

re·al·ist (rē′əl ist) *n.* **1** a person interested in what is real and practical rather than what is imaginary or theoretical. **2** a writer or artist who represents nature, life, people, etc. objectively and factually. **3** a person who believes in realism.

re·al·is·tic (rē′əl is′tik) *adj.* **1** like the real thing; lifelike. **2** of or having to do with realism in literature or art. **3** seeing things as they really are; practical. **4** of or having to do with realists or realism. —**re′al·is′ti·cal·ly,** *adv.*

re·al·i·ty (rē al′ə tē) *n., pl.* **-ties. 1** the quality or state of being real: *He was convinced of the reality of what he had seen.* **2** a real

re′a·dapt′   re′ad·just′   re′ad·mit′   re′af·firm′   re′a·lign′ment
re′a·dap·ta′tion   re′ad·just′ment   re′ad·mit′tance   re′af·fir·ma′tion
re·add′   re′ad·mis′sion   re′a·dopt′   re′a·lign′

thing, fact, or event: *the terrible realities of war. Her dream became a reality.* **3** actual existence; the true state of affairs: *They said his writing was just an attempt to escape from reality.*
in reality, really; actually; in fact: *We thought he was serious, but in reality he was joking.*

re·al·i·za·tion (rē′əl ə zā′shən *or* rē′əl ī zā′shən) *n.* **1** the action of realizing or the state of being realized: *the explorers had a full realization of the dangers they might face. For years they saved, waiting for the realization of their hopes.* **2** something that is realized: *The farm was the realization of all his dreams.*

re·al·ize (rē′əl īz′) *v.* **-ized, -iz·ing. 1** understand clearly; be fully aware of: *She realizes how hard you worked.* **2** make real; bring into actual existence: *Her uncle's present made it possible for her to realize her dream of going to college.* **3** cause to seem real. **4** change (property) into money: *Before going to England to live, he realized all his property in Canada.* **5** obtain as a return or profit: *He realized $10 000 from his investment.* **6** bring as a return or profit. Also, **realise.**

re·al·ly (rē′əl ē) *adv.* **1** actually; in fact: *things as they really are. He really didn't know who it was.* **2** without question; truly: *a really magnificent house.* **3** an expression of surprise, disbelief, or disapproval: *Really, Don? I don't believe it!*

realm (relm) *n.* **1** kingdom. **2** range; domain: *the realm of science. Such an occurrence is outside the realm of possibility.* [ME < OF *reialme* < *reial* regal < L *regalis.* See REGAL.]

real·tor (rē′əl tər *or* rē′əl tôr′) *n.* a member of an organization of persons engaged in the business of buying and selling real estate.

re·al·ty (rē′əl tē) *n.* real estate. [< *real*[1] (def. 3) + *-ty*[2]]

ream[1] (rēm) *n.* **1** a quantity of paper of the same size and quality, usually consisting of 500 sheets, but sometimes 480 or 516. **2** Usually, **reams,** *pl. Informal.* a very large quantity: *He took reams of notes. Abbrev.:* rm. [ME < OF *rayme* < Sp. < Arabic *rizmah* bundle]

ream[2] (rēm) *v.* **1** enlarge or shape (a hole). **2** remove with a reamer. [origin uncertain; perhaps akin to OE *rȳman* enlarge < *rūm* room]

A reamer for removing burrs from the inside of a cut pipe

ream·er (rēm′ər) *n.* **1** a tool for enlarging or shaping a hole. **2** a utensil for squeezing the juice out of oranges, lemons, etc.

reap (rēp) *v.* **1** cut (grain). **2** gather (a crop). **3** cut grain or gather a crop from: *to reap fields.* **4** get as a return or reward: *Kind acts often reap happy smiles.* **5** get a return. [OE *repan*]

reap·er (rēp′ər) *n.* **1** a person or machine that cuts grain or gathers a crop. **2** a person who reaps.

rear[1] (rēr) *n., adj.* —*n.* **1** the back part; the part opposite the front; back: *the rear of the house.* **2** the space or position at the back: *He moved toward the rear.* **3** *Slang.* buttocks. **4** the last part of an army, fleet, etc.; the part farthest from the battlefront.
at or **in the rear of,** behind.
bring up the rear, come or be last: *We filed through the woods, with me bringing up the rear.*
—*adj.* at or in the back. [var. of *arrear*]

rear[2] (rēr) *v.* **1** make grow; help to grow; bring up: *He was reared in the city.* **2** set up; build: *to rear a temple.* **3** raise; lift up: *to rear one's head.* **4** especially of a horse, rise on the hind legs; rise: *The horse reared as the fire engine dashed past.* **5** extend to a great height: *Mountain peaks reared up above the valley.* [OE *rǣran* raise, causative of *rīsan* rise]

rear–admiral 1 *Canadian Forces.* in Maritime Command, the equivalent of a major-general. See chart at **rank**[1]. **2** a naval officer of similar rank in other countries. *Abbrev.:* R.Adm., RAdm, or R.A.

rear guard that part of an army that protects the rear.

hat, āge, fär; let, ēqual, tèrm; it, īce
hot, ōpen, ôrder; oil, out; cup, pùt, rüle,
əbove, takən, pencəl, lemən, circəs

ch, child; ng, long; sh, ship
th, thin; ŦH, then; zh, measure

re·arm (rē ärm′) *v.* especially of a nation or a military force, arm again with new or better weapons.

re·ar·ma·ment (rē är′mə mənt) *n.* rearming or being rearmed.

rear·most (rēr′mōst) *adj.* farthest in the rear; last.

re·ar·range (rē′ə rānj′) *v.* **-ranged, -rang·ing. 1** arrange in a new or different way: *to rearrange furniture.* **2** arrange again.
—**re′ar·range′ment,** *n.* —**re′ar·rang′er,** *n.*

rear·view mirror (rēr′vyü′) a mirror on an automobile, etc. attached so as to give a view of the area to the rear.

rear·ward (rēr′wərd) *adv. or adj.* toward or in the rear.

rea·son (rē′zən) *n., v.* —*n.* **1** a cause or motive for an action, feeling, etc.; ground: *I have my own reasons for doing this.* **2** a justification; explanation: *What is your reason for doing such poor work?* **3** the ability or power to think and draw conclusions. **4** right thinking; good sense. **5** sanity.
bring to reason, cause to be reasonable.
by reason of, on account of; because of.
in reason, within reasonable and sensible limits.
stand to reason, be reasonable and sensible: *It stands to reason that he would resent your insults.*
—*v.* **1** think; think logically: *Man can reason.* **2** draw conclusions or inferences from facts or premises. **3** consider; discuss; argue.
reason away, get rid of by reasoning.
reason out, think through and come to a conclusion; think out. [ME < OF *raison* < L *ratio.* Doublet of RATIO, RATION.]
—**rea′son·er,** *n.*

☛ *Syn. n.* **1. Reason, cause, motive** = the ground or occasion for an event, action, etc. **Reason** applies to a ground or occasion that explains something that has happened, or one given as explanation, which may or may not be the true cause or motive: *The reason he went to the city was to attend university.* **Cause** applies to a person, thing, incident, or condition that directly brings about an action or happening: *The cause of death was given as poisoning.* **Motive** applies to the feeling or desire that makes a person do what he does: *His motive was to regain his health.*

☛ *Usage.* **The reason is, the reason was,** etc. should be followed by **that,** not by **because.** Instead of *His reason for being late is because his car would not start,* say: *His reason for being late is that his car would not start.* Or avoid the word **reason** and say: *He was late because his car would not start.*

rea·son·a·ble (rē′zən ə bəl *or* rēz′nə bəl) *adj.* **1** according to reason; not absurd: *a reasonable explanation, a reasonable theory.* **2** fair or moderate; not extreme: *a reasonable request, a reasonable price.* **3** not high in price; inexpensive: *I expected the dress to be expensive, but it was really very reasonable.* **4** ready to listen to reason; sensible: *She's a reasonable person. Be reasonable; it can't possibly work that way.* **5** having the ability to reason.
—**rea′son·a·ble·ness,** *n.* —**rea′son·a·bly,** *adv.*

☛ *Syn.* **1. Reasonable, rational** = according to reason. **Reasonable,** describing people or their actions, words, plans, or procedures, emphasizes showing good judgment and being governed by reason in deciding and choosing: *He took a reasonable view of the dispute and offered a solution that was fair, sensible, and practical.* **Rational** emphasizes having or showing the power to think logically and to draw conclusions that guide in doing or saying what is wise, sensible, or reasonable: *His approach to the problem was rational.*

rea·son·ing (rē′zən ing *or* rēz′ning) *n.* **1** the process of drawing conclusions from facts. **2** reasons, arguments, etc. resulting from or used in this process.

re·as·sem·ble (rē′ə sem′bəl) *v.* **-bled, -bling.** come or bring together again.

re·as·sur·ance (rē′ə shü′əns) *n.* **1** reassuring or being reassured. **2** reinsurance.

re·as·sure (rē′ə shür′) *v.* **-sured, -sur·ing. 1** restore to confidence: *The captain's confidence during the storm reassured the passengers.* **2** assure again or anew. **3** insure again.
—**re′as·sur′ing·ly,** *adv.*

Ré·au·mur (rā′ə myür′; *French,* rā ō MYR′) *adj.* of, based on, or according to the Réaumur scale for measuring temperature, in which the freezing point of water is 0 degrees and the boiling point is 80 degrees. [< René de *Réaumur* (1683-1757), a French physicist]

reave (rēv) v. **reaved**, or **reft**, **reav·ing**. *Archaic.* deprive by force; strip; rob: *Reft of his livelihood, he had nowhere to go.* [OE *rēafian*]
☛ *Hom.* **reeve.**

re·bate (rē′bāt or rē bāt′) n., v. **-bat·ed**, **-bat·ing.** —n. the return of part of the money paid; partial refund; discount. —v. give as a rebate. [ME < OF *rabattre* beat down < *re-* back + *abattre* abate < *a-* (< L *ad-*) + *battre* beat < L *batuere*]

re·bec or **re·beck** (rē′bek) n. a musical instrument, resembling a violin, used in the Middle Ages. [< F *rebec*, var. of OF *rebebe*, ult. < Arabic *rabāb*]

reb·el (n. reb′əl; v. ri bel′) n., v. **re·belled**, **re·bel·ling.** —n. 1 a person who opposes or takes up arms against a government or ruler. 2 (adjl.) of, having to do with, or made up of persons who take up arms against a government or ruler: *a rebel stronghold, a rebel army.* 3 a person who resists authority or control: *She always was a rebel; her family never understood her.*
—v. 1 use force or arms to oppose a government or an authority: *The people rebelled when the new tax was imposed. The troops rebelled against their commander.* 2 resist authority or control: *He rebelled against his parents.* 3 feel or express a great dislike: *We rebelled at the thought of having to stay home all weekend.* [ME < OF < L *rebellare*, ult. < *re-* again + *bellum* war. Doublet of REVEL.]

re·bel·lion (ri bel′yən) n. 1 organized resistance against the authority of a government; a revolt. 2 an act of resistance against any authority; a revolt or fight against any restriction. [< L *rebellio, -onis* < *rebellis* rebel < *rebellare.* See REBEL, v.]
☛ *Syn.* See note at **revolt.**

re·bel·lious (ri bel′yəs) adj. 1 defying authority; acting like a rebel. 2 hard to manage; hard to treat. —**re·bel′lious·ly**, adv. —**re·bel′lious·ness**, n.

re·birth (rē′bėrth′ or rē bėrth′) n. 1 being born again; reincarnation. 2 a new spiritual life; spiritual renewal. 3 revival; reawakening: *the rebirth of nationalism, the rebirth of hope.*

re·born (rē bôrn′) adj. born again, renewed, or revived.

re·bound (v. ri bound′; n. rē′bound′ or ri bound′) v., n. —v. 1 spring back. 2 resound. —n. 1 a springing back. 2 *Basketball.* a ball that bounds off the backboard when a scoring attempt has been missed.
on the rebound, in a state of shock caused by the abrupt ending of a love affair. [ME < OF *rebondir* < *re-* back (< L) + *bondir* bound, resound, ? < VL *bombitire* < L *bombus* booming sound < Gk. *bombos*]

re·broad·cast (rē brod′kast′ or -brôd′kast′) v. **-cast** or **-cast·ed**, **-cast·ing**; n. —v. 1 broadcast again at a later time or date. 2 relay (a television or radio program) as it is being received from another station. —n. a relayed or repeated television or radio broadcast.

re·buff (ri buf′) n., v. —n. a blunt or sudden rejection of a person or animal that makes advances, offers help or sympathy, makes a request, etc.; snub. —v. give a rebuff to. [< F < Ital. *ribuffo*]

re·build (rē′bild′) v. **-built**, **-build·ing.** build again or anew.

re·built (rē′bilt′) v. pt. and pp. of **rebuild.**

re·buke (ri byūk′) v. **-buked**, **-buk·ing**; n. —v. express disapproval of; reprove. —n. an expression of disapproval; scolding. [ME < ONF *rebuker* < *re-* back + *buchier* strike] —**re·buk′er**, n. —**re·buk′ing·ly**, adv.
☛ *Syn.* v. See note at **reprove.**

re·bus (rē′bəs) n. a puzzle in which a word or phrase is represented by pictures, letters, or signs suggesting the original sounds. A picture of a cat on a log is a rebus for *catalogue.* [< L *rebus* by means of objects]

re·but (ri but′) v. **-but·ted**, **-but·ting.** contradict or oppose by formal argument presenting evidence on the other side; try to disprove: *Each team in the debate was given two minutes to rebut the other's arguments.* [ME < OF *reboter* < *re-* back + *boter* butt³ < Gmc.]

re·but·tal (ri but′əl) n. the act of rebutting.

re·but·ter (ri but′ər) n. 1 a person who rebuts. 2 an argument that rebuts.

rec (rek) n. *Informal.* recreation.

rec. 1 receipt. 2 recipe. 3 record; recorder.

re·cal·ci·trance (ri kal′sə trəns) n. a refusal to submit, conform, or comply.

re·cal·ci·tran·cy (ri kal′sə trən sē) n. recalcitrance.

re·cal·ci·trant (ri kal′sə trənt) adj., n. —adj. resisting authority or control; disobedient. —n. one who is recalcitrant. [< L *recalcitrans, -antis*, ppr. of *recalcitrare* kick back, ult. < *re-* back + *calx, calcis* heel]

re·call (v. ri kol′ or -kôl′; n. rē′ kol′ or -kôl′, ri kol′ or -kôl′) v., n. —v. 1 call back to mind; remember. 2 call back; order back: *The ambassador was recalled.* 3 bring back: *recalled to life.* 4 take back; withdraw: *The order has been given and cannot be recalled.* —n. 1 a recalling to mind. 2 a calling back; ordering back. 3 a signal used in calling back men, ships, etc. 4 a taking back; revocation; annulment. 5 the removal of a public official from office by the vote of the people: *There is no longer provision for recall in Canada.*
☛ *Syn.* v. 1. See note at **remember.**

re·cant (ri kant′) v. 1 take back formally or publicly; withdraw or renounce (a statement, opinion, purpose, etc.). 2 renounce an opinion or allegiance: *Though he was tortured to make him change his religion, the prisoner would not recant.* [< L *recantare*, ult. < *re-* back + *canere* sing]

re·can·ta·tion (rē′kan tā′shən) n. the act or action of recanting.

re·cap¹ (v. rē′kap′ or rē kap′; n. rē′kap′) v. **-capped**, **-cap·ping**; n. —v. 1 put a strip of rubber or similar material on (a worn surface of an automobile tire), by using heat and pressure to make a firm union. 2 put a cap or lid on again: *to recap a bottle of ginger ale.* —n. a tire repaired in this manner.

re·cap² (v. rē′kap′ or rē kap′; n. rē′kap′) v. **-capped**, **-cap·ping**; n. *Informal.* —v. recapitulate. —n. recapitulation.

re·ca·pit·u·late (rē′kə pich′ə lāt′) v. **-lat·ed**, **-lat·ing.** repeat or recite the main points of; tell briefly; sum up. [< L *recapitulare* < *re-* again + *capitulum* chapter, section, dim. of *caput* head]

re·ca·pit·u·la·tion (rē′kə pich′ə lā′shən) n. 1 a brief statement of the main points; summary. 2 *Music.* a repetition, usually in a later movement or section of the initial theme of a composition.

re·cap·ture (rē kap′chər) v. **-tured**, **-tur·ing**; n. —v. 1 capture or take again. 2 bring back; recall: *The picture album recaptured the days of the horse and buggy.* —n. a taking or being taken again.

re·cast (v. rē kast′; n. rē′kast′) v. **-cast**, **-cast·ing**; n. —v. 1 cast again or anew: *recast a bell.* 2 make over; remodel: *recast a sentence.* —n. a recasting.

recd. or **rec'd** received.

re·cede (ri sēd′) v. **-ced·ed**, **-ced·ing.** 1 move back or away. 2 slope backward: *He has a chin that recedes.* 3 withdraw: *He receded from the agreement.* [< L *recedere* < *re-* back + *cedere* go]

re·ceipt (ri sēt′) n., v. —n. 1 a written statement that money, a package, a letter, etc. has been received. 2 the act or fact of receiving or being received: *The goods will be sent on receipt of payment. She wrote to acknowledge receipt of the package.* 3 Usually, **receipts,** pl. money, etc. received: *The expenses were greater than the receipts.* 4 *Archaic.* recipe.
—v. write on or stamp (a bill, etc.) to indicate that something has been received or paid for: *He asked them to receipt the bill.* [ME < ONF < L *recepta*, fem. pp. of *recipere* receive. See RECEIVE.]

re·ceiv·a·ble (ri sēv′ə bəl) adj. 1 fit for acceptance: *Gold is receivable all over the world.* 2 on which payment is to be received. *Bills receivable* is the opposite of *bills payable.* 3 to be received.

re·ceive (ri sēv′) v. **-ceived**, **-ceiv·ing.** 1 take (something offered or sent); take into one's hands or possession: *to receive gifts.* 2 have (something) bestowed, conferred, etc.: *to receive a name.* 3 be given; get: *to receive a letter from home.* 4 take, accept, admit, or get something: *Everyone will receive as he deserves.* 5 take; support; bear; hold: *The boat received a heavy load.* 6 take or let into the mind: *to receive new ideas.* 7 accept as true or valid: *a theory widely received.* 8 agree to listen to: *to receive confession.* 9 experience; suffer; endure: *to receive a blow.* 10 let into one's house, society, etc.: *The people of the neighborhood were glad to receive the new couple.* 11 admit to a place; give shelter to: *receive strangers.* 12 admit to a state or condition: *to receive a person into the Christian faith.* 13 be at home to friends and visitors: *She receives on Tuesdays.* 14 *Radio and television.* change electromagnetic waves into sound or picture signals. [ME < ONF < L *recipere* < *re-* back + *capere* take]
☛ *Syn.* 1. **Receive, accept** = take what is given, offered, or delivered. **Receive** carries no suggestion of positive action or of activity of the mind or will on the part of the receiver and means nothing more than to take to oneself or take in what is given or given out: *He received a prize.* **Accept** always suggests being willing to take what is offered, or giving one's consent: *She received a gift from him, but refused to accept it.*

re·ceiv·er (ri sēv′ər) n. 1 a person who receives. 2 anything that receives. 3 the part of a telephone that receives electrical impulses and converts them into sound. 4 a device in a telephone, radio, or television set that converts electromagnetic waves into sound or

picture signals. **5** *Law.* one appointed to take charge of the property of others. **6** a person who knowingly receives stolen goods or harbors offenders.

re·ceiv·er·ship (ri sēv′ər ship′) *n.* **1** the position of a receiver in charge of the property of others. **2** the condition of being in the control of a receiver.

receiving blanket a small, lightweight blanket for wrapping a newborn baby.

receiving line a group of people who stand in a row at wedding receptions or other formal occasions in order to welcome each guest individually.

re·cen·cy (rē′sən sē) *n.* the fact or condition of being recent.

re·cent (rē′sənt) *adj., n.* —*adj.* **1** that has happened or been done not long ago: *a recent quarrel, a recent cold spell.* **2** made, begun, or originated not long ago; new: *an information pamphlet for recent parents. Her recent promotion has gone to her head.* **3** of or designating a time or period comparatively near to the present: *recent history, the most recent ice age.* **4 Recent,** of, having to do with, or designating the most recent geological epoch (including the present time) or the rocks or plant and animal life characteristic of this period. See chart at **geology.**
—*n.* **the Recent,** the Recent geological epoch or its rock series. [< L *recens, -entis*] —**re′cent·ness,** *n.*

re·cent·ly (rē′sənt lē) *adv.* lately; not long ago.

re·cep·ta·cle (ri sep′tə kəl) *n.* **1** any container or place used to put things in to keep them conveniently. Bags, baskets, and vaults are all receptacles. **2** *Botany.* the base of the flower to which all the parts of the flower are attached. See **flower** for picture. **3** a wall socket for an electrical plug. [< L *receptaculum,* ult. < *recipere* receive. See RECEIVE.]

re·cep·tion (ri sep′shən) *n.* **1** the act of receiving: *calm reception of bad news.* **2** the fact of being received. **3** a manner of receiving: *a warm reception.* **4** a gathering to receive and welcome people. **5** the quality of the sound in a radio or of the sound and picture signals in a television set. [< L *receptio, -onis* < *recipere.* See RECEIVE.]

re·cep·tion·ist (ri sep′shən ist) *n.* a person employed in an office to welcome visitors, direct them where to go, give out information, etc.

re·cep·tive (ri sep′tiv) *adj.* able, quick, or willing to receive ideas, suggestions, or impressions, etc.: *a receptive mind.*
—**re·cep′tive·ly,** *adv.* —**re·cep′tive·ness,** *n.*

re·cep·tiv·i·ty (rē′sep tiv′ə tē) *n.* the ability or readiness to receive.

re·cep·tor (ri sep′tər) *n. Physiology.* a cell or group of cells sensitive to stimuli; a sense organ. [< L *receptor* receiver]

re·cess (*n.* rē′ses for 1, ri ses′ or rē′ses for 2 and 3; *v.* ri ses′) *n., v.* —*n.* **1** time during which work stops: *There will be a short recess before the next meeting.* **2** a part in a wall or other surface set back from the rest; alcove; niche. **3** an inner place or part; quiet, secluded place: *the recesses of a cave, the recesses of one's secret thoughts.*
—*v.* **1** take a recess: *The convention recesses until afternoon.* **2** put in a recess; set back. **3** make a recess in. [< L *recessus* a retreat < *recedere* recede. See RECEDE.]

re·ces·sion[1] (ri sesh′ən) *n.* **1** going backward; moving backward. **2** sloping backward. **3** withdrawal. **4** a period of temporary business decline, shorter and less extreme than a depression. [< L *recessio, -onis* < *recedere* recede. See RECEDE.]

re·ces·sion[2] (ri sesh′ən) *n.* a ceding back to a former owner. [< re- + cession]

re·ces·sion·al (ri sesh′ən əl) *n., adj.* —*n.* a hymn or other piece of music sung or played while the clergy and the choir leave at the end of a church service. —*adj.* **1** of or having to do with recession. **2** being a hymn, etc. that serves as a recessional.

re·ces·sive (ri ses′iv) *adj.* **1** tending to go back; receding. **2** *Biology.* of or designating a gene in one of a pair of chromosomes that is dominated by the corresponding gene in the other chromosome and is therefore latent and not expressed as a trait in an organism. Compare **dominant.**

Rech·a·bite (rek′ə bīt′) *n.* **1** in the Old Testament, a member of a Jewish family that refused to drink wine (Jer. 35:2-19). **2** a total abstainer from alcohol, especially a member of a fraternal benefit organization affiliated to the Independent Order of Rechabites, founded in England in 1835.

re·cher·ché (rə sher′shā; *French,* rə sher shā′) *adj.* **1** sought out or devised with care; rare; choice. **2** too studied; far-fetched. [< F *recherché* sought after < *re-* again + *chercher* search]

re·cid·i·vism (rē sid′ə viz′əm) *n.* a tendency to chronic relapse

hat, āge, fär; let, ēqual, tėrm; it, īce
hot, ōpen, ôrder; oil, out; cup, pút, rüle,
əbove, takən, pencəl, lemən, circəs

ch, child; ng, long; sh, ship
th, thin; ₸H, then; zh, measure

into crime or antisocial behavior. [< L *recidivus* < *recidere* fall back < L *re-* back + *cadere* fall]

re·cid·i·vist (rē sid′ə vist′) *n., adj.* —*n.* a habitual criminal. —*adj.* of or having to do with recidivism or recidivists. —**re·cid′i·vis′tic,** *adj.*

rec·i·pe (res′ə pē) *n.* **1** a set of directions for preparing something to eat. **2** a set of directions for preparing anything by combining various ingredients: *a recipe for making soap.* **3** a means of reaching some state or condition: *a recipe for happiness.* [< L *recipe* take!, imperative of *recipere* take, receive. See RECEIVE.]

re·cip·i·ent (ri sip′ē ənt) *n., adj.* —*n.* a person or thing that receives something: *The recipients of the prizes had their names printed in the paper.* —*adj.* receiving or willing to receive. [< L *recipiens, -entis,* ppr. of *recipere.* See RECEIVE.]

re·cip·ro·cal (ri sip′rə kəl) *adj., n.* —*adj.* **1** in return: *a reciprocal gift.* **2** move or cause to move with an alternating backward and forward motion: *a reciprocating valve.* **3** inversely proportional; inverse. **4** *Grammar.* expressing mutual action or relation. In *The two children like each other, each other* is a reciprocal pronoun.
—*n.* **1** a number so related to another that when multiplied together they give 1. The reciprocal of 3 is ⅓, and the reciprocal of ⅓ is 3. **2** something that is reciprocal. [< L *reciprocus* returning]

re·cip·ro·cal·ly (ri sip′rə kə lē *or* ri sip′rə klē) *adv.* in a reciprocal way; each to the other; mutually.

re·cip·ro·cate (ri sip′rə kāt′) *v.* **-cat·ed, -cat·ing. 1** give, do, feel, or show in return: *She loves me, and I reciprocate her love.* **2** move or cause to move with an alternating backward and forward motion. [< L *reciprocare* < *reciprocus* returning]
—**re·cip′ro·ca′tion,** *n.* —**re·cip′ro·ca′tor,** *n.*

reciprocating engine an engine in which the back-and-forth motion of a piston is converted into a circular motion of the crankshaft by means of a connecting rod. Most internal-combustion engines are of this type.

rec·i·proc·i·ty (res′ə pros′ə tē) *n.* **1** a reciprocal state; mutual action, influence, or dependence. **2** a mutual exchange, especially an exchange of special privileges in regard to trade between two countries, institutions, etc.

re·cit·al (ri sīt′əl) *n.* **1** the act of reciting; a telling of facts in detail: *Her recital of her experiences in the hospital bored her hearers.* **2** a story; account. **3** a program of music or dance given by a single performer or several individual performers, or by a small ensemble. **4** a public performance given by a number of music or dance pupils to show their skill.

rec·i·tan·do (rä chē tän′dō) *adv. Music.* after the manner of a recitative. [Ital.]

rec·i·ta·tion (res′ə tā′shən) *n.* **1** reciting; a telling of facts in detail. **2** a reciting of a prepared lesson by pupils before a teacher. **3** a repeating of something from memory, especially before an audience. **4** a piece repeated from memory. [< L *recitatio, -onis* < *recitare.* See RECITE.]

rec·i·ta·tive (res′ə tā′tiv *or* ri sī′tə tiv) *adj.* of or having to do with recital; reciting: *a recitative account of the event.*

rec·i·ta·tive[2] (res′ə tə tēv′) *n. Music.* **1** a style halfway between speaking and singing. Operas often contain passages of recitative. **2** a passage, part, or composition in this style. [< Ital. *recitativo*]

re·cite (ri sīt′) *v.* **-cit·ed, -cit·ing. 1** tell in detail: *He recited the day's adventures.* **2** mention in order; enumerate: *They recited a long list of grievances.* **3** repeat a poem, etc. before an audience. **4** repeat or answer questions about: *to recite a lesson.* [< L *recitare* < *re-* again + *citare* appeal to] —**re·cit′er,** *n.*

reck (rek) *v. Archaic.* **1** care; heed. **2** be important or interesting; matter. [OE *reccan*]
➤ *Hom.* **wreck.**

reck·less (rek′lis) *adj.* rash; heedless; careless: *Reckless of consequences, the boy played truant. Reckless driving causes many automobile accidents.* [OE *receleās*] —**reck′less·ly,** *adv.*
—**reck′less·ness,** *n.*
➤ *Syn.* See note at **rash.**

re·chal′lenge   re·charge′   re·char′ter   re·chew′   re·cir′cle
re·chan′nel   re·chart′   re·check′   re·chris′ten   re·cir′cu·late′

reck·on (rek′ən) v. **1** find the number or value of; count: *Reckon the cost before you decide.* **2** consider; judge; account: *He is reckoned the best player in the league.* **3** *Informal.* think; suppose. **4** depend; rely: *You can reckon on our help.* **5** settle accounts.
reckon on, count on, take into account: *He didn't reckon on breaking his leg when he decided to try skiing.*
reckon up, count up.
reckon with, take into account; face: *We are going to have to reckon with higher prices for food.*
[OE (*ge*)*recenian*] —**reck′on·er,** n.

reck·on·ing (rek′ən ing *or* rek′ning) n. **1** the act or an instance of computing; a count or calculation: *By my reckoning, we still have about seven kilometres to go.* **2** the settlement of an account. **3** a bill, especially at an inn or tavern. **4** the calculation of the position of a ship. **5** the position calculated.

re·claim (ri klām′) v. **1** make available for cultivation, etc.: *to reclaim a swamp.* **2** rescue or bring back from wrong conduct, vice, etc.; reform. **3** recover from discarded or waste products: *to reclaim tin from tin cans.* **4** demand or obtain the return of: *The library sent a notice reclaiming the book.* [ME < OF < L *reclamare* cry out against < *re-* back + *clamare* cry out] —**re·claim′a·ble,** adj. —**re·claim′er,** n.
☛ *Syn.* **1.** See note at **recover.**

re–claim (rē′klam′) v. claim back or again: *He had trouble re-claiming the money.*

rec·la·ma·tion (rek′lə mā′shən) n. reclaiming or being reclaimed: *the reclamation of deserts by irrigation.*

re·cline (ri klīn′) v. **-clined, -clin·ing. 1** lean back or lie down: *to recline on a couch.* **2** lay back or down: *He reclined his head on the pillow.* [< L *reclinare* < *re-* back + *-clinare* lean]

rec·luse (n. rek′lüs *or* ri klüs′; adj. ri klüs′) n., adj. —n. a person who lives shut up or withdrawn from the world. —adj. shut up or apart from the world. [ME < OF < L *reclusus* shut up, pp. of *recludere* < *re-* back + *claudere* shut]

re·clu·sive (ri klü′siv) adj. having or showing a tendency to withdraw from society: *She became reclusive in her old age and rarely had any visitors.*

rec·og·ni·tion (rek′əg nish′ən) n. **1** a knowing again; recognizing; being recognized: *By a good disguise he escaped recognition.* **2** acknowledgment: *We insisted on complete recognition of our rights.* **3** notice. **4** a favorable notice: *The actor soon won recognition from the public.* **5** formal approval or sanction. [< L *recognitio, -onis*]

rec·og·niz·a·ble (rek′əg nīz′ə bəl) adj. capable of being recognized. —**rec′og·niz′a·bly,** adv.

re·cog·ni·zance (ri kog′nə zəns) n. *Law.* **1** a bond binding a person to perform some particular act, such as appearing in court on a particular day or keeping the peace. If no surety in the form of money or property is required, a person is said to be released on his own recognizance. **2** the sum of money to be forfeited if the required act is not performed. [ME < OF *recognoissance* < *reconoistre* recognize. See RECOGNIZE. Doublet of RECONNAISSANCE.]

rec·og·nize (rek′əg nīz′) v. **-nized, -niz·ing. 1** know again: *I could scarcely recognize my old friend.* **2** identify: *to recognize a person from a description.* **3** acknowledge acquaintance with; greet: *to recognize a person on the street.* **4** acknowledge; accept; admit: *He recognized his duty to defend his country.* **5** take notice of: *Anyone who wishes to speak in a public meeting should stand up and wait till the chairman recognizes him.* **6** show appreciation of. **7** acknowledge and agree to deal with: *For some years certain nations did not recognize the new government.* [ME < OF *reconoistre* < L *recognoscere* < *re-* again + *com-* (intensive) + (*g*)*noscere* learn. Doublet of RECONNOITRE.] —**rec′og·niz′er,** n.

re·coil (v. ri koil′; n. ri koil′ *or* rē′koil) v., n. —v. **1** draw back; shrink back: *Most people would recoil at seeing a snake in their path.* **2** spring back: *The gun recoiled after I fired.* **3** react: *Revenge often recoils on the avenger.* —n. **1** the act or action of recoiling. **2** the distance or force with which a gun, spring, etc. springs back. [ME < OF *reculer*, ult. < L *re-* back + *culus* rump]

rec·ol·lect (rek′ə lekt′) v. call back to mind; remember. [from the same source as *re-collect*, but distinguished in meaning and pronunciation]
☛ *Syn.* See note at **remember.**

re–col·lect (rē′kə lekt′) v. **1** collect again. **2** recover control of

(oneself). [originally < L *recollectus*, pp. of *recolligere* < *re-* again + *colligere* collect, but later taken as < *re-* + *collect*, and pronounced accordingly]

rec·ol·lec·tion (rek′ə lek′shən) n. **1** the act or power of recalling to mind. **2** memory; remembrance. **3** something remembered.
☛ *Syn.* **2.** See note at **memory.**

re·com·bi·nant (rē kom′bə nənt) adj. showing genetic recombination: *recombinant DNA.*

re·com·bi·na·tion (rē′kom bə nā′shən) n. *Genetics.* the formation of new combinations of genes in a zygote that are different from the gene combinations of either parent, occurring especially as a result of the interchange of paired genes during meiosis. Recombination is an important natural means of producing variation in species.

rec·om·mend (rek′ə mend′) v. **1** speak in favor of; suggest favorably. **2** advise. **3** make pleasing or attractive: *The position of the camp recommends it as a summer home.* **4** hand over for safekeeping. [< Med.L *recommendare* < L *re-* again + *commendare* commend] —**rec′om·mend′er,** n.

rec·om·men·da·tion (rek′ə men dā′shən) n. **1** the act of recommending. **2** something that recommends a person or thing or that expresses praise: *She got a very good recommendation from her former boss.* **3** something recommended. *The doctor's recommendation was that the child stay in bed for a few days.*

rec·om·men·da·to·ry (rek′ə men′də tô′rē) adj. serving to recommend; recommending.

re·com·mit (rē′kə mit′) v. **-mit·ted, -mit·ting. 1** commit again. **2** refer again to a committee.

re·com·mit·ment (rē′kə mit′mənt) n. recommitting or being recommitted.

re·com·mit·tal (rē′kə mit′əl) n. recommitment.

rec·om·pense (rek′əm pens′) v. **-pensed, -pens·ing;** n. —v. **1** pay (a person); pay back; reward. **2** make a fair return for (an action, anything lost, damage done, etc.). —n. **1** a payment or reward: *He asked for fair recompense for the work he had done.* **2** a return for anything lost, damaged, etc.; amends: *He demanded recompense for the broken window.* [< LL *recompensare*, ult. < L *re-* back + *com-* with, against + *pendere* weigh out in payment]

rec·on·cil·a·bil·i·ty (rek′ən sī′lə bil′i tē) n. the quality of being reconcilable.

rec·on·cil·able (rek′ən sī′lə bəl) adj. capable of being reconciled: *The two points of view are not reconcilable.*

rec·on·cile (rek′ən sīl′) v. **-ciled, -cil·ing. 1** make friends again. **2** settle (a quarrel, disagreement, etc.). **3** make agree; bring into harmony: *It is impossible to reconcile his story with the facts.* **4** make satisfied or content with: *It is hard to reconcile oneself to being sick for a long time.* [< L *reconciliare* < *re-* back + *concilium* bond of union] —**rec′on·cil′a·ble,** adj. —**rec′on·cil′er,** n.

rec·on·cile·ment (rek′ən sīl′mənt) n. reconciliation.

rec·on·cil·i·a·tion (rek′ən sil′ē ā′shən) n. reconciling or being reconciled: *the reconciliation of opposite points of view. They had hopes of a reconciliation between the brothers.*

rec·on·cil·i·a·to·ry (rek′ən sil′ē ə tô′rē) adj. tending to reconcile.

rec·on·dite (rek′ən dīt′ *or* ri kon′dīt) adj. **1** hard to understand; profound. **2** little known; obscure. [< L *reconditus*, pp. of *recondere* store away, ult. < *re-* back + *com-* up + *dare* put]

re·con·di·tion (rē′kən dish′ən) v. restore to a good or satisfactory condition by repairing or replacing parts, etc.: *The motor has been completely reconditioned.*

re·con·nais·sance (ri kon′ə səns) n. an examination or survey, especially for military purposes. [< F *reconnaissance* (< OF *recognoissance*). Doublet of RECOGNIZANCE.]

rec·on·noi·tre (rek′ə noi′tər *or* rē′kə noi′tər) v. **-tred, -tring. 1** approach and examine or observe in order to learn something; make a survey of (the enemy, the enemy's strength or position, a region, etc.) in order to gain information for military purposes. **2** approach a place and make a first survey of it: *It seemed wise to reconnoitre before entering the town.* Also, **reconnoiter.** [< F *reconnoître*, earlier form of *reconnaître* (< OF *reconoistre*). Doublet of RECOGNIZE.] —**rec′on·noi′trer,** n.

re·con·sid·er (rē′kən sid′ər) v. consider again with a view to changing or reversing a position or decision: *The assembly voted to reconsider the bill. They have said they won't go, but we're hoping they will reconsider.* —**re′con·sid·er·a′tion,** n.

---

re·con·sti·tute (rē kon′stə tyüt′ or rē kon′stə tüt′) v. **-tut·ed, -tut·ing.** constitute anew; especially, restore a condensed or dehydrated substance to its original liquid state by adding water: *reconstituted orange juice.*

re·con·struct (rē′kən strukt′) v. **1** construct again; rebuild; make over. **2** go back over and organize all the information or evidence on an event to try to discover exactly what happened: *When the police reconstructed the crime, they realized who the murderer must be.*

re·con·struc·tion (rē′kən struk′shən) n. **1** the act of reconstructing. **2** the thing reconstructed.

re·con·struc·tive (rē′kən struk′tiv) adj. having to do with or involved in reconstruction: *Their reconstructive efforts were hampered by lack of money.*

re·cord (v. ri kôrd′; n. adj. rek′ərd) v., n. —v. **1** set down in writing so as to keep for future use: *Listen to the speaker and record what he says.* **2** put in some permanent form; keep for remembrance: *History is recorded in books.* **3** put on a phonograph disk, or on phonographic tape or wire. **4** tell; indicate: *The thermometer records temperatures.*
—n. **1** the thing written or kept. **2** an official written account: *The secretary kept a record of what was done at the meeting.* **3** a thin, flat disk with narrow spiral grooves on its surface that reproduces sounds when played on a record player. **4** the known facts about what a person, animal, ship, etc. has done: *She has a fine record at school.* **5** a criminal record: *They say he has a record.* **6** a remarkable performance or event, going beyond others of the same kind, especially the best achievement in a sport: *to hold the record for the high jump.* **7** (adj.) unequalled; greater, higher, better, etc. than ever before: *a record wheat crop.* **8** a recording or being recorded: *What happened is a matter of record.*
break a record, improve on a record previously set in some athletic event, etc.
go on record, state publicly.
off the record, not to be recorded or quoted: *The Prime Minister was speaking off the record.*
on record, written down, printed, or otherwise made available: *The facts of the murder are now on record.*
[ME < OF < L *recordari* remember, ult. < *re-* back + *cor, cordis* heart, mind]

record changer a device on a record player that permits several records to be played one after the other automatically.

record club a business organization that regularly supplies selected records to its subscribers.

A recorder

re·cord·er (ri kôr′dər) n. **1** a person who records, especially one whose work is making and keeping written accounts. **2** an apparatus or machine that records. **3** tape-recorder. **4** *Brit.* a barrister or solicitor appointed as judge of a crown court. **5** a musical instrument resembling a flute but having the mouthpiece on the end rather than on the side.

re·cord·ing (ri kôr′ding) n. **1** a sound record made on disk or tape. **2** the original transcription of any sound or combination of sounds.

record player an instrument for playing back the sounds recorded on records, or discs, especially a small, portable one. It consists basically of a turntable, a needle (or stylus) that follows the grooves in the record, a pickup arm that converts the vibrations of the needle back into sound, and an amplifier and loudspeaker to make the sounds audible. Also called **phonograph.**

re·count[1] (ri kount′) v. tell in detail; give an account of: *He recounted all the happenings of the day.* [ME < ONF *reconter* < *re-* again + *conter* relate, count[1]]

re·count[2] (rē′kount′ or rē kount′) n. a second count, as of votes.

re–count (rē′kount′) v. count again.

re·coup (ri küp′) v. **1** make up for: *He recouped his losses.* **2** repay. [< F *recouper* < *re-* back + *couper* cut]

re·course (rē′kôrs or ri kôrs′) n. **1** the act of turning to a person, organization, course of action, etc. when in need of help or protection: *to have recourse to weapons. We had recourse to a doctor who lived nearby.* **2** a person, organization, course of action,

hat, āge, fär; let, ēqual, tèrm; it, īce
hot, ōpen, ôrder; oil, out; cup, pu̇t, rüle,
abōve, takən, pencəl, lemən, circəs
ch, child; ng, long; sh, ship
th, thin; ŦH, then; zh, measure

etc. turned to for help or protection: *The child's recourse was always her mother.* **3** the right to collect payment from the maker or endorser of a cheque or similar negotiable instrument. [ME < OF < L *recursus* retreat, ult. < *re-* back + *currere* run]

re·cov·er (ri kuv′ər) v. **1** get back (something lost, taken away, or stolen). **2** make up for (something lost or damaged): *recover lost time.* **3** bring back to life, health, one's senses, or normal condition. **4** get well; get back to a normal condition. **5** get back to the proper position or condition: *He started to fall but recovered himself.* **6** *Law.* **a** obtain by judgment in a court. **b** obtain judgment in one's favor in a court. **7** rescue; deliver. **8** regain in usable form; reclaim. Many useful substances are now recovered from materials that used to be thrown away. [ME < OF < L *recuperare.* Doublet of RECUPERATE.] —**re·cov′er·er,** n.
► *Syn.* **1. Recover, reclaim, retrieve** = get or bring something back. **Recover** = get something back again in one's possession after losing it: *He recovered the stolen furs.* **Reclaim** = bring back into usable or useful condition from a lost state: *Part of his farm is reclaimed swamp.* **Retrieve** = recover by effort or search: *The rescuers retrieved the victims of the mine disaster.*

re·cov·er (rē′kuv′ər) v. cover again or anew; especially, provide a piece of upholstered furniture with a new covering.

re·cov·er·y (ri kuv′ər ē or ri kuv′rē) n., pl. **-er·ies. 1** the act of recovering. **2** a coming back to health or normal condition. **3** the getting back of something that was lost, taken away, or stolen. **4** a getting back to a proper position or condition: *He started to fall, but made a quick recovery.* **5** the obtaining of some property or right by the judgment of a law court. **6** the act of locating and repossessing a missile, nose cone, etc. after a flight in space.

recovery room in a hospital, a room in which patients are placed immediately after an operation.

rec·re·an·cy (rek′rē ən sē) n. **1** cowardice. **2** unfaithfulness or treason.

rec·re·ant (rek′rē ənt) adj., n. —adj. **1** cowardly. **2** disloyal or traitorous. —n. **1** coward. **2** traitor. [ME < OF *recreant* confessing oneself beaten, ult. < L *re-* back + *credere* believe]

rec·re·ate (rek′rē āt′) v. **-at·ed, -at·ing. 1** refresh with games, pastimes, exercises, etc. **2** take recreation. [ult. < L *recreare* restore < *re-* again + *creare* create]

re·cre·ate (rē′krē āt′) v. **-at·ed, -at·ing.** create anew.

rec·re·a·tion (rek′rē ā′shən) n. **1** a refreshing of the body and spirit after working, through play or amusement. **2** a form of play or amusement that serves as recreation: *Her favorite recreation is tennis.*

rec·re·a·tion·al (rek′rē ā′shən əl) adj. of or having to do with recreation.

recreation room 1 in a hotel, apartment building, community centre, etc., a room for recreation such as playing games, lounging, dancing, and other informal activities. **2** in a private home, a family room; rec room.

rec·re·a·tive (rek′rē ā′tiv) adj. refreshing; restoring.

re·crim·i·nate (ri krim′ə nāt′) v. **-nat·ed, -nat·ing.** accuse (someone) in return: *Tom said Harry had lied, and Harry recriminated by saying Tom had lied too.* [< Med.L *recriminare,* ult. < L *re-* back + *crimen* charge]

re·crim·i·na·tion (ri krim′ə nā′shən) n. an accusing in return; counter accusation.

re·crim·i·na·tive (ri krim′ə nə tiv or ri krim′ə nā′tiv) adj. recriminatory.

re·crim·i·na·to·ry (ri krim′ə nə tô′rē) adj. of or involving recrimination.

rec room (rek) *Informal.* a room in a house, usually in the basement, used for recreation and relaxation; a family room.

re·cru·desce (rē′krü des′) v. **-desced, -desc·ing.** become active again or break out afresh; flare up.

re·cru·des·cence (rē′krü des′əns) n. breaking out afresh after a period of being inactive or dormant; renewed activity: *a sudden recrudescence of a polio epidemic.* [< L *recrudescere,* ult. < *re-* again + *crudus* raw]

re·cru·des·cent (rē′krü des′ənt) *adj.* breaking out again.

re·cruit (ri krüt′) *n., v.* —*n.* **1** a newly enlisted member of the armed forces. **2** a new member of any group or class. —*v.* **1** get people to join one of the armed forces. **2** strengthen or supply (armed forces) with new personnel. **3** get (new members). **4** increase or maintain the number of. **5** renew health, strength, or spirits. **6** renew; get a sufficient number or amount of; replenish. [< F *recruter* < *recrue* recruit(ing), new growth < *recrû*, pp. of *recroître* < *re-* again (< L *re-*) + *croître* grow < L *crescere*] —**re·cruit′er**, *n.* —**re·cruit′ment**, *n.*

rect. **1** receipt. **2** rector; rectory.

rec·tal (rek′təl) *adj.* of or having to do with the rectum.

rec·tan·gle (rek′tang′gəl) *n.* **1** a four-sided plane figure with four right angles; a right-angle parallelogram. Squares and oblongs are rectangles. See **quadrilateral** for picture. **2** a rectangle that is not square; oblong. [< F < LL *rectangulum* < L *rectus* right + *angulus* angle]

rec·tan·gu·lar (rek tang′gyə lər) *adj.* **1** shaped like a rectangle. **2** having one or more right angles. **3** placed at right angles. —**rec·tan′gu·lar·ly**, *adv.*

rec·ti·fi·er (rek′tə fī′ər) *n.* **1** a person or thing that makes right, corrects, adjusts, etc. **2** *Electricity.* a device for changing alternating current into direct current.

rec·ti·fy (rek′tə fī′) *v.* **-fied, -fy·ing. 1** make right; put right; adjust; remedy: *The storekeeper admitted his mistake and was willing to rectify it.* **2** *Electricity.* change (an alternating current) into a direct current. **3** purify; refine: *rectify a liquor by distilling it several times.* [< LL *rectificare* < L *rectus* right + *facere* make] —**rec′ti·fi·able**, *adj.* —**rec′ti·fi·ca′tion**, *n.*

rec·ti·lin·e·ar (rek′tə lin′ē ər) *adj.* **1** in, moving in, or forming a straight line. **2** bounded or formed by straight lines. **3** characterized by straight lines. [< L *rectus* straight + E *linear*]

rec·ti·tude (rek′tə tyüd′ *or* rek′tə tüd′) *n.* **1** upright conduct or character; honesty; righteousness. **2** correctness. [< LL *rectitudo* < L *rectus* straight]

rec·to (rek′tō) *n., pl.* **-tos. 1** the front of a sheet of printed paper; the side that is to be read first. **2** the right-hand page of an open book. Compare **verso.**

rec·tor (rek′tər) *n.* **1** *Anglican Church of Canada, Church of England.* a member of the clergy who has charge of a parish. **2** *Roman Catholic Church.* a priest who has charge of a college or a religious house. **3** the head or principal of certain schools, colleges, or universities. [< L *rector* ruler < *regere* to rule]

rec·tor·ate (rek′tər it) *n.* the position, rank, or term of a rector.

rec·to·ry (rek′tə rē *or* rek′trē) *n., pl.* **-ries. 1** the residence of a rector or pastor. **2** *Esp.Brit.* a rector's benefice with all its rights, tithes, and lands.

rec·tum (rek′təm) *n.* the lowest part of the large intestine. See **alimentary canal** for picture. [< NL *rectum*, for L *intestinum rectum* straight intestine]

re·cum·ben·cy (ri kum′bən sē) *n.* a recumbent position or condition.

re·cum·bent (ri kum′bənt) *adj.* lying down, reclining, or leaning. [< L *recumbens, -entis*, ppr. of *recumbere* recline] —**re·cum′bent·ly**, *adv.*

re·cu·per·ate (ri kü′pər āt′ *or* ri kyü′pər āt′) *v.* **-at·ed, -at·ing. 1** get back to a former state or condition, especially, recover from sickness or exhaustion: *She is at home, recuperating from surgery.* **2** get back; regain: *to recuperate one's health. He worked hard to recuperate his losses after the fire.* [< L *recuperare* recover. Doublet of RECOVER.]

re·cu·per·a·tion (ri kü′pər ā′shən *or* ri kyü′pər ā′shən) *n.* recovery from sickness, exhaustion, loss, etc.

re·cu·per·a·tive (ri kü′pər ə tiv *or* -ā′tiv, ri kyü′pər ə tiv *or* -ā′tiv) *adj.* **1** of or having to do with recuperation: *She has remarkable recuperative powers.* **2** aiding recuperation; helping to restore health, strength, etc.

re·cur (ri kėr′) *v.* **-curred, -cur·ring. 1** come up again; occur again; be repeated: *A leap year recurs every four years.* **2** return in thought or speech: *Old memories constantly recurred to him. He recurred to the matter of cost.* [< L *recurrere* < *re-* back + *currere* run]

re·cur·rence (ri kėr′əns) *n.* an occurring again; repetition; return: *More care in the future will prevent recurrence of the mistake.*

re·cur·rent (ri kėr′ənt) *adj.* **1** recurring; occurring again and again; repeated: *recurrent attacks of hay fever.* **2** of certain nerves and blood vessels, turned back so as to run in the opposite direction. [< L *recurrens, -entis*, ppr. of *recurrere.* See RECUR.] —**re·cur′rent·ly**, *adv.*

re·curve (rē kėrv′) *v.* **-curved, -curv·ing.** curve back; bend back.

rec·u·san·cy (rek′yə zən sē *or* ri kyü′zən sē) *n.* the act or state of being recusant.

rec·u·sant (rek′yə zənt *or* ri kyü′zənt) *n., adj.* —*n.* **1** a person who refuses to submit to an established authority. **2** *Historical.* in England, a Roman Catholic who refused to attend the services of the Church of England. —*adj.* of or like a recusant; refusing to submit. [< L *recusans, -antis*, ppr. of *recusare* refuse, ult. < *re-* back + *causa* cause]

red (red) *n., adj.* **red·der, red·dest.** —*n.* **1** the color of blood, glowing coals, rubies, etc. the color of the visible spectrum having the longest light waves, at the end opposite to violet. **2** a red pigment or dye. **3** red cloth or clothing. **4** a red or reddish person, animal, or thing. **5 Red,** a radical; revolutionary: *Communists are often referred to as Reds.* **6** *Cdn.* a Liberal.
in the red, operating at a loss; in debt: *We'll be in the red soon if we don't cut down our expenses.*
see red, *Informal.* become very angry: *She sees red as soon as you mention the new by-law.*
—*adj.* **1** of or having the color of blood; being like it; suggesting it: *red ink, red hair, a red fox.* **2** sore; inflamed: *red eyes.* **3** blushing. **4** radical; revolutionary. **5** of or having to do with Liberals. [OE *rēad*] —**red′ly**, *adv.* —**red′ness**, *n.*
☛ *Hom.* read².

red- form of re- in some cases before vowels, as in *redeem.*

re·dac·tion (ri dak′shən) *n.* **1** the preparation of another person's writings for publication; revising; editing. **2** the form or version of a work as prepared by revision or editing. [< L *redactio, -onis* < *redactus*, pp. of *redigere* reduce < *red-* back + *agere* bring]

red alert the final stage of alert, when an attack by an enemy is expected at any moment.

re·dan (ri dan′) *n.* a fortification with two walls forming an angle that points outward. [< F *redan* a double notching, ult. < L *re-* again + *dens* tooth]

red·bird (red′bėrd′) *n.* any of various birds with mainly red plumage, such as the cardinal or the scarlet tanager.

red blood cell one of the cells found in the blood of vertebrates that carry oxygen to the tissues of the body. Red blood cells contain hemoglobin and give blood its red color.

red-blood·ed (red′blud′id) *adj.* full of life and spirit; vigorous; lusty.

red·breast (red′brest′) *n.* robin.

red·bud (red′bud′) *n.* any of a genus (*Cercis*) of north temperate shrubs and small trees of the pea family often cultivated for their small rosy-pink or purplish flowers which appear before the leaves. There are two North American species but only one (*C. canadensis*) extends into Canada, occurring in extreme southern Ontario. See also **Judas tree.**

red·cap (red′kap′) *n.* a porter at a railway station, bus station, etc., usually wearing a red cap as part of his uniform.

red carpet a carpet, traditionally red, laid out at formal receptions for royalty or other important persons.
roll out the red carpet, welcome royally and treat with special consideration.

red-car·pet (red′kär′pət) *adj. Informal.* showing special courtesy: *They got the red-carpet treatment.*

red cedar 1 a small, pyramid-shaped juniper (*Juniperus virginiana*) found in southern Ontario and the eastern United States. Also called **red juniper, juniper. 2** western red cedar. **3** the wood of either of these trees.

Red Chamber a name sometimes given to the Canadian Senate because of the color of the rugs, draperies, etc. of the room in which the Senate meets.

red clover a clover (*Trifolium pratense*) native to Europe and Asia, having heads of fragrant, purplish-red flowers. It is widely cultivated for forage and hay and also as a cover crop.

red·coat (red′kōt′) *n.* **1** *Historical.* a British soldier. **2** a member of the RCMP.

red corpuscle red blood cell.

Red Cross 1 a group of societies in over 100 countries, that work to relieve human suffering in time of war or peace. Co-operation among the national societies takes place through the League of Red Cross Societies. Major projects of the Canadian Red

Cross, which is made up mostly of volunteers, are the free blood-transfusion service and the water safety program. The badge of most societies is a red cross on a white background, but societies in Moslem countries have a red crescent, and are called Red Crescent societies. **2** a national society that is a branch of this organization: *the Canadian Red Cross.* **3 red cross,** a red Greek cross on a white ground, the emblem of the Red Cross. **4** the cross of Saint George, England's national emblem.

redd (red) *n.* a depression made on the bed of a river or stream by the female of salmon, trout, etc. for laying eggs in. [origin uncertain]

red deer 1 a deer (*Cervus elaphus*) of Europe, Asia, and N Africa, about 120—135 cm tall at the shoulder, having a smooth, reddish coat, a buff-colored patch on the rump, and a mane of dark, shaggy hair around the neck and shoulders. **2** the white-tailed deer of North America, especially in its reddish summer coat. **3** *Cdn. Historical.* the North American elk; wapiti.
➤ *Usage.* (def. 3). The name **red deer** was used for the elk by English explorers to western Canada, and many authorities today in fact consider the elk and European red deer to belong to the same species.

red·den (red′ən) *v.* **1** make or become red: *The sky was just beginning to redden when we left home.* **2** blush: *She reddened with embarrassment.*

red·dish (red′ish) *adj.* somewhat red.

rede (rēd) *v., n. Archaic or dialect.* —*v.* **1** advise. **2** interpret; explain. **3** tell. —*n.* **1** advice; counsel. **2** an interpretation, account, or story. [OE *rædan.* Cf. READ¹.]

re·deem (ri dēm′) *v.* **1** buy back: *The property was redeemed when the loan was paid back.* **2** pay off: *We redeemed the mortgage.* **3** convert (certificates, coupons, etc.) into cash or goods. **4** carry out; make good; fulfill: *We redeem a promise by doing what we said we would.* **5** *Christianity.* of Christ, set (the human soul) free from the consequences of sin; save from damnation. **6** make up for; balance: *A very good feature will sometimes redeem several bad ones.* **7** reclaim (land). [< L *redimere* < *red-* back + *emere* buy]

re·deem·a·ble (ri dēm′ə bəl) *adj.* **1** capable of being redeemed. **2** that will be redeemed or paid: *bonds redeemable in ten years.*

re·deem·er (ri dēm′ər) *n.* **1** a person who redeems. **2 Redeemer,** Jesus Christ.

re·demp·tion (ri demp′shən) *n.* **1** the act or process, or an instance of redeeming: *redemption from sin, the redemption of a captive, the redemption of a loan.* **2** the state of being redeemed. [< L *redemptio, -onis* < *redimere* redeem. See REDEEM. Doublet of RANSOM.]

re·demp·tive (ri demp′tiv) *adj.* serving to redeem.

re·demp·to·ry (ri demp′tə rē) *adj.* redemptive.

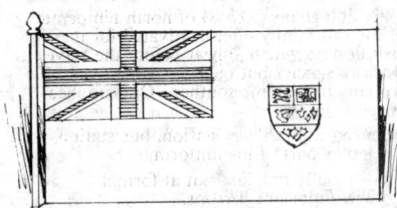

The Canadian Red Ensign

Red Ensign the distinctive Canadian flag until 1965, having a red ground with the arms of Canada in the middle of the outer half and the Union Jack in the upper corner near the staff. It is based on the Red Ensign of the British Merchant Marine. Also called **Canadian Red Ensign.**

re·de·ploy (rē di ploi′) *v.* change the position (of troops) from one theatre of war to another. —**re′de·ploy′ment,** *n.*

re·de·vel·op (rē′di vel′əp) *n.* **1** develop again. **2** improve buildings or land. **3** *Photography.* put through a stronger developer a second time, to intensify the image. —**re′de·vel′op·ment,** *n.*

red·eye (red′ī′) *n. Cdn. Slang.* a drink made of beer and tomato juice.

red fire a chemical that burns with a red light, used in fireworks, signals, etc.

red·fish (red′fish′) *n.* **1** any of various reddish-colored marine food fishes (family Scorpaenidae) of the Atlantic coasts of North America and Europe. **2** *Cdn.* kokanee.

hat, āge, fär; let, ēqual, tėrm; it, īce
hot, ōpen, ôrder; oil, out; cup, pút, rüle;
əbove, takən, pencəl, lemən, circəs
ch, child; ng, long; sh, ship
th, thin; ᴛʜ, then; zh, measure

red flag 1 a symbol of rebellion, revolution, etc. **2** a sign of danger. **3** anything that stirs up anger.

red fox a fox (*Vulpes vulpes*) found throughout the northern hemisphere, having mainly reddish-brown fur.

red–hand·ed (red′han′did) *adj.* **1** having hands red with blood. **2** in the very act of crime: *a man caught red-handed in robbery.* —**red′-hand′ed·ly,** *adv.* —**red′-hand′ed·ness,** *n.*

red hat 1 a cardinal's hat. **2** the position or rank of a cardinal.

red·head (red′hed′) *n.* **1** a person having red hair: *All three of their children are redheads.* **2** a North American diving duck (*Aythya americana*) the male of which has a reddish-brown head, blue bill, black breast, and grey back, sides, and wings. It closely resembles the canvasback but has a high, rounded forehead.

red·head·ed (red′hed′id) *adj.* **1** having red hair. **2** having a red head.

red herring 1 the common smoked herring. **2** something used to draw attention away from the real issue.

red hot *Informal.* hot dog.

red–hot (red′hot′) *adj.* **1** red with heat; very hot. **2** very enthusiastic; excited; violent. **3** fresh from the source.

red·in·gote (red′ing gōt′) *n.* **1** a man's fitted, double-breasted coat with full skirts reaching below the knee, worn in the 18th and 19th centuries. **2** a woman's lightweight coat similar to this. [< F < E *riding coat*]

red·in·te·grate (red in′tə grāt′) *v.* **-grat·ed, -grat·ing. 1** make whole again; restore to a perfect state; renew; re-establish. **2** become whole again; be renewed. [< L *redintegrare,* ult. < *red-* again + *integer* whole] —**red·in′te·gra′tion,** *n.*

re·di·rect (rē′də rekt′ *or* -dī rekt′) *v., adj.* —*v.* **1** direct again or anew: *to redirect a letter.* **2** give a new direction to: *to redirect the activities of an organization.* —*adj. U.S. Law.* of or having to do with the re-examination of a witness. —**re′di·rec′tion,** *n.*

re·dis·tri·bute (rē′dis trib′yət) *v.* **-uted, -ut·ing.** change the distribution of.

re·dis·tri·bu·tion (rē′dis trə byü′shən) *n.* **1** a distribution made again or anew. **2** the revision, made every ten years, of the number of seats in the Canadian House of Commons to which each province is entitled on the basis of its population.

red juniper red cedar (def. 1).

red lead red oxide of lead, used in paint, in making cement for pipes, and in making glass. *Formula:* Pb_3O_4

red–let·ter (red′let′ər) *adj.* **1** marked by red letters. **2** memorable; especially happy.

red light *Informal.* any warning signal or instruction to stop, exercise caution, etc.

red–light (red′līt′) *adj.* **1** of or having to do with a red light. **2** characterized by a concentration of brothels or other places of low repute: *a red-light district.*

red line either of two red lines drawn across the ice at each end of a hockey rink as an extension of the goal line.

red man *Archaic.* a North American Indian.
➤ *Usage.* See note at **redskin.**

red mullet mullet (def. 2).

red·neck (red′nek′) *n. Derogatory slang.* a very conservative person whose attitudes and reactions are characterized by bigotry and philistinism.

re·do (rē dü′) *v.* do again; do over.

red·o·lence (red′ə ləns) *n.* the quality of being redolent.

red·o·lent (red′ə lənt) *adj.* **1** having a pleasant smell; fragrant. **2** smelling strongly; giving off an odor: *a house redolent of fresh paint.* **3** suggesting thoughts or feelings: *Ivanhoe is a name redolent of romance.* [< L *redolens, -entis,* ppr. of *redolere* emit scent < *red-* back + *olere* to smell]

---

re·dec′o·rate′
re·dec·o·ra′tion
re·ded′i·cate′
re·ded·i·ca′tion
re′de·fine′

re′def·i·ni′tion
re′de·lib′er·a′tion
re′de·liv′er
re′de·liv′er·y
re′dem′on·strate

re′dem·on·stra′tion
re′de·pos′it
re′de·scribe′
re′de·sign′
re·di′al

re′di·gest′
re′di·ges′tion
re·dis′count
re′dis·cov′er
re′dis·cov′er·y

re′dis·til′
re′dis·til·la′tion

red–osier dogwood (red′ō′zhər) *Cdn.* a North American shrub (*Cornus stolonifera*) common throughout Canada, having bright-red twigs and branchlets, white flowers, and whitish fruit.

re·dou·ble (rē dub′əl) *v.* **-bled, -bling. 1** double again. **2** increase greatly; double: *When he saw land ahead, the swimmer redoubled his speed.* **3** repeat; echo. **4** double back: *The fox redoubled on his trail to escape the hunters.* [< F *redoubler*]

re·doubt (ri dout′) *n.* a small fort standing alone. [< F *redoute* < Ital. < VL *reductus* retreat < L *reducere*. See REDUCE.]

re·doubt·a·ble (ri dout′ə bəl) *adj.* inspiring or worthy of fear, awe, or great respect; formidable: *a redoubtable warrior, a redoubtable opponent.* [ME < OF *redoutable* < *redouter* dread < *re-* again + *douter* doubt < L *dubitare*] —**re·doubt′a·bly,** *adv.*

re·dound (ri dound′) *v.* come back as a result; contribute: *The number of scholarships we gained redound to the honor of our school.* [ME < OF < L *redundare* overflow, ult. < *red-* back + *unda* wave]

red pepper 1 a seasoning having a very strong, burning taste, made from the dried, ground fruit of a pepper (def. 4), or capsicum; cayenne. **2** a capsicum bearing pungent, red fruits used to make red pepper. **3** the fruit itself.

red pine a medium-tall pine (*Pinosa resinosa*) of northeastern North America having long needles and egg-shaped cones without prickles. The wood of the red pine is used especially for poles, piles, and railway ties.

red·poll (red′pōl′) *n.* any of several small finches (genus *Acanthis*) that breed in arctic and northern alpine regions, having greyish-brown streaked plumage and a red or pinkish crown, especially the **common redpoll** (*A. flammea*).

re·draft (*v.* rē draft′; *n.* rē′draft′) *v., n.* —*v.* draft again or anew. —*n.* a second draft.

re·dress (*v.* ri dres′; *n.* rē′dres *or* ri dres′) *v., n.* —*v.* **1** set right; repair; remedy. **2** adjust evenly again. —*n.* a setting right; reparation; relief: *Any man deserves redress if he has been wronged.* [< F *redresser* < *re-* again + *dresser* straighten, arrange] —**re·dress′a·ble,** *adj.*

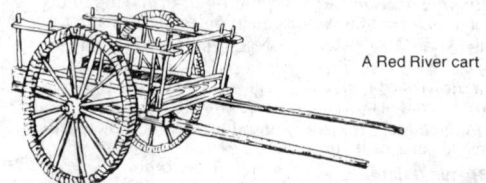

A Red River cart

Red River cart *Cdn. Historical.* a strong, two-wheeled cart pulled by oxen or horses. Red River carts were much used during pioneer days in the West.

Red River Rebellion the uprising in 1869-70 of mainly Métis settlers in the Red River region against the takeover of their territory by the government of Canada from the Hudson's Bay Company. The Métis' main objection was that it was done without consultation with the Red River settlers or assurance that their rights and way of life would be protected.

Red River Settlement the colony that was founded on the Red River by Lord Selkirk in 1812. It was made up of Scottish and Irish settlers.

red salmon *Cdn.* sockeye.

red shift a displacement of the spectral lines of a celestial body toward the red end of the visual spectrum, caused by the Doppler effect. The existence of a red shift in the light emitted by stars of distant galaxies, which suggests that they are receding from our galaxy, is the main evidence for the theory of the expansion of the universe.

red·skin (red′skin′) *n. Offensive.* a North American Indian.
☛ *Usage.* The association of North American Indians with red skin derives from early references to the now extinct Beothuks of Newfoundland, who painted their bodies with ochre. To apply the idea of redness to other Indian peoples was always incorrect and now seems insulting.

red snapper any of several reddish marine food fishes (genus *Lutjanus*).

red spruce 1 *Cdn.* a medium-sized spruce (*Picea rubens*) found mainly in the Maritimes and S Quebec, having narrow, egg-shaped cones and shiny, yellowish-green, often curved needles. **2** the soft, light wood of this tree.

red squirrel 1 a reddish-brown North American squirrel (*Tamiasciurus hudsonicus*) found throughout Canada and the N United States, considerably smaller than the grey or black squirrel. **2** a reddish-brown Eurasian squirrel (*Sciurus vulgaris*).

red·start (red′stärt′) *n.* **1** any of a genus (*Phoenicurus*) of small European thrushes, especially *P. phoenicurus*, the male of which is grey with a brownish-red breast and tail and a black throat. **2** any of a genus (*Setophaga*) of wood warblers, especially *S. ruticilla*, found throughout most of North America, the male of which has orange-and-black upper parts and white under parts. [< *red* + *start* tail]

red tape strict attention to form and detail, especially in government business, causing delay and irritation. [so called because official documents used to be tied with red tape]

red tide *Cdn.* **1** an area of sea water having a reddish coloration due to the presence of large numbers of micro-organisms (especially of genera *Gonyaulax* or *Gymnodinium*) that are constituents of plankton and that in large numbers are poisonous to many forms of marine life. **2** a population of such micro-organisms.

red·top (red′top′) *n.* any of various grasses (genus *Agrostis*) having panicles of tiny reddish-colored flowers. Some redtops are important forage and pasture grasses.

re·duce (ri dyüs′ *or* ri düs′) *v.* **-duced, -duc·ing. 1** make less; make smaller; decrease: *to reduce expenses, to reduce one's weight.* **2** become less; especially, become slimmer by dieting: *His doctor told him he would have to reduce.* **3** make lower in degree, intensity, etc.; weaken; dilute. **4** bring down; lower: *Misfortune reduced that poor woman to begging.* **5** bring to a certain state, form, or condition; change: *The teacher soon reduced the noisy class to order.* **6** change to another form: *to reduce a verbal statement to writing.* **7** conquer; subdue: *The army reduced the fort by a sudden attack.* **8** restore to its proper place or normal condition. A doctor can reduce a fracture or dislocation. **9** *Chemistry.* **a** combine with hydrogen. **b** remove oxygen from. **c** change (a compound) so that the valence of the positive element is lower. **10** *Mathematics.* simplify (an expression, formula, etc.). **11** smelt: *to reduce the ores of silver or copper.* [< L *reducere* < *re-* back + *ducere* bring]

re·duc·er (ri dyüs′ər *or* ri düs′ər) *n.* **1** one that reduces. **2** a threaded cylindrical piece for connecting pipes of different sizes.

re·duc·i·ble (ri dyüs′ə bəl *or* ri düs′ə bəl) *adj.* that can be reduced: *⁴/₈ is reducible to ¹/₂.*

reducing agent *Chemistry.* any substance that reduces or removes the oxygen in a compound.

re·duc·ti·o ad ab·sur·dum (ri duk′tē ō *or* ri duk′shē ō ad′ab sèr′dəm) *Latin.* a reduction to absurdity; a method of proving something false by showing that conclusions to which it leads are absurd.

re·duc·tion (ri duk′shən) *n.* **1** reducing or being reduced. **2** the amount by which a thing is reduced: *The reduction in cost was $5.* **3** a form of something produced by reducing; copy of something on a smaller scale. **4** *Chemistry.* a reaction in which each of the atoms affected gains one or more electrons. The atom or group of atoms that lose electrons become oxidized. [< L *reductio, -onis* < *reducere*. See REDUCE.]

re·dun·dance (ri dun′dəns) *n.* redundancy.

re·dun·dan·cy (ri dun′dən sē) *n., pl.* **-cies. 1** more than is needed. **2** a redundant thing, part, or amount. **3** the use of too many words for the same idea.

re·dun·dant (ri dun′dənt) *adj.* **1** extra; not needed. **2** that says the same thing again; using too many words for the same idea; wordy: *"We two both had an apple each" is a redundant sentence.* [< L *redundans, -antis,* ppr. of *redundare*. See REDOUND.] —**re·dun′dant·ly,** *adv.*

re·du·pli·cate (*v.* ri dyü′plə kāt′ *or* ri dü′plə kāt′; *adj.* ri dyü′plə kit *or* ri dü′plə kit) *v.* **-cat·ed, -cat·ing;** *adj.* —*v.* double; repeat. —*adj.* doubled or repeated. [< L *reduplicare* < *re-* again + *duplicare* double < *duplex, duplicis* double]

re·du·pli·ca·tion (ri dyü′plə kā′shən *or* ri dü′plə kā′shən) *n.* **1** a reduplicating or being reduplicated; doubling; repetition. **2** something resulting from repeating; a duplicate; copy: *To the prisoner each day seemed a reduplication of the preceding day.*

re·du·pli·ca·tive (ri dyü′plə kə tiv *or* -kā′tiv, ri dü′plə kə tiv or -kā′tiv) *adj.* tending to reduplicate; having to do with or marked by reduplication.

red·wing (red′wing′) *n.* **1** a European thrush (*Turdus iliacus*) having mainly brown plumage with red on the underside of the wings and on the flanks. **2** red-winged blackbird.

red-winged blackbird a North American blackbird (*Agelaius phoeniceus*), the male of which has black plumage with a bright red patch, edged on one side with yellow, on each wing.

red·wood (red′wud′) *n.* **1** a giant coniferous tree (*Sequoia sempervirens*) native to the Pacific coast of North America from California to Oregon, highly valued for timber. The redwood is considered to be the tallest tree in the world, often more than 90 metres tall, and also one of the longest lived, some specimens being over 2000 years old. See also **sequoia**. **2** the brownish-red, light wood of this tree. **3** any of various other trees having wood that is reddish or that yields a red dye; also, the wood of any of these trees.

re–echo (rē ek′ō) *v.* **-ech·oed, -ech·o·ing**; *n.* **-ech·oes**. —*v.* echo back. —*n.* the echo of an echo.

reed (rēd) *n.* **1** any of various tall water or marsh grasses (especially genus *Phragmites*) having long, jointed, hollow stems. **2** a stalk or stalks of any of these grasses, especially as used for thatching, basketry, pens, etc. **3** something made from a reed or reeds, such as an arrow or a musical pipe. **4** a thin piece of wood, metal, cane or plastic in a musical instrument that produces sound when vibrated by a current of air. **5** a wind instrument or organ pipe that produces sound by means of a reed or reeds. **6** (*adj.*) producing tones by means of reeds: *a reed organ*. **7** a device on a loom, consisting of vertical parallel wires, that serves to space the warp yarns evenly. [OE *hrēod*]
☛ *Hom.* **read**[1].

reed·bird (rēd′bèrd′) *n.* bobolink.

reed instrument a musical instrument that produces sound by means of a vibrating reed or reeds. Oboes, clarinets, and saxophones are reed instruments.

reed mace *Brit.* cat-tail; bulrush (def. 1).

reed organ an organ producing tones by means of small metal reeds. Two common forms are the harmonium, in which the air is forced outward through the reeds, and the American organ, in which the air is sucked inward.

reed·y (rē′dē) *adj.* **reed·i·er, reed·i·est**. **1** full of reeds. **2** made of a reed or reeds. **3** like a reed or reeds. **4** sounding like a reed instrument: *a thin, reedy voice*. —**reed′i·ness**, *n.*

reef[1] (rēf) *n.* **1** a narrow ridge of rock, sand, or coral at or near the surface of the water: *The ship was wrecked on a hidden reef.* **2** a vein or lode in mining. [ult. < ON *rif*]

reef[2] (rēf) *n., v.* —*n.* the part of a sail that can be rolled or folded up to reduce its size. —*v.* **1** reduce the size of (a sail) by rolling or folding up a part of it. **2** reduce the length of (a topmast, bowsprit, etc.) by lowering, etc. [ME < ON *rif* rib, reef. Cf. REEF[1].]

reef·er[1] (rē′fər) *n.* **1** a person who reefs. **2** a short coat of thick cloth, worn especially by sailors and fishermen. **3** a full-length, usually double-breasted, coat. [< *reef*[2]]

reef·er[2] (rē′fər) *n. Slang.* a cigarette containing marijuana. [? < *reef*[2], since such cigarettes are rolled by hand]

reef·er[3] (rē′fər) *n. Slang.* a refrigerated shipping container, railway car, truck trailer, or van. [< *refrigerator*]

reef knot square knot. See **knot** for picture.

reek (rēk) *n., v.* —*n.* **1** a strong, unpleasant smell; vapor. **2** the condition of reeking: *in a reek of a sweat*.
—*v.* **1** send out vapor or a strong, unpleasant smell. **2** be wet with sweat or blood. **3** be filled with something unpleasant or offensive: *a government reeking with corruption*. **4** give out strongly or unmistakably: *His manner reeks arrogance*. [OE *rēc*]
☛ *Hom.* **wreak**.

reel[1] (rēl) *n., v.* —*n.* **1** a frame turning on an axis, for winding thread, yarn, a fish line, rope, wire, etc. **2** a spool; roller. **3** something wound on a reel: *two reels of motion-picture film*. **4** a length of motion-picture film on a reel.
off the reel, *Informal.* quickly and easily.
—*v.* **1** wind on a reel. **2** draw with a reel or by winding: *to reel in a fish*.
reel off, say, write, or make in a quick, easy way: *My grandfather can reel off stories by the hour.*
[OE *hrēol*]
☛ *Hom.* **real**[1].

reel[2] (rēl) *v., n.* —*v.* **1** sway, swing, or rock under a blow, shock, etc. **2** sway in standing or walking. **3** be in a whirl; be dizzy. **4** go

hat, āge, fär; let, ēqual, tèrm; it, īce
hot, ōpen, ôrder; oil, out; cup, pùt, rüle,
ə above, takən, pencəl, lemən, circəs
ch, child; ng, long; sh, ship
th, thin; ŦH, then; zh, measure

with swaying or staggering movements. **5** sway; stagger; waver: *Our regiment reeled when the cavalry attacked it.*
—*n.* a reeling or staggering movement. [special use of *reel*[1]]
☛ *Syn. v.* **2. Reel, stagger** = stand or move unsteadily. **Reel** particularly suggests dizziness and unsteadiness, a swaying on one's feet and danger of toppling over at any moment: *Sick and faint, he reeled when he tried to cross the room.* **Stagger** particularly suggests being unable to keep one's balance, reeling to one side and the other or walking in a zigzag way: *The boy staggered in with the wood.*

reel[3] (rēl) *n.* **1** a lively dance. Two kinds are the Highland reel and the Virginia reel. **2** the music for a reel. [special use of *reel*[2]]
☛ *Hom.* **real**[1].

re·en·force or **re-en·force** (rē′in fôrs′) See **reinforce**.
—**re′en·force′ment** or **re′-en·force′ment**, *n.*

re·en·try (rē en′trē) *n., pl.* **-tries**. an entering again or returning, especially of a rocket or spacecraft into the earth's atmosphere after flight in outer space.

reeve[1] (rēv) *n.* **1** *Cdn.* in Ontario and some western provinces, the elected head of a rural municipal council; in Ontario, also the elected head of a village or township council. **2** *Historical.* bailiff; steward; overseer. [OE (*ge*)*rēfa*]
☛ *Hom.* **reave**.

reeve[2] (rēv) *v.* **reeved** or **rove, reev·ing**. **1** pass (a rope) through a hole, ring, etc. **2** fasten by placing through or around something. [? < Du. *reven* reef a sail]
☛ *Hom.* **reave**.

reeve·ship (rēv′ship′) *n.* the office or position of reeve.

ref. **1** referee. **2** reference; referred. **3** reformation. **4** refund.

re·face (rē fās′) *v.* **-faced, -fac·ing**. **1** mend or repair the face or surface of stone, walls, etc. **2** replace the facing in a garment.

re·fec·tion (ri fek′shən) *n.* **1** refreshment by food or drink. **2** a meal; repast. [< L *refectio, -onis* < *reficere*. See REFECTORY.]

re·fec·to·ry (ri fek′tə rē) *n., pl.* **-ries**. a room for meals, especially in a monastery, convent, or school. [< LL *refectorium*, ult. < L *reficere* refresh < *re-* again + *facere* make]

re·fer (ri fèr′) *v.* **-ferred, -fer·ring**. **1** direct attention to or speak about: *The article often refers us to the dictionary.* **2** relate; apply: *The rule refers only to special cases.* **3** send or direct for information, help, or action: *We referred him to the boss.* **4** turn for information or help: *Writers often refer to a dictionary.* **5** hand over; submit: *Let's refer the dispute to the umpire.* **6** consider as belonging or due; assign: *Many people refer their failures to bad luck instead of to poor work.* [< L *referre* < *re-* back + *ferre* take]
☛ *Syn.* **1. Refer, allude** = speak of something in a way to turn attention to it. **Refer** = make direct and specific mention. **Allude** = mention incidentally or call attention indirectly: *She never referred to the incident in her writing, but often alluded to it in conversation.*

ref·er·ee (ref′ər ē′) *n., v.* **-eed, -ee·ing**. —*n.* **1** a judge of play in certain games and sports including hockey, football, and boxing. **2** a person to whom something is referred for decision or settlement.
—*v.* act as referee; act as referee in.

ref·er·ence (ref′ər əns) *n., adj.* —*n.* **1** referring or being referred. **2** a directing of attention: *This history contains many references to larger histories.* **3** a statement, book, etc. to which attention is directed: *You will find that reference on page 16.* **4** something used for information or help: *A dictionary is a book of reference.* **5** a person who can give information about another person's character or ability. **6** a statement about someone's character or ability: *The boy had excellent references from men for whom he had worked.* **7** relation; respect; regard: *This test is to be taken by all pupils without reference to age or grade.*
in or **with reference to**, about; concerning.

re·dye′	re′e·mer′gent	re′en·gage′ment	re′e·rect′	re′ex·am′ine
re·ed′it	re′em′i·grate	re′en·list′	re′e·rec′tion	re′ex·ca·va′tion
re·ed′u·cate′	re′em·pha′sis	re′en·list′ment	re′es·tab′lish	re′ex·change′
re·ed′u·ca′tion	re′em′pha·size′	re′en·slave′	re′es·tab′lish·ment	re′ex·hib′it
re′e·lect′	re′em·ploy′	re′en·slave′ment	re′e·val′u·ate′	re′ex·hi·bi′tion
re′e·lec′tion	re′em·ploy′ment	re·en′ter	re′e·val′u·a′tion	re′ex·port′
re′em·bark′	re′en·act′	re·en′trance	re′e·vap′o·rate′	re′ex·por·ta′tion
re′e·merge′	re′en·act′ment	re′e·quip′	re′e·vap′o·ra′tion	re·fash′ion
re′e·mer′gence	re′en·gage′	re′e·quip′ment	re′ex·am′i·na′tion	re·fas′ten

make reference to, mention.
—*adj.* used for information or help: *a reference library.*

ref·er·end (ref′ər ənd) *n.* a person or object referred to; referent.

ref·er·en·dum (ref′ər en′dəm) *n., pl.* **-dums, -da** (-də). **1** the process of submitting a law already passed by the law-making body to a direct vote of the citizens for approval or rejection. British Columbia and Alberta have provision for a referendum. **2** the submitting of any matter to a direct vote. [< L *referendum* that which must be referred < *referee*. See REFER.]

ref·er·ent (ref′ər ənt) *n., adj.* —*n.* **1** a person who is consulted. **2** an idea, person, or thing to which reference is made in an example, statement, etc. —*adj.* containing a reference; referring.

re·fer·ral (ri fer′əl) *n.* **1** a referring or directing to a specific person, place, or group. **2** the person thus referred to.

re·fill (*v.* rē fil′; *n.* rē′fil′) *v., n.* —*v.* fill again. —*n.* something to refill a thing. —**re·fill′a·ble,** *adj.*

re·fine (ri fīn′) *v.* **-fined, -fin·ing. 1** make free from impurities. Sugar, oil, and metals are refined before being used. **2** make or become fine, polished, or cultivated. **3** change or remove by polishing, purifying, etc. **4** make very fine, subtle, or exact. **refine on** or **upon, a** improve. **b** excel.
[< *re- + fine* make fine] —**re·fin′er,** *n.*

re·fined (ri fīnd′) *adj.* **1** freed from impurities: *refined sugar.* **2** freed or free from grossness, coarseness, crudeness, vulgarity, etc. **3** having or showing cultivated feeling, taste, manners, etc.; polished: *a refined voice, refined manners.* **4** fine; subtle: *refined distinctions.* **5** minutely precise: *refined measurements.*

re·fine·ment (ri fīn′mənt) *n.* **1** fineness of feeling, taste manners, or language. **2** the act or result of refining: *Gasoline is produced by the refinement of petroleum.* **3** an improvement. **4** a fine point; subtle distinction. **5** an improved, higher, or extreme form of something.

re·fin·er·y (ri fīn′ər ē *or* ri fīn′rē) *n., pl.* **-er·ies.** a building and machinery for purifying metal, sugar, petroleum, etc.

re·fit (*v.* rē fit′; *n.* rē′fit′) *v.* **-fit·ted, -fit·ting;** *n.* —*v.* **1** fit, prepare, or equip for use again: *to refit an old ship.* **2** get fresh supplies. —*n.* a fitting, preparing, or equipping for use again: *The ship went to the dry dock for a refit.*

re·flate (rē flāt′) *v.* **-flat·ed, -flat·ing.** *Economics.* cause the reflation of: *to reflate a depressed economy.* [back formation < *reflation*]

re·fla·tion (rē flā′shən) *n. Economics.* an increase in the supply of money and credit following a period of deflation, for the purpose of stimulating the economy and increasing employment. [*re-* + in*flation*]

re·flect (ri flekt′) *v.* **1** turn back or throw back (light, heat, sound, etc.): *The sidewalks reflect heat on a hot day.* **2** give back an image; give back a likeness or image of: *A mirror reflects your face and body.* **3** reproduce or show like a mirror: *The newspaper reflected the owner's opinions.* **4** think; think carefully: *Take time to reflect before doing important things.* **5** cast blame, reproach, or discredit: *Bad behavior reflects on home training.* **6** serve to cast or bring: *A brave act reflects credit on the person who performs it.* [< L *reflectere < re-* back + *flectere* bend]
☛ *Syn.* **4.** See note at **think.**

reflecting telescope a type of optical telescope in which the light rays entering it are brought to a focus by means of a concave mirror. Compare **refracting telescope.**

re·flec·tion (ri flek′shən) *n.* **1** reflecting or being reflected. **2** something reflected. **3** a likeness; image: *You can see your reflection in a mirror.* **4** thinking; careful thinking: *On reflection, the plan seemed too dangerous.* **5** an idea or remark resulting from careful thinking; idea; remark. **6** a remark, action, etc. that casts blame or discredit. **7** blame; discredit. **8** See **angle of reflection.**

re·flec·tive (ri flek′tiv) *adj.* **1** reflecting: *the reflective surface of polished metal.* **2** thoughtful: *a reflective look.* —**re·flec′tive·ly,** *adv.* —**re·flec′tive·ness,** *n.*

re·flec·tor (ri flek′tər) *n.* **1** any thing, surface, or device that reflects light, heat, sound, etc., especially a piece of glass or metal, usually concave, for reflecting light in a required direction. **2** reflecting telescope.

re·flex (*adj., n.* rē′fleks; *v.* ri fleks′) *adj., n., v.* —*adj.* **1** not voluntary; coming as a direct response to a stimulation of some sensory nerve cells. Sneezing is a reflex act. **2** bent or turned back. **3** of an angle, more than 180° and less than 360°.

—*n.* **1** an automatic action in direct response to a stimulation of certain nerve cells. Sneezing and shivering are reflexes. **2** something reflected; an image; reflection: *A law should be a reflex of the will of the people.*
—*v.* bend back; turn back. [< L *reflexus,* pp. of *reflectere.* See REFLECT.]

re·flex·ive (ri flek′siv) *adj., n. Grammar.* —*adj.* indicating that an action turns back on the subject. —*n.* a reflexive verb or pronoun. *Example: In* The boy hurt himself, hurt *and* himself *are* reflexives. —**re·flex′ive·ly,** *adv.*
☛ *Usage.* **Reflexive pronouns.** Personal pronouns plus the suffix **-self** or **-selves** (**myself, yourself, himself,** etc.) are called **reflexive pronouns** when they appear in constructions such as: *He shaves himself. She bought herself two hats.* They are called reflexive because they indicate that the direct or indirect object of a verb is the same as the subject and so reflects the subject). The same words are called **intensive pronouns** when they serve to emphasize, as in *He himself did it.*

ref·lu·ent (ref′lü ənt) *adj.* flowing back; ebbing. [< L *refluens, -entis,* ppr. of *refluere* flow back < *re-* back + *fluere* flow]

re·flux (rē′fluks) *n.* the ebb of a tide. [< *re- + flux*]

re·for·est (rē fôr′ist) *v.* replant with trees.

re·for·est·a·tion (rē fôr is tā′shən) *n.* a replanting or being replanted with trees.

re·form (ri fôrm′) *v., n.* —*v.* **1** make better: *Prisons should try to reform criminals instead of just punishing them.* **2** improve by removing faults or abuses: *to reform a city administration.* **3** correct one's own faults; improve one's behavior: *The boy promised to reform if given another chance.* **4** crack and refine (petroleum, etc.). —*n.* an improvement, especially one made by removing faults or abuses; a change to improve conditions: *The new government put through many reforms.* [< L *reformare,* ult. < *re-* again + *forma* form] —**re·form′a·ble,** *adj.*

Re·form (ri fôrm′) *adj.* **1** of or having to do with the liberal branch of Judaism, as contrasted with the Orthodox and Conservative branches. **2** *Cdn. Historical.* of or having to do with the Reform Party.

re–form (rē fôrm′) *v.* **1** form again. **2** take a new shape.

ref·or·ma·tion (ref′ər mā′shən) *n.* **1** a reforming or being reformed; change for the better; improvement. **2 Reformation,** the 16th-century religious movement in Europe that began with the aim of reforms in the Roman Catholic Church and ended with the establishment of certain Protestant churches.

re·form·a·tive (ri fôr′mə tiv) *adj.* tending toward or inducing reform.

re·form·a·to·ry (ri fôr′mə tô′rē) *adj., n., pl.* **-ries.** —*adj.* serving to reform; intended to reform. —*n.* an institution for reforming young offenders against the laws; a prison for juveniles.

Re·formed (ri fôrmd′) *adj.* of or designating the Protestant churches, especially the Calvinist as distinct from the Lutheran.

re·form·er (ri fôr′mər) *n.* a person who reforms, or tries to reform, some state of affairs, custom, etc.; a supporter of reforms.

re·form·ism (ri fôrm′iz əm) *n.* a policy or doctrine advocating reform, especially political, social, or religious reform.

re·form·ist (ri fôrm′ist) *n., adj.* —*n.* a person who favors or supports reformism. —*adj.* of or having to do with reformists or reformism.

Reform Party *Cdn. Historical.* the party that opposed Tory rule in Upper Canada and the Maritimes in the 19th century, advocating a greater measure of responsible government and other reforms. Joseph Howe was a prominent leader of this party.

reform school reformatory.

re·fract (ri frakt′) *v.* bend (a ray) from a straight course. Water refracts light. See chart at **angle of refraction.** [< L *refractus,* pp. of *refringere* break up < *re-* back + *frangere* break]

refracting telescope a type of optical telescope in which the light rays entering it are brought to a focus by a lens or set of lens. Compare **reflecting telescope.**

The refraction of light rays entering the water makes the straw appear to be broken at the water line.

re·frac·tion (ri frak′shən) *n.* **1** the bending of a ray of light when

it travels from one medium to another at an oblique angle, due to a slight change in the velocity of the light. When a ray of light crosses the boundary from air into water, the higher density of the water causes the wavelength to become shorter and the ray to turn slightly toward the perpendicular. See also **angle of refraction.** 2 the bending or turning of any other electromagnetic radiation, such as sound, when it passes from one medium into another of different density. 3 the ability of the eye to refract light, permitting the formation of an image on the retina. 4 the determination of the condition of an eye with respect to this ability. 5 *Astronomy.* the apparent change in the position of a heavenly body in the sky, due to the refraction of light rays from it as they enter the earth's atmosphere.

re·frac·tive (ri frak′tiv) *adj.* 1 having power to refract. 2 having to do with or caused by refraction. —**re·fract′ive·ly,** *adv.* —**re·fract′ive·ness,** *n.*

refractive index a measure of the extent to which a given medium refracts light; the ratio of the velocities of light in two given media. The **absolute refractive index,** which is the ratio of the speed of light in a vacuum to that in a given medium, is always greater than one.

re·frac·tor (ri frak′tər) *n.* 1 anything that refracts. 2 refracting telescope.

re·frac·to·ry (ri frak′tə rē) *adj., n.* —*adj.* 1 hard to manage; stubborn; obstinate: *Mules are refractory.* 2 not yielding readily to treatment: *He had a refractory cough.* 3 hard to melt, reduce, or work. Some ores are more refractory than others. —*n.* 1 an ore, cement, ceramic material, or similar substance that is hard to melt, reduce, or work. 2 a brick made of refractory material, used for lining furnaces, etc. —**re·frac′to·ri·ly,** *adv.* —**re·frac′to·ri·ness,** *n.*

re·frain[1] (ri frān′) *v.* hold oneself back: *Refrain from crime.* [ME < OF < L *refrenare* < *re-* back + *frenum* bridle]

☛ *Syn.* **Refrain, abstain** = keep oneself from (doing) something. **Refrain** emphasizes checking an impulse, and means voluntarily not doing something one would like to do: *He politely refrained from saying what he thought of her hat.* **Abstain** emphasizes holding oneself back by force of will, and means deliberately doing without something one believes harmful or wrong, especially certain pleasures: *He is abstaining from alcohol.*

re·frain[2] (ri frān′) *n.* 1 a phrase or verse repeated regularly in a song or poem; chorus. 2 the music for a refrain. [ME < OF *refrain,* ult. < VL *refrangere* break off, for L *refringere.* See REFRACT.]

re·fran·gi·bil·i·ty (ri fran′jə bil′ə tē) *n.* 1 the property of being refrangible. 2 the amount of refraction (of light rays, etc.) that is possible.

re·fran·gi·ble (ri fran′jə bəl) *adj.* capable of being refracted: *Rays of light are refrangible.* [< *re-* + L *frangere* to break] —**re·fran′gi·ble·ness,** *n.*

re·fresh (ri fresh′) *v.* make fresh again; renew: *He refreshed his memory by a glance at the book. She refreshed herself with a cup of tea.* [ME < OF *refrescher* < *re-* again + *fresche* fresh < Gmc.]

re·fresh·er (ri fresh′ər) *adj., n.* —*adj.* helping to renew knowledge or abilities, or to bring a person needed new knowledge. —*n.* a person or thing that refreshes.

re·fresh·ing (ri fresh′ing) *adj.* 1 that refreshes. 2 welcome as a pleasing change. —**re·fresh′ing·ly,** *adv.*

re·fresh·ment (ri fresh′mənt) *n.* 1 a refreshing or being refreshed. 2 anything that refreshes. 3 **refreshments,** *pl.* food or drink: *to serve refreshments at a party.*

re·frig·er·ant (ri frij′ər ənt) *adj., n.* —*adj.* 1 refrigerating; cooling. 2 reducing bodily heat or fever. —*n.* something that cools, etc. Ice is a refrigerant.

re·frig·er·ate (ri frij′ər āt′) *v.* -**at·ed,** -**at·ing.** make or keep cold or cool. [ult. < L *refrigerare,* ult. < *re-* again + *frigus, -goris* cold]

re·frig·er·a·tion (ri frij′ər ā′shən) *n.* the act or process of cooling or keeping cold.

re·frig·er·a·tor (ri frij′ər ā′tər) *n.* an appliance, closet, or room equipped for keeping things, especially food and drink, cool.

reft (reft) *v. Archaic.* a pt. and a pp. of reave.

re·fu·el (rē fyü′əl) *v.* -**elled** or -**eled,** -**el·ling** or -**el·ing.** 1 supply with fuel again. 2 take on a fresh supply of fuel.

ref·uge (ref′yüj) *n.* 1 shelter or protection from danger, trouble, etc.; safety: *The cat took refuge in a tree.* 2 any person, thing, or action providing or seeming to provide safety, security, or comfort: *A deserted farmhouse was their refuge from the storm.* [ME < OF < L *refugium* < *re-* back + *fugere* flee]

ref·u·gee (ref′yə jē′ or ref′yə jē′) *n.* a person who flees for refuge or safety, especially to a foreign country, in time of persecution, war, etc. [< F *réfugié*]

re·ful·gence (ri ful′jəns) *n.* radiance; brightness.

re·ful·gent (ri ful′jənt) *adj.* shining brightly; radiant; splendid: *a*

hat, āge, fär; let, ēqual, tèrm; it, īce
hot, ōpen, ôrder; oil, out; cup, pùt, rüle,
ə above, takən, pencəl, lemən, circəs
ch, child; ng, long; sh, ship
th, thin; ᴛʜ, then; zh, measure

refulgent sunrise. [< L *refulgens, -entis,* ppr. of *refulgere* < *re-* back + *fulgere* shine] —**re·ful′gent·ly,** *adv.*

re·fund[1] (*v.* ri fund′; *n.* rē′fund) *v., n.* —*v.* pay back: *If these shoes do not wear well, the shop will refund your money.* —*n.* 1 the return of money paid. 2 the money paid back. [< L *refundere* < *re-* back + *fundere* pour] —**re·fund′er,** *n.*

re·fund[2] (rē fund′) *v.* change (a debt, loan, etc.) into a new form. [< *re-* + *fund*]

re·fur·bish (rē fėr′bish) *v.* polish up again; do up anew; brighten; renovate.

re·fus·al (ri fyüz′əl) *n.* 1 the act of refusing: *His refusal to play the game provoked the other boys.* 2 the right to refuse or take a thing before it is offered to others: *Give me the refusal of the car till tomorrow.*

re·fuse[1] (ri fyüz′) *v.* -**fused,** -**fus·ing.** 1 decline to accept; reject: *to refuse an offer.* 2 deny (a request, demand, invitation); decline to give or grant: *to refuse admittance.* 3 decline (to do something): *to refuse to discuss the question.* 4 decline to accept or consent: *She is free to refuse.* [ME < OF *refuser* < L *refuses,* pp. < *refundere.* See REFUND[1].]

☛ *Syn.* **1. Refuse, decline, reject** = not accept something offered. **Refuse** is the blunt term, implying a direct and sometimes an ungracious denial: *He refused to go with me.* **Decline** is more polite, implying a reluctant rather than a direct denial: *He declined my invitation.* **Reject** is more emphatic than **refuse,** implying a very positive and brusque denial: *He rejected my friendly advice.*

ref·use[2] (ref′yüs) *n., adj.* —*n.* useless stuff; waste; rubbish. —*adj.* rejected as worthless or of little value; discarded. [ME, probably < OF *refuse,* ppr. of *refuser.* See REFUSE[1].]

ref·u·ta·ble (ref′yə tə bəl *or* ri fyü′tə bəl) *adj.* able to be refuted.

ref·u·ta·tion (ref′yə tā′shən) *n.* disproof of a claim, opinion, or argument.

re·fute (ri fyüt′) *v.* -**fut·ed,** -**fut·ing.** prove (a claim, opinion, or argument) to be false or incorrect. [< L *refutare* < OL *re-* back + *futare* cause to fall] —**re·fut′er,** *n.*

☛ *Usage.* See note at **confute.**

reg. 1 register; registered. 2 registrar; registry. 3 regular; regularly. 4 region.

re·gain (ri gān′) *v.* 1 get again; recover: *to regain health.* 2 get back to; reach again: *to regain the shore.*

re·gal (rē′gəl) *adj.* 1 belonging to a monarch; royal. 2 kinglike; fit for a monarch; stately; splendid; magnificent. [ME < L *regalis* < *rex, regis* king. Doublet of ROYAL, REAL[2], RIAL.] —**re′gal·ly,** *adv.*

☛ *Syn.* **1.** See note at **royal.**

re·gale[1] (ri gāl′) *v.* -**galed,** -**gal·ing.** 1 entertain agreeably; delight with something pleasing: *The old sailor regaled the boys with sea stories.* 2 entertain with a choice repast; feast. [< F *régaler,* ult. < MDu. *wale* wealth] —**re·gale′ment,** *n.* —**re·gal′er,** *n.*

re·gale[2] (ri gāl′) *n. Cdn. Historical.* 1 an extra ration, especially of liquor, given to the employees of a fur company for a festive occasion such as Christmas. 2 a party, celebration, etc. held on such an occasion. 3 a ration of liquor given to boatmen at the start or finish of an arduous journey. [< Cdn.F < MF *régale* pleasure, festivity]

re·ga·li·a (ri gā′lē ə *or* ri gāl′yə) *n.pl.* 1 the emblems of royalty. Crowns, sceptres, etc. are regalia. 2 the emblems or decorations of any society, order, etc. 3 clothes, especially fine clothes: *in party regalia.* [< L *regalia* royal things, neut. pl. of *regalis.* See REGAL.]

re·gal·i·ty (rē gal′ə tē) *n., pl.* -**ties.** 1 royalty; sovereignty; kingship. 2 a right or privilege having to do with a king. 3 a kingdom.

re·gard (ri gärd′) *v., n.* —*v.* 1 consider; think of: *He is regarded as the best doctor in town.* 2 show thought or consideration for; care for; respect: *She always regards her parents' wishes.* 3 heed: *None regarded her screams.* 4 look at; look closely at; watch: *He regarded me sternly.* 5 look closely.

as regards, as for; concerning; relating to: *As regards money, I have enough.*

—*n.* 1 consideration; thought; care: *Have regard for the feelings of others.* 2 a look; steady look. 3 esteem; favor; good opinion.

4 regards, *pl.* good wishes; an expression of esteem. **5** a point; particular matter.
in regard to, about; concerning; relating to.
without regard to, not considering.
with regard to, about; concerning; relating to.
[< F *regarder* < *re-* back + *garder* guard]
☛ *Syn. n.* **1.** See note at **respect.**

re·gard·ful (ri gärd′fəl) *adj.* **1** heedful; observant; mindful. **2** considerate; respectful. —**re·gard′ful·ly,** *adv.*

re·gard·ing (ri gär′ding) *prep.* with regard to; concerning; about: *a prophecy regarding the future.*

re·gard·less (ri gärd′lis) *adj., adv.* —*adj.* with no heed; careless. —*adv.* Informal. in spite of what happens: *We plan to leave on Monday, and we will leave then, regardless.* —**re·gard′less·ly,** *adv.* —**re·gard′less·ness,** *n.*
☛ *Usage.* The form **irregardless** is not logical since it literally means 'not regardless'. As a result, it is generally considered to be non-standard and should be avoided in both speech and writing.

re·gat·ta (ri gat′ə) *n.* **1** a boat race. **2** a series of boat races: *the annual regatta of the yacht club.* [< dial. Ital.]

re·gen·cy (rē′jən sē) *n., pl.* **-cies.** **1** the position, office, or function of a regent or group of regents: *The Queen Mother held the regency till the young king became of age.* **2** a body of regents. **3** a government consisting of regents. **4** the time during which there is a regency. **5 Regency, a** in Great Britain, the period from 1811 to 1820 during which George, Prince of Wales, acted as regent for King George III. **b** *Architecture and design.* a style characterized by graceful, elegant lines, developed in England during the Regency. **c** in France, the period from 1715 to 1723 during which Philip, Duke of Orleans, acted as regent for King Louis XV.

re·gen·er·a·cy (ri jen′ər ə sē) *n.* a regenerate state.

re·gen·er·ate (*v.* ri jen′ər āt′; *adj.* ri jen′ər it) *v.* **-at·ed, -at·ing;** *adj.* —*v.* **1** give a new and better spiritual life to. **2** improve the moral condition of; put new life and spirit into. **3** reform. **4** grow again; form (new tissue, a new part, etc.) to replace what is lost. If a young crab loses a claw, it can regenerate a new one. **5** *Physics.* cause (a substance) to return intermittently to its original state or condition. **6** *Electronics.* amplify by transferring a portion of the power from the output to the input.
—*adj.* **1** born again spiritually. **2** made over in better form; formed anew morally. [< L *regenerare* make over ult. < *re-* again + *genus, -neris* birth] —**re·gen′er·a′tor,** *n.*

re·gen·er·a·tion (ri jen′ər ā′shən) *n.* regenerating or being regenerated.

re·gen·er·a·tive (ri jen′ər ə tiv *or* ri jen′ər ā′tiv) *adj.* regenerating; tending to regenerate. —**re·gen′er·a′tive·ly,** *adv.*

re·gent (rē′jənt) *n., adj.* —*n.* **1** a person who rules in the name of a sick or absent sovereign or a sovereign who is not yet grown up: *The regent ruled for seven years until the boy king came of age.* **2** a member of a governing board. Many universities have boards of regents. —*adj.* acting as a regent (*used after a noun*): *a queen regent.* [< L *regens, -entis,* ppr. of *regere* rule]

re·gent·ship (rē′jənt ship′) *n.* the position of a regent.

reg·gae (reg′ā) a style of music that developed in Jamaica in the mid 1970's, that is a blend of calypso and rock rhythms in 4/4 time with accented second and last beats.

reg·i·cid·al (rej′ə sī′dəl) *adj.* of, having to do with, or involving regicide.

reg·i·cide (rej′ə sīd′) *n.* **1** the crime of killing a monarch. **2** a person who commits regicide. [< L *regi-,* stem of *rex* king + E *-cide*[l]]

re·gime *or* **ré·gime** (ri zhēm′; *French,* rā zhēm′) *n.* **1** a system of government or rule. **2** a prevailing system; a regular pattern of action, behavior, etc. **3** a system of living; regimen. [< F < L *regimen.* Doublet of REGIMEN.]

reg·i·men (rej′ə mən *or* rej′ə men′) *n.* **1** a set of rules or habits of diet, exercise, or manner of living intended to improve health, reduce weight, etc. **2** the act of governing; government; rule. **3** *Grammar.* the influence of one word in determining the case or mood of another; government. [< L *regimen* < *regere* rule. Doublet of REGIME.]

reg·i·ment (*n.* rej′ə mənt; *v.* rej′ə ment′) *n., v.* —*n.* **1** in the army, a unit consisting of several companies of soldiers organized into one large group, usually commanded by a colonel. A regiment is larger than a battalion and smaller than a brigade. **2** a large number.
—*v.* **1** form into a regiment or organized group. **2** assign to a regiment or group. **3** treat in a strict or uniform manner. A totalitarian state regiments its citizens. [< LL *regimentum* rule < L *regere* to rule]

reg·i·men·tal (rej′ə men′təl) *adj., n.* —*adj.* of a regiment; having to do with a regiment. —*n.* **regimentals,** *pl.* military uniform. —**reg′i·men′tal·ly,** *adv.*

reg·i·men·ta·tion (rej′ə men tā′shən) *n.* **1** a formation into organized or uniform groups. **2** making uniform. **3** a subjection to control. In time of war there may be regimentation of our work, play, food, and clothing.

re·gion (rē′jən) *n.* **1** any large part of the earth's surface: *the region of the equator.* **2** a place; space; area: *an unhealthful region.* **3** a part of the body: *the region of the heart.* **4** a sphere; domain: *the region of art, the region of imagination.* **5** *Cdn.* in Ontario, a geographical division for purposes of government, having wider powers than those of a county. Regions were established in 1973 in some parts of the province by combining counties and townships to provide for more effective planning. [< L *regio, -onis* direction < *regere* direct]

re·gion·al (rē′jən əl) *adj.* of or in a particular region: *a regional storm.* —**re′gion·al·ly,** *adv.*

re·gion·al·ism (rē′jən əl iz′əm) *n.* **1** concern with and loyalty to one's own geographical region within a country, rather than the country as a whole; regional patriotism. **2** in art and literature, emphasis on and reflection of the peculiar characteristics of a particular locale or region. **3** a linguistic feature or a custom, etc. that is characteristic of a particular geographical region. **4** the division of a country, etc. into partially autonomous administrative areas called regions.

re·gion·al·ist (rē′jə nə list′) *n., adj.* —*n.* a person who favors or advocates regionalism. —*adj.* of or having to do with regionalism or regionalists. —**re′gion·al·is′tic,** *adj.*

reg·is·ter (rej′is tər) *n., v.* —*n.* **1** a list; record: *A register of attendance is kept in our school.* **2** a book in which a list or record is kept: *a hotel register.* **3** anything that records. A cash register shows the amount of money taken in. **4** a registration or registry. **5** a registrar. **6** an opening in a wall or floor with an arrangement to regulate the amount of cooled or heated air that passes through. **7** the range of a voice or an instrument. **8** the set of pipes of an organ stop. **9** *Printing.* the exact fit or correspondence of lines, columns, colors, etc. **10** the exact adjustment of the focus in a camera. **11** a customs document declaring the nationality of a ship.
—*v.* **1** write in a list or record: *to register the names of the new members.* **2** have one's name written in a list or record: *You must register if you want to attend the conference.* **3** indicate; record: *The thermometer registers 28 degrees.* **4** show (surprise, joy, anger, etc.) by the expression on one's face or by actions. **5** have (a letter, parcel, etc.) recorded in a post office, paying extra postage for special care in delivery. **6** *Printing.* **a** make (lines, columns, colors, etc.) fit or correspond exactly. **b** fit or correspond exactly. [ME < Med.L *registrum* < L *regestrum,* neut. pp. of *regerere* record < *re-* back + *gerere* carry]

registered mail a postal service that provides proof that a letter or parcel has been sent and delivered and also guarantees compensation if the mail is not delivered. Every article of registered mail is recorded at the post office where it is mailed and must be signed for by the receiver.

reg·is·tra·ble (rej′is trə bəl) *adj.* that can be registered.

reg·is·trant (rej′is trənt) *n.* a person who registers or has registered: *a registrant for a trademark, registrants for a conference.*

reg·is·trar (rej′is trär′) *n.* **1** an official who keeps a register; an official recorder. **2** in some universities, colleges, etc., the officer in charge of admissions, examinations, and general regulations. [var. of *registrer* < *register*]

reg·is·tra·tion (rej′is trā′shən) *n.* **1** the act of registering. **2** an entry in a register. **3** the number of people registered. **4** a document certifying an act of registering.

reg·is·try (rej′is trē) *n., pl.* **-tries.** **1** a registering; registration. **2** a place where a register is kept; an office of registration. **3** a book in which a list or record is kept.

reg·nant (reg′nənt) *adj.* **1** ruling. **2** exercising sway or influence; predominant. **3** prevalent; widespread. [< L *regnans, -antis,* ppr. of *regnare* rule < *regnum* kingdom]

re·gress (*v.* ri gres′; *n.* rē′gres) *v., n.* —*v.* **1** go back; move in a backward direction. **2** return to an earlier or less advanced state. —*n.* a going back; movement backward. [< L *regressus,* pp. of *regredi* < *re-* back + *gradi* go] —**re·gres′sor,** *n.*

re·gres·sion (ri gresh′ən) *n.* **1** the act of going back; backward movement. **2** *Psychology.* a way of trying to escape difficult

problems by casting off responsibility and assuming other characteristics of childhood. **3** *Biology.* the reversion of offspring toward a more general condition. **4** *Statistics.* the tendency of one variable that is correlated with another to revert to the general type and not to equal the amount of deviation of the second variable.

re·gret (ri gret′) *v.* **-gret·ted, -gret·ting;** *n.* —*v.* **1** feel regret about. **2** feel sorry; mourn. —*n.* **1** the feeling of being sorry; sorrow; sense of loss. **2 regrets,** *pl.* a polite reply declining an invitation. [ME < OF *regreter* < Gmc.; cf. ON *gráta* weep] —**re·gret′ter,** *n.*

☛ *Syn. n.* **1. Regret, remorse** = a feeling of sorrow for a fault or wrongdoing. **Regret** suggests a troubled mind and a feeling of being dissatisfied and sorry about something one has or has not done: *With regret he remembered his forgotten promise.* **Remorse** suggests the mental torment of a gnawing conscience and deep sorrow for a wrong that can never be undone: *The boy was filled with remorse for the worry he had caused his mother.*

re·gret·ful (ri gret′fəl) *adj.* feeling or expressing regret. —**re·gret′ful·ly,** *adv.* —**re·gret′ful·ness,** *n.*

re·gret·ta·ble (ri gret′ə bəl) *adj.* that should be or is regretted. —**re·gret′ta·bly,** *adv.*

re·group (rē′grüp′) *v.* **1** form into a new arrangement or grouping: *to regroup military forces. You can regroup two bags of six oranges each to make three bags of four oranges each.* **2** in subtraction, decrease the digit in one column of the minuend by 1 in order to increase the value in the column on the right by 10: *To subtract 8 from 64, regroup 64 as 5 tens and 14 ones.*

Regt. **1** regiment. **2** regent.

reg·u·lar (reg′yə lər) *adj., n.* —*adj.* **1** fixed by custom or rule; usual; normal: *Six o'clock was his regular hour of rising.* **2** following some rule or principle; according to rule: *A period is the regular ending for a sentence.* **3** coming, acting, or done again and again at the same time: *Saturday is a regular holiday.* **4** steady; habitual: *A regular customer is one who shops frequently at the same store.* **5** even in size, spacing, or speed; well-balanced: *regular features, regular teeth.* **6** symmetrical. **7** having all its angles equal and all its sides equal. **8** *Botany.* having all the same parts of a flower alike in shape and size. **9** orderly; methodical: *lead a regular life.* **10** properly fitted or trained: *The maid did the cooking while the regular cook was sick.* **11** *Grammar.* of a noun, verb, etc., changing according to the usual pattern of the language to show tense, number, person, etc. **12** *Informal.* thorough; complete: *a regular bore.* **13** *Informal.* fine; agreeable; all right: *He's a regular fellow.* **14** permanently organized. The regular army is under the direct control of the federal government. **15** of or belonging to the permanent armed forces of a country. **16** belonging to a religious order bound by certain rules. The regular clergy live in religious communities.
—*n.* **1** a full-time member of a group: *The fire department was made up of regulars and volunteers.* **2** a person who makes the armed forces a full-time career. **3** a person belonging to a religious order bound by certain rules. **4** a regular customer, contributor, etc. **5** in sports, a player on the regular team. [ME < OF < L *regularis* < *regula* RULE.] —**reg′u·lar·ly,** *adv.*

☛ *Syn. adj.* **4.** See note at **steady.**

reg·u·lar·i·ty (reg′yə lar′ə tē *or* reg′yə ler′ə tē) *n.* order; system; steadiness; the condition of being regular.

reg·u·late (reg′yə lāt′) *v.* **-lat·ed, -lat·ing. 1** control by rule, principle, or system: *Good schools regulate the behavior of students.* **2** put in condition to work properly. **3** keep at some standard: *This instrument regulates the temperature of the room.* [< LL *regulare* < L *regula* See RULE.]

reg·u·la·tion (reg′yə lā′shən) *n., adj.* —*n.* **1** control by rule, principle, or system. **2** a rule; law: *traffic regulations.* —*adj.* **1** according to or required by a regulation; standard: *Soldiers wear a regulation uniform.* **2** usual; ordinary.

reg·u·la·tive (reg′yə lə tiv *or* reg′yə lā′tiv) *adj.* regulating.

reg·u·la·tor (reg′yə lā′tər) *n.* **1** a person or thing that regulates. **2** a device in a clock or watch to make it go faster or slower. **3** a very accurate clock used as a standard of time.

reg·u·la·to·ry (reg′yə lə tô′rē) *adj.* regulating.

re·gur·gi·tate (rē gėr′jə tāt′) *v.* **-tat·ed, -tat·ing. 1** of liquids, gases, undigested foods, etc., rush, surge, or flow back. **2** bring undigested food back from the stomach to the mouth: *Some birds regurgitate food to feed their young.* [< Med.L *regurgitare,* ult. < L *re-* back + *gurges, -gitis* whirlpool] —**re·gur′gi·ta′tion,** *n.*

re·ha·bil·i·tate (rē′hə bil′ə tāt′) *v.* **-tat·ed, -tat·ing. 1** restore to a good condition; make over in a new form: *The old house is to be rehabilitated.* **2** restore to former standing, rank, rights, privileges,

hat, āge, fär; let, ēqual, tėrm; it, īce
hot, ōpen, ôrder; oil, out; cup, pút, rüle,
əbove, takən, pencəl, lemən, circəs

ch, child; ng, long; sh, ship
th, thin; ᴛʜ, then; zh, measure

reputation, etc.: *The former criminal completely rehabilitated himself and was trusted and respected by all.* [< Med. L *rehabilitare,* ult. < L *re-* again + *habilis* fit] —**re·ha·bil′i·ta′tion,** *n.*

re·ha·bil·i·ta·tive (rē′hə bil′ə tə tiv *or* rē′hə bil′ə tā′tiv) *adj.* of or having to do with rehabilitation.

re·hash (*v.* rē hash′; *n.* rē′hash) *v., n.* —*v.* deal with again; work up (old material) into a new form: *The question had been rehashed again and again.* —*n.* **1** the act of rehashing. **2** something old put into a different form: *That composition is simply a rehash of an article in the encyclopedia.*

re·hears·al (ri hėr′səl) *n.* **1** the act of rehearsing. **2** a performance beforehand for practice or drill.

re·hearse (ri hėrs′) *v.* **-hearsed, -hears·ing. 1** practise (a play, part, etc.) for a public performance. **2** drill or train (a person, etc.) by repetition. **3** tell in detail; repeat: *She rehearsed all the happenings of the day from beginning to end.* [ME < OF *rehercier* < *re-* again + *hercier* harrow, ult. < L *hirpex, hirpicis* rake]

Reich (rīH) *n. German.* empire, a term applied to the Holy Roman Empire, 962-1806 (**First Reich**); the German Empire, 1871-1918 (**Second Reich**); and Germany under Adolf Hitler, 1933-1945 (**Third Reich**).

reichs·mark (rīHs′märk′) *n.* **-marks** or **-mark.** the basic unit of money of Germany from 1924 to 1948. [< G]

Reichs·tag (rīHs′täk′) *n.* the former elective legislative assembly of the German Empire and Republic. It was established in 1871 but, under Hitler, gradually lost its powers.

re·i·fi·ca·tion (rē′ə fə kā′shən) *n.* the act, process, or result of reifying.

re·i·fy (rē′ə fī′) *v.* **-fied, -fy·ing.** think of (an abstract concept or idea) as a real or material thing.

reign (rān) *n., v.* —*n.* **1** the period of power of a ruler: *Queen Victoria's reign lasted sixty-four years.* **2** the royal power; rule: *The reign of a wise ruler benefits his country.* **3** existence everywhere; prevalence.
—*v.* **1** be a ruler: *A king reigns over his kingdom.* **2** exist everywhere; prevail: *Silence reigned on the lake, except for the sound of our paddles in the water.* [ME < OF < L *regnum* < *regere* rule]

☛ *Hom.* **rain, rein.**

Reign of Terror in France, a period of the Revolution from about March, 1793, to July, 1794, during which thousands of people were executed.

re·im·burse (rē′im bėrs′) *v.* **-bursed, -burs·ing.** pay back: *His employer reimbursed him for his travelling expenses.* [< *re-* + obs. *imburse* < Med.L *imbursare* < L *in-* into + LL *bursa* purse; patterned on F *rembourser*] —**re·im·burse′ment,** *n.*

re·im·port (*v.* rē′im pôrt′; *n.* rē im′pôrt) *v., n.* —*v.* import something previously exported: *Raw materials are sometimes exported from Canada and later reimported in the form of manufactured goods.* —*n.* reimportation.

re·im·por·ta·tion (rē′im pôr tā′shən) *n.* **1** an importing of something previously exported. **2** the goods reimported.

rein (rān) *n., v.* —*n.* **1** a long, narrow strap or line fastened to the bit of a bridle, by which to guide and control an animal. A driver or rider of a horse holds the reins in his hands. See **harness** for picture. **2** a means of control and direction: *to seize the reins of government.*
draw rein, a tighten the reins. **b** slow down; stop.
give rein to, let move or act freely, without guidance or control: *give rein to one's feelings.*
keep a tight rein on, keep under close supervision and control.
—*v.* **1** check or pull with reins. **2** guide and control: *Rein your tongue.*
rein in or **up,** cause to stop or to go slower. [ME < OF *rene,* ult. < L *retinere* hold back. See RETAIN.]

☛ *Hom.* **rain, reign.**

re·in·car·nate (rē′in kär′nāt) *v.* **-nat·ed, -nat·ing.** give a new body to (a soul).

re·grow′	re·hard′en	re·hem′	re′im·plant′	re′im·pris′on·ment
re·growth′	re·har′ness	re·hire′	re′im·pose′	
re·han′dle	re·hear′	re·house′	re′im·po·si′tion	
re·hang′	re·heat′	re′ig·nite′	re′im·pris′on	

re·in·car·na·tion (rē'in kär nā'shən) *n.* **1** a rebirth of the soul in a new body. **2** a new incarnation or embodiment.

rein·deer (rān'dēr') *n., pl.* **-deer.** a large deer (*Rangifer tarandus*) of arctic and subarctic regions, both sexes of which have large, branching antlers. Reindeer have been domesticated since early times in N Europe and Asia. In North America this animal is known as the caribou. See also **caribou.** [ME < ON *hreindýri* < *hreinn* reindeer + *dýr* animal]

reindeer moss a grey, tufted, and branched lichen (*Cladonia rangiferina*) found in arctic and subarctic regions and providing the major food for reindeer (caribou) and musk-oxen and also sometimes used for human food.

re·in·force (rē'in fôrs') *v.* **-forced, -forc·ing. 1** strengthen with new force or materials: *to reinforce an army or a fleet, to reinforce a garment with an extra thickness of cloth, to reinforce a wall or a bridge.* **2** strengthen: *to reinforce an argument, a plea, an effect, a stock, a supply, etc.* [< *re-* + *enforce*]

reinforced concrete concrete with metal embedded in it to make the structure stronger.

re·in·force·ment (rē'in fôrs'mənt) *n.* **1** the act of reinforcing or being reinforced. **2** something that reinforces. **3 reinforcements,** *pl.* extra personnel and equipment, especially troops, warships, military aircraft, etc.

re·in·state (rē'in stāt') *v.* **-stat·ed, -stat·ing.** restore to a former position or condition; establish again. —**re'in·state'ment,** *n.*

re·in·sure (rē'in shūr') *v.* insure again; insure under a contract by which a first insurer relieves himself from the risk and transfers it to another insurer.

reis (rās) *n. pl.* of **real³.** [< Pg.]

re·it·er·ate (rē it'ər āt') *v.* **-at·ed, -at·ing.** say or do several times; repeat (an action, demand, etc.) again and again: *The boy did not move, though the teacher reiterated her command.* [< L *reiterare,* ult. < *re-* again + *iterum* again] —**re·it'er·a'tion,** *n.*
☛ *Syn.* See note at **repeat.**

re·ject (*v.* ri jekt'; *n.* rē'jekt) *v., n.* —*v.* **1** refuse to take, use, believe, consider, grant, etc.: *He rejected our help. He tried to join the army but was rejected.* **2** throw away as useless or unsatisfactory: *Reject all apples with soft spots.* **3** vomit.
—*n.* a rejected person or thing: *The rejects were sold at a lower price.* [< L *rejectus,* pp. of *reicere. rejicere* < *re-* back + *jacere* throw] —**re·ject'er,** *n.*
☛ *Syn. v.* **1.** See note at **refuse.**

re·jec·tion (ri jek'shən) *n.* **1** the act of rejecting or the state of being rejected. **2** the thing rejected.

re·joice (ri jois') *v.* **-joiced, -joic·ing. 1** be glad; be filled with joy. **2** make glad; fill with joy. [ME < OF *rejoïss-,* a stem of *rejoïr,* ult. < L *re-* again + *gaudere* be glad] —**re·joic'er,** *n.*

re·joic·ing (ri jois'ing) *n.* the feeling or expression of joy.

re·join¹ (rē join') *v.* **1** join again; unite again. **2** join the company of (somebody) again. [< *re-* + *join*]

re·join² (ri join') *v.* answer; reply: *"Not on your life," he rejoined.* [< F *rejoindre* < *re-* back + *joindre* join]

re·join·der (ri join'dər) *n.* an answer to a reply; response. [< F *rejoindre,* infin. used as n.]

re·ju·ve·nate (ri jū'və nāt') *v.* **-nat·ed, -nat·ing.** make young or vigorous again; give youthful qualities to. [< *re-* < L *juvenis* young] —**re·ju've·na'tion,** *n.* —**re·ju've·na'tor,** *n.*

rel. 1 relative; relatively; relating. **2** religion.

re–laid (rē lād') *v.* pt. and pp. of **re-lay.**

re–lapse (*v.* ri laps'; *usually, n.* rē'laps) *v.* **-lapsed, -laps·ing.** —*v.* fall or slip back into a former state, way of acting, etc.: *After one cry of surprise, she relapsed into silence.* —*n.* a falling or slipping back into a former state, way of acting, etc.: *He seemed to be getting over his illness but had a relapse.* [< L *relapsus,* pp. of *relabi* < *re-* back + *labi* slip]

re·late (ri lāt') *v.* **-lat·ed, -lat·ing. 1** give an account of; tell: *The traveller related his adventures.* **2** connect in thought or meaning: *Better and best are related to good.* **3** be connected in any way: *We are interested in what relates to ourselves.* [< L *relatus,* pp. of referre < *re-* back + *ferre* bring]

re·lat·ed (ri lāt'id) *adj.* **1** connected. **2** belonging to the same family; connected by a common origin: *English and Dutch are closely related languages.* —**re·lat'ed·ness,** *n.*

re·la·tion (ri lā'shən) *n.* **1** a connection in thought or meaning: *Your answer has no relation to the question.* **2** connections or dealings between persons, groups, countries, etc.: *The relation of mother and child is the closest in the world.* **3 relations,** *pl.* dealings; affairs: *Our firm has business relations with his firm.* **4** a person who belongs to the same family as another, such as father, brother, aunt, etc.; relative. **5** the act or instance of telling; account. **6** *Mathematics.* a property, as of equality or inequality, by which an ordered pair of quantities, expressions, etc. is associated.
in or **with relation to,** concerning; with respect to: *We must plan in relation to the future.* [< L *relatio, -onis* < *relatus.* See RELATE.]

re·la·tion·al (ri lā'shən əl) *adj.* **1** that relates. **2** having to do with relations.

re·la·tion·ship (ri lā'shən ship') *n.* **1** connection. **2** the condition of belonging to the same family.

rel·a·tive (rel'ə tiv) *n., adj.* —*n.* **1** a person who belongs to the same family as another, such as father, brother, aunt, etc. **2** a relative pronoun.
—*adj.* **1** related or compared to each other: *Before ordering our dinner, we considered the relative merits of fried chicken and roast beef.* **2** depending on a relation to something else: *East is a relative term; for example, Regina is east of Vancouver but west of Toronto.* **3** *Grammar.* introducing a subordinate clause; referring to another person or thing. *Example. In* The man who wanted it is gone, who *is a relative pronoun, and* who wanted it *is a relative clause.*
relative to, a about; concerning: *a letter relative to my proposal.* **b** in proportion to: *He is strong relative to his size. This subject is little understood relative to its importance.*
[ME < LL *relativus* < L *relatus.* See RELATE.]
☛ *Usage.* **Relative clauses.** A relative clause is an adjective clause introduced by a relative pronoun, **that, which,** or **who,** or a relative adverb, **where, when, why:** *The ball* that has been lost *was found by the caddy. Mike's plane,* which was lost in the storm, *landed safely in a field. They asked for a student* who would volunteer to play Santa Claus. *That is the place* where he lived. See also **restrictive clause.**
☛ *Usage.* **Relative pronouns.** The relative pronouns are **that, which (of which, whose)** and **who (whose, whom).** They introduce relative clauses and refer to an antecedent in the main clause: *A man* who was there *gave us the details. Our team,* which scored first, *had the advantage.* **Who** refers to persons; **which,** to animals or things; and **that,** to persons, animals, or things.

relative density the ratio of the density of any substance to the density of a particular substance used as a standard. For solids and liquids, the standard is water; for gases, it is air.

relative humidity the ratio between the amount of water vapor actually present in the air and the amount it would take to saturate the air at the same temperature, expressed as a percentage. At 15°C, if the air contains 10 grams of water vapor per cubic metre, its relative humidity is about 80%; at 30°C with the same amount of water vapor, the air has a relative humidity of about 33%, because warmer air can hold more water vapor. Compare **absolute humidity.**

rel·a·tive·ly (rel'ə tiv lē) *adv.* in a relative manner; in relation to something else; comparatively: *a relatively small difference.*

rel·a·tiv·i·ty (rel'ə tiv'ə tē) *n.* **1** the state or quality of being relative. **2** *Physics.* the character of being relative rather than absolute, as ascribed to motion or velocity. **3** a theory formulated by Albert Einstein in the equation $E = mc^2$ (energy = mass × the square of the speed of light). The **special theory of relativity** is based on the hypothesis that the speed of light is the same when measured by two observers even though one observer is moving at a constant velocity with respect to the other. The **general theory of relativity** is an extension of the special theory to relate the measurements of observers who are accelerated with respect to each other.

re·la·tor (ri lā'tor) *n.* a person who relates or narrates. [< L]

re·lax (ri laks') *v.* **1** loosen up; make or become less stiff or firm: *Relax your muscles to rest them.* **2** make or become less strict or severe; lessen in force: *Discipline is relaxed on the last day of school.* **3** relieve or be relieved from work or effort; give or take recreation or amusement: *Take a vacation and relax.* **4** weaken: *Don't relax your efforts because the examinations are over.* [ME < L *relaxare,* ult. < *re-* back + *laxus* loose. Doublet of RELEASE.] —**re·lax'er,** *n.*

---

re'in·cor'po·rate'	re'in·fes·ta'tion	re'in·stal·la'tion	re'in·ter·ro·ga'tion	re'in·voke'
re'in·cor'po·ra'tion	re'in·flame'	re'in·te·grate'	re'in·tro·duce'	re·is'sue
re'in·duce'	re'in·form'	re'in·te·gra'tion	re'in·tro·duc'tion	re·judge'
re'in·duct'	re'in·sert'	re'in·vest'	re'in·vest'ment	re·kin'dle
re'in·duc'tion	re'in·ser'tion	re'in·vest'ment	re'in·ves'ti·gate'	re·la'bel
re'in·fect'	re'in·spect'	re'in·ter'pret	re'in·ves'ti·ga'tion	
re'in·fec'tion	re'in·spec'tion	re'in·ter·pre·ta'tion	re'in·vig'or·ate'	
re'in·fest'	re'in·stall'	re'in·ter'ro·gate'	re'in·vig'or·a'tion	

re·lax·ant (ri lak′sənt) *n., adj.* —*n.* a substance that relaxes, especially a drug used to relax muscles. —*adj.* of, having to do with, or producing relaxation.

re·lax·a·tion (rē′lak sā′shən) *n.* **1** a loosening: *the relaxation of the muscles.* **2** a lessening of strictness, severity, force, etc.: *the relaxation of discipline.* **3** a relief from work or effort; recreation; amusement. **4** the state or condition of being relaxed.

re·lax·ed·ly (ri lak′sid lē) *adv.* in a relaxed manner.

re·lay (*n.* rē′lā; *v.* ri lā′ *or* rē′lā) *n., v.* —*n.* **1** a fresh supply: *New relays of men were sent to the battle front.* **2 a** a relay race. **b** one part of a relay race. **c relays,** a meeting, or a part of a meeting, at which relay races are run. **3** the act of passing on a ball, puck, etc. from one player to another. **4** an electromagnetic device in which a weak current controls a stronger current. A relay is used in transmitting telegraph or telephone messages over long distances. **5** a device that extends or reinforces the action or effect of an apparatus. **6 a** one of several persons or groups taking on a job, mission, etc. in turn. **b** a system of working, sending messages, etc. by the use of several people or groups acting in turn. —*v.* **1** take and carry farther: *Messengers will relay your message.* **2** transmit by an electrical relay. **3** receive and then pass to another: *to relay a phone message, to relay a thrown ball.* [ME < OF *relai* reserve pack of hounds, etc., ult. < *re-* back + *laier* leave < Gmc.]

re·lay (rē lā′) *v.* **-laid, -lay·ing.** lay again.

re·lay race (rē′lā) a race in which each member of a team runs, swims, etc. only a certain part of the distance.

re·lease (ri lēs′) *v.* **-leased, -leas·ing;** *n.* —*v.* **1** let go; let loose: *The prisoner was released.* **2** set free; relieve: *The nurse is released from duty at seven o'clock.* **3** give up (legal right, claim, etc.); make over to another (property, etc.) **4** permit to be published, shown, sold, etc. —*n.* **1** a letting go; setting free. **2** freedom; relief. **3** a device for releasing a part or parts of a mechanism. **4** *Law.* **a** the legal surrender of right, estate, etc. to another. **b** a document that accomplishes this. **5** an authorization for publication, exhibition, sale, etc. **6** an article, statement, etc. distributed for publication. [ME < OF *relaissier* < L *relaxare.* Doublet of RELAX.] —**re·leas′er,** *n.*

☞ *Syn. v.* **1. Release, free** = set loose from something that holds back or keeps confined. **Release** emphasizes relaxing the hold on the person or thing: *He released the brakes of the truck.* **Free,** more general in meaning and application, emphasizes giving freedom by removing or unfastening whatever is holding: *He freed the bird from the cage.*

re·lease (rē lēs′) *v.* **-leased, -leas·ing.** lease again.

rel·e·gate (rel′ə gāt′) *v.* **-gat·ed, -gat·ing. 1** send away, usually to a lower position or condition. **2** send into exile; banish. **3** hand over (a matter, task, etc.). [< L *relegare* < *re-* back + *legare* despatch < *legatus* having a commission < *lex, legis* law] —**rel′e·ga′tion,** *n.*

re·lent (ri lent′) *v.* become less harsh or strict; be more tender and merciful. [ult. < L *re-* again + *lentus* slow]

re·lent·less (ri lent′lis) *adj.* without pity; unyielding; harsh: *The storm raged with relentless fury.* —**re·lent′less·ly,** *adv.*

rel·e·vance (rel′ə vəns) *n.* the condition of being relevant; being applicable or to the point.

rel·e·van·cy (rel′ə vən sē) *n.* relevance.

rel·e·vant (rel′ə vənt) *adj.* bearing upon or connected with the matter in hand; to the point: *relevant questions.* [< L *relevans, -antis* refreshing, ppr. of *relevare,* ult. < *re-* back + *levis* light] —**rel′e·vant·ly,** *adv.*

☞ *Syn.* See note at **pertinent.**

re·li·a·bil·i·ty (ri lī′ə bil′ə tē) *n.* the quality of being reliable; trustworthiness; dependability.

re·li·a·ble (ri lī′ə bəl) *adj.* worthy of trust; that can be depended on: *reliable sources of news.* —**re·li′a·bly,** *adv.*

☞ *Syn.* **Reliable, trustworthy** = worthy of being depended on or trusted. **Reliable** suggests that the person or thing it describes can safely be believed or trusted, and counted on to do or be what is expected, wanted, or needed: *I have always found this to be a reliable brand of canned goods.* **Trustworthy,** usually describing a person, suggests that he is fully deserving of complete confidence in his truthfulness, honesty, good judgment, justice, etc.: *He is a trustworthy news commentator.*

re·li·ance (ri lī′əns) *n.* **1** trust; dependence: *A child has reliance on his mother.* **2** confidence.

re·li·ant (ri lī′ənt) *adj.* **1** relying; trusting or depending. **2** confident.

rel·ic (rel′ik) *n.* **1** a thing, custom, etc. that remains from the past: *This ruined bridge is a relic of pioneer days.* **2** something belonging to a holy person, kept as a sacred memorial. **3** an object having interest because of its age or its associations with the past; keepsake; souvenir. **4 relics,** *pl.* remains; ruins. [ME < OF *relique* < L *reliquiae,* pl., remains]

hat, āge, fär; let, ēqual, tėrm; it, īce
hot, ōpen, ôrder; oil, out; cup, pùt, rüle,
əbove, takən, pencəl, lemən, circəs
ch, child; ng, long; sh, ship
th, thin; ŦH, then; zh, measure

rel·ict (rel′ikt) *n.* **1** widow. **2** a plant or animal surviving from an earlier period. [< Med.L *relicta,* originally fem. pp. of L *relinquere.* See RELINQUISH.]

Reliefs (def. 9). The picture on the left is a detail from an ancient Greek sculpture in high relief; the picture on the right is a detail from an ancient Indic sculpture in low relief.

re·lief (ri lēf′) *n.* **1** the lessening of, or freeing from, a pain, burden, difficulty, etc. **2** something that lessens or frees from pain, burden, difficulty, etc.; aid; help. **3** help, in the form of money or food, given to poor people. **4** something that makes a pleasing change or lessens strain. **5** a release from a post of duty, often by the coming of a substitute: *This nurse is on duty from seven in the morning until seven at night, with only two hours' relief.* **6** a change of persons on duty. **7** a person or persons relieving others from duty: *The sentry was waiting for his relief.* **8** *Sculpture, painting, etc.* a projection of figures and designs from a flat surface. **9** a figure or design standing out from the surface from which it is cut, shaped, or stamped. **10** the appearance of standing out given to a drawing or painting by use of shadow, shading, color, or line. **11** differences in height between the summits and lowlands of a region. **12** strong, clear manner; distinctness.
in relief, standing out from a surface.
on relief, receiving money to live on from public funds.
[ME < AF *relef* < *relever.* See RELIEVE.]

relief map a map that shows the different heights of a surface by using shading, colors, etc., or solid materials such as clay.

re·lieve (ri lēv′) *v.* **-lieved, -liev·ing. 1** make less; make easier; reduce the pain or trouble of: *These pills will relieve a headache.* **2** set free: *Your coming relieves me of the bother of writing a long letter.* **3** bring aid to; help: *Soldiers were sent to relieve the fort.* **4** give variety or a pleasing change to: *The black dress was relieved by red trimming.* **5** free (a person on duty) by taking his place. **6** make stand out more clearly. [ME < OF *relever* < L *relevare* lighten. See RELEVANT.] —**re·liev′er,** *n.*

re·lie·vo (ri lē′vō) *n., pl.* **-vos.** *Sculpture, painting, etc.* relief. [< Ital. *rilievo*]

re·li·gion (ri lij′ən) *n.* **1** belief in or worship of God or gods. **2** a particular system of religious belief and worship: *the Christian religion, the Moslem religion.* **3** a matter of conscience: *She makes a religion of keeping her house neat.* [< L *religio, -onis* respect for what is sacred, probably originally, care (for worship and traditions) < *relegere* go through again < *re-* again + *legere* read]

re·li·gi·os·i·ty (ri lij′ē os′ə tē) *n.* an affectation of religious feelings.

re·li·gious (ri lij′əs) *adj., n., pl.* **re·li·gious.** —*adj.* **1** of religion; connected with religion. **2** much interested in religion; devoted to the worship of God or gods. **3** belonging to an order of monks, nuns, friars, etc. **4** of or connected with such an order. **5** strict; very careful: *We paid religious attention to the doctor's orders.* —*n.* **1** a monk, nun, friar, etc.; member of a religious order. **2** such persons collectively. [ME < OF < L *religiosus* < *religio.* See RELIGION.] —**re·li′gious·ly,** *adv.* —**re·li′gious·ness,** *n.*

re·lin·quish (ri ling′kwish) *v.* give up; let go: *The small dog relinquished his bone to the big dog. She has relinquished all hope of going to Europe this year.* [ME < OF *relinquiss-,* a stem of

relinquir < L *relinquere* < *re-* behind + *linquere* leave]
—**re·lin′quish·er,** *n.*

re·lin·quish·ment (ri ling′kwish mənt) *n.* giving up; abandonment; surrender.

rel·i·quar·y (rel′ə kwer′ē) *n., pl.* **-quar·ies.** a small box or other receptacle for a relic or relics. [< MF *reliquaire* < *relique.* See RELIC.]

rel·ique (rel′ik; *French* rə lēk′) *n.* relic. [<F]

rel·ish (rel′ish) *n., v.* —*n.* **1** a pleasant taste; a good flavor: *Hunger gives relish to simple food.* **2** something to add flavor to food. Olives and pickles are relishes. **3** a kind of pickle made of chopped cucumbers, etc. **4** a slight dash (of something). **5** a liking; appetite; enjoyment: *The hungry boy ate with a great relish. The teacher has no relish for John's jokes.*
—*v.* like; enjoy: *A cat relishes cream. He did not relish the prospect of staying after school.* [earlier *reles* < OF *reles* remainder < *relesser, relaissier.* See RELEASE.]

re·live (rē liv′) *v.* **-lived, -living.** experience (an event, etc.) again, especially in one's imagination.

re·luc·tance (ri luk′təns) *n.* **1** a reluctant feeling or action; unwillingness. **2** slowness in action because of unwillingness.

re·luc·tan·cy (ri luk′tən sē) *n.* reluctance.

re·luc·tant (ri luk′tənt) *adj.* **1** unwilling; showing unwillingness. **2** slow to act because unwilling: *He was very reluctant to give his money away.* [< L *reluctans, -antis* struggling against, ppr. of *reluctari,* ult. < *re-* back + *lucta* wrestling] —**re·luc′tant·ly,** *adv.*
☞ *Syn.* **1. Reluctant, loath** = unwilling to do something. **Reluctant** suggests struggling against doing something one finds disagreeable or unpleasant, disapproves of, is afraid of, etc.: *He was reluctant to leave her, but he had no choice.* **Loath** suggests unwillingness because one feels the thing to be done is extremely disagreeable or hateful: *His parents were loath to believe their son would steal.*

re·ly (ri lī′) *v.* **-lied, -ly·ing.** depend; trust: *Rely on your own efforts.* [ME < OF *relier* < L *religare* bind fast < *re-* back + *ligare* bind]
☞ *Syn.* **Rely, depend** = have confidence in someone or something. **Rely** means count on, or put one's trust in, someone or something one has reason to believe will never fail to do what is expected or wanted: *He relies on his parents' advice.* **Depend** suggests confidently taking it for granted, with or without reason, that a person or thing will give the help or support expected or needed: *She depends on her friends to make her decisions.*

rem (rem) *n.* the unit for measuring the harm caused by radiation on human tissue. It is equal to the effect of one roentgen of X rays. [< *roentgen* + *equivalent* + *man*]

REM rapid eye movement.

re·main (ri mān′) *v., n.* —*v.* **1** continue in a place; stay: *We remained at the lake till September.* **2** continue; last; keep on: *The town remains the same year after year.* **3** be left: *A few apples remain on the trees.*
—*n.* **remains,** *pl.* **a** what is left. **b** a dead body. **c** a writer's works not yet published at the time of his death. **d** things left from the past, such as a building, a monument, or parts of an animal or plant: *the remains of an ancient civilization, fossil remains.* [ME < OF *remainder* < L *remanere* < *re-* back + *manere* stay]
☞ *Syn. v.* **1.** See note at **stay.**

re·main·der (ri mān′dər) *n., v.* —*n.* **1** the part left over; the rest: *After studying an hour, she spent the remainder of the afternoon in play.* **2** *Arithmetic.* **a** a number left over after subtracting one number from another: *In 9 – 2, the remainder is 7.* **b** a number left over after dividing one number by another: *In 14 ÷ 3, the quotient is 4 with a remainder of 2.* **3** a copy or a number of copies of a book left in the publisher's hands after sales have dropped considerably or ceased, which the publisher sells at greatly reduced prices.
—*v.* sell (a book or books) as a remainder. [ME < OF *remaindre,* infin. used as n. See REMAIN.]

re·mand (ri mand′) *v., n.* —*v.* **1** send back. **2** **a** send back (a prisoner or an accused person) into custody. **b** send back a case to the court it came from for further action there. —*n.* the act of remanding. [ME < LL *remandare* < L *re-* back + *mandare* order]

re·mark (ri märk′) *v., n.* —*v.* **1** say; speak; comment. **2** observe; notice. —*n.* **1** something said in a few words; short statement. **2** the act of noticing; observation. [< F *remarquer* < *re-* again + *marquer* mark]

re·mark·a·ble (ri mär′kə bəl) *adj.* worthy of notice; unusual.
—**re·mark′a·ble·ness,** *n.* —**re·mark′a·bly,** *adv.*

re·match (re′mach′) *n.* a second match between the same contestants.

re·me·di·a·ble (re mē′dē ə bəl) *adj.* that can be remedied or cured. —**re·me′di·a·bly,** *adv.*

re·me·di·al (ri mē′dē əl) *adj.* intended as a remedy or cure; curing; helping. [< LL *remedialis* < L *remedium.* See REMEDY.]
—**re·me′di·al·ly,** *adv.*

rem·e·di·less (rem′ə dē lis) *adj.* without remedy; incurable; irreparable.

rem·e·dy (rem′ə dē) *n., pl.* **-dies;** *v.* **-died, -dy·ing.** —*n.*
1 anything used to cure or relieve illness: *Aspirin and mustard plaster are two old cold remedies.* **2** anything intended to put right something bad or wrong: *The free movie was a remedy for the children's bad spirits.* [ME < AF *remedie* < L *remedium.* See *v.*]
—*v.* put right; make right; cure. [ME < L *remediare* < *remedium* < *me-* again + *mederi* heal]
☞ *Syn. v.* See note at **cure.**

re·mem·ber (ri mem′bər) *v.* **1** have (something) come into the mind again; call to mind; recall. **2** keep in mind; take care not to forget. **4** have memory: *Dogs remember.* **5** make a gift to; reward; tip: *Grandfather remembered us all in his will.* **6** mention (a person) as sending friendly greetings; recall to the mind of another. [ME < OF *remembrer* < L *rememorari,* ult. < *re-* again + *memor* mindful of]
☞ *Syn.* **1. Remember, recall, recollect** = think of something again by an act of memory. **Remember** emphasizes having something once known or experienced come back into one's mind, sometimes by a conscious effort but often through no act of will: *Do you remember that?* **Recall** emphasizes being able to remember, consciously calling back: *Yes, I recall the incident.* **Recollect,** more formal, particularly suggests a thinking process requiring a conscious or special effort to recall something that has been forgotten: *Now I recollect what he said.*

re·mem·brance (ri mem′brəns) *n.* **1** the power to remember; memory. **2** the act of remembering or a state of being remembered. **3** a keepsake; any thing or action that makes one remember a person, place, or event; souvenir. **4 remembrances,** *pl.* greetings.

Remembrance Day November 11, the day set aside to honor the memory of those killed in World Wars I and II.

re·mem·branc·er (ri mem′brən sər) *n.* a person or thing that reminds one; reminder.

re·mind (ri mīnd′) *v.* make (one) think (of something); cause to remember.

re·mind·er (ri mīn′dər) *n.* something to help one remember.

rem·i·nisce (rem′ə nis′) *v.* **-nisced, -nisc·ing.** talk or think about past experiences or events.

rem·i·nis·cence (rem′ə nis′əns) *n.* **1** remembering; recalling past happenings, etc. **2** Often, **reminiscences,** *pl.* an account of something remembered; recollection: *reminiscences of the war.* **3** something that makes one remember or think of something else. [< L *reminiscentia,* ult. < *reminisci* remember < *re-* again + *men-* think]

rem·i·nis·cent (rem′ə nis′ənt) *adj.* **1** recalling past events, etc.: *reminiscent talk.* **2** awakening memories of something else; suggestive: *a manner reminiscent of a statelier age.*
—**rem′i·nis′cent·ly,** *adv.*

re·miss (ri mis′) *adj.* careless; slack; neglectful; negligent: *A police officer who fails to report a crime is remiss in his duty.* [< L *remissus,* pp. of *remittere* < *re-* back + *mittere* let go]
—**re·miss′ness,** *n.*

re·mis·si·ble (ri mis′ə bəl) *adj.* that can be remitted.

re·mis·sion (ri mish′ən) *n.* **1** a letting off (from debt, punishment, etc.): *The bankrupt sought remission of his debts.* **2** pardon; forgiveness: *Remission of sins is promised to those who repent.* **3** a lessening or abatement (of pain, of the effects or symptoms of a disease, etc.).

re·mit (ri mit′) *v.* **-mit·ted, -mit·ting. 1** send money to a person or place: *Enclosed is our bill; please remit.* **2** send (money due). **3** refrain from carrying out; refrain from exacting; cancel: *The king remitted the prisoner's punishment.* **4** pardon; forgive: *power to remit sins.* **5** make less; decrease: *After we had rowed the boat into calm water, we remitted our efforts.* **6** become less. **7** send back (a case) to a lower court for further action. [ME < L *remittere* send back, let go. See REMISS.] —**re·mit′ter,** *n.*

re·mit·tal (ri mit′əl) *n.* remission.

re·mit·tance (ri mit′əns) *n.* **1** the act of sending money to someone at a distance. **2** the money that is sent.

remittance man someone who lives abroad on money sent from his relatives at home.

re·mit·tent (ri mit′ənt) *adj.* lessening for a time; lessening at

re·list′　　re′lo·ca′tion　　re′make′　　re·mar′ry　　re′melt′
re·load′　　re·lock′　　　　re′man·u·fac′ture　　re·meas′ure　　re′mix′
re′lo·cate′　　re·made′　　re·mar′riage　　re·meas′ure·ment

rem·nant (rem′nənt) *n.* **1** a small part left. **2** a piece of cloth, ribbon, lace, etc. left after the rest has been used or sold: *She bought a remnant of silk at the sale.* [ME < OF *remenant,* ppr. of *remenoir* remain < L *remanere.* See REMAIN.]

re·mod·el (rē mod′əl) *v.* **-elled** or **-eled, -el·ling** or **-el·ing.** **1** model again. **2** make over; change or alter: *The old barn was remodelled into a house.*

re·mon·e·tize (rē mun′ə tīz′ *or* rē mon′ə tīz′) *v.* **-tized, -tiz·ing.** restore to use as legal tender: *remonetize silver.* —**re·mon′e·ti·za′tion,** *n.*

re·mon·strance (ri mon′strəns) *n.* a protest; complaint. [< Med.L *remonstrantia* < *remonstrare.* See REMONSTRATE.]

re·mon·strant (ri mon′strənt) *adj., n.* —*adj.* remonstrating; protesting. —*n.* a person who remonstrates.

re·mon·strate (ri mon′strāt *or* rem′ən strāt′) *v.* **-strat·ed, -strat·ing.** speak, reason, or plead in complaint or protest: *The foreman remonstrated with the worker about his slackness.* [< Med.L *remonstrare* point out, ult. < L *re-* back + *monstrum* sign] —**re·mon′stra·tor,** *n.*

re·mon·stra·tion (rē′mon strā′shən *or* rem′ən strā′shən) *n.* the act of remonstrating.

re·mon·stra·tive (ri mon′strə tiv) *adj.* remonstrating.

rem·o·ra (rem′ə rə) *n.* any of a family (Echeneidae) of fishes of warm seas having the front dorsal fin modified into a flat sucking disk on the head, by means of which they attach themselves to larger fish or to ships, rocks, etc. [< L *remora* hindrance < re- + *mora* delay; from the idea that these fish delayed ships. 16c. See MORATORIUM]

re·morse (ri môrs′) *n.* deep, painful regret for having done wrong: *Because he felt remorse for his crime, the thief confessed.* [< L *remorsus* tormented, ult. < *re-* back + *mordere* bite] ☛ *Syn.* See note at **regret.**

re·morse·ful (ri môrs′fəl) *adj.* feeling or expressing remorse. —**re·morse′ful·ly,** *adv.* —**re·morse′ful·ness,** *n.*

re·morse·less (ri môrs′lis) *adj.* without remorse; pitiless; cruel. —**re·morse′less·ly,** *adv.* —**re·morse′less·ness,** *n.*

re·mote (ri mōt′) *adj.* **-mot·er, -mot·est.** **1** far away from a given place or time: *Dinosaurs lived in remote ages.* **2** out of the way; secluded: *a remote village.* **3** distantly related or connected: *a remote relative.* **4** slight; faint: *I haven't the remotest idea what you mean.* [ME < L *remotus,* pp. of *removere* remove. See REMOVE.] —**re·mote′ly,** *adv.* —**re·mote·ness,** *n.* ☛ *Syn.* **1.** See note at **distant.**

remote control **1** control from a distance, usually by electrical impulses or radio signals. **2** the device used for operating a remote-control system.

re·mount (*v.* rē mount′; *n.* rē′mount *or* rē mount′) *v., n.* —*v.* **1** mount again. **2** furnish with fresh horses. —*n.* a fresh horse, or a supply of fresh horses, for use.

re·mov·al (ri mü′vəl) *n.* **1** a removing; taking away: *We paid ten dollars for garbage removal.* **2** a change of place: *The store announces its removal to larger quarters.* **3** a dismissal from an office or position.

re·move (ri müv′) *v.* **-moved, -mov·ing;** *n.* —*v.* **1** move from a place or position; take off; take away: *Remove your hat.* **2** get rid of; put an end to: *to remove all doubt.* **3** kill. **4** dismiss from an office or position: *to remove an official for taking bribes.* **5** go away; move oneself to another place. —*n.* **1** a moving away. **2** a step or degree of distance: *His cruelty was only one remove from crime.* [ME < OF < L *removere* < *re-* back + *movere* move] —**re·mov′a·ble,** *adj.* —**re·mov′er,** *n.*

re·moved (ri müvd′) *adj.* **1** distant; remote. **2** separated by one or more steps or degrees of relationship.

re·mu·ner·ate (ri myü′nər āt′) *v.* **-at·ed, -at·ing.** pay for work, services, trouble, etc.; reward. [< L *remunerare,* ult. < *re-* back + *munus* gift] ☛ *Syn.* See note at **pay.**

re·mu·ner·a·tion (ri myü′nər ā′shən) *n.* a reward; pay; payment.

re·mu·ner·a·tive (ri myü′nər ə tiv *or* ri myü′nər ā′tiv) *adj.* paying; profitable. —**re·mu′ner·a·tive·ly,** *adv.*

Re·mus (rē′məs) *n. Roman mythology.* the twin brother of Romulus.

ren·ais·sance (ren′ə säns′, ren′ə säns′, *or* ri nā′səns) *n.* **1** a revival; new birth. **2 the Renaissance, a** the great revival of art, literature, and classical learning in Europe during the 14th, 15th, and 16th centuries. **b** the period of time when this revival occurred

---

hat, āge, fär; let, ēqual, tèrm; it, īce
hot, ōpen, ôrder; oil, out; cup, pùt, rüle,
əbove, takən, pencəl, lemən, circəs
ch, child; ng, long; sh, ship
th, thin; ᴛʜ, then; zh, measure

---

c in art, architecture, etc., a style developed in this period and characterized by the simplicity, elegance, and proportion of classical Greek and Roman models. [< F *renaissance* < *renaître* be born again; ult. < L *renasci.* See RENASCENT.]
☛ *Usage.* **Renaissance.** The word is capitalized when it refers to the period of history: *art of the Renaissance.* It is not capitalized when it refers to a revival: *a renaissance of interest in old-time melodramas.*

re·nal (rē′nəl) *adj.* **1** of or having to do with the kidneys. **2** near the kidney: *the renal arteries.* [< L *renalis* < *ren* kidney]

re·name (rē nām′) *v.* **-named, -nam·ing.** give a new name to; name again.

re·nas·cence (ri nas′əns *or* ri nā′səns) *n.* **1** a revival; new birth; renewal. **2** a being renascent. **3 the Renascence,** the Renaissance.

re·nas·cent (ri nas′ənt *or* ri nā′sənt) *adj.* being born again; reviving; springing again into being or vigor. [< L *renascens, -entis,* ppr. of *renasci* < *re-* again + *nasci* be born]

ren·coun·ter (ren koun′tər) *n.* **1** a hostile meeting; conflict; battle; duel. **2** a chance meeting. [< F *rencontre* < *rencontrer* meet < *re-* again + *encontrer* encounter]

rend (rend) *v.* **rent, rend·ing.** **1** pull apart violently; tear: *Wolves will rend a lamb.* **2 split:** *Lightning rent the tree.* **3** disturb violently: *His mind was rent by doubt.* **4** *Archaic.* remove with force or violence: *He rent the sword from the knight's hand.* [OE *rendan*]

ren·der (ren′dər) *v.* **1** cause to become; make: *An accident has rendered him helpless.* **2** give; do: *She rendered us a great service by her help.* **3** offer for consideration, approval, payment, etc.; hand in; report: *The treasurer rendered an account of all the money spent.* **4** give in return: *Render thanks for kindness.* **5** pay as due: *The conquered rendered tribute to the conqueror.* **6** bring out the meaning of; represent; perform: *The actor rendered the part of Hamlet well.* **7** play or sing (music). **8** change from one language to another; translate. **9** give up; surrender. **10** melt (fat, etc.); clarify or extract by melting. Fat from pigs is rendered into lard. [ME < OF *rendre* < L *reddere* give as due, pay < *re-* as due + *dare* give; influenced by L *prendere* take]

ren·dez·vous (ron′də vü′; French, rän dā vü′) *n., pl.* **-vous** (-vüz′); *v.* **-voused** (-vüd′), **-vous·ing** (-vü′ing). —*n.* **1** an appointment or engagement to meet at a fixed place or time; meeting by agreement. **2** a meeting place; gathering place: *The family had two favorite rendezvous, the library and the garden.* **3** a place agreed on for a meeting at a certain time, especially of ships, troops, or aircraft. —*v.* **1** meet or come together at a rendezvous. **2** bring together at a rendezvous. [< F *rendezvous* < *rendez-vous* betake yourself!]

ren·di·tion (ren dish′ən) *n.* **1** the act of rendering. **2** a performance of a dramatic part, musical composition, etc. **3** translation. [< MF *rendition* < OF *rendre.* See RENDER.]

ren·e·gade (ren′ə gād′) *n.* **1** a deserter from a religious faith, a political party, etc.; traitor. **2** an outlaw. **3** (*adj.*) deserting; disloyal; like a traitor. [< Sp. *renegado* < Med.L *renegatus,* pp. of *renegare* deny. See RENEGE.]

re·nege (ri neg′, ri nāg′, *or* ri nig′) *v.* **-neged, -neg·ing,** *n.* —*v.* **1** *Card games.* fail to play a card of the suit that is led, although you have one. It is against the rules to renege. **2** *Informal.* back out; fail to keep a promise. —*n. Card games.* a failure to follow suit when able to do so. [< Med.L *renegare* < L *re-* back + *negare* deny] —**re·neg′er,** *n.*

re·new (ri nyü′ *or* -nü′) *v.* **1** make new again; make like new; restore. **2** make spiritually new. **3** begin again; get again; say, do, or give again: *to renew an attack, one's youth, one's vows, one's efforts.* **4** replace by new material or a new thing of the same sort; fill again. **5** give or get for a new period: *We renewed our lease for another year.* **6** renew a lease, note, etc. —**re·new′a·ble,** *adj.* —**re·new′er,** *n.*
☛ *Syn.* **1. Renew, restore, renovate** = put back in a new or former condition. **Renew** = put back in a condition like new something that has lost its freshness, force, or vigor: *He renewed the finish of the table.* **Restore** = put back in its original, former, or normal condition something that has been damaged, worn out, partly ruined, etc.: *That old pioneer fort has been restored.* **Renovate** = put in good condition or make like new by cleaning, repairing, redecorating, etc.: *The store was renovated.*

re·new·al (ri nyü′əl *or* ri nü′əl) *n.* **1** renewing or being renewed.

---

re·mort′gage   re·mould′

2 something renewed, such as a magazine subscription.

re·new·ed·ly (ri nyü′id lē *or* ri nü′id lē) *adv.* anew.

ren·i·form (ren′ə fôrm′ *or* rē′nə fôrm′) *adj.* suggesting a kidney in shape or outline: *The marsh marigold has reniform leaves.* See **leaf** for picture. [< L *ren, renis* kidney + E *-form*]

ren·net (ren′it) *n.* a substance containing rennin, used for making cheese and junket. [ME *rennet < renne(n)* run, OE *rinnan*]

ren·nin (ren′ən) *n.* an enzyme in the gastric juice that coagulates or curdles milk. [< *rennet*]

re·nounce (ri nouns′) *v.* **-nounced, -nounc·ing. 1** give up entirely, especially by making a formal declaration: *He renounced his claim to the money.* **2** make formal surrender. **3** cast off; refuse to recognize as one's own: *He renounced his wicked son.* **4** *Card games.* play a card of a different suit from that led. [ME < OF *renoncer* < L *renuntiare*, ult. < *re-* back + *nuntius* message] **—re·nounce′ment,** *n.*

ren·o·vate (ren′ə vāt′) *v.* **-vat·ed, -vat·ing.** make new again; make like new; restore to good condition: *to renovate a garment or a house.* [< L *renovare*, ult. < *re-* again + *novus* new] **—ren′o·va′tor,** *n.*
☛ *Syn.* See note at **renew.**

ren·o·va·tion (ren′ə vā′shən) *n.* a restoration to good condition; renewal.

re·nown (ri noun′) *n.* the condition of being widely known; fame. [ME < AF *renoun*, ult. < L *re-* repeatedly + *nomen* name]

re·nowned (ri nound′) *adj.* famed.
☛ *Syn.* See note at **famous.**

rent¹ (rent) *n., v.* —*n.* **1** a payment, especially when made regularly, for the right to occupy or use another's land, buildings, goods, etc. **2** *Economics.* what is paid for the use of natural resources.
for rent, available in return for rent paid: *That vacant apartment is for rent.*
—*v.* **1** pay at regular times for the use of (property): *We rent a house from Mr. Smith.* **2** receive regular pay for the use of (property): *He rents several other houses.* **3** be leased or let for rent: *This house rents for $550.00 a month.* [ME < OF *rente*, ult. < L *reddere* render. See RENDER.] **—rent′a·ble,** *adj.* **—rent′er,** *n.*

rent² (rent) *n., adj., v.* —*n.* a torn place; tear; split. —*adj.* torn; split. —*v.* pt. and pp. of **rend.** [originally *v.*, var. of *rend*]

rent·al (ren′təl) *n., adj.* —*n.* **1** an amount received or paid as rent: *The monthly rental of her house is $500.* **2** something rented or able to be rented. —*adj.* **1** of or in rent. **2** that is rented: *a rental car.* [< AF]

ren·tier (ron tyä′; *French,* raṅ tyä′) *n.* a person whose principal income is in the form of rent, dividends, interest, etc. [< F < *rente* revenue + *-ier -er²*]

re·nun·ci·ate (ri nun′sē āt′) *v.* **-at·ed, -at·ing.** give up formally; renounce; disclaim.

re·nun·ci·a·tion (ri nun′sē ā′shən) *n.* a giving up of a right, title, possession, etc.; renouncing. [< L *renuntiatio, -onis < renuntiare.* See RENOUNCE.]

re·o·pen (rē ō′pən) *v.* **1** open again. **2** bring up again for discussion: *The matter is settled and cannot be reopened.*

re·or·der (rē ôr′dər) *v., n.* —*v.* **1** put in order again; rearrange. **2** give a second or repeated order for goods; order again. —*n.* a second or repeated order for goods.

re·or·gan·i·za·tion (rē′ôr gən ə zā′shən *or* rē′ôr gən ī zā′shən) *n.* the act of reorganizing or the state of being reorganized.

re·or·gan·ize (rē ôr′gən īz′) *v.* **-ized, -iz·ing. 1** organize anew; form again; arrange in a new way: *Classes will be reorganized after the first four weeks.* **2** form a new company to operate (a business in the hands of a receiver). **—re′or·gan·iz′er,** *n.*

rep¹ (rep) *n.* a heavy, ribbed fabric of wool, silk, cotton, etc. Also, **repp.** [< F *reps* < E *ribs*]

rep² (rep) *n.* representative: *The company has hired several new sales reps.*

rep³ (rep) *n. Informal.* repertory (theatre).

rep. 1 report; reported; reporter. **2** representative.

Rep. 1 Representative. **2** Republican; Republic.

re·paid (ri pād′) *v.* pt. and pp. of **repay.**

re·pair¹ (ri per′) *v., n.* —*v.* **1** put in good condition again; mend: *He repairs shoes.* **2** make up for: *How can I repair the harm done?* —*n.* **1** the act or work of repairing: *Repairs on the school building are made during the summer.* **2** an instance or piece of repairing. **3** a condition fit to be used: *Keeping highways in repair is a provincial responsibility.* **4** a condition with regard to the need for repairs: *The house was in bad repair.* [ME < L *reparare* < *re-* again + *parare* prepare] **—re·pair′a·ble,** *adj.* **—re·pair′er,** *n.*
☛ *Syn. v.* **1.** See note at **mend.**

re·pair² (ri per′) *v.* go (to a place): *After dinner we repaired to the balcony.* [ME < OF *repairer* < LL *repatriare* return to one's own country. Doublet of REPATRIATE.]

re·pair·man (ri per′man′ *or* ri per′mən) *n., pl.* **-men.** a man whose work is repairing machines, etc.

rep·a·ra·ble (rep′ə rə bəl) *adj.* that can be repaired or remedied. [< L *reparabilis*] **—rep′a·ra·bly,** *adv.*

rep·a·ra·tion (rep′ə rā′shən) *n.* **1** a giving of satisfaction or compensation for wrong or injury done. **2** a compensation for wrong or injury. **3** Usually, **reparations,** *pl.* compensation demanded from a defeated enemy for the devastation of territory during war. **4** repairing or being repaired; restoration to good condition. [< LL *reparatio, -onis < reparare.* See REPAIR¹.]

rep·ar·tee (rep′ər tē′) *n.* **1** a witty reply or replies. **2** talk characterized by clever and witty replies. **3** cleverness and wit in making replies. [< F *repartie < repartir* reply, ult. < L *re-* back + *pars, partis* part]

re·pass (rē pas′) *v.* **1** pass back. **2** pass again.

re·past (ri past′) *n.* **1** a meal; food. **2** a taking of food; eating: *a brief repast.* [ME < OF *repast*, ult. < L *re-* again + *pascere* feed]

re·pa·tri·ate (*v.* rē pā′trē āt′ *or* rē pat′rē āt′; *n. usually* rē pā′trē it *or* rē pat′trē it) *v.* **-at·ed, -at·ing.** —*v.* send back or restore to one's own country: *After peace was declared, refugees and prisoners of war were repatriated.* —*n.* a person who is sent back to his own country. [< LL *repatriare*, ult. < L *re-* back + *patria* native land. Doublet of REPAIR².] **—re·pa′tri·a′tion,** *n.*

re·pay (ri pā′) *v.* **-paid, -pay·ing. 1** pay back; give back: *He repaid the money he had borrowed.* **2** make return for: *No thanks can repay such kindness.* **3** make return to: *The boy's success repaid the teacher for her efforts.* [< MF *repaier < re-* back (< L) + *paier* pay < L *pacare* pacify < *pax, pacis* peace] **—re·pay′ment,** *n.*

re·pay·a·ble (ri pā′ə bəl) *adj.* that can be repaid; that must be repaid.

re·peal (ri pēl′) *v., n.* —*v.* take back; withdraw; do away with: *A law may be repealed by act of Parliament.* —*n.* the act of repealing; withdrawal; abolition: *He voted for the repeal of that law.* [ME < AF *repeler*, alteration of OF *rapeler < re-* back + *apeler* call < L *ad-* up + *pellare* call]

re·peat (ri pēt′) *v., n.* —*v.* **1** do or make again: *to repeat an error.* **2** say again: *to repeat a word for emphasis.* **3** say over; recite: *to repeat a poem from memory.* **4** say after another says: *Repeat the oath after me.* **5** tell to another or others: *I promised not to repeat the secret.* **6** *U.S.* vote more than once in an election.
repeat oneself, say what one has already said.
—*n.* **1** the act of repeating. **2** a thing repeated: *We saw the repeat on television.* **3** *Music.* **a** a passage to be repeated. **b** a sign indicating this, usually a row of dots. Coming after a double bar line, it indicates the beginning of the passage to be repeated; before a double bar line, it indicates the end of the passage. [< L *repetere* attack again < *re-* again + *petere* aim at]
☛ *Syn. v.* **1, 2. Repeat, reiterate** = do or say again. **Repeat** is the common word meaning "say, do, make, or perform something over again, once or many times": *The Glee Club will repeat the program next week.* **Reiterate,** more formal, means "repeat again and again something said or a statement, objection, accusation, etc. made": *For months we reiterated our requests for better bus service.*

re·peat·ed (ri pēt′id) *adj.* said, done, made, or happening a number of times: *repeated offers, repeated calls for help.*

re·peat·ed·ly (ri pēt′id lē) *adv.* again and again; more than once.

re·peat·er (ri pēt′ər) *n.* **1** a gun that fires several shots without reloading. **2** a watch or clock that, if a spring is pressed, strikes again the hour it struck last. **3** *U.S.* a person who votes more than once in an election. **4** a student who takes a course again or fails to pass on to the next grade. **5** *Informal.* a person who is repeatedly sent to prison or a reformatory; habitual criminal. **6 a** a device that amplifies voice sounds in telephonic communication. **b** a similar device for amplifying and relaying radio, telegraph, and radar signals. **7** any person or thing that repeats.

---

re·nom′i·nate′	re·num′ber	re′oc·cur′rence	re′o·ri·en·ta′tion	re·pa′per
re·nom·i·na′tion	re′oc·cu·pa′tion	re·of′fer	re·pack′	re·pave′
re′no·ti·fi·ca′tion	re·oc′cu·py′	re·oil′	re·pack′age	
re′no·ti·fy′	re′oc·cur′	re·o′ri·ent	re·paint′	

repeating decimal a decimal in which there is an indefinite repetition of the same figure or series of figures. *Examples*: .3333+, .2323+.

repeating rifle a rifle that fires several shots without reloading.

re·pel (ri pel′) *v.* **-pelled, -pel·ling. 1** force back; drive back; drive away: *They repelled the enemy.* **2** keep off or out; fail to mix with: *Oil and water repel each other. This tent repels moisture.* **3** force apart or away by some inherent force. Particles with similar electric charges repel each other. **4** be displeasing to; cause disgust in. **5** cause dislike; displease. **6** reject. [ME < L *repellere* < *re-* back + *pellere* drive]

re·pel·lent (ri pel′ənt) *adj., n.* —*adj.* **1** unattractive; disagreeable. **2** repelling; driving back. —*n.* something that repels, especially a substance used to keep away insects, such as mosquitoes or blackflies.

re·pent (ri pent′) *v.* **1** feel sorrow or remorse for one's sins or errors. **2** feel remorse for; regret: *to repent one's choice.* [ME < OF *repentir*, ult. < L *re-* repeatedly + *paenitere* cause to regret] —**re·pent′er**, *n.*

re·pent·ance (ri pen′təns) *n.* **1** sorrow for doing wrong. **2** sorrow; regret.

re·pent·ant (ri pen′tənt) *adj.* repenting; feeling repentance or regret; sorry for wrongdoing. [< OF *repentant*, ppr. of *repentir.* See REPENT.] —**re·pent′ant·ly**, *adv.*

re·per·cus·sion (rē′pər kush′ən) *n.* **1** an indirect influence or reaction from an event. **2** a sound flung back; echo. **3** a springing back; rebound; recoil. [< L *repercussio, -onis,* ult. < *re-* back + *per-* thoroughly + *quatere* beat]

rep·er·toire (rep′ər twär′) *n.* the list of plays, operas, parts, pieces, etc. that a company, an actor, a musician, or a singer is prepared to perform. [< F < LL *repertorium.* Doublet of REPERTORY.]

rep·er·to·ry (rep′ər tô′rē) *n., pl.* **-ries. 1** a catalogue or list of things; repertoire. **2** a store or stock of things ready for use. **3** storehouse. **4** the production system of a repertory theatre: *The company is performing three plays in repertory.* [< LL *repertorium* inventory, ult. < *reperire* find, get < *re-* again + *parere* get. Doublet of REPERTOIRE.]

repertory theatre 1 a theatre in which a company of actors, singers, or dancers present a repertoire of productions for a season. **2** a theatre in which one company presents a different production at regular intervals, such as every week, every two weeks, or every month.

rep·e·ti·tion (rep′ə tish′ən) *n.* **1** the act of repeating; doing again; saying again: *Repetition helps learning. Any repetition of the offence will be punished.* **2** the thing repeated. [< L *repetitio, -onis* < *repetere.* See REPEAT.]

rep·e·ti·tious (rep′ə tish′əs) *adj.* full of repetitions; repeating in a tiresome way. —**rep′e·ti′tious·ly**, *adv.* —**rep′e·ti′tious·ness**, *n.*

re·pet·i·tive (ri pet′ə tiv) *adj.* of or characterized by repetition. —**re·pet′i·tive·ly**, *adv.* —**re·pet′i·tive·ness**, *n.*

re·phrase (rē frāz′) *v.* **-phrased, -phras·ing.** phrase again; phrase in a new or different way: *to rephrase a speech, to rephrase a melody.*

re·pine (ri pīn′) *v.* **-pined, -pin·ing.** be discontented; fret; complain. [< *re-* + *pine²*]

re·place (ri plās′) *v.* **-placed, -plac·ing. 1** fill or take the place of. **2** get another in place of. **3** put back; put in place again. —**re·place′a·ble**, *adj.* —**re·plac′er**, *n.*

☛ *Syn.* **1. Replace, supersede, supplant** = take the place of another. **Replace** means take or fill as substitute or successor the place formerly held by another: *When one of the players on the team was hurt, another replaced him.* **Supersede**, a formal word chiefly used of things, especially suggests causing what is replaced to be put aside as out-of-date, no longer useful, etc.: *Buses are superseding streetcars.* **Supplant** when used of a person especially suggests forcing him out and taking over his place by scheming or treachery: *The dictator supplanted the president.*

re·place·ment (ri plās′mənt) *n.* **1** the act of replacing or the state of being replaced. **2** something or someone that replaces. **3** a person who takes the place of another, such as a member of the armed forces assigned to a particular unit to fill a vacancy.

re·play (*v.* rē′plā′; *n.* rē′plā′) *v., n.* —*v.* play (a match, etc.) again. —*n.* **1** a match thus played. **2** a repeated, often slow-motion, showing of part of a television sportscast.

re·plen·ish (ri plen′ish) *v.* fill again; provide a new supply for: *Her wardrobe needs replenishing. Please replenish the fire.* [ME < OF *repleniss-*, a stem of *replenir*, ult. < L *re-* again + *plenus* full] —**re·plen′ish·er**. *n.*

hat, āge, fär; let, ēqual, tèrm; it, īce
hot, ōpen, ôrder; oil, out; cup, pút, rüle,
əbove, takən, pencəl, lemən, circəs

ch, child; ng, long; sh, ship
th, thin; ₮H, then; zh, measure

re·plen·ish·ment (ri plen′ish mənt) *n.* **1** replenishing or being replenished. **2** a fresh supply.

re·plete (ri plēt′) *adj.* abundantly supplied; filled. [ME < L *repletus,* pp. of *replere* < OF *re-* again + *plere* fill]

re·ple·tion (ri plē′shən) *n.* fullness; excessive fullness.

re·plev·in (ri plev′ən) *n., v.* —*n. Law.* **1** the recovery by a person of goods allegedly taken from him, upon his giving security that the case shall be tried in court and the goods returned if he is defeated. **2** the writ by which the goods are thus recovered. —*v.* recover (goods) by replevin. [ME < AF *replevine,* ult. < OF *re-* again + *plevir* pledge]

rep·li·ca (rep′lə kə) *n.* a copy; reproduction: *The artist made a replica of his picture.* [< Ital. *replica* < *replicare* reproduce < L *replicare* unroll. See REPLY.]

rep·li·cate (*v.* rep′lə kāt′; *adj., n.* rep′lə kit) *v.* **-cat·ed, -cat·ing;** *adj., n.* —*v.* **1** duplicate or repeat: *to replicate an experiment.* **2** fold or bend (something) back on itself. —*adj. Botany.* folded back on itself: *a replicate leaf.* —*n.* any of several identical experiments, procedures, etc.

rep·li·ca·tion (rep′lə kā′shən) *n.* **1** the act or process of duplicating or repeating: *the replication of an experiment, the replication of a document.* **2** a copy; reproduction. **3** a reply, especially a rejoinder to an answer. **4** *Law.* the plaintiff's reply to a defendant's plea or counterclaim.

rep·li·ca·tive (rep′lə kā′tiv) *adj.* of, having to do with, or involving replication.

re·ply (ri plī′) *v.* **-plied, -ply·ing;** *n., pl.* **-plies.** —*v.* **1** answer by words or action; answer: *Has she replied to your letter? The rebels replied with a burst of gunfire.* **2** give as an answer: *He replied, "I have no intention of going."* —*n.* a response or answer. [ME < OF *replier* < L *replicare* unroll < *re-* back + *plicare* fold]
☛ *Syn. v.* **1.** See note at **answer.**

re·port (ri pôrt′) *n., v.* —*n.* **1** an account or statement of facts: *a news report.* **2** an account officially expressed, generally in writing: *an annual report.* **3** the sound of a shot or an explosion. **4** common talk; rumor: *Report has it that our neighbors are leaving town.* **5** reputation. —*v.* **1** make a report of; announce. **2** give a formal account of; state officially. **3** take down in writing; write an account of. **4** make a report. **5** act as reporter. **6** repeat or give an account of; describe; tell: *The radio reports the news and weather.* **7** present; present oneself: *Report for duty at 9 a.m.* **8** announce as a wrongdoer; denounce: *report one to the police.* [ME < OF *report* < *reporter* < L *reportare* < *re-* back + *portare* carry]

re·port·a·ble (ri pôr′tə bəl) *adj.* capable of being reported; worth reporting.

re·port·age (ri pôr′tij *or* rə pôr täzh′) *n.* **1** the act or process of reporting news or other factual information, especially in a journalistic style. **2** something reported, such as a news story or other factual account.

report card a report sent regularly by a school to parents or guardians, showing the quality of a student's work.

re·port·ed·ly (ri pôr′təd lē) *adv.* according to reports or rumors: *Several firms are reportedly interested in the new design.*

re·port·er (ri pôr′tər) *n.* **1** a person who reports. **2** a person who gathers news for a newspaper, radio station, etc. **3** a person authorized to write the official reports of law cases.

rep·or·to·ri·al (rep′ər tôr′ē əl) *adj.* of or having to do with reporters or reporting.

re·pose¹ (ri pōz′) *n., v.* **-posed, -pos·ing.** —*n.* **1** rest or sleep: *Do not disturb her repose.* **2** quietness; ease: *She has repose of manner.* **3** peace; calmness. —*v.* **1** lie at rest: *The cat reposed upon the cushion.* **2** lie in a grave. **3** rest from work or toil; take a rest. **4** be supported. **5** depend; rely (on). [< F *repos* < *reposer* < LL *repausare* cause to rest < *re-* again + *pausare* pause]

re·pose² (ri pōz′) *v.* **-posed, -pos·ing.** put; place: *We repose complete confidence in his honesty.* [< L *repositus,* pp. of *reponere* < *re-* back + *ponere* place; modelled on verbs ending in *-pose*]

re·peo′ple   re·pin′   re·plant′   re·pol′ish   re·pop′u·late′
re·pho′to·graph′   re·plan′

re·pose·ful (ri pōz′fəl) *adj.* calm; quiet. —**re·pose′ful·ly,** *adv.* —**re·pose′ful·ness,** *n.*

re·pos·i·to·ry (ri poz′ə tô′rē) *n., pl.* **-ries. 1** a place or container where things are stored or kept: *The box was the repository for old magazines.* **2** a person to whom something is confided or entrusted. [< L *repositorium* < *reponere* replace. See REPOSE[2].]

re·pos·sess (rē′pə zes′) *v.* possess again; get possession of again.

re·pos·ses·sion (rē′pə zesh′ən) *n.* the act of repossessing.

re·pous·sé (rə pü sā′) *adj., n.* —*adj.* **1** raised in relief by hammering on the reverse side. A repoussé design can be made on thin metal. **2** ornamented or made in this manner. —*n.* repoussé work. [< F *repoussé* < *re-* back + *pousser* push]

repp (rep) See **rep**[1].

repr. 1 reprinted. **2** represent; represented.

rep·re·hend (rep′ri hend′) *v.* reprove; rebuke; blame. [ME < L *reprehendere*, originally, pull back < *re-* back + *prehendere* grasp]

rep·re·hen·si·ble (rep′ri hen′sə bəl) *adj.* deserving reproof, rebuke, or blame. —**rep′re·hen′si·bly,** *adv.*

rep·re·hen·sion (rep′ri hen′shən) *n.* reproof; rebuke; blame. [< L *reprehensio, -onis* < *reprehendere.* See REPREHEND.]

rep·re·sent (rep′ri zent′) *v.* **1** stand for; be a sign or symbol of: *The stars on this map represent the cities.* **2** act in place of; speak and act for: *People are elected to represent us in the government.* **3** act the part of: *Each child will represent an animal at the party.* **4** show in a picture, statue, carving, etc.; give a likeness of; portray: *This painting represents the Fathers of Confederation.* **5** be a type of; be an example of: *A log represents a very simple kind of boat.* **6** describe; set forth: *He represented the plan as safe.* **7** bring before the mind; make one think of: *His fears represented the undertaking as impossible.* [< L *repraesentare* < *re-* back + *praesentare* present[2]]

rep·re·sen·ta·tion (rep′ri zen tā′shən) *n.* **1** the act of representing. **2** the condition or fact of being represented: *"Taxation without representation is tyranny."* **3** representatives considered as a group. **4** a likeness; picture; model. **5** symbol; sign. **6** a performance of a play; presentation. **7** the process of forming mental images or ideas. **8** a protest; complaint. **9** an account; statement: *false representations.*

rep·re·sen·ta·tion·al (rep′ri zen tā′shə nəl) *adj.* **1** *Art.* of or having to do with a style that attempts to portray people, things, etc. as they are. **2** of or having to do with representation. —**rep′re·sen·ta′tion·al·ly,** *adv.*

rep·re·sent·a·tive (rep′ri zen′tə tiv) *n., adj.* —*n.* **1** a person appointed or elected to act or speak for others: *He is the club's representative at the convention.* **2 Representative,** in the United States, a member of the House of Representatives. **3** a typical example; type: *The tiger is a representative of the cat family.* —*adj.* **1** having its citizens represented by chosen persons: *a representative government.* **2** representing: *Images representative of animals were made by the children.* **3** serving as an example of; typical: *Oak, birch, and maple are representative North American hardwoods.* —**rep′re·sent′a·tive·ly,** *adv.*

re·press (ri pres′) *v.* **1** prevent from acting; check: *She repressed her desire to laugh.* **2** keep down; put down: *The dictator repressed the revolt.* **3** *Psychoanalysis.* force (a painful or undesirable memory or impulse) from the conscious mind into the unconscious mind. [< L *repressus,* pp. of *reprimere* < *re-* back + *premere* press] —**re·press′er,** *n.*

re·press·i·ble (ri pres′ə bəl) *adj.* that can be repressed.

re·pres·sion (ri presh′ən) *n.* **1** the act of repressing or the state of being repressed. **2** *Psychoanalysis.* a defence mechanism by which unacceptable or painful impulses, emotions, or memories are put out of the conscious mind, their energy or effect remaining (according to Freudian theory) in the unconscious, where it influences personality and behavior.

re·pres·sive (ri pres′iv) *adj.* tending to repress; having power to repress. —**re·pres′sive·ly,** *adv.* —**re·pres′sive·ness,** *n.*

re·prieve (ri prēv′) *v.* **-prieved, -priev·ing;** *n.* —*v.* **1** delay the execution of (a person condemned to death). **2** give relief from any hardship or trouble. —*n.* **1** a delay in carrying out a punishment, especially of the death penalty. **2** a temporary relief from any hardship or trouble. [earlier *repry* < F *repris,* pp. of *reprendre* take back < L *reprehendere* (see REPREHEND); influenced by ME *repreve,* var. of *reprove* in sense of "retest"]

rep·ri·mand (rep′rə mand′) *n., v.* —*n.* a severe or formal

reproof. —*v.* reprove severely or formally. [< F *réprimande* < *réprimer* repress < L *reprimere.* See REPRESS.]

re·print (*v.* rē print′; *n.* rē′print′) *v., n.* —*v.* print again; print a new impression of. —*n.* **1** reprinting; a new impression of printed work. **2** *Philately.* a stamp printed from the original plate after the issue has been discontinued.

re·pris·al (ri prīz′əl) *n.* **1** any measure, economic or military, taken in retaliation by one nation against another. **2** any act of retaliation by one person against another. [ME < OF *reprisaille,* ult. < L *reprehendere* reprehend. See REPREHEND.]

re·prise (rə prēz′) *n. Music.* a repetition or return to a previous theme or subject. [< OF *reprise* < *reprendre* take back]

re·proach (ri prōch′) *n., v.* —*n.* **1** blame. **2** disgrace. **3** any object of blame, censure, or disapproval. **4** an expression of blame, censure, or disapproval. —*v.* **1** blame. **2** disgrace. [< F *reproche* < *reprocher* < VL *repropriare* lay at the door of, ult. < L *re-* again + *prope* near]
☛ *Syn.* **1.** See note at **blame.**

re·proach·ful (ri prōch′fəl) *adj.* full of reproach; expressing reproach. —**re·proach′ful·ly,** *adv.* —**re·proach′ful·ness,** *n.*

re·proach·less (ri prōch′lis) *adj.* without reproach; irreproachable.

rep·ro·bate (rep′rə bāt′) *n., adj., v.* **-bat·ed, -bat·ing.** —*n.* an unprincipled scoundrel. —*adj.* morally abandoned; unprincipled: *reprobate acts.* —*v.* disapprove; condemn; censure. [< LL *reprobatus,* pp. of *reprobare* reprove < L *re-* dis- + *probare* approve < *probus* good. Doublet of REPROVE.]

rep·ro·ba·tion (rep′rə bā′shən) *n.* disapproval; condemnation; censure.

re·pro·duce (rē′prə dyüs′ *or* rē′prə düs′) *v.* **-duced, -duc·ing. 1** produce again: *A radio reproduces sound.* **2** make a copy of: *to reproduce a memo on a photocopier.* **3** produce offspring: *Most plants reproduce by seeds.* —**re′pro·duc′er,** *n.*

re·pro·duc·i·ble (rē′prə dyüs′ə bəl *or* rē′prə düs′ə bəl) *adj.* that can be reproduced.

re·pro·duc·tion (rē′prə duk′shən) *n.* **1** reproducing or being reproduced. **2** a copy. **3** the process by which offspring are produced.

re·pro·duc·tive (rē′prə duk′tiv) *adj.* **1** that reproduces. **2** for or concerned with reproduction. —**re′pro·duc′tive·ly,** *adv.* —**re′pro·duc′tive·ness,** *n.*

re·proof (ri prüf′) *n.* words of blame or disapproval; blame. [ME < OF *reprove* < *reprover;* influenced in form by *proof.* See REPROVE.]

re·prov·a·ble (ri prüv′ə bəl) *adj.* deserving reproof.

re·prov·al (ri prüv′əl) *n.* a reproving or reproof.

re·prove (ri prüv′) *v.* **-proved, -prov·ing.** find fault with; blame: *Reprove the boy for teasing the cat.* [ME < OF *reprover* < LL *reprobare.* Doublet of REPROBATE.] —**re·prov′er,** *n.* —**re·prov′ing·ly,** *adv.*
☛ *Syn.* **Reprove, rebuke** = criticize or blame someone for a fault. **Reprove** suggests expressing disapproval or blame directly to the person at fault, usually with the purpose or hope of correcting the fault: *The principal reproved the students who had been smoking in the locker room.* **Rebuke** means reprove sharply and sternly, with authority and often in public: *The sergeant rebuked the patrolmen who had been neglecting duty.*

rep·tile (rep′tīl) *n., adj.* —*n.* any of a class (Reptilia) of cold-blooded animals that breathe by means of lungs and have a body covered by horny scales and that, unlike amphibians, do not undergo metamorphosis. Present-day reptiles include crocodiles, alligators, lizards, snakes, and turtles; extinct reptiles include the dinosaurs. —*adj.* reptilian. [ME < LL *reptile,* originally neut. adj. < L *repere* crawl]

rep·til·i·an (rep til′ē ən) *adj., n.* —*adj.* **1** of, having to do with, or characteristic of reptiles. **2** mean, contemptible, or grovelling. —*n.* reptile.

re·pub·lic (ri pub′lik) *n.* **1** a nation or state in which the citizens elect representatives to manage the government, the head of which is usually a president rather than a monarch. **2** any body of persons or things: *the republic of authors and scholars.* [< L *res publica* public interest, state]

re·pub·li·can (ri pub′lə kən) *adj., n.* —*adj.* **1** of a republic; like that of a republic. **2** favoring a republic. **3 Republican,** *U.S.* of or having to do with the Republican Party.
—*n.* **1** a person who favors a republic. **2 Republican,** *U.S.* a member of the Republican Party.

re·pub·li·can·ism (ri pub′lə kən iz′əm) *n.* **1** republican government. **2** republican principles; adherence to republican

principles. **3 Republicanism,** *U.S.* the principles or policies of the Republican Party.

Republican Party in the United States, one of the two main political parties.

re·pub·li·ca·tion (rē′pub lə kā′shən) *n.* **1** publication anew. **2** a book, etc. published again.

re·pu·di·ate (ri pyü′dē āt′) *v.* **-at·ed, -at·ing. 1** refuse to accept; reject: *to repudiate a doctrine.* **2** refuse to acknowledge or pay: *to repudiate a debt.* **3** cast off; disown: *to repudiate a son.* [< L *repudiare* < *repudium* divorce, probably originally, a spurning < *re-* back, away + *pod-* kick (related to *pes, pedis* foot)] —**re·pu′di·a·tor,** *n.*

re·pu·di·a·tion (ri pyü′dē ā′shən) *n.* the act of repudiating; fact or condition of being repudiated.

re·pug·nance (ri pug′nəns) *n.* strong dislike, distaste, or aversion.

re·pug·nan·cy (ri pug′nən sē) *n.* repugnance.

re·pug·nant (ri pug′nənt) *adj.* **1** distasteful; disagreeable; offensive: *Work is repugnant to lazy people.* **2** objecting; averse; opposed: *Segregation is repugnant to our idea of equality.* [ME < L *repugnans, -antis,* ppr. of *repugnare* resist < *re-* back + *pugnare* fight] —**re·pug′nant·ly,** *adv.*

re·pulse (ri puls′) *v.* **-pulsed, -puls·ing;** *n.* —*v.* **1** drive back; repel. **2** refuse to accept; reject: *She coldly repulsed the plan.* —*n.* **1** a driving back; being driven back: *After the second repulse, the enemy surrendered.* **2** a refusal; rejection. [< L *repulsus,* pp. of *repellere* repel. See REPEL.]

re·pul·sion (ri pul′shən) *n.* **1** a strong dislike or aversion. **2** a repulse; repelling or being repelled.

re·pul·sive (ri pul′siv) *adj.* **1** causing strong dislike or aversion: *Snakes are repulsive to some people.* **2** tending to drive back or repel. —**re·pul′sive·ly,** *adv.* —**re·pul′sive·ness,** *n.*

rep·u·ta·ble (rep′yə tə bəl) *adj.* having a good reputation; well thought of; in good repute. —**rep′u·ta·bly,** *adv.*

rep·u·ta·tion (rep′yə tā′shən) *n.* **1** what people think and say the character of a person or thing is; character in the opinion of others: *He had the reputation of being very bright.* **2** a good name; high standing in the opinion of others: *The scandal ruined his reputation.* **3** fame: *She has an international reputation.*

re·pute (ri pyüt′) *n., v.* **-put·ed, -put·ing.** —*n.* **1** reputation. **2** a good reputation. —*v.* suppose to be; consider generally: *He is reputed the richest man in the city.* [< L *reputare* < *re-* over + *putare* think]

re·put·ed (ri pyüt′id) *adj.* accounted or generally supposed to be such: *the reputed author of a book.*

re·put·ed·ly (ri pyüt′id lē) *adv.* by repute; supposedly.

re·quest (ri kwest′) *v., n.* —*v.* **1** ask for; ask as a favor: *He requested a loan from the bank.* **2** ask: *He requested her to go with him.* —*n.* **1** the act of asking: *She did it at our request.* **2** what is asked for: *He granted my request.* **3** the state of being asked for or sought after: *She is such a good dancer that she is in great request.* **by request,** in response to a request. [ME < OF *requester* < *requeste* < VL *requaesita* < *requaerere* < L *re-* again + *quaerere* ask] ☛ *Syn. v.* **1.** See note at **ask.**

Req·ui·em or **req·ui·em** (rek′wē əm or rē′kwē əm) *n.* **1** a Mass or similar religious service sung for the dead. **2 a** the music for such a service. **b** a musical composition of similar theme and style. **3** any hymn or other composition for the dead. [< L *requiem,* accus. of *requies* rest; the first word of the Mass for the dead]

re·qui·es·cat in pa·ce (rek′wē es′kat in pä′chā) *Latin.* "May he (or she) rest in peace," a wish or prayer for the dead. *Abbrev.:* R.I.P. [< L *requiescat* may he (or she) rest, ult. < *re-* again + *quies* rest; *in pace* in peace < *pax, pacis* peace]

re·quire (ri kwīr′) *v.* **-quired, -quir·ing. 1** have need for; need; want: *The government requires more money.* **2** command; order; demand: *The rules require us all to be present.* [ME < OF < L *requirere* < *re-* again + *quaerere* ask. Related to REQUEST.] ☛ *Syn.* **2.** See note at **demand.**

re·quire·ment (ri kwīr′mənt) *n.* **1** a need; something needed: *Patience is a requirement in teaching.* **2** a demand; something demanded: *He has filled all requirements for graduation.*

req·ui·site (rek′wə zit) *adj., n.* —*adj.* required by circumstances; needed; necessary: *the qualities requisite for a leader, the number*

Republican Party   957   resemblance

hat, āge, fär; let, ēqual, tėrm; it, īce
hot, ōpen, ôrder; oil, out; cup, pút, rüle,
əbove, takən, pencəl, lemən, circəs
ch, child; ng, long; sh, ship
th, thin; ₮H, then; zh, measure

of votes requisite for election. —*n.* the thing needed: *Food and air are requisites for life.* [ME < L *requisitus,* pp. of *requirere.* See REQUIRE.] —**req′ui·site·ly,** *adv.* —**req′ui·site·ness,** *n.*

req·ui·si·tion (rek′wə zish′ən) *n., v.* —*n.* **1** the act of requiring. **2** a demand made, especially a formal written demand: *the requisition of supplies for troops.* **3** the state of being required for use or called into service: *The car was in constant requisition for errands.* **4** an essential condition; requirement. —*v.* **1** demand or take by authority: *to requisition supplies or labor.* **2** make demands upon: *The army requisitioned the village for food.*

re·quit·al (ri kwīt′əl) *n.* a repayment; payment; return: *What requital can we make for all his kindness to us?*

re·quite (ri kwīt′) *v.* **-quit·ed, -quit·ing. 1** pay back; make return for: *The Bible tells us to requite evil with good.* **2** make return to: *The knight requited the boy for his warning.* [< *re-* + *quite,* var. of *quit*]

rere·dos (rēr′dos) *n.* a screen or a decorated part of the wall behind an altar. [ME < AF **reredos,* ult. < *rere* rear[1] + *dos* back < L *dossus,* var. of *dorsum*]

re·route (rē rüt′ *or* -rout′) *v.* **-rout·ed, -rout·ing.** send by a new or different route.

re·run (*v.* rē run′; *n.* rē′run′) *v.* **-ran, -run·ning;** *n.* —*v.* run again. —*n.* **1** running again. **2** a television program or motion-picture film that is shown again.

re·sale (rē′sāl′ *or* rē sāl′) *n.* **1** the act of selling again. **2** a selling at retail: *The store has a 20 percent markup over the wholesale price for resale.*

re·scind (ri sind′) *v.* deprive of force; repeal; cancel: *to rescind a law.* [< L *rescindere* < *re-* back + *scindere* cut]

re·scis·sion (ri sizh′ən) *n.* the act of rescinding. [< LL *rescissio, -onis* < L *rescindere.* See RESCIND.]

re·script (rē′skript) *n.* **1** a written answer to a question or petition. **2** an edict; decree; an official announcement. **3** rewriting. [< L *rescriptum,* originally neut. pp. of *rescribere* write in reply < *re-* back + *scribere* write]

res·cue (res′kyü) *v.* **-cued, -cu·ing;** *n.* —*v.* **1** save from danger, capture, harm, etc.; free; deliver. **2** *Law.* take (a person) forcibly or unlawfully from a jail, the police, etc.; take (property) unlawfully from legal custody. —*n.* **1** the act of saving or freeing from danger, capture, harm, etc. **2** *Law.* the forcible or unlawful taking of a person or thing from the care of the law. [ME < OF *rescoure,* ult. < L *re-* back + *ex* out + *quatere* shake] —**res′cu·er,** *n.*
☛ *Syn. v.* **1.** Rescue, deliver = save or free from danger, harm, or restraint. **Rescue** suggests saving, by quick and forceful action, a person from immediate or threatened danger or harm, such as death, injury, attack, capture, confinement, etc.: *Searchers rescued the boys lost in the mountains.* **Deliver** suggests setting someone free from something holding him in captivity or under its power or control, such as prison, slavery, oppression, suffering, temptation, evil, etc.: *Advancing troops delivered the prisoners.*

re·search (ri sėrch′ *or* rē′sėrch) *n., v.* —*n.* a careful hunting for facts or truth; inquiry; investigation: *Medical research has done much to lessen disease.* —*v.* **1** carry out research. **2** inquire into (something) thoroughly; investigate. [< MF *recherche* < *re-* again + *cerche* search]

re·search·er (ri sėr′chər *or* rē′sėr chər) *n.* a person who carries out research; investigator.

re·seat (rē sēt′) *v.* **1** seat again. **2** provide with a new seat or seats.

re·sec·tion (ri sek′shən) *n.* the removal of an organ, bone, part, etc. by surgery.

re·sem·blance (ri zem′bləns) *n.* a similar appearance; likeness: *Twins often show great resemblance.* [< AF]
☛ *Syn.* **Resemblance, similarity** = likeness to another or between two persons or things. **Resemblance** emphasizes looking alike or having some of the same external features or superficial qualities: *There is some resemblance between the accounts of the fire, but all the important details are different.* **Similarity** especially suggests being of the same kind or nature, having some of the same

---

re′pub·li·ca′tion	re·quick′en	re′re·lease′	re·sched′ule	re·seg′re·gate′
re·pub′lish	re·read′	re′re·vise′	re·score′	re′seg·re·ga′tion
re·pur′chase	re·cord′	re·roll′	re·screen′	re·sell′
re·pur′i·fi·ca′tion	re·reg′is·ter	re·sad′dle	re·seal′	
re′pur′i·fy	re′reg·is·tra′tion	re·say′	re·seed′	

essential qualities and usually a strong resemblance: *The similarity between the two reports suggests that one person wrote both.*

re·sem·ble (ri zem′bəl) *v.* **-bled, -bling.** be like; be similar to; have likeness to in form, figure, or qualities. [ME < OF *resembler*, ult. < L *re-* again + *similis* similar] —**re·sem′bler,** *n.*

re·sent (ri zent′) *v.* feel injured and angry at; feel indignation at: *Our cat seems to resent having anyone sit in its chair.* [< F *ressentir*, ult. < L *re-* back + *sentire* feel] —**re·sent′er,** *n.*

re·sent·ful (ri zent′fəl) *adj.* feeling resentment; injured and angry; showing resentment. —**re·sent′ful·ly,** *adv.* —**re·sent′ful·ness,** *n.*

re·sent·ment (ri zent′mənt) *n.* the feeling that one has at being wronged or insulted; indignation.

re·ser·pine (ri sèr′ pēn, ri sèr′pən, *or* res′ər pin) *n.* a drug extracted from the roots of a SE Asian shrub of the dogbane family, used to lower blood pressure and as a sedative and tranquillizer. *Formula:* $C_{33}H_{40}N_2O_9$

res·er·va·tion (rez′ər vā′shən) *n.* **1** keeping back; hiding in part; something not expressed: *She outwardly approved of the plan with the mental reservation that she would change it to suit herself.* **2** a limiting condition: *The committee accepted the plan with reservations plainly stated.* **3** land set aside for a special purpose; reserve. **4** an arrangement to keep a thing for a person; securing of accommodations, etc.: *We make reservations in advance for rooms at a hotel, seats at a theatre or on an airliner, etc.* **5** something reserved. **6** in Canada, the provision made for the withholding of royal assent to a bill, federal or provincial, until it has been re-examined.

re·serve (ri zèrv′) *v.* **-served, -serv·ing;** *n.* —*v.* **1** keep or hold back; retain: *to reserve the right to withdraw an offer after a certain time, to reserve criticism.* **2** set apart or save for future use. **3** set aside or have set aside for the use of a particular person or persons: *to reserve a table for two.* —*n.* **1** something kept back or set aside for future use or contingency: *a reserve of strength, a small cash reserve.* **2** *Finance.* capital or assets that can be turned into cash quickly to meet liabilities, contingencies, etc. **3** Often, **reserves,** *pl.* **a** a part of a military force kept ready to help the main force in battle. **b** a part of the armed forces of a nation that in peace time is not on full-time, active duty. **4** a tract of public land set apart by the government for a specific purpose, especially for the preservation of wild animals and plants; preserve. **5** a tract of land set apart, usually by treaty, for the exclusive use of Amerindian peoples. **6** a person kept available to act as a substitute: *He is a reserve for the basketball team.* **7** the act of reserving. **8** the fact or condition of being reserved: *We still have a bit of cash in reserve.* **9** (*adjl.*) kept in reserve; being a reserve. **10** restraint, formality, or coolness of manner. **11** an exception or qualification to the acceptance of some idea, belief, etc. [ME < OF < L *reservare* < *re-* back + *servare* keep] —**re·serv′er,** *n.*

reserve army the militia: *Members of the reserve army are not full-time soldiers.*

re·served (ri zèrvd′) *adj.* **1** kept in reserve; kept by special arrangement: *reserved seats.* **2** set apart. **3** self-restrained in action or speech. **4** disposed to keep to oneself.

re·serv·ed·ly (ri zèr′vid lē) *adv.* in a reserved manner.

re·serv·ist (ri zèr′vist) *n.* a member of the reserve.

res·er·voir (rez′ər vwär′ *or* rez′ər vwôr′) *n.* **1** a place where water is collected and stored for use: *This reservoir supplies the entire city.* **2** anything to hold a liquid: *A fountain pen has an ink reservoir.* **3** a place where anything is collected and stored: *His mind was a reservoir of facts.* **4** a great supply. [< F *réservoir* < *réserver* reserve]

re·set (*v.* rē set′; *n.* rē′set′) *v.* **-set, -set·ting;** *n.* —*v.* set again: *The diamonds were reset in platinum. John's broken arm had to be reset.* —*n.* **1** the act of resetting. **2** the thing reset.

re·shape (rē shāp′) *v.* **-shaped, -shap·ing.** shape anew; form into a new or different shape.

re·side (ri zīd′) *v.* **-sid·ed, -sid·ing. 1** live (*in* or *at*) for a long time; dwell. **2** be (*in*); exist (*in*): *Her charm resides in her happy smile.* [< L *residere* < *re-* back + *sedere* sit, settle] —**re·sid′er,** *n.*

res·i·dence (rez′ə dəns) *n.* **1** a place where a person lives; house; home. **2** residing; living; dwelling. **3** a period of residing in a place. **4** a building in which students, nurses, etc. live.

in residence, a living in a place: *The owner of the house is not in*

residence. **b** living in an institution while on duty or doing active work: *a doctor in residence.*

res·i·den·cy (rez′ə dən sē) *n., pl.* **-cies. 1** residence. **2** *Historical.* the official residence in India of a representative of the Governor General at a native court.

res·i·dent (rez′ə dənt) *n., adj.* —*n.* **1** a person living in a place, not a visitor. **2** a resident physician, especially one who has completed internship. **3** an official sent to live in a foreign land to represent his country. **4** *Historical.* a representative of the British Governor General of India at a native court.
—*adj.* **1** staying; dwelling in a place. A resident owner lives on his property. **2** living in a place while on duty or doing active work. **3** not migratory: *English sparrows are resident birds.* [ME < L *residens, -entis,* ppr. of *residere.* See RESIDE.]

res·i·den·tial (rez′ə den′shəl) *adj.* **1** of, having to do with, or allocated or zoned for homes or residences: *They live in a good residential district.* **2** designating a school that provides living accommodation for students. **3** used as a residence: *a residential hotel.* **4** of or having to do with residence: *a residential qualification for schoolteachers.*

residential school *Cdn. North.* a boarding school operated or subsidized by the federal government to accommodate students, especially Indian and Inuit students, attending classes at a considerable distance from their homes.

re·sid·u·al (ri zij′ü əl) *adj., n.* —*adj.* **1** of or forming a residue; remaining; left over. **2** *Geology.* resulting in the weathering of rock: *residual clay soil, a residual deposit.* —*n.* **1** the amount left over; remainder. **2** a residual quantity. **3** a fee paid to a performer or writer for each rerun of a radio or television broadcast, etc.

re·sid·u·ar·y (ri zij′ü er′ē) *adj.* entitled to the remainder of an estate.

res·i·due (rez′ə dyü′ *or* rez′ə dü′) *n.* what remains after a part is taken; remainder: *The syrup had dried up, leaving a sticky residue.* **2** *Law.* the part of a testator's estate that is left after all debts, charges, and particular devises and bequests have been satisfied: *Mr. Smith's will directed that the residue of his property should go to his son.* **3** *Chemistry.* an atom or group of atoms considered as a radical or part of a molecule. [< F < L *residuum,* neut. adj., left over. Doublet of RESIDUUM.]

re·sid·u·um (ri zij′ü əm) *n., pl.* **-sid·u·a** (-zij′ü ə). what is left at the end of any process; residue; remainder. [< L. Doublet of RESIDUE.]

re·sign (ri zīn′) *v.* **1** take oneself out of a job, position, etc.; leave; depart (*often used with* from): *He resigned in a fit of rage. She has resigned from the club.* **2** give up: *She resigned her seat in Parliament.* **3** give in or yield, often unwillingly, but without complaint (*used with a reflexive pronoun*): *He had to resign himself to a week in bed when he hurt his back.* [ME < OF < L *resignare* unseal, ult. < *re-* back + *signum* seal]

☞ *Usage.* **Resign** is often followed by **from,** though sometimes the object follows without the **from:** *He resigned from the editorship of the magazine.* Or: *He resigned the editorship of the magazine.*

res·ig·na·tion (rez′ig nā′shən) *n.* **1** the act of resigning. **2** a written statement giving notice that one resigns. **3** patient acceptance; quiet submission: *She bore the pain with resignation.*

re·signed (ri zīnd′) *adj.* showing or feeling resignation; accepting, often unwillingly; submissive: *resigned to an unhappy fate.*

re·sign·ed·ly (ri zīn′id lē) *adv.* in a resigned manner; with resignation.

re·sil·i·ence (ri zil′ē əns *or* ri zil′yəns) *n.* **1** the power of springing back; elasticity; a resilient quality or nature: *Rubber has resilience.* **2** buoyancy; cheerfulness.

re·sil·i·en·cy (ri zil′ē ən sē *or* ri zil′yən sē) *n.* resilience.

re·sil·i·ent (ri zil′ē ənt *or* ri zil′yənt) *adj.* **1** springing back; returning to the original form or position after being bent, compressed, or stretched: *resilient steel, resilient turf.* **2** buoyant; cheerful: *a resilient nature that throws off trouble.* [< L *resiliens, -entis,* ppr. of *resilire* rebound < *re-* back + *salire* jump]

res·in (rez′ən) *n., v.* —*n.* **1** a sticky, yellow or brown substance that flows from certain plants and trees, especially the pine and fir. It is used in medicine and varnish. The harder portion of resin remaining after heating is called rosin. **2** any similar substance that is made synthetically. Artificial resins are used in the manufacture of plastics. —*v.* rub, coat, or treat with resin. [< L *resina*]

res·in·ous (rez′ə nəs) *adj.* **1** of resin. **2** like resin; containing resin; full of resin.

re·sist (ri zist′) *v.* **1** act against (something); strive against;

re·send′   re·sew′   re·ship′ment   re·shuf′fle   re·sil′ver
re·set′tle   re·sharp′en   re·shoot′
re·set′tle·ment   re·ship′   re·show′

oppose: *The window resisted his efforts to open it.* 2 act against something; oppose something: *Do not resist.* 3 strive successfully against; keep from: *I could not resist laughing.* 4 withstand the action or effect of (something harmful or hurtful): *A healthy body resists disease.* [< L *resistere* < *re-* back + *sistere* make a stand] —**re·sist′er**, *n.*

☛ *Syn.* 1. See note at **oppose**.

re·sist·ance (ri zis′təns) *n.* 1 the act of resisting: *The bank clerk made no resistance to the robbers.* 2 the power to resist: *She has little resistance to germs and so is often ill.* 3 a thing or act that resists; an opposing force; opposition. An airplane can overcome the resistance of the air and go in the desired direction, while a balloon simply drifts. 4 *Electricity.* the property of a conductor that opposes the passage of a current and changes electric energy into heat. The elements of electric stoves have high resistance. Copper has a low resistance. 5 a conductor, coil, etc. that offers resistance. 6 Usually, **Resistance,** people in a country occupied or controlled by another country who secretly organize and fight for their freedom: *the French Resistance in World War II.*

resistance coil a coil or wire made of metal that has a high resistance, used especially for measuring resistance, reducing voltage or amperage, and producing heat.

re·sist·ant (ri zis′tənt) *adj.* resisting.

re·sist·i·bil·i·ty (ri zis′tə bil′ə tē) *n.* the quality of being resistible.

re·sist·i·ble (ri zis′tə bəl) *adj.* capable of being resisted.

re·sist·less (ri zist′lis) *adj.* that cannot be resisted: *A resistless impulse made him wander over the earth.*

re·sis·tor (ri zis′tər) *n.* a conducting body or device used in an electric circuit, etc. because of its resistance.

re·sole (rē sōl′) *v.* **-soled, -sol·ing.** put a new sole on (a shoe, etc.).

re·sol·u·ble¹ (ri zol′yə bəl) *adj.* capable of being resolved.

re·sol·u·ble² (rē sol′yə bəl) *adj.* capable of being dissolved again.

res·o·lute (rez′ə lüt′) *adj.* 1 determined; firm: *He was resolute in his attempt to climb to the top of the mountain.* 2 bold: *A soldier must be resolute in battle.* 3 indicating firmness, boldness, etc.: *a resolute air.* [< L *resolutus,* pp. of *resolvere* resolve. See RESOLVE.] —**res′o·lute·ly,** *adv.*

res·o·lu·tion (rez′ə lü′shən) *n.* 1 something decided on; thing determined: *He made a resolution to get up early.* 2 the quality or power of holding firmly to a purpose; determination. 3 a formal expression of opinion, especially as agreed upon by a group: *The club passed a resolution thanking the consultant for her help.* 4 the act or an instance of determining or solving: *the resolution of a problem.* 5 the act or process of breaking or separating into parts. 6 *Medicine.* a return to a normal condition, especially the subsiding of inflammation, as in a lung. 7 *Music.* the progression of a chord from dissonance to consonance. 8 the power of a telescope, etc. to produce separate images of closely adjacent objects or sources of light.

re·solve (ri zolv′) *v.* **-solved, -solv·ing;** *n.* —*v.* 1 make up one's mind firmly; determine: *He resolved to do better work in the future.* 2 express (a decision) formally, especially by vote: *It was resolved by the committee that the project be dropped.* 3 separate into parts or elements: *to resolve a chemical compound.* 4 answer and explain: *Her letter resolved all our doubts.* 5 solve: *to resolve a problem.* 6 change: *The assembly resolved itself into committees.* 7 *Medicine.* cause (inflammation) to subside. 8 *Music.* **a** follow (a dissonant tone or chord) by another to produce consonance. **b** of a dissonant tone or chord, progress to consonance. 9 make distinguishable or visible the separate adjacent parts of, as by means of a telescope: *to resolve a cluster of stars with a high-powered telescope.* —*n.* 1 something determined: *a resolve to do better.* 2 firmness in carrying out a purpose; determination. [< L *resolvere* < *re-* un- + *solvere* loosen] —**re·solv′a·ble,** *adj.* —**re·solv′er,** *n.*

☛ *Syn. v.* 1. See note at **decide**.

re·solved (ri zolvd′) *adj.* determined; resolute.

re·solv·ed·ly (ri zol′vid lē) *adv.* in a determined manner; with resolution.

res·o·nance (rez′ə nəns) *n.* 1 a resounding quality; being resonant: *the resonance of an organ.* 2 *Physics.* a reinforcing and prolonging of sound by reflection or by vibration of other objects. The sounding board of a piano gives it resonance. 3 *Electricity.* the condition of a circuit adjusted to allow the greatest flow of current at a certain frequency. A radio set must be in resonance to receive music or speech from a radio station.

res·o·nant (rez′ə nənt) *adj.* 1 resounding; continuing to sound;

hat, āge, fär; let, ēqual, tėrm; it, īce
hot, ōpen, ôrder; oil, out; cup, pút, rüle,
əbove, takən, pencəl, lemən, circəs
ch, child; ng, long; sh, ship
th, thin; ŦH, then; zh, measure

echoing: *a resonant tone.* 2 tending to increase or prolong sound: *a guitar has a resonant body.* 3 of or in resonance. [< L *resonans, -antis,* ppr. of *resonare,* ult. < *re-* back + *sonus* sound] —**res′o·nant·ly,** *adv.*

res·o·nate (rez′ə nāt′) *v.* **-nat·ed -nat·ing.** resound; exhibit resonance. [< L *resonare.* Doublet of RESOUND.]

res·o·na·tor (rez′ə nā′tər) *n.* 1 something that produces resonance; an appliance for increasing sound by resonance. 2 a device for detecting electromagnetic radiation, as radio broadcasting waves. [< NL]

re·sorb (ri sôrb′ *or* re zôrb′) *v.* absorb again.

res·or·cin (rez ôr′sən) *n.* resorcinol. [< *res(in)* + *orcin,* a chemical compound (< NL *orcina*)]

res·or·cin·ol (rez ôr′sə nol′ *or* rez ôr′sə nōl′) *n.* a colorless crystalline substance that is used in medicine as an antiseptic, and in making dyes, drugs, etc. *Formula:* $C_6H_4(OH)_2$ [< *resorcin + -ol*]

re·sorp·tion (ri sôrp′shən *or* ri zôrp′shən) *n.* the action or process of resorbing.

re·sort (ri zôrt′) *v., n.* —*v.* 1 go; go often: *Many people resort to the beaches in hot weather.* 2 turn for help: *to resort to violence.* —*n.* 1 an assembling; going to often: *A park is a place of popular resort in good weather.* 2 a place people go to, usually for relaxation or recreation: *There are many summer resorts in the mountains.* 3 the act of turning for help: *The resort to force is a poor substitute for persuasion.* 4 a person or thing turned to for help. [ME < OF *resortir* < *re-* back + *sortir* go out]

re·sound (ri zound′) *v.* 1 give back sound; echo: *The hills resounded when he shouted.* 2 give back (sound); echo (sound). 3 sound loudly: *Radios resound from every house.* 4 be filled with sound: *The room resounded with the children's shouts.* 5 repeat loudly: *to resound a hero's praise.* 6 be much talked about. [< L *resonare,* ult. < *re-* back + *sonus* sound. Doublet of RESONATE.] —**re·sound′ing·ly,** *adv.*

re·source (ri zôrs′ *or* ri sôrs′) *n.* 1 any supply that will meet a need: *We have resources of money, of quick wit, and of strength.* 2 **resources,** *pl.* the actual and potential wealth of a country; natural resources. 3 any means of getting success or getting out of trouble: *Climbing a tree is a cat's resource when chased by a dog.* 4 skill in meeting difficulties, getting out of trouble, etc. [< F *resource,* ult. < L *re-* again + *surgere* rise]

re·source·ful (ri zôrs′fəl *or* ri sôrs′-) *adj.* good at thinking of ways to do things; quick-witted. —**re·source′ful·ly,** *adv.* —**re·source′ful·ness,** *n.*

resp. 1 respectively. 2 respondent.

re·spect (ri spekt′) *n., v.* —*n.* 1 honor; esteem: *Children should show respect to those who are older and wiser.* 2 consideration; regard: *Show respect for other people's property.* 3 **respects,** *pl.* expressions of respect; regards. 4 a point; matter; detail: *The plan is unwise in many respects.* 5 relation; reference.
in respect of, with reference or comparison to.
in respect that, because of the fact that; since.
with respect to, with relation, reference, or regard to (something): *We must plan with respect to the future.*
—*v.* 1 feel or show honor or esteem for: *We respect an honest person.* 2 show consideration for: *Respect the ideas and feelings of others.* 3 relate to; refer to; be connected with. [< L *respectus* < *respicere* look back, have regard for < *re-* back + *specere* look] —**re·spect′er,** *n.*

☛ *Syn. n.* 2. **Respect, regard** = consideration, felt or shown, for someone or something of recognized worth or value. **Respect** emphasizes recognizing or judging the worth or value of someone or something and paying the consideration or honor due: *A soldier may feel respect for an officer he dislikes.* **Regard** emphasizes seeing that a person or thing is entitled to consideration, appreciation, or admiration, and usually suggests a kindly, friendly, or sympathetic feeling: *A person who reads another's mail has no regard for other people's privacy.*

re·spect·a·bil·i·ty (ri spek′tə bil′ə tē) *n., pl.* **-ties.** 1 the quality or condition of being respectable. 2 respectable social standing.

re·spect·a·ble (ri spek′tə bəl) *adj.* 1 worthy of respect; having a good reputation: *Respectable citizens obey the laws.* 2 having fair social standing; honest and decent: *His parents were poor, but*

respectable, people. 3 fairly good; moderate in size or quality: *John's record in his career was respectable but not brilliant.* **4** good enough to use; fit to be seen. —**re·spect′a·bly,** *adv.*

re·spect·ful (ri spekt′fəl) *adj.* showing respect; polite. —**re·spect′ful·ly,** *adv.* —**re·spect′ful·ness,** *n.*

re·spect·ing (ri spek′ting) *prep.* regarding; about; concerning: *A discussion arose respecting the merits of different automobiles.*

re·spec·tive (ri spek′tiv) *adj.* belonging to each; particular; individual: *The wrestlers returned to their respective corners.*

re·spec·tive·ly (ri spek′tiv lē) *adv.* as regards each one in his turn or in the order mentioned: *Brown, Smyth, and Jones are 27, 43, and 35 years old respectively.*

re·spell (rē′spel′) *v.* spell again or in a different way; especially, spell in a phonetic alphabet or writing system of another language.

res·pi·ra·tion (res′pə rā′shən) *n.* **1** the act of inhaling and exhaling; breathing. **2** *Biology.* the processes by which an animal, plant, or living cell secures oxygen from the air or water, distributes it, combines it with substances in the tissues, and gives off carbon dioxide.

res·pi·ra·tor (res′pə rā′tər) *n.* **1** a device worn over the nose and mouth to prevent inhaling harmful substances. **2** a device used to help a person breathe.

res·pi·ra·to·ry (res′pə rə tô′rē) *adj.* having to do with or used for breathing. The lungs are respiratory organs.

re·spire (ri spīr′) *v.* **-spired, -spir·ing.** inhale and exhale; breathe. [< L *respirare* < *re-* regularly + *spirare* breathe]

res·pite (res′pit *or* res′pīt) *n., v.* **-pit·ed, -pit·ing.** —*n.* **1** a time of relief and rest; lull: *A thick cloud brought a respite from the glare of the sun.* **2** a putting off; delay, especially in carrying out a sentence of death; reprieve. —*v.* give a respite to. [ME < OF < VL *respectus* delay < LL *respectus* expectation < L *respectare* wait for. Related to RESPECT.]

re·splend·ence (ri splen′dəns) *n.* splendor; great brightness; gorgeous appearance.

re·splend·en·cy (ri splen′dən sē) *n.* resplendence.

re·splend·ent (ri splen′dənt) *adj.* very bright; shining; splendid: *The queen was resplendent with jewels.* [ME < L *resplendens, -entis,* ppr. of *resplendere* glitter < *re-* back + *splendere* shine] —**re·splend′ent·ly,** *adv.*

re·spond (ri spond′) *v.* **1** answer; reply. **2** act in answer; react: *A dog responds to kind treatment by loving its master.* [ME < OF < L *respondere* < *re-* in return + *spondere* promise]
☞ *Syn.* **1.** See note at **answer.**

re·spond·ent (ri spon′dənt) *adj., n.* —*adj.* answering; responding. —*n.* **1** a person who responds. **2** a defendant, especially in a divorce case.

re·sponse (ri spons′) *n.* **1** an answer by word or act. **2** a set of words said or sung by the congregation or choir in a religious service, in answer to the minister. **3** *Psychology or physiology.* any activity or behavior resulting from stimulation; reaction. [< L *responsum,* originally neut. pp. of *respondere* respond. See RESPOND.]

re·spon·si·bil·i·ty (ri spon′sə bil′ə tē) *n., pl.* **-ties. 1** a being responsible; obligation: *A little child does not feel much responsibility.* **2** something for which one is responsible: *Keeping house and caring for the children are her responsibilities.*

re·spon·si·ble (ri spon′sə bəl) *adj.* **1** obliged or expected to account (*for*): *Each pupil is responsible for the care of the books given him. The government is responsible to the people for its proper conduct of the country's affairs.* **2** deserving credit or blame: *The bad weather is responsible for the small attendance.* **3** trustworthy; reliable: *A responsible person should take care of the money.* **4** involving obligation or duties: *The Prime Minister holds a very responsible position.* **5** able to tell right from wrong; able to think and act reasonably: *Babies are not responsible.* —**re·spon′si·ble·ness,** *n.* —**re·spon′si·bly,** *adv.*

responsible government 1 a form of government in which a cabinet, selected from the members of an elected legislature, acts as the executive, taking decisions for which it is then held collectively responsible and accountable to the legislature. **2 Responsible Government,** this system of government as it existed in Canada from 1848-1867.

re·spon·sive (ri spon′siv) *adj.* **1** making answer; responding: *a responsive glance.* **2** easily moved; responding readily: *having a responsive nature, be responsive to kindness.* **3** using or containing

responses: *responsive reading in church in which minister and congregation read in turn.* —**re·spon′sive·ly,** *adv.* —**re·spon′sive·ness,** *n.*

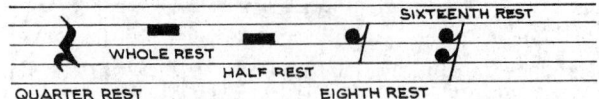

Musical rests (def. 7). A whole rest has the same duration as a whole note, a half rest the same as a half note, and so on.

rest¹ (rest) *n., v.* —*n.* **1** sleep; repose: *a good night's rest.* **2** ease after work or effort; freedom from activity: *Allow an hour for rest.* **3** freedom from anything that tires, troubles, disturbs, or pains; respite: *The medicine gave the sick man a short rest from pain.* **4** the absence of motion: *The driver brought the car to rest.* **5** a support: *a rest for a billiard cue.* **6** a place of rest: *sailors' rest.* **7** *Music.* **a** a measured period of silence. **b** a mark used in a musical score to indicate a period of silence of specific duration. **8** *Reading.* a pause. **9** death; the grave.
at rest, a asleep. **b** not moving: *The lake was at rest.* **c** free from pain, trouble, etc.: *The injured man is now at rest.* **d** dead.
lay to rest, bury: *Lay his bones to rest.*
—*v.* **1** be still; sleep: *Lie down and rest.* **2** be free from work, trouble, pain, etc.: *He was able to rest during his holidays.* **3** stop moving; cause to stop moving: *The ball rested at the bottom of the hill.* **4** give rest to; refresh by rest: *Stop and rest your horse.* **5** lie, recline, sit, lean, etc. for rest or ease: *He spent the whole day resting in a chair.* **6** be supported: *The ladder rests against the wall.* **7** fix or be fixed: *Our eyes rested on the open book.* **8** be at ease: *Don't let her rest until she promises to visit us.* **9** become inactive; let remain inactive: *Let the matter rest. Rest the matter there.* **10** place for support; lay; lean: *to rest one's head in one's hands.* **11** rely (*on*); trust (*in*); depend; be based: *Our hope rests on you.* **12** cause to rely or depend; base: *We rest our hope on you.* **13** be found; be present: *In a democracy, government rests with the people.* **14** be dead; lie in the grave. **15** *Law.* end voluntarily the introduction of evidence in (a case): *The lawyer rested his case.* **16** of agricultural land, be unused for crops, especially in order to restore fertility. [OE *restan*]
☞ *Hom.* **wrest.**

rest² (rest) *n., v.* —*n.* what is left; those that are left. —*v.* continue to be: *You may rest assured that I will keep my promise.* [< F *reste,* ult. < L *restare* be left < *re-* back + *stare* stand]
☞ *Hom.* **wrest.**

re·state (rē stāt′) *v.* **-stat·ed, -stat·ing. 1** state again or anew. **2** state in a new way.

re·state·ment (rē stāt′mənt) *n.* **1** a statement made again. **2** a new statement.

res·tau·rant (res′tə ront *or* res′tront) *n.* a place to buy and eat a meal. [< F *restaurant,* originally ppr. or *restaurer* restore]

res·tau·ra·teur (res′tə rə tėr′) *n.* the owner or manager of a restaurant. [< F]

rest cure a treatment for mental or nervous disorders, consisting of rest and seclusion, a healthful diet, massage, etc.

rest·ful (rest′fəl) *adj.* **1** full of rest; giving rest. **2** quiet; peaceful. —**rest′ful·ly,** *adv.* —**rest′ful·ness,** *n.*

res·ti·tu·tion (res′tə tyü′shən *or* res′tə tü′shən) *n.* **1** the giving back of what has been lost or taken away. **2** the act of making good any loss, damage, or injury: *It is only fair that those who do the damage should make restitution.* [< L *restitutio, -onis,* ult. < *re-* again + *statuere* set up]

res·tive (res′tiv) *adj.* **1** restless; uneasy. **2** hard to manage. **3** refusing to go ahead; balky. [ME < OF *restif* motionless < *rester* < L *restare.* See REST².] —**res′tive·ly,** *adv.* —**res′tive·ness,** *n.*

rest·less (rest′lis) *adj.* **1** unable to rest; uneasy: *The dog seemed restless as if he sensed some danger.* **2** without rest or sleep; not restful: *The sick child passed a restless night.* **3** rarely or never still or quiet; always moving. —**rest′less·ly,** *adv.* —**rest′less·ness,** *n.*

re·stock (rē stok′) *v.* supply with a new stock; replenish.

res·to·ra·tion (res′tə rā′shən) *n.* **1** the act of restoring or the condition of being restored: *the restoration of health, the restoration of a monarch.* **2** something restored. **3 Restoration,** in England: **a** the re-establishment of the monarchy in 1660 under Charles II. **b** the period from 1660 to 1688 during which Charles II and James II reigned.

re·stor·a·tive (ri stôr′ə tiv) *adj., n.* —*adj.* capable of restoring:

tending to restore health or strength. —*n.* something that restores health and strength.

re·store (ri stôr′) *v.* **-stored, -stor·ing. 1** bring back; establish again: *to restore order.* **2** bring back to a former condition or to a normal condition: *The old house has been restored.* **3** give back; put back: *The thief was forced to restore the money to its owner.* [ME < OF < L *restaurare*] **—re·stor′er,** *n.*
☞ *Syn.* **2.** See note at **renew.**

re·strain (ri strān′) *v.* **1** hold back; keep down; keep in check; keep within limits: *She could not restrain her curiosity.* **2** keep in prison; confine. [ME < OF *restreindre, restraindre* < L *restringere* restrict. See RESTRICT.] **—re·strain′a·ble,** *adj.* **—re·strain′er,** *n.*
☞ *Syn.* **1.** See note at **check.**

re·strain·ed·ly (ri strān′id lē *or* ri strānd′lē) *adv.* in a restrained manner; with restraint.

re·straint (ri strānt′) *n.* **1** restraining or being restrained. **2** a means of restraining: *A horse's bridle is a restraint.* **3** control of natural feeling; reserve. [ME < OF *restraint(e)* < *restraindre.* See RESTRAIN.]

restraint of trade *Business.* the limitation or prevention of free competition.

re·strict (ri strikt′) *v.* **1** keep within limits; confine: *Our club membership is restricted to twelve.* **2** put limitations on: *to restrict the meaning of a word.* [< L *restrictus,* pp. of *restringere* < *re-* back + *stringere* draw tight]

re·stric·tion (ri strik′shən) *n.* **1** something that restricts; limiting condition or rule: *The restrictions on the use of the new gymnasium are these: no hard-soled boots or shoes; no fighting; no damaging of property.* **2** restricting or being restricted: *This part is open to the public without restriction.*

re·stric·tive (ri strik′tiv) *adj.* restricting; limiting: *Some laws are prohibitive; some are only restrictive.* **—re·stric′tive·ly,** *adv.*

restrictive clause *Grammar.* an adjectival clause that is an essential and inseparable part of the sentence in which it appears.
☞ *Usage.* A **restrictive clause** restricts the noun it modifies in that it identifies or defines the member of the class of things being referred to and is for this reason an inseparable part of the noun construction; such clauses are never set off by commas, nor is there any perceptible pause before or after them in speech. *Example:* The man *who came to dinner* stayed for a month. A **non-restrictive clause** contains nothing more than descriptive detail and for this reason is merely a clause inserted into the main construction; such clauses must be set off from the main clause by commas and there is a perceptible pause, usually accompanied by a change in voice pitch, before and after them in speech. *Example:* The principal of the high school, *who is a most interesting man,* came to our house for dinner last evening.

re·string (rē string′) *v.* **-strung, -string·ing.** put a new string or new strings on.

rest room a public washroom, or toilet, as in a theatre or service station.

re·sult (ri zult′) *n., v.* —*n.* **1** that which happens as the outcome of something: *The result of the fall was a broken leg.* **2** a good or useful result: *We want results, not talk.* **3** *Mathematics.* a quantity, value, etc. obtained by calculation. **4** an outcome: *the result of a game.* —*v.* **1** be a result; follow as a consequence: *Sickness often results from eating too much.* **2** have as a result; end: *Eating too much often results in sickness.* [< L *resultare* rebound, ult. < *re-* back + *salire* spring]
☞ *Syn. n.* **1.** See note at **effect.**

re·sult·ant (ri zul′tənt) *adj., n.* —*adj.* resulting. —*n.* **1** a result. **2** *Physics or Mathematics* any force that has the same effect as two or more forces acting together.

re·sume (ri züm′ *or* ri zyüm′) *v.* **-sumed, -sum·ing. 1** begin again; go on: *Resume reading where we left off.* **2** get or take again: *Those standing may resume their seats.* [< L *resumere* < *re-* again + *sumere* take up] **—re·sum′a·ble,** *adj.*

rés·u·mé (rez′ů mā′; *French,* rā zý mā′) *n.* **1** a short account of a person's education, employment history, etc., prepared for submission with a job application. **2** any summary, as of events, etc. [< F *résumé,* originally pp. of *résumer* resume]

re·sump·tion (ri zump′shən) *n.* the act of resuming: *the resumption of duties after absence.* [ME < LL *resumptio, -onis* < L *resumere.* See RESUME.]

re·sur·face (rē sėr′fis) *v.* **-faced, -fac·ing.** provide with a new or different surface.

re·surge (ri sėrj′) *v.* **-surged, -surg·ing.** rise again. [< L *resurgere* < *re-* again + *surgere* rise]

re·sur·gence (ri sėr′jəns) *n.* a rising again.

re·sur·gent (ri sėr′jənt) *adj.* rising or tending to rise again.

re·sur·rect (rez′ə rekt′) *v.* **1** raise from the dead; bring back to

---

hat, āge, fär; let, ēqual, tèrm; it, īce
hot, ōpen, ôrder; oil, out; cup, pů t, rüle,
əbove, takən, pencəl, lemən, circəs
ch, child; ng, long; sh, ship
th, thin; ᴛʜ, then; zh, measure

life. **2** bring back to sight or into use: *resurrect an old custom.* [< *resurrection*]

res·ur·rec·tion (rez′ə rek′shən) *n.* **1** a coming to life again; rising from the dead. **2 Resurrection,** the rising of Christ after His death and burial. **3** the state of being alive again after death. **4** a restoration from decay, disuse, etc. [< L *resurrectio, -onis,* ult. < *re-* again + *surgere* rise]

re·sus·ci·tate (ri sus′ə tāt′) *v.* **-tat·ed, -tat·ing.** bring or come back to life or consciousness; revive. [< L *resuscitare,* ult. < *re-* again + *sub-* up + *citare* rouse < *ciere* stir up] **—re·sus′ci·ta′tion,** *n.*

re·sus·ci·ta·tive (ri sus′ə tə tiv *or* ri sus′ə tā′tiv) *adj.* helping to resuscitate.

re·sus·ci·ta·tor (ri sus′ə tā′tər) *n.* **1** an apparatus for forcing air or oxygen into the lungs of a person who has stopped breathing, in order to revive him. **2** a person who resuscitates.

ret (ret) *v.* **ret·ted, ret·ting.** expose (flax, hemp, etc.) to moisture or soak in water, in order to soften by partial rotting. [< MDu. *reten*]

ret. 1 retain. **2** retired. **3** return.

re·tail (*n., adj., adv., v.* **1** *and* **2** rē′tāl; *v.* **3** ri tāl′) *n., adj., v., adv.* —*n.* the sale of goods in small quantities directly to the final consumer: *Most stores sell at retail.* Compare **wholesale.** —*adj.* **1** in small lots or quantities: *The retail price of this jewellery is 70 percent higher than the wholesale price.* **2** selling in small quantities: *the retail trade, a retail merchant.* —*v.* **1** sell in small quantities. **2** be sold in small quantities: *a dress retailing at $50.00.* **3** tell over again: *She retails everything she hears about her acquaintances.* —*adv.* from a retail merchant or dealer: *He has to buy his supplies retail.* [ME < OF *retail* scrap, ult. < *re-* back + *taillier* cut, ult. < L *talea* rod]

re·tail·er (rē′tāl ər) *n.* a retail merchant or dealer.

re·tain (ri tān′) *v.* **1** continue to have or hold; keep: *She retained control of the business until she died. Porcelain retains heat longer than metal does.* **2** keep in mind; remember. **3** employ by payment of a fee: *He retained the best lawyer in the city.* [ME < OF < L *retinere* < *re-* back + *tenere* hold]
☞ *Syn.* **1.** See note at **keep.**

re·tain·er¹ (ri tān′ər) *n.* **1** a person or attendant, especially one who serves a person of rank or one who is a long-time family servant. **2** a device that holds in place or holds back a part of a machine. **3** a device that keeps teeth in place after orthodontic treatment. [< *retain*]

re·tain·er² (ri tān′ər) *n.* a fee paid to secure services: *This lawyer receives a retainer before he begins work on a case.* [< F *retenir,* n. use of infin. *retenir* retain]

retaining wall a wall built to hold back or confine a bank of earth, loose stones, etc.

re·take (*v.* rē tāk′; *n.* rē′tāk′) *v.* **-took, -tak·en, -tak·ing;** *n.* —*v.* **1** take again. **2** take back. —*n.* the act or process: *a retake of a scene in a motion picture.*

re·tal·i·ate (ri tal′ē āt′) *v.* **-at·ed, -at·ing.** repay one injury, etc. with another; return like for like: *If we insult them, they will retaliate.* [< L *retaliare* < *re-* in return + *tal-* pay; influenced by *talis* such]

re·tal·i·a·tion (ri tal′ē ā′shən) *n.* **1** the repaying a wrong, injury, etc. with another; return of like for like. **2** the thing done to retaliate.

re·tal·i·a·tive (ri tal′ē ə tiv *or* ri tal′ē ā′tiv) *adj.* disposed to retaliate; retaliatory.

re·tal·i·a·to·ry (ri tal′ē ə tô′rē) *adj.* returning like for like, especially one injury for another.

re·tard (ri tärd′) *v.* make slow; delay the progress of; keep back; hinder: *Bad roads retarded the car.* [< L *retardare,* ult. < *re-* back + *tardus* slow] **—re·tard′er,** *n.*

re·tard·ant (ri tärd′ənt) *n., adj.* —*n.* something, often a chemical, that slows up or delays an effect or an action. —*adj.* holding back; tending to delay or make slower.

---

re·straight′en   re·stuff′   re′sub·scribe′   re′sur·vey′   re·swal′low
re·stud′y   re′sub·mit′   re·sum′mon

re·tar·da·tion (rē′tär dā′shən) *n.* **1** the act or an instance of retarding. **2** the extent to which something is retarded. **3** a significant, or noticeable, limitation or slowness of intellectual and social development. **4** something that retards; hindrance.

re·tard·ed (ri tärd′əd) *adj., n. —adj.* **1** held back; hindered. **2** noticeably limited or slow in intellectual and social development.

retch (rech) *v.* make efforts to vomit; make movements like those of vomiting. [OE *hrǣcan* clear the throat]

ret'd 1 returned. **2** retired.

re·ten·tion (ri ten′shən) *n.* **1** retaining or being retained. **2** the power to retain. **3** the ability to remember. [< L *retentio, -onis* < *retinere* retain. See RETAIN.]

re·ten·tion·ist (ri ten′shə nist′) *n.* a person who supports the retention of a policy or practice, especially capital punishment.

re·ten·tive (ri ten′tiv) *adj.* **1** able to hold or keep. **2** able to remember. **—re·ten′tive·ly,** *adv.* **—re·ten′tive·ness,** *n.*

re·ten·tiv·i·ty (rē′ten tiv′ə tē) *n.* **1** the power to retain; retentiveness. **2** the power of retaining magnetization after the magnetizing force has ceased to operate.

re·think (rē thingk′) *v.* **-thought, -think·ing.** think over again, especially with a view to changing one's ideas, tactics, etc.: *We will have to rethink our energy strategy.*

ret·i·cence (ret′ə səns) *n.* a tendency to be silent or say little; reserve in speech.

ret·i·cent (ret′ə sənt) *adj.* disposed to keep silent or say little; not speaking freely; reserved in speech. [< L *reticens, -entis,* ppr. of *reticere* keep silent < *re-* back + *tacere* be silent] **—ret′icently,** *adv.* ☛ *Syn.* See note at **silent.**

re·tic·u·lar (ri tik′yə lər) *adj.* **1** netlike. **2** intricate; entangled.

re·tic·u·late (*adj.* ri tik′yə lit *or* ri tik′yə lāt′; *v.* ri tik′yə lāt′) *adj., v.* **-lat·ed, -lat·ing. —adj.** netlike; covered with a network. Reticulate leaves have the veins arranged like the threads of a net. **—v. 1** cover or mark with a network. **2** form a network.

re·tic·u·la·tion (ri tik′yə lā′shən) *n.* **1** a reticulated formation, arrangement, or appearance; network. **2** one of the meshes of a network. [< L *reticulatio, -onis,* ult. < *reticulum,* dim. of *rete* net]

ret·i·cule (ret′ə kyül′) *n. Archaic.* a woman's small purse or handbag. [< F < L *reticulum,* dim. of *rete* net. Doublet of RETICULUM.]

re·tic·u·lum (ri tik′yə ləm) *n., pl.* **-la** (-lə). **1** a network; any reticulated system or structure. **2** *Zoology.* the second stomach of cud-chewing mammals. [< L. Doublet of RETICULE.]

ret·i·na (ret′ə nə) *n., pl.* **-nas, -nae** (-nē′ *or* -nī′). a membrane at the back of the eyeball, composed of layers of nervous tissue and containing light-sensitive rods and cones. The membrane receives images and passes them on to the optic nerve. See **eye** for picture. [< Med.L *retina* < L *retinacula,* pl., band, reins < *retinere* retain. See RETAIN.]

ret·i·nal (ret′ə nəl) *adj.* of or on the retina.

ret·i·nue (ret′ə nyü′) *n.* a group of attendants or retainers; following: *The king's retinue accompanied him on the journey.* [ME < OF *retenue,* originally fem. pp. of *retenir* retain < L *retinere.* See RETAIN.]

re·tire (ri tīr′) *v.* **-tired, -tir·ing. 1** give up an office, occupation, etc.: *The teacher expects to retire at 65.* **2** remove from an office, occupation, etc. **3** go away, especially to be quiet: *She retired to a convent.* **4** withdraw; draw back; send back: *The government retires worn or torn dollar bills from use.* **5** go back; retreat: *The enemy retired before the advance of our troops.* **6** go to bed: *We retire early.* **7** take up and pay off (bonds, loans, etc.). **8** *Baseball and cricket.* put out (a batter, side, etc.). [< F *retirer* < *re-* back + *tirer* draw] ☛ *Syn.* **3.** See note at **depart.**

re·tired (ri tīrd′) *adj.* **1** withdrawn from one's profession or occupation: *a retired sea captain.* **2** reserved; retiring: *a shy, retired nature.* **3** secluded; shut off; hidden: *a retired spot.*

re·tir·ee (ri tī rē′) *n.* a person who has retired from his occupation or profession.

re·tire·ment (ri tīr′mənt) *n.* **1** the act of retiring or the state of being retired; especially, withdrawing or being retired from an occupation or profession. **2** the age at which a person normally retires from work: *Several people in our department will reach retirement within the next year.* **3** (*adjl.*) of, having to do with, or designed for people who are retired: *a retirement village.* **4** seclusion or privacy: *She lives in retirement, neither making nor receiving visits.* **5** a secluded or private place.

re·tir·ing (ri tīr′ing) *adj.* shrinking from society or publicity; reserved; shy: *a retiring nature.* **—re·tir′ing·ly,** *adv.*

re·took (rē tůk′) *v.* pt. of **retake.**

re·tort¹ (ri tôrt′) *v., n. —v.* **1** reply quickly or sharply. **2** return in kind; turn back on: *to retort insult for insult or blow for blow.* **—n.** a sharp or witty reply. [< L *retortus,* pp. of *retorquere* throw back < *re-* back + *torquere* twist]

re·tort² (ri tôrt′ *or* rē′tôrt′) *n.* a container used for distilling or decomposing substances by heat. [< Med.L *retorta,* originally fem. pp. of L *retorquere.* See RETORT¹.]

re·touch (rē tuch′) *v.* improve (a photographic negative, etc.) by making slight changes.

re·trace (ri trās′) *v.* **-traced, -trac·ing.** go back over: *We retraced our steps to where we started.* [< F *retracer* < *re-* back + *tracer* trace] **—re·trace′a·ble,** *adj.*

re–trace (rē trās′) *v.* **-traced, -trac·ing.** trace over again: *Re-trace these drawings.* [< *re-* + *trace*]

re·tract (ri trakt′) *v.* **1** draw back or in: *Cats can retract their claws.* **2** withdraw; take back: *to retract an offer, to retract an opinion.* [< L *retractare,* ult. < *re-* back + *trahere* draw] **—re·tract′a·ble,** *adj.*

re·trac·ta·tion (rē′trak tā′shən) *n.* a retracting of a promise, statement, etc.

re·trac·tile (ri trak′tīl *or* ri trak′təl) *adj.* capable of being drawn back or in.

re·trac·tion (ri trak′shən) *n.* **1** a drawing or being drawn back or in. **2** a taking back; withdrawal of a promise, statement, etc. **3** retractile power.

re·trac·tive (ri trak′tiv) *adj.* tending or serving to retract.

re·trac·tor (ri trak′tər) *n.* **1** a person or thing that draws back something. **2** a muscle that retracts an organ, protruded part, etc. **3** a surgical instrument or device for drawing and holding back an organ or part.

re·tread (*v.* rē tred′; *n.* rē′tred′) *v.* **-tread·ed, -tread·ing;** *n. —v.* put a new tread on. **—n.** a retreaded tire.

re·treat (ri trēt′) *v., n. —v.* go back; move back; withdraw: *Seeing the big dog, the tramp retreated rapidly.* **—n. 1** the act of going back or withdrawing: *The army's retreat was orderly.* **2** a signal for retreat: *The drums beat a retreat.* **3** a signal on a bugle or drum, given in the army at sunset. **4** a safe, quiet place; place of rest or refuge. **5** an asylum for mentally ill people and for habitual drunkards. **6** a period of withdrawal from regular life, singly or in a group, devoted to prayer, meditation, and other religious exercises.

beat a retreat, run away; retreat: *We dropped the apples and beat a hasty retreat when the farmer shouted at us.* [ME < OF *retraite,* orig. pp. of *retraire* < L *retrahere* retract < *re-* back + *trahere* draw. Related to RETRACT.]

re·trench (ri trench′) *v.* **1** cut down; reduce (expenses, etc.). **2** reduce expenses: *In hard times, we must retrench.* [< MF *retrencher* < *re-* back + *trencher* cut]

re·trench·ment (ri trench′mənt) *n.* **1** a reduction of expenses. **2** a cutting down; cutting off.

ret·ri·bu·tion (ret′rə byü′shən) *n.* **1** a deserved punishment; return for evil done, or sometimes, for good done. **2** the act of punishing or, sometimes, rewarding. [< L *retributio, -onis,* ult. < *re-* back + *tribuere* assign]

re·trib·u·tive (ri trib′yə tiv) *adj.* paying back, especially bringing or inflicting punishment in return for some evil, wrong, etc. **—re·trib′u·tive·ly,** *adv.*

re·trib·u·to·ry (ri trib′yə tô′rē) *adj.* retributive.

re·triev·al (ri trēv′əl) *n.* the act of retrieving.

re·trieve (ri trēv′) *v.* **-trieved, -triev·ing. 1** get again; recover: *to retrieve a lost pocketbook.* **2** bring back to a former or better condition; restore: *to retrieve one's fortunes.* **3** make good; make amends for; repair: *to retrieve a mistake, to retrieve a loss or defeat.* **4** find and bring back killed or wounded game: *Some dogs can be trained to retrieve.* [ME < OF *retreuv-,* a stem of *retrouver* < *re-* again + *trouver* find] **—re·triev′a·ble,** *adj.* ☛ *Syn.* **1.** See note at **recover.**

re·triev·er (ri trēv′ər) *n.* **1** any of several breeds of medium-sized to large dog often trained to retrieve game from land or water. See also **Labrador retriever, golden retriever. 2** any person or thing that retrieves.

re·teach′ re·tes′ti·fy′ re·train′ re′trans·la′tion re·tri′al
re·tell′ re·thread′ re·trans·fer′ re′trans·mis′sion
re·test′ re·tie′ re′trans·late′ re′trans·mit′

retro– *prefix.* backward; back; behind, as in *retrogress, retro-rocket.* [< L *retro-* < *retro,* adv.]

ret·ro·ac·tive (ret'rō ak'tiv) *adj.* acting back; having an effect on what is past. A retroactive law applies to events that occurred before the law was passed. —**ret'ro·ac'tive·ly,** *adv.*

ret·ro·cede[1] (ret'rə sēd') *v.* **-ced·ed, -ced·ing.** go back; recede. [< L *retrocedere* < *retro-* backward + *cedere* go]

ret·ro·cede[2] (ret'rə sēd') *v.* **-ced·ed, -ced·ing.** cede back (territory, etc.). [< *retro-* + *cede*]

ret·ro·flex (ret'rə fleks') *adj., v.* —*adj.* **1** bent backward. **2** having the tip raised and bent backward. **3** made by raising the tip of the tongue and bending it backward: *a retroflex vowel in "hurt."* —*v.* pronounce with the tip of the tongue raised and bent backward. [< L *retroflexus,* pp. of *retroflectere* < *retro-* back + *flectere* bend]

ret·ro·flex·ion (ret'rə flek'shən) *n.* a bending backward.

ret·ro·grade (ret'rə grād') *adj., v.* **-grad·ed, -grad·ing.** —*adj.* **1** moving backward; retreating. —*v.* **1** move or go backward. **2** fall back toward a worse condition; grow worse; decline. [< L *retrogradus* < *retrogradi,* ult. < *retro-* backward + *gradi* go]

ret·ro·gress (ret'rə gres' *or* ret'rə gres') *v.* **1** move backward; go back. **2** become worse. [< L *retrogressus,* pp. of *retrogradi.* See RETROGRADE.]

ret·ro·gres·sion (ret'rə gresh'ən) *n.* **1** a backward movement. **2** a becoming worse; a falling off; decline.

ret·ro·gres·sive (ret'rə gres'iv) *adj.* **1** moving backward. **2** becoming worse. —**ret'ro·gres'sive·ly,** *adv.*

ret·ro–rock·et (ret'rō rok'it) *n.* a rocket that fires in a direction opposite to that of the motion of a spacecraft or satellite, thus acting as a brake.

ret·ro·spect (ret'rə spekt') *n., v.* —*n.* a survey of past time, events, etc.; thinking about the past.
in retrospect, when looking back.
—*v.* think of (something past). [ult. < L *retrospectus* < *retro-* back + *specere* look]

ret·ro·spec·tion (ret'rə spek'shən) *n.* the act or an instance of looking back on things past; a survey of past events or experiences.

ret·ro·spec·tive (ret'rə spek'tiv) *adj., n.* —*adj.* **1** looking back on things past; surveying past events or experiences. **2** applying to the past; retroactive. —*n.* an art exhibition reviewing the work of an artist or group of artists over a number of years. —**ret'ro·spec'tive·ly,** *adv.*

ret·rous·sé (ret'rü sā') *adj.* turned up: *a retroussé nose.* [< F]

ret·si·na (ret'si nə *or* ret sē'nə) *n.* a resin-flavored Greek wine.

ret·ting (ret'ing) *n.* the process of wetting flax, hemp, etc., and allowing it to decay until the fibres can be easily separated from the woody parts of the stalks. [see RET]

re·turn (ri tėrn') *v., n., adj.* —*v.* **1** go back; come back: *My brother will return this summer.* **2** bring, give, send, hit, put, or pay back: *Return that book to the library.* **3** yield; provide: *The concert returned about $150 over expenses.* **4** report or announce officially: *The jury returned a verdict of guilty.* **5** reply: *"No!" he returned crossly.* **6** elect to a lawmaking body. **7** *Card games.* lead (the suit led by one's partner).
—*n.* **1** a going or coming back; happening again. **2** something returned. **3** a bringing back; giving back; sending back; hitting back; putting back: *a poor return for kindness.* **4** Often, **returns,** *pl.* a profit; an amount received. **5** a report; account: *election returns.* **6** a reply.
in return, as a return: *They let us use their garden, and in return we give them some of the produce.*
—*adj.* **1** of or having to do with a return: *a return ticket.* **2** sent, given, done, etc. in return: *a return game.* **3** repeated: *a return engagement.* **4** causing or allowing the return of some part of a device to its normal or starting position: *a return spring, a return valve.* [ME < OF *retourner* < *re-* back + *tourner* turn]

re·turn·a·ble (ri tėr'nə bəl) *adj.* **1** that can be returned. **2** meant or required to be returned.

returned man *Cdn.* a war veteran.

re·turn·ee (ri tėr'nē') *n.* a person who has returned, especially one who has returned to his own country after capture in a war or service abroad.

returning officer in Canada, the official who is responsible for the entire election procedure in a particular constituency, from preparing the voters' list and the ballots to the proclamation of the winning candidate. In federal elections, returning officers are appointed by the Governor General in Council.

return trip a trip to a place and back again; a round trip.

hat, āge, fär; let, ēqual, tėrm; it, īce
hot, ōpen, ôrder; oil, out; cup, put, rüle, above, takən, pencəl, lemən, circəs
ch, child; ng, long; sh, ship
th, thin; ᴛʜ, then; zh, measure

re·tuse (ri tyüs' *or* ri tüs') *adj.* especially of leaves or flower petals, having a rounded apex with a small notch in the middle. See **leaf** for picture. [< L *retusus,* pp. of *retundere* blunt, beat back < *re-* back + *tundere* beat]

re·u·ni·fi·ca·tion (rē'yü nə fə kā'shən) *n.* **1** the act or process of reunifying. **2** the state of being reunified.

re·u·ni·fy (rē yü'nə fī') *v.* **-fied, -fy·ing.** restore unity to; bring back together again.

re·un·ion (rē yün'yən) *n.* **1** a coming together again: *the reunion of parted friends.* **2** a social gathering of persons who have been separated or who have interests in common: *We have a family reunion every summer.*

re·u·nite (rē'yü nīt') *v.* **-nit·ed, -nit·ing.** **1** bring together again: *Mother and child were reunited after years of separation.* **2** come together again.

rev (rev) *n., v.* **revved, rev·ving.** *Informal.* —*n.* a revolution (of an engine or motor). —*v.* increase the speed of (an engine or motor).

rev. **1** revenue. **2** reverse. **3** review. **4** revised; revision. **5** revolution.

Rev. Reverend.

re·val·ue (rē val'yü) *v.* **-val·ued, -val·u·ing.** value again or anew. —**re'val·u·a'tion,** *n.*

re·vamp (rē vamp') *v.* patch up; repair.

re·veal (ri vēl') *v.* **1** make known something hidden, secret, or mysterious: *Never reveal my secret.* **2** display; show: *Her smile revealed her even teeth.* [ME < L *revelare,* ult. < *re-* back + *velum* veil] —**re·veal'er,** *n.*
☛ *Syn.* **1. Reveal, disclose** = make known something hidden or secret. **Reveal** has a basic sense of uncovering or unveiling, and suggests making known something that has been hidden or screened: *At the new school he revealed an aptitude for science.* **Disclose** has a basic sense of unclosing, and emphasizes making known something that has been kept secret: *She disclosed that she had been married for a month.*

rev·eil·le (rə val'ē) *n.* **1** a signal on a bugle or drum to waken military personnel in the morning. The bugler blows reveille. **2** the time when this signal is sounded. [< F *réveillez(-vous)* awaken!, ult. < L *re-* again + *ex-* up + *vigil* awake]
☛ *Pronun.* The pronunciation (rev'ə lē) is American.

rev·el (rev'əl) *v.* **-elled** or **-eled, -el·ling** or **-el·ing;** *n.* —*v.* **1** take great pleasure (*in*): *The children revel in country life.* **2** make merry. —*n.* a noisy good time; merrymaking. [ME < OF *reveler* be disorderly, make merry < L *rebellare.* Doublet of REBEL, v.] —**rev'el·ler** or **rev'el·er,** *n.*

rev·e·la·tion (rev'ə lā'shən) *n.* **1** the act of making known: *The revelation of the thieves' hiding place by one of their own number caused their capture.* **2** the thing made known: *Her true nature was a revelation to me.* **3** *Theology.* God's disclosure of Himself and of His will to His creatures. [ME < LL *revelatio, -onis* < *revelare* reveal. See REVEAL.]

rev·e·la·to·ry (rev'ə lə tôr'ē) *adj.* **1** making known; revealing. **2** concerning religious revelation.

rev·el·ry (rev'əl rē) *n., pl.* **-ries.** boisterous revelling or festivity; wild merrymaking.

rev·e·nant (rev'ə nənt *or* rev'ə nän'; *French,* rəv nän') *n.* **1** a person who returns after a long absence. **2** a person who returns after death; ghost. [< F *revenant* ghost < *revenir* to come back]

re·venge (ri venj') *n., v.* **-venged, -veng·ing.** —*n.* **1** harm done in return for a wrong; vengeance; returning evil for evil: *a blow struck in revenge.* **2** a desire for vengeance: *She said nothing but there was revenge in her heart.* **3** a chance to win in a return game after losing a game.
—*v.* **1** do harm in return for: *His family vowed to revenge his death.* **2** take vengeance on behalf of (someone or oneself): *He vowed to revenge himself on them for the betrayal.*
be revenged, get revenge: *He swore to be revenged on his brother's murderers.*
[ME < MF *revenge* < OF *revengier,* ult. < L *re-* back + *vindicare* avenge < *vindex, -icis* defender]
☛ *Syn.* **Revenge, avenge. Revenge** may be noun or verb, but **avenge** is always a verb. As a verb, **revenge** suggests getting even with someone else, often in a

mean or savage way: *The gangsters revenged the murder of one of their gang.*
Avenge suggests more the morally righteous equalizing of wrongs: *We avenged the insult to our family.*

re·venge·ful (ri venj′fəl) *adj.* feeling or showing a strong desire for revenge. —**re·venge′ful·ly,** *adv.*

rev·e·nue (rev′ə nyü′) *n.* 1 money coming in; income: *The government gets revenue from taxes.* 2 a particular item of income. 3 a source of income. [< F *revenue,* originally fem. pp. of *revenir* < L *re-* back + *venire* come]

revenue stamp a stamp to show that money has been paid to the government as a tax on something.

re·ver·ber·ant (ri vėr′bər ənt) *adj.* reverberating.

re·ver·ber·ate (ri vėr′bər āt′) *v.* **-at·ed, -at·ing.** 1 echo back: *His voice reverberates from the high ceiling.* 2 cast or be cast back; reflect (light or heat). [< L *reverberare* beat back, ult. < *re-* back + *verber* a blow]

re·ver·ber·a·tion (ri vėr′bər ā′shən) *n.* 1 an echoing back of sound; echo. 2 a reflection of light or heat. 3 that which is reverberated.

re·ver·ber·a·to·ry (ri vėr′bər ə tô′rē) *adj.* characterized by or produced by reverberations; deflected.

re·vere (ri vēr′) *v.* **-vered, -ver·ing.** love and respect deeply; honor greatly; show reverence for. [< L *revereri* < *re-* back + *vereri* stand in awe of, fear]

☛ *Syn.* **Revere, reverence** = feel deep respect and honor for someone or something. **Revere** means to regard with deep respect mixed with love someone of very noble character or something associated with such a person: *People revered the great philosopher.* **Reverence** means to regard with deep respect mixed with wonder, awe, and love something, such as tradition, law, object (seldom a person), considered as almost sacred and not to be violated, injured, or profaned: *We reverence the memory of our heroes.*

rev·er·ence (rev′ər əns or rev′rəns) *n., v.* **enced, -enc·ing.** —*n.* 1 a feeling of deep respect, mixed with wonder, awe, and love. 2 a deep bow. 3 **Reverence,** a title used in speaking of or to a clergyman.
—*v.* regard with reverence. [ME < L *reverentia* < *reverens.* See REVERENT.]
☛ *Syn. v.* See note at **revere.**

rev·er·end (rev′ər ənd or rev′rənd) *adj., n.* —*adj.* worthy of great respect. —*n.* 1 **Reverend,** a title for a member of the clergy. 2 *Informal.* a member of the clergy. [ME < L *reverendus* be respected < *revereri.* See REVERE.]
☛ *Usage.* **Reverend,** usually preceded by **the,** is normally followed by the person's first name or initials: *the Reverend James Shaw, the Reverend J.T. Shaw.* However, it is acceptable to say *the Reverend Mr. Shaw,* but not *the Reverend Shaw.* The abbreviation (**Rev.**) is used in newspapers and in more-or-less informal writing: *the Reverend James Shaw, Rev. J. T. Shaw.*

rev·er·ent (rev′ər ənt or rev′rənt) *adj.* feeling reverence; showing reverence. [ME < L *reverens, -entis,* ppr. of *revereri* revere. See REVERE.] —**rev′er·ent·ly,** *adv.*

rev·er·en·tial (rev ər en′shəl) *adj.* reverent. —**rev·er·en′tial·ly,** *adv.*

rev·er·ie (rev′ər ē) *n.* 1 dreamy thoughts; dreamy thinking of pleasant things: *He loved to indulge in reveries about the future.* 2 the condition of being lost in dreamy thoughts. 3 a fantastic idea; ridiculous fancy. 4 *Music.* a composition suggesting a dreamy or musing mood. Also, **revery.** [< F *rêverie* < *rêver* to dream]

re·vers (rə vėr′ or rə ver′) *n., pl.* **re·vers** (rə vėrz′ or rə verz′). a part of the front of a garment, especially a coat lapel, that is turned back to show the facing or lining. [< F *revers* reverse]

re·ver·sal (ri vėr′səl) *n.* a change to the opposite; a reversing or being reversed.

re·verse (ri vėrs′) *n., adj., v.* **-versed, -vers·ing.** —*n.* 1 the opposite or contrary: *She did the reverse of what I ordered.* 2 **a** the gear or gears that reverse the movement of machinery. **b** the arrangement of such a gear or gears. **c** the position of the control that moves such a gear or gears. 3 movement in an opposite direction; a backward or contrary movement. 4 a change to bad fortune; check; defeat: *He used to be rich, but he met with reverses.* 5 the back: *His name is on the reverse of the medal.*
—*adj.* 1 turned backward; opposite or contrary in position or direction: *the reverse side of a phonograph record.* 2 acting in a manner opposite or contrary to that which is usual. 3 causing an opposite or backward movement.
—*v.* 1 turn the other way; turn inside out; turn upside down. 2 *Dancing.* turn in a direction opposite to the usual one. 3 change to the opposite; repeal. [ME < L *reversus,* pp. of *revertere* turn around. See REVERT.] —**re·vers′er,** *n.*

☛ *Syn. v.* 1. **Reverse, invert** = turn something the other way. **Reverse** is the more general in application, meaning "to turn to the other side or in an opposite position, direction, order, etc.": *In this climate one needs a coat that can be reversed when it begins to rain.* **Invert** means to turn upside down: *Invert the glasses to let them drain.*

re·verse·ly (ri vėrs′lē) *adv.* 1 in a reverse position, direction, or order. 2 on the other hand; on the contrary.

re·vers·i·bil·i·ty (ri vėr′sə bil′ə tē) *n.* the fact or quality of being reversible.

re·vers·i·ble (ri vėr′sə bəl) *adj., n.* —*adj.* 1 that can be reversed; that can reverse. 2 of a fabric, finished on both sides so that either can be used as the outer side. —*n.* a garment made so that either side may be worn exposed. —**re·vers′i·bly,** *adv.*

re·ver·sion (ri vėr′zhən or ri vėr′shən) *n.* 1 a return to a former condition, practice, belief, etc.; return. 2 *Law.* **a** the return of property to the grantor or his heirs. **b** the right to possess a certain property under certain conditions. 3 *Biology.* a return to certain characteristics that have not been present for two or more generations. [ME < L *reversio, -onis* < *revertere* turn around. See REVERT.]

re·ver·sion·al (ri vėr′zhən əl or ri vėr′shən əl) *adj.* of, having to do with, or involving a reversion.

re·ver·sion·ar·y (ri vėr′zhən er′ē or ri vėr′shən er′ē) *adj.* reversional.

re·vert (ri vėrt′) *v.* 1 go back; return: *If a man dies without heirs, his property reverts to the government.* 2 *Biology.* return to certain characteristics that have not been present for two or more generations. [ME < OF < L *revertere* < *re-* back + *vertere* turn]

rev·er·y (rev′ər ē) *n., pl.* **-er·ies.** reverie.

re·vet (ri vet′) *v.* **re·vet·ted, re·vet·ting.** face (a wall, embankment, etc.) with masonry or other material. [< F *revêtir* clothe, ult. < L *re-* again + *vestis* garment]

re·vet·ment (ri vet′mənt) *n.* a retaining wall; a facing of stone, brick, cement, etc. [< F *revêtement*]

re·view (ri vyü′) *v., n.* —*v.* 1 study again; look at again: *He reviewed the scene of the crime.* 2 look back on: *Before falling asleep, Helen reviewed the day's happenings.* 3 examine again; look at with care; examine. A superior court may review decisions of a lower court. 4 inspect formally: *The Admiral reviewed the fleet.* 5 examine to give an account of: *Mr. Brown reviews books for a living.* 6 review books, etc.
—*n.* 1 a studying again. 2 a looking back on; survey. 3 a re-examination. 4 an examination; inspection. 5 a critical account of a book, play, etc. giving its merits and faults. 6 a magazine containing articles on subjects of current interest, including accounts of books, etc.: *a law review, a motion-picture review.* 7 revue. [< F *revue,* originally fem. pp. of *revoir* see again, ult. < L *re-* again + *videre* see]
☛ *Hom.* **revue.**

☛ *Syn. n.* 5. **Review, criticism** = an article or account criticizing a book, play, art exhibit, etc. **Review** applies particularly to an account giving some idea of what the book or play, etc. is about, its good and bad points, and the reviewer's critical or personal opinion: *That magazine contains good reviews of the new movies.* **Criticism** applies particularly to an article or essay giving a critical judgment based on deep and thorough study and definite critical standards of what is good and bad in books, music, pictures, etc.: *an anthology of recent Shakespeare criticism.*

re·view·er (ri vyü′ər) *n.* 1 a person who reviews. 2 a person who writes articles discussing books, plays, etc.

reviewing stand a raised platform for those reviewing a formal parade of troops, a flypast, etc.

re·vile (ri vīl′) *v.* **-viled, -vil·ing.** call bad names; abuse with words: *The tramp reviled the man who drove him off.* [ME < OF *reviler* despise < *re-* again + *vil* vile < L *vilis* cheap] —**re·vil′er,** *n.*

re·vile·ment (ri vīl′mənt) *n.* 1 the act of reviling. 2 reviling speech.

re·vise (ri vīz′) *v.* **-vised, -vis·ing;** *n.* —*v.* 1 read carefully and correct or improve; look over and change: *She has revised the poem she wrote.* 2 change; alter: *to revise one's opinion.*
—*n.* 1 the process of revising. 2 a revised form or version. 3 *Printing.* a proof sheet printed after corrections have been made. [< F *reviser,* ult. < L *re-* again + *videre* see] —**re·vis′er,** *n.*

Revised Standard Version an American Protestant revision of the Bible. The New Testament was published in 1946 and the complete Bible in 1952. *Abbrev.:* RSV or R.S.V.

Revised Version the revised form of the Authorized Version of the Bible. The New Testament was published in 1881 and the Old Testament in 1885. *Abbrev.:* RV or R.V.

re·vi·sion (ri vizh′ən) *n.* 1 the act or work of revising. 2 a revised form: *a revision of a book.*

re·vi·sion·ism (ri vizh′ə niz′əm) *n.* the proposals or beliefs of revisionists.

re·vi·sion·ist (ri vizh′ə nist′) *n.* **1** one who supports or favors revision. **2** a reviser, especially one of those responsible for the Revised Version of the Bible. **3** a communist who believes that the doctrines of Marxism may be interpreted flexibly and revised in the light of national circumstances.

re·vi·so·ry (ri vī′zə rē) *adj.* of or having to do with revision.

re·viv·al (ri vīv′əl) *n.* **1** a bringing or coming back to life or consciousness. **2** a restoration to vigor or health. **3** a bringing or coming back to style, use, activity, etc.: *the revival of a play of years ago.* **4** an awakening or increase of interest in religion. **5** special services or efforts made to awaken or increase interest in religion.

re·viv·al·ist (ri vīv′əl ist) *n.* a person who holds special services to awaken interest in religion.

re·vive (ri vīv′) *v.* **-vived, -viv·ing. 1** bring back or come back to life or consciousness: *to revive a half-drowned person.* **2** bring or come back to a fresh, lively condition: *Flowers revive in water.* **3** make or become fresh; restore: *Hot coffee revived the cold, tired man.* **4** bring back or come back to notice, use, fashion, memory, activity, etc.: *An old play is sometimes revived on the stage.* [< L *revivere* < *re-* again + *vivere* live] —**re·viv′er,** *n.*

re·viv·i·fy (rē viv′ə fī′) *v.* **-fied, -fy·ing.** restore to life; give new life to. —**re·viv′i·fi·ca′tion,** *n.* —**re·viv′i·fi′er,** *n.*

rev·o·ca·ble (rev′ə kə bəl) *adj.* that can be repealed, cancelled, or withdrawn. —**rev′o·ca·ble·ness,** *n.* —**rev′o·ca·bly,** *adv.*

rev·o·ca·tion (rev′ə kā′shən) *n.* a repeal; cancelling; withdrawal: *the revocation of a law.*

rev·o·ca·to·ry (rev′ə kə tô′rē) *adj.* revoking; recalling; repealing.

re·voke (ri vōk′) *v.* **-voked, -vok·ing;** *n.* —*v.* **1** take back; repeal; cancel; withdraw: *The government revoked the bill before it was voted on.* **2** *Card games.* fail to follow suit when one can and should; renege. —*n. Card games.* a failure to follow suit when one can and should. [ME < OF < L *revocare* < *re-* back + *vocare* call]

re·volt (ri vōlt′) *n., v.* —*n.* the act or state of rebelling: *The town is in revolt.* —*v.* **1** turn away from and fight against a leader; rise against the government's authority: *The people revolted against the dictator.* **2** turn away with disgust: *to revolt at a bad smell.* **3** cause to feel disgust. [< F < Ital. *rivolta,* ult. < L *revolvere* revolve. See REVOLVE.] —**re·volt′er,** *n.*

☛ *Syn. n.* **Revolt, insurrection, rebellion** = a rising up in active resistance against authority. **Revolt** emphasizes casting off allegiance and refusing to accept existing conditions or control: *The revolt of the French mob that stormed the Bastille developed into revolution.* **Insurrection** suggests an armed uprising of a group or section against established authority, often to seize control for their own class or party: *The leader of the insurrection became dictator.* **Rebellion** applies to open armed resistance organized to force the government to do something or to overthrow it: *A rebellion may become civil war.*

re·volt·ing (ri vōl′ting) *adj.* disgusting; repulsive. —**re·volt′ing·ly,** *adv.*

rev·o·lu·tion (rev′ə lü′shən) *n.* **1** a complete, often violent, overthrow of an established government or political system: *The 1917 revolution ended the monarchy in Russia.* **2** a complete change: *Plastics have brought about a revolution in industry.* **3** a movement in a circle or curve around some point: *One revolution of the earth around the sun takes a year.* **4** the act or fact of turning round a centre or axis; rotation: *The revolution of the earth causes day and night.* **5** a single complete turn around a centre: *The wheel of the motor turns at a rate of more than one thousand revolutions a minute.* **6** the time or distance of one revolution. **7** a complete cycle or series of events: *The revolution of the four seasons fills a year.* [ME < OF < L *revolutio, -onis* < *revolvere* revolve. See REVOLVE.]

rev·o·lu·tion·ar·y (rev′ə lü′shən er′ē) *adj., n., pl.* **-ar·ies.** —*adj.* **1** of or involving a revolution (defs. 1 and 2). **2** bringing or causing great changes. —*n.* a revolutionist.

Revolutionary War in the United States the war from 1775 to 1783 by which the thirteen American colonies won independence from Great Britain.

rev·o·lu·tion·ist (rev′ə lü′shən ist) *n.* a person who advocates, or takes part in, a revolution.

rev·o·lu·tion·ize (rev′ə lü′shən īz′) *v.* **-ized, -iz·ing.** change completely; produce a very great change in: *Mechanization revolutionized farm life.*

hat, āge, fär; let, ēqual, tèrm; it, īce
hot, ōpen, ôrder; oil, out; cup, pút, rüle,
əbove, takən, pencəl, lemən, circəs
ch, child; ng, long; sh, ship
th, thin; ŦH, then; zh, measure

re·volve (ri volv′) *v.* **-volved, -volv·ing. 1** move in a circle; move in a curve round a point: *The moon revolves around the earth.* **2** turn round a centre or axis; rotate: *The wheels of a moving car revolve.* **3** cause to move round. **4** turn over in the mind; consider from many points of view: *He wishes to revolve the problem before giving an answer.* **5** move in a complete cycle or series of events: *The seasons revolve.* [ME < L *revolvere* < *re-* back + *volvere* roll] —**re·volv′a·ble,** *adj.*

☛ *Syn.* **1.** See note at **turn.**

re·volv·er (ri vol′vər) *n.* **1** a pistol with a revolving cylinder in which the cartridges are contained, that can be fired several times without reloading. See **firearm** for picture. **2** a person or thing that revolves.

re·vue (ri vyü′) *n.* a theatrical entertainment with singing, dancing, parodies of recent plays, humorous treatments of happenings and fads of the year, etc. [< F. See REVIEW.]

☛ *Hom.* **review.**

re·vul·sion (ri vul′shən) *n.* **1** a strong feeling of disgust or distaste: *The stench of rotting vegetables filled us with revulsion.* **2** a sudden, violent change of feeling: *He suddenly felt a revulsion from the long solitude.* **3** a drawing or being drawn back and away, especially suddenly or violently. [< L *revulsio, -onis,* ult. < *re-* back + *vellere* tear away]

Rev. Ver. Revised Version.

re·ward (ri wôrd′) *n., v.* —*n.* **1** a return made for something done. **2** a money payment given or offered for capture of criminals, the return of lost property, etc. —*v.* **1** give a reward to. **2** give a reward for. [ME < ONF *reward* < *rewarder,* dial. var. of *regarder* < *re-* back + *garder* guard. Cf. REGARD.]

re·wire (rē wīr′) *v.* **-wired, -wir·ing. 1** put new wires on or in. **2** telegraph again.

re·word (rē wėrd′) *v.* change the wording of; express differently.

re·work (rē wėrk′) *v.* work anew; revise or reprocess.

re·write (*v.* rē rīt′, *n.* rē′rīt′) *v.* **-wrote, -writ·ten, -writ·ing;** *n.* —*v.* **1** write again; write in a different form; revise. **2** write (a news story) from material supplied in a form that cannot be used as copy. —*n.* something rewritten, especially for publication.

Reyn·ard (ren′ərd *or* rā′närd) *n.* **1** a fox that is the main character in a group of medieval fables about animals. **2** reynard, any fox. [ME < OF *Renart, Renard* < Gmc.]

Rf rutherfordium.

RF, R.F., *or* **r.f.** radio frequency.

r.h. **1** right hand. **2** relative humidity.

Rh **1** Rh factor. **2** rhodium.

R.H. **1** Royal Highness. **2** Royal Highlanders.

Rhad·a·man·thine (rad′ə man′thin) *adj.* **1** of or having to do with Rhadamanthus. **2** incorruptibly and sternly just.

Rhad·a·man·thus (rad′ə man′thəs) *n. Greek mythology.* a son of Zeus and brother of King Minos of Crete. Because he was such a just man during his life, he was made one of the three judges in Hades after his death.

rhap·sod·ic (rap sod′ik) *adj.* rhapsodical.

rhap·sod·i·cal (rap sod′ə kəl) *adj.* of, having to do with, or characteristic of rhapsody; extravagantly enthusiastic; ecstatic. —**rhap·sod′i·cal·ly,** *adv.*

rhap·so·dist (rap′sə dist) *n.* a person who talks or writes with extravagant enthusiasm.

rhap·so·dize (rap′sə dīz′) *v.* **-dized, -diz·ing.** talk or write with extravagant enthusiasm.

rhap·so·dy (rap′sə dē) *n., pl.* **-dies. 1** an utterance or writing marked by extravagant enthusiasm: *She went into rhapsodies over the garden.* **2** *Music.* an instrumental composition following no regular form: *Liszt's Hungarian rhapsodies.* **3** an epic poem, or a part of such a poem, suitable for recitation at one time. [< L < Gk.

re·vis′it	re·wa′ter	re·weld′	re·work′
re′vi·tal·i·za′tion	re·wax′	re·win′	re·wrap′
re·vi′tal·ize′	re·weave′	re·wind′	
re·vote′	re·weigh′	re·word′	
re·wake′			
re·wak′en			
re·warm′			
re·wash′			

rhapsōidia verse-composition, ult. < *rhaptein* to switch]

rhe·a (rē′ə) *n.* either of two species constituting a family (Rheidae) of large, flightless birds of South America, resembling ostriches but smaller and having three toes instead of two and a completely feathered head and neck. This family of birds constitutes the order Rheiformes.

Rhein·gold (rīn′gōld′) *n. German and Norse mythology.* a magic hoard of gold owned by the Nibelungs and later by Siegfried. Also, **Rhinegold.**

Rhen·ish (ren′ish) *adj., n.* —*adj.* of the river Rhine or the regions near it. —*n.* Rhine wine. [< L *Rhenus* Rhine]

rhe·ni·um (rē′nē əm) *n.* a rare, hard, greyish metallic chemical element that has chemical properties similar to those of manganese. *Symbol*: Re; *at.no.* 75; *at.wt.* 186.2. [< L *Rhenus* Rhine]

rhe·o·stat (rē′ə stat′) *n.* an instrument for regulating the strength of an electric current by introducing different amounts of resistance into the circuit. [< Gk. *rheos* current + *statos* standing still]

Rhe·sus factor (rē′səs) Rh factor.

rhe·sus monkey (rē′səs) a small monkey (*Macaca mulatta*) of S Asia much used in biological and medical research. The rhesus monkey is a macaque. [from a character in the *Iliad*]

rhet·o·ric (ret′ə rik) *n.* **1** the art of using words effectively in speaking or writing. **2** a book about this art. **3** language used to persuade or influence others: *The crowd was impressed by the speaker's rhetoric.* [ME < L < Gk. *rhētorikē* (*technē*) art of an orator < *rhētōr* orator]

rhe·tor·i·cal (ri tôr′ə kəl) *adj.* **1** of or having to do with rhetoric. **2** using rhetoric. **3** intended especially for display; artificial. **4** oratorical. —**rhe·tor′i·cal·ly,** *adv.*

rhetorical question a question asked only for effect, not for information, and not expecting an answer.

rhet·o·ri·cian (ret′ə rish′ən) *n.* **1** a person skilled in rhetoric. **2** a person given to display in language.

rheum (rüm) *n.* **1** a watery discharge, such as mucus, tears, or saliva. **2** a cold; catarrh. [ME < OF < L < Gk. *rheuma* a flowing < *rhein* flow]
☛ *Hom.* **room.**

rheu·mat·ic (rü mat′ik) *adj., n.* —*adj.* **1** of rheumatism. **2** having rheumatism; liable to have rheumatism. **3** causing rheumatism. **4** caused by rheumatism.
—*n.* **1** a person who has rheumatism. **2 rheumatics,** *pl. Informal.* rheumatism.
[ME < L < Gk. *rheumatikos* < *rheuma.* See RHEUM.]

rheumatic fever an acute disease occurring usually in children, characterized by fever, swelling, pain in the joints, and inflammation of the heart.

rheu·ma·tism (rü′mə tiz′əm) *n.* any of various painful conditions of the joints, muscles, or connective tissue, characterized by inflammation, stiffness, etc. Bursitis and arthritis are forms of rheumatism. [< L < Gk. *rheumatismos,* ult. < *rheuma* rheum. See RHEUM.]

rheu·ma·toid (rü′mə toid′) *adj.* **1** resembling or affected by rheumatism: *rheumatoid arthritis.* **2** having rheumatism.
—**rheu′ma·toi′dal·ly,** *adv.*

rheumatoid arthritis a persistent disease that produces swelling and inflammation of the joints and is often progressively crippling.

rheum·y (rü′mē) *adj.* **1** full of rheum. **2** causing rheum; damp and cold.
☛ *Hom.* **roomy.**

Rh factor a substance often found in the blood of human beings and the higher mammals. Blood containing this substance (**Rh positive**) does not combine favorably with blood lacking it (**Rh negative**). Also called **Rhesus factor.** [first discovered in the blood of the rhesus monkey]

rhi·nal (rī′nəl) *adj.* of or having to do with the nose; nasal. [< Gk. *rhis, rhinos* nose]

Rhine·gold (rīn′gōld′) See **Rheingold.**

rhine·stone (rīn′stōn′) *n.* an imitation diamond, made of glass. [translation of F *caillou du Rhin*]

Rhine wine (rīn) a wine produced in the valley of the Rhine. Most Rhine wines are white wines.

rhi·ni·tis (rī nī′tis) *n.* inflammation of the nose or its mucous membrane. [< NL < Gk. *rhis, rhinos* nose + *itis*]

rhi·no (rī′nō) *n., pl.* -**nos.** rhinoceros.

rhi·noc·er·os (rī nos′ər əs) *n., pl.* -**os·es** or (esp. collectively) -**os.** any of a small family (Rhinocerotidae) of large, hoofed,

plant-eating mammals of Africa and Asia having very thick, hairless skin, a massive body, short, thick legs with three-toed feet, and one or two large horns growing upright on the snout. [ME < L < Gk. *rhinokerōs,* ult. < *rhis* nose + *keras* horn]

rhi·nol·o·gist (rī nol′ə jist) *n.* a physician specializing in rhinology.

rhi·nol·o·gy (rī nol′ə jē) *n.* the branch of medicine that deals with the nose and its diseases. [< Gk. *rhis, rhinos* nose + E -*logy*]

rhi·no·plas·ty (rī′nə plas′tē) *n.* plastic surgery involving the nose.

rhi·zoid (rī′zoid) *adj., n.* —*adj.* rootlike. —*n.* one of the rootlike filaments in mosses, etc., by which the plant is attached to the substratum. [< Gk. *rhiza* root + *eidos* form]

rhi·zome (rī′zōm) *n.* a rootlike stem lying along or under the ground, that usually produces roots below and shoots from the upper surface; rootstock. [< Gk. *rhizōma,* ult. < *rhiza* root]

rhi·zo·pod (rī′zə pod′) *n.* any of a subclass (Rhizopoda) of protozoans, including the amoebas, that form temporary projections of protoplasm for moving about and taking in food. [< NL *rhizopoda,* pl. < Gk. *rhiza* root + *pous, podos* foot]

rho (rō) *n.* the 17th letter of the Greek alphabet (P, ρ).

Rhode Island Red (rōd) a breed of American chicken that has reddish feathers and a black tail.

Rho·de·sian man (rō dē′zhən) an early type of man (*Homo rhodesiensis,* also classified as *Homo sapiens rhodesiensis*) of late Pleistocene times in Africa, characterized by long limb bones and a large face with prominent brow ridges. [< Northern *Rhodesia,* former name of Zambia, in Africa]

Rhodesian ridge·back (rij′bak′) a breed of large African hunting dog having a short coat with a ridge of hair growing forward along the backbone.

Rhodes Scholar (rōdz) a holder of any of a number of scholarships awarded annually to students from certain Commonwealth countries, South Africa, and the United States for study at Oxford University in England. [< Cecil *Rhodes* (1853-1902), a British colonial statesman who provided for these scholarships in his will.]

rho·di·um (rō′dē əm) *n.* a greyish-white metallic chemical element, forming salts that give rose-colored solutions. It is similar to aluminum. *Symbol*: Rh; *at.no.* 45; *at.wt.* 102.905 [< Gk. *rhodon* rose]

rho·do·den·dron (rō′də den′drən) *n.* any of a very large genus (*Rhododendron*) of shrubs and small trees of the heath family, found mainly in the cooler regions of the northern hemisphere and the mountains of S Asia, having showy, bell-shaped or funnel-shaped flowers and evergreen or deciduous leaves. Some rhododendrons are widely cultivated as garden plants. [< NL < Gk. *rhododendron* < *rhodon* rose + *dendron* tree]

rho·do·lite (rō′də līt′) *n.* a pink or violet variety of garnet used as a gemstone.

rho·do·nite (rō′də nīt′) *n.* a reddish, translucent mineral consisting mainly of manganese silicate, that occurs in metamorphic rocks and is often used as an ornamental stone. *Formula:* Mn Si O_3

rho·dor·a (rō dôr′ə) *n.* any of a genus (Rhodora) of shrubs of the heath family native to eastern Canada and New England, having pink or red flowers that appear before or with the leaves. [< NL *Rhodora,* the genus name]

rhomb (rom *or* romb) *n.* rhombus.

rhom·bic (rom′bik) *adj.* **1** having the form of a rhombus. **2** having a rhombus as base or cross section. **3** bounded by rhombuses. **4** *Chemistry.* having to do with a system of crystallization characterized by three unequal axes intersecting at right angles.

rhom·boid (rom′boid) *n., adj.* —*n.* a parallelogram that is not a rectangle. See **quadrilateral** for picture. —*adj.* shaped like a rhombus or rhomboid. [< LL < Gk. *rhomboeidēs*]

rhom·boi·dal (rom boi′dəl) *adj.* rhomboid.

rhom·bus (rom′bəs) *n., pl.* -**bus·es,** -**bi** (-bī *or* -bē). a parallelogram with equal sides. See **quadrilateral** for picture. [< L < Gk. *rhombos*]

rhon·cus (rong′kəs) *n., pl.* -**chi** (-kī *or* -kē) a coarse rattling or whistling sound resembling a snore, caused by obstruction in the breathing passages. [< L *rhoncus* a snoring, croaking, perhaps related to Gk. *rhenchos* < *renkein* to snore]

rhu·barb (rü′bärb) *n.* **1** any of several plants (genus *Rheum*) of the buckwheat family, especially a common garden plant (*R. rhaponticum*) having large, heart-shaped leaves and long, thick, red-and-green, juicy leafstalks with an acid taste that are used for pies, preserves, etc. The leaves of rhubarb are poisonous. **2** the leafstalks of garden rhubarb. **3** the dried rhizomes and roots of any of several Asian rhubarbs, used as a laxative. **4** *Slang.* a heated

dispute. [ME < OF < Med.L *rheubarbarum*, ult. < Gk. *rhēon barbaron* foreign rhubarb]

rhumb (rum *or* rumb) *n. Nautical.* any of the 32 points of the compass. [ult. (< F, Sp., *or* Pg.) < L *rhombus* < Gk. *rhombos* rhombus]

rhum·ba (rum′bə) *n., v.* **-baed, -ba·ing.** See **rumba.**

rhyme (rīm) *v.* **rhymed, rhym·ing;** *n.* —*v.* **1** sound alike in the last part: Long *and* song *rhyme.* Go to bed *rhymes with* sleepy head. **2** put or make into rhyme: *to rhyme a translation.* **3** make rhymes: *He enjoys rhyming.* **4** use (a word) with another that rhymes with it: *to rhyme* love *with* dove. —*n.* **1** an agreement in the final sounds of words or lines. **2** a word or line having the same last sound as another: Cat *is a rhyme for* mat. **3** verses or poetry with some of the lines ending in similar sounds. **without rhyme or reason,** having no system or sense.

Also, **rime.** [ME < OF *rime* < L < Gk. *rhythmos* rhythm. Doublet of RHYTHM.] —**rhym′er,** *n.*

☛ *Hom.* **rime.**
☛ *Spelling.* **Rhyme, rime.** The simpler spelling, **rime,** seems to be becoming gradually more common. It was the original spelling in English.

rhyme·ster (rīm′stər) *n.* a maker of rather poor rhymes or verse. Also, **rimester.**

rhythm (riᴛн′əm) *n.* **1** a movement having a regular repetition of a beat, accent, stress, rise and fall, etc.: *the rhythm of dancing, skating, swimming, the rhythm of the tides, the rhythm of one's heartbeats.* **2** the repetition of an accent; arrangement of beats in a line of poetry: *The rhythms of "The Lord's Prayer," and "O Canada" are different.* **3** a grouping by accents or beats: *triple rhythm.* **4** *Music.* the pattern of movement produced by the combination of accent, metre, and tempo. **5** *Biology.* a pattern of involuntary behavior, action, etc. occurring regularly and periodically. [< L < Gk. *rhythmos* < *rhein* flow. Doublet of RHYME.]

rhythm and blues a style of music that developed in black urban areas of the SW United States in the 1930's and that was basically blues sung, often shouted, to the accompaniment of large bands with saxophones, guitars, etc., and strong rhythm sections.

rhyth·mic (riᴛн′mik) *adj.* rhythmical.

rhyth·mi·cal (riᴛн′mə kəl) *adj.* having rhythm; of or having to do with rhythm. —**rhyth′mi·cal·ly,** *adv.*

rhythm method a form of birth control involving abstention from sexual intercourse during the estimated period of ovulation.

RI Rhode Island.

R.I. **1** Queen and Empress (for L *Regina et Imperatrix*). **2** King and Emperor (for L *Rex et Imperator*). **3** Rhode Island.

ri·al (rē′əl) *n.* **1** the basic unit of money in Iran, divided into 100 dinars. **2** the basic unit of money in Oman, divided into 1000 baizas. **3** the basic unit of money in Saudi Arabia, divided into 100 halalas. See table at **money. 4** a unit of money in the Yemen Arab Republic, equal to ¹⁄₁₀₀ of a riyal. **5** a coin or note worth one rial. [< Persian < Arabic *riyal* < Sp. *real.* Doublet of REAL², REGAL, ROYAL]

Ri·al·to (ri al′tō) *n.* **1** in Venice: **a** a former business district. **b** a famous bridge that crosses the Grand Canal. **2 rialto,** *Business.* a place of exchange; market place.

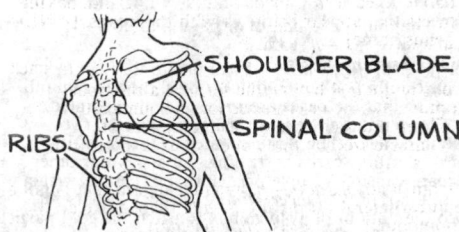

SHOULDER BLADE

SPINAL COLUMN

RIBS

rib (rib) *n., v.* **ribbed, rib·bing.** —*n.* **1** one of the curved bones extending from the backbone and enclosing the upper part of the body. **2** one of a number of similar pieces forming a frame. An umbrella has ribs. **3** a thick vein of a leaf. **4** a ridge in a knitted or woven fabric. **5** a cut of meat containing a rib: *a rib of beef.* **6** one of the arches forming the supports for a vault. **7** *Informal.* **a** a joke. **b** a teasing or mocking; a satire on or a parody of something. **tickle the ribs,** cause laughter, as a joke. —*v.* **1** furnish or strengthen with ribs. **2** mark with riblike ridges. **3** *Informal.* tease. [OE *ribb*]

rib·ald (rib′əld) *adj.* offensive in speech; coarsely mocking; irreverent; indecent; obscene. [ME < OF *ribauld* < *riber* to be wanton < Gmc.] —**rib′ald·ly,** *adv.*

rib·ald·ry (rib′əld rē) *n.* ribald language.

rib·band *or* **rib·and** (rib′ənd) *n. Archaic.* ribbon.

hat, āge, fär; let, ēqual, tèrm; it, īce
hot, ōpen, ôrder; oil, out; cup, pụt, rüle,
əbove, takən, pencəl, lemən, circəs

ch, child; ng, long; sh, ship
th, thin; ᴛн, then; zh, measure

ribbed (ribd) *adj.* having ribs or ridges.

rib·bing (rib′ing) *n.* **1** ribs collectively; a group or arrangement of ribs. **2** *Informal.* teasing.

rib·bon (rib′ən) *n.* **1** a strip or band of silk, satin, velvet, etc. **2** anything like such a strip: *a typewriter ribbon.* **3 ribbons,** *pl.* torn pieces; shreds: *Her dress was torn to ribbons by the thorns and briars she had come through.* **4** a small badge of cloth worn as a sign of membership in an order, decoration for bravery, etc.: *the ribbon of the Victoria Cross.* [ME < OF *riban* < Gmc.] —**rib′bon·like′,** *adj.*

ribbon worm any of a phylum (Nemertea, also called Rhynchocoela) of mostly marine worms having a long, soft, often flattened, and often vividly colored body and a long, threadlike "tongue" that can be shot out to capture prey. Ribbon worms range in length from several centimetres to over 25 metres.

rib cage the cagelike structure formed by the ribs, that encloses the lungs, heart, etc.

ri·bo·fla·vin (rī′bō flā′vən) *n.* a constituent of the vitamin B complex, present in liver, eggs, milk, spinach, etc.; lactoflavin. It is sometimes called vitamin B₂ or G. [< *ribose* + L *flavus* yellow]

ri·bo·nu·cle·ic acid (rī′bō nyü klē′ik *or* -nü klē′ik) an acid found in the nuclei and other parts of cells that helps promote the synthesis of cell proteins. *Abbrev.:* RNA

ri·bose (rī′bōs) *n.* a type of sugar made up of five carbon atoms to the molecule, instead of the six that make up glucose. [< alteration of E *arabinose* (sugar), prepared from gum *arabic*]

rib–tick·ler (rib′tik′lər) *n. Informal.* a joke or funny story.

rice (rīs) *n., v.* **riced, ric·ing.** —*n.* **1** an annual cereal grass (*Oryza sativa*) cultivated throughout the world, from tropical to warm temperate regions, for its starchy, edible seeds. **2** the oblong seeds, or grain, of this plant, a major staple food. —*v.* reduce (cooked potatoes, etc.) to a form resembling cooked rice, as by forcing through a sieve or ricer. [ME < OF < Ital. *riso,* ult. < Gk. *oryza* < Iranian]

rice paper **1** a thin paper made from the straw of rice. **2** paper made from the pith of certain other plants.

ric·er (rī′sər) *n.* a utensil for ricing cooked potatoes, etc. by pressing them through small holes.

rich (rich) *adj., n.* —*adj.* **1** having much money or property: *a rich man.* **2** well supplied; abounding: *Canada is rich in nickel and oil.* **3** abundant: *a rich supply.* **4** producing or yielding abundantly; fertile: *rich soil, a rich mine.* **5** valuable; having great worth: *a rich harvest.* **6** costly; elegant: *rich dress.* **7** having many desirable elements or qualities. **8** of foods, made with plenty of butter, eggs, flavoring, etc. **9** of colors, sounds, smells, etc., deep; full; vivid: *a rich red, a rich tone.* **10** of wine, etc., strong and finely flavored: *a rich, mellow sherry.* **11** of a fuel mixture, containing a high proportion of fuel to air. **12** *Informal.* very amusing; ridiculous. —*n.* **the rich,** *pl.* rich people. [OE *rīce* < Gmc. < Celtic] —**rich′ly,** *adv.* —**rich′ness,** *n.*

☛ *Syn. adj.* **1. Rich, wealthy** = having much money or property. **Rich** = having more than enough money, possessions, or resources for all normal needs and desires: *They own the mill in our town and are considered rich.* **Wealthy** = very rich, having a great store of money, property, and valuable possessions or resources: *Wealthy people are often patrons of the arts.*

rich·es (rich′iz) *n.pl.* wealth; abundance of property; much money, land, goods, etc. [ME < OF *richesse,* taken as plural of *riche* rich < Gmc. Akin to RICH.]

Rich·ter scale (rik′tər) a scale for measuring the intensity of an earthquake in terms of the vibrations produced at its centre. Each whole number on the scale, beginning with 1, represents a magnitude 10 times greater than the preceding one. An earthquake of magnitude 1 can be detected only by instruments; a magnitude of 7 indicates a major earthquake: *The most powerful earthquakes so far recorded registered 8.6 on the Richter scale.* [after Charles F. Richter, American seismologist, born 1900]

rick (rik) *n., v.* —*n.* a stack of hay, straw, etc., especially one made so that the rain will run off it. —*v.* form into a rick or ricks. [OE *hrēac*]

rick·ets (rik′its) *n.* a disease of childhood, caused by lack of vitamin D or calcium, that results in softening and, sometimes, bending of the bones; rachitis. [apparently alteration of *rachitis,* influenced by *wrick* wrench, strain]

rick·ett·si·a (rik et′sē ə) *n., pl.* **-si·as** or **-si·ae** (-sē ē). any of a family (Rickettsiaceae, especially genus *Rickettsia*) of parasitic micro-organisms intermediate between bacteria and viruses, which usually live in lice, fleas, ticks, and other arthropods, and cause diseases such as typhus in human beings. [after Howard T. *Ricketts* (1871-1910), U.S. pathologist. 20 c.]

rick·et·y (rik′ə tē) *adj.* **1** liable to fall or break down; shaky: *a rickety old chair.* **2** having rickets; suffering from rickets. **3** feeble in the joints. **—rick′et·i·ness,** *n.*

rick·ey (rik′ē) *n.* **1** a drink made of sugar, lime, carbonated water, and gin or some other alcoholic liquor. **2** a similar, non-alcoholic drink.

rick·rack (rik′rak′) *n.* a flat, narrow, zigzag braid used for trimming. [? reduplication of *rack*[1]]

rick·shaw or **rick·sha** (rik′sho or rik′shô) *n.* a small, two-wheeled hooded carriage for usually one passenger, pulled by one or more men. Rickshaws were originally used in Japan.

ric·o·chet (rik′ə shā′) *n., v.* **-chet·ted** or **-cheted** (-shād′), **-chet·ting** or **-chet·ing** (-shā′ing). **—n.** the skipping or rebounding of a projectile, such as a bullet, after striking a surface at an angle: *the ricochet of a bullet from a post, the ricochet of a flat stone on the water.* **—v.** of a projectile, skip on or rebound from a surface. [< F]

ric·tus (rik′təs) *n.* **1** the width or gape of an open mouth or beak. **2** a fixed, gaping grimace or grin. [< NL < L *rictus* open mouth, pp. of *ringi* open the mouth, gape. 18 c.]

rid[1] (rid) *v.* **rid** or **rid·ded, rid·ding.** make free (from): *What will rid a house of rats?*
be rid of, be freed from.
get rid of, a get free from: *I can't get rid of this cold.* **b** do away with: *Poison will get rid of the rats in the barn.* [OE (ge)*ryddan* clear land] **—rid′der,** *n.*

rid[2] (rid) *v. Archaic.* a pt. and a pp. of **ride.**

rid·dance (rid′əns) *n.* a clearing away or out; removal.
good riddance, an expression of relief that something or somebody has been removed.

rid·den (rid′ən) *v.* a pp. of **ride.**

rid·dle[1] (rid′əl) *n., v.* **-dled, -dling. —n. 1** a puzzling or misleading question, statement, or problem, usually amusing and often involving a play on words. *Example:* Q.: *When is a door not a door?* A.: *When it is ajar.* **2** a person or thing that is hard to understand, explain, etc.: *His disappearance remains a riddle.* **—v. 1** speak in riddles. **2** solve or explain (a riddle or question). [OE *rǣdels* < *rǣdan* guess, explain; ME *redels* taken as pl.]

rid·dle[2] (rid′əl) *v.* **-dled, -dling;** *n.* **—v. 1** make many holes in: *The door of the fort was riddled with bullets.* **2** sift: *to riddle gravel.* **—n.** a coarse sieve. [OE *hriddel* sieve]

ride (rīd) *v.* **rode** or (*Archaic*) **rid, rid·den** or (*Archaic*) **rid, rid·ing;** *n.* **—v. 1** sit on a horse or other animal and make it go. **2** sit on a bicycle, etc. and make it go. **3** be carried along by anything: *to ride on a train.* **4** admit of being ridden: *a horse that rides easily.* **5** ride over, along, or through: *to ride a mountain trail.* **6** be mounted on; be carried on: *The eagle rides the winds.* **7** do or perform: *to ride a race.* **8** move on; float; float along: *The ship rode the waves.* **9** *Informal.* make fun of; tease. **10** cause to ride or be carried: *to ride a man on a rail as punishment.* **11** control, dominate, or tyrannize over: *to be ridden by foolish fears.*
let ride, leave undisturbed or inactive: *Let the matter ride until the next meeting.*
ride down, a knock down. **b** overcome. **c** overtake by riding. **d** exhaust by riding.
ride high, enjoy success; do very well.
ride out, a withstand (a gale, etc.) without damage. **b** endure successfully.
ride up, slide up out of place: *That coat rides up at the back.*
—n. 1 a trip on the back of a horse, in a carriage, car, train, boat, etc. **2** a path, road, etc. made for riding. **3** a mechanical amusement, such as a merry-go-round, Ferris wheel, etc. **4** a turn on a merry-go-round, Ferris wheel, roller coaster, etc.
take for a ride, *Slang.* **a** murder. **b** cheat.
[OE *rīdan*]
☛ *Syn.* n. **1. Ride, drive** = a trip by some means of transportation. **Ride** emphasizes being carried along in or by something, as on horseback, in a boat, train, bus, etc., or in a car if one is going nowhere in particular or is strictly a passenger: *Let's go for a ride in my new car.* **Drive** emphasizes causing to move in a particular direction, and applies only to a trip in a horse-drawn or motor vehicle that one controls or operates or helps to direct: *Let's take a drive into the country.*

Ri·deau Hall (rē′dō) the official residence of the Governor General of Canada, situated in Ottawa.

rid·er (rīd′ər) *n.* **1** a person who rides: *The Calgary Stampede is famous for its riders.* **2** anything added to a record, document,

legislative bill, or statement after it was considered to be completed. **—rid′er·less,** *adj.*

ridge (rij) *n., v.* **ridged, ridg·ing. —n. 1** the long and narrow upper part of something: *the ridge of an animal's back.* **2** the line where two sloping surfaces meet: *the ridge of a roof.* **3** a long, narrow chain of hills or mountains. **4** any raised, narrow strip: *the ridges on corduroy cloth, the ridges in ploughed ground.* **—v. 1** form or make into ridges. **2** cover or mark with ridges. [OE *hrycg*]

ridge·pole (rij′pōl′) *n.* the horizontal timber along the top of a roof or tent. See **frame** for picture.

ridg·y (rij′ē) *adj.* rising in a ridge or ridges.

rid·i·cule (rid′ə kyūl′) *v.* **-culed, -cul·ing. —v.** laugh at; make fun of. **—n.** laughter in mockery; words or actions that make fun of somebody or something. [< F < L *ridiculum,* neut. of *ridiculus.* see RIDICULOUS.]
☛ *Syn.* v. **Ridicule, deride, mock** = make fun of someone or something and cause him or it to be laughed at. **Ridicule** emphasizes making fun of a person or thing, in either a good-natured or an unkind way, with the intention of making him or it seem little and unimportant: *Boys may ridicule their sisters' friends.* **Deride** emphasizes laughing in contempt and holding up to scorn: *Some people deride patriotic rallies and parades.* **Mock** means to ridicule, often by imitating, in a scornful way: *The impudent boys mocked the teacher.*

ri·dic·u·lous (ri dik′yə ləs) *adj.* deserving ridicule; absurd; laughable. [< L *ridiculus* < *ridere* laugh] **—ri·dic′u·lous·ly,** *adv.* **—ri·dic′u·lous·ness,** *n.*
☛ *Syn.* **Ridiculous, absurd, preposterous** = not sensible or reasonable. **Ridiculous** emphasizes the laughable effect produced by something out of keeping with good sense: *His attempts to be the life of the party were ridiculous.* **Absurd** emphasizes the contrast with what is true or sensible: *His belief that he was too clever to be caught in his wrong-doing was absurd.* **Preposterous** adds to **absurd** the idea of being contrary to reality: *The bandit made the preposterous suggestion that he would drop his gun if the policeman first dropped his.*

rid·ing (rī′ding) *n.* **1** *Cdn.* a political division represented by a Member of Parliament or a Member of the Legislative Assembly; constituency. **2** *Brit.* formerly, an administrative division: *the West Riding of Yorkshire.* [ME *thriding* < ON *thrithjungr* one third; the *th-* was lost as a result of the previous *-t* or *-th* in the compounds *East Thriding, North Thriding, West Thriding*]

riding boot a high boot worn by riders.

riding crop a short whip with a loop on one end instead of a lash.

riding habit a dress or suit worn by riders.

ri·el (rē el′) *n.* the basic unit of money in Kampuchea. See table at **money.** [origin unknown]

Riel Rebellions (rē el′ or rē′əl) the Red River Rebellion and the Northwest Rebellion. [after Louis David *Riel* (1844-1885), leader of the Métis]

rife (rīf) *adj.* **1** happening often; common; numerous; widespread. **2** well supplied; full; abounding: *The land was rife with rumors of war.* [OE *rīfe*]

riff (rif) *n., v. Jazz.* **—n.** a continuously repeated instrumental phrase, supporting a solo improvisation or forming the basis of a tune. **—v.** play a riff or riffs. [prob. shortened and altered form of *refrain.* 20c.]

Riff (rif) *n., pl.* **Riffs, Riff,** or **Riff·i** (rif′ē) a member of a Berber people of the Rif, a mountainous region in northern Morocco, along the Mediterranean coast.

Riff·i·an (rif′ē ən) *adj., n.* **—adj.** of or having to do with the Riffs or the region they live in. **—n.** Riff.

rif·fle (rif′əl) *v.* **-fled, -fling;** *n.* **—v. 1** leaf or flip through (a stack of paper, the pages of a book, etc.) quickly by sliding the thumb along the edges, so that the pages are momentarily separated. **2** shuffle cards by bending the edges slightly so that the two divisions slide into each other. **3** cause water to run in riffles. **—n. 1** the act of shuffling cards by riffling. **2 a** a shoal or other object in a stream causing a ripple or a stretch of choppy water. **b** the ripple itself; a rapid. **3** *Placer mining.* the slat or bars set diagonally into the bottom of a sluice box to catch the gold particles in gravel, water, etc. [? variant of *ripple* or *ruffle*[1]]

riff·raff (rif′raf′) *n., adj.* **—n. 1** worthless people. **2** trash. **—adj.** worthless. [ME < OF *rif et raf* every scrap < *rifler* rifle[2] + *raffler* carry off (related to RAFFLE)]

ri·fle[1] (rī′fəl) *n., v.* **-fled, -fling. —n. 1** a gun having spiral grooves in its barrel to spin the bullet as it is fired. See **firearm** for picture. **2** such a gun that is fired from the shoulder. **—v.** cut spiral grooves in (a gun). [ult. < F *rifler* scratch, groove, rifle[2]]

ri·fle[2] (rī′fəl) *v.* **-fled, -fling. —v. 1** search and rob; ransack and rob. **2** steal; take away. **3** strip bare: *The boys rifled the apple tree.* [ME < OF *rifler* < Gmc.] **—ri′fler,** *n.*

ri·fle·man (rī′fəl mən) *n., pl.* **-men. 1** a soldier armed with a rifle. **2** a man who uses a rifle.

rifle pit a pit or short trench that shelters riflemen firing at an enemy.

rifle range 1 a place for practice in shooting with a rifle. **2** the distance that a rifle will shoot a bullet.

ri·fling (rī′fling) *n.* **1** the act or process of cutting spiral grooves in a gun barrel. **2** the system of spiral grooves in a rifle.

rift (rift) *n., v.* —*n.* **1** a gap, split, or break: *a rift in the clouds.* **2** a breach in relations between individuals, groups, or nations; estrangement. —*v.* break or cause to break open or split.

rig¹ (rig) *v.* **rigged, rig·ging;** *n.* —*v.* **1** equip (a ship) with masts, sails, ropes, etc. **2** move (a shroud, boom, stay, etc.) to its proper place. **3** equip (used with **out**): *to rig out a football team.* **4** *Informal.* clothe; dress (usually used with **out** or **up**): *On Halloween the children rig themselves up in queer clothes.* **5** get ready for use. **6** put together in a hurry or by using odds and ends (often used with **up**): *The girls rigged up a tent, using a rope and a blanket.*
—*n.* **1** the arrangement of masts, sails, ropes, etc. on a ship. A schooner has a fore-and-aft rig; that is, the sails are set lengthwise on the ship. **2** *Informal.* clothing or costume, especially when unusual, showy, etc.: *John's rig consisted of a silk hat and overalls.* **3** an outfit; equipment. **4** the machinery or installation used for locating and extracting petroleum or natural gas from the earth: *a drill rig, an oil rig.* **5** *Informal.* **a** an automobile, truck, etc. **b** a carriage, with its horse or horses. [ME < Scand.; cf. Danish *rigge*]

rig² (rig) *n., v.* **rigged, rig·ging.** —*n.* a trick, prank, or swindle. —*v.* **1** arrange dishonestly for one's own advantage: *to rig a race.* **2** arrange unfavorably.

rig·a·ma·role (rig′ə mə rōl′) *n.* rigmarole.

–rigged (rigd) *combining form.* of a sailing vessel, having a specified kind of rigging, as in *square-rigged.*

rig·ger (rig′ər) *n.* **1** a person who rigs. **2** a person who rigs ships, or works with hoisting tackle, etc. **3** *Informal.* a person who manipulates something fraudulently.

rig·ging (rig′ing) *n.* **1** the ropes, chains, etc. on a ship, used to support and work the masts, yards, sails, etc. **2** tackle; equipment.

right (rīt) *adj., adv., n., v.* —*adj.* **1** good; just; lawful: *He did the right thing when he told the truth.* **2** correct; true: *the right answer.* **3** proper; fitting: *He always managed to say the right thing at the right time.* **4** favorable: *If the weather is right, we'll go.* **5** healthy; normal: *My head doesn't feel right.* **6** meant to be seen; most important: *the right side of cloth.* **7** of the side that is turned to the east when the main side faces north; opposite left: *You have a right hand and a left hand. The right bank of a river is the one to the right as one faces downstream.* **8** Often, **Right,** *Politics.* of, having to do with, supporting, or belonging to the right; rightist. **9** straight: *a right line.* **10** formed by a line drawn to another line or surface by the shortest course: *a right angle, a right cone.* **11** *Archaic.* rightful; real: *the right owner.*
—*adv.* **1** in a way that is good, just, or lawful: *He acted right when he told the truth.* **2** correctly; truly: *She guessed right.* **3** properly; well: *It's faster to do a job right the first time.* **4** favorably: *turn out right.* **5** in a good or suitable condition: *Put things right.* **6** on or to the right hand: *Turn right.* **7** exactly; just; precisely: *Put it right here.* **8** (used in some titles) very: *Right Honourable.* **9** *Archaic or informal.* extremely: *I am right glad to see you.* **10** in a straight line; directly: *Look me right in the eye.* **11** completely: *His hat was knocked right off.* **12** yes; very well: *"Come at once," his mother called. "Right," he replied.*
right away, at once; immediately: *He promised to do it right away.*
right now, immediately; at the present time: *Stop that right now! They're playing in the yard right now.*
right off, at once; immediately.
—*n.* **1** that which is right: *Do right, not wrong.* **2** a just claim, title, or privilege: *the right to vote.* **3** fair treatment; justice. **4** the right side or hand: *Turn to your right. The school is on the right.* **5** a blow struck with the right hand. **6** the **Right** or the **right,** *Politics.* **a** a group or party generally supporting capitalism and private enterprise and opposed to socialism, government regulation of business, etc. **b** a group or party that tend to oppose political and social change; advocates or supporters of conservatism or reaction. **c** especially in some European legislatures, the members occupying the seats to the right of the presiding officer by virtue of their conservative or reactionary views. **7** *Business.* **a** the privilege of subscribing for a stock or bond. **b** a certificate granting such a privilege.
by right or **by rights,** rightly; properly; correctly.
in the right, right.
to rights, *Informal.* in or into proper condition, order, etc.
—*v.* **1** make correct: *to right errors.* **2** do justice to: *to right the oppressed.* **3** get or put into proper position: *The ship righted as the wave passed.*
right about! turn in the opposite direction.
[OE *riht*] —**right′er,** *n.* —**right′ness,** *n.*
▸ *Hom.* **rite, wright, write.**

right about–face (rīt′ə bout′fās′) a turn in the opposite direction.

hat, āge, fär; let, ēqual, tėrm; it, īce
hot, ōpen, ôrder; oil, out; cup, put, rüle,
əbove, takən, pencəl, lemən, circəs

ch, child; ng, long; sh, ship
th, thin; ŦH, then; zh, measure

right angle an angle of 90 degrees. See **angle** for picture.

right–an·gled (rīt′ang′gəld) *adj.* containing a right angle or right angles; rectangular.

right·eous (rī′chəs) *adj.* **1** doing right; virtuous; behaving justly. **2** morally right or justifiable: *righteous indignation.* [OE *rihtwīs < riht* right + *wīs* way, manner] —**right′eous·ly,** *adv.*

right·eous·ness (rī′chəs nis) *n.* upright conduct; virtue; the state or condition of being right and just.

right face a turn to the right.

right·ful (rīt′fəl) *adj.* **1** according to law; by rights: *the rightful owner of this dog.* **2** just and right; proper. —**right′ful·ly,** *adv.* —**right′ful·ness,** *n.*

right–hand (rīt′hand′) *adj.* **1** on or to the right. **2** of, for, or with the right hand. **3** most helpful or useful: *one's right-hand man.*

right–hand·ed (rīt′han′did) *adj.* **1** using the right hand more easily and readily than the left. **2** done with the right hand. **3** made to be used with the right hand. **4** turning from left to right: *a right-handed screw.* —**right′-hand′ed·ly,** *adv.*

Right Honourable a title given to all members of the United Kingdom Privy Council. The Prime Minister of Canada has this title. *Abbrev.:* Rt. Hon.

right·ist (rīt′ist) *n., adj.* —*n. Politics.* **1** a person who supports or favors the right. **2** a member of a conservative or reactionary organization. —*adj. Informal.* having conservative or reactionary ideas.

right·ly (rīt′lē) *adv.* **1** justly; fairly. **2** correctly. **3** properly; suitably. [OE *rihtlīce*]

right–mind·ed (rīt′mīn′did) *adj.* having right opinions or principles. —**right′-mind′ed·ly,** *adv.* —**right′-mind′ed·ness,** *n.*

right of way 1 the right to go first; precedence over all others. **2** the right to pass over property belonging to someone else. **3** a strip of land on which a road, railway, power line, etc. is built.

right triangle a triangle, one of whose angles is a right angle.

right whale 1 a large, thickset, black baleen whale (*Balaena glacialis*) of the northern hemisphere having a large head and a thick lower lip that curves upward in a high bow on each side and a very thick layer of blubber. **2** any other whale of the same family (Balaenidae). Right whales lack the throat grooves of other baleen whales. [probably from the fact that these whales are large and slow moving and therefore "right" for hunting in the early days of whaling with sailing ships and hand harpoons]

right wing 1 the more conservative or reactionary faction of an assembly, group, or party. **2** *Hockey, lacrosse, etc.* **a** the playing position to the right of centre on a forward line. **b** the player in this position. —**right′-wing′,** *adj.* —**right′-wing′er,** *n.*

rig·id (rij′id) *adj.* **1** stiff; firm; not bending: *a rigid support.* **2** strict; not changing: *Our club has few rigid rules.* **3** severely exact; rigorous: *a rigid examination.* [< L *rigidus < rigere* be stiff] —**rig′id·ly,** *adv.* —**rig′id·ness,** *n.*
▸ *Syn.* **1.** See note at **stiff. 3.** See note at **strict.**

ri·gid·i·ty (ri jid′ə tē) *n.* **1** stiffness; firmness. **2** strictness; severity.

rig·ma·role (rig′mə rōl′) *n.* **1** a fussy or complicated procedure. **2** meaningless or incoherent talk. [earlier *ragman roll < ragman* list, catalogue (origin uncertain) + *roll*]

rig·or or **rig·our** (rig′ər) *n.* **1** strictness; severity. **2** harshness: *the rigor of a long, cold winter.* **3** logical exactness: *the rigor of scientific method.* **4** stiffness; rigidity, especially in body tissues or organs. **5** a shivering accompanied by a feeling of chilliness, often preceding a fever. [ME < OF < L *rigor < rigere* be stiff]

rig·or mor·tis (rig′ər môr′tis) the stiffening of the muscles after death. [< L *rigor mortis* stiffness of death]

rig·o·ro·so (rig ə rō′sō) *adj. Music.* in exact rhythm; in the strict timing. [< Ital.]

rig·or·ous (rig′ər əs) *adj.* **1** very severe; strict: *the rigorous discipline in the army.* **2** harsh: *a rigorous climate.* **3** thoroughly logical and scientific; exact: *the rigorous methods of science.* —**rig′or·ous·ly,** *adv.*
▸ *Syn.* **1.** See note at **strict.**

rig·our (rig′ər) See **rigor.**

Rig-Ve·da (rig′vā′də *or* rig′vē′də) *n.* the oldest and most

important of the ancient sacred writings of Hinduism, consisting of about 1000 hymns dating from about 1500 B.C.

rile (rīl) v. **riled, ril·ing. 1** make angry or irritated. **2** roil. [var. of *roil*]

rill (ril) n. a tiny stream; little brook. [cf. Du. *ril* groove, furrow]

rim (rim) n., v. **rimmed, rim·ming.** —n. an edge, border, or margin on or around anything: *the rim of a wheel, the rim of a cup.* —v. **1** form or put a rim around: *Wildflowers and grasses rimmed the little pool.* **2** surround: *The well was rimmed with grass.* [OE *rima*] —**rim′less,** adj.

rime¹ (rīm) v. **rimed, rim·ing.** n. rhyme.
☞ *Hom.* **rhyme.**
☞ *Usage.* See note at **rhyme.**

rime² (rīm) n., v. **rimed, rim·ing.** —n. white frost; hoarfrost. —v. cover with rime. [OE *hrīm*]
☞ *Hom.* **rhyme.**

rime·ster (rīm′stər) See **rhymester.**

rim·rock (rim′rok′) n. *Cdn. Esp.West.* **1** an outcropping or ridge of rock, especially one that once formed the bank of a stream. **2** the crest of a range of hills or mountains.

rim·y (rīm′ē) adj. **rim·i·er, rim·i·est.** covered with rime or hoarfrost; frosty.

rind (rīnd) n. the hard or firm outer covering (of oranges, melons, cheeses, etc.). The bark of a tree or plant may be called the rind. [OE]

rin·der·pest (rin′dər pest′) n. an acute and usually fatal infectious disease of cattle, sheep, etc., caused by a virus. [< G < *rinder* cattle + *pest* pestilence]

ring¹ (ring) n., v. **ringed, ring·ing.** —n. **1** a circle. One can tell the age of a tree by counting the rings in a cross-section of its trunk; one ring grows every year. **2** a thin circle of metal or other material: *a napkin ring, rings on her fingers.* **3** persons or things arranged in a circle. **4** the outer edge or border of a coin, plate, wheel, or anything round. **5** an enclosed space for races, games, circus performances, showing livestock, etc. The ring for a prize fight is square. **6** prize fighting. **7** a competition; rivalry; contest: *in the ring for election to the House.* **8** a group of people combined for a selfish or bad purpose: *A ring of crooks controlled the smuggling operation.* **9** an enclosed area for the showing and judging of livestock.
run rings around, *Informal.* do much better than; outclass or surpass with ease.
—v. **1** put a ring around; enclose; form a circle around. **2** *Sports.* toss a horseshoe, ring, etc. around (a certain mark or post). **3** provide with a ring. **4** put a ring in the nose of (an animal). **5** form a ring or rings. **6** cut away the bark in a ring around (a tree or branch). [OE *hring*] —**ring′less,** adj.
☞ *Hom.* **wring.**

ring² (ring) v. **rang, rung, ring·ing.** n. —v. **1** give forth a clear sound, as a bell does: *The bells rang. Their laughter rang out.* **2** cause to give forth such a sound: *Ring the bell.* **3** cause a bell or buzzer to sound: *I had to ring twice before anyone came.* **4** make (a sound) by ringing: *The bells rang a joyous peal.* **5** call to church, prayers, etc. by ringing bells. **6** announce or proclaim by ringing; usher; conduct: *Ring out the old year; ring in the new.* **7** proclaim or repeat loudly everywhere: *to ring a person's praises.* **8** give back sound; echo or resound: *The mountains rang with the roll of thunder.* **9** be filled with report or talk. **10** sound: *His words rang true.* **11** have a sensation of as of sounds of bells: *My ears are ringing.* **12** call on the telephone (often used with **up**): *I'll ring you when I get home.* **13** summon by means of a bell or buzzer (used with **for**): *to ring for the steward.* **14** record (a specified amount) on a cash register (used with **up**).
ring off, end a telephone call.
—n. **1** the act of ringing. **2** the sound of a bell or buzzer: *I didn't hear the ring.* **3** a sound like that of a bell: *the ring of steel on steel.* **4** a characteristic sound or quality: *the ring of truth.* **5** a call on the telephone: *Give me a ring tonight.* [OE *hringan*] —**ring′ing·ly,** adv.
☞ *Hom.* **wring.**

ring·bolt (ring′bōlt′) n. a bolt with a ring fitted in its head.

ringed (ringd) adj. **1** having or wearing a ring or rings. **2** marked or decorated with a ring or rings. **3** surrounded by a ring or rings. **4** formed of or with rings; ringlike.

ringed seal a small earless seal (*Phoca hispida*) found in arctic and subarctic waters around the world, having a mainly brown or black coat with irregular cream-colored rings. The ringed seal is the cornerstone of the traditional economy of the coastal Inuit, supplying them with food, clothing, blubber for lamps, and bone for tools, etc.

ring·er¹ (ring′ər) n. **1** a person or thing that encircles, surrounds

with a ring, etc. **2** a quoit, horseshoe, etc. thrown so as to fall over a peg. [< *ring¹*]
☞ *Hom.* **wringer.**

ring·er² (ring′ər) n. **1** a person or thing that rings; device for ringing a bell. **2** *Slang.* a player who is not an eligible member of the team that he is playing on. **3** *Slang.* a person or thing very much like another.
be a (dead) ringer for, be the image of. [< *ring²*]
☞ *Hom.* **wringer.**

ring·ette (ring et′) n. an ice game similar to hockey, played on skates by two teams of six persons each, using straight sticks to try to shoot a rubber ring into the opposing team's goal.

ring·git (ring′git) n. **1** the basic unit of money in Malaysia, divided into 100 sen. See table at **money. 2** a coin or note worth one ringgit. [< Malay]

ring·lead·er (ring′lēd′ər) n. a person who leads others in opposition to authority or law. [< the phrase *to lead the ring* to be first]

ring·let (ring′lit) n. **1** a long curl: *She wears her hair in ringlets.* **2** a little ring: *Drops of rain made ringlets in the pond.*

ring·mas·ter (ring′mas′tər) n. a man in charge of the performances in the ring of a circus.

ring–neck (ring′nek′) n. **1** a type of green snake that has a yellow ring round its neck. **2** any of various types of birds having a colored ring round the neck, such as the ring-necked duck.

Ring of the Nibelungs *Germanic mythology.* the magic ring made from the Rheingold by dwarf Alberich, leader of the Nibelungs.

ring ouzel a large European thrush (*Turdus torquatus*), the male having blackish plumage with a white crescent on the upper part of the breast.

ring·side (ring′sīd′) n. **1** a place just outside the ring at a circus, prize fight, etc. **2** a place affording a close view.

ring·worm (ring′wèrm′) n. a contagious disease of the skin, hair, and nails, caused by fungi and characterized by ring-shaped patches.

rink (ringk) n. **1** a sheet of ice for skating or playing hockey. **2** a smooth floor for roller skating. **3** a sheet of ice for curling. **4** a curling team of four players. **5** a building in which there is a rink; arena. [< Scottish < OF *renc* course, rank¹ < Gmc.]

rink rat *Cdn. Slang.* a young person who helps with the chores around a hockey rink, often in return for free skating, free admission to hockey games, etc.

rinse (rins) v. **rinsed, rins·ing;** n. —v. **1** cleanse by washing lightly, especially by allowing water, etc. to run through, over, etc. (often used with **out**): *He rinsed his coffee cup under the tap. I usually rinse my mouth out after eating.* **2** remove (dirt, etc.) by rinsing: *to rinse the sand out of a swimsuit.* **3** give (laundry, dishes, etc.) a final washing in clear water to remove soap or detergent. **4** treat (hair) with a rinse.
—n. **1** the act or process of rinsing. **2** the liquid used in rinsing. **3** a preparation to add temporary lustre or color to the hair. [ME < OF *reincier,* ult. < L *recens* fresh]

ri·ot (rī′ət) n., v. —n. **1** a wild, violent public disturbance; disorder caused by an unruly crowd or mob. **2** a loud outburst: *to break out in a riot of laughter.* **3** loose living; wild revelling. **4** a bright display: *The garden was a riot of color.* **5** *Informal.* a very amusing person or performance: *He was a riot at the party.*
read the riot act, a give orders for disturbance to cease. **b** reprimand severely.
run riot, a act without restraint. **b** of plants, grow wildly or luxuriantly: *The weeds have run riot in our garden.* **c** run wild.
—v. **1** behave in a wild, disorderly way. **2** revel. [ME < OF *riote* dispute, ult. < L *rugire* roar] —**ri′ot·er,** n.

ri·ot·ous (rī′ət əs) adj. **1** taking part in a riot. **2** boisterous; disorderly: *He was expelled from school for riotous conduct. Sounds of riotous glee came from the yard.* —**ri′ot·ous·ly,** adv.

rip¹ (rip) v. **ripped, rip·ping;** n. —v. **1** cut roughly; tear apart; tear off: *Rip the cover off this box.* **2** become torn apart: *The sheet will rip if you pull on it like that.* **3** cut or pull out (the stitches of a seam). **4** saw (wood) along the grain, as opposed to across the grain. **5** *Informal.* move fast or violently. **6** *Informal.* utter violently (used with **out**): *He ripped out an angry oath.*
rip into, *Informal.* attack violently.
rip off, *Slang.* **a** take advantage of; exploit or cheat. **b** steal.
—n. **1** a torn place. **2** a seam unstitched in a garment. **3** tearing. [ME *rippe(n)*]
☞ *Syn. v.* **1.** See note at **tear.**

rip² (rip) n. **1** a stretch of rough water made by cross currents meeting. **2** a swift current made by the tide. [? special use of *rip¹*]

rip³ (rip) n. *Informal.* **1** a worthless or dissolute person. **2** a worthless worn-out horse. [? alteration of *rep,* short for *reprobate*]

R.I.P. may he or she (they) rest in peace (for L *requiescat*, or *requiescant, in pace*).

ri·par·i·an (rə per′ē ən *or* rī per′ē ən) *adj.* of or on the bank of a river, a lake, etc.: *riparian rights, riparian property.* [< L *riparius* < *ripa* riverbank]

rip cord a cord that, when pulled, opens a parachute.

ripe (rīp) *adj.* **rip·er, rip·est. 1** full-grown and ready to be gathered and eaten: *ripe fruit.* **2** resembling ripe fruit in ruddiness and fullness. **3** fully developed; mature: *a ripe cheese, ripe in knowledge.* **4** ready to break or be lanced: *a ripe boil.* **5** ready: *ripe for mischief.* **6** far enough along. **7** advanced in years. [OE *rīpe*] —**ripe′ly,** *adv.* —**ripe′ness,** *n.*

rip·en (rī′pən) *v.* **1** become ripe. **2** make ripe.

rip–off (rip′of′) *n. Slang.* **1** the act or an instance of exploiting or cheating: *Thirty dollars a ticket for that show is a rip-off.* **2** something that is grossly overpriced: *The exhibition midway was a big rip-off this year.* **3** the act or an instance of stealing.

ri·poste (rə pōst′) *n., v.* **-post·ed, -post·ing.** —**1** *Fencing.* a quick thrust given after parrying a lunge. **2** a quick, sharp reply or return. —*v.* make a riposte; reply; retaliate. [< F < Ital. *risposta* reply, ult. < L *respondere* respond. See RESPOND.]

rip·per (rip′ər) *n.* **1** one that rips. **2** a tool for ripping.

rip·ping (rip′ing) *adj. Brit. Slang.* fine; splendid.

rip·ple (rip′əl) *n., v.* **-pled, -pling.** —*n.* **1** a very little wave: *Throw a stone into still water and watch the ripples spread in rings.* **2** anything that seems like a little wave: *ripples in cardboard.* **3** a sound that reminds one of little waves: *a ripple of laughter in the crowd.* **4** a riffle (def. 2). —*v.* **1** make a sound like rippling water. **2** form or have little waves. **3** flow with little waves on the surface. **4** make little waves on: *A breeze rippled the quiet waters.* [origin uncertain]
☛ *Syn. n.* **1.** See note at **wave.**

rip·ply (rip′lē) *adj.* characterized by ripples; rippling.

rip·rap (rip′rap′) *n., v.* **-rapped, -rap·ping.** —*n.* **1** a wall or foundation of broken stones thrown together irregularly. **2** the broken stones so used. —*v.* build or strengthen with loose, broken stones. [varied reduplication of *rap[1]*]

rip·roar·ing (rip′rôr′ing) *adj. Slang.* hilarious; uproarious.

rip·saw (rip′so′ *or* -sô′) *n.* a saw for cutting wood along the grain, not across the grain. [< *rip[1]*, v. + *saw[1]*]

rip·snort·er (rip′snôrt′ər) *n. Slang.* an exciting, intense, or wild person or thing: *a ripsnorter of a storm.*

rip·snort·ing (rip′snôrt′ing) *adj.* **Slang.** exciting, intense, or wild: *a ripsnorting party.*

rip·tide (rip′tīd′) *n.* a strong current of churning water caused by one tide meeting another.

Rip Van Win·kle (rip′van wing′kəl) **1** the hero of a story by Washington Irving. He falls asleep and wakes 20 years later to find everything changed. **2** someone who is ignorant of present-day conditions.

rise (rīz) *v.* **rose, ris·en, ris·ing;** *n.* —*v.* **1** get up from a lying, sitting, or kneeling position: *to rise from a chair.* **2** get up from sleep or rest: *to rise at dawn.* **3** go up; come up; ascend: *The kite rises in the air.* **4** extend upward: *The tower rises to a height of 30 metres.* **5** slope upward: *Hills rise in the distance.* **6** cause to rise; cause to rise above the horizon by approaching nearer to it. **7** go higher; increase: *Prices are rising.* **8** advance to a higher level of action, thought, feeling, expression, rank, position, etc.: *He rose from errand boy to president.* **9** become louder or of higher pitch. **10** appear above the horizon: *The sun rises in the morning.* **11** start; begin: *The river rises from a spring. Quarrels often rise from trifles.* **12** comes into being or action: *The wind rose rapidly.* **13** be built up, erected, or constructed: *Houses are rising on the edge of the town.* **14** become more animated or more cheerful: *His spirits rose.* **15** revolt; rebel: *The slaves rose against their masters.* **16** grow larger and lighter: *Yeast makes dough rise.* **17** come to life again. **18** end a meeting or session; adjourn: *The House rose for the summer.* **19** be able to cope or deal with; respond adequately (*used with* **to**): *They rose to the occasion.*
—*n.* **1** an upward movement; ascent: *the rise of a balloon.* **2** the coming of a fish to the surface of the water to seize bait, etc. **3** an upward slope: *The rise of that hill is gradual.* **4** a piece of rising or high ground; hill. **5** the vertical height of a step, slope, arch, etc. **6** an increase. **7** an advance in rank, power, etc. **8** an increase in loudness or in pitch. **9** a coming above the horizon. **10** an origin; beginning; start: *the rise of a ritzy, the rise of a storm, the rise of a new problem.*
get a rise out of (someone), get an expected reaction, as of anger, protest, or incredulity, from (someone) by means of a calculated question, comment, etc.
give rise to, start; begin; cause; bring about: *The circumstances of*

hat, āge, fär; let, ēqual, tèrm; it, īce
hot, ōpen, ôrder; oil, out; cup, pút, rüle,
əbove, takən, pencəl, lemən, circəs

ch, child; ng, long; sh, ship
th, thin; ᴛʜ, then; zh, measure

his disappearance gave rise to the fear that he might have been kidnapped.
[OE *rīsan*]
☛ *Usage.* **Rise.** *v.* **1, 2.** In referring to people, **arise** is formal and poetic; **rise** is rather formal; **get up,** the most frequent, is general and informal.

ris·en (riz′ən) *v.* pp. of **rise.**

ris·er (rī′zər) *n.* **1** a person or thing that rises: *an early riser.* **2** the vertical part of a step.

ris·i·bil·i·ty (riz′ə bil′ə tē) *n., pl.* **-ties. 1** an ability or inclination to laugh. **2** Often, **risibilities,** *pl.* desire to laugh; sense of humor.

ris·i·ble (riz′ə bəl) *adj.* **1** able or inclined to laugh. **2** of laughter; used in laughter. **3** causing laughter; amusing; funny. [< LL *risibilis,* ult. < L *ridere* laugh]

ris·ing (rī′zing) *n., adj.* —*n.* **1** the act of ascending; coming up. **2** the act of getting up. **3** a rebellion; revolt.
—*adj.* that rises.

risk (risk) *n., v.* —*n.* **1** a chance of harm or loss; danger. **2** *Insurance.* **a** a person or thing described with reference to the chance of loss from insuring him or it. **b** an insurance obligation or possible loss. **c** the amount of possible loss. **3** a person or thing that cannot be relied on.
run a risk or **take a risk,** expose oneself to the chance of harm or loss.
—*v.* **1** expose to the chance of harm or loss: *A soldier risks his life.* **2** take the risk of: *They risked getting wet.* [< F *risque* < Ital. *risco* < *risciare* dare, originally, skirt cliffs in sailing < Gk. *rhiza* base, root]

risk capital capital not covered by collateral and invested in the hope of profit but at the risk of loss.

risk·y (ris′kē) *adj.* **risk·i·er, risk·i·est. 1** full of risk; dangerous. **2** somewhat improper; risqué. —**risk′i·ly,** *adv.* —**risk′i·ness,** *n.*

ri·sot·to (ri zot′ō; *Italian,* rē sôt′tō) *n.* an Italian dish consisting of rice cooked in oil and chicken broth, served with cut-up chicken, tomato sauce, cheese, and spices. [< Ital.]

ris·qué (ris kā′) *adj.* suggestive of indecency; somewhat improper: *a risqué situation in a play.* [< F *risqué,* pp. of *risquer* to risk]

ris·sole (ris′ōl; *French,* rē sôl′) *n.* a fried ball or cake of meat or fish mixed with bread crumbs, egg, etc. [< F]

rit. or **ritard.** ritardando.

ri·tar·dan·do (rē′tär dän′dō) *adj., adv., n. Music.* —*adj.* becoming gradually slower. —*adv.* gradually more slowly. —*n.* a gradual decrease in tempo. *Abbrev.:* rit. or ritard. [< Ital. *ritardando* < *ritardare* retard]

rite (rīt) *n.* **1** a solemn ceremony. Secret societies have their special rites. **2** a particular form or system of ceremonies: *the Latin rite.* [< L *ritus*]
☛ *Hom.* **right, wright, write.**
☛ *Syn.* **1.** See note at **ceremony.**

rit·u·al (rich′ü əl) *n., adj.* —*n.* **1** a form or system of rites. The rites of baptism, marriage, and burial are parts of the ritual of most churches. **2** a book containing rites or ceremonies. **3** the carrying out of rites. **4** any set or formal procedure, act, etc., that is followed consistently.
—*adj.* of or having to do with rites; done as a rite: *a ritual dance.* [< L *ritualis* < *ritus* rite]

rit·u·al·ism (rich′ü əl iz′əm) *n.* **1** a fondness for ritual; insistence upon ritual. **2** the study of ritual practices or religious rites.

rit·u·al·ist (rich′ü əl ist) *n.* **1** a person who practises or advocates observance of ritual. **2** a person who studies or knows much about ritual practices or religious rites.

rit·u·al·is·tic (rich′ü əl is′tik) *adj.* **1** having to do with ritual or ritualism. **2** fond of ritual. —**rit′u·al·is′ti·cal·ly,** *adv.*

rit·u·al·ize (rich′ü ə līz′) *v.* **-ized, -iz·ing.** make a ritual of.

rit·u·al·ly (rich′ü əl ē) *adv.* with or according to a ritual.

ritz·y (rit′sē) *adj.* **ritz·i·er, ritz·i·est.** *Slang.* elegant or luxurious; posh: *a ritzy nightclub.* [after the *Ritz* hotels established by Swiss hotelier César *Ritz* (1850-1918). 20 c.]

riv. river.

ri·val (rī′vəl) *n., adj., v.* **-valled** or **-valed, -val·ling** or **-val·ing.** —*n.* **1** a person who wants and tries to get the same thing as another;

one who tries to equal or do better than another; competitor. **2 a** thing that will bear comparison with something else; equal; match: *Her beauty has no rival.*
—*adj.* wanting the same thing as another; competing: *The rival store tried to get the other's trade.*
—*v.* **1** try to equal or outdo: *The stores rival each other in beautiful window displays.* **2** equal; match: *The sunset rivalled the sunrise in beauty.* [< L *rivalis* using the same stream < *rivus* stream]

ri·val·ry (rī′vəl rē) *n., pl.* **-ries.** the action, position, or relation of a rival or rivals; competition: *There is rivalry among business firms for trade.*

rive (rīv) *v.* **rived, rived** or **riv·en, riv·ing.** tear apart; split; cleave. [ME < ON *rifa*]

riv·en (riv′ən) *adj., v.* —*adj.* torn apart; split. —*v.* a pp. of **rive.**

riv·er¹ (riv′ər) *n.* **1** a large natural stream of water that flows into a lake, ocean, etc. **2** any abundant stream or flow: *rivers of blood.* [ME < OF *rivere* < L *riparius* of a riverbank < *ripa* bank]

riv·er² (rīv′ər) *n.* a person or thing that rives. [< *rive*]

river basin land that is drained by a river and its tributaries.

riv·er·head (riv′ər hed′) *n.* the source of a river.

river horse hippopotamus.

riv·er·ine (riv′ər īn′ or riv′ər ēn′) *adj.* **1** of or having to do with a river. **2** located on or living near a river: *a riverine town.*

riv·er·side (riv′ər sīd′) *n.* **1** the bank of the river. **2** (*adj.*) on the bank of a river: *The riverside path is much used.*

riv·et (riv′it) *n.* a metal bolt having a head at one end, the other end made to be hammered into a head once it is in position.
—*v.* **1** fasten with a rivet or rivets. **2** flatten (the end of a bolt) so as to form a head. **3** fasten or fix firmly: *Their eyes were riveted on the speaker.* [ME < OF *rivet* < *river* fix < VL *ripare* come to shore < L *ripa* bank] —**riv′et·er,** *n.*

Riv·i·er·a (riv′e er′ə) *n.* a section of France and Italy along the Mediterranean Sea, famous as a resort area.

riv·u·let (riv′yə lit) *n.* a very small stream. [< Ital. *rivoletto*, ult. < L *rivus* stream]

ri·yal (rē äl′) *n.* **1** the basic unit of money in Yemen Arabic Republic, divided into 100 rials. See table at **money. 2** rial (def. 3). **3** a note worth one riyal. [< Arabic *riyal* < Sp. *real*]

rm. **1** room. **2** ream.

R.M. **1** rural municipality. **2** Royal Marines.

Rn radon.

RN or **R.N.** **1** registered nurse. **2** Royal Navy.

RNA ribonucleic acid.

roach¹ (rōch) *n.* cockroach.

roach² (rōch) *n., pl.* **roach** or **roach·es. 1** a European freshwater fish related to the carp. **2** any of various similar fishes, such as the North American sunfish. [ME < OF *roche*]

roach³ (rōch) *v., n.* —*v.* of hair, etc., trim the top so that the part that is left stands upright. —*n.* hair, nap, etc. that has been trimmed short. [origin uncertain]

roach⁴ (rōch) *n. Slang.* the butt of a marijuana cigarette.

road (rōd) *n.* **1** a highway between places; way made for trucks or automobiles to travel on: *The road from here to the city is being paved.* **2** a way, route, or course: *Our road went through the woods. He was soon on the road to ruin.* **3** railway. **4** Also, **roads,** a place near the shore where ships can ride at anchor. **5** roadbed.
hold the road, drive or travel on a road easily, smoothly, and safely.
on the road, a travelling, especially as a salesman. **b** of a theatre company, etc., on tour.
take to the road, a go on the road; begin to travel. **b** *Historical.* become a highwayman.
[OE *rād* a riding, journey]
☛ *Hom.* **rode.**

road agent *Esp.U.S. Historical.* a highwayman.

road allowance *Cdn.* land reserved by the government as public property to be used for roads. The road allowance includes the road and a certain amount of land on either side of it.

road·bed (rōd′bed′) *n.* the foundation of a road or of a railway.

road·block (rōd′blok′) *n.* **1** a road barricade set up by police to prevent wanted men from escaping: *A roadblock was set up to stop the car thief.* **2** an obstacle placed across a road. **3** any obstacle to progress.

road hog *Informal.* a driver who obstructs traffic by keeping his vehicle in the middle of the road, refusing to let other vehicles pass.

road·house (rōd′hous′) *n.* a restaurant in the country where people can stop for refreshments and, sometimes, entertainment.

road metal broken stone, cinders, etc. used for roads and roadbeds.

road roller a machine or vehicle used in building or repairing roads, having large, smooth, heavy rollers for levelling and compressing road surfaces.

road runner a long-tailed bird of the deserts of the SW United States that is related to the cuckoo. It usually runs instead of flying.

road show a play, opera, ballet, etc. that travels from city to city.

road·side (rōd′sīd′) *n.* **1** the side of a road. **2** (*adj.*) beside a road: *a roadside inn.*

road·stead (rōd′sted) *n.* road (def. 4).

road·ster (rōd′stər) *n.* **1** an open automobile of the 1920's and 1930's, especially a sporty style seating two or four passengers. **2** a horse for riding or driving on roads.

road·way (rōd′wā′) *n.* **1** road. **2** the part of a road used by vehicles.

road·wor·thy (rōd′wèr′ᴛHē) *adj.* of vehicles, suitable for use on the road. —**road′wor′thi·ness,** *n.*

roam (rōm) *v., n.* —*v.* **1** go about with no special plan or aim; wander: *to roam through the fields.* **2** wander over. —*n.* a walk or trip with no special aim; wandering. —**roam′er,** *n.*
☛ *Syn. v.* **1.** Roam, rove, ramble = wander. **Roam** suggests going about here and there as one pleases over a wide area, with no special plan or aim: *The photographer roamed about the world.* **Rove** usually adds the suggestion of a definite purpose, though not of a settled destination: *Submarines roved the ocean.* **Ramble** particularly suggests straying from a regular path or plan and wandering about aimlessly for one's own pleasure: *We rambled through the shopping district.*

roan (rōn) *adj., n.* —*adj.* yellowish brown or reddish brown sprinkled with grey or white.
—*n.* **1** an animal of this color, especially a horse. **2** a soft, flexible leather made from sheepskin, used in bookbinding. **3** a roan color. [< F < Sp. *roano*, probably < Gmc.]

roar (rôr) *v., n.* —*v.* **1** make a loud, deep sound; make a loud noise: *The lion roared.* **2** utter loudly: *to roar out an order.* **3** make or put by roaring: *The crowd roared itself hoarse.* **4** laugh loudly. **5** move with a roar: *The train roared past us.*
—*n.* a loud, deep sound; loud noise. [OE *rārian*] —**roar′er,** *n.*

roar·ing (rôr′ing) *adj., n.* —*adj.* **1** emitting roars; bellowing. **2** riotous; noisy; boisterous. **3** successful; booming: *a roaring business.*
—*n.* **1** the act of one that roars. **2** a loud, full cry; bellowing. **3** a disease of horses, characterized by loud breathing. —**roar′ing·ly,** *adv.*

roaring forties the rough, stormy region in the North Atlantic Ocean that lies between 40 degrees and 50 degrees latitude.

roast (rōst) *v., n., adj.* —*v.* **1** cook (meat, etc.) by dry heat; cook in an oven, before or over an open fire, or in embers; bake. **2** prepare by heating: *to roast coffee, to roast a metal ore.* **3** make or become very hot. **4** be baked. **5** *Informal.* **a** make fun of; ridicule. **b** reprove; criticize severely.
—*n.* **1** a piece of roasted meat; a piece of meat to be roasted. **2** an informal outdoor meal, at which some food is cooked over an open fire: *a wiener roast.*
—*adj.* roasted: *roast beef.*
[ME < OF *rostir* < Gmc.]

roast·er (rōs′tər) *n.* **1** a pan used in roasting. **2** a chicken, young pig, etc. fit to be roasted. **3** a person or thing that roasts.

rob (rob) *v.* **robbed, rob·bing. 1** take away from by force or threats; steal from: *He was robbed of all his money.* *Bandits robbed the bank.* **2** steal: *They said they would not rob again.* **3** take away some characteristic; keep from having or doing: *The disease has robbed him of his strength.*
rob Peter to pay Paul, take something away from one to pay, satisfy, or advance another. [ME < OF *rober* < Gmc.]

rob·ber (rob′ər) *n.* a person who robs.
☛ *Syn.* See note at **thief.**

rob·ber·y (rob′ər ē or rob′rē) *n., pl.* **-ber·ies.** an act of robbing; theft. [ME < OF *roberie* < *rober.* See ROB.]

robe (rōb) *n., v.* **robed, rob·ing.** —*n.* **1** a long, loose outer garment. **2** a garment that shows rank, office, etc.: *a judge's robe, the king's robes of state.* **3** a covering or wrap: *He had a robe over his lap.* **4** *Cdn. Historical.* the dressed skin of a buffalo or other animal, used especially for protection against moisture and cold. **5** a bathrobe or dressing gown.
—*v.* put a robe on; dress. [ME < OF *robe*, originally, plunder, booty. Cf. ROB.]

rob·in (rob′ən) *n.* **1** a large North American thrush (*Turdus migratorius*) having greyish-brown upper parts and a brick-red breast and abdomen. **2** a small Eurasian thrush (*Erithacus rubecula*), the well-known **robin redbreast** of Britain, the male of which has a brownish back, orange-red throat and breast, and

greyish abdomen. [ME < OF *Robin*, dim. of Robert]

Robin Goodfellow Puck, a mischievous fairy of English folklore.

Robin Hood *English legend.* the brave, chivalrous leader of an outlaw band of Sherwood Forest, who robbed the rich to help the poor.

robin's-egg blue greenish blue.

ro·bot (rō′bot *or* rō′bət) *n.* **1** a machine-made man; a mechanical device that does some of the work of human beings. **2** a person who acts or works in a dull, mechanical way. [invented by Karel Capek (1890-1938), a Czech writer, for his play, *R.U.R.*; suggested by Czech *robota* work, *robotnik* serf]

ro·bust (rō bust′ *or* rō′bust) *adj.* **1** strong and healthy; sturdy: *a robust person, a robust mind.* **2** suited to or requiring bodily strength: *robust exercises.* **3** rough; rude. [< L *robustus*, originally, oaken < *robur* oak] —**ro·bust′ly**, *adv.* —**ro·bust′ness**, *n.*
☞ *Syn.* **1.** See note at **strong.**

ro·bus·tious (rō bus′chəs) *adj. Archaic or humorous.* **1** rough; rude; boisterous. **2** robust; strong; stout.

roc (rok) *n. Arabian legend.* a bird of enormous size and strength. [< Arabic *rokh, rukhkh* < Persian]

Ro·chelle salt (rō shel′) a colorless or white crystalline compound, potassium sodium tartrate, used as a laxative. *Formula:* $KNaC_4H_4O_6 \cdot 4H_2O$ [< La *Rochelle*, a city in France]

roch·et (roch′it) *n.* a vestment of linen or lawn resembling a surplice, worn by bishops and abbots. [ME < OF *rochet*, ult. < Gmc.]

rock¹ (rok) *n.* **1** a large mass of stone. **2** any piece of stone; a stone. **3** *Geology.* **a** the mass of mineral matter of which the earth's crust is made up. **b** a particular layer or kind of such matter. **4** something firm like a rock; support; defence. **5** anything that suggests or acts as a rock. **6** a curling stone. **7** rock candy. **8** *Slang.* a precious stone, especially a diamond. **9 rocks,** *pl. Slang.* money. **on the rocks, a** wrecked; ruined. **b** *Informal.* bankrupt. **c** of alcoholic drinks, with ice but without water or mixes: *whisky on the rocks.* [ME < OF *roque* < VL *rocca*]

rock² (rok) *v., n.* —*v.* **1** move backward or forward, or from side to side; sway. **2** move or shake violently: *The earthquake rocked the houses.* **3** move powerfully with emotion. **4** put (to sleep, rest, etc.) with swaying movements. **5** *Informal.* disturb; shake; upset: *The family was rocked by the news.*
rock the boat, *Informal.* make trouble; especially, disturb or upset a stable situation.
—*n.* **1** a rocking movement. **2** a kind of lively popular music with a very heavy, regular beat and much repetition, usually played with electronically amplified instruments. Rock often has elements of jazz or country and folk music. **3** (*adj.*) of, having to do with, or being this type of music. [OE *roccian*]
☞ *Syn. v.* **1.** See note at **swing.**

rock-and-roll (rok′ən rōl′) *n.* **1** a style of popular music with a heavy beat, an early form of rock. **2** a lively style of dancing to such music, characterized by improvisation and exaggerated movements. Also, **rock'n'roll.**

rock bottom the very bottom; lowest level.

rock-bot·tom (rok′bot′əm) *adj.* down to the very bottom; very lowest.

rock-bound (rok′bound′) *adj.* surrounded by rocks; rocky.

rock burst a violent falling in of rocks from the walls of a mine.

rock candy sugar in the form of large, hard crystals.

Rock Cornish a chicken that is a cross between a Cornish chicken and a white Plymouth Rock. Rock Cornish chickens are usually killed young and eaten as broilers.

rock crystal a colorless, transparent variety of quartz, often used for jewellery, ornaments, etc.

rock·er (rok′ər) *n.* **1** one of the curved pieces on which a cradle, rocking chair, etc. rocks. **2** rocking chair. **3** a cradle used in placer mining.

rock·er·y (rok′ər ē) *n., pl.* **rock·er·ies.** an ornamental garden, or part of a garden, consisting of an arrangement of rocks and earth for growing plants and flowers; a rock garden. Rockeries are often built on slopes.

rock·et (rok′it) *n., v.* —*n.* **1** a projectile consisting of a tube open at one end and filled with some substance that burns rapidly, creating expanding gases that propel the tube and whatever is attached to it at great speed. Rockets are used for fireworks and signalling and for propelling rockets used as weapons, and for carrying satellites into outer space. **2** a spacecraft, missile, etc., propelled by such a projectile.
—*v.* **1** go like a rocket; rise or move extremely fast. **2** fly straight up rapidly. **3** put into orbit with a rocket. [(? < F) < Ital. *rochetta*,

hat, āge, fär; let, ēqual, tèrm; it, īce
hot, ōpen, ôrder; oil, out; cup, pùt, rüle,
əbove, takən, pencəl, lemən, circəs
ch, child; ng, long; sh, ship
th, thin; ᴛʜ, then; zh, measure

probably dim. of *rocca* distaff (from the similarity in shape) < Gmc.]

rock·et·ry (rok′it rē) *n.* the designing and firing of rockets, missiles, etc.

rock garden rockery.

rock·hound (rok′hound′) *n. Informal.* a person who collects rocks as a hobby.

rocking chair a chair mounted on rockers, or on springs, so that it can rock back and forth.

rocking horse a toy horse on rockers for children to ride.

rock'n'roll (rok′ən rōl′) *n.* rock-and-roll.

rock ptarmigan a brown-and-white Arctic ptarmigan, or grouse, that turns white in winter.

rock rabbit 1 pika. **2** hyrax.

rock-ribbed (rok′ribd′) *adj.* **1** having ridges of rock. **2** unyielding.

rock salt common salt as it occurs in the earth in large crystals.

rock tripe *Cdn.* any of various grey or brown lichens (especially of genus *Umbilicaria*) that grow attached to rocks; they are edible when cooked and are often used as emergency food by northern travellers, etc.

rock-weed (rok′wēd′) *n.* any of various coarse seaweeds growing on rocks near the shore.

rock wool a fibrous, wool-like material made by blowing a jet of steam or air through molten slag or rock. It is used especially for insulation and packing.

rock·y¹ (rok′ē) *adj.* **rock·i·er, rock·i·est. 1** full of rocks: *a rocky shore.* **2** made of rock. **3** like rock; hard; firm. [< *rock*¹]

rock·y² (rok′ē) *adj.* **rock·i·er, rock·i·est. 1** likely to rock; shaky: *That table is a bit rocky; put a piece of wood under the short leg.* **2** unpleasantly uncertain. **3** *Informal.* sickish; weak; dizzy. [< *rock*²]
—**rock′i·ly**, *adv.* —**rock′i·ness**, *n.*

Rocky Mountain goat mountain goat.

Rocky Mountain juniper a small, bushy juniper (*Juniperus scopularum*) found in southern Alberta and British Columbia and the W United States.

Rocky Mountain sheep bighorn.

ro·co·co (rō kō′kō *or* rō′kə kō′) *n., adj.* —*n.* **1** *Architecture and design.* a style developed in France in the first half of the 18th century, marked by elaborate ornamentation. **2** *Literature.* a style of florid, ornamental writing. **3** *Music.* a style characterized by graceful, gay ornamentations.
—*adj.* of or having to do with rococo. [< F *rococo*, ? < *rocaille* shellwork < *roc* rock]

rod (rod) *n.* **1** a thin, straight bar of metal or wood. **2** a thin, straight stick, either growing or cut off. **3** anything resembling a rod in shape. **4** a stick used to beat or punish. **5** punishment. **6** a long, light pole. **7** a long, springy, tapered piece of wood, metal, plastic, etc. to which a reel may be attached, used for fishing. **8** a unit for measuring length, equal to 5½ yards (about 5.03 metres). **9** a stick used to measure with. **10** *Slang.* pistol. **11** a branch of a family or tribe: *the rod of Jesse.* **12** a staff or wand carried as a symbol of one's position. **13** power; authority; tyranny. **14** divining rod. **15** one of the microscopic sense organs in the retina of the eye that are sensitive to dim light. **16** a cylindrical or rod-shaped bacterium; bacillus.
spare the rod, fail to punish.
[OE *rodd*]

rode (rōd) *v.* pt. of **ride.**
☞ *Hom.* **road.**

ro·dent (rō′dənt) *n.* **1** any of an order (Rodentia) of relatively small gnawing mammals having a single pair of continually growing incisors in both the upper and lower jaws. The order includes beavers, squirrels, rats, and mice. **2** (*adj.*) of or like a rodent. [< L *rodens, -entis,* ppr. of *rodere* gnaw]

ro·de·o (rō′dē ō *or* rō dā′ō) *n., pl.* **-de·os. 1** a contest or exhibition of skill in roping cattle, riding horses, etc. **2** *Esp.U.S.* the driving together of cattle; roundup. [< Sp. *rodeo* < *rodear* go around]

rod·o·mon·tade (rod′ə mon tād′ *or* rod′ə mon täd′) *n.* vain boasting; bragging. [< F < Ital. *rodomontata* < *Rodomonte,* a

braggart king in a work of Lodovico Ariosto (1474-1533), an Italian poet < dial. *rodare* roll away (ult. < L *rota* wheel) + *monte* mountain < L *mons, montis*]

roe (rō) *n.* fish eggs. [ME *rowe*]
— Hom. **row.**

roe·buck (rō′buk′) *n.* a male roe deer.

roe deer (rō) a small deer (*Capreolus capreolus*) of Europe and Asia, having forked antlers. [OE *rā*]

roent·gen (rent′gən) *n.* the unit for measuring the effect of X rays or gamma rays. It is the quantity of radiation required to produce one electrostatic unit of electrical charge in one cubic centimetre of dry air under normal temperature and pressure. [after Wilhelm Konrad *Roentgen* (1845-1923), a German physicist, who discovered X rays]

Roentgen ray X ray.

ro·ga·tion (rō gā′shən) *n.* **1** *Christianity.* a solemn prayer or supplication, especially as chanted on the three days before Ascension Day (*usually used in the plural*). **2** in ancient Rome: **a** the proposal of a law by consuls or tribunes to be approved by the people. **b** a law so proposed. [< L *rogatio, -onis < rogare* ask]

rog·a·tor·y (rog′ə tôr′ē) *adj.* questioning or asking questions, as in legal investigations: *a rogatory commission.*

rog·er (roj′ər) *interj. Informal.* message received and understood; O.K. [< the signaller's word for the letter *r*, for "received"]

rogue (rōg) *n., v.* **rogued, ro·guing.** —*n.* **1** a tricky, dishonest, or worthless person; rascal. **2** a mischievous person. **3** an animal with a savage nature that lives apart from the herd: *rogue elephant.* **4** *Biology.* an individual, usually a plant, that varies from the standard.
—*v.* **1** eliminate defective plants from. **2** cheat. **3** be a rogue; act like a rogue. [? short for earlier *roger* beggar]

ro·guer·y (rō′gər ē) *n., pl.* **-guer·ies. 1** the conduct of rogues; dishonest trickery. **2** playful mischief.

rogues′ gallery a collection of photographs of known criminals.

ro·guish (rō′gish) *adj.* **1** dishonest; rascally; having to do with or like rogues. **2** playfully mischievous. —**ro′guish·ly,** *adv.* —**ro′guish·ness,** *n.*

roil (roil) *v.* **1** make (a liquid) cloudy or muddy by stirring up sediment. **2** agitate or disturb. **3** especially of a liquid, be agitated or turbulent. **4** rile (def. 1). [< F *rouiller* rust, earlier, make muddy < OF *rouil* mud, rust, ult. < L *robigo* rust]

rois·ter (rois′tər) *v.* be boisterous; revel noisily; swagger. [< MF *ruistre* rude, ult. < L *rus* the country] —**rois′ter·er,** *n.*

Ro·land (rō′lənd) *n.* one of Charlemagne's legendary chiefs, famous for his strength and courage. He and another hero, Oliver, once fought for five days without either gaining the advantage.
a Roland for an Oliver, one thing thought to be a full match for another.

role or **rôle** (rōl) *n.* **1** a performer's part in a play, opera, etc.: *the leading role.* **2** a part played in real life: *He played an important role in the development of art in Canada.* [< F *rôle* the roll (of paper, etc.) on which a part is written]
— Hom. **roll.**
— *Spelling.* **Role, rôle.** The spelling with the circumflex is still preferred by some people, especially in formal usage.

roll (rōl) *v., n.* —*v.* **1** move along by turning over and over: *A ball rolls.* **2** wrap or become wrapped around on itself or on some other thing: *Roll the string into a ball.* **3** move or be moved on wheels: *The car rolled along.* **4** move smoothly; sweep along: *Waves roll in on the beach.* **5** turn around; revolve. **6** of a heavenly body, etc. perform a periodical revolution in an orbit. **7** move from side to side: *The ship rolled in the waves.* **8** turn over, or over and over: *The horse rolled in the dust.* **9** walk with a swaying gait. **10** rise and fall again and again: *rolling country.* **11** *Archaic.* travel; wander; roam. **12** make flat or smooth with a roller; spread out with a rolling pin, etc. **13** put ink, paint, etc. on with a roller. **14** make deep, loud sounds: *Thunder rolls.* **15** beat (a drum) with rapid continuous strokes. **16** utter with full, flowing sound: *The organ rolled out the stirring hymn.* **17** utter with a trill: *to roll one's r's.* **18** *Informal.* have more than enough: *be rolling in money.* **19 a** cast dice. **b** turn up (a number) on a dice: *to roll a five.* **20** *Slang.* rob (a person who is drunk or helpless), especially by turning him over to search through his pockets.
roll back, a cause (prices, wages, etc.) to return to a lower level. **b** *Informal.* set back; cause to fall behind.
roll up, increase; pile up or become piled up. —*n.* **1** something rolled up; a cylinder formed by rolling, (often forming a definite measure): *rolls of paper.* **2** a more or less rounded, cylindrical, or rolled-up mass. **3** continued motion up and down, or from side to side. **4** a rapid continuous beating on a drum. **5** a deep, loud sound:

the roll of thunder. **6** the act of rolling. **7** a motion like that of waves; undulation. **8** a roller, especially a revolving wheel-like tool used by bookbinders. **9** a record; list; list of names: *Call the roll.* **10 a** a small piece of dough which is cut, shaped, and often doubled or rolled over and then baked: *a dinner roll.* **b** a cake rolled up after being spread with something: *jelly roll.* **11** *Slang.* paper money rolled up. **12** *Slang.* money; funds. **13** a part which is rolled or turned over: *the roll in a hem.* **14** a rich or rhythmical flow of words: *the roll of a verse.* **15** a rolling gait; swagger: *walk with a roll.*
strike (someone) **off the rolls,** expel from membership.
[ME < OF *roller*, ult. < L *rota* wheel]
— Hom. **role.**
— *Syn.* n. **9.** See note at **list.**

roll·a·way (rōl′ə wā′) *n.* a folding bed having rollers so that it can be easily stored.

roll call 1 the calling of a list of names, as of soldiers, pupils, etc. to find out who are present. **2** the time of day for such a calling.

rolled oats hulled, steamed oats that have been pressed flat between rollers.

roll·er (rōl′ər) *n.* **1** anything that rolls; a cylinder on which something is rolled along or rolled up. **2** a cylinder of metal, stone, wood, etc. used for smoothing, pressing, crushing, etc. **3** a covered cylinder used for applying paint, ink, etc. **4** a long rolled bandage. **5** a long, swelling wave. **6** a person who rolls something. **7** a variety of canary that has a trilling voice. **8** a variety of tumbler pigeon.

roller bearing a bearing in which the shaft turns on rollers to lessen friction.

roller coaster a railway built for amusement, on which small cars roll up and down steep inclines, round sharp corners, etc.

roller skate one of a pair of skates equipped with small wheels, used on floors, roads, sidewalks, etc.

roll·er·skate (rōl′ər skāt′) *v.* **-skat·ed, -skat·ing.** move on roller skates.

rol·lick (rol′ik) *v.* frolic; be merry; enjoy oneself in a free, hearty way. [origin uncertain]

rol·lick·ing (rol′ik ing) *adj.* frolicking; jolly; lively. —**rol′lick·ing·ly,** *adv.*

rol·lick·some (rol′ik səm) *adj.* rollicking.

rolling mill 1 a factory where metal is rolled into sheets and bars. **2** a machine for rolling metal.

rolling pin a cylinder of wood, porcelain, plastic, etc. for rolling out dough.

rolling stock the locomotives and cars of a railway.

roll-top (rōl′top′) *adj.* having a top that rolls back: *a roll-top desk.*

ro·ly-po·ly (rō′lē pō′lē) *adj., n., pl.* **-lies.** —*adj.* short and plump: *a roly-poly child.* —*n.* **1** a short, plump person or animal. **2** a pudding made of jam or fruit spread on a rich dough, rolled up and cooked. [apparently < *roll*]

rom. *Printing.* roman (type).

Rom. 1 Roman. **2** Romania; Romanian. **3** Romance.

Ro·ma·ic (rō mā′ik) *n., adj.* —*n.* the everyday spoken language of modern Greece. —*adj.* of or having to do with this language.

ro·maine (rō mān′) *n.* a variety of lettuce (*Lactuca sativa longifolia*) having long green leaves with crinkly edges, which are joined loosely at the base. [< F *romaine*, fem. adj., Roman]

ro·man (rō mäN′) *n. French.* **1** a romantic novel. **2** a metrical romance of medieval French literature.

Ro·man (rō′mən) *n., adj.* —*n.* **1** a native or inhabitant of ancient or modern Rome. **2 roman,** roman print or type.
—*adj.* **1** of or having to do with ancient or modern Rome or its people. **2** of or having to do with the Roman Catholic Church. **3** *Architecture.* of or having to do with a style developed by the ancient Romans, characterized by massive walls and pillars, rounded arches and vaults, domes, and pediments. **4 roman,** of or designating an upright style of type, the one most commonly used in printing. The capital letters of roman type are modelled on those used in ancient Roman inscriptions. Compare **italic.** [OE < L *Romanus < Roma* Rome]

roman à clef (ro mäN ä klā′) *pl.* **ro·mans à clef** (ro mäN zä klā′) *French.* a novel featuring real people or events slightly disguised, as with fictitious names.

Roman candle a kind of firework consisting of a tube that shoots out sparks and balls of fire.

Roman Catholic 1 a member of the Catholic Church that follows the Latin rite, as distinguished from the Eastern rites. **2** Catholic (def. 1). **3** of or having to do with Roman Catholics or Roman Catholicism.

Roman Catholicism the doctrines, faith, practices, and system of government of the Roman Catholic Church.

ro·mance (*n.* rō mans′ or rō′mans; *v.* rō mans′) *n., v.* **-manced,**

-manc·ing. —*n.* **1** a love story. **2** a medieval story or poem telling of heroes and strange and exciting adventures. **3** any story of adventure, especially when set in a remote time or place, or involving heroes, strange happenings, etc. **4** a quality or aura of real events or conditions that suggests such stories, characterized by excitement, noble deeds, etc.: *the romance of an explorer's life.* **5** an interest in or inclination for adventure, mystery, love, etc. **6** a love affair. **7** a false or extravagant account. **8** *Music.* a short, lyrical composition.
—*v.* **1** make up extravagant or romantic stories. **2** think or talk in a romantic way. **3** exaggerate or lie. [ME < OF *romanz,* ult. < VL *romanice* in a Romance language < L *Romanus* Roman < *Roma* Rome]

Ro·mance (rō mans′ *or* rō′mans) *adj.* of or having to do with languages that developed from Latin, the language of the Romans. French, Italian, Spanish, Portuguese, Romanian, and Provençal are Romance languages.

ro·manc·er (rō man′sər) *n.* **1** a writer of romance. **2** a person who makes up false or extravagant stories.

Roman Empire the empire of ancient Rome that lasted from 27 B.C. to A.D. 395, when it was divided into the **Eastern Roman Empire** and the **Western Roman Empire.**

Ro·man·esque (rō′mən esk′) *n., adj.* —*n.* *Architecture.* a style characterized by massiveness and round arches and vaults, developed in Europe during the early Middle Ages, between the periods of Roman and Gothic architecture. —*adj.* of, in, or having to do with this style of architecture.

Ro·ma·ni·an (rō mā′nē ən) *n., adj.* —*n.* **1** a native or inhabitant of Romania, a country in SE Europe. **2** the Romance language of the Romanians. —*adj.* of or having to do with Romania, its people, or their language. Also, **Rumanian, Roumanian.**

Ro·man·ic (rō man′ik) *adj.* **1** Romance. **2** Roman. [< L *Romanicus*]

Ro·man·ist (rō′mən ist) *n.* **1** *Derogatory.* a member of the Roman Catholic Church. **2** a student of Roman law, institutions, etc.

Ro·man·ize (rō′mən īz′) *v.* **-ized, -iz·ing. 1** make or become Roman in character. **2** make or become Roman Catholic. **3** write or print in or convert to roman characters. —**Ro′man·i·za′tion,** *n.*

Roman law the laws of the ancient Romans. Roman law is the basis of civil law in many countries.

Roman nose a nose having a prominent bridge.

ROMAN NUMERALS

ROMAN	I	V	X	L	C	D	M
ARABIC	1	5	10	50	100	500	1000

EXAMPLES: XXIII=23, MDCCLXI=1761

Roman numerals the system of numerals used by the ancient Romans. The values of the numerals are added together, except when a numeral is followed by another of greater value, in which case the smaller one is subtracted from the larger one. *Examples:* XI = 10 + 1 = 11; IX = 10 − 1 = 9; XIX = 10 + (10 − 1) = 19.

Ro·ma·no (rō mä′nō) *n.* a hard, sharp Italian cheese similar to Parmesan, but somewhat sharper. [< Ital.]

Ro·ma·nov or **Ro·ma·noff** (rō′mə nof′ *or* rō mä′nof) *n.* the royal family of Russia from 1613 to 1917.

Roman rite the system of ceremonies used in the Roman Catholic Church in celebrating the Mass and administering the sacraments.

ro·man·tic (rō man′tik) *adj., n.* —*adj.* **1** characteristic of romances or romance; appealing to fancy and the imagination: *romantic tales of love and war.* **2** having ideas or feelings suited to romance: *a romantic schoolgirl.* **3** suited to a romance: *What a romantic wood! Fairies might live here!* **4** fond of making up fanciful stories. **5** Often, **Romantic.** of or having to do with art, music, and literature appealing to the emotions and the imagination in subject and style; not classical: *The novel* Jane Eyre *and Chopin's music are romantic. Romantic* writing usually tells about the unusual and adventurous aspects of life and uses complete freedom of form and expression. **6** of or having to do with romanticists or romanticism.
—*n.* **1** romanticist. **2** a romantic person. [< F *romantique* < earlier *romant* a romance, var. of OF *romanz.* See ROMANCE.] —**ro·man′ti·cal·ly,** *adv.*

ro·man·ti·cism (rō man′tə siz′əm) *n.* **1** a romantic spirit or tendency. **2** a style or movement in literature and art that prevailed in W Europe in the late 18th and early 19th centuries, characterized by a highly imaginative and emotional treatment of life, nature, and the supernatural. **3** *Music.* a style characterized by melodic inventiveness and rich harmonies.

ro·man·ti·cist (rō man′tə sist) *n.* a follower of romanticism in

hat, āge, fär; let, ēqual, tėrm; it, īce
hot, ōpen, ôrder; oil, out; cup, pùt, rüle,
əbove, takən, pencəl, lemən, circəs

ch, child; ng, long; sh, ship
th, thin; ŦH, then; zh, measure

literature, art, or music. Scott and Wordsworth were romanticists.

ro·man·ti·cize (rō man′tə sīz′) *v.* **-cised, -ciz·ing. 1** make romantic; give a romantic character to. **2** be romantic; act, talk, or write in a romantic manner.

Romantic Movement the tendency toward romanticism in the literature, art, and music of the late 18th century and early 19th century.

Rom·a·ny (rom′ə nē) *n., pl.* **-nies;** *adj.* —*n.* **1** Gypsy. **2** the Indic language of the Gypsies. —*adj.* belonging or having to do with the Gypsies or their language. [< Romany *Romani,* fem. and pl. of *Romano,* adj. < *Rom* gypsy, man, husband]

ro·maunt (rō mont′ *or* rō mônt′) *n. Archaic.* a romance; a romantic poem or tale. [ME < OF *romaunt,* var. of *romant,* var. of *romanz.* See ROMANCE.]

Rom. Cath. Roman Catholic.

Rome (rōm) *n.* **1** the Roman Catholic Church. **2** the governing authority of the Roman Catholic Church: *The marriage was annulled by Rome.*

Ro·me·o (rō′mē ō′) *n.* **1** the hero of Shakespeare's tragedy *Romeo and Juliet,* who killed himself for love. **2** any young and romantic lover.

romp (romp) *v., n.* —*v.* **1** play in a rough, boisterous way; rush, tumble, and punch in play. **2 a** run or go quickly and easily. **b** win easily.
—*n.* **1** a rough, lively play or frolic: *A pillow fight is a romp.* **2** *Archaic.* tomboy. **3** a swift but effortless victory in which all the others are left behind, as in racing: *to win in a romp.* [ult. var. of *ramp,* v.] —**romp′er,** *n.*

romp·ers (romp′ərz) *n.pl.* a loose outer garment, worn by young children.

Rom·u·lus (rom′yə ləs) *n. Roman legend.* the founder and first king of Rome. As children, he and his brother Remus were nursed by a wolf. Romulus slew Remus for leaping derisively over the walls of his new city of Rome.

ron·deau (ron′dō *or* ron dō′) *n., pl.* **ron·deaux** (ron′dōz *or* ron dōz′). a short poem with thirteen (or ten) lines. The opening words are used in two places as a refrain. The poem "In Flanders Fields" is a rondeau. [< MF *rondeau,* var. of *rondel* < OF *rondel.* Doublet of RONDEL.]

ron·del (ron′dəl *or* ron′del) *n.* a short poem, usually with fourteen lines and two rhymes. The initial couplet is repeated in the middle and at the end. [ME < OF *rondel,* originally dim. of *rond* round < L *rotundus.* Doublet of RONDEAU.]

ron·do (ron′dō *or* ron dō′) *n., pl.* **-dos.** *Music.* a composition or movement having one principal theme to which return is made after the introduction of each subordinate theme. [< Ital. < F *rondeau* rondeau]

rood (rüd) *n.* **1** a unit for measuring land area, equal to ¼ acre (about 1012 m²). **2** *Archaic.* the cross on which Christ died. **3** a representation of the cross; crucifix. [OE *rōd*]
☞ Hom. **rude.**

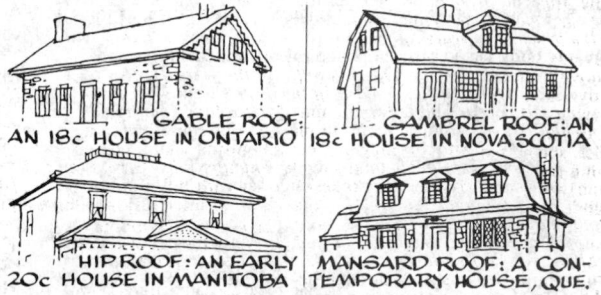

GABLE ROOF: AN 18c HOUSE IN ONTARIO

GAMBREL ROOF: AN 18c HOUSE IN NOVA SCOTIA

HIP ROOF: AN EARLY 20c HOUSE IN MANITOBA

MANSARD ROOF: A CONTEMPORARY HOUSE, QUE.

roof (rüf) *n., pl.* **roofs** or **rooves;** *v.* **1** the top covering of a building. **2** something that in form or position resembles the roof of a building: *the roof of a cave, the roof of a car, the roof of the mouth.* **3** a house; home: *live together under the same roof.*
raise the roof, *Informal.* make a disturbance; create an uproar or confusion.

—v. provide or cover with or as if with a roof. [OE *hrōf*]

roof·er (rüf'ər) *n.* a person who makes or repairs roofs.

roof garden 1 a garden on the flat roof of a building. 2 a roof or top storey of a building, ornamented with plants, etc. and used for a restaurant, theatre, etc.

roof·ing (rüf'ing) *n.* material used for roofs. Shingles are a common roofing for houses.

roof·less (rüf'lis) *adj.* 1 having no roof. 2 having no home or shelter.

roof·top (rüf'top') *n.* the top of the roof.

roof·tree (rüf'trē') *n.* the horizontal timber along the top of the roof.

rook[1] (rük) *n., v.* —*n.* 1 a common European bird (*Corvus frugilegus*) closely related to the North American crow. 2 *Slang.* a person who cheats at cards, dice, etc. —*v. Slang.* cheat. [OE *hrōc*]

rook[2] (rük) *n. Chess.* one of the pieces with which the game is played, also called a castle. [ME < OF *roc*, ult. < Persian *rukh*]

rook·er·y (rük'ər ē) *n., pl.* -er·ies. 1 a breeding place of rooks; a colony of rooks. 2 a breeding place or colony where other birds or animals are crowded together: *a rookery of seals.* 3 a crowded, dirty, and poor tenement house or group of such houses.

rook·ie (rük'ē) *n. Informal.* a beginner, such as a recruit or a new player on a team. [? alteration of *recruit*]

room (rüm *or* rùm) *n., v.* —*n.* 1 a part of a house, or other building, with walls separating it from the rest of the building of which it is a part. 2 **rooms,** *pl.* lodgings. 3 the people in a room. 4 the space occupied by, or available for, something: *There is little room to move in a crowd.* 5 scope or opportunity: *room for improvement, room for advancement.* —*v.* 1 rent a room; lodge: *The two girls roomed together.* 2 provide with a room. [OE *rūm*]
☞ *Hom.* rheum.

–roomed *combining form.* having a specified number of rooms: *a six-roomed house.*

room·er (rü'mər) *n.* a person who lives in a rented room or rooms in another's house.
☞ *Hom.* rumor.

room·ette (rü met') *n.* a small private bedroom on some railway cars.

room·ful (rüm'fùl *or* rùm'-) *n., pl.* -fuls. 1 enough to fill a room. 2 the people or things in a room.

rooming house a house with rooms to rent.

room–mate (rüm'māt') *n.* a person who shares a room with another or others.

room service in a hotel, lodge, etc., a special service by which one may order food or drink to be brought to one's room.

room·y (rü'mē) *adj.* room·i·er, room·i·est. having plenty of room; large; spacious. —**room'i·ness,** *n.*
☞ *Hom.* rheumy.

roost (rüst) *n., v.* —*n.* 1 a bar, pole, or perch on which birds rest or sleep. 2 a place for birds to roost in. 3 a place to rest or stay: *a robber's roost in the mountains.*
come home to roost, have unforeseen and unfavorable consequences for the originator; boomerang: *The stories he spread came home to roost when everyone thought they were about him.*
rule the roost, *Informal.* be master.
—*v.* 1 sit or sleep on a roost: *roosting birds.* 2 settle down, as for the night. [OE *hrōst*]

roost·er (rüs'tər) *n.* a male domesticated fowl; cock.

GRASS (FIBROUS) **CARROT** (TAPROOT) **ORCHID** (AERIAL)

The two main types of root (fibrous roots and taproot) are shown at the left. The specialized aerial roots of an orchid are shown above.

root[1] (rüt) *n., v.* —*n.* 1 the part of a plant that grows downward, usually into the ground, to hold the plant in place, absorb water and mineral foods from the soil, and often to store food material. 2 any underground part of a plant. 3 something like a root in shape,

position, use, etc.: *the root of a tooth, the roots of the hair.* 4 a thing from which other things grow and develop; cause; source: *"The love of money is the root of all evil."* 5 the essential part; core or base: *to get to the root of a problem.* 6 an ancestor or antecedent: *searching for one's roots.* 7 **roots,** *pl.* a sense of belonging to a particular place or community: *a person without roots.* 8 *Mathematics.* **a** the quantity that produces another quantity when multiplied by itself a certain number of times. 2 is the square root of 4 and the cube root of 8 ($2 \times 2 = 4$, $2 \times 2 \times 2 = 8$). **b** the quantity that satisfies an equation when substituted for an unknown quantity. In the equation $x^2 + 2x - 3 = 0$, 1 and –3 are the roots. 9 a word or word element from which others are derived. *Example:* Room is the root of roominess, roomer, room-mate, and roomy. 10 *Music.* the fundamental tone of a chord.
take root, a send out roots and begin to grow. **b** become firmly fixed.
—*v.* 1 send out roots and begin to grow; become fixed in the ground: *Some plants root more quickly than others.* 2 fix firmly: *He was rooted to the spot by surprise.* 3 become firmly fixed.
root out or **up,** get rid of completely: *to root out corruption in government.*
[OE *rōt* < ON *rót*; akin to L *radix*] —**root'like',** *adj.* —**root'er,** *n.*
☞ *Hom.* route.

root[2] (rüt) *v.* 1 dig with the snout: *Pigs like to root in gardens.* 2 poke; pry; search. [OE *wrōtan*] —**root'er,** *n.*
☞ *Hom.* route.

root[3] (rüt) *v. Informal.* cheer or support a contestant, etc. enthusiastically. [probably < earlier *rout* shout, roar < ON *rauta*] —**root'er,** *n.*
☞ *Hom.* route.

root beer a soft drink flavored with the juice of the roots of certain plants such as sarsaparilla and sassafras.

root canal 1 the central passage in the root of a tooth, containing blood vessels and nerves. 2 root-canal treatment.

root hair a hairlike outgrowth from a root that absorbs water and dissolved minerals from the soil.

root·less (rüt'ləs) *adj.* having no roots: *a rootless transient.* —**root'less·ness,** *n.*

root·let (rüt'lit) *n.* a little root; a small branch of a root.

root·stock (rüt'stok') *n.* rhizome.

root·worm (rüt'wèrm') *n.* any of various insect larvae or worms that feed on plant roots.

rooves (rüvz) *n.* a pl. of **roof.**

rope (rōp) *n., v.* roped, rop·ing. —*n.* 1 a strong, thick line or cord made by twisting smaller cords together. 2 lasso. 3 a number of things twisted or strung together: *a rope of pearls, a rope of onions.* 4 a cord or noose for hanging a person. 5 death by being hanged. 6 a sticky, stringy mass: *Molasses candy forms a rope.*
give (someone) rope, *Informal.* let a person act freely.
know the ropes, a know the various ropes of a ship. **b** *Informal.* know about a business or activity.
the end of (one's) rope, the end of one's resources, endurance, etc.
—*v.* 1 tie, bind, or fasten with a rope. 2 enclose or mark off with a rope. 3 catch (a horse, calf, etc.) with a lasso. 4 form a sticky, stringy mass: *Cook the syrup until it ropes when you lift it with a spoon.*
rope in, *Slang.* get or lead in by tricking.
[OE *rāp*]

rope·danc·er (rōp'dan'sər) *n.* a person who dances, walks, etc. on a rope stretched high above the floor or ground.

rope·walk (rōp'wok' *or* -wôk') *n.* a place where ropes are made. A ropewalk is usually a long, low shed.

rope·walk·er (rōp'wok'ər *or* -wôk'ər) *n.* a person who walks on a rope stretched high above the floor or ground.

rope·way (rōp'wā') *n.* an aerial cable along which passengers or freight may be carried.

rop·y (rōp'ē) *adj.* rop·i·er, rop·i·est. 1 forming sticky threads; stringy. 2 like a rope or ropes. —**rop'i·ly,** *adv.* —**rop'i·ness,** *n.*

roque (rōk) *n.* a form of croquet played on a hard court and modified from ordinary croquet so as to demand greater skill. [abstracted from *croquet*]

Roque·fort (rōk'fərt) *n.* a strongly flavored French cheese made of goats' milk, veined with mould.

ror·qual (rôr'kwəl) *n.* any of a genus (*Balaenoptera*) of baleen whales of the same family (Balaenopteridae) as the humpback, having a long, streamlined body with a small dorsal fin and numerous grooves or furrows running along the throat to the belly; especially, *B. physalus,* found in almost all oceans and also called **fin whale** or **finback.** See also **blue whale.** [< F < Norwegian *röyrkval,* literally, red whale]

Ror·schach test (rôr'shäk) a psychological test that indicates personality traits, based on the subject's interpretation of ten

different ink-blot designs. [after Hermann *Rorschach* (1884-1922), a Swiss psychiatrist]

ro·sa·ceous (rō zā′shəs) *adj.* **1** belonging to the rose family. **2** like a rose. **3** rose-colored. [< L *rosaceus* < *rosa* rose¹]

ro·sa·ry (rō′zə rē) *n., pl.* **-ries. 1** a string of beads for keeping count in saying a series of prayers. **2** a series of prayers. **3** a rose garden; rose bed. [< Med.L. *rosarium* < L *rosarium* rose garden; ult. < *rosa* rose¹]

rose¹ (rōz) *n., adj., v.* **rosed, ros·ing.** —*n.* **1** any of a genus (*Rosa*) of shrubs of the northern hemisphere, having compound leaves, showy flowers, and, usually, prickly stems. There are many cultivated species and varieties of rose. Wild roses have flowers with five petals. **2** the flower of any of these shrubs. **3** (*adj.*) designating a large family (Rosaceae) of herbs, shrubs, and trees, found especially in temperate regions, that includes some of the most important fruit-bearing and ornamental shrubs and trees. Raspberries, strawberries, cherries, plums, peaches, hawthorns, brambles, and roses belong to the rose family. **4** a medium to dark, slightly purplish pink. **5** something shaped like a rose or suggesting a rose, such as a rosette, compass card, the sprinkling nozzle of a watering can, or a gem cut with faceted top and flat base. **6** a woman of great beauty, loveliness, or excellence.
under the rose, in secret; privately.
—*adj.* of the color rose.
—*v.* make rosy. [OE < L *rosa*] —**rose′like′,** *adj.*

rose² (rōz) *v.* pt. of **rise.**

ro·sé or **Ro·sé** (rō zā′) *n.* a light, pink table wine. [< F]

ro·se·ate (rō′zē it *or* rō′zē āt′) *adj.* **1** rose-colored; rosy. **2** cheerful; optimistic.

rose·bud (rōz′bud′) *n.* the bud of a rose.

rose·bush (rōz′bùsh′) *n.* a shrub that bears roses; a rose plant.

rose-col·ored or **rose-col·oured** (rōz′kul′ərd) *adj.* **1** pinkish red. **2** bright; cheerful; optimistic.

rose geranium a geranium (*Pelargonium graveolens*) having small pink flowers and rose-scented, lobed leaves. The oil of the leaves of some varieties of rose geranium is used in perfumes as a substitute for attar of roses.

rose leaf a petal of a rose.

rose mallow 1 any of several species of hibiscus having large red, pink, or white flowers, especially *Hibiscus moscheutos*, native to marshy areas of E North America, from which many cultivated varieties have been derived. **2** hollyhock.

rose·mar·y (rōz′mer′ē) *n., pl.* **-mar·ies.** a European evergreen shrub (*Rosmarinus officinalis*) widely cultivated for its fragrant, greyish-green leaves which are used as a flavoring and which yield an essential oil used in perfumes. Rosemary is a traditional symbol of remembrance. [ME < L *ros maris,* literally, dew of the sea; associated with *rose* and *Mary*]

rose of Sharon 1 a shrub or small tree (*Hibiscus syriacus*) of the mallow family native to Asia, commonly cultivated for its large, bell-shaped, usually rose, purple, or white flowers. **2** a Eurasian shrub (*Hypericum calycinum*) closely related to the St.-John's-worts, cultivated for its large yellow flowers.

Ro·set·ta stone (rō zet′ə) a slab of black basalt found in 1799 near the mouth of the Nile. A decree carved on it in two kinds of ancient Egyptian writing and in Greek provided the most important key to the understanding of Egyptian hieroglyphics. [< *Rosetta* (< Arabic *Rashid*), a town near one of the mouths of the Nile]

ro·sette (rō zet′) *n.* an ornament, object, or arrangement shaped like a rose. Rosettes made of ribbon are given as prizes at livestock shows. Carved or moulded rosettes are used in architecture. [< F *rosette,* dim. of *rose* rose¹]

rose water water containing oil of roses, used as a perfume and in cooking.

rose window a circular window, usually of stained glass, especially one with a pattern radiating from a centre.

rose·wood (rōz′wùd′) *n.* **1** the hard, dark-reddish wood of any of various tropical trees (especially of genus *Dalbergia*) of the pea family valued for fine furniture, panelling, etc. **2** any of the trees having such wood.

Rosh Ha·sha·nah or **Ha·sha·na** (rosh′hə shä′nə; *Hebrew,* rōsh′hä shä nä′) the Jewish New Year, falling usually in late September or early October. [< Hebrew *rōsh* head + *hash-shānāh* the year]

Ro·si·cru·cian (rō′zə krü′shən) *n., adj.* —*n.* **1** a member of a secret society, especially prominent in the 17th and 18th centuries, that claims to have a special and secret knowledge of nature and religion. **2** a member of any of various similar societies founded later. —*adj.* of or having to do with the Rosicrucians. [< Latinized version of Christian *Rosenkreuz* (1387-1484), the name of the supposed founder of the order]

hat, āge, fär; let, ēqual, tèrm; it, īce
hot, ōpen, ôrder; oil, out; cup, pùt, rüle,
əbove, takən, pencəl, lemən, circəs
ch, child; ng, long; sh, ship
th, thin; ŦH, then; zh, measure

ros·i·ly (rō′zə lē) *adv.* **1** with a rosy tinge or color. **2** brightly; cheerfully.

ros·in (roz′ən) *n., v.* —*n.* a hard, yellow substance that remains when turpentine is evaported from pine resin. Rosin is rubbed on violin bows and on the shoes of acrobats, ballet dancers, boxers, etc. to keep them from slipping. —*v.* cover or rub with rosin. [ME var. of *resin*]

Ros·i·nan·te (roz′ə nan′tē) *n.* **1** in Cervantes' *Don Quixote,* the hero's thin and worn-out horse. **2** any very poor, thin, or worn-out horse.

ros·ter (ros′tər) *n.* **1** a list of people's names and the duties assigned to them. **2** any list. [< Du. *rooster*]

ros·tral (ros′trəl) *adj.* of or having to do with a rostrum.

ros·trum (ros′trəm) *n., pl.* **-trums, -tra** (-trə). **1** a platform for public speaking. **2** the beak of an ancient war galley. **3** a beaklike part. [< L *rostrum* beak < *rodere* gnaw; with reference to the speakers' platform in the Roman forum, which was decorated with the beaks of captured war galleys]

ros·y (rō′zē) *adj.* **ros·i·er, ros·i·est. 1** like a rose; rose red; pinkish red. **2** made of roses. **3** bright; cheerful: *a rosy future.* —**ros′i·ness,** *n.*

rot (rot) *v.* **rot·ted, rot·ting;** *n.* —*v.* **1** decay; spoil. **2** cause to decay. **3** moisten or soak (flax, etc.) in order to soften; ret. **4** lose vigor; degenerate.
—*n.* **1** the process of rotting; decay. **2** rotten matter. **3** a liver disease of animals, especially of sheep, caused by a liver fluke and marked by anemia, weakness, and swollen jaws. **4** any of various diseases of plants marked by decay and caused by bacteria or fungi, as crown rot. **5** *Slang.* nonsense; rubbish. [OE *rotian*].
☛ *Hom.* **wrought** (rot).
☛ *Syn. v.* **1.** See note at **decay.**

Ro·tar·i·an (rō ter′ē ən) *n., adj.* —*n.* a member of a Rotary Club. —*adj.* of, belonging, or having to do with Rotary Clubs.

ro·ta·ry (rō′tə rē) *adj., n.* —*adj.* **1** turning like a top or a wheel; rotating. **2** having parts that rotate. **3** of an airplane engine, having radially arranged cylinders that revolve around a common fixed crankshaft. **4** of or operating under the rotary system.
—*n.* **1** traffic circle. **2** the rotary system: *All classes are on rotary this year.* [< Med.L *rotarius* < L *rota* wheel]

Rotary Club an association of business and professional men formed with the purpose of serving their community. Rotary Clubs form an international organization.

rotary system a method of operation in schools, under which students move to different rooms (and specialist teachers) for different subjects.

ro·tate (rō′tāt *or* rō tāt′) *v.* **-tat·ed, -tat·ing. 1** move around a centre or axis; turn in a circle; revolve. Wheels, tops, and the earth rotate. **2** change in a regular order; take turns or cause to take turns: *Farmers rotate crops.* [< L *rotare* < *rota* wheel]
☛ *Syn.* **1.** See note at **turn.**

ro·ta·tion (rō tā′shən) *n.* **1** the act or process of moving around a centre or axis; turning in a circle; revolving. The earth's rotation causes night and day. **2** a change in a regular order. **3** a system of taking turns; changing in regular succession: *The job of classroom roll call is done in rotation.*

ro·ta·tion·al (rō tā′shən əl) *adj.* of or with rotation.

rotation of crops the varying of the crops grown in the same field to keep the soil from losing its fertility.

ro·ta·tor (rō′tā tər) *n.* **1** a person or thing that rotates. **2** *Physiology.* a muscle that turns a part of the body. [< L]

ro·ta·to·ry (rō′tə tô′rē) *adj.* **1** rotating; rotary. **2** causing rotation. **3** passing or following from one to another in a regular order.

rote (rōt) *n.* a set, routine way of doing things.
by rote, by memory, without thought of the meaning: *to learn a lesson by rote.* [ME; origin uncertain]
☛ *Hom.* **wrote.**

ro·te·none (rō′tə nōn′) *n.* a white crystalline compound obtained from various plant roots, used as an insecticide and fish poison although it is harmless to mammals or birds. *Formula:* $C_{23}H_{22}O_6$ [origin unknown]

rot·gut (rot′gut′) *n. Slang.* raw, cheap alcoholic liquor.

rot·hole (rot′hōl′) *n. Cdn.* a soft place in the ice over a lake, river, etc.

ro·ti·fer (rō′tə fər) *n.* any of a phylum (Rotifera) of minute or microscopic, multicellular, aquatic invertebrates having at one end of the body a disk with one or more rings of cilia. Some authorities classify the rotifers as a class within the phylum Aschelminthes, which also includes the nematodes. [< NL *Rotifera*, pl. < *rota* wheel + *ferre* carry]

ro·tis·se·rie (rō tis′ə rē) *n.* **1** a rotating spit used in an oven, under a broiler, or over an open fire, for roasting meat or fowl. **2** a portable oven containing such a device. **3** a shop or restaurant where meats or poultry cooked on a rotisserie are sold. [< F *rotisserie* < *rôtir* to roast]

ro·to·gra·vure (rō′te grə vyür′ *or* -grä′vyür) *n.* **1** a process of printing from an engraved copper cylinder on which the pictures, letters, etc. have been depressed instead of raised. **2** a print or section of a newspaper made by this process. [< L *rota* wheel + E *gravure*]

ro·tor (rō′tər) *n.* **1** the rotating part of a machine or apparatus. **2** a system of rotating blades by which a helicopter is enabled to fly. See **helicopter** for picture. [shortened form of *rotator*]

ROTP or **R.O.T.P.** Regular Officer Training Plan.

rot·ten (rot′ən) *adj.* **1** decayed; spoiled: *a rotten egg.* **2** foul; bad-smelling: *rotten air.* **3** not in good condition; unsound; weak: *rotten ice.* **4** corrupt; dishonest. **5** *Slang.* bad; nasty. [ME < ON *rotinn*] —**rot′ten·ly,** *adv.* —**rot′ten·ness,** *n.*

rotten borough **1** in England before 1832, a borough that had only a few voters, but kept the privilege of sending a member to Parliament. **2** an electoral district having an insufficient number of voters to justify the representation it has.

ro·tund (rō tund′) *adj.* **1** round; plump. **2** sounding rich and full; full-toned: *a rotund voice.* [< L *rotundus,* ult. < *rota* wheel. Doublet of ROUND.] —**ro·tund′ly,** *adv.*

ro·tun·da (rō tun′də) *n.* **1** a circular building or part of a building, especially one with a dome. **2** a large, circular room with a high ceiling. **3** a large room or area with a high ceiling, such as the lobby of a hotel or the concourse of a railway station. [< L *rotunda,* fem. of *rotundus.* See ROTUND.]

ro·tun·di·ty (rō tun′də tē) *n., pl.* **-ties. 1** roundness; plumpness. **2** something round. **3** rounded fullness of tone.

rou·ble (rü′bəl) *n.* **1** the basic unit of money in the Soviet Union, divided into 100 kopeks. See table at **money. 2** a coin or note worth one rouble. Also, **ruble.** [< Russian]

rou·é (rü ā′ *or* rü′ā) *n.* a dissipated man; rake. [< F *roué,* originally pp. of *rouer* break on the wheel < *roue* wheel < L *rota;* first applied to an 18th-century group of profligates]

rouge (rüzh) *n., v.* **rouged, roug·ing.** —*n.* **1** a red or reddish powder, paste, or liquid for coloring the cheeks or lips. **2** a red powder, chiefly ferric oxide, used for polishing metal, jewels, etc. **3** *Cdn. Football.* **a** a play in which the team receiving a punt behind its own goal line is liable or unwilling to carry the ball back into the field of play, thus conceding a point to the opposition. **b** the single point conceded on such a play.
—*v.* **1** color with rouge. **2** *Cdn. Football.* **a** score a rouge. **b** tackle (a defending player) in the end zone so as to score a rouge: *Jones rouged Smith on the last play.* [< F *rouge* red]

rouge et noir (rü zhā nwär′) a gambling game played with cards. [< F *rouge et noir* red and black]

rough (ruf) *adj., n., v., adv.* —*adj.* **1** not smooth; not level; not even: *rough boards, rough bark.* **2** without polish or fine finish: *rough diamonds.* **3** without luxury and ease: *rough life in camp.* **4** not completed or perfected; done as a first try; without details: *a rough drawing, a rough idea.* **5** coarse and tangled: *a dog with a rough coat of hair.* **6** likely to hurt others; harsh; rude; not gentle: *rough manners.* **7** disorderly; riotous: *a rough crowd.* **8** *Informal.* unpleasant; hard; severe: *He was in for a rough time.* **9** requiring merely strength rather than intelligence or skill: *rough work.* **10** stormy: *rough weather.* **11** violently disturbed or agitated: *a rough sea.* **12** harsh, sharp, or dry to the taste: *rough wines.* **13** *Phonetics.* pronounced with much breath; aspirated.
—*n.* **1** a coarse, violent person. **2** rough ground. **3** a rough thing or condition. **4** *Golf.* ground where there is long grass, etc. on a course.
in the rough, not polished or refined; coarse; crude.
—*v.* **1** make rough; roughen. **2** become rough. **3** treat roughly. **4** *Sports.* illegally check, tackle, etc. an opposing player with unnecessary roughness. **5** shape or sketch roughly: *to rough out a plan, to rough in the outlines of a face for a drawing.*
rough it, live without comforts and conveniences.

—*adv.* in a rough manner; roughly: *Those boys play too rough for me.* [OE *rūh*] —**rough′ness,** *n.*
☛ *Hom.* **ruff.**

rough·age (ruf′ij) *n.* **1** rough or coarse material. **2** the coarser parts or kinds of food which stimulate the movement of food and waste products through the intestines. Bran, fruit skins, and certain fruits are roughage.

rough-and-read·y (ruf′ən red′ē) *adj.* **1** rough and crude, but good enough for the purpose; crude but effective. **2** showing rough vigor rather than refinement.

rough-and-tum·ble (ruf′ən tum′bəl) *adj.* showing confusion and violence; with little regard for rules; unrestrainedly vigorous; boisterous.

rough·cast (ruf′kast′) *n., v.* **-cast, -cast·ing.** —*n.* **1** a coarse plaster for outside surfaces. **2** rough form. —*v.* **1** cover or coat with coarse plaster. **2** make, shape, or prepare in a rough form: *roughcast a story.*

rough-dry (ruf′drī′) *v.* **-dried, -dry·ing.** dry (clothes) after washing without ironing them.

rough·en (ruf′ən) *v.* **1** make rough. **2** become rough.

rough fish a fish that has no commercial value and is also not valued as a sport fish.

rough-hew (ruf′hyü′) *v.* **-hewed, -hewed** or **-hewn, -hew·ing. 1** hew (timber, stone, etc.) without smoothing or finishing. **2** shape crudely; give crude form to.

rough·house (ruf′hous′) *n., v.* **-housed, -hous·ing.** *Slang.* —*n.* boisterous play; rowdy conduct; disorderly behavior. —*v.* **1** act in a boisterous, disorderly way. **2** disturb by such conduct.

rough·ing (ruf′ing) *n. Sports.* the illegal act or practice of checking, tackling, etc. an opposing player with unnecessary roughness: *a penalty for roughing.*

rough·ly (ruf′lē) *adv.* **1** in a rough manner. **2** approximately.

rough·neck (ruf′nek′) *n.* **1** *Informal.* a rough, coarse, bad-mannered person; a rowdy. **2** *Slang.* a member of an oil-drilling crew.

rough·rid·er (ruf′rīd′ər) *n.* **1** a man used to tough, hard riding. **2** a person who breaks in and rides rough, wild horses.

rough·shod (ruf′shod′) *adj.* having horseshoes equipped with sharp calks to prevent slipping.
ride roughshod over, domineer; show no consideration for; treat roughly.

rou·lade (rü läd′) *n.* **1** *Music.* a rapid succession of tones sung to a single syllable. **2** a slice of meat rolled about a filling of minced meat and cooked. [< F *roulade* < *rouler* roll]

rou·lette (rü let′) *n.* **1** a gambling game in which the players bet on the turn of a wheel. **2** a small wheel with sharp teeth for making lines of marks, dots, or perforations. [< F *roulette,* ult. < *roue* < L *rota* wheel]

Rou·ma·ni·an (rü mā′nē ən *or* rü mān′yən) *adj. or n.* Romanian.

round (round) *adj., n., v., adv., prep.* —*adj.* **1** shaped like a ball, a ring, a cylinder, or the like; having a circular or curved outline or surface. **2** plump: *Her figure was short and round.* **3** making or requiring a circular movement: *The waltz is a round dance.* **4** full; complete: *a round dozen.* **5** large: *a good round sum of money.* **6** general; approximate; to the nearest unit, ten, hundred, etc.: *The cost of the whole trip should be $500 in round figures. 3974 in round numbers would be 4000.* **7** plainly expressed; plain-spoken; frank: *The boy's father scolded him in good round terms.* **8** with a full tone: *a mellow, round voice.* **9** vigorous; brisk: *a round trot.*
—*n.* **1** anything shaped like a ball, circle, cylinder, etc. The rungs of a ladder are sometimes called rounds. **2** a fixed course ending where it begins: *The watchman makes his rounds of the building every hour.* **3** a movement in a circle or about an axis: *the earth's yearly round.* **4** a series of duties, events, etc.); routine: *a round of pleasures, a round of duties.* **5** the distance between any limits; range; circuit: *the round of human knowledge.* **6** a section of a game or sport: *a round in a boxing match, a round of cards.* **7** the firing of a number or group of rifles, guns, etc. at the same time. **8** the bullets, powder, etc. for such a shot. **9** a single bullet, artillery shell, etc. **10** an act that a number of people do together: *a round of applause, a round of cheers.* **11** a dance in which the dancers move in a circle. **12** *Music.* a short song, sung by several persons or groups beginning one after the other: *"Three Blind Mice" is a round.* **13 rounds,** the ringing of a set of bells from the highest tone through the major scale to the lowest tone. **14** a form of sculpture in which the figures are apart from any background. **15** a cut of beef just above the hind leg. See **beef** for picture.
go the round, be passed, told, shown, etc. by many people from one to another.
in the round, a in a form of sculpture in which the figures are apart from any background. **b** in the open; showing all sides or aspects.

make or **go the rounds,** go about from place to place in a certain course or through a certain area.
—*v.* **1** make or become round: *The carpenter rounded the corners of the table.* **2** go wholly or partly around: *They rounded the island. The ship rounded Cape Horn.* **3** take a circular course; make a complete or partial circuit: *The car rounded the corner.* **4** turn around; wheel about: *The bear rounded and faced the hunters.* **5** fill (*out*); complete: *to round out a paragraph, to round out a career.* **6** *Phonetics.* utter (a vowel) with a circular opening of the lips: *The rounded vowels include* (ō) *and* (ü).
round in, in nautical use, haul in.
round off, a make or become round. **b** finish; complete: *round off a meal with a light dessert.* **c** generalize a number by expressing it in the nearest unit, ten, hundred, etc.; generalize a number: *The total was 361, but he rounded it off to 350. Please round the answer off to two decimal places.*
round on, turn on to attack, or as if to attack.
round out, complete: *to round out a paragraph, to round out a career.*
round to, in nautical use, come head up to the wind.
round up, draw or drive together.
—*adv.* **1** in a circle; with a whirling motion: *Wheels go round.* **2** on all sides; in every direction: *The travellers were compassed round by dangers.* **3** in circumference: *The pumpkin measures 105 centimetres round.* **4** by a longer road or way: *We went round by the candy store on our way home.* **5** from one to another: *A report is going round that the stores will close.* **6** through a recurring interval of time: *Summer will soon come round again.* **7** about; around: *He doesn't look fit to be round.* **8** here and there: *I am just looking round.* **9** for all: *There is just enough cake to go round.*
—*prep.* **1** on all sides of: *Bullets whistled round him, but he was not hit.* **2** so as to encircle or surround: *They built a fence round the yard.* **3** so as to make a turn to the other side of: *He walked round the corner.* **4** to all or various parts of: *We took our cousins round the town.* **5** about; around: *Stand still and look round you.* **6** here and there in: *There are boxes for mail all round the city.*
get or **come round** (someone), **a** outwit him. **b** wheedle him. [ME < OF *roont* (fem. *roonde*) < L *rotundus.* Doublet of ROTUND.] —**round′ness,** *n.*

☛ *Usage.* **Round, around.** In informal usage **round** and **around** are used interchangeably, with a definite tendency to use **round.** In formal English there is some tendency to keep **around** to mean "here and there or in every direction" and **round** for "in a circular motion or in a reverse motion": *I have looked all around. There aren't any around here. He is going round the world. Everyone turned round.*

round·a·bout (round′ə bout′) *adj., n.* —*adj.* indirect: *a roundabout route. I heard about it in a roundabout way.*
—*n.* **1** an indirect way, course, or speech. **2** a short, tight jacket for men or boys. **3** *Brit.* merry-go-round. **4** *Esp.Brit.* a traffic circle.

round dance 1 a dance performed by couples and characterized by circular or revolving movements. **2** a dance performed by dancers in a circle.

roun·del (round′dəl) *n.* **1** a small round ornament, window, panel, tablet, etc. **2** rondel. **3** rondeau. [ME < OF *rondel.* See RONDEL.]

roun·de·lay (roun′də lā′) *n.* **1** a song in which a phrase or a line is repeated again and again. **2** a dance in which the dancers move in a circle. [< MF *rondelet,* dim. of *rondel* (see RONDEL); influenced by *lay⁴*]

Round·head (round′hed′) *n.* in England, a supporter of Oliver Cromwell during the civil wars from 1642 to 1651. The Roundheads wore their head cut short in contrast to the long curls of their opponents, the Cavaliers.

round·house (round′hous′) *n.* **1** a circular building for storing or repairing locomotives, built about a turntable. **2** a cabin on the after part of a ship's quarterdeck. **3** *Informal.* a punch or blow delivered with a wide swing. **4** (*adj.*) of or designating such a punch or style of punching: *taking a roundhouse swing.*

round·ish (roun′dish) *adj.* somewhat round.

round·ly (round′lē) *adv.* **1** in a round manner or form. **2** plainly, severely, or fully: *He was roundly scolded for getting in so late.*

round number 1 a whole number without a fraction. **2** a number in even tens, hundreds, thousands, etc. 3874 in round numbers would be 3900 or 4000.

round robin 1 a petition, protest, etc. with the signatures written in a circle, so that it is impossible to tell who signed first. **2** any petition. **3** *Sports.* a system of scheduling a number of games, in which every competing player or team is matched with every other one.

round–shoul·dered (round′shōl′dərd) *adj.* having the shoulders bent forward.

round steak a cut of beef just above the hind leg.

round table 1 a group of persons assembled for an informal discussion, etc. **2 Round Table, a** the table around which King Arthur and his knights sat. **b** King Arthur and his knights.

round trip a trip to a place and back.

hat, āge, fär; let, ēqual, tèrm; it, īce
hot, ōpen, ôrder; oil, out; cup, pût, rüle,
əbove, takən, pencəl, lemən, circəs

ch, child; ng, long; sh, ship
th, thin; ŦH, then; zh, measure

round·up (round′up′) *n.* **1 a** the act of driving or bringing cattle or horses together from long distances. **b** the people and horses that take part in a roundup. **2** a gathering together of people or things: *a roundup of criminals, a roundup of late news, a roundup of old friends.*

round·wood (round′wûd′) *n.* timber that is used in the round without being squared or cut into lumber, such as logs, poles, and pulpwood.

round·worm (round′wèrm′) *n.* nematode.

roup (rüp) *n.* **1** either of two diseases of poultry characterized by hoarseness and a discharge of mucus from the eyes, nostrils, and throat. One form of roup is contagious and is often fatal. **2** hoarseness or huskiness. [origin uncertain]

rouse¹ (rouz) *v.* **roused, rous·ing;** *n.* —*v.* **1** arouse; wake up: *I was roused by the telephone.* **2** stir up; excite: *He was roused to anger by the insult.* —*n.* **1** the act of rousing. **2** a signal for rousing or for action. [origin uncertain] —**rous′er,** *n.*

rouse² (rouz) *n. Archaic.* a drinking party; carouse. [? short for *carouse*]

rous·ing (rou′zing) *adj.* **1** able to rouse or stir; lively; brisk: *a rousing speech, a rousing response.* **2** *Informal.* extraordinary; exceptional: *a rousing falsehood.* —**rous′ing·ly,** *adv.*

roust·a·bout (roust′ə bout′) *n. Informal.* an unskilled laborer on wharves, ships, ranches, circuses, etc. [< *roust* move, stir + *about*]

rout¹ (rout) *v.* —*n.* **1** the flight in disorder of a defeated army: *The enemy's retreat soon became a rout.* **2** a complete defeat. **3** *Archaic.* a crowd; band. **4** a group of followers. **5** a noisy, disorderly crowd; mob; rabble. **6** a riot; disturbance. **7** *Archaic.* a large evening party. —*v.* **1** put to flight: *Our soldiers routed the enemy.* **2** defeat completely: *The home team routed the visitors with a score of ten to one.* [ME < OF *route* detachment, ult. < L *rumpere* break]
☛ *Hom.* **route** (rout).

rout² (rout) *v.* **1** dig (*out*); get by searching. **2** put (*out*); force (*out*): *The farmer routed his sons out of bed at five o'clock.* **3** dig with the snout, as pigs do. **4** poke; search; rummage. [var. of *root²*]
☛ *Hom.* **route** (rout).

route (rüt *or* rout) *n., v.* **rout·ed, rout·ing.** —*n.* **1** a way to go; road. **2** a fixed, regular course or area assigned to a person making deliveries, sales, etc.: *a newspaper route, a milk route.* —*v.* **1** arrange the route for. **2** send by a certain route. [ME < OF < L *rupta* (*via*) (a way) opened up, (a passage) forced < *rumpere* break]
☛ *Pronun.* **Route.** The pronunciation (rüt) is the preferred form in Canada but (rout) is in common use, especially with reference to newspaper and delivery routes.

rout·er (rou′tər) *n.* a tool or machine for cutting grooves in or hollowing out wood or metal.

rou·tine (rü tēn′) *n., adj.* —*n.* **1** a fixed, regular method of doing things; habitual doing of the same things in the same way: *Getting up and going to bed are parts of your daily routine.* **2** an act or skit that is part of some entertainment. —*adj.* **1** using routine: *routine methods, a routine operation.* **2** average or ordinary; run-of-the-mill: *a routine show with routine performances.* [< F *routine* < *route* route] —**rou·tine′ly,** *adv.*

rove¹ (rōv) *v.* **roved, rov·ing.** wander; wander about; roam: *He loved to rove over the fields and woods.* [origin uncertain]
☛ *Syn.* See note at **roam.**

rove² (rōv) *v.* a pt. and a pp. of **reeve².**

rov·er¹ (rō′vər) *n.* **1** a wanderer or roamer. **2** *Lacrosse.* a player who holds no special position but who may rove over the entire field. **3 Rover,** a member, aged 17 to 23, of the Boy Scouts. [< *rove¹*]

rov·er² (rō′vər) *n.* **1** pirate. **2** a pirate ship. [< MDu. *rover* < *roven* rob]

row¹ (rō) *n.* **1** a line of people or things: *a row of potatoes.* **2** a street with a line of buildings on either side.
hard row to hoe, a difficult thing to do. [OE *rāw*]
☛ *Hom.* **roe.**

row² (rō) *v., n.* —*v.* **1** move a boat by means of oars: *Row to the island.* **2** move (a boat, etc.) by the use of oars: *We had to row the dinghy.* **3** carry in a rowboat: *We were rowed to the shore.* **4** perform (a race, etc.) by rowing. **5** row against in a race.

—*n.* **1** the act of using oars. **2** a trip in a rowboat. [OE *rōwan*] —**row′er**, *n.*
☛ *Hom.* **roe.**

row³ (rou) *n., v.* —*n.* **1** a noisy quarrel; disturbance; clamor. **2** *Informal.* a squabble. —*v.* **1** *Informal.* quarrel noisily; make noise. **2** *Informal.* scold. [origin uncertain]

row·an (rō′ən *or* rou′ən) *n.* **1** a mountain ash, especially the European mountain ash (*Sorbus aucuparia*). **2** the fruit of a rowan. [< Scand.; cf. Norwegian *raun*]

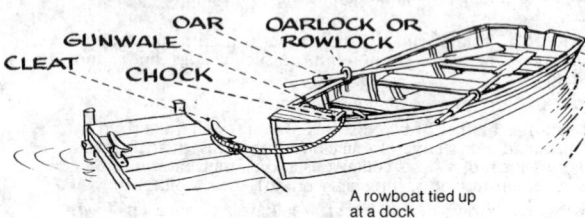

OAR
GUNWALE   OARLOCK OR
          ROWLOCK
CLEAT
     CHOCK

A rowboat tied up
at a dock

row·boat (rō′bōt′) *n.* a small boat moved by oars.

row·dy (rou′dē) *n., pl.* **-dies;** *adj.* **-di·er, -di·est.** —*n.* a rough, disorderly, quarrelsome person. —*adj.* rough; disorderly; quarrelsome. [probably < *row³*] —**row′di·ly**, *adv.* —**row′di·ness**, *n.*

row·dy·ish (rou′dē ish) *adj.* like a rowdy; rough and disorderly; quarrelsome.

row·dy·ism (rou′dē iz′əm) *n.* disorderly, quarrelsome conduct; rough, noisy behavior: *rowdyism at Halloween.*

row·el (rou′əl) *n., v.* **-elled** *or* **-eled, -el·ling** *or* **-el·ing.** —*n.* a small wheel having sharp points, attached to the end of a spur. See **spur** for picture. —*v.* use a rowel on. [ME < OF *roel*, ult. < L *rota* wheel]

row house one of several houses built together in a row and constituting one building.

row·lock (rō′lok′) *n.* a device, usually a swivelling, U-shaped metal piece, attached to the top of the gunwale of a boat to serve as support for an oar in rowing. Also called **oarlock.** See **rowboat** for picture.

roy·al (roi′əl) *adj., n.* —*adj.* **1** of or having to do with kings and queens: *the royal family.* **2** belonging to a king or queen: *royal power.* **3** favored or encouraged by a king or queen; serving a king or queen: *the Royal Society of Canada.* **4** from or by a king or queen: *a royal command.* **5** of a kingdom or its government. **6** appropriate for a king or queen; splendid: *a royal welcome.* **7** like a king or queen; noble; majestic. **8** fine; excellent; supreme. **9** rich and bright: *royal blue.*
—*n.* **1** a small mast or sail set above the topgallant. **2** *Printing.* a size of paper (20 × 25 inches). [ME < OF *roial* < L *regalis.* Doublet of REAL², REGAL, RIAL.] —**roy′al·ly**, *adv.*
☛ *Syn. adj.* **1, 2. Royal, regal, kingly** = of or belonging to a monarch or monarchs. **Royal** is the most general in application, describing people or things associated with or belonging to a king or queen: *Sherwood Forest is a royal forest.* **Regal** emphasizes the majesty and stateliness or pomp and magnificence of the office, but is now used chiefly of people or things showing these qualities: *The general has a regal bearing.* **Kingly** emphasizes the personal character, actions, purposes or feelings of or worthy of a king: *Tempering justice with mercy is a kingly virtue.*

royal assent the signature of the Queen or her representative giving approval to a bill that has been passed by Parliament or by a legislative assembly. A bill does not become law until royal assent has been given.

Royal Canadian Legion a Canadian organization of former military personnel, especially war veterans, and nowadays also the families of such personnel. It sponsors numerous community services and undertakes welfare work for veterans and their families.

Royal Canadian Mounted Police the federal police force of Canada. The Royal Canadian Mounted Police also act as provincial police in most Canadian provinces. *Abbrev.:* RCMP *or* R.C.M.P.

royal commission *Cdn.* **1** any investigation by a person or persons commissioned by the Crown to inquire into some matter on behalf of the federal or a provincial government and to make a report recommending appropriate action. **2** the person or persons so commissioned.

royal flush *Poker.* a straight flush consisting of the Ace, King, Queen, Jack, and ten of one suit.

roy·al·ism (roi′əl iz′əm) *n.* adherence to a king or to a monarchy.

roy·al·ist (roi′əl ist) *n., adj.* —*n.* **1** a supporter of a king or of a royal government. **2 Royalist,** **a** in England, a supporter of Charles I during the civil wars from 1642 to 1651. **b** in the United States, a supporter of George III during the Revolution; loyalist. **c** in France, Spain, etc., a supporter of the monarchy. —*adj.* of or having to do with royalism or royalists.

royal palm any of several palm trees (genus *Roystonea*), especially a tropical American species (*R. regia*) having a tall, whitish trunk and pinnate leaves, widely cultivated for ornament.

royal poinciana a tropical tree (*Delonix regia*) of the pea family having wide-spreading limbs forming an umbrella-shaped crown and bearing large clusters of brilliant scarlet or orange flowers. It is a native of Madagascar but is widely cultivated throughout the tropics.

roy·al·ty (roi′əl tē) *n., pl.* **-ties.** **1** a royal person; royal persons. Kings, queens, princes, and princesses are royalty. **2** the rank or dignity of a king or queen; royal power. **3** kingliness; royal quality; nobility. **4** a royal right or privilege. **5** a share of the receipts or profits paid to an owner of a patent or copyright; payment for the use of any of various rights. [ME < OF *roialte* < *roial.* See ROYAL.]

rpm *or* **r.p.m.** revolutions per minute.

rps *or* **r.p.s.** revolutions per second.

R.R. **1** rural route: *His address is R.R. 1, Kingston, Ontario.* **2** railroad. **3** Right Reverend.

R.S.F.S.R. Russian Soviet Federated Socialist Republic.

RSV *or* **R.S.V.** Revised Standard Version.

R.S.V.P. *or* **r.s.v.p.** please reply (for F *répondez s'il vous plaît*).

rt. right.

Rt.Hon. Right Honourable.

Rt.Rev. Right Reverend.

Ru ruthenium.

rub (rub) *v.* **rubbed, rub·bing;** *n.* —*v.* **1** move (one thing) back and forth (against another); move (two things) together: *Rub your hands to warm them.* **2** move one's hands or an object over the surface of; push and press along the surface of: *The nurse rubbed my back.* **3** press along the surface of, in moving; chafe or grate: *That door rubs against the floor. The back of the shoe rubs on my heel.* **4** make or bring to some condition by rubbing: *to rub silver bright, to rub one's hands dry.* **5** remove or be removed by rubbing: *The spot won't rub off. He rubbed the skin off his hand in the fall.* **6** make an image of an engraved or textured surface by rubbing charcoal, graphite, etc. over a piece of paper placed on top of the surface. **7** admit of rubbing. **8** *Informal.* keep going with difficulty: *Money is scarce, but we'll rub along.*
rub down, rub (the body); massage.
rub it in, *Informal.* keep on mentioning something unpleasant.
rub off on, cling to; become part of; take hold of: *Some of his gall has rubbed off on his son.*
rub out, **a** erase: *to rub out a mistake.* **b** *Slang.* kill: *He was rubbed out by another gangster.*
rub the right way, please; pacify.
rub the wrong way, annoy; irritate.
—*n.* **1** the act of rubbing. **2** something that rubs or hurts the feelings: *He didn't like her mean rub at his slowness.* **3** a spot or area roughened by rubbing. **4** a difficulty: *The rub came when both boys wanted to sit with the driver.* [ME *rubbe(n)*]

rub·a·boo *or* **rub·ba·boo** (rub′ə bü′) *n. Cdn.* a soup made by boiling pemmican in water with flour and other ingredients. [< Cdn.F *rababou* < Algonquian]

rub·ber¹ (rub′ər) *n.* **1** an elastic substance obtained from the milky juice (latex) of various tropical plants, especially the rubber tree. It is airtight, water resistant, and does not conduct electricity. **2** synthetic rubber. **3** a waterproof overshoe. **4** eraser: *Some pencils have a rubber on one end.* **5** any of various other things made of rubber or a similar substance. **6** a person or thing that rubs. **7** (*adj.*) made of rubber: *a rubber tire.* [< *rub*] —**rub′ber·like′**, *adj.*

rub·ber² (rub′ər) *n. Card games.* **1** a series of two games out of three, or three games out of five, won by the same side. **2** the deciding game in such a series. [origin uncertain]

rubber band a circular strip of rubber, used to hold things together.

rubber ice *Cdn.* especially in the North, thin, flexible ice on the surface of seas, lakes, etc.

rub·ber·ize (rub′ər īz′) *v.* **-ized, -iz·ing.** cover or treat with rubber.

rub·ber·neck (rub′ər nek′) *n., v. Slang.* —*n.* a person who stares and gapes, especially a tourist or sightseer. —*v.* stare; gape.

rubber plant **1** a tropical Asian plant (*Ficus elastica*) of the mulberry family having large, thick, glossy leaves. The rubber plant becomes a tall tree in its native environment but is cultivated in dwarf form as a house plant in North America and Europe. **2** any of

various plants that yield rubber. Compare **rubber tree.**

rubber stamp **1** a stamp made of rubber, used with ink for printing dates, signatures, etc. **2** *Informal.* a person or group that approves or endorses something without thought or without power to refuse.

rub·ber–stamp (rub'ər stamp') *v.* **1** print or sign with a rubber stamp. **2** *Informal.* approve or endorse (a policy, bill, etc.) without thought or without power to refuse.

rubber tree a widely cultivated, tropical American tree (*Hevea brasiliensis*) of the spurge family that yields a latex that is the main commercial source of rubber. Compare **rubber plant.**

rub·ber·y (rub'ər ē) *adj.* like rubber; elastic; tough.

rub·bing (rub'ing) *n.* an image of an engraved or textured surface, such as a brass inscription or rock carving, made by rubbing charcoal, graphite, etc. over a piece of paper placed on top of the surface.

rub·bish (rub'ish) *n.* **1** worthless or useless stuff; waste; trash. **2** silly words and thoughts; nonsense. [ME *robys*; origin uncertain]

rub·ble (rub'əl) *n.* **1** rough, broken stones, bricks, etc., especially from collapsed or demolished buildings. **2** masonry made of this. [ME *robel*; origin uncertain]

rub·down (rub'doun') *n.* a rubbing of the body; massage.

rube (rüb) *n. Derogatory slang.* a rustic; an unsophisticated person. [< *Reuben*, a traditional rural name]

ru·be·fa·cient (rü'bə fā'shənt) *adj., n.* —*adj.* producing redness or irritation, especially of the skin: *a rubefacient ointment.* —*n.* a rubefacient medication or substance, such as a mustard plaster. [< L *rubefaciens, -facientis*, pp. of *rubefacere* < *rubeus* red + *facere* to make]

ru·bel·la (rü bel'ə) *n.* German measles.

ru·be·o·la (rü bē'ə lə) *n.* measles. [< NL *rubeola*, dim. of *rubeus* red]

Ru·bi·con (rü'bə kon') *n.* a point, decision, etc. from which one cannot turn back.
cross (or **pass**) **the Rubicon,** make an important and irrevocable decision.
[< *Rubicon*, a small river in E Italy, in ancient times forming part of the boundary between the Roman republic and its provinces. By crossing the Rubicon into the republic in 49 B.C., Julius Caesar broke the law forbidding a general to lead his troops out of the province in which he was stationed, and so committed himself to the civil war that ended with him as master of Rome.]

ru·bi·cund (rü'bə kund') *adj.* reddish; ruddy. [< L *rubicundus* < *rubere* be red]

ru·bi·cun·di·ty (rü'bə kun'də tē) *n.* a rubicund quality or state.

ru·bid·i·um (rü bid'ē əm) *n.* a silver-white metallic chemical element resembling potassium. *Symbol:* Rb; *at.no.* 37; *at.wt.* 85.47. [< NL < L *rubidus* red < *rubere* be red; its spectrum has red lines.]

ru·ble (rü'bəl) See **rouble.**

ru·bric (rü'brik) *n.* **1** a title or heading of a chapter, a law, etc. written or printed in red or in special lettering. **2** a direction for conducting of religious services inserted in a prayer book, ritual, etc. **3** any heading, rule, or guide. [< L *rubrica* red coloring matter < *ruber* red]

ru·bri·cal (rü'brə kəl) *adj.* **1** red; marked with red; printed or written in special lettering. **2** of, having to do with, or according to religious rubrics. —**ru'bri·cal·ly,** *adv.*

ru·bri·cate (rü'brə kāt') *v.* -cat·ed, -cat·ing. **1** mark or color with red. **2** furnish with rubrics. **3** regulate by rubrics.

ru·by (rü'bē) *n., pl.* -bies; *adj.* —*n.* **1** a clear, hard, red precious stone that is a variety of corundum. **2** a piece of this stone, or a gem made from it. **3** a deep, glowing red. —*adj.* deep, glowing red: *ruby lips, ruby wine.* [ME < OF *rubi*, ult. (cf. Med.L *rubinus*) < L *rubeus* red] —**ru'by-like',** *adj.*

ruche (rüsh) *n.* a pleated piece or fill of lace, ribbon, net, etc. used as trimming for women's dresses, blouses, etc. [< F *ruche*, originally, beehive]

ruch·ing (rüsh'ing) *n.* a trimming made of ruches.

ruck (ruk) *n.* a crowd; the great mass of common or inferior people or things. [ME *ruke* heap, stack < Scand.; cf. Norwegian dial. *ruka.*]

ruck·sack (ruk'sak' or rük'sak') *n.* knapsack. [< G *Rucksack,* literally, back sack]

ruck·us (ruk'əs) *n. Slang.* a noisy disturbance or uproar; row. [? blend of *ruction* and *rumpus*]

ruc·tion (ruk'shən) *n. Informal.* a disturbance; quarrel; row. [? alteration of *insurrection*]

rud·der (rud'ər) *n.* **1** a hinged, flat piece of wood or metal that projects into the water at the rear end of a boat or ship, by which

hat, āge, fär; let, ēqual, tèrm; it, īce
hot, ōpen, ôrder; oil, out; cup, pùt, rüle,
əbove, takən, pencəl, lemən, circəs

ch, child; ng, long; sh, ship
th, thin; ŦH, then; zh, measure

the vessel is steered. The rudder is controlled by a tiller, wheel, or other apparatus. **2** a similar piece on an aircraft hinged vertically to the rear of the fin and used for right-and-left steering. See **airplane** for picture. **3** a person or thing that guides or steers. [OE *rōthor*] —**rud'der·less,** *adj.*

rud·dy (rud'ē) *adj.* -di·er, -di·est; *adv.* —*adj.* **1** red or reddish: *a ruddy glow.* **2** rosy and glowing, as with good health: *After skiing all afternoon the boys had ruddy cheeks.* **3** *Slang.* bloody. —*adv. Slang.* very; surely; extremely. [OE *rudig*] —**rud'di·ly,** *adv.* —**rud'di·ness,** *n.*

ruddy duck a small, freshwater duck (*Oxyura jamaicensis*) that ranges from Canada south to the West Indies and Colombia. In breeding season the male has mainly reddish-brown plumage with a black head, white cheeks, and blue bill.

rude (rüd) *adj.* rud·er, rud·est. **1** impolite; not courteous: *It is rude to stare at people.* **2** roughly made or done; without finish or polish; coarse; crude: *rude tools, a rude cabin.* **3** rough in manner or behavior; violent; harsh: *Rude hands seized the child and threw him into the car.* **4** harsh to the ear; unmusical. **5** not having learned much; uncivilized; rather wild; barbarous. **6** belonging to the poor or to uncultured people; simple; without luxury or elegance. **7** not fully or properly developed. **8** robust; sturdy; vigorous: *rude health, rude strength.* [< L *rudis*] —**rude'ly,** *adv.* —**rude'ness,** *n.*
☛ *Hom.* **rood.**

ru·di·ment (rü'də mənt) *n.* **1** a part to be learned first; beginning: *the rudiments of grammar.* **2** something in an early stage of development. **3** an organ or part incompletely developed in size or structure: *the rudiments of wings on a baby chick.* **4** an organ or part, such as the appendix, that does not develop completely and has no function. [< L *rudimentum* < *rudis* rude]

ru·di·men·ta·ry (rü'də men'tə rē or rü'də men'trē) *adj.* **1** to be learned or studied first; elementary. **2** in an early stage of development; undeveloped.
☛ *Syn.* **1.** See note at **elementary.**

rue[1] (rü) *v.* rued, ru·ing. **1** be sorry for; regret (something). **2** *Archaic.* feel sorrow. [OE *hrēowan*]

rue[2] (rü) *n.* **1** any of a genus (*Ruta*) of aromatic Eurasian plants, especially *R. graveolens*, having small yellow flowers and strong-smelling, evergreen leaves that yield a bitter oil formerly used in medicine. **2** (*adj.*) designating the family (Rutaceae) of shrubs, trees, and herbs that includes rue as well as the citrus trees and the kumquats. [ME < OF < L *ruta*, ? < Gk. *rhytē*]

rue·ful (rü'fəl) *adj.* **1** sorrowful; unhappy; mournful: *a rueful expression.* **2** causing sorrow or pity: *a rueful sight.* —**rue'ful·ly,** *adv.* —**rue'ful·ness,** *n.*

A ruff

ruff[1] (ruf) *n.* **1** a deep frill, stiff enough to stand out, worn around the neck by men and women in the 15th century. **2** a collar of specially marked feathers or hairs on the neck of a bird or animal. [akin to RUFFLE[1]]
☛ *Hom.* **rough.**

ruff[2] (ruf) *v., n. Card games.* —*v.* trump. —*n.* the act of trumping. [< MF *roffle* < OF *roffle, fonfle,* cf. Ital. *ronfa* a card game]
☛ *Hom.* **rough.**

ruffed (ruft) *adj.* having a ruff.

ruffed grouse *Cdn.* a North American grouse (*Bonasa umbellus*) having a small crest, a black or reddish-brown ruff on either side of the neck, a fanlike tail, and barred and mottled brown plumage.

ruf·fi·an (ruf'ē ən) *n., adj.* —*n.* a rough, brutal, or cruel person. —*adj.* rough; brutal; cruel. [< MF]

ruf·fi·an·ism (ruf′ē ən iz′əm) *n.* brutal conduct; ruffianly conduct or character.

ruf·fi·an·ly (ruf′ē ən lē) *adj.* like a ruffian; violent; lawless.

A blouse with a ruffle around the neck

ruf·fle¹ (ruf′əl) *v.* **-fled, -fling;** *n.* —*v.* **1** make rough or uneven; wrinkle: *A breeze ruffled the lake. The hen ruffled her feathers at the sight of the dog.* **2** gather into a ruffle. **3** trim with ruffles. **4** disturb; annoy: *Nothing can ruffle her calm temper.* **5** become ruffled. **6** shuffle (playing cards). —*n.* **1** a roughness or unevenness in some surface; wrinkling. **2** a strip of cloth, ribbon, or lace gathered or pleated along one edge or along the middle and attached along this gathered or pleated line to a garment, curtain, etc. for decoration. **3** a disturbance; annoyance. **4** disorder; confusion. [ME; origin uncertain]

ruf·fle² (ruf′əl) *n., v.* **-fled, -fling.** —*n.* a low, steady beat of a drum. —*v.* beat (a drum) in this way. [? imitative]

ru·fous (rü′fəs) *adj.* reddish or reddish brown. [< L *rufus*]

rug (rug) *n.* **1** a heavy fabric floor covering. **2** a thick, warm cloth used as covering: *He wrapped his woollen rug around him.* [< Scand.; cf. Norwegian dial. *rugga* coarse covering]

rug·by (rug′bē) *n.* **1** *Cdn.* a game played by teams of twelve men who carry, pass, or kick an oval ball towards the opposing team's goal; football. **2** rugger. [< *Rugby*, a famous school for boys in Rugby, England]

☛ *Usage.* **Rugby, rugger, soccer.** Though still heard in Canada, the term **rugby** (or **rugby football**) is being displaced by the American term **football.** As such, it is distinct from **rugger**, played with 15 players a side, and **soccer**, played with 11 players of whom only the goalie can play the ball with his hands.

rug·ged (rug′id) *adj.* **1** rough; wrinkled; uneven: *rugged ground.* **2** strong; vigorous; sturdy: *The pioneers were rugged people.* **3** strong and irregular: *rugged features.* **4** harsh; stern; severe: *rugged times.* **5** rude; unpolished; unrefined: *rugged manners.* **6** stormy: *rugged weather.* **7** rough or harsh to the ear. [< Scand.; cf. Swedish *rugga* roughen. Cf. RUG.] —**rug′ged·ly,** *adv.*

rug·ger (rug′ər) *n.* a game played by teams of fifteen men who kick or pass an oval ball toward the opposing team's goal. [< *rugby*]

☛ *Usage.* See **rugby** for note.

ru·in (rü′ən) *n., v.* —*n.* **1** a building, wall, etc. that has fallen to pieces: *That ruin was once a famous castle.* **2** **ruins,** *pl.* that which is left after destruction, decay, or downfall, especially of a building, wall, etc. that has fallen to pieces: *the ruins of an ancient city.* **3** very great damage; destruction; overthrow; decay: *His enemies planned the duke's ruin.* **4** a condition of destruction, decay, or downfall: *The house had gone to ruin and neglect.* **5** the cause of destruction, decay, or downfall: *Drink was his ruin.* **6** bankruptcy. —*v.* **1** bring to ruin; destroy; spoil. **2** be destroyed; come to ruin. **3** make bankrupt. [ME < OF < L *ruina* a collapse < *ruere* collapse]

☛ *Syn. n.* **2. Ruin, destruction** = very great damage or complete loss. **Ruin** emphasizes falling to pieces or falling down, and applies to damage that impairs or ends its soundness, value, or beauty, whether caused by decay or by a destructive force: *Proper care protects property from ruin.* **Destruction** emphasizes breaking to pieces or tearing down, and applies to damage caused by a wrecking or injuring force: *The storm caused widespread destruction.* —*v.* **1.** See note at **spoil.**

ru·in·a·tion (rü′ə nā′shən) *n.* ruin; destruction; downfall.

ru·in·ous (rü′ə nəs) *adj.* **1** bringing ruin; causing destruction. **2** fallen into ruins; ruined: *a building in ruinous condition.* —**ru′in·ous·ly,** *adv.*

rule (rül) *n., v.* **ruled, rul·ing.** —*n.* **1** a statement of what to do and not to do; a law; principle governing conduct, action, arrangement, etc.: *Obey the rules of the game.* **2** Law. an order by a court, based upon a principle of law. **3** a set of rules; code. A religious order lives under a certain rule. **4** control; government: *In a democracy the people have the rule.* **5** a period of power of a ruler; reign: *The B.N.A. Act was passed during the rule of Queen Victoria.* **6** a regular method; what usually happens or is done; what is usually true: *Fair weather is the rule in summer.* **7** ruler (def. 2). **8** Printing.

a thin, type-high strip of metal, for printing a line or lines. **as a rule,** usually. **work to rule** See **work.** —*v.* **1** make a rule; decide. **2** make a formal decision: *The judge ruled against them.* **3** exercise the highest authority; control; govern; direct. **4** prevail; be current: *Prices of wheat and corn ruled high all the year.* **5** mark with lines. **6** mark off. **rule out,** eliminate or exclude. [ME < OF *riule* < L *regula* straight stick < *regere* guide. Doublet of RAIL¹.] —**rul′a·ble,** *adj.*

☛ *Syn. v.* **3. Rule, govern** = direct or control by the exercise of authority or power. **Rule** emphasizes having complete control over others through supreme or absolute power, both to make laws or give commands and to force obedience: *He tries to rule his family as a dictator rules a nation.* **Govern** emphasizes directing and keeping under control by the active use of authority or power, usually for the good of the thing, person, or nation governed: *Parents govern a child until he develops the power to govern himself.*

rule book a book of rules, especially those for some games or sport: *The National Hockey League Rule Book.*

rule of three *Mathematics.* a method of finding the fourth term in proportion when three are given.

rule of thumb **1** a rule based on experience or practice rather than on scientific knowledge. **2** a rough, practical method of procedure.

rul·er (rü′lər) *n.* **1** a person who rules. **2** a straight strip of wood, metal, etc. marked in units, such as centimetres, used in drawing lines or in measuring.

rul·ing (rü′ling) *n., adj.* —*n.* **1** a decision of a judge or court. **2** ruled lines. —*adj.* **1** that rules; governing; controlling. **2** predominating; prevalent.

rum¹ (rum) *n.* **1** an alcoholic liquor made from sugar cane, molasses, etc. **2** any alcoholic liquor. [short for *rumbullion* rum; origin uncertain]

rum² (rum) *adj.* *Esp.Brit. Slang.* odd; strange. [origin uncertain]

Rum. Rumania; Rumanian.

Ru·ma·ni·an (rü mā′nē ən *or* rü mān′yən) *n. or adj.* Romanian.

rum·ba (rum′bə) *n., v.* **-baed, -ba·ing.** —*n.* **1** a dance that originated among the black people of Cuba, having a complex, syncopated rhythm in 2/4 or 4/4 time. **2** music for this dance. —*v.* dance a rumba. Also, **rhumba.** [< Sp. *rumba*, probably < African lang.]

rum·ble (rum′bəl) *v.* **-bled, -bling;** *n.* —*v.* **1** make a deep, heavy, continuous sound. **2** move with such a sound. **3** utter with such a sound. —*n.* **1** a deep, heavy, continuous sound: *We hear the far-off rumble of thunder.* **2** *Slang.* a teenage gang fight. **3** the rear part of an automobile or carriage containing an extra seat or a place for baggage. [ME *romble(n)*, ? imitative]

rumble seat in certain old-fashioned types of automobile, an extra, open seat behind and outside the cab, or top.

ru·men (rü′mən) *n., pl.* **ru·mi·na** (rü′mə nə). **1** the first stomach of an animal that chews the cud. **2** the cud of such an animal. [< L *rumen* gullet]

ru·mi·nant (rü′mə nənt) *n., adj.* —*n.* an animal that chews the cud. Cows, sheep, and camels are ruminants. —*adj.* **1** belonging to the group of ruminants. **2** meditative; reflective. [< L *ruminans, -antis,* ppr. of *ruminare* chew a cud < *rumen* gullet]

ru·mi·nate (rü′mə nāt′) *v.* **-nat·ed, -nat·ing. 1** chew food for a second time; chew the cud. **2** chew again: *A cow ruminates its food.* **3** ponder; meditate: *He ruminated on the strange events of the past week.* [< L *ruminare* chew the cud < *rumen* gullet] —**ru′mi·nat′ing·ly,** *adv.*

ru·mi·na·tion (rü′mə nā′shən) *n.* **1** the act or process of chewing the cud. **2** meditation; reflection.

ru·mi·na·tive (rü′mə nə tiv *or* rü′mə nā′tiv) *adj.* meditative; inclined to ruminate. —**ru′mi·na·tive·ly,** *adv.*

rum·mage (rum′ij) *v.* **-maged, -mag·ing;** *n.* —*v.* **1** search thoroughly by moving things about: *I rummaged in my drawer for a pair of gloves.* **2** pull from among other things; bring to light. —*n.* a rummaging search. [< MF *arrumage* < *arrumer* stow cargo < *rum,* var. of *run* hold of a ship < Gmc.] —**rum′mag·er,** *n.*

☛ *Syn. v.* **1.** See note at **search.**

rummage sale a sale of odds and ends, old clothing etc., usually held to raise money for charity.

rum·my¹ (rum′ē) *adj.* **-mi·er, -mi·est.** *Slang.* odd; strange; queer. [< *rum²*]

rum·my² (rum′ē) *n.* a kind of card game in which points are scored by assembling sets of three or four cards of the same rank or sequences of three or more cards of the same suit. [origin uncertain]

rum·my³ (rum′ē) *n.* *Slang.* drunkard.

ru·mor *or* **ru·mour** (rü′mər) *n., v.* —*n.* **1** a story or statement talked of as news without any proof that it is true. **2** vague, general

talk: *Rumor has it that Bill will marry Joan.* —*v.* tell or spread by rumor. [ME < OF < L]

☛ **Hom. roomer.**

rump (rump) *n.* **1** the hind part of the body of an animal, where the legs join the back. **2** a cut of beef from this part. See **beef** for picture. **3** the corresponding part of the human body; buttocks. **4** an unimportant or inferior part; remnant. [ME < Scand.; cf. Danish *rumpe*]

rum·ple (rum′pəl) *v.* **-pled, -pling;** *n.* —*v.* crumple; crush; wrinkle: *rumpled clothing.* —*n.* a wrinkle; crease. [cf. MDu. *rompel*]

rum·pus (rum′pəs) *n. Informal.* a noisy disturbance or uproar; row. [origin uncertain]

rumpus room rec room.

rum·run·ner (rum′run′ər) *n.* a person or ship that smuggles alcoholic liquor into a country.

run (run) *v.* **ran, run, run·ning;** *n.* —*v.* **1** move the legs quickly; go faster than walking: *A horse can run faster than a man.* **2** go hurriedly; hasten: *Run for help.* **3** flee: *Run for your life.* **4** cause to run; cause to move: *to run a horse up and down.* **5** perform by, or as by, running: *to run errands.* **b** carry or take by, or as by, running: *Can you run this book over to the library for me?* **6** go; move; keep going: *This train runs to Calgary.* **7** go on; proceed: *House prices are running very high these days.* **8** creep; trail; climb: *Vines run along the sides of the road.* **9** go along (a way, path, etc.): *to run the course until the end.* **10** pursue; chase (game, etc.): *to run a fox.* **11** pass or cause to pass quickly: *A thought ran through my mind. Time runs on.* **12** trace; draw: *Run that report back to its source.* **13** stretch; extend: *Shelves run along the walls.* **14** drive; force; thrust: *He ran a splinter into his hand.* **15** flow; flow with: *The streets ran oil after an oil truck overturned.* **16** discharge fluid, mucus, or pus: *My nose runs.* **17** get; become: *Never run into debt. The well ran dry.* **18** have a specified character, quality, form, size, etc.: *These potatoes run large.* **19** spread: *The color ran when the dress was washed.* **20** continue; last: *a lease to run two years.* **21** have currency or be current; occur: *The story runs that school will close early today.* **22** have legal force. **23** take part in a race or contest. **24 a** be a candidate for election. **b** put up as a candidate. **25** enter (a horse, etc.) in a race. **26** expose oneself to: *to run a risk.* **27** move easily, freely, or smoothly; keep operating: *A rope runs in a pulley.* **28** cause to move easily, freely, or smoothly; cause to keep operating: *to run a machine.* **29** be worded or expressed: *How does the first verse run?* **30** conduct; maintain; manage: *to run a business.* **31** go about, proceed, or grow without restraint: *Children were allowed to run about the streets.* **32** drop stitches, ravel. **33** get past or through: *Enemy ships tried to run the blockade.* **34** smuggle: *to run rum.* **35** publish (an advertisement, story, etc.) in a newspaper: *He ran an ad in the evening paper.* **36** soften; become liquid; melt: *The wax ran when the candles were lit.* **37** shape by melting: *run bullets through a mould.* **38** pass to or from the sea; migrate, as for spawning: *The salmon are running.* **39** return often to the mind: *That tune has been running in my head.* **40** make an unbroken sequence of (shots, strokes, etc.) in billiards, pool, etc.

run across, meet by chance.
run away with, go far better than others in.
run down, a cease to go; stop working. **b** pursue till caught or killed; hunt down. **c** knock down by running against. **d** speak disparagingly against. **e** decline or reduce in vigor or health. **f** fall off, diminish, or decrease; deteriorate. **g** *Baseball.* put a base runner out after trapping him between bases.
run for it, run for safety.
run in, a *Informal.* arrest and put in jail. **b** pay a short visit.
run into, a meet by chance. **b** crash into; collide with.
run off, a cause to be run or played. **b** print; duplicate. **c** run away; flee.
run out, come to an end; become exhausted.
run out of, use up; have no more: *I can't bake a cake because we have run out of sugar.*
run over, a ride or drive over: *The car ran over some glass.* **b** overflow: *Coffee ran over into the saucer.* **c** go through quickly: *Please run over these figures to check my addition.*
run through, a consume or spend rapidly or recklessly: *The spendthrift ran through his inheritance in a year.* **b** pierce. **c** review; rehearse: *The teacher ran through the homework assignment a second time.*
run up, a *Informal.* make quickly. **b** collect; accumulate: *Don't run up a big bill.*

—*n.* **1** the act of running; *to set out at a run.* **2** a spell or period of causing (a machine, etc.) to operate; the amount of anything produced in such a period: *During a run of eight hours the factory produced a run of 100 cars.* **3** a spell of causing something liquid to run or flow, or the amount that runs: *the run of sap from maple trees.* **4** a trip, especially a journey over a certain route: *The ship reached port after a six weeks' run.* **5** *Baseball* or *cricket.* the unit of score. **6** a period; a continuous spell or course; continuous extent: *a run of bad luck.* **7** a succession of performances: *This play has had*

---

hat, āge, fär; let, ēqual, tèrm; it, īce
hot, ōpen, ôrder; oil, out; cup, půt, rüle,
əbove, takən, pencəl, lemən, circəs

ch, child; ng, long; sh, ship
th, thin; ŦH, then; zh, measure

a two-year run. **8** an onward movement; progress; course; trend: *the run of events.* **9** a continuous series or succession of something; succession of demands: *a run on the bank to draw out money.* **10** *Music.* a rapid succession of tones. **11** the usual kind: *the common run of mankind.* **12** freedom to go over or through, or to use: *The guests were given the run of the house.* **13** a flow or rush of water; small stream. **14** a number of fish moving together, especially a periodic movement to spawning grounds: *a run of salmon.* **15** a track, pipe, or trough, etc.: *a ski run.* **16** a stretch or enclosed space for animals: *a chicken run.* **17** a place where stitches have slipped out or become undone: *a run in a stocking.* **18** a landing of smuggled goods. **19** the extreme after part of a ship's bottom.

a run for (one's) **money, a** strong competition. **b** satisfaction for one's efforts.
in the long run, on the whole; in the end.
on the run, a hurrying: *The butcher had so many orders that he was on the run all day.* **b** in retreat or rout: *Victory is ours; the enemy is on the run.*
[ME *rinne, renne,* ? < *runnon,* pp. of OE *rinnan* run]

run·a·bout (run′ə bout′) *n.* **1** a light automobile or carriage with a single seat. **2** a small motorboat. **3** a person who runs about from place to place.

run·a·gate (run′ə gāt′) *n. Archaic.* **1** runaway. **2** a vagabond; wanderer. [< *run* + *agate* away; influenced by ME *renegat* renegade]

run·a·round (run′ə round′) *n.* **1** *Slang.* a series of excuses, evasions, or deceptions: *They gave him the runaround.* **2** *Printing.* type set narrower than the full width of a column or page, to permit the insertion of an illustration, etc.

run·a·way (run′ə wā′) *n.* **1** a person or animal that runs away. **2** a horse, vehicle, etc. that runs out of control. **3** (*adj.*) being a runaway: *a runaway horse.* **4** the act or an instance of running away or out of control. **5** (*adj.*) resulting from a running away, or done by runaways: *a runaway marriage.* **6** (*adj.*) easily won or accomplished: *a runaway victory.*

run·ci·nate (run′sə nit *or* run′sə nāt′) *adj.* of a leaf, having large lobes or teeth pointing toward the base: *Dandelion leaves are runcinate.* See **leaf** for picture. [< L *runcina* plane (but taken as "saw") < Gk. *rhykanē*; influenced by L *runcare* clear (of thorns, etc.)]

run·down (run′doun′) *n.* an account; summary: *Give me a rundown on what happened.*

run–down (run′doun′) *adj., n.* —*adj.* **1** tired; sick. **2** falling to pieces; partly ruined: *a run-down building.* **3** that has stopped going or working.
—*n.* **1** a brief summary. **2** *Baseball.* the act of putting a base runner out after trapping him between bases.

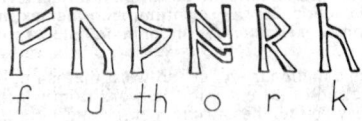

The first six letters of the English runic alphabet

rune¹ (rün) *n.* **1** any letter of an ancient Germanic alphabet. **2** a mark that looks like a rune and has some mysterious, magic meaning. [< ON *rún*]

rune² (rün) *n.* an old Scandinavian poem or song. [< Finnish *runo* < ON *rún*]

rung¹ (rung) *v.* a pt. and a pp. of **ring²**.

☛ **Hom. wrung.**

rung² (rung) *n.* **1** a rod or bar used as a step of a ladder. **2** a crosspiece set between the legs of a chair or as part of the back or arm of a chair. **3** a spoke of a wheel. **4** a bar of wood resembling a spoke in shape and use. [OE *hrung*]

☛ **Hom. wrung.**

ru·nic¹ (rü′nik) *adj.* consisting of runes; written in runes; marked with runes. [< *rune¹*]

ru·nic² (rü′nik) *adj.* like a rune. [< *rune²*]

run–in (run′in′) *n. Informal.* a sharp disagreement; an argument or quarrel.

run·let (run′lit) *n.* a small stream.

run·nel (run′əl) *n.* a small stream or brook. [OE *ryne* < *rinnan* run]

run·ner (run′ər) *n.* **1** a person or animal that runs. **2** messenger: *a runner for a bank.* **3** a person who runs or works a machine, etc. **4** either of the narrow pieces on which a sleigh or sled slides. **5** the blade of a skate. **6** a long, narrow strip: *We have a runner of carpet in our hall, and runners of linen and lace on our dressers.* **7** a smuggler; person or ship that tries to evade somebody. **8** a slender stem that grows along the ground and takes root, thus producing new plants. Strawberry plants spread by runners.

run·ner–up (run′ər up′) *n.* the person, player, or team that takes second place in a contest.

run·ning (run′ing) *n., adj.* —*n.* **1** the act of a person or thing that runs. **2** a flow of liquid; a discharge. **3** management or care: *the running of a business.* **4** operation: *the running of a machine.*
be in the running, have a chance to win.
be out of the running, have no chance to win.
—*adj.* **1** cursive: *a running hand.* **2** discharging matter: *a running sore.* **3** flowing: *running water.* **4** liquid. **5** going or carried on continuously: *a running commentary.* **6** current: *the running month.* **7** repeated continuously: *a running pattern.* **8** following in succession: *for three nights running.* **9** prevalent. **10** moving or proceeding easily or smoothly. **11** moving when pulled or hauled: *a running rope.* **12** slipping or sliding easily: *a running knot or noose.* **13** of plants, creeping or climbing. **14** that is measured in a straight line. **15** of the normal run of a train, bus, etc.: *the running time between towns.* **16** performed with or during a run: *a running leap.*

running board a metal step beneath the doors of early automobiles.

running gear the wheels and axles of an automobile, locomotive, or other vehicle.

running head a heading printed at the top of each page of a book, etc.

running knot a knot made to slip along the rope or cord around which it is tied; slip-knot.

running mate *Esp.U.S.* a candidate running jointly with another, but for a less important office, such as a candidate for vice-president.

running noose a noose with a running knot.

running stitch a series of short, even stitches all taken with one passage of the needle.

run·ny (run′ē) *adj.* **1** having a tendency to flow: *The pie filling is a bit runny.* **2** of the nose, continuously discharging mucus.

run–off (run′of′) *n.* **1** something that runs off. **2** the running off of water during the spring thaw or after a heavy rain. **3** a final, deciding race or contest.

run–of–the–mill (run′əv ᵺə mil′) *adj.* average or commonplace; ordinary: *a run-of-the-mill design.*

run–on (run′on′) *adj., n.* —*adj.* **1** *Printing.* **a** continued to the end, without a break. **b** of or having to do with copy to be set immediately after the preceding material, without any paragraph break or other indentation. **2** *Poetry.* continuing to the next line without punctuation. —*n.* **1** *Printing.* run-on material. **2** a run-on entry in a dictionary.

run–on entry in a dictionary, a derived word that is not defined but is shown at the end of the entry for the word from which it is formed. *Rurally* may be found as a run-on entry under *rural.*

runt (runt) *n.* an animal, person, or plant that is smaller than the usual size. [origin uncertain]

runt·y (run′tē) *adj.* **runt·i·er, runt·i·est.** stunted; dwarfish.

run·way (run′wā′) *n.* **1** a strip having a level surface on which aircraft land and take off. **2** a channel, track, groove, trough, etc. along which something moves, slides, etc. **3** the beaten track of deer or other animals. **4** an enclosed place for animals to run in.

ru·pee (rü pē′) *n.* **1** the basic unit of money in India and Pakistan, divided into 100 paise (India) or paisas (Pakistan). **2** the basic unit of money in Mauritius and Sri Lanka, divided into 100 cents. **3** the basic unit of money in Nepal, divided into 100 pice. See table at **money. 4** a coin or note worth one rupee. [< Hind. *rupiyah* < Skt. *rupya* wrought silver]

Ru·pert's Land (rü′pərts) the name given to the territories granted to the Hudson's Bay Company by Charles II in 1670. Rupert's Land, so named because Prince Rupert was the first governor of the Company, included all the land watered by rivers flowing into Hudson Bay.

ru·pi·ah (rü pē′ə) *n.* **1** the basic unit of money in Indonesia, divided into 100 sen. See table at **money. 2** a note worth one rupiah. [< Indonesian < Hind. *rupiyah.* See RUPEE.]

rup·ture (rup′chər) *n., v.* **-tured, -tur·ing.** —*n.* **1** the tearing apart of body tissue: *the rupture of a muscle or blood vessel.* **2** hernia. **3** a breaking off of friendly relations; especially, a break between nations that threatens to lead to war. **4** any breaking apart or break of relations: *the rupture of a marriage.*
—*v.* **1** burst or break: *A heart muscle has ruptured. He ruptured his spleen.* **2** suffer or cause to suffer a breaking apart of friendly relations: *Their friendship has ruptured. She ruptured the family peace.* [< L *ruptura* < *rumpere* burst]

ru·ral (rür′əl) *adj.* **1** in, of, having to do with, or like the country or the people who live in the country: *a rural upbringing, a rural riding.* **2** of or having to do with agriculture: *rural economy.* [< L *ruralis* < *rus, ruris* country] —**ru′ral·ly,** *adv.*
☛ *Syn.* Rural, rustic, pastoral = of, relating to, or characteristic of the country. **Rural** expresses an objective attitude toward the country and country life as distinguished from towns and cities and city life, but is sometimes used to suggest pleasant country scenes: *Rural life is healthful and quiet.* **Rustic** suggests simplicity, lack of refinement, or roughness and clumsiness, especially in appearance, manners, etc.: *The cottage has a rustic charm.* **Pastoral** has poetic associations, suggesting shepherds, grazing flocks, green pastures, and a simple, peaceful life: *He paints pastoral pictures.*

rural dean *Esp.Brit.* a priest of the highest rank in a district outside the cathedral city. He acts as the local deputy of a bishop or archdeacon.

rural municipality *Cdn.* in certain provinces, a municipal district in a rural area, administered by an elected reeve and council. *Abbrev.:* R.M.

rural route **1** a postal service by which mail is delivered by car or truck to the mailboxes of individual farms or country residences or businesses from a local post office. **2** any one route or circuit in this service: *There are four rural routes from this post office.* *Abbrev.:* R.R.

Rus. Russia; Russian.

ruse (rüz *or* rüs) *n.* a trick; stratagem. [< F *ruse* < *ruser* dodge]
☛ *Syn.* See note at **stratagem.**

rush¹ (rush) *v., n., adj.* —*v.* **1** move with speed or force: *We rushed along.* **2** attack with much speed and force: *They rushed the enemy.* **3** come, go, pass, act, etc. with speed or haste: *He rushes into things without knowing anything about them.* **4** send, push, force, etc. with speed or haste: *Rush this order, please.* **5** urge to hurry: *Don't rush me.* **6** *Informal.* **a** lavish much and frequent attention on: *He rushed the girl all summer.* **b** attempt to persuade to join a fraternity or sorority. **7** advance (a football) by running. —*n.* **1** the act of rushing: *the rush of the flood.* **2** busy haste; hurry: *the rush of city life.* **3** a great or sudden effort of many people to go somewhere or get something: *the Christmas rush. Few people got rich in the Klondike gold rush.* **4** an eager demand; pressure: *A sudden rush of business kept everyone working hard.* **5** *Football.* an attempt to carry the ball through the opposing line. **6** *Informal.* the lavishing of much attention, as in courting. **7 rushes,** *pl.* the first prints of film shot for a motion picture.
with a rush, suddenly; quickly.
—*adj.* requiring haste: *A rush order must be filled at once.* [originally, force out of place by violent impact; cf. OE *hrȳsc* a blow] —**rush′er,** *n.*

rush² (rush) *n.* **1** any of a genus (*Juncus*) of marsh plants having round, pithy stems, grasslike leaves, and clusters of tiny, greenish or brownish flowers. The stems of some rushes are widely used for chair bottoms, mats, baskets, etc. The pith of the stems was also formerly used for wicks in candles. **2** (*adj.*) designating the family (Juncaceae) of perennial, flowering marsh plants that includes these rushes, found in temperate and cold regions, and having slender leaves that are either grasslike or round and clusters of small flowers. **3** any of various other flowering marsh plants, especially of the sedge family, having round stems or hollow, stemlike leaves often used to make chair bottoms, mats, etc. **4** the stem or hollow leaf of a rush, used for baskets, etc. **5** (*adj.*) made of or with rushes. **6** *Archaic.* something of little or no value: *not worth a rush.* [OE *rysc*] —**rush′like′,** *adj.*

rush hour the time of day when traffic is heaviest or when trains, buses, etc. are most crowded. —**rush′-hour′,** *adj.*

rush seat a seat for a stage show, sports event, etc. that is sold on the day of the performance or event.

rush·y (rush′ē) *adj.* **rush·i·er, rush·i·est. 1** abounding in or covered with rushes. **2** made of rushes.

rus in ur·be (rus′in ėr′bē; *Latin,* rùs′in ür′bā) *Latin.* the country in the city.

rusk (rusk) *n.* **1** a piece of bread or cake toasted in the oven. **2** a kind of light, soft, sweet biscuit. [< Sp., Pg. *rosca* roll]

Russ (rus) *adj.* or *n., pl.* **Russ** or **Russes.** *Archaic.* Russian.

Russ. Russia; Russian.

rus·set (rus′it) *adj.* reddish brown. —*n.* **1** a reddish brown. **2** a coarse, russet-colored cloth. Peasants used to make and wear russet. **3** a kind of apple having a rough, brownish skin. [ME < OF *rousset,* ult. < L *russus* red]

rus·sia (rush′ə) *n.* Russia leather.

Russia leather a fine, smooth leather, usually dyed dark red, made from skins treated with birchbark oil. Russia leather is used especially for bookbinding.

Rus·sian (rush′ən) *n., adj.* —*n.* **1** a native or inhabitant of Russia (the Soviet Union or the former Russian Empire); especially, a member of the dominant Slavic people of Russia. **2** a person descended from these people. **3** the Slavic language of the Russians, which is the official language of the Soviet Union. —*adj.* of or having to do with Russia, its people, or their language.

Russian Church a branch of the Orthodox Eastern Church, until 1918 the national church of Russia.

Rus·sian·ize (rush′ən īz′) *v.* **-ized, -iz·ing.** make or become Russian in customs, language, etc.

Russian Revolution the revolution in which Russian workers, sailors, and soldiers, led by Lenin, overthrew the government of the Czar in 1917 and established the Soviet Union.

Russian thistle a common annual weed (*Salsola pestifer,* also classified as *S. kali* var. *tenuifolia*) of the goosefoot family, introduced to North America from Europe and Asia, having very narrow leaves ending in a sharp point and tiny flowers that grow from the leaf axils. When the plant is mature, the leaves become very stiff and prickly and the nearly ball-shaped plant breaks off at ground level and is rolled by the wind, scattering its seed as it goes.

Russian wolfhound borzoi.

rust (rust) *n., v., adj.* —*n.* **1** the reddish-brown or orange coating that forms on iron or steel when exposed to air or moisture. **2** any film or coating on any other metal due to oxidization, etc. **3** a harmful growth, habit, influence, or agency. **4** a plant disease that spots leaves and stems. **5** a reddish brown or orange. —*v.* **1** become covered with rust. **2** coat with rust. **3** spoil by not using. **4** become spoiled by not being used: *Don't let your mind rust during vacation.* **5** have or cause to have the disease rust. —*adj.* reddish brown or orange. [OE *rust,* var. of *rūst*]

rus·tic (rus′tik) *adj., n.* —*adj.* **1** belonging to or suitable for the country; rural: *rustic furnishings.* **2** simple; plain: *His rustic speech and ways made him uncomfortable in the city school.* **3** rough; awkward. **4** made of branches with the bark still on them: *rustic arches in a garden.* —*n.* a country person. [< L *rusticus* < *rus* country] —**rus′ti·cal·ly,** *adv.*

☛ **Syn. adj. 1.** See note at **rural.**

rus·ti·cate (rus′tə kāt′) *v.* **-cat·ed, -cat·ing. 1** go to or live in the country. **2** send to the country. **3** *Brit.* send (a student) away from a university or college temporarily as a punishment. [< L *rusticari* < *rusticus* rustic. See RUSTIC.]

rus·ti·ca·tion (rus′tə kā′shən) *n.* **1** the act of rusticating or the state of being rusticated. **2** residence in the country. **3** *Brit.* the temporary dismissal of a student from a university or college as a punishment.

rus·tic·i·ty (rus tis′ə tē) *n., pl.* **-ties. 1** a rustic quality, characteristic, or peculiarity. **2** rural life.

rust·i·ly (rus′tə lē) *adv.* in a rusty state; in such a manner as to suggest rustiness.

rus·tle (rus′əl) *n., v.* **-tled, -tling.** —*n.* a light, soft sound of things gently rubbing together, such as leaves make when moved by the wind. —*v.* **1** make this sound. **2** move or stir (something) so that it makes such a sound: *We could hear him rustling papers in the next room.* **3** *Informal.* steal (cattle, etc.). **4** *Informal.* act, do, or get with energy or speed: *We'll have to rustle if we want to finish in time.* **rustle up, a** gather; find. **b** get ready; prepare: *The cook rustled up some food.* [OE *hrūxlian* make noise]

rus·tler (rus′lər) *n.* **1** *Informal.* a cattle thief. **2** an active, energetic person. **3** a person or thing that rustles.

rust·less (rust′lis) *adj.* free from rust; resisting rust.

rust·proof (rust′prüf′) *adj., v.* —*adj.* resisting rust. —*v.* treat with a preparation that resists rust.

rust·y (rus′tē) *adj.* **rust·i·er, rust·i·est. 1** covered with rust; rusted: *a rusty knife.* **2** made by rust. **3** colored like rust. **4** faded: *a*

hat, āge, fär; let, ēqual, tèrm; it, īce
hot, ōpen, ôrder; oil, out; cup, pút, rüle,
əbove, takən, pencəl, lemən, circəs

ch, child; ng, long; sh, ship
th, thin; ŦH, then; zh, measure

rusty black. **5** weakened or deficient from lack of use or practice: *My mother says her biology is rusty.* **6** out of practice. —**rust′i·ness,** *n.*

rut¹ (rut) *n., v.* **rut·ted, rut·ting.** —*n.* **1** a track made in the ground, especially by a wheel. **2** a channel or groove in which something runs. **3** a fixed or established way of acting, especially a dull routine: *She decided to change jobs because she felt she was getting into a rut.* —*v.* make a rut or ruts in: *The road to the cottage was deeply rutted.* [? var. of *route*]

rut² (rut) *n., v.* **rut·ted, rut·ting.** —*n.* **1** the sexual excitement of deer, goats, sheep, etc. occurring at regular intervals. **2** the period during which this excitement lasts. —*v.* be in rut. [ME < OF *ruit* < L *rugitus* bellowing < *rugire* bellow]

ru·ta·ba·ga (rü′tə bā′gə *or* rü′tə bag′ə) *n.* a turnip (*Brassica napobrassica*) with a very large yellowish root. [< Swedish (dial.) *rotabagge,* literally, root bag]

ruth (rüth) *n. Archaic.* **1** pity; compassion. **2** sorrow. [ME *rewthe* < *rewen* rue¹ < OE *hrēowan*]

Ruth (rüth) *n.* in the Bible, a Moabite woman who left her own people to go to Bethlehem with her mother-in-law, Naomi, to whom she was devoted. Her story is told in the Book of Ruth.

ru·the·ni·um (rü thē′nē əm) *n.* a hard, brittle, greyish metallic element of the platinum group. *Symbol:* Ru; *at.no.* 44; *at.wt.* 101.07. [< NL < Med.L *Ruthenia* Russia; because it was discovered in the Urals]

ruth·er·for·di·um (ruŦH′ər fôr′dē əm) *n.* a very unstable, artificially created, radio-active element. *Symbol:* Rf; *at.no.* 104; *at.wt.* (261); *half-life* approx. 70 seconds. [after Ernest *Rutherford* (1871-1973), British physicist, who discovered the aromatic nucleus] Also called **kurchatovium.**

☛ *Usage.* No name has yet been officially adopted internationally for element 104. Scientists in the Soviet Union and the United States both claim priority in synthesizing this element. **Rutherfordium** is the name proposed by the U.S. group and **kurchatovium** the one proposed by the Soviet group.

ruth·less (rüth′lis) *adj.* having no pity; showing no mercy; cruel. —**ruth′less·ly,** *adv.* —**ruth′less·ness,** *n.*

ru·tile (rü′til *or* rü′tēl) *n.* a lustrous, reddish-brown or black, crystalline form of titanium dioxide, widely occurring in igneous and metamorphic rocks. It is an important ore of titanium. *Formula:* TiO_2 [< F < G *Rutil* < L *rutilus* reddish]

rut·ty (rut′ē) *adj.* **-ti·er, -ti·est.** full of ruts. —**rut′ti·ness,** *n.*

RV *pl.* **RV's.** recreation vehicle.

RV or **R.V.** Revised Version.

Rx or **rx 1** in medical prescriptions, take (for L *recipe*). **2** tens of rupees.

-ry *noun-forming suffix.* **1** the occupation or work of a——, as in *dentistry, chemistry.* **2** the act of a——, as in *mimicry.* **3** the quality, state, or condition of a——, as in *rivalry.* **4** a group of——s, considered collectively, as in *peasantry.* [short form of *-ery*]

Ry. railway.

rye (rī) *n.* **1** a cereal grass (*Secale cereale*) widely grown in northern Europe and northern North America for grain and straw. **2** the seeds, or grain, of this plant, used for bread or for fodder. **3** flour made from this grain. **4** bread made from rye flour: *He ordered a corned beef on rye.* **5** whisky made from rye. **6** in Canada, a blended whisky made from rye and other grains; Canadian whisky. [OE *ryge*]

☛ **Hom. wry.**

rye-grass (rī′gras′) *n.* any of several grasses (genus *Lolium*) native to Europe and Northern Africa, widely cultivated as a pasture grass in western Europe, Britain, New Zealand, and along the Atlantic and Pacific coasts of North America.

S s

s or **S** (es) *n., pl.* **s's** or **S's. 1** the nineteenth letter of the English alphabet. **2** any speech sound represented by this letter. **3** a person or thing identified as *s*, especially the nineteenth in a series. **4** something shaped like the letter S. **5** (*adj.*) of or being an S or s.

's¹ an abbreviation of *is*, *has*, or *does*, added to the preceding pronoun or noun. *Examples*: *He's here. He's given the books away. What's that mean?*

's² an abbreviation of *us*, used with *let*. *Example*: *Let's go.*

–s¹ *suffix.* **1** used to form the plural of most nouns, as in *hats, boys, dogs, houses, monkeys, taxis, handfuls.* **2** used to form certain adverbs. *Examples*: *always, mornings,* in *You will always find him home mornings.*

–s² *suffix.* used to form the third person singular of verbs in the present indicative, as in *tells, drives, loses.* [OE *-es*]

–'s a suffix used to form the possessive case of nouns in the singular and also of plural nouns not ending in *s*, as in *boy's, man's, child's, men's, children's.* [OE *-(e)s*]

s. 1 shilling(s). **2** son. **3** second. **4** singular.

S 1 south; southern. **2** sulphur. **3** the sea element of the Canadian Forces.

S. 1 south; southern. **2** Saint. **3** School. **4** Saturday. **5** Sunday. **6** September. **7** Section. **8** Sea. **9** Senate. **10** Signor.

S.A. 1 South America. **2** South Africa. **3** South Australia. **4** Salvation Army.

Sab. Sabbath.

Sab·ba·tar·i·an (sab'ə ter'ē ən) *n., adj.* —*n.* **1** a person who observes Saturday as the Sabbath. **2** a person who favors a very strict observance of the Sabbath. —*adj.* of or having to do with the Sabbath or its observance.

Sab·ba·tar·i·an·ism (sab'ə ter'ē ən iz'əm) *n.* **1** the observance of Saturday as the Sabbath. **2** very strict observance of the Sabbath.

Sab·bath (sab'əth) *n.* **1** the seventh day of the week, Saturday, observed as a day of rest and worship by Jews and members of some Christian denominations. **2** Sunday, observed as a day of rest and worship by most Christians. **3** (*adj.*) of or belonging to the Sabbath. **4** sabbath, any day or period of rest. [< L < Gk. *sabbaton* < Hebrew *shabbāth* < *shābath* to rest]
➤ *Syn. n.* **1.** See note at **Sunday.**

sab·bat·ic (sə bat'ic) *adj.* sabbatical.

sab·bat·i·cal (sə bat'ə kəl) *adj., n.* —*adj.* **1** of, having to do with, or suitable for the Sabbath: *sabbatical laws.* **2** of or having to do with sabbatical leave. —*n.* sabbatical leave. [< Gk. *sabbatikos* < *sabbaton.* See SABBATH.]

sabbatical leave a leave of absence for a year or half year given to teachers, usually in a university and especially once in seven years, for study and travel.

sa·ber (sā'bər) See **sabre.**

Sa·bine (sā'bīn *or* sab'īn) *n., adj.* —*n.* **1** a member of an ancient people in central Italy who were conquered by the Romans in the third century B.C. **2** the Italic language of the Sabines. —*adj.* of or having to do with the Sabines or their language. [< L *Sabinus*]

sa·ble (sā'bəl) *n., adj.* —*n.* **1** a small flesh-eating mammal (*Martes zibellina*) of the forests of N Asia, closely related to the martens, having glossy, dark-brown or black fur. **2** the fur of the sable, one of the most costly furs. **3** any of various related animals, such as the North American marten, or their fur. **4** (*adj.*) made of the fur of a sable. **5** the color of sable fur, usually a dark brown. —*adj.* **1** of the color of sable. **2** *Poetic.* black or very dark: *sable garments of mourning.* [ME < OF *sable*, ult. < Slavic]

sa·ble·fish (sā'bəl fish') *n., pl.* **-fish** *or* **-fish·es.** blackcod.

sab·ot (sab'ō *or* sab'ət; *French*, sä bō') *n.* **1** a shoe hollowed out of a single piece of wood, worn by peasants in France, Belgium, etc. **2** a coarse leather shoe having a thick wooden sole. [< F *sabot* < OF *çabot*, alteration of *çavate* old shoe < Arabic *sabbāt*; influenced by OF *bote* boot]

sab·o·tage (sab'ə täzh') *n., v.* **-taged, -tag·ing.** —*n.* **1** the destruction of machinery or tools, a hindering of a manufacturing process, waste of materials, etc. by workers as a threat or act of protest against an employer. **2** damage or destruction by civilians or enemy agents to interfere with a military operation or war effort.

Sabotage may be carried out by civilians against conquerors of their country or by enemy agents or by sympathizers within a country at war. **3** any destruction or damage intended to hinder or hurt. —*v.* commit sabotage on or against; damage or destroy deliberately: *The group was accused of trying to sabotage the negotiations for a new labor contract.* [< F *sabotage* < *saboter* bungle, walk noisily < *sabot.* See SABOT.]

sab·o·teur (sab'ə tèr') *n.* a person who commits sabotage. [< F]

sa·bra (sä'brə) *n.* a person born in Israel; native Israeli. [< Hebrew *sābrāh* cactus, thought of as being tough and prickly outside but soft inside]

sa·bre (sā'bər) *n., v.* **-bred, -bring.** —*n.* **1** a heavy, curved sword having a sharp point and cutting edge. See **sword** for picture. **2** a light sword used in fencing or duelling, having a tapering, flexible blade with a full cutting edge along one side. A sabre is heavier than a foil. —*v.* strike, wound, or kill with a sabre. Also, **saber.** [< F *sabre*, alteration of *sable*, ult. < Hungarian *száblya* < *szabni* cut]

sabre saw a hand-held power saw for light work, having a narrow blade that moves back and forth at high speed.

sabre–toothed tiger any of a number of extinct tigerlike mammals of the cat family having very long, curved upper canine teeth.

sac (sak) *n.* a baglike part in an animal or plant, often containing liquids: *the sac of a honeybee.* [< F < L *saccus* sack¹. See SACK¹.] —**sac'like'**, *adj.*
➤ *Hom.* **sack, sacque.**

Sac (sak, sok, *or* sôk) *n.* Sauk.
➤ *Hom.* **sack, sacque.**

SAC *U.S.* Strategic Air Command.

sac·cha·rin (sak'ə rin) *n.* a very sweet substance obtained from coal tar, used as a calorie-free substitute for sugar. Saccharin is very much sweeter than cane sugar. *Formula*: $C_7H_5NO_3S$

sac·cha·rine (sak'ə rin *or* sak'ə rēn') *adj.* **1** of, like, or containing sugar: *a saccharine taste.* **2** too sweet. **3** unpleasantly friendly or agreeable; ingratiating: *a saccharine smile.* [< Med.L *saccharum* sugar < Gk. *sakcharon* ult. < Skt. *çarkarā*, originally, gravel, grit] —**sac'cha·rine·ly**, *adv.*

sac·er·do·tal (sas'ər dō'təl) *adj.* of priests or the priesthood; priestly. [< L *sacerdotalis* < *sacerdos, -otis* priest < *sacra* rites + verb stem *dot-* put, set < *dare* give]

sac·er·do·tal·ism (sas'ər dō'təl iz'əm) *n.* **1** the character, system, or practices of the priesthood. **2** a religious doctrine that emphasizes the necessity of having priests as mediators between God and mankind. **3** excessive respect for or belief in the authority and power of priests.

sa·chem (sā'chəm) *n.* **1** among Algonquian peoples, a ruler or chief, especially the chief of a confederacy of tribes. The position of sachem was a hereditary one. **2** any North American Indian leader or chief. [< Algonquian. Related to SAGAMORE.]

sa·chet (sa shā'; *esp.Brit.*, sash'ā) *n.* **1** a small bag or pad containing perfumed powder, used especially for scenting linens and clothes. **2** the powder in such a bag or pad. **3** a small packet of shampoo, etc. [< F *sachet*, dim. of *sac* sack¹]

sack¹ (sak) *n., v.* —*n.* **1** a large bag, usually made of coarse cloth. Sacks are used for holding grain, flour, potatoes, and coal. **2** the amount that a sack can hold. **3** a sack and its contents. **4** *U.S.* any bag or its contents: *a sack of candy.* **5** a woman's loose-fitting dress. **6 the sack,** *Informal.* dismissal from a job, etc.: *He got the sack for always coming to work late.*
hit the sack, *Slang.* go to bed: *I'm about ready to hit the sack.*
hold the sack, *Informal.* be left empty-handed.
—*v.* **1** put into a sack or sacks. **2** discharge from employment; fire. [OE *sacc* < L *saccus* < Gk. *sakkos* < Hebrew *saq*]
➤ *Hom.* **sac, sacque.**
➤ *Syn. n.* **1.** See note at **bag.**

sack² (sak) *v., n.* —*v.* plunder or pillage: *The invaders sacked the town.* —*n.* a plundering of a captured city. [< F *sac* < Ital. *sacco* < VL *saccare* take by force < Gmc.; influenced by L *saccus* sack¹] —**sack'er**, *n.*
➤ *Hom.* **sac, sacque.**

sack³ (sak) *n.* dry sherry or other strong, light-colored wine. [< F (*vin*) *sec* dry (wine) < L *siccus*]
☞ *Hom.* **sac, sacque.**

sack·but (sak′but′) *n.* **1** a musical wind instrument of the Middle Ages, the ancestor of the trombone. **2** an ancient harplike stringed instrument mentioned in the Bible. The English name for this instrument is the result of a mistranslation of an Aramaic word. [< F *saquebute* < *saquer* pull + *bouter* push]

sack·cloth (sak′kloth′) *n.* **1** coarse cloth for making sacks. **2** a garment of such cloth worn as a sign of mourning or penance.

sack coat a man's loose-fitting jacket or suit coat having a straight-cut back.

sack·ful (sak′ful) *n., pl.* **-fuls.** enough to fill a sack.

sack·ing (sak′ing) *n.* coarse cloth, such as burlap, for making sacks, etc.

sacque (sak) *n.* See **sack¹** (defs. 5, 6). [var. of *sack¹*]
☞ *Hom.* **sac, sack.**

sac·ra·ment (sak′rə mənt) *n.* **1** in Christian churches, any of certain formal religious ceremonies established or recognized by Jesus, considered especially sacred. Baptism is a sacrament. **2** Often, **Sacrament,** the elements of the Eucharist; the consecrated bread and wine or the bread alone. **3** something especially sacred; a sacred sign, token, or symbol. **4** a solemn promise; oath. [< L *sacramentum,* ult. < *sacer* holy]

sac·ra·men·tal (sak′rə men′təl) *adj., n.* —*adj.* **1** of, having to do with, or used in a sacrament: *sacramental wine.* **2** especially sacred. —*n. Roman Catholic Church.* a ceremony similar to, but not included among, the sacraments. The use of holy water is a sacramental. —**sac′ra·men′tal·ly,** *adv.*

sa·cred (sā′krid) *adj.* **1** belonging to or dedicated to God or a god; set apart for worship: *the sacred altar, a sacred grove.* **2** coming from God; worthy of religious reverence; holy: *the sacred Scriptures.* **3** connected with religion; religious: *sacred music.* **4** worthy of the highest respect: *the sacred memory of a dead hero.* **5** dedicated to some person, object, or purpose: *This monument is sacred to the memory of the Unknown Soldier.* **6** that must not be violated or disregarded: *sacred oaths.* [originally pp. of ME *sacre(n)* sanctify < L *sacrare* < *sacer* holy] —**sa′cred·ly,** *adv.* —**sa′cred·ness,** *n.*
☞ *Syn.* **1.** See note at **holy.**

Sacred College the College of Cardinals.

sacred cow a person or thing so highly regarded as to be beyond criticism. [an allusion to the traditional Hindu veneration of the cow.]

sac·ri·fice (sak′rə fīs′) *n., v.* **-ficed, -fic·ing.** —*n.* **1** the act of offering to a god. **2** the thing offered: *The ancient Hebrews killed animals on the altars as sacrifices to God.* **3** the act or an instance of giving up or destroying one thing for the sake of something else: *the sacrifice of one's life for an ideal, the sacrifice of an ideal for commercial gain.* **4** a loss from selling something below its value: *He will sell his house at a sacrifice because he needs the money.* **6** *Baseball.* a bunt or fly that helps a runner to advance although the batter is put out. —*v.* **1** give or offer to a god. **2** give up, suffer the loss of, or injure or destroy for a particular belief or purpose: *to sacrifice one's life for another person, to sacrifice business for pleasure.* We decided to sacrifice part of the garden for a patio. **3** offer or make a sacrifice. **4** sell at a loss. **5** *Baseball.* help (a runner) to advance by a sacrifice. [ME < OF < L *sacrificium,* ult. < *sacra* rites + *facere* perform] —**sac′ri·fic′er,** *n.*

sac·ri·fi·cial (sak′rə fish′əl) *adj.* of, having to do with, involving, or used in a sacrifice. —**sac′ri·fi′cial·ly,** *adv.*

sac·ri·lege (sak′rə lij) *n.* an intentional injury to anything sacred; disrespectful treatment of anyone or anything sacred: *Robbing the church is considered a sacrilege.* [ME < OF < L *sacrilegium* temple robbery < *sacrum* sacred object + *legere* pick up]

sac·ri·le·gious (sak′rə lij′əs) *adj.* **1** injurious or insulting to sacred persons or things; involving sacrilege. **2** guilty of sacrilege. —**sac′ri·le′gious·ly,** *adv.*

sac·ris·tan (sak′ris tən) *n.* the person in charge of the sacred vessels, robes, etc. of a church. [ME < Med.L *sacristanus,* ult. < L *sacer* holy. Doublet of SEXTON.]

sac·ris·ty (sak′ris tē) *n., pl.* **-ties.** the place where the sacred vessels, robes, etc. of a church are kept. [< Med.L *sacristia,* ult. < L *sacer* holy]

sac·ro·il·i·ac (sak′rō il′ē ak′) *adj., n.* —*adj.* of, having to do with, or designating the part of the body where the sacrum and ileum meet. —*n.* the joint or part of the body where the sacrum and ileum meet. See **pelvis** for picture.

sac·ro·sanct (sak′rō sangkt′) *adj.* **1** most holy or sacred; not to be violated. **2** *Informal.* very much revered; not to be scorned or laughed at: *That old car of his is sacrosanct to him.* [< L *sacrosanctus,* ult. < *sacer* sacred + *sancire* consecrate]

sac·ro·sanc·ti·ty (sak′rō sangk′tə tē) *n.* the fact or state of being sacrosanct; an especial sacredness.

sa·crum (sā′krəm *or* sak′rəm) *n., pl.* **-cra** (-krə) *or* **-crums.** the triangular bone at the lower end of the spine, formed by the joining of several vertebrae and serving as the back of the pelvis. See **pelvis** and **spinal column** for pictures. [< L (*os*) *sacrum* sacred (bone)]

sad (sad) *adj.* **sad·der, sad·dest. 1** feeling or expressing sorrow or grief: *a sad look, a sad child.* **2** characterized by sorrow or grief: *a sad life, a sad occasion.* **3** causing sorrow or grief; distressing: *a sad disappointment.* **4** dark or dull in color; not cheerful-looking: *He always dressed in sad greys and browns.* **5** *Informal.* shocking; hopeless; pitiable: *This is a sad mess.* [OE *sæd* sated] —**sad′ly,** *adv.*
☞ *Syn.* **1.** Sad, dejected, depressed = unhappy and low in spirits. Sad, the general word, meaning "not glad, cheerful, or happy," particularly suggests feeling sorrowful or mournful, but not the cause or degree of the feeling: *Moonlight makes her sad.* Dejected suggests casting down of the spirits by some disappointing, discouraging, or frustrating happening or situation: *She is dejected over his leaving.* Depressed suggests sinking into a low-spirited, discouraged, or gloomy state as the result of an experience or physical, mental, or other condition: *He is depressed by his failure.*

sad·den (sad′ən) *v.* make or become sad: *It saddened him to think that he might never see them again.*

A western saddle   An English saddle

sad·dle (sad′əl) *n., v.* **-dled, -dling.** —*n.* **1** a seat, usually padded and leather-covered, for a rider on an animal such as a horse. **2** a seat for a rider on a bicycle, etc. **3** the part of a harness that holds the shafts, or to which a checkrein is attached. See **harness** for picture. **4** a colored marking on the back of an animal: *a white dog with a black saddle and black ears.* **5** anything shaped or used like a saddle. **6** a ridge between two mountain peaks. **7** a cut of meat consisting of the upper back portion of an animal, including both loins: *a saddle of venison.*
in the saddle, *Informal.* in a position of control.
—*v.* **1** put a saddle on. **2** burden: *He is saddled with a big house that he does not need or want.* **3** put (something) as a burden (*on*): *They saddled the hardest part of the job on me.* [OE *sadol*]

sad·dle·bag (sad′əl bag′) *n.* **1** one of a pair of bags laid over an animal's back behind the saddle. **2** a similar bag hanging over the rear wheel of a bicycle or motorcycle.

sad·dle·bow (sad′əl bō′) *n.* the front part of a saddle, which sticks up.

sad·dle·cloth (sad′əl kloth′) *n.* a cloth put between an animal's back and the saddle.

saddle horse a horse for riding.

sad·dler (sad′lər) *n.* a person who makes or sells saddles and harness.

sad·dler·y (sad′lər ē) *n., pl.* **-dler·ies. 1** the work of a saddler. **2** the shop of a saddler. **3** saddles, harness, and other equipment for horses.

sad·dle·tree (sad′əl trē′) *n.* the frame of a saddle.

Sad·du·cee (saj′ù sē′) *n.* a member of an ancient Jewish sect that accepted the Mosaic law and believed in immortality but denied the resurrection of the dead and the existence of angels. [OE *sadducēas,* pl. < LL < LGk. *Saddoukaios* < Hebrew *Tsaddûq* Zadok, a Hebrew high priest in the time of David]

sa·dhu (sä′dü) *n.* a Hindu holy man.

sad·i·ron (sad′i′ərn) *n.* a heavy, solid flatiron pointed at both ends, used for ironing clothes. [< *sad,* in obs. or dial. sense of "firm, solid" + *iron*]

sa·dism (sā′diz əm *or* sad′iz əm) *n.* **1** delight in cruelty; getting pleasure from inflicting physical or mental pain on another person or on an animal. **2** a form of sexual perversion in which sexual gratification is obtained by inflicting pain on one's partner. Compare **masochism.** [< F; from Comte Donatien de *Sade* (1740-1814), who wrote of this condition]

sa·dist (sā′dist *or* sad′ist) *n.* one who practises sadism.

sa·dis·tic (sə dis′tik) *adj.* of, having to do with, or showing sadism: *a sadistic streak, a sadistic act.* —**sa·dis′tic·al·ly,** *adv.*

sad·ness (sad′nis) *n.* sorrow; grief.

sa·do·mas·och·ism (sā′dō mas′ə kiz′əm or sad′ō-) n. the combination of sadism and masochism in a single personality or in a relationship between persons.

sa·do·mas·och·ist (sā′dō mas′ə kist′ or sad′ō-) n. a person who is given to sadomasochism.

sa·do·mas·och·is·tic (sā′dō mas′ə kis′tik or sad′ō-) adj. of, having to do with, or exhibiting sadomasochism: a sadomasochistic relationship.

sad sack Esp.U.S. Slang. a bewildered, incompetent person, especially a soldier who blunders his way through the mazes of army life. [from a character in a U.S. comic strip by Sgt. George Baker]

sa·fa·ri (sə fä′rē) n., pl. -ris. 1 a journey or hunting expedition in E Africa. 2 any long trip or expedition. [< Arabic]

safe (sāf) adj. saf·er, saf·est; n. —adj. 1 free from harm or danger: Keep money in a safe place. 2 not harmed: He returned from war safe and sound. 3 out of danger; secure: We feel safe with the dog in the house. 4 put beyond power of doing harm: a criminal safe in prison. 5 cautious; careful: a safe guess, a safe move. 6 that can be depended on: a safe guide. 7 Baseball. (of a batter or base runner) reaching a base or home plate without being out. —n. 1 a box or place that can be locked, used for keeping things safe; especially, a heavy steel or iron chest or room for money, jewels, documents, etc. 2 Slang. condom. [ME < OF sauf < L salvus] —safe′ly, adv. —safe′ness, n.
☛ Syn. adj. 1. Safe, secure = free from danger. Although often used interchangeably, safe emphasizes being not exposed to danger, harm, or risk: The children are safe in their own yard. Secure emphasizes being protected or guarded against loss, attack, injury, or other anticipated or feared danger or harm: A child feels secure with his mother.

safe-con·duct or **safe conduct** (sāf′kon′dukt) n. 1 the privilege of passing safely through a region, especially in time of war. 2 a paper granting this privilege.

safe·crack·er (sāf′krak′ər) n. a thief who specializes in safecracking.

safe·crack·ing (sāf′krak′ing) n. the act or practice of breaking open safes and stealing the contents.

safe–deposit box (sāf′di poz′it) Esp.U.S. safety deposit box.

safe·guard (sāf′gärd′) v., n. —v. 1 keep safe; guard against hurt or danger; protect: Pure food laws safeguard our health. 2 guard; convoy. —n. 1 a protection; defence: Keeping clean is a safeguard against disease. 2 a guard; convoy. [ME < OF sauvegarde < sauve, fem. of sauf safe (< L salvus) + garde guard < Gmc.]

safe·keep·ing (sāf′kēp′ing) n. keeping safe; protection; care.

safe·ty (sāf′tē) n., pl. -ties. 1 the quality or state of being safe; freedom from harm or danger: They did not stop running until they had reached safety. 2 a device on a firearm, machine, etc. designed to prevent injury through accidental or careless operation. 3 (adj.) designed to give extra safety; designed to protect against harm through accident or misuse: a safety lamp, safety glass, a safety belt. 4 Football. safety touch.

safety belt 1 seat belt. 2 a strap used by window cleaners, loggers, linemen, etc. to prevent falling.

safety deposit box a box in the vault of a bank, etc. for the storage of valuables, such as original documents, bonds, jewellery, etc.

safety glass glass that resists shattering, made of two or more layers of glass joined together by a layer of transparent plastic.

safety island a marked area or a platform built in a thoroughfare for the convenience of pedestrians boarding and getting off buses, streetcars, etc.

safety lamp 1 a miner's lamp in which the flame is kept from setting fire to explosive gases by a piece of wire gauze. 2 an electric lamp similarly protected.

safety match a match that will ignite only when rubbed on a specially prepared surface.

safety pin a pin bent back on itself to form a spring and having a guard that covers the point in order to prevent injury or accidental unfastening.

safety razor a razor having a replaceable blade that is protected and angled to reduce the risk of cutting one's skin.

safety touch Cdn. Football. the act of putting a ball down behind one's own goal line after a player on one's own team has made it go there. It counts two points for the other team.

safety valve 1 a valve in a steam boiler, etc. that opens and lets steam or fluid escape when the pressure becomes too great. 2 something that helps a person get rid of anger, nervousness, etc. in a harmless way.

saf·flow·er (saf′lou′ər) n. 1 an annual herb (Carthamus tinctorius) of the composite family having large, red or orange flower heads yielding a red dye and seeds that are rich in oil. 2 a red dye prepared from the flower heads.

hat, āge, fär; let, ēqual, tėrm; it, īce
hot, ōpen, ôrder; oil, out; cup, pút, rüle,
əbove, takən, pencəl, lemən, circəs
ch, child; ng, long; sh, ship
th, thin; ᴛʜ, then; zh, measure

safflower oil an edible oil obtained from safflower seeds.

saf·fron (saf′rən) n., adj. —n. 1 a purple-flowered autumn crocus (Crocus sativus) native to the Old World. 2 the dried orange-colored stigmas of this crocus, used to flavor and color candy, drinks, etc. 3 a medium orange or orange yellow. —adj. medium orange or orange yellow. [< F safran, ult. < Arabic za'faran]

S.Afr. 1 South Africa. 2 South African.

sag (sag) v. sagged, sag·ging; n. —v. 1 sink under weight or pressure; bend down in the middle. 2 hang down unevenly: Your dress sags in the back. 3 become less firm or elastic; yield through weakness, weariness, or lack of effort; droop; sink. 4 decline in price. 5 of a ship, drift from her course. —n. 1 the act, state, or degree of sagging. 2 the place where anything sags. [cf. Du. zakken sink]

sa·ga (sä′gə) n. 1 a type of prose story of heroic deeds written in Iceland or Norway in the Middle Ages. 2 any extended story of adventure or heroic deeds. [< Scand. Akin to sᴀw³.]

sa·ga·cious (sə gā′shəs) adj. 1 wise in a keen, practical, farsighted way; shrewd. 2 resulting from or showing wisdom or sagacity. [< L sagax, acis] —sa·ga′cious·ly, adv. —sa·ga′cious·ness, n.
☛ Syn. 1. See note at shrewd.

sa·gac·i·ty (sə gas′ə tē) n., pl. -ties. keen, sound judgment; mental acuteness; shrewdness.

sag·a·more (sag′ə môr′) n. 1 among Algonquian peoples, an elected ruler or chief of a tribe, especially one subordinate to a sachem. 2 sachem. [earlier sagamo < Algonquian. Related to sᴀᴄʜᴇᴍ.]

sage¹ (sāj) adj. sag·er, sag·est; n. —adj. 1 wise: a sage adviser. 2 showing wisdom or good judgment: a sage reply. 3 Obsolete. solemn. —n. a very wise man. [ME < OF sage, ult. < L sapere be wise] —sage′ly, adv. —sage′ness, n.
☛ Syn. adj. 1, 2. See note at wise.

sage² (sāj) n. 1 any of a genus (Salvia) of plants of the mint family; especially, scarlet sage (S. splendens), grown for its brilliant red flowers, and garden sage (S. officinalis), grown for its aromatic leaves. 2 the dried leaves of the garden sage, used mainly as a seasoning for meats. 3 sagebrush. [ME < OF sauge < L salvia. Doublet of sᴀʟᴠɪᴀ.]

sage·brush (sāj′brush′) n. any of several shrubs (genus Artemisia) of the composite family native to the dry plains of W North America. Common sagebrush (A. tridentata) has greyish-green leaves and a smell like sage.

sage grouse a very large grouse (Centrocercus urophasianus) common on the plains of W North America. The males perform an elaborate courtship dance.

sage hen 1 sage grouse. 2 a female sage grouse.

Sag·it·tar·i·us (saj′ə ter′ē əs) n. 1 Astronomy. a southern constellation thought of as having the shape of a centaur drawing a bow. 2 Astrology. a the ninth sign of the zodiac. The sun enters Sagittarius about November 23. See zodiac for picture. b a person born under this sign. [< L Sagittarius, literally, the Archer < sagitta arrow]

sag·it·tate (saj′ə tāt′) adj. especially of a leaf, shaped like an arrowhead. See leaf for picture. [< NL sagittatus < L sagitta arrow]

sa·go (sā′gō) n., pl. -goes. a powdered or granulated starch prepared from the pith of a sago palm, used in making puddings and as a stiffening agent for textiles. [< Malay sagu]

sago palm 1 any of various tropical Asian palms (especially of genera Metroxylon and Arenga) that yield the starch sago. 2 any of several cycads that yield sago, especially Cycas revoluta, also cultivated as a conservatory plant.

Sa·har·an (sə her′ən or sə här′ən) adj., n. —adj. of or having to do with the Sahara Desert, or the people inhabiting it. —n. a native or inhabitant of the Sahara Desert.

sa·hib (sä′ib or sä′hib) n. sir; master (used as a title of respect by Indians in colonial India when speaking to or of a European). [< Hind. < Arabic çāhib lord]

said (sed) v., adj. —v. pt. and pp. of say. —adj. named or mentioned before: the said witness.

sail (sāl) *n., pl.* **sails** or (def. 4) **sail;** *v.* —*n.* **1** a piece of cloth spread to the wind to make a vessel move through the water. **2** the sails of a ship collectively. **3** a ship: *a fleet numbering thirty sail.* **4** something like a sail, such as the part of an arm of a windmill that catches the wind. **5** a trip on a boat with sails: *Let's go for a sail.*
in sail, in a ship with sails.
make sail, a spread out the sails of a ship. **b** begin a trip by water.
set sail, begin a trip by water.
take in sail, a lower or lessen the sails of a ship. **b** lessen one's hopes, ambitions, etc.
under sail, moving with the sails spread out.
—*v.* **1** travel on water by the action of wind on sails. **2** travel on a ship of any kind: *He is sailing to Europe on the Queen Elizabeth II.* **3** move smoothly like a ship with sails: *The hawk sailed by. Mrs. Grand sailed into the room.* **4** to sail upon, over, or through: *to sail the seas.* **5** manage a ship or boat: *The boys are learning to sail.* **6** manage or navigate (a ship or boat). **7** begin a trip by water: *We sail at 2 p.m.* **8** travel through the air: *The football sailed over the goal post.*
sail into, *Slang.* **a** attack; beat. **b** criticize; scold.
[OE *segl*]
☞ *Hom.* **sale.**

sail·board·ing (sāl′bôr′ding) *n.* windsurfing.

sail·boat (sāl′bōt′) *n.* a boat that is moved by a sail or sails. See **schooner** and **sloop** for pictures.

sail·cloth (sāl′kloth′) *n.* **1** canvas or other material used for making sails. **2** a similar material used in making clothes, curtains, etc.

sail·er (sāl′ər) *n.* a ship described in terms of its sailing power: *the best sailer in the fleet, a fast sailer.*
☞ *Hom.* **sailor.**

sail·fish (sāl′fish′) *n., pl.* **-fish** or **-fishes.** any of a genus (*Istiophorus*) of large, blue and silver fishes of the open sea, found in tropical and temperate waters, having an elongated, spearlike upper jaw and a large, high, sail-like dorsal fin. Sailfishes belong to the same family (Istiophoridae) as the marlins.

sail·ing (sāl′ing) *n.* the act of a person or thing that sails.

sail·or (sāl′lər) *n.* **1** a member of the crew of a ship or boat, especially one who is not an officer. **2** a person serving in the navy, especially one below the rank of petty officer. **3** a person whose hobby or pastime is sailing: *She's a keen sailor.* **4** any person who travels by water, especially with reference to his liability to seasickness: *I'm a bad sailor.* **5** sailor hat. **6** sailor suit. **7** sailor collar. —**sail′or·like′,** *adj.*
☞ *Hom.* **sailer.**

sailor collar a large, flat collar resembling the collar of a traditional sailor's blouse, having squared corners at the back and tapering to a point at the bottom of a V neck at the front.

sailor hat a flat-crowned hat with a wide brim slightly turned up all around.

sail·or·ly (sāl′ər lē) *adj.* like or suitable for a sailor.

sailor suit a child's suit resembling the traditional middy blouse and pants worn by sailors. Sailor suits are usually navy and white.

sail·plane (sāl′plān′) *n.* a light glider that can stay aloft for a long time supported by air currents.

sain (sān) *v. Archaic.* **1** make the sign of the cross on. **2** protect by prayer, etc. **3** bestow divine favor on. [OE *segnian* < L *signare* mark < *signum* sign]

saint (sānt) *n., v.* —*n.* **1** a very holy person. **2** a person who has gone to heaven. **3** *Roman Catholic Church.* a person who has been canonized. **4** a person who is very humble, patient, etc., like a saint. **5** angel. **6 Saint,** Mormon. **7** (*adj.*) **Saint,** holy or sacred (*used as a title before the name of a canonized person or an archangel*): *Saint Francis, St. Michael.*
—*v.* **1** make a saint of; canonize. **2** call or consider a saint.
—*adj.* holy; sacred. [ME < OF < L *sanctus* consecrated]
—**saint′like′,** *adj.*
☞ *Usage.* **Saint.** Entries commonly written in the abbreviated form, such as *St. Elmo's Fire* and *St. John's-wort* will be found in their alphabetical places after **St.**

Saint Agnes' Eve (ag′nəs) the night of January 20, when a girl was supposed to see a vision of her future husband if she performed certain ceremonies.

Saint Ber·nard (bər närd′ *or* bėr′nərd) a breed of big, powerful working dog, often tan and white, having a large head. These intelligent dogs were first bred by the monks of the St. Bernard hospice in the Alps to rescue travellers lost in the snow.

saint·ed (sān′tid) *adj.* **1** declared to be a saint. **2** thought of as a saint; gone to heaven. **3** sacred; very holy. **4** saintly.

saint·hood (sānt′hùd) *n.* **1** the character or status of a saint. **2** saints as a group.

Saint–Jean Baptiste Society (saN′zhäN′bä tēst′) *Cdn.* an organization in the Province of Quebec that is dedicated to the preserving and fostering of French culture in Canada. [< *Saint Jean Baptiste* St. John the Baptist, patron saint of Quebec]

saint·ly (sānt′lē) *adj.* **-li·er, -li·est.** like a saint; very holy or very good. —**saint′li·ness,** *n.*

Saint Nicholas 1 the patron saint of Russia and Greece, and of children, sailors, travellers, etc. Nicholas was a bishop in Asia Minor in the 4th century A.D. **2** Santa Claus.

saint·ship (sānt′ship) *n.* sainthood.

Saint Vi·tus's dance (vī′təs iz). See **St. Vitus's dance.**

saith (seth) *v. Archaic.* 3rd pers. sing., present tense, of **say.** *She saith* means *she says.*

saithe (sāth) *n. Esp.Brit.* pollock (def. 1). [< ON *seithr*]

sake¹ (sāk) *n.* **1** benefit; account; interest: *Don't go to any trouble just for my sake. For your own sake, drive carefully.* **2** purpose; aim: *He moved to the country for the sake of peace and quiet. For the sake of argument, let us suppose that the Tories win the election.*
for goodness' (or **Pete's, Heaven's, gosh,** etc.) **sake** or **sakes,** *Informal.* an exclamation of impatience, annoyance, surprise, etc.
for old times' sake, in memory of former days. [OE *sacu* cause at law]

sa·ke² (sak′ē *or* sä′kē) *n.* a Japanese fermented alcoholic drink made from rice. [< Japanese]

sal (sal) *n. Pharmacology.* salt (def. 2): *sal volatile.* [< L]

sa·laam (sə läm′) *n., v.* —*n.* **1** a salutation or greeting used especially among Moslems, meaning literally, "Peace." **2** a very low bow, made with the palm of the right hand placed on the forehead. **3** any ceremonial or respectful greeting or bow.
—*v.* **1** greet with a salaam. **2** make a salaam. [< Arabic *salām* peace]

sal·a·bil·i·ty (sā′lə bil′ə tē) *n.* a salable condition or quality.

sal·a·ble (sā′lə bəl) *adj.* that can be sold; fit to be sold; easily sold. Also, **saleable.**

sa·la·cious (sə lā′shəs) *adj.* **1** lustful; lecherous. **2** of writings, pictures, etc., erotic or lewd; tending to arouse sexual desire. [< L *salax, -acis*] —**sa·la′cious·ly,** *adj.* —**sa·la′cious·ness,** *n.*

sa·lac·i·ty (sə las′ə tē) *n.* a salacious quality.

sal·ad (sal′əd) *n.* **1** raw, leafy, green vegetables, such as lettuce, spinach, endive, etc., often mixed with other raw vegetables such as tomatoes, celery, sweet peppers, mushrooms, etc. and served with a dressing. **2** a similar cold dish made with cooked meat, fish, vegetables, eggs, potatoes, or fruits, etc., served with a dressing. **3** any leafy, green vegetable eaten raw, especially lettuce. [ME < OF < Provençal *salada,* ult. < L *sal* salt]

salad days days of youthful inexperience.

salad dressing a sauce for use in or on a salad.

sal·al (sal al′) *n. Cdn.* **1** a small evergreen shrub (*Gaultheria shallon*) native to the Pacific coast, having glossy leaves, showy, white flowers, and edible, purplish berries. Salal is closely related to wintergreen. **2** the berry of this shrub. [< Chinook Jargon (*klkwu*)-*shala*]

sal·a·man·der (sal′ə man′dər) *n.* **1** any of an order (Urodela, also called Caudata) of tailed amphibians resembling lizards but having moist, scaleless skin and often weak or rudimentary legs and having an aquatic larval stage during which they breathe by gills; especially, any of several species of the family Salamandridae, such as the European **fire salamander** (*Salamandra salamandra*). **2** *Mythology and legend.* a reptile able to live in fire. **3** in the ancient Greek theory of the four elements, the spirit that inhabited fire. [ME < OF < L < Gk. *salamandra*]

sa·la·mi (sə lä′mē) *n.* a highly seasoned sausage of pork and beef or beef alone, often flavored with garlic. Salami may be eaten dried or fresh. [< Ital. *salami,* pl. of *salame,* ult. < L *sal* salt]

sal ammoniac ammonium chloride.

sal·a·ried (sal′ə rēd *or* sal′rēd) *adj.* receiving a salary.

sal·a·ry (sal′ə rē *or* sal′rē) *n., pl.* **-ries.** fixed pay for regular work, usually paid every two weeks or monthly. Compare **wage.** [ME < AF < L *salarium* soldier's allowance for salt < *sal* salt]
☞ *Syn.* **Salary** and **wages** both refer to a fixed amount paid for regular work. **Salary** is used more for professional and office work, and for pay spoken of as covering a longer period of time: *The young engineer was paid a salary of $20 000.* **Wages** is used more for manual and physical work, and for pay spoken of as covering an hour, day, or week: *The minimum wage was fixed at $3.50 an hour.*

sal·chow (sal′kôv) *n. Figure skating.* a jump that includes a full turn in mid-air. [< Ulrich *Salchow,* a Swedish skating champion]

sale (sāl) *n.* **1** the act of selling; exchange of goods for money: *Did*

he make the sale? That was the last sale of the day. **2 sales,** pl. the amount sold; gross receipts: Today's sales were larger than yesterday's. **3** the chance to sell; demand; market. **4** a selling at lower prices than usual: This store is having a sale on suits. **5** auction. **6 sales,** the work involved in selling (used with a singular verb): His first job was in sales.

for sale, to be sold; available for buying: There are several nice houses for sale in this area.

on sale, **a** offered at a reduced price: All the winter boots are on sale now. **b** for sale: Tickets for the concert will be on sale here on Monday.

[OE sala]

☛ Hom. **sail.**

sale·a·ble (sā′lə bəl) adj. salable.

sal·e·ra·tus (sal′ə rā′təs) n. sodium bicarbonate or potassium bicarbonate used as a leavening agent in cooking.

sales·clerk (sālz′klėrk′) n. a person whose work is selling goods in a store.

sales·girl (sālz′gėrl′) n. saleswoman.

sales·la·dy (sālz′lā′dē) n., pl. **-dies.** saleswoman.

sales·man (sālz′mən) n., pl. **-men. 1** a man whose work is selling goods in a store; salesclerk. **2** sales representative.

sales·man·ship (sālz′mən ship′) n. the skill or technique of selling.

sales·peo·ple (sālz′pē′pəl) n.pl. salespersons.

sales·per·son (sālz′pėr′sən) n. **1** salesclerk. **2** sales representative.

sales representative a person employed as representative of a company to sell its goods or services in a certain territory.

sales·room (sālz′rüm′ or -rum′) n. a room where things are sold or shown for sale.

sales tax a tax on the amount received for articles sold.

sales·wom·an (sālz′wûm′ən) n., pl. **-wom·en.** a woman whose work is selling, especially in a store.

sal·i·cin (sal′ə sin) n. a bitter, white crystalline compound of glucose, obtained from the bark of various willows and poplars. It is used in medicine as a tonic and to reduce fever. Formula: $C_{13}H_{18}O_7$ [< F salicine < L salix, salicis willow]

Sal·ic law (sal′ik or sā′lik) Historical. **1** the code of laws of the Franks. **2** in France and Spain, a law excluding females from succession to the crown. [< Med.L. Salicus < LL Salii the Salian Franks, a tribe of Franks who dwelt in the regions of the Rhine near the North Sea]

sal·i·cyl·ate (sal′ə sil′āt or sə lis′ə lāt′) n. salt or ester of salicylic acid.

sal·i·cyl·ic (sal′ə sil′ik) adj. of or having to do with salicin.

salicylic acid a white crystalline compound used as a mild antiseptic and preservative, and as a medicine for rheumatism, gout, etc. Aspirin is a common preparation of salicylic acid. Formula: $C_7H_6O_3$ [< salicin]

sa·li·ence (sā′lē əns or sal′yəns) n. **1** the quality or state of being salient. **2** a striking part or feature.

sa·li·en·cy (sā′lē ən sē or sal′yən sē) n. salience.

sa·li·ent (sā′lē ənt or sal′yənt) adj., n. —adj. **1** standing out; easily seen or noticed; prominent; striking: the salient features in a landscape, the salient points in a speech. **2** pointing outward; projecting: a salient angle. **3** Heraldry. standing with forepaws raised as if jumping: a lion salient. —n. **1** a salient angle or part. **2** the part of a fort or line of trenches that projects toward the enemy. [< L saliens, -entis, ppr. of salire leap] —**sa′li·ent·ly,** adv.

sa·line (sā′līn) adj., n. —adj. **1** of salt; like salt; salty. **2** containing common salt or any other salts. —n. **1** a salt spring, well, or marsh. **2** a substance containing common salt or any other salts. [< L sal salt]

sa·lin·i·ty (sə lin′ə tē) n. saltiness; saline quality.

Salisbury steak (solz′ber′ē or sôlz′ber′ē) chopped beef shaped before cooking into a patty about twice the size of a hamburger, usually served with a gravy.

Sa·lish (sā′lish) n. **1** a group of North American Indians of British Columbia and the NW United States. In Canada a division is made between the **Coast Salish** and the **Interior Salish. 2** a member of this group. **3** any of the related languages of this group.

Sa·lish·an (sā′lish ən) adj., n. —adj. of or having to do with the Salish Indians or their languages. —n. Salish.

sa·li·va (sə lī′və) n. the liquid that the salivary glands secrete into the mouth to keep it moist, aid in chewing, and start digestion. [< L]

sal·i·var·y (sal′ə ver′ē) adj. of or producing saliva.

hat, āge, fär; let, ēqual, tėrm; it, īce
hot, ōpen, ôrder; oil, out; cup, put, rüle,
ə above, takən, pencəl, lemən, circəs

ch, child; ng, long; sh, ship
th, thin; ₮н, then; zh, measure

salivary gland any of various glands that secrete saliva into the mouth. The salivary glands of human beings and most other vertebrates are digestive glands that secrete saliva containing enzymes, salts, albumin, etc.

sal·i·vate (sal′ə vāt′) v. **-vat·ed, -vat·ing. 1** secrete saliva, especially an excessive amount. **2** produce an excessive flow of saliva in. [< L salivare < saliva saliva]

sal·i·va·tion (sal′ə vā′shən) n. **1** the secretion of saliva. **2** an abnormally large flow of saliva.

sal·let (sal′it) n. a light, rounded medieval helmet, with or without a visor. [< F < Ital. < L caelata, fem. pp. of caelare chisel < caelum chisel]

sal·low[1] (sal′ō) adj., v. —adj. of or having a pallid, yellowish complexion: a sallow face. He still looks quite sallow after his illness. —v. make or become yellow. [OE salo] —**sal′low·ness,** n.

sal·low[2] (sal′ō) n. **1** willow. **2** a willow twig. [OE sealh]

sal·low·ish (sal′ō ish) adj. somewhat sallow.

sal·ly (sal′ē) n., pl. **-lies;** v. **-lied, -ly·ing.** —n. **1** a sudden attack on an enemy made from a defensive position; sortie. **2** a sudden rushing forth. **3** a going forth; trip; excursion. **4** a sudden start into activity. **5** an outburst. **6** a witty remark. —v. **1** go suddenly from a defensive position to attack an enemy. **2** rush forth suddenly; go out. **3** set out briskly. **4** go on an excursion or trip. **5** of things, issue forth. [< F saillie, ult. < L salire leap]

Sally Ann (sal′ē an′) Informal. Salvation Army.

Sal·ly Lunn (sal′ē lun′) a slightly sweetened tea cake, served hot with butter. [after Sally Lunn, a woman who sold such cakes in Bath, England, at the end of the 18th century]

sal·ma·gun·di (sal′mə gun′dē) n. **1** a dish of chopped meat, anchovies, eggs, onions, oil, etc. **2** any mixture or medley of things, qualities, etc. [< F salmigondis, ult. < Ital. salami conditi pickled sausages]

sal·mi (sal′mē) n. a highly seasoned stew, especially of game. [< F salmi, short for salmigondis salmagundi]

salm·on (sam′ən) n., pl. **-on** or **-ons;** adj. —n. **1** any of various saltwater and freshwater fishes (family Salmonidae) that are highly prized as food and game fish, especially the Atlantic salmon or any species of Pacific salmon. —adj. having the color yellowish pink. [ME samon < OF < L salmo, -onis, probably "leaper" < salire leap]

sal·mon·ber·ry (sam′ən ber′ē) n., pl. **-ries. 1** a showy shrub (Rubus spectabilis) of the Pacific coast having red flowers and edible, salmon-colored, raspberrylike fruit. **2** the fruit of the salmonberry.

sal·mo·nel·la (sam′ən el′ə or sal′mə nel′ə) n., pl. **-lae** (-ī or -ē) or **-las.** any of various bacteria causing food poisoning, typhoid, and other infectious diseases. [< NL Salmonella, the genus name < Daniel E. Salmon (1850-1914), American pathologist]

salm·o·noid (sam′ə noid′ or sal′mə noid′) adj., n. —adj.. of or belonging to a family of fishes including the salmon and trout. —n. a salmonoid fish.

salmon pink yellowish pink.

salmon trout lake trout.

Sal·o·me (sə lō′mē) n. in the Bible, the daughter of Herodias, whose dancing so pleased Herod that he granted her request for the head of John the Baptist (Matthew 14:3-11).

sa·lon (sə lon′ or sal′on; French, sä lôn′) n., pl. **-lons. 1** a large room for receiving or entertaining guests. **2** an assembly of guests in such a room. **3** a place used to exhibit works of art. **4** an exhibition of works of art. **5** a business establishment that provides services such as hairdressing and manicuring. [< F < Ital. salone < sala hall < Gmc.]

sa·loon (sə lün′) n. **1** a place where alcoholic drinks are sold and drunk; bar. **2** a large room for general or public use: Concerts are often held in the saloon of the steamship. The ship's passengers ate in the dining saloon. **3** Also, **saloon car.** Brit. sedan. [< F salon salon. See SALON.]

sa·loon·keep·er (sə lün′kēp′ər) n. a person who keeps a saloon (def. 1).

sal·pi·glos·sis (sal′pə glos′is) n. any of a genus (Salpiglossis) of herbs of the nightshade family native to Chile, having brilliantly

colored, funnel-shaped flowers. [< NL *Salpiglossis*, the genus name < Gk. *salpinx, -pingos* trumpet + *glossa* tongue, referring to the shape of the stigma]

sal·si·fy (sal′sə fē *or* sal′sə fī′) *n.* **1** a European biennial plant of the composite family having a long, fleshy, edible root. **2** the root of this plant, eaten as a vegetable. Salsify has an oysterlike flavor. [< F *salsifis* < Ital. *sassefrica* < L *saxifraga*. Doublet of SAXIFRAGE.]

sal soda washing soda; crystallized sodium carbonate.

salt (solt *or* sôlt) *n., adj., v.* —*n.* **1** a white crystalline compound found in the earth and in sea water; sodium chloride. Salt is used to season and preserve food. **2** a usually crystalline chemical compound derived from an acid by replacing the hydrogen wholly or partly by a metal or an electropositive radical. Baking soda is a salt. **3** that which gives liveliness, piquancy, or pungency to anything. **4** saltcellar. **5** *Informal.* sailor. **6** salts, *pl.* **a** a salt prepared for use as a laxative: *Epsom salts, Rochelle salts.* **b** smelling salts. **above** or **below the salt,** in a superior or inferior position. **eat (someone's) salt,** be someone's guest. **salt of the earth,** a person, or people, considered to be especially fine, noble, etc. **with a grain of salt,** with some reservation or allowance: *The policeman took their story with a grain of salt.* **worth (one's) salt,** worth one's support, wages, etc. —*adj.* **1** containing salt: *salt water.* **2** tasting like salt. **3** overflowed with or growing in salt water: *salt marshes, salt grasses.* **4** cured or preserved with salt: *salt pork.* **5** sharp; pungent; to the point; lively: *salt speech.* —*v.* **1** mix or sprinkle with salt. **2** cure or preserve with salt. **3** provide or feed with salt: *to salt cattle.* **4** make pungent; season: *conversation salted with wit.* **5** *Chemistry.* **a** treat with any salt. **b** add a salt to (a solution) in order to precipitate a dissolved substance. **salt a mine,** put ore, gold dust, etc. into a mine to create a false impression of value. **salt away** or **down, a** pack with salt to preserve: *The fish were salted down in a barrel.* **b** store away: *The miser salted a lot of money away.* [OE *sealt*]

sal·tant (sal′tənt) *adj.* dancing; leaping. [< L *saltans, -antis,* ppr. of *saltare* dance]

salt–cel·lar (solt′sel′ər *or* sôlt′-) *n.* a shaker or dish for holding salt, used on the table. [ME *saltsaler* < *salt,* n. + obs. *saler* saltcellar < OF *salier,* masc., *saliere,* fem. < L *salarius,* adj. of salt < *sal* salt]

salt chuck *Cdn.* on the west coast and in the Northwest, the sea; saltwater.

salt·chuck·er (solt′chuk′ər *or* sôlt′-) *n.* a saltwater fisherman or angler.

salt·ed (sol′tid *or* sôl′tid) *adj.* **1** seasoned, cured, or preserved with salt. **2** experienced; hardened.

salt·er (sol′tər *or* sôl′tər) *n.* **1** a person who makes or sells salt. **2** a person who salts meat, fish, etc.

sal·tie or **sal·ty** (sol′tē *or* sôl′tē) *n. Informal.* a saltwater vessel, especially a freighter, sailing the Great Lakes.

salt·ine (sol tēn′ *or* sôl tēn′) *n.* a thin, crisp, salted cracker.

salt·ish (sol′tish *or* sôl′tish) *adj.* rather salty.

salt lick **1** a place where common salt occurs naturally on the surface of the ground and where animals go to lick it up. **2** a block of salt placed in a pasture for cattle, etc. to lick.

salt·pe·tre (solt′pē′tər *or* sôlt′-) *n.* **1** a mineral used in making gunpowder, in explosives, etc.; potassium nitrate; nitre. **2** a kind of fertilizer; sodium nitrate. Also, **saltpeter.** [ME < OF *salpetre* < Med.L *sal petrae* salt of rock < Gk. *petra* rock]

salt pork fatty pork that has been cured in salt.

salt rheum *Informal.* a skin eruption; eczema.

salt·shak·er (solt′shā′kər *or* sôlt′-) *n.* a container for salt, having a perforated top for sprinkling the salt.

salt·wa·ter (solt′wo′tər *or* sôlt′wô′tər) *adj.* **1** of, containing, or having to do with salt water or the sea: *a saltwater solution, saltwater fishing.* **2** living or found in the sea: *saltwater fish.*

salt·wort (solt′wèrt *or* sôlt′-) *n.* any of several plants (genus *Salsola*) of the goosefoot family found on seashores and in salt marshes, especially a European species (*S. kali*), also occurring on the E coast of North America. See also **Russian thistle.** **2** glasswort.

salt·y (sol′tē *or* sôl′tē) *adj.* **salt·i·er, salt·i·est. 1** containing or tasting of salt: *Sweat and tears are salty. The soup is too salty.* **2** to the point; witty and a bit improper: *a salty remark.* **3** suggesting the sea or nautical life: *a salty breeze.* —**salt′i·ly,** *adv.* —**salt′i·ness,** *n.*

sa·lu·bri·ous (sə lü′brē əs) *adj.* healthful. [< L *salubris < salus*

good health] —**sa·lu′bri·ous·ly,** *adv.* —**sa·lu′bri·ous·ness,** *n.*

sa·lu·bri·ty (sə lü′brə tē) *n.* healthfulness.

sa·lu·ki (sə lü′kē) *n.* a breed of sporting dog, having the sleek build of a greyhound, short, silky hair, and fringed ears and tail. It is probably the oldest known breed of dog, familiar to ancient Egyptians, Arabs, and Hebrews. [< Arabic *salugi,* of *Satuq,* an ancient city of Arabia]

sal·u·tar·y (sal′yə ter′ē) *adj.* **1** beneficial: *The teacher gave the boy salutary advice.* **2** good for the health; wholesome: *Walking is a salutary exercise.* [< L *salutaris < salus, salutis* good health]

sal·u·ta·tion (sal′yə tā′shən) *n.* **1** a greeting; saluting: *The man raised his hat in salutation.* **2** something uttered, written, or done to salute. Most letters begin with a salutation, such as "Dear Sir" or "My Dear Mrs. Jones."

sa·lu·ta·to·ry (sə lü′tə tô′rē) *adj.* expressing greeting; welcoming.

sa·lute (sə lüt′) *v.* **-lut·ed, -lut·ing;** *n.* —*v.* **1** honor in a formal manner by raising the hand to the head, by firing guns, by dipping flags, etc.: *The soldier saluted the officer.* **2** meet with kind words, cheers, a bow, a kiss, etc.; greet. **3** make a bow, gesture, etc. to. **4** come to; meet: *Shouts of welcome saluted their ears.* **5** make a salute. —*n.* **1** the act of saluting; a sign of welcome, farewell, or honor. **2** the position of the hand, gun, etc. in saluting. [ME < L *salutare* greet < *salus, salutis* good health] —**sa·lut′er,** *n.*

Salv. Salvador.

Sal·va·do·ran (sal′və dôr′ən) *n., adj.* —*n.* a native or inhabitant of El Salvador, a country in Central America. —*adj.* of or having to do with El Salvador or its people.

sal·vage (sal′vij) *n., v.* **-vaged, -vag·ing.** —*n.* **1** the act or process of rescuing a ship or its cargo from wreck, capture, etc. **2** payment made or due for such saving or rescuing. **3** the property saved or rescued. **4** the act of saving or rescuing anything from wreckage, destruction, etc. **5** anything saved or rescued for use, such as scrap metal, wood, etc.: *They used mostly salvage to build their cabin.* **6** the act of saving or rescuing from harm or ruin. —*v.* **1** save or rescue from wreckage, destruction, etc.: *We salvaged quite a few parts from the engine of the old car.* **2** save or rescue from harm or ruin: *to salvage one's dignity.* [< F *salvage,* ult. < L *salvus* safe] —**sal′vag·er,** *n.*

sal·va·tion (sal vā′shən) *n.* **1** saving or being saved. **2** a person or thing that saves. Christians believe that Christ is the salvation of the world. **3** a saving of the soul; deliverance from sin and from punishment for sin. [ME < OF < LL *salvatio, -onis,* ult. < L *salvus* safe]

Salvation Army an international organization to spread the Christian religion and to help the poor and unfortunate, founded in England in 1865 by William Booth (1829-1912).

salve¹ (sav) *n., v.* **salved, salv·ing.** —*n.* **1** a soft, greasy, ointment to put on wounds and sores to soothe or heal them. **2** something soothing; balm: *The kind words were a salve to his hurt feelings.* —*v.* **1** put salve on. **2** soothe; smooth over: *He salved his conscience by the thought that his lie harmed no one.* [OE *sealf*]

salve² (salv) *v.* **salved, salv·ing.** save from loss or destruction; salvage. [< *salvage*]

sal·ver (sal′vər) *n.* a tray, especially a silver one for serving drinks, for presenting letters or visiting cards, etc. [< F < Sp. *salva,* originally, foretasting, ult. < L *salvus* safe]

sal·vi·a (sal′vē ə) *n.* any of a large genus (*Salvia*) of herbs and shrubs of the mint family, especially a popular garden plant (*S. splendens*), also called **scarlet sage,** having showy spikes of scarlet flowers. Garden sage is also a salvia. [< L *salvia,* probably < *salvus* healthy; with reference to its supposed healing properties. Doublet of SAGE².]

sal·vo (sal′vō) *n., pl.* **-vos** or **-voes. 1** the discharge of several guns at the same time, as a broadside or as a salute. **2** a load of bombs or missiles released at the same time from an aircraft. **3** a round of cheers or applause. [< Ital. *salva,* ult. < L *salve* hail!, be in good health!]

sal vo·la·ti·le (sal′ və lat′ə lē) **1** an aromatic solution of ammonium carbonate and alcohol, used to relieve faintness, etc. **2** ammonium carbonate. *Formula:* NH₄CO₃. [< NL *sal volatile* volatile salt. 17 c.]

sal·vor (sal′vər) *n.* a person who salvages or takes part in salvaging a vessel or its cargo.

sam·a·ra (sam′ə rə *or* sə mer′ə) *n.* any dry fruit that has a winglike extension and does not split open when ripe. The fruit of the maple tree is a double samara with one seed in each half. See **fruit** for picture. [< L *samara* elm seed]

Sa·mar·i·tan (sə mar′ə tən *or* sə mer′ə tən) *n., adj.* —*n.* **1** a native or inhabitant of Samaria, a district in the northern part of

ancient Palestine. **2** See **Good Samaritan.** —*adj.* of or having to do with Samaria or its people.

sa·mar·i·um (sə mer′ē əm) *n.* a rare, lustrous, grey metallic element used especially in alloys that form permanent magnets. *Symbol:* Sm; *at.no.* 62; *at.wt.* 150.35. [< *samar(skite)*, a mineral < G *Samarskit*, after Col. *Samarski*, a Russian]

sam·ba (sam′bə) *n., v.* **-baed, -ba·ing.** —*n.* **1** a Brazilian dance of African origin. **2** the music for this dance. —*v.* dance the samba. [< Pg.]

Sam Browne belt (sam′broun′) a leather belt having a supporting piece passing over the right shoulder, worn by army officers, etc. [after Sir *Samuel J. Browne*, a British army officer (1824-1901)]

same (sām) *adj., pron.* —*adj.* **1** not another; identical: *We came back the same way we went.* **2** just alike; not different: *Her name and mine are the same.* **3** unchanged: *He is the same kind old man.* **4** just spoken of; aforesaid: *The boys were talking about an eccentric man. This same man wore his hair very long and was always dressed in white.* —*pron.* the same person or thing.
all the same, notwithstanding; nevertheless.
just the same, a in the same manner. **b** nevertheless.
the same, in the same manner: *Sea and see are pronounced the same.* [OE]
☛ *Syn. adj.* **1, 2. Same, identical** means not different from another or each other. Both may mean that what is described is not another person or thing but the one already mentioned or otherwise suggested: *That is the same* (or *identical*) *man I saw yesterday.* When describing two or more people or things, **same** means alike, of one kind, appearance, size, or quality, etc.: *He always has the same lunch.* **Identical** means absolutely alike, agreeing exactly in every detail: *Their cars are identical.*

same·ness (sām′nis) *n.* **1** the state of being the same; an exact likeness; identity or uniformity. **2** a lack of variety; tiresomeness; monotony.

S.Amer. South America; South American.

Sa·mi·an (sā′mē ən) *n., adj.* —*n.* a native or inhabitant of Samos, a Greek island in the Aegean Sea. —*adj.* of or having to do with Samos or its people.

sam·i·sen (sam′ə sen′) *n.* a Japanese musical instrument resembling a banjo, having three strings and played with a plectrum. [< Japanese < Chinese *san hsien*]

sam·ite (sam′īt or sā′mīt) *n.* a heavy, rich silk fabric, sometimes interwoven with gold, worn in the Middle Ages. [ME < OF < Med.Gk. *hexamiton* < Gk. *hex* six + *mitos* thread]

Sa·mo·an (sə mō′ən) *n., adj.* —*n.* **1** a native or inhabitant of Samoa, a group of islands in the South Pacific. **2** the Polynesian language of the Samoans. —*adj.* of or having to do with Samoa, its people, or their language.

sam·o·var (sam′ə vär′ or sam′ə vär′) *n.* a metal urn with a tap, used for heating water for tea. [< Russian *samovar*, literally, self-boiler]

Sam·o·yed (sam′ə yed′) *n.* a Siberian breed of large work dog, having a long-haired, white or cream-colored coat, and used in arctic regions to guard reindeer herds and to pull sleds. [< Russian *samoed*, prob. < Lapp *Sáme-Aednàma* of Lapland]

sam·pan (sam′pan) *n.* a type of small boat sculled by one or more oars at the stern, usually having a single sail and a cabin made of mats. Sampans are used in the rivers and coastal waters of China, SE Asia, and Japan. [< Chinese < Pg.; origin uncertain]

sam·phire (sam′fīr) *n.* **1** a plant (*Crithmum maritimum*) of the parsley family found on rocky coasts of Europe, having fleshy divided leaves. **2** glasswort. [earlier *sampere* < F (*herbe de*) *Saint Pierre* (herb of) St. Peter]

sam·ple (sam′pəl) *n., v.* **-pled, -pling.** —*n.* **1** a part or single item taken to represent a larger whole or a group; a part or item shown or presented as evidence of what the rest is like: *The display samples are not for sale. We sent a sample of the soil to the university for testing.* **2** (*adj.*) serving as a sample: *a sample copy.* —*v.* take a sample of, especially in order to test quality, etc.: *We sampled the cake and found it very good.* [var. of *essample*, var. of *example*]
☛ *Syn. n.* See note at **example.**

sam·pler (sam′plər) *n.* **1** a person who samples. **2** a piece of cloth embroidered with letters, verses, etc. in various stitches to show skill in needlework. **3** a book, kit, etc. providing a collection of samples. [< OF *essamplaire* < LL *exemplarium* < L *exemplum* example]

sam·pling (sam′pling) *n.* a small part or number selected for the purpose of testing or analysing.

Sam·son (sam′sən) *n.* **1** in the Bible, a judge of Israel who had very great strength. He confided to Delilah that his strength was in his hair, and she cut if off while he slept, so that his enemies, the

samarium **993** **sand**

hat, āge, fär; let, ēqual, tèrm; it, īce
hot, ōpen, ôrder; oil, out; cup, pùt, rüle,
əbove, takən, pencəl, lemən, circəs
ch, child; ng, long; sh, ship
th, thin; ҭ н, then; zh, measure

Philistines, could overcome him (Judges 13-16). **2** any man of great strength.

sam·u·rai (sam′ù rī′) *n., pl.* **-rai. 1** in feudal Japan, the military class, consisting of the retainers of the great nobles. **2** a member of this class. [< Japanese]

san (san) *n. Informal.* sanatorium, especially one for the treatment of tuberculosis: *She spent six months in the san.*

San (sän *or* san) *adj.* Spanish and Italian. Saint (def. 7).

san·a·tive (san′ə tiv) *adj.* healing; having power to cure. [ME < LL *sanativus*, ult. < L *sanus* healthy]

san·a·to·ri·um (san′ə tôr′ē əm) *n., pl.* **-ri·ums** or **-ri·a** (-rē ə). **1** an establishment for the treatment of the sick, especially persons with long-term or chronic diseases, such as tuberculosis. **2** a health resort. [< NL *sanatorium*, neut. of LL *sanatorius* health-giving, ult. < L *sanus* healthy]

san·be·ni·to (san′bə nē′tō) *n.* **1** a yellow penitential garment with a red St. Andrew's Cross before and behind, worn by a confessed heretic under trial by the Inquisition. **2** a black garment ornamented with flames, devils, etc., worn by a condemned heretic at an auto-da-fé. [< Sp. *San Benito* St. Benedict, from its resemblance to the cloak, or scapular, he introduced]

sanc·ti·fi·ca·tion (sangk′tə fə kā′shən) *n.* sanctifying or being sanctified; consecration; purification from sin.

sanc·ti·fied (sangk′tə fīd′) *adj.* **1** consecrated. **2** sanctimonious.

sanc·ti·fy (sangk′tə fī′) *v.* **-fied, -fy·ing. 1** make holy: *A life of sacrifice had sanctified her.* **2** set apart as sacred; observe as holy: *"Lord, sanctify this our offering to Thy use."* **3** make free from sin. **4** justify; make right. [ME < OF < L *sanctificare* < *sanctus* holy + *facere* make] —**sanc′ti·fi′er,** *n.*

sanc·ti·mo·ni·ous (sangk′tə mō′nē əs) *adj.* making a show of holiness; putting on airs of sanctity; pretending to be pious. —**sanc′ti·mo′ni·ous·ly,** *adv.* —**sanc′ti·mo′ni·ous·ness,** *n.*

sanc·ti·mo·ny (sangk′tə mō′nē) *n.* a show of holiness; airs of sanctity; hypocrisy in religious matters. [< L *sanctimonia* < *sanctus* holy]

sanc·tion (sangk′shən) *n., v.* —*n.* **1** permission with authority; approval: *We have the sanction of the law to play ball in this park.* **2** a solemn ratification. **3 a** a provision of a law enacting a penalty for disobedience to it or a reward for obedience. **b** the penalty or reward. **4** an action by several nations toward another, such as a blockade, economic restrictions, etc., intended to force it to obey international law. **5** a consideration that leads one to obey a rule of conduct. **6** a binding force. —*v.* **1** authorize; approve; allow: *Her conscience does not sanction stealing.* **2** confirm. [< L *sanctio, -onis* < *sancire* ordain] —**sanc′tion·er,** *n.*
☛ *Syn.* **1.** See note at **approve.**

sanc·ti·ty (sangk′tə tē) *n., pl.* **-ties. 1** holiness; saintliness; godliness. **2** the fact or quality of being inviolable or sacred; being hallowed: *the sanctity of a church, the sanctity of the home.* **3 sanctities,** *pl.* **a** sacred obligations, feelings, etc. **b** objects possessing sanctity. [< L *sanctitas* < *sanctus* holy]

sanc·tu·ar·y (sangk′chü er′ē) *n., pl.* **-ar·ies. 1** a sacred place. A church is a sanctuary. **2** the part of a church around the altar. **3** a place of refuge or protection: *This island is maintained as a bird sanctuary.* **4** a refuge or protection: *The lost travellers found sanctuary in a deserted hut.* **5** the temple at Jerusalem. **6** the sacred place where the ark of the covenant was kept in the temple at Jerusalem. [ME < OF < L *sanctuarium*, ult. < *sanctus* holy]

sanc·tum (sangk′təm) *n., pl.* **-tums** or (rare) **-ta** (-tə). **1** a sacred place. **2** a private room or office where a person can be undisturbed. [< L *sanctum*, originally neut. adj., holy]

sanc·tum sanc·to·rum (sangk′təm sangk tô′rəm) **1** *Latin.* holy of holies. **2** an especially private place.

Sanc·tus (sangk′təs) *n.* **1** a hymn beginning "Sanctus, Sanctus, Sanctus" in Latin and "Holy, holy, holy, Lord God of hosts" in English, ending the preface of the Mass or Eucharistic service. **2** the musical setting of this. [< L *sanctus*, holy; first word of this hymn]

sand (sand) *n., v., adj.* —*n.* **1** tiny grains of worn-down or disintegrated rock finer than gravel but coarser than silt: *Sand is found along seashores and in deserts.* **2 sands,** *pl.* a tract or region

composed mainly of sand: *the sands of the desert.* **3** the sand in an hourglass thought of as moments or particles of time: *The sands of time will run out.* **4** *Slang.* courage; pluck; grit. **5** a very light greyish brown.
—*v.* **1** sprinkle with sand: *to sand an icy walk.* **2** fill up or cover with sand. **3** clean, smooth, or polish by rubbing with an abrasive such as sandpaper. **4** mix with sand, especially to adulterate.
—*adj.* very light greyish-brown. [OE]

san·dal (san'dəl) *n.* a kind of open shoe consisting of a sole kept on the foot by means of any of various arrangements of straps over the toes or instep and often around the heel and ankle. See **shoe** for picture. [ME < L < Gk. *sandalion*]

san·dalled or **san·daled** (san'dəld) *adj.* wearing sandals.

san·dal·wood (san'dəl wůd') *n.* **1** the fragrant, hard, light-colored heartwood of any of several evergreen trees (genus *Santalum*) of S Asia, especially **white sandalwood** (*S. album*), used in cabinetwork and for ornamental carved objects such as boxes and fans, and also burned as incense. **2** a tree that yields this wood. The sandalwood is partially parasitic on the roots of other trees. **3** any of various other, similar trees. [< *sandal* (< Med.L *sandalum*, ult. < Skt. *çandana*) + *wood*]

sand·bag (sand'bag') *n., v.* **-bagged, -bag·ging.** —*n.* **1** a bag filled with sand. Sandbags are used to form temporary dams, protective walls for trenches used in battle, and as ballast on balloons. **2** a small bag of sand used as a club. —*v.* **1** furnish with sandbags. **2** hit or stun with, or as if with, a sandbag.

sand·bank (sand'bangk') *n.* a ridge of sand.

sand bar a ridge of sand in a river or along a shore formed by the action of tides or currents.

sand·blast (sand'blast') *n., v.* —*n.* **1** a blast of air or steam containing sand, used to clean, grind, cut, or decorate hard surfaces such as glass, stone, or metal. **2** the apparatus used to apply such a blast. A sandblast is often used in cleaning the outside of buildings. —*v.* use a sandblast on.

sand·box (sand'boks') *n.* a box for holding sand, especially for children to play in.

sand cherry **1** any of several North American shrubs (genus *Prunus*) of the rose family, especially common in the Prairie Provinces. **2** the edible, purplish or black berry of any of these shrubs.

sand dollar any of various flat, thin-edged, disk-shaped marine invertebrates (order Clypeasteroida) found in shallow, sandy-bottomed, coastal waters. Sand dollars are flat sea urchins.

sand·er (san'dər) *n.* **1** a truck having a device for spreading sand on icy roads. **2** the device itself. **3** a tool or machine for cleaning, smoothing, or polishing by means of sandpaper or some similar material. **4** any person or thing that sands.

sand flea **1** any of various tiny terrestrial crustaceans (order Amphipoda, especially family Talidridae) found in the sand of seashores, that hop like fleas. **2** chigoe.

sand fly **1** any of various small two-winged flies (genus *Phlebotomus*), the females of which have mouthparts adapted for sucking blood. Sand flies sometimes transmit diseases. **2** any of various other small two-winged flies.

sand·glass (sand'glas') *n.* hourglass.

sand·hill crane (sand'hil') a crane (*Grus canadensis*) of central and eastern North America, mainly bluish grey with a bare reddish patch on the forehead and upper face. The sandhill crane resembles the great blue heron.

sand·hog (sand'hog') *n.* a person who works under compressed air in underground or underwater construction, as in a caisson or tunnel.

sand·man (sand'man') *n. Folklore.* a man said to make children sleepy by sprinkling sand on their eyes.

sand·pa·per (sand'pā'pər) *n., v.* —*n.* a strong paper with a layer of sand or some other rough material glued on it, used for smoothing, cleaning, or polishing. —*v.* smooth, clean, or polish with sandpaper.

sand·pip·er (sand'pīp'ər) *n.* **1** any of numerous small or medium-sized shore birds (especially of genera *Actitus* and *Erolia*) having slender legs and long toes, a long, slender bill, and spotted or streaked, brownish or greyish plumage. **2** (*adj.*) designating the worldwide family (Scolopacidae) of shore birds that includes the sandpipers, curlews, snipes, and woodcocks.

sand·spit (sand'spit') *n.* a stretch of low, sandy land jutting out into water.

sand·stone (sand'stōn') *n.* a kind of sedimentary rock consisting of grains of sand held together by a natural cementing material.

sand·storm (sand'stôrm') *n.* a storm of wind that carries clouds of sand.

sand·wich (sand'wich) *n., v.* —*n.* **1** two or more slices of bread with meat, jelly, cheese, or some other filling between them. **2** something formed by similar arrangement: *an ice-cream sandwich.* —*v.* put or squeeze (*between*): *When he went to get his car, he found it sandwiched between two trucks.* [after John Montagu, the fourth Earl of *Sandwich* (1718-1792)]

sandwich board a pair of signboards, usually hinged at the top, designed to be hung from a person's shoulders with one board in front and the other behind, and used for advertising or picketing.

sandwich man a man carrying a sandwich board.

sand·wort (sand'wèrt') *n.* any of a genus (*Arenaria*) of herbs of the pink family that grow in low tufts or mats in sandy soil and have many very small, white or purplish flowers.

sand·y (san'dē) *adj.* **sand·i·er, sand·i·est. 1** containing, consisting of, or covered with sand: *Most of the shore is rocky, but there is a sandy beach.* **2** of the color of sand: *sandy hair.* **3** like sand in texture, etc. —**sand'i·ness,** *n.*

sane (sān) *adj.* **san·er, san·est. 1** having a healthy mind; especially, in law, able to make rational judgments and to appreciate the effects of one's actions. **2** showing good sense; reasonable or sensible: *a sane foreign policy.* **3** regulated by reason; rational. [< L *sanus* healthy] —**sane'ly,** *adv.* —**sane'ness,** *n.*
☞ **Hom. seine.**

San·for·ize (san'fər īz') *v.* **-ized, -iz·ing.** *Trademark.* shrink (cotton or linen cloth) by a patented process before it is made into clothing. [after *Sanford* L. Cluett (born 1874), the inventor]

sang (sang) *v.* pt. of **sing.**

sang–froid (säN frwä') *n. French.* coolness of mind; calmness; composure. [literally, cold blood]

san·gui·nar·i·a (sang'gwə ner'ē ə) *n.* **1** bloodroot. **2** a drug derived from the bloodroot, used as a stimulant, emetic, etc. [< NL]

san·gui·nar·y (sang'gwə ner'ē) *adj.* **1** with much blood or bloodshed; bloody: *a sanguinary battle.* **2** delighting in bloodshed; bloodthirsty. [< L *sanguinarius* < *sanguis, sanguinis* blood] —**san'gui·nar'i·ness,** *n.*

san·guine (sang'gwin) *adj.* **1** cheerful and hopeful; optimistic; confident: *a sanguine disposition. They were sanguine of success.* **2** having a healthy, red color; ruddy: *a sanguine complexion.* **3** in the physiology of the Middle Ages, having a temperament in which blood predominates over other humors; having an active circulation, ruddy complexion, and a cheerful and ardent disposition. **4** *Archaic.* sanguinary. [ME < OF < L *sanguineus* < *sanguis, sanguinis* blood] —**san'guine·ly,** *adv.*

san·guin·e·ous (sang gwin'ē əs) *adj.* **1** of or like blood; bloody. **2** blood-red. **3** sanguinary; bloodthirsty.

San·he·drim (san'hē drim') *n.* Sanhedrin.

San·he·drin (san'hē drin') *n.* the supreme council and highest religious and legal authority of the ancient Jewish nation. [< Late Hebrew < Gk. *synedrion* council, literally, sitting together < *syn-* together + *hedra* seat]

san·i·tar·i·an (san'ə ter'ē ən) *n., adj.* —*n.* a person familiar with, or engaged in, sanitary work. —*adj.* sanitary.

san·i·tar·i·um (san'ə ter'ē əm) *n., pl.* **-i·ums** or **-i·a** (-ē ə). sanatorium. [< NL < L *sanitas* health < *sanus* healthy]

san·i·tar·y (san'ə ter'ē) *adj.* **1** of or having to do with health and the conditions that affect health: *The city is looking for a more sanitary method of waste disposal.* **2** free from dirt or anything bad for health: *The top of the picnic table was not very sanitary.* [< F *sanitaire,* ult. < L *sanus* healthy] —**san'i·tar'i·ness,** *n.*

sanitary napkin or **pad** a disposable absorbent pad worn on the outside of the body to absorb the discharge from menstruation.

san·i·ta·tion (san'ə tā'shən) *n.* the working out and practical application of sanitary measures, such as disposal of garbage and government inspection of food.

san·i·tize (san'ə tīz') *v.* **-tized, -tiz·ing.** make sanitary by cleaning, sterilizing, etc.: *The lining of these shoes has been sanitized.*

san·i·ty (san'ə tē) *n.* **1** soundness of mind; especially, in law, the ability to make rational judgments and appreciate the effects of one's actions. **2** soundness of judgment; sensibleness; reasonableness. [< L *sanitas* < *sanus* healthy]

sank (sangk) *v.* pt. of **sink.**

sans (sanz; *French,* säN) *prep.* without: *"sans teeth, sans eyes, sans taste, sans everything."* [ME < OF *sanz,* ult. < L *sine* without, prob. influenced by L *absentia* (abl.) in the absence (of)]

sans–cu·lotte (sanz'kyü lot') *n.* **1** *Historical.* in France, a contemptuous term for a republican of the poorer classes, adopted

by the revolutionaries of the French Revolution as a designation of honor. **2** any extreme republican or revolutionary. [< F *sans-culotte* without knee breeches]

San·sei (san′sā′) *n., pl.* **-sei** or **-seis.** a native-born Canadian or United States citizen whose grandparents were Japanese immigrants; an offspring of Nisei parents. [< Japanese *san* third + *sei* generation]

San·skrit (san′skrit) *n.* the ancient literary language of India. [< Skt. *samskrta* prepared, cultivated (applied to the literary language as contrasted with the vernacular language). Cf. PRAKRIT.]

sans pa·reil (sän pä rā′) *French.* without equal.

sans-ser·if (sanz′ser′if) *n. Printing.* any style of type having no serifs. [< F *sans* without + E *serif*]

sans sou·ci (sän sü sē′) *French.* without care or worry.

San·ta (san′tə *for n.* san′tə or sän′tä *for adj.*) *n., adj.* —*n.* Santa Claus. —*adj. Spanish and Italian.* Saint (def. 7) (*feminine form*): *Santa Maria.*

Santa Claus (kloz′ or klôz′) Saint Nicholas, the saint of Christmas giving; according to the modern conception, a jolly old man with a white beard, dressed in a fur-trimmed red suit. [< Du. dial. *Sante Klaas* Saint Nicholas]

sap¹ (sap) *n.* **1** the liquid that circulates through a plant as blood does in animals. Rising sap carries water and salt from the roots; sap travelling downward carries sugar, gums, resins, etc. **2** any body fluid essential to life or health. **3** vital spirit; health and vigor: *the sap of youth.* **4** *Slang.* a silly, stupid person; fool. [OE *sæp*]

sap² (sap) *v.* **sapped, sap·ping;** *n.* —*v.* **1** weaken or use up; undermine: *The extreme heat sapped their strength.* **2** dig under or wear away the foundation of: *The walls of the boathouse had been sapped by the waves.* **3** dig protected trenches. **4** approach (the enemy's position) by means of such trenches. **5** make a tunnel under.
—*n.* **1** the making of trenches to approach a besieged place or an enemy's position. **2** a trench protected by the earth dug up; trench dug to approach the enemy's position. [< MF *sappe*, n., < *sapper*, v. < Ital. *zappare* < *zappa* spade, hoe]

sap·head (sap′hed′) *n. Slang.* a silly, stupid person.

sa·pi·ence (sā′pē əns or sap′ē əns) *n.* wisdom.

sa·pi·en·cy (sā′pē ən sē) *n.* sapience.

sa·pi·ent (sā′pē ənt or sa′pē ənt) *adj.* wise; sage. [< L *sapiens, -entis,* ppr. of *sapere* be wise] —**sa′pi·ent·ly,** *adv.*

sap·less (sap′lis) *adj.* **1** without sap; withered. **2** without energy or vigor.

sap·ling (sap′ling) *n.* **1** a young tree. **2** a young person.

sap·o·dil·la (sap′ə dil′ə) *n.* **1** a large evergreen tree (*Achras zapota*) of tropical America, the latex of which yields chicle. **2** the large, edible fruit of this tree, having a rough, brown skin and yellowish pulp that tastes somewhat like that of a pear. **3** (*adj.*) designating a family of tropical plants, most of which are trees, including the sapodilla and numerous other trees of economic importance as sources of latex. [< Sp. *zapotilla,* ult. < Nahuatl]

sap·o·na·ceous (sap′ə nā′shəs) *adj.* soapy. [< Med.L *saponaceus* < L *sapo, saponis* soap]

sa·pon·i·fi·ca·tion (sə pon′ə fə kā′shən) *n.* saponifying or being saponified. [< F]

sa·pon·i·fy (sə pon′ə fī′) *v.* **-fied, -fy·ing.** **1** make (a fat or oil) into soap by treating it with an alkali. **2** be saponified; become soap. **3** decompose (an ester of an acid) into an alcohol and a salt of the acid. [< NL *saponificare* < L *sapo, saponis* soap + *facere* make]

sap·o·nin (sap′ə nin) *n.* any of various glucose derivatives found in certain plants, that form a lather with water and are used in detergents and as foaming and emulsifying agents. [< F *saponine* < L *sapo, sapon-* soap. 19c.]

sap·o·nite (sap′ə nīt) *n.* a hydrated silicate of magnesium and aluminum that occurs in amorphous masses in veins and cavities of metamorphic rocks such as serpentine. It is a soft mineral with a soapy feel. < Swedish *saponit* < L *sapo, saponis* soap. 19c.]

sap·per (sap′ər) *n.* a soldier employed in the construction of trenches, fortifications, etc. [< *sap²*]

Sap·phic (saf′ik) *adj., n.* —*adj.* **1** of or having to do with Sappho. **2** having to do with certain poetic metres, or a stanza form, used by or named after *Sappho.* —*n.* a Sapphic stanza or strophe.

sap·phire (saf′īr) *n., adj.* —*n.* **1** a transparent, bright-blue or colorless precious stone that is a variety of corundum. **2** a gem made from this stone. **3** a bright blue.
—*adj.* bright-blue. [ME < OF < L < Gk. *sappheiros* < Semitic; cf. Hebrew *sappīr* < Skt. *çani-priya* dear to the planet Saturn]

Sap·pho (saf′ō) *n.* a Greek lyric poetess of Lesbos, an island in the Aegean Sea, who lived about 600 B.C.

sap·py (sap′ē) *adj.* **-pi·er, -pi·est.** **1** full of sap. **2** vigorous, energetic. **3** *Slang.* silly; foolish. —**sap′pi·ness,** *n.*

hat, āge, fär; let, ēqual, tèrm; it, īce
hot, ōpen, ôrder; oil, out; cup, put, rüle,
əbove, takən, pencəl, lemən, circəs
ch, child; ng, long; sh, ship
th, thin; ᵺ, then; zh, measure

sap·ro·phyte (sap′rō fīt′) *n.* an organism that lives on decaying organic matter; especially, a plant, such as any of several species of fungi. [< Gk. *sapros* rotten + E *-phyte*]

sap·ro·phyt·ic (sap′rō fit′ik) *adj.* of or like a saprophyte; living on dead organic matter. —**sap·ro·phyt′i·cal·ly,** *adv.*

sap·sa·go (sap′sə gō′ or sap sā′gō) *n.* a hard, greenish, skim-milk cheese of Swiss origin, flavored and colored with sweet clover. [alteration of G *Schabziger* < *schaben* to grate + dialect *Ziger* a kind of cheese]

sap·suck·er (sap′suk′ər) *n.* either of two North American woodpeckers (*Sphyrapicus varius* or *S. thyroideus*) that drill holes in trees to feed on sap and insects.

sap·wood (sap′wud′) *n.* the sap-carrying tissue between the bark and the heartwood of most trees. The sapwood is softer and usually lighter in color than the heartwood.

sar·a·band (sar′ə band′ or ser′ə band′) *n.* **1** a slow and stately Spanish dance. **2** the music for this dance. [< F < Sp. *zarabanda*]

Sar·a·cen (sar′ə sən or ser′ə sən) *n.* **1** especially in the Middle Ages, a Moslem, either Arab or Turkish. **2** in earlier times, an Arab. —*adj.* of or having to do with the Saracens.

Sar·a·cen·ic (sar′ə sen′ik or ser′ə sen′ik) *adj.* of or having to do with the Saracens.

sa·ran (sə ran′) *n.* a synthetic polymer of vinyl chloride and a radical derived from ethylene, manufactured as a thin, flexible sheet or film or as a textile fibre. Saran is highly resistant to rotting, soiling, and damage and is used in clothing, automobile seat covers, insect screens, etc. [< *Saran,* a trademark, coined by Dow Chemical Company]

sar·casm (sär′kaz əm) *n.* **1** a sneering or cutting remark; an ironical taunt. **2** the act of making fun of a person to hurt his feelings; bitter irony: *Her sarcasm was obvious when she called the frightened boy a hero.* [< LL < Gk. *sarkasmos* < *sarkazein* sneer, strip off flesh < *sarx, sarkos* flesh]
☛ *Usage.* See note at **irony.**

sar·cas·tic (sär kas′tik) *adj.* **1** characterized by sarcasm: *a sarcastic remark.* **2** using or tending to use sarcasm: *He gets sarcastic when his feelings are hurt.* —**sar·cas′ti·cal·ly,** *adv.*

Sar·cee (sär′sē) *n., pl.* **-cee** or **-cees;** *adj.* —*n.* **1** a member of an Amerindian people formerly living in the region of the upper Athabasca River in Alberta, now living mainly near Calgary. **2** the Athapascan language of the Sarcee. —*adj.* of or having to do with the Sarcee or their language.

sarce·net (särs′net) *n.* a soft, thin silk fabric. Also, **sarsenet.** [ME < AF *sarzinett,* dim. of *Sarzin* Saracen]

sar·co·ma (sär kō′mə) *n., pl.* **-mas** or **-ma·ta** (-mə tə). a cancerous tumor that develops in connective tissue, bone, or muscle. [< NL < Gk. *sarkōma,* ult. < *sarx, sarkos* flesh]

sar·coph·a·gus (sär kof′ə gəs) *n., pl.* **-gi** (-jī′ or -jē′) or **-gus·es.** a stone coffin, especially one ornamented with sculpture and inscriptions. [< L < Gk. *sarkophagos,* originally, flesh-eating (stone) < *sarx, sarkos* flesh + *phagein* eat]

sard (särd) *n.* **1** a deep-brownish-red variety of chalcedony, a quartz mineral used as a gem stone since ancient times. Sard is traditionally classified as a variety of carnelian. **2** a gem made from this stone. [< L *sarda;* cf. Gk. *sardios* (*lithos*) stone from Sardis in Lydia]

sar·dine (sär dēn′) *n., pl.* **-dines** or (esp. collectively) **-dine. 1** any of various food fishes (especially of genera *Sardina, Sardinops,* or *Sardinella*) of the herring family. Some species of small or young sardines are commonly preserved and canned in oil. **2** such a fish or any of various other small, herringlike fishes when preserved and canned in oil.
packed like sardines, very much crowded.
[ME < OF < Ital. < L *sardina* < *sarda* sardine < Gk., perhaps < *Sardō* Sardinia]

Sar·din·i·an (sär din′ē ən) *n., adj.* —*n.* **1** a native or inhabitant of Sardinia, a large island off the SW coast of Italy. **2** the Romance language of the Sardinians. —*adj.* of or having to do with Sardinia, its people, or their language.

sar·don·ic (sär don′ik) *adj.* bitterly mocking or cynical and disdainful: *He listened to their naïve proposal with a sardonic smile.* [< F < L < Gk. *sardonios,* a supposed Sardinian plant that produced hysterical convulsions] —**sar·don′i·cal·ly,** *adv.*

sar·do·nyx (sär′də niks) *n.* **1** a variety of onyx containing layers of sard. **2** a piece of this stone, or a gem made from it. [ME < L < Gk. *sardonyx*, probably < *sardios* sard + *onyx* onyx]

sar·gas·so (sär gas′ō) *n.* gulfweed. [< Pg. *sargasso* < *sarga*, a type of grape]

sar·gas·sum (sär gas′əm) *n.* gulfweed; sargasso. [< NL *sargassum*, name of genus]

A sari

sa·ri (sä′rē) *n., pl.* **-ris.** a garment worn by women especially in India and Pakistan, consisting of a long piece of light fabric, usually cotton or silk, draped around the body so that one end forms a long skirt and the other end hangs loosely over the shoulder or is draped over the head. [< Hind.]

sa·rong (sə rong′) *n.* **1** a rectangular piece of cloth, usually a brightly colored printed material, worn as a skirt by men and women in the Malay Archipelago, Sri Lanka, and some parts of India. **2** a fabric used to make this garment. [< Malay *sārung*]

sar·sa·pa·ril·la (sas′pə ril′ə *or* sär′sə pə ril′ə) *n.* **1** any of several tropical American prickly climbing plants (genus *Smilax*) of the lily family. **2** the dried roots of any of these plants, from which a flavoring agent is prepared that is used in various carbonated drinks, such as root beer. **3** a carbonated drink flavored with sarsaparilla or something like it. **4** any of various plants resembling sarsaparilla, especially the North American **wild sarsaparilla** (*Aralia nudicaulis*) of the ginseng family. [< Sp. < *zarza* bramble + *parrilla*, dim. of *parra* vine]

sarse·net (särs′net) See **sarcenet.**

Sar·si (sär′sē) See **Sarcee.**

sar·to·ri·al (sär tô′rē əl) *adj.* of tailors, tailoring, or tailored clothes: *His clothes were a sartorial triumph.* [< L *sartorius* of a tailor, ult. < *sarcire* patch] **—sar·to′ri·al·ly,** *adv.*

sash[1] (sash) *n.* a long, broad strip of cloth or ribbon, worn as an ornament round the waist or over one shoulder. [earlier *shash* < Arabic *shāsh* turban]

sash[2] (sash) *n., v.* **—n.** **1** the frame which holds the glass in a window or door. **2** the frame together with its pane or panes of glass, usually forming a movable part of a window: *She raised the sash to let in the spring air.* **—v.** furnish with a sash or sashes. [alteration of *chassis*, taken as pl.]

sa·shay (sa shā′) *v., n. Informal.* **—v.** move or walk casually in a bold or swaggering manner: *He sashayed up to the front door as if he owned the place.* **—n.** an excursion or trip. [alteration of *chassé* a gliding dance step < F]

Sask. Saskatchewan.

Sas·katch·e·wan·i·an (sas kach′ə won′ē ən) *n., adj.* **—n.** a native or long-term resident of Saskatchewan. **—adj.** of or having to do with Saskatchewan.

sas·ka·toon (sas′kə tün′) *n. Cdn.* **1** a North American shrub (*Amelanchier alnifolia*) of the rose family found from western Ontario to the Yukon and south to Colorado, having tiny white flowers that bloom in May and edible purple berries. **2** the sweet, juicy berry of this shrub. Saskatoons are harvested wild in western Canada and used especially in pies and preserves. [< Algonquian (Cree) *misaskwatomin* < *misaskwat* tree of many branches + *min* fruit]

Sas·quatch (sas′kwach) *n. Cdn.* a wild hairy monster of subhuman appearance, supposed to inhabit certain western mountain regions. [< Salish *se′sxac*]

sass (sas *or* sos) *n., v. Informal.* **—n.** back talk; impudence or cheekiness. **—v.** be saucy; be impudent or cheeky. [var. of *sauce*]

sas·sa·fras (sas′ə fras′) *n.* **1** an aromatic, North American tree (*Sassafras albidum*) of the laurel family, having small clusters of yellow flowers and bluish-black berries. **2** the aromatic dried bark of its root, used in medicine, as a flavoring in candy, soft drinks, etc. [< Sp. *sasafras*]

Sas·se·nach (sas′ə naн′ *or* sas′ə nak′) *n. Scottish and Irish.* **1** Englishman. **2** the English people as a whole. [< Irish *sasenach* Saxon < ML *Saxonicus*. Related to SAXON.]

sas·sy (sas′ē) *adj.* **-si·er, -si·est.** *Dialect.* saucy.

sa·stru·gi (sə strü′gē) *n. Cdn. Esp.North.* ridges of hard-packed snow, formed by the wind and often attaining a height of more than one metre. Also, **zastrugi.** [< Russian]

sat (sat) *v.* pt. and pp. of **sit.**

Sat. Saturday.

Sa·tan (sā′tən) *n.* Lucifer; the Devil. [OE < LL < Gk. < Hebrew *sātān* enemy, plotter < *sātan* plot against]

sa·tang (sa tang′)′ *n., pl.* **-tang.** a unit of money in Thailand, equal to ¹⁄₁₀₀ of a baht. See table at **money.** [< Thai *satān*]

sa·tan·ic (sā tan′ik) *adj.* **1** of or having to do with Satan: *satanic magic.* **2** showing extreme viciousness or cruelty; very wicked: *a satanic act of revenge.* **—sa·tan′i·cal·ly,** *adv.*

Sa·tan·ism (sā′tə niz′əm) *n.* **1** devil worship, especially a French cult of the 1890's that professed worship of Satan. **2** the beliefs or rites of devil worship. **3** wickedness; a malicious or diabolical disposition.

satch·el (sach′əl) *n.* a small bag, often having a shoulder strap, for carrying books, clothes, etc. [ME < OF < L *saccellus*, double dim. of *saccus* sack[1]. See SACK[1].]

sate[1] (sāt) *v.* **sat·ed, sat·ing.** **1** satisfy fully (any appetite or desire). **2** supply with more than enough, so as to disgust or weary. [alteration of *sade* (OE *sadian* glut; cf. SAD) under influence of L *satiare* satiate. See SATIATE.]
➤ *Syn.* **2.** See note at **satiate.**

sate[2] (sat *or* sāt) *v. Archaic.* a pt. and a pp. of **sit.**

sa·teen (sa tēn′) *n.* a fabric, usually cotton, woven in a satin weave and having a smooth, lustrous face. [var. of *satin*]

sat·el·lite (sat′ə līt′) *n.* **1** a small planet that revolves around a larger planet, especially around one of the nine major planets of the solar system. **2** a man-made object or vehicle sent into an orbit around the earth or other heavenly body. **3** a follower or attendant upon a person of importance. **4** a subservient follower. **5** a country that is nominally independent but actually controlled by a more powerful country. **6** a town or city situated near a large city and partially dependent on it. **7** (*adj.*) of, having to do with, or being a satellite: *a satellite nation.* [< L *satelles, -itis* attendant]

sa·ti·a·ble (sā′shē ə bəl *or* sā′shə bəl) *adj.* that can be satiated.

sa·ti·ate (sā′shē āt′) *v.* **-at·ed, -at·ing.** **1** feed fully; satisfy fully. **2** weary or disgust with too much. [< L *satiare* < *satis* enough] **—sa′ti·a′tion,** *n.*
➤ *Syn.* **2.** Satiate, sate, surfeit = fill with more than enough to satisfy. Satiate, formal, chiefly means "feed, literally or figuratively, to excess. Too much," to the point where something that did please or was wanted no longer gives pleasure: *Children who are given every toy they want eventually tire of them; others may become satiated.* Sate, chiefly literary, usually means "satisfy a desire or appetite" so fully that it dies: *Will nothing sate his lust for power?* Surfeit emphasizes excess, overeating or oversupplying to the point of making sick or disgusted: *He surfeited them with candy and sodas.*

sa·ti·e·ty (sə tī′ə tē) *n.* the feeling of having had too much; disgust or weariness caused by excess; a satiated condition. [< F < L *satietas* < *satis* enough]

sat·in (sat′ən) *n.* **1** a soft fabric, usually of silk or rayon, woven in a satin weave, having a smooth, lustrous face and a dull back. **2** a smoothness or glossiness like that of satin: *the satin of the silver bowl.* **3** (*adj.*) of or like satin: *a satin dress, a satin finish on a silver bowl.* [ME < OF < Arabic *zaitūnī*]

satin stitch an embroidery stitch using long stitches placed closely together, producing a solid embroidered surface resembling the smooth finish of satin. See **embroidery** for picture.

satin weave a weave in which the crosswise threads alternately cross over a number of lengthwise threads and under a single thread, producing a soft, luxurious fabric with a smooth, glossy surface. See **weave** for picture.

sat·in·wood (sat′ən wud′) *n.* **1** an East Indian tree (*Chloroxylon swietenia*) of the mahogany family (or, according to some authorities, the rice family) having hard, yellowish-brown wood with a satiny lustre. **2** the wood of this tree, used for fine furniture, farm tools, etc.

sat·in·y (sat′ən ē) *adj.* like satin in smoothness and gloss.

sat·ire (sat′īr) *n.* **1** a literary genre characterized by the use of irony to attack a vice or foolishness. **2** a literary work in this genre. Jonathan Swift's *Gulliver's Travels* is a satire. **3** the use of irony, often biting or bitter, to attack vice or foolishness. [< L *satira*, var. of (*lanx*) *satura* mixed (dish) < *satur* full]
➤ *Usage.* See note at **irony.**

sa·tir·ic (sə tir′ik) *adj.* **1** of or having to do with satire: *satiric verse.* **2** satirical.

sa·tir·i·cal (sə tir′ə kəl) *adj.* **1** containing, showing, or reflecting satire: *a satirical smile, a satirical letter.* **2** fond of using satire: *a satirical columnist.* —**sa·tir′i·cal·ly,** *adv.*

sat·i·rist (sat′ə rist) *n.* a writer of satires; a person who uses satire. The follies and vices of their own times are the chief subjects of satirists.

sat·i·rize (sat′ə rīz′) *v.* **-rized, -riz·ing.** criticize or ridicule by means of satire: *Her novel satirizes Canadian attitudes toward the United States.*

sat·is·fac·tion (sat′is fak′shən) *n.* **1** a fulfilment; satisfying. **2** the condition of being satisfied or pleased and contented. **3** anything that makes us feel pleased or contented. **4** a response, information, etc. that fully meets doubts, objections, demands, etc. **5** the payment of debt; the discharge of obligation; a making up for wrong or injury done.
give satisfaction, a satisfy. **b** *Historical.* accept a challenge to a duel from a person one has wronged.
[ME < OF < L *satisfactio, -onis* < *satisfacere.* See SATISFY.]

sat·is·fac·to·ry (sat′is fak′tə rē *or* -fak′trē) *adj.* satisfying; good enough to satisfy. —**sat′is·fac′to·ri·ly,** *adv.* —**sat′is·fac′to·ri·ness,** *n.*

sat·is·fy (sat′is fī′) *v.* **-fied, -fy·ing. 1** give enough to; fulfil (desires, hopes, demands, etc.); put an end to (needs, wants, etc.): *He satisfied his hunger with a sandwich and milk.* **2** fully meet (an objection, doubt, demand, etc.). **3** make contented; please: *Are you satisfied now?* **4** give satisfaction. **5** pay; make right: *After the accident he satisfied all claims for the damage he had caused.* **6** set free from doubt; convince: *He was satisfied that it was an accident.* **7** make up for a wrong or injury. [ME < OF < L *satisfacere* < *satis* enough + *facere* do] —**sat′is·fy′ing·ly,** *adv.*
☛ *Syn.* **1. Satisfy, content** = meet, wholly or partly, a person's desires and wants. **Satisfy** suggests giving enough to fulfil a person's desires, hopes, needs, etc.: *The little mongrel satisfied the boy's desire for a dog.* **Content** suggests giving enough to please a person and keep him from feeling deprived: *A letter from her once a week contented him.*

sa·trap (sā′trap *or* sat′rap) *n.* **1** a ruler, often a tyrant, who is subordinate to a higher ruler. **2** in ancient Persia, a governor of a province. [ME < L < Gk. *satrapēs* < OPersian *kshathra-pāwan* guardian of the realm]

sa·trap·y (sā′trə pē *or* sat′rə pē) *n., pl.* **-trap·ies.** the province, position, or authority of a satrap.

sat·u·ra·ble (sach′ə rə bəl) *adj.* that can be saturated.

sat·u·rate (sach′ə rāt′) *v.* **-rat·ed, -rat·ing. 1** fill completely with moisture; soak: *Saturate the peat moss with water before planting the bulbs in it.* **2** fill or imbue: *a ceremony saturated with tradition.* **3** *Military.* overwhelm with heavy bombing or shelling. **4** cause (a substance, air, vapor, etc.) to absorb or unite with the greatest possible amount of another substance: *to saturate air with water vapor.* [< L *saturare* glut < *satur* full]

sat·u·rat·ed (sach′ə rā′təd) *adj.* **1** thoroughly wet. **2** of a solution, containing the maximum amount of dissolved substance that can normally be dissolved at a given temperature and pressure. **3** of an organic compound, containing no double or triple bonds and thus not able to unite directly with other compounds or elements. **4** of a color, containing little or no white; pure and rich.

sat·u·ra·tion (sach′ə rā′shən) *n.* **1** the act or process of saturating. **2** the state or condition of being saturated. **3** the degree of difference of a color from a grey of the same lightness; the degree of a color's chromatic purity. The less white a color contains, the greater its saturation.

saturation point 1 the point at which a substance can absorb no more of another substance. **2** the stage beyond which no more can be accepted, endured, etc. **3** a condition in which a market is supplied with as much of a particular commodity as it can absorb.

Sat·ur·day (sat′ər dē *or* sat′ər dā′) *n.* the seventh day of the week, following Friday. [OE *Sæterdæg, Sætern(es)dæg,* translation of L *Saturni dies* day of Saturn (the planet)]

Sat·urn (sat′ərn) *n.* **1** *Roman mythology.* the god of agriculture, ruler of the world until overthrown by his son Jupiter. He corresponds to the Greek god Cronus. **2** the second largest planet in the solar system, the sixth in distance from the sun. The planet has at least 10 satellites and is surrounded by seven thin concentric rings composed of particles that may be chunks of ice. [< L *Saturnus,* associated by the Romans with *satio* sowing, ult. < *serere* to sow]

Sat·ur·na·li·a (sat′ər nā′lē ə *or* -nāl′yə) *n.pl.* **1** the ancient Roman festival of Saturn, celebrated in December with much feasting and merrymaking. **2 saturnalia,** a period of unrestrained revelry and licence (*used with a singular or plural verb*). [< L]

Sat·ur·na·li·an (sat′ər nā′lē ən *or* -nāl′yən) *adj.* **1** of or having to do with the Roman Saturnalia. **2 saturnalian,** riotously merry; revelling without restraint.

Sa·tur·ni·an (sə tėr′nē ən) *adj.* **1** of or having to do with the god Saturn, whose reign is referred to as the "golden age."

2 prosperous, happy, or peaceful. **3** of or having to do with a form of verse used in early Roman poetry. **4** of or having to do with the planet Saturn.

sat·ur·nine (sat′ər nīn′) *adj.* gloomy, grave, or taciturn: *a saturnine disposition.* [< *Saturn*; those born under the planet's sign are supposed to be morose] —**sat′ur·nine·ly,** *adv.*

sat·yr (sat′ər *or* sā′tər) *n.* **1** *Greek mythology.* any of a class of minor woodland gods who were companions of Bacchus and indulged in merrymaking and lechery. In early Greek art they were pictured as men with the ears and tail of a horse. In later Roman art they became partially assimilated with the Roman fauns, and were represented as having the ears, tail, horns, and legs of a goat. **2** a lecherous man. **3** any of numerous usually brownish butterflies (family Satyridae) often having eyelike spots on the wings. [ME < L < Gk. *satyros*]

sauce (sos *or* sôs) *n., v.* **sauced, sauc·ing.** —*n.* **1** something, usually a liquid, served with food to make it taste better. We eat mint sauce with lamb, egg sauce with fish, and many different sauces with puddings. **2** stewed fruit: *cranberry sauce, applesauce.* **3** something that adds interest or relish. **4** *Informal.* sauciness. —*v.* **1** prepare with sauce; season. **2** give interest or flavor to. **3** *Informal.* be saucy to. [ME < OF < L *salsa,* fem. adj., salted, ult. < *sal, salis* salt]

sauce·box (sos′boks′ *or* sôs′-) *n. Informal.* an impertinent person.

sauce·pan (sos′pan′ *or* sôs′-) *n.* a deep cooking utensil of metal, glass, ceramic, etc., usually having a lid and a long handle at the side, and used for cooking on top of the stove.

sau·cer (so′sər *or* sô′sər) *n.* **1** a shallow dish to set a cup on. **2** any small, round, shallow dish, such as a dish put under a flowerpot to catch excess water. **3** something round and shallow like a saucer. [ME *saucer* sauce dish < OF *saucier* < *sauce.* See SAUCE.] —**sau′cer·like′,** *adj.*

sau·cy (so′sē *or* sô′sē) *adj.* **-ci·er, -ci·est. 1** showing lack of respect; rude. **2** pert; smart: *a saucy hat.* [< *sauce*] —**sau′ci·ly,** *adv.* —**sau′ci·ness,** *n.*
☛ *Syn.* **1.** See note at **impertinent.**

sauer·kraut (sour′krout′) *n.* cabbage cut fine, salted, and allowed to ferment; cabbage pickled in brine. [< G *Sauerkraut* < *sauer* sour + *Kraut* cabbage]

sau·ger (so′gər *or* sô′gər) *n.* a North American freshwater fish of the perch family (*Stizostedion canadense*) that is a popular food and game fish. It is closely related to the walleye. [origin uncertain; ? < North American Indian]

Sauk (sok *or* sôk) *n., pl.* **Sauk** *or* **Sauks. 1** a member of an Amerindian people formerly living in the Fox River valley in Wisconsin. **2** a dialect of Fox spoken by the Sauks. Also, **Sac.**

sault (sü) *n. Cdn.* a waterfall or rapids (*now used mainly in place names*). [obs. spelling of F *saut* leap, jump, falls < L *saltus* < *salire* to leap]
☛ *Hom.* **sou, sue.**

sau·na (son′ə, sô′nə, *or* sou′nə) *n.* **1** a steam bath in which the steam is usually produced by pouring water over hot stones. **2** a house or other structure used for such baths. [< Finnish]

saun·ter (son′tər *or* sôn′tər) *v., n.* —*v.* walk along slowly and quietly; stroll: *saunter through the park.* —*n.* **1** a leisurely or careless gait. **2** a stroll. [origin uncertain] —**saun′ter·er,** *n.*

sau·ri·an (sôr′ē ən) *n., adj.* —*n.* **1** any of a suborder (Sauria) of reptiles commonly known as lizards. Geckos, horned toads, chameleons, etc. are saurians. **2** any of various reptiles resembling the lizards, such as the crocodiles. —*adj.* of, designating, or like lizards. [< NL *sauria,* pl. < Gk. *sauros* lizard]

sau·ry (sôr′ē) *n., pl.* **-ry** *or* **-ries.** any of a family (Scomberesocidae) of long, slender fishes found in tropical and temperate seas, having a pointed, beaklike snout. [< NL < Gk. *sauros* lizard]
☛ *Hom.* **sorry.**

sau·sage (so′sij *or* sô′sij) *n.* chopped pork, beef, or other meats, seasoned and stuffed into a thin casing or skin. [ME < ONF *saussiche* < LL *salsicia,* ult. < L *sal, salis* salt]

sau·té (so tā′) *adj., n., v.* **-téed, -té·ing.** —*adj.* fried quickly in a little fat, over a high heat.
—*n.* a dish of food prepared in this way.

hat, āge, fär; let, ēqual, tėrm; it, īce
hot, ōpen, ôrder; oil, out; cup, put, rüle,
əbove, takən, pencəl, lemən, circəs
ch, child; ng, long; sh, ship
th, thin; ᴛʜ, then; zh, measure

—*v.* fry quickly in a little fat. [< F *sauté*, pp. of *sauter* jump < L *saltare* hop, frequentative of *salire* leap]

sau·terne (sō tėrn′) *n.* **1** a French white table wine. **2** any wine of the same type. [< *Sauternes*, a district in S France, where the grapes are grown]

sauve qui peut (sōv kē pœ′) *French.* a general rout; hasty flight. [literally, let (everyone) save (himself) who can]

sav·age (sav′ij) *adj., n., v.* **-aged, -ag·ing.** —*adj.* **1** of animals, not tamed or under human control; wild and fierce: *Savage beasts of the jungle.* **2** of geographical features, wild and rugged: *Savage mountain scenery.* **3** ferocious or brutal: *He was the victim of a savage attack by a mugger.* **4** enraged; furiously angry. **5** not having an advanced or complex culture; uncivilized; primitive: *a savage people.* —*n.* **1** a fierce, brutal, or cruel person. **2** a crude or boorish person. **3** a person belonging to a primitive society. —*v.* attack fiercely or brutally: *The child was savaged by a dog.* [ME < OF *sauvage* < LL *salvaticus*, ult. < L *silva* forest] —**sav′age·ly,** *adv.* —**sav′age·ness,** *n.*
☛ *Syn. adj.* 3. See note at **fierce.**

sav·age·ry (sav′ij rē) *n., pl.* **-ries.** **1** the quality or condition of being savage: *The savagery of their attack took the enemy by surprise.* **2** an act of cruelty or brutality. **3** a primitive state: *a people living in savagery.*

sa·van·na or **sa·van·nah** (sə van′ə) *n.* **1** a treeless plain. **2** a region of tropical or sub-tropical grassland having a scattering of trees. **3** especially in the Maritimes, a swamp or tract of peat bog; muskeg. [< earlier Sp. *zavana* < Arawakan]

sa·vant (sə vänt′ or sav′ənt) *n.* a man of learning. [< earlier F ppr. of *savoir* know < L *sapere* be wise]

save¹ (sāv) *v.* **saved, sav·ing;** *n.* —*v.* **1** make safe from harm, danger, loss, etc.; rescue: *to save a drowning man.* **2** keep safe from harm, danger, hurt, loss, etc.; protect: *to save one's honor.* **3** lay aside; store up: *She saves pieces of string.* **4** keep from spending or wasting: *Save your strength.* **5** avoid expense or waste: *She saves in every way she can.* **6** prevent; make less: *to save work, to save trouble, to save expense.* **7** treat carefully to lessen wear, weariness, etc.: *Large print saves one's eyes.* **8** set free from sin and its consequences. —*n.* the act of saving, especially by preventing an opponent from scoring. [ME < OF < LL *salvare* < L *salvus* safe] —**sav′er,** *n.*

save² (sāv) *prep., conj.* —*prep.* except; but: *He works every day of the week save Sunday.* —*conj. Archaic.* unless. [var. of *safe,* in sense of "not being involved"]

sav·in (sav′ən) *n.* **1** a shrubby Eurasian juniper (*Juniperus sabina*) having dark foliage that yields an oil formerly used in medicine. **2** the oil obtained from this shrub. **3** any of several related shrubs. Also, **savine.** [ult. < L *sabina,* originally adj., Sabine]

sav·ing (sā′ving) *adj., n., prep., conj.* —*adj.* **1** that saves. **2** tending to save up money; avoiding waste; economical. **3** making a reservation: *a saving clause.* —*n.* **1** an act or way of saving money, time, etc.: *It will be a saving to take this short cut.* **2** that which is saved. **3 savings,** *pl.* money saved. —*prep.* **1** save; except. **2** with all due respect to or for. —*conj.* except.

saving grace a redeeming quality or feature.

savings account an account in a bank, trust company, or credit union on which interest is paid.

sav·ior or **sav·iour** (sāv′yər) *n.* **1** a person who saves or rescues. **2 the Saviour** or **the Savior,** Jesus Christ. [ME < OF < LL *salvator* < *salvare.* See SAVE¹.]
☛ *Spelling.* See note at **-or.**

sa·voir–faire (sav′wär fer′) *n.* the knowledge of just the right thing to do or say, especially in social situations. [< F *savoir-faire,* literally, knowing how to act]

sa·voir–vi·vre (sav′wär vē′vʀ) *n.* knowledge of the world and of the usages of polite society; good breeding. [< F *savoir-vivre,* literally, knowing how to live]

sa·vor or **sa·vour** (sā′vər) *n., v.* —*n.* **1** a taste or smell; flavor: *The soup has a savor of onion.* **2** a distinctive quality; noticeable trace: *There is a savor of conceit in everything he says.* —*v.* **1** taste or smell (*of*): *That sauce savors of lemon.* **2** enjoy the savor of; perceive or appreciate by taste or smell: *He savored the soup with pleasure.* **3** give flavor to; season. **4** have the quality or nature (*of*): *a request that savors of a command.* [ME < OF < L *sapor*] —**sa′vor·er** or **sa′vour·er,** *n.* —**sa′vor·less** or **sa′vour·less,** *adj.*

sa·vor·y¹ or **sa·vour·y** (sā′vər ē) *adj.* **-vor·i·er** or **-vour·i·er,**

-vor·i·est or **-vour·i·est;** *n., pl.* **-vor·ies** or **-vour·ies.** —*adj.* **1** pleasing in taste or smell especially because of the seasoning: *The savory smell of roasting turkey greeted us as we entered the house.* **2** having a salt or piquant flavor and not a sweet one: *There were both sweet and savory relishes on the table.* **3** morally acceptable: *His reputation was not particularly savory.* —*n.* a small portion of highly seasoned food served at the beginning or end of a dinner to stimulate the appetite or digestion. [ME < OF *savoure,* ult. < L *sapor* taste] —**sa′vor·i·ness** or **sa′vour·i·ness,** *n.*

sa·vor·y² (sā′vər ē) *n., pl.* **-vor·ies.** any of a genus (*Satureia*) of fragrant herbs of the mint family, used for seasoning food; especially, summer savory. [ME *saverey,* ult. < L *satureia*]

sa·voy (sə voi′) *n.* a variety of cabbage having a compact head and wrinkled leaves. [< *Savoie* Savoy, a region in E France]

Sa·voy (sə voi′) *n.* the French noble family that ruled Italy from 1861 to 1946.

Sa·voy·ard (sə voi′ərd) *n., adj.* —*n.* **1** a native or inhabitant of Savoy, a region in E France. **2** an actor, producer, or warm admirer of Gilbert and Sullivan's operas, many of which were first produced at the Savoy Theatre, London. —*adj.* **1** of Savoy or its people. **2** of or having to do with the Savoy Theatre, London.

sav·vy (sav′ē) *v.* **-vied, -vy·ing;** *n. Slang.* —*v.* know; understand. —*n.* understanding; intelligence; sense. [< Sp. or Pg. *sabe* (you) know, both ult. < L *sapere* be wise. 18c.]

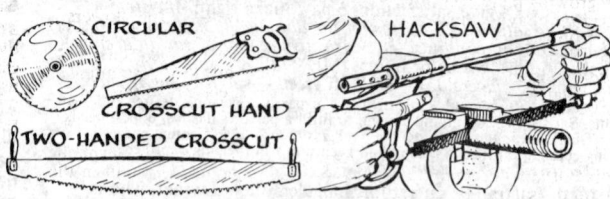

Saws. The circular saw (upper left) is mounted in a frame and turned by a motor. The other three are used by hand.

saw¹ (so *or* sô) *n., v.* **sawed, sawed** or **sawn, saw·ing.** —*n.* **1** a tool for cutting hard material such as wood or metal, consisting of a blade or disk with sharp teeth on the edge, especially such a tool operated by hand. **2** a device or machine that includes such a tool. —*v.* **1** cut with a saw. **2** make with a saw. **3** use a saw. **4** be sawed: *Pine saws more easily than oak.* **5** cut as if with a saw; move through as if sawing. [OE *sagu*] —**saw′er,** *n.*

saw² (so *or* sô) *v.* pt. of see¹.

saw³ (so *or* sô) *n.* a wise saying; proverb: *"A stitch in time saves nine"* is a familiar saw. [OE *sagu.* Related to SAY.]

saw·buck (so′buk′ *or* sô′-) *n.* **1** sawhorse. **2** *Slang.* a ten-dollar bill. [< Du. *zaagbok*]

saw·dust (so′dust′ *or* sô′-) *n.* the particles of wood produced in sawing.

sawed–off (sod′of′ *or* sôd′of′) **1** designating a shotgun with the end of the barrel cut off. **2** *Slang.* of less than average height; short.

saw·fish (so′fish′ *or* sô′-) *n., pl.* **-fish** or **-fish·es.** any of a family (Pristidae) of sharklike rays found in warm coastal waters, having an elongated, bladelike snout with strong teeth along the edges on both sides.

saw·fly (so′flī′ *or* sô′-) *n., pl.* **-flies.** any of a superfamily (Tenthredinoidea) of insects belonging to the same order as ants, bees, and wasps, the adult female having a sawlike part on its egg-laying organ which it uses to cut slits in plants, depositing its eggs in these openings. Adult sawflies can be distinguished from bees and wasps by their thick bodies.

SAWHORSES

saw·horse (so′hôrs′ *or* sô′-) *n.* a frame on which wood is placed for sawing.

saw·mill (so′mil′ *or* sô′-) *n.* **1** a place where timber is sawed into

planks, boards, etc. by power-driven machines. **2** a large machine for sawing.

sawmill burner a conical furnace for burning sawdust at a sawmill.

sawn (son *or* sôn) *v.* a pp. of **saw**[1].

saw-off (so′of′ *or* sô′-) *n. Cdn. Slang.* **1** *Politics.* **a** an arrangement between two parties by which one agrees not to enter a candidate in one riding if the other agrees not to enter a candidate in a different riding. **b** an arrangement by which one party agrees after an election to drop charges of corruption against another if the second party will make a similar agreement. **2** the repayment of a debt; any act of compensation. **3** any arrangement by which one concession is balanced against another. **4** *Sports and games.* a tie.

saw-whet owl (so′wet′ *or* -hwet′, sô′wet′ *or* -hwet′) a small North American owl (*Aegolius acadicus*) having dark-brown plumage on the head, back, and wings, and white on the breast and abdomen, and having a characteristic rasping, metallic call.

saw·yer (soi′yər, so′yər, *or* sô′yər) *n.* a person whose work is sawing timber. [< *saw*[1] + -*yer*, as in *lawyer*]

sax·horn (saks′hôrn′) *n.* any of a family of trumpet-like, valved brass instruments ranging from soprano to bass, used especially in military-style brass bands. [after Adolphe *Sax*, 1814-1894, the inventor]

sax·i·frage (sak′sə frij *or* sak′sə frāj′) *n.* **1** any of various low-growing plants (family Saxifragaceae, especially genus *Saxifraga*) having clusters of white, pink, yellow, or purple flowers and having thick fleshy leaves often growing in rosettes from the base of the plant. Some species are cultivated for rock gardens. **2** (*adj.*) designating the family (Saxifragaceae) of mostly perennial herbs that includes the saxifrages and, in some classifications, gooseberries, currants, and mock oranges. [ME < LL *saxifraga*, ult. < *saxum* rock + *frangere* break. Doublet of SALSIFY.]

Sax·on (sak′sən) *n., adj.* —*n.* **1** a member of an ancient Germanic people of NW Germany. They invaded and conquered Britain in the fifth and sixth centuries A.D., settling in western and southern England. **2** the language of the Saxons. **3** Anglo-Saxon. **4** a native of Saxony, a region in East Germany.
—*adj.* **1** of or having to do with the early Saxons or their language. **2** Anglo-Saxon. **3** English. **4** of or having to do with Saxony. [< L *Saxo*, pl. *Saxones* < Gmc.]

A saxophone

sax·o·phone (sak′sə fōn′) *n.* any of a group of musical wind instruments ranging from soprano to bass, having a curved metal body, keys for the fingers, and a single-reed mouthpiece. [after Adolphe *Sax* (1814-1894), the inventor]

sax·o·phon·ist (sak′sə fōn′ist) *n.* a person who plays the saxophone, especially a skilled player.

sax·tu·ba (saks′tyü′bə *or* -tü′bə) *n.* a brass saxhorn. [< *sax*horn + *tuba*]

say (sā) *v.* **said, say·ing;** *n.* —*v.* **1** speak: *What did you say?* **2** put into words; express; declare: *Say what you think. What does that sign say?* **3** recite; repeat: *Say your prayers.* **4** suppose; take as an estimate: *You can learn in, say, ten lessons.* **5** express an opinion: *It is hard to say which dress is prettier.*
go without saying, be extremely obvious: *It goes without saying that he will be furious when he gets the bill.*
that is to say, in other words.
to say nothing of, without mentioning: *The hotel itself cost a lot, to say nothing of the meals.*
—*n.* **1** what a person says or has to say: *I have had my say.* **2** the chance to say something. **3** power; authority: *Who has the say in this matter?* [OE *secgan*] —**say′er,** *n.*

say·est (sā′ist) *v. Archaic.* 2nd pers. sing., present tense, of **say.** *Thou sayest* means *you* (sing.) *say.*

say·ing (sā′ing) *n.* something said, especially a wise statement that is often repeated: *I remember a saying of my father's. "Haste makes waste" is a saying.*

says (sez) *v.* 3rd pers. sing., present tense, of **say.**

say-so (sā′sō′) *n. Informal.* **1** an unsupported statement: *Don't*

hat, āge, fär; let, ēqual, tèrm; it, īce
hot, ōpen, ôrder; oil, out; cup, put, rüle,
above, takən, pencəl, lemən, circəs

ch, child; ng, long; sh, ship
th, thin; ŦH, then; zh, measure

do it just on his say-so; he might not know what he's talking about. **2** authority or power to decide; say: *She has no say-so in the matter.*

sayst (sāst) *v. Archaic.* sayest.

sb. substantive.

Sb antimony (for L *stibium*).

'sblood (zblud) *interj. Archaic.* 'God's blood' used as an oath.

sc. **1** scene. **2** science. **3** scilicet.

s.c. small capitals.

Sc **1** scandium. **2** strato-cumulus.

Sc. Scottish; Scotland.

SC **1** *Cdn.* Star of Courage. **2** South Carolina.

S.C. **1** Social Credit. **2** Supreme Court. **3** Security Council (United Nations). **4** South Carolina.

scab (skab) *n., v.* **scabbed, scab·bing.** —*n.* **1** the crust that forms over a sore or wound during healing. **2** a skin disease in animals, especially sheep. **3** any of several fungous diseases of plants, usually producing dark, crustlike spots. **4** *Slang.* a workman who will not join a trade union or who takes a striker's place. **5** *Slang.* a rascal; scoundrel.
—*v.* **1** become covered with a scab. **2** *Slang.* act or work as a scab. [< Scand.; cf. Danish *skab*]

scab·bard (skab′ərd) *n.* a sheath or case for the blade of a sword, dagger, etc. See **sword** for picture. [ME < AF *escaubers*, pl. < Gmc.]

scab·by (skab′ē) *adj.* **-bi·er, -bi·est. 1** covered with or consisting of scabs: *scabby skin.* **2** having scab (def. 2). **3** *Informal.* low; mean: *a scabby trick.* —**scab′bi·ly,** *adv.* —**scab′bi·ness,** *n.*

sca·bies (skā′bēz *or* skā′bē ēz) *n.* a contagious skin infection caused by a mite (*Sarcoptes scabiei*), the female of which burrows beneath the outer layer of skin, laying its eggs there, and producing a skin eruption that is intensely itchy; the itch. [< L *scabies* itch < *scabere* scratch]

sca·bi·o·sa (skā′bē ō′sə) *n.* scabious[2].

sca·bi·ous[1] (skā′bē əs) *adj.* of, having to do with, or like scabies. [< L *scabiosus* mangy, rough < *scabies.* See SCABIES.]

sca·bi·ous[2] (skā′bē əs) *n.* any of a genus (*Scabiosa*) of annual and perennial Mediterranean plants of the teasel family having dense, dome-shaped heads of various colors. [< ML *scabiosa* (*herba*) (herb) for scabies, originally adj. fem. of *scabiosus* scabious < L *scabies.* See SCABIES.]

scab·land (skab′land′) *n.* a region stripped of topsoil by floods, characterized by low, rocky hills.

scab rock **1** an area of scabland. **2** the bare rock at the surface of scabland.

sca·brous (skā′brəs) *adj.* **1** rough with very small points or projections. **2** full of difficulties; harsh. **3** hard to treat with decency; indelicate. [< LL *scabrosus* < L *scaber* scaly]

scads (skadz) *n.pl. Slang.* a large quantity. [origin uncertain]

scaf·fold (skaf′əld) *n., v.* —*n.* **1** a temporary structure for holding workers when working at a height above the ground or floor during the construction, repair, etc. of a building. **2** a raised platform used as a base for a gallows or guillotine. **3** any raised framework or platform.
—*v.* furnish or support with a scaffold. [ME < var. of OF *eschaffault*, from same source as *catafalque*]

scaf·fold·ing (skaf′əl ding) *n.* **1** a scaffold or system of scaffolds. **2** materials for building scaffolds.

scal·a·wag (skal′ə wag′) *n. Informal.* a good-for-nothing person; scamp; rascal. [origin uncertain]

scald[1] (skold *or* skôld) *v., n.* —*v.* **1** burn with or as if with hot liquid or steam. **2** pour boiling liquid over; use boiling liquid on: *The scald on her hand came from lifting a pot cover carelessly.* **3** heat or be heated almost to boiling, but not quite.
—*n.* a burn caused by hot liquid or steam. [< dial. OF *escalder* < LL *excaldare* < L *ex-* very + *calidus* hot]

scald[2] (skold, skôld, *or* skäld) See **skald.**

scale[1] (skāl) *n., v.* **scaled, scal·ing.** —*n.* **1** one of the thin, flat, hard plates forming the outer covering of some fishes, snakes, and lizards. **2** a thin layer or piece like a scale: *Scales of skin peeled off*

after she had scarlet fever. **3** tartar coating that forms on teeth. **4** the oxide coating that forms on the inside of a boiler, kettle, etc. **5** scale leaf. **6** scale insect.
—*v.* **1** remove scale or scales from. **2** come off in thin pieces or a thin layer: *The paint is starting to scale.* **3** remove in thin layers. **4** cover with scale or scales. **5** become coated with scale. [ME < OF *escale* < Gmc.] —**scal′er**, *n.* —**scale′less**, *adj.* —**scale′like′**, *adj.*

scale² (skāl) *n., v.* **scaled, scal·ing.** —*n.* **1** either of the two dishes or pans of a balance. **2** Usually, **scales**, *pl.* **a** a balance. **b** any instrument for weighing. **3 Scales**, *pl. Astronomy or astrology.* Libra.
tip the scales at, have as one's mass; weigh: *She tips the scales at 65 kilograms.*
tip or **turn the scale** or **scales,** be the deciding factor; decide: *His year of experience tipped the scales in his favor and he got the job.*
—*v.* **1** have as one's mass; weigh: *He scales 80 kilograms.* **2** weigh on scales: *The produce is scaled and packaged on the premises.* [ME < ON *skál* bowl. Akin to SHALE, SHELL.] —**scal′er**, *n.*

scale³ (skāl) *n., v.* **scaled, scal·ing.** —*n.* **1** a series of steps or degrees; scheme of graded amounts: *The scale of wages in this factory ranges from thirty dollars to sixty dollars a day.* **2** a series of marks made along a line at regular distances, for use in measuring: *A thermometer has a scale.* **3** an instrument marked in this way, used for measuring, etc. **4** the size of a plan, map, drawing, or model compared with what it represents: *a map drawn to a scale of one centimetre for each ten kilometres.* **5** relative size or extent: *to entertain on a large scale.* **6** a system of numbering. The decimal scale counts by tens, as in cents, dimes, dollars. **7** *Music.* a specific series of tones ascending or descending in pitch.
—*v.* **1** climb: *They scaled the wall by ladders.* **2** reduce by a certain proportion (*used with* **down**): *All prices were scaled down 10 percent.* **3** make according to a scale. [ME < L *scala* ladder, ult. < *scandere* climb] —**scal′er**, *n.*

scale insect any of numerous small plant-eating insects constituting several families within the order Homoptera, the wingless females of which typically secrete a protective scale around themselves and their eggs.

scale leaf a modified plant leaf that covers a dormant bud in winter and falls away when growth begins again.

sca·lene (skā lēn′ *or* skā′lēn) *adj.* **1** of a triangle, having three unequal sides. **2** of a cone or cylinder, having its axis not perpendicular to the base. [< LL < Gk. *skalēnos* limping, uneven]

scaling ladder a ladder for climbing high walls.

scal·lion (skal′yən) *n.* **1** a kind of onion that does not form a large bulb. **2** shallot. **3** leek. [ME < AF *scal(o)un* < L (*caepa*) *Ascalonia* (onion) from Ascalon, in Palestine]

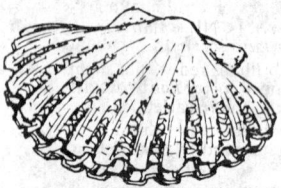

A Eurasian scallop
(*Pecten jacobaeus*)

A collar with
a scalloped edge

scal·lop (skol′əp *or* skal′əp) *n., v.* —*n.* **1** any of a family (Pectinidae) of bivalve molluscs resembling clams but having a fan-shaped shell with ridges that form a wavy edge around the shell. **2** the large, edible adductor muscle of certain species of scallop. **3** a single valve of the shell of a scallop. Scallops are often used as dishes for baking or serving food. Pilgrims returning from Palestine formerly wore scallops as the sign of their pilgrimage. **4** one of a series of curves forming an edge, especially on cloth.
—*v.* **1** *Cooking.* bake with sauce, bread crumbs etc. in a scallop shell or other low dish; escallop: *scalloped oysters.* **2** decorate or finish (an edge, as of cloth) with a series of scallops: *to scallop the hem of a tablecloth.* Sometimes, **scollop.** [ME < OF *escalope* shell < Gmc.]

scalp (skalp) *n., v.* —*n.* **1** the skin on the top and back of the head, usually covered with hair. **2** part of this skin with the hair attached, taken from a conquered enemy and kept as a token of victory. The taking of scalps was formerly practised among certain Amerindian and European peoples. **3** any trophy or token of victory.
—*v.* **1** cut or tear the scalp from. **2** *Informal.* buy and sell (stocks, etc.) to make small, quick profits. **3** *Informal.* buy (tickets) to

theatre productions, games, etc. and resell at greatly increased prices. [ME < Scand.; cf. ON *skálpr* sheath]

scal·pel (skal′pəl) *n.* a small, sharp, straight knife used in surgery and dissections. [< L *scalpellum*, dim. of *scalprum* knife < *scalpere* carve]

scalp·er (skal′pər) *n. Informal.* one who scalps, especially one who scalps stocks, tickets, etc.

scal·y (skā′lē) *adj.* **scal·i·er, scal·i·est.** **1** having scales like a fish. **2** covered or encrusted with a layer of something like scales: *This iron pipe is scaly with rust.* **3** like or suggesting scales. **4** infested with scale insects. **5** *Slang.* mean, stingy, or shabby: *a scaly lot of ruffians.* —**scal′i·ness,** *n.*

scaly anteater pangolin.

scamp¹ (skamp) *n.* **1** a rascal; rogue; worthless person. **2** a mischievous person, especially a child. [< dial. *scamp* roam, probably < *scamper*]

scamp² (skamp) *v.* do (work, etc.) in a hasty, careless manner.

scam·per (skam′pər) *v., n.* —*v.* **1** run or move away quickly. **2** run about playfully. —*n.* playful running about: *Let the dog out for a scamper.* [ult. < OF *escamper* run away, ult. < L *ex-* out of + *campus* field]

scam·pi (skam′pē *or* skäm′pē) *n.pl.* large shrimps or prawns, especially when used in Italian dishes. [< Ital., pl. of *scampo* prawn]

scan (skan) *v.* **scanned, scan·ning;** *n.* —*v.* **1** look at closely; examine with care: *His mother scanned his face to see if he was telling the truth.* **2** *Informal.* glance at; look over hastily: *She took a few minutes to scan the newspaper headlines.* **3** find or test (the metre of a poem) by marking the lines off into feet. *Example:*

Tíger! | Tíger! | búrning | bríght |
In the | foörests | of the | níght. |

4 read or recite (poetry) so as to emphasize the metre. **5** fit a particular metrical pattern: *Your poem is good, but this line does not scan.* **6** *Electronics.* pass a rapidly moving beam of light or electrons over (a scene, picture, etc.) in order to sense and transmit or reproduce an image of it, as for television. **7** search (an area) with radar. **8** *Computer science.* use a computer to search through (a file of stored information) in order to retrieve specific items from the file.
—*n.* the act or process, or an instance of scanning. [ME < LL *scandere* scan verses < L *scandere* climb] —**scan′ner,** *n.*

Scand. Scandinavia; Scandinavian.

scan·dal (skan′dəl) *n.* **1** a shameful action, condition, or event that brings disgrace or offends public opinion: *It was a scandal for the city official to take tax money for his own use.* **2** damage to someone's reputation; disgrace. **3** public talk about a person that will hurt his reputation; malicious gossip.
be the scandal of, scandalize.
[ME < ONF < L < Gk. *skandalon* trap. Doublet of SLANDER.]

scan·dal·ize (skan′dəl īz′) *v.* **-ized, -iz·ing.** offend by doing something thought to be wrong or improper; shock.

scan·dal·mon·ger (skan′dəl mung′gər *or* -mong′gər) *n.* a person who spreads scandal and malicious gossip.

scan·dal·ous (skan′dəl əs) *adj.* **1** bringing disgrace; shameful; shocking: *scandalous behavior.* **2** consisting of or spreading scandal or slander; slandering: *a scandalous piece of gossip.* —**scan′dal·ous·ly,** *adv.*

scandal sheet a newspaper or periodical that features sensational stories and malicious gossip.

Scan·di·na·vi·an (skan′də nā′vē ən *or* -nāv′yən) *n., adj.* —*n.* **1** a native or inhabitant of Scandinavia, a region including Denmark, Norway, Sweden, and, often, Iceland. **2** a person of Scandinavian descent. **3** the northern Germanic languages spoken by the people of Scandinavia.
—*adj.* of or having to do with Scandinavia, its people, or their languages.
☛ *Usage.* The terms **Scandinavian** and **Scandinavia** have sometimes been used to include Finland, but Finland is historically distinct from the Scandinavian countries, having a very different language and different cultural traditions.

scan·di·um (skan′dē əm) *n.* a rare metallic chemical element. *Symbol*: Sc; *at.no.* 21; *at.wt.* 44.956. [< NL < L *Scandia* Scandinavia]

scan·sion (skan′shən) *n.* the analysis of the metre of poetry or a particular poem. [< L *scansio, -onis* < *scandere* scan]

scant (skant) *adj., v., adv.* —*adj.* **1** not enough in size, amount, or quantity: *making do with scant provisions.* **2** scarcely full or complete; not coming quite up to a particular measure: *He takes a scant teaspoon of sugar in his tea. You have a scant hour in which to pack.*
scant of, short of; having not enough: *She was scant of breath.*
—*v.* make scant; limit or cut down; stint: *Don't scant the butter if you want a rich cake.*

—*adv. Dialect.* scarcely; barely; hardly. [ME < ON *skamt*, neut. adj., short]

scant·ling (skant′ling) *n.* **1** a small beam or piece of timber, especially one used as an upright piece in the frame of a building. **2** the dimensions of stone or timber used in building: *timber of small scantling.* **3** the set of standard dimensions of parts of a structure, especially a ship: *The two ships were built to the same scantling.* [var. of ME *scantillon* < OF *escantillon*, ult. probably < LL *cantus* corner < Gk. *kanthos* corner of the eye]

scant·y (skan′tē) *adj.* **scant·i·er, scant·i·est. 1** not enough: *His scanty clothing did not keep out the cold.* **2** barely enough; meagre: *a scanty harvest.* [< *scant*, adj.] —**scant′i·ly,** *adv.* —**scant′i·ness,** *n.*
☛ **Syn. Scanty, sparse, meagre** = less than is needed or normal. **Scanty** emphasizes falling short of the amount or measure necessary to satisfy a need or come up to a standard: *The scanty rainfall is causing a water shortage.* **Sparse** emphasizes a thin scattering of what there is, particularly of numbers or units: *He carefully combs his sparse hair.* **Meagre** emphasizes thinness, a lack of something necessary for fullness, completeness, richness, body, strength, etc.: *His meagre soil produces meagre crops.*

scape¹ (skāp) *n., v.* **scaped, scap·ing.** See **'scape.**

scape² (skāp) *n.* **1** *Botany.* a leafless flower stalk rising from the ground, such as that of the dandelion. **2** something like a stalk, such as the shaft of a feather or the shaft of a column. [< L *scapus* stalk; cf. dial. Gk. *skapos* branch]

'scape (skāp) *n., v.* **'scaped, 'scap·ing.** *Archaic.* escape. [var. of *escape*]

scape·goat (skāp′gōt′) *n., v.* —*n.* **1** a person or thing made to bear the blame for the mistakes or sins of others. **2** in the Bible, a goat on which the sins of the people were laid by the ancient Jewish high priests on the Day of Atonement. The goat was then driven into the wilderness (Leviticus 16:5-22). —*v.* make a scapegoat of. [< *scape*, var. of *escape* + *goat*]

scape·grace (skāp′grās′) *n.* a reckless, good-for-nothing person; scamp.

s.caps small capitals.

scap·u·la (skap′yə lə) *n., pl.* **-lae** (-lē′ *or* -lī′) *or* **-las.** a shoulder blade. See **rib** for picture. [< LL]

scap·u·lar (skap′yə lər) *adj., n.* —*adj.* of the shoulder or shoulder blade.
—*n.* **1** *Roman Catholic Church.* a loose, sleeveless garment hanging from the shoulders, worn by certain religious orders. **2** a symbol of devotion or association with a religious order, consisting of two small pieces of cloth joined by shoulder pieces and worn to hang down over the chest and back. **3** a bird's feather growing where the wing joins the body, or near there. [ME < LL, ult. < L *scapulae* shoulders]

scar¹ (skär) *n., v.* **scarred, scar·ring.** —*n.* **1** the mark left by a healed cut, wound, burn, or sore. **2** any mark like this. A fallen leaf leaves a scar where it joined the stem. **3** a lasting effect from grief, etc.: *War leaves deep scars on the minds of those who endure it.* —*v.* **1** of a wound, etc., form a scar; heal over. **2** make a scar on: *The door was badly scarred by the fire.* [ME < OF *escare* < L < Gk. *eschara* scab, hearth] —**scar′less,** *adj.*

scar² (skär) *n.* **1** a steep, rocky place on the side of a mountain; precipice; cliff. **2** a low rock in the sea. Also, **scaur.** [ME < ON *sker* reef]

scar·ab (skar′əb *or* sker′əb) *n.* **1** a large black beetle (*Scarabaeus sacer*) regarded as sacred by the ancient Egyptians. **2** an image of this beetle, used in ancient Egypt as a charm, ornament, etc. **3** any beetle of the same family (Scarabaeidae), including June bugs, dung beetles, and the cockchafer. [< MF < L *scarabaeus* < Gk.]

scar·a·bae·us (skar′ə bē′əs *or* -bē′əs) *n.* **-bae·us·es** *or* **-bae·i** (-bē′ī). scarab.

scar·a·mouch (skar′ə mouch′ *or* sker′ə-, skar′ə müsh′ *or* sker′ə-) *n.* **1** braggart. **2** rascal. **3** Scaramouch, a stock character in traditional Italian comedy: *Scaramouch was a braggart and coward.* [< F < Ital. *scaramuccia* skirmish. Akin to SKIRMISH.]

scarce (skers) *adj.* **scarc·er, scarc·est;** *adv.* —*adj.* hard to get; rare: *Good cooks are scarce.*
make (oneself) scarce, *Informal.* **a** go away. **b** stay away.
scarce as hen's teeth, *Informal.* very scarce.
—*adv.* scarcely. [ME < ONF *escars* < VL *excarpsus*, ult. < L *ex-* out + *carpere* pluck] —**scarce′ness,** *n.*
☛ **Syn. adj. 1.** See note at **rare.**

scarce·ly (skers′lē) *adv.* **1** only just; barely; hardly: *scarcely old enough for school. We could scarcely see through the fog.* **2** decidedly not: *He can scarcely have said that.* **3** very probably not: *I will scarcely pay that much.*
☛ **Syn. 1.** See note at **hardly.**
☛ **Usage.** See note at **hardly.**

scar·ci·ty (sker′sə tē) *n., pl.* **-ties.** too small to supply; lack; rarity.

scare (sker) *v.* **scared, scar·ing;** *n.* —*v.* **1** make or become frightened: *The dog's barking scared the children. She doesn't scare*

hat, āge, fär; let, ēqual, tèrm; it, īce
hot, ōpen, ôrder; oil, out; cup, pút, rüle,
əbove, takən, pencəl, lemən, circəs
ch, child; ng, long; sh, ship
th, thin; ₮H, then; zh, measure

easily. **2** frighten (*off* or *away*): *The watchdog scared away the robbers by barking.*
scare up, *Informal.* get or get together quickly: *We made camp and then tried to scare up some food.*
—*n.* **1** a fright: *I got a real scare when the lights went out.* **2** a state of alarm or panic: *There was a polio scare last summer. The flight was delayed because of a bomb scare.* [ME < ON *skirra* < *skjarr* timid]
☛ **Syn. v. 1.** See note at **frighten.**

scare·crow (sker′krō′) *n.* **1** an object, usually a figure of a man dressed in old clothes, set in a field to frighten birds away from crops. **2** a person who is thin and gaunt or who dresses like a scarecrow. **3** anything that fools people into being frightened.

scared (skerd) *adj.* filled with fear; afraid.

scare·mon·ger (sker′mung′gər) *n.* one who spreads unfounded rumors; alarmist.

scarf¹ (skärf) *n., pl.* **scarves** *or,* rarely, **scarfs. 1** a square or strip of cloth worn about the neck, shoulders, head, or waist. **2** a necktie with hanging ends. **3** a long strip of cloth used as a decorative cover for a dresser, table, etc.; runner. **4** a sash worn across the chest to indicate membership in some ceremonial order. [probably < dial. OF *escarpe* < Gmc.]

scarf² (skärf) *n., pl.* **scarfs;** *v.* —*n.* **1** a joint made by cutting away part of the ends of beams, etc. so that they overlap and fit tightly together without increasing the overall thickness. See **joint** for picture. **2** an end cut in this way. **3** *Whaling.* a cut made along the body of a whale in preparation for removing the blubber.
—*v.* **1** join by a scarf. **2** cut a scarf on (a piece of wood). **3** *Whaling.* cut scarfs and remove the blubber from the body of (a whale). [ME < Scand.; cf. Swedish *skarv*]

scarf·pin (skärf′pin′) *n.* an ornamental pin worn in a scarf or necktie.

scarf·skin (skärf′skin′) *n.* the outer layer of skin; epidermis.

scar·i·fi·ca·tion (skar′ə fə kā′shən *or* sker′ə-) *n.* **1** scarifying. **2** a scratch or scratches made by scarifying.

scar·i·fy (skar′ə fī′ *or* sker′ə fī′) *v.* **-fied, -fy·ing. 1** make scratches or cuts in the surface of (the skin, etc.), as for vaccination. **2** criticize severely; hurt the feelings of. **3** loosen (soil) without turning it over. [< LL < L *scarifare* < Gk. *skariphasthai* scratch < *skariphos* stylus] —**scar′i·fi′er,** *n.*

scar·la·ti·na (skär′lə tē′nə) *n.* scarlet fever. [< NL < Ital. *scarlattina*, fem. of *scarlattino*, dim. of *scarlatto* scarlet]

scar·let (skär′lit) *n., adj.* —*n.* **1** a light, brilliant red with a slight tinge of orange. **2** cloth or clothing having this color: *The Mounties look impressive in their scarlets.* —*adj.* of the color scarlet. [ME < OF *escarlate,* ? ult. < Persian *saqirlat* rich cloth]

scarlet fever a contagious disease characterized by a scarlet rash, sore throat, and fever.

scarlet runner a tropical American perennial climbing bean plant (*Phaseolus multiflorus,* also called *P. coccineus*) having large scarlet flowers and long green pods. The scarlet runner is widely grown as an annual plant in temperate climates, both for ornament and for its edible pods and seeds.

scarlet sage a popular garden plant (*Salvia splendens*) having spikes of scarlet flowers.

scarlet tanager a tanager (*Piranga olivacea*) of central and E North America, the adult male having a bright red body with black wings and tail in spring and summer, the red changing to olive green in fall and winter. The female is mainly olive green and pale yellow.

scarp (skärp) *n., v.* —*n.* **1** a steep slope. **2** the inner slope or side of a ditch surrounding a fortification. —*v.* make into a steep slope; slope steeply. [< Ital. *scarpa* < Gmc.]

scarves (skärvz) *n.* a pl. of **scarf¹.**

scar·y (sker′ē) *adj.* **scar·i·er, scar·i·est.** *Informal.* **1** causing fright or alarm: *a scary movie.* **2** easily frightened.

scat¹ (skat) *interj., v.* **scat·ted, scat·ting.** *Informal.* —*interj.* an impatient exclamation used especially to drive away an animal. —*v.* beat it; get away fast: *He told the boys to scat.* [< *scatter*]

scat² (skat) *n., v.* **scat·ted, scat·ting.** *Music.* —*n.* jazz singing with meaningless syllables instead of words. In scat, the voice is used as an instrument. —*v.* sing scat.

scathe (skā₮H) *v.* **scathed, scath·ing;** *n.* —*v.* **1** blast or sear with

invective; wither with satire. **2** injure or destroy by fire, lightning, etc.; scar; scorch. **3** *Archaic.* injure; damage.
—*n.* **1** hurt; harm. **2** *Archaic.* a matter for sorrow or regret. **3** *Obsolete.* an injury. [ME < ON *skathi* injury]

scathe·less (skāᴛʜ′lis) *adj.* without harm; unhurt.

scath·ing (skā′ᴛʜing) *adj.* extremely severe: *scathing criticism.* —**scath′ing·ly,** *adv.*

scat·o·log·i·cal (skat′ə loj′ə kəl) *adj.* of or having to do with scatology.

sca·tol·o·gy (skə tol′ə jē) *n.* **1** the study of excrement, used in paleontology, for medical diagnosis, etc. **2** abnormal interest in excrement, excretory functions, etc. **3** obscene literature. [< Gk. *skōr, skatos* excrement + E *-logy*]

scat·ter (skat′ər) *v.* **—v. 1** throw here and there; sprinkle: *Scatter ashes on the icy sidewalk.* **2** separate and drive off in different directions: *The police scattered the mob.* **3** separate and go in different directions: *The hens scattered.* **4** *Physics.* reflect or refract (a beam of radiation) irregularly and in all directions. **—n. 1** the act or fact of scattering. **2** something that is scattered. **3** a small number occurring or distributed irregularly or here and there: *a scatter of houses in the valley.* [ME; probably var. of SHATTER] —**scat′ter·er,** *n.*
☞ *Syn. v.* **2. Scatter, dispel, disperse** = separate and drive away. **Scatter** means to separate and drive off in different directions a group or mass of people or objects: *The wind scattered my papers.* **Dispel** applies only to things that cannot be touched, such as clouds and feelings, and means "drive away as if by scattering in the air": *The wind dispelled the fog.* **Disperse** means the same as **scatter,** but is more formal and may suggest even spreading in every direction: *Storms dispersed the convoy.*

scat·ter·brain (skat′ər brān′) *n.* a thoughtless, frivolous person.

scat·ter·brained (skat′ər brānd′) *adj.* frivolous; thoughtless; not able to think steadily.

scat·tered (skat′ərd) *adj.* not occurring together or in great numbers; few and far apart: *scattered instances of violence. We heard scattered shouts in the distance.*

scat·ter·gun (skat′ər gun′) *n.* **1** shotgun. **2** (*adj.*) suggesting the effect of a load of shot from a scattergun: *a scattergun blast of sixty-seven different policy proposals.*

scat·ter·ing (skat′ər ing) *n., adj.* **—n. 1** a small number or quantity occurring or situated at irregular intervals: *a scattering of cheers, a scattering of villages.* **2** the act or process of scattering. **—adj.** widely separated; occurring here and there.

scatter rug a small rug.

scaup (skop *or* skôp) *n.* either of two diving ducks (*Aythya affinis* or *A. marila*), the adult male having black-and-white plumage and the female brownish plumage. Both species of scaup are found in Canada. [*scaup,* var. of dial. *scalp,* a bank providing a bed for shellfish]

scaur (skôr) *n.* scar². [var. of *scar*²]

scav·enge (skav′ənj) *v.* **-enged, -eng·ing. 1 a** clean streets and waterways by collecting garbage, rubbish, etc. **b** pick over, feed on, use or sell garbage, rubbish, etc. **2** salvage something usable from discarded materials, rubbish, etc.: *to scavenge usable wood scraps. He makes a living by scavenging.* **3** of an animal, feed on garbage or other dead or decaying matter. **4** expel exhaust gas from the cylinder of an internal combustion engine. **5** chemically remove impurities from molten metal. [back formation < *scavenger*]

scav·en·ger (skav′ən jər) *n.* **1** an animal that feeds on dead animals or other decaying matter. Vultures and jackals are scavengers. **2** a person who cleans streets, taking away dirt and rubbish. **3** a person who searches through discarded material for something of value. [alteration of *scavager,* literally, inspector < *scavage* toll < OF *scawager* < *escauwer* inspect < Flemish *scauwen*]

sce·nar·i·o (si ner′ē ō′ *or* si nä′rē ō′) *n., pl.* **-nar·i·os. 1** an outline of a motion picture, giving the main facts about the scenes, persons, and acting. **2** an outline of any play, opera, etc. **3** an outline of a course of action or sequence of events, proposed as a possible outcome of a real or imagined situation: *In our revolution scenario, the rebels are bound to be defeated within a week.* [< Ital. *scenario,* ult. < L *scena* scene. See SCENE.]

sce·nar·ist (si ner′ist *or* si nä′rist) *n.* a person who writes scenarios.

scene (sēn) *n.* **1** the time, place, circumstances, etc. of a play or story: *The scene of the novel is Quebec City in the year 1759.* **2** the place where anything is carried on or takes place: *the scene of an accident, the scene of my childhood.* **3** the painted screens, hangings, etc. used on a stage to represent places: *The scene represents a city street.* **4** a part of an act of a play: *The king comes to the castle in Act I, Scene 2.* **5** a particular incident of a play: *the*

trial scene *in* The Merchant of Venice. **6** an action, incident, situation, etc. occurring in reality or represented in literature or art: *He has painted a series of pictures called "Scenes of My Boyhood."* **7** a view; picture: *The white sailboats on the blue water made a pretty scene.* **8** a show of strong feeling in front of others; exhibition; display: *The child kicked and screamed and made such a scene that his mother was ashamed of him.* **9** *Informal.* sphere of activity; the context or environment in which an activity takes place.

behind the scenes, a out of sight of the audience. **b** privately; secretly; not publicly: *A lot of planning for the Festival was done behind the scenes.*

make the scene, *Slang.* appear at a place.
[< F *scène* < L < Gk. *skēnē,* originally, tent, where actors changed costumes]
☞ *Hom.* **seen.**
☞ *Syn.* **6.** See note at **view.**

scen·er·y (sēn′ər ē *or* sēn′rē) *n., pl.* **-er·ies. 1** *Theatre.* the painted hangings, fittings, etc. used to represent places. **2** the general appearance of the natural features of a place: *mountain scenery.*

sce·nic (sē′nik *or* sen′ik) *adj.* **1** of or having to do with natural scenery; having much fine scenery: *The scenic splendors of Lake Louise are famous.* **2** belonging to the stage of a theatre; of or having to do with stage effects: *The production of the musical comedy was a scenic triumph.* **3** *Art.* representing an action, incident, situation, etc.

scenic dome a transparent dome at the top of a railway car, designed for better viewing of the passing scenery.

sce·nog·ra·phy (sē nog′rə fē) *n.* **1** the representing of objects according to the rules of perspective. **2** scene painting.

scent (sent) *n., —n.* **1** a smell, especially an agreeable one: *the scent of new-mown hay, the scent of roses.* **2** the sense of smell: *The bloodhounds have a keen scent.* **3** a smell left in passing: *The dogs followed the fox by its scent.* **4** any means by which a person or thing can be traced: *The police picked up the thief's scent again where he had stopped for gas.* **5** perfume.
—v. 1 become aware of through smell: *The dog immediately scented the rabbit and dashed off after it.* **2** hunt by using the sense of smell: *The dog scented about till he found the trail.* **3** use the sense of smell on: *to scent the air for signs of rain.* **4** apply perfume to: *She scented her handkerchief. This tobacco has been scented.* **5** fill with odor: *Lilacs scented the air.* **6** get or have a suspicion, or inkling, of: *They scented trouble and left quickly.* [ME < OF *sentir* smell < L *sentire* feel]
☞ *Hom.* **cent, sent.**
☞ *Syn.* See note at **smell.**

scent·less (sent′lis) *adj.* having no smell.

scep·ter (sep′tər) See **sceptre.**

scep·tered (sep′tərd) See **sceptred.**

scep·tic *or* **skep·tic** (skep′tik) *n.* **1** a person who questions the truth of a particular theory or apparent fact; doubter. **2** a person who doubts or questions the possibility or certainty of our knowledge of anything. **3** a person who doubts the truth of religious doctrines. [< L < Gk. *skeptikos* reflective < *skeptesthai* reflect]

scep·ti·cal *or* **skep·ti·cal** (skep′tə kəl) *adj.* having to do with, characteristic of, or marked by scepticism: *They showed him all their data, but he remained sceptical about the plan.* —**scep·ti·cal·ly** *or* **skep·ti·cal·ly,** *adv.*

scep·ti·cism *or* **skep·ti·cism** (skep′tə siz′əm) *n.* **1** a sceptical attitude; a general tendency to doubt or doubt about a particular idea or thing. **2** doubt or unbelief with regard to religion. **3** the doctrine that nothing can be proved absolutely.

scep·tre (sep′tər) *n., v.* **-tred, -tring. —n. 1** the rod or staff carried by a ruler as a symbol of royal power or authority. **2** royal or imperial power or authority. **—v.** furnish with a sceptre. Also, **scepter.** [ME < OF < L < Gk. *skēptron* staff]

scep·tred (sep′tərd) *adj.* **1** furnished with or bearing a sceptre. **2** invested with regal authority; regal. Also, **sceptered.**

sch. school.

scha·den·freu·de (shä′dən froi′də) *n. German.* pleasure taken in the misfortunes and unhappiness of another. [G < *Schaden* harm + *Freude* joy]

sched·ule (skej′ül *or* shej′ül) *n., v.* **-uled, -ul·ing. —n. 1** a written or printed statement of details; list. A railway timetable is a schedule of the coming and going of trains. **2** a listing of the games to be played by the teams in the league. **3** the time or times fixed for doing something, arrival at a place, etc.: *The bus was an hour behind schedule.*
—v. 1 make a schedule of; enter in a schedule. **2** plan or arrange (something) for a definite time or date: *The convention has been scheduled for early fall.* [ME < OF < LL *schedula,* dim. of L *scheda, schida* sheet of papyrus < Gk. *schidē* split piece of wood]

schef·fler·a (shə fler′ə) *n.* any of a genus (*Schefflera*) of tropical and subtropical plants of the ginseng family, some of which are grown as house plants in temperate regions.

Sche·her·a·za·de (shə her′ə zä′də *or* shə hĕr′ə zä′də) *n.* in the *Arabian Nights*, the narrator of the tales, a young bride of the murderous Sultan, who saves her own life by keeping the Sultan interested in her stories.

sche·ma (skē′mə) *n.*, *pl.* **-ma·ta** (-mə tə). **1** an outline, synopsis, plan, or scheme. **2** *Kantian philosophy.* the general idea or concept of things that are common to all members of a class. [< L < Gk. *schēma*, *-atos* figure, appearance]

sche·mat·ic (skē mat′ik) *adj.* having to do with or having the nature of a diagram, plan, or scheme; diagrammatic. —**sche·mat·i·cal·ly**, *adv.*

sche·ma·tize (skē′mə tīz′) *v.* **-tized, -tiz·ing.** reduce to or represent as a formula or scheme: *to schematize the metre of a poem.*

scheme (skēm) *n.*, *v.* **schemed, schem·ing.** —*n.* **1** a program of action; plan: *He has a scheme for extracting gold from sea water.* **2** a plot: *a scheme to cheat the government.* **3** a system of connected things, parts, thoughts, etc.; design: *The color scheme of the room is blue and gold.* **4** a diagram, outline, or table. —*v.* plan or plot: *Those men were scheming to bring the jewels into the country without paying duty.* [< L < Gk. *schēma*, *-atos* figure, appearance] —**schem′er**, *n.*
☛ *Syn. v.* See note at **plot.**

schem·ing (skēm′ing) *adj.* given to forming sly or tricky schemes; deceitful and crafty. —**schem′ing·ly**, *adv.*

scher·zan·do (sker tsän′dō) *adj.*, *adv.*, *n. Music.* —*adj.* playful; sportive. —*adv.* playfully; sportively. —*n.* a playful movement or passage; composition to be played or sung in this manner. [< Ital. *scherzando* < *scherzare* to play, sport < *scherzo*. See SCHERZO.]

scher·zo (sker′tsō) *n.*, *pl.* **-zos, -zi** (-tsē). *Music.* a light and playful composition or part of a sonata, concerto, or symphony. [< Ital. < G *Scherz* joke]

Schick test (shik) a test to determine susceptibility to or immunity from diphtheria, made by injecting a dilute diphtheria toxin under the skin. If the skin becomes inflamed as a result, the person is not immune to the disease. [after Dr. Béla *Schick* of Vienna (born 1877)]

schil·ling (shil′ing) *n.* **1** the basic unit of money in Austria, divided into 100 groschen. See table at **money.** **2** a coin worth one schilling. [< G]

schip·per·ke (skip′ər kē′) *n.* a Belgian breed of small, sturdy, black watchdog having erect ears and no tail. [< Du *schipperke*, dim. of *schipper* skipper, since originally used on boats as a watchdog]

schism (siz′əm, shiz′əm, *or* skiz′əm) *n.* **1** the division or separation of a group into opposing factions. **2** a division within or separation from an established church on account of some difference of opinion of faith or discipline. **3** the offence of promoting or causing such a division or separation. **4** a faction formed by schism. **5** discord; strife. [ME < OF < LL < Gk. *schisma* < *schizein* split]

schis·mat·ic (siz mat′ik *or* shiz mat′ik) *adj.*, *n.* —*adj.* **1** causing or likely to cause schism. **2** inclined toward, or guilty of, schism. —*n.* a person who tries to cause a schism or takes part in a schism.

schis·mat·i·cal (siz mat′ə kəl *or* shiz-) *adj.* schismatic.

schist (shist) *n.* a crystalline metamorphic rock that splits easily into layers. [< F < L < Gk. *schistos* cleft < *schizein* split]

schist·ose (shis′tōs) *adj.* of or like schist; having the structure of schist.

schis·to·some (shis′tə sōm′ *or* skis′tə sōm′) *n.* any of a genus (*Schistosoma*) of blood flukes, some of which cause bilharzia in man.

schis·to·so·mi·a·sis (shis′tə sō mī′ə səs *or* skis′-) *n.* bilharzia.

schiz·o (skit′sō *or* skiz′ō) *n.*, *pl.* **-os.** *Slang.* a schizophrenic.

schizo– *combining form.* divided; split: *schizophrenia = a split personality.* [< Gk. *schizein* split]

schiz·o·carp (skiz′ō kärp′) *n.* a dry compound fruit that splits when ripe into two or more closed parts containing one seed each. See **fruit** for picture. [< *schizo–* + Gk. *karpos* fruit]

schiz·oid (skit′soid) *adj.*, *n.* —*adj.* characterized by, tending toward, or resulting from schizophrenia: *schizoid tendencies. He's a bit schizoid.* —*n.* a schizoid person.

schiz·o·phre·ni·a (skit′sə frē′nē ə) *n.* a mental disorder characterized by dissociation from reality and deterioration of personality. [< NL < Gk. *schizein* split + *phrēn* mind]

schiz·o·phren·ic (skit′sə fren′ik) *adj.*, *n.* —*adj.* of, having to do

hat, āge, fär; let, ĕqual, tėrm; it, īce
hot, ōpen, ôrder; oil, out; cup, pút, rüle, əbove, takən, pencəl, lemən, circəs

ch, child; ng, long; sh, ship
th, thin; ŦH, then; zh, measure

with, or suffering from schizophrenia. —*n.* a person suffering from schizophrenia.

schle·miel (shlə mēl′) *n. Slang.* a gullible, inept person; a bungler or fool. Also, **schlemihl.** [< Yiddish < Hebrew *Shelumiel*; cf. Numbers 7:36]

schlep *or* **schlepp** (shlep) *v.* **schlepped, schlep·ping;** *n. Slang.* —*v.* haul or lug (something or oneself): *I don't want to schlep the suitcase all over town.* —*n.* **1** a stupid or ineffectual person. **2** a difficult or tiresome undertaking, journey, etc.: *It was a long schlep.* [< Yiddish < MHG *sleppen* drag, haul]

schlock (shlok) *n.*, *adj. Slang.* —*n.* something that is shoddy or inferior. —*adj.* shoddy or inferior: *a schlock movie.* [< Yiddish *shlak* cheap merchandise, prob. < MHG *slag, slak* a blow. Akin to SLAY.]

schmaltz *or* **schmalz** (shmolts) *n. Slang.* extreme sentimentalism, especially in music or art. [< G *Schmaltz* melted fat]

schmaltz·y *or* **schmalz·y** (shmolt′sē) *adj. Slang.* of or having to do with schmaltz; overly sentimental.

schmo *or* **schmoe** (shmō) *n. Slang.* a foolish or unsophisticated person; jerk. Also, **shmo.** [< Yiddish]

schnapps *or* **schnaps** (shnäps) *n.* **1** Hollands. **2** any of various distilled liquors. [< G]

schnau·zer (shnou′zər *or* shnout′zer) *n.* any of three breeds of terrier originally developed in Germany, having a short, wiry coat, small ears, bushy eyebrows, and a beard. The three breeds are the **standard schnauzer, giant schnauzer,** and **miniature schnauzer.** [< G *Schnauzer* < *Schnauze* snout]

schnit·zel (shnit′səl) *n.* a breaded and seasoned veal cutlet. [< G]

schnook (shnúk) *n. Slang.* a dull or stupid person. [origin unknown]

schnor·kel (shnôr′kəl) *n.* snorkel.

schnoz·zle (shnoz′əl) *n. Slang.* nose.

schol·ar (skol′ər) *n.* **1** a learned person; a person having much knowledge. **2** a pupil at school; learner. **3** a student who is given money by some institution to help him continue his studies; the holder of a scholarship: *a Rhodes scholar.* [ME < AF < LL *scholaris* < L *schola* school[1]. See SCHOOL[1].]
☛ *Syn.* **2.** See note at **student.**

schol·ar·ly (skol′ər lē) *adj.*, *adv.* —*adj.* **1** of, like, or fit for a scholar: *scholarly habits.* **2** having much knowledge; learned. **3** fond of learning; studious. **4** thorough and orderly in methods of study: *a scholarly book.* —*adv.* in a scholarly manner. —**schol′ar·li·ness**, *n.*

schol·ar·ship (skol′ər ship′) *n.* **1** the possession of knowledge gained by study; quality of learning and knowledge: *The painstakingly thorough treatment of events showed the excellence of the historian's scholarship.* **2** a grant of money or other aid to help a student continue his studies. **3** a fund to provide this money.

scho·las·tic (skə las′tik) *adj.*, *n.* —*adj.* **1** of schools, scholars, or education; academic: *scholastic achievements or methods; scholastic life.* **2** of or like scholasticism. —*n.* **1** Often, **Scholastic.** a person who favors scholasticism. **2** in the Middle Ages, a theologian and philosopher. [< L *scholasticus* < Gk. *scholastikos*, ult. < *scholē* school[1]]

scho·las·ti·cal·ly (skə las′tik lē) *adv.* in a scholastic way or manner; in scholastic respects.

scho·las·ti·cism (skə las′tə siz′əm) *n.* **1** in the Middle Ages, a system of theological and philosophical teaching based chiefly on the authority of the church fathers and of Aristotle, and characterized by a formal method of discussion. **2** an adherence to traditional doctrines and methods.

scho·li·ast (skō′lē ast′) *n.* an ancient or medieval grammarian who wrote comments upon the classics; one who made scholia. [< LL < Gk. *scholiastēs*]

scho·li·um (skō′lē əm) *n.*, *pl.* **-li·a** (-lē ə). **1** an explanatory note or comment, especially an annotation by an ancient grammarian upon a passage in the Greek or Latin classics. **2** a note added by way of illustration or amplification. [< Med.L < Gk. *scholion*, dim. of *scholē* discussion]

school[1] (skül) *n.*, *v.* —*n.* **1** a place for teaching and learning. **2** instruction in school; education received at school: *Most children*

start school when they are about five years old. **3** a regular course of meetings of teachers and pupils for instruction. **4** a session of such a course. **5** those who are taught and their teachers. **6** any place, situation, experience, etc. as a source of instruction or training: *the school of adversity.* **7** a group of people holding the same beliefs, working in the same style, etc.: *the Dutch school of painting, a gentleman of the old school.* **8** a particular department or group in a university. **9** a room, rooms, buildings, or group of buildings in a university, set apart for the use of one department: *a school of dentistry.* **10** a place of training or discipline. **11** (*adj.*) of or having to do with a school or schools.
—*v.* **1** educate in a school; teach. **2** train; discipline: *School yourself to control your temper.* [OE *scōl* < L < Gk. *scholē*, originally, leisure]

school² (skül) *n., v.* —*n.* a large group of the same kind of fish or water animals swimming together. —*v.* swim together in a school. [ME < MDu. *schole* a crowd. Akin to SHOAL².]

school age **1** the age at which a child begins to go to school. **2** the years during which going to school is compulsory or customary.

school board a group of people, usually elected, who manage the schools in a designated area; a board of education.

school·book (skül′bůk′) *n.* a book for study in schools.

school·boy (skül′boi′) *n.* a boy attending school.

school·child (skül′chīld′) *n.* a child who goes to school.

school·fel·low (skül′fel′ō) *n.* a companion at school.

school·girl (skül′gėrl′) *n.* a girl attending school.

school guard **1** a member of a school patrol. **2** a person whose job is to escort schoolchildren across busy streets near schools.

school·house (skül′hous′) *n.* a small building used as a school, especially in a village.

school·ing (skü′ling) *n.* **1** instruction in school; education received at school. **2** the cost of instruction.

school·m'am (skül′mäm or skül′mam′) *n.* *Informal.* schoolmarm.

school·man (skül′mən) *n., pl.* **-men.** **1** Usually, **Schoolman,** a teacher of philosophy and theology in a medieval European university; scholastic. **2** a teacher or scholar.

school·marm (skül′märm′) *n.* *Informal.* **1** a female schoolteacher, especially in a rural or village school. **2** a very strict conservative teacher or similar person of either sex.

school·mas·ter (skül′mas′tər) *n.* **1** a man who teaches in or manages a school. **2** any person or thing that teaches or disciplines.

school·mate (skül′māt′) *n.* a companion at school.

school·mis·tress (skül′mis′tris) *n.* a woman who teaches in or manages a school.

school patrol a group of older schoolchildren who escort younger ones across busy streets.

school·room (skül′rüm′ or -rům′) *n.* a room in which pupils are taught.

school·teach·er (skül′tēch′ər) *n.* a person who teaches in a school.

school trustee an elected member of a school board, or board of education.

school·yard (skül′yärd′) *n.* a piece of ground around or near a school, used for play, games, etc.

school year that part of the year during which school is in session.

FOREMAST
JIB
BOWSPRIT
MAINSAIL
MAINMAST
SHROUDS
STAYS

The *Bluenose,* a famous Canadian schooner

schoon·er (skü′nər) *n.* **1** a ship with two or more masts and fore-and-aft sails. **2** *Informal.* a large glass for beer. [< *scoon* skim, probably < Scand.]

schoon·er-rigged (skü′nər rigd′) *adj.* having fore-and-aft sails.

schot·tische (shot′ish) *n.* **1** a dance in 2/4 time, resembling the polka. **2** the music for such a dance. [< G *Schottische,* literally, Scottish]

schuss (shůs) *n., v.* **schussed, schuss·ing.** *Skiing.* —*n.* **1** a straight, downhill run at high speed. **2** a straight, downhill course for making such a run. —*v.* make such a run. [< G]

schwa (shwo or shwä) *n.* **1** an unstressed vowel sound such as that of the *a* in *about,* the *u* in *circus,* or the *o* in *lemon;* neutral vowel. **2** the symbol (ə) used to represent this sound. [< G < Hebrew *sh'wa*]

sci. **1** science. **2** scientific.

sci·at·ic (sī at′ik) *adj.* **1** of, having to do with, or in the region of the hip. **2** of, having to do with, or caused by sciatica. [< Med.L *sciaticus,* alteration of L *ischiadicus* < Gk. < *ischion* hip joint]

sci·at·i·ca (sī at′ə kə) *n.* pain along the path of the sciatic nerve and its branches; neuralgia of the hips and legs. [< Med.L *sciatica,* fem. of *sciaticus.* See SCIATIC.]

sciatic nerve a large nerve that begins in the pelvis and runs down along the back of the thigh.

sci·ence (sī′əns) *n.* **1** knowledge of general facts, laws and relationships that is obtained through systematic observation and experiment, especially as applied to the physical world and the phenomena associated with it: *new discoveries in science, natural science.* **2** a branch of such knowledge. Biology and chemistry are sciences. **3** any branch of knowledge arranged in an orderly system and considered as an object of study: *Economics is a social science.* **4** a technique, skill, etc. that can be studied in a systematic way: *the science of boxing. Photography is both an art and a science.* [ME < OF < L *scientia* knowledge < *scire* know]

science fiction a type of fiction based on actual or fanciful elements of science.

sci·en·tif·ic (sī′ən tif′ik) *adj.* **1** using the facts and laws of science: *a scientific method, a scientific farmer.* **2** of or having to do with science; used in science: *scientific books, scientific instruments.* [< LL *scientificus* < *scientia* knowledge + *facere* make] —**sci′en·tif′i·cal·ly,** *adv.*

scientific method the principles and procedures of scientific investigation, including: (1) the recognition and description of a particular problem, (2) the collection of data related to this problem, through observation and experimentation, (3) the interpretation of the data and formulation of a hypothesis to describe the event, law, or relationship discovered, and (4) the testing of the hypothesis by more observation and experimentation.

sci·en·tist (sī′ən tist) *n.* **1** a person who is trained in science, especially a natural science, and whose work is scientific investigation. **2** **Scientist,** Christian Scientist.

sci–fi (sī′fī′) *Informal.* **1** science fiction. **2** (*adj.*) of, having to do with, or designating science fiction: *sci-fi fans. He has a huge sci-fi collection.*

scil·i·cet (sil′ə set′) *adv.* to wit; namely. [< L *scilicet* < *scire* know + *licet* it is allowed]

scil·la (sil′ə) *n.* any of a genus (*Scilla*) of Old World, bulbous herbs of the lily family having narrow leaves and small bell-shaped flowers. See also **squill** (def. 2).

scim·i·tar (sim′ə tər or sim′ə tär′) *n.* a short, curved sword having a cutting edge on the convex side, formerly used especially by Arabs and Turks. See **sword** for picture. [< Ital. *scimitarra*]

scin·til·la (sin til′ə) *n.* a spark or trace: *There is not a scintilla of evidence against him.* [< L *scintilla* spark. Doublet of TINSEL.]

scin·til·late (sin′tə lāt′) *v.* **-lat·ed, -lat·ing.** sparkle; flash: *The snow scintillates like diamonds in the sun.* [< L *scintillare* < *scintilla* spark]

scin·til·la·tion (sin′tə lā′shən) *n.* **1** sparkling; flashing. **2** a spark; flash.

sci·o·lism (sī′ə liz′əm) *n.* superficial knowledge. [< LL *sciolus* knowing little, ult. < *scire* know]

sci·o·list (sī′ə list) *n.* a person who pretends to have more knowledge than he really has.

sci·on (sī′ən) *n.* **1** a bud or branch cut for grafting or planting. **2** descendant. Also, **cion.** [ME < OF *cion,* probably ult. < L *secare* to cut]

scis·sion (sizh′ən or sish′ən) *n.* the act of cutting, dividing, or splitting; division; separation. [ME < LL *scissio, -onis* < *scindere* split]

scis·sor (siz′ər) *v.* cut with scissors.

scis·sors (siz′ərz) *n.* **1** a tool or instrument for cutting that has two sharp blades so fastened that their edges slide against each other (*usually used with a plural verb*). **2** *Gymnastics.* a forward and

backward movement of the legs suggesting the action of scissors (*used with a singular or plural verb*). **3** *Wrestling.* a hold in which the opponent's body or head is held with the legs (*used with a singular verb*). [ME < OF *cisoires*, pl., < LL *cisorium*, sing., tool for cutting, ult. < L *caedere* cut; confused with < *scissor* cutter < *scindere* cleave, split]

scler·a (sklēr′ə) *n.* the tough, fibrous, white outer membrane covering all of the eyeball except the part covered by the cornea. See **eye** for picture.

scle·rom·e·ter (sklə rom′ə tər) *n.* an instrument for measuring the hardness of a substance, especially a mineral. [< Gk. *sklēros* hard + E -*meter*]

scle·ro·sis (sklə rō′sis) *n., pl.* -**ses** (-sēz). **1** a hardening of a tissue or part of the body by an increase of connective tissue or the like at the expense of more active tissue. **2** a hardening of a tissue or cell wall of a plant by thickening or the formation of wood. [< Med.L < Gk. *sklērōsis* < *sklēros* hard]

scle·rot·ic (sklə rot′ik) *adj., n.* —*adj.* **1** having to do with or being the sclera. **2** of, having to do with, or affected with sclerosis. —*n.* sclera. [< NL *scleroticus* < Gk. *sklēros* hard]

scoff[1] (skof) *v., n.* —*v.* make fun to show one does not believe something; mock. —*n.* **1** mocking words or acts. **2** something ridiculed or mocked. [ME < Scand.; cf. Danish *skuffe* deceive] —**scoff′er,** *n.* —**scoff′ing·ly,** *adv.*

☛ *Syn. v.* **Scoff, jeer, sneer** = show scorn or contempt for someone or something by mocking or biting words or by laughter. **Scoff** emphasizes speaking in an insultingly contemptuous or mocking way about something others respect or believe in: *He scoffs at religion.* **Jeer** implies a louder and coarser or more sarcastic way of making fun and, particularly, suggests mocking laughter: *The mob jeered when the speaker got up to talk.* **Sneer** emphasizes an insultingly contemptuous facial expression or tone of voice, or a slighting and hinting way of speaking: *He sneers at everything sentimental.*

scoff[2] (skof) *v., n. Slang.* —*v.* eat, especially greedily. —*n.* food; a meal.

scold (skōld) *v., n.* —*v.* **1** find fault with and criticize severely or angrily; rebuke with severe or angry words: *His mother scolded him for tearing his jacket.* **2** find fault; talk angrily: *He's always scolding.* —*n.* a person, especially a woman, who makes a habit of scolding. [ME, probably < ON *skáld* poet, in sense of "lampooner"] —**scold′er,** *n.*

☛ *Syn. v.* **1. Scold, upbraid, chide** = find fault with someone. **Scold** particularly suggests cross and impatient, often loud and insistent, finding fault or expressing disapproval in angry or abusive words, not always with good reason: *That woman is always scolding the children in our neighborhood.* **Upbraid,** more formal, always suggests a definite fault or offence, and emphasizes angrily and sharply or severely blaming and trying to shame: *He upbraided them for tormenting animals.* **Chide** usually suggests milder words of disapproval, or blame intended to correct: *He chided her for carelessness.*

scol·lop (skol′əp) *n.* or *v.* scallop.

sconce[1] (skons) *n.* a bracket projecting from a wall, used to hold a candle or other light. [ME < Med.L *sconsa,* ult. < L *abscondere* hide]

sconce[2] (skons) *n. Archaic.* **1** the head, especially the top of the head. **2** sense; wit. [? jocular use of *sconce*[1]]

scone (skon *or* skōn) *n.* a thick, flat cake cooked on a griddle or in an oven. [probably < MDu. *schoon(brot)* fine (bread)]

scoop (sküp) *n., v.* —*n.* **1** a tool like a small shovel, having a short handle and a deeply concave blade for dipping out or shovelling up things. **2** the part of a dredge, shovel, etc. that holds coal, sand, etc. **3** the amount taken up at one time by a scoop. **4** a place or thing hollowed out. **5** the action or process of scooping. **6** *Slang.* **a** the publishing of a piece of news before a rival newspaper does. **b** the piece of news as published. —*v.* **1** take up or out with a scoop, or as a scoop does. **2** hollow out; dig out; make by scooping: *The children scooped holes in the sand.* **3** *Slang.* publish a piece of news before a rival newspaper does. [partly < MDu. *schoepe* bucket, partly < MDu. *schoppe* shovel]

scoop·ful (sküp′fůl′) *n., pl.* -**fuls.** as much as a scoop can hold.

scoot (süt) *v., n.* —*v. Informal.* go quickly; dart: *She scooted out the side door just as I came in the front.* —*n.* **1** *Informal.* the act of scooting. **2** *Cdn.* a strong-hulled, flat-bottomed boat, driven by an aircraft propeller or an engine mounted toward the stern, designed for travelling on water, through slob ice, or over ice or snow. [probably < Scand.; cf. ON *skióta* shoot. Akin to SHOOT.]

scoot·er[1] (skü′tər) *n., v.* —*n.* **1** a child's vehicle consisting of a long footboard with a wheel at the front and the back, steered by raised handlebars and moved by pushing against the ground with one foot. **2** a light, two-wheeled motor vehicle having a footboard and handlebars somewhat like a child's scooter and equipped with a seat; motor scooter. **3** a sailboat with runners, for use on either water or ice. —*v.* go or travel by scooter. [< *scoot*]

scoot·er[2] (skü′tər) *n.* scoter.

scope (skōp) *n.* **1** the amount the mind can take in; extent of

hat, āge, fär; let, ēqual, tèrm; it, īce
hot, ōpen, ôrder; oil, out; cup, pút, rüle,
əbove, takən, pencəl, lemən, circəs

ch, child; ng, long; sh, ship
th, thin; ʇH, then; zh, measure

one's view: *Very hard words are not within the scope of a child's understanding.* **2** the area over which any activity extends: *This subject is not within the scope of our investigation.* **3** space; opportunity: *Football gives scope for courage and quick thinking.* [< Ital. *scopo,* ult. < Gk. *skopos* aim, object]

☛ *Syn.* **1.** See note at **range.**

–**scope** *combining form.* an instrument or other means for viewing or observing, as in *stethoscope, telescope.* [< NL -*scopium* < Gk. -*scopion* < *skopeein* look at]

sco·pol·a·mine (skō pol′ə mēn′) *n.* a drug obtained from the roots of certain plants of the nightshade family, used as a sedative or truth serum or, with morphine, to relieve pain. *Formula:* $C_{17}H_{21}NO_4$ [< NL *Scopolia,* a genus of plants (named after Giacomo A. *Scopoli* (1723-1788), an Italian naturalist) + E *amine*]

scor·bu·tic (skôr byü′tik) *adj.* **1** having to do with or of the nature of scurvy. **2** affected with scurvy. [< NL *scorbuticus* < *scorbutus* scurvy < F *scorbut* < Gmc.]

scorch (skôrch) *v., n.* —*v.* **1** burn slightly; burn on the outside: *The cake tastes scorched. The maid scorched the shirt in ironing it.* **2** parch with intense heat; dry up; wither: *grass scorched by the sun.* **3** criticize with harsh or sarcastic words. **4** *Informal.* drive or ride very fast. —*n.* a slight burn. [ME; cf. *skorken* < ON *skorpna* dry up]

☛ *Syn.* **1.** See note at **burn.**

scorched–earth policy (skôrcht′ẻrth′) a military policy of destroying all crops, buildings, etc. in the course of a retreat, so as to leave nothing useful for the enemy.

scorch·er (skôr′chər) *n.* **1** *Informal.* a very hot day. **2** *Informal.* a person who drives or rides very fast. **3** a scathing criticism. **4** a person or thing that scorches.

score (skôr) *n., v.* **scored, -scor·ing.** —*n.* **1** *Game, contest, etc.* the record of points made: *The score was 9 to 2 in our favor.* **2** an amount owed; debt; account: *He paid his score at the inn.* **3** a group or set of twenty; twenty. **4 scores,** *pl.* a large number, but less than hundreds: *Scores died in the epidemic.* **5** a written or printed piece of music arranged for different instruments or voices: *the score of a musical comedy.* **6** a cut; scratch; stroke; mark; line: *The slave's back showed scores made by the whip.* **7** the act of making or winning a point; successful stroke, rejoinder, etc. **8** an account; reason; ground: *Don't worry on that score.* **9 the score,** *Informal.* the truth about anything or things in general; the facts: *The new man doesn't know what the score is yet.*

on the score of, because of; on account of.

pay off *or* **settle a score,** get even for an injury or wrong.

—*v.* **1 a** *Game, contest, etc.* make as points. **b** keep a record of (the number of points made in a game, contest, etc.). **c** be counted as in the score. **d** make as an addition to the score; gain; win: *He scored five runs for our team.* **2** keep a record of as an amount owed; mark; set down: *The innkeeper scored on a slate the number of meals each person had.* **3** achieve a success; succeed. **4 a** *Music.* arrange (a composition) for different instruments or voices. **b** write out (music) in score. **5** cut; scratch; mark; line: *Mistakes are scored in red ink.* **6** *Informal.* blame or scold severely. [OE < ON *skor* notch] —**score′less,** *adj.* —**scor′er,** *n.*

score·board (skôr′bôrd′) *n.* a large board for posting the score and, sometimes, other details of a game or other sporting event.

score·card (skôr′kärd′) *n.* a card for keeping the score of a game, match, etc. Also, **score card.**

sco·ri·a (skô′rē ə) *n., pl.* -**ri·ae** (-rē ē′ *or* rē ī′). **1** refuse left from ore after the metal has been melted out; slag. **2** solidified lava having a great many cavities, like a very coarse pumice. [< L < Gk. *skōria* < *skōr* dung]

sco·ri·a·ceous (skô′rē ā′shəs *or* skô′rē ā′shəs) *adj.* like or consisting of scoria.

scorn (skôrn) *v., n.* —*v.* **1** look down upon; think of as mean or low; despise: *He scorned their attempts at reconciliation. She scorns her critics as being out-of-date and incompetent.* **2** reject or refuse as low or wrong: *The judge scorned to take a bribe.* —*n.* **1** a feeling that a person, animal, or act is mean or low; contempt: *We feel scorn for a traitor.* **2** an object of scorn. [ME < OF *escarnir* < Gmc.] —**scorn′er,** *n.*

☛ *Syn. n.* **1. Scorn, contempt, disdain** = a feeling that a person or thing is mean, low, or worthless. **Scorn,** which expresses the strongest feeling, adds to this basic meaning the idea of disgust mixed with anger, sometimes shown by unkind and bitter laughter: *We feel scorn for a person who avoids his*

responsibilities. **Contempt** adds to the basic meaning the idea of disgust mixed with strong disapproval: *We feel contempt for a coward.* **Disdain** adds the idea of feeling oneself above anything mean or low and rejecting it: *We feel disdain for a person who cheats.*

scorn·ful (skôrn′fəl) *adj.* showing contempt; mocking; full of scorn. —**scorn′ful·ly,** *adv.* —**scorn′ful·ness,** *n.*

Scor·pi·o (skôr′pē ō′) *n.* **1** *Astronomy.* a southern constellation thought of as having the shape of a scorpion. **2** *Astrology.* **a** the eighth sign of the zodiac. The sun enters Scorpio about October 24. See **zodiac** for picture. **b** a person born under this sign. [< L *scorpio* scorpion]

scor·pi·on (skôr′pē ən) *n.* **1** any of an order (Scorpionida) of arachnids having six pairs of appendages, the first two pairs adapted for grasping and tearing apart prey and the others used for walking, and having a segmented abdomen that tapers to form a tail with a poisonous stinger at the tip. **2** in the Bible, a whip or scourge, probably studded with metal points (1 Kings 12:11). **3 Scorpion,** *Astronomy or astrology.* Scorpio. [< L *scorpio, -onis,* ult. < Gk. *skorpios*]

scot (skot) *n. Historical.* a tax or levy assessed or paid. [ME < ON *skit.* Related to SHOT.]

Scot (skot) *n.* **1** a native or inhabitant of Scotland, a division of Great Britain. **2** a person of Scottish descent. [OE *Scottas,* pl., Irishmen, Scotsmen < LL *Scottus* Irishman]

Scot. Scotland; Scottish; Scotch.

scotch (skoch) *v.* **1** wound so as to cripple or make temporarily harmless: *to scotch a snake without killing it.* **2** stamp out; stifle; crush: *to scotch a rumor.* **3** cut; score; gash. [origin uncertain]

Scotch (skoch) *n., adj.* —*n.* **1** a kind of whisky made in Scotland. **2** Scottish. —*adj.* Scottish.

Scotch fir Scots pine.

Scotch–I·rish (skoch′ī′rish) *adj., n.* —*adj.* **1** of, having to do with, or designating the population of Ulster that is descended from Scottish settlers. **2** of, having to do with, or designating the descendants of those members of this group who emigrated from Ulster to North America in the early 19th century. **3** of both Scottish and Irish descent. —*n.* a person of both Scottish and Irish descent.

Scotch·man (skoch′mən) *n., pl.* **-men.** Scot.

Scotch pine Scots pine.

Scotch tape **1** *Trademark.* a transparent, self-sealing, adhesive plastic tape for patching, sealing, etc. **2** any similar transparent tape.

Scotch terrier Scottish terrier.

Scotch whisky a whisky distilled from barley malt in Scotland.

sco·ter (skō′tər) *n.* any of a small genus (*Melanitta*) of diving ducks found along the northern coasts and large lakes and rivers of North America and Europe, the adult male having mostly black plumage, the female mostly brown. [? < dial. *scote,* var. of *scoot*]

scot–free (skot′frē′) *adj. or adv.* completely free from injury, punishment, penalty, etc.: *His partner was convicted of fraud but he got off scot-free.* See also **scot.**

Sco·tia (skō′shə) *n. Poetic.* Scotland. [< Med.L]

Scot·land Yard (skot′lənd) **1** the headquarters of the police of London, England, properly called **New Scotland Yard.** **2** the London police, especially the department that does detective work. [< the building in which the London police headquarters was formerly located, in Great Scotland Yard]

Scots (skots) *n., adj.* —*n.* any of the dialects of English spoken in Scotland. —*adj.* of, having to do with, or characteristic of Scotland, its people, their English dialects, or their Gaelic language.

Scots fir Scots pine.

Scots–Gael·ic (skots′gāl′ik *or* -gal′ik) *n.* the Celtic language of the Scottish Highlanders.

Scots·man (skots′mən) *n., pl.* **-men.** a native or inhabitant of Scotland; a Scot.

Scots pine **1** a pine (*Pinus sylvestris*) native to N Europe and Asia but now widely planted in Canada, having spreading branches and short, twisted, bluish-green needles. **2** the hard, yellowish wood of this tree, valuable for timber. Also called **Scotch pine, Scotch fir, Scots fir.**

Scots·wom·an (skots′wùm′ən) *n., pl.* **-wom·en.** a woman who is a native of Scotland.

Scot·ti·cism (skot′ə siz′əm) *n.* a word, expression, pronunciation, etc. that is characteristic of Scottish English.

Scot·tish (skot′ish) *adj., n.* —*adj.* of, having to do with, or characteristic of Scotland, its people, or their English dialects or

Gaelic language; Scots. —*n.* **1 the Scottish,** *pl.* **a** the people of Scotland. **b** people of Scottish descent. **2** Scots.

Scottish deerhound deerhound.

Scottish terrier an old Scottish breed of short-legged terrier having rough, wiry hair and pointed, standing ears.

scoun·drel (skoun′drəl) *n.* a mean or wicked person; a person without principles; villain. [? < OF *escondre* hide, abscond < L *ex-* from + *condere* hide]

scoun·drel·ly (skoun′drəl ē) *adj.* **1** having the character of a scoundrel. **2** having to do with or characteristic of a scoundrel.

scour¹ (skour) *v., n.* —*v.* **1** clean or polish by vigorous rubbing: *Scour the frying pan with cleanser.* **2** remove dirt and grease by washing: *Raw wool is usually scoured before it is made into yarn.* **3** clear of dirt, weeds, etc.: *The current scoured mud and sand out of the channel.* **4** dig or dig out by the action of running water: *The stream had scoured a channel.* —*n.* the act of scouring. [prob. < MDu. < OF *escurer,* ult. < L *ex-* completely + *cura* care] —**scour′er,** *n.*

scour² (skour) *v.* **1** move quickly over: *Men scoured the country round about for the lost child.* **2** look into every part of; search: *scour one's memory for a forgotten date.* **3** go swiftly in search or pursuit. [ME, probably < OF *escourre* run forth, ult. < L *ex-* out + *currere* run]

scourge (skėrj) *n., v.* **scourged, scourg·ing.** —*n.* **1** a whip. **2** any means of punishment. **3** some thing or person that causes great trouble or misfortune. In former times, an outbreak of disease was called a scourge. —*v.* **1** whip severely; flog. **2** punish severely. **3** put great hardship or suffering on; afflict or oppress. [ME < AF *escorge,* ult. < L *ex-* out + *corrigia* whip]

scour·ings (skour′ingz) *n.pl.* **1** dirt or other material removed by scouring or cleaning. **2** the lowest level or class of society; rabble: *the scourings of the slums.*

scout¹ (skout) *n., v.* —*n.* **1** a person sent to find out what the enemy is doing. A scout usually wears a uniform; a spy does not. **2** a warship, aircraft, etc. used to find out what the enemy is doing. **3** a person sent out to get information, especially about one's opponents, competitors, etc. **4** a person who looks for promising recruits for a film studio, sports team, etc. **5** the act of scouting. **6 Scout,** a member of the Boy Scouts. **7** *Slang.* a fellow; person: *He's a good scout.* —*v.* **1** act as a scout. **2** hunt around to find something: *Go and scout for firewood.* **3** observe or examine to get information. [ME < OF *escoute* act of listening, listener < *escouter* listen < L *auscultare*] —**scout′er,** *n.*

scout² (skout) *v.* **1** refuse to believe in; reject with scorn: *He scouted the idea of a dog with two tails.* **2** scoff. [< Scand.; cf. ON *skúta* taunt]

scout car **1** a police car that patrols streets and roads, maintaining contact with the station by radio telephone. **2** a lightly armored military reconnaissance vehicle. **3** a wide-tracked vehicle designed for use on northern muskeg.

Scout·er (skout′ər) *n.* an adult working directly with a group of Boy Scouts or Wolf Cubs.

Scout·ing (skout′ing) *n.* the activities, programs, or principles of the Boy Scouts.

Scout·mas·ter (skout′mas′tər) *n.* Troop Scouter.

scow (skou) *n.* a large, flat-bottomed boat used especially to carry bulk freight, such as sand or coal, and usually either towed by a tug or pushed with a pole, like a raft. [< Du. *schouw*]

scowl (skoul) *v., n.* —*v.* **1** draw the eyebrows down and together and tighten the mouth, especially as an expression of anger or sullenness; frown: *He scowled at us and asked what we were doing there.* **2** express with a scowl: *She scowled her displeasure.* —*n.* an angry or sullen look. [ME *skoul*; akin to Danish *skule* cast down the eyes] —**scowl′er,** *n.*
☛ **Syn.** *v.* **1.** See note at **frown.**

scrab·ble (skrab′əl) *v.* **-bled, -bling**; *n.* —*v.* **1** scratch or scrape about with hands, claws, etc.; scramble. **2** struggle or scramble feverishly, desperately, etc.: *scrabble for scraps of food, scrabble for a living.* **3** scrawl; scribble. —*n.* **1** a scraping; scramble. **2 Scrabble,** *Trademark.* a game played with small wooden or plastic squares with different letters on them, arranged to form words somewhat as in a crossword puzzle. [< Du. *schrabbelen,* frequentative of *schrabben* scratch]

scrag (skrag) *n., v.* **scragged, scrag·ging.** —*n.* **1** a skinny or scrawny person or animal. **2** a lean, bony cut of meat, especially the lean end of a neck of mutton or veal. **3** *Slang.* the neck. —*v.* **1** *Slang.* put to death by hanging or garrotting. **2** *Slang.* wring the neck of. [< Scand.; cf. dial. Swedish *skragge* old and torn thing]

scrag·gly (skrag′lē) *adj.* **-gli·er, -gli·est.** rough, irregular, or

ragged: *a scraggly garden. The child's hair was scraggly and matted.*

scrag·gy (skrag′ē) *adj.* **-gi·er, -gi·est. 1** lean; thin. **2** scraggly. **—scrag′gi·ness,** *n.*

scram (skram) *v.* **scrammed, scram·ming.** *Slang.* go away: *Scram! You're in the way here. He told the kids to scram.* [short for *scramble*]

scram·ble (skram′bəl) *v.* **-bled, -bling;** *n.* —*v.* **1** make one's way by climbing; crawling, etc.: *It took us half an hour to scramble up the rocky hill.* **2** struggle with others for something: *The boys scrambled to get the football.* **3** collect in a hurry or without method. **4** mix together in a confused way. **5** fry (eggs) with the whites and yolks mixed together. **6** *Military. Slang.* get a crew or aircraft into the air hurriedly, usually to intercept unidentified planes. **7** *Telecommunications.* break up or mix (a message or signal) so that it cannot be received and understood without special equipment. —*n.* **1** a climb or walk over rough ground. **2** a struggle to possess: *the scramble for wealth.* **3** any disorderly struggle or activity. **4** *Military. Slang.* the act or process of scrambling. [var. of *scrabble*] **—scram′bler,** *n.*

scran·nel (skran′əl) *adj. Archaic.* **1** thin, meagre, or slight. **2** harsh; unmelodious. [< Scand.; cf. dial. Norwegian *skran* lean, shrivelled]

scrap¹ (skrap) *n., v.* **scrapped, scrap·ping.** —*n.* **1** a small discarded or leftover piece of food: *The cook gave the scraps to the dog.* **2** a small detached or separated bit or piece: *scraps of paper, fabric scraps.* **3** a bit of something written, printed, etc.: *She read out scraps from the letter.* **4** material or articles discarded as useless and fit only to be broken down, melted, etc. and reprocessed: *a yard full of iron scrap.* **5** (*adj.*) in the form of scrap or scraps: *She buys scrap metal.* **6 scraps,** *pl.* cracklings. —*v.* **1** throw aside as worn out or useless: *They decided to scrap their old chesterfield.* **2** condemn or abandon as useless, not worth the effort, etc.: *The missile project was scrapped.* [ME < ON *scrap* < *scrapa* scrape]

scrap² (skrap) *n., v.* **scrapped, scrap·ping.** —*n. Informal.* a fight or quarrel. —*v. Informal.* have a scrap; fight or quarrel. [var. of *scrape*] **—scrap′per,** *n.*

scrap·book (skrap′bŭk′) *n.* a book in which pictures or clippings are pasted and kept.

scrape (skrāp) *v.* **scraped, scrap·ing;** *n.* —*v.* **1** rub with something sharp or rough; make smooth or clean thus: *Scrape your muddy shoes with this old knife.* **2** remove by rubbing with or against something sharp or rough: *The man scraped some paint off the table when he pushed it through the doorway.* **3** scratch or graze by rubbing against something rough: *She fell and scraped her knee on the sidewalk.* **4** rub with a harsh sound; rub harshly: *Don't scrape your feet on the floor. The branch of the tree scraped against the window.* **5** give a harsh sound; grate. **6** dig: *The child scraped a hole in the sand.* **7** collect with difficulty or a little at a time: *John has scraped together enough money for his first year at university.* **8** draw one foot back along the ground in making a bow.
scrape acquaintance, take the trouble to get acquainted.
scrape along, through, or **by,** barely get through or manage with difficulty: *That family can just scrape along but never asks for charity. He scraped through the examination.* —*n.* **1** the act of scraping. **2** a scraped place. **3** a harsh, grating sound: *the scrape of the bow of a violin.* **4** a position hard to get out of; difficulty. [ME < ON *skrapa*]

scrap·er (skrā′pər) *n.* an instrument or tool for scraping: *We removed the loose paint with a scraper.*

scrap·ing (skrā′ping) *n.* **1** the act of a person or thing that scrapes. **2** the sound produced by this: *We could hear the scraping of the shovel against the sidewalk.* **3** Usually, **scrapings,** *pl.* that which is scraped off, together, or up: *Put the scrapings into this box.*

scrap iron or **metal** broken or waste pieces of old iron or other metal collected for reworking: *He buys scrap iron.*

scrap·per (skrap′ər) *n. Informal.* a person or animal that fights readily or effectively: *The way she took on that bully showed that she was a scrapper.*

scrap·ple (skrap′əl) *n.* scraps of pork boiled with corn meal, made into cakes, sliced, and fried. [< *scrap¹*]

scrap·py¹ (skrap′ē) *adj.* **-pi·er, -pi·est.** made up of odds and ends; fragmentary; disconnected. [< *scrap¹*]

scrap·py² (skrap′ē) *adj.* **-pi·er, -pi·est.** *Informal.* fond of fighting. [< *scrap²*] **—scrap′pi·ness,** *n.*

scratch (skrach) *v., n., adj.* —*v.* **1** break, mark, or cut slightly with something sharp or rough: *Your shoes have scratched the chair.* **2** tear or dig with the nails or claws: *The cat scratched him.* **3** rub or scrape to relieve itching: *He scratched his head.* **4** rub or scrape with a harsh noise: *He scratched his fingernail along the*

hat, āge, fär; let, ēqual, tèrm; it, īce
hot, ōpen, ôrder; oil, out; cup, pùt, rüle,
əbove, takən, pencəl, lemən, circəs
ch, child; ng, long; sh, ship
th, thin; ŦH, then; zh, measure

chalkboard. **5** scribble. **6** strike out; draw a line through; cancel. **7** withdraw from a race or contest: *The horse was scratched because of an injury.* **8** gather by effort; scrape. —*n.* **1** a mark made by scratching. **2** a very slight cut on the skin. **3** the sound of scratching: *the scratch of a pen.* **4** the starting place of a race or contest. **5** the act of scratching. **6** *Slang.* money.
from scratch, with no advantages; from the beginning: *He lost his notes and so had to start his project again from scratch.*
up to scratch, up to standard; in good condition. —*adj.* **1** made up from whatever is on hand: *a scratch meal, a scratch football team.* **2** done by or dependent on chance: *a scratch shot.* [alteration of earlier *scrat,* influenced by obs. *cratch*; origin uncertain]

scratch hit *Baseball.* a poorly hit ball that is credited as a base hit.

scratch pad a pad of paper used for rough work or casual writing.

scratch paper paper used for rough work or casual writing.

scratch·y (skrach′ē) *adj.* **scratch·i·er, scratch·i·est. 1** that scratches or scrapes: *a scratchy rosebush.* **2** giving a prickly feeling; irritating: *This woollen dress is scratchy.* **3** making a scratching noise: *a scratchy pen.* **4** consisting of or made with scratches: *a scratchy drawing.* **—scratch′i·ly,** *adv.* **—scratch′i·ness,** *n.*

scrawl (skrol) *v., n.* —*v.* write or draw poorly, carelessly, or hastily: *He scrawled a note on the back of an envelope.* —*n.* **1** poor, careless, or hasty handwriting: *I could hardly read her scrawl.* **2** something scrawled, such as a hastily or badly written letter or note. [? < obs. *scrawl* spread the arms, gesticulate (of uncertain origin)] **—scrawl′er,** *n.*

scraw·ny (skro′nē or skrô′nē) *adj.* **-ni·er, -ni·est.** *Informal.* lean; thin; skinny: *Turkeys have scrawny necks.* [< Scand.; cf. dial. Norwegian *skran*]

scream (skrēm) *v., n.* —*v.* **1** give voice to a loud, sharp, piercing cry. *People scream in fright, in anger, and in sudden pain.* **2** produce a loud, shrill, harsh noise: *The siren screamed.* **3** utter or speak very loudly: *"That's wet paint!" he screamed. We had to scream to hear each other above the music.* **4** laugh loudly or uncontrollably: *The audience screamed at his antics.* **5** produce an extremely startling effect: *"War declared!" the headlines screamed.* —*n.* **1** a loud, sharp, piercing cry. **2** a loud, shrill, harsh noise. **3** *Informal.* something or somebody extremely funny. [ME, ? < ON *skræma* scare]

➤ **Syn.** *v.* **1. Scream, shriek** = make a loud, sharp, piercing sound. **Scream** means to give out suddenly a loud, high-pitched, piercing cry expressing fear, pain, or almost hysterical anger or joy: *She screamed when she saw the child fall.* **Shriek** suggests a more high pitched, wild, hair-raising and back-tingling cry, expressing extreme terror, horror, agony, or uncontrolled rage or laughter: *The prisoner shrieked when he was tortured.*

scream·er (skrē′mər) *n.* **1** a person or thing that screams. **2** any of three species making up a family (Anhimidae) of large South American marsh birds having a plump body with mainly grey or black plumage, spurs on the front edge of the wings, and a very loud, trumpeting call. The closest relatives of the screamers are ducks, geese, and swans. **3** a large and sensational headline.

scream·ing (skrē′ming) *adj.* **1** that screams. **2** evoking screams of laughter: *a screaming farce.* **3** startling: *screaming headlines, screaming colors.*

scream·ing·ly (skrē′ming lē) *adv.* to an extreme degree: *screamingly funny.*

scree (skrē) *n.* a steep slope of loose, fragmented rock lying below a cliff or bluff. [< ON *skritha* glide]

screech¹ (skrēch) *v.* or *n.* scream; shriek. [ME *scritch,* imitative] **—screech′er,** *n.*

screech² (skrēch) *n. Cdn. Slang. Esp.Newfoundland.* a potent dark rum. [ult. < Scottish dial. *screigh* whisky, influenced by *screech¹*]

screech owl 1 any of several small New World owls (genus *Otus*) having hornlike tufts of feathers on the head. Screech owls have a mournful, wailing, whistling call. **2** *Esp.Brit.* any owl that screeches, as distinguished from one that hoots.

screech·y (skrē′chē) *adj.* **screech·i·er, screech·i·est.** screeching.

screed (skrēd) *n.* **1** a long speech or piece of writing. **2** a strip of plaster (or wood) of the proper thickness, applied to the wall as a guide in plastering. [ME var. of OE *scrēade* shred]

screen (skrēn) *n., v.* —*n.* **1** a covered frame that hides, protects, or separates. **2** wire woven together with small openings in between the strands: *We have screens at our windows to keep out flies.* **3** an ornamental partition. **4** anything like a screen: *A screen of trees hides our house from the road.* **5** a flat surface on which a slide or film is projected. **6** motion pictures collectively or the motion picture industry: *a star of stage and screen.* **7** the surface at the wide end of a cathode-ray tube on which the image appears: *a television screen, a radar screen.* **8** a sieve for sifting sand, gravel, coal, seed, etc. **9** a body of soldiers detached toward the enemy to protect an army. **10** an escort of destroyers, etc. to protect battleships, aircraft carriers, etc., especially against submarine attack. **11** *Photo-engraving.* a transparent plate with fine lines that cross at right angles, used to produce the minute dots in a half-tone. —*v.* **1** shelter, protect, or hide with, or as with, a screen: *She screened her face from the fire with a fan. The mother tried to screen her guilty son.* **2** show (a motion picture) on a screen. **3** photograph with a motion-picture camera. **4** adapt (a story, etc.) for reproduction as a motion picture. **5** be suitable for reproducing on a motion picture screen. **6** sift with a screen. **7** examine carefully to test quality, suitability, etc.: *Applicants for this job must be carefully screened.* **8** print with a screen or by the silk-screen process. [ME < OF *escren* < Gmc.] —**screen′a·ble,** *adj.* —**screen′er,** *n.* —**screen′like′,** *adj.*

screen·ing (skrē′ning) *n.* **1** a fine wire mesh for making screens, filters, etc. **2 screenings,** *pl.* the matter separated out by sifting through a sieve or screen.

screen·play (skrēn′plā′) *n.* a story or play written for production as a motion picture, including description of characters and scenes, dialogue, etc.

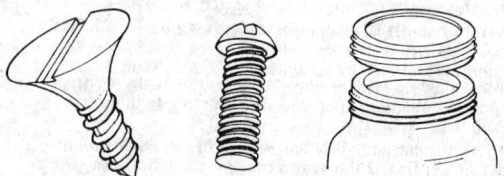

Screw (defs. 1 and 2): from left to right, a screw for use in wood, a bolt with a screw thread, and a jar with a screw top.

screw (skrü) *n., v.* —*n.* **1** a fastening device like a nail but having a ridge twisted evenly round its length and a slot or recess in the head: *Turn the screw to the right to tighten it.* **2** a simple machine consisting of a spiral ridge around a cylinder that acts to exert pressure in any of various ways. Certain kinds of jack use a screw as the means for exerting the force to raise an object. **3** a part into which this cylinder fits and advances. **4** something that resembles a screw. **5** a spiral or screwing motion. **6** *Informal.* a very stingy person; miser. **7** screw propeller. **8** *Slang.* a guard in a prison.

have a screw loose, *Slang.* be crazy or eccentric.
put the screws on, *Informal.* use pressure or force to get something. —*v.* **1** turn as one turns a screw; twist: *Screw the lid on the jar.* **2** turn like a screw; be fitted for being put together or taken apart by a screw or screws. **3** twist or contort. **4** fasten or tighten with a screw or screws. **5** force, press, or stretch tight by using screws. **6** force to do something; force (prices) down; force (people) to tell or to give up; force people to tell or give up something. **7** gather for an effort: *He finally screwed up enough courage to dive.*

screw up, *Slang.* make a mess of; botch; bungle.
[ME < OF *escroue* nut, screw (def. 3) < VL *scroba* < L *scrobis* ditch, vulva, influenced by L *scrofa* a sow]

screw·ball (skrü′bol′ or -bôl′) *n., adj.* —*n.* **1** *Slang.* an eccentric or crazy person. **2** *Baseball.* a pitch thrown with a break or spin opposite to that of a curve. —*adj. Slang.* eccentric or crazy: *That was a screwball thing to do.*

screw·driv·er (skrü′driv′ər) *n.* a tool for putting in or taking out screws by turning them.

screw propeller a device consisting of a revolving hub with radiating, slightly twisted blades, used for propelling a steamship, aircraft, etc.

screw thread the spiral ridge of a screw.

screw·y (skrü′ē) *adj. Slang.* crazy or eccentric.

scrib·ble (skrib′əl) *v.* **-bled, -bling;** *n.* —*v.* **1** write or draw carelessly or hastily. **2** make meaningless marks. —*n.* something scribbled. [ME < Med.L *scribillare,* ult. < L *scribere* write]

scrib·bler (skrib′lər) *n.* **1** a person who scribbles. **2** a pad of paper or a book in which to make notes, do rough work, etc. **3** an

author of little or no importance.

scribe (skrīb) *n., v.* **scribed, scrib·ing.** —*n.* **1** a person who copies manuscripts. Before printing was invented, there were many scribes. **2** a member of the class of professional interpreters of the Jewish law. **3** a writer; author (often used humorously). **4** a public clerk or secretary.
—*v.* mark or cut with something sharp. [ME < L *scriba* < *scribere* write]

scrib·er (skrīb′ər) *n.* a tool for marking on wood, metal, etc.

scrim (skrim) *n.* lightweight, loosely woven cotton or linen fabric having a mesh weave, used for curtains. [origin uncertain]

scrim·mage (skrim′ij) *n., v.* **-maged, -mag·ing.** —*n.* **1** a rough fight or struggle. **2** *Football.* a play that takes place when the two teams are lined up and the ball is snapped back. —*v.* **1** take part in a rough fight or struggle. **2** *Football.* take part in a scrimmage. [ult. var. of *skirmish*]

scrimp (skrimp) *v.* **1** be very economical; stint; skimp: *They had to scrimp for several years to save enough for a good down payment on a house.* **2** make too small, short, or scant; be very sparing of: *to scrimp food.* **3** treat stingily or very economically. [origin uncertain]

scrimp·y (skrim′pē) *adj.* **scrimp·i·er, scrimp·i·est.** too small; too little; scanty; meagre. —**scrimp′i·ly,** *adv.* —**scrimp′i·ness,** *n.*

scrim·shaw (skrim′sho′) *n., v.* —*n.* **1** the art or practice of drawing on or carving pieces of whalebone or ivory, as traditionally done by sailors in their leisure time. **2** an article produced in this way. **3** such articles collectively.
—*v.* produce scrimshaw (from).

scrip¹ (skrip) *n.* **1** a certificate, coupon, voucher, etc. establishing the bearer's right to something. **2** *Cdn.* a certificate issued following the Riel Rebellions to Métis as compensation for lands, entitling the holder to 240 acres of land (**land-scrip**) or to a choice between $240 cash (**money-scrip**) and 240 acres of land. **3** a short piece of writing, such as a certificate or schedule. [var. of *script*]

scrip² (skrip) *n. Archaic.* a small bag. [ME < OF *escrepe* < Gmc.]

script (skript) *n., v.* —*n.* **1** written letters, figures, signs, etc.; handwriting: *German script.* **2** *Printing.* a style of type that looks like handwriting. **3** the written text of a play, an actor's part, a radio or television broadcast, a motion picture, etc.
—*v. Informal.* write a script for (a radio or television show, film, etc.). [< L *scriptum,* originally neut. pp. of *scribere* write]

scrip·to·ri·um (skrip tôr′ē əm) *n., pl.* **-ri·ums, -ri·a** (-rē ə). a writing room; especially a room in a medieval monastery set apart for writing or copying manuscripts. [< Med.L *scriptorium,* ult. < L *scribere* write]

scrip·tur·al or **Scrip·tur·al** (skrip′chər əl) *adj.* of, according to, contained in, or based on the Scriptures. —**scrip′tur·al·ly,** *adv.*

Scrip·ture (skrip′chər) *n.* **1** the Bible. **2 the Scriptures** or **the Holy Scriptures,** *pl.* the Bible. **3 scripture,** any sacred writing. [ME < L *scriptura* a writing < *scribere* write]

script·writ·er (skript′rīt′ər) *n.* a person who writes scripts for motion pictures or radio or television programs.

scriv·ner (skriv′nər) *n. Archaic.* **1** a public writer of letters or documents for others; scribe or clerk. **2** notary. [ME < obs. *scrivein* < OF *escrivein,* ult. < L *scribere* write]

scrod (skrod) *n.* a young cod, especially one split for cooking. [< MDu. *schrode* piece cut off]

scrof·u·la (skrof′yə lə) *n.* tuberculosis of the lymph nodes, especially in the neck, and sometimes of the bones and joint surfaces, characterized by swelling and formation of pus. [< Med.L *scrofula,* sing. < L *scrofulae,* pl. < *scrofa* a sow; ? from fanciful comparison of glandular swellings to little pigs]

scrof·u·lous (skrof′yə ləs) *adj.* **1** of, having to do with, or affected with scrofula. **2** resembling scrofula. **3** of literature, etc., morally degenerate.

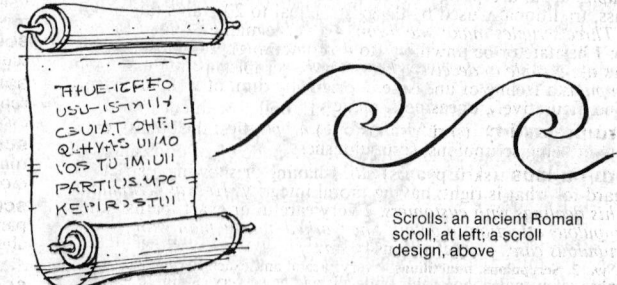

Scrolls: an ancient Roman scroll, at left; a scroll design, above

scroll (skrōl) *n.* **1** a roll of parchment or paper, especially one with

writing on it. **2** a list of names, events, etc.; roll; schedule: *to be entered in the scrolls of history.* **3** an ornament resembling a partly unrolled sheet of paper, or having a spiral or coiled form. **4** the curved head of a violin, etc. [alteration of *scrow* (influenced by roll), ult. < OF *escroe* scrap < Gmc.] —**scroll′·like′**, *adj.*

scroll saw a very narrow saw for cutting thin wood in curved or ornamental patterns.

scroll·work (skrōl′wêrk′) *n.* decorative work characterized by scrolls, especially such work done in wood with a scroll saw.

Scrooge (skrüj) *n.* **1** in Dickens' story *A Christmas Carol,* an embittered old miser. **2** any mean or stingy person.

scro·tal (skrō′təl) *adj.* of or having to do with the scrotum.

scro·tum (skrō′təm) *n., pl.* **-ta** (-tə) *or* **-tums.** in most male mammals, the pouch of skin that contains the testicles. [< L]

scrounge (skrounj) *v.* **scrounged, scroung·ing.** *Informal.* **1** find or collect by hunting around: *They're out scrounging kindling for the fire.* **2** get by begging; mooch; cadge: *He was always scrounging cigarettes.* **3** take without permission; pilfer: *to scrounge bricks from a construction site.* **4** look around for something; forage: *She scrounged around in the drawer, looking for a pencil.* [< dial. *scrunge* steal] —**scroung′er,** *n.*

scrub¹ (skrub) *v.* **scrubbed, scrub·bing;** *n.* —*v.* **1** wash or clean by rubbing hard with a brush or cloth: *to scrub the kitchen floor.* **2** remove (dirt, a spot, etc.) by rubbing with a brush or cloth. **3** rub hard in cleaning: *He had to scrub to get the ink off.* **4** wash the hands and arms before performing a surgical operation (*usually used with* **up**). **5** *Informal.* call off, especially at the last minute: *The launching was scrubbed.* **6** remove impurities from (a gas or vapor): *to scrub the air emissions of a lead smelter.* —*n.* the act or an instance or scrubbing. [? < MDu. *schrubben*]

scrub² (skrub) *n., adj.* —*n.* **1** low, stunted trees or shrubs. **2** any person, animal, or thing below the usual size: *He is a little scrub of a man.* **3** *Sports.* a player not on the regular team, etc. —*adj.* **1** small; poor; inferior. A scrub ball team is made up of inferior, substitute, or untrained players. **2** of or for players not on the regular team. [ME; var. of *schrobbe,* OE *scrybb* brushwood. See SHRUB¹.]

scrub·ber (skrub′ər) *n.* **1** an apparatus for purifying a gas or vapor. **2** any person or thing that scrubs.

scrub·by (skrub′ē) *adj.* **-bi·er, -bi·est. 1** low; stunted; small; below the usual size: *scrubby trees.* **2** covered with scrub: *scrubby land.* **3** shabby; mean. —**scrub′bi·ness,** *n.*

scrub pine *Cdn.* any of various small or scrubby pines, such as the jack pine or whitebark pine.

scruff (skruf) *n.* the back of the neck or the skin at the back of the neck: *She picked up the kitten by the scruff of the neck.* [alteration of *scuff,* of the same meaning (of uncertain origin)]

scruf·fy (skruf′ē) *adj.* unkempt, slovenly, or shabby: *That scruffy little kid is John's brother.*

scrum (skrum) *n. Esp.Brit.* a scrummage; scrimmage.

scrum·mage (skrum′ij) *n. Esp.Brit. Rugger.* a formation in which the forwards of each side bend down and lock together in two or three ranks, each side pushing against the other when the ball is placed in the middle. [var. of *scrimmage*]

scrump·tious (skrump′shəs) *adj. Informal.* splendid; first-rate: *a scrumptious meal.* [? alteration of *sumptuous*]

scrunch (skrunch) *v., n.* —*v.* **1** crunch, crush, or crumple: *He scrunched the paper into a tiny ball.* **2** hunch or squeeze: *We scrunched down behind the fence and waited.* **3** move with or make a scrunching sound: *They scrunched over the snow.* —*n.* the act or sound of scrunching. [imitative]

scru·ple (skrü′pəl) *n., v.* **-pled, -pling.** —*n.* **1** a feeling of doubt about what one ought to do: *No scruple ever holds him back from prompt action.* **2** a feeling of uneasiness which keeps a person from doing something that might be morally or ethically wrong: *He had scruples about accepting the free tickets.* **3** a unit for measuring mass, traditionally used by druggists, equal to 20 grains (about 1.3 g): *Three scruples make one dram.* **4** a very small amount. —*v.* **1** hesitate or be unwilling (to do something): *A dishonest man does not scruple to deceive others.* **2** have scruples. [< MF < L *scrupulus* a feeling of uneasiness, originally dim. of *scrupus* sharp stone; figuratively, uneasiness, anxiety]

scru·pu·los·i·ty (skrü′pyə los′ə tē) *n., pl.* **-ties.** the quality or state of being scrupulous; scrupulousness.

scru·pu·lous (skrü′pyə ləs) *adj.* **1** having or showing a strict regard for what is right; having moral integrity: *He was scrupulous in his dealings with customers.* **2** very careful or exact; painstaking: *scrupulous attention to detail. She worked out the plan with scrupulous care.* —**scru′pu·lous·ly,** *adv.*

☛ **Syn. 2. Scrupulous, punctilious** = very careful and exact. **Scrupulous** emphasizes attending thoroughly to details and being very careful to follow strictly and exactly what one knows is right or true: *She takes scrupulous care of the children's health.* **Punctilious,** a formal word, emphasizes paying special

hat, āge, fär; let, ēqual, tèrm; it, īce
hot, ōpen, ôrder; oil, out; cup, pùt, rüle,
above, takən, pencəl, lemən, circəs

ch, child; ng, long; sh, ship
th, thin; ŦH, then; zh, measure

and scrupulously exact, often excessive, attention to fine points of laws, rules, and requirements for conduct, behavior, or performance of duties: *He is punctilious about returning borrowed books.*

scru·pu·lous·ness (skrü′pyə ləs nəs) *n.* the quality or state of being scrupulous.

scru·ti·neer (skrü′tə nēr′) *n., v.* —*n.* a person who represents the interests of a particular candidate or party at a polling station on election day in order to ensure that the voting procedure and counting of ballots are properly carried out. —*v.* act as a scrutineer. [< *scrutin(y)* + *-eer*]

scru·ti·nize (skrü′tə nīz′) *v.* **-nized, -niz·ing.** examine closely; inspect carefully: *The jeweller scrutinized the diamond for flaws.* —**scru′ti·niz′er,** *n.* —**scru′ti·niz′ing·ly,** *adv.*

scru·ti·ny (skrü′tə nē) *n., pl.* **-nies. 1** a close examination; careful inspection: *His work looks all right at first glance, but it will never bear scrutiny.* **2** a looking searchingly at something; searching gaze. **3** an official examination of the votes cast at an election. [ME < LL *scrutinium* < L *scrutari* ransack]

scu·ba (skü′bə) *n.* a portable apparatus used for breathing while swimming underwater or diving. [< *s*elf-*c*ontained *u*nderwater *b*reathing *a*pparatus]

scuba diver a person who uses scuba gear to breathe while swimming under water or diving.

scud (skud) *v.* **scud·ded, scud·ding;** *n.* —*v.* run or move swiftly: *Clouds scudded across the sky, driven by the high wind.* —*n.* **1** the action of scudding. **2** clouds or spray driven by the wind. [? var. of *scut* a short tail, especially of a rabbit or deer; first applied to a running of a hare; cf. Norwegian *skudda* push]

scuff (skuf) *v., n.* —*v.* **1** walk without lifting the feet; shuffle. **2** wear or injure the surface of by hard use: *to scuff one's shoes.* —*n.* **1** the act of scuffing. **2** the sound made by scuffing. **3** a slipper having a toe piece but no covering for the heel. [var. of *scuffle*]

scuf·fle (skuf′əl) *v.* **-fled, -fling;** *n.* —*v.* **1** struggle or fight in a rough, confused manner, but not violently: *The children scuffled for first place in the lineup.* **2** shuffle. —*n.* **1** a confused, rough struggle or fight. **2** a shuffling. [< Scand.; cf. Swedish *skuffa* push] —**scuf′fler,** *n.*

A girl sculling a boat   A man in a racing scull

scull (skul) *n., v.* —*n.* **1** an oar worked with a side twist over the end of a boat to make it go. **2** one of a pair of oars used, one on each side, by a single rower. **3** the act of propelling by sculls. **4** a light racing boat for one or more rowers using sculls; sculler. —*v.* propel (a boat), by a scull or by sculls. [ME; origin unknown]

scull·er (skul′ər) *n.* **1** a person who sculls. **2** a boat propelled by sculling.

scull·er·y (skul′ər ē *or* skul′rē) *n., pl.* **-ler·ies.** *Esp.Brit.* a small room where the dirty, rough work of a kitchen is done. [ME < OF *escuelerie,* ult. < L *scutella,* dim. of *scutra* platter]

scul·lion (skul′yən) *n. Archaic.* **1** a servant who does the dirty, rough work in a kitchen. **2** a low, contemptible person. [ME < OF *escouillon* swab, cloth < *escouve* broom < L *scopa*]

scul·pin (skul′pin) *n.* any of a family (Cottidae) of scaleless or partially scaled, chiefly marine fishes having a large, spiny head. [? alteration of *scorpene* < L *scorpaena* < Gk. *skorpaina,* kind of fish < *skorpios* scorpion]

sculpt (skulpt) *v. Informal.* carve; sculpture: *to sculpt a statue.*

sculp·tor (skulp′tər) *n.* a person who makes figures by carving,

modelling, casting, etc.; artist in sculpture. Sculptors work in marble, wood, bronze, etc. [< L *sculptor*, late var. of *scalptor* < *scalpere* carve]

sculp·tress (skulp′tris) *n.* a woman who sculptures; a female artist in sculpture.

sculp·tur·al (skulp′chər əl) *adj.* of, having to do with, or like sculpture: *The fine use of light and shadow gave the painting a sculptural quality.* **-sculp′tur·al·ly,** *adv.*

sculp·ture (skulp′chər) *n., v.* **-tured, -tur·ing.** —*n.* **1** the art or process of carving, modelling, or welding hard or plastic substances into figures. Sculpture includes carving statues from stone or wood, casting in bronze, working in metal, and modelling in clay, soap, plastics, or wax. **2** sculptured work; a piece of such work. —*v.* **1** carve, model, or weld into a three-dimensional work of art. **2** change or shape by erosion: *snowbanks sculptured into strange shapes by the wind.* **3** decorate with sculpture. [ME < L *sculptura*, late var. of *scalptura* < *scalpere* carve]

sculp·tured (skulp′chərd) *adj.* **1** carved, moulded, cast, etc., in sculpture. **2** covered or ornamented with sculpture.

scum (skum) *n., v.* **scummed, scum·ming.** —*n.* **1** a surface film formed when certain liquids are boiled: *The scum had to be skimmed from the top of the boiling maple syrup.* **2** the layer of algae or other matter that forms on the top of still water. **3** low, worthless people; rabble. —*v.* **1** form scum or become covered with scum. **2** remove scum from; skim. [ME < MDu. *schuum*]

scum·my (skum′ē) *adj.* **-mi·er, -mi·est. 1** consisting of or covered with scum. **2** low; worthless.

scun·ner[1] (skun′ər) *n. Cdn. Newfoundland.* the assistant to the master of the watch on a boat. [< *scun*, var. of *scan*]

scun·ner[2] (skun′ər) *n., v.* —*n.* a strong dislike or prejudice: *I immediately took a scunner to him.* —*v.* feel a strong dislike or disgust.

scup (skup) *n., pl.* **scup** or **scups. 1** a common porgy (*Stenotomus chrysops*) of the Atlantic coast of the United States, valued as a panfish. **2** any of various other North American porgies. [< Algonquian]

scup·per (skup′ər) *n., v.* —*n.* an opening in the side of a ship to let water run off the deck. —*v. Slang.* catch by surprise and kill or destroy. [origin uncertain]

scurf (skėrf) *n.* **1** small scales of dead skin; dandruff. **2** any scaly matter on a surface. [ME < Scand.; cf. Icelandic *skurfa* skurf]

scurf·y (skėr′fē) *adj.* **scurf·i·er, scurf·i·est.** of, like, or covered with scurf. **-scurf′i·ness,** *n.*

scur·ril·i·ty (skə ril′ə tē) *n., pl.* **-ties. 1** the quality or state of being scurrilous. **2** indecent or abusive language. **3** an indecent or coarse remark.

scur·ri·lous (skėr′ə ləs) *adj.* **1** using coarse or indecent language; foulmouthed: *a scurrilous rabblerouser.* **2** containing obscenities and abuse: *a scurrilous political pamphlet, a scurrilous attack.* [< L *scurrilis* < *scurra* buffoon] **-scur′ri·lous·ly,** *adv.* **-scur′ri·lous·ness,** *n.*

scur·ry (skėr′ē) *v.* **-ried, -ry·ing;** *n., pl.* **-ries.** —*v.* run quickly; hurry: *We could hear the mice scurrying about in the walls.* —*n.* a hasty running; hurrying. [? < *hurry-scurry*, varied reduplication of *hurry*]

S–curve (es′kėrv′) *n.* a curve in the shape of the letter S.

scur·vy (skėr′vē) *n., adj.* **-vi·er, -vi·est.** —*n.* a disease caused by lack of vitamin C, characterized by swollen and bleeding gums, livid spots on the skin, and prostration. Scurvy used to be common among sailors when they had little to eat except bread and salt meat. —*adj.* low; mean; contemptible: *a scurvy fellow, a scurvy trick.* [< *scurf*] **-scur′vi·ly,** *adv.* **-scur′vi·ness,** *n.*

scut (skut) *n.* a short tail, especially that of a rabbit or deer. [cf. Icelandic *skutr* stern]

scu·tate (skyü′tāt) *adj.* **1** *Zoology.* having shieldlike plates or large scales of bone, shell, etc. **2** *Botany.* round. Nasturtiums have scutate leaves. [< L *scutatus* having a shield < *scutum* shield]

scutch (skuch) *v., n.* —*v.* separate (flax or cotton fibre) from woody parts by beating; make fibre ready for use by beating. —*n.* scutcher. [origin uncertain]

scutch·eon (skuch′ən) *n.* escutcheon.

scutch·er (skuch′ər) *n.* an implement for scutching.

scute (skyüt) *n.* scutum.

scu·tel·la (skyü tel′ə) *n. pl.* of **scutellum.**

scu·tel·late (skyü′tə lāt′ or skyü tel′āt) *adj. Biology.* **1** having scutella. **2** formed into a scutellum.

scu·tel·lum (skyü tel′əm) *n., pl.* **-tel·la.** *Zoology and botany.* a small plate, scale, or other shieldlike part. [< NL *scutellum*, dim. of L *scutum* shield]

scut·tle[1] (skut′əl) *n.* a kind of bucket for holding or carrying coal. [< L *scutella* platter]

scut·tle[2] (skut′əl) *v.* **-tled, -tling;** *n.* scamper; scurry. [var. of *scuddle*, frequentative of *scud*] **-scut′tler,** *n.*

scut·tle[3] (skut′əl) *n., v.* **-tled, -tling.** —*n.* **1** a small opening with a lid or cover, especially in the deck or side of a ship. **2** the lid or cover for any such opening. —*v.* **1** cut a hole or holes through the bottom or sides of (a ship) to sink it. **2** cut a hole or holes in the deck of (a ship) to salvage the cargo. **3** ruin or destroy (an undertaking, hope, etc.): *The minister's premature statement to the press scuttled the conference.* [? < F < Sp. *escotilla* hatchway]

scut·tle·butt (skut′əl but′) *n.* **1** a drinking fountain or a cask containing drinking water on a ship. **2** *Slang.* rumor and stories not based on fact.

scu·tum (skyü′təm) *n., pl.* **-ta** (-tə). a shieldlike part of bone, shell, etc., as on the body of certain reptiles or insects. [< L *scutum* shield]

Scyl·la (sil′ə) *n.* **1** a dangerous rock opposite the whirlpool Charybdis, at the extreme southwestern tip of Italy. **2** a mythical monster with six heads and twelve arms that lived on this rock and snatched sailors from ships.
between Scylla and Charybdis, between two dangers, of which the avoiding of one means being faced with the other.

A scythe

scythe (sīŦH) *n., v.* **scythed, scyth·ing.** —*n.* an implement used for cutting grass, grain, etc., consisting of a long, slightly curved blade set at an angle on the end of a long handle. —*v.* cut with a scythe. [OE *sīthe*; spelling influenced by L *scindere* cut]

Scyth·i·an (sith′ē ən) *n., adj.* —*n.* **1** a native or inhabitant of Scythia, an ancient region in SE Europe. **2** the extinct Iranian language of the Scythians. —*adj.* of or having to do with Scythia, its people, or their language.

s.d. 1 sine die. **2** several dates.

SD South Dakota.

S.D. 1 School District. **2** South Dakota.

S.Dak. South Dakota.

'sdeath (zdeth) *interj. Archaic.* "God's death," used as an oath.

Se selenium.

SE or **S.E.** southeast; southeasterly.

sea (sē) *n.* **1** the great body of salt water that covers almost three fourths of the earth's surface; the ocean. **2** any large body of salt water, smaller than an ocean, partly or wholly enclosed by land: *the North Sea, the Mediterranean Sea.* **3** a large lake of fresh water. **4** a large, heavy wave: *A high sea swept away the ship's masts.* **5** the swell of the ocean. **6** an overwhelming amount or vast expanse: *a sea of trouble, a sea of faces.*
at sea, a out on the sea. **b** *Informal.* puzzled; confused: *His complicated explanation left me even more at sea about the problem.*
follow the sea, be a sailor.
go to sea, a become a sailor. **b** begin a voyage.
put to sea, begin a voyage.
[OE *sǣ*]
☛ *Hom.* see.

sea anchor a device, such as a large canvas funnel or bag, dragged in the water to slow a vessel, keep it from drifting, or keep it heading into the wind.

sea anemone any of numerous flowerlike, often bright-colored polyps (order Actiniaria) found especially in warm seas, having a fleshy, cylinder-shaped body with a mouth opening at the upper end surrounded by many tentacles.

sea bass any of various marine fishes belonging to the same family (Serranidae) as the groupers and jewfish, found especially along the Atlantic coast of North America and including some important food and game fishes, such as the **black sea bass** (*Centropristes striatus*).

sea·bed (sē′bed′) *n.* the bed or bottom of the sea.

sea bird any bird that spends most of its time on or near the open sea. Gulls, cormorants, murres, and puffins are sea birds.

sea biscuit hardtack.

sea·board (sē′bôrd′) *n., adj.* —*n.* the land near the sea; seacoast; seashore: *the Atlantic seaboard.* —*adj.* bordering on the sea.

sea bread hardtack; ship biscuit.

sea bream any of various marine fishes (family Sparidae) found especially in warm eastern Atlantic and Mediterranean waters, such as the **red sea bream** (*Pagellus centrodontus*), highly valued as a food fish. Fishes of this family found along the western Atlantic coasts are usually known as porgies.

sea breeze a breeze blowing from the sea toward the land.

sea butterfly any of a subclass (Opisthobranchia) of mostly very small marine gastropods, having a pair of winglike lobes that are used for swimming.

sea cadet a person under military age who is undertaking basic naval training in an organization subsidized by the armed forces.

sea·coast (sē′kōst′) *n.* land along the sea.

sea·cock (sē′kok′) *n.* any cock or valve on a ship that opens through the hull to the sea.

sea cow 1 a manatee, dugong, or any similar mammal living in the sea. 2 walrus.

sea cucumber any of a class (Holothuroidea) of marine invertebrates found in all oceans, having a long, flexible, cylindrical body.

sea dog 1 a sailor having long experience at sea. 2 any of various seals.

sea eagle any of various large, fish-eating eagles, such as the bald eagle.

sea element *Cdn.* the branch of the Canadian Forces having to do with ships of war and their officers and personnel, formerly known as the Royal Canadian Navy.

sea elephant elephant seal.

sea·far·er (sē′fer′ər) *n.* a traveller on the sea, especially a sailor.

sea·far·ing (sē′fer′ing) *adj., n.* —*adj.* going, travelling, or working on the sea: *He had been a seafaring man all his life.* —*n.* 1 the calling or profession of a sailor. 2 the act or fact of travelling by sea.

sea-flea (sē′flē′) *n.* a tiny, one-man speedboat driven by a powerful motor and used especially for racing, so called because it skims the surface of the water.

sea foam 1 foam of the sea. 2 meerschaum.

sea·food (sē′füd′) *n.* edible saltwater fish and shellfish.

sea·fowl (sē′foul′) *n., pl.* -**fowls** or (esp. collectively) -**fowl.** any bird that lives on or near the sea.

sea·girt (sē′gėrt′) *adj. Poetic.* surrounded by the sea.

sea–go·ing (sē′gō′ing) *adj.* 1 going by sea; seafaring. 2 fit for going to sea.

sea green light bluish-green.

sea gull any of various large gulls, especially the herring gull.

Atlantic sea horses
(*Hippocampus hudsonius*)—
about 10 cm long

sea horse 1 any of a number of small marine fishes (family Syngnathidae) found in warm seas, having rings of scales around the body, a forward-curled, prehensile tail, and a horselike head set at an angle to the body. Sea horses swim in an upright position. 2 *Archaic.* walrus. 3 a mythical sea creature having the foreparts of a horse and the hind parts of a fish. Sea horses were the steeds of the sea gods.

sea king a Scandinavian pirate chief of the Middle Ages. [translation of Old Icelandic *sækonungr*]

seal¹ (sēl) *n., v.* —*n.* 1 a design stamped on a piece of wax, etc. to show ownership or authenticity; a paper, circle, mark, etc. representing it. The official seal is attached to important government papers. 2 a stamp for marking things with such a design: *a seal with one's initials on it.* 3 a piece of wax, paper,

hat, āge, fär; let, ēqual, tėrm; it, īce
hot, ōpen, ôrder; oil, out; cup, pút, rüle,
əbove, takən, pencəl, lemən, circəs
ch, child; ng, long; sh, ship
th, thin; ŦH, then; zh, measure

metal, etc. on which the design is stamped. 4 something that fastens or closes something tightly. 5 something that secures; a pledge: *under seal of secrecy.* 6 something that settles or determines: *the seal of authority.* 7 a mark; sign. 8 a special kind of stamp: *Christmas seals, Easter seals.* 9 a small quantity of water left in a trap to prevent the escape of foul air from a sewer or drain. 10 **the seals,** the symbols of public office.
set (one's) **seal to, a** put one's seal on. **b** approve.
—*v.* 1 mark (a document) with a seal; make binding or certify by affixing a seal: *The treaty was signed and sealed by both governments.* 2 stamp as an evidence of standard measure or quality or legal size: *to seal weights and measures.* 3 close tightly; shut; fasten: *Seal the letter before mailing it. She sealed the jars of fruit. Her promise sealed her lips.* 4 close up the cracks of: *They sealed the log cabin with clay.* 5 fix firmly. 6 settle; determine: *The judge's word sealed the prisoner's fate.* 7 give a sign that (something) is true: *to seal a promise with a kiss. They sealed their bargain by shaking hands.* 8 set apart; destine; decide beyond recall: *The king's fate was sealed.* [ME < AF *seal,* ult. < L *sigillum,* dim. of *signum* sign] —**seal′a·ble,** *adj.*

seal² (sēl) *n., pl.* **seals** or **seal** (*for I*); *v.* —*n.* 1 any of numerous carnivorous aquatic mammals comprising two families (Phocidae and Otariidae) of pinnipeds found especially in cold seas, having a streamlined, fur-covered body, limbs modified into flippers, and a thick layer of fat, or blubber, under the skin that provides insulation, acts as a food reserve, and makes the animals more buoyant. See also **hair seal, eared seal.** 2 the pelt of a seal, especially a fur seal; sealskin. 3 leather made from the skin of a seal.
—*v.* hunt seals. [OE *seolh*] —**seal′like′,** *adj.*

seal·ant (sē′lənt) *n.* a substance used for sealing, especially any of various substances used for waterproofing wood, joints in a pipe, etc.

sea lavender any of several perennial plants (genus *Limonium*) found in temperate coastal regions, having dense spikes of small white, pink, or mauve flowers.

sea legs *Informal.* legs accustomed to walking steadily on a rolling or pitching ship.
get (one's) **sea legs,** *Informal.* become accustomed to the motion of a ship, especially after an initial period of seasickness.

seal·er¹ (sē′lər) *n.* 1 something that seals, especially a substance applied to a porous surface such as wood to prevent paint or varnish from soaking in. 2 a glass jar that can be sealed, usually one holding about a litre or half a litre, used for home preserving of food. 3 an official appointed to examine and test weights and measures. [< *seal¹*]

seal·er² (sē′lər) *n.* 1 a person who hunts seals. 2 a ship used for hunting seals. [< *seal²*]

seal·er·y (sē′lər ē) *n., pl.* -**er·ies.** 1 the act or trade of hunting for seals. 2 a place where seals are hunted.

sea level the level of the surface of the sea, especially when halfway between mean high and low water. Mountains, plains, ocean beds, etc. are measured as so many metres above or below sea level.

sea lily any of numerous crinoids that in the adult stage are attached to the sea bottom by a long stalk. Some sea lilies may grow to a length of 60 cm.

sealing wax a substance used for sealing letters, etc., consisting of a mixture of resin, shellac, turpentine, and pigment that is hard at normal temperatures but becomes soft when heated.

sea lion any of several large eared seals of the Pacific Ocean, having small external ears and a coat of short, coarse hair that lacks a distinct undercoat. The northern sea lion (*Eumetopias jubata*) is found in the coastal waters of British Columbia.

seal ring a finger ring engraved with a design so that it can be used as a seal.

seal·skin (sēl′skin′) *n.* 1 the pelt or fur of a fur seal, prepared for use. 2 a garment made of this fur.

Sea·ly·ham (sē′lē ham *or* sē′lē əm) *n.* a breed of small terrier originally developed in Wales, having short legs, a rough, shaggy coat, and a square jaw. [< *Sealyham,* a Welsh estate where the breed was originated]

seam (sēm) *n., v.* —*n.* 1 the join formed when two pieces of cloth, canvas, leather, etc. are sewn together. 2 any join where edges

come together: *The seams of the boat must be filled in if they leak. The seams of the carpet hardly show.* **3** any mark or line like a seam. **4** *Geology.* a layer; stratum: *a seam of coal.* —*v.* **1** join by sewing or as if by sewing. **2** mark with lines or wrinkles: *Years of exposure to the harsh climate had seamed his face.* **3** develop cracks or fissures. [OE *sēam*] —**seam′less,** *adj.*

☛ *Hom.* **seem.**

sea·man (sē′mən) *n., pl.* **-men. 1** a sailor, especially one who sails the ocean. **2** a sailor who is not an officer.

☛ *Hom.* **semen.**

sea·man·like (sē′mən līk′) *adj.* like or fit for a good seaman; having or showing seamanship.

sea·man·ship (sē′mən ship′) *n.* skill in handling and navigating a ship.

sea·mark (sē′märk′) *n.* **1** a lighthouse, beacon, or other landmark that can be seen from the sea, used as a guide for a ship's course. **2** a line on the shores that shows the limit of the tide.

seam·er (sē′mər) *n.* **1** a person or thing that seams. **2** a machine that joins two pieces of metal.

sea mew a sea gull, especially *Larus canus;* mew².

sea mile nautical mile (about 1.85 km).

sea monster 1 a huge fish, cetacean, or the like. **2** a fabulous marine animal of terrifying proportions and shape.

seam·stress (sēm′stris) *n.* a woman who sews, especially one whose occupation is sewing. Also, **sempstress.**

seam·y (sē′mē) *adj.* **seam·i·er, seam·i·est. 1** least attractive or pleasant; sordid or squalid: *the seamy side of life.* **2** showing seams; especially, showing the rough edges of the seams on the inside of a garment, etc. —**seam′i·ness,** *n.*

sé·ance (sā′äns; *French,* sā äNs′) *n.* **1** a meeting of people trying to communicate with spirits of the dead by the help of a medium. **2** any session or meeting of an organization. [< F *séance* < *seoir* sit < L *sedere*]

sea otter a large marine otter (*Enhydra lutris*) of N Pacific coastal waters having large, flipperlike hind feet and a thick, reddish-brown or dark-brown coat. It was hunted almost to extinction for its fur and is now a rare and protected species.

sea·plane (sē′plān′) *n.* an airplane that can take off from and come down on water.

sea·port (sē′pôrt′) *n.* **1** a port or harbor on the seacoast. **2** a city or town with a harbor that ships can reach from the sea.

sea power 1 naval strength: *The United States possesses great sea power.* **2** a nation having great naval strength: *Canada is not one of the world's major sea powers.*

sea purse the horny case or pouch produced by certain species of fish, such as some sharks, to protect their eggs and anchor them to rocks, weeds, etc.

sear (sēr) *v., n., adj.* —*v.* **1** burn or char the surface of: *The hot iron seared his flesh.* **2** make hard or unfeeling: *Years of cruelty had seared his heart.* **3** dry up; wither. **4** become dry, burned, or hard. —*n.* a mark made by searing. —*adj.* *Archaic.* dried up; withered. [OE *sēarian,* v. < *sēar,* adj.]

☛ *Hom.* **seer, sere.**

☛ *Syn. v.* **1.** See note at **burn.**

search (sėrch) *v., n.* —*v.* **1** try to find by looking; seek; look for: *We searched all day for the lost cat.* **2** look through; go over carefully; examine, especially for something concealed: *The police searched the prisoner to see if he had a gun.* **3** look through (writings, records, etc.) in order to discover if certain things are there: *to search land titles.* **4** examine by probing: *The doctor searched the wound for the bullet.* **5** *Archaic.* pierce or penetrate. **search out, a** look for. **b** find by searching. —*n.* the act of searching; examination. **in search of,** trying to find; looking for: *They went in search of buried treasure.*

[ME < OF *cerchier,* ult. < L *circus* circle] —**search′a·ble,** *adj.* —**search′er,** *n.*

☛ *Syn. v.* **2. Search, explore, rummage** = look through a place or thing for something. **Search** = look carefully through something, trying to find what is there or hunting for something lost or hidden: *Men searched the woods for the murderer.* **Explore** = search into a region, field of interest, etc. to discover the facts about it, its nature, condition, quality, etc.: *Geologists explored the newly discovered mineral deposit.* **Rummage** = search thoroughly a ship, house, trunk, etc. by moving or searching among the contents: *He rummaged through the drawers looking for a map.*

search·ing (sėr′ching) *adj.* **1** examining carefully; thorough: *a searching gaze or look, a searching examination.* **2** piercing; penetrating: *a searching wind.* —**search′ing·ly,** *adv.*

search·light (sėrch′līt′) *n.* **1** a device that can throw a bright,

far-reaching beam of light in any direction desired. **2** the beam of light.

search warrant a legal document authorizing the search of a house or building for stolen or contraband goods, persons wanted by the police, etc.

sea robber pirate.

sea robin any of a family (Triglidae) of bottom-living marine fishes having a bony, armored head and fan-shaped pectoral fins with a few elongated rays that are used as feelers and for walking along the bottom of the sea. Some sea robins, such as the **northern sea robin** (*Prionotus carolinus*) of the North American Atlantic coast, can produce sounds with the muscular vibration of their swim bladders.

sea room space at sea free from obstruction, in which a ship can easily sail, tack, turn around, etc.

sea rover 1 a pirate. **2** a pirate ship.

sea-run (sē′run′) *adj.* anadromous.

sea·scape (sē′skāp′) *n.* **1** a picture, often a painting, showing scenery on the sea. **2** a view of scenery on the sea. [modelled on *landscape*]

Sea Scout a member of the Boy Scouts, aged 11 to 14, belonging to a program that emphasizes activities involving boats, boating, swimming, rescue work, and the lore of the sea.

sea serpent 1 a huge snakelike sea monster often reported as having been seen in the sea, but never proven to exist. **2** sea snake.

sea-shell (sē′shel′) *n.* the shell of any sea mollusc, such as an oyster, conch, abalone, etc.

sea·shore (sē′shôr′) *n.* the land along the sea; the beach at the seaside.

sea·sick (sē′sik′) *adj.* suffering from seasickness.

sea·sick·ness (sē′sik′nis) *n.* **1** nausea and dizziness caused by the pitching and rolling of a ship at sea. **2** *Informal.* nausea and dizziness caused by any similar motion, as when travelling in a motor vehicle or aircraft or swinging in a hammock; motion sickness.

sea·side (sē′sīd′) *n.* **1** the land along the sea; seacoast; seashore. **2** (*adj.*) beside the sea: *a seaside inn.*

sea snake any of a family (Hydrophidae) of poisonous aquatic snakes having a laterally compressed, rudderlike tail, found in tropical seas, especially in the Indian and W Pacific oceans.

sea·son (sē′zən) *n., v.* —*n.* **1** one of the four periods of the year: spring, summer, autumn, or winter. **2** a period of the year with reference to the particular conditions of weather, temperature, etc., that characterize it. **3** any period of time marked by something special: *the Christmas season, the harvest season.* **4** the time when something is occurring, active, at its best, or in fashion: *the baseball season.* **5** a period of time: *a season of rest.* **6** the period of the year when a place is most frequented or active: *the Paris season.* **7** a suitable or fit time. **for a season,** for a time. **in good season,** early enough. **in season, a** at the right or proper time. **b** in the time or condition for eating, hunting, etc. **c** early enough. **in season and out of season,** at all times. **out of season,** not in season. —*v.* **1** improve the flavor of: *season soup with salt.* **2** give interest or character to: *season conversation with wit.* **3** make fit for use by a period of keeping or treatment: *Wood is seasoned for building by drying and hardening it.* **4** become fit for use. **5** accustom; make used: *Soldiers are seasoned to battle by experience in war.* **6** make less severe; soften: *Season justice with mercy.* [ME < OF *seson* < L *satio, -onis* a sowing, ult. < *serere* sow] —**sea′son·er,** *n.*

☛ *Usage.* **Seasons.** The names **spring, summer, fall, autumn,** and **winter** are not capitalized.

sea·son·a·ble (sē′zən ə bəl *or* sēz′nə bəl) *adj.* **1** suitable to the season: *Hot weather is seasonable in July.* **2** coming at the right or proper time: *The second expedition brought seasonable aid to the men who had survived the first.* —**sea′son·a·ble·ness,** *n.* —**sea′son·a·bly,** *adv.*

sea·son·al (sē′zən əl) *adj.* **1** of, having to do with, or occurring in a particular season: *seasonal variations in the weather, seasonal rains.* **2** depending on or affected by the season: *seasonal unemployment, a seasonal worker.* —**sea′son·al·ly,** *adv.*

sea·son·ing (sē′zən ing *or* sēz′ning) *n.* **1** something that is added to food to give extra flavor. Salt, pepper, spices, and herbs are used as seasonings. **2** anything that adds interest or character: *conversation with a seasoning of wit.*

season ticket a ticket that gives its holder the right to attend a series of games or entertainments, or to make a daily trip to a railway, bus, etc. for a stated period of time.

sea squirt any of a class (Ascidiacea) of minute invertebrates found in all seas from near the shore down to the greatest depths,

characterized by a saclike body having openings through which water passes. Most sea squirts are free-swimming as larvae but sedentary as adults.

sea star starfish.

seat¹ (sēt) *n., v.* —*n.* **1** something to sit on. **2** a place to sit. **3** a place in which one has the right to sit: *We have reserved seats in the first balcony.* **4** a right to sit as a member of a legislature, city council, stock exchange, etc: *The Liberals lost ten seats in the last election.* **5** that part of a chair, bench, stool, etc. on which one sits. **6** that part of the body on which one sits, or the clothing covering it. **7** a manner of sitting on horseback. **8** that on which anything rests; base.
—*v.* **1** set or place on a seat: *to seat a person on a chair.* **2** have seats for (a specified number): *That stadium seats thirty thousand people.* **3** provide with a seat or seats. **4** put a seat on.
be seated, a sit down. **b** be sitting. **c** be situated.
[ME < ON *sæti*]

seat² (sēt) *n., v.* —*n.* **1** an established place or centre: *A university is a seat of learning. The seat of our government is in Ottawa.* **2** the throne of a king, etc.; the authority or dignity of a king, etc. **3** a residence; home: *The family seat of the Percys is in Northumberland.* **4** location; situation; site: *the seat of a disease.*
—*v.* fix in a particular or proper place; settle; locate. [OE *sǣte*]

seat belt a belt or arrangement of straps in an automobile or aircraft, designed to hold an occupant in the seat in case of a crash, jolt, bump, etc.

seat·ing (sēt'ing) *n.* **1** upholstery for covering seats. **2 a** the arrangement of seats for a dinner party, in a theatre, etc. **b** the seats themselves. **3 a** a support on which something rests: *the seating of a valve.* **b** something resting on such a support.

sea trout 1 any of various trouts or chars that spend part of their lives in the sea. **2** any of several weakfishes, especially *Cynoscion nebulosus*, which is also called **spotted sea trout.**

sea urchin any of a class (Echinoidea) of marine invertebrates typically having a spherical or slightly flattened body with a rigid outer shell of fused plates bearing rows of movable spines.

sea wall a strong wall or embankment made to prevent the waves from wearing away the shore, to act as a breakwater, etc.

sea·ward (sē'wərd) *adv., adj., n.* —*adv. or adj.* toward the sea: *Our house faces seaward.* —*n.* the direction toward the sea: *The island lies one kilometre to seaward.*

sea·wards (sē'wərdz) *adv.* seaward.

sea·way (sē'wā') *n.* **1** a way or route over the ocean. **2** the progress of a ship through the waves. **3** a rough sea. **4** an inland waterway that connects with the open sea and is deep enough to permit ocean shipping: *the St. Lawrence Seaway.*

sea·weed (sē'wēd') *n.* any plant or plants growing in the sea, especially a sea alga such as kelp.

sea wind a wind blowing from the sea toward the land.

sea·wor·thy (sē'wèr'ᴙē) *adj.* fit for sailing on the sea; able to stand storms at sea. —**sea'wor'thi·ness,** *n.*

se·ba·ceous (si bā'shəs) *adj.* **1** of, having to do with, or being fat; fatty. **2** producing sebum: *sebaceous glands.* [< L *sebaceus* < *sebum* grease]

se·ba·go (si bā'gō) *n.* ouananiche. [< Lake *Sebago,* Maine]

se·bum (sē'bəm) *n.* the oily substance produced by the sebaceous glands to lubricate the skin and hair.

sec. 1 secretary. **2** second(s). **3** section(s). **4** secant. **5** according to (for L *secundum*). **6** secondary.

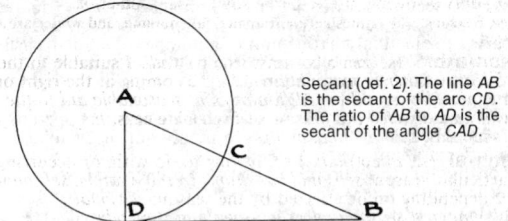
Secant (def. 2). The line *AB* is the secant of the arc *CD.* The ratio of *AB* to *AD* is the secant of the angle *CAD.*

se·cant (sē'kənt *or* sē'kant) *n., adj.* —*n.* **1** *Geometry.* a line that intersects a curve at two or more points. **2** *Trigonometry.* **a** a straight line drawn from the centre of a circle through one extremity of an arc to the tangent from the other extremity of the same arc. **b** the ratio of the length of this line to the length of the radius of the circle. **c** the ratio of the length of the hypotenuse of a right-angled triangle to the length of the side adjacent to an acute angle. See **sine¹** for picture. —*adj.* intersecting. [< L *secans, -antis,* ppr. of *secare* cut]

hat, āge, fär; let, ēqual, tèrm; it, īce
hot, ōpen, ôrder; oil, out; cup, pút, rüle,
əbove, takən, pencəl, lemən, circəs
ch, child; ng, long; sh, ship
th, thin; ᴙ, then; zh, measure

se·ca·teurs (se'kə tèrz') *n.pl. Esp.Brit.* pruning shears or clippers. [< F < L *secare* cut]

se·cede (si sēd') *v.* **-ced·ed, -ced·ing.** withdraw formally from an organization, especially a church or a political federation. [< L *secedere* < *se-* apart + *cedere* go] —**se·ced'er,** *n.*

se·ces·sion (si sesh'ən) *n.* a formal withdrawing from an organization, especially a church or a political federation. [< L *secessio, -onis* < *secedere.* See SECEDE.]

se·ces·sion·ism (si sesh'ən iz'əm) *n.* the principles or policy of those in favor of secession.

se·ces·sion·ist (si sesh'ən ist) *n.* **1** a person who believes that secession is a right. **2** a person who takes part in a secession.

se·clude (si klüd') *v.* **-clud·ed, -clud·ing.** shut off or keep apart from others; isolate: *He has secluded himself and no longer accepts visitors.* [< L *secludere* < *se-* apart + *claudere* shut]

se·clud·ed (si klüd'id) *adj.* shut off from others; undisturbed.

se·clu·sion (si klü'zhən) *n.* **1** keeping apart or being shut off from others; retirement: *She lives in seclusion, apart from her friends.* **2** a secluded place. [< Med.L *seclusio, -onis* < L *secludere.* See SECLUDE.]

se·clu·sive (si klü'siv) *adj.* **1** fond of seclusion. **2** tending to seclude. —**se·clu'sive·ly,** *adv.* —**se·clu'sive·ness,** *n.*

sec·ond¹ (sek'ənd; *so* sek'ənd *for v. def. 3*) *adj., adv., n., v.* —*adj.* **1** next after the 1st; 2nd: *the second seat from the front.* **2** next below the first in rank, authority, etc.: *the second officer on a ship.* **3** another; other: *Napoleon has been called a second Caesar.* **4** *Music.* being or having to do with a part subordinate to and usually lower than the first in an ensemble composition: *second soprano.*
at second hand, not directly from the source or first owner; not primarily or originally: *a report received at second hand.*
—*adv.* in the second group, division, rank, etc.; secondly.
—*n.* **1** a person or thing that is second. **2 seconds,** *pl.* articles below first quality. Seconds have some defect or other. **3** a person who supports or aids another; backer: *The prize fighter had a second.* **4** *Music.* **a** the second, usually lower, part in a composition for ensemble performance. **b** a voice or instrument rendering such a part. **c** a tone on the next degree from a given tone. **d** the interval between the two. **e** the harmonic combination of such tones. **f** the second note in a scale. **5** a forward gear or speed of a motor vehicle having a ratio to the engine speed between that of low and high.
—*v.* **1 a** support; back up; assist: *to second another person's idea.* **b** attend (a boxer or duellist). **2** express approval or support of: *One member made a motion to adjourn the meeting, and another seconded it.* **3** assign (a person, especially a member of the armed forces) temporarily to some office outside his regular appointment. [ME < OF < L *secundus < sequi* follow] —**sec'ond·er,** *n.*

sec·ond² (sek'ənd) *n.* **1** an SI unit for measuring time. There are sixty seconds in one minute, sixty minutes in one hour, and twenty-four hours in one day. The second is one of the seven base units in the SI. *Symbol:* s **2** any short period of time: *I'll be with you in a second.* **3** a unit used with the SI for measuring plane angles: There are sixty seconds in one minute and sixty minutes in one degree. *Symbol: "* [ME < OF < Med.L *secunda (minuta)* second (minute), i.e., the result of the second division of the hour into sixty parts]

Second Advent Second Coming.

sec·ond·ar·y (sek'ən der'ē) *adj., n., pl.* **-ar·ies.** —*adj.* **1** next after the first in order, place, time, etc. **2** not main or chief; having less importance. **3** not original; derived. **4** *Electricity.* noting or having to do with a coil or circuit in which a current is produced by induction. **5** *Chemistry.* involving the substitution of two atoms or groups. **6** *Geology.* produced from another mineral by decay, alteration, etc.
—*n.* **1** a person or thing that is secondary, second in importance, or subordinate. **2** a secondary stress. **3** *Electricity.* a coil or circuit in which a current is produced by induction. —**sec'ond·ar·i·ly,** *adv.*

secondary accent secondary stress.

secondary feather feather used in flying, situated on the second segment of a bird's wing.

secondary school a school attended after elementary or junior high school; a high school or collegiate institute.

secondary stress 1 a stress accent that is weaker than the

strongest stress in a word (primary stress), but stronger than weak stress. The second syllable of *ab·bre′vi·a′tion* has a secondary stress. **2** a mark, such as (′), used to show where this stress falls.

second childhood a period or state of mental decline associated with old age; dotage.

sec·ond–class (sek′ənd klas′) *adj., adv. —adj.* **1** of, having to do with, or belonging to a class ranking next below the first or highest. **2** having to do with or designating the grade of travel accommodation next below the best: *a second-class ticket, a second-class railway car.* **3** of inferior grade or quality. **4** not enjoying the full rights of the majority: *second-class citizens.* **5** designating a mail classification that includes newspapers and periodicals sent to subscribers.
—adv. **1** with second-class accommodation: *to travel second-class.* **2** by second-class mail.

Second Coming *Christianity.* the return of Christ to earth as judge at the end of the world.

second growth **1** a crop of grass or hay that comes up after the first crop has been cut; aftergrass. **2** a new growth of trees in an area where virgin forest has been cut or burned. **3** any new growth in an area that has been cleared of vegetation.

second hand a hand on a clock or watch, pointing to the seconds.

sec·ond–hand (sek′ənd hand′) *adj.* **1** not original; obtained from another: *second-hand information.* **2** not new; used already by someone else: *second-hand clothes.* **3** dealing in used goods: *a second-hand bookshop.*

second lieutenant the lowest-ranking commissioned officer in the armed forces. See chart at **rank¹.** *Abbrev.:* 2Lt. or 2Lt

sec·ond·ly (sek′ənd lē) *adv.* in the second place.

second nature a habit, quality, knowledge, etc. that a person has acquired and had for so long that it seems to be almost a part of his nature.

second person the form of a pronoun or verb used to indicate the person spoken to. *You* and *your* are used for the second person.

sec·ond–rate (sek′ənd rāt′) *adj.* of inferior quality or value; mediocre: *a second-rate diamond, a second-rate author.*

second sight the power to see distant objects or future events; clairvoyance.

second wind **1** a recovery or renewal of breath and energy following the initial feeling of exhaustion during an effort, as in running a race. **2** any recovery or renewal of energy: *The rise in steel production faltered in early spring and then got its second wind.*

se·cre·cy (sē′krə sē) *n., pl.* **-cies. 1** the condition of being secret. **2** the condition of being kept secret. **3** the act or habit of keeping things secret: *They relied on her secrecy.* [< secret, adj.]

se·cret (sē′krit) *adj., n. —adj.* **1** kept from the knowledge of others: *a secret marriage.* **2** keeping to oneself what one knows: *Be as secret as the grave.* **3** known only to a few: *a secret society.* **4** kept from sight; hidden: *a secret drawer.* **5** retired; secluded: *a secret place.* **6** working or acting in secret: *a secret agent, secret police.* **7** very hard to understand or discover.
—n. **1** something secret or hidden; mystery. **2** something known only to a few. **3** a hidden cause or reason.
in secret, in private; not openly.
[< F *secret* < L *secretus,* pp. of *secernere* set apart < *se-* apart + *cernere* separate. Doublet of SECRETE.] **—se′cret·ly,** *adv.*
☛ **Syn.** *adj.* **1. Secret, covert, clandestine** = done, made, or carried on without the knowledge of others. **Secret** is the general word describing something hidden or kept from sight or knowledge: *They have secret plans.* **Covert,** formal, suggests being done or kept under cover, and describes looks, meanings, or actions that are disguised or not open: *A hint is a covert suggestion.* **Clandestine,** formal, describes something underhand or with an unlawful or wicked purpose: *He feared someone would learn of his clandestine trips.*

secret agent an agent of a government secret service.

sec·re·tar·i·al (sek′rə ter′ē əl) *adj.* of a secretary; having to do with a secretary: *She learned to do stenography, typewriting, and other secretarial work.*

sec·re·tar·i·at (sek′rə ter′ē it *or* sek′rə ter′ē at′) *n.* **1** the office or position of secretary, especially of a secretary or secretary-general as the administrative head of an organization. **2** the administrative unit controlled by a secretary or secretary-general: *the United Nations Secretariat.* **3** a group of secretaries. **4** a place where a secretary or secretary-general transacts business. [< F *secrétariat*]

sec·re·tar·y (sek′rə ter′ē) *n., pl.* **-tar·ies. 1** someone who writes letters, keeps records, etc. for a person, company, club, etc.: *Our club has a secretary who keeps the minutes of the meeting.* **2** in

some countries, a person who administers a department of the government. **3** a diplomatic agent, usually of lower rank in an embassy or legation, often designated as first secretary, second secretary, etc. **4** a writing desk with a set of drawers, often having shelves for books. [ME < LL *secretarius* confidential officer < L *secretum,* n., secret, originally pp., neut. of *secretus.* See SECRET.]

secretary bird a large, long-legged African bird of prey (*Sagittarius serpentarius*) that feeds mainly on reptiles, so called because its crest suggests pens stuck over the ear.

sec·re·tar·y–gen·er·al (sek′rə ter′ē jen′ə rəl *or* -jen′rəl) *n., pl.* **sec·re·tar·ies–gen·er·al.** the chief or senior secretary; the administrator or head of a secretariat: *the Secretary-General of the United Nations.*

se·crete (si krēt′) *v.* **-cret·ed, -cret·ing. 1** keep secret; hide. **2** produce and release: *Glands in the mouth secrete saliva.* [< L *secretus.* Doublet of SECRET.] **—se·cre′tor,** *n.*

se·cre·tion (si krē′shən) *n.* **1** a substance that is secreted by some part of an animal or plant. Bile is the secretion of the liver. **2** the producing and releasing of such a substance. **3** concealing; hiding.

se·cre·tive (sē′krə tiv *or* si krē′tiv *for I;* si krē′tiv *for 2*) *adj.* **1** having the habit of secrecy; not frank and open. **2** causing or aiding secretion. **—se·cre′tive·ly,** *adv.* **—se·cre′tive·ness,** *n.*

se·cre·to·ry (si krē′tə rē) *adj., n., pl.* **-ries. —adj.** secreting; of or causing secretion. **—n.** an organ of the body that secretes.

secret police in a dictatorship or similar regime, a special government police force that operates secretly to control and suppress activities considered subversive.

secret service **1** the branch of a government that makes secret investigations. **2** an official service that is secret.

secret society **1** an association of which some ceremonies and activities are known only to members. **2** an organization to promote some cause by secret methods, its members being sworn to observe secrecy.

sect (sekt) *n.* **1** a group of people having the same principles, beliefs, or opinions. **2** a group of people forming part of a larger religious body but rejecting some of the larger body's beliefs or customs: *The Protestant church used to have many different sects.* [< L *secta* party, school, probably < *sectari* keep following, intensive of *sequi* follow]

sect. section; sectional.

sec·tar·i·an (sek ter′ē ən) *adj., n. —adj.* **1** of or having to do with a sect. **2** characteristic of one sect only; strongly prejudiced in favor of a certain sect. **—n.** **1** a devoted member of a sect, especially a narrow-minded or strongly prejudiced member. **2** a member of a religious group separated from an established church.

sec·tar·i·an·ism (sek ter′ē ən iz′əm) *n.* the spirit or tendencies of sectarians; adherence or too great devotion to a particular sect.

sec·ta·ry (sek′tə rē) *n., pl.* **-ries.** a member of a particular sect, especially a member of a religious group separated from an established church. [< Med.L *sectarius* < L *secta.* See SECT.]

sec·tile (sek′tīl *or* sek′təl) *adj.* capable of being cut smoothly by a knife.

sec·tion (sek′shən) *n., v. —n.* **1** a part; division; slice: *Divide the cake into sections. His section of the family estate was larger than his brother's.* **2** a division of a book, etc.: *Chapter X has seven sections.* **3** a region; part of a country, city, etc.: *The city has a business section and a residential section.* **4** a division of a company, office, or other organization. **5** a military formation that is smaller than a platoon and usually commanded by a corporal. **6** the act of cutting. **7** a view of a thing as it would appear if cut straight through; cross section. **8** a district or tract of land one mile square; 640 acres (about 260 ha): *He farms two sections near Regina.* **9** one of the parts of something that is built of a number of similar parts: *the sections of a bookcase.* **10** a thin slice of a tissue, mineral, etc. cut off for microscopic examination. **11** a part of a railway line kept up by one group of workmen. **12** a part of a sleeping car containing an upper and a lower berth. **13** one of two or more trains operating on the same schedule. **14** *Bookbinding.* a number of sheets folded together to form a unit.
—v. cut or divide into sections: *to section an orange.* [< L *sectio, -onis* < *secare* cut]

sec·tion·al (sek′shən əl) *adj.* **1** having to do with a particular section; local. **2** made of sections: *a sectional bookcase.* **—sec′tion·al·ly,** *adv.*

sec·tion·al·ism (sek′shən el iz′əm) *n.* excessive regard for sectional interests; sectional prejudice or hatred.

sec·tion·al·ize (sek′shən əl īz′) *v.* **-ized, -iz·ing. 1** make sectional. **2** divide into sections.

sec·tor (sek′tər) *n.* **1** *Geometry.* the part of a circle between two radii and the included arc. See **circle** for picture. **2** *Military.* a clearly defined area that a given unit protects or covers with fire;

the part of a front held by a unit. **3** an instrument consisting of two rulers connected by a joint. A sector is used in measuring or drawing angles. [< LL < L *sector* cutter < *secare* cut]

sec·u·lar (sek′yə lər) *adj., n.* —*adj.* **1** worldly, not religious or sacred: *secular music, a secular education.* **2** living in the world; not belonging to a religious order: *the secular clergy, a secular priest.* **3** occurring once in an age; lasting for an age or century. **4** lasting through long ages; going on from age to age. —*n.* a secular priest. [< L *saecularis* < *saeculum* age, world] —**sec′u·lar·ly,** *adv.*

sec·u·lar·ism (sek′yə lər iz′əm) *n.* **1** scepticism in regard to religion. **2** opposition to the introduction of religion into public schools or other public affairs.

sec·u·lar·ist (sek′yə lər ist) *n.* a believer in secularism.

sec·u·lar·i·ty (sek′yə lar′ə tē *or* -ler′ə tē) *n.* a secular spirit or quality; worldliness.

sec·u·lar·ize (sek′yə lər īz′) *v.* **-ized, -iz·ing.** **1** make secular or worldly; separate from religious connection or influence: *to secularize the schools.* **2** transfer (property) from the possession of the church to that of the government. —**sec′u·lar·i·za′tion,** *n.* —**sec′u·lar·iz′er,** *n.*

se·cure (si kyūr′) *adj., v.* **-cured, -cur·ing.** —*adj.* **1** safe against loss, attack, escape, etc.: *to keep a prisoner secure within a dungeon. This is a secure hiding place. Land in a growing city is a secure investment.* **2** sure; certain; that can be counted on: *We know in advance that our victory is secure.* **3** free from care or fear: *He hoped for a secure old age.* **4** firmly fastened; not likely to give way: *The boards of this bridge do not look secure.* —*v.* **1** make safe; protect: *Every loan was secured by bonds or mortgages.* **2** make oneself safe; be safe: *We must secure against the dangers of the coming storm.* **3** make (something) sure or certain. **4** make firm or fast: *Secure the locks on the windows.* **5** get; obtain: *Secure your tickets early.* [< L *securus* < *se-* free from + *cura* care. Doublet of SURE.] —**se·cur′a·ble,** *adj.* —**se·cur′er,** *n.* —**se·cure′ly,** *adv.* —**se·cure′ness,** *n.*
☛ *Syn. adj.* **1.** See note at **safe.**

se·cu·ri·ty (si kyūr′ə tē) *n., pl.* **-ties.** **1** freedom from danger, care, or fear; feeling or condition of being safe. **2** certainty. **3** carelessness; overconfidence. **4** something that secures or makes safe: *My watchdog is a security against burglars.* **5 securities,** *pl.* bonds, stocks, etc.: *These railway securities can be sold for $5000.* **6** something given as a guarantee that a person will be able to pay back a loan or fulfil some duty, promise, etc. A life-insurance policy may serve as security for a loan. **7** a person who agrees to be responsible for another.

Security Council in the United Nations, a permanent body whose function is to maintain world peace. It has five permanent members—France, the United Kingdom, the People's Republic of China, the U.S.S.R., and the United States—and ten non-permanent members.

secy. secretary.

se·dan (si dan′) *n.* **1** a closed automobile seating four or more persons. **2** sedan chair. [origin uncertain]

sedan chair an enclosed chair carried on poles by two men.

se·date (si dāt′) *adj.* quiet; calm; serious: *She is a very sedate person and would rather read or sew than play.* [< L *sedatus,* pp. of *sedare* calm] —**se·date′ly,** *adv.* —**se·date′ness,** *n.*

se·da·tion (si dā′shən) *n.* **1** the producing of a relaxed state by means of a sedative; treatment with sedatives. **2** a relaxed or painless state produced or as if produced by a sedative.

sed·a·tive (sed′ə tiv) *n., adj.* —*n.* **1** a medicine that lessens pain or excitement. **2** anything soothing or calming. —*adj.* **1** lessening pain or excitement. **2** soothing; calming.

sed·en·tar·y (sed′ən ter′ē) *adj.* **1** used to sitting still much of the time: *Sedentary people get little physical exercise.* **2** that keeps one sitting still much of the time: *Bookkeeping is a sedentary occupation.* **3** moving little and rarely. **4** fixed to one spot. **5** not migratory. Pigeons are sedentary birds. [< L *sedentarius,* ult. < *sedere* sit] —**sed·en·tar′i·ly,** *adv.* —**sed·en·tar′i·ness,** *n.*

Se·der (sā′dər) *n., pl.* **Se·ders** *or* **Se·dar·im** (sə där′im). the religious rites and feast held in Jewish homes on the first two nights of Passover. [< Hebrew]

sedge (sej) *n.* any of a large family (Cyperaceae) of grasslike plants that grow in marshes, bogs, and shallow water, having solid, often triangular stems, long, narrow leaves, and spikelets of tiny, petal-less flowers; especially any of the genus *Carex.* [OE *secg*]

sedged (sejd) *adj.* **1** made of sedge. **2** abounding or bordered with sedge.

sedg·y (sej′ē) *adj.* **1** abounding in or covered with sedge; bordered with sedge: *a sedgy brook.* **2** like sedge.

sed·i·ment (sed′ə mənt) *n.* **1** any matter that settles to the bottom of a liquid; dregs. **2** *Geology.* earth, stones, etc., deposited

hat, āge, fär; let, ēqual, tėrm; it, īce
hot, ōpen, ôrder; oil, out; cup, pút, rüle,
əbove, takən, pencəl, lemən, circəs

ch, child; ng, long; sh, ship
th, thin; ŦH, then; zh, measure

by water, wind, or ice: *Each year the Nile overflows and deposits sediment on the land.* [< F < L *sedimentum* < *sedere* settle]

sed·i·men·tal (sed′ə men′təl) *adj.* sedimentary.

sed·i·men·ta·ry (sed′ə men′tə rē *or* sed′ə men′trē) *adj.* **1** of or having to do with sediment. **2** *Geology.* designating rock that is made up of sediment, fragments of older rock, or organic materials. Shale is a kind of sedimentary rock.

sed·i·men·ta·tion (sed′ə men tā′shən) *n.* a depositing of sediment.

se·di·tion (si dish′ən) *n.* speech or action causing discontent or rebellion against the government; incitement to discontent or rebellion. [ME < L *seditio, -onis* < *sed-,* var. of *se-* apart + *ire* go]

se·di·tion·ar·y (si dish′ən er′ē) *adj., n., pl.* **-ar·ies.** —*adj.* having to do with or involving sedition. —*n.* one guilty of sedition.

se·di·tious (si dish′əs) *adj.* **1** stirring up discontent or rebellion. **2** taking part in sedition; guilty of sedition. **3** having to do with sedition. —**se·di′tious·ly,** *adv.* —**se·di′tious·ness,** *n.*

se·duce (si dyüs′ *or* si düs′) *v.* **-duced, -duc·ing.** **1** persuade or entice (a person to whom one is not married) to engage in sexual intercourse. **2** lead away from virtue or right action; tempt into wrongdoing. **3** attract or lure. **4** win over; beguile; entice. [< L *seducere* < *se-* aside + *ducere* lead] —**se·duc′er,** *n.*

se·duce·ment (si dyüs′mənt *or* si düs′mənt) *n.* seduction.

se·duc·i·ble (si dyüs′ə bəl *or* si düs′ə bəl) *adj.* that can be seduced.

se·duc·tion (si duk′shən) *n.* **1** the act of seducing; the fact or condition of being seduced. **2** something that seduces; temptation; attraction. [< L *seductio, -onis* < *seducere.* See SEDUCE.]

se·duc·tive (si duk′tiv) *adj.* alluring; captivating; charming. —**se·duc′tive·ly,** *adv.* —**se·duc′tive·ness,** *n.*

se·du·li·ty (si dyü′lə tē *or* si dü′lə tē) *n.* the quality of being sedulous; diligent application or care.

sed·u·lous (sej′ə ləs) *adj.* hard-working; diligent; painstaking. [< L *sedulus* < *se dolo* without deception] —**sed′u·lous·ly,** *adv.* —**sed′u·lous·ness,** *n.*

se·dum (sē′dəm) *n.* any of a genus (*Sedum*) of plants of the same family as the houseleeks, having fleshy leaves and clusters of white, pink, or yellow flowers. Some sedums are cultivated as garden flowers. [< L *sedum* house leek]

see[1] (sē) *v.* **saw, seen, see·ing.** **1** perceive with the eyes; look at: *See that black cloud.* **2** use the eyes to see things: *to see a tennis match.* **3** have the power of sight: *The blind do not see.* **4** perceive with the mind; understand: *I see what you mean.* **5** find out; learn: *I will see what needs to be done.* **6** take care; make sure: *See that you lock the back door.* **7** think; consider: *You may go if you see fit to do so.* **8** have knowledge or experience of: *That coat has seen hard wear.* **9** attend; escort; go with: *to see a girl home.* **10** meet; have a talk with: *He wishes to see you alone.* **11** call on: *I went to see a friend.* **12** receive a visit from: *She is too ill to see anyone.* **13** visit; attend: *We saw the Canadian National Exhibition.* **14** *Poker, etc.* meet (a bet) by staking an equal sum.
see after, take care of.
see into, understand the real character or hidden purpose of.
see off, go with to the starting place of a journey.
see (one's) way, see the possibility of doing something.
see out, go through with; finish.
see through, a understand the real character or hidden purpose of. **b** go through with; finish. **c** watch over or help through a difficulty: *His friends saw him through his financial difficulties.*
see to, look after; take care of.
[OE *sēon*]
☛ *Hom.* sea.
☛ *Syn.* **1. See, perceive, observe** = become aware of something through sight. **See,** the general word, means "be conscious of what is before the eyes," with or without trying: *We saw someone standing in the doorway.* **Perceive,** the formal substitute for **see,** emphasizes using the mind as well as the eyes and consciously noticing or recognizing what is seen: *We perceived the figure to be your mother.* **Observe** suggests directing the attention as well as the eyes to what is seen: *We observed a change in her.*

see[2] (sē) *n.* **1** the position or authority of a bishop. **2** the district under a bishop's authority; diocese; bishopric. [ME < OF *sie* < L *sedes* abode; OF form influenced by forms like *siet* sits < L *sedet*]
☛ *Hom.* sea.

seed (sēd) *n., pl.* **seeds** or **seed;** *adj., v.* —*n.* **1** the thing from which a flower, vegetable, or other plant grows; a small, grainlike fruit. Farmers often save part of a crop for the seeds. **2** a bulb, sprout, or any part of a plant from which a new plant will grow. **3** seeds collectively. **4** the source or beginning of anything: *seeds of trouble.* **5** children; descendants: *The Jews are the seed of Abraham.* **6** semen; sperm. **7** a minute bubble arising in glass during fusion. **go to seed, a** come to the time of yielding seeds: *Dandelions' heads turn white when they go to seed.* **b** come to the end of vigor, usefulness, prosperity, etc.: *After the mines closed, the town went to seed.* —*adj.* of or containing seeds; used for seeds. —*v.* **1** sow with seeds; scatter seeds over: *The farmer seeded his field with corn.* **2** sow (seeds). **3** produce seeds; shed seeds. **4** remove the seeds from: *She seeded the grapes for the salad.* **5** *Sports.* **a** schedule (tournament players or teams) so that the best ones will not meet each other in the early matches. **b** rank (a player) in relation to other contestants: *the top-seeded contestant.* **6** scatter dry ice or other chemicals into clouds from an airplane in an effort to produce rain artificially. [OE *sǣd*] —**seed′less,** *adj.* —**seed′like′,** *adj.*
☛ *Hom.* **cede.**

seed·bed (sēd′bed′) *n.* **1** soil that is specially prepared for nurturing plants from seed. **2** any place conducive to growth and development; breeding ground.

seed capsule seed vessel.

seed·case (sēd′kās′) *n.* any pod, capsule, or other dry, hollow fruit that contains seeds.

seed·er (sē′dər) *n.* **1** one that seeds. **2** a machine or device for planting seeds. **3** a machine or device for removing seeds.

seed leaf the embryo leaf in the seed of a plant; cotyledon.

seed·ling (sēd′ling) *n., adj.* —*n.* **1** a young plant grown from a seed. **2** a young tree less than one metre high. —*adj.* **1** developed or raised from seed. **2** like a small seed; existing in a rudimentary state.

seed pearl a very small pearl.

seed plant any plant that bears seeds. Most seed plants have flowers and produce seeds in fruits; some, such as the pines, form seeds on cones.

seeds·man (sēdz′mən) *n., pl.* **-men. 1** a sower of seed. **2** a dealer in seed.

seed tree a tree providing seed for natural reproduction.

seed vessel any pod, capsule, or other hollow fruit that contains seeds; pericarp.

seed·y (sē′dē) *adj.* **seed·i·er, seed·i·est. 1** full of seed. **2** gone to seed. **3** *Informal.* shabby; no longer fresh or new: *seedy clothes.* —**seed′i·ly,** *adv.* —**seed′i·ness,** *n.*

see·ing (sē′ing) *conj.* in view of the fact; considering: *Seeing that coaxing won't work, we'll have to try something else.*

Seeing Eye an organization that breeds and trains dogs as guides for blind people.

seeing–eye dog a dog trained as a guide for blind people.

seek (sēk) *v.* **sought, seek·ing. 1** try to find; look for: *We are seeking a new home.* **2** hunt; search: *to seek for something lost.* **3** try to get: *Friends sought his advice.* **4** try; attempt: *He seeks to make peace with his enemies.* **5** go to: *Being sleepy, he sought his bed.* [OE *sēcan*] —**seek′er,** *n.*

seem (sēm) *v.* **1** appear; appear to be: *He seemed a very old man.* **2** appear to oneself: *I still seem to hear the music.* **3** appear to exist: *There seems no need to wait longer.* **4** appear to be true or to be the case of: *It seems likely to rain. This, it seems, is your idea of cleaning a room.* [ME < ON *sæma* < *sæmr* seemly]
☛ *Hom.* **seam.**
☛ *Syn.* **1. Seem, appear** = give the impression or have the outward look of being something that (it) may or may not be in fact or reality. Although the two words are often used interchangeably, **seem** particularly suggests showing signs or giving other indications that point to a conclusion and serve as the basis of an opinion arrived at: *He seems to be sick. His efforts seem in vain.* **Appear** particularly suggests the way the thing looks on the surface or is seen or perceived by the observer: *He does appear pale, but to me he appears able to work.*

seem·ing (sē′ming) *adj., n.* —*adj.* apparent; that appears to be: *a seeming advantage.* —*n.* appearance: *It was worse in its seeming than in reality.* —**seem′ing·ly,** *adv.*

seem·ly (sēm′lē) *adj.* **-li·er, -li·est;** *adv.* —*adj.* **1** suitable or proper: *He thought their behavior was not seemly.* **2** having a pleasing appearance. —*adv.* properly; becomingly; fittingly. [ME < ON *sæmiligr*] —**seem′li·ness,** *n.*
☛ *Syn.* See note at **fitting.**

seen (sēn) *v.* pp. of **see¹.**
☛ *Hom.* **scene.**

seep (sēp) *v.* ooze; trickle; leak: *Water seeps through sand.* [apparently < MDu. *sipen;* akin to OE *sipian* to leak]

seep·age (sē′pij) *n.* **1** a seeping; slow leakage. **2** moisture or liquid that seeps: *a centimetre of seepage in the basement.*

seep·er (sē′pər) *n.* a pit for collecting water that seeps into cellars, etc.; sump.

seer (sēr) *n.* a person who foresees or foretells future events; prophet.
☛ *Hom.* **sear, sere.**

seer·ess (sēr′is) *n.* a woman who is a seer.

seer·suck·er (sēr′suk′ər) *n.* a thin cotton, rayon, nylon, etc. fabric, usually with alternate plain and crinkled stripes. [< Hind. < Persian *shir o shakkar,* literally, milk and sugar]

see·saw (sē′so′ *or* -sô′) *n., v.* —*n.* **1** teeter-totter. **2** continuous motion up and down or back and forth: *the seesaw of a pitching ship.* —*v.* **1** teeter-totter. **2** move continuously up and down or back and forth. [varied reduplication of *saw¹*]

seethe (sēṪH) *v.* **seethed, seeth·ing. 1** bubble and foam: *Water seethed under the falls.* **2** be excited; be disturbed. **3** soak; steep. **4** *Archaic.* boil. [OE *sēothan* boil]
☛ *Syn.* **1.** See note at **boil.**

see–through (sē′thrü′) *adj.* especially of fabric or a garment, sheer or transparent: *a see-through blouse.*

seg·ment (seg′mənt) *n., v.* —*n.* **1** a part cut, marked, or broken off; division; section: *Some oranges are easily pulled apart into segments.* **2** *Geometry.* **a** a part of a circle, sphere, etc. cut off by a line or plane: *A segment of a circle is an area that is bounded or cut off by a chord.* See **circle** for picture. **b** any of the finite sections of a divided line. **3** *Biology.* one of a series of parts having a more or less similar structure: *a segment of a tapeworm.* —*v.* divide into segments. [< L *segmentum* < *secare* cut]

seg·men·tal (seg men′təl) *adj.* **1** composed of segments. **2** of or having to do with segments. **3** having the form of a segment of a circle. —**seg·men′tal·ly,** *adv.*

seg·men·tar·y (seg′mən ter′ē) *adj.* segmental.

seg·men·ta·tion (seg′mən tā′shən) *n.* **1** a division into segments. **2** *Biology.* the growth and division of a cell into two, four, eight cells, and so on.

seg·re·gate (*v.* seg′rə gāt′; *adj.* seg′rə git *or* seg′rə- gāt′) *v.* **-gat·ed, -gat·ing;** *adj.* —*v.* **1** separate from others; set apart; isolate: *The doctor segregated the child with mumps to protect the other patients.* **2** separate from the rest and collect in one place. **3** separate or keep apart one racial group from another or from the rest of society especially in schools, separate public facilities, etc. —*adj.* segregated. [< L *segregare* < *se-* apart from + *grex, gregis* herd]

seg·re·ga·tion (seg′rə gā′shən) *n.* **1** a separation from others; setting apart; isolation. **2** the separation of one radical group from another or from the rest of society, especially in schools, theatres, etc. **3** a thing separated or set apart; isolated part, group, etc.

seg·re·ga·tion·ist (seg′rə gā′shən ist) *n.* a person who believes in the keeping apart of one race from another in housing, schools, etc.

seg·re·ga·tive (seg′rə gā′tiv) *adj.* **1** tending to segregate. **2** keeping apart from others; unsociable.

Seid·litz powder (sed′lits) a laxative consisting of two powders, one tartaric acid and the other a mixture of sodium bicarbonate and Rochelle salt. These are dissolved separately, and the solutions are mixed and drunk while effervescing. [after *Seidlitz,* a village in Czechoslovakia]

seif (sīf) *n.* a long, crescent-shaped dune stretching in the direction of the wind that caused it. [< Arabic *saif* sword, from its shape]

sei·gneur or **seign·ior** (sēn yèr′; *French,* se nyœr′) *n. Historical.* **1** *Cdn.* in French Canada, a person granted a seigneury; landowner. **2** a feudal lord or landowner. A **grand seigneur** was a person of high rank. [< F *seigneur* < OF *seignor* < *accus.* of L *senior.* See SENIOR. Doublet of SIEUR.]

sei·gneu·ri·al (sēn yèr′ē əl) *adj.* of or having to do with a seigneur.

sei·gneur·y or **seign·ior·y** (sēn′yər ē; *French,* se nyœ rē′) *n., pl.* **-ior·ies.** *Historical.* **1** *Cdn.* in French Canada, a tract of land or an estate originally granted to an individual by the King of France. **2** power or authority of a seigneur. **3** a feudal lord's domain. **4** a group of lords. [ME < OF *seignorie* < *seignor.* See SEIGNEUR.]

seign·ior·age (sēn′yər ij) *n.* **1** *Historical.* something claimed by a sovereign or superior as a prerogative. **2** a charge for coining gold or silver.

sei·gnio·ri·al (sēn yôr′ē əl) *adj.* seigneurial.

seine (sān) *n., v.* **seined, sein·ing.** —*n.* a fishing net that hangs straight down in the water. A seine has floats at the upper edge and sinkers at the lower. —*v.* fish or catch with a seine: *to seine for herring.* [OE *segne* < L *sagena* < Gk. *sagēnē*]
☛ *Hom.* **sane.**

sein·er (sā′nər) *n.* **1** a fishing boat equipped with a seine. **2** a person who fishes with a seine.

seishe (sāsh) *n.* an occasional rhythmic rising and falling of the level of water in a lake, lasting briefly and usually attributed to local changes in atmospheric pressure. [< Swiss French]

seism (sī′zəm) *n.* earthquake.

seis·mic (sīz′mik *or* sīs′mik) *adj.* **1** of or having to do with shocks or tremors in the earth caused by earthquakes, explosions, etc.: *seismic waves.* **2** of or having to do with earthquakes: *seismic safety.* **3** having to do with or involved in the study of earth shocks or tremors: *seismic crews, a seismic survey.* [< Gk. *seismos* earthquake < *seiein* shake]

seismo– *combining form.* earthquake, as in *seismograph.* [< Gk. *seismos*]

seis·mo·gram (sīz′mə gram′ *or* sīs′mə-) *n.* a record of an earthquake obtained by a seismograph.

seis·mo·graph (sīz′mə graf′ *or* sīs′mə-) *n.* an instrument for recording the direction, intensity, and duration of earthquakes.

seis·mo·graph·ic (sīz′mə graf′ik *or* sīs′mə-) *adj.* **1** of a seismograph. **2** of seismography.

seis·mog·ra·phy (sīz mog′rə fē *or* sīs-) *n.* **1** the art of using the seismograph in recording earthquakes. **2** the branch of seismology dealing especially with the mapping and description of earthquakes.

seis·mo·log·i·cal (sīz′mə loj′ə kəl *or* sīs′mə-) *adj.* of or having to do with seismology.

seis·mol·o·gist (sīz mol′ə jist *or* sīs-) *n.* a person who is trained in seismology, especially one whose work it is.

seis·mol·o·gy (sīz mol′ə jē *or* sīs-) *n.* the study of earthquakes and other movements of the earth's crust.

seis·mom·e·ter (sīz mom′ə tər *or* sīs-) *n.* seismograph.

sei whale (sā *or* sī) a small, grey or bluish rorqual (*Balaenoptera borealis*) found in most oceans.

seize (sēz) *v.* **seized, seiz·ing.** **1** take hold of suddenly; clutch; grasp: *When she lost her balance, she seized his arm.* **2** grasp with the mind: *to seize an idea, the point, etc.* **3** take possession of by force: *The soldiers seized the city.* **4** take possession of or come upon suddenly: *A fever seized him.* **5** take possession of by legal authority. **6** *Law.* put in possession of; possess. **7** bind; lash; make fast: *to seize one rope to another.* **8** of a moving part of an engine or other mechanism, get stuck or jammed (*often used with* **up**): *The valve has seized up.*
seize on *or* **upon,** **a** take hold of suddenly. **b** take possession of. [ME < OF *seisir*, ult. < Gmc.]
☛ *Syn.* **1. Seize, grasp, clutch** = take hold of something. **Seize** emphasizes taking hold suddenly and with force: *The dog seized the sausages.* **Grasp** emphasizes seizing and holding firmly with the fingers, claws, or talons closed around the object: *The eagle grasped the rat.* **Clutch** suggests grasping eagerly, sometimes greedily, and tightly as in a clenched fist: *The child clutched his toy.*

seiz·ing (sē′zing) *n.* **1** a binding, lashing, or fastening together with several turns of small rope, cord, etc. **2** a fastening made in this way. **3** a small rope, cord, etc. used for making such fastenings.

sei·zure (sē′zhər) *n.* **1** the act of seizing. **2** the condition of being seized. **3** a short period of unconsciousness which occurs suddenly and is accompanied by a general, more-or-less violent, contraction of the muscles. **4** any sudden onset of disease: *heart seizure.*

se·lah (sē′lə) *n.* a Hebrew word occurring frequently in the Psalms and Habakkuk in the Bible, the meaning of which is unknown, but is thought to be a direction to musicians.

sel·dom (sel′dəm) *adv.* rarely; not often: *He is seldom ill.* [OE *seldum*]

se·lect (si lekt′) *v., adj.* —*v.* choose; pick out: *Select the book you want.*
—*adj.* **1** picked as best; chosen specially: *A few select officials were admitted to the conference.* **2** choice; superior: *That store carries a very select line of merchandise.* **3** careful in choosing; particular as to friends, company, etc.: *She belongs to a very select club.* [< L *selectus*, pp. of *seligere* < *se-* apart + *legere* choose] —**se·lect′ly,** *adv.* —**se·lect′ness,** *n.*

se·lec·tion (si lek′shən) *n.* **1** the act or process of selecting or the state of being selected: *the selection of a hat.* **2** one or more persons or things that have been selected: *My dessert selection was an apple strudel.* **3** a range of things from which one may select: *The shop offered a very good selection of children's books.* **4** the natural or artificial process by which certain animals or plants survive and are perpetuated while others are not.

se·lec·tive (si lek′tiv) *adj.* **1** selecting; having the power to

---

hat, āge, fär; let, ēqual, tèrm; it, īce
hot, ōpen, ôrder; oil, out; cup, pùt, rüle,
əbove, takən, pencəl, lemən, circəs

ch, child; ng, long; sh, ship
th, thin; ŦH, then; zh, measure

---

select. **2** having to do with selection. **3** responding to oscillations of a certain frequency only. When a selective radio is tuned to one station, those on other wave lengths are excluded.

se·lec·tiv·i·ty (si lek tiv′ə tē) *n.* **1** the quality of being selective. **2** the property of a circuit, instrument, etc. by virtue of which it responds to electric oscillations of a particular frequency; especially, the ability of a radio receiving set to receive certain frequencies or waves to the exclusion of others.

se·lec·tor (si lek′tər) *n.* **1** a person who selects. **2** a mechanical or electrical device that selects.

Se·le·ne (sə lē′nē) *n. Greek mythology.* the goddess of the moon.

sel·e·nite (sel′ə nīt′ *or* sə lē′nīt) *n.* a variety of gypsum, found in transparent crystals and foliated masses. [< L < Gk. *selenitēs* (*lithos*) (stone) of the moon < *selēnē* moon; its brightness was supposed to vary with the moon]

se·le·ni·um (sə lē′nē əm) *n.* a non-metallic chemical element resembling sulphur in chemical properties. Because its electrical resistance varies with the amount of light, selenium is used in photo-electric cells. *Symbol:* Se; *at.no.* 34; *at.wt.* 78.96. [< NL < Gk. *selēnē* moon]

self (self) *n., pl.* **selves;** *adj., pron., pl.* **selves.** —*n.* **1** one's own person: *his very self.* **2** one's own welfare, interests, etc.: *A selfish person puts self first.* **3** the nature, character, etc. of a person or thing: *She does not seem like her former self.*
—*adj.* being the same throughout; all of one kind, quality, color, material, etc.
—*pron. Informal.* myself; himself; herself; yourself: *a cheque made payable to self.* [OE]
☛ *Usage.* **Self** as a suffix forms the reflexive and intensive pronouns: **myself, yourself, himself, herself, itself, oneself, ourselves, yourselves, themselves.** These are used as reflexive objects (*I couldn't help myself*) or for emphasis (*I can do that myself*).
☛ *Usage.* The pronominal use of *self* (*payable to self, a room for self and wife*) is widely regarded as non-standard.

self– *prefix.* **1** of or over oneself, etc., as in *self-conscious, self-control.* **2** by or in oneself, etc., as in *self-inflicted, self-evident.* **3** to or for oneself, etc., as in *self-addressed, self-respect.* **4** automatic; automatically, as in *self-starter, self-closing.* [< *self*]

self-a·base·ment (self′ə bās′mənt) *n.* abasement of self.

self-ab·hor·rence (self′ab hôr′əns) *n.* abhorrence of self.

self-ab·ne·ga·tion (self′ab′nə gā′shən) *n.* self-denial.

self-ab·sorp·tion (self′ab sôrp′shən *or* -ab zôrp′shən) *n.* absorption in one's own thoughts, affairs, etc.

self-act·ing (self′ak′ting) *adj.* working of itself: *a self-acting machine.*

self-ad·dressed (self′ə drest′) *adj.* addressed to oneself: *a self-addressed envelope.*

self-as·ser·tion (self′ə sèr′shən) *n.* an insistence on one's own wishes, opinions, claims, etc.

self-as·ser·tive (self′ə sèr′tiv) *adj.* putting oneself forward; insisting on one's own wishes, opinions, etc. —**self′-as·ser′tive·ly,** *adv.*

self-as·sur·ance (self′ə shür′əns) *n.* self-confidence.

self-as·sured (self′ə shürd′) *adj.* self-confident; sure of oneself.

self-cen·tred (self′sen′tərd) *adj.* **1** occupied with one's own interests and affairs. **2** selfish. **3** being a fixed point around which other things move.

self-col·ored *or* **self-col·oured** (self′kul′ərd) *adj.* **1** of one uniform color. **2** of the natural color.

self-com·mand (self′kə mand′) *n.* control of oneself.

self-com·mun·ion (self′kə myün′yən) *n.* communion with oneself.

self-com·pla·cence (self′kəm plā′səns) *n.* self-complacency.

self-com·pla·cen·cy (self′kəm plā′sən sē) *n.* the state or quality of being self-satisfied.

self-com·pla·cent (self′kəm plā′sənt) *adj.* pleased with oneself; self-satisfied. —**self′-com·pla′cent·ly,** *adv.*

self-con·ceit (self′kən sēt′) *n.* conceit; too much pride in oneself or one's ability.

self-con·cept (self′kon′sept) *n.* one's conception of one's own basic character and nature.

self–con·fi·dence (self′kon′fə dəns) *n.* belief in one's own ability, power, judgment, etc.; confidence in oneself.

self–con·fi·dent (self′kon′fə dənt) *adj.* believing in one's own ability, power, judgment, etc. —**self′-con′fi·dent·ly,** *adv.*

self–con·scious (self′kon′shəs) *adj.* conscious of how one is appearing to others; embarrassed, especially by the presence of other people and their attitude toward one; shy. —**self′-con′scious·ly,** *adv.* —**self′-con′scious·ness,** *n.*

self–con·se·quence (self′kon′sə kwens′ or -kon′sə kwəns) *n.* a sense of one's own importance.

self–con·sist·ent (self′kən sis′tənt) *adj.* consistent with oneself or itself; having its parts or elements in agreement. —**self′-con·sist′ent·ly,** *adv.*

self–con·tained (self′kən tānd′) *adj.* 1 saying little; reserved. 2 containing in oneself or itself all that is necessary; independent of what is external. 3 having all its working parts contained in one case, cover, or framework: *A watch is self-contained.* 4 of an apartment, etc., having all facilities (bathroom, kitchen, etc.) within itself, and having a private entrance.

self–con·tra·dic·tion (self′kon′trə dik′shən) *n.* 1 a contradiction of oneself or itself. 2 a statement containing elements that are contradictory.

self–con·tra·dic·to·ry (self′kon′trə dik′tə rē) *adj.* contradicting oneself or itself. —**self′-con′tra·dic′to·ri·ly,** *adv.*

self–con·trol (self′kən trōl′) *n.* control of one's own actions, feelings, etc.

self–crit·i·cism (self′krit′ə siz′əm) *n.* criticism of oneself.

self–de·cep·tion (self′di sep′shən) *n.* the act or an instance of deceiving oneself as to one's true motives, feelings, etc.

self–de·cep·tive (self′di sep′tiv) *adj.* deceiving oneself. —**self′-de·cep′tive·ly,** *adv.*

self–de·fence (self′di fens′) *n.* defence of one's own person, property, reputation, etc. Also, **self-defense.**

self–de·ni·al (self′di nī′əl) *n.* a sacrifice of one's own desires and interests; going without things one wants.

self–de·ny·ing (self′di nī′ing) *adj.* unselfish; sacrificing one's own wishes and interests.

self–de·struct (self′di strukt′) *v. Informal.* of a mechanism, machine, etc., automatically destroy itself: *The tape-recorder will self-destruct if it is tampered with.*

self–de·ter·mi·na·tion (self′di tėr′mə nā′shən) *n.* 1 direction from within only, without influence or force from without. 2 the deciding by the people of a nation what form of government they are to have, without reference to the wishes of any other nation.

self–de·ter·min·ing (self′di tėr′mən ing) *adj.* determining one's own acts; having the power of self-determination.

self–de·vo·tion (self′di vō′shən) *n.* self-sacrifice.

self–dis·ci·pline (self′dis′ə plin) *n.* careful control and training of oneself.

self–dis·cov·er·y (self′dis kuv′ə rē) *n.* the act or process of discovering one's own real nature, character, etc.; the achievement of self-knowledge.

self–ed·u·cat·ed (self′ej′ə kā′tid) *adj.* self-taught; educated by one's own efforts.

self–ef·face·ment (self′ə fās′mənt) *n.* the act or habit of modestly keeping oneself in the background.

self–em·ployed (self′em ploid′) *adj.* not employed by others; working for oneself: *Doctors, lawyers, and farmers are usually self-employed.*

self–es·teem (self′əs tēm′) *n.* 1 thinking well of oneself; self-respect. 2 thinking too well of oneself; conceit.

self–ev·i·dent (self′ev′ə dənt) *adj.* evident by itself; needing no proof. —**self′-ev′i·dent·ly,** *adv.*

self–ex·am·i·na·tion (self′eg zam′ə nā′shən) *n.* examination into one's own state, conduct, motives, etc.

self–ex·ist·ent (self′eg zis′tənt) *adj.* 1 existing independently of any other cause. 2 having an independent existence.

self–ex·plan·a·to·ry (self′eks plan′ə tôr′ē) *adj.* explaining itself; that needs no explanation; obvious.

self–ex·pres·sion (self′eks presh′ən) *n.* an expression of one's personality.

self–fill·ing (self′fil′ing) *adj.* that can fill itself.

self–gov·erned (self′guv′ərnd) *adj.* having self-government.

self–gov·ern·ing (self′guv′ər ning) *adj.* that governs itself.

self–gov·ern·ment (self′guv′ərn mənt or -guv′ər mənt) *n.* 1 government of a group by its own members: *self-government through elected representatives.* 2 self-control.

self–heal (self′hēl′) *n.* a low-growing European herb (*Prunella vulgaris*) of the mint family having blue or purple flowers, formerly believed to possess healing powers.

self–help (self′help′) *n.* a helping oneself; getting along without assistance from others.

self–im·age (self′im′əj) *n.* one's opinion or general view of oneself.

self–im·por·tance (self′im pôr′təns) *n.* a having or showing too high an opinion of one's own importance; conceit; behavior showing conceit.

self–im·por·tant (self′im pôr′tənt) *adj.* having or showing too high an opinion of one's own importance. —**self′-im·por′tant·ly,** *adv.*

self–im·posed (self′im pōzd′) *adj.* imposed on oneself by oneself.

self–im·prove·ment (self′im prüv′mənt) *n.* an improvement of one's character, mind, etc. by one's own efforts.

self–in·duced (self′in dyüst′ or -in düst′) *adj.* 1 induced by itself; induced by oneself. 2 produced by self-induction.

self–in·duc·tion (self′in duk′shən) *n. Electricity.* the inducing of a current in a circuit by a varying current in that circuit.

self–in·dul·gence (self′in dul′jəns) *n.* a gratification of one's own desires, passions, etc. with too little regard for the welfare of others.

self–in·dul·gent (self′in dul′jənt) *adj.* characterized by self-indulgence. —**self′-in·dul′gent·ly,** *adv.*

self–in·flict·ed (self′in flik′tid) *adj.* inflicted on oneself by oneself.

self–in·ter·est (self′in′trist or -in′tər ist) *n.* 1 an interest in one's own welfare with too little care for the welfare of others; selfishness. 2 personal advantage.

self·ish (sel′fish) *adj.* 1 caring too much for oneself; caring too little for others. A selfish person puts his own interests first. 2 showing care solely or chiefly for oneself: *selfish motives.* —**self′ish·ly,** *adv.* —**self′ish·ness,** *n.*

self–knowl·edge (self′nol′ij) *n.* knowledge of one's own character, ability, etc.

self·less (self′lis) *adj.* having no regard or thought for self; unselfish. —**self′less·ly,** *adv.* —**self′less·ness,** *n.*

self–love (self′luv′) *n.* 1 love of oneself; selfishness. 2 conceit.

self–made (self′mād′) *adj.* 1 made by oneself. 2 successful through one's own efforts: *A self-made man is one who has succeeded in business, etc., without the usual formal training or education.*

self–mov·ing (self′mü′ving) *adj.* that can move by itself.

self–or·dained (self′ôr dānd′) *adj.* ordained by oneself.

self–per·pet·u·at·ing (self′pər pech′ü ā′ting) *adj.* that can be continued or renewed indefinitely without outside action or influence: *a self-perpetuating oligarchy.*

self–pit·y (self′pit′ē) *n.* pity for oneself.

self–pol·li·na·tion (self′pol′ə nā′shən) *n.* the transfer of pollen from a stamen to a pistil of the same flower.

self–pos·sessed (self′pə zest′) *adj.* having or showing control of one's feelings and acts; not excited, embarrassed, or confused; calm.

self–pos·ses·sion (self′pə zesh′ən) *n.* the control of one's feelings and actions; composure; calmness.

self–praise (self′prāz′) *n.* praise of oneself.

self–pres·er·va·tion (self′prez′ər vā′shən) *n.* the preservation of oneself from harm or destruction.

self–pro·pelled (self′prə peld′) *adj.* propelled by an engine, motor, etc., within itself: *a self-propelled missile.*

self–re·cord·ing (self′ri kôr′ding) *adj.* that makes a record of its own operations; recording automatically.

self–reg·is·ter·ing (self′rej′is tər ing) *adj.* registering automatically.

self–reg·u·lat·ing (self′reg′yə lāt′ing) *adj.* regulating oneself or itself.

self–re·li·ance (self′ri lī′əns) *n.* a reliance on one's own acts, abilities, etc.

self–re·li·ant (self′ri lī′ənt) *adj.* having or showing self-reliance. —**self′-re·li′ant·ly,** *adv.*

self–re·proach (self′ri prōch′) *n.* blame by one's own conscience.

self–re·spect (self′ri spekt′) *n.* respect for oneself; proper pride.

self·re·spect·ing (self′ri spek′ting) *adj.* having self-respect; properly proud.

self·re·straint (self′ri stränt′) *n.* self-control.

self·right·eous (self′rī′chəs) *adj.* thinking that one is more moral than others; thinking that one is very good and pleasing to God. —**self′-right′eous·ly,** *adv.* —**self′-right′eous·ness,** *n.*

self·sac·ri·fice (self′sak′rə fīs′) *n.* the sacrifice of one's own interests and desires, for one's duty, another's welfare, etc.

self·sac·ri·fic·ing (self′sak′rə fīs′ing) *adj.* unselfish; giving up things for someone else.

self·same (self′sām′) *adj.* the very same: *We study the selfsame books that you do.* [< *self,* adj. + *same*]

self·sat·is·fac·tion (self′sat′is fak′shən) *n.* satisfaction with oneself; complacence.

self·sat·is·fied (self′sat′is fīd′) *adj.* pleased with oneself; complacent.

self·seek·er (self′sē′kər) *n.* a person who seeks his own interests too much.

self·seek·ing (self′sē′king) *adj., n.* —*adj.* selfish. —*n.* selfishness.

self·serv·ice (self′sėr′vis) *n.* the serving of oneself in a restaurant, store, etc.

self·start·er (self′stär′tər) *n.* **1** an electric motor or other device used to start an engine automatically. **2** *Informal.* a person who has initiative: *Wanted: a proven self-starter for unusual sales opportunities.*

self·styled (self′stīld′) *adj.* called by oneself: *a self-styled leader whom no one follows.*

self·suf·fi·cien·cy (self′sə fish′ən sē) *n.* **1** the ability to supply one's own needs. **2** *Archaic.* conceit; self-assurance.

self·suf·fi·cient (self′sə fish′ənt) *adj.* **1** asking and needing no help; independent. **2** *Archaic.* having too much confidence in one's own resources, powers, etc.; conceited. —**self′-suf·fi′cient·ly,** *adv.*

self·suf·fic·ing (self′sə fīs′ing) *adj.* sufficing in or for oneself or itself; self-sufficient.

self·sup·port (self′sə pôrt′) *n.* unaided support of oneself.

self·sup·port·ing (self′sə pôr′ting) *adj.* earning one's expenses; getting along without help.

self·sus·tain·ing (self′sə stā′ning) *adj.* self-supporting.

self·taught (self′tot′ *or* -tôt′) *adj.* taught by oneself without aid from others.

self·will (self′wil′) *n.* insistence on having one's own way.

self·willed (self′wild′) *adj.* insisting on having one's own way; objecting to doing what others ask or command.

self·wind·ing (self′wīn′ding) *adj.* that is wound automatically.

sell (sel) *v.* **sold, sell·ing;** *n.* —*v.* **1** exchange for money or other payment: *sell a house.* **2** deal in; keep for sale: *The butcher sells meat.* **3** be on sale; be sold: *This model sells for $95.* **4** give up; betray: *The traitor sold his country for money.* **5** be or cause to be accepted, approved, or adopted: *to sell an idea to the public. That book will never sell.* **6** *Slang.* cheat; trick; hoax.
sell off, dispose of by sale.
sell on, a inspire with the desire to buy or possess something: *He has sold me on a convertible as opposed to a sedan.* **b** *Informal.* show or convince of the value, truth, etc. of something: *For a time she was sold on folk music.*
sell out, a sell all that one has of; get rid of by selling. **b** *Informal.* betray, especially by a secret bargain.
—*n. Slang.* a cheat; trick; hoax. [OE *sellan*]
☛ *Hom.* **cell.**

sell·er (sel′ər) *n.* **1** a person who sells. **2** a thing considered with reference to its sale: *This book is a best seller.*
☛ *Hom.* **cellar.**

seller's market an economic situation in which the seller has the advantage because goods are scarce and prices tend to be high. Compare **buyer's market.**

sell·out (sel′out′) *n.* **1** *Informal.* a selling out. **2** *Informal.* a performance of a play, sports event, etc. for which all seats are sold.

selt·zer (selt′sər) *n.* **1** a bubbling mineral water containing salt, sodium, calcium, and magnesium carbonates. **2** an artificial water of similar composition. [< G *Selterser* < *Selters,* Germany, where it is found]

sel·vage *or* **sel·vedge** (sel′vij) *n.* the edge of a fabric finished off to prevent ravelling; border; edge. [< *self* + *edge*; because it serves itself as an edge]

selves (selvz) *n.* pl. of **self:** *He had two selves—a friendly self and a shy self.*

Sem. 1 Seminary. **2** Semitic.

hat, āge, fär; let, ēqual, tėrm; it, īce
hot, ōpen, ôrder; oil, out; cup, pút, rüle,
əbove, takən, pencəl, lemən, circəs

ch, child; ng, long; sh, ship
th, thin; ᴛʜ, then; zh, measure

se·man·tic (sə man′tik) *adj.* **1** having to do with meaning. **2** having to do with semantics.

se·man·ti·cist (sə man′tə sist′) *n.* a person trained in semantics.

se·man·tics (sə man′tiks) *n.* the scientific study of the meanings, and the development of meanings, of words. [< LL *semanticus* < Gk. *sēmantikos* having meaning, ult. < *sēma* sign]

sem·a·phore (sem′ə fôr′) *n., v.* **-phored, -phor·ing.** —*n.* **1** an apparatus for signalling; upright post or structure with movable arms, an arrangement of lanterns, flags, etc. used in railway signalling. **2** a system of signals for sending messages by using different positions of the arms or flags, or by using other mechanical devices: *Many Boy Scouts learn semaphore.* —*v.* signal by semaphore. [< Gk. *sēma* signal + *-phoros* carrying]

sem·blance (sem′bləns) *n.* **1** the outward appearance: *His story had the semblance of truth, but was really false.* **2** likeness: *These clouds have the semblance of a huge head.* [ME < OF *semblance* < *sembler* seem, ult. < L *similis* similar]

se·men (sē′mən) *n.* the thick, whitish fluid produced by the reproductive organs of male animals and containing the male reproductive cells, or sperm. [< L *semen* seed]
☛ *Hom.* **seaman.**

se·mes·ter (sə mes′tər) *n.* a half of a school year. [< G < L *semestris* semi-annual, ult. < *sex* six + *mensis* month]

semi- *prefix.* **1** half: *semicircle = half circle.* **2** partly; incompletely: *semicivilized = partly civilized.* **3** twice. Semi——ly means in each half of a —, or twice in a —: *semi-annually = every half year, or twice a year.* [< L]
☛ *Usage.* **Semi-** usually is hyphenated before root words beginning with a vowel and before proper nouns and proper adjectives: *semi-annual, semi-invalid, semi-Christian.* In other cases a hyphen is optional, though one's own usage should be consistent.
☛ *Pronun.* See note at **anti-.**

sem·i·an·nu·al (sem′ē an′yü əl) *adj.* **1** occurring every half year. **2** lasting a half year.

sem·i·an·nu·al·ly (sem′ē an′yü əl ē) *adv.* twice a year.

sem·i·ar·id (sem′ē ar′id *or* -er′id) *adj.* having very little rainfall.

sem·i·breve (sem′ē brēv′) *n. Music.* the longest note in common use; a whole note.

sem·i·cir·cle (sem′ē sėr′kəl) *n.* half a circle: *We sat in a semicircle around the fire.*

sem·i·cir·cu·lar (sem′ē sėr′kyə lər) *adj.* having the form of half a circle.

semicircular canal any of three curved, tubelike canals in the inner part of the ear that help us keep our balance. See **ear** for picture.

sem·i·civ·i·lized (sem′ē siv′ə līzd′) *adj.* partly civilized.

sem·i·co·lon (sem′ē kō′lən) *n.* a mark of punctuation (;) that shows a separation less marked than that shown by a period.

sem·i·con·duct·or (sem′ē kən duk′tər) *n.* any of a group of solids, such as silicon and germanium, that are poor conductors at low temperatures, but good conductors at high temperatures.

sem·i·con·scious (sem′ē kon′shəs) *adj.* half-conscious; not fully conscious. —**sem′i·con′scious·ly,** *adj.* —**sem′i·con′scious·ness,** *n.*

sem·i·dai·ly (sem′ē dā′lē) *adv.* twice a day.

sem·i·dark·ness (sem′ē därk′nəs) *n.* partial darkness.

sem·i·de·tached (sem′ē di tacht′) *adj.* partly detached, used especially of either of two houses joined by a common wall but separated from other buildings.

sem·i·de·vel·oped (sem′ē di vel′əpt) *adj.* not fully developed.

sem·i·di·vine (sem′ē də vīn′) *adj.* partly divine.

sem·i·fi·nal *or* **sem·i·fi·nal** (sem′ē fī′nal) *n., adj.* —*n.* one of the two rounds, matches, etc. that settles who will play in the final one, which follows. —*adj.* designating or having to do with such a round, match, game, etc.: *a semifinal score.*

sem·i·flu·id (sem′ē flü′id) *adj., n.* —*adj.* imperfectly fluid; extremely viscous. —*n.* a substance neither solid nor liquid; one that flows but is very thick: *A soft-boiled egg is a semifluid.*

sem·i·for·mal (sem′ē fôr′məl) *adj., n.* —*adj.* designed for or

designating a somewhat formal social occasion: *a semiformal gown, a semiformal dinner party.* —*n.* a semiformal gown.

sem·i·liquid (sem′ē lik′wid) *adj. or n.* semifluid.

sem·i·lu·nar (sem′ē lü′nər) *adj.* shaped like a half moon.

sem·i·month·ly (sem′ē munth′lē) *adj., adv., n., pl.* **-lies.** —*adj.* occurring or appearing twice a month.
—*adv.* twice a month.
—*n.* something that occurs or appears twice a month; a magazine or paper published twice a month.

sem·i·nal (sem′ə nəl) *adj.* **1** of or having to do with semen or seed. **2** contaning semen or seed. **3** having to do with reproduction. **4** like seed; having the possibility of future development: *seminal ideas.* [ME < L *seminalis* < *semen* seed]

sem·i·nar (sem′ə när′) *n.* **1** a group of college or university students doing research under direction. **2** a course of study or work for such a group. **3** a meeting of such a group. **4** a specialized conference or short, intensive course of study. [< G < L *seminarium* plant nursery, hotbed < *semen* seed. Doublet of SEMINARY.]

sem·i·nar·i·an (sem′ə ner′ē ən) *n.* a student at a seminary.

sem·i·nar·y (sem′ə ner′ē) *n., pl.* **-nar·ies. 1** a school, especially one beyond high school. **2** an academy or boarding school, especially one for young women. **3** a school or college for training students to be priests, ministers, etc. **4** a place for instruction, training, or development. [< L *seminarium.* Doublet of SEMINAR.]

sem·i·na·tion (sem′ə nā′shən) *n.* sowing; propagation; dissemination.

sem·i·nif·er·ous (sem′ə nif′ər əs) *adj.* **1** bearing or producing seed. **2** conveying or containing semen.

sem·i·of·fi·cial (sem′ē ə fish′əl *or* -ō fish′əl) *adj.* partly official; having some degree of authority.

sem·i·per·me·a·ble (sem′ē pėr′mē ə bəl) *adj.* partly permeable; able to be penetrated or passed through by some substances but not by others.

sem·i·pre·cious (sem′ē presh′əs) *adj.* of gemstones, having less commercial value than precious stones. Amethysts and garnets are semiprecious stones; diamonds and rubies are precious stones.

sem·i·pri·vate (sem′ē prī′vət) *adj.* of a hospital room, designed to accommodate from two to four patients.

sem·i·qua·ver (sem′ē kwā′vər) *n. Music.* a sixteenth note.

Se·mir·a·mis (sə mir′ə mis) *n.* an Assyrian princess who lived about 800 B.C. According to legend, she was famous for her beauty and wisdom, and was said to have founded Babylon.

sem·i·skilled (sem′ē skild′) *adj.* partly skilled.

sem·i·sol·id (sem′ē sol′id) *adj., n.* —*adj.* partly solid. —*n.* a partly solid substance.

Sem·ite (sem′īt *or* sē′mīt) *n.* **1** a member of any people speaking a Semitic language as their native tongue: *Jews and Arabs are Semites.* **2** a descendant of Shem.

Se·mit·ic (sə mit′ik) *adj., n.* —*adj.* of or having to do with the Semites or their languages. —*n.* a group of languages including Hebrew, Arabic, Aramaic, Phoenician, and Assyrian.

Sem·i·tism (sem′ə tiz′əm *or* sē′mə tiz′əm) *n.* **1** Semitic character, especially the ways, ideas, influence, etc. of the Jews. **2** a Semitic word or idiom.

sem·i·tone (sem′ē tōn′) *n. Music.* the smallest interval of the modern scale; a half tone; half step.

sem·i·trail·er (sem′ē trāl′ər) *n.* a large trailer used for carrying freight, having wheels at the back but supported in front by the truck tractor to which it is hitched.

sem·i·trop·i·cal (sem′ē trop′ə kəl) *adj.* halfway between tropical and temperate: *Mexico is a semitropical country.*

sem·i·vow·el (sem′ē vou′əl) *n.* **1** *Phonetics.* a gliding sound that is pronounced like a vowel but cannot by itself form a syllable. **2** a letter or character representing such a sound. *W* and *y* are semivowels in *win* and *yet.*

sem·i·week·ly (sem′ē wēk′lē) *adj., adv., n., pl.* **-lies.** —*adj.* occurring or appearing twice a week.
—*adv.* twice a week.
—*n.* something that occurs or appears twice a week; a magazine or paper published twice a week.

sem·i·year·ly (sem′ē yēr′lē) *adj., adv., n., pl.* **-lies.** —*adj.* occurring or appearing twice a year.
—*adv.* twice a year.
—*n.* something that occurs or appears twice a year.

sem·o·li·na (sem′ə lē′nə) *n.* the coarsely ground hard parts of wheat remaining after the fine flour has been sifted through, used in

making puddings, macaroni, etc. [< Ital. *semolino,* ult. < L *simila* fine flour]

sem·pi·ter·nal (sem′pi tėr′nəl) *adj.* everlasting; eternal. [ME < LL *sempiternalis,* ult. < L *semper* forever]

semp·stress (sem′stris *or* semp′stris) *n.* seamstress.

sen (sen) *n., pl.* **sen. 1** a unit of money in Indonesia, equal to ¹/₁₀₀ of a rupiah. **2** a unit of money in Malaysia, equal to ¹/₁₀₀ of a ringgit. **3** a coin worth one sen. [< Japanese]

Sen. 1 Senate; Senator. **2** Senior.

sen·ate (sen′it) *n.* **1** a governing or lawmaking assembly: *the senate of a university.* The highest council of state in ancient Rome was called the senate. **2** the upper and smaller branch of an assembly or parliament that makes laws. **3 Senate,** the upper and smaller branch of a parliament or legislature. The Canadian Senate, which consists of 104 members, is made up of representatives from each province. [ME < OF < L *senatus* < *senex* old man]

sen·a·tor (sen′ə tər) *n.* a member of a senate. [< L]

sen·a·to·ri·al (sen′ə tôr′ē əl) *adj.* **1** of or befitting a senator or senators. **2** consisting of senators. **3** entitled to elect a senator: *a senatorial district.*

sen·a·tor·ship (sen′ə tər ship′) *n.* the position, duties, etc. of a senator.

send (send) *v.* **sent, send·ing. 1** cause to go from one place to another: *to send a child on an errand.* **2** cause (a person) to do something, go somewhere, etc. for a period of time: *They sent all their children to university.* **3** refer (a reader) to some author, authority, etc.: *to send a reader to the dictionary.* **4** cause to be carried: *to send a letter.* **5** cause to come, occur, be, etc.: *Send help at once. The earthquake sent destruction to the village.* **6** despatch a message or messenger: *Send for a doctor.* **7** drive; impel; throw: *He sent the ball into the rough.* **8** send forth; emit: *The volcano sent clouds of smoke into the air.* **9 a** transmit (radio signals, etc.). **b** transmit (a current, electromagnetic wave, etc.) by means of pulsation. **10** *Slang.* excite greatly or inspire, especially by jazz.
send around, have something circulate.
send away for, mail a request for.
send packing, send away or force to leave quickly.
[OE *sendan*] —**send′er,** *n.*

sen·dal (sen′dəl) *n.* **1** a silk fabric used during the Middle Ages. **2** a garment made of it. [ME < OF *cendal,* ult. < Gk. *sindon* fine cloth]

send–off (send′of′) *n.* **1** a friendly demonstration in honor of a person setting out on a journey, course, career, etc. **2** *Informal.* a start given to a person or thing.

Sen·e·ca (sen′ə kə) *n., pl.* **Seneca** *or* **Senecas;** *adj.* —*n.* **1** a member of an Amerindian tribe living mainly in New York State. The Seneca belonged to the Iroquois Confederacy. **2** the Iroquoian language of the Seneca. —*adj.* of or having to do with the Seneca or their language.

Sen·e·gal·ese (sen′ə gol ēz′ *or* sen′ə gôl ēz′) *n., pl.* **-ese;** *adj.* —*n.* a native or inhabitant of Senegal, a republic in W Africa. —*adj.* of or having to do with Senegal or its people.

se·nes·cence (sə nes′əns) *n.* the fact or condition of growing old.

se·nes·cent (sə nes′ənt) *adj.* growing old; beginning to show old age. [< L *senescens, -entis,* ppr. of *senescere* grow old, ult. < *senex* old]

sen·es·chal (sen′ə shəl) *n.* in the Middle Ages, a steward in charge of a royal palace, nobleman's estate, etc. Seneschals often had the powers of judges and magistrates. [ME < OF; from a Gmc. compound meaning "old servant"]

se·nile (sen′īl *or* sē′nīl) *adj.* **1** of, having to do with, or characteristic of old age. **2** having to do with, characteristic of, or showing the mental confusion, memory loss, etc., often associated with old age. **3** *Geology.* having reached an advanced stage of erosion; made flat or level by the action of water, wind, etc.: *a senile valley.* [< L *senilis* < *senex* old] —**se′nile·ly,** *adv.*

se·nil·i·ty (sə nil′ə tē) *n.* the quality or state of being senile.

sen·ior (sēn′yər) *adj., n.* —*adj.* **1** older or elderly: *a senior citizen.* **2** the older; designating a father whose son has the same given name: *John Parker, Senior.* **3** higher in rank or longer in service: *Mr. Jones is the senior member of the firm of Jones and Brown.* **4** of or having to do with a graduating class.
—*n.* **1** an older person: *Paul is his brother's senior by two years.* **2** a person of higher rank or longer service. **3** a member of the graduating class of a high school or college. [< L *senior,* comparative of *senex* old. Doublet of SIRE.]

senior citizen any member of the community who is of advanced age.

senior high school a school attended after junior high school.

sen·ior·i·ty (sē nyôr′ə tē) *n., pl.* **-ties. 1** superiority in age or standing; the state or fact of being older: *Harry felt that two years'*

seniority gave him the right to advise his brother. **2** priority or precedence in office or service: *A captain has seniority over a lieutenant.*

sen·na (sen′ə) *n.* **1** any of various cassias, especially either of two species *Cassia angustifolia* and *C. acutifolia*) used in medicine. **2** the dried leaves or roots of a senna, used as a laxative. [< NL < Arabic *sana*]

sen·night (sen′īt *or* sen′it) *n. Archaic.* seven nights and days; a week. [OE *seofon nihta* seven nights]

sen·nit (sen′it) *n.* a kind of flat, braided cordage used on shipboard, formed by plaiting strands of rope yarn or other fibre. [? < *seven + knit*]

se·ñor (sā nyôr′) *n., pl.* **-ño·res** (-nyō′rās). *Spanish.* **1** Mr.; Sir. **2** gentleman.

se·ño·ra (sā nyō′rä) *n. Spanish.* **1** Mrs.; Madame. **2** lady.

se·ño·ri·ta (sā′nyō rē′tä) *n. Spanish.* **1** Miss. **2** a young lady.

sen·sa·tion (sen sā′shən) *n.* **1** the action of the senses; power to see, hear, feel, taste, smell, etc.: *A dead body is without sensation.* **2** a feeling: *Ice gives a sensation of coldness; sugar, of sweetness.* **3** strong or excited feeling: *The announcement of war caused a sensation throughout the country.* **4** the cause of such feeling: *The first manned orbit of the earth was a great sensation.* [< LL *sensatio, -onis,* ult. < L *sensus.* See SENSE.]
☛ *Syn.* 1. See note at **sense.**

sen·sa·tion·al (sen sā′shən əl *or* sen sāsh′nəl) *adj.* **1** arousing strong or excited feeling: *The player's sensational catch made the crowd cheer wildly.* **2** trying to arouse strong or excited feeling: *a sensational newspaper story.* **3** of the senses; having to do with sensation. **4** of, based on, or adhering to sensationalism in philosophy. —**sen·sa′tion·al·ly,** *adv.*

sen·sa·tion·al·ism (sen sā′shən əl iz′əm *or* sen sāsh′nəl iz′əm) *n.* **1** sensational methods; sensational writing, language, etc. **2** *Philosophy.* the theory or doctrine that all ideas are derived solely through sensation.

sen·sa·tion·al·ist (sen sā′shən əl ist *or* sen sāsh′nəl ist) *n.* **1** a sensational writer, speaker, etc.; one who tries to make a sensation. **2** a believer in philosophical sensationalism.

sense (sens) *n., v.* **sensed, sens·ing.** —*n.* **1** one of the special functions or mechanisms of the body by which humans and animals perceive the world around them and become aware of changes within themselves. Sight, hearing, touch, taste, and smell are the five senses. **2** the ability to perceive. **3** a sensation felt through one of these senses: *a sense of pain.* **4** a mental feeling: *The extra lock on the door gave him a sense of security.* **5** the faculties of the mind or soul, compared or contrasted with the bodily senses: *moral sense.* **6** an understanding; appreciation: *Everyone thinks he has a sense of humor.* **7** Usually, **senses,** *pl.* normal, sound condition of mind. **8** the judgment; intelligence: *He had the good sense to keep out of foolish quarrels. Common sense could have prevented the accident.* **9** the recognition (of a duty, virtue, etc.) as incumbent upon one or as fitting and proper: *a sense of justice.* **10** the ability to judge things: *a sense of direction, a sense of beauty.* **11** a meaning: *He was a gentleman in every sense of the word.* **12** discourse that has a satisfactory or intelligible meaning: *to speak or write sense.* **13** the general opinion: *The sense of the assembly was clear even before the vote.*
in a sense, in some respects; to some degree.
make sense, have a meaning; be understandable or reasonable: *Cow cat bless Monday does not make sense.*
—*v.* **1** be aware; feel: *She sensed that he was tired.* **2** *Informal.* understand. [ME < L *sensus < sentire* perceive]
☛ *Syn. n.* 1, 2. **Sense, sensation, sensibility** = the power or act of feeling or perceiving. **Sense** applies especially to the power of the mind to respond to a stimulus or influence outside itself, but implies awareness or full consciousness of something existing rather than bodily reaction: *He has a sense of well-being.* **Sensation** applies to physical feeling, particularly the response to stimulation of a bodily organ like the eyes or nerves: *He has no sensation in his feet.* **Sensibility** applies to the capacity for feeling or perceiving physically or, especially, emotionally: *He has no sensibility to pain.* **6.** See note at **meaning.**

sense·less (sens′lis) *adj.* **1** unconscious: *A blow on the head knocked him senseless.* **2** foolish; stupid. **3** meaningless: *senseless words.* —**sense′less·ly,** *adv.* —**sense′less·ness,** *n.*

sense organ the eye, ear, or other part of the body by which a person or an animal receives sensations of colors, sounds, smells, etc.

sen·si·bil·i·ty (sen′sə bil′ə tē) *n., pl.* **-ties.** **1** the ability to feel or perceive: *Some drugs lessen a person's sensibilities.* **2** sensitiveness. **3** fineness of feeling: *She has an unusual sensibility for colors.* **4** Usually, **sensibilities,** *pl.* sensitive feelings. **5** a tendency to feel hurt or offended too easily. **6** awareness; consciousness.
—**sen′si·bly,** *adv.*
☛ *Syn.* 1. See note at **sense.**

sen·si·ble (sen′sə bəl) *adj.* **1** having or showing good judgment; wise. **2** aware; conscious: *I am sensible of your kindness.* **3** that can be noticed. **4** that can be perceived by the senses. **5** large enough to

hat, āge, fär; let, ēqual, tėrm; it, īce
hot, ōpen, ôrder; oil, out; cup, pút, rüle,
above, takən, pencəl, lemən, circəs

ch, child; ng, long; sh, ship
th, thin; ŦH, then; zh, measure

be perceived or considered; considerable: *a sensible reduction in expenses.* **6** sensitive. [ME < LL *sensibilis,* ult. < L *sentire* feel]
☛ *Syn.* 1. **Sensible, practical** = having or showing good sense. **Sensible** emphasizes having and using common sense and good judgment in acting and speaking, and particularly suggests natural intelligence: *He is too sensible to do anything foolish.* **Practical** emphasizes using common sense in everyday affairs, and particularly suggests being given to action rather than thought or imagination and concerned with the usefulness, application, and results of knowledge, principles, and methods: *He is a practical man and does not understand dreamers and scientists.*

sen·si·tive (sen′sə tiv) *adj.* **1** receiving impressions readily: *The eye is sensitive to light.* **2** easily affected or influenced: *The mercury in the thermometer is sensitive to changes in temperature.* **3** easily hurt or offended. **4** of or connected with the senses or sensation. **5** *Medicine.* unusually susceptible, as to a serum. **6** *Biology.* able to respond to stimulation by various external agents, as light, gravity, etc. **7** *Botany.* responding to external stimuli by moving, as the leaves of a sensitive plant, etc. **8** involving classified documents, etc. [ME < Med.L *sensitivus* < L *sensus.* See SENSE.] —**sen′si·tive·ly,** *adv.* —**sen′si·tive·ness,** *n.*
☛ *Syn.* 2. **Sensitive, susceptible** = easily affected or influenced. **Sensitive** particularly suggests having, by nature or because of a physical or emotional condition, a specially keen or delicate capacity for feeling (physical or mental) or for responding or reacting to an external action, force, or influence: *Sensitive people are quickly touched by something beautiful or sad.* **Susceptible** particularly suggests having a nature, character, or makeup that makes a person or thing unable to resist an influence and easily acted on: *Susceptible people are easily tricked.*

sensitive plant **1** either of two tropical American mimosas (*Mimosa pudica* and *M. sensitiva*) cultivated as house and greenhouse plants in temperate regions for their foliage, which folds up and droops when touched. **2** any of various other plants showing sensitiveness to touch.

sen·si·tiv·i·ty (sen′sə tiv′ə tē) *n., pl.* **-ties.** the state or quality of being sensitive.

sen·si·tize (sen′sə tīz′) *v.* **-tized, -tiz·ing.** **1** make sensitive. Camera films have been sensitized to light. **2** *Medicine.* make unusually sensitive to a protein or other substance by repeated injections. —**sen′si·tiz′er,** *n.*

sen·sor (sen′sər) *n.* a device for receiving and transmitting a physical stimulus such as heat, light, or pressure: *Sensors were applied to the astronaut's body to record his pulse, temperature, etc.*
☛ *Hom.* **censer, censor.**

sen·so·ri·al (sen sôr′ē əl) *adj.* sensory.

sen·so·ri·um (sen sô′rē əm) *n., pl.* **-ri·ums, -ri·a** (-rē ə). **1** the supposed seat of sensation in the brain. **2** the whole sensory apparatus of the body. **3** the brain or mind (an unscientific use of the word). [< LL *sensorium,* ult. < L *sentire* feel]

sen·so·ry (sen′sə rē) *adj.* **1** of or having to do with sensation. The eyes and ears are sensory organs. **2** of nerves, ganglia, etc., conveying an impulse from the sense organs to a nerve centre.

sen·su·al (sen′shü əl) *adj.* **1** having to do with the bodily senses rather than with the mind or soul: *sensual pleasures.* **2** caring too much for the pleasures of the senses. **3** lustful; lewd. **4** indicative of a sensual disposition: *sensual lips.* **5** of or having to do with the senses or sensation. [ME < LL *sensualis* < L *sensus.* See SENSE.] —**sen′su·al·ly,** *adv.*
☛ *Syn.* 1, 2. **Sensual, sensuous** = of or concerned with the senses. **Sensual** describes things that give pleasurable satisfaction to the bodily senses and appetites and applies to people who indulge their desires and feelings for pure physical pleasure, almost always suggesting baseness or excess: *A glutton derives sensual pleasure from eating.* **Sensuous,** always favorable, describes people highly sensitive to beauty and the pleasure of the senses and feelings and applies to things that give pleasure through the senses: *She derives sensuous delight from old church music.*

sen·su·al·ism (sen′shü əl iz′əm) *n.* sensuality.

sen·su·al·ist (sen′shü əl ist) *n.* a person who indulges too much in the pleasures of the senses: *Gluttons and drunkards are sensualists.*

sen·su·al·i·ty (sen′shü al′ə tē) *n., pl.* **-ties.** **1** a sensual nature. **2** an excessive indulgence in the pleasures of the senses. **3** lewdness.

sen·su·al·ize (sen′shü əl īz′) *v.* **-ized, -iz·ing.** make sensual.

sen·su·ous (sen′shü əs) *adj.* **1** of or derived from the senses; having an effect on the senses; perceived by the senses: *the*

sensuous thrill of a warm bath, a sensuous love of color. **2** enjoying the pleasures of the senses. —**sen′su·ous·ly,** *adv.* —**sen′su·ous·ness,** *n.*
☛ *Syn.* 1, 2. See note at **sensual.**

sent (sent) *v.* pt. and pp. of **send.**
☛ *Hom.* cent, scent.

sen·tence (sen′təns) *n., v.* -**tenced, -tenc·ing.** —*n.* **1** a word or group of words making a grammatically complete statement, question, request, command or exclamation. A sentence usually consists of a subject and a predicate with a finite verb.
2 *Mathematics.* a group of symbols that expresses a complete idea or a requirement. *Examples:* 4 + 2 = 6 (a **closed sentence** expressing a complete idea); $x + 2 = 6$ (an **open sentence** expressing a requirement). **3** *Law.* **a** a decision by a judge on the punishment of a criminal. **b** the punishment itself. **4** a short, wise saying; proverb. —*v.* pronounce punishment on: *The judge sentenced the thief to five years in prison.* [< F < L *sententia,* originally, opinion < *sentire* feel]

sen·ten·tial (sen ten′shəl) *adj.* **1** having to do with or of the nature of a judicial sentence. **2** having to do with a grammatical sentence.

sen·ten·tious (sen ten′shəs) *adj.* **1** full of meaning; saying much in few words. **2** speaking as if one were a judge settling a question. **3** inclined to make wise sayings; abounding in proverbs. [ME < OF < Med.L. *sententiosus* < *sententia.* See SENTENCE.]
—**sen·ten′tious·ly,** *adv.* —**sen·ten′tious·ness,** *n.*

sen·tience (sen′shəns *or* sen′shē əns) *n.* a capacity for feeling: *Some people believe in the sentience of flowers.*

sen·tient (sen′shənt *or* sen′shē ənt) *adj., n.* —*adj.* that can feel; having feeling. —*n.* one that feels. [< L *sentiens, -entis,* ppr. of *sentire* feel]

sen·ti·ment (sen′tə mənt) *n.* **1** a mixture of thought and feeling. Admiration, patriotism, and loyalty are sentiments. **2** feeling, especially refined or tender feeling. **3** a thought or saying that expresses feeling. **4** a mental attitude. **5** a personal opinion. [ME < OF < Med.L *sentimentum* < L *sentire* feel]
☛ *Syn.* 2. Sentiment, sentimentality = refined or tender feeling, or a quality or characteristic showing or produced by such feeling. **Sentiment,** usually used in a good sense, suggests genuine, sincere, and refined, delicate, or tender feeling: *Christmas and birthdays are times for sentiment.* **Sentimentality** suggests affected or false, excessive or exaggerated feeling, sickening tenderness, or weakly emotional show, and therefore is used unfavorably or contemptuously: *Sentimentality towards criminals is as dangerous as it is disgusting.*

sen·ti·men·tal (sen′tə men′təl) *adj.* **1** having or showing much tender feeling: *sentimental poetry.* **2** likely to act from feelings rather than from logical thinking. **3** of sentiment; dependent on sentiment: *She values her mother's gift for sentimental reasons.* **4** having too much sentiment. —**sen·ti·men′tal·ly,** *adv.*

sen·ti·men·tal·ism (sen′tə men′təl iz′əm) *n.* **1** a tendency to be influenced by sentiment rather than reason. **2** an excessive indulgence in sentiment. **3** a feeling expressed too openly or commonly or sentimentally.

sen·ti·men·tal·ist (sen′tə men′təl ist) *n.* a sentimental person; one who indulges in sentimentality.

sen·ti·men·tal·i·ty (sen′tə men tal′ə tē) *n., pl.* -**ties. 1** a tendency to be influenced by sentiment rather than reason. **2** an excessive indulgence in sentiment. **3** a feeling expressed too openly or sentimentally.
☛ *Syn.* 2. See note at **sentiment.**

sen·ti·men·tal·ize (sen′tə men′təl īz′) *v.* -**ized, -iz·ing. 1** indulge in sentiment; affect sentiment. **2** make sentimental. **3** be sentimental about.

sen·ti·nel (sen′tə nəl) *n., v.* -**nelled** or -**neled, -nel·ling** or -**nel·ing.** —*n.* **1** a person stationed to keep watch and guard against surprise attack. **2** a person or thing that watches, or stands as if watching, like a sentinel: *The tree stood like a sentinel against the sky.*
stand sentinel, act as a sentinel; keep watch.
—*v.* **1** stand guard over; watch as a sentinel. **2** furnish with or as if with a sentinel or sentinels. **3** post as a sentinel. [< F < Ital. *sentinella* < LL *sentinare* avoid danger wisely < L *sentire* feel]

sen·try (sen′trē) *n., pl.* -**tries.** a person, especially a soldier, stationed at a place to keep watch and guard against surprise attacks, etc.
stand sentry, watch; guard: *We stood sentry over the sleepers.* [? abbreviation of *centrinel,* var. of *sentinel*]

sentry box a small roofed structure for sheltering a sentry.

sep. **1** sepal(s). **2** separate.

Sep. **1** September. **2** Septuagint.

se·pal (sē′pəl) *n. Botany.* one of the leaflike divisions of the calyx, or outer covering, of a flower. In a carnation, the sepals

make a green cup at the base of the flower. In a tulip, the sepals are colored like the petals. See **flower** for picture. [< NL *sepalum,* short for L *separatum petalum* separate petal, coined by H.J. de Necker in 1790]

sep·a·ra·bil·i·ty (sep′ə rə bil′ə tē *or* sep′rə bil′ə tē) *n.* the quality of being separable.

sep·a·ra·ble (sep′ə rə bəl *or* sep′rə bəl) *adj.* that can be separated. —**sep′a·ra·bly,** *adv.*

sep·a·rate (*v.* sep′ə rāt′; *adj., n.* sep′ə rit *or* sep′rit) *v.* -**rat·ed, -rat·ing;** *adj., n.* —*v.* **1** be between; keep apart; divide: *The Atlantic Ocean separates North America from Europe.* **2** take apart; part; disjoin: *to separate church and state.* **3** live apart or cause to live apart. A husband and wife may be separated by agreement or by order of a court. **4** divide into parts or groups; divide or part (a mass, compound, whole) into elements, sizes, etc.: *to separate a tangle of string.* **5** draw, come, or go apart; become disconnected or disunited; part company; withdraw (from): *After classes the students separated in all directions. The rope separated under the strain.* **6** put apart; take away: *Separate your books from mine.*
—*adj.* apart from others; divided; not joined; individual; single: *separate clubs. These are two separate questions. Our teeth are separate.*
—*n.* something separate. [< L *separare* < *se-* apart + *parare* get]
—**sep′a·rate·ly,** *adv.*
☛ *Syn. v.* 2. Separate, divide = part or put apart two or more people, things, or elements. **Separate** emphasizes parting or causing to be apart people or things that have been together, whether or not actually connected or united: *We have decided to separate the twins for the summer.* **Divide** emphasizes separating, breaking up, cutting, etc. a mass, body, or whole into individuals, parts, or sections: *The instructor divides the class for field trips.*

separate school **1** *Cdn.* a school for children belonging to a religious minority in a particular district, operated by a school board elected by the minority rate-payers and financed by taxes imposed on them by the board as well as by grants from the provincial Department of Education. It is under the jurisdiction of the Department of Education and follows the same basic curriculum as that laid down for public schools. **2** a Roman Catholic parochial school. **3** *Rare.* a school that is not part of the public school system; a private or independent school.

sep·a·ra·tion (sep′ə rā′shən) *n.* **1** the act of separating; dividing; taking apart. **2** the condition of being separated. **3** the line or point where things separate: *They soon came to the separation of the path into two tracks.* **4** the living apart of husband and wife by agreement or by order of a court.

sep·a·ra·tism (sep′ə rə tiz′əm *or* sep′rə tiz′əm) *n.* **1** a principle or policy for separation, secession, or segregation. **2 Separatism, *Cdn.* advocacy or support of the withdrawal of a province from Confederation.

sep·a·ra·tist (sep′ə rə tist *or* sep′rə tist) *n.* **1** an advocate or supporter of separatism. **2 Separatist,** *Cdn.* an advocate or supporter of the withdrawal of a province from Confederation.

sep·a·ra·tive (sep′ə rə tiv, sep′rə tiv *or* sep′ə rā′tiv) *adj.* tending to separate; causing separation.

sep·a·ra·tor (sep′ə rā′tər) *n.* a person or thing that separates, especially a machine for separating cream from milk, wheat from chaff or dirt, etc. [< L]

Se·phar·dic (si fär′dik) *adj.* of, having to do with, or descended from the Sephardim.

Se·phar·dim (si fär′dim) *n.pl.* Spanish or Portuguese Jews and their descendants, as distinguished from the Ashkenazim of central and eastern Europe.

se·pi·a (sē′pē ə) *n., adj.* —*n.* **1** a brown paint or ink prepared from the inky fluid of cuttlefish. **2** a dark brown. **3** a drawing, photograph, etc. in tones of brown.
—*adj.* **1** dark brown. **2** done in sepia: *a sepia print.* [< L < Gk.]

se·poy (sē′poi) *n. Historical.* a native of India who was a soldier in the British army in India. [< Pg. < Hind. < Persian *sipāhī* soldier < *sipāh* army]

sep·sis (sep′sis) *n.* a toxic condition resulting from the absorption of any of various pus-forming bacteria or their toxins into the blood or tissues from a wound, etc. Blood poisoning, or septicemia, is a type of sepsis. [< NL < Gk. *sēpsis* putrefaction < *sēpein* rot]

Sept. **1** September. **2** Septuagint.

sep·tal (sep′təl) *adj.* of or having to do with a septum.

Sep·tem·ber (sep tem′bər) *n.* the ninth month. September has 30 days. [< L *September* < *septem* seven; from the order of the Roman calendar]

sep·te·nar·y (sep′tə ner′ē) *adj., n., pl.* -**nar·ies.** —*adj.* **1** of or having to do with the number seven. **2** forming a group of seven. **3** septennial.
—*n.* **1** the number seven. **2** a group or set of seven things. **3** a period of seven years. [< L *septenarius* seven-year period < *septum* seven + *annus* year]

sep·ten·ni·al (sep ten'ē əl) *adj.* **1** lasting seven years. **2** occurring every seven years. [< L *septennium* seven-year period < *septem* seven + *annus* year] —**sep·ten'ni·al·ly,** *adv.*

sep·tet or **sep·tette** (sep tet') *n.* **1** *Music.* **a** a composition for seven voices or instruments. **b** seven singers or players. **2** any group of seven. [< G < L *septem* seven; modelled after *duet*]

sep·tic (sep'tik) *adj., n.* —*adj.* **1** causing infection or putrefaction. **2** caused by infection or putrefaction. —*n.* a substance that causes or promotes sepsis. [< L < Gk. *sēptikos* < *sēpein* rot]

sep·ti·ce·mi·a or **sep·ti·cae·mi·a** (sep'tə sē'mē ə) *n.* a disease caused by the presence of micro-organisms and their toxins in the bloodstream; blood poisoning. [< NL < Gk. *sēptikos* septic (ult. < *sēpein* rot) + *haima* blood]

septic tank a tank in which sewage is acted on by bacteria.

sep·til·lion (sep til'yən) *n.* **1** in Canada, the United States and France, 1 followed by 24 zeros. **2** in Great Britain, 1 followed by 42 zeros. [< F *septillion* < L *septem* seven), modelled after *million* million]

sep·tu·a·ge·nar·i·an (sep'chü ə jə ner'ē ən *or* sep'tyü-) *adj., n.* —*adj.* of the age of 70 years, or between 70 and 80 years old. —*n.* a person who is 70 or between 70 and 80 years old. [< L *septuagenarius,* ult. < *septuaginta* seventy]

sep·tu·ag·e·nar·y (sep'chü aj'ə ner'ē *or* sep'tyü-) *adj., n., pl.* **-nar·ies.** septuagenarian.

Sep·tu·a·ges·i·ma (sep'chü ə jes'ə mə *or* sep'tyü-) *n.* the third Sunday before Lent. [< L *septuagesima,* literally, seventieth]

Sep·tu·a·gint (sep'chü ə jint' *or* sep'tyü-) *n.* the Greek translation of the Old Testament that was made before the time of Christ. [< L *septuaginta* seventy; because it was supposed to have been done in seventy days by seventy scholars who were brought to Alexandria by Ptolemy II of Egypt]

sep·tum (sep'təm) *n., pl.* **-ta** (-tə). a dividing wall; partition. There is a septum of bone and cartilage between the nostrils. The inside of a green pepper is divided into chambers by septa. [< L *saeptum* a fence < *saepire* hedge in]

sep·tu·ple (sep tyü'pəl *or* sep tü'pəl, sep'tup əl *or* sep'tə pəl) *adj., v.* **-pled, -pling.** —*adj.* seven times as great; seven-fold. —*v.* make seven times as great. [< LL *septuplus* < L *septem* seven + *-plus* -fold]

sep·ul·cher (sep'əl kər) See **sepulchre.**

se·pul·chral (sə pul'krəl) *adj.* **1** of sepulchres or tombs. **2** of burial: *sepulchral ceremonies.* **3** deep and gloomy; dismal; suggesting a tomb.

sep·ul·chre or **sep·ul·cher** (sep'əl kər) *n., v.* **-chred, -chring.** —*n.* a place of burial; tomb. —*v.* bury a dead body in a sepulchre. [ME < OF < L *sepulcrum* < *sepelire* bury]

sep·ul·ture (sep'əl chər) *n. Archaic.* **1** burial. **2** a place of burial; sepulchre. [ME < OF < L *sepultura* < *sepelire* bury]

seq. **1** sequel. **2** the following. [< L *sequens,* ppr. of *sequi* follow]

se·quel (sē'kwəl) *n.* **1** that which follows; a continuation. **2** something that follows as a result of some earlier happening; result. **3** a complete story continuing an earlier one about the same people. [ME < L *sequela* < *sequi* follow]

se·que·la (si kwē'lə) *n., pl.* **-lae** (-lē *or* -lī). **1** anything following or resulting. **2** *Medicine.* a disease or morbid condition that is the result of a previous disease. [< L. See SEQUEL.]

se·quence (sē'kwəns) *n., v.* **-quenced, -quenc·ing.** —*n.* **1** the coming of one thing after another; succession; order of succession: *Arrange the names in alphabetical sequence.* **2** a connected series: *a sequence of lessons on one subject.* **3** something that follows; result: *Crime has its sequence of misery.* **4** *Card games.* a set of three or more cards of the same suit following one after another in order of value. **5 a** a part of a motion picture consisting of an episode without breaks. **b** any group of scenes of a motion picture taken as a unit. **6** *Music.* a series of melodic or harmonic phrases repeated three or more times at successive pitches upward or downward. —*v.* arrange in a sequence. [ME < LL *sequentia,* ult. < L *sequi* follow]

☛ *Syn.* **1.** See note at **series.**

se·quent (sē'kwənt) *adj., n.* —*adj.* **1** following; subsequent. **2** following in order; consecutive. **3** following as a result; consequent. —*n.* that which follows; result; consequence. [< L *sequens, -entis,* ppr. of *sequi* follow]

se·quen·tial (si kwen'shəl) *adj.* **1** sequent. **2** forming a sequence or connected series; characterized by a regular sequence of parts. —**se·quen'tial·ly,** *adv.*

se·ques·ter (si kwes'tər) *v.* **1** remove or withdraw from public use or from public view: *The shy old lady sequestered herself from all strangers.* **2** take away (property) for a time from an owner until a debt is paid or some claim is satisfied. **3** seize by authority; take and keep: *The soldiers sequestered food from the people they*

hat, āge, fär; let, ēqual, tèrm; it, īce
hot, ōpen, ôrder; oil, out; cup, pút, rüle,
abóve, takən, pencəl, lemən, circəs

ch, child; ng, long; sh, ship
th, thin; ᴛн, then; zh, measure

conquered. [ME < LL *sequestrare* < *sequester* trustee, mediator < *sequi* follow]

se·ques·trate (si kwes'trāt) *v.* **-trat·ed, -trat·ing.** **1** confiscate. **2** *Archaic.* sequester. —**se·ques'tra·tor,** *n.*

se·ques·tra·tion (sē'kwes trā'shən *or* si kwes'trā'shən) *n.* **1 a** the seizing and holding of property until legal claims are satisfied. **b** a writ authorizing this. **2** a forcible or authorized seizure; confiscation. **3** a separation or withdrawal from others; seclusion.

se·quin (sē'kwin) *n.* **1** a small spangle used to ornament dresses, scarfs, etc. **2** any of various former Italian gold coins. [< F < Ital. *zecchino* < *zecca* mint < Arabic *sikka* a stamp]

se·quoi·a (si kwoi'ə) *n.* either of two giant, very long-lived, coniferous evergreen trees, the redwood and the big tree, found in the coastal regions of the SW United States. Each is the only living member of its genus, and both belong to the same family (Taxodiaceae) as the bald cypress. See also **big tree, redwood.** [< NL *sequoia* < *Sequoya* (Cherokee *Sikwayi*) (1770?-1843), an Indian who invented the Cherokee system of writing]

se·rac (sā rak') *n.* a large block or pinnacle-like mass of ice on a glacier, formed by the intersection of two or more crevasses. [< Swiss F *sérac,* a kind of white cheese]

se·ragl·io (sə ral'yō) *n., pl.* **-ragl·ios.** **1** the women's quarters of a Moslem house or palace; harem. **2** in Turkey, a palace. [< Ital. *serraglio,* ult. < L *serare* lock up; influenced by Turkish *serāī* palace]

se·ra·pe (sə rä'pē) *n.* a shawl or blanket, often having bright colors, worn by Indians in Spanish-American countries. [< Mexican Sp. *serape or sarape*]

ser·aph (ser'əf) *n., pl.* **-aphs** *or* **-a·phim.** one of the highest order of angels. [< *seraphim,* pl., < LL < Hebrew]
☛ *Hom.* **serif.**

se·raph·ic (sə raf'ik) *adj.* **1** of seraphs. **2** like a seraph; angelic. —**se·raph'i·cal·ly,** *adv.*

ser·a·phim (ser'ə fim') *n.* a pl. of **seraph.**

Se·ra·pis (sə rā'pis) *n. Egyptian mythology.* a god of the lower world, the dead Apis.

Serb (sèrb) *n., adj.* —*n.* **1** a native or inhabitant of Serbia, a constituent republic of Yugoslavia. **2** Serbian. —*adj.* Serbian. [< *Serbian*]

Ser·bi·an (sèr'bē ən) *n., adj.* —*n.* **1** the Slavic language spoken by the Serbs, very closely related to Croatian. **2** Serb (def. 1). —*adj.* of or having to do with Serbia, its people, or their language.

Ser·bo-Cro·a·tian (sèr'bō krō ā'shən) *n., adj.* —*n.* the Slavic language of the Serbs and Croats, consisting of Serbian, written with the Cyrillic alphabet, and Croatian, written with the Latin alphabet. Serbo-Croatian is the most common of the three official languages of Yugoslavia. —*adj.* of or having to do with this language or the people who speak it.

sere (sēr) *adj.* dried up; withered. [var. of *sear*]
☛ *Hom.* **sear, seer.**

ser·e·nade (ser'ə nād') *n., v.* **-nad·ed, -nad·ing.** —*n.* **1** music played or sung outdoors at night, especially by a lover under his lady's window. **2** a piece of music suitable for such a performance. **3** an instrumental composition having several movements. —*v.* **1** sing or play a serenade to. **2** sing or play a serenade. [< F < Ital. *serenata,* ult. < L *serenus* serene] —**ser'e·nad'er,** *n.*

ser·en·dip·i·tous (ser'ən dip'ə təs) *adj.* possessing or characterized by serendipity: *serendipitous inspiration.*

ser·en·dip·i·ty (ser'ən dip'ə tē) *n.* the faculty of accidentally making fortunate discoveries; happening upon things, information, etc. by chance. [coined by Horace Walpole from *Serendip* in the title of the Persian fairy tale *The Three Princes of Serendip,* whose heroes make many fortunate discoveries accidentally. 18c.]

se·rene (sə rēn') *adj.* **1** peaceful; calm: *a serene smile.* **2** clear; bright; not cloudy: *a serene sky.* [< L *serenus*] —**se·rene'ly,** *adv.*
☛ *Syn.* **1.** See note at **peaceful.**

se·ren·i·ty (sə ren'ə tē) *n., pl.* **-ties.** **1** quiet peace; calmness. **2** clearness; brightness.

serf (sèrf) *n.* **1** especially in medieval Europe, a person who worked on a feudal estate and passed with the land from one owner

to another. **2** a person treated almost like a slave; a person who is mistreated, underpaid, etc. [< F < L *servus* slave] —**serf′like′**, *adj.*

☛ *Hom.* **surf.**

serf·dom (sèrf′dəm) *n.* **1** the condition of a serf. **2** the custom of having serfs. Serfdom existed all over Europe in the Middle Ages and lasted in Russia till the middle of the 19th century.

serge (sèrj) *n.* a kind of woollen or silk cloth having slanting lines or ridges on its surface. [ME < OF *serge*, ult. < L *serica* (*vestis*) silken (garment) < Gk. *sērikē* < *Sēres* the Chinese. Cf. SILK.]

☛ *Hom.* **surge.**

ser·gean·cy (sär′jən sē) *n., pl.* **-cies.** the position, rank, or duties of a sergeant.

ser·geant (sär′jənt) *n.* **1** *Canadian Forces.* a non-commissioned officer ranking next above a master corporal and below a warrant officer. **2** a non-commissioned officer of similar rank in the armed forces of other countries. **3** a police officer, senior to a constable. **4** sergeant at arms. *Abbrev.:* Sgt. or Sgt Also, *esp.Brit.* **serjeant.** [ME < OF *sergent* < L *serviens, -entis*, ppr. of *servire* serve]

sergeant at arms or **ser·geant–at–arms** (sär′jənt ət ärmz′) *n., pl.* **ser·geants at arms** or **ser·geants-at-arms.** an officer who keeps order in a legislature, law court, etc.

ser·geant–ma·jor (sär′jənt mā′jər) *n.* **1** in the army, a non-commissioned officer senior to a staff sergeant and junior to a warrant officer. **2** in the Royal Canadian Mounted Police, a non-commissioned officer senior to a staff sergeant. *Abbrev.:* S.M. or Sgt.Maj.

Sergt. Sergeant.

se·ri·al (sēr′ē əl) *n., adj.* —*n.* a story presented one part at a time in a magazine, on radio or television, etc. —*adj.* **1** published, broadcast, or televised one part at a time: *a serial publication, a serial story.* **2** of, having to do with, or arranged in a series: *books arranged in serial order.* [< NL *serialis* < L *series.* See SERIES.]

☛ *Hom.* **cereal.**

se·ri·al·ize (sēr′ē ə līz′) *v.* **-ized, -iz·ing.** present in the form of a serial: *a novel serialized in a magazine.* Also, *esp.Brit.,* **serialise.** —**se′ri·al·i·za′tion,** *n.*

se·ri·al·ly (sēr′ē əl ē) *adv.* **1** in a series. **2** as a serial.

serial number an individual number given to a person, article, etc., as a means of easy identification.

se·ri·ate (sēr′ē it *or* sēr′ē āt′) *adj.* arranged or occurring in one or more series.

se·ri·a·tim (sēr′ē ā′tim *or* ser′ē ā′tim) *adv.* in a series; one after another. [< Med.L]

ser·i·cul·ture (ser′ə kul′chər) *n.* the raising and care of silkworms for the production of raw silk. [< F *séri(ci)culture* < L *sericum* silk + *cultura* culture]

se·ries (sēr′ēz) *n., pl.* **-ries. 1** a number of similar things in a row: *A series of rooms opened off the long hall.* **2** a number of things placed one after another. **3** a number of things, events, etc. coming one after the other: *A series of rainy days spoiled their vacation.* **4** coins, stamps, etc. of a particular issue, ruler, country, etc. **5** written or artistic works that are produced one after another, usually having a common subject or purpose, and often by a single author, artist, or composer. **6** *Electricity.* an arrangement in which the positive pole or terminal of one battery, etc. is connected to the negative pole or terminal of the next. [< L *series* < *serere* join]

☛ *Syn.* **1. Series, sequence, succession** = a number of things, events, etc. arranged or coming one after another in some order. **Series** applies to a number of similar things with the same purpose or relation to each other: *He gave a series of lectures on Mexico.* **Sequence** implies a closer or unbroken connection, in thought, between cause and effect, in numerical or alphabetical order, etc.: *He reviewed the sequence of events leading to peace.* **Succession** emphasizes following in order of time, sometimes place, usually without interruption: *He had a succession of colds.*

☛ *Usage.* **Series.** Commas are used between the members of a series of three or more short items, although usage is divided over the insertion of a comma before the last item of the series. Since this comma is sometimes needed to avoid confusion, it is better to use it all the time: *He forgot to pack his toothbrush, comb, and shaving equipment.*

se·ries–wound (sēr′ēz wound′) *adj. Electricity.* wound so that the field magnet coils are connected in series with the armature and carry the same current.

ser·if (ser′if) *n. Printing.* a thin or smaller line used to finish off a main stroke of a letter, as at the top and bottom of M. [? < Du. *schreef* stroke, line < *schrijven* write < L *scribere*]

☛ *Hom.* **seraph.**

ser·i·graph (ser′ə graf′) *n.* an original color print produced by a silk-screen process.

se·ri·o–com·ic (sēr′ē ō kom′ik) *adj.* partly serious and partly comic.

se·ri·ous (sēr′ē əs) *adj.* **1** thoughtful; grave: *a serious face.* **2** in

earnest; not joking; sincere: *He was serious about the subject.* **3** needing thought; important: *Choice of one's life work is a serious matter.* **4** important because it may do much harm; dangerous: *The badly injured man was in a serious condition.* [< LL *seriosus* < L *serius* earnest] —**se′ri·ous·ly,** *adv.* —**se′ri·ous·ness,** *n.*

☛ *Hom.* **cereus.**

☛ *Syn.* **1.** See note at **grave.**

ser·mon (sèr′mən) *n.* **1** a public talk on religion or something connected with religion. Ministers preach sermons in church. **2** a serious talk, often long and tiresome, about morals, conduct, duty, etc.: *After the guests left, the boy got a sermon on table manners from his father.* [ME < OF < L *sermo, -onis* a talk, originally, a stringing together of words < *serere* join]

ser·mon·ize (sèr′mən īz′) *v.* **-ized, -iz·ing. 1** give a sermon; preach. **2** preach or talk seriously to; lecture. —**ser′mon·iz′er,** *n.*

Sermon on the Mount Christ's sermon to His disciples, as reported in Matthew 5-7 and Luke 6:20-49.

se·ro·log·i·cal (sēr′ə loj′ə kəl) *adj.* of or having to do with serology. —**se′ro·log′i·cal·ly,** *adv.*

se·rol·o·gist (si rol′ə jist) *n.* a person trained in serology, especially one whose work it is.

se·rol·o·gy (si rol′ə jē) *n.* the study of the use of serums in curing or preventing disease. [< *sero-* (< L *serum* whey) + *-logy*]

ser·o·to·nin (ser′ə tō′nən) *n.* a compound that is synthesized in the hypothalmus region of the brain and that can produce muscle contraction and an increase in body temperature and is associated with the regulation of emotion. *Formula:* $C_{10}H_{12}N_2O$ [< *sero-* (< L *serum* whey) + *ton(ic)* + *-in*]

se·rous (sēr′əs) *adj.* **1** of serum; having to do with serum. **2** like serum; watery. Tears are drops of a serous fluid. [< L *serosus* < *serum* whey]

ser·pent (sèr′pənt) *n.* **1** a snake, especially a big snake. **2** a sly, treacherous person. **3** Serpent, the Devil; Satan. [< L *serpens, -entis*, originally ppr. of *serpere* creep]

ser·pen·tine (*adj.* sèr′pən tīn′ *or* sèr′pən tēn′; *n.* sèr′pən tēn′) *adj., n.* —*adj.* **1** of or like a serpent. **2** winding; twisting: *the serpentine course of a creek.* **3** cunning; sly; treacherous: *a serpentine suggestion.* —*n.* a mineral consisting chiefly of a hydrous silicate of magnesium, usually green, and sometimes spotted like a serpent's skin. *Formula:* $Mg_3Si_2O_5(OH)_4$ [< LL *serpentinus* < L *serpens, -entis* serpent]

ser·rate (ser′āt *or* ser′it) *adj., v.* **-rat·ed, -rat·ing.** —*adj.* **1** of a leaf, having a margin with sawlike notches angled toward the tip. See **leaf** for picture. **2** having a notched edge; serrated. —*v.* notch like a saw; make serrations in or on. [< L *serratus* < *serra* a saw]

ser·rat·ed (ser′āt id) *adj.* having a notched edge; toothed.

ser·ra·tion (se rā′shən) *n.* **1** a serrated edge or formation. **2** one of its series of notches.

ser·ried (ser′ēd) *adj.* crowded closely together. [< F *serré*, pp. of *serrer* press close]

ser·ru·late (ser′yə lāt′ *or* ser′ə lāt′) *adj.* very finely notched: *a serrulate leaf.* [< NL *serrulatus* < L *serrula*, dim. of *serra* a saw]

se·rum (sēr′əm) *n., pl.* **se·rums** *or* **se·ra** (sēr′ə). **1** the clear, pale-yellow, watery part of the blood that separates from the clot when blood coagulates. **2** a liquid used to prevent or cure a disease, usually obtained from the blood of an animal that has been made immune to the disease. Diphtheria antitoxin is a serum. **3** any watery animal liquid, such as lymph. **4** whey. [< L *serum* whey]

ser·val (sèr′vəl) *n.* a medium-sized wildcat (*Felis serval*) of the African bush having long legs, large ears, and a tawny coat with black spots and stripes. [< NL < Pg. (*lobo*) *cerval* lynx, ult. < L *cervus* stag]

serv·ant (sèr′vənt) *n.* **1** a person employed in a household. **2** a person employed by another. Policemen and firemen are public servants. **3** a person devoted to any service: *Ministers are the servants of God.* [ME < OF *servant*, ppr. of *servir* serve. See SERVE.] —**serv′ant·less,** *adj.*

serve (sèrv) *v.* **served, serv·ing;** *n.* —*v.* **1** give service to; work for or in: *A slave serves his master.* **2** give service; work; perform official duties: *He served as butler. She served three years in the armed forces.* **3** wait on at table; bring food or drink to: *An old waiter served us.* **4** put (food or drink) on the table: *The maid served the first course.* **5** supply; furnish; supply with something needed: *The dairy serves us with milk. The men were served with a round of ammunition.* **6** help; aid: *Let me know if I can serve you in any way.* **7** be useful; be what is needed; be of use: *Boxes served as seats.* **8** be useful to; fulfil: *This will serve my purpose.* **9** be favorable or suitable; be favorable or suitable to; satisfy: *The ship will sail when the wind and tide serve.* **10** treat: *The prisoner was poorly served.* **11** pass; spend: *The thief served a term in prison.* **12** *Law.* **a** deliver (an order from a court, etc.). **b** present (someone) with an order

from a court, etc.: *He was served with a notice to appear in court.*
13 act as a server at Mass. **14** *Tennis, badminton, etc.* put (the ball or shuttlecock) in play by hitting. **15** operate (a gun, etc.).
16 *Nautical.* bind or wind (a rope, etc.) with fine cord or wire to strengthen or protect it.
serve (someone) **right,** be just what one deserves: *The punishment served him right.*
—*n. Tennis, badminton, etc.* **1** the act or way of serving a ball or shuttlecock. **2** a player's turn to serve. [ME < OF *servir* < L *servire* < *servus* slave]

serv·er (sėr′vər) *n.* **1** a person who serves. **2** a tray for dishes. **3** any of various pieces of tableware for serving food: *a cake or pie server.* **4** *Roman Catholic Church.* a person who assists the priest at Mass; acolyte.

serv·ice (sėr′vis) *n., adj., v.* **-iced, -ic·ing.** —*n.* **1** a helpful act or acts; aid; conduct that is useful to others: *He performed many services for his country.* **2** supply; arrangements for supplying something useful or necessary: *The bus service was good.*
3 occupation or employment as a servant: *go into service.* **4** work done for others; performance of duties; work: *Mrs. Brown no longer needs the services of a doctor.* **5** advantage; benefit; use: *This coat has given me great service. Every available truck was pressed into service.* **6** a department of government or public employment; the persons engaged in it: *the civil service.* **7** duty in the navy, army, air force, etc.: *active service.* **8** a religious meeting, ritual, or ceremony: *We attend church services twice a week.* **9** regard; respect; devotion. **10** the manner of serving food; the food served. **11** a set of dishes, etc.: *a silver tea service.* **12** *Law.* the serving of a process or writ upon a person. **13** *Tennis, squash, badminton, etc.* **a** the act or manner of serving the ball or shuttlecock. **b** a player's turn to serve. **14** *Nautical.* a fine cord or wire wound about a rope, etc. to strengthen or protect it. **15 services,** **a** work done in the service of others; helpful labor, as opposed to production, manufacturing, construction work, etc.: *goods and services.* **b** arrangements or installations for public use, such as electricity, water supply, and sewers. **16 the service** or **the services,** the navy, army, or air force.
at (someone's) **service,** ready to do what someone wants.
in service, in working order; functioning: *We'll call you as soon as the line is in service again. Is their telephone in service?*
of service, helpful; useful.
out of service, not in working order; not functioning: *This elevator is out of service.*
—*adj.* **1** belonging to or assisting household servants, tradespeople, etc.: *a service door, service pantry.* **2** belonging to a branch of the armed forces, especially on active duty: *a service cap.* **3** used for ordinary occasions: *a service uniform.*
—*v.* **1** make fit for service; keep fit for service: *The mechanic serviced our automobile.* **2** provide with a service or with services: *Two trains serviced the town.* [ME < OF < L *servitium* < *servus* slave]

serv·ice·a·bil·i·ty (sėr′vis ə bil′ə tē) *n.* being serviceable.

serv·ice·a·ble (sėr′vis ə bəl) *adj.* **1** useful for a long time; able to stand much use. **2** capable of giving good service; useful. **3** *Archaic.* willing to be useful. —**serv′ice·a·ble·ness,** *n.*
—**serv′ice·a·bly,** *adv.*

serv·ice·ber·ry (sėr′vis ber′ē) *n.* any of several North American shrubs or small trees (genus *Amelanchier*) of the rose family having showy white flowers and sweet, purplish, edible berries. Also called **shadbush.** See also **saskatoon.**

service centre 1 a stopping area adjoining an expressway, consisting of a service station, restaurant, toilet facilities, etc.
2 *Cdn.* a town or city serving as a shopping and distribution centre for the surrounding region: *In summer our small town is the service centre for a large resort area.*

service club 1 a men's organization, such as the Rotary or the Kiwanis, formed to promote the welfare of its community and further the interests of its members. **2** a recreation centre for military personnel.

serv·ice·man (sėr′vis man′ *or* ser′vis mən) *n., pl.* **-men. 1** a member of the armed forces. **2** a man whose job is to maintain and repair machines, appliances, etc.

service road 1 access road. **2** a road, generally paralleling an expressway, to carry local traffic and to provide access to adjoining property.

service station 1 a place for supplying automobiles with gasoline, oil, water, etc. **2** a place where repairs, parts, adjustments, etc. can be obtained for mechanical or electrical devices.

service vote *Cdn.* in an election, the votes of members of the armed forces who are on duty away from their home ridings. These votes are tallied separately and reported some time after the general count of votes.

serv·ice·wom·an (sėr′vis wú′mən) *n., pl.* **serv·ice·wom·en.** a female member of the armed forces.

hat, āge, fär; let, ēqual, tėrm; it, īce
hot, ōpen, ôrder; oil, out; cup, pút, rüle,
ə above, takən, pencəl, lemən, circəs

ch, child; ng, long; sh, ship
th, thin; ᴛʜ, then; zh, measure

ser·vi·ette (sėr′vē et′) *n.* a piece of cloth or paper used at meals for protecting the clothing or for wiping the lips or fingers. [< F *serviette* < *servir* serve]

ser·vile (sėr′vil *or* sėr′vəl) *adj.* **1** fawning or submissive: *servile flattery.* **2** of or having to do with slaves: *a servile revolt, servile work.* **3** fit for a slave. **4** yielding through fear, lack of spirit, etc.: *An honest judge cannot be servile to public opinion.* [ME < L *servilis* < *servus* slave] —**ser′vile·ly,** *adv.* —**ser′vile·ness,** *n.*

ser·vil·i·ty (sėr vil′ə tē) *n., pl.* **-ties.** an attitude or behavior fit for a slave; servile yielding.

serv·ing (sėr′ving) *n.* portion of food served to a person at one time; helping.

ser·vi·tor (sėr′və tər) *n.* a servant; attendant. [ME < OF < LL *servitor* < L *servire* serve. See SERVE.]

ser·vi·tude (sėr′və tyüd′ *or* sėr′və tüd′) *n.* **1** slavery; bondage. **2** forced labor as a punishment: *The criminal was sentenced to five years' servitude.* **3** *Law.* **a** the condition of property subject to a right of enjoyment possessed by some person other than its owner, or attaching to some other property. **b** such a right of enjoyment. [ME < OF < L *servitudo* < *servus* slave]

ses·a·me (ses′ə mē) *n.* **1** a tropical annual plant (*Sesamum indicum*) widely cultivated for its small, oval, oily seeds. **2** the seeds of this plant, used to flavor bread, etc. and also as a source of oil. **3** See **open sesame.** [< Gk. < Semitic]

ses·qui·cen·ten·ni·al (ses′kwi sen ten′ē əl) *n., adj.* —*n.* a 150th anniversary or its celebration. —*adj.* having to do with, or marking the completion of, a period of a century and a half. [< L *sesqui-* one and a half + E *centennial*]

ses·qui·pe·da·li·an (ses′kwi pə dā′lē ən) *adj., n.* —*adj.* **1** of a word, very long; containing many syllables. **2** using long words. —*n.* a very long word. [< L *sesquipedalis* half a yard long < *sesqui* one and a half + *pes, pedis* foot]

ses·sile (ses′il *or* ses′əl) *adj.* **1** *Botany.* attached by a base instead of by a stem, as a leaf having no petiole or a flower having no peduncle or pedicel. **2** *Zoology.* sedentary; fixed to one spot; not able to move around, as barnacles and sponges. [< L *sessilis* sitting < *sedere* sit]

ses·sion (sesh′ən) *n.* **1** a sitting or meeting of a court, council, legislature, etc.: *a session of Parliament.* **2** a series of such sittings. **3** the term or period of such sittings: *This year's session of Parliament was unusually long.* **4** a period of meetings, classes, etc.: *Our school has two sessions, one in the morning and one in the afternoon. He attended the university during the summer session.* **5** any meeting: *a heated session with the head of the department.*
in session, meeting: *The teachers were in session all Saturday morning.* [ME < L *sessio, -onis* < *sedere* sit]
☛ *Hom.* **cession.**

ses·sion·al (sesh′ən əl) *adj.* **1** of a session; having to do with sessions. **2** occurring every session.

sessional indemnity in certain provinces of Canada, the remuneration paid each session to a Member of the Legislative Assembly.

ses·terce (ses′tėrs) *n.* an ancient Roman coin of small value. [< L *sestertius*, originally, adj., two and a half < *semis* half unit (< *semi-* half + *as* unit) + *tertius* third]

ses·ter·ti·um (ses tėr′shē əm) *n., pl.* **-ti·a** (-shē ə). an ancient Roman unit of money equal to a thousand sesterces. [erroneously formed as a singular to L *sestertia*, short for *milia sestertium* thousands of sesterces]

ses·tet (ses tet′) *n.* **1** *Music.* sextet. **2** the last six lines of certain sonnets. [< Ital. *sestetto*, ult. < L *sex* six]

set (set) *v.* **set, set·ting; adj., n.** —*v.* **1** put in some place; put; place: *Set the box on its end.* **2 a** put in the right place, position, or condition: *to set a broken bone.* **b** arrange (the hair) when damp to make it take a certain position. **3** adjust according to a standard: *to set a clock.* **4** put in some condition or relation: *A spark set the woods on fire. The slaves were set free.* **5** put (a price, etc.); fix the value of at a certain amount or rate: *He set the value of the watch at $500.* **6** put as the measure of esteem of a person or thing: *to set great store by a thing.* **7** post, appoint, or station for the purpose of performing some duty: *to set a detective on a person.* **8** fix; arrange; appoint: *to set a time limit for taking an examination.* **9** provide for

others to follow: *to set a good example.* **10** put in a fixed, rigid, or settled state: *to set one's jaw.* **11** make or become firm or hard; become fixed: *Jelly sets as it cools.* **12** put in a frame or other thing that holds: *to set a diamond in gold.* **13** adorn; ornament: *a bracelet set with diamonds.* **14** go down; sink: *The sun sets in the west.* **15** put (a hen) to sit on eggs to hatch them; place (eggs) under a hen to be hatched. **16** plant or transplant (a seedling, shoot, etc.). **17** of a dog, indicate the position of game by standing stiffly and pointing with the nose. **18** hang or fit in a particular manner: *That coat sets well.* **19** have a direction; tend: *The current sets to the south.* **20** begin to move. **21** make an attack. **22** encourage to attack; cause to be hostile. **23** begin to apply; begin to apply oneself: *Have you set to work?* **24** form fruit in the blossom. **25** *Music.* **a** adapt; fit: *to set words to music.* **b** arrange (music) for certain voices or instruments. **26** *Printing.* put (type) in the order required. **27** make (a color of fabrics, etc.) fast.

set about, start work upon; begin: *Set about your washing.*

set against, a make unfriendly toward. **b** balance; compare.

set apart, reserve.

set aside, a put to one side. **b** put by for later use. **c** discard, dismiss, or leave out; reject; annul.

set back, a stop; hinder; check: *The job was set back because of the accident.* **b** *Informal.* cost (a person) so much: *The new car set him back a lot of money.*

set bread, mix batter or dough and leave it to rise.

set down, a deposit or let alight; put down: *set down a suitcase. The bus set him down near the town.* **b** put down in writing or printing. **c** consider; ascribe: *Your failure in the test can be set down to too much haste.*

set forth, a make known; express; declare. **b** start out: *We set forth on our trip.*

set in, a begin. **b** blow or flow towards the shore.

set off, a explode. **b** start to go: *set off for home.* **c** emphasize or enhance by contrast: *The green dress set off her red hair.* **d** balance; compensate: *His losses were set off by some gains.* **e** mark off; separate from the others: *One sentence was set off from the rest by quotation marks.*

set on or **set upon, a** attack: *The dog set on him.* **b** urge to attack.

set out, a start to go. **b** spread out to show, sell, or use. **c** plant. **d** plan; intend (to do something). **e** put down.

set to, a begin: *Set to work.* **b** begin fighting: *The two boys set to.*

set up, a build. **b** begin; start. **c** put up; raise in place, position, power, pride, etc. **d** claim; pretend. **e** make ready; prepare; arrange. **f** establish.

set up for, claim or pretend to be.

—*adj.* **1** fixed or appointed beforehand; established: *a set time, set rules.* **2** fixed; rigid: *a set smile. He has set opinions.* **3** firm; hard. **4** resolved; determined: *He is set on going today.* **5** *Informal.* stubbornly fixed; obstinate.

—*n.* **1** a number of things or persons belonging together: *a set of dishes.* **2** *Mathematics.* a specified collection of elements, especially a collection having some feature or features in common: *the set of all right triangles, the set of even integers.* **3** a device for receiving or sending by radio, television, telephone, telegraph, etc. **4 a** the complete scenery for a play, act, scene, etc. **b** the physical setting for a scene in a motion picture, television show, etc. **5** the way a thing is put or placed; form; shape: *His jaw had a stubborn set.* **6** the way in which anything fits: *the set of a coat.* **7** a direction; tendency; course; drift: *the set of a current. The set of opinion was toward building a new bridge.* **8** a warp; bend; displacement: *a set to the right.* **9** a slip or shoot for planting. **10** a young fruit just formed from a blossom. **11** the act or manner of setting. **12** *Tennis.* a group of six or more games. To win a set, one side must win at least two more than the other side. **13** a snare or trap. **14** the direction in which a current flows or a wind blows. **15** *Square dancing.* **a** a group of four couples. **b** the figures of a square dance. **16** the pointing of a dog, such as a setter, in the presence of game. [OE *settan*]

☛ *Syn. v.* **1.** See note at **put.**

☛ *Usage.* **Set, sit.** People and things sit (pt., *sat*) or they are set (pt., *set*), meaning "placed": *I like to sit in a hotel lobby. I have sat in this same seat for a long time. She set the soup down with a flourish. The post was set one metre into the ground.*

Set (set) *n.* the ancient Egyptian god of evil. He was represented as having an animal's head with a pointed snout.

se·ta (sē′tə) *n., pl.* **se·tae** (-tē *or* -tī). any slender, stiff, bristle-like structure. Earthworms have two pairs of setae in each segment. [< L *saeta*]

set·back (set′bak′) *n.* **1** a check to progress; reverse. **2** a steplike setting back of the upper storeys of a tall building in order to give better light and air in the street. **3** a lessening in the thickness of a wall. **4** a flat, plain projection of a wall.

set–off (set′of′) *n.* **1** a setting out on a trip; a start; departure. **2** a thing used to set off or adorn; ornament; decoration. **3** something

that counterbalances or makes up for something else; a compensation; offset. **4** a settlement of a debt by means of a claim in the debtor's favor. **5** a claim so used.

set·screw (set′skrü′) *n.* a machine screw used to fasten gears, pulleys, etc. to a shaft.

set·tee (se tē′) *n.* a sofa or long bench with a back and, usually, arms. [< *set*]

set·ter (set′ər) *n.* **1** any of several breeds of hunting dog usually trained to locate game and indicate its presence by pointing. Setters were originally trained to crouch when they had located game. **2** a person who sets or arranges things: *a setter of type, a setter of jewels.*

set·ting (set′ing) *n.* **1** a frame or other thing in which something is set. The mounting of a jewel is its setting. **2** the scenery of a play; a set. **3** the place, time, etc. of a play or story. **4** the surroundings; background: *a scenic mountain setting.* **5** the music composed to go with a story, poem, etc. **6** the eggs that a hen sets on for hatching. **7** the act of one that sets. **8** the dishes or cutlery required to set one place at a table.

set·tle¹ (set′əl) *v.* -tled, -tling. **1** determine; decide; agree (upon): *Have you settled on a time for leaving?* **2** put or be put in order; arrange: *I must settle all my affairs before going away for the winter.* **3** pay; arrange payment: *to settle a bill.* **4** take up residence (in a new country or place): *to settle in Manitoba.* **5** establish colonies or communities in: *The French settled Quebec.* **6** set or be set in a fairly permanent position, place, or way of life: *We are settled in our new home.* **7** put or come to rest in a particular place; put in or come to a definite condition: *His cold settled in his lungs.* **8** arrange in or come to a desired or comfortable position: *The cat settled herself in the chair.* **9** make or become quiet: *A vacation will settle your nerves.* **10** go down; sink: *The end of that wall has settled five centimetres.* **11** of liquid, make or become clear: *A beaten egg or cold water will settle coffee.* **12** of dregs, sink or cause to sink to the bottom. **13** make or become firm and compact: *to settle the contents of a barrel.*

settle down, a live a more regular life. **b** direct steady effort or attention. **c** calm down; become quiet.

settle up, pay a bill or bills; make payment.

settle upon or **on,** give (property, etc.) to by law.

[OE *setlan* < *setl* settle²]

☛ *Syn.* **1.** See note at **fix.**

set·tle² (set′əl) *n.* a long wooden seat with arms and a high back, and often having a boxlike base that can be used as a storage chest. [OE *setl*]

set·tle·ment (set′əl mənt) *n.* **1** the act of settling or the state of being settled. **2** establishment in life. **3** a deciding; determining: *settlement of a date.* **4** a putting in order; arrangement. **5** a payment: *Settlement of all claims against the firm will be made shortly.* **6** the settling of persons in a new region: *The settlement of the English along the Atlantic Coast of North America gave England claim to that section.* **7** a region settled in this way: *England had many settlements along the Atlantic Coast.* **8** a group of buildings and the people living in them: *The explorers spent the night in an Indian settlement.* **9** a place in a poor, neglected neighborhood where work for its improvement is carried on. **10** the settling of property upon someone: *She received $200 000 by a marriage settlement.* **11** the amount so given. **12** a gradual sinking or subsidence of a structure, etc.

set·tler (set′lər) *n.* **1** a person who settles. **2** a person who settles in a new region.

set·tlings (set′lingz) *n.pl.* sediment.

set–to (set′tü′) *n., pl.* -tos. *Informal.* a fight; dispute.

set–up (set′up′) *n.* **1** an arrangement of apparatus, machinery, etc. **2** the arrangement of an organization. **3** *Slang.* **a** a contest or match where the outcome is assured. **b** anything that is very easy to do or whose outcome is readily predictable. **4** one's manner of holding the head and body; carriage; bearing.

sev·en (sev′ən) *n., adj.* —*n.* **1** one more than six; 7: *Ten minus three equals seven.* **2** the numeral 7: *This 7 looks like a 1.* **3** the seventh in a set or series; especially, a playing card having seven spots: *She led with a seven of spades.* **4** a set or series of seven persons or things: *She arranged the cards in sevens.* —*adj.* **1** one more than six; 7: *They stayed seven days.* **2** being seventh in a set or series (used mainly after the noun): *Lesson Seven was boring.* [OE *seofon*]

sev·en·fold (sev′ən fōld′) *adv., adj.* —*adv.* **1** seven times as much or as many. **2** seven times as much or as often; in the proportion of seven to one. —*adj.* **1** seven times as much or as many. **2** having seven parts.

Seven Hills the hills upon and about which Rome was built.

seven seas all the seas and oceans of the world, traditionally believed to be the Arctic, Antarctic, North Atlantic, South Atlantic, North Pacific, South Pacific, and Indian oceans: *to sail the seven seas.*

sev·en·teen (sev′ən tēn′) *n., adj.* —*n.* **1** seven more than ten;

17: *Seventeen plus three is twenty.* **2** the numeral 17: *I think it's a 17, not an 11.* **3** the seventeenth in a set or series. **4** a set or series of seventeen persons or things.
—*adj.* **1** seven more than ten; 17: *It costs about seventeen dollars.* **2** being seventeenth in a set or series (*used after the noun*): *Chapter Seventeen looks interesting.* [OE *seofontēne*]

sev·en·teenth (sev′ən tēnth′) *adj. or n.* **1** next after the 16th; last in a series of 17; 17th. **2** one or being one of 17 equal parts.

sev·enth (sev′ənth) *adj., n.* —*adj.* **1** next after the sixth; last in a series of 7; 7th. **2** being one of 7 equal parts.
—*n.* **1** the next after the sixth; the last in a series of 7. **2** one of 7 equal parts. **3** *Music.* **a** the interval between two tones that are seven degrees apart. **b** the combination of two such tones.

Seventh Day Adventist a member of a Christian group that believes that the second coming of Christ is near at hand. Seventh Day Adventists keep the sabbath on Saturday, the seventh day.

seventh heaven **1** the highest part of heaven. **2** the highest place or condition of joy and happiness.

sev·enth·ly (sev′ənth lē) *adv.* in the seventh place.

sev·en·ti·eth (sev′ən tē ith) *adj., n.* **1** next after the 69th; last in a series of 70; 70th. **2** one, or being one, of 70 equal parts.

sev·en·ty (sev′ən tē) *n., pl.* **-ties**; *adj.* —*n.* **1** seven times ten; 70. **2 seventies,** *pl.* the years from seventy through seventy-nine, especially of a century or of a person's life: *He was still skiing regularly well into his seventies.* —*adj.* being seven times ten; 70. [OE *seofontig*]

Seven Wonders of the World the seven structures of the ancient world considered by ancient and medieval scholars to be most remarkable. They are the Egyptian Pyramids, the Mausoleum at Halicarnassus, the Temple of Artemis (Diana) at Ephesus, the walls and hanging gardens of Babylon, the Colossus of Rhodes, the statue of Zeus by Phidias at Olympia, and the Pharos (lighthouse) at Alexandria.

Seven Years' War a war fought between Great Britain and France and their allies, 1756-1763, in Europe, North America, India, etc. In Canada, the French were defeated by the British in 1759, with the result that Canada became a British colony. In North America, the war was known also as the **French and Indian War.**

sev·er (sev′ər) *v.* **1** cut apart; cut off: *sever a rope. The axe severed his head from his body.* **2** part; divide; separate: *a church severed into two factions. The rope severed and the swing fell down.* **3** break off: *The two countries severed relations.* [ME < OF *sevrer,* ult. < L *separare* separate. See SEPARATE.] —**sev′er·a·ble,** *adj.*

sev·er·al (sev′ər əl or sev′rəl) *adj.* —*adj.* **1** being more than two or three but not many; some; a few: *to gain several kilograms.* **2** individual; different: *The boys went their several ways, each on his own business.* **3** considered separately; single: *The several steps in the process of making paper were shown in a movie.* —*n.* more than two or three but not many; some; a few: *Several have given their consent.* [ME < AF *several,* ult. < L *separ* distinct < *separare* separate. See SEPARATE.]

sev·er·al·ly (sev′ər əl ē or sev′rəl ē) *adv.* **1** separately; singly; individually: *Consider these points, first severally and then collectively.* **2** respectively. **3** *Archaic.* apart from others; independently.

sev·er·al·ty (sev′ər əl tē or sev′rəl tē) *n., pl.* **-ties. 1** the state of being separate or distinct. **2** the condition of being held or owned by separate or individual rights. **3** land so held.

sev·er·ance (sev′ər əns or sev′rəns) *n.* **1** a severing or being severed; separation; division. **2** a breaking off: *the severance of diplomatic relations between two countries.*

severance pay additional pay, based on seniority, granted to employees that are leaving a business, company, etc.

se·vere (sə vēr′) *adj.* **-ver·er, -ver·est. 1** very strict; stern; harsh: *The judge imposed a severe sentence on the criminal.* **2** serious; grave: *a severe illness.* **3** very plain or simple; without ornament: *Her severe dress made her look old.* **4** sharp; violent: *a severe criticism, a severe storm.* **5** difficult: *a series of severe tests.* **6** rigidly exact, accurate, or methodical: *severe reasoning.* [< L *severus*] —**se·vere′ly,** *adv.* —**se·vere′ness,** *n.*

se·ver·i·ty (sə ver′ə tē) *n., pl.* **-ties. 1** strictness; sternness; harshness. **2** violence; sharpness: *the severity of storms, pain, disease, grief, etc.* **3** simplicity of style or taste; plainness. **4** seriousness; gravity. **5** accuracy; exactness. **6** something severe.

Sè·vres (sev′rə) *n.* **1** a choice and costly kind of porcelain. **2** something made of this porcelain. [< *Sèvres,* a town in N France, where this porcelain is made]

sew (sō) *v.* **sewed, sewn** or **sewed, sew·ing. 1** work with needle and thread. **2** fasten with stitches.
sew up, **a** close with stitches: *The doctor sewed up the wound.* **b** *Informal.* make certain.
[OE *seowian*]
☞ *Hom.* **so, sow.**

hat, āge, fär; let, ēqual, tėrm; it, īce
hot, ōpen, ôrder; oil, out; cup, put, rüle,
əbove, takən, pencəl, lemən, circəs
ch, child; ng, long; sh, ship
th, thin; ᴛʜ, then; zh, measure

sew·age (sü′ij) *n.* the waste matter that passes through sewers.

sew·er¹ (sü′ər) *n.* a pipe or channel to carry off waste water and refuse. Sewers are usually underground. [ME < OF *sewiere* sluice from a pond, ult. < L *ex* by + *aqua* water]

sew·er² (sō′ər) *n.* a person or thing that sews. [< *sew*]

sew·er³ (sü′ər) *n.* in medieval England, a head servant in charge of arranging the table and serving the meals. [ME < AF *asseour,* literally, seater, ult. < L *ad-* by + *sedere* sit]

sew·er·age (sü′ər ij) *n.* **1** the removal of waste matter by sewers. **2** a system of sewers. **3** sewage.

sew·ing (sō′ing) *n., adj.* —*n.* **1** work done with a needle and thread. **2** something to be sewn. —*adj.* for sewing: *a sewing room.*

sewing circle a group of women who meet regularly to sew for their church, for charity, etc.

sewing machine a machine for sewing or stitching cloth.

sewn (sōn) *v.* a pp. of **sew.**
☞ *Hom.* **sown.**

sex (seks) *n., v.* —*n.* **1** either of the two categories, male and female, into which human beings, animals, and plants are divided according to their function in the reproductive process. **2** the fact or condition of being male or female: *without regard to age or sex. Give age, sex, and place of birth.* **3** the attraction of one sex for the other: *Sex makes the world go round. She oozes sex from every pore.* **4** behavior motivated by such attraction. **5** sexual intercourse. **6** the genitals. **7** (*adj.*) of or having to do with sex: *sex education.* —*v.* **1** determine the sex of (young chickens, kittens, puppies, etc.). **2** make sexually more interesting or appealing (*usually used with* **up**): *You could put a slit in the side of the skirt to sex it up.* **3** excite or arouse sexually (*usually used with* **up**). [< L *sexus*] —**sex′less,** *adj.*

sex·a·ge·nar·i·an (sek′sə jə ner′ē ən) *adj., n.* —*adj.* of the age of 60 years, or between 60 and 70 years old. —*n.* a person aged 60, or between 60 and 70. [< L *sexagenarius,* ult. < *sexaginta* sixty]

sex·ag·e·nar·y (seks aj′ə ner′ē) *adj., n., pl.* **-nar·ies.** —*adj.* **1** of or having to do with the number 60; composed of or going by sixties. **2** sexagenarian. —*n.* a sexagenarian.

Sex·a·ges·i·ma (sek′sə jes′ə mə) *n.* the second Sunday before Lent. [< L *sexagesima,* literally, sixtieth]

sex·a·ges·i·mal (sek′sə jes′ə məl) *adj., n.* —*adj.* having to do with or based upon the number 60. A sexagesimal fraction is one whose denominator is 60 or a power of 60. —*n.* a sexagesimal fraction.

sex appeal attraction for the opposite sex.

sex·ism (sek′siz əm) *n.* prejudice or discrimination against a person or group of persons on the basis of their sex.

sex·ist (sek′sist) *n.* **1** characterized by prejudice or discrimination on the basis of sex: *a sexist attitude, a sexist statement.* **2** a person who has such an attitude.

sext (sekst) *n.* **1** the fourth of the seven canonical hours set aside for prayer and meditation. **2** the office or service for this hour, originally fixed for noon, the sixth hour after sunrise. [< L *sexta* (*hora*) sixth (hour) < *sex* six; because it originally came at the sixth hour of the day (noon)]

sex·tan (seks′tən) *n., adj.* —*n.* a fever or ague characterized by paroxysms that recur every sixth day. —*adj.* **1** of such a fever or ague. **2** recurring every sixth day. [< NL *sextana* (*febris* fever) < L *sex* six]

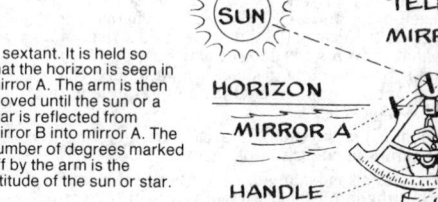

A sextant. It is held so that the horizon is seen in mirror A. The arm is then moved until the sun or a star is reflected from mirror B into mirror A. The number of degrees marked off by the arm is the altitude of the sun or star.

sex·tant (seks′tənt) *n.* **1** an instrument used by navigators,

surveyors, etc. for measuring the angular distance between two objects. Sextants are used at sea to measure the altitude of the sun, a star, etc. in order to determine the latitude and longitude. **2** one sixth of a circle. [< L *sextans, -antis* a sixth < *sex* six]

sex·tet or **sex·tette** (seks tet′) *n.* **1** *Music.* **a** a composition for six voices or instruments. **b** six singers or players. **2** any group of six. [alteration of *sestet,* after L *sex* six]

sex·til·lion (seks til′yən) *n.* **1** in Canada, the United States and France, 1 followed by 21 zeros. **2** in Great Britain, 1 followed by 36 zeros. [< F *sextillion* (< L *sextus* sixth), modelled after *million* million]

sex·ton (seks′tən) *n.* a person employed as caretaker of a church and its adjacent property. A sexton's duties sometimes include ringing the church bell for services, etc. and digging graves. [ME < OF *secrestein* < Med.L *sacristanus* sacristan. Doublet of SACRISTAN.]

sex·tu·ple (seks tyü′pəl or seks tü′pəl, seks′tup əl or seks′tə pəl) *adj., n., v.* **-pled, -pling.** —*adj.* **1** consisting of six parts; sixfold. **2** six times as great. **3** *Music.* characterized by six beats to the measure.
—*n.* a number or amount six times as great as another.
—*v.* make or become six times as great. [< L *sextus* sixth; modelled after *quadruple*]

sex·tu·plet (seks tu′plit or seks tü′plit, seks′tup lit′ or seks′tə plit′) *n.* **1** one of six children, animals, etc. born of the same mother at the same time. **2** a group of six things. [< *sextuple,* modelled after *triplet*]

sex·u·al (sek′shü əl) *adj.* **1** of or having to do with sex or the sexes: *sexual distinctions.* **2** of or having to do with relations between the sexes: *sexual conflict, sexual morality.* **3** *Biology.* having or involving sex: *sexual reproduction.* [< LL *sexualis* < L *sexus* sex] —**sex′u·al·ly,** *adv.*

sex·u·al·i·ty (sek′shü al′ə tē) *n.* **1** sexual character; possession of sex. **2** attention to sexual matters.

sexual intercourse a joining of the sexual organs of a male and a female human being, usually with the transfer of semen from the male to the female.

sex·y (sek′sē) *adj.* **sex·i·er, sex·i·est.** *Informal.* **1** sexually provocative or stimulating: *a sexy dress, sexy beauties.* **2** especially concerned with sexual functions: *a sexy novel.*

sf. sforzando.

sfor·zan·do (sfôr tsän′dō) *adj., adv., n. Music.* —*adj.* with special, usually sudden, emphasis.
—*adv.* in a sforzando manner.
—*n.* a tone or chord performed in this way. *Abbrev.:* sf. or sfz. [< Ital. *sforzando* forcing]

S.F.S.R. Soviet Federated Socialist Republic.

sfz. sforzando.

s.g. specific gravity.

Sgt. or **Sgt** sergeant.

Sgt.Maj. sergeant-major.

sh or **'sh** (sh) *interj.* a shortening of **hush,** used to urge silence.

shab·by (shab′ē) *adj.* **-bi·er, -bi·est. 1** much worn: *His old suit looks shabby.* **2** wearing old or much worn clothes. **3** poor or neglected; run-down: *a shabby old house.* **4** not generous; mean; unfair: *It is shabby not to speak to an old friend because he is poor.* [< dial. *shab* scab, OE *sceabb*] —**shab′bi·ly,** *adv.* —**shab′bi·ness,** *n.*

shack (shak) *n., v.* —*n.* **1** a roughly built hut or cabin: *The boys made a shack in the backyard.* **2** a house in bad condition. —*v.* **shack up,** *Slang.* live with a person of the opposite sex in a common-law union.
[? < Mexican Sp. *jacal* wooden hut < Nahuatl *xacalli*]

shack·le (shak′əl) *n., v.* **-led, -ling.** —*n.* **1** a metal band fastened around the ankle or wrist of a prisoner, slave, etc. Shackles are usually fastened to each other, the wall, floor, etc. by chains. **2** the link fastening together the two rings for the ankles and wrists of a prisoner. **3** anything that prevents freedom of action, thought, etc. **4** something for fastening or coupling. **5 shackles,** *pl.* fetters; chains. —*v.* **1** put shackles on. **2** restrain; hamper. **3** fasten or couple with a shackle. [OE *sceacel*] —**shack′ler,** *n.*

shack·town (shak′toun′) *n.* a residential area consisting of roughly built huts or cabins; a collection of shacks.

shad (shad) *n., pl.* **shad** or **shads.** any of several saltwater fishes (genus *Alosa*) of the herring family that ascend rivers in the spring to spawn. The American shad (*A. sapidissima*) of the N Atlantic coast is a valuable food fish. [OE *sceadd*]

shad·ber·ry (shad′ber′ē) *n., pl.* **-ries.** *Cdn. Esp.Maritimes.* **1** the

---

fruit of the shadbush. **2** shadbush; serviceberry. [? because the bush flowers at the season when shad appear in Atlantic rivers]

shad·blos·som (shad′blos′əm) *n.* shadbush.

shad·bush (shad′bush′) *n. Cdn. Esp.Maritimes.* serviceberry.

shad·dock (shad′ək) *n.* **1** a SE Asian citrus tree (*Citrus grandis,* also called *C. Maxima*) bearing very large, usually pear-shaped, edible, yellow fruit with a tart flavor. **2** the fruit of this tree. [after Captain *Shaddock,* its first western cultivator]

shade (shād) *n., v.* **shad·ed, shad·ing.** —*n.* **1** a partly dark place, not in the sunshine. **2** a slight darkness or coolness afforded by something that cuts off light: *the shade of a tree.* **3** a place or condition of comparative obscurity. **4 the shades,** darkness of evening or night. **5** something that shuts out light; a blind: *Pull down the shades of the windows.* **6** lightness or darkness of color: *silks in all shades of blue.* **7** the dark part of a picture. **8** a very small difference, amount, or degree: *a shade too long.* **9** a darkening look, feeling, etc.; shadow; cloud: *A shade of doubt troubled her.* **10** a ghost; spirit: *the shades of departed heroes.*
in or **into the shade, a** out of the light. **b** in or into a condition of being unknown or unnoticed.
—*v.* **1** screen from light; darken. **2** make darker than the rest. **3** make dark or gloomy. **4** show small differences; change little by little: *This scarf shades from deep rose to pale pink.* **5** lessen slightly: *Can't you shade the price for me?* [OE *sceadu*]
—**shade′less,** *adj.*
☛ *Syn. n.* 6. See note at **color.**

shad-fly (shad′flī′) *n. Cdn. Maritimes.* any of various winged insects that appear in the spring, especially the mayfly.

shad·ing (shā′ding) *n.* **1** a covering from the light. **2** the use of black or color to give the effect of shade in a picture. **3** a slight variation or difference of color, character, etc.

shad·ow (shad′ō) *n., v.* —*n.* **1** the shade made by some person, animal, or thing. **2** shade; darkness; partial shade. **3 the shadows,** darkness after sunset. **4** the dark part of a place or picture. **5** a little bit; small degree; slight suggestion: *There's not a shadow of a doubt about his guilt.* **6** ghost. **7** a faint image or likeness: *You look worn to a shadow.* **8** a reflected image. **9** protection; shelter. **10** a person who follows another closely and secretly. **11** a constant companion; follower. **12** sadness; gloom. **13** obscurity. **14** a gloomy or troubled look or expression.
under or **in the shadow of,** very near to.
—*v.* **1** protect from light; shade: *The grass is shadowed by huge oaks.* **2** cast a shadow on. **3** represent faintly (often used with **forth**). **4** follow closely and secretly. **5** make sad or gloomy. **6** represent in a prophetic way. [from oblique case forms of OE *sceadu* shade]
—**shad′ow·er,** *n.*

shad·ow·box (shad′ō boks′) *v.* engage in shadowboxing.

shadow box 1 a boxlike frame, having artificial lighting, in which an object, painting, piece of stained glass, etc. may be attractively presented. **2** a device to shade a surface on which a film is to be projected in daylight.

shad·ow·box·ing (shad′ō bok′sing) *n.* **1** boxing before a mirror or with an imaginary opponent for exercise or training. **2** engaging in cautious preliminaries before taking positive action in an argument, struggle, campaign, etc.

shadow cabinet the senior, policy-making members of an opposition or minority party in a legislature.

shad·ow·graph (shad′ō graf′) *n.* **1** a picture produced by throwing a shadow on a lighted screen. **2** radiograph.

shad·ow·less (shad′ō lis) *adj.* having or casting no shadow.

shad·ow·y (shad′ō ē) *adj.* **1** having much shadow or shade; shady. **2** like a shadow; dim, faint, or slight: *He saw a shadowy outline on the window curtain.* **3** not real; ghostly. —**shad′ow·i·ly,** *adv.* —**shad′ow·i·ness,** *n.*

shad·y (shā′dē) *adj.* **shad·i·er, shad·i·est. 1** in the shade; shaded. **2** giving shade. **3** *Informal.* of doubtful honesty, character, etc.: *He has engaged in rather shady occupations.*
on the shady side of, older than; beyond the age of: *on the shady side of thirty.*
—**shad′i·ly,** *adv.* —**shad′i·ness,** *n.*

shaft (shaft) *n.* **1** in a machine, a cylindrical bar that rotates or supports rotating parts. **2** a deep passage sunk in the earth. The entrance to a mine is called a shaft. **3** a well-like passage; a long, narrow space: *an elevator shaft.* **4** the long, slender stem of an arrow, spear, lance, etc. **5** an arrow, spear, lance, etc. **6** something aimed at a person as one might aim an arrow or spear: *shafts of ridicule.* **7** a ray or beam of light. **8** a wooden pole by means of which a horse is harnessed to a carriage, etc. **9** column. **10** the main part of a column. See **column** for picture. **11** flagpole. **12** the long, straight handle of a hammer, axe, golf club, etc. **13** stem; stalk. **14** the rib of a feather. [OE *sceaft*] —**shaft′like′,** *adj.*

shag¹ (shag) *n.* **1** a mass or growth of long, rough, matted hair, wool, etc. **2** a long, rough, matted nap or fibre. **3** cloth, a rug, etc.

having a long, rough nap. **4** coarsely shredded tobacco. **5** cormorant. [OE *sceacga*]

shag² (shag) *v.* **shagged, shag·ging. 1** *Informal.* retrieve and return (a ball). **2** *Slang.* leave at once; go away.

shag·a·nap·pi (shag′ə nap′ē) *n.* **1** thongs, straps, lines, or cords made from rawhide. **2** an Indian pony; cayuse. [< Algonquian]

shag·bark (shag′bärk′) *n.* **1** a North American hickory (*Carya ovata*) having rough, loose, grey bark and large, sweet-tasting, edible nuts. Also called **shagbark hickory. 2** the nut of this tree. Shagbarks have fairly thin shells and are considered the best hickory nuts. **3** the wood of this tree.

shag·gy (shag′ē) *adj.* **-gi·er, -gi·est. 1** covered with a thick, rough mass of hair, wool, etc.: *a shaggy dog.* **2** long, thick, and rough: *shaggy eyebrows.* **3** having a long, rough nap; of coarse texture. **4** rough, coarse, or unkempt: *The dog had shaggy hair.* [< *shag*] —**shag′gi·ly,** *adv.* —**shag′gi·ness,** *n.*

shaggy–dog story a joke in which the humor depends on a long recital of trivial incidents building up to an absurd and unexpected ending. [from an original story of this type about a shaggy dog]

sha·green (shə grēn′) *n.* a kind of untanned leather with a granular surface, made from the skin of the horse, ass, shark, seal, and other animals. [< F *chagrin* < Turkish *saghri* rump of a horse, leather from this]

Shah (shä) *n.* a title of an Iranian male ruler. [< Persian]

shake (shāk) *v.* **shook, shak·en, shak·ing;** *n.* —*v.* **1** move quickly backwards and forwards, up and down, or from side to side: *to shake a rug.* **2** bring, throw, force, rouse, scatter, etc. by or as if by such movement: *to shake snow off one's clothes.* **3** be shaken: *Sand shakes off easily.* **4** clasp (hands) in greeting, congratulating, etc.: another: *to shake hands.* **5** tremble: *He is shaking with cold.* **6** make tremble: *The explosion shook the town.* **7** totter; waver: *His courage began to shake.* **8** cause to totter or waver: *to shake the very foundations of society.* **9** disturb; make less firm: *His lie shook my faith in his honesty.* **10** trill. **11** *Informal.* get rid of: *Can't you shake him?* **12** mix (dice) before throwing.
shake down, a bring or throw down by shaking. **b** cause to settle down. **c** bring into working order. **d** *Slang.* get money from dishonestly.
shake off, get rid off.
shake up, a shake hard. **b** stir up. **c** jar in body or nerves.
—*n.* **1** the act or fact of shaking: *a shake of the head.* **2** *Informal.* earthquake. **3** a drink made by shaking the ingredients together: *a milk shake.* **4** *Slang.* a moment: *I'll be there in two shakes.* **5** *Music.* a rapid alternation of a note with a tone above or below it; a trill. **6** a crack in a growing tree; fissure. **7** a long, rough shingle or board: *a barn roofed with cedar shakes.*
no great shakes, *Informal.* not unusual, extraordinary, or important. [OE *sceacan*] —**shak′a·ble** or **shake′a·ble,** *adj.*
☛ *Hom.* sheik.
☛ *Syn. v.* **5. Shake, tremble, quiver** = move with unsteady, irregular, rapid, and repeated movements from side to side or up and down. **Shake,** the general word, suggests a rapid, irregular, more or less violent, or abrupt motion: *He shook with laughter.* **Tremble,** used chiefly of people or animals, suggests uncontrollable, continued shaking with quick, short movements, caused by fear, strong feeling, cold, etc.: *In his excitement his hands trembled.* **Quiver** suggests a slight trembling or vibrating motion: *The dog's nostrils quivered at the scent.*

shake–down¹ (shāk′doun′) *n.* **1** a makeshift bed: *We made a shake-down of straw and blankets on the floor.* **2** the process of shaking down. **3** a bringing into proper condition or working order by practice: *The warship was given a shake-down by a trial voyage.*

shake–down² (shāk′doun′) *n. Slang.* an exaction of money, etc. by compulsion, especially as in various forms of graft. [from shaking a tree for fruit, or, possibly, the pockets of one's victim held upside down]

shak·en (shā′kən) *v.* pp. of **shake.**

shak·er (shā′kər) *n.* **1** a person who shakes something. **2** a machine or utensil used in shaking: *a cocktail shaker.* **3** a container having a perforated top, used for dispensing small amounts of pepper, salt, etc. **4 Shaker,** a member of an American religious sect, so called from body movements that formed part of their worship. Shakers owned all their property in common.

Shake·spear·e·an or **Shake·spere·an** (shāk spēr′ē ən) *adj., n.* —*adj.* of, having to do with, or suggestive of William Shakespeare (1564-1616), or his works. —*n.* a specialist in the study of the works of Shakespeare.

Shake·spear·i·an or **Shake·sper·i·an** (shāk spēr′ē ən) *adj.* or *n.* Shakespearean.

shake–up (shāk′up′) *n. Informal.* a sudden and complete change; drastic rearrangement of policy, personnel, etc.: *a shake-up in the government.*

shaking palsy Parkinson's disease.

shak·o (shak′ō) *n., pl.* **shak·os.** a high, stiff military hat with a

hat, āge, fär; let, ēqual, tėrm; it, īce
hot, ōpen, ôrder; oil, out; cup, pút, rüle,
əbove, takən, pencəl, lemən, circəs
ch, child; ng, long; sh, ship
th, thin; ₮H, then; zh, measure

plume or other ornament. See **hat** for picture. [< Hungarian *csákó* peaked (cap) < G *Zacke* point, spike]

Shak·ti (shuk′tē) *n.* one of the three great divinities of classical Hinduism, the mother goddess who stands for nature in all its aspects, the main object of worship among Hindus in northeastern India.

shak·y (shā′kē) *adj.* **shak·i·er, shak·i·est. 1** shaking: *a shaky voice.* **2** liable to break down; weak: *a shaky porch.* **3** not to be depended on; not reliable: *a shaky business firm, a shaky knowledge of art.* —**shak′i·ly,** *adv.* —**shak′i·ness,** *n.*

shale (shāl) *n.* a fine-grained sedimentary rock formed from clay that has been subjected to great pressure. Shale splits easily into thin layers. [OE *scealu* shell] —**shal′y,** *adj.*

shall (shal; *unstressed,* shəl) *v.pt.* **should,** *pres. sing. or pl.* **shall.** an auxiliary verb used: **1** in questions to ask what one is to do: *Shall we go? Shall I wait?* **2** in statements, especially with the second and third persons, to show obligation or express a command: *You shall pay attention.* **3** in statements to indicate simple future time: *I shall go tomorrow if I cannot make it today.* [OE *sceal*]
☛ *Usage.* See note at **will.**

shal·loon (sha lün′) *n.* a twilled woollen cloth, used chiefly for linings. [< F *chalon* < *Chalons-sur-Marne,* a city in NE France]

shal·lop (shal′əp) *n. Archaic.* a small, light, open boat propelled by sail or oars. [< F *chaloupe* < Du. *sloepe.* Doublet of SLOOP.]

shal·lot (shə lot′) *n.* **1** a small perennial herb (*Alium ascalonicum*) related to and resembling the onion, but having a bulb composed of sections or cloves. **2** a bulb or clove of this plant, used for seasoning. It is stronger in flavor than an onion, but milder than garlic. [ult. < F *eschalotte,* alteration of OF *eschaloigne* scallion < L (*caepa*) *Ascalonia* (onion) from Ascalon, in Palestine]

shal·low (shal′ō) *adj., n., v.* —*adj.* **1** not deep: *shallow water, a shallow dish.* **2** lacking depth of thought, knowledge, feeling, etc.: *a shallow mind.*
—*n.* Usually, **shallows,** *pl.* a shallow place: *The boys splashed in the shallows of the pond.*
—*v.* make or become less deep. [ME *shalowe,* related to OE *sceald,* adj., shallow] —**shal′low·ly,** *adv.*

shalt (shalt) *v. Archaic.* 2nd pers. sing., present tense, of **shall.** *Thou shalt* means *You* (sing.) *shall.*

shal·y (shā′lē) *adj.* of, like, or containing shale.

sham (sham) *n., adj., v.* **shammed, sham·ming.** —*n.* **1** a pretence; fraud. **2** a counterfeit; imitation. **3** a person who is a fraud. **4** a cover or the like to give a thing a different outward appearance: *a pillow sham.*
—*adj.* pretended; feigned; being an imitation: *The soldiers fought a sham battle for practice.*
—*v.* **1** pretend; feign: *He shammed sickness so he wouldn't have to work.* **2** create a false imitation of. [originally dial. var. of *shame*] —**sham′mer,** *n.*

sha·man (shā′mən, shä′mən, *or* sham′ən) *n.* a medicine man or priest believed to have the power to influence spirits for good or evil. [< Russian *shaman* < Tungus *saman* < Pali *samana* < Sanskrit *sramana* Buddhist monk; (literally) self-tormentor < *sramati* he tires]

sha·man·ism (shā′mə niz′əm, shä′mə niz′əm, *or* sham′ə niz′əm) *n.* **1** a religion of the Ural-Altaic peoples of N Asia and Europe, characterized by belief in spirits, demons, and gods that can be influenced only by the shamans. **2** any of various similar religions, as among some Amerindian or Inuit peoples.

sha·man·is·tic (shā′mə nis′tik, shä′mə nis′tik, *or* sham′ə nis′tik) *adj.* of or having to do with shamans or shamanism.

sham·a·teur (sham′ə chər, sham′ə chür, sham′ə tyür′ *or* sham′ə tėr′) *n. Slang. Sports.* a player who is classed as an amateur but is paid as if he were professional. [blend of *sham* and *amateur*]

sham·a·teur·ism (sham′ə chər iz′əm, sham′ə chür iz′əm, sham′ə tyür iz′əm *or* sham′ə tėr iz′əm) *n. Slang. Sports.* **1** the practice of using shamateurs. **2** the fact or condition of being a shamateur.

sham·ble (sham′bəl) *v.* **-bled, -bling;** *n.* —*v.* walk awkwardly or unsteadily: *The tired old man shambles.* —*n.* a shambling walk. [probably ult. special use of *shamble,* sing. of *shambles;* with reference to the straddling legs of a bench]

sham·bles (sham′bəlz) *n.pl. or sing.* **1** slaughterhouse. **2** a place of butchery or of great bloodshed. **3** *Informal.* confusion; mess; general disorder: *The room was a shambles.* [OE sc(e)amel < L *scamellum*, dim. of *scamnum* bench; originally, a table on which meat is sold]

shame (shām) *n., v.* **shamed, sham·ing.** —*n.* **1** a painful feeling of having done something wrong, improper, or silly: *to blush with shame.* **2** a disgrace; dishonor. **3** a fact to be sorry about: *It is a shame to be so wasteful.* **4** a person or thing to be ashamed of; cause of disgrace. **5** a sense of what is decent or proper.
for shame! shame on you!
put to shame, a disgrace; make ashamed. **b** surpass; make dim by comparison: *His careful work put all the rest to shame.* —*v.* **1** cause to feel shame. **2** drive or force by shame. **3** bring disgrace upon. [OE *sceamu*]

shame·faced (shām′fāst′) *adj.* **1** bashful; shy. **2** showing shame and embarrassment. [originally < *shamefast* (OE sc(e)amfæst, apparently, fixed in shame), taken as from *shame*, n. + *face*]

shame·ful (shām′fəl) *adj.* causing shame; bringing disgrace. **shame′ful·ly,** *adv.* —**shame′ful·ness,** *n.*

shame·less (shām′lis) *adj.* **1** without shame. **2** not modest. —**shame′less·ly,** *adv.* —**shame′less·ness,** *n.*

sham·my (sham′ē) *n., pl.* **-mies.** chamois.

sham·poo (sham pü′) *v.* **-pooed, -poo·ing;** *n.* —*v.* **1** wash (the hair, the scalp, a rug, etc.) with a soapy or oily preparation. **2** *Archaic.* massage. —*n.* **1** a washing of the hair, the scalp, a rug, etc. with such a preparation. **2** a preparation used for shampooing. **3** *Archaic.* massage. [< Hind. *chhāmpo*, literally, press!] —**sham·poo′er,** *n.*

sham·rock (sham′rok) *n.* **1** any of various plants having leaves composed of three rounded leaflets, such as wood sorrel or any of several clovers. The shamrock, the national emblem of Ireland and an international symbol of St. Patrick's Day, is said to have been chosen by St. Patrick to symbolize the Trinity, but the identity of the actual species has never been established. **2** a leaf of any of these plants, or a symbolic depiction or representation of such a leaf. [< Irish *seamróg*, dim. of *seamair* clover]

sha·mus (shā′məs *or* shä′məs) *n. Slang.* a detective, especially a private detective. [< Yiddish *shames* sexton, caretaker < Hebrew *shammash*]

shang·hai (shang′hī *or* shang hī′) *v.* **-haied, -hai·ing. 1** make unconscious by drugs, liquor, etc. and put on a ship to serve as a sailor. **2** bring by trickery or force. [with reference to the practice of securing sailors by kidnapping or other violent and illegal means for long voyages, often to *Shanghai*, China]

Shang·hai (shang′hī′) *n.* one of a long-legged breed of domestic fowls. [< *Shanghai*, a seaport in China]

Shan·gri-La *or* **Shan·gri·la** (shang′gri lä′) *n.* an idyllic earthly paradise. [an inaccessible land in *Lost Horizon*, a novel by James Hilton (1900-1954), an English author]

shank (shangk) *n.* **1** the part of the leg between the knee and the ankle. **2** the corresponding part in animals. See **beef** and **lamb** for pictures. **3** the whole leg. **4** any part like a leg, stem, or shaft. The shank of a fish-hook is the straight part between the hook and the loop. **5** *Printing.* the body of a type. **6** the narrow part of a shoe, connecting the broad part of the sole with the heel. **7** the latter end or part of anything.
go or **ride on shank's mare,** walk.
[OE *sceanca*]

shan't (shant) shall not.

shan·tung (shan′tung *or* shan tung′) *n.* **1** a heavy pongee, a kind of soft silk. **2** a similar fabric of cotton, rayon, etc. [< *Shantung*, a province in NE China]

shan·ty¹ (shan′tē) *n., pl.* **-ties.** *Cdn.* **1** a roughly built hut or cabin. **2** the log-built living quarters of a gang of loggers. [< Cdn.F *chantier* loggers' headquarters < F *chantier* timber yard, dock < L *cantherius* framework, beast of burden; perhaps also from or influenced by Irish *sean tig* hut]

shan·ty² (shan′tē) *n., pl.* **-ties.** a song sung by sailors in rhythm with the motions made during their work. Also, **chantey, chanty.** [var. of *chantey* < F *chanter* sing]

shan·ty·man (shan′tē man′ *or* -mən) *n., pl.* **-men.** *Cdn. Historical.* one living and working in a logging camp; logger.

shape (shāp) *n., v.* **shaped, shap·ing.** —*n.* **1** the outward contour or outline; the form of a person or thing; figure: *the shape of a triangle. All circles have the same shape; rectangles have different shapes.* **2** an assumed appearance: *A witch was supposed to take the shape of a cat or a bat.* **3** something seen, or thought to be seen, though having no definite or describable form: *A white shape*

stood at his bedside. **4** condition: *He exercises to keep in shape.* **5** a definite form; proper arrangement; order: *Take time to get your thoughts into shape.* **6** a kind; sort: *dangers of every shape.* **7** mould; pattern. **8** something shaped: jelly, pudding, etc. shaped into a mould.
take shape, have or take on a definite form.
—*v.* **1** form into a shape: *The child shapes clay into balls.* **2** take shape; assume form: *His plan is shaping well.* **3** adapt in form: *That hat is shaped to your head.* **4** give definite form or character to: *events that shape people's lives.* **5** direct; plan; devise; aim: *to shape one's course in life.* **6** express in words: *to shape a question.* **7** mould; pattern.
shape up, a take on a certain form or appearance; develop. **b** show a certain tendency.
[OE (ge)sceap, n. *sceapen*, v., pp. of *scieppan* create] —**shap′er,** *n.*
☛ *Syn. n.* **1.** See note at **form**.

SHAPE (shāp) Supreme Headquarters Allied Powers Europe.

shape·less (shāp′lis) *adj.* **1** without definite shape. **2** having an unattractive shape. —**shape′less·ly,** *adv.* —**shape′less·ness,** *n.*

shape·ly (shāp′lē) *adj.* **-li·er, -li·est.** having a pleasing shape; well-formed. —**shape′li·ness,** *n.*

shape-up (shāp′up′) *n. Informal.* a system of hiring longshoremen whereby the men line up each workday to be selected for work by the foreman.

shard (shärd) *n.* **1** a broken piece; fragment. **2** a piece of broken earthenware or pottery. **3** the hard case that covers a beetle's wing. Also, **sherd.** [OE *sceard*]

share¹ (sher) *n., v.* **shared, shar·ing.** —*n.* **1** a part belonging to one individual; portion; part: *Do your share of the work.* **2** a part of anything owned in common with others: *One of the boys offered to sell his share in the boat.* **3** each of the parts into which the ownership of a company or corporation is divided: *The ownership of this company is divided into several million shares.*
go shares, share in something.
on shares, sharing in the risks and profits.
—*v.* **1** use together; enjoy together; have in common: *The sisters share a room.* **2** divide into parts, each taking a part: *The child shared his candy with his sister.* **3** have a share; take part: *Everyone shared in making the picnic a success.* [OE *scearu* division] —**shar′er,** *n.*
☛ *Syn. v.* **1. Share, participate, partake** = use, enjoy or have something in common with another. **Share** means either to give or take a part, and emphasizes the idea of common possession, enjoyment, use, etc.: *He shares a room with his brother.* **Participate,** more formal, followed by **in,** means "take part together with others in an idea, feeling, or action": *He participated in the discussion.* **Partake,** now formal and usually followed by **of,** means "take a share of food, pleasure, qualities, etc.": *He partook of our meal.*

share² (sher) *n.* ploughshare. [OE *scear*]

share·crop (sher′krop′) *v.* **-cropped, -crop·ping.** farm or raise a crop as a sharecropper.

share·crop·per (sher′krop′ər) *n.* a person who farms land for the owner in return for part of the crops.

share·hold·er (sher′hōl′dər) *n.* a person owning shares of stock.

shark¹ (shärk) *n.* any of an order (Selachii) of cartilaginous fishes having a torpedo-shaped body, a tough, grey or whitish hide covered with tiny tubercles, two dorsal fins, and five to seven gill slits on either side of the head. Most sharks are marine and most are carnivorous. See also **basking shark, dogfish, white shark.** [origin uncertain] —**shark′like′,** *adj.*

shark² (shärk) *n.* **1** a dishonest person who preys on others: *a loan shark.* **2** *Slang.* a person unusually good at something; an expert: *a shark at mathematics.* [< G *Schork,* var. of *Schurke* scoundrel]

shark·skin (shärk′skin′) *n.* cloth made from fine threads of wool, rayon, or cotton, used in suits.

sharp (shärp) *adj., adv., n., v.* —*adj.* **1** having a thin cutting edge or a fine point: *a sharp knife, a sharp pencil.* **2** having a point; not rounded: *a sharp nose, a sharp corner on a box.* **3** with a sudden change of direction: *a sharp turn.* **4** very cold: *sharp weather, a sharp morning.* **5** severe; biting: *sharp words.* **6** causing a sensation like a cut or pinprick; affecting the senses keenly: *a sharp taste, a sharp noise, a sharp pain.* **7** clear; distinct: *the sharp contrast between black and white.* **8** quick; brisk: *a sharp walk or run.* **9** fierce; violent: *a sharp struggle.* **10** keen; eager: *a sharp desire, a sharp appetite.* **11** being aware of things quickly: *a sharp eye, sharp ears.* **12** watchful; wide-awake: *a sharp watch.* **13** quick in mind; clever: *a sharp boy.* **14** shrewd; artful; almost dishonest: *sharp practice. He is sharp at a bargain.* **15** high in pitch; shrill. **16** *Music.* **a** above the true pitch. **b** raised a half step in pitch: *F sharp.* **c** of a key, having sharps in the signature. **17** of a consonant, pronounced with breath and not with voice; voiceless. **18** *Slang.* attractive; striking in looks, value, etc.: *a sharp car. His new suit looks sharp.*
—*adv.* **1** promptly, exactly: *Come at one o'clock sharp.* **2** in a sharp manner; in an alert manner; keenly: *Look sharp!* **3** suddenly: *to pull a horse up sharp.*

—n. 1 *Music.* **a** a tone one half step, or half note, above a given tone. **b** such a tone or note. **c** the sign (♯) that stands for such a tone. 2 a swindler; sharper. 3 *Informal.* expert. 4 **sharps,** *pl.* the hard part of wheat requiring a second grinding.
—v. *Music.* make or sound sharp. [OE *scearp*] —**sharp′ly,** *adv.* —**sharp′ness,** *n.*

☛ *Syn. adj.* 13. Sharp, keen, acute, used figuratively to describe a person or the mind, means "quickly aware or penetrating." **Sharp** emphasizes being well suited to cutting or piercing through things, and suggests cleverness, shrewdness, or quickness to see and take advantage, sometimes dishonestly: *He is a sharp lawyer.* **Keen** emphasizes being shaped to slash through things, and suggests clear-sightedness, vigor, and quickness of perception and thinking: *He has a keen mind.* **Acute,** literally meaning "coming to a sharp point," suggests penetrating perception, insight, or understanding: *He is an acute interpreter of current events.*

sharp·en (shär′pən) *v.* 1 make sharp: *to sharpen a pencil. Sharpen your wits.* 2 become sharp: *Her voice sharpened as she became angry.* —**sharp′en·er,** *n.*

sharp·er (shär′pər) *n.* 1 a swindler; cheat. 2 a gambler who makes a living by cheating at cards, etc.

sharp–eyed (shärp′īd′) *adj.* 1 having keen sight: *a sharp-eyed person.* 2 watchful; very observant; vigilant.

sharp·ie (shär′pē) *n.* a long, flat-bottomed boat having one or two masts, each rigged with a triangular sail.

sharp·shoot·er (shärp′shüt′ər) *n.* a person who shoots very well, especially with a rifle.

sharp–sight·ed (shärp′sī′tid) *adj.* 1 having sharp sight. 2 sharp-witted. —**sharp′-sight′ed·ly,** *adv.* —**sharp′-sight′ed·ness,** *n.*

sharp–tailed grouse a medium-sized grouse (*Pedioecetes phasianellus*) of central and W North America, so called because of its short, pointed tail.

sharp–wit·ted (shärp′wit′id) *adj.* having or showing a quick, keen mind.

Shas·ta daisy (shas′tə) a chrysanthemum (*Chrysanthemum maximum*) widely cultivated in numerous varieties for its large, daisylike, white flowers. [< Mount *Shasta* in N. California]

shat (shat) *v. Vulgar slang.* a pt. of **shit.**

shat·ter (shat′ər) *v., n.* —*v.* 1 break into pieces: *A stone shattered the window.* 2 disturb greatly; destroy: *The great mental strain shattered his mind. Her hopes were shattered.* —*n.* **shatters,** *pl.* fragments. [ME *schater(en);* probably var. of *scatter*] —**shat′ter·er,** *n.* —**shat′ter·ing·ly,** *adv.*

☛ *Syn. v.* 1. See note at **break.**

shave (shāv) *v.* **shaved, shaved** or **shav·en, shav·ing;** *n.* —*v.* 1 remove hair with a razor; cut hair from (the face, chin, etc.) with a razor. 2 cut off (hair) with a razor. 3 cut off in thin slices; cut in thin slices. 4 cut very close. 5 come very close to; graze: *The car shaved the corner.*
—*n.* 1 the cutting off of hair with a razor. 2 a tool for shaving, scraping, removing thin slices, etc. 3 a shaving; thin slice. 4 a narrow miss or escape: *The shot missed him, but it was a close shave.* [OE *sceafan*]

shave·ling (shāv′ling) *n. Archaic.* 1 *Derogatory.* a tonsured monk, friar, or priest. 2 a youth.

shav·en (shā′vən) *adj., v.* —*adj.* 1 shaved. 2 closely cut. 3 tonsured.
—*v.* a pp. of **shave.**

shav·er (shā′vər) *n.* 1 a person who shaves. 2 an instrument for shaving. 3 *Informal.* a youngster; a small boy.

Sha·vi·an (shā′vē ən) *adj., n.* —*adj.* of, having to do with, or characteristic of George Bernard Shaw (1856-1950), an Irish dramatist and critic. —*n.* a devoted admirer of Shaw or his works.

shav·ing (shā′ving) *n.* 1 Often, **shavings,** *pl.* a very thin piece or slice. Shavings of wood are cut off by a plane. 2 the act or process of cutting hair from the face, chin, legs, etc. with a razor.

shawl (shol or shôl) *n.* a square or oblong piece of cloth to be worn about the shoulders or head. [< Persian]

shawm (shom or shôm) *n.* a medieval musical instrument resembling an oboe. [ME < OF *chalemie,* var. of *chalemel,* ult. < L < Gk. *kalamos* reed]

Shaw·nee (sho nē′ or shô nē′) *n., pl.* **-nee** or **-nees.** 1 a member of an Amerindian people formerly living in Tennessee and South Carolina, now in Oklahoma. 2 the Algonquian language of the Shawnee.

shay (shā) *n. Informal.* a chaise, a light carriage with two wheels and one seat. [< *chaise,* taken as pl.]

she (shē) *pron., subj.* **she,** *obj.* **her,** *poss.* **hers,** *pl. subj.* **they,** *pl. obj.* **them,** *pl. poss.* **theirs;** *n., pl.* **she′s.** —*pron.* 1 the girl, woman, or female animal already referred to and identified. 2 anything personified as feminine and already referred to and identified: *She was a fine old ship.* —*n.* any girl, woman, or female animal: *Is it a he or a she?* [probably OE demonstrative pronoun *sīo, sēo, sīe*]

hat, āge, fär; let, ēqual, tèrm; it, īce
hot, ōpen, ôrder; oil, out; cup, pùt, rüle,
əbove, takən, pencəl, lemən, circəs
ch, child; ng, long; sh, ship
th, thin; ŦH, then; zh, measure

sheaf (shēf) *n., pl.* **sheaves.** 1 a bundle of cut grain bound in the middle for drying, loading, and stacking. 2 a bundle of like things laid or otherwise kept together lengthwise: *a sheaf of arrows.* 3 any bundle or lot of things: *a sheaf of notes.* [OE *scēaf*]

shear (shēr) *v.* **sheared** or **(archaic) shore, sheared** or **shorn, shear·ing;** *n.* —*v.* 1 cut with shears or scissors. 2 cut the wool or fleece from: *The farmer sheared his sheep.* 3 cut close; cut off; cut. 4 to strip or deprive as if by cutting: *The assembly had been shorn of its legislative powers.* 5 break by a force causing two parts or pieces to slide on each other in opposite directions: *Too much pressure on the handles of the scissors sheared off the rivet holding the blades together.*
—*n.* 1 the act or process of shearing. 2 that which is taken off by shearing. 3 one blade of a pair of shears. 4 **shears** (def.1). 5 a force causing two parts or pieces to slide on each other in opposite directions. [OE *sceran*] —**shear′er,** *n.*

☛ *Hom.* **sheer.**

shears (shērz) *n.pl. or sing.* 1 large scissors. 2 any cutting instrument resembling scissors. 3 apparatus for hoisting heavy weights, consisting of two or more poles fastened together at the top to support a block and tackle. [OE *scēar*]

shear·wa·ter (shēr′wot′ər or -wô′tər) *n.* any of various oceanic birds (family Procellariidae) belonging to the same order as petrels and albatrosses, having long, narrow, pointed wings, a hooked bill, and mainly dark plumage, and having the habit of skimming the surface of the water in flight. [< *shear,* v. + *water,* n.]

shear zone *Geology.* a belt of rock crushed and metamorphosed by compression.

sheath (shēth) *n., pl.* **sheaths** (shēŦHz). 1 a case or covering for the blade of a sword, knife, etc. 2 any similar covering, especially on an animal or plant. 3 a woman's dress, having a fitted bodice and straight skirt, usually worn unbelted. [OE *scēath*]

sheathe (shēŦH) *v.* **sheathed, sheath·ing.** 1 put (a sword, etc.) into a sheath. 2 enclose in a case or covering: *a mummy sheathed in linen, doors sheathed in metal.*

sheath·ing (shēŦH′ing) *n.* a casing; covering. The first covering of boards on a house is sheathing.

sheath knife a knife carried in a sheath.

sheave¹ (shēv) *v.* **sheaved, sheav·ing.** gather and tie into a sheaf or sheaves. [< *sheaf*]

sheave² (shēv or shiv) *n.* a wheel with a grooved rim; the wheel of a pulley. [var. of *shive,* ME *schive*]

sheaves (shēvz *for I;* shēvz or shivz *for 2*) *n.* 1 pl. of **sheaf.** 2 pl. of **sheave.**

She·ba (shē′bə) *n.* 1 an ancient country in S Arabia. 2 **Queen of,** a biblical queen who visited Solomon to test his wisdom (I Kings 10:1-13).

she·bang (shə bang′) *n. Slang.* 1 an outfit; concern. 2 an affair; event. [origin uncertain]

She·bat (shə bät′ or shə vät′) *n.* in the Hebrew calendar, the eleventh month of the ecclesiastical year, and the fifth month of the civil year.

she·been (shi bēn′) *n. Irish dialect.* a place where liquor is sold without a licence. [< Irish *síbín*]

shed¹ (shed) *n.* a building used for shelter, storage, etc., usually having only one storey: *a tool shed.* [OE *sced* shelter]

shed² (shed) *v.* **shed, shed·ding.** 1 pour out; let fall: *He shed his blood for his country. The girl shed tears.* 2 throw off; cast aside: *A snake sheds its skin. The umbrella sheds water.* 3 throw off a covering, hair, etc.: *That snake has just shed.* 4 scatter abroad; give forth: *The sun sheds light. Flowers shed perfume.* 5 cause to flow: *He shed his enemy's blood.*
shed blood, destroy life; kill.
shed (one's) blood or **(one's) own blood,** sacrifice one's life. [OE *scēadan*]

she'd (shēd; *unstressed,* shid) 1 she had. 2 she would.

shed·der (shed′ər) *n.* 1 a person or thing that sheds. 2 a crab or lobster beginning to shed its shell.

sheen (shēn) *n.* brightness; lustre: *Satin and polished silver have a sheen.* [OE *scēne* bright]

sheen·y (shē′nē) *adj.* bright; lustrous.

sheep (shēp) *n., pl.* **sheep. 1** any of a genus (*Ovis*) of hoofed cud-chewing bovid mammals (related to goats, cattle, etc.) native to mountainous regions of North America and Europe, especially one species (*O. aries*) raised in many breeds for its wool, meat, and hide. See also **Dall sheep, aoudad. 2** a person who is weak, timid, or easily led.
make or **cast sheep's eyes at,** look at in a yearning, loving way.
separate the sheep from the goats, distinguish the better, superior, etc. people from the rest.
[OE *scēap*] —**sheep′like′,** *adj.*

sheep·cote (shēp′kōt′) *n.* a shelter for sheep.

sheep-dip (shēp′dip′) *n.* **1** a liquid disinfectant and insecticide in which sheep are immersed to destroy parasites, etc. in their fleece. **2** a trough, etc. filled with such a substance.

sheep·dog (shēp′dog′) *n.* **1** a dog trained to watch or herd sheep. **2** See **old English sheepdog** and **Shetland sheepdog.**

sheep·fold (shēp′fōld′) *n.* a pen for sheep.

sheep·herd·er (shēp′hėr′dər) *n. Esp.U.S.* a person who watches and tends large numbers of sheep while they are grazing on the unfenced land.

sheep·hook (shēp′hůk′) *n.* a shepherd's staff.

sheep·ish (shē′pish) *adj.* **1** awkwardly bashful or embarrassed: *a sheepish smile.* **2** like a sheep; timid; weak; stupid. —**sheep′ish·ly,** *adv.* —**sheep′ish·ness,** *n.*

sheep·man (shēp′man′) *n., pl.* **-men. 1** a person who owns and raises sheep. **2** sheepherder.

sheep range a tract of land on which sheep are pastured.

sheep·shank (shēp′shangk′) *n.* a kind of knot, hitch, or bend made on a rope to shorten it temporarily. See **knot** for picture.

sheeps·head (shēps′hed′) *n.* a food fish (*Archosargus rhomboidalis*) of the Atlantic coast of the United States related to the porgies and sea breams.

sheep·skin (shēp′skin′) *n.* **1** the skin of a sheep, especially with the wool on it. **2** leather or parchment made from the skin of a sheep. **3** *Informal.* diploma.

sheep sorrel a perennial herb (*Rumex acetosella*) of the northern hemisphere, having sour-tasting, narrow leaves, usually lobed at the base, and small, reddish flowers.

sheep·walk (shēp′wok′ *or* -wôk′) *n.* sheep range.

sheer¹ (shēr) *adj., adv., n.* —*adj.* **1** very thin; almost transparent: *a sheer white dress.* **2** unmixed with anything else; complete: *sheer weariness.* **3** straight up and down; steep: *From the top of the wall there was a sheer drop of 50 metres to the water below.* —*adv.* **1** completely; quite. **2** very steeply. —*n.* a dress of transparent material. [OE *scīr* bright; probably from ON *skærr* bright] —**sheer′ness,** *n.*
☛ *Hom.* **shear.**

sheer² (shēr) *v., n.* —*v.* turn from a course; turn aside; swerve. —*n.* **1** a turning of a ship from its course. **2** the upward curve of a ship's deck or lines from the middle toward each end. **3** the position in which a ship at anchor is placed to keep her clear of the anchor. [var. of *shear, v.,* in the sense of "part"]
☛ *Hom.* **shear.**

sheer legs shears (def. 3).

sheer·ly (shēr′lē) *adv.* absolutely; thoroughly; quite.

sheet¹ (shēt) *n., v.* —*n.* **1** a large piece of cloth, usually cotton or partly cotton, used to sleep on or under. **2** a broad, thin piece of anything: *a sheet of glass.* **3** a single piece of paper. **4** newspaper. **5** a broad, flat surface: *a sheet of water.* **6** the ice surface on which a game of curling is played. **7** *Poetic.* a sail. —*v.* furnish or cover with a sheet. [OE *scēte*]

sheet² (shēt) *n., v.* —*n.* **1** a rope that controls the angle at which a sail is set. **2** **sheets,** *pl.* the space at the bow or stern of an open boat. —*v.*
sheet home, stretch (a square sail) as flat as possible by pulling hard on the sheets fastened to it. [OE *scēata*]

sheet anchor **1** a large anchor used only in emergencies. **2** the chief support or source of security. [origin uncertain]

sheet bend a kind of knot to fasten two ropes together. See **knot** for picture.

sheet·ing (shē′ting) *n.* **1** cloth of cotton, linen, nylon, etc. for bed sheets. **2** a lining or covering of timber or metal, used to protect a surface.

sheet iron iron in sheets or thin plates.

sheet lightning lightning in broad flashes.

sheet metal metal in thin pieces or plates.

sheet music music printed on unbound sheets of paper.

Sheffield plate (shef′ēld) an especially durable silver plate made by rolling out sheets of copper and silver fused together. [< *Sheffield,* a city in England]

sheik or **sheikh** (shēk *or* shāk) *n.* **1** an Arab chief or head of a family, village, or tribe. **2** a Moslem religious leader. **3** a title of respect used by Moslems. **4** *Slang.* a man supposed to be irresistibly fascinating to women; a great lover. [< Arabic *shaikh,* originally, old man]
☛ *Hom.* **chic** (shēk), **shake** (shāk).

sheik·dom or **sheikh·dom** (shēk′dəm) *n.* the territory ruled by a sheik.

shek·el (shek′əl) *n.* **1** a unit for measuring mass, used by the ancient Babylonians, Phoenicians, and Hebrews; equal to about 14 g. **2** a silver or gold coin of the ancient Hebrews weighing one shekel. **3** the basic unit of money in Israel, divided into 10 pounds. See table at **money. 4 shekels,** *pl.* money or riches. [< Hebrew]

shel·drake (shel′drāk′) *n., pl.* **-drakes** or (esp. collectively) **-drake. 1** shelduck. **2** merganser. [< obs. *sheld* variegated + *drake*]

shel·duck (shel′duk′) *n.* any of several Old World ducks (tribe Tadornini), somewhat gooselike in appearance and having a short bill and typically brightly colored plumage, such as the black-and-white **common shelduck** (*Tadorna tadorna*) of Europe.

shelf (shelf) *n., pl.* **shelves. 1** a thin, flat piece of wood, or other material, fastened to a wall or frame to hold things, such as books, dishes, etc. **2** anything like a shelf.
on the shelf, put aside as no longer useful or desirable. [probably < LG *schelf*]

shell (shel) *n., v.* —*n.* **1** a hard outside covering of an animal. Oysters, turtles, and beetles all have shells. **2** the hard outside covering of a nut, seed, fruit, etc. **3** the hard outside covering of an egg. **4** the outer part or appearance; outward show: *Going to church is the mere shell of religion.* **5** any framework or outside covering of a structure. **6** a long, narrow racing boat of light wood, rowed by a crew using long oars. **7** a hollow case of pastry or the lower crust of a pie. **8** a cartridge used in a rifle or shotgun. **9** a metal projectile filled with explosives that is fired by artillery and explodes on impact. **10** a cartridgelike firework that explodes in the air. **11** *Physics.* an orbit of electrons about the nucleus of an atom in which the electrons all have approximately the same amount of energy. **12** a woman's sleeveless and usually collarless knitted or crocheted top or blouse.
come out of (one's) **shell,** stop being shy or reserved; join in conversation, etc. with others.
retire into (one's) **shell,** become shy and reserved; refuse to join in conversation, etc. with others.
—*v.* **1** take out of a shell: *shell peas.* **2** fall or come out of the shell. **3** come away or fall off as an outer covering does. **4** separate (the grains of corn) from a cob. **5** bombard by artillery fire: *The enemy shelled the town.*
shell out, *Informal.* **a** give something away: *On Halloween the children cry: "Shell out!"* **b** hand over (money); pay up: *He shelled out $15 for the roses.*
[OE *sciell*] —**shell′-like′,** *adj.*

she'll (shēl: *unstressed,* shil) she will.

shel·lac (shə lak′) *n., v.* **-lacked, -lack·ing.** —*n.* **1** purified lac (a resin), used for making varnishes, leather polishes, etc. **2** a varnish for wood or metal, consisting of shellac dissolved in alcohol. —*v.* **1** coat or treat with shellac. **2** *Informal.* defeat completely. [< *shell* + *lac¹*; translation of F *laque en écailles* lac in thin plates]

shell·bark (shel′bärk′) *n.* shagbark.

shell·er (shel′ər) *n.* **1** a person who shells something. **2** a tool or machine used in shelling.

shell·fire (shel′fīr′) *n.* bombardment by explosive shells or projectiles.

shell·fish (shel′fish′) *n., pl.* **-fish** or **-fish·es.** any aquatic invertebrate animal having a shell, especially edible molluscs or crustaceans, such as oysters, clams, crabs, and lobsters. [OE *scilfisc*]

shell ice *Cdn.* in the North, a formation of ice remaining as a shell, after the water over which it was formed has receded.

shell·proof (shel′prüf′) *adj.* secure against shells, bombs, etc.

shell shock any of the many types of mental disorders formerly thought to result from prolonged exposure to exploding shells, bombs, etc.

shell·shocked (shel′shokt′) *adj.* suffering from shell shock.

shell·y (shel′ē) *adj.* **shell·i·er, shell·i·est. 1** abounding in shells. **2** consisting of a shell or shells. —**shell-like,** *adj.*

shel·ter (shel′tər) *n., v.* —*n.* **1** something that covers or protects

from weather, danger, or attack: *Trees are a shelter from the sun.* **2** protection; refuge: *We took shelter from the storm in a barn.* —*v.* **1** protect; shield; hide: *shelter runaway slaves.* **2** find shelter; take shelter: *The sheep sheltered from the hot sun in the shade of the haystack.* [? < ME *sheltrum* < OE *scildtruma* a guard < *scild* shield + *truma* a band of men] —**shel′ter·er,** *n.* —**shel′ter·ing·ly,** *adv.* —**shel′ter·less,** *adj.*

shel·ter·belt (shel′tər belt′) *n.* a barrier of trees or shrubs that functions as protection against the wind and rain and serves to lessen erosion.

shelter tent a small tent, usually made of pieces of waterproof cloth that fasten together.

shelve (shelv) *v.* **shelved, shelv·ing. 1** place on a shelf: *to shelve books.* **2** furnish with a shelf or shelves. **3** set aside or postpone: *to shelve an issue.* **4** cause (a person) to retire from active service or employment. **5** of ground, etc., slope gradually. [ult. < *shelf*]

shelves (shelvz) *n.* pl. of **shelf.**

shelv·ing (shel′ving) *n.* **1** wood, metal, etc. for shelves. **2** shelves collectively.

Shem (shem) *n.* in the Bible, the oldest of the three sons of Noah, regarded as the ancestor of the Semitic peoples.

Shem·ite (shem′īt) *n.* Semite.

she·nan·i·gan (shə nan′ə gən) *n.* **Informal.** Usually, **shenanigans,** *pl.* mischief or trickery. [origin uncertain]

shent (shent) *adj.* Archaic. **1** shamed. **2** blamed; scolded. **3** defeated. **4** ruined. **5** damaged. [pp. of *shend* revile, OE *scendan*]

She·ol (shē′ōl) *n.* **1** a Hebrew name for the abode of the dead. **2 sheol,** *Informal.* hell. [< Hebrew]

shep·herd (shep′ərd) *n., v.* —*n.* **1** a man who takes care of sheep. **2** a person who cares for and protects. **3** a spiritual guide; pastor.
the Good Shepherd, Jesus Christ.
—*v.* **1** take care of. **2** guide; direct: *The teacher shepherded the children safely out of the burning building.* [OE *scēaphierde* < *scēap* sheep + *hierde* herder < *heord* a herd]

shepherd dog sheep dog.

shep·herd·ess (shep′ər dis) *n.* a woman who takes care of sheep.

Shepherd Kings the Hyksos.

shep·herd's purse a common, weedy plant (*Capsella bursa pastoris*) of the mustard family having tiny white flowers and flattened, triangular pods.

Sher·a·ton (sher′ə tən) *adj., n.* —*adj.* of, like, or having to do with a light, graceful style of furniture characterized by straight lines and little ornamentation. —*n.* **1** this style of furniture. **2** a piece of furniture in this style. [< Thomas *Sheraton* (1751-1806), an English maker and designer of furniture]

sher·bet (shèr′bət) *n.* **1** a frozen dessert made of fruit juice, sugar, water, gelatin, and sometimes, milk or egg white. **2** *Brit.* a cold drink made of water, sugar, and fruit juice or flavoring. **3** a stemmed glass with a wide bowl, used for serving desserts. [< Turkish, Persian < Arabic *sharibah* to drink]

sherd (shèrd) *n.* shard.

she·reef (shə rēf′) See **sherif.**

she·rif (shə rēf′) *n.* **1** a descendant of Mohammed through his daughter Fatima. **2** an Arab prince or ruler; especially the chief magistrate of Mecca or (formerly) the sovereign of Morocco. [< Arabic *sharif* exalted]

sher·iff (sher′if) *n.* **1** in Canada, an official whose job is to enforce certain court orders, such as evicting persons for failure to pay rent and escorting convicted persons to prison. **2** in the United States, the most important law enforcing officer of a county. **3** in England and Wales, the chief executive officer of a county or shire, nominally responsible for the administration of justice, the conduct of parliamentary elections, etc. [OE *scīrgerēfa* < *scīr* shire + *gerēfa* reeve[1]]

Sher·pa (shèr′pə) *n.* a member of a Himalayan people living on the Tibet-Nepal border, famous as mountain climbers and guides.

sher·ry (sher′ē) *n., pl.* **-ries. 1** a strong Spanish wine fortified with brandy and ranging in flavor from very dry to sweet. It varies in color from pale yellow to brown. **2** any similar wine. [earlier *sherris* (taken as pl.) wine from *Xeres,* a Spanish town]

Sher·wood Forest (shèr′wùd) a royal forest near Nottingham, where Robin Hood is said to have lived.

she's (shēz) *unstressed* shiz) **1** she is. **2** she has.

Shet·land (shet′lənd) *n.* **1** Shetland pony. **2** Shetland sheepdog. **3** Shetland wool. [< *Shetland* Islands, a group of British islands northeast of Scotland]

Shetland pony a small, sturdy, rough-coated pony, originally from the Shetland Islands.

hat, āge, fär; let, ēqual, tèrm; it, īce
hot, ōpen, ôrder; oil, out; cup, pùt, rüle,
above, takən, pencəl, lemən, circəs
ch, child; ng, long; sh, ship
th, thin; ŦH, then; zh, measure

Shetland sheepdog a breed of small dog that looks like a miniature collie, originally bred in the Shetland Islands for herding sheep.

Shetland wool a fine, hairy, strong worsted spun from the wool of Shetland sheep, widely used in knitting shawls, sweaters, etc.

shew (shō) *n.* or *v.* **shewed, shewn, shew·ing.** *Archaic.* show.

shew·bread (shō′bred′) *n.* the unleavened bread placed near the altar every Sabbath by the ancient Jewish priests as an offering to God. Also, **showbread.**

shib·bo·leth (shib′ə lith) *n.* **1** any peculiarity of speech, habit, or custom considered distinctive of a particular group, class, etc. **2** any test word, password, watchword, or pet phrase of a political party, a class, sect, etc. [< Hebrew *shibbōleth* stream; used as a password by the Gileadites to distinguish the fleeing Ephraimites, because they could not pronounce *sh* (Judges 12:4-6).]

shied (shīd) *v.* pt. and a pp. of **shy.**

shield (shēld) *n., v.* —*n.* **1** a piece of armor carried on the arm to protect the body in battle. **2** any person or thing that protects: *She held up a newspaper as a shield against the sun.* **3** something shaped like a shield. **4** a covering for moving parts of machinery. **5 a** any substance to protect against exposure to radiation, especially in nuclear reactors, as lead or water. **b** a barrier built out of one of these substances. **6 a** a framework pushed ahead in a tunnel to prevent the earth from caving in while the tunnel is being lined. **b** a movable framework protecting a miner at his work. **7 a** steel screen or plate attached to a cannon, howitzer, etc. to protect the crew, mechanism, etc. **8 a** a policeman's badge. **b** an escutcheon. **9** a piece of fabric, often rubberized, worn inside a dress or other garment at the armpit. **10** *Zoology.* a protective plate covering a part, as a scute, carapace, or plastron. **11 the Shield,** the Canadian Shield.
—*v.* **1** be a shield to; protect; defend. **2** serve as a shield. [OE *sceld*]

shift (shift) *v., n.* —*v.* **1** change from one place, position, person, sound, etc. to another; change: *The wind has shifted to the southeast. He shifted the heavy bag from one hand to the other.* **2** be rather dishonest; scheme. **3** manage to get along; contrive: *When his parents died, Tom had to shift for himself.* **4** *Archaic or dialect.* change the clothes of. **5** get rid of. **6** change the position of (the gears of an automobile).
—*n.* **1** a change of direction, position, attitude, etc.: *a shift of the wind, a shift in policy.* **2** a group of workers who work during the same period of time: *The night shift comes on at 11 o'clock.* **3** the time during which such a group works: *I usually work the day shift.* **4** a way of getting on; scheme; trick: *The lazy girl tried every shift to avoid doing her work.* **5 a** *Archaic.* a woman's chemise. **b** a woman's dress having straight, loose-fitting lines. **6** *Football.* a change in the arrangement of the players before a ball is put into play. **7** *Geology.* a slight fault or dislocation in a seam or stratum. **8** *Linguistics.* a sound change that affects the phonetic and phonemic system of a language or language group.
make shift, a manage to get along. **b** manage with effort or difficulty. **c** do as well as one can.
[OE *sciftan* arrange] —**shift′er,** *n.*

shift·less (shift′lis) *adj.* lazy; inefficient. —**shift′less·ly,** *adv.* —**shift′less·ness,** *n.*

shift·y (shift′tē) *adj.* **shift·i·er, shift·i·est. 1** tricky; sly; not straightforward. **2** resourceful. **3** *Sports.* fast and tricky in playing style. —**shift′i·ly,** *adv.* —**shift′i·ness,** *n.*

shill (shil) *n., v.* **Slang.** —*n.* a person who acts as a decoy or confederate of a barker, peddler, or gambler in order to influence bystanders to bid, buy, bet, etc. —*v.* work as a shill; act as a decoy or lure. [origin unknown]

shil·le·lagh or **shil·la·lah** (shə lā′lē or shə lā′lə) *n.* *Irish.* a stick to hit with; cudgel. [< *Shillelagh,* a village in the Irish Republic]

shil·ling (shil′ing) *n.* **1** a former unit of money in the United Kingdom, equal to 1/20 of a pound. **2** the basic unit of money in Kenya, Somalia, Tanzania, and Uganda, divided into 100 cents. See table at **money. 3** a coin or note worth one shilling. [OE *scilling*]

shil·ly–shal·ly (shil′ē shal′ē) *adj., v.* **-lied, -ly·ing;** *n.* —*adj.* vacillating; wavering; hesitating; undecided.
—*v.* be undecided; vacillate; hesitate.

—*n.* an inability to decide; hesitation. [varied reduplication of *shall I*?]

shi·ly (shī′lē) See **shyly.**

shim (shim) *n., v.* **shimmed, shim·ming.**—*n.* a thin strip of metal or wood used to fill up space, make something level, etc.—*v.* put a shim or shims in. [origin uncertain]

shim·mer (shim′ər) *v., n.*—*v.* gleam faintly: *The satin shimmers.* —*n.* a faint gleam or shine. [OE *scimrian*]

shim·mer·y (shim′ər ē) *adj.* shimmering; gleaming softly.

shim·my (shim′ē) *n., pl.* **-mies;** *v.* **-mied, -my·ing.**—*n.* 1 *Slang.* a jazz dance with much shaking of the body. 2 an unusual shaking or vibration, especially of the front wheels of a car, truck, etc. 3 *Informal.* chemise. —*v.* 1 dance the shimmy. 2 shake; vibrate. [var. of *chemise* (taken as pl.)]

shin (shin) *n., v.* **shinned, shin·ning.**—*n.* 1 the front part of the leg from the knee to the ankle. See **leg** for picture. 2 in beef cattle, the lower part of the foreleg.—*v.* climb up or down a rope, pole, etc. by gripping alternately with the hands and feet: *shin up a tree.* [OE *scinu*]

shin·bone (shin′bōn′) *n.* the front bone of the leg below the knee; tibia.

shin·dig (shin′dig′) *n. Informal.* a merry or noisy dance, party, etc. [? variant of *shindy,* suggesting a dig, or blow, on the shin]

shin·dy (shin′dē) *n., pl.* **-dies.** *Slang.* disturbance; rumpus. [origin uncertain]

shine (shīn) *v.* **shone** or (esp. for def. 3) **shined, shin·ing;** *n.*—*v.* 1 send out light; be bright with light; reflect light; glow: *The sun shines.* 2 do very well; be brilliant; excel: *Mary shines in French.* 3 make bright; polish: *shine shoes.* 4 cause to shine: *shine a light.* **shine up to,** *Slang.* try to please and get the friendship of. —*n.* 1 light; brightness. 2 a lustre; polish; gloss, as of silk. 3 fair weather; sunshine: *rain or shine.* 4 polish put on shoes. 5 *Slang.* a fancy; liking. 6 *Slang.* a trick; prank. **take a shine to,** *Slang.* become fond of; like. [OE *scīnan*]

shin·er (shī′nər) *n.* 1 any of numerous small freshwater cyprinid fishes (especially genus *Notropis*) of North America. 2 *Slang.* a black eye. 3 a person or thing that shines.

shin·gle¹ (shing′gəl) *n., v.* **-gled, -gling.**—*n.* 1 a thin piece of wood, etc. used for roofing, etc. Shingles are laid in overlapping rows with the thicker ends exposed. 2 *Informal.* a small signboard, especially for a doctor's or lawyer's office. 3 a short haircut. **hang out (one's) shingle,** *Informal.* of lawyers, doctors, and dentists, open an office. —*v.* 1 cover with shingles: *to shingle a roof.* 2 cut (the hair) short. [var. of earlier *shindle* < L *scindula*]

shin·gle² (shing′gəl) *n.* 1 loose stones or pebbles such as lie on the seashore; coarse gravel. 2 a beach or other place covered with such pebbles. [origin uncertain; cf. Norwegian *singling* small, round pebble]

shin·gles (shing′gəlz) *n. sing. or pl.* a virus disease that causes painful irritation of a group of nerves and an outbreak of itching spots or blisters. [ME < Med.L *cingulus,* var. of L *cingulum* girdle < *cingere* gird]

shin·gly (shing′glē) *adj.* consisting of or covered with small, loose stones or pebbles.

shin·ing (shī′ning) *adj.* 1 that shines; bright. 2 brilliant; outstanding.—**shin′ing·ly,** *adv.*

shin·ny¹ (shin′ē) *n., pl.* **-nies;** *v.* **-nied, -ny·ing.** *Cdn.*—*n.* 1 a simple kind of hockey, played on the ice with skates, or without skates on the street or in a field. 2 the stick used in this game. 3 *Slang.* the game of ice hockey. —*v.* play shinny. [< *shin*]

shin·ny² (shin′ē) *v.* **-nied, -ny·ing.** *Informal.* shin; climb.

shin·plas·ter (shin′plas′tər) *n.* 1 *Cdn. Historical. Informal.* a banknote worth 25 cents, issued in 1870, 1900, and 1923. 2 a piece of paper currency of any of various small denominations, issued privately or by a government; especially, such a note devalued by inflation or poor security.

Shin·to (shin′tō) *n., adj.*—*n.* 1 the main religion of Japan, primarily a system of nature worship and ancestor worship. 2 an adherent of this religion.—*adj.* of or having to do with Shinto. [< Japanese < Chinese *shin tao* way of the gods]

Shin·to·ism (shin′tō iz′əm) *n.* the Shinto religion.

shin·y (shī′nē) *adj.* **shin·i·er, shin·i·est.** 1 shining; bright: *a shiny*

new nickel. 2 worn to a glossy smoothness: *a coat shiny from hard wear.*—**shin′i·ness,** *n.*

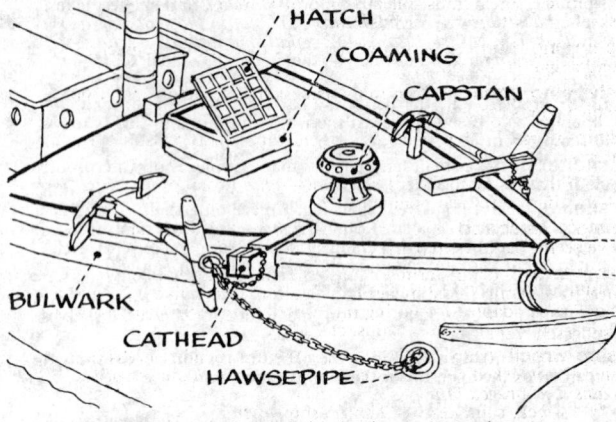

The forward part of a sailing ship, showing the capstan, anchor, etc.

ship (ship) *n., v.* **shipped, ship·ping.**—*n.* 1 any large vessel for travel on water, such as a steamship, frigate, or galley. 2 a large sailing vessel, especially one with three or more masts. 3 an airship, airplane, spacecraft, etc. 4 the officers and crew of a vessel. **about ship!** turn the ship round! put the ship on the other tack! **when (someone's) ship comes home** or **in,** when someone's fortune is made; when one has money. —*v.* 1 put, take, or receive on board a ship. 2 go on board a ship. 3 travel on a ship; sail. 4 send or carry from one place to another by a ship, train, truck, etc.: *Did he ship it by express?* 5 engage for service on a ship: *to ship a new crew.* 6 take a job on a ship: *He shipped as cook.* 7 take in (water) over the side, as a vessel does when the waves break over it. 8 fix (something) in a ship or boat in its proper place for use: *to ship a rudder.* [OE *scip*]

-ship *suffix.* 1 the office, position, or occupation of —, as in *authorship, kingship.* 2 the quality, state, or condition of being —, as in *kinship, partnership.* 3 the act, acts, power, or skill of —, as in *horsemanship, workmanship.* 4 the relation between —s, as in *comradeship.* [OE *-scipe*]

ship biscuit a kind of hard biscuit formerly used on shipboard; hardtack.

ship·board (ship′bôrd′) *n.* a ship. **on shipboard,** on or inside a ship.

ship bread ship biscuit; hardtack.

ship·break·er (ship′brāk′ər) *n.* a person who breaks up or contracts to break up ships no longer seaworthy.

ship·break·ing (ship′brāk′ing) *n.* the work or business of a shipbreaker.

ship·build·er (ship′bil′dər) *n.* a person who designs or constructs ships.

ship·build·ing (ship′bil′ding) *n.* 1 the designing or building of ships. 2 the art of building ships. 3 (*adj.*) of or used in shipbuilding; having to do with shipbuilding.

ship canal a canal wide and deep enough for ships.

ship·lap (ship′lap′) *n.* 1 a flush, overlapping joint between boards, formed by cutting corresponding rabbets in the adjoining edges and lapping the boards to the depth of the rabbets. 2 boards thus rabbeted.

ship·load (ship′lōd′) *n.* a full load for a ship.

ship·man (ship′mən) *n., pl.* **-men.** 1 *Archaic.* sailor. 2 the master of a ship.

ship·mas·ter (ship′mas′tər) *n.* a master, commander, or captain of a ship.

ship·mate (ship′māt′) *n.* 1 a fellow sailor on a ship. 2 a person who sails on the same ship; fellow passenger.

ship·ment (ship′mənt) *n.* 1 the act of shipping goods. 2 goods sent at one time to a person, firm, etc.

ship money in England, a tax to provide money for the building and maintenance of naval ships, levied at various times until it was abolished in 1641.

ship of the desert a camel.

ship of the line *Historical.* a sailing warship carrying 74 or more guns, corresponding to the modern battleship.

ship·own·er (ship′ō′nər) *n.* a person who owns a ship or ships.

ship·per (ship′ər) *n.* a person who ships goods.

ship·ping (ship′ing) *n.* **1** the act or business of sending goods by water, rail, etc. **2** ships collectively. **3** their total tonnage. **4** the ships of a nation, city, or business.

shipping clerk a person whose work is to see to the packing and shipment of goods.

shipping room a room in a business house, factory, etc. from which goods are sent.

ship–rigged (ship′rigd′) *adj.* rigged with square sails on all three masts.

ship·shape (ship′shāp′) *adj., adv.*—*adj.* in good order; trim. —*adv.* in a trim, neat manner.

ship's husband a person who has general care of a ship in port, overseeing supplies, repairs, entering and clearing procedures, etc.

ship·worm (ship′wėrm′) *n.* any of various marine bivalve molluscs (family Teredinidae) having a long, wormlike body and a small shell adapted for boring into wood. Shipworms can do great damage to wooden piers, ships, etc.

ship·wreck (ship′rek′) *n., v.*—*n.* **1** the destruction or loss of a ship. **2** a wrecked ship. **3** destruction; ruin: *The shipwreck of his plans discouraged him.* —*v.* **1** wreck; ruin; destroy. **2** suffer shipwreck.

ship·wright (ship′rīt′) *n.* a person who builds or repairs ships.

ship·yard (ship′yärd′) *n.* a place near the water where ships are built or repaired.

shire (shīr) *n.* one of the counties into which Great Britain is divided. [OE *scīr*]

Shire (shīr) *n.* shire horse.

shire horse any of the largest breed of draft horses having very hairy legs, said to descend from the war horses of the Middle Ages. [< the *Shires*, midland counties of England where they are chiefly raised]

shire·town (shīr′toun′) *n. Cdn.* in the Maritimes, a county seat.

shirk (shėrk) *v., n.*—*v.* avoid or get out of doing (work, duty, etc.).—*n.* a person who shirks or does not do his share. [< G *Schurke* rascal]—**shirk′er,** *n.*

shirr (shėr) *v., n.*—*v.* **1** draw up or gather (cloth) on parallel threads. **2** bake (eggs) in a shallow dish with butter, etc.—*n.* a shirred arrangement of cloth, etc. [origin unknown]

shirt (shėrt) *n.* **1** a boy's or man's garment for the upper part of the body, made of a light material such as cotton, a cotton blend, or silk, and typically having a collar, sleeves, a front opening with buttons, and a tail that is tucked into the pants. **2** a similar garment for girls and women. **3** an undergarment for the upper part of the body.
keep (one's) **shirt on,** *Slang.* stay calm; keep one's temper.
lose (one's) **shirt,** *Slang.* lose everything one owns.
[OE *scyrte*. Cf. SKIRT.]—**shirt′less,** *adj.*

shirt·band (shėrt′band′) *n.* the neckband or other band of a shirt.

shirt·ing (shėr′ting) *n.* cloth for shirts.

shirt–sleeve (shėrt′slēv′) *adj. Informal.* characterized by informality: *shirt-sleeve diplomacy.*

shirt–tail (shėrt′tāl′) *n.* **1** the part of a shirt extending below the waist, usually worn tucked into the pants or skirt. **2** (*adj.*) distantly related: *a shirt-tail cousin.*

shirt·waist (shėrt′wāst′) *n.* **1** a woman's tailored blouse similar in style to a man's shirt; shirt (def. 2). **2** shirtwaist dress.

shirtwaist dress a tailored dress having a bodice similar in style to a man's shirt.

shish·ka·bob (shish′kə bob′) *n.* shish kebab.

shish ke·bab (shish′kə bob′) cubes of lamb, beef, or other meat, marinated and cooked with mushrooms, tomatoes, onions, etc. on a skewer or spit. [< Armenian *shish kabab*]

shiv (shiv) *n. Slang.* a knife or razor, especially when used as an offensive weapon. A switchblade is a kind of shiv. [perhaps < earlier *chive* file, knife < Romany]

shiv·a (shiv′ə) *n. Judaism.* a period of seven days' mourning for a dead relative. [< Hebrew *shib'ah* seven]

Shi·va (shē′və) *n.* one of the three great divinities of classical Hinduism, the creator and destroyer, a remote, austere god who remains in a state of constant meditation, worshipped as the highest god by many Hindus. Also, **Siva.**

shiv·a·ree (shiv′ə rē′) *n.* **1** a celebration held to do honor to a newly married couple; charivari. **2** a noisy serenade for a newly married couple, often performed in a spirit of mockery. **3** any noisy celebration. [var. of *charivari*]

---

hat, āge, fär; let, ēqual, tėrm; it, īce
hot, ōpen, ôrder; oil, out; cup, pùt, rüle,
əbove, takən, pencəl, lemən, circəs

ch, child; ng, long; sh, ship
th, thin; ŦH, then; zh, measure

shiv·er¹ (shiv′ər) *v., n.*—*v.* shake with cold, fear, etc.—*n.* a shaking from cold, fear, etc. [ME *schiveren*; origin uncertain] —**shiv′er·er,** *n.*
☛ *Syn. v.* **Shiver, shudder, quake** = shake or tremble. **Shiver,** used chiefly of people and animals, suggests a quivering of the flesh: *He crept shivering into bed.* **Shudder** especially suggests sudden sharp shivering of the whole body in horror or extreme disgust: *He shuddered at the ghastly sight.* **Quake** suggests violent trembling with fear or cold, or shaking and rocking from a violent disturbance: *The house quaked on its foundations.*

shiv·er² (shiv′ər) *v., n.*—*v.* break into small pieces: *He shivered the mirror with a hammer.*—*n.* a small piece; splinter. [origin uncertain]

shiv·er·y (shiv′ər ē *or* shiv′rē) *adj.* **1** quivering from cold, fear, etc.; shivering. **2** inclined to shiver from cold. **3** chilly. **4** causing shivers.

shmo (shmō) *n.* schmo.

shoal¹ (shōl) *n., adj., v.*—*n.* **1** a place in a sea, lake, or stream where the water is shallow. **2** a sandbank or sand bar that makes the water shallow: *The ship was wrecked on the shoals.* —*adj.* shallow. —*v.* become shallow. [OE *sceald* shallow]

shoal² (shōl) *n., v.*—*n.* a large number; crowd: *a shoal of fish.* —*v.* form into a shoal; crowd together. [OE *scolu*]

shoal·y (shō′lē) *adj.* full of shoals or shallow places.

shoat (shōt) *n.* a young pig able to feed itself. Also, **shote.** [origin uncertain]

shock¹ (shok) *n., v.*—*n.* **1** a sudden, violent shake, blow or crash: *the shock of an earthquake. The two trains collided with a terrible shock.* **2** a sudden and violent emotional or mental disturbance: *His death was a great shock to his family.* **3** something that causes such a disturbance. **4** condition of physical collapse or depression, together with a sudden drop in blood pressure, often resulting in unconsciousness. Shock may set in after a severe injury, great loss of blood, or a sudden emotional disturbance. **5** a sudden stimulation of the nerves and muscles produced by an electric current passing through the body. **6** *Informal.* shock absorber (def. 2).
—*v.* **1** strike together violently. **2** cause to feel surprise, horror, or disgust: *That child's bad language shocks everyone.* **3** collide with a shock. **4** give an electric shock to. [probably < F *choc,* n., *choquer,* v.]—**shock′er,** *n.*

shock² (shok) *n. or v.* stook. [ME < LG or MDu. *schok*] —**shock′er,** *n.*

shock³ (shok) *n.* a thick, bushy mass: *He has a shock of red hair.* [? < *shock²*]

shock absorber **1** anything that absorbs or lessens shocks. **2** a device used on automobiles to absorb or lessen the shocks caused by rough roads. **3** a similar device on the landing gear of aircraft.

shock–head·ed (shok′hed′id) *adj.* having a thick, bushy mass of hair.

shock·ing (shok′ing) *adj.* **1** causing intense and painful surprise: *shocking news.* **2** offensive; disgusting; revolting: *a shocking sight.* **3** *Informal.* very bad: *shocking manners.*—**shock′ing·ly,** *adv.*

shock–proof (shok′prüf′) *adj.* **1** able to endure or resist shock. **2** protected against electric shock.

shock therapy the treatment of mental disorder through shock induced by chemical or electrical means.

shock treatment **1** shock therapy. **2** any act intended to shock.

shock troops troops chosen and specially trained for making attacks.

shock wave **1** a disturbance of the atmosphere created by the movement of an aircraft, rocket, etc. at a velocity greater than that of sound. **2** a similar effect caused by an explosion.

shod (shod) *v.* pt. and pp. of **shoe.**

shod·dy (shod′ē) *n., pl.* **-dies;** *adj.* **-di·er, -di·est.**—*n.* **1** an inferior kind of wool made of woollen waste, old rags, yarn, etc. **2** cloth made of woollen waste. **3** anything inferior made to look like what is better.
—*adj.* **1** made of woollen waste. **2** pretending to be better than it is: *a shoddy necklace.* **3** mean; shabby: *shoddy treatment, a shoddy trick.* [origin uncertain]—**shod′di·ly,** *adv.*—**shod′di·ness,** *n.*

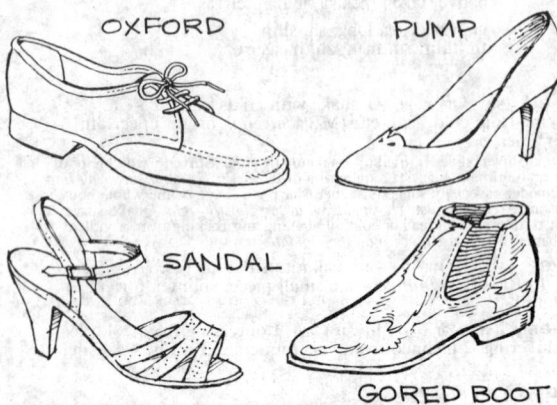

OXFORD PUMP

SANDAL

GORED BOOT

Some current shoe styles

shoe (shü) *n., v.* **shod, shoe·ing.** —*n.* **1** an outer covering for a person's foot, usually consisting of a firm or thick sole and separate heel and a thinner, flexible upper part of leather, cloth, or a synthetic material resembling leather. **2** anything like a shoe in shape or use. **3** a horseshoe. **4** a ferrule; metal band, etc. to protect the end of a staff, pole, etc. **5** the part of a brake that presses on a wheel. **6** the outer case of an automobile tire. **7** a sliding plate or contact by which an electric car takes current from the third rail.
fill (another person's) **shoes,** take another person's place.
in (another person's) **shoes,** in another's place, situation, or circumstances. *I wouldn't like to be in the murderer's shoes right now.*
the shoe is on the other foot, the situation is reversed.
where the shoe pinches, where the real trouble or difficulty lies.
—*v.* **1** furnish with a shoe or shoes: *A blacksmith shoes horses.* **2** protect or arm at the point; edge or face with metal: *a stick shod with steel.* [OE *scōh*] —**shoe′less,** *adj.*
☛ *Hom.* **shoo.**

shoe·black (shü′blak′) *n.* a person who cleans and polishes shoes to earn money.

shoe·horn (shü′hôrn′) *n.* a piece of metal, horn, etc. inserted at the heel of a shoe to make it slip on easily.

shoe·lace (shü′lās′) *n.* a cord, braid, or leather strip for fastening a shoe.

shoe·mak·er (shü′māk′ər) *n.* a person who makes or repairs shoes.

shoe·mak·ing (shü′māk′ing) *n.* the making or repairing of shoes.

shoe·shine (shü′shīn′) *n.* **1** the shining or polishing of shoes. **2** the polished look of shined shoes. **3** shoeblack.

shoe·string (shü′string′) *n.* **1** shoelace. **2** *Informal.* a very small amount of money used to start or carry on a business, investment, etc.: *The firm is paying its way, but it is operating on a shoestring.*

shoe tree a device with a shaped front for keeping a shoe in shape when it is not being worn.

sho·far (shō′fär) *n., pl.* **sho·froth** (shō′frōt *or* shō frōt′) *or* **sho*fars.** *Judaism.* a musical horn made from a ram's horn, sounded in the synagogue as part of the ritual marking Rosh Hashanah and Yom Kippur. The use of the shofar dates back to the time of the ancient Hebrews.

sho·gun (shō′gun *or* shō′gün) *n.* the former hereditary commander in chief of the Japanese army. The shoguns were the real rulers of Japan for hundreds of years until 1867. [< Japanese < Chinese *chiang chun* army leader]

sho·gun·ate (shō′gun it, shō′gun āt′, shō′gün it, *or* shō′gün āt′) *n.* **1** the position, rank, or rule of a shogun. **2** government by shoguns.

shone (shon) *v.* pt. and a pp. of **shine.**

shoo (shü) *interj., v.* **shooed, shoo·ing.** —*interj.* an exclamation used to scare away hens, birds, etc. —*v.* **1** scare or drive away: *Shoo those flies away from the sugar.* **2** exclaim or call "shoo".
☛ *Hom.* **shoe.**

shoo·in (shü′in′) *n. Informal.* **1** a person who will win easily;

sure winner. **2** a contest or match considered easy to win.

shook¹ (shük) *n.* a set of pieces, cut and ready to assemble, that are used in making boxes, barrels, articles of furniture, etc. [origin uncertain]

shook² (shük) *v.* pt. of **shake.**

shoon (shün) *n. Archaic.* a pl. of **shoe.**

shoot (shüt) *v.* **shot, shoot·ing;** *n.* —*v.* **1** hit, wound, or kill with a bullet, arrow, etc.: *shoot a rabbit.* **2** send with force or speed at or as if at a target: *He shot question after question at us.* **3** fire or use a weapon, such as a gun, bow, catapult, etc. **4** of a gun, etc., send a bullet: *This gun shoots straight.* **5** kill game in or on: *shoot a farm.* **6** *Informal.* terrorize, destroy, or wreck by shooting (used with **up**): *to shoot up a town.* **7** move suddenly and swiftly: *A car shot by us. Flames shot up from the burning house. Pain shot up his arm. He shot back the bolt.* **8** pass quickly along, through, over, or under: *shoot Niagara Falls in a barrel.* **9** grow quickly by or as if by putting out shoots; grow bigger or taller quickly (used with **up, forth,** etc.): *The grain is really shooting up in the warm weather. He shot up three centimetres last summer.* **10** take (a picture) with a camera; photograph. **11** project sharply: *a cape that shoots out into the sea.* **12** dump; empty out. **13** vary with some different color, etc.: *Her dress was shot with threads of gold.* **14** measure the altitude of: *shoot the sun.* **15** send (a ball, etc.) toward the goal, pocket, etc. **16** propel (a marble), as from the thumb and forefinger. **17** cast or toss (the dice) in playing craps. **18** open, loosen, remove, etc. by setting off a charge of an explosive: *shoot an oil well.* **19** *Informal.* give an injection to. **20** *Slang.* take (a drug) by injection (often used with **up**): *He shoots heroin.*
shoot at or **for,** *Informal.* aim at; aspire to.
shoot down, kill or destroy by shooting: *He was shot down in cold blood. They shot down two enemy aircraft.*
—*n.* **1** shooting practice. **2** a trip, party, or contest for shooting. **3 a** the act of sprouting or growing. **b** a new part growing out; young bud or stem. **4** a sloping trough for conveying coal, grain, water, etc. to a lower level; chute. [OE *scēotan*] —**shoot′er,** *n.*
☛ *Hom.* **chute.**

shooting gallery a long room or deep booth fitted with targets for practice in shooting.

shooting iron *Informal.* a firearm or gun, especially a pistol or rifle.

shooting star **1** a meteor resembling a star seen falling or darting through the sky. **2** any of a genus (*Dodecatheon*) of plants of the primrose family found especially in W North America, having clusters of rose, purple, or white flowers whose petals and sepals turn backward.

shoot·out or **shoot-out** (shüt′out′) *n.* **1** a decisive gun battle: *a shootout between rebels and militia.* **2** any desperate and decisive contest, quarrel, or argument.

shop (shop) *n., v.* **shopped, shop·ping.** —*n.* **1** a place where things are sold; store. **2** a place where things are made or repaired: *He works in a carpenter's shop.* **3** a place where a certain kind of work is done: *a barber shop.*
set up shop, start work or business.
shut up shop, give up work or business.
talk shop, talk about one's work or profession.
—*v.* visit stores to look at or to buy things. [OE *sceoppa*]

shop·girl (shop′gèrl′) *n.* a girl who works in a shop or store.

sho·phar (shō′fär) See **shofar.**

shop·keep·er (shop′kēp′ər) *n.* a person who carries on business in a shop or store.

shop·lift·er (shop′lif′tər) *n.* a person who steals goods from a store while pretending to be a customer.

shop·lift·ing (shop′lif′ting) *n.* the act of stealing goods from a store while pretending to be a customer.

shop·man (shop′mən) *n., pl.* **-men.** shopkeeper.

shop·per (shop′ər) *n.* **1** a person who visits stores to look at or buy things. **2** a person hired to buy goods at retail for another, especially one hired by a retail store to buy items of merchandise from competitive stores in order to determine how similar items offered by it compare in price and quality.

shop·ping (shop′ing) *n.* the buying of groceries, clothes, etc.: *Mother does her shopping on Wednesdays and Saturdays.*
go shopping, go to the store or stores in order to buy groceries, clothes, etc.

shopping centre **1** a concentration of retail stores, usually in a suburban residential district, built as a unit and having ample parking, spacious walks, etc. **2** the street or streets of a town where the main stores and shops are concentrated. **3** a town, city, etc. serving as retail and distribution centre for the surrounding region.

shopping mall a large shopping centre, especially one that is roofed and contains one or more department stores.

shopping plaza *Cdn.* shopping centre (def. 1).

shop steward a union worker elected by fellow workers to represent them in dealings with management and to maintain union rules.

shop·talk (shop′tok′ or -tôk′) n. 1 the informal language of an occupation. 2 the discussion of business or professional matters, especially outside of office hours.
☛ *Usage.* **Shoptalk** (def. 1) is a less formal term for **jargon** (def. 3) and refers to a private or restricted aspect of language. It is appropriate to use shoptalk when writing for and about people in a particular walk of life. In speaking or writing for a wider audience, shoptalk terms can be useful for the sake of realism if their meaning is explained or clear from the context. Otherwise, they should be avoided.

shop·worn (shop′wôrn′) adj. 1 soiled by being displayed or handled in a store. 2 no longer new, interesting, or appealing: *shopworn slogans, shopworn ideas.*

shore¹ (shôr) n. 1 the land at the edge of a sea, lake, etc. 2 the land near a sea: *There is good farmland on the western shore of the island.* 3 **shores,** pl. land: *foreign shores.* 4 *Law.* the land between high-water and low-water marks.
in shore, in or on the water, near to the shore or nearer to the shore.
off shore, in or on the water, not far from the shore.
[ME; ? < LG or MDu. *schore*]

shore² (shôr) n., v. **shored, shor·ing.** —n. a prop placed against or beneath something to support it. —v. prop up or support with shores. [ME; ? < MDu. *schore* prop] —**shor′er,** n.

shore³ (shôr) v. *Archaic.* a pt. of **shear.**

shore·less (shôr′lis) adj. 1 having no shore. 2 boundless.

shore·line (shôr′līn′) n. the line where shore and water meet.

shore pine a form of the lodgepole pine found along the Pacific coast.

shore·ward (shôr′wərd) adv. or adj. toward the shore.

shor·ing (shôr′ing) n. the shores or props for supporting a building, ship, etc.

shorn (shôrn) v., adj. —v. a pp. of **shear.** —adj. 1 sheared. 2 deprived.

short (shôrt) adj., adv., n., v. —adj. 1 not long; of small extent from end to end: *a short distance, a short time, a short street.* 2 not long for its kind: *a short tail.* 3 not tall: *a short man, short grass.* 4 not coming up to the right amount, measure, standard, etc.: *The cashier is short in his accounts.* 5 not having enough; scanty: *The prisoners were kept on short allowance of food.* 6 so brief as to be rude: *He was so short with me that I felt hurt.* 7 of vowels or syllables, occupying a relatively short time in utterance. The vowels are considered as short in *fat, net, pin, not, up.* 8 breaking or crumbling easily. Pastry is made short with lard and butter. 9 not possessing at the time of sale the stocks or commodities that one sells. 10 denoting or having to do with sales of stocks or commodities that the seller does not possess. 11 depending for profit on a decline in prices.
make short work of, deal with quickly.
run short, a not have enough. **b** not be enough.
short of, a not up to; less than: *Nothing short of your best work will satisfy me.* **b** not having enough of. **c** on the near side of.
—adv. 1 so as to be or make short. 2 abruptly; suddenly: *The horse stopped short.* 3 briefly. 4 on the near side of an intended or particular point: *stop short of actual crime.*
cut short, end suddenly.
fall short, a fail to reach. **b** be insufficient.
sell short, sell without possessing at the time the stocks, etc. that are being sold: *It is risky to sell short.*
—n. 1 something short. 2 a short circuit. 3 a person who has sold short; a sale by selling short; sold short. 4 any short motion picture as a cartoon, newsreel, etc., especially one shown on the same program with a full-length picture (feature). 5 *Baseball.* the position of shortstop: *play short.* 6 **shorts,** pl. **a** short pants that reach no lower than the knees. **b** a pair of short underpants worn by men or boys. **c** a baby's short clothes. **d** mixture of bran and coarse meal.
for short, to make shorter.
in short, briefly.
—v. short-circuit. [OE *sceort*] —**short′ness,** n.
☛ *Syn. adj.* 1. **Short, brief** = of small extent. **Short** may describe either space or time, but when describing time it often suggests cutting or stopping short before finishing: *Because he was late, he could take only a short walk today.* **Brief** almost always describes time and means "coming to an end quickly," and therefore when applied to speeches or writing is more likely to suggest leaving out unimportant or unnecessary details than cutting off the end: *A brief essay is short but to the point.*

short·age (shôr′tij) n. 1 too small an amount; a lack: *There is a shortage of grain because of poor crops.* 2 the amount by which something is deficient.

short·bread (shôrt′bred′) n. a cake or cookie that is rich in butter and crumbles easily.

short·cake (shôrt′kāk′) n. 1 a cake made of rich biscuit dough

hat, āge, fär; let, ēqual, tèrm; it, īce
hot, ōpen, ôrder; oil, out; cup, pùt, rüle,
əbove, takən, pencəl, lemən, circəs

ch, child; ng, long; sh, ship
th, thin; ŦH, then; zh, measure

and shortening, covered or filled with berries or other fruit. 2 a sweet cake filled or spread with fruit. 3 shortbread.

short·change (shôrt′chānj′) v. **-changed, -chang·ing.** *Informal.* 1 give less than the right change to. 2 cheat. —**short′-chang′er,** n.

short circuit an electrical circuit, formed accidentally or intentionally, that by-passes the main circuit. An accidental short circuit, in which worn or faulty wires touch each other, may blow a fuse or cause a fire.

short-cir·cuit (shôrt′sèr′kit) v. 1 develop or bring about a short circuit. 2 get around or avoid; bypass: *to short-circuit the usual administrative procedure.* 3 frustrate or hinder: *to short-circuit a plan.*

short·com·ing (shôrt′kum′ing) n. a fault; defect.

short·cut (shôrt′kut′) n., v. **-cut, -cut·ting.** —n. 1 a quicker or less distant route: *We took a shortcut through the field.* 2 a method, procedure, etc. that is simpler or quicker than the standard one: *shortcuts in cooking.* —v. use or take a shortcut.

short·en (shôr′tən) v. 1 make shorter; cut off. 2 become shorter. 3 make rich with butter, lard, etc. 4 take in (sail). —**short′en·er,** n.
☛ *Syn.* 1. **Shorten, curtail, abbreviate** = make shorter. **Shorten** is the general word, meaning "reduce the length or extent of something": *The new highway shortens the trip.* **Curtail,** more formal, means "cut something short by taking away or cutting off a part," and particularly suggests causing loss or incompleteness: *Bad news made him curtail his trip.* **Abbreviate,** used chiefly of words and phrases, means "shorten by leaving out syllables, letters, or sounds," sometimes by using initial letters or substitutions: *Abbreviate kilogram to kg after numerals.*

short·en·ing (shôrt′ning) n. butter, lard, or other fat, used in baking to make pastry, cake, etc. crisp or crumbly.

short·fall (shôrt′fol′ or shôrt′fôl′) n. 1 the act or an instance of falling short; failure to meet a need or reach a goal: *The chairman of the fund-raising campaign has predicted a shortfall.* 2 the amount of such a failure; deficiency.

short·hand (shôrt′hand′) n. 1 a method of rapid writing which uses symbols or a combination of letters and symbols to represent sounds. 2 writing in such symbols. 3 (*adj.*) using or written in shorthand.

short·hand·ed (shôrt′han′did) adj. 1 not having enough workers or helpers. 2 *Hockey, etc.* playing without the services of one or more players as a result of penalties. 3 playing with less than a full side because of injuries.

short·horn (shôrt′hôrn′) n. a breed of cattle having short horns, raised for both beef and milk.

short·ish (shôr′tish) adj. rather short.

short-lived (shôrt′livd′ or -līvd′) adj. living only a short time; lasting only a short time.

short·ly (shôrt′lē) adv. 1 in a short time; before long; soon. 2 in a few words; briefly. 3 briefly and rudely.

short-or·der (shôrt′ôr′dər) adj. in a restaurant, etc., having to do with the cooking of foods that require little time to prepare: *a short-order cook.*

short-range (shôrt′rānj′) adj. not reaching far: *short-range plans.*

short shrift 1 short time for confession and absolution. 2 little mercy, respite, or delay.

short-sight·ed (shôrt′sīt′id) adj. 1 near-sighted; not able to see far. 2 a lacking in foresight; not prudent. b characterized by or proceeding from lack of foresight: *a short-sighted strategy.* —**short′-sight′ed·ly,** adv. —**short′-sight′ed·ness,** n.

short-staffed (shôrt′staft′) adj. not having enough staff; short of the regular or necessary number of people.

short·stop (shôrt′stop′) n. *Baseball.* a player stationed between second base and third base.

short story a prose story with a full plot, but of much less length than a novel.

short-tailed weasel (shôrt′tāld′) ermine (def. 1).

short-tem·pered (shôrt′tem′pərd) adj. easily made angry; quick-tempered.

short-term (shôrt′tèrm′) adj. 1 lasting or intended for a short period of time: *our short-term plans.* 2 falling due in a short time.

short ton 2000 pounds avoirdupois (about 0.9 tonnes).

short–waist·ed (shôrt'wās'tid) *adj.* having a high waistline; short from neck to waistline.

short wave a high-frequency radio wave having a wave length of 60 metres or less.

short–wave (shôrt'wāv') *v.* -waved, -wav·ing. transmit by short waves: *The Prime Minister's speech was short-waved overseas.*

short–wind·ed (shôrt'win'did) *adj.* getting out of breath too quickly; having difficulty in breathing.

Sho·sho·ne·an (shō shō'nē ən) *n.* a language group of North American Indians of the Western United States that includes Comanche, Hopi, etc.

shot[1] (shot) *n., pl.* **shots** or (for def. 3) **shot**; *v.* **shot·ted, shot·ting.** —*n.* **1** the discharge of a gun or cannon: *He heard two shots.* **2** the act of shooting. **3** small pellets of lead or steel that make up the charge of a shotgun cartridge. **4** a single ball of lead for a gun or cannon. **5** an attempt to hit by shooting: *That was a good shot.* **6** the distance a weapon can shoot; range: *They were within rifle shot of the fort.* **7** a person who shoots: *He is a good shot.* **8** *Informal.* an injection, as of a vaccine or drug: *a polio shot.* **9** a sharp or critical remark. **10** an attempt; try: *I'm not very good at puzzles, but I'll take a shot at it.* **11** a bet or guess. **12** *Track and field.* a heavy metal ball that is put (or thrown) for distance. **13** snapshot. **14** a single sequence of a motion picture taken with one camera without a break. **15** *Informal.* a single drink of alcoholic liquor. **16** *Informal.* a dose. **17** *Mining.* a blast. **18** an amount to be paid: *She offered to pay the shot.* Compare **scot.**
a long shot, an attempt at something difficult.
call the shots, *Informal.* be in a position of control in an organization, enterprise, etc.
like a shot, very quickly and, especially, eagerly.
not by a long shot, not at all.
put the shot, cast the ball, in the track-and-field event of shot-put.
shot in the arm, *Informal.* something that stimulates or revives; an incentive; spur.
—*v.* load or weight with shot. [OE *sceot*]

shot[2] (shot) *v., adj.* —*v.* pt. and pp. of **shoot.**
—*adj.* **1** of a fabric, woven so as to show changing colors; iridescent: *shot taffeta, blue silk shot with gold.* **2** streaked with a contrasting color: *black hair shot with grey.* **3** permeated or infused (*often used with* **through**): *a clever speech, shot through with humor.* **4** *Informal.* worn out, ruined, exhausted, etc.: *This old dictionary is just about shot. He said his nerves were shot.*

shote (shōt) See **shoat.**

shot·gun (shot'gun') *n.* **1** a large firearm having a long barrel with a smooth bore and firing cartridges filled with shot. **2** (*adj.*) of, having to do with, or produced by a shotgun: *a shotgun blast.* **3** (*adj.*) involving compulsion. **4** (*adj.*) covering a broad field; indiscriminate or haphazard: *a shotgun approach to criticism.*

shotgun marriage or **wedding** *Informal.* a marriage or wedding enforced or arranged on account of pregnancy.

shot–put (shot'pút') *n.* an athletic event or contest in which contestants send a heavy metal ball (the shot) as far as possible with one overhand throw from the shoulder.

shot rock or **shot–rock** (shot'rok') *n. Curling.* the stone nearest the centre of the target; the stone that counts towards the score.

should (shúd; *unstressed,* shəd) *v.* **1** a word used: **a** to express obligation or duty: *Everyone should learn to swim. I really should do my homework before I go out.* **b** to suggest that the speaker is uncertain about a thing or unwilling to believe something: *I don't see why you should think that. It's strange that they should be so late.* **c** to express a possible action in the future: *If we should go, we'll call you.* The statement *I will be there in an hour* is a promise; *I should be there in an hour* means that the speaker is not sure and therefore is not willing to promise. **d** to express a belief: *She should be there by now.* **2** pt. of **shall** (def. 3): *I hoped I should see you.* [OE *sceolde*]

shoul·der (shōl'dər) *n., v.* —*n.* **1** the part of the body to which an arm of a human being, a foreleg of an animal, or a wing of a bird is attached. **2 shoulders,** *pl.* the two shoulders and the upper part of the back. **3** the part of a garment covering this. **4** a cut of meat including the upper foreleg and adjacent parts. See **lamb** and **pork** for pictures. **5** a shoulderlike part or projection: *He grasped the shoulder of the rock.* **6** the edge of a road or highway, often unpaved: *Do not drive on the shoulder.* **7** *Printing.* the flat surface on a type extending beyond the base of the letter. **8** the angle between the face and flank of a bastion in a fortification.
put (one's) shoulder to the wheel, make a great effort.
shoulder to shoulder, **a** side by side; together. **b** with united effort.
straight from the shoulder, frankly; directly.

—*v.* **1** take upon or support with the shoulder or shoulders: *shoulder a tray.* **2** bear (a burden, blame, etc.); assume (responsibility, expense, etc.). **3** push with the shoulders: *He shouldered his way through the crowd.*

shoulder arms, hold a rifle almost upright with the barrel resting in the hollow of the shoulder and the butt in the hand. [OE *sculdor*] —**shoul'der·like,** *adj.*

shoulder bag a handbag with a long strap by which it can be hung from the shoulder.

shoulder blade the flat triangular bone in the upper back behind either shoulder; scapula. See **rib** for picture.

shoulder knot a knot of ribbon or lace worn on the shoulder.

shoulder strap a strap worn over the shoulder to hold a garment up.

should·n't (shúd'ənt) should not.

shouldst (shúdst) *v. Archaic.* 2nd pers. sing., past tense, of **shall.** *Thou shouldst* means *you* (sing.) *should.*

shout (shout) *v., n.* —*v.* **1** call or cry loudly and vigorously. **2** talk or laugh very loudly. **3** express by a shout or shouts: *The crowd shouted its approval.*
shout a person down, silence a person by very loud talk.
—*n.* **1** a loud, vigorous call or cry. **2** a loud outburst of laughter.
give (someone) a shout, call or telephone someone: *Give me a shout when you're ready.*
[ME *schoute;* ? ult. var. of *scout*[2]] —**shout'er,** *n.*

shove (shuv) *v.* **shoved, shov·ing;** *n.* —*v.* **1** push; move forward or along by the application of force from behind. **2** push roughly or rudely; jostle.
shove off, **a** push away from the shore; row away. **b** *Slang.* leave; start.
—*n.* push. [OE *scūfan*] —**shov'er,** *n.*
☛ *Syn. v.* **1.** See note at **push.**

shov·el (shuv'əl) *n., v.* **-elled** or **-eled, -el·ling** or **-el·ing.** —*n.* **1** a tool with a longish handle and broad, concave blade, used to lift and throw loose matter: *a coal shovel.* **2** a part of a machine having a similar use. **3** shovelful. **4** shovel hat.
—*v.* **1** lift and throw with a shovel. **2** make with a shovel: *They shovelled a path through the snow.* **3** work with a shovel. **4** throw in large quantities: *The hungry man greedily shovelled the food into his mouth.* [OE *scofl*]

shov·el·board (shuv'əl bôrd) See **shuffleboard.**

shov·el·er (shuv'əl ər) See **shoveller.**

shov·el·ful (shuv'əl fül') *n., pl.* **-fuls.** as much as a shovel can hold.

shovel hat a hat having a broad brim turned up at the sides and projecting with shovel-like curves in front and behind. Some clergymen of the Church of England wear shovel hats. See **hat** for picture.

shov·el·ler or **shov·el·er** (shuv'əl ər) *n.* **1** a duck (*Anas clypeata,* also classified as *Spatula clypeata*) of ponds and marshes of the northern hemisphere, having a large, broad bill, and the male having a green head, white breast, and chestnut body. **2** a person or thing that shovels.

show (shō) *v.* **showed, shown** or **showed, show·ing;** *n.* —*v.* **1** let be seen; put in sight: *She showed her new hat.* **2** reveal; manifest; disclose: *He showed himself a generous man by giving to charity.* **3** be in sight; appear; be seen: *Anger showed in his face.* **4** point out: *A boy showed us the way to town.* **5** direct; guide: *Show him out.* **6** make clear; explain. **7** make clear to; explain to: *Show us how to do the problem. He showed that it was true.* **9** grant; give: *to show mercy, to show favor.* **10** display. **11** display for effect. **12** of a list, instrument, etc., indicate: *a watch showing twelve o'clock.* **13** *Sports.* **a** finish among the first three in a race. **b** finish third in a race or competition, especially in a horse race. Compare **win** (def. 1) and **place** (def. 8b). **14** *Informal.* appear in or present a theatrical performance: *We are showing at the Centennial Hall.*
show off, **a** make a show of; display; act or talk for show: *He was showing off his new bike.* **b** make a vain display; act in such a way as to attract attention: *That boy is always showing off.*
show up, **a** expose. **b** stand out: *He is very tall and shows up in any crowd.* **c** *Informal.* put in an appearance: *The Prime Minister showed up at the first concert.*
—*n.* **1** a display: *The jewels made a fine show.* **2** a display for effect. **3** any kind of public exhibition or display: *a horse show.* **4** a showing: *The club voted by a show of hands.* **5** an appearance: *There is some show of truth in his excuse.* **6** a false appearance: *He hid his treachery by a show of friendship.* **7** a trace; indication: *a show of oil in a region.* **8** *Informal.* an entertainment, such as a stage play or motion picture: *a motion-picture show.* **9** a motion-picture theatre. **10** an object of scorn; something odd; queer sight: *Don't make a show of yourself.* **11** *Informal.* a chance; opportunity. **12** *Sports.* third place in a race or competition, especially in a horse race.

for show, for effect; to attract attention: *Some houses are furnished for show, not comfort.*
[OE *scēawian* look at]
☛ *Syn. n.* **1. Show, display** = a public exhibiting. **Show** suggests something exposed to sight or put forward unconsciously, by oversight, or intentionally for others to look at: *That was a disgraceful show of temper.* **Display** suggests something spread out or unfolded to be seen clearly, or arranged so as to call attention to its fineness, beauty, strength, or other qualities: *That florist has the most beautiful displays in the city.*

show bill a poster, placard, etc. advertising a show.

show·biz (shō′biz′) *n. Slang.* show business.

show·boat (shō′bōt′) *n.* a steamboat with a theatre for plays. Showboats carry their own actors and make frequent stops to give performances.

show·bread (shō′bred′) See **shewbread.**

show business all the occupations and businesses that make up the entertainment industry, including theatre, film, television, and radio. —**show′-bus′i·ness,** *adj.*

show·case (shō′kās′) *n.* **1** a glass case to display and protect articles in stores, museums, etc. **2** anything that displays: *Quebec City is a showcase of Canadian history.*

show·down (shō′doun′) *n.* **1** a forced disclosure of facts, purposes, methods, etc. **2** *Card games.* the displaying of the hands of the players at the end of a round.

show·er (shou′ər) *n., v.* —*n.* **1** a brief fall of rain. **2** anything like a fall of rain: *a shower of hail, a shower of tears, a shower of sparks from an engine.* **3** a party for giving presents to a woman about to be married, or on some other special occasion. **4** a bath in which water is sprayed over the body from above in small jets. **5** the apparatus for such a bath.
—*v.* **1** rain for a short time. **2** wet with a shower; spray; sprinkle. **3** have a shower bath. **4** come or fall in a shower. **5** send in a shower; pour down: *They showered gifts upon her.* [OE *scur*]

shower bath a shower (defs. 4 and 5).

show·er·y (shou′ər ē) *adj.* **1** raining in showers. **2** having many showers. **3** like a shower.

show·man (shō′mən) *n., pl.* -**men.** **1** a person who manages a show. **2** a person skilled in presenting things in a dramatic and exciting way.

show·man·ship (shō′mən ship′) *n.* **1** the management of shows. **2** skill in managing shows or in publicity.

shown (shōn) *v.* a pp. of **show.**

show-off (shō′of′) *n.* **1** a showing off. **2** *Informal.* a person who shows off; a person who is always calling attention to himself.

show-piece (shō′pēs′) *n.* anything displayed as an outstanding example of its kind.

show-place (shō′plās′) *n.* any place considered worth exhibiting because of its superior beauty, interest, etc.

show-room (shō′rüm′ *or* -rum′) *n.* a room used for the display of goods or merchandise.

show window a window in the front of a store, where things are shown for sale.

show·y (shō′ē) *adj.* **show·i·er, show·i·est. 1** making a display; striking; conspicuous: *A peony is a showy flower.* **2** too bright and gay to be in good taste. **3** ostentatious. —**show′i·ly,** *adv.* —**show′i·ness,** *n.*

shrank (shrangk) *v.* a pt. of **shrink.**

shrap·nel (shrap′nəl) *n.* **1** a shell filled with fragments of metal and powder, set to explode in the air and scatter the fragments over a wide area. **2** the fragments scattered by such a shell. [after the inventor, Henry *Shrapnel* (1761-1842), a British army officer]

shred (shred) *n., v.* **shred·ded** *or* **shred, shred·ding.** —*n.* **1** a very small piece torn off or cut off; a very narrow strip; scrap: *The wind tore the sail to shreds.* **2** a particle; fragment; bit: *There's not a shred of evidence that he took the money.* —*v.* tear or cut into small pieces. [OE *scrēade*]

shrew (shrü) *n.* **1** any of a family (Soricidae) of small, mouselike mammals found almost throughout the world, having a long, pointed snout, short, velvety fur, and tiny, beadlike eyes. Shrews are extremely active and often ferocious, attacking animals larger than themselves, such as mice. **2** a bad-tempered and quarrelsome woman. [OE *scrēawa*]

shrewd (shrüd) *adj.* **1** having or showing a keen, practical mind; astute and penetrating: *a shrewd observer, a shrewd comment.* **2** *Archaic.* sharp or biting: *a shrewd wind.* **3** *Archaic.* spiteful or mischievous. [earlier *shrewed,* < *shrew,* v., in sense of "scold"] —**shrewd′ly,** *adv.* —**shrewd′ness,** *n.*
☛ *Syn.* **1. Shrewd, sagacious, astute** = having a sharp or keen mind and good judgment, especially in practical affairs. **Shrewd** emphasizes sharpness and ability to see below the surface of things, and suggests natural cleverness in practical affairs or, sometimes, craftiness: *He is a shrewd businessman.* **Sagacious** emphasizes a keen or penetrating understanding of practical affairs and the ability to arrive at wise decisions: *The company director was a*

hat, āge, fär; let, ēqual, tèrm; it, īce
hot, ōpen, ôrder; oil, out; cup, pút, rüle,
əbove, takən, pencəl, lemən, circəs

ch, child; ng, long; sh, ship
th, thin; ŦH, then; zh, measure

sagacious man. **Astute** adds to **shrewd** the idea of having unusual power to see through and understand things and being hard to fool: *He is an astute diplomat.*

shrew·ish (shrü′ish) *adj.* scolding; bad-tempered. —**shrew′ish·ly,** *adv.* —**shrew′ish·ness,** *n.*

shrew·mouse (shrü′mous′) *n., pl.* -**mice.** shrew.

shriek (shrēk) *n., v.* —*n.* **1** a loud, sharp, shrill sound: *We heard the shriek of the engine's whistle.* **2** a loud, shrill laugh. —*v.* **1** make such a sound. People sometimes shriek because of terror, anger, pain, or amusement. **2** utter loudly and shrilly. [< ON *skrækja*]
☛ *Syn. v.* **1.** See note at **scream.**

shriev·al·ty (shrēv′əl tē) *n., pl.* -**ties.** the office, term of office, or jurisdiction of a sheriff.

shrieve (shrēv) *n. Obsolete.* sheriff. [var. of *sheriff*]

shrift (shrift) *n. Archaic.* **1** confession to a priest, followed by the imposing of penance and the granting of absolution. **2** the act of shriving. [OE *scrift* < L *scriptus* written]

shrike (shrīk) *n.* any of a family (Laniidae) of mainly Old World songbirds having a strong, hooked bill and feeding on insects and small birds and mammals, which they often impale on thorns, barbed wire, etc. Two species of shrike are found in Canada. [OE *scrīc*]

shrill (shril) *adj., v., n., adv.* —*adj.* **1** having a high pitch; high and sharp in sound; piercing: *Crickets, locusts, and katydids make shrill noises.* **2** full of shrill sounds.
—*v.* **1** make a shrill sound. **2** sound sharply.
—*n.* a shrill sound.
—*adv.* with a shrill sound. [ME *shrille*] —**shrill′ness,** *n.* —**shril·ly,** *adv.*

shrimp (shrimp) *n., pl.* **shrimp** *or* **shrimps. 1** any of a suborder (Natantia) of mostly marine decapod crustaceans having a relatively slender, laterally compressed body encased in a thin, semi-transparent shell, well-developed swimmerets on the abdomen, a fanlike tail, and long antennae; especially, any of the smaller members of this group (genera *Crangon, Peneus,* etc.), usually from four to eight centimetres long. Compare **prawn. 2** any of various other, shrimplike crustaceans. **3** *Usually derogatory.* a very small or weak person. [ME *shrimpe;* cf. MHG *schrimpen* shrink up] —**shrimp′like′,** *adj.*

shrine (shrīn) *n., v.* **shrined, shrin·ing.** —*n.* **1** a case, box, etc. holding a holy object. **2** the tomb of a saint, etc. **3** a place of worship: *a wayside shrine.* **4** a place or object considered as sacred because of its memories, history, etc.
—*v.* enclose in a shrine or something like a shrine. [OE *scrīn* < L *scrinium* case]

shrink (shringk) *v.* **shrank** *or* **shrunk, shrunk** *or* **shrunk·en, shrink·ing;** *n.* —*v.* **1** draw back: *The dog shrank from the whip. A shy person shrinks from making new acquaintances.* **2** become smaller: *His wool sweater shrank when it was washed.* **3** make smaller; cause to contract: *Hot water shrinks wool.*
—*n.* the act or process of shrinking. [OE *scrincan*] —**shrink′a·ble,** *adj.* —**shrink′er,** *n.*
☛ *Syn. v.* **1. Shrink, flinch** = draw back from something painful, unpleasant, etc. **Shrink** suggests instinctive drawing back physically or mentally, by or as if by contracting or drawing away some part of the body in fear, horror, or sensitiveness, from something painful or disagreeable: *He shrank from admitting his guilt.* **Flinch** suggests drawing back or turning away in spite of one's desire or determination not to, from danger, an unpleasant or difficult task or duty, or, especially, pain: *He could bear torture without flinching.*
☛ *Usage.* See note at **shrunk.**

shrink·age (shringk′ij) *n.* **1** the fact or process of shrinking. **2** the amount or degree of shrinking: *a shrinkage of two centimetres in the length of a sleeve.*

shrink-wrap (shrink′rap′) *v.* -**wrapped, -wrap·ping;** *n.* —*v.* wrap (merchandise) tightly in a thin, clear plastic film that shrinks closely around the contours of the article as it is sealed. —*n.* such wrapping.

shrive (shrīv) *v.* **shrove** *or* **shrived, shriv·en** *or* **shrived, shriv·ing.** *Archaic.* **1** hear the confession of, impose penance on, and grant absolution to. **2** make confession. **3** hear confessions.
shrive oneself, confess to a priest and do penance.
[OE *scrīfan* < L *scribere* write]

shriv·el (shriv′əl) *v.* -**elled** *or* -**eled, -el·ling** *or* -**el·ing. 1** dry up; wither; shrink and wrinkle: *The hot sunshine shrivelled the grass.*

2 waste away; become useless. **3** make helpless or useless. [origin unknown]

shriv·en (shriv′ən) *v.* a pp. of **shrive.**

The *Nonsuch*, a 17th-century square-rigged ketch. Its successful Atlantic voyage in 1668 resulted in the formation of the Hudson's Bay Company. The detail at left shows how shrouds are attached.

shroud (shroud) *n., v.* —*n.* **1** a cloth or garment in which a dead person is wrapped for burial. **2** something that covers, conceals, or veils: *The fog was a shroud over the city.* **3** one of a set of supporting ropes running from a masthead to the side of a ship. —*v.* **1** wrap for burial. **2** cover; conceal; veil: *The earth is shrouded in darkness.* [OE *scrūd*]

shrove (shrōv) *v.* a pt. of **shrive.**

Shrove·tide (shrōv′tīd′) *n.* the three days, **Shrove Sunday, Shrove Monday,** and **Shrove Tuesday,** before Ash Wednesday, the first day of Lent. Shrovetide is a time for confession, absolution, rejoicing, and feasting.

shrub¹ (shrub) *n.* a woody plant smaller than a tree, usually with many separate stems starting from or near the ground; bush. [OE *scrybb* brush] —**shrub′like′**, *adj.*

shrub² (shrub) *n.* a drink made from fruit juice, sugar, and, usually, rum or brandy. [< Arabic *shurb* drink]

shrub·ber·y (shrub′ər ē *or* shrub′rē) *n., pl.* **-ber·ies. 1** shrubs collectively. **2** a place planted with shrubs.

shrub·by (shrub′ē) *adj.* **-bi·er, -bi·est. 1** like shrubs. **2** covered with shrubs. **3** consisting of shrubs.

shrug (shrug) *v.* **shrugged, shrug·ging;** *n.* —*v.* raise (the shoulders) as an expression of dislike, doubt, indifference, impatience, etc. —*n.* a raising of the shoulders in this way. [ME *schrugge(n)* shiver; origin uncertain]

shrunk (shrungk) *v.* a pp. and a pt. of **shrink.**

☞ *Usage.* **Shrunk, shrunken.** The preferred past participle is **shrunk:** *The shirt has shrunk.* The form **shrunken,** the original past participle, is generally used as the adjective, especially before nouns: *a shrunken face.*

shrunk·en (shrungk′ən) *adj., v.* —*adj.* grown smaller; shrivelled. —*v.* a pp. of **shrink.**

☞ *Usage.* See note at **shrunk.**

shuck¹ (shuk) *n., v.* —*n.* a husk; pod. —*v.* **1** remove the shucks from. **2** *Informal.* take or throw off (clothing, etc.): *He shucked his jacket at the door.* [origin uncertain] —**shuck′er,** *n.*

shucks (shuks) *interj. Informal.* an exclamation of disgust, regret, impatience, etc.

shud·der (shud′ər) *v., n.* —*v.* tremble with horror, fear, cold, etc.: *She shudders at the sight of a snake.* —*n.* a trembling; quivering. [ME *shodder(en)*, frequentative of OE *scūdan* shake] —**shud′der·ing·ly,** *adv.*

☞ *Syn. v.* See note at **shiver.**

shuf·fle (shuf′əl) *v.* **-fled, -fling;** *n.* —*v.* **1** walk without lifting the feet: *The old man shuffles feebly along.* **2** scrape or drag (the feet). **3** dance with a shuffle. **4** mix (cards, etc.) so as to change the order. **5** push about; thrust or throw with clumsy haste: *He shuffled on his clothes and ran out of the house.* **6** move this way and that: *shuffle a stack of papers.* **7** act or answer in a tricky way.

shuffle off, get rid of.

—*n.* **1** a scraping or dragging movement of the feet. **2** a dance with a shuffle. **3** a shuffling of cards. **4** the right or turn to shuffle (cards). **5** a movement this way and that. **6** a trick; unfair act; evasion: *Through some legal shuffle he secured a new trial.* [? < LG *schuffeln.* Akin to SHOVE.] —**shuf′fler,** *n.*

shuf·fle·board (shuf′əl bôrd′) *n.* a game played by pushing large wooden or iron disks along a surface to certain spots. Also, **shovelboard.**

shun (shun) *v.* **shunned, shun·ning.** keep away from; avoid. [OE *scunian*] —**shun′ner,** *n.*

shun·pike (shun′pīk′) *n. Slang.* a quiet by-road, used by motorists to avoid major highways. [< *shun* + *turnpike*; originally, in the United States, a road used to avoid paying tolls on a turnpike]

shun·pik·ing (shun′pīk′ing) *n.* the practice of using quiet by-roads for motoring, rather than fast major highways.

shunt (shunt) *v., n.* —*v.* **1** move out of the way; turn aside. **2** sidetrack; put aside; get rid of. **3 a** switch (a train) from one track to another. **b** switch (anything) to another route or place. **4** *Electricity.* carry (a part of a current) by means of a shunt. —*n.* **1** a turning aside; shift. **2** a railway switch. **3** *Electricity.* a wire or other conductor joining two points in a circuit and forming a path through which a part of the current will pass. [ME; ? < *shun*] —**shunt′er,** *n.*

shush (shush) *v., interj.* —*v.* tell or cause to become silent; silence (someone); hush (*often used with* **up**). *interj.* quiet! hush!

shut (shut) *v.* **shut, shut·ting;** *adj.* —*v.* **1** close (a receptacle or opening) by pushing or pulling a lid, door, or other such part into place: *to shut a box, to shut a window.* **2** close (the eyes, a knife, a book, etc.) by bringing parts together. **3** close or lock the doors and windows of (*often used with* **up**): *After Thanksgiving we shut our cottage up for the winter.* **4** become shut; be closed: *The door doesn't shut properly.* **5** enclose or exclude; keep from going out or coming in (*used with* **in, out,** etc.): *He was shut in prison. They shut the cat out.*

shut down, a close by lowering. **b** close (a factory, etc.) for a time; stop work. **c** settle down so as to cover or envelop. **d** *Informal.* put a stop or check on.

shut off, close; obstruct; check; bar.

shut out, *Sports.* defeat (a team) without allowing it to score.

shut up, *Informal.* stop talking.

—*adj.* **1** closed; fastened up; enclosed. **2** *Phonetics.* formed by completely stopping the mouth passage. [OE *scyttan* bolt up]

shut–down (shut′doun′) *n.* a shutting down; a closing of a factory, etc. for a time.

shut–eye (shut′ī′) *n. Slang.* sleep.

shut–in (shut′in′) *adj., n.* —*adj.* confined. —*n.* a person who is kept from going out by sickness, weakness, etc.

shut–out (shut′out′) *n.* **1** *Sports.* the defeat of a team without allowing it to score. **2** a lockout.

shut·ter (shut′ər) *n., v.* —*n.* **1** a movable cover for a window. **2** a movable cover, slide, etc. for closing an opening. The device that opens and closes in front of the film or plate in a camera is a shutter. **3** a person or thing that shuts. —*v.* put a shutter or shutters on or over. [< *shut*]

shut·tle (shut′əl) *n., v.* **-tled, -tling.** —*n.* **1** a device used in weaving for carrying the weft between the warp threads, from one side of the web to the other. **2** a similar device on which thread is wound for tatting, etc. **3** a device on a sewing machine that carries the lower thread back and forth to loop with the upper thread in making a stitch. **4** any of various other devices or things that go back and forth. **5** a bus, train, aircraft, etc. that runs back and forth regularly over a short distance. **6** the route travelled by such a vehicle. **7** (*adj.*) of, involving, or designating such a vehicle or route: *a shuttle bus, a shuttle service.* —*v.* **1** move quickly to and fro. **2** of ships, aircraft, buses, etc., ply between two points: *This bus shuttles between Toronto and Hamilton.* [OE *scutel* a dart < *scēotan* shoot]

shut·tle·cock (shut′əl kok′) *n.* **1** a cone-shaped ring of feathers or light plastic with a cork or similar base, used in the game of badminton. **2** a cork with feathers stuck in one end, which is hit back and forth by a small racket, called a battledore, in the game of battledore and shuttlecock.

shy¹ (shī) *adj.* **shy·er** *or* **shi·er, shy·est** *or* **shi·est;** *v.* **shied, shy·ing;** *n., pl.* **shies.** —*adj.* **1** uncomfortable in company; bashful: *John is shy and dislikes parties.* **2** easily frightened away; timid: *A deer is a shy animal.* **3** cautious; wary. **4** not having enough; short; scant: *This store is shy on children's clothing.*

be shy (of), *Informal.* having little; lacking: *We are shy of butter. The team is shy of a goalkeeper.*

fight shy of, keep away from; avoid.

—*v.* **1** start back or aside suddenly: *The horse shied at the newspaper blowing along the ground.* **2** shrink.

—*n.* a sudden start to one side. [OE *scēoh*] —**shy′ly,** *adv.* —**shy′ness,** *n.*

☞ *Syn. adj.* **1. Shy, bashful** = uncomfortable in the presence or company of others. **Shy** suggests a lack of self-confidence that makes a person shrink from making friends or going up to others, and is shown by a reserved or timid manner: *People who appear snobbish are often really shy.* **Bashful** suggests shrinking by nature from being noticed, shown by awkward and embarrassed

behavior in the presence of strangers: *The boy was too bashful to ask her to dance.*

shy² (shī) *v.* **shied, shy·ing;** *n., pl.* **shies.** —*v.* throw; fling: *The boy shied a stone at the tree.*
—*n.* **1** a throw; fling. **2** *Informal.* a verbal attack; sarcastic or taunting remark. **3** *Informal.* a try; fling. [origin uncertain]

Shy·lock (shī′lok) *n.* **1** in Shakespeare's *The Merchant of Venice,* a relentless and revengeful moneylender. **2** any person who lends money at exorbitant interest and insists on prompt payment.

shy·ster (shī′stər) *n. Informal.* a lawyer or other person who uses improper or questionable methods in his business or profession. [origin uncertain]

si (sē) *n. Music.* ti. [see GAMUT]

Si silicon.

SI Système international d'unités (International System of Units), the system adopted by Canada as the official system of measurement. See **metric system.**

si·al (sī′əl) *n.* the upper layer of the earth's continental crust, composed of comparatively light rocks, such as granite, that are rich in silica and aluminum. [< *si*licon + *al*uminum. 20c.]

si·al·ic (sī al′ik) *adj.* of, having to do with, or being sial.

Si·a·mese (sī′ə mēz′) *adj., n., pl.* **-mese.** —*adj.* Thai. —*n.* **1** Thai. **2** a breed of cat having a lithe, sinuous body and short hair, always dark at the ears, feet, and tail.

Siamese twins twins joined together at birth. [< Eng and Chan (1811-1874), twin boys born in Siam, who were joined together at the chest]

sib (sib) *adj., n.* —*adj.* related by blood; closely related; akin.
—*n.* **1** a kinsman or relative. **2** one's kin. **3** a brother or sister. [OE *sibb*]

Si·be·ri·an (sī bēr′ē ən) *n., adj.* —*n.* a native or inhabitant of Siberia, a part of the Soviet Union extending across northern Asia. —*adj.* of or having to do with Siberia or its people.

Siberian husky a breed of medium-sized working dog originally developed in Siberia, having a brush tail and a thick coat of black, tan, or grey with white markings. It is much used in the North.

sib·i·lance (sib′ə ləns) *n.* the state or quality of having a hissing sound.

sib·i·lan·cy (sib′ə lən sē) *n.* sibilance.

sib·i·lant (sib′ə lənt) *adj., n.* —*adj.* hissing. —*n.* a hissing sound, letter, or symbol. The sounds represented by *s* and *sh* are sibilants. [< L *sibilans, -antis,* ppr. of *sibilare* hiss]

sib·i·late (sib′ə lāt′) *v.* **-lat·ed, -lat·ing. 1** utter a hissing sound. **2** pronounce with a hissing sound. [< L *sibilare* hiss]

sib·ling (sib′ling) *n.* a brother or sister. [< *sib* + *-ling*]

sib·yl (sib′əl) *n.* **1** in ancient times, any of several prophetesses that the Greeks and Romans consulted about the future. **2** a prophetess; fortuneteller; witch. [< L < Gk. *sibylla*]

sib·yl·line (sib′ə līn′, sib′ə lēn′, or sib′ə lin) *adj.* **1** of or like a sibyl; prophetic; mysterious. **2** said or written by a sibyl.

Sibylline Books a collection of prophecies and advice venerated and consulted by the ancient Romans.

sic¹ (sik) *adv. Latin.* so; thus.
☛ *Hom.* **sick.**
☛ *Usage.* Sic is used, usually in square brackets, to emphasize that a strange or incorrect word or form in a quoted passage is recorded just as it is in the original: *The picture caption read "Victoria, capitol [sic] of British Columbia."*

sic² (sik) *v.* **sicked, sick·ing.** sick².
☛ *Hom.* **sick.**

sic·ca·tive (sik′ə tiv) *adj., n.* —*adj.* drying. —*n.* a drying substance, especially a dryer used in painting. [< LL *siccativus* < L *siccare* make dry < *siccus* dry]

Si·cil·ian (sə sil′yən) *n., adj.* —*n.* **1** a native or inhabitant of Sicily, an island near the SW tip of Italy. **2** a dialect of Italian spoken in Sicily. —*adj.* of or having to do with Sicily, its people, or their dialect.

sick¹ (sik) *adj.* **1** in poor health; having some disease; ill. **2** of or for a sick person; connected with sickness. **3** showing sickness: *a sick look.* **4** (*noml.*) **the sick,** people who are sick. **5** feeling nausea; inclined to vomit. **6** weary or disgusted (*usually followed by* **of**): *He is sick of school. I'm sick of hearing that same old excuse.* **7** affected with sorrow or longing: *sick at heart.* **8** not in the proper condition. **9** pale; wan. **10** morbid; sadistic; cruel: *a sick joke, sick humor.* [OE *sēoc*]
☛ *Hom.* **sic.**
☛ *Syn.* Sick (def. 1) and ill (def. 1) have the same meaning. Ill is used in more formal contexts. In British use, and sometimes in Canada, ill is the general word and sick means simply 'nauseated' or 'sick to the stomach.'

sick² or **sic²** (sik) *v.* **sicked, sick·ing. 1** set upon or attack. **2** incite to set upon or attack (*used with* **on**). [var. of *seek*]

hat, āge, fär; let, ēqual, tèrm; it, īce
hot, ōpen, ôrder; oil, out; cup, pút, rüle,
əbove, takən, pencəl, lemən, circəs

ch, child; ng, long; sh, ship
th, thin; ᴛʜ, then; zh, measure

sick bay **1** a place used as a hospital on a ship. **2** a room or rooms set apart for the care of the sick or injured.

sick·bed (sik′bed′) *n.* the bed of a sick person.

sick·en (sik′ən) *v.* **1** become sick: *The bird sickened when kept in the cage.* **2** make sick: *The sight of blood sickened him.*

sick·en·ing (sik′ən ing *or* sik′ning) *adj.* **1** making sick; causing nausea, faintness, disgust, or loathing. **2** becoming sick.
—**sick′en·ing·ly,** *adv.*

sick headache a headache accompanied by nausea; migraine.

sick·ish (sik′ish) *adj.* **1** somewhat sick. **2** somewhat sickening.
—**sick′ish·ly,** *adv.* —**sick′ish·ness,** *n.*

A sickle

sick·le (sik′əl) *n., v.* **-led, -ling.** —*n.* a tool consisting of a short, curved blade on a short handle, used for cutting grass, etc. —*v.* mow or cut with a sickle. [OE *sicol* < L *secula*; related to *secare* cut]

sick·ly (sik′lē) *adj.* **-li·er, -li·est;** *adv.* —*adj.* **1** often sick; not strong; not healthy. **2** of or having to do with sickness: *Her skin is a sickly yellow.* **3** causing sickness: *That place has a sickly climate.* **4** faint; weak; pale. **5** weak; mawkish: *sickly sentimentality.* —*adv.* in a sick manner. —**sick′li·ness,** *n.*

sick·ness (sik′nis) *n.* **1** the condition of being sick; illness; disease. **2** nausea; vomiting.

sick parade in the armed forces, the appearance of persons requiring medical attention before the medical officer or his staff.

sic tran·sit glo·ri·a mun·di (sik′tran′sit glô′rē ə mun′dī or mún′dē) *Latin.* so passes away the glory of the world.

side (sīd) *n., adj., v.* **sid·ed, sid·ing.** —*n.* **1** a surface or line bounding a thing: *the sides of a square.* **2** one of the two surfaces of an object that is not the front, back, top, or bottom: *There is a door at the side of the house.* **3** either of the two surfaces of paper, cloth, etc.: *Write only on one side of the paper.* **4** a particular surface: *the outer and inner sides of a hollow ball, the side of the moon turned toward the earth.* **5** either the right or the left part of a thing; either part or region beyond a central line: *the east side of a city, our side of the street, turn to one side.* **6** either the right or the left part of the body of a person or an animal: *a pain in one's side.* **7** the slope of a hill or bank. **8** a bank or shore of a river. **9** an aspect or view of someone or something: *the better side of one's nature, the bright side of a difficulty.* **10** a group of persons opposed to another group: *Both sides are ready for the contest.* **11** a team. **12** the position, course, attitude, or part of one person or party against another: *It is pleasant to be on the winning side of a dispute.* **13** a part of a family; line of descent; *The man is English on his mother's side.* **14** *Billiards. Brit.* a spinning motion given a ball by hitting it quickly on the side. **15** *Esp.Brit. Slang.* pretentious airs.
by (someone's) **side,** near someone: *He wanted his family by his side.*
on the side, *Informal,* in addition to one's ordinary duties.
side by side, a beside one another. **b** equally: *Hourly earnings of our employees rank side by side with those in similar industries.*
split (one's) **sides,** laugh very hard.
take sides, place oneself with one person or group against another.
—*adj.* **1** at one side; on one side: *the side aisles of a theatre.* **2** from one side: *a side view.* **3** toward one side: *a side glance.* **4** less important: *a side issue.*
—*v.* take the part of; favor one among opposing or differing groups or persons: *The sisters always side with each other* (*used with* **with**). [OE *sīde*]

side arms weapons, such as a sword, revolver, bayonet, etc., carried at the side or on a belt.

side·board (sīd′bôrd′) *n.* **1** a piece of dining-room furniture having drawers and shelves for holding silver and linen, and space on top for dishes. **2** an additional and removable board placed on

the side of a truck, wagon, etc. to increase the height of, or form, a side.

side boards *Hockey.* the fence surrounding the playing surface; the boards (def. 13b).

side·burns (sīd′bėrnz′) *n.pl.* hair growing down in front of the ears, especially when the chin is shaved. [alteration of *burnsides*, from Ambrose E. *Burnside* (1824-1881), an American general who wore thick side whiskers]

side·car (sīd′kär′) *n.* 1 a small, one-wheeled car for a passenger, baggage, etc. attached to the side of a motorcycle. 2 a cocktail made with Cointreau, brandy, and lemon juice in approximately equal parts.

side channel a small offshoot of a river, sometimes running for some distance before rejoining the main stream, sometimes coming to a dead end, and usually shallow, narrow, and sluggish.

–sided *adjective-forming suffix.* having a side or sides, as in *three-sided.*

side dish a dish served in addition to the main dish of a course.

side effect an incidental consequence of a course of action, treatment, etc., especially an undesirable reaction to a drug.

side·hill (sīd′hil′) *n.* hillside.

side·kick (sīd′kik′) *n. Slang.* a partner or assistant.

side light 1 light coming from the side. 2 incidental information about a subject. 3 either of two lights carried by a moving ship at night, a red one on the port side and a green one on the starboard side. 4 a window or other opening for light in the side of a building, ship, etc. 5 a window at the side of a door or of another window.

side·line (sīd′līn′) *v.* **-lined, -lin·ing.** —*n.* 1 a line at the side of something. 2 *Football, etc.* a line that marks the limit of play on the side of the field. 3 Often, **sidelines,** *pl.* the space just outside these lines: *They watched the game from the sidelines.* 4 a a line of goods, trade, etc. that is additional, auxiliary, and secondary to the basic one or ones. b any enterprise, business, etc. carried on apart from that in which one is chiefly or officially employed.
on the sidelines, inactive; not taking an active part in a game, enterprise, etc.
—*v.* put on the sidelines; make inactive.

side·long (sīd′lông′) *adj. or adv.* to one side; toward the side.

side·man (sīd′man′) *n.* an instrumentalist in a jazz group or dance band other than the leader or a soloist.

side·piece (sīd′pēs′) *n.* a piece forming a side or part of a side, or fixed by the side, of something.

si·de·re·al (sī dēr′ē əl) *adj.* 1 of or having to do with the stars. 2 *Astronomy.* measured by the apparent daily motion of the stars. A **sidereal year** is about twenty minutes longer than a solar year. [< L *sidereus* astral < *sidus, sideris* star]

sid·er·ite (sīd′ər īt′) *n.* 1 an iron ore composed of iron carbonate. Siderite occurs in various forms and colors. 2 a meteorite consisting mainly of iron. *Formula:* $FeCO_3$ [< L < Gk. *sidērītēs* < *sidēros* iron]

side·road (sīd′rōd′) *n. Cdn.* in Ontario, a road built along the side line of a concession, connecting concession roads and usually running north-south.

side road 1 a secondary road, often unpaved, leading to a main road or highway. 2 *Cdn.* See **sideroad.**

side·sad·dle (sīd′sad′əl) *n.* 1 a woman's saddle so made that both of the rider's legs are on the same side of the horse. 2 (*advl.*) on or as if on a sidesaddle.

side·show (sīd′shō′) *n.* 1 a small show in connection with a principal one: *the side shows of a circus.* 2 any minor proceeding or affair connected with a more important one.

side·slip (sīd′slip′) *n., v.* **-slipped, -slip·ping.** —*n.* 1 a slip or skid to one side. 2 the slipping to one side of an aircraft. —*v.* slip or skid to one side.

sides·man (sīdz′mən) *n., pl.* **-men.** 1 *Anglican church.* an assistant to a churchwarden. 2 *Obsolete.* a person who takes sides.

side step 1 a step or stepping to one side. 2 a step at the side of a ship, vehicle, etc.

side–step (sīd′step′) *v.* **-stepped, -step·ping.** 1 step aside. 2 avoid by stepping aside; evade: *He never side-stepped a responsibility.* —**side′-step′per,** *n.*

side·swipe (sīd′swīp′) *v.* **-swiped, -swip·ing;** *n.* —*v.* hit with a sweeping blow along the side. —*n.* a sweeping blow along the side.

side·track (sīd′trak′) *n., v.* —*n.* 1 a railway siding. 2 turning or being turned aside: *Stick to the business at hand and avoid sidetracks.* —*v.* 1 switch (a train, etc.) to a siding.

2 put aside; turn aside: *The teacher refused to be sidetracked by questions on other subjects.*

side trip a short, extra trip not included in the main itinerary of a journey or voyage.

side·walk (sīd′wok′ *or* -wôk′) *n.* a place to walk at the side of a street, usually paved.

sidewalk bicycle a child's bicycle that has an extra small wheel on either side of the rear wheel.

side·ward (sīd′wərd) *adj. or adv.* toward one side.

side·wards (sīd′wərdz) *adv.* sideward.

side·way (sīd′wā′) *adv., adj., n.* —*adv. or adj.* sideways. —*n.* 1 a side street, not a main road; byway. 2 sidewalk.

side·ways (sīd′wāz′) *adv. or adj.* 1 toward one side: *to walk sideways.* 2 from one side: *a sideways glimpse.* 3 with one side toward the front: *to stand sideways, to place a book sideways on a shelf.*

side–wheel (sīd′wēl′ *or* -hwēl′) *adj.* of or designating a steamboat having a paddle wheel on each side.

side–wheel·er (sīd′wē′lər *or* -hwē′lər) *n.* a side-wheel steamboat.

side whisker 1 a hair growing long on the side of the face. 2 **side whiskers,** *pl.* the whiskers that grow on the cheek or side of the face.

side·wise (sīd′wīz′) *adv. or adj.* sideways.

sid·ing (sīd′ing) *n.* 1 a short railway track to which cars can be switched from a main track. 2 the boards forming the sides of a wooden building.

si·dle (sī′dəl) *v.* **-dled, -dling;** *n.* —*v.* move sideways, especially shyly or stealthily: *The little boy shyly sidled up to the visitor.* —*n.* a movement sideways. [< *sideling* sidelong]

Si·do·ni·an (sī dō′nē ən) *n., adj.* —*n.* a native or inhabitant of Sidon, a town on the SW coast of Lebanon. —*adj.* of or having to do with Sidon or its people.

siege (sēj) *n., v.* **sieged, sieg·ing.** —*n.* 1 the surrounding of a fortified place by an army trying to capture it; a besieging or being besieged. 2 any long or persistent effort to overcome resistance; any long-continued attack: *a siege of illness.*
lay siege to, a besiege. **b** attempt to win or get by long and persistent effort.
—*v.* besiege. [ME < OF *siege,* ult. < L *sedere* sit]
☛ *Syn. n.* **1. Siege, blockade** = a military operation to cut off normal communications and supplies of a place. **Siege,** chiefly a land operation, means surrounding a city or fortified place, cutting off all movement to and from it, and usually assaulting it: *The British had barely laid siege to Detroit in 1812 when it surrendered.* **Blockade** applies to an operation, chiefly but not always naval, to close a harbor, coast, or city and cut off its supplies by controlling ship movements or other transportation to and from it, but does not suggest attacking it: *The air lift defeated the blockade of Berlin.*

Siege Perilous *Arthurian legend.* a vacant seat at the Round Table, which could be taken only by the knight who was destined to find the Holy Grail.

Sieg·fried (sēg′frēd) *n. Germanic legend.* a hero who killed a dragon and bathed in its blood to make himself invulnerable. He won the treasure of the Nibelungs.

sie·mens (sē′mənz) *n.* an SI unit for measuring electrical conductance. One siemens is the conductance between two points of a conductor when a current of one ampere produces one volt of electromotive force. *Symbol:* S

Si·en·ese (sē′ə nēz′) *n., pl.* **-ese;** *adj.* —*n.* a native or inhabitant of Siena, a city and province in central Italy. —*adj.* of or having to do with Siena.

si·en·na (sē en′ə) *n.* 1 a yellowish-brown coloring matter (**raw sienna**) made from earth containing iron. 2 a reddish-brown coloring matter (**burnt sienna**) made by roasting earth containing iron. 3 a yellowish brown or reddish brown. [short for Ital. *terra di Sien(n)a* earth of Siena, a city in Italy]

si·er·ra (sē er′ə) *n.* a chain of hills or mountains with jagged peaks. [< Sp. *sierra,* literally, saw < L *serra*]

si·es·ta (sē es′tə) *n.* a nap or rest taken at noon or in the afternoon. [< Sp. < L *sexta (hora)* sixth (hour), noon]

sieur (syœr) *n. French.* formerly, a title of respect for a man; Sir. [< F < VL *seiorem* < L *seniorem,* accus. of *senior* senior. Doublet of SEIGNIOR and SEIGNEUR.]

sieve (siv) *n., v.* **sieved, siev·ing.** —*n.* a utensil having holes that let liquids and small pieces pass through, but not large pieces: *Shaking flour through a sieve removes lumps.* —*v.* put through a sieve. [OE *sife*] —**sieve′like′,** *adj.*

sif·fleur (sē flėr′) *n. Cdn.* hoary marmot. [< Cdn.F]

sift (sift) *v.* 1 separate large pieces from small by shaking in a sieve: *Sift the gravel and put the larger stones in a separate pile.* 2 put through a sieve: *Sift sugar onto the top of the cake.* 3 use a

sieve. **4** fall through, or as if through, a sieve: *The snow sifted softly down.* **5** examine very carefully: *The jury sifted the evidence to decide if the man was guilty.* [OE *siftan* < *sife* sieve] —**sift′er**, *n.*

sigh (sī) *v., n.* —*v.* **1** draw in and let out a very long, deep, loud breath because one is sad, tired, relieved, etc. **2** say or express with a sigh. **3** make a sound like a sigh: *The wind sighed in the treetops.* **4** wish very much; long: *She sighed for home and friends.* **5** lament with sighing: *sigh over one's unhappy fate.*
—*n.* the act or sound of sighing. [ME *sighe(n)*, ult. < OE *sīcan*] —**sigh′er**, *n.* —**sigh′ing·ly**, *adv.*

sight (sīt) *n., v.* —*n.* **1** the power of seeing; vision: *Birds have better sight than dogs.* **2** the act or fact of seeing; look: *love at first sight.* **3** the range or field of vision: *Land was in sight.* **4** the thing seen; view: *The vase of flowers was a pretty sight.* **5** something worth seeing: *see the sights of the city.* **6** something that looks bad, ridiculous, or odd: *Her clothes were a sight.* **7** a device on a gun, surveying instrument, etc. used in taking aim or observing. **8** an observation taken with a telescope or other instrument; aim with a gun, etc. **9** a way of looking or thinking; regard: *The old doll was precious in the little girl's sight.* **10** *Informal.* a great deal: *That's a sight more money than I can afford.*
at sight, as soon as seen: *She reads music at sight.*
catch sight of, see: *I caught sight of him.*
in sight of, where one can see or be seen by: *We live in sight of the school.*
know by sight, know sufficiently to recognize when seen: *I've never met him but I know him by sight.*
on sight, as soon as seen; at sight.
out of sight of, a where one cannot see: *out of sight of land.* **b** where one cannot be seen by: *out of sight of the neighbors.*
sight unseen, not seen beforehand: *He bought the radio sight unseen.*
—*v.* **1** see: *At last Columbus sighted land.* **2** take a sight or observation of. **3** aim by means of sights. **4** adjust the sight (of a gun, etc.). **5** provide with sights. [OE *(ge)siht*]
☛ *Hom.* cite, site.

sight draft a written order from one bank to another, requiring a certain amount of money to be paid on demand.

sight·less (sīt′lis) *adj.* **1** blind. **2** *Poetic.* invisible.

sight·ly (sīt′lē) *adj.* **-li·er, -li·est. 1** pleasing to the sight. **2** affording a fine view. —**sight′li·ness**, *n.*

sight·see·ing (sīt′sē′ing) *n.* the act of going around to see objects or places of interest.

sight·se·er (sīt′sē′ər) *n.* a person who goes around to see objects or places of interest.

sig·ma (sig′mə) *n.* **1** the 18th letter of the Greek alphabet (Σ, σ or, when final, ς = English S, s). **2** something shaped like an S. **3** something shaped like a C.

sig·moid (sig′moid) *adj., n.* —*adj.* **1** having a double curve like the letter S. **2** having a single curve like the letter C. **3** of or having to do with the sigmoid flexure.
—*n.* sigmoid flexure. [< Gk. *sigmoeidēs* < *sigma* sigma + *eidos* form]

sigmoid flexure the S-shaped curve of the large intestine between the descending colon and the rectum. See **alimentary canal** for picture.

sign (sīn) *n., v.* —*n.* **1 a** any mark used to mean, represent, or point out something. **b** *Mathematics.* a mark or symbol used to indicate an operation to be performed on a quantity or number, a relation of quantities or numbers, etc. The four signs of the arithmetic operations are addition (+), subtraction (−), multiplication (×), division (÷). The sign (=) means "equals." The sign (+) and (−) in algebra and higher mathematics define positive and negative numbers. **c** *Music.* a flat, sharp, or other symbol used in notation to give directions, indicate tonality, etc. **2** a motion or gesture used to mean, represent, or point out something: *A nod is a sign of agreement. We talked to the deaf man by signs.* **3** an inscribed board, space, etc. serving for advertisement, information, etc.: *The sign reads, "Keep off the grass."* **4** an indication; trace; evidence: *signs of life. The hunter found signs of deer.* **5** an indication of a coming event: *The robin is a sign of spring.* **6** *Astrology.* any of the twelve divisions of the zodiac.
—*v.* **1** attach one's name to: *Sign this letter.* **2** attach one's name to show authority, agreement, obligation, etc.; write one's name: *Sign on the dotted line.* **3** write: *Sign your initials here.* **4** hire by a written agreement: *to sign a new player.* **5** accept employment: *They signed for three years.* **6** give a sign to; signal: *to sign someone to enter.* **7** communicate by gesture: *to sign assent.* **8** mark with a sign.
sign away, assign.
sign in, indicate by signing a register, etc. that one is present.
sign off, a in radio and television, stop broadcasting. **b** bring a letter, speech, lecture, etc. to a close.
sign on or **sign up, a** accept a job by putting one's name to an agreement. **b** hire in this way. **c** enlist in the armed services.

hat, āge, fär; let, ēqual, tèrm; it, īce
hot, ōpen, ôrder; oil, out; cup, pùt, rüle,
əbove, takən, pencəl, lemən, circəs

ch, child; ng, long; sh, ship
th, thin; ᴛʜ, then; zh, measure

sign out, indicate by signing a register, etc. that one will not be present.
sign over, hand over by signing one's name.
[ME < OF < L *signum*] —**sign′a·ble**, *adj.* —**sign′er**, *n.*
☛ *Hom.* sine, syne.

☛ *Syn. n.* **4.** See note at **mark**. **5.** **Sign**, **omen** = an indication of something about to happen. **Sign** applies to something that can be seen, felt, or otherwise perceived as objective evidence that some particular happening can reasonably be expected: *Those big black clouds are signs of a storm.* **Omen** applies to a thing or event that, particularly from a religious or superstitious point of view, is seen as extraordinary and as a promise of something good or bad to come: *He believed his dream was an omen of death.*

sig·nal (sig′nəl) *n., v.* **-nalled** or **-naled, -nal·ling** or **-nal·ing.** —*n.* **1** a sign, token, etc. that gives information or notice of something: *A flashing red light is a warning signal.* **2** a sign agreed upon or understood as the occasion of concerted action: *to give the signal to advance.* **3** anything that produces a response or action: *The defeat of the government was the signal for a mass uprising.* **4** *Radio, television, etc.* **a** a wave, current, impulse, etc. serving to convey sounds and images. **b** a sound or image so conveyed. **5** *Bridge, etc.* a bid or play designed to give information to one's partner. **6 signals**, *pl. Football.* the numbers called by an offensive back, usually the quarterback, designating a particular play, or by a member of the defensive team to direct the positions of the players. **7** (*adj.*) used as a signal or in signalling. **8** (*adj.*) remarkable; striking; notable.
—*v.* **1** make a signal or signals (to): *He signalled the car to stop by raising his hand.* **2** make known by a signal or signals: *A bell signals the end of a class period.* [< F *signal*, ult. < L *signum* sign] —**sig′nal·ler** or **sig′nal·er**, *n.*

signal fire a fire used in giving a signal.

signal flag a flag used in giving a signal.

Signal Hill the hill overlooking the entrance to St. John's harbor in Newfoundland, where Marconi received the first transatlantic signal in 1901.

sig·nal·ize (sig′nəl īz′) *v.* **-ized, -iz·ing. 1** make stand out; make notable: *The present century has been signalized by many great inventions.* **2** point out; mention specially; draw attention to. **3 a** make signals to; communicate with by signal. **b** announce by a signal or signals.

sig·nal·ler or **sig·nal·er** (sig′nəl ər) *n.* **1** a soldier in the infantry, artillery, etc. who looks after communications within the regiment. **2** signalman.

sig·nal·ly (sig′nəl ē) *adv.* remarkably; strikingly; notably.

sig·nal·man (sig′nəl mən or -man′) *n., pl.* **-men. 1** a railway employee in charge of the signals. **2** a person who sends or receives signals, as in the armed forces.

sig·na·to·ry (sig′nə tôr′ē) *n., pl.* **-ries;** *adj.* —*n.* a signer of a document. —*adj.* signing: *signatory delegates.*

sig·na·ture (sig′nə chər or sig′nə chür′) *n.* **1** a person's name written by himself. **2** a writing of one's name. **3** *Music.* the signs printed at the beginning of a staff to show the key and time of a piece of music. **4** *Printing.* **a** a letter or number printed at the bottom of the first page of every sheet, telling how it is to be folded and arranged in pages. **b** a sheet with such a mark, especially when folded. **5** a tune, song, or slogan, used to identify a radio or television program. **6** *Pharmacy.* that part of a prescription that gives the directions to be marked on the container of the medicine. [< LL *signatura*, ult. < L *signum* sign]

sign·board (sīn′bôrd′) *n.* a board having a sign, notice, advertisement, inscription, etc. on it.

sig·net (sig′nit) *n.* a small seal: *The order was sealed with the king's signet.* [ME < OF *signet*, ult. < L *signum* seal]

signet ring a finger ring containing a signet.

sig·nif·i·cance (sig nif′ə kəns) *n.* **1** importance; consequence: *The chairman wanted to see him on a matter of significance.* **2** meaning: *Do you understand the significance of this picture?* **3** expressiveness; significant quality: *the significance of her smile.*

sig·nif·i·cant (sig nif′ə kənt) *adj.* **1** full of meaning; important; of consequence: *July 1, 1867, is a significant date for Canadians.* **2** having a meaning; expressive: *Smiles are significant of pleasure.* **3** having or expressing a hidden or special meaning: *A significant nod from his friend warned him to stop talking.* [< L *significans,*

-antis, ppr. of *significare* signify. See SIGNIFY.] —**sig·nif′i·cant·ly,** *adv.*

☛ *Syn.* **1.** See note at **expressive.**

sig·ni·fi·ca·tion (sig′nə fə kā′shən) *n.* **1** the meaning; sense. **2** the act or process of signifying. Signification relies largely upon words and gestures.

sig·nif·i·ca·tive (sig nif′ə kə tiv *or* sig nif′ə kā′tiv) *adj.* **1** serving to signify; having a meaning. **2** significant or suggestive.

sig·ni·fy (sig′nə fī′) *v.* **-fied, -fy·ing. 1** be a sign of; mean: *"Oh!" signifies surprise.* **2** make known by signs, words, or actions: *He signified his consent with a nod.* **3** have importance; be of consequence; matter: *What a fool says does not signify.* [ME < OF < L *significare* < *signum* sign + *facere* make]

si·gnior (sē′nyôr) See **signor.**

sign language language in which movements and positions of the hands and fingers stand for words, ideas, etc.

sign manual 1 a person's signature, especially that of a sovereign or magistrate on an official document. **2** a distinctively individual sign, stamp, or quality.

sign of the cross a hand gesture indicating the shape of a cross, made by a Christian priest in blessing or by any person as an act of reverence.

sign of the zodiac any of the twelve divisions of the zodiac. Each of them is named after a constellation.

si·gnor (sē′nyôr; *Italian,* sē nyôr′) *n. Italian.* Mr. *Abbrev.:* S. or Sr.

si·gno·ra (sē nyô′rə; *Italian,* sē nyô′rä) *n., pl.* **-re** (-rä). *Italian.* **1** Mrs. **2** lady.

si·gno·re (sē nyô′rä) *n., pl.* **-ri** (-rē). *Italian.* **1** gentleman. **2** sir (def. 1).

si·gno·ri·na (sē′nyô rē′nə; *Italian,* sē′nyô rē′nä) *n., pl.* **-ne** (-nä). *Italian.* **1** Miss. **2** a young lady.

si·gno·ry (sēn′yə rē) *n., pl.* **-ries. 1** lordship; rule. **2** domain. **3** a governing body. Venice was ruled by a signory. [ME < OF *signorie,* var. of *seignorie* (see SEIGNIORY); influenced by Ital. *signoria*]

sign·post (sīn′pōst′) *n.* **1** a post having a sign, notice, or direction on it; guidepost. **2** anything that marks, points, guides, or from which bearings may be taken, conclusions drawn, etc.

Sikh (sēk) *n., adj.* —*n.* a member of a religious sect, founded in N India in the early 16th century as an offshoot of Hinduism, that teaches monotheism and rejection of the caste system. —*adj.* of or having to do with the Sikhs or their religion. [< Hind. *sikh* disciple]

Sikh·ism (sē′kiz′əm) *n.* the beliefs and doctrines of the Sikhs.

si·lage (sī′lij) *n.* green fodder for farm animals, preserved and stored in a silo; ensilage. [< *ensilage,* after *silo*]

si·lence (sī′ləns) *n., v.* **-lenced, -lenc·ing;** *interj.* —*n.* **1** the absence of sound or noise; stillness. **2** a state of keeping still; not talking. **3 a** an omission of mention or notice in a narrative. **b** the omission or neglect to write, communicate, or reply (about something); secrecy: *Silence in matters of public interest is intolerable in a free society.*
in silence, without saying anything: *They finished their work in silence.*
—*v.* **1** stop the speech or noise of; make silent; quiet: *They asked him to silence the noisy children.* **2** make silent by persuasion, restraint, force, etc.: *Her strong arguments soon silenced the opposition. The new government attempted to silence the press.* **3** stop (enemy guns, etc.) from firing by destroying or disabling with return fire.
—*interj.* be silent! [ME < OF < L *silentium,* ult. < *silere* be silent]

si·lenc·er (sī′lən sər) *n.* **1** a person or thing that silences. **2** a muffler on an internal-combustion engine. **3** a device for deadening the sound of a firearm.

si·lent (sī′lənt) *adj.* **1** quiet; still; noiseless: *a silent house, the silent hills.* **2** not speaking; saying little or nothing: *You're very silent today.* **3** not spoken; not said out loud: *a silent prayer, silent disapproval.* **4** of a letter in a word, not pronounced in speech. The *l* in *folk* and the *b* in *lamb* are silent. **5** not active; taking no open or active part. A **silent partner** has no share in managing a business. **6** omitting mention of something, as in a narrative: *The book is silent on the question of motive for his actions.* **7** designating a motion picture without spoken dialogue: *The first movies were silent.* [< L *silens, -entis,* ppr. of *silere* be silent] —**si′lent·ly,** *adv.* —**si′lent·ness,** *n.*

☛ *Syn.* **2. Silent, taciturn, reticent** = saying little or nothing. **Silent** especially means "not talkative," characteristically speaking only when necessary or saying very little, but also means saying nothing on some particular occasion for some special reason: *He is a silent, thoughtful boy.* **Taciturn** means "not

fond of talking," being by nature inclined to be silent avoid avoid conversation: *He is a taciturn man who dislikes parties.* **Reticent** means "not saying all one knows, disposed to keep silent," especially about private affairs: *He is reticent about his early life.*

Si·le·nus (sī lē′nəs) *n. Greek mythology.* the foster father and companion of Dionysus and leader of the satyrs. He is represented as a short, stout, drunken old man.

si·le·sia (sī lē′shə *or* sə lē′shə) *n.* a fine, light, smooth cotton cloth used for lining. [< *Silesia,* a region in central Europe where it was originally made]

Si·le·sian (sī lē′shən *or* sə lē′shən, sī lē′zhən *or* sə lē′zhən) *n., adj.* —*n.* a native or inhabitant of Silesia, a region in central Europe, now divided between East Germany, Czechoslovakia, and Poland. —*adj.* of or having to do with Silesia.

si·lex (sī′leks) *n.* **1** silica. **2** a strong, heat-resistant glass that is mostly quartz. **3 Silex,** *Trademark.* a coffee maker made of such glass. [< L *silex* flint]

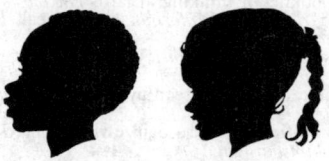

Silhouettes of children's heads

sil·hou·ette (sil′ü et′) *n., v.* **-et·ted, -et·ting.** —*n.* **1** an outline portrait cut out of black paper or filled in with some single color. **2** a dark image outlined against a lighter background. **3** the contour of a garment, figure, etc.: *Her dress has the new, slim silhouette.*
in silhouette, shown in outline, or in black against a white background.
—*v.* show in outline: *The mountain was silhouetted against the sky.* [after Etienne de *Silhouette* (1709-1767), a French minister of finance]

sil·i·ca (sil′ə kə) *n.* silicon dioxide, a compound that occurs in crystalline form as in quartz and non-crystalline form as in opal, and that also forms the main ingredient of sand. *Formula:* SiO_2 [< NL < L *silex, -licis* flint]

silica gel a non-crystalline form of silica resembling sand, but having many fine pores that make it highly absorbent. Silica gel is used as a drying and deodorizing agent in air conditioners, etc.

sil·i·cate (sil′ə kit *or* sil′ə kāt′) *n.* any of many insoluble compounds of silicon, oxygen, and a metal or metals that make up the largest class of minerals. Silicates are found widely in rocks of the earth and are used in building materials such as glass, bricks, and cement.

si·li·ceous *or* **si·li·cious** (sə lish′əs) *adj.* of, having to do with, containing, or resembling silica or a silicate. [< L *siliceus* of flint < *silex, -licis* flint]

si·lic·ic (sə lis′ik) *adj.* of, having to do with, or derived from silica or silicon.

si·lic·i·fy (sə lis′ə fī′) *v.* **-fied, -fy·ing. 1** convert into or impregnate with silica. **2** become silica or be impregnated with it. —**si·lic′i·fi·ca′tion,** *n.*

sil·i·con (sil′ə kən) *n.* a non-metallic element that occurs naturally only in compounds and is the most abundant element, next to oxygen, in the earth's crust. Silicon combines with oxygen to form silica. *Symbol:* Si; *at.no.* 14; *at.wt.* 28.086. [< *silica*]

sil·i·cone (sil′ə kōn′) *n.* any of a large group of organic silicon compounds that are water-resistant and are good insulators for heat, cold, or electricity. Silicones are used to make lubricants, synthetic rubber, waterproof polishes, etc.

silicone rubber a synthetic rubber made from certain silicones, having great tensile strength and elasticity over a wide range of temperatures.

sil·i·co·sis (sil′ə kō′sis) *n.* a disease of the lungs caused by continually breathing air filled with dust from quartz or silicates. [< *silic-* flint, silica (< L *silex, -licis* flint) + *-osis* diseased condition]

silk (silk) *n.* **1** a fine, soft, tough protein fibre produced by silkworms for their cocoons and used to make textiles. **2** any of various similar fibres produced by other insect larvae, usually for cocoons. **3** thread, yarn, or cloth made from the silk produced by silkworms. **4** silklike fibre, thread, or cloth made artificially. **5** a garment of silk or silklike cloth, such as the gown worn by a King's or Queen's Counsel. **6** anything like silk in softness, lustre, etc.: *corn silk.* **7** silks, *pl.* the blouse and cap worn by a jockey or harness race driver, and the colors of which identify the owner of the horse. **8** (*adj.*) of, like, or having to do with silk: *silk thread, a silk finish.* **9** parachute.

take silk, become a king's or queen's counsel.
[OE *sioloc* < Slavic < Gk. *sērikos* < *Sēres* the Chinese]
—**silk´like´,** adj.

silk·en (sil´kən) adj. **1** made of silk: *a silken dress.* **2** like silk;
smooth, soft, and glossy: *silken hair.* **3** of a voice, manner, etc.,
smoothly agreeable and polite, especially when suggesting
insincerity or an ulterior motive: *He spoke in silken tones.* **4** clothed
in silk: *silken legs.*

silk–screen (silk´skrēn´) n., v. —n. **1** a method of color printing
in which a screen of silk or similar material is prepared as a stencil
and the coloring matter is forced through the mesh in all the areas
of the design to be printed. **2** a print produced by this process.
3 (adj.) having to do with or produced by this process.
—v. produce (a print) by means of silk-screen.

silk–stock·ing (silk´stok´ing) adj., n. —adj. **1** dressing
fashionably and elegantly; especially, formerly, wearing silk
stockings. **2** aristocratic or wealthy: *He caters to the silk-stocking
trade.* —n. a wealthy or aristocratic person.

silk·worm (silk´wėrm´) n. **1** the hairless, yellowish larva of an
Asiatic moth (*Bombyx mori*) that produces the silk used for textiles.
The silkworm feeds mainly on mulberry leaves. **2** any of various
other moth caterpillars that spin cocoons of silk. [OE *seolcwyrm*]

silk·y (sil´kē) adj. **silk·i·er, silk·i·est. 1** of or like silk; smooth,
soft, glossy, etc.: *Some cats have silky fur.* **2** of a voice, manner,
etc., smooth and extremely polite, especially so as to suggest
insincerity or an ulterior motive: *a silky voice describing the
features of a new luxury-model car.* —**silk´i·ly,** adv. —**silk´i·ness,** n.

sill (sil) n. **1** a horizontal piece of wood, block of stone, etc. that
forms the bottom of a window or door frame. See **frame** for picture.
2 a large, wooden beam on which the wall of a house, etc. rests.
3 *Geology.* a mass or sheet of igneous rock that has come between
layers of other rock while molten and has solidified there. [OE *syll*]

sil·la·bub (sil´ə bub´) n. a dessert made of cream, eggs, and wine
sweetened and flavored. Also, **syllabub.** [origin uncertain]

sil·li·ness (sil´ē nis) n. **1** foolishness; being silly. **2** a silly act,
thing, etc.

sil·ly (sil´ē) adj. **-li·er, -li·est. 1** without sense or reason; foolish.
2 *Archaic.* simple; innocent; harmless. **3** *Informal.* stunned; dazed.
[OE *sælig* happy < *sæl* happiness]
☛ *Syn.* **1.** See note at **foolish.**

si·lo (sī´lō) n., pl. **-los. 1** an airtight building or pit in which green
fodder for farm animals is stored. **2** a vertical underground shaft in
which missiles, nuclear rockets, etc. are housed ready for
launching. [< Sp. < L < Gk. *siros* graincellar]

silt (silt) n., v. —n. very fine earth, sand, etc. carried by moving
water and deposited as sediment: *The river mouth is being choked
up with silt.* —v. make or become choked or filled with silt or mud.
[ME; cf. Danish, Norwegian (dial.) *sylt* salt marsh. Akin to SALT.]

silt·stone (silt´stōn´) n. a kind of fine-grained sedimentary rock
formed from silt that has been subjected to great pressure.

silt·y (sil´tē) adj. **silt·i·er, silt·i·est.** of, like, or full of silt.

Si·lu·ri·an (sə lür´ē ən *or* sī lür´ē ən) adj., n. *Geology.* —adj.
of or having to do with an early Paleozoic period or the rocks
formed during it. The earliest vertebrates appeared toward the end
of the Silurian period. See chart at **geology.** —n. **1** an early period of
the Paleozoic era, beginning approximately 375 million years ago.
2 the rocks formed during this period. [< L *Silures,* an ancient
people of SE Wales where rock of this period occurs abundantly]

sil·va (sil´və) n. **1** the forest trees of a particular region or time.
2 a treatise on forest trees, or a descriptive list or catalogue of
trees. [< L *silva* forest]

sil·van (sil´vən) See **sylvan.**

sil·ver (sil´vər) n., adj., v. —n. **1** a white metallic element that is a
precious metal. It takes a high polish, it can be moulded, stretched,
hammered, or drawn thin without breaking, and it is the best
conductor of heat and electricity. Silver is used for jewellery,
cutlery, dishes, coins, etc. *Symbol:* Ag; *at.no.* 47; *at.wt.* 107.870.
2 coins, especially those made of silver or having a silvery color:
Do you have any silver? **3** cutlery, dishes, etc. made of or plated
with silver; silverware: *I spent half an hour polishing the silver.*
4 any cutlery. **5** the color of silver. **6** something having the color of
silver. **7** a soft, lustrous, light grey or white: *She wore a silver
gown.*
—adj. **1** made of, plated with, or containing silver: *a silver spoon,
silver thread.* **2** of, having to do with, or resembling silver: *a silver
sheen, silver shoes. The back of a mirror has a silver coating.*
3 having the color of silver: *silver buttons.* **4** of a soft, lustrous, light
grey or white color: *silver hair.* **5** having a clear, ringing sound.
6 eloquent: *a silver tongue.* **7** designating the 25th anniversary of an
event.
—v. **1** cover or coat with silver or something like silver: *to silver a
spoon, to silver a mirror.* **2** give a sheen to, like that of a silver:
Moonlight silvered the lake. **3** make or become white or very light

grey: *Her hair had silvered since he had last seen her.* [OE *siolfor*]

Silver Age 1 *Classical mythology.* the second age of mankind,
inferior to the Golden Age. **2 silver age,** a period following and
inferior to a period of brilliance.

sil·ver·ber·ry (sil´vər ber´ē) n. *Cdn.* wolf willow.

silver birch 1 a Eurasian birch (*Betula pendula*) having
silvery-white bark and drooping branches, widely cultivated as an
ornamental tree. Also called **weeping birch. 2** any of various other
birches having white bark.

sil·ver·fish (sil´vər fish´) n., pl. **-fish** or **-fish·es. 1** a
quick-moving, wingless insect (*Lepisma saccharina*), a species of
bristletail having a body covered with silvery scales, often found in
buildings where it feeds on food scraps and on sized papers and
fabrics. **2** a silvery variety of goldfish. **3** any of various
silvery-colored fishes, such as the tarpon.

silver fox 1 a color phase of the red fox of North America, in
which the fur is black but tipped with white. **2** the fur of this fox.

sil·ver·jar (sil´vər jär´) n. *Cdn.* **1** a young ringed seal. **2** its fur.

silver leaf silver beaten into very thin sheets.

silver lining the brighter side of a gloomy or unfortunate
situation.

silver maple a maple (*Acer saccharinum*) found especially in
southern central and eastern Canada, having deeply lobed leaves
that are light green above and silvery underneath. The silver maple
is a popular shade and ornamental tree.

sil·vern (sil´vərn) adj. *Archaic.* of or like silver.

silver nitrate a white crystalline salt obtained by treating silver
with nitric acid, used in medicine as an antiseptic, in photography,
dyeing, etc. *Formula:* $AgNO_3$

silver paper paper covered or coated on one side with a metallic
layer resembling silver. Silver paper is used as decoration in
greeting cards, as a wrapping for chocolate bars, etc.

silver plate 1 dishes, cutlery, etc. made of silver or of copper,
etc. plated with silver. **2** a plating of silver.

sil·ver–plate (sil´vər plāt´) v. coat (another metal or a metal
object) with silver, especially by electroplating: *silver-plated cutlery.*

silver screen 1 a screen with a silverlike coating on which
motion pictures are shown. **2** motion pictures.

sil·ver·side (sil´vər sīd´) n. any of a family (Atherinidae) of
mostly small marine and freshwater fishes having a silver stripe
along each side of the body. Also called **silversides.**

sil·ver·sides (sil´vər sīdz´) n., pl. **-sides.** silverside.

sil·ver·smith (sil´vər smith´) n. an artist or craftsman who
makes and repairs articles of silver.

silver thaw *Cdn.* **1** a storm of quick-freezing rain. **2** the glitter
ice found after such a rain, encrusting trees, rocks, and other
surfaces.

sil·ver·tip (sil´vər tip´) n. *Cdn.* a color phase of the grizzly bear
found in the Rocky Mountain region, in which the pelage is dark
brown with the long hairs of the back and shoulders tipped with
white.

sil·ver·tongued (sil´vər tungd´) adj. eloquent.

sil·ver·ware (sil´vər wer´) n. articles, especially cutlery or
dishes, made of or plated with silver.

silver wedding the 25th anniversary of a wedding.

sil·ver·y (sil´vər ē) adj. **1** having a lustre or sheen like that of
silver: *silvery moonbeams, a silvery gown.* **2** having a soft, clear
resonance; melodious: *silvery laughter, a silvery voice.* **3** containing
or consisting of silver. —**sil´ver·i·ness,** n.

sil·vi·cul·ture (sil´və kul´chər) n. the branch of forestry dealing
with the cultivation and care of forests. [< F < L *silva* forest +
cultura culture] —**sil´vi·cul´tur·al,** adj.

Sim·e·on (sim´ē ən) n. **1** in the Bible, a son of Jacob and Leah
(Gen. 29:33). **2** one of the twelve tribes of Israel.

sim·i·an (sim´ē ən) adj., n. —adj. of, having to do with, or like
apes or monkeys. —n. an ape or monkey. [< L *simia* ape,
apparently < Gk. (name) *Simias* < *simos* snub-nosed]

sim·i·lar (sim´ə lər) adj. **1** having characteristics in common;
much the same as; like or alike: *A creek and a brook are similar.
Your desk is similar to mine.* **2** *Geometry.* of figures, having the

hat, āge, fär; let, ēqual, tėrm; it, īce
hot, ōpen, ôrder; oil, out; cup, put, rüle,
above, takən, pencəl, lemən, circəs

ch, child; ng, long; sh, ship
th, thin; ᴛʜ, then; zh, measure

same shape but not necessarily the same size: *similar triangles.* [< F *similaire* < L *similis* like] —**sim′i·lar·ly,** *adv.*

sim·i·lar·i·ty (sim′ə lar′ə tē *or* -ler′ə tē) *n., pl.* **-ties.** the state of being similar; a likeness; resemblance.
☛ *Syn.* See note at **resemblance.**

sim·i·le (sim′ə lē) *n.* a figure of speech that expresses a comparison between two unlike things, usually introduced by *like* or *as. Examples: a face like marble. He had a mind as sharp as a tack. She could run like the wind.* Compare **metaphor.** [< L *simile,* neut. adj., like]
☛ *Usage.* See note at **metaphor.**

si·mil·i·tude (sə mil′ə tyüd′ *or* sə mil′ə tüd′) *n.* **1** a similarity or likeness: *similitude of structure.* **2** *Archaic.* a parable, allegory, or simile. **3** *Archaic.* counterpart or image. [< L *similitudo* < *similis* like]

sim·mer (sim′ər) *v., n.* —*v.* **1** keep or stay at or just below the boiling point: *The stew should be simmered for two hours.* **2** be on the point of bursting or breaking out; be in an inner turmoil: *He simmered with indignation, but said nothing.*
simmer down, calm down; cool down: *She told the excited child to simmer down.*
—*n.* a degree of heat at or just below the boiling point: *Keep the sauce at a simmer.* [earlier *simper,* ? imitative]
☛ *Syn. v.* **2.** See note at **boil.**

si·mo·ni·a·cal (sī′mə nī′ə kəl *or* sim′ə nī′ə kəl) *adj.* **1** guilty of simony. **2** of, having to do with, or involving simony.
—**si′mo·ni′a·cal·ly,** *adv.*

Si·mon Le·gree (sī′mən lə grē′) a severe or too-demanding employer, officer, overseer, etc. [< *Simon Legree,* a brutal slave dealer in the novel *Uncle Tom's Cabin* by Harriet Beecher Stowe]

si·mon–pure (sī′mən pyür′) *adj. Informal.* **1** real; genuine; authentic; true: *simon-pure maple sugar.* **2** morally incorruptible: *He's not as simon-pure as he pretends.* **3** *Slang.* a legitimate non-professional athlete. [< *Simon Pure,* the name of a Quaker in Mrs. Centlivre's comedy *A Bold Stroke for a Wife* (1717), whose identity is questioned but proved genuine]

si·mo·ny (sī′mə nē *or* sim′ə nē) *n.* the buying or selling of ecclesiastical positions, promotions, etc. [< LL *simonia,* from *Simon* Magus, a Samaritan magician, who tried to buy the power of conferring the Holy Spirit (Acts 8: 9-24)]

si·moom (sə müm′) *n.* a hot, dry, suffocating, usually sand-laden, wind or whirlwind of the deserts of the Arabian peninsula and N Africa, occurring mainly in spring and summer. [< Arabic *semūm*]

si·moon (sə mün′) *n.* simoom.

simp (simp) *n. Slang.* a simpleton; fool. [< *simpleton*]

sim·per (sim′pər) *v., n.* —*v.* **1** smile in a silly, affected way. **2** express by a simper; say with a simper. —*n.* a silly, affected smile. [cf. G *zimper(lich)* affected, coy]

sim·ple (sim′pəl) *adj.* **-pler, -plest;** *n.* —*adj.* **1** easy to do or understand: *a simple problem, simple language.* **2** not divided into parts; single; not compound. An oak leaf is a simple leaf. "John called his dog" is a simple sentence. **3** having few parts; not complex; not involved; elementary: *a simple one-celled animal.* **4** with nothing added; bare; mere: *My answer is the simple truth.* **5** without ornament; not rich or showy; plain: *simple clothes.* **6** natural; not affected; not showing off: *She has a pleasant, simple manner.* **7** honest; sincere: *a simple heart.* **8** not subtle; not sophisticated; innocent; artless: *a simple child.* **9** common; ordinary: *a simple citizen.* **10** humble: *His parents were simple people.* **11** dull; stupid; weak in mind.
—*n.* **1** a foolish, stupid person. **2** something simple. **3** a plant used in medicine; the medicine made from it. [ME < OF < L *simplex*]
—**sim′ple·ness,** *n.*
☛ *Syn. adj.* **1.** See note at **easy.**

simple closed curve *Geometry.* a closed plane curve that does not cross itself.

simple fraction a fraction in which both the numerator and the denominator are whole numbers. *Examples:* 1/3, 3/4, 219/125. Compare **complex fraction.**

sim·ple–heart·ed (sim′pəl här′tid) *adj.* having or showing a simple, unaffected, sincere nature.

simple interest interest paid only on the principal of a loan, etc., as opposed to compound interest which is paid on the principal and other interest already added to it.

simple machine any of several elementary devices for transmitting a force or changing its direction in order to overcome a resistance and lessen work. Usually considered as the six basic types are the lever, pulley, wheel and axle, inclined plane, screw, and wedge.

sim·ple–mind·ed (sim′pə mīn′did) *adj.* **1** natural and inexperienced; artless; unsophisticated: *a simple-minded approach to a complex problem.* **2** foolish or feeble-minded.
—**sim′ple–mind′ed·ly,** *adv.* —**sim′ple–mind′ed·ness,** *n.*

simple sentence a sentence consisting of one main clause. *Examples: The whistle blew. We got back yesterday.*

sim·ple·ton (sim′pəl tən) *n.* a silly person; fool. [< *simple*]

sim·plic·i·ty (sim plis′ə tē) *n., pl.* **-ties. 1** the state or quality of being simple in form or structure; freedom from complexity: *the simplicity of a design. They appreciated the simplicity of the directions he had given them.* **2** absence of luxury, ornamentation, etc.; plainness: *simplicity of dress, the simplicity of a lifestyle.* **3** absence of show or pretence; sincerity or naturalness: *The old man answered all their questions with simplicity.* **4** lack of shrewdness; ignorance or dullness: *His simplicity made him easy to fool.* [< L *simplicitas* < *simplex, -icis* simple]

sim·pli·fi·ca·tion (sim′plə fə kā′shən) *n.* **1** the act or process of simplifying: *The simplification of the plan will take some time.* **2** something that has been simplified: *This is a simplification of an earlier model.*

sim·pli·fy (sim′plə fī′) *v.* **-fied, -fy·ing.** make simple or simpler; make plainer, easier, or more streamlined: *to simplify a design. The plot of your story is a little confusing, and should be simplified.* [< F *simplifier* < Med.L *simplificare* < L *simplus* simple + *facere* make] —**sim′pli·fi′er,** *n.*

sim·plis·tic (sim plis′tik) *adj.* simplified to such an extent as to be misleading; given a false simplicity by ignoring some important aspects: *Her interpretation of the issue of international disarmament is biassed and simplistic.* —**sim·plis′ti·cal·ly,** *adv.*

sim·ply (sim′plē) *adv.* **1** in a simple manner: *to dress simply. She explained the procedure simply and clearly.* **2** merely; only: *The baby did not simply cry, he yelled. He thinks of his car as simply a means of transportation.* **3** really; absolutely: *simply perfect.*

sim·u·la·cra (sim′yə lā′krə) *n.* pl. of **simulacrum.**

sim·u·la·crum (sim′yə lā′krəm) *n., pl.* **-cra** *or* **-crums. 1** a faint, shadowy, or unreal likeness; mere semblance: *The dictator permitted only a simulacrum of democracy.* **2** an image. [< L *simulacrum,* ult. < *similis* like]

sim·u·late (sim′yə lāt′) *v.* **-lat·ed, -lat·ing;** *adj.* —*v.* **1** pretend; feign: *Anne simulated interest to please her friend.* **2** act like; look like; imitate: *Certain insects simulate leaves.* —*adj. Archaic.* simulated. [< L *simulare* < *similis* like] —**sim′u·la′tor,** *n.*

sim·u·lat·ed (sim′yə lāt′əd) *adj.* made to look genuine or real: *simulated pearls.*

sim·u·la·tion (sim′yə lā′shən) *n.* **1** a pretence; feigning. **2** an imitation; an acting or looking like: *a harmless insect's simulation of a poisonous one.*

sim·u·la·tive (sim′yə lə tiv *or* sim′yə lā′tiv) *adj.* simulating.

sim·ul·cast (sim′əl kast′ *or* sī′məl kast′) *v.* **-cast** *or* **-cast·ed, -cast·ing;** *n.* —*v.* broadcast a program over radio and television at the same time or over more than one radio or television station at the same time: *CBC FM Radio and Television will simulcast the concert live from the civic auditorium.* —*n.* a broadcast made in this way. [< *simul*taneous + broad*cast*]

si·mul·ta·ne·ous (sim′əl tā′nē əs *or* sī′məl tā′nē əs) *adj.* existing, done, or happening at the same time: *The two simultaneous shots sounded like one.* [< Med.L *simultaneus* simulated; confused in sense with L *simul* at the same time]

si·mul·ta·ne·ous·ly (sim′əl tā′nē əs lē *or* sī′məl-) *adv.* at once; at the same time; together.

sin (sin) *n., v.* **sinned, sin·ning.** —*n.* **1 a** a breaking of the law of God deliberately. **b** the state or condition resulting from this. **2** any act regarded as immoral or bad; wrongdoing: *It's a sin to waste food.* —*v.* **1** break the law of God. **2** do wrong. [OE *synn*]

SIN (sin) *Cdn.* Social Insurance Number.

Si·nai (sī′nī) *n.* Mount, in the Bible, the mountain, of uncertain identity, from which the law was given to Moses.

Sin·bad (sin′bad) *n.* in *The Arabian Nights,* a sailor who had seven extraordinary voyages.

sin bin *Cdn. Slang. Hockey.* the penalty box.

since (sins) *prep., conj., adv.* —*prep.* **1** (from a past time) continuously till now: *The package has been ready since noon.* **2** at any time between (some past time or event and the present): *We have not seen you since Saturday.*
—*conj.* **1** in the course of the period following the time when: *He has written home only once since he left us.* **2** continuously or counting from the time when: *Charles has worked hard since he left school.* **3** because: *Since you feel tired, you should rest.*
—*adv.* **1** from then till now: *He got sick last Saturday and has been in bed ever since.* **2** at some time between a particular past time and the present: *At first he refused but has since accepted.* **3** before

now; ago: *I heard that old joke long since.* [ME *sinnes, sithenes* < OE *siththan* then, later < *sīth* late]

➨ *Usage.* See note at **because**.

sin·cere (sin sēr′) *adj.* **-cer·er, -cer·est.** free from pretence or deceit; genuine in feeling; honest and straightforward: *a sincere expression of sympathy, a sincere person.* [< L *sincerus*]
—**sin·cere′ly,** *adv.*

sin·cer·i·ty (sin ser′ə tē) *n., pl.* **-ties.** freedom from pretence or deceit; honesty.

Sind·bad (sin′bad) *n.* Sinbad.

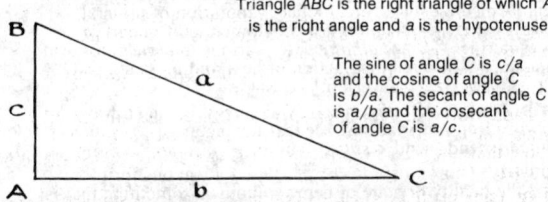

Triangle *ABC* is the right triangle of which *A* is the right angle and *a* is the hypotenuse.

The sine of angle *C* is *c/a* and the cosine of angle *C* is *b/a.* The secant of angle *C* is *a/b* and the cosecant of angle *C* is *a/c.*

sine[1] (sīn) *n. Trigonometry.* the ratio of the length of the side opposite an acute angle to the length of the hypotenuse. In the diagram, the sine of angle a = BC/AB; the sine of angle b = AC/AB. [< L *sinus* bend, bosom < Med.L translation of Arabic *jaib* sine, bosom]

➨ *Hom.* **sign, syne.**

si·ne[2] (sin′ē *or* sī′nē) *prep. Latin.* without.

si·ne·cure (sī′nə kyūr′ *or* sin′ə kyūr′) *n.* **1** an extremely easy job; a position requiring little or no work and usually paying well. **2** an ecclesiastical benefice without parish duties. [< Med.L (*beneficium*) *sine cura* (benefice) without care (of souls)]

si·ne·cur·ist (sī′nə kyūr′ist *or* sin′ə kyūr′ist) *n.* a person who has a sinecure.

si·ne di·e (sin′ē dē′ā *or* sī′nē dī′ē) *Latin.* without a day fixed for future action: *The committee adjourned sine die.* [literally: without day]

si·ne qua non (sin′ē kwä′nōn′ *or* sī′nē kwä non′) something essential; an indispensable condition or thing: *It was a sine qua non that all parties concerned should be included in the negotiations.* [< LL *sine qua non* without which not]

sin·ew (sin′yü) *n.* **1** a tough, strong band or cord that joins muscle to bone; tendon. **2** strength; energy: *moral sinew.* **3** Usually, **sinews,** *pl.* a means of strength or power; mainstay: *Guns are the sinews of war.* —*v.* strengthen by furnishing with sinews. [OE *sionu*]

sin·ew·y (sin′yü ē) *adj.* **1** strong and muscular: *The blacksmith had broad shoulders and sinewy arms.* **2** vigorous; forcible: *sinewy arguments, sinewy prose.* **3** of meat, having many or large sinews; tough; stringy. —**sin′ew·i·ness,** *n.*

sin·fo·ni·a (sin′fə nē′ə; *Italian,* sēn′fō nē′ä) *n., pl.* **-ni·e** (-nē′ā). **1** symphony. **2** an orchestral overture, especially in an 18th century Italian opera. [< Ital.]

sin·fo·niet·ta (sin′fən yet′ə; *Italian,* sēn′fō nyet′tä) *n.* **1** a short instrumental piece modelled on the symphony. **2** a small orchestra, usually consisting chiefly or entirely of strings. [< Ital. *sinfonietta* < dim. of *sinfonia* symphony]

sin·ful (sin′fəl) *adj.* characterized by sin or having a tendency to sin. —**sin′ful·ly,** *adv.* —**sin′ful·ness,** *n.*

sing (sing) *v.* **sang** *or* (*archaic*) **sung, sung, sing·ing;** *n.* —*v.* **1** make music with the voice: *She often sings on television.* **2** utter musically: *He almost seemed to sing his lines from the play.* **3** chant; intone: *The priest sings Mass.* **4** make pleasant musical sounds: *Birds sing.* **5** cause something to happen with or by singing: *Sing the baby to sleep.* **6** tell in song or poetry: *Homer sang of Troy.* **7** tell of in song or poetry: *They sang the deeds of heroes.* **8** proclaim: *sing a person's praises.* **9** make a ringing, whistling, humming, or buzzing sound: *The teakettle sang.* **10** have the sensation of a ringing, buzzing, or humming sound: *A bad cold made his ears sing.* **11** admit of being sung: *This arrangement of the song sings more easily than that one.* **12** *Slang.* reveal; inform; tell all.

sing out, call loudly; shout.

—*n.* **1** a singing, ringing, or whistling sound: *the sing of a bullet in flight.* **2** a singing, especially in a group. [OE *singan*] —**sing′a·ble,** *adj.*

sing. singular.

singe (sinj) *v.* **singed, singe·ing;** *n.* —*v.* **1** burn a little; scorch: *He got too close to the fire and singed his eyebrows.* **2** expose the carcass of a chicken, etc. to flame for a very short while to burn off down, fuzz, etc. **3** burn the ends of hair after a haircut.

hat, āge, fär; let, ēqual, tėrm; it, īce
hot, ōpen, ôrder; oil, out; cup, pút, rüle,
above, takən, pencəl, lemən, circəs
ch, child; ng, long; sh, ship
th, thin; ŦH, then; zh, measure

singe (one's) wings, be slightly harmed by, especially by some risky venture.
—*n.* a slight burn. [OE *sengan*]

sing·er (sing′ər) *n.* **1** a person who sings, especially one who sings well or whose profession is singing: *He's an opera singer.* **2** a bird having a varied and musical call: *Our canary is a fine singer.*

Sin·gha·lese (sing′gə lēz′) *n. or adj.* Sinhalese.

sin·gle (sing′gəl) *adj., n., v.* **-gled, -gling.** —*adj.* **1** one and no more; only one: *Please give me a single piece of paper.* **2** for only one; individual: *The sisters share one room with two single beds in it.* **3** without others; alone: *He came to the party single.* **4** not married: *a single man.* **5** having only one on each side: *The knights engaged in single combat.* **6** of a flower, having only one set of petals. There are both single and double varieties of roses. **7** not double; not multiple: *single houses.* **8** sincere; honest; genuine: *She showed single devotion to her religion.*
—*n.* **1** a single thing or person. **2** *Baseball.* a hit that allows the batter to reach first base only. **3** *Cricket.* a hit for which one run is scored. **4** a game for two people only. **5** *Football.* a single point scored by kicking into or beyond the end zone; rouge. **6 singles,** *pl.* a game played with only one person on each side.
—*v.* **1** pick from among others: *The teacher singled Harry out for praise.* **2** *Baseball.* make a hit that allows the batter to reach first base. [ME < OF < L *singulus*]

➨ *Syn. adj.* **1. Single, sole, only** = one alone. **Single** emphasizes the idea of one and no more: *She buys a single new dress each year.* **Sole** adds the idea of being by itself, the single one (or group) that there is or that is to be considered: *My sole purpose is to help you.* **Only,** often a less emphatic substitute for **sole,** emphasizes the idea of being by itself, without others of its kind: *He is an only child.* In addition, both **sole** and **only** can sometimes be used with plural nouns: *the sole survivors, our only friends.*

single bed a bed wide enough for one person: *The hotel room had two single beds.*

sin·gle–breast·ed (sing′gəl bres′tid) *adj.* of a coat, jacket, etc., overlapping across the breast just enough to fasten with only one button or row of buttons.

single file *n., adv.* —*n.* a line of persons or things arranged one behind another. —*adv.* in a line, one behind the other: *We walked single file along the narrow path.*

sin·gle–foot (sing′gəl füt′) *n., v.* —*n.* the gait of a horse in which one foot is put down at a time; rack. —*v.* of a horse, go at a single-foot.

sin·gle–hand·ed (sing′gəl han′did) *adj., adv.* —*adj.* **1** without help from others; working alone: *a single-handed effort.* **2** using or requiring only one hand: *a single-handed sword.* —*adv.* without help: *She built all the cupboards single-handed.*
—**sin′gle–hand′ed·ly,** *adv.*

sin·gle–heart·ed (sing′gəl här′tid) *adj.* having or showing sincerity of heart or purpose. —**sin′gle–heart′ed·ly,** *adv.* —**sin′gle–heart′ed·ness,** *n.*

sin·gle–mind·ed (sing′gəl mīn′did) *adj.* **1** having or showing sincerity and devotion to one purpose or aim. **2** sincere and guileless. —**sin′gle–mind′ed·ly,** *adv.* —**sin′gle–mind′ed·ness,** *n.*

sin·gle–ness (sing′gəl nis) *n.* the state or quality of being single: *singleness of purpose. After years of singleness she decided to get married.*

sin·gle–space (sing′gəl spās′) *v.* type with no blank lines between lines of print: *Quotations set off within an essay should always be single-spaced.*

sin·gle·stick (sing′gəl stik′) *n.* **1** a stick held in one hand, used in a type of fencing. **2** the act of fencing with such a stick.

sin·glet (sing′glit) *n.* a kind of undershirt or jersey worn by men.

sin·gle·ton (sing′gəl tən) *n.* **1** something occurring singly or apart from others; especially, a child or animal born alone, without a twin. **2** a playing card that is the only one of a suit in a person's hand. **3** *Hockey, etc.,* a single point.

sin·gle–track (sing′gəl trak′) *adj.* **1** of a railway, etc., having only a single track. **2** *Informal.* preoccupied or able to deal with only one thing at a time; one-track.

sin·gle·tree (sing′gəl trē′) *n.* the swinging bar of a carriage or wagon, to which the traces are fastened. [var. of *swingletree*]

sin·gly (sing′glē) *adv.* **1** as a single person or thing; separately: *Misfortunes never come singly.* **2** one by one; one at a time in

sequence: *Let us consider each point singly.* **3** by one's own efforts; without help; single-handed.

sing·song (sing′sông′) *n., adj., v.* —*n.* **1** a monotonous, up-and-down rhythm. **2** a monotonous tone or sound in speaking. **3** a monotonous or jingling verse. **4** a gathering for community singing.
—*adj.* monotonous in rhythm: *a singsong recitation of the multiplication table.*
—*v.* recite or speak in a singsong way.

sin·gu·lar (sing′gyə lər) *adj., n.* —*adj.* **1** extraordinary; unusual: *"Treasure Island" is a story of singular interest to boys.* **2** strange; queer; peculiar: *The detectives were greatly puzzled by the singular nature of the crime.* **3** being the only one of its kind: *an event singular in history.* **4** *Grammar.* signifying or denoting reference to only one person, thing, instance, etc. *Boy is singular; boys is plural.* **5** *Archaic.* individual or separate.
—*n. Grammar.* **1** the singular form of a word. **2** a word or construction in the singular. [< L *singularis* < *singulus* single]
—**sin′gu·lar·ly,** *adv.*

sin·gu·lar·i·ty (sing′gyə lar′ə tē *or* sin′gyə ler′ə tē) *n., pl.* **-ties.**
1 peculiarity; oddness; strangeness: *The singularity of the stranger's appearance attracted much attention.* **2** something singular; peculiarity; oddity: *One of the giraffe's singularities is the length of its neck.*

Sin·ha·la (sin′hə lä′ *or* sin′ə lä′) *n.* the Indic language of the Sinhalese, which is the official language of Sri Lanka.

Sin·ha·lese (sin′hə lēz′) *n., pl.* **-lese;** *adj.* —*n.* **1** a number of a people who make up the majority of the population of Sri Lanka. **2** Sinhala. —*adj.* of or having to do with the Sinhalese or their language. [< Skt. *Sinhala* Ceylon + E *-ese*]

sin·is·ter (sin′is tər) *adj.* **1** showing or suggesting ill will or evil; wicked or malignant: *a sinister look, a sinister plan, a sinister motive.* **2** giving a warning of bad fortune or trouble; ominous: *a sinister sky, sinister rumblings of rebellion.* **3** extremely unfortunate; disastrous: *He met a sinister fate.* **4** of or on the left. **5** *Heraldry.* of or on the left-hand side of a shield, etc. from the point of view of the person bearing it; on the right of a person viewing it. [< OF *sinistre or* L *sinister* on or to the left. In foretelling the future, the left side was considered by the Romans to be unlucky or ill-fated.

sin·is·tral (sin′is trəl) *adj.* **1** of or having to do with the left side; left; left-handed. **2** of a spiral shell, having the whorl raising from right to left as viewed from the outside.

sink (singk) *v.* **sank** *or* **sunk, sunk, sink·ing;** *n.* —*v.* **1** go down; fall slowly; go lower and lower: *The sun is sinking. She sank to the floor in a faint.* **2** make go down; make fall: *Lack of rain sank the water level of the lake.* **3** go under: *The ship is sinking.* **4** make go under: *The submarine sank two ships.* **5** become lower or weaker: *The wind has sunk.* **6** make lower; reduce: *She sank her voice to a whisper.* **7** pass gradually (into a state of sleep, silence, oblivion, etc.). **8** go or cause to go deeply: *Let the lesson sink into your mind.* **9** make by digging or drilling: *The men are sinking a well.* **10** set into a hole dug or drilled: *to sink a pipe.* **11** insert or fasten into a hollow space, etc.: *a stone sunk into the wall.* **12** become worse: *His spirits sank.* **13** invest (money) unprofitably. **14** keep quiet about; conceal: *to sink evidence.* **15** fall in; become hollow: *The sick man's cheeks have sunk.* **16 a** *Basketball.* score. **b** *Golf.* hit (the ball) into a hole or score by doing so with (a stroke).
—*n.* **1** a shallow basin or tub with a drainpipe. **2** a drain; sewer. **3** a place where dirty water or any filth collects. **4** a place of vice or corruption. **5** a low-lying area in land where waters collect, or where they disappear by sinking downward or by evaporation. [OE *sincan*] —**sink′a·ble,** *adj.*
☛ *Hom.* **sync.**

sink·er (singk′ər) *n.* **1** a person or thing that sinks, especially a lead weight for sinking a line or net for fishing. **2** *U.S. Slang.* a doughnut or a dumpling.

sink·hole (singk′hōl′) *n.* **1** the hole in a sink etc. for waste to pass through. **2** a hollow or cavity in limestone, etc. through which surface water drains into an underground passage or cavern. **3** a hollow place where water collects. **4** a place of vice and corruption.

sinking fund a fund set up by a government, corporation, etc. to offset a borrowing. Certain sums of money are regularly set aside to accumulate at interest so that when the debt, such as a debenture, matures, there will be enough money to pay it off.

sin·less (sin′lis) *adj.* without sin; free from sin. —**sin′less·ly,** *adv.* —**sin′less·ness,** *n.*

sin·ner (sin′ər) *n.* a person who sins or does wrong.

Sinn Fein (shin′fān′) a political organization in Ireland, founded about 1905, for the complete political separation of Ireland from Great Britain. [< Irish *Sinn Féin* we ourselves]

Sino– **1** often **sino-,** Chinese: *Sinology means the study of Chinese culture, etc.* **2** (sī′nō) Chinese and —: *Sino-Japanese means Chinese and Japanese.*

si·nol·o·gist *or* **Si·nol·o·gist** (sī nol′ə jist′) *n.* a person versed in sinology.

si·nol·o·gy *or* **Si·nol·o·gy** (sī nol′ə jē) *n.* the study of Chinese literature, art, culture, etc.

Si·no–Ti·bet·an (sī′nō tə bet′ən) *n.* a family of languages that includes Burmese, Thai, and Tibetan, as well as most of the languages of China.

sin·ter (sin′tər) *n., v.* —*n.* **1** a crust or deposit of silica or calcium carbonate formed on rocks, etc. by the evaporation of mineral springs, geysers, etc. **2** *Metallurgy.* a conglomerate of materials fused by sintering. —*v. Metallurgy.* fuse (various materials) to form larger masses by the combined action of heat and pressure. [< G *Sinter* dross, slag; origin uncertain]

sin·u·ate (sin′yü āt′) *adj.* especially of leaves, having a wavy margin, with deep indentations. See **leaf** for picture. [< L *sinuatus,* pp. of *sinuare* bend, wind < *sinus* a curve]

sin·u·os·i·ty (sin′yü os′ə tē) *n., pl.* **-ties.** **1** a sinuous form or character; the quality or state of being sinuous. **2** something that is sinuous; a curve or bend.

sin·u·ous (sin′yü əs) *adj.* **1** having many curves or turns; winding: *The motion of a snake is sinuous.* **2** indirect; devious. **3** morally crooked. [< L *sinuosus* < *sinus* curve] —**sin′u·ous·ly,** *adv.* —**sin′u·ous·ness,** *n.*

si·nus (sī′nəs) *n.* **1** *Anatomy.* **a** a cavity or hollow in the body, especially one of the cavities in the bones of the skull that connect with the nose. **b** a large channel for venous blood. **2** *Medicine.* a long, narrow channel leading from an abscess and serving for the discharge of pus. **3** *Botany.* a curve or indentation between the lobes of a leaf. **4** any curved hollow or cavity. [< L]

si·nus·i·tis (sī′nə sī′tis) *n.* the inflammation of a sinus of the skull.

Si·on (sī′ən) *n.* Zion.

Siou·an (sü′ən) *n., adj.* —*n.* **1** a stock or family of languages spoken by Amerindian peoples of central and eastern North America. **2** a member of any of these peoples speaking one of these languages, including the Assiniboines and the Dakota. —*adj.* of, having to do with, or designating these peoples or their languages.

Sioux (sü) *n., pl.* **Sioux** (sü *or* süz) *or adj.* **1** Dakota. **2** Siouan.

sip (sip) *v.* **sipped, sip·ping;** *n.* —*v.* drink little by little: *She sipped her tea.* —*n.* a very small drink: *She took a sip.* [OE *sypian* take in moisture]
☛ *Syn. v.* See note at **drink.**

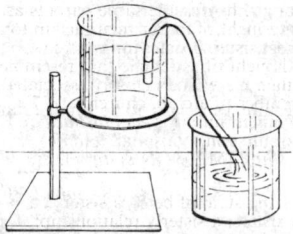
A siphon (def. 1).

si·phon (sī′fən) *n., v.* —*n.* **1** a bent tube through which liquid can be drawn over the edge of one container into another at a lower level by air pressure. **2** a bottle for soda water, having a tube through which the liquid is forced out by the pressure of the gas in the bottle. **3** a tube-shaped organ of some shellfish for drawing in and expelling water, etc.
—*v.* **1** draw off by means of a siphon or pass through a siphon: *He siphoned water from the rain barrel onto the garden.* **2** draw off as if with a siphon. Also, **syphon.** [< L < Gk. *siphon* pipe]

si·phon·al (sī′fən əl) *adj.* of or having to do with a siphon.

sir (sèr; *unstressed,* sər) *n.* **1** a respectful or formal term of address used to a man (*used only alone, never with a name*): *Excuse me, sir.* **2** **Sir,** the title used before the given name or full name of a knight or baronet: *Sir Wilfrid Laurier.* **3** *Archaic.* a term of respect used before a man's given name or the title of his office or profession: *sir priest, sir knight.* [var. of *sire*]
☛ *Usage.* **Sir** (def. 2) is usually used with a person's given name plus his surname or with a given name alone, but not with the surname only. Thus *Sir Winston Churchill* might have been addressed or referred to as *Sir Winston,* but not *Sir Churchill.*

sir·dar (sèr′där *or* sər där′) *n.* **1** a leader or military commander in India and Pakistan. **2** *Historical.* the British commander of the Egyptian army. [< Hind. *sardar* chief < Persian]

sire (sīr) *n., v.* **sired, sir·ing.** —*n.* **1** *Poetic* or *archaic*. a father or male ancestor. **2** the male parent of an animal, especially a domestic animal: *The sire of Danger, a great racehorse, was Lightning.* **3** *Archaic*. a respectful form of address for a king or a great noble: *"I'm killed, Sire!" said the messenger to King Richard.* —*v.* be the father of; beget (used especially for male domestic animals): *Lightning sired Danger.* [ME < OF < VL *seior* < L *senior*, nom., older. Doublet of SENIOR.]

si·ren (sī′rən) *n.* **1** a device that produces a loud, penetrating sound, used as a warning of the approach of an ambulance, police vehicle, etc. or as a warning of an air raid. **2** *Greek mythology.* one of a group of human or partly human female creatures who by their sweet, enchanting singing lured sailors to destruction upon the rocks where the sirens lived. **3** a dangerously seductive woman; temptress. **4** (*adj.*) of a siren or like that of a siren; enchanting. [ME < OF < L < Gk. *seirēn*] —**si′ren·like′,** *adj.*

si·ren·ic (sī ren′ik) *adj.* sirenlike; seductive; alluring.

Sir·i·us (sir′ē əs) *n.* the brightest (fixed) star in the sky; the Dog Star. [< L < Gk. *Seirios*]

sir·loin (sėr′loin) *n.* a choice cut of beef from the part of the loin in front of the rump. See **beef** for picture. [obs. *surloin* < var. of OF *surlonge* < *sur* over (< L *super*) + *longe* loin, ult. < L *lumbus*]

si·roc·co (sə rok′ō) *n., pl.* **-cos.** **1** a hot, dry, southerly wind of N Africa that often picks up moisture as it crosses the Mediterranean, reaching Sicily and S Italy as a hot, oppressively humid wind. **2** any hot oppressive wind. [< F < Ital. < Arabic *šarūq* < *šarq* east]

sir·rah (sir′ə) *n. Archaic.* fellow, used as a term of address to men and boys when speaking contemptuously, angrily, impatiently, etc. [var. of *sir*]

Sir Rog·er de Cov·er·ley (sėr roj′ər də kuv′ər lē) **1** a country squire in Addison's *Spectator*. **2** an old-fashioned country dance, similiar to the Virginia reel.

sir·up (sėr′əp *or* sir′əp) See **syrup.**

sir·up·y (sėr′əp ē *or* sir′əp ē) See **syrupy.**

sis (sis) *n. Informal.* sister. [short for *sister*]

sis·al (sis′əl *or* sī′səl) *n.* **1** a strong white fibre, used for making rope, twine, etc. **2** a West Indian plant (*Agave sisalana*) of the amaryllis family from whose leaves this fibre is prepared. [< *Sisal*, a town in Yucatán, Mexico]

sisal hemp sisal.

sis·kin (sis′kən) *n.* a yellowish-green Eurasian finch (*Carduelis spinus*). See also **pine siskin.**

sis·si·fied (sis′ə fīd′) *adj. Informal.* effeminate or cowardly.

sis·sy (sis′ē) *n., pl.* **-sies.** *Informal.* **1** an effeminate boy or man. **2** a cowardly or very timid person: *Don't be such a sissy; there's nothing to be afraid of.* [dim. of *sis*]

sis·ter (sis′tər) *n.* **1** a woman or girl having the same parents as another person; a woman or girl thought of in her relationship to other children of her parents. **2** half sister. **3** sister-in-law. **4** stepsister. **5** a quality or thing thought of as female that resembles or is closely connected with another. **6** a woman closely associated with another, such as a fellow member of a club, church, etc. **7** a member of a religious order of women; nun: *Sisters of Charity.* **8** *Esp.Brit.* a senior nurse or head nurse in a hospital. **9** (*adj.*) related as if by sisterhood: *sister ships.* [ME < ON *systir*; cf. OE *sweostor*] —**sis′ter·less,** *adj.*

sis·ter·hood (sis′tər hùd′) *n.* **1** the state of being a sister. **2** a spiritual bond, like that between sisters; a sisterly relationship: *A feeling of sisterhood had developed between them over the years.* **3** an association or society of women with some common aim, characteristic, set of beliefs, etc. Nuns form a sisterhood.

sis·ter–in–law (sis′tər in lo′ *or* -lô′) *n., pl.* **sis·ters·in·law.** **1** the sister of one's husband or wife. **2** the wife of one's brother. **3** the wife of one's brother-in-law.

sis·ter·ly (sis′tər lē) *adj.* of, having to do with, or like a sister: *sisterly advice.* —**sis′ter·li·ness,** *n.*

Sis·tine (sis′tēn) *adj.* **1** of or having to do with any of the five popes named Sixtus. **2** of or having to do with the Sistine Chapel, the chapel of the Pope in the Vatican, decorated with frescoes by Michaelangelo and other great artists. [< Ital. *sistino*]

sis·trum (sis′trəm) *n., pl.* **-tra** *or* **-trums.** a metal percussion instrument consisting of a frame with rings that rattle when shaken, used especially in ancient Egypt, in the worship of Isis. [ME < L < Gk. *seistron* < *seiein* to shake. See SEISMIC.]

Sis·y·phe·an (sis′ə fē′ən) *adj.* **1** of or having to do with Sisyphus. **2** futile, laborious, and unending.

Sis·y·phus (sis′ə fəs) *n. Greek legend.* a king of Corinth condemned in Hades for his misdeeds and punished by eternally having to roll a large stone up a steep hill, from which it always rolled down again.

sit (sit) *v.* **sat, sit·ting. 1** rest on the buttocks, with the weight off

hat, āge, fär; let, ēqual, tėrm; it, īce
hot, ōpen, ôrder; oil, out; cup, pùt, rüle,
above, takən, pencəl, lemən, circəs
ch, child; ng, long; sh, ship
th, thin; ŦH, then; zh, measure

the feet: *She sat in a chair.* **2** seat; cause to sit: *The woman sat the little boy down hard.* **3** bear oneself on; sit on: *He sat his horse well.* **4** be in a certain place or position: *The clock has sat on that shelf for years.* **5** have a seat in an assembly, etc.; be a member of a council: *to sit in Parliament.* **6** hold a session: *The court sits next month.* **7** place oneself as required for some purpose or activity; seat oneself; pose: *to sit for a portrait.* **8** be in a state of rest; remain inactive. **9** press or weigh: *Care sat heavy on his brow.* **10** perch: *The birds were sitting on the fence rail.* **11** baby-sit. **12** cover eggs so that they will hatch; brood. **13** fit: *Her coat sits well.*

sit down, take a seat; put oneself in a sitting position.

sit in, a take part in (a game, conference, etc.). **b** take part in a sit-in.

sit on *or* **upon, a** sit in judgment or council on. **b** have a seat on a jury, commission, etc. **c** think about; consider over a period of time. **d** *Slang.* check, rebuke, or snub.

sit out, a remain seated during (a dance). **b** stay through; wait through; *to sit out a storm. They sat out the performance although the singing was poor.* **c** stay later than (another).

sit up, a raise the body to a sitting position. **b** keep such a position. **c** stay up instead of going to bed. **d** *Informal.* start up in surprise.

[OE *sittan*]
☛ *Usage.* See note at **set.**

si·tar (si tär′) *n.* a lutelike instrument having a very long neck and a varying number of strings. The sitar was developed in India.

sit·com (sit′kom′) *n. Informal.* situation comedy.

sit–down strike (sit′doun′) a strike in which employees stop working but stay in their place of employment until an agreement is reached.

site (sīt) *n., v.* **sit·ed, sit·ing.** —*n.* **1** the ground on which a structure or group of structures is, was, or will be located: *the site of the new civic centre.* **2** the location or scene of something: *a company site. They visited the site of the Battle of Queenston Heights.* —*v.* choose a position for; locate; place: *They sited the new building on a hill.* [< L *situs*]
☛ *Hom.* **cite, sight.**

sith (sith) *adv., prep., conj. Archaic.* since. [OE *sīth* after]

sit–in (sit′in′) *n.* a form of protest in which a group of people occupy a public place and remain seated there for a long time.

sit·ka spruce (sit′kə) **1** a very tall spruce (*Picea sitchensis*) found along the Pacific coast of North America, having stiff, very sharp, yellowish-green needles and long, cylinder-shaped cones. The sitka spruce is the largest of the spruces, usually between 38 and 50 metres high. **2** the light, soft wood of this tree. [< *Sitka*, a town in Alaska]

si·tol·o·gy (sī tol′ə jē) *n.* the science of food or diet; dietetics. [< Gk. *sitos* food + E *-logy*]

sit·ter (sit′ər) *n.* **1** baby-sitter. **2** any person or thing that sits, especially a brooding hen.

sit·ting (sit′ing) *n.* **1** the act of one that sits. **2** a single time of remaining seated; one uninterrupted occasion of sitting: *The portrait took five sittings. He read eight chapters at one sitting.* **3** a meeting or session of a legislature, court, etc. **4** the number of eggs on which a bird sits. **5** one or two or more consecutive fixed hours for serving a particular meal, when all cannot be served at once, as on a train, ship, etc.: *the second sitting for dinner.*

sitting duck *Informal.* an easy target or mark.

sitting room a room furnished with comfortable chairs, chesterfields, etc.; parlor.

sit·u·ate (sich′ü āt′) *v.* **-at·ed, -at·ing;** *adj.* —*v.* put in a certain place; locate. —*adj. Archaic.* situated. [< LL *situatus,* pp. of *situare* < L *situs* location]

sit·u·at·ed (sich′ü āt′id) *adj.* **1** having a location or site: *Montreal is well situated.* **2** having a certain financial or social position: *The doctor was quite well situated.*

sit·u·a·tion (sich′ü ā′shən) *n.* **1** circumstances: *Act reasonably in all situations.* **2** site; location; place: *Our house has a beautiful situation on a hill.* **3** a place to work; job. **4** a critical state of affairs in a play, novel, etc.
☛ *Syn.* **3.** See note at **position.**

sit·u·a·tion·al (sich′ü ā′shə nəl) *adj.* of or having to do with situations.

situation comedy a radio or television comedy series consisting of unconnected, usually weekly episodes featuring the same cast of characters in each episode.

sit·up (sit′up′) *n.* a conditioning exercise that consists of raising the body from a lying to a sitting position without using the hands for support.

si·tus (sī′təs) *n.* a position, situation, or location, especially the proper or original position, as of a part of the body or organ. [< L]

sitz bath (sits) **1** a small tub for bathing in a sitting position. **2** a bath so taken, especially as part of medical treatment. [< G *Sitzbad* < *Sitz* seat + *Bad* bath]

sitz·mark (sits′märk′) *n.* a hole or furrow in the snow made by a skier who has fallen backwards. [< G *Sitzmarke* < *Sitz* a sitting, seat + *Marke* sign]

SIU Seamen's International Union.

Si·va (sē′və or shē′və) *n. Hinduism.* Shiva. [< Skt.]

Si·van (sē vän′) *n.* in the Hebrew calendar, the third month of the ecclesiastical year, and the ninth month of the civil year.

si·wash (sī′wosh) *n., adj., v. Cdn.* —*n.* **1** a heavy sweater knitted of raw, unbleached wool, usually having a colored design or motif knitted into the centre of the back and each side front. Siwashes are very common for outdoor wear in the West. **2** Usually, **Siwash,** *Slang.* a mean, contemptible person. **3** *Siwash, Slang.* a North American Indian.
—*adj.* **1** of or having to do with North American Indians. **2** *Slang.* especially on the West Coast, unsuitable, inferior, or worthless: *siwash coffee, a siwash arrangement.*
—*v.* **1** *Informal.* camp out, travelling light and using only natural shelter. **2** *Slang.* prohibit from buying liquor. [< Chinook Jargon < F *sauvage* person of the wilds]
☛ *Usage.* The term **Siwash** as applied to an Indian, is now considered offensive, whether or not it is intended to be insulting.

six (siks) *n., adj.* —*n.* **1** one more than five. **2** the numeral 6: *Is that supposed to be a 6 or a 9?* **3** the sixth in a set or series; especially, a playing card or side of a die having six spots: *If you throw a six, you get another turn.* **4** one of the sections into which a pack of Wolf Cubs or Brownies is divided. **5** any set or series of six persons or things: *He arranged the ten chips as a six and a four.*
at sixes and sevens, in confusion or disagreement.
—*adj.* **1** being one more than five. **2** being sixth in a set or series (*used mainly after the noun*): *I'm bogged down in Chapter Six.* [OE *siex* six]

six-eight (siks′āt′) *adj. Music.* indicating or having six eighth notes in a bar or measure, the first and fourth of which are accented.

six·er (siks′ər) *n.* the leader of a six of Wolf Cubs or Brownies.

six·fold (siks′fōld′) *adj., adv.* —*adj.* **1** six times as much or as many. **2** having six parts. —*adv.* six times as much or as many.

six-gun (siks′gun′) *n.* six-shooter.

Six Nations a federation of Iroquois Indian tribes called the **Five Nations** until the Tuscarora tribe joined in about 1722.

six·pence (siks′pəns) *n. Historical.* **1** a sum of six British pennies. **2** a British coin having a value of six pennies under the old system of pounds, shillings, and pence. It has not been minted since 1970.

six·pen·ny (siks′pen′ē or siks′pə nē) *adj.* **1** *Brit.* worth or costing sixpence. **2** of little worth; cheap. **3** designating a kind of nail about 5 cm long, once costing six pennies per 100.

six-shoot·er (siks′shü′tər) *n.* a revolver that can fire six shots without being reloaded.

six·teen (siks′tēn′) *n., adj.* —*n.* **1** six more than ten; 16: *I got sixteen out of twenty.* **2** the numeral 16: *Is that a 91 or a 16?* **3** the sixteenth in a set or series. **4** a set or series of sixteen persons or things.
—*adj.* **1** being six more than ten. **2** being sixteenth in a set or series of sixteen persons or things. [OE *sixtēne*]

six·teenth (siks′tēnth′) *adj. or n.* **1** next after the 15th; last in a series of 16; 16th. **2** one or being one of 16 equal parts.

sixteenth note *Music.* a note one sixteenth of the time value of a whole note. See **note** for picture.

sixteenth rest *Music.* a rest lasting one sixteenth as long as a whole rest.

sixth (siksth) *adj. or n.* **1** next after the fifth; last in a series of six; 6th. **2** one or being one of six equal parts.

sixth·ly (siksth′lē) *adv.* in the sixth place.

sixth sense an unusual power of perception, beyond the common five senses; intuition.

six·ti·eth (siks′tē ith) *adj. or n.* **1** next after the 59th; last in a

series of 60; 60th. **2** one or being one of 60 equal parts.

six·ty (siks′tē) *n., pl.* **-ties;** *adj.* —*n.* **1** six times ten; 60. **2** **sixties,** *pl.* the years from sixty through sixty-nine, especially of a century or of a person's life: *Rock music became popular in the sixties.*
—*adj.* being six times ten. [OE *siextig, sixtig*]

six·ty·fold (siks′tē fōld′) *adj. or adv.* sixty times as much or as many.

sixty-fourth note (siks′tē fôrth′) *Music.* a note having the time value of one sixty-fourth of a whole note. See **note** for picture.

sixty-fourth rest *Music.* a rest lasting one sixty-fourth of a whole rest.

siz·a·ble (sī′zə bəl) *adj.* fairly large. Also, **sizeable.** —**siz′a·bly,** *adv.* —**siz′a·ble·ness,** *n.*

siz·ar (sī′zər) *n. Brit.* a student who pays reduced rates in the colleges of Cambridge University in Cambridge, England, and Trinity College in Dublin, Irish Republic. [< *size*[1]]

size[1] (sīz) *n., v.* **sized, siz·ing.** —*n.* **1** the amount of surface or space a thing takes up. **2** an extent; amount; magnitude: *the size of an industry.* **3** one of a series of measures: *His shoes are size 10. The size of card I want is 7 x 12 centimetres.* **4** *Informal.* the actual condition; true description. **5** (*adj.*) sized (*used only in compounds*): *He cut the meat into bite-size pieces.*
of a size, of the same size.
—*v.* **1** arrange according to size or in sizes. **2** make of certain size.
size up, *Informal.* **a** form an opinion of; estimate. **b** come up to some size or grade.
[ult. var. of *assize,* in sense of "to set a standard of weights and measures"]
☛ *Syn. n.* **1, 2.** Size, volume, bulk = the measure of something. **Size** applies particularly to the dimensions (length, width, and height or depth) of something, but also to the extent of surface occupied or the number of individuals included: *What is the size of your herd?* **Volume** is used of something measured by the cubic metres, etc. it occupies, especially something that rolls or flows: *The volume of water confined by the new dam is tremendous.* **Bulk** refers to size or quantity measured in three dimensions, and often suggests largeness: *Let the dough double in bulk.*

size[2] (sīz) *n., v.* **sized, siz·ing.** —*n.* a sticky preparation made from materials like glue, starch, or resin, and used as a glaze or filler for cloth, paper, plaster, leather, etc. —*v.* coat or treat with size. [< F *assise* a sitting, fixing, layer]

size·a·ble (sī′zə bəl) See **sizable.**

sized (sīzd) *adj.* **1** having a specified size or bulk (*used in compounds*): *giant-sized.* **2** ranked or arranged according to size.

siz·ing (sī′zing) *n.* size[2].

siz·zle (siz′əl) *v.* **-zled, -zling;** *n.* —*v.* **1** make a hissing sound, as fat does when it is frying or burning. **2** be very hot: *sizzle with anger.* —*n.* a hissing sound. [imitative]

S.J. or **s.j.** Society of Jesus.

SJAA or **S.J.A.A.** St. John Ambulance Association.

SJAB or **S.J.A.B.** St. John Ambulance Brigade.

SK Saskatchewan (*used esp. in computerized address systems*).

skald (skold or skäld) *n.* an ancient Scandinavian poet and singer. Also, **scald.** [< ON *skáld.* Cf. SCOLD.]

skat (skät) *n.* a card game for three players. [< G < Ital. *scarto* discard, n.]

skate[1] (skāt) *n., v.* **skat·ed, skat·ing.** —*n.* **1** a boot with a metal blade, or runner, attached to the sole, designed for gliding over ice. **2** the runner itself, together with its frame, especially when forming a separate part that is attached to a shoe or boot by means of clamps, straps, etc. **3** roller skate.
—*v.* glide or move along on skates. [< Du. *schaats* < OF *escache* stilt < Gmc.] —**skat′er,** *n.*

skate[2] (skāt) *n., pl.* **skate** or **skates.** any of a family (Rajidae) of large, bottom-dwelling, egg-laying rays found in tropical and temperate seas, having very broad fins, giving them a diamond shape from above, and, in some species, having weak electric organs in the tail. [ME < ON *skata*]

skate·board or **skate board** (skāt′bôrd′) *n.* a small, narrow board of wood or plastic, usually about 45-50 cm long, shaped somewhat like a surfboard, but equipped with a pair of roller-skate wheels at each end and used for coasting along streets, sidewalks, etc.

skate·board·er (skāt′bôrd′ər) *n.* one who uses a skate board.

skate·board·ing (skāt′bôrd′ing) *n.* the act or practice of going on a skate board for sport.

skating rink **1** a smooth sheet of ice for skating. **2** a smooth floor for roller skating.

skean or **skene** (skēn) *n.* a dagger formerly used in Ireland and Scotland. [< Irish *scian,* Scots Gaelic *sgian*]

ske·dad·dle (ski dad′əl) *v.* **-dled, -dling.** *Informal.* run away; scatter in flight. [origin uncertain]

skee (skē) *n., pl.* **skees** or **skee;** *v.* **skeed, skee·ing.** *Rare.* ski.

skeet (skēt) *n. Trapshooting.* a type of target practice using clay pigeons that are released into the air so as to imitate the flight of birds. [ult. < ON *skjóta* to shoot]

skeet·er (skē′tər) *n. Informal.* **1** mosquito. **2** a small sailboat used on ice; iceboat.

skein (skān) *n.* **1** a loosely coiled bundle of yarn or thread. **2** a confused tangle. **3** a flock of geese in flight. [ME < OF *escaigne*; ult. origin uncertain]

skel·e·tal (skel′ə təl) *adj.* of, having to do with, attached to, or forming a skeleton.

skel·e·ton (skel′ə tən) *n.* **1** the framework of bones and cartilage of a vertebrate animal that supports the soft tissues and protects the internal organs. **2** a very thin person or animal: *He was just a skeleton after his long illness.* **3** the basic framework or structure of something: *The steel skeleton of an office tower, the skeleton of a story.* **4** (*adj.*) of, like, or having the characteristics of a skeleton; basic or essential: *A skeleton crew remained on board while the ship was at the dock.*
skeleton in the closet, something shameful that is kept secret, as in a family.
[< NL *sceleton* < Gk. *skeleton,* neut., adj., dried up]

skel·e·ton·ize (skel′ə tən īz′) *v.* **-ized, -iz·ing. 1** make a skeleton of. **2** outline; sketch out; draft in outline: *a skeletonized report.* **3** greatly reduce the numbers of.

skeleton key a key made to open many locks.

skelp¹ (skelp) *n., v. Scottish.* —*n.* a slapping or smacking noise; spank. —*v.* **1** spank; slap. **2** move quickly; hurry. [probably imitative]

skelp² (skelp) *n.* a strip of iron or steel used in the making of pipes or tubes. [origin unknown]

skep·tic (skep′tik) *n.* or *adj.* sceptic.

skep·ti·cal (skep′tə kəl) *adj.* sceptical.

skep·ti·cism (skep′tə siz′əm) *n.* scepticism.

sker·ry (sker′ē) *n., pl.* **-ries.** *Esp.Scottish.* a small, rocky island or reef. [< Orkney dialect < ON *sker* reef. See SCAR².]

sketch (skech) *n., v.* —*n.* **1** a rough, quickly done drawing, painting, or design. **2** an outline; plan. **3** a short, light description, story, play, etc.: *a vaudeville sketch. Sunshine Sketches of a Little Town is a collection of short stories by Stephen Leacock.* —*v.* **1** make a sketch or sketches: *We spent the afternoon sketching.* **2** make a sketch of; draw or describe roughly. [< Du. *schets* < Ital. *schizzo* < L < Gk. *schedios* impromptu, ult. < *schesthai* be near] —**sketch′er,** *n.*

sketch·book (skech′bùk′) *n.* a book of or for rough, quick drawings.

sketch·y (skech′ē) *adj.* **sketch·i·er, sketch·i·est. 1** like a sketch; having or giving only outlines or main features. **2** incomplete; slight; imperfect: *a sketchy meal.* —**sketch′i·ly,** *adv.* —**sketch′i·ness,** *n.*

skew (skyü) *adj., n., v.* —*adj.* **1** twisted to one side; slanting. **2** having a part that deviates from a straight line, right angle, etc. **3** unsymmetrical.
—*n.* a slant; twist.
—*v.* **1** slant; twist. **2** give a slanting form, position, or direction to. **3** turn aside; swerve. **4** represent unfairly; distort. [ME < ONF *eskiuer* shy away from, eschew < Gmc.]

skew·back (skyü′bak′) *n.* **1** a sloping surface against which the end of an arch rests. **2** a stone, course of masonry, or the like, with such a surface.

skew·er (skyü′ər) *n., v.* —*n.* **1** a long pin of wood or metal stuck through meat to hold it together while it is cooking. **2** something shaped or used like a long pin. —*v.* **1** fasten with a skewer or skewers. **2** pierce with or as if with a skewer. [earlier *skiver*, origin uncertain]

ski (skē; *Norwegian,* shē) *n., pl.* **skis** or **ski;** *v.* **skied, ski·ing.** —*n.* **1** one of a pair of long pieces of wood, metal, plastic, etc. that can be fastened to boots to enable a person to glide over snow. **2** a ski-like device fastened to the undercarriage of an aircraft and used in place of wheels for landing on snow, mud, sand, etc. **3** water ski. —*v.* **1** glide over the snow on skis. **2** water-ski. [< Norwegian] —**ski′er,** *n.*

skid (skid) *v.* **skid·ded, skid·ding;** *n.* —*v.* **1** slip or slide sideways out of control, while moving: *The car skidded on the slippery road.* **2** prevent from going round by means of a skid. **3** slide along without going round, as a wheel does when held by a skid. **4** slide on a skid or skids.
—*n.* **1** a slip or slide sideways out of control: *His car went into a skid.* **2** a piece of wood or metal used to prevent a wheel from going round. **3** a piece of timber, or a runner, on which something heavy may slide. **4** a frame on which heavy articles may be piled for moving to another position, often by lifting with a crane. **5** a runner

on the bottom of an airplane to enable the airplane to slide along the ground when landing.
on the skids, *Slang.* headed for dismissal, failure, or other disaster. [cf. O Frisian *skīd* stick of wood]

skid·doo (ski dü′) *v. Slang.* get out; be off; scat. [? < *skedaddle*]

ski·doo (ski dü′ *or* skē′dü) *n. or v. Cdn.* snowmobile (defs. 1 and 2). [< *Ski-Doo,* a trademark]

skid road 1 *Cdn.* in lumbering, a road of greased skids, over which logs were dragged by teams of mules, oxen, or horses. **2** skid row.

skid row a run-down district of cheap hotels and bars, used as a hangout by vagrants, petty criminals, etc.

skies (skīz) *n. pl.* of **sky.**

skiff (skif) *n.* **1** a small, light rowboat with a rounded bottom and flat stern. **2** a small, light boat with a centreboard and a single sail. [< F < Ital. *schifo* < Gmc.]

ski·jor·ing (skē′jôr′ing) *n.* a sport in which a person on skis is pulled along by a horse or vehicle. [< Norwegian *skikjøring* < *ski* ski + *kjøring* driving] **ski′jor·er,** *n.*

ski jump 1 a jump made by a person on skis. **2** a place for making such a jump.

skil·fish (skil′fish) *n.* sablefish. [< Haida *sqil* fish]

skil·ful or **skill·ful** (skil′fəl) *adj.* **1** having skill; expert. **2** showing skill. —**skil′ful·ness** or **skill′ful·ness,** *n.*

skil·ful·ly or **skill·ful·ly** (skil′fəl ē) *adv.* with skill; expertly.

ski lift a mechanism for transporting skiers to the top of a slope, usually by means of a chair running on a suspended cable.

skill (skil) *n.* **1** ability gained by practice or knowledge; expertness: *It takes skill to tune a piano.* **2** an ability or technique that can be learned: *One must master the basic language skills.* **3** an art or craft that is learned through training or experience: *the skill of carpentry.* [ME < ON *skil* distinction]

skilled (skild) *adj.* **1** having skill; trained; experienced: *a skilled workman.* **2** showing skill; requiring skill: *Bricklaying is skilled labor.*
➤ *Syn.* **1.** See note at **expert.**

skil·let (skil′it) *n.* **1** a shallow pan with a long handle, used for frying; frying pan. **2** *Esp.Brit.* a long-handled cooking pot or kettle, often having legs. [ME *skelet;* origin uncertain]

skill·ful (skil′fəl) See **skilful.**

skill·ful·ly (skil′fəl ē) See **skilfully.**

skim (skim) *v.* **skimmed, skim·ming;** *n.* —*v.* **1** remove from the top: *to skim the cream from the milk.* **2** take something from the top of: *She skims the milk to get cream.* **3** move lightly over: *The pebble I threw skimmed the little waves. The skaters skimmed the ice.* **4** glide along: *The swallows were skimming by.* **5** send skimming: *You can skim a flat stone over the water.* **6** read rapidly or superficially; read with omissions, especially in order to get the general sense or purpose: *It took me an hour to skim the book.* **7** become covered with a thin layer of ice, scum, etc. **8** cover with a thin layer of ice, scum, etc.
—*n.* **1** that which is skimmed off. **2** the act of skimming. [ME < OF *escumer* < *escume* scum < Gmc.]

skim·mer (skim′ər) *n.* **1** a person or thing that skims; especially a long-handled, shallow ladle with small holes, used in skimming liquids. **2** any of several sea birds (genus *Rhynchops*) that skim along the surface of water to get food. **3** a straw hat with a flat crown and wide brim.

skim milk milk from which the cream has been removed.

Ski·mo (skē′mō) *n. Derogatory slang.* in the North, an Eskimo.

ski·mo·bile (skē′mə bēl′) *n.* a vehicle resembling a small automobile but running on tracks, designed for carrying skiers to the top of a slope.

skimp (skimp) *v.* **1** supply in too small an amount: *Don't skimp the butter in making a cake.* **2** be very saving or economical: *She had to skimp to send her son to university.* **3** do imperfectly. [? alteration of *scrimp*]

skimp·y (skimp′ē) *adj.* **skimp·i·er, skimp·i·est. 1** scanty; not enough. **2** too saving or economical. —**skimp′i·ly,** *adv.* —**skimp′i·ness,** *n.*

skin (skin) *n., v.* **skinned, skin·ning.** —*n.* **1** the outer layer of

skee   **1051**   **skin**

Pronunciation key:

hat, āge, fär; let, ēqual, tèrm; it, īce
hot, ōpen, ôrder; oil, out; cup, pùt, rüle,
ə above, takən, pencəl, lemən, circəs
ch, child; ng, long; sh, ship
th, thin; ŦH, then; zh, measure

tissue of a human or animal body, especially when relatively soft and flexible. **2** the skin of a fur-bearing animal, together with its covering of fur; hide or pelt. **3** any outer or surface layer, as the rind of a fruit, a sausage casing, etc. **4** a container made of skin for holding liquids. **5** the outer covering of a structure such as an aircraft or ship. **6** *Slang.* swindler. **7** *Slang.* skinflint.
by the skin of (one's) **teeth,** very narrowly; barely.
in or **with a whole skin,** safe and sound.
save (one's) **skin,** escape without harm.
—*v.* **1** take the skin off: *Jack skinned his knees when he fell. The hunter skinned the deer.* **2** shed skin. **3** be covered with skin. **4** cover with skin. **5** *Slang.* swindle (someone) of money, etc.; cheat. **6** *Slang.* slip away.
skin alive, *Slang.* **a** torture; flay. **b** scold severely. **c** defeat completely.
[ME < ON *skinn*]
☛ *Syn. n.* **2. Skin, hide, pelt** = the outer covering of the body of an animal. **Skin** is the general word applying to this covering of a person or animal: *The skin of a calf makes soft leather.* **Hide** applies especially to the tough skin of a large animal, raw or tanned: *The hide of cows is tough.* **Pelt** applies especially to the skin of a fur- or wool-bearing animal before dressing or tanning: *Trappers sell pelts of foxes; stores sell dressed skins.*

skin-deep (skin′dēp′) *adj.* **1** of a wound, etc., no deeper than the skin. **2** of an emotion, impression, quality, etc., not deep or lasting in effect; of no real significance.

skin-di-ver (skin′dī′vər) *n.* a person engaged in skin diving.

skin diving swimming under water, using a face mask and flippers, usually with a snorkel or scuba gear, and, in cold water, a rubber or rubberized suit to protect the body against the cold.

skin flick *Slang.* a motion picture that exploits nudity and explicit sex.

skin-flint (skin′flint′) *n.* a mean, stingy person.

skin-ful (skin′fùl) *n., pl.* **-fuls. 1** as much as a skin container can hold. **2** *Informal.* as much as the stomach can hold; especially, as much wine, liquor, etc. as a person can take.

skin game *Informal.* a game or action in which the outcome is rigged; swindle.

skin graft a piece of skin taken from another part of the body or another person to replace skin that has been burned or otherwise damaged or destroyed.

skin grafting the action or process of making a skin graft; the surgical transplanting of skin.

skink (skink) *n.* any of a family (Scinidae) of mostly small lizards having a long, round body with small, smooth scales, and short limbs or no limbs at all. [< L < Gk. *skinkos*]

skin-less (skin′ləs) *adj.* without a skin or casing: *skinless weiners.*

skin-ner (skin′ər) *n.* **1** a person who prepares or deals in skins or furs. **2** a person who drives draft animals, especially mules.

skin-ny (skin′ē) *adj.* **-ni-er, -ni-est. 1** having too little flesh; too thin or lean: *She was always skinny as a child, but usually healthy.* **2** like skin. —**skin′ni-ness,** *n.*

skin-ny–dip (skin′ē dip′) *v.* **-dipped, -dip-ping.** *Informal.* swim in the nude.

skin-tight (skin′tīt′) *adj.* of clothes, fitting closely to the body.

skip¹ (skip) *v.* skipped, skip-ping; *n.* —*v.* **1** leap lightly; spring; jump: *Lambs skipped in the fields.* **2** leap lightly over: *The girls skipped rope.* **3** move along by stepping and hopping first with one foot, then with the other. **4** send bounding along a surface: *Boys like to skip stones on the lake.* **5** go bounding along a surface. **6** pass over; fail to notice; omit: *Answer the questions in order without skipping.* **7** change quickly from one task, subject, etc. to another. **8** *Informal.* leave in a hurry: *He skipped town to avoid meeting his enemies.* **9** be promoted past the next regular grade in school. **10** *Informal.* stay away from: *to skip classes.*
—*n.* **1** a light spring, jump, or leap. **2** a gait, especially of children, in which hops and steps are alternated. **3** the act of passing over or omitting. **4** something that is omitted. [ME < Scand.; cf. MSwedish *skuppa*]

skip² (skip) *n., v.* —*n.* the captain of a curling team or a lawn bowling team. —*v.* act as a skip. [short for *skipper*]

skip³ (skip) *n.* *Mining or quarrying.* a huge bucket or cage in which heavy loads of men or materials may be raised or lowered to and from ground level.

skip-jack (skip′jak′) *n., pl.* **skip-jacks.** any of various fishes that leap out of the water or play on the surface of the water, such as any of several tunas.

ski pole either of a pair of light poles used in skiing, having a leather strap and hand grip at one end and a pointed metal tip at the

other with a disk slightly above the tip to keep the pole from sinking into the snow.

skip-per¹ (skip′ər) *n.* **1** the captain of a ship, especially of a small trading or fishing boat. **2** any captain or leader. [ME < MDu. *schipper* < *schip* ship]

skip-per² (skip′ər) *n.* **1** any of a large family (Hesperiidae) of small, butterfly-like insects belonging to the same order as butterflies and moths, having a heavy body and threadlike antennae with a hook at the end. **2** any of various skipping insects. **3** saury. **4** any person or thing that skips. [< *skip*]

skirl (skèrl) *v., n.* —*v.* **1** of bagpipes, sound loudly and shrilly. **2** play a bagpipe. —*n.* the sound of a bagpipe. [probably Scand.; cf. dial. Norwegian *skrylla*]

skir-mish (skèr′mish) *n., v.* —*n.* **1** a minor fight in war between small groups of soldiers, ships, aircraft, etc. **2** a minor conflict, argument, contest, etc. —*v.* take part in a skirmish. [ME < OF *eskirmiss-* a stem of *eskirmir*, originally, ward off < Gmc.]

skir-mish-er (skèr′mish ər) *n.* a person who engages in a skirmish, especially one of a group of soldiers sent out in advance of an army to clear the way for the main attack or to prevent a surprise attack by the enemy, etc.

skirt (skèrt) *n.* **1** a women's and girls' garment for the lower body that hangs freely from the waist and may be wide or narrow, long or short: *She wore a skirt and blouse.* **2** the free-hanging part of a dress, jumper, cassock, etc. that extends from the waist down. **3** a cloth facing or hanging that resembles a skirt: *a dressing table with a skirt.* **4** a border; edge. **5** the rim or outer edge of an area. **6** one of the flaps hanging from the sides of a saddle. **7** *Slang.* a woman or girl.
—*v.* **1** extend along or form a border or edge: *The road skirts the lake.* **2** pass along the border or edge: *The boys skirted the forest because they did not want to go through it.* **3** avoid or evade: *to skirt an issue.* [ME < ON *skyrta* shirt]

skirt-ing (skèr′ting) *n.* cloth for making skirts.

skit (skit) *n.* a short dramatic sketch that contains humor or satire. [cf. ON *skyti* shooter]

ski tow a motorized conveyor for towing skiers to the top of a slope on their skis, usually consisting of an endless moving rope or cable which the skiers hang onto.

skit-ter (skit′ər) *v.* **1** move lightly or quickly; skim or skip along a surface. **2** *Fishing.* draw a lure over the surface of the water with a skipping motion. [akin to *skittish*]

skit-tish (skit′ish) *adj.* **1** apt to start, jump, or run; easily frightened: *a skittish horse.* **2** fickle; changeable. **3** coy. [< *skit*] —**skit′tish-ly,** *adv.* —**skit′tish-ness,** *n.*

skit-tle (skit′əl) *n.* **1 skittles,** *pl.* a game in which the players try to knock down nine wooden pins by rolling or throwing wooden disks or balls at them. **2** one of the pins used in this game.
beer and skittles, pure amusement; fun and games: *Life isn't all beer and skittles.*
[< Scand.; cf. Danish *skyttel* shuttle]

skiv-vy (skiv′ē) *n., pl.* **-vies.** *Brit. Slang.* a female domestic servant, especially a scullery maid. [origin uncertain]

skoal (skōl) *interj.* a drinking toast meaning: "To your health!" or "Cheers!" [< ON *skál* bowl]

skoo-kum (skü′kəm) *adj., n. Cdn. West Coast and Northwest.* —*adj.* powerful, big, or brave: *a skookum bacon-and-egg breakfast.* —*n.* an evil genius or spirit. [< Chinook Jargon]

skookum chuck *Cdn. West Coast and Northwest.* **1** a swift current; white water; rapids. **2** tidal rapids.

Skt. Sanskrit.

sku-a (skyü′ə) *n.* **1** a gull-like bird (*Catharacta skua*) resembling and related to the jaegers, but larger and more robust and without the elongated central tail feathers of the jaegers. The breeding range of the skua includes both the arctic and antarctic regions. Also called **great skua.** **2** *Esp.Brit.* any bird of the family Stercorariidae, including the jaegers. [< Faroese (lang. of the Faroe Islands) *skúgvur* < ON *skúfr*]

skul-dug-ger-y (skul dug′ər ē *or* skul dug′rē) *n.* *Informal.* trickery; dishonesty. [origin uncertain]

skulk (skulk) *v., n.* —*v.* **1** move in a stealthy, furtive manner; slink: *The burglar skulked around the house, looking for an easy way in.* **2** sneak away or keep out of sight to avoid danger, work, etc.: *He skulked at home to avoid facing the bully.* —*n.* a person who skulks. [ME < Scand.; cf. Danish *skolke*] —**skulk′er,** *n.* —**skulk′ing-ly,** *adv.*
☛ *Syn. v.* **1.** See note at **lurk.**

skull (skul) *n.* **1** the bones of the head; the part of the skeleton of a vertebrate animal that encloses and protects the brain and organs of sight, hearing, and smell. **2** the head, thought of as the seat of intelligence: *It's impossible to get anything into his thick skull.* [ME *scolle*; cf. dial. Norwegian *skul* shell]

skull and crossbones a picture of a human skull above two crossed bones, often used on pirates' flags as a symbol of death, and now often used on the labels of poisonous drugs, etc.

skull·cap (skul′kap′) *n.* a close-fitting cap with no brim.

skunk (skungk) *n., v.* —*n.* **1** any of various small, black-and-white, New World mammals of the weasel family noted for their ability to defend themselves by ejecting an extremely bad-smelling, oily liquid from a pair of anal glands. The commonest and best-known species is *Mephitis mephitis*, also called the **striped skunk**, having a white patch on the top of the head that continues along the back as a single or double band of white, often extending to the long, bushy tail. **2** the fur of a skunk. **3** a despicable person. —*v. Slang.* hold scoreless; defeat utterly. [< Algonquian]

skunk cabbage **1** a low-growing, perennial swamp herb (*Symplocarpus foetidus*) of the arum family found in E North America, having large, broad leaves and a purplish-spotted spathe, and giving off a strong, offensive odor when bruised. **2** a similar and related plant (*Lysichitum americanum*) of W North America.

sky (skī) *n., pl.* **skies**; *v.* **skied** or **skyed, sky·ing.** —*n.* **1** the space high above the earth, appearing as a great arch or dome covering the world; the region of the clouds or the upper air; the heavens: *a blue sky, a cloudy sky. A vapor trail stretched across the sky.* **2** heaven. **3** climate or weather: *warm tropical skies.*
out of a clear sky, suddenly; unexpectedly.
to the skies, very highly; extravagantly: *The review praised him to the skies.*
—*v.* hit, throw, or raise high into the air. [ME *ski(es)* cloud(s) < ON *ský*]

sky blue a light, clear blue. —**sky′-blue′,** *adj.*

sky·cap (skī′kap′) *n.* a porter at an airport. [adapted from *redcap*]

sky·div·er (skī′dī′vər) *n.* a person who engages in sky-diving.

sky–div·ing (skī′dī′ving) *n.* the sport of jumping from an airplane at a moderate height and making certain manoeuvres while falling free before opening one's parachute.

Skye terrier or **Skye** (skī) *n.* a breed of small terrier originally developed in Scotland, having short legs, a long body, and long, shaggy hair. [< the Isle of *Skye* near Scotland]

sky·ey (skī′ē) *adj.* of or like the sky.

sky–high (skī′hī′) *adv.* or *adj.* **1** to a great height; high up in the air: *to throw something sky-high.* **2** to a high degree or level: *Prices have gone sky-high in the last month.* **3** to bits; completely apart: *The warehouse was blown sky-high.*

sky·jack (skī′jak′) *v.* take over an aircraft by force, causing it to be flown to a place other than its destination. [blend of *sky* + *hijack*] —**sky′jack·er,** *n.*

sky·lark (skī′lärk′) *n., v.* —*n.* an Old World lark (*Alauda arvensis*) having inconspicuous, brown-streaked plumage and famous for the beautiful song of the male, produced while the bird is soaring at great heights. The skylark was introduced into southern British Columbia and has become established there. —*v.* frolic or play pranks.

sky·light (skī′līt′) *n.* a window in a roof.

sky·line (skī′līn′) *n.* **1** the line at which earth and sky seem to meet; horizon. **2** the outline of buildings, mountains, trees, etc. as seen against the sky, from a distance.

sky pilot *Slang.* a member of the clergy, especially a chaplain.

sky·rock·et (skī′rok′it) *n., v.* —*n.* a firework that can be shot high into the air, where it bursts in a shower of sparks and stars; rocket. —*v.* rise or increase suddenly and quickly, like a skyrocket: *Prices were skyrocketing. The actor had skyrocketed to fame with his first movie.*

sky·sail (skī′sāl′ or skī′səl) *n.* in a square-rigged ship, a light sail set at the top of the mast above the royal.

sky·scrap·er (skī′skrā′pər) *n.* an extremely tall building.

sky·ward (skī′wərd) *adv.* or *adj.* toward the sky.

sky·wards (skī′wərdz) *adv.* skyward.

sky·way (skī′wā′) *n.* **1** a route used by aircraft; air lane. **2** a stretch of elevated highway. **3** a covered walkway between upper storeys of two buildings or towers.

sky·writ·ing (skī′rī′ting) *n.* **1** the tracing of words, etc. against the sky from an airplane by means of smoke or some similar substance. **2** the letters, words, etc. so traced.

S.L. or **S/L** Squadron Leader.

slab (slab) *n., v.* **slabbed, slab·bing.** —*n.* **1** a broad, flat, thick piece (of stone, wood, meat, etc.): *This sidewalk is made of slabs of stone. The hungry boy ate a slab of cheese as big as his hand.* **2** the piece of wood cut from the outside of a log in squaring it. **3** *Baseball. Slang.* the place where the pitcher stands to deliver the ball.

hat, āge, fär; let, ēqual, tèrm; it, īce
hot, ōpen, ôrder; oil, out; cup, pụt, rüle,
əbove, takən, pencəl, lemən, circəs
ch, child; ng, long; sh, ship
th, thin; ŦH, then; zh, measure

—*v.* **1** make into slabs. **2** cut the outside pieces from (a log). **3** lay or cover with slabs. [ME *slabbe*; origin uncertain]

slab·ber (slab′ər) *v.* or *n.* slobber.

slack¹ (slak) *adj., n., v., adv.* —*adj.* **1** not tight or firm; loose: *The rope hung slack.* **2** careless: *She is a slack housekeeper.* **3** slow: *The horse was moving at a slack pace.* **4** not active; not brisk; dull: *Business is slack at this season.*
—*n.* **1** the part that hangs loose: *He pulled in the slack of the rope.* **2** a dull season; quiet period. **3** a stopping of a strong flow of the tide or a current of water. **4 slacks,** *pl.* trousers, especially for informal wear.
—*v.* **1** make slack; let up on. **2** be or become slack; let up. **3** slake (lime).
slack off, a loosen. **b** lessen one's efforts.
slack up, slow down; go more slowly.
—*adv.* in a slack manner. [OE *slæc*] —**slack′ly,** *adv.* —**slack′ness,** *n.*

slack² (slak) *n.* dirt, coal dust, and small pieces of coal left after coal has been screened. [ME *slac*; cf. G *Schlacke*]

slack·en (slak′ən) *v.* **1** make or become slower; slow down: *Don't slacken now; we're almost finished. The work slackened as the temperature climbed.* **2** become less active; vigorous, brisk, etc.: *His business slackens in winter.* **3** make or become looser: *Slacken the rope. The rope slackened as the boat neared the pier.*

slack·er (slak′ər) *n. Informal.* a person who shirks work or evades his duty.

slack–jawed (slak′jod′ or -jôd′) *adj.* having a loose-hanging jaw or a partly open mouth.

slacks (slaks) *n.pl.* trousers designed for casual wear.

slack water the time between tides when the water does not move either way.

slag (slag) *n., v.* **slagged, slag·ging.** —*n.* **1** the rough, hard, waste left after metal is separated from ore by melting. **2** a light, spongy lava. —*v.* form slag; change into slag. [< MLG *slagge*]

slag·gy (slag′ē) *adj.* of, like, or having to do with slag.

slain (slān) *v.* pp. of **slay.**

slake (slāk) *v.* **slaked, slak·ing.** **1** satisfy (thirst, revenge, wrath, etc.). **2** cause to be less active, intense, etc. **3** put out (a fire). **4** a change (lime) from CaO to $Ca(OH)_2$ (**slaked lime**) by leaving it in the moist air or putting water on it. Plaster contains slaked lime and sand. **b** be changed thus. **5** *Rare.* become less active, vigorous, intense, etc. [OE *slacian* < *slæc* slack]

sla·lom (slä′ləm or slal′əm) *n., v.* —*n. Skiing.* a zigzag race downhill on a course set between a series of posts. —*v.* ski on such a course. [< Norwegian]

slam¹ (slam) *v.* **slammed, slam·ming;** *n.* —*v.* **1** shut with force and noise; close with a bang: *He slammed the window down. The door slammed.* **2** throw, push, hit, or move hard with force. **3** *Informal.* criticize harshly.
—*n.* **1** a violent and noisy closing, striking, etc.; bang: *John threw his books down with a slam.* **2** *Informal.* a harsh criticism. [? < Scand.; cf. Icel. and dial. Norwegian *slamra* slam]

slam² (slam) *n.* **1** *Bridge.* the winning of 12 (**little** or **small slam**) or all 13 (**grand slam**) tricks. **2** in certain other card games, the winning of all the tricks in one hand. [origin uncertain]

slam·mer (slam′ər) *n. Slang.* Usually, **the slammer,** jail or prison. [< slam¹]

slan·der (slan′dər) *n., v.* —*n.* **1** *Law.* **a** the act or practice of making false oral statements meant to do harm to the reputation of another. **b** such a statement. Compare **libel. 2** the spreading of false statements intended to damage someone's reputation; calumny. —*v.* speak or spread slander against. [ME < OF *esclandre* scandal < L *scandalum.* Doublet of SCANDAL.] —**slan′der·er,** *n.*

slan·der·ous (slan′dər əs or slan′drəs) *adj.* using or containing slander: *a slanderous remark.* —**slan′der·ous·ly,** *adv.*

slang (slang) *n., v.* —*n.* **1** vocabulary and usage that differ from the standard, consisting mainly of new, usually colorful, humorous, or vigorous words or phrases, or such meanings for existing words or phrases. Slang is often adopted by a particular group of people to set themselves apart from others; it often passes quickly out of use because it depends on novelty for much of its effect. **2** jargon;

shoptalk: *In the slang of the Canadian fur trade, stealing furs from a warehouse was called* indoor trapping. —v. attack with abusive language; rail at; scold. [origin uncertain]

☞ *Usage.* Slang is not usually considered acceptable in formal speech or writing, and should be avoided even in informal situations when one is communicating with people outside one's own group. See also the notes at **standard** and **informal.**

slang·y (slang′ē) *adj.* **slang·i·er, slang·i·est.** using or containing much slang: *The writing is too slangy for an essay.* —**slang′i·ly,** *adv.* —**slang′i·ness,** *n.*

slank (slangk) *v. Archaic.* a pt. of **slink.**

slant (slant) *v., n.* —*v.* **1** slope: *Most handwriting slants to the right.* **2** interpret or present from a particular angle to appeal to a particular group or interest: *a magazine slanted toward the teenage audience.* **3** distort on purpose to give a certain impression; falsify: *The newspaper slanted the story by leaving out some of the facts.* —*n.* **1** a slanting or oblique direction or position; a slope: *The greenhouse roof has a sharp slant.* **2** (adjl.) sloping: *a slant roof.* **3** a peculiar or personal attitude or viewpoint: *His reminiscences provide us with an interesting slant on the political scene of the sixties.* [var. of ME *slent* to slant < Scand.; cf. Norwegian *slenta*] —**slant′ing·ly,** *adv.*

☞ *Syn. v.* See note at **slope.**

slant·ways (slant′wāz′) *adv.* slantwise.

slant·wise (slant′wīz′) *adv., adj.* —*adv.* in a slanting manner; obliquely. —*adj.* slanting; oblique.

slap (slap) *n., v.* **slapped, slap·ping;** *adv.* —*n.* **1** a blow with the open hand or with something flat. **2** sharp words of blame; a direct insult or rebuff. —*v.* **1** strike with the open hand or with something flat. **2** put, dash, or cast with force: *She slapped the book down on the table.* **3** beat or hit with a slapping sound: *waves slapping against the dock.* —*adv.* **1** *Informal.* straight; directly: *The thief ran slap into a policeman.* **2** *Informal.* suddenly. [< LG *slappe*]

slap–bang (slap′bang′) *adv., adj.* —*adv.* **1** speedily; immediately. **2** thoughtlessly; in a headlong manner. —*adj.* headlong; thoughtless; slapdash.

slap·dash (slap′dash′) *adv., adj., n.* —*adv. Informal.* hastily and carelessly. —*adj.* hasty and careless. —*n.* hasty, careless action, methods, or work.

slap·hap·py (slap′hap′ē) *adj. Slang.* **1** cheerfully irresponsible and foolish; recklessly carefree. **2** punch-drunk.

slap·shot (slap′shot′) *n. Hockey. Cdn.* a fast, not always accurate, shot made with a powerful swinging stroke.

slap·stick (slap′stik′) *n., adj.* —*n.* **1** two long, narrow boards fastened so as to slap together loudly when a clown, actor, etc. hits somebody with it. **2** comedy full of broad humor and rough play. —*adj.* characterized by broad humor and rough play: *slapstick comedy.*

slash (slash) *v., n.* —*v.* **1** cut with a sweeping stroke of a sword, knife, etc.; gash: *He slashed the bark off the tree with his knife.* **2** make a slashing stroke. **3** cut or slit to let a different cloth or color show through. **4** whip severely; lash. **5** criticize sharply, severely, or unkindly. **6** cut down severely; reduce a great deal: *His salary was slashed when business became bad.* **7** cut out parts of (a book, etc.); change greatly (a book, etc.). —*n.* **1** a sweeping, slashing stroke: *the slash of a sword, the slash of the rain.* **2** a cut or wound made by such a stroke; gash. **3** a sharp cutting down; great reduction: *a slash in prices.* **4** an ornamental slit in a garment that lets a different cloth or color show through. **5** an open space in a forest, usually littered with chips, broken branches, etc. **6** a litter of chips, broken branches, etc. [ME *slasche(n)*; cf. OF *esclachier* break] —**slash′er,** *n.*

slat¹ (slat) *n., v.* **slat·ted, slat·ting.** —*n.* a long, thin, narrow piece of wood or metal. —*v.* provide or build with slats. [ME < OF *esclat* split piece < Gmc.]

slat² (slat) *v.* **slat·ted, slat·ting;** *n. Archaic.* —*v.* **1** hurl; dash; fling. **2** slap; strike; beat. —*n.* a sharp blow or slap. [< ON *sletta* slap]

slate¹ (slāt) *n., v.* **slat·ed, slat·ing;** *adj.* —*n.* **1** a fine-grained, bluish-grey rock formed from the compression of layers of shale or clay that splits easily into thin, smooth layers. Slate is used to cover roofs. **2** a thin piece of slate or material like slate, especially one used for writing on, or as a roofing tile: *Children used to do their schoolwork on slates they carried with them.* **3** a dark bluish-grey. **4** a list of candidates, officers, etc. to be considered for appointment, nomination, etc.
a clean slate, a record not marked by mistakes, dishonor, etc.: *He is entering public office with a clean slate.*
—*v.* **1** cover with slate. **2** list as a candidate: *He is slated for the office of club president.*

—*adj.* dark bluish-grey. [ME < OF *esclate*, var. of *esclat* slat < Gmc.] —**slate′like′,** *adj.*

slate² (slāt) *v.* **sla·ted, sla·ting. 1** beat violently. **2** criticize severely. [? var. of *slat²*]

slat·er (slā′tər) *n.* **1** a person who covers roofs, etc. with slates. **2** wood louse.

slath·er (slaᴛʜ′ər) *n., v. Informal.* —*n.* **slathers,** a great quantity: *slathers of bacon and eggs.* —*v.* spread thickly or lavishly. [origin unknown]

slat·tern (slat′ərn) *n.* a woman who is dirty, careless, or untidy in her dress, her ways, her housekeeping, etc. [< Brit. dial. *slatter* slop; origin uncertain; cf. LG *slattje* slattern]

slat·tern·ly (slat′ərn lē) *adj.* slovenly; untidy. —**slat′tern·li·ness,** *n.*

slat·y (slā′tē) *adj.* **slat·i·er, slat·i·est. 1** of or containing slate. **2** slate-colored.

slaugh·ter (slo′tər *or* slô′tər) *n., v.* —*n.* **1** the killing of an animal or animals for food; butchering. **2** brutal killing; much or needless killing. —*v.* **1** butcher. **2** kill brutally; massacre. [ME < Scand.; cf. ON *slátr* butcher-meat < *slá* slay] —**slaugh′ter·er,** *n.*

slaughter house (slo′tər hous′ *or* slô′tər-) a place where animals are killed for food; abattoir.

slaugh·ter·ous (slot′ər əs *or* slô′tər əs) *adj.* murderous; destructive.

Slav (slav *or* släv) *n., adj.* —*n.* a member of any of a group of E European peoples who speak Slavic languages, such as Russians, Poles, Czechs, Slovaks, and Bulgarians. —*adj.* Slavic. [< Med.L *Slavus, Sclavus.* Cf. SLAVE.]

Slav. Slavic; Slavonic; Slavonian.

slave (slāv) *n., v.* **slaved, slav·ing.** —*n.* **1** a person who is the property of another. Slaves used to be bought and sold like cattle. **2** a person who is controlled or ruled by some desire, habit, or influence: *A drunkard is a slave to drink.* **3** a person who works like a slave. **4** an ant that is captured and forced to work for other ants. **5 a** an electronic device that receives and relays radio signals transmitted by a master control, as in loran navigation. **b** a mechanical or electric device for manipulating objects by remote control. —*v.* work like a slave. [ME < OF < Med.L *Sclavus* Slav (captive) < LGk. *Sklabos,* ult. < Slavic *slovo.* Cf. SLOVENE.] —**slave′like′,** *adj.*

Slave (slāv) *n., pl.* **Slaves** *or* **Slave;** *adj.* —*n.* **1** a member of an Amerindian people in the Northwest Territories between the rockies and Great Slave Lake. **2** the Athapascan language of the Slaves. —*adj.* of or having to do with the Slaves or their language. Also, **Slavey.** [translation of Cree *awokanak* slaves]

slave driver 1 a person who supervises slaves at work. **2** an employer, supervisor, etc. who is excessively harsh or demanding.

slave·hold·er (slāv′hōl′dər) *n.* an owner of slaves.

slave·hold·ing (slāv′hōl′ding) *adj., n.* —*adj.* owning slaves. —*n.* the owning of slaves.

slav·er¹ (slā′vər) *n.* **1** a dealer in slaves. **2** a ship used in the slave trade. [< *slave*]

slav·er² (slav′ər) *v., n.* —*v.* **1** let saliva run from the mouth; drool. **2** *Archaic.* cover or wet with saliva. —*n.* saliva running from the mouth. [ME < Scand.; cf. Icel. *slafra.* Related to SLOBBER.]

slav·er·y (slā′vər ē *or* slāv′rē) *n.* **1** the condition of being a slave. Many Africans were captured by Europeans and sold into slavery in America. **2** the custom of owning slaves: *They fought against slavery.* **3** a condition like that of a slave: *slavery to the dictates of fashion.* **4** hard work like that of a slave: *He said the job was pure slavery.*

slave trade traffic in slaves; the buying and selling of slaves for profit.

slav·ey (slā′vē) *n., pl.* **-eys.** *Informal.* a maid of all work.

Slav·ey (slā′vē) *n. or adj.* Slave.

Slav·ic (slav′ik *or* släv′ik) *adj., n.* —*adj.* of or having to do with the Slavs or their languages. —*n.* the branch of the Indo-European family of languages that includes Bulgarian, Czech, Polish, Russian, Serbo-Croatian, Slovak, etc.

slav·ish (slā′vish) *adj.* **1** of or having to do with a slave or slaves. **2** like or characteristic of a slave; weakly submissive and servile: *a slavish personality, a slavish follower.* **3** lacking originality and independence: *a slavish translation of the original, slavish reliance on a pattern.* —**slav′ish·ly,** *adv.* —**slav′ish·ness,** *n.*

Sla·vo·ni·an (slə vō′nē ən) *adj., n.* —*adj.* **1** of or having to do with Slavonia, a region in N Yugoslavia, or its people. **2** *Archaic.* Slavic. —*n.* **1** a native or inhabitant of Slavonia. **2** *Archaic.* Slavic.

Sla·von·ic (slə von′ik) *adj. or n.* Slavic.

slaw (slo *or* slô) *n.* coleslaw. [< Du. *sla*, contraction of *salade* salad]

slay (slā) *v.* **slew** *or* **slayed** (for 2), **slain**, **slay·ing. 1** kill with violence, especially in battle: *Many soldiers were slain on that hill.* **2** *Slang.* amuse greatly: *That comedian just slays me.* [OE *slēan.* Akin to SLY.] —**slay′er,** *n.*
☞ *Hom.* sleigh.
☞ *Syn.* See note at kill.

sld. sailed.

sleave (slēv) *v.* **sleaved, sleav·ing;** *n.* —*v.* divide or separate into smaller threads. —*n.* a small silk thread made by separating a thicker thread. [OE *slǣfan,* as in *tōslǣfan* divide]

slea·zy (slē′zē) *adj.* **-zi·er, -zi·est. 1** flimsy and poor: *sleazy cloth.* **2** *Informal.* shoddy, squalid, or mean: *a sleazy, run-down hotel.* [origin uncertain] —**slea′zi·ness,** *n.*

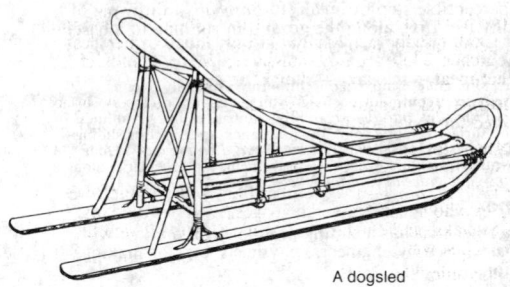
A dogsled

sled (sled) *n., v.* **sled·ded, sled·ding.** —*n.* **1** a small, low vehicle having runners instead of wheels, used especially for carrying loads over ice and snow. Before the snowmobile, the common means of winter transportation in the North was a sled pulled by a team of dogs. **2** sleigh (def. 2). —*v.* ride or carry on a sled. [< MDu. *sledde*]

sled·ding (sled′ing) *n.* **1** the act of riding or coasting on a sled. **2** the condition of the snow or ice as a surface for a sled: *The new snow made for good sledding.* **3** advance toward a goal; progress: *He found it tough sledding at first because everything was strange to him.*

sled dog a dog trained and used to draw a sled, especially in the Arctic.

sledge¹ (slej) *n., v.* **sledged, sledg·ing.** —*n.* **1** a low, heavy vehicle mounted on runners, used for carrying loads and drawn over snow or ice or dragged over the ground by draft animals. **2** *Esp.Brit.* a sled or sleigh. —*v.* ride or carry on a sledge. [MDu. *sledse*]

sledge² (slej) *n.* sledgehammer. [OE *slecg*]

sledge·ham·mer (slej′ham′ər) *n., v.* —*n.* **1** a large, heavy hammer, usually swung with both hands. **2** (*adj.*) powerful or crushing: *sledgehammer sarcasm.* —*v.* hit with, or as if with, a sledgehammer.

sleek (slēk) *adj., v.* —*adj.* **1** smooth and glossy; looking highly polished: *sleek hair.* **2** having a well-groomed, well-fed appearance: *a sleek cat. He was looking very sleek and healthy after his holiday.* **3** too smooth in speech, manners, etc.; slick. **4** trim and elegant: *a sleek ship.*
—*v.* make smooth and glossy: *He sleeked down his hair.* [var. of *slick*] —**sleek′ly,** *adv.* —**sleek′ness,** *n.*

sleep (slēp) *v.* **slept, sleep·ing;** *n.* —*v.* **1** rest the body and mind; be without ordinary consciousness. **2** be in a condition like sleep: *The seeds sleep in the ground all winter.* **3** pass in sleeping. **4** provide with or offer sleeping accommodation for: *a hotel that sleeps 500 people.* **5** provide space for sleeping: *This room sleeps two.*
sleep away, pass or spend in sleeping: *He slept away the whole morning.*
sleep in, a remain in bed later than usual: *We always sleep in on a Sunday morning.* **b** sleep late or oversleep: *He was late because he slept in.* **c** live at one's place of work: *The maid slept in.*
sleep like a log, sleep soundly or heavily.
sleep off, get rid of by sleeping: *She was sleeping off a headache.*
sleep on, put off deciding on: *He said he would sleep on the idea.*
—*n.* **1** a condition in which body and mind are very inactive, occurring naturally and regularly in all animals. **2** a period spent in sleeping. **3** a state or condition like sleep. **4** mucus that is sometimes secreted by the eyes during sleep, and that collects and hardens especially in the inner corners of the eyes.
last sleep, death.
put to sleep, put an animal, especially a pet, to death humanely: *We had to put our dog to sleep because she was old and sick.*
[OE *slǣpan*]

hat, āge, fär; let, ēqual, tèrm; it, īce
hot, ōpen, ôrder; oil, out; cup, put, rüle,
above, takən, pencəl, lemən, circəs

ch, child; ng, long; sh, ship
th, thin; ŦH, then; zh, measure

sleep·er (slē′pər) *n.* **1** a person or animal that sleeps: *They made their way silently past the sleepers. He's a sound sleeper.* **2** a railway sleeping car. **3** a horizontal beam, especially one on or near the ground, that supports a structure. **4** *Brit.* a tie to support a railway track. **5** someone or something that is unexpectedly successful, especially a book, play, or motion picture that is an unexpected hit or winner: *Her first play was the sleeper of the season.* **6** a small, plain gold ring worn instead of an earring in a newly pierced ear lobe to prevent the hole from growing closed. **7 sleepers,** one-piece pyjamas for children, extending from the neck and covering the feet.

sleeping bag a zippered bag for sleeping in, usually waterproof and warmly lined, used especially when camping.

sleeping car a railway sleeping car with berths or small rooms for passengers to sleep in.

sleeping partner a partner who takes no active part in managing the business; a silent partner.

sleeping pill a pill or capsule containing a drug that causes sleep.

sleeping sickness a disease causing fever, inflammation of the brain, sleepiness, and usually death.

sleeping tablet sleeping pill.

sleep·less (slēp′lis) *adj.* **1** not able to sleep. **2** not providing or producing sleep: *sleepless nights.* **3** continually active or watchful: *a sleepless sentry, a sleepless memory.* —**sleep′less·ly,** *adv.* —**sleep′less·ness,** *n.*

sleep·walk (slēp′wok′ *or* -wôk′) *v.* walk about while asleep.

sleep·walk·er (slēp′wok′ər *or* -wôk′ər) *n.* a person who walks about while asleep.

sleep·walk·ing (slēp′wok′ing *or* -wôk′ing) *n.* the act or practice of walking while asleep.

sleep·y (slē′pē) *adj.* **sleep·i·er, sleep·i·est. 1** ready to go to sleep; inclined to sleep. **2** not active; quiet. **3** inducing sleep; soporific: *a warm, sleepy day.* —**sleep′i·ly,** *adv.* —**sleep′i·ness,** *n.*
☞ *Syn.* **Sleepy, drowsy** = ready or inclined to sleep. **Sleepy** is the general word describing people or things, particularly suggesting being ready to fall asleep or having a tendency to sleep: *He never gets enough rest and is always sleepy.* **Drowsy** particularly suggests being heavy or dull with sleepiness: *After lying in the sun, he became drowsy.*

sleep·y·head (slē′pē hed′) *n.* a person who is sleepy or not paying attention: *Wake up, sleepyhead!*

sleet (slēt) *n., v.* —*n.* **1** partly frozen rain, often mixed with snow. **2** a mixture of snow and rain. **3** a fall or shower of sleet. —*v.* be the case that sleet is falling (*used with the subject* it): *It began to sleet.* [ME *slete*]

sleet·y (slē′tē) *adj.* **sleet·i·er, sleet·i·est.** of, like, or characterized by sleet. —**sleet′i·ness,** *n.*

sleeve (slēv) *n., v.* **sleeved, sleev·ing.** —*n.* **1** the tubelike part of a garment that extends from the shoulder and covers the arm or part of the arm. **2** a tube or tubelike machine part enclosing a rod or another tube. **3** a paper or plastic cover for a phonograph record.
have up (one's) sleeve, have in reserve, concealed but ready for use when needed: *She had one more trick up her sleeve.*
laugh in or **up (one's) sleeve** See **laugh.**
—*v.* provide with a sleeve or sleeves. [OE *slīefe*]

sleeved (slēvd) *adj.* having sleeves of a specified kind (*used especially in compounds*): *a long-sleeved shirt.*

sleeve·less (slēv′lis) *adj.* without sleeves: *a sleeveless dress.*

Sleighs: at the right, a cutter; at the left, a children's sleigh

sleigh (slā) *n., v.* —*n.* **1** a light carriage mounted on runners, used

for carrying persons over snow or ice, and usually drawn by a horse or horses. A cutter is a kind of sleigh. 2 a small, low vehicle consisting of a platform of boards on narrow metal runners, used as a plaything for going over snow or ice and coasting down snow-covered hills. —v. travel or ride in a sleigh. [< Du. *slee*, var. of *slede* sled]
☛ Hom. **slay.**

sleigh·ing (slā'ing) n. 1 riding in a sleigh. 2 the conditions for sleighing: *The warm rain spoiled the sleighing.*

sleight (slīt) n. 1 skill; dexterity. 2 a clever trick. [ME < ON *slǽgth* < *slǽgr* sly. See SLY.]
☛ Hom. **slight.**

sleight of hand 1 skill and quickness in moving the hands, as in juggling or conjuring tricks. 2 a display of skill and quickness with the hands; a trick or juggling act requiring such skill.

slen·der (slen'dər) adj. 1 gracefully narrow and slight of frame; slim: *a tall, slender girl, a slender hand.* 2 long and thin; not wide or big around in proportion to length or height: *a slender sapling. A pencil is a slender piece of wood.* 3 scanty; meagre; not adequate: *a slender meal, a slender income, a slender hope.* [ME *slendre, sclendre*; origin uncertain] —**slen'der·ly,** adv. —**slen'der·ness,** n.
☛ Syn. **Slender, slim** = thin, not big around. **Slender,** describing a person or thing and meaning tall or long and thin, suggests good proportions, gracefulness, and beauty: *Many girls want to be slender. The legs of those chairs are slender.* **Slim** emphasizes lack of flesh and lightness or weakness of frame or build: *He is a slim boy who may fill out as he becomes older.*

slen·der·ize (slen'dər īz') -ized, -iz·ing. 1 make slender. 2 cause to look slender or less stout: *a slenderizing dress.*

slept (slept) v. pt. and pp. of **sleep.**

sleuth (slūth) n., v. —n. *Informal.* detective. —v. be or act like a detective. [ME < ON *slóth* trail]

sleuth·hound (slūth'hound') n. 1 bloodhound. 2 *Informal.* detective.

slew[1] (slū) v. pt. of **slay.**
☛ Hom. **slough, slue.**

slew[2] (slū) v., n. —v. 1 turn or swing on a pivot or as if on a pivot: *He slewed around in his seat to get a better look. We slewed the telescope around to the east.* 2 skid or turn sharply: *The car slewed around the curve. She slewed the car to the right to avoid the dog.* —n. a turn, twist, or skid. Also, **slue.** [origin uncertain]
☛ Hom. **slough, slue.**

slew[3] (slū) n. slough[1].
☛ Hom. **slough, slue.**

slew[4] (slū) n. *Informal.* a lot; a large number or amount: *There was a whole slew of people waiting at the stage door.* [< Irish Gaelic *sluagh* host, crowd]
☛ Hom. **slough, slue.**

slice (slīs) n., v. **sliced, slic·ing.** —n. 1 a thin, flat, broad piece cut from something, especially food: *a slice of bread, meat, or cake.* 2 a knife or spatula with a thin, broad blade. 3 a part; share: *He wanted a slice of the profits.* 4 *Sports.* a hit made so that the ball curves away. Compare **hook** (def. 9). —v. 1 cut into slices: *He sliced the loaf of bread.* 2 cut off as a slice: *I sliced a piece of the meatloaf for myself.* 3 cut or pass through like a knife: *A bullet sliced the air by his head. The plough sliced through the earth.* 4 *Sports.* hit a ball so that it curves away. Compare **hook** (def. 10). [ME < OF *esclice* thin chip < Gmc.]

slic·er (slī'sər) n. a person or thing that slices, especially a mechanical device for slicing food: *a meat slicer.*

slick (slik) adj., v., n., adv. —adj. 1 sleek; smooth: *slick hair.* 2 slippery; greasy: *a road slick with ice or mud.* 3 *Informal.* clever; ingenious. 4 smooth in speech, manners, etc., especially in a tricky or deceitful way. 5 *Informal.* of or like that of a smooth, tricky person; cunningly made up: *a slick excuse.* —v. make sleek or smooth. —n. 1 a smooth spot or surface, especially a patch of oil, etc. on water or a paved road. 2 *Informal.* a magazine printed on heavy, glossy paper. 3 a a tool used for scraping and smoothing leather. b a trowel for smoothing the top of a mould in casting metals. —adv. in a slick manner; slickly. [ME *slike*, adj. OE *slician* make smooth] —**slick'ly,** adv. —**slick'ness,** n.

slick·er (slik'ər) n. 1 a long, loose, waterproof coat. 2 *Slang.* a sly, tricky person.

slick–lick·er (slik'lik'ər) n. a device for removing large oil slicks from water, consisting basically of a large conveyor belt covered with absorbent material like towelling that soaks up the oil.

slid (slid) v. pt. and pp. of **slide.**

slide (slīd) v. **slid, slid·ing,** n. —v. 1 move smoothly over a surface: *The bureau drawers slide in and out.* 2 move easily or quietly or secretly: *The thief slid behind the curtains.* 3 pass without

heeding or being heeded. 4 pass by degrees; slip: *He has slid into bad habits.* 5 pass or put quietly or secretly: *He slid a gun into his pocket.* 6 slip in an uncontrolled manner: *The car slid into the ditch.* 7 *Music.* pass or progress from tone to tone without perceptible step or break. 8 *Baseball.* launch a slide for a base or home plate.
let slide, neglect; not bother about: *He has been letting his business slide lately.*
—n. 1 the act of sliding: *The children each take a slide in turn.* 2 a smooth surface for sliding on. 3 a track, rail, etc. on which something slides. 4 something that works by sliding. 5 the U-shaped tube of a trumpet or trombone that is pushed in or out to change the pitch of the tones. 6 a a mass of earth, snow, etc. sliding down. b the sliding down of such a mass. 7 a small, thin sheet of glass on which objects are placed for microscopic examination. 8 a small transparent photograph made of glass or film: *Slides are put in a projector and shown on a screen.* 9 *Music.* a rapid ascending or descending series of three or more notes, composed of grace notes which ornament the last or principal note. b a passing from tone to tone without perceptible step or break. 10 *Baseball.* a throwing of the body, usually feet first, along the ground in running to a base, so as to avoid being tagged, to break up a double play, etc. [OE *slīdan*] —**slid'er,** n.
☛ Syn. v. 1. **Slide, slip, glide** = move along smoothly, especially over a surface. **Slide** emphasizes continuous contact with a smooth or slippery surface: *The boat slid down the bank into the water.* **Slip** emphasizes the smoothness or slipperiness of the surface or absence of any hindrance, and suggests sliding suddenly without intention: *One of the climbers slipped on the rocks.* **Glide** emphasizes continuous, smooth, even, easy movement, not necessarily along a surface: *The swans glide gracefully on the lake.*

slide fastener zipper.

slide rule a ruler that has a sliding middle strip, marked with logarithmic scales, used by engineers, physicists, etc. for making rapid calculations.

slid·ing (slī'ding) adj. moving or operating on a track or groove: *a sliding door.*

sliding scale a scale or standard, as for wages, tariffs, or fees, that is adjusted to fit certain conditions or situations. Wages based on a sliding scale are adjusted according to the cost of living.

slight (slīt) adj., v., n. —adj. 1 not much; not important; small: *I have a slight headache.* 2 not big around; slender: *She is a slight girl.* 3 frail; flimsy: *a slight excuse.* —v. treat as of little value; pay too little attention to; neglect: *She felt slighted because she was not asked to the party.* —n. slighting treatment; an act showing neglect or lack of respect. [OE *-sliht* level, as in *eorthslihtes* level with the ground] —**slight'ness,** n.
☛ Hom. **sleight.**
☛ Syn. v. **Slight, overlook, neglect** = pay too little or no attention to someone or something needing or deserving it. **Slight** emphasizes intentionally treating a person, thing, work, or duty as of too little importance to deserve consideration or attention: *He slights his cousins because they are poor.* **Overlook** emphasizes unintentionally failing to see something needing attention, because of other concerns, haste, carelessness, etc.: *He overlooked the telephone bill.* **Neglect** emphasizes failing to give enough or deserved attention or care to a person, work, or duty: *He neglects his teeth.*

slight·ing (slī'ting) adj. that detracts; contemptuous; disrespectful: *a slighting remark.* —**slight'ing·ly,** adv.

slight·ly (slīt'lē) adv. to a slight degree; somewhat; a little: *I knew him slightly.*

sli·ly (slī'lē) See **slyly.**

slim (slim) adj. **slim·mer, slim·mest;** v. **slimmed, slim·ming.** —adj. 1 slender; gracefully thin: *a slim girl, a slim waist.* 2 small or scanty; slight: *There is a slim chance that she will get the letter in time. His chances of escape were slim.* —v. make or become slender or more slender: *He is trying to slim down. A girdle is designed to slim the figure.* [< Du. *slim* bad] —**slim'ly,** adv. —**slim'ness,** n.
☛ Syn. 1. See note at **slender.**

slime (slīm) n., v. **slimed, slim·ing.** —n. 1 a soft, sticky mud or something like it. 2 a sticky substance given off by snails, slugs, fish, etc. 3 disgusting filth. —v. 1 cover or smear with, or as with, slime. 2 clear (skins, fish, etc.) of slimy matter by scraping. [OE *slīm*]

slim·y (slī'mē) adj. **slim·i·er, slim·i·est.** 1 covered with slime. 2 of or like slime. 3 disgusting; vile; filthy. 4 using sly or crafty flattery, insinuation, etc. —**slim'i·ly,** adv. —**slim'i·ness,** n.

sling (sling) n., v. **slung, sling·ing.** —n. 1 a strip of leather with a string fastened to each end, for throwing stones. 2 a throw; hurling. 3 a hanging loop of cloth fastened around the neck to support an injured arm or hand. 4 a loop of rope, band, chain, etc. by which heavy objects are lifted, carried, or held: *The men lowered the boxes into the cellar by a sling. Rifles have slings.* —v. 1 throw with a sling. 2 throw; cast; hurl; fling. 3 raise, lower, etc. with a sling. 4 hang in a sling; hang so as to swing loosely: *The soldier's gun was slung over his shoulder.* 5 *Slang.* mix; serve: *to sling hash.* [ME, perhaps < ON *slyngva*]

sling·er (sling'ər) *n.* **1** a fighter armed with a sling. **2** a worker in charge of slings used in hoisting, etc. **3** a person who slings.

sling·shot (sling'shot') *n.* **1** a Y-shaped stick wtih a band of rubber between its prongs, used to shoot pebbles, etc.; catapult. **2** sling (def. 1).

slink¹ (slingk) *v.* **slunk** or *(Archaic)* **slank, slunk, slink·ing.** move in a sneaking, guilty manner; sneak: *After stealing the meat, the dog slunk away.* [OE *slincan*] —**slink'ing·ly,** *adv.*

slink² (slingk) *v.* **slinked** or **slunk, slink·ing;** *n., adj.* —*v.* of animals, give birth to prematurely.
—*n.* any animal born prematurely.
—*adj.* born prematurely. [< *slink¹*]

slink·y (slingk'ē) *adj.* **1** furtive; sneaking. **2** of clothing, tight-fitting in an alluring, graceful way: *a slinky gown.* —**slink'i·ly,** *adv.* —**slink'i·ness,** *n.*

slip¹ (slip) *v.* **slipped, slip·ping;** *n.* —*v.* **1** go or move smoothly, quietly, easily, or quickly: *She slipped out of the room. Time slips by. The ship slips through the waves. The drawer slips into place.* **2** slide; move out of place: *The knife slipped and cut him.* **3** slide suddenly without wanting to: *He slipped on the icy sidewalk.* **4** cause to slip; put, pass, or draw smoothly, quietly, or secretly: *He slipped back the bolt. She slipped the ring from her finger. Slip the note into Mary's hand.* **5** put or take (something) easily or quickly: *Slip on your coat. Slip off your shoes.* **6** pass without notice; pass through neglect; escape: *Don't let this opportunity slip.* **7** get loose from; get away from; escape from: *The dog has slipped his collar. Your name has slipped my mind.* **8** let go; release: *He slipped the hound. The ship has slipped anchor and is off.* **9** make a mistake or error. **10** fall off; decline; deteriorate: *New car sales have slipped.*
let slip, tell without meaning to: *He let the secret slip in a careless moment.*
slip one over on, *Informal.* get the advantage of, especially by trickery.
slip up, *Informal.* make a mistake or error.
—*n.* **1** the act or fact of slipping. **2** something that covers and can be slipped on or over; covering: *Pillows are covered by slips.* **3** a dress-length or skirt-length under-garment of nylon, silk, etc. worn by women and girls. **4** a mistake; error: *He makes slips in grammar. That remark was a slip of the tongue.* **5** a space for ships between wharves or in a dock. **6** an inclined platform alongside the water, on which ships are built or repaired. **7** a leash for a dog. **8** *Cricket.* **a** the position of a player behind and to the side of the wicketkeeper. **b** the player in this position.
give (someone) the slip, *Informal.* escape from or get away from (someone): *She gave her creditors the slip.* [probably < MLG *slippen*]
☛ *Syn. v.* **1.** See note at **slide.**

slip² (slip) *n., v.* **slipped, slip·ping.** —*n.* **1** a small stem or shoot cut from a plant, used to grow a new plant, either by rooting in water or earth or by grafting; cutting; scion. **2** a long, narrow strip of paper, wood, etc.: *a sales slip.* **3** a young, slender person: *She is just a slip of a girl.*
—*v.* take a stem or shoot from (a plant) to grow a new plant. [probably < MDu. or MLG *slippen* cut]

slip·cov·er (slip'kuv'ər) *n.* **1** a removable cloth cover for a chair, chesterfield, etc. **2** a dust jacket for a book.

slip·knot (slip'not') *n.* **1** a knot made to slip along the rope or cord around which it is made. **2** a knot that can be undone by a pull. See **knot** for picture.

slip noose a noose made with a slip knot.

slip-on (slip'on') *adj., n.* —*adj.* **1** that can be put on or taken off easily or quickly. **2** that must be put on or taken off over the head. —*n.* a slip-on glove, blouse, sweater, etc.

slip·page (slip'ij) *n.* **1** the act or fact of slipping. **2** the loss in time, distance, or amount between a standard and what is achieved, between theoretical and actual speed, power, output, etc.

slip·per (slip'ər) *n., v.* —*n.* a light, soft shoe that is easily slipped on and off the foot, especially one worn while resting indoors. —*v.* strike with a slipper, as a punishment. —**slip'per·less,** *adj.*

slip·pered (slip'ərd) *adj.* wearing slippers.

slip·per·y (slip'ər ē or slip'rē) *adj.* **-per·i·er, -per·i·est. 1** causing or likely to cause sliding and slipping because of smoothness, greasiness, etc.: *Wet or icy streets are slippery. A waxed floor is slippery.* **2** slipping away easily; hard to hold firmly: *Wet soap is slippery.* **3** difficult to handle or pin down: *a slippery situation, a slippery concept.* **4** not to be depended on; tricky or deceitful: *a slippery character.* [< obs. *slipper* slippery, OE *slipor*]
—**slip'per·i·ly,** *adv.* —**slip'per·i·ness,** *n.*

slippery elm 1 an elm (*Ulmus fulva*) of E North America having an inner bark that becomes slimy or slippery when moistened. **2** the inner bark of this tree.

slip·shod (slip'shod') *adj.* **1** careless in dress, habits, speech, etc.; untidy; slovenly. **2** shuffling: *a slipshod gait.* **3** wearing shoes worn down at the heel.

hat, āge, fär; let, ēqual, tèrm; it, īce
hot, ōpen, ôrder; oil, out; cup, pùt, rüle,
əbove, takən, pencəl, lemən, circəs
ch, child; ng, long; sh, ship
th, thin; ᴛʜ, then; zh, measure

slip·stitch (slip'stich') *n.* an almost invisible kind of stitch used for sewing folded edges, such as hems, made by alternately taking a stitch inside the folded edge and a very tiny stitch in the body of the article being sewn.

slip·stream (slip'strēm') *n.* **1** a backward-moving stream of air created beside a rapidly moving object, such as an aircraft or a motor vehicle. **2** the area of decreased air pressure immediately behind such a moving object.

slipt (slipt) *v. Archaic.* a pt. of **slip.**

slip-up (slip'up') *n. Informal.* a mistake; error.

slit (slit) *v.* **slit, slit·ting;** *n.* —*v.* **1** make a long, straight cut in; cut open: *She used a paper knife to slit the envelope open.* **2** cut lengthwise into strips: *to slit leather into thongs.* —*n.* a straight, narrow cut or opening: *the slit in a letter box, a slit for a buttonhole. His eyes were just slits.* [ME *slitte(n)*] —**slit'ter,** *n.*

slith·er (sliᴛʜ'ər) *v., n.* —*v.* **1** slide unsteadily down or along a loose or gravelly surface: *We slithered down the embankment to the road.* **2** move or go with a gliding or sliding motion: *The snake slithered away into the grass.* —*n.* a slithering movement. [OE *slidrian*]

slit skirt a narrow skirt having a slit, or vent, in the lower part of the seam at one or both sides or at the front or back, for ease in walking.

sliv·er (sliv'ər) *n., v.* —*n.* **1** a long, thin piece that has been split off, broken off, or cut off; splinter: *a sliver of wood, a sliver of glass.* **2** a loose fibre of wool, cotton, etc. obtained by carding or combing. —*v.* split or break into slivers. [ult. < OE *slīfan* split]

sliv·o·vitz (sliv'ə vits or slē'və vits) *n.* a usually colorless plum brandy made especially in E Europe.

slob (slob) *n.* **1** an untidy or boorish person. **2** *Cdn.* slob ice. **3** *Irish.* mud. [probably < Irish *slab,* var. of *slaba* mud < Gmc.]

slob·ber (slob'ər) *v., n.* —*v.* **1** let liquid run out from the mouth; drool: *The dog slobbered all over my skirt.* **2** wet or smear with saliva, etc. **3** speak in a silly, sentimental way.
—*n.* **1** saliva or other liquid running out from the mouth. **2** silly, sentimental talk or emotion. [probably ult. < Du. *slobberen*]

slob·ber·y (slob'ər ē) *adj.* **1** slobbering. **2** disagreeably wet; sloppy. —**slob'ber·i·ness,** *n.*

slob ice *Cdn.* a mass of densely packed chunks of heavy, sludgy ice, especially sea ice.

sloe (slō) *n.* **1** the blue-black, tart, plumlike fruit of the blackthorn. **2** blackthorn. [OE *slāh*]

sloe-eyed (slō'īd') *adj.* having very dark eyes.

sloe gin a liqueur made of gin and flavored with sloes.

slog (slog) *v.* **slogged, slog·ging;** *n. Informal.* —*v.* **1** plod heavily: *We slogged through the snow to the cabin.* **2** work hard and steadily: *She slogged away at the hard assignment.* **3** hit hard.
—*n.* **1** a spell of hard, steady work. **2** a hard blow. [var. of *slug²*]

slo·gan (slō'gən) *n.* **1** a word or phrase used by a business, club, political party, etc. to advertise its purpose; motto: *"Service with a smile" was the store's slogan.* **2** war cry. [< Scots Gaelic *sluagh-ghairm* < *sluagh* army + *gairm* cry]

A sloop

GAFF

BOOM

sloop (slüp) *n.* a sailboat having one mast, a mainsail, a jib, and sometimes other sails. [< Du. *sloep,* earlier *sloepe.* Doublet of SHALLOP.]

sloop of war *Historical.* a small warship having guns on the upper deck only.

slop[1] (slop) v. **slopped, slop·ping;** n. —v. **1** spill liquid upon; spill; splash. **2** splash through mud, slush, or water.
slop over, Slang. show too much feeling, enthusiasm, etc.
—n. **1** liquid spilled or splashed about. **2** Often, **slops,** pl. **a** partially liquid kitchen waste. On a farm, slops are often fed to pigs, etc. **b** any liquid or partially liquid waste. **3** a thin liquid mud or slush. **4** weak liquid food, such as gruel. [ME *sloppe* a mud hole; origin uncertain]

slop[2] (slop) n. Usually, **slops,** pl. **1** cheap ready-made clothing. **2** clothes, bedding, etc. supplied to sailors on a ship. **3** loose trousers; wide baggy breeches. [OE *slop,* as in *oferslop* overgarment]

slope (slōp) v. **sloped, slop·ing;** n. —v. **1** lie at an angle or slant; be inclined up or down: *a sloping roof. The land slopes toward the sea.* **2** cause to slant: *He sloped the ground so that rainwater would run away from the basement wall.* —n. **1** any line, surface, land, etc. that goes up or down at an angle: *If you roll a ball up a slope, it will roll down again.* **2** the amount of slope. [OE *-slopen,* pp. of *-slūpan* slip]
☛ *Syn. v.* **1. Slope, slant** = go off at an angle from a straight line or level surface. **Slope** is used chiefly of a surface that goes up or down from a level, usually gradually unless sharpness, steepness, etc. is stated: *The fields slope up to the foothills.* **Slant** is the general word and means "turn or go off noticeably in any degree up, down, or to one side from a line straight up and down or across": *That picture slants to the left.*

slop·py (slop'ē) adj. **-pi·er, -pi·est. 1** very wet; slushy: *sloppy ground, sloppy weather.* **2** splashed or soiled with liquid: *a sloppy table.* **3** Informal. careless; slovenly: *to do sloppy work, to use sloppy English.* **4** Informal. weak; silly: *sloppy sentiment.* **5** loose or baggy; ill-fitting: *sloppy trousers.* —**slop'pi·ly,** adv. —**slop'pi·ness,** n.

slop·shop (slop'shop') n. a store where cheap ready-made clothing is sold.

slosh (slosh) n., v. —n. **1** slush. **2** Informal. a watery or weak drink. —v. **1** splash in slush, mud, or water. **2** go about idly. [? blend of *slop* and *slush*]

sloshed (slosht) adj. Slang. drunk.

slot[1] (slot) n., v. **slot·ted, slot·ting.** —n. **1** a small, narrow opening or groove: *Vending machines have coin slots. We have a letter slot in our front door.* **2** a place or position in a series or scheme: *The new comedy series has a good time slot.* **3** Hockey. **the slot,** the area on the ice two or three paces in front of the goal crease. An offensive forward tries to occupy the slot so as to be in a good position to score when the puck is passed to him.
—v. **1** make a slot or slots in. **2** place in a series or scheme: *The new show will be slotted after the six o'clock news.* [ME < OF *esclot* the hollow between the breasts]

slot[2] (slot) n. a track or trail left by an animal, especially a deer. [< OF *esclot* hoof print, probably < ON *slóth* trail. Akin to SLEUTH.]

sloth (slōth *or* sloth) n. **1** unwillingness to work or exert oneself; laziness; indolence: *His sloth keeps him from engaging in sports.* **2** any of several slow-moving edentate mammals (family Bradypodidae) of Central and South America that dwell in trees, hanging upside down by all four feet from tree branches and feeding on leaves and fruits. [< *slow*]

sloth bear a long-haired bear (*Melursus ursinus*) of S India and Sri Lanka, having a long, flexible snout adapted for feeding on termites.

sloth·ful (slōth'fəl *or* sloth'fəl) adj. unwilling to work or exert oneself; lazy; idle. —**sloth'ful·ly,** adv. —**sloth'ful·ness,** n.

slot machine a coin-operated machine, especially a gambling machine in which one pulls a handle to try to match up a series of symbols.

slouch (slouch) v., n. —v. **1** stand, sit, walk, or move in an awkward, drooping manner: *The weary man slouched along.* **2** droop or bend downward.
—n. **1** a bending forward of head and shoulders; an awkward, drooping way of standing, sitting, or walking. **2** a drooping or bending downward of the brim of a hat, etc. **3** an awkward, slovenly, or inefficient person. [origin uncertain]

slouch hat a soft hat, usually with a broad brim that bends down easily.

slouch·y (slouch'ē) adj. **slouch·i·er, slouch·i·est.** not erect in posture or gait; slouching: *a slouchy walk.*

slough[1] (slü *for 1 - 4; usually slou for 5*) n. **1** Cdn. Western Canada. a body of fresh water formed by rain or melted snow. **2** a soft, deep, muddy place; mud hole. **3** a backwater or side channel of a stream. **4** on the Pacific coast, a shallow or marshy inlet of the sea. **5** a state of hopeless discouragement or degradation. [OE *slōh*]
☛ *Hom.* **slew, slue** (slü).

slough[2] (sluf) n., v. —n. **1** the old skin shed, or cast off, by a snake. **2** a layer of dead skin or tissue that drops or falls off as a wound, sore, etc. heals. **3** anything that has been shed or cast off: *the slough of outmoded ideas, the slough of grief.*
—v. **1** drop off; throw off; shed: *The snake sloughed its skin.* **2** be shed or cast; drop or fall: *A scab sloughs off when new skin takes its place.* **3** cast off as undesirable, bothersome, etc. (*usually used with* **off**): *to slough off a heavy backpack. He sloughed off his depression and started anew.* **4** Card games. discard (a losing card). [ME *slugh(e), slouh* < Gmc.; cf. G *Schlauch* skin, bag]

slough of despond (slou) a state of hopeless dejection; deep despondency.

slough·y[1] (slou'ē) adj. **slough·i·er, slough·i·est.** soft and muddy; full of soft, deep mud. [< *slough*[1]]

slough·y[2] (sluf'ē) adj. of dead skin; covered with dead skin. [< *slough*[2]]

Slo·vak (slō'vak) n. **1** a member of a Slavic people living mainly in Slovakia, a region in E Czechoslovakia. **2** the Slavic language of the Slovaks. —adj. of or having to do with Slovakia, the Slovaks, or their language. [< Czech *Slovák,* originally *Slav*]

Slo·vak·i·an (slō vak'ē ən) adj. or n. Slovak.

slov·en[1] (sluv'ən) n., adj. —n. a person who is untidy, dirty, or careless in dress, appearance, habits, work, etc. —adj. slovenly. [? ult. < Flemish *sloef* dirty, Du. *slof* careless]

slov·en[2] (sluv'ən) n. Cdn. in the Atlantic Provinces, a long, low wagon having a high driver's box; dray. [origin uncertain]

Slo·vene (slō'vēn) n., adj. —n. **1** a member of a Slavic group of people living in Slovenia, a region in NW Yugoslavia. The Slovenes are closely related to the Croats, Serbians, and other southern Slavs. **2** their language. —adj. of or having to do with Slovenia, its people, or their language; Slovenian. [< G < OSlavic *Slovĕne,* literally, speaker < *slovo* word; distinguished from Germans who were called "mutes"]

Slo·ve·ni·an (slō vē'nē ən *or* slō vēn'yən) adj. or n. Slovene.

slov·en·ly (sluv'ən lē) adj. **-li·er, -li·est;** adv. —adj. untidy, dirty, or careless in dress, appearance, habits, work, etc. —adv. in a slovenly manner: *He dresses very slovenly.* —**slov'en·li·ness,** n.

slow (slō) adj., v., adv. —adj. **1** taking a long time; taking longer than usual; not fast or quick: *a slow journey.* **2** behind time; running at less than proper speed: *a slow runner.* **3** indicating time earlier than the correct time: *a slow clock.* **4** causing a low or lower rate of speed: *slow ground, a slow track.* **5** burning or heating slowly or gently: *a slow flame.* **6** sluggish; naturally inactive: *a slow pupil.* **7** dull; not interesting: *a slow party.* **8** not brisk; slack: *Business is slow.* **9** behind the times; not smart or up-to-date: *a slow town.* **10** of time, passing slowly or heavily.
—v. **1** make slow or slower; reduce the speed of: *slow down a car.* **2** become slow; go slower: *Slow up when you drive through a town.* —adv. in a slow manner. [OE *slāw*] —**slow'ly,** adv. —**slow'ness,** n.
☛ *Syn. adj.* **1. Slow, leisurely, deliberate** = taking a long time to do something or to happen. **Slow,** the general term, suggests taking longer than usual or necessary: *We took the slow train.* **Leisurely** suggests slowness because of having plenty of time: *I like leisurely meals.* **Deliberate,** describing people or their acts, suggests slowness due to care, thought, or self-control: *His speech is deliberate.*
☛ *Usage.* **Slow** and **slowly** are both used as adverbs. In most written English **slowly** is preferred, except in certain set phrases (such as *go slow, drive slow*). There is a distinction between *The buses are running slow* (late) and *This bus is going slowly.*

slow·down (slō'down') n. a slowing down: *There has been a slowdown in housing construction lately. The employees' protest took the form of a work slowdown.*

slow match a fuse that burns very slowly, used for setting fire to gunpowder, dynamite, etc.

slow–mo·tion (slō'mō'shən) adj. **1** moving at less than normal speed. **2** showing action at much less than its actual speed.

slow–poke (slō'pōk') n. Informal. a person who moves, works, or acts very slowly.

slow time standard time, as opposed to daylight saving time, which is often called fast time: *We go back on slow time in fall.*

slow–wit·ted (slō'wit'id) adj. slow at thinking; dull; stupid.

slow·worm (slō'wèrm') n. blindworm.

sloyd (sloid) n. a system of manual training by means of graded courses in woodworking, etc., originating in Sweden. Also, **sloid, slojd.** [< Swedish *slöjd* skill]

S.Lt or **SLt** sub-lieutenant.

slub (slub) v. **slubbed, slub·bing;** n. —v. twist (wool, yarn, etc.) slightly before spinning. —n. **1** a slightly twisted piece of cotton, silk, or wool. **2** an uneven lump in a strand of yarn. [cf. MDu. *slubbe*]

sludge (sluj) n. **1** soft mud; mire. **2** a soft, thick, muddy mixture, deposit, sediment, etc., such as that produced in sewage treatment

processes. 3 small pieces of newly formed sea ice. [origin uncertain]

sludg·y (sluj′ē) *adj.* **sludg·i·er, sludg·i·est.** like or containing sludge.

slue¹ (slü) *v.* **slued, slu·ing;** *n.* See **slew².**
☞ *Hom.* **slough¹** (slü).

slue² (slü) *n.* slough¹.
☞ *Hom.* **slew.**

slug¹ (slug) *n.* **1** any of various mainly terrestrial gastropod molluscs resembling snails but having no shell or only a rudimentary shell. **2** any of various other invertebrates having a soft, slimy body, such as the caterpillars of certain moths. **3** *Informal.* a slow-moving person, animal, or vehicle. **4** bullet. **5** a roughly shaped, roundish lump of metal. **6** a small disk, such as one used illegally instead of a coin in a coin-operated machine. **7** *Printing.* **a** a strip of metal used to space lines of type. A slug is thicker than a printer's lead. **b** a line of type cast in one piece by a linotype machine. [ME *slugg* sluggard, ? < Scand.; cf. dial. Swedish *slogga* be sluggish]

slug² (slug) *v.* **slugged, slug·ging;** *n. Informal.* —*v.* hit hard with the fist, a bat, or a blunt weapon. —*n.* **1** a hard blow. **2** *Slang.* a drink; shot: *a slug of whisky.* [origin uncertain] —**slug′ger,** *n.*

slug·gard (slug′ərd) *n., adj.* —*n.* a person who is habitually lazy and idle. —*adj.* lazy; idle. [ME < *slug* be slothful + *-ard,* personal suffix with derogatory sense, as in *drunkard.* See SLUG¹.]

slug·gish (slug′ish) *adj.* **1** slow; lacking energy or vigor: *a sluggish mind.* **2** very slow in movement, growth or flow: *a sluggish river, sluggish blood circulation. The economy has been sluggish for the past few months.* **3** lazy or idle. [< *slug¹*] —**slug′gish·ly,** *adv.* —**slug′gish·ness,** *n.*

sluice (slüs) *n., v.* **sluiced, sluic·ing.** —*n.* **1** a structure having a gate for holding back or controlling the water of a canal, river, or lake. **2** a gate that holds back or controls the flow of water. When the water behind a dam gets too high, the sluices are opened. **3** the water held back or controlled by such a gate. **4** something that controls the flow or passage of anything: *War opens the sluices of hatred and bloodshed.* **5** a long, sloping trough through which water flows, used to wash gold from sand, dirt, or gravel. **6** a channel for carrying off overflow or surplus water.
—*v.* **1** let out or draw off (water) by opening a sluice. **2** flow or pour in a stream: *Water sluiced down the channel.* **3** flush or cleanse with a rush of water; pour or throw water over. **4** wash (gold) from sand, dirt, or gravel in a sluice. **5** send (logs, etc.) along a channel of water. [ME < OF *escluse,* ult. < L *ex-* out + *claudere* shut]

sluice–box (slüs′boks′) *n. Placer mining. Historical.* a long sluice fitted with riffles, in which gold is separated from gravel, muck, etc.

sluice gate a gate to control the flow of water in a sluice.

slum (slum) *n., v.* **slummed, slum·ming.** —*n.* Often, **slums,** *pl.* a district or area in a city characterized by overpopulation, poor housing and sanitation, and social problems. —*v.* visit slums or other places considered inferior to one's usual surroundings, especially out of curiosity or for amusement. [origin uncertain]

slum·ber (slum′bər) *v., n.* —*v.* **1** sleep, especially in a peaceful manner. **2** pass in sleep: *to slumber away the morning hours.* **3** be inactive, dormant, or negligent: *The volcano had slumbered for years. The incident awakened his slumbering conscience.*
—*n.* **1** sometimes, **slumbers,** *pl.* sleep: *The child was deep in slumber. Her slumbers were interrupted by the sound of a siren.* **2** an inactive, dormant, or negligent state or condition. [ult. < OE *slūma,* n.] —**slum′ber·er,** *n.*

slum·ber·ous (slum′bər əs *or* slum′brəs) *adj.* **1** sleepy; heavy with drowsiness: *slumberous eyelids.* **2** causing or inducing sleep. **3** characterized by or suggestive of a state of sleep or inactivity: *the slumberous calm of a summer evening.* —**slum′ber·ous·ly,** *adv.*

slum·brous (slum′brəs) *adj.* slumberous. —**slum′brous·ly,** *adv.*

slum·lord (slum′lôrd′) *n. Informal.* an absentee owner of slum property, especially one who charges exorbitant rent.

slum·mer (slum′ər) *n.* a person who visits slums for charitable purposes, curiosity, etc.

slum·my (slum′ē) *adj.* of, having to do with, or like a slum.

slump (slump) *v., n.* —*v.* **1** drop or fall suddenly: *He slumped to the floor in a dead faint.* **2** have or assume a drooping posture: *The bored students slumped in their seats, waiting for the bell.* **3** go into a marked decline: *Business has slumped.*
—*n.* **1** a great or sudden decline in prices, activity, etc. **2** a long period during which a person is not working or performing as well as usual: *The team's pitcher is in a slump and they have lost several games in a row.* [? imitative]

slung (slung) *v.* pt. and pp. of **sling.**

slung shot a piece of metal, stone, etc. fastened to a short strap, chain, etc., used as a weapon.

hat, āge, fär; let, ēqual, tėrm; it, īce
hot, ōpen, ôrder; oil, out; cup, pùt, rüle,
əbove, takən, pencəl, lemən, circəs
ch, child; ng, long; sh, ship
th, thin; ᴛʜ, then; zh, measure

slunk (slungk) *v.* a pt. and a pp. of **slink.**

slur (slėr) *v.* **slurred, slur·ring;** *n.* —*v.* **1** pass lightly over; go through hurriedly or in a careless way. **2** pronounce indistinctly: *Many persons slur "How do you do?"* **3** speak or write sounds, letters, etc. so indistinctly that they run into each other. **4** *Music.* **a** sing or play (two or more tones of different pitch) without a break; run together in a smooth, connected manner. **b** mark with a slur. **5** harm the reputation of; insult; slight.
—*n.* **1** a slurred pronunciation, sound, etc. **2** *Music.* **a** a slurring of tones. **b** a curved mark (⌢)(⌣) indicating this. **3** a blot or stain (upon reputation); an insulting or slighting remark: *Malicious rumor left a slur on his good name.* [ME *slor* mud]

slurp (slėrp) *v., n. Informal.* —*v.* eat or drink noisily or with a sucking sound. —*n.* a slurping sound. [< Du. *slurpen* lap]

slur·ry (slėr′ē) *n., pl.* **-ries;** *v.* —*n.* a thin mixture of water and an insoluble substance such as cement, mud, or clay. —*v.* make into a slurry. [related to SLUR]

slush (slush) *n.* **1** partly melted snow; snow and water mixed. **2** soft mud. **3** *Informal.* silly, sentimental talk, writing, etc. **4** grease. [origin uncertain]

slush fund money collected or set aside for dishonest purposes, such as bribery or improper political or business lobbying.

slush hole *Cdn.* especially in the North, a patch of rotten ice on the surface of a lake or river.

slush·y (slush′ē) *adj.* **slush·i·er, slush·i·est.** **1** covered with slush; having much slush: *a slushy sidewalk.* **2** made up of or like slush: *slushy snow.* —**slush′i·ness,** *n.*

slut (slut) *n.* **1** a slovenly, untidy woman; slattern. **2** a woman of loose morals. **3** *Archaic.* a bold or saucy girl. [ME *slutte, slotte;* origin uncertain]

slut·tish (slut′ish) *adj.* having to do with, like, or characteristic of a slut. —**slut′tish·ly,** *adv.* —**slut′tish·ness,** *n.*

sly (slī) *adj.* **sly·er** *or* **sli·er, sly·est** *or* **sli·est;** *n.* —*adj.* **1** clever in deceiving or tricking: *The sly cat stole the meat while the cook's back was turned.* **2** not straightforward or open; cleverly underhanded; crafty: *Her sly questions were intended to get them to reveal more than they realized. They had developed a sly scheme for taking over control of the organization.* **3** playfully mischievous or knowing: *a sly wink.*
—*n.*

on the sly, in a way meant to avoid notice; secretly: *They got their information on the sly.*
[ME *slēgh* skilful < ON *slǣgr,* originally, able to strike < *slá* slay] —**sly′ly,** *adv.* —**sly′ness,** *n.*
☞ *Syn. adj.* **2. Sly, cunning** = having or showing ability to get what one wants by secret or indirect means. **Sly** emphasizes lack of frankness and straightforwardness, and suggests stealthy actions or secrecy and deceit in dealing with others: *That sly girl managed to get her best friend's job.* **Cunning** emphasizes an instinctive cleverness in getting the better of others by tricks or schemes, unfair dealing, or cheating: *They were cunning enough to get complete control of the company.*

Sm samarium.

S.M. Sergeant-Major.

smack¹ (smak) *n., v.* —*n.* **1** a slight taste or flavor: *The sauce had a smack of nutmeg.* **2** a trace; suggestion: *The old sailor still had a smack of the sea about him.* **3** heroin.
—*v.* have a smack: *The Irishman's speech smacked of the Old Country.* [OE *smæcc*]

smack² (smak) *v., n., adv.* —*v.* **1** open (the lips) quickly so as to make a sharp sound. **2** kiss loudly. **3** slap. **4** crack (a whip, etc.).
—*n.* **1** a sharp sound made by opening the lips quickly. **2** a loud kiss. **3** a slap or crack.
—*adv. Informal.* suddenly and sharply; with or as if with a smack. [ult. imitative]

smack³ (smak) *n.* **1** a small sailboat with one mast. **2** a similar fishing boat with a well for keeping fish alive. [probably < Du. *smak*]

smack·er (smak′ər) *n.* **1** one that smacks. **2** *Informal.* a resounding kiss; smack. **3** *Slang.* dollar.

smack·ing (smak′ing) *adj.* lively, brisk, or strong.

small (smol *or* smôl) *adj., adv., n.* —*adj.* **1** not large; little; not large as compared with other things of the same kind: *a small house.* **2** not great in amount, degree, extent, duration, value,

strength, etc.: *a small dose, small hope of success. The cent is our smallest coin.* **3** not important: *a small matter.* **4** not prominent; of low social position; humble; poor: *People great and small mourned Laurier's death.* **5** having little land, capital, etc.: *a small farmer, a small dealer.* **6** gentle; soft; low: *a small voice, a small crumbling sound.* **7** mean: *A man with a small nature is not generous.* **8** of letters, not capital.

feel small, be ashamed or humiliated.

—*adv.* **1** into small pieces. **2** in low tones.

sing small, change to a humble tone or manner.

—*n.* **1** something that is small; a small, slender, or narrow part or thing: *the small of the back.* **2 smalls,** *pl. Esp.Brit. Informal.* small articles of clothing, especially underwear. [OE *smæl*] —**small′ness,** *n.*

☛ *Syn. adj.* **1.** See note at **little.**

small arms weapons easily carried by a person, and held in the hand or hands while being fired: *Rifles and revolvers are classed as small arms.*

small beer **1** weak beer. **2** matters of little or no consequence.

small capital a type of capital letter about the same height as a lower case x in the same type size and face. Small capitals are often used for acronyms or abbreviations in printed materials. *Examples:* A.D. 1066, UNICEF Christmas cards.

small change **1** coins of small value, such as nickels, dimes, etc. **2** anything small and unimportant.

small claims court a court with limited jurisdiction for dealing in an informal and inexpensive way with civil cases involving small claims for breach of contract or debt.

small·clothes (smol′klōz′ *or* -klōᵺz′, smôl′klōz′ *or* -klōᵺz′) *n. pl.* knee breeches, especially, close-fitting ones.

small fry **1** babies or children; small or young creatures. **2** small fish. **3** unimportant people or things.

small hours the early hours of the morning.

small intestine the long, narrow part of the intestine where most of the absorption of digested food takes place, extending from the stomach to the large intestine. In adults the small intestine is more than six metres long. See **alimentary canal** for picture.

small·ish (smol′ish *or* smôl′ish) *adj.* somewhat small.

small letter a lower-case letter, not a capital.

small–mind·ed (smol′mīn′did *or* smôl′-) *adj.* petty or mean. —**small′-mind′ed·ness,** *n.*

small potatoes *Informal.* an unimportant person or thing or group of persons or things: *The last deal was just small potatoes, compared with what she's planning now.*

small·pox (smol′poks′ *or* smôl′-) *n.* an acute, contagious virus disease characterized by fever and blisterlike eruptions on the skin that usually leave permanent pitlike scars, called pockmarks.

small–scale (smol′skāl′ *or* smôl′-) *adj.* **1** small in operation or scope; limited: *He runs a small-scale import business.* **2** of a map, etc., drawn to a small scale, not permitting much detail.

small talk light, informal conversation; chit-chat.

small–time (smol′tīm′ *or* smôl′-) *adj. Slang.* minor, petty, or insignificant: *a small-time crook. His business ventures are strictly small-time.*

small–town (smol′toun′ *or* smôl′-) *adj.* **1** of or coming from a small town. **2** narrow; provincial: *small-town bigotry.*

smarm (smärm) *v. Brit. Informal.* act in a toadying or obsequiously flattering way. [var. of dial. *smalm* plaster down]

smarm·y (smärm′ē) *adj. Brit. Informal.* obsequiously flattering; toadying.

smart (smärt) *v., n., adj., adv.* —*v.* **1** feel sharp pain: *His eyes smarted.* **2** cause sharp pain: *The cut smarts.* **3** feel distress or irritation: *He smarted from the scolding.* **4** suffer: *He will smart for this.*

—*n.* a sharp pain.

—*adj.* **1** sharp; severe: *He gave the horse a smart blow.* **2** keen; active; lively: *They walked at a smart pace.* **3** clever; bright: *a smart child.* **4** fresh and neat; in good order: *He looked smart in his uniform.* **5** stylish; fashionable. **6** *Informal or dialect.* fairly large; considerable. **7** witty, humorous, or clever in an annoying way. —*adv.* in a smart manner. [OE *smeortan,* v., *smeart,* adj.] —**smart′ly,** *adv.* —**smart′ness,** *n.*

smart al·eck *or* **al·ec** (al′ik) an obnoxious person who tries to show that he is cleverer or more knowledgeable than others. —**smart′-a′leck·y** *or* **smart′-a′leck** *or* **-a′lec,** *adj.*

smart·en (smär′tən) *v.* **1** improve in appearance; brighten. **2** make or become brisker.

smart·weed (smärt′wēd′) *n.* any of several weedy plants (genus

Polygonum) of the buckwheat family typically having lance-shaped leaves and erect or drooping spikes of tiny greenish, pink, or white flowers, and some of which have a stinging, acid taste.

smash (smash) *v., n.* —*v.* **1** break into pieces with violence and noise: *to smash a window.* **2** destroy; shatter; ruin: *to smash an argument.* **3** be broken to pieces: *The dishes smashed on the floor.* **4** become ruined. **5** rush violently; crash: *The car smashed into a tree.* **6** crush; defeat: *to smash an attack.* **7** in tennis or baseball, hit (a ball) with a hard, fast, overhand stroke. **8** *Informal.* hit a hard blow.

—*n.* **1** the action or an instance of smashing: *The two cars collided with a terrific smash.* **2** the sound of a smash: *We heard the smash of broken glass but couldn't see anything.* **3** (*advl.*) with a smash: *I drove smash into the fence.* **4** a crushing defeat; disaster. **5** a business failure; bankruptcy. **6** *Tennis or baseball.* a hard, fast overhand stroke. **7** *Informal.* a hard blow. **8** a drink made of water, mint, sugar, and brandy or other alcoholic liquor. **9** *Informal.* a smash hit.

to smash, **a** into broken pieces; into bits. **b** to ruin.

[a blend of *smack²* and *mash*]

☛ *Syn. v.* **1.** See note at **break.**

smashed (smasht) *adj. Slang.* very drunk or high on drugs.

smash hit a very successful play, motion picture, recording, etc.

smash·ing (smash′ing) *adj. Informal.* fine; excellent; splendid.

smash–up (smash′up′) *n.* **1** a bad collision of motor vehicles. **2** complete collapse or failure; ruin.

smat·ter (smat′ər) *n.* smattering. [cf. Swedish *smattra* rattle]

smat·ter·ing (smat′ər ing) *n.* a slight or superficial knowledge of a language or a subject: *He has a smattering of Italian that he picked up on a visit to Italy last summer.*

smear (smēr) *v., n.* **1** cover or stain with anything sticky, greasy, or dirty: *Her fingers were smeared with jam.* **2** rub or spread (oil, grease, paint, etc.). **3** blur or make a streak across (a drawing, writing, etc.): *The corner of the painting was smeared a bit while it was still wet.* **4** receive a mark or stain; be smeared: *Wet paint smears easily.* **5** harm the reputation of; slander: *She attempted to smear her opponent by suggesting that he had accepted bribes while in office.*

—*n.* **1** mark or stain left by smearing. **2** a small amount of something, such as blood, spread on a slide for examination with a microscope. **3** a charge or accusation, usually without any basis, against a person, group, etc.: *the smear was unsuccessful.* **4** (*adj.*) of or characterized by such charges or accusations: *a smear campaign.* [OE *smerian, smirian < smeoru* grease]

smear·y (smēr′ē) *adj.* **smear·i·er, smear·i·est.** **1** smeared. **2** tending to smear. —**smear′i·ness,** *n.*

smell (smel) *v.* **smelled** *or* **smelt, smell·ing;** *n.* —*v.* **1** perceive with the nose: *I smell smoke in the air.* **2** detect or recognize smells. **3** give out a smell. **4** give out a bad smell; have a bad smell. **5** find a trace or suggestion of: *We smelled trouble.* **6** have the smell (*of*); have the trace (*or*): *The plan smells of trickery.* **7** hunt or find by smelling or as if by smelling: *The dog will smell out a thief.*

smell up, *Informal.* cause to have a bad smell: *That garbage is smelling up the whole house.*

—*n.* **1** the act of smelling; sniff. **2** the sense of smelling: *Smell is keener in dogs than in people.* **3** the quality in a thing that affects the sense of smell: *the smell of burning cloth.* **4** a trace; suggestion. [ME *smelle(n);* origin uncertain] —**smell′er,** *n.*

☛ *Syn. n.* **3. Smell, odor, scent** = the property or quality of a thing that affects the sense organs of the nose. **Smell** is the general word, used especially when the effect on the sense organs is emphasized, but often suggests that the effect is unpleasant: *He never got used to the farmyard smells.* **Odor** is often interchanged with **smell,** but is neutral and applies particularly to the actual property or quality itself, as belonging to and coming from what is smelled: *I find the odor of hay especially pleasing.* **Scent** also emphasizes the actual property or quality, but is usually used when the effect is pleasant or favorable: *She loves the scent of roses.*

smelling salts a form of ammonia that, when inhaled, helps to relieve faintness, headaches, etc.

smell·y (smel′ē) *adj.* **smell·i·er, smell·i·est.** giving off a strong, unpleasant odor.

smelt¹ (smelt) *v.* **1** melt (ore) in order to get the metal out of it. **2** obtain (metal) from ore by melting. **3** refine (impure metal) by melting. [< MDu. *or* MLG *smelten*]

smelt² (smelt) *n., pl.* **smelt** *or* **smelts.** **1** any of various small, edible fishes (family Osmeridae) having a long, slender, silvery body and two dorsal fins. The **rainbow smelt** (*Osmerus mordax*), found in the Great Lakes and along northern and arctic coasts, is a commercially important food fish. **2** (*adj.*) designating the family (Osmeridae) that includes the smelts and the oolichan and caplin. [OE]

smelt³ (smelt) *v.* a pt. and a pp. of **smell.**

smelt·er (smel′tər) *n.* **1** a person whose work or business is smelting ores or metals. **2** an establishment or plant where smelting is done.

smid·gen or **smid·gin** (smij′ən) *n. Informal.* a tiny piece or amount; mite. [origin uncertain]

smi·lax (smī′laks) *n.* 1 any of a genus (*Smilax*) of woody or herbaceous, often prickly, vines found in warm and tropical regions, having clusters of yellowish-green or white flowers and bluish-black or red berries. 2 a twining plant (*Asparagus asparagoides*) of the lily family having shiny, bright-green, flattened, leaflike stems. It is often cultivated by florists. [< L < Gk.]

smile (smīl) *v.* **smiled, smil·ing;** *n.* —*v.* 1 look pleased or amused; show pleasure, favor, kindness, amusement, etc. by an upward curve of the mouth. 2 look pleasant or agreeable; look with favor. 3 bring, put, drive, etc. by smiling: *Smile your tears away.* 4 give (a smile): *She smiled a sunny smile.* 5 express by a smile: *She smiled consent.* 6 show scorn, disdain, etc. by a curve of the mouth: *She smiled bitterly.*
—*n.* 1 the act of smiling. 2 a favoring look or regard; a pleasant look or aspect. [ME *smile(n)*] —**smil′er,** *n.* —**smil′ing·ly,** *adv.*

smirch (smėrch) *v., n.* —*v.* 1 make dirty; soil or stain with soot, dirt, dust, etc. 2 bring dishonor or disgrace on; sully: *to smirch one's reputation.* —*n.* 1 a dirty mark; a smear or stain. 2 dishonor or disgrace. [ME *smorch;* ? < OF *esmorcher* torture, ult. < L *ex-* (intensive) + LL *mordicare* bite]

smirk (smėrk) *v., n.* —*v.* smile in a knowing, self-satisfied way. —*n.* a knowing or self-satisfied smile. [OE *smearcian* smile]

smit (smit) *v.* a pp. and an obsolete pt. of **smite.**

smite (smīt) *v.* **smote, smit·ten** or **smit, smit·ing.** 1 *Archaic or poetic.* strike or hit hard: *The hero smote the giant with his sword.* 2 have a sudden, strong effect on: *The thief's conscience smote him.* 3 *Archaic or poetic.* come with force (*upon*): *The waves smote upon the shore.* *The sound of a blacksmith's hammer smote upon their ears.* 4 *Archaic or poetic.* strike down; punish severely, or destroy. [OE *smītan*] —**smit′er,** *n.*

smith (smith) *n.* 1 a person who makes or shapes things out of metal (*used mainly in compounds*): *a goldsmith, a tinsmith.* 2 blacksmith. [OE]

smith·er·eens (smiɪH′ər ēnz′) *n.pl. Informal.* small pieces; bits: *The plate was smashed to smithereens.* [apparently from Irish *smidirín* fragments. Akin to SMITE.]

smith·y (smith′ē or smiɪH′ē) *n., pl.* **smith·ies.** the workshop of a smith, especially a blacksmith. [ME < ON *smithja.* Akin to SMITH.]

smit·ten (smit′ən) *adj., v.* —*adj.* 1 hard hit; struck: *sudden sparks from smitten steel.* 2 suddenly and strongly affected: *smitten with terror.* 3 *Informal.* very much in love: *He's really smitten.*
—*v.* pp. of **smite.**

smock (smok) *n., v.* —*n.* a loose, coatlike outer garment, usually of cotton, worn to protect clothing. —*v.* ornament with smocking: *The little girl's dress was smocked from the neckline to the waist.* [OE *smocc*]

smock·ing (smok′ing) *n.* decorative stitching used on clothing, made by gathering material closely with rows of stitches in a honeycomb pattern.

smog (smog) *n.* a combination in the air of smoke or other chemical fumes and fog. [a blend of *smoke* and *fog*]

smoke (smōk) *n., v.* **smoked, smok·ing.** —*n.* 1 the visible mixture of gases and particles of carbon that rises when anything burns; a cloud from anything burning. 2 something resembling this. 3 something unsubstantial, quickly passing, or without result. 4 that which is smoked; a cigar, cigarette, pipe, etc. 5 the act or period of smoking tobacco.
—*v.* 1 give off smoke, steam, etc.: *The fireplace smokes.* 2 draw the smoke from (a pipe, cigar, or cigarette) into the mouth and puff it out again. 3 preserve or flavor (meat, fish, etc.) by exposing to smoke. 4 drive out or away by smoke, or as if by smoke. 5 make, bring, pass, etc. by smoking. 6 color, darken, or stain with smoke. 7 *Archaic.* find out; suspect; notice.
smoke out, a drive out with smoke. **b** find out and make known. [OE *smoca*]

smoke bomb a kind of bomb containing chemicals that give out dense smoke when the bomb bursts.

smoke drift a cloud of smoke seen at a distance and indicating a forest fire.

smoke·house (smōk′hous′) *n.* a building where meat or fish is treated with smoke to preserve and flavor it.

smoke·jump·er (smōk′jump′ər) *n.* a person who is trained and equipped to fight forest fires and who is parachuted into an area where there is a fire.

smoke·less (smōk′lis) *adj.* having or producing no smoke: *Anthracite coal burns with an almost smokeless flame.*

smokeless powder a substitute for ordinary gun powder that gives off little or no smoke when it explodes.

smok·er (smōk′ər) *n.* 1 a person who smokes tobacco. 2 a railway car or compartment where smoking is permitted. 3 an

hat, āge, fär; let, ēqual, tėrm; it, īce
hot, ōpen, ôrder; oil, out; cup, pu̇t, rüle,
əbove, takən, pencəl, lemən, circəs

ch, child; ng, long; sh, ship
th, thin; ɪH, then; zh, measure

informal gathering of men for smoking, card-playing, and other entertainment.

smoke screen 1 a mass of thick smoke used to hide a ship, aircraft, etc. from the enemy. 2 anything that hides or obscures a plan, project, etc.: *a smoke screen of false information.*

smoke·stack (smōk′stak′) *n.* 1 a tall chimney. 2 a pipe that discharges smoke, etc.: *the smokestack of a boat.*

smoke tree either of two small trees (genus *Cotinus*) of the cashew family having large, feathery clusters of tiny flowers that from a distance look like puffs of smoke. One species (*C. americanus*) is native to North America; the other (*C. coggygria*) is Eurasian.

smok·y (smōk′ē) *adj.* **smok·i·er, smok·i·est.** 1 giving off much smoke: *a smoky fire.* 2 full of smoke. 3 darkened or stained with smoke. 4 like smoke or suggesting smoke: *a smoky grey, a smoky taste.* —**smok′i·ly,** *adv.* —**smok′i·ness,** *n.*

smol·der (smōl′dər) See **smoulder.**

smolt (smōlt) *n.* a young salmon or sea trout, usually two or three years old, that has turned silvery in color and is preparing to migrate from a stream or lake to the sea or from a stream to a large lake. Compare **parr.** [ME. Probably related to SMELT[2].]

smooch (smüch) *v., n. Slang.* —*v.* kiss or pet. —*n.* a kiss.

smooth (smüɪH) *adj., v., adv., n.* —*adj.* 1 having an even surface, like glass, silk, or still water; flat; level: *smooth stones.* 2 free from unevenness or roughness: *smooth sailing, a smooth voyage.* 3 without lumps: *smooth sauce.* 4 without hair: *a smooth face.* 5 without trouble or difficulty; easy: *a smooth course of affairs.* 6 calm; serene: *a smooth temper.* 7 polished; pleasant; polite: *That salesman is a smooth talker.* 8 not harsh in sound or taste: *smooth verses, smooth wine.*
—*v.* 1 make smooth or smoother: *Smooth this dress with a hot iron. He smoothed out the ball of crushed paper and read it.* 2 make easy.
smooth away, get rid of (troubles, difficulties, etc.).
smooth down, calm; soothe.
smooth over, make (something) seem less wrong, unpleasant, or noticeable: *The teacher tried to smooth over the argument between the two boys.*
—*adv.* in a smooth manner.
—*n.* 1 the act of smoothing. 2 a smooth part or place. [OE *smōth*] —**smooth′er,** *n.* —**smooth′ly,** *adv.* —**smooth′ness,** *n.*

smooth·bore (smüɪH′bôr′) *adj., n.* —*adj.* of a gun, having no grooves on the inside of the barrel; not rifled. —*n.* a gun having a barrel with a smooth bore.

smooth·faced (smüɪH′fāst′) *adj.* 1 having a smooth face; beardless or clean-shaven: *a smooth-faced youth.* 2 having a smooth surface: *smooth-faced brick.* 3 having the appearance of being agreeable and sincere: *a smooth-faced hypocrite.*

smooth·ie or **smooth·y** (smü′ɪHē) *n., pl.* **smooth·ies.** *Slang.* a smooth, persuasive, often insincere person.

smooth–spo·ken (smüɪH′spō′kən) *adj.* speaking easily and pleasantly; polished in speech.

smooth–tongued (smüɪH′tungd′) *adj.* speaking smoothly and agreeably; suave and plausible: *a smooth-tongued liar.*

smor·gas·bord (smôr′gəs bôrd′) *n.* a buffet meal, featuring a large variety of meats, salads, etc. [< Swedish *smörgåsbord* hors d'oeuvres < *smörgås* open sandwich + *bord* table]

smote (smōt) *v.* a pt. of **smite.**

smoth·er (smuɪH′ər) *v., n.* —*v.* 1 make unable to get air; kill by depriving of air: *The murderer smothered his victim with a pillow.* 2 be unable to breathe freely; suffocate: *We almost smothered in that stuffy room.* 3 cover thickly: *In the fall the grass is smothered with leaves.* 4 deaden or put out by covering thickly: *The fire is smothered by ashes.* 5 keep back; check; suppress: *He smothered a sharp reply.* 6 cook in a covered pot or baking dish: *smothered chicken, smothered cabbage.*
—*n.* 1 a cloud of dust, smoke, spray, etc. 2 anything that smothers. 3 the condition of being smothered. [ME *smorther,* n., based on OE *smorian* suffocate] —**smoth′er·er,** *n.*

smoth·er·y (smuɪH′ər ē) *adj.* tending to smother; full of dust, smoke, spray, etc.

smoul·der or **smol·der** (smōl′dər) *v., n.* —*v.* 1 burn and

smoke without flame: *The fire smouldered most of the night.* **2** exist or continue in a suppressed condition: *The people's discontent smouldered for years before it broke out into open rebellion.* **3** show suppressed feeling: *The man's eyes smouldered with anger.*
—*n.* a slow, smoky burning without flame. [ME *smolderen*; akin to Du. *smeulen*]

smudge (smuj) *n., v.* **smudged, smudg·ing.** —*n.* **1** a dirty mark; smear. **2** a smoky fire made to drive away insects or to protect plants from frost. —*v.* **1** mark with dirty streaks; smear: *The child's drawing was smudged.* **2** use a smudge or smudges, especially in an orchard. [origin uncertain]

smudg·y (smuj′ē) *adj.* **smudg·i·er, smudg·i·est.** smudged; marked with smudges. —**smudg′i·ly,** *adv.* —**smudg′i·ness,** *n.*

smug (smug) *adj.* **smug·ger, smug·gest. 1** too pleased with one's own goodness, cleverness, respectability, etc.; self-satisfied; complacent: *Nothing disturbs the smug beliefs of some narrow-minded people.* **2** sleek; neat; trim. [originally, neat, spruce; probably < Du. or LG *smuk* spruce, adj.] —**smug′ly,** *adv.* —**smug′ness,** *n.*

smug·gle (smug′əl) *v.* **-gled, -gling. 1** secretly bring into or take out of a country something that is prohibited by law or without paying the duty required: *to smuggle heroin, to smuggle watches.* **2** bring, take, put, etc. secretly: *Rob tried to smuggle his puppy into the house.* [< LG *smuggeln*] —**smug′gler,** *n.*

smut (smut) *n., v.* **smut·ted, smut·ting.** —*n.* **1** soot, dirt, etc. **2** a place soiled with smut. **3** indecent or obscene talk, writing, or pictures. **4** any of various plant diseases caused by fungi of the order Ustilaginales, affecting mainly cereal grasses and characterized by the formation of sooty masses of spores on the affected plant parts. **5** any fungus causing such a disease.
—*v.* **1** soil or be soiled with smut. **2** affect (a plant or crop) with smut. **3** of a plant or crop, become affected with smut. [OE *smitte*; influenced by *smudge, smutch*]

smutch (smuch) *n.* or *v. Archaic.* smudge. [origin uncertain. Related to SMUDGE.]

smut·ty (smut′ē) *adj.* **-ti·er, -ti·est. 1** soiled with smut, soot, etc.; dirty. **2** indecent or obscene with smut. **3** of a plant, affected with smut. —**smut′ti·ness,** *n.*

Sn tin (for L *stannum*).

snack (snak) *n., v.* —*n.* a light meal: *He eats a snack before going to bed.* —*v.* eat a snack. [< MLG *snakken*]

snack bar a counter where light meals, coffee, etc. are served.

snaf·fle (snaf′əl) *n., v.* **-fled, -fling.** —*n.* a slender, jointed bit used on a bridle. —*v.* **1** control or manage by a snaffle. **2** *Informal.* pilfer; steal. [cf. Du. *snavel* beak]

sna·fu (sna fü′) *adj., n., v.* **-fued, -fu·ing.** *Slang.* —*adj.* being in a characteristic state of confusion and disorder.
—*n.* confusion; chaos.
—*v.* put into disorder and confusion. [from the initial letters of "situation normal—all fouled up"]

snag (snag) *n., v.* **snagged, snag·ging.** —*n.* **1** a tree or branch held fast in a river or lake. Snags are dangerous to boats. **2** any sharp or rough projecting point, such as the broken end of a branch. **3** the stump of a tooth; projecting tooth. **4** a hidden or unexpected obstacle: *He had to drop his plans because of a snag.* **5** a pulled or broken thread in fabric.
—*v.* **1** hinder. **2** run or catch on a snag. **3** clear of snags. **4** tear or pull (fabric) so as to make a snag. [? < Scand.; cf. dial. Norwegian *snage* point of land]

snag·gle·tooth (snag′əl tüth′) *n., pl.* **-teeth.** a tooth that grows apart from or beyond the others.

snag·gle-toothed (snag′əl tütht′) *adj.* having uneven, broken, or projecting teeth.

snag·gy (snag′ē) *adj.* **-gi·er, -gi·est. 1** having snags: *a snaggy tree, a snaggy river.* **2** projecting sharply or roughly.

snail (snāl) *n.* **1** any gastropod mollusc having an external, spirally coiled shell, especially those species that live on land or in fresh water. **2** a lazy or slow-moving person or animal. [OE *snegel*]

snake (snāk) *n., v.* **snaked, snak·ing.** —*n.* **1** any of a large suborder (Serpentes, also called Ophidia) of reptiles having an extremely elongated, scaly-skinned body, no legs, no movable eyelids, and no external ears, and moving by means of undulations of the body. Snakes and lizards constitute the order Squamata. **2** a sly, treacherous person. **3** a long, flexible metal rod used to clear drainpipes of obstructions.
—*v.* **1** move, wind, or curve like a snake. **2** *Informal.* drag; haul. **3** *Informal.* jerk. [OE *snaca*] —**snake′like′,** *adj.*

snake·bird (snāk′bėrd′) *n.* any of a genus (*Anhinga*, constituting the family Anhingidae) of large aquatic birds found in tropical and warm temperate regions, having a long, straight, pointed bill, a long, slender neck and a long, broad tail. Snakebirds belong to the same order as pelicans and cormorants.

snake·bite (snāk′bīt′) *n.* **1** the bite of a snake, especially a poisonous one. **2** the condition resulting from the bite of a poisonous snake.

snake charmer a person who entertains an audience by demonstrating an apparent power to hypnotize, or charm, poisonous snakes.

snake dance 1 an informal single-file procession of people who join hands and dance in a weaving path through buildings, streets, etc., especially as part of an athletic victory celebration. **2** a ceremonial dance among certain peoples in which snakes are handled, invoked, etc. The Hopi Indian people of the SW United States have a traditional snake dance.

snake fence a fence made of horizontal tiers of wooden rails laid zigzag so that their ends overlap at an angle.

snake in the grass a person who seems to be a friend but is actually faithless; a secret enemy.

snake pit 1 a pit filled with snakes. **2** a place of utter confusion and distress; especially, a mental hospital that is overcrowded and where patients are not properly cared for.

snake·root (snāk′rüt′) *n.* any of various plants whose roots have at some time been used as a remedy for snakebite. Two North American species are **black snakeroot** (*Sanicula marilandica*) and **white snakeroot** (*Eupatorium urticaefolium*).

snake·skin (snāk′skin′) *n.* **1** the skin of a snake. **2** a leather made from it.

snak·y (snāk′ē) *adj.* **snak·i·er, snak·i·est. 1** of or like a snake or snakes. **2** curving, turning, or twisting, suggesting the movements of a snake: *a snaky path up the hillside.* **3** having many snakes. **4** sly; venomous; treacherous. —**snak′i·ly,** *adv.* —**snak′i·ness,** *n.*

snap (snap) *v.* **snapped, snap·ping;** *n.* —*v.* **1** make or cause to make a sudden, sharp sound: *This wood snaps as it burns. She snapped her fingers in time to the music.* **2** move, shut, catch, etc. with a snap: *He snapped the lid shut. The latch snapped into place.* **3** break suddenly with a sharp sound: *The violin string snapped.* **4** become suddenly unable to endure a strain: *His nerves snapped.* **5** make a sudden, quick bite or snatch: *The dog snapped at the child's hand. The dog snapped up the meat.* **6** seize eagerly: *She snapped at the chance to go to Europe.* **7** speak sharply or impatiently: *"Silence!" snapped the captain. Don't snap at him; he doesn't understand what you want.* **8** move quickly and sharply: *The soldiers snapped to attention. Her eyes snapped with anger.* **9** take a snapshot of. **10** *Football.* pass the ball between the legs.
snap back, make a quick recovery.
snap out of it, *Slang.* change one's attitude, habit, etc. suddenly.
—*n.* **1** a sudden, sharp breaking of something hard or brittle: *the snap of a branch.* **2** the quick, sharp sound of a snap: *The box shut with a snap.* **3** a quick, sudden bite or snatch. **4** quick, sharp speech. **5** *Informal.* the quality or condition of being energetic, lively, and alert. **6** (*adj.*) made or done quickly or unexpectedly: *A snap judgment is often wrong. The government called a snap election.* **7** dome fastener: *The jacket closes with snaps.* **8** a snapping of the fingers, especially as a sign of disregard, contempt, etc. **9** a thin, crisp cookie: *a gingersnap, lemon snaps.* **10** *Informal.* snapshot. **11** *Informal.* snapdragon. **12** *Slang.* a very easy job, piece of work, etc.: *The exam was a snap.* **13** *Slang.* (*adj.*) very easy: *a snap assignment.* **14** *Football.* **a** the act of passing the ball between the legs by the centre. **b** the player in the middle of the line of scrimmage; the centre.
not a snap, not at all.
[< MDu. or MLG *snappen*]

snap·drag·on (snap′drag′ən) *n.* **1** any of several plants (genus *Antirrhinum*) of the figwort family having showy, two-lipped, white, yellow, red, pink, or purple flowers. Most garden snapdragons are varieties of *A. majus*, native to the Mediterranean. **2** an old game in which people try to snatch raisins from burning brandy.

snap fastener dome fastener.

snap·per (snap′ər) *n.* **1** any of a family (Lutjanidae) of mostly large marine fishes found in warm and tropical waters, including some important food fishes. **2** snapping turtle. **3** a person or thing that snaps.

snapping beetle click beetle.

snapping turtle any of a family (Chelydridae, comprising two species) of large, edible, freshwater turtles of North and Central America having powerful, hooked jaws. The **common snapping turtle** (*Chelydra serpentina*) is found from Canada south to Central America.

snap·pish (snap′ish) *adj.* **1** quick and sharp in speech or manner; curt and irritable: *He's very snappish today.* **2** apt to bite or snap. —**snap′pish·ly,** *adv.* —**snap′pish·ness,** *n.*

snap·py (snap′ē) *adj.* **-pi·er, -pi·est. 1** *Informal.* brisk and

vigorous: *We went at a snappy pace.* **2** *Informal.* sharply chilly: *a snappy fall day.* **3** *Informal.* smart; stylish: *a snappy sports jacket. He's a snappy dresser.* **4** snappish.
make it snappy, *Informal.* be quick about it; hurry: *We're waiting, so make it snappy with your phone call.*

—**snap′pi·ly,** *adv.* —**snap′pi·ness,** *n.*

snap·shot (snap′shot′) *n.* an informal photograph, such as one taken by an amateur photographer with a hand-held camera, often without regard to artistic or creative effects.

snap shot *Cdn. Hockey.* an expert wrist shot quickly made and aimed at the goal.

snare¹ (sner) *n., v.* **snared, snar·ing.** —*n.* **1** a noose for catching small animals and birds. **2** something that acts as a temptation and by which one is entangled; trap: *It is easy to be caught in the snare of popularity.* —*v.* catch with a snare. [ME < ON *snara*] —**snar′er,** *n.*

☛ *Syn. n.* **1.** See note at **trap.**

snare² (sner) *n.* one of the twisted gut or rawhide strings or spiralled lengths of wire stretched across the bottom of a snare drum. [probably < MDu. or MLG]

snare drum a small drum having lengths of wire, gut, or rawhide stretched across the bottom to make a rattling sound when the drum is struck. See **drum** for picture.

snark·y (snär′kē) *adj. Slang.* showing annoyance in a sarcastic and snappish way: *He made some snarky comments about the way the meeting was conducted.*

snarl¹ (snärl) *v.* **1** of a dog, etc., growl while baring and snapping the teeth: *The dog snarled at the stranger.* **2** speak harshly in a sharp, menacing tone. **3** say or express with a snarl: *to snarl a threat.*
—*n.* the act or sound of snarling. [earlier *snar*, cf. MDu. or MLG *snarren* rattle. Akin to SNORE.] —**snarl′er,** *n.* —**snarl′ing·ly,** *adv.*

snarl² (snärl) *n., v.* —*n.* **1** a tangle, especially of hair, thread, yarn, etc.: *She combed the snarls out of her hair.* **2** confusion and disorder: *His legal affairs were in a snarl.* —*v.* **1** tangle or become tangled. **2** complicate or confuse: *Traffic soon became snarled when the traffic lights broke down.* [ult. < *snare¹* or its source]

snarl·y¹ (snär′lē) *adj.* **snarl·i·er, snarl·i·est.** inclined to snarl or growl; bad-tempered; cross. [< *snarl¹*]

snarl·y² (snär′lē) *adj.* **snarl·i·er, snarl·i·est.** tangled; full of snarls. [< *snarl²*]

snatch (snach) *v., n.* —*v.* **1** seize suddenly; grasp hastily: *She snatched her jacket and ran.* **2** take suddenly: *He snatched off his hat and bowed.* **3** save or attain by quick action: *They snatched victory from what seemed to be sure defeat.* **4** *Slang.* kidnap. **5** *Weightlifting.* lift (a weight) with a snatch.
snatch at, a try to seize or grasp: *He snatched at the railing to keep himself from falling.* **b** eagerly take advantage of: *He snatched at the chance to travel.*
—*n.* **1** the act of snatching: *The boy made a snatch at the ball.* **2** a short time: *He had a snatch of sleep sitting in his chair.* **3** a small amount; bit; scrap: *to hear snatches of conversation.* **4** *Slang.* the act of kidnapping. **5** *Weightlifting.* a lift in which the weight is raised from the floor to an overhead position in a single quick movement. [cf. MDu. *snakken*] —**snatch′er,** *n.*

snatch·y (snach′ē) *adj.* done or occurring in snatches; disconnected; irregular. —**snatch′i·ly,** *adv.*

snath (snath) *n.* the long wooden handle of a scythe. [var. of *snead*, OE *snǣd*]

snathe (snāᴛʜ) *n.* snath.

snaz·zy (snaz′ē) *adj. Slang.* attractive in a showy and stylish way: *a snazzy new car, a snazzy outfit.* [? blend of *snappy* and *jazzy*]

sneak (snēk) *v.* **sneaked** or (*informal*) **snuck, sneak·ing;** *n.* —*v.* **1** move in a stealthy, sly way: *The man sneaked about the barn watching for a chance to steal the dog.* **2** get, put, pass, etc. in a stealthy, sly way. **3** *Informal.* steal. **4** act in a mean, contemptible, cowardly way.
sneak out of, avoid by slyness.
—*n.* **1** the act of sneaking. **2** a person who sneaks; a sneaking, cowardly, contemptible person. **3** (*adj.*) stealthy; underhand; sneaking: *a sneak thief, a sneak attack.* [cf. OE *snīcan*]

sneak·er (snē′kər) *n.* **1** a light shoe with a cloth upper and pliable rubber sole, used for sports like tennis, badminton, etc. or for general casual wear. **2** a person that sneaks; sneak.

sneak·ing (snē′king) *adj.* **1** that one cannot justify or does not like to confess: *I have a sneaking suspicion that she doesn't know what she's talking about. He had a sneaking admiration for his adventuresome but irresponsible brother.* **2** mean and underhand; furtive and cowardly: *sneaking treachery, a sneaking manner.* —**sneak′ing·ly,** *adv.*

sneak preview a special single showing of a new motion picture in advance of regular distribution in order to test audience reaction.

hat, āge, fär; let, ēqual, tèrm; it, īce
hot, ōpen, ôrder; oil, out; cup, pút, rüle,
above, takən, pencəl, lemən, circəs

ch, child; ng, long; sh, ship
th, thin; ᴛʜ, then; zh, measure

sneak thief a person who takes advantage of open doors, windows, or other easy opportunities to steal.

sneak·y (snē′kē) *adj.* **sneak·i·er, sneak·i·est.** sly, mean, or underhand. —**sneak′i·ness,** *n.*

sneer (sner) *v., n.* —*v.* **1** smile, laugh, speak, etc. in such a way as to show contempt or scorn: *They sneered at his attempts to curry favor with the boss. She sneers at any expression of sentiment.* **2** say or express with scorn or contempt: *"Bah!" he sneered with a curl of his lip.* —*n.* a look or words expressing scorn or contempt. [ME *snere(n)*. Akin to SNORE, SNARL¹.] —**sneer′er,** *n.* —**sneer′ing·ly,** *adv.*

☛ *Syn. v.* **1.** See note at **scoff.**

sneeze (snēz) *v.* **sneezed, sneez·ing;** *n.* —*v.* expel air suddenly and violently through the nose and mouth by an involuntary spasm.
not to be sneezed at, *Informal.* not to be disregarded or despised; not to be made light of: *A saving of ten dollars is not to be sneezed at.*
—*n.* a sudden, violent expelling of air through the nose and mouth. [ME *snese(n)*, var. of earlier *fnese(n)*, OE *fnēosan*] —**sneez′er,** *n.*

snell (snel) *n.* a short piece of gut, etc. by which a fish-hook is fastened to a longer line. [? < Du. *snel*; cf. G *schnellen* snap]

snick¹ (snik) *v., n.* —*v.* **1** cut slightly; snip or nick. **2** *Cricket.* give (a ball) a light, glancing blow. —*n.* **1** a small cut; a nick. **2** *Cricket.* a light, glancing blow given to the ball by the batsman, or the ball so hit. [back formation from *snickersnee*]

snick² (snik) *v., n.* —*v.* make or cause to make a clicking sound. —*n.* a slight, sharp sound; click. [imitative]

snick·er (snik′ər) *n., v.* —*n.* a half-suppressed and usually disrespectful laugh; sly or silly laugh; giggle. —*v.* laugh in this way. [imitative]

snick·er·snee (snik′ər snē′) *n.* a heavy knife or short sword. [< earlier *snick or snee,* alteration of *stick or snee* < Du. *steken* to thrust + *snijen* to cut]

snide (snīd) *adj., n.* —*adj.* **1** spitefully or slyly sarcastic: *When he did not get the part in the play, he started making snide remarks about the director.* **2** mean or cheap: *a snide trick.* **3** counterfeit; false; bogus: *a snide gem.*
—*n.* counterfeit jewellery. [? < Du. or G; cf. G *schneidend* cutting, sarcastic] —**snide′ly,** *adv.* —**snide′ness,** *n.*

snies (snīz) *n.* pl. of **sny.**

sniff (snif) *v., n.* —*v.* **1** draw air through the nose in short, quick breaths that can be heard. **2** smell with sniffs: *The dog sniffed suspiciously at the stranger.* **3** try the smell of: *to sniff a new perfume.* **4** draw in through the nose with the breath: *He sniffed the steam to clear his head.* **5** show contempt by or as if by sniffing: *to sniff at an inexpensive gift.* **6** suspect; detect: *The police sniffed a plot and broke up the meeting.*
—*n.* **1** the act or sound of sniffing: *a loud sniff.* **2** a single breathing in of something; breath. [ME. Related to SNIVEL, SNUFF.]

snif·fle (snif′əl) *v.* **-fled, -fling;** *n.* —*v.* **1** sniff again and again: *The child stopped crying, but kept on sniffling.* **2** breathe audibly through a partly clogged nose. —*n.* **1** the act or sound of sniffling. **2 the sniffles,** a head cold marked by a runny nose and sniffling. —**snif′fler,** *n.*

sniff·y (snif′ē) *adj.* **sniff·i·er, sniff·i·est.** *Informal.* **1** inclined to sniff. **2** contemptuous; scornful; disdainful.

snif·ter (snif′tər) *n.* **1** a pear-shaped glass having a short stem and used especially for brandy, the narrow top serving to retain the aroma of the liquor. **2** a small drink of liquor. [< dial. *snift* sniff]

snig·ger (snig′ər) *n. or v.* snicker.

snip (snip) *v.* **snipped, snip·ping;** *n.* —*v.* cut with a small, quick stroke or series of strokes with scissors: *She snipped the thread.*
—*n.* **1** the act of snipping: *With a few snips she cut out a paper doll.* **2** a small piece cut off: *Pick up the snips of cloth and thread from the floor.* **3** any small piece; bit; fragment. **4** *Informal.* **a** a small and unimportant person. **b** a cheeky, impertinent person. **5 snips,** *pl.* hand shears for cutting metal. [< Du. or LG *snippen*]

snipe (snīp) *n., pl.* **snipe** or **snipes;** *v.* **sniped, snip·ing.** —*n.* any of several shore birds of the sandpiper family found in most parts of the world, having a long bill used in digging for worms in the mud, eyes set far back in the head, short legs with long toes, and a very short tail. Only one species (*Capella gallinago*) is found in North America. Snipe are important game birds in Europe. —*v.* **1** hunt snipe. **2** shoot as a sniper does.

snipe at, attack suddenly or unexpectedly, especially by words. [ME < ON -*snipe*, originally, snapping bird]

snip·er (snī'pər) *n.* a person who shoots from a concealed place at one enemy or target at a time, as a sportsman shoots at game.

snip·pet (snip'it) *n.* **1** a small piece snipped off; bit; scrap; fragment: *snippets of information.* **2** *Informal.* a small or unimportant person.

snip·py (snip'ē) *adj.* **-pi·er, -pi·est. 1** *Informal.* sharp; curt. **2** *Informal.* haughty; disdainful. **3** made up of scraps or fragments. **—snip'pi·ness,** *n.*

snit (snit) *n. Informal.* a state of agitation, especially of peevish annoyance.

snitch[1] (snich) *v. Slang.* snatch; steal. [origin unknown] **—snitch·er,** *n.*

snitch[2] (snich) *v., n. Slang.* **—v.** be an informer; tell tales. **—n.** informer. [original meaning "nose"; origin uncertain] **—snitch'er,** *n.*

sniv·el (sniv'əl) *v.* **-elled** or **-eled, -el·ling** or **-el·ing;** *n.* **—v. 1** cry with sniffling. **2** put on a show of grief; whine. **3** run at the nose; sniffle. **—n. 1** pretended grief or crying; whining. **2** a running from the nose; sniffling. [ME <OE *snyflan* < *snofl* mucus] **—sniv'el·ler** or **sniv'el·er,** *n.*

snob (snob) *n.* **1** a person who cares too much for rank, wealth, and position, being too anxious to please or imitate people above him and too ready to ignore those below him. **2** a person who is contemptuous of the popular taste in some field, and is attracted to esoteric or learned things for their own sake. [origin uncertain]

snob·ber·y (snob'ər ē *or* snob'rē) *n., pl.* **-ber·ies.** snobbishness.

snob·bish (snob'ish) *adj.* **1** of or like a snob. **2** looking down on those in a lower position. **—snob'bish·ly,** *adv.* **—snob'bish·ness,** *n.*

snood (snüd) *n., v.* **—n. 1** a pouch, often of net, for loosely holding a woman's long hair at the nape of the neck. It is tied on or attached with hairpins, etc. **2** a headband or ribbon formerly worn around the hair by young unmarried women in Scotland. **—v.** confine or bind (the hair) with a snood. [OE *snōd*]

snook·er (snúk'ər *or* snü'kər) *n., v.* **—n.** a type of pool played with 15 red balls and six other balls of different colors. **—v. 1** leave (one's opponent) a shot in which he cannot aim directly at the object ball but must reach it off the cushion. **2** place (someone) in a difficult or frustrating situation; thwart. [origin unknown. 19c.]

snoop (snüp) *v., n. Informal.* **—v.** go about in a sneaking, prying way; prowl; pry. **—n.** a person who snoops. [< Du. *snoepen* eat in secret] **—snoop'er,** *n.*

snoose (snüs) *n.* a kind of snuff, prepared damp and in grated form, used for chewing. Also, **Copenhagen snuff.** [< Danish, Swedish, etc. *snus,* shortening of *snutstobak* < *snusa, snuse* sniff + *tobak* tobacco]

snoot (snüt) *n. Slang.* **1** the nose. **2** the face. [originally a Scottish var. of *snout*]

snoot·y (snü'tē) *adj.* **snoot·i·er, snoot·i·est.** *Informal.* snobbish; conceited.

snooze (snüz) *v.* **snoozed, snooz·ing;** *n. Informal.* **—v.** take a nap; sleep; doze. **—n.** a nap; doze. [origin uncertain]

snore (snôr) *v.* **snored, snor·ing;** *n.* **—v. 1** breathe during sleep with a harsh, rough sound. **2** pass in snoring: *The lazy man snored away the afternoon.* **—n.** the sound made in snoring. [ME *snore(n),* ? imitative] **—snor'er,** *n.*

snor·kel (snôr'kəl) *n., v.* **-kelled** or **-keled, -kel·ling** or **kel·ing. —n. 1** a shaft admitting air and discharging gases that allows submarines to remain submerged for a long time. See **submarine** for picture. **2** a curved tube which enables swimmers to breathe under water while using a snorkel. **—v.** swim or stay underwater, using a snorkel to breathe. [< LG slang *snorkel* nose < MLG **snorkeln,* frequentative of *snorken* snore; because the snorkel is the nose of the submarine and its intake valve makes a snoring sound]

snort (snôrt) *v., n.* **—v. 1** force the breath violently through the nose with a loud, harsh sound: *The horse snorted.* **2** make a sound like this: *The engine snorted.* **3** show contempt, defiance, anger, etc. by snorting. **4** say or express with a snort: *"Indeed!" snorted my aunt.* **—n. 1** the act or sound of snorting. **2** *Slang.* a small, quick drink, especially of liquor taken neat. [< *snore*] **—snort'er,** *n.*

snot (snot) *n.* **1** *Vulgar.* mucus from the nose. **2** *Slang.* a mean or contemptible person. [OE *gesnot*]

snot·ty (snot'ē) *adj., n., pl.* **-ties. —adj. 1** *Vulgar.* dirty with snot. **2** *Slang.* mean or contemptible. **3** *Slang.* insolent or arrogant. **—n. Brit. Slang.** midshipman.

snout (snout) *n.* **1** the projecting part of an animal's head that contains the nose, mouth, and jaws. Pigs, dogs, and crocodiles have snouts. **2** anything like an animal's snout. **3** *Informal.* a person's nose, especially a large or ugly one. [ME *snoute*; akin to G *Schnauze*]

snout beetle weevil (def. 1).

snow (snō) *n., v.* **—n. 1** water vapor frozen into crystals in the upper atmosphere and falling to earth in the form of individual crystals or large flakes consisting of many crystals together. **2** a fall of snow. **3** *Poetic.* pure whiteness. **4** something resembling or suggesting snow. **5** *Slang.* cocaine or heroin. **6** *Cdn.* snow apple. **7** a pattern of dots on a television screen caused by atmospheric interference with the signals. **—v. 1** be the case that snow is falling (*used with the subject* it): *It has been snowing since last night.* **2** fall or scatter like snow: *It was snowing apple blossom petals in the garden.* **3** cover, block up, shut in, etc. with snow or as if with snow (*used with* in, up, under, *etc., and usually used in the passive*): *The town was snowed in for a week after the blizzard. He is snowed under with work. The car was completely snowed under.* **4** *Slang.* deceive, mislead, or charm by glib or elaborate talk. [OE *snāw*]

snow angel a shaped depression resembling a traditional angel figure, made by lying down in soft snow and moving the outstretched arms and legs over the surface of the snow to form the shape of wings and gown.

snow apple *Cdn.* a fine eating apple having crisp, white flesh and a deep-red skin.

snow·ball (snō'bol' *or* -bôl') *n., v.* **—n. 1** a rounded mass of snow that has been pressed or rolled together, often used for throwing in play. **2** any of several cultivated viburnums, especially a sterile variety of *V. opulus,* having large, showy, spherical clusters of white flowers. **—v. 1** throw snowballs at. **2** increase, expand, or accumulate at an accelerating rate: *Demands for an independent investigation are snowballing.*

snow·bank (snō'bangk') *n.* a large mass or drift of snow.

snow·ber·ry (snō'ber'ē) *n., pl.* **-ries. 1** any of several shrubs (genus *Symphoricarpos*) of the honeysuckle family having white berries, especially a small, pink-flowered, North American species (*S. albus*). **2** any of various other shrubs having white berries. **3** the berry of any of these shrubs.

snow·bird (snō'bėrd') *n. Cdn.* **1** snow bunting. **2** junco.

snow–blind (snō'blīnd') *adj.* suffering from snow blindness.

snow blindness *Cdn.* a painful inflammation of the eyes caused by overexposure to the glare of sunlight on wide expanses of snow or ice, and resulting in temporary, partial or complete, blindness.

snow–blink (snō'blingk') *n.* the glare caused by the reflection of the sun's rays off snow.

snow–blow·er (snō'blō'ər) *n. Cdn.* a machine that clears snow by drawing it in by means of a large fan and blowing it out in another direction.

snow boot a waterproof boot, usually well-lined, for use in snow.

snow–bound (snō'bound') *adj.* shut in by snow; snowed in.

snow bunting *Cdn.* a small songbird (*Plectrophenax nivalis*) of the same family as grosbeaks, goldfinches, and sparrows that breeds in the Arctic and winters in northern temperate regions, having mostly white plumage with back and wings black in breeding season and mainly rusty brown in winter. The snow bunting is a common sight in most of southern Canada in winter; in the Arctic, it is a harbinger of spring.

snow–capped (snō'kapt') *adj.* having its top covered with snow.

snow devil a whirling column of snow sucked up in a vortex by the wind.

snow·drift (snō'drift') *n.* **1** a mass or bank of snow piled up by the wind. **2** snow driven before the wind.

snow·drop (snō'drop') *n.* any of a genus (*Galanthus*) of spring-blooming, bulbous Eurasian herbs of the amaryllis family, especially *G. nivalis,* having drooping, white, bell-shaped flowers.

snow·fall (snō'fol' *or* -fôl') *n.* **1** a fall of snow. **2** the amount of snow falling within a certain time and area: *The snowfall at Banff in that one storm was 30 centimetres.*

snow fence *Cdn.* a lath and wire fence erected in winter alongside roads, etc. to prevent snow from drifting.

snow fencing *Cdn.* **1** the material of which snow fences are made. **2** snow fence.

snow·flake (snō'flāk') *n.* a single feathery crystal, or flake, of snow.

snow goose *Cdn.* a wild goose (*Chen caerulescens*) that breeds in the Arctic, the adult typically white with black wing tips and having a pinkish bill with a blackish patch on each side and reddish legs and feet. Some ornithologists, especially in Europe, classify the

snow goose as *Anser caerulescens.* See also **blue goose.**

snow·i·ness (snō′ē nis) *n.* **1** the state or quality of being snowy. **2** whiteness.

snow job *Slang.* an intensive effort to persuade or deceive by flattering, glib, or elaborate talk.

snow knife *Cdn.* a knife about 35 cm long, having a broad, curved blade and used chiefly for cutting snow blocks for igloos.

snow leopard a large mammal (*Panthera uncia*) of the cat family found in the mountains of central Asia, having a long, thick, greyish coat marked with dark spots arranged in rosettes. It is closely related to the leopard.

snow lily *Cdn.* glacier lily.

snow line a height on mountains, etc. above which there is snow all year round.

snow·man (snō′man′) *n., pl.* **-men.** a mass of snow made into a figure shaped somewhat like a man.

snow·melt (snō′melt′) *n.* liquid resulting from the melting of snow.

A snowmobile

snow·mo·bile (snō′mə bēl′) *n., v.* **-biled, -bil·ing.** *Cdn.* —*n.* **1** a small, open motor vehicle for travelling over snow and ice, equipped with skis at the front, by which it is steered, and a caterpillar track beneath the body. Snowmobiles are used as a means of transportation, especially in the North, and also for sport. **2** a large, closed-in vehicle similar to this, but having two tracks and designed to carry a number of persons, goods, etc.; bombardier. **3** (*adj.*) designed for wear when snowmobiling: *a snowmobile suit.* —*v.* travel by snowmobile; ride or drive a snowmobile. —**snow′mo·bil′er,** *n.*

snow·plough or **snow·plow** (snō′plou′) *n.* a machine for clearing away snow from streets, railway tracks, etc. by means of a large blade that pushes the snow as the machine moves forward.

snow·shed (snō′shed′) *n.* a long shed built over a railway track or a highway to protect it from snowslides.

snow·shine (snō′shīn′) *n.* snowblink.

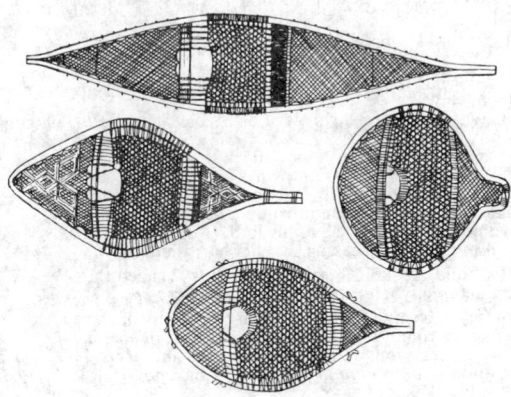

Four different types of snowshoe; clockwise from the top: Cree, beavertail, swallowtail, Ojibwa

snow·shoe (snō′shü′) *n., v.* **-shoed, -shoe·ing.** —*n.* a light, wooden frame with strips of leather stretched across it. Trappers in the far North wear snowshoes on their feet to keep from sinking in deep, soft snow. —*v.* walk or travel on snowshoes. —**snow′sho·er,** *n.*

snowshoe hare *Cdn.* a medium-sized hare (*Lepus americanus*) common throughout the forested regions of N North America, having grizzled brown fur in summer which, throughout most of the animal's range, turns to white in winter; and having very large, broad hind feet which in winter are very heavily furred, giving the animal its common name. Also called **snowshoe rabbit, varying hare.**

hat, āge, fär; let, ēqual, tėrm; it, īce hot, ōpen, ôrder; oil, out; cup, pùt, rüle, əbove, takən, pencəl, lemən, circəs

ch, child; ng, long; sh, ship th, thin; ᴛʜ, then; zh, measure

snowshoe rabbit *Cdn.* snowshoe hare.

snow shovel a shovel having a large, square blade with a straight edge and slightly curved sides for clearing snow.

snow·slide (snō′slīd′) *n.* **1** the sliding down of a mass of snow on a steep slope. **2** the mass of snow that slides.

snow snake 1 a North American Indian game in which a wooden stick is slid as far as possible along a smooth patch of ice or snow, or along a furrow in snow. **2** the stick used in this game.

snow·storm (snō′stôrm′) *n.* a storm accompanied by falling snow.

snow thrower snowblower.

snow tire a tire for motor vehicles, having a deeply cut tread to provide extra traction when driving in snow or mud.

snow·white (snō′wīt′ *or* -hwīt′) *adj.* white as snow.

snow·y (snō′ē) *adj.* **snow·i·er, snow·i·est. 1** having snow. **2** covered with snow. **3** like snow; white as snow: *She has snowy hair.* **4** having a blurred and dotted pattern: *The TV picture is snowy.* —**snow′i·ly,** *adv.*

snub (snub) *v.* **snubbed, snub·bing;** *n.* —*v.* **1** treat coldly or with contempt. **2** check or stop (a rope or cable) running out by winding it round a post or other object. **3** check or stop the motion of (a boat, horse, etc.) in this way. —*n.* **1** cold or contemptuous treatment; a rebuff or slight. **2** a sudden check or stop. [ME < ON *snubba* reprove]

snub·ber (snub′ər) *n.* **1** a person that snubs. **2** a device for snubbing a rope, cable, etc. **3** an early type of shock absorber for automobiles.

snub·by (snub′ē) *adj.* **-bi·er, -bi·est.** short and turned up at the top.

snub nose a short, turned-up nose.

snub–nosed (snub′nōzd′) *adj.* **1** having a short, turned-up nose. **2** of a handgun, having a short barrel.

snuck (snuk) *v. Informal.* a pt. and a pp. of **sneak.**
☛ *Usage.* Though it is widely used, especially in such phrases as **snuck in** and **snuck up on,** many people regard this form as nonstandard.

snuff¹ (snuf) *v., n.* —*v.* **1** draw in through the nose; draw up into the nose: *He snuffs up salt and water to cure a cold.* **2** sniff; smell: *The dog snuffed at the track of the fox.* **3** take powdered tobacco into the nose by snuffing; use snuff. —*n.* powdered tobacco that is snuffed into the nose.
up to snuff, a *Informal.* in perfect order or condition; as good as expected. **b** *Slang.* not easily deceived.
[< MDu. *snuffen* sniff]

snuff² (snuf) *v., n.* —*v.* **1** cut or pinch off the burned wick of a candle. **2** put out (a candle); extinguish.
snuff out, a put out; extinguish. **b** put an end to suddenly and completely: *to snuff out all hope of freedom.* —*n.* the burned part of a candlewick. [ME; origin uncertain; cf. G *Schnuppe,* n.]

snuff·box (snuf′boks′) *n.* a small box for holding snuff.

snuf·fer (snuf′ər) *n.* **1** a device for extinguishing a candle, consisting of a small, cone-shaped metal cup, usually at the end of a handle, that is inverted over the flame. **2 snuffers,** *pl.* an instrument like a pair of scissors for trimming the wick of a burning candle or extinguishing the candle.

snuf·fle (snuf′əl) *v.* **-fled, -fling;** *n.* —*v.* **1** breathe noisily through a partly clogged nose. **2** smell; sniff. **3** speak, sing, etc. through the nose or with a nasal tone. —*n.* **1** the act or sound of snuffling. **2** the nasal tone of voice of a person who snuffles. **3 the snuffles,** *Informal.* **a** a fit of snuffling; stuffed-up condition of the nose, caused by a cold, hay fever, etc. **b** a respiratory disease of animals. [ult. < *snuff¹* or its source] —**snuf′fler,** *n.*

snuff·y (snuf′ē) *adj.* **snuff·i·er, snuff·i·est. 1** like snuff. **2** soiled or stained with snuff. **3** having the habit of using snuff. **4** disagreeable; cross. —**snuf′fi·ly,** *adv.*

snug (snug) *adj.* **snug·ger, snug·gest;** *v.* **snugged, snug·ging;** *adv.* —*adj.* **1** comfortable; warm; sheltered: *The cat has found a snug corner behind the stove.* **2** neat; trim; compact: *The cabins on the boat are snug.* **3** well-built; seaworthy: *a snug ship.* **4** fitting closely: *That coat is a little too snug.* **5** small but sufficient: *A snug income*

enables him to live in comfort. **6** hidden; concealed: *He lay snug until the searchers passed by.*
—*v.* make snug.
—*adv.* in a snug manner. [cf. Swedish *snygg* neat, trim] —**snug′ly,** *adv.* —**snug′ness,** *n.*
☛ *Syn. adj.* **1. Snug, cosy** = comfortable. **Snug** emphasizes the comfort and security of a small space, warm and sheltered from the weather, or of a quiet and peaceful life, protected from disturbance or excitement: *The children were snug in their beds.* **Cosy** emphasizes warmth, shelter, and ease, often affection or friendliness, making for comfort and contentment: *She was sitting in a cosy corner by the fire.*

snug·ger·y (snug′ər ē) *n., pl.* **-ger·ies.** a snug place, position, room, etc.

snug·gies (snug′ēz) *n.pl.* women's warm underwear.

snug·gle (snug′əl) *v.* **-gled, -gling. 1** lie or press closely for warmth or comfort or from affection; nestle; cuddle. **2** draw closely. [< *snug*]

snye or **sny** (snī) *n., pl.* **snyes** or **snies.** *Cdn.* a side channel of a stream. [< Cdn.F *chenail;* cf. F *chenal* channel]

so¹ (sō; *unstressed before consonants,* sə) *adv., conj., interj., pron.* —*adv.* **1** in this way; in that way; in the same way; as shown: *Hold your pen so.* **2** in such a way as stated: *Is that really so?* **3** to this degree; to that degree: *Do not walk so fast.* **4** to such a degree; to the same degree: *He was not so cold as she was.* **5** very: *You are so kind.* **6** very much: *My head aches so.* **7** for this reason; for that reason; accordingly; therefore: *The dog was hungry; so we fed it.* **8** likewise; also: *She likes dogs; so does he.*
and so, **a** likewise; also. **b** accordingly.
or so, more or less: *It cost a dollar or so.*
so as, with the aim or purpose: *We went to bed early so as to get enough sleep.*
so that, **a** with the result that. **b** with the purpose that. **c** provided that; if.
—*conj.* **1** with the result that; in order that: *Go away so I can rest.* **2** with the purpose or intention that: *I did the work so he would not need to.* **3** *Archaic.* on the condition that; if: *So it be done, I care not who does it.*
—*interj.* **1** well! **2** let it be that way! all right! **3** is that true? **4** what now? so what?
—*pron.* **1** more or less; approximately that: *a kilogram or so.* **2** the same: *He is unconscious and will probably remain so for some time.* **3** whatever has been or is going to be said; this; that. [OE *swā*]
☛ *Hom.* **sew, sow¹.**

so² (sō) *n. Music.* a syllable used for the fifth tone of an eight-tone scale; sol. [see GAMUT]
☛ *Hom.* **sew, sow¹.**

s.o. or **so** *Baseball.* **1** struck out. **2** strike out.

So. South; Southern.

soak (sōk) *v., n.* —*v.* **1** make very wet; wet through. **2** let remain in water or other liquid until wet through. **3** become very wet; remain until wet through. **4** make its way; enter; go: *Water will soak into the earth.* **5** absorb or suck (*used with* up): *A sponge will soak up water. We soaked up the sunshine. She would read for hours, soaking up knowledge.* **6** *Slang.* drink heavily. **7** *Slang.* punish severely; strike hard. **8** *Slang.* make pay too much; charge or tax heavily.
—*n.* **1** the act or process of soaking. **2** the state of being soaked. **3** the liquid in which anything is soaked. **4** *Slang.* a heavy drinker. [OE *socian*]
☛ *Syn. v.* **1.** See note at **wet.**

so–and–so (sō′ənd sō′) *n., pl.* **-sos. 1** a person or thing not named. **2** *Informal.* an unpleasant or distasteful person.

soap (sōp) *n., v.* —*n.* **1** a substance used for washing, usually made of a fat and caustic soda or potash. **2** *Slang.* money, especially money as used for bribery. **3** *Slang.* soap opera.
no soap, *Slang.* **a** no; nothing doing. **b** no results; nothing accomplished.
—*v.* rub with soap. [OE *sāpe*] —**soap′less,** *adj.*

soap·ber·ry (sōp′ber′ē) *n., pl.* **-ries. 1** any of a genus (*Sapindus*) of mainly tropical woody plants or trees bearing fruit that is used as a soap substitute. **2** the fruit or nut of a soapberry. **3** (*adj.*) designating a family (Sapindaceae) of mainly tropical woody plants, shrubs, and trees, including the soapberries, litchi, etc. **4** *Cdn.* a low shrub (*Shepherdia canadensis*) of the oleaster family, found throughout Canada and the N United States.

soap·box (sōp′boks′) *n., v.* —*n.* **1** a box, especially of wood, in which soap is packed. **2** an empty box used as a temporary platform by agitators or other speakers addressing gatherings in the open air.
—*v.* address an audience in the open air.

soap bubble a bubble made with soapy water.

soap opera a radio or television drama presented in serial form, usually featuring emotional domestic situations.

soap·stone (sōp′stōn′) *n.* a heavy, soft stone that feels somewhat like soap; steatite: *Eskimo carvings are often made of soapstone.*

soap·suds (sōp′sudz′) *n.pl.* bubbles and foam made with soap and water.

soap·wort (sōp′wèrt′) *n.* a tall European perennial herb (*Saponaria officinalis*) of the pink family having clusters of fragrant pink or white flowers and leaves containing a lathering juice that has been used as a soap substitute.

soap·y (sōp′ē) *adj.* **soap·i·er, soap·i·est. 1** covered with soap or soapsuds. **2** containing soap: *soapy water.* **3** like soap; smooth and slippery or greasy: *Soapstone feels soapy.* —**soap′i·ly,** *adv.* —**soap′i·ness,** *n.*

soar (sôr) *v.* **1** fly at a great height; fly upward: *The eagle soared without flapping its wings.* **2** rise beyond what is common and ordinary; aspire: *His ambition soared to the throne.* **3** reach in soaring. **4** fly or move through the air by means of rising air currents. A glider can soar for a great distance. [ME < OF *essorer,* ult. < L *ex-* out + *aura* breeze < Gk.]
☛ *Hom.* **sore.**

sob (sob) *v.* **sobbed, sob·bing;** *n.* —*v.* **1** cry or sigh with short, quick breaths. **2** put, send, etc. by sobbing: *She sobbed herself to sleep.* **3** make a sound like a sob: *The wind sobbed.* **4** say or express with sobs: *She sobbed out her story.*
—*n.* **1** a catching of short, quick breaths because of grief, etc. **2** the sound of this. [ME *sobbe(n),* perhaps ult. imitative]

so·ber (sō′bər) *adj., v.* —*adj.* **1** not drunk. **2** temperate; moderate: *The Puritans led sober, hard-working lives.* **3** quiet; serious; solemn: *a sober expression.* **4** calm; sensible: *The judge's sober opinion was not influenced by prejudice or strong feeling.* **5** free from exaggeration: *sober facts.* **6** quiet in color: *dressed in sober grey.*
—*v.* make or become sober.
sober down, become quiet, serious, or solemn.
sober up or **off,** recover from too much alcoholic drink. [ME < OF < L *sobrius*] —**so′ber·ly,** *adv.* —**so′ber·ness,** *n.*
☛ *Syn. adj.* **3.** See note at **grave.**

so·ber–mind·ed (sō′bər mīn′did) *adj.* having or showing a sober mind; self-controlled; sensible. —**so′ber–mind′ed·ly,** *adv.* —**so′ber–mind′ed·ness,** *n.*

so·ber·sid·ed (sō′bər sīd′id) *adj.* of a serious or earnest disposition.

so·ber·sides (sō′bər sīdz′) *n., pl.* **-sides.** a serious or earnest person.

so·bri·e·ty (sə brī′ə tē) *n., pl.* **-ties. 1** soberness. **2** temperance in the use of alcoholic liquors. **3** moderation. **4** quietness; seriousness. [< L *sobrietas*]

so·bri·quet (sō′brə kā′ or sō′brə ket′) *n.* a nickname. Also, **soubriquet.** [< F]

sob sister *Informal.* a person, often a woman reporter, who writes or tells sob stories.

sob story *Informal.* a story that is excessively pathetic or sentimental.

Soc. **1** Society. **2** Socialist.

soc·age or **soc·cage** (sok′ij) *n.* feudal tenure of land under which the tenant paid a definite rent or did a definite amount of work, but gave no military service to his lord. [ME < AF *socage* < *soc* < Med.L *soca* < OE *sōcn* seeking, inquiry, jurisdiction]

so–called (sō′kold′ or -kôld′) *adj.* **1** called thus. **2** called thus improperly or incorrectly: *Her so-called friend dislikes her.*

soc·cer (sok′ər) *n.* a game played between two teams of eleven players each, using a round ball; association football. In soccer, only the goalkeeper may touch the ball with hands and arms. [< *assoc.,* abbreviation of *association* (*football*); for the ending cf. *Rugger* for *Rugby*]
☛ *Usage.* See note at **rugby.**

so·cia·bil·i·ty (sō′shə bil′ə tē) *n., pl.* **-ties.** one's social disposition or behavior.

so·cia·ble (sō′shə bəl) *adj., n.* —*adj.* **1** liking company; friendly: *The Smiths are a sociable family and entertain a great deal.* **2** marked by conversation and companionship: *We had a sociable afternoon together.* **3** of animals or plants, naturally inclined to be in company with others of the same species; social.
—*n. Esp.U.S.* an informal social gathering; a social. [< L *sociabilis* < *sociare* associate < *socius.* See SOCIAL.] —**so′cia·bly,** *adv.*
☛ *Syn. adj.* **1.** See note at **social.**

so·cial (sō′shəl) *adj., n.* —*adj.* **1** of or dealing with human beings in their relations to each other; having to do with the life of human beings in a community: *social problems. History and geography are social sciences.* **2** living, or liking to live, with others: *Human*

beings are social creatures. **3** for companionship or friendliness; having to do with companionship or friendliness: *a social club.* **4** liking company: *She has a social nature.* **5** connected with fashionable society: *a social leader.* **6** of animals, living together in organized communities. Ants and bees are social insects. —*n.* an informal social gathering or party. [< L *socialis* < *socius* companion, originally adj., sharing in]

☛ *Syn. adj.* **4. Social, sociable** = pertaining to, characterized by, or inclined to companionship and friendliness. **Social,** now rarely describing a person, emphasizes human relations and, when particularly describing groups, occasions, activities, etc., means pertaining to or being for companionship or for mingling with others: *He has too little social life.* **Sociable,** usually describing persons, means liking company and being inclined to seek and enjoy companionship and friendly relations even with strangers: *He is a likable, sociable person.*

Social Credit Party a Canadian political party, founded in Alberta in the 1930's. Its traditional policies are based on certain economic theories originally developed by Major C. H. Douglas (1878-1952).

Social Credit Rally a Canadian political party formed in 1962 from the Quebec wing of the Social Credit Party. [translation of F *Ralliement des Créditistes*]

social disease any disease communicated by sexual intercourse; venereal disease.

social insurance benefits, such as old-age pension, family allowance, unemployment insurance, etc., provided by a government.

Social Insurance Number *Cdn.* a nine-digit number by which the federal government identifies an individual for purposes of income tax, unemployment insurance, old-age pension, etc. *Abbrev.*: SIN

so·cial·ism (sō′shəl iz′əm) *n.* a political and economic theory or system in which the means of production and distribution are owned, managed, or controlled by a central, democratically elected authority. Compare **capitalism** and **communism.**

so·cial·ist (sō′shəl ist) *n., adj.* —*n.* a person who favors and supports socialism. —*adj.* socialistic.

so·cial·is·tic (sō′shəl is′tik) *adj.* **1** of or having to do with socialism or socialists. **2** advocating or supporting socialism. —**so′cial·is′ti·cal·ly,** *adv.*

Socialist Party a political party that favors and supports socialism.

so·cial·ite (sō′shəl īt′) *n.* a person who is prominent in society.

so·ci·al·i·ty (sō′shē al′ə tē) *n., pl.* **-ties. 1** social activity; social intercourse. **2** social nature or tendencies: *The congregating of people in cities and towns shows sociality.*

so·cial·ize (sō′shəl īz′) *v.* **-ized, -iz·ing. 1** make social; make fit for living with others. **2** adapt to community needs. **3** establish or regulate in accordance with socialism. —**so′cial·i·za′tion,** *n.*

socialized medicine the provision of medical care and hospital services for all classes of society, especially through government subsidy and administration.

so·cial·ly (sō′shəl ē) *adv.* **1** in a social way or manner; in relation to other people. **2** as a member of society or of a social group: *He is an able man, but socially he is a failure.*

social register a list of people who are prominent in fashionable society.

social science the study of people, their activities, and their customs in relationship to others. History, sociology, economics, and civics are social sciences.

social security *Esp.U.S.* social insurance.

social service social work.

social studies a course of study in elementary and secondary schools that includes elements of history, geography, sociology, civics, economics, etc.

social work work directed toward the betterment of social conditions in a community. Social work includes such services as medical clinics, counselling for families, and recreational activities.

social worker a person employed by a community or government to do social work.

so·ci·e·tal (sə sī′ə təl) *adj.* of or having to do with human society. —**so·ci′e·tal·ly,** *adv.*

so·ci·e·ty (sə sī′ə tē) *n., pl.* **-ties. 1** a group of persons joined together for a common purpose or by a common interest. A club, a fraternity, a lodge, or an association may be called a society. **2** all the people of a particular place and time who have developed organized cultural and social patterns and institutions: *Drug-control laws are passed for the good of society. Magic plays an important part in primitive society.* **3** people thought of as a group because of common economic position, similar interests, etc.: *in cultivated society.* **4** company; companionship: *I enjoy his society.* **5** the fashionable or privileged people in a community: *a leader of*

hat, āge, fär; let, ēqual, tėrm; it, īce
hot, ōpen, ôrder; oil, out; cup, put, rüle,
above, takan, pencal, lemon, circas

ch, child; ng, long; sh, ship
th, thin; ŦH, then; zh, measure

society. **6** *Ecology.* **a** an interdependent community of organisms, especially of a single species. **b** a natural group of plants of a single species forming a community within a larger ecological comunity. [< L *societas* < *socius* companion]

Society of Friends a Christian sect founded by George Fox in England in 1650; Quakers.

Society of Jesus a Roman Catholic religious order, founded by Saint Ignatius Loyola in 1534. Its members are called Jesuits. *Abbrev.*: S.J.

so·ci·o·e·co·nom·ic (sō′sē ō- *or* sō′shē ō ē′kə nom′ik *or* -ek′ə nom′ik) *adj.* of or having to do with social and economic matters: *a socio-economic study on poverty in big cities.*

so·ci·o·log·i·cal (sō′sē ə loj′ə kəl *or* sō′shē ə loj′ə kəl) *adj.* **1** of or having to do with human society or problems relating to it: *The care of the poor is a sociological problem.* **2** of sociology.

so·ci·o·log·i·cal·ly (sō′sē ə loj′ik lē *or* sō′shē ə loj′ik lē) *adv.* according to sociology.

so·ci·ol·o·gist (sō′sē ol′ə jist *or* sō′shē ol′ə jist) *n.* a student of human society and its problems; person skilled in sociology.

so·ci·ol·o·gy (sō′sē ol′ə jē *or* sō′shē ol′ə jē) *n.* the study of the nature, origin, and development of human society and community life; the science of social facts. Sociology deals with social conditions, such as crime or poverty, and social institutions, such as marriage or the church. [< L *socius* companion + E -*logy*]

so·ci·o·path (sō′sē ə path′ *or* sō′shē ə path′) *n.* a person in whom mental illness leads to a lack of social or moral responsibility.

sock¹ (sok) *n., v.* —*n.* **1** a cloth foot covering, usually knitted, worn inside a shoe and extending above the ankle, sometimes to the knee. **2** a light shoe worn by actors in ancient Greek and Roman comedy. **3** windsock. —*v.*

sock in, *Informal.* close (an airfield) to takeoffs and landings by aircraft because of bad weather (*usually used in the passive*). [< L *soccus*]

sock² (sok) *v., n., adv. Slang.* —*v.* strike or hit hard. —*n.* a hard blow. —*adv.* squarely; right. [origin uncertain]

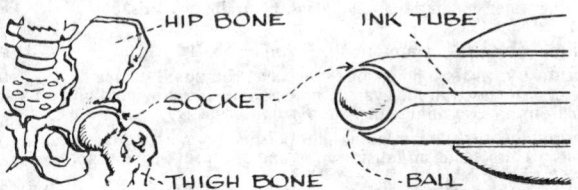

The ball-and-socket joint of the hip   The ball and socket forming the tip of a ball-point pen

sock·et (sok′it) *n.* **1** a hollow part or piece for receiving and holding something. A candlestick has a socket in which to set a candle. Eyes are set in sockets. An electric light has a socket into which the bulb is screwed. **2** a connecting place for electric wires and plugs. [ME < AF *soket* < *soc* ploughshare < Celtic]

sock·eye (sok′ī′) *n., pl.* **sock·eye** *or* **sock·eyes.** *Cdn.* a small Pacific salmon (*Oncorhynchus nerka*) found along the coasts of British Columbia and Alaska, greenish blue and metallic green in color and having red, oily flesh highly valued for its flavor. The sockeye changes color to a bright red in spawning season. [< Salish *suk-kegh* red fish, altered by folk etymology]

So·crat·ic (sō krat′ik) *adj.* of or having to do with Socrates (469-399 B.C.), a famous Athenian philosopher, his philosophy, followers, etc.

Socratic method the use of a series of questions to lead a pupil to think, to make an opponent contradict himself, etc.

So·cred (sō′kred′) *n. Cdn. Informal.* **1** the Social Credit Party. **2** a member of this party.

sod (sod) *n., v.* **sod·ded, sod·ding.** —*n.* **1** ground covered with grass. **2** a piece or layer of ground containing the grass and its roots.

under the sod, dead and buried.
—v. cover with sods. [< MDu. or MLG *sode*]

so·da (sō′də) *n.* 1 any of several substances containing sodium, such as sodium carbonate, sodium bicarbonate, caustic soda (NaOH), or sodium oxide (Na_2O). Soda is used in the manufacture of soap and glass. Washing soda (sal soda) is used in cleaning. Baking soda is used in cooking and as a medicine. 2 soda water. 3 soda water flavored with fruit juice or syrup, and often containing ice cream. [< Med.L]

soda ash partly purified sodium carbonate.

soda biscuit a simple, light, thin biscuit made with little or no sugar or shortening.

soda cracker soda biscuit.

soda fountain 1 an apparatus for holding soda water, syrups, ice, etc. and having taps for drawing off the liquids. 2 a counter with places for holding soda water, flavored syrups, ice cream, etc. 3 a store having such a counter.

soda jerk or **jerker** *Slang.* a person who serves at a soda fountain.

so·da·lite (sō′də līt′) *n.* an opaque silicate of sodium and aluminum with chlorine, found in igneous rock and often colored blue. *Formula:* $Na_4Al_3Si_3O_{12}Cl$

so·dal·i·ty (sō dal′ə tē) *n., pl.* **-ties.** 1 fellowship; friendship. 2 an association, society, or fraternity. 3 *Roman Catholic Church.* a society having religious or charitable purposes. [< L *sodalitas* < *sodalis* sociable]

soda water water charged with carbon dioxide to make it bubble and fizz, often served with the addition of syrup, ice cream, etc.

sod·bust·er (sod′bust′ər) *n. Cdn. Slang.* a prairie farmer, especially one of the early homesteaders.

sod·den (sod′ən) *adj.* 1 soaked through: *His clothing was sodden with rain.* 2 heavy and moist: *This bread is sodden because it was not baked well.* 3 dull-looking; stupid. [old pp. of *seethe*]
—**sod′den·ly,** *adv.* —**sod′den·ness,** *n.*

so·dic (sō′dik) *adj.* of, having to do with, or containing sodium.

so·di·um (sō′dē əm) *n.* a soft, silver-white metallic element which reacts violently with water and occurs in nature only in compounds. Salt and soda contain sodium. *Symbol:* Na; *at.no.* 11; *at.wt.* 22.9898 [< *soda*]

sodium bicarbonate a powdery white salt used in cooking, medicine, etc.; baking soda; bicarbonate of soda. *Formula:* $NaHCO_3$

sodium carbonate a salt that occurs in a powdery white form and in a hydrated crystalline form; washing soda. It is used for softening water, making soap and glass, neutralizing acids, etc. *Formula:* Na_2CO_3

sodium chloride common salt. *Formula:* NaCl

sodium cyanide a poisonous substance, composed of fine white crystals, used in the cyanide process for extracting gold and silver from ores, in fumigating, etc. *Formula:* NaCN

sodium fluoride a crystalline salt, poisonous in large quantities, used as an insecticide and disinfectant and as a preventive of tooth decay. *Formula:* NaF

sodium hydroxide a white solid that is a strong, corrosive alkali; caustic soda. *Formula:* NaOH

sodium hypochlorite a crystalline salt, used as an insecticide, a disinfectant, in household bleaches, etc. *Formula:* $NaClO \cdot 5H_2O$

sodium iodide a white, odorless salt, used for the treatment of nervous disorders, in animal fodder, in photography, etc. *Formula:* NaI

sodium nitrate a colorless crystalline substance used in making fertilizers, explosives, etc.; Chile saltpetre. *Formula:* $NaNO_3$

sodium nitrite a white or yellowish salt made by heating sodium nitrate, used especially in the manufacture of dyes and as a meat preservative. *Formula:* $NaNO_2$

sodium pentothal a barbiturate used as an anesthetic and in the treatment of mental illness. *Formula:* $C_{11}H_{17}N_2O_2SNa$

Sod·om (sod′əm) *n.* 1 an ancient city near the Dead Sea that, according to the account in the Bible, was destroyed by fire from heaven because of the wickedness of its inhabitants (Gen. 18 and 19). 2 any extremely wicked or corrupt place.

sodomite (sod′ə mīt′) *n.* 1 a person who practises sodomy. 2 **Sodomite,** a native or inhabitant of Sodom.

sod·o·my (sod′ə mē) *n.* abnormal sexual relations, especially between two males or between a human being and an animal. [ME < OF *sodomie* < LL < *Sodom*]

sod turning (sod′tèrn′ing) *n.* the breaking of ground for digging the foundations of a building.

so·ev·er (sō ev′ər) *adv.* 1 in any case; in any way; in any degree: *no matter how long soever the work may take.* 2 of any kind; at all: *He has no home soever.*

–soever *suffix.* in any way; of any kind; at all; ever, as in *whosoever, whatsoever, whensoever, wheresoever, howsoever.*

so·fa (sō′fə) *n.* a long, upholstered seat or couch having a back and arms; chesterfield. [< F < Arabic *ṣuffah*]

sof·fit (sof′it) *n. Architecture.* the under surface or face of an architrave, arch, or the like. See **arch** for picture. [< Ital. *soffitto,* ult. < L *sub-* under + *figere* fix]

soft (soft) *adj., adv., n., interj.* —*adj.* 1 not hard; yielding readily to touch or pressure: *a soft pillow.* 2 not hard compared with other things of the same kind: *Pine wood is soft. Copper and lead are softer than steel.* 3 not hard or sharp; gentle and graceful: *soft shadows, soft outlines.* 4 fine in texture; not rough or coarse; smooth: *soft skin.* 5 not loud: *a soft voice.* 6 quietly pleasant; mild; not harsh: *soft air.* 7 not glaring or harsh: *soft light.* 8 gentle; kind; tender: *a soft heart.* 9 weak; unmanly: *The army had become soft from idleness and luxury.* 10 silly. 11 *Phonetics.* of the English consonants *c* and *g,* pronounced as fricatives or affricates, as in *city* and *gem,* rather than as stops, as in *corn* and *get.* 12 *Informal.* easy; easy-going: *a soft job, a soft person.* 13 of water, comparatively free from certain mineral salts that prevent soap from lathering. 14 of a drug, considered not seriously addictive or harmful to health. Marijuana is called a soft drug. Compare **hard** (def. 14). 15 of currency, not supported by gold or silver or not easily convertible in other currencies, and therefore likely to fluctuate or depreciate in value. Compare **hard** (def. 15).
—*adv.* softly; quietly; gently.
—*n.* that which is soft; soft part.
—*interj. Archaic.* hush! stop! [OE *sōfte*] —**soft′ly,** *adv.*

soft–ball (soft′bol′ *or* -bôl′) *n.* 1 a modified kind of baseball game that uses a larger and softer ball. 2 the ball used in that game.

soft–boiled (soft′boild′) *adj.* of eggs, boiled only a little so that the yolk is still soft.

soft–bound (soft′bound′) *adj., n.* —*adj.* of a book or edition, having covers of cardboard or a similar flexible material and usually sold more cheaply than a hardbound book; paperback; softcover.
—*n.* a book or edition bound in this way.

soft coal bituminous coal.

soft–cov·er (soft′kuv′ər) *adj. or n.* softbound.

soft drink a refreshing cold drink that is non-alcoholic, such as ginger ale, orangeade, etc.

soft·en (sof′ən) *v.* 1 make softer: *Hand lotion softens the skin.* 2 become softer: *Soap softens in water.* 3 lessen the ability of (a country, region, etc.) to resist invasion or attack through preliminary bombing, etc. 4 decrease; decline. —**soft′en·er,** *n.*

soft goods clothing, textiles, etc.; dry goods.

soft–head·ed (soft′hed′id) *adj. Informal.* silly; stupid; foolish.

soft–heart·ed (soft′här′tid) *adj.* gentle; kind; tender.
—**soft′-heart′ed·ly,** *adv.* —**soft′-heart′ed·ness,** *n.*

soft·ness (soft′nis) *n.* the state of being soft; ease; comfort; mildness; gentleness; weakness.

soft palate the fleshy back part of the roof of the mouth.

soft–ped·al (soft′ped′əl) *v.* **-alled** or **-aled, -al·ling** or **-al·ing.** 1 use a pedal on a piano, organ, etc. to soften musical tones. 2 make quieter, less noticeable, or less strong.

soft sell *Informal.* a sales approach that uses indirect persuasive tactics rather than pushing, aggressive ones.

soft–shell clam (soft′shel′) any of several marine clams (genus *Mya*) having a thin, crumbly shell, especially an edible species (*M. arenaria*) of the Atlantic coasts of North America and Europe.

soft shoe 1 a type of tap dancing using shoes without metal taps. 2 the style of shoe used for this.

soft–shoe (soft′shü′) *v.* **-shoed, -shoe·ing.** *Informal.* dance the soft shoe.

soft soap 1 a liquid or partly liquid soap. 2 *Informal.* flattery.

soft–soap (soft′sōp′) *v. Informal.* flatter. —**soft′-soap′er,** *n.*

soft–spo·ken (soft′spō′kən) *adj.* 1 speaking with a soft voice. 2 spoken softly.

soft spot 1 a feeling of tenderness or affection: *She still had a soft spot in her heart for her first boyfriend.* 2 a vulnerable spot or point: *a soft spot in an otherwise strong argument.*

soft touch *Informal.* a person who lends or gives money easily.

soft·ware (soft′wer′) *n. Computer science.* the standard programming procedures and specific programs associated with a computer system. Compare **hardware** (def. 3).

soft wheat a wheat that has a high starch and low gluten content.

soft·wood (sôft′wŭd′) *n.* **1** wood that is easily cut. **2** a tree that has needles or does not have broad leaves. Pines and firs are softwoods; oaks and maples are hardwoods. **3** the wood of such a tree.

soft·y (sôf′tē) *n., pl.* **soft·ies.** *Informal.* **1** a soft, silly, or weak person. **2** one who is easily imposed upon.

sog·gy (sog′ē) *adj.* **-gi·er, -gi·est. 1** thoroughly wet; soaked: *a soggy washcloth.* **2** damp and heavy: *soggy bread.* [< dial. *sog* bog, swamp < Scand.; cf. ON *soggr* damp] —**sog′gi·ness,** *n.*

soh (sō) *n. Music.* sol.

soi–di·sant (swä dē zäɴ′) *adj. French.* **1** calling oneself thus; self-styled. **2** so-called; pretended.

soi·gné (swä nyā′) *adj.* feminine form **soignée.** *French.* well-groomed; elegant.

soil¹ (soil) *n.* **1** ground; earth; dirt: *A farmer tills the soil.* **2** something thought of as a place for growth. **3** one's land; country. [ME < AF < L *solium* seat, influenced by L *solum* soil]

soil² (soil) *v., n.* —*v.* **1** make dirty: *He soiled his clean clothes.* **2** become dirty: *White shirts soil easily.* **3** spot; stain: *The splashing paint soiled the wall.* **4** disgrace; dishonor: *His actions have soiled the family name.* **5** corrupt morally. —*n.* a spot; stain. [ME < OF *soillier,* ult. < L *suile* pigsty < *sus* pig]

soi·ree or **soi·rée** (swä rā′) *n.* an evening party or social gathering. [< F *soirée* < *soir* evening]

so·journ (*v.* sō jėrn′ *or* sō′jėrn; *n.* sō′jėrn) *v., n.* —*v.* stay for a time: *The Israelites sojourned in the land of Egypt.* —*n.* a brief stay. [ME < OF *sojorner,* ult. < L *sub* under + *diurnus* of the day] —**so·journ′er,** *n.*

sol¹ (sōl) *n. Music.* **1** the fifth tone of an eight-tone major scale. **2** the tone G. See **do²** for picture. [see GAMUT.]
☛ *Hom.* **sole, soul.**

sol² (sōl) *n.* **1** the basic unit of money in Peru, divided into 100 centavos. See table at **money. 2** a coin worth one sol. [< Sp.]
☛ *Hom.* **sole, soul.**

sol. solution; soluble.

Sol (sol) *n.* **1** *Roman mythology.* the god of the sun, corresponding to the Greek god Helios. **2** the sun.

Sol. 1 Solomon. **2** Solicitor.

sol·ace (sol′is) *n., v.* **-aced, -ac·ing.** —*n.* a comfort; relief: *She found solace from her troubles in music.* —*v.* comfort; relieve: *He solaced himself with a book.* [ME < OF < L *solacium* < *solari* console] —**sol′ac·er,** *n.*

so·lar (sō′lər) *adj.* **1** of the sun: *a solar eclipse.* **2** having to do with the sun: *solar research.* **3** coming from the sun: *solar heat.* **4** measured or determined by the earth's motion in relation to the sun. A solar year is about 365¼ days long. **5** working by means of the sun's light or heat. A solar battery traps sunlight and converts it into electrical energy. [ME < L *solaris* < *sol* sun]

solar cell a small device for converting sunlight into electrical energy. It consists of thin wafers of a semiconductor, such as silicon, to which traces of certain other substances have been added. Sunlight striking the semiconductor produces charges which flow from the cell as an electric current.

solar collector a device, such as a glass-covered metal pan or plate that has been painted dull black, used to trap heat from sunlight. Solar collectors are used together with a storage device and a distribution system to provide heating for buildings, etc.

solar day the period of time from when the sun is at the meridian at any place on earth until the next time it reaches the same meridian.

solar flare an eruption of gases on the sun, usually associated with sunspots, which produces ultra-violet radiation and causes ionization in the upper atmosphere.

solar house a house designed to obtain part or all of its space and water heating directly from the sun by means of solar collectors, large windows facing the winter sun, etc.

so·lar·i·um (sə ler′ē əm) *n., pl.* **-lar·i·a** (-ler′ē ə). a room, porch, etc. where people can lie or sit in the sun. [< L *solarium* < *sol* sun]

solar plex·us (plek′səs) **1** the network of nerves situated at the upper part of the abdomen, behind the stomach and in front of the aorta. **2** *Informal.* the pit of the stomach.

solar system the sun and all the planets, satellites, comets, etc. that revolve around it.

solar wind the continuous flow of charged particles from the sun into space.

solar year the period of time required for the earth to make one revolution around the sun, which equals about 365¼ days.

hat, āge, fär; let, ēqual, tėrm; it, īce
hot, ōpen, ôrder; oil, out; cup, pūt, rüle,
əbove, takən, pencəl, lemən, circəs

ch, child; ng, long; sh, ship
th, thin; ŦH, then; zh, measure

sold (sōld) *v.* pt. and pp. of **sell.**

sol·der (sod′ər) *n., v.* —*n.* **1** a metal or alloy that can be melted and used for joining or mending metal surfaces, parts, etc. **2** anything that unites firmly or joins closely. —*v.* **1** fasten, mend, or join with solder. **2** unite firmly; join closely. **3** mend; repair; patch. [ME < OF *soldure,* ult. < L *solidus* solid] —**sol′der·er,** *n.*

sol·dier (sōl′jər) *n., v.* —*n.* **1** a person who serves in an army. **2** a private or a noncommissioned officer. **3** a person having skill or experience in war. **4** a person who serves in any cause: *soldiers of Christ.* **5** in colonies of certain ants or termites, an individual having a large head and powerful jaws, adapted for defending the colony. —*v.* **1** act or serve as a soldier. **2** *Archaic.* shirk work, especially on pretence of illness. [ME < OF *soldier* < *soulde* pay < L *solidus,* a Roman coin]

sol·dier·ly (sōl′jər lē) *adj.* like or suitable for a soldier.

soldier of fortune a man serving or ready to serve as a soldier under any government for money, adventure, or pleasure; military adventurer.

sol·dier·y (sōl′jər ē) *n., pl.* **-dier·ies. 1** soldiers collectively. **2** a body of soldiers. **3** military training or knowledge.

sol·do (sōl′dō) *n., pl.* **-di** (-dē). a former Italian copper coin worth 1/20 of a lira. [< Ital. < L *solidus.* See SOLIDUS.]

sole¹ (sōl) *adj.* **1** one and only; single: *the sole heir.* **2** only: *We three were the sole survivors.* **3** of or for only one person or group and not others; exclusive: *the sole right of use.* **4** alone: *a sole undertaking.* [ME < OF < L *solus*]
☛ *Hom.* **sol, soul.**
☛ *Syn.* **1, 2.** See note at **single.**

sole² (sōl) *n., v.* **soled, sol·ing.** —*n.* **1** the bottom or under surface of the foot. **2** bottom of a shoe, slipper, boot, etc. **3** a piece of leather, rubber, etc. cut to fit the bottom of a shoe, slipper, boot, etc. **4** the under surface; under part; bottom. —*v.* put a sole on. [ME < OF *sole,* ult. < L *solea* < *solum* bottom, ground]
☛ *Hom.* **sol, soul.**

sole³ (sōl) *n., pl.* **sole** or **soles. 1** any of a family (Soleidae) of flatfishes including some species highly valued as food fishes, such as the **European sole** (*Solea solea*), also called **Dover sole. 2** any of various similar flatfishes belonging to other families. [ME < MF < L *solea,* originally, sole²]
☛ *Hom.* **sol, soul.**

sol·e·cism (sol′ə siz′əm) *n.* **1** a violation of the grammatical or other accepted usages of language; a mistake in using words. *I done it* is a solecism. **2** a mistake in social behavior; breach of good manners or etiquette. [< L < Gk. *soloikismos,* supposedly < *Soloi,* a Greek colony in Cilicia, an ancient region in Asia Minor]

sol·e·cis·tic (sol′ə sis′tik) *adj.* of, having to do with, or involving a solecism or solecisms. —**sol′e·cis′ti·cal·ly,** *adv.*

sole·ly (sōl′lē) *adv.* **1** as the only one or ones; alone: *You will be solely responsible.* **2** only; purely; entirely: *He does it solely for convenience.*

sol·emn (sol′əm) *adj.* **1** serious; grave; earnest: *a solemn face.* **2** causing serious or grave thoughts: *The organ played solemn music.* **3** done with form and ceremony. **4** connected with religion; sacred. [ME < OF < L *sollemnis*] —**sol′emn·ly,** *adv.* —**sol′emn·ness,** *n.*

so·lem·ni·ty (sə lem′nə tē) *n., pl.* **-ties. 1** a solemn feeling; seriousness; impressiveness. **2** Often, **solemnities,** *pl.* a solemn, formal ceremony: *The solemnities were concluded with a prayer by the college chaplain.*

sol·em·nize (sol′əm nīz′) *v.* **-nized, -niz·ing. 1** observe with ceremonies: *Christian churches solemnize the resurrection of Christ at Easter.* **2** hold or perform (a ceremony or service): *The marriage was solemnized in the cathedral.* **3** make serious or grave. —**sol′em·ni·za′tion,** *n.*

so·le·noid (sō′lə noid′) *n. Electricity.* a spiral or cylindrical coil of wire that acts like a magnet when a current passes through it. [< F < Gk. *sōlēn* pipe]

sol–fa (sōl′fä′) *n., v.* **-faed** (-fäd), **-fa·ing.** *Music.* —*n.* **1** tonic sol-fa. **2** (*adj.*) of or having to do with tonic sol-fa: *sol-fa notation, sol-fa syllables.* —*v.* use the sol-fa syllables in singing. [< Ital. *solfa* < *sol* + *fa.* See GAMUT.]

sol·feg·gio (sol fej′ō) n., pl. **-gios.** 1 an exercise for the voice in which the sol-fa syllables are used. 2 the use of the sol-fa syllables. [< Ital. *solfeggio* < *solfa.* See SOL-FA.]

so·lic·it (sə lis′it) v. 1 ask earnestly; try to get: *The tailor sent around cards soliciting trade.* 2 make appeals or requests: *to solicit for contributions.* 3 influence to do wrong; tempt; entice: *To solicit a judge means to offer him bribes.* 4 accost a person with immoral offers. [ME < L *sollicitare* < *sollicitus.* See SOLICITOUS.]
☛ *Syn.* 1. See note at **ask.**

so·lic·i·ta·tion (sə lis′ə tā′shən) n. 1 an earnest request; entreaty. 2 an urging to do wrong; temptation; enticement.

so·lic·i·tor (sə lis′ə tər) n. 1 a person who entreats or requests. 2 a person who seeks trade or business. 3 a lawyer, especially one who does not plead in court. In England, a solicitor prepares a case and a barrister pleads it. In Canada, the same person may be both solicitor and barrister. 4 a lawyer for a town, city, etc.

solicitor general *pl.* **solicitors general.** 1 in Canada: **a** the federal cabinet minister having primary responsibility for law enforcement and correctional services, including the RCMP and the Canadian Penitentiary Service. **b** in Alberta, the cabinet minister responsible for correctional services. **c** in Ontario, the cabinet minister responsible for the police. Compare **attorney general. Crown, the other being the attorney general.** 2 a law officer ranking next below an attorney general. Also, **solicitor-general,** *pl.* **solicitors-general.**

so·lic·it·ous (sə lis′ə təs) adj. 1 showing care or concern; anxious; concerned: *Parents are solicitous for their children's progress.* 2 desirous; eager: *solicitous to please.* [< L *sollicitus* < OL *sollus* all + *citus* stirred up, pp. of *ciere* arouse] —**so·lic′it·ous·ly,** adv. —**so·lic′it·ous·ness,** n.

so·lic·i·tude (sə lis′ə tyüd′ *or* sə lis′ə tüd′) n. anxious care; anxiety; concern.
☛ *Syn.* See note at **care.**

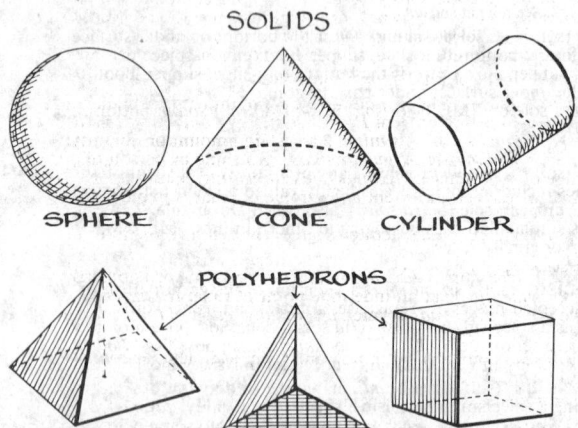

SOLIDS

SPHERE   CONE   CYLINDER

POLYHEDRONS

PYRAMID   TETRAHEDRON   CUBE

sol·id (sol′id) adj., n. —adj. 1 not a liquid or a gas: *Water becomes solid when it freezes.* 2 not hollow: *A bar of iron is solid; a pipe is hollow.* 3 hard; firm: *They were glad to leave the boat and put their feet on solid ground.* 4 strongly made or put together: *This is not a very solid table.* 5 alike throughout: *The cloth is a solid blue.* 6 firmly united: *The country was solid for peace.* 7 serious; not superficial or trifling: *a background of solid study.* 8 genuine; real: *solid comfort.* 9 that can be depended on: *He is a solid citizen.* 10 having good judgment; sound; sensible; intelligent: *a solid book by a solid thinker.* 11 financially sound or strong: *a solid business.* 12 whole; entire: *I waited three solid hours.* 13 undivided; continuous: *a solid row of houses.* 14 *Printing.* having the lines of type not separated by leads; having few open spaces. 15 having length, breadth, and thickness: *A cylinder is a solid figure.* 16 written without a hyphen. *Earthworm* is a solid compound. 17 *Informal.* on a friendly, favorable, or advantageous footing: *to get in solid with one's employer.* 18 thorough; downright; vigorous; substantial: *a good solid blow.* 19 *Slang.* good; excellent; first-rate. —n. 1 a substance that is not a liquid or a gas. 2 a body that has length, breadth, and thickness. A cube is a solid. [ME, ult. < L *solidus*] —**sol′id·ly,** adv. —**sol′id·ness,** n.
☛ *Syn.* adj. 3. See note at **firm.**

sol·i·dar·i·ty (sol′ə dar′ə tē *or* sol′ə der′ə tē) n., pl. **-ties.** unity of fellowship arising from common responsibilities and interests. [< F *solidarité*]

solid geometry the branch of mathematics that deals with objects having the three dimensions of length, breadth, and thickness.

so·lid·i·fy (sə lid′ə fī′) v. **-fied, -fy·ing.** 1 make or become solid; harden: *Extreme cold will solidify water. Jelly solidifies as it gets cold.* 2 make or become firmly united. 3 make or become crystallized. —**so·lid′i·fi·ca′tion,** n.

so·lid·i·ty (sə lid′ə tē) n., pl. **-ties.** the state or quality of being solid; firmness; hardness; density.

sol·id–state (sol′id stāt′) adj. 1 of or having to do with the study of the properties of solid materials, especially of their molecular structure, the movement of their electrons, etc. The transistor was developed as a result of research in solid-state physics. 2 utilizing the electrical, magnetic, etc. properties of solid materials, especially semiconductor materials: *a solid-state radio receiver.*

sol·i·dus (sol′ə dəs) n., pl. **-di** (-dī *or* -dē). 1 a Roman gold coin introduced by Constantine, later called a bezant. 2 a sloping line (/) used as a dividing line in writing dates (20/7/82), fractions (2/3), etc. and to indicate alternative words (and/or), ratios (km/h), etc. [< L *solidus* (*nummus*) solid (coin)]

sol·i·fluc·tion *or* **sol·i·flux·ion** (sol′ə fluk′shən) n. the movement of soil and rock waste caused by weather. [< L *solum* ground, earth + E *fluxion*]

so·lil·o·quize (sə lil′ə kwīz′) v. **-quized, -quiz·ing.** 1 talk to oneself. 2 speak a soliloquy. —**so·lil′o·quiz′er,** n.

so·lil·o·quy (sə lil′ə kwē) n., pl. **-quies.** 1 the act of talking to oneself. 2 a speech made by an actor to himself when alone on the stage. A soliloquy may be used to impart knowledge to the audience, to reveal a character's true motives, etc. [< LL *soliloquium* < L *solus* alone + *loqui* speak]

sol·ip·sism (sol′ip siz′əm) n. 1 the theory that the only thing the self can know is its own existence and experiences. 2 the theory that the only reality is the self.

sol·ip·sist (sol′ip sist′) n., adj. —n. a person who follows or believes in solipsism. —adj. solipsistic.

sol·ip·sis·tic (sol′ip sis′tik) adj. of or having to do with solipsism or solipsists.

sol·i·taire (sol′ə ter′) n. 1 any of various card games played by one person. 2 a diamond or other gem set by itself. [< F < L *solitarius.* Doublet of SOLITARY.]

sol·i·tar·y (sol′ə ter′ē) adj., n., pl. **-tar·ies.** —adj. 1 alone; single; only: *A solitary rider was seen in the distance.* 2 without companions; away from people; lonely: *He leads a solitary life in his hut in the mountains. The house is in a solitary spot many kilometres from a town.* 3 a *Zoology.* living alone, rather than in colonies: *the solitary bee.* b *Botany.* growing separately; not forming clusters: *a solitary stipule.*
—n. 1 a person living alone, away from people. 2 solitary confinement: *The prisoner was put in solitary.* [< L *solitarius,* ult. < *solus* alone. Doublet of SOLITAIRE.] —**sol′i·tar′i·ly,** adv. —**sol′i·tar′i·ness,** n.

solitary confinement the keeping of a prisoner in complete isolation from others, often as a penalty for misbehavior while in prison.

sol·i·tude (sol′ə tyüd′ *or* sol′ə tüd′) n. 1 the condition of being alone: *He likes company and hates solitude.* 2 a lonely place. 3 loneliness. [< L *solitudo* < *solus* alone]
☛ *Syn.* 1. **Solitude, isolation** = a state of being alone. **Solitude,** applying to a state of being either where there are no other people for company or cut off either voluntarily or involuntarily from those around, emphasizes aloneness, the fact or feeling of being entirely by oneself, without companions: *Both the prospector in the desert and the shy person in the city live in solitude.* **Isolation** emphasizes being separated from others or standing apart from the rest of the world: *A single mountain peak rose in splendid isolation.*

sol·mi·za·tion (sol′mə zā′shən) n. *Music.* the system of singing the syllables *do, re, mi, fa, sol, la, ti, do* to the tones of the eight-tone scale; sol-fa. [< F *solmisation,* ult. < *sol* + *mi.* See GAMUT.]

so·lo (sō′lō) n., pl. **-los;** adj., v. **-loed, -lo·ing.** —n. 1 a piece of music arranged for one voice or instrument. 2 anything done without a partner, companion, instructor, etc.
—adj. 1 arranged for and performed by one voice or instrument: *a solo part.* 2 playing the solo part: *a solo violin.* 3 without a partner, companion, instructor, etc.; alone: *a solo flight, a solo dance.*
—v. make a solo flight in an airplane. [< Ital. *solo* alone < L *solus*]

so·lo·ist (sō′lō ist) n. a person who performs a solo.

Sol·o·mon (sol′ə mən) n. 1 in the Bible, a king of Israel and son of David, famous for his wisdom and for the great temple which he had built in Jerusalem (I Kings 3:5-28). 2 any man of great wisdom.

A Solomon's seal (def. 1).

hat, āge, fär; let, ēqual, tėrm; it, īce
hot, ōpen, ôrder; oil, out; cup, pů̇t, rüle,
əbove, takən, pencəl, lemən, circəs

ch, child; ng, long; sh, ship
th, thin; ᴛʜ, then; zh, measure

Solomon's seal 1 the Star of David, especially as a medieval mystical symbol. 2 any of several perennial plants (genus *Polygonatum*) of the lily family having greenish or white flowers and a white underground stem marked with prominent, seal-like leaf scars.

So·lon (sō′lən *or* sō′lon) *n.* 1 a wise man; sage. 2 *Informal.* a member of a legislature. [< *Solon* (638?–558? B.C.), a wise Athenian lawgiver]

so long *Informal.* goodbye; farewell.

sol·stice (sol′stis) *n.* 1 either of the two times in the year when the sun is at its greatest distance from the celestial equator. In the Northern Hemisphere, June 21 or 22, the **summer solstice**, is the longest day of the year and December 21 or 22, the **winter solstice**, is the shortest. 2 either of the two points reached by the sun at these times. 3 a turning or culminating point; furthest limit; crisis. [ME < OF < L *solstitium*, ult. < *sol* sun + *sistere* stand still]

sol·sti·tial (sol stish′əl) *adj.* having to do with a solstice.

sol·u·bil·i·ty (sol′yə bil′ə tē) *n., pl.* **-ties.** 1 a quality that substances have of dissolving or being dissolved easily: *the solubility of sugar in water.* 2 a quality that problems, difficulties, questions, etc. have of being solved or explained.

sol·u·ble (sol′yə bəl) *adj.* 1 that can be dissolved or made into liquid: *Salt is soluble in water.* 2 that can be solved: *soluble puzzles.* [< L *solubilis* < *solvere* dissolve]—**sol′u·bly,** *adv.*

sol·ute (sol′yüt *or* sō′lüt) *n.* a solid, gas, etc. dissolved in a liquid to make a solution: *Salt is a solute in sea water.* [< L *solutus*, pp. of *solvere* dissolve, loosen]

so·lu·tion (sə lü′shən) *n.* 1 the solving of a problem: *The solution of the problem required many hours.* 2 an explanation or answer: *The police are seeking a solution of the crime.* 3 the process of dissolving; changing of a solid or gas to a liquid by treatment with a liquid. 4 a liquid or mixture formed by dissolving. 5 a separating into parts. 6 the condition of being dissolved: *Sugar and salt can be held in solution in water.* [ME < OF < L *solutio, -onis* a loosing < *solvere* loosen]

solv·a·ble (sol′və bəl) *adj.* 1 capable of being solved. 2 capable of being dissolved.

solve (solv) *v.* **solved, solv·ing.** find the answer to; clear up; explain: *The mystery was never solved. He has solved all the problems in the lesson.* [ME < L *solvere* loosen]—**solv′er,** *n.*

sol·ven·cy (sol′vən sē) *n., pl.* **-cies.** the ability to pay all one owes.

sol·vent (sol′vənt) *adj., n.—adj.* 1 able to pay all that one owes: *A bankrupt firm is not solvent.* 2 especially of a liquid, able to dissolve another substance.—*n.* 1 a substance, usually a liquid, that can dissolve other substances: *Water is a solvent of sugar and salt.* 2 a thing that solves. [< L *solvens, -entis*, ppr. of *solvere* loosen, pay]

so·ma¹ (sō′mə) *n., pl.* **so·ma·ta** (sō′mə tə). all the tissues and organs of an animal or plant except the germ cells. [< NL < Gk. *sōma* body]

so·ma² (sō′mə) *n.* 1 an intoxicating or hallucinogenic drink prepared from the juice of a plant, used in ancient Vedic rituals. 2 the plant from whose juice this drink was prepared, variously identified as a species of milkweed or a mushroom.

So·ma·li (sə mä′lē) *n., pl.* **-li** *or* **-lis;** *adj.—n.* 1 a member of a people inhabiting Somalia, a country in NE Africa. The Somalis are apparently of mixed African and Mediterranean descent. 2 the Afro-Asiatic language of the Somalis.—*adj.* of or having to do with Somalia, the Somalis, or their language.

so·mat·ic (sō mat′ik) *adj.* 1 of or having to do with the body. 2 having to do with the cavity of the body, or its walls. 3 having to do with the soma. [< Gk. *sōmatikos* < *sōma, -atos* body]

somatic cell any of the cells of an animal or plant body other than the reproductive, or germ, cells. Compare **germ cell.**

som·bre (som′bər) *adj.* 1 dark; gloomy: *A cloudy winter day is sombre.* 2 melancholy; dismal: *His losses made him very sombre.* Also, **somber.** [< F *sombre*, probably ult. < L *sub-* under + *umbra* shade]—**som′bre·ly,** *adv.*—**som′bre·ness,** *n.*

som·brer·o (som brer′ō) *n., pl.* **-brer·os.** a broad-brimmed hat with a high crown worn especially in Mexico and the SW United States. See **hat** for picture. [< Sp. *sombrero*, ult. < L *sub-* under + *umbra* shade]

some (sum; *unstressed,* səm) *adj., pron., adv.—adj.* 1 certain, but not known or not named: *Some people sleep more than others.* 2 a number of: *He left the city some years ago.* 3 a quantity of: *Drink some milk.* 4 a; any: *Ask some girl to come here.* 5 about: *Some twenty people saw it.* 6 *Informal.* big; good: *That was some storm!*
—*pron.* 1 certain unnamed persons or things: *Some think so.* 2 a certain number or quantity: *Jack ate some and threw the rest away.*
—*adv.* 1 *Informal.* to some degree or extent; somewhat: *He is some better today.* 2 *Informal.* to a great degree or extent: *That's going some!* [OE *sum*]
☞ *Hom.* **sum.**

–some¹ *adjective-forming suffix.* 1 tending to, as in *frolicsome, meddlesome.* 2 causing, as in *awesome, troublesome.* 3 to a considerable degree, as in *lonesome.* [OE *-sum*]

–some² *suffix.* a group of, as in *twosome, foursome.* [< *some*]

some·bod·y (sum′bud′ē *or* -bod′ē) *pron., n., pl.* **-bod·ies.**
—*pron.* a person not known or named; some person; someone.—*n.* a person of importance: *She acts as if she were somebody since she won the prize.*

some·day (sum′dā′) *adv.* at some future time.

some·how (sum′hou′) *adv.* in a way not known or not stated; in one way or another: *I'll finish this work somehow.*
somehow or other, in one way or another.

some·one (sum′wun′ *or* sum′wən) *pron.* some person; somebody.

some·place (sum′plās′) *adv.* in or to some place; somewhere.

som·er·sault (sum′ər solt′ *or* -sôlt′) *n., v.—n.* a complete roll of the body, forward or backward, bringing the feet over the head.
—*v.* roll in this way. Also, **summersault.** [ME *sombresault* < Provençal *sobresaut*, ult. < L *supra* over + *saltus* jump]

som·er·set (sum′ər set′) *n. or v.* somersault.

some·thing (sum′thing′) *n., adv.—n.* 1 some thing; a particular thing not named or not known: *I've got something important to tell you. He has something on his mind.* 2 a certain amount or quantity; part; little: *Something yet of doubt remains.* 3 a thing or person of some value or importance: *He thinks he's something.* 4 a thing or person that is to a certain extent an example of what is named: *He was something of a violinist.*
—*adv.* somewhat; to some extent or degree: *He is something like his father.*

some·time (sum′tīm′) *adv., adj.—adv.* 1 at one time or another: *Come over sometime.* 2 at an indefinite point of time: *It happened sometime last March.—adj.* former: *a sometime pupil of the school.*

some·times (sum′tīmz′) *adv.* now and then; at times: *He comes to visit sometimes.*

some·way (sum′wā′) *adv.* in some way.

some·what (sum′wot′ *or* -hwot′) *adv., n.—adv.* to some extent or degree; slightly: *somewhat round.—n.* some part or amount; a bit: *It was somewhat of a struggle. Somewhat of the fun is lost when you hear a joke the second time.*

some·where (sum′wer′ *or* -hwer′) *adv.* 1 in or to some place; in or to one place or another: *He lives somewhere in the neighborhood.* 2 at some time: *It happened somewhere in the last century.*

some·while (sum′wīl′ *or* -hwīl′) *adv.* 1 at times. 2 *Rare.* for some time. 3 sometime. 4 formerly.

some·whith·er (sum′wiᴛʜ′ər *or* -hwiᴛʜ′ər) *adv. Rare.* to some place.

som·nam·bu·lant (som nam′byə lənt) *adj.* sleepwalking or having the habit of sleepwalking.

som·nam·bu·late (som nam′byə lāt) *v.* **-at·ed, -at·ing.** walk about while asleep; sleepwalk.—**som·nam′bu·la′tion,** *n.*—**som·nam′bu·la′tor,** *n.*

som·nam·bu·lism (som nam′byə liz′əm) *n.* sleepwalking. [< L *somnus* sleep + *ambulare* walk]

som·nam·bu·list (som nam′byə list) *n.* sleepwalker.

som·nam·bu·lis·tic (som nam′byə lis′tik) *adj.* having to do with sleepwalking or sleepwalkers.—**som·nam′bu·lis′ti·cal·ly,** *adv.*

som·nif·er·ous (som nif′ər əs) *adj.* 1 causing sleep. 2 sleepy.

[< L *somnifer* < *somnus* sleep + *ferre* bring]—**som·nif′er·ous·ly**, *adv.*

som·no·lence (som′nə ləns) *n.* sleepiness; drowsiness.

som·no·lent (som′nə lənt) *adj.* sleepy; drowsy. [< L *somnolentus* < *somnus* sleep]—**som′no·lent·ly**, *adv.*

Som·nus (som′nəs) *n. Roman mythology.* the god of sleep.

son (sun) *n.* **1** a male child or person spoken of in relation to either or both of his parents. **2** a male descendant. **3** son-in-law. **4** a boy or man attached to a country, a cause, etc. as a child is to its parents: *sons of liberty.* **5** anything thought of as a son in relation to its origin. **6** a term of address to a boy or from an older person, priest, etc. **7** the Son, Jesus Christ. [OE *sunu*]—**son′less**, *adj.*
☛ **Hom. sun.**

so·nance (sō′nəns) *n.* a sonant quality or state.

so·nant (sō′nənt) *adj., n.—adj.* **1** of sound; having sound; sounding. **2** *Phonetics.* pronounced with the vocal cords vibrating; voiced.—*n. Phonetics.* a sound pronounced with the vocal cords vibrating; a voiced sound. (z) and (v) are sonants; (s) and (f) are not. [< L *sonans, -antis*, ppr. of *sonare* to sound < *sonus*, n., sound]

so·nar (sō′när) *n.* a device using the reflection of underwater sound waves for navigation, range finding, detecting submerged objects, etc. [< *so*und *na*vigation *a*nd *r*anging]

so·na·ta (sə nä′tə) *n.* a musical composition for one or two instruments, having three or four movements in contrasted rhythms but related keys: *a piano sonata.* [< Ital. *sonata*, literally, sounded (on an instrument, as distinguished from sung), ult. < L *sonus* sound]

sonata form a musical structure used especially for the first movement of a sonata, symphony, concerto, etc. The sonata form usually has three main divisions, exposition, development, and recapitulation, often followed by a coda.

son·a·ti·na (son′ə tē′nə) *n.* a short or simplified sonata. [< Ital. *sonatina*, dim. of *sonata* sonata]

song (song) *n.* **1** something to sing; a short poem set to music. **2 a** poetry: *fame celebrated in song.* **b** poetry that has a lyrical quality: *a song of childhood.* **3** a piece of music for, or as if for, a poem that is to be sung. **4** the act or practice of singing: *The canary burst into song.* **5** any sound like singing: *the cricket's song, the song of the teakettle, the song of the brook.* **6** a mere trifle; low price: *to buy things for a song.*
for a song, very cheaply: *I bought the bike for a song at an auction.*
song and dance, *Slang.* **a** an explanation or account, not necessarily true, and often intended to impress or deceive. **b** fuss; disturbance; turmoil: *He made a great song and dance about having to do the job.*
[OE *sang*]—**song′like**, *adj.*

song·bird (song′bèrd′) *n.* **1** a bird that sings. **2** a passerine bird, especially any species of the suborder Oscines, having vocal organs specialized for producing varied and, in many cases, melodic calls.

song·less (song′lis) *adj.* not able to sing.

Song of Solomon a book of the Bible consisting of a collection of love poems traditionally attributed to King Solomon.

Song of Songs Song of Solomon.

song sparrow a small North American sparrow (*Melospiza melodia*) having black, brown, and white plumage and noted for its pleasing song.

song·ster (song′stər) *n.* **1** singer. **2** a writer of songs or poems. **3** songbird. [OE *sangestre*]

song·stress (song′stris) *n.* **1** a woman singer. **2** a woman writer of songs or poems; poetess. **3** a female songbird.

song thrush a common Old World thrush (*Turdus philomelos*) that is noted for its singing, having plumage that is brown above and white below, with a spotted breast. Also called **mavis.**

son·ic (son′ik) *adj.* **1** of, having to do with, or using sound waves. **2** of or having to do with the speed of sound in air (331 metres per second or about 1192 kilometres per hour at 0° Celsius). [< L *sonus* sound]

sonic barrier the sudden increase in aerodynamic resistance experienced by an aircraft when it approaches the speed of sound (331 m/s or about 1192 km/h at 0°C).

sonic boom the sound, like that of an explosion, of the shock wave formed in front of an aircraft travelling above the speed of sound.

sonic mine a container holding an explosive charge that is put under water and exploded by propeller vibrations; acoustic mine.

so·nif·er·ous (sō nif′ər əs) *adj.* carrying or producing sound. [< L *sonus* sound + E *-ferous*]

son-in-law (sun′in lo′ *or* -lô′) *n., pl.* **sons-in-law.** the husband of one's daughter.

son·net (son′it) *n.* a poem having 14 lines, usually in iambic pentameter, and a certain arrangement of rhymes. Elizabethan and Italian sonnets differ in the arrangement of the rhymes. [< F < Ital. < Provençal *sonet*, ult. < L *sonus* sound]

son·net·eer (son′ə tēr′) *n., v.—n.* a writer of sonnets.—*v.* write sonnets.

son·ny (sun′ē) *n., pl.* **-nies.** *Informal.* a word used in speaking to a young boy: *Say, sonny, can you tell me how to get to the city hall from here?*

so·no·buoy (sō′nə boi′ *or* -bü′ē) *n.* a buoy equipped with devices for detecting underwater sounds and transmitting them by radio. [< L *sonus* sound + E *buoy*]

Son of God Jesus Christ.

so·nom·e·ter (sō nom′ə tər) *n.* **1** an instrument used in measuring the pitch of musical tones or for experimenting with vibrating strings. **2** an instrument used for testing a person's hearing. [< L *sonus* sound + E *-meter*]

so·nor·i·ty (sə nôr′ə tē) *n., pl.* **-ties.** the state or quality of being sonorous.

so·no·rous (sə nô′rəs) *adj.* **1** giving out or having a deep, loud sound. **2** full and rich in sound. **3** having an impressive sound; high-sounding: *sonorous phrases, a sonorous style.* [< L *sonorus*, ult. < *sonor* sound]—**so·no′rous·ly**, *adv.*

son·ship (sun′ship) *n.* the state of being a son.

Sons of Freedom a sect of Doukhobors located, for the most part, in British Columbia.

soon (sün) *adv.* **1** in a short time; before long: *I will see you again soon.* **2** before the usual or expected time; early: *Why have you come so soon?* **3** promptly; quickly: *As soon as I hear, I will let you know.* **4** readily; willingly: *The brave soldier would as soon die as yield to the enemy.*
had sooner, would more readily; prefer to.
[OE *sōna* at once]
☛ *Usage.* **Sooner than.** After **no sooner** the connective used is **than**, not **when:** *The fly had no sooner hit the water than* (not *when*) *a huge trout snapped at it.*

soot (sut) *n., v.—n.* a black substance in the smoke from burning coal, wood, oil, etc. Soot makes smoke dark and collects on the inside of chimneys.—*v.* cover or blacken with soot. [OE *sōt*]—**soot′less**, *adj.*

sooth (süth) *n., adj. Archaic.—n.* truth.—*adj.* true. [OE *sōth*]

soothe (süᴛн) *v.* **soothed, sooth·ing.** **1** quiet; calm; comfort: *The mother soothed the crying child.* **2** make less painful; relieve; ease. [OE *sōthian*]—**sooth′ing·ly**, *adv.*

sooth·er (sü′ᴛнər) *n.* **1** a person or thing that soothes. **2** a baby's pacifier.

sooth·ly (süth′lē) *adv. Archaic.* truly; in truth.

sooth·say·er (süth′sā′ər) *n.* a person who claims to foretell the future; person who makes prophecies. [< *sooth* + *sayer*]

sooth·say·ing (süth′sā′ing) *n.* **1** the foretelling of future events. **2** a prediction of prophecy.

soot·y (sut′ē) *adj.* **soot·i·er, soot·i·est.** **1** covered or blackened with soot. **2** dark-brown or black; dark-colored.—**soot′i·ly**, *adv.* —**soot′i·ness**, *n.*

sop (sop) *n., v.* **sopped, sop·ping.—n.** **1** a piece of food dipped or soaked in milk, broth, etc. **2** something given to soothe or quiet; bribe. **3** a person or thing that is thoroughly soaked.
—*v.* **1** dip or soak. **2** take up (water, etc.); wipe; mop: *Please sop up that water with a cloth.* **3** be drenched. **4** soak thoroughly; drench. **5** soak in or through. [OE *sopp*]

sop. soprano.

soph·ic (sof′ik) *adj.* of, having to do with, or teaching wisdom. [< Gk. *sophikos* < *sophos* wise, clever]

soph·ism (sof′iz əm) *n.* a clever but misleading or specious argument; an argument based on false or unsound reasoning. [ME < OF < L < Gk. *sophisma*, ult. < *sophos* clever]

soph·ist (sof′ist) *n.* **1** Usually, **Sophist,** one of a group of professional teachers of ancient Greece who gave instruction in rhetoric, grammar, science, the nature of virtue, the history of society, and other teachings designed especially to promote success in public life. The Sophists were accused of not really seeking the truth, but being only interested in success in debate, even at the expense of honesty. **2** a person who reasons cleverly but falsely. **3** in early use, a philosopher or sage.

so·phis·tic (sə fis′tik) *adj.* sophistical.

so·phis·ti·cal (sə fis′tə kəl) *adj.* **1** clever but misleading; based

on false or unsound reasoning. **2** using clever but misleading arguments; reasoning falsely or unsoundly.—**so·phis′ti·cal·ly,** *adv.*

so·phis·ti·cate (*v.* sə fis′tə kāt′; *n.* sə fis′tə kāt′ *or* sə fis′tə kət) *v.* **-cat·ed, -cat·ing;** *n.*—*v.* **1** make experienced in worldly ways; cause to lose one's natural simplicity and frankness. **2** mislead (a person) or corrupt (an argument, etc.) by using sophistry. **3** of instruments, devices, etc., make more complex and refined.
—*n.* a sophisticated person. [ME < Med.L *sopohisticare* < L < Gk. *sophistikos* sophistical, ult. < *sophos* clever]

so·phis·ti·cat·ed (sə fis′tə kāt′id) *adj.* **1** refined, cultured, and experienced in worldly ways: *a sophisticated writer.* **2** appealing to sophisticated people: *a sophisticated novel, a sophisticated little restaurant.* **3** lacking natural simplicity, frankness, etc.; too refined, worldly-wise, etc. **4** of mechanical or electronic devices, complex and advanced in design: *sophisticated missiles.*

so·phis·ti·ca·tion (sə fis′tə kā′shən) *n.* **1** the act, process, or result of sophisticating. **2** the quality or state of being sophisticated.

soph·ist·ry (sof′is trē) *n.,* *pl.* **-ries. 1** unsound reasoning. **2** a clever but misleading argument.

soph·o·more (sof′ə môr′) *n.,* *adj.*—*n.* a student in the second year of college.—*adj.* of or having to do with second-year college students. [earlier *sophomer,* originally, taking part in dialectic exercises < *sophom,* var. of *sophism*]

soph·o·mor·ic (sof′ə môr′ik) *adj.* **1** of, having to do with, or like a sophomore or sophomores. **2** conceited and pretentious but crude and ignorant.

so·po·rif·er·ous (sop′ə rif′ər əs *or* sō′pə rif′ər əs) *adj.* bringing sleep; causing sleep. [< L *soporifer* < *sopor* deep sleep + *ferre* bring]

so·po·rif·ic (sop′ə rif′ik *or* sō′pə rif′ik) *adj.,* *n.*—*adj.* **1** causing or tending to cause sleep. **2** sleepy; drowsy.—*n.* a drug that causes sleep. [< L *sopor* deep sleep + *facere* make]

sop·ping (sop′ing) *adj.* soaked; drenched.

sop·py (sop′ē) *adj.* **-pi·er, -pi·est. 1** soaked; very wet: *soppy ground, soppy weather.* **2** *Informal.* silly; sentimental.

so·pra·no (sə pran′ō *or* sə prä′nō) *n.,* *pl.* **-pran·os. 1** the highest singing voice for women, girls, or boys. **2** a singer who has such a voice. **3** the part sung by a soprano. Soprano is the highest part in standard four-part harmony for male and female voices. **4** an instrument having the highest range in a family of musical instruments. **5** (*adj.*) having to do with, having the range of, or designed for a soprano. **6** a high-pitched voice. [< Ital. *soprano* < *sopra* above < L *supra*]

Sor·bonne (sôr bon′ *or* sôr′bon) *n.* the seat of the faculties of letters and science of the University of Paris.

sor·cer·er (sôr′sər ər) *n.* a man who practices magic with the aid of evil spirits; magician.

sor·cer·ess (sôr′sər is) *n.* a woman who practises magic with the aid of evil spirits; witch.

sor·cer·y (sôr′sər ē) *n.,* *pl.* **-cer·ies.** magic performed with the aid of evil spirits; witchcraft. [ME < OF *sorcerie,* ult. < L *sors* lot]

sor·did (sôr′did) *adj.* **1** dirty; filthy: *The poor family lived in a sordid hut.* **2** mean; low; base; contemptible. **3** caring too much for money; meanly selfish; greedy. [< L *sordidus* dirty < *sordere* be dirty < *sordes* dirt]—**sor′did·ly,** *adv.*—**sor′did·ness,** *n.*

sore (sôr) *adj.* **sor·er, sor·est;** *n.,* *adv.*—*adj.* **1** painful; aching; tender; smarting: *a sore throat, a sore finger.* **2** sad; distressed: *The suffering of the refugees made her heart sore.* **3** easily angered or offended; irritable; touchy. **4** *Informal.* offended; angered; vexed: *He is sore at missing the game.* **5** causing pain, misery, anger, or offence; vexing: *Their defeat is a sore subject with the members of the team.* **6** severe; distressing: *Your going away is a sore grief to us.*
—*n.* **1** a painful place on the body where the skin or flesh is broken or bruised. **2** a cause of pain, sorrow, sadness, anger, offence, etc.
—*adv. Archaic.* in a sore manner. [OE *sār*]—**sore′ly,** *adv.*
—**sore′ness,** *n.*
☛ *Hom.* **soar.**

sore·head (sôr′hed′) *n. Informal.* a person who is easily angered or offended.

sor·ghum (sôr′gəm) *n.* **1** any of an Old World genus (*Sorghum*) of annual and perennial cereal grasses, especially a cornlike African species (*S. vulgare*) widely cultivated in many varieties as a cereal crop, as a source of edible oil, starch, and syrup, and for fodder. **2** syrup made from the juice of cultivated sorghum. [< NL < Ital. < L *syricum* Syrian]

so·ror·i·ty (sə rôr′ə tē) *n.,* *pl.* **-ties. 1** sisterhood. **2** a club or society of women or girls. There are student sororities in many

---

hat, āge, fär; let, ēqual, tèrm; it, īce
hot, ōpen, ôrder; oil, out; cup, pút, rüle,
əbove, takən, pencəl, lemən, circəs

ch, child; ng, long; sh, ship
th, thin; ᵺ, then; zh, measure

North American colleges. [probably < Med.L *sororitas* < L *soror* sister]

sor·rel¹ (sôr′əl) *adj.,* *n.*—*adj.* reddish brown.—*n.* **1** a reddish brown. **2** a reddish-brown horse. [ME < OF *sorel* < *sor* yellowish-brown]

sor·rel² (sôr′əl) *n.* any of several plants (genus *Rumex*) of the buckwheat family, especially *R. acetosa,* found throughout temperate North America and Eurasia, having sour-tasting, arrow-shaped leaves that are used as a vegetable or as salad greens or as a flavoring in sauces and soups. [ME < OF *surele* < *sur* sour < Gmc.]

sor·row (sôr′ō) *n.,* *v.*—*n.* **1** grief; sadness; regret. **2** a cause of grief, sadness, or regret; trouble; suffering; misfortune: *Her sorrows have aged her.*—*v.* **1** feel or show grief, sadness, or regret. **2** be sad; feel sorry; grieve. [OE *sorg*]—**sor′row·er,** *n.*—**sor′row·less,** *adj.*
☛ *Syn. n.* **1. Sorrow, grief, distress** = mental suffering caused by loss or trouble. **Sorrow** suggests deep sadness or mental pain caused by the loss of someone or something dear or the experiencing or doing of something bad or wrong: *The dope addict became a criminal and brought great sorrow to his mother.* **Grief** emphasizes deeply or keenly felt sorrow or very painful regret: *Her grief when he died was unbearable.* **Distress** particularly suggests the strain or pressure of pain (physical or mental), grief, fear, anxiety, etc. caused by any trouble: *War causes widespread distress.*

sor·row·ful (sôr′ə fəl) *adj.* **1** full of sorrow; feeling sorrow; sad. **2** showing sorrow. **3** causing sorrow.—**sor′row·ful·ly,** *adv.*
—**sor′row·ful·ness,** *n.*

sor·ry (sôr′ē) *adj.* **-ri·er, -ri·est. 1** feeling pity, regret, sympathy, etc.; sad: *I am sorry that you are sick.* **2** wretched; poor; pitiful: *The blind beggar in his ragged clothes was a sorry sight.*
be sorry, ask pardon, as in making an apology.
[OE *sārig* < *sār* sore]—**sor′ri·ly,** *adv.*—**sor′ri·ness,** *n.*
☛ *Hom.* **saury.**

sort (sôrt) *n.,* *v.*—*n.* **1** a kind; class: *What sort of work does he do?* **2** a character; quality; nature. **3** a person or thing of a certain kind or quality: *He is a good sort.* **4** *Printing.* a letter or pieces in a font of type. **5** a way; fashion; manner.
of sorts, a of one kind or another. **b** of a poor or mediocre quality.
out of sorts, ill, cross, or uncomfortable.
sort of (*used adverbially*), *Informal.* somewhat; rather.
—*v.* **1** arrange by kinds or classes; arrange in order: *Sort these cards according to their colors.* **2** separate from others (*used with* out): *The farmer sorted out the best apples for eating.* **3** *Archaic.* agree; accord. [ME < OF *sorte,* ult. < L *sors, sortis,* originally, lot]
—**sort′er,** *n.*
☛ *Syn. n.* **1.** See note at **kind².**
☛ *Usage.* See note at **kind².**

sor·tie (sôr′tē) *n.* **1** a sudden attack by troops from a defensive position. **2** a single round trip of a military aircraft against an enemy. [< F *sortie* < *sortir* go out]

so·rus (sô′rəs) *n.,* *pl.* **so·ri** (-rī *or* -rē). *Botany.* any of the dotlike clusters of spores on the back of the frond of a fern. [< NL < Gk. *sōros* heap]

S O S (es′ō′es′) **1** a signal of distress consisting of the letters *s o s* of the Morse code (···———···), used in wireless telegraphy. **2** *Informal.* any urgent call for help.
☛ *Usage.* SOS is a code signal only; it is not an abbreviation.

so-so (sō′sō′) *adj.,* *adv.*—*adj.* neither very good nor very bad.—*adv.* passably; indifferently; tolerably.

sos·te·nu·to (sos′tə nü′tō) *adj.,* *adv., n. Music.*—*adj.* **1** sustained; held. **2** prolonged; played or sung at a gradually decreasing tempo.
—*adv.* in a sostenuto manner.
—*n.* a sostenuto note, movement, or passage; composition to be played or sung in this manner. [< Ital. *sostenuto,* pp. of *sostenere* sustain < L *sustinere.* See SUSTAIN.]

sot (sot) *n.* drunkard. [OE < Med.L *sottus*]
☛ *Hom.* **sought.**

sot·tish (sot′ish) *adj.* **1** stupid and foolish from drinking too much alcoholic liquor; drunken. **2** of a sot; like a sot.—**sot′tish·ly,** *adv.*
—**sot′tish·ness,** *n.*

sot·to vo·ce (sot′ō vō′chē; *Italian,* sōt′tō vō′chä) **1** in a low tone. **2** aside; privately. [< Ital. *sotto voce,* literally, below (normal) voice]

sou (sü) *n.* **1** a former French coin, worth 5 centimes or ¹/₂₀ of a

franc. **2** anything of little value. [< F *sou* ult. < L *solidus,* a Roman coin]
☛ *Hom.* **sault, sue.**

sou·brette (sü bret′) *n.* **1** a maidservant or lady's maid in a play or opera, especially one displaying coquetry, pertness, and a spirit of intrigue; a lively or pert young woman character. **2** an actress or singer taking such a part. [< F < Provençal *soubreto* coy < *soubra* set aside]

sou·bri·quet (sü′brə kā′ *or* sü′brə ket′) *n.* sobriquet.

souf·flé (sü flā′ *or* sü′flā) *n., adj.* —*n. French.* a frothy baked dish, usually made light by beaten eggs: *cheese soufflé.* —*adj.* puffed up: *potatoes soufflé.* [< F *soufflé,* originally pp. of *souffler* puff up]

sough (sou *or* suf) *v., n.* —*v.* make a rustling or murmuring sound: *The pines soughed when the wind blew.* —*n.* a rustling or murmuring sound. [OE *swōgan*]

sought (sot *or* sôt) *v.* pt. and pp. of **seek.**
☛ *Hom.* **sot.**

soul (sōl) *n., adj.* —*n.* **1** the spiritual part of a person, regarded as the source of thought, feeling, and action, and considered as separate from the body. Many religions believe that the soul and the body are separated in death and that the soul lives forever. **2** energy of mind or feelings; spirit: *She puts her whole soul into her work.* **3** a cause of inspiration and energy: *Florence Nightingale was the soul of the movement to reform nursing.* **4** the essential part: *Brevity is the soul of wit.* **5** a person: *Don't tell a soul.* **6** an embodiment: *He is the soul of honor.* **7** the spirit of a dead person. **8** among North American blacks, a consciousness of and sense of pride in their African heritage.
upon my soul! an exclamation of surprise, wonder, etc.
—*adj.* **1** of, having to do with, or reflecting the cultural heritage of American blacks: *soul food.* **2** *Music.* designating a style of rhythm and blues that incorporates elements of black gospel music. [OE *sāwol*]
☛ *Hom.* **sol, sole.**

soul·ful (sōl′fəl) *adj.* **1** full of feeling; deeply emotional. **2** expressing or suggesting a deep feeling. —**soul′ful·ly,** *adv.* —**soul′ful·ness,** *n.*

soul·less (sōl′lis) *adj.* having no soul; without spirit or noble feelings. —**soul′less·ly,** *adv.*

soul–search·ing (sōl′ser′ching) *n.* a deep and honest effort, especially during a crisis, to evaluate one's own motives, beliefs, etc. so as to assess one's conduct and attitudes.

sound¹ (sound) *n., v.* —*n.* **1** what is or can be heard; auditory sensation. **2** the vibrations causing this sensation. Sound travels in waves. **3** a noise, note, tone, etc. whose quality indicates its source or nature; *the sound of fighting.* **4** the distance within which a noise may be heard. **5** one of the simple elements composing speech: *a vowel sound.* **6** the effect produced on the mind by what is heard: *a warning sound, a queer sound.* **7** mere noise without meaning.
within sound, near enough to hear.
—*v.* **1** make a sound or noise: *The trumpet sounds for battle. The wind sounds like an animal howling.* **2** pronounce: *Sound each syllable.* **3** be pronounced: *"Rough" and "ruff" sound alike.* **4** be heard as a sound; issue or pass as sound; be mentioned. **5** be filled with sound. **6** cause to sound: *"Sound the trumpets; beat the drums."* **7** test by noting sounds: *to sound a person's lungs.* **8** order or direct by a sound: *to sound a retreat.* **9** make known; announce; utter: *The trumpets sounded the call to arms. Everyone sounded his praises.* **10** seem: *That excuse sounds queer.* [ME < OF *son,* n., *soner,* v. (< L *sonare*) < L *sonus*] —**sound′er,** *n.*

sound² (sound) *adj., adv.* —*adj.* **1** free from injury, decay, or defect: *a sound ship, sound fruit.* **2** free from disease; healthy: *a sound body and mind.* **3** strong; safe; secure: *a sound business firm.* **4** solid: *sound rock.* **5** correct; right; reasonable; reliable: *sound advice.* **6** without any legal defect: *a sound title.* **7** having orthodox or conventional ideas: *politically sound.* **8** thorough; hearty: *a sound whipping, a sound sleep.*
—*adv.* deeply; thoroughly: *sound asleep.* [OE *(ge)sund*] —**sound′ly,** *adv.* —**sound′ness,** *n.*
☛ *Syn. adj.* **6.** See note at **valid.**

sound³ (sound) *v., n.* —*v.* **1** measure the depth of (water) by letting down a weight fastened to the end of a line. **2** examine or test by a line arranged to bring up a sample. **3** inquire into the feelings, inclination, etc. of (a person); examine indirectly; investigate. **4** go toward the bottom; dive: *The whale sounded.* **5** examine with a sound.
sound out, inquire into a person's feelings, opinions, etc.; examine indirectly: *John sounded her out on the project, but she didn't seem interested.*
—*n.* a long, slender instrument used by doctors in examining body

cavities. [ME < OF *sonder,* probably < Gmc. source of *sound⁴*]
—**sound′er,** *n.*

sound⁴ (sound) *n.* **1** a narrow passage of water joining two larger bodies of water or separating an island and the mainland: *Queen Charlotte Sound.* **2** an arm of the sea: *Howe Sound.* **3** the air bladder of a fish. [OE *sund* swimming; partly < ON *sund* strait]

sound barrier sonic barrier.

sound·board (sound′bôrd′) *n.* a thin, resonant piece of wood forming part of a musical instrument, as in a violin or piano, to increase the fullness of its tone.

sound effects noises, as of rain, traffic, crowds, doorbells, etc., called for in the script of a play or motion picture.

sound·er¹ (soun′dər) *n.* **1** a person or thing that makes a sound. **2** an electromagnetic receiving instrument that converts a telegraphic message into sound. [< *sound¹*]

sound·er² (soun′dər) *n.* a person or thing that measures the depth of water. [< *sound³*]

sound·ing¹ (soun′ding) *adj.* **1** giving forth sound, especially resonant or sonorous sound: *sounding brass.* **2** pompous; bombastic: *sounding rhetoric.* [< *sound¹*]

sound·ing² (soun′ding) *n.* **1** the act of measuring the depth of water by letting down a weight fastened to the end of a line. **2** the depth of water found by measuring in this way. **3** investigation. **4** examination with a sound or probe. **5 soundings,** *pl.* **a** the depths of water found by a line and weight. **b** a place where the water is shallow enough for a sounding line to touch bottom. [< *sound³*]

sounding board **1** soundboard. **2** a structure used to direct sound toward an audience. **3** a means of bringing opinions, etc. out into the open.

sounding line a line having a weight fastened to the end, used to measure the depth of water.

sound·less¹ (sound′lis) *adj.* without sound; making no sound. [< *sound¹*] —**sound′less·ly,** *adv.*

sound·less² (sound′lis) *adj.* so deep that the bottom cannot be reached. [< *sound³*]

sound·proof (sound′prüf′) *adj., v.* —*adj.* not letting sound pass through. —*v.* make soundproof.

sound track a recording of the sounds of words, music, etc. made along one edge of a motion-picture film.

sound waves the progressive vibrations by which sounds are transmitted.

soup (süp) *n., v.* —*n.* **1** a liquid food made by boiling meat, vegetables, fish, etc. **2** *Slang.* a heavy, wet fog or cloud formation: *to fly on instruments through soup.* **3** *Slang.* power; horsepower.
in the soup, *Informal.* in difficulties; in trouble.
—*v.*
soup up, *Slang.* increase the power, capacity, or efficiency of: *to soup up an engine.*
[< F *soupe* < Gmc.]

soup·çon (süp′son; *French,* süp sôn′) *n. French.* a slight trace or flavor; very small amount. [< F *soupçon* suspicion]

soup kitchen a place that serves food free or at a very low charge to poor or unemployed people or to victims of a flood, fire, or other disaster.

soup·y (sü′pē) *adj.* **soup·i·er, soup·i·est.** like soup.

sour (sour) *adj., v., n., adv.* —*adj.* **1** having the basic taste sensation produced by acids; sharp and biting: *Lemon juice is sour. Most green fruit is sour.* **2** fermented; spoiled. Sour milk is healthful, but most foods are not good to eat when they have become sour. **3** having a sour or rank smell. **4** disagreeable; bad-tempered; peevish: *a sour face.* **5** unusually acid: *sour soil.* **6** cold and wet; damp: *sour weather.*
go sour, fall below usual standards of excellence or interest; fall off. —*v.* **1** make or become sour; turn sour. **2** make or become peevish, bad-tempered, or disagreeable. **3** fall below usual standards of excellence or interest.
sour on, take a dislike for.
—*n.* **1** something sour. **2** a sour, alcoholic drink, such as whisky and lemon juice: *a whisky sour.*
—*adv.* in a sour manner. [OE *sūr*] —**sour′ly,** *adv.* —**sour′ness,** *n.*
☛ *Syn. adj.* **4. Sour, tart, acid** used figuratively to describe a person's looks, disposition, words, manner of expression, etc. means "resembling vinegar or lemons in harshness or sharpness." **Sour** emphasizes harsh, forbidding, or irritable qualities, and suggests bad temper or a disagreeable mood, surly rudeness, grouchiness, or sullenness: *That janitor has a sour disposition.* **Tart** emphasizes sharp and stinging qualities: *His tart answer made her cry.* **Acid** emphasizes biting, sarcastic, severely critical qualities: *I read an acid comment on the political situation.*

source (sôrs) *n.* **1** a beginning of a brook or river; fountain; spring. **2** a place from which anything comes or is obtained. **3** a person, book, statement, etc. that supplies information. [ME < OF *sourse,* ult. < L *surgere* rise, surge]

sour·dough (sour′dō′) *n. Cdn.* **1** dough containing active yeast, saved from one baking for the next. Prospectors and pioneers used sourdough for making bread to avoid the need for fresh yeast. **2** (*adj.*) made with sourdough: *sourdough bread.* **3** a prospector or pioneer in northwestern Canada or Alaska. **4** any old resident, experienced hand, etc.; person who is not a tenderfoot.

sour grapes something that a person pretends not to want because he cannot have it. [< Aesop's fable of the fox and the grapes]

sour·puss (sour′pùs′) *n. Slang.* a person who looks gloomy, grumpy, or ill-tempered, especially habitually.

sour·sop (sour′sop′) *n.* **1** a small, tropical American evergreen tree (*Annona muricata*) of the custard-apple family having leaves with a spicy smell and large, spiny fruit with tart, edible flesh. **2** the fruit of this tree.

souse (sous) *v.* **soused, sous·ing;** *n.* —*v.* **1** plunge into liquid; drench; soak in a liquid. **2** soak in vinegar, brine, etc.; pickle. **3** *Slang.* make or become drunk. —*n.* **1** a plunging into a liquid; drenching. **2** liquid used for pickling. **3** something soaked or kept in pickle, especially the head, ears, and feet of a pig. **4** *Slang.* drunkard. [ME; ult. < OF *sous* pickled pork, ult. < Gmc. **sult-, *salt-* salt]

sou·tache (sü′tash *or* sü tash′) *n.* a narrow braid used for trimming. [< F < Hungarian *sujtás* trimming]

sou·tane (sü tän′) *n.* a cassock. [< F < Ital. *sottana,* ult. < L *sub* under]

south (south) *n., adj., adv.* —*n.* **1** the direction to the right as one faces the rising sun; direction opposite to north. **2** Also, **South,** the part of any country toward the south. —*adj.* **1** toward the south. **2** from the south. **3** in the south. **4 South,** designating the southern part of a geographical area having a proper name: *South America, South Europe.* **5** south of, farther south than. —*adv.* toward the south: *The journey south took two days.* [OE *sūth*]

South African *n., adj.* —*n.* a native or inhabitant of the Republic of South Africa, a country in southern Africa. —*adj.* of or having to do with South Africa or its people.

South African Dutch Afrikaans.

South American *n., adj.* —*n.* a native or inhabitant of the continent of South America. —*adj.* of or having to do with South America or its people.

south–bound (south′bound′) *adj.* going toward the south.

South·down (south′doun′) *n.* an English breed of small, hornless sheep raised for mutton. [< *South Downs,* an area in S England where this breed originated]

south·east (south′ēst′) *n., adj., adv.* —*n.* **1** the direction or compass point halfway between south and east. **2** a place that is in the southeast part or direction. —*adj. or adv.* **1** of, at, in, to, or toward the southeast: *the southeast corner of the house, to walk southeast.* **2** coming from the southeast: *a southeast wind.*

south·east·er (south′ēs′tər) *n.* a wind or storm from the southeast.

south·east·er·ly (south′ēs′tər lē) *adj. or adv.* **1** toward the southeast. **2** from the southeast.

south·east·ern (south′ēs′tərn) *adj.* of, at, in, to, or from the southeast.

south·east·ward (south′ēst′wərd) *adv., adj., n.* —*adv. or adj.* toward the southeast. —*n.* southeast.

south·east·ward·ly (south′ēst′wərd lē) *adj., adv.* —*adj.* **1** toward the southeast. **2** of winds, from the southeast. —*adv.* toward the southeast.

south·east·wards (south′ēst′wərdz) *adv.* southeastward.

south·er (souŦH′ər) *n.* a wind or storm from the south.

south·er·ly (suŦH′ər lē) *adj. or adv.* **1** toward the south. **2** from the south.

south·ern (suŦH′ərn) *adj.* **1** toward the south: *a southern view.* **2** from the south: *a southern breeze.* **3** of or in the south or the southern part of the country. **4 Southern,** of, in, or having to do with the South. [OE *sūtherne*]

Southern Cross a southern constellation of four bright stars in the form of a cross, used in finding the direction south.

South·ern·er (suŦH′ər nər) *n.* a native or inhabitant of the South.

south·ern·ly (suŦH′ərn lē) *adj.* southerly.

south·ern·most (suŦH′ərn mōst′) *adj.* farthest south.

south·ing (souŦH′ing) *n.* **1** a movement toward the south. **2** a distance due south.

hat, āge, fär; let, ēqual, tėrm; it, īce
hot, ōpen, ôrder; oil, out; cup, pút, rüle,
əbove, takən, pencəl, lemən, circəs

ch, child; ng, long; sh, ship
th, thin; ŦH, then; zh, measure

south·land (south′lənd *or* -land′) *n.* land in the south; the southern part of a country.

south·most (south′mōst′) *adj.* farthest south.

south–paw (south′po′ *or* -pô′) *n., adj. Slang.* —*n.* **1** a left-handed baseball pitcher. **2** any left-handed person. —*adj.* left-handed.

South Pole the southern end of the earth's axis.

south·ron (suŦH′rən) *adj., n., pl.* **-rons** *or* **-ron.** *Archaic. Esp.Scottish.* —*adj.* southern. —*n.* **1** Southerner. **2** a native of the south of Great Britain; Englishman. **3 the southron,** Englishmen.

South Sea Islander a native or inhabitant of the South Sea Islands, islands in the S Pacific Ocean.

south–south·east (south′south′ēst′) *n., adj., adv.* —*n.* the direction or compass point midway between south and southeast. —*adj. or adv.* in, toward, or from this direction.

south–south·west (south′south′west′) *n., adj., adv.* —*n.* the direction or compass point midway between south and southwest. —*adj. or adv.* in, toward, or from this direction.

south·ward (south′wərd) *adv., adj., n.* —*adv. or adj.* toward the south; south. —*n.* a southward part, direction, or point.

south·ward·ly (south′wərd lē) *adj., adv.* —*adj.* **1** toward the south. **2** of winds, coming from the south. —*adv.* toward the south.

south·wards (south′wərdz) *adv.* southward.

south·west (south′west′) *n., adj., adv.* —*n.* **1** the direction halfway between south and west. **2** a place that is in the southwest part or direction. —*adj. or adv.* of, at, in, to, toward, or from the southwest.

south·west·er (south′wes′tər *or* sou′wes′tər) *n.* **1** a wind or storm from the southwest. **2** a waterproof hat having a broad brim at the back to protect the neck, worn especially by seamen. See **hat** for picture.

south·west·er·ly (south′wes′tər lē) *adj. or adv.* toward or from the southwest.

south·west·ern (south′wes′tərn) *adj.* of, at, in, to, toward, or from the southwest.

south·west·ward (south′west′wərd) *adv., adj., n.* —*adv. or adj.* toward the southwest. —*n.* southwest.

south·west·ward·ly (south′west′wərd lē) *adj., adv.* —*adj.* **1** toward the southwest. **2** of winds, from the southwest. —*adv.* toward the southwest.

south·west·wards (south′west′wərdz) *adv.* southwestward.

sou·ve·nir (sü′və nēr′ *or* sü′və nēr′) *n.* something to remind one of a place, person, or occasion; a keepsake. [< F *souvenir,* originally infinitive, < L *subvenire* come to mind < *sub-* up + *venire* come]

sou'west·er (sou′wes′tər) *n.* southwester.

sov·er·eign (sov′rən) *n., adj.* —*n.* **1** a king or queen; a supreme ruler; monarch. **2** a person, group, or nation having supreme control or dominion; ruler; governor; lord; master: *sovereign of the seas.* **3** a former British gold coin, worth one pound. —*adj.* **1** having the rank or power of a sovereign. **2** greatest in rank or power: *a sovereign court.* **3** independent of the control of other governments. **4** above all others; supreme; greatest: *Character is of sovereign importance.* **5** excellent or powerful: *a sovereign cure for colds.* [ME < OF *soverain,* ult. < L *super* over]

sov·er·eign·ly (sov′rən lē) *adv.* **1** so as to exceed all others; exceedingly. **2** chiefly; especially. **3** effectually; efficaciously. **4** as a sovereign.

sov·er·eign·ty (sov′rən tē) *n., pl.* **-ties. 1** supreme power or authority. **2** freedom from outside control; independence in exercising power or authority: *Countries that are satellites lack full sovereignty.* **3** a state, territory, community, etc., that is independent or sovereign. **4** rank, power, or jurisdiction of a sovereign.

sovereignty association *Cdn.* a policy proposed in the late

1970's by the Quebec government, under which the province would become an independent state but would remain associated with Canada.

so·vi·et (sō′vē et′ *or* sō′vē it) *n., adj.* —*n.* **1** a council; assembly. **2** Often, **Soviet,** in the Soviet Union: **a** either of two elected assemblies (**village soviets, town soviets**). **b** any of the higher elected assemblies. The highest assembly of all is the **Supreme Soviet. 3** any council like a Russian soviet.
—*adj.* **1** of or having to do with soviets. **2 Soviet,** of or having to do with the Soviet Union. [< Russian *soviet* council]

so·vi·et·ism (sō′vē it iz′əm) *n.* **1** a system of government by means of soviets. **2** communism.

so·vi·et·ize (sō′vē et īz′) *v.* **-ized, -iz·ing.** bring under a soviet type of government; change to a soviet government.

sov·ran (sov′rən) *n. or adj. Poetic.* sovereign.

sow[1] (sō) *v.* **sowed, sown** *or* **sowed, sow·ing. 1** plant seed or a crop: *It was time to begin sowing. They sowed more oats than wheat.* **2** plant seed in: *to sow a field with rye.* **3** introduce or implant: *to sow discontent.* [OE *sāwan*] —**sow′er,** *n.*
☛ *Hom.* **sew, so.**

sow[2] (sou) *n.* a fully grown female pig. [OE *sugu or sū*]

sow bug (sou) wood louse.

sown (sōn) *v.* a pp. of **sow**[1].
☛ *Hom.* **sewn.**

soy (soi) *n.* **1** soya sauce. **2** soybean. [< Japanese, short for *shoyu* < Chinese *shi-yu < shi,* a type of bean + *yu* oil]

soy·a (soi′ə) *n.* soy.

soya bean soybean.

soya sauce any of several thin, dark-brown sauces made from soybeans fermented in brine, used as a flavoring, especially in Chinese and Japanese cooking.

soy·bean (soi′bēn′) *n.* **1** an annual bean (*Glycine max*) native to E Asia, widely cultivated for its protein-rich seeds and for forage and soil improvement. **2** the seed of this plant, used for food and livestock feed and yielding an oil used as a cooking oil and for making margarine, etc., as well as for resins, paints, chemicals, etc.

soy sauce soya sauce.

sp. 1 special. **2** specific. **3** species. **4** spelling. **5** spirits.

Sp. Spain; Spanish; Spaniard.

SP *U.S. Shore Patrol.*

spa (spä) *n.* **1** a mineral spring. **2** a place where there is a mineral spring, especially a health resort at such a place. **3** any fashionable resort. [< *Spa,* a resort city in Belgium]

space (spās) *n., v.* **spaced, spac·ing.** —*n.* **1** the unlimited room or expanse extending in all directions and in which all things exist: *The earth moves through space.* **2** extent of area or volume: *We have plenty of space in this house.* **3** a limited place or area: *a parking space.* **4** outer space. **5** a distance; a stretch: *The road is bad for the space of ten kilometres.* **6** a length of time: *He has not seen his brother for the space of ten years.* **7** *Archaic.* an interval of time; a while. **8** a time in which to do something; opportunity. **9** accommodations on a train, etc. **10** a part of a surface; a blank between words, etc.: *Fill in the spaces as directed.* **11** a extent or room in a periodical, book, letter, etc. available for, or occupied by, written or printed matter. **b** *Advertising.* the part of a page or number of lines in a periodical, newspaper, etc. available or used for advertising. **12** *Printing.* one of the blank types used to separate words, etc. **13** *Music.* one of the intervals between the lines of a staff.
—*v.* **1** fix the space or spaces of; divide into spaces. **2** separate by spaces: *Space your words evenly when you write.* [ME < OF *espace* < L *spatium*]

space age the current period of history, thought of as being marked by man's first efforts to explore and conquer space.

space·craft (spās′kraft′) *n., pl.* **space·craft.** any manned or unmanned vehicle designed for flight in outer space.

space·less (spās′lis) *adj.* **1** independent of space; infinite. **2** occupying no space.

space·man (spās′man′) *n., pl.* **-men. 1** astronaut. **2** any person, especially a scientist, concerned with space flight.

spac·er (spās′ər) *n.* **1** a device for spacing words, etc. as in a typesetting machine. **2** an instrument by which to reverse a telegraphic current to increase the speed of transmission.

space ship *or* **space·ship** (spās′ship′) *n.* spacecraft.

space station an artificial earth satellite to be used as an observatory or as a launching site for space ships.

space suit an airtight suit designed to protect astronauts from

radiation, heat, lack of oxygen, etc., the condition of the earth's atmosphere being maintained within the suit.

space·ward (spās′wərd) *adv.* toward outer space.

spac·ing (spā′sing) *n.* **1** the fixing or arranging of spaces. **2** the manner in which spaces are arranged: *uneven spacing.* **3** space or spaces in printing or other work.

spa·cious (spā′shəs) *adj.* **1** having or affording much space or room; large; roomy: *The rooms of the palace were spacious.* **2** of great extent or area; extensive; vast. **3** broad in scope or range; not limited or narrow; expansive: *a spacious mind.* [< L *spatiosus* < *spatium* space] —**spa′cious·ly,** *adv.* —**spa′cious·ness,** *n.*

spade[1] (spād) *n., v.* **spad·ed, spad·ing.** —*n.* a tool for digging, having a relatively flat blade which can be pressed into the ground with the foot, and a long handle with a grip or crosspiece at the top. **call a spade a spade,** call a thing by its real name; speak plainly and frankly.
—*v.* dig with a spade. [OE *spadu;* akin to L *spatha.* See SPADE[2].]

spade[2] (spād) *n.* **1** a black figure (♠) used on playing cards. **2** a playing card bearing such figures. **3 spades,** *pl.* the suit of playing cards bearing such figures, usually the highest ranking suit in card games. [< Ital. *spada* < L < Gk. *spathē* sword, broad blade]

SPATHE
SPADIX

A jack-in-the-pulpit (left) and a calla lily (right)

spa·dix (spā′diks) *n., pl.* **spa·dix·es** *or* **spa·di·ces** (spā′də sēz′ *or* spā dī′sēz). *Botany.* a spike composed of minute flowers on a fleshy stem. A spadix is usually enclosed in a petal-like leaf called a spathe, as in the jack-in-the-pulpit and the calla lily. [< L < Gk. *spadix* palm branch]

spa·ghet·ti (spə get′ē) *n.* **1** long, slender sticks made of pasta, soft when cooked: *Spaghetti is thinner than macaroni.* **2** *Electricity.* an insulating cloth or plastic tube used for covering bare wire or holding a group of insulated wires together. [< Ital. *spaghetti,* pl. dim. of *spago* cord]

spake (spāk) *v. Archaic.* a pt. of **speak.**

spall (spol *or* spôl) *n., v.* —*n.* a chip, splinter, or small piece of stone. —*v.* **1** break up roughly, or chip, especially to prepare ore for sorting. **2** chip off, especially at the edges. A stone may spall under pressure.

Sp.Am. Spanish American.

span[1] (span) *n., v.* **spanned, span·ning.** —*n.* **1** the distance between two supports: *The arch had a span of fifteen metres.* **2** the part between two supports: *The bridge crossed the river in three spans.* **3** a short space of time: *"A life's but a span."* **4** the full extent: *the span of a bridge, the span of memory.* **5** wingspan. **6** a unit for measuring length based on the distance between the tip of the thumb and the tip of the little finger of a spread-out hand; about 23 cm.
—*v.* **1** measure by the hand spread out: *This post can be spanned by one's two hands.* **2** encircle or encompass (the waist, wrist, etc.) with the hand or hands. **3** extend over: *A bridge spanned the river.* **4** provide with something that extends over or across: *to span a river with a bridge.* [OE *spann*]

span[2] (span) *n.* a pair of horses, mules, etc. harnessed and driven together. [< Du. or LG *span* < *spannen* stretch, yoke]

span[3] (span) *v. Archaic.* a pt. of **spin.**

span·dex (span′deks) *n.* a very light, synthetic elastic fibre used especially in swimsuits and women's undergarments.

span·drel (span′drəl) *n. Architecture.* **1** the triangular space between the curve of an arch and the rectangular moulding or framework enclosing the arch. **2** the space between the curves of two adjacent arches and the moulding above them. See **arch** for picture. Also, **spandril.** [ME *spandrell* < AF *spaundre,* short for OF *espander* expand < L *expandere.* Cf. EXPAND and SPAWN.]

spang (spang) *adv. Informal.* directly, with a smack; exactly on the mark. [perhaps < dial. *spang* a jerk, smack]

span·gle (spang′gəl) *n., v.* **-gled, -gling.** —*n.* **1** a small piece of glittering metal, plastic, etc. used for decoration: *The dress was covered with spangles.* **2** any small, bright bit.
—*v.* **1** decorate with spangles. **2** sprinkle with, or as if with, small,

bright bits: *The sky is spangled with stars.* **3** glitter. [dim. of earlier *spang*, probably < MDu. *spange* brooch]

Span·iard (span'yərd) *n.* a native or inhabitant of Spain, a country in SW Europe.

span·iel (span'yəl) *n.* **1** any of several breeds of dog, usually of small or medium size, having long, silky hair and drooping ears. **2** a person who yields too easily to others. [ME < OF *espagneul,* originally, Spanish < L *Hispania* Spain]

Span·ish (span'ish) *n., adj.* —*n.* **1 the Spanish,** *pl.* the people of Spain, a country in SW Europe. **2** the Romance language of Spain and most countries of South America. —*adj.* of or having to do with Spain, Spaniards, or Spanish.

Span·ish–A·mer·i·can (span'ish ə mer'ə kən) *adj., n.* —*adj.* **1** of or having to do with Spain and America, or with Spain and the United States. **2** of, having to do with, or designating the parts of America where Spanish is the prevailing language. —*n.* **Spanish American,** a native or inhabitant of a Spanish-American country, especially a person of Spanish descent.

Spanish Armada the great fleet sent by Philip II of Spain to attack England in 1588.

Spanish bayonet any of several yuccas, especially a treelike species (*Yucca aloifolia*) having stiff, spearlike, spine-tipped leaves and clusters of white flowers.

Spanish fly a bright-green blister beetle (*Lytta vesicatoria*) of S Europe. The crushed wing cover of these beetles are a source of a substance used in medicine as a counterirritant and diuretic and, formerly, as an aphrodisiac.

Spanish Inquisition **1** the body of men appointed during the Renaissance by the Roman Catholic Church to suppress heresy in Spain. It was put under state control at the end of the 15th century and was very active during the 16th century. **2** the activities of this body of men.

Spanish Main *Historical.* **1** the mainland of America adjacent to the Caribbean Sea, especially between the mouth of the Orinoco River and the Isthmus of Panama. **2** in later use, the Caribbean Sea.

Spanish moss a greyish-green air plant (*Tillandsia usneoides*) of the pineapple family found in tropical and warm temperate America, that grows as very long, beardlike masses hanging from trees.

Spanish onion a large, mild, juicy onion often eaten raw in sandwiches, hamburgers, salads, etc.

spank¹ (spangk) *v., n.* —*v.* strike, usually on the buttocks, with the open hand, a slipper, etc., especially as a punishment. —*n.* a blow with the open hand, a slipper, etc.; slap. [imitative]

spank² (spangk) *v. Informal.* go quickly and vigorously; move at a speedy rate. [probably back formation < *spanking*]

spank·er (spangk'ər) *n.* **1** a fore-and-aft sail on the mast nearest the stern. See **brig** for picture. **2** *Informal.* a fast horse. **3** *Informal.* anything large, large, unusual for its kind, etc. [apparently < *spanking* or *spank²* move fast]

spank·ing (spangk'ing) *adj., adv., n.* —*adj.* **1** brisk; lively; vigorous: *a spanking breeze, a spanking team of horses.* **2** *Informal.* unusually fine, great, large, etc.: *a spanking new car.* —*adv. Informal.* extremely; exceptionally: *a spanking good time.* —*n.* a series of slaps with the open hand, a slipper, etc., especially on the buttocks, as a punishment for children. [cf. Danish *spanke* strut]

span·less (span'lis) *adj.* that cannot be spanned.

span·ner (span'ər) *n.* **1** one that spans: *the spanners of a bridge.* **2** *Esp.Brit.* a tool for holding and turning a nut, bolt, etc.; wrench.

spar¹ (spär) *n., v.* **sparred, spar·ring.** —*n.* **1** a stout pole used to support or extend the sails of a ship; mast, yard, boom, etc. of a ship. **2** the main beam of an airplane wing. —*v.* provide (a ship) with spars. [ME *sparre*, akin to OE *spere* spear; cf. ON *sparri,* MDu. *sparre*]

spar² (spär) *v.* **sparred, spar·ring;** *n.* —*v.* **1** box with feinting movements or light blows, as when training. **2** dispute or wrangle. **3** of a gamecock, fight with the feet or spurs. —*n.* **1** a sparring movement. **2** a boxing match. **3** a dispute. [< MF *esparer* kick < Ital. *sparare* fling < *s-,* intensive (< L *ex-*) + *parare* parry]

spar³ (spär) *n.* a shiny, crystalline mineral that splits into flakes easily. [OE *spær-;* cf. *spæren* gypsum]

spar deck the upper deck extending from one end of a ship to the other.

spare (sper) *v.* **spared, spar·ing;** *adj.* **spar·er, spar·est;** *n.* —*v.* **1** show mercy to; refrain from harming or destroying: *He spared his enemy.* **2** show mercy; refrain from doing harm. **3** show consideration for; save from labor, pain, etc.: *We walked uphill to spare the horse.* **4** get along without; do without: *Father couldn't spare the car, so John had to walk. "Spare the rod and spoil the child."* **5** make (a person, etc.) free from (something); relieve or

hat, āge, fär; let, ēqual, tèrm; it, īce
hot, ōpen, ôrder; oil, out; cup, pût, rüle,
əbove, takən, pencəl, lemən, circəs
ch, child; ng, long; sh, ship
th, thin; ŦH, then; zh, measure

exempt (a person, etc.) from (something): *He did the work to spare you the trouble.* **6** use in small quantities or not at all; be saving of: *We spared no expense.* **7** have free or available for use: *Can you spare the time? I have no money to spare.* **8** be saving. —*adj.* **1** free for other use: *spare time.* **2** extra; in reserve: *a spare tire.* **3** thin; lean: *The minister was a tall, spare man.* **4** small in quantity; meagre; scanty: *a spare diet.* —*n.* **1** an extra or duplicate person or thing: *We have five tires, including a spare.* **2** Bowling. the knocking down of all the pins with two rolls of a ball. [OE *sparian*] —**spare′ness,** *n.* —**spar′er,** *n.*

spare·ly (sper′lē) *adv.* sparingly; scantily; thinly; leanly.

spare·rib (sper′rib′) *n.* a rib of meat, especially pork, having less meat than the ribs near the loins. See **pork** for picture. [transposition of *ribspare* < MLG *ribbespēr* rib cut]

spar·ing (sper′ing) *adj.* **1** that spares. **2** avoiding waste; economical; frugal: *a sparing use of sugar.* —**spar′ing·ly,** *adv.* —**spar′ing·ness,** *n.*

spark¹ (spärk) *n., v.* —*n.* **1** a small particle of flame: *The burning wood threw off sparks.* **2** Electricity. **a** a flash given off when electricity jumps across an open space. An electric spark explodes the gas in the engine of an automobile. **b** the discharge occurring at the same time. **3** a flash; gleam: *a spark of light.* **4** a small amount: *I haven't a spark of interest in the plan.* **5** a trace of life or vitality. **6** a glittering bit. —*v.* **1** flash; gleam. **2** send out small bits of fire; produce sparks. **3** operate properly in forming sparks, as the ignition in an internal-combustion engine. **4** stir to activity; stimulate: *to spark a revolt, to spark sales, ideas, etc.* [OE *spearca*]

spark² (spärk) *n., v.* —*n.* **1** a suitor or lover. **2** *Rare.* a dashing, showy young man. —*v.* **1** court; woo. **2** *Informal.* pet or neck: *young lovers sparking on the river bank.* [? < ON *sparkr* lively] —**spark′er,** *n.*

spark coil *Electricity.* an induction coil for producing sparks.

spar·kle (spär′kəl) *v.* **-kled, -kling;** *n.* —*v.* **1** send out little sparks: *The fireworks sparkled.* **2** shine; glitter; flash; gleam: *The diamonds sparkled.* **3** be brilliant; be lively: *His wit sparkles.* **4** bubble: *Ginger ale sparkles.* **5** cause to sparkle. —*n.* **1** a little spark. **2** a shine; glitter; flash; gleam: *I like the sparkle of her eyes.* **3** brilliance; liveliness: *We admired the sparkle of his wit.* [< *spark¹*]
➤ *Syn. n.* 2. See note at **flash.**

spar·kler (spär′klər) *n.* **1** a person or thing that sparkles. **2** a firework that sends out little sparks. **3** *Informal.* a sparkling gem, especially a diamond.

spark plug **1** a device in the cylinder of a gasoline engine by which the mixture of gasoline and air is exploded by an electric spark. See **cylinder** for picture. **2** *Informal.* a person who gives energy or enthusiasm to others.

spar·row (spar′ō *or* sper′ō) *n.* **1** any of a genus (*Passer*) of small, dull-colored weaverbirds, especially the English sparrow. See **English sparrow.** **2** any of various North American finches having brown and grey streaked plumage. See **chipping sparrow, song sparrow.** [OE *spearwa*]

sparrow hawk **1** a small North American falcon (*Falco sparverius*) having mainly reddish-brown upper parts and white or buff under parts, spotted and barred with black, and feeding on large insects, such as grasshoppers and caterpillars, and on mice and some small birds. **2** any of several small hawks, especially an Old World species (*Accipiter nisus*) that feeds exclusively on small birds, especially sparrows.

sparse (spärs) *adj.* **spars·er, spars·est. 1** thinly scattered; occurring here and there: *a sparse population, sparse hair.* **2** scanty; meagre. [< L *sparsus,* pp. of *spargere* scatter] —**sparse′ly,** *adv.* —**sparse′ness,** *n.*
➤ *Syn. 1.* See note at **scanty.**

spar·si·ty (spär′sə tē) *n.* a sparse or scattered condition; sparseness.

Spar·ta·cus (spär′tə kəs) *n.* a Thracian slave and gladiator in Italy (died 71 B.C.) who led an insurrection of slaves that lasted from 73 to 71 B.C.

Spar·tan (spär′tən) *n., adj.* —*n.* **1** a native or inhabitant of Sparta, a city in ancient Greece. The Spartans were noted for their simplicity of life, severity, courage, and brevity of speech. **2** a

person who is courageous, self-denying, disciplined, etc.
—*adj.* **1** of or having to do with Sparta or its people. **2** like that of the Spartans: *Spartan courage, Spartan endurance.* **3** characterized by sternness, frugality, simplicity, self-discipline, etc.: *a Spartan upbringing.*

Spar·tan·ism (spär′tən iz′əm) *n.* **1** the beliefs and methods of ancient Sparta. **2** any discipline, method, etc. like that of the ancient Spartans.

spasm (spaz′əm) *n.* **1** a sudden, involuntary contraction of a muscle or muscles. **2** any sudden, brief fit or spell of unusual energy or activity: *a spasm of temper, a spasm of industry.* [< L < Gk. *spasmos* < *spaein* draw up, tear away]

spas·mod·ic (spaz mod′ik) *adj.* **1** having to do with spasms; resembling a spasm: *a spasmodic cough.* **2** sudden and violent, but brief; occurring very irregularly. **3** having or showing bursts of excitement. **4** disjointed; choppy: *a spasmodic style, spasmodic writing.* [< Med.L *spasmodicus* < Gk. *spasmōdēs* < *spasmos.* See SPASM.] —**spas·mod′i·cal·ly,** *adv.*

spas·tic (spas′tik) *adj., n.* —*adj.* **1** caused by a spasm or spasms. **2** of, having to do with, or characterized by spasms. —*n.* a person suffering from a disorder involving continuous contraction of a muscle or muscles. [< L < Gk. *spastikos* < *spaein* draw up]

spat¹ (spat) *n., v.* **spat·ted, spat·ting.** —*n.* **1** a slight quarrel. **2** a light blow; slap. —*v.* **1** *Informal.* have a slight quarrel. **2** slap lightly. [? imitative]

spat² (spat) *v.* a pt. and a pp. of spit¹.

spat³ (spat) *n.* a short, usually cloth, gaiter covering the ankle and instep, worn by men especially in the late 19th and early 20th centuries and also by women in the early 20th century. [short for *spatterdash*]

spat⁴ (spat) *n., v.* **spat·ted, spat·ting.** —*n.* the spawn of oysters; young oyster. —*v.* of oysters, spawn. [origin uncertain. Perhaps related to SPIT¹.]

spate (spāt) *n.* **1** a flood; downpour. **2** a sudden outburst: *a spate of words, a spate of advertising.* [ME; related to OE *spātan* spit]

spathe (spāŦH) *n. Botany.* a large bract or pair of bracts that enclose a flower cluster. The calla lily has a white spathe around a yellow flower cluster. See **spadix** for picture. [< Gk. *spathē* palm branch, oar blade]

spa·tial (spā′shəl) *adj.* **1** of or having to do with space. **2** existing in space. **3** occupying or taking up space. [< L *spatium* space]

spa·tial·ly (spā′shəl ē) *adv.* in spatial respects; so far as space is concerned; in space.

spa·tio-tem·po·ral (spā′shē ō tem′pər əl) *adj.* of both space and time. [< L *spatium* space + E *temporal*]

spat·ter (spat′ər) *v., n.* —*v.* **1** scatter or dash in drops or particles: *to spatter mud.* **2** fall in drops or particles: *Rain spatters on the sidewalk.* **3** strike in a shower; strike in a number of places: *Bullets spattered the wall.* **4** splash or spot with mud, paint, etc. **5** stain with slander, disgrace, etc. —*n.* **1** spattering: *a spatter of hail.* **2** the sound of spattering. **3** a splash or spot. [cf. Du. or LG *spatten* splash; akin to Flemish *spatteren* spatter]

spat·ter·dash (spat′ər dash′) *n.* a high leather legging worn especially in the 18th. century as protection from mud when riding, etc.

spat·ter·dock (spat′ər dok′) *n.* any of several water lilies (genus *Nuphar*), especially a common, yellow species (*N. advenum*) of E North America. [< obs. *splatterdock* < *splatter* + *dock⁴*]

spat·u·la (spach′ə lə) *n.* a tool with a broad, flat, flexible blade, used for mixing drugs, in cooking and baking, for spreading paints, etc. [< L *spatula*, dim. of *spatha* flat blade < Gk. *spathē*]

spat·u·late (spach′ə lit *or* spach′ə lāt′) *adj.* **1** shaped like a spatula; rounded somewhat like a spoon. **2** *Botany.* having a broad, rounded end and a narrow base: *a spatulate leaf.* **3** wide at the tips: *spatulate fingers.*

spav·in (spav′ən) *n.* a disease of horses in which a bony swelling forms at the hock, causing lameness. [ME < OF *espavain*, probably < Gmc.]

spav·ined (spav′ənd) *adj.* having spavin; lame.

spawn (spon *or* spôn) *n., v.* —*n.* **1** the eggs of fish, frogs, shellfish, etc. **2** young fish, frogs, etc. when newly hatched from such eggs. **3** offspring, especially a large number of offspring. **4** a product; result. **5** the mass of white, threadlike fibres from which fungi grow; mycelium, especially as prepared for growing mushrooms. —*v.* **1** of fish, etc., produce eggs: *Salmon spawn in the rivers of British Columbia.* **2** give birth to; bring forth in great quantity: *The comedian spent ten minutes spawning poor jokes.* [ME < OF

espandre < L *expandere* spread out. Doublet of EXPAND.] —**spawn′er,** *n.*

spay (spā) *v.* remove the ovaries of (a female cat, dog, etc.). [ME < AF *espeir*, ult. < OF *espee* sword < L *spatha.* See SPADE².]

SPCA or **S.P.C.A.** Society for the Prevention of Cruelty to Animals.

speak (spēk) *v.* **spoke** or *(archaic)* **spake, spok·en** or *(archaic)* **spoke, speak·ing.** **1** say words; talk: *A cat cannot speak. Speak distinctly.* **2** give a speech or lecture: *Who is going to speak at the forum? She spoke to them about law reform.* **3** tell; express; make known: *Speak the truth.* **4** use or know how to use in speaking: *I couldn't understand what they said because they were speaking Gaelic. Do you speak Swedish?* **5** express an idea, feeling, etc.; communicate: *Their eyes spoke. His expression spoke deep sorrow.* **6** make a plea, request, application, etc. (used with **for**): *to speak for seats ahead of time.* **7** serve as spokesman; represent (used with **for**): *She spoke for us all.* **8** make a statement or mention (used with **of, about,** etc.): *They spoke of renovating their house.* **9** give forth a characteristic sound: *The cannon spoke.* **10** be an indication or evidence: *His clothing speaks of wealth. It was an unselfish action that spoke well for her.* **11** of dogs, bark when told: *Speak for the candy, Fido.* **12** *Archaic.* show to be; characterize as: *His conduct speaks him honorable.*
so to speak, to speak in such a manner.
speak out or **up, a** speak loudly and clearly. **b** speak freely and without restraint: *They were all too frightened to speak out.*
to speak of, of a significant nature (used with negatives): *I have no complaints to speak of.*
[OE *specan*]

☛ *Syn.* **Speak, talk** = say or use words. **Speak** emphasizes the uttering of clear and distinct speech sounds and the saying of words, and does not necessarily or always suggest a definite hearer or audience or that the sounds and words are logically or grammatically connected: *Some children learn to speak much earlier than others.* **Talk** emphasizes using words in connected speech to make known ideas or give information, commonly to a listener, but often particularly suggests more or less meaningless continued speaking: *Some people are always talking.*

speak·eas·y (spēk′ēz′ē) *n., pl.* **-eas·ies.** *Esp.U.S. Slang.* during the era of prohibition, a place where alcoholic liquors were sold contrary to law.

speak·er (spē′kər) *n.* **1** a person who speaks, especially one who speaks before an audience: *Our next speaker is Professor Chapman.* **2 Speaker,** a person who presides over an assembly: *the Speaker of the House of Commons.* **3** loudspeaker.

Speaker of the House 1 in Canada and the United Kingdom, the presiding officer of the House of Commons. **2** in the United States, the presiding officer of the House of Representatives.

speak·er·ship (spē′kər ship′) *n.* the position of presiding officer.

speak·ing (spē′king) *n., adj.* —*n.* the act, utterance, or discourse of a person who speaks. —*adj.* **1** that speaks; giving information as if by speech: *a speaking example of a thing.* **2** used in, suited to, or involving speech: *within speaking distance, a speaking part in a play.* **3** permitting conversation: *a speaking acquaintance with a person.* **4** highly expressive: *speaking eyes.* **5** life-like: *a speaking likeness.*

spear¹ (spēr) *n., v.* —*n.* a weapon having a long shaft and a sharp-pointed head. —*v.* **1** pierce with a spear: *The Indian speared a fish.* **2** pierce or stab with anything sharp. **3** *Hockey.* check (an opponent) illegally by stabbing with the point of the stick blade. **4** *Football.* block (an opponent) with the helmet instead of with the body. [OE *spere*] —**spear′er,** *n.*

spear² (spēr) *n., v.* —*n.* a sprout or shoot of a plant: *a spear of grass.* —*v.* sprout or shoot into a long stem. [var. of *spire¹*; influenced by *spear¹*]

spear·head (spēr′hed′) *n., v.* —*n.* **1** the sharp-pointed striking end of a spear. **2** the part, person, or group that comes first in an attack, undertaking, etc.: *She was the spearhead of the project to make the park here.* —*v.* go first in an attack, undertaking, etc.: *Tanks spearheaded the army's advance.*

spear·man (spēr′mən) *n., pl.* **-men.** a soldier armed with a spear.

spear·mint (spēr′mint′) *n.* a European mint (*Mentha spicata*) widely cultivated for its aromatic leaves which yield an oil used for flavoring. [< *spear¹* + *mint¹*; from the shape of the inflorescence]

spear·side the paternal side or branch of a family. Compare **distaff side.**

spec. 1 special. **2** specification. **3** speculation.

spe·cial (spesh′əl) *adj., n.* —*adj.* **1** of a particular kind; distinct from others; not general: *This desk has a special lock.* **2** more than ordinary; unusual; exceptional: *Today's topic is of special interest.* **3** held in unusually high regard; valued in an exceptional way: *a special friend, a special favorite.* **4** for a particular person, thing,

purpose, etc.: *The railway ran special trains on holidays. Send the letter by a special messenger.*
—*n.* **1** a special train, car, bus, etc. **2** any special person or thing. **3** a special edition of a newspaper. **4** in a store, restaurant, etc., a product that is specially featured; bargain: *a weekend special.* **5** a specially produced television show, not one of the regular daily or weekly programs. [ME < L *specialis* < *species* appearance. Doublet of ESPECIAL.]

☛ *Syn. adj.* **1. Special, particular** = not general, but belonging or relating to one person, thing, or group, as distinguished from others. **Special** emphasizes the idea of qualities making one different from others of its kind, or other kinds, and giving it a character, nature, use, etc. of its own: *Babies need special food.* **Particular** emphasizes the idea of pertaining to one considered as an individual, apart from all others of the same kind or covered by a general statement: *These synonym studies give both the general and particular meanings of words.*

special delivery the delivery of a letter or package by a special messenger rather than by the regular postman. Special delivery mail is handled faster and delivered sooner than regular mail.

spe·cial·ism (spesh′əl iz′əm) *n.* devotion or restriction to one particular branch of study, business, etc.

spe·cial·ist (spesh′əl ist) *n.* a person who devotes or restricts himself to one particular branch of study, business, etc.: *Dr. White is a specialist in diseases of the nose and throat.*

spe·ci·al·i·ty (spesh′ē al′ə tē) *n., pl.* **-ties. 1** a special or particular character. **2** a special quality or characteristic; the distinctive characteristic or feature of a thing. **3** a special point; particular; detail. **4** a special pursuit, branch, product, etc.; speciality.

spe·cial·ize (spesh′əl īz′) *v.* **-ized, -iz·ing. 1** pursue some special branch of study, work, etc.: *Many students specialize in engineering.* **2** adapt to special conditions; give special form, use, duty, etc. to; limit. **3** develop in a special way; take on a special form, use, etc. **4** mention specially; specify. **5** go into particulars. —**spe′cial·i·za′tion,** *n.*

spe·cial·ly (spesh′əl ē) *adv.* in a special manner or degree; particularly; unusually.

☛ *Usage.* See note at **especially.**

spe·cial·ty (spesh′əl tē) *n., pl.* **-ties. 1** a special study; special line of work, profession, trade, etc.: *Repairing watches is his specialty.* **2** a product, article, etc. to which special attention is given: *This store makes a specialty of children's clothes.* **3** a special character; special quality. **4** a special or particular characteristic; peculiarity. **5** a special point or item; particular; detail. [ME < OF (*e*)*specialte* < L *specialitas* < *specialis.* See SPECIAL.]

spe·cie (spē′shē) *n.* money in the form of coins; metal money. Silver dollars are specie. [< L (*in*) *specie,* abl. of *species* kind]

spe·cies (spē′sēz *or* spē′shēz) *n., pl.* **-cies. 1** *Biology.* the narrowest major category in the classification of plants and animals. See chart at **classification. 2** kind or sort: *A species of advertisement.* **3** *Roman Catholic or Orthodox Eastern Church.* the consecrated bread and wine of the Eucharist. **4** *Obsolete.* an outward appearance or form. **5 the species,** the human race. [< L *species,* originally, appearance. Doublet of SPICE.]

specif. specifically.

spe·cif·ic (spə sif′ik) *adj., n.* —*adj.* **1** definite; precise; particular: *There was no specific reason for the quarrel.* **2** characteristic: *A scaly skin is a specific feature of snakes.* **3** curing some particular disease. **4** produced by some special cause. **5** *Biology.* of or having to do with a species.
—*n.* **1** any specific statement, quality, etc. **2** a cure for some particular disease: *Quinine is a specific for malaria.* [< LL *specificus* constituting a species < L *species* sort + *facere* make] —**spe·cif′ic·ness,** *n.*

spe·cif·i·cal·ly (spə sif′ik lē) *adv.* in a specific manner; definitely; particularly: *The doctor told Kate specifically not to eat eggs.*

spec·i·fi·ca·tion (spes′ə fə kā′shən) *n.* **1** the act of specifying; a definite mention: *Mary made careful specification of the kinds of cake and candy for her party.* **2** Usually, **specifications,** *pl.* a detailed description of the dimensions, materials, etc. for a building, road, dam, boat, etc.: *The repairs had not been done according to specifications.* **3** something specified; a particular item, article, etc. **4** *Patent law.* a detailed statement of particulars.

specific duty a customs duty on a specified article or quantity of articles, regardless of its market value.

specific gravity relative density. *Abbrev.:* s.g. *or* sp.gr.

specific heat 1 a number that expresses the ratio of the quantity of heat needed to raise the temperature of a given substance one degree to that needed to raise the temperature of an equal mass of water one degree: *The specific heat of aluminum is about 0.2.* **2** specific heat capacity.

specific heat capacity the quantity of heat needed to raise the temperature of one unit of a substance one degree.

hat, āge, fär; let, ēqual, tèrm; it, īce
hot, ōpen, ôrder; oil, out; cup, pu̇t, rüle,
əbove, takən, pencəl, lemən, circəs

ch, child; ng, long; sh, ship
th, thin; ŦH, then; zh, measure

specific impulse a measure of the efficiency of a rocket engine. It is the thrust delivered in a given time per unit weight of propellant expended.

spec·i·fy (spes′ə fī′) *v.* **-fied, -fy·ing. 1** mention or name definitely; state or describe in detail: *Did you specify any particular time for us to call?* **2** include in the speculations: *The contractor would have used cement blocks, but bricks were specified.* [ME < OF < LL *specificare* < *specificus.* See SPECIFIC.]

spec·i·men (spes′ə mən) *n., adj.* —*n.* **1** one of a group or class taken to show what the others are like; a single part, thing, etc. regarded as an example of its kind: *The statue was a fine specimen of Greek sculpture.* **2** *Informal.* a human being; person: *The tramp was a queer specimen.* —*adj.* taken or regarded as a specimen. [< L *specimen* < *specere* view]

spe·ci·os·i·ty (spē′shē os′ə tē) *n., pl.* **-ties. 1** the quality of being specious. **2** a specious act, appearance, remark, etc.

spe·cious (spē′shəs) *adj.* **1** seeming desirable, reasonable, or probable, but not really so; apparently good or right, but without real merit: *The teacher saw through John's specious excuse.* **2** make a good outward appearance in order to deceive: *His dishonest actions showed him to be nothing but a specious hypocrite.* [< L *speciosus* < *species* appearance] —**spe′cious·ly,** *adv.* —**spe′cious·ness,** *n.*

speck (spek) *n., v.* —*n.* **1** a small spot; stain: *Can you clean the specks off this wallpaper?* **2** a tiny bit; particle: *I have a speck in my eye.* —*v.* mark with specks: *This fruit is badly specked.* [OE *specca*]

speck·le (spek′əl) *n., v.* **-led, -ling.** —*n.* a small spot or mark: *This hen is grey with white speckles.* —*v.* mark with speckles.

speckled char *or* **trout** brook trout.

specs (speks) *n.pl. Informal.* spectacles.

spec·ta·cle (spek′tə kəl) *n.* **1** something to look at; sight: *The children at play among the flowers made a charming spectacle.* **2** a public show or display: *The big army parade was a fine spectacle.* **3** a person or thing set before the public view as an object of curiosity, contempt, wonder, or admiration. **4 spectacles,** *pl.* **a** a pair of glasses to help a person's sight or to protect the eyes. **b** a means or medium through which anything is viewed or regarded; point of view.

make a spectacle of oneself, behave foolishly or crudely in public. [ME < L *spectaculum,* ult. < *specere* view]

spec·ta·cled (spek′tə kəld) *adj.* **1** provided with or wearing spectacles. **2** having a marking resembling spectacles: *a spectacled snake.*

spec·tac·u·lar (spek tak′yə lər) *adj., n.* —*adj.* **1** making a great display: *The television program included a spectacular scene of a storm.* **2** having to do with a spectacle or show. —*n.* a spectacular display or show: *a TV spectacular.*

spec·tac·u·lar·ly (spek tak′yə lər lē) *adv.* **1** in a spectacular manner or degree. **2** as a spectacle.

spec·ta·tor (spek′tā tər *or* spek tā′tər) *n.* a person who watches without taking part; onlooker: *Thousands of spectators lined the streets, waiting for the parade to come by.* [< L *spectator* < *spectare* watch < *specere* view]

spectator sport a sport that attracts many spectators who do not practise the sport themselves: *Hockey and football are spectator sports.*

spec·ter (spek′tər) See **spectre.**

spec·tra (spek′trə) *n.* a pl. of **spectrum.**

spec·tral (spek′trəl) *adj.* **1** of or like a spectre; ghostly: *He saw the spectral form of the headless horseman.* **2** of or produced by the spectrum: *spectral colors.*

spec·tre (spek′tər) *n.* **1** ghost. **2** something causing terror or dread. Also, **specter.** [< L *spectrum* appearance. See SPECTRUM.]

☛ *Syn.* **1.** See note at **ghost.**

spec·tro·scope (spek′trə skōp′) *n.* an instrument for obtaining and examining the spectrum of radiation from any source by the passage of rays through a prism or a grating.

spec·tro·scop·ic (spek′trə skop′ik) *adj.* **1** of, made by, or done with a spectroscope. **2** using a spectroscope. —**spec′tro·scop′i·cal·ly,** *adv.*

spec·tros·co·py (spek tros′kə pē *or* spek′trə skō′pē) *n.* **1** a

science having to do with the examination and analysis of spectra.
2 the use of the spectroscope.

spec·trum (spek'trəm) n., pl. **-tra** (-trə) or **-trums. 1** the band of colors formed when a beam of light is broken up by being passed through a prism or by some other means. A rainbow has all the colors of the spectrum: red, orange, yellow, green, blue, indigo, and violet. **2** the band of colors formed when any radiant energy is broken up. The ends of such a spectrum are not visible to the eye, but are studied by photography, heat effects, etc. **3** *Radio.* the wave-length range between 30 000 metres and 3 centimetres. **4** range; scope; compass: *the spectrum of political thought.* [< L *spectrum* appearance < *specere* view]

spec·u·lar (spek'yə lər) adj. **1** of or like a mirror; reflecting. **2** having to do with a speculum. [< L *specularis* < *speculum* mirror. See SPECULUM.]

spec·u·late (spek'yə lāt') v. **-lat·ed, -lat·ing. 1** reflect; meditate; consider: *The philosopher speculated about time and space.* **2** guess; conjecture: *She refused to speculate about the possible winner.* **3** buy or sell when there is a large risk, with the hope of making a profit from future price changes. **4** take part or invest in a risky business enterprise or transaction, in the hope of making large profits. [< L *speculari* < *specula* watchtower < *specere* look]

spec·u·la·tion (spek'yə lā'shən) n. **1** thought; reflection: *Former speculations about electricity were often mere guesses.* **2** a guessing; conjecture. **3** the act of buying or selling where there is a risk, with the hope of making a profit from future price changes: *His speculations in stocks made him poor.* **4** a taking part in any risky business enterprise, transaction, etc.

spec·u·la·tive (spek'yə lə tiv *or* spek'yə lā'tiv) adj. **1** thoughtful; reflective. **2** theoretical rather than practical. **3** risky. **4** of or involving speculation in land, stocks, etc. **—spec'u·la·tive·ly,** adv. **—spec'u·la·tive·ness,** n.

spec·u·la·tor (spek'yə lā'tər) n. **1** a person who speculates, usually in business. **2** a person who buys tickets for shows, games, etc. in advance, hoping to sell them later at a higher price. [< L *speculator* explorer, spy]

spec·u·lum (spek'yə ləm) n., pl. **-la** (-lə) or **-lums. 1** a mirror of polished metal. A reflecting telescope contains a speculum. **2** a surgical instrument for enlarging an opening in order to examine a cavity. [< L *speculum* mirror < *specere* view]

sped (sped) v. a pt. and a pp. of **speed.**

speech (spēch) n. **1** the act of speaking; talk. **2** the power of speaking: *Animals lack speech.* **3** a manner of speaking: *The sailor's speech showed that he was a Newfoundlander.* **4** what is said; the words spoken: *We made the usual farewell speeches.* **5** a public talk. **6** a number of lines spoken by an actor in a single sequence. **7** particular language or dialect: *His native speech was French.* **8** the study and practice of the spoken language: *take a course in speech.* [OE *spǣc*]
☞ *Syn.* **5. Speech, address, oration** = a talk made to an audience. **Speech** is the general word applying to a prepared or unprepared, formal or informal talk made for some purpose: *Most after-dinner speeches are interesting.* **Address** suggests a prepared formal speech, usually of some importance or given on an important occasion: *Who gave your commencement address?* **Oration** applies to a formal address on a special occasion, and particularly suggests artistic style, dignity, and eloquence: *a funeral oration.*

speech community any group of people sharing the same language or dialect.

Speech from the Throne a statement of government policy for the coming year read to the opening session of a legislature by the sovereign or his representative.

speech·i·fy (spē'chə fī') v. **-fied, -fy·ing.** *Humorous or contemptuous.* make a speech or speeches. **—speech'i·fi'er,** n.

speech·less (spēch'lis) adj. **1** not able to speak: *George was speechless with anger.* **2** silent: *Her frown gave a speechless reply.* **—speech'less·ness,** n.
☞ *Syn.* **1.** See note at **dumb.**

speech·less·ly (spēch'lis lē) adv. **1** without speaking. **2** so as to be speechless.

speed (spēd) n., v. **speed** or **speed·ed, speed·ing. —n. 1** swift or rapid movement. **2** a rate of movement; velocity: *a speed of 100 kilometres per hour. The boys ran at full speed.* **3** an arrangement of gears to give a certain rate of movement: *a ten-speed bike. Most cars with standard transmissions have three forward speeds.* **4** *Slang.* any of various amphetamines used as mood-elevating drugs, especially methamphetamine. **5** *Archaic.* good luck; success. **—v. 1** go quickly: *The boat sped over the water.* **2** make go quickly: *speed a horse.* **3** send quickly. **4** go faster than is safe or lawful: *The car was caught speeding near the school zone.* **5** help forward; promote: *to speed an undertaking.* **6** *Archaic.* succeed. **7** *Archaic.* give success to: *God speed you.*

speed up, go or cause to go more quickly; increase in speed. [OE *spēd*]
☞ *Syn.* n. **1.** See note at **hurry.**

speed·boat (spēd'bōt') n. a motorboat built to go at high speeds.

speed·er (spē'dər) n. **1** a person or thing that goes at a fast pace, especially one who indulges in speeding. **2** a small trolley powered by a gasoline engine, used on railway tracks by maintenance crews.

speed·ing (spē'ding) n. the act of driving faster than the legal speed limit.

speed limit the top speed at which vehicles are allowed to travel on a particular road.

speed·om·e·ter (spē dom'ə tər *or* spi dom'ə tər) n. an instrument to indicate the speed of an automobile or other vehicle.

speed trap a section of road or highway where police set up a means of catching persons who are speeding.

speed–up (spēd'up') n. an increase in speed: *a speed-up in manufacturing.*

speed·way (spēd'wā') n. a road or track for fast driving.

speed·well (spēd'wel') n. any of a genus (*Veronica*) of annual and perennial plants found chiefly in north temperate regions. Some speedwells are cultivated in gardens for their blue, pink, or white flowers.

speed·y (spē'dē) adj. **speed·i·er, speed·i·est.** fast; rapid; quick; swift: *speedy workers, a speedy change, speedy progress, a speedy decision.* **—speed'i·ly,** adv. **—speed'i·ness,** n.

spe·le·ol·o·gist (spē'lē ol'ə jist) n. a person trained in speleology, especially one whose work it is.

spe·le·ol·o·gy (spē'lē ol'ə jē) n. the scientific study of caves, including the geology, flora and fauna, etc. [< L *spelaeum* < Gk. *spēlaion* + *-logy*]

spell¹ (spel) v. **spelled** or **spelt, spell·ing. 1** write or say the letters of (a word) in order. **2** write or say the letters of words in order: *She cannot spell well.* **3** make up or form (a word): *C-a-t spells cat.* **4** mean: *Delay spells danger.* [ME < OF *espeller* < Gmc.]

spell² (spel) n. **1** a word or set of words having magic power. **2** fascination; charm.
cast a spell on, put under the influence of magic power; fascinate.
under a spell, controlled by a spell; spellbound: *The explorer's story held the children under a spell.* [OE *spell* story]

spell³ (spel) n., v. **spelled, spell·ing. —n. 1** a period of work or duty: *The sailor's spell at the wheel was four hours.* **2** a period or time of anything: *a spell of coughing, a spell of hot weather.* **3** the relief of one person by another in doing something. **4** *Informal.* an attack or fit of illness or nervous excitement. **5** *Informal.* a brief period: *to rest for a spell.*
—v. 1 *Informal.* work in place of (another) for a while: *to spell another person at rowing a boat.* **2** give a time of rest to. [OE *spelian, v.*]

spell·bind (spel'bīnd') v. **-bound, -bind·ing.** make spellbound; fascinate; enchant.

spell·bind·er (spel'bīn'dər) n. a speaker or writer who can hold his audience spellbound.

spell·bound (spel'bound') adj. too interested to move; fascinated; enchanted. [< *spell²* + *bound¹*]

spell·er (spel'ər) n. **1** a person who spells words in a particular manner: *I'm not a very good speller.* **2** a book for teaching spelling.

spell·ing (spel'ing) n. **1** the writing or saying of the letters of words in order. **2** the way a word is spelled: *Many English words have more than one spelling.*

spelling bee a spelling contest.

spelt¹ (spelt) v. a pt. and a pp. of **spell¹.**

spelt² (spelt) n. an old species of wheat (*Triticum spelta*) no longer much cultivated. [< LL *spelta*]

spel·ter (spel'tər) n. zinc, usually in the form of small bars. [origin uncertain; cf. LG *spialter*]

spe·lunk·er (spi lung'kər) n. a person who studies and explores caves as a hobby. [< L *spelunca* cave < Gk. *spēlaion* + E *-er²*]

spe·lunk·ing (spi lung'king) n. the act or hobby of studying and exploring caves.

spen·cer (spen'sər) n. a short fitted or semi-fitted jacket for men or women. [after George John *Spencer*, the second Earl Spencer (1758-1834)]

Spen·ce·ri·an¹ (spen sēr'ē ən) adj. of or having to do with Herbert Spencer (1820-1903), an English philosopher, or his philosophy.

Spen·ce·ri·an² (spen sēr'ē ən) adj. of or having to do with a system of penmanship, characterized by clearly formed, rounded

letters slanting to the right. [< Platt R. *Spencer* (1800-1864), an American penmanship expert who originated it + *-ian*]

spend (spend) *v.* **spent, spend·ing. 1** pay out: *She spent ten dollars today.* **2** pay out money: *Earn before you spend.* **3** use; use up: *Don't spend any more time on that job.* **4** pass (time, etc.): *to spend a day at the beach.* **5** wear out; exhaust: *The storm has spent its force.* **6** waste; squander: *He spent his fortune on horse racing.* **7** lose, as for a cause. [OE *-spendan* (as in *forspendan* use up) < L *expendere.* Doublet of EXPEND.] —**spend′er,** *n.*

☞ *Syn.* **1. Spend, expend, disburse** = pay out money, time, effort, etc. **Spend** is the common word, meaning "pay out money, or other resources for some thing or purpose": *He spends all he earns.* **Expend,** more formal, emphasizes the idea of using up by spending sums or amounts, commonly large, that reduce or exhaust a fund: *She expends her energy on parties.* **Disburse,** formal or financial, means "pay out from a fund for expenses": *The treasurer reports what he disburses.*

spend·thrift (spend′thrift′) *n., adj.* —*n.* a person who wastes money. —*adj.* extravagant with money; wasteful.

Spen·se·ri·an (spen sêr′ē ən) *adj.* of, having to do with, or characteristic of Edmund Spenser (1552?-1599), an English poet, or his work.

Spenserian stanza the stanza used by Edmund Spenser in his *Faerie Queene,* consisting of eight iambic pentameter lines and a final alexandrine, with three rhymes arranged thus: ababbcbcc.

spent (spent) *v., adj.* —*v.* pt. and pp. of **spend.** —*adj.* **1** used up. **2** worn out; tired: *a spent swimmer, a spent horse.*

sperm¹ (spêrm) *n.* **1** the mature male reproductive cell produced by almost all animals and plants that reproduce sexually; a male gamete. The sperm of mammals are very tiny and consist of a head that contains the genes and a thin tail by which they propel themselves inside the female reproductive tract. **2** semen. [ME < LL < Gk. *sperma* seed < *speirein* sow¹]

sperm² (spêrm) *n.* **1** spermaceti. **2** sperm whale. **3** sperm oil. [short for *spermaceti,* etc.]

sper·ma·cet·i (spêr′mə set′ē *or* spêr′mə sē′tē) *n.* a whitish, waxy substance obtained from the oil in the head of the sperm whale and used in making fine candles, ointments, cosmetics, etc. [< Med.L *sperma ceti* sperm of a whale < LL *sperma* sperm, seed < Gk., and L *cetus* large sea animal < Gk. *kētos*]

sper·mat·ic (spêr mat′ik) *adj.* **1** of or having to do with sperm; seminal; generative. **2** having to do with a sperm gland.

sper·ma·to·phyte (spêr′mə tə fīt′) *n.* any plant that reproduces by means of seeds, including the angiosperms (flowering plants) and the gymnosperms (conifers, etc.). Spermatophytes constitute a major plant group which in earlier classification systems constitute a division, or phylum, (Spermatophyta) of the plant kingdom. [< Gk. *sperma, -atos* seed + E *-phyte*]

sper·ma·to·zo·on (spêr′mə tə zō′ən) *n., pl.* **-zo·a** (-zō′ə). a sperm, especially of an animal. [< Gk. *sperma, -atos* seed + *zōion* animal]

sperm oil a light-yellow oil from the sperm whale, used for lubricating.

sperm whale a large toothed whale (*Physeter catodon,* constituting the family Physeteridae) having a very large, blunt-nosed head which has a cavity containing spermaceti. Sperm whales have long been hunted for spermaceti and also for ambergris and sperm oil.

spew (spyü) *v.* **1** vomit: *The dog spewed on the rug.* **2** cast forth; throw out: *The volcano was spewing lava. He spewed out a stream of insults.* [OE *spīwan*] —**spew′er,** *n.*

sp. gr. specific gravity.

sphag·num (sfag′nəm) *n.* peat moss. [< NL < Gk. *sphagnos,* a kind of moss]

sphal·er·ite (sfal′ə rīt′ *or* sfa′lə rīt′) *n.* a native zinc sulphide, found in both crystalline and massive forms; blende. *Formula:* ZnS [< Gk. *sphaleros* deceptive, slippery < *sphallen* overthrow, baffle + E *-ite¹*]

sphe·noid (sfē′noid) *adj., n.* —*adj.* **1** wedge-shaped. **2** *Anatomy.* of or having to do with a compound bone of the base of the skull. —*n. Anatomy.* this bone. [< NL < Gk. *sphenoeidēs* < *sphēn* wedge + *eidos* form]

sphere (sfēr) *n.* **1** *Geometry.* a round solid figure bounded by a surface that is at all points equally distant from the centre. See **solid** for picture. **2** an object approximately like this in form; ball; globe. **3** the place or field in which a person or thing exists, acts, works, etc.: *His sphere is advertising. People used to say that woman's sphere was the home.* **4** a range; extent; region: *Great Britain's sphere of influence.* **5** any of the stars or planets. The earth, sun, and moon are spheres. **6** a supposed hollow globe, with the earth at its centre, enclosing the stars, sun, and planets. **7** any one of a series of such globes, one inside another, in which the stars and planets were supposed to be set. Movement of the spheres was

hat, āge, fär; let, ēqual, tèrm; it, īce
hot, ōpen, ôrder; oil, out; cup, pùt, rüle,
əbove, takən, pencəl, lemən, circəs
ch, child; ng, long; sh, ship
th, thin; ᴛʜ, then; zh, measure

believed to cause the stars and planets to revolve around the earth. **8** the heavens; the sky. [< L < Gk. *sphaira*]

spher·i·cal (sfer′ə kəl) *adj.* **1** shaped like a sphere. **2** of or having to do with a sphere or spheres.

spher·i·cal·ly (sfer′ik lē) *adv.* **1** in the form of a sphere, or of part of a sphere. **2** so as to be spherical.

sphe·ric·i·ty (sfi ris′ə tē) *n., pl.* **-ties.** spherical form; roundness.

sphe·roid (sfēr′oid) *n.* a body shaped somewhat like a sphere.

sphe·roi·dal (sfi roi′dəl) *adj.* shaped somewhat like a sphere.

spher·ule (sfer′ül) *n.* a small sphere or spherical body.

sphinc·ter (sfingk′tər) *n. Anatomy.* a ringlike muscle that surrounds an opening or passage of the body, and can contract to close it. [< LL < Gk. *sphinktēr* < *sphingein* squeeze]

sphinx (sfingks) *n., pl.* **sphinx·es. 1** a statue of a lion's body with the head of a man, ram, or hawk: *There are many sphinxes in Egypt.* **2 Sphinx,** *Greek mythology.* a monster with the head of a woman, the body of a lion, and wings. The Sphinx proposed a riddle to every passer-by and killed those unable to guess the answer. **3** a puzzling or mysterious person. [< L < Gk.]

sphinx moth hawk moth.

sphygmo- *combining form.* the pulse; pulsation, as in *sphygmograph.* [< Gk. *sphygmos* throbbing, heartbeat < *sphyzein* throb, beat]

sphyg·mo·gram (sfig′mə gram′) *n.* a diagram of the pulse beats as recorded by a sphygmograph.

sphyg·mo·graph (sfig′mə graf′) *n.* an instrument that records the rate, strength, etc. of the pulse. [< Gk. *sphygmos* pulse + E *-graph*]

sphyg·moid (sfig′moid) *adj.* pulselike.

sphyg·mo·ma·nom·e·ter (sfig′mō mə nom′ə tər) *n. Medicine.* an instrument for measuring blood pressure, especially in an artery. [< *sphygmo-* + Gk. *manos* at intervals + E *-meter*]

spi·ca (spī′kə) *n., pl.* **spi·cae** (spī′sē). **1** *Botany.* a spike. **2** *Surgery.* spiral bandages with reversed turns. **3 Spica,** a very bright star in the constellation Virgo. [< L *spica* ear of grain]

spi·cate (spī′kāt) *adj.* **1** *Botany.* **a** having spikes. **b** arranged in spikes. **2** *Zoology.* having the form of a spike; pointed. [< L *spicatus,* pp. of *spicare* furnish with spikes < *spica* spike²]

spice (spīs) *n., v.* **spiced, spic·ing.** —*n.* **1** any of various seasonings obtained from plants and used to flavor food: *Pepper, cinnamon, cloves, ginger, and nutmeg are common spices.* **2** such substances considered collectively or as a material. **3** a spicy, fragrant odor. **4** something that adds flavor or interest. **5** a slight touch or trace: *a spice of wickedness.*
—*v.* **1** put spice in; season. **2** add flavor or interest to. [ME < OF *espice,* ult. < L *species* sort. Doublet of SPECIES.]

spic·er·y (spī′sər ē) *n., pl.* **-er·ies. 1** spices. **2** a spicy flavor or fragrance.

spick–and–span (spik′ənd span′) *adj.* **1** neat and clean; spruce or smart: *a spick-and-span room, apron, or uniform.* **2** fresh; new. [short for *spick-and-span-new: spick,* var. of *spike¹; span-new* < ON *spán-nýr* < *spánn* chip + *nýr* new]

spic·u·late (spik′yə lāt′ *or* spik′yə lit) *adj.* **1** having spicules; consisting of spicules. **2** having the form of a spicule.

spic·ule (spik′yəl) *n.* **1** a small, slender, sharp-pointed piece, usually bony or crystalline. **2** *Zoology.* one of the small, slender, calcareous or siliceous bodies that form the skeleton of a sponge. **3** *Botany.* a small spike of flowers; spikelet. **4** a small solar prominence. [< L *spiculum,* dim. of *spicum,* var. of *spica* ear of grain]

spic·y (spī′sē) *adj.* **spic·i·er, spic·i·est. 1** flavored with spice. **2** having a taste or smell like that of spice: *spicy apples.* **3** lively; keen: *spicy conversation.* **4** somewhat improper: *Some of his stories were a bit spicy.* **5** producing spices; abounding with spices. —**spic′i·ly,** *adv.* —**spic′i·ness,** *n.*

spi·der (spī′dər) *n.* **1** any of an order (Araneida, also called Araneae) of arachnids found throughout the world, having an unsegmented body with two main divisions, four pairs of walking legs and organs for producing silk which is used for making nests, webs to catch prey, or cocoons for their eggs. **2** any of various implements, tools, or machine parts having radiating arms, spokes,

etc. **3** a cast-iron frying pan of a type originally made with short legs to stand over an open fire. [OE *spīthra* < *spinnan* spin] —**spi′der·like′**, *adj.*

spider web a web spun by a spider. See **web** for picture.

spi·der·wort (spī′dər wėrt′) *n.* **1** any of a genus (*Tradescantia*) of perennial plants having somewhat grasslike leaves and clusters of purple, blue, or white flowers. The wandering Jew is a spiderwort. **2** (*adj.*) designating a family (Commelinaceae) of mainly tropical plants that includes the spiderworts, all having jointed and often branching stems with parallel-veined leaves.

spi·der·y (spī′dər ē) *adj.* **1** long and thin like a spider's legs. **2** suggesting a spider's web: *spidery handwriting.* **3** full of, or infested with, spiders.

spiel[1] (spēl) *n., v. Slang.* —*n.* talk; speech; harangue, especially of a cheap, noisy nature. —*v.* talk; speak. [< G *spielen* play]

spiel[2] or **'spiel** (spēl) *n. Cdn.* bonspiel.

spiel·er[1] (spē′lər) *n. Slang.* a person who spiels, especially one who exaggerates and has a lot to say.

spiel·er[2] or **'spiel·er** (spē′lər) *n. Cdn.* a person who takes part in a bonspiel.

spiff·y (spif′ē) *adj.* **spiff·i·er, spiff·i·est.** *Slang.* smart; neat; trim. [< dial. E *spiff* dandified (person)]

spig·ot (spig′ət) *n.* **1** a valve for controlling the flow of water or other liquid from a pipe, tank, barrel, etc. **2** a tap or faucet. **3** a peg or plug used to stop the small hole of a cask, barrel, etc.; bung. [ME; ? via OF < base of *spike*]

spike[1] (spīk) *n., v.* **spiked, spik·ing.** —*n.* **1** a large, strong nail. **2** a sharp-pointed object or part, especially one made of metal: *a fence with spikes at the top.* **3** one of a set of metal projections on the sole and sometimes the heel of a shoe to improve traction. **4 spikes,** *pl.* a pair of shoes having such spikes.
spike (someone's) guns, obstruct or defeat someone.
—*v.* **1** fasten with spikes: *The men spiked the rails to the ties when laying the track.* **2** provide or equip with spikes: *Runners wear spiked shoes to keep from slipping.* **3** pierce or injure with a spike. **4** make (a cannon) useless by driving a spike into the touchhole. **5** put an end or stop to; make useless; block: *to spike an attempt.* **6** *Slang.* add liquor to (a drink, etc.). [ME < Scand. < L *spica*; cf. Swedish *spik* nail] —**spik′er,** *n.* —**spike′like′,** *adj.*

spike[2] (spīk) *n.* **1** an ear of grain. **2** a long, pointed flower cluster. See **inflorescence** for picture. [ME < L *spica*]

spike heel a high, thin heel on a woman's dress shoe.

spike·let (spīk′lit) *n.* a small or secondary spike, especially one of the small spikes that make up a spike, or head, of grain or grass. Each spikelet of wheat may produce one or more kernels.

spike·nard (spīk′nərd *or* spīk′närd) *n.* **1** a sweet-smelling ointment used in ancient times. **2** a fragrant East Indian plant (*Nardostachys jatamansi*) of the valerian family from which this ointment was probably obtained. [ME < Med.L *spica nardi* ear of nard]

spik·y (spī′kē) *adj.* **1** having spikes; set with sharp, projecting points. **2** having the shape of a spike.

spile (spīl) *n., v.* **spiled, spil·ing.** —*n.* **1** a peg or plug of wood used to stop the small hole of a cask or barrel. **2** a spout for drawing off sap from sugar maple trees. **3** a heavy stake or beam driven into the ground as a support.
—*v.* **1** stop up (a hole) with a plug. **2** furnish with a spout. **3** furnish, strengthen, or support with stakes or piles. [cf. MDu. or MLG *spile*]

spill[1] (spil) *v.* **spilled** or **spilt, spill·ing;** *n.* —*v.* **1** let (liquid or any matter in loose pieces) run or fall: *to spill milk or salt.* **2** fall or flow out: *Water spilled from the pail.* **3** scatter. **4** shed (blood). **5** *Informal.* cause to fall from a horse, car, boat, etc. **6** let wind out of (a sail). **7** *Slang.* make known; tell.
—*n.* **1** spilling. **2** the quantity spilled. **3** *Informal.* a fall. [OE *spillan*] —**spill′er,** *n.*

spill[2] (spil) *n.* **1** splinter. **2** a piece of wood or paper used to light candles, etc. [? ult. var. of *spile*]

spill·age (spil′ij) *n.* **1** a spilling of liquid, food, etc. **2** that which is spilled; the quantity spilled.

spil·li·kin (spil′ə kin) *n.* jackstraw. [< *spill*[2]]

spill·way (spil′wā′) *n.* a channel or passage for the escape of surplus water from a dam, river, etc.

spilt (spilt) *v.* a pt. and a pp. of **spill**[1].

spin (spin) *v.* **spun** or (*archaic*) **span, spun, spin·ning;** *n.* —*v.* **1** turn or make turn rapidly: *The wheel spins round. The boy spins his top.* **2** feel as if one were whirling around; feel dizzy: *My head is spinning.* **3** draw out and twist (cotton, flax, wool, etc.) into thread. **4** make (thread, yarn etc.) by drawing out and twisting cotton,

wool, flax, etc. **5** make (a thread, web, cocoon, etc.) by giving out from the body sticky material that hardens into thread. A spider spins a web. **6** make (glass, gold, etc.) into thread. **7** run, ride, drive, etc. rapidly. **8** produce; tell: *The old sailor used to spin yarns about adventures at sea.*
spin out, make long and slow; draw out; prolong: *Try not to spin out your story.*
—*n.* **1** the action of spinning. **2** a ride, run, or drive, especially a short one: *Get your bicycle and come for a spin with me.* **3** a rapid turning around of an aircraft as it falls. **4** *Physics.* **a** the rotation of an elementary particle about its axis, producing a spin energy which is expressed as a quantum number value. Spin is a property by which particles may be differentiated. **b** a quantum number representing this energy. It may be integral (0, 1, or 2) or half integral. Electrons have a spin of ½. [OE *spinnan*]

spin·ach (spin′ich *or* spin′ij) *n.* **1** a plant (*Spinacia oleracea*) of the goosefoot family cultivated for its large, dark-green, edible leaves. **2** the leaves of this plant, eaten cooked as a vegetable or raw in salads. [< OF (*e*)*spinache* < Med.L < Sp. *espinaca* < Arabic]

spi·nal (spī′nəl) *adj., n.* —*adj.* **1** of, having to do with, or located near the backbone. **2** of, having to do with, or affecting the spinal cord. **3** resembling a spine in form or function: *a spinal ridge or hill.* —*n.* an anesthetic for the lower part of the body. [< LL *spinalis* < L *spina.* See **SPINE.**]

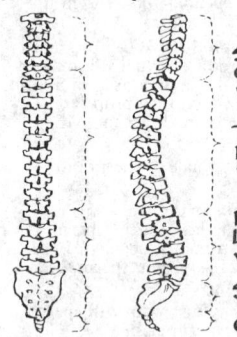

SEVEN CERVICAL VERTEBRAE

TWELVE DORSAL VERTEBRAE

FIVE LUMBAR VERTEBRAE

SACRUM

COCCYX

The human spinal column, seen from the back (far left) and the side (near left)

spinal column in human beings and other vertebrates, the series of small bones along the middle of the back, that encloses and protects the spinal cord and provides support for the body. The many bones of the spinal column, called vertebrae, are held together by muscles and tendons that allow movement in different directions.

spinal cord the thick, whitish cord of nerve tissue that extends from the brain down through most of the backbone and from which nerves to various parts of the body branch off. See **brain** for picture.

spin·dle (spin′dəl) *n., v.* **-dled, -dling.** —*n.* **1** a rod or pin used in spinning to twist, wind, and hold thread. **2** a unit for measuring length of yarn, equal to 15 120 yards (about 13 825 metres) for cotton and 14 400 yards (about 13 167 metres) for linen. **3** any rod or pin that turns around, or on which something turns. Axles and shafts are spindles. **4** one of the turned or circular supporting parts of a balustrade or stair rail. **5** *Biology.* a spindle-shaped bundle of fibres that form during the process of cell division, along which the chromosomes move to opposite ends of the parent cell.
—*v.* especially of a shoot, stem, or plant, grow tall and thin. [OE *spinel*; related to *spinnan* spin]

spin·dle-leg·ged (spin′dəl leg′id *or* -legd′) *adj.* having long, thin legs.

spin·dle·legs (spin′dəl legz′) *n.pl.* **1** long, thin legs. **2** *Informal.* a person with long, thin legs (*used with a singular verb*): *Spindlelegs, as the boys call John, is a good basketball player.*

spin·dle-shanked (spin′dəl shangkt′) *adj.* spindle-legged.

spin·dle-shanks (spin′dəl shangks′) *n.pl.* spindlelegs.

spin·dling (spin′dling) *adj.* spindly.

spin·dly spin′dlē) *adj.* **-dli·er, -dli·est.** very long and slender; too tall and thin.

spin·drift (spin′drift′) *n.* spray blown or dashed up from the waves. Also, **spoondrift.** [var. of *spoondrift*]

spine (spīn) *n.* **1** spinal column; backbone. **2** something that looks like a backbone or functions as a main support. **3** *Botany.* a stiff, sharp-pointed growth of woody tissue on a plant, such as a cactus or hawthorn. **4** a stiff, sharp-pointed projection on an animal body, such as any of the quills on a porcupine's tail or any of the rigid rays of a fish's fin. **5** spicule. **6** the back portion of a book where the pages are held together, or the part of the cover over this. **7** courage, determination, etc., as that by which a person is

supported in the face of danger or adversity: *Threats merely stiffened his spine.* [< L *spina*, originally, thorn] —**spine′like′**, *adj.*

spined (spīnd) *adj.* having a spine or spines.

spi·nel (spi nel′ *or* spin′əl) *n.* a crystalline mineral, consisting chiefly of oxides of magnesium and aluminum, that occurs in various colors. Transparent spinel is used for jewellery. [< F < Ital. *spinella*, ult. < L *spina* thorn]

spine·less (spīn′lis) *adj.* **1** without spines or sharp-pointed processes: *a spineless cactus.* **2** having no backbone: *All insects are spineless.* **3** having a weak spine; limp. **4** without moral force, resolution, or courage; weak-willed; feeble. —**spine′less·ly**, *adv.* —**spine′less·ness**, *n.*

spin·et (spin′it *or* spi net′) *n.* **1** a former musical keyboard instrument like a small harpsichord. **2** a compact upright piano. [< F < Ital. *spinetta*, probably named after Giovanni *Spinetti*, an Italian inventor]

spin·i·fex (spin′ə feks′) *n.* **1** any of a genus (*Spinifex*) of Australian grasses having sharp-pointed leaves and spiny seeds, often planted on sand dunes because their long underground stems anchor the sand. **2** any of various similar Australian grasses, especially of genus *Triodia.* [< NL < L *spina* thorn + *facere* to make]

spin·na·ker (spin′ə kər) *n.* a large, triangular sail carried by yachts on the side opposite the mainsail when running before the wind. [supposedly from *Sphinx*, a yacht on which first used, perhaps influenced by *spanker*]

spin·ner (spin′ər) *n.* a person, animal, or thing that spins.

spin·ner·et (spin′ər et′) *n.* the organ by which spiders, silkworms, etc. spin their threads. [dim. of *spinner*]

spin·ney (spin′ē) *n., pl.* **-neys.** *Esp.Brit.* a thicket; a small wood and its undergrowth, especially one preserved for sheltering game birds. [< OF *espinnei*, ult. < L *spina* thorn]

spin·ning (spin′ing) *adj., n.* —*adj.* that spins. —*n.* the act of one that spins.

spinning jenny an early type of spinning machine having more than one spindle, whereby one person could spin a number of threads at the same time.

spinning wheel an apparatus for spinning cotton, flax, wool, etc. into thread or yarn, consisting of a large wheel, operated by hand or foot, and a single spindle.

spin·off (spin′of′) *n.* a by-product or fringe benefit of an operation, activity, product, etc.

spi·nose (spī′nōs) *adj.* full of spines or thorns; spiny. [< L *spinosus* < *spina* thorn]

spi·nous (spī′nəs) *adj.* **1** resembling a spine or thorn; spinelike. **2** having spines; spinose.

spin·ster (spin′stər) *n.* **1** an unmarried woman (*used especially in legal documents*). **2** an elderly woman who has never married. **3** *Archaic.* a woman whose occupation is spinning. [ME *spinster* < *spin* + *-ster*]

spin·ster·hood (spin′stər hùd′) *n.* the state of being a spinster.

spi·nule (spī′nyəl *or* spin′yəl) *n.* a small, sharp-pointed spine.

spin·y (spī′nē) *adj.* **spin·i·er, spin·i·est. 1** covered with spines; having spines; thorny: *a spiny cactus, a spiny porcupine.* **2** spinelike. **3** difficult; troublesome. —**spin′i·ness**, *n.*

spiny anteater echidna.

spi·ra·cle (spī′rə kəl *or* spîr′ə kəl) *n.* **1** a small body opening in certain animals, used for respiration. Rays and sharks have spiracles on the top of the head, through which they take in water for their gills. Insects and spiders breathe through a series of spiracles on the side of the body. The blowhole of a whale is a spiracle. **2** a vent or air hole, such as an opening in the ground through which underground vapors are given off. [< L *spiraculum* < *spirare* breathe]

spi·rae·a (spī rē′ə) See **spirea.**

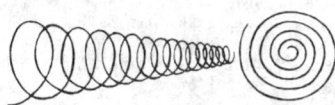

Spirals

spi·ral (spī′rəl) *n., adj., v.* **-ralled** *or* **-raled, -ral·ling** *or* **-ral·ing.** —*n.* **1** a plane curve formed by a point moving around a fixed central point in a continuously increasing or decreasing arc. **2** helix. **3** an object having the form of a spiral, such as a watch spring. **4** a single coil of a spiral. **5** a flight or course in the form of a spiral. **6** a constant increasing or decreasing of two or more interdependent quantities: *an inflationary spiral.* —*adj.* having the form or shape of a spiral: *a spiral spring, the spiral stripes on a barber pole.*

hat, āge, fär; let, ēqual, tèrm; it, īce
hot, ōpen, ôrder; oil, out; cup, pùt, rüle,
above, takən, pencəl, lemən, circəs
ch, child; ng, long; sh, ship
th, thin; ŦH, then; zh, measure

—*v.* **1** move in a spiral: *The flaming airplane spiralled to earth.* **2** form into a spiral. [< Med.L *spiralis* < L *spira* a coil < Gk. *speira*] —**spi′ral·ly**, *adv.*

spiral nebula a cluster of stars in the apparent form of a spiral.

spi·rant (spī′rənt) *n. Phonetics.* a consonant uttered with an audible expulsion of breath, such as (f) or (v); fricative. [< L *spirans, -antis*, ppr. of *spirare* breathe]

spire¹ (spīr) *n., v.* **spired, spir·ing.** —*n.* **1** the top part of a tower or steeple that narrows to a point. **2** anything tapered and pointed: *The sunset shone on the rocky spires of the mountains.* —*v.* **1** shoot up. **2** furnish with a spire. [OE *spīr*] —**spire′like′**, *adj.*

spire² (spīr) *n.* **1** a coil; spiral. **2** a single twist of a coil or spiral. [< L < Gk. *speira* coil]

spi·re·a *or* **spi·rae·a** (spī rē′ə) *n.* any of a genus (*Spiraea*) of shrubs and herbs of the rose family, including many varieties and hybrids cultivated for their showy clusters of small white, pink, or red flowers. [< L < Gk. *speiraia*, apparently < *speira* coil. 17c.]

spi·ril·lum (spī ril′əm) *n., pl.* **-ril·la** (-ril′ə). any of a genus (*Spirillum*) of rigid, spiral-shaped, gram-negative bacteria. [< NL *spirillum* < L *spira* spire² < Gk. *speira*]

spir·it (spir′it) *n., v.* —*n.* **1** the immaterial part of man; the soul: *Many religions teach that at death the spirit leaves the body.* **2** man's moral, religious, or emotional nature. **3** a supernatural being, such as a god, a ghost, or a fairy. **4 the Spirit, a** God. **b** the Holy Ghost. **5** Often, **spirits**, *pl.* a state of mind; disposition; temper: *He is in good spirits.* **6** a person; personality: *Montcalm was a noble spirit.* **7** an influence that stirs up and rouses: *A spirit of reform marked the nineteenth century.* **8 spirits**, *pl.* liveliness; cheerfulness. **9** courage; vigor; liveliness: *That race horse has spirit.* **10** enthusiasm and loyalty. **11** the real meaning or intent: *The spirit of a law is more important than its words.* **12** Often, **spirits**, *pl.* **a** a solution in alcohol: *spirits of camphor.* **b** an alcoholic drink made by distilling the juice of certain fruits, grains, roots, etc.; liquor: *He drinks beer but no spirits.*
out of spirits, sad; gloomy.
—*v.* **1** carry (away or off) secretly: *The child has been spirited away.* **2** stir up; encourage; cheer. **3** conjure (up). [< L *spiritus*, originally, breath < *spirare* breathe. Doublet of ESPRIT, SPRITE.]

spir·it·ed (spir′ə tid) *adj.* full of energy and spirit; lively; dashing: *a spirited race horse.* —**spir′it·ed·ly**, *adv.* —**spir′it·ed·ness**, *n.*

spir·it·ism (spir′ə tiz′əm) *n.* spiritualism.

spir·it·less (spir′it lis) *adj.* without spirit or courage; depressed.

spirit level an instrument used to find out whether a surface is level. When the bubble of air in the glass tube of a spirit level is exactly at the middle of the tube, the surface is level.

spir·i·to·so (spir′ə tō′sō) *adj., adv. Music.* —*adj.* spirited; lively. —*adv.* with spirit; in a lively manner. [< Ital.]

spir·i·tu·al (spir′i chü əl) *adj., n.* —*adj.* **1** of or having to do with the spirit as distinct from the body or material things: *man's spiritual nature.* **2** sacred; religious: *spiritual songs.* **3** of the church, as opposed to secular institutions: *lords spiritual, spiritual authority.* **4** of or having to do with spirits; supernatural. **5** of, having to do with, or involving spiritualism.
—*n.* a deeply emotional religious song or hymn with a jazz rhythm: *Spirituals developed from the folk music of the black people in the S United States.* —**spir′i·tu·al·ly**, *adv.*

spir·i·tu·al·ism (spir′i chü əl iz′əm) *n.* **1** the belief that spirits of the dead communicate with the living, especially through persons called mediums. **2** emphasis or insistence on the spiritual; the doctrine that spirit alone is real.

spir·i·tu·al·ist (spir′i chü əl ist) *n.* a person who believes that the dead communicate with the living.

spir·i·tu·al·is·tic (spir′i chü əl is′tik) *adj.* of or having to do with spiritualism or spiritualists.

spir·i·tu·al·i·ty (spir′i chü al′ə tē) *n., pl.* **-ties.** a devotion to spiritual things; spiritual quality.

spir·i·tu·al·i·za·tion (spir′i chü əl ə zā′shən *or* -ī zā′shən) *n.* **1** spiritualizing. **2** the state of being spiritualized.

spir·i·tu·al·ize (spir′i chü əl īz′) *v.* **-ized, -iz·ing.** make spiritual.

spir·i·tu·el *or* **spir·i·tu·elle** (spir′i chü el′) *adj.* showing a refined mind or wit. [< F *spirituel*, ult. < L *spiritus*. See SPIRIT.]

spir·i·tu·ous (spir′i chü əs) *adj.* **1** containing alcohol. **2** distilled, not fermented.

spi·ro·chete (spī′rə kēt) *n.* any of an order (Spirochaetales) of flexible, spiral-shaped bacteria, including the species that causes syphilis. [< NL < Gk. *speira* coil + *chaitē* hair]

spi·ro·gy·ra (spī′rə jī′rə) *n.* any of several algae that grow in scumlike masses in freshwater ponds or tanks. [< NL < Gk. *speira* coil + *gyros* circle]

spi·rom·e·ter (spī rom′ə tər) *n.* an instrument for measuring the capacity of the lungs, by the amount of air that can be breathed out after the lungs have been filled as full as possible. [< L *spirare* breathe + E *-meter*]

spirt (spėrt) See **spurt.**

spir·y (spī′rē) *adj.* **1** having the form of a spire; tapering. **2** having many spires.

spit[1] (spit) *v.* **spat** or **spit, spit·ting;** *n.* —*v.* **1** eject saliva from the mouth. **2** eject from the mouth. **3** throw out: *The gun spits fire.* **4** spit (at, on, etc.) a person or thing to express hatred or contempt. **5** make a spitting noise: *The cat spits when angry.* **6** sputter. **7** rain or snow slightly. —*n.* **1** the liquid produced in the mouth; saliva. **2** the noise or act of spitting. **3** a frothy or spitlike secretion given off by some insects. **4** a light rain or snow. **the spit of,** *Informal.* just like. See **spit and image.** [OE *spittan*] —**spit′ter,** *n.*

spit[2] (spit) *n., v.* **spit·ted, spit·ting.** —*n.* **1** a sharp-pointed, slender rod or bar on which meat is roasted. A spit is turned so that the meat is cooked evenly. **2** a narrow point of land running into the water. —*v.* **1** run a spit through; put on a spit. **2** pierce; stab. [OE *spitu*]

spit and image *Informal.* exact or perfect likeness: *In that dress she looked the spit and image of her grandmother.*

spit and polish *Informal.* a high standard of cleanliness or smartness. [from the soldier's practice of using spit in polishing boots, etc.]

spit·ball (spit′bol′ or -bôl′) *n.* **1** a small ball of chewed-up paper, used as a missile. **2** *Baseball.* a curve resulting from the pitcher's moistening one side of the ball with saliva, now illegal.

spit curl *Informal.* a small wisp of hair that is dampened, curled, and pressed against the cheek, temple, etc.

spite (spīt) *n., v.* **spit·ed, spit·ing.** —*n.* ill will; a grudge. **in spite of,** not prevented by; notwithstanding: *We decided to go in spite of the rain.* —*v.* show ill toward; annoy: *He left his yard dirty to spite the people who lived next door.* [shortened from ME *despit* despite] —**spite′less,** *adj.*

☛ *Syn. n.* **1. Spite, malice, grudge** = ill will against another. **Spite** suggests envy or a mean disposition, and applies to active ill will shown by doing mean, petty things to hurt or annoy: *She ruined his flowers out of spite.* **Malice** emphasizes actual wish or intention to injure, and suggests hatred or, especially, a disposition that delights in doing harm or seeing others hurt: *Gossips are motivated by malice.* **Grudge** suggests wishing to get even for real or imagined injury, and applies to ill will nursed over a long time: *She bears grudges.*

spite·ful (spīt′fəl) *adj.* full of spite; eager to annoy; behaving with ill will and malice. —**spite′ful·ly,** *adv.* —**spite′ful·ness,** *n.*

spit·fire (spit′fīr′) *n.* **1** a person, especially a woman or girl, who has a quick and fiery temper. **2** something that sends forth fire, such as a cannon or some kinds of fireworks.

spitting image *Informal.* See **spit and image.**

spit·tle (spit′əl) *n.* saliva; spit. [< *spit*]

spit·toon (spi tün′) *n.* a receptacle or container for spitting into.

spitz (spits) *n.* any of various types of small dog having long, thick hair, erect ears, and a pointed muzzle, especially a white variety of Pomeranian. [< G *spitz* pointed]

spiv (spiv) *n. Brit. Slang.* a man who avoids honest work and makes a living by dubious, usually illegal, means, especially by buying and selling goods on the black market. [prob. a dial. var. of *spiff* dandified person; see SPIFFY. 20c.]

splake (splāk) *n., pl.* **splake** or **splakes.** *Cdn.* a fertile hybrid game fish, produced by fertilizing lake trout eggs with sperm from brook (or speckled) trout. [*speckled* + *lake* trout]

splash (splash) *v., n.* —*v.* **1** cause (water, mud, etc.) to fly about. **2** dash liquid about: *The baby likes to splash in his tub.* **3** cause to scatter a liquid about: *He splashed the oars as he rowed.* **4** dash in scattered masses or drops: *The waves splashed on the beach.* **5** wet, spatter, or soil. **6** fall, move, or go with a splash or splashes: *He splashed across the brook.* **7** mark with spots or patches. **8** display (a picture or story) prominently in a newspaper or magazine: *The scandal was splashed all over the front page.* —*n.* **1** the action or sound of splashing; splashing: *The splash of the wave knocked him over. The boat upset with a loud splash.* **2** a spot of liquid splashed on something. **3** a spot; patch: *The dog is white with brown splashes.* **make a splash,** *Informal.* attract attention; cause excitement. [alteration of *plash,* n., OE *plæsc* puddle]

splash·down (splash′down′) *n.* the landing of a capsule or other spacecraft in the ocean after re-entry.

splash·er (splash′ər) *n.* **1** one that splashes. **2** something that protects from splashes.

splash·y (splash′ē) *adj.* **splash·i·er, splash·i·est. 1** making a splash. **2** full of irregular spots or streaks. **3** *Informal.* attracting attention; causing excitement.

splat (splat) *n.* a broad, flat piece of wood, especially such a piece forming the central upright part of the back of a chair. [origin uncertain; ? < ME *splat* to split open; cut up]

splat·ter (splat′ər) *v. or n.* splash; spatter. [blend of *spatter* and *splash*]

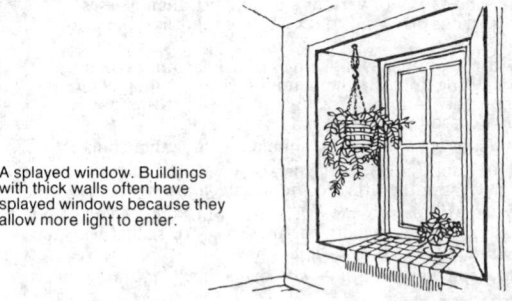

A splayed window. Buildings with thick walls often have splayed windows because they allow more light to enter.

splay (splā) *v., adj., n.* —*v.* **1** spread out. **2** spread; flare. **3** make slanting. —*adj.* **1** wide and flat. **2** awkward and clumsy. —*n.* **1** a spread; flare. **2** a slanting surface; surface that makes an oblique angle with another. [< *display*]

splay·foot (splā′füt′) *n., pl.* **-feet.** a broad, flat foot, especially one turned outward.

splay-foot·ed (splā′füt′id) *adj.* **1** having splayfeet. **2** awkward; clumsy.

spleen (splēn) *n.* **1** a vascular ductless organ located at the left of the stomach in mammals and serving to store blood, destroy worn-out red blood cells, form lymphocytes, filter bacteria, etc. **2** a similar organ in other vertebrates. **3** *Obsolete.* the organ believed to be the seat of certain emotions, especially low spirits, bad temper, and spite. **4** ill humor, especially when mingled with spite: *to vent one's spleen on others.* **5** *Archaic.* melancholy. [ME < L < Gk. *splēn*]

splen·dent (splen′dənt) *adj.* shining; gleaming; brilliant; splendid. [ME < L *splendens, -entis,* ppr. of *splendere* be bright]

splen·did (splen′did) *adj.* **1** brilliant; glorious; magnificent; grand: *a splendid sunset, a splendid palace, splendid jewels, a splendid victory.* **2** very good; fine; excellent: *a splendid chance.* [< L *splendidus < splendere* be bright] —**splen′did·ly,** *adv.* —**splen′did·ness,** *n.*

☛ *Syn.* **1.** See note at **magnificent.**

splen·dif·er·ous (splen dif′ər əs) *adj. Informal.* splendid; magnificent. [< LL *splendifer,* for L *splendorifer* (< *splendor, -oris* splendor + *ferre* to bear) + E *-ous*]

splen·dor or **splen·dour** (splen′dər) *n.* **1** great brightness; brilliant light. **2** a magnificent show; pomp; glory. [ME < L *splendor < splendere* be bright]

sple·net·ic (spli net′ik) *adj., n.* —*adj.* **1** having to do with the spleen. **2** bad-tempered; irritable; peevish. —*n.* a person who is splenetic in disposition. [< LL *spleneticus < L sp. splēnitis* disease of the spleen < *splēn* spleen] —**sple·net′i·cal·ly,** *adv.*

splen·ic (splen′ik or splē′nik) *adj.* of or having to do with the spleen. [< L < Gk. *splēnikos < splēn* spleen]

A spliced rope

splice (splīs) *v.* **spliced, splic·ing;** *n.* —*v.* **1** join together (ropes, etc.) by weaving together ends that have been untwisted. **2** join together (two pieces of timber) by overlapping. **3** join together (film, tape, wire, etc.). **4** *Slang.* marry.

—*n.* **1** a joining of ropes, timbers, tapes, etc. by splicing. **2** a joint made in such a way. **3** *Slang.* a marriage; wedding. [< MDu. *splissen*] —**splic′er,** *n.*

spline (splīn) *n., v.* **splined, splin·ing.** —*n.* **1** a long, narrow, relatively thin strip of wood or metal; slat. **2** a long, flexible strip of wood or the like used in drawing curves. **3** a flat, rectangular piece or key fitting into a groove or slot between parts of a machine. **4** the groove for such a key.
—*v.* **1** fit with a spline or key. **2** provide with a groove for a spline or key. [origin uncertain]

splint (splint) *n., v.* —*n.* **1** a rigid arrangement of wood, metal, plaster, etc. to hold a broken or dislocated bone in place until it is put in a cast or, sometimes, until it heals. **2** a thin strip of wood, such as is used in making baskets. **3** a thin metal strip or plate. Old armor often had overlapping splints to protect the elbow, knee, etc. and allow easy movement. **4** a hard, bony growth on the splint bone of a horse, mule, etc.
—*v.* **1** secure, hold in position, or support by means of a splint or splints. **2** support as if with splints. [< MDu. or MLG *splinte*]

splint bone one of the two smaller bones on either side of the cannon of a horse, etc.

splin·ter (splin′tər) *n., v.* —*n.* **1** a thin, sharp piece of wood, bone, glass, etc.: *He got a splinter in his hand. The mirror broke into splinters.* **2** a splinter group or party. —*v.* split or break into splinters. [< MDu.]

splinter group or **party** a body formed by a small dissenting group that has broken away from a political party, religious organization, etc.

splin·ter·y (splin′tər ē) *adj.* **1** apt to splinter: *splintery wood.* **2** of or like a splinter. **3** rough and jagged, as if from splintering. **4** full of splinters. **5** characterized by the production of splinters.

split (split) *v.* **split, split·ting;** *n., adj.* —*v.* **1** break or cut from end to end, or in layers. **2** separate into parts; divide: *The huge tree split when it was struck by lightning. The two men split the cost of the dinner between them.* **3** divide into different groups, factions, parties, etc. **4** divide (a molecule) into two or more individual atoms. **5** divide (an atomic nucleus) into two portions of approximately equal mass by forcing the absorption of a neutron. **6** issue a certain number of new shares of (stock) for each share currently held. **7** *Slang.* leave; depart: *We'd better split.*
split hairs, make distinctions that are too fussy: *It is splitting hairs to complain of having just 59 minutes instead of an hour in the pool.*
split (one's) **vote** or **ticket,** *Esp.U.S.* vote for candidates of different political parties.
—*n.* **1** the act or process of splitting. **2** a narrow break, gap, or tear caused by splitting. **3** a breach or division created in a group. **4** a faction formed in this way. **5** *Slang.* a portion or share, especially of loot. **6** a confection consisting of fruit, such as a banana, split lengthwise with ice cream, whipped cream, nuts, etc. **7** *Informal.* a bottle of mineral water, etc. half the usual size. **8** *Informal.* a drink of liquor half the usual size. **9** Often, **splits,** *pl.* an exercise in which one lands on the floor with the legs stretched out in opposite directions.
—*adj.* divided or separated from end to end. [< MDu. *splitten*] —**split′ter,** *n.*

split infinitive in grammar, an infinitive having an adverb between *to* and the verb. *Example: He wants to never work, but to always play.*
☛ *Usage.* **Split infinitive.** Awkward split infinitives should be avoided. Awkward: *After a while I was able to, although not very accurately, distinguish the good customers from the sulky ones.* Improved: *After a while I was able to distinguish, though not very accurately, the good customers from the sulky ones.*

split personality 1 schizophrenia. **2** a personality characterized by two seemingly independent, contradictory patterns of behavior.

split–sec·ond (split′sek′ənd) *adj.* extremely quick; happening in a flash; instantaneous.

split·ting (split′ing) *adj.* **1** that splits. **2** very painful; aching severely: *a splitting headache. My head is splitting.*

splotch (sploch) *n., v.* —*n.* a large, irregular spot; splash. —*v.* make splotches on. [? blend of *spot* and *blotch*]

splotch·y (sploch′ē) *adj.* marked with splotches.

splurge (splėrj) *n., v.* **splurged, splurg·ing.** *Informal.* —*n.* **1** a showing off; an ostentatious display. **2** a lavish or extravagant expenditure: *He made a big splurge for his daughter's wedding.*
—*v.* **1** show off. **2** spend money extravagantly.

splut·ter (splut′ər) *n., v.* —*v.* **1** talk in a hasty, confused way. People sometimes splutter when they are excited. **2** make spitting or popping noises; sputter: *The baked apples are spluttering in the oven.* —*n.* spluttering. [? var. of *sputter*] —**splut′ter·er,** *n.*

Spode or **spode** (spōd) *n.* a type of fine pottery or porcelain. [after Josiah *Spode* (1754-1827), a famous potter of Staffordshire, England]

hat, āge, fär; let, ēqual, tėrm; it, īce
hot, ōpen, ôrder; oil, out; cup, pùt, rüle,
əbove, takən, pencəl, lemən, circəs
ch, child; ng, long; sh, ship
th, thin; ᴛʜ, then; zh, measure

spoil (spoil) *v.* **spoiled** or **spoilt, spoil·ing;** *n.* —*v.* **1** damage; injure; destroy: *He spoils a dozen pieces of paper before he writes a letter.* **2** be damaged; become bad or unfit for use: *The fruit spoiled because I kept it too long.* **3** injure the character or disposition of, especially by being too kind, generous, etc.: *That child is being spoiled by too much attention.* **4** *Archaic.* despoil, plunder, rob, or pillage: *The Romans spoiled the Egyptians.*
be spoiling for, *Informal.* be longing for (a fight, etc.).
—*n.* **1** Often, **spoils,** *pl.* **a** plunder taken in time of war; things won: *The soldiers carried the spoils back to their own land.* **b** any goods, property, etc., seized by force or similar means after a struggle. **2** an object of plundering; prey. **3 spoils,** *pl. U.S.* government offices and positions regarded as being at the disposal of the successful political party. [ME < OF *espoillier*, ult. < L *spolium* booty, spoil]
☛ *Syn. v.* **1. Spoil, ruin** = damage beyond repair or recovery. **Spoil** emphasizes damage that so reduces or weakens the value, strength, beauty, usefulness, etc. of something as to make the thing useless or bring it to nothing: *Her friend's unkind comments spoiled her pleasure in her new dress.* **Ruin** emphasizes bringing to an end the value, soundness, beauty, usefulness, health and happiness, etc. of someone or something through a destructive force or irretrievable loss: *He ruined his eyes by reading in a poor light.*

spoil·er (spoil′ər) *n.* **1** a person or thing that spoils. **2** a person who takes spoils.

spoil·sport (spoil′spôrt′) *n.* a person who spoils or prevents the fun of others.

spoils system *U.S.* the system or practice in which public offices with their salaries and advantages are at the disposal of the victorious political party for its own purposes and in its own (rather than the public) interest.

spoilt (spoilt) *v.* a pt. and a pp. of **spoil.**

spoke[1] (spōk) *v.* **1** pt. of **speak. 2** *Archaic.* a pp. of **speak.**

spoke[2] (spōk) *n., v.* —*n.* **1** one of the bars running from the centre of a wheel to the rim. See **wheel** for picture. **2** a rung of a ladder.
put a spoke in someone's wheel, stop or hinder someone.
—*v.* provide with spokes. [OE *spāca*]

spo·ken (spō′kən) *v., adj.* —*v.* a pp. of **speak.** —*adj.* **1** expressed with the mouth; uttered; told: *the spoken word.* **2** speaking in a certain way: *a soft-spoken man.*

spoke·shave (spōk′shāv′) *n.* a cutting tool having a blade with a handle at each end.

spokes·man (spōks′mən) *n., pl.* **-men.** a person who speaks for another or others: *Mr. Smith was the spokesman for the factory workers.*

spo·li·ate (spō′lē āt′) *v.* **-at·ed, -at·ing.** rob; plunder; despoil. [< L *spoliatus,* ult. < *spolium* booty]

spo·li·a·tion (spō′lē ā′shən) *n.* **1** a plundering; robbery. **2** the plundering of neutrals at sea in time of war. **3** *Law.* **a** an act of destroying a document, or of tampering with it so as to destroy its value as evidence. **b** the destruction of a ship's papers, especially to conceal an illegal act. [ME < L *spoliatio, -onis,* ult. < *spolium* booty]

spon·da·ic (spon dā′ik) *adj.* of or having to do with a spondee; constituting a spondee; consisting of or characterized by a spondee or spondees.

spon·dee (spon′dē) *n. Prosody.* a foot or measure consisting of two long or accented syllables. The spondee is used to vary other metres. "Sŏ strōde | hĕ báck | slŏw to | thĕ wóund | ĕd Kíng" has spondees for the first two feet. [ME < L < Gk. *spondeios* < *spondē* libation; originally used in songs accompanying libations]

sponge (spunj) *n., v.* **sponged, spong·ing.** —*n.* **1** any of a phylum (Porifera) of aquatic multicellular invertebrate animals, usually living in colonies permanently attached to rocks in the sea, and certain species of which have a fibrous, porous, elastic internal skeleton. **2** a piece of the skeleton of such sponges, which readily absorbs water and is used for bathing, scrubbing, etc. **3** a product resembling this skeletal material, made of rubber or cellulose, etc. **4** something like a sponge, such as a gauze pad used in surgery. **5** a wipe or rub with a sponge. **6** a mop for cleaning the bore of a cannon. **7** yeast dough, especially before kneading. **8** a light, porous, steamed or baked pudding. **9** See **spongecake. 10** *Informal.* sponger. **11** *Informal.* a person who drinks heavily.
throw or **toss in the sponge** or **throw up the sponge,** give up; admit defeat.

—*v.* **1** wipe or rub with a wet sponge; make clean or damp in this way. **2** remove or wipe (away or off) with a sponge: *Sponge the mud spots off the car.* **3** absorb. **4** rub or wipe (out) as if with a sponge; remove all traces of; obliterate; efface. **5** gather sponges. **6** *Informal.* live or profit at the expense of another in a mean way: *That lazy man won't work; he just sponges on his family.* [< L < Gk. *spongia*] —**sponge′like′**, *adj.*

sponge bath a washing of the body with a wet sponge or cloth without getting into water.

sponge cake a light, spongy cake made with eggs, sugar, flour, etc. but no shortening.

spong·er (spun′jər) *n.* **1** a person who sponges. **2** a machine for sponging cloth. **3** a person or vessel engaged in gathering sponges. **4** *Informal.* a person who gets by at the expense of others.

sponging house *Historical.* in England, a house kept by a sheriff's officer for the confinement of arrested debtors before they were put in prison.

spon·gy (spun′jē) *adj.* **-gi·er**, **-gi·est**. **1** like a sponge; soft, light, and full of holes: *spongy moss, spongy dough.* **2** full of holes. —**spon′gi·ness**, *n.*

spon·son (spon′sən) *n.* **1** a part projecting from the side of a ship or boat, used for support or protection. **2** an air-filled section on either side of an airplane, canoe, etc. to steady it. [? shortening and alteration of *expansion*]

spon·sor (spon′sər) *n., v.* —*n.* **1** a person or group that supports or is responsible for a person or thing: *the sponsor of a law, the sponsor of a student applying for a scholarship. I will serve as his sponsor for admission to our club.* **2** a person who takes vows for an infant at baptism; a godfather or godmother. **3** a company, store, or organization that pays the cost of a radio or television program for purposes of advertising, public relations, etc. **4** a person who pledges or gives a certain amount of financial assistance to an organization. —*v.* act as sponsor for. [< L < *spondere* give assurance]

spon·so·ri·al (spon sô′rē əl) *adj.* of or having to do with a sponsor.

spon·sor·ship (spon′sər ship′) *n.* the position, duties, etc. of a sponsor.

spon·ta·ne·i·ty (spon′tə nē′ə tē) *n., pl.* **-ties**. **1** the state, quality, or fact of being spontaneous. **2** a spontaneous action, movement, etc.

spon·ta·ne·ous (spon tā′nē əs) *adj.* **1** caused by natural impulse or desire; not forced or compelled; not planned beforehand: *Both sides burst into spontaneous cheers at the skilful play.* **2** happening without external cause or help; caused entirely by inner forces: *The eruption of a volcano is spontaneous.* **3** growing or produced naturally; not planted, cultivated, etc. [< LL *spontaneus* < L *sponte* of one's own accord] —**spon·ta′ne·ous·ly**, *adv.* —**spon·ta′ne·ous·ness**, *n.*
☛ *Syn.* **1.** See note at **voluntary**.

spontaneous abortion miscarriage (def. 2).

spontaneous combustion the bursting into flame of a substance as a result of the heat produced by chemical action within the substance itself.

spoof (spüf) *n., v. Slang.* —*n.* **1** a trick or hoax. **2** a light satirical parody; take-off. —*v.* **1** play tricks; fool. **2** make a light satirical parody on. [coined by Arthur Roberts (1852-1933), a British comedian] —**spoof′er**, *n.*

spook[1] (spük) *n. Informal.* a ghost; spectre. [< Du. *spook*]

spook[2] (spük) *v.* startle game or fish.

spook·y (spü′kē) *adj.* **spook·i·er**, **spook·i·est**. *Informal.* like or suggesting spooks; weird; scary.

spool (spül) *n., v.* —*n.* **1** a cylinder of plastic, wood, or metal on which thread, wire, etc. is wound. **2** something like a spool in shape or use. —*v.* wind on a spool. [< MDu. *spoele*]

spoon (spün) *n., v.* —*n.* **1** a utensil consisting of a small, shallow bowl at the end of a handle. Spoons are used to take up or stir food or drink. **2** something shaped like a spoon. **3** *Golf.* a kind of club having a wooden head. **4** a shiny, curved bait having hooks attached for catching fish.
born with a silver spoon in one's mouth, born lucky or rich.
—*v.* **1** take up in a spoon. **2** hollow out or form in the shape of the bowl of a spoon. **3** *Slang.* kiss and caress amorously, especially in a way considered foolish or sentimental. **4** troll for or catch (fish) with a spoon bait. **5** *Sports.* hit a ball upward in a weak or feeble manner. [OE *spōn* chip, shaving] —**spoon′like′**, *adj.*

spoon·bill (spün′bil′) *n.* any of a small subfamily (Plataleinae, of the family Threskiornithidae) of tropical and subtropical wading

birds having long legs and a long bill with a broad, horizontally flattened tip.

spoon·drift (spün′drift′) *n.* spindrift. [< *spoon* sail before the wind (of uncertain origin) + *drift*]

spoon·er·ism (spü′nə riz′əm) *n.* an unintentional, often humorous, transposing of the first letters or sounds of successive words. *Example:* kinkering kongs *for* conquering kings. [after Rev. William A. *Spooner* (1844-1930), of New College, Oxford, who was famous for such mistakes]

spoon–feed (spün′fēd′) *v.* **-fed**, **-feed·ing**. **1** feed with a spoon. **2** spoil; coddle; overprotect: *Industry is being spoon-fed with government grants.*

spoon·ful (spün′fùl′) *n., pl.* **-fuls.** as much as a spoon can hold.

spoon·y (spü′nē) *adj.* **spoon·i·er**, **spoon·i·est**; *n., pl.* **spoonies.** *Informal.* —*adj.* amorously sentimental; demonstratively fond. —*n.* **1** a sentimental or overfond lover. **2** simpleton. —**spoon′i·ly**, *adv.* —**spoon′i·ness**, *n.*

spoor (spür *or* spôr) *n., v.* —*n.* the trail of a wild animal; track. —*v.* track by or follow a spoor. [< Afrikaans *spoor* < MDu.; cf. OE *spor* footprint]

spo·rad·ic (spə rad′ik) *adj.* **1** appearing or happening at intervals in time: *sporadic outbursts.* **2** being or occurring apart from others; isolated. **3** appearing in scattered instances: *sporadic cases of scarlet fever.* **4** occurring singly, or widely apart in locality: *sporadic genera of plants.* [< Med.L < Gk. *sporadikos* scattered, ult. < *spora* a sowing]

spo·rad·i·cal (spə rad′ə kəl) *adj.* sporadic.

spo·rad·i·cal·ly (spə rad′ik lē) *adv.* here and there; now and then; separately.

spo·ran·gi·a (spə ran′jē ə) *n.* pl. of **sporangium.**

spo·ran·gi·um (spə ran′jē əm) *n., pl.* **-gi·a** (-jē ə). *Botany.* a receptacle in which asexual spores are produced; spore case. The little brown spots sometimes seen on the under side of ferns are sporangia. [< NL < Gk. *spora* seed + *angeion* vessel]

spore (spôr) *n.* **1** *Biology.* a single cell that becomes free and is capable of developing into a new plant or animal. Ferns produce spores. **2** a germ or seed. [< NL < Gk. *spora* seed]

spo·ro·phyl or **spo·ro·phyll** (spô′rə fil′) *n. Botany.* any leaf that bears spores or spore cases. [< Gk. *spora* seed + *phyllon* leaf]

spo·ro·phyte (spô′rə fīt′) *n.* the spore-producing form or generation of a plant that reproduces by alternation of generations. It develops from the union of gametes and is the dominant form of higher plants. Compare **gametophyte.** [< Gk. *spora* seed + E *-phyte*]

spor·ran (spôr′ən) *n.* in Scottish Highland dress, a large purse, commonly of fur or leather, hanging from the belt in front. See **kilt** for picture. [< Scots Gaelic *sporan*]

sport (spôrt) *n., v.* —*n.* **1** a game, contest or other pastime requiring some skill and a certain amount of exercise. Baseball and fishing are outdoor sports; bowling and basketball are indoor sports. **2** amusement or recreation: *That was great sport.* **3** (*adj.*) suitable for sports. **4** playful joking; fun: *to say a thing in sport.* **5** ridicule. **6** the object of a joke; plaything: *His hat blew off and became the sport of the wind.* **7** sportsman. **8** *Informal.* a person who behaves in a sportsmanlike manner; good fellow: *be a sport.* **9** *Informal.* gambler. **10** *Slang.* a flashy or showy person. **11** *Biology.* an animal or plant that varies suddenly or in a marked manner from the normal type. A white blackbird would be a sport.
make sport of, make fun of; laugh at; ridicule: *Don't make sport of his mistakes.*
—*v.* **1** amuse oneself; play: *Lambs sport in the fields.* **2** jest. **3** *Informal.* display: *sport a new hat.* **4** *Biology.* become or produce a sport. [ult. short for *disport*]
☛ *Syn. n.* **1.** See note at **play**.

sport·ful (spôrt′fəl) *adj.* playful.

sport·ing (spôr′ting) *adj.* **1** of, interested in, or engaging in sports. **2** playing fair: *Letting the little boy throw first was a sporting gesture.* **3** willing to take a chance. **4** *Informal.* involving risk; uncertain. —**sport′ing·ly**, *adv.*

spor·tive (spôr′tiv) *adj.* playful; merry: *The old dog seemed as sportive as the puppy.* —**spor′tive·ly**, *adv.* —**spor′tive·ness**, *n.*

sports (spôrts) *adj.* of sports; suitable for sports: *a sports dress.*

sports car **1** any low, fast, two-seater car, usually one having an open top. **2** any car appealing to driving enthusiasts and designed for high speeds and manoeuvrability.

sports·cast (spôrts′kast′) *n.* a radio or television broadcast of a sports event or of news or discussion of sports events. —**sports′cas′ter**, *n.*

sports·man (spôrts′mən) *n., pl.* **-men.** **1** a person who takes part in sports, especially hunting, fishing, or racing. **2** a person who plays fair. **3** a person who is willing to take a chance.

sports·man·like (spôrts′mən lĭk′) *adj.* like or befitting a sportsman; fair and honorable.

sports·man·ship (spôrts′mən ship′) *n.* 1 the qualities or conduct of a sportsman; fair play. 2 ability in sports.

sports·wear (spôrts′wer′) *n.* clothing designed for casual wear or recreation.

sports·writ·er (spôrts′rīt′ər) *n.* a newspaper or magazine writer who reports sporting events.

sport·y (spôr′tē) *adj.* **sport·i·er, sport·i·est.** *Informal.* 1 sportsmanlike; sporting. 2 gay or fast; flashy. 3 smart in dress, appearance, manners, etc. —**sport′i·ly,** *adv.* —**sport′i·ness,** *n.*

spor·ule (spôr′yəl) *n. Botany.* a small spore, especially a spore of certain fungi.

spot (spot) *n., v.* **spot·ted, spot·ting.** —*n.* 1 a small discoloring or disfiguring mark made by a foreign substance; stain; speck: *a spot of ink on the paper.* 2 a stain or blemish on character or reputation; moral defect; fault; flaw: *His character is without spot.* 3 a small part of a surface differing in some way from the rest, as in color, material, or finish: *His tie is blue with white spots.* 4 a place: *From this spot you can see the ocean.* 5 *Informal.* a small amount; a little bit: *a spot of lunch.* 6 *Informal.* a position or place with reference to employment, radio or television scheduling, etc. 7 *Informal.* spotlight. 8 *(adj.)* on hand; ready: *a spot answer.* 9 *Botany.* a plant disease; leaf spot. 10 a figure or dot on a playing card, domino, or die to show its kind and value.

hit the spot, *Informal.* be just right; be satisfactory.

in a spot, in a difficult situation.

in spots, a in one spot, part, place, point, etc. and another: *an argument weak in spots.* **b** at times; by snatches.

on the spot, a at the very place. **b** at once. **c** in trouble or difficulty: *He put me on the spot by asking a question I could not answer.*

—*v.* 1 make spots on: *to spot a dress.* 2 become spotted; have spots: *This silk will spot.* 3 stain, sully, or tarnish (character, reputation, etc.): *He spotted his reputation by lying repeatedly.* 4 place in a certain spot; scatter in various spots: *Lookouts were spotted all along the coast.* 5 *Informal.* pick out; find out; recognize: *The teacher spotted every mistake.* [ME, perhaps < G; cf. MDu. *spotte,* ON *spotti*]

spot announcement a brief advertisement or announcement made between radio or television programs or at some point during a program.

spot cash money paid just as soon as goods are delivered or work is done.

spot check 1 a brief, rough sampling. 2 a checkup made without warning.

spot fire jump fire.

spot·less (spot′lis) *adj.* without a spot or blemish. —**spot′less·ly,** *adv.* —**spot′less·ness,** *n.*

spot·light (spot′līt′) *n., v.* **-light·ed** or **-lit, light·ing.** —*n.* 1 a strong light thrown upon a particular place or person. 2 a lamp that gives such a light: *a spotlight in a theatre.* 3 anything that focusses attention on a person or thing; public notice. —*v.* 1 light up with a spotlight or spotlights. 2 call attention to; give public notice to.

spot·ted (spot′id) *adj.* 1 stained with spots: *a spotted wall.* 2 marked with spots: *a spotted dog.* 3 sullied: *a spotted reputation.*

spotted fever any of various fevers characterized by spots on the skin, especially cerebrospinal fever or typhus fever.

spot·ter (spot′ər) *n.* 1 a person who makes or removes spots. 2 a device for making or removing spots. 3 a person who observes a wide area of enemy terrain in order to locate, and direct artillery fire against, any of various targets. 4 a civilian who watches for enemy aircraft over a city, town, etc. 5 a person employed to keep watch on employees, customers, etc. for evidence of dishonesty or other misconduct. 6 any person, aircraft, device, etc. that looks, watches, or observes for some specialized purpose or detail. 7 a machine that automatically sets up the pins in a bowling alley; pinspotter.

spot·ty (spot′ē) *adj.* **-ti·er, -ti·est.** 1 having spots; spotted. 2 not of uniform quality; irregular: *His work was spotty.* —**spot′ti·ly,** *adv.* —**spot′ti·ness,** *n.*

spous·al (spouz′əl) *n., adj. Archaic.* —*n.* Usually, **spousals,** *pl.* the ceremony of marriage. —*adj.* of or having to do with marriage. [ME *spousaille* < MF *espousaille*]

spouse (spous *or* spouz) *n.* a husband or wife. [ME < OF < L *sponsus, sponsa,* pp. of *spondere* bind oneself]

spout (spout) *v., n.* —*v.* 1 throw out (a liquid) in a stream or spray: *A whale spouts water when it breathes.* 2 flow out with force: *Water spouted from a break in the pipe.* 3 *Informal.* speak in loud tones with affected emotion: *The old-fashioned actor spouted his lines.* 4 *Slang.* pawn.

—*n.* 1 a stream or jet. 2 a pipe for carrying off water: *Rain runs down a spout from our roof to the ground.* 3 a tube or lip by which

hat, āge, fär; let, ēqual, tèrm; it, īce
hot, ōpen, ôrder; oil, out; cup, pùt, rüle,
əbove, takən, pencəl, lemən, circəs
ch, child; ng, long; sh, ship
th, thin; ŦH, then; zh, measure

liquid is poured. A teakettle, a coffee pot, and a syrup jug have spouts. 4 a column of spray thrown into the air by a whale in breathing. 5 *Archaic.* **a** a lift in a pawnshop used for transferring pawned articles to a storeroom. **b** *Slang.* pawnshop.

up the spout, *Slang.* **a** in pawn. **b** ruined; done for. [cf. MDu. *spouten*] —**spout′er,** *n.* —**spout′less,** *adj.*

S.P.Q.R. the Senate and the People of Rome (for L *Senatus Populusque Romanus*).

sprad·dle (sprad′əl) *v.* **-dled, -dling.** 1 spread or stretch the legs apart; straddle. 2 sprawl. [probably a blend of *sprawl* and *straddle*]

sprain (sprān) *v., n.* —*v.* injure (a joint or muscle) by a sudden twist or wrench: *He sprained his ankle.* —*n.* an injury caused by a sudden twist or wrench. [origin uncertain]

sprang (sprang) *v.* pt. of **spring.**

sprat (sprat) *n.* 1 a small food fish (*Clupea sprattus*) of the herring family that is common along the atlantic coasts of Europe. 2 any of various small or young fishes related to the sprat. [OE *sprott*]

sprawl (sprol *or* sprôl) *v., n.* —*v.* 1 lie or sit with the limbs spread out, especially ungracefully: *The people sprawled on the beach in their bathing suits.* 2 crawl or move awkwardly. 3 spread out or develop in an irregular and straggling way: *sprawling suburbs. His handwriting sprawled across the page.* 4 cause to sprawl. —*n.* the act or position of sprawling. [OE *sprēawlian*]

spray¹ (sprā) *n., v.* —*n.* 1 liquid going through the air in small drops: *We were wet with the sea spray.* 2 something like this: *A spray of bullets hit the target.* 3 an instrument that sends a liquid out as spray. —*v.* 1 sprinkle; scatter a liquid in a mist or small drops: *Spray this paint on the far wall.* 2 scatter spray on or over: *We spray apple trees to keep the fruit free of disease.* 3 direct numerous small missiles, etc. upon: *The soldiers sprayed the enemy with bullets.* [? < MDu. *sprayen*] —**spray′er,** *n.*

spray² (sprā) *n.* 1 a small branch or piece of some plant with its leaves, flowers, or fruit: *a spray of lilacs, a spray of ivy, a spray of berries.* 2 a floral arrangement or an ornament like this. [cf. Danish *sprag*]

spray gun device used to spray paint, insecticide, or other liquids.

spread (spred) *v.* **spread, spread·ing;** *n., adj.* —*v.* 1 cover or cause to cover a large or larger area; stretch out; unfold; open: *to spread rugs on the floor, to spread one's arms, a fan that spreads when shaken.* 2 cause (a job or other activity) to be continued over a period of time: *He spread his reading assignment over several days.* 3 move further apart: *The rails of the track have spread. He spread the end of the rivet with a hammer.* 4 lie or cause to lie; extend: *Fields or corn spread out before us.* 5 make widely or generally prevalent; propagate: *to spread a religion.* 6 scatter; distribute: *He spread the news. The sickness spread rapidly.* 7 cover with a thin layer: *She spread each slice with butter.* 8 put as a thin layer: *He spread jam on his bread.* 9 be put as a thin layer: *This paint spreads evenly.* 10 set (a table) for a meal. 11 put food on (a table).

spread (oneself), *Informal.* **a** try hard to make a good impression. **b** display one's abilities fully. **c** brag.

—*n.* 1 the act of spreading: *Doctors fight the spread of disease.* 2 the width; extent; amount of or capacity for spreading: *the spread of a bird's wings, the spread of elastic.* 3 a stretch; expanse. 4 a the difference between what something is bought for and what it is sold to another for. **b** the difference between any two prices, rates, etc. 5 a cloth covering for a bed or table. 6 *Informal.* the food put on the table; feast. 7 something for spreading on bread, crackers, etc., such as butter or jam. 8 the area of land owned by a rancher. 9 a piece of advertising, a news story, etc. occupying a large number of adjoining columns: *The advertisement was a three-column spread.* 10 two facing pages of a newspaper, magazine, etc. viewed as a single unit in make-up.

—*adj.* stretched out; expanded; extended. [OE *sprǣdan*] —**spread′er,** *n.*

spread eagle a boastful person.

spread–ea·gle (spred′ē′gəl) *adj., v.* **-gled, -gling.** —*adj.* having the form of an eagle with wings spread out. —*v.* stretch out flat and sprawling; lie with arms and legs outstretched.

spree (sprē) *n.* 1 a lively frolic; a jolly time. 2 a period during which a person drinks alcoholic liquor to excess; bout of drinking.

3 a period of intense interest in an activity. [origin uncertain]

sprig (sprig) *n., v.* **-sprigged, sprig·ging.** —*n.* **1** a shoot, twig, or small branch: *He wore a sprig of lilac in his buttonhole.* **2** an ornament or design shaped like a sprig. **3** a scion or offspring of some person, class, institution, etc. **4** a young man; stripling. **5** a small, headless nail.
—*v.* **1** decorate (pottery, fabrics, etc.) with designs representing sprigs. **2** strip a sprig or sprigs from (a plant, tree, etc.). **3** fasten with sprigs or brads. [ME *sprigge*]

spright·ly (sprīt'lē) *adj.* **-li·er, -li·est.** lively and quick. [< *spright*, var. of *sprite*] —**spright'li·ness,** *n.*

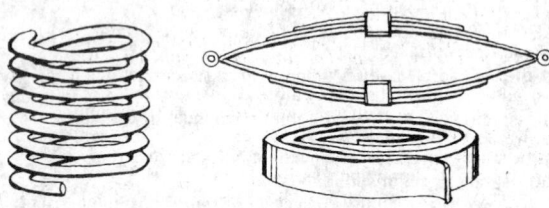

Metal springs of three different types

spring (spring) *v.* **sprang** or **sprung, sprung, spring·ing;** *n., adj.*
—*v.* **1** move or rise rapidly or suddenly; leap; jump: *The boy sprang to his feet.* **2** fly back or away as if by elastic force: *The door sprang to.* **3** cause to spring; cause to act by a spring: *spring a trap.* **4** be flexible, resilient, or elastic; be able to spring: *This branch springs enough to use as a snare.* **5** come from some source; arise; grow: *Plants sprang up from the seeds we planted.* **6** derive by birth or parentage; be descended; be the issue of: *spring from New England stock.* **7** begin to move, act, grow, etc. suddenly; burst forth: *Sparks sprang from the fire. Towns sprang up where oil was discovered.* **8** bring out, produce, or make suddenly: *spring a surprise on someone.* **9** crack, slit, warp, bend, strain, or break: *Frost had sprung the rock wall.* **10** force to ᴏpen, slip into place, etc. by or as if by bending: *The burglar was able to spring the lock quite easily.* **11** rouse (partridges, etc.) from cover. **12** *Slang.* secure the release of (a person) from prison by bail or otherwise.
spring a leak, crack and begin to let water through.
spring a mine, cause the gunpowder or other explosive in a mine to explode.
—*n.* **1** leap or jump: *a spring over the fence.* **2** an elastic device that returns to its original shape after being pulled or held out of shape: *Beds have wire springs. The spring in a clock makes it go.* **3** elastic quality: *The old man's knees have lost their spring.* **4** a flying back from a forced position. **5** the season after winter (in North America, March, April, May) when plants begin to grow. **6** a small stream of water flowing naturally from the earth. **7** a source; origin; cause. **8** the first and freshest period: *the spring of life.* **9** a crack, bend, strain, or break. **10** spring salmon.
—*adj.* **1** having a spring or springs. **2** of, having to do with, characteristic of, or suitable for the season of spring. Spring wheat is wheat sown in spring. **3** from a spring. Spring water often contains healthful minerals. [OE *springan*] —**spring'like',** *adj.*

spring·al (spring'əl) *n. Archaic.* springald.

spring·ald (spring'əld) *n. Archaic.* youth; young fellow. [< *spring* (n. def. 8)]

spring beauty any of a genus (*Claytonia*) of perennial plants of the purslane family having succulent leaves and white or pinkish, star-shaped flowers that bloom in spring.

spring·board (spring'bôrd') *n.* **1** a flexible board used to give added spring in diving, jumping, or vaulting. **2** anything that gives one a good start toward a goal or purpose: *Hard work was his springboard to success.*

spring·bok (spring'bok') *n., pl.* **-boks** or (esp. collectively) **-bok.** a small, graceful antelope (*Antidorcas marsupialis*) of semiarid regions of southern Africa, known for its habit of suddenly leaping straight up into the air. [< Afrikaans *springbok* springing buck < Du. *springen* leap + *bok* antelope]

spring chicken 1 a young chicken used for frying or broiling. **2** *Slang.* a young or inexperienced person: *She's no spring chicken.*

springe (sprinj) *n., v.* **springed, spring·ing.** —*n.* a snare for catching small game. —*v.* catch in a snare. [OE *sprengan* cause to spring]

spring·er (spring'ər) *n.* **1** a person or thing that springs. **2** *Architecture.* a place where the vertical support of an arch ends and the curve begins. See **arch**[1] for picture. **3** springer spaniel. **4** springbok.

springer spaniel either of two breeds of large spaniel often trained as bird dogs. The **English springer spaniel** has a white coat with liver, black, or tan markings; the **Welsh springer spaniel** is lighter in build and has a red and white coat. [so called because it was originally used to spring (def. 11) game]

spring fever a listless, lazy feeling felt by some people, caused by the first sudden warm weather of spring.

spring·halt (spring'holt' *or* -hôlt') *n.* stringhalt.

spring lock a lock that fastens automatically by a spring.

spring salmon *Cdn.* the largest Pacific salmon (*Oncorhynchus tshawytscha*), found from California to Alaska, mainly dark greenish-blue and silver in color and having red, white, or sometimes, pink flesh. Spring salmon are very highly valued as food fish.

spring·tail (spring'tāl') *n.* any of an order (Collembola) of small, primitive, wingless insects found throughout the world, having a forked, taillike appendage which they use for leaping.

spring·tide (spring'tīd') *n.* springtime.

spring tide 1 the high tide at its highest level. It comes at the time of the new moon or the full moon. **2** any great flood, swell, or rush.

spring·time (spring'tīm') *n.* **1** the season of spring. **2** the first or earliest period: *the springtime of life.*

spring·y (spring'ē) *adj.* **spring·i·er, spring·i·est. 1** yielding; flexible; elastic. **2** jaunty; gay; full of bounce: *a springy personality.* **3** having many springs of water. **4** spongy with moisture, as soil in the area of a subterranean spring or springs. —**spring'i·ly,** *adv.* —**spring'i·ness,** *n.*

sprin·kle (spring'kəl) *v.* **-kled, -kling;** *n.* —*v.* **1** scatter in drops or tiny bits. **2** scatter (something) in drops or tiny bits: *He sprinkled ashes on the icy sidewalk.* **3** spray or cover with small drops: *to sprinkle flowers with water.* **4** dot or vary with something scattered here and there. **5** rain a little.
—*n.* **1** the act of sprinkling. **2** a sprinkling; small quantity. **3** a light rain. [ME *sprenklen* or *sprinklen*; cf. Du. *sprenkelen*] —**sprin'kler,** *n.*

sprin·kling (spring'kling) *n.* a small number or quantity scattered here and there.

sprint (sprint) *v., n.* —*v.* run at top speed, especially for a short distance. —*n.* a short race or dash at full speed. [ME *sprente(n)*] —**sprint'er,** *n.*

sprit (sprit) *n.* a small pole that supports and stretches a sail. [OE *sprēot*]

sprite (sprīt) *n.* an elf; fairy; goblin. [ME < OF *esprit* spirit < L *spiritus.* Doublet of ESPRIT, SPIRIT.]

sprit·sail (sprit'sāl'; sprit'səl) *n.* a sail supported and stretched by a sprit.

sprock·et (sprok'it) *n.* **1** one of a set of projections on the rim of a wheel, arranged so as to fit into the links of a chain. The sprockets keep the chain from slipping. **2** Also, **sprocket wheel,** a wheel made with sprockets. [origin uncertain]

sprout (sprout) *v., n.* **1** begin to grow; shoot forth: *Seeds sprout. Buds sprout in the spring.* **2** cause to grow: *The rain has sprouted the corn.* **3** develop rapidly. **4** *Informal.* remove sprouts from: *He sprouted the potatoes twice every winter.*
—*n.* **1** a small shoot or bud of a plant. **2** a small boy. **3** sprouts, *pl.* Brussels sprouts. [OE *-sprūtan,* as in *āsprūtan*]

spruce[1] (sprüs) *n.* **1** any of a genus (*Picea*) of evergreen tree of the pine family found throughout the northern areas of the world, having hanging cones and short, needle-like leaves growing singly along the stems. There are five species of spruce native to Canada. **2** the wood of any of these trees. [ME *Spruce,* var. of *Pruce* Prussia, perhaps because the trees first came from there]

spruce[2] (sprüs) *adj.* **spruc·er, spruc·est;** *v.* **spruced, spruc·ing.**
—*adj.* neat; trim: *John looked very spruce in his new suit.* —*v.* make spruce or make oneself spruce (*usually used with* **up**): *The new slipcovers spruce up the living room. He spruced up before going in for the interview.* [? < *Spruce leather* a superior type of leather formerly imported from Prussia and popular in the 16th century. See SPRUCE[1].] —**spruce'ly,** *adv.* —**spruce'ness,** *n.*

spruce beer a fermented drink made with an extract of spruce twigs and sugar (or molasses) boiled together.

spruce budworm a moth (*Choristoneura fumiferana*) whose larva feeds on the young needles of spruce and fir and is one of the most serious periodic pests of these trees in Canada and the N United States.

spruce grouse bush partridge.

sprung (sprung) *v.* a pt. and pp. of **spring.**

spry (sprī) *adj.* **spry·er, spry·est** or **spri·er, spri·est.** active; lively; nimble: *The spry old lady travelled everywhere.* [? < Scand.; cf. Swedish *sprugg* active]

spud (spud) *n., v.* **spud·ded, spud·ding.** —*n.* 1 a tool with a narrow blade, for digging up or cutting the roots of weeds. 2 a tool resembling a chisel, for removing bark. 3 *Informal.* potato. —*v.* 1 dig up or remove with a spud. 2 make a hole as the first stage in drilling an oil well (*often used with* **in**): *The new well was spudded in two weeks ago.* [cf. Danish *spyd* spear]

Spud Island *Cdn. Slang.* Prince Edward Island.

Spud Islander *Cdn. Slang.* a Prince Edward Islander.

spue (spyü) *v.* **spued, spu·ing.** See **spew.**

spume (spyüm) *n., v.* **spumed, spum·ing.** —*n. or v.* foam; froth. [< L *spuma*]

spu·mo·ne (spə mō′nē; *Italian,* spü mō′nä) *n.* a type of Italian ice cream, usually containing fruit, nuts, etc. [< Ital.]

spum·y (spyü′mē) *adj.* **spum·i·er, spum·i·est.** covered with, consisting of, or resembling spume; foamy; frothy.

spun (spun) *v.* pt. and pp. of **spin.**

spun glass glass made into threads.

spunk (spungk) *n.* 1 *Informal.* courage; pluck; spirit; mettle. 2 a spark. 3 tinder or punk. **get** (one's) **spunk up,** *Informal.* show courage, pluck, or spirit. [< Irish or Scots Gaelic *sponnc* < L *spongia* sponge < Gk.]

spunk·y (spungk′ē) *adj.* **spunk·i·er, spunk·i·est.** *Informal.* courageous; plucky; spirited. —**spunk′i·ly,** *adv.* —**spunk′i·ness,** *n.*

spun rayon a yarn made from rayon threads. When woven, spun rayon often resembles linen cloth.

spun silk silk waste spun into yarn.

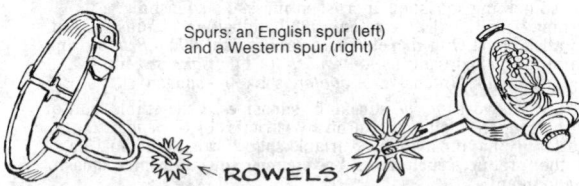

Spurs: an English spur (left) and a Western spur (right)

ROWELS

spur (spėr) *n., v.* **spurred, spur·ring.** —*n.* 1 a pricking device worn on a horseman's heel for urging a horse on. 2 anything that urges on: *Ambition was the spur that made him work.* 3 something like a spur; a point sticking out. A cock has spurs on his legs. 4 a ridge projecting from or subordinate to the main body of a mountain or mountain range. 5 any short branch: *a spur of a railway.* **on the spur of the moment,** on a sudden impulse; without previous thought or preparation. **win** (one's) **spurs,** make a reputation for oneself; attain distinction. —*v.* 1 prick with spurs. 2 go or ride quickly. 3 strike or wound with a spur or spurs. 4 urge on: *Pride spurred the boy to fight.* 5 provide with a spur or spurs. **spur on,** encourage. [OE *spura*]

spurge (spėrj) *n.* 1 any of a large genus (*Euphorbia*) of plants having a bitter, milky juice and clusters of small flowers. Some species and varieties of spurge are grown as garden flowers. The poinsettia is a spurge. 2 (*adj.*) designating a family (Euphorbiaceae) of plants found in most temperate and tropical regions that includes spurge, croton, rubber, and cassava. Most plants of the spurge family have milky juice. [ME < OF *espurge,* ult. < L *ex* out + *purgare* purge]

spur gear 1 a spur wheel. 2 gearing using such wheels.

spu·ri·ous (spyür′ē əs) *adj.* 1 not coming from the right source; not genuine; false; sham: *a spurious document.* 2 *Botany.* superficially resembling but differing in form and structure. 3 illegitimate. [< L *spurius*] —**spu′ri·ous·ly,** *adv.* —**spu′ri·ous·ness,** *n.*

spurn (spėrn) *v., n.* —*v.* 1 refuse with scorn; scorn: *The judge spurned the bribe.* 2 oppose with scorn: *They spurned at restraint.* 3 strike with the foot; kick away. —*n.* 1 disdainful rejection; contemptuous treatment. 2 a kick. [OE *spurnan*]

spurred (spėrd) *adj.* having spurs or a spur.

spurt (spėrt) *v., n.* —*v.* 1 flow suddenly in a stream or jet; gush out; squirt: *Blood spurted from the wound.* 2 cause to gush out. 3 put forth great energy for a short time; show great activity for a short time: *The runners spurted near the end of the race.* —*n.* 1 a sudden rushing forth; jet: *Spurts of flame broke out all over the building.* 2 a great increase of effort or activity for a short time. 3 a sudden outburst of feeling, etc. 4 a sudden rise in prices, improvement in prices, etc. Also, **spirt.** [var. of *sprit,* OE *spryttan*]

spur track a branch railway track connected with the main track at one end only.

hat, āge, fär; let, ēqual, tėrm; it, īce
hot, ōpen, ôrder; oil, out; cup, pùt, rüle,
əbove, takən, pencəl, lemən, circəs
ch, child; ng, long; sh, ship
th, thin; ₮H, then; zh, measure

spur wheel a wheel with projecting teeth on the rim placed parallel to the axis; the simplest form of gearwheel or cogwheel.

sput·nik (sput′nik *or* sut′nik) *n.* any of a series of earth satellites put into orbit by the Soviet Union. Sputnik I, launched in 1957, was the first artificial satellite to orbit the earth. [< Russian *sputnik* companion, satellite]

sput·ter (sput′ər) *v., n.* —*v.* 1 make spitting or popping noises: *fat sputtering in the frying pan. The firecrackers sputtered.* 2 throw out (drops of saliva, bits of food, etc.) in excitement or in talking too fast. 3 say (words or sounds) in haste and confusion. —*n.* 1 confused talk. 2 a sputtering; sputtering noise. [probably echoic; cf. Du. *sputtern*] —**sput′ter·er,** *n.*

spu·tum (spyü′təm) *n., pl.* **-ta** (-tə). 1 saliva; spit. 2 what is coughed up from the lungs and spat out. [< L]

spy (spī) *n., pl.* **spies;** *v.* **spied, spy·ing.** —*n.* 1 a person who keeps secret watch on the actions of others. 2 a person paid by a government to get secret information about the government plans, military strength, etc. of another country. —*v.* 1 keep secret watch, especially for a hostile purpose (*usually used with* **on**): *They had two men spying on the house.* 2 by a spy; engage in espionage: *The punishment for spying in wartime is death.* 3 catch sight of; see: *They spied a car in the distance.* 4 find out or try to find out by careful observation; search (*often used with* **out**): *to spy out all the happenings in the neighborhood.* [ME < OF *espie,* n., *espier,* v.< Gmc.]

spy·glass (spī′glas′) *n.* a small telescope.

spy·mas·ter (spī′mas′tər) *n.* a person who directs the activities of, and acts as a clearing agent for, a spy ring.

spy ring an organized group of spies.

sq. 1 square. 2 the following (for L *sequens*). 3 sequence.

sq. ft. square foot (or feet).

sq. in. square inch(es).

sq. mi. square mile(s).

sqq. the following ones (for L *sequentia*).

squab (skwob) *n., adj.* —*n.* 1 a very young bird, especially a young pigeon. 2 a short, stout person. 3 a thick, soft cushion. 4 a sofa; couch. —*adj.* 1 newly hatched. 2 short and stout. [cf. dial. Swedish *sqvabb* loose or fat flesh, dial. Norwegian *skvabb* soft wet mass]

squab·ble (skwob′əl) *n., v.* **-bled, -bling.** —*n.* a petty, noisy quarrel: *Children's squabbles.* —*v.* take part in a petty, noisy quarrel. [? imitative] —**squab′bler,** *n.*

squad (skwod) *n.* 1 the smallest unit of military personnel, grouped especially for drill, inspection, or work. 2 *U.S.* the smallest tactical unit in the United States army. 3 any small group of persons working together. [< F < Ital. *squadra* square]

squad car scout car.

squad·ron (skwod′rən) *n.* 1 a part of a naval fleet used for special service. 2 a cavalry unit consisting of two or more troops, together with headquarters and supporting units. 3 an air-force unit larger than a flight and smaller than a group. 4 any group. [< Ital. *squadrone* < *squadra* square]

squadron leader 1 the leader of a squadron of cavalry, tanks, or airplanes. 2 an air-force officer ranking next above a flight lieutenant and below a wing commander. *Abbrev.:* S.L. or S/L

squal·id (skwol′id) *adj.* 1 filthy, degraded, and wretched, especially as a result of poverty or neglect. 2 sordid. [< L *squalidus* < *squalere* be filthy] —**squal′id·ness,** *n.*

squall¹ (skwol *or* skwôl) *n.* 1 a sudden, violent gust of wind, often with rain, snow, or sleet. 2 *Informal.* trouble. [cf. Swedish *skval-regn* sudden downpour of rain]

squall² (skwol *or* skwôl) *v., n.* —*v.* cry out loudly; scream violently: *The baby squalled.* —*n.* a loud, harsh cry: *The parrot's squall was heard all over the house.* [< Scand.; cf. ON *skvala* cry out] —**squall′er,** *n.*

squall·y (skwol′ē *or* skwôl′ē) *adj.* **squal·i·er, squal·i·est.** 1 disturbed by sudden and violent gusts of wind: *squally weather.* 2 blowing in squalls. 3 *Informal.* threatening; troublous.

squal·or (skwol′ər) *n.* the quality or state of being squalid; misery and dirt. [< L]

squama (skā′mə) *n.*, *pl.* **-mae** (-mē *or* -mī). *Biology.* a scale or scale-like part: *a squama of bone.* [< L]

squa·mate (skwā′māt) *adj.* having scales; covered with scales.

squa·mose (skwā′mōs) *adj.* squamous.

squa·mous (skwā′məs) *adj.* furnished with, covered with, or formed of scales; characterized by the development of scales; scale-like. [< L *squamosus*]

squan·der (skwon′dər) *v.* spend foolishly; waste: *He squandered his money in gambling.* [origin uncertain] —**squan′der·er,** *n.*

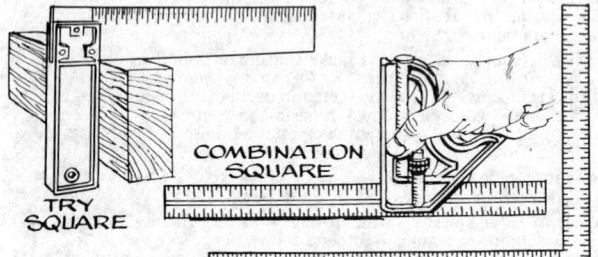

COMBINATION SQUARE

TRY SQUARE

STEEL SQUARE

Carpenter's squares

square (skwer) *n.*, *adj.* **squar·er, squar·est;** *v.* **squared, squar·ing; adv. —n. 1** a plane figure with four equal sides and four right angles. See **quadrilateral** for picture. **2** anything of or near this shape. **3** a space in a city or town bounded by streets on four sides: *This square is filled with stores.* **4** the distance along one side of such a space; block. **5** an open space in a city or town bounded by streets on four sides, often planted with grass, trees, etc. **6** any similar open space, such as the meeting of streets. **7** the buildings surrounding such a place. **8** a parade ground. **9** an instrument having two straight edges that meet to form a right angle, used in carpentry, etc. for drawing and testing right angles. **10** *Mathematics.* the product obtained when a number is multiplied by itself. 16 is the square of 4. **11** *Slang.* a person who is not in tune with the latest fashions in popular entertainment, culture, etc.
on the square, a at right angles. **b** *Informal.* justly; fairly; honestly. **out of square,** not at right angles; out of order; incorrect or incorrectly.
—*adj.* **1** having four equal sides and four right angles. **2** of a specified length on each side of a square: *a room five metres square.* **3** having breadth more nearly equal to length or height than is usual: *a square jaw.* **4** forming a right angle: *a square corner.* **5** straight; level; even. **6** leaving no balance; even: *make accounts square.* **7** just; fair; honest: *a square deal.* **8** straightforward; direct: *a square refusal.* **9** *Informal.* satisfying: *a square meal.* **10** squared: *a square centimetre.* **11** multiplied by itself. **12** solid and strong. **13** *Slang.* not up to date; old-fashioned.
—*v.* **1** make square; make rectangular; make cubical. **2** mark out in squares. **3** bring to the form of a right angle. **4** make straight, level, or even: *to square a picture on the wall.* **5** adjust; settle: *Let us square our accounts.* **6** agree; conform: *His acts do not square with his promises.* **7** regulate. **8** *Mathematics.* **a** find the equivalent in square measure. **b** multiply (a number) by itself: *25 squared makes 625.* **9** *Sports.* bring (the score of a game or contest) to equality; tie: *to square the score with a touchdown in the third quarter.* **10** *Slang.* win over, conciliate, or secure the silence or consent of, especially by bribery; bribe.
square away, a of a ship, set the sails so that it will stay before the wind. **b** prepare; put in order; get ready.
square off, *Informal.* put oneself in a position of defence or attack.
square (oneself), *Informal.* **a** make up for something one has said or done. **b** get even.
square the circle, a find a square equal in area to a circle. **b** try to do something impossible.
square up, a adjust; settle. **b** take up a fighting stance; get ready to fight.
—*adv.* **1** *Informal.* fairly or honestly. **2** so as to be square; in square or rectangular form; at right angles. [ME < OF *esquar(r)e,* ult. < L *es* outr + *quadrus* square] —**square′ly,** *adv.*

square dance a dance performed by a set of couples arranged in some set form. The quadrille and Virginia reel are square dances.

square–dance (skwer′dans′) *v.* **-danced, -danc·ing.** take part in a square dance. —**square′danc′er,** *n.*

square deal *Informal.* fair and honest treatment.

square flipper *Cdn.* the bearded seal.

square knot a knot firmly joining two loose ends of rope or cord. Each end is formed into a loop which both encloses and passes through the other. See **knot** for picture.

square meal a substantial or satisfying meal.

square measure a unit or measure of units for measuring area. The hectare is a square measure.

square–rigged (skwer′rigd′) *adj.* having the principal sails set at right angles across the masts. See **brig** for picture.

square–rig·ger (skwer′rig′ər) *n.* a square-rigged ship.

square root *Mathematics.* a number that produces a given number when multiplied by itself: *If the given number is 16, the square root is 4.*

square sail a four-sided sail.

square shooter *Informal.* a fair and honest person.

square·tail (skwer′tāl′) *n. Cdn.* **1** the speckled trout or the rainbow trout. **2** a prairie chicken. **3** a sharp-tailed grouse.

square timber *Cdn. Historical.* squared logs such as those rafted to the Quebec timber coves for export.

square-toed (skwer′tōd′) *adj.* **1** having a broad, square toe: *a square-toed boot.* **2** old-fashioned and homely in habits, ideas, etc.

squar·ish (skwer′ish) *adj.* nearly square; having breadth more nearly equal to length or height than is usual.

squash[1] (skwosh) *v.*, *n.* —*v.* **1** press until soft or flat; crush: *The boy squashed the bug. Carry the cream puffs carefully, for they squash easily.* **2** make a squashing sound; move with a squashing sound: *We heard him squash through the mud and slush.* **3** put an end to; stop by force: *The police squashed the riot.* **4** *Informal.* silence with a crushing argument, reply, etc. **5** crowd; squeeze. —*n.* **1** something squashed; a crushed mass. **2** a squashing; a squashing sound. **3** a game resembling handball and tennis, played in a walled court with rackets and a rubber ball. **4** *Esp.Brit.* a drink containing crushed fruit: *lemon squash.* [< OF *esquasser,* ult. < L *ex* out + *quassare,* intensive of *quatere* shake] —**squash′er,** *n.*

squash[2] (skwosh) *n.*, *pl.* **squash** *or* **squash·es. 1** the edible fruit of *Cucurbita maxima* and certain bushy varieties of *C. pepo* of the gourd family, having a greatly variable shape, size, and color. **2** a plant that produces such fruits. See **summer squash, winter squash.** [< Algonquian]

squash bug a dark-brown or black North American bug (*Anasa tristis* of family Coreidae) that is a pest of squash, pumpkin, and related plants.

squash·y (skwosh′ē) *adj.* **squash·i·er, squash·i·est. 1** easily squashed: *squashy cream puffs.* **2** soft and wet: *squashy ground.* **3** having a crushed appearance. [< *squash*[1]] —**squash′i·ly,** *adv.* —**squash′i·ness,** *n.*

squat (skwot) *v.* **squat·ted** *or* **squat, squat·ting;** *adj.*, *n.* —*v.* **1** crouch on the heels. **2** sit on the ground or floor with the legs drawn up closely beneath or in front of the body. **3** seat (oneself) with the legs drawn up. **4** settle on another's land without title or right. **5** settle on public land to acquire ownership of it under government regulation.
—*adj.* **1** crouching: *We saw a squat figure in front of the fire.* **2** short and thick; low and broad: *The burglar was a squat, dark man. I like that squat teapot.*
—*n.* the act of squatting; squatting posture. [ME < OF *esquatir* crush, ult. < L *ex-* out + *coactus* forced, pp. of *cogere* < *co-* together + *agere* drive]

squat·ter (skwot′ər) *n.* **1** a person who settles on another's land without right. **2** a person who settles on public land to acquire ownership of it. **3** a person, animal, etc. that crouches or squats.

squat·ty (skwot′ē) *adj.* **-ti·er, -ti·est.** short and thick; low and broad.

squaw (skwo *or* skwô) *n.* **1** an Amerindian woman or wife. [< Algonquian; cf. Cree *es-quayo* woman]
Usage. This term, an Anglicized form of an Algonquian word, came to be used by English speakers to refer to any Amerindian woman. The term was meaningless, however, to people speaking other Amerindian languages and came to be resented by them as an English word. Moreover, since it often had derogatory implications, it is no longer considered acceptable usage.

squaw·fish (skwo′fish′ *or* skwô′-) *n.*, *pl.* **-fish** *or* **-fishes.** any of a genus (*Ptychocheilus*) of relatively large cyprinid fishes found in the rivers and lakes of W North America, especially the **northern squawfish** (*P. oregonensis*) of British Columbia, the Peace River region, and the NW United States.

squawk (skwok *or* skwôk) *v.* —*v.* **1** make a loud, harsh sound: *Chickens and ducks squawk when frightened.* **2** utter harshly and loudly. **3** *Slang.* complain loudly. —*n.* **1** a loud, harsh sound. **2** *Slang.* a loud complaint. [imitative] —**squawk′er,** *n.*

squawk box *Slang.* a loudspeaker of a public address system.

squaw man *Derogatory.* a white man married to or living with

an Indian woman, especially such a man who has abandoned white customs.

squaw winter in the North, an early spell of winter weather, often coming before an Indian summer.

squeak (skwēk) *v., n.* —*v.* **1** make a short, sharp, shrill sound: *A mouse squeaks.* **2** cause to squeak. **3** utter with a squeak. **4** *Slang.* **a** turn informer; squeal. **b** confess. **5** *Informal.* get or pass (by or through) with difficulty.
—*n.* **1** a short, sharp, shrill sound. **2** *Informal.* a chance to get by or through; chance of escape: *a narrow squeak.* [ME; probably echoic; cf. Swedish *sqväka* croak] —**squeak′er,** *n.*

squeak·er (skwē′kər) *n. Informal.* a game, fight, or other contest won by a narrow margin.

squeak·y (skwē′kē) *adj.* **squeak·i·er, squeak·i·est.** squeaking. —**squeak′i·ly,** *adv.* —**squeak′i·ness,** *n.*

squeal (skwēl) *v., n.* —*v.* **1** make a long, sharp, shrill cry: *A pig squeals when it is hurt.* **2** utter sharply and shrilly. **3** *Slang.* turn informer.
—*n.* **1** a long, sharp, shrill cry. **2** *Informal.* an act of informing against another. **3** *Informal.* an act of complaining loudly. [imitative] —**squeal′er,** *n.*

squeam·ish (skwē′mish) *adj.* **1** too proper; modest, etc.; easily shocked. **2** too particular; too scrupulous. **3** slightly sick at one's stomach; sickish. **4** easily turned sick. [var. of earlier *squeamous* < AF *escoymous*] —**squeam′ish·ly,** *adv.* —**squeam′ish·ness,** *n.*

squee·gee (skwē′jē) *n., v.* **-geed, -gee·ing.** —*n.* **1** an implement edged with rubber or the like, for sweeping water from wet decks, scraping water off windows after washing, cleaning a sink, etc. **2** any of various similar devices. **3** *Photography.* a device with a roller for pressing water from prints, etc.
—*v.* sweep, scrape, or press with a squeegee. [? < *squeege,* var. of *squeeze*]

squeeze (skwēz) *v.* **squeezed, squeez·ing;** *n.* —*v.* **1** press hard: *Don't squeeze the kitten; you will hurt it.* **2** hug: *She squeezed her child.* **3** force by pressing: *I can't squeeze another thing into my trunk.* **4** burden; oppress: *Heavy taxes squeezed the people.* **5** get by pressure, force, or effort: *The dictator squeezed money from the people.* **6** *Informal.* put pressure on or try to influence (a person or persons) to do something, especially pay money. **7** yield to pressure: *Sponges squeeze easily.* **8** force a way: *He squeezed through the crowd.* **9** press (the hand) in friendship or affection. **10** *Bridge.* compel (an opponent) to discard or unguard a valuable card.
—*n.* **1** the act or an instance of squeezing: *a squeeze of the hand.* **2** a hug. **3** a crush; crowd. **4** a small quantity or amount squeezed out. **5** something made by pressing; cast; impression. **6** *Informal.* a situation from which escape is difficult. **7** *Informal.* pressure used to extort a favor, money, etc. **8** a squeeze play in baseball or bridge. **9** *Business.* pressure resulting from shortages.
tight squeeze, *Informal.* a difficult situation.
[ult. < OE *cwȳsan*] —**squeez′er,** *n.*

squeeze play **1** *Baseball.* a play executed when a runner on third base starts for home as soon as the pitcher begins to pitch. **2** *Bridge.* a play or series of plays in which the holder of a card that may win a trick is compelled to discard it or to unguard another possible winner. **3** *Informal.* an attempt to force somebody into a difficult situation or to make him act against his wishes.

squelch (skwelch) *v., n.* —*v.* **1** cause to be silent; crush: *She squelched him with a look of contempt.* **2** strike or press on with crushing force. **3** walk in mud, water, wet shoes, etc., making a splashing sound. **4** make the sound of one doing so.
—*n.* **1** a crushing retort. **2** a splashing sound made by walking in mud, water, wet shoes, etc. [earlier *quelch,* blend of *quell* and *crush*] —**squelch′er,** *n.*

squib (skwib) *n., v.* **squibbed, squib·bing.** —*n.* **1** a short, witty attack in speech or writing; sharp sarcasm. **2** a brief item in a newspaper used mainly to fill space. **3** a small firework that burns with a hissing noise and finally explodes. **4** a broken firecracker.
—*v.* **1** say, write, or publish a squib or squibs. **2** assail or attack with squibs; lampoon. **3** set off or fire a squib. [origin uncertain]

squid (skwid) *n., pl.* **squid** or **squids;** *v.* **squid·ded, squid·ding.**
—*n.* any of various 10-armed marine cephalopod molluscs (genera *Loligo, Omnastrephes, Architeuthis,* etc.), having an elongated body, a pair of triangular tail fins, and a mouth surrounded by 10 sucker-bearing arms, two of which are long tentacles used to capture prey. —*v.* fish with a squid as bait. [< *squit,* dial. var. of *squirt*]

squid·jig·ger (skwid′jig′ər) *n. Cdn.* especially in Newfoundland: **1** a device for catching squid, made of several hooks so joined that their points form a compact circle which is pulled or jerked through the water. **2** a person who engages in squidjigging.

squid·jig·ging (skwid′jig′ing) *n. Cdn.* especially in Newfoundland, the act or process of fishing for squid with a squidjigger.

hat, āge, fär; let, ēqual, tèrm; it, īce
hot, ōpen, ôrder; oil, out; cup, pùt, rüle,
əbove, takən, pencəl, lemən, circəs

ch, child; ng, long; sh, ship
th, thin; ŦH, then; zh, measure

squiffed (skwift) *adj. Slang.* squiffy.

squif·fy (skwif′ē) *adj. Slang.* drunk; intoxicated. [origin uncertain]

squig·gle (skwig′əl) *n., v.* **-gled, -gling.** —*n.* a twist, curve, or wriggle. —*v.* **1** make with crooked or twisted strokes; scrawl. **2** writhe; squirm; wriggle. [probably a blend of *squirm* and *wiggle*]

squill (skwil) *n.* **1** a Mediterranean plant (*Urginea maritima*) of the lily family having spikes of small white flowers and a bulb that is used in medicine. Also **sea squill. 2** scilla, especially any of several species cultivated in rock gardens, etc. for their spring-blooming, usually blue, flowers. [< L *squilla,* var. of *scilla* < Gk. *skilla*]

squint (skwint) *v., n.* —*v.* **1** look or peer with the eyes partly closed: *He squinted at the sign.* **2** have a squint: *She used to squint before she got glasses.* **3** look sideways or askance. **4** cause (an eye) to squint. **5** incline; tend.
—*n.* **1** a tendency to look with the eyes partly closed. **2** cross-eye; strabismus. **3** the act or an instance of squinting. **4** inclination; tendency.
—*adj.* **1** looking sideways or askance. **2** of the eyes, having a squint. [< *asquint,* of uncertain origin] —**squint′er,** *n.*

squire (skwīr) *n., v.* **squired, squir·ing.** —*n.* **1** in England, a country gentleman; especially, the chief landowner in a district. **2** *Historical.* a young man of noble family who attended a knight till he himself was made a knight. **3** attendant. **4** a woman's escort.
—*v.* **1** formerly, attend as squire. **2** escort (a woman). [ult. var. of *esquire*] —**squire′like,** *adj.*

squirm (skwèrm) *v., n.* —*v.* **1** wriggle; writhe; twist: *The restless boy squirmed in his chair.* **2** show great embarrassment, annoyance, confusion, etc. —*n.* a wriggle; writhe; twist. [? imitative]

squirm·y (skwèr′mē) *adj.* **squirm·i·er, squirm·i·est.** squirming; wriggling.

squir·rel (skwèr′əl *or* skwir′əl) *n., v.* **squir·relled** or **squir·reled, squir·rel·ling** or **squir·rel·ing.** —*n.* **1** any of numerous small, quick-moving, arboreal rodents (genera *Sciurus* and *Tamiascurus* of family Sciuridae) having a long, bushy tail and feeding mainly on nuts and seeds. See also **grey squirrel, red squirrel. 2** any other rodent of the family Sciuridae, especially a flying squirrel or a ground squirrel. **3** the fur of a squirrel.
—*v.* store or hide for future use (*usually used with* **away**): *He had vast supplies of paper squirreled away in the closet.* [ME < AF *esquirel* < L *sciurus* < Gk. *skiouros* < *skia* shadow + *oura* tail]

squir·rel·ly (skwèr′əl ē *or* skwir′əl ē) *adj. Slang.* **1** crazy. **2** mentally unbalanced, especially as a result of long isolation in the bush; bushed.

squirt (skwèrt) *v., n.* —*v.* **1** force out (liquid) through a narrow opening: *squirt water through a tube.* **2** come out in a jet or stream: *Water squirted from a hose.* **3** wet or soak by shooting liquid in a jet or stream: *The elephant squirted me with its trunk.*
—*n.* **1** the act of squirting. **2** a jet of liquid, etc. **3** a small pump, syringe, or other device for squirting a liquid. **4** *Informal.* an insignificant person who is impudent or self-assertive. **5** a young boy. [ME; probably echoic; cf. LG *swirtjen,* alteration of earlier *swirt* young or small < LG or Du. *swirtjen*] —**squirt′er,** *n.*

squirt gun water pistol.

squish (skwish) *v., n.* —*v.* **1** make a soft splashing sound when walking in mud, water, wet shoes, etc. **2** *Informal.* squash; squeeze. —*n.* a squishing sound. [imitative alteration of *squash*] —**squish′y,** *adj.*

sq. yd. square yard(s).

Sr strontium.

Sr. 1 Senior. **2** Sir. **3** Sister. **4** Señor.

S.R.O. standing room only.

SS[1] (es′es′) *n. Historical.* a select military unit in the Nazi Party whose members served as Hitler's bodyguard, concentration camp guards, security police, etc. [< G, short for *Schutzstaffel*]

SS[2] **1** steamship. **2** *Typing.* single space.

SS. Saints.

S.S. 1 steamship. **2** Sunday school. **3** Secretary of State. **4** separate school. **5** school section. **6** staff sergeant.

SSE or **S.S.E.** south-southeast.

SST supersonic transport.

SSW or **S.S.W.** south-southwest.

st. 1 street. 2 stet. 3 stone (weight). 4 stanza. 5 statue. 6 stitch. 7 strophe.

St. 1 Street. 2 Saint. 3 Strait.

sta. station; stationary.

stab (stab) *v.* **stabbed, stab·bing;** *n.* —*v.* 1 pierce or wound with a pointed weapon. 2 thrust with a pointed weapon; aim a blow. 3 penetrate suddenly and sharply; pierce. 4 wound sharply or deeply in the feelings: *The mother was stabbed to the heart by her son's thoughtlessness.*
stab in the back, attempt to injure in a sly, treacherous manner; slander.
—*n.* 1 a thrust or blow made with a pointed weapon; any thrust. 2 a wound made by stabbing. 3 an injury to the feelings. 4 *Informal.* an attempt.
have or **make a stab at,** try; attempt.
[ult. related to *stub*] —**stab′ber,** *n.*

Sta·bat Ma·ter (stä′bät mä′tər *or* stä′bat mā′tər) 1 a celebrated 13th century Latin hymn about the Virgin Mary at the Cross. 2 a musical setting of this hymn. 3 any of certain other Latin hymns beginning with the same words. 4 a musical setting of any of these hymns. [< L *Stabat Mater* the Mother was standing, the first two words of the hymn]

sta·bile (stā′bīl *or* stā′bəl, stab′īl *or* stab′əl) *adj., n.* —*adj.* 1 *Medicine.* **a** not affected by average heat. **b** of or having to do with the method of electrotherapy in which one electrode is kept stationary over the part to be treated. 2 stable; fixed. —*n. Art.* a stationary, abstract sculpture made of cut or shaped metal, wood, etc.

sta·bil·i·ty (stə bil′ə tē) *n., pl.* **-ties.** 1 the condition of being fixed in position; firmness. 2 permanence. 3 steadfastness of character, purpose, etc. 4 the tendency of an object to return to its original position.

sta·bi·li·za·tion (stā′bə lə zā′shən *or* -lī zā′shən) *n.* a stabilizing; the state of being stabilized.

sta·bi·lize (stā′bə līz′) *v.* **-lized, liz·ing.** 1 make stable or firm. 2 prevent changes in; hold steady: *stabilize prices.* 3 keep (a ship, aircraft, spacecraft, etc.) steady by special construction or automatic devices.

sta·bi·liz·er (stā′bə līz′ər) *n.* 1 a person or thing that makes something stable. 2 a device for keeping a ship, aircraft, spacecraft, etc. steady. See **airplane** for picture.

sta·ble¹ (stā′bəl) *n., v.* **-bled, -bling.** —*n.* 1 a building fitted with stalls, rack and manger, etc. in which horses are kept. 2 a barn, shed, or other building in which any domestic animals, such as cattle, goats, etc. are kept. 3 a group of animals housed in such a building. 4 Often, **stables,** *pl.* the buildings and grounds where race horses are quartered and trained. 5 a group of race horses belonging to one owner. 6 the persons caring for such a group. 7 *Informal.* a group of athletes, artists, writers, etc. who work under the same management.
—*v.* 1 put or keep in a stable. 2 lodge in a stable. [ME < OF < L *stabulum*]

sta·ble² (stā′bəl) *adj.* 1 not likely to move or change; firm; steady. 2 lasting without change; permanent. 3 able to return to its original position. 4 of a chemical compound, not easily decomposed. [ME < AF < L *stabilis*] —**sta′bly,** *adv.*

sta·ble·boy (stā′bəl boi′) *n.* a boy who works in a stable.

sta·bling (stāb′ling) *n.* 1 the act or fact of accommodating horses in a stable. 2 a stable or stable buildings.

stab·lish (stab′lish) *v. Archaic.* establish.

stacc. staccato.

stac·ca·to (stə kä′tō) *adj., adv., n.* —*adj.* 1 *Music.* of a note or a passage, short and sharp. 2 disconnected; abrupt: *staccato speech.* —*adv.* in a staccato manner.
—*n.* 1 *Music.* a staccato passage or composition; a piece to be played or sung staccato. 2 a disconnected, abrupt quality or manner. *Abbrev.:* stacc. [< Ital. *staccato,* literally, detached]

stack (stak) *n., v.* —*n.* 1 a large, round or conical pile of hay, straw, etc. arranged for storage in the open air. 2 an orderly pile of anything: *a stack of wood, a stack of coins.* 3 a number of rifles arranged to form a cone or pyramid. 4 Often, **stacks,** *pl. Informal.* a large quantity: *stacks of work.* 5 a number of chimney flues or pipes forming a single structure. 6 a chimney or ship's funnel. 7 Usually, **stacks,** *pl.* a compactly arranged bookshelves for the storage of large numbers of books, as in a library. **b** the part of a library in which the main collection of books is shelved. 8 *Brit.* a unit for measuring a quantity of firewood, equal to about 3.06 cubic metres. 9 an arrangement of aircraft circling an airport at different altitudes, waiting for clearance to land. 10 *Computer science.* a computer memory or part of a memory for temporary storage.

blow (one's) stack, *Slang.* lose one's temper.
—*v.* 1 pile or arrange in a stack: *to stack hay or firewood. We stacked the books on the floor.* 2 load with something: *The table was stacked with records.* 3 arrange (a deck of playing cards, etc.) secretly in order to cheat. 4 assign (aircraft approaching an airport) to circling patterns at different altitudes above the airport to wait for clearance to land.
stack up, *Informal.* measure up.
[ME < ON *stakkr*] —**stack′er,** *n.*

Stad·a·con·a (stad′ə kōn′ə) *n.* the name of the Iroquois village on the site of the present city of Quebec when it was visited by Jacques Cartier in 1535.

stad·hold·er (stad′hōl′dər) *n.* 1 the chief magistrate of the former republic of the United Provinces of the Netherlands. 2 *Historical.* the viceroy or governor of a province in the Netherlands. [< Du. *stadhouder* < *stad* place, city + *houder* holder]

sta·di·a¹ (stā′dē ə) *n.* an instrument for measuring distances or heights by means of angles. A surveyor's transit is one kind of stadia. [? ult. < *stadium,* or its source]

sta·di·a² (stā′dē ə) *n.* a pl. of **stadium.**

sta·di·um (stā′dē əm) *n., pl.* **-di·ums** or **-di·a.** 1 an oval or U-shaped structure with rows of seats around a large, open space for games, concerts, etc. 2 an ancient Greek running track for foot races, with rows of seats along each side and at one end. The stadium of Athens is about 185 m long. [< L < Gk. *stadion,* ancient Greek measure of length, equal at Athens to about 185 m]

stadt·hold·er (stat′hōl′dər) *n.* stadholder.

staff (staf) *n., pl.* **staves** or **staffs** *for 1 and 2,* **staffs** *for 3-6; v.* —*n.* 1 a stick, pole, or rod used as a support, as an emblem of office, as a weapon, etc.: *The flag hangs on a staff.* 2 something that supports or sustains: *Bread is called the staff of life.* 3 a group assisting a chief; a group of assistants working with their chief as a unit. 4 *Military.* a group of officers that assists a commanding officer in planning and supervisory operations. 5 a similar group assisting or attending a governor, president, or other executive. 6 *Music.* the five lines and four spaces between them on which the notes, rests, etc. are written.
—*v.* provide with officers or employees. [OE *stæf*]

staf·fer (staf′ər) *n.* a member of a staff, as of a newspaper, government department, etc.

staff officer a military officer who assists in planning and supervising operations.

staff sergeant 1 in the army and air force, a noncommissioned officer junior to a warrant officer. 2 in the Royal Canadian Mounted Police, a noncommissioned officer senior to a corporal and junior to a sergeant major. *Abbrev.:* S.S.

stag (stag) *n., adj., adv.* —*n.* 1 an adult male deer, especially the male of the European red deer. 2 *Informal.* **a** a man who goes to a dance, party, etc. without a female partner. **b** a dinner party, etc. attended by men only.
—*adj. Informal.* attended by, or for men only: *a stag dinner.*
—*adv. Informal.* unaccompanied by a person of the opposite sex: *He went stag to the party.* [OE *stagga*]

stag beetle any of a family (Lucanidae) of beetles, the males of which have antlerlike mandibles.

stage (stāj) *n., v.* **staged, stag·ing.** —*n.* 1 one step or degree in a process; period of development. An insect passes through several stages before it is full-grown. 2 the raised platform in a theatre on which the actors perform. 3 the theatre; the drama; an actor's profession: *Shakespeare wrote for the stage.* 4 the scene of action: *Queenston Heights was the stage of a famous battle.* 5 a section of a rocket or missile having its own motor and fuel. 6 a stagecoach; bus. 7 a place of rest on a journey; a regular stopping place. 8 the distance between two places of rest on a journey; the distance between stops. 9 a platform; flooring. 10 a scaffold. 11 any platform raised high or built off the ground for the safe drying of fish, meat, etc.
by or **in easy stages,** a little at a time; slowly; often stopping: *We made the long journey in easy stages.*
on the stage, being an actor or actress.
—*v.* 1 put on a stage; arrange: *The play was excellently staged.* 2 be suited to the theatre: *That scene will not stage well.* 3 arrange to have an effect; plan and carry out: *The angry people staged a riot.* 4 travel by stagecoach. 5 carry out or do by stages: *staged disarmament.* 6 burn out and detach from a rocket or missile: *to stage a motor or a fuel tank.* 7 place on a stage for drying. 8 *Esp.military.* establish a position or base as a stop in a planned movement or operation. [ME < OF *estage,* ult. < L *stare* stand] —**stage′like′,** *adj.*

stage·coach (stāj′kōch′) *n.* a large, four-wheeled, horse-drawn coach formerly used for carrying passengers, mail, and parcels over a regular route.

stage·craft (stāj′kraft′) *n.* skill in, or the art of writing, adapting, or presenting plays.

stage director 1 a stage manager, especially a chief, or executive, stage manager. 2 *Esp.U.S.* director.

stage door an outside door of a theatre leading to the dressing rooms, stage, etc., used by actors, stage hands, etc.

stage fright a nervous fear experienced when appearing before an audience.

stage·hand (stāj′hand′) *n.* a person whose work is moving scenery, arranging lights, etc. in a theatre.

stage–man·age (stāj′man′əj) *v.* **-aged, -ag·ing. 1** act as stage manager (for a theatrical production). **2** arrange, direct, or present for a particular effect, especially from behind the scenes: *A few revolutionaries had stage-managed the whole crisis.*

stage manager *Theatre.* the person responsible for the arrangement of the stage, including the placing and changing of scenery, props, etc. and for the proper running of each performance.

stag·er (stā′jər) *n.* **1** a person of long experience. **2** a horse used for drawing a stagecoach.

stage–struck (stāj′struk′) *adj.* extremely interested in acting; wanting very much to become an actor or actress.

stage whisper 1 a loud whisper on a stage meant for the audience to hear. **2** a whisper meant to be heard by others than the person addressed.

stag·ey (stā′jē) See **stagy.**

stag·ger (stag′ər) *v., n.* **1** sway or reel (from weakness, a heavy load, or drunkenness). **2** cause to sway or reel: *The blow staggered him for a moment.* **3** become unsteady; waver. **4** hesitate. **5** cause to hesitate or become confused. **6** confuse or astonish greatly: *We were staggered by the news of the air disaster.* **7** make helpless. **8** arrange in a zigzag or irregular order or way: *The rows of seats in the theatre were staggered so that each person could see past the one in front.* **9** arrange at intervals, often to prevent congestion or confusion: *The school was so crowded that classes had to be staggered. Vacations were staggered so that only one person was away at a time.*
—*n.* **1** the act or an instance of staggering. **2** a staggered arrangement. **3 staggers,** a disease of the central nervous system that affects horses and some other domestic animals and is characterized by a staggering or swaying gait (*used with a singular verb*). Also called **blind staggers.**
[ult. < ON *stakra*] —**stag′ger·er,** *n.* —**stag′ger·ing·ly,** *adv.*
☛ *Syn. v.* **1.** See note at **reel².**

stag·hound (stag′hound′) *n.* a breed of hounds resembling the foxhound but larger, formerly used for hunting deer, etc.

stag·ing (stā′jing) *n.* **1** a temporary platform or structure of posts and boards for support, as in building; scaffolding. **2** the act or process of putting a play on the stage. **3** a travelling by stages or by stagecoach. **4** the business of running stagecoaches.

stag·nan·cy (stag′nən sē) *n.* a stagnant condition.

stag·nant (stag′nənt) *adj.* **1** not running or flowing: *stagnant air, stagnant water.* **2** foul from standing still: *a stagnant pool of water.* **3** not active; sluggish; dull. [< L *stagnans, -antis,* ppr. of *stagnare.* See STAGNATE.] —**stag′nant·ly,** *adv.*

stag·nate (stag′nāt) *v.* **-nat·ed, -nat·ing. 1** be stagnant; become stagnant. **2** make stagnant. [< L *stagnare* < *stagnum* standing water]

stag·na·tion (stag nā′shən) *n.* a becoming or making stagnant; stagnant condition.

stag·y (stā′jē) *adj.* **stag·i·er, stag·i·est. 1** of or having to do with the stage. **2** suggestive of the stage; theatrical. **3** artificial; pompous; affected. —**stag′i·ly,** *adv.* —**stag′i·ness,** *n.*

staid (stād) *adj., v.* —*adj.* having a settled, quiet character; sober; sedate. —*v. Archaic.* a pt. and a pp. of **stay¹.** [originally pp. of *stay¹* in sense of "restrain"] —**staid′ly,** *adv.* —**staid′ness,** *n.*

stain (stān) *v., n.* —*n.* **1** a discoloration; soil; spot. **2** a natural spot or patch of color different from the ground. **3** a cause of reproach, infamy, or disgrace; a moral blemish; stigma: *a stain on one's character or reputation.* **4** a liquid dye used to color or darken wood, fabric, etc. **5** a dye or pigment used to make transparent or very small structures visible, or to differentiate tissue elements by coloring, for microscopic study.
—*v.* **1** discolor; spot: *The tablecloth is stained where food has been spilled.* **2** take, or receive, a stain; admit of staining. **3** bring reproach or disgrace on (a person's reputation, honor, etc.); blemish; soil. **4** corrupt morally; taint with guilt or vice; defile. **5** color: *to stain a microscopic specimen.* [earlier *distain* < OF *desteindre* take out the color, ult. < L *dis-* off + *tingere* dye] —**stain′a·ble,** *adj.* —**stain′er,** *n.*

stained glass 1 glass colored by metallic oxides, used in church windows, etc. **2** a window or windows made of many pieces of

hat, āge, fär; let, ēqual, tėrm; it, īce
hot, ōpen, ôrder; oil, out; cup, pùt, rüle,
əbove, takən, pencəl, lemən, circəs

ch, child; ng, long; sh, ship
th, thin; ᴛʜ, then; zh, measure

stained glass, usually painted to represent figures, scenes, etc. and joined together by grooved strips of lead.

stained–glass (stānd′glas′) *adj.* **1** of or having to do with stained glass: *stained-glass windows; a stained-glass designer.* **2** *Informal.* having or revealing a superficial or oversentimental attitude to religion; sanctimonious: *stained-glass piety.*

stain·less (stān′lis) *adj.* without stain; spotless. —**stain′less·ly,** *adv.* —**stain′less·ness,** *n.*

stainless steel steel containing chromium, nickel, or some other metal that makes it resistant to rust and corrosion.

stair (ster) *n.* **1** one of a series of steps for going from one level or floor to another. **2** Usually, **stairs,** *pl.* a set of such steps; stairway: *the top of the stairs.*
below stairs, a servant's quarters. **b** downstairs.
[OE *stæger*] —**stair′less,** *adj.*
☛ *Hom.* **stare.**

stair·case (ster′kās′) *n.* a flight of stairs with its framework; stairs.

stair·way (ster′wā′) *n.* a flight or flights of steps; stairs.

stair·well (ster′wel′) *n.* a vertical space or shaft containing a staircase.

stake (stāk) *n., v.* **staked, stak·ing.** —*n.* **1** a stick or post pointed at one end for driving into the ground. **2** Often, **stakes,** *pl.*
a something that is risked for gain or loss: *They played for high stakes.* **b** the prize in a race or contest: *The stakes were divided among three winners.* **3** an interest or share in something, especially a commercial undertaking. **4** *Informal.* grubstake.
at stake, to be won or lost; risked: *His honor is at stake.*
pull up stakes, *Informal.* move away: *After seven years of drought, they finally pulled up stakes and left the farm.*
—*v.* **1** fasten to a stake or with a stake. **2** mark with stakes; mark the boundaries of: *The miner staked his claim.* **3** risk (money or something valuable) on the result of a game or on any chance. **4** risk the loss of; hazard. **5** *Informal.* grubstake. **6** *Informal.* assist (a person) with money or other resources (to something): *I'll stake you to a dinner if you'll come.* **7** put or keep under police surveillance (*used with* out). [OE *staca*] —**stak′er,** *n.*
☛ *Hom.* **steak.**

stake driver a bittern (*Botaurus lentiginosus*), so called from its deep, hollow cry, suggesting the sound of a stake being pounded into mud.

stake·hold·er (stāk′hōl′dər) *n.* the person who takes care of what is bet and pays it to the winner.

stake–out (stāk′out′) *n. Informal.* surveillance by police of a building or area where criminal activity is expected or where a criminal suspect is believed to be.

stak·ey (stā′kē) *adj. Cdn. Slang.* with money available; having money to spend.

Sta·kha·no·vism (stə kä′nə viz′əm) *n.* in the Soviet Union, a system of rewarding individual enterprise (in factories, etc.) and thereby increasing output. It is a form of piecework. [< Aleksey G. *Stakhanov,* a coal miner whose record output in two shifts in 1935 was taken as a model for the system + *-ism*]

Sta·kha·no·vite (stə kä′nə vīt′) *n.* a worker who increases his output under Stakhanovism.

sta·lac·tite (stə lak′tīt *or* stal′ək tīt′) *n.* an icicle-shaped mass of calcium carbonate hanging from the roof of a limestone cave, formed by dripping water. Compare **stalagmite.** [< NL *stalactites* < Gk. *stalaktos* dripping < *stalassein* trickle]

sta·lag (stal′ag *or* stä′lag; *German,* shtä′läk′) *n.* a German camp for prisoners of war. [< G *Stalag* < *Sta(mm)lag(er)* base camp]

sta·lag·mite (stə lag′mīt *or* stal′əg mīt′) *n.* a cone-shaped mass of calcium carbonate formed on the floor of a limestone cave by water dripping from the roof. Compare **stalactite.** [< NL *stalagmites* < Gk. *stalagmos* a drop < *stalassein* trickle]

stale¹ (stāl) *adj.* **stal·er, stal·est;** *v.* **staled, stal·ing.** —*adj.* **1** not fresh: *stale bread.* **2** of a carbonated beverage, beer, etc., flat. **3** no longer new or interesting: *a stale joke.* **4** out of condition as a result of overtraining or excessive exertion over a period of time: *The horse has gone stale from too much running.* **5** temporarily lacking in vigor, nimbleness, etc., especially as a result of overactivity.
—*v.* **1** make stale. **2** become stale. [ME; origin uncertain; cf. MDu. *stel* stale] —**stale′ly,** *adv.* —**stale′ness,** *n.*

stale² (stāl) v. **staled, stal·ing;** n. —v. of horses and cattle, urinate. —n. the urine of horses and cattle. [origin uncertain; cf. OF *estaler*, Du. and MHG *stallen*]

stale·mate (stāl′māt′) n., v. **-mat·ed, -mat·ing.** —n. **1** Chess. the position of the pieces when no move can be made without putting the king in check. **2** any position in which no action can be taken; a complete standstill. —v. **1** put in a position in which no action can be taken; bring to a complete standstill. **2** chess, subject to a stalemate. [ME *stale* stalemate (probably < AF *estale* standstill < Gmc.) + *mate* < *checkmate*]

Sta·lin·ism (stal′ə niz′əm or stä′lə niz′əm) n. the theory or system of Communism practised under Joseph Stalin (1879-1953), chief minister of the Soviet Union from 1924 to 1953, especially as characterized by coercion and severe oppression of opposition.

Sta·lin·ist (stal′ə nist or stä′lə nist) n., adj. —n. a follower or believer in Stalinism. —adj. of, having to do with, or characteristic of Stalinism.

stalk¹ (stok or stôk) n. **1** the stem or main axis of a plant. **2** any slender, supporting or connected part of a plant. A flower or leaf blade may have a stalk. **3** any similar part of an animal. The eyes of a crayfish are on stalks. **4** any slender upright support. [ME *stalke*; ? dim. of OE *stalu* wooden upright, related to OE *stela* stalk, support]
☞ *Hom.* stock (stok).

stalk² (stok or stôk) v., n. —v. **1** approach or pursue without being seen or heard: *The hunters stalked the lion.* **2** spread silently and steadily: *Disease stalked through the land.* **3** walk proudly or haughtily. —n. **1** a haughty gait. **2** an act of stalking. [OE *-stealcian*, as in *bestealcian* steal along] —**stalk′er,** n.
☞ *Hom.* stock (stok).

stalk·ing–horse (stok′ing hôrs′ or stôk′ing-) n. **1** a horse or figure of a horse, behind which a hunter conceals himself in stalking game. **2** anything used to hide plans or acts; a pretext.

stall¹ (stol or stôl) n., v. —n. **1** a place in a stable for one animal. **2** a small place for selling things. At the public market different things are sold in different stalls under one big roof. **3** a seat in the choir of a church. **4** Brit. a seat in the front part of a theatre. **5** one of the sheaths for the fingers in a glove. **6** any of various other sheaths or receptacles. —v. **1** live in a stall, stable, kennel, etc. **2** put or keep in a stall. **3** stop or bring to a standstill, usually against one's wish: *He stalled the engine of his automobile.* **4** come to a stop because of too heavy a load or too little fuel. **5** stick fast in mud, snow, etc. **6** of an aircraft, lose so much speed that it cannot be controlled. [OE *steall*] —**stall′-like′,** adj.

stall² (stol or stôl) n., v. Informal. —n. a pretext to prevent action, the accomplishment of a purpose, etc. —v. **1** pretend; evade; deceive. **2** put off; delay: *You have been stalling long enough.* [< AF *estal* decoy < Gmc.; cf. OHG *stal* place, stall. Akin to STALL¹.]

stal·lion (stal′yən) n. an uncastrated male horse, especially one kept for breeding purposes. [ME < OF *estalon* < Gmc.]

stall shower a small boothlike enclosure in which one may take a shower bath.

stal·wart (stol′wərt or stôl′wərt) adj., n. —adj. **1** strongly built. **2** strong and brave. **3** firm; steadfast: *a stalwart friend.* —n. **1** a stalwart person. **2** a loyal supporter. [OE *stælwierthe* serviceable < *stathol* position + *wierthe* worthy] —**stal′wart·ly,** adv. —**stal′wart·ness,** n.

sta·men (stā′mən) n. the male reproductive organ of a flower, consisting of a threadlike stem called a filament and an anther. The anther of the stamen produces pollen grains that become sperm. See **flower** for picture. [< L *stamen* warp, thread]

stam·i·na (stam′ə nə) n. enduring strength or energy: *A long-distance runner needs stamina.* [< L *stamina* threads (of life, spun by the Fates)]

stam·i·nate (stam′ə nit or stam′ə nāt′) adj. Botany. **1** having stamens but no pistils. **2** having a stamen or stamens; producing stamens.

stam·mer (stam′ər) v., n. —v. **1** repeat the same sound in an effort to speak; hesitate in speaking: *She stammers whenever she is nervous.* **2** utter in this manner: *to stammer an excuse.* —n. a stammering; stuttering: *John has a nervous stammer.* [OE *stamerian*] —**stam′mer·er,** n. —**stam′mer·ing·ly,** adv.
☞ *Syn. v.* **1. Stammer, stutter** = speak in a stumbling or jerky way or by repeating the same sound. Although they are often used interchangeably, **stammer** usually suggests a plainly seen, painful effort to form and give voice to sounds and words, and speaking with breaks or silences in or between words, especially when extremely embarrassed or through fear or emotional disturbance. **Stutter** more often suggests a habit of repeating rapidly or jerkily the same sound, especially initial consonants such as (s), (p), etc.

stamp (stamp) v., n. —v. **1** bring down (one's foot) with force: *to stamp on a spider, to stamp one's foot in anger.* **2** fix firmly or deeply: *His words were stamped on my mind.* **3** pound; crush; trample; tread: *to stamp the snow from one's boots. She stamped out the fire.* **4** mark with an instrument that cuts, shapes, or impresses a design. **5** impress, mark, or cut out (a design, characters, words, etc.) on something, especially to indicate genuineness, quality, inspection, etc. **6** impress with an official stamp or mark: *to stamp a deed.* **7** show to be of a certain quality or character; indicate: *His speech stamps him as an educated man.* **8** put a stamp or stamps on.
stamp out, a put out by stamping. **b** put an end to by force. —n. **1 a** a small piece of paper with a gummed back, put on letters, papers, parcels, etc. to show that the required postage has been paid. **b** a similar piece of paper used for any of various purposes: *a trading stamp.* **2** the act of stamping. **3** a mark printed by a machine to show that postage has been, or will be, paid. **4** a heavy metal piece used to crush or pound rock, etc. **5** a mill or machine that crushes rock, etc. **6** an instrument that cuts, shapes, or impresses a design on (paper, wax, metal, etc.); a thing that puts a mark on. **7** the mark made with such an instrument. **8** an official mark certifying quality, genuineness, validity, etc. **9** an official mark or seal. **10** impression; marks: *Her face bore the stamp of suffering.* **11** kind; type: *Men of his stamp are rare.* [ME *stampe(n)*] —**stamp′er,** n.

stam·pede (stam pēd′) n., v. **-ped·ed, -ped·ing.** —n. **1** a sudden scattering or headlong flight of a frightened herd of cattle or horses. **2** any headlong flight of a large group: *a stampede of a panic-stricken crowd from a burning building.* **3** a general rush: *a stampede to newly discovered gold fields.* **4** Cdn. a rodeo, often accompanied by other amusements usually found at a fair: *the Calgary stampede.* —v. **1** scatter or flee in a stampede. **2** make a general rush. **3** cause to stampede. [< Mexican Sp. *estampida* (in Sp. *estampida* uproar) < *estampar* stamp, ult. < Gmc.] —**stam·ped′er,** n.

stamping ground or **grounds** a favorite or much-frequented place: *He was happy to return to his old stamping ground.*

stamp pad a pad soaked with ink for use with a rubber or metal stamp.

stance (stans) n. **1** Golf, etc. the position of the feet of a player when making a stroke. **2** manner of standing; posture: *an erect stance.* **3** Scottish. **a** a standing place, station, or postion. **b** a site. [< OF *estance*, ult. < L *stare* stand]

stanch¹ (stonch) See **staunch¹.** —**stanch′er,** n.

stanch² (stonch) See **staunch².** —**stanch′ly,** adv. —**stanch′ness,** n.

stan·chion (stan′shən) n., v. —n. **1** an upright bar, post, or rod used as a support. **2** a device for loosely restraining cattle in a stall, consisting of a pair of upright metal bars set into a supporting framework, that are fastened about the animal's neck. —v. **1** provide, strengthen, or support with a stanchion or stanchions. **2** confine (a cow) by a stanchion. [< OF *estanchon*, ult. < L *stare* stand]

stand (stand) v. **stood, stand·ing;** n. —v. **1** be upright on one's feet: *Don't stand if you are tired, but sit down.* **2** have a specified height when upright: *He stands 180 centimetres in his socks.* **3** rise to one's feet: *He stood when she entered the room.* **4** be set upright; be placed; be located: *The box stands over there.* **5** set upright or in an indicated position, condition, etc.: *Stand the box here.* **6** be in a certain place, rank, scale, etc.: *He stood first in his class for service to the school.* **7** take or keep a certain position: *"Stand back!" called the policeman to the crowd.* **8** take a way of thinking or acting: *to stand for fair play, stand on one's rights.* **9** be in a special condition: *He stands innocent of any wrong. The poor man stands in need of food and clothing.* **10** be unchanged; hold good; remain the same: *The rule against lateness will stand.* **11** stay in place; last: *The old house has stood for a hundred years.* **12** gather and stay: *Tears stood in her eyes.* **13** bear; endure: *Those plants cannot stand cold; they die in winter.* **14** be submitted to (a trial, test, ordeal, etc.); undergo: *Stand a rigid examination.* **15** withstand: *cloth that will stand wear.* **16** Informal. bear the expense of: *to stand treat.* **17** hold a specified course: *The ship stood out to sea.* **18** of a dog, point. **19** stop moving; halt: *"Stand!" cried the sentry.* **20** become or remain still or motionless; not move or be operated: *The pumps were allowed to stand.* **21** of plants, grow erect: *corn standing in the fields.* **22** of an account, score, etc., show a (specified) position of the parties concerned: *The score stands in his favor.*
stand a chance, have a chance.
stand behind, support; vouch for; guarantee.
stand by, a be near. **b** side with; help; support: *to stand by a friend.* **c** keep; maintain. **d** be or get ready for use, action, etc.: *The radio operator was ordered to stand by.*
stand down, step off or retire for a time from a place or post.
stand easy, stand completely at ease.
stand for, a represent; mean. **b** be on the side of; take the part of;

uphold: *Our school stands for fair play.* **c** be a candidate for; run for; make oneself available for election: *to stand for parliament.* **d** *Informal.* put up with: *The teacher said she would not stand for talking during class.* **e** sail or steer toward.
stand in, *Informal.* **a** be associated or friendly; be on good terms. **b** serve as a substitute for somebody.
stand off, a *Informal.* keep off; keep away. **b** hold oneself aloof, especially from an offer or appeal, friendship, etc. **c** in nautical use, take a position or course away from.
stand on, a be based on; depend on. **b** demand; assert; claim.
stand out, a project: *His ears stood out.* **b** be noticeable or prominent: *Certain facts stand out.* **c** refuse to yield: *to stand out against popular opinion.* **d** refuse to come in or join others. **e** endure to the end: *to stand out the war.*
stand over, be left for later consideration, treatment, or settlement.
stand to, serve at one's post.
stand up, a get to one's feet; rise: *He stood up and began to speak.* **b** endure; last: *That fabric won't stand up under hard wear.* **c** *Informal.* break a date with; fail to meet: *He has never forgiven her for standing him up.*
stand up for, take the part of; defend; support: *to stand up for a friend.*
stand up to, meet or face boldly: *The young boy stood up to the bully.*
stand up with, *Informal.* act as best man, bridesmaid, etc. to.
—*n.* **1** the act of standing. **2** a halt; stop. **3** a stop for defence, resistance, etc.: *We made a last stand against the enemy.* **4** a halt on a theatrical tour to give a performance: *a one-night stand.* **5** a town where such a halt is made. **6** a place where a person stands; position. **7** a raised place where people can sit or stand. **8** a moral position with regard to other persons, a question, etc.: *to take a new political stand.* **9** a station for a row of vehicles available for hire: *a stand for taxis.* **10** the place where a witness stands or sits to testify in court. **11** something to put things on or in: *Leave your wet umbrella in the stand in the hall.* **12** a stall, booth, table, etc., for a small business: *a newspaper stand.* **13** a standing growth of plants, such as trees or a crop: *a fine stand of timber, a stand of wheat.* [OE *standan*]
☞ *Syn. v.* **13.** See note at **bear.**

stand·ard (stan'dərd) *n., adj.* —*n.* **1** anything taken as a basis of comparison; model: *Your work is not up to standard.* **2** a rule, test, or requirement. **3** an authorized weight or measure. **4** a commodity serving as a basis of value in a monetary system: *the gold standard.* **5** the legally prescribed proportion of metal and alloy to be used in coins. **6** the lowest level or grade of excellence of produce, a product, etc. **7** a flag, emblem, or support: *The dragon was the standard of China.* **8** an upright support: *The floor lamp has a long standard.* **9** a tree or shrub with one tall, straight stem. —*adj.* **1** of the accepted or normal size, amount, power, quality, etc.: *the standard rate of pay, a standard gauge.* **2** used as a standard; according to rule. **3** having recognized excellence or authority: *Scott and Dickens are standard authors.* **4** of a usable or serviceable grade or quality; not of good or fine quality: *standard quality sheets.* **5** designating or characterized by the vocabulary, pronunciation, syntax, etc. accepted by the majority of educated native speakers as appropriate for almost any situation. Standard English includes both formal and informal levels, but not slang. Standard Canadian English differs somewhat from standard American or British English. [ME < OF *estandart* < Gmc.]
☞ *Syn. n.* **1. Standard, criterion** = something used to measure or judge a person or thing. **Standard** applies to a rule, principle, ideal, pattern, or measure generally accepted for use as a basis of comparison in determining the quality, value, quantity, social or moral or intellectual level, etc. of something: *That school has high standards of teaching.* **Criterion,** formal, means a standard used as a test in judging the true nature, goodness, or worth of a person, thing, or accomplishment: *Popularity is not everybody's criterion of a good motion picture.*
☞ *Usage.* **Standard English** is the kind of English that educated people use in public and accept as appropriate for almost any situation. It includes **formal** and **informal** levels of language, but not **slang.** See also the note at **informal.**

standard atmosphere a unit for measuring atmospheric pressure, equal to the mean pressure at sea level at a temperature of 15°C. One standard atmosphere is about 101.3 kPa. *Symbol:* atm

stand·ard-bear·er (stan'dərd ber'ər) *n.* **1** an officer or soldier who carries a flag or standard. **2** a person who carries a banner in a procession. **3** a conspicuous leader of a movement, political party, etc.

stand·ard–bred (stan'dərd bred') *adj., n.* —*adj.* **1** of horses, poultry, etc., bred to meet set standards of excellence for a breed, species, etc. **2** of a horse, bred for drawing light vehicles or for use in harness races. —*n.* a breed of horses noted as trotters and pacers and much used in harness racing.

stand·ard·i·za·tion (stan'dər də zā'shən *or* stan'dər dī zā'shən) *n.* standardizing or being standardized.

stand·ard·ize (stan'dər dīz') *v.* **-ized, -iz·ing. 1** make standard in size, shape, weight, quality, strength, etc: *Many of the parts of an automobile engine are standardized to fit a number of different makes.* **2** regulate by a standard. **3** test by a standard.

hat, āge, fär; let, ēqual, tèrm; it, īce
hot, ōpen, ôrder; oil, out; cup, pút, rüle,
əbove, takən, pencəl, lemən, circəs

ch, child; ng, long; sh, ship
th, thin; ᴛʜ, then; zh, measure

standard of living the way of living that a person or community considers necessary to provide enough material things for comfort, happiness, etc.

standard time the time officially adopted for a region or country, based on the distance from Greenwich, England. The world is divided into 24 standard time zones.

stand–by (stand'bī') *n., pl.* **-bys. 1** a person or thing that can be relied upon; chief support; ready resource. **2** a ship kept in readiness for emergencies. **3** an order or signal for a boat to stand by. **4** any person or thing held in reserve. **5** a person waiting to board an aircraft, bus, etc. if space becomes available.

stand·ee (stan dē') *n.* a person who has to stand in a theatre, bus, etc. for lack of seats.

stand–in (stand'in') *n.* **1** a person whose work is occupying the place of an actor or actress while the lights, cameras, etc. are being arranged. **2** a person or thing that takes the place of another; substitute: *He acted as a stand-in for his boss at the meeting.*

stand·ing (stan'ding) *n., adj.* —*n.* **1** position; reputation: *men of good standing.* **2** length of service, experience, residence, etc., especially as determining position, wages, etc. **3** duration: *a feud of long standing between two families.* **4** the act of standing; place of standing.
—*adj.* **1** straight up; erect: *a standing position, standing timber.* **2** done from an erect position: *a standing jump, a standing ovation.* **3** permanent, fixed, or long-term; always operative or ready: *a standing invitation, a standing army, a standing order.* **4** not flowing; stagnant: *standing water.*

standing room 1 space to stand in. **2** space to stand in after all the seats are taken.

stand–off (stand'of') *n., adj.* —*n.* **1** a standing off or apart; reserve; aloofness. **2** a tie or draw in a game. —*adj.* standing off or apart; reserved; aloof.

stand–off·ish (stand'of'ish) *adj.* reserved; aloof.

stand–out (stand'out') *n. Informal.* a thing or person that is outstanding in appearance or performance.

stand·pat (stand'pat') *adj. Informal.* standing firm for things as they are; opposing any change.

stand·pat·ter (stand'pat'ər) *n. Informal.* a person who stands firm for things as they are and opposes any change, especially in politics.

stand·pipe (stand'pīp') *n.* a large vertical pipe or tower to hold water.

stand·point (stand'point') *n.* a point of view; mental attitude.

stand·still (stand'stil') *n.* a complete stop; halt; pause.

stand–up (stand'up') *adj.* **1** having an erect or upright position: *a stand-up collar.* **2** done or taken in a standing position: *a stand-up lunch.* **3** made for or to allow a standing position: *a stand-up lunch counter.* **4** of or designating a comedian who performs alone, standing and talking to the audience.

stan·hope (stan'hōp *or* stan'əp) *n.* a kind of light, open, one-seated, horse-drawn carriage with two or four wheels. [after Fitzroy *Stanhope* (1787-1864), a British clergyman]

stank (stangk) *v.* pt. of **stink.**

Stanley Cup 1 the cup presented annually to the winning team in a special end-of-season competition between National Hockey League clubs. **2** the competition, or playoffs, for this trophy. [< Sir Frederick Arthur *Stanley,* 16th Earl of Derby (1841-1908), Governor General of Canada, 1888-93]

stan·nate (stan'āt) *n.* a salt of stannic acid.

stan·nic (stan'ik) *adj.* **1** of or having to do with tin. **2** containing tin with a valence of four. [< LL *stannum* tin]

stan·nous (stan'əs) *adj.* **1** of or having to do with tin. **2** containing tin with a valence of two.

stannous chloride a crystalline compound of tin dissolved with hydrochloric acid, used to silver mirrors and to galvanize tin, as a reducing agent for some chemicals, etc. *Formula:* $SnCl_2$

St. Anthony's fire (an'thə nēz *or* an'tə nēz) any of various inflammations of the skin, such as erysipelas.

stan·za (stan'zə) *n.* **1** a group of lines of poetry, commonly four or more, arranged according to a fixed plan. **2** *Sports.* any period of time in, or division of, a game, as an inning in baseball or a quarter

in football. [< Ital. *stanza*, originally stopping place, ult. < L *stare* stand]

stan·za·ic (stan zā′ik) *adj.* of, having to do with, or designating verse composed in stanzas.

sta·pes (stā′pēz) *n.* the stirrup bone, the innermost of the three small bones in the middle ear. See **ear** for picture. [< Med.L *stapes* stirrup]

staph (staf) *n. Informal.* staphylococcus or staphylococci.

staph·y·lo·coc·cal (staf′ə lə kok′əl) *adj.* 1 of or having to do with staphylococcus. 2 caused by staphylococcus.

staph·y·lo·coc·cus (staf′ə lə kok′əs) *n., pl.* -coc·ci (-kok′ī or -kok′sī). any of a genus (*Staphylococcus*) of round or oval, gram-positive bacteria, occurring in irregular clusters and also singly or in pairs, and including many species that are pathogenic. [< NL *Staphylococcus*, the genus name < Gk. *staphylē* bunch of grapes + *kokkos* grain]

sta·ple¹ (stā′pəl) *n., v.* -pled, -pling. —*n.* 1 a U-shaped piece of metal with pointed ends. Staples are driven into doors, wood, etc. to hold hooks, pins, or bolts. 2 a similar device for fastening papers, etc., together, being a small piece of thin wire in the form of a square, short-armed U, the ends of which are driven through the layers of material and clinched on the other side. —*v.* fasten with a staple or staples. [OE *stapol* post]

sta·ple² (stā′pəl) *n., adj., v.* -pled, -pling. —*n.* 1 the most important or principal article grown or manufactured in a place: *Wheat is the staple in Saskatchewan.* 2 any major article of trade. 3 a chief element or material. 4 a raw material. 5 a fibre of cotton, wool, etc. 6 a short fibre that must be spun to form a yarn. 7 *Archaic.* the principal market of a place; the chief centre of trade. —*adj.* 1 most important; principal: *The weather is a staple subject of conversation.* 2 established in commerce: *a staple trade.* 3 regularly produced in large quantities for the market. —*v.* sort according to fibre: *staple wool.* [ME < OF *estaple* mart < Gmc.]

sta·pler¹ (stā′plər) *n.* a machine for driving wire staples into papers, cardboard, etc. [< *staple¹*]

sta·pler² (stā′plər) *n.* a person who sorts and grades fibres of wool, cotton, etc. [< *staple²*]

star (stär) *n., v.* starred, star·ring; *adj.* —*n.* 1 any of the heavenly bodies, especially one that is not the moon, a planet, a comet, or a meteor, appearing as bright points in the sky at night. 2 *Astrology.* a planet or constellation of the zodiac, considered as influencing people and events. 3 a conventional plane figure having five points, or sometimes six, like these: ☆ ✩ 4 something having or suggesting this shape, used as a mark of excellence, designation of rank, badge of honor, etc. 5 an asterisk (*). 6 a person of brilliant qualities: *an athletic star.* 7 a famous person in some art, profession, etc., especially one who plays the lead in a performance: *a motion-picture star.* 8 *(adj.)* chief; best; leading; excellent: *the star player on a football team.* 9 fate; fortune.
see stars, *Informal.* see flashes of light as a result of a hard blow on the head.
thank (one's) (lucky) stars, be thankful for one's good luck.
—*v.* 1 mark or ornament with stars: *Nan's card was starred for perfect attendance.* 2 mark with an asterisk. 3 single out for special notice or recommendation. 4 be prominent; be a leading performer; excel: *She has starred in many motion pictures.* 5 present as a star. [OE *steorra*]

star·board (stär′bərd *or* -bôrd′) *n., adj., v.* —*n.* the right side of a ship or aircraft, facing forward. See **aft** for picture. —*adj.* on the right side of a ship or aircraft. —*v.* turn (the helm) to the right. [OE *stēorbord* the side from which a vessel was steered < *stēor* steering paddle + *bord* side (of a ship)]

starch (stärch) *n., v.* —*n.* 1 a white, tasteless, odorless, carbohydrate found in many vegetables, including potatoes, and cereal crops, such as wheat, rice, and corn. 2 a preparation of this substance used to stiffen clothes, curtains, etc. 3 a similar preparation produced artificially. 4 **starches,** *pl.* foods containing much starch. 5 a stiff, formal manner; stiffness. 6 *Informal.* vigor; energy.
take the starch out of, *Informal.* cause to lose courage, confidence, or determination.
—*v.* stiffen (clothes, curtains, etc.) with starch. [OE *stercan* make rigid (in *stercedferhth* stouthearted) < *stearc* stiff, strong]

Star Chamber or **star chamber** 1 *Historical.* in England, an arbitrary, secret court that existed by statute and became notorious for its harsh methods of trial. It was established in 1487 and abolished in 1641. 2 any similar court, committee, or group.

starch·y (stär′chē) *adj.* **starch·i·er, starch·i·est.** 1 like starch;

containing starch. 2 stiffened with starch. 3 stiff in manner; formal. —**starch′i·ness,** *n.*

star–crossed (stär′krost′) *adj.* ill-fated; doomed to failure and unhappiness: *star-crossed lovers.*

star·dom (stär′dəm) *n.* 1 the condition or fact of being a star actor or performer. 2 star actors or performers as a group.

star dust 1 masses of stars that look so small as to suggest particles of dust. 2 particles of matter falling from space to the earth. 3 *Informal.* glamour; happy enchantment.

stare (ster) *v.* stared, star·ing; *n.* —*v.* 1 look long and directly with the eyes wide open. A person stares in wonder, surprise, stupidity, curiosity, or from mere rudeness. 2 bring to a named condition by staring: *stare someone into confusion.* 3 gaze at. 4 be very striking or glaring: *His eyes stared with anger.*
stare down or **stare out of countenance,** confuse or embarrass by staring.
stare (someone) in the face, a be very evident; force itself on the notice of: *His spelling mistake was staring him in the face.* **b** very likely or certain to happen soon.
stare (someone) up and down, gaze at or survey from head to foot.
—*n.* a long and direct look with the eyes wide open. [OE *starian*]
—**star′er,** *n.*
☛ *Hom.* **stair.**
☛ *Syn. v.* 1. See note at **gaze.**

star·fish (stär′fish′) *n., pl.* -fish *or* -fish·es. any of a class (Asteroidea) of marine invertebrate animals having a flattened, fleshy, spiny body with five or more arms radiating from a central disk.

star·flow·er (stär′flou′ər) *n.* 1 any of several low-growing perennial plants (genus *Trientalis*) of the primrose family having a whorl of leaves at the top of the stem and small, white, star-shaped flowers. 2 star-of-Bethlehem.

star·gaze (stär′gāz′) *v.* -gazed, -gaz·ing. 1 gaze at the stars. 2 be absent-minded; daydream. —**star′gaz′er,** *n.*

star·ing (ster′ing) *adj.* 1 very conspicuous; too bright; glaring. 2 gazing with a stare; wide-open.

stark (stärk) *adj., adv.* —*adj.* 1 downright; complete: *That fool is talking stark nonsense.* 2 stiff: *The dog lay stark in death.* 3 bare; barren; desolate: *a stark landscape.* 4 harsh; stern. 5 *Archaic.* strong; sturdy.
—*adv.* 1 entirely; completely. 2 in a stark manner. [OE *stearc* stiff, strong] —**stark′ly,** *adv.*

stark·ers (stär′kərz) *adj. Esp.Brit. Slang.* stark-naked (*used only after the noun modified*).

stark–naked (stärk′nā′kəd) *adj.* completely naked.

star·less (stär′lis) *adj.* without stars; without starlight.

star·let (stär′lit) *n.* 1 a young actress or singer who is being trained for leading roles in motion pictures or television. 2 a little star.

star·light (stär′līt′) *n., adj.* —*n.* light from the stars. —*adj.* lighted by the stars.

star·like (stär′līk′) *adj.* 1 shaped like a star. 2 shining like a star.

star·ling (stär′ling) *n.* any of a family (Sturnidae) of Old World songbirds, especially a common dark-brown or glossy-black, short-tailed bird (*Sturnus vulgaris*) that is native to Europe but has become naturalized in North America, Australia, and New Zealand, and is often considered a pest. [OE *stærling*]

star·lit (stär′lit′) *adj.* lighted by the stars: *a starlit night.*

star–of–Beth·le·hem (stär′əv beth′lē əm *or* -beth′lə hem′) *n.* any of several bulbous herbs (genus *Ornithogalum*) of the lily family, especially (*O. umbellatum*), having narrow leaves and clusters of white, star-shaped flowers.

Star of Bethlehem in Christian use, the star that heralded Christ's birth.

Star of Courage *Cdn.* a decoration awarded for an act of outstanding courage involving personal risk. It is one of a series of three Canadian bravery decorations, the other two being the Cross of Valour (the highest award) and the Medal of Bravery. *Abbrev.:* SC

Star of David a six-pointed star or hexagram formed by two superimposed, often interlaced, equilateral triangles. It is an ancient decorative motif and mystical symbol and it also figured as a Christian symbol in the Middle Ages. From about the 17th century it became a symbol of Judaism and is featured on the flag of Israel. Also called **Magen David.** Compare **Solomon's seal.**

starred (stärd) *adj.* 1 decorated with stars. 2 marked with a star or stars. 3 presented as a star actor or performer. 4 influenced by the stars or by fate.

star·ry (stär′ē) *adj.* -ri·er, -ri·est. 1 lighted by stars; containing many stars: *a starry sky.* 2 shining like stars: *starry eyes.* 3 like a star in shape. 4 of or having to do with stars. —**star′ri·ly,** *adv.* —**star′ri·ness,** *n.*

star·ry–eyed (stär′ē īd′) *adj.* tending to be too optimistic or idealistic; romantically naïve.

Stars and Stripes the flag of the United States.

star sapphire 1 a sapphire which reflects light in the shape of a brilliant star as a result of its crystalline structure. 2 a gem made from such a stone.

star–stud·ded (stär′stud′əd) *adj.* filled or covered with stars: *a star-studded sky. They are planning a new production of the play, with a star-studded cast.*

start (stärt) *v., n.* —*v.* 1 get in motion; set out; begin a journey: *The train started on time.* 2 begin: *to start a book.* 3 set moving, going, acting, etc.; cause to set out; cause to begin: *to start an automobile, to start a fire.* 4 give a sudden, involuntary jerk or twitch; move suddenly: *He started in surprise.* 5 come, rise, or spring out suddenly: *Tears started from her eyes.* 6 burst or stick out: *eyes seeming to start from their sockets.* 7 rouse: *to start a rabbit.* 8 become loose. 9 cause to become loose: *to start a run in a stocking.*

start in or **start out,** begin to do something.

start up, a rise suddenly; spring up. b come suddenly into being or notice. c cause (an engine) to begin operating. d begin to do something.

—*n.* 1 the beginning of a movement, action, process of development or construction, etc.: *to make an early start. We were all there at the start. There has been a decrease in housing starts.* 2 a setting in motion; signal to start. 3 a sudden movement; jerk. 4 a surprise; fright. 5 a beginning ahead of others; advantage: *He got the start of his rivals.* 6 a chance of starting a career, etc.: *His father gave him a start.* 7 a spurt of activity: *to work by fits and starts.* 8 the place, line, etc. where a race begins. [var. of OE *styrtan* leap up]

☛ *Syn. v.* 2, 3. See note at **begin.**

start·er (stär′tər) *n.* 1 a person or thing that starts. 2 a person who gives the signal for starting. 3 an electric motor used to start an internal-combustion engine; self-starter. 4 a special kind of food for baby chicks and animals. 5 the first in a series of things. 6 a chemical agent or bacterial culture used to start a reaction, especially in the formation of acid in making cheese, vinegar, etc.

for starters, *Slang.* first of all; to begin with.

starting point a place of starting; beginning.

star·tle (stär′təl) *v.* -**tled, -tling;** *n.* —*v.* 1 frighten suddenly; surprise. 2 move suddenly in fear or surprise. —*n.* a sudden shock of surprise or fright. [OE *steartlian* struggle]

star·tling (stär′tling) *adj.* surprising; frightening. —**star′tling·ly,** *adv.*

star·va·tion (stär vā′shən) *n.* 1 starving. 2 the condition of suffering from extreme hunger; being starved.

starve (stärv) *v.* **starved, starv·ing.** 1 die because of hunger. 2 suffer severely because of hunger. 3 weaken or kill with hunger. 4 force or subdue by lack of food: *They starved the enemy into surrendering.* 5 *Informal.* feel hungry. 6 have a strong desire or craving. 7 weaken or destroy by lack of something needed.

starve down or **out,** force or subdue from lack of food.

starve for, suffer from lack of: *to starve for news. That child is starving for affection.* [OE *steorfan* die]

starve·ling (stärv′ling) *adj., n.* —*adj.* starving; hungry. —*n.* a person or animal that is suffering from lack of food.

stash (stash) *v., n. Slang.* —*v.* hide or put away for safe-keeping or future use. —*n.* 1 a place where something is hidden away or stored. 2 something hidden away or stored: *a small stash of money.* [origin uncertain]

sta·sis (stā′sis *or* stas′is) *n., pl.* -**ses** (-sēz) 1 a slowing or stopping of the normal flow of circulating blood or other fluid in the body. 2 a state of balance or motionlessness. [< NL *stasis* < Gk. *stasis* a standing < *sta-*, a root of *histanai* stand]

stat. 1 statute. 2 statuary; statue.

stat·a·ble (stā′tə bəl) *adj.* that can be stated.

state (stāt) *n., v.* **stat·ed, stat·ing.** —*n.* 1 the condition of a person or thing: *He is in a state of poor health. Ice is water in a solid state.* 2 a particular condition of mind or feeling: *a state of uncertainty, a state of excitement.* 3 a person's position in life; rank: *humble state.* 4 ceremonious and luxurious style; pomp and dignity: *living in state.* 5 (*adj.*) of or for very formal and ceremonious occasions: *state robes.* 6 nation. 7 Also, **State,** one of several organized political groups of people that together form a nation: *The State of Alaska is one of the United States.* 8 the territory of a state. 9 the civil government; the highest civil authority: *affairs of state.* 10 (*adj.*) of or having to do with civil government or authority: *state control.*

in or **into a state,** *Informal.* in or into a very agitated or excited condition.

lie in state, of the body of a monarch, political leader, etc., lie in an open coffin for public view before burial.

starry-eyed   1097   station

hat, āge, fär; let, ēqual, tèrm; it, īce
hot, ōpen, ôrder; oil, out; cup, put, rüle,
əbove, takən, pencəl, lemən, circəs

ch, child; ng, long; sh, ship
th, thin; ᴛʜ, then; zh, measure

—*v.* 1 tell in speech or writing; express; say: *to state one's views.* 2 settle; fix. [< L *status* condition, position < *stare* stand; common in L phrase *status rei publicae* condition of the republic. Doublet of ESTATE.]

☛ *Syn. n.* 1. **State, condition** = the form or way in which something exists, especially as affected by circumstances. **State** is the general word, sometimes used in a very general way without reference to anything concrete, more often referring to the circumstances in which a person or thing exists or to his (its) nature or form at a certain time: *The state of the world today should interest every serious person.* **Condition** applies to a particular state thought of especially as produced by circumstances or other causes: *The condition of the patient is critical.*

state·craft (stāt′kraft′) *n.* 1 statesmanship. 2 crafty statesmanship.

stat·ed (stā′tid) *adj.* 1 said; told. 2 fixed; settled.

state·hood (stāt′hud) *n.* the condition of being a state.

state·house (stāt′hous′) *n. U.S.* the building in which the legislature of a state meets; the capitol of a state.

state·less (stāt′lis) *adj.* 1 without nationality; without citizenship in any country. 2 without states or boundaries: *a stateless world.*

state·ly (stāt′lē) *adj.* -**li·er, -li·est.** dignified; imposing; grand; majestic. —**stat′li·ness,** *n.*

☛ *Syn.* See note at **grand.**

state·ment (stāt′mənt) *n.* 1 the act of stating; the manner of stating something. 2 something stated; report. 3 a summary of an account, showing the amount owed or due. 4 a sentence that states something or makes an assertion; declarative sentence.

state·room (stāt′rüm′ *or* -rum′) *n.* a private room on a ship or, formerly, on a railway train.

state's evidence *U.S.* 1 evidence brought forward by the government in a criminal case. 2 testimony given in court by a criminal against his associates in a crime.

turn state's evidence, testify in court against one's associates in a crime. Compare **Queen's evidence.**

States–Gen·er·al (stāts′jen′ər əl *or* -jen′rəl) *n.* 1 in France, the legislative body before 1789, consisting of representatives of the three estates, the clergy, the nobility, and the middle class; Estates-General. 2 in the Netherlands, the lawmaking body made up of two houses.

State·side or **state·side** (stāt′sīd′) *adj. or adv. Informal.* in, into, to, toward, or of the United States, especially the continental U.S.

states·man (stāts′mən) *n., pl.* -**men.** a person skilled in the management of public or national affairs.

☛ *Syn.* See note at **politician.**

states·man·like (stāts′mən līk′) *adj.* having the qualities of a statesman.

states·man·ly (stāts′mən lē) *adj.* like, worthy of, or befitting a statesman.

states·man·ship (stāts′mən ship′) *n.* the qualities of a statesman; skill in the management or ownership of public or national affairs.

state socialism a form of socialism in which government control, management, or ownership is used to improve social conditions.

states·wom·an (stāts′wùm′ən) *n., pl.* -**wom·en.** a woman skilled in the management of public or national affairs.

stat·ic (stat′ik) *adj., n.* —*adj.* 1 at rest; standing still: *Civilization does not remain static, but changes constantly.* 2 having to do with bodies at rest or with forces that balance each other. 3 acting by weight without producing motion: *static pressure.* 4 *Electricity.* having to do with stationary charges that balance each other. Static electricity can be produced by rubbing a glass rod with a silk cloth. 5 of or having to do with atmospheric electricity that interferes with radio reception.

—*n.* 1 atmospheric electricity. 2 interference, especially with radio signals, due to such electricity. [< Gk. *statikos* causing to stand, ult. < *stēnai* stand] —**stat′i·cal·ly,** *adv.*

stat·ics (stat′iks) *n.* the branch of mechanics that deals with the study of bodies at rest and the action of forces that balance each other to produce equilibrium.

sta·tion (stā′shən) *n., v.* —*n.* 1 a place to stand in; a place that a person, army unit, or naval fleet is appointed to occupy in the

performance of some duty; an assigned post: *The policeman took his station at the corner.* **2** a building or place used for a definite purpose: *a police station.* **3** the place or equipment for sending out or receiving programs, messages, etc. by radio or television. **4** a regular stopping place: *a railway station.* **5** a military camp or establishment. **6** social position; rank. **7** *Australian.* a ranch or large farm.
—*v.* **1** give a position or place to; place: *He stationed himself just outside the hotel.* **2** post or assign to a military camp or establishment. [< L *statio, -onis* < *stare* stand]

station agent a person in charge of a railway station.

sta·tion·ar·y (stā′shən er′ē) *adj.* **1** having a fixed station or place; not movable: *A factory engine is stationary.* **2** standing still; not moving. **3** not changing in size, number, activity, etc.: *The population of this town has been stationary for ten years at about 5000 people.* [< L *stationarius* < *statio.* See STATION.]
☛ *Hom.* **stationery.**
☛ *Usage.* Do not confuse **stationary** and **stationery. Stationary**, with an **a** in the second last syllable, is an adjective. **Stationery**, including 'writing material', is a noun.

sta·tion·er (stā′shən ər) *n.* a person who sells paper, pens, pencils, inks, etc. [< Med.L *stationarius* shopkeeper, originally, stationary, as distinct from a roving peddler]

sta·tion·er·y (stā′shən er′ē) *n.* material for writing; paper, cards, and envelopes.
☛ *Hom.* **stationary.**
☛ *Usage.* See note at **stationary.**

station house a building used as a station, especially a police station.

sta·tion·mas·ter (stā′shən mas′tər) *n.* the person in charge of a railway station.

Stations of the Cross *Roman Catholic Church.* **1** fourteen scenes from the Passion of Christ, usually painted or sculpted and ranged round the walls of a church. **2** the prayers, devotions, etc. performed in sequence at these stations.

station wagon a closed automobile that can serve both as a passenger car and as a light truck.

stat·ism (stāt′iz əm) *n.* **1** a highly centralized governmental control of the economy, information media, etc. of a state or nation. **2** advocacy of the sovereignty of a state, especially of a state of a republic.

stat·ist (stāt′ist) *n.* **1** statistician. **2** one advocating statism.

sta·tis·tic (stə tis′tik) *adj., n.* —*adj.* statistical. —*n.* an item, element, etc. in a set of statistics.

sta·tis·ti·cal (stə tis′tə kəl) *adj.* of or having to do with statistics; consisting of or based on statistics.

sta·tis·ti·cal·ly (stə tis′tik lē) *adv.* in a statistical manner; according to statistics.

stat·is·ti·cian (stat′is tish′ən) *n.* a person trained in the science of statistics, especially one whose work it is.

sta·tis·tics (stə tis′tiks) *n.pl.* **1** numerical facts about people, the weather, business conditions, etc. Statistics are collected and classified systematically. **2** the science of collecting and classifying such facts in order to show their significance (*used with a singular verb*). [ult. < G < NL *statisticus* political, ult. < L *status* state. See STATE.]

sta·tor (stā′tər) *n.* a stationary unit that encloses rotating parts of a turbine, electric generator or motor, etc. [< NL < L *stator* sustainer < *sistere* cause to stand < *stare* to stand]

stat·o·scope (stat′ə skōp′) *n.* **1** a form of aneroid barometer for registering very small variations of atmospheric pressure. **2** an instrument for detecting a small rise or fall of an aircraft. [< Gk. *statos* standing still + E -*scope*]

stat·u·ar·y (stach′ü er′ē) *n., pl.* **-ar·ies;** *adj.* —*n.* **1** statues collectively. **2** the art of making statues. **3** sculptor.
—*adj.* of or for statues: *statuary marble.*

stat·ue (stach′ü) *n.* an image of a person or animal carved in stone, wood, etc., cast in bronze or modelled. [< F < L *statua,* ult. < *stare* stand]

stat·u·esque (stach′ü esk′) *adj.* like a statue in dignity, formal grace, or classic beauty.

stat·u·ette (stach′ü et′) *n.* a small statue. [< F *statuette,* dim. of *statue* statue]

stat·ure (stach′ər) *n.* **1** height: *A man 185 centimetres tall is above average stature.* **2** development; physical, mental, or moral growth. **3** reputation or distinction: *He is a man of great stature in his line of business.* [ME < OF < L *statura* < *stare* stand]

sta·tus (stā′təs *or* stat′əs) *n.* **1** condition; state: *Diplomats are interested in the status of world affairs.* **2** one's social or

professional standing; position; rank: *his status as a doctor.* **3** legal position. [< L *status* < *stare* stand]

status quo (kwō) **1** the way things are; the existing state of affairs. **2** status quo ante. [< L *status quo* the state in which]

status quo an·te (an′tē) *Latin.* the way in which (things were) previously.

status symbol a material possession, such as a car or boat, ownership of which is supposed to indicate a certain social rank or status.

stat·u·ta·ble (stach′ə tə bəl) *adj.* statutory. —**stat′u·ta·bly,** *adv.*

stat·ute (stach′üt) *n.* **1** a law enacted by a legislative body. **2** a law; decree; a formally established rule. **3** *International Law.* an instrument annexed or subsidiary to an international agreement, especially a treaty. [< OF *estatut,* ult. < L *statuere* establish, ult. < *stare* stand]
☛ *Syn.* **1.** See note at **law.**

statute book a collection or record of statutes.

statute law written law; law expressed or stated by statutes.

statute mile a unit for measuring distance on land, equal to 5280 feet (about 1.61 km).

statute of limitations *Law.* any statute that specifies a certain period of time after which legal action cannot be brought or offences punished.

Statute of Westminster an act of the British Parliament, passed in 1931, by which Canada and other dominions were granted the authority to make their own laws.

stat·u·to·ry (stach′ə tô′rē) *adj.* **1** having to do with a statute. **2** fixed by statute. **3** punishable by statute. —**stat′u·to·ri·ly,** *adv.*

staunch¹ (stonch *or* stônch) *v.* **1** stop a flow of blood, etc. **2** stop the flow of blood from a wound. **3** cease flowing. Also, **stanch.** [ME < OF *estanchier* < VL *extanicare* press together, literally, un-thin < L *ex-* un- + Celtic *tan-* thin] —**staunch′er,** *n.*

staunch² (stonch *or* stônch) *adj.* **1** firm; strong. **2** loyal; steadfast. **3** watertight: *a staunch boat.* Also, **stanch.** [ME < OF *estanche,* fem. < *estanchier.* See STAUNCH¹.] —**staunch′ly,** *adv.* —**staunch·ness,** *n.*

stave (stāv) *n., v.* **staved** *or* **stove, stav·ing.** —*n.* **1** one of the curved pieces of wood that form the sides of a barrel, tub, etc. **2** a stick or staff. **3** a rung of a ladder. **4** a verse or stanza of a poem, song, etc. **5** *Music.* the staff.
—*v.* **1** break a hole in (a barrel, boat, etc.). **2** become smashed or broken in. **3** furnish with staves.
stave off, put off; keep back; delay or prevent: *The lost campers ate birds' eggs to stave off starvation.*
[< *staves,* pl. of *staff*]
☛ *Usage.* **Staved, stove.** The variant past tense and past participle **stove** is used chiefly with reference to the breaking of boats and the like: *The waves stove (or staved) the boat in,* but *He staved off his creditors.*

staves (stāvz) *n.* **1** pl. of **staff. 2** pl. of **stave.**

stay¹ (stā) *v., n.* —*v.* **1** continue to be as indicated; remain: *to stay clean. Stay here till I call you.* **2** live for a while; dwell: *She is staying with her aunt while her mother is ill.* **3** stop; halt: *We have no time to stay.* **4** pause; wait: *"Time and tide stay for no man."* **5** wait for; await. **6** put an end to for a while; satisfy (hunger, appetite, etc.). **7** put off; hold back; delay; restrain; check: *The chief stayed judgment till he could hear both sides.* **8** endure: *unable to stay to the end of a race.*
stay put, remain in the same place or condition; remain stationary, fixed, or established: *Stay put till I get there. This label won't stay put.*
—*n.* **1** a staying; a stop; time spent: *a pleasant stay in the country.* **2** a check; restraint: *a stay on his activity.* **3** *Law.* a delay in carrying out the order of a court: *The judge granted the condemned man a stay for an appeal.* **4** *Informal.* staying power; endurance. [< OF *ester* stand < L *stare*] —**stay′er,** *n.*
☛ *Syn. v.* **1. Stay, remain** = continue in some (stated) place, position, state, condition, relation, action, etc. **Stay** emphasizes the idea of keeping on in the present or in some specified place, state, condition, etc. without leaving or stopping: *He decided to stay in school another year.* **Remain,** often used interchangeably with **stay,** emphasizes keeping on in the same place or state, without changing in condition, quality, or form: *This room remains cool all summer.*

stay² (stā) *n., v.* **stayed, stay·ing.** —*n.* **1** a support; prop; brace. **2** a thin, flat strip of plastic, bone, etc. used to stiffen a corselet, corset, shirt collar, etc. **3 stays,** *pl.* corset.
—*v.* **1** support; prop; hold up. **2** strengthen mentally or spiritually; fix or rest in dependence or reliance. [probably ult. < OF *estayer* < Gmc.] —**stay′er,** *n.*

stay³ (stā) *n., v.* **stayed, stay·ing.** —*n.* **1** a strong rope, chain, or wire attached to something to steady it: *The mast of a ship is held in place by stays.* See **shroud** for picture. **2** any rope or chain similarly used.
in stays, of a ship, in the act of changing from one tack to another.
—*v.* **1** support or secure with stays. **2** of a ship, change to the other tack. [OE *stæg*]

stay–at–home (stā′ət hōm′) *n., adj.* —*n.* a person who prefers to stay home rather than go out or travel for fun and recreation. —*adj.* of or characteristic of someone who prefers to stay at home rather than go out, travel, etc.

staying power the ability to endure: *He doesn't work very fast, but he has great staying power.*

stay·sail (stā′sāl′ *or* stā′səl) *n.* a sail fastened on a stay or rope.

S.T.B. Bachelor of Sacred Theology (for L *Sacrae Theologiae Baccalaureus*).

stbd. starboard.

St. Bernard a Saint Bernard dog.

Ste. Sainte.

stead (sted) *n.* a place: *The sales manager could not come, but sent his assistant in his stead.*
stand (someone) **in good stead,** be of advantage or service to someone.
[OE *stede*]

stead·fast (sted′fast′ *or* sted′fəst) *adj.* **1** loyal; unwavering. **2** firmly fixed; not moving or changing. Also, **stedfast.** [OE *stedefæst* < *stede* place + *fæst* fast¹, firm] —**stead′fast·ly,** *adv.* —**stead′fast·ness,** *n.*

stead·y (sted′ē) *adj.* **stead·i·er, stead·i·est;** *v.* **stead·ied, stead·y·ing;** *interj., adv., n., pl.* **stead·ies.** —*adj.* **1** changing little; uniform; regular: *steady progress.* **2** firmly fixed; firm; not swaying or shaking: *to hold a ladder steady.* **3** not easily excited; calm: *steady nerves.* **4** resolute; steadfast: *steady friendship.* **5** having good habits; reliable: *a steady young man.* **6** of a ship, keeping nearly upright in a heavy sea. **7** *Informal.* being one's regular girl friend or boy friend: *Mary was his steady girl.*
—*v.* **1** make steady; keep steady. **2** become steady. **3** make regular in character and conduct.
—*interj.* **1** be calm! don't get excited! **2** *Nautical.* hold the helm as it is! keep on course! —*adv.*
go steady, a *Informal.* date one person or each other only. **b** go carefully.
—*n. Informal.* a regular girlfriend or boyfriend; a person who is being courted regularly by the same person. [< *stead*] —**stead′i·ly,** *adv.* —**stead′i·ness,** *n.*
☛ *Syn. adj.* **1. Steady, regular** = constant or uniform in acting, doing, moving, happening. **Steady** particularly suggests uninterrupted or unchanging movement, action, progress, or direction: *He has been unable to find steady work.* **Regular** emphasizes a fixed, usual, or uniform procedure, practice, program, or pattern: *He is a regular subscriber to several magazines.*

stead·y–state (sted′ē stāt′) *adj.* maintaining the same basic condition; unchanging in quality, structure, behavior, etc.: *a steady-state current.*

steady–state theory the theory that the universe has now the same basic form as always, matter being continuously created to replace that which is naturally destroyed.

steak (stāk) *n.* **1** a thick slice of meat from a beef carcass, usually broiled or fried; beef steak. **2** a similar slice of other meat or of fish for broiling or frying: *ham steak, salmon steak.* **3** ground meat shaped and cooked somewhat like a steak: *hamburger steak.* [ME < ON *steik*]
☛ *Hom.* **stake.**

steal (stēl) *v.* **stole, sto·len, steal·ing;** *n.* —*v.* **1** take (something) that does not belong to one; take dishonestly: *to steal money.* **2** take, get, or do secretly: *to steal a look at someone.* **3** take, get, or win by art, charm, or gradual means: *She steals all hearts.* **4** move secretly or quietly: *She stole out of the house.* **5** move slowly or gently: *The years steal by.* **6** *Baseball.* run to (a base) without being helped by a hit or error.
—*n.* **1** *Informal.* the act of stealing. **2** *Informal.* the thing stolen. **3** *Informal.* something obtained very cheaply or very easily: *At that price the car is a steal.* **4** *Informal.* a dishonest or unethical transaction at a great profit. **5** *Baseball.* a safe advance from one base to another by stealing. [OE *stelan*] —**steal′er,** *n.*
☛ *Hom.* **steel.**
☛ *Syn. v.* **1. Steal, pilfer, filch** = take dishonestly or wrongfully and secretly something belonging to someone else. **Steal** is the general and most common word: *Thieves stole the silver.* **Pilfer,** more formal, means "steal and carry away in small amounts": *In many supermarkets hidden guards watch for people who pilfer food.* **Filch** particularly suggests stealthy or furtive pilfering, usually of objects of little value: *The boys filched some candy from the counter.*

stealth (stelth) *n.* a secret or sly action: *He obtained the letter by stealth, taking it while his sister's back was turned.* [< *steal*]

stealth·y (stel′thē) *adj.* **stealth·i·er, stealth·i·est.** done in a secret manner; secret; sly: *The cat crept in a stealthy way toward the bird.* —**stealth′i·ly,** *adv.* —**stealth′i·ness,** *n.*

steam (stēm) *n., v.* —*n.* **1** the invisible vapor or gas into which water is changed when it is heated to the boiling point. Compare **water vapor. 2** the white cloud or mist formed when the invisible vapor from boiling water condenses as it cools. **3 a** the vapor from boiling water, kept under pressure to generate mechanical power and for heating and cooking: *Engines powered by steam were*

hat, āge, fär; let, ēqual, tėrm; it, īce
hot, ōpen, ôrder; oil, out; cup, pùt, rüle,
əbove, takən, pencəl, lemən, circəs
ch, child; ng, long; sh, ship
th, thin; ᵺ, then; zh, measure

formerly used to run threshing machines, tractors, etc. **b** the power thus generated. **4** *Informal.* power or energy.

full steam ahead, with all possible power or energy: *They went full steam ahead as soon as they got final approval.*

let off steam, *Informal.* **a** get rid of excess energy: *He took the kids to the playground so they could let off steam.* **b** relieve one's feelings of anger, frustration, etc.: *Wait till we get home before you let off steam.*

run out of steam, *Informal.* lose power, energy, or effectiveness; collapse.
—*v.* **1** give off steam: *The soup was steaming. Their mitts were steaming on the radiator.* **2** become covered with steam (*usually used with* **up**): *The windshield had steamed up inside the car.* **3** rise as vapor: *Mist was steaming off the lake.* **4** expose to the action of steam; prepare, treat, etc. with steam: *to steam oneself for a cold, to steam a pudding, to steam a letter open.* **5** move or travel by the power of steam: *The ship steamed away.* **6** *Informal.* be angry; fume: *She was steaming by the time he got there, half an hour late.*

steamed up, *Informal.* **a** angry, fuming: *He gets all steamed up about nothing.* **b** full of energy and enthusiasm: *She's steamed up now about her science project.*
[OE *stēam*] —**steam′like′,** *adj.*

steam bath a kind of bath taken in a steam-filled room or chamber: *A steam bath is usually followed by massage.*

steam·boat (stēm′bōt′) *n.* a boat propelled by a steam engine.

steam boiler a boiler in which water is heated to make steam.

steam box steam chest.

steam chest a chamber through which the steam of an engine passes from the boiler to the cylinder.

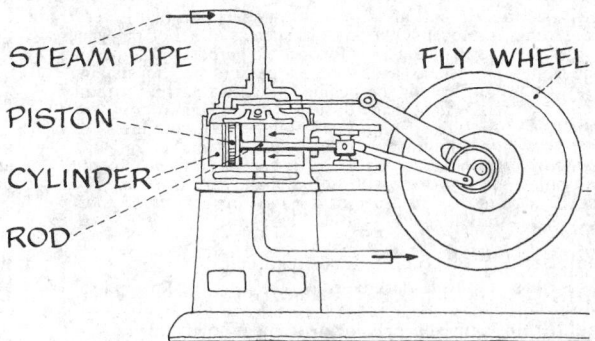

A steam engine. The pressure of the steam forced into the cylinder pushes the piston back and forth. This causes the rod to turn a shaft that passes on motion to wheels or other parts. The weight of the heavy flywheel attached to the shaft keeps the shaft turning evenly.

steam engine an engine operated by steam, typically one in which a sliding piston in a cylinder is moved by the expansive action of steam generated in a boiler.

steam·er (stē′mər) *n.* **1** a steamboat; steamship. **2** an engine run by steam. **3** a container in which something is steamed or kept warm.

steamer rug a blanket, especially one used to keep a person warm in a chair on the deck of a ship.

steam fitter a man who installs and repairs steam pipes, radiators, boilers, etc.

steam heat heat given off by steam in radiators and pipes.

steam iron an electric iron in which water is heated to produce steam that is released through holes in the undersurface to dampen cloth while pressing it.

steam–roll·er (stēm′rōl′ər) *n., v.* —*n.* **1** a road roller, especially one powered by steam. **2** an overpowering force used to crush opposition. **3** (*adj.*) designating or using a relentlessly overpowering force.
—*v.* **1** override by crushing power or force; crush: *to steam-roller all opposition.* **2** force by this means: *to steam-roller a bill through*

Parliament. **3** make level, smooth, etc. with a steam-roller.

steam·ship (stēm′ship′) *n.* a ship propelled by a steam engine.

steam shovel a machine for digging, formerly always operated by steam, but now often by an internal-combustion engine.

steam·tight (stēm′tīt′) *adj.* so tight that no steam can get in or out: *a steamtight valve.*

steam turbine a turbine moved by steam.

steam·y (stē′mē) *adj.* **steam·i·er, steam·i·est. 1** of steam; like steam. **2** full of steam; giving off steam; rising in steam. —**steam′i·ly,** *adv.* —**steam′i·ness,** *n.*

ste·ap·sin (stē ap′sən) *n. Biochemistry.* an enzyme in the pancreatic juice that converts fats into more easily digested fatty acids and glycerin. [blend of *stea(rin)* and *(pe)psin*]

ste·a·rate (stē′ə rāt′) *n.* a salt of stearic acid.

ste·ar·ic (stē ar′ik, stē er′ik, *or* stēr′ik) *adj.* having to do with stearin, suet, or fat. [< F *stéarique* < Gk. *stear* fat]

stearic acid a solid, white substance obtained from certain fats and used in making candles. *Formula:* $C_{18}H_{36}O_2$

ste·a·rin (stē′ə rin *or* stēr′in) *n.* **1** a colorless, odorless substance that is the chief constituent of many animal and vegetable fats. **2** a mixture of fatty acids used for making candles, solid alcohol, etc. [< F *stéarine* < Gk. *stear* fat]

ste·a·rine (stē′ə rin *or* stē′ə rēn′, stēr′in *or* stēr′ēn′) *n.* stearin.

ste·a·tite (stē′ə tīt′) *n.* a rock composed of impure talc; soapstone. [< L *steatitis* < Gk. *stear, -atos* fat]

ste·a·tit·ic (stē′ə tit′ik) *adj.* composed of soapstone; like soapstone.

ste·a·to·sis (stē ə tō′sis) *n.* **1** fatty degeneration. **2** any disease of the sebaceous glands. [< NL < Gk. *stear, -atos* fat + NL *-osis* -osis]

sted·fast (sted′fast′ *or* sted′fəst) *adj.* steadfast. —**sted′fast·ly,** *adv.*

steed (stēd) *n.* a horse, especially a high-spirited riding horse. [OE *stēda*]

steel (stēl) *n., v.* —*n.* **1** an alloy of iron and carbon that is very hard, strong, and tough. Other metals, such as nickel or manganese, may be added to the basic alloy for specific purposes. **2** something made from steel, such as: **a** a sword. **b** a piece of steel for making sparks. **c** a rod of steel for sharpening knives. **d** a narrow strip of steel in a corset. **3** (*adj.*) made of steel. **4** steel-like hardness or strength: *nerves of steel.* **5** (*adj.*) resembling steel in hardness, color, etc. **6** *Cdn.* **a** a railway track: *Steel has been laid for 200 kilometres north.* **b** the railway line: *They arranged to meet at steel.* —*v.* **1** point, edge, or cover with steel. **2** make hard or strong like steel: *He tried to steel his heart against the sufferings of the poor.* [OE *stēle*] —**steel′less,** *adj.* —**steel′-like′,** *adj.*
☞ *Hom.* **steal.**

steel band a band composed of steel drums.

steel blue a lustrous dark blue, like the color of tempered steel. —**steel′-blue′,** *adj.*

steel drum a tuned percussion instrument originating in Trinidad, made from an oil drum by cutting off one end and part of the sides and shaping the other end into sections (called notes), each tuned to a specific note. Steel drums may be tuned for a soprano, tenor, or bass range.

steel·head *or* **steel·head trout** (stēl′hed′) *n., pl.* **-head or -heads.** a large, silvery variety or stock of the rainbow trout as found in Pacific coastal rivers, on returning from the sea, and also found in the Great Lakes. See also **rainbow trout** and **Kamloops trout.**

steel mill a place where steel is made.

steel wool fine steel threads or shavings in a pad, etc., used for cleaning or polishing.

steel·work·er (stēl′wèr′kər) *n.* a person who works in a place where steel is made.

steel·works (stēl′wèrks′) *n.pl. or sing.* a place where steel is made.

steel·y (stē′lē) *adj.* **steel·i·er, steel·i·est. 1** made of steel. **2** like steel in color, strength, or hardness. —**steel′i·ness,** *n.*

steel·yard (stēl′yärd *or* stil′yərd) *n.* a portable balance for weighing, having a horizontal bar on a pivot with a movable weight at the longer end and, at the shorter, a hook for holding the object to be weighed. It is designed to be suspended from a hook or from the user's hand. [< *steel* + *yard²*, in the sense of "rod"]

steen·bok (stēn′bok′ *or* stän′bok′) *n.* steinbok. [< Afrikaans *stenbok* < *steen* stone + *bok* buck]

steep¹ (stēp) *adj., n.* —*adj.* **1** having a sharp slope; almost straight up and down: *The hill is steep.* **2** *Informal.* unreasonable: *a steep price.* **3** of a story, etc., exaggerated; incredible.
—*n.* a steep slope. [OE *stēap*] —**steep′ly,** *adv.* —**steep′ness,** *n.*
☞ *Syn. adj.* **1. Steep, abrupt, precipitous** = having a slope almost straight up and down. **Steep** suggests having a very sharp slope that is hard to go up: *I do not like to drive up a steep hill.* **Abrupt** emphasizes being very steep and sudden, with no slope toward the sharp angle from which the surface goes up or down: *From the rim they made their way down the abrupt sides of the canyon.* **Precipitous** suggests something as abrupt and straight up and down as a precipice: *The climbers will attempt to scale the precipitous eastern slope of the peak.*

steep² (stēp) *v., n.* —*v.* **1** soak (something), especially so as to soften, cleanse, or extract an essence. **2** undergo such soaking: *Let the tea steep for five minutes.* **3** make thoroughly wet; saturate or immerse: *a sword steeped in blood.* **4** imbue; permeate (*usually used in the passive*): *ruins steeped in gloom, a mind steeped in hatred.*
—*n.* **1** the process of steeping or the state of being steeped. **2** the liquid or bath in which something is steeped. [probably < OE *stēap* bowl] —**steep′er,** *n.*

stee·ple (stē′pəl) *n.* **1** a high tower rising above the roof of a church, etc., and usually having a spire at the top. **2** such a tower, together with the spire or other structure surmounting it. [OE *stēpel* < *stēap* steep] —**stee′ple·like′,** *adj.*

stee·ple·bush (stē′pəl bùsh′) *n.* hardhack, a shrub that has flowers in steeple-shaped clusters.

stee·ple·chase (stē′pəl chās′) *n., v.* **-chased, -chas·ing.** —*n.* **1** a horse race over a course having ditches, hedges, and other obstacles. **2** a cross-country foot race. —*v.* ride or run in a steeplechase. —**stee′ple·chas·er,** *n.*

stee·ple·jack (stē′pəl jak′) *n.* a man who climbs steeples, tall chimneys, etc. to paint, make repairs, etc.

steer¹ (stēr) *v., n.* —*v.* **1** guide the course of: *to steer a ship, to steer a sled, to steer an automobile, to steer an airplane.* **2** guide; lead; conduct; pilot: *to steer a person through a crowd.* **3** set and follow: *He steered a course for home.* **4** be guided: *This car steers easily.* **5** guide a ship: *The pilot steered for the harbor.* **6** direct one's way or course.
steer clear of, keep away from; avoid.
—*n. Slang.* an idea or a suggested course of action. [OE *stēoran*] —**steer′er,** *n.*

steer² (stēr) *n.* a full-grown, castrated male of cattle, less than four years old. Steers are usually raised for their meat. Compare **ox.**

steer·age (stēr′ij) *n.* **1** the part of a passenger ship occupied by passengers travelling at the cheapest rate. **2** the act of steering. **3** the manner in which a ship is affected by the helm.

steer·age·way (stēr′ij wā′) *n.* the amount of forward motion a ship must have before it can be steered.

steering gear the apparatus for steering an automobile, ship, etc.

steering wheel the wheel that is turned to steer an automobile, ship, etc.

steers·man (stērz′mən) *n., pl.* **-men.** a person who steers a ship.

steg·o·sau·rus (steg′ə sô′rəs) *n., pl.* **-ri** (-rī *or* -rē). any of a genus (*Stegosaurus*) of large, plant-eating dinosaurs of the late Jurassic period having two rows of large, triangular, bony plates along the back. [< NL < Gk. *stegos* roof + *sauros* lizard]

stein (stīn) *n.* a beer mug. [< G *Stein* stone]

stein·bok (stīn′bok′) *n.* **1** a small, reddish-brown African antelope (*Raphicerus campestris*), the male of which has small, straight horns. **2** ibex.

ste·le (stē′lē) *n., pl.* **-lae** (-lē *or* -lī) **or -les. 1** an upright slab or pillar of stone bearing an inscription, sculptural design, etc. **2** a prepared surface on the face of a building, a rock, etc. bearing an inscription or the like. [< Gk.]

stel·lar (stel′ər) *adj.* **1** of or having to do with the stars; of a star; like a star. **2** chief: *a stellar role.* **3** of or having to do with a star performer. [< L *stellaris* < *stella* star]

stel·late (stel′āt *or* stel′it) *adj.* spreading out like the points of a star; star-shaped. [< L *stellatus* < *stella* star]

Steller's jay (stel′ərz) a large, crested jay (*Cyanocitta stelleri*) of W North America, having dark-blue and black plumage. [< Georg Wilhelm *Steller* (1709-1745), a German naturalist]

Steller's sea cow a huge, extinct sea mammal of the N Pacific Ocean, belonging to the same order as the dugong and manatee. It was discovered in the mid 18th century and within 30 years was hunted to extinction. [see STELLER'S JAY]

Stel·lite (stel′īt) *n. Trademark.* an extremely hard, rust-resisting alloy of cobalt, chromium, and tungsten, widely used in the making of cutting tools.

St. El·mo's fire (el′mōz) a fiery light due to a discharge of atmospheric electricity, often seen on masts, towers, etc.

St. Elmo's light St. Elmo's fire.

PEDICEL
PETIOLE
MAIN STEM
STIPULES
NODES

A wild rose

hat, āge, fär; let, ēqual, tėrm; it, īce
hot, ōpen, ôrder; oil, out; cup, pút, rüle,
əbove, takən, pencəl, lemən, circəs

ch, child; ng, long; sh, ship
th, thin; ᴛʜ, then; zh, measure

stem¹ (stem) *n., v.* **stemmed, stem·ming.** —*n.* **1** the main part of a plant usually above the ground, that develops buds and shoots. **2** the part of a flower, a fruit, or a leaf that joins it to the plant or tree. **3** anything like or suggesting the stem of a plant: *the stem of a goblet, the stem of a pipe, etc.* **4** the line of descent of a family. **5** *Grammar.* the part of a word to which endings are added and inside which changes are made. *Run* is the stem of *running, runner, ran,* etc. **6** the bow or front end of a boat.
from stem to stern, from one end of the ship to the other.
—*v.* **1** remove the stem from (a leaf, fruit, etc.). **2** grow out; develop; come from: *The difficulty stems from his failure to plan properly.* **3** originate or spring: *Newspapers stemmed from the invention of the printing press.* [OE *stemn*] —**stem′like′,** *adj.*

stem² (stem) *v.* **stemmed, stem·ming. 1** stop; check; dam up. **2** make progress against: *stem the swift current.* [< ON *stemma*]

stem·less (stem′lis) *adj.* having no stem; having no visible stem.

stemmed (stemd) *adj.* **1** having a stem. **2** having the stem removed.

stem·mer (stem′ər) *n.* a person or thing that removes stems from leaves, fruit, etc.

stem·ware (stem′wer′) *n.* goblets or drinking glasses having stems, used for wine, liqueurs, etc.

stem-wind·ing (stem′wīn′ding) *adj.* of a watch, winding by turning a knob on the stem.

stench (stench) *n.* a very bad smell; stink. [OE *stenc*; related to *stincan* smell]

sten·cil (sten′səl) *n., v.* **-cilled** or **-ciled, -cil·ling** or **-cil·ing.** —*n.* **1** a thin sheet of metal, paper, etc. having letters or designs cut through it. When it is laid on a surface and ink or color is spread on, these letters or designs are made on the surface. **2** the letters or designs so made. —*v.* mark, paint, or make with a stencil: *The curtains have a stencilled border.* [ult. < OF *estanceler* ornament with colors, ult. < L *scintilla* spark]

sten·o (sten′ō) *n., pl.* **-os.** *Informal.* stenographer.

sten·o·graph (sten′ə graf′) *n., v.* —*n.* **1** a writing in shorthand. **2** any of various keyboard instruments, resembling a typewriter, used for writing in shorthand. —*v.* write in shorthand.

ste·nog·ra·pher (stə nog′rə fər) *n.* a person whose chief work is taking dictation and transcribing it on a typewriter, etc.

sten·o·graph·ic (sten′ə graf′ik) *adj.* **1** of, having to do with, or produced by stenography. **2** of style, concise.

sten·o·graph·i·cal·ly (sten′ə graf′ik lē) *adv.* by means of stenography.

ste·nog·ra·phy (stə nog′rə fē) *n.* shorthand. [< Gk. *stenos* narrow + E *-graphy*]

ste·no·sis (stə nō′sis) *n., pl.* **-ses** (-sēz) an abnormal narrowing or constriction of a canal or passage in the body, especially a constriction of a heart valve.

ste·not·ic (stə not′ik) *adj.* of or having to do with stenosis.

Sten·o·type (sten′ə tīp′) *n.* **1** *Trademark.* a kind of typewriter used in stenotypy. **2 stenotype,** a letter or group of letters used for a sound, word, or phrase in stenotypy. [< Gk. *stenos* narrow + E *type*]

sten·o·typ·y (sten′ə tīp′ē or stə not′ə pē) *n.* **1** a form of shorthand that uses ordinary letters. **2** the use of a stenotype machine to record speeches, etc.

Sten·tor (sten′tôr) *n. Greek legend.* a Greek herald in the Trojan War, whose voice was as loud as the voices of fifty men.

sten·to·ri·an (sten tô′rē ən) *adj.* very loud or powerful in sound. [< *Stentor*]

step (step) *n., v.* **stepped, step·ping.** —*n.* **1** a movement made by lifting the foot and putting it down again in a new position; one motion of the leg in walking, running, dancing, etc. **2** the distance covered by one such movement: *She was three steps away when he called her back.* **3** a short distance; little way: *The school is only a*

step away. **4** a way of walking, dancing, etc.: *a slow step.* **5** a sequence of steps taken in a particular manner and forming a unit or pattern of a particular dance: *a cha-cha step.* **6** a place for the foot in going up or coming down. A stair or a rung of a ladder is a step. **7** the sound made by putting the foot down. **8** a footprint: *steps in the mud.* **9** an action: *Taking steps to reduce absenteeism.* **10** a degree in a series; grade in rank. **11** *Music.* **a** a degree of the staff or the scale. **b** the interval between two successive degrees of the scale. **12** a part like a step; support, frame, etc. for holding the end of something upright: *the step of a mast.* **13 steps,** *pl.* a stepladder.
in step, a keeping one's pace uniform with that of another or others or in time with music. **b** making one's actions or ideas agree with those of another person or persons; in agreement.
keep step, move at the same pace as another person or persons or in time with music.
out of step, a not keeping pace with others or in time to music. **b** not in harmony or accord.
step by step, little by little; slowly.
take steps, adopt, put into effect, or carry out measures considered to be necessary, desirable, etc.: *Steps have already been taken to deal with the emergency.*
watch (one's) **step,** be careful.
—*v.* **1** move the legs as in walking, running, dancing, etc.: *Step lively!* **2** walk a short distance: *Step this way.* **3** put the foot down: *to step on a worm.* **4** make or arrange like a flight of steps. **5** set (a mast); fix or place in a support. **6** *Informal.* go fast.
step down, a come down. **b** surrender or resign from an office or position: *He stepped down from the presidency.* **c** decrease: *to step down the rate of flow in a pipeline.*
step in, come in; intervene; take part.
step off, measure by taking steps: *Step off the distance from the door to the window.*
step on it, *Informal.* go faster; hurry up.
step out, *Informal.* go out for entertainment.
step up, a go up. **b** make go higher, faster, etc.; increase: *to step up production, to step up the pressure in a boiler.* [OE *steppan*]

step– *prefix.* related by the remarriage of a parent, not by blood, as in *stepmother, stepsister,* etc. [OE *stēop-*]

step·broth·er (step′bruᴛʜ′ər) *n.* a stepfather's or stepmother's son by a former marriage.

step·child (step′chīld′) *n., pl.* **-chil·dren.** a child of one's husband or wife by a former marriage.

step·dame (step′dām′) *n. Archaic.* stepmother.

step·daugh·ter (step′do′tər or -dô′tər) *n.* a daughter of one's husband or wife by a former marriage.

step–down (step′doun′) *adj.* **1** serving or causing to decrease gradually. **2** *Electricity.* lowering the voltage of a current, especially by means of a transformer.

step·fa·ther (step′fo′ᴛʜər) *n.* a man who has married one's mother after the death or divorce of one's natural father.

step–in (step′in′) *adj.* of garments, shoes, etc., put on by being stepped into.

step·lad·der (step′lad′ər) *n.* a portable ladder with narrow flat steps fixed to a hinged, free-standing supporting frame.

step·moth·er (step′muᴛʜ′ər) *n.* a woman who has married one's father after the death or divorce of one's natural mother.

step–out well (step′out′) a gas or oil well dug near the site of another that has already been proved productive, giving further proof of reserves in the area.

step–par·ent (step′per′ənt) *n.* a stepfather or stepmother.

steppe (step) *n.* **1** one of the vast, treeless plains in SE Europe and in Asia. **2** a vast, treeless plain. [< Russian *step*]

step·per (step′ər) *n.* a person or animal that steps, especially in a particular manner: *a high stepper.*

step·ping–stone (step′ing stōn′) *n.* **1** a stone or one of a line of stones in shallow water, a marshy place, etc. used in crossing. **2** a stone for use in mounting or ascending. **3** anything serving as a means of advancing or rising.

step·sis·ter (step′sis′tər) *n.* a stepfather's or stepmother's daughter by a former marriage.

step·son (step′sun′) *n.* a son of one's husband or wife by a former marriage.

step–up (step′up′) *adj., n.* —*adj.* **1** serving or causing to increase gradually. **2** *Electricity.* increasing the voltage of a current, especially by means of a transformer. —*n.* an increase: *a step-up in production.*

step·wise (step′wīz′) *adv.* in a step or steps.

–ster *suffix.* **1** one that —s, as in *fibster.* **2** one that makes —, as in *maltster, rhymester.* **3** one that is —, as in *youngster.* **4** special meanings, as in *gangster, roadster, teamster.* [OE -*estre*, -*istre*]

ster. sterling.

ste·ra·di·an (stə rā′dē ən) *n.* an SI unit for measuring solid angles, equal to the angle from the centre of a sphere which cuts off an area on the surface of the sphere equal to the square of the radius. The steradian is used mostly in mathematics; it is one of the two supplementary units in the SI. See **radian** for picture. *Symbol:* sr

stere (stēr) *n.* a unit of volume sometimes used for measuring stacked timber, equal to one cubic metre. [< F < Gk. *stereos* solid]

ster·e·o (ster′ē ō′ or stēr′ē ō′) *n., adj.* —*n.* **1** stereophonic reproduction. **2** a set or apparatus for stereophonic reproduction. **3** *Informal.* a radio, record player, or tape-recorder equipped with a stereophonic system. **4** stereotype. —*adj.* **1** stereophonic. **2** produced for use with stereophonic equipment.

stereo– *combining form.* solid or three-dimensional, as in *stereoscope.* [< Gk. *stereos* solid]

ster·e·o·phon·ic (ster′ē ə fon′ik or stēr′ē ə-) *adj.* in sound reproduction, of or produced by the use of two or more microphones, recording channels, loudspeakers, etc. in order to give a three-dimensional effect. —**ster′e·o·phon′i·cal·ly,** *adv.*

ster·e·op·ti·con (ster′ē op′tə kən or -op′tə kən) *n.* an improved form of magic lantern, having a powerful light that projects pictures upon a screen. [< NL < Gk. *stereos* solid + *optikos* relating to vision]

ster·e·o·scope (ster′ē ə skōp′ or stēr′ē ə-) *n.* an instrument through which two pictures of the same object or scene are viewed, one by each eye. The picture thus viewed appears to have three dimensions.

ster·e·o·scop·ic (ster′ē ə skop′ik or stēr′ē ə-) *adj.* having to do with stereoscopes.

ster·e·o·scop·i·cal·ly (ster′ē ə skop′ik lē or stēr′ē ə-) *adv.* by means of a stereoscope.

ster·e·o·type (ster′ē ə tīp′ or stēr′ē ə-) *n., v.* -**typed,** -**typ·ing.** —*n.* **1** *Printing.* a one-piece plate of type metal cast from a mould made from a surface of composed type. **2** the method or process of making such plates. **3** something that has a fixed form, as if cast from a mould; especially, a kind of oversimplified mental picture shared by many people in a group: *He fits the stereotype of the insecure bully.* **4** a person or group that represents such a mental picture: *The novel's hero is a stereotype of the ambitious young man.* —*v.* **1** *Printing.* **a** make a stereotype of. **b** print from stereotypes. **2** have or show a mental stereotype of. —**ster′e·o·typ′er,** *n.*

ster·e·o·typed (ster′ē ə tīpt′ or stēr′ē ə-) *adj.* **1** printed from a stereotype. **2** not original or individual; too conventional and rigid.

ster·e·o·typ·ic (ster′ē ə tip′ik or stēr′ē ə-) *adj.* stereotypical.

ster·e·o·typ·i·cal (ster′ē ə kəl or stēr′ē ə-) *adj.* of, having to do with, or representing a mental stereotype.

ster·e·o·typ·y (ster′ē ə tip′ē or stēr′ē ə-) *n.* **1** the process of making stereotype plates. **2** printing from stereotype plates.

ster·ile (ster′īl or ster′əl) *adj.* **1** free from living micro-organisms, especially potentially harmful ones: *sterile surgical instruments.* **2** of animals or plants, failing or not able to reproduce; barren. **3** not producing crops or vegetation: *sterile land.* **4** *Botany.* **a** of a plant, not bearing fruit or spores. **b** of a flower, producing only stamens, or producing neither stamens nor pistils. **5** not producing results: *sterile hopes.* [< L *sterilis*] —**ster′ile·ly,** *adv.*

ste·ril·i·ty (stə ril′ə tē) *n., pl.* -**ties.** barrenness; a sterile condition or character.

ster·i·li·za·tion (ster′ə lə zā′shən or -lī zā′shən) *n.* a sterilizing or being sterilized: *the sterilization of dishes by boiling them.*

ster·i·lize (ster′ə līz′) *v.* -**lized,** -**liz·ing.** **1** free from living germs: *The water had to be sterilized by boiling to make it fit to drink.* **2** deprive of fertility. **3** make unproductive, unprofitable, or useless. —**ster′i·liz′er,** *n.*

ster·ling (stėr′ling) *n., adj.* —*n.* **1** British money, especially the pound as the standard British monetary unit in international trade: *to pay in sterling.* **2** sterling silver or things made of it.

—*adj.* **1** of or payable in British money. **2** designating a silver alloy of a standard quality, that is not less than 92.5 percent pure silver, the remaining 7.5 percent usually being copper. **3** made of sterling silver. **4** of dependable excellence. [probably ult. < OE *steorra* star (as on certain early coins)]

stern[1] (stėrn) *adj.* **1** severe; strict; harsh: *a stern master, a stern frown.* **2** hard; not yielding; firm: *stern necessity.* **3** grim: *stern mountains.* [OE *stirne*] —**stern′ly,** *adv.* —**stern′ness,** *n.*

stern[2] (stėrn) *n.* the rear of a ship or boat. See **aft** for picture. [probably < ON *stjórn* steering]

ster·nal (stėr′nəl) *adj.* of or having to do with the breastbone or sternum. [< NL *sternalis*]

stern chase a chase in which the pursuing ship follows in the wake of the other.

stern chaser a gun in the stern of a ship for protection against an enemy ship following in its wake.

stern·most (stėrn′mōst) *adj.* **1** nearest the stern. **2** farthest in the rear.

stern·post (stėrn′pōst′) *n.* the principal piece of timber or iron in the stern of a ship. Its lower end is fastened to the keel, and it usually supports the rudder.

stern sheets the space at the stern of an open boat.

ster·num (stėr′nəm) *n., pl.* -**na** (-nə) or **nums.** breastbone. [< NL < Gk. *sternon* chest]

ster·nu·ta·tion (stėr′nyə tā′shən or stėr′nə tā′shən) *n.* the act of sneezing. [< L *sternutatio, -onis* < *sternutare* sneeze, frequentative of *sternuere* sneeze]

ster·nu·ta·tive (stėr nyü′tə tiv or stėr nü′tə tiv) *adj.* causing sneezing.

stern·ward (stėrn′wərd) *adv.* toward the stern; astern.

stern·wards (stėrn′wərdz) *adv.* sternward.

stern·way (stėrn′wā′) *n.* the backward movement of a ship.

stern–wheel·er (stėrn′wē′lər or -hwē′lər) *n.* a steamboat driven by a paddle wheel at the stern or rear.

ster·oid (ster′oid or stēr′oid) *n. Biochemistry.* any of a large group of organic compounds, including the sterols, the bile acids, and the sex hormones, distributed widely in living plant and animal cells. [< *sterol* + -*oid*]

ster·ol (ster′ol or stēr′ol) *n. Biochemistry.* any of various complex organic alcohols distributed widely in living plant and animal cells. [contraction of *cholesterol*]

ster·to·rous (stėr′tə rəs) *adj.* making a heavy snoring sound: *stertorous breathing.* [< NL *stertor* snoring < L *stertere* snore] —**ster′to·rous·ness,** *n.*

stet (stet) *n., v.* stet·ted, stet·ting. —*n.* "let it stand," a direction on printer's proof, a manuscript, etc. to retain cancelled matter (usually accompanied by a row of dots under or beside the matter). —*v.* mark for retention. [< *stet* let it stand]

steth·o·scope (steth′ə skōp′) *n.* an instrument used by doctors for listening to sounds in the lungs, heart, etc. [< Gk. *stēthos* chest + E -*scope*]

steth·o·scop·ic (steth′ə skop′ik) *adj.* **1** having to do with the stethoscope or its use. **2** made or obtained by the stethoscope. —**steth′o·scop′i·cal·ly,** *adv.*

stet·son or **Stet·son** (stet′sən) *n.* a broad-brimmed, high-crowned, soft felt hat worn especially in western Canada and the SW United States. [< Trademark]

ste·ve·dore (stē′və dôr′) *n., v.* -**dored,** -**dor·ing.** —*n.* a man who loads and unloads ships. —*v.* load or unload (a vessel or cargo). [< Sp. *estivador,* ult. < L *stipare* pack down]

stew (styü or stü) *v., n.* —*v.* **1** cook by slow boiling or simmering. **2** *Informal.* worry; fret. **stew in** (one's) **own juice,** suffer the consequence of one's actions. —*n.* **1** a dish, usually consisting of meat, vegetables, etc., cooked by slow boiling or simmering: *beef stew.* **2** any food cooked in this way. **3** *Informal.* a state of worry; fret. [ME < OF *estuver* < VL *extufare* < L *ex-* out + Gk. *typhos* vapor]

stew·ard (styü′ərd or stü′ərd) *n.* **1** a man who looks after the needs of persons in a club or on a ship, train, aircraft, etc., especially one in charge of food and table service. **2** a man who manages another's property: *He is the steward of that great estate.* **3** a person appointed to manage a dinner, ball, show, etc. **4** shop steward. [OE *stigweard* < *stig* hall + *weard* keeper, ward]

stew·ard·ess (styü′ər dis or stü′ər dis) *n.* a woman who performs the duties of a steward, especially a flight attendant on a commercial airliner.

stew·ard·ship (styü′ərd ship′ or stü′ərd-) *n.* **1** the position, duties, and responsibilities of a steward. **2** management for others.

stew·pan (styü′pan′ or stü′-) *n.* a pan for stewing; saucepan.

sthen·ic (sthen′ik) *adj.* **1** having to do with vigor or nervous

energy. 2 *Medicine.* accompanied by an unhealthy increase in vital processes, such as circulation and respiration. [< NL *sthenicus* < Gk. *sthenos* strength]

stib·i·um (stib′ē əm) *n.* antimony. [< L < Gk. *stibi* < Egyptian]

stich (stik) *n.* a line of poetry; verse: *a Biblical stich.* [< Gk. *stichos* line < *steichein* march in a line]

stich·ic (stik′ik) *adj.* of, having to do with, or designating verse composed in lines that are metrically the same. The alliterative form is basically stichic rather than stanzaic.

stick¹ (stik) *n., v.* **sticked, stick·ing.** —*n.* 1 a long, thin piece of wood. 2 such a piece of wood shaped for a special use: *a walking stick, a hockey stick.* 3 something like a stick in shape: *a stick of candy.* 4 *Informal.* a stiff, awkward, or stupid person. 5 a lever used to work certain main controls of an airplane. 6 *Nautical.* a mast or yard. 7 *Informal.* a portion of alcoholic liquor added to a drink. 8 *Printing.* **a** a small metal tray in which type is set by hand. **b** the amount of type so set. 9 **the sticks,** *pl. Informal.* the outlying districts; backwoods.

shake a stick at, *Informal.* take notice of: *There was not enough snow to shake a stick at.*

—*v.* furnish with a stick or sticks to support or prop. [OE *sticca*]

stick² (stik) *v.* **stuck, stick·ing;** *n.* —*v.* 1 pierce with a pointed instrument; thrust (a point) into; stab. 2 kill by stabbing or piercing. 3 fasten by thrusting the point or end into or through something: *He stuck a flower in his buttonhole.* 4 put in a place or position: *Don't stick your head out of the car window.* 5 be thrust; extend (from, out, through, up, etc.): *His arms stick out of his coat sleeves.* 6 fasten; attach: *Stick a stamp on the letter.* 7 set into or adorn the surface of: *to stick a ham with cloves.* 8 keep close: *The boy stuck to his mother's heels.* 9 be or become fastened; become fixed; be at a standstill: *Our car stuck in the mud.* 10 bring to a stop: *Our work was stuck by the breakdown of the machinery.* 11 keep on; hold fast: *to stick to a task, to stick to one's friends when they are in trouble.* 12 *Informal.* puzzle. 13 be puzzled; hesitate. 14 *Slang.* **a** impose upon; cheat. **b** leave (a person) with, especially something to pay. 15 *Informal.* stand or put up with; tolerate: *I won't stick his insults much longer.*

stick around, *Informal.* stay or wait nearby.

stick at, hesitate or stop for: *He sticks at nothing to get his own way.*

stick by or **to,** remain resolutely faithful or attached to; refuse to desert: *He sticks by his friends when they are in trouble.*

stick it out, *Informal.* put up with unpleasant conditions, circumstances, etc.; endure: *Try to stick it out for a few more days.*

stick out, a stand out; be plain. **b** *Informal.* put up with until the end.

stick together, keep or cling together; stay united; support each other or one another.

stick up, *Slang.* hold up; rob.

stick up for, *Informal.* support; defend.

—*n.* 1 a thrust. 2 a sticky condition. 3 a standstill; stop. [OE *stician*]

☞ *Syn. v.* 7, 8. **Stick, adhere** = cling or become firmly or closely attached to another or each other. **Stick,** the common and general word, particularly suggests being fastened together or to another person or thing by or as if by something gummy: *Flies stick to flypaper.* **Adhere,** a more formal word sometimes used as a dignified substitute for **stick,** means cling fast or remain firmly attached to someone or something, by itself or of its own accord: *Adhesive tape does not adhere well to his skin.*

stick·er (stik′ər) *n.* 1 a person or thing that sticks. 2 a label or slip of paper for sticking to something. 3 a burr; thorn. 4 *Informal.* a puzzle.

stick figure a simple figure of a person or animal drawn with straight lines except for a circle representing the head.

stick·han·dle (stik′han′dəl) *v.* **-dled, -dling.** *Cdn.* 1 *Hockey.* manoeuvre the puck by deft handling of the stick, especially to avoid opposing checkers. 2 manoeuvre skilfully, especially in difficult circumstances: *to stickhandle a proposal through various government committees.* —**stick′han′dler,** *n.* —**stick′han′dling,** *n.*

Stick Indian *Cdn.* 1 an Indian from the bush country of the interior of British Columbia and the Yukon, originally so called by Indians of the Pacific coast. 2 **stick Indian,** *West Coast. Derogatory slang.* a backwoods Indian; an Indian ignorant of city ways. [< Chinook Jargon *stik* woods, bush]

sticking plaster cloth coated with a sticky substance, used to cover and close slight cuts and wounds.

sticking point 1 the place where a thing stops and holds. 2 any factor that prevents the solution of a problem: *When the contract was being reviewed, the sticking point proved to be shorter hours.*

stick insect any of a family (Phasmidae) of chiefly tropical, plant-eating insects having a very long, twiglike body and long, thin legs. Most stick insects are wingless.

stick-in-the-mud (stik′in ᴛʜə mud′) *n. Informal.* 1 a person who prefers the old to the new; a conservative; fogey. 2 a person who lacks initiative or resourcefulness.

hat, āge, fär; let, ēqual, tèrm; it, īce
hot, ōpen, ôrder; oil, out; cup, pùt, rüle,
əbove, takən, pencəl, lemən, circəs

ch, child; ng, long; sh, ship
th, thin; ᴛʜ, then; zh, measure

stick·le (stik′əl) *v.* **-led, -ling.** 1 make objections about trifles; insist stubbornly. 2 feel difficulties about trifles; have objections; scruple. [probably ult. < OE *stihtan* arrange]

stick·le·back (stik′əl bak′) *n., pl.* **-back** or **-backs.** any of a family (Gasterosteidae) of small, scaleless fishes found in fresh and salt water in northern regions, having a row of sharp spines on the back. The male builds an elaborate nest for the eggs. [ME *styklylbak* < OE *sticel* prick, sting + *bæc* back]

stick·ler (stik′lər) *n.* 1 a person who contends stubbornly or insists on trifles. 2 something that puzzles.

stick·man (stik′man′) *n., pl.* **-men.** *Slang.* 1 a croupier at a casino or gambling house. 2 *Sports.* a person who handles a stick or bat. 3 a stick figure.

stick·pin (stik′pin′) *n.* a pin worn for ornament.

stick·shift (stik′shift′) *n.* a gearshift lever that sticks upward from the floor of a motor vehicle.

stick-up (stik′up′) *n. Slang.* a holdup; robbery.

stick·y (stik′ē) *adj.* **stick·i·er, stick·i·est.** 1 that sticks: *sticky glue.* 2 that makes things stick; covered with adhesive matter: *sticky flypaper.* 3 *Informal.* unpleasantly humid: *sticky weather.* 4 *Informal.* puzzling; difficult: *a sticky problem.* 5 *Slang.* unpleasant; extremely disagreeable. —**stick′i·ly,** *adv.* —**stick′i·ness,** *n.*

sticky bun a sweet bun having a layer of sugar on top.

sties (stīz) *n.* pl. of **sty.**

stiff (stif) *adj., adv., n.* —*adj.* 1 not easily bent: *a stiff collar.* 2 hard to move: *stiff hinges.* 3 not able to move easily: *He was stiff and sore.* 4 drawn tight; tense: *a stiff cord.* 5 not fluid; firm: *stiff jelly.* 6 dense; compact: *stiff soil.* 7 not easy or natural in manner; formal: *a stiff style of writing. He gave a stiff bow.* 8 lacking grace of line, form, or arrangement: *stiff geometrical designs.* 9 resolute; steadfast; unyielding: *a stiff resistance.* 10 strong and steady in motion: *a stiff breeze.* 11 hard to deal with; hard: *a stiff examination.* 12 harsh or severe: *a stiff penalty.* 13 strong: *a stiff drink.* 14 *Informal.* more than seems suitable: *a stiff price.*

—*adv.* 1 in a stiff manner; stiffly: *He walks very stiff.* 2 completely; utterly: *We were bored stiff.*

—*n. Slang.* 1 a dead body; corpse. 2 a drunken person. 3 a man; fellow: *He hired a couple of stiffs to do the job for him.* 4 a tramp or hobo. 5 a very formal, priggish, or dull person. [OE *stīf*]
—**stiff′ly,** *adv.* —**stiff′ness,** *n.*

☞ *Syn. adj.* 1. **Stiff, rigid** = not easily bent or capable of being bent or turned without breaking. **Stiff,** the general word, describes anything so firm or solid that it does not bend easily or cannot be bent without injury: *Library books need stiff covers.* **Rigid** describes something so stiff and hard that it will not bend at all and cannot be bent without breaking: *The bodies of animals become rigid after death.*

stiff·en (stif′ən) *v.* 1 make stiff. 2 become stiff: *The jelly will stiffen as it cools. Pat stiffened with anger. The wind was stiffening as the storm approached.* —**stiff′en·er,** *n.*

stiff·en·ing (stif′ən ing *or* stif′ning) *n.* 1 a making or becoming stiff. 2 something used to stiffen.

stiff-necked (stif′nekt′) *adj.* 1 having a stiff neck. 2 stubborn; obstinate.

sti·fle (stī′fəl) *v.* **-fled, -fling.** 1 stop the breath of; smother: *The smoke stifled the firemen.* 2 be unable to breathe freely: *I am stifling in this close room.* 3 keep back; suppress; stop: *to stifle a cry, to stifle a yawn, to stifle business activity, to stifle a rebellion.* [ME *stuffle(n), stiffle(n)* < *stuffe(n)* stuff, stifle; influenced by ON *stifla* dam up]

stig·ma (stig′mə) *n., pl.* **stig·mas** or **stig·ma·ta.** 1 a mark of disgrace; a stain or reproach on one's reputation. 2 a distinguishing mark or sign. 3 a small spot or mark; a spot in the skin that bleeds or turns red. 4 *Botany.* the part of the pistil of a plant that receives the pollen. See **flower** for picture. 5 **stigmata,** *pl.* marks or wounds like the five wounds on the crucified body of Christ, said to appear supernaturally on the bodies of certain persons. 6 *Archaic.* a special mark burned on a slave or criminal. [< L < Gk.]

stig·ma·ta (stig′mə tə *or* stig mä′tə) *n.* pl. of **stigma.**

stig·mat·ic (stig mat′ik) *adj., n.* —*adj.* of or having to do with a stigma; like that of a stigma; marked by a stigma. —*n.* a person bearing marks suggesting the wounds of Christ.

stig·ma·tism (stig′mə tiz′əm) *n.* 1 the absence of astigmatism. 2 a condition in which the person has the stigmata.

stig·ma·tize (stig′mə tīz′) v. **-tized, -tiz·ing. 1** set some mark of disgrace upon; reproach. **2** brand. **3** produce stigmas on. **—stig′ma·ti·za′tion,** n. **—stig′ma·tiz′er,** n.

stile (stīl) n. **1** a step or steps for getting over a fence or wall. **2** a turnstile. **3** a vertical piece in a door, panelled wall, etc. [OE *stigel*; related to *stīgan* climb]
☛ *Hom.* **style.**

sti·let·to (stə let′ō) n., pl. **-tos** or **-toes. 1** a dagger with a narrow blade tapering to a sharp point. **2** a small, sharp-pointed instrument for making eyelet holes in embroidery. [< Ital. *stiletto*, ult. < L *stilus* pointed instrument]

still¹ (stil) adj., v., n., adv., conj. **—adj. 1** remaining in the same position or at rest; motionless; stationary: *stand, sit, or lie still.* **2** quiet; tranquil; undisturbed: *The lake is still now.* **3** soft; low; subdued: *a still, small voice.* **4** not bubbling: *still wine.*
—v. 1 make calm or quiet: *to still a crying child.* **2** become calm or quiet. **3** relieve or allay: *to still someone's fears.*
—n. 1 *Poetic.* silence: *the still of the night.* **2** a photograph of a person or other subject at rest. **3** an individual picture, or frame, from a motion picture.
—adv. 1 at this or that time: *He came yesterday and he is still here.* **2** up to this time or that time: *The matter is still unsettled.* **3** in the future as in the past: *It will still be here.* **4** even; yet: *still more, still worse.* **5** yet; nevertheless: *Proof was given, but they still doubted.* **6** without moving; quietly. **7** *Archaic or poetic.* steadily; constantly; always.
—conj. yet; nevertheless: *He is dull; still he tries hard.* [OE *stille*]
☛ *Syn. adj.* **1. Still, quiet** = without noise or activity. **Still** particularly suggests being silent and at rest, and sometimes emphasizes absence of sound, sometimes absence of motion: *It was very late and the night was still. Her hands are never still.* **Quiet** particularly suggests being calm and peaceful or restful, without disturbance, excited activity, or noise: *He lives in a quiet little town.*

still² (stil) n. **1** an apparatus for distilling liquids especially alcoholic liquors. **2** a place where alcoholic liquors are distilled; distillery. [n. use of *still*, short form of *distil*]

still·born (stil′bôrn′) adj. **1** dead when born. **2 a** destined never to be realized: *stillborn hopes.* **b** that fails utterly to attract an audience: *a stillborn book or play.*

still hunt a quiet or secret pursuit.

still life pl. **still lifes 1** fruit, flowers, furniture, pottery, dead animals, etc. shown in a picture. **2** a picture showing such things.

still–life (stil′līf′) adj. of or having to do with still life.

still·ness (stil′nis) n. **1** quiet; silence. **2** the absence of motion; calm.

Still·son wrench (stil′sən) *Trademark.* a wrench with an adjustable L-shaped jaw, used for turning pipes and other round objects.

stil·ly (adj. stil′ē; adv. stil′lē) adj. **-li·er, -li·est,** adv. **—adj.** *Poetic.* quiet; still; calm. **—adv.** calmly; quietly.

stilt (stilt) n. **1** one of a pair of poles to stand on and hold while walking, each with a support for the foot at some distance above the ground. **2** a long post or pole used to support a house, shed, etc. above the water. **3** any of various shore birds of warm regions belonging to the same family (Recurvirostridae) as avocets, having a long, straight bill and very long, thin legs. [ME *stilte*] **—stilt′like′,** adj.

stilt·ed (stil′tid) adj. **1** stiffly dignified or formal: *stilted conversation.* **2** raised above the ordinary level. **—stilt′ed·ly,** adv.

Stil·ton cheese (stil′tən) a rich, white cheese veined with mould when well ripened. [< Stilton, a village in Huntingdonshire, England, where it was first made]

stim·u·lant (stim′yə lənt) n., adj. **—n. 1** a food, drug, medicine, etc. that temporarily increases the activity of some part of the body. Tea and coffee are stimulants. **2** something that spurs one on or stirs one up; a motive, influence, etc. that rouses one to action: *Hope is a stimulant.* **—adj.** stimulating. [< L *stimulans, -antis,* ppr. of *stimulare.* See STIMULATE.]

stim·u·late (stim′yə lāt′) v. **-lat·ed, -lat·ing. 1** spur on; stir up; rouse to action: *Praise stimulated her to work hard.* **2** increase temporarily the functional activity of (a nerve, organ, or other part of the body). **3** excite with alcoholic liquor; intoxicate. **4** act as a stimulant or a stimulus. [< L *stimulare* < *stimulus* goad] **—stim′u·lat′er, stim′u·la′tor,** n.

stim·u·la·tion (stim′yə lā′shən) n. a stimulating; being stimulated: *Lazy people need some stimulation to make them work.*

stim·u·la·tive (stim′yə lə tiv or stim′yə lā′tiv) adj., n. **—adj.** tending to stimulate; stimulating. **—n.** a stimulating thing; stimulus.

stim·u·li (stim′yə lī′ or stim′yə lē′) n. pl. of **stimulus.**

stim·u·lus (stim′yə ləs) n., pl. **-li. 1** something that stirs to action or effort: *Ambition is a great stimulus.* **2** *Physiology.* something that excites some part of the body to activity. [< L *stimulus,* originally, goad]

sting (sting) v. **stung, sting·ing;** n. **—v. 1** prick with a sharp-pointed organ: *Bees, wasps, and hornets sting.* **2** hurt sharply: *He was stung by the mockings of the other children.* **3** cause a feeling like that of a sting: *Mustard stings.* **4** of certain plants, etc., produce irritation, rash, or inflammation in (a person's skin) by contact. **5** affect with a tingling pain, burning sensation, sharp hurt, etc.: *stung by a spark.* **6** drive or stir up as if by a sting: *Their ridicule stung him into making a sharp reply.* **7** *Slang.* impose upon; charge too much.
—n. 1 the wound caused by stinging: *Put mud on the sting to take away the pain.* **2** stinger. **3** a sharp pain: *The ball team felt the sting of defeat.* **4** something that causes sharp pain. **5** something that drives or urges sharply. **6** a stinging quality; capacity to sting or hurt. [OE *stingan*] **—sting′ing·ly,** adv. **—sting′less,** adj.

sting·a·ree (sting′ə rē′) n. sting ray. [alteration of *sting ray*]

sting·er (sting′ər) n. **1** the sharp part of an insect or animal that pricks or wounds and often poisons. **2** anything that stings. **3** *Informal.* a stinging blow, remark, etc.

sting·ray (sting′rā′) n. any of a family (Dasyatidae) of rays having winglike fins that give them a round or diamond-shaped outline and having a long, thin whiplike tail with one or more poisonous spines near the base of the tail that can inflict a very painful wound which is sometimes fatal to human beings. Sting-rays bear live young.

stin·gy (stin′jē) adj. **-gi·er, -gi·est. 1** mean about spending, lending, or giving money; not generous: *He tried to save money without being stingy.* **2** scanty; meagre. [related to STING.] **—stin′gi·ly,** adv. **—stin′gi·ness,** n.

stink (stingk) n., v. **stank** or **stunk, stunk, stink·ing. —n. 1** a bad smell. **2** *Slang.* a great deal of complaint or criticism: *There was a stink about the new dates for exams. She's sure to raise a stink about the shoddiness of the work.*
—v. 1 have a bad smell. **2** cause to have a very bad smell (*usually used with up*): *That fish is stinking up the whole house.* **3 a** have a very bad reputation; be in great disfavor. **b** savor offensively (*of*): *His remark stinks of treason.* **4** *Informal.* be of poor quality or unattractive in some way: *His performance stank. That idea stinks.* **stink out,** drive out with stinking smoke or fumes. [OE *stincan* to smell] **—stink′ing·ly,** adv.

stink·bug (stingk′bug′) n. any of various plant-eating, heteropterous bugs having a disagreeable odor, especially any of the family Pentatomidae.

stink·er (sting′kər) n. **1** a person or thing that stinks. **2** *Slang.* a low, mean, contemptible person. **3** *Slang.* something unpleasant or contemptible.

stink·weed (stink′wēd′) n. **1** a Eurasian annual herb (*Thlaspi arvense*) of the mustard family that has become naturalized as a common weed in North America, having white flowers and irregularly toothed leaves that give off a disagreeable odor when crushed. **2** any of various other plants having a disagreeable odor.

stint (stint) v., n. **—v. 1** keep on short allowance; be saving or careful in using or spending; limit: *The parents stinted themselves of food to give it to their children.* **2** be saving; get along on very little. **3** *Archaic.* stop.
—n. 1 limit; limitation: *That generous man gives without stint.* **2** an amount or share set aside. **3** a task assigned: *Washing the breakfast dishes was her daily stint.* **4** *Archaic.* a stop. [OE *styntan* blunt] **—stint′er,** n. **—stint′ing·ly,** adv.

stipe (stīp) n. **1** *Botany.* a stalk; stem: *the stipe of a mushroom, the stipe of a fern.* **2** *Zoology.* a stalk or stalklike part. [< F < L *stipes* trunk]

sti·pel (stī′pəl) n. *Botany.* a secondary stipule situated at the base of a leaflet of a compound leaf. [< NL *stipella,* dim. of L *stipula.* See STIPULE.]

sti·pend (stī′pend) n. **1** in some professions, fixed or regular pay; salary: *A magistrate receives a stipend.* **2** a regular allowance paid under the terms of a scholarship. [< L *stipendium* < *stips* wages, originally, coin + *pendere* weigh out]

sti·pen·di·ar·y (stī pen′dē er′ē) adj., n., pl. **-ar·ies. —adj. 1** receiving a stipend. **2** paid for by a stipend. **3** of or having to do with a stipend. **4** performing services for regular pay. **—n.** a person who receives a stipend; a salaried clergyman, judge, etc.

stip·ple (stip′əl) v. **-pled, -pling;** n. **—v. 1** paint, draw, or engrave in dots. **2** produce a stippled effect on. **—n. 1** the method of painting, drawing, or engraving by stippling. **2** the effect produced by this method. **3** stippled work. [< Du. *stippelen*] **—stip′pler,** n.

stip·pling (stip′ling) n. the act, method, or work of a person or thing that stipples.

stip·u·lar (stip′yə lər) adj. **1** of or having to do with stipules. **2** stipule-like; having stipules.

stip·u·late¹ (stip′yə lāt′) v. **-lat·ed, -lat·ing.** arrange definitely; demand as a condition of agreement: *He stipulated that he should receive a month's vacation every year if he took the job.* [< L *stipulari* stipulate] —**stip′u·la′tor,** n.

stip·u·late² (stip′yə lit or stip′yə lāt′) adj. having stipules. [< *stipule*]

stip·u·la·tion (stip′yə lā′shən) n. **1** a definite arrangement; agreement. **2** a condition in an agreement or bargain.

stip·ule (stip′yül) n. one of the pair of little leaflike parts at the base of a leaf stem. See **stem** for picture. [< L *stipula* stem; related to *stipes* trunk. Doublet of STUBBLE.]

stir¹ (stèr) v. **stirred, stir·ring;** n. —v. **1** move: *The wind stirred the leaves.* **2** move about: *No one was stirring in the house.* **3** mix by moving around with a spoon, fork, stick, etc.: *to stir sugar into one's coffee.* **4** be mixed with a spoon, etc.: *This dough stirs hard.* **5** set going; affect strongly; excite: *John stirs the other children to mischief.* **6** become active, much affected, or excited: *The countryside was stirring with new life.*
stir oneself, move briskly; bestir.
stir up, a rouse to action, activity, or emotion; incite; stimulate. **b** excite; provoke; induce: *stir up a mutiny.*
—n. **1** a movement. **2** a state of motion, activity, briskness, bustle, etc. **3** excitement. **4** *Archaic.* a public disturbance, tumult, or revolt. **5** the act of stirring. **6** a jog; thrust; poke. [OE *styrian*] —**stir′rer,** n.
☛ *Syn.* n. **2.** Stir, bustle, ado = excitement or excited activity. **Stir** particularly suggests a disturbance, especially where there has been quiet, and a great deal of excitement: *There was a stir in the courtroom.* **Bustle** suggests a great deal of noisy, excited, energetic activity: *All the week before the class picnic, studying gave way to the bustle of preparations.* **Ado** suggests much needless or pointless busyness and fuss, especially over something not worth it: *They made much ado about a comfortable bed for the kitten.*

stir² (stèr) n. *Slang.* prison. [origin uncertain]

stir–cra·zy (stèr′krā′zē) adj. *Slang.* mentally disturbed on account of long imprisonment, or from subjection to endless, restricted routines.

stirps (stèrps) n., pl. **stir·pes** (stèr′pēz). **1** stock; family. **2** *Law.* the person from whom a family is descended. [< L *stirps,* originally, stem]

stir·ring (stèr′ing) adj. **1** moving; active; lively: *stirring times.* **2** rousing; exciting: *a stirring speech.* —**stir′ring·ly,** adv.

stir·rup (stèr′əp or stir′əp) n. **1** one of a pair of foot supports that hang from a saddle. See **saddle** for picture. **2** a piece resembling a stirrup used as a support or clamp. [OE *stigrap* < *stige* climbing + *rāp* rope]

stirrup bone the stapes of the ear.

stirrup cup 1 a cup of wine or other liquor offered to a rider mounted for departure. **2** any farewell drink.

stitch (stich) n., v. —n. **1** in sewing, embroidering, etc., a movement of a threaded needle through the cloth and back out again. **2** *Surgery.* a similar movement through skin, etc. **3** in knitting, crocheting, etc., a single turn or twist of yarn around a knitting needle or crochet hook. **4** the loop of thread, etc. made by a stitch: *The doctor will take the stitches out of the wound tomorrow.* **5** a particular method of making stitches: *a buttonhole stitch.* **6** a small piece of cloth or clothing. **7** *Informal.* a small bit: *The lazy boy wouldn't do a stitch of work.* **8** a sudden, sharp pain.
in stitches, laughing uncontrollably.
—v. **1** make stitches in; fasten with stitches. **2** sew. [OE *stice* puncture] —**stitch′er,** n.

stitch·ing (stich′ing) n. **1** the act or work of one who stitches. **2** stitches collectively.

stith·y (stiŦH′ē or stith′ē) n., pl. **stith·ies. 1** anvil. **2** a forge; smith. [ME < ON *stethi*]

sti·ver (stī′vər) n. **1** a former unit of money in the Netherlands, equal to ¹⁄₂₀ of a guilder. **2** a coin worth one stiver. **3** something having little value. [< Du. *stuiver*]

St. James Street *Cdn.* **1** in Montreal, a street on which is located the city's principal banking firms. **2** the financial or moneyed interests of Montreal.

St.–John's–wort (sānt jonz′wèrt′) n. any of numerous shrubs or perennial herbs (genus *Hypericum*) of temperate regions, including some that are cultivated as garden flowers. See also **rose of Sharon** (def. 2).

sto·a (stō′ə) n. **1** *Greek architecture.* a portico, usually detached and of considerable length and used as a promenade or meeting place. **2 the Stoa,** the Porch, a public walk at Athens, where Zeno, the philosopher who founded Stoicism, taught. [< Gk.]

stoat (stōt) n. **1** ermine (def. 1). **2** any weasel having a black-tipped tail, especially in its brown summer coat. [ME *stote;* origin uncertain]

stock (stok) n., v. —n. **1** a supply or store of goods, materials, equipment, etc. regularly kept on hand for sale or for use as needed; inventory: *a large stock of information. The store has*

already received most of its spring stock. We keep a stock of canned foods at the cottage in case of emergency. **2** (adjl.) kept regularly in stock and available: *stock sizes.* **3** cattle or other farm animals; livestock: *purebred Jersey stock.* **4** (adjl.) for livestock or for the raising of livestock: *a stock farm.* **5** (adjl.) in common use; commonplace or trite: *a stock response. The weather is a stock topic of conversation.* **6** the capital of a company or corporation, divided into portions or shares of uniform amount which are represented by transferable certificates. The holder of one of these is considered a part owner, rather than a creditor, of the company. The profits of a company are divided among the owners of stock. **7** shares in the ownership of an incorporated business. The holder of stock in a company owns a part of that company in proportion to the amount of stock he holds. **8** (adjl.) of, having to do with, or dealing with stock or stocks: *a stock exchange, a stock broker.* **9** *Brit.* a debt owed by a government to individual lenders who receive a fixed rate of interest. **10** the estimation in which a person or thing is held: *to set great stock by a remedy.* **11** a group having a common origin; family or race: *She is of Loyalist stock.* **12** an original ancestor of a family, tribe, or race. **13** a part used as a support or handle; a part or framework to which other parts are attached: *the wooden stock of a rifle, the stock of a whip.* **14 stocks,** pl. **a** a wooden frame having holes for the feet and, sometimes, for the hands, into which people were formerly locked in public as a punishment for minor offences. **b** a frame of timbers on which a ship rests during construction. **15** raw material used to manufacture something: *All the cabinetmaker's wood was kiln-dried stock.* **16** a particular kind of paper: *The advertisement was printed on heavy stock.* **17** liquid in which meat or fish has been cooked, used as a base for soups, sauces, etc.: *chicken stock.* **18** a stiff band of cloth worn around the neck by men especially in the nineteenth century: *A stock is still worn as part of a riding habit for both men and women.* **19** *Theatre.* **a** the repertoire of plays produced by a company at a single theatre. **b** a stock company, or such companies and their activities as a category or type of theatrical production (used without an article): *She is playing in summer stock.* **20** the trunk of a tree or the main stem of a plant. **21** stump. **22** *Archaic.* a person or thing that is stupid or lifeless: *"You stocks and stones!"* **23** *Horticulture.* **a** a tree or plant that furnishes cuttings for grafting. **b** the stem in which a graft is inserted. **24** the crosspiece of an anchor. See **anchor** for picture. **25** any of a genus (*Matthiola*) of plants of the mustard family having flowers that are usually fragrant.
in stock, available for sale or use; on hand.
on the stocks, being built.
out of stock, sold out or used up; not immediately available for sale or use.
take stock, a find out how much stock there is on hand. **b** make an estimate or examination: *We decided to stop and take stock of our situation before continuing with the scheme.*
take stock in, a *Informal.* take an interest in; consider important; trust: *She takes no stock in his promises.* **b** take shares in (a company).
—v. **1** supply or furnish: *to stock a lake with fish, to stock a farm. Our camp is well stocked for the week.* **2** lay in a supply (used with up): *to stock up on firewood for the winter.* **3** keep regularly for use or sale: *Our corner store stocks school supplies.* **4** fasten to or provide with a stock. **5** of a plant, send out shoots. [OE *stocc*]
☛ *Hom.* stalk (stok).

stock·ade (stok ād′) n., v. **-ad·ed, -ad·ing.** —n. **1** an enclosure for defence made of large, strong upright posts placed closely together in the ground: *A heavy stockade protected the trading post from attack.* **2** a fort, camp, etc. surrounded by a stockade. **3** a pen or other enclosed space made with upright posts, stakes, etc.
—v. protect, fortify, or surround with a stockade. [< F *estacade,* ult. < Provençal *estaca* stake < Gmc.]

stock·bro·ker (stok′brō′kər) n. a person who buys and sells securities for customers.

stock·bro·ker·age (stok′brō′kər ij) n. the business of a stockbroker.

stock car 1 a railway freight car for livestock. **2** an automobile of a standard make that has been altered in various ways for use in racing.

stock company 1 a company whose capital is divided into shares. **2** *Theatre.* a company employed more or less permanently

under the same management, usually at one theatre, to perform many different plays.

stock dove a wild pigeon (*Columba oenas*) of Europe.

stocker (stok′ər) *n.* a young motherless or stray calf; dogie.

stock exchange 1 a place where stocks and bonds are bought and sold. 2 an association of brokers and dealers in stocks and bonds.

stock·fish (stok′fish′) *n.* fish preserved by splitting and drying in the air without salt.

stock·hold·er (stok′hōl′dər) *n.* an owner of stocks or shares in a company.

stock·i·net (stok′ə net′) *n.* an elastic, machine-knitted fabric used for making underwear, etc.

stock·ing (stok′ing) *n.* 1 a close-fitting, knitted covering of nylon, cotton, wool, etc. for the foot and leg. 2 sock. 3 something suggesting a stocking, especially a patch of different color on the leg of an animal.
in (one's) **stocking feet,** wearing socks or stockings but no shoes: *Don't run around in your stocking feet; the floor's too dirty. He's 188 cm tall in his stocking feet.* [< *stock* stocking, OE *stocc*] —**stock′ing·less,** *adj.*

stocking cap tuque (def. 1).

stock in trade 1 the stock of a dealer or company; goods kept for sale. 2 tools or other materials needed to carry on a trade or business. 3 any resources, practices, etc. that are characteristic of a particular person, group, or business: *His stock in trade is a slightly rumpled look and a charming smile that audiences love.*

stock·job·ber (stok′job′ər) *n.* 1 *Often derogatory.* a stockbroker, especially one who deals in questionable stocks. 2 a stockbroker who buys and sells securities for other brokers but not for the public.

stock–keep·er (stok′kē′pər) a person in charge of a stock of materials or goods in a warehouse, etc. The stock-keeper keeps an inventory of goods on hand, received, or shipped.

stock·man (stok′mən) *n., pl.* **-men.** 1 a man who owns or manages livestock. 2 stock-keeper.

stock market 1 a place where stocks and bonds are bought and sold; stock exchange. 2 the buying and selling in such a place. 3 the prices of stocks and bonds across a country: *The stock market is falling.*

stock·pile (stok′pīl′) *n., v.* **-piled, -pil·ing.** —*n.* a supply of raw materials, manufactured items, etc. built up and held in reserve in case of a shortage or emergency: *a stockpile of weapons, a stockpile of canned goods.* —*v.* collect or bring together such a reserve supply: *to stockpile nuclear weapons.*

stock·pot (stok′pot′) *n.* a pot in which soup stock is prepared: *They keep all leftover bones for the stockpot.*

stock raising the raising of livestock.

stock·room (stok′rüm′ or -rum′) *n.* 1 a room where stock is kept. 2 a room in a hotel, etc. where sales representatives can show their samples.

stock–still (stok′stil′) *adj.* motionless: *She stood stock-still and listened.*

stock·tak·ing (stok′tā′king) *n.* 1 the act of checking the supply of goods on hand: *The store will be closed two days for stocktaking.* 2 any review of one's position, qualifications, progress, etc.

stock·y (stok′ē) *adj.* **stock·i·er, stock·i·est.** having a solid, sturdy, somewhat thick form or build: *a stocky child, a stocky stem.* —**stock′i·ly,** *adv.* —**stock′i·ness,** *n.*

stock·yard (stok′yärd′) *n.* a place with pens and sheds for cattle, sheep, hogs, and horses. Livestock is kept in a stockyard before being slaughtered or sent to market.

stodg·y (stoj′ē) *adj.* **stodg·i·er, stodg·i·est.** 1 dull or uninteresting; tediously commonplace: *a stodgy style of writing.* 2 very old-fashioned; out-of-date: *He's very stodgy and set in his ways.* 3 of food, heavy and indigestible. 4 heavily built and slow-moving: *A stodgy figure came lumbering through the fog.* [< *stodge* stuff; origin unknown] —**stodg′i·ly,** *adv.* —**stodg′i·ness,** *n.*

sto·gie or **sto·gy** (stō′gē) *n., pl.* **-gies.** a long, slender, cheap cigar. [< *Conestoga,* a town in Pennsylvania]

Sto·ic (stō′ik) *n., adj.* —*n.* 1 a member of a school of philosophy founded by Zeno (336?-264? B.C.), a Greek philosopher. This school taught that virtue is the highest good and that human beings should be free from passion and unmoved by life's happenings. 2 stoic, a person who remains calm, represses feelings, and is indifferent to pleasure and pain. —*adj.* 1 having to do with the philosophy of the Stoics, or with its followers. 2 stoic, stoical. [< L *stoicus* < Gk. *stoikos,* literally, pertaining to a stoa]

sto·i·cal (stō′ə kəl) *adj.* like a stoic; self-controlled; indifferent to pleasure and pain. —**sto′i·cal·ly,** *adv.*

Sto·i·cism (stō′ə siz′əm) *n.* 1 the philosophy of the Stoics. 2 stoicism, patient endurance; indifference to pleasure and pain.

stoke (stōk) *v.* **stoked, stok·ing.** 1 stir up and feed fuel to: *to stoke a fire in a fireplace, to stoke a furnace.* 2 tend a boiler, furnace, etc.
stoke up, a put fuel on (a fire) or in (a furnace). **b** *Informal.* give or feed in abundance, in order to renew energy, make able to act, etc.; fill (*with*). [< *stoker*]

stoke·hold (stōk′hōld′) *n.* the place in a steamship where the furnaces, boilers, etc. are.

stoke·hole (stōk′hōl′) *n.* 1 the hole through which fuel is put into a furnace. 2 the space in front of a boiler or furnace of a ship from which the fires are tended.

stok·er (stō′kər) *n.* 1 a person who tends the fires of a furnace or boiler, especially on a steamship. 2 a mechanical device for tending and feeding a furnace. [< Du. *stoker* < *stoken* stoke]

STOL short takeoff and landing.

stole[1] (stōl) *v.* pt. of **steal.**

stole[2] (stōl) *n.* 1 a long, narrow strip of silk or other material worn around the neck by a minister or priest during certain religious functions. See **vestment** for picture. 2 a woman's long, wide scarf or wrap worn around the shoulders with the ends hanging down in front: *a mink stole, a knitted stole.* 3 a long, loose robe worn by women in ancient Rome. [OE < L < Gk. *stolē* robe]

sto·len (stō′lən) *v.* pp. of **steal.**

stol·id (stol′id) *adj.* having or showing no emotion; hard to arouse; not excitable: *stolid opposition to new ideas. Her stolid presence was a comfort during the uproar.* [< L *stolidus*] —**stol′id·ly,** *adv.*

sto·lid·i·ty (stə lid′ə tē) *n., pl.* **-ties.** the quality or state of being stolid.

sto·lon (stō′lon) *n.* 1 *Botany.* a slender horizontal branch growing from the base of a plant that takes root at the tip and produces a new plant; runner. Strawberry plants have stolons. 2 *Zoology.* a stemlike growth, as in certain polyps, that produces buds from which new individuals grow. [< L *stolo, -onis* a shoot]

sto·ma (stō′mə) *n., pl.* **sto·ma·ta.** 1 *Botany.* one of the very tiny openings in the surface of a leaf, etc., through which water vapor and gases pass in and out. 2 *Zoology.* a small, mouthlike opening in lower animals. 3 a permanent artificial opening between a cavity or canal of the body and the surface or between two cavities or canals. [< NL < Gk. *stoma, -atos* mouth]

stom·ach (stum′ək) *n., v.* —*n.* 1 a large internal organ, the part of the alimentary canal in which the first stage of digestion takes place. Food passes into the stomach from the esophagus and from the stomach into the intestines. See **alimentary canal** for picture. 2 a cavity in an invertebrate animal having a similar function. 3 the lower part of the front of the body; abdomen: belly: *My stomach aches. He was hit in the stomach.* 4 desire for food; appetite: *no stomach for dinner.* 5 any desire or liking: *I had no stomach for a fight. He's got no stomach for that kind of behavior.*
—*v.* 1 eat or keep on one's stomach: *She can't stomach spinach.* 2 put up with; bear; endure: *He can't stomach arrogance.* [ME < OF < L < Gk. *stomachos* < *stoma* mouth]

stom·ach·ache (stum′ək āk′) *n.* a steady pain in the abdomen.

A 17th-century stomacher

stom·ach·er (stum′ək ər) *n.* a stiff, often elaborately decorated panel laced over the front of a tight-fitting bodice, worn by men. Stomachers were worn by men and women in the 16th century and by women also in the 17th and 18th centuries.

stom·ach·ic (stō mak′ik) *adj., n.* —*adj.* 1 of or having to do with the stomach. 2 beneficial to the stomach, digestion, or appetite. —*n.* a medicine for the stomach.

sto·ma·ta (stō′mə tə or stom′ə tə) *n.* pl. of **stoma.**

sto·mate (stō′māt) *adj., n.* —*adj.* having stomata or a stoma. —*n.* stoma.

sto·ma·ti·tis (stō′mə tī′tis *or* stom′ə-) *n.* any of various types of inflammation of the mouth. [< NL *stomatis* < Gk. *stoma, -atos* mouth + NL *-itis*]

stomp (stomp) *v., n.* —*v.* tread heavily or stamp with the foot or feet. —*n.* **1** the act of stomping. **2** a popular dance of the 1930's, marked by lively music and stamping of the feet. [var. of *stamp*]

stone (stōn) *n., pl.* **stones** *or* (for def. 9) **stone**; *v.* **stoned, ston·ing.** —*n.* **1** hard mineral matter that is not metal; rock. Stone is much used in building. **2** a small piece of rock. **3** a piece of rock of definite size, shape, etc. used for a particular purpose: *His grave is marked by a fine stone.* **4** (*adj.*) having to do with or made of stone: *a stone wall.* **5** a gem; jewel. **6** a stonelike concretion, usually of mineral salts or cholesterol, which sometimes forms in the kidneys or gall bladder, causing sickness and pain; calculus. **7** the single seed, usually covered by a hard shell, found inside such fruits as peaches, plums, cherries, and avocadoes; pit. **8** a curling stone. **9** *Brit.* a unit of mass equal to about 6.34 kg: *He weighed more than fourteen stone.* **10** (*adj.*) made of stoneware: *a stone bottle.*
cast the first stone, be the first to criticize.
leave no stone unturned, do everything that can be done.
—*v.* **1** put stone on; pave, build, line, etc. with stone. **2** rub with or on a stone. **3** throw stones at; drive by throwing stones; kill by throwing stones: *Saint Stephen was stoned.* **4** take stones or seeds out of: *to stone cherries or plums.* [OE *stān*] —**stone′like′,** *adj.*

Stone Age the earliest known period of any human culture, characterized by the use of tools and weapons made of stone. The Stone Age is usually divided into the Paleolithic, Mesolithic, and Neolithic periods.

stone-blind (stōn′blīnd′) *adj.* totally blind.

stone·boat (stōn′bōt′) *n.* a low kind of sledge often having runners made of logs, used for transporting stones taken from fields and for other heavy hauling.

stone–broke (stōn′brōk′) *adj. Slang.* not having any money at all.

stone bruise a bruise caused by a stone, especially one on the sole of the foot.

stone–cold (stōn′kōld′) *adj., adv.* —*adj.* cold as stone; completely cold: *By the time he got back, his soup was stone-cold.* —*adv.* absolutely; quite; completely: *He claimed he was stone-cold sober.*

stone·crop (stōn′krop′) *n.* any of various sedums found in rocky places, having yellow, red, or white flowers. [OE *stāncrop*]

stone·cut·ter (stōn′kut′ər) *n.* **1** a person who cuts or carves stone. **2** a machine for cutting or dressing stone.

stoned (stōnd) *adj.* **1** having the stones, or pits, removed: *stoned peaches.* **2** *Slang.* high on or stupefied with drugs or alcohol.

stone–dead (stōn′ded′) *adj.* completely dead; lifeless.

stone–deaf (stōn′def′) *adj.* totally deaf.

stone fruit any fruit that has a layer of pulp outside a hard shell containing a seed; any drupe. Peaches, cherries, olives, etc. are stone fruits.

stone–ground (stōn′ground′) *adj.* of whole-grain flour, made by grinding the whole kernels of grain between millstones, instead of processing the grain to separate the bran from the pulp and then adding bran again after grinding.

stone marten **1** a marten (*Martes foina*) of Europe and Asia that has a patch of white fur on the throat and breast. **2** the fur of this animal.

stone·ma·son (stōn′mā′sən) *n.* a person who cuts stone or builds walls, etc. of stone.

Stone sheep *Cdn.* a dark-brown or black subspecies of the Dall sheep, found in the mountains of northern British Columbia. [after Andrew J. *Stone,* an American naturalist]

Stone's sheep Stone sheep.

stone's throw a short distance.

stone·wall (stōn′wol′ *or* -wôl′) *v.* meet questions, probes, etc. with complete lack of co-operation or response; engage in obstructive or delaying tactics: *to stonewall an official inquiry. The government was accused of stonewalling the opposition.*
—**stone′wal′ler,** *n.*

stone·ware (stōn′wer′) *n.* **1** a hard, non-porous, opaque pottery fired at a temperature that is higher than that for earthenware, but lower than that for porcelain. **2** articles made of stoneware. **3** (*adj.*) made of stoneware.

stone·work (stōn′wèrk′) *n.* **1** work in stone. **2** the part of a building made of stone.

stone·work·er (stōn′wèr′kər) *n.* a person who shapes or cuts stone for use in buildings, sculpture, etc.; stonecutter.

Ston·ey (stō′nē) *n., pl.* **Ston·ey, Ston·eys,** *or* **Ston·ies.** Assiniboine.

ston·y (stō′nē) *adj.* **ston·i·er, ston·i·est. 1** having many stones:

---

hat, āge, fär; let, ēqual, tèrm; it, īce
hot, ōpen, ôrder; oil, out; cup, put, rüle,
əbove, takən, pencəl, lemən, circəs

ch, child; ng, long; sh, ship
th, thin; ғн, then; zh, measure

The beach is stony. **2** hard like stone. **3 a** without expression or feeling: *a stony stare.* **b** cold and unfeeling: *a stony heart.* **c** of fear, grief, etc., petrifying, stupefying. **4** *Slang.* stone-broke. —**ston′i·ly,** *adv.* —**ston′i·ness,** *n.*

Ston·y (stō′nē) *n.* **Ston·y** *or* **Ston·ies.** See Stoney.

ston·y–broke (stō′nē brōk′) *adj. Slang.* stone-broke.

ston·y–heart·ed (stō′nē här′təd) *adj.* pitiless and unfeeling; cold-hearted; cruel.

stood (stud) *v.* pt. and pp. of **stand.**

stooge (stüj) *n., v.* **stooged, stoog·ing.** *Informal.* —*n.* **1** a person on the stage who asks questions of a comedian and is the butt of the comedian's jokes. **2** a person who follows and flatters another; hanger-on. —*v.* be or act as a stooge (for). [origin uncertain]

Stooks of wheat

stook (stuk) *n., v.* —*n.* an upright arrangement of sheaves, intended to speed up drying in the field. —*v.* build such arrangements of sheaves. [ME *stouke*; cf. MLG *stuke* pile of sheaves, bundle] —**stook′er,** *n.*

stook threshing the practice of threshing in the field from the stooks rather than first hauling the sheaves to the barn.

stool (stül) *n., v.* —*n.* **1** a separate seat for one person, having three or four legs or a central pedestal and having no back or arms. **2** a low bench used to rest the feet on or to kneel on; footstool. **3** a seat to be used as a toilet. **4** waste matter from the bowels. **5** the stump or root of a plant from which shoots grow. **6** a cluster of shoots growing from such a base. **7** stool pigeon.
—*v.* send out shoots. [OE *stōl*] —**stool′-like′,** *adj.*

stool·ie (stü′lē) *n. Slang.* stool pigeon.

stool pigeon **1** a pigeon used to lead other pigeons into a trap. **2** *Slang.* a spy for the police; informer. [prob. from the former practice of tying the decoy bird to a stool (defs. 5 and 6)]

stoop¹ (stüp) *v., n.* —*v.* **1** bend forward: *to stoop over a desk.* **2** carry the head and shoulders bent forward. **3** descend from a superior rank or position; condescend: *She would never stoop to speak to the workers.* **4** lower oneself morally; demean oneself: *He stooped to cheating his customers in trying to save his business.* **5** swoop down like a hawk attacking prey. **6** *Archaic.* submit; yield.
—*n.* **1** an act of bending forward. **2** a forward bend of the head and shoulders, especially when habitual: *She walks with a noticeable stoop.* **3** a lowering of oneself; condescension or a demeaning of oneself. **4** the descent of a hawk, etc. on its prey. [OE *stūpian*]
—**stoop′er,** *n.*
☛ **Hom. stoup.**

stoop² (stüp) *n.* a porch or platform at the entrance of a house. [< Du. *stoep*]
☛ **Hom. stoup.**

stop (stop) *v.* **stopped** *or* (*poetic*) **stopt, stop·ping;** *n.* —*v.* **1** keep from moving, acting, doing, being, etc.: *to stop a clock, to stop a speaker.* **2** cut off; withhold: *to stop supplies.* **3** put an end to; interrupt; check: *to stop a noise.* **4** stay; remain: *to stop at a hotel.* **5** leave off moving, acting, doing, being, etc.; cease: *All work stopped.* **6** close by filling; fill holes in; close: *to stop a hole, a leak, a wound.* **7** close (a vessel) with a cork, plug, or the like; shut up (something) in a closed vessel or place: *to stop a bottle.* **8** block; obstruct: *A fallen tree stopped traffic.* **9** check (a blow, stroke, etc.); parry; ward off. **10** defeat by a knockout. **11** *Games.* defeat. **12** punctuate. **13** *Music.* **a** close (a finger hole, etc.) in order to produce a particular note from a wind instrument. **b** press down (a string of a violin, etc.) to alter the pitch of tone produced. **14** instruct a bank not to honor (a cheque, bill, etc.) when presented.
stop off, *Informal.* stop for a short stay.
stop over, a make a short stay. **b** *Informal.* stop in the course of a trip.
—*n.* **1** the act of stopping, closing up, blocking, or checking: *We put a stop to his tricks.* **2** a stay or staying; a halt: *We made a stop for*

lunch. **3** being stopped. **4** the place where a stop is made. **5** anything that stops; obstacle. **6** any piece or device that serves to check or control movement or action in a mechanism. **7** any of several punctuation marks: *A period is a full stop.* **8** a word used in telegrams, cables, etc. instead of a period. **9** *Music.* **a** the closing of a finger hole or aperture in the tube of a wind instrument, or the act of pressing with the finger on a string of a violin, etc. so as to alter the pitch of its tone. **b** a key or other device used for this purpose. **c** in organs, a graduated set of pipes of the same kind, or the knob or handle that controls them. **10** *Photography.* the aperture of a lens, or the f number indicating this. **11** *Phonetics.* **a** a sudden, complete stopping of the breath stream, usually followed by its sudden release. **b** a consonant that involves such a stopping; a plosive. *Examples: the sounds for* p, t, k, b, d, *and* g (*as in* go).

pull out all the stops, do something in the biggest way possible; exert maximum effort.

put a stop to, stop; end.

[OE *stoppian,* ult. < L *stuppa* tow < Gk. *styppē*]

☛ *Syn. v.* **1. Stop, arrest, check** = keep someone or something from continuing an action, movement, progress, etc. **Stop** is the general word, and means "bring advance or movement to an end": *He stopped the car.* **Arrest** emphasizes stopping and holding firmly back progress, development, or action that is already advancing: *Jonathan's tuberculosis was arrested early.* **Check** suggests stopping or arresting suddenly, sharply, or with force, sometimes only temporarily: *An awning over the sidewalk checked his fall and saved his life.*

☛ *Syn.* **5. Stop, cease, pause** = leave off. **Stop,** the general word, means "leave off," particularly doing, acting, moving, or going ahead: *The train stopped. He stopped breathing.* **Cease** is more formal and literary, but means "come to an end," and therefore is used of things that were existing or lasting, or to emphasize that action or movement has stopped permanently: *All life has ceased. He has ceased to breathe.* **Pause** means "stop for a time," but suggests going on again: *He paused to tie his shoe.*

stop·cock (stop′kok′) *n.* a cock or valve for regulating the flow of a gas or liquid in a pipe, etc.

stope (stōp) *n., v.* **stoped, stop·ing.** —*n.* a steplike excavation formed in a mine as ore is extracted in successive layers. —*v.* mine by cutting stopes. [probably related to STEP, n.]

stop·gap (stop′gap′) *n.* **1** anything that fills the place of something lacking; a temporary substitute. **2** (*adj.*) serving as a stopgap: *stopgap legislation.*

stop·light (stop′līt′) *n.* **1** a traffic light or signal. **2** brake light.

stop·log (stop′log′) *n.* a block of wood or concrete used to control an outlet in a dam.

stop·off (stop′of′) *n. Informal.* stopover.

stop order an order to a broker to buy or sell commodities, stocks, etc. whenever the market reaches a set price.

stop·o·ver (stop′ō′vər) *n.* **1** a stopping over in the course of a journey, especially with the privilege of proceeding later on the ticket originally issued for the journey. **2** a place where such a stop is made: *Our first stopover was Regina.*

stop·page (stop′ij) *n.* **1** stopping or being stopped. **2** a block; obstruction.

stop·per (stop′ər) *n., v.* —*n.* **1** a plug or cork for closing a bottle, tube, etc. **2** a person or thing that brings to a halt or causes to stop functioning; a check. —*v.* close or fit with a stopper: *to stopper a flask.*

stop·ple (stop′əl) *n., v.* **-pled, -pling.** —*n.* a stopper for a bottle, etc. —*v.* close or fit with a stopper. [? < *stop*]

stop street a side street from which vehicles may not enter a main street without first stopping. Compare **through street.**

stopt (stopt) *v. Poetic.* a pt. and a pp. of **stop.**

stop·watch (stop′woch′) *n.* a watch having a hand that can be stopped or started at any instant. A stopwatch indicates fractions of a second and is used for timing races and contests.

stor·age (stôr′ij) *n.* **1** the act or fact of storing goods, data, etc. **2** the condition of being stored. **Cold storage** is used to keep eggs and meat from spoiling. **3** a place or space for storing: *She has put her furniture in storage. This house has very little storage.* **4** the cost of storing. **5** the production by electric energy of chemical reactions that can be reversed to produce electricity, especially that occurring in and exemplified by the charging of a storage battery.

storage battery a device for producing electric current, consisting of a group of electrochemical cells that can be recharged; battery (def. 2).

store (stôr) *n., v.* **stored, stor·ing.** —*n.* **1** a place where goods are kept for sale. **2** a thing or things laid up for use; supply; stock. **3** *Esp.Brit.* a place where supplies are kept for future use; storehouse. **4** (*adj.*) not homemade: *store bread.* **5** *Archaic.* quantity; abundance: *We wish them store of happy days.*

in store, on hand; in reserve; saved for the future.

mind the store, *Informal.* look after or keep a check on things.

set store by, value; esteem: *She sets great store by her mother's opinion.*

—*v.* **1** supply or stock. **2** put away for future use; lay up. **3** put in a warehouse or place used for preserving. [ME < OF *estorer* construct, restore, store < L *instaurare* restore, originally, establish < *in* upon + *staurus* pillar] —**stor′er,** *n.*

store–bought (stôr′bot′ *or* -bôt′) *adj. Archaic or dialect* (*often used facetiously*). bought at a store instead of being homemade: *store-bought cookies, a store-bought dress.* Also, **store-boughten.**

store·front (stôr′frunt′) *n.* **1** the front of a store or shop: *All the storefronts were newly painted.* **2** (*adj.*) of a business office, social service, etc., situated at street level in a business district and providing direct access for the public: *a storefront legal office.* **3** (*adj.*) operating a storefront business or service: *a storefront lawyer.*

store·house (stôr′hous′) *n.* **1** a place where things are stored; warehouse. **2** an abundant supply or source: *A library is a storehouse of information.*

store·keep·er (stôr′kēp′ər) *n.* a person who has charge of a store or stores.

store·room (stôr′rüm′ *or* -rùm′) *n.* a room where things are stored.

sto·rey (stôr′ē) *n., pl.* **-reys** *or* **-ries. 1** a level or floor of a house or other building. **2** the set of rooms or apartments on one level or floor. Also, **story.** [? ult. special use of *story* in sense of "row of historical statues across a building front"]

sto·reyed (stôr′ēd) *adj.* having storeys, especially of a specified number (*usually used in compounds*): *a two-storeyed house.* Also, **storied.**

sto·ried (stôr′ēd) *adj.* **1** celebrated in story or history: *the storied Klondike.* **2** ornamented with designs representing happenings in history or legend: *storied tapestry.* [< *story*¹]

stork (stôrk) *n.* **1** any of a family (Ciconiidae) of large, long-legged wading birds found mainly in warm parts of the Old World, having a long neck, a long, heavy bill, and, typically, white-and-black plumage. The Eurasian **white stork** (*Ciconia ciconia*), which often nests on rooftops, has long been a symbol of good fortune among the peoples of Europe; according to folklore it brings new babies into the home. **2** the process or fact of childbirth: *It was a close race with the stork, but we reached the hospital in time.* [OE *storc*] —**stork′like′,** *adj.*

storm (stôrm) *n., v.* —*n.* **1** a very strong wind, especially one with a velocity of about 100 to 120 km/h; windstorm. **2** a violent outbreak of rain with strong winds and, usually, thunder and lightning: *The clouds threatened an approaching storm.* **3** any heavy and especially sudden fall of snow, sleet, hail, etc. together with a strong wind. **4** anything like a storm: *a storm of arrows.* **5** a violent outburst or disturbance: *a storm of tears, a storm of angry words.* **6** a violent attack: *The castle was taken by storm.* **7** a storm window or storm door.

storm in a teacup, *Esp.Brit.* great excitement or commotion over something unimportant.

—*v.* **1** be a storm: *It stormed for three days.* **2** be violent; rage. **3** speak loudly and angrily. **4** rush violently: *to storm out of the room.* **5** attack violently: *The troops stormed the city.* [OE]

storm cellar a cellar for shelter during cyclones, tornadoes, etc.

storm centre 1 the moving centre of a cyclone, where the pressure is lowest and the wind is comparatively calm. **2** any centre of trouble, tumult, etc.

storm door an extra door fixed outside of a regular door as protection against cold, wind, etc. in winter.

storm petrel stormy petrel (def. 1).

storm trooper a member of the Nazi private army formed by Adolf Hitler around 1923 and disbanded in 1934.

storm window an extra window fixed on the outside of a regular window as protection against cold, wind, etc. in winter.

storm·y (stôr′mē) *adj.* **storm·i·er, storm·i·est. 1** having storms; likely to have storms; troubled by storms. **2** rough and disturbed; violent: *They had stormy quarrels.* —**storm′i·ly,** *adv.* —**storm′i·ness,** *n.*

stormy petrel 1 any of several small, black-and-white petrels, sea birds whose presence is supposed to give warning of a storm; especially, a petrel (*Hydrobates pelagicus*) of the N Atlantic and Mediterranean. **2** anyone believed likely to cause trouble or to indicate trouble.

Stor·thing *or* **Stor·ting** (stôr′ting′) *n.* the national parliament of Norway. [< Norwegian *storting,* earlier *storthing* < *stor* great + *thing* assembly]

sto·ry¹ (stôr′ē) *n., pl.* **-ries;** *v.* **-ried, -ry·ing.** —*n.* **1** an account of some happening or group of happenings: *Tell us the story of your life.* **2** such an account, either true or made-up, intended to interest the reader or hearer; tale. **3** *Informal.* falsehood. **4** stories as a branch of literature: *a character famous in story.* **5** the plot of a

play, novel, etc. **6** a newspaper article, or material for such an article. **7** *Archaic.* history: *well-read in story.*
—*v. Archaic.* tell the history or story of. [ME < AF *estorie* < L < Gk. *historia* history. Doublet of HISTORY.] —**sto′ry·less,** *adj.*

☛ *Syn. n.* **2. Story, anecdote, tale** = a spoken or written account of some happening or happenings. **Story** applies to any such account, true or made-up, long or short, in prose or verse, intended to interest another: *I like stories about science.* **Anecdote** applies to a brief story about a single actual incident, usually funny or with an interesting point, often in the life of a famous person: *He knows many anecdotes about life at sea.* **Tale** applies to a longer story told as if giving true facts about some happening or situation but usually made-up or exaggerated: *He reads tales of frontier days.*

sto·ry² (stôr′ē) *n., pl.* **-ries.** See **storey.**

sto·ry·book (stôr′ē bùk′) *n.* **1** a book containing one or more stories or tales, especially for children. **2** (*adjl.*) of or like that of a storybook; romantic: *a storybook hero, a storybook ending.*

sto·ry·tell·er (stôr′ē tel′ər) *n.* **1** a person who tells stories. **2** *Informal.* a person who tells falsehoods; liar.

sto·ry·tell·ing (stôr′ē tel′ing) *n. or adj. Informal.* **1** telling stories. **2** telling falsehoods; lying.

sto·tin·ka (stō ting′ka) *n., pl.* **-ki** (-kē). a unit of money in Bulgaria, equal to ¹/₁₀₀ of a lev. [< Bulgarian]

stoup (stüp) *n.* **1** a drinking vessel of varying size, such as a cup, flagon, or tankard. **2** the amount it holds. **3** a basin for holy water at the entrance of a church. [< ON *staup*]
☛ *Hom.* **stoop.**

stout (stout) *adj., n.* —*adj.* **1** bulky; somewhat fat: *He's getting stout.* **2** thick or thick; solid; substantial: *a stout ship, a stout walking stick. The fort has stout walls.* **3** brave; bold: *He has a stout heart.* **4** not yielding; stubborn; determined: *stout resistance.* **5** characterized by endurance or staying power: *a stout horse, a stout engine.*
—*n.* **1** a strong, dark-brown beer brewed with roasted malt. **2** a stout person. [ME < OF *estout* strong < Gmc. root *stolt-* proud < L *stultus* foolish] —**stout′ly,** *adv.* —**stout′ness,** *n.*
☛ *Syn. adj.* **1.** See note at **fat.**

stout–heart·ed (stout′här′tid) *adj.* brave; bold; courageous. —**stout′-heart′ed·ly,** *adv.* —**stout′-heart′ed·ness,** *n.*

stove¹ (stōv) *n.* **1** an apparatus for cooking and heating, using electricity or burning a fuel such as gas, oil or wood. **2** a kiln or a similar heating device or chamber. [OE *stofa* warm bathing room < VL *stufa* < *extufare* sweat out, ult. < L *ex-* out + Gk. *typhos* vapor. Related to STEW.]

stove² (stōv) *v.* a pt. and a pp. of **stave.** See note at **stave.**

stove·pipe (stōv′pīp′) *n.* **1** a sheet metal pipe of large diameter connected to a fuel-burning stove, used to carry smoke and gases from the stove to a chimney. **2** *Informal.* a tall silk hat.

stow (stō) *v.* **1** pack: *The cargo was stowed in the ship's hold.* **2** pack things closely in; fill by packing: *They stowed the little cabin with supplies for the trip.* **3** *Slang.* stop: *Stow the chatter.*
stow away, hide on a ship, aircraft, etc. to avoid paying the fare or to escape. [ult. < OE *stōw* place] —**stow′er,** *n.*

stow·age (stō′ij) *n.* **1** stowing or being stowed: *The stowage of all their equipment took them two hours.* **2** a room or place for stowing: *The boat has stowage fore and aft.* **3** capacity for stowing: *Our boat has stowage for a three-day cruise.* **4** what is stowed. **5** the charge for stowing something.

stow·a·way (stō′ə wā′) *n.* a person who hides on a ship, aircraft, etc. to get a free passage or to escape.

str. 1 steamer. **2** strait.

stra·bis·mal (strə biz′məl) *adj.* strabismic.

stra·bis·mic (strə biz′mik) *adj.* **1** cross-eyed. **2** of or having to do with strabismus.

stra·bis·mus (strə biz′məs) *n.* a disorder of vision due to the turning of one eye or both eyes from the normal position so that both cannot be directed at the same point or object at the same time; squint; cross-eye. [< NL < Gk. *strabismos,* ult. < *strabos* squint-eyed]

strad·dle (strad′əl) *v.* **-dled, -dling;** *n.* —*v.* **1** sit or stand with one's legs on either side of something: *He straddled the chair. She stood straddling the row of lettuce as she hoed.* **2** be or lie across something: *A footbridge straddled the brook. A pair of large glasses straddled his nose.* **3** be or be spread apart: *His legs straddled as he floundered through the snow.* **4** avoid committing oneself on an issue; favor or appear to favor both sides: *She is still straddling the question, but will soon have to decide one way or the other.*
—*n.* the act of straddling or the position of a person who straddles. [< var. of dial. *striddle,* frequentative of *stride*] —**strad′dler,** *n.*

Strad·i·var·i·us (strad′ə ver′ē əs) *n.* a violin, viola, or cello made by Antonio Stradivari (1644-1737), a violin-maker of Cremona, Italy. These instruments are famous for their exquisite tone.

strafe (strāf *or* straf) *v.* **strafed, straf·ing.** bombard or shell

hat, āge, fär; let, ēqual, tèrm; it, īce
hot, ōpen, ôrder; oil, out; cup, pút, rüle;
əbove, takən, pencəl, lemən, circəs
ch, child; ng, long; sh, ship
th, thin; ŦH, then; zh, measure

heavily; especially, rake enemy ground positions with machine-gun fire from low-flying aircraft. [from a German slogan of World War I, *Gott strafe England!* May God punish England!] —**straf′er,** *n.*

strag·gle (strag′əl) *v.* **-gled, -gling. 1** wander in a scattered fashion: *Cows straggled along the lane.* **2** stray from the rest. **3** spread in an irregular, rambling manner: *Vines straggled over the old wall.* [? related to STRETCH.] —**strag′gler,** *n.*

strag·gly (strag′lē) *adj.* spread out in an irregular, rambling way; straggling.

straight (strāt) *adj., adv., n.* —*adj.* **1** without a bend or curve; direct: *a straight line, a straight path.* **2 a** frank; honest; upright: *straight conduct.* **b** right; correct: *straight thinking.* **3** in proper order or condition: *Keep your accounts straight.* **4** continuous: *in straight succession.* **5** thoroughgoing or unreserved: *a straight Tory.* **6** unmodified; undiluted: *a straight comedy, straight whisky.* **7** *Informal.* reliable: *a straight tip.* **8** *Poker.* made up of a sequence of five cards: *a straight flush.* **9** serious rather than comic; natural rather than eccentric: *a straight part in a play.* **10** *Slang.* conventional in behavior, dress, views, etc. **11** *Slang.* heterosexual.
—*adv.* **1** in a line; directly: *Walk straight.* **2** in an erect position; upright: *Stand up straight.* **3** frankly; honestly; uprightly: *Live straight.* **4** continuously: *Drive straight on.* **5** without delay. **6** without qualification of any kind.
straight off, at once.
—*n.* **1** the condition of being straight; straight form, position, or line. **2** a straight part, as of a racecourse. **3** *Poker.* a sequence of five cards. **4** *Slang.* a person who is conventional. **5** *Slang.* a heterosexual person. [OE *streht,* pp. of *streccan* stretch] —**straight′ly,** *adv.* —**straight′ness,** *n.*
☛ *Hom.* **strait.**

straight angle an angle of 180°.

straight–arm (strāt′ärm′) *v., n. Football.* —*v.* prevent (an opponent) from making a tackle by holding one's arm straight in front. —*n.* the act of straight-arming.

straight·a·way (strāt′ə wā′) *n., adj., adv.* —*n.* a straight course; especially, the straight part of a closed race course or a straight stretch of highway: *They were now on a straightaway, making excellent time.* —*adj.* in a straight course. —*adv.* as quickly as possible; at once; immediately: *The captain read the letter and burned it straightaway.*

straight·edge (strāt′ej′) *n.* a strip of wood or metal having one edge accurately straight, used in obtaining or testing straight lines and level surfaces.

straight·en (strāt′ən) *v.* **1** make straight or become straight: *Straighten your shoulders.* **2** put in the proper order or condition (*usually used with* **up** *or* **out**): *He straightened up his room. We have to straighten out our accounts to see how much we owe.* **3** *Informal.* make or become better in behavior, etc.; reform (*usually used with* **out** *or* **up**): *His parents have tried to straighten him out but he still keeps getting into trouble.* —**straight′en·er,** *n.*

straight face an expressionless face, especially one showing no trace of amusement: *He kept a straight face through the whole ridiculous story.*

straight–faced (strāt′fāst′) *adj.* keeping a straight face.

straight flush *Poker.* a sequence of five cards of the same suit, ranking higher than four of a kind.

straight·for·ward (strāt′fôr′wərd) *adj.* **1** honest; frank: *a straightforward person, a straightforward answer.* **2** without complications; clear-cut and precise: *The plan was straightforward.* **3** going straight ahead; direct. **4** (*advl.*) in a straightforward manner; openly or directly: *She talks very straightforward.*
—**straight′for′ward·ly,** *adv.* —**straight′for′ward·ness,** *n.*

straight·for·wards (strāt′fôr′wərdz) *adv.* straightforward.

straight–out (strāt′out′) *adj. Informal.* out-and-out; complete; thorough.

straight·way (strāt′wā′) *adv. Archaic.* at once; immediately; straightaway.

strain¹ (strān) *v., n.* —*v.* **1** draw tight; stretch: *The weight strained the rope.* **2** pull hard: *The dog strained at his leash.* **3** stretch more than one should: *She strained the truth in telling the story.* **4** use to the utmost: *She strained her eyes to see.* **5** injure by too much effort or by stretching: *The runner strained his heart.* **6** be injured by too much effort. **7** make a very great effort. **8** press or

pour through a material or device that allows only liquid to pass through it: *Consommé is a soup that has been strained.* **9** drip through. **10** press closely; squeeze; hug.
—*n.* **1 a** force or weight that stretches. **2 a** too much muscular or physical effort. **b** an injury caused by too much effort or by stretching. **3** any severe, trying, or wearing pressure: *the strain of worry.* **4** the effect of such pressure on the body or mind. [ME < OF < L *stringere* draw tight]

strain² (strān) *n.* **1** a line of descent; race; stock; breed: *The Irish strain in him explains his sense of humor.* **2** a group of animals or plants that form a part of a breed, race, or variety. **3** an inherited quality: *There is a strain of musical talent in that family.* **4** a trace or streak: *That horse has a mean strain.* **5** Often, **strains,** *pl.* a part of a piece of music; melody; song. **6** a manner or style of doing or speaking: *He wrote in a playful strain.* [var. of OE *strēon* gain, begetting]

strained (strānd) *adj.* **1** produced by efforts; forced; not natural: *a strained laugh. Their first meeting after the quarrel was strained.* **2** dangerously tense; near open conflict: *strained relations between the two nations.*

strain·er (strā′nər) *n.* a utensil or device for straining, filtering, or sifting: *A filter, a sieve, and a colander are strainers.*

strait (strāt) *n., adj.* —*n.* **1** a narrow channel connecting two larger bodies of water. **2 straits,** *pl.* difficulty; need; distress. —*adj. Archaic.* **1** narrow; limited; confining. **2** strict: *The nun took strait vows.* [ME < OF *estreit* < L *strictus* drawn tight. Doublet of STRICT.] —**strait′ly,** *adv.* —**strait′ness,** *n.*
☛ *Hom.* straight.

strait·en (strā′tən) *v.* **1** restrict or limit in range, scope, or amount: *a mind straitened by prejudice.* **2** *Archaic.* make or become narrow.
in straitened circumstances, needing money badly.

strait–jack·et (strāt′jak′ət) *n., v.* —*n.* **1** a strong, tight garment used to bind the arms in keeping a violent person from harming himself or others. **2** anything that hampers or confines: *a legal straitjacket. She felt that the school system should break out of the straitjacket of tradition.* —*v.* confine in or as if in a straitjacket.

strait–laced (strāt′lāst′) *adj.* very strict in matters of conduct; prudish.

strake (strāk) *n.* a single breadth of planks or metal plates along the side of a ship from the bow to the stern. [related to *stretch;* influenced by *streak*]

stra·mo·ni·um (strə mō′nē əm) *n.* **1** a drug prepared from the dried leaves of jimsonweed or another plant of the same genus, used especially in the treatment of asthma. **2** jimsonweed. [< NL]

strand¹ (strand) *v., n.* —*v.* **1** leave in a helpless position: *He was stranded a thousand kilometres from home with no money.* **2** run aground; drive on the shore: *The ship was stranded on the rocks.* —*n. Poetic.* a shore; land bordering a sea, lake, or river. [OE]

strand² (strand) *n.* **1** one of the threads, strings, or wires that are twisted together to make a rope or cable: *This is a rope of three strands.* **2** a fibre, hair, etc. **3** a string of beads, pearls, etc. [ME < OF *estran* < Gmc.]

strange (strānj) *adj.* **strang·er, strang·est. 1** unusual; queer; peculiar: *It was a strange accident: he was unhurt, but the driver was killed. She had the strangest laugh. It's strange that you didn't get the book, because I left it right on your desk.* **2** not known, seen, or heard of before; unfamiliar: *strange faces, a strange language. The procedure was entirely strange to him.* **3** unaccustomed; inexperienced (*used with* **to**): *She made the mistake because she is still strange to the job.* **4** *Archaic.* foreign; alien: *travelling in strange lands.*
feel strange, feel out of place; feel awkward: *He still feels strange in his brother-in-law's home.*
make strange, of a baby or small child, show fear or distress at the presence of someone unknown or not very well known: *She hardly ever makes strange.*
[ME < OF *estrange* < L *extraneus* foreign. Doublet of EXTRANEOUS.] —**strange′ly,** *adv.* —**strange′ness,** *n.*
☛ *Syn. adj.* **1. Strange, odd, peculiar** = unusual or out of the ordinary. **Strange** always suggests the idea of something unfamiliar and outside the usual, ordinary, expected, or natural order: *A strange quiet pervaded the city.* **Odd** suggests a strangeness that is puzzling, or a quality different from the normal or regular: *That is an odd color.* **Peculiar** particularly suggests a quality or character so individual as to be uncommon and seem strange or odd: *Raising frogs is a peculiar way to make a living.*

stran·ger (strān′jər) *n.* **1** a person not known, seen, or heard of before: *She is a stranger to me.* **2** a person new to a place; one who is not yet well acquainted with a place or its inhabitants, etc.; newcomer: *He is a stranger in this area.* **3** a person or thing that is unaccustomed to or not at home in something; one that has no experience of something (*used with* **to**): *He is no stranger to hard*

work. **4** a person from another country; foreigner or alien. **5** *Archaic.* visitor; guest.

stran·gle (strang′gəl) *v.* **-gled, -gling. 1** kill by squeezing the throat to stop the breath: *The infant Hercules strangled a snake with each hand.* **2** suffocate; choke: *His high collar seemed to be strangling him. She almost strangled on a piece of meat that caught in her throat.* **3** choke down; suppress; keep back: *to strangle an impulse to laugh.* [ME < OF *estrangler* < L *strangulare* < Gk. *strangalaein,* ult. < *strangos* twisted. Doublet of STRANGULATE.] —**stran′gler,** *n.*

stran·gle·hold (strang′gəl hōld′) *n.* **1** *Wrestling.* an illegal hold by which an opponent is choked. **2** a controlling or dominant position that chokes opposition, freedom of movement, etc.; an unshakable or deadly grip: *One company had a stranglehold on the market.*

stran·gu·late (strang′gyə lāt′) *v.* **-lat·ed, -lat·ing. 1** *Medicine.* become compressed or constricted so as to stop circulation. **2** strangle; choke. [< LL *strangulare.* Doublet of STRANGLE.]

stran·gu·la·tion (strang′gyə lā′shən) *n.* **1** the act of strangling or the state of being strangled. **2** the state of strangulating or being strangulated.

strap (strap) *n., v.* **strapped, strap·ping.** —*n.* **1** a narrow strip of leather, cloth, or other material that bends easily: *She wore a sun dress with narrow shoulder straps. The box was strengthened by straps of steel.* **2** a narrow strip of leather to sharpen razors on; strop. **3** a looped band suspended from an overhead bar in a bus, train, etc. for standing passengers to hold on to.
—*v.* **1** fasten with a strap. **2** punish by beating with a strap. **3** sharpen on a strap or strop. **4** bind or support (an injured limb, etc.) with adhesive plaster. [var. of *strop*]

strap–hang·er (strap′hang′ər) *n. Informal.* a passenger in a streetcar, subway train, bus, etc. who cannot get a seat and stands holding on to a strap or bar.

strap·less (strap′lis′) *adj.* having no shoulder straps; leaving the shoulders and arms completely bare: *a strapless evening gown.*

strapped (strapt) *adj. Informal.* without money; having no ready cash: *I'm strapped, so I won't be able to go to the movie after all.*

strap·per (strap′ər) *n.* **1** a person or thing that straps. **2** *Informal.* a tall, robust person.

strap·ping (strap′ing) *adj., n.* —*adj. Informal.* tall, strong, and healthy: *a fine, strapping girl.* —*n.* a beating with a strap as punishment.

stra·ta (strā′tə *or* strat′ə) *n.* pl. of **stratum.**

strat·a·gem (strat′ə jəm) *n.* **1** a scheme or trick for deceiving and outwitting the enemy in war. **2** any clever scheme or trick designed to achieve a goal: *He got the position by an unusual stratagem.* **3** skill in using such schemes or tricks: *The plan requires stratagem to be effective.* [< F < L < Gk. *stratēgēma,* ult. < *stratēgos* general. See STRATEGY.]
☛ *Syn.* **Stratagem, artifice, ruse** = a scheme or device to trick or mislead others. **Stratagem** applies to a plan to gain one's own ends or to defeat those of others by skilful deception: *The general planned a stratagem to trap the enemy.* **Artifice** applies to a clever trick or device, sometimes mechanical, to gain one's ends by misleading, and usually deceiving, others: *Motion pictures often employ artifices to get realistic effects.* **Ruse** applies to a trick or device to gain one's ends indirectly by deceiving others about one's real purpose: *His appointment was simply a ruse to leave early.*

stra·te·gic (strə tē′jik) *adj.* **1** of, having to do with, or based on strategy: *a strategic retreat, a strategic move. The booth was in a strategic location, just inside the entrance to the fair grounds.* **2** important in or necessary to strategy: *Each element of the armed forces is a strategic link in our national defence. He went over the strategic points again at the end of his talk.* **3** having to do with or designating materials essential for warfare. **4** specially trained or made for destroying enemy bases, industry, or communications behind the lines of battle: *a strategic bomber.*

stra·te·gi·cal (strə tē′jə kəl) *adj.* strategic. —**stra·te′gi·cal·ly,** *adv.*

stra·te·gics (strə tē′jiks) *n.* strategy.

strat·e·gist (strat′ə jist) *n.* a person skilled in strategy.

strat·e·gy (strat′ə jē) *n., pl.* **-gies. 1** the science and art of war; the overall planning and directing of the military operations of a nation or group of nations at war with another, including political and economic decisions affecting the nation or nations as a whole. **2** a plan based on this. **3** any skilful plan: *She needed a strategy to gain time until she was ready to move.* **4** the skilful planning and management of something: *Strategy is important in an election campaign.* [< Gk. *stratēgia* < *stratēgos* general < *stratos* army + *agein* lead]

strath (strath) *n. Scottish.* a wide valley. [< Scots Gaelic *srath*]

strath·spey (strath′spā′ *or* strath′spā′) *n.* **1** a lively Scottish dance resembling a slow reel. **2** the music for this dance. [< *Strath Spey,* a district in Scotland]

strat·i·fi·ca·tion (strat′ə fə kā′shən) *n.* **1** an arrangement in layers or strata. **2** *Geology.* **a** the formation of strata; deposition or occurrence in strata. **b** stratum.

strat·i·fy (strat′ə fī′) *v.* **-fied, -fy·ing.** arrange, form, or deposit in layers or strata. [< Med.L *stratificare* < L *stratum* (see STRATUM) + *facere* make]

stra·tig·ra·pher (strə tig′rə fər) *n.* a person trained in stratigraphy, especially one whose work it is.

strat·i·graph·ic (strat′ə graf′ik) *adj.* of or having to do with stratigraphy. —**strat′i·graph′i·cal·ly,** *adv.*

stra·tig·ra·phy (strə tig′rə fē) *n.* **1** the branch of geology that deals with the origin, composition, and arrangement of the strata of a region, country, etc. **2** the order and arrangement of strata. [< *stratum* covering, layer + E *-graphy*]

stra·to–cu·mu·lus (strā′tō kyū′myə ləs *or* strat′ō-) *n.* a low, often extensive cloud layer consisting of rounded masses or rolls showing dark patches on the underside where the masses are thickest. [< L *stratus* a spreading out + E *cumulus*]

strat·o·sphere (strat′ə sfēr′) *n.* the region of the earth's atmosphere just above the troposphere, characterized by concentration of ozone, chiefly horizontal winds, and temperature that increases with altitude. It extends to a height of about 50 kilometres, where the mesosphere begins. [< L *stratus* a spreading out + E *sphere*]

strat·o·spher·ic (strat′ə sfer′ik) *adj.* of or having to do with the stratosphere.

strat·o·vi·sion (strat′ə vizh′ən) *n.* a method of using aircraft in the stratosphere to transmit telecasts. [< *strato-* (*sphere*) + (*tele*)*vision*]

stra·tum (strā′təm *or* strat′əm) *n., pl.* **stra·ta** *or* **stra·tums. 1** a horizontal layer of material, especially one of several parallel layers placed one upon another. **2** a layer of sedimentary rock or earth, usually one of a series of distinct, more or less horizontal, layers in the earth's crust, representing continuous periods of deposition. **3** a similar distinct horizontal region or section of the sea or atmosphere. **4** a single layer of tissue or cells. **5** a socioeconomic level of society, comprising persons of similar education, culture, etc.: *Professional people, such as doctors and lawyers, represent one stratum of society.* [< NL < L *stratum,* neut. pp. of *sternere* spread out]

stra·tus (strā′təs *or* strat′əs) *n., pl.* **-ti** (-tī *or* -tē). a very low, sheetlike layer of grey cloud resembling fog, from which rain may fall as drizzle. [< L *stratus* a spreading out < *sternere* spread]

straw (stro *or* strô) *n.* **1** the stalks or stems of grain after drying and threshing. Straw is used for bedding for horses and cows, for making hats, and for many other purposes. **2** a pale-yellow color, similar to that of straw. **3** a single stem or stalk, especially of a grass. **4** (*adj.*) made of straw: *a straw hat.* **5** a slender tube made of waxed paper, plastic, etc., used for sucking up drinks. **6** a bit; trifle: *He doesn't care a straw.* **7** (*adj.*) of little value or consequence; worthless.
catch at a straw, try anything in desperation.
straw in the wind, something taken as an indication of a trend. [OE *strēaw*]

straw·ber·ry (stro′ber′ē *or* strô′-) *n., pl.* **-ries. 1** the small, juicy, edible, red fruit of any of several plants (genus *Fragaria*) of the rose family. A strawberry is not a fruit in the botanical sense; the juicy part is an enlarged flower receptacle and the actual fruits are the tiny, seedlike achenes on its surface. **2** a plant that produces strawberries. There are many varieties of cultivated strawberry.

strawberry blonde 1 reddish blonde. **2** a woman or girl with reddish blonde hair.

strawberry mark a small, reddish birthmark.

straw·board (stro′bôrd′ *or* strô′-) *n.* coarse cardboard made of straw pulp, used for boxes, packing, etc.

straw boss *Informal.* an assistant foreman.

straw flower (stro′flou′ər *or* strô′flou′ər) *n.* an Australian annual herb (*Helichrysum bracteatum*) of the composite family, widely grown for its yellow, orange, red, or white, papery flowers which can be dried for use in permanent bouquets.

straw–hat (stro′hat′ *or* strô′-) *n.* of or concerning plays, musical shows, etc. performed in resort and suburban areas during the summer. [from the wearing of straw hats in summer]

straw man 1 a weak opposing argument or view put forward by a speaker or writer for the purpose of attacking and easily overcoming it. **2** a token candidate or opponent who is put in for appearances by one party or side, but who does not expect to win.

straw vote an unofficial poll or vote taken to find out how a group of people feel about a particular candidate or issue.

straw·y (stro′ē *or* strô′ē) *adj.* **1** of, containing, or resembling straw. **2** strewed or thatched with straw.

stray (strā) *v., n., adj.* —*v.* **1** lose one's way or get separated from

stratification 1111 street

hat, āge, fär; let, ēqual, tėrm; it, īce
hot, ōpen, ôrder; oil, out; cup, pút, rüle,
əbove, takən, pencəl, lemən, circəs
ch, child; ng, long; sh, ship
th, thin; ŧH, then; zh, measure

a group. **2** move or wander aimlessly or without conscious control: *Her eyes strayed around the room as she listened.* **3** turn from the right course; go wrong.
—*n.* **1** a person or thing that has strayed, such as a domestic animal wandering at large: *Our dog is a stray that we picked up a year ago.* **2** Usually, **strays,** *pl.* electromagnetic waves that interfere with radio reception; static.
—*adj.* **1** wandering or lost: *a stray cat.* **2** occurring here and there or now and then; scattered or isolated: *We could hear stray snatches of song from across the lake. There were a few stray fishermen's huts along the beach.* **3** unwanted or wasted: *stray magnetic fields.* [ME < OF *estraier,* originally adj. < VL *stratarius* roaming the streets < LL (*via*) *strata.* See STREET.] —**stray′er,** *n.*
☛ *Syn. v.* **1.** See note at **wander.**

streak (strēk) *n., v.* —*n.* **1** a long, thin mark or line of a different color or texture: *He has a streak of dirt on his face. We saw a streak of lightning.* **2** layer: *Side bacon has streaks of fat and streaks of lean.* **3** a vein; strain; element: *He has a streak of humor, though he looks very serious.* **4** *Informal.* a brief period; spell: *a streak of luck.*
like a streak, *Informal.* very fast; at full speed: *The dog heard the whistle and was off like a streak.*
—*v.* **1** make streaks in or on: *hair streaked by the sun.* **2** become streaked. **3** *Informal.* move very fast; go at full speed. **4** *Informal.* run naked through a crowd or in a public place. [OE *strica*] —**streak′er,** *n.*

streak·y (strē′kē) *adj.* **streak·i·er, streak·i·est. 1** marked with streaks; streaked: *The wall is streaky where the paint did not cover properly.* **2** occurring in streaks: *streaky clouds near the horizon. The color is streaky and faded.* **3** varying or uneven in quality, character, activity, etc.: *A streaky performance.* —**streak′i·ly,** *adv.* —**streak′i·ness,** *n.*

stream (strēm) *n., v.* —*n.* **1** a body of flowing water in a channel or bed, especially a narrow river or a brook. **2** any flow or current of water or other liquid. **3** a steady flow or current, like that of a liquid: *a stream of light, a stream of fresh air.* **4** a continuous series or succession: *a stream of words, a stream of cars.*
on stream, in or into production: *The refinery went bankrupt only a few months after it had gone on stream.*
—*v.* **1** move in a stream: *The sunlight streamed in the window. Tears streamed from his eyes. Soldiers streamed out of the fort.* **2** give off or produce a stream: *Her eyes streamed with tears. The wound streamed blood.* **3** be very wet; drip or run with water, etc.: *streaming windows, a streaming umbrella.* **4** extend or float at full length: *The flag streamed in the wind. Her long hair streamed out behind her as she ran.* [OE *strēam*] —**stream′like,** *adj.*
☛ *Syn. n.* **1. Stream, current** = a flow of liquid or something fluid. **Stream** emphasizes the idea of a continuous flow, as of water in a river or from a spring or tap: *Because of the lack of rain, many streams dried up.* **Current** emphasizes the strong or rapid, onward movement in a certain direction, and applies particularly to the more swiftly moving part of a stream, ocean, body of air, etc.: *He let his boat drift with the current.* —*v.* **1.** See note at **flow.**

stream·er (strē′mər) *n.* **1** any long, narrow, flowing thing: *Streamers of ribbon hung from her hat. Streamers of light are in the northern sky.* **2** a long, narrow flag. **3** a newspaper headline that runs all the way across the page.

stream·flow (strēm′flō′) *n.* the velocity and volume of water flowing at a given time in a channel or stream.

stream·let (strēm′lit) *n.* a small stream.

stream·line (strēm′līn′) *n., v.* **-lined, -lin·ing.** —*n.* the path of a fluid particle past a solid body in a smooth flow. **2** a shape, or contour, designed to offer as little resistance as possible for motion through air or water.
—*v.* **1** give such a contour to; design or construct with a streamline: *They began to streamline cars in the 1930's.* **2** bring up to date, modernize: *to streamline the curriculum.* **3** organize to make simpler or more efficient: *to streamline a procedure.*

stream·lined (strēm′līnd′) *adj.* **1** having a contour designed to offer as little resistance as possible for motion through air or water: *The first streamlined car was the 1933 Chrysler.* **2** organized and efficient: *a streamlined program.* **3** without extra bulk, etc.: *a streamlined figure.*

stream of consciousness an individual's mental processes or experiences considered as flowing in an unbroken stream.

street (strēt) *n.* **1** a public road in a small or large community,

usually having sidewalks and buildings along the sides. **2** the part of such a road for automobiles, trucks, etc.: *Don't play in the street.* **3** people who live in the buildings on a street: *The whole street was against the new bylaw.* **4** (*adj.*) of, on, or near the street: *The camera department is on the street level of the store.* **5** (*adj.*) of clothing, suitable for everyday wear in public: *She changed into her street clothes before leaving the hospital.* **6** **the street,** an environment or way of life associated with a part of a city characterized by poverty, crime, prostitution, etc., where survival depends on toughness, scepticism, and self-reliance. **7** (*adj.*) of, having to do with, or characteristic of such an environment or way of life: *a street kid, street language.*

the man in the street, the typical person; the average person.

on or **in the street,** homeless or without a job: *You'll be out in the street if you don't pay your rent soon. He was on the street for three months before he found another job.*

[OE *strǣt* < LL (*via*) *strata* paved (road), pp. of L *sternere* lay out] —**street′like′,** *adj.*

street Arab a homeless child that wanders about the streets.

TROLLEY

A streetcar

street·car (strēt′kär′) *n.* a large electrically powered vehicle that runs on rails on city streets and is used for public transportation.

street·light (strēt′līt′) *n.* a powerful light, usually mounted on a pole, that is one of a series used to provide illumination for the streets of a town or city.

street·walk·er (strēt′wok′ər *or* -wôk′ər) *n.* prostitute.

street·wise (strēt′wīz′) *adj. Informal.* knowledgeable in the ways of the street (def. 6); shrewd, sceptical, etc.

strength (strength) *n.* **1** the capacity to exert or produce force; power or vigor: *Samson was a man of great strength.* **2** the capacity to resist force or strain: *the strength of a rope, the strength of a wall. He doesn't have enough strength of mind to stick to a diet.* **3** the capacity to resist attack: *the strength of a fort, the strength of an argument.* **4** the number of effective soldiers, warships, team members, etc.; power measured in numbers: *Our team was not at full strength for the game.* **5** intensity: *the strength of a beverage, the strength of a sound.* **6** a person or thing that gives strength or firmness; support: *He said his children were his strength when his wife died.* **7** the existence of a firm or rising level of stock or commodity prices on an exchange, etc.

on the strength of, relying or depending on; with the support or help of: *We hired the man on the strength of your recommendation.* [OE *strengthu* < *strang* strong]

☛ *Syn.* **1.** See note at **power.**

strength·en (streng′thən) *v.* make or become stronger. —**strength′en·er,** *n.*

stren·u·ous (stren′yü əs) *adj.* **1** requiring or marked by much energy or effort: *Squash is a strenuous game. We had a strenuous day moving into the new house.* **2** full of energy; persistently active and vigorous: *strenuous efforts. He was faced with strenuous opposition.* [< L *strenuus*] —**stren′u·ous·ly,** *adv.* —**stren′u·ous·ness,** *n.*

☛ *Syn.* **1, 2.** See note at **vigorous.**

strep (strep) *n. Informal.* streptococcus.

strep·to·coc·cal (strep′tə kok′əl) *adj.* of, having to do with, or caused by streptococci: *streptococcal organisms.*

strep·to·coc·cus (strep′tə kok′əs) *n., pl.* **-coc·ci** (-kok′ī or -kok′sī). any of a group of spherical bacteria that multiply by dividing in only one direction, usually forming chains. Many serious infections and diseases are caused by streptococci. [< NL < Gk. *streptos* curved + *kokkos* grain]

strep·to·my·cin (strep′tō mī′sən) *n.* a powerful antibiotic drug similar to penicillin, effective against tuberculosis, typhoid fever, and certain other bacterial infections. Formula: $C_{21}H_{39}N_7O_{12}$ [< Gk. *streptos* curved + *mykēs* fungus]

stress (stres) *n., v.* —*n.* **1** constraining force; physical, mental, or emotional pressure: *under the stress of hunger, the stresses of urban living.* **2** a state or condition resulting from such pressure or strain: *suffering from stress.* **3** *Physics.* **a** a force exerted when one body or body part pushes against, pulls, or twists another body or body part: *Stresses must be carefully balanced in building*

a bridge. **b** the intensity of such a force per unit area. It is usually measured in pascals. **c** deformation or strain caused by such a force. **4** emphasis or special importance given to something: *The course lays stress on basic computational skills.* **5** emphasis placed on a syllable of a word or a word in an utterance, making it louder or more forceful than the ones surrounding it. In the word *farmer* the stress is on the first syllable; the second syllable has no stress. When an English word has more than one stress, there is always one that is the strongest (**primary stress**) and one or more that are somewhat weaker (**secondary stress**). In the word *institutionalize* the first and last syllables have secondary stresses and the third syllable has the primary stress. **6** a mark written or printed to show which syllable or syllables of a word are uttered more loudly or forcefully than the surrounding ones. In this dictionary ′ is a primary stress and ′ is a secondary stress; both are placed after the syllable concerned. *Examples:* leg′en·dar′y, in′sti·tu′tion·al·ize′, ne′o·clas′si·cist′, cat′walk′. **7** *Prosody.* **a** emphasis or prominence given to a syllable or word as part of a metrical pattern. **b** a syllable given such emphasis. **8** *Music.* accent.

—*v.* **1** give emphasis or importance to: *to stress safety on the job.* **2** pronounce with stress: *Accept is stressed on the second syllable.* **3** place under stress. [partly < *distress,* partly < OF *estrece* narrowness, oppression, ult. < L *strictus,* pp. of *stringere* draw tight]

stretch (strech) *v., n.* —*v.* **1** draw out; extend to full length: *The blow stretched him out on the ground.* **2** continue over a distance; extend from one place to another; fill space; spread: *The forest stretches for miles. We stretched a wire across the path.* **3** extend one's body or limbs. **4** straighten out. **5** reach out; hold out: *He stretched out his hand for the money.* **6** draw out to greater size: *Stretch the shoe a little.* **7** become longer or wider without breaking: *Rubber stretches.* **8** draw tight; strain: *He stretched the violin string until it broke.* **9** make great effort. **10** extend beyond proper limits: *He stretched the law to suit his purpose.* **11** *Informal.* exaggerate: *to stretch the truth.*

—*n.* **1** an unbroken length; extent: *A stretch of sand hills lay between the road and the ocean.* **2** a continuous length of time. **3** *Slang.* a term of imprisonment. **4** *Racing.* one of the two straight sides of a course, especially the part between the last turn and the finish line. **5** the action of stretching or the state of being stretched. **6** a capacity for stretching: *a textile fabric with stretch.* **7** (*adj.*) capable of being stretched; elastic: *a stretch fabric for swimsuits, a stretch wig.* [OE *streccan*]

stretch·er (strech′ər) *n.* **1** a frame or other device for stretching something: *a glove stretcher.* **2** a frame having a canvas or similar covering and either wheels or carrying handles on which to move the sick, wounded, or dead. **3** *Masonry.* a brick or stone laid horizontally with its length along the length of a wall. Compare **header** (def. 3).

stretcher case a person who has to be carried on a stretcher because of serious injury or illness: *Several bus passengers were hurt in the accident, but there were no stretcher cases.*

strew (strü) *v.* **strewed, strewn** or **strewed, strew·ing. 1** scatter; sprinkle: *The pages were strewn all over the floor. He strewed shredded coconut on the cake.* **2** cover with something scattered or sprinkled. **3** be scattered over; be sprinkled over: *Litter strewed the sidewalk.* [OE *strēowian*]

strewn (strün) *n.* pp. of **strew.**

stri·a (strī′ə) *n., pl.* **-ae** (-ē *or* -ī). **1** a slight furrow or channel. **2** a linear marking; a narrow stripe or streak, as of color or texture, especially one of a number in parallel arrangement. **3** *Architecture.* a fillet between the flutes of columns, etc. [< L]

stri·at·ed (strī′āt id) *adj.* striped, streaked, or furrowed: *the striated plumage of a bird, a striated muscle.* [< L *striatus,* pp. of *striare* furrow, channel < *stria* furrow, channel]

stri·a·tion (strī ā′shən) *n.* **1** a striated condition or appearance. **2** a stria; one of a number of parallel striae.

strick·en (strik′ən) *adj., v.* —*adj.* **1** affected or overwhelmed by disease, trouble, sorrow, etc.: *a stricken conscience. Help was rushed to the fire-stricken city.* **2** hit or wounded by or as if by a missile.

stricken in years, old. —*v.* a pp. of **strike.**

strict (strikt) *adj.* **1** enforcing a rule or set of rules with great care: *The teacher was strict but not unfair.* **2** requiring complete obedience: *They were under strict orders not to leave the barracks.* **3** exact; precise: *a strict translation. He wasn't trespassing in the strict sense of the word.* **4** complete; absolute: *It was told to him in strict confidence. She lives in strict seclusion.* **5** very careful in following a standard or principle: *a strict Catholic.* **6** *Archaic.* close; tight. [< L *strictus,* pp. of *stringere* bind tight. Doublet of STRAIT.] —**strict′ly,** *adv.* —**strict′ness,** *n.*

☛ *Syn.* **1, 2.** **Strict, rigid, rigorous** = severe and unyielding or harsh and stern. **Strict** emphasizes showing or demanding a very careful and close following of a rule, standard, or requirement: *Our supervisor is strict and insists that we follow instructions.* **Rigid** emphasizes being firm and unyielding, not changing or relaxing for anyone or under any conditions: *He maintains a rigid working*

schedule. **Rigorous** emphasizes the severity, harshness, or sternness of the demands made, conditions imposed, etc.: *We believe in rigorous enforcement of the laws.*

stric·ture (strik′chər) *n.* **1** an unfavorable criticism; critical remark. **2** an abnormal narrowing of some duct or tube of the body. **3** something that binds or limits; restriction. [< L *strictura* < *stringere* bind tight]

strid·den (strid′ən) *v.* pp. of **stride.**

stride (strīd) *v.* **strode, strid·den, strid·ing;** *n.* —*v.* **1** walk with long steps. **2** pass with one long step: *He strode over the brook.* **3** *Archaic or poetic.* bestride or straddle. —*n.* **1** a long step: *With two strides he was at the door.* **2** the distance covered by such a step. **3** a striding gait: *The child could not keep up with her father's stride.*

hit (one's) **stride,** reach one's normal speed or level of efficiency: *By the second day of working together they had hit their stride and were making good progress.*

take in stride or **in** (one's) **stride,** do or handle without difficulty or hesitation; cope with easily: *He took the defeat in stride. The award came as a surprise, but she took it in her stride.*

[OE *strīdan*] —**strid′er,** *n.*

☛ *Syn. v.* **1.** See note at **walk.**

stri·dence (strī′dəns) *n.* the quality or state of being strident.

stri·den·cy (strī′dən sē) *n.* stridence.

stri·dent (strī′dənt) *adj.* **1** making or having a harsh sound; grating or shrill: *a strident voice, the strident sound of a power saw.* **2** commanding attention in an unpleasant, irritating way: *strident colors. They agreed with his argument, but they didn't like the strident tone of the letter.* [< L *stridens, -entis,* ppr. of *stridere* sound harshly] —**stri′dent·ly,** *adv.*

strid·u·lant (strij′ə lənt) *adj.* stridulating.

strid·u·late (strij′ə lāt′) *v.* **-lat·ed, -lat·ing.** produce a shrill, grating sound, as a cricket or katydid does, by rubbing together certain parts of the body. [< NL *stridulare* < L *stridulus* producing a harsh or grating sound < *stridere* sound harshly]

strid·u·la·tion (strij′ə lā′shən) *n.* the action or sound of stridulating.

strife (strīf) *n.* **1** the act or fact of quarrelling or fighting; bitter or violent conflict: *The relationship between the brothers had always been full of strife.* **2** a struggle or contest between rivals. [ME < OF *estrif* < Gmc.]

strig·il (strij′əl) *n.* in ancient Greece and Rome, a scraper for the skin, used after physical exercise, a bath, etc. [< L *strigilis*; related to *stringere* draw tight, strip off, scrape]

strike (strīk) *v.* **struck, struck** or **strick·en, strik·ing;** *n.* —*v.* **1** hit; deal a blow to: *to strike a person in anger.* **2** deal; give: *to strike a blow in self-defence.* **3** make by stamping; printing, etc.: *to strike a medal.* **4** set or be set on fire by hitting or rubbing: *to strike a match.* **5** affect the mind or feeling of; impress: *The plan strikes me as silly.* **6** sound: *The clock strikes twelve times at noon.* **7** overcome, as by death, disease, suffering, fear, etc.: *They were struck with terror.* **8** make an attack: *The enemy will strike at dawn.* **9** occur to: *An amusing thought struck her.* **10** find or come upon (ore, oil, water, etc.). **11** stop work to get better pay, shorter hours, etc.: *The coal miners struck.* **12** cross; rub: *Strike out the last word. Strike his name off the list.* **13** take away by a blow; take away: *Strike off his head.* **14** go: *We struck into a gallop. We walked along the road one kilometre, then struck out across the fields.* **15** assume: *He struck an attitude.* **16** enter or cause to enter; send or take root; fasten or be fastened: *The roots of oaks strike deep.* **17** get by figuring: *Strike an average.* **18** enter upon; make; decide: *The employer and the workmen have struck an agreement.* **19** lower or take down (a sail, flag, tent, etc.). **20** make level; make level with the top edge of a measure. **21** of a snake, etc., wound with fangs or sting. **22** take hold of the bait: *The fish are striking well today.* **23** collide with: *The car struck a fence.* **24** fall on; touch; reach; catch: *The sun struck his eyes.* **25** come across; come upon; find: *to strike an amusing book.* **26** remove (a scene) from the stage; remove the scenery, etc. of (a play).

strike a balance, find the difference between the credit and debit sides of an account.

strike home, a make an effective thrust or stroke with a weapon or tool. **b** make a strong impression: *The words of warning struck home.*

strike it rich, *Informal.* **a** find rich ore, oil, etc. **b** have a sudden or unexpected great success.

strike off, to take or remove by or as if by a stroke.

strike out, a cross out; rub out. **b** in baseball, fail to hit three times: *The batter struck out.* **c** in baseball, cause to fail to hit three times: *The pitcher struck out six men.* **d** in swimming, use arms and legs to move forward. **e** hit from the shoulder. **f** make a start by personal effort or enterprise.

strike up, a begin: *The two boys struck up a friendship.* **b** begin to play, sing, or sound: *to strike up a song.*

—*n.* **1** the act or fact of finding rich ore in mining, oil in boring,

---

hat, āge, fär; let, ēqual, tėrm; it, īce
hot, ōpen, ôrder; oil, out; cup, pút, rüle,
əbove, takən, pencəl, lemən, circəs

ch, child; ng, long; sh, ship
th, thin; ᴛʜ, then; zh, measure

etc.; sudden success. **2** a general quitting of work in order to force an employer or employers to agree to the workers' demands for higher wages, shorter hours, etc. **3** the act of striking. **4** *Baseball.* **a** the failure of the batter to make a proper hit. **b** a pitched ball that passes above the plate at a height between the level of the batter's shoulders and that of his knees. **5** *Bowling.* **a** an upsetting of all the pins with the first ball bowled. **b** the score so made. **6** a number of coins made at one time. **7** a taking hold of the bait. **8** a metal piece in a doorjamb, into which the latch of a lock fits when the door closes. **9** an attack.

on strike, having stopped work to get more pay, shorter hours, etc.: *Most of the workers voted to go on strike.*

[OE *strican* rub, stroke]

strike-bound (strīk′bound′) *adj.* immobilized by a labor strike.

strike·break·er (strīk′brā′kər) *n.* a person actively involved in trying to break up a strike, especially one hired to replace a striking employee.

strike·break·ing (strīk′brā′king) *n.* forceful measures taken to break up a strike.

strike·out (strīk′out′) *n. Baseball.* **1** an out made by a pitcher throwing three strikes against the batter. **2** the act of striking out.

strik·er (strī′kər) *n.* **1** a person or thing that strikes. **2** a worker who is on strike.

strik·ing (strī′king) *adj.* **1** attracting attention because of some unusual quality; remarkable: *a striking use of color, a striking dress.* **2** that strikes or is on strike: *The striking workers have rejected the latest offer.* —**strik′ing·ness,** *n.*

strik·ing·ly (strī′king lē) *adv.* in a way that attracts attention.

string (string) *n., v.* **strung, strung** or *(rare)* **stringed, string·ing.** —*n.* **1** a thin strip or line of twisted fibre; fine cord. **2** a piece of this. **3** a series of objects threaded or hung on a string: *a string of pearls, a string of fish.* **4** a length of wire or catgut for a musical instrument: *the strings of a violin.* **5 strings,** pl. *Music.* **a** violins, cellos, and other stringed instruments collectively. **b** the section of an orchestra composed of stringed instruments. **6** anything used for tying: *apron strings.* **7** a cordlike part of a plant, especially the tough fibre connecting the two halves of a string bean pod. **8** a series or sequence of like things in a line or as if in a line: *a string of cars, a string of victories.* **9** *Informal.* a condition; proviso: *an offer with a string attached to it.* **10** the race horses belonging to a particular stable or owner. **11** a group of persons or things under the same ownership or management or associated with the same person, etc.: *a string of restaurants, a string of boyfriends.*

have or **keep** (someone) **on a string,** dominate or control someone completely.

have two strings to (one's) **bow,** have more than one way of doing or getting something.

pull strings, use one's influence, especially secretly: *There were more qualified applicants, but he got the job because she pulled some strings for him.*

pull the strings, direct the actions of others, often secretly: *He is supposed to be retired, but he still pulls the strings on all the company's big deals.*

—*v.* **1** thread or hang on a string: *to string beads.* **2** furnish with a string or strings: *to string a violin, to string a bow. He had his tennis racket strung.* **3** tie or hang with a string or rope: *We dry herbs by stringing them from the rafters in the barn.* **4** extend or stretch from one point to another: *to string a cable.* **5** tune the strings of an instrument. **6** make tense; key up: *The news had got them all strung up.* **7** remove the stringy fibres from: *We sat there stringing beans.* **8** form into a string or strings. **9** move, lie, or arrange in a line or series. **10** *Slang.* fool or deceive (often used with **along**): *Are you stringing me?*

string along, *Informal.* **a** go along; follow: *He asked if he could string along with them.* **b** agree or accept: *stringing along with the majority opinion.*

string out, prolong; stretch; extend: *The program was strung out too long.*

string up, *Informal.* kill by hanging: *The horse thief was caught and strung up from the nearest tree.*

[OE *streng*] —**string′less,** *adj.* —**string′like′,** *adj.*

string bean 1 a green bean or wax bean, especially a variety having stringlike fibres connecting the two halves of the pod. **2** *Informal.* a tall, very thin person.

string bog *Cdn.* a series or chain of small sink holes, as distinguished from a large swamp or bog.

string·course (string′kôrs′) *n. Architecture.* a horizontal band running around a structure, usually raised and decorated.

stringed instrument a musical instrument having strings, played by striking, by plucking, or with a bow. The violin, piano, harp, and guitar are stringed instruments.

strin·gen·cy (strin′jən sē) *n., pl.* **-cies.** the state or quality of being stringent.

strin·gent (strin′jənt) *adj.* **1** strict; severe: *stringent laws.* **2** lacking ready money; tight: *a stringent market for loans.* **3** convincing; forcible: *stringent arguments.* [< L *stringens, -entis,* ppr. of *stringere* bind tight] —**strin′gent·ly,** *adv.*

string·er (string′ər) *n.* **1** a person or thing that strings. **2 a** a long, horizontal supporting timber in a building. **b** a stringpiece. **3** a part-time or local correspondent for a newspaper or magazine. **4** a newspaper correspondent paid on the basis of lineage. **5** a member of a team ranked according to ability; person ranked according to ability: *a first-stringer.* **6** a heavy, horizontal timber or girder supporting the ties of a railroad trestle or bridge or the flooring of a wooden bridge. **7** *Geology.* a narrow vein of a mineral.

string·halt (string′holt′ *or* -hôlt′) *n.* a lame condition of one or both hind legs of a horse, caused by spasms of the muscles that make the legs jerk when the horse walks. Also, **springhalt.**

string·piece (string′pēs′) *n.* a long, horizontal beam used to strengthen or connect parts of a framework.

string quartet 1 a quartet of performers on stringed instruments. **2** the instruments themselves, usually consisting of two violins, a viola, and a cello. **3** a composition for string quartet.

string tie a short, narrow necktie.

string·y (string′ē) *adj.* **string·i·er, string·i·est. 1** like, containing, or consisting of fibres or strings: *tough, stringy meat. Her hair was long and stringy.* **2** forming strings: *a stringy syrup.* **3** lean and sinewy; wiry: *a boy of about sixteen, tall and stringy.* —**string′i·ness,** *n.*

strip¹ (strip) *v., n.* —*v.* **stripped** *or (rare)* **stript, strip·ping. 1** remove the clothing, covering, or outer layer from: *to strip a bed, to strip a baby for a bath, to strip a banana, to strip a table for refinishing.* **2** undress: *He stripped down to his shorts.* **3** perform a striptease. **4** tear or pull off; remove: *to strip wallpaper from a wall, to strip the fruit from a tree.* **5** make bare; clear out or empty: *to strip a house of its furniture, to strip a forest of its timber.* **6** take away the titles, rights, etc. of. **7** deprive of or rob: *to be stripped of one's pride.* **8** break or damage the thread or teeth of (a gear, screw, etc.). **9** milk (a cow) thoroughly. —*n.* the act or an instance of undressing or of performing a striptease. [OE *-strīpan,* as in *bestrīepan* plunder]

strip² (strip) *n.* **1** a long, narrow, flat piece of material: *a strip of metal, a strip of paper. He tore the cloth into strips for a bandage. The bark came off in strips.* **2** a long, narrow tract of land, forest, etc. **3** airstrip. **4** comic strip. [probably < MLG *strippe* strap]

strip cropping *or* **planting** the planting of alternate rows of crops having strong and weak root systems, done along the contours of a slope to lessen soil erosion.

stripe¹ (strip) *n., v.* **striped, strip·ing.** —*n.* **1** a long, narrow band of different color or texture: *A tiger has black stripes. The wallpaper is white with green stripes.* **2** fabric, wallpaper, etc. having a pattern of parallel stripes: *She used a stripe for the slip covers.* **3** stripes, *pl.* a number or combination of strips of braid on the sleeve of a uniform to show rank, length of service, etc. **4** a sort; type: *Men of a different stripe.* —*v.* mark with stripes. [< MDu.]

stripe² (strip) *n.* a stroke or lash with a whip. [probably a special use of *stripe¹*]

striped (stript) *adj.* having stripes; marked with stripes.

strip·ling (strip′ling) *n.* an adolescent boy; youth. [< *strip²* + *-ling*]

strip mine a mine operated by digging out layers of earth on the surface to expose the ore.

strip mining the act or work of operating a strip mine.

stripped-down (stript′down′) *adj.* reduced to essentials.

strip·per (strip′ər) *n.* **1** a person or thing that strips. **2** an oil well producing several hours daily and requiring time to rebuild pressure before the oil flows again. **3** a striptease dancer.

strip poker a type of poker in which the loser of each hand must take off a piece of clothing.

strip·tease (strip′tēz′) *n.* **1** an entertainment in which a performer, usually a woman, slowly undresses before an audience, to the accompaniment of music. **2** (*adj.*) of, having to do with, or featuring striptease: *a striptease act, a striptease club.* —**strip′teas′er,** *n.*

strive (strīv) *v.* **strove** *or* **strived, striv·en, striv·ing. 1** try hard; make a great effort: *to strive for self-control.* **2** fight or contend; vie: *The swimmer strove against the tide. The wrestlers strove with each other.* [ME < OF *estriver* < Gmc.]

striv·en (striv′ən) *v.* pp. of **strive.**

strobe (strōb) *n.* **1** strobe light. **2** stroboscope.

strobe light an apparatus for producing very brief, brilliant flashes of light, either by means of a neon or xenon-filled tube in which rapid electric discharges produce flashes of light or by means of a steady, intense light with a rotating perforated disk in front of it. Strobe lights are used in photography, theatre, discothèques, etc. [short for *stroboscope*]

strob·ile (strob′il *or* strob′əl) *n. Botany.* any seed-producing cone, such as a pine cone, or a compact mass of scale-like leaves that produce spores, such as the cone of the club moss. [< LL < Gk. *strobilos* pine cone < *strobos* a whirling around]

strob·o·scope (strō′bə skōp′) *n.* an instrument for studying periodic motion by the illumination of a moving body in flashes or at intervals. [< G *Stroboskop* < Gk. *strobos* a whirling + G *-skop,* equivalent to E *-scope*]

strob·o·scop·ic (strō′bə skop′ik) *adj.* of or having to do with stroboscopes.

strode (strōd) *v.* pt. of **stride.**

stroke¹ (strōk) *n., v.* **stroked, strok·ing.** —*n.* **1** an act of striking; blow: *The house was hit by a stroke of lightning.* **2** a sound made by striking: *We arrived on the stroke of three.* **3** a piece of luck, fortune, etc.: *a stroke of bad luck.* **4 a** a single complete movement to be made again and again, especially of a moving part or parts, in one direction. **b** the distance travelled by this part. **5** *Tennis, golf, etc.* the hitting of a ball. **6** a throb or pulsing, as of the heart. **7** a movement or mark made by a pen, pencil, brush, etc.: *He writes with a heavy down stroke.* **8** a vigorous attempt to attain some object: *a bold stroke for freedom.* **9** a feat or achievement: *a stroke of genius.* **10** an act, piece, or amount of work, etc.: *a stroke of work.* **11** a sudden inability to feel or move, with partial or complete loss of consciousness, caused by injury to the brain when a blood vessel breaks or becomes blocked by a clot. **12** a sudden attack of any of various illnesses (*used only in compounds*): *heat stroke, sunstroke.* **13** a sudden action like a blow in its effect, as in causing pain, injury, or death: *a stroke of fate, the stroke of death.* **14** *Swimming.* **a** one of a series of propelling movements, involving the pull of one arm (or both together) with one or more kicks. **b** a style or method of swimming: *He swims a fast stroke.* **15** *Rowing.* **a** a single pull of the oar. **b** the style or rate of pulling the oars: *He rows with a strong stroke.* **c** the rower seated nearest the stern of the boat, who sets the time for the other oarsmen. **d** the position of this rower.

keep stroke, make strokes at the same time.

—*v.* **1** act as the stroke of (a rowing crew): *Who stroked the Vancouver crew?* **2** mark with a stroke or strokes, especially in order to cancel. [related to STRIKE or its source] —**strok′er,** *n.*

☛ *Syn. n.* **1.** See note at **blow.**

stroke² (strōk) *v.* **stroked, strok·ing;** *n.* —*v.* move the hand gently over: *She stroked the kitten.*

stroke the wrong way, **a** stroke (an animal) in the direction contrary to that in which the fur naturally lies. **b** ruffle or irritate (a person), especially by going counter to his wishes.

—*n.* a stroking movement. [OE *strācian*]

stroke oar 1 the oar nearest the stern of the boat. **2** the rower who pulls the oar nearest the stern of the boat, setting the time of the stroke for the other rowers; stroke¹ (def. 15c).

stroll (strōl) *v., n.* —*v.* **1** take a quiet walk for pleasure; walk. **2** go from place to place: *strolling musicians, strolling gypsies.* **3** stroll along or through: *Every evening they strolled the path by the river.* —*n.* a leisurely walk. [origin uncertain]

stroll·er (strō′lər) *n.* **1** a person who strolls: *The park was filled with strollers.* **2** a wanderer; a vagabond; an actor who goes from place to place in search of work. **3** a kind of light carriage for wheeling a young child, in which the child can sit upright.

strong (strong) *adj., adv.* —*adj.* **1** having much force or power: *a strong wind, strong muscles, a strong nation.* **2** able to last, endure, resist, etc.: *a strong fort, a strong rope.* **3** not easily influenced, changed, etc.; firm: *a strong will.* **4** of great force or effectiveness: *strong arguments.* **5** having a certain number: *A group that is 100 strong has 100 in it.* **6** having a particular quality or property in high degree: *a strong poison, a strong acid, a strong tea.* **7** containing much alcohol: *a strong drink.* **8** having much flavor or odor: *strong seasoning, strong perfume.* **9** having an unpleasant taste or smell: *strong butter.* **10** intense: *a strong light.* **11** vigorous, forceful: *a strong speech.* **12** hearty; zealous: *a strong dislike.* **13** *Grammar.* of or designating a verb or class of verbs inflected by a vowel change

within the stem of the word. *Examples: find, found; give, gave, given; sing, sang, sung.* **14** *Phonetics.* of a syllable, stressed. —*adv.* in a strong manner: *They're still going strong.* [OE *strang*] —**strong′ly,** *adv.*

☛ *Syn. adj.* **1. Strong, sturdy, robust** = having or showing much power, force, or vigor. **Strong** is the general word, describing people, animals, plants, or things, and especially suggesting great power or force in acting, resisting, or enduring: *Fishermen need strong backs and arms.* **Sturdy** suggests power coming from good, solid construction and unyielding strength: *Children need sturdy clothes.* **Robust** emphasizes healthy vigor of mind or body and a toughness of muscles or spirit: *Sports make children robust.*

strong–arm (strong′ärm′) *adj., v. Informal.* —*adj.* having or using force or violence: *strong-arm tactics.* —*v.* use force or violence on.

strong·box (strong′boks′) *n.* a strongly made box for holding valuables.

strong drink alcoholic drink; liquor.

strong·hold (strong′hōld′) *n.* **1** a fort or fortress. **2** a secure place or centre: *a stronghold of freedom. The city is the stronghold of the Conservative party in the province.*

strong·man (strong′man′) *n., pl.* **-men. 1** a muscular man who performs feats of strength in a carnival, circus, etc. **2** a leader who obtains power by force and suppression; dictator.

strong–mind·ed (strong′mīn′did) *adj.* having a strong mind; mentally vigorous. —**strong′-mind′ed·ly,** *adv.* —**strong′-mind′ed·ness,** *n.*

strong wood or **woods** *Cdn.* forest; big trees. [translation of F *bois fort* (s)]

stron·ti·um (stron′tē əm *or* stron′shē əm) *n.* a soft, silver-white metallic element which occurs only in combination with other elements. Strontium is used in making alloys and in fireworks and signal flares. *Symbol:* Sr; *at.no.* 38; *at.wt.* 87.62. [< NL *strontium* < *Strontian,* a parish in Scotland, the site of lead mines where strontium was first discovered]

strontium 90 a radio-active isotope of strontium that occurs in the fallout from nuclear explosions. Strontium 90 is dangerous because it is absorbed by bones and tissues and may replace the calcium in the body.

strop (strop) *n., v.* **stropped, strop·ping.** —*n.* a leather strap used for sharpening razors. —*v.* sharpen on a strop. [ME; ult. < L *stroppus* band < Gk. *strophos*]

stro·phe (strō′fē) *n.* **1** a part of an ancient Greek ode sung by the chorus when moving from right to left. **2** a series of lines forming a division of a poem and having metrical structure which is repeated in a second group of lines (the antistrophe), especially in ancient Greek choral and lyric poetry. **3** any of two or more metrically corresponding series of lines forming divisions of a lyric poem; stanza. [< Gk. *strophē,* originally, a turning (i.e., a section sung by the chorus while turning)]

stroph·ic (strof′ik *or* strō′fik) *adj.* of or having to do with a strophe.

stroud (stroud) *n. Cdn.* **1** a heavy woollen cloth popular in the North as material for blankets, leggings, capotes, etc. **2** a garment or blanket made of this material. [< *Stroud,* England, where it was first made]

strove (strōv) *v.* pt. of **strive.**

strow (strō) *v.* **strowed, strown** or **strowed, strow·ing.** *Archaic.* strew.

strown (strōn) *v. Archaic.* pp. of **strow.**

struck (struk) *v., adj.* —*v.* pt. and pp. of **strike.** —*adj.* closed or affected in some way by a strike of workers.

struc·tur·al (struk′chər əl) *adj.* **1** of or having to do with building. **Structural steel** is steel made into beams, girders, etc. **2** of or having to do with structure or structures: *The geologist showed the structural difference in rocks of different ages.* **3** of or proceeding from structural linguistics: *structural grammar.* **4** *Biology.* of or having to do with the organic structure of an animal or plant; morphological. **5** *Geology.* having to do with the structure of rock, the earth's crust, etc. **6** *Chemistry.* of or showing the placement or manner of attachment of the atoms that make up a particular molecule.

struc·tur·al·ism (struk′chər ə liz′əm) *n.* any theory or study that tends to emphasize structure more than function, especially in psychology, linguistics, etc.

struc·tur·al·ist (struk′chər ə list) *n.* one who believes in or follows structuralism.

structural linguistics a branch of linguistic study in which languages are analysed and described in terms of their structural elements and the patterns in which these combine.

struc·tur·al·ly (struk′chər əl ē) *adv.* with regard to structure: *The design is structurally sound, but it is not very attractive.*

struc·ture (struk′chər) *n., v.* **-tured, -tur·ing.** —*n.* **1** a building; something built. **2** anything composed of parts arranged together:

hat, āge, fär; let, ēqual, tèrm; it, īce
hot, ōpen, ôrder; oil, out; cup, pút, rüle,
əbove, takən, pencəl, lemən, circəs

ch, child; ng, long; sh, ship
th, thin; ͭ͟H, then; zh, measure

The human body is a wonderful structure. **3** the manner of building; the way parts are put together; construction: *The structure of the apartment building was excellent.* **4** the arrangement or interrelation of parts, elements, etc. forming something, especially as it determines its special character or nature: *the structure of a molecule, the structure of a sentence, a complex economic structure.* —*v.* **1** make into a structure; build; fabricate. **2** organize; put together in a systematic way. [< L *structura* < *struere* arrange]

☛ *Syn.* **1.** See note at **building.**

stru·del (strü′dəl; *German,* shtrü′dəl) *n.* a pastry, made of very thin dough rolled up around a filling and baked: *Apple strudel has an apple filling.* [< G]

strug·gle (strug′əl) *v.* **-gled, -gling;** *n.* —*v.* **1** move one's arms and legs about violently in an effort to get free: *The child struggled to get down from her mother's lap.* **2** make strong efforts against difficulties; try hard: *For years she had to struggle to make a living. He struggled to control his anger.* **3** move or make one's way with great effort: *She struggled through the hedge. The old man struggled to his feet.* —*n.* **1** great effort or hard work: *It was always a struggle for him to express himself.* **2** fighting; conflict: *a struggle for control of the seas.* [ME *strugle(n), strogele(n);* origin uncertain] —**strug′gler,** *n.*

strum (strum) *v.* **strummed, strum·ming;** *n.* —*v.* **1** play by brushing the fingers across the strings of: *to strum a guitar. We heard him strumming on his banjo.* **2** produce music in this way: *to strum a tune.* —*n.* the act or an instance or the sound of strumming: *the strum of a banjo.* [? imitative] —**strum′mer,** *n.*

stru·ma (strü′mə) *n., pl.* **-mae** (-mē *or* -mī). **1** scrofula. **2** goitre. **3** *Botany.* a cushionlike swelling on an organ. [< NL < L]

strum·pet (strum′pit) *n.* prostitute. [ME; origin uncertain]

strung (strung) *v.* pt. and pp. of **string.**

strut¹ (strut) *v.* **strut·ted, strut·ting;** *n.* —*v.* walk in a stiff, erect manner, suggesting vanity or self-importance: *He strutted about the room in his new jacket.* —*n.* a strutting walk. [OE *strūtian*] —**strut′ter,** *n.*

☛ *Syn. v.* **Strut, swagger** = walk or hold oneself with an air of importance. **Strut** emphasizes putting on an air of dignity by sticking the chest out and holding the head and body stiffly and proudly, to show how important one is: *The little boy put on his father's medals and strutted around the room.* **Swagger** emphasizes showing off how much better one is than others by strutting boldly, rudely, or insultingly: *After being put on probation again, the boys swaggered out of the courtroom.*

strut² (strut) *n., v.* **strut·ted, strut·ting.** —*n.* a supporting bar fitted into a framework, designed to resist pressure of its length; brace. See **truss** for picture. —*v.* brace or support by a strut or struts. [ult. related to STRUT¹.]

strych·nine (strik′nēn *or* strik′nin; *sometimes* strik′nīn) *n.* a bitter, poisonous compound consisting of colorless crystals obtained from nux vomica and related plants. Strychnine is used in small doses as a stimulant for the central nervous system. *Formula:* $C_{21}H_{22}N_2O_2$ [< F < L < Gk. *strychnos* nightshade]

Stu·art (styü′ərt *or* stü′ərt) *n.* **1** the royal family that ruled Scotland from 1371 to 1603 and England and Scotland from 1603 to 1649 and from 1660 to 1714. **2** a member of this family.

stub (stub) *n., v.* **stubbed, stub·bing.** —*n.* **1** a short piece that is left: *the stub of a pencil, a cigarette stub.* **2** the short piece of a ticket or of each leaf in a chequebook, etc. kept as a record. **3** something short and blunt; especially, something cut short or stunted in growth: *a stub of a tail.* —*v.* **1** strike (one's toe) against something. **2** clear (land) of tree stumps. **3** dig up by the roots. **4** put out (a cigarette or cigar) by crushing the burning end in an ashtray, etc. (*often used with* out). [OE]

stub·ble (stub′əl) *n.* **1** the lower ends of stalks of grain that are left in the ground after the grain is cut. **2** any short, rough growth like this, especially a very short growth of beard. [ME < OF *stuble* < LL *stupula,* var. of L *stipula* stem. Doublet of STIPULE.]

stub·ble–jump·er (stub′əl jump′ər) *n. Cdn. Slang, often derogatory.* a prairie farmer.

stub·bly (stub′lē) *adj.* **1** covered with stubble. **2** resembling stubble; bristly: *a stubbly mustache.*

stub·born (stub′ərn) *adj.* **1** too fixed or unyielding in purpose or opinion; pigheaded: *He's just too stubborn to admit he was wrong.*

2 determined; dogged; resolute: *a stubborn fight for freedom, stubborn courage.* **3** hard to deal with or manage: *a stubborn cough. Facts are stubborn things; they can't be changed.* [probably ult. < *stub*] —**stub′born·ly,** *adv.* —**stub′born·ness,** *n.*
☛ *Syn.* **1.** See note at **obstinate.**

stub·by (stub′ē) *adj.* **-bi·er, -bi·est. 1** short and thick or short and blunt, like a stub: *stubby fingers, a stubby pencil.* **2** short, dense, and stiff: *a stubby beard.* **3** having many stubs or stumps. —**stub′bi·ly,** *adv.* —**stub′bi·ness,** *n.*

stuc·co (stuk′ō) *n.* **-coes, -cos;** *v.* **-coed, -co·ing.** —*n.* **1** a hard, rough, strong material usually made of cement, sand, and a small amount of lime, used as a covering for the outer walls of buildings. **2** a fine plaster used for moulding into architectural decorations. **3** stuccowork. —*v.* cover or decorate with stucco. [< Ital. < Gmc.; cf. OHG *stukki* crust]

stuc·co·work (stuk′ō wėrk′) *n.* work done in stucco.

stuck (stuk) *v.* pt. and pp. of **stick²**.

stuck–up (stuk′up′) *adj. Informal.* too proud; conceited; haughty.

stud¹ (stud) *n., v.* **stud·ded, stud·ding.** —*n.* **1** a head of a nail, a knob, etc. sticking out from a surface: *The belt was ornamented with silver studs.* **2** a kind of small button used to fasten the collar or front of a man's shirt. **3** one of a row of upright posts, usually wooden, which form part of the frame to which boards or laths are nailed in making a wall of a building. See **frame** for picture. **4** a projecting pin on a machine. **5** a crosspiece put in each link of a chain cable to strengthen it. **6** stud poker. —*v.* **1** set with studs or something like studs: *He plans to stud the sword hilt with jewels.* **2** be set or scattered over: *Little islands stud the harbor.* **3** set like studs; scatter at intervals: *Stooks of wheat were studded over the field.* **4** provide with studs. [OE *studu*]

stud² (stud) *n.* **1** a male animal, especially a stallion, kept for breeding. **2** a group of horses or, sometimes, other animals, kept mainly for breeding. **3** a place where such animals are kept. **4** (adjl.) of, having to do with, or kept as a stud. **5** *Slang.* a virile man, especially one who is sexually promiscuous.
at stud, of a male animal, available for breeding. [OE *stōd*]

stud·book (stud′bŭk′) *n.* a book giving the pedigrees of thoroughbred horses.

stud·ding (stud′ing) *n.* **1** the studs forming the framework of a wall. **2** lumber for studs.

stud·ding·sail (stud′ing sāl′ *or* stun′səl) *n.* a light sail set at the side of a square sail. [origin unknown]

stu·dent (styü′dənt *or* stü′dənt) *n.* **1** a person who is studying in a school, college, or university. **2** a person who studies; one who investigates or observes systematically: *a student of human nature.* [< L *studens, -entis,* ppr. of *studere,* originally, be eager]
☛ *Syn.* **1, 2. Student, pupil, scholar** = a person who is studying or being taught. **Student,** emphasizing the idea of studying, applies to anyone who loves to study or studies a subject, but especially to someone attending a high school, college, or university: *Several high-school students were there.* **Pupil,** emphasizing personal supervision by a teacher, applies especially to a child in an elementary school or to someone studying personally with a teacher: *She was the pupil of a famous opera singer.* **Scholar** now applies chiefly to a learned person who is an authority in some field or to a student who has a scholarship: *He is a distinguished medieval scholar.*

student body all the students at a school, etc. collectively.

stud·horse (stud′hôrs′) *n.* a stallion kept for breeding.

stud·ied (stud′ēd) *adj.* **1** produced or marked by deliberate effort or design; intentional: *studied politeness. What she said to me was studied insult.* **2** prepared or planned carefully and thoughtfully: *a studied essay.* —**stud′ied·ly,** *adv.* —**stud′ied·ness,** *n.*
☛ *Syn.* See note at **elaborate.**

stu·di·o (styü′dē ō′ *or* stü′dē ō′) *n., pl.* **-di·os. 1 a** the workroom of a painter, sculptor, photographer, etc. **b** a room in which a music teacher, dramatic coach, etc. gives lessons. **2** a place where music, dancing, etc. is taught. **3** a place where motion pictures are made. **4** a place from which a radio or television program is broadcast. [< Ital. < L *studium* study, enthusiasm. Doublet of ÉTUDE, STUDY.]

studio couch a couch, usually without a back or arms, that can be converted into a bed.

stu·di·ous (styü′dē əs *or* stü′dē əs) *adj.* **1** fond of study: *He's very studious.* **2** thoughtful and painstaking; deliberate and careful: *He made a studious effort to please his customers.* **3** taking care; anxiously careful (*of*): *She was always studious of her mother's comfort.* —**stu′di·ous·ly,** *adv.* —**stu′di·ous·ness,** *n.*

stud poker a type of poker in which one or more cards are dealt face down on the first round and the rest dealt face up, or alternating rounds of cards dealt face up and face down. Betting is done on each round of open cards.

stud·y (stud′ē) *n., pl.* **stud·ies;** *v.* **stud·ied, stud·y·ing.** —*n.* **1** the effort to learn by reading or thinking. **2** a careful examination; investigation. **3** a subject studied; branch of learning; something investigated or to be investigated. **4** a room for study, reading, writing, etc. **5** a literary or artistic work that deals in careful detail with one particular subject. **6** a sketch for a picture, story, etc. **7** *Music.* a composition designed primarily for practice in a particular technical problem; a concert version of this, often of great difficulty and brilliance. **8** an earnest effort, or the object of endeavor or effort: *Her constant study is to please her parents.* **9** deep thought; reverie: *She was in a brown study.* **10 studies,** a person's work as a student: *to return to one's studies after a vacation.*
—*v.* **1** try to learn or gain knowledge by means of books, observation, or experiment: *to study history. He studies most of the time.* **2** examine carefully: *We studied the map to find the shortest road home.* **3** consider with care; think (out); plan: *The prisoner studied ways to escape.* **4** give care and thought to; try hard: *The grocer studies to please his customers.* **5** memorize or try to memorize: *to study one's part in a play.* [ME < AF < L *studium,* originally, eagerness. Doublet of ÉTUDE, STUDIO.]
☛ *Syn. v.* **3.** See note at **consider.**

stuff (stuf) *n., v.* —*n.* **1** what a thing is made of; material. **2** a woollen fabric. **3** a thing or things; substance: *The doctor rubbed some kind of stuff on the burn.* **4** goods; belongings: *He was told to move his stuff out of the room.* **5** silly writing, talk, or thoughts; nonsense. **6** inward qualities; character.
—*v.* **1** pack full; fill. To stuff a ballot box means to put in more votes than there are rightful voters. **2** stop or block up: *My nose is stuffed by a cold.* **3** fill the skin of (a dead animal) to make it look as it did when alive. **4** fill (a chicken, turkey, etc.) with seasoned bread crumbs, etc. **5** force; push; thrust: *He stuffed his clothes into the drawer.* **6** eat too much. [ME < OF *estoffe,* ? ult. < L *stuppa* tow², oakum < Gk. *stypē*]

stuffed shirt *Informal.* a pompous, conceited person, especially one who is old-fashioned or conservative.

stuff·ing (stuf′ing) *n.* **1** any soft material used to fill or stuff cushions, upholstered furniture, toys, etc. **2** seasoned bread crumbs, etc. for stuffing a chicken, turkey, etc. for cooking.

stuff·y (stuf′ē) *adj.* **stuff·i·er, stuff·i·est. 1** lacking fresh air: *a stuffy room.* **2** lacking freshness or interest; dull: *a stuffy conversation.* **3** stopped up: *I've got a stuffy nose from hay fever.* **4** prim and proper; narrow-minded and stodgy: *Don't be so stuffy; it was only a harmless joke.* **5** angry or sulky. —**stuff′i·ly,** *adv.* —**stuff′i·ness,** *n.*

stul·ti·fi·ca·tion (stul′tə fə kā′shən) *n.* the act of stultifying or the state of being stultified.

stul·ti·fy (stul′tə fī′) *v.* **-fied, -fy·ing. 1** cause to appear foolish or absurd; reduce to foolishness or absurdity. **2 a** make futile. **b** make passive or weak by requiring absolute obedience or conformity: *the stultifying atmosphere of a prison or dictatorship.* [< LL *stultificare* < L *stultus* foolish + *facere* make] —**stul′ti·fi′er,** *n.*

stum·ble (stum′bəl) *v.* **-bled, -bling;** *n.* —*v.* **1** trip by striking the foot against something: *She stumbled, but did not fall.* **2** walk unsteadily, stumbling often: *The tired hikers stumbled along.* **3** speak or act in a hesitating, faltering way: *The frightened boy stumbled through his recitation.* **4** make a mistake; do wrong. **5** come by accident or chance: *While in the country, she stumbled upon some fine antiques.* **6** *Archaic.* cause to stumble or pause. —*n.* the act or an instance of stumbling. [cf. Norwegian *stumla*] —**stum′bler,** *n.* —**stum′bling·ly,** *adv.*

stum·bling–block (stum′bling blok′) *n.* an obstacle or hindrance; something that causes difficulty or slows down progress.

stump (stump) *n., v.* —*n.* **1** the lower end of a tree trunk left after the tree has fallen or been cut down. **2** anything left after the main or important part is removed: *The dog wagged its stump of a tail.* **3** a person with a short, thick build. **4** a place where a political speech is made. **5** a heavy step. **6** the sound made by stiff walking or heavy steps. **7** a wooden leg. **8** *Slang.* leg. **9** a tight roll of paper or other material pointed at the ends and used to soften pencil marks in drawing. **10** *Cricket.* one of the three upright sticks of a wicket.
up a stump, *Informal.* unable to act, answer, etc.; impotent; baffled. —*v.* **1** remove stumps from (land). **2** reduce to a stump; cut off. **3** go about or travel through (an area), making speeches: *All the candidates are out stumping the riding this week.* **4** walk in a heavy, clumsy way. **5** *Informal.* make unable to answer, do, etc: *The first question was easy but the second one stumped him.* **6** *Cricket.* put a batsman out by knocking down the bails while he is out of his ground. [cf. MLG *stump*] —**stump′er,** *n.* —**stump′like′,** *adj.*

stump speaker a person who makes political speeches from a platform, etc.

stump speech a political speech.

stump·y (stum′pē) *adj.* **stump·i·er, stump·i·est. 1** short and thick. **2** having many stumps. —**stump′i·ly,** *adv.* —**stump′i·ness,** *n.*

stun (stun) *v.* **stunned, stun·ning;** *n.* —*v.* **1** make senseless; knock unconscious: *He was stunned by the fall.* **2** bewilder; shock; overwhelm: *She was stunned by the news of her friend's death.* —*n.* **1 a** the act of stunning or dazing. **b** the condition of being stunned. **2** a thing that stuns; stunner. [OE *stunian* crash, resound; influenced by OF *estoner* resound, stun, ult. < L *ex-* + *tonare* thunder]

stung (stung) *v.* pt. and pp. of **sting.**

stunk (stungk) *v.* a pt. and pp. of **stink.**

stun·ner (stun′ər) *n.* **1** a person, thing, or blow that stuns. **2** *Informal.* a very striking or attractive person or thing.

stun·ning (stun′ing) *adj.* **1** that stuns: *a stunning blow.* **2** very attractive or good-looking; strikingly pretty: *a stunning girl, a stunning new hat.* **3** excellent or delightful; first-rate; splendid: *a stunning performance.* —**stun′ning·ly,** *adv.*

stun·sail (stun′səl) *n.* studdingsail.

stunt[1] (stunt) *v., n.* —*v.* check in growth or development: *Lack of proper food stunts a plant.* —*n.* a check in growth or development. [OE *stunt* foolish]

stunt[2] (stunt) *n., v. Informal.* —*n.* a feat or act intended to thrill an audience or to attract attention; an act showing boldness or skill: *Circus riders perform stunts on horseback.* —*v.* perform such feats. [probably a var. of *stint* task]

stunt man (stunt′man′) *n., pl.* **-men.** a professional acrobat who doubles for an actor or actress in dangerous scenes.

stu·pa (stü′pə) *n.* a large, dome-shaped mound erected as a shrine by Buddhists. [< Skt. *stupa* heap]

stupe (styüp *or* stüp) *n.* a small, hot, wet cloth, or compress, of soft material, used in dressing a wound, to stimulate circulation, etc. [ME < L *stupa* coarse flax < Gk. *stypē*]

stu·pe·fa·cient (styü′pə fā′shənt *or* stü′pə fā′shənt) *adj., n.* —*adj.* stupefying. —*n.* a drug or agent that produces stupor. [< L *stupefaciens, -entis,* ppr. of *stupefacere.* See STUPEFY.]

stu·pe·fac·tion (styü′pə fak′shən *or* stü′pə fak′shən) *n.* stupefying or being stupefied.

stu·pe·fy (styü′pə fī′ *or* stü′pə fī′) *v.* **-fied, -fy·ing. 1** make stupid, dull, or senseless: *stupefied by a drug.* **2** overwhelm with shock or amazement; astound: *They were stupefied by the calamity.* [< L *stupefacere* < *stupere* be amazed + *facere* make] —**stu′pe·fi′er,** *n.*

stu·pen·dous (styü pen′dəs *or* stü pen′dəs) *adj.* **1** amazing; marvellous: *Niagara Falls is a stupendous sight.* **2** unusually large or great: *a stupendous meal, a stupendous structure.* [< L *stupendus* < *stupere* be amazed] —**stu·pen′dous·ly,** *adv.* —**stu·pen′dous·ness,** *n.*

stu·pid (styü′pid *or* stü′pid) *adj., n.* —*adj.* **1** not intelligent; dull: *a stupid person.* **2** not interesting: *a stupid book.* **3** showing lack of intelligence or good sense: *That was a stupid thing to do.* **4** dazed: *He was still stupid from the effect of the sedative.* —*n. Informal.* a stupid person. [< L *stupidus* < *stupere* be dazed] —**stu′pid·ness,** *n.*

☛ *Syn. adj.* **1. Stupid, dull** = having or showing little intelligence. **Stupid,** describing people or what they say or do, particularly suggests being by nature lacking in good sense or ordinary intelligence: *Running away from an accident is stupid.* **Dull** particularly suggests a mind slow in understanding and lacking in sharpness and alertness, either by nature or because of overwork, poor health, etc., and needing to be stirred up and made more lively: *The mind becomes dull if the body gets no exercise.*

stu·pid·i·ty (styü pid′ə tē *or* stü pid′ə tē) *n., pl.* **-ties. 1** the quality or state of being stupid. **2** a stupid act, idea, etc.

stu·pid·ly (styü′pid lē *or* stü′pid lē) *adv.* **1** in a stupid manner. **2** to an extent or degree that is stupid. **3** so as to be or appear stupid.

stu·por (styü′pər *or* stü′pər) *n.* **1** loss or lessening of the power to feel: *The man lay in a stupor, unable to tell what had happened to him.* **2** mental or moral numbness; torpor. [< L *stupere* be dazed]

stur·dy (stėr′dē) *adj.* **-di·er, -di·est. 1** strong; stout: *sturdy legs.* **2** not yielding; firm: *sturdy resistance, sturdy defenders.* [ME < OF *esturdi* violent, originally, dazed] —**stur′di·ly,** *adv.* —**stur′di·ness,** *n.*

☛ *Syn.* **1.** See note at **strong.**

stur·geon (stėr′jən) *n., pl.* **-geon** *or* **-geons.** any of a family (Acipenseridae) of sharklike, bony fishes found in north temperate waters, having a heavy, almost cylindrical body with several longitudinal rows of bony plates, and a small mouth on the underside of the head. Sturgeon are valued as a source of caviar and isinglass. [ME < AF *esturgeon,* ult. < Gmc.]

stut·ter (stut′ər) *v., n.* —*v.* **1** repeat (the same sound) in an effort to speak. *Example: C-c-c-can't they go?* **2** say, speak, or sound with a stutter: *to stutter a reply.* —*n.* the act or habit of stuttering. [<

hat, āge, fär; let, ēqual, tėrm; it, īce
hot, ōpen, ôrder; oil, out; cup, pút, rüle,
əbove, takən, pencəl, lemən, circəs

ch, child; ng, long; sh, ship
th, thin; ᵺ, then; zh, measure

dial. *stut;* cf. Du. *stotteren*] —**stut′ter·er,** *n.* —**stut′ter·ing·ly,** *adv.*
☛ *Syn. v.* See note at **stammer.**

St. Vi·tus's dance (vī′təs iz) a disorder of the nervous system with involuntary spasms of the muscles of the face and the arms and legs; chorea.

sty[1] (stī) *n., pl.* **sties. 1** a pen for pigs. **2** any filthy place. [OE *stig*]

sty[2] *or* **stye** (stī) *n., pl.* **sties** *or* **styes.** a small, inflamed swelling on the edge of the eyelid. A sty is like a small boil. [probably < ME *styanye* (taken to mean "sty on eye"), ult. < OE *stīgend* rising + *ēage* eye]

Styg·i·an (stij′ē ən) *adj.* **1** of or having to do with the river Styx or the lower world. **2** dark; gloomy. **3** of an oath, completely binding; inviolable like the oath by the Styx, which the gods themselves feared to break. [< L *Stygius* < Gk. *Stygios* < *Styx, Stygos* Styx]

style (stīl) *n., v.* **styled, styl·ing.** —*n.* **1** fashion: *dresses in the latest styles.* **2** a manner; method; way: *the Gothic style of architecture.* **3** a way of writing or speaking. **4** a fashionable, elegant, or admirable way or manner: *She dresses in style.* **5** literary or artistic excellence. **6** an official name; title: *Salute him with the style of King.* **7** stylus (def. 1). **8** something like this in shape or use. **9** a pointer on a dial, chart, etc. **10** *Botany.* the stemlike part of the pistil of a flower containing the stigma at its top. See **flower** for picture. **11** the rules of spelling, punctuation, etc. used by printers. —*v.* **1** give a distinctive design or manner to; design, fashion, or arrange: *dresses styled in Paris. She uses a blow dryer to style her hair.* **2** name; call: *Joan of Arc was styled "the Maid of Orleans."* [ME < OF < L *stilus,* originally, pointed writing instrument; influenced in modern spelling by Gk. *stylos* column. Doublet of STYLUS.] —**style′less,** *adj.*
☛ *Hom.* **stile.**
☛ *Syn. n.* **1.** See note at **fashion.**

style·book (stīl′bûk′) *n.* **1** a book containing rules of punctuation, capitalization, etc., used by printers, editors, etc. **2** a book showing fashions in dress, etc.

styl·ish (stī′lish) *adj.* fashionable; smart: *a stylish new coat.* —**styl′ish·ly,** *adv.* —**styl′ish·ness,** *n.*

styl·ist (stī′list) *n.* **1** a person, especially a writer, who has or aims at a good style or whose work is characterized by a particular style: *His editorials read well because he is a stylist.* **2** a person who designs or advises concerning fashionable interior decoration, clothes, etc.

sty·lis·tic (stī lis′tik) *adj.* of or having to do with artistic or literary style.

sty·lis·ti·cal·ly (stī lis′tik lē) *adv.* as regards style; in matters of style.

styl·ize (stī′līz) *v.* **-ized, -iz·ing.** make or design according to a particular or standard style or pattern rather than according to nature: *Our new bedroom wallpaper has tiny stylized tulips.* —**styl′i·za′tion,** *n.* —**styl′iz·er,** *n.*

sty·lo·graph (stī′lə graf′) *n.* a fountain pen in which the writing point consists of a small metal tube. [< *stylus* + *-graph*]

sty·lo·graph·ic (stī′lə graf′ik) *adj.* of or having to do with a stylograph.

sty·lus (stī′ləs) *n.* **1** a pointed instrument used in ancient times for writing on wax or clay tablets. **2** a needle-like device of jewel, steel, etc. attached to the cartridge on the pickup arm of a phonograph, and which rests in the groove of a record, transmitting the vibration to the cartridge; needle. **3** a similar device used for cutting the grooves on the original disc when recording music, etc. **4** a pointed instrument used for marking, engraving, or writing, as on a mimeograph stencil, the drum of an oscillograph, etc. [< L *stilus.* Doublet of STYLE.]

sty·mie (stī′mē) *n., v.* **-mied, -mie·ing.** —*n.* **1** *Golf.* a situation on a putting green in which an opponent's ball is directly between the player's ball and the hole. **2** a situation in which one is blocked or frustrated. —*v.* **1** *Golf.* hinder with a stymie. **2** block completely: *He was stymied by the last question on the exam and gave up on it.* [? < Scots *stymie* a person having poor eyesight]

styp·tic (stip′tik) *adj., n.* —*adj.* able to stop or check bleeding; astringent. —*n.* something that stops or checks bleeding by contracting the tissue. Alum is a common styptic. [< L < Gk. *styptikos < styphein* constrict]

styptic pencil a small stick of alum or other styptic substance, used on slight wounds to stop bleeding.

sty·rene (stī′rēn) *n.* an aromatic liquid hydrocarbon used mainly in making synthetic rubber and plastics. *Formula:* C_8H_8 [< L *styrax* an aromatic resin < Gk.]

sty·ro·foam (stī′rə fōm) *n.* **1** a kind of lightweight, firm polystyrene plastic used for insulation, packaging, etc. **2 Styrofoam,** *Trademark.* a brand of such plastic.

Styx (stiks) *n. Greek mythology.* a river in the lower world. The souls of the dead were ferried across it into Hades. [< L < Gk. *Styx* (related to *stygeein* hate)]

sua·sion (swā′zhən) *n. Rare.* persuasion: *Moral suasion is an appeal to one's sense of what is right.* [ME < L *suasio, -onis* < *suadere* persuade]

sua·sive (swā′siv) *adj. Rare.* persuasive. —**sua′sive·ly,** *adv.* —**sua′sive·ness,** *n.*

suave (swäv) *adj.* smoothly agreeable or polite. [< F < L *suavis* agreeable] —**suave′ly,** *adv.* —**suave′ness,** *n.*

sua·vi·ty (swä′və tē *or* swav′ə tē) *n., pl.* **-ties.** a smoothly agreeable quality of behavior; smooth politeness.

sub (sub) *n., adj., v.* **subbed, sub·bing.** *Informal.* —*n. or adj.* **1** substitute. **2** submarine. **3** subordinate. —*v.* act as a substitute.

sub– *prefix.* **1** under; below, as in *subway, submarine.* **2** further or again, as in *subdivide, sublease.* **3** near; bordering upon, as in *subarctic.* **4** nearly; almost, as in *subarid.* **5** secondary, subordinate, or assistant, as in *substation, subhead.* **6** resulting from further division; subordinate portion of, as in *subcommittee, subspecies.* **7** in a comparatively small degree or proportion; somewhat, as in *subacid.* Also, **suc–** before *c*; **suf–** before *f*; **sug–** before *g*; **sum–** in some cases before *m*; **sup–** before *p*; **sur–** before *r*; **sus–** in some cases before *c, p, t.* [< L *sub,* prep.]

sub. **1** substitute. **2** subscription. **3** suburban; suburbs. **4** subaltern.

sub·ac·id (sub′as′id) *adj.* moderately acid. Oranges are a subacid fruit.

sub·a·gent (sub′ā′jənt) *n.* a person employed as the agent of an agent; a subordinate or deputy agent.

sub·al·tern (sub′əl tərn, sə bol′tərn *or* sə bôl′tərn) *adj., n.* —*adj.* **1** lower in rank or status. **2** *Logic.* of a proposition, particular in relation to a given universal proposition. —*n. Esp.Brit.* lieutenant. [< LL *subalternus* < L *sub-* under + *alternus* alternate]

sub·a·quat·ic (sub′ə kwat′ik *or* -ə kwot′ik) *adj.* somewhat or partly aquatic: *subaquatic plants.*

sub·a·que·ous (sub ā′kwē əs *or* sub ak′wē əs) *adj.* **1** under water; suitable for use under water. **2** formed under water. **3** living under water.

sub·arc·tic (sub ärk′tik *or* sub är′tik) *adj., n.* —*adj.* of, having to do with, or like the region just south of the Arctic Circle. —*n.* the region just south of the Arctic Circle.

sub·ar·id (sub ar′id *or* sub′er′id) *adj.* moderately arid.

sub·a·tom·ic (sub′ə tom′ik) *adj.* having to do with the inside of the atom or with particles smaller than atoms.

sub–base·ment (sub′bās′mənt) *n.* a storey below the main basement of a building.

sub·ce·les·tial (sub′sə les′chəl) *adj.* beneath the heavens; earthly; terrestrial.

sub·cel·lar (sub′sel′ər) *n.* a cellar beneath another cellar.

sub·class (sub′klas′) *n.* **1** a secondary category in the classification of plants and animals, that is a grouping within a class and includes one or more orders. **2** a primary division within a class; especially, in mathematics, a subset.

sub·com·mit·tee (sub′kə mit′ē) *n.* a small committee chosen from a larger general committee for some special duty.

sub·com·pact (sub′kom′pakt) *n.* the smallest of the four basic sizes of automobile.

sub·con·scious (sub kon′shəs) *adj.* **1** existing in the mind and affecting thoughts, attitudes, or behavior but not consciously felt: *a subconscious motive, subconscious inhibitions.* **2** not completely conscious or aware: *In his subconscious state, he thought he heard a knocking.* **3** (*nom.*) thoughts, feelings, etc. existing in the mind but not consciously recognized. —**sub·con′scious·ly,** *adv.*

sub·con·scious·ness (sub kon′shəs nis) *n.* **1** the quality or state of being not completely conscious. **2** the subconscious.

sub·con·ti·nent (sub kon′tə nent) *n.* **1** a very large land mass that is smaller than the land masses usually called continents. Greenland is a subcontinent. **2** a large section of a continent that

has considerable geographical or political independence: *the Indian sub-continent.* —**sub′con·ti·nen′tal,** *adj.*

sub·con·tract (*n.* sub′kon′trakt; *v.* sub kon′trakt *or* sub′kən trakt′) *n., v.* —*n.* **1** a contract under a previous contract; contract for carrying out a previous contract or a part of it: *The contractor for the new school building gave my father the subcontract to install the plumbing.* —*v.* make a subcontract: *The plumbing for the new school was subcontracted to my father.*

sub·con·trac·tor (sub′kon′trak tər *or* sub′kon trak′tər) *n.* a person or company that contracts to carry out part or all of a contract made by someone else.

sub·cul·ture (sub′kul′chər) *n.* **1** an element or cultural group within a larger culture, but distinguished from it by features of belief, custom, conduct, background, etc.: *the subculture of organized crime.* **2** a culture of bacteria, etc. derived from another culture.

sub·cu·ta·ne·ous (sub′kyə tā′nē əs) *adj.* **1** under the skin. **2** living under the skin. **3** placed or performed under the skin. —**sub′cu·ta′ne·ous·ly,** *adv.*

sub·dea·con (sub′dē′kən) *n.* a member of the clergy next below a deacon in rank.

sub·di·vide (sub′də vīd′) *v.* **-vid·ed, -vid·ing. 1** divide again; divide into smaller parts. **2** divide (land) into lots for houses, buildings, etc.: *A developer bought the farm and subdivided it into building lots.* —**sub′di·vid′er,** *n.*

sub·di·vi·sion (sub′də vizh′ən) *n.* **1** a division into smaller parts. **2** a part of a part. **3** a tract of land divided into building lots. **4** the houses, community, etc. established on such a tract.

sub·dom·i·nant (sub dom′ə nənt) *n., adj.* —*n. Music.* the fourth tone of a scale; the tone next below the dominant. —*adj.* of or having to do with this tone.

sub·due (səb dyü′ *or* səb dü′) *v.* **-dued, -du·ing. 1** conquer: *The Spaniards subdued the Indian peoples of South America.* **2** keep down; hold back; suppress: *to subdue a desire to laugh.* **3** tone down; soften or reduce: *to subdue a fever. They pulled down the blinds to subdue the light.* [ME *sodewe* < OF *soduire* deceive < L *subducere* draw away < *sub-* from under + *ducere* lead; influenced in meaning by L *subdere* subdue < *sub-* under + *dare* put] —**sub·du′a·ble,** *adj.* —**sub·du′er,** *n.*

sub·dued (səb dyüd′ *or* səb düd′) *adj.* **1** lacking in intensity or strength: *subdued colors.* **2** quietened down; less spirited or lively than usual: *He was quiet and subdued all afternoon.*

sub·en·try (sub′en′trē) *n.* an entry listed under a main entry: *In this dictionary, idioms are included as subentries under the entry word.*

su·be·re·ous (sü bēr′ē əs) *adj.* corky; like cork. [< L *subereus* < *suber* cork]

sub·fam·i·ly (sub′fam′ə lē *or* -fam′lē) *n., pl.* **-lies. 1** a secondary category in the classification of plants and animals, that is a grouping within a family and includes one or more genera. **2** a group of languages within a language family.

sub·fusc *or* **sub·fusk** (sub fusk′) *adj.* **1** darkish; dull in color: *subfusc woods at twilight.* **2** not distinctive; monotonous; drab: *rows of subfusc city houses.* [< L *subfuscus* < *sub-* under + *fuscus* dark]

sub·ge·nus (sub′jē′nəs) *n., pl.* **sub·gen·er·a** (sub jen′ər ə *or* sub′jen′ər ə) **or sub·ge·nus·es.** a secondary category in the classification of plants and animals, that is a grouping within a genus and includes one or more species.

sub·group (sub′grüp′) *n.* a subordinate group; a division of a group.

sub·head (sub′hed′) *n.* **1** the title, or heading, of a subdivision of an article, chapter, etc. **2** a subordinate title, headline, etc.: *Newspaper articles often have a subhead underneath the headline.*

sub·head·ing (sub′hed′ing) *n.* subhead.

sub·hu·man (sub hyü′mən) *adj.* **1** below the human race or type; less than human. **2** almost human: *subhuman primates.*

su·bi·to (sü′bē tō′) *adv. Music.* suddenly; quickly; abruptly. [< Ital.]

subj. **1** subject; subjective; subjectively. **2** subjunctive.

sub·ja·cent (sub jā′sənt) *adj.* **1** situated below; underlying. **2** being in a lower situation, though not directly beneath. [< L *subjacens, -entis,* ppr. of *subjacere* < *sub-* below + *jacere* lie]

sub·ject (*n., adj.* sub′jikt; *v.* səb jekt′) *n., adj., v.* —*n.* **1** something thought about, discussed, etc. **2** something learned or taught; a course of study, field of learning, etc.: *English, history, mathematics, and biology are required subjects in this school.* **3** a person under the power, control, or influence of another: *the Queen's subjects.* **4** a person or thing that undergoes or experiences something. **5** *Grammar.* the word or group of words in a sentence about which something is said in the predicate. In the sentence *His little brother went to find him, His little brother* is the subject; in *Their travellers' cheques were stolen, Their travellers' cheques* is

the subject. **6 a** the theme of a book, poem, or other literary work. **b** a figure, scene, object, incident, etc. chosen by an artist for representation. **c** *Music.* the theme or melody on which a composition or movement is based. **7** *Philosophy.* **a** the substance of anything as opposed to its qualities. **b** mind or self opposed to everything outside the mind. **8** *Logic.* **a** that term of a proposition of which the other term is affirmed or denied. **b** the thing about which such affirmation or denial is made.
—*adj.* under some power or influence: *A colony is a subject nation.*
subject to, a under the power or influence of: *We are subject to our country's laws.* **b** likely to have: *Many children are subject to colds.* **c** depending on; on the condition of: *I bought the car subject to your approval.*
—*v.* **1** bring under some power or influence: *Rome subjected all Italy to her rule.* **2** cause to undergo or experience something: *The savages subjected their captives to torture.* **3** lay open or expose; make liable (*to*): *Credulity subjects one to impositions.* [ME < OF < L *subjectus,* pp. of *subjicere, subicere* place under < *sub-* under + *jacere* throw]
☛ *Syn. n.* **1. Subject, topic** = the main thing or idea thought, talked, or written about, as in a conversation, lecture, essay, book. **Subject** is the general word: *He tried to change the subject. Juvenile delinquency is a broad subject.* **Topic** often applies to a subject having to do with a current event or problem, but particularly means a limited and definitely stated subject that is, or is to be, discussed in a lecture, essay, etc. or some part of it: *"The plan for a recreation centre" is today's topic.*

sub·jec·tion (səb jek′shən) *n.* **1** the act of bringing under some power or influence: *The new dictator's first concern was the subjection of the rebel forces.* **2** the condition of being under some power or influence: *They lived in subjection to an old aunt.*

sub·jec·tive (səb jek′tiv) *adj., n.* —*adj.* **1** originating or existing in the mind; belonging to the person thinking rather than to the object thought of: *Ideas and opinions are subjective; facts are objective.* **2** about the thoughts and feelings of the speaker, writer, painter, etc.; personal: *a subjective poem.* **3** *Philosophy.* **a** of or relating to reality as perceived by the mind, as distinct from reality as independent of the mind. **b** influenced by an individual's state of mind: *a subjective perception or apprehension.* **c** having to do with the substance of anything, as opposed to its qualities and attributes. **4** *Grammar.* of, having to do with, or being the grammatical form of an English pronoun that shows that it is the subject of a sentence. There are six English pronouns with special subjective forms: *I, we, he, she, they,* and *who.*
—*n.* **1** the subjective form: *The English subjective corresponds roughly to the nominative case in German and Latin.* **2** a word or construction word in the subjective form. *I* and *who* are subjectives.
—**sub·jec′tive·ly,** *adv.* —**sub·jec′tive·ness,** *n.*

sub·jec·tiv·i·ty (sub′jek tiv′ə tē) *n.* the quality or condition of being subjective: *The subjectivity of his account of the war makes it unreliable as a source of information.*

subject matter the thing or things discussed or considered in a book, speech, debate, etc.

sub·join (səb join′) *v.* add at the end; append. [< MF *subjoindre* < L *subjungere* < *sub-* under + *jungere* join]

sub ju·di·ce (sub′jü′də sē) before a judge or court; under judicial consideration. [< L]

sub·ju·gate (sub′jə gāt′) *v.* -**gat·ed, -gat·ing. 1** subdue; conquer. **2** bring under complete control; make subservient or submissive. [ME < LL *subjugare* < *sub-* under + *jugum* yoke] —**sub′ju·ga′tor,** *n.*

sub·ju·ga·tion (sub′jə gā′shən) *n.* conquest; subjection.

sub·junc·tive (səb jungk′tiv) *n., adj. Grammar.* —*n.* **1** a set of verb forms used to express a state or act as possible, conditional, desirable, doubtful, etc. rather than as fact. The subjunctive is not used much in modern English, normally being replaced by other constructions. **2** a verb form in the subjunctive. In *God bless the Queen! Come what may, we will see it through,* and *If I were you I'd try again,* the verb forms *bless, come,* and *were* are subjunctives.
—*adj.* of, having to do with, or designating the subjunctive. [< LL *subjunctivus,* ult. < L *sub-* under + *jungere* join]

sub·king·dom (sub′king′dəm) *n.* a secondary category in the classification of plants and animals, that is a grouping within a kingdom and includes one or more phyla.

sub·lease (*n.* sub′lēs′; *v.* sub lēs′ or sub′lēs′) *n., v.* -**leased, -leas·ing.** —*n.* a lease of all or part of some property by the person who rents the property himself from the owner. —*v.* grant or take a sublease of.

sub·let (sub let′) *v.* -**let, -let·ting. 1** rent to another some property that has been rented to oneself: *She sublet her apartment while she was away last summer.* **2** give part of a contract to another; subcontract: *The contractor for the whole building sublet the contract for the plumbing.*

sub–lieu·ten·ant (sub′lef ten′ənt; *esp.U.S.,* sub′lü ten′ənt) *n.* **1** *Canadian Forces.* in Maritime Command, the equivalent of a lieutenant. See chart at **rank¹. 2** a naval officer of similar rank in other countries. *Abbrev:* S.Lt., SLt. or Sub.Lt.

hat, āge, fär; let, ēqual, tèrm; it, īce
hot, ōpen, ôrder; oil, out; cup, pùt, rüle,
above, takən, pencəl, lemən, circəs

ch, child; ng, long; sh, ship
th, thin; ᴛн, then; zh, measure

sub·li·mate (*v.* sub′lə māt′; *adj. n.* sub′lə mit or sub′lə māt′) *v.* -**mat·ed, -mat·ing; adj., n.** —*v.* **1** change the natural expression of an impulse or desire into one considered more socially or personally acceptable: *to sublimate one's aggressiveness.* **2** *Chemistry.* sublime (a solid substance). **3** *Archaic.* refine or improve.
—*adj.* sublimated.
—*n.* a substance produced by the process of subliming: *Frost and snow are sublimates; they form directly from water vapor in the air.* [< L *sublimare,* originally, raise < *sublimis* lofty]

sub·li·ma·tion (sub′lə mā′shən) *n.* **1** the act or process of sublimating or subliming. **2** the resulting product or state.

sub·lime (sə blīm′) *adj., v.* -**limed, -lim·ing.** —*adj.* **1** noble; majestic; lofty or exalted: *the sublime Dante, the sublime beauty of the Rocky Mountains.* **2** (*noml.*) **the sublime,** that which is lofty, noble, exalted, etc. **3** perfect; supreme: *She carried on with sublime indifference to what people might say.*
—*v.* **1** subject a solid substance to the action of heat to produce a vapor which is then condensed to a solid again: *Some substances can be purified by subliming them.* **2** pass directly from a solid state to a vapor: *Some substances that will sublime are arsenic, camphor, and dry ice.* **3** make higher or nobler; make sublime. [ME < OF, ult. < L *sublimis,* originally, sloping up < *sub-* up + *limen* lintel] —**sub·lime′ly,** *adv.*

sub·lim·i·nal (sub lim′ə nəl) *adj.* **1** existing or acting below the threshold of conscious awareness: *the subliminal self. The committee protested against the use of subliminal advertising on television.* **2** too weak or small to be felt or noticed. [< *sub-* + L *limen, liminis* threshold] —**sub·lim′i·nal·ly,** *adv.*

sub·lim·i·ty (səb lim′ə tē) *n., pl.* -**ties. 1** the quality or state of being sublime; lofty excellence or grandeur. **2** something sublime.

sub·lin·gual (sub ling′gwəl or -ling′gyə wəl) *adj., n.* —*adj.* located beneath or on the under side of the tongue. —*n.* a sublingual gland, artery, etc.

Sub.Lt. sub-lieutenant.

sub·lu·nar (sub lü′nər) *adj.* sublunary.

sub·lu·nar·y (sub′lü ner′ē or sub lü′nər ē) *adj.* beneath the moon; earthly. [< NL *sublunaris,* ult. < L *sub-* under + *luna* moon]

sub·ma·chine gun (sub′mə shēn′) a lightweight automatic or semi-automatic gun, designed to be fired from the shoulder or hip.

sub·mar·gin·al (sub mär′jə nəl) *adj.* **1** *Biology.* near the margin of an organ or part. **2** below a required minimum standard: *submarginal living conditions.* **3** of land, etc., not productive enough to be worth cultivating, developing, etc.

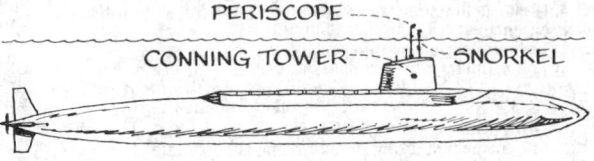

A submarine

sub·ma·rine (*n., v.* sub′mə rēn′; *adj.* sub′mə rēn′) *n., v.* -**rined, -rin·ing; adj.** —*n.* **1** a boat that can operate under water, used in warfare for discharging torpedoes, etc. **2** a large sandwich consisting of a long roll that is split lengthwise and filled with a variety of cold meats, cheese, tomatoes, onions, coleslaw, etc.
—*v.* attack or sink by a submarine.
—*adj.* **1** of or carried out by a submarine or submarines: *submarine tactics, submarine warfare.* **2** placed, growing, or used below the surface of the sea: *submarine plants.*

sub·mar·i·ner (sub mar′ə nər, sub mer′ə nər, or sub′mə rēn′ər) *n.* a member of the crew of a submarine.

sub·max·il·lar·y (sub mak′sə ler′ē) *adj., n., pl.* -**lar·ies.** —*adj.* **1** of, having to do with, or situated under the lower jaw. **2** of or having to do with either of the salivary glands situated beneath the lower jaw, one on either side. —*n.* a submaxillary part, especially the lower jawbone.

sub·merge (səb mėrj′) *v.* -**merged, -merg·ing. 1** put under water;

cover with water: *A big wave submerged us. At high tide this path is submerged.* 2 cover; bury: *His talent was submerged by his shyness.* 3 sink under water; go below the surface. 4 sink out of sight. [< L *submergere* < *sub-* under + *mergere* plunge]

sub·mer·gence (səb mèr′jəns) *n.* the act of submerging or the state of being submerged.

sub·merse (səb mèrs′) *v.* **-mersed, -mers·ing.** submerge. [< L *submersus*, pp. of *submergere*. See SUBMERGE.]

sub·mers·i·ble (səb mèr′sə bəl) *adj., n.* —*adj.* that can be submerged. —*n.* a ship or craft that can operate under water for research, exploration, etc.

sub·mer·sion (səb mèr′zhən *or* səb mèr′shən) *n.* submergence.

sub·mi·cro·scop·ic (sub′mī krə skop′ik) *adj.* too small to be seen through an ordinary microscope; visible only by means of an electron microscope.

sub·mis·sion (səb mish′ən) *n.* 1 the act of submitting; a yielding to the power, control, or authority of another. 2 obedience or humbleness: *an attitude of submission. The slave bowed in submission.* 3 a referring or being referred to the consideration or judgment of another or others. 4 a petition; a formal request. 5 a report. [ME < L *submissio, -onis* < *submittere.* See SUBMIT.]

sub·mis·sive (səb mis′iv) *adj.* yielding to the power, control, or authority of another; obedient; humble. —**sub·mis′sive·ly,** *adv.* —**sub·mis′sive·ness,** *n.*

sub·mit (səb mit′) *v.* **-mit·ted, -mit·ting.** 1 yield to the power, control, or authority of another or others; surrender; yield: *The thief submitted to arrest by the police.* 2 refer to the consideration or judgment of another or others: *The secretary submitted a report of the last meeting. She submitted a bid on the contract for the new shopping centre.* 3 offer as an opinion; propose or affirm: *We submit that the proposed expansion of the airport is unnecessary.* [ME < L *submittere* < *sub-* under + *mittere* let go]
☛ *Syn.* 1. See note at **yield.**

sub–mul·ti·ple (sub′mul′tə pəl) *n.* a number or quantity contained exactly within another number or quantity. The millimetre is a sub-multiple of the metre.

sub·nor·mal (sub′nôr′məl) *adj.* 1 lower or smaller than normal: *subnormal temperatures.* 2 below normal, especially in mental ability. —**sub′nor′mal·ly,** *adv.*

sub–or·bit·al (sub′ôr′bit əl) *adj.* 1 not in or going into a complete orbit: *The new space capsule was tested in a sub-orbital flight.* 2 *Anatomy.* situated below the orbit of the eye: *a sub-orbital nerve.*

sub·or·der (sub′ôr′dər *or* sub′ôr′dər) *n.* a secondary category in the classification of plants and animals, that is a grouping within an order and includes one or more families.

sub·or·di·nate (*adj., n.* sə bôr′də nit; *v.* sə bôr′də nāt′) *adj., n., v.* **-nat·ed, -nat·ing.** —*adj.* 1 inferior in rank: *In the armed forces, lieutenants are subordinate to captains.* 2 inferior in importance; secondary: *a subordinate position.* 3 under the control or influence of something else. 4 *Grammar.* of, having to do with, or designating a clause that depends for its complete sense on a main clause. A subordinate clause functions as an adjective, adverb, or noun in a complex sentence.
—*n.* a subordinate person or thing.
—*v.* make subordinate: *The host politely subordinated his wishes to those of his guests.* [< Med.L *subordinatus,* pp. of *subordinare,* ult. < L *sub-* under + *ordo, ordinis* order] —**sub·or′di·nate·ly,** *adv.*

sub·or·di·na·tion (se bôr′də nā′shən) *n.* 1 the act of subordinating or the quality or state of being subordinate. 2 a subordinate position or importance. 3 a submission to authority; willingness to obey; obedience.

sub·orn (sə bôrn′) *v.* 1 persuade by bribery or other means to do something illegal; especially, to give false testimony in court: *A friend of the accused was charged with suborning a witness.* 2 obtain by bribery or other means: *to suborn perjury.* [< L *subornare* < *sub-* secretly + *ornare* equip] —**sub·orn′er,** *n.*

sub·or·na·tion (sub′ôr nā′shən) *n.* the obtaining by a bribe or other means of an illegal act; especially, the crime of getting someone to commit perjury.

subornation of perjury the criminal offence of causing or persuading a person to commit perjury.

sub·phy·lum (sub′fī′ləm) *n.* a secondary category in the classification of plants and animals, that is a grouping within a phylum and includes one or more classes.

sub·plot (sub′plot′) *n.* a subordinate plot within the main plot of a novel, film, play, etc.

sub·poe·na (sə pē′nə) *n., v.* **-naed, -na·ing.** —*n. Law.* a written order, or summons, requiring a person to be present in court for a specified purpose at a specified time. Rarely (esp.U.S.), **subpena.** —*v.* summon with a subpoena. [< NL *sub poena* under penalty]

sub·ro·gate (sub′rə gāt′) *v.* **-gated, -gat·ing.** *Law.* substitute (one person or thing) for another in respect of a right or claim. [< L *subrogare* < *sub-* in place of + *rogare* ask]

sub·ro·ga·tion (sub′rə gā′shən) *n. Law.* the substitution of one person or thing for another, especially the substitution of one party for another as creditor, with the transference of all the rights and duties of the original creditor.

sub ro·sa (sub′rō′zə) in strict confidence; privately. [< *sub rosa* under the rose; the rose was an ancient symbol of secrecy]

sub·scribe (səb skrīb′) *v.* **-scribed, -scrib·ing.** 1 promise to give or pay (a sum of money): *He subscribed $75 to the hospital fund.* 2 arrange to receive a periodical or a service regularly for a given length of time (*used with* **to**): *He subscribes to several magazines.* 3 write (one's name) at the end of a document, etc.; sign one's name. 4 write one's name at the end of; show one's consent or approval by signing: *Thousands of citizens subscribed the petition.* 5 give one's consent or approval; agree: *He will not subscribe to anything unfair.* [ME < L *subscribere* < *sub-* under + *scribere* write] —**sub·scrib′er,** *n.*

sub·script (sub′skript) *n., adj.* —*n.* a small number, letter, etc. written immediately below or below and to one side of another number, letter, etc. *Example:* In H_2SO_4 the 2 and the 4 are subscripts. —*adj.* written underneath or low on the line. [< L *subscriptus,* pp. of *subscribere.* See SUBSCRIBE.]

sub·scrip·tion (səb skrip′shən) *n.* 1 subscribing. 2 a sum of money subscribed: *His subscription to the Fresh Air Fund was $25. We are raising a subscription for a new arena.* 3 something obtained by subscribing, especially a magazine, etc. or a service paid for in advance for a specific period of time. 4 something written at the end of a thing; signature. 5 a signing, as of one's name on a document.

sub·sec·tion (sub′sek′shən *or* sub sek′shən) *n.* a part of a section.

sub·se·quence (sub′sə kwəns) *n.* 1 the quality or state of being subsequent. 2 a subsequent event or circumstance.

sub·se·quent (sub′sə kwənt) *adj.* coming after; following; later: *Subsequent events proved him right. That problem is dealt with in a subsequent chapter. The package arrived on the day subsequent to her call.* —**sub′se·quent·ly,** *adv.* [< L *subsequens, -entis,* ppr. of *subsequi* < *sub-* up + *sequi* follow]

sub·serve (səb sèrv′) *v.* **-served, -serv·ing.** be of use or service in helping along (a purpose, action, etc.); promote: *Chewing food well subserves digestion.* [< L *subservire* < *sub-* under + *servire* serve]

sub·ser·vi·ence (səb sèr′vē əns) *n.* 1 tame submission; slavish obedience; servility. 2 usefulness in a subordinate place or function.

sub·ser·vi·en·cy (səb sèr′vē ən sē) *n.* subservience.

sub·ser·vi·ent (səb sèr′vē ənt) *adj.* 1 tamely submissive; slavishly polite and obedient; servile. 2 useful as a means to help a purpose or end; servicable. [< L *subserviens, -entis,* ppr. of *subservire* < *sub-* under + *servire* serve] —**sub·ser′vi·ent·ly,** *adv.*

sub·set (sub′set′) *n. Mathematics and logic.* a set whose members are also members of another set or series: *The set of dogs is a subset of the set of mammals.*

sub·side (səb sīd′) *v.* **-sid·ed, -sid·ing.** 1 sink to a lower level: *After the rain stopped, the flood waters subsided.* 2 grow less; die down; become less active: *The storm finally subsided.* 3 fall to the bottom; settle. [< L *subsidere* < *sub-* down + *sidere* settle]

sub·sid·ence (səb sīd′ens *or* sub′sə dəns) *n.* the act or process of subsiding.

sub·sid·i·ar·y (səb sid′ē er′ē) *adj., n., pl.* **-ar·ies.** —*adj.* 1 useful to assist or support; auxiliary; supplementary. 2 subordinate; secondary. 3 of, having to do with, or maintained by a subsidy. —*n.* 1 a thing or person that assists or supplements. 2 a company having over half of its stock owned or controlled by another company: *The bus line was a subsidiary of the railway.* [< L *subsidiarius* < *subsidium* reserve troops]

sub·si·dize (sub′sə dīz′) *v.* **-dized, -diz·ing.** 1 aid or assist with a grant of money: *The government subsidizes shipping lines and airlines that carry mail.* 2 buy the aid or assistance of with a grant of money. —**sub′si·diz′er,** *n.*

sub·si·dy (sub′sə dē) *n., pl.* **-dies.** a grant or contribution of money, especially one made by a government. [< L *subsidium* aid, reserve troops]

sub·sist (səb sist′) *v.* 1 keep alive; live: *While the hikers were stranded they subsisted on berries.* 2 continue to be; exist: *Many superstitions still subsist.* [< L *subsistere* < *sub-* up to + *sistere* stand]

sub·sist·ence (səb sis′təns) *n.* 1 existence; continuance. 2 the state or fact of keeping alive; living. 3 a means of keeping alive;

livelihood: *The sea provides a subsistence for fishermen.*

sub·soil (sub′soil′) *n.* the layer of earth that lies just under the surface soil.

sub·son·ic (sub son′ik) *adj.* having to do with or designed for use at a speed less than that of sound.

sub·spe·cies (sub′spē′sēz or -spē′shēz) *n., pl.* **-cies.** a geographical grouping within an animal or plant species based on inherited biological differences. Subspecies often develop when groups of a particular species have been isolated from each other for many generations. The grizzly is a subspecies of the brown bear.

subst. 1 substitute. 2 substantive.

sub·stance (sub′stəns) *n.* 1 what a thing consists of; matter; material: *Ice and water are the same substance in different forms.* 2 the real, main, or important part of anything: *The substance of an education is its effect on your life, not just the learning of lessons.* 3 the real meaning: *Give the substance of the speech in your own words.* 4 solid quality; body: *Pea soup has more substance than bouillon.* 5 wealth; property. 6 a particular kind of matter: *The little pond is covered with a green substance.* 7 *Philosophy.* **a** something that underlies all phenomena, and in which accidents or attributes inhere. **b** something that subsists by itself; a separate or distinct thing.
in substance, a essentially; mainly. **b** really; actually.
[ME < OF < *substantia* < *substare* stand firm < *sub-* up to + *stare* stand]
☛ *Syn.* **1. Substance, matter, material** = what a thing consists or is made of. **Substance** suggests "what a thing consists of," as apart from the form in which it exists, and applies both to things existing in the physical world and to those given actual form only in the mind: *The substance of the plan is good.* **Matter** applies to substance that occupies space and that physical objects consist of: *Matter may be gaseous, liquid, or solid.* **Material** applies particularly to matter from which something is made: *Wood is an important building material.*

sub·stan·dard (sub stan′dərd or sub stan′dərd) *adj.* 1 falling short of a minimum standard of quality: *The substandard sheets are being sold at very low prices.* 2 of language, differing from the standard usage of a group, especially by falling short of what is considered grammatical or acceptable by educated people: *Words like* ain't *and constructions like* them books *are considered substandard by many people.*

sub·stan·tial (səb stan′shəl) *adj.* 1 real; actual: *People and things are substantial; dreams and ghosts are not.* 2 large; important; ample: *John has made a substantial improvement in health.* 3 strong; firm; solid: *The house is substantial enough to last a hundred years.* 4 in the main; in essentials: *The stories told by the two boys were in substantial agreement.* 5 well-to-do; wealthy. 6 of real or solid worth or value; weighty; sound: *substantial criticism, substantial evidence.* [ME < L *substantialis* < *substantia.* See SUBSTANCE.] —**sub·stan′tial·ly,** *adv.*

sub·stan·ti·al·i·ty (səb stan′shē al′ə tē) *n., pl.* **-ties.** the quality or state of being substantial.

sub·stan·ti·ate (səb stan′shē āt′) *v.* **-at·ed, -at·ing.** 1 establish by evidence; prove: *to substantiate a rumor, a claim, a theory, etc.* 2 give concrete or substantial form to.

sub·stan·ti·a·tion (səb stan′shē ā′shən) *n.* a substantiating or being substantiated; embodiment; proof.

sub·stan·ti·val (sub′stən tī′vəl) *adj.* of, having to do with, or being a substantive. —**sub·stan·ti′val·ly,** *adv.*

sub·stan·tive (sub′stən tiv) *n., adj.* —*n. Grammar.* a noun or pronoun or an adjective, phrase, or clause used as a noun. —*adj.* 1 *Grammar.* **a** used as a noun. **b** showing or expressing existence. The verb *be* is the substantive verb. 2 independent. 3 real; actual. 4 having a firm or solid basis. [ME < LL *substantivus,* ult. < *substare.* See SUBSTANCE.] —**sub′stan·tive·ly,** *adv.*

sub·sta·tion (sub′stā′shən) *n.* a branch station; subordinate station: *Besides the main post office in our city, there are six substations.*

sub·sti·tute (sub′stə tyüt′ or sub′stə tüt′) *n., v.* **-tut·ed, -tut·ing.**
—*n.* 1 a person or thing used or taking the place of another: *Margarine is a common substitute for butter. We were taught by a substitute today because our teacher was sick.* 2 (*adj.*) taking the place of or put in for another: *a substitute teacher.* —*v.* 1 put in the place of another: *We substituted brown sugar for molasses in these cookies.* 2 take the place of another. [ME < L *substitutus,* pp. of *substituere* < *sub-* instead + *statuere* establish]

sub·sti·tu·tion (sub′stə tyü′shən or sub′stə tü′shən) *n.* 1 the substituting of one person or thing for another. 2 something that functions as a substitute.

sub·sti·tu·tion·al (sub′stə tyü′shən əl or sub′stə tü′shən əl) *adj.* 1 having to do with or characterized by substitution. 2 acting or serving as a substitute. —**sub′sti·tu′tion·al·ly,** *adv.*

sub·sti·tu·tive (sub′stə tyü′tiv or sub′stə tü′tiv) *adj.* 1 having to do with or involving substitution. 2 serving as, or capable of serving as, a substitute.

sub·stra·ta (sub strā′tə or -strat′ə) *n.* pl. of **substratum.**

hat, āge, fär; let, ēqual, tèrm; it, īce
hot, ōpen, ôrder; oil, out; cup, put, rüle,
əbove, takən, pencəl, lemən, circəs
ch, child; ng, long; sh, ship
th, thin; ғн, then; zh, measure

sub·stra·tum (sub strā′təm or -strat′əm) *n., pl.* **-stra·ta** or **-stra·tums.** 1 a layer lying under another. 2 a layer of earth lying just under the surface soil; subsoil. 3 a basis; foundation: *The story has a substratum of truth.* 4 *Biology.* the base or matter of which an organism develops. [< NL *substratum,* neut. of L *substratus,* pp. of *substernere* < *sub-* under + *sternere* spread]

sub·struc·tur·al (sub struk′chər əl) *adj.* of, having to do with, or like a substructure.

sub·struc·ture (sub′struk′chər or sub struk′chər) *n.* a structure forming a foundation.

sub·sume (səb süm′) *v.* **-sumed, -sum·ing.** incorporate (an idea, term, proposition, etc.) within a more general or comprehensive one; bring under a broader category or classification: *Your suggestion has been subsumed under point 4 of the committee's recommendations.* [< NL *subsumere* < L *sub-* under + *sumere* assume]

sub·teen (sub′tēn′) *n. Informal.* 1 a boy or girl who is almost a teenager. 2 (*adj.*) of or for subteens.

sub·ten·an·cy (sub ten′ən sē) *n., pl.* **-cies.** a status, right or holding of a subtenant.

sub·ten·ant (sub ten′ənt or sub′ten′ənt) *n.* a tenant of a tenant; one who rents land, a house, or the like, from a tenant.

sub·tend (səb tend′) *v.* 1 *Geometry.* **a** define by marking off the endpoints of: *A chord subtends an arc of a circle.* **b** of a line, arc, etc., be opposite to an angle: *The hypotenuse subtends the right angle of a right-angled triangle. An arc of a circle subtends the central angle of the arc.* 2 *Botany.* underlie, usually so as to enclose or surround: *a flower subtended by a leafy bract.* [< L *subtendere* < *sub-* under + *tendere* stretch]

sub·ter·fuge (sub′tər fyüj′) *n.* a trick, excuse, or expedient used to escape something unpleasant: *The girl's headache was only a subterfuge to avoid taking the examination.* [< LL *subterfugium,* ult. < L *subter-* from under + *fugere* flee]

sub·ter·ra·ne·an (sub′tə rā′nē ən) *adj.* 1 underground: *A subterranean passage led from the castle to a cave.* 2 carried on secretly; hidden. [< L *subterraneus* < *sub-* under + *terra* earth]

sub·ter·ra·ne·ous (sub′tə rā′nē əs) *adj.* subterranean. —**sub′ter·ra′ne·ous·ly,** *adv.*

sub·tile (sut′əl) *adj. Archaic.* subtle. [ME < OF *subtil,* learned borrowing < L *subtilis.* See SUBTLE.] —**sub′tile·ly,** *adv.* —**sub′tile·ness,** *n.*

sub·til·i·ty (sub til′ə tē) *n., pl.* **-ties.** *Archaic.* subtlety.

sub·til·ty (sut′əl tē or sub′təl tē) *n., pl.* **-ties.** subtlety.

sub·ti·tle (sub′tī′təl) *n., v.* **-tled, -tling.** —*n.* 1 an additional or subordinate title of a book, article, etc. 2 a piece of dialogue or description printed on the film and shown between the scenes of a silent motion picture or as part of the scenes of a foreign-language motion picture. —*v.* give a subtitle to.

sub·tle (sut′əl) *adj.* 1 delicate; thin; fine: *a subtle odor of perfume.* 2 faint; mysterious: *a subtle smile.* 3 having a keen, quick mind; discerning; acute: *She is a subtle observer.* 4 sly; crafty; tricky: *a subtle scheme to get some money.* 5 skilful; clever; expert. 6 working unnoticeably or secretly; insidious: *a subtle poison or drug.* [ME < OF *soutil* < L *subtilis,* originally, woven underneath] —**sub′tly,** *adv.* —**sub′tle·ness,** *n.*

sub·tle·ty (sut′əl tē) *n., pl.* **-ties.** 1 the quality or state of being subtle. 2 something subtle, especially a fine distinction: *He did not understand all the subtleties of the author's argument.*

sub·ton·ic (sub ton′ik) *n. Music.* the seventh tone of a scale; tone next below the upper tonic.

sub·top·ic (sub′top′ik) *n.* one of the secondary topics into which a main topic is divided.

sub·to·tal (sub′tō′təl) *n.* the total of a group of figures that form part of a series of figures to be added.

sub·tract (səb trakt′) *v.* 1 take away (a number or quantity) from a larger number or quantity: *Subtract 2 from 10 and you have 8.* 2 take away (a part) from a whole. [< L *subtractus,* pp. of *subtrahere* < *sub-* from under + *trahere* draw] —**sub·tract′er,** *n.*
☛ *Syn.* **1, 2. Subtract, deduct** = take away. **Subtract** = to take away from a whole, but in present usage is almost never used except in its mathematical sense, commonly meaning "to take away one number from another": *He subtracted 89 from 200.* **Deduct** = take away a quantity or amount from a total

or whole: *He deducted the price of the cup I broke from the amount he owed me. He deducted 89 cents from $2.00.*

sub·trac·tion (səb trak'shən) *n.* the act or process of subtracting; especially, subtracting one number or quantity from another; the process of finding the difference between two numbers or quantities. 10 − 2 = 8 is a simple subtraction.

sub·trac·tive (səb trak'tiv) *adj.* **1** tending to subtract; having power to subtract. **2** to be subtracted; having the minus sign (−).

sub·tra·hend (sub'trə hend') *n.* a number or quantity to be subtracted from another. In 10 − 2 = 8, the subtrahend is 2. [< L *subtrahendus* < *subtrahere*. See SUBTRACT.]

sub·trop·i·cal (sub'trop'ə kəl) *adj.* bordering on the tropics; nearly tropical.

sub·trop·ics (sub'trop'iks or sub'trop'iks) *n.pl.* the region bordering on the tropics.

sub·urb (sub'èrb) *n.* **1** a district, town, or village just outside or near a city or town. **2 the suburbs,** the residential section or sections on the outskirts of a city or town. [ME < L *suburbium* < *sub-* below + *urbs* city]

sub·ur·ban (sə bėr'bən) *adj., n.* —*adj.* **1** having to do with a suburb; in a suburb: *We have an excellent suburban train service.* **2** characteristic of a suburb or its inhabitants. —*n.* suburbanite.

sub·ur·ban·ite (sə bėr'bən īt') *n.* a person who lives in a suburb.

sub·ur·bi·a (sə bėr'bē ə) *n.* **1** the suburbs of a city. **2** the residents of the suburbs, thought of as a distinct social class. **3** the values, attitudes, etc. thought to be characteristic of residents of the suburbs.

sub·ven·tion (səb ven'shən) *n.* **1** money granted to aid or support some cause, institution, or undertaking; subsidy. **2 a** the providing of help, support, or relief. **b** an instance of this. [ME < OF < LL *subventio, -onis* < L *subvenire* come to one's aid < *sub-* under + *venire* come]

sub·ver·sion (səb vėr'zhən or səb vėr'shən) *n.* subverting or being subverted; overthrow; especially, an attempt to overthrow a government by working against it secretly from within the country. [ME < OF < LL *subversio, -onis* < L *subvertere*. See SUBVERT.]

sub·ver·sive (səb vėr'siv) *adj., n.* —*adj.* tending or designed to overthrow or destroy a government, institution, etc.: *a subversive scheme.* —*n.* a person who seeks to overthrow or undermine (a government, etc.). —**sub·ver'sive·ly,** *adv.*

sub·vert (səb vėrt') *v.* **1** ruin; overthrow; destroy: *Dictators subvert democracy.* **2** undermine the principles of; corrupt. [ME < OF < L *subvertere* < *sub-* up from under + *vertere* turn] —**sub·vert'er,** *n.*

sub·way (sub'wā') *n.* **1** an electric railway running for all or most of its length beneath the surface of the streets in a city. **2** a road running under another road or under a railway track; an underpass. **3** an underground passage for pipes, etc.

suc– *prefix.* the form of sub- occurring before *c,* as in *succeed.*

suc·ceed (sək sēd') *v.* **1** turn out well; have success: *His plans succeeded.* **2** accomplish what is attempted or intended: *The attack succeeded beyond all expectations.* **3** come next after; follow; take the place of: *Diefenbaker succeeded St. Laurent as Prime Minister of Canada.* **4** come into possession of an office, title, or property through right of birth, etc. (used with **to**): *The Prince of Wales succeeds to the throne of England.* [ME < L *succedere* < *sub-* up (to) + *cedere* go] —**suc·ceed'er,** *n.*
☛ *Syn.* 3. See note at **follow.**

suc·cess (sək ses') *n.* **1** a favorable result; a wished-for ending; good fortune. **2** the gaining of wealth, position, etc.: *He has had little success in life.* **3** a person or thing that succeeds. **4** the result; outcome; fortune: *What success did you have in finding a new cook?* [< L *successus* < *succedere*. See SUCCEED.]

suc·cess·ful (sək ses'fəl) *adj.* **1** having success; ending in success. **2** prosperous; fortunate. —**suc·cess'ful·ly,** *adv.*

suc·ces·sion (sək sesh'ən) *n.* **1** a number of persons or things following one after the other; series: *a succession of capable leaders, a succession of misfortunes.* **2** the act or process of following one after the other. **3** the right of succeeding to an office, property, or rank: *There was a dispute about the rightful succession to the throne.* **4** the order of persons having such a right: *The king's oldest son is next in succession to the throne.*
in succession, one after another: *We visited our sick friend several days in succession.*
☛ *Syn.* 1. See note at **series.**

succession duty a tax payable on the value of all property or interest acquired by inheritance.

suc·ces·sive (sək ses'iv) *adj.* coming one after another;

following in order; consecutive: *It rained for three successive days.* —**suc·ces'sive·ly,** *adv.*
☛ *Syn.* **Successive, consecutive** = following one after another without interruption or a break. **Successive** emphasizes the idea of coming one after another in order or without interruption: *He has worked on three successive Saturdays.* **Consecutive** emphasizes the closeness of the connection or the idea of following immediately or continuously: *He worked three consecutive days last week.*

suc·ces·sor (sək ses'ər) *n.* a person or thing that comes next after another in a series; especially, a person who succeeds to an office, position, ownership of property, or title. [< L]

suc·cinct (sək singkt') *adj.* marked by clear, brief expression; concise: *She gave a succinct account of her meeting with the director.* [ME < L *succinctus,* pp. of *succingere* tuck up clothes for action < *sub-* up + *cingere* gird] —**suc·cinct'ly,** *adv.* —**suc·cinct'ness,** *n.*

suc·cor or **suc·cour** (suk'ər) *n.* **1** help; aid; relief: *to give succor in time of need.* **2** a person or thing that gives help or aid. —*v.* help or assist a person or animal in distress or need; relieve: *to succor the wounded.* [ME < OF *sucurs,* ult. < L *succurrere* run to help < *sub-* up (to) + *currere* run]
☛ *Hom.* **sucker.**

suc·co·ry (suk'ə rē) *n.* chicory.

suc·co·tash (suk'ə tash') *n.* a dish made of cooked sweet corn and lima beans or green beans, often with cream, butter, and green onions. It was originally a North American Indian dish. [< Algonquian]

suc·cour (suk'ər) See **succor.**

suc·cu·lence (suk'yə ləns) *n.* juiciness.

suc·cu·len·cy (suk'yə lən sē) *n.* succulence.

suc·cu·lent (suk'yə lənt) *adj.* **1** juicy: *a succulent fruit.* **2** full of vigor and richness; not dull. **3** of a plant, having thick, fleshy tissues adapted for storing water, either in the stem, as cactuses, or in the leaves, as argives. Most succulents are native to desert or semi-arid regions. —*n.* a succulent plant. [< L *succulentus* < *succus* juice] —**suc'cu·lent·ly,** *adv.*

suc·cumb (sə kum') *v.* **1** give way to superior force, etc. or to overwhelming desire; yield: *He succumbed to temptation and stole the money. After several days of fighting, the garrison succumbed.* **2** die or die of: *She succumbed to her injuries two days after being admitted to hospital.* [ME < L *succumbere* < *sub-* down + *-cumbere* lie]

such (such) *adj., pron.* —*adj.* **1** of that kind; of the same kind or degree: *I have never seen such a sight.* **2** of the kind that; of a particular kind: *She wore such thin clothes it is no wonder she caught cold.* **3** of the kind already spoken of or suggested: *The ladies took only tea and coffee and such drinks.* **4** so great, so bad, so good, etc.: *He is such a liar.* **5** a certain one or ones not named or identified; some; certain: *The bank was robbed in such and such a town by such and such persons.*
such as, a the kind or degree that; of a particular kind: *Her behavior was such as might be expected of a young child.* **b** of a particular character or kind: *The food, such as it was, was plentiful.* **c** for example: *members of the dog family, such as the wolf, fox, and jackal.*
—*pron.* one or more persons or things of a certain kind: *The box contains blankets and towels and such.*
as such, a as being what is indicated or implied: *A leader, as such, deserves respect.* **b** in or by itself; intrinsically considered: *Mere good looks, as such, will not take you far.*
[OE *swylc, swelc* < *swa* so + *līc* like]

such·like (such'līk') *adj., pron.* —*adj.* of such kind; of a like kind. —*pron.* persons or things of the same kind: *deceptions, disguises, and suchlike.*

suck (suk) *v., n.* —*v.* **1** draw into the mouth: *Lemonade can be sucked through a straw.* **2** draw something from with the mouth: *to suck oranges.* **3** draw milk from the breast or a bottle. **4** draw or be drawn by sucking: *He sucked at his pipe.* **5** drink; take; absorb: *Plants suck up moisture from the earth. A sponge sucks in water.* **6** draw in; swallow: *The whirlpool sucked down the boat.* **7** draw air instead of water: *The pump sucked noisily.* **8** hold in the mouth to draw on, moisten, or dissolve: *The child sucked a lollipop.* —*n.* **1** the act of sucking. **2** a sucking force or sound. [OE *sūcan*]

suck·er (suk'ər) *n., v.* —*n.* **1** an animal or thing that sucks. **2** any of a family (Catostomidae) of freshwater fishes found mainly in North America, having a soft, thick-lipped, toothless mouth, usually on the under surface of the head. **3** in some animals, an organ for sucking or holding fast by a sucking force. **4** *Botany.* **a** a shoot growing from an underground stem or root. **b** an adventitious shoot from the trunk or a branch of a tree or plant. **5** the piston of a suction pump. **6** the valve of such a piston. **7** *Slang.* a person easily deceived. **8** a lump of hard candy, usually on a stick.
—*v.* **1** remove suckers from (corn, tobacco, etc.). **2** form suckers. **3** *Slang.* treat as a fool or simpleton; deceive; dupe.
☛ *Hom.* **succor.**

hat, āge, fär; let, ēqual, tėrm; it, īce
hot, ōpen, ôrder; oil, out; cup, pu̇t, rüle,
əbove, takən, pencəl, lemən, circəs
ch, child; ng, long; sh, ship
th, thin; ᴛʜ, then; zh, measure

suck·le (suk′əl) *v.* **-led, -ling. 1** feed with milk from the breast, udder, etc.: *The cat suckles her kittens.* **2** suck at the breast. **3** nourish; bring up. [< *suck*]

suck·ling (suk′ling) *n.* a young animal or child that has not yet been weaned.

su·cre (sü′krā) *n.* **1** the basic unit of money in Ecuador, divided into 100 centavos. See table at **money. 2** a coin worth one sucre. [Antonio José de *Sucre* (1793-1830), a South American general and liberator]

su·crose (sü′krōs) *n.* sugar obtained from sugar cane, sugar beets, etc. *Formula*: $C_{12}H_{22}O_{11}$ [< F *sucre* sugar]

suc·tion (suk′shən) *n.* **1** the production of a vacuum by removing all or part of the air in a space with the result that atmospheric pressure forces fluid or gas into the vacant space or causes surfaces to stick together: *Lemonade is drawn through a straw by suction.* **2** the force caused by sucking out or removing part of the air in a space. **3** the act or process of sucking. **4** (*adjl.*) causing a suction; working by suction: *a suction valve.* [< L *suctio, -onis* < *sugere* suck]

suction cup a cuplike device of rubber, etc., designed to adhere to smooth surfaces by creating a vacuum when pressed against them and then released: *Toy arrows are often tipped with suction cups.*

suc·to·ri·al (suk tô′rē əl) *adj.* adapted for sucking or suction.

Su·da·nese (sü′də nēz′) *n., pl.* **-nese;** *adj.* —*n.* a native or inhabitant of Sudan, a country in NE Africa, or of the Sudan, a vast grassy region in Africa south of the Sahara desert. —*adj.* of or having to do with Sudan, the Sudan, or the Sudanese.

Sudan grass (sü dan′) a variety of sorghum widely grown for hay and fodder.

su·da·to·ri·um (sü′də tô′rē əm) *n., pl.* **-ri·a** (-rē ə). a hot-air bath for inducing sweating. [< L *sudatorium*, ult. < *sudor* sweat]

sud·den (sud′ən) *adj., n.* —*adj.* **1** not expected: *The army made a sudden attack on the fort.* **2** found or hit upon unexpectedly; abrupt: *a sudden turn in a road, a sudden shift in foreign policy.* **3** quick; rapid: *The cat made a sudden jump at the mouse.*
—*n.*
all of a sudden, in a sudden manner: *All of a sudden he stopped and listened.*
[ME < AF *sodein* < L *subitaneus* < *subitus* sudden] **—sud′den·ly,** *adv.* **—sud′den·ness,** *n.*

sudden death 1 instant or unexpected death. **2** *Sports.* an extra game played to break a tie, or an extra period of play for the same purpose, ending as soon as either side scores.

su·dor·if·er·ous (sü′dər if′ər əs) *adj.* secreting sweat: *sudoriferous glands.*

su·dor·if·ic (sü′dər if′ik) *adj., n.* —*adj.* **1** causing or promoting sweat. **2** secreting sweat. —*n.* a sudorific agent or remedy. [< NL *sudorificus* < L *sudor* sweat + *facere* make]

suds (sudz) *n.pl., v.* —*n.* **1** soapy water. **2** the bubbles and foam on soapy water. **3** any froth or foam. **4** *Slang.* beer.
—*v.* **1** *Informal.* form suds: *This shampoo doesn't suds well.* **2** wash in suds: *Just suds the stockings and hang them to dry.* [? < MDu. *sudse* bog]

sud·sy (sud′zē) *adj.* full of suds; frothy: *sudsy dishwater.*

sue (sü) *v.* **sued, su·ing. 1** *Law.* **a** start a lawsuit against: *He sued the railway because his cow was killed by the engine.* **b** take action: *to sue for damages.* **2** beg or ask (*for*); plead: *Messengers came suing for peace.* **3** *Archaic.* court; woo.
sue out, apply for and get (a writ, pardon, etc.) from a law court.
[ME < AF *suer*, ult. < L *sequi* follow] **—su′a·ble,** *adj.*
☛ *Hom.* **sault, sou.**

suede or **suède** (swād) *n.* **1** a kind of soft leather that has a velvety nap on one or both sides. **2** a kind of cloth with a short nap that looks and feels much like suede. **3** (*adjl.*) made of suede. [< F (*de*) *Suède* (from) Sweden]

su·et (sü′it) *n.* the hard fat about the kidneys and loins of cattle or sheep. Suet is used in cooking and to make tallow. [ME < AF **suet*, dim. of *sue*, OF *sieu* tallow < L *sebum*]

su·et·y (sü′it ē) *adj.* **1** like suet. **2** containing suet.

suf– *prefix.* the form of **sub-** occurring before *f*, as in *suffer* and *suffice.*

suf. or **suff.** suffix.

suf·fer (suf′ər) *v.* **1** have pain, grief, injury, etc.: *Sick people suffer.* **2** have or feel (pain, grief, etc.). **3** experience harm, loss, etc.: *His business suffered greatly during the war.* **4** allow; permit: *"Suffer little children to come unto me."* **5** bear with patiently; endure: *I will not suffer such insults.* [ME < AF < L *sufferre* < *sub-* up + *ferre* bear] **—suf′fer·er,** *n.*

suf·fer·a·ble (suf′ər ə bəl *or* suf′rə bəl) *adj.* that can be endured or allowed. **—suf′fer·a·bly,** *adv.*

suf·fer·ance (suf′ər əns *or* suf′rəns) *n.* **1** permission or consent not actually given but only implied by a failure to object or prevent: *They managed to get their supplies through with the sufferance of the neutral country.* **2** the power to bear or endure; patient endurance.
on sufferance, allowed or tolerated, but not really wanted: *Our cousin came with us to the party on sufferance.*

suf·fer·ing (suf′ər ing *or* suf′ring) *n.* pain, trouble, or distress.

suf·fice (sə fīs′) *v.* **-ficed, -fic·ing. 1** be enough; be sufficient: *The money will suffice for one year.* **2** satisfy; make content: *A small amount sufficed him.*
suffice it to say, it is enough if I say only (*that*): *Suffice it to say that he was very upset.*
[ME < OF < L *sufficere* < *sub-* up (to) + *facere* make]

suf·fi·cien·cy (sə fish′ən sē) *n., pl.* **-cies. 1** a sufficient amount; a large enough supply: *The ship had a sufficiency of provisions for a voyage of two months.* **2** the quality or state of being sufficient; adequacy: *They questioned the sufficiency of the preparations.*

suf·fi·cient (sə fish′ənt) *adj.* **1** as much as is needed; enough: *sufficient proof.* **2** *Archaic.* competent; able. [ME < L *sufficiens, -entis*, ppr. of *sufficere.* See SUFFICE.] **—suf·fi′cient·ly,** *adv.*
☛ *Syn.* **1.** See note at **enough.**

suf·fix (*n.* suf′iks; *v.* sə fiks′) *n., v.* —*n.* **1** *Grammar.* **a** a syllable or syllables put at the end of a word to form another word of different meaning or function, as in bad*ly*, good*ness*, spoon*ful*, amaze*ment*. **b** an inflectional ending, as in talk*s*, talk*ed*, talk*ing*. Compare **prefix. 2** something added at the end of something else.
—*v.* add or attach as a suffix. [< NL < L *suffixum*, neut. pp. of *suffigere* < *sub-* upon + *figere* fasten]

suf·fix·al (suf′iks əl) *adj.* having to do with or of the nature of a suffix.

suf·fo·cate (suf′ə kāt′) *v.* **-cat·ed, -cat·ing. 1** kill by stopping the breath. **2** have or cause to have difficulty in breathing: *the suffocating smell of sulphur. I was suffocating in that hot, smoky room.* **3** die for lack of air in the lungs: *The victims of the fire had not burned to death but had suffocated.* **4** be or cause to be unable to develop: *He longed to escape the suffocating environment of his home town.* [< L *suffocare*, originally, narrow up < *sub-* up + *foces*, dial. var. of *fauces* throat, narrow entrance]
—suf′fo·cat′ing·ly, *adv.*

suf·fo·ca·tion (suf′ə kā′shən) *n.* suffocating or being suffocated.

suf·fo·ca·tive (suf′ə kā′tiv) *adj.* stifling.

Suf·folk (suf′ək) *n.* **1** any of an English breed of hornless sheep raised especially for meat. **2** any of an English breed of heavy-bodied, chestnut-colored work horses. [< *Suffolk*, a county in England]

suf·fra·gan (suf′rə gən) *n.* **1** a bishop consecrated to assist another bishop. **2** (*adjl.*) assisting. **3** any bishop considered in relation to his archbishop. [ME < OF *suffragan*, ult. < L *suffragium* suffrage. See SUFFRAGE.]

suf·frage (suf′rij) *n.* **1** the right to vote; franchise: *Alberta granted suffrage to women in 1916.* **2** a vote, especially a vote in support of a person or proposal. **3** a casting of votes. **4** a short prayer of supplication. [ME < L *suffragium* supporting vote < *sub-* nearby + *frag-* applause (related to *fragor* din, crash, originally, a breaking)]

suf·fra·gette (suf′rə jet′) *n. Historical.* a militant female advocate of suffrage for women.

suf·fra·gist (suf′rə jist) *n.* a person who favors giving suffrage to more people, especially to women.

suf·fuse (sə fyüz′) *v.* **-fused, -fus·ing.** overspread or flood with color, light, a fluid, etc.: *At twilight the sky was suffused with color. Her eyes were suffused with tears.* [< L *suffusus*, pp. of *suffundere* < *sub-* (up from) under + *fundere* pour]

suf·fu·sion (sə fyü′zhən) *n.* **1** suffusing or being suffused. **2** that with which anything is overspread: *a suffusion of light or color.*

sug– *prefix.* the form of **sub-** occurring before *g*, as in *suggest.*

sug·ar (shu̇g′ər) *n., v.* —*n.* **1** a sweet substance consisting entirely or mainly of sucrose and obtained especially from sugar cane or sugar beets. Sugar is much used as a sweetener and preservative of foods and as a source of carbohydrate for the diet. **2** any of the class of carbohydrates to which this substance belongs: *grape sugar, milk sugar. Glucose and levulose are sugars.* **3** a sugar

bowl, especially as forming a set with a cream jug. **4** sweet or honeyed words; flattery. **5** *Informal.* sweetheart; darling. **6** *Slang.* money.

—*v.* **1** mix or sprinkle with sugar; put sugar in or on: *She sugared her tea. We sugared the buns before baking them.* **2** form sugar: *Honey sugars if kept too long.* **3** make maple sugar by boiling maple syrup until it is thick enough to crystallize (*usually used with* **off**). **4** make more pleasant or agreeable: *He sugared his criticism of the team with some praise for the individual players.* [ME < OF *sucre* < Med.L < Arabic *sukkar* < Persian < Skt. *sarkara*, originally, grit]

sugar beet a variety of beet having a large white root with high sugar content, grown commercially for the sugar it yields.

sugar bush a grove of sugar maples.

sugar cane a very tall, coarse, perennial grass (*Saccharum officinarum*) having a strong, jointed stem and flat leaves, widely cultivated in warm regions as a source of sugar.

sug·ar–coat (shug′ər kōt′) *v.* **1** cover with sugar. **2** cause to seem more pleasant or agreeable.

sug·ar–coat·ing (shug′ər kōt′ing) *n.* **1** a covering of sugar. **2** anything that makes something seem more pleasant or agreeable.

sugar corn sweet corn.

sugar cube a cake of sugar in cube form.

sugar daddy *Slang.* a wealthy old or middle-aged man who lavishes gifts and money on a younger woman in return for her favors.

sugaring off *Cdn.* **1** the converting of maple syrup into sugar by boiling it until it crystallizes. **2** a gathering of friends and neighbors to assist in this process and enjoy a party afterwards.

sugar loaf **1** a cone-shaped mass of sugar. **2** something shaped like a sugar loaf, such as a hill or mountain.

sug·ar–loaf (shug′ər lōf′) *adj.* shaped like a sugar loaf.

sugar maple *Cdn.* a large maple (*Acer saccharum*) of E North America, a valuable timber tree having large, lobed leaves that turn bright crimson, scarlet, or yellow in fall, and yielding a sweet sap that is the main source of maple syrup and maple sugar. The sugar maple is one of the largest Canadian maples, usually about 24 to 27 metres high, but sometimes reaching a height of 35 metres.

sugar of lead lead acetate.

sugar of milk lactose, the sugar that occurs in milk.

sug·ar·plum (shug′ər plum′) *n.* a piece of candy; bonbon.

sugar shanty a hut or cabin used for making maple sugar.

sug·ar·y (shug′ər ē) *adj.* **1** consisting of, containing, or like sugar. **2** too sweet, pleasant, or agreeable: *sugary compliments, a sugary voice.* —**sug′ar·i·ness,** *n.*

sug·gest (sə jest′ *or* səg jest′) *v.* **1** bring to mind; call up the thought of: *The thought of summer suggests swimming, tennis, and hot weather.* **2** propose: *John suggested a swim, and we all agreed.* **3** provide the motive for; prompt. **4** show in an indirect way; hint: *His yawns suggested that he would like to go to bed.* [< L *suggestus*, pp. of *suggerere* put under, supply, suggest < *sub-* up + *gerere* bring] —**sug′gest·er,** *n.*

sug·gest·i·bil·i·ty (sə jes′tə bil′ə tē *or* səg jes′tə bil′ə tē) *n.* the quality or condition of being suggestible.

sug·gest·i·ble (sə jes′tə bəl *or* səg jes′tə bəl) *adj.* **1** easily influenced by suggestion. **2** that can be suggested.

sug·ges·tion (sə jes′chən *or* səg jes′chən) *n.* **1** suggesting: *The trip was made at his suggestion.* **2** the thing suggested: *The picnic was an excellent suggestion.* **3** the calling up of one idea by another because they are connected or associated in some way. **4** a very small amount; slight trace: *She spoke English with just a suggestion of an accent.* **5** *Psychology.* **a** the insinuation of an idea, belief, or impulse into the mind, especially a hypnotized person's mind, with avoidance of normal critical thought, contrary ideas, etc. **b** the idea, belief, or impulse so insinuated.

sug·ges·tive (sə jes′tiv *or* səg jes′tiv) *adj.* **1** tending to suggest ideas, acts, or feelings: *a mild breeze suggestive of spring.* **2** tending to suggest something improper or indecent; risqué: *a suggestive remark.* —**sug·ges′tive·ness,** *n.*
☛ *Syn.* **1.** See note at **expressive.**

su·i·cid·al (sü′ə sīd′əl) *adj.* **1** having to do with suicide. **2** tending to consider committing suicide: *He had been suicidal for some time.* **3** ruinous to one's own interests; disastrous to oneself: *It would be suicidal for a store to sell many things below cost.* —**su′i·cid′al·ly,** *adv.*

su·i·cide¹ (sü′ə sīd′) *n., v.* **-cid·ed, -cid·ing.** —*n.* **1** the killing of oneself on purpose. **2** the destruction of one's own interests or prospects.

commit suicide, kill oneself on purpose.
—*v. Informal.* commit suicide. [< NL *suicidium* < L *sui* of oneself + *-cidium* act of killing]

su·i·cide² (sü′ə sīd′) *n.* a person who kills himself on purpose. [< NL *suicida* < L *sui* of oneself + *-cida* killer]

su·i ge·ne·ris (sü′ē jen′ə ris *or* sü′ī) *Latin.* of his, her, its, or their peculiar kind; unique.

suit (süt) *n., v.* —*n.* **1** a set of clothes to be worn together: *A man's suit consists of a coat and pants and, often, a vest. The knight wore a suit of armor.* **2** *Law.* a case in a court; application to a court for justice: *He started a suit to collect damages for his injuries.* **3** one of the four sets of cards (spades, hearts, diamonds, and clubs) in a deck. **4** a request; asking; wooing: *His suit was successful and she married him.*

follow suit, **a** play a card of the same suit as that first played. **b** follow the example of another.
—*v.* **1** provide with clothes. **2** make suitable; make fit: *to suit the punishment to the crime.* **3** be suitable for; agree with: *The Canadian climate suits apples and wheat, but not oranges and tea.* **4** be agreeable or convenient to; please; satisfy: *Which date suits best?* **5** be becoming to: *That hat suits you.*

suit (oneself), do as one pleases.
[ME < AF *siute* < VL *sequita* < L *sequi* follow. Doublet of SUITE.]

suit·a·bil·i·ty (süt′ə bil′ə tē) *n.* the quality or state of being suitable.

suit·a·ble (süt′ə bəl) *adj.* right for the occasion, purpose, condition, etc.; fitting; appropriate: *The park gives the children a suitable playground.* —**suit′a·ble·ness,** *n.* —**suit′a·bly,** *adv.*
☛ *Syn.* See note at **fit.**

suit·case (süt′kās′) *n.* a more or less rigid, flat, rectangular travelling bag.

suit coat *or* **suit-coat** (süt′kōt′) *n.* the long-sleeved upper part, or jacket, of a suit.

suite (swēt) *n.* **1** a set of connected rooms to be used as a unit by one person or group: *a suite in a hotel. She lives in a large suite above a store.* **2** a set of furniture that matches. **3** any set or series of like things. **4** *Music.* **a** an instrumental composition consisting of a series of connected movements: *suite for strings.* **b** a set of dance tunes. **5** a group of attendants: *The queen travelled with a suite of twelve.* [< F < OF < VL *sequita.* Doublet of SUIT.]
☛ *Hom.* **sweet.**

suit·ing (süt′ing) *n.* cloth for making suits.

suit·or (süt′ər) *n.* **1** a man who is courting a woman. **2** *Law.* a person bringing a suit in a court. **3** anyone who sues or petitions.

su·ki·ya·ki (sü′kē yä′kē) *n.* a Japanese dish consisting mainly of fried meat, onions, and other vegetables. [< Japanese]

sul·fa (sul′fə) See **sulpha.**
☛ *Spelling.* Compounds and derivatives beginning with **sulf-** are entered under their **sulph-** forms.

sulk (sulk) *v., n.* —*v.* hold oneself aloof in a sullen manner; be sulky: *The child stood sulking in a corner.* —*n.* **1** a fit of sulking; a sulky mood: *She was in a sulk because nothing was going her way.* **2 sulks,** *pl.* ill humor shown by sulking: *He has the sulks.* [< *sulky*]

sulk·y¹ (sul′kē) *adj.* **sulk·i·er, sulk·i·est.** silent and bad-humored because of resentment; sullen: *She became sulky when she could not have her own way.* [cf. OE *āsolcen* lazy] —**sulk′i·ly,** *adv.* —**sulk′i·ness,** *n.*
☛ *Syn. adj.* See note at **sullen.**

sulk·y² (sul′kē) *n., pl.* **-ies.** a very light, two-wheeled carriage for one person. [? < *sulky,* possibly because the rider is alone]

sul·len (sul′ən) *adj.* **1** silent because of bad humor or anger: *The sullen child refused to answer my question.* **2** showing bad humor or anger. **3** gloomy; dismal: *The sullen skies threatened rain.* [ME < OF *solain,* ult. < L *solus* alone] —**sul′len·ly,** *adv.* —**sul′len·ness,** *n.*
☛ *Syn.* **1. Sullen, sulky, glum** = silent and bad-humored or gloomy. **Sullen** suggests an ill-natured refusal to talk or be co-operative because of anger or bad humor or disposition: *It is disagreeable to have to sit at the breakfast table with a sullen person.* **Sulky** suggests moody or childish sullenness because of resentment or discontent: *Children sometimes become sulky when they are jealous.* **Glum** carries less suggestion of bad humor or bad temper, and emphasizes a dismal silence because of low spirits or some depressing condition or happening: *He is glum about world affairs.*

sul·ly (sul′ē) *v.* **-lied, -ly·ing;** *n., pl.* **-lies.** soil; stain; tarnish. [OE *sōlian* < *sōl* dirty]

sul·pha *or* **sul·fa** (sul′fə) *adj.* of or having to do with sulpha drugs.

sul·pha·di·a·zine *or* **sul·fa·di·a·zine** (sul′fə dī′a zēn′ *or* -dī′ə zin) *n.* a sulpha drug used mainly in treating meningitis, pneumonia, and infections of the intestines.

sulpha drug *or* **sulfa drug** any of a group of synthetic organic drugs, such as sulphanilamide, or a drug derived from it, that are used in treating various infections or diseases caused by bacteria.

sul·pha·nil·a·mide or **sul·fa·nil·a·mide** (sul'fə nil'ə mīd' or sul'fə nil'ə mid) *n.* a white, crystalline, synthetic compound derived from coal tar, from which most sulpha drugs are derived. *Formula:* $C_6H_8N_2O_2S$

sul·phate or **sul·fate** (sul'fāt) *n.* a salt or ester of sulphuric acid.

sul·phide or **sul·fide** (sul'fīd) *n.* any compound of sulphur with another element or radical.

sul·phite or **sul·fite** (sul'fīt) *n.* a salt or ester of sulphurous acid.

sul·phon·a·mide or **sul fon'ə mīd** or sul fon'ə mid, sul'fə nam'īd or sul'fə nam'id) *n.* **1** any of a group of sulpha drugs, derived from sulphanilimide, that check bacterial infection. **2** *Chemistry.* **a** an organic compound that contains the univalent radical. *Formula:* -SO₂NH₂ **b** the radical itself. Also, **sulfonamide**. [< *sulfonyl* + *-amide*]

sul·phur or **sul·fur** (sul'fər) *n., v.* —*n.* **1** a light-yellow, non-metallic chemical element that burns with a blue flame and a stifling odor: *Sulphur is used mainly in making gunpowder and matches, in vulcanizing rubber, and in treating skin diseases. Symbol:* S; *at.no.* 16; *at.wt.* 32.064. **2** (*adj.*) containing sulphur. **3** any of various butterflies (family Pieridae) having yellow or orange wings with black borders. —*v.* treat with sulphur or a compound of sulphur.

sul·phu·rate or **sul·fu·rate** (sul'fə rāt' or sul'fyə rāt') *v.* -rat·ed, -rat·ing. combine, treat, or impregnate with sulphur, the fumes of burning sulphur, etc.

sul·phu·ra·tion or **sul·fu·ra·tion** (sul'fə rā'shən or sul'fyə rā'shən) *n.* **1** the act or process of treating with sulphur. **2** the state of being treated or impregnated with sulphur.

sulphur dioxide or **sulfur dioxide** a heavy, colorless gas that has a sharp odor, used as a bleach, disinfectant, preservative, and refrigerant. *Formula:* SO₂

sul·phu·re·ous or **sul·fu·re·ous** (sul fyür'ē əs) *adj.* **1** of, containing, or like sulphur. **2** sulphur-colored; greenish yellow.

sul·phu·ret·ed or **sul·fu·ret·ed** (sul'fyə ret'id) See **sulphuretted**.

sul·phu·ret·ted or **sul·fu·ret·ted** (sul'fyə ret'id) *adj.* **1** combined with sulphur. **2** containing sulphur or a compound of sulphur.

sul·phu·ric or **sul·fu·ric** (sul fyür'ik) *adj.* **1** of or having to do with sulphur. **2** containing sulphur, especially with a higher valence than sulphurous compounds.

sulphuric acid or **sulfuric acid** a heavy, colorless, oily, very strong acid; oil of vitriol. Sulphuric acid is used in making explosives, in refining petroleum, etc. *Formula:* H₂SO₄

sul·phur·ous or **sul·fur·ous** (sul'fər əs or sul'fyə rəs; *in chemistry, also,* sul fyür'əs) *adj.* **1** of or having to do with sulphur. **2** containing sulphur, especially with a lower valence than sulphuric compounds. **3** like sulphur, especially sulphur that is burning. **4** of or like the fires of hell; hellish. **5** violent, fiery, or scathing.

sulphurous acid or **sulfurous acid** a weak, unstable, colorless acid known only in solution or in the form of its salts, used as a bleach, reducing agent, etc. *Formula:* H₂SO₃

sul·phur·y or **sul·fur·y** (sul'fər ē) *adj.* of or like sulphur.

Sul·pi·cian (sul pish'ən) *n.* a priest of a Roman Catholic order founded in 1642 to conduct seminaries of theology. [< F *sulpicien* < St. *Sulpice*, Paris, the founder's parish + *-en* -an]

sul·tan (sul'tən) *n.* **1** the ruler of a Moslem country. Turkey was ruled by a sultan until 1922. **2** an absolute ruler. [ult. < Arabic *sultān* ruler]

sul·tan·a (sul tan'ə or sul tä'nə) *n.* **1** the wife of a sultan. **2** the mother, sister, or daughter of a sultan. **3** a small, seedless raisin. **4** the small, seedless, pale-yellow grape from which these raisins are prepared. Sultanas are also cultivated for wine. [< Ital.]

sul·tan·ate (sul'tən āt') *n.* **1** the position, authority, or period of rule of a sultan. **2** the territory ruled over by a sultan.

sul·try (sul'trē) *adj.* -tri·er, -tri·est. **1** of weather or atmosphere, uncomfortably hot, humid, and close. **2** very hot; fiery: *the sultry sun.* **3** having or showing passion or sensuality: *a sultry glance.* [< obs. *sulter*, v.; akin to *swelter*] —**sul'tri·ness**, *n.*

sum (sum) *n., v.* —*n.* **1** an amount of money: *He paid a huge sum for that bicycle.* **2** the number or quantity obtained by adding two or more numbers or quantities together. **3** *Informal.* a problem in arithmetic: *She's very good at sums.* **4** the whole or total amount: *Winning the prize seemed to her the sum of happiness.*

in sum, a in a few words; briefly. **b** to conclude in a few words; in short.

—*v.* find the total of.

sum up, a express or tell briefly; summarize: *to sum up the main points of a lesson.* **b** collect or add up into a whole. **c** review and

chief points of evidence to a jury before the jury retires to consider a verdict. **d** form or express an idea of the qualities or character of; size up. [< L *summa*, originally fem. adj., highest]
☛ *Hom.* **some**.
☛ *Syn. n.* 2. See note at **number**.

sum– *prefix.* the form of **sub-** occurring in some cases before *m*, as in *summon*.

su·mac (shü'mak or sü'mak) *n.* **1** any of a genus (*Rhus*) of trees, shrubs, and vines having compound leaves that turn a brilliant red in the fall. Some species, such as the poison sumac, have leaves that are poisonous to the touch. **2** a common sumac (*Rhus typhina*) also called **staghorn sumach**, having cone-shaped clusters of red fruit, native to eastern Canada and often planted as an ornamental tree. **3** the dried, powdered leaves and flowers of various sumacs, used in tanning and dyeing. Also, **sumach**. [ME < OF < Arabic *summāq*]

Su·ma·tran (sü mä'trən or sü mat'rən) *n., adj.* —*n.* a native or inhabitant of Sumatra, an island in Indonesia. —*adj.* of or having to do with Sumatra or its people.

Su·me·ri·an (sü mėr'ē ən or sü mer'ē ən) *n., adj.* —*n.* **1** a member of an ancient non-Semitic people who were the earliest known inhabitants of Sumer, a region in the valley of the Euphrates River. **2** the extinct language of the Sumerians, of no known relationship to any other language. —*adj.* of or having to do with the Sumerians or their language.

sum·ma cum lau·de (sùm'ə kùm'lou'dā or sum'ə kum'lô'dē) *Latin.* with the highest honor. [< L]

sum·ma·ri·ly (sum'ə rə lē or sə mer'ə lē) *adv.* in a summary manner; briefly or without delay.

sum·ma·ri·za·tion (sum'ər ə zā'shən or sum'ər ī zā'shən) *n.* **1** the act of summarizing. **2** summary.

sum·ma·rize (sum'ə rīz') *v.* -rized, -riz·ing. make or be a summary; express briefly: *The review summarized the plot of the novel.*

sum·ma·ry (sum'ə rē) *n., pl.* -ries; *adj.* —*n.* a brief statement giving the main points: *The history book had a summary at the end of each chapter.*
—*adj.* **1** concise and comprehensive; brief. **2** direct and prompt; without delay or formality: *a summary dismissal. The soldier took summary vengeance on his betrayers.* **3** of legal proceedings, carried out without the formalities or complexities of the usual process of law. [< L *summarium* < *summa* sum]
☛ *Hom.* **summery**.
☛ *Syn. n.* **Summary, digest** = a brief presentation of facts or subject matter. **Summary** applies to a brief statement, in one's own words, giving only the main points of an article, chapter, book, speech, subject, proposed plan, etc.: *Give a summary of today's lesson.* **Digest**, applying particularly to a collection of materials in condensed form, sometimes applies to a shortened form of an article, etc., leaving out less important details but keeping the original order, emphasis, and words: *Some magazines contain digests of books.*

summary offence *Law.* a criminal offence that is less serious than an indictable offence. In Canada, a summary offence in most cases carries a maximum penalty of a $500 fine or six months' imprisonment, or both. Also called **summary conviction offence**.

sum·ma·tion (sum ā'shən) *n.* **1** the process of finding the sum or total; addition. **2** the total. **3** *Law.* the final charge of a judge to the jury before it considers the verdict.

sum·mer (sum'ər) *n., v.* —*n.* **1** the warmest season of the year; season of the year between spring and autumn. **2** a year of age: *a girl of seventeen summers.* **3** a period or stage of maturity or fulfilment: *He was in the summer of his life.* **4** (*adj.*) of or in summer: *the summer sun, summer holidays.* **5** (*adj.*) fit for or used in summer: *summer clothes, a summer cottage.*
—*v.* **1** pass or spend the summer: *to summer at the seashore.* **2** keep or feed during the summer: *The cattle were summered on the mountain.* [OE *sumor*]

summer cottage a house, usually small and simply furnished and equipped, built near a body of water and used for holidaying during summer.

summer fallow land ploughed and left unseeded for a season or more, in order to destroy weeds, improve the soil, etc.; fallow.

sum·mer-fal·low (sum'ər fal'ō or, *esp. in the Prairie Provinces,* sum'ər fol'ō) *v.* prepare land as summer fallow.

sum·mer·house (sum′ər hous′) *n.* a small building in a park or garden in which to sit in warm weather. Summerhouses often have no walls.

summer resort a place where people go for summer holidays.

sum·mer·sault (sum′ər solt′ *or* -sôlt′) See **somersault**.

summer savory a European herb (*Satureja hortensis*) of the mint family widely grown for its leaves, which are used as a flavoring in cooking meats and vegetables.

summer school a school or university session held in summer, usually over a period of four to six weeks, offering a selection of regular courses, each compressed into daily classes of several hours. —**sum′mer-school′**, *adj.*

summer solstice in the northern hemisphere, the time when the sun is farthest north from the equator, about June 21 or 22.

summer squash 1 the fruit of any of several bushy varieties of a plant (*Cucurbita pepo*) of the gourd family, smaller than pumpkins and winter squashes and varying greatly in shape and color. Summer squashes are used as a cooked vegetable in summer, before they are fully ripe, when their skins are soft; they cannot be stored like winter squashes. 2 a plant that produces such fruits.

sum·mer·time (sum′ər tīm′) *n.* 1 the summer season; summer. 2 any period in which energy is greatest or talent most productive: *in the summertime of life.*

sum·mer·y (sum′ər ē) *adj.* of, like, or fit for summer: *a summery breeze. She wore a light, summery dress.*
☛ Hom. **summary**.

sum·mit (sum′it) *n.* 1 the highest point; top; peak: *the summit of a mountain.* 2 the highest degree or state: *The summit of her ambition was to be a foreign correspondent.* 3 *Informal.* a conference at the highest level. 4 (*adj.*) of, having to do with, or being a discussion between heads of government: *a summit conference.*
at the summit, at the level of diplomacy involving heads of government; at the highest level.
[ME < OF *somete*, ult. < L *summus* highest]
☛ Syn. 1. See note at **top**.

sum·mon (sum′ən) *v.* 1 call with authority or urgency; order to come; send for: *to summon citizens to defend their country. A telegram summoned Bill home.* 2 call together: *to summon an assembly.* 3 order or notify formally to appear in court, especially to answer a charge. 4 call upon: *to summon a fort to surrender.* 5 stir to action; rouse: *Jack summoned his courage and entered the deserted house.* [< L *summonere* hint to < *sub-* secretly + *monere* warn] —**sum′mon·er**, *n.*
☛ Syn. 1. See note at **call**.

sum·mons (sum′ənz) *n., pl.* -**mons·es**; *v.* —*n.* 1 an urgent or authoritative call for the presence or attendance of a person. 2 *Law.* **a** an order or notice to a person from an authority to appear before a court or judge on or before a certain date, especially to answer as a defendant to a charge made against him. **b** the writ (**writ of summons**) by which such an order is made: *The policeman handed her a summons.* 3 something that summons; a message or signal to come or appear: *He heard the summons of his friend's car horn.* —*v. Informal.* summon to court. [ME < OF *somonse* < *somondre* summon, ult. < L *summonere*. See SUMMON.]

sum·mum bo·num (sum′əm bō′nəm) *Latin.* the highest or chief good.

sump (sump) *n.* 1 a pit or reservoir for collecting water, oil, sewage, etc. 2 a pool at the bottom of a mine, where water collects and from which it is pumped. [ME < MDu. *somp* or MLG *sump* swamp]

sump pump a pump for removing collected water, sewage, etc. from a sump.

sump·ter (sump′tər) *n.* pack animal. [ME < OF *sommetier*, ult. < L *sagma, -atos* pack-saddle < Gk.]

sump·tu·ar·y (sump′chü er′ē) *adj.* having to do with the regulating of expenses; especially, limiting personal expenditure on moral or religious grounds to prevent extravagance: *sumptuary laws.* [< L *sumptuarius* < *sumptus* expense < *sumere* spend]

sump·tu·ous (sump′chü əs) *adj.* costly; magnificent; rich: *The king gave a sumptuous banquet.* [< L *sumptuosus* < *sumptus* expense < *sumere* spend] —**sump′tu·ous·ly**, *adv.* —**sump′tu·ous·ness**, *n.*

sum total 1 the total amount added up. 2 the total result; everything included.

sun (sun) *n., v.* **sunned, sun·ning.** —*n.* 1 the brightest heavenly body in the sky; the star around which the earth and planets revolve. The sun provides light, heat, and energy for the solar system. 2 the light and warmth of the sun: *to sit in the sun.* 3 any

heavenly body made up of burning gas and having satellites. Many stars are suns and have their worlds that travel around them. 4 something like the sun in brightness or splendor; something that is a source of light, honor, glory, or prosperity. 5 a figure, image, ornament, etc. made to resemble the sun, as a heraldic bearing, usually charged with human features, or a kind of circular firework. 6 *Archaic.* day. 7 *Archaic.* year.
from sun to sun, from sunrise to sunset.
in the sun, in a position easily seen; in the public eye.
under the sun, on earth; in the world.
—*v.* 1 expose to the sun's rays. 2 warm or dry in the sunshine. [OE *sunne*]
☛ Hom. **son**.

Sun. Sunday.

sun·baked (sun′bākt′) *adj.* 1 baked by exposure to the sun: *sunbaked bricks.* 2 hardened, dried out, or cracked, etc. by too much sunlight: *sunbaked soil.*

sun·bath *or* **sun bath** (sun′bath′) *n.* an exposure of the body to sunshine or a sunlamp.

sun·bathe (sun′bāŦн′) *v.* -**bathed, -bath·ing.** take a sunbath; bask in the sun. —**sun′bath′er**, *n.*

sun·beam (sun′bēm′) *n.* a ray of sunlight.

sun·bird (sun′bėrd′) *n.* any of a family (Nectariniidae) of small, tropical Old World songbirds having a long, slender, downward-curving bill and a tube-shaped tongue adapted for feeding on nectar, the males having bright-colored plumage.

sun·bon·net (sun′bon′it) *n.* a large bonnet that shades the face and neck.

sun·burn (sun′bėrn′) *n., v.* -**burned** *or* -**burnt, -burn·ing.** —*n.* an inflammation of the skin caused by too much exposure to the rays of the sun: *A sunburn can be very painful.* —*v.* get or cause to get a sunburn: *Her skin sunburns very quickly.*

sun·burnt (sun′bėrnt′) *v.* a pt. and a pp. of **sunburn.**

sun·burst (sun′bėrst′) *n.* 1 the sun shining suddenly through a break in clouds. 2 a brooch with jewels arranged to look like the sun with its rays. 3 any such pattern or design.

sun·dae (sun′dē *or* -dā) *n.* a serving of ice cream with syrup, crushed fruits, nuts, etc. poured over it. [probably < *Sunday,* originally the only day on which it was served]
☛ Hom. **Sunday**.

Sun·day (sun′dē *or* -dā) *n.* 1 the first day of the week, observed in Canada and many other countries as the general day of rest and relaxation: *Most stores and businesses are closed on Sundays. Sunday is the traditional day of rest and worship among most Christians.* 2 (*adj.*) of, having to do with, or taking place on Sunday: *Sunday Mass.* 3 (*adj.*) associated with Sunday, especially as a special day or a day of leisure and recreation: *a Sunday painter, Sunday drivers, Sunday clothes. n.*
a month of Sundays, an indefinitely long time: *That wouldn't happen again in a month of Sundays.*
[OE *sunnandæg*, translation of L *dies solis* day of the sun]
☛ Hom. **sundae**.

Sunday best *Informal.* best clothes.

Sunday school 1 a school held by a church on Sundays for teaching religion, especially to children. 2 its members.

sun·deck (sun′dek′) *n.* 1 a passenger ship's upper deck. 2 a balcony, terrace, or other area in or on a building, beside a swimming pool, etc., designed for lounging and sunbathing.

sun·der (sun′dər) *v., n. Archaic or poetic.* —*v.* break or cause to break apart; sever or separate. —*n.*
in sunder, apart: *Lightning tore the tree in sunder.*
[OE *sundrian* < *sundor* apart]

sun·dew (sun′dyü′ *or* -dü′) *n.* 1 any of a genus (*Drosera*) of insect-eating bog plants found throughout the world, having leaves covered with hairs with glands at the tips. The glands produce a sticky, glistening substance resembling dewdrops that attracts and captures insects. 2 (*adj.*) designating a small family (Droseraceae) of insect-eating plants which includes the sundews and three other groups of plants. The Venus's-flytrap is a member of the sundew family.

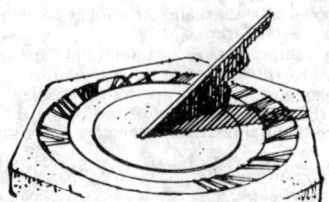

A garden sundial

sun·di·al (sun′dī′əl *or* sun′dīl′) *n.* an instrument for telling the

time of day by the position of the shadow of a rod or pointer cast by the sun on a usually horizontal disk marked off in hours.

sun·dog (sun′dog′) *n.* **1** parhelion. **2** a small halo or incomplete rainbow near the horizon.

sun·down (sun′doun′) *n.* sunset.

sun·down·er (sun′doun′ər) *n. Australian slang.* a tramp who arrives about sunset wanting food and lodging.

sun–dried (sun′drīd′) *adj.* dried by exposure to the sun: *sun-dried apples.*

sun·dry (sun′drē) *adj., pron., n.* —*adj.* several; various: *From sundry hints, he guessed he was to be given a bicycle on his birthday.*
—*pron.* an indefinite number (*now used only in the idiom* **all and sundry**).
all and sundry, everybody; one and all: *He sent out invitations to all and sundry to visit him in his new house.*
—*n.* **sundries,** *pl.* sundry things; miscellaneous items not named. [OE *syndrig* separate < *sundor* apart]

sun·fast (sun′fast′) *adj.* made to resist fading by sunlight: *sunfast colors.*

sun·fish (sun′fish′) *n., pl.* **-fish** or **-fish·es. 1** any of various small, North American freshwater fishes (family Centrarchidae, especially genus *Lepomis*) having a deep, compressed usually brightly colored body and a long dorsal fin. Some species are valued as food and game fish. **2** (*adj.*) designating the family of freshwater fishes that comprises the sunfishes, basses, and crappies. **3** any of a family (Molidae) of large ocean fishes, especially one species (*Mola mola*) having a scaleless, silvery, compressed body that is about as deep as it is long, giving the fish a chopped-off look. Sunfish often rest on the surface of the water in the sun.

sun·flow·er (sun′flou′ər) *n.* **1** a very tall annual plant (*Helianthus annuus*) of the composite family having large leaves and a very large, flat flower head surrounded by rays of long yellow petals. The sunflower is native to North and South America, but is widely cultivated throughout the world, especially for its seeds and the oil they yield. **2** any of a number of other annual or perennial plants of the same genus, such as the prairie sunflower (*H. petiolaris*).

sung (sung) *v.* a pt. and pp. of **sing**.

sun·glass·es (sun′glas′iz) *n.pl.* eyeglasses with tinted lenses designed to protect the eyes from direct sunlight or glare.

sun·god (sun′god′) *n.* a god who personifies the sun or is associated with it.

sunk (sungk) *v.* pp. and archaic pt. of **sink**.

sunk·en (sungk′ən) *adj.,* —*adj.* **1** sunk: *a sunken ship.* **2** submerged: *a sunken rock.* **3** situated or constructed below the general level: *a sunken garden, a sunken living room.* **4** fallen in; hollow: *sunken eyes.*
—*v. Archaic.* a pp. of **sink**.

sun·lamp (sun′lamp′) *n.* an electric lamp that gives out ultraviolet rays, used for therapy or for producing an artificial suntan.

sun·less (sun′lis) *adj.* without sunlight; dark: *a sunless day, sunless caverns.*

sun·light (sun′līt′) *n.* the light of the sun.

sun·lit (sun′lit′) *adj.* lighted by the sun.

sun·ny (sun′ē) *adj.* **-ni·er, -ni·est. 1** having much sunshine: *a sunny day.* **2** exposed to, lighted by, or warmed by the direct rays of the sun: *a sunny room.* **3** like the sun. **4** bright; cheerful; happy.
—**sun′ni·ly,** *adv.* —**sun′ni·ness,** *n.*

sunny side 1 the side of a house, street, etc. on which the sun shines or is shining. **2** the cheerful or optimistic aspect of something: *She usually looks on the sunny side of things.*
on the sunny side of, somewhat younger than (an age given in round numbers): *He's still on the sunny side of 50.*
sunny side up, of an egg, fried on one side only and with the yolk unbroken: *I like my eggs sunny side up.*

sun parlor or **parlour** a room with many windows to let in sunlight.

sun porch a porch enclosed largely by glass or screen, designed to admit plenty of sunlight.

sun·proof (sun′prüf′) *adj.* impervious to or unaffected by the rays of the sun: *These sunproof curtains will not fade.*

sun·rise (sun′rīz′) *n.* **1** the appearance of the sun above the horizon in the morning. **2** the often rosy color of the sky that accompanies its appearance. **3** the time of day when the sun rises; the beginning of day.

sun·roof (sun′rüf′) *n.* **1** an automobile roof having a panel that can be opened to admit air and sunlight. **2** the panel that opens.

sun·room (sun′rüm′ *or* -rùm′) *n.* a room with many windows to let in sunlight.

hat, āge, fär; let, ēqual, tėrm; it, īce
hot, ōpen, ôrder; oil, out; cup, put, rüle,
əbove, takən, pencəl, lemən, circəs

ch, child; ng, long; sh, ship
th, thin; ᴛн, then; zh, measure

sun·screen (sun′skrēn′) *n.* something that gives protection from the sun; especially, a substance put on the skin to block ultraviolet rays and prevent sunburn.

sun·set (sun′set′) *n.* **1** the setting of the sun; the last appearance of the sun in the evening. **2** the often red, pink, etc. color of the sky accompanying the disappearance of the sun. **3** the time of day when the sun sets; the close of day. **4** any decline or close: *Old age is often thought of as the sunset of life.*

sun·shade (sun′shād′) *n.* an umbrella, parasol, awning, etc. used to provide protection from the sun.

sun·shine (sun′shīn′) *n.* **1** the shining of the sun; light or rays of the sun. **2** brightness; cheerfulness; happiness.

sun·shin·y (sun′shīn′ē) *adj.* **-shin·i·er, -shin·i·est. 1** having much sunshine. **2** bright; cheerful; happy.

sun·spot (sun′spot′) *n.* one of the dark spots that appear from time to time on the surface of the sun. Sunspots are usually visible only with a telescope.

sun·stroke (sun′strōk′) *n.* a heatstroke caused by overexposure to direct sunlight. Sunstroke is serious because the body's sweating system has stopped functioning and can no longer cool the body.

sun·suit (sun′süt′) *n.* an abbreviated one-piece or two-piece garment worn by women and children for sunbathing.

sun·tan (sun′tan′) *n., adj.* —*n.* **1** a bronzed coloring of a person's skin resulting from exposure to the sun. **2** a light yellowish brown; khaki. —*adj.* light yellowish-brown; khaki.

sun·tanned (sun′tand′) *adj.* having a suntan; browned by the sun: *suntanned vacationers.*

sun time *Informal.* standard time.

sun–up (sun′up′) *n.* sunrise.

sun·ward (sun′wərd) *adv.* or *adj.* toward the sun.

sun·wards (sun′wərdz) *adv.* sunward.

sup¹ (sup) *v.* **supped, sup·ping.** eat the evening meal; take supper: *He supped alone on bread and milk.* [ME < OF *soper.* See SUPPER.]

sup² (sup) *v.* **supped, sup·ping;** *n.* sip. [OE *sūpan*]

sup– *prefix.* the form of **sub–** occurring before *p,* as in *suppress.*

sup. 1 supra. **2** superior. **3** superlative. **4** supply. **5** supplement. **6** supreme.

su·per (sü′pər) *n., adj.* —*n. Informal.* **1** a supernumerary. Mobs on the stage are usually made up of supers. **2** superintendent. —*adj. Slang.* excellent; wonderful.

super– *prefix.* **1** over; above, as in *superimpose, superstructure.* **2** besides; extra, as in *superadd, supertax.* **3** in high proportion; to excess; exceedingly, as in *superabundant, supersensitive.* **4** surpassing, as in *superman, supernatural.* [< L *super* over, above]

super. 1 superfine. **2** superintendent. **3** superior. **4** supernumerary.

su·per·a·ble (sü′pər ə bəl) *adj.* capable of being overcome; surmountable. [< L *superabilis* < *superare* overcome < *super* over] —**su′per·a·bly,** *adv.*

su·per·a·bound (sü′pər ə bound′) *v.* **1** be very abundant. **2** be too abundant.

su·per·a·bun·dance (sü′pər ə bun′dəns) *n.* a greater amount than is needed; surplus; excess: *a superabundance of rain.*

su·per·a·bun·dant (sü′pər ə bun′dənt) *adj.* more than is needed; excessive. —**su′per·a·bun′dant·ly,** *adv.*

su·per·add (sü′pər ad′) *v.* add besides; add further: *A toothache was superadded to her other troubles.* [< L *superaddere* < *super–* besides + *addere* add]

su·per·an·nu·ate (sü′pər an′yü āt′) *v.* **-at·ed, -at·ing. 1** retire on a pension on reaching a certain age or owing to ill-health. **2** make old-fashioned or out-of-date. [earlier *superannate* < Med.L *superannatus* more than a year old < L *super annum* beyond a year; influenced in spelling by L *annuus* annual]

su·per·an·nu·at·ed (sü′pər an′ü āt′id) *adj.* **1** retired on a pension. **2** too old for work, service, etc. **3** old-fashioned; out-of-date.

su·per·an·nu·at·ion (sü′pər an′yü ā′shən) *n.* **1** the process of superannuating or the state of being superannuated. **2** a pension or allowance granted to a superannuated person.

su·perb (sù pėrb′) *adj.* **1** grand; stately; majestic; magnificent;

splendid: *The mountain scenery in the Rockies is superb. The queen's jewels were superb.* **2** rich; elegant; sumptuous: *a superb dinner.* **3** very fine; first-rate; excellent: *The actor gave a superb performance.* [< L *superbus* < *super-* above] —**su·perb′ly,** *adv.*
☛ *Syn.* **1.** See note at **magnificent**.

su·per·car·go (sü′pər kär′gō) *n., pl.* **-goes** or **-gos.** an officer on a merchant ship, who has charge of the cargo and the business affairs of the voyage. [earlier *supracargo* < Sp. *sobrecargo*]

su·per·charge (sü′pər chärj′) *v.* **-charged, -charg·ing. 1** charge with excessive vigor, emotion, etc.: *The atmosphere at the trial was supercharged with tension.* **2** augment the power or efficiency of an engine, vehicle, etc. by fitting it with a supercharger.

su·per·charg·er (sü′pər chär′jər) *n.* in an internal-combustion engine, a blower, pump, etc. for forcing more of the mixture of air and gasoline vapor into the cylinders than the action of the pistons would draw. It is designed to increase the power or efficiency of an engine.

su·per·cil·i·ar·y (sü′pər sil′ē er′ē) *adj.* of, having to do with, or near the eyebrow; over the eye. [< NL *superciliaris* < L *supercilium* eyebrow < *super-* above + *cel-* cover]

su·per·cil·i·ous (sü′pər sil′ē əs) *adj.* showing scorn or indifference because of a feeling of superiority; haughty, proud, and contemptuous; disdainful: *supercilious politeness, a supercilious desk clerk.* [< L *superciliosus* < *supercilium* eyebrow. See SUPERCILIARY.] —**su′per·cil′i·ous·ly,** *adv.*
☛ *Syn.* See note at **proud**.

su·per·class (sü′pər klas′) *n.* a secondary category in the classification of plants and animals, including one or more classes within a phylum or division. It is usually a narrower classification than a subphylum.

su·per·con·duc·tive (sü′pər kən duk′tiv) *adj.* showing superconductivity.

su·per·con·duc·tiv·i·ty (sü′pər kon′duk tiv′ə tē) *n.* the property of being able to conduct electricity without resistance, found in lead and tin and some other metals at temperatures near absolute zero (−273.16°C).

su·per·con·duc·tor (sü′pər kən duk′tər) *n.* a superconductive metal.

su·per·dom·i·nant (sü′pər dom′ə nənt) *n. Music.* the sixth tone in a scale; the tone next above the dominant.

su·per·em·i·nent (sü′pər em′ə nənt) *adj.* of superior eminence, rank, or dignity; standing out or rising above others. —**su′per·em′i·nent·ly,** *adv.*

su·per·er·o·ga·tion (sü′pər er′ə gā′shən) *n.* the doing of more than what is required by duty. [< LL *supererogatio, -onis* < L *super-* over + *erogare* pay out]

su·per·e·rog·a·to·ry (sü′pər ə rog′ə tô′rē) *adj.* **1** doing more than what is required by duty: *a supererogatory act of assistance.* **2** unnecessary; superfluous: *a supererogatory explanation of what everyone had seen quite clearly.*

su·per–family (sü′pər fam′ə lē or -fam′lē) *n.* a secondary category in the classification of plants and animals, including one or more families within an order. It is usually a narrower classification than a suborder.

su·per·fi·cial (sü′pər fish′əl) *adj.* **1** of, on, or affecting the surface: *superficial burns, superficial measurement.* **2** concerned with or understanding only what is on the surface; not thorough; shallow or casual: *a superficial person, a superficial reading.* **3** of or having to do with outward appearance only; general or external: *a superficial resemblance.* [< L *superficialis* < *superficies* surface < *super-* above + *facies* form] —**su′per·fi′cial·ly,** *adv.*

su·per·fi·ci·al·i·ty (sü′pər fish′ē al′ə tē) *n., pl.* **-ties. 1** the quality or state of being superficial. **2** something superficial.

su·per·fi·cial·ness (sü′pər fish′əl nəs) *n.* the quality or state of being superficial.

su·per·fi·ci·es (sü′pər fish′ē ēz′) *n., pl.* **-fici·es. 1** surface. **2** the surface area. **3** the outward appearance. [< L *superficies* upper side, surface < *super-* over + *facies* form]

su·per·fine (sü′pər fīn′) *adj.* **1** very fine in texture or size; extra fine: *superfine cotton, superfine sugar.* **2** too refined or subtle: *superfine distinctions.* **3** of commercial goods, etc. very high in quality: *superfine craftsmanship, superfine china.* —**su′per·fine′ly,** *adv.* —**su′per·fine′ness,** *n.*

su·per·flu·id (sü′pər flü′id) *n., adj.* —*n.* a liquid, such as liquid helium, that has no viscosity when reduced to temperatures approaching absolute zero. —*adj.* extraordinarily fluid; having superfluidity.

su·per·flu·id·i·ty (sü′pər flü id′ə tē) *n.* extraordinary fluidity, as found in superfluids.

su·per·flu·i·ty (sü′pər flü′ə tē) *n., pl.* **-ties. 1** a greater amount than is needed; excess. **2** something not needed: *Luxuries are superfluities.*

su·per·flu·ous (sü pèr′flü əs) *adj.* **1** more than is sufficient or necessary: *In writing telegrams omit superfluous words.* **2** uncalled for; irrelevant: *a superfluous remark.* [< L *superfluus,* ult. < *super-* over + *fluere* flow] —**su·per′flu·ous·ly,** *adv.*

su·per·heat (sü′pər hēt′) *v.* **1** heat a liquid above its boiling point without producing vaporization. **2** heat (steam) apart from water until it resembles a dry or perfect gas. **3** overheat.

su·per·heat·er (sü′pər hēt′ər) *n.* a device for superheating steam.

su·per·het·er·o·dyne (sü′pər het′ər ə dīn′) *adj., n.* —*adj.* of or having to do with a kind of radio reception in which signals are received at a supersonic frequency and combined with locally produced oscillations of a lower supersonic frequency before being rectified and amplified. —*n.* a superheterodyne radio receiving set.

su·per·high·way (sü′pər hī′wā′) *n.* a high-speed expressway or freeway divided by a median and having two or more traffic lanes in each direction.

su·per·hu·man (sü′pər hyü′mən) *adj.* **1** above or beyond ordinary human power, experience, etc.: *By a superhuman effort, the hunter choked the leopard to death.* **2** above or beyond what is human: *Angels are superhuman beings.* —**su′per·hu′man·ly,** *adv.*

su·per·im·pose (sü′pər im pōz′) *v.* **-posed, -pos·ing. 1** put on top of something else. **2** put or join as an addition.

su·per·im·po·si·tion (sü′pər im pə zi′shən) *n.* superimposing or being superimposed.

su·per·in·cum·bent (sü′pər in kum′bənt) *adj.* lying or resting and exerting pressure on something else: *a superincumbent stratum of rock.*

su·per·in·duce (sü′pər in dyüs′ or -in düs′) *v.* **-duced, -duc·ing.** bring in or develop as an addition.

su·per·in·duc·tion (sü′pər in duk′shən) *n.* the act or superinducing or the state of being superinduced.

su·per·in·tend (sü′pər in tend′ or sü′prin tend′) *v.* oversee and direct (work or workers), act as a superintendent of; supervise. [< LL *superintendere* < L *super-* above + *intendere* direct]

su·per·in·tend·ence (sü′pər in ten′dəns or sü′prin ten′dəns) *n.* guidance and direction; supervision.

su·per·in·tend·en·cy (sü′pər in ten′dən sē or sü′prin-) *n., pl.* **-cies.** the position, authority, or work of a superintendent.

su·per·in·tend·ent (sü′pər in ten′dənt or sü′prin ten′dənt) *n.* **1** a person who oversees, directs, or manages: *a superintendent of schools, a superintendent of a factory.* **2** a police officer of high rank. **3** a person in charge of the maintenance of an apartment building, office building, etc. *Abbrev.:* Supt. or supt.

su·pe·ri·or (sə pēr′ē ər or sü pēr′ē ər) *adj., n.* —*adj.* **1** very good; excellent: *superior work in school.* **2** higher in quality; better; greater: *The last brand of coffee we tried was superior to this.* **3** higher in position, rank, importance, etc.: *a superior officer.* **4** above yielding or giving in (to): *superior to flattery.* **5** showing a feeling of being above others; proud: *superior airs, superior manners.* **6** *Printing.* written above and beside a letter or symbol: *a superior number.* **7** *Botany.* growing above some other part or organ, as: **a** the ovary when situated above or free from the (inferior) calyx. **b** the calyx when adherent to the sides of the (inferior) ovary and thus seeming to rise from its top.
—*n.* **1** a person who is higher in rank or more accomplished than another: *A captain is a lieutenant's superior.* **2** the head of a monastery or convent. **3** *Printing.* a superior letter or figure; superscript. [ME < OF < L *superior,* comparative of *superus,* adj., above < *super,* prep., above]

superior court a court of law having absolute jurisdiction to administer justice according to the law, as distinguished from courts of limited jurisdiction, such as county or district courts. Superior courts in Canada include the Supreme Court of Canada and the supreme courts of the provinces.

su·pe·ri·or·i·ty (sə pēr′ē ôr′ə tē or sü pēr′ē ôr′ə tē) *n.* the quality or state of being superior: *He was convinced of the superiority of the new data processing system over the old one.*

superiority complex a feeling of being superior to other people; an exaggerated feeling of self-importance.

superl. superlative.

su·per·la·tive (sə pèr′lə tiv or sü pèr′lə tiv) *adj., n.* —*adj.* **1** of the highest kind; above all others; supreme: *King Solomon had superlative wisdom.* **2** exaggerated; excessive; hyperbolic: *Such superlative praise could not be sincere.* **3** *Grammar.* expressing the highest degree of comparison of an adjective or adverb. *Fairest, best,* and *most slowly* are the superlative forms of *fair, good,* and *slowly.*
—*n.* **1** a person or thing above all others; supreme example.

2 *Grammar.* **a** the third of three degrees of comparison, used when qualities are being compared. **b** the form or combination of words that shows this degree.
talk in superlatives, exaggerate.
[ME < MF < LL *superlativus,* ult. < *super-* beyond + *latus,* pp. *ferre* carry] —**su·per'la·tive·ly,** *adv.* —**su·per'la·tive·ness,** *n.*

su·per·man (sü′pər man′) *n., pl.* **-men. 1** a man having superhuman powers. **2** the ideal man as conceived by the German philosopher Friedrich W. Nietzsche (1844-1900), who would be above the weaknesses of ordinary humans and have superior physical and intellectual powers.

su·per·mar·ket (sü′pər mär′kit) *n.* a large self-service store selling groceries and household articles.

su·per·nal (sŭ pėr′nəl) *adj.* **1** heavenly; divine. **2** of, coming from, or in the sky. **3** lofty. [< L *supernus* < *super* above] —**su·per′nal·ly,** *adv.*

su·per·na·tant (sü′pər nā′tənt) *adj.* floating above or on the surface: *oil supernatant on water.*

su·per·na·tion·al (sü′pər nash′ə nəl *or* -nash′nəl) *adj.* above or independent of limitations imposed by national sovereignty; having to do with or involving more than one nation: *Europe may one day become a supernational state.*

su·per·nat·u·ral (sü′pər nach′rəl *or* -nach′ə rəl) *adj., n.* —*adj.* of, having to do with, or caused by some agency or force outside the known laws of nature; especially, of, having to do with, or caused by God or a god or other spirit: *a supernatural event, supernatural powers.* —*n.* **the supernatural,** supernatural agencies, influences, or phenomena. —**su′per·nat′u·ral·ly,** *adv.*

su·per·nat·u·ral·ism (sü′pər nach′rəl iz′əm *or* -nach′ə rəl iz′əm) *n.* **1** the quality or state of being supernatural. **2** a belief in supernatural force or agencies as producing effects in the universe.

su·per·no·va (sü′pər nō′və) *n.* a star that has exploded, becoming up to a hundred million times brighter than the sun for a few days, and leaving behind a large, expanding shell of gases and debris (the **supernova remnant**), which may radiate light, radio waves, and X rays for hundreds or thousands of years.

su·per·nu·mer·a·ry (sü′pər nyü′mər er′ē *or* -nü′mər er′ē) *adj., n., pl.* **-ar·ies.** —*adj.* more than the usual or necessary number; extra. —*n.* **1** an extra person or thing. **2** *Theatre.* a person who appears on the stage but has no lines to speak: *In addition to the regular actors, there were 20 supernumeraries for the mob scene.* [< LL *supernumerarius* excessive in number < L phrase *super numerum* beyond the number]

su·per·or·der (sü′pər ôr′dər) *n.* a secondary category in the classification of plants and animals, including one or more orders within a class. It is usually a narrower classification than a subclass.

su·per·phos·phate (sü′pər fos′fāt) *n.* **1** an acid phosphate. **2** any of various fertilizing materials composed chiefly of soluble phosphates.

su·per·pose (sü′pər pōz′) *v.* **-posed, -pos·ing. 1** *Geometry.* place (a figure) upon another so that the two coincide. **2** superimpose. [< F *superposer* < *super-* above + *poser* (see POSE¹)]

su·per·po·si·tion (sü′pər pə zish′ən) *n.* superposing or being superposed.

su·per·pow·er (sü′pər pou′ər) *n.* **1** an extremely powerful nation; especially, one of a very small number of nations that dominate the world and compete with each other for economic or political control of blocs of less powerful nations. **2** extensive or extraordinary power.

su·per·sat·u·rate (sü′pər sach′ə rāt′) *v.* **-rat·ed, -rat·ing.** add to beyond the ordinary saturation point; saturate abnormally. A **supersaturated solution** is one in which more of a substance is dissolved than the solvent will hold under normal conditions.

su·per·sat·u·ra·tion (sü′pər sach′ə rā′shən) *n.* **1** the act of supersaturating. **2** an unstable condition of a vapor or solution, in which the density of the vapor or dissolved substance is in excess of that which is normally in equilibrium under the given conditions.

su·per·scribe (sü′pər skrīb′) *v.* **-scribed, -scrib·ing. 1** write (words, letters, one's name, etc.) at the top of, above, or on the outside of something: *Her name was superscribed on the document.* **2** write something at the top of or over: *to superscribe a document or a monument.* [< LL < L *superscribere* write over (as a correction) < *super-* above + *scribere* write]

su·per·script (sü′pər skript′) *adj., n.* —*adj.* written above. —*n.* a number, letter, etc. written directly above or above and to one side of another letter, number, etc. *Example:* In $a^3 \times b^n$, the ³ and the ⁿ are superscripts. [< LL *superscriptus,* pp. of *superscribere.* See SUPERSCRIBE.]

su·per·scrip·tion (sü′pər skrip′shən) *n.* **1** the act of writing above, on, or outside of something. **2** something written above or on the outside. **3** an address on a letter or parcel.

su·per·sede (sü′pər sēd′) *v.* **-sed·ed, -sed·ing. 1** cause to be set

hat, āge, fär; let, ēqual, tèrm; it, īce
hot, ōpen, ôrder; oil, out; cup, pùt, rüle,
above, takən, pencəl, lemən, circəs

ch, child; ng, long; sh, ship
th, thin; ᴛʜ, then; zh, measure

aside as obsolete or inferior; displace: *Electric lights had superseded gas lights in most homes by the 1920's.* **2** fill the place of; succeed: *Mrs. McKenzie has superseded Mr. Mossop as principal of the school.* **3** set aside or ignore in promotion; promote another over the head of. [< L *supersedere* be superior to, refrain from < *super-* above + *sedere* sit] —**su′per·sed′er,** *n.*
☛ *Syn.* **1, 2.** See note at **replace.**

su·per·sen·si·tive (sü′pər sen′sə tiv) *adj.* extremely or morbidly sensitive. —**su′per·sen′si·tive·ly,** *adv.* —**su′per·sen′si·tive·ness,** *n.*

su·per·son·ic (sü′pər son′ik) *adj.* **1** having a frequency above the human ear's audibility limit of about 20 kilohertz. **2** of, having to do with, or produced by waves or vibrations of such frequency. **3** of, having to do with, or being a speed greater than the speed of sound in air (about 1200 kilometres per hour at sea level). **4** capable of moving at a speed greater than the speed of sound: *supersonic aircraft.*

su·per·sti·tion (sü′pər stish′ən) *n.* **1** an unreasoning and abject fear of what is unknown or mysterious. **2** a belief or practice founded on ignorant fear or mistaken reverence: *A common superstition considers it bad luck to sleep in a room numbered 13.* [ME < OF < L *superstitio, -onis,* ? originally a standing over, as in wonder or awe < *super-* above + *stare* stand]

su·per·sti·tious (sü′pər stish′əs) *adj.* having to do with, caused by, or showing superstition: *He was superstitious about the number 13.* —**su′per·sti′tious·ly,** *adv.*

su·per·stra·tum (sü′pər strā′təm *or* -strat′əm) *n., pl.* **-stra·ta or -stra·tums.** a stratum lying over another.

su·per·struc·ture (sü′pər struk′chər) *n.* **1** all of a building above the foundation. **2** the parts of a ship above the main deck. **3** a structure built on something else. **4** a concept, etc. based on a more general or fundamental one.

su·per·tank·er (sü′pər tang′kər) *n.* a very large tanker.

su·per·tax (sü′pər taks′) *n.* a tax in addition to an ordinary tax; surtax.

su·per·ton·ic (sü′pər ton′ik) *n. Music.* the second tone of a scale, that is, the next above the tonic.

su·per·vene (sü′pər vēn′) *v.* **-vened, -ven·ing.** come as something additional or interrupting. [< L *supervenire* < *super-* upon + *venire* come]

su·per·ven·tion (sü′pər ven′shən) *n.* the act or fact of supervening.

su·per·vise (sü′pər vīz′) *v.* **-vised, -vis·ing.** look after and direct (work or workers, a process, etc.); oversee; superintend; manage: *He supervised the planning of the year's activities.* [< Med.L *supervisus* < L *super-* over + *videre* see]

su·per·vi·sion (sü′pər vizh′ən) *n.* the act, process, or occupation of supervising: *He built the boat under his father's supervision.*

su·per·vi·sor (sü′pər vī′zər) *n.* a person who supervises: *The music supervisor had charge of the school orchestra.*

su·per·vi·so·ry (sü′pər vī′zə rē) *adj.* of or having to do with supervision or a supervisor: *supervisory duties. She was employed in a supervisory capacity.*

su·pine (*adj.* sü pīn′; *n.* sü′pīn) *adj., n.* —*adj.* **1** lying on the back with the face upwards: *The patient was placed in a supine position.* Compare **prone. 2** morally or mentally inactive or passive; sluggish: *supine indifference.* —*n.* Latin grammar. a verbal noun formed from the stem of the past participle. [< L *supinus*] —**su·pine′ly,** *adv.*

supp (sup) *n. Informal.* a supplemental examination.

supp. *or* **suppl.** supplement; supplementary.

sup·per (sup′ər) *n.* **1** the evening meal; the third main meal of the day: *We usually have supper at 6 o'clock.* **2** *Esp.Brit.* a light meal eaten late in the evening, as after going to the theatre. **3** the food served at this meal: *I enjoyed supper.* **4** an informal public social event that takes place in the evening, featuring a meal and often held to raise money: *a church supper.* [ME < OF *soper,* originally infinitive, sup¹ < Gmc.] —**sup′per·less,** *adj.*

sup·plant (sə plant′) *v.* **1** take the place of; displace or set aside: *Machinery has supplanted hand labor in the making of shoes.* **2** take the place of by unfair or treacherous means: *The rebels*

plotted to supplant the legal government. **3** remove from its position; get rid of; oust. [ME < OF < L *supplantare* trip up < *sub-* under + *planta* sole of the foot]
☛ **Syn. 1, 2.** See note at **replace.**

sup·ple (sup′əl) *adj.* **-pler, -plest;** *v.* **-pled, -pling.** —*adj.* **1** capable of being bent or folded without breaking or cracking: *a supple birch tree, supple leather.* **2** able to move and bend or twist easily and gracefully: *a supple dancer.* **3** readily adaptable to different ideas, circumstances, people, etc.; yielding: *a supple mind.*
—*v.* make or become supple. [ME < OF < L *supplex* submissive < *supplicare.* See SUPPLICATE.] —**sup′ple·ly,** *adv.* —**sup′ple·ness,** *n.*

sup·ple·ment (*n.* sup′lə mənt; *v.* sup′lə ment′) *n., v.* —*n.* **1** something added to complete a thing, or to make it larger or better: *a diet supplement. The newspaper has a supplement every Saturday.* **2** *Geometry.* an angle or arc that together with a given angle or arc equals 180°. The supplement of a 60° angle is a 120° angle. —*v.* supply what is lacking in; add to; complete: *to supplement one's income.* [< L *supplementum,* ult. < *sub-* up + *-plere* fill]
☛ **Syn.** *n.* **1. Supplement, appendix** = something added to a book or paper to complete or improve it. **Supplement** applies to a section added later or printed separately to give completeness by bringing the information up to date, correcting mistakes, or presenting special features: *This world history has a supplement covering recent events.* **Appendix** applies to a section added at the end of a book to give extra information that is useful for reference but not necessary for completeness: *The appendix contains a list of dates.* —*v.* See note at **complement.**

sup·ple·men·tal (sup′lə men′təl) *adj., n.* —*adj.* supplementary. —*n.* supplemental examination.

supplemental examination an examination held for students who have failed the regular examination.

sup·ple·men·ta·ry (sup′lə men′tə rē *or* sup′lə men′trē) *adj.* added to supply what is lacking; additional: *The new members of the class received supplementary instruction.*

supplementary angle *Geometry.* either of two angles or arcs which together equal 180° (*usually used in the plural*). A 45° angle and a 135° angle are supplementary angles.

sup·ple·men·ta·tion (sup′lə men tā′shən) *n.* **1** the act or process of supplementing. **2** an additional supplement.

sup·pli·ance (sup′lē əns) *n.* supplication.

sup·pli·ant (sup′lē ənt) *adj., n.* —*adj.* **1** asking humbly and earnestly; entreating: *a suppliant petitioner.* **2** expressing supplication: *suppliant gestures. They raised suppliant hands.* —*n.* a person who asks humbly and earnestly: *She knelt as a suppliant at the altar.* [< F *suppliant,* ppr. of *supplier* < L *supplicare.* See SUPPLICATE.] —**sup′pli·ant·ly,** *adv.*

sup·pli·cant (sup′lə kənt) *n. or adj.* suppliant. [< L *supplicans, -antis,* ppr. of *supplicare.* See SUPPLICATE.]

sup·pli·cate (sup′lə kāt′) *v.* **-cat·ed, -cat·ing. 1** beg humbly and earnestly: *The mother supplicated the judge to spare her son.* **2** beg humbly for (something); seek by entreaty: *to supplicate a blessing.* **3** pray humbly. [< L *supplicare* < *sub-* down + *plicare* bend] —**sup′pli·cat′ing·ly,** *adv.* —**sup′pli·ca′tor,** *n.*

sup·pli·ca·tion (sup′lə kā′shən) *n.* **1** the act of supplicating. **2** a humble and earnest request or prayer: *Their supplications were granted.*

sup·pli·ca·to·ry (sup′lə kə tô′rē) *adj.* supplicating.

sup·ply¹ (sə plī′) *v.* **-plied, -ply·ing;** *n., pl.* **-plies.** —*v.* **1** furnish; provide: *The city supplies books for the children.* **2** make up for (a loss, lack, absence, etc.): *to supply a deficiency.* **3** satisfy (a want, need, etc.): *There was just enough to supply the demand.* **4** fill (a place, vacancy, pulpit, etc.) as a substitute.
—*n.* **1** a quantity ready for use; stock; store: *Our school gets its supply of paper from the city.* **2** the quantity of an article in the market ready for purchase: *a supply of coffee.* **3 supplies,** *pl.* the food, equipment, etc., necessary for an army, expedition, or the like. **4** (*adj.*) of or having to do with such supplies or their management: *supply routes, a supply officer.* **5** a person, such as a teacher or a member of the clergy, who supplies a vacancy or substitute. **6** (*adj.*) serving as a substitute: *a supply teacher.* **7** the act of supplying. **8** a sum of money provided by parliament, or a like body, to meet the expenses of government.
in (short, good, etc.) **supply,** available to a specified extent: *Apples are in short supply this year.*
on supply, serving or available to serve as a substitute.
[ME < OF < L *supplere* < *sub-* up + *-plere* fill] —**sup·pli′er,** *n.*

sup·ply² (sup′lē) *adv.* in a supple manner.

sup·port (sə pôrt′) *v.* —*v.* **1** keep from falling; hold up: *Walls support the roof.* **2** give strength or courage to; keep up; help: *Hope supports us in trouble.* **3** provide for: *She supported her nephew while he was at university.* **4** supply funds or means for; bear the

expense of: *to support the expenses of government.* **5** maintain, keep up, or keep going: *This city supports two orchestras.* **6** be in favor of; back; second: *He supports the Liberals.* **7** bear; bear prove; bear out: *The facts support his claim.* **8** in military use, assist or protect (another unit) in combat: *Artillery fire supported the infantry attack.* **9** put up with; bear; endure: *She couldn't support life without friends.* **10** *Theatre.* **a** act with (a leading actor); assist; attend. **b** act (a part or character) with success.
—*n.* **1** the act of supporting or the condition of being supported; help; aid: *He needs the support of a scholarship.* **2** maintenance: *the support of a family.* **3** a person or thing that supports; prop: *The neck is the support of the head.* **4** *Military.* **a** assistance or protection given by one element or unit to another. **b** a unit that helps another in combat. Aircraft may be used as a support for infantry. **c** the part of any unit held back at the beginning of an attack as reserve. [ME < OF < L *supportare* bring up < *sub-* up + *portare* carry] —**sup·port′er,** *n.*
☛ **Syn.** *v.* **1, 2. Support, maintain, uphold** = hold up or keep up, literally or figuratively. **Support** suggests bearing the weight, serving as a prop, or giving needed strength to prevent something or someone from falling or sinking: *Team-mates supported the injured player.* **Maintain** suggests keeping up in a state or condition by providing what is needed to prevent loss of strength, value, etc.: *Provincial governments maintain the highways.* **Uphold** chiefly suggests giving aid or moral support to a person, cause, belief, etc.: *He upheld his brother's honor.* —*n.* **2.** See note at **living.**

sup·port·a·ble (sə pôr′tə bəl) *adj.* capable of being supported; bearable or endurable. —**sup·port′a·bly,** *adv.*

sup·port·ive (sə pôr′tiv) *adj.* offering or furnishing support: *supportive testimony, a supportive friend.*

sup·pose (sə pōz′) *v.* **-posed, -pos·ing. 1** consider as a possibility; assume for the sake of argument: *Suppose it doesn't work; what will we do then?* **2** think probable; believe: *I suppose she will come as usual. I suppose I'll be left with the dishes again.* **3** involve as necessary; imply; presuppose: *An invention supposes an inventor.* **4** presume the existence or presence of: *The author of the story supposes a race of intelligent beings living in another galaxy.* [ME < OF *supposer* < *sub-* under + *poser* (see POSE¹)] —**sup·pos′a·ble,** *adj.*

sup·posed (sə pōzd′) *adj.* **1** accepted as real or true, but mistakenly or without proof or evidence; believed or imagined: *a supposed insult. We need to take a closer look at the supposed improvements in the postal system.* **2** designed or intended: *What is that supposed to mean?* **3** obliged or expected (*to*): *I was supposed to bring the cake, but I forgot.* **4** permitted; allowed (*to*) (*used only in the negative*): *You are not supposed to jump on the bed.*

sup·pos·ed·ly (sə pōz′id lē) *adv.* according to what is supposed or was supposed: *He was supposedly sleeping but we discovered that he was out.*

sup·pos·ing (sə pōz′ing) *conj.* in the event that; assuming that: *Supposing it rains, shall we go?*

sup·po·si·tion (sup′ə zish′ən) *n.* **1** the act of supposing. **2** something supposed; assumption: *He entered the campaign on the supposition that his friends would support him.* [ME < OF < Med.L *suppositio, -onis,* ult. < L *sub-* under + *ponere* place]

sup·po·si·tion·al (sup′ə zish′ən əl) *adj.* of or based on supposition; hypothetical; supposed.

sup·pos·i·ti·tious (sə poz′ə tish′əs) *adj.* **1** put in place of another with intent to defraud; counterfeit: *supposititious writings, a supposititious heir.* **2** hypothetical; supposed. [< L *suppositicius,* ult. < *sub-* under + *ponere* place] —**sup·pos′i·ti′tious·ly,** *adv.*

sup·pos·i·to·ry (sə poz′ə tô′rē) *n., pl.* **-ries.** a medicated preparation in the form of a cone or cylinder to be put into the rectum or other opening of the body. [< LL *suppositorium* (thing) placed underneath, ult. < L *sub-* under + *ponere* place]

sup·press (sə pres′) *v.* **1** put an end to; stop by force; put down: *The troops suppressed the rebellion by firing on the mob.* **2** keep in; hold back; check: *She suppressed a yawn.* **3** hide; refuse to make known: *The government was accused of suppressing important facts.* **4** stop or prohibit the publication or circulation of: *The book was suppressed because it contained libelous statements.* **5** hinder or restrain the flow or growth of: *to suppress bleeding.* [ME < L *suppressus,* pp. of *supprimere* < *sub-* down + *premere* press] —**sup·press′er** or **sup·pres′sor,** *n.*

sup·press·i·ble (sə pres′ə bəl) *adj.* that can be suppressed.

sup·pres·sion (sə presh′ən) *n.* **1** suppressing or being suppressed: *the suppression of a revolt, the suppression of an impulse to cough, the suppression of facts.* **2** the conscious controlling or inhibiting of a thought or feeling.

sup·pres·sive (sə pres′iv) *adj.* tending to suppress; causing suppression.

sup·pu·rate (sup′yə rāt′) *v.* **-rat·ed, -rat·ing.** form or discharge pus; fester. [< L *suppurare* < *sub-* under + *pus* pus]

sup·pu·ra·tion (sup′yə rā′shən) *n.* **1** the formation or discharge of pus. **2** pus.

sup·pu·ra·tive (sup′yə rā′tiv) *adj., n.* —*adj.* 1 promoting suppuration. 2 suppurating. —*n.* a medicine or application that promotes suppuration.

su·pra (sü′prə) *adv.* 1 above. 2 in a book, manuscript, etc., before; previously. [< L]

supra– *prefix.* above, over, beyond, or greater than, as in *suprarenal.* [< L]

su·pra·na·tion·al (sü′prə nash′ə nəl *or* -nash′nəl) *adj.* supernational.

su·pra·re·nal (sü′prə rē′nəl) *adj., n.* —*adj.* situated above or on the kidney; especially, adrenal. —*n.* a suprarenal part, especially an adrenal gland. [< supra- above + L *renes* kidneys]

su·pra·seg·men·tal (sü′prə seg men′təl) *adj. Phonetics.* of, having to do with, or designating significant features that accompany a sound or sequence of sounds in an utterance, such as in English, stress and pitch.

su·prem·a·cy (sə prem′ə sē *or* sü prem′ə sē) *n.* 1 the quality or state of being supreme. 2 supreme authority or power.

su·preme (sə prēm′ *or* sü prēm′) *adj.* 1 highest in rank or authority: *a supreme ruler.* 2 of or belonging to a person or thing that is supreme: *supreme authority.* 3 highest in degree or quality; greatest; utmost: *supreme disgust, supreme courage.* 4 last; final: *To give one's life is to make the supreme sacrifice.* [< L *supremus,* ult. < *super* above] —**su·preme′ly,** *adv.*

Supreme Being God.

Supreme Court 1 in Canada: **a** the highest appeal court of Canada in civil and criminal matters. It consists of nine judges and hears appeals from the provincial courts of appeal and from the federal court dealing with matters of taxation, copyright, etc. **b** the highest appeal or trial court in some provinces. 2 a similar court in other countries.

Supt. or **supt.** superintendent.

sur–¹ *prefix.* upon, over, or above, as in *surcharge, surcoat, surtax.*

sur–² *prefix.* the form of sub- occurring before *r,* as in *surreptitious.*

sur. 1 surplus. 2 surcharge. 3 surname.

su·rah (sür′ə) *n.* a soft, twilled silk, rayon, etc. [< *Surat,* a city in W India]

sur·cease (sėr sēs′) *n. Archaic.* end; cessation. [ME < OF *sursis,* pp. of *surseoir* refrain < L *supersedere.* See SUPERSEDE.]

sur·charge (*n.* sėr′chärj′; *v.* sər chärj′) *n., v.* **-charged, -charg·ing.** —*n.* 1 an extra charge: *The express company made a surcharge for delivering the trunk outside of the city limits.* 2 an additional and usually excessive load, burden, or supply: *a surcharge of punishment.* 3 an additional mark printed on a postage stamp to change its value, date, etc. 4 a stamp bearing such a mark. —*v.* 1 charge extra. 2 overcharge. 3 overload: *a heart surcharged with grief.* 4 print a surcharge on (a postage stamp). [< F *surcharger* < *sur-* over (< L *super-*) + *charger* charge < L *carricare* to load < *carrus* load]

sur·cin·gle (sėr′sing gəl) *n.* a strap or belt around a horse's body to keep a saddle, blanket, or pack in place. [ME < OF *surcengle* < *sur-* over (< L *super-*) + *cengle* girdle < L *cingula* < *cingere* gird]

sur·coat (sėr′kōt′) *n.* an outer coat or cloak, especially such a garment once worn by knights over their armor. [ME < OF *surcote* < *sur-* over (< L *super-*) + *cote* coat < Gmc.]

surd (sėrd) *n., adj.* 1 *Phonetics.* a voiceless sound. 2 *Mathematics.* a quantity that cannot be expressed in whole numbers. *Example:* √2. —*adj.* 1 *Phonetics.* uttered without vibration of the vocal cords; unvoiced or voiceless. 2 *Mathematics.* that cannot be expressed in whole numbers. [< L *surdus* unheard]

sure (shür) *adj.* **sur·er, sur·est;** *adv.* —*adj.* 1 free from doubt; certain; having ample reason for belief; confident; positive: *He is sure of success in the end. I am sure of his guilt.* 2 safe; reliable; to be trusted: *a sure messenger.* 3 never missing, slipping, etc.; unfailing; unerring: *sure aim, a sure touch.* 4 certain to be or to happen: *The army faced sure defeat. He is sure to win the prize.* 5 *Archaic.* secure or safe.
be sure, be careful; do not fail: *Be sure to lock the door when you leave.*
for sure, *Informal.* **a** surely; certainly: *He's coming for sure.* **b** sure; certain: *That's for sure.*
make sure, a act so as to make something certain. **b** get sure knowledge.
to be sure, surely; certainly.
—*adv. Informal.* surely; certainly. [ME < OF *sur* < L *securus.* Doublet of SECURE.] —**sure′ness,** *n.*
☛ *Syn. adj.* 1. **Sure, certain, confident** = having no doubt about a person, fact, statement, action, etc. **Sure** emphasizes being free from doubt in one's own mind: *Police are sure he was murdered.* **Certain,** often interchangeable with **sure,** more definitely suggests positive reasons or proof to support one's trust or belief: *They have been certain since they uncovered new evidence.* **Confident**

suggests a strong and unshakable belief: *They are confident they will solve the case soon.*
☛ *Usage.* **Sure** is primarily an adjective: *a sure footing. Are you sure?* As an adverb, **sure** is often used in informal speech instead of **surely** or as an equivalent of **certainly** or **yes**: *Sure, I'm coming. That sure is interesting.* In writing, this usage should be used only in dialogue or in very informal situations.

sure–fire (shür′fīr′) *adj. Informal.* that will not fail; certain: *a sure-fire formula.*

sure–foot·ed (shür′füt′id) *adj.* not liable to stumble, slip, or fall. —**sure′-foot′ed·ness,** *n.*

sure·ly (shür′lē) *adv.* 1 undoubtedly; certainly: *Half a loaf is surely better than none.* 2 really (*used to emphasize or intensify a statement*): *Surely you can't be serious!* 3 without mistake; without missing, slipping, etc.; firmly: *The goat leaped surely from rock to rock.* 4 without fail: *slowly but surely.*

Sû·re·té (shür′ə tā′; *French,* sʏr tā′) *n.* in France, the criminal investigation section of the police department. [< F]

sur·e·ty (shür′ə tē) *n., pl.* **-ties.** 1 security against loss, damage, or failure to do something: *An insurance company gives surety against loss by fire.* 2 a person who agrees to be legally responsible for another: *He was surety for his brother's appearance in court on the day set for the trial.* 3 *Archaic.* a sure thing; certainty.

sur·e·ty·ship (shür′ə tē ship′) *n.* the obligation of a person to answer for the debt, fault, or conduct of another.

surf (sėrf) *n.* 1 the waves or swell of the sea breaking on the shore or upon shoals, reefs, etc. 2 the deep pounding or thundering sound of this. —*v.* travel or ride on the crest of a wave, especially with a surfboard. —**surf′er,** *n.* [earlier *suff*; possibly var. of *sough*]
☛ *Hom.* **serf.**

sur·face (sėr′fis) *n., v.* **-faced, -fac·ing.** —*n.* 1 the outside of anything: *the surface of a golf ball, the surface of a mountain.* 2 the top of the ground or soil, or of a body of water or other liquid: *The stone sank below the surface.* 3 any face or side of a thing: *A cube has six surfaces.* 4 that which has length and breadth but no thickness: *a plane surface in geometry.* 5 the outward appearance: *He seems rough, but you will find him very kind below the surface.* 6 (*adj.*) of, on, or having to do with the surface: *a surface view, surface mail, surface travel.* —*v.* 1 put a surface on; make smooth: *to surface a road.* 2 bring or come to the surface: *to surface a submarine. The submarine surfaced.* [< F *surface* < *sur-* above (< L *super-*) + *face* face, ult. < L *facies* form] —**sur′fac·er,** *n.*

surface mail 1 mail transported by land and sea, rather than by air. 2 the system of sending surface mail.

surface tension an elastic-like property of the surface of a liquid that makes it tend to contract, caused by the forces of attraction between the molecules of the liquid.

surf·board (sėrf′bôrd′) *n.* a more-or-less oblong board on which a person may stand or lie in order to ride on the crest of a wave as it comes in to the beach.

surf·boat (sėrf′bōt′) *n.* a strong boat specially made for use in heavy surf.

surf duck scoter.

sur·feit (sėr′fit) *n., v.* —*n.* 1 a grossly excessive amount of something; too much; excess: *A surfeit of food makes one sick. A surfeit of advice annoys me.* 2 disgust or nausea caused by this; painful satiety. 3 an abnormal physical condition caused by gluttony, intemperance, etc. —*v.* 1 feed or cause to take too much, so as to cause nausea or disgust. 2 take too much of something; indulge too much. [ME < OF *surfait,* originally pp., overdone < *sur-* over (< L *super-*) + *faire* do < L *facere*]
☛ *Syn. v.* See note at **satiate.**

surf·ing (sėrf′ing) *n.* the sport of using a surfboard to ride toward shore on the crest of a wave. —**surf′er,** *n.*

surf·y (sėr′fē) *adj.* 1 having much surf or heavy surf. 2 forming or resembling surf.

surge (sėrj) *v.* **surged, surg·ing;** *n.* —*v.* 1 rise and fall in waves or billows: *the surging sea.* 2 move as a wave; roll, swell, or sweep forward: *A great wave surged over us. Joy surged through him when he saw her. The crowd surged out of the arena.* —*n.* 1 the swelling and rolling of the sea. 2 a swelling, rolling, or

sweeping forward like a wave: *A surge of anger swept over her.* **3** a sudden increase: *a surge of power.* [ult. (probably through OF *surgeon* a spring) < L *surgere* rise < *sub-* up + *regere* reach]
☞ *Hom.* **serge.**

sur·geon (sėr′jən) *n.* a physician, especially one who specializes in surgery. [ME < AF *surgien,* OF *cirurgien* < *cirurgie.* See SURGERY. Doublet of CHIRURGEON.]

sur·ger·y (sėr′jər ē) *n., pl.* **-ger·ies. 1** the treatment of disease, injury, etc. by using the hands or instruments to mend or remove an organ, tissue, or part, or to remove foreign matter in the body: *The fracture was a serious one that required surgery.* **2** the branch of medicine that deals with such treatment. **3** an operating room. **4** *Brit.* a doctor's or dentist's office. [ME < OF *surgerie, cirurgerie* < *cirurgie* < L < Gk. *cheirourgia,* ult. < *cheir* hand + *ergon* work]

sur·gi·cal (sėr′jə kəl) *adj.* **1** of or having to do with surgeons or surgery; *a surgical specialist.* **2** used in surgery: *surgical instruments.* **3** resulting from surgery: *surgical fever.* —**sur′gi·cal·ly,** *adv.*

sur·ly (sėr′lē) *adj.* **-li·er, -li·est.** bad-tempered and unfriendly; rude; gruff: *a surly answer.* [ult. < *sir,* in sense of "lord"] —**sur′li·ly,** *adv.* —**sur′li·ness,** *n.*

sur·mise (*v.* sər mīz′; *n.* sər mīz′ *or* sėr′mīz) *v.* **-mised, -mis·ing;** *n.* —*v.* guess: *We surmised that the delay was caused by some accident.* —*n.* **1** the formation of an idea with little or no evidence; a guessing: *His guilt was a matter of surmise; there was no proof.* **2** a guess. [ME < OF *surmise* accusation, ult. < *sur-* upon (< L *super-*) + *mettre* put < L *mittere* send]
☞ *Syn. v.* See note at **guess.**

sur·mount (sər mount′) *v.* **1** overcome: *He surmounted many difficulties.* **2** be at or on the top of: *mountain peaks surmounted with snow.* **3** go up and across; get up and over: *to surmount a hill.* **4** place something on top of; cap. [ME < OF *surmonter* < *sur-* over (< L *super-*) + *monter* mount < L *mons, montis* mountain] —**sur·mount′a·ble,** *adj.*

sur·name (sėr′nām′) *n., v.* **-named, -nam·ing.** —*n.* **1** the name that members of a family have in common; family name; last name: *Kahn is the surname of Nathan Kahn.* **2** *Archaic.* name added to a person's real name: *William I of England had the surname "the Conqueror."* —*v.* give an added name to; call by a surname: *Simon was surnamed Peter.* [< F *surnom* < *sur-* over (< L *super-*) + *nom* name < L *nomen;* influenced by E *name*]

sur·pass (sər pas′) *v.* **1** do or be better or greater than; be superior to: *The experience surpassed anything he had known before. She surpasses all the other team members in her ability to score.* **2** be too much or too great for; go beyond the range or capacity of: *The magnificence of the sight surpassed description.* [< F *surpasser* < *sur-* beyond + *passer* pass] —**sur·pass′a·ble,** *adj.* —**sur·pass′ing·ly,** *adv.*
☞ *Syn.* **1.** See note at **excel.**

A clergyman wearing a surplice

sur·plice (sėr′plis) *n.* a loose, white, usually knee-length gown having very wide sleeves, worn over the clothing by the clergy and choir members during a service. [ME < AF *surpliz,* OF *surpelice* < *sur-* over (< L *super-*) + *pelice* fur garment, ult. < L *pellis* hide]

sur·plus (sėr′pləs *or* sėr′plus) *n.* **1** an amount over and above what is needed; an extra quantity left over; excess. **2** an excess of assets over liabilities. **3** (*adj.*) more than is needed; forming a surplus: *The store's surplus stock was put on sale at the end of the season.* [ME < OF *surplus* < *sur-* over (< L *super-*) + *plus* more < L *plus*]

sur·plus·age (sėr′plus ij) *n.* **1** surplus; excess. **2** unnecessary words; irrelevant material.

sur·prise (sər prīz′ *or* sə prīz′) *n., v.* **-prised, -pris·ing.** —*n.* **1** a feeling caused by something unexpected. **2** something unexpected.

3 (*adj.*) that is not expected; surprising: *a surprise party, a surprise visit.* **4** catching unprepared; coming upon suddenly; a sudden attack.
take by surprise, a catch unprepared; come on suddenly and unexpectedly. **b** astonish.
—*v.* **1** cause to feel surprised; astonish. **2** catch unprepared; come upon suddenly; attack suddenly: *The enemy surprised the fort.* **3** lead or bring (a person, etc.) unawares: *The news surprised her into tears.* **4** find or discover (something) by a sudden or unexpected question, attack, etc.; detect or elicit: *to surprise the truth of the matter from him.* [ME < OF *surprise,* pp. fem. of *surprendre* < *sur-* over (< L *super-*) + *prendre* take < L *prehendere*]
☞ *Syn. v.* **1. Surprise, astonish, amaze** = strike a person with a sudden feeling of perplexity, confusion, or wonder. **Surprise,** the general word, suggests the sudden feeling caused by something unexpected or out of the ordinary: *His answer surprised her.* **Astonish** suggests the stronger feeling caused by something too extraordinary to be possible: *He astonished many people by failing in college work after getting high grades in high school.* **Amaze** emphasizes the idea of bewildered wonder: *New scientific discoveries constantly amaze us.*

sur·pris·ing (sər prī′zing *or* sə prī′zing) *adj.* causing surprise: *a surprising recovery.* —**sur·pris′ing·ly,** *adv.*

sur·re·al·ism (sə rē′əl iz′əm) *n.* a style in art and literature characterized by the attempt to portray the functioning of the subconscious mind, especially as in dreams, often by combining conventional and unconventional elements or by distorting the conventional. [< F *surréalisme*]

sur·re·al·ist (sə rē′əl ist) *n., adj.* —*n.* an artist or writer who uses surrealism. —*adj.* of or having to do with surrealism or surrealists.

sur·re·al·is·tic (sə rē′əl is′tik) *adj.* **1** of or having to do with surrealism or surrealists. **2** having a strange and unreal quality, like a surrealist painting: *a surrealistic experience.* —**sur·re′al·is′ti·cal·ly,** *adv.*

sur·ren·der (sə ren′dər) *v., n.* —*v.* **1** give up control or possession of, especially under compulsion or demand from another: *to surrender a fort to an invader, to surrender an office. As the storm increased, the men on the raft surrendered all hope.* **2** give oneself up; stop resisting; give in to a demand for submission: *The captain had to surrender when the ammunition ran out.* **3** give in to an emotion, etc. (*used with a reflexive pronoun*): *to surrender oneself to grief.* **4** cancel (an insurance policy) in return for a cash sum.
—*n.* the act or an instance of surrendering. [ME < AF *surrendre* < OF *sur-* over (< L *super-*) + *rendre* render < L *reddere* give as due, pay]

surrender value the value of an insurance policy in terms of the cash payable to the holder if the policy is cancelled, or surrendered.

sur·rep·ti·tious (sėr′əp tish′əs) *adj.* **1** done, made, or acquired secretly; secret and stealthy or unauthorized: *a surreptitious wink, a surreptitious gift.* **2** acting in a secret or stealthy way: *He was very surreptitious in his movements.* [< L *surrepticius,* ult. < *sub-* secretly + *rapere* snatch] —**sur′rep·ti′tious·ly,** *adv.* —**sur′rep·ti′tious·ness,** *n.*

sur·rey (sėr′ē) *n., pl.* **-reys.** a light, four-wheeled, horse-drawn carriage having two seats and, usually, a flat top. [< *Surrey,* a county in SE England]

sur·ro·gate (sėr′ə gāt′ *or* sėr′ə git) *n.* **1** a person who acts for or takes the place of another; substitute or deputy. **2** (*adj.*) of, having to do with, or acting as a surrogate: *surrogate parents, a surrogate pleasure.* [< L *surrogatus,* pp. of *surrogare* substitute < *sub-* instead + *rogare* ask for]

surrogate court a court of law that deals with wills and other matters relating to the estates of deceased persons.

sur·ro·gate·ship (sėr′ə gāt ship′ *or* sėr′ə git-) *n.* the office or authority of a surrogate.

sur·round (sə round′) *v., n.* —*v.* **1** come or be all around; shut in on all sides; enclose: *News reporters surrounded the minister as she emerged from the legislature. The little girl was surrounded by her toys. Police surrounded the house.* **2** extend around the outside or edge of: *A high fence surrounds the field. The inscription on the medal was surrounded by a design of flowers.* **3** be or form part of the environment of: *Love and goodwill surrounded him.* **4** cause to be surrounded by: *The invalid's family surrounded him with every comfort. The king surrounded himself with flatterers.*
—*n.* something that surrounds, such as a border or edging. [ME < AF *surounder* surpass < LL *superundare* overflow < L *super-* over + *unda* wave; influenced in meaning by *round*]

sur·round·ings (sə roun′dingz) *n.pl.* surrounding things, conditions, etc.

sur·tax (sėr′taks′) *n.* an additional or extra tax: *A surtax was temporarily levied by the government on incomes above $60 000.* [< F *surtaxe* < *sur-* over + *taxe* tax]

sur·tout (sèr tüt′ or sèr tü′) n. a man's overcoat. [< F surtout < sur- over + tout all]

sur·veil·lance (sər vā′ləns) n. 1 a watch kept over a person: She has been under police surveillance for several weeks. 2 supervision. [< F surveillance < sur- over (< L super-) + veiller watch < L vigilare]

sur·vey (v. sər vā′; n. sèr′vā) v., n., pl. -veys. —v. 1 look over; take a general view of: She surveyed the scene before her. They surveyed the wreckage. 2 examine or inspect the condition, situation, etc. of: He surveyed the alternatives open to him and decided he had to act at once. 3 determine the exact boundaries and contours of (an area of land) by measuring distances, angles, etc.: The land is being surveyed for subdivision into building lots. 4 survey land: He spent the summer surveying. —n. 1 a general or comprehensive study or view of something: His book includes a survey of twentieth century Canadian poetry. 2 an inspection or investigation of the condition, situation, etc. of something: Our first survey of the house showed us that it needed a lot of repairs. A recent survey shows that public opinion on the issue has changed. 3 a written statement or description of the result of such an investigation or examination: The government survey of food prices has just been published. 4 the act or an instance of surveying land. 5 a map or plan of such a survey. 6 Cdn. a a tract of land divided into building lots; subdivision. b the houses or community built on such land. [ME < AF surveier, ult. < L super- over + videre see]

sur·vey·ing (sər vā′ing) n. 1 the science or technique of measuring the boundaries and contours of particular areas on, above, or beneath the earth's surface by using the principles of geometry. 2 the act or business of making such measurements.

sur·vey·or (sər vā′ər) n. a person who surveys, especially one whose work is making land surveys.

sur·vey·or·ship (sər vā′ər ship′) n. the position of a surveyor.

surveyor's measure a system for measuring land area, formerly used by surveyors. The basic unit was the chain, a unit of length equal to 66 feet or about 20 metres, which was divided into 100 links each equal to about 20 centimetres.

625 square links	= 1 square pole	
16 square poles	= 1 square chain	
10 square chains	= 1 acre	
640 acres	= 1 section (or 1 square mile)	
36 sections	= 1 township	

sur·viv·al (sər vī′vəl) n. 1 the act or fact of surviving; continuing to live, or exist: He had little chance of survival when his food ran out. 2 a person, thing, custom, belief, etc. that has lasted from an earlier time. 3 (adjl.) of, having to do with, or assisting survival: survival techniques, a survival kit.

survival of the fittest the process or result of natural selection.

sur·vive (sər vīv′) v. -vived, -viv·ing. 1 continue to live or exist; live on: The family survived in spite of terrible hardship. Several of the original buildings still survive. 2 live longer than; outlive: He survived his wife by three years. 3 continue to live or exist after: Ten of the crew survived the shipwreck. The roses did not survive the winter. [ME < AF survivre < sur- over (< L super-) + vivre live < L vivere]

sur·vi·vor (sər vī′vər) n. a person or thing that survives.

sus– prefix. the form of sub- (from the form subs-) occurring in some cases before c, p, t, as in susceptible, suspend, sustain.

sus·cep·ti·bil·i·ty (sə sep′tə bil′ə tē) n., pl. -ties. 1 the quality or state of being susceptible: susceptibility to disease. 2 Physics. the capacity of a substance to be magnetized, measured by the ratio of the magnetization to the magnetizing force. Symbol: k 3 susceptibilities, pl. sensitive feelings.

sus·cep·ti·ble (sə sep′tə bəl) adj. 1 capable of receiving or undergoing a process or operation; allowing (used with of): a statement not susceptible of proof. Oak is susceptible of high polish. 2 open or liable to an influence, stimulus, etc.; readily affected (used with to): He is susceptible to flattery. Children are susceptible to many diseases. 3 sensitive and impressionable; easily influenced by emotions or emotions: Tales of adventure appealed to her susceptible nature. [< LL susceptibilis, ult. < L sub- up + capere take] —sus·cep′ti·bly, adv.
► Syn. 1. See note at sensitive.

sus·pect (v. səs pekt′; n. sus′pekt; adj. sus′pekt or səs pekt′) v., n., adj. —v. 1 imagine to be so; have an impression of the presence or existence of: The old fox suspected danger and did not touch the trap. 2 tend to believe to be guilty, false, bad, etc. without proof: The policeman suspected him. 3 feel no confidence in; doubt: The judge suspected the truth of the thief's excuse. 4 be suspicious: I'm sure she suspects. 5 be inclined to think or believe that: I suspect he was just trying to be funny. —n. a person suspected: The police have arrested two suspects. —adj. open to or viewed with suspicion; suspected or deserving to

hat, āge, fär; let, ēqual, tèrm; it, īce
hot, ōpen, ôrder; oil, out; cup, pút, rüle,
əbove, takən, pencəl, lemən, circəs
ch, child; ng, long; sh, ship
th, thin; ₮H, then; zh, measure

be suspected: That version of the story is suspect. [ME < OF suspect, adj. (F suspecter, v.) < L suspectus, pp. of suspicere < sub- under + specere look]

sus·pend (səs pend′) v. 1 hang from a support above so as to be free on all sides: The lamp was suspended from the ceiling. 2 hold, keep, or stay in place somewhere between the top and bottom: We saw the smoke suspended in the still air. 3 stop for a while: to suspend work on the project, to suspend hostilities. 4 make temporarily inoperative: to suspend a law. 5 defer (sentence on a convicted person) under certain conditions. 6 remove or exclude for a while from some privilege or job: to suspend a member of a team, to be suspended from school. 7 keep undecided; put off: to suspend judgment. 8 stop payment or be unable to pay one's debts.
suspend payment, declare inability to pay one's debts; fail. [ME < L suspendere < sub- up + pendere hang]

suspended sentence Law. a sentence given to a convicted person, that remains unenforced subject to the person's good behavior for a certain length of time.

sus·pend·ers (səs pen′dərz) n. 1 straps worn over the shoulders to hold up the trousers; braces. 2 garters worn by men to hold up their socks and by women to hold up their stockings.

sus·pense (səs pens′) n. 1 the condition of being uncertain about an outcome or decision: The detective story kept me in suspense until the very end. They were kept in suspense while the doctors deliberated. 2 a feeling of anxiety, or excitement resulting from such uncertainty: They had a long night of suspense before her fever broke. We all felt the suspense as we waited for the announcement of the winner. 3 (adjl.) producing suspense, especially pleasant excitement: a suspense novel. [ME < OF (en) suspens (in) abeyance, ult. < L suspendere. See SUSPEND.]

sus·pen·sion (səs pen′shən) n. 1 the act of suspending or the state or period of being suspended. 2 a support on which something is suspended. 3 an arrangement of springs, etc. for supporting the body of an automobile, railway car, etc. 4 Chemistry. a mixture in which very small particles of a solid remain suspended without dissolving. 5 Electricity. a wire or filament for supporting the moving parts of various instruments. 6 the method or mechanism by which the pendulum or balance wheel is suspended in a clock or watch. 7 Music. a a prolonging of one or more tones of a chord into the following chord, usually producing a temporary discord. b the tone or tones so prolonged.

suspension bridge a bridge having its roadway hung on cables or chains between towers. See bridge¹ for picture.

sus·pen·sive (səs pen′siv) adj. 1 inclined to suspend judgment; undecided in mind. 2 having to do with or characterized by suspense, uncertainty, or apprehension. 3 having the effect of temporarily stopping something: a suspensive veto. 4 involving such suspension.

sus·pen·so·ry (səs pen′sə rē) adj., n., pl. -ries. —adj. supporting or suspending: a suspensory muscle. —n. a muscle, ligament, bandage, etc. that holds up or supports a part of the body.

sus·pi·cion (səs pish′ən) n. 1 the act or an instance of suspecting: His suspicion of the stranger turned out to be well founded. 2 the feeling or state of mind of a person who suspects: an atmosphere of suspicion. He had a suspicion that the document was forged. 3 the condition of being suspected: She tried to protect herself by diverting suspicion to someone else. 4 a slight trace; suggestion: She speaks with just a suspicion of an accent.
above suspicion, so honest, honorable, etc. as not to be suspected of wrongdoing: They said their old servants were all above suspicion.
on suspicion, because of being suspected: He was arrested on suspicion of robbery.
under suspicion, suspected; believed guilty but not proven to be so. [ME < L suspicio, -onis < suspicere. See SUSPECT.]
► Syn. n. 1. **Suspicion, distrust, doubt** = lack of trust or confidence in someone. **Suspicion** suggests fearing, or believing without enough or any proof, that someone or something is guilty, wrong, false, etc.: Suspicion points to him, but the evidence is circumstantial. **Distrust** emphasizes lack of confidence or trust, especially in a person, and may suggest certainty of guilt, falseness, etc.: Even his mother feels distrust. **Doubt** emphasizes lack of certainty, and suggests inability to make a decision: He must be proved guilty beyond reasonable doubt.

sus·pi·cious (səs pish′əs) adj. 1 causing one to suspect: A man was seen loitering near the house in a suspicious manner. They left under suspicious circumstances. 2 feeling suspicion; distrustful; suspecting: It was the way he said it that made me suspicious.

3 tending to suspect; prone to distrust: *She has a very suspicious nature. Our dog is suspicious of strangers.* **4** showing suspicion: *The dog gave a suspicious sniff at my leg.* —**sus·pi′cious·ly,** *adv.* —**sus·pi′cious·ness,** *n.*

sus·pi·ra·tion (sus′pə rā′shən) *n.* a sigh.

sus·pire (səs pīr′) *v.* **-pired, -pir·ing.** take a long, deep breath; especially, sigh. [< L *suspirare* < *sub-* up + *spirare* breathe]

sus·tain (səs tān′) *v.* **1** keep up; keep going: *Hope sustains him in his misery.* **2** supply with food, provisions, etc.: *to sustain an army.* **3** hold up; support: *Arches sustain the weight of the roof.* **4** bear; endure: *The sea wall sustains the shock of the waves.* **5** suffer; experience: *to sustain a great loss.* **6** allow; admit; favor: *The court sustained his suit.* **7** agree with; confirm: *The facts sustain his theory.* [ME < OF < L *sustinere* < *sub-* up + *tenere* hold] —**sus·tain′a·ble,** *adj.* —**sus·tain′er,** *n.*

sustained yield in the management of forests, fisheries, etc., the principles of maintaining a steady yield by keeping annual growth or increase at least as high as annual output.

sustaining program or **programme** a radio or television program having no sponsor but maintained at the expense of a station or network.

sus·te·nance (sus′tə nəns) *n.* **1** a means of sustaining life; food or provisions: *He has gone for a week without sustenance.* **2** the means of living; support: *He gave money for the sustenance of a poor family.* **3** sustaining or being sustained; especially, supplying or being supplied with food or provisions. [ME < OF *sustenance* < *sustenir* sustain < L *sustinere.* See SUSTAIN.]

sut·ler (sut′lər) *n. Historical.* a person who followed an army and sold provisions, etc. to the soldiers. [< earlier < Du. *soeteler* < *soetelen* ply a low trade]

sut·tee (su tē′ *or* sut′ē) *n.* **1** a Hindu widow who threw herself on the burning funeral pile of her husband and was burned with him. **2** the Hindu custom of a widow burning herself with the body of her husband. [< Hind. < Skt. *satī* faithful wife]

su·ture (sü′chər) *n., v.* **-tured, -tur·ing.** —*n.* **1** the act or process of joining together the edges of a cut or wound by stitching. **2** a length of material, such as gut, thread, or wire, used in stitching wounds. **3** one of the stitches closing a wound. **4** a joining of parts by or as if by sewing, or into joint or line formed in this way. **5** the line where the edges of two bones form a rigid joint, as between the bones of the skull. **6** *Biology.* the line between adjoining parts in a plant or animal such as that along which clamshells join or pea pods split.
—*v.* join or unite by suture or as if by a suture. [< L *sutura* < *suere* sew]

su·ze·rain (sü′zə rin *or* sü′zə rān′) *n.* **1** a feudal lord. **2** a state or government exercising political control over the foreign affairs of a dependent state. [< F *suzerain* < *sus* above (< L *sursum* upward), modelled on *souverain* sovereign]

su·ze·rain·ty (sü′zə rin tē *or* sü′zə rān tē) *n., pl.* **-ties.** the position or authority of a suzerain.

s.v. under the following word or heading (for L *sub verbo* or *sub voce* under the word).

svelte (svelt) *adj.* slender; lithe. [< F < Ital. *svelto,* pp. < L *ex-* out + *vellere* pluck]

Sw. Swedish; Sweden.

SW or **S.W.** southwest.

swab (swob) *n., v.* **swabbed, swab·bing.** —*n.* **1** a mop for cleaning decks, floors, etc. **2** a bit of absorbent material usually attached to the end of a small stick, used for cleansing or removing material from some part of the body or for applying medicine to it. **3** a specimen taken with a swab for examination for bacteria, etc. **4** a sponge attached to a handle, used for cleaning the bore of a firearm. **5** *Slang.* a clumsy or contemptible person.
—*v.* **1** clean with or as if with a swab. **2** apply medication to with a swab: *to swab a person's throat.* Also, **swob.** [< *swabber*]
☛ *Hom.* **swob.**

swab·ber (swob′ər) *n.* **1** a person who uses a swab. **2** a swab. [< Du. *zwabber* < *zwabben* swab]

Swa·bi·an (swä′bē ən *or* swä′bē ən) *adj., n.* —*adj.* of or having to do with Swabia, a former duchy in SW Germany. —*n.* a native or inhabitant of Swabia.

swad·dle (swod′əl) *v.* **-dled, -dling;** *n.* —*v.* **1** wrap a baby with swaddling clothes. **2** wrap tightly with bandages or thick layers of clothes; swathe. —*n.* the cloth used for swaddling. [OE *swæthel* band, bandage. Related to SWATHE¹.]

swaddling clothes 1 long, narrow strips of cloth formerly used for wrapping a newborn infant. **2** anything that restrains freedom of thought or action.

swag (swag) *n., v.* —*n.* **1** *Slang.* things stolen; booty or spoils acquired dishonestly. **2** *Australian.* a bundle of personal belongings such as that carried by a tramp, a traveller in the bush, etc. **3** an ornamental festoon of flowers, leaves, draperies, etc.
—*v.* **1** lurch or sag. **2** arrange in or adorn with ornamental festoons. [special use of *swag,* v., sway, probably < Scand.; cf. dial. Norwegian *svagga* sway]

swage (swāj) *n., v.* **swaged, swag·ing.** —*n.* **1** a tool for bending metal. **2** a die or stamp for giving a particular shape to metal by hammering, stamping, etc. —*v.* bend or shape by using a swage. [ME < OF *souage*]

swag·ger (swag′ər) *v., n., adj.* —*v.* **1** walk with a bold, defiant, or superior air; strut about or show off in a vain or insolent way: *The bully swaggered into the schoolyard.* **2** boast or brag noisily. **3** influence or force by bluster; bluff.
—*n.* a swaggering way of walking or acting.
—*adj. Informal.* elegantly stylish: *swagger clothes.* [< *swag*]
—**swag′ger·er,** *n.* —**swag′ger·ing·ly,** *adv.*
☛ *Syn. v.* **1.** See note at **strut.**

swagger stick a short, light stick or cane, sometimes carried by military officers.

Swa·hi·li (swä hē′lē) *n., pl.* **-li** or **-lis;** *adj.* —*n.* **1** a member of a Bantu-speaking people of Zanzibar and the nearby African coast. **2** a Bantu language spoken originally in Zanzibar and the nearby coast of Africa, characterized by a large proportion of words of Arabic origin. Swahili is the common language of trade in Tanzania, Kenya, Zaire, and Uganda. [literally, people of the coast < Arabic *sawâhil,* pl. of *sâhil* coast]

swain (swān) *n. Archaic or poetic.* **1** a suitor; lover. **2** a young man who lives in the country. [ME < ON *sveinn* boy]

swale (swāl) *n.* a low, wet piece of land; low place. [ME, probably < Scand.; cf. ON *svalr* cool]

swal·low¹ (swol′ō) *v., n.* —*v.* **1** pass (food, drink, etc.) from the mouth to the stomach by the action of muscles in the throat. **2** perform the act of swallowing: *It hurts when I swallow.* **3** *Informal.* believe (a statement, etc.) readily or gullibly: *She'll never swallow that story.* **4** accept meekly, without protest or resentment: *to swallow an affront.* **5** take back; retract: *She threatened to make him swallow his words.* **6** keep back; repress: *to swallow one's tears, to swallow resentment.* **7** engulf, absorb, or destroy, as if by swallowing (*usually used with* **up**): *Several small countries were swallowed up by the imperial forces. The waves swallowed the swimmer.* **8** pronounce or speak (words or sounds) indistinctly.
—*n.* **1** the act of swallowing. **2** the amount swallowed at one time. **3** *Rare.* gullet. [OE *swelgan*] —**swal′low·er,** *n.*

Barn swallows—
about 18 cm long
including the tail

swal·low² (swol′ō) *n.* any of a family (Hirundinidae) of small, swift-flying birds found in many parts of the world, having long, narrow, pointed wings, a long, more or less forked tail, and a short, broad bill that can open very wide to catch insects in flight. [OE *swealwe*]

swal·low·tail (swol′ō tāl′) *n.* **1** a deeply forked tail, such as that of a swallow. **2** something shaped like or suggesting a swallowtail. **3** swallow-tailed coat. **4** any of various mostly brightly colored butterflies (family Papilionidae) having a taillike extension at the end of each hind wing. See also **tiger swallowtail.**

swal·low–tailed (swol′ō tāld′) *adj.* having a tail or end that is deeply forked or extends into long, tapering points.

swallow–tailed coat (swol′ō tāld′) a man's formal coat cut away in the front and extending at the back in two long tapering pieces; tailcoat.

swam (swam) *v.* pt. of **swim.**

swa·mi (swä′mē) *n., pl.* **-mis.** the title of a Hindu religious teacher. [< Hind. < Skt. *svāmin*]

swamp (swomp) *n., v.* —*n.* **1** an area of wet land sometimes partially covered with water, especially such an area having trees and shrubs as well as grasses and sedges. **2** (*adj.*) of, for use in, or found in swamps: *swamp grasses.*
—*v.* **1** cover or fill with water; flood or soak: *A huge wave swamped the boat. All our provisions were swamped.* **2** fill with

water and sink: *Our boat swamped in the storm.* **3** overwhelm as by a flood; make helpless with too much or too many of something: *swamped with work. The lottery winner was swamped with letters asking for money.*

swamp cypress bald cypress.

swamp·land (swomp′land′) *n.* a tract of land covered by swamps.

swamp rabbit in the North, muskrat prepared as food.

swamp·y (swomp′ē) *adj.* **swamp·i·er, swamp·i·est. 1** of, containing, or consisting of a swamp or swamps: *swampy meadowland.* **2** like a swamp; soft and wet: *The yard was swampy after the heavy rain.*

Swampy Cree one of the two main divisions of Cree Indians, scattered in groups over the woodlands of northwestern Ontario. Also, **Woodland Cree.**

swan (swon) *n.* **1** any of a small subfamily (Cygninae) of large, typically pure-white, aquatic birds of the same family as ducks and geese, having webbed feet, a long, slender neck that is curved back in swimming but stretched out straight in flight, and a very long, convoluted windpipe that allows them to make a variety of far-reaching calls. Many authorities classify the North American species in a separate genus (*Olor*), but others place them in the genus *Cygnus*, together with all other species except the South American **coscoroba swan** (*Coscoroba coscoroba*). See also **trumpeter swan, whistling swan. 2** a poet or singer. Shakespeare is sometimes called the Swan of Avon. **3 Swan,** *Astronomy.* Cygnus. [OE] —**swan′like′,** *adj.*

swan dive a graceful dive in which the legs are held straight from the toes to the hips, the back is arched, and the arms are spread like the wings of a gliding bird. The diver's arms come forward and together just before entering the water.

swang (swang) *v. Archaic or dialect.* a pt. of **swing.**

swank (swangk) *Slang.* —*v.* show off; swagger: *She was swanking around in her new outfit.*
—*n.* **1** swaggering behavior, speech, etc. **2** style and dash; smartness; elegance. **3** (*adj.*) swanky: *Their apartment is very swank.* [cf. OE *swancor* lithe]

swank·y (swangk′ē) *adj.* **swank·i·er, swank·i·est.** stylish and dashing; smart; elegant: *a swanky car.* —**swank′i·ly,** *adv.* —**swank′i·ness,** *n.*

swan's–down (swonz′doun′) *n.* **1** the soft down of a swan, used for trimming, powder puffs, etc. **2** a fine, thick, soft cloth made of a mixture of cotton or silk with wool. **3** a very soft, absorbent cotton flannel.

swan song 1 the song that a swan is said to sing just before it dies. **2** a person's farewell performance or final statement, composition, painting, etc.

swap (swop) *v.* **swapped, swap·ping;** *n. Informal.* —*v.* exchange; barter; trade. —*n.* a trading; trade. Also, **swop.** [ME *swappe* strike, strike the hands together; probably imitative; the modern meaning arose from the practice of "striking hands" as a sign of agreement in bargaining] —**swap′per,** *n.*

sward (swôrd) *n.* a grassy surface; turf. [OE *sweard* skin]

sware (swer) *v. Archaic.* a pt. of **swear.**
☛ *Hom.* **swear.**

swarm¹ (swôrm) *n.* **1** a large group of honeybees, led by a queen bee, leaving a hive to start a new colony elsewhere. **2** a colony of bees settled together in a hive. **3** a large number of insects, birds, people, etc. clustered together and usually moving about: *a swarm of children, swarms of migrating birds.* **4** a group of free-swimming, single-celled organisms, especially zoospores.
—*v.* **1** of honeybees, flying off together to start a new colony. **2** fly or move about in great numbers; throng: *The mosquitoes swarmed about us.* **3** be crowded or overrun; teem: *The plaza was swarming with shoppers. Our camp swarmed with mosquitoes.* **4** of zoospores, etc., escape from the parent organism in a swarm, with characteristic movement. [OE *swearm*: akin to L *susurrus* hum, Skt. *svara* voice]
☛ *Syn. n.* **4.** See note at **crowd.**

swarm² (swôrm) *v.* climb; shin. [origin uncertain]

swart (swôrt) *adj. Archaic.* dark; swarthy. [OE *sweart*]

swarth·y (swôr′гне or swôr′thē) *adj.* **swarth·i·er, swarth·i·est.** having a dark skin. [earlier *swarty < swart + -y¹*] —**swarth′i·ly,** *adv.* —**swarth′i·ness,** *n.*
☛ *Syn.* See note at **dusky.**

swash (swosh) *v., n.* —*v.* **1** dash (water, etc.) about; splash. **2** move with a splashing, washing sound: *The water swashed against the boat.* **3** swagger.
—*n.* **1** a swashing action or sound: *the swash of waves against a boat.* **2** the act of swaggering. **3** a narrow channel of water cutting through a sandbank or between a sandbank and the shore. **4** the

hat, āge, fär; let, ēqual, tėrm; it, īce
hot, ōpen, ôrder; oil, out; cup, pút, rüle,
əbove, takən, pencəl, lemən, circəs

ch, child; ng, long; sh, ship
th, thin; ʈʜ, then; zh, measure

ground under water or over which water washes. [probably imitative]

swash·buck·ler (swosh′buk′lər) *n.* a swaggering swordsman, bully, or boaster. [< *swash* + *buckler*]

swash·buck·ling (swosh′buk′ling) *n. or adj.* swaggering; bullying; boasting.

Swastikas: on the left, a traditional Amerindian swastika; on the right, a Nazi Party armband with a swastika

swas·ti·ka (swos′tə kə) *n.* an ancient symbol or ornament consisting of a cross with equal arms that are continued at the ends at right angles, all in the same direction. The Nazis adopted the swastika with the arms bent in a clockwise direction. [< Skt. *svastika < svasti* luck < *su* well + *asti*, n., being < *as* be]

swat (swot) *v.* **swat·ted, swat·ting;** *n. Informal.* —*v.* hit with a smart or violent blow: *to swat a fly.* —*n.* a smart or violent blow. [originally var. of *squat*] —**swat′ter,** *n.*

swatch (swoch) *n.* a sample of cloth or other similar material. [origin uncertain]

swath (swoth) *n., v.* —*n.* **1** the space covered by a single cut of a scythe or by one cut of a mowing machine. **2** a row of grass, grain, etc. cut by a scythe or mowing machine. **3** a long, wide strip or belt.
cut a (wide) swath, a make a destructive sweep: *The aggressive new company cut a swath through its competitors.* **b** make a forceful impression or effective display: *He cuts a wide swath in this town.*
—*v.* cut grain with a swather. [OE *swæth* track, trace]

swathe¹ (swāʈʜ *or* swōʈʜ) *v.* **swathed, swath·ing;** *n.* —*v.* **1** wrap up closely or completely: *swathed in a blanket.* **2** bind with bandages; bandage: *to swathe an injured arm.* **3** envelop or surround like a wrapping: *The mountain top was swathed in cloud.* —*n.* a wrapping or bandage. [OE *swathian*]

swathe² (swōʈʜ *or* swāʈʜ) *n.* swath.

swath·er (swoth′ər) *n.* a machine used for cutting grain that is not dry or is mixed with weeds.

sway (swā) *v., n.* —*v.* **1** swing slowly back and forth or from side to side from a base or pivot: *The tower of dominoes swayed and fell. The trees swayed in the wind.* **2** move or bend slowly down or to one side, as if from weight or pressure: *He suddenly felt dizzy and swayed against the wall.* **3** cause to sway: *The wind sways the grass.* **4** change in opinion, feeling, etc.: *Nothing could sway him after he made up his mind.* **5** *Archaic or poetic.* govern or rule.
—*n.* **1** a swaying: *the sway of a branch in the wind.* **2** a controlling influence or power: *under the sway of a violent emotion. The rebel leader held sway over a large territory.* [ME < Scand.; akin to ON *sveigja*]
☛ *Syn. v.* **1.** See note at **swing.**

sway·back (swā′bak′) *adj.* **1** an abnormally hollow or sagging back in horses, etc., especially as a result of strain or overwork. **2** an abnormal forward curve of the middle of the spine in human beings.

sway·backed (swā′bakt′) *adj.* having a swayback.

swear (swer) *v.* **swore, sworn, swear·ing. 1** make a solemn promise before a judge, coroner, etc.: *A witness at a trial has to swear to tell the truth.* **2** declare, calling God to witness; make solemn oath; declare on oath. **3** bind by an oath; require to promise: *Members of the club were sworn to secrecy.* **4** admit to office or service by administering an oath to: *to swear a witness.* **5** promise on oath or solemnly to observe to do something: *I swear to obey the rules of this club.* **6** bring, set, take, etc. by swearing: *to swear a person's life away.* **7** utter (an oath). **8** use profane language; curse.
swear by, a name as one's witness in taking an oath. **b** have great confidence in.

swear in, admit to office or service by giving an oath: *to swear in a jury.*

swear off, promise to give up: *to swear off smoking.*

swear out, get (a warrant for arrest) by taking an oath that a certain charge is true.
[OE *swerian*] —**swear'er,** *n.*
☞ *Hom.* sware.
☞ *Syn.* 8. See note at curse.

swear·word (swer'werd') *n.* a word or phrase used in cursing; a profane or obscene word or phrase.

sweat (swet) *n., v.* **sweat** or **sweat·ed, sweat·ing.** —*n.* **1** moisture coming through the pores of the skin. **2** a fit or condition of sweating: *He was in a cold sweat from fear.* **3** *Informal.* a condition of anxiety, impatience, or anything that might make a person sweat: *We were all in a sweat over the big test we would get on Monday.* **4** moisture given out by something or gathered on its surface: *The water pipes were covered with sweat.* **5** an exuding of moisture from something, or the process of producing an exudation, as part of certain industrial processes, as tanning. **6** anything that causes sweat; hard work or strenuous exertion; labor.
by the sweat of (one's) **brow,** by one's own efforts and hard work.
old sweat, *Informal.* an old soldier.
—*v.* **1** give out moisture through the pores of the skin. **2** cause to sweat: *He sweated his horse by riding him too hard.* **3** cause to give off moisture; ferment: *to sweat hides or tobacco in preparing them for use.* **4** come out in drops; ooze. **5** send out in drops. **6** wet or stain with sweat. **7** get rid of by sweating or as if by sweating: *to sweat off excess weight, to sweat out a hard test.* **8** give out moisture; collect or gather moisture on the surface: *A pitcher of ice water sweats on a hot day.* **9** cause to work hard and under bad conditions: *That employer sweats his workers.* **10** *Informal.* work very hard. **11** suffer severely, especially as a penalty: *The prisoner sweated under the severe questioning.* **12** be annoyed or vexed; fume: *sweat over a delay.* **13** *Slang.* deprive of or cause to give up something, especially money; rob; fleece. **14** heat (solder) till it melts; join (metal parts) by heating. **15** heat (metal) in order to remove an easily fusible constituent.
sweat it out, *Informal.* wait anxiously or nervously for something to happen.
[ME *swete,* n., v. < OE *swǣtan,* v.]
☞ *Syn.* n. **1. Sweat, perspiration** = moisture coming through the pores of the skin. **Sweat** is the direct native English word, used always when speaking of animals or things and often of people, especially when the moisture is flowing freely or is mixed with grime or blood: *Sweat streamed down the horse's flanks. The rider's shirt was stained with sweat.* **Perspiration** is applicable only when speaking of human beings: *Tiny drops of perspiration formed at her temples.*

sweat·band (swet'band') *n.* **1** a band, usually of leather, lining the inside edge of a hat or cap to protect it from sweat. **2** a cloth band tied around the head or wrist to absorb sweat.

sweat·box (swet'boks') *n.* **1** a boxlike device used to sweat certain commodities before use or sale, as figs, hides, etc. **2** *Slang.* a very small cell in which a prisoner is confined as a special punishment.

sweat·er (swet'ər) *n.* a knitted or crocheted outer garment for the upper body, made of wool, acrylic, nylon, etc.; a pullover or cardigan.

sweat gland a small gland, just under the skin, that secretes sweat.

sweat pants long, loose pants made of a warm, absorbent fabric such as fleece-lined cotton, and having a string-tied or elasticized waist and knitted cuffs at the ankles, worn for warm-up exercises, etc.

sweat shirt a long-sleeved, collarless pullover, made of a warm, absorbent fabric such as fleece-lined cotton, worn for outdoor sports, warm-up exercises, etc.

sweat·shop (swet'shop') *n.* a place where workers are employed at low pay for long hours under bad conditions.

sweat suit a suit consisting of a sweat shirt and sweat pants, worn especially by athletes, etc. while exercising.

sweat·y (swet'ē) *adj.* **sweat·i·er, sweat·i·est. 1** sweating; covered with sweat. **2** causing sweat: *sweaty work, sweaty weather.* **3** of or like sweat: *a sweaty odor.* —**sweat'i·ly,** *adv.* —**sweat'i·ness,** *n.*

Swed. Sweden; Swedish.

Swede (swēd) *n.* **1** a native or inhabitant of Sweden, a country in N Europe. **2** a person of Swedish descent. **3 swede,** rutabaga (introduced to Scotland from Sweden in the 18th century). [< MLG or MDu.]

Swe·den·bor·gi·an (swē'dən bôr'jē ən) *n., adj.* —*n.* a believer in the religious doctrines of Emanuel Swedenborg (1688-1772), a Swedish philosopher, scientist, and mystic. —*adj.* having to do with Swedenborg, his doctrines, or his followers.

Swede·saw (swēd'sô' *or* -sô') *n. Cdn.* a handsaw having a bow-like tubular frame, the blade being kept taut by the tension of the bow. It is used for pruning trees, sawing pulpwood, etc. [apparently < *Swedish saw;* cf. *Swedish fiddle* or *violin,* originally, loggers' slang for a large crosscut saw]

Swed·ish (swē'dish) *n., adj.* —*n.* **1 the Swedish,** *pl.* the people of Sweden. **2** the North Germanic language of Sweden. —*adj.* of or having to do with Sweden, its people, or their language.

sweep (swēp) *v.* **swept, sweep·ing;** *n.* —*v.* **1** clean or clear with a broom, brush, etc.; use a broom or something similar to remove dirt: *Sweep the steps.* **2** move, drive, or take away with or as with a broom, brush, etc.: *The wind sweeps the snow into drifts.* **3** remove with a sweeping motion; carry along: *A flood swept away the bridge.* **4** trail upon: *Her dress sweeps the ground.* **5** pass over with a steady, searching movement: *Her fingers swept the strings of the harp. His eye swept the sky, searching for signs of rain.* **6** range over; scour: *Enthusiasm for the candidate swept the country.* **7** move swiftly; pass swiftly: *Pirates swept down on the town.* **8** move with purpose and dignity: *The lady swept out of the room.* **9** move or extend in a long course or curve: *The shore sweeps to the south for some distance.*
—*n.* **1** the act of sweeping; clearing away; removing: *He made a clean sweep of all his debts.* **2** a steady, driving motion or swift onward course of something: *The sweep of the wind kept the trees from growing tall.* **3** a smooth, flowing motion or line; dignified motion: *the sweep of verse.* **4** a curve; bend: *the sweep of a road.* **5** a swinging or curving motion: *He cut the grass with strong sweeps of his scythe.* **6** a continuous extent; stretch: *The house looked upon a wide sweep of farming country.* **7** the reach; range; extent: *The mountain is beyond the sweep of your eye.* **8** a winning of all the games in a series, match, contest, etc.; complete victory. **9** an act of surveying, reconnoitring, attacking, etc. carried out over a definite area: *The bombers cleared the coast by aerial sweeps.* **10** a person who sweeps chimneys, streets, etc. **11** any implement for sweeping, such as a broom; sweeper. **12** a long oar. **13** a long pole which pivots on a high post and is used to raise or lower a bucket in a well. **14** a sweepstakes contest. [OE (*ge*)*swēpa* sweepings]

sweep·er (swē'pər) *n.* **1** a person or thing that sweeps: *a carpet sweeper.* **2** *Cdn.* a tree that has been undermined by the current of a river or stream so that some of its leaves and branches hang down into the water, though its roots remain anchored to the bank.

sweep·ing (swē'ping) *adj., n.* —*adj.* **1** passing or extending over a wide space: *a sweeping glance.* **2** having wide range; extensive; thoroughgoing: *sweeping reforms.* **3** not considering exceptions or limitations; indiscriminate: *a sweeping statement.*
—*n.* **1** the act or work of a person or thing that sweeps: *The porch needs a good sweeping.* **2 sweepings,** *pl.* things that have been swept up; refuse: *Put the sweepings in that box.* —**sweep'ing·ly,** *adv.*

sweep·stake (swēp'stāk') *n.* sweepstakes.

sweep·stakes (swēp'stāks') *n.sing. or pl.* **1** a form of lottery for gambling on horse races, etc. Each person pays a specified sum to draw a ticket bearing the name of one of the competitors in a race or contest; the money paid in goes to the holder or holders of tickets on the winner of the race or contest. **2** the race or contest. **3** a race or contest in which the prize or prizes derive from a pooling of the stakes of the contestants, with or without additional contributions by the sponsor or sponsors of the contest. **4** a prize in any such race or contest. [ME, literally a person who takes, or sweeps, all the prizes]

sweet (swēt) *adj., n., adv.* —*adj.* **1** having a taste like sugar or honey. **2** pleasing to the sense of smell; fragrant, like roses, perfume, etc.: *The air was sweet with the scent of lilacs. Vanilla has a sweet smell.* **3** pleasing to the ear; harmonious: *sweet music.* **4** attractive, charming, kind, etc.: *She had a sweet smile. He's a sweet child. It's sweet of you to help.* **5** very pleasurable; gratifying or satisfying: *sweet praise, sweet dreams of success. Revenge is sweet.* **6** fresh; not sour, fermented or spoiled: *sweet cider. Is the milk still sweet?* **7** not salty: *sweet butter.* **8** of soil, not too acid. **9** dear; darling. **10** of a wine, not dry. **11** easily managed, handled, or dealt with: *a sweet ship.* **12** *Chemistry.* free from corrosive salt, sulphur, acid, etc. or unpleasant gases and odors. **13** *Music.* of or designating jazz characterized by a regular beat and straightforward melody, with little improvisation.
be sweet on, *Informal.* be in love with.
—*n.* **1** sweetheart; darling. **2 the sweet,** that which is sweet: *to take the bitter with the sweet.* **3 sweets,** *pl.* food, such as candy, cake, etc., containing a lot of sugar or other sweetening agent: *I like sweets.* **4** *Esp.Brit.* a sweetmeat or a sweet dessert: *Would you like a sweet?*
—*adv.* in a sweet manner; sweetly. [OE *swēte*] —**sweet'ly,** *adv.* —**sweet'ness,** *n.*
☞ *Hom.* suite.

sweet alyssum a common, low-growing garden plant (*Lobularia maritima*) of the mustard family native to Europe,

having clusters of small, white or mauve flowers. Sweet alyssum is popular for flower borders, window boxes, etc.

sweet-and-sour (swēt′ən sour′) *adj.* of food, prepared with a sauce containing sugar together with vinegar or lemon juice: *sweet-and-sour pork.*

sweet basil basil (def. 1): *Sweet basil is the only basil used in cooking.*

sweet bay **1** laurel (def. 1). **2** a small tree (*Magnolia virginiana*) native to the SE United States, having fragrant, creamy-white flowers.

sweet·bread (swēt′bred′) *n.* the pancreas or thymus of a calf, lamb, etc. used as meat.

sweet·bri·er (swēt′brī′ər) *n.* a wild rose (*Rosa rubiginosa*; also called *R. eglanteria*) native to Europe and Asia but now naturalized in E North America, having fragrant leaves and having fragrant pink flowers. Sometimes, **sweetbriar.**

sweet cider unfermented cider.

sweet clover any of a genus (*Melilotus*) of plants of the pea family, having small flowers and leaflets in groups of three. It is widely grown to improve the soil and for use as hay.

sweet corn any of several varieties of corn having kernels with a high sugar content, that are eaten as a vegetable when young and tender, in the milky stage. Sweet corn is the common table corn.

sweet·en (swē′tən) *v.* **1** make sweet. **2** become sweet. **3** make pleasant or agreeable.

sweet·en·er (swē′tən ər *or* swēt′nər) *n.* something that sweetens, especially an artificial substitute for sugar or honey, such as saccharin.

sweet·en·ing (swēt′ən ing *or* swēt′ning) *n.* something that sweetens.

sweet fern a North American shrub (*Comptonia asplenifolia*), also called *C. peregrina*) of the wax-myrtle family having long, scented, fernlike leaves.

sweet flag a tall, perennial marsh plant (*Acorus calamus*) of the arum family, found in north temperate regions, having tiny flowers, long, sword-shaped leaves, and a thick fragrant underground stem.

sweet gale a low-growing shrub (*Myrica gale*) of the wax-myrtle family found along river banks and in marshy places in North America, Europe, and Asia. The wood and leaves of the sweet gale are fragrant when crushed.

sweet grass any of various sweet-smelling grasses, such as *Hierochloe odorata*, found throughout North America and Eurasia.

sweet gum **1** a tall shade and timber tree (*Liquidambar styraciflua*) of E North America having star-shaped leaves that turn scarlet or gold in the fall. The bark of the sweet gum yields a fragrant, pleasant-tasting liquid balsam, or gum, used in medicines and in making perfumes, etc. **2** the hard, fine-grained wood of this tree, highly valued for making fine furniture, mouldings, etc.

sweet·heart (swēt′härt′) *n.* **1** a loved one; lover. **2** darling.

sweetheart neckline a neckline for women's clothing that is low in front and scalloped in the shape of the top of a heart.

sweet·ie (swē′tē) *n. Informal.* sweetheart.

sweetie pie *Informal.* sweetheart.

sweet·ing (swēt′ing) *n.* **1** a sweet apple. **2** *Archaic.* sweetheart.

sweet·ish (swēt′ish) *adj.* somewhat sweet.

sweet marjoram a garden herb (*Majorana hortensis*, sometimes classified as *Origanum hortensis*) of the mint family, having aromatic leaves commonly used as a seasoning in cookery.

sweet·meat (swēt′mēt′) *n.* an article of food prepared with much sugar or honey; especially, candy or candied or crystallized fruit.

sweet nothings trivial endearments exchanged by lovers.

sweet pea **1** an annual climbing plant (*Lathyrus odoratus*) of the pea family, native to Italy but long cultivated in many parts of the world, having fragrant flowers of many different colors. **2** the flower of this plant.

sweet pepper **1** the large, fleshy, green or red fruit of a pepper (def. 4), or capsicum, having a mild, somewhat sweet taste. It is eaten raw in salads or cooked as a vegetable. **2** a plant that bears this fruit.

sweet potato **1** a perennial tropical vine (*Ipomoea batatas*) of the morning glory family widely cultivated in tropical and warm temperate regions, having a large tuberous root that is used for food. **2** its sweet, starchy root, ranging in color from white to orange inside and light brown to rose outside. Sweet potatoes are usually served as a cooked vegetable.

sweet-sop (swēt′sop′) *n.* **1** a small tropical American tree (*Annona squamosa*) of the custard-apple family widely cultivated in

hat, āge, fär; let, ēqual, tėrm; it, īce
hot, ōpen, ôrder; oil, out; cup, pût, rüle,
ə above, takən, pencəl, lemən, circəs
ch, child; ng, long; sh, ship
th, thin; ŦH, then; zh, measure

tropical regions for its yellowish-green, edible fruit. **2** the fruit of this tree having soft, sweet, pale-yellow pulp.

sweet spirit of nitre a medicine used as sedative, as a means of increasing sweating, etc.

sweet talk flattery.

sweet-talk (swēt′tok′ *or* -tôk′) *v. Informal.* coax or flatter.

sweet-tem·pered (swēt′tem′pərd) *adj.* having or showing a gentle or pleasant nature; amiable.

sweet tooth a fondness or craving for sweet foods.

sweet william *or* **sweet William** a widely cultivated pink (*Dianthus barbatus*) having flat clusters of small, fragrant, showy flowers often spotted or banded in different colors.

swell (swel) *v.* **swelled, swelled** *or* **swol·len, swell·ing;** *n., adj.* —*v.* **1** grow or make larger in size, amount, degree, force, etc.: *Bread dough swells as it rises. The river is swollen by rain. His head is swollen where he bumped it. Savings may swell into a fortune. The sound swelled from a murmur to a roar.* **2** be larger or thicker in a particular place; stick out; cause to stick out: *A barrel swells in the middle.* **3** rise or cause to rise above the level: *Rounded hills swell gradually from the village plain.* **4** *Informal.* become or make proud or conceited.
—*n.* **1** the act of swelling; increase in amount, degree, force, etc. **2** the condition of being swollen. **3** a part that swells out. **4** a piece of higher ground; a rounded hill. **5** a long, unbroken wave or waves. **6** a swelling tone or sound. **7** *Music.* **a** a crescendo followed by a diminuendo. **b** the signs for this (< >). **8** a device in an organ, etc. to control the volume of sound. **9** *Informal. Esp.Brit.* a fashionable person.
—*adj.* **1** *Informal.* stylish; grand. **2** *Slang.* excellent; first-rate. [OE *swellan*]
☛ *Syn. v.* **1.** See note at **expand.**

swell·ing (swel′ing) *n.* **1** a swollen part: *There is a swelling on his head where he bumped it.* **2** the condition of being swollen; an increase in size.

swel·ter (swel′tər) *v., n.* —*v.* suffer from heat, as by sweating freely, feeling faint, etc. —*n.* a sweltering condition or atmosphere. [frequentative of obs. *swelt*, OE *sweltan* die] —**swel′ter·ing·ly,** *adv.*

swept (swept) *v.* pt. and pp. of **sweep.**

swept-back (swept′bak′) *adj.* of the wings of an aircraft, slanting backward from the base to the tip.

swerve (swėrv) *v.* **swerved, swerv·ing;** *n.* —*v.* turn aside sharply from a straight course or line: *The road swerves to the right here and goes around the lake. He swerved the car to avoid hitting the child.* —*n.* the act or instance of turning aside sharply: *The swerve of the ball made it hard to hit.* [OE *sweorfan* rub, file]

swift (swift) *adj., n.* —*adj.* **1** moving or able to move very fast: *a light, swift sailboat. He took the swiftest horse.* **2** coming or happening quickly: *a swift response.* **3** quick or prompt to act, etc.: *He is swift to repay a kindness.* **4** (*advl.*) in a swift manner; swiftly: *a swift-flowing river.*
—*n.* **1** any of a family (Apodidae) of small, mostly dull-colored birds noted for their speed in flight, having long, narrow wings that when closed extend well past the tip of the tail. Swifts resemble swallows when in flight, but are not related to them. **2** any of various small North American lizards (genera *Sceloporus* and *Uta*) that run quickly. —**swift′ness,** *n.* [OE] —**swift′ly,** *adv.*

swift-foot·ed (swift′fût′id) *adj.* able to run swiftly.

swig (swig) *n., v.* **swigged, swig·ging.** *Informal.* —*n.* a big or hearty drink or swallow, especially of liquor. —*v.* drink heartily or greedily. [origin uncertain] —**swig′ger,** *n.*

swill (swil) *n., v.* —*n.* **1** kitchen scraps and other vegetable refuse, especially when partly liquid; garbage; slops. Swill is sometimes fed to pigs. **2** a deep drink, especially of liquor; swig.
—*v.* **1** drink greedily or in great quantity; guzzle. **2** feed with swill: *to swill the pigs.* **3** wash by flooding with water. [OE *swilian*]

swim (swim) *v.* **swam, swum, swim·ming;** *n.* —*v.* **1** make oneself move in water by movements of the arms and legs, tail, or fins: *I'm learning to swim.* **2** cross by swimming: *to swim a river. I swam four lengths of the pool.* **3** make (a person or animal) swim: *He swam his horse across the stream.* **4** float on a liquid: *There were some bits of parsley swimming in the soup.* **5** be covered or flooded with a liquid: *a roast swimming in gravy, eyes swimming*

with tears. The floor was swimming with water. **6** go smoothly; glide. **7** have a feeling of floating or reeling; be dizzy: *The heat and noise made my head swim.*
—*n.* **1** the act or a period of swimming: *We went for a swim.* **2** the distance covered or to be covered in swimming: *a four-kilometre swim.* **3** (*adj.*) of, having to do with, or involving swimming: *a swim meet.*
in the swim, in the main current of activity in fashion, business, politics, etc.: *He's socially very active and likes to be in the swim.* [OE *swimman*]

swim bladder the air bladder of a fish.

swim·mer (swim′ər) *n.* a person or animal that swims.

swim·mer·et (swim′ər et′) *n. Zoology.* one of a number of abdominal limbs or appendages in many crustaceans, usually adapted for swimming and thus distinguished from other limbs adapted for walking or grasping. [dim. of *swimmer*]

swim·ming (swim′ing) *n., adj.* —*n.* **1** the practice or sport of swimming: *Tom is an expert at both swimming and diving.* **2** the act of swimming: *Can you reach the island by swimming?* **3** a state of dizziness or giddiness; vertigo.
—*adj.* **1** of or for swimming or swimmers: *a swimming teacher, a swimming pool.* **2** filled with tears; watery: *swimming eyes.* **3** faint; dizzy: *a swimming sensation.*

swim·ming·ly (swim′ing lē) *adv.* with great ease or success: *Everything went swimmingly at our party.*

swimming pool a large tank of concrete, plastic, etc., built into or on the ground for swimming or bathing in.

swim·suit (swim′süt′) *n.* a close-fitting garment worn for swimming or bathing; bathing suit.

swin·dle (swin′dəl) *v.* **-dled, -dling;** *n.* —*v.* **1** take money or property from by deceit or fraud; cheat: *They said he had swindled them. He swindled them out of their savings.* **2** get money or property by deceit or fraud: *She had swindled $200 from him.* —*n.* an act of swindling; a cheating or defrauding: *The whole deal was a swindle.* [< *swindler*]

swin·dler (swin′dlər) *n.* a person who cheats or defrauds. [< G *Schwindler* < *schwindeln* be dizzy, act thoughtlessly, cheat]

swine (swīn) *n., pl.* **swine.** **1** pig; hog. **2** a coarse or beastly person. [OE *swīn*]

swine·herd (swīn′hėrd′) *n.* a person who tends swine.

swing (swing) *v.* **swung, swung, swing·ing;** *n.* —*v.* **1** move freely to and fro in an arc or circle from an upper or overhead support that remains still: *A pendulum swings. His arms swung as he walked. Monkeys swing through the trees.* **2** move on or as if on hinges or a pivot: *The screen door was swinging in the wind. The gate swung slowly shut. She swung around and confronted them.* **3** cause to swing: *to swing a golf club. He swung his arms. She swung the car into the driveway.* **4** carry or transport something that is suspended: *The crane swung the cargo into the hold.* **5** move or transport something with a sweeping motion: *I swung the suitcase up onto the rack.* **6** move or cause to move to and fro on a swing, in a hammock, etc.: *Several children were swinging in the playground. He was swinging his little sister.* **7** be suspended or hang freely: *The microphone swung from an overhead track.* **8** *Slang.* be put to death by hanging. **9** hang so as to swing; suspend: *We swung the hammock between two trees.* **10** *Informal.* manage successfully: *We didn't think he'd be able to swing the deal.* **11** move with a free, rhythmic motion: *The soldiers came swinging down the street.* **12** *Music.* play or sing a melody in the style of swing. **13** *Slang.* follow a lifestyle that emphasizes unrestrained enjoyment of the fashionable social pleasures: *He is quiet at work, but they say after hours he swings.* **14** *Slang.* of a place, occasion, etc., be lively, exciting, and unrestrained: *The party was swinging by the time they got there. The town really swings these days.*
—*n.* **1** a swinging movement, stroke, or blow: *One swing of the axe split the log in two. He took a swing at me but missed.* **2** the width or manner of a swing: *a wide swing. She has an excellent swing.* **3** a seat hung from ropes or chains, on which one may swing for pleasure. **4** a swinging gait, movement, or rhythm. **5** freedom of action. **6** the normal rhythm or sequence of activity: *to get into the swing of a new job.* **7** *Music.* a style of jazz that evolved in the 1930's, characterized by a smooth but lively rhythm with more syncopation than in ragtime. Swing was usually played by large bands. **8** (*adj.*) of, having to do with, or playing music in this style: *a swing band.* **9** a trip around a country, region, etc.; tour: *a swing through the Maritimes.* **10** *Cdn.* in the North: **a** a train of sleighs or freight canoes, so called because they move, or swing, over a certain route in periodic trips. **b** a train of freight sleighs drawn by tractors; cat-train. **11** *Cdn.* a cowhand who rides out to the side of a herd to keep it from spreading.

in full swing, going on actively and completely; without restraint: *By five the party was in full swing.*
[OE *swingan* beat] —**swing′er,** *n.*

☛ *Syn. v.* **1. Swing, sway, rock** = move back and forth or from side to side. **Swing** applies to the movement of something attached at one side or the end or ends, and often but not always suggests a regular or rhythmical movement: *The lantern hanging overhead swung in the wind.* **Sway** suggests the unsteady swinging motion of something that bends or gives easily at any pressure: *The branches sway in the breeze.* **Rock** may suggest a gentle motion, but more often suggests the violent swaying of something shaken hard: *The house rocked in the storm.*

swing·er (swing′ər) *n. Slang.* a person who follows a lifestyle that emphasizes unrestrained enjoyment of fashionable social pleasures: *a couple of swingers in an expensive sportscar.*

swin·gle (swing′gəl) *n., v.* **-gled, -gling.** —*n.* a wooden instrument shaped like a large knife, for beating flax or hemp and scraping from it the woody or coarse portions. —*v.* clean (flax or hemp) by beating and scraping. [OE *swingel* < *swingan* beat]

swin·gle·tree (swing′gəl trē′) *n.* singletree.

swing music jazz music, especially for dancing, in which the players improvise freely on the original melody.

swing shift in factories, etc., the working hours between the day and night shifts, usually from 4 p.m. to midnight.

swin·ish (swī′nish) *adj.* of, characteristic of, or like swine; hoggish, beastly, or coarse: *swinish behavior.* —**swin′ish·ly,** *adv.* —**swin′ish·ness,** *n.*

swink (swingk) *n., v. Archaic.* —*n.* labor; toil. —*v.* work hard; labor; toil. [OE *swine, swincan*]

swipe (swīp) *n., v.* **swiped, swip·ing.** —*n. Informal.* a sweeping stroke; hard blow: *He made two swipes at the golf ball without hitting it.*
take a swipe at, *Informal.* try to hit; aim a blow at: *He took a swipe at me, but I ducked.* —*v.* **1** *Informal.* strike with a sweeping blow. **2** *Slang.* steal. [cf. OF *swipu* scourge]

swirl (swėrl) *v., n.* —*v.* **1** move or drive along with a twisting motion; whirl: *dust swirling in the air, a stream swirling over rocks.* **2** have a twisting shape or pattern. —*n.* **1** a swirling movement or mass; eddy. **2** something having a twisting shape or pattern: *a swirl of whipped cream.* [ME (Scottish); ? < Scand.; cf. Norwegian dial. *svirla* whirl] —**swirl′er,** *n.*

swish (swish) *v., n., adj.* —*v.* **1** move, pass, or swing with a light hissing or brushing sound: *The whip swished through the air.* **2** make such a sound: *Her long skirt swished as she danced across the floor.* **3** cause to swish: *She swished the stick through the branches. The horse swished its tail.*
—*n.* a swishing movement or sound: *the swish of little waves on the shore.* —*adj. Esp.Brit. Slang.* smart; posh. [? imitative]

Swiss (swis) *n., pl.* **Swiss;** *adj.* —*n.* **1** a native or inhabitant of Switzerland, a small country in W Europe. **2** a person of Swiss descent. **3** Usually, **swiss,** a fine, sheer, crisp, usually cotton fabric originally from Switzerland, often having a pattern of woven or flocked dots or figures.
—*adj.* of or having to do with Switzerland or its people. [< F *Suisse*]

Swiss chard a variety of white beet whose leaves and stalks are eaten as a vegetable.

Swiss cheese a firm pale-yellow or whitish cheese having a mild, slightly nutty flavor and many large holes that form as the cheese ripens.

Swiss Guards a body of soldiers who act as bodyguard to the Pope in the Vatican.

Swiss steak a cut of steak prepared by pounding it with flour and seasonings, browning it, and then cooking it slowly in a sauce with onions and, sometimes, tomatoes, sweet peppers, etc.

switch (swich) *n., v.* —*n.* **1** a device for making or breaking a connection in an electric circuit. **2** a pair of movable rails by which a train can shift from one track to another. **3** a turn; change; shift: *a switch of votes to another candidate.* **4** a slender stick used in whipping. **5** a stroke; lash: *The big dog knocked a vase off the table with a switch of its tail.* **6** anything resembling a switch in appearance or use. **7** a long tress of hair, often artificial, bound at one end, used to add bulk or length to a woman's hair for some hairstyles. **8** an exchange.
—*v.* **1** connect, disconnect, or change the path of (an electric circuit) by means of a switch. **2** start or stop the electric current to (an appliance, lamp, etc.) by operating a switch: *I switched on the radio. Don't forget to switch the light off.* **3** move (a train, railway car, etc.) from one track to another by means of a switch. **4** turn aside; change course or direction: *He was driving on the outside lane but suddenly switched.* **5** shift or divert (something): *She quickly switched the subject.* **6** exchange: *The children switched hats.* **7** strike with a switch. **8** move or swing like a switch: *a horse switching its tail.* [probably < var. of LG *swutsche*] —**switch′er,** *n.*

switch·back (swich′bak′) *n., v.* —*n.* **1** a railway or road

climbing a steep grade in a zigzag course. **2** *Esp.Brit.* roller coaster. —*v.* take a zigzag course.

switch·blade (swich′blād′) *n.* a pocket knife whose blade springs open at the press of a button or knob.

switch·board (swich′bôrd′) *n.* a panel containing the necessary switches, meters, etc. for opening, closing, combining, or controlling electric circuits. A telephone switchboard has plugs for connecting one line to another.

switch·gear (swich′gēr′) *n.* an apparatus for operating switches in electrical circuits.

switch·man (swich′mən) *n., pl.* **-men.** a person in charge of one or more railway switches.

switch·o·ver (swich′ō′vər) *n.* the act of changing over; a turning to something new.

switch·yard (swich′yärd′) *n.* a railway yard where cars are switched from one track to another, put together to make trains, etc.

swiv·el (swiv′əl) *n., v.* **-elled** or **-eled, -el·ling** or **-el·ing.** —*n.* **1** a fastening joining two parts so that one part may turn without moving the other. **2** swivel gun. —*v.* **1** turn on a swivel or as if on a swivel: *She swivelled the chair around. He swivelled his eyes in our direction.* **2** fasten or support by a swivel. [ult. < OE *swīfan* move]

swivel chair a chair that turns on a swivel in its base.

swivel gun a gun mounted on a swivel so that it can be turned in any direction.

swiz·zle (swiz′əl) *n., v.* **-zled, -zling.** —*n.* any of various alcoholic mixed drinks, especially one made with rum or other liquor, ice, bitters, and sugar. —*v.* drink alcoholic liquor habitually and excessively. [apparently var. of earlier *switchel*; origin unknown]

swizzle stick a small stick of plastic, glass, etc. used to stir alcoholic drinks.

swob (swob) *n., v.* **swobbed, swob·bing.** See **swab.** —**swob′ber,** *n.*

swol·len (swō′lən) *adj., v.* —*adj.* swelled: *a swollen ankle.* —*v.* a pp. of **swell.**

swoln (swōln) *adj. Archaic.* swollen.

swoon (swün) *v., n.* —*v.* **1** faint. **2** of sound, fade or die away gradually. —*n.* a loss of consciousness: *He fell in a swoon.* [ult. < OE *geswōgen* in a swoon]

swoop (swüp) *v., n.* —*v.* **1** move with a rush; especially, make a sudden, swift attack (*usually used with* **down**): *The eagle swooped down on the mouse. The horsemen swooped down on the village and burned it.* **2** seize; snatch (*used with* **up**): *She swooped the puppy up in her arms.* —*n.* the act or an instance of swooping. [ult. < OE *swāpan* sweep] —**swoop′er,** *n.*

swoosh (swüsh) *v.* **1** move with or make a sound like a rush of liquid or air: *The car swooshed by.* **2** the act or an instance of swooshing: *We heard a swoosh as the water rushed into the tank.*

swop (swop) *v.* **swopped, swop·ping;** *n.* See **swap.** —**swop′per,** *n.*

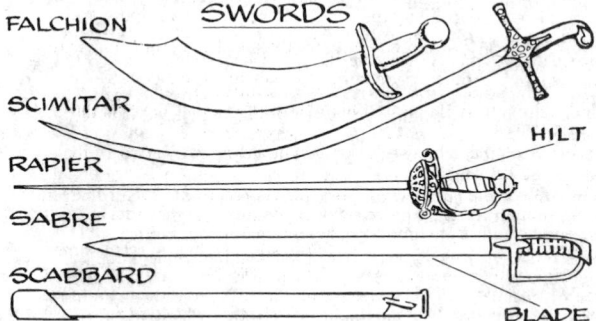

SWORDS
FALCHION
SCIMITAR
RAPIER
SABRE
SCABBARD
HILT
BLADE

sword (sôrd) *n.* **1** a hand weapon, usually metal, with a long sharp blade fixed in a handle or hilt. **2** something resembling a sword, such as the elongated upper jawbone of the swordfish. **3** a symbol of power or authority. **4** a symbol of honor or authority: *the sword of justice.* **5 the sword,** war or military power: *The pen is mightier than the sword. The conqueror ruled by the sword.*

at sword's points, very unfriendly; ready to fight or quarrel.

cross swords, a fight or quarrel: *I wouldn't want to cross swords with him; he's mean.*

draw the sword, begin a war.

put to the sword, kill, especially in war: *He put his captives to the sword.*

[OE *sweord*] —**sword′like′,** *adj.*

sword dance any dance performed with swords or over swords laid on the ground.

hat, āge, fär; let, ēqual, tėrm; it, īce
hot, ōpen, ôrder; oil, out; cup, put, rüle,
əbove, takən, pencəl, lemən, circəs

ch, child; ng, long; sh, ship
th, thin; ᴛʜ, then; zh, measure

sword·fish (sôrd′fish′) *n., pl.* **-fish** or **-fish·es.** a very large food and game fish (*Xiphias gladius*) found in tropical and temperate seas throughout the world, having a tall, scaleless back fin, a crescent-shaped tail fin and a very long, flat, swordlike upper jawbone with which it slashes and pierces its prey. It comprises the family Xiphiidae, distantly related to the martins and tunas.

sword grass any of various grasses or plants having swordlike leaves.

sword knot a looped strap, ribbon, etc. attached to the hilt of a sword, serving as a means of supporting it from the wrist or as an ornament.

Sword of Damocles an imminent danger. See **Damocles.**

sword·play (sôrd′plā′) *n.* the action, practice, or art of wielding a sword, especially in fencing.

swords·man (sôrdz′mən) *n., pl.* **-men. 1** a person skilled in using a sword. **2** a person using a sword.

swords·man·ship (sôrdz′mən ship′) *n.* skill in using a sword.

sword·tail (sôrd′tāl′) *n.* any of several small, tropical freshwater fishes (genus *Xiphophorus*), especially a brightly colored Central American species (*X. helleri*) having a long, swordlike extension on the tail fin. Swordtails are bred in many colors for keeping in aquariums.

swore (swôr) *v.* pt. of **swear.**

sworn (swôrn) *v., adj.* —*v.* pp. of **swear.** —*adj.* **1** having taken an oath; bound by an oath. **2** declared, promised, etc. with an oath.

swot (swot) *v.* **swot·ted, swot·ting;** *n. Slang.* —*v.* study very hard. —*n.* **1** hard work, especially hard study at schoolwork. **2** a person who studies hard and constantly. [apparently Scottish variant of *sweat*]

swound (swound) *v.* or *n. Archaic.* swoon; faint.

'swounds (zwoundz *or* zoundz) *interj. Archaic.* a shortened form of *God's wounds,* used as an oath.

swum (swum) *v.* pp. of **swim.**

swung (swung) *v.* pt. and pp. of **swing.**

sy- the form of **syn-** before *s* plus a consonant, as in *system.*

syb·a·rite (sib′ə rīt′) *n.* a person who cares very much for luxury and pleasure. [< *Sybarite,* an inhabitant of *Sybaris,* an ancient Greek city in Italy known for its luxury]

syb·a·rit·ic (sib′ə rit′ik) *adj.* luxurious; voluptuous.

syc·a·more (sik′ə môr′) *n.* **1** any of a genus (*Platanus*) of trees comprising the North American and Eurasian plane tree family (Platanaceae); especially, a large North American hardwood tree (*P. occidentalis*) having broad, lobed leaves, spreading branches, and brownish outer bark that flakes off in large, irregular patches, revealing the whitish inner bark. **2** a large Eurasian maple (*Acer pseudoplatanus*) having spreading branches and broad leaves. It is also called the sycamore maple. **3** a fig tree (*Ficus sycamorus*) of Egypt and Asia Minor having a sweetish, edible fruit. It is the sycamore mentioned in the Bible. [ME < OF < L *sycomorus* < Gk. *sykomoros*]

syc·o·phan·cy (sik′ə fən sē) *n., pl.* **-cies.** servile, self-seeking flattery.

syc·o·phant (sik′ə fənt) *n.* a servile, self-seeking flatterer; toady. [< L < Gk. *sykophantēs* informer, slanderer (originally, one who makes the insulting gesture of the "fig," i.e., sticking the thumb between index and middle finger) < *sykon* fig, vulva + *phainein* show]

syc·o·phan·tic (sik′ə fan′tik) *adj.* having to do with, characteristic of, or acting as a sycophant. —**syco′phan′ti·cal·ly,** *adv.*

sy·e·nite (sī′ə nīt′) *n.* a grey crystalline rock composed of feldspar and hornblende. [< L < Gk. *Syēnitēs* (*lithos*) (stone) from *Syēnē* (now Aswan), a city in Egypt]

syl- the form of **syn-** before *l,* as in *syllogism.*

syl. or **syll. 1** syllable. **2** syllabus.

syl·lab·ic (sə lab′ik) *adj., n.* —*adj.* **1** of, having to do with, based on, or consisting of syllables. **2** forming a syllable or the nucleus of a syllable. The second *l* in *little* is syllabic; it forms a separate syllable. **3** pronounced syllable by syllable. **4** *Prosody.* designating verse based on the number of syllables in a line rather than on the arrangement of stresses or quantities.

—n. **1** a syllabic speech sound. **2** a written sign or character representing a syllable. —**syl·lab′i·cal·ly,** adv.

syl·lab·i·cate (sə lab′ə kāt′) v. **-cat·ed, -cat·ing.** form or divide into syllables; syllabicate.

syl·lab·i·ca·tion (sə lab′ə kā′shən) n. the process of dividing into syllables; division into syllables.

syl·lab·i·fi·ca·tion (sə lab′ə fə kā′shən) n. syllabication.

syl·lab·i·fy (sə lab′ə fī′) v. **-fied, -fy·ing.** syllabicate.

syl·la·bize (sil′ə bīz′) v. **-bized, -biz·ing. 1** form or divide into syllables. **2** utter with careful distinction of syllables.

syl·la·ble (sil′ə bəl) n., v. **-bled, -bling.** —n. **1** a word or part of a word spoken as a unit, usually consisting of a vowel sound alone or a vowel sound with one or more consonant sounds. *See* is a word of one syllable, consisting of a consonant sound (s) plus a vowel sound (ē). *Syllable* is a word of three syllables (sil′ə bəl). **2** in writing or printing, a letter or group of letters corresponding roughly to a syllable of spoken language. The syllables of the entry word *syllable* in this dictionary are separated by dots: **syl·la·ble.** A word that has to be broken at the end of a line is usually hyphenated between two syllables. **3** the slightest bit or detail of something: *He promised not to breathe a syllable of the secret to anyone.* —v. pronounce or utter in or as if in syllables. [ME < OF < L < Gk. *syllabē,* originally, a taking together < *syn-* together + *labein* take]

syl·la·bub (sil′ə bub′) See **sillabub.**

syl·la·bus (sil′ə bəs) n., pl. **-bus·es, -bi** (-bī′ or -bē′). a brief statement of the main points of a speech, a book, a course of study, etc. [< NL *syllabus,* erroneous reading of L and Gk. *sittyba* parchment label]

syl·lo·gism (sil′ə jiz′əm) n. **1** a form of argument or reasoning consisting of two statements and a conclusion drawn from them. *Example: All trees have roots; an oak is a tree; therefore, an oak has roots.* **2** a reasoning in this form; deduction. **3** a specious or very subtle argument; a deviously crafty piece of reasoning. [< L < Gk. *syllogismos,* originally, inference, ult. < *syn-* together + *logos* a reckoning]

syl·lo·gis·tic (sil′ə jis′tik) adj. of, having to do with, or using syllogisms. —**syl′lo·gis′ti·cal·ly,** adv.

syl·lo·gize (sil′ə jīz′) v. **-gized, -giz·ing. 1** argue or reason by syllogisms. **2** deduce by syllogism.

sylph (silf) n. **1** a slender, graceful girl or woman. **2** in the ancient Greek theory of the four elements, the spirit that inhabited the air. [< NL *sylphes,* pl.; a coinage of Paracelsus (1493?-1541), a Swiss alchemist and physician] —**sylph′like′,** adj.

syl·va (sil′və) See **silva.**

syl·van (sil′vən) adj. **1** of, having to do with, or characteristic of the woods. **2** living or situated in the woods: *a sylvan retreat.* [< L *silvanus < silva* forest]

syl·vat·ic (sil vat′ik) adj. **1** of, belonging to, or found in woods; sylvan: *sylvatic animals.* **2** of or carried by insects or animals that are found in woods or forests: *sylvatic plague.*

syl·vi·cul·ture (sil′və kul′chər) n. silviculture.

syl·vite (sil′vīt) n. a mineral, potassium chloride, occurring in cubic crystals, an important source of potassium. *Formula:* Cl [< NL (*sal digestivus*) *sylvii* digestive salt of *Sylvius* (probably after François de la Boe *Sylvius* (1614-1672), a Flemish anatomist) + E -*ite*[1]]

sym– prefix. the form of **syn-** occurring before *b, m, p,* as in *symbol, symmetry, sympathy.*

sym. **1** symbol. **2** symmetrical. **3** symphony. **4** symptom.

sym·bi·o·sis (sim′bī ō′sis or sim′bē ō′sis) n. the association or living together of two unlike organisms in a relationship that benefits each of them. The lichen, which is composed of an alga and a fungus, is an example of symbiosis; the alga provides the food, and the fungus provides water and protection. [< NL < Gk. *symbiōsis,* ult. < *syn-* together + *bios* life]

sym·bi·ot·ic (sim′bī ot′ik or sim′bē ot′ik) adj. having to do with or living in symbiosis.

sym·bol (sim′bəl) n., v. **-boled, -bol·ing** or **-bolled, -bol·ling.** —n. **1** something that stands for or represents an idea, quality, condition, or other abstraction: *The lion is the symbol of courage; the lamb, of meekness; the olive branch, of peace; the cross, of Christianity.* **2** a letter, figure, or sign conventionally used in writing or printing, standing for a process, object, quantity, relation, etc.: *The marks +, −, ×, and ÷ are symbols for add, subtract, multiply, and divide.* —v. symbolize. [< L < Gk. *symbolon* token, ult.

< *syn-* together + *ballein* throw]
☛ *Hom.* **cymbal.**
☛ *Syn.* n. **1.** See note at **emblem.**

sym·bol·ic (sim bol′ik) adj. **1** used as a symbol: *The maple leaf is symbolic of Canada.* **2** of, expressed by, or using symbols: *Writing is a symbolic form of expression.* —**sym·bol′i·cal·ly,** adv.

sym·bol·i·cal (sim bol′ə kəl) adj. symbolic.

symbolic logic a method in formal logic that uses a formalized language, or calculus, to represent terms and relationships, permitting a precision in the formulation and analysis of propositions that is not possible in ordinary language.

sym·bol·ism (sim′bəl iz′əm) n. **1** the use of conventional or traditional signs, etc. to represent things, especially things that are abstract or invisible; representation by symbols. **2** a system of symbols: *The cross, the crown, the lamb, and the lily are parts of Christian symbolism.* **3** a symbolic meaning or character. **4** a movement in art and literature seeking to express ideas, feelings, or states of mind through the symbolic use of objects, shapes, words, etc.

sym·bol·ist (sim′bəl ist) n. **1** a person who uses symbols or symbolism. **2** an artist or writer who makes much use of colors, sounds, etc. as symbols. **3** a person who is skilled in the study or interpretation of symbols.

sym·bol·is·tic (sim′bəl is′tik) adj. of symbolism or symbolists.

sym·bol·i·za·tion (sim′bəl ə zā′shən or -ī zā′shən) n. a symbolizing; representation by symbols.

sym·bol·ize (sim′bəl īz′) v. **-ized, -iz·ing. 1** be a symbol of; stand for; represent: *A dove symbolizes peace.* **2** represent or express by a symbol or symbols: *We symbolize the chemical composition of water by the formula H_2O.* **3** use symbols. —**sym′bol·iz′er,** n.

sym·bol·o·gy (sim bol′ə jē) n. **1** the science or study of symbols. **2** the use of symbols; symbolism. [< NL *symbologia* < Gk. *symbolon* + NL -*logia* -logy. See SYMBOL.]

sym·met·ric (si met′rik) adj. symmetrical.

sym·met·ri·cal (si met′rə kəl) adj. **1** having or showing symmetry: *a symmetrical design, a symmetrical curve. The tree on our front lawn has an almost symmetrical crown.* **2** of a flower: **a** having the same number of parts in each whorl. **b** divisible vertically into similar halves. **3** *Chemistry.* having a structural formula characterized by symmetry. **4** *Logic and mathematics.* of propositions, equations, etc., so constituted that the truth or value is not changed by interchanging the terms. **5** of a disease, affecting corresponding organs or parts at the same time, such as both arms or both lungs or both ears equally. —**sym·met′ri·cal·ly,** adv.

sym·me·trize (sim′ə trīz′) v. **-trized, -triz·ing.** reduce to symmetry; make symmetrical.

sym·me·try (sim′ə trē) n., pl. **-tries. 1** a regular, balanced arrangement on opposite sides of a line or plane, or around a centre or axis. **2** pleasing proportions between the parts of a whole; well-balanced arrangement of parts; harmony. **3** *Botany.* agreement in number of parts along the cycles of organs that compose a flower. [< L < Gk. *symmetria < syn-* together + *metron* measure]

sym·pa·thet·ic (sim′pə thet′ik) adj. **1** having or showing kind feelings toward others; sympathizing. **2** inclined to agree or approve; favorably inclined: *They are sympathetic to our idea.* **3** enjoying the same things and getting along well together; congenial: *He enjoys the skating club because he finds most of the members sympathetic.* —**sym′pa·thet′i·cal·ly,** adv.

sym·pa·thize (sim′pə thīz′) v. **-thized, -thiz·ing. 1** feel or show sympathy: *sympathize with a child who has hurt himself.* **2** share in or agree with a feeling or opinion: *My mother sympathizes with my plan to be a doctor.* **3** enjoy the same things and get along well together. **4** respond sympathetically to some influence or to some disorder of the body. [< F *sympathiser < sympathie* sympathy] —**sym′pa·thiz′ing·ly,** adv.

sym·pa·thiz·er (sim′pə thīz′ər) n. a person who sympathizes; especially, a person who is favorably inclined toward a particular belief or person.

sym·pa·thy (sim′pə thē) n., pl. **-thies. 1** a sharing of another's sorrow or trouble: *We feel sympathy for a person who is ill.* **2** an agreement in feeling; the condition or fact of having the same feeling: *The sympathy between the twins was so great that they always smiled or cried at the same things.* **3** agreement; approval; favor: *He is in sympathy with my plan.* **4 a** an affinity between certain things, whereby they are similarly or correspondingly affected by the same influence. **b** an action or response induced by such a relationship. [< L < Gk. *sympatheia < syn-* together + *pathos* feeling]
☛ *Syn.* **1.** See note at **pity.**

sym·pet·al·ous (sim pet′əl əs) adj. gamopetalous.

sym·phon·ic (sim fon′ik) adj. **1** of, having to do with, or having

the character of a symphony: *a symphonic composition.* **2** of or having to do with harmony of sounds; harmonious.

symphonic poem *Music.* a free-form composition for symphony orchestra, usually consisting of only one movement and usually descriptive or rhapsodic in character, often attempting to translate a literary or pictorial idea.

sym·pho·ni·ous (sim fō′nē əs) *adj.* harmonious.

sym·pho·ny (sim′fə nē) *n., pl.* **-nies. 1** a long and elaborate musical composition for a full orchestra. A symphony is usually in the form of a sonata, with three or four movements that are different in rhythm and speed but related in key. **2** symphony orchestra. **3** *Informal.* a concert given by a symphony orchestra. **4** a harmony of sounds. **5** a harmony of colors: *In autumn the woods are a symphony in red, brown, and yellow.* [ME < OF < L < Gk. *symphōnia* harmony, concert, band < *syn-* together + *phōnē* voice, sound]

symphony orchestra a large orchestra for playing symphonies and similar works, made up of brass, woodwind, percussion, and stringed instruments.

sym·phy·sis (sim′fə sis) *n., pl.* **-ses. 1** *Anatomy.* **a** a union of two bones or other parts originally separate, especially of two similar bones on opposite sides of the body, such as the pubic bones or the two halves of the lower jawbone. **b** the line of junction thus formed. **2** *Botany.* a fusion of parts of a plant that are normally separate. [< Gk. *symphysis* growing together < *symphyein* to unite < *syn* together + *phyein* grow]

sym·po·si·um (sim pō′zē əm) *n., pl.* **-si·ums** or **-si·a** (-zē ə). **1** a collection of the opinions of several persons on some subject: *This magazine contains a symposium on sports.* **2** a formal meeting at which several specialists give their views on a subject. **3** in ancient Greece, an after-dinner drinking party. [< L < Gk. *symposion* < *syn-* together + *posis* drinking]

symp·tom (simp′təm) *n.* **1** something that indicates the existence of something else; sign: *symptoms of discontent.* **2** a noticeable change in the normal working of the body that indicates or accompanies disease or injury: *The doctor made his diagnosis after studying the patient's symptoms.* [< LL < Gk. *symptōma* a happening, ult. < *syn-* together + *piptein* fall]

symp·to·mat·ic (simp′tə mat′ik) *adj.* **1** being a sign; indicative or characteristic: *Riots are symptomatic of political or social unrest.* **2** indicating or accompanying a disease, etc.: *The infection caused a symptomatic fever.* **3** having to do with symptoms of disease, etc. —**symp′to·mat′i·cal·ly,** *adv.*

syn– *prefix.* with, jointly, or at the same time, as in *synchronous, synopsis,* and *synthesis.* Also: **sy-** before *s* plus a consonant; **syl-** before *l;* **sym-** before *b, m, p.* [< Gk. *syn* with, together]

syn. synonym; synonymous.

syn·a·gogue (sin′ə gog′) *n.* **1** a building used by a Jewish congregation as a house of worship and religious instruction. **2** a Jewish congregation or assembly. **3** Judaism as a whole. [ME < LL < Gk. *synagōgē,* literally, assembly, ult. < *syn-* together + *agein* bring]

syn·apse (si naps′ or sin′aps) *n. Physiology.* a place where a nerve impulse passes from one nerve cell to another. [< Gk. *synapsis* conjunction < *syn-* together + *haptein* fasten]

sync (singk) *n., v.* **synced, sync·ing.** *Informal.* —*n.* synchronization of sound and action or of speech and lip movement, as in television or motion pictures.
in sync, synchronized.
out of sync, not synchronized. —*v.* synchronize.
☛ *Hom.* **sink.**

syn·chro·mesh (sing′krə mesh′) *n.* in an automobile, a gear or system of gears so constructed as to mesh with a minimum of friction and noise when the driver shifts from one speed to another. [< *synchro*nous + *mesh*]

syn·chro·nal (sing′krə nəl) *adj.* synchronous.

syn·chron·ic (sin kron′ik or sing kron′ik) *adj.* **1** concerned with a subject or with phenomena from a strictly descriptive point of view without reference to historical causes or antecedents: *synchronic linguistics.* Compare **diachronic. 2** synchronous.

syn·chro·nism (sing′krə niz′əm) *n.* **1** the quality or state of being synchronous. **2** an arrangement of historical events or persons according to their dates.

syn·chro·nize (sing′krə nīz′) *v.* **-nized, -niz·ing. 1** happen at the same time; be simultaneous; coincide. **2** make occur or operate at the same time or speed: *to synchronize all the clocks in the building, to synchronize the flash with the camera shutter, to synchronize the sound with the action in a motion picture.* **3** establish or show the correspondence of the dates of (events). [< Gk. *synchronizein* < *synchronos* synchronous. See SYNCHRONOUS.] —**syn′chro·ni·za′tion,** *n.* —**syn′chro·niz′er,** *n.*

hat, āge, fär; let, ēqual, tèrm; it, īce
hot, ōpen, ôrder; oil, out; cup, pút, rüle,
əbove, takən, pencəl, lemən, circəs

ch, child; ng, long; sh, ship
th, thin; ŧH, then; zh, measure

syn·chro·nous (sing′krə nəs) *adj.* **1** occurring or existing at exactly the same time; simultaneous. **2** moving or taking place at the same rate and exactly together. **3** *Physics.* having coincident periods, or coincident periods and phases, as an alternating electric current. [< LL < Gk. *synchronos* < *syn-* together + *chronos* time] —**syn′chro·nous·ly,** *adv.*

syn·chro·tron (sing′krə tron′) *n.* a type of accelerator that accelerates electrified particles by means of a varying magnetic field and an alternating high-frequency electric field. [< *synchro*nous + *-tron* as in electron]

syn·cli·nal (sin klī′nəl or sing′klə nəl) *adj.* **1** sloping downward from opposite directions so as to form a trough or inverted arch. **2** of, having to do with, or containing a syncline. [< Gk. *synklinein* lean, incline < *syn-* together + *klinein* bend]

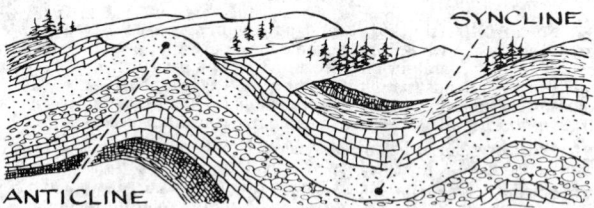

Layers of sedimentary rock forming synclines and anticlines

syn·cline (sing′klīn) *n. Geology.* a downward fold, or trough, of stratified rock, in which the layers slope upward in opposite directions from the centre. Compare **anticline.**

syn·co·pate (sing′kə pāt′) *v.* **-pat·ed, -pat·ing. 1** *Music.*
a change a regular rhythm by beginning a note on an unaccented beat and holding it into an accented one or beginning it midway through a beat and continuing it midway into the next one.
b introduce such shifted accents into a passage or piece of music. **2** *Linguistics.* shorten a word by syncope. [< LL *syncopare* < *syncope.* See SYNCOPE.]

syn·co·pa·tion (sing′kə pā′shən) *n.* **1** *Music.* **a** the action or art of syncopating a musical rhythm or piece of music: *Syncopation is much used in jazz.* **b** a syncopated rhythm, piece of music, etc. **2** *Linguistics.* syncope.

syn·co·pe (sing′kə pē′) *n.* **1** *Linguistics.* the contraction of a word by the loss or omission of a sound or sounds from the middle, as *batt'ry* for *battery.* **2** a temporary loss of consciousness due to an inadequate supply of blood to the brain, caused by illness, extreme pain or emotion, etc.; fainting. [< LL < Gk. *synkopē,* originally, a cutting off, ult. < *syn-* together + *koptein* cut]

syn·cret·ic (sin kret′ik) *adj.* of or having to do with syncretism; characterized by syncretism.

syn·cre·tism (sing′krə tiz′əm) *n.* **1** a tendency or effort to reconcile different religious or philosophical beliefs, or to absorb some of the tenets of one into the system of another. **2** *Linguistics.* the fusion of originally different inflectional categories. **3** the doctrines of George Calixtus (1586-1656), a Lutheran who aimed at uniting Protestant sects and, eventually, all Christendom. [< NL < Gk. *synkrētismos* (< *synkrētizein* combine, ally, apparently originally as in a union or federation of Cretan communities < *Krēs, Krētos* Crete)]

syn·cre·tis·tic (sing′krə tis′tik) *adj.* of, having to do with, or characterized by syncretism.

syn·cre·tize (sing′krə tīz′) *v.* **-tized, -tiz·ing.** combine or attempt to combine different systems, philosophical or religious beliefs, etc. [< NL *syncretizare* < Gk. *synkrētizein.* See SYNCRETISM.]

syn·dic (sin′dik) *n.* **1** a person who manages the business affairs of a university or other corporation. **2** a government official or chief magistrate. [< LL < Gk. *syndikos* advocate < *syn-* together + *dikē* justice]

syn·di·cal·ism (sin′də kəl iz′əm) *n.* a movement in industrial unions aimed at taking control of industry and government by direct means such as a general strike.

syn·di·cal·ist (sin′də kəl ist) *n.* a person who favors or supports syndicalism.

syn·di·cate (*n.* sin′də kit; *v.* sin′də kāt′) *n., v.* **-cat·ed, -cat·ing.** —*n.* **1** a combination of persons or companies to carry out some undertaking, especially one requiring a large capital investment. **2** an agency that sells special articles, photographs, etc. to a large number of newspapers or magazines for publication at the same time. **3** a group of businesses, especially newspapers, under one management. **4** an association or combination of criminals controlling organized crime. —*v.* **1** combine into a syndicate. **2** manage by a syndicate. **3** publish through a syndicate. [< F *syndicat* < *syndic* < LL *syndicus.* See SYNDIC.]

syn·di·ca·tion (sin′də kā′shən) *n.* the act of syndicating or the condition of being syndicated.

syn·drome (sin′drōm) *n.* **1** *Medicine.* a number of symptoms that taken together indicate the presence of a specific condition or disease. **2** any set of ideas, attitudes, or customs that together indicate a state of mind, pattern of behavior, etc.: *the beatnik syndrome.* [< NL < Gk. *syndromē,* literally, a running together < *syn-* with + *dromos* course, related to *dramein* run]

syne (sīn) *adv., prep.,* or *conj. Scottish.* since.
☛ *Hom.* sign, sine.

syn·ec·do·che (si nek′də kē′) *n.* a figure of speech by which a part is put for the whole, or the whole for a part, the special for the general, or the general for the special. *Examples: a factory employing 500 hands (persons); to eat of the* tree *(its fruit); a* Solomon *(wise man); a* marble *(a statue) on its pedestal.* [< LL < Gk. *synekdochē,* ult. < *syn-* with + *ek-* out + *dechesthai* receive]

syn·er·gism (sin′ər jiz′əm) *n.* synergy. [< NL *syn- ergismus* < Gk. *synergéin* work together. See SYNERGY.]

syn·er·gy (sin′ər jē) *n., pl.* **-ies.** the combined or co-operative action of two or more agents, groups, or parts, etc. that together increase each other's effectiveness: *the synergy of the muscles of the body.* [< NL < Gk. *synergia* joint work < *syn- ergéin* work together < *syn-* together + *ergon* work]

syn·od (sin′əd) *n.* **1** an assembly called together under authority to discuss and decide church affairs; a church council. **2** a court of the Presbyterian Church ranking next above the presbytery. **3** an assembly; convention; council. [< LL < Gk. *synodos* assembly, meeting < *syn-* together + *hodos* a going]

syn·od·al (sin′əd əl) *adj.* of, having to do with, or made by a synod: *a synodal assembly, a synodal decree.*

syn·od·ic (si nod′ik) *adj.* synodical.

syn·od·i·cal (si nod′ə kəl) *adj.* **1** having to do with the conjunctions of the heavenly bodies. The synodical period of the moon is the time between one new moon and the next. **2** synodal.

syn·o·nym (sin′ə nim′) *n.* **1** one of two or more words of a language having the same or nearly the same meaning. *St. Vitus's dance* and *chorea* are synonyms. *Sharp* is a synonym for one meaning of *keen; enthusiastic* is a synonym for another meaning of *keen.* Compare **antonym. 2** a word or expression generally accepted as another name for something: *Churchill's name has become a synonym for patriotic devotion to one's country.* [ME < LL < Gk. *synōnymon,* originally adj., neut. of *synōnymos* synonymous. See SYNONYMOUS.]

syn·on·y·mous (si non′ə məs) *adj.* having the same or nearly the same meaning. The words *velocity* and *speed* are synonymous. [< Med.L < Gk. *synōnymos* < *syn-* together + dial. *onyma* name] —**syn·on′y·mous·ly,** *adv.*

syn·on·y·my (si non′ə mē) *n., pl.* **-mies. 1** the quality or state of being synonymous. **2** the study of synonyms. **3** the use of synonyms together in discourse for emphasis or amplification. *Example: in any shape or form.* **4** a set, list, or system of synonyms.

syn·op·sis (si nop′sis) *n., pl.* **-ses** (-sēz). a brief statement giving a general view of some subject, book, play, etc.; summary. [< LL < Gk. *synopsis* < *syn-* together + *opsis* a view]

syn·op·size (si nop′sīz) *v.* make a synopsis of.

syn·op·tic (si nop′tik) *adj.* **1** giving a general view. **2** Often, **Synoptic.** taking a common view. *Matthew, Mark,* and *Luke* are called the **Synoptic Gospels** because they are much alike in content, order, and statement.

syn·op·ti·cal (si nop′tə kəl) *adj.* synoptic.

syn·op·ti·cal·ly (si nop′tik lē) *adv.* in a synoptic manner; so as to give a general view.

syn·o·vi·a (si nō′vē ə) *n. Physiology.* a lubricating liquid secreted by certain membranes, such as those of the joints. [< NL *synovia;* coinage of Paracelsus (1493?-1541), a Swiss alchemist and physician]

syn·o·vi·al (si nō′vē əl) *adj.* consisting of, containing, or secreting synovia: *synovial fluid, a synovial membrane.*

syn·o·vi·tis (sin′ə vī′tis) *n.* inflammation of a synovial membrane.

syn·tac·tic (sin tak′tik) *adj.* of, having to do with, or according to the rules of syntax.

syn·tac·ti·cal (sin tak′tə kəl) *adj.* syntactic. —**syn·tac′ti·cal·ly,** *adv.*

syn·tax (sin′taks) *n. Grammar.* **1** the way in which words are arranged to form sentences, clauses, or phrases; sentence structure. **2** the patterns of such arrangement in a given language. **3** the use or function of a word, phrase, or clause in a sentence. **4** the part of grammar dealing with the construction of phrases, clauses, and sentences. [< LL < Gk. *syntaxis,* ult. < *syn-* together + *tassein* arrange]

syn·the·ses (sin′thə sēz) *n.* pl. of **synthesis.**

syn·the·sis (sin′thə sis) *n., pl.* **-ses. 1** a combination of parts or elements into a whole. Compare **analysis. 2** the combination produced in this way. **3** *Chemistry.* the formation of a compound by the chemical union of chemical elements, combination of simpler compounds, etc. Alcohol, ammonia, rubber, etc. can be artificially produced by synthesis. **3** *Philosophy and logic.* **a** the combination or unification of particular phenomena, observed or hypothesized, into a general body or abstract whole. **b** as used by the German philosopher Immanuel Kant (1724-1804), the action of the understanding in combining and unifying the isolated data of sensation into a cognizable whole. **c** deductive reasoning. **d** the third and highest stage in the Hegelian dialect, the combination of thesis and antithesis for a new, higher truth. [< L < Gk. *synthesis* < *syn-* together + *tithenai* put]

syn·the·size (sin′thə sīz′) *v.* **-sized, -siz·ing. 1** combine into a complex whole by synthesis. **2** form or produce by synthesis: *to synthesize rubber.* —**syn′the·si·za′tion,** *n.*

syn·the·siz·er (sin′thə sīz′ər) *n.* **1** a person or thing that synthesizes. **2** an electronic device that simulates and blends conventional and ultrasonic sounds.

syn·thet·ic (sin thet′ik) *adj., n.* —*adj.* **1** having to do with synthesis: *synthetic chemistry.* **2** made by chemical synthesis: *synthetic rubies, synthetic silk.* **3** *Linguistics.* designating a language characterized by the use of affixes and inflectional endings rather than by the use of separate words, such as auxiliary verbs and prepositions, to express the same concepts. Latin is a synthetic language, while English is analytic. For example, the Latin *amabitur* expresses in one word the English *he will be loved.* **4** not real or genuine; artificial: *synthetic affection.* —*n.* a substance or material made by chemical synthesis. Synthetics are very common for clothing, etc. because they are easy to care for.
☛ *Syn.* **2.** See note at **artificial.**

syn·thet·i·cal (sin thet′ə kəl) *adj.* synthetic. —**syn·thet′i·cal·ly,** *adv.*

synthetic rubber any of numerous elastic substances resembling natural rubber, made from various chemicals, such as butadiene and styrene (for general-purpose synthetic rubber); ethylene, propylene, etc. (for polyurethane rubber); or oxygen and silicon (for silicone rubber).

syph·i·lis (sif′ə lis) *n.* a contagious venereal disease caused by a spirochete (*Trepenema pallidum*), characterized by a long progress in three main stages over many years and finally, if untreated, causing bones, muscles, and nerve tissue to degenerate. Syphilis is usually transmitted through sexual intercourse. It is not hereditary, but can be transmitted inside the womb from mother to child. [< NL *syphilis* < *Syphilus,* the hero of a Latin poem describing the disease, written in 1530 by Fracastoro, a physician and poet of Verona, Italy]

syph·i·lit·ic (sif′ə lit′ik) *adj., n.* —*adj.* **1** having to do with syphilis. **2** affected with syphilis. —*n.* a person affected with syphilis.

sy·phon (sī′fən) See **siphon.**

Syr·i·ac (sir′ē ak) *n.* a dialect of Aramaic spoken in ancient Syria and surviving as a liturgical language used in a number of Eastern churches.

Syr·i·an (sir′ē ən) *n., adj.* —*n.* **1** a native or inhabitant of Syria, a country in SW Asia on the Mediterranean. **2** a native or inhabitant of ancient Syria, a region between the E Mediterranean coast and the desert of N Arabia. —*adj.* of or having to do with modern or ancient Syria or its people.

sy·rin·ga (sə ring′gə) *n.* **1** mock orange. **2** lilac. *Syringa* is the scientific name for the genus of shrubs and trees commonly called lilacs; unfortunately, botanists chose a name that was already in use as a common name for the unrelated mock orange, thus creating some confusion. [< NL *syringa* < Gk. *syrinx, -ingos* shepherd's pipe]

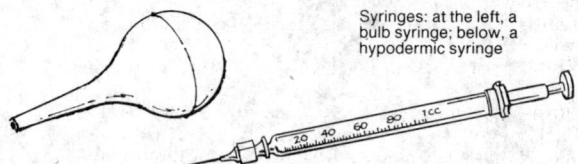
Syringes: at the left, a bulb syringe; below, a hypodermic syringe

hat, āge, fär; let, ēqual, tèrm; it, īce
hot, ōpen, ôrder; oil, out; cup, put, rule,
above, takən, pencəl, lemən, circəs

ch, child; ng, long; sh, ship
th, thin; ŦH, then; zh, measure

sy·ringe (sə rinj′) *n., v.* **-ringed, -ring·ing.** —*n.* **1** a device consisting of a narrow tube with a nozzle at one end and a compressible rubber bulb at the other, for drawing in a quantity of fluid and then forcing it out in a stream. Syringes are used to clean wounds, inject fluids into body cavities, etc. **2** a similar device consisting of a hollow needle attached to a hollow barrel with a plunger, used for injecting medicine under the skin, withdrawing body fluids, etc; hypodermic syringe. —*v.* clean, wash, inject, etc. by means of a syringe. [< Gk. *syrinx, -ingos* pipe]

syr·inx (sir′ingks) *n., pl.* **sy·rin·ges** (sə rin′jēz) **or syr·inx·es. 1** the vocal organ of birds, situated where the trachea divides into the right and left bronchi. **2** panpipe. [< L < Gk. *syrinx* shepherd's pipe]

syr·up (sèr′əp *or* sir′əp) *n.* **1** a thick solution of sugar and water, usually combined with flavoring or medicine: *cough syrup.* **2** condensed juice of a plant or fruit; especially, sugar cane juice that remains uncrystallized in the refining of sugar, or the juice condensed from the sap of the sugar maple. **3** *Informal.* excessive sweetness of style or manner. [ME < OF *sirop* < Arabic *sharāb* drink] —**syr′up·like′,** *adj.*

syr·up·y (sèr′əp ē *or* sir′əp ē) *adj.* **1** of, like, or suggesting syrup in consistency or sweetness. **2** excessively sweet in style or manner; cloying.

sys·tem (sis′təm) *n.* **1** a set of things or parts forming a whole: *a mountain system, a railway system, the digestive system.* **2** an ordered group of facts, principles, beliefs, etc.: *a system of government, a system of education.* **3** a theory or hypothesis, especially of the relationship of the heavenly bodies by which their observed movements and phenomena are explained: *the Copernican system.* **4** a plan; scheme; method: *a system for betting.* **5** an orderly way of getting things done. **6** *Biology.* **a** a set of organs or parts in an animal body of the same or similar structure, or subserving the same function: *the nervous system, the respiratory system.* **b** the animal body as an organized whole; the organism in relation to its vital processes or functions: *to take food into the system.* **7** a group of heavenly bodies forming a whole that follows certain natural laws. **8** the world; universe. **9** *Geology.* a major division of rocks including two or more series, and formed during a geological period. **10** *Chemistry.* **a** an assemblage of substances which are in, or tend to approach, equilibrium. **b** a substance, or an assemblage of substances, considered as a separate entity for the purpose of restricted study. **11** *Music.* a set of staves linked by a brace. [< LL < Gk. *systēma* < *syn-* together + *stēsai* cause to stand] —**sys′tem·less,** *adj.*

sys·tem·at·ic (sis′tə mat′ik) *adj.* **1** based on, involving, or forming a system: *a systematic investigation, a systematic classification.* **2** orderly and methodical: *She is a systematic worker.*

sys·tem·at·i·cal (sis′təm at′ə kəl) *adj.* systematic.

sys·tem·at·i·cal·ly (sis′tə mat′ik lē) *adv.* in a systematic manner.

sys·tem·a·tize (sis′təm ə tīz′) *v.* **-tized, -tiz·ing.** arrange according to a system; make into a system: *to systematize one's methods.* —**sys′tem·a·ti·za′tion,** *n.* —**sys′tem·a·tiz′er,** *n.*

sys·tem·ic (sis tem′ik) *adj.* **1** of, having to do with, or affecting the body as a whole. **2** of or having to do with the general blood circulation, except for that supplied to the lungs through the pulmonary artery. **3** of an insecticide, fungicide, etc., entering the tissues of a plant and making the plant itself poisonous to pests. **4** a systemic pesticide.

sys·tem·ize (sis′təm īz′) *v.* **-ized, -iz·ing.** systematize. —**sys′tem·i·za′tion,** *n.*

systems analysis the process or profession of using mathematical techniques to break down a complex activity into basic elements in order to discover ways for the goal or purpose of the activity to be accomplished most efficiently. Systems analysis is used for business organizations, technical procedures, etc.

systems analyst a person whose work is systems analysis.

sys·to·le (sis′tə lē′) *n. Physiology.* the normal rhythmical contraction of the heart. [< NL < Gk. *systolē* contraction < *syn-* together + *stellein* wrap]

sys·tol·ic (sis tol′ik) *adj.* of or having to do with a contraction of the heart.

syz·y·gy (siz′ə jē) *n., pl.* **-gies.** either of the two points (opposition or conjunction) in the orbit of the moon or a planet when it lies approximately in a straight line with the earth and the sun. [< LL *syzygia* < Gk. < *syzygos* yoked, paired < *syn-* together + *zygon* yoke]

Tt

t or **T** (tē) *n., pl.* **t's** or **T's. 1** the twentieth letter of the English alphabet. **2** any speech sound represented by this letter. **3** a person or thing identified as *t*, especially the twentieth in a series. **4** something shaped like the letter T. **5** (*adj.*) of or being a T or t. **to a T,** exactly; perfectly: *That suits me to a T.*

t 1 tonne(s). **2** *t*, temperature (common, or Celsius). **3** *t*, time.

t. 1 teaspoon(s). **2** *Grammar.* tense. **3** transitive. **4** ton(s). **5** territory. **6** tenor. **7** in the time of (for L *tempore*). **8** town. **9** township. **10** telephone. **11** terminal. **12** troy weight.

T 1 tritium. **2** *T*, temperature (thermodynamic). **3** *T*, torque. **4** *T*, period (one cycle of time).

T. 1 territory. **2** Tuesday. **3** Testament. **4** tablespoon(s).

Ta tantalum.

tab (tab) *n., v.* **tabbed, tab·bing.** —*n.* **1** a small flap, strap, loop, or piece: *He wore a fur cap with tabs over the ears.* **2** a small projection or attached piece on a card or folder used as a filing aid. Tabs may be labelled, numbered, color-coded, etc. **3** *Informal.* a bill or check; a statement of costs: *to pay the tab.*
keep tab, tabs, or **a tab on,** *Informal.* keep track of; keep watch on: *He was asked to keep tab on his little brother.*
—*v.* **1** put a tab on (something): *to tab index cards.* **2** name or mark; identify: *He was very quickly tabbed as a show-off.* [origin uncertain]

tab·ard (tab′ərd) *n.* **1** a short, loose coat worn by a herald, emblazoned with his sovereign's coat of arms. **2** a short surcoat or tunic, worn over armor by a knight, having short sleeves and open sides, and emblazoned with the knight's coat of arms. **3** a coarse, loose outer garment formerly worn out of doors by the lower classes and also by monks and foot soldiers. **4** a similar modern garment, sleeveless or short-sleeved and often open at the sides. [ME < OF *tabart*]

Ta·bas·co (tə bas′kō) *n. Trademark.* a kind of peppery sauce, used on fish, meat, etc. and prepared from the fruit of a kind of hot red pepper. [< *Tabasco*, a state in Mexico]

tab·by (tab′ē) *n., pl.* **-bies;** *adj.* —*n.* **1** a domestic cat having a grey or brownish coat with dark stripes. **2** any cat, especially a female. **3** *Esp.Brit. Derogatory.* **a** a woman who gossips. **b** old maid. **4** silk taffeta with a watered, or moiré, finish.
—*adj.* brown or grey with dark stripes. [< F < Arabic *'attābiy* (def. 4), from a section of Baghdad where such cloth was first made]

tab·er·nac·le (tab′ər nak′əl) *n.* **1 Tabernacle,** the covered wooden framework carried by the Israelites for use as a place of worship during their journey from Egypt to Palestine. **2** a Jewish temple. **3** a building used as a place of worship for a large group of people. **4** the human body thought of as the temporary dwelling of the soul. **5** *Archaic.* a temporary dwelling; tent. **6** a tomb, shrine, etc. with a canopy. **7** a small chest or cupboard in a church, often built into the altar, for keeping consecrated bread. [< L *tabernaculum* tent < *taberna* cabin]

tab·la (tä′blə) *n.* a musical instrument consisting of a pair of small, tuned hand drums. [< Hindi or Urdu < Arabic *ṭabla* drum]

ta·ble (tā′bəl) *n., v.* **-bled, -bling.** —*n.* **1** a piece of furniture having a smooth, flat top on legs. **2** the food put on a table to be eaten: *Mrs. Brown sets a good table.* **3** the persons seated at a table. **4** a flat surface; plateau. **5** *Architecture.* a flat, vertical, usually rectangular surface forming a distinct feature in a wall. **6** a horizontal moulding, especially a cornice. **7** the flat surface of a jewel. **8** very condensed tabulated information; a list: *The table of contents is in the front of the book.* **9** a thin, flat piece of wood, stone, metal, etc.; a tablet: *The Ten Commandments were written on tables of stone.* **10** matter inscribed or written on tables. **11** the **tables,** certain laws cut or carved on thin, flat pieces of stone.
on the table, of a bill, motion, etc.: **a** before a committee, legislative body, etc. for discussion. **b** *Esp.U.S.* put off or shelved.
set or **lay the table,** arrange cutlery, dishes, etc. on the table for a meal.
turn the tables, reverse conditions or circumstances completely: *The enemy troops had advanced, but our sudden attack turned the tables on them.*
—*v.* **1** put on a table. **2** make a list or condensed statement. **3** present (a motion, report, etc.) for consideration. **4** *Esp.U.S.* put off discussion of (a bill, motion, etc.); shelve. [ME < OF < L *tabula* plank, tablet]

tab·leau (tab′lō) *n., pl.* **-leaux** or **-leaus. 1** a striking scene; picture. **2** a representation of a picture, statue, scene, etc. by a person or group posing in appropriate costume. [< F *tableau* picture, dim. of *table* table]

tab·leaux (tabl′lōz) *n. pl.* of **tableau.**

ta·ble·cloth (tā′bəl kloth′) *n.* a cloth for covering a table.

ta·ble d'hôte (tä′bəl dōt′ *or* tä′əl dōt′; *French;* täbl′ dōt′) *pl.* **ta·bles d'hôte. 1** in a restaurant, hotel, etc., a complete meal with specified courses, offered at a fixed price and, often, served at a set time. **2** (*adj.*) designating such a meal. Compare **à la carte.** [< F *table d'hôte,* literally, host's table]

ta·ble–hop·ping (tā′bəl hop′ing) *n.* going from table to table in a club, restaurant, etc., in order to visit with friends. —**table-hop,** *v.*

table knife a knife usually having a rounded tip, designed for use at the table, for cutting food on one's plate, etc.

ta·ble·land (tā′bəl land′) *n.* a plateau that rises sharply from a lowland area or the sea.

table linen tablecloths, napkins, etc.

table salt ordinary, refined salt, such as that put in saltshakers for adding to food at the table.

ta·ble·spoon (tā′bəl spün′) *n.* **1** a spoon larger than a teaspoon or dessert spoon, used to serve vegetables, etc. **2** a standard unit of measurement in cookery, equal to three teaspoons, or about 15 mL. *Abbrev.:* T., tbs., or tbsp. **3** tablespoonful: *The recipe calls for a tablespoon of sugar.*

ta·ble·spoon·ful (tā′bəl spün fül′) *n., pl.* **-fuls.** the amount that a tablespoon can hold.

tab·let (tab′lit) *n.* **1** a small, flat slab of stone, wood, ivory, etc. used in ancient times to write or draw on. **2** a number of sheets of writing paper fastened together at one edge; a pad of paper. **3** a small, flat surface with an inscription. **4** a small, flat piece of medicine, candy, etc.: *vitamin tablets.* [< F *tablette < table* table]

table talk *Informal.* conversation at or as at meals.

table tennis an indoor game resembling tennis, played on a table with small wooden paddles and a very light, hollow, plastic ball.

ta·ble·top (tā′bəl top′) *n.* **1** the top of a table: *The tabletop was scarred with cigarette burns.* **2** (*adj.*) of a machine, instrument, or apparatus, designed to be used on a table; not having its own stand or support: *a tabletop loom.*

ta·ble·ware (tā′bəl wer′) *n.* the dishes, knives, forks, spoons, etc. used at meals.

table wine a red or white still wine for drinking with meals, usually containing between 9 and 15 percent alcohol.

tab·loid (tab′loid) *n.* **1** a newspaper, usually having a page that is half the ordinary size and that presents the news through pictures and short articles. **2** (*adj.*) condensed. [< *tablet*]

ta·boo (tə bü′) *adj., v.* **-booed, -boo·ing;** *n., pl.* **-boos.** —*adj.* **1** forbidden by custom or tradition; banned: *Eating human flesh is taboo in most cultures.* **2** set apart as sacred, unclean, or cursed, and forbidden to general use.
—*v.* forbid; prohibit; ban.
—*n.* **1** a prohibition; ban. **2 a** the system or act of setting things apart as sacred, unclean, or cursed. **b** the fact or condition of being so placed. **c** the prohibition or interdict itself. [< Tongan (lang. of the Tonga Islands in the S Pacific) *tabu*]
☛ *Usage.* **Taboo, tabu. Taboo** is more generally used than **tabu,** except in anthropology.

ta·bor (tā′bər) *n.* a small drum, used especially in the Middle Ages to accompany a pipe or fife played by the same person. [ME < OF *tabur,* of Oriental origin; cf. Persian *tabīrah* drum]

tab·o·ret or **tab·ou·ret** (tab′ə ret′ *or* tab′ə ret′) *n.* **1** a small, low stand or table. **2** a stool. **3** a frame for embroidery. **4** *Archaic.* a small tabor. [< F *tabouret*]

ta·bu (tə bü′) *adj., v.* **-bued, -bu·ing;** *n., pl.* **-bus.** See **taboo.**
☛ *Usage.* See note at **taboo.**

tab·u·lar (tab′yə lər) *adj.* **1** of, having to do with, or arranged in tables or lists; especially, written or printed in columns and rows. **2** flat like a table: *a tabular rock.* [< L *tabularis* relating to a board or plate < *tabula* plank, tablet]

tab·u·la ra·sa (tab′yü lə rä′sə) *pl.* **tab·u·lae ra·sae** (-ē *or* -ī).

Latin. **1** in some philosophical thought, the human mind, as at birth, before any outside impressions are received. **2** a clean slate. [literally, a scraped, or erased, slate]

tab·u·late (*v.* tab′yə lāt′; *adj.* tab′yə lit *or* tab′yə lāt′) *v.* **-lat·ed, -lat·ing;** *adj.* —*v.* arrange (facts, figures, etc.) in tables or lists. —*adj.* having a flat surface.

tab·u·la·tion (tab′yə lā′shən) *n.* an arrangement in tables or lists.

tab·u·la·tor (tab′yə lā′tər) *n.* **1** a person or machine that tabulates. **2** a device on a typewriter for making even paragraph and column indentions.

tac·a·ma·hac (tak′ə mə hak′) *n.* **1** a strong-smelling gum resin used in incenses, ointments, etc. **2** any of several trees yielding this gum, such as the balsam poplar. [< Sp. *tacamahaca* < Nahuatl]

tach·isme *or* **tach·ism** (tash′iz əm; *French,* tä shēsm′) *n.* a style of abstract painting based on the dribbling or splashing of paint on canvas to see what form it will take. [< F *tachisme* < *tache* blot + *-isme* -ism]

tach·iste *or* **tach·ist** (tash′ist; *French,* tä shēst′) *adj., n.* —*adj.* using the technique of tachisme. —*n.* a painter using this technique.

ta·chom·e·ter (tə kom′ə tər) *n.* an instrument for measuring speed of rotation, especially that of the crankshaft of a motor vehicle engine. A tachometer measures engine rpm (revolutions per minute). [< Gk. *tachos* speed + E *-meter*]

tac·it (tas′it) *adj.* **1** unspoken; silent: *a tacit prayer.* **2** implied or understood without being openly expressed: *His eating the food was a tacit confession that he liked it.* **3** *Law.* existing out of custom or from silent consent but not expressly stated. [< L *tacitus,* pp. of *tacere* be silent] —**tac′it·ly,** *adv.* —**tac′it·ness,** *n.*

tac·i·turn (tas′ə tèrn′) *adj.* speaking very little; not fond of talking. [< L *taciturnus* < *tacitus* tacit. See TACIT.] —**tac′i·turn·ly,** *adv.*

☛ *Syn.* See note at **silent.**

tac·i·tur·ni·ty (tas′ə tèr′nə tē) *n.* the habit of keeping silent; disinclination to talk much.

tack[1] (tak) *n., v.* —*n.* **1** any of various types of very short, sharp nail with a flat head, used for fastening upholstery, carpets, etc. in place, pinning paper to a drawing board, notices on a bulletin board, etc. **2** a sewing stitch used as a temporary fastening. **3** *Nautical.* **a** a zigzag course against the wind. **b** the movement of a boat or ship in relation to the direction of the wind. When on port tack, a ship has the wind on her left. **c** a zigzag movement; one of the movements in a zigzag course. **d** a rope to hold in place a corner of some sails. **e** the corner to which this is fastened. **4** a course of action or conduct: *To demand what he wanted was the wrong tack to take with his father.* —*v.* **1** fasten with tacks. **2** sew with temporary stitches. **3** attach; add: *He tacked the postscript to the end of the letter.* **4** *Nautical.* **a** sail in a zigzag course against the wind. **b** change from one tack to another. **5** move along any zigzag route. **6** change one's attitude, conduct, or course of action. **7** use indirect methods. [< dial. OF *taque* nail < Gmc.] —**tack′er,** *n.*

tack[2] (tak) *n. Informal.* food, especially coarse or disagreeable food. [origin unknown]

tack[3] (tak) *n.* **1** equipment for saddle horses, such as bridles and saddles. **2** (*adj.*) of or for such equipment: *a tack room.* [< *tackle*]

tack·le (tak′əl) *n., v.* **-led, -ling.** —*n.* **1** equipment; apparatus; gear. Fishing tackle means the rod, line, hooks, etc. **2** a set of ropes and pulleys for lifting, lowering, or moving heavy things. The sails of a ship are raised and moved by tackle. **3** the act of tackling. **4** *Football.* a player between the guard and the end on either side of the line. —*v.* **1** try to deal with: *Everyone has his own problems to tackle.* **2** lay hold of; seize: *John tackled the runner and pulled him to the ground.* **3** *Football.* seize and stop (an opponent having the ball) by bringing to the ground. **4** *Soccer.* obstruct (an opponent) in order to get the ball away from him. **5** fasten or attach by means of tackle. [ME < MDu. or MLG *takel*] —**tack′ler,** *n.*

tack·y[1] (tak′ē) *adj.* sticky. [< *tack*]

tack·y[2] (tak′ē) *adj.* **tack·i·er, tack·i·est.** *Informal.* **1** shabby or shoddy; of poor quality or appearance: *a row of tacky little houses.* **2** cheap and vulgar; in bad taste: *a tacky magazine, a tacky costume.* [origin uncertain; cf. dial. G *tacklig* untidy]

tac·o·nite (tak′ə nīt′) *n.* a kind of rock consisting of about 30 percent iron ore. [< *Taconic* Mts. (Mass. and Vt.)]

tact (takt) *n.* a keen sense of the right or fitting thing to say or do so as to avoid hurting someone's feelings; sensitivity in dealing with people. [< L *tactus* sense of feeling < *tangere* touch]

tact·ful (takt′fəl) *adj.* **1** having tact. **2** showing tact. —**tact′ful·ly,** *adv.* —**tact′ful·ness,** *n.*

tac·tic (tak′tik) *n.* a device or procedure for accomplishing a goal.

tac·ti·cal (tak′tə kəl) *adj.* **1** of or having to do with tactics; especially, having to do with the disposal of naval, military, or air forces in action against an enemy. **2** organized for or used in action against enemy troops, rather than against enemy bases, industry, etc., behind the lines of battle: *a tactical bomber.* **3** having or showing cleverness and skill in planning or manoeuvring: *a tactical statesman.* —**tac′ti·cal·ly,** *adv.*

tac·ti·cian (tak tish′ən) *n.* a person skilled or trained in tactics.

tac·tics (tak′tiks) *n.pl.* **1** the science and art of managing naval, ground, or air forces in active combat (*used with a singular verb*). **2** the operations themselves: *The generals' tactics were successful.* **3** any procedures, or devices to gain advantage or success: *Those are dangerous tactics to use. When his coaxing failed, the little boy changed his tactics and began to cry.* [< NL *tactica* < Gk. *taktikē* (*technē*) the art of arranging < *tassein* arrange]

tac·tile (tak′tīl *or* tak′təl) *adj.* **1** of, having to do with, or perceived by the sense of touch: *a tactile organ, a tactile impression.* **2** that can be felt by touch; tangible: *Heat and cold are tactile qualities.* [< L *tactilis* < *tangere* touch]

tac·til·i·ty (tak til′ə tē) *n.* the capability of being felt by touch.

tact·less (takt′lis) *adj.* **1** without tact: *a tactless person.* **2** showing no tact: *a tactless reply.* —**tact′less·ly,** *adv.* —**tact′less·ness,** *n.*

tac·tu·al (tak′chü əl) *adj.* **1** of or having to do with the sense of touch; tactile. **2** arising from the sense of touch; giving sensations of touch. [< L *tactus.* See TACT.] —**tac′tu·al·ly,** *adv.*

tad (tad) *n. Informal.* **1** a young boy. **2** a small amount; bit: *Move the picture to the right just a tad.*

tad·pole (tad′pōl′) *n.* the aquatic larva of a frog or toad, having a short, round body, gills, and a long tail with a fin along each side. [ME *tad* toad + *pol* poll (head); apparently "a toad that is all head"]

tael (tāl) *n.* **1** any of various units of mass used in E Asia, varying in value from about 30 to 70 grams. **2** *Historical.* a Chinese unit of money equal to the value of one tael of silver. [< Pg. < Malay *tahil* mass]

ta·en (tān) *Poetic.* taken.

taf·fe·ta (taf′ə tə) *n.* a stiff cloth of silk, rayon, linen, etc. in a plain weave having a smooth, glossy surface on both sides. [ME < OF < Persian *taftah* silk or linen < *tāftan* shine]

taff·rail (taf′rāl′) *n.* **1** a rail around a ship's stern. **2** the upper part of the stern of a wooden ship. [< Du. *tafereel* panel, dim. of *tafel* table]

taf·fy (taf′ē) *n.* **1** a kind of hard but chewy candy made of brown sugar or molasses boiled down, often with butter, and pulled to make it porous. **2** *Cdn.* maple-syrup candy, often made by pouring the syrup over snow so that it hardens in brittle sheets. **3** toffee. **4** *Informal.* flattery. [var. of *toffee*]

Taf·fy (taf′ē) *n., pl.* **-fies.** *Slang.* Welshman. [< Welsh pronunciation of *Dafydd* David]

tag[1] (tag) *n., v.* **tagged, tag·ging.** —*n.* **1** a piece of card, paper, leather, etc. to be tied or fastened to something: *Each coat in the store has a tag with the price marked on it.* **2** a small hanging piece; a loosely attached piece; a loose end. **3** a tab or loop by which a coat is hung up. **4** a metal or plastic covering for the end of a shoelace. **5** a quotation, moral, etc. added for ornament or effect. **6** a piece of cardboard, etc., sometimes with a piece of string attached, sold by charitable organizations, etc. to raise money. **7** the last line or lines of a song, play, actor's speech, etc. **8** *Fishing.* a small piece of bright material such as tinsel, wrapped around the shank of the hook near the tail of an artificial fly. —*v.* **1** add for ornament or effect. **2** furnish with a tag or tags. **3** mark; label; identify: *to tag suitcases and trunks.* **4** accompany, by or as if by following or trailing behind (*usually used with* **along**): *children tagging along behind the parade. She sneaked out of the house because she didn't want her brother to tag along.* **5** sell tags: *She tagged for the Cancer Society.* [ME *tagge* ? < Scand.; cf. Swedish *tagg* bark, tooth, and Norwegian *tagge* tooth]

tag[2] (tag) *n., v.* **tagged, tag·ging.** —*n.* **1** a children's game in which the player who is "it" chases the others until he touches one. The one touched is then "it" and must chase the others. **2** *Baseball.* the act of touching a base runner with the ball, or a base with the foot while holding the ball. —*v.* **1** touch or tap with the hand. **2** *Baseball.* put out a base runner with a touch of the ball. [origin uncertain]

Ta·ga·log (tä gä′log *or* tag′ə log′) *n.* **1** a member of a Malay people living in the Philippines, especially Luzon. **2** the language of this people, the official language of the Philippines. It is related to Indonesian and to Malay.

tag day a day on which tags (def. 6) are sold on behalf of a charitable organization, etc.

tag end 1 a loosely hanging or attached bit or end. **2** the last part of something.

tag line 1 a punch line. **2** a slogan or catch phrase. **3** a last line or phrase in a play, speech, etc.

Ta·hi·ti·an (tə hē′shən *or* tə hē′tē ən) *n., adj.* —*n.* **1** a native or inhabitant of Tahiti, an island country in the S Pacific. **2** the Polynesian language of the Tahitians. —*adj.* of or having to do with Tahiti, its people, or their language.

Tahl·tan (täl′tən) *n., adj.* —*n.* a member of an Athapascan people of NW British Columbia. —*adj.* of or having to do with the Tahltans.

tai·ga (tī′gə) *n.* the moist evergreen forest of the subarctic regions, as in Siberia and northern Canada. The taiga begins at the southern edge of the arctic tundra. [< Russian]

tail (tāl) *n., v.* —*n.* **1** a thin part that extends from the back of certain animals. **2** something like an animal's tail: *the tail of a kite.* **3** the after portion of an airplane. **4** *Astronomy.* the luminous train extending from the head of a comet. **5** the hind part of anything; back; rear; conclusion: *the tail of a cart.* **6** a long braid or tress of hair. **7** a part at the end of anything; conclusion: *towards the tail of his letter.* **8** (*adj.*) at the tail, back, or rear. **9** (*adj.*) coming from behind: *a strong tail wind.* **10** *Slang.* a person who follows another to watch and report on his movements. **11 tails,** *pl.* **a** the reverse side of a coin. **b** *Informal.* a man's coat with long tails, worn on formal occasions.
at the tail of, following.
turn tail, run away from danger, trouble, etc.
twist the lion's tail, *Esp.Brit.* humiliate Britain.
with (one's) tail between (one's) legs, afraid; dejected; humiliated.
—*v.* **1** furnish with a tail. **2** form a tail. **3** follow close behind; form the tail of. **4** *Slang.* follow closely and secretly, especially in order to watch or to prevent escaping. **5 a** occur less and less; gradually stop; diminish; subside; die away. **6** fall behind; lag; straggle. **6** join (one thing) to the end of another; fasten timber by an end.
tail off, *Informal.* run away.
[OE *tægel*] —**tail′less,** *adj.*
☛ *Hom.* tale.

tail·board (tāl′bôrd′) *n.* a board at the back end of a vehicle such as a cart, wagon, or truck, that can be let down or removed when loading or unloading.

tail·coat (tāl′kōt′) *n.* a man's formal coat cut away at the front and extending at the back in two long, tapering pieces, or tails.

tail end 1 the rear or bottom end: *the tail end of the parade.* **2** the concluding period: *the tail end of the school year.*

tail·gate (tāl′gāt′) *n., v.* **-gated, -gat·ing.** —*n.* **1** a tailboard, especially on a truck or station wagon. **2** the lower gate of a canal lock. —*v.* of a driver or a motor vehicle, follow another vehicle too closely.

tail·ing (tāl′ing) *n.* **1** the part of a projecting stone or brick put in a wall. **2 tailings,** *pl.* leavings; remainders, especially waste matter left over after the mining or milling of ore.

tail lamp tail light.

tail–light (tāl′līt′) *n.* a light, usually red, at the back end of an automobile, wagon, train, etc.

tai·lor (tā′lər) *n., v.* —*n.* a person whose business is making or repairing clothes, especially men's clothes. —*v.* **1** make clothes, especially clothes that are cut and shaped to fit the body and that are finely finished. **2** make or adjust to suit a particular need: *The standard house design can be tailored to suit the individual buyer.* [ME < AF *taillour*, ult. < L *taliare* cut < L *talea* rod, cutting]

tai·lor·bird (tā′lər bėrd′) *n.* any of a small genus (*Orthotomus*) of Old World warblers of tropical Asia that stitch the edges of large leaves together with plant fibres to form a support and camouflage for their nests.

tai·lored (tā′lərd) *adj.* **1** made by a tailor. **2** having simple, shaped, straight fitted lines; not loose, draped, frilly, etc.: *a tailored shirt or suit, a tailored bedspread.*

tai·lor·ing (tā′lər ing) *n.* **1** the business or work of a tailor. **2** the workmanship or skill of a tailor: *expert tailoring.*

tai·lor–made (tā′lər mād′) *adj., n.* —*adj.* **1** made by a tailor or as if by a tailor: *His suit was tailor-made.* **2** of women's clothes, simple, trim, and well-fitting; tailored. **3** made especially to suit a particular person, object, or purpose: *a tailor-made course of study.* **4** *Slang.* of cigarettes, factory made rather than rolled by hand. —*n. Slang.* a cigarette made in a factory rather than rolled by hand.

tailor's chalk a usually thin, flat piece of hard chalk or soapstone, used in sewing for making temporary guide marks on cloth.

tail·piece (tāl′pēs′) *n.* **1** a piece forming the end or added at the end. **2** *Printing.* a small decorative engraving placed at the end of a

hat, āge, fär; let, ēqual, tèrm; it, īce
hot, ōpen, ôrder; oil, out; cup, pút, rüle,
əbove, takən, pencəl, lemən, circəs

ch, child; ng, long; sh, ship
th, thin; ŦH, then; zh, measure

chapter, etc. **3** in a violin, etc. a triangular piece of ebony or other wood to which the lower ends of strings are fastened. **4** a short beam or rafter inserted in a wall and supported by a header.

tail pipe a pipe leading from the muffler to the rear of a motor vehicle, through which exhaust gases are discharged.

tail·race (tāl′rās′) *n.* **1** the part of a millrace below the wheel. **2** a channel for floating away refuse and residue from a mine.

tail·spin (tāl′spin′) *n.* **1** a downward spin of an aircraft with the nose pointed down. **2** a state of panic or confusion: *The news threw the whole household into a tailspin.*

tail wind a wind blowing in the direction of the course of an aircraft, ship, etc.; a wind coming from behind: *We made very good time because we had a tail wind all the way.*

taint (tānt) *n., v.* —*n.* **1** a spot or trace of infection, decay, or corruption. **2** a moral blemish; a trace of discredit or dishonor: *a taint of vice. There was no taint of self-interest in his transactions.* —*v.* **1** give a taint to; infect, spoil, or contaminate: *tainted meat. Her reputation had been tainted by a questionable business deal.* **2** become tainted; become infected or corrupted: *Meat taints quickly if not kept cold.* [ME; partly var. of *attaint*, partly < OF *teint*, pp. of *teindre* dye < L *tingere*]

ta·ka (tä′kä) *n.* the basic unit of money in Bangladesh. See table at **money.**

take (tāk) *v.* **took, tak·en, tak·ing;** *n.* —*v.* **1** lay hold of; grasp: *He took her by the hand.* **2 a** seize; catch; capture: *to take a wild animal in a trap.* **b** come upon suddenly: *to be taken by surprise.* **3** have the proper effect; catch hold; lay hold: *The fire has taken. The vaccination took.* **4** accept: *Take my advice. The man won't take a cent less for the car.* **5** get; receive; assume the ownership or possession of: *She took the gifts and opened them.* **6 a** win: *He took first prize.* **b** receive (something bestowed, conferred, administered, etc.): *to take a degree in science.* **7** receive in an indicated manner; react to someone or something: *to take it all in good fun.* **8** receive into the body; swallow; inhale, drink: *to take food, to take snuff.* **9** absorb: *Wool takes a dye well.* **10** stick to a surface; stick; adhere: *This ink doesn't take on glossy paper.* **11** get; have: *to take a seat.* **12** use; make use of: *to take medicine.* **13** indulge in: *to take a rest, to take a vacation.* **14** of fish, seize the bait. **15 a** submit to; put up with: *to take hard punishment.* **b** study: *to take physiology.* **16** need; require: *It takes time and patience to learn how to drive an automobile.* **17** choose; select: *Take the shortest way home.* **18** remove: *Please take the waste basket away and empty it.* **19** remove by death: *Pneumonia took him.* **20** remove something; detract: *Her paleness takes from her beauty.* **21** subtract: *If you take 2 from 7, you have 5.* **22** lead: *Where will this road take me?* **23** go with; escort: *Take her home.* **24** carry: *Take your lunch along.* **25** do; make; obtain by some special method: *Please take my photograph.* **26** form and hold in mind; feel: *Mary takes pride in her schoolwork.* **27** find out: *The doctor took his temperature.* **28** of ice, to form, become thick enough to support people. **29 a** understand: *I take the meaning.* **b** understand the acts or words of; interpret: *How did you take his remark?* **30** suppose: *I take it the train was late.* **31** regard; consider: *Let us take an example.* **32** assume: *She took charge of the household.* **33** engage; hire; lease: *to take a house.* **34** write down; record: *to take dictation.* **35** receive and pay for regularly: *to take a newspaper.* **36** photograph: *to take a scene of a movie.* **37** become affected by: *to take a cold.* **38** *Grammar.* be used with: *A plural noun takes a plural verb.* **39** please; attract; charm: *The song took our fancy.* **40** win favor: *Do you think the new play will take?* **41** go: *The car took to the woods.* **42** become: *He took sick.* **43** begin to grow; strike root. **44** attempt to get over, through, around, etc.: *My horse took the fence easily.* **45** *Baseball.* of a batter, let (a pitched ball) pass without swinging at it. **46** *Cricket.* **a** catch and put out. **b** capture (a wicket), especially by striking it with the ball. **47** photograph: *to take a scene of a movie.* **48** *Slang.* copulate with (a woman). **49** *Slang.* swindle; cheat.
take aback, See **aback.**
take after, a be like; resemble: *Mary takes after her mother.* **b** chase in order to try to seize or capture: *The dog took after the rabbit.* **c** follow (someone's) example.
take against, take sides against; oppose.
take amiss, a misinterpret. **b** be offended at.
take back, a withdraw; retract. **b** remind of the past: *The letter took her back ten years.*
take down, a write down. **b** lower the price of.
take for, suppose to be.

take in,   **a** receive; admit: *to take in boarders.* **b** make smaller. **c** understand. **d** deceive; trick; cheat: *I was taken in by the strange boy's friendly manner; in fact, he wasn't friendly at all.* **e** include: *It's too late to take in Helen's party now.*

take it on the chin, *Informal.* take a beating.

take it or leave it, accept or reject without modification.

take it out of, **a** *Informal.* exhaust; fatigue. **b** take (something) from a person in compensation; exact satisfaction from.

take it out on, *Informal.* relieve one's anger or annoyance by scolding or hurting.

take kindly to, look favorably upon; be friendly toward.

take lying down, *Informal.* take without a protest.

take off, **a** leave the ground or water: *Three airplanes took off at the same time.* **b** *Informal.* give an amusing imitation of; mimic. **c** *Informal.* leave quickly; rush away: *He took off at the first sign of trouble.*

take on, **a** engage; hire. **b** undertake to deal with: *to take on an opponent.* **c** *Informal.* show great excitement, grief, etc. **d** acquire: *to take on the appearance of health.*

take out, **a** remove; get rid of. **b** borrow (a book, etc.) from a library or similar collection. **c** apply for and obtain (a licence, patent, etc.). **d** escort. **e** destroy.

take over, **a** take the ownership or control of. **b** adapt.

take (one's) time, not hurry.

take to, form a liking for; become fond of: *She has really taken to skiing. They took to each other right away.*

take up, **a** soak up; absorb: *A sponge takes up liquid.* **b** make smaller. **c** begin to do, play, etc.; undertake: *He took up piano lessons in the summer.* **d** pay off. **e** lift. **f** establish a homestead; settle on: *He took up land in Alberta.* **g** collect. **h** adopt (an idea, purpose, etc.). **i** secure the loose end of (a stitch). **j** reprove; rebuke: *to take someone up short.* **k** reduce or remove (lost motion, etc.); tighten.

take (someone) up on, accept.

take up with, *Informal.* begin to associate or be friendly with.
—*n.* **1** the amount or number taken: *a great take of fish.* **2** the act of taking. **3** that which is taken. **4** *Slang.* receipts; profits: *the box-office tibus.* **5** the act of transplanting or grafting. **6** in motion pictures: **a** a scene or sequence photographed at one time. **b** the act or process of making a photograph or scene in a motion picture. **7 a** the act or process of making a recording for a record, tape, etc. **b** a record or tape of this.

on the take, *Slang.* taking bribes.

[OE < ON *taka*] —**tak′er,** *n.*

take–home pay (tāk′hōm′) the balance remaining after taxes, insurance payments, etc. have been deducted from one's wages or salary.

tak·en (tā′kən) *v.* pp. of **take.**

take·off (tāk′of′) *n.* **1** *Informal.* a mocking but generally good-humored imitation: *The highlight of the evening was his clever takeoff on the Prime Minister.* **2** the act of leaving the ground or other surface, as in jumping or flying: *The plane was on the runway and ready for takeoff.* **3** the place or point at which a person or thing leaves the ground, etc.

take·out (tāk′out′) *adj., n.* —*adj.* **1** of or designating prepared food packaged in disposable containers and sold by a restaurant, etc. to be eaten away from the premises: *a takeout dinner.* **2** designating a restaurant, etc. that sells such food.
—*n.* **1** *Curling.* a shot that hits an opposing stone so as to remove it from the house. **2** *Bridge.* a bid that releases a partner from a double or other bid. **3** any act of taking out.

take·o·ver (tāk′ō′vər) *n.* a taking over; seizure of ownership or control: *a takeover of a country by the army, the takeover of one business enterprise by a larger one.*

tak·est (tā′kist) *v. Archaic.* 2nd pers. sing., present tense, of **take.** *Thou takest* means *you* (sing.) *take.*

tak·eth (tā′kith) *v. Archaic.* 3rd pers. sing., present tense, of **take.** *He taketh* means *he takes.*

take–up (tāk′up′) *n.* **1** the action of taking up, as by absorbing, gathering, reeling in, etc. **2** a device for taking in or tightening.

tak·ing (tā′king) *adj., n.* —*adj.* attractive, charming, or winning: *a taking smile.*
—*n.* **1** the act of a person or thing that takes. **2** something that is taken, such as a catch of fish. **3 takings,** *pl.* money taken in; receipts.

talc (talk) *n.* **1** a soft, smooth, white, grey, or greenish mineral with a soapy feel, used in making talcum or face powder, lubricants, etc. Talc consists of hydrated magnesium silicate. *Formula:* $Mg_3Si_4O_{10}(OH)_2$ **2** talcum powder. [< Med.L *talcum* < Arabic *talq* < Persian *talk*]

tal·cum (tal′kəm) *n.* **1** talcum powder. **2** talc.

talcum powder a powder made of purified white talc, often perfumed, for use on the face and body.

tale (tāl) *n.* **1** a series of happenings or events related; recital or account: *They listened in shocked silence to his tale of the day's events.* **2** a story of true, legendary, or fictitious events, especially when imaginatively treated: *tales of dragons. The old sea captain told the children tales of his adventures.* **3** a malicious piece of gossip or scandal, either true or false: *He's always telling tales.* **4** *Archaic.* a tally or total.

tell tales out of school, reveal confidential matters.

tell the tale, **a** show the true state of affairs; be revealing. **b** be effective; work. **c** *Esp.Brit. Slang.* tell a story intended to attract pity.

[OE *talu*]

☛ *Hom.* **tail.**

☛ *Syn.* **1.** See note at **story.**

tale·bear·er (tāl′ber′ər) *n.* a person who spreads gossip or scandal; telltale.

tale·bear·ing (tāl′ber′ing) *n.* the spreading of gossip or scandal.

tal·ent (tal′ənt) *n.* **1** a special natural ability; ability: *a talent for music.* **2** general intelligence or ability: *a person of talent.* **3** a person or persons having talent: *They were looking for local talent.* **4** any of various units of mass or money used among the ancient Greeks, Romans, Assyrians, etc. [ME < OF < L *talentum* (def. 4) < Gk. *talanton*]

☛ *Syn.* **1.** See note at **ability.**

tal·ent·ed (tal′ən tid) *adj.* having great natural ability; gifted: *a talented musician.*

talent scout a person who looks for and recruits people having talent in a particular field of activity, especially in the public entertainment field.

talent show a show made up of separate performances of singing, dancing, etc. by amateurs looking for recognition as performers.

tales·man (tālz′mən *or* tā′lēz mən) *n., pl.* **-men.** *Law.* a person chosen to fill a vacancy on a jury caused by the absence or disqualification of one of the original jury members. [MF < Med.L *tales* (de circumstantibus) such (of the bystanders) + *man*]

tale·tell·er (tāl′tel′ər) *n.* talebearer.

tal·i·pot (tal′ə pot′) *n.* a tall palm tree (*Corypha umbraculifera*) of S India, Sri Lanka, and Burma, having large, fan-shaped leaves used for making fans and umbrellas, for covering houses, and in place of paper for writing. [< Singhalese talapata < Skt. *tāla* fan palm + *pattra* leaf]

tal·is·man (tal′is mən *or* tal′iz mən) *n., pl.* **-mans. 1** a stone, ring, etc. engraved with figures or characters supposed to have magic power; charm. **2** anything that acts as a charm. [< F < Arabic < LGk. *telesma* < Gk. *telesma* initiation into the mysteries < *teleein* perform < *telos* completion]

tal·is·man·ic (tal′is man′ik *or* tal′iz man′ik) *adj.* having to do with or serving as a talisman. —**tal′is·man′i·cal·ly,** *adv.*

talk (tok *or* tôk) *v., n.* —*v.* **1** use words; speak: *A child learns to talk.* **2** exchange words; converse: *The two ministers talked for an hour.* **3** use in speaking: *to talk sense, to talk French.* **4** bring, put, drive, influence, etc. by talk: *to talk a person to sleep. We talked him out of trying to hitchhike home.* **5** discuss: *to talk politics, to talk business.* **6** consult; confer: *to talk with one's doctor.* **7** communicate: *to talk in sign language.* **8** make sounds that suggest speech: *The birds were talking loudly.* **9** gossip; rumor: *She talked behind their backs.*

talk around, discuss at length without coming to the point or to a conclusion.

talk away, **a** spend (time) in talking; pass by talking. **b** remove or take away by talking: *He talked away his fears.*

talk back, *Informal.* answer rudely or disrespectfully.

talk big, *Slang.* talk boastfully; brag.

talk down, **a** make silent by talking louder or longer. **b** speak condescendingly (to). **c** belittle; disparage: *He talks down his competitor's products.* **d** give (a pilot) radio instructions for landing because of instrument failure or poor visibility.

talk of or about, **a** mention. **b** consider with a view to doing.

talk off (or out of) the top of (one's) **head,** *Informal.* utter one's immediate thoughts or ideas without consideration.

talk out, **a** resolve (a problem, etc.) by means of discussion. **b** in Parliament, discuss (a bill) until the time for adjournment and so prevent its being put to a vote.

talk over, **a** discuss; consider together. **b** persuade or convince by arguing.

talk tall, *Slang.* exaggerate.

talk up, talk earnestly in favor of; campaign for.
—*n.* **1** the use of words; spoken words; speech; conversation. **2** an informal speech. **3** a way of talking: *baby talk.* **4** a conference; council. **5** gossip or rumor: *There is talk of a quarrel between them.* **6** a subject for talk or gossip: *She is the talk of the town.*

7 *Informal.* boastful or empty words: *His threat was just talk.* [ME *talke(n),* ult. related to *tell*] *v.*

☛ *Syn.* **1.** See note at **speak.**

talk·a·thon (tok′ə thon′ *or* tôk′ə thon′) *n.* an extra-long public discussion or session of speech-making: *The city council's evening meeting turned into an all-night talkathon.*

talk·a·tive (tok′ə tiv *or* tôk′ə tiv) *adj.* having the habit of talking a great deal; fond of talking. —**talk′a·tive·ly,** *adv.* —**talk′a·tive·ness,** *n.*

☛ *Syn.* **Talkative, loquacious** = talking much. **Talkative** the common word, emphasizes a fondness for talking and a tendency to talk a great deal: *He is a talkative old man who knows everybody in town.* **Loquacious,** a formal word, adds the idea of talking smoothly and easily and suggests a steady stream of words: *The president of the club is a loquacious person.*

talk·er (tok′ər *or* tôk′ər) *n.* **1** a person who talks. **2** a talkative person.

talk·fest (tok′fest′) *n. Slang.* gabfest.

talk·ie (tok′ē *or* tôk′ē) *n. Informal.* a talking picture.

talking picture an early name for a motion picture with synchronized sound.

talking point an important point in a discussion or argument; a point to be emphasized or that serves as a basis for discussion: *These facts may not prove our case but at least they are a talking point.*

talk·ing–to (tok′ing tü′ *or* tôk′-) *n., pl.* **-tos.** *Informal.* a scolding.

talk show a radio or television show featuring interviews with well-known people or people who have some special interest or cause.

talk·y (tok′ē *or* tôk′ē) *adj.* **1** talkative. **2** containing too much talk or dialogue: *a talky novel.*

tall (tol *or* tôl) *adj.* **1** of considerable height; high: *Mountains are tall.* **2** higher than the average or than surrounding things: *The trees in the valley were very tall. She is a tall woman.* **3** of a particular height: *He is 185 centimetres tall.* **4** *Informal.* high or large in amount or degree: *That's a tall order.* **5** *Informal.* hard to believe; exaggerated: *a tall tale.* [OE *(ge)tæl* prompt, active] —**tall′ness,** *n.*

☛ *Syn.* **1.** See note at **high.**

tall·ish (tol′ish *or* tôl′ish) *adj.* quite tall.

tal·low (tal′ō) *n.* the hard, white, rendered fat of cattle and sheep, used mainly for making candles, soap, lubricants, etc. Tallow is produced by melting suet. —*v.* smear or grease with tallow. [ME *talgh*]

tal·low·y (tal′ō ē) *adj.* **1** like tallow; fat; greasy. **2** yellowish white; pale.

tall story *or* **tale** *Informal.* an unlikely or exaggerated story.

tal·ly (tal′ē) *n., pl.* **-lies;** *v.* **-lied, -ly·ing.** —*n.* **1** an account, reckoning or score: *the tally of a game.* **2** something on which a score or account is kept. **3** a specific number or a mark representing such a number, used as a unit in counting: *The ballots were counted in tallies of 20.* **4** a mark, label, or ticket used for identification or classification: *He checked the tallies on the crates.* **5** *Sports.* a scoring point; a run, goal, etc. **6** something corresponding to or duplicating something else, such as the counterfoil of a cheque. **7** correspondence or agreement. **8** *Historical.* **a** a stick of wood in which notches were cut to represent numbers and which was then split lengthwise so both parties of a transaction had a record of the amount involved. **b** a notch made in such a stick. —*v.* **1** mark on a tally; count up: *to tally a score.* **2** *Sports.* make scoring points; score: *We tallied seven goals in our last game.* **3** provide with an identifying mark, label, or ticket. **4** agree; correspond: *Your account tallies with mine.* [ME < AF *tallie,* ult. < L *talea* rod]

tal·ly·ho (interj. tal′ē hō′; *n.* tal′ē hō *or* tal′ē hō′ *for 1,* tal′ē hō′ *for 2*) *interj., n., pl.* **-hos;** —*interj.* the cry of a hunter to encourage the hounds when the fox is sighted. —*n.* **1** a sounding of this cry by a hunter. **2** a coach drawn by four horses; four-in-hand. [apparently alteration of F *taïaut,* OF *taho, tietau*]

tally sheet a sheet on which a record or score is kept, especially a record of votes.

tally stick tally (def. 1).

Tal·mud (tal′məd *or* täl′mùd) *n.* the body of traditional Jewish civil and canonical law, made up of the Mishnah and the Gemara. [< Hebrew *talmūd* instruction]

Tal·mud·ic (tal mud′ik *or* täl mùd′ik) *adj.* of or having to do with the Talmud.

Tal·mud·ist (tal′məd ist *or* täl′mùd ist) *n.* **1** one of the writers or compilers of the Talmud. **2** a person who accepts the doctrines of the Talmud. **3** a person who knows much about the Talmud.

tal·on (tal′ən) *n.* **1** a claw, especially of a bird of prey. **2** a human finger or hand resembling a claw in appearance or when thought of as grasping. [ME < OF *talon* heel, ult. < L *talus* ankle]

hat, āge, fär; let, ēqual, tèrm; it, īce
hot, ōpen, ôrder; oil, out; cup, pùt, rüle,
əbove, takən, pencəl, lemən, circəs

ch, child; ng, long; sh, ship
th, thin; ᴛʜ, then; zh, measure

ta·lus¹ (tā′ləs) *n., pl.* **-li** (-lī *or* -lē). the highest tarsal bone in the foot, situated just below the bottom ends of the lower leg bones and joined to them. The talus and the ends of the lower leg bones form the ankle (def. 3). [< L]

ta·lus² (tā′ləs) *n.* **1** a slope. **2** a sloping side or face of a wall, rampart, parapet, or other fortification. **3** *Geology.* a sloping mass of rocky fragments lying at the base of a cliff or the like. [< F < L *talutium* a sign of the presence of a gold mine near the surface < Celtic]

tam (tam) *n.* **1** tam-o′-shanter. **2** beret.

ta·ma·le (tə mä′lē) *n.* a Mexican food made of minced meat seasoned with red peppers, rolled in corn meal, wrapped in cornhusks, and roasted or steamed. [< Am.Sp. < Nahuatl *tamalli*]

tam·a·rack (tam′ə rak′) *n.* **1** a small or medium-sized larch (*Larix laricina*) found mainly in muskeg and swamp areas throughout most of Canada. Tannin, used in tanning leather, can be extracted from the bark of the tamarack. **2** the wood of this tree. [< Algonquian]

tam·a·rind (tam′ə rind′) *n.* **1** a tropical evergreen tree (*Tamarindus indica*) of the pea family native to E Africa, having hard yellowish wood, yellow flowers with reddish veins, and fruit with an acid pulp. **2** the fruit, used in foods, drinks, and medicine. [ult. < Arabic *tamr-hindi* date of India]

tam·a·risk (tam′ə risk′) *n.* any of a genus (*Tamarix*) of shrubs and small trees of warm and tropical regions having small, scalelike leaves and long, feathery clusters of tiny pink or white flowers, often grown as ornamentals or windbreaks along exposed seashores, on salt flats, and in deserts, where few other plants can flourish. [ME < LL *tamariscus,* var. of L *tamarix*]

tam·bac (tam′bak) *n.* tombac.

tam·ba·la (täm bä′lə) *n., pl.* **-la** *or* **-las.** a unit of money in Malawi, equal to ¹⁄₁₀₀ of a kwacha.

tam·bour (tam′bür) *n., v.* —*n.* **1** a drum. **2** a pair of embroidery hoops; frame for holding in place cloth to be embroidered. **3** embroidery done on this. —*v.* embroider on a tambour. [< F]

tam·bour·a (tam bür′ə) *n.* a musical instrument of India, resembling a lute but having no frets, used to produce a drone accompaniment. [< Persian < Arabic *ṭanbūr*]

tam·bou·rine (tam′bə rēn′) *n.* a small, shallow drum with one head and with jingling metal disks around the side, played by shaking, striking with the knuckles, or rubbing with the thumb. [< F *tambourin,* dim. of *tambour* drum]

tame (tām) *adj.* **tam·er, tam·est;** *v.* **tamed, tam·ing.** —*adj.* **1** of an animal, changed by man from a wild state to a being able to be handled or managed in order to serve as beasts of burden, sources of food or clothing, pets, etc. **2** gentle and easy to control; docile. **3** without spirit; dull and lifeless: *a tame story, a tame election campaign.* —*v.* **1** make or become tame, or domesticated: *to tame a horse. White rats tame easily.* **2** make submissive or docile: *Severe discipline had finally tamed him.* **3** tone down or mitigate: *He was told to tame his language.* [OE *tam*] —**tame′a·ble, tam′a·ble,** *adj.* —**tame′ly,** *adv.* —**tame′ness,** *n.* —**tam′er,** *n.*

tame·less (tām′lis) *adj.* not tamed or not capable of being tamed.

Tam·il (tam′əl) *n., adj.* —*n.* **1** a member of a people of mainly Dravidian ancestry living especially in S India and in Sri Lanka. **2** the Dravidian language of the Tamils. —*adj.* of or having to do with the Tamils or their language.

Tam·muz (täm′müz) *n.* **1** in the Hebrew calendar, the 4th month of the ecclesiastical year and 10th month of the civil year. **2** *Babylonian mythology.* a god of agriculture, whose annual rebirth and return to the earth symbolized spring and its new growth. Also, **Thammuz.** [< Hebrew]

tam-o′-shan·ter (tam′ə shan′tər) *n.* a type of peakless woollen cap originating in Scotland, having a tight headband, a flat, loose, round crown, and, frequently, a pompom. See **cap** for picture. [from the name of the hero in a poem by Burns]

tamp (tamp) *v.* **1** pack down firmly by a series of taps or blows. **2** in blasting, fill (the hole containing explosive) with dirt, etc. [? < *tampion*]

tam·per (tam′pər) *v.* interfere with or alter in an improper way, so as to damage or weaken (*used with* **with**): *The lock had been*

tampered with but not broken. It was obvious that someone had tampered with the evidence. [ult., var. of *temper*] —**tam′per·er,** *n.*
☛ *Syn.* **1.** See note at **meddle.**

tam·pi·on (tam′pē ən) *n.* **1** a wooden plug placed in the muzzle of a gun to keep out dampness and dust. **2** a plug for the top of an organ pipe. [< F *tampon,* ult. < *taper* plug < Gmc.]

tam·pon (tam′pon) *n., v.* —*n.* a plug of cotton or other absorbent material inserted into a wound or body cavity to stop bleeding or to absorb blood, etc. —*v.* plug with a tampon: *to tampon a wound.* [< F. See TAMPION.]

tan (tan) *v.* **tanned, tan·ning;** *n., adj.* —*v.* **1** make (hide) into leather by treating it with a solution containing tannin or a similar chemical agent to preserve it and keep it soft and flexible. **2** make light skin brown by exposure to the sun or a sunlamp: *He was deeply tanned after a summer spent out of doors.* **3** become tanned: *My sister tans more quickly than I do.* **4** *Informal.* spank or thrash in punishment.
—*n.* **1** a medium, or light, slightly reddish, brown. **2** the brown color acquired by light skin from exposure to the sun or a sunlamp. **3** the liquid used in tanning hides, or the active ingredient in it, such as tannin. **4** tanbark. **5** the astringent acid in it; tannin. —*adj.* having the color tan: *tan shoes.* [< Med.L *tannare*]

tan or **tan.** tangent.

tan·a·ger (tan′ə jər) *n.* any of a family (Thraupidae) of small to medium-sized, mostly bright-colored American songbirds found mainly in woodlands. Most tanagers are found only in the tropics, but three species, including the scarlet tanager, are regular summer visitors in Canada. [< NL < Tupi *tangara*]

tan·bark (tan′bärk′) *n.* any bark rich in tannin, crushed or cut into small pieces and used in tanning hides. Used tanbark is often used to cover circus rings, race-tracks, etc.

tan·dem (tan′dəm) *adv., adj., n.* —*adv.* one behind the other: *to drive horses tandem.*
—*adj.* having animals, seats, parts, etc. arranged one behind the other.
—*n.* **1** a team of horses harnessed tandem. **2** a two-wheeled carriage drawn by horses harnessed tandem. **3** a bicycle with two seats and two sets of pedals, one behind the other. **4** a truck or other vehicle with two attached units, as a cab for pulling and a trailer to carry the load.
in tandem, a one ahead of the other; in tandem formation: *mounted in tandem.* **b** closely together; in partnership or co-operation: *working in tandem.*
[< L *tandem* at length < *tam* so]

tang¹ (tang) *n., v.* —*n.* **1** a strong, distinctive taste or flavor or smell: *the tang of blue cheese, the tang of sea air.* **2** a distinctive or characteristic quality or property: *We need a slogan with more tang.* **3** a slight touch or suggestion; trace. **4** a long, slender projecting point, shank, or prong forming the part of a chisel, file, sword, etc. that fits into the handle.
—*v.* **1** provide with a spike, flange, or other tang. **2** give a distinct taste or flavor to. [ME < ON *tangi* point]

tang² (tang) *n., v.* —*n.* a sharp, ringing sound. —*v.* make a sharp, ringing sound. [imitative]

Tang or **T'ang** (tang) *n.* a Chinese dynasty, A.D. 618-906, a period during which China expanded and her art and science flourished.

Tan·gan·yi·kan (tang′gən yē′kən) *n., adj.* —*n.* a native or inhabitant of Tanganyika, a former state in E Africa, now a part of the Republic of Tanzania. —*adj.* of or having to do with Tanganyika or its people.

tan·gen·cy (tan′jən sē) *n.* the quality or state of being tangent.

tan·gent (tan′jənt) *adj., n.* —*adj.* **1** touching. **2** *Geometry.* touching at one point only and not intersecting. These circles are tangent: ◯.
—*n.* **1** a tangent line, curve, or surface. **2** *Trigonometry.* in a right triangle, the ratio of the length of the side opposite to an (acute) angle to the length of the side (not the hypotenuse) adjacent to the angle. **3** *Geometry.* the part of a line tangent to a curve from the point of tangency to the axis of abscissas. *Abbrev.:* tan or tan.
fly off or **go off at a tangent,** change suddenly from one course of action or thought to another.
[< L *tangens, -entis,* ppr. of *tangere* touch]

tan·gen·tial (tan jen′shəl) *adj.* **1** of or having to do with a tangent. **2** being a tangent. **3** in the direction of a tangent. **4** diverging. **5** slightly connected. —**tan·gen′tial·ly,** *adv.*

tan·ge·rine (tan′jə rēn′ or tan′jə rēn′) *n., adj.* —*n.* **1** any of several varieties of mandarin orange having a reddish-orange skin and easily separated segments. **2** any mandarin orange. **3** a reddish-orange color.

—*adj.* having the color tangerine. [< F *Tanger* Tangiers, a seaport in Morocco]

tan·gi·bil·i·ty (tan′jə bil′ə tē) *n.* the quality or state of being tangible.

tan·gi·ble (tan′jə bəl) *adj., n.* —*adj.* **1** capable of being touched or felt by touch: *A chair is a tangible object.* **2** real; actual; definite: *tangible evidence.* **3** whose value can be accurately appraised: *Real estate is tangible property.*
—*n.*
tangibles, *pl.* things whose value is easily appraised; material assets. [< LL *tangibilis* < *tangere* touch] —**tan′gi·bly,** *adv.*

tan·gle (tang′gəl) *v.* **-gled, -gling;** *n.* —*v.* **1** twist and twine together in a confused mass. **2** become tangled: *Her hair tangles easily because it is fine and curly.* **3** involve in something that hampers or obstructs (*often used with* up): *He has tangled himself in a complicated business deal.* **4** get into a fight or argument (*with*): *Don't tangle with him.*
—*n.* **1** a twisted or confused mass; a snarl or jumble: *a tangle of contradictory statements.* **2** a complicated, confused, or bewildered state or condition: *Her business affairs are in a dreadful tangle. My mind was in such a tangle I didn't hear a word he said.* **3** a matted bit of hair. [probably var. of *tagle* entangle < Scand.; cf. dial. Swedish *taggla* disorder] —**tan′gle·ment,** *n.*

tan·gled (tang′gəld) *adj.* **1** confused, disordered, or snarled: *a tangled pile of stockings, tangled hair.* **2** very involved or complicated: *a tangled web of lies, tangled relationships.*

tan·gly (tang′glē) *adj.* full of tangles; tangled.

tan·go (tang′gō) *n., pl.* **-gos;** *v.* **-goed, -go·ing.** —*n.* **1** a Latin American ballroom dance of African origin, in 2/4 or 4/4 time and characterized by dips and slow glides. **2** the music for this dance.
—*v.* dance the tango. [< Sp.]

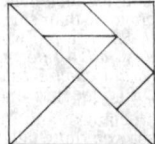

A tangram

tan·gram (tang′grəm) *n.* a Chinese puzzle consisting of a square cut into five triangles, a square, and a rhomboid, which can be combined so as to form a great variety of figures. [? < Chinese *t'ang* Chinese + E *-gram*; cf. *anagram, cryptogram,* etc.]

tang·y (tang′ē) *adj.* having a strong taste or flavor.

tank (tangk) *n., v.* —*n.* **1** a large container for liquid or gas: *an oil tank.* **2** as much as a tank will hold; tankful: *They used up almost a tank of gas just driving around.* **3** an armored, enclosed combat vehicle carrying machine guns and, usually, an artillery piece and moving on tracks. **4** *Brit.* or *U.S. Dialect.* a pool or pond, especially one made as a swimming pool or reservoir.
—*v.* put or store in a tank. [? < Pg. *tanque* < L *stagnum* pool]

tank·age (tangk′ij) *n.* **1** the capacity of a tank or tanks. **2** storage in tanks. **3** the price charged for storage in tanks. **4** the waste matter left over from the rendering of fat in slaughterhouse tanks, dried and ground and used as fertilizer or feed.

tank·ard (tangk′ərd) *n.* a large, usually silver or pewter drinking mug with a handle and, often, a hinged cover. [ME; cf. MF *tanquart,* MDu. *tanckaert*]

tank car a railway car with a tank for carrying liquids or gases.

tank·er (tangk′ər) *n.* a ship, aircraft, or truck having a tank or tanks for carrying oil, gasoline, or other liquid freight.

tank farm a tract of land containing many large tanks for the storing of oil.

tank·ful (tangk′fùl) *n., pl.* **-fuls.** as much as will fill a tank.

tank top a sleeveless, low-necked T-shirt.

tank truck a truck equipped with a large tank for carrying oil, gasoline, or other liquid freight.

tan·nate (tan′āt) *n.* a salt of tannic acid.

tan·ner¹ (tan′ər) *n.* a person whose work is tanning hides.

tan·ner² (tan′ər) *n.* *Brit. Slang.* sixpence.

tan·ner·y (tan′ər ē) *n., pl.* **-ner·ies.** a place where hides are tanned.

tan·nic (tan′ik) *adj.* of or obtained from tanbark or tannin.

tannic acid tannin.

tan·nin (tan′ən) *n.* an acid obtained from the bark or galls of oaks, etc. and from certain plants, used in tanning, dyeing, making ink, and in medicine. [< F *tanin*]

tan·ning (tan′ing) *n.* **1** the process or art of converting hide or

skins into leather. **2** a making brown, as by exposure to sun.
3 *Informal.* a severe spanking or thrashing.

tan·sy (tan′zē) *n., pl.* **-sies. 1** a coarse, strong-smelling,
bitter-tasting perennial herb (*Tanacetum vulgare*) native to Europe,
now common in North America, having large toothed leaves and
small, yellow flowers. Tansy was formerly much used as a food
seasoning and medicine. **2** any of numerous other plants of the same
genus. [ME < OF < LL < Gk. *athanasia*, originally, immortality]

tan·ta·lize (tan′tə līz′) *v.* **-lized, -liz·ing.** torment or tease by
keeping something desired in sight but out of reach, or by holding
out hopes that are repeatedly disappointed. [< *Tantalus*]
—tan′ta·li·za′tion, *n.* **—tan′ta·liz′er,** *n.* **—tan′ta·liz′ing·ly,** *adv.*

tan·ta·lum (tan′tə ləm) *n.* a rare, hard, greyish metallic chemical
element that is resistant to acids. It is used in alloys for making
surgical instruments. *Symbol:* Ta; *at.no.* 73; *at.wt.* 180.948. [<
Tantalus; because it will not absorb acid]

Tan·ta·lus (tan′tə ləs) *n. Greek mythology.* a Greek king
punished in Hades by having to stand up to his chin in water, under
branches laden with fruit. Whenever he tried to eat or drink, the
fruit or water withdrew from his reach.

tan·ta·mount (tan′tə mount′) *adj.* having the same force, effect,
etc.; equivalent (*to*): *His silence when questioned was tantamount
to an admission of guilt.* [< n. < v. < AF *tant amunter* amount to
as much < *tant* as much (< L *tantum*) + *amunter,* OF *amonter.*
See AMOUNT.]
☞ **Syn.** See note at **equal.**

tan·tar·a (tan tar′ə, tan ter′ə, *or* tan′tə rə) *n.* **1** a blast of a
trumpet or horn. **2** any similar sound. [imitative]

tan·trum (tan′trəm) *n.* a violent, childish outburst of bad temper.
[origin uncertain]

Tan·za·ni·an (tan′zə nē′ən) *n., adj.* **—n.** a native or inhabitant of
Tanzania, a country in E Africa. **—adj.** of or having to do with
Tanzania or its people.

Tao·ism (tou′iz əm) *n.* **1** a 2500-year-old Chinese philosophy that
conceives of nature as being ordered by the balance between
positive and negative forces produced by the universal creative
spirit **Tao. 2** a religion that was developed from this philosophy,
with influence from Confucianism and Buddhism. Taoism is
characterized by the worship of many gods and a belief in magic. [<
Chinese *tao* the way]

Tao·ist (tou′ist) *n., adj.* **—n.** a believer in Taoism. **—adj.** of or
having to do with Taoism or Taoists.

tap¹ (tap) *v.* **tapped, tap·ping;** *n.* **—v. 1** strike lightly: *to tap on a
window.* **2** cause to strike lightly: *She tapped her foot on the floor.*
3 make, put, etc. by light blows: *to tap a rhythm, to tap time, to tap
the ashes out of a pipe.* **4** repair with a tap (def. 3). **5** select or
designate, especially for membership in a society or club.
—n. 1 a light blow: *There was a tap at the door.* **2** the sound of a
light blow. **3** a piece of leather, etc. added to the sole or heel of a
shoe to repair it. **4** a small steel plate on a shoe to reduce wear or to
make a louder tap in tap-dancing. **5** tap-dancing. [ME < OF *taper,*
imitative] **—tap′per,** *n.*

tap² (tap) *n., v.* **tapped, tap·ping. —n. 1** a device for turning on
and off the flow of fluid in a pipe. **2** a stopper or plug to close a
hole in a cask containing liquid. **3** a certain kind or quality of liquor.
4 *Informal.* taproom. **5 a** an electric connection on a coil somewhere
other than at the end. **b** the place where an electric connection is or
can be made. **6** any long, tapering cylinder, especially a taproot. **7** a
tool for cutting threads of internal screws. **8** a wire tapping.
on tap, a ready to be let out of a keg or barrel and served. **b** ready
for use; on hand.
—v. 1 make a hole in to let out liquid: *They tapped the sugar
maples when the sap began to flow.* **2** draw the plug from: *to tap a
cask.* **3** furnish with a tap. **4** let out (liquid) by piercing or by
drawing a plug. **5** let out liquid from by surgery. **6** make resources,
reserves, etc. available; penetrate to; open up: *This highway taps
a large district.* **7** make a connection with (a telephone line) in order
to eavesdrop. **8** make an internal screw thread in. **9** *Slang.* ask (a
person) for money, help, etc. [OE *tæppa*] **—tap′per,** *n.*

ta·pa (tä′pə) *n.* **1** an unwoven cloth of the Pacific islands, made
by steeping and beating the inner bark of a mulberry tree. **2** this
bark. [< Polynesian]

tap dance a dance in which the steps are accented by loud taps
of the foot, toe, or heel.

tap-dance (tap′dans′) *v.* **-danced, -danc·ing.** dance a tap dance.
—tap′-danc′er, *n.*

tape (tāp) *n., v.* **taped, tap·ing. —n. 1** a long, narrow, woven strip
of cotton, linen, etc. Tape is used to make loops and bind seams.
2 a long, narrow strip of other material. Surveyors measure with a
steel tape. Stock quotations are printed on paper tape. **3** such a strip
coated with a sticky substance to make it adhere to a surface:
Scotch tape. **4** strip, string, etc. stretched across a race track at the
finish line. **5** magnetic tape. **6** tape recording.

hat, āge, fär; let, ēqual, tèrm; it, īce
hot, ōpen, ôrder; oil, out; cup, pút, rüle,
əbove, takən, pencəl, lemən, circəs

ch, child; ng, long; sh, ship
th, thin; ŦH, then; zh, measure

—v. 1 fasten with tape; wrap with tape. **2** attach a tape or tapes to.
3 measure with a tape measure. **4** record on tape. [ME *tape,* var. of
tappe, OE *tæppe*] **—tape′like′,** *adj.*

tape deck an apparatus for making and playing tape recordings,
especially a separate component of a stereo system.

tape grass a freshwater plant (*Vallisneria spiralis*) of warm
temperate regions having long, ribbonlike leaves that are entirely
submerged. Also called **eelgrass, wild celery.**

tape·line (tāp′līn′) *n.* tape measure.

tape measure a long, narrow strip of flexible steel or of cloth,
paper, etc., marked off in millimetres, centimetres, etc. for
measuring length or distance.

tap·er (tā′pər) *v., n.* **—v. 1** become gradually smaller toward one
end: *The church spire tapers to a point.* **2** grow less gradually;
diminish: *His business gradually tapered to nothing as people
moved away.*
taper off, gradually reduce; leave off or stop: *She thought she could
taper off smoking rather than quit outright. He has been a heavy
drinker but is trying to taper off.*
—n. 1 a gradual lessening in thickness, diameter, or width toward
one end: *pant legs with a slight taper.* **2** a gradual decrease of force,
capacity, etc. **3** a figure that tapers to a point; a slender cone or
pyramid; spire. **4** a slender candle. **5** a long wick coated with wax,
used to light candles, lamps, etc. [OE *tapor*] **—ta′per·ing·ly,** *adv.*

tape-re·cord (tāp′ri kôrd′) *v.* record on magnetic tape.

tape-re·cord·er (tāp′ri kôr′dər) *n.* a device for recording sound
on magnetic tape and also playing back the recorded sound. In
recording, the sound is converted into electric waves which
magnetize the tape. When the recording is played back, the
magnetic patterns on the tape create electric waves which are
amplified and changed into sound.

tape recording 1 the recording of sound, etc. on magnetic tape.
2 a tape on which such a recording has been made.

tap·es·tried (tap′is trēd) *adj.* covered or decorated with a
tapestry or tapestries: *tapestried walls.*

tap·es·try (tap′is trē) *n., pl.* **-tries. 1** heavy, thick, handwoven
fabric having designs or pictures woven into it, used to hang on
walls, cover furniture, etc. **2** a machine-made fabric woven to
resemble tapestry. [ME < OF *tapisserie,* ult. < *tapis* < L < Gk.
tapētion, dim. of *tapēs* carpet, covering]

tape·worm (tāp′wèrm′) *n.* any of numerous flatworms (class
Cestoda) that in the adult stage live as parasites in the intestines of
human beings and other vertebrates.

tap·ing (tā′ping) *n.* **1** tape recording. **2** data on punched or
magnetic tape, for use in a computer, etc.

tap·i·o·ca (tap′ē ō′kə) *n.* **1** a starchy food in the form of white
grains prepared from the root of the cassava plant. Tapioca is used
especially for puddings and as a thickener for foods. **2** pudding, etc.
made from tapioca. [ult. < Tupi-Guarani *tipioca*]

ta·pir (tā′pər) *n.* any of a genus (*Tapirus*) of heavy, thick-skinned,
woodland mammals having four toes on the front feet and three on
the hind feet, and a long, tapered, flexible snout with the nostrils at
the end. They belong to the same order (Perissodactyla) as horses
and rhinoceroses. [< Tupi *tapira*]

tap·is (tap′ē *or* tap′is) *n. Archaic.* a carpet or tapestry.
on the tapis, being given attention; under discussion. [< F *tapis.* See
TAPESTRY.]

tap·pet (tap′it) *n.* a projecting machine part, cam, etc. that
intermittently comes in contact with another part to which it
communicates, or from which it receives, an intermittent motion.
[< *tap¹*]

tap·room (tap′rüm′ *or* -rùm′) *n.* a room where alcoholic liquor is
sold; barroom.

tap·root (tap′rüt′) *n.* the main root of certain plants, such as the
dandelion or carrot, that grows straight downward in smaller roots
branching out from it. See **root¹** for picture.

taps (taps) *n.* (*usually used with a singular verb*) *U.S.* the last
bugle call at night, serving as a signal that all lights in soldiers'
quarters are to be put out. Taps is also played at military funerals
and memorial services. Compare **last post.** [prob. shortened from
taptoo, an earlier form of **tattoo¹**. See TATTOO¹]

tap·ster (tap′stər) n. a person who draws and serves liquor in a tavern or barroom. [OE tæppestre, fem.]

tar¹ (tär) n., v. **tarred, tar·ring.** —n. **1** a thick, brown or black, sticky substance obtained by the distillation of wood or coal. **2** a similar, condensible substance found in the smoke from burning tobacco. **3** (adj.) of, like, or covered with tar: tar paper.
—v. **1** cover or smear with tar: a tarred roof. **2** smear or besmirch as if with tar: tarred by his own bad reputation.
tar and feather, smear heated tar on and then cover with feathers as a punishment.
tarred with the same brush (or **stick**), having similar faults or defects.
tar with (a specified) **brush,** disgrace in a specified way; stigmatize. [OE teoru]

tar² (tär) n. Informal. sailor. [special use of tar¹ or short for tarpaulin]

Ta·ra (tä′rə, tar′ə, or ter′ə) n. **Hill of Tara,** the home of the ancient Irish kings.

ta·ra·did·dle or **tar·ra·did·dle** (tar′ə did′əl or ter′ə did′əl) n. Informal. **1** a petty lie; fib. **2** twaddle.

tar·an·tel·la (tar′ən tel′ə or ter′ən tel′ə) n. **1** a rapid, whirling southern Italian dance in 6/8 time, usually performed by couples. **2** the music for this dance. [< Ital. tarantella < Taranto, a city in S Italy; influenced by Ital. tarantola tarantula]

ta·ran·tu·la (tə ran′chü lə) n., pl. **-las, -lae** (-lē or -lī). **1** a large, hairy, southern European wolf spider (Lycosa tarentula) whose bite is painful, but not serious. Its bite was formerly believed to cause an uncontrollable desire to dance. **2** any large hairy spider thought of as poisonous; especially any of a family (Theraphosidae) of spiders found in tropical America, Mexico, and the southern United States, some species reaching a body length of about 8 cm. The bite of some South American tarantulas can be dangerous but all the species found in the United States are harmless to human beings. [< Med.L tarantula,ult. < L Tarentum Taranto. See TARANTELLA.]

tar·boosh (tär büsh′) n. a close-fitting, brimless cap like a fez, worn by Moslem men either alone or as the inner part of a turban. [< Arabic tarbūsh]

tar·dy (tär′dē) adj. **-di·er, -di·est. 1** after the proper or desired time; late: a tardy attempt at reform. **2** slow or sluggish: tardy growth, a tardy pace. [< F tardif, ult. < L tardus] —**tar′di·ly,** adv. —**tar′di·ness,** n.
☛ Syn. 2. See note at **late.**

tare¹ (ter) n. **1** any of several vetches, especially the common vetch (Vicia sativa). Tare is grown for fodder and for enriching the soil. **2** the seed of a vetch. **3** in the Bible, an injurious weed, possibly the darnel. [cf. MDu. tarwe wheat]
☛ Hom. **tear².**

tare² (ter) n. a deduction made from the gross mass of something in a container to allow for the mass of the container. [< F tare, ult. < Arabic ṭarhah < ṭaraha reject]
☛ Hom. **tear².**

targe (tärj) n. Archaic. a shield or buckler. [ME < OF < Gmc.]

tar·get (tär′git) n., v. —n. **1** a mark for shooting at. **2** something aimed at, as in a wartime operation: The bomber's target was a bridge. **3** a goal or objective: The target for the fund-raising drive was $10 000. **4** an object of scorn or abuse: His absent-mindedness made him a target for their practical jokes. **5** a shield, especially a small, round one; buckler. **6** the plate opposite the cathode in an X-ray tube, upon which the cathode rays impinge and produce X rays. **7** any substance, object, or surface bombarded by high-energy nuclear particles, electrons, etc., such as the plate in a television camera tube that receives the image from the screen plate. **8** a disk-shaped signal on a railway switch that shows whether the switch is open or closed.
on target, to the purpose; to the point; appropriate or valid: Her criticism of the book was right on target.
—v. **1** make or put up as a target. **2** guide to a target. [ME targete, dim. of targe < OF < Gmc.]

tar·iff (tar′if or ter′if) n., v. —n. **1** a list or schedule of duties or taxes imposed by a government on imports and, sometimes, exports. **2** any duty or tax in such a list or schedule: There is a very high tariff on jewellery. **3** a schedule of rates or prices of a business, etc.: This hotel has the highest tariff in town.
—v. **1** make subject to a tariff; set a tariff on. **2** list the tariff or tariffs on. [< Ital. tariffa arithmetic < Arabic tar′īf information]

tar·la·tan (tär′lə tən) n. a thin, sheer, usually heavily-sized muslin used for costumes and trimming, for stiffening garments, etc. [< F tarlatane]

tar·mac (tär′mak) n. **1** the paved area of an airport, including the aprons and runways. **2** a paved road or other surface. **3** Tarmac,

Trademark. a paving material consisting of crushed stone bound with coal tar. [< tar¹ + macadam. 20c.]

tarn (tärn) n. Brit. a small mountain lake or pool. [ME < ON tjörn]

tar·nish (tär′nish) v., n. —v. **1** dull the lustre or brightness of: The salt tarnished the silver salt shaker. **2** lose lustre and brightness, especially through exposure to the air or certain chemical substances: This silver does not tarnish. **3** bring disgrace upon; sully: His involvement in that business deal has tarnished his reputation. **4** grow less appealing; become uninviting; pall; fade.
—n. **1** the condition of being tarnished or the film or coating characteristic of this condition: We took the tarnish off with silver polish. **2** any unattractiveness, especially mild disgrace; blot. [< F ternir < terne dark, ? < Gmc.]

ta·ro (tä′rō) n., pl. **-ros. 1** a tropical plant (Colocasia esculenta) of the same family as the jack-in-the-pulpit, grown in the Pacific islands for its edible starchy roots. **2** the root of the taro. [< Polynesian]

tar·ot (tar′ət or ter′ət, tar′ō or ter′ō) n. **1** a pack of 14th-century Italian playing cards, consisting of 78 cards including 22 trumps, often used by fortunetellers. **2** tarots, the game played with these cards. [< F < Ital. tarocchi]

tarp (tärp) n. Informal. tarpaulin.

tar paper heavy paper coated with tar to make it waterproof, for use on roofs, outer walls, etc.

tar·pau·lin (tär po′lən or tär pô′lən) n. **1** a sheet of waterproofed canvas or other coarse strong cloth, used to protect goods against the weather. **2** a sailor's hat made of this or similar material. **3** Archaic. sailor; tar. [< tar¹ + pall in sense of "covering"]

Tar·pei·an Rock (tär pē′ən) in Rome, the rock on the Capitoline Hill from which persons convicted of treason were hurled. [< Tarpeia, a legendary Roman maiden]

tar·pon (tär′pon) n., pl. **-pon** or **-pons.** a large, silver-colored game fish (Tarpon atlanticus) found in the warmer parts of the Atlantic Ocean. [origin uncertain]

tar·ra·did·dle (tar′ə did′əl or ter′ə did′əl) See **taradiddle.**

tar·ra·gon (tar′ə gən or ter′ə gən) n. **1** a perennial Old World herb (Artemesia dracunculus) of the composite family widely cultivated for its aromatic leaves, which are used as seasoning in salads, sauces, etc. **2** the leaves of this plant.

tar·ry¹ (tar′ē or ter′ē) v. **-ried, -ry·ing. 1** stay or lodge for a time: He tarried at the inn till he felt well again. **2** delay in going or coming, or in doing; be tardy: Why do you tarry so long? **3** Archaic. wait for. [OE tergan vex, irritate; meaning influenced by OF targer delay, ult. < L tardare] —**tar′ri·er,** n.

tar·ry² (tär′ē) adj. **-ri·er, -ri·est.** of, like, or covered with tar: a tarry smell. The dog's feet were tarry from the new pavement. [< tar¹]

tar·sal (tär′səl) adj., n. —adj. of or having to do with the tarsus. —n. a tarsal bone or cartilage.

tar sands Cdn. a deposit of bitumen mixed with sand, clay, and various minerals, having the appearance and texture of asphalt paving, and found near the surface or hundreds of metres deep. The bitumen in the tar sands can be processed into a lighter, liquid form which is called synthetic crude oil to distinguish it from the traditional petroleum occurring naturally in a liquid state.

tar·sus (tär′səs) n., pl. **-si** (-sī or -sē). **1** the group of bones between the lower leg bones and the metatarsal bones, forming the ankle and the back half of the foot. The tarsus contains seven bones, including the talus and the heel bone. See **leg** for picture. **2** the corresponding part in the hind leg of a four-footed animal, forming the backward-bending joint between the lower thigh and the shank. **3** the shank of a bird's leg. **4** the last segment of an insect's leg. **5** the small plate of connective tissue in the eyelid. [< NL < Gk. tarsos sole of the foot, originally, crate]

tart¹ (tärt) adj. **1** having a pleasantly sharp, sour taste: a tart apple. **2** having a sharp, cutting quality: a tart reply. [OE teart] —**tart′ly,** adv. —**tart′ness,** n.
☛ Syn. 2. See note at **sour.**

tart² (tärt) n., v. —n. **1** a piece of pastry filled with cooked fruit, jam, etc. In Canada and the United States, a tart is small and usually open at the top; in the British Isles, any shallow fruit pie is a tart. **2** Slang. prostitute. —v. Informal. dress or decorate in a cheap and gaudy way (used with **up**): The resort was all tarted up for the tourist season. [ME < OF tarte]

tar·tan¹ (tär′tən) n. **1** a plaid pattern for cloth originating in Scotland and designed with the stripes in varying widths and colors to distinguish the different families, or clans: The main color in the Douglas tartan is green. **2** a similar pattern designed as an official symbol of a group, etc.: The colors of Canada's Maple Leaf tartan represent the colors of maple leaves in different seasons. **3** cloth woven with such a pattern, especially woollen cloth in a twill

weave: *I bought a length of tartan.* **4** a garment made of such cloth: *He wore his tartan.* **5** (*adj.*) made of tartan: *a tartan skirt.* **6** (*adj.*) of or like tartan: *a tartan design.* [? < MF *tiretaine* linsey-woolsey]

tar·tan² (tär′tən) *n.* a single-masted vessel with a lateen sail and a jib, used in the Mediterranean. [< F < Ital. *tartana*]

tar·tar (tär′tər) *n.* **1** an acid substance derived from grape juice that collects as a crustlike deposit on the inside of wine casks. Purified tartar is called cream of tartar. *Formula*: $KHC_4H_4O_6$ **2** a hard deposit on the teeth, consisting of proteins from saliva, calcium carbonate or other salts, and, usually, food particles; dental calculus. [ME < OF *tartre* < Med.L < Med.Gk. *tartaron*]

Tar·tar (tär′tər) *n.* **1** a member of a Turkic people living mainly in the southwestern U.S.S.R. **2** the Turkic language of the Tartars. **3** a member of any of various groups of Asian nomads of ancient and medieval times; especially, a Mongol people that formed part of the hordes of Genghis Khan. **4** (*adj.*) of or having to do with the Tartars. **5** *tartar*, a violent-tempered or savage person.
catch a tartar, meet with or oppose a person who is unexpectedly stronger than oneself.
[ME < Med.L *Tartarus* < Persian *Tātār*, influenced in form by L *Tartarus* Hades]

tartar emetic a poisonous, white, crystalline tartrate of potassium and antimony, used in medicine to cause vomiting and sweating, as a mordant in dyeing, etc. *Formula*: $K(SbO)C_4H_4O_6·½H_2O$

tar·tar·ic (tär tar′ik *or* tär ter′ik) *adj.* of, having to do with, containing, or derived from tartar.

tartaric acid a colorless crystalline acid found in many plants, especially grapes. Tartaric acid is usually obtained commercially from tartar and is used in food and medicines, in photography, etc. *Formula*: $C_4H_6O_6$

tartar sauce a sauce made of mayonnaise with chopped pickles, olives, capers, etc.

Tar·ta·rus (tär′tə rəs) *n.* Greek mythology. **1** the abyss below Hades, where Zeus hurled the Titans, who had rebelled against him. **2** a place of punishment in Hades for the spirits of the worst sinners. **3** Hades. [< L < Gk. *Tartaros*]

Tar·ta·ry (tär′tə rē) *n.* the kingdom of the Tartars in the late Middle Ages which, at its greatest, under Genghis Khan, extended from SW Russia east to the Pacific.

tart·let (tärt′lit) *n.* a small tart.

tar·trate (tär′trāt) *n.* a salt or ester of tartaric acid.

Tar·zan (tär′zan *or* tär′zən) *n.* a masculine figure of heroic proportions, especially one noted for great strength and agility. [after the hero of a series of novels by Edgar Rice Burroughs (1875-1950)]

task (task) *n., v.* —*n.* **1** work to be done; a piece of work that has been assigned or undertaken: *One of his tasks was to take the garbage out.* **2** something hard or unpleasant that has to be done: *She was left with the task of breaking the news to her mother.*
take to task, reprove: *The teacher took him to task for not studying harder.*
—*v.* **1** assign a task to: *They tasked her with the organization of the membership drive.* **2** put a strain on; burden; tax. [ME < ONF *tasque*, var. of *tasche* < VL *tasca*, var. of *taxa* < Med.L *taxare*. See TAX.] —**task′er**, *n.*

task force a temporary group, specially organized under one leader for a particular task: *A naval task force was sent to turn away the spy ship. The mayor set up a task force to study the effects of the proposed expressway.*

task·mas·ter (task′mas′tər) *n.* a person who sets tasks for others to do; especially, one who is very demanding or severe.

Tas·ma·ni·an (taz mā′nē ən *or* taz mān′yən) *n., adj.* —*n.* a native or inhabitant of Tasmania, an island state of Australia just south of Victoria. —*adj.* of or having to do with Tasmania or its people.

Tass (tas) *n.* the official news agency of the Soviet Union.

tas·sel (tas′əl) *n., v.* -**selled** or -**seled**, -**sell·ing** or -**sel·ing**. —*n.* **1** a hanging bunch of equal-sized lengths of yarn, cord, strung beads, etc. fastened together at the top and used to ornament curtains, etc. **2** something resembling a tassel, such as the group of flower spikelets at the top of the main stem of a corn plant. —*v.* **1** put tassels on; ornament with tassels. **2** form or produce tassels, as corn does. [ME < OF *tassel*; ult. origin uncertain]

taste (tāst) *n., v.* **tast·ed**, **tast·ing**. —*n.* **1** what is special about something to the sense organs of the mouth; flavor: *Sweet, sour, salt, and bitter are four important tastes.* **2** the sensation produced in these organs. **3** the sense by which the flavor of things is perceived: *Her taste is unusually keen.* **4** a little bit; sample: *to take a taste of a cake.* **5** a liking: *Suit your own taste.* **6** the ability to perceive and enjoy what is beautiful and excellent. **7** a manner or style that shows such ability: *Their house is furnished in excellent taste.* **8** the prevailing typical style in an age, class, or country: *in*

hat, āge, fär; let, ēqual, tėrm; it, īce
hot, ōpen, ôrder; oil, out; cup, put, rüle,
əbove, takən, pencəl, lemən, circəs
ch, child; ng, long; sh, ship
th, thin; ₮H, then; zh, measure

the Moorish taste. **9** any little exposure to or experience (*of*): *brief tastes of joy.* **10** the act of tasting or the fact of being tasted.
a bad or nasty taste in the mouth, an unpleasant feeling or memory left by a distasteful experience; bad aftertaste.
to (someone's) taste, in harmony with one's preferences; to one's liking; pleasing: *That style of furniture is not to his taste.*
to taste, in the amount that suits one's palate: *Add salt and pepper to taste.*
—*v.* **1** try the flavor of (something) by taking a little into the mouth. **2** get the flavor of by the sense of taste: *She tasted almond in the cake.* **3** have a particular flavor: *The soup tastes of onion.* **4** eat or drink a little bit of. **5** eat or drink a little bit. **6** experience; have: *to taste freedom.* **7** have experience: *to taste of pleasure.* [ME < OF *taster*, originally, feel] —**tast′a·ble**, *adj.*
☛ *Syn.* **n. 1. Taste, flavor** = the property or quality of a thing that affects the sense organs of the mouth. **Taste** is the general word: *Mineral oil has no taste.* **Flavor** refers to characteristic taste belonging to a thing, or a specially noticeable quality in the taste: *These berries have no flavor, but merely a sweet taste.*

taste bud any of certain small groups of cells, most of which are in the outer layer of the tongue, that are sense organs of taste.

taste·ful (tāst′fəl) *adj.* **1** having or showing good taste: *tasteful furnishings.* **2** pleasing to the taste; tasty: *tasteful food.*
—**taste′ful·ly,** *adv.* —**taste′ful·ness,** *n.*

taste·less (tāst′lis) *adj.* **1** not appealing to the sense of taste; without flavor; bland: *The meat was dry and tasteless.* **2** having or showing a lack of sensitivity to beauty and artistic worth: *a tasteless choice of accessories.* **3** showing a lack of sensitivity to what is appropriate or proper: *She made a tasteless remark about his having gained weight.* —**taste′less·ly,** *adv.* —**taste′less·ness,** *n.*

tast·er (tās′tər) *n.* **1** a person who tastes; especially, one whose work is testing the quality of tea, wine, etc. by tasting it. **2** a utensil or container used in tasting or sampling. **3** *Historical.* a person who ate a bit of food before it was touched by his master or employer as a precaution against poison.

tast·y (tās′tē) *adj.* **tast·i·er, tast·i·est. 1** pleasing to the taste; appetizing; flavorful: *That cake is very tasty.* **2** *Rare.* tasteful. —**tast′i·ly,** *adv.* —**tast′i·ness,** *n.*

tat (tat) *v.* **tat·ted, tat·ting. 1** do tatting; work at tatting. **2** make by tatting: *to tat a lace edging.* [? back formation from *tatting*]

ta·ta·mi (tä tä′mē) *n., pl.* **-mi** *or* **-mis.** a floor mat woven of straw, used especially in Japanese homes for sitting or lying on. [< Japanese]

Ta·tar (tä′tər) *n. or adj.* Tartar.

Ta·ta·ry (tä′tə rē) *n.* Tartary.

tat·ter (tat′ər) *n., v.* —*n.* **1** a torn piece left hanging; shred: *After the storm the flag hung in tatters upon the mast.* **2 tatters,** *pl.* torn or ragged clothing. —*v.* tear or wear to pieces; make or become ragged. [ult. < Scand.; cf. ON *tötturr* rag]

tat·ter·de·mal·ion (tat′ər dē māl′yən *or* -mal′yən) *n.* a person in tattered clothes; ragamuffin. [< *tatter* + *-demalion*, of uncertain origin]

tat·tered (tat′ərd) *adj.* **1** torn or ragged; in tatters: *a tattered dress.* **2** wearing torn or ragged clothes: *a tattered urchin.*

tat·ting (tat′ing) *n.* **1** the act or process of making a delicate kind of lace by looping and knotting cotton or linen thread by hand, using a small shuttle. **2** the lace made in this way. [? < Brit. dial. *tat* tangle]

tat·tle (tat′əl) *v.* **-tled, -tling;** *n.* —*v.* **1** reveal secrets; tell tales. **2** betray; give away (*used with* **on**): *He tattled on his sister and she was punished.* **3** talk idly or foolishly; gossip. **4** say or reveal by tattling: *They tattled the story to the principal.*
—*n.* idle talk or gossip. [cf. MDu. *tatelen* stutter] —**tat′tler,** *n.*

tat·tle·tale (tat′əl tāl′) *n.* a person who tells secrets, especially to get other people into trouble.

tat·too¹ (ta tü′) *n., pl.* **-toos;** *v.* **-tooed, -too·ing.** —*n.* **1** a signal on a bugle or drum calling soldiers to their quarters at night. **2** a series of raps, taps, etc.: *The hail beat a loud tattoo on the roof.* **3** a military display, especially music and parading by show units. —*v.* tap continuously; drum: *tattooing with one's fingers on the table.* [< Du. *taptoe* < *tap* tap of a barrel + *toe* pull to, shut]

tat·too² (ta tü′) *v.* **-tooed, -too·ing;** *n., pl.* **-toos.** —*v.* **1** mark (the skin) with designs or patterns by pricking it and putting in colors.

2 mark (a design) on the skin in this way: *The sailor had a ship tattooed on his arm.* —*n.* **1** a mark or design made by tattooing. **2** the act or practice of tattooing the skin. [< Polynesian *tatau*] —**tat·too′er**, *n.*

tat·ty (tat′ē) *n.* shabby or tacky: *a row of tatty little houses.*

tau (to, tô, *or* tou) *n.* the 19th letter (*T*, τ = English T, t) of the Greek alphabet.

tau cross a cross shaped like the Greek letter tau, sometimes having broadened ends. See **cross** for picture.

taught (tot *or* tôt) *v.* pt. and pp. of **teach**.
☞ *Hom.* taut.

taunt (tont *or* tänt) *v.*, *n.* —*v.* **1** tease or reproach in a scornful or insulting way; jeer at; mock: *At school she had been taunted with being poor. They taunted him with cowardice.* **2** get or drive by taunts: *They taunted him into taking the dare.* —*n.* a scornful or insulting remark. [obs. phrase *taunt (pour taunt)*, var. of F *tant pour tant* tit for tat]

taupe (tōp) *n. or adj.* medium brownish-grey. [< F *taupe*, originally, mole < L *talpa*]
☞ *Hom.* tope.

tau·rine (tôr′īn *or* tôr′in) *adj.* **1** of or like a bull; bovine. **2** of or having to do with Taurus. [< L *taurinus* < *taurus* bull]

Tau·rus (tô′rəs) *n.* **1** *Astronomy.* a northern constellation thought of as having the shape of a bull. **2** *Astrology.* **a** the second sign of the zodiac. The sun enters Taurus about April 20. See **zodiac** for picture. **b** a person born under this sign. [< L *taurus* bull]

taut (tot *or* tôt) *adj.* **1** tightly drawn; having no slack: *a taut rope.* **2** strained; tense: *taut nerves, a taut smile.* **3** of a ship, etc., in neat condition; tidy. [earlier *taught*, apparently var. of *tight*] —**taut′ly**, *adv.* —**taut′ness**, *n.*
☞ *Hom.* taught.
☞ *Syn.* **1.** See note at **tight**.

tau·tog (to′tog *or* tô tog′) *n.* a food and game fish (*Tautoga onitis*) of the wrasse family found mainly along the Atlantic coast of the United States; blackfish. [< Algonquian]

tau·to·log·i·cal (to′tə loj′ə kəl *or* tô′tə loj′ə kəl) *adj.* characterized by or using tautology; redundant. —**tau′to·log′i·cal·ly**, *adv.*

tau·tol·o·gous (to tol′ə gəs *or* tô tol′ə gəs) *adj.* tautological.

tau·tol·o·gy (to tol′ə jē *or* tô tol′ə jē) *n., pl.* **-gies**. **1** the saying of a thing over again in other words without making it clearer or more forceful; redundancy. *Example*: *the modern student of today.* **2** *Logic.* a statement that is true by virtue of its form. *Example*: *She is either married or not.* **3** an instance of tautology. [< LL < Gk. *tautologia*, ult. < *to auto* the same (thing) + *legein* say]

tav·ern (tav′ərn) *n.* **1** a place where alcoholic drinks are sold and drunk. **2** *Archaic.* an inn. *Hotels have taken the place of the old taverns.* [ME < OF < L *taberna*, originally, rude dwelling]

taw (to *or* tô) *n.* **1** in the game of marbles, a large fancy marble used for shooting. **2** a game of marbles played with taws. **3** the line from which the players shoot their marbles. [origin uncertain]

taw·dry (to′drē *or* tô′drē) *adj.* **-dri·er, -dri·est**. showy and cheap. [ult. alteration of *St. Audrey*, from cheap laces sold at St. Audrey's fair in Ely, England] —**taw′dri·ly**, *adv.* —**taw′dri·ness**, *n.*

taw·ny (to′nē *or* tô′nē) *adj.* **-ni·er, -ni·est**; *n., pl.* **-nies**. —*adj.* brownish yellow: *the tawny coat of a lion.* —*n.* a brownish yellow. [ME < OF *tane*, pp. of *taner* tan] —**taw′ni·ness**, *n.*

tax (taks) *n., v.* —*n.* **1** money paid by people for the support of the government, for public works, etc.: *Taxes are paid to the federal, provincial, and municipal governments.* **2** burden, duty, or demand that oppresses; strain: *Climbing stairs is a tax on a weak heart.* —*v.* **1** put a tax on. **2** lay a heavy burden on; be hard for: *Reading in a poor light taxes the eyes.* **3** accuse or charge (used with **with**): *The office manager taxed Rob with having neglected his work.* **4** *Law.* examine and fix (the costs of a lawsuit, etc.). [< Med.L *taxare* impose a tax < L *taxare* estimate, assess, charge < Gk. *taxai*, aorist infin. of *tassein* assign] —**tax′er**, *n.* —**tax′less**, *adj.*

tax·a·bil·i·ty (tak′sə bil′ə tē) *n.* the state of being taxable.

tax·a·ble (tak′sə bəl) *adj.* liable to be taxed; subject to taxation: *Churches are not taxable.*

tax·a·tion (taks ā′shən) *n.* **1** the act of taxing: *Taxation is necessary to provide roads, schools, and police protection.* **2** the amount people pay for the support of the government.

tax—ex·empt (taks′eg zempt′) *adj.* free from taxes; not taxed.

tax·i (tak′sē) *n., pl.* **tax·is**; *v.* **tax·ied, tax·i·ing** *or* **tax·y·ing**. —*n.* an automobile driven for hire, usually having a meter for recording the fare. —*v.* **1** ride in a taxi. **2** of an aircraft, move across the

ground or water under its own power: *An airplane taxis down the runway before takeoff and taxis to the terminal building after landing.* **3** cause an aircraft to move in this way: *The pilot taxied the plane out onto the tarmac.* [short for *taxicab*]

tax·i·cab (tak′sē kab′) *n.* taxi. [contraction of *taximeter cab*. See TAXIMETER.]

tax·i·der·mal (tak′sə dėr′məl) *adj.* of or having to do with taxidermy.

tax·i·der·mist (tak′sə dėr′mist) *n.* a person trained in taxidermy, especially one whose work it is.

tax·i·der·my (tak′sə dėr′mē) *n.* the art of preparing the skins of animals and stuffing and mounting them in lifelike form. [< Gk. *taxis* arrangement (< *tassein* arrange) + *derma* skin]

tax·i·me·ter (tak′sē mē′tər) *n.* a device fitted to a hired vehicle for showing the fare as it accumulates. [< F *taximètre* < *taxe* fare < *mètre* meter]

taxi stand a place where taxis may park while waiting to be hired: *There is a taxi stand in front of the railway station.*

tax·o·nom·ic (tak′sə nom′ik) *adj.* of or having to do with taxonomy.

tax·on·o·mist (taks on′ə mist) *n.* a person knowledgable about taxonomy.

tax·on·o·my (taks on′ə mē) *n.* **1** the study of the principles of scientific classification. **2** *Biology.* the classification of animals and plants according to natural relationships based on structure, patterns of change and variation, etc. The basic categories, from the most general to the most specific are *kingdom*, *phylum* (or for plants, *division*), *class*, *order*, *family*, *genus*, and *species*. [< F *taxonomie* < Gk. *taxis* arrangement (< *tassein* arrange) + *-nomos* assigning]

tax·pay·er (taks′pā′ər) *n.* a person who pays a tax or taxes or is required by law to do so.

tax·pay·ing (taks′pā′ing) *adj.* paying a tax or taxes: *the taxpaying public.*

tax rate the rate of taxation on property, income, etc.

Tb terbium.

TB *Informal.* tuberculosis.

T-bone (tē′bōn′) *n.* a beefsteak taken from the middle part of the loin, containing a T-shaped bone and a bit of tenderloin.

tbs. or **tbsp.** tablespoon; tablespoons.

Tc technetium.

TD or **td** touchdown.

te (tē) *n. Music.* ti.

Te tellurium.

tea (tē) *n.* **1** a dark-brown or greenish drink made by pouring boiling water over the crushed, dried leaves of a tropical or subtropical Asian evergreen shrub (*Camellia sinensis*). **2** the dried and prepared leaves from which this drink is made. Most tea comes from China, Japan, and India. **3** the shrub itself. **4** *Esp.Brit.* a meal in the late afternoon or early evening, at which tea is commonly served. **5** an afternoon reception at which tea is served. **6** a hot drink made from herbs, meat broth, etc.: *mint tea, fruit tea, beef tea.*
another cup of tea, *Informal.* a very different sort of thing.
(one's) cup of tea, *Informal.* just what one likes.
[< dial. Chinese *t'e*]
☞ *Hom.* tee, ti.

tea bag a small paper or gauze bag containing enough tea leaves for one or two cups of tea.

tea ball a hollow, perforated metal or china ball which is filled with tea leaves and put in hot water to make tea.

tea caddy or **canister** a small can or tin-lined box for keeping tea fresh.

tea·cart (tē′kärt′) *n.* a tea wagon.

teach (tēch) *v.* **taught, teach·ing**. **1** show or explain how to do: *We taught our dog a new trick. His mother taught him to drive.* **2** make understand or know about: *She taught him honesty. That experience taught me not to believe everything I hear.* **3** give instruction to: *He taught my sister last year.* **4** give lessons in: *She teaches mathematics.* **5** give instruction; act as teacher: *He taught for 40 years.* [OE *tæcan* show]
☞ *Syn.* **1, 2. Teach, instruct** = give or convey knowledge or information to someone. **Teach** emphasizes causing or enabling a person to learn something by giving information, explanation, and training, by showing how as well as what to learn, and by guiding the learner's studies: *Some children learn to read by themselves, but most need to be taught.* **Instruct** emphasizes providing, in a systematic way, the necessary information or knowledge about a subject: *He instructs classes in chemistry.*
☞ *Usage.* See note at **learn**.

teach·a·bil·i·ty (tēch′ə bil′ə tē) *n.* the fact or quality of being teachable.

teach·a·ble (tēch′ə bəl) *adj.* capable of being taught.
—**teach′a·ble·ness**, *n.*

teach·er (tēch′ər) *n.* a person trained to teach, especially one who teaches in a school or college.

teach·er·age (tēch′ər əj) *n. Historical.* in rural areas and small towns, a house owned by a board of education for the use of the schoolteacher.

teach·ing (tēch′ing) *n.* 1 the work or profession of a teacher. 2 the act of one who teaches. 3 what is taught; doctrine or precept: *the teachings of the church.*

teaching machine a mechanical or electronic apparatus containing graded educational material and operated by a student so that he can learn at his own pace.

tea cloth 1 *Brit.* a dish towel. 2 a decorative cloth for a tea table.

tea cosy a hatlike insulated covering for putting over a teapot to keep the tea hot.

tea·cup (tē′kup′) *n.* 1 a cup used with a saucer for drinking tea, coffee, etc. A teacup is usually smaller than a mug or a measuring cup. 2 as much as a teacup holds; teacupful.
storm in a teacup See **storm.**

tea·cup·ful (tē′kup fül′) *n., pl.* **-fuls.** as much as a teacup holds.

tea·house (tē′hous′) *n.* a place where tea and other light refreshments are served. There are many teahouses in Japan and China.

teak (tēk) *n.* 1 a tall East Indian tree (*Tectona grandis*) of the verbena family, one of the most valuable timber trees in the world. 2 the fragrant yellowish-brown wood of this tree, used for building ships and bridges, making fine furniture, flooring and panelling, etc. Teak is valued mainly for its hardness and durability; beams of teak have lasted more than 1000 years. [< Pg. < Malayalam *tēkka*]

tea·ket·tle (tē′ket′əl) *n.* a covered kettle with a spout and handle, used for boiling water to make tea, etc.

teak·wood (tēk′wüd′) *n.* the wood of the teak tree.

teal (tēl) *n., pl.* **teal** or **teals.** 1 any of several small freshwater ducks (genus *Anas*) of America, Europe, and Asia. The two commonest Canadian teals are the blue-winged teal (*A. discors*) and green-winged teal (*A. carolinensis*). 2 teal blue. [ME *tele*; cf. Du. *taling, teling*]

teal blue a medium to dark greenish-blue.

team (tēm) *n., v.* —*n.* 1 a group of people forming one of the sides in a game or competition: *a debating team, a football team.* 2 a group of people working or acting together; crew: *He was on the clean-up team.* 3 two or more horses or other animals harnessed together to work. —*v.* 1 join together in a team (*usually used with* **up**): *We teamed up to clean the classroom after the party.* 2 drive a team. 3 work, carry, haul, etc. with a team. [OE *tēam*]
☞ *Hom.* **teem.**

team·mate (tēm′māt′) *n.* a fellow member of a team.

team·ster (tēm′stər) *n.* 1 a truck driver. 2 a person who drives a team of horses, especially as an occupation.

team teaching a system of teaching in which several teachers co-ordinate the instruction of a group of students. Team teaching may involve bringing together different subject areas or different aspects of one subject.

team·work (tēm′wėrk′) *n.* the acting together of a number of people to make the work of the group successful and effective: *Football calls for teamwork.*

tea·pot (tē′pot′) *n.* a container with a handle and a spout for making and serving tea.
tempest in a teapot See **tempest.**

tear¹ (tēr) *n., v.* —*n.* 1 **tears,** *pl.* a salty liquid secreted by a gland in the eyelid that serves to lubricate and wash the eye and that overflows the eyelids, especially in weeping: *He had tears in his eyes. We laughed till the tears came.* **b** the act of weeping: *Tears will not help. She broke into tears.* 2 a drop of the liquid secreted by the eyes: *There was a tear on the baby's cheek.* 3 something suggesting a tear: *a tear of dew.* —*v.* of an eye or the eyes, fill with tears: *The bitter wind made her eyes tear.* [OE *tēar*]
☞ *Hom.* **tier.**

tear² (ter) *v.* **tore, torn, tear·ing;** *n.* —*v.* 1 pull apart by force: *to tear a box open.* 2 make by pulling apart: *She tore a hole in her dress.* 3 make a hole or a rent in by a pull: *The nail tore her coat.* 4 pull hard; pull violently: *He tore down the enemy's flag.* 5 cut badly; wound: *The jagged stone tore his skin.* 6 rend; divide: *The political party was torn by two factions.* 7 remove by effort: *He could not tear himself from that spot.* 8 make miserable; distress: *She was torn by grief.* 9 become torn: *Lace tears easily.*
10 *Informal.* move with great force or haste: *An automobile came tearing along.* 11 hurry; rush; dash.
tear down, a pull down; raze; destroy: *The city tore down a whole*

hat, āge, fär; let, ēqual, tèrm; it, īce
hot, ōpen, ôrder; oil, out; cup, pút, rüle,
əbove, takən, pencəl, lemən, circəs
ch, child; ng, long; sh, ship
th, thin; ᴛʜ, then; zh, measure

block of houses. **b** bring about the wreck of; discredit; ruin: *She tried to tear down his reputation.*
tear into, attack or criticize severely.
—*n.* 1 a torn place. 2 the act or process of tearing. 3 a hurry; rush; dash. 4 *Slang.* a spree. 5 a fit of violent anger. [OE *teran*]
☞ *Hom.* **tare¹, tare².**
☞ *Syn. v.* 1. **Tear, rip** = pull apart by force, especially something that is in one piece. **Tear** = pull apart or into pieces in such a way as to leave rough or ragged edges: *He tore the letter into tiny pieces.* **Rip** = tear or cut roughly or quickly and with force, usually along a joining: *She ripped the hem in her skirt.*

tear bomb (tēr) a bomb that sends forth tear gas.

tear·drop (tēr′drop′) *n.* 1 a single tear. 2 something shaped like a tear or a falling drop, especially a gem.

tear·ful (tēr′fəl) *adj.* 1 flowing with or accompanied by tears: *a tearful face, a tearful goodbye.* 2 causing tears; sad. —**tear′ful·ly,** *adv.* —**tear′ful·ness,** *n.*

tear gas (tēr) a gas that irritates the eyes, causing tears and temporary blindness, used especially in breaking up riots.

tear–gas (tēr′gas′) *v.* **-gassed, -gas·sing.** 1 use tear gas. 2 subdue with tear gas.

tear·jerk·er (tēr′jėr′kər) *n. Informal.* a story, motion picture, etc. calculated to play on the emotions of the audience or reader.

tear·less (tēr′lis) *adj.* without tears; not crying.

tea·room (tē′rüm′ *or* -rùm′) *n.* a room or shop where tea, coffee, and light meals are served.

tea rose 1 any of several varieties of cultivated hybrid rose typically having a scent resembling that of dried tea leaves. The original hybrid (*Rosa odorata*) from which they are derived no longer exists. See also **hybrid tea rose.** 2 a yellowish-pink color.

tear·y (tēr′ē) *adj.* tearful.

tease (tēz) *v.* **teased, teas·ing;** *n.* —*v.* 1 bother or annoy by means of jokes, questions, requests, etc.: *The other boys teased Jim about his curly hair.* 2 beg: *The child teases for every little thing that he sees.* 3 comb out or card wool, etc. 4 raise nap on (cloth). 5 comb hair by holding it up and working the short hairs toward the scalp. —*n.* 1 a person or thing that teases. 2 the act of teasing or the state of being teased. [OE *tǣsan*] —**teas′ing·ly,** *adv.*
☞ *Syn. v.* 1. **Tease, plague, pester** = vex or torment by continuous or persistent annoyance. **Tease** emphasizes driving a person or animal to lose patience and flare up in irritation or anger, either by persistent begging or asking or by unkind jokes or tricks: *The children teased the dog until he bit them.* **Plague** emphasizes the presence of someone or something thought of as a trial or affliction: *Her little brother plagues her.* **Pester** emphasizes continued repetition of nuisances or petty vexations: *He pesters his mother for candy.*

tea·sel (tē′zəl) *n., v.* **-selled** or **-seled, -sel·ling** or **-sel·ing.** —*n.* 1 any of several Old World biennial plants (genus *Dipsacus*), especially **fuller's teasel** (*D. fullonum*), having prickly leaves and heads of small flowers with sharp, stiff, hooked bracts. 2 a dried flower head of teasel, especially fuller's teasel, formerly much used in the textile industry for raising a nap on woollen cloth. 3 a mechanical device used for the same purpose.
—*v.* raise a nap on (cloth) with teasels. Also, **teazel.** [OE *tǣsel*]

teas·er (tē′zər) *n.* 1 a person or thing that teases. 2 *Informal.* an annoying problem; a puzzling task.

tea service a set of silver, china, etc. for serving tea, usually consisting of a teapot, hot water pitcher, cream jug, sugar bowl, and, sometimes, a coffee pot.

tea set 1 a set of china dishes for serving tea, etc., usually consisting of a teapot, sugar bowl, cream jug, teacups, saucers, and small plates. 2 tea service.

tea·spoon (tē′spün′) *n.* 1 a spoon smaller than a dessert spoon and larger than a coffee spoon, commonly used to stir tea or coffee, eat desserts, etc. 2 a standard unit of measurement in cooking, equal to one third of a tablespoon, or about 5 mL. *Abbrev.:* t. or tsp. 3 teaspoonful: *I put in a teaspoon of salt.*

tea·spoon·ful (tē′spün fül′) *n., pl.* **-fuls.** the amount that a teaspoon can hold. 1 teaspoonful = ⅓ tablespoon.

teat (tēt *or* tit) *n.* of female mammals, the nipple of a breast or udder, from which the young suck milk. [ME < OF *tete* < Gmc.]

tea towel a towel for drying dishes that have been washed.

tea wagon a small table on wheels used in serving tea, etc.

tea·zel (tē′zəl) See **teasel.**

Te·bet *or* **Te·beth** (tā vāth′ *or* tā′vəs) *n.* in the Hebrew

calendar, the tenth month of the ecclesiastical year, and the fourth month of the civil year.

tech (tek) *n. Informal.* technical school or college.

tech. 1 technical; technician. 2 technological; technologist; technology.

tech·ne·ti·um (tek nē'shē əm) *n.* a silver-grey, artificially produced, radio-active metallic element. *Symbol:* Tc; *at.no.* 43; *at.wt.* (97); *half-life* 2.6 million years. [< Gk. *technētos* artificial < *technē* art, because this was the first artificial element]

tech·nic (tek'nik) *n.* 1 technique. 2 **technics**, technology (*used with a singular or plural verb*). 3 **technics**, *pl.* technical details, points, terms, etc. [< Gk. *technikos* < *technē* art, skill, craft]

tech·ni·cal (tek'nə kəl) *adj.* 1 of or having to do with a mechanical or industrial art or with applied science: *a technical school. Technical training is needed for many jobs in industry.* 2 of or having to do with the special facts or characteristics of a science or art; specialized: *Electrolysis, tarsus, and enzyme are technical words.* 3 treating a subject technically; using technical terms: *The book gets very technical after the first chapter.* 4 strictly according to the rules or principles of a certain science, art, game, etc.: *a technical victory, a technical distinction.* 5 of or having to do with technique: *Her singing shows technical skill but her voice is weak.* [< *technic*] —**tech'ni·cal·ly**, *adv.* —**tech'ni·cal·ness**, *n.*

tech·ni·cal·i·ty (tek'nə kal'ə tē) *n., pl.* **-ties.** 1 a technical matter, point, detail, term, etc.; especially one that only a specialist is likely to be aware of or to appreciate: *She was acquitted on a legal technicality.* 2 the quality or state of being technical: *The technicality of the article soon discouraged him.*

technical knockout *Boxing.* a knockout called by the referee when he considers a fighter, though not knocked out, to be too severely injured to continue the match. *Abbrev.:* TKO, T.K.O., t.k.o.

technical school a school that provides training for work in industry, agriculture, etc.

tech·ni·cian (tek nish'ən) *n.* 1 a person trained or skilled in the technical details of a subject: *an electrical technician, a laboratory technician.* 2 a person skilled in the technique of an art: *a superb technician at the keyboard.*

tech·ni·col·or or **tech·ni·col·our** (tek'nə kul'ər) *adj.* highly colorful; vivid. [< *Technicolor*, trademark for a process for making motion pictures in color]

Tech·ni·col·or (tek'nə kul'ər) *n. Trademark.* a process for making motion pictures in color, in which three single-color films, made at the same time but each showing tones of a different primary color, are combined into one full-color print.

tech·nics (tek'niks) *n.* 1 the study or science of an art or of arts in general, especially of the mechanical or industrial arts. 2 a technic or technique.

tech·nique (tek nēk') *n.* 1 a method or way of performing the technical details of an art; technical skill: *The pianist's technique was brilliant, but her interpretation of the piece lacked warmth.* 2 a special method or system used to accomplish something: *a new technique for removing tonsils.* [< F]

tech·noc·ra·cy (tek nok'rə sē) *n.* governmental, social, and industrial management according to the findings of engineers and usually administered by technologists. [< Gk. *technē* craft + *kratos* rule, power]

tech·no·crat (tek'nə krat') *n.* a person in favor of technocracy.

tech·no·crat·ic (tek'nə krat'ik) *adj.* having to do with technocracy or technocrats.

tech·no·log·ic (tek'nə loj'ik) *adj.* technological.

tech·no·log·i·cal (tek'nə loj'ə kəl) *adj.* of, having to do with, or resulting from technology: *a technological age, technological advances.* —**tech'no·log'i·cal·ly**, *adv.*

tech·nol·o·gist (tek nol'ə jist) *n.* a person skilled in a branch of technology.

tech·nol·o·gy (tek nol'ə jē) *n.* 1 scientific knowledge applied to practical uses; applied science: *Engineering is a branch of technology.* 2 the system by which society is provided with the things needed to sustain life or desired for comfort. 3 technical language. [< Gk. *technologia* systematic treatment < *technē* art + *-logos* treating of]

tech·y (tech'ē) *adj.* **tech·i·er, tech·i·est.** See **tetchy.**

tec·ton·ic (tek ton'ik) *adj.* 1 of or having to do with the architecture or construction of a building; structural. 2 *Geology.* of or having to do with structures that build up on the earth's crust. [< LL *tectonicus* < Gk. *tektonikos* of building < *tektōn* carpenter] —**tec·ton'i·cal·ly**, *adv.*

tec·ton·ics (tek ton'iks) *n.* 1 the art or science of design and building; construction. 2 the geological study of the earth's crust.

ted (ted) *v.* **ted·ded, ted·ding.** spread out (hay) for drying. [ME < ON *tethja* spread manure]

ted·der (ted'ər) *n.* a machine for stirring and spreading out hay to speed up drying.

teddy bear a stuffed toy made to look somewhat like a bear cub.

ted·dy-boy or **Ted·dy-boy** (ted'ē boi') *n. Brit. Slang.* an idle young ruffian, sometimes delinquent, who dresses in a flashy manner. [from the fancy clothes worn by such persons, cut in the style of Edward VII, nicknamed *Teddy*]

Te De·um (tē dē'əm) 1 a hymn of praise and thanksgiving sung in Christian churches at morning service and also on special occasions. 2 the music for this hymn. [< L *Te Deum (landamus)* (We praise) thee, God, the first words of the hymn]

te·di·ous (tē'dē əs or tē'jəs) *adj.* long and tiring: *a tedious lecture.* [ME < LL *taediosus* < L *taedium* tedium. See TEDIUM.] —**te'di·ous·ly**, *adv.* —**te'di·ous·ness**, *n.*
☞ *Syn.* See note at **tiresome.**

te·di·um (tē'dē əm) *n.* the quality or state of being tedious; tiresomeness; tediousness. [< L *taedium* < *taedet* it is wearisome]

tee (tē) *n., v.* **teed, tee·ing.** —*n.* 1 *Curling.* the centre circle of the target toward which the stones are aimed; the centre of the house; button. 2 the target in various other games, such as quoits. 3 *Golf.* **a** an area from which a player makes the first stroke in playing a hole. **b** a little mound of sand or dirt or a short wooden or plastic peg on which a golf ball is placed when a player drives. —*v. Golf.* place (the ball) in position for hitting it on, or as if on, a tee (*often used with* up).
tee off, **a** drive (a golf ball) from a tee. **b** begin; start. **c** *Slang.* make angry or annoyed: *The whole thing really teed me off.* [origin uncertain]
☞ *Hom.* **tea, ti.**

tee line *Curling.* the line that runs through the centre of the house, parallel to the hog line.

teem¹ (tēm) *v.* 1 abound; swarm: *The swamp teemed with mosquitoes.* 2 be fertile, fruitful, or prolific. [OE *tēman* < *tēam* progeny]
☞ *Hom.* **team.**

teem² (tēm) *v.* pour; come down in torrents. [ME < ON *tœma* empty]
☞ *Hom.* **team.**

teen (tēn) *n., adj.* —*n.* 1 **teens,** *pl.* of a century or a person's age, the years from thirteen to nineteen: *He was still in his teens when he got married. The songs in this book date from the teens and twenties.* 2 *Informal.* teenager: *a club for teens.* —*adj. Informal.* teenage.

teen·age (tēn'āj') *adj.* of, for, being, or having to do with teenagers: *a teenage club, teenage boys.*

teen·ag·er (tēn'āj'ər) *n.* a person in his or her teens.

teens (tēnz) *n.pl.* the years of life from 13 to 19 inclusive.

tee·ny (tē'nē) *adj.* **-ni·er, -ni·est.** *Informal.* tiny; wee: *a teeny bit of sugar.*

tee·ny-bop·per (tē'nē bop'ər) *n.* 1 a young girl, usually about 11 to 13 years of age, who follows the latest fads in popular music, clothes, etc. 2 any girl of about this age.

tee·pee (tē'pē) *n.* a cone-shaped tent used mainly by the Plains Indians, consisting of a frame of poles spread out at the ground and joined at the top, covered with animal skins, canvas, etc. Teepees were originally covered with buffalo hide. Compare **wigwam.** [< Dakota *tipi*] Also, **tepee, tipi.**

tee·ter (tē'tər) *n., v.* —*n.* 1 a swaying movement; reeling. 2 a teeter-totter. —*v.* 1 rock unsteadily; sway: *to teeter on stilts.* 2 balance on a teeter-totter. [var. of dial. *titter* totter, probably < ON *titra* shake]

tee·ter-tot·ter (tē'tər to'tər) *n., v.* —*n.* 1 a long plank balanced on a raised central support, used especially by children in a game in which they sit at opposite ends and move alternately up and down; seesaw. 2 the game of teeter-tottering. —*v.* play by moving up and down on a teeter-totter: *We watched the children teeter-tottering in the playground.*

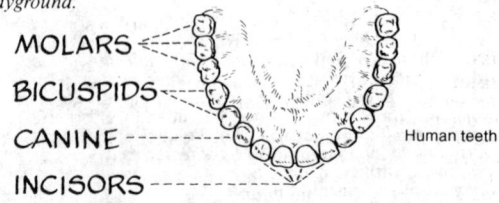

MOLARS

BICUSPIDS

CANINE

INCISORS

Human teeth

teeth (tēth) *n.* pl. of **tooth.**

by the skin of (one's) **teeth,** very narrowly; barely: *He escaped by the skin of his teeth.*

grit or **set** (one's) **teeth,** prepare to endure something without complaining.

in the teeth or **in** (someone's) **teeth, a** in direct opposition or conflict. **b** to one's face or openly.

in the teeth of, a straight against; in the face of: *He advanced in the teeth of the gale.* **b** in defiance of; in spite of.

put teeth in or **into,** put force into.

set (one's) **teeth,** prepare to do or endure something with firmness.

show (one's) **teeth,** show anger; threaten.

throw in (someone's) **teeth,** blame or reproach someone for: *He threw the lie in her teeth.*

to the teeth, to the limit of what is possible; to the utmost: *She was armed to the teeth.*

teethe (tēᴛʜ) *v.* **teethed, teeth·ing.** cut one's first teeth; grow primary teeth: *The baby is teething.*

teeth·er (tē′ᴛʜər) *n.* an object of hard rubber, plastic, etc. for babies to bite on when they are teething.

teeth·ing (tēᴛʜ′ing) *n.* the developing or cutting of teeth; dentition.

teething ring a teether in the shape of a ring.

tee·to·tal (tē tō′təl) *adj.* **1** of, having to do with, or practising total abstinence from alcoholic liquor. **2** *Informal.* absolute, complete, or entire. [< *total,* with initial letter repeated]

tee·to·tal·er (tē tō′təl ər) See **teetotaller.**

tee·to·tal·ism (tē tō′təl iz′əm) *n.* the principle or practice of total abstinence from alcoholic liquor.

tee·to·tal·ler or **tee·to·tal·er** (tē tō′təl ər) *n.* a person who never drinks alcoholic liquor.

tee·to·tum (tē tō′təm) *n.* a top spun with the fingers. [< *totum* (< L *totum* all, the whole), with the initial letter repeated]

Tef·lon (tef′lon) *n. Trademark.* a tough synthetic resin used in making bearings, etc. and as a coating on the inside of cooking utensils, the bottom of steam irons, etc. to prevent sticking.

teg·u·lar (teg′yə lər) *adj.* **1** having to do with or resembling a tile. **2** consisting of tiles. **3** arranged like tiles. [< L *tegula* tile]

teg·u·ment (teg′yə mənt) *n. Rare.* integument. [< L *tegumentum* < *tegere* cover]

te–hee (tē hē′) *interj., n., v.* **-heed, -hee·ing.** —*interj.* a word representing the sound of a tittering laugh. —*n.* **1** the sound of a tittering laugh. **2** a titter; snicker; giggle. —*v.* titter; snicker; giggle. [imitative]

tek·tite (tek′tīt) *n.* a small, rounded, glassy body thought to be of meteoric origin. Tektites are found in large quantities in certain parts of the world. [< Gk. *tēktos* molten + E *-ite¹.* 20c.]

tel. **1** telephone. **2** telegram. **3** telegraph.

tel·a·mon (tel′ə mon′) *n., pl.* **tel·a·mon·es** (tel′ə mō′nēz). a supporting column carved in the form of a man. Compare **caryatid.** [< L < Gk. *telamōn* bearer, supporter < *tlēnai* to bear]

Tel·Au·to·graph (tel ot′ə graf′ or -ô′tə graf′) *n. Trademark.* a telegraphic device for reproducing handwriting, pictures, etc. The movements of a pen at one end are reproduced by a pen at the other end.

tele– or **tel–** *prefix.* **1** over, from, or to a long distance, as in *telegraph, telephone.* **2** of, in, or by television, as in *telecast.* [< Gk. *tēle* far]

tel·e·cast (tel′ə kast′) *v.* **-cast** or **-cast·ed, -cast·ing.** *n.* —*v.* broadcast by television. —*n.* **1** a television program. **2** a television broadcast. [< *tele*vision + *broadcast*] —**tel′e·cast′er,** *n.*

tel·e·com (tel′ə kom′) *n.* telecommunication.

tel·e·com·mu·ni·ca·tion (tel′ə kə myü′nə kā′shən) *n.* **1** communication at a distance, especially by means of a system using electromagnetic impulses, as in radio, radar, telegraphy, or television. **2** Usually, **telecommunications,** the science that deals with such communication (*used with a singular or plural verb*).

tel·e·con (tel′ə kon′) *n.* **1** a device that flashes messages sent by teletype from long distances onto a screen, thus enabling groups in widely scattered places to hold conferences. **2** a conference held by means of a telecon. [< radio *tele*type + *con*ference]

tel·e·gen·ic (tel′ə jen′ik) *adj.* appearing attractive on television; suitable for televising. [< *tele*vision + photo*genic*]

tel·e·gram (tel′ə gram′) *n.* a message sent by telegraph.

tel·e·graph¹ (tel′ə graf′) *n., v.* —*n.* an apparatus, system, or process for sending or receiving coded messages by electricity, especially over a wire.

—*v.* **1** send by telegraph: *They telegraphed the news of the escape.* **2** send a telegram to: *She telegraphed us yesterday.* **3** send by means of an order made by telegraph: *to telegraph flowers.* **4** *Informal.* **a** in boxing, indicate unintentionally that one is about to punch. **b** give away an intention in advance.

hat, āge, fär; let, ēqual, tėrm; it, īce
hot, ōpen, ôrder; oil, out; cup, pút, rüle,
əbove, takən, pencəl, lemən, circəs

ch, child; ng, long; sh, ship
th, thin; ᴛʜ, then; zh, measure

tel·e·graph² (tel′ə graf′) *v. Cdn. Informal.* especially in Quebec, vote illegally by impersonating another voter. [< Cdn.F]

te·leg·ra·pher (tə leg′rə fər) *n.* a person whose work is sending and receiving messages by telegraph.

tel·e·graph·ic (tel′ə graf′ik) *adj.* of, having to do with, or transmitted by telegraph: *a telegraphic message.* —**tel′e·graph′i·cal·ly,** *adv.*

te·leg·ra·phy (tə leg′rə fē) *n.* the making or operating of telegraphs.

tel·e·ki·ne·sis (tel′ə ki nē′sis or tel′ə kī nē′sis) *n.* **1** the moving of an object by means of the power of thought alone, without physical contact. **2** the ability to bring about such movement.

tel·e·ki·net·ic (tel′i ki net′ik or tel′i kī net′ik) *adj.* having to do with, characterized by, or caused by telekinesis.

tel·e·mark (tel′ə märk′) *n. Skiing.* a stop or turn made by advancing and turning the outside ski. [< *Telemark,* a region in Norway]

te·lem·e·ter (*n.* tə lem′ə tər; *v.* tel′ə mē′tər) *n., v.* —*n.* **1** a device used in rockets, etc. for measuring heat, radiation, speed, etc. and transmitting the information, especially by radio, to a distant station where it is recorded. **2** range finder. —*v.* measure and transmit by telemeter.

tel·e·met·ric (tel′ə met′rik) *adj.* of or having to do with telemeters or telemetry.

te·lem·e·try (tə lem′ə trē) *n.* **1** the use of telemeters for measuring and transmitting information. **2** the equipment used in this process: *The ground telemetry indicated that the retrorockets on the space capsule had been fitted.*

tel·e·o·log·i·cal (tel′ē ə loj′ə kəl or tē′lē ə loj′ə kəl) *adj.* **1** of or having to do with teleology. **2** relating to final causes. **3** having to do with design or purpose in nature.

tel·e·ol·o·gy (tel′ē ol′ə jē or tē′lē ol′ə jē) *n.* **1** the fact or quality of being purposeful. **2** purpose or design as shown in nature. **3** the doctrine that mechanisms alone cannot explain the facts of nature, and that purposes have causal power. **4** the doctrine that all things in nature were made to fulfil a plan or design. [< NL *teleologia* < Gk. *telos* end + *-logos* treating of]

tel·e·path·ic (tel′ə path′ik) *adj.* **1** of or having to do with telepathy. **2** by telepathy.

tel·e·path·i·cal·ly (tel′ə path′ik lē) *adv.* by telepathy.

te·lep·a·thist (tə lep′ə thist) *n.* **1** a student of or believer in telepathy. **2** a person who has telepathic power.

te·lep·a·thy (tə lep′ə thē) *n.* the communication of one mind with another without using speech, hearing, sight, or any other sense used normally to communicate.

tel·e·phone (tel′ə fōn′) *n., v.* **-phoned, -phon·ing.** —*n.* an apparatus, system, or process for transmitting sound or speech over distances by converting it into electrical impulses that are sent through a wire.

—*v.* **1** talk through a telephone; communicate by telephone: *Wait till he's finished telephoning.* **2** make a telephone call to: *Did you telephone her?* **3** send by telephone: *to telephone a message.* —**tel′e·phon′er,** *n.*

telephone book telephone directory.

telephone booth a small enclosure in a public place containing a telephone that is usually coin-operated.

telephone directory a book containing an alphabetical list of names of telephone subscribers, together with their addresses and telephone numbers.

tel·e·phon·ic (tel′ə fon′ik) *adj.* of, having to do with, or sent by telephone. —**tel′e·phon′i·cal·ly,** *adv.*

te·leph·o·ny (tə lef′ə nē) *n.* the making or operating of telephones.

tel·e·pho·to (tel′ə fō′tō) *adj., n.* —*adj.* of or designating a system of lenses for a camera designed to produce a large image of a distant object. —*n.* **1** a telephoto lens. **2** a photograph taken with a camera having a telephoto lens. **3 Telephoto,** *Trademark.* **a** a device for sending photographs by telegraphy. **b** a picture sent in this way.

tel·e·pho·to·graph (tel′ə fō′tə graf′) *n., v.* —*n.* **1** a picture taken with a camera having a telephoto lens. **2** a picture sent by

telegraphy. —v. 1 take a picture with a camera having a telephoto lens. 2 send such a picture.

tel·e·pho·to·graph·ic (tel′ə fō′tə graf′ik) *adj.* of, having to do with, or designating the process of telephotography.

tel·e·pho·tog·ra·phy (tel′ə fə tog′rə fē) *n.* 1 the method or process of photographing distant objects by using a camera with a telephoto lens. 2 the method or process of sending and reproducing pictures by telegraph.

tel·e·print·er (tel′ə print′ər) *n. Esp.Brit.* teletypewriter.

Tel·e·promp·ter (tel′ə promp′tər) *n. Trademark.* a device consisting of a moving band that gives a prepared speech line, used by speakers who are being televised. [< *tele*vision *prompter*]

tel·e·ran (tel′ə ran′) *n.* a system of air navigation by which radar mappings and other data are collected by ground stations and transmitted to aircraft by means of television. [short for *Tele*(vision) *R*(adar) *A*(ir) *N*(avigation)]

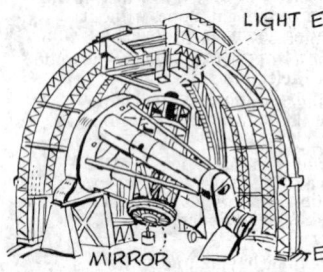

LIGHT ENTERS

A large reflecting telescope in an observatory. A large concave mirror at the bottom reflects light from the object being studied to one or more flat mirrors and then to a set of magnifying lenses called the eyepiece.

MIRROR   EYEPIECE

tel·e·scope (tel′ə skōp′) *n., v.* **-scoped, -scop·ing.** —*n.* 1 an instrument for directly viewing distant objects, using lenses or mirrors or both to make the object appear nearer and larger, telescope. 2 radio telescope.
—*v.* 1 slide one within the other like the sections of a hand telescope: *Built-in radio aerials are made so that they can be telescoped.* 2 force or be forced one into the other as in a collision: *When the two trains collided, the force of the crash telescoped the first few cars.* 3 shorten; condense. [< NL *telescopium,* ult. < Gk. *tēle* far + *-skopion* instrument for observing < *skopeein* watch]

tel·e·scop·ic (tel′ə skop′ik) *adj.* 1 of or having to do with a telescope. 2 obtained or seen by means of a telescope: *a telescopic view of the moon.* 3 visible only through a telescope: *telescopic stars.* 4 far-seeing: *telescopic vision.* 5 consisting of parts that slide inside one another like the tubes of some telescopes: *a telescopic antenna.*

tel·e·scop·i·cal·ly (tel′ə skop′ik lē) *adv.* 1 in a telescopic manner. 2 by a telescope.

tel·e·thon (tel′ə thon′) *n.* a television program lasting a very long time and, usually, serving to solicit funds for charity. [< *tele-* + *-thon* as in *marathon*]

tel·e·type (tel′ə tīp′) *n., v.* **-typed, -typ·ing.** —*n.* 1 teletypewriter. 2 Teletype, *Trademark.* a brand of teletypewriter. 3 the process or a system of communication by means of a teletypewriter: *to transmit information by teletype.* 4 a message sent by Teletype.
—*v.* send (a message) by means of a teletypewriter.

tel·e·type·writ·er (tel′ə tīp′rīt′ər) *n.* a telegraphic transmitting and receiving device resembling a typewriter, that converts a message typed on it into electric impulses which are transmitted through a telephone system to another device like it which decodes and prints out the message.

tel·e·view (tel′ə vyü′) *v.* watch by means of television.
—**tel′e·view′er,** *n.*

tel·e·vise (tel′ə vīz′) *v.* **-vised, -vis·ing.** pick up and transmit by television: *All the games are being televised.*

tel·e·vi·sion (tel′ə vizh′ən) *n.* 1 the process of transmitting the image of an object, scene, or event by radio or wire so that a person in some other place can see it at once. In television, waves of light from an object are changed into electric waves that are transmitted by radio or wire, and then changed back into waves of light that produce an image of the object on a screen. 2 the apparatus on which these pictures may be seen. 3 the business of television broadcasting; the television industry. *Abbrev:* TV or T.V.

tel·ex (tel′eks) *n., v.* —*n.* 1 an international service for telegraphic communication by means of teletypewriters connected with the regular telephone system. 2 a teletypewriter used by a subscriber to this service. 3 a message sent or received through this service.
—*v.* 1 send (a message) by telex. 2 send a telex to.

Tel·i·don (tel′ə don′) *n. Cdn.* a two-way graphics communications system through which a wide range of information in the form of words or static or moving images can be transmitted from remote computer data bases to television sets in homes or offices. The user calls up the desired information by means of a decoder or terminal in the form of a keyboard or a calculator-like key pad.

tell (tel) *v.* **told, tell·ing.** 1 put in words; say: *Tell the truth.* 2 tell to; inform: *Tell us about it.* 3 make known: *Don't tell where the money is.* 4 tell something; give an account or description (*of*): *telling of all the places she had visited.* 5 act as a talebearer; reveal (something secret or private): *Promise not to tell.* 6 recognize, know, or distinguish: *He couldn't tell which house it was. We could tell something was wrong.* 7 order or direct: *Tell him to stop!* 8 be evidence or an indication (*of*): *Her clenched hands told of her anger, though she said nothing.* 9 count (votes, etc.). 10 have effect or force: *Every blow told.*
all told, counting everyone or everything; altogether: *We'll be 15 people all told.*
I (can) tell you, yes indeed; I emphasize: *I tell you, he knows all about it.*
let me tell you, yes indeed; I emphasize.
tell apart, distinguish one from the other or others: *Nobody could tell the sisters apart.*
tell me another, *Slang.* that's hard to believe: *You made that table? Tell me another!*
tell off, a count off; count off and detach for some special duty. **b** *Informal.* rebuke strongly; castigate: *His father told him off for staying out late.*
tell on, a inform on; tell tales about. **b** have a harmful effect on; break down: *The strain told on the man's health.*
tell (one's) beads See **bead.**
tell time, know what time it is by the clock: *a child learning to tell time.*
you're telling me, *Slang.* I agree with you!
[OE *tellan*]

tell·a·ble (tel′ə bəl) *adj.* capable or worthy of being told.

tell·er (tel′ər) *n.* 1 a person who tells a story. 2 a cashier in a bank. A teller in a bank takes in, gives out, and counts money. 3 a person appointed to count votes.

tell·ing (tel′ing) *adj.* having a marked effect or great force; impressive or effective: *a telling blow.* —**tell′ing·ly,** *adv.*

tell·tale (tel′tāl′) *n.* 1 a person who tells tales on others; tattletale; talebearer. 2 (*adj.*) revealing thoughts, actions, etc. that are supposed to be secret: *telltale fingerprints, a telltale blush.* 3 any of various devices that indicate or record something: *A time clock is sometimes called a telltale.*

tel·lu·ride (tel′yə rīd′ *or* tel′yə rid) *n.* a compound of tellurium with an electropositive element or a radical.

tel·lu·ri·um (te lür′ē əm) *n.* a rare, silver-white chemical element resembling sulphur in its chemical properties and usually occurring in nature combined with gold, silver, or other metals. Symbol: Te; *at.no.* 52; *at.wt.* 127.60. [< NL < L *tellus, -uris* earth]

tel·lu·rom·e·ter (tel′yə rom′ə tər) *n.* an electronic instrument for measuring distance by timing a radio microwave from one point to another and back. [< *tellur-* earth < L *tellus, telluris* + E *-meter*]

tel·ly (tel′ē) *n. Brit. Informal.* 1 television. 2 **tellies,** *pl.* television programs.

Tel·u·gu (tel′ə gü′) *n.* a Dravidian language, spoken in southeastern India.

te·mer·i·ty (tə mer′ə tē) *n.* reckless boldness; rashness. [< L *temeritas* < *temere* heedlessly]

temp. 1 temperature. 2 temporary. 3 in the time of (for L *tempore*).

tem·per (tem′pər) *n., v.* —*n.* 1 a state of mind; disposition; condition: *She was in a good temper.* 2 an angry state of mind: *In her temper she broke a vase.* 3 a calm or controlled state of mind: *He became angry and lost his temper.* 4 the degree of hardness, toughness, etc. of a substance: *The temper of the clay was right for shaping.* 5 a substance added to something to modify its properties or qualities.
—*v.* 1 moderate; soften: *Temper justice with mercy.* 2 bring to a proper or desired condition of hardness, toughness, etc. by mixing or preparing. A painter tempers colors by mixing them with oil. Steel is tempered by heating it and working it till it has the proper degree of hardness and toughness. 3 *Music.* tune or adjust the pitch of (an instrument, a voice, etc.). [OE *temprian* < L *temperare,* originally, observe due measure < *tempus, -poris* time, interval]
☞ *Syn. n.* 1. See note at **disposition.**

tem·per·a (tem′pər ə) *n. Painting.* 1 a method in which colors are mixed with white of egg or some similar substance instead of oil. 2 the paint used. [< Ital.]

tem·per·a·ment (tem′pər ə mənt *or* tem′prə mənt) *n.* 1 an individual's usual way of thinking, feeling, and acting; natural

disposition: *a person of shy temperament, the artistic temperament.*
2 great or extreme sensitivity, especially when characterized by irritability or an unwillingness to submit to ordinary rules and restraints: *Temperament is often attributed to actors and artists.*
3 *Music.* the adjustment of the intervals, as in tuning a piano, to produce 12 equally spaced semitones of the octave, so as to fit the instrument for use in all keys. [< L *temperamentum* < *temperare.* See TEMPER.]

☛ *Syn.* **1.** See note at **disposition.**

tem·per·a·men·tal (tem′pər ə men′təl *or* tem′prə men′təl) *adj.*
1 of, having to do with, or due to temperament (def. 1); constitutional: *Cats have a temperamental dislike for water.*
2 extremely sensitive and excitable or unpredictable in behavior: *a temperamental actress. When he gets temperamental like that, it's impossible to reason with him.* —**tem′per·a·men′tal·ly,** *adv.*

tem·per·ance (tem′pər əns *or* tem′prəns) *n.* **1** moderation in action, speech, habits, etc. **2** moderation in the use of alcoholic drinks. **3** the principle and practice of not using alcoholic drinks at all. [ME < AF *temperaunce* < L *temperantia* < *temperare.* See TEMPER.]

tem·per·ate (tem′pər it *or* tem′prit) *adj.* **1** not very hot and not very cold: *a temperate climate, the temperate regions of the world.*
2 having to do with or found in regions with a moderate climate: *temperate plants.* **3** self-restrained; moderate: *He spoke in a calm, temperate manner.* **4** moderate in using alcoholic drinks; abstemious. [< L *temperatus,* pp. of *temperare.* See TEMPER.] —**tem′per·ate·ly,** *adv.* —**tem′per·ate·ness,** *n.*

☛ *Syn.* **2.** See note at **moderate.**

Temperate Zone *or* **temperate zone** either of two regions comprising the middle latitudes north and south of the equator, between the tropics and the polar regions, forming part of a now obsolete classification system for world climate zones. See also **Frigid Zone, Torrid Zone.**

tem·per·a·ture (tem′pə rə chər *or* tem′prə chər) *n.* **1** the degree of heat or cold measured on a scale. The temperature of freezing water is zero degrees Celsius. **2** the degree of heat contained in a living body. The normal temperature of the human body is about 37 degrees Celsius. **3** a level of body heat that is above normal; fever: *He stayed home all day because he had a temperature.* [< L *temperatura,* ult. < *tempus, -poris* time, season]

tem·pered (tem′pərd) *adj.* **1** softened; moderated: *justice tempered with mercy.* **2** having a particular disposition (*used in compounds*): *an even-tempered person.* **3** treated by tempering; brought to a desired condition of hardness and toughness: *a sword of tempered steel.* **4** *Music.* of a scale, interval, etc., tuned or adjusted in pitch according to equal temperament.

tem·pest (tem′pist) *n.* **1** a violent windstorm, usually accompanied by rain, hail or snow. **2** a violent disturbance; uproar; tumult: *a tempest of cheers.*
tempest in a teapot, great excitement or commotion over something unimportant.
[ME < OF *tempest(e)* < var. of L *tempestas* < *tempus* time, season]

tem·pes·tu·ous (tem pes′chü əs) *adj.* **1** stormy: *a tempestuous night.* **2** violent: *a tempestuous argument.* —**tem·pes′tu·ous·ly,** *adv.* —**tem·pes′tu·ous·ness,** *n.*

Tem·plar (tem′plər) *n.* **1** a member of a religious and military order founded among the Crusaders about 1118 to protect the Holy Sepulchre and pilgrims to the Holy Land. **2** Often, **templar,** *Brit.* a lawyer or law student having chambers in the Temple, London, a building which formerly belonged to the Templars. [< Med.L *templarius* < L *templum* temple¹]

tem·plate (tem′plit) *n.* **1** a thin piece of wood, metal, plastic, or cardboard used as a pattern in cutting an object or shape out of wood, metal, cloth, etc. **2** a stout, short piece of wood or stone placed horizontally under a beam or girder to distribute downward thrust, as over a doorway. **3** a wedge or block to support a ship's keel. Also, **templet.** [< var. of *templet;* probably influenced by PLATE.]

tem·ple¹ (tem′pəl) *n.* **1** a building used for religious services or worship. **2** Often, **Temple,** any of three religious buildings built in succession by the Jews in ancient Jerusalem. **3** synagogue. **4** a Mormon church. **5** a place in which God is thought of as residing. [OE *temp(e)l* < L *templum*]

tem·ple² (tem′pəl) *n.* **1** the flattened part on either side of the forehead. **2** either of the side supports of a pair of eyeglasses passing above and behind the ears. [ME < OF *temple,* ult. < L *tempus*]

tem·ple³ (tem′pəl) *n.* a device in a loom for keeping the web stretched to the correct width during weaving. [ME *temple* < MF, prob. < L *templus* small timber]

tem·plet (tem′plit) *n.* template. [< F *templet, templette,* dim. of *temple* temple³]

hat, āge, fär; let, ēqual, têrm; it, īce
hot, ōpen, ôrder; oil, out; cup, pùt, rüle,
əbove, takən, pencəl, lemən, circəs

ch, child; ng, long; sh, ship
th, thin; ŦH, then; zh, measure

tem·po (tem′pō) *n., pl.* **-pos, -pi** (-pē). **1** *Music.* **a** the time or rate of speed of a composition or passage: *The tempo of this piece is very fast. He didn't play it at the correct tempo.* **b** (*adjl.*) indicating a specific tempo: *a tempo mark.* **2** characteristic rate of activity or motion; pace: *the fast tempo of modern life.* [< Ital. *tempo* time < L *tempus.* Doublet of TENSE².]

tem·po·ral¹ (tem′pə rəl *or* tem′prəl) *adj.* **1** of, having to do with, or designating time or earthly life, as opposed to eternity. **2** of or having to do with secular things; worldly: *temporal concerns.*
3 *Grammar.* **a** expressing time, as an adverb or a clause. **b** of tense. [ME < OF < L *temporalis* < *tempus, -poris* time] —**tem′po·ral·ly,** *adv.*

tem·po·ral² (tem′pə rəl *or* tem′prəl) *adj.* of or having to do with the temples of the head: *the temporal artery.* [ME < OF < L *temporalis* < *tempus, -poris* temple²]

tem·po·ral·i·ty (tem′pə ral′ə tē) *n., pl.* **-ties. 1** Usually, **temporalities,** *pl.* secular possessions of a church, especially revenues or properties. **2** the quality or state of being temporal.

tem·po·rar·y (tem′pə rer′ē) *adj., n.* —*adj.* lasting or used for a short time only; not permanent: *a temporary shelter, a temporary inconvenience.* —*n.* a person employed for a short time: *They hired several temporaries last summer.* [< L *temporarius* < *tempus, -poris* time] —**tem′po·rar′i·ly,** *adv.* —**tem′po·rar′i·ness,** *n.*

☛ *Syn.* **Temporary, transient** = lasting or staying only for a time. **Temporary** emphasizes existing or being used or in effect for a time, and describes either something meant only for the time being or something liable to come to an end at any time: *He has a temporary job. Our school is a temporary building.* **Transient** emphasizes quick passing, and describes something that stays or lasts only a short time: *His nervousness was transient, and passed when he began to speak.*

tem·po·ri·za·tion (tem′pə rə zā′shən *or* -rī zā′shən) *n.* the act or practice of temporizing; a compromise.

tem·po·rize (tem′pə rīz′) *v.* **-rized, -riz·ing. 1** evade immediate action or decision in order to gain time, avoid trouble, etc. **2** fit one's acts to the time or occasion. **3** make or discuss terms; negotiate. [< MF *temporiser,* ult. < L *tempus, -poris* time] —**tem′po·riz′er,** *n.*

tempt (tempt) *v.* **1** make, or try to make a person do something wrong by promising pleasure or some advantage: *He was tempted to steal.* **2** appeal to strongly; be very attractive to: *sweets that tempt one's appetite.* **3** cause to feel strongly inclined (*usually used in the passive*): *After three failures he was tempted to quit.*
4 provoke or defy: *It would be tempting fate to take that old car on the road.* **5** *Archaic.* test: *God tempted Abraham by asking him to sacrifice his son.* [< L *temptare* try] —**tempt′a·ble,** *adj.*

temp·ta·tion (temp tā′shən) *n.* **1** the act of tempting or the state of being tempted: *No temptation could make her false to her friend.*
2 something that tempts: *The money lying on the counter was a temptation to him.*

tempt·er (temp′tər) *n.* **1** a person who tempts. **2 the Tempter,** the Devil; Satan.

tempt·ing (temp′ting) *adj.* that tempts; alluring; inviting. —**tempt′ing·ly,** *adv.*

tempt·ress (temp′tris) *n.* a woman who tempts.

tem·pu·ra (tem pùr′ə *or* tem′pù rə) *n.* a dish of deep-fried shrimp, vegetables, etc. [< Japanese]

tem·pus fu·git (tem′pəs fyü′jit) *Latin.* time flies.

ten (ten) *n., adj.* —*n.* **1** one more than nine; 10. **2** the numeral 10: *That's a 10, not a 16.* **3** the tenth in a set or series; especially, a playing card having ten spots: *She played a ten of clubs.* **4** a ten-dollar bill. **5** a set or series of ten persons or things: *I got my ten right.*
—*adj.* **1** being one more than nine. **2** being tenth in a set or series (*used mainly after the noun*): *Chapter Ten will be discussed tomorrow.* [OE *tīen, tēn*]

ten. tenor.

ten·a·bil·i·ty (ten′ə bil′ə tē) *n.* the fact or quality of being tenable.

ten·a·ble (ten′ə bəl) *adj.* capable of being held or defended: *a tenable position, a tenable theory.* [< F *tenable* < *tenir* hold < L *tenere*] —**ten′a·bly,** *adv.*

te·na·cious (ti nā′shəs) *adj.* **1** holding fast; not readily letting go: *a tenacious grip, the tenacious jaws of a bulldog. He is tenacious of his rights and will fight to the end.* **2** stubborn or persistent; not

readily giving up: *a tenacious salesman, tenacious courage.*
3 especially good at remembering: *a tenacious memory.* **4** tending to stick or cling: *tenacious burrs.* **5** holding fast together; not easily pulled apart; tough: *a tenacious metal.* [< L *tenax, -acis* < *tenere* hold] —**te·na′cious·ly**, *adv.*

te·na·cious·ness (ti nā′shəs nəs) *n.* tenacity.

te·nac·i·ty (ti nas′ə tē) *n.* the quality or state of being tenacious.

ten·an·cy (ten′ən sē) *n., pl.* **-cies. 1** the state of being a tenant; occupying and paying rent for land or buildings. **2** the length of time a tenant occupies a property. **3** the period of holding an office or position: *a long tenancy as mayor.*

ten·ant (ten′ənt) *n., v.* —*n.* **1** a person paying rent for the temporary use of the land or buildings of another person: *They have tenants on the second floor of their house.* **2** a person or thing that occupies: *Birds are tenants of the trees.* —*v.* hold or occupy as a tenant; inhabit. [< F *tenant,* originally ppr. of *tenir* hold < L *tenere*] —**ten′ant·less**, *adj.*

ten·ant·ry (ten′ənt rē) *n., pl.* **-ries. 1** all the tenants on an estate. **2** tenancy.

tench (tench) *n., pl.* **tench** or **tench·es.** a European freshwater game fish (*Tinca tinca*) that is noted for the length of time it can live out of water. The tench is a cyprinid. [ME < OF *tenche* < LL *tinca*]

Ten Commandments in the Bible, the ten rules for living and for worship that God gave to Moses on Mount Sinai (Exod. 20:2-17; Deut. 5:6-21).

tend¹ (tend) *v.* **1** have an inclination or tendency: *She tends to use large canvases for her paintings. He tends to dress conservatively.* **2** move or extend; be directed: *The coastline tends to the south here.* [ME < OF *tendre* < L *tendere* stretch, aim. Doublet of TENDER².]

tend² (tend) *v.* **1** take care of; look after; attend to: *He tends shop for his father. A shepherd tends his flock.* **2** serve; wait upon. **3** *Nautical.* stand by and watch over (a line, anchor cable, etc.) to prevent fouling. **4** *Informal.* pay attention (*to*): *Just tend to your work and never mind what everyone else is doing.* [< *attend*]

tend·ance (ten′dəns) *n.* attention; care.

tend·en·cy (ten′dən sē) *n., pl.* **-cies. 1** an inclination or leaning toward a particular kind of action, behavior, etc.: *a tendency to favor pastel colors, a tendency to reject new ideas without considering them.* **2** a natural disposition to move, proceed, or act in some direction or toward some point, end, or result: *Wood has a tendency to swell if it gets wet.* [< Med.L *tendentia* < L *tendere.* See TEND¹.]
☛ *Syn.* **2.** See note at **direction.**

ten·den·tious (ten den′shəs) *adj.* having or promoting a particular aim or point of view; biassed: *tendentious writings.* [< Med.L *tendentia.* See TENDENCY.] —**ten·den′tious·ly**, *adv.* —**ten·den′tious·ness,** *n.*

ten·der¹ (ten′dər) *adj.* **1** not hard or tough; soft: *tender meat.* **2** not strong and hardy; delicate: *tender young grass.* **3** kind; affectionate; loving: *She spoke tender words to the child.* **4** not rough or crude; gentle: *With tender, loving hands, the mother bathed her baby.* **5** young; immature: *at the tender age of two.* **6** sensitive; painful; sore: *a tender wound.* **7** feeling pain or grief easily: *She has a tender heart and would never hurt anyone.* **8** considerate; careful: *He handles people in a tender manner.* **9** requiring careful or tactful handling: *a tender situation.* [ME < OF *tendre* < L *tener*] —**ten′der·ly**, *adv.* —**ten′der·ness,** *n.*

ten·der² (ten′dər) *v., n.* —*v.* **1** offer formally: *He tendered his thanks.* **2** *Business.* make an offer to buy, supply, etc.: *Several firms tendered for the contract.* **3** *Law.* offer (money, goods, etc.) in payment of a debt or other obligation.
—*n.* **1** a formal offer: *She refused his tender of marriage.* **2** the thing offered. Money that may be offered as payment for a debt is called legal tender. **3** *Business.* an offer to buy, supply, etc. **4** *Law.* an offer of money, goods, etc. in payment of a debt, etc. [< OF *tendre* < L *tendere* extend. Doublet of TEND¹.] —**ten′der·er**, *n.*
☛ *Syn. v.* **1.** See note at **offer.**

tend·er³ (ten′dər) *n.* **1** a small boat carried or towed by a big one and used for landing passengers. **2** a small ship used for carrying supplies and passengers to and from larger ships. **3** the car attached behind a steam locomotive and used for carrying coal, oil, water, etc. **4** a person or thing that tends another. [< *tend²*]

ten·der·foot (ten′dər fut′) *n., pl.* **-foots** or **-feet.** *Informal.* **1** a newcomer to the pioneer life of the West. **2** a person not used to rough living and hardships. **3** an inexperienced person; beginner. **4** a young person in the first stage of being a Boy Scout or Girl Guide.

ten·der-heart·ed (ten′dər här′tid) *adj.* kindly; sympathetic. —**ten′der-heart′ed·ly**, *adv.* —**ten′der-heart′ed·ness,** *n.*

ten·der·ize (ten′də rīz′) *v.* **-ized, -iz·ing.** make (meat) tender; soften.

ten·der·loin (ten′dər loin′) *n.* **1** a tender part of the loin of beef or pork. **2** a district of a city noted for its high level of vice, crime, and corruption. (Originally applied to an area of New York City, from the rich living supposed to be gained there by corrupt policemen.)

ten·di·nous (ten′də nəs) *adj.* **1** of or like a tendon. **2** consisting of tendons. [< F *tendineux* < *tendon* tendon < Med.L. See TENDON.]

ten·don (ten′dən) *n.* a tough, strong band or cord of tissue that joins a muscle to a bone or some other part; sinew. [< Med.L *tendo, -onis* < Gk. *tenōn;* influenced by L *tendere* stretch]

ten·dril (ten′drəl) *n.* **1** a threadlike part of a climbing plant that attaches itself to something and helps support the plant. **2** something resembling such a part of a plant: *tendrils of hair curling about a child's face.* [< F *tendrillon,* ult. < L *tener* tender]

ten·e·brous (ten′ə brəs) *adj.* dark; gloomy; dim. [< L *tenebrosus* < *tenebrae* darkness]

ten·e·ment (ten′ə mənt) *n.* **1** any house or building to live in; a dwelling house. **2** a part of a house or building occupied by a tenant as a separate dwelling. **3** a building, especially in a poor section of a city, divided into sets of rooms for separate families. **4** an abode; habitation. [ME < OF *tenement,* ult. < L *tenere* hold]

ten·et (ten′it; *esp.Brit.,* tē′nit) *n.* a doctrine, principle, belief, or opinion held as true. [< L *tenet* he holds]

ten·fold (ten′fōld′) *adj. or adv.* ten times as much or as many.

ten–gallon hat a large, wide-brimmed hat, often worn by cowboys. [< Sp. *galón* braid, cowboy hats being originally decorated with a number of braids; confused with *gallon,* as if in reference to the hat's size]

Tenn. Tennessee.

ten·nis (ten′is) *n.* **1** a game played on a special court by two or four players who knock a ball back and forth over a net with a racket (**tennis racket**). **2** lawn tennis. **3** court tennis. [ME < AF *tenetz* hold!, ult. < L *tenere*]

tennis court a place prepared and marked out to play tennis on.

ten·on (ten′ən) *n., v.* —*n.* the end of a piece of wood cut so as to fit into a hole (the mortise) in another piece and so form a joint. See **joint** for picture. —*v.* **1** cut so as to form a tenon. **2** fit together with tenon and mortise. [ME < OF, ult. < L *tenere* hold]

ten·or (ten′ər) *n.* **1** the general tendency or direction; a settled course: *The calm tenor of her life has never been disturbed by excitement or trouble.* **2** the general meaning or drift: *I understand French well enough to get the tenor of his lecture.* **3** *Law.* **a** the exact words or intent and meaning of a document, etc. as distinguished from their effect. **b** an exact copy. **4** the highest ordinary, or natural, adult male singing voice. Compare **countertenor. 5** a singer who has such a voice. **7** the part sung by a tenor. Tenor is the second lowest part, above bass, in a standard four-part harmony for men's and women's voices. **7** an instrument having a range next above that of the bass in a family of musical instruments. **8** (*adj.*) having to do with, having the range of, or designed for a tenor. **9** a high-pitched male voice. [ME < OF < L *tenor,* originally, a holding on < *tenere* hold]

ten·pen·ny (ten′pen′ē *or* ten′pən ē) *adj.* **1** *Brit.* worth or costing ten pennies. **2** designating a kind of large-sized nail, once costing ten pennies per hundred.

ten·pin (ten′pin′) *n.* **1** tenpins, a bowling game similar to fivepins, but using a larger ball (about 70 cm in circumference) to knock over 10 pins instead of five (*used with a singular verb*). **2** one of the pins used in this game.

tense¹ (tens) *adj.* **tens·er, tens·est;** *v.* **tensed, tens·ing.** —*adj.* **1** stretched tight; strained to stiffness: *a tense rope, a face tense with pain.* **2** strained; keyed up: *tense feelings, a tense moment.* —*v.* stretch tight; stiffen: *He tensed his muscles for the leap.* [< L *tensus,* pp. of *tendere* stretch] —**tense′ly**, *adv.* —**tense′ness,** *n.*

tense² (tens) *n.* **1** a set of verb forms to show the time, duration, etc. of the action or state expressed by the verb. The simple past tense in English is used to express an action or state that is completed or ended. **2** a form of a verb indicating a particular time, etc. of an action or state. The simple past tense of *go* is *went.* [ME < OF *tens* time < L *tempus.* Doublet of TEMPO.] —**tense′less,** *adj.*

ten·si·ble (ten′sə bəl) *adj.* capable of being stretched. [< Med.L *tensibilis* < L *tendere* stretch]

ten·sile (ten′sīl *or* ten′səl) *adj.* **1** of or having to do with tension: *Steel has great tensile strength.* **2** capable of being stretched; ductile. [< NL *tensilis* < L *tendere* stretch]

ten·sil·i·ty (ten sil′ə tē) *n.* a tensile quality; ductility.

ten·sion (ten′shən) *n.* **1** a stretching. **2** a stretched condition: *The tension of the spring is caused by the weight.* **3** mental strain: *A mother feels tension when her baby is sick.* **4** a strained condition:

political tension. **5** a stress caused by the action of a pulling force. An elevator exerts tension on the cables supporting it. **6** a device to control the pull or strain on something. The tension in a sewing machine may be adjusted to hold the thread tight or loose. **7** voltage: *high-tension wires.* **8** the pressure of a gas. [< LL *tensio, -onis* < L *tendere* stretch]

ten·sion·al (ten′shən əl) *adj.* of or having to do with tension.

ten·si·ty (ten′sə tē) *n.* a tense quality or state.

ten·sor (ten′sər *or* ten′sôr) *n.* **1** *Physiology.* a muscle that stretches or tightens some part of the body. **2** *Mathematics.* a vector that can only be defined by reference to more than three components. [< NL]

ten–strike (ten′strīk′) *n.* **1** *Tenpins.* the stroke that knocks down all the pins. **2** *Informal.* any completely successful stroke or act.

tent (tent) *n., v.* —*n.* **1** a movable shelter, usually made of canvas and often supported by one or more poles and ropes or wires. **2** a tentlike device to regulate the temperature and humidity of the air in treating certain respiratory diseases. —*v.* **1** camp out or live in a tent. **2** cover with a tent. [ME < OF *tente,* ult. < L *tendere* stretch] —**tent′like′,** *adj.*

ten·ta·cle (ten′tə kəl) *n.* **1** a long, slender, flexible growth on the head or around the mouth of an animal, used to touch, hold, or move; feeler. **2** a sensitive, hairlike growth on a plant. **3** something that resembles a tentacle in its reach and grasp: *The tentacles of a dictator's power reach into every home.* [< NL *tentaculum* < L *tentare* try. See TENTATIVE.]

ten·tac·u·lar (ten tak′yə lər) *adj.* of, forming, or resembling tentacles.

tent·age (tent′ij) *n.* **1** a supply or number of tents. **2** equipment for tents.

ten·ta·tive (ten′tə tiv) *adj.* done as a trial or experiment; experimental: *a tentative plan.* [< Med.L *tentativus* < L *tentare* try out, intensive of *tendere* stretch, aim; associated in L with *temptare* feel out] —**ten′ta·tive·ly,** *adv.* —**ten′ta·tive·ness,** *n.*

tent caterpillar the larva of any of various moths (family Lasiocampidae), especially *Malacosoma americanum,* that feeds on the leaves of deciduous trees. Tent caterpillars live in colonies in huge, tentlike webs which they spin in the crotches of trees in early spring.

ten·ter (ten′tər) *n., v.* —*n.* a framework on which cloth is stretched so that it may set or dry evenly without shrinking. —*v.* stretch (cloth) on a tenter. [ult. < L *tentus,* pp. of *tendere* stretch]

ten·ter·hook (ten′tər hùk′) *n.* one of the hooks or bent nails that hold the cloth stretched on a tenter.
on tenterhooks, in painful suspense; anxious.

tenth (tenth) *adj. or n.* **1** next after the 9th; last in a series of ten; 10th. **2** one, or being one, of 10 equal parts.

tenth·ly (tenth′lē) *adv.* in the tenth place.

tent stitch petit point (def. 1).

ten·u·i·ty (ten yü′ə tē *or* ti nü′ə tē) *n.* a rarefied condition; thinness; slightness.

ten·u·ous (ten′yü əs) *adj.* **1** thin; slender. **2** not dense: *tenuous air.* **3** having slight importance; not substantial. [< L *tenuis* thin] —**ten′u·ous·ly,** *adv.* —**ten′u·ous·ness,** *n.*

ten·ure (ten′yər) *n.* **1** a holding; possessing. **2** the length of time of holding or possessing: *The tenure of office of the president of our club is one year.* **3** the manner of holding land, buildings, etc. from a feudal lord or superior. **4** the conditions, terms, etc. on which anything is held or occupied. **5** permanent status in one's job, granted to a teacher, especially a university professor, after certain specified conditions of length of service, performance, etc. have been met. [ME < OF *tenure,* ult. < L *tenere* hold]

te·nu·to (te nü′tō) *adj. Music.* held; not a note, or to be held to its full time value. [< Ital. *tenuto,* pp. of *tenere* hold < L]

te·pee (tē′pē) See teepee.

tep·id (tep′id) *adj.* slightly warm; lukewarm. [< L *tepidus*] —**te′pid·ly,** *adv.* —**tep′id·ness,** *n.*

te·pid·i·ty (ti pid′ə tē) *n.* lukewarmness; tepid condition.

te·qui·la (tə kē′lə) *n.* **1** a Mexican agave (*Agave tequilana*) from which mescal is made. **2** a strong alcoholic liquor made by redistilling mescal. [< Am.E < Am.Sp. < *Tequila,* a town in Mexico]

ter. **1** territory; territorial. **2** terrace.

ter·a·to·gen (ter′ə tə jən *or* tə rat′ə jən) an agent, such as a chemical, that produces or tends to produce malformations in a fetus. [< Gk. *teras, teratos* monster + *-gen*]

ter·a·to·gen·e·sis (ter′ə tō jen′ə sis) *n.* the production of malformations in fetuses.

ter·a·to·gen·ic (ter′ə tə gèn′ik) *adj.* being a teratogen.

ter·bi·um (tèr′bē əm) *n.* a rare metallic chemical element of the

hat, āge, fär; let, ēqual, tèrm; it, īce
hot, ōpen, ôrder; oil, out; cup, pùt, rüle,
əbove, takən, pencəl, lemən, circəs

ch, child; ng, long; sh, ship
th, thin; ŧH, then; zh, measure

yttrium group. *Symbol:* Tb; *at.no.* 65; *at.wt.* 158.924. [< *terb-,* abstracted from *Ytterby,* a town in Sweden]

ter·cel (tèr′səl) *n.* a male falcon or goshawk, especially a male peregrine falcon as used in falconry. Compare **falcon** (def. 2). [ME < OF *tercel,* ult. < L *tertius* third]

ter·cen·te·nar·y (tèr′sen ten′ə rē *or* tèr′sen tē′nə rē) *adj. or n., pl.* **-nar·ies.** tricentennial. [< L *ter* three times + E *centenary*]

ter·cen·ten·ni·al (tèr′sen ten′ē əl) *adj. or n.* tricentennial.

ter·cet (tèr′sit *or* tèr set′) *n.* **1** a group of three lines rhyming together, or connected by rhyme with the adjacent group or groups of three lines. **2** *Music.* triplet. [< F < Ital. *terzetto,* ult. < L *tertius* third]

te·re·do (tə rē′dō) *n., pl.* **-dos.** shipworm, especially any of the genus *Teredo.* [< L < Gk. *terēdōn < tereein* bore]

ter·gi·ver·sate (tèr′jə vər sāt′) *v.* **-sat·ed, -sat·ing. 1** change one's attitude or opinions with respect to a cause or subject; turn renegade. **2** shift or shuffle; evade. [< L *tergiversatus,* ult. < *tergum* back + *vertere* turn] —**ter′gi·ver·sa′tor,** *n.* —**ter′gi·ver·sa′tion,** *n.*

term (tèrm) *n., v.* —*n.* **1** a word or phrase used in a recognized and definite sense in some particular subject, science, art, business, etc.: *medical terms, terms about radio.* **2** a word or expression: *an abstract term, a term of reproach.* **3** a set period of time; the length of time that a thing lasts: *a president's term of office.* **4** one of the long periods into which the school year may be divided: *the fall term.* **5** *Law.* one of the periods of time when certain courts are in session. **6** *Mathematics.* **a** one of the members in a proportion or ratio. **b** one or more numerals or symbols that make a product. Terms in an algebraic expression are always separated by + or −. The expressions x and xy each consist of one term; $xy + ab$ is an expression consisting of two terms. **7** *Logic.* **a** a word or words that form the subject or predicate of a proposition. **b** one of the three parts of a syllogism. **8** *Archaic.* a boundary; end; limit. **9 terms,** *pl.* **a** conditions: *the terms of a treaty.* **b** a way of speaking: *flattering terms.* **c** personal relations: *on good terms, on speaking terms.*
bring to terms, compel to agree, assent, or submit; force to come to terms.
come to terms, reach an agreement.
terms of reference, the matters referred to a person, committee, etc. for study; instructions indicating the scope of an inquiry.
—*v.* name; call; describe as: *He might be termed handsome.* [ME < OF *terme* < L *terminus* end, boundary line. Doublet of TERMINUS.]

ter·ma·gan·cy (tèr′mə gən sē) *n.* shrewishness.

ter·ma·gant (tèr′mə gənt) *n., adj.* —*n.* a violent, quarrelling, scolding woman. —*adj.* violent; quarrelling; scolding. [ME < OF *Tervagan,* a fictitious Moslem deity]

ter·mi·na·bil·i·ty (tèr′mə nə bil′ə tē) *n.* the fact or quality of being terminable.

ter·mi·na·ble (tèr′mə nə bəl) *adj.* **1** that can be ended: *The contract was terminable by either party.* **2** coming to an end after a certain time: *a loan terminable in ten years.* —**ter′mi·na·ble·ness,** *n.* —**ter′mi·na·bly,** *adv.*

ter·mi·nal (tèr′mə nəl) *adj., n.* —*adj.* **1** at the end; forming the end part. A terminal flower or bud is one growing at the end of a stem, branch, etc. **2** coming at the end: *a terminal examination.* **3** having to do with a term. **4** at the end of a railway line: *a terminal station.* **5** having to do with the handling of freight at a terminal. **6** marking a boundary, limit, or end. **7** of a disease, incurable and fatal: *terminal cancer.*
—*n.* **1** the end part. **2** either end of a railway line, airline, shipping route, etc. where sheds, hangars, garages, offices, etc., and stations to handle freight and passengers are located; terminus. **3** a device for making an electrical connection: *the terminals of a battery.* **4** an apparatus, such as a visual display unit, by which a user can give information to or receive information from a computer, communications system, etc. [< L *terminalis < terminus* end]

ter·mi·nal·ly (tèr′mə nəl ē) *adv.* **1** at the end. **2** with respect to a termination.

ter·mi·nate (tèr′mə nāt′) *v.* **-nat·ed, -nat·ing. 1** bring to an end; put an end to: *to terminate a partnership.* **2** come to an end: *His contract terminates soon.* **3** occur at or form the end of; bound; limit. [< L *terminare < terminus* end] —**ter′mi·na′tor,** *n.*

ter·mi·na·tion (tèr′mə nā′shən) *n.* **1** an ending; end. **2** an end part. **3** the ending of a word; suffix. *Example: In* gladly, *the adverbial termination is* -ly.

ter·mi·na·tive (tèr′mə nə tiv *or* tèr′mə nā′tiv) *adj.* tending or serving to terminate.

ter·mi·no·log·i·cal (tèr′mə nə loj′ə kəl) *adj.* of or having to do with terminology.

ter·mi·nol·o·gy (tèr′mə nol′ə jē) *n., pl.* **-gies.** the special words or terms used in a science, art, business, etc.: *medical terminology.* [< G *Terminologie* < Med.L *terminus* term + Gk. *-logos* treating of]

term insurance life insurance that expires at the end of a specified period of time.

ter·mi·nus (tèr′mə nəs) *n., pl.* **-nus·es** *or* **-ni** (-nī′ *or* -nē′). **1** either end of a railway line, bus line, etc.; terminal. **2** a city or station at the end of a railway line, bus line, etc. **3** an ending place; final point; goal; end. **4** a stone, post, etc. marking a boundary or limit. [< L *terminus.* Doublet of TERM.]

ter·mite (tèr′mīt) *n.* any of an order (Isoptera) of antlike, social insects, found chiefly in tropical regions, having a soft, pale-colored body and a broad abdomen. Termites eat cellulose, the main constituent of wood, and can be very destructive if they invade buildings. [< NL *termes, -itis,* special use of L *termes* woodworm]

tern (tèrn) *n.* any of a subfamily (Sterninae) of typically grey-and-white, aquatic birds related to and resembling gulls, but usually smaller and having a pointed bill and, usually, a deeply forked tail. [< Scand.; cf. Danish *terne*]
☛ *Hom.* turn.

ter·na·ry (tèr′nə rē) *adj.* consisting of three; involving three; triple. [< L *ternarius,* ult. < *ter* three times]

ter·nate (tèr′nit *or* tèr′nāt) *adj.* **1** consisting of three. **2** arranged in threes. **3** *Botany.* **a** consisting of three leaflets. **b** having leaves arranged in whorls of three.

Terp·sich·o·re (tèrp sik′ə rē′) *n. Greek mythology.* the Muse of dancing.

terp·si·cho·re·an (tèrp′sə kə rē′ən) *adj.* having to do with dancing: *the terpsichorean art.*

terr. **1** territory. **2** terrace.

A series of terraces on a mountainside in Peru

ter·race (ter′is) *n., v.* **-raced, -rac·ing.** —*n.* **1** a flat level of land like a large step, especially one of a series of such levels on a slope. **2** a street along the side or top of a slope. **3** a row of houses on such a street. **4** a paved outdoor space adjoining a house, used for lounging, dining, etc. **5** the flat roof of a house, especially a house of Spanish or Oriental style.
—*v.* form into a terrace or terraces; furnish with terraces. [< OF *terrace,* ult. < L *terra* earth]

ter·ra cot·ta (ter′ə kot′ə) **1** a kind of hard, brownish-red earthenware, used for vases, statuettes, decorations on buildings, etc. **2** a piece of this earthenware, or something made from it. **3** a dull brownish-red. [< Ital. *terra cotta* < *terra* earth + *cotta* baked]

ter·ra fir·ma (ter′ə fèr′mə) solid earth; dry land. [< L]

ter·rain (te rān′ *or* ter′ān) *n.* land; a tract of land, especially considered as to its extent and natural features in relation to its use in warfare. [< F *terrain,* ult. < L *terra* land]

Ter·ra·my·cin (ter′ə mī′sin) *n. Trademark.* an antibiotic derived from a soil micro-organism, used in the treatment of syphilis, some rheumatic diseases, certain bacterial infections, etc. *Formula:* $C_{22}H_{24}N_2O_9 \cdot 2H_2O$

ter·ra·pin (ter′ə pin) *n.* any of various small, edible turtles (family Emydidae) occurring in fresh or brackish water. See also **diamondback terrapin.** [< Algonquian]

ter·rar·i·um (tə rer′ē əm) *n., pl.* **-i·ums,** *or* **-i·a** (-ē ə) a glass or plastic enclosure in which plants or small land animals are kept. [< NL *terrarium* < L *terra* land]

ter·raz·zo (te rät′sō) *n.* a floor made of small pieces of marble embedded in cement. [< Ital. *terrazzo* terrace, balcony < *terra* earth]

ter·res·tri·al (tə res′trē əl) *adj.* **1** of the earth; having to do with the earth. **2** of land, not water or air: *Islands and continents make up the terrestrial parts of the earth.* **3** living on the ground, not in the air or water or in trees: *terrestrial animals.* **4** growing on land; growing in the ground: *terrestrial plants.* **5** worldly; earthly. [ME < L *terrestris* < *terra* earth]
☛ *Syn.* **5.** See note at **earthly.**

terrestrial globe **1** the earth. **2** a sphere with the map of the earth on it.

ter·ret (ter′it) *n.* one of the round loops or rings on the saddle of a harness, through which the driving reins pass. [var. of *toret* < OF *toret* < *tour* < L *tornus.* See TOUR.]

ter·ri·ble (ter′ə bəl) *adj.* **1** causing great fear; dreadful; awful: *a terrible leopard.* **2** distressing; severe: *the terrible suffering caused by war.* **3** *Informal.* extremely bad, unpleasant, etc.: *She has a terrible temper.* [< L *terribilis* < *terrere* terrify] —**ter′ri·ble·ness,** *n.*

ter·ri·bly (ter′ə blē) *adv.* **1** *Informal.* extremely: *We were terribly afraid. I'm terribly sorry I stepped on your toe.* **2** in a terrible manner: *The ogre frowned terribly.*

ter·ri·er (ter′ē ər) *n.* any of several breeds of dog, such as the Airedale, fox terrier, or Scotch terrier, having either a short-haired, smooth coat or a long-haired, rough coat. Terriers were formerly used to pursue burrowing animals. [< F *terrier,* ult. < L *terra* earth]

ter·rif·ic (tə rif′ik) *adj.* **1** causing great fear; terrifying. **2** *Informal.* very unusual; remarkable; extraordinary: *A terrific hot spell ruined many of the crops.* **3** *Slang.* very good; wonderful: *He is a terrific football player. The party was terrific.* [< L *terrificus* < *terrere* terrify + *-ficus* making] —**ter·rif′i·cal·ly,** *adv.*

ter·ri·fied (ter′ə fīd′) *adj.* filled with great fear; frightened.
☛ *Syn.* See note at **afraid.**

ter·ri·fy (ter′ə fī′) *v.* **-fied, -fy·ing.** fill with great fear; frighten very much. [< L *terrificare* < *terrere* terrify + *facere* make]

ter·ri·to·ri·al (ter′ə tôr′ē əl) *adj., n.* —*adj.* **1** of or having to do with territory: *Many wars have been fought for territorial gain.* **2 Territorial,** of or having to do with a Territory: *the Territorial Council.* **3** of or restricted to a particular territory or region. **4** Also, **Territorial,** *Brit.* organized for home defence.
—*n.* **Territorial,** *Brit.* a soldier of a Territorial force.
—**ter′ri·to′ri·al·ly,** *adv.*

Territorial Council **1** in the Yukon Territory, an elected body consisting of seven members and responsible for local government. **2** the Council of the Northwest Territories.

ter·ri·to·ry (ter′ə tôr′ē) *n., pl.* **-ries. 1** land: *Much territory in Africa is desert.* **2** a region; an area of land: *The company leased a large territory for oil explorations.* **3** land under the rule or control of a distant government: *The British Empire included many territories.* **4 Territory, a** in Canada, a region having its own elected council and administered by a commissioner appointed by the federal government: *the Northwest Territories, the Yukon Territory.* **b** a region having similar status in some other countries. **5** a region assigned to a salesman or agent. **6** the facts investigated by some branch of science or learning: *the territory of biochemistry.* [ME < L *territorium* < *terra* land]

ter·ror (ter′ər) *n.* **1** great fear. **2** a cause of great fear. **3** *Informal.* a person or thing that causes much trouble and unpleasantness. **4 the Terror,** Reign of Terror. [ME < OF < L *terror* < *terrere* terrify]

ter·ror·ism (ter′ər iz′əm) *n.* **1** the act of terrorizing; use of terror. **2** the condition of fear and submission produced by frightened people. **3** a method of opposing a government internally through the use of terror.

ter·ror·ist (ter′ər ist) *n.* **1** a person who uses or favors terrorism. **2** (*adj.*) of, having to do with, or like terrorists: *a terrorist bomb; terrorist tactics.*

ter·ror·is·tic (ter′ər is′tik) *adj.* using or favoring methods that inspire terror.

ter·ror·i·za·tion (ter′ər ə zā′shən *or* -ī zā′shən) *n.* the act of terrorizing or the state of being terrorized; rule by terror.

ter·ror·ize (ter′ər īz′) *v.* **-ized, -iz·ing. 1** fill with terror. **2** rule or subdue by causing terror. —**ter′ror·iz′er,** *n.*

ter·ror-strick·en (ter′ər strik′ən) *adj.* terrified.

ter·ry (ter′ē) *n., pl.* **-ries.** a rough cloth made of uncut looped yarn. [? < F *tiré* drawn]

terry cloth terry.

terse (tèrs) *adj.* **ters·er, ters·est. 1** brief and to the point: *a terse account of a voyage; a terse writer.* **2** abrupt or curt. [< L *tersus,* pp. of *tergere* rub, polish] —**terse′ly,** *adv.* —**terse′ness,** *n.*

ter·tian (tėr′shən) *n., adj.* —*n.* a fever or ague that reaches a peak every other day. —*adj.* recurring every other day. [ME < L *tertiana* (*febris* fever) < *tertius* third]

Ter·ti·ar·y (tėr′shē er′ē *or* tėr′shə rē) *adj., n., pl.* **-ar·ies.** —*adj.* 1 *Geology.* of or having to do with the Tertiary or the rocks formed during it. 2 tertiary, of the third order, rank, formation, etc.; third. —*n.* 1 *Geology.* **a** the third chief period of time in the formation of the earth's surface, beginning approximately 60 million years ago. During this period the great mountain systems, such as the Rockies, Alps, Himalayas, and Andes, appeared and rapid development of mammals occurred. See chart at **geology. b** the rocks formed during this period. 2 tertiary, one of a bird's flight feathers. [< L *tertiarius* < *tertius* third]

ter·ti·um quid (ter′shē əm kwid′) *Latin.* something related in some way to two things, but distinct from both; something intermediate between two things. [*literally,* third thing]

ter·y·lene (ter′ə lēn′) *n.* 1 Terylene, *Trademark.* a crease-resistant synthetic polyester fibre, much used for shirts, dresses, suits, etc. and often mixed with wool or other yarns. 2 any fibre of this kind.

ter·za ri·ma (tėr′tsä rē′mä) an Italian form of iambic verse consisting of ten-syllable or eleven-syllable lines arranged in tercets, the middle line of each tercet rhyming with the first and third lines of the following tercet. Shelley's *Ode to the West Wind* is in terza rima. [< Ital. *terza rima* < *terza* third + *rima* rhyme]

tes·sel·late (*v.* tes′ə lāt′; *adj.* tes′ə lit *or* tes′ə lāt′) *v.* **-lat·ed, -lat·ing;** *adj.* —*v.* make of small squares or blocks, or in a checkered pattern. —*adj.* made in small squares or blocks or in a checkered pattern. [< L *tessellatus,* ult. < *tessera.* See TESSERA.]

tes·ser·a (tes′ər ə) *n., pl.* **tes·ser·ae** (tes′ər ē′ *or* tes′ər ī′). 1 a small piece of marble, glass, etc. used in mosaic work. 2 a small square of bone, wood, etc. used in ancient times as a token, tally, ticket, die, etc. [< L < Gk. *tessera* piece having four corners < *tessares* four]

test (test) *n., v.* —*n.* 1 an examination; trial: *People who want to drive an automobile must pass a test. The teacher gave the class a test in arithmetic.* 2 a means of trial: *Trouble is a test of character.* 3 *Chemistry.* **a** an examination of a substance to see what it is or what it contains. **b** a process or substance used in such an examination. —*v.* put to a test; try out: *He tested the boy's honesty by leaving money on the table.* [ME < OF *test* vessel used in assaying < L *testum* earthen vessel] —**test′a·ble,** *adj.* ☛ *Syn. n.* 1. See note at **trial.**

test. 1 testamentary. 2 testator.

Test. Testament.

tes·ta (tes′tə) *n., pl.* **-tae** (-tē *or* -tī). 1 *Zoology.* a shell; the hard covering of certain animals. 2 *Botany.* the hard outside coat of a seed. [< L *testa* earthen vessel]

tes·ta·cy (tes′tə sē) *n.* the leaving of a will at death.

tes·ta·ment (tes′tə mənt) *n.* 1 written instructions telling what to do with a person's property after his death; a will. 2 **Testament, a** a main division of the Christian Bible; the Old Testament or the New Testament. **b** *Informal.* New Testament. [ME < L *testamentum,* ult. < *testis* witness]

tes·ta·men·ta·ry (tes′tə men′tə rē *or* tes′tə men′trē) *adj.* 1 of or having to do with a testament or will. 2 given, done, or appointed by a testament or will. 3 in a testament or will.

tes·tate (tes′tāt) *adj.* having made and left a valid will. [< L *testatus,* pp. of *testari* make a will < *testis* witness]

tes·ta·tor (tes tā′tər *or* tes′tā tər) *n.* 1 a person who makes a will. 2 a person who has died leaving a valid will.

tes·ta·trix (tes tā′triks) *n., pl.* **-tri·ces** (-trə sēz′). 1 a woman who makes a will. 2 a woman who has died leaving a valid will.

test ban an agreement between nations to ban the testing of nuclear weapons.

test case *Law.* a case whose outcome may set a precedent.

test–drive (test′drīv′) *v.* **-drove, -driv·en, -driv·ing.** drive a car or other vehicle to test it. —**test′-driv′er,** *n.*

test·er[1] (tes′tər) *n.* a person or thing that tests. [< *test*]

tes·ter[2] (tes′tər) *n.* canopy. [probably < OF *testre,* ult. < VL *testa* head < L *testa* earthen pot]

tes·tes (tes′tēz) *n. pl.* of **testis.**

tes·ti·cle (tes′tə kəl) *n.* the male reproductive organ of most animals, which produces sperm. In most mammals, the testicles are contained in an external pouch called the scrotum. [< L *testiculus,* dim. of *testis.* See TESTIS.]

tes·ti·fy (tes′tə fī′) *v.* **-fied, -fy·ing.** 1 give evidence; bear witness: *The excellence of Shakespeare's plays testifies to his genius.* 2 give evidence of; bear witness to: *The firm testified their appreciation of her work by raising her pay.* 3 declare solemnly; affirm. 4 *Law.* declare or give evidence under oath before a judge, coroner, etc.:

hat, āge, fär; let, ēqual, tėrm; it, īce
hot, ōpen, ôrder; oil, out; cup, put, rüle, əbove, takən, pencəl, lemən, circəs
ch, child; ng, long; sh, ship
th, thin; ₮H, then; zh, measure

The police testified that the speeding car had crashed into the truck. The witness was unwilling to testify. [ME < L *testificari* < *testis* witness + *facere* make] —**tes′ti·fi′er,** *n.*

tes·ti·mo·ni·al (tes′tə mō′nē əl) *n., adj.* —*n.* 1 a certificate of character, conduct, qualifications, value, etc.; recommendation: *The boy looking for a job has testimonials from his teachers and former employer. Advertisements of patent medicines often contain testimonials from people who have used them.* 2 something given or done to show esteem, admiration, gratitude, etc.: *The members of the church collected money for a testimonial to their retiring pastor.* —*adj.* given or done as a testimonial.

tes·ti·mo·ny (tes′tə mō′nē *or* tes′tə mo′nē) *n., pl.* **-nies.** 1 a statement used for evidence or proof: *A witness gave testimony that Mr. Doe was at home at 9 p.m.* 2 evidence: *The pupils presented their teacher with a watch in testimony of their respect and affection.* 3 an open declaration or profession of one's faith. 4 *Archaic.* the Ten Commandments. 5 testimonies, *pl.* the laws of God; the Scriptures. [ME < L *testimonium* < *testis* witness] ☛ *Syn.* 1, 2. See note at **evidence.**

tes·tis (tes′tis) *n., pl.* **-tes.** testicle. [< L *testis* witness (of virility)]

tes·tos·ter·one (tes tos′tər ōn′) *n.* a male steroid hormone produced mainly by the testicles. It is also extracted from animal testicles or made synthetically for use in medicine. *Formula:* $C_{19}H_{28}O_2$ [< *testes* + *sterol*]

test pilot a pilot employed to test new or experimental aircraft by subjecting them to greater than normal stress.

test tube a thin glass tube closed at one end, used in making chemical tests.

tes·tu·do (tes tyü′dō *or* tes tü′dō) *n., pl.* **-di·nes** (-də nēz′). 1 in ancient Rome: **a** a movable shelter with a strong and usually fireproof arched roof, used for protection in siege operations. **b** a shelter formed by a body of troops overlapping their shields above their heads. 2 some other sheltering contrivance. [< L *testudo,* literally, tortoise < *testa* shell]

tes·ty (tes′tē) *adj.* **-ti·er, -ti·est.** easily irritated; impatient. [ME < AF *testif* headstrong < OF *teste* head < L *testa* pot] —**tes′ti·ly,** *adv.* —**tes′ti·ness,** *n.*

tet·a·nus (tet′ə nəs) *n.* 1 a disease caused by certain bacilli usually entering the body through wounds, characterized by violent spasms, stiffness of many muscles, and even death. Tetanus of the lower jaw is called lockjaw. 2 *Physiology.* a condition of prolonged contraction of a muscle. [ME < L < Gk. *tetanos* < *teinein* stretch]

tet·a·ny (tet′ə nē) *n. Medicine.* a type of disorder marked by muscular spasms. [< F *tetanie*]

tetch·y (tech′ē) *adj.* **tetch·i·er, tetch·i·est.** irritable; touchy. Also, **techy.** [? < ME *teche, tache* fault < OF *teche* mark, quality]

tête-à-tête (tāt′ə tāt′) *adv., adj., n.* —*adv.* two together in private: *They dined tête-à-tête.* —*adj.* of or for two people in private. —*n.* 1 a private conversation between two people. 2 an S-shaped seat built so that two people can sit facing one another. [< F *tête-à-tête* head to head]

teth·er (te₮H′ər) *n., v.* —*n.* a rope or chain for fastening an animal so that it can graze only within certain limits. **at the end of** (one's) **tether,** *Informal.* at the end of one's resources or endurance: *After the class had gone wild for an hour, the teacher was at the end of her tether.* —*v.* fasten with a tether. [ME < ON *tjothr*]

tetra– *combining form.* four, as in *tetrahedron.* [< Gk. *tetra-,* combining form of *tessares* four]

tet·ra·chord (tet′rə kôrd′) *n. Music.* a series of four notes in the diatonic scale, the first and last notes of the series being a perfect fourth apart; half an octave. [< L < Gk. *tetrachordos* producing four tones < *tessares* four + *chordē* string]

tet·ra·cy·cline (tet′rə sī′klēn) *n.* an antibiotic derived from a soil bacterium (*Streptomyces viridifaciens*) or synthetically produced, effective against a wide variety of disease bacteria and viruses. *Formula:* $C_{22}H_{24}N_2O_8$ [< *tetra-* + *cycl(ic)* + *-in*]

tet·rad (tet′rad) *n.* 1 a group or collection of four. 2 *Chemistry.* an atom, element, or radical with a valence of four. 3 *Biology.* a group of four chromosomes formed when a pair of chromosomes splits during meiosis. [< Gk. *tetros, tetrados* a group of four]

tet·ra·eth·yl lead (tet′rə eth′əl) a colorless, poisonless liquid used as an antiknock in gasoline.

tet·ra·he·dral (tet′rə hē′drəl *or* tet′rə hed′rəl) *adj.* **1** of, having to do with, or being a tetrahedron. **2** having four sides.

tet·ra·he·dron (tet′rə hē′drən *or* tet′rə hed′rən) *n., pl.* **-drons, -dra** (-drə). a polyhedron having four faces. The most common tetrahedron is a pyramid whose base and three sides are equilateral triangles. See **solid** for picture. [< LGk. *tetraedron* < Gk. *tessares* four + *hedra* seat, base]

te·tral·o·gy (te tral′ə jē) *n., pl.* **-gies.** a series of four connected dramas, operas, etc. [< Gk. *tetralogia* < *tessares* four + *logos* discourse]

te·tram·e·ter (te tram′ə tər) *adj., n.* —*adj.* consisting of four measures or feet. —*n.* a line of verse having four measures or feet. *Example:*
The stag | at éve | had drúnk | his fíll.
[< L < Gk. *tetrametron* < *tessares* four + *metron* measure]

tet·rarch (tet′rärk *or* tē′trärk) *n.* **1** in ancient Rome, the ruler of a part (originally a fourth part) of a province. **2** any subordinate ruler. [< L < Gk. *tetrarchēs* < *tessares* four + *archos* ruler]

tet·rar·chy (tet′rär kē *or* tē′trär kē) *n., pl.* **-chies.** **1** government or jurisdiction of a tetrarch. **2** the territory governed by a tetrarch. **3** government by four persons. **4** a set of four rulers. **5** a country divided into four governments.

tet·ra·va·lent (tet′rə vā′lənt *or* te trav′ə lənt) *adj. Chemistry.* **1** having a valence of four. **2** having four valences. [< *tetra-* + L *valens, -entis,* ppr. of *valere* be worth]

te·trox·ide (te trok′sīd) *n.* any oxide having four atoms of oxygen in each molecule. [< *tetr-,* var. of *tetra-* + *oxide*]

tet·ter (tet′ər) *n.* an itching skin disease. Eczema is a tetter. [OE *teter*]

Teut. **1** Teutonic. **2** Teuton.

Teu·ton (tyü′tən *or* tü′tən) *n.* **1** a member of an ancient Germanic or Celtic people of N Europe. **2** a member of any of the N European peoples speaking a Germanic language, especially a German. [< L *Teutones, Teutoni,* pl.]

Teu·ton·ic (tyü ton′ik *or* tü ton′ik) *adj., n.* —*adj.* **1** of or having to do with the ancient Teutons. **2** of, having to do with, or designating the Germanic languages or the people who speak them. **3** German. —*n.* Germanic.

Tex. Texas.

Tex·an (tek′sən) *adj., n.* —*adj.* of or having to do with Texas or its people. —*n.* a native or inhabitant of Texas.

Tex·as gate (tek′səs) in the West, an opening in a fence, designed to let people and vehicles through but hinder cattle, horses, or deer, the surface being made of metal tubes, often revolving, or rails, bars, etc. laid crosswise.

text (tekst) *n.* **1** the main body of reading matter in a book: *This history contains 300 pages of text and about 50 pages of notes, explanations, and questions for study.* **2** the original words of a writer: *Always quote the exact words of a text.* **3** any one of the various wordings of a poem, play, etc. **4** a short Biblical passage used as the subject of a sermon : *The minister preached on the text "Judge not, that ye be not judged."* **5** topic; subject. **6** textbook. [ult. < L *textus,* originally, texture < *texere* weave] —**text′less,** *adj.*

text·book (tekst′búk′) *n.* a book used as a basis of instruction or as a standard reference in a particular course of study.

tex·tile (teks′tīl *or* teks′təl) *n., adj.* —*n.* **1** a woven or knit fabric. **2** material suitable for weaving.
—*adj.* **1** woven: *Linen is a textile material.* **2** suitable for weaving: *Cotton, silk, and wool are common textile materials.* **3** of or having to do with weaving: *the textile art.* **4** of or having something to do with the making, selling, etc. of textiles: *the textile business.* [< L *textilis* < *texere* weave]

tex·tu·al (teks′chü əl) *adj.* of or having to do with the text: *A misprint is a textual error.*

textual criticism the analysis of a manuscript or printed text to correct the additions, errors, or omissions of copyists, printers, etc. in order to establish the original text: *textual criticism of the Bible.*

tex·tu·al·ly (teks′chü əl ē) *adv.* in regard to the text.

tex·tur·al (teks′chər əl) *adj.* of texture; having to do with texture. —**tex′tur·al·ly,** *adv.*

tex·ture (teks′chər) *n., v.* **-tured, -tur·ing.** —*n.* **1** the arrangement of threads in a woven fabric: *Burlap has a much coarser texture than a linen handkerchief.* **2** the arrangement of the parts of anything; structure; constitution; make-up: *Sandstone and granite have very different textures.* **3** *Painting, sculpture, etc.* the

representation of the structure and minute moulding of a surface, especially of the skin, as distinct from its color. **4** the musical quality of combined voices, instruments, etc.: *the harsh texture of brass instruments.*
—*v.* give a texture to. [< L *textura* < *texere* weave]

tex·tured (teks′chərd) *adj.* **1** having a certain texture. **2** bulky; looped: *textured wool.*

T-group (tē′grüp′) *n.* a group of people organized under the leadership of a psychologist, etc. for the development of self awareness and sensitivity towards others through group interaction. [< training group]

Th thorium.

Th. **1** Thursday. **2** Thomas.

Thai (tī) *n., adj.* —*n.* **1** a native or inhabitant of Thailand, a country in SE Asia. **2** the official language of Thailand. —*adj.* of or having to do with Thailand, its people, or their language.

thal·a·mus (thal′ə məs) *n., pl.* **-mi** (-mī′ *or* -mē′). **1** a part of the brain where a nerve emerges or appears to emerge. The **optic thalami** are two large, oblong masses of grey matter forming a part of the midbrain. **2** the receptacle or torus of a flower. [< L *thalamus* inside room < Gk. *thalamos*]

tha·ler (tä′lər) *n., pl.* **-ler.** a former German silver coin. Also, **taler.** [< G *Taler,* earlier *Thaler.* Akin to DOLLAR.]

Tha·li·a (thə lī′ə) *n. Greek mythology.* **1** the Muse of comedy and idyllic poetry. **2** one of the three Graces.

thal·id·o·mide (thə lid′ə mīd′) *n.* a drug formerly used as a tranquillizer. Its use by pregnant women was found to cause malformation of their babies. *Formula:* $C_{13}H_{10}N_2O_4$
thalidomide baby, a malformed baby born to a woman who had taken thalidomide during pregnancy.

thal·li·um (thal′ē əm) *n.* a rare metallic chemical element that is soft and malleable. *Symbol:* Tl; *at.no.* 81; *at.wt.* 204.37. [< NL < Gk. *thallos* green shoot (its spectrum is marked by a green band)]

thal·lo·phyte (thal′ə fīt′) *n.* any of the group (Thallophyta) of lower plants having a relatively simple, undifferentiated body (called a thallus) without true stems, roots, or leaves. Modern classification systems utilizing this grouping regard the Thallophyta as constituting a subkingdom that includes the algae, bacteria, and fungi. [< Gk. *thallos* green shoot + E *-phyte*]

thal·lus (thal′əs) *n., pl.* **thal·li** (thal′ī *or* thal′ē) **or thal·lus·es.** a plant body lacking differentiation into true stems, roots, and leaves, characteristic of algae, fungi, and lichens. [< NL < Gk. *thallos* green shoot]

Tham·muz (täm′müz) *n.* Tammuz.

than (ᴛʜan; *unstressed,* ᴛʜən) *conj., prep.* **1** in comparison with; compared to that which: *This train is faster than that one.* **2** except; besides; other than: *How else can we come than on foot?*
than whom, compared with whom.
[OE]
☛ *Usage.* **Than** acts usually as a conjunction joining comparative adjectives and adverbs (as well as adverbs expressing a difference or exception, such as **rather, otherwise,** and **else**) with the second part of the comparison: *nicer than usual; otherwise than he did; more quickly than yesterday.* The part of speech, case, tense, etc. of the word following **than** depends on its function in the clause containing it, whether the clause itself is completely expressed or not. Compare:
Cindy likes Jane better *than* (she likes) *me.* (comparing objects)
Cindy likes Jane better *than I* (do). (comparing subjects)
I am taller *than he* (is). (comparing subjects)
In informal speech, however, in sentences such as the last, the objective case is often used even by educated speakers, making **than** into a preposition: I am taller *than him.* In a few special constructions **than** acts regularly as a preposition:
We can drive no further *than Montreal.*
We read about Eisenstein, *than whom* there was no greater film director.
☛ *Usage.* See also the note at **then.**

thane (thān) *n.* **1** in Anglo-Saxon England, a man who ranked between an earl and an ordinary freeman. Thanes held lands of the king or lord and gave military service in return. **2** in Scotland, a baron or lord; chief of a clan. Also, **thegn.** [OE *thegn*]

thank (thangk) *v., n.* —*v.* **1** say that one is pleased and grateful for something given or done; express gratitude to: *He thanked them for their hospitality.* **2** consider or hold responsible: *We can thank the previous committee for the financial mess we're in now. You have only yourself to thank if you run out of gas.*
thank goodness (or **heavens, God,** etc.), an expression of relief or satisfaction: *Thank goodness, they arrived safely.*
thank you, the standard courteous expression of appreciation: *"It's a lovely present. Thank you."*
—*n.* **thanks, a** the act of thanking; an expression of gratitude: *to give thanks for a favor, to give thanks before a meal.* **b** a feeling of kindness and gratitude: *You have our heartful thanks.*
thanks to, owing to; because of: *Thanks to his efforts, we won the game. The fair was a disaster, thanks to the storm.*

—*interj.* **thanks,** *Informal.* thank you: *Thanks. I appreciate your help.* [OE *thanc,* originally, thought]

thank·ful (thangk′fəl) *adj.* feeling or expressing thanks; grateful.
☛ *Syn.* See note at **grateful.**

thank·ful·ly (thangk′fəl ē) *adv.* with thanks; gratefully.

thank·ful·ness (thangk′fəl nis) *n.* a thankful feeling; gratitude.

thank·less (thangk′lis) *adj.* 1 not likely to be rewarded with thanks; not appreciated: *Giving advice is usually a thankless act.* 2 not feeling or expressing thanks; without a desire to do a favor in return: *The thankless woman did nothing for the neighbor who had helped her.* —**thank′less·ly,** *adv.* —**thank′less·ness,** *n.*

thanks·giv·ing (thangks giv′ing) *n.* 1 a giving of thanks. 2 an expression of thanks: *They offered thanksgiving for the bountiful harvest.* 3 **Thanksgiving,** Thanksgiving Day.

Thanksgiving Day 1 in Canada, the second Monday in October, a day set apart as a statutory holiday on which to give thanks for God's goodness and for the harvest. 2 in the United States, the fourth Thursday in November, a holiday observed for similar reasons.

that (ᴛʜat; *unstressed,* ᴛʜət) *adj., pl.* **those;** *pron., pl.* (for def. 1) **those;** *conj., adv.* —*adj.* pointing out, indicating, or emphasizing some person, thing, idea, etc. already mentioned or understood, especially one some distance away in place or time. When used with *this, that* refers to something far or farther away and *this* refers to something near. *Examples: Do you know that boy over there? I will not allow that piano to be misused. That route is shorter than this one. What was that noise?*
—*pron.* 1 some person, thing, idea, etc. already mentioned or understood, often one that is to be emphasized or contrasted with another nearer in place or time: *That is a better drawing than this. That's the spirit! That's not fair. After that they went home. What was that?* 2 which, who, or whom: *Is he the man that trains dogs? Bring the box that's in the kitchen.* 3 when; at or in which: *The year that we went to England, they had a terrible drought.*
at that, *Informal.* **a** with no more talk, work, etc.: *Let's just leave it at that.* **b** on reconsideration: *We may need more money at that.*
in that, because: *His plan is superior in that it is more practical.*
that's that, *Informal.* that is finished, settled, or decided: *We're not going, and that's that.*
—*conj.* 1 to introduce a noun clause and connect it with the preceding verb: *I know that 6 and 4 are 10.* 2 to show purpose: *He ran fast that he might not be late.* 3 to show result: *He ran so fast that he was five minutes early.* 4 to show cause: *I wonder what happened, not that I care.* 5 to express a wish: *Oh, that she were here!* 6 to show anger, surprise, etc.: *That one so fair should be so false!*
—*adv.* to such an extent or degree; so. *He cannot stay up that late.* [OE *þæt*]
☛ *Usage.* **That** (pron., def. 4), **who, which. That** as a relative pronoun refers to persons or things, **who** to persons, **which** usually to things: *The people who* (or *that*) *were in the auditorium listened to the speech in silence. He solved in five minutes a problem that* (or *which*) *I had struggled with for five hours.* **That** usually introduces clauses that are restrictive; **which** introduces clauses that are non-restrictive. Restrictive: *The book that she selected for her report was the longest in the list.* Non-restrictive: *The privilege of free speech, which we hold so dear, is now endangered.*

thatch (thach) *n., v.* —*n.* 1 straw, rushes, palm leaves, etc. used as a roof or covering. 2 a roof or covering of thatch. 3 *Informal.* the hair covering the head.
—*v.* roof or cover with thatch. [OE *þæc*]

thau·ma·tur·gy (tho′mə tėr′jē *or* thô′mə tėr′jē) *n.* the working of wonders or miracles; magic. [< Gk. *thaumatourgia,* ult. < *thauma* marvel + *-orgos* working < *ergon* work]

thaw (tho *or* thô) *v., n.* —*v.* 1 melt (ice, snow, or anything frozen); free from frost: *Salt was put on the sidewalk to thaw the ice.* 2 become warm enough to melt ice, snow, etc.: *If the sun stays out, it will probably thaw today.* 3 become free of frost, ice, etc.: *The ground has begun to thaw. The pond thaws in April.* 4 make or become less stiff and formal in manner; soften: *His shyness thawed under her kindness.*
—*n.* 1 thawing. 2 a period of weather above the freezing point (0° C); time of melting. 3 a becoming less stiff and formal in manner; softening. [OE *thawian*] —**thaw′er,** *n.*
☛ *Syn. v.* 1. See note at **melt.**

the[1] (*unstressed before a consonant,* ᴛʜə; *when stressed, and always before vowels,* ᴛʜē) *definite article.* The word *the* shows that a certain one (or ones) is meant. Various special uses are: 1 to mark a noun as indicating something well-known or unique: *the* (ᴛʜə) *prodigal son, the* (ᴛʜē) *Alps.* 2 denoting the time in question or under consideration, now or then present: *the hour of victory. Was that the moment to act?* 3 with or as part of a title: *the Duke of Wellington.* 4 to mark a noun as indicating the best known or most important of its kind: *the* (ᴛʜē) *place to dine.* 5 to mark a noun as being used generically: *The dog is a quadruped.* 6 to indicate a part of the body or a personal belonging: *to hang the head in shame.*

hat, āge, fär; let, ēqual, tèrm; it, īce
hot, ōpen, ôrder; oil, out; cup, pùt, rüle,
əbove, takən, pencəl, lemən, circəs
ch, child; ng, long; sh, ship
th, thin; ᴛʜ, then; zh, measure

7 before adjectives used as nouns: *to visit the sick.* 8 distributively, to denote any one separately: *candy at five dollars the kilogram.* [OE *þē, the*]
☛ *Usage.* **The.** Repetition of the article before the various nouns of a series emphasizes their distinctness: *The color, the fragrance, and the patterns of these flowers make them universal favorites.* Compare: *The color, fragrance, and patterns of these flowers make them universal favorites.*

the[2] (ᴛʜə *or* ᴛʜē) *adv.* The word *the* is used to modify an adjective or adverb in the comparative degree: 1 signifying "in or by that," "on that account," "in some or any degree": *If you start now, you will be back the sooner.* 2 used correlatively, in one instance with relative force and in the other with demonstrative force, and signifying "by how much ... by so much," "in what degree ... in that degree": *the more the merrier, the sooner the better.* [OE *þȳ*]

the·a·tre (thē′ə tər) *n.* 1 a place where plays and other stage performances are acted or where motion pictures are shown. 2 a place that looks like a theatre in its arrangement of seats: *the operating theatre of a hospital.* 3 a place where some action proceeds; scene of action: *France has too often been a theatre of war.* 4 a plays; the writing and producing of plays; the drama. **b** a play, situation, dialogue, etc. considered as to its effectiveness on the stage: *This scene is bad theatre.* Sometimes, **theater.** [ME < OF < L < Gk. *theatron,* ult. < *thea* view]

the·a·tre·go·er (thē′ə tər gō′ər) *n.* one who goes to the theatre, especially one who goes frequently.

the·a·tre–in–the–round (thē′ə tər in ᴛʜə round′) *n.* 1 a theatre having the stage situated in the centre, surrounded with seats on all sides. 2 the presentation of plays in such theatres.

the·at·ric (thē at′rik) *adj.* theatrical.

the·at·ri·cal (thē at′rə kəl) *adj., n.* —*adj.* 1 of or having to do with the theatre or actors: *theatrical performances, a theatrical company.* 2 suggesting a theatre or acting; for display or effect; artificial. —*n.* **theatricals,** *pl.* **a** dramatic performances, especially as given by amateurs. **b** matters having to do with the stage and acting. **c** actions of a theatrical or artificial character. —**the·at′ri·cal·ly,** *adv.*
☛ *Syn. adj.* 2. See note at **dramatic.**

the·at·ri·cal·i·ty (thē at′rə kal′ə tē) *n.* the quality of being theatrical.

The·ban (thē′bən) *n., adj.* —*n.* a native or inhabitant of the city of Thebes in ancient Greece or the city of Thebes in ancient Egypt. —*adj.* of or having to do with either city or its inhabitants.

thee (ᴛʜē) *pron. Archaic or poetic.* the objective form of **thou:** *"Hail to thee, blithe Spirit!"* [OE *thē*]
☛ *Usage.* See note at **thou.**

theft (theft) *n.* 1 the act of stealing: *The man was put in prison for theft.* 2 an instance of stealing: *The theft of the jewels caused much excitement.* [OE *thēoft* < *thēof* thief]

thegn (thān) *n.* thane.

the·in (thē′ən) *n.* theine.

the·ine (thē′ēn *or* thē′ən) *n.* caffeine. [< NL *thea* tea + *-ine*[2]]

their (ᴛʜer; *unstressed,* ᴛʜər) *adj.* 1 a possessive form of **they:** of, belonging to, or made or done by them or themselves: *They did their best. They all raised their hands. That's their house.* 2 **Their,** a word used as part of any of certain formal titles when using the title to refer to the people holding it: *Their Majesties are resting.* [ME < ON *their(r)a*]
☛ *Hom.* **there, they're.**
☛ *Usage.* **Their, theirs** are the possessive forms of **they. Their** is a determiner and is always followed by a noun: *This is their farm.* **Theirs** is a pronoun and stands alone: *This farm is theirs.*

theirs (ᴛʜerz) *pron.* a possessive form of **they:** that which belongs to them: *The painting isn't theirs, it's just rented.*
☛ *Hom.* **there's.**
☛ *Usage.* See note at **their.**

the·ism (thē′iz əm) *n.* 1 a belief in one God, the creator and ruler of the universe. 2 belief in a deity or deities; religious faith or conviction. [< Gk. *theos* god]

the·ist (thē′ist) *n.* a believer in theism.

the·is·tic (thē is′tik) *adj.* of or having to do with theism or theists. —**the·is′ti·cal·ly,** *adv.*

them (ᴛʜem; *unstressed,* ᴛʜəm) *pron.* the objective form of **they.**

The books were a gift, but I don't really like them. [ME *theim* < ON]

the·mat·ic (thē mat′ik) *adj.* of or having to do with a theme or themes.

theme (thēm) *n.* **1** a topic; subject: *Patriotism was the speaker's theme.* **2** a short written composition. **3** *Music.* **a** the principal melody in a composition. **b** a short melody repeated in different forms in an elaborate composition. **4** a melody used to identify a particular radio or television program. [ME < L < Gk. *thema*, literally, something set down]

them·selves (ᴛʜᴇm selvz′ *or* ᴛʜəm selvz′) *pron.* **1** a reflexive pronoun, the form used instead of **they** or **them** when referring to the subject of the sentence: *They hurt themselves in climbing down.* **2** a form of **they** or **them** used for emphasis: *They did it themselves.* **3** their normal or usual selves: *They were ill and were not themselves.*

then (ᴛʜen) *adv., n., adj.* —*adv.* **1** at that time: *Prices were lower then.* **2** soon afterwards: *The noise stopped, and then began again.* **3** next in time or place: *First comes spring, then summer.* **4** at another time: *Now one boy does best and then another.* **5** also; besides: *The dress seems too good to throw away, and then it is very attractive.* **6** in that case; therefore: *If Harry broke the window, then he should pay for it.*
but then, but at the same time; but on the other hand.
there and then, at that time and place; at once and on the spot.
—*n.* that time: *By then we shall know the result.*
—*adj.* being at that time in the past; existing then: *the then Prime Minister.* [OE *thænne*]

thence (thens *or* ᴛʜens) *adv.* **1** from that place; from there: *A few kilometres thence was a river.* **2** for that reason; therefore: *You didn't work, thence no pay.* **3** from that time; from then: *a year thence.* [ME *thennes* < OE *thanan(e)*]

thence·forth (thens′fôrth′ *or* ᴛʜens′-) *adv.* from then on; from that time forward: *Women were given the same rights as men. Thenceforth they could vote.*

thence·for·ward (thens′fôr′wərd *or* ᴛʜens′-) *adv.* thenceforth.

theo– *combining form.* God; a god or gods: *theology* = study of God; *theogony* = study of the origin of the gods.

the·oc·ra·cy (thē ok′rə sē) *n., pl.* -**cies. 1** a system of government in which God, or a god, is recognized as the supreme civil ruler and His laws are taken as the laws of the state. **2** a system of government by priests. **3** a country governed by a theocracy. [< Gk. *theokratia* < *theos* god + *kratos* rule]

the·o·crat (thē′ə krat′) *n.* **1** a ruler, or member of a governing body, in a theocracy. **2** a person who favors theocracy.

the·o·crat·ic (thē′ə krat′ik) *adj.* **1** of or having to do with theocracy. **2** having a theocracy. —**the′o·crat′i·cal·ly,** *adv.*

the·od·o·lite (thē od′ə līt′) *n.* a surveying instrument for measuring horizontal and vertical angles. [< NL *theodelitus*; ult. origin unknown]

the·og·o·ny (thē og′ə nē) *n., pl.* -**nies. 1** the origin of the gods. **2** an account of this; genealogical account of the gods. [< Gk. *theogonia* < *theos* god < *gonos* begetting, descent]

the·o·lo·gian (thē′ə lō′jən *or* thē′ə lō′jē ən) *n.* a person skilled or trained in theology.

the·o·log·i·cal (thē′ə loj′ə kəl) *adj.* **1** of or having to do with theology. A theological school trains young men for the ministry. **2** referring to the nature and will of God. —**the′o·log′i·cal·ly,** *adv.*

the·ol·o·gy (thē ol′ə jē) *n., pl.* -**gies. 1** the study of the nature of God and His relations to man and the universe. **2** the study of religion and religious beliefs. **3** a system of religious beliefs. [< L < Gk. *theologia* < *theos* god + *-logos* treating of]

the·o·rem (thē′ə rəm) *n.* **1** *Mathematics.* **a** a statement to be proved. **b** a statement of relations that can be expressed by an equation or formula. **2** any statement or rule that can be proved to be true. [< L < Gk. *theōrēma* < *theōreein* consider. See THEORY.]

the·o·ret·ic (thē′ə ret′ik) *adj.* theoretical.

the·o·ret·i·cal (thē′ə ret′ə kəl) *adj.* **1** planned or worked out in the mind, not from experience; based on theory, not on fact; limited to theory. **2 a** dealing with theory only; not practical. **b** having the object of knowledge as its end; concerned with knowledge only, not with accomplishing anything or producing anything; purely scientific.

the·o·ret·i·cal·ly (thē′ə ret′ik lē) *adv.* in theory; according to theory; in a theoretical manner.

the·o·re·ti·cian (thē′ə rə tish′ən) *n.* a person who knows much about the theory of an art, science, etc.

the·o·rist (thē′ə rist) *n.* a person who forms theories.

the·o·rize (thē′ə rīz′) *v.* -**rized,** -**riz·ing.** form a theory or theories; speculate. —**the′o·riz′er,** *n.*

the·o·ry (thē′ə rē) *n., pl.* -**ries. 1** an explanation based on thought or speculation. **2** an explanation based on observation and reasoning: *the theory of evolution, Einstein's theory of relativity.* **3** the principles or methods of a science or art rather than its practice: *the theory of music.* **4** an idea or opinion about something. **5** thought or fancy as opposed to fact or practice. **6** *Mathematics.* a set of theorems which constitute a connected, systematic view of some branch of mathematics: *the theory of probabilities.* [< LL < Gk. *theōria* < *theōreein* consider < *theōros* spectator < *thea* a sight + *horaein* see]
☛ *Syn.* **1. Theory, hypothesis** = an explanation based on observation and thought. **Theory** applies to an explanation that has been tested and confirmed as a general principle explaining a large number of related facts, occurrences, or other phenomena in nature, mechanics, etc.: *Einstein's theory of relativity explains the motion of moving objects.* **Hypothesis** applies to a proposed explanation for a certain group of facts, admittedly unproved but accepted for the time being as highly probable or as an experimental guide: *Archaeological discoveries strengthened the hypothesis that Troy had once existed.*

the·o·soph·ic (thē′ə sof′ik) *adj.* of or having to do with theosophy.

the·o·soph·i·cal (thē′ə sof′ə kəl) *adj.* theosophic.

the·os·o·phist (thē os′ə fist) *n.* a person who believes in theosophy.

the·os·o·phy (thē os′ə fē) *n.* a philosophy or religion that claims to have a special insight into the divine nature through spiritual self-development. Modern theosophy includes many of the teachings of Buddhism and Brahmanism. [< Med.L < LGk. *theosophia,* ult. < Gk. *theos* god + *sophos* wise]

ther·a·peu·tic (ther′ə pyü′tik) *adj.* of or having to do with the treatment or curing of disease; curative. [< NL *therapeuticus,* ult. < Gk. *therapeuein* cure, treat < *theraps* attendant]

ther·a·peu·ti·cal (ther′ə pyü′tə kəl) *adj.* therapeutic. —**ther′a·peu′ti·cal·ly,** *adv.*

ther·a·peu·tics (ther′ə pyü′tiks) *n.* a branch of medicine that deals with the treating or curing of disease; therapy.

ther·a·peu·tist (ther′ə pyü′tist) *n.* a person who specializes in therapeutics.

ther·a·pist (ther′ə pist) *n.* therapeutist.

ther·a·py (ther′ə pē) *n., pl.* -**pies.** the treatment of diseases or disorders (*often used in compounds*): *physiotherapy, hydrotherapy. These exercises are good therapy for your back.* [< NL < Gk. *therapeia* < *therapeuein.* See THERAPEUTIC.]

there (ᴛʜer; *unstressed,* ᴛʜər) *adv., n., interj.* —*adv.* **1** in or at that place: *Sit there.* **2** to or into that place: *Go there at once.* **3** at that point in an action, speech, etc.: *You have done enough, you may stop there.* **4** in that matter, particular, or respect: *You are mistaken there.* **5** *There* is used in sentences in which the verb comes before the subject: *There are three new houses on our street. Is there a drugstore near here?* **6** *There* is used to call attention to some person or thing: *There goes the bell.*
all there, *Informal.* **a** wide-awake; alert. **b** not crazy; sane.
—*n.* that place: *From there go on to Hamilton.*
—*interj. There* is also used to express satisfaction, triumph, dismay, encouragement, comfort, etc.: *There, there! Don't cry.* [OE *thǽr*]
☛ *Usage. There* (*adv.* def. 5). **There** is often used at the beginning of a sentence as a temporary substitute for the real subject, which follows the verb: *There is only one book on your desk.* When the subject is singular, a singular verb is used after **there:** *There was much work to be done.* When the subject is plural, a plural verb is usual: *There are many answers in the back of the book.*

there·a·bout (ᴛʜer′ə bout′) *adv.* thereabouts.

there·a·bouts (ᴛʜer′ə bouts′) *adv.* **1** near that place: *She's from Nova Scotia; Halifax, or thereabouts.* **2** near that time. **3** near that number or amount.

there·af·ter (ᴛʜer af′tər) *adv.* **1** after that; afterward. **2** accordingly.

there·at (ᴛʜer at′) *adv.* **1** when that happened; at that time. **2** because of that; because of it. **3** at that place.

there·by (ᴛʜer bī′ *or* ᴛʜer′bī′) *adv.* **1** by means of that; in that way: *He wished to travel and thereby study the customs of other countries.* **2** in connection with that: *Calgary won the game, and thereby hangs a tale.* **3** near there.

there·for (ᴛʜer fôr′) *adv.* for that; for this; for it: *He promised to give a building for a hospital and as much land as should be necessary therefor.*

there·fore (ᴛʜer′fôr′) *adv.* for that reason; as a result of that; consequently. [ME *therfore* < *ther* there + *fore,* var. of *for* for]
☛ *Syn.* **Therefore, consequently** indicate a logical or causal relationship between two groups of words by connecting to one statement a group of words stating a conclusion or result. **Therefore** indicates formally and precisely that the second group of words states the necessary conclusion to be drawn from the first: *He was the only candidate; therefore, he was elected.* **Consequently,** also formal, indicates a reasonable conclusion, but may also be used to connect a statement

of effect or result: *He is the popular candidate; consequently, he will be elected. I overslept and, consequently, was late.*

there·from (ᴛнer frum′ *or* -frum′) *adv.* from that; from this; from it.

there·in (ᴛнer in′) *adv.* 1 in that place; in it. 2 in that matter; in that way; in that respect.

there·in·to (ᴛнer in′tü *or* ᴛнer′in tü′) *adv.* 1 into that place; into it. 2 into that matter.

there'll (ᴛнerl) 1 there will. 2 there shall.

there·of (ᴛнer ov′ *or* ᴛнer uv′) *adv.* 1 of that; of it. 2 from it; from that source.

there·on (ᴛнer on′) *adv.* 1 on that; on it. 2 immediately after that.

there's (ᴛнerz) there is.

there·to (ᴛнer tü′) *adv.* 1 to that; to it: *The castle stands on a hill, and the road thereto is steep and rough.* 2 in addition to that; also.

there·to·fore (ᴛнer′tə fôr′) *adv.* before that time; until then.

there·un·der (ᴛнer un′dər) *adv.* 1 under that; under it. 2 under the authority of that; according to that.

there·un·to (ᴛнer un′tü *or* ᴛнer′un tü′) *adv.* to that; to it.

there·up·on (ᴛнer′ə pon′) *adv.* 1 immediately after that. 2 because of that; therefore. 3 on that; on it.

there·with (ᴛнer wiᴛн′ *or* -wiᴛн′) *adv.* *Archaic.* 1 with that; with it. 2 immediately after that; then.

there·with·al (ᴛнer wiᴛн′ol *or* ᴛнer′wiᴛн ôl′) *adv.* 1 with that; with this; with it. 2 in addition to that; also.

ther·mal (ᴛнer′məl) *adj., n.* —*adj.* 1 of, having to do with, caused by, or producing heat or warmth. 2 warm or hot: *thermal springs.* 3 designed to conserve heat or warmth: *thermal underwear.* —*n.* a bubble, or column, of rising air currents that are warmer than the surrounding air. Thermals are used by gliders to gain altitude. [< Gk. *thermē* heat] —**ther′mal·ly,** *adv.*

thermal barrier the point of speed beyond which an aircraft is subjected to dangerously high temperatures as a result of friction with the atmosphere.

thermal spring a natural spring whose water is warmer than the surrounding atmosphere; hot spring.

ther·mic (ᴛнer′mik) *adj.* of or having to do with heat; thermal.

ther·mis·tor (ᴛнer mis′tər) *n.* a very small electronic resistor used to measure or regulate heat through changes in conductivity.

thermo– *or* **therm–** *combining form.* heat, as in *thermodynamics.* [< Gk. *thermē*]

ther·mo·cline (ᴛнer′mō klīn′) *n.* a layer of water below the surface layer in the ocean or a lake, characterized by a marked decrease in temperature with increase in depth. [< *thermo-* + (*in*)*cline*]

ther·mo·dy·nam·ic (ᴛнer′mō dī nam′ik) *adj.* 1 of or having to do with thermodynamics. 2 using force due to heat or to the conversion of heat into mechanical energy.

ther·mo·dy·nam·ics (ᴛнer′mō dī nam′iks) *n.* the branch of physics that deals with the relations between heat and mechanical energy or work.

thermodynamic temperature temperature considered as a basic physical quantity that is a measure of the thermal energy possessed by a body, expressed in units (kelvins). *Symbol: T* See also **absolute zero.**

ther·mo·e·lec·tric (ᴛнer′mō i lek′trik) *adj.* of or having to do with thermo-electricity.

ther·mo·e·lec·tri·cal (ᴛнer′mō i lek′trə kəl) *adj.* thermo-electric.

ther·mo·e·lec·tric·i·ty (ᴛнer′mō i lek′tris′ə tē *or* -ē′lek tris′ə tē) *n.* electricity produced directly by heat.

ther·mo·gram (ᴛнer′mə gram′) *n.* 1 the record produced by a thermograph. 2 a photographic image produced by thermography.

ther·mo·graph (ᴛнer′mə graf′) *n.* a type of thermometer that includes a system for recording temperature variations over a period of time on a graph.

ther·mog·ra·phy (ᴛнer mog′rə fē) *n.* 1 the technique or process of producing a photographic image of an object by means of a camera that measures the heat emitted by it. Thermography is used in the diagnosis of cancerous tumors, etc. 2 a printing or writing process involving the use of heat, especially one that produces raised printing.

ther·mo·karst (ᴛнer′mō kärst′) *n.* the melting of permafrost with a high ice content and the resultant collapse of the ground, producing deep gullies, trenches, or sinks. Thermokarst is often produced by the removal of insulating plant and soil cover. [< *thermo* + *karst*]

hat, āge, fär; let, ēqual, tėrm; it, īce
hot, ōpen, ôrder; oil, out; cup, pút, rüle,
əbove, takən, pencəl, lemən, circəs

ch, child; ng, long; sh, ship
th, thin; ᴛн, then; zh, measure

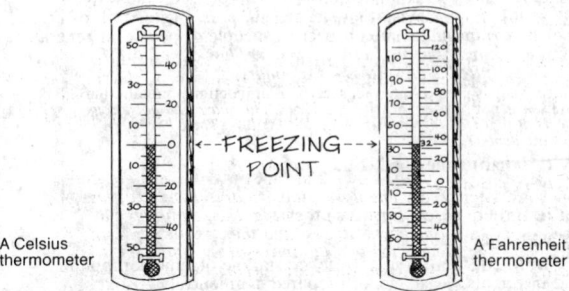

←--FREEZING--→
POINT

A Celsius thermometer · A Fahrenheit thermometer

ther·mom·e·ter (thər mom′ə tər) *n.* an instrument for measuring temperature, usually by means of the expansion and contraction of mercury or alcohol in a capillary tube and bulb.

ther·mo·nu·cle·ar (ᴛнer′mō nyü′klē ər *or* -nü′klē ər) *adj.* of or designating the fusion of atoms (as in the hydrogen bomb) through very high temperature: *a thermonuclear reaction.*

ther·mo·plas·tic (ᴛнer′mō plas′tik) *adj., n.* —*adj.* becoming soft and capable of being moulded when heated. —*n.* a thermoplastic material, especially one of certain synthetic resins.

ther·mos (ᴛнer′məs) *n.* 1 **Thermos,** *Trademark.* a double-walled bottle or flask made with a vacuum between its inner and outer walls, used to keep a beverage, soup, etc. hot or cold for a long time; vacuum bottle. 2 a bottle or flask of this kind. [< Gk. *thermos* hot]

Thermos bottle or **flask** thermos.

ther·mo·set (ᴛнer′mō set′) *adj., n.* —*adj.* thermosetting. —*n.* a thermosetting material, especially a plastic.

ther·mo·set·ting (ᴛнer′mō set′ing) *adj.* becoming hard and permanently set after being heated: *thermosetting plastics.*

ther·mo·sphere (ᴛнer′mə sfėr′) *n.* the layer of the earth's atmosphere lying above the mesosphere, extending from about 85 km to about 450 km above the earth's surface, where the exosphere begins, and characterized by an increase in temperature with increasing altitude. This is also the region of meteors and aurorae.

ther·mo·stat (ᴛнer′mə stat′) *n.* 1 an automatic device for regulating temperature. In most thermostats, the expansion and contraction of a metal, liquid, or gas opens and closes an electric circuit by which an appliance or device, such as an air conditioner or oil furnace, is made to work or to stop working. 2 a similar device that responds to temperature changes, such as one that will activate a sprinkler system or fire alarm if the temperature increases beyond a certain point. [< *thermo-* + Gk. *-statēs* that stands]

ther·mo·stat·ic (ᴛнer′mə stat′ik) *adj.* of, having to do with, or like a thermostat.

ther·mo·stat·i·cal·ly (ᴛнer′mə stat′ik lē) *adv.* by means of a thermostat.

the·sau·rus (thi sô′rəs) *n., pl.* **-ri** (-rī *or* -rē). 1 a dictionary or encyclopedia, especially a dictionary in which words are grouped by their semantic relationships; a book of synonyms and antonyms. 2 *Rare.* a treasury or storehouse. [< L < Gk. *thesauros.* Doublet of ᴛREASURE.]

these (ᴛнēz) *adj. or pron.* pl. of **this.** [OE *thǣs,* var. of *thās.* Cf. ᴛHOSE.]

the·sis (thē′sis) *n., pl.* **-ses** (-sēz′). 1 a proposition or statement to be proved or to be maintained against objections. 2 an essay; an essay presented by a candidate for a diploma or degree. [< L < Gk. *thesis,* originally, a setting down]

Thes·pi·an (thes′pē ən) *adj., n.* —*adj.* 1 having to do with Thespis, a Greek tragic poet who lived about 534 B.C. 2 of or having to do with the drama or tragedy; dramatic; tragic. —*n.* an actor or actress. [< *Thespis,* a Greek poet]

Thes·sa·li·an (the sā′lē ən) *n., adj.* —*n.* a native or inhabitant of Thessaly, a district in E Greece. —*adj.* of or having to do with Thessaly or its people.

Thes·sa·lo·ni·an (thes′ə lō′nē ən) *n., adj.* —*n.* a native or

inhabitant of Thessalonica (in modern times, Salonika), a seaport in NE Greece. —*adj.* of or having to do with Thessalonica or its people.

the·ta (thā′tə *or* thē′tə) *n.* the eighth letter (θ, Θ) of the Greek alphabet, pronounced as the English "th" in *thin.*

thews (thyūz *or* thūz) *n.pl.* **1** muscles. **2** sinews. [ME *theawes* good quality; strength < OE *thēaw* habit]

they (THā) *pron., pl., subj.* **they,** *obj.* **them,** *poss.* **theirs. 1** pl. of **he, she,** or **it. 2** *Informal.* some unspecified people or people in general: *They say he's really a very serious person. They don't have Boxing Day in the United States.* [ME < ON *their*]
☛ *Usage.* **They** is used in informal speech as an indefinite pronoun but generally it is not so used in writing. Spoken: *They have had no serious accidents at that crossing for over two years.* Written: *There have been no serious accidents…*

they'd (THād) **1** they had. **2** they would.

they'll (THāl) they will.

they're (THer; *unstressed,* THər) they are.

they've (THāv) they have.

thi·a·min (thī′ə min) *n.* a white, crystalline organic compound found in cereals, yeast, etc. or prepared synthetically. Also, **thiamine.** *Formula:* $C_{12}H_{17}ClN_4OS$

thi·a·mine (thī′ə min *or* thī′ə mēn′) *n.* thiamin.

Thib·e·tan (ti bet′ən) *adj. or n.* Tibetan.

thick (thik) *adj., adv., n.* —*adj.* **1** of an object or substance, filling much space from one surface to the other; not thin: *The castle has thick stone walls.* **2** measuring between two opposite surfaces or an object or substance: *three centimetres thick.* **3** set close together; dense: *thick hair.* **4** many and close together; abundant: *bullets thick as hail.* **5** filled; covered: *thick with flies.* **6** like glue or syrup, not like water; rather dense of its kind: *Thick liquids pour much more slowly than thin liquids.* **7** not clear; foggy: *The weather was thick and the airports were shut down.* **8** not clear in sound; hoarse: *a thick voice.* **9** stupid; dull: *He has a thick head.* **10** *Informal.* very friendly; intimate. **11** *Informal.* too much to be endured.
thick skin, the ability to take criticism, etc. without being affected by it.
—*adv.* thickly.
lay it on thick, *Informal.* praise or blame too much.
—*n.* the part that is thickest, most crowded, most active, etc.: *in the thick of the fight.*
through thick and thin, in good times and bad: *A true friend stays loyal through thick and thin.*
[OE *thicce*] —**thick′ly,** *adv.*

thick·en (thik′ən) *v.* **1** make or become thick or thicker. **2** of the plot of a play, novel, etc., become more complex or intricate. —**thick′en·er,** *n.*

thick·en·ing (thik′ən ing *or* thik′ning) *n.* **1** a material or ingredient used to thicken something. **2** a thickened part. **3** the act or process of making or becoming thick or thicker.

thick·et (thik′it) *n.* a dense growth of shrubs, bushes, or small trees. [OE *thiccet* < *thicce* thick]

thick–head·ed (thik′hed′id) *adj.* stupid; dull. —**thick′–head′ed·ness,** *n.*

thick·ish (thik′ish) *adj.* somewhat thick.

thick·ness (thik′nis) *n.* **1** the quality or state of being thick. **2** the distance between opposite surfaces; the third measurement of a solid, not length or breadth. **3** the thick part. **4** a layer: *The pad was made up of three thicknesses of blotting paper.*

thick·set (thik′set′) *adj., n.* —*adj.* **1** closely placed, planted, etc.: *a thickset hedge.* **2** thick in form or build: *a thickset man.* —*n. Archaic.* thicket.

thick–skinned (thik′skind′) *adj.* **1** having a thick skin. **2** not readily affected by criticism, rebuff, insults, etc.; insensitive.

thick–wit·ted (thik′wit′id) *adj.* stupid; dull.

thief (thēf) *n., pl.* **thieves.** a person who steals, especially one who steals secretly and without using force. [OE *thēof*]
☛ *Syn.* **Thief, robber** = someone who steals. **Thief** applies to someone who takes and, usually, carries away something belonging to another, in a secret or stealthy way: *A thief stole the little boy's bicycle from the yard.* **Robber** applies to one who takes another's property by force or threats of violence: *The robbers bound and gagged the night watchman.*

thieve (thēv) *v.* **thieved, thiev·ing.** steal. [OE *thēofian* < *thēof* thief]

thiev·er·y (thēv′ər ē *or* thēv′rē) *n., pl.* **-er·ies.** the act of stealing; theft.

thieves (thēvz) *n.* pl. of **thief.**

thiev·ish (thēv′ish) *adj.* **1** having the habit of stealing; likely to

steal. **2** like a thief; stealthy; sly. —**thiev′ish·ly,** *adv.* —**thiev′ish·ness,** *n.*

thigh (thī) *n.* the part of the leg between the hip and the knee. See **leg** for picture. [OE *thēoh*]

thigh·bone (thī′bōn′) *n.* the bone of the leg between the hip and the knee; femur. See **leg** for picture.

thill (thil) *n.* either of the shafts between which a single animal drawing a vehicle is placed. [ME *thille*]

thim·ble (thim′bəl) *n.* **1** a small cap of metal, bone, plastic, etc. worn on the finger to protect it when pushing the needle in sewing. **2** a short metal tube. **3** a metal ring fitted in a rope, to save wear on the rope. [OE *thȳmel* < *thūma* thumb]

thim·ble·ber·ry (thim′bəl ber′ē) *n., pl.* **-ries.** any of several plants closely related to and resembling the raspberry, especially a tall, thornless shrub (*Rubus parviflorus*) of central and western North America, having large, very broad, lobed leaves, white flowers, and red, thimble-shaped, edible fruit.

thim·ble·ful (thim′bəl ful′) *n., pl.* **-fuls.** as much as a thimble will hold; a very small quantity.

thim·ble·rig (thim′bəl rig′) *n., v.* **-rigged, rig·ging.** —*n.* a swindling game in which the operator apparently covers a small ball or pea with one of three thimble-like cups, and then, moving the cups about, offers to bet that no one can tell under which cup the ball or pea lies. —*v.* cheat by or as by the thimblerig. —**thim′ble·rig′ger,** *n.*

thin (thin) *adj.* **thin·ner, thin·nest;** *adv., v.* **thinned, thin·ning.** —*adj.* **1** of an object or substance, filling little space from one surface to the other; not thick: *thin paper, thin wire, a thin layer of dust.* **2** having little flesh or fat; slender or lean: *a long, thin face. He is dieting to get thin again. She is still thin after her illness.* **3** not set close together; scanty: *He has thin hair.* **4** not dense: *The air on the top of those high mountains is thin.* **5** few and far apart; not abundant: *The actors played to a thin audience.* **6** not like glue or syrup; like water; of less substance than usual: *thin milk.* **7** not deep or strong: *a shrill, thin voice.* **8** having little depth, fullness, or intensity: *a thin color.* **9** easily seen through; flimsy: *a thin excuse.*
thin skin, the condition of being easily affected by criticism, etc.
—*adv.* in a thin manner.
—*v.* **1** make or become thin: *to thin paint.* **2** make less crowded or close by removing individuals: *to thin a row of beets.* **3** of a crowd, become less numerous. [OE *thynne*] —**thin′ly,** *adv.* —**thin′ner,** *n.* —**thin′ness,** *n.*
☛ *Syn. adj.* **2. Thin, lean, gaunt** = having little flesh. **Thin** emphasizes its basic meaning of being not thick through, but sometimes suggests lack of the normal or usual amount of flesh, as from sickness, strain, lack of food, etc.: *She has a thin face.* **Lean** emphasizes lack of fat, and suggests natural thinness with firm, solid flesh: *The forest ranger is lean and brown.* **Gaunt** adds to **thin** the idea of showing the bones, and often suggests a starved or worn look: *Gaunt, bearded men stumbled into camp.*

thine (THīn) *pron., adj. Archaic or poetic.* —*pron.* the possessive form of **thou:** *"For Thine is the kingdom."* —*adj.* the form of **thy** used before a vowel or *h*: *"Drink to me only with thine eyes."* [OE *thīn*]
☛ *Usage.* See note at **thou.**

thing (thing) *n.* **1** any object or substance: *All the things in the house were burned. Put these things away.* **2** whatever is spoken or thought of; any act, deed, fact, event, happening, idea, or opinion: *A strange thing happened. It was a good thing to do.* **3** a person or creature (referred to with pity, scorn, condescension, etc.): *a silly old thing, a mean thing, a dear little thing, a poor thing.* **4 the thing,** anything considered desirable, suitable, appropriate, etc.: *the latest thing in swimsuits, the thing to do.* **5 things,** *pl.* **a** belongings; possessions: *Take your things.* **b** clothes and wearing apparel generally: *Put on your things.* **6** *Informal.* a person's special interest or strong point: *She decided to just do her own thing instead of joining the tour.*
do (one's) thing, *Informal.* express one's personality by doing what one does well or enjoys most.
know a thing or two, *Informal.* be experienced or wise.
make a good thing of, *Informal.* profit from.
see things, have hallucinations.
[OE]

thing·a·ma·jig (thing′ə mə jig′) *n. Informal.* thingumbob.

thing·um·a·bob (thing′ə mə bob′) *n. Informal.* thingumbob.

thing·um·bob (thing′əm bob′) *n. Informal.* something whose name one forgets or does not bother to mention.

think (thingk) *v.* **thought, think·ing;** *n.* —*v.* **1** use the mind to generate and shape ideas, link concepts, assess ideas of others, etc. **2** have in the mind: *He thought that he would go.* **3** have one's thoughts full of: *He thinks nothing but sports.* **4** have an idea: *He had thought of her as still a child.* **5** have an opinion; believe: *Do what you think fit.* **6** reflect; consider: *I must think before answering.* **7** imagine: *You can't think how surprised I was.* **8** remember: *I can't think of his name.* **9** intend: *He thinks to escape punishment.* **10** expect: *I did not think to find you here.*

think aloud, say what one is thinking.

think better of, a change one's mind about; reconsider: *He was going to confront them immediately, but then thought better of it and decided to collect more evidence first.* **b** have a more favorable opinion of (a person, idea, etc.): *She thought better of him for his apology.*

think out, a plan or discover by thinking. **b** solve or understand by thinking: *Bill thought out the reasons for his dad's anger.* **c** think through to the end.

think out loud, say what one is thinking.

think over, consider carefully: *Think it over before you decide.*

think through, think about until one reaches an understanding or conclusion.

think twice, think again before acting; hesitate.

think up, plan or discover by thinking: *We will have to think up a better strategy.* —*n. Informal.* **1** the act or a period of pondering or assessing: *to sit down for a long think on the matter.* **2** (*adj.*) of, involving, or designed for contemplation or assessment: *a think session.* [OE *thencan*] —**think′er,** *n.*

☛ *Syn.* **1. Think, reflect, meditate** = use the powers of the mind. **Think** is the general word meaning to use the mind to form ideas, reach conclusions, understand what is known, etc.: *I must think about your offer before I accept it.* **Reflect** suggests quietly and seriously thinking over a subject, by turning the thoughts (back) upon it: *They need time to reflect on their problems.* **Meditate** suggests focussing one's thoughts on a subject from every point of view, to understand all its sides and relations: *He meditated on the nature of truth.*

think·a·ble (thingk′ə bəl) *adj.* capable of being thought; conceivable.

think·ing (thingk′ing) *adj.* **1** that thinks; reasoning. **2** thoughtful or reflective.

put on (one's) **thinking cap,** take time for thinking over something. —*n.* thought.

think tank *Informal.* a centre for technological research, often engaged in government and defence projects.

thin·nish (thin′ish) *adj.* somewhat thin.

thin–skinned (thin′skind′) *adj.* **1** having a thin skin. **2** easily affected by criticism, rebuff, etc.; too sensitive; touchy.

third (thèrd) *adj., n.* —*adj.* **1** next after the second; last in a series of three; 3rd. **2** being one of three equal parts. —*n.* **1** the next after the second; the last in a series of three. **2** one of three equal parts: *The pizza was divided into thirds.* **3** *Music.* **a** a tone three degrees from another tone. **b** the interval between such tones. **c** the combination of such tones. **4** in automobiles and similar machines, the forward gear or speed next above second; high gear in a three-gear system. [OE *thirda,* var. of *thridda < thrēo* three]

third–class (thèrd′klas′) *adj., adv.* —*adj.* **1** of or belonging to a class after the second. **2** of or having to do with the class of mail that includes unsealed greeting cards, printed circulars, books, etc. —*adv.* by third-class mail.

third degree the use of severe treatment by the police to force a person to give information to make a confession.

third estate persons not in the nobility or clergy; common people.

third eyelid nictitating membrane.

third·ly (thèrd′lē) *adv.* in the third place.

third party 1 a person or group affected by the actions of two major parties in a contract, arrangement, etc. **2** in a two-party political system, any party other than the two major ones.

third person the form of a pronoun or verb used to refer to a person who is neither the person speaking nor the one spoken to. *He, she, it,* and *they* are pronouns of the third person.

third rail a rail parallelling the ordinary rails of a railway. It carries a powerful electric current and is used on some railways instead of an overhead wire.

third–rate (thèrd′rāt′) *adj.* **1** of the third class. **2** distinctly inferior.

Third World the underdeveloped countries of the world, especially those emerging in Africa and Asia since World War II.

thirst (thèrst) *n., v.* —*n.* **1** a dry, uncomfortable feeling in the mouth or throat caused by having had nothing to drink; desire or need for something to drink. **2** a strong desire: *a thirst for adventure.* —*v.* **1** feel thirsty; be thirsty. **2** have a strong desire. [OE *thurst*]

thirst·y (thèrs′tē) *adj.* **thirst·i·er, thirst·i·est. 1** feeling thirst; having thirst. **2** without water or moisture; dry. **3** having a strong desire; eager. —**thirst′i·ly,** *adv.* —**thirst′i·ness,** *n.*

thir·teen (thèr′tēn′) *n., adj.* —*n.* **1** three more than ten; 13: *He counted fourteen people, but I counted thirteen.* **2** the numeral 13: *The 13 is very faint.* **3** the thirteenth in a set or series. **4** a set or series of thirteen persons or things. —*adj.* **1** three more than ten; 13. **2** being thirteenth in a set or series (*used after the noun*): *Section thirteen.* [OE *thrēotēne*]

---

hat, āge, fär; let, ēqual, tèrm; it, īce
hot, ōpen, ôrder; oil, out; cup, pùt, rüle,
əbove, takən, pencəl, lemən, circəs

ch, child; ng, long; sh, ship
th, thin; ᴛʜ, then; zh, measure

Thirteen Colonies See **colony** (def. 7).

thir·teenth (thèr′tēnth′) *adj. or n.* **1** next after the 12th; last in a series of thirteen; 13th. **2** one, or being one, of 13 equal parts.

thir·ti·eth (thèr′tē ith) *adj. or n.* **1** next after the 29th; last in a series of thirty; 30th. **2** one, or being one, of 30 equal parts.

thir·ty (thèr′tē) *adj., n., pl.* **-ties.** —*adj.* being three times ten; 30. —*n.* **1** three times ten; 30. **2** **thirties,** *pl.* the years from thirty through thirty-nine, especially of a century or of a person's life: *His grandfather still vividly remembered the drought of the thirties.* [OE *thrītig*]

thirty–second note *Music.* a note equal to one thirty-second of a whole note; demisemiquaver. See **note** for picture.

thirty–second rest *Music.* a rest lasting as long as a thirty-second note.

this (ᴛʜis) *adj., pl.* **these;** *pron., pl.* **these;** *adv.* —*adj.* pointing out, indicating, or emphasizing some person, thing, idea, etc. already mentioned or understood, especially one present or near in place or time. When used with *that, this* refers to something near and *that* refers to something far or farther away. *Examples: I liked this book a lot. This dress is nicer than that one. I'd rather do it this way.* —*pron.* some person, thing, idea, etc. already mentioned or understood, often one that is to be emphasized or contrasted with another nearer in place or time: *This is a better drawing than that. "What's this?" she asked, holding up my torn sweater. After this we'd better go home.* —*adv.* to such an extent or degree; so: *You can have this much.* [OE]

☛ *Usage.* **This,** like **that,** is regularly used to refer to the idea of a preceding clause or sentence: *He had always had his own way at home, and this made him a poor room-mate.*

this·tle (this′əl) *n.* **1** any of numerous plants of the composite family (especially of genus *Cirsium*) having prickly leaves and stem and showy heads of purple, pink, or yellow flowers. Some thistles, such as the common, or bull, thistle (*Cirsium vulgare*) and the Canada thistle (*C. arvense*) are troublesome weeds. **2** any of various other prickly plants. [OE *thistel*]

this·tle·down (this′əl doun′) *n.* the down or fluff from the ripe flower head of a thistle.

this·tly (this′lē) *adj.* **1** like thistles; prickly. **2** having many thistles.

thith·er (thiᴛʜ′ər) *adv., adj.* —*adv.* to or toward that place; there. —*adj.* on that side; farther. [OE *thider*]

thith·er·ward (thiᴛʜər wərd) *adv.* thither.

tho' (ᴛʜō) *conj. or adv. Informal.* though.

thole (thōl) *n.* a wooden peg or either of a pair of pegs set into the top of the gunwale on each side of a boat to serve as a support for an oar in rowing. [OE *tholl*]

thole·pin (thōl′pin′) *n.* thole.

Thomp·son submachine gun (tomp′sən) *Trademark.* a .45-calibre, air-cooled, automatic weapon that can be carried and operated by one man. Also, **Tommy gun.** [< General John T. Thompson (1860-1940), U.S. Army, one of the inventors]

thong (thong) *n.* **1** a narrow strip of leather, etc., especially one used as a fastening. **2** the lash of a whip. **3** a kind of sandal held on the foot by a narrow piece of leather, plastic, etc. that passes between the toes. [OE *thwang*]

Thor (thôr) *n. Norse mythology.* the god of thunder, war, and agriculture.

tho·rac·ic (thô ras′ik) *adj.* of or having to do with the thorax. The thoracic cavity contains the heart and lungs.

thoracic duct the main duct of the lymphatic system, extending from below the diaphragm up through the thorax to the base of the neck, where it opens into a large vein below the left clavicle.

tho·rax (thô′raks) *n., pl.* **-rax·es, -ra·ces** (-rə sēz′). **1** the part of the body between the neck and the abdomen. **2** the second division of an insect's body, between the head and the abdomen. See **insect** for picture. [< L < Gk.]

tho·rite (thô′rīt) *n.* a mineral consisting essentially of a silicate of thorium.

tho·ri·um (thô′rē əm) *n.* a radio-active metallic chemical element

present in certain rare minerals. *Symbol*: Th; *at.no.* 90; *at.wt.* 232.038. [< NL *thorium* < *Thor*]

thorn (thôrn) *n.* **1** a sharp-pointed, woody growth on a stem or branch of a plant, especially a tree or shrub. **2** a plant having thorns, such as a hawthorn.
thorn in the flesh or **side,** a cause of discomfort or irritation. [OE]

thorn apple 1 the fruit of a hawthorn; haw. **2** hawthorn. **3** jimsonweed or any other plant of the same genus.

thorn·y (thôr′nē) *adj.* **thorn·i·er, thorn·i·est. 1** full of thorns. **2** troublesome; annoying.

tho·ron (thô′ron) *n.* a radio-active, gaseous isotope of radon, formed in the disintegration of thorium. [< *thor(ium)* + *-on*, as in *neon*]

thor·ough (thėr′ō *or* thėr′ə) *adj., adv., prep.* —*adj.* **1** being all that is needed; complete: *a thorough search.* **2** doing all that should be done and neglecting nothing: *The doctor was very thorough in his examination of the patient.* —*adv. or prep. Archaic.* through. Also, **thoro.** [OE *thuruh*, var. of *thurh* through] —**thor′ough·ly,** *adv.* —**thor′ough·ness,** *n.*

thor·ough·bred (thėr′ə bred′) *adj., n.* —*adj.* **1** of pure breed or stock. **2** of persons, well-bred; thoroughly trained. **3** of or having to do with the Thoroughbreds.
—*n.* **1 Thoroughbred,** a breed of horse, used especially in racing, originally derived from a domestic English stock in the female line and an Arabian or Turkish stock in the male line. **2** a purebred or pedigreed animal. **3** a well-bred person.

thor·ough·fare (thėr′ə fer′) *n.* **1** a passage, road, or street open at both ends. **2** a main road; highway: *The Queen Elizabeth Way is a well-known thoroughfare between Toronto and Niagara Falls.*
no thoroughfare, do not go through.

thor·ough·go·ing (thėr′ə gō′ing) *adj.* thorough; complete.

thorp (thôrp) *n. Archaic.* a village; a small town. [OE]

those (ᴛʜōz) *adj. or pron.* pl. of **that.** [OE *thās* these]

thou (ᴛʜou) *pron. Archaic or poetic.* you (sing.); the one spoken to: *"O wild West Wind, thou breath of Autumn's being."* [OE *thū*]
☛ *Usage.* **Thou, thee, thine, thy** and **thyself** are used today only in religious language, as for addressing God, and in poetry. In Old English they were the general words used for addressing one person. See also note at **ye.**

though (ᴛʜō) *conj., adv.* —*conj.* **1** in spite of the fact that; notwithstanding the fact that: *Though it was pouring, the girls went to school.* **2** yet; still; nevertheless: *He is better, though not yet cured.* **3** even if; granting or supposing that: *Though I fail, I shall try again.*
as though, as if; as it would be if: *You look as though you are tired.* —*adv. Informal.* however: *I am sorry about our quarrel; you began it, though.* [ME *thoh* < ON *thó,* with *-h* from OE *thēah*]

thought (thot *or* thôt) *n., v.* —*n.* **1** what one thinks; an idea; notion: *Her thought was to have a picnic.* **2** the power or process of thinking; mental activity: *Thought helps us solve problems.* **3** reasoning: *He applied thought to the problem.* **4** the intellectual activity or mental product characteristic of the thinkers of a specified group, time, or place: *in modern scientific thought, 16th-century thought.* **5** consideration; attention; care; regard: *Show some thought for others.* **6** intention: *His thought was to avoid controversy.* **7** a little bit; trifle: *Be a thought more polite.*
—*v.* pt. and pp. of **think.** [OE *thōht*]
☛ *Syn. n.* **1.** See note at **idea.**

thought control the strict limiting or regimentation of ideas, reasoning, etc. to make them conform to those of a particular group, government, etc.

thought·ful (thot′fəl *or* thôt′fəl) *adj.* **1** deep in thought; thinking: *He was thoughtful for a while and then replied, "No."* **2** careful; showing careful thought: *a thoughtful plan.* **3** careful of others; considerate: *She is always thoughtful of her mother.*
—**thought′ful·ly,** *adv.* —**thought′ful·ness,** *n.*
☛ *Syn.* **3. Thoughtful, considerate** = giving careful attention to the comfort or feelings of others. **Thoughtful** emphasizes concerning oneself with the comfort and welfare of others and doing, without being asked, things that will add to their well-being or happiness: *A thoughtful neighbor, knowing the girl was sick and alone, took her some hot food.* **Considerate** emphasizes concerning oneself with the feelings and rights of others and trying to spare them from discomfort, pain, or unhappiness: *She is considerate enough to tell her parents where she goes.*

thought·less (thot′lis *or* thôt′lis) *adj.* **1** without thought; doing things without thinking; careless. **2** showing little or no care or regard for others; not considerate. **3** stupid. —**thought′less·ly,** *adv.* —**thought′less·ness,** *n.*

thought–out (thot′out′ *or* thôt′-) *adj.* carefully considered; deliberate.

thou·sand (thou′zənd) *n. or adj.* ten hundred; 1000. [OE *thūsend*]

thou·sand·fold (thou′zənd fōld′) *adj., adv., or n.* a thousand times as much or as many.

thou·sandth (thou′zəndth) *adj. or n.* **1** the last in a series of a thousand. **2** one, or being one, of a thousand equal parts.

Thra·cian (thrā′shən) *n., adj.* —*n.* a native or inhabitant of ancient Thrace, a region in the E part of the Balkan peninsula. —*adj.* of or having to do with ancient Thrace or its people.

thral·dom (throl′dəm *or* thrôl′dəm) See **thralldom.**

thrall (throl *or* thrôl) *n.* **1** a person in bondage; slave. **2** thralldom; bondage; slavery. [OE < ON *thrǽll*]

thrall·dom or **thral·dom** (throl′dəm *or* thrôl′dəm) *n.* bondage; slavery.

thrash (thrash) *v.* **1** beat: *The man thrashed the boy for stealing the apples.* **2** move violently; toss: *Unable to sleep, the patient thrashed about in his bed.* **3** thresh.
thrash out, settle by thorough discussion: *to thrash out a problem.*
thrash over, go over again and again.
[var. of *thresh*]

thrash·er (thrash′ər) *n.* **1** any of several North American songbirds (esp. genus *Toxostoma*) belonging to the same family as the mockingbird, having a long tail and long bill. Thrashers are noted for their song. **2** a person or thing that thrashes.

thread (thred) *n., v.* —*n.* **1** cotton, silk, flax, etc. spun out into a fine cord: *Thread is used for sewing.* **2** something long and slender like a thread: *Threads of gold could be seen in the ore.* **3** a continuing or connecting element: *He lost the thread of their conversation when he heard the phone ring.* **4** the sloping ridge that winds around a bolt, screw, pipe, joint, etc.: *The thread of a nut interlocks with the thread of a bolt.* **5** a tenuous or slender assurance or support: *a thread of hope.* **6 threads,** *pl. Slang.* clothes, especially an outfit or suit.
hang by or **on a thread,** be in a precarious position.
—*v.* **1** pass a thread through: *She threaded her needle. Mary threaded a hundred beads.* **2** form into a thread: *Cook the syrup until it will thread.* **3** pass like a thread through; pervade. **4** make one's way through; make (one's way) carefully; go on a winding course: *He threaded his way through the crowd.* **5** cut threads into a bolt, screw, pipe, joint, etc. [OE *thrǽd*] —**thread′like′,** *adj.*

thread·bare (thred′ber′) *adj.* **1** having the nap worn off; worn so much that the threads show: *a threadbare coat.* **2** wearing clothes worn to the threads; shabby. **3** old and worn; stale.

thread·worm (thred′wėrm′) *n.* any of various long, thin nematode worms, especially the pinworm.

thread·y (thred′ē) *adj.* **1** consisting of or resembling a thread. **2** fibrous; stringy or viscid. **3** of the pulse, thin and feeble. **4** of the voice, etc., lacking in fullness. —**thread′i·ness,** *n.*

threat (thret) *n.* **1** a statement of what will be done to hurt or punish someone. **2** a sign or cause of possible harm or unpleasantness: *Those black clouds are a threat of rain.* [OE *thrēat* troop, throng; coercion]

threat·en (thret′ən) *v.* **1** make a threat against; say what will be done to hurt or punish: *to threaten a person with imprisonment.* **2** be a sign of (possible evil or harm, etc.): *Black clouds threaten rain.* **3** be a threat. **4** utter threats: *Do you mean to threaten?* **5** be a cause of possible evil or harm to: *A flood threatened the city.* [OE *thrēatnian* urge; coerce] —**threat′en·er,** *n.* —**threat′en·ing·ly,** *adv.*
☛ *Syn.* **1. Threaten, menace** = promise or warn of harm, injury, or punishment. **Threaten** emphasizes trying to force or influence someone to do (or not to do) something, by stating that some harm or hurt will be inflicted to punish disobedience or to get even: *He threatened to shoot her if she screamed.* **Menace** emphasizes showing by a look, position, movement, etc. an intention to harm: *He menaced her with a gun.*

three (thrē) *n., adj.* —*n.* **1** one more than two; 3: *I bought two T-shirts and he bought three.* **2** the numeral 3: *There's a 3 at the bottom of the page.* **3** the third in a set or series; especially, a playing card or side of a die having three spots: *the three of hearts.* **4** a set or series of three persons or things: *The soldiers marched past in threes.*
—*adj.* **1** one more than two; 3. **2** being third in a set or series (*used mainly after the noun*): *Have you read Chapter Three?* [OE *thrēo*]

three–D or **3–D** (thrē′dē′) *adj., n.* —*adj.* being three-dimensional or producing a three-dimensional effect. —*n.* a motion picture, etc. having a three-dimensional effect.

three–deck·er (thrē′dek′ər) *n.* **1** a ship having three decks. **2** anything having three storeys, layers, or parts: *a three-decker sandwich.*

three–di·men·sion·al (thrē′di men′shən əl *or* -dī men′shən əl) *adj.* **1** of, having, or having to do with the three dimensions of width, depth, and height. **2** of a motion picture, etc., producing an effect of depth by stereoscopic means. **3** of a character in a novel, play, etc., being true to life.

three·fold (thrē′fōld′) *adj., adv., n.* —*adj.* **1** three times as much or as many. **2** having three parts. —*adv. or n.* three times as much or as many.

three–four (thrē′fôr′) *adj. Music.* indicating or having three quarter notes in a bar or measure, the first of which is accented, as in a waltz.

three–mile limit the traditional limit of a nation's territorial waters, according to international law, being three nautical miles (almost 6 km) from shore. This was extended to 12 nautical miles (about 22 km) by international agreement in 1982.

three·pence (thrup′əns *or* threp′əns) *n. Brit.* the sum of three pence.

three·pen·ny (thrup′ən ē, threp′ən ē, *or* thrē′pen′ē) *adj., n.* —*adj.* **1** *Brit.* worth or costing three pence. **2** of little worth; cheap. —*n.* threepenny bit.

threepenny bit *Brit.* a former British coin worth three pence.

three–ply (thrē′plī′) *adj.* having three thicknesses, layers, folds, or strands.

three–quar·ter (thrē′kwôr′tər) *adj.* three-four: *three-quarter time.*

three R's reading, writing, and arithmetic.

three·score (thrē′skôr′) *adj.* three times twenty; 60.

three·some (thrē′səm) *n.* **1** a group of three people. **2** any game played by three people. **3** the players in such a game.

thren·o·dy (thren′ə dē) *n., pl.* **-dies.** a song of lamentation, especially at a person's death. [< Gk. *thrēnōidia* < *thrēnos* lament + *ōidē* song]

thresh (thresh) *v.* **1** separate the grain or seeds from (wheat, etc.). *Nowadays most farmers use a machine to thresh their wheat.* **2** toss about; move violently; thrash.

thresh out, settle by thorough discussion.

thresh over, go over again and again. [OE *threscan*]

thresh·er (thresh′ər) *n.* **1** a person who threshes. **2** a machine used for separating the grain or seeds from the stalks and other parts of wheat, oats, etc. **3** a large shark (*Alopias vulpinus*) having a tail with a very long upper lobe.

threshing machine a machine for separating the grain, or seeds, from the stalks and other parts of wheat, oats, etc.

thresh·old (thresh′ōld *or* thresh′hōld) *n.* **1** a piece of wood or stone under a door. **2** doorway. **3** the point of entering; a beginning point: *The scientist was on the threshold of an important discovery.* **4** *Psychology and physiology.* the limit below which a given stimulus ceases to be perceptible, or the point beyond which two stimuli cannot be differentiated. [OE *thresch(w)old*]

threw (thrü) *v.* pt. of **throw.**
☞ *Hom.* **through.**

thrice (thrīs) *adv.* **1** three times. **2** every; extremely. [ME *thries* < OE *thriga* thrice]

thrid (thrid) *v.* **thrid·ded, thrid·ding.** *Archaic or dialect.* thread.

thrift (thrift) *n.* **1** the absence of waste; economical management; the habit of saving: *By thrift she managed to get along on her small salary.* **2** any of several perennial plants (genus *Armeria*) related to the sea lavender, especially *A. maritima,* native to mountainous, marshy, and sandy coastal regions of Eurasia and North America, having clusters of pink or white flowers. [< *thrive*]

thrift·less (thrift′lis) *adj.* without thrift; wasteful. —**thrift′less·ly,** *adv.* —**thrift′less·ness,** *n.*

thrift·y (thrif′tē) *adj.* **thrift·i·er, thrift·i·est. 1** careful in spending; economical; saving. **2** *Rare.* thriving or prosperous: *a thrifty plant, a thrifty farm.* —**thrift′i·ly,** *adv.* —**thrift′i·ness,** *n.*
☞ *Syn.* **1.** See note at **economical.**

thrill (thril) *n., v.* —*n.* **1** a shivering, exciting feeling. **2** a vibrating or quivering; throbbing; tremor.
—*v.* **1** give a shivering, exciting feeling to: *Stories of adventure thrilled him.* **2** have a shivering, exciting feeling. **3** quiver; tremble: *Her voice thrilled with terror.* [var. of *thirl* < OE *thyrlian* pierce < *thurh* through] —**thrill′ing·ly,** *adv.*

thrill·er (thril′ər) *n.* **1** a person or thing that thrills. **2** *Informal.* a sensational story, play, or motion picture, especially one involving a murder.

thrips (thrips) *n., pl.* **thrips.** any of numerous small or minute insects (order Thysanoptera) having long, narrow wings fringed with hairs, and mouthparts adapted for sucking plant juices. Many thrips are serious plant pests. [< L < Gk. *thrips* woodworm]

thrive (thrīv) *v.* **throve** *or* **thrived, thrived** *or* **thriv·en, thriv·ing. 1** grow vigorously and well; flourish: *thriving crops. The garden is thriving under his care.* **2** be successful; prosper: *Her business is thriving.* [ME < ON *thrífa(sk)*] —**thriv′ing·ly,** *adv.*

thriv·en (thriv′ən) *v.* a pp. of **thrive.**

---

hat, āge, fär; let, ēqual, tèrm; it, īce
hot, ōpen, ôrder; oil, out; cup, pùt, rüle,
əbove, takən, pencəl, lemən, circəs

ch, child; ng, long; sh, ship
th, thin; ᴛʜ, then; zh, measure

thro' (thrü) *prep., adv., or adj. Esp.U.S.* through.

throat (thrōt) *n.* **1** the front of the neck. **2** the passage from the mouth to the stomach or the lungs. **3** any narrowed opening or passage: *the throat of a mine.*

jump down (someone's) **throat,** *Informal.* attack or criticize a person with sudden violence.

lump in (one's) **throat, a** a feeling of inability to swallow. **b** a feeling of being about to cry: *The story brought a lump to his throat.*

stick in (one's) **throat,** be hard or unpleasant to say: *The apology stuck in his throat.* [OE *throte*]

throat·ed (thrōt′id) *adj.* having a throat, especially of a specified kind (*usually used in compounds*): *a ruby-throated hummingbird.*

throat·y (thrō′tē) *adj.* **throat·i·er, throat·i·est. 1** produced or uttered from far back in the throat; low-pitched and resonant: *a throaty voice.* **2** deep and resonant as if produced far back in the throat. —**throat′i·ness,** *n.*

throb (throb) *v.* **throbbed, throb·bing;** *n.* —*v.* **1** beat more rapidly or strongly than normally: *Our hearts were still throbbing from the long climb up the hill.* **2** beat or vibrate steadily. **3** quiver; tremble: *They were throbbing with excitement.*
—*n.* **1** an abnormally rapid or strong beat: *the throb of our hearts.* **2** a steady beat or vibration: *She felt the throb of the little plane's engine.* **3** a quiver; tremble. [ME *throbbe(n)*; ? imitative] —**throb′bing·ly,** *adv.*

throe (thrō) *n.* Usually, **throes,** *pl.* **1** a violent pang or pangs; great pain: *the throes of death, the throes of childbirth.* **2** a hard or agonizing struggle: *a poet in the throes of creation, the throes of revolution.* [? a fusion of OE *thrōwian* suffer, and *thrāwan* twist; throw]
☞ *Hom.* **throw.**

throm·bo·sis (throm bō′sis) *n.* the formation of a blood clot in a blood vessel or in the heart. [< NL < Gk. *thrombōsis,* ult. < *thrombos* clot]

throm·bus (throm′bəs) *n., pl.* **-bi** (-bī *or* -bē). a blood clot causing thrombosis.

throne (thrōn) *n., v.* **throned, thron·ing;** —*n.* **1** the chair on which a king, queen, bishop, or other person of high rank sits during ceremonies. **2** the power or authority of a king, queen, etc. **3** the person who sits on a throne; sovereign.
—*v.* enthrone. [ME < OF < L < Gk. *thronos*]

throng (throng) *n., v.* —*n.* a crowd; multitude. —*v.* **1** crowd; fill with a crowd. **2** come together in a crowd; go or press in large numbers. [OE (ge)*thrang*]
☞ *Syn. n.* See note at **crowd.**

thros·tle (thros′əl) *n.* a thrush, especially the song thrush. [OE]

throt·tle (throt′əl) *n., v.* **-tled, -tling.** —*n.* **1** a valve regulating the flow of steam, gasoline vapor, etc. to an engine; especially, the valve controlling the gasoline vapor entering the cylinders of an internal combustion engine. **2** a lever or pedal working such a valve. The throttle of a car is called an accelerator. **3** throat or windpipe.
—*v.* **1** lessen the speed of an engine by closing a throttle (*often used with* **down** *or* **back**): *to throttle down a steam engine.* **2** stop the breath of by pressure on the throat; choke; strangle: *The thief throttled the dog to keep it from barking.* **3** stop or check the expression or action of; suppress: *Increased tariffs soon throttled trade between the two countries.* [ME; perhaps dim. of *throat*]

through (thrü) *prep., adv., adj.* —*prep.* **1** from end to end of; from side to side of; between the parts of; from beginning to end of: *The soldiers marched through the town. The men cut a tunnel through a mountain.* **2** here and there in; over; around: *We travelled through Quebec, visiting many old towns.* **3** because of; by reason of: *The woman refused help through pride.* **4** by means of: *He became rich through hard work and ability.* **5** having reached the end of; finished with: *We are through school at three o'clock.* **6 a** during the whole of; throughout: *to work from dawn through the day and into the night.* **b** during and until the finish of: *to help a person through hard times.*
—*adv.* **1** from end to end; from side to side; between the parts: *The bullet hit the wall and went through.* **2** completely; thoroughly: *He walked home in the rain and was wet through.* **3** from beginning to end: *She read the book through.* **4** along the whole distance; all the way: *The train goes through to Vancouver.*

through and through, completely; thoroughly.
—*adj.* **1 a** going all the way without change: *a through train from Montreal to Vancouver.* **b** for the whole distance or journey: *a through ticket.* **c** going straight on without stopping: *through traffic.* **2** having reached the end; finished: *I am almost through.* **3** passing or extending from one end, side, surface, etc. to the other. [earlier *thourgh,* OE *thurh*]

☞ *Syn. prep.* **3, 4.** See note at **by.**

through·out (thrü out′) *prep., adv.* —*prep.* all the way through; through all; in every part or during the whole course of: *Dominion Day is celebrated throughout Canada. She skied almost every weekend throughout the winter.* —*adv.* in or to every part or from beginning to end: *The house is well built throughout. He remained stubborn throughout.*

through·put (thrü′pùt′) *n.* the handling or processing of goods or material: *The elevator's records show that the throughput of wheat has increased over last year.*

through street a street on which traffic is given the right of way at intersections. Compare **stop street.**

through·way (thrü′wā′) *n.* a thoroughfare, especially an expressway.

throve (thrōv) *v.* pt. of **thrive.**

throw (thrō) *v.* **threw, thrown, throw·ing;** *n.* —*v.* **1** cast; toss; hurl: *to throw a ball. The fire hose threw water on the fire.* **2** bring to the ground: *His horse threw him.* **3** put carelessly or in haste: *Throw some clothes on and run.* **4** put or move quickly or by force: *to throw oneself into a fight, to throw a man into prison.* **5** put into a certain condition: *to throw a person into confusion.* **6** turn, direct, or move, especially quickly: *She threw a glance at each car that passed us.* **7** move (a lever, etc.) that connects or disconnects parts of a switch, clutch, or other mechanism. **8** connect or disconnect thus. **9** shed. A snake throws its skin. **10** of some animals, bring forth (young). **11** *Informal.* let an opponent win (a race, game, etc.), often for money. **12** make a specified cast with dice. **13** twist (silk) into threads. **14** shape on a potter's wheel: *to throw a bowl from a ball of clay.* **15** *Informal.* give (a party, etc.). **16** project or direct: *The lamp threw his shadow on the wall.*

throw away, a get rid of; discard. **b** waste: *to throw away an opportunity.* **c** fail to use.

throw back, revert to an ancestral type.

throw cold water on, discourage by being indifferent or unwilling.

throw in, add as a gift: *Our grocer often throws in an extra apple.*

throw off, a get rid of. **b** cause to lose: *to throw a hound off the scent.* **c** *Informal.* produce (a poem, etc.) in an offhand manner.

throw (oneself) at, try very hard to get the love, friendship, or favor of.

throw open, a open suddenly or widely. **b** remove all obstacles or restrictions from.

throw out, a get rid of; discard. **b** reject. **c** expel. **d** *Baseball.* put out (a base runner) by throwing the ball to a base.

throw over, give up; discard; abandon.

throw up, a *Informal.* vomit. **b** give up; abandon: *He threw up his plan to go to Europe.* **c** build rapidly.

—*n.* **1** the act or an instance of throwing: *That was a good throw.* **2** the distance a thing is or may be thrown: *a record throw. The river is just a stone's throw from the house.* **3** a light cover or wrap, such as a blanket or shawl. **4** the act or result of casting dice: *a throw of six.* **5** a venture or risk. **6** *Geology.* the vertical displacement of part of a bed of rock, produced by a fault. [OE *thrāwan* twist] —**throw′er,** *n.*

☞ *Hom.* **throe.**

☞ *Syn. v.* **1. Throw, toss, cast** = send something through the air by a sudden twist or quick movement of the arm. **Throw** is the general word: *The children threw pillows at each other.* **Toss** means throw lightly or carelessly with the palm up: *Please toss me the matches.* **Cast** is literary or archaic in the literal meaning of "throw" (except in special uses, as in games, voting, fishing, sailing—*They cast anchor*) but it is often used figuratively: *She cast dignity to the winds, and ran.*

throw·a·way (thrō′ə wā′) *n.* **1** a free handbill or leaflet carrying advertising or other information; handout. **2** anything designed to be discarded after use. **3** (*adjl.*) meant to be discarded or thrown away after use; disposable: *throwaway bottles.* **4** (*adjl.*) of a remark, a line of dialogue, etc., spoken or delivered in an offhand or casual way: *a throwaway line in a play.*

throw·back (thrō′bak′) *n.* **1** a reversion to an ancestral type or character. **2** an instance of such a reversion: *The boy seemed to be a throwback to his great-grandfather.*

thrown (thrōn) *v.* pp. of **throw.**

thrum[1] (thrum) *v.* **thrummed, thrum·ming;** *n.* —*v.* **1** play on a stringed instrument by plucking the strings, especially in an idle, mechanical, or unskilful way: *to thrum a guitar.* **2** of a guitar, etc. or its strings, sound when thrummed on. **3** drum or tap idly with the

fingers: *to thrum on a table.* **4 a** recite or tell in a monotonous way. **b** hum over (a melody).
—*n.* the sound made by thrumming. [imitative] —**thrum′mer,** *n.*

thrum[2] (thrum) *n.* **1** an end of the warp thread left unwoven on the loom after the web is cut off. **2** loose thread or yarn. **3** a tuft or fringe. [OE *thrum;* in *tungethrum* tongue ligament]

thrush[1] (thrush) *n.* any of a subfamily (Turdinae, of the family Muscicapidae) of songbirds found throughout the world, especially those species having brownish plumage with a spotted breast. This group includes some of the finest singers among birds, such as the nightingale and the hermit thrush. Some authorities classify thrushes as a separate family (Turdidae). [OE *thrȳsce*]

thrush[2] (thrush) *n.* **1** a contagious disease, especially of very young babies, in which white blisters form in the mouth and throat and on the lips. Thrush is caused by a fungus (*Candida albicans*). **2** a diseased condition of a horse's foot.

thrust (thrust) *v.* **thrust, thrust·ing;** *n.* —*v.* **1** push with force: *He thrust his hands into his pockets. She thrust her brother aside and grabbed the plate of cookies.* **2** drive into or cause to pierce by pushing; stab: *He thrust his fork into the potato.* **3** put forth; extend: *The tree thrust its roots deep into the ground.*
—*n.* **1** a sudden or forceful push: *With a quick thrust, she hid the book behind the pillow.* **2** a push or lunge with a pointed weapon: *A thrust with the pin broke the balloon.* **3** a military attack. **4** *Mechanics.* the continuous sideways force of one part of a structure against another, such as the pressure of an arch against a pillar. **5** the endwise push exerted by the rotation of a propeller, producing forward motion. **6** the force exerted by a high-speed jet of gas, etc. ejected to the rear, as in a jet engine, producing forward motion. **7** main purpose or direction: *the thrust of an argument.* [ME < ON *thrȳsta*] —**thrust′er,** *n.*

thru·way (thrü′wā′) *n. Esp. U.S.* throughway.

thud (thud) *n., v.* **thud·ded, thud·ding.** —*n.* **1** a dull sound caused by a blow or fall: *The book hit the floor with a thud.* **2** a blow or thump. —*v.* hit, move, or strike with a thud. [? ME *thudden* < OE *thyddan* strike]

thug (thug) *n.* **1** a ruffian; cutthroat; gangster. **2** *Historical.* in India, a member of a religious organization of robbers and murderers. [< Hind. < Skt. *sthaga* rogue] —**thug′gish,** *adj.*

thug·ger·y (thug′ər ē) *n.* violent or brutal acts or behavior.

Thu·le (thü′lē) *n.* **1** the part of the world that the ancient Greeks and Romans regarded as farthest north, that is, some island or region north of Britain. **2** an Inuit culture of N Greenland, lasting from about A.D. 500 to 1400. **3** See **ultima Thule.** [< L < Gk. *Thoulē*]

thu·li·um (thü′lē əm *or* thyül′ē əm) *n.* a metallic element of the rare-earth group. *Symbol:* Tm; *at.no.* 69; *at.wt.* 168.934. [< NL *thulium* < *Thule*]

thumb (thum) *n., v.* —*n.* **1** the short finger of the human hand that is nearest the wrist and can be opposed to the other fingers. **2** the part of a glove, mitten, etc. that covers the thumb.

all thumbs, very clumsy, awkward, etc.: *I'm all thumbs when it comes to tying bows.*

thumbs down, a a sign of disapproval, rejection, or disappointment, made by closing the hand and pointing the thumb downward: *She just gave us a thumbs down when we asked how she liked the slogan.* **b** an expression of disapproval, rejection, or disappointment: *The principal turned thumbs down on the proposal for another field trip.*

thumbs up, a a sign of acceptance or satisfaction, made by closing the hand and pointing the thumb up: *He smiled and signalled thumbs up as he came out of the employment office.* **b** an expression of satisfaction: *"Thumbs up!" he called as he came out of the examination room.*

under (someone's) thumb, under someone's control or influence: *He's got them all under his thumb and they'll do anything he tells them.*

—*v.* **1** leaf through or turn the pages of a book, magazine, etc. rapidly. **2** soil or wear by repeated thumbing or as if by thumbing: *The books were badly thumbed.* **3** *Informal.* ask for or get a free ride by signalling with the thumb to passing motorists: *He thumbed a ride into town when his car broke down.* **4** travel by thumbing rides; hitchhike: *She thumbed her way from Calgary to Winnipeg.*

thumb off, *Hockey.* indicate by a jerk of the thumb that a given player has been penalized for an infraction of the rules and that he is to take his place in the penalty box.

thumb (one's) nose, express scorn or defiance by or as if by placing one's thumb on the end of one's nose and extending the fingers: *The rude little girl thumbed her nose at a passer by. He thumbed his nose at the promise of success and went on his way.* [OE *thūma*] —**thumb′like′,** *adj.*

thumb·nail (thum′nāl′) *n.* the nail of the thumb.

thumbnail sketch 1 a small or quickly drawn picture: *a thumbnail sketch of a child at play.* **2** a short description.

thumb·screw (thum′skrü′) *n.* **1** a screw made so that its head can be easily turned with the thumb and a finger. **2** an instrument of torture for squeezing the thumbs.

thumb·tack (thum′tak′) *n.* a tack having a broad, flat head, designed to be pressed into a surface with the thumb.

thump (thump) *v., n.* —*v.* **1** strike with something thick and heavy: *He thumped the table with his fist.* **2** strike against (something) heavily and noisily: *The shutters thumped the wall in the wind.* **3** make a dull sound; pound: *The hammer thumped against the wood.* **4** beat violently or heavily: *His heart always thumped as he walked past the cemetery at night.* **5** beat or thrash severely. —*n.* **1** a blow with something thick and heavy; a heavy knock. **2** the dull sound made by a blow, knock, or fall. [imitative] —**thump′er,** *n.*

thump·ing (thump′ing) *adj. Informal.* great; huge; whopping.

thun·der (thun′dər) *n., v.* —*n.* **1** the loud noise that often follows a flash of lightning. It is caused by a disturbance of the air resulting from the discharge of electricity. **2** any noise like thunder: *the thunder of Niagara Falls, a thunder of applause.* **3** a threat or denunciation. **4** thunderbolt.
steal (someone's) **thunder,** make someone's idea, method, etc. less effective by using it first or doing something better or more startling: *The Liberals stole the Tories' thunder by announcing their election plans first.* —*v.* **1** give forth thunder: *We heard it thunder in the distance.* **2** make a noise like thunder. **3** utter very loudly; roar: *to thunder a reply.* **4** utter a threat or denunciation loudly, violently, or impressively: *The newspaper article thundered against the injustices of the political system.* [OE *thunor*] —**thun′der·er,** *n.*

thun·der·bird (thun′dər bėrd′) *n.* in the mythology of several North American Indian peoples, a huge bird that creates thunder with its beating wings and lightning with its flashing eyes. Carved representations of the thunderbird are often found on totem poles of the Pacific Coast peoples.

thun·der·bolt (thun′dər bōlt′) *n.* **1** a flash of lightning and the thunder that follows it. **2** something sudden, startling, and terrible: *The news of his death came as a thunderbolt.*

thun·der·clap (thun′dər klap′) *n.* **1** a loud crash of thunder. **2** something sudden or startling.

thun·der·cloud (thun′dər kloud′) *n.* a dark, electrically charged cloud that brings thunder and lightning.

Thun·der·er (thun′dər ər) *n.* Jupiter; Zeus.

thun·der·head (thun′dər hed′) *n.* one of the round, swelling masses of cumulus clouds often appearing before thunderstorms and frequently developing into thunderclouds.

thun·der·ing (thun′dər ing *or* thun′dring) *adj.* **1** making thunder; extremely loud. **2** *Informal.* unusual; superlative; extremely big or great. —**thun′der·ing·ly,** *adv.*

thun·der·ous (thun′dər əs *or* thun′drəs) *adj.* **1** producing thunder. **2** making a noise like thunder. —**thun′der·ous·ly,** *adv.*

thun·der·show·er (thun′dər shou′ər) *n.* a shower accompanied by thunder and lightning.

thun·der·squall (thun′dər skwol′ *or* -skwôl′) *n.* a squall accompanied by thunder and lightning.

thun·der·storm (thun′dər stôrm′) *n.* a storm accompanied by thunder and lightning and, usually, by heavy rain.

thun·der·struck (thun′dər struk′) *adj.* overcome, as if hit by a thunderbolt; astonished; amazed.

thu·ri·ble (thür′ə bəl) *n.* censer. [ME < L *t(h)uribulum* < *t(h)us, thuris* incense < Gk. *thyos* burnt sacrifice]

Thu·rin·gi·an (thü rin′jē ən *or* thyü rin′jē ən) *adj., n.* —*adj.* **1** of or having to do with Thuringia, a former state in southern East Germany, or its people. **2** *Geology.* of or having to do with the upper division of the Permian period in Europe. —*n.* **1** a native or inhabitant of Thuringia. **2** a member of a Germanic tribe living in central Germany till the 6th century.

Thurs. *or* **Thur.** Thursday.

Thurs·day (thėrz′dē *or* -dā) *n.* the fifth day of the week, following Wednesday. [OE < ON *Thórsdagr*, literally, day of Thor, translation of LL *dies Jovis* day of Jupiter (or Jove)]

thus (₮HUs) *adv.* **1** in this way; in the way just indicated or about to be indicated: *He spoke thus.* **2** accordingly; consequently; therefore: *Thus we decided that he was wrong.* **3** to this extent or degree; so: *thus far.* [OE]

thwack (thwak) *v., n.* —*v.* strike vigorously with a stick or something flat. —*n.* a sharp blow with a stick or something flat. [probably imitative]

thwart (thwôrt) *v., n., adj., adv.* —*v.* hinder, defeat, or frustrate; keep from doing something: *The boy's lack of money thwarted his plans for a trip. The enemy's attack was thwarted.*

---

hat, āge, fär; let, ēqual, tėrm; it, īce
hot, ōpen, ôrder; oil, out; cup, pút, rüle,
əbove, takən, pencəl, lemən, circəs
ch, child; ng, long; sh, ship
th, thin; ₮H, then; zh, measure

—*n.* **1** a seat across a boat, on which a rower sits. **2** a brace in a canoe. See **canoe** for picture.
—*adj.* lying or situated across something else; transverse or oblique.
—*adv.* across; athwart. [ME < ON *thvert*, adv., across, originally neut. of adj. *thverr* transverse]
☛ *Syn. v.* See note at **frustrate.**

thy (₮HĪ) *adj. Archaic or poetic.* the possessive form of **thou** used before a noun: *"Thy kingdom come, Thy will be done."* [OE *thīn*]
☛ *Usage.* See note at **thou.**

thyme (tīm) *n.* any of several herbs or small shrubs (genus *Thymus*) of the mint family having aromatic leaves, especially a garden herb (*T. vulgaris*), whose dried leaves and flowering tops are used as seasoning. [ME < MF *thym* < L *thymum* < Gk. *thymon*]
☛ *Hom.* **time.**

thy·mol (thī′mōl *or* thī′mol) *n.* a crystalline substance obtained from thyme, etc. or made synthetically, used as an antiseptic. *Formula:* $C_{10}H_{13}OH$

thy·mus (thī′məs) *n.* a ductless glandlike body situated near the base of the neck, present in the young of most vertebrates but becoming very small or disappearing altogether in adults. The thymus is thought to function in the development of the body's immune system. [< NL < Gk. *thymos*]

thy·roid (thī′roid) *n.* **1** the thyroid gland. **2** a medicine made from the thyroid glands of certain animals, used in the treatment of goitre, obesity, etc. **3** the thyroid cartilage. **4** (*adj.*) of or having to do with the thyroid gland or thyroid cartilage. [ult. < Gk. *thyreoeidēs* shieldlike < *thyreos* oblong shield (< *thyra* door) + *eidos* form]

thyroid cartilage the principal cartilage of the larynx, which in human beings forms the Adam's apple.

thyroid gland an important ductless gland in the neck of vertebrates producing a hormone that regulates growth and metabolism.

thy·rox·in (thī rok′sən) *n.* thyroxine.

thy·rox·ine (thī rok′sēn) *n.* an amino acid that is the active hormone produced by the thyroid gland. Thyroxine is also prepared synthetically or obtained from the thyroid glands of animals and is used in the treatment of thyroid disorders. *Formula:* $C_{15}H_{11}I_4NO_4$

thyrse (thėrs) *n. Botany.* a compound inflorescence (flower cluster), as in the grape and lilac, composed of two simple types of inflorescence: the main axis is a raceme and the secondary axes are cymes. [< F < NL *thyrsus* thyrsus. 17c.]

thyr·sus (thėr′səs) *n., pl.* **-si** (-sī *or* -sē). **1** *Greek mythology.* a staff or spear tipped with an ornament like a pine cone and sometimes wrapped round with ivy and vine branches, borne by Dionysus (Bacchus) and his followers. **2** thyrse. [< L < Gk. *thyrsos* staff, stem. 18c.]

thy·self (₮HĪ self′) *pron. Archaic or poetic.* the reflexive form of **thou:** *"Thou shalt love thy neighbour as thyself."*
☛ *Usage.* See note at **thou.**

ti (tē) *n. Music.* **1** the seventh tone of an eight-tone major scale. **2** the tone B. See **do²** for picture. [see GAMUT.]
☛ *Hom.* **tea, tee.**

Ti titanium.

ti·ar·a (tē ä′rə *or* tī er′ə) *n.* **1** a band of gold, jewels, flowers, etc., worn around the head by women as an ornament. **2** *Roman Catholic Church.* **a** the triple crown of the Pope. **b** the position or authority of the Pope. **3** in ancient Persia, a headdress for men. [< L < Gk.]

Ti·bet·an (ti bet′ən) *n., adj.* —*n.* **1** a member of an Asiatic people who are the original inhabitants of Tibet, a region in SW China. **2** a native or inhabitant of Tibet. **3** the language of Tibet, belonging to the Sino-Tibetan language family.
—*adj.* of or having to do with Tibet, its people, or their language.

tib·i·a (tib′ē ə) *n., pl.* **-i·ae** (-ē ē′ *or* -ē ī′) *or* **i·as. 1** *Anatomy.* the inner and thicker of the two bones of the leg from the knee to the ankle; shinbone. See **leg** for picture. **2** in animals or birds, a corresponding bone. **3** the fourth joint of the leg of an insect. **4** in ancient times, a flute. [< L]

tib·i·al (tib′ē əl) *adj.* of or having to do with the tibia.

tic (tik) *n.* a habitual, involuntary twitching of the muscles, especially those of the face. [< F]
☛ *Hom.* tick.

tick¹ (tik) *n., v.* —*n.* **1** a sound made by a clock or watch. **2** a sound like it. **3** *Informal.* a moment; instant. **4** a small mark used in checking, usually √ or /.
—*v.* **1** make a tick. **2** mark off: *The clock ticked away the minutes.* **3** mark an item in a list, etc. with a tick; check (*usually used with* **off**): *He ticked off the groceries he had already bought.*
tick off, *Slang.* scold; tell off: *She got ticked off for being late again.*
tick over, of an automobile engine, etc., run gently; idle.
what makes (someone) **tick,** what motivates a person to act or behave in a certain way: *He's very quiet. I wonder what makes him tick.*
[probably ult. imitative]
☛ *Hom.* tic.

tick² (tik) *n.* **1** any of a large group of small arachnids comprising two families (Ixodidae, the **hard ticks,** and Argasidae, the **soft ticks**), having sucking mouthparts with which they feed on the blood of dogs, cattle, human beings, etc. Some ticks carry infectious diseases. **2** any of various species of usually wingless insect that live as parasites on cattle, sheep, birds, etc. [OE *ticia*]
☛ *Hom.* tic.

tick³ (tik) *n.* **1** the cloth covering of a mattress or pillow. **2** *Informal.* ticking. [probably ult. < L *theca* case < Gk. *thēkē*]
☛ *Hom.* tic.

tick·er (tik′ər) *n.* **1** something that ticks, especially a clock or watch. **2** a telegraphic instrument that records stock market reports or news on a paper tape. **3** *Slang.* the heart.

ticker tape a paper tape on which a ticker records its information.

tick·et (tik′it) *n., v.* —*n.* **1** a card or other piece of paper showing that a fee or fare has been paid: *a theatre ticket, an airline ticket, a lottery ticket.* **2** an official notification that a person is charged with a traffic violation: *a parking ticket, a ticket for speeding.* **3** a label or tag attached to an article for sale, showing its size, price, etc. **4** *U.S.* the list of candidates to be voted for that belong to one political party. **5** *Slang.* a certificate: *a chief engineer's ticket.*
that's the ticket, *Informal.* that's the correct or desirable thing.
—*v.* **1** put a ticket on; mark with a ticket: *All articles in the store are ticketed with the price.* **2** describe or mark as if by a ticket; label; designate; characterize. **3** furnish with a ticket, such as a railway or airline ticket. **4** give or attach a ticket to, indicating a traffic violation: *She was ticketed for speeding.* [< F *étiquette* ticket < Gmc.]

ticket of leave *Brit. Archaic.* a permit giving a convict his liberty before his sentence has expired, provided he obeys certain conditions.

tick·ing (tik′ing) *n.* a strong cotton or linen cloth, used to cover mattresses and pillows and to make tents and awnings. [< *tick³*]

tick·le¹ (tik′əl) *v.* **-led, -ling;** *n.* —*v.* **1** touch lightly causing little thrills, shivers, or wriggles. **2** have a feeling like this; cause to have such a feeling: *My nose tickles.* **3** excite pleasantly; amuse: *The story tickled him.* **4** play, stir, get, etc. with light touches or strokes. **5** refresh or jog (the memory).
—*n.* **1** a tingling or itching feeling. **2** the act of tickling. [ME *tik(e)le(n)*]

tick·le² (tik′əl) *n. Cdn. esp.Newfoundland.* **1** a narrow channel between an island and the mainland or, sometimes, between islands. **2** a narrow entrance to a harbor. [origin unknown]

tick·ler (tik′lər) *n.* **1** a person or device that tickles. **2** *Informal.* a memorandum book, card index, or other device kept as a reminder. **3** *Informal.* a difficult or puzzling problem.

tick·lish (tik′lish) *adj.* **1** sensitive to tickling. **2** requiring careful handling; delicate, precarious, or risky: *a ticklish situation. A canoe is a ticklish craft.* **3** easily annoyed or offended: *a proud man and a ticklish fellow.* —**tick′lish·ly,** *adv.* —**tick′lish·ness,** *n.*

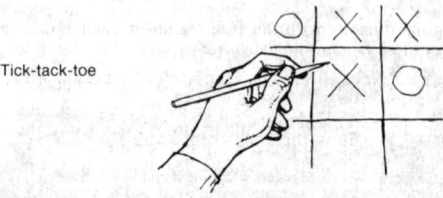

Tick-tack-toe

tick–tack–toe (tik′tak tō′) *n.* a game in which two players

alternately put circles or crosses in a figure of nine squares, each player trying to be the first to fill three spaces in a row with his mark.

tick–tock (tik′tok′) *n., v.* —*n.* the sound made by a clock or watch. —*v.* make this sound; tick: *A tall clock tick-tocked on the stair.*

t.i.d. three times a day (for L *ter in die*).

tid·al (tī′dəl) *adj.* **1** of, having to do with, caused by, or having tides: *tidal waters, a tidal breeze.* **2** dependent on the state of the tide as to time of arrival and departure: *a tidal steamer.*

tidal wave **1** a large wave or sudden increase in the level of water along a shore, caused by unusually strong winds. **2** a destructive ocean wave which is caused by an underwater earthquake. **3** any great movement or manifestation of feeling, opinion, or the like: *a tidal wave of popular indignation.*

tid·bit (tid′bit′) *n.* a very pleasing bit of food, news, etc. Also, **titbit.** [< *tid* nice + *bit* morsel]

tid·dle·dy·winks (tid′əl dē wingks′) *n.* tiddlywinks.

tid·dly·winks (tid′lē wingks′) *n.* a game in which the players try to make small colored disks jump into a cup by pressing on their edges with a larger disk (*used with a singular verb*). [origin uncertain]

tide¹ (tīd) *n., v.* **tid·ed, tid·ing.** —*n.* **1** the rise and fall of the ocean, usually taking place about every twelve hours, caused by the attraction of the moon and the sun. **2** anything that rises and falls like the tide: *the tide of popular opinion.* **3** a stream; current; flood. **4** a season; time (*usually used in compounds*): *Eastertide.*
turn the tide, change from one condition to the opposite.
—*v.* drift with the tide; especially, get (a ship) into or out of a harbor, etc. with the help of the tide.
tide over, help to overcome a difficulty, etc.: *He said five dollars would tide him over until payday.*
[OE *tīd,* originally, time] —**tide′less,** *adj.*

tide² (tīd) *v.* **tid·ed, tid·ing.** *Archaic.* betide; happen. [OE *tīdan*]

tide·mark (tīd′märk′) *n.* a mark left by the tide at its highest point, or, sometimes, at its lowest point.

tide·wa·ter (tīd′wo′tər *or* -wô′tər) *n.* **1** water having tides. **2** water brought by tides; water flooding land at high tide. **3** a low-lying seacoast.

tide·way (tīd′wā′) *n.* **1** a channel through which a tide runs. **2** the current or ebb and flow in such a channel. **3** the tidal part of a river.

ti·dings (tī′dingz) *n.pl.* news; information. [OE *tīdung* < *tīdan* happen, tide²]

ti·dy (tī′dē) *adj.* **-di·er, -di·est;** *v.* **-died, -dy·ing;** *n., pl.* **-dies.** *adj.* **1** neat and in order: *a tidy room.* **2** inclined to keep things neat and in order: *a tidy person.* **3** *Informal.* fairly large; considerable; substantial: *He already has a tidy sum saved up toward a stereo.* **4** *Informal.* fairly good; acceptable; satisfactory: *They've worked out a tidy solution.*
—*v.* put in order; make tidy (*often used with* **up**): *She quickly tidied the room. We tidied up before we left.*
—*n.* a small decorative cover used to protect the back or arms of a chair, chesterfield, etc. [ult. < OE *tīd* time] —**ti′di·ly,** *adv.*
—**ti′di·ness,** *n.*
☛ *Syn. adj.* **1.** See note at **neat.**

tie (tī) *v.* **tied, ty·ing;** *n.* —*v.* **1** fasten, attach, or close with cord, ribbon, rope, or the like: *Tie the package securely and tie a label on it. She tied the dog to the fence. Tie your shoes. He tied down the tarpaulin to keep it from flapping.* **2** arrange to form a bow or knot: *to tie a scarf.* **3** make by tying: *to tie a knot, to tie a fishing fly.* **4** be capable of being tied: *This paper ribbon doesn't tie very well.* **5** close or join by means of cord, ribbon, etc.: *The apron ties at the back.* **6** restrain or limit: *He did not want to be tied to a steady job.* **7** connect or join in any way: *When the river was low, a narrow strip of sand tied the island to the shore.* **8** make the same score; be equal in points: *The two teams tied.* **9** make the same score as: *Halifax tied Charlottetown in the last game of the series.* **10** *Music.* connect (notes) by a tie.
tie down, a confine or restrict: *She's tied down with a full-time job and night school.* **b** fasten or hold down by tying.
tie in, a connect: *Where does this line tie in with the main circuit?* **b** co-ordinate or relate: *The illustrations tie in very well with the story.*
tie into, *Informal.* start in on vigorously: *She forgot everything else and tied into her food.*
tie one on, *Slang.* get drunk: *He really tied one on last night.*
tie up, a confine in bonds; bind with cord, etc.: *The thieves tied him up and left him.* **b** hinder or stop the progress of: *The stalled truck tied up traffic for half an hour.* **c** invest or place money or property in such a way as to make it unavailable for other uses: *Since his money was tied up in real estate, he was unable to buy the bonds.* **d** have one's program full; be very busy: *He's tied up and can't make it to the dinner.* **e** take for oneself so as to make unavailable for others: *Don't tie up the phone too long.* **f** complete

a sale; bring to completion; conclude: *They've nearly got the details tied up.*
—*n.* **1** a cord, ribbon, etc. used for fastening parts together, especially one already attached: *An apron has ties. I don't like shoes with ties.* **2** a shaped, folded length of cloth worn under a shirt collar and knotted in front, either to form a bow or, more often, so that the two ends hang straight down: *He always wears a shirt and tie to work.* **3** anything that unites or binds; a bond or obligation: *family ties.* **4** one of the parallel wooden beams placed crosswise at intervals on a railway bed to form a foundation and support for the rails. **5** a connecting beam or rod, as in a framework supporting a roof, etc. **6** equality in points, votes, etc.: *The game ended in a tie, 3 to 3.* **7** *Music.* a curved line joining two notes of the same pitch to show that they are to be played or sung without a break between them. **8** a shoe fastened by means of a shoelace (*usually used in the plural*). [OE *tīgan* < *tēag* rope]
☞ *Syn. n.* 5. See note at **bond.**

tie-and-dye (tī'ən dī') *n.* tie-dye.

tie·back (tī'bak') *n.* **1** a cord, ribbon, strip of cloth, etc., usually decorative, used to drape a curtain to the side of a window instead of allowing it to hang straight down. **2 tiebacks,** *pl.* curtains having tiebacks.

tie beam a timber or piece serving as a tie; especially, a horizontal beam connecting the lower ends of two opposite principal rafters, thus forming the base of a roof truss. See **truss** for picture.

tie breaker a contest or game held to determine a winner from among contestants with equal scores.

tie clip a long clip, usually having an ornamental face, used to clip a necktie to the front of a shirt.

tie·dye (tī'dī') *n.*, *v.* **-dyed, dye·ing.** —*n.* **1** a method of dyeing cloth in patterns by tying parts of the cloth with string so that they will not absorb the dye. **2** a design made in this way. **3** cloth decorated with such a design.
—*v.* dye cloth or a garment in this way: *to tie-dye a scarf.*

tie-in (tī'in') *n.* a link; association; connection: *There was no tie-in between the murder and the robbery.*

tie·pin (tī'pin') *n.* a pin, usually having an ornamental head and a protective sheath for the point, used to hold a necktie or cravat in place.

tier[1] (tēr) *n.*, *v.* —*n.* one of a series of rows arranged one above another: *tiers of seats in a football stadium.* —*v.* arrange in tiers. [< F *tire*, originally, order < *tirer* draw]
☞ *Hom.* **tear**[1].

ti·er[2] (tī'ər) *n.* a person or thing that ties. [< *tie*]

tierce (tērs) *n.* **1** a cask of varying sizes, for provisions. **2** a sequence of three playing cards of the same suit. **3** *Fencing.* the third position. **4** *Music.* a third. **5** the service for the third canonical hour. [ME < OF < L *tertius* third]

tier·cel (tēr'səl) *n.* tercel.

tie tack a kind of pin to hold a necktie in place, having an ornamental head with a short stud behind it that is passed through the tie and shirt and held in place with a small clasp on the inside.

tie-up (tī'up') *n.* **1** a stopping of work or action on account of a strike, storm, accident, etc. **2** *Informal.* a connection; relation.

tiff (tif) *n.*, *v.* —*n.* **1** a slight quarrel. **2** a slight fit of ill humor or peevishness; a pet. —*v.* have or be in a tiff. [origin uncertain]

tif·fin (tif'ən) *n. Esp.Brit.* a light meal, especially at mid-day; lunch. [Anglo-Indian for *tiffing* < *tiff* drink, of uncertain origin]

ti·ger (tī'gər) *n.* **1** a large, fierce Asiatic mammal (*Panthera tigris*) of the cat family, that has dull-yellow fur striped with black. **2** a fierce and wild person: *He becomes a tiger if you criticize his work.* **3** a vigorous or energetic person: *a tiger for work.* **4** *Informal.* an extra yell at the end of a cheer. [< L < Gk. *tigris*] —**ti'ger·like'**, *adj.*

tiger beetle any of a large family (Cicindelidae) of beetles found mostly in warm regions, having large, strong jaws and noted for their voracity in going after prey, especially as larvae.

tiger cat **1** any of various medium-sized wild members of the cat family resembling the tiger, such as the ocelot or serval. **2** a striped domestic cat.

ti·ger-eye (tī'gər ī') *n.* tiger's-eye.

ti·ger·ish (tī'gər ish) *adj.* like a tiger; wild and fierce.

tiger lily **1** a commonly grown garden lily (*Lilium tigrinum*) native to China and Japan, having large, black-spotted orange flowers. **2** any of various lilies with similar flowers, such as the prairie lily.

tiger moth any of a large family (Arctiidae) of nocturnal moths, especially any of the genus *Arctia*, typically having conspicuously spotted or striped wings.

ti·ger's-eye (tī'gərz ī') *n.* a golden-brown semiprecious stone

hat, āge, fär; let, ēqual, tėrm; it, īce
hot, ōpen, ôrder; oil, out; cup, put, rüle,
əbove, takən, pencəl, lemən, circəs

ch, child; ng, long; sh, ship
th, thin; ᴛʜ, then; zh, measure

with a changeable lustre, composed chiefly of quartz, colored with iron oxide.

tiger swallowtail a large butterfly, (*Papilio glaucus*) a species of swallowtail found in eastern North America, having yellow wings with black stripes and margins.

tight (tīt) *adj., adv.* —*adj.* **1** firm; held firmly; packed or put together firmly: *a tight knot.* **2** drawn; stretched: *a tight canvas.* **3** fitting closely; close: *Since she gained weight, her skirt has a tight fit.* **4** well-built; trim; neat: *a tight craft.* **5** not letting water, air, or gas in or out: *The caulking on the boat is tight.* **6** not wasteful of words; terse; concise: *tight writing, a tight style.* **7** hard to deal with or manage; difficult: *His lies got him in a tight place.* **8** *Informal.* almost even; close: *It was a tight race.* **9 a** hard to get; scarce: *Money for mortgages is tight just now.* **b** characterized by scarcity or eager demand: *a tight money market.* **10** *Informal.* stingy. **11** *Informal.* drunk. **12** strict; severe: *to rule with a tight hand.*
—*adv.* closely; securely; firmly: *The rope was tied too tight.*
sit tight, *Informal.* **a** keep the same position, opinion, etc. **b** let matters take their own course; refrain from action.
[OE *getyht*, pp. of *tyhtan* stretch] —**tight'ly,** *adv.* —**tight'ness,** *n.*
☞ *Syn. adj.* 2. **Tight, taut** = drawn or stretched so as to be not loose or slack. **Tight,** the general word, emphasizes the idea of drawing closely together or of being drawn over or around something so firmly that there is no looseness: *You need a tight string around that package.* **Taut** emphasizes stretching until the thing described would break, snap, or tear if pulled more tightly, and is used chiefly as a nautical or mechanical term or to describe or suggest strained nerves or muscles: *The covering on a drum must be taut.*

tight·en (tī'tən) *v.* **1** make tight or tighter. **2** become tight or tighter. —**tight'en·er,** *n.*

tight-fist·ed (tīt'fis'tid) *adj.* stingy.

tight-lipped (tīt'lipt') *adj.* **1** keeping the lips firmly together, as in determination or when controlling strong emotion: *She stood there in tight-lipped fury.* **2** saying little or nothing; reluctant to speak: *He's very tight-lipped; you won't get any information out of him.*

tight·rope (tīt'rōp') *n.* **1** a rope or wire stretched tight some distance above the ground, for acrobats to perform on. **2 a** dangerous or extremely delicate situation: *She was on a tightrope now; one wrong word and she would lose their confidence.*

tights (tīts) *n.pl.* a close-fitting, usually knitted, garment covering the lower body and each leg and foot separately, worn by acrobats, dancers, etc. or as stockings in cold weather.

tight squeeze a difficult situation; narrow escape.

tight·wad (tīt'wod') *n. Slang.* a stingy person.

ti·gress (tī'gris) *n.* **1** an adult female tiger. **2** a woman thought of as being like a tiger in fierceness or wildness.

ti·grish (tī'grish) *adj.* tigerish.

tike (tīk) See **tyke.**

til (til) *n.* See **tilde** (def. 2).

til·bu·ry (til'bər ē) *n.*, *pl.* **-ries.** a light, two-wheeled, horse-drawn carriage without a top. [< name of a British coach designer]

til·de (til'də; *Spanish,* tēl'dä) *n.* **1** a diacritical mark (˜) used in Spanish over *n* when it is pronounced *ny*, as in *cañon* (kä nyōn'). **2** the same mark, used in Portuguese over certain vowels to indicate that they are nasalized, as in *São* (soun). The Portuguese name for this mark is **til.** [< Sp. < L *titulus* title]

tile (tīl) *n.*, *v.* **tiled, til·ing.** —*n.* **1** a thin piece of baked clay, stone, etc. Tiles are used for covering roofs and floors, and for ornamenting. **2** a thin square of plastic, rubber, etc. used for surfacing floors, walls, or ceilings. **3** a short porous pipe, usually earthenware, used for draining land. **4** tiles collectively. **5** (*adj.*) covered with or made of tile: *a tile floor.* **6** *Informal.* a stiff hat; high silk hat.
—*v.* put tiles on or in; cover with tile. [OE *tigele* < L *tegula*]

til·er (tī'lər) *n.* a person who makes or lays tiles.

til·ing (tī'ling) *n.* **1** tiles collectively. **2** the work of a person who tiles. **3** a surface or structure consisting of tiles.

till[1] (til) *prep., conj.* —*prep.* up to the time of; until: *The child played till eight.* —*conj.* up to the time when; until: *Walk till you come to a white house.* [OE *til*]
☞ *Usage.* **Till, until.** These two words are not distinguishable in meaning, though **until** is usually considered the more formal word and is normally used at the beginning of sentences: *Until he left high school, he never took any job. He*

didn't take any job till (or *until*) *he left high school.* Otherwise, one may choose between the two forms on the basis of stress and rhythm.

till² (til) *v.* cultivate; plough; harrow, etc.: *Farmers till the land.* [OE *tilian*] —**till′a·ble,** *adj.*

till³ (til) *n.* **1** a drawer or box for money, especially in a store, etc.: *The till is under the counter.* **2** cash register. [ult. < OE *-tyllan* draw, as in *betyllan* lure]

till⁴ (til) *n.* glacial drift composed of clay, stones, gravel, boulders, etc. mixed together. [origin unknown]

till·age (til′ij) *n.* **1** the cultivation of land. **2** tilled land.

till·er¹ (til′ər) *n.* a bar or handle used to turn the rudder in steering a boat. [ME < OF *telier* weaver's beam, ult. < L *tela* web, loom]

till·er² (til′ər) *n.* **1** a person who tills the land. **2** a machine for tilling; cultivator. [< *till²*]

til·li·cum (til′lə kəm) *n.* on the Pacific coast and in the Northwest, a friend; pal. [< Chinook Jargon *tilikum* kin, people, especially as distinguished from tribal chiefs]

tilt (tilt) *v., n.* —*v.* **1** slant or cause to slant; incline: *She tilted the board to allow the water to run off. The table is liable to tilt.* **2** take part in a jousting match, especially one in which the competitors ride toward each other along either side of a barrier to prevent the collision of the horses. **3** attack or overthrow a person in such a match. **4** thrust or aim: *to tilt a lance.* **5** attack or charge (*used with* at): *tilting at injustice.* **6** forge or work (steel, etc.) with a tilt hammer.

tilt at windmills See **windmill.**

—*n.* **1** slope or slant: *the tabletop has a slight tilt.* **2** the act of tilting. **3** a jousting match, especially one in which the competitors ride toward each other along either side of a barrier. **4** the barrier itself. **5** the ground or yard where such contests were held; the lists. **6** a debate or dispute.

full tilt, at full speed or with full force: *The car ran full tilt against the tree.* [ult. < OE *tealt* shaky]

tilth (tilth) *n.* **1** the cultivation of land. **2** tilled land. **3** the condition of tilled soil: *a garden in bad tilth.* [OE *tilth < tilian* till²]

tilt hammer a drop hammer consisting of a heavy head at the end of a pivot, used in drop-forging.

tim·bal (tim′bəl) *n.* kettledrum. [< F *timbale,* ult. < Arabic *at-tabl* the drum]

tim·bale (tim′bəl) *n.* **1** a food consisting of minced meat, fish, vegetables, etc. prepared with a sauce and cooked in a mould. **2** a cup-shaped pastry mould. [< F *timbale,* originally, *timbal.* See TIMBAL.]

tim·ber (tim′bər) *n., v.* —*n.* **1** wood suitable for building and making things. **2** a large squared piece of wood ready to use in building or forming part of a structure. Beams and rafters are timbers. **3** a curved piece forming a rib of a ship. **4** trees that are growing and suitable for cutting: *Half of his land is covered with timber.* **5** logs, green or cured, cut from such trees.

—*v.* cover, support, or furnish with timber. [OE]

☛ *Hom.* **timbre.**

tim·bered (tim′bərd) *adj.* **1** made or furnished with timber. **2** covered with growing trees.

timber hitch a knot used to fasten a rope around a spar, post, etc. See **knot¹** for picture.

tim·ber·ing (tim′bər ing) *n.* **1** building material of wood. **2** timbers collectively. **3** an arrangement or structure of timbers.

tim·ber·land (tim′bər land′) *n.* land with trees that are, or will be, used for timber.

timber limit *Cdn.* **1** timberline. **2** *Logging.* a tract of land in which a person or company has the right to fell trees and remove timber; concession.

tim·ber·line (tim′bər līn′) *n.* a limit on mountains and in high latitudes beyond which trees will not grow because of climatic conditions such as extreme cold and strong winds. In Canada, the country north of the timberline is called the Barrens.

timber raft *Logging.* a collection of logs lashed together for floating downstream.

timber wolf *Cdn.* a large grey wolf (*Canis lupus*), especially any of several subspecies found in wooded regions of Canada and Alaska.

tim·bre (tim′bər *or* tam′bər; *French,* taNbr) *n.* the quality in sounds that distinguishes a certain voice, instrument, etc. from other voices, instruments, etc. Notes of the same pitch and loudness may differ in timbre. [< MF *timbre,* ult. < Gk. *tympanon* kettledrum. Doublet of TYMPAN, TYMPANUM.]

☛ *Hom.* **timber** (tim′bər).

tim·brel (tim′brəl) *n. Archaic.* tambourine. Timbrels are mentioned in the Bible. [dim. of ME *timbre* < OF *timbre,* a kind of tambourine. See TIMBRE.]

time (tīm) *n., v.* **timed, tim·ing;** *adj.* —*n.* **1** all the days there have been or ever will be; the past, present, and future: *We measure time in years, months, days, hours, minutes, seconds, etc.* **2** a part of time: *A minute is a short time.* **3** a period of time; epoch: *the time of the Stuarts of England.* **4** a term of imprisonment, enlistment, apprenticeship, etc.: *to complete one's time.* **5** a long time: *What a time it took you!* **6** some point in time; a particular point in time: *What time is it?* **7** the right part or point of time: *It is time to eat.* **8** an occasion: *This time we will succeed.* **9** a way of reckoning time: *daylight-saving time.* **10** times, *pl.* **a** conditions of life: *War brings hard times.* **b** multiplied by (*prepositional use*): *Four times three is twelve.* **c** multiplied instances: *five times as much.* **11** amount of time: *I have some time for rest.* **12** an experience during a certain time: *She had a good time at the party.* **13** rate of speed; tempo. **14** *Music.* **a** the length of a note or rest. **b** the grouping of such notes into rhythmic beats, divided into bars or measures of equal length. **c** the tempo of a composition. **d** the rhythm of a composition: *waltz time, march time.* **15** the amount of time that one has worked or should work. **16** the pay for this. **17** leisure: *to have time to read.* **18** *Military.* a rate of stepping; pace: *to march in quick time.*

about time, at or near the proper time: *It's about time to go home.*

against time, trying to finish before a certain time.

at the same time, however; nevertheless.

at times, now and then; once in a while.

behind the times, old-fashioned; out of date.

do or **serve time,** *Informal.* be imprisoned as a criminal: *a man doing time for bank robbery.*

for the time being, for the present; for now.

from time to time, now and then; once in a while: *From time to time we visited Uncle Jim's fruit farm.*

in good time, a at the right time: *We reached the theatre in good time for the first act.* **b** soon; quickly.

in no time, shortly; before long.

in time, a after a while. **b** soon enough: *We got there just in time, before the bank closed.* **c** *Music.* in the right rate of movement.

keep time, a of a watch or clock, go correctly. **b** sound or move at the right rate: *The marchers kept time to the martial music.*

make time, go with speed.

on time, a at the right or specified time, or hour; not late: *He's never on time. Be sure you're on time, so we can start promptly at 8.* **b** with time in which to pay; on credit: *He bought a car on time.*

pass the time away, occupy oneself during the day: *She passed the time away by knitting.*

tell time, read the clock; tell what time it is by the clock.

time after time or **time and again,** again and again.

time of life, age: *a foolish thing to do at his time of life.*

time out of mind, beyond memory or record.

—*v.* **1** measure the time of: *to time a race.* **2** fix, set, or regulate the length of in time: *to time an exposure correctly.* **3** set, regulate, or adjust: *to time an alarm clock.* **4** do in rhythm with; set the time of: *The dancers timed their steps to the music.* **5** choose the moment or occasion for: *The demonstrators timed their march through the business section so that most shoppers would see them.*

—*adj.* **1** of or having to do with time. **2** provided with a clocklike mechanism so that it will explode or ignite at a given moment: *a time bomb.* **3** *Business.* having to do with purchases to be paid for at a future date. [OE *tīma*]

☛ *Hom.* **thyme.**

time and motion study a systematic study of the methods and body motions used and the amount of time taken to do the various steps in a certain job, conducted to establish the most effective way of doing it.

time bomb a bomb equipped with a timing device, so that it can be set to explode at a certain moment.

time capsule a container with documents and other items representative of the current civilization, that is buried or sealed into the cornerstone of a building, etc., to be discovered in a future age.

time·card (tīm′kärd′) *n.* a card used with a time clock for recording the arrival and departure times of an employee.

time clock a clock with a device to stamp an employee's timecard with the time he arrives or leaves.

time–con·sum·ing (tīm′kən süm′ing *or* -kən syüm′ing) *adj.* taking up or requiring a great deal of time: *The calculations weren't hard, but they were time-consuming.*

time draft a draft to be paid at the future time stated in the draft.

time exposure **1** the exposure of a photographic film for a certain time, usually longer than a half second. **2** a photograph taken in this way.

time fuse a fuse that will burn for a certain time.

time–hon·ored or **time–hon·oured** (tīm′on′ərd) *adj.*

honored because old and established: *a time-honored custom.*

time immemorial 1 a period in time so distant that it is before the beginning of records or known chronology. **2** *Law.* the time before legal records were known. In England, it is fixed by law as the time prior to 1189, the beginning of Richard I's reign.

time·keep·er (tīm′kē′pər) *n.* a measurer of time; a person or thing that keeps time: *The factory timekeeper keeps account of the hours of work done. My watch is an excellent timekeeper.*

time·less (tīm′lis) *adj.* **1** never ending; eternal. **2** referring to no special time.

time·ly (tīm′lē) *adj.* **-li·er, -li·est.** at the right time: *The timely arrival of the police stopped the riot.* —**time′li·ness,** *n.*
☛ *Syn.* **Timely, opportune** = well-timed or especially suited to the time or occasion. **Timely** describes something perfectly suited to the time or circumstance, coming or happening just at a time to be useful or valuable: *Saturday's paper contained a timely article on wise buying and foolish spending.* **Opportune** describes either the moment or occasion most favorable for doing something, or an event or action happening or done at exactly the right and most advantageous moment: *The invitation came at an opportune moment.*

time of day the time as shown by the clock.
give the time of day to, notice or acknowledge.
know the time of day, know what is going on or the current state of affairs.
pass the time of day, exchange greetings or brief conversation.

time·piece (tīm′pēs′) *n.* a clock or watch.

tim·er (tī′mər) *n.* **1** a device for indicating or recording intervals of time, such as a stop watch. **2** a device similar to a clock that can be set to indicate, by means of a buzzer, etc., when a specific period of time has elapsed, or to start or stop another device or mechanism automatically at a predetermined time: *a timer on a stove.* **3** an automatic device in the ignition system of an internal-combustion engine that causes the spark for igniting the charge to occur just at the time required. **4** timekeeper.

time·sav·er (tīm′sā′vər) *n.* a person or thing that saves time.

time·sav·ing (tīm′sā′ving) *adj.* that saves time: *timesaving household appliances.*

time·serv·er (tīm′sèr′vər) *n.* a person who for selfish purposes shapes his conduct to conform with the opinions of the time or of the persons in power.

time·serv·ing (tīm′sèr′ving) *n., adj.* —*n.* the practice or behavior of a timeserver. —*adj.* having or showing a lack of integrity or independent thinking: *a timeserving little wretch.*

time–shar·ing (tīm′sher′ing) *n. Computer science.* a system in which different users at separate terminals can have access to a single computer at virtually the same time, due to the high speed at which the computer operates.

time signature *Music.* a symbol, usually in the form of a fraction, that is printed or written at the beginning of a composition or where the time changes. The numerator of the fraction indicates the number of beats in a bar or measure; the denominator gives the length of the note that receives one beat. A special symbol is sometimes used to indicate 4/4 time.

time·ta·ble (tīm′tā′bəl) *n.* **1** a table showing the times when trains, buses, airplanes, or boats arrive and depart. **2** any list or schedule showing a planned sequence; especially, a list showing the times of different classes for students.

time–test·ed (tīm′tes′təd) *adj.* having a value or effectivensss that has been proven over a long period of time: *a time-tested recipe for bread.*

time–worn (tīm′wôrn′) *adj.* **1** worn by long existence or use: *They walked up the timeworn steps of the old house.* **2** hackneyed or trite: *a timeworn excuse.*

The Canadian time zones

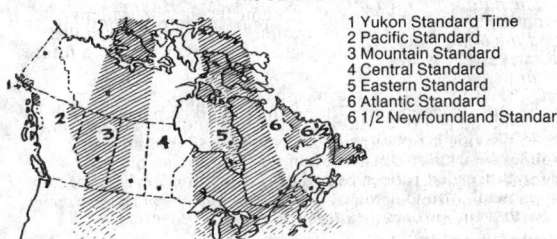

1 Yukon Standard Time
2 Pacific Standard
3 Mountain Standard
4 Central Standard
5 Eastern Standard
6 Atlantic Standard
6 1/2 Newfoundland Standard

time zone a geographical region within which the same standard of time is used. The world is divided into 24 time zones, beginning and ending at the International Date Line.

tim·id (tim′id) *adj.* **1** lacking courage or self-confidence; easily frightened. **2** showing lack of self-confidence or determination: *a*

---

hat, āge, fär; let, ēqual, tèrm; it, īce
hot, ōpen, ôrder; oil, out; cup, pùt, rüle,
əbove, takən, pencəl, lemən, circəs
ch, child; ng, long; sh, ship
th, thin; ℔, then; zh, measure

timid voice, a timid excuse. [< L *timidus* < *timere* to fear]
—**tim′id·ly,** *adv.* —**tim′id·ness,** *n.*
☛ *Syn.* **Timid, cowardly** = lacking courage. **Timid** emphasizes the idea of being always ready to be afraid, especially of anything new, different, uncertain, or unknown: *He does not like his job, but is too timid to try to find another.* **Cowardly** emphasizes the idea of a weak and dishonorable lack of courage in the presence of danger or trouble: *Leaving his wife because she was hopelessly sick was a cowardly thing to do.*

ti·mid·i·ty (tə mid′ə tē) *n.* the quality of being timid: *Her timidity prevents her from asking questions.*

tim·ing (tī′ming) *n.* **1** the choice or regulation of the speed, co-ordination, or moment of occurrence of something so as to produce the best possible effect: *The timing of the engine is off. Timing is very important in a golf swing. Her timing couldn't have been worse—she asked for the car just after her mother had discovered the mess in the living room.* **2** the measurement and recording of time taken by an action or process. Timing is often done with a stopwatch.

Ti·mis·ka·ming (tə mis′kə ming) *adj., n. Geology.* —*adj.* of or having to do with the more recent period of the Archeozoic era. —*n.* **1** the more recent period of the Archeozoic era. **2** the rocks or rock formations of this period.
[< *Timiskaming,* Ontario]

Ti·mon (tī′mən) *n.* a hater of mankind. [after the hero of Shakespeare's play, *Timon of Athens,* noted for his dislike of mankind]

tim·or·ous (tim′ər əs) *adj.* **1** easily frightened; timid: *a timorous child.* **2** marked or caused by fear or lack of self-confidence: *The puppy's timorous advances were ignored.* [ME < OF < Med.L *timorosus* < L *timor* fear] —**tim′or·ous·ly,** *adv.* —**tim′or·ous·ness,** *n.*

tim·o·thy (tim′ə thē) *n.* a perennial European grass (*Phleum pratense*) having long, cylindrical flower spikes, widely cultivated in temperate regions for hay and as a pasture grass. [< *Timothy Hanson,* an early American cultivator]

tim·pa·ni (tim′pə nē) *n.* a set of kettledrums played by one person in an orchestra or band (*sometimes used with a singular verb*). [< Ital., pl. of *timpano* kettledrum < L *tympanum* drum. See TYMPANUM.]

tim·pa·nist (tim′pə nist) *n.* a person who plays the timpani in an orchestra or band.

tin (tin) *n., v.* **tinned, tin·ning.** —*n.* **1** a soft, silver-white metallic element used as a coating on other metals and in making alloys. *Symbol:* Sn; *at.no.* 50; *at.wt.* 118.69. **2** thin sheets of iron or steel coated with tin. **3** (*adj.*) made of tin: *tin cans, a tin box.* **4** any box, can, pan, or other container made of tin or tin plate: *Sardines are packed in tins.* **5** such a container together with its contents: *a tin of peas.* **6** any of various kinds of metal containers, especially pans used for baking: *a cake tin, a muffin tin.* —*v.* **1** cover or plate with tin or a tin alloy. **2** *Esp.Brit.* put up in tin cans or tin boxes; can. [OE]

tin·a·mou (tin′ə mü′) *n.* any of a family (Tinamidae) of brown or grey game birds of Central and South America having small, weak wings and a very short tail. Tinamous resemble grouse, but are most closely related to the rheas and ostriches. [< F < Carib]

tinct (tingkt) *adj., n. Archaic.* —*adj.* tinged. —*n.* a tint; tinge. [< L *tinctus,* pp. of *tingere* tinge]

tinc·ture (tingk′chər) *n., v.* **-tured, -tur·ing.** —*n.* **1** a solution of medicine in alcohol: *tincture of iodine.* **2** a trace or tinge of something. **3** a slight color or flavor.
—*v.* **1** give a trace or tinge to; affect slightly with a certain quality (*used with* **with**): *Everything he says is tinctured with conceit.* **2** color or flavor slightly. [< L *tinctura* < *tingere* tinge]

tin·der (tin′dər) *n.* **1** anything that catches fire easily. **2** material used to catch fire from a spark. Before matches were invented people carried a box holding tinder, flint, and steel. [OE *tynder*]

tin·der·box (tin′dər boks′) *n.* **1** a box formerly used for holding tinder, flint, and steel for making a fire. **2** an object, structure, etc. that is highly inflammable. **3** a situation or place likely to burst into conflict or violence of some kind.

tine (tīn) *n.* a sharp, projecting point or prong: *the tines of a fork.* [OE *tind*]

tin foil 1 very thin sheeting of tin, aluminum, or an alloy of tin

and lead, used for wrapping food products, for insulation, etc. 2 silver paper.

ting (ting) n., v. —n. a light, clear ringing sound, as that made by crystal goblets striking each other lightly. —v. make or cause to make such a sound: *The glass tinged when I touched it with the spoon.* [imitative]

tinge (tinj) v. **tinged, tinge·ing** or **ting·ing;** n. —v. 1 color slightly: *A drop of ink will tinge a glass of water.* 2 add a trace of some quality to; change slightly: *Sad memories tinged their present joy.* —n. 1 a slight coloring or tint. 2 a very small amount; trace. [< L *tingere*]

tin·gle (ting'gəl) v. **-gled, -gling;** n. —v. 1 have a pricking or stinging feeling, especially from excitement: *He tingled with delight on his first train trip.* 2 cause this feeling in: *Shame tingled his cheeks.* 3 be thrilling: *The newspaper story tingled with excitement.* 4 tinkle; jingle. —n. 1 a pricking, stinging feeling. 2 a tinkle; jingle. [probably var. of *tinkle*]

tink·er¹ (tingk'ər) n., v. —n. 1 a person who mends pots, pans, etc., usually one who travels from place to place to practise his trade. 2 a clumsy or unskilful worker. —v. 1 work as a tinker. 2 work with, adjust, or repair in an unskilled or experimental way: *Someone has been tinkering with my bicycle. She likes to tinker with old radios and TV sets.* 3 work at or keep busy with in an irregular or purposeless way: *to tinker with a new idea.* [? ult. < *tin*]

tink·er² (tingk'ər) n. *Cdn. Atlantic Provinces.* the razorbill or the common murre. [prob. < *tinkershere,* Brit. name for guillemot, meaning dark or black (tinker's hue)]

tinker's damn or **dam** a most contemptible or useless thing. [? from tinkers' reputation for cursing]

tin·kle (ting'kəl) v. **-kled, -kling;** n. —v. 1 make short, light, ringing sounds: *Little bells tinkle.* 2 cause to tinkle. 3 indicate, make known, etc. by tinkling: *The little clock tinkled out the hours.* —n. a series of short, light, ringing sounds: *the tinkle of bells.* [ult. imitative]

tin·man (tin'mən) n., pl. **-men.** tinsmith.

tin·ner (tin'ər) n. 1 a person who works in a tin mine; a tin miner. 2 tinsmith.

tin·ny (tin'ē) adj. **-ni·er, -ni·est.** 1 of or containing tin. 2 shrill or thin in sound: *a tinny voice, the tinny music of an old juke box.* 3 thin and cheap; of poor quality: *tinny cutlery, tinny jewellery.* 4 tasting of tin: *The salmon tastes tinny.* —**tin'ni·ness,** n.

tin–pan alley 1 a district or area of a city serving as a centre for composers and publishers of popular music. 2 the people concerned with writing and publishing popular music.

tin plate thin sheets of iron or steel coated with tin. Ordinary tin cans are made of tin plate.

tin–plate (tin'plāt') v. **-plat·ed, -plat·ing.** coat or plate metal with tin.

tin–pot (tin'pot') adj. *Informal. Esp.Brit.* inferior; petty.

tin·sel (tin'səl) n., v. **-selled** or **-seled, -sel·ling** or **-sel·ing,** —n. 1 thin sheets, strips, or threads of a metallic substance, used to add glitter to cloth, yarn, or decorations. 2 something like tinsel; something showy and attractive, but not worth much. 3 cloth woven with threads of gold, silver, or copper. 4 (*adj.*) made of or decorated with tinsel. 5 (*adj.*) showy but cheap; gaudy. —v. decorate or trim with or as if with tinsel. [< F *étincelle* spark < L *scintilla.* Doublet of SCINTILLA.] —**tin'sel·like',** adj.

tin·smith (tin'smith') n. a person who works with tin or other light metal; maker of tinware.

tint (tint) n., v. —n. 1 a variety of a color, especially one mixed with white. 2 a suggestion of or tendency toward a different color: *white with a bluish tint.* 3 a delicate or pale color. 4 a preparation for coloring hair; —v. put a tint on; color: *to tint a black-and-white photograph, to tint one's hair.* [earlier *tinct* < L *tinctus* a dyeing < *tingere* dye]

tin·tin·nab·u·la·tion (tin'tə nab'yə lā'shən) n. the ringing of bells. [ult. < L *tintinnabulum* bell]

tin·type (tin'tīp') n. a photograph taken on a sheet of enamelled tin or iron.

tin·ware (tin'wer') n. articles made of or lined with tin.

ti·ny (tī'nē) adj. **-ni·er, -ni·est.** very small; wee. [ME *tine;* origin uncertain]

–tion suffix. 1 the act or process of —ing, as in *addition, opposition.* 2 the condition of being —ed, as in *exhaustion.* 3 the

result of —ing, as in *reflection.* [< L *-tio, -onis* < *-t-* of pp. stem + *-io* (cf. *-ion*)]

tip¹ (tip) n., v. **tipped, tip·ping.** —n. 1 the end part; end; point: *the tips of the fingers.* 2 a small piece put on the end of something: *a rubber tip for a cane.* —v. 1 put a tip on; furnish with a tip: *spears tipped with steel.* 2 cover or adorn at the tip: *mountains tipped with snow. Sunlight tips the steeple.* [ME *tippe;* ? < MDu. *tip* point]

tip² (tip) v. **tipped, tip·ping;** n. —v. 1 slope; slant: *She tipped the table toward her.* 2 upset; overturn: *He tipped over the milk jug. We fell in the water when the canoe tipped.* 3 take off (a hat) in greeting: *Men used to tip their hats when meeting a woman.* 4 empty out; dump. —n. 1 the act of tipping: *a tip of the hat.* 2 a slope; slant. [ME. *tipen;* of certain origin]

tip³ (tip) n., v. **tipped, tip·ping.** —n. 1 a small present of money in return for service: *He gave the waiter a tip.* 2 a piece of secret or confidential information: *Fred had a tip that the black horse would win the race.* 3 a useful hint, suggestion, etc: *a book of tips on caring for your pet.* —v. 1 give a small present of money to: *She tipped the porter.* 2 give a tip: *He always tips too much.* 3 give secret information or a warning to (*usually used with* **off**): *Someone tipped off the criminal and he escaped before the police arrived.* [origin uncertain]

tip⁴ (tip) n., v. **tipped, tip·ping.** —n. a slight, sharp blow; tap. —v. hit lightly and sharply; tap.

ti·pi (tē'pē) See teepee.

tip–off (tip'of') n. *Informal.* 1 a piece of secret information. 2 a warning.

tip·pet (tip'it) n. 1 a scarf for the neck and shoulders with ends hanging down in front. 2 a long, narrow strip of cloth hanging from a sleeve, hood, or cape, worn especially in the 16th century. [probably < *tip¹*]

tip·ple (tip'əl) v. **-pled, -pling;** n. —v. drink alcoholic liquor often. —n. an alcoholic liquor. [origin uncertain; cf. Norwegian *tipla* drip, tipple]

tip·pler (tip'lər) n. a habitual drinker of alcoholic liquor.

tip·py (tip'ē) adj. liable to tip; unsteady or shaky: *Kayaks are tippy craft.*

tip·staff (tip'staf') n., pl. **-staves** or **-staffs.** 1 a staff tipped with metal, formerly carried by constables and other officers of the law. 2 an official who carried such a staff.

tip·ster (tip'stər) n. *Informal.* a person who makes a business of furnishing private or secret information for use in betting, speculation, etc. [< *tip* a hint + *-ster*]

tip·sy (tip'sē) adj. **-si·er, -si·est.** 1 tipping easily; unsteady; tilted. 2 somewhat intoxicated but not thoroughly drunk. [< *tip²*] —**tip'si·ly,** adv. —**tip'si·ness,** n.

tip·toe (tip'tō) n., v. **-toed, -toe·ing.** —n. the tips of the toes. **on tiptoe, a** walking on the balls and toes of the feet: *He crossed the room on tiptoe to avoid waking her.* **b** eager: *The children were on tiptoe for vacation to begin.* —v. walk on the balls and toes of the feet, with the heels raised off the ground: *She tiptoed quietly up the stairs.*

tip·top (tip'top') n., adj. —n. the very top; highest point. —adj. 1 at the very top or highest point. 2 *Informal.* first-rate; excellent. [< *tip* end + *top*]

ti·rade (tī'rād or tə rād') n. a long, vehement, usually scolding, speech. [< F < Ital. *tirata* < *tirare* shoot]

ti·rail·leur (tē rä yœr') n. *French.* skirmisher; sharpshooter. [< F *tirailleur* < *tirer* shoot]

tire¹ (tīr) v. **tired, tir·ing.** 1 lower or use up the strength of; make weary: *The hard work tired him.* 2 become weary: *He tires easily.* 3 wear down the patience, interest, or appreciation of: *Dull filing jobs tired the office boy.* **tire out,** make very weary. [OE *tȳrian*]

tire² (tīr) n., v. **tired, tir·ing.** —n. 1 a circular rubber tube or ring fitted around the rim of a wheel, as of an automobile, aircraft, or bicycle, to provide a smooth ride and to increase traction. An automobile tire usually consists of an air-filled casing of cord covered with treaded rubber. See **wheel** for picture. 2 a band of rubber or metal around a wheel: *The wagon had iron tires.* —v. furnish with a tire or tires. [< *attire,* in sense of "covering"]

tire³ (tīr) n., v. **tired, tir·ing.** *Archaic.* —n. headdress; attire. —v. attire or adorn. [short for *attire*]

tired (tīrd) adj. 1 weary; wearied; exhausted. 2 trite: *the same tired old arguments.* **tired of,** no longer interested in; bored with: *I'm tired of hearing about their holidays.* [< *tire¹*] —**tired'ly,** adv. —**tired'ness,** n.

Syn. Tired, weary, exhausted = having one's physical or mental strength, energy, and power of endurance lowered or drained by hard or long-continued work, strain, etc. **Tired** is the general and least precise word: *I am tired, but I must get back to work.* **Weary** suggests feeling worn out and unable or unwilling to go on: *Weary shoppers waited for buses and streetcars.* **Exhausted** emphasizes being without enough energy or endurance left to be able to go on: *Exhausted by play, the child could not eat.*

–tired *combining form.* having a tire or tires of a specified kind: *a wagon with rubber-tired wheels.* [< *tire²*]

tire·less¹ (tīr′lis′) *adj.* **1** never becoming tired; requiring little rest: *a tireless worker.* **2** never stopping: *tireless efforts.* —**tire′less·ly,** *adv.* —**tire′less·ness,** *n.*

tire·less² (tīr′lis) *adj.* having no tire or tires.

Ti·re·si·as (tī rē′sē əs or tə rē′sē əs) *n. Greek legend.* a soothsayer from Thebes who was blinded by Athena because he saw her bathing. In compensation she gave him power to foresee future events, an understanding of birds' language, and a staff to serve as eyes.

tire·some (tīr′səm) *adj.* tiring, because boring: *a tiresome speech.* —**tire′some·ly,** *adv.* —**tire′some·ness,** *n.*

Syn. Tiresome, tedious = tiring or boring, or both. **Tiresome** describes a person or thing that tires or bores one quickly because he or it is dull and uninteresting: *Our neighbor is good-hearted, but I find her tiresome.* **Tedious** adds the idea of being long or slow or too much the same or, when describing a person, speaking or writing at too great length: *Weeding a garden is tedious work. He is a tedious speaker.*

tire·wom·an (tīr′wūm′ən) *n., pl.* **-wom·en.** *Archaic.* a lady's maid.

tiring room *Archaic.* a dressing room, especially in a theatre. [< *attiring room*]

ti·ro (tī′rō) *n., pl.* **-ros.** See **tyro.**

Ti·ro·le·an (tə rō′lē ən or tir′ə lē′ən) See **Tyrolean.**

Tir·o·lese (tir′ə lēz′) See **Tyrolese.**

'tis (tiz) it is.

Tish·ri (tish′rē) *n.* in the Hebrew calendar, the seventh month of the ecclesiastical year, and the first month of the civil year.

tis·sue (tish′ü) *n.* **1** a mass of similar cells that together form some part of an animal or a plant: *muscle tissue, skin tissue.* **2** a thin, light cloth. **3** a web; network: *Her whole story was a tissue of lies.* **4** tissue paper. **5** a thin, soft paper that absorbs moisture easily: *toilet tissue, cleansing tissue.* **6** a piece or a sheet of this paper: *There are 450 tissues in each box.* [ME < OF *tissu,* originally pp. of *tistre* weave < L *texere*]

tissue paper a very thin, crisp paper, used mainly for wrapping.

tit¹ (tit) *n. Esp.Brit.* **1** any bird of the titmouse family, especially the Old World members of the genus *Parus,* such as the **great tit** (*Parus major*) of Europe, NW Africa, and Asia. **2** any of various similar small birds. [ME; cf. Icelandic *tittr* titmouse]

tit² (tit) *n.* **1** *Slang.* breast. **2** nipple; teat. [OE *titt*]

ti·tan (tī′tən) *n.* **1** **Titan,** *Greek mythology.* one of a family of giants who ruled the world until they were overthrown by the gods of Olympus. **2** a person or thing of great size, power, or strength. **3** (*adj.*) having great size, strength or power; titanic. [< L < Gk.]

ti·tan·ic (tī tan′ik) *adj.* **1** Usually, **Titanic,** of or like the Titans. **2** having or showing great size, strength, or power; colossal: *titanic energy.*

ti·ta·ni·um (tī tā′nē əm or ti tā′nē əm) *n.* a light, strong, silvery or grey metallic element that occurs in ilmenite and rutile, used especially in steel alloys for aircraft parts. *Symbol:* Ti; *at.no.* 22; *at.wt.* 47.90. [< *Titan*]

ti·tan·o·there (tī′tə nə thēr′) *n.* any of various extinct, rhinoceros-like mammals (order Perissodactyla) that flourished in North America from the Eocene to the Oligocene epochs, having a large, bulky body, a massive skull often having large horns over the snout, hoofed feet, and a very small, primitive brain. [< Gk. *Titan* Titan + *thērion* beast]

tit·bit (tit′bit′) *n.* tidbit.

tit for tat blow for blow; like for like. [? < *tip for tap*]

tithe (tīŦH) *n., v.* **tithed, tith·ing.** —*n.* **1** one tenth. **2** Often, **tithes,** *pl.* a tax or a donation of one tenth of the yearly produce of land, animals, and personal work, paid for the support of the church and the clergy. **3** a very small part. **4** any small tax, levy, etc. —*v.* **1** put a tax or a levy of a tenth on. **2** pay a tithe on. **3** give one tenth of one's income to the church or to charity. [OE *teogotha* tenth]

ti·tian (tish′ən) *n. or adj.* auburn; golden red. [< *Titian* (1477-1576), an Italian painter, who used this color in his paintings]

tit·il·late (tit′ə lāt′) *v.* **-lat·ed, -lat·ing. 1** excite pleasantly; stimulate agreeably. **2** tickle. [< L *titillare*]

tit·il·la·tion (tit′ə lā′shən) *n.* **1** pleasant excitement; agreeable stimulation. **2** a tickling.

---

hat, āge, fär; let, ēqual, tèrm; it, īce
hot, ōpen, ôrder; oil, out; cup, pút, rüle,
əbove, takən, pencəl, lemən, circəs

ch, child; ng, long; sh, ship
th, thin; ŦH, then; zh, measure

tit·i·vate or **tit·ti·vate** (tit′ə vāt′) *v.* **-vat·ed, -vat·ing.** *Informal.* dress or spruce up; make smart. [? ult. < *tidy*] —**tit′i·va′tion** or **tit′ti·va′tion,** *n.*

tit·lark (tit′lärk′) *n.* pipit. [< *tit¹* + *lark¹*]

ti·tle (tī′təl) *n., v.* **-tled, -tling.** —*n.* **1 a** the name of a book, poem, picture, song, etc. **b** a title page. **c** a descriptive heading or caption, as of a chapter or section of a book, etc. **2** a name showing a person's rank, occupation, or condition in life. *Examples:* king, duke, lord, countess, captain, doctor, professor, Madame, and Miss. **3** a first place position; championship: *the tennis title.* **4** *Law.* **a** the legal right to the possession of property. **b** the evidence showing such a right. **5** a book; volume: *There are 5000 titles in our library.* **6** a recognized right; claim. —*v.* call by a title; name. [ME < OF < L *titulus.* Doublet of TITTLE.]

Syn. *n.* 1. See note at **name.**

ti·tled (tī′təld) *adj.* having a title, such as that of a duke, countess, lord, dame, etc.: *She married a titled diplomat.*

title deed a document showing that a person owns certain property.

title page the page at the beginning of a book that contains the title, the author's name, etc.

title role or **rôle** the part or character for which a play is named. Hamlet and Othello are title roles.

tit·mouse (tit′mous′) *n., pl.* **-mice. 1** any of various small, active, insect-eating songbirds (family Paridae), such as the **tufted titmouse** (*Parus bicolor*), which is closely related to the chickadees. **2** (*adj.*) designating the family (Paridae) of songbirds that includes the titmice and chickadees. See also **tit¹.** [ME *titmose* < *tit* a small creature + *mose* titmouse + OE *māse*; influenced by *mouse*]

Ti·to·ism (tē′tō iz′əm) *n.* the principles and practices of Marshal Tito (1892-1980), president of Yugoslavia, from 1953 until his death, especially a form of Communism that asserts national rather than international interests and does not accept Soviet domination.

ti·trate (tī′trāt or tit′rāt) *v.* **-trat·ed, -trat·ing. 1** analyse (a solution) by titration. **2** be subjected to titration. [< F *titrer* < *titre* quality]

ti·tra·tion (tī trā′shən or ti trā′shən) *n.* the process of determining the amount of some substance present in a solution by measuring the amount of a different substance that must be added to cause a chemical change.

ti·tre (tī′tər or tē′tər) *n. Chemistry.* **1** a standard amount or strength of a solution as established by titration. **2** the minimum quantity of a standard solution needed to produce a given result in titration. Also, **titer.** [< OF *titre* the proportion of gold or silver in an alloy; originally, learned borrowing < L *titulus* inscription]

tit·ter (tit′ər) *v., n.* —*v.* **1** laugh or giggle in a partly checked way: *Some people in the audience tittered nervously when the actor forgot his lines.* **2** say with such a laugh or giggle: *"He's got his sweater on inside out," she tittered.* —*n.* a tittering laugh or giggle. —**tit′ter·er,** *n.*

tit·tle (tit′əl) *n.* **1** a very little bit; particle; whit. **2** a small stroke or mark over a letter in writing or printing. The dot over an *i* is a tittle. [ME < Med.L *titulus* diacritical mark < L *titulus* title. Doublet of TITLE.]

tit·tle–tat·tle (tit′əl tat′əl) *n. or v.* **-tled, -tling.** gossip. [varied reduplication of *tattle*]

tit·u·lar (tich′ü lər or tit′yə lər) *adj.* **1** in title or name only: *He is a titular prince without any power.* **2** having a title; titled. **3** having to do with a title. [< L *titulus* title] —**tit′u·lar·ly,** *adv.*

tiz·zy (tiz′ē) *n., pl.* **-zies.** *Slang.* a very excited state; dither. [origin uncertain]

TKO, T.K.O., or **t.k.o.** technical knockout.

Tl thallium.

Tlin·git (tling′git) *n., pl.* (def. 1) **Tlin·git** or **Tlin·gits;** *adj.* —*n.* **1** a member of a group of Amerindian peoples of the northern Pacific coast. **2** the group of Athapascan languages spoken by these peoples. —*adj.* of or having to do with the Tlingit or their languages.

Tm thulium.

tme·sis (tmē′sis) *n. Grammar.* the separation of a compound

word by an intervening word or words, as in *to us-ward* for *toward us.* [< LL < Gk. *tmēsis,* originally, a cutting < *temnein* cut]

tn. ton(s).

TN Tennessee.

TNT or **T.N.T.** (tē'en'tē') **1** trinitrotoluene. **2** *Informal.* anything dangerous or explosive.

to (tü; *unstressed,* tu *or* tə) *prep., adv.* —*prep.* **1** in the direction of: *Go to the right.* **2** as far as; until: *rotten to the core, faithful to the end.* **3** for; for the purpose of: *He came to the rescue.* **4** toward or into the position, condition, or state of: *He went to sleep.* **5** so as to produce, cause, or result in: *To her horror, the bear kept advancing towards her.* **6** into: *She tore the letter to pieces.* **7** by: *a fact known to few.* **8** along with; with: *We danced to the music.* **9** compared with: *Those dogs are as different as black is to white. The score was 9 to 5.* **10** in agreement or accordance with: *It is not to my liking.* **11** as seen or understood by: *a symptom alarming to the doctor.* **12** belonging with; of: *the key to my room.* **13** in honor of: *Drink to the King.* **14** on; against: *Fasten it to the wall.* **15** about; concerning: *What did he say to that?* **16** included, contained, or involved in: *seven apples to the kilogram.* **17** *To* is used to show action toward: *Give the book to me. Speak to her.* **18** *To* is used with some infinitive forms of verbs: *He likes to read. The birds began to sing. "To err is human; to forgive, divine."* —*adv.* **1** forward: *He wore his cap wrong side to.* **2** together; touching; closed: *The door slammed to.* **3** to action or work: *We turned to gladly.* **4** to consciousness: *She came to.*
to and fro, first one way and then back again; back and forth. [OE *tō*]
☛ Hom. **too, two.**

toad (tōd) *n.* **1** any of numerous small amphibians (especially family Bufonidae) resembling frogs, but living mostly on land and having a more squat body, weaker hind legs, and rough, dry, often warty skin. Toads return to water to breed. **2** a contemptible or disgusting person. [OE *tāde*]

toad·eat·er (tōd'ēt'ər) *n.* a servile flatterer; toady. [originally, a quack doctor's attendant who pretended to eat toads, which were thought to be poisonous, to prove the efficacy of his master's "cure"]

toad·fish (tōd'fish') *n.* any of a family (Batrachoididae) of saltwater fishes having a thick head, a wide mouth, and slimy skin usually without scales.

toad·flax (tōd'flaks') *n.* any of several plants (genus *Linaria*) of the same family as the snapdragon, especially *L. vulgaris,* which has yellow-and-orange flowers.

toad·stool (tōd'stül') *n.* a mushroom, especially a poisonous mushroom.

toad·y (tō'dē) *n., pl.* **toad·ies;** *v.* **toad·ied, toad·y·ing.** —*n.* a fawning flatterer. —*v.* **1** act like a toady. **2** fawn upon; flatter. [short for *toadeater*]

toad·y·ism (tō'dē iz'əm) *n.* the action or behavior of a toady; interested flattery; mean servility.

to-and-fro (tü'ən frō') *adj.* back-and-forth.

toast¹ (tōst) *n.* —*v.* a slice or slices of bread browned by heat. —*v.* **1** brown by heat. **2** heat thoroughly. [ME < OF *toster,* ult. < L *torrere* parch]

toast² (tōst) *n.* **1** a tribute to a person or thing by a company of people, in which the people raise their drinking glasses, express a wish for the health or success of the person or thing, and take a drink together: *The chairman proposed a toast to the Queen.* **2** a call for or the act of making such a tribute. **3** the person or thing honored in such a way. **4** a person having many admirers: *She was the toast of the town.* —*v.* drink a toast to: *The guests toasted the bride and groom.* [from the custom of putting spiced toast into drinks for flavoring]

toast·er (tōs'tər) *n.* a device or electrical appliance for toasting bread, etc.

toast·mas·ter (tōst'mas'tər) *n.* **1** a person who presides at a dinner and introduces the speakers. **2** a person who proposes toasts.

to·bac·co (tə bak'ō) *n., pl.* **-cos** or **-coes. 1** a plant (*Nicotiana tabacum*) of the nightshade family, widely cultivated in many varieties for its leaves, from which cigarettes, cigars, etc. are made. **2** the prepared leaves of this plant. **3** the products made from such leaves: *Does this store sell tobacco?* **4** the practice of using tobacco for smoking, etc.: *She has sworn off tobacco.* **5** any plant of the genus *Nicotiana,* which includes several species grown for their sweet-smelling flowers. [< Sp. *tabaco* < Carib]

Tobacco Nation the Petun Indians, an Iroquoian people once inhabiting SW Ontario.

to·bac·co·nist (tə bak'ə nist) *n.* a dealer in tobacco.

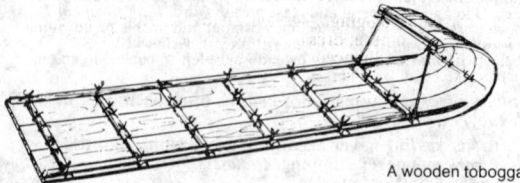
A wooden toboggan

to·bog·gan (tə bog'ən) *n., v. Cdn.* —*n.* a long, light, narrow sleigh with a flat bottom and no runners, and having the front end curved up and back. —*v.* **1** ride or carry on a toboggan: *We went tobogganing yesterday. The supplies were tobogganed to camp.* **2** decline sharply and rapidly in value: *House prices tobogganed.* [< Cdn.F *tabagane* < Algonquian; cf. Micmac *tobākun*]

to·by or **To·by** (tō'bē) *n., pl.* **to·bies** or **To·bies.** a small, fat jug or mug in the form of a fat man wearing a long coat and a three-cornered hat. [< *Toby,* proper name, short for *Tobias*]

toc·ca·ta (tə kä'tə) *n. Music.* a composition for the piano, organ, or other keyboard instrument, often intended to exhibit the player's technique. [< Ital. *toccata,* originally pp. of *toccare* touch]

toc·sin (tok'sən) *n.* **1** an alarm sounded on a bell; a warning signal. **2** a bell used to sound an alarm. [< F < Provençal *tocasenh* < *tocar* strike, touch + *senh* bell]

to·day (tə dā') *n., adv.* —*n.* the present day, time, or period: *The photographer of today has many types of camera to choose from.* —*adv.* **1** on or during this day: *I have to go to the dentist today.* **2** at the present time or period; these days: *Most Canadian homes today have a refrigerator.* Also, **to-day.** [OE *tō dæge* on (the) day]

tod·dle (tod'əl) *v.* **-dled, -dling;** *n.* —*v.* walk with short, unsteady steps, as a baby does. —*n.* a toddling way of walking. [origin unknown]

tod·dler (tod'lər) *n.* a young child, especially one between the ages of one and two or three.

tod·dy (tod'ē) *n., pl.* **-dies. 1** the fresh or fermented sap of various palm trees, especially of the East Indies. **2** a usually hot drink made of an alcoholic liquor such as whisky or brandy mixed with water, sugar, and spices. [< Hind. *tārī* palm sap < *tār* palm]

to-do (tə dü') *n., pl.* **-dos.** *Informal.* fuss; flurry; excitement: *There was a great to-do when the new puppy arrived.*

toe (tō) *n., v.* **toed, toe·ing.** —*n.* **1** one of the five end parts of the foot. **2** the part of a stocking, shoe, etc. that covers the toes. **3** the forepart of a foot or hoof. **4** anything resembling a toe: *the toe and heel of a golf club.*
on (one's) toes, ready for action; alert.
—*v.* **1** touch or reach with the toes: *to toe a line.* **2** turn the toes in walking, standing, etc.: *to toe in, to toe out.* **3** furnish with a toe or toes. **4** drive (a nail) slantwise. **5** fasten by nails driven slantwise.
toe in, adjust the front wheels of an automobile, etc. so that they point forward and slightly inward.
toe the line, a have one's toes on the starting line of a race. **b** obey rules, conform to a doctrine, etc. strictly.
[OE *tā*] —**toe'less,** *adj.* —**toe'-like',** *adj.*
☛ Hom. **tow.**

toea (tō'ä) *n.* a unit of money in Papua New Guinea, equal to ¹⁄₁₀₀ of a kina. [< a Pupan language]

toed (tōd) *adj.* **1** having a specified number or kind of toes (used only in compounds): *square-toed shoes. The camel is a two-toed animal.* **2** of a nail, driven slantwise. **3** fastened by nails driven slantwise.

toe·hold (tō'hōld') *n.* **1** a small place of support for the toes when climbing: *The climber cut toeholds in the glacier as he went.* **2** any means of support in progressing, especially at the start of a venture, etc.: *She opened a small neighborhood store to get a toehold in the business.* **3** *Wrestling.* a hold in which an opponent's foot is bent back or twisted.

toe–in (tō'in) *n.* the adjustment of the front wheels of a motor vehicle so that they are not perfectly parallel but point slightly inward at the front. This makes for better steering and helps equalize wear on the tires.

toe·nail (tō'nāl') *n.* **1** the nail growing on a toe. **2** *Carpentry.* a nail driven obliquely.

toe rubber a very low rubber overshoe worn by men, covering only the toe, heel, and sole of the shoe.

toff (tof) *n. Esp.Brit. Slang.* **1** a rich, important, or aristocratic man; a nob. **2** a richly or elegantly dressed man; a dandy. [? < *tuft,* formerly a nobleman or other privileged undergraduate at Oxford University who wore a gold tassel in his cap]

tof·fee (tof'ē) *n., pl.* **-fees. 1** a hard but chewy candy made from

sugar or syrup boiled with butter at a high temperature. **2** taffy. Also, **toffy** (pl. **-fies**). [origin uncertain]

tog (tog) *n., v.* **togged, tog·ging. —n. 1** a garment. **2 togs,** *pl. Informal.* clothes. **—v.** clothe; dress. [apparently a shortening of obs. *togman*; probably influenced by L *toga*]

A Roman toga of the first century A.D.

to·ga (tō′gə) *n., pl.* **-gas, -gae** (-jē). **1** in ancient Rome, the loose flowing outer garment worn by citizens. A toga was made of a single piece of cloth with no sleeves or armholes, covering the whole body except for the right arm. **2** a robe of office. [< L]

to·gaed (tō′gəd) *adj.* wearing a toga.

to·geth·er (tə geŦH′ər) *adv.* **1** in company or association; with each other: *They walked down the road together. I like navy and red together. They worked together for many years.* **2** in or into one unit, mass, piece, etc.: *She mixed the two colors together.* **3** considered as a whole: *All the dimes and nickles together don't even make up three dollars. All together, there were 25 people at the party.* **4** in or into one gathering, company, or collection: *They get together every Friday to play bridge.* **5** in or into harmony or agreement: *Let's get together on our basic requirements.* **6** at the same time: *Day and night cannot occur together.* **7** without a stop or break; continuously: *He worked for days together.*
together with, along with.
[OE *tōgædere* < *tō* to + *gædere* together]
☛ *Usage.* **Together with.** In formal writing a singular subject followed by "together with—" still takes a singular verb: *My uncle, together with my two cousins, was there to meet me.* Compare this with: *My uncle and my two cousins were there to meet me.*

to·geth·er·ness (tə geth′ər nis) *n.* the condition of being closely associated or united, especially in family or social activities.

tog·ger·y (tog′ər ē) *n. Informal.* **1** garments; clothes. **2** a clothing store.

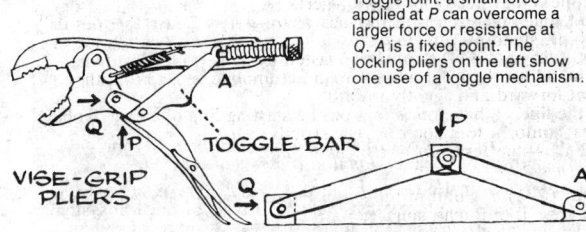

Toggle joint: a small force applied at *P* can overcome a larger force or resistance at *Q. A* is a fixed point. The locking pliers on the left show one use of a toggle mechanism.

tog·gle (tog′əl) *n., v.* **-gled, -gling. —n. 1** a pin, bolt, or rod put through the eye of a rope or the link of a chain to keep it in place, to hold two ropes together, to serve as a hold for the fingers, etc. **2** an oblong piece that is attached crosswise by its centre and is passed through a loop or hole to act as a fastening for a coat, etc. **3** a toggle joint, or a device furnished with one.
—v. fasten or furnish with a toggle or toggles. [cf. *tug,* v.]

toggle joint a knee-like joint that transmits pressure at right angles.

toggle switch an electric switch having a projecting lever that is pushed through a small arc to open or close the circuit.

togue (tōg) *n. Cdn. Maritimes.* lake trout. [< Cdn.F < Algonquian]

toil¹ (toil) *n., v.* **—n.** hard work; labor: *to succeed finally after years of toil.*
—v. 1 work hard: *to toil with one's hands for a living.* **2** move with difficulty, pain or weariness: *They toiled up the hill.* **3** *Archaic.* bring, achieve, or obtain by hard work or effort. [ME < AF *toiler* < OF *toeillier* drag about, make dirty < L *tudiculare* stir up < *tudicula* olive press < *tundere* pound] **—toil′er,** *n.*
☛ *Syn. n.* **1.** See note at **work.**

hat, āge, fär; let, ēqual, tėrm; it, īce
hot, ōpen, ôrder; oil, out; cup, pu̇t, rüle,
əbove, takən, pencəl, lemən, circəs
ch, child; ng, long; sh, ship
th, thin; ŦH, then; zh, measure

toil² (toil) *n.* **1** *Archaic.* a net for trapping game. **2 toils,** *pl.* anything that holds one fast; a snare or trap: *caught in the toils of the law.* [< F *toile,* literally, cloth < L *tela* web < *texere* weave]

toi·let (toi′lit) *n.* **1** a fixture, usually a porcelain bowl flushed by water, into which waste matter from the body is passed. **2** a room containing a toilet. **3** (*adj.*) for a toilet: *a toilet brush.* **4** the act or process of washing, dressing, and grooming oneself: *She took an hour to complete her toilet.* **5** (*adj.*) of or for use in the process of dressing and grooming: *Combs and brushes are toilet articles.* **6** *Archaic.* dressing table. **7** *Archaic.* attire or costume: *Her toilet was elaborate.*
go to the toilet, *Informal.* urinate or defecate: *The child said he had to go to the toilet.*
[< F *toilette,* dim. of *toile.* See TOIL².]

toilet paper thin, soft, absorbent paper for use in a toilet, especially for cleaning the body after passing waste matter.

toi·let·ry (toi′lit rē) *n.* Usually, **toiletries,** *pl.* soap, face powder, perfume or cologne, shaving cream, etc. used in washing and grooming oneself.

toilet soap mild soap that is usually perfumed and colored.

toi·lette (toi let′; *French,* twä let′) *n.* **1** the process of washing, dressing, and grooming oneself. **2** fashionable attire or costume. [< F]

toilet tissue toilet paper.

toi·let–train·ing (toi′lət trā′ning) *n.* the process of training a child to control bladder and bowel movements and to use a toilet.
—toi′let-train′, *v.*

toilet water a fragrant liquid, weaker than perfume, used after bathing, as a cologne in grooming, etc.

toil·some (toil′səm) *adj.* requiring hard work; laborious; wearisome.

toil·worn (toil′wôrn′) *adj.* worn by toil; showing the affects of toil: *toilworn hands.*

To·kay (tō kā′) *n.* **1** a rich, sweet, golden wine made in Hungary. **2** a similar wine made elsewhere. **3** a variety of large, reddish, sweet grape used for making such wine. [< *Tokay,* a town in N Hungary, where this wine was first made]

to·ken (tō′kən) *n.* **1 a** a mark or sign: *Black is a token of mourning.* **b** something that serves to prove; an evidence: *His actions are a token of his sincerity.* **c** a characteristic mark or indication: *the tokens of a good horse, the tokens of a disease.* **2** a sign of friendship; keepsake: *She received many birthday tokens.* **3** a piece of metal, plastic, etc. stamped for a higher value than of the material, often made and sold for use as a single bus or train fare, etc. **4** a piece of metal, plastic, etc. indicating a right or privilege: *This token will admit you to the swimming pool.* **5** something that is a sign of genuineness or authority. **6** (*adj.*) serving only as a symbol; having no real significance; nominal: *a token payment, token resistance.* **7** *Archaic.* a signal.
by the same token, for the same reason; similarly.
in token of, as a token of; to show.
[OE *tācen*]
☛ *Syn.* **1.** See note at **mark.**

to·ken·ism (tō′kə niz′əm) *n.* the practice or policy of making only a nominal or partial effort, especially in providing equal opportunity to disadvantaged or minority groups: *Putting a few women on boards of directors is just tokenism.*

told (tōld) *v.* pt. and pp. of **tell.**
all told, including all.

To·le·do (tə lē′dō) *n.* a fine sword or sword blade made in Toledo, a city in central Spain.

tol·er·a·ble (tol′ər ə bəl *or* tol′rə bəl) *adj.* **1** that can be endured: *The pain has not disappeared, but it has become tolerable.* **2** fairly good: *She is in tolerable health.* [ME < OF < L *tolerabilis* < *tolerare* tolerate] **—tol′er·a·bly,** *adv.* **—tol′er·a·ble·ness,** *n.*

tol·er·ance (tol′ər əns) *n.* **1** a willingness to be tolerant and patient toward people whose opinions or ways differ from one's own. **2** the power of enduring or resisting the action of a drug, poison, etc. **3** the action of tolerating. **4** an allowed amount of variation from a standard, as in the mass of coins or the dimensions of a machine or part.
☛ *Syn.* **1.** See note at **toleration.**

tol·er·ant (tol′ər ənt) *adj.* **1** willing to let other people do as they

think best; willing to allow beliefs and actions of which one does not approve: *A more tolerant person would not have walked out in the middle of the meeting.* **2** easy-going; not readily saying no: *The teacher was tolerant toward the high-spirited children.* **3** able to endure or resist the action of a drug, poison, etc. —**tol′er·ant·ly,** *adv.*

tol·er·ate (tol′ə rāt′) *v.* **-at·ed, -at·ing. 1** allow; permit: *He was an informal teacher, but would never tolerate insolence.* **2** bear; endure; put up with: *They tolerated the grouchy old man because he was their employer.* **3** endure or resist the action of (a drug, poison, etc.). [< L *tolerare*]

tol·er·a·tion (tol′ər ā′shən) *n.* **1** the act or practice of tolerating. **2** the recognition of a person's rights, especially the freedom to worship as he thinks best without loss of civil rights or social privileges.

☛ *Usage.* **Toleration** (def. 1) and **tolerance** (def. 1) are associated with the verb **tolerate,** but differ in meaning. **Toleration** = the act of allowing or putting up with actions, beliefs, or people one does not like or approve of, often because of indifference or a desire to avoid conflict: *Toleration of dishonest officials encourages corruption.* **Tolerance** = the state or quality of being willing to let others think, live, or worship according to their own beliefs and to refrain from judging, harshly or with blind prejudice: *Through tolerance we learn to understand people.*

toll[1] (tōl) *v., n.* —*v.* **1** sound (a church bell, etc.) with single strokes slowly and regularly repeated: *Bells were tolled all over the country at the king's death.* **2** of a bell, sound with slow, single strokes: *The bell tolled.* **3** call, announce, etc. by tolling: *The bells tolled the death of the king.*
—*n.* **1** the stroke or sound of a bell being tolled. **2** the act or fact of tolling. [related to OE *-tyllan* draw. See TILL[3].]

toll[2] (tōl) *n., v.* —*n.* **1** a tax or fee paid for some right or privilege: *We pay a toll when we use the bridge.* **2** a charge for a certain service. There is a toll on long-distance telephone calls. **3** something paid, lost, suffered, etc.: *Automobile accidents take a heavy toll of human lives.*
—*v. Rare.* collect as a toll or collect a toll from. [OE *toll,* var. of *toln* < L < Gk. *telōnion* toll house, ult. < *telos* tax]

toll[3] (tōl) *v., n. Hunting.* —*v.* **1** lure game by using a call or other sound. **2** make such a call or sound. —*n.* a call or sound thus made. [ME; cf. OE *talu* talk. Akin to TALE.]

toll bar a barrier, especially a gate, across a road or bridge where toll is taken.

toll bridge a bridge at which a toll is charged.

toll call a long-distance telephone call.

toll·er (tō′lər) *n. Cdn.* Nova Scotia duck tolling retriever.

toll·gate (tōl′gāt′) *n.* a gate where toll is collected.

toll·keep·er (tōl′kēp′ər) *n.* a person who collects the toll at a tollgate.

toll road a road on which tolls are charged; turnpike.

Tol·tec (tol′tek) *n.* **1** a North American Indian people supposed to have ruled in Mexico before the Aztecs. **2** one of this people.

to·lu (tō lü′) *n.* a fragrant balsam obtained from a South American tree, used in medicine, perfume, etc. [< Santiago de *Tolú,* a city in Colombia]

tol·u·ene (tol′yü ēn′) *n.* a colorless liquid hydrocarbon resembling benzene and obtained from coal tar and coal gas. It is used as a solvent and for making explosives and dyes. *Formula:* $C_6H_5CH_3$ [< *tolu* + *-ene,* as in *benzene*]

tol·u·ol (tol′yü ol′ *or* tol′yü ōl′) *n.* a commercial grade of toluene.

tom (tom) *n.* the male of some animals; male: *a tom turkey. This cat is a tom.* [< *Tom,* used as a type name for a common man. cf. TOMCAT.]

tom·a·hawk (tom′ə hok′ *or* -hôk′) *n., v.* —*n.* a light axe used by many North American Indian peoples as a weapon and as a tool. **bury the tomahawk,** stop fighting; make peace.
—*v.* strike or kill with a tomahawk. [< Algonquian]

to·ma·to (tə mā′tō, tə mä′tō, *or* tə mat′ō) *n., pl.* **-toes. 1** a juicy, pulpy, red or yellow fruit commonly eaten as a vegetable, either raw or cooked. **2** the widely cultivated perennial plant (*Lycopersicon esculentum*) this fruit grows on, having hairy leaves and stems and small, yellow flowers. [< Sp. < Nahuatl *tomatl*]

tomb (tüm) *n., v.* —*n.* **1** a vault or chamber for the dead, often built partly or completely above ground. **2** grave. **3** a monument or tombstone to commemorate the dead. **4 the tomb,** death. —*v. Rare.* entomb. [ME < AF < LL < Gk. *tymbos* mound]

tom·bac, tom·back, or **tom·bak** (tom′bak) *n.* any of several alloys consisting of zinc, copper, and sometimes arsenic,

used to make cheap jewellery, art objects, etc. Also, **tambac.** [< F *tombac* < Pg. *tambaca* < Malay < Skt. *tamraka*]

tom·boy (tom′boi′) *n.* a girl who is more active and enjoys rougher games than most girls.

tomb·stone (tüm′stōn′) *n.* a stone that marks a tomb or grave.

tom·cat (tom′kat′) *n.* a male cat. [< *tom* + *cat,* after *Tom the Cat,* hero of "The Life and Adventures of a Cat" (1760)]

tom·cod (tom′kod′) *n.* any of several small saltwater fishes (genus *Microgadus*) resembling and related to the cod.

Tom, Dick, and Harry people in general; everyone.

tome (tōm) *n.* a book, especially a large and scholarly book. [< F < L < Gk. *tomos,* originally, piece cut off]

tom·fool (tom′fül′) *n., adj.* —*n.* a silly fool; stupid person. —*adj.* very stupid or foolish: *That was a tomfool thing to do.*

tom·fool·er·y (tom′fül′ər ē) *n., pl.* **-er·ies.** silly behavior; nonsense.

Tom·my or **tom·my** (tom′ē) *n., pl.* **-mies.** a nickname for a British soldier. [< *Thomas Atkins,* a fictitious name used since 1815 in British army regulations to represent a private soldier.]

Tommy At·kins (at′kinz) *n.* a nickname for a British soldier. [< *Thomas Atkins,* a name used for privates in the sample forms given in the official regulations of the British Army from 1815 on]

tommy cod *Cdn.* tomcod.

Tommy gun or **tommy gun** *Informal.* a Thompson submachine gun.

tom·my·rot (tom′ē rot′) *n. Slang.* nonsense; rubbish; foolishness. [origin uncertain]

to·mor·row (tə môr′ō) *n., adv.* —*n.* **1** the day after today. **2** the indefinite future: *the world of tomorrow.* —*adv.* on the day after today. Also, **to-morrow.** [ME *to morowe*]

Tom Thumb 1 in the children's story, a dwarf no bigger than his father's thumb. **2** any very small thing or person.

tom·tit (tom′tit′) *n. Esp.Brit.* any of various small birds, especially a titmouse.

tom–tom (tom′tom′) *n.* a usually long, narrow drum beaten with the hands; especially, any of various such drums of India or Africa. [< Hind. *tam-tam;* of imitative origin]

ton (tun) *n.* **1** either of two formerly standard units for measuring mass: the **short ton,** used in Canada, the United States, etc., equal to 2000 pounds (about 907 kg) and the **long ton,** used in the United Kingdom, equal to 2240 pounds (about 1016 kg). **2** a unit for measuring the internal capacity of a ship, equal to 100 cubic feet (about 2.8 m³); in full, **register ton. 3** a unit for measuring the cargo or carrying capacity of a ship, equal to 40 cubic feet (about 1.1 m³); in full, **freight ton** or **measurement ton. 4** a unit for measuring the amount of water a ship will displace, equal to 35 cubic feet (about 1 m³), which is approximately equal to a long ton mass of sea water; in full, **displacement ton. 5** *Informal.* a very large number or amount: *These books weigh a ton. He's got tons of records.* [var. of *tun*]
☛ *Hom.* **tonne, tun.**

ton·al (tō′nəl) *adj.* **1** of or having to do with tones or tone. **2** characterized by tonality: *tonal music.* —**ton′al·ly,** *adv.*

to·nal·i·ty (tō nal′ə tē) *n., pl.* **-ties. 1** *Music.* **a** the relations existing between the tones that make up a scale or musical system. **b** a particular arrangement of tones in a scale or musical system; key. **2** in painting, etc., the overall tone or color scheme of a picture: *The colors in the painting are sombre, but the tonality is good.*

tone (tōn) *n., v.* **toned, ton·ing.** —*n.* **1** any sound considered with reference to its quality, pitch, strength, source, etc.: *sweet, shrill, or loud tones.* **2** the quality of sound: *a voice silvery in tone.* **3** *Music.* **a** a sound of definite pitch and character. **b** the difference in pitch between two notes. C and D are one tone apart. **4** a manner of speaking or writing: *We disliked the haughty tone of her letter.* **5** a spirit; character; style: *tone of elegance.* **b** mental or emotional state; mood; disposition: *a healthful tone of mind.* **6** a normal, healthy condition; vigor. **7** the effect of color and of light and shade in a painting, drawing, etc.: *I like the soft green tone of that painting.* **8** a shade of color: *This room is furnished in tones of brown.* **9** *Linguistics.* **a** the pitch of the voice as it is high or low, or as it rises and falls, regarded as a distinctive feature of a language. **b** any of the tonal levels distinctive in a language. **c** the pronunciation characteristic of a particular person, group of people, area, etc.; accent.
—*v.* **1** harmonize: *This rug tones in well with the wallpaper and furniture.* **2** give a tone to. **3** change the tone of.
tone down, soften.
tone up, give more sound, color, or vigor to; strengthen.
[ME < OF < L < Gk. *tonos,* originally, a stretching, taut string]

tone arm the part of a record player that carries the pickup and needle. The tone arm moves on a pivot.

toned (tōnd) *adj.* having a tone, especially of a specified kind (*used especially in compounds*): *a sweet-toned voice.*

tone–deaf (tōn′def′) *adj.* not able to accurately distinguish differences in musical pitch.

tone·less (tōn′lis) *adj.* 1 lacking in expression or variation of tone: *He spoke in a toneless voice.* 2 having no tone. —**tone′less·ly,** *adv.* —**tone′less·ness,** *n.*

tone poem symphonic poem.

to·nette (tō net′) *n.* a simple flutelike instrument having easy finger guides and range slightly more than an octave, used for basic education in music.

tong¹ (tong) *n.* 1 in China, an association or club. 2 a secret organization or club in North American Chinese communities. [< Chinese *t'ang, t'ong,* originally, meeting hall]

tong² (tong) *v.* 1 seize, gather, hold, or handle with tongs. 2 use tongs; work with tongs. [OE *tang*]

tongs (tongz) *n.pl.* a tool for seizing, holding, or lifting, usually consisting of two long arms joined like a pair of scissors, or by a spring piece.

tongue (tung) *n., v.* **tongued, tongu·ing.** —*n.* 1 the movable fleshy organ in the mouth of human beings and most vertebrates. The tongue is used for tasting and taking and swallowing food and also, in man, for talking. See **windpipe** for picture. 2 an animal's tongue used as food. 3 the power of speech: *You are silent—have you lost your tongue?* 4 a way of speaking; speech; talk: *a flattering tongue.* 5 the language of a people: *the English tongue.* 6 something shaped or used like a tongue. 7 the strip of material under the laces of a shoe. 8 a narrow strip of land running out into water. 9 a tapering jet of flame. 10 the pin of a buckle, brooch, etc. 11 the pole by which a team of horses draws a wagon. 12 a projecting strip along the edge of a board for fitting into a groove in another board. 13 the pointer of a dial, balance, etc. 14 the clapper of a bell. 15 in a wind musical instrument, a vibrating reed, etc. 16 the short movable rail of a railway switch.
give tongue, of hounds, etc., bark or bay.
hold (one's) **tongue,** keep silent.
on the tip of (one's) **tongue, a** almost spoken. **b** ready to be spoken.
—*v.* 1 modify tones of (a flute, cornet, etc.) with the tongue. 2 use the tongue. 3 furnish (a board) with a tongue. [OE *tunge*] —**tongue′less,** *adj.* —**tongue′like′,** *adj.*

tongue–and–groove joint (tung′ən grüv′) *Carpentry.* a joint made by fitting a projecting strip, or tongue, along one edge of a board into a groove in another board. See **joint** for picture.

tongue–in–cheek (tung′in chēk′) *adj.* meant to be ironic or facetious: *a tongue-in-cheek criticism.*

tongue–lash·ing (tung′lash′ing) *n.* a severe scolding: *Her mother gave her a tongue-lashing for letting her ice cream drip all over the carpet.* —**tongue-lash,** *v.*

tongue–tie (tung′tī′) *n., v.* **-tied, -ty·ing.** —*n.* a condition in which the motion of the tongue is impeded by an abnormal shortness of the folded membrane below it. —*v.* make (someone) unable to speak, because of amazement, fear, shyness, etc.

tongue–tied (tung′tīd) *adj.* 1 unable to speak because of shyness or embarrassment. 2 having the motion of the tongue hindered or limited because the membrane that connects its lower side to the bottom of the mouth is abnormally short.

tongue twister a phrase or sentence having a sequence of similar consonants or consonant groups that is difficult to say quickly without getting the sounds mixed up. *Example: She sells sea shells on the seashore.*

tongue–twist·ing (tung′twis′ting) *adj.* of or like a tongue twister; difficult to say quickly without a mistake.

ton·ic (ton′ik) *n., adj.* —*n.* 1 anything that gives strength; a medicine to give strength: *Cod-liver oil is a tonic.* 2 *Music.* the first note of a scale; keynote. 3 tonic water: *gin and tonic.*
—*adj.* 1 restoring to health and vigor; giving strength; bracing: *The mountain air is tonic.* 2 a having to do with muscular tension. b characterized by continuous contraction of the muscles: *a tonic convulsion.* 3 *Music.* a having to do with a tone or tones. b of or based on a keynote. 4 *Linguistics.* a having to do with tone or accent in speaking. b of a language, using tone distinctively. 5 of speech sounds, accented or stressed. [< Gk. *tonikos < tonos* tone. See TONE.]

to·nic·i·ty (tō nis′ə tē) *n.* 1 the quality or condition of being tonic. 2 the property of possessing bodily tone; the normal elastic tension of muscles, arteries, etc.

tonic sol–fa a system of teaching music, especially sight-singing and notation, in which the notes of a major scale are sung to sol-fa syllables with *do* as the tonic or keynote.

tonic water a type of flavored carbonated water.

---

hat, āge, fär; let, ēqual, tėrm; it, īce
hot, ōpen, ôrder; oil, out; cup, pút, rüle,
above, takən, pencəl, lemən, circəs

ch, child; ng, long; sh, ship
th, thin; ᴛʜ, then; zh, measure

to·night (tə nīt′) *adv., n.* —*adv.* on or during the present or the coming night or evening. —*n.* the present or the coming night or evening: *I wish tonight would come.* Also, **to-night.** [OE *tō niht*]

ton·ite (tō′nīt) *n.* an explosive used in blasting, consisting of guncotton and barium nitrate. [< *ton-,* abstracted from L *tonare* thunder]

ton·nage (tun′ij) *n.* 1 the internal capacity of a ship expressed in tons of 100 cubic feet, or register tons (about 2.8 m³). A ship with a tonnage of 500 has an internal capacity of 50 000 cubic feet. 2 ships in terms or their total carrying capacity of the total amount carried: *the tonnage of Canada's navy.* 3 a duty or tax on ships at so much a ton. 4 total mass in tons shipped or carried.

tonne (tun) *n.* a unit used with the SI for measuring mass, equal to one thousand kilograms. A very small car has a mass of about one tonne. *Symbol:* t
☞ *Hom.* **ton, tun.**

ton·neau (tun ō′) *n., pl.* **-neaus** or **-neaux** (-ōz′). the part of an automobile that contains the back seats. [< F *tonneau,* literally, cask, ult. < Gmc.]

ton·sil (ton′səl) *n.* either of the two oval masses of lymphatic tissue on the inner sides of the throat, at the back of the mouth. [< L *tonsillae,* pl., dim. of *toles,* pl., goiter]

ton·sil·lar or **ton·sil·ar** (ton′sə lər) *adj.* of or having to do with the tonsils.

ton·sil·lec·to·my (ton′sə lek′tə mē) *n., pl.* **-mies.** a removal of the tonsils by surgery. [< L *tonsil + -ectomy*]

ton·sil·li·tis (ton′sə lī′tis) *n.* inflammation of the tonsils. [< NL < L *tonsillae* tonsils + -*itis*]

ton·so·ri·al (ton sô′rē əl) *adj. Facetious.* of or having to do with a barber or his work. [< L *tonsorius,* ult. < *tondere* shear]

ton·sure (ton′shər) *n., v.* **-sured, -sur·ing.** —*n.* 1 the act or the rite of clipping the hair or of shaving a part or the whole of the head of a person entering the priesthood or an order of monks. 2 the shaved part of the head of a priest or monk. 3 the state of being so shaved.
—*v.* shave the head of. [ME < L *tonsura < tondere* shear, shave]

ton·tine (ton′tēn *or* ton tēn′) *n.* 1 a form of annuity or insurance in which subscribers share the benefits on such terms that the share of any member who dies or defaults is distributed among the other members until the whole goes to the last surviving member or until a specified expiration date, when the whole is divided among the remaining members. 2 the total fund accumulated in such a scheme. 3 the share of each member. 4 the members collectively. [< F *tontine < Lorenzo Tonti,* an Italian banker, who introduced this system into France in about 1653]

too (tü) *adv.* 1 also; besides: *The dog is hungry, and thirsty too.* 2 beyond what is desirable, proper, or right; more than enough: *My dress is too long for you. He ate too much. The summer passed too quickly.* 3 very; exceedingly: *I am only too glad to help you. I didn't do too well on the exam.* 4 indeed; most definitely (*used to contradict a negative statement*): *I didn't take it. You did too!* [var. of *to*]
☞ *Hom.* **to, two.**

took (tùk) *v.* pt. of **take.**

tool (tül) *n., v.* —*n.* 1 a knife, hammer, saw, shovel, or any instrument used in doing work. 2 anything used to achieve some purpose: *Books are a scholar's tools.* 3 a person used by another like a tool: *He is a tool of the departmental boss.* 4 a part of a machine that cuts, bores, smooths, etc. 5 the whole of such a machine.
—*v.* 1 work, shape, or cut with a tool: *He tooled beautiful designs in leather with a knife.* 2 ornament by cutting, pressing, etc. with a tool: *to tool leather.* 3 *Slang.* drive or ride, especially fast: *tooling along the highway in a beat-up old car.*
tool up, install equipment for a certain task; prepare for a specific job: *The factory is tooling up for the production of new cars.* [OE *tōl*]
☞ *Hom.* **tulle.**

☞ *Syn. n.* 1. **Tool, implement** = an instrument or other article used in doing work. **Tool** indicates an instrument or simple device especially suited or designed to make a particular kind of work easier, but applies particularly to something held and worked by the hands in doing manual work: *Plumbers, mechanics, carpenters, and shoemakers need tools.* **Implement** is a general

word meaning a tool, instrument, utensil, or mechanical device needed to do something: *Hoes and tractors are agricultural implements.*

tool·ing (tü′ling) *n.* 1 ornamentation made with a hand tool; especially, lettering or designs made on leather. 2 any work done with a tool. 3 the assembly of machine tools in a factory.

tool·mak·er (tül′māk′ər) *n.* 1 a man who makes tools. 2 a man who makes, repairs, or maintains machine tools.

tool·push·er (tül′pŭsh′ər) *n.* a foreman of a drilling operation in the oil industry. Also, **toolpush.**

toot¹ (tüt) *n., v.* —*n.* the sound of a horn, whistle, etc. —*v.* 1 give forth a short blast: *He heard the train toot three times.* 2 sound a horn, whistle, etc. in short blasts: *to toot a horn. She tooted as she drove past the house.* [probably ult. imitative] —**toot′er,** *n.*

toot² (tüt) *n. Slang.* a drinking spree; binge: *go on a toot.* [earlier, a large drink < obs. *toot,* v., drink copiously; origin unknown]

tooth (tüth) *n., pl.* **teeth;** *v.* —*n.* 1 one of the hard, bonelike parts in the mouth, used for biting and chewing. See **teeth** for picture. 2 something like a tooth. Each one of the projecting parts of a comb, rake, or saw is a tooth. 3 a taste; liking: *have no tooth for fruit.*
fight tooth and nail, fight fiercely, with all one's force.
long in the tooth, ageing or old.
—*v.* 1 furnish with teeth; put teeth on. 2 cut teeth on the edge of; indent. [OE *tōth*] —**tooth′like′,** *adj.*

tooth·ache (tüth′āk′) *n.* a pain in a tooth or the teeth.

tooth·brush (tüth′brush′) *n.* a small brush for cleaning the teeth.

toothed (tütht *or* tüᴛʜd) *adj.* 1 having teeth, especially of a certain kind or number (*often used in compounds*): *yellow-toothed.* 2 notched or indented: *a toothed blade.*

tooth·less (tüth′lis) *adj.* without teeth.

tooth·paste (tüth′pāst′) *n.* a paste for use in cleaning the teeth.

tooth·pick (tüth′pik′) *n.* a small, pointed piece of wood, plastic, etc., for removing bits of food from between the teeth.

tooth powder a powder for cleaning the teeth.

tooth·some (tüth′səm) *adj.* pleasing to the taste; tasting good.

too·tle (tü′təl) *v.* -tled, -tling; *n.* —*v.* toot softly and continuously, as on a whistle. —*n.* the act of tootling. [frequentative of TOOT¹.]

top¹ (top) *n., v.* **topped, top·ping.** —*n.* 1 the highest point or part: *the top of a mountain.* 2 the upper end or surface: *the top of a table.* 3 the highest or leading place, rank, etc.: *He is at the top of his class.* 4 one that occupies the highest or leading position: *He is the top in his profession.* 5 the highest point, pitch, or degree: *The boy was yelling at the top of his voice.* 6 the best or most important part: *the top of the morning.* 7 the part of a plant that grows above ground, especially a plant with edible roots: *carrot tops.* 8 the head. 9 the cover of an automobile, carriage, etc. 10 the upper part of a shoe or boot. 11 a lid or cap: *Put the top back on the bottle.* 12 a piece of clothing for the upper part of the body: *She wore white shorts and a pink top.* 13 (*adj.*) having to do with, situated at, or forming the top: *the top shelf.* 14 (*adj.*) highest in degree; greatest: *at top speed.* 15 (*adj.*) chief; foremost: *top honors.* 16 on a ship, a platform around the top of a lower mast. See **mast¹** for picture. 17 *Golf.* a stroke above the centre of a ball. 18 a tent used as a covering for a circus or other performance. 19 *Baseball.* the first half of an inning.
blow (one's) top, *Slang.* **a** lose one's temper; get very excited. **b** become insane.
from top to toe, a from head to foot. **b** completely.
on top, with success; with victory: *to come out on top.*
over the top, a over the front of a trench to attack. **b** over a target or limit: *We aimed for 50 subscriptions to our magazine, but we went over the top and collected 73.*
—*v.* 1 put a top on: *to top a box.* 2 be on top of; be the top of: *A church tops the hill.* 3 reach the top of: *They topped the mountain.* 4 rise high; rise above: *The sun topped the horizon.* 5 be higher than; be greater than. 6 do better than; outdo; excel: *His story topped all the rest.* 7 *Golf.* hit (a ball) above centre. 8 remove the top of (a plant, etc.). 9 in chemical distillation, remove the part that volatilizes first; skim.
top off, a finish; end. **b** complete; put the finishing touches to: *We topped off the evening with an excellent dinner.* **c** *Slang.* in the West, begin to tame or break (a horse).
[OE *topp*]
☞ *Syn. n.* 1. **Top, summit, crown** = the highest point or part of something. **Top** is the general word: *Please loosen the top of this jar.* **Summit** is the highest point of a hill, mountain, or pass, but is often used figuratively to mean the highest level that can be reached, or reached toward, by effort: *At last he attained the summit of his ambition.* **Crown,** used figuratively, means the highest degree of perfection or completion or highest state of something: *A Nobel Prize is the crown of success.*

top² (top) *n.* a rounded or cone-shaped toy having a point at one end on which it is made to spin.
sleep like a top, sleep soundly.
[OE *topp*]

to·paz (tō′paz) *n.* 1 a mineral that is a silicate of aluminum, occurring usually in transparent or translucent crystals in various colors. Transparent yellow or brownish topaz is used as a gem. *Formula:* $Al_2SiO_4(F, OH)_2$ 2 a gem made from this stone. 3 any of various yellow gemstones, such as a yellow sapphire. [ME < OF < L < Gk. *topazos*]

top boot a high boot usually having the upper part of the top in a different color or material and made to look as if turned down.

top brass *Slang.* 1 high-ranking officers of the armed forces. 2 high-ranking officials of any organization.

top·coat (top′kōt′) *n.* 1 an overcoat, especially a lightweight one. 2 the fur of an animal that covers its back and sides. 3 a finishing coating of paint, etc.

top dog *Informal.* the best, most successful or most important individual or group. [from the position of the winning dog in a dogfight]

top drawer *Informal.* the highest level of excellence, importance, good breeding, etc.: *a family in the top drawer of society.*

tope (tōp) *v.* **toped, top·ing.** drink excessively or habitually; tipple. [origin uncertain]
☞ *Hom.* **taupe.**

top·er (tōp′ər) *n.* a person who drinks a great deal of alcoholic liquor. [< *tope* drink habitually; origin uncertain]

top–flight (top′flīt′) *adj.* superior; of the highest excellence.

top·gal·lant (top′gal′ənt *or* tə gal′ənt) *n., adj.* —*n.* the mast or sail above the topmast; the third section of a mast above the deck. —*adj.* next above the topmast.

top hat a tall, black silk hat worn by men in formal clothes. See **hat** for picture.

top–heav·y (top′hev′ē) *adj.* 1 too heavy at the top. 2 overcapitalized, as a business corporation. 3 having too many officials of high rank: *a department top-heavy with full professors.*

To·phet (tō′fit) *n.* hell. [< Hebrew *Topheth,* a proper name]

to·pi·ar·y (tō′pěr er′ē) *adj., n., pl.* -ar·ies. —*adj. Gardening.* 1 trimmed or clipped into figures or designs: *topiary shrubs.* 2 of or having to do with such trimming. —*n.* 1 the art or practice of such trimming. 2 a topiary garden. [< F *topiare,* ult. < L *topia* fancy gardening < Gk. *topos* place]

top·ic (top′ik) *n.* 1 a subject that people think, write, or talk about: *The main topics at the dinner party were the weather and the election.* 2 a short phrase or sentence used in an outline to give the main point of a part of a speech, writing, etc. [sing. of *topics* < L *topica* < Gk. (*ta*) *topika,* a study of logical and rhetorical commonplaces (by Aristotle) < *topos* place]
☞ *Syn.* 1. See note at **subject.**

top·i·cal (top′ə kəl) *adj.* 1 having to do with topics of the day; of current or local interest. 2 of or using topics; having to do with the topics of a speech, writing, etc. 3 of or designed for a particular part of the body; local: *a topical medicine.*

top·knot (top′not′) *n.* 1 a knot or tuft of hair on the top of the head of a person or animal. 2 a plume or crest of feathers on the head of a bird.

top·less (top′ləs) *adj.* 1 having no top: *a topless table.* 2 wearing no clothes on the upper part of the body: *a topless waitress.* 3 *Informal.* of a restaurant, etc., featuring topless waitresses, dancers, etc. 4 *Archaic.* so high or tall that the top cannot be seen.

top–lev·el (top′lev′əl) *adj. Informal.* of the highest importance, authority, etc.: *top-level decisions.*

top·loft·y (top′lof′tē) *adj. Informal.* lofty in character or manner; haughty; pompous; pretentious.

top·mast (top′mast′ *or* top′məst) *n.* the second section of a mast above the deck. See **mast¹** for picture.

top·most (top′mōst′) *adj.* highest.

top–notch (top′noch′) *adj. Informal.* first-rate; best possible.

to·pog·ra·pher (tə pog′rə fər) *n.* a person trained in topography, especially one whose work it is.

top·o·graph·ic (top′ə graf′ik) *adj.* topographical.

top·o·graph·i·cal (top′ə graf′ə kəl) *adj.* of or having to do with topography. A topographical map shows mountains, rivers, etc. —**top′o·graph′i·cal·ly,** *adv.*

to·pog·ra·phy (tə pog′rə fē) *n., pl.* -phies. 1 the art or practice of detailed description or mapping of the natural and man-made features of a region or place. 2 a detailed description of the surface features of a place or region. 3 the surface features of a place or region. The topography of a region includes hills, valleys, streams,

lakes, bridges, tunnels, roads, etc. **4** topographical surveying. [< LL < Gk. *topographia* < *topos* place + *graphein* write]

to·pon·o·my (tə pon′ə mē) *n.* **1** the study of the place names of a region, country, etc. **2** a register of such names. [< Gk. *topos* place + *onyma* name]

top·per (top′ər) *n.* **1** *Slang.* an excellent, first-rate person or thing. **2** *Informal.* top hat. **3** *Informal.* topcoat.

top·ping (top′ing) *adj., n.* —*adj. Brit. Informal.* excellent; first-rate. —*n.* **1** something that forms a top, such as a garnish placed on food to add flavor or for decoration: *pudding with a topping of whipped cream, a cake with a crumb topping.* **2 toppings,** *pl.* branches, stems, etc. cut off in topping trees or plants.

top·ple (top′əl) *v.* **-pled, -pling. 1** fall forward; tumble down: *The chimney toppled over on the roof.* **2** throw over or down; overturn: *The wrestler toppled his opponent.* **3** hang over in an unsteady way: *beneath toppling crags.* [frequentative of *top*, *v.* < *top¹*, *n.*]

tops (tops) *adj., n. Slang.* —*adj.* of the highest degree in quality, excellence, popularity, etc. (*never used before a noun*): *She's tops in her field.* —*n.*
the tops, an excellent person or thing of its kind.

top·sail (top′sāl′ *or* top′səl) *n.* the second sail above the deck on a mast.

top–se·cret (top′sē′krit) *adj.* of utmost secrecy; extremely confidential.

top·side (top′sīd′) *n., adv.* —*n.* **1** Often, **topsides,** *pl.* **a** the top or upper portion of a ship's sides above the water line. **b** the upper part of a ship, as distinct from the hold, engine room, etc. **2** *Brit.* the outer side of a joint of beef. —*adv.* Often, **topsides, 1** to or on the bridge or an upper deck; on deck. **2** *Informal.* on top; up above.

top·soil (top′soil′) *n.* surface soil suitable for growing plants in: *People buy topsoil for gardens and lawns.*

top·stitch (top′stich′) *v.* decorate or finish with topstitching.

top·stitch·ing (top′stich′ing) *n.* a decorative line of stitching on the outside of a garment near an edge or seam: *The jacket has topstitching around the collar and down the front.*

top·sy–tur·vy (top′sē tėr′vē) *adv., adj., n., pl.* **-vies.** —*adv. or adj.* **1** upside down. **2** in confusion or disorder. —*n.* confusion; disorder. [probably ult. < *top¹* + *tirve* overturn, related to OE *tearflian* roll over]

toque (tōk) *n.* **1** a hat with no brim or with very little brim. **2** tuque. [< F]

to·rah *or* **to·ra** (tô′rə) *n.* **1** in Jewish usage, a doctrine, teaching, or law. **2 the Torah,** the law of Moses; Pentateuch. [< Hebrew]

torch (tôrch) *n.* **1** a light to be carried around or stuck in a holder on a wall. A piece of pine wood makes a good torch. **2** a device for producing a very hot flame, used especially to burn off paint, to solder metal, and to melt metal; blowtorch. **3** *Brit.* flashlight. **4** something thought of as a source of enlightenment: *the torch of civilization.*
carry a (or the) torch, a *Slang.* be in love; especially, suffer unrequited love: *He has been carrying the torch for her for months.* **b** *Informal.* crusade for; support a cause.
[ME < OF *torche*, probably ult. < L *torquere* twist] —**torch′like′,** *adj.*

torch·bear·er (tôrch′ber′ər) *n.* **1** one who carries a torch. **2** one who spreads the light of knowledge, civilization, etc. **3** *Informal.* one who is prominent in support of a crusade, a cause, or an individual.

torch·light (tôrch′līt′) *n.* the light of a torch or torches.

tor·chon lace (tôr′shon) **1** a handmade linen lace with loosely twisted threads in simple open patterns. **2** a machine-made imitation of this in linen or cotton. [< F *torchon* dish cloth]

tore (tôr) *v.* pt. of **tear².**

tor·e·a·dor (tôr′ē ə dôr′) *n.* bullfighter. [< Sp. *toreador*, ult. < *toro* bull < L *taurus*]

The torii marking the entrance to the Shinto shrine of Itsukushima on the island of Itsukushima, Japan. It is made of camphor wood.

to·ri·i (tô′rē ē′) *n., pl.* **-ri·i.** in Japan, a gateway at the entrance to

hat, āge, fär; let, ēqual, tėrm; it, īce
hot, ōpen, ôrder; oil, out; cup, pút, rüle,
əbove, takən, pencəl, lemən, circəs

ch, child; ng, long; sh, ship
th, thin; ᴛʜ, then; zh, measure

a Shinto temple, built of two uprights and two crosspieces. [< Japanese]

tor·ment (*v.* tôr ment′; *n.* tôr′ment) *v., n.* —*v.* **1** cause very great pain to. **2** worry or annoy very much: *He torments everyone with silly questions.*
—*n.* **1** a cause of very great pain. Instruments of torture were torments. **2** very great pain. **3** a cause of very much worry or annoyance. [ME < OF *tormenter*, ult. < L *tormentum*, originally, twisted sling < *torquere* twist]
☛ **Syn.** *v.* **1. Torment, torture** = cause physical or mental pain or suffering that is hard to bear. **Torment** = hurt or harm again and again and cause sharp, severe pain that continues or is constantly repeated: *He is tormented by a racking cough.* **Torture** = torment so severely that the victim twists and turns in agony, and often suggests a deliberate purpose, such as love of cruelty, hatred, attempt to force a confession, etc.: *We do not believe in torturing prisoners.*

tor·men·tor *or* **tor·ment·er** (tôr men′tər) *n.* a person or thing that torments.

torn (tôrn) *v.* pp. of **tear².**

tor·na·do (tôr nā′dō) *n., pl.* **-does** *or* **-dos. 1** a violent, destructive kind of cyclone only a few hundred metres to a few kilometres wide, seen as a slender, funnel-shaped, whirling cloud that moves across the land. **2** any whirlwind or hurricane. **3** a violent outburst. [alteration of Sp. *tronada* < *tronar* thunder]

tor·pe·do (tôr pē′dō) *n., pl.* **-does;** *v.* **-doed, -do·ing.** —*n.* **1** a large, cigar-shaped shell that contains explosives and travels by its own power. Torpedoes are sent under water to blow up enemy ships. **2** a submarine mine, shell, etc. that explodes when hit. **3** an explosive put on a railway track that makes a loud noise for a signal when a wheel of the engine runs over it. **4** a kind of firework that explodes when it is thrown against something hard. **5** an electric ray, especially any of the genus *Torpedo.*
—*v.* **1** attack or destroy with a torpedo. **2** set off a torpedo in or against. **3** bring completely to an end; destroy: *torpedo a peace conference.* [< L *torpedo* the electric ray (a fish), originally, numbness < *torpere* be numb]

torpedo boat a small, fast warship designed for firing torpedoes.

tor·pid (tôr′pid) *adj.* **1** lacking in vigor; dull or sluggish: *a torpid mind.* **2** dormant, as a hibernating animal. **3** numb. [< L *torpidus* < *torpere* be numb] —**tor′pid·ly,** *adv.* —**tor′pid·ness,** *n.*

tor·pid·i·ty (tôr pid′ə tē) *n.* the quality or state of being torpid.

tor·por (tôr′pər) *n.* **1** a state of being dormant or inactive. **2** sluggishness or dullness. [< L *torpor* < *torpere* be numb]

torque (tôrk) *n.* **1** a force that produces rotation. The engine of a motor vehicle transmits torque to the axle. **2** a necklace of twisted metal, especially such necklaces worn by the ancient Celts. [< L *torques* twisted neck chain < *torquere* twist]

tor·re·fy (tôr′ə fī′) *v.* **-fied, -fy·ing.** dry or parch with heat: *a torrefied drug, torrefied ores.* [< L *torrefacere* < *torrere* parch + *facere* make]

tor·rent (tôr′ənt) *n.* **1** a violent, rushing stream of liquid, especially water or lava. **2** any violent, rushing stream or flood: *a torrent of abuse.* [< L *torrens, -entis* boiling, parching]

tor·ren·tial (tô ren′shəl) *adj.* of, caused by, or like a torrent: *torrential rains, a torrential flow of words.* —**tor·ren′tial·ly,** *adv.*

tor·rid (tôr′id) *adj.* **1** very hot: *a torrid climate.* **2** passionate; intense: *torrid love letters.* [< L *torridus* < *torrere* parch]

tor·rid·i·ty (tô rid′ə tē) *n.* extreme heat.

Torrid Zone the region comprising the low latitudes, between the Tropic of Cancer and the Tropic of Capricorn, forming part of a now obsolete classification system for world climate zones. See also **Frigid Zone, Temperate Zone.**

tor·sion (tôr′shən) *n.* **1** the act or process of twisting or wrenching by turning one end of something while the other end is held fast or twisted in the opposite direction. **2** the state of being twisted. **3** the torque exerted by a body being twisted. [ME < OF < LL *torsio, -onis* < L *torquere* twist]

tor·sion·al (tôr′shən əl) *adj.* of, having to do with, or resulting from torsion.

tor·so (tôr′sō) *n., pl.* **-sos. 1** the trunk or body of a statue without any head, arms, or legs. **2** the trunk of the human body. **3** something left mutilated or unfinished. [< Ital. *torso*, originally, stalk < L < Gk. *thyrsos* wand]

tort (tôrt) *n. Law.* any civil, as opposed to criminal, wrong (except for certain cases involving a breach of contract) for which the law requires damages: *If a person's automobile breaks a fence, he has committed a tort against the owner.* [ME < OF < Med.L *tortum* injustice < L *torquere* turn awry, twist]

tor·ti·col·lis (tôr′tə kol′əs) *n. Medicine.* wryneck.

tor·til·la (tôr tē′yə) *n.* especially in Spanish America, a thin, flat, round corn cake. [< Sp.]

tor·toise (tôr′təs) *n., pl.* **-toise** or **-tois·es. 1** a turtle, especially any land-dwelling turtle of the family Testudinidea. **2** a very slow person or thing. [ME < Med.L *tortuca*, ult. < L *torquere* twist]

tortoise beetle any of various small, often brilliantly colored, leaf-eating beetles (family Chrysomelidae) shaped somewhat like turtles.

tor·toise–shell (tôr′təs shel′ *or* tôr′təs shel′) *n.* **1** the mottled yellow-and-brown shell of some species of turtle, such as the hawksbill turtle, used for ornaments, combs, etc. **2** (*adj.*) made of or resembling tortoise-shell. **3** a breed of domestic cat, having a mottled black-and-cream coat. **4** any of various butterflies (genus *Nymphalis*) having orange-and-black wings.

tor·tu·ous (tôr′chü əs) *adj.* **1** full of twists, turns, or bends; twisting; winding; crooked. **2** mentally or morally crooked; not straightforward; devious or indirect: *tortuous reasoning.* [ME < AF < L *tortuosus*, ult. < *torquere* twist] —**tor′tu·ous·ly,** *adv.* —**tor′tu·ous·ness,** *n.*

tor·ture (tôr′chər) *n., v.* **-tured, -tur·ing.** —*n.* **1** the act or fact of inflicting extreme pain, especially to make people give evidence about crimes, or to make them confess. **2** extreme pain. **3** something that causes extreme pain. **4** a violent and continuous twisting, pushing, or shaking that taxes a thing to the limit: *the torture of a boat by pounding waves.*
—*v.* **1** cause extreme pain to, especially in order to obtain evidence, a confession, etc. **2** twist the meaning of. **3** twist or force out of its natural form: *Winds tortured the trees.* **4** puzzle or perplex greatly. [< LL *tortura* < L *torquere* twist] —**tor′tur·er,** *n.*
☛ *Syn. v.* **1.** See note at **torment.**

tor·tur·ous (tôr′chər əs) *adj.* full of, involving, or causing torture.

to·rus (tô′rəs) *n., pl.* **to·ri** (tô′rī *or* tô′rē). **1** *Architecture.* a large convex moulding, commonly forming the lowest member of the base of a column. **2** *Botany.* the receptacle of a flower. **3** *Anatomy.* a rounded ridge; a protuberant part. [< L *torus,* originally, cushion, swelling]

To·ry (tô′rē) *n., pl.* **-ries;** *adj.* —*n.* **1** in Canada, a member or supporter of the Progressive Conservative Party: *His mother is a Tory.* **2** in Britain, originally, a member of the political party that favored royal power and the established church and that opposed change. Strictly speaking, there is no Tory party in modern Britain, although members of the Conservative Party are often called Tories. **3** *U.S.* during the American Revolution, a person who supported continued allegiance to Britain; Loyalist. **4** Often, **tory,** a person who has extremely conservative political or economic principles. —*adj.* of or having to do with the Tories or their policies: *a strong Tory opposition.* [< Irish *tóraí* persecuted person (used of Irishmen dispossessed by the English in the 17th c.), outlaw, originally meaning "pursuer"]

To·ry·ism (tô′rē iz′əm) *n.* **1** the principles and practices of the Tories. **2** the fact or state of being a Tory.

toss (tos) *v., n.* —*v.* **1** throw lightly with the palm upward; cast; fling: *toss a ball.* **2** throw about; pitch about: *The ship was tossed by the heavy waves.* **3** lift quickly; throw upward: *She tossed her head. He was tossed by the bull.* **4** mix the ingredients of lightly: *to toss a salad.* **5** throw a coin to decide something by the side that falls upward. **6** throw oneself about in bed; roll restlessly. **7** fling oneself: *He tossed out of the room in anger.*
toss off, a do or make quickly and easily. **b** drink all at once: *He tossed off a whole glass of whisky.*
—*n.* **1** the distance to which something is or can be tossed. **2** a throw; tossing. [? < Scand.; cf. dial. Norwegian *tossa* strew]
☛ *Syn. v.* **1.** See note at **throw.**

toss–up (tos′up′) *n.* **1** a tossing of a coin to decide something. **2** an even chance: *It was a toss-up whether he or his brother would get the nomination.*

tost (tost) *v. Poetic.* a pt. and a pp. of **toss.**

tot (tot) *n.* **1** a little child. **2** *Esp.Brit.* a small portion of alcoholic liquor. [origin uncertain]

to·tal (tō′təl) *adj., n., v.* **-talled** or **-taled, -tal·ling** or **-tal·ing.**
—*adj.* **1** whole, especially having all parts or elements included: *The total cost of the furnishings will be $10 000.* **2** complete; absolute: *The lights went out and we were in total darkness.*

—*n.* the whole amount; sum: *His expenses reached a total of $100.*
—*v.* **1** find the sum of; add: *Total that column of figures.* **2** reach an amount of; amount to: *The money spent yearly on chewing gum totals millions of dollars.* **3** *Slang.* wreck completely: *Her car was totalled in the accident.* [ME < OF < Med.L *totalis* < L *totus* all] —**to′tal·ly,** *adv.*

to·tal·i·sa·tor (tō′tə lə zā′tər *or* tō′tə lī zā′tər) See **totalizator.**

to·tal·i·tar·i·an (tō tal′ə ter′ē ən) *adj., n.* —*adj.* **1** of, having to do with, or designating a form of government in which a centralized state authority permits no competing political group and exercises strict control over economic, social, and cultural aspects of life. **2** supporting or favoring such a form of government. —*n.* a person who supports or practises totalitarianism.

to·tal·i·tar·i·an·ism (tō tal′ə ter′ē ən iz′əm) *n.* **1** a totalitarian system of government. **2** the political principle that the individual citizen should be under the complete control of a government or ruler.

to·tal·i·ty (tō tal′ə tē) *n., pl.* **-ties. 1** a total number or amount; whole; sum. **2** the quality or state of being total; entirety. **3** the total eclipse of the sun or moon or the period during which this takes place.

to·tal·i·za·tor (tō′tə lə zā′tər *or* tō′tə lī zā′tər) *n.* an apparatus for registering and indicating totals of operations, measurements, etc., especially one used for pari-mutuel betting at horse races.

to·tal·ly (tō′təl ē) *adv.* wholly; entirely; completely: *The experiment was totally successful.*

total recall the ability to remember clearly every detail about an experience or situation in the past.

total war a war in which all the resources of a nation are used, and in which attack is made not only on the armed forces of the opponent, but also (subject to certain limitations) on all its people and property.

tote[1] (tōt) *v.* **tot·ed, tot·ing;** *n.* —*v. Informal.* carry; haul. —*n.* **1** a carrying or hauling. **2** the distance of this; a haul: *a long tote.* [origin uncertain]

tote[2] (tōt) *n. Slang.* totalizator.

tote bag a large handbag of canvas, straw, vinyl, etc., usually open at the top, used for carrying small packages, clothing, etc.

to·tem (tō′təm) *n.* **1** among Amerindian peoples of the northern Pacific coast, an animal or plant taken as the emblem of a tribe, clan, or family. **2** among many peoples throughout the world, a creature or object that is associated with their ancestral traditions and is looked on with awe and reverence by a tribe, clan, etc.: *Many peoples never kill the animals that are their totems.* **3** a representation of a totem, usually carved or painted. **4** anything that is used as an emblem or symbol. [< Algonquian]

to·tem·ic (tō tem′ik) *adj.* of or having to do with a totem or totemism.

to·tem·ism (tō′təm iz′əm) *n.* **1** belief in a mystical relationship or kinship between human beings and animals and plants, usually taking the form of a special reverence felt by a people or a person for particular creatures or objects. **2** the use of totems to distinguish tribes, clans, or families.

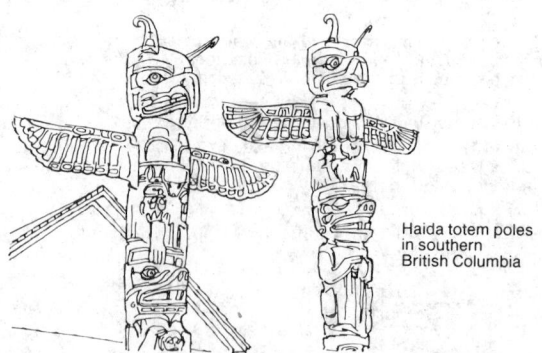

Haida totem poles in southern British Columbia

totem pole a large upright log carved and painted with representations of totems, traditionally erected by many of the Amerindian peoples of the northern Pacific coast. Totem poles served as a record of the ancestry of a family and sometimes also of historical or mythological happenings.

toth·er (tuᴛн′ər) *adj.* or *pron. Dialect.* the other. [ME *thet other* the other, pronounced as *the tother*]

tot·ter (tot′ər) *v., n.* —*v.* **1** walk with shaky, unsteady steps. **2** tremble or rock as if about to fall: *The old wall tottered in the*

storm and fell. **3** become unstable; be about to fall or collapse: *The old regime was already tottering before the revolution broke out.* —*n.* an unsteady way of walking. [ME; ? < Scand.; cf. dial. Norwegian *totra* quiver] —**tot′ter·er,** *n.*

tot·ter·y (tot′ər ē) *adj.* tottering; shaky.

Toucan: a keel-billed toucan (*Ramfastos sulfuratus*), about 50 cm long including the tail. It is mainly black with a yellow face, throat, and chest.

tou·can (tü′kan *or* tü kän′) *n.* any of a family (Ramphastidae) of bright-colored birds of tropical America, having a large but very light beak. [< Carib]

touch (tuch) *v., n.* —*v.* **1** put the hand or some other part of the body on or against: *She touched the pan to see whether it was still hot.* **2** put against; make contact with: *He touched the post with his umbrella.* **3** be against; come against: *Your sleeve is touching the butter.* **4** be in contact: *Our hands touched.* **5 a** border on: *a country that touches the mountains on the north.* **b** in geometry, be tangent to. **6** strike lightly or gently: *She touched the strings of the harp.* **7** injure slightly: *The flowers were touched by the frost.* **8** affect with some feeling: *The sad story touched us.* **9** affect in some way by contact: *a metal so hard that a file cannot touch it.* **10** *Informal.* make slightly insane. **11** have to do with; concern: *The matter touches your interest.* **12** speak of; deal with; refer to; treat lightly: *Our conversation touched on many subjects.* **13** handle; use: *He won't touch liquor or tobacco.* **14** reach; come up to: *His head almost touches the top of the doorway. Nobody in our class can touch her in music.* **15** stop at; visit in passing: *The ship touched port.* **16** make a brief stop: *Most ships touch at that port.* **17** *Slang.* borrow from: *to touch a man for a quarter.* **18** compare with; rival: *No one in our class can touch her in music.* **19** mark slightly or superficially, as with some color: *a sky touched with pink.* **20** mark, draw, or delineate, as with strokes of the brush, pencil, etc.
touch down, a land an aircraft. **b** *Football.* touch the ground with (the ball) behind the opposing team's goal line.
touch off, a represent exactly or cleverly. **b** cause to go off; fire: *The new tax touched off a rebellion.*
touch on or **upon, a** speak of; treat lightly: *Our conversation touched on many subjects.* **b** come close to.
touch up, a change a little; improve: *He touched up a photograph.* **b** rouse.
—*n.* **1** a touching or being touched: *A bubble bursts at a touch.* **2** the sense by which a person perceives things by feeling, handling, or coming against them: *The blind have a keen touch.* **3** a coming or being in contact: *the touch of their hands.* **4** communication or connection: *A newspaper keeps one in touch with the world. He has been out of touch with his mother since he left home.* **5** a slight amount; little bit: *We had a touch of frost.* **6** a stroke with a brush, pencil, pen, etc.: *With a few skilful touches the artist finished my picture.* **7** a detail in any artistic work: *a story with charming poetic touches.* **8** a manner of striking, or depressing, keys on a keyboard: *a pianist with an excellent touch. She types with an uneven touch.* **9** of a keyboard instrument or machine, the resistance that the keys offer to the fingers: *A piano should not have too light a touch.* **10** a distinctive manner or quality: *The work showed an expert's touch.* **11** a slight attack: *a touch of fever.* **12 a** an official mark put on gold, etc. after testing. **b** a stamp for impressing such a mark. **c** the quality so tested. **13** quality in general. **14** any test. **15** *Slang.* **a** the act of soliciting or getting money as a loan or a gift from a person. **b** money got in this way. **c** a person from whom one has got or expects to get money in this way: *He's a soft touch.* **16** *Football, soccer, etc.* the part of the field, including the sidelines, lying outside of the field of play. [ME < OF *tuchier* < VL *toccare* strike (as a bell); originally imitative] —**touch′a·ble,** *adj.* —**touch′er,** *n.*

touch and go an uncertain or risky situation: *So far it's been touch and go, but we're still hoping for the best.*

touch–and–go (tuch′ən gō′) *adj.* uncertain; risky.

touch·back (tuch′bak′) *n.* *American football.* the act of touching the ball to the ground behind one's own goal line when driven there by the other side.

touch·down (tuch′doun′) *n.* **1** *Football.* **a** the act of scoring by being in possession of the ball on or behind the opponents' goal line. **b** the score made in this way. **2** the landing or moment of landing of an aircraft.

tou·ché (tü shā′) *n., interj.* —*n.* a touch by an opponent's

hat, āge, fär; let, ēqual, tèrm; it, īce
hot, ōpen, ôrder; oil, out; cup, pút, rüle,
ə*bove, tak*ə*n, penc*ə*l, lem*ə*n, circ*ə*s

ch, child; ng, long; sh, ship
th, thin; ᵺ, then; zh, measure

weapon in fencing. —*interj.* an exclamation acknowledging a clever reply or a point well made in discussion. [< F]

touched (tucht) *adj.* **1** stirred emotionally, especially by gratitude or sympathy; moved: *He was touched by their offer to help.* **2** *Informal.* slightly unbalanced mentally.

touch football a variety of football, usually played informally and without protective equipment, in which the person carrying the ball is touched rather than tackled.

touch·hole (tuch′hōl′) *n.* the small opening in early cannon or firearms through which the gunpowder inside was set on fire.

touch·ing (tuch′ing) *adj., prep.* —*adj.* arousing tender feeling. —*prep.* concerning; about. —**touch′ing·ly,** *adv.*

touch·line (tuch′līn′) *n.* *Rugger and soccer.* a line along one side of the playing field; sideline.

touch–me–not (tuch′mē not′) *n.* any of several wild species of impatiens, such as *Impatiens capensis* or *I. pallida*, found in wet places and woods in North America and Europe.

touch·stone (tuch′stōn′) *n.* **1** a dark stone containing silica, such as jasper or basalt, formerly used to test the purity of gold or silver by the color of the streak produced on the stone by rubbing it with the metal. **2** any test or standard for determining the genuineness or value of something: *His work has for many years been the touchstone of excellence in architecture.*

touch–ty·ping (tuch′tī′ping) *n.* a method of typing without looking at the keyboard by always using a particular finger to strike a particular key. —**touch–type,** *v.*

touch–typ·ist (tuch′tīp′ist) *n.* a person skilled in touch-typing.

touch–wood (tuch′wùd′) *n.* **1** a substance prepared from certain types of fungus (e.g. genus *Formes*) found on tree trunks, used as tinder. **2** punk[1].

touch·y (tuch′ē) *adj.* **touch·i·er, touch·i·est. 1** apt to take offence at trifles; too sensitive. **2** requiring skill in handling; ticklish; precarious: *It was a touchy situation; he didn't know whether to stay or leave.* **3** of a part or the body, very sensitive to touch: *The skin around the wound is very touchy.* —**touch′i·ly,** *adv.* —**touch′i·ness,** *n.*

tough (tuf) *adj., n.* —*adj.* **1** bending without breaking: *Leather is tough.* **2** hard to cut, tear, or chew: *The steak was so tough he couldn't eat it.* **3** stiff; sticky: *tough clay.* **4** strong; hardy: *a tough plant. Donkeys are tough little animals and can carry big loads.* **5** hard; difficult: *tough work.* **6** hard to bear; bad; unpleasant: *A spell of tough luck discouraged him.* **7** hard to influence; stubborn: *a tough customer.* **8** severe; violent; strenuous: *Football is a tough game.* **9** rough; disorderly: *a tough neighborhood.* —*n.* a rough person; rowdy. [OE *tōh*] —**tough′ly,** *adv.* —**tough′ness,** *n.*

tough·en (tuf′ən) *v.* **1** make tough or tougher. **2** become tough or tougher. —**tough′en·er,** *n.*

tou·la·di (tü′lə dē′) *n., pl.* **-adi** or **-adis.** *Cdn.* lake trout. [< Cdn. F *touladi* < Algonquian (Micmac)]

tou·pee (tü pā′) *n.* a wig or patch of false hair worn to cover a bald spot. [< F *toupet* < OF *toupe* tuft < Gmc.]

tour (tür) *n., v.* —*n.* **1** a long journey through a country or countries, in which one returns to the starting point: *a European tour.* **2** a regular spell or turn of work or duty, or the length of time such a spell lasts: *Her last tour of duty was in France.* **3** a short trip or walk around, as for inspection: *a tour of the boat.*
on tour, of a theatre company, orchestra, entertainer, etc., travelling from place to place, fulfilling engagements: *The choir is on tour for six months of the year.*
the grand tour, a tour through France, Germany, Italy, and Switzerland. The grand tour was formerly considered essential as the finishing course in the education of British young men of good family.
—*v.* **1** travel from place to place: *He's touring next winter with the Canadian Opera Company.* **2** travel through: *Last year they toured Europe.* **3** *Theatre.* take (a play, etc.) on tour. **4** go through (a building or other structure) to see its different parts, exhibits, etc.: *to tour a museum, to tour a manufacturing plant.* [< F < L *tornus* turner's wheel, lathe < Gk. *tornos.* Related to TURN.]

tour de force (tür′də fôrs′) *pl.* **tours de force** (tür′də fôrs′). **1** a notable feat of strength, skill, or ingenuity. **2** something done that is merely clever or ingenious: *His later work showed that his first*

novel was little more than a tour de force. [< F, literally, feat of strength]

touring car an open automobile, especially of the 1920's and 1930's, usually seating five or six people.

tour·ism (tür′iz əm) *n.* **1** touring or travelling as a pastime or recreation. **2** the business of providing services for tourists.

tour·ist (tür′ist *or* tür′ist) *n.* **1** a person travelling for pleasure. **2** tourist class. **3** (*adj.*) of or for tourists.

tourist class the lowest class of accommodation for passengers on a ship, train, etc.; economy class.

tourist court *Esp.U.S.* motel.

tourist trap a place or business establishment that exploits tourists.

tour·ist·y (tür′is tē) *adj. Informal, often derogatory.* **1** like or characteristic of a tourist: *She was wearing a very touristy outfit.* **2** catering to or often visited by tourists: *They tried to avoid the touristy places on their trip.*

tour·ma·lin (tür′mə lin) *n.* tourmaline.

tour·ma·line (tür′mə lin *or* tür′mə lēn) *n.* **1** a complex silicate of aluminum and boron occurring in various colors. The transparent varieties of tourmaline are used for gems. **2** a gem made from this stone. [< F < Singhalese *toramalli*]

tour·na·ment (tėr′nə mənt *or* tür′nə mənt) *n.* **1** a series of contests testing the skill of many persons: *a golf tournament. His uncle won the chess tournament.* **2** in the Middle Ages: **a** a contest between two groups of knights on horseback who fought for a prize. **b** a series of knightly jousts, sports, etc. occurring at one time at a particular place. [ME < OF *torneiement* < *tornei.* See TOURNEY.]

tour·ney (tėr′nē *or* tür′nē) *n., pl.* **-neys;** *v.* **-neyed, -ney·ing.** —*n.* tournament. —*v.* take part in a tournament. [ME < OF *tornei,* ult. < L *tornus.* See TURN.]

tour·ni·quet (tür′nə ket′ *or* tür′nə kā′, tėr′nə ket′ *or* tėr′nə kā′) *n.* a device for stopping bleeding by compressing a blood vessel. A bandage tightened by twisting with a stick may be used as a tourniquet. [< F *tourniquet* < *tourner* to turn]

tour·tière (tür tyer′) *n. Cdn.* a pie made with ground pork, often mixed with some veal or chicken, associated especially with French Canada. [Cdn.F]

tou·sle (tou′zəl) *v.* **-sled, -sling;** *n.* —*v.* put into disorder; make untidy; muss: *She tousled her brother's hair to tease him.* —*n.* a disordered or tangled mass of hair, etc. [ME *touse(n)*]

tout (tout) *v., n. Informal.* —*v.* **1** try to get (customers, jobs, votes, etc.). **2** urge betting on (a race horse) by claiming to have special information. **3** *Esp.Brit.* spy out (information about race horses) for use in betting. **4** praise highly and insistently. —*n.* a person who touts. [< var. of OE *tȳtan* peep out] —**tout′er,** *n.*

tout à fait (tü′tä fe′) *French.* entirely; completely.

tout de suite (tüt swēt′) *French.* immediately; at once.

tout en·sem·ble (tü tän sänbl′) *French.* **1** all together. **2** the general effect; the assemblage of parts or details, considered as forming a whole.

tout le monde (tü lə mônd′) *French.* the whole world; everybody.

tow¹ (tō) *v., n.* —*v.* pull by a rope, chain, etc.: *The tug is towing three barges.* —*n.* **1** the act or an instance of towing: *He charges seven dollars for a tow.* **2** the fact or condition of being towed. **3** that which is towed: *Each tug had a tow of three barges.* **4** something used for towing: *a ski tow.*
in tow, a in the state of being towed: *The launch had a sailboat in tow.* **b** under protection or guidance: *He was taken in tow by his aunt as soon as he arrived.* **c** under someone's influence; in the position of follower or dependent: *The movie producer arrived at the reception with several admirers in tow.*
[OE *togian* drag]
☛ *Hom.* **toe.**

tow² (tō) *n.* **1** the coarse, broken fibres of flax, hemp, etc., prepared for spinning. **2** (*adj.*) made from tow. [OE *tōw-* a spinning]
☛ *Hom.* **toe.**

tow·age (tō′ij) *n.* **1** towing or being towed. **2** a charge for towing.

to·ward (*prep.* tôrd *or* tə wôrd′; *adj.* tôrd) *prep., adj.* —*prep.* **1** in the direction of: *He walked toward the north.* **2** with respect to; regarding; about; concerning: *What is his attitude toward war?* **3** near: *It must be toward four o'clock.* **4** as a help to; for: *Will you give something toward our new hospital?*

—*adj.* **1** about to happen; impending. **2** *Archaic.* promising, hopeful, or apt; docile. [OE *tōweard* < *tō* to + *-weard* -ward]

to·wards (tôrdz *or* tə wôrdz′) *prep.* toward.

tow·boat (tō′bōt′) *n.* tugboat.

tow·el (tou′əl) *n., v.* **-elled** *or* **-eled, -el·ling** *or* **-el·ing.** —*n.* an absorbent piece of cloth or paper for wiping and drying something wet.
throw *or* **toss in the towel,** *Informal.* admit defeat.
—*v.* dry with a towel. [ME < OF *toaille* < Gmc.]

tow·el·ling *or* **tow·el·ing** (tou′əl ing) *n.* material used for towels, especially cotton or linen.

tow·er (tou′ər) *n., v.* —*n.* **1** a high structure that may be completely walled in or may consist only of a framework of metal or wood, and that may stand alone or form part of a church, castle, etc.: *a lookout tower, a bell tower, a water tower.* **2** a fortress or prison consisting of or including a tower: *the Tower of London.* **3** a very tall building; highrise: *an office tower.* **4** a person or thing that acts as a defence, protection, or support: *He proved to be a tower of strength during the emergency.*
—*v.* rise or reach to a great height: *He was a giant of a man, towering over all his friends.* [ME < OF < L *turris*]

tow·er·ing (tou′ər ing) *adj.* **1** very high. **2** very tall: *a towering basketball player.* **3** very great: *Making electricity from atomic power is a towering achievement.* **4** very violent: *a towering rage.*

Tower of London (lun′dən) an ancient palace-fortress in London. The present building dates back to William the Conqueror. It has been used as a palace, prison, mint, and arsenal.

tow·er·y (tou′ər ē) *adj.* **1** having towers. **2** towering; lofty.

tow·head (tō′hed′) *n.* **1** a person having light, pale-yellow hair. **2** a head of light-colored hair.

tow·head·ed (tō′hed′id) *adj.* having light, pale-yellow hair.

tow·hee (tou′hē *or* tō′hē) *n.* **1** a long-tailed North American finch (*Pipilo erythrophthalmus*) having a call that sounds somewhat like its name. The male has a black head and back, reddish sides, and a white abdomen. Also called **rufous-sided towhee.** **2** any of various other North American finches (genera *Pipilo* and *Chlorura*). [imitative of its call]

tow·line (tō′līn′) *n.* a rope, chain, etc. for towing.

town (toun) *n.* **1** a large group of houses, stores, schools, churches, etc. that together with the people living there forms a community with fixed boundaries and its own local government. A town is usually smaller than a city but larger than a village. **2** any large place with many people living in it: *Toronto is an exciting town.* **3** the people of a town: *The whole town was having a holiday.* **4** the part of a town or city where the stores and office buildings are: *Let's go into town.*
go to town, *Informal.* **a** achieve success. **b** do or go through thoroughly: *The hungry girls really went to town on that pie.*
in town, in a specified town or city: *He is not in town today.*
on the town, a out on the town. **b** *Brit. Archaic.* supported by a town; on charity.
out of town, happening, located, etc. outside a specified town or city: *The restaurant is a short distance out of town.*
out on the town, out for entertainment and pleasure as available in a city or town.
paint the town red, *Slang.* go on a wild spree or party; celebrate in a noisy manner.
[OE *tūn*]

town clerk an official who keeps the records of a town.

town crier a public crier in a city or town.

town hall the headquarters of a town's government.

town house a house in town, belonging to a person who also has a house in the country.

town·house (toun′hous′) *n.* a house that is one of a row of attached houses two or more storeys high, each having its own entrance from the street and a small yard.

town meeting a general meeting of the inhabitants of the town.

towns·folk (tounz′fōk′) *n.pl.* the people of a town.

town·ship (toun′ship) *n.* **1** in Canada and the United States, a division of a county having certain powers of government; municipality. **2** a land-survey area on which later subdivisions may be based. In the Prairie Provinces, a township is an area of 36 square miles (about 93 km²), divided into 36 sections. *Abbrev.:* Tp., tp., *or* twp. [OE *tunscipe* < *tūn* town + *-scipe* -ship]

town·site (toun′sīt′) *n.* **1** the site of a town. **2** a piece of land being developed or to be developed as a town.

towns·man (tounz′mən) *n., pl.* **-men. 1** a native or resident of a city or town. **2** a person who lives in one's own town.

towns·peo·ple (tounz′pē′pəl) *n.pl.* the people of a town.

towns·wom·an (tounz′wùm′ən) *n., pl.* **-wom·en. 1** a woman who is a native or inhabitant of a city or town. **2** a woman who lives in one's own town.

tow·path (tō′path′) *n.* a path along the bank of a canal or river for use in towing boats.

tow·rope (tō′rōp′) *n.* a rope used for towing.

tow truck a truck equipped for towing away disabled or illegally parked vehicles.

tox·a·phene (tok′sə fēn′) *n.* a chlorinated camphene insecticide used for forage crops. *Formula:* $C_{10}H_{10}Cl_8$ [< Trademark]

tox·e·mi·a (toks ē′mē ə) *n.* a form of blood poisoning, especially one in which the toxins produced by certain micro-organisms enter the blood. Also, **toxaemia.** [< NL *toxaemia* < L *toxicum* poison (See TOXIC) + Gk. *haima* blood]

tox·e·mic (toks ē′mik) *adj.* **1** of or having to do with toxemia. **2** suffering from toxemia. Also, **toxaemic.**

tox·ic (tok′sik) *adj.* **1** of, having to do with, or caused by a poison or toxin: *a toxic reaction.* **2** poisonous: *Automobile exhaust fumes are toxic.* [< Med.L *toxicus* < L *toxicum* poison < Gk. *toxikon* (*pharmakon*) (poison) for shooting arrows < *toxon* bow]
—tox′i·cal·ly, *adv.*

tox·ic·i·ty (toks is′ə tē) *n., pl.* **-ties.** the quality or state of being toxic.

tox·i·co·log·i·cal (tok′sə kə loj′ə kəl) *adj.* of or having to do with the science of poisons.

tox·i·col·o·gist (tok′sə kol′ə jist) *n.* a person trained in toxicology, especially one whose work it is.

tox·i·col·o·gy (tok′sə kol′ə jē) *n.* the science that deals with poisons, their effects, antidotes, detection, etc. [< Gk. *toxikon* poison (see TOXIC) + E *-logy*]

tox·i·co·sis (tok′si kō′sis) *n.* any disease or diseased condition brought on by poisoning.

tox·in (tok′sən) *n.* any poisonous product of animal or vegetable metabolism, especially one of those produced by bacteria. The symptoms of a disease caused by bacteria, such as diphtheria, are due to toxins. [< *toxic*]

toy (toi) *n., v.* **—***n.* **1** something for a child to play with; plaything. **2** (*adj.*) made for use as a toy; especially, being a small model of a real thing: *a toy truck, a toy soldier.* **3** something that resembles a child's toy in being small or having little real value, usefulness, or importance, etc.: *That little calculator is nothing but a toy.* **4** (*adj.*) designating a small variety of certain breeds of dog: *a toy poodle, a toy terrier.* **5** a small breed or variety of dog: *Pekinese, pugs, and chihuahuas are toys.*
—*v.* handle or deal with in a light, careless, or trifling way (*used with* **with**): *She toyed with her beads as she talked. He has been toying with the idea of writing a book but so far has not done anything about it.* [ME *toye* play, n.; cf. Du. *tuig* tools, stuff, and G *Zeug* stuff]

to·yon (tō′yən) *n.* a shrub (*Photinia arbutifolia*) of the rose family found along the Pacific coast of North America, whose evergreen leaves and scarlet berries look much like holly. [< Am.Sp. *tollon*]

t.p. title page.

Tp. or **tp. 1** township. **2** troop.

tr. 1 transitive. **2** transpose. **3** translation; translator. **4** train.

trace¹ (trās) *n., v.* **traced, trac·ing. —***n.* **1** a sign or evidence of the existence, presence, or action of something in the past; vestige: *The explorer found traces of an ancient city.* **2** a footprint or other mark left; track; trail: *We saw traces of rabbits on the snow.* **3** a very small amount; little bit: *There wasn't a trace of grey in her hair.* **4** something marked out or drawn. **5** *Chemistry.* an indication of an amount of some constituent in a compound, usually too small to be measured.
—*v.* **1** follow by means of marks, tracks, or signs: *to trace deer.* **2** follow the course of; follow a trail of evidence to: *He traced the river to its source. He traced his family back through eight generations.* **3** find signs of; observe. **4** mark out; draw: *The spy traced a plan of the fort.* **5** copy by following the lines of: *He put thin paper over the map and traced it.* **6** decorate with tracery. **7** write, especially by forming the letters carefully or laboriously. **8** record in the form of a curving, wavy, or broken line, as a cardiograph, seismograph, etc. [ME < OF *tracier* < VL *tractiare,* ult. < L *trahere* drag]
☛ *Syn. n.* **1. Trace, vestige** = a mark or sign of what has existed or happened. **Trace** applies to any noticeable sign or mark left by something that has happened or been present: *The campers removed all traces of their fire.* **Vestige,** sometimes used as a more formal substitute especially when referring to something no longer present or existing, applies particularly to an actual remnant of something that existed in the past: *Some of our common social manners are vestiges of very old customs.*

trace² (trās) *n.* either of the two straps, ropes, or chains by which an animal pulls a wagon, carriage, etc. See **harness** for picture.

hat, āge, fär; let, ēqual, tèrm; it, īce
hot, ōpen, ôrder; oil, out; cup, pùt, rüle,
above, takən, pencəl, lemən, circəs

ch, child; ng, long; sh, ship
th, thin; ŦH, then; zh, measure

kick over the traces, throw off control; become unruly. [ME < OF *traiz,* pl. of *trait,* ult. < L *trahere* drag]

trace·a·bil·i·ty (trā′sə bil′ə tē) *n.* the quality or condition of being traceable.

trace·a·ble (trā′sə bəl) *adj.* capable of being traced.
—trace′a·bly, *adv.*

trace element any element occurring in very small amounts, especially such an element occurring in an organism and necessary to the physiological and biological processes of the organism.

trac·er (trā′sər) *n.* **1** a person whose work is tracing missing persons or property. **2** an inquiry sent from place to place to trace a missing person, letter, parcel, etc. **3** a person whose work is tracing patterns, designs, markings, etc. **4** a device or machine for making tracings of drawings, plans, etc. **5** a bullet or shell containing a substance that marks its course with a trail of smoke or fire. **6** *Chemistry.* an element (**tracer element**) or atom (**tracer atom**), usually radio-active, used in a chemical or biological process to permit the course of the process to be traced.

trac·er·y (trā′sər ē *or* trās′rē) *n., pl.* **-er·ies. 1** ornamental open-work in stone, consisting of branching or interlacing lines, especially such ornament at the top of a window in Gothic architecture. **2** any decorative pattern or natural outline suggesting this: *the tracery in a butterfly's wing. Tracery is sometimes used in embroidery.*

tra·che·a (trā′kē ə *or* trə kē′ə) *n., pl.* **tra·che·ae** (trā′kē ī *or* trə kē′ē *or* -ī). **1** the tube extending from the larynx to the bronchi; windpipe. **2** *Zoology.* one of the air-carrying tubes of the respiratory system of insects and other arthropods. **3** *Botany.* a vessel or duct serving to carry water and dissolved minerals. [< LL *trachia,* ult. < Gk. *tracheia* (*artēria*), literally, rough (artery)]

tra·che·al (trā′kē əl *or* trə kē′əl) *adj.* of or having to do with the trachea.

tra·che·o·phyte (trā′kē ə fīt′) *n.* any of a division (Tracheophyta) of plants, including club mosses, horsetails, ferns, and flowering plants, all having a vascular system for conducting food and a life cycle showing alternation of generations. [< NL *Tracheophyta* (division name) < *trache-* + Med.L *trachea* trachea + Gk. *phyton* plant]

tra·che·ot·o·my (trā′kē ot′ə mē) *n.* a surgical operation that involves cutting an opening into the trachea. [< Gk. *tracheia* trachea + *tomia* cutting]

tra·cho·ma (trə kō′mə) *n.* a contagious disease of the eye caused by a virus (*Chlamydia trachomatis*) and characterized by inflamed granulations on the inner surface of the eyelids. [< NL < Gk. *trachōma* roughness < *trachys* rough]

trac·ing (trā′sing) *n.* **1** a copy of a map, drawing, etc. made by following its lines on a transparent sheet that has been placed over it. **2** a line made by a recording instrument that registers movement. An electrocardiograph makes tracings of the contractions of the heart, which are used to diagnose heart disease.

track (trak) *n., v.* **—***n.* **1** the pair of parallel steel rails on which a locomotive, etc. runs: *The train disappeared down the track.* **2** a mark or marks left by something that has passed by: *The tires left tracks on the new asphalt. We followed the deer's tracks along the river.* **3** a path or trail: *A track runs through the woods to the farmhouse.* **4** a course for running or racing: *The school has an oval track.* **5** the sport made up of contests in running. See **track and field. 6** (*adj.*) of or for use in such sports: *track shoes.* **7** a line of motion or travel: *the track of a bullet.* **8** a course of action or way of doing: *going on in the same track year after year.* **9** a sequence or succession of events, thoughts, etc. **10** a path on a magnetic tape, disc, etc. on which sound or information is recorded. **11** a band on a phonograph record. **12** an endless belt of linked steel treads by which a bulldozer, tank, etc. moves over the ground.
in (one's) tracks, *Informal.* right where one is: *He saw the bear and stopped in his tracks.*
keep track of, keep within one's sight, knowledge, or attention: *The noise of the crowd made it difficult to keep track of what was going on.*
lose track of, fail to keep track of.
make tracks, *Informal.* go very fast; run away.
off the track, off the subject; wrong.
on the track, on the subject; right.
the beaten track, the ordinary or usual way.

—v. **1** follow by means of footprints, marks, smell, etc.: *The hunter tracked the bear and killed it.* **2** trace in any way: *to track down a criminal.* **3** make footprints or other marks on (a floor, etc.): *Don't track the floor.* **4** bring (snow or mud) into a place on one's feet: *to track mud into the house.* **5** follow and plot the course of, as by radar. **6** *Cdn.* draw or lead a canoe, boat, scow, etc. through rapids, shallows, or other difficult stretches of water by means of lines running from the craft to people on the bank or shore. [ME < OF *trac*, probably < Gmc.] —**track′er**, *n.*

track·age (trak′ij) *n.* **1** all the tracks of a railway. **2** the right of one railway to use the tracks of another. **3** the charge for this.

track and field the group of competitive athletic events performed on a running track and field next to it, including running, jumping, pole-vaulting, and throwing: *John doesn't play hockey but he's good at track and field. Joan entered several track-and-field events.* —**track-and-field**, *adj.*

tracking station any of several telemeter stations built to track the orbit of a satellite.

track·less (trak′lis) *adj.* **1** without a track; without tracks. **2** without paths or trails.

track meet a series or group of contests in track-and-field events.

tract[1] (trakt) *n.* **1** a stretch of land, water, etc.; extent; area: *A tract of desert land has little value to farmers.* **2** a system of related parts or organs in the body. The stomach and intestines are part of the digestive tract. **3** *Archaic.* a period of time. [< L *tractus*, originally, hauling < *trahere* drag. Doublet of TRAIT.]

tract[2] (trakt) *n.* a pamphlet on a religious or political subject intended to support or speak out against a particular cause or point of view. [apparently < L *tractatus* a handling, ult. < *trahere* drag]

trac·ta·bil·i·ty (trak′tə bil′ə tē) *n.* the quality or condition of being tractable.

trac·ta·ble (trak′tə bəl) *adj.* **1** easily managed or controlled; easy to deal with; docile: *Dogs are more tractable than mules.* **2** easily worked: *Copper and gold are tractable.* [< L *tractabilis* < *tractare.* See TREAT.] —**trac′ta·ble·ness**, *n.* —**trac′ta·bly**, *adv.*

trac·tile (trak′tīl or trak′təl) *adj.* capable of being drawn out to a greater length.

trac·tion (trak′shən) *n.* **1** the friction between a body and the surface on which it moves enabling the body to move without slipping: *Wheels slip on ice because there is too little traction.* **2** the kind of power used by a locomotive, streetcar, etc.: *Some railways use electric traction.* **3** the act or process of pulling a load or vehicle over a surface, or the state of being pulled. **4** the pulling of leg or arm muscles, etc. by means of a special device to relieve pressure, bring a fractured bone into place, etc., or the state of tension produced by such a device: *He spent several months in traction as a result of the accident.* [< Med.L *tractio, -onis* < L *trahere* drag]

traction engine a steam engine on wheels, used for pulling wagons, ploughs, etc. along roads or over fields.

trac·tive (trak′tiv) *adj.* pulling; used for pulling.

trac·tor (trak′tər) *n.* **1** a vehicle with a powerful gasoline or diesel engine, having four wheels or running on continuous tracks, used for pulling farm implements, wagons, etc. **2** a powerful truck having a cab for the driver, a short chassis, and no body, used to pull a large trailer or semitrailer along the highway. **3** an aircraft having the propeller in front of the engine. [< Med.L *tractor* < L *trahere* drag]

tractor swing a cat train.

trac·tor–trail·er (trak′tər trā′lər) *n.* a very large truck, consisting of a tractor (def. 2) together with a trailer or semitrailer, used for hauling freight.

tractor train a cat train.

trade (trād) *n., v.* **trad·ed**, **trad·ing.** —*n.* **1** the process of buying and selling; exchange of goods; commerce: *Canada has trade with many foreign countries.* **2** an exchange: *an even trade.* **3** *Informal.* a bargain; business deal: *He made a good trade.* **4** a kind of work; business, especially one requiring skilled mechanical work: *He is learning the carpenter's trade.* **5** people in the same kind of work or business: *the building trade.* **6** *Informal.* customers: *That store has a lot of trade.* **7 the trades**, *pl.* the trade winds.
—*v.* **1** buy and sell; exchange goods; be in commerce: *Canada trades with many foreign countries.* **2** make an exchange: *to trade seats.* **3** bargain; deal. **4** be a customer: *We've been trading at that grocery store for years.*

trade in, give an automobile, radio, etc. as part payment for something else: *She traded her old car in for a new one.*
trade off, get rid of by trading.
trade on, take advantage of: *She traded on her father's good name.*

[ME < MDu. or MLG *trade* track]

☛ *Syn. n.* **1. Trade, commerce** = the buying and selling or exchanging of goods or other commodities. **Trade** applies to the actual buying and selling, or exchange, between countries or within a country: *The Government has drawn up new agreements for trade with various countries.* **Commerce** is more general, applying to the whole business of the exchange of commodities, including both trade and transportation, especially as conducted on a large scale between different states or countries.

trade agreement 1 an agreement between nations to promote trade between them. **2** an agreement for a specified time between labor and management concerning job conditions.

trade balance the difference between the value of a country's imports and its exports; balance of trade.

trade barrier anything that restricts or limits international trade: *Tariffs or embargoes are trade barriers.*

trade book a book published for sale to the general public, through retail stores, as opposed to textbooks or other specialized books sold by mail order, etc.

trade edition an edition of a book designed for sale to the general public through retail stores, as opposed to a school text edition, etc.

trade-in (trād′in′) *n.* **1** something, such as a used appliance or car, given or accepted as part payment for a new thing of the same kind. **2** the value or price allowed by the seller on a trade-in: *The dealer gave her $600 trade-in on her old car.* **3** (*adj.*) of or as a trade-in: *My car has a trade-in value close to zero.*

trade·mark (trād′märk′) *n., v.* —*n.* a mark, picture, symbol, or name that identifies a product or service as being produced or sold by a particular company, and that is protected by law. A trademark may legally be applied only to goods or services produced or sold by the company that owns it. —*v.* **1** distinguish by means of a trademark. **2** register the trademark of.

trade name a distinctive name that identifies a product or service as being produced or sold by a particular company; brand name.

trad·er (trā′dər) *n.* **1** a person who trades; merchant. **2** a ship used in trading. **3** a person who buys and sells stocks and securities for himself rather than for customers. **4** an item of which a collector has another copy; a duplicate.

trade school a school where trades are taught.

trades·man (trādz′mən) *n., pl.* **-men.** a storekeeper; shopkeeper.

trades·peo·ple (trādz′pē′pəl) *n.pl.* storekeepers; shopkeepers.

trades union *Esp.Brit.* trade union.

trade union an association of workers in any trade or craft or group of allied trades to protect and promote their interests; labor union.

trade unionism 1 the system of having trade unions. **2** the principles, methods or practices of trade unions.

trade unionist 1 a member of a trade union. **2** a person who favors trade unionism.

trade wind a tropical wind blowing steadily toward the equator from about 30° north latitude to about 30° south latitude. North of the equator, it blows from the northeast; south of the equator, from the southeast.

trading post a store or station of a trader, especially in a remote place: *The Hudson's Bay Company operates trading posts in the North.*

trading stamp a stamp offered by a merchant to purchasers and redeemable, in certain quantities, for goods to be selected from a special list.

tra·di·tion (trə dish′ən) *n.* **1** the handing down of beliefs, opinions, customs, stories, etc. from one generation to another. **2** the body of beliefs, opinions, customs, etc. handed down in this way: *a culture strongly steeped in tradition.* **3** an established custom or practice: *The navy has many old traditions.* **4** *Theology.* **a** in Jewish usage, the unwritten laws and doctrines received from Moses. **b** in Christian usage, the oral teachings of Christ and the apostles, not recorded in the Scriptures. **c** in Moslem usage, the sayings and deeds of Mohammed not recorded in the Koran. [< L *traditio, -onis* < *tradere* hand down < *trans-* over + *dare* give. Doublet of TREASON.]

tra·di·tion·al (trə dish′ən əl or trə dish′nəl) *adj.* of, based on, or handed down by tradition: *The coronation is a traditional ceremony. They prefer traditional furniture to modern furniture.* —**tra·di·tion·al·ly**, *adv.*

tra·duce (trə dyüs′ or trə düs′) *v.* **-duced, -duc·ing.** speak evil of (a person) falsely; slander. [< L *traducere* parade in disgrace < *trans-* across + *ducere* lead] —**tra·duc′er**, *n.*

traf·fic (traf′ik) *n., v.* **-ficked, -fick·ing.** —*n.* **1** the people, automobiles, wagons, ships, etc. coming and going along a way of travel. **2** a buying and selling; commerce; trade. **3 a** the business done by a railway line, a steamship line, etc. **b** the number of

passengers or the amount of freight carried. **4** the total amount of business done by any company or industry within a certain time. **5** intercourse; dealings.
—*v.* **1** carry on trade; buy; sell exchange: *The men trafficked with the natives for ivory.* **2** have social dealings with; have to do with: *He refuses to traffic with strangers.* [< MF < Ital. *traffico* < *trafficare* < *tras-* across (< L *trans-*) + *ficcare* shove, poke, ult. < L *figere* fix]

traffic circle a type of intersection in which traffic from different roads moves in a single direction around a circular island.

traffic island a usually raised area in a road or street designed to direct the flow of traffic into particular lanes, protect pedestrians, etc.

traf·fick·er (traf′ik ər) *n.* a person who buys and sells, especially one who deals illicitly in drugs or other goods.

traffic light an electrically operated device for controlling traffic at intersections, consisting of a standard series of colored lights. A green light means go ahead, an orange light means caution, and a red one means stop.

trag·a·canth (trag′ə kanth′) *n.* **1** a gum obtained from certain Asian or eastern European shrubs (genus *Astragalus*) of the pea family used for stiffening cloth, thickening medicines, etc. **2** a plant yielding this gum. [< L < Gk. *tragakantha*, literally, goat's thorn < *tragos* goat + *akantha* thorn]

tra·ge·di·an (trə jē′dē ən) *n.* **1** a writer of tragedies. **2** an actor who specializes in tragic roles.

tra·ge·di·enne (trə jē′dē en′) *n.* an actress who specializes in tragic roles. [< F]

trag·e·dy (traj′ə dē) *n., pl.* **-dies. 1** a serious play having, usually, a central character and an unhappy or disastrous ending. In many tragedies the hero experiences great mental suffering and, finally, meets his death. *Hamlet* is a tragedy. **2 a** the branch of drama that includes such plays. **b** the writing of such plays. **3** a novel, long poem, etc. similar to a tragic play. **4** a very sad or terrible happening: *The father's death was a tragedy to his family.* [ME < OF < L < Gk. *tragōidia* < *tragos* goat (connection obscure) + *ōidē* song]

trag·ic (traj′ik) *adj.* **1** of or having to do with tragedy: *a tragic actor, a tragic poet.* **2** very sad or dreadful: *a tragic death, a tragic event.* [< L < Gk. *tragikos*] —**trag′i·cal·ly**, *adv.*

trag·i·cal (traj′ə kəl) *adj.* tragic.

tragic flaw a flaw in the character of a tragic hero that brings about his downfall.

trag·i·com·e·dy (traj′ē kom′ə dē) *n., pl.* **-dies. 1** a play having both tragic and comic elements. *The Merchant of Venice* is a tragicomedy. **2** an incident or situation in which serious and comic elements are blended. [< F < LL *tragicomoedia* < L *tragicocomoedia* < *tragicus* tragic + *comoedia* comedy]

trag·i·com·ic (traj′ē kom′ik) *adj.* having both tragic and comic elements.

trag·i·com·i·cal (traj′ē kom′ə kəl) *adj.* tragicomic.

trail (trāl) *n., v.* —*n.* **1** a path across a wild or unsettled region. **2** a track or smell: *The dogs found the trail of a rabbit.* **3** anything that follows along behind: *The car left a trail of dust behind it.* **4** the lower end of a gun carriage.
—*v.* **1** pull or drag or be pulled or dragged along behind: *The child trailed a toy horse after him. Her dress trails on the ground.* **2** hang down or float loosely from something. **3** follow the trail or track of; track: *to trail a bear or thief.* **4** carry or bring by or as if by dragging: *to trail snow into a house.* **5** bring or have floating after itself: *a car trailing dust.* **6** follow along behind; follow: *The dog trailed him constantly.* **7** *Sports.* be behind in a game or competition: *trailing by seven points.* **8** move or extend in a long, uneven line: *ivy trailing over an old wall, refugees trailing from their ruined village.* **9** mark out (a trail or track): *to trail a path through the jungle.* **10** go along slowly or wearily: *children trailing to school.* **11** become gradually less (*used with* **off** *or* **away**): *Her voice trailed off into silence.* [ME < OF *trailler* tow, ult. < L *tragula* dragnet]

trail·bla·zer (trāl′blā′zər) *n.* **1** a person who blazes a trail. **2** a person who pioneers or prepares the way to something new.

trail·er (trā′lər) *n.* **1** a small or large vehicle having one or more pairs of wheels, designed to be pulled along by a truck, tractor, automobile, etc., and used for transporting goods, animals, a boat or snowmobile, etc. **2** a closed-in vehicle having one or more pairs of wheels, designed to be pulled by an automobile or truck and equipped for use as a dwelling or place of business; a camper, mobile home, etc.: *We have a trailer that we take to the lake every summer. Large trailers are often called mobile homes.* **3** a short film made up of selected scenes from a motion picture, shown to advertise the motion picture. **4** a trailing plant. **5** a person or animal that follows a trail.

---

hat, āge, fär; let, ēqual, tėrm; it, īce
hot, ōpen, ôrder; oil, out; cup, pùt, rüle,
əbove, takən, pencəl, lemən, circəs

ch, child; ng, long; sh, ship
th, thin; ŦH, then; zh, measure

trailer camp or **park** an area equipped to accommodate trailers (def. 2), often having electricity, running water, etc.

trailing arbutus a trailing plant (*Epigaea repens*) of the heath family found in the woodlands of eastern North America, having evergreen leaves and clusters of fragrant, pink or white flowers very early in spring; mayflower. The trailing arbutus is the provincial flower of Nova Scotia.

train¹ (trān) *n., v.* —*n.* **1** a connected line of railway cars pulled by an engine. **2** a line of people, animals, wagons, trucks, etc. moving along together. **3** a collection of vehicles, animals, and men accompanying an army to carry supplies, baggage, ammunition, or any equipment or materials. **4** a part of a dress, cloak, or gown that trails behind the wearer: *Two attendants carried the queen's train.* **5** something that is drawn along behind; a trailing part. **6** a tail: *the train of a peacock, the train of a comet.* **7** a group of followers. **8 a** a series; succession: *a long train of misfortunes.* **b** a continuous course: *a train of thought.* **c** a succession of results or conditions following some event: *The flood brought starvation and disease in its train.* **9** a series of happenings; succession of results. **10** a line of gunpowder that acts as a fuse. **11** a series of connected parts, such as wheels and pinions, through which motion is transmitted in a machine.
in train, in proper order, arrangement, or sequence; in process.
train of thought, a succession of thoughts passing through one's mind at a particular time: *From the way the speaker paused, it was obvious that he had lost his train of thought.*
—*v.* **1** bring up; rear; teach: *to train a child.* **2** make skilful by teaching and practice: *to train as a nurse.* **3** discipline and instruct (an animal) to be useful, obedient, perform tricks, race, etc.: *to train a horse.* **4** make fit by exercise and diet: *Runners train for races.* **5** make oneself fit. **6** point; aim: *to train cannon upon a fort.* **7** bring into a particular position: *Train the vine around this post.* [ME < OF *trainer* < VL *traginare*, ult. < L *trahere* drag]

train² (trān) *n. Cdn.* a large, toboggan-shaped sled. [< Cdn.F *traîne sauvage* toboggan < F *traîneau* sled]

train·ee (trā nē′) *n.* one who is receiving training.

train·er (trā′nər) *n.* **1** a person who trains individual athletes or sports teams. **2** a person who trains racehorses, circus beasts, or other animals. **3** a device, machine, etc. used in training: *The pilot was flying a single-engined trainer.*

train·ing (trā′ning) *n.* **1** practical education in some art, profession, etc.: *training for teachers.* **2** the development of strength and endurance. **3** a good condition maintained by exercise, diet, etc.

training camp a session of intensive training undertaken by a team or an athlete at a place away from home base in preparation for a regular season or for a special contest or event.

training school **1** an institution for the custody and education of juvenile offenders. Training schools in Canada are operated by a provincial government or by a private organization under a provincial charter. **2** trade school.

training wheels small wheels attached on either side of the rear wheel of a bicycle to steady the vehicle for a child learning to ride.

train·load (trān′lōd′) *n.* as much as a train can hold or carry.

train·man (trān′mən) *n., pl.* **-men.** a man who works on a railway train, especially a brakeman.

train oil oil obtained from a sea animal, especially a whale. [< obs. *train* train oil < MLG *trān* or MDu. *traen* tear, drop; cf. G *Träne*]

traipse (trāps) *v.* **traipsed, traips·ing;** *n. Informal.* —*v.* walk, wander, or tramp: *I traipsed all over town looking for a gift.* —*n.* a walk, especially a long or tiring one. [probably < OF *trapasser*, var. of *trespasser*. See TRESPASS.]

trait (trāt *or* trā) *n.* a quality of mind, character, etc.; distinguishing feature; characteristic: *Courage, love of justice, and common sense are desirable traits.* [< F *trait* < L *tractus* < *trahere* drag. Doublet of TRACT¹.]
☞ *Hom.* tray (trā).
☞ *Syn.* See note at **feature**.

trai·tor (trā′tər) *n.* **1** a person who betrays his country or ruler; one who commits treason. **2** a person who betrays a trust, duty, friend, etc. [ME < OF *traitor*, ult. < L *traditor*, ult. < *trans-* over + *dare* give]

trai·tor·ous (trā′tər əs) *adj.* like a traitor; treacherous; faithless. —**trai′tor·ous·ly,** *adv.* —**trai′tor·ous·ness,** *n.*

trai·tress (trā′tris) *n.* a woman who commits treason.

tra·jec·to·ry (trə jek′tə rē *or* trə jek′trē) *n., pl.* **-ries.** the curved path of something moving through space, such as a bullet from a gun or a planet in its orbit. [< Med.L *trajectorius* throwing across, ult. < L *trans-* across + *jacere* throw]

tram (tram) *n.* **1** *Esp.Brit.* streetcar. **2** tramway. **3** a truck or car on which loads are carried in coal mines. [< MDu. or MLG *trame* beam]

tram·car (tram′kär′) *n. Brit.* streetcar.

tram·mel (tram′əl) *n., v.* **-melled** *or* **-meled, -mel·ling** *or* **-mel·ing.** —*n.* **1** Usually, **trammels,** *pl.* anything that hinders or restrains: *A large bequest freed the artist from the trammels of poverty.* **2** a fine net to catch fish, birds, etc. **3** a hook in a fireplace to hold pots, kettles, etc. over the fire. **4** a shackle for controlling the motions of a horse and teaching him to amble. —*v.* **1** hinder; restrain. **2** entangle. [ME *tramayle* a kind of net < OF < LL *trimaculum* (spelled *tremaculum*) < L *tri-* three + *macula* mesh] —**tram′mel·ler** *or* **tram′mel·er,** *n.*

tra·mon·tane (trə mon′tān *or* tram′ən tān′) *adj., n.* —*adj.* **1** having to do with, coming from, or located on the other side of the mountains, especially beyond the Alps; transalpine: *a tramontane wind.* **2** foreign. —*n.* **1** one who lives on the other side of the mountains, especially the Alps. **2** foreigner. **3** a cold wind blowing from a mountain range. [< Ital. *tramontana* < L *transmontanus* < *trans* across + *montanus* mountain]

tramp (tramp) *v., n.* —*v.* **1** walk heavily: *He tramped across the room in his heavy boots.* **2** step heavily (*on*): *He tramped on the flowers.* **3** go on foot; walk: *We tramped through the streets.* **4** travel through on foot: *to tramp the streets.* **5** walk steadily; march: *We tramped all day.* **6** go or wander as a tramp. —*n.* **1** the sound of heavy footsteps: *Hear the tramp of the parade.* **2** a long, steady walk; hike. **3** a person who goes about on foot, living by begging, doing odd jobs, etc. **4** a freighter that takes a cargo when and where it can. [? < LG *trampen*] —**tramp′er,** *n.*

tram·ple (tram′pəl) *v.* **-pled, -pling;** *n.* —*v.* **1** crush, kill, or destroy by treading on heavily: *The cattle broke through the fence and trampled the farmer's crops.* **2** hurt or violate, as if by treading on (*often used with* **on** *or* **upon**): *to trample on someone's rights.* —*n.* the act or sound of trampling: *We heard the trample of many feet.* [< *tramp*] —**tram′pler,** *n.*

tram·po·line (tram′pə lēn′ *or* tram′pə lin) *n.* an apparatus for tumbling, acrobatics, etc. consisting of a taut piece of canvas or other sturdy fabric attached by springs to a metal frame.

tram·way (tram′wā′) *n.* **1** *Esp.Brit.* a track for streetcars. **2** *Mining.* **a** a track or roadway for carrying ore from mines. **b** a cable or system of cables on which suspended cars carry ore, etc.

trance (trans) *n., v.* **tranced, tranc·ing.** —*n.* **1** a state of unconsciousness resembling sleep. A person may be in a trance from illness, from the influence of some other person, or from his own will. **2** a dreamy, absorbed condition that is like a trance: *The old man sat before the fire in a trance, thinking of his past life.* **3** a high emotion; rapture. —*v.* hold in a trance; enchant. [ME < OF *transe,* ult. < L *trans-* across + *ire* go] —**trance′like′,** *adj.*

tran·quil (trang′kwəl) *adj.* calm; peaceful; quiet: *a tranquil mood, the tranquil evening air.* [< L *tranquillus*] —**tran′quil·ly,** *adv.*

tran·quil·i·ty *or* **tran·quil·i·ty** (trang kwil′ə tē) *n.* calmness; peacefulness; quiet.

tran·quil·ize *or* **tran·quil·ize** (trang′kwəl īz′) *v.* **-lized, -ized, -liz·ing** *or* **-iz·ing.** **1** make tranquil; especially, reduce mental tension and anxiety by the use of drugs. **2** become tranquil.

tran·quil·liz·er *or* **tran·quil·iz·er** (trang′kwəl īz′ər) *n.* a person or thing that tranquillizes; especially, any of several drugs used to reduce mental tension and anxiety, control certain psychoses, etc.

trans– *prefix.* **1** across, over, or through, as in *transcontinental, transmit.* **2** beyond; on the other side of, as in *Transjordan, transcend.* **3** across, etc.; and also beyond, on the other side of, as in *transarctic, transequatorial, transmarine, transoceanic, transpolar,* and many other geographical terms, such as *trans-African.* **4** into a different place, condition, etc., as in *transform, transmute.* [< L *trans,* prep.]

trans. **1** transitive. **2** transportation. **3** transactions. **4** translation. **5** transferred. **6** transpose.

trans·act (tran zakt′ *or* tran sakt′) *v.* manage, negotiate, or carry on (business, etc.): *He transacts business with stores all over the country.* [< L *transactus,* pp. of *transigere* accomplish < *trans-* through + *agere* drive]

trans·ac·tion (tran zak′shən *or* tran sak′shən) *n.* **1** the act of or an instance of transacting: *Mr. Smith attends to the transaction of important matters himself.* **2** a piece of business: *A record is kept of all the firm's transactions.* **3** **transactions,** *pl.* a record of what is done at the meetings of a society, club, etc. [ME < LL *transactio, -onis* < *transigere.* See TRANSACT.]

trans·ac·tor (tran zak′tər *or* tran sak′tər) *n.* a person who transacts business affairs.

trans·al·pine (tranz al′pīn *or* trans-) *adj.* across or beyond the Alps, especially as viewed from Italy.

trans·at·lan·tic (trans′ət lan′tik *or* tranz′-) *adj.* **1** crossing or extending across the Atlantic ocean. **2** having to do with crossing the Atlantic ocean: *transatlantic air fares.* **3** on the other side of the Atlantic ocean.

trans–Can·a·da (trans′kan′ə də) *adj.* **1** extending right across Canada, from the Atlantic to the Pacific oceans: *the trans-Canada microwave system.* **2** (*noml.*) **Trans-Canada,** the Trans-Canada Highway, a series of paved roads extending across Canada through each province and conforming to agreed standards of construction.

Trans–cau·ca·sian (trans′ko kā′zhən *or* -kô kā′zhən) *n., adj.* —*n.* a native or inhabitant of Transcaucasia, a region in the SW Soviet Union, in and to the south of the Caucasus Mountains. —*adj.* of or having to do with Transcaucasia or its inhabitants.

tran·scend (tran send′) *v.* **1** go beyond the limits or powers of; exceed: *The grandeur of Niagara Falls transcends description.* **2** be higher or greater than; surpass; excel. **3** of God, be above and independent of (the physical universe). **4** be superior or extraordinary. [ME < L *transcendere* < *trans-* beyond + *scandere* climb]

tran·scend·ence (tran sen′dəns) *n.* the state or quality of being transcendent.

tran·scend·ent (tran sen′dənt) *adj.* **1** surpassing ordinary limits; excelling; superior; extraordinary. **2** existing apart from the universe. **3** *Philosophy.* **a** transcending the Aristotelian categories or predicaments, especially as considered by the medieval scholastics. **b** in Kantian philosophy, not realizable in human experience. —**tran·scend′ent·ly,** *adv.*

tran·scen·den·tal (tran′sen den′təl) *adj.* **1** transcendent. **2** supernatural. **3** obscure; incomprehensible; fantastic. **4** *Philosophy.* **a** explaining matter and objective things as products of the mind that is thinking about them; idealistic. **b** implied in and necessary to human experience. —**tran′scen·den′tal·ly,** *adv.*

tran·scen·den·tal·ism (tran′sen den′təl iz′əm) *n.* **1** a transcendental quality, thought, language, or philosophy. **2** any philosophy based upon the doctrine that the principles of reality are to be discovered by a study of the processes of thought, not from experience. **3** obscurity; incomprehensibility; fantasy.

tran·scen·den·tal·ist (tran′sen den′təl ist) *n.* a person who believes in transcendentalism.

trans·con·ti·nen·tal (trans′kon tə nen′təl) *adj.* **1** crossing or extending across a continent: *a transcontinental railway.* **2** (*noml.*) a train that crosses a continent. **3** on the other side of a continent.

tran·scribe (tran skrīb′) *v.* **-scribed, -scrib·ing.** **1** copy in writing or in typewriting: *The account of the trial was transcribed from the stenographer's shorthand notes.* **2** set down in writing or print: *His entire speech was transcribed in the newspapers, word for word.* **3** arrange (a musical composition) for a different instrument or voice. **4** *Radio and television.* make a recording of (a program, commercial, etc.), especially for broadcasting at a later time. **5** broadcast a program, commercial, etc. that has been previously recorded. **6** *Phonetics.* record (speech) in a system of phonetic symbols; represent (a speech sound) by a phonetic symbol. [< L *transcribere* < *trans-* over + *scribere* write] —**tran·scrib′er,** *n.*

tran·script (tran′skript) *n.* **1** a written or typewritten copy: *They were waiting for a transcript of the tapes.* **2** any copy or reproduction: *The university requires a transcript of your high-school grades.* [< L *transcriptum,* pp. neut. of *transcribere.* See TRANSCRIBE.]

tran·scrip·tion (tran skrip′shən) *n.* **1** the act or process of transcribing. **2** a transcript; copy. **3** an arrangement of a musical composition for a different instrument or voice. **4** a recording of a program, commercial, etc. made for broadcasting on radio or television. **5** the act or practice of broadcasting such a recording. **6** *Phonetics.* a written representation of speech in a system of phonetic symbols.

trans·duce (trans dyüs′ *or* tranz-, trans düs′ *or* tranz-) *v.* **-duced, -duc·ing.** transfer or convert one form of energy into another. [< L *transducere* < *trans-* + *ducere* lead]

trans·duc·tion (trans duk′shən *or* tranz-) *n.* **1** *Biology.* the transfer of genes or chromosomes from one cell to another by

means of a bacterial virus. **2** *Physics.* the transfer of one form of energy to another.

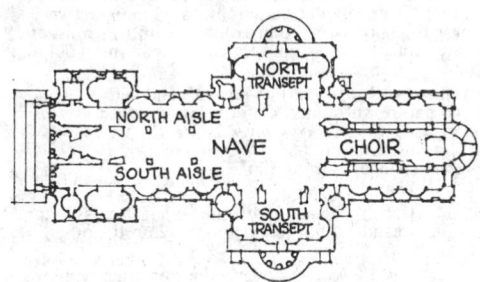

Plan of St. Paul's Cathedral in London, England

tran·sept (tran′sept) *n.* **1** the part of a cross-shaped church at right angles to the long main part. **2** either projecting end of this part. [< Med.L *transeptum*, ult. < L *trans-* across + *saeptum* fence]

trans·fer (*v.* trans fer′ or trans′fer; *n.* trans′fer) *v.* **-ferred, -fer·ring;** *n.* —*v.* **1** convey or remove from one person or place to another; hand over: *This farm has been transferred from father to son for generations. My trunks were transferred by express.* **2** convey (a drawing, design, pattern) from one surface to another. **3** make over (a title, right, or property) by deed or legal process: *to transfer a bond by endorsement.* **4** change from one streetcar, bus, train, etc. to another without having to pay another fare. —*n.* **1** transferring or being transferred. **2** a drawing, pattern, etc. printed from one surface onto another. **3** a ticket allowing a passenger to continue his journey on another streetcar, bus, train, etc. **4** a point or place for transferring. **5 a** the act of turning the ownership of a share of stock or registered bond over to someone else. **b** a document ordering this. **6** the making over to another of title, right, or property by deed or legal process. [ME < L *transferre* < *trans-* across + *ferre* bear] —**trans·fer′rer,** *n.*

trans·fer·a·bil·i·ty (trans fer′ə bil′ə tē or trans′fər ə bil′ə tē) *n.* the quality of being transferable.

trans·fer·a·ble (trans fer′ə bəl or trans′fər ə bəl) *adj.* capable of being transferred.

trans·fer·ee (trans′fər ē′) *n.* **1** a person who has been or is being transferred. **2** a person to whom something, especially property, is transferred.

trans·fer·ence (trans fer′əns or trans′fər əns) *n.* **1** the act of transferring or the state of being transferred. **2** *Psychoanalysis.* a revival of emotions previously experienced and repressed, as toward a parent, with a new person as the object.

trans·fig·u·ra·tion (trans fig′ər ā′shən or -fig′yər ā′shən) *n.* **1** a change in form or appearance; transformation. **2 the Transfiguration, a** in the Bible, the change in the appearance of Christ on the mountain (Matt. 17; Mark 9). **b** a Christian festival held on August 6 in honor of this.

trans·fig·ure (trans fig′ər or -fig′yər) *v.* **-ured, -ur·ing. 1** change in form or appearance, especially for the better: *New paint had transfigured the old house.* **2** change so as to glorify; exalt. [ME < L *transfigurare* < *trans-* across + *figura* figure]

trans·fix (trans fiks′) *v.* **1** pierce through: *The hunter transfixed the lion with a spear.* **2** fasten by piercing through with something pointed. **3** make motionless (with amazement, terror, etc.). [< L *transfixus,* pp. of *transfigere* < *trans-* through + *figere* fix]

trans·form (trans fôrm′) *v.* **1** change considerably or radically in form, appearance, function, condition, or character: *The blizzard transformed the bushes into glittering mounds of snow. His face was transformed by a sudden smile. The witch transformed the brothers into pigs.* **2** *Physics.* change (one form of energy) into another. *A generator transforms mechanical energy into electricity.* **3** change the voltage, etc. of (an electric current). **4** *Mathematics.* change (a figure, term, etc.) to another differing in form but having the same value or quantity. [ME < L *transformare* < *trans-* across + *forma* form]

☛ *Syn.* **1, 2. Transform, transmute, convert** = change the form, nature, substance, or state of something. **Transform** suggests a thoroughgoing or fundamental change in the appearance, shape, or nature of a thing or person: *Responsibility transformed him from a happy-go-lucky youth into a capable leader.* **Transmute,** formal, implies a complete change in nature or substance, especially a change to a higher level or kind: *He thus transmuted disapproval into admiration.* **Convert** suggests turning from one state or condition to another, especially for a new use or purpose: *convert boxes into furniture.*

trans·for·ma·tion (trans′fər mā′shən) *n.* **1** the act or process of transforming or the state of being transformed: *the transformation of a caterpillar into a butterfly.* **2** the result of transforming.

hat, āge, fär; let, ēqual, tèrm; it, īce
hot, ōpen, ôrder; oil, out; cup, put, rüle,
above, takən, pencəl, lemən, circəs
ch, child; ng, long; sh, ship
th, thin; ᴛʜ, then; zh, measure

trans·form·er (trans fôr′mər) *n.* a device for changing the voltage of an electric current. North American electrical appliances cannot be used in Europe without a transformer because the voltage there is much higher than in North America.

trans·fuse (trans fyüz′) *v.* **-fused, -fus·ing. 1** pour from one container into another. **2** transfer (blood) from one person or animal to another. **3** inject (a solution) into a blood vessel. **4** infuse; instil: *The speaker transfused his enthusiasm into the audience.* [ME < L *transfusus,* pp. of *transfundere* < *trans-* across + *fundere* pour]

trans·fu·sion (trans fyü′zhən) *n.* **1** the act or process of transfusing; especially, the process of transfusing blood or blood plasma into a blood vessel of a person or animal. **2** an instance of transfusing blood: *He has received three transfusions.*

trans·gress (trans gres′ or tranz-) *v.* **1** break a law, command, etc.; sin: *He knew he had transgressed.* **2** go contrary to; sin against: *to transgress the divine law.* **3** go beyond (a boundary or limit): *The interviewer's questions transgressed the bounds of good taste.* [< L *transgressus,* pp. of *transgredi* go beyond < *trans-* across + *gradi* to step]

trans·gres·sion (trans gresh′ən or tranz-) *n.* a transgressing; breaking a law, command, etc.; sin. [< L *transgressio, -onis,* originally, a going over < *transgredi.* See TRANSGRESS.]

trans·gres·sor (trans gres′ər or tranz-) *n.* a person who transgresses; sinner.

tran·ship (tran ship′) *v.* **-shipped, -ship·ping.** transship. —**tran·ship′ment,** *n.*

trans·hu·mance (trans hyü′məns) *n.* the moving of livestock to more suitable pastures as the seasons change. [< F < Sp., ult. < L *trans-* + *humus* ground]

tran·si·ence (tran′zē əns) *n.* the quality or state of being transient.

tran·si·en·cy (tran′zē ən sē) *n.* transience.

tran·si·ent (tran′zē ənt) *n.* —*adj.* **1** passing soon; fleeting; not lasting; transitory. **2 a** passing through and not staying long: *a transient guest in a hotel.* **b** serving transient guests, customers, etc.: *a transient hotel.* —*n.* **1** a visitor or boarder who stays for a short time. **2** a tramp or hobo. [< L *transiens, -entis,* ppr. of *transire* pass through < *trans-* through + *ire* go] —**tran′si·ent·ly,** *adv.*

☛ *Syn. adj.* **1.** See note at **temporary.**

tran·sis·tor (tran zis′tər) *n.* **1** a small electronic device, similar to an electron tube in use, that amplifies electricity by controlling the flow of electrons. Transistors are used in computers, radios, television sets, etc. **2** a portable radio that has transistors instead of tubes. [< L *trans-* + *sistere* send, convey]

tran·sis·tor·ize (tran zis′tə rīz′) *v.* **-ized, -iz·ing.** equip with transistors.

tran·sit (tran′sit or tran′zit) *n., v.* **-it·ed, -it·ing.** —*n.* **1** the act or process of passing across or through. **2** the process of carrying or being carried across or through: *The goods were damaged in transit.* **3** transportation by trains, buses, etc. **4** transition or change. **5** *Surveying.* an instrument used for measuring angles. It includes a telescope and levels and scales for measuring angles both vertically and horizontally. **6** *Astronomy.* **a** the apparent passage of a heavenly body across the meridian of a place. **b** the passage of a small heavenly body across the disk of a larger one. **7** rapid transit. —*v.* **1** pass through, over, or across. **2** turn (the telescope of a transit) around its horizontal transverse axis to point in the opposite direction. [< L *transitus* < *transire.* See TRANSIENT.]

transit instrument or **telescope 1** *Astronomy.* a telescope so fixed that it can move only in the plane of the meridian along which it is located, used to determine the time of a heavenly body's transit. **2** a surveyor's transit.

tran·si·tion (tran zish′ən) *n.* **1** a change or passing from one condition, place, form, stage, etc. to another: *a transition from poverty to wealth and power, a period of transition in history.* **2** *Music.* **a** a change of key. **b** a passage linking one section, subject, etc. of a composition with another. **3** in writing, a word, phrase, sentence, etc. serving to link ideas or to lead smoothly from one topic to the next. [< L *transitio, -onis* < *transire.* See TRANSIENT.]

tran·si·tion·al (tran zish′ən əl) *adj.* of, having to do with, or involving transition: *a transitional stage in his life.* —**tran·si′tion·al·ly,** *adv.*

tran·si·tive (tran′sə tiv or tran′zə tiv) adj., n. —adj. **1** Grammar. of a verb, taking a direct object. Bring and raise are transitive verbs. Compare **intransitive**. **2** transitional. —n. Grammar. a transitive verb. —**tran′si·tive·ly,** adv. —**tran′si·tive·ness,** n.
☛ Usage. See note at **verb.**

tran·si·to·ry (tran′sə tôr′ē or tran′zə tôr′ē) adj. passing soon or quickly; lasting only a short time. —**tran′si·to′ri·ly,** adv. —**tran′si·to′ri·ness,** n.

trans·late (trans lāt′ or tranz-) v. -lat·ed, -lat·ing. **1** change from one language into another: to translate a book from French into English. **2** change into other words, especially in order to explain the meaning of: to translate a scientific treatise for the layman. **3** change from one place, position, or condition to another. **4** Theology. take to heaven, especially without death. **5** Physics. move (a body) from one point or place to another without rotation. **6** retransmit (a telegraphic message), as by a relay. [ME < L translatus, pp. to transferre. See TRANSFER.] —**trans·lat′a·ble,** adj.

trans·la·tion (trans lā′shən or tranz-) n. **1** translating or being translated: Her translation of the German novel was very successful. **2** the result of translating; a version. **3** the automatic retransmission of a long-distance telegraph message by means of a relay. **4** Physics. motion in which there is no rotation; onward movement that is not rotary or reciprocating.

trans·la·tor (trans lā′tər or tranz-) n. a person who translates, especially from one language into another.

trans·lit·er·ate (trans lit′ər āt′ or tranz-) v. -at·ed, -at·ing. change (letters, words, etc.) into corresponding characters of another alphabet or language: We transliterate the Greek χ as ch and φ as ph. [< trans- + L litera letter]

trans·lit·er·a·tion (trans lit′ər ā′shən or tranz-) n. the act of transliterating; the rendering of a letter or letters of one alphabet by equivalents in another.

trans·lu·cence (trans lü′səns or tranz-) n. the quality or state of being translucent.

trans·lu·cen·cy (trans lü′sən sē or tranz-) n. **1** translucence. **2** something that is translucent.

trans·lu·cent (trans lü′sənt or tranz-) adj. letting light through without being transparent: Frosted glass is translucent. [< L translucens, -entis, ppr. of translucere < trans- through + lucere shine] —**trans·lu′cent·ly,** adv.

trans·ma·rine (trans′mə rēn′ or tranz′-) adj. across or beyond the sea.

trans·mi·grate (trans mī′grāt or tranz-) v. -grat·ed, -grat·ing. **1** of the soul, pass at death into another body. **2** move from one place or country to another; migrate. [< L transmigrare < trans-across + migrare move]

trans·mi·gra·tion (trans′mī grā′shən or tranz′-) n. **1** in certain religions, the passing of the soul at death into another body. **2** the going from one place or country to another; migration.

trans·mis·si·ble (trans mis′ə bəl or tranz-) adj. capable of being transmitted: Scarlet fever is a transmissible disease.

trans·mis·sion (trans mish′ən or tranz-) n. **1** a sending over; passing on or along; letting through: Mosquitoes are the only means of transmission of malaria. **2** something transmitted. **3** of a motor vehicle, the part that transmits power from the engine to the driving axle. **4** the passage through space of radio waves from the transmitting station to the receiving station: When radio transmission is good, distant stations can be received. [< L transmissio, -onis < transmittere. See TRANSMIT.]

trans·mit (trans mit′ or tranz-) v. -mit·ted, -mit·ting. **1** send over; pass on; pass along; let through: I will transmit the money by special messenger. Rats transmit disease. **2** Physics. **a** cause (light, heat, sound, etc.) to pass through a medium. **b** convey (force or movement) from one part of a body or mechanism to another. **c** of a medium, allow (light, heat, etc.) to pass through: Glass transmits light. **3** the passage through space of radio waves from the transmitting station to the receiving station: When transmission is good, distant radio stations can be heard. [< L transmittere < trans- across + mittere send]

trans·mit·tal (trans mit′əl or tranz-) n. transmitting.

trans·mit·ter (trans mit′ər or tranz-) n. **1** the part of a telephone into which one speaks and which contains a device that converts the sound waves of speech into corresponding electric waves. **2** the part of a telegraph by which a message is sent. **3** in radio and television broadcasting, the apparatus that generates and modulates radio-frequency waves and sends them to the station's antenna. **4** any person or thing that transmits.

trans·mon·tane (trans mon′tān or tranz-) adj. beyond a mountain or mountain range; tramontane.

trans·mu·ta·tion (trans′myü tā′shən or tranz′-) n. **1** a change into another nature, substance, or form. **2** Physics and chemistry. the conversion of atoms of one element into atoms of a different element or a different isotope, either naturally, as by radio-active disintegration, or artificially, as by bombardment with neutrons, etc. **3** Alchemy. the (attempted) conversion of a baser metal into gold or silver.

trans·mute (trans myüt′ or tranz-) v. -mut·ed, -mut·ing. **1** change from one nature, substance, or form into another: We can transmute water power into electrical power. **2** Chemistry and physics. subject to transmutation. [< L transmutare < trans-thoroughly + mutare change] —**trans·mut′er,** n.
☛ Syn. See note at **transform.**

trans·o·ce·an·ic (trans′ō shē an′ik or tranz′-) adj. **1** crossing or extending across the ocean: a transoceanic airline. **2** on the other side of the ocean.

tran·som (tran′səm) n. **1** a window over a door or other window, usually hinged for opening. **2** a horizontal crossbar in a window, over a door, or between a door and a window above it. [ME; ult. < L transtrum; originally, crossbeam]

tran·son·ic (tran son′ik) adj. of, having to do with, or designed for operation at speeds close to the speed of sound in air, which is about 1190 km/h at sea level.

trans·pa·cif·ic (trans′pə sif′ik or tranz′-) adj. **1** crossing or extending across the Pacific ocean. **2** having to do with crossing the Pacific ocean: transpacific air fares. **3** on the other side of the Pacific ocean.

trans·par·ence (trans per′əns or trans par′əns) n. transparency.

trans·par·en·cy (trans per′ən sē or trans par′ən sē) n., pl. -cies. **1** the quality or state of being transparent. **2** something transparent; especially, a photograph, picture, or design on glass or clear plastic made visible by light shining through from below or behind.

trans·par·ent (trans per′ənt or trans par′ənt) adj. **1** transmitting light so that something behind or beyond can be distinctly seen: Window glass is transparent. **2** of fabrics, etc., so fine, or open in weave that something on the other side can be seen quite clearly; sheer. **3** easily seen through or detected; obvious: The excuse he gave was transparent. **4** free from deceit or guile; frank: He had led a simple and transparent life. [< Med.L transparens, -entis, ppr. of transparere show light through < L trans- through + parere appear] —**trans·par′ent·ly,** adv.

tran·spi·ra·tion (tran′spə rā′shən) n. the act or process or an instance of transpiring; especially, the passage of moisture through the pores of the skin or surface of plant leaves.

tran·spire (tran spīr′) v. -spired, -spir·ing. **1** take place; happen. **2** leak out; become known. **3** pass off or send off in the form of vapor through a wall or surface, as from the human body or from leaves. [< F < L trans- through + spirare breathe]
☛ Usage. **Transpire.** The meaning "happen, take place" was once regarded as not being in good use, but **transpire** in this sense is fairly common in cultivated English today.

trans·plant (v. trans plant′; n. trans′plant′) v., n. **1** plant again in a different place: We start the flowers indoors and then transplant them to the garden. **2** remove from one place to another: The colony was transplanted to a more healthful location. **3** transfer (skin, an organ, etc.) from one person or animal to another, or from one part of the body to another: transplant a kidney. **4** bear transplanting: Poppies do not transplant well and should be planted where they are to grow.
—n. **1** the transfer of an organ, etc. from one person or animal to another, or from one part of the body to another: a heart transplant. **2** something transplanted. [ME < LL transplantare < trans- across + plantare plant] —**trans·plant′a·ble,** adj. —**trans·plant′er,** n.

trans·plan·ta·tion (trans′plan tā′shən) n. **1** transplanting or being transplanted. **2** something that has been transplanted.

tran·spond·er (tran spon′dər) n. a type of transmitting and receiving system for radio or radar signals that automatically transmits signals when it receives a predetermined signal. [< transmitter + responder]

trans·port (v. trans pôrt′; n. trans′pôrt) v., n. —v. **1** carry from one place to another: Wheat is transported from the farm to the mills. **2** carry away by strong feeling: She was transported with joy by the good news. **3** send away to another country as a punishment.
—n. **1** a carrying from one place to another: Trucks are much used for transport. **2** a large truck used to carry freight long distances by road. **3** a ship used to carry men and supplies. **4** an airplane that transports passengers, mail, freight, etc. **5** a strong feeling: a transport of rage. **6** a transported convict. [ME < L transportare < trans- across + portare carry] —**trans·port′er,** n.
☛ Syn. v. **1.** See note at **carry.**

trans·port·a·bil·i·ty (trans pôr′tə bil′ə tē) n. the fact or property of being transportable.

trans·port·a·ble (trans pôr′tə bəl) adj. **1** capable of being

transported. 2 involving, or liable to, punishment by transportation: *a transportable offence.*

trans·por·ta·tion (trans′pər tā′shən) *n.* 1 transporting or being transported: *The railway allows free transportation for a certain amount of a passenger's baggage.* 2 a means of transport. 3 the cost of transport; a ticket for transport. 4 a sending away or being sent to another country as a punishment.

trans·pos·al (trans pōz′əl) *n.* transposition.

trans·pose (trans pōz′) *v.* **-posed, -pos·ing.** 1 change the position or order of; interchange. 2 change the usual order of (letters, words, or numbers); invert. *Example: Up came the wind, and off went his hat.* 3 *Music.* **a** change the key of. **b** play in another key. 4 *Algebra.* transfer (a term) to the other side of an equation, changing plus to minus or minus to plus. [< F *transposer* < *trans-* across (< L) + *poser* put (see POSE¹)] —**trans·pos′er,** *n.*

trans·po·si·tion (trans′pə zish′ən) *n.* 1 the act of transposing or the state of being transposed. 2 something transposed, such as a piece of music transposed into a different key.

trans·pro·vin·cial (trans prə vin′shəl) *adj.* crossing or extending across a province: *transprovincial bus service.*

trans·ship (trans ship′ *or* tran ship′) *v.* **-shipped, -ship·ping.** transfer from one ship, train, car, etc. to another. Also, **tranship.** —**trans·ship′ment,** *n.*

trans·son·ic (trans son′ik) *adj.* moving at a speed close to the speed of sound.

tran·sub·stan·ti·a·tion (tran′səb stan′shē ā′shən) *n.* 1 a changing of one substance into another. 2 *Roman Catholic Church and Orthodox Eastern Church.* the miraculous changing of the substance of the bread and wine of the Eucharist into the substance of the body and blood of Christ, only the appearance of the bread and wine remaining. [< Med.L *transubstantiatio, -onis* < *transubstantiare* transmute < L *trans-* over + *substantia* substance]

trans·ver·sal (trans vėr′səl *or* tranz-) *adj., n.* —*adj.* transverse. —*n. Geometry.* a line intersecting two or more other lines.

trans·verse (trans vėrs′ *or* tranz-, trans′vėrs *or* tranz′-) *adj., n.* —*adj.* 1 lying or placed across or crosswise: *The transverse beams in the barn were walnut.* 2 *Geometry.* designating the axis that passes through the foci of a hyperbola. —*n.* a transverse part or piece. [< L *transversus,* pp. of *transvertere* < *trans-* across + *vertere* turn]

trans·verse·ly (trans vėrs′lē *or* tranz-) *adv.* across; athwart; crosswise; from side to side.

trans·vest·ism (trans vest′iz əm *or* tranz-) *n.* the practice of being a transvestite. [< G *Transvestismus* < L *trans-* + *vestire* dress]

trans·vest·ite (trans vest′īt *or* tranz-) *n.* a person who seeks or derives sexual pleasure from wearing clothing normally associated with the opposite sex.

Tran·syl·va·ni·an (tran′səl vā′nē ən *or* -səl vān′yən) *n., adj.* —*n.* a native or inhabitant of Transylvania, a region in W Romania. —*adj.* of or having to do with Transylvania or its people.

trap¹ (trap) *n., v.* **trapped, trap·ping.** —*n.* 1 a device for catching animals, lobsters, birds, etc. 2 a trick or other means for catching someone off guard: *He knew that the question was a trap.* 3 trapdoor. 4 a bend in a pipe for holding a small amount of water to prevent the escape of air, gas, etc. 5 speed trap. 6 a light two-wheeled carriage. 7 a device to throw clay pigeons, etc. into the air to be shot at. 8 *Slang.* mouth: *Shut your trap!* 9 **traps,** *pl.* drums, cymbals, bells, gongs, etc. —*v.* 1 catch in a trap. 2 set traps for animals; especially engage in trapping animals for their fur. 3 provide with a trap. 4 stop with a trap: *a gutter to trap rainwater.* [OE *træppe*]
► *Syn.* n. 1, 2. **Trap, snare** = something that catches or is contrived to catch an animal or person. **Trap** figuratively suggests a situation deliberately set to catch someone by surprise and destroy them or trick him into doing or saying something: *Suspecting a trap, the detachment of soldiers withdrew.* **Snare** figuratively applies to a desperate situation someone gets entangled in unawares, or a device to lure him into getting caught: *The detectives used marked money as a snare for the thief.*

trap² (trap) *v.* **trapped, trap·ping;** *n.* —*v.* cover with trappings. —*n.* **traps,** *pl. Informal.* belongings; baggage. [ME, alteration of OF *drap* cloth < Med.L *drappus,* of uncertain origin]

trap·door (trap′dôr′) *n.* a hinged or sliding door in a floor, ceiling, or roof, as to provide access to an attic or cellar.

trapes (trāps) See **traipse.**

tra·peze (trə pēz′) *n.* a short horizontal bar hung by ropes like a swing, used in gymnastics and acrobatics. [< F < LL < Gk. *trapezion,* dim. of *trapeza* table < *tra-* (unique for *tetra-*) four + *peza* foot. Doublet of TRAPEZIUM.]

tra·pe·zi·um (trə pē′zē əm) *n., pl.* **-zi·ums, -zi·a** (-zē ə). 1 a four-sided plane figure having no sides parallel. See **quadrilateral** for picture. 2 *Brit.* trapezoid. [< LL < Gk. *trapezion,* originally, little table. Doublet of TRAPEZE.]

hat, āge, fär; let, ēqual, tėrm; it, īce
hot, ōpen, ôrder; oil, out; cup, pút, rüle,
əbove, takən, pencəl, lemən, circəs

ch, child; ng, long; sh, ship
th, thin; ᴛʜ, then; zh, measure

tra·pe·zi·us (trə pē′zē əs) *n., pl.* **-zi·i** (-zē ī′ *or* -zē ē′). *Anatomy.* either of two large, flat, triangular muscles in the back of the neck and upper shoulders, that together resemble a trapezium or similar four-sided figure. [< LL < L < Gk.]

trap·e·zoid (trap′ə zoid′) *n.* 1 a four-sided plane figure having two sides parallel and two sides not parallel. See **quadrilateral** for picture. 2 *Brit.* trapezium. [< NL < Gk. *trapezoeides* < *trapeza* table + *eidos* form]

trap·line (trap′līn′) *n. Cdn.* 1 a series of traps set and maintained by a trapper who periodically goes over the line, removing trapped animals and resetting the traps. 2 the way or route along which such a series of traps is set.

trap·per (trap′ər) *n.* a person who traps wild animals for food or for their fur.

trap·pings (trap′ingz) *n.pl.* 1 ornamental coverings for a horse. 2 things worn; ornamental dress: *the trappings of a king and his court.* 3 outward appearances: *He had all the trappings of a cowboy, but he couldn't even ride a horse.* [< trap²]

Trap·pist (trap′ist) *n., adj.* —*n. Roman Catholic Church.* a monk belonging to an extremely austere branch of the Cistercian order established in 1664. —*adj.* of or having to do with the Trappists. [< F *trappiste,* from the monastery of *La Trappe* in N France]

trap·shoot·er (trap′shüt′ər) *n.* a person who takes part in trapshooting.

trap·shoot·ing (trap′shüt′ing) *n.* the sport or art of shooting at clay pigeons, etc. thrown into the air.

trash (trash) *n.* 1 discarded or worthless stuff; rubbish. 2 worthless or inferior writing: *That novel is trash; I can't imagine how it ever got published.* 3 a person of worthless character or such persons as a group; riffraff. [< Scand.; cf. dial. Norwegian *trask*]

trash·y (trash′ē) *adj.* **trash·i·er, trash·i·est.** like or containing trash; of inferior quality: *a trashy magazine.* —**trash′i·ly,** *adv.* —**trash′i·ness,** *n.*

trau·ma (tro′mə, trô′mə, *or* trou′mə) *n., pl.* **-ma·ta** (-mə tə) **or -mas.** 1 an injury to living tissue; wound. 2 *Psychiatry.* **a** an emotional shock that has lasting effects on the victim. **b** a state of emotional disturbance resulting from an injury or mental shock. [< Gk. *trauma, -atos* wound]

trau·mat·ic (tro mat′ik, trô mat′ik, *or* trou mat′ik) *adj.* 1 of, having to do with, or produced by a trauma. 2 *Informal.* shocking or unpleasant: *It was a traumatic experience to run into his old enemy after all those years.* —**trau·mat′i·cal·ly,** *adv.*

trav·ail (trav′āl) *n., v.* —*n.* 1 hard work; toil. 2 trouble or pain. 3 the pains of childbirth; labor pains. —*v.* 1 suffer the pains of childbirth. 2 work hard. [ME < OF *travail,* ult. < LL *tripalium* (spelled *trepalium*) torture device, probably ult. < L *tri-* three + *palus* stake]

trave (trāv) *n.* 1 a wooden frame to hold a horse while being shod. 2 *Architecture.* **a** a crossbeam. **b** a division in a ceiling, etc. made of crossbeams. [ME < OF < L *trabs, trabis* beam]

trav·el (trav′əl) *v.* **-elled** *or* **-eled, -el·ling** *or* **-el·ing;** *n.* —*v.* 1 go from one place to another; journey: *to travel across the country.* 2 go from place to place selling things: *He travels for a large firm.* 3 move; proceed; pass: *Light and sound travel in waves.* 4 walk or run: *A deer travels a considerable distance in a day.* 5 pass through or over: *to travel a road.* —*n.* 1 going in aircraft, trains, ships, cars, etc. from one place to another; journeying. 2 movement in general. 3 the length of stroke, speed, way of working, etc. of a part of a machine. 4 **travels,** *pl.* **a** journeys. **b** a book about one's experiences, visits, etc. while travelling. [var. of *travail*]

trav·elled *or* **trav·eled** (trav′əld) *adj.* 1 that has done much travelling. 2 much used by travellers: *It was a well-travelled road.*

trav·el·ler *or* **trav·el·er** (trav′əl ər *or* trav′lər) *n.* 1 a person who travels or is travelling. 2 sales representative: *He's a traveller for a drug company.*

traveller's cheque *or* **traveler's cheque** a cheque that is signed by the buyer and must be signed again by him at the time of cashing.

travelling bag *or* **traveling bag** handbag (def. 2).

---

travelling fellowship or **traveling fellowship** a fellowship that enables the one receiving it to travel for purposes of study.

travelling salesman or **traveling salesman** a person whose work is going from place to place, usually in an assigned area, selling things for a company.

trav·e·log (trav′ə log′) *Esp.U.S.* See **travelogue**.

trav·e·logue (trav′ə log′) *n.* 1 a lecture describing travel, usually accompanied by pictures. 2 a motion picture depicting travel. [< *travel* + *-logue*, as in *dialogue*]

trav·erse (*v., adv.* trav′ərs or trə vėrs′; *n., adj.* trav′ərs) *v.* -ersed, -ers·ing; *n., adj., adv.* —*v.* 1 pass across, over, or through: *The caravan traversed the desert.* 2 lie, extend, or stretch across; cross; intersect. 3 walk or move in a crosswise direction; move back and forth: *That horse traverses.* 4 go to and fro over or along (a place, etc.). 5 ski diagonally across (a slope). 6 read, examine, or consider carefully. 7 move sideways; turn from side to side. 8 *Fencing.* glide the blade along that of the opponent's foil, toward the hilt, while applying pressure. 9 turn big guns to right or left. 10 turn on a pivot, or as if on a pivot. 11 oppose; hinder; thwart. 12 examine carefully. —*n.* 1 the act of crossing. 2 something put or lying across. 3 an earth wall protecting a trench or an exposed place in a fortification. 4 in a church, etc., a gallery running from side to side. 5 a distance across. 6 a sideways motion of a ship, part in a machine, mountain climbers, etc. 7 the zigzag line taken by a ship because of contrary winds or currents. 8 a line that crosses other lines. 9 opposition; an obstacle; hindrance. 10 a a changing the direction of a gun to the right or left. b the amount of such change. 11 *Law.* a formal denial of something alleged to be a fact by the opposing side. —*adj.* lying across; being across. —*adv.* across; crosswise. [ME < OF *traverser* < LL *transversare* < L *transversus*. See TRANSVERSE.] —**trav′ers·a·ble,** *adj.* —**trav′ers·er,** *n.*

trav·er·tin (trav′ər tin) *n.* travertine.

trav·er·tine (trav′ər tin or trav′ər tēn′) *n.* a form of limestone deposited by springs, etc., used as building material. [< Ital. *travertino,* var. of *tivertino,* ult. < L *Tibur,* an ancient town in Latium]

trav·es·ty (trav′is tē) *n., pl.* -ties; *v.* -tied, -ty·ing. —*n.* 1 an imitation of a serious literary work in such a way as to make it seem ridiculous. 2 any treatment or imitation that makes a serious thing seem ridiculous. —*v.* make (a serious subject or matter) ridiculous; imitate in an absurd or grotesque way. [< F *travesti* disguised, ult. < L *trans-* over + *vestire* dress < *vestis* garment]

Two kinds of travois

tra·vois (trə voi′ or trav′woi; *French,* trä vwä′) *n., pl.* **-vois.** 1 *Cdn. Historical.* a simple wheel-less vehicle used by Indian peoples of the plains, made of two shafts or poles, to which was attached a platform or net for holding the load: *A travois was dragged by a horse or dog hitched to the shafts.* 2 a sled used for transporting logs. [< Cdn.F. alteration of F *travail* frame to hold a horse being shod]

trawl (trol or trôl) *n., v.* —*n.* 1 a strong net dragged along the bottom of the sea. 2 a line supported by buoys and having attached to it many short lines with baited hooks. —*v.* 1 fish with a net by dragging it along the bottom of the sea. 2 fish with lines supported by buoys. 3 catch with a trawl: *to trawl fish.* [< MDu. *traghel* < L *tragula* dragnet]

trawl·er (trol′ər or trôl′ər) *n.* 1 a boat used in trawling. 2 a person who fishes by trawling.

tray (trā) *n.* 1 a flat, open holder or container with a low rim around it: *We carried the dishes into the dining room on a tray. The sewing basket has an accessory tray that can be lifted out.* 2 a tray together with its contents. [OE *trēg*]
☛ *Hom.* **trait.**

treach·er·ous (trech′ər əs) *adj.* 1 not to be trusted; not faithful; disloyal: *The treacherous soldier carried reports to the enemy.* 2 having a false appearance of strength, security, etc.; not reliable; deceiving: *Thin ice is treacherous.* —**treach′er·ous·ly,** *adv.* —**treach′er·ous·ness,** *n.*

treach·er·y (trech′ər ē) *n., pl.* -er·ies. 1 a breaking of faith; treacherous behavior; deceit. 2 treason. [ME < OF *trecherie* < *trechier* cheat]
☛ *Syn.* 1. See note at **disloyalty.**

trea·cle (trē′kəl) *n.* 1 *Esp.Brit.* molasses. 2 a compound formerly much used as an antidote for poison or poisonous bites. [ME *triacle* antidote for bites < OF < L < Gk. *thēriakē,* ult. < *thēr* wild beast]

tread (tred) *v.* trod, trod·den or trod, tread·ing; *n.* —*v.* 1 walk; step; set the foot down: *Don't tread on the flower beds.* 2 set the feet on; walk on or through; step on: *to tread the streets.* 3 press under the feet; trample on; crush: *to tread grapes.* 4 make, form, or do by walking: *Cattle had trodden a path to the pond.* 5 follow; pursue: *to tread the path of virtue.* 6 treat with cruelty; oppress. 7 of a male bird, copulate with (a female).
tread on (someone's) toes, offend or annoy one.
tread the boards, be an actor or actress; play a part in a play.
tread water, keep afloat in water, with the body upright and the head above the surface, by slowly moving the legs as if bicycling. —*n.* 1 the act or sound of treading: *We heard the tread of marching feet.* 2 a way of walking: *He walks with a heavy tread.* 3 the horizontal part of a step. 4 the width of this, from front to back. 5 the part of something, such as a wheel or shoe, that touches the ground. 6 the raised pattern on the surface of a tire: *The tread on the back tires is almost gone.* 7 either of the tracks of a caterpillar tractor or similar vehicle. 8 the part of a rail or rails that the wheels touch. 9 the distance between the two front or rear wheels of a motor vehicle: *a car with a wide tread.* 10 *Rare.* footprint. [OE *tredan*] —**tread′er,** *n.*

trea·dle (tred′əl) *n., v.* -dled, -dling. —*n.* a rocking lever or pedal worked by the foot to drive a machine, such as a sewing machine, grindstone, or lathe. —*v.* work a treadle. [OE *tredel* < *tredan* tread]

tread·mill (tred′mil′) *n.* 1 an apparatus for producing motion by having a person or animal walk on the moving steps of a wheel or of a sloping, endless belt. 2 any wearisome or monotonous round of work or life that seems to go nowhere.

treas. treasurer; treasury.

trea·son (trē′zən) *n.* 1 the act or fact of betraying one's country or ruler. Helping the enemies of one's country is treason. 2 *Rare.* the betrayal of a trust, duty, friend, etc.; treachery. [ME < AF *treson* < L *traditio.* Doublet of TRADITION.]
☛ *Syn.* 1. See note at **disloyalty.**

trea·son·a·ble (trē′zən ə bəl or trēz′nə bəl) *adj.* having to do with, consisting of, or involving treason. —**trea′son·a·ble·ness,** *n.* —**trea′son·a·bly,** *adv.*

trea·son·ous (trē′zən əs or trēz′nəs) *adj.* treasonable.

treas·ure (trezh′ər) *n., v.* -ured, -ur·ing. —*n.* 1 wealth or riches stored up; valuable things. 2 any thing or person that is much loved or valued. —*v.* 1 value highly. 2 put away for future use; store up. [ME < OF *tresor* < L < Gk. *thēsauros.* Doublet of THESAURUS.]

treas·ur·er (trezh′ər ər) *n.* a person in charge of the finances of a club, society, corporation, government body, etc.

treas·ure–trove (trezh′ər trōv′) *n.* 1 money, jewels, or other treasure that a person finds, especially if the owner of it is not known. 2 any valuable discovery. [< AF *tresor trové* treasure found]

treas·ur·y (trezh′ər ē) *n., pl.* -ur·ies. 1 the place where money is kept; especially, one where public revenues are deposited and kept. 2 money owned; funds: *We paid for the party out of the club treasury.* 3 a government department that has charge of the collection, management and expenditure of public revenues. 4 a place where treasure or anything valuable is kept. 5 a book, person, etc. thought of as a valued source: *a treasury of adventure stories. He is a treasury of information on rocks.*

Treasury bench or **benches** in the House of Commons or in a legislature, the front benches to the Speaker's right, occupied by the ministers of the government.

treat (trēt) *v., n.* —*v.* 1 act toward; handle: *He treats his dog gently. My father treats our new car with care.* 2 think of; consider; regard: *He treats his mistake as a joke.* 3 deal with to relieve or cure: *The dentist is treating my tooth.* 4 deal with to bring about some special result: *to treat a metal plate with acid in engraving.* 5 deal with; discuss: *Her talk treated of recent political developments in Europe. This magazine treats the progress of*

medicine. **6** express in literature, music, or art: *to treat a theme realistically*. **7** deal with a subject. **8** discuss terms; arrange terms: *Messengers came to treat for peace.* **9** entertain by giving food, drink, or amusement: *He treated us to lunch.* **10** pay the cost of entertainment: *I'll treat today.*
—*n.* **1** a gift of food, drink, or amusement: *"This is my treat,"* she said, as she paid for the tickets. **2** anything that gives pleasure: *Being in the country is a treat to her.* [ME < OF *traitier* < L *tractare*, originally, drag violently, handle, frequentative of *trahere* drag] —**treat′er,** *n.*

treat·a·ble (trēt′ə bəl) *adj.* capable of being treated; that will respond to treatment: *a treatable disease.*

trea·tise (trē′tis) *n.* a book or writing dealing formally and systematically with some subject. [ME < AF *tretiz,* ult. < L *tractare* treat. See TREAT.]

treat·ment (trēt′mənt) *n.* **1** the act or process of treating. **2** a way of treating. **3** something done or used to treat something else, such as a disease: *We read about old treatments for colds.*

trea·ty (trē′tē) *n., pl.* **-ties. 1** an agreement, especially one between nations, signed and approved by each nation. **2** the document embodying such an agreement. **3** *Cdn.* one of a number of official agreements between the federal government and certain Indian bands whereby the Indians give up their land rights except for reserves and accept treaty money and other kinds of government assistance. **4** treaty money.
take treaty or **take the treaty,** *Cdn.* of an Indian band or people, accept the terms of treaty with the federal government.
[ME < AF *trete,* OF *traitie* < L *tractatus* discussion < *tractare.* See TREAT.]

treaty Indian *Cdn.* a member of an Indian band or people living on a reserve and receiving treaty money and other treaty rights.

treaty money *Cdn.* an annual payment made by the federal government to treaty Indians.

treaty rights *Cdn.* the rights guaranteed to Indians in their treaties with the federal government.

tre·ble (treb′əl) *adj., v.* **-bled, -bling;** *n.* —*adj.* **1** three times; threefold; triple. **2** *Music.* having to do with, having the range of, or designed for the treble. **3** of a voice or sound, shrill and high-pitched.
—*v.* make or become three times as much: *She trebled her income when she changed to a career in advertising.*
—*n.* **1** *Music.* **a** the highest voice part in choral music, especially for a boys' choir; soprano. **b** a singer who sings such a part. **c** the upper half of the whole musical range of a voice or instrument. Compare **bass¹** (def. 5). **d** an instrument having the highest range in a family of musical instruments. **2** a shrill, high-pitched voice or sound. [ME < OF < L *triplus* triple. Doublet of TRIPLE.]

treble clef *Music.* a symbol (𝄞) indicating that the pitch of the notes on a staff is above middle C.

tre·bly (treb′lē) *adv.* three times.

tree (trē) *n., v.* **treed, tree·ing.** —*n.* **1** a large perennial plant having a woody trunk, branches, and leaves. **2** less accurately, any of certain other plants that resemble trees in form or size. **3** a piece or structure of wood, etc. for some special purpose: *a clothes tree, a shoe tree.* **4** anything suggesting a tree and its branches. **5** See **family tree. 6** *Archaic.* a gallows. **7** *Archaic.* the cross on which Christ died.
up a tree, a chased up a tree. **b** *Informal.* in a difficult position.
—*v.* **1** furnish with a tree (beam, bar, wooden handle, etc.). **2** stretch (a shoe) on a tree. **3** assume a treelike or branching form. **4** chase up a tree: *The cat was treed by a dog.* **5** take refuge in a tree. **6** *Informal.* put into a difficult position. [OE *trēo*]

treed (trēd) *adj.* planted or covered with trees: *treed lands.*

tree farm a privately owned area in which trees are grown under a system of forest management.

tree farmer a person engaged in tree farming.

tree farming the management of a tree farm.

tree fern any of numerous tropical ferns (especially of family Cyatheaceae) that grow to the size of a tree, with a trunklike stem and large fronds at the top.

tree frog 1 any of a large family (Hylidae) of frogs found mainly in the New World, most of which live in trees. Tree frogs have sucker-like, sticky disks on the tips of their toes which help them in climbing. **2** any of various other frogs and toads that live in trees.

tree house a structure, such as a playhouse, built in the branches of a tree.

tree line a limit on mountains and in high latitudes beyond which trees will not grow because of the cold, etc.; timberline.

treen (trēn) *n.* the art and craft of making treenware. Canadian treen ranges from the late 17th century to recent times. [< *tree* wood]

hat, āge, fär; let, ēqual, tėrm; it, īce
hot, ōpen, ôrder; oil, out; cup, put, rüle,
əbove, takən, pencəl, lemən, circəs

ch, child; ng, long; sh, ship
th, thin; ŦH, then; zh, measure

tree·nail (trē′nāl′, tren′əl, *or* trun′əl) *n.* a round pin of hard wood for fastening timbers together. Also, **trenail.**

treen·ware (trēn′wer′) *n.* household utensils and objects carved from wood, as used by the early settlers.

tree of heaven an Asian ailanthus (*Ailanthus altissima*) that is widely grown as an ornamental and shade tree.

tree toad tree frog.

tree·top (trē′top′) *n.* the top of a tree.

tre·foil (trē′foil) *n.* **1** any of various herbs having leaves made up of three leaflets, especially clover. **2** a leaf made up of three leaflets. **3** an ornamental figure shaped like such a leaf. [ME < AF < L *trifolium* < *tri-* three + *folium* leaf]

trek (trek) *v.* **trekked, trek·king;** *n.* —*v.* **1** travel, especially slowly and for a long distance or under difficult conditions; migrate. **2** *Informal.* go; proceed: *to trek down to the office.* **3** especially in South Africa, travel by ox wagon.
—*n.* **1** a journey, especially a slow or difficult one. **2** a journey by ox wagon. **3** a stage of such a journey, from one stopping place to the next. [< Du. *trekken,* originally, draw, pull]

trel·lis (trel′is) *n., v.* —*n.* **1** a frame of light strips of wood or metal crossing one another with open spaces in between; lattice, especially one supporting growing vines. **2** a summerhouse or other structure with sides of lattice.
—*v.* **1** furnish with a trellis. **2** support on a trellis. **3** cross or interlace like a trellis; interweave. [ME < OF *trelis,* ult. < L *trilix* triple-twilled < *tri-* three + *licium* thread]

trel·lis·work (trel′is wėrk′) *n.* trellises; latticework.

trem·a·tode (trem′ə tōd′ *or* trē′mə tōd′) *n.* any of a class (Trematoda) of flatworms that live as parasites in or on other animals; fluke. [< NL < Gk. *trēmatōdēs* holed < *trēma, -atos* hole]

trem·ble (trem′bəl) *v.* **-bled, -bling;** *n.* —*v.* **1** shake because of fear, excitement, weakness, cold, etc. **2** feel fear, anxiety, etc: *She trembled for their safety. He trembled at the thought of having to ask for the money.* **3** move gently.
—*n.* a trembling or quivering: *There was a tremble in her voice as she began to recite.* [ME < OF *trembler,* ult. < L *tremulus.* See TREMULOUS.] —**trem′bling·ly,** *adv.*
☛ *Syn. v.* **1.** See note at **shake.**

trembling aspen a North American poplar (*Populus tremuloides*) found throughout the forested regions of Canada, having finely toothed, rounded, hairless leaves that flutter in the slightest breeze. See also **aspen.**

trem·bly (trem′blē) *adj.* trembling; tremulous: *His voice was trembly with fear.*

tre·men·dous (tri men′dəs) *adj.* **1** dreadful; awful. **2** *Informal.* very great; enormous: *a tremendous house.* **3** *Informal.* especially good: *We saw a tremendous movie yesterday.* [< L *tremendus,* literally, to be trembled at < *tremere* tremble] —**tre·men′dous·ly,** *adv.*

trem·o·lo (trem′ə lō′) *n., pl.* **-los. 1** *Music.* a trembling or vibrating quality, as produced by singing by a wavering in pitch or on a stringed instrument by a rapid repeating of a tone with fast strokes of the bow. The tremolo is used to express emotion. **2** in an organ, a device used to produce this quality. [< Ital. *tremolo* < L *tremulus.* Doublet of TREMULOUS.]

trem·or (trem′ər) *n.* **1** an involuntary shaking or trembling as from physical weakness, emotional upset, or disease: *a nervous tremor in the voice.* **2** a thrill of emotion or excitement. **3** a shaking movement. An earthquake is called an earth tremor. [< L]

trem·u·lous (trem′yə ləs) *adj.* **1** trembling; quivering. **2** timid; fearful. [< L *tremulus* < *tremere* tremble. Doublet of TREMOLO.] —**trem′u·lous·ly,** *adv.* —**trem′u·lous·ness,** *n.*

tre·nail (trē′nāl′, tren′əl, *or* trun′əl) See **treenail.**

trench (trench) *n., v.* —*n.* **1** a long, narrow cut in the ground; especially one having the excavated earth thrown up in front, used as a defence for soldiers in battle. **2** a long, narrow, deep area in the ocean floor.
—*v.* **1** surround or fortify with a trench or trenches. **2** dig a trench in. **3** dig ditches. **4** make a cut in.
trench on or **upon, a** trespass upon. **b** come close to; border on: *The demagogue's speech trenched closely on treason.*
[ME < OF *trenche,* n., *trenchier,* v., to cut, apparently ult. < L *truncare* lop off < *truncus* mutilated]

trench·an·cy (tren′chən sē) *n.* the quality or state of being trenchant.

trench·ant (tren′chənt) *adj.* **1** sharp; keen; cutting: *trenchant wit.* **2** vigorous; effective: *a trenchant policy.* **3** clear-cut; distinct: *in trenchant outline against the sky.* [ME < OF *trenchant,* ppr. of *trenchier* cut. See TRENCH.] —**trench′ant·ly,** *adv.*

trench coat a loose-fitting raincoat worn with a belt, often double-breasted and usually having wide lapels and epaulettes. The classic trench coat is a beige or camel color.

trench·er (tren′chər) *n.* a wooden platter formerly used for serving food, especially meat. [ME < OF *trencheoir* knife, ult. < *trenchier* cut. See TRENCH.]

trench·er·man (tren′chər mən) *n., pl.* **-men. 1** a heavy eater; a person who has a hearty appetite. **2** *Archaic.* a hanger-on; sponger.

trench fever an infectious fever that is transmitted by lice, particularly common among soldiers in the trenches during the First World War.

trench mouth a contagious disease of the gums and, sometimes, the inside of the lips and cheeks, etc., caused by bacteria, and characterized by foul-smelling breath.

trend (trend) *n., v.* —*n.* **1** the general direction; a course or tendency: *a western trend, the trend of modern living.* **2** a current style in fashion, etc. —*v.* have a general direction; tend; run: *The road trends to the north.* [OE *trendan*]
☛ *Syn. n.* See note at **direction.**

trend·y (tren′dē) *adj. Informal.* following the very latest fashions or trends: *a trendy boutique, trendy styles.*

Trent (trent) *n.* **Council of,** the council of the Roman Catholic Church held at Trent, Italy, from time to time, between 1545 and 1563. It defined Catholic doctrines, corrected certain abuses within the church, and organized the Catholic opposition to the Protestant movement.

tre·pan (tri pan′) *n., v.* **-panned, -pan·ning.** —*n.* **1** an early form of the trephine. **2** a boring instrument, used for sinking shafts. —*v.* **1** operate on with a trepan (trephine). **2** bore through with a trepan; cut a disk out of with a trepan or similar tool. [ME < OF < Med.L < Gk. *trypanon* < *trypaein* bore < *trypē* hole]

tre·pang (tri pang′) *n.* **1** any of various large, edible sea cucumbers found especially on the coral reefs of the SW Pacific Ocean, that are boiled, dried, and smoked for use in soup, especially in E Asia. **2** the body wall of any of these sea cucumbers, prepared for use as food. [< Malay *tripang*]

tre·phine (tri fīn′ *or* tri fēn′) *n., v.* **-phined, -phin·ing.** —*n.* a cylindrical saw with a removable centre pin, used to cut out circular pieces from the skull. —*v.* operate on with a trephine. [earlier *trafine,* alteration by inventor Woodall of *trapan* (var. of *trepan*) after L *tres fines* three ends]

trep·i·da·tion (trep′ə dā′shən) *n.* **1** nervous dread; apprehension; fear. **2** a trembling. [< L *trepidatio, -onis,* ult. < *trepidus* alarmed]

tres·pass (tres′pəs *or* tres′pas) *v., n.* —*v.* **1** go on somebody's property without any right: *The farmer put up "No Trespassing" signs to keep people off his property.* **2** go beyond the limits of what is right, proper, or polite: *I won't trespass on your time any longer.* **3** do wrong; sin.
—*n.* **1** the act or fact of trespassing. **2** a wrong; a sin. **3** *Law.* **a** an unlawful act done against the person, property, or rights of another. **b** an action to recover damages for such an injury. [ME < OF *trespasser* < *tres-* across (< L *trans-*) + *passer* pass, ult. < L *passus* step] —**tres′pass·er,** *n.*
☛ *Syn. v.* **1, 2.** See note at **intrude.**

tress (tres) *n.* **1** a lock, curl, or braid of hair. **2** **tresses,** *pl.* a woman's or girl's hair, especially when long: *She had thick, dark brown tresses.* [< ME < OF *tresce,* probably < Gmc.]

tres·tle (tres′əl) *n.* **1** a structure, such as a sawhorse, used to support a table top, platform, etc. **2** a framework used as a bridge to support a road, railway tracks, etc. [ME < OF *trestel* crossbeam, ult. < L *transtrum*]

tres·tle·tree (tres′əl trē′) *n.* either of two horizontal, fore-and-aft timbers or bars secured to a ship's masthead, one on each side, in order to support the crosstrees.

tres·tle·work (tres′əl wèrk′) *n.* a system of connected trestles supporting a bridge, etc.

trews (trüz) *n.pl. Scottish.* tight-fitting tartan trousers. [< Irish *trius* < *triubhas.* Cf. TROUSERS.]

trey (trā) *n.* a card, die, or domino, etc. having three spots. [ME < OF *trei* < L *tres* three]

tri– *prefix.* **1** three; having three; having three parts, as in *triangle.* **2** three times; into three parts, as in *trisect.* **3** containing three

atoms, etc. of the substance specified, as in *trioxide.* **4** once in three; every third, as in *trimonthly.* [< L or Gk.]

tri·ad (trī′ad) *n.* **1** a group of three, especially of three closely related persons or things. **2** *Music.* a chord of three tones, especially one consisting of the root tone plus the third and fifth tones above it. **3** *Chemistry.* an element, atom, or radical with a valence of three. [< LL *trias, -adis* < Gk. *trias, -ados* < *treis* three]

tri·age (trī′ij *or* trē äzh′) *n.* **1** the sorting of a large number of battle casualties, accident victims, etc. by a system of priorities which ensures that those with the best chance of benefiting from treatment are looked after first. **2** the allocation of a scarce commodity, such as food, by a similar method, giving priority to those who will derive the greatest benefit from it. [< F < *trier* to sort, sift. 18c. See TRY]

tri·al (trī′əl) *n.* **1** the process of examining and deciding a case in court: *The suspected thief was arrested and brought to trial.* **2** *(adj.)* of or having to do with a trial in a law court: *trial testimony.* **3** the process of trying or testing: *He gave the machine another trial.* **4** *(adj.)* for a try or test: *a trial run, a trial model.* **5** experimentation by investigation, tentative action, use, etc.; experiment: *to learn by trial and error.* **6** the condition of being tried or tested: *He is employed on trial.* **7** *(adj.)* that is on trial: *a trial employee.* **8** a trouble or hardship. **9** a cause of trouble or hardship: *She is a trial to her big sister.* **10** an attempt; effort. **11** a preliminary competition in field or track events at a track meet. [< AF *trial* < *trier* try]
☛ *Syn. n.* **3. Trial, test, experiment** = a way of discovering or proving something. **Trial** applies to the process of discovering the qualities of something and establishing its worth, genuineness, strength, effect, etc.: *He gave the new toothpaste a trial.* **Test** applies to a trial to end uncertainty about quality, genuineness, or presence, as by thorough examination: *The new plane passed all tests.* **Experiment** applies to a process to find out something still unknown or to test conclusions, a hypothesis, etc.: *Experiments indicate the new drug will cure infections.*

trial and error the process of arriving at a solution of a problem by trying several ways and learning from the errors so made.

trial balance in bookkeeping, a comparison of debit and credit totals in a ledger. If they are not equal, there is an error.

trial jury a jury selected to hear evidence in a criminal or civil trial and sworn to give a verdict on the basis of facts found from the evidence. In a criminal trial, the jury gives a verdict as to the guilt or innocence in law of the accused. In a civil trial it decides in favor of the plaintiff or the defendant. Also called **petit jury.**

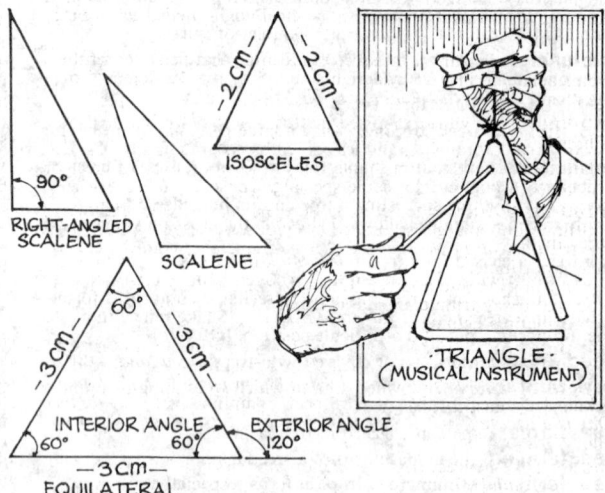

ISOSCELES
RIGHT-ANGLED SCALENE
90°
SCALENE
INTERIOR ANGLE 60° 60°
EXTERIOR ANGLE 120°
—3cm—
EQUILATERAL
·TRIANGLE· (MUSICAL INSTRUMENT)

tri·an·gle (trī′ang gəl) *n.* **1** a plane figure having three sides and three angles. **2** any object, part, or area having three sides or three angles: *Our backyard is a triangle.* **3** a musical instrument consisting of a steel rod bent in a triangle with one corner open, that produces a light ringing sound when struck with a small steel rod. **4** an instrument for drafting, consisting of a flat right-angled triangle of wood, plastic, etc. **5** a situation involving three persons or points of view, especially an emotional relationship involving two men and one woman or two women and one man, with attendant complications: *the eternal triangle.* **6** a group of three. [ME < L *triangulum* < *tri-* three + *angulus* corner]

tri·an·gu·lar (trī ang′gyə lər) *adj.* **1** of, having to do with, or

shaped like a triangle: *a triangular piece of cloth.* **2** concerned with three persons, groups, etc.

tri·an·gu·late (*v.* trī ang′gyə lāt′; *adj.* trī ang′yə lit or trī ang′gyə lāt′) *v.* **-lat·ed, -lat·ing;** *adj.* —*v.* **1** divide into triangles. **2** survey or map out (a region) by dividing (it) into triangles and measuring their angles. **3** find by trigonometry: *to triangulate the height of a mountain.* **4** make triangular. —*adj.* **1** composed of or marked with triangles. **2** triangular.

tri·an·gu·la·tion (trī ang′gyə lā′shən) *n.* **1** a survey or measurement done by means of trigonometry. **2** a division into triangles.

Tri·as·sic (trī as′ik) *n., adj. Geology.* —*n.* **1** the earliest period of the Mesozoic era, beginning approximately 200 million years ago. **2** the rocks formed during this period. See **geology** for chart. —*adj.* of or having to do with the Triassic period or the rocks formed during it. [< G *Trias,* the name for a certain series of strata containing three types of deposit < LL *trias.* See TRIAD.]

trib·al (trīb′əl) *adj.* of, having to do with, or characteristic of a tribe: *tribal customs, tribal lore.*

trib·al·ism (trīb′ə liz′əm) *n.* tribal organization and culture.

trib·a·lize (trīb′ə līz′) *v.* **-lized, -liz·ing. 1** divide or organize into tribes. **2** confer tribal status on.

trib·al·ly (trīb′əl ē) *adv.* according to tribe; by tribe or tribes: *a tribally organized society.*

tri·bas·ic (trī bās′ik) *adj. Chemistry.* **1** of an acid, having three atoms of hydrogen replaceable by basic atoms or radicals. **2** having three atoms or radicals of a univalent metal. **3** having three basic hydroxyl (OH) radicals.

tribe (trīb) *n.* **1** a group of families, clans, etc. united by race, custom, etc. under one leader or ruling group. **2** a group of people having a common interest, profession, etc.: *the tribe of artists, the whole tribe of gossips.* **3** a minor category in the classification of animals and plants ranking between a genus and a subfamily or family. **4** any group, class, or kind of animals, plants, or things. [< L *tribus*]

tribes·man (trībz′mən) *n., pl.* **-men.** a member of a tribe.

trib·u·la·tion (trib′yə lā′shən) *n.* great trouble or affliction, especially as a result of persecution or oppression: *the tribulations of the early Christians.* [ME < OF < LL *tribulatio, -onis,* ult. < L *tribulum* threshing sledge]

tri·bu·nal (tri byü′nəl or trī byü′nəl) *n.* **1** a court of justice; a place of judgment: *He was brought before the tribunal for trial.* **2** a place where judges sit in a law court. **3** something by or in which judgment is rendered; judicial or deciding authority: *the tribunal of the polls, the tribunal of the press.* [< L *tribunal* < *tribunus.* See TRIBUNE¹.]

trib·une¹ (trib′yün) *n.* **1** in ancient Rome, an official chosen by the plebeians to protect their rights and interests. **2** a defender of the people. [ME < L *tribunus* < *tribus* tribe]

trib·une² (trib′yün) *n.* a raised platform or dais. [< Ital. *tribuna* tribunal]

trib·une·ship (trib′yün ship′) *n.* the position, duties, or term of a tribune.

trib·u·tar·y (trib′yə ter′ē) *n., pl.* **-tar·ies;** *adj.* —*n.* **1** a stream that flows into a larger stream or body of water: *The Ottawa River is a tributary of the St. Lawrence River.* **2** a person, country, etc. that pays tribute. —*adj.* **1** flowing into a larger stream or body of water. **2** paying or required to pay tribute. **3** paid as tribute; of the nature of tribute. **4** contributing; helping.

trib·ute (trib′yüt) *n.* **1** money paid by one nation to another for peace or protection or because of some agreement. **2** any forced payment: *The pirates demanded tribute from passing ships.* **3** an acknowledgement of thanks or respect; compliment: *Remembrance Day is a tribute to our dead soldiers.* [ME < L *tributum* < *tribuere* allot < *tribus* tribe]

trice¹ (trīs) *v.* **triced, tric·ing.** haul up and fasten with a rope: *to trice up a sail.* [ME < MDu. *trisen* hoist < *trise* pulley]

trice² (trīs) *n. Archaic* (*except in* **in a trice**). a very short time; moment; instant: *In a trice, he was through the window and in the room.* [abstracted from phrase *at a trice* at a pull. Cf. TRICE¹.]

tri·cen·te·nar·y (trī′sen ten′ə rē or trī′sen tē′nə rē) *adj. or n., pl.* **-nar·ies.** tricentennial.

tri·cen·ten·ni·al (trī′sen ten′ē əl, -sen ten′yəl or -sen tēn′yəl) *adj., n.* —*adj.* having to do with a period of 300 years. —*n.* **1** a period of 300 years. **2** a 300th anniversary.

tri·ceps (trī′seps) *n. Physiology.* the large muscle at the back of the upper arm. It extends, or straightens, the arm. [< NL < L *triceps* three-headed < *tri-* three + *caput* head]

tri·chi·na (tri kī′nə) *n., pl.* **-nae** (-nē or -nī). a tiny nematode worm (*Trichinella spiralis*) that occurs as a parasite in the intestines

hat, āge, fär; let, ēqual, tèrm; it, īce

hot, ōpen, ôrder; oil, out; cup, pùt, rüle, əbove, takən, pencəl, lemən, circəs

ch, child; ng, long; sh, ship

th, thin; ᵀH, then; zh, measure

and muscles of certain mammals, including man. Trichinae usually get into the human body from pork that is infected with the larvae and is not cooked long enough to destroy them. [< NL < Gk. *trichinē,* fem. adj., of hair < *thrix, trichos* hair]

trich·i·no·sis (trik′ə nō′sis) *n.* a disease due to the presence of trichinae in the intestines and muscular tissues. [< NL]

trich·i·nous (trik′ə nəs) *adj.* **1** having trichinosis; infected with trichinae. **2** of, having to do with, or involving trichinae or trichinosis: *a trichinous infection.*

trick (trik) *n., v.* —*n.* **1** something done to deceive or cheat: *The false message was a trick to get him to leave the house.* **2** something pretended or unreal; illusion: *Those two lines are really the same length, but a trick of vision makes one of them look longer.* **3** a clever act; a feat of skill: *We enjoyed the tricks of the trained animals.* **4** the best way of dealing with or doing something: *the trick of making pies.* **5** a piece of mischief; prank: *Stealing John's lunch was a mean trick.* **6** a peculiar habit or way of acting: *He has a trick of pulling at his collar.* **7** single round of certain card games. **8** a turn or period of duty at a job, especially at steering a ship.

do or **turn the trick,** do what one wants done.
—*v.* **1** deceive; cheat: *We were tricked into buying a poor car.* **2** play pranks. **3** dress or adorn, especially in an ornate or fanciful way (*used with* **out** or **up**): *She was tricked out in her mother's clothes.* [ME < OF *trique*]

☞ *Syn.* **1.** See note at **cheat.**

trick·er·y (trik′ər ē or trik′rē) *n., pl.* **-er·ies.** the act or practice of deceiving or cheating; fraud.

trick·le (trik′əl) *v.* **-led, -ling;** *n.* —*v.* **1** flow or fall in drops or in a small stream: *Tears trickled down her cheeks. The brook trickled through the valley.* **2** cause to flow in drops or in a small stream: *He trickled the water into the container.* **3** come, go, pass, etc. slowly and unevenly: *An hour before the show people began to trickle into the theatre.*
—*n.* **1** a small flow or stream. **2** the act of trickling. [ME *strikle* < *strike* flow, move, strike < OE *strīcan*]

trick or treat a call used by children dressed in costumes at Halloween, going from door to door and begging for candy or other gifts under the threat of playing tricks if they are refused.

trick·ster (trik′stər) *n.* a cheat; deceiver.

trick·sy (trik′sē) *adj.* **1** mischievous; playful; frolicsome. **2** tricky. —**trick′si·ness,** *n.*

trick·y (trik′ē) *adj.* **trick·i·er, trick·i·est. 1** full of tricks; deceiving; cheating. **2** not reliable; difficult to handle: *Our back door has a tricky lock.* —**trick′i·ly,** *adv.* —**trick′i·ness,** *n.*

tri·col·or or **tri·col·our** (trī′kul′ər) *adj., n.* —*adj.* having three colors. —*n.* a flag having three colors, especially the flag of France, which has three equal vertical stripes of blue, white, and red. [< F (*drapeau*) *tricolore* tricolored (flag)]

tri·cot (trē′kō) *n.* **1** a knitted wool, cotton, or synthetic fabric made by hand or machine. **2** a kind of woollen cloth. **3** a close-fitting garment worn by ballet dancers. [< F *tricot,* ult. < Gmc.]

tri·co·tine (trik′ə tēn′) *n.* a kind of twilled woollen cloth.

tri·cus·pid (trī kus′pid) *adj., n.* —*adj.* having three points or cusps: *a tricuspid tooth.* —*n.* a tricuspid tooth. [< L *tricuspis, -idis* three-pointed < *tri-* three + *cuspis* tip]

tri·cy·cle (trī′sə kəl or trī′sik′əl) *n.* **1** a three-wheeled vehicle usually worked by pedals attached to the large single wheel in front, now used especially by small children. **2** a three-wheeled motor vehicle designed for use by a disabled person. [< F *tricycle* < *tri-* three (< L or Gk.) + *cycle,* ult. < Gk. *kyklos* ring, circle]

tri·dent (trī′dənt) *n., adj.* —*n.* a three-pronged spear, especially as the identifying attribute of Poseidon (Neptune), the ancient Greek and Roman god of the sea. —*adj.* three-pronged. [< L *tridens, -entis* < *tri-* three + *dens* tooth]

tri·den·tate (trī den′tāt) *adj.* having three teeth or teethlike points; three-pronged.

tried (trīd) *adj., v.* —*adj.* tested; proved. —*v.* pt. and pp. of **try.**

tri·en·ni·al (trī en′ē əl) *adj., n.* —*adj.* **1** lasting three years. **2** occurring every three years. —*n.* **1** an event that occurs every three years. **2** the third anniversary of an event. [< L *triennium* three-year period < *tri-* three + *annus* year] —**tri·en′ni·al·ly,** *adv.*

tri·er (trī′ər) *n.* a person or thing that tries.

tri·fle (trī′fəl) *n., v.* **-fled, -fling.** —*n.* **1** something having little value or importance. **2** a small amount; a little bit. **3** a small amount of money. **4** a rich dessert made of sponge cake, whipped cream, custard, fruit, wine, etc.
—*v.* **1** talk or act lightly, not seriously: *Don't trifle with serious matters.* **2** play or toy (*with*): *He trifled with his pencil while he was talking to me.* **3** spend (time, effort, money, etc.) on things having little value: *She had trifled away the whole morning.* [ME < OF *trufle*; origin uncertain]
☛ *Syn. v.* **1. Trifle, dally** = treat a person or thing without seriousness. **Trifle** means "talk or act lightly, or playfully," especially about something deserving serious treatment or respect: *He is not a man to be trifled with.* **Dally** emphasizes amusing oneself by playing, especially at love or with thoughts, or by flirting with danger or temptation: *I have dallied with the idea of taking a trip.*

tri·fler (trī′flər) *n.* a frivolous or shallow person.

tri·fling (trī′fling) *adj.* **1** having little value; not important; small. **2** frivolous; shallow. —**tri′fling·ly,** *adv.*

tri·fo·li·ate (trī fō′lē it *or* trī fō′lē āt′) *adj.* **1** of a plant, having leaves or leaflike parts in groups of three. Clover is a trifoliate plant. **2** of a leaf, composed of three leaflets. [< *tri-* + L *foliatus* leaved < *folium* leaf]

tri·fo·ri·um (trī fō′rē əm) *n., pl.* **-ri·a** (-rē ə). a gallery above a side aisle or transept in a church. [< Med.L *triforium,* apparently < L *tri-* three + *foris* door]

trig (trig) *adj.* neat; trim; smart-looking. [ME < ON *tryggr* trusty]

trig. trigonometry; trigonometric.

trig·ger (trig′ər) *n., v.* **-gered, -ger·ing.** —*n.* **1** the small lever pulled back by the finger in firing a gun. See **firearm** for picture. **2** any lever that releases a spring, catch, etc. when pulled or pressed. **3** anything that sets off or initiates something else.
quick on the trigger, a quick to shoot. **b** *Informal.* quick to act; mentally alert.
—*v.* **1** set off: *The explosion was triggered by a spark.* **2** cause to start; begin: *The fiery speech triggered an outburst of violence.* [ult. < Du. *trekker < trekken* pull]

trig·ger–hap·py (trig′ər hap′ē) *adj. Informal.* shooting or inclined to shoot at the slightest provocation.

tri·glyph (trī′glif) *n. Doric architecture.* the part of a frieze between two metopes, consisting typically of a rectangular block with two vertical grooves and a half groove at each side. See **order** for picture. [< L < Gk. *triglyphos < tri* three + *glyphē* carving]

trigon. **1** trigonometry; trigonometric.

trig·o·no·met·ric (trig′ə nə met′rik) *adj.* of or having to do with trigonometry.

trig·o·no·met·ri·cal (trig′ə nə met′rə kəl) *adj.* trigonometric.

trig·o·no·met·ri·cal·ly (trig′ə nə met′rik lē) *adv.* by or according to trigonometry.

trig·o·nom·e·try (trig′ə nom′ə trē) *n.* the branch of mathematics that deals with the relations between the sides and angles of triangles and the calculations based on these. The principles of trigonometry are used in surveying, navigation, and engineering. [< NL *trigonometria,* ult. < Gk. *tri-* three + *gōnia* angle + *metron* measure]

tri·graph (trī′graf) *n.* three letters used to spell a single sound. *Example:* the *eau* in *beau.*

tri·he·dral (trī hē′drəl *or* trī hed′rəl) *adj.* of or having to do with a trihedron; formed by three planes meeting at a point.

tri·he·dron (trī hē′drən *or* trī hed′rən) *n., pl.* **-drons, -dra** (-drə). a figure formed by three planes meeting at a point. [< *tri-* + Gk. *hedra* seat, base]

trike (trīk) *n. Informal.* tricycle.

tri·lat·er·al (trī lat′ər əl) *adj.* having three sides. [< L *trilaterus* < *tri-* three + *latus, lateris* side]

tri·lin·gual (trī ling′gwəl *or* trī ling′yə wəl) *adj.* **1** able to speak three languages: *a trilingual person.* **2** using or involving three languages.

trill (tril) *v., n.* —*v.* **1** sing, play, sound, or speak with a quivering, vibrating sound. **2** sing or play with a trill. **3** *Phonetics.* pronounce with rapid vibration of the tongue, etc. Many Scots trill the sound of *r.*
—*n.* **1** the act or sound of trilling. **2** *Music.* a quick alternating of two notes a tone or a half tone apart. **3** *Phonetics.* **a** a rapid vibration of the tongue, etc. **b** a consonant pronounced by such a vibration. The (r) of most Highland Scots is a trill. [< Ital. *trillare* < ....c.]

....on (tril′yən) *n. or adj.* **1** in Canada and the United States, 1 ....d by 12 zeros; 1 000 000 000 000. **2** in the British Isles,

France, Germany, etc., 1 followed by 18 zeros. [< F *trillion < tri-* three, modelled on *million* million]

tril·li·um (tril′ē əm) *n.* any of a genus (*Trillium*) of small plants of the lily family having a short stem with a whorl of three leaves and a single flower with three narrow green sepals and three white, pink, or reddish petals. The white trillium (*T. grandiflorum*) is the provincial flower of Ontario. [< NL *trillium < L tri-* three]

tri·lo·bate (trī lō′bāt *or* trī′lə bāt′) *adj.* especially of a leaf, having three lobes.

tri·lo·bite (trī′lə bīt′) *n.* any of a large group (Trilobata) of extinct marine arthropods that flourished in the Paleozoic era, having a segmented outside skeleton divided by two deep, lengthwise furrows into three lobes. The relationship of trilobites to other arthropods is still unclear. [< NL *trilobita,* < Gk. *tri-* three + *lobos* lobe]

tril·o·gy (tril′ə jē) *n., pl.* **-gies.** three plays, operas, novels, etc. that fit together to make a related series. Any section of a trilogy is itself a complete work. [< Gk. *trilogia < tri-* three + *logos* story]

trim (trim) *v.* **trimmed, trim·ming;** *adj.* **trim·mer, trim·mest;** *n., adv.* —*v.* **1** put in good order; make neat by cutting away parts: *The lumber has to be trimmed for the carpenter. The gardener trimmed the hedge.* **2** remove (parts that are not needed): *He trimmed dead leaves off the plants.* **3** decorate: *The children trimmed the Christmas tree.* **4** balance (a boat, airplane, etc.) by arranging the load carried. **5** be or keep in balance. **6** arrange (the sails) to fit wind and direction. **7** change (opinions, views, etc.) to suit circumstances. **8** *Informal.* defeat heavily; beat. **9** *Informal.* scold.
—*adj.* **1** neat or spruce in appearance: *A trim maid appeared.* **2** that is or appears to be well designed and maintained: *a trim little ketch.*
—*n.* **1** good condition or order: *to get in trim for a race.* **2** condition; order: *That ship is in poor trim for a voyage.* **3** trimming: *the trim on a dress.* **4** equipment; outfit. **5** the position of a ship or aircraft when properly balanced. **6** the position or angle of the sails, yards, etc. in relation to the direction of the wind. **7** the visible woodwork inside a building. **8** woodwork used as a finish or ornament on the outside of a building. **9** the upholstery, handles, and accessories inside an automobile. **10** the chrome, color scheme, etc. decorating the outside of an automobile. **11** a display in a store window.
—*adv.* in a trim manner. [OE *trymman* strengthen, make ready]
—**trim′ly,** *adv.* —**trim′ness,** *n.*
☛ *Syn. adj.* See note at **neat.**

tri·ma·ran (trī′mə ran′) *n.* a boat with three hulls side by side. [< *tri-* + cata*maran*]

tri·mes·ter (trī mes′tər) *n.* **1** a third part of a school year. **2** a three-month period; a quarter of a year. [< F *trimestre* < L *trimestris < tri-* + *mensis* month]

trim·e·ter (trim′ə tər) *n. Prosody.* —*n.* a line of verse having three metrical feet. —*adj.* consisting of three feet or measures. [< L < Gk. *trimetros < tri-* three + *metron* measure]

trim·mer (trim′ər) *n.* **1** a person or thing that trims: *a hat trimmer, a window trimmer.* **2** a person who changes his opinions, actions, etc. to suit circumstances.

trim·ming (trim′ing) *n.* **1** something added as a decoration or accessory: *I'm putting red and blue trimming on my costume.* **2** *Informal.* a decisive defeat. **3** *Informal.* a scolding or thrashing. **4** act of a person or thing that trims. **5** **trimmings,** *pl.* **a** parts cut away in trimming. **b** *Informal.* garnishes, side dishes, and other accompaniments to a main dish: *We ate turkey with all the trimmings.*

tri·month·ly (trī munth′lē) *adj.* occurring every three months.

tri·mor·phism (trī môr′fiz əm) *n.* **1** *Mineralogy.* the occurrence in the same compound of three different forms of a crystalline substance. **2** *Botany.* the occurrence in the same species or individual plant of three different types of leaf, flower, etc. **3** *Zoology.* the occurrence in one species of three types distinct in size, color, structure, etc. [< Gk. *trimorphis < tri-* + *morphē* form + E *-ism*]

trim size the finished size of a book or book page, after all extra margins have been trimmed off.

tri·nal (trī′nəl) *adj.* composed of three parts; threefold.

trine (trīn) *adj., n.* —*adj.* **1** threefold; triple. **2** *Astrology.* of or having to do with the aspect of two planets 120 degrees distant from each other. —*n.*
Trine, the Trinity. [< L *trinus* triple]

Trin·i·dad·i·an (trin′i dad′ē ən *or* trin′i dā′dē ən) *n., adj.* —*n.* a native or inhabitant of Trinidad, an island in the West Indies. —*adj.* of or having to do with Trinidad or its people.

Trin·i·tar·i·an (trin′ə ter′ē ən) *adj., n.* —*adj.* **1** believing in the Trinity. **2** having to do with the Trinity. —*n.* a person who believes in the Trinity.

tri·ni·tro·tol·u·ene (trī nī′trō tol′yü ēn′) *n.* a powerful explosive formed from toluene, usually known as TNT. *Formula:*

CH₃C₆H₂(NO₂)₃ [< *trinitro-*, a combining form meaning "of three nitro-groups" (NO₂) + *toluene*]

tri·ni·tro·tol·u·ol (trī nī′trō tol′yü ōl′) *n.* trinitrotoluene.

Trin·i·ty (trin′ə tē) *n.* **1** *Christianity.* the union of Father, Son, and Holy Ghost in one divine nature. **2** *Informal.* Trinity Sunday. **3 trinity, a** a group of three closely related persons or things. **b** the state of being threefold. [ME < OF < L *trinitas* < *trinus* triple]

Trinity Sunday the eighth Sunday after Easter, observed as a feast to honor the Trinity.

trin·ket (tring′kit) *n.* **1** any small, fancy article, bit of jewellery, etc. **2** a trifle. [ME *trenket* little knife < ONF; ? < OF *trenchier*, *tranchier* cut]

tri·no·mi·al (trī nō′mē əl) *n.* **1** *Mathematics.* an expression consisting of three terms connected by plus or minus signs. *Example:* a + *bx*² − 2 **2** *Biology.* the name of an animal or plant consisting of three words. —*adj.* consisting of three terms. [< *tri-* + -*nomial*, modelled after *binomial*]

tri·o (trē′ō) *n., pl.* **-tri·os. 1** a musical composition for three voices or instruments. **2** the second section or theme of a march, scherzo, etc., often quiet and lyrical in character. **3** a group of three singers or players performing together. **4** any group of three persons or things. [< Ital. *trio*, ult. < L *tres* three]

tri·ode (trī′ōd) *n. Electronics.* a vacuum tube that has an anode, a cathode, and a controlling grid.

tri·o·let (trī′ə lit) *n.* a poem having eight lines and only two rhymes. Lines 1, 4, and 7 are the same. Lines 2 and 8 are the same. [< F]

tri·ox·ide (trī ok′sīd *or* trī ok′sid) *n.* any oxide having three atoms of oxygen in each molecule.

trip (trip) *n., v.* **tripped, trip·ping.** —*n.* **1** a journey; voyage: *We took a trip to Europe.* **2** a stumble; slip. **3** the act of catching a person's foot to throw him down. **4** a mistake; blunder. **5** a light, quick tread; stepping lightly. **6** a projecting part, catch, etc. on a mechanism or machine for starting or checking some movement. **7** *Slang.* the mental state or experience induced by hallucinogenic drugs, such as LSD. —*v.* **1** stumble: *to trip on the stairs.* **2** cause to stumble and fall: *The loose board tripped him.* **3** make a mistake; do something wrong: *He tripped on that difficult question.* **4** cause to make a mistake or blunder: *The difficult question tripped him.* **5** overthrow by catching in a mistake or blunder; outwit. **6** detect in an inconsistency or inaccuracy: *The examining board tripped him up several times.* **7** take light, quick steps: *She tripped across the floor.* **8** tip; tilt. **9** release the catch of (a wheel, clutch, etc.). **10** activate a mechanism or machine by releasing a catch. **11** move past or be released by the pallet, as a cog on an escapement wheel of a watch or clock. **12** journey. [ME < OF *tripper* < Gmc.]
► **Syn.** *n.* **1. Trip, journey, voyage** = a travelling from one place to another. **Trip** is the general word, usually suggesting return to the starting place, but not suggesting the length, purpose, manner, or means of travel: *How was your trip? He took a trip to Honolulu.* **Journey** applies especially to a long or very tiring trip by land to a place for a definite purpose: *He decided to make the journey to Mexico by car.* **Voyage** applies to a trip, usually long, by water: *The voyage to the Islands will be restful.*

tri·par·tite (trī pär′tīt) *adj.* **1** divided into or composed of three parts. **2** having three corresponding parts or copies. **3** made or shared by three parties: *a tripartite treaty.* [< L *tripartitus* < *tri-* three + *partitus*, pp. of *partiri* divide]

tripe (trīp) *n.* **1** the walls of the first and second stomachs of an ox, etc. used as food. **2** *Slang.* something foolish, worthless, or trashy. [ME < OF *tripe* entrails < Arabic *tharb*]

trip·ham·mer (trip′ham′ər) *n.* a heavy, power-driven hammer, operated by a tripping device by which it is raised and allowed to fall repeatedly.

triph·thong (trif′thong *or* trip′thong) *n.* a union of three vowel sounds pronounced in one syllable. [< *diphthong*, with substitution of *tri-* for *di-*]

tri·plane (trī′plān′) *n.* an airplane having three sets of wings, one above another.

tri·ple (trip′əl) *adj., n., v.* **-pled, -pling.** —*adj.* **1** including three; having three parts: *the triple petals of the trillium.* **2** three times as much or as many: *She has triple the foreign stamps I have.* —*n.* **1** a number, amount, etc. that is three times as much or as many. **2** *Baseball.* a three-base hit. —*v.* **1** make or become three times as much or as many. **2** *Baseball.* hit a triple. [< L *triplus* < *tres* three + -*plus* fold. Doublet of TREBLE.]

triple crown 1 *Horse racing.* a championship won by a horse that in a single season wins the three classic races for its category. **2** a similar championship in football, etc.

triple play *Baseball.* a play that puts three men out.

tri·plet (trip′lit) *n.* **1** one of three children born at the same time from the same mother. **2** a group of three similar or equal things.

hat, āge, fär; let, ēqual, tèrm; it, īce
hot, ōpen, ôrder; oil, out; cup, pùt, rüle,
above, takən, pencəl, lemən, circəs

ch, child; ng, long; sh, ship
th, thin; ŦH, then; zh, measure

3 *Music.* a group of three notes to be performed in the time of two notes having the same time value. **4** three successive lines of poetry, usually rhyming and equal in length. [< *triple*]

triple time *Music.* time or rhythm having three beats to the measure.

tri·plex (trip′leks) *adj., n.* —*adj.* triple; threefold. —*n.* **1** *Music.* triple time. **2** *Cdn.* a three-storey building having three apartments. [< L *triplex* < *tri-* three + *plic-* fold]

trip·li·cate (*v.* trip′lə kāt′; *adj., n.* trip′lə kit) *v.* **-cat·ed, -cat·ing;** *adj., n.* —*v.* make threefold; triple. —*adj.* triple; threefold. —*n.* one of three things exactly alike. **in triplicate,** in three copies exactly alike. [< L *triplicare* < *triplex* threefold]

trip·li·ca·tion (trip′lə kā′shən) *n.* **1** triplicating or being triplicated. **2** something triplicated.

tri·ply (trip′lē) *adv.* in a triple manner; three times.

trip·man (trip′man′) *n., pl.* **-men.** *Cdn. Historical.* a temporary hand hired for duty on a canoe or other trip; a voyageur.

tri·pod (trī′pod) *n.* **1** a support or stand having three legs, as for a camera, telescope, etc. **2** a stool or other article having three legs. [< L < Gk. *tripous, -odos* < *tri-* three + *pous* foot]

Tri·pol·i·tan (tri pol′ə tən) *n., adj.* —*n.* a native or inhabitant of Tripoli, a region in Libya. —*adj.* of or having to do with Tripoli or its inhabitants.

trip·per (trip′ər) *n.* **1** a person or thing that trips; especially, a device in a machine that releases a catch, etc. or one that operates a railway signal. **2** *Esp. Brit.* a person who takes a trip or short excursion.

trip·ping (trip′ing) *adj.* light and quick. —**trip′ping·ly,** *adv.*

trip·tych (trip′tik) *n.* **1** a set of three panels side by side, having pictures, carvings, etc. on them; especially, an altarpiece consisting of a central panel and two smaller, hinged side panels that fold over it. **2** a hinged, three-leaved writing tablet used in ancient Rome. [< Gk. *triptychos* three-layered < *tri-* three + *ptyx* fold]

tri·reme (trī′rēm) *n.* an ancient Greek or Roman warship having three rows of oars, one above the other, on each side. [< L *triremis* < *tri-* three + *remus* oar]

tri·sect (trī sekt′) *v.* **1** divide into three parts. **2** *Geometry.* divide into three equal parts. [< *tri-* + L *sectus*, pp. of *secare* cut] —**tri·sec′tion,** *n.*

tri·ser·vice *or* **tri-ser·vice** (trī sèr′vis) *adj.* of, for, or involving the land, maritime, and air forces or elements of the Canadian Forces.

Tris·tan (tris′tən) *n.* Tristram.

Tris·tram (tris′trəm) *n. Arthurian legend.* one of the most famous knights of the Round Table. His love for Iseult, wife of King Mark, is the subject of many stories and poems.

tri·syl·lab·ic (trī′sə lab′ik *or* tris′ə lab′ik) *adj.* having three syllables. —**tri′syl·lab′i·cal·ly,** *adv.*

tri·syl·la·ble (trī sil′ə bəl *or* tri sil′ə bəl) *n.* a word of three syllables. *Educate* is a trisyllable.

trite (trīt) *adj.* **trit·er, trit·est.** ordinary; commonplace; no longer interesting: *The movie turned out to be very trite, so we left early.* [< L *tritus*, pp. of *terere* rub away] —**trite′ly,** *adv.* —**trite′ness,** *n.*

trit·i·ca·le (trit′ə kā′lē *or* trit′ə kä′lē) *n.* a fertile hybrid cereal grain, a cross between wheat and rye that has a high protein content and a high yield. [NL < *Tritic*um, genus of wheat + *Secale*, genus of rye. 20c.]

trit·i·um (trit′ē əm *or* trish′ē əm) *n.* a radio-active isotope of hydrogen that occurs in minute amounts in natural water, having a mass three times that of ordinary hydrogen. Tritium is used with deuterium in a hydrogen bomb. *Symbol:* T or ³H [< NL < Gk. *tritos* third]

tri·ton¹ (trī′tən) *n.* any of a family (Cymatiidae) of marine gastropod molluscs found mainly in tropical waters, having an elongated, often brightly coloured, spiral shell. [< *Triton*]

tri·ton² (trī′ton) *n.* the nucleus of a tritium atom. [< *tritium* + -*on*, as in *electron*]

Tri·ton (trī′tən) *n. Greek mythology.* a sea god and a son of

Poseidon, represented as having the head and body of a man and the tail of a fish, and carrying a conch shell.

trit·u·rate (trich′ə rāt′) *v.* **-rat·ed, -rat·ing;** *n.* —*v.* rub, crush, or grind into a very fine powder. —*n.* any substance that is ground into a very fine powder. [< LL *triturare* thresh, ult. < L *terere* rub]

trit·u·ra·tion (trich′ə rā′shən) *n.* **1** the act or process of triturating or the state of being triturated. **2** a triturated powder, especially one consisting of a powdered medicinal substance mixed with lactose.

tri·umph (trī′umf) *n., v.* —*n.* **1** the state of being victorious or successful: *a final triumph over the enemy. They returned home in triumph.* **2** a great success or achievement: *a triumph of modern science.* **3** joy because of victory or success. **4** in ancient Rome, a procession in honor of a victorious general.
—*v.* **1** gain victory; win success: *Our team triumphed over theirs.* **2** exult or rejoice because of victory or success: *They triumphed in their success.* [< L *triumphus*]
☛ *Syn. n.* **1.** See note at **victory.**

tri·um·phal (trī um′fəl) *adj.* of, having to do with, or for a triumph; celebrating a victory.

tri·um·phant (trī um′fənt) *adj.* **1** victorious; successful. **2** rejoicing because of victory or success. —**tri·um′phant·ly,** *adv.*

tri·um·vir (trī um′vər) *n., pl.* **-virs** or **-vi·ri** (-və rī′ or -və rē′). **1** in ancient Rome, one of three men who shared the same public office. **2** one of any three persons sharing power or authority. [< L *triumvir*, abstracted from phrase *trium virorum* "of three men"]

tri·um·vi·rate (trī um′və rit or trī um′və rāt′) *n.* **1** the position or term of office of a triumvir. **2** government by three persons together. **3** any association of three in office or authority. **4** any group of three.

tri·une (trī′yün) *adj.* three in one: *the triune God.* [< *tri-* + L *unus* one]

tri·u·ni·ty (trī yü′nə tē) *n.* the state of being triune.

tri·va·lence (trī vā′ləns or triv′ə ləns) *n.* the state or quality of being trivalent.

tri·va·len·cy (trī vā′lən sē or triv′ə lən sē) *n.* trivalence.

tri·va·lent (trī vā′lənt or triv′ə lənt) *adj.* having a valence of three. [< *tri-* + L *valens, -entis,* ppr. of *valere* be worth]

triv·et (triv′it) *n.* a stand or support usually having three legs or feet. Trivets are used over fire and under hot platters, etc. [< L *tri-* three + OE *-fēte* footed]

triv·i·a (triv′ē ə) *n.pl.* trifles; unimportant matters (*sometimes used with a singular verb*). [? < *trivial*]

triv·i·al (triv′ē əl) *adj.* **1** minor; not important; trifling; insignificant. **2** *Archaic.* not new or interesting; ordinary. [< L *trivialis* vulgar, originally, of the crossroads, ult. < *tri-* three + *via* road] —**triv′i·al·ly,** *adv.*

triv·i·al·i·ty (triv′ē al′ə tē) *n., pl.* **-ties. 1** the quality or state of being trivial. **2** something trivial; trifle.

triv·i·um (triv′ē əm) *n., pl.* **-i·a** (-ē ə). in the Middle Ages, grammar, rhetoric, and logic, the first group of the seven liberal arts; opposed to *quadrivium.* [< Med.L *trivium* a triple way < L *tri-* + *via* way]

tri·week·ly (trī wēk′lē) *adv., n., pl.* **-lies;** *adj.* —*adv.* **1** once every three weeks. **2** three times a week. —*n.* newspaper or magazine published triweekly. —*adj.* occurring or appearing triweekly.

tro·cha·ic (trō kā′ik) *adj., n.* —*adj.* of trochees. —*n.* a line or poem in trochees.

tro·che (trō′kē; *Brit.,* trōsh) *n.* a small, usually round, medicinal lozenge. [< obs. *trochisk* < F < LL *trochiscus* < Gk. *trochiskos,* dim. of *trochos* wheel]

tro·chee (trō′kē) *n. Prosody.* a foot or measure consisting of two syllables, the first accented and the second unaccented or the first long and the second short. *Example:*

Sing a | song of | sixpence.

[< L < Gk. *trochaios,* originally, running < *trochos* a course < *trechein* run]

trod (trod) *v.* a pt. and a pp. of **tread.**

trod·den (trod′ən) *v.* a pp. of **tread.**

trode (trōd) *v. Archaic.* a pt. of **tread.**

trog·lo·dyte (trog′lə dīt′) *n.* **1** a member of a prehistoric people who lived in caves. **2** a person who is antisocial or lives in seclusion. **3** an anthropoid ape. [< L < Gk. *trōglodytēs* < *trōglē* cave + *dyein* go in]

troi·ka (troi′kə) *n.* **1** a Russian vehicle, especially a sleigh, drawn by three horses abreast. **2** the horses themselves. **3** triumvirate. [< Russian < *troie* three together]

Tro·jan (trō′jən) *n., adj.* —*n.* **1** a native or inhabitant of Troy, an ancient city in NW Asia Minor. **2** a person who shows courage or energy: *They all worked like Trojans.* —*adj.* of or having to do with Troy or its people. [< L *Trojanus* < *Troja, Troia* Troy < Gk.]

Trojan horse 1 *Greek mythology.* a huge wooden horse in which the Greeks concealed soldiers and had them brought into Troy during the Trojan War. **2** any person or group stationed inside a country, institution, etc. to sabotage or otherwise disrupt its activities from within.

Trojan War *Greek legend.* a ten years' war carried on by the Greeks against Troy to get back Helen, wife of King Menelaus of Sparta. Helen had been carried off by Paris, son of King Priam of Troy.

troll[1] (trōl) *v., n.* —*v.* **1** fish with a moving line, usually by trailing the line behind the boat near the surface: *He trolled for bass.* **2** fish in (water) in this way: *to troll a lake.* **3** *Archaic.* **a** sing in a full, rolling voice. **b** sing as a round is sung. **4** revolve or cause to revolve; roll.
—*n.* **1** a lure or a lure and line used in trolling. **2** *Archaic.* a song whose parts are sung in succession; round. **3** the act or an instance of trolling. [ME *trollen* stroll < OF *troller* wander < Gmc.]
—**troll′er,** *n.*

troll[2] (trōl) *n. Scandinavian folklore.* any of a race of supernatural beings, thought of as giants or, more recently, as dwarfs. [< ON]

trol·ley (trol′ē) *n., pl.* **-leys. 1** a pulley moving against a wire to carry electricity to a streetcar, electric engine, etc. See **streetcar** for picture. **2** trolley bus. **3** streetcar. **4** a basket, carriage, etc., suspended from a pulley running on an overhead track. **5** *Brit.* a truck pushed by hand; handcart. [probably < *troll*[1] in sense of "roll"]

trolley bus an electrically powered bus having two overhead trolleys and running on tires like a motor bus.

trolley car streetcar.

trol·lop (trol′əp) *n.* **1** an untidy or slovenly woman. **2** a morally loose woman; slut. **3** prostitute. [probably < *troll*[1]]

A trombone

trom·bone (trom′bōn or trom bōn′) *n.* a musical wind instrument resembling a trumpet and having either a sliding piece or, less often, valves for varying the pitch. [< Ital. *trombone* < *tromba* trumpet < Gmc.]

trom·bon·ist (trom′bōn ist or trom bōn′ist) *n.* a person who plays the trombone; especially a skilled player.

troop (trüp) *n., v.* —*n.* **1** a group or collection of people or animals: *a troop of deer. A troop of children burst into the kitchen.* **2** a formation of armored or cavalry forces smaller than a squadron; also, a similar group in other army units. **3 troops,** *pl.* armed forces; soldiers. **4** a group of Boy Scouts or Girl Guides made up of several patrols: *He belongs to the 4th Kingston troop.*
—*v.* **1** gather or move in a troop or band: *We all trooped into the living room to sing happy birthday.* **2** carry (the colors) before a formation of troops as part of an official ceremony. **3** walk; go: *The young boys trooped off after the older ones.* [< F *troupe,* ult. < LL *troppus* herd < Gmc.]
☛ *Hom.* **troupe.**

troop·er (trü′pər) *n.* **1** a soldier in a cavalry regiment or an armored regiment. **2** a cavalry horse. **3** troopship. **4** a mounted police officer. **5** *U.S.* a state police officer.
☛ *Hom.* **trouper.**

troop leader 1 the person in charge of a military troop. **2** the senior boy or girl of a troop of Boy Scouts or Girl Guides.

Troop Scouter an adult responsible for the operation of a troop of Boy Scouts.

troop·ship (trüp′ship′) *n.* a ship used to carry soldiers; transport.

trope (trōp) *n.* **1** the use of a word or phrase in a sense different from its ordinary meaning; figurative use of a word of phrase. **2** a word or phrase so used; figure of speech. *Example:*

All in a hot and copper sky,
The bloody sun at noon. . . .

[< L < Gk. *tropos* turn]

tro·phied (trō′fēd) *adj.* decorated with trophies: *trophied walls.*

tro·phy (trō′fē) *n., pl.* **-phies.** **1** something taken or won in war, hunting, etc., especially if displayed as a memorial or souvenir: *The hunter kept the lion's skin as a trophy.* **2** a prize, often in the form of a silver cup, awarded in sports or other competitions: *He kept his tennis trophy on the mantelpiece.* **3** in ancient Greece and Rome, captured arms, flags, etc. of a defeated enemy set up on the field of battle or in a public place as a memorial of victory. **4** a representation of such a memorial on a medal or in the form of a monument. **5** anything serving as a remembrance. [< F *trophée* < L *trophaeum,* for *tropaeum* < Gk. *tropaion* < *tropē* rout, originally, turn]

trop·ic (trop′ik) *n.* **1** either of two parallels of latitude, one 23°27′ north and the other 23°27′ south of the equator. The northern parallel is the tropic of Cancer and the southern parallel is the tropic of Capricorn. **2 the tropics** or **Tropics,** *pl.* the region between these parallels. The equator runs through the middle of the tropics, which include the hottest parts of the earth. **3** (*adj.*) of or belonging to the tropics. **4** either of two corresponding circles in the celestial sphere, the limits reached by the sun in its apparent journey north and south. [< L *tropicus* < Gk. *tropikos* pertaining to a turn < *tropē* a turn, a change]

trop·i·cal[1] (trop′ə kəl) *adj.* **1** of, characteristic of, or found in the tropics: *tropical fruits, tropical diseases, a tropical climate.* **2** suitable for or used in the tropics: *tropical suiting.* **3** like the tropics; especially, very hot or sultry. **—trop′i·cal·ly,** *adv.*

trop·i·cal[2] (trop′ə kəl) *adj.* **1** having to do with or involving a trope or tropes. **2** of the nature of a trope or tropes; metaphorical; figurative.

tropic bird any of a very small family (Phaethontidae) of web-footed birds of warm seas having white plumage with black markings and having long, streamer-like tail feathers. They belong to the same order as pelicans and cormorants.

Tropic of Cancer the parallel of latitude at 23°27′ north of the equator, that marks the northern limit of the part of the earth where the sun is directly overhead at some time during the year. See **equator** for picture.

Tropic of Capricorn the parallel of latitude at 23°27′ south of the equator, that marks the southern limit of the part of the earth where the sun is directly overhead at some time during the year. See **equator** for picture.

tro·pism (trō′piz əm) *n. Biology.* the tendency of an animal or plant to turn or move in response to a stimulus. [< Gk. *tropē* a turning]

tro·pis·tic (trō pis′tik) *adj.* of or having to do with a tropism.

trop·o·sphere (trop′ə sfēr′) *n.* the lowest layer of the atmosphere, extending about 10 to 16 kilometres from the earth upward to the stratosphere. The troposphere is characterized by winds, cloud formation, and a rapid decrease in temperature with increase in altitude. [< Gk. *tropē* a turn, a change + E *sphere*]

trop·o·spher·ic (trop′ə sfēr′ik *or* -sfēr′ik) *adj.* of or having to do with the troposphere.

trop·po (trop′ō; *Italian,* trôp′pō) *adv. Italian.* too much. *Example: allegro ma non troppo,* fast but not too fast.

trot (trot) *v.* **trot·ted, trot·ting;** *n.* **—v. 1** of horses, etc., go at a gait between a walk and a run by lifting the right forefoot and the left hind foot at about the same time and then the other two feet in the same way. **2** ride a horse at such a gait: *We trotted along the path.* **3** cause to trot: *to trot a horse.* **4** of a person, run at a moderate pace: *The child trotted along after her mother.* **trot out,** *Informal.* bring out for others to see. **—n. 1** the gait of a trotting animal or person: *We started off at a trot.* **2** the action or exercise of trotting: *to go for a trot.* **3** a brisk, steady movement. **4** the sound of trotting. **5** a single face in a program of harness racing. [ME < OF *trotter* < Gmc.]

troth (troth *or* trōth) *n., v.* **—n. 1** faithfulness; loyalty. **2** a promise, especially a promise or engagement to marry. **3** truth. **by my troth** or **in troth,** truly; upon my word: *By my troth, I'll see him revenged.* **plight** (one's) **troth,** pledge one's word, especially in an engagement to marry. **—v.** pledge; betroth. [OE *trēowth* < *trēow* faith]

trot·line (trot′līn′) *n. Fishing.* a long line with short lines and baited hooks attached at regular intervals.

Trot·sky·ism (trot′skē iz′əm) *n.* the social, political, and economic principles of Leon Trotsky (1879-1940), a Russian revolutionary leader, especially the principle that world-wide communist revolution must be put before everything else, including Soviet growth and development.

Trot·sky·ite (trot′skē īt′) *n.* a follower of Leon Trotsky; a believer in Trotskyism.

trot·ter (trot′ər) *n.* **1** an animal that trots, especially a horse bred

hat, āge, fär; let, ēqual, tèrm; it, īce
hot, ōpen, ôrder; oil, out; cup, pût, rüle,
əbove, takən, pencəl, lemən, circəs
ch, child; ng, long; sh, ship
th, thin; ᴛʜ, then; zh, measure

and trained for harness racing. **2** a sheep's or pig's foot used for food.

trou·ba·dour (trü′bə dôr′ *or* trü′bə dür′) *n.* one of a class of medieval lyric poets of southern France, northern Spain, and northern Italy who wrote poems of chivalry and courtly love. The troubadours had great social influence and were often of knightly rank. [< F < Provençal *trobador,* ult. < LL *tropus* song, mode (in music) < Gk. *tropos* mode, style (in music), originally, a turn]

trou·ble (trub′əl) *n., v.* **-bled, -bling.** **—n. 1** distress; worry or difficulty: *That dog has caused them a lot of trouble. We're still having trouble with the furnace.* **2** a distressing or annoying fact, event, or experience: *His life was full of troubles.* **3** an occasion or cause of affliction, distress, vexation, etc.: *Is she a trouble to you?* **4** public disturbance or unrest: *There was some trouble on the picket line.* **5** extra work; bother; effort: *She took the trouble to make extra copies.* **6** illness or disease: *She has stomach trouble.* **7** faulty operation; malfunction: *They were delayed because of engine trouble.* **8 the trouble,** the cause of annoyance, worry, etc.: *The trouble is that he never bothers to let us know. She's just too easygoing; that's the trouble.*
in or **into trouble, a** in or into a situation in which one is caught in wrongdoing and is liable to be blamed, punished, etc.: *They're very mischievous and are always getting into trouble. Her boyfriend is in trouble with the police.* **b** *Informal.* pregnant without being married.
make trouble, cause problems or unpleasantness: *Mind your own business and don't make trouble.*
—v. 1 cause distress or worry to: *The lack of business troubled him.* **2** require extra work or effort of: *May I trouble you to do something for me?* **3** cause oneself inconvenience or effort: *Don't trouble to come to the door; I can let myself out.* **4** cause pain or discomfort to; afflict: *His arthritis is troubling him again. The baby has been troubled with colds.* [ME < OF *truble* < *trubler* trouble, ult. < L *turba* turmoil]

trou·ble·mak·er (trub′əl mā′kər) *n.* a person who causes trouble, especially one who deliberately causes disagreement between people.

trou·ble·mak·ing (trub′əl mā′king) *n., adj.* **—n.** the actions of a troublemaker. **—adj.** causing or making trouble.

trou·ble·shoot (trub′əl shüt′) *v.* **-shot, -shoot·ing.** work as a troubleshooter: *She troubleshoots for a large construction firm.*

trou·ble–shoot·er (trub′əl shü′ter) *n.* **1** a person employed to discover and eliminate causes of trouble in equipment, machinery, etc. **2** a person who is skilled in mediating diplomatic or political disputes.

trou·ble·some (trub′əl səm) *adj.* causing trouble; annoying. **—trou′ble·some·ly,** *adv.* **—trou′ble·some·ness,** *n.*

trou·blous (trub′ləs) *adj. Archaic or poetic.* **1** disturbed; restless: *troublous times.* **2** troublesome.

trough (trof) *n.* **1** a long, narrow container for holding food or water for animals: *a watering trough.* **2** a container shaped like this: *The baker uses a trough for kneading dough.* **3** a channel for carrying water; gutter. **4** a long hollow between two ridges, etc.: *the trough between two waves.* **5** *Meteorology.* a long, narrow area of relatively low barometric pressure. **6** *Geology.* a basin-shaped depression; the lowest part of a synclinal fold. [OE *trōh*] **—trough′like′,** *adj.*

trounce (trouns) *v.* **trounced, trounc·ing.** **1** beat; thrash. **2** *Informal.* defeat severely in a contest, game, etc. [origin uncertain]

troupe (trüp) *n., v.* **trouped, troup·ing.** **—n.** a troop, band, or company, especially a group of actors, singers, or acrobats. **—v.** tour or travel with a troupe. [< F]
☛ *Hom.* troop.

troup·er (trü′pər) *n.* **1** a member of a theatrical troupe. **2** an old, experienced actor.
☛ *Hom.* trooper.

trou·pi·al (trü′pē əl) *n.* any of several small or medium-sized New World orioles, especially an orange-and-black species (*Icterus icterus*) of Central and South America.

trou·sers (trou′zərz) *n.pl.* **1** pants (defs. 1 and 2). **2** (*adj.*) **trouser,** of, having to do with, or designed for trousers: *trouser cuffs.* [< *trouse* < Irish *triús*]

trous·seau (trü′sō *or* trü sō′) *n., pl.* **trous·seaux** *or* **trous·seaus**

(trü′sōz *or* trü sōz′). a bride's outfit of clothes, linen, etc. [< F *trousseau*, originally, bundle]

trout (trout) *n., pl.* **trout** *or* **trouts**. **1** any of several food and game fishes (genus *Salmo*) of the salmon family found mainly in northern lakes and rivers. Trout belonging to this group, such as the rainbow trout, are often called true trout to distinguish them from char. **2** any of several species of char (genus *Salvelinus*), also of the salmon family, such as the lake trout or brook trout. [OE *truht* < LL *tructa, trocta,* probably < Gk. *trōktēs,* literally, gnawer < *trōgein* gnaw]

trow (trō) *v. Archaic.* believe; think. [OE *truwian*]

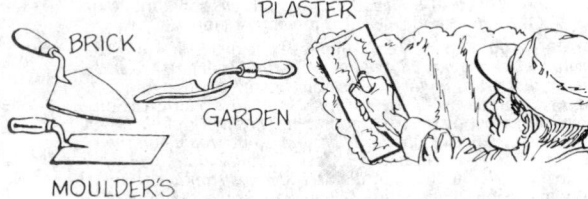

Several different types of trowel

trow·el (trou′əl) *n.* **1** a hand tool with a thin, flat blade, used for smoothing or spreading plaster, mortar, etc. **2** a garden hand tool similar to a scoop, used for taking up plants, loosening dirt, etc. [ME < OF *truele* < LL *truella,* dim. of L *trua* skimmer]

troy (troi) *adj.* expressed in troy weight: *a troy ounce.* [< *Troyes,* a city in France]

troy weight a system of units for measuring mass, traditionally used for weighing gems and precious metals. One pound troy weight is equal to about 0.373 kilograms.

24 grains	=	1 pennyweight
20 pennyweight	=	1 ounce
12 ounces	=	1 pound

Trp. or **trp.** troop.

trs. transpose.

tru·an·cy (trü′ən sē) *n., pl.* **-cies.** the act or habit of staying away from school without permission; truant behavior.

tru·ant (trü′ənt) *n., adj.* —*n.* a person who neglects work, especially a student who stays away from school without permission; truant behavior.
play truant, neglect one's work or duty; especially, stay away from school without permission.
—*adj.* **1** being a truant; especially, staying away from school without permission. **2** of, like, or characteristic of a truant: *truant habits.* **3** wandering. [ME < OF *truant,* probably < Celtic]

truant officer a school official employed to investigate and deal with cases of truancy.

truce (trüs) *n.* **1** a stop in fighting by agreement between opposing armed forces, either temporary or permanent. **2** a rest from quarrelling, turmoil, trouble, etc. [ME *trewes,* pl. of *trewe,* OE *trēow* faith, treaty]

truck¹ (truk) *n., v.* —*n.* **1** a motor vehicle designed primarily for carrying heavy things or animals rather than people. **2** any of various strongly built carts, wagons, etc. used, especially formerly, for a similar purpose. **3** a small vehicle, sometimes with a motor, for carrying trunks, boxes, etc.: *Jim uses a truck in the warehouse. The redcap is coming with a truck.* **4** a swivelling frame with two or more pairs of wheels supporting each end of a railway car, locomotive, etc. **5** a low, flat car. **6** on a ship or boat, a wooden disk at the top of a flagstaff or mast with holes for the ropes. **7** (*adj.*) of, for, or used on a truck.
—*v.* **1** carry on a truck. **2** drive a truck. **3** engage in trucking goods, especially as a business; operate a trucking business. [? < L *trochus* iron hoop < Gk. *trochos* wheel]

truck² (truk) *n., v.* —*n.* **1** vegetables raised for market. **2** small articles of little value; odds and ends. **3** *Informal.* rubbish. **4** *Informal.* dealings: *He wanted no truck with peddlers.* **5** exchange; barter. **6** the payment of wages in goods, etc. rather than in money. —*v.* make an exchange; swap or barter. [ME < OF *troquer*]

truck·age (truk′ij) *n.* **1** carrying of goods, etc. by trucks. **2** the charge for carrying by truck.

truck·er¹ (truk′ər) *n.* **1** a person who drives a truck. **2** a person whose business is carrying goods, etc. by trucks.

truck·er² (truk′ər) *n.* **1** a market gardener; truck farmer. **2** a person who barters or travels as a peddler.

truck farm a farm where vegetables are raised for market; market garden. —**truck farmer,** *n.* **truck farming,** *n.*

truck·le¹ (truk′əl) *v.* **-led, -ling.** give up or submit tamely (*usually used with* **to**): *to truckle to one's superiors.* [< obsolete *truckle* to sleep in a truckle bed; with reference to its low position] —**truck′ler,** *n.* —**truck′ling·ly,** *adv.*

truck·le² (truk′əl) *n., v.* **-led, -ling.** —*n.* **1** a small wheel; caster. **2** truckle bed. —*v.* move or roll on truckles, or casters. [< L *trochlea* < Gk. *trochilea* sheaf of a pulley]

truckle bed trundle bed.

truck·man (truk′mən) *n., pl.* **-men.** trucker.

truc·u·lence (truk′yə ləns *or* trü′kyə ləns) *n.* the quality or state of being truculent.

truc·u·len·cy (truk′yə lən sē *or* trü′kyə lən sē) *n.* truculence.

truc·u·lent (truk′yə lənt *or* trü′kyə lənt) *adj.* **1** showing a readiness to fight or quarrel; arrogant and hostile: *a truculent attitude.* **2** fierce and cruel: *at the mercy of a truculent ruffian.* **3** of speech or writing, ruthless and scathing; harsh: *truculent satire.* [< L *truculentus* < *trux, trucis* fierce] —**truc′u·lent·ly,** *adv.*

trudge (truj) *v.* **trudged, trudg·ing;** *n.* —*v.* walk, especially wearily or with effort: *The tired hikers trudged home.* —*n.* a hard or weary walk: *It was a long trudge up the hill.* [origin uncertain] —**trudg′er,** *n.*

trudg·en stroke (truj′ən) *Swimming.* a stroke using a double overarm stroke together with a scissors movement of the legs. [after John *Trudgen* (1852-1902), a British swimmer]

true (trü) *adj.* **tru·er, tru·est;** *n., v.* **trued, tru·ing;** *adv.* —*adj.* **1** agreeing with fact; not false: *It is true that 6 and 4 are 10.* **2** real; genuine: *true gold, true kindness.* **3** faithful; loyal: *a true patriot.* **4** agreeing with a standard; right; proper; correct; exact; accurate: *a true copy, a true voice, true to type.* **5** representative of the class named: *A sweet potato is not a true potato.* **6** rightful; lawful: *the true heir to the property.* **7** reliable; sure: *a true sign.* **8** accurately formed, fitted, or placed: *a true angle.* **9** steady in direction, force, etc.; unchanging: *The arrow made a true course through the air.* **10** *Archaic.* truthful. **11** honest.
come true, happen as expected; become real.
—*n.* **1** that which is true. **2** exact or accurate formation, position, or adjustment: *A slanting door is out of true.*
—*v.* make true; shape, place, or make in the exact position, form, etc. required.
—*adv.* **1** in a true manner; truly; exactly: *His words ring true.* **2** in agreement with the ancestral type: *breed true.* [OE *trīewe, trēowe*] —**true′ness,** *n.*
☛ *Syn. adj.* **1.** See note at **real.**

true bill *Esp.U.S. Law.* the endorsement made by a grand jury when satisfied that a bill of indictment is supported by enough evidence to justify the case being brought to trial.

true–blue (trü′blü′) *adj.* staunch and unchanging; very loyal: *She's a true-blue conservative.*

true–heart·ed (trü′här′tid) *adj.* faithful; loyal.

true–love (trü′luv′) *n.* a faithful lover; sweetheart.

truelove knot a kind of bowknot that is hard to untie, standing for true and lasting love.

true–lover's knot truelove knot.

truf·fle (truf′əl *or* trü′fəl) *n.* any of several European underground fungi (genus *Tuber*) valued as food. [probably ult. < F *truffe*]

tru·ism (trü′iz əm) *n.* a statement that is obviously true, especially one that is too obvious to mention, such as "You're only young once."

trull (trul) *n. Archaic.* prostitute; strumpet. [? < G *Trulle*]

tru·ly (trü′lē) *adv.* **1** in a true manner; exactly; rightly; faithfully. **2** in fact; really.

trump¹ (trump) *n., v.* —*n.* **1** *Card games.* **a** any playing card of a suit that for the duration of a deal or game ranks higher than the other suits. **b** Often, **trumps,** *pl.* the suit itself. **2** any resource or advantage held back until needed. **3** *Informal.* a fine, dependable person.
—*v.* **1** *Card games.* **a** take (a trick, card, etc.) with a trump: *He trumped my king.* **b** play a trump when another suit was led: *We didn't expect him to trump.* **2** be better than; surpass; beat.
trump up, think up or invent falsely: *He trumped up an excuse for being late.*
[alteration of *triumph*]

trump² (trump) *n., v. Archaic or poetic.* —*n.* **1** a trumpet. **2** the sound of a trumpet. —*v.* trumpet. [ME < OF *trompe* < Gmc.]

trump card **1** any playing card of a suit that for a particular hand ranks higher than the other suits. **2** a decisive fact, argument, etc., especially one that is held in reserve until needed; clincher.

trumped–up (trumpt′up′) *adj.* invented in order to deceive; fraudulent: *trumped-up charges.*

trump·er·y (trump′ər ē *or* trump′rē) *n., pl.* **-er·ies;** *adj.* —*n.* something showy but without value; worthless ornaments; useless stuff; rubbish; nonsense. —*adj.* showy but without value; trifling; worthless; useless; nonsensical. [< F *tromperie* < *tromper* deceive]

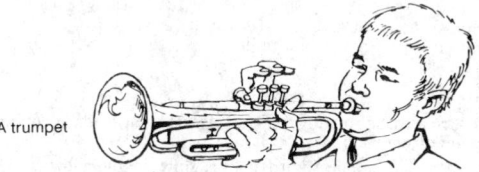

A trumpet

trump·et (trum′pit) *n., v.* —*n.* **1** a musical wind instrument having a looped tube that is bell-shaped at one end and has three valves to vary the pitch. The trumpet has a sharp, clear tone and can produce great volume. **2** anything shaped like a trumpet: *Some people used ear trumpets before small hearing aids were invented.* **3** a sound like that of a trumpet. **4** a trumpeter (def. 1).
blow (one's) own trumpet, talk boastfully; praise oneself.
—*v.* **1** blow a trumpet. **2** make a sound like a trumpet: *The elephant trumpeted in fright.* **3** proclaim loudly or widely: *He'll trumpet that story all over town.* [ME < OF *trompette,* dim. of *trompe.* See TRUMP.]

trumpet creeper 1 a climbing woody vine (*Campsis radicans*) native to the warm regions of the western hemisphere, having clusters of large red, trumpet-shaped flowers. **2** (adjl.)
trumpet-creeper, designating the family (Bignoniaceae) of mostly trees, shrubs, and vines that includes the trumpet creeper, bignonia, and catalpa.

trum·pet·er (trum′pə tər) *n.* **1** a person who blows a trumpet. **2** any of a genus (*Psophia,* comprising the family Psophidae) of large birds living mainly on the ground in the tropical rain forests of South America, having a long neck and legs, short tail and wings, and mainly black plumage. Trumpeters have a loud, deep call. **3** trumpeter swan. **4** a breed of domestic pigeon.

trumpeter swan the largest swan (*Olor buccinator,* also classified as *Cygnus buccinator*), found in western Canada and the NW United States, weighing up to 18 kg and with a wingspread of often more than 2.5 m, having a deep, very far-carrying, trumpetlike call.

trumpet flower 1 any of various plants having trumpet-shaped flowers, such as the trumpet creeper. **2** the flower of any of these plants.

trumpet vine trumpet creeper.

trun·cate (trung′kāt) *v.* **-cat·ed, -cat·ing;** *adj.* —*v.* shorten by cutting off the top or end of. —*adj.* **1** *Biology.* having a blunt or square end: *the truncate leaf of the tulip tree.* See **leaf** for picture. **2** truncated. [< L *truncare* < *truncus* maimed] —**trun·ca′tion,** *n.*

trun·cat·ed (trung′kā tid) *adj.* **1** *Geometry.* of a cone, pyramid, etc., having the top or apex cut off. **2** cut short: *a truncated version of a speech.*

trun·cheon (trun′chən) *n., v.* —*n.* **1** *Esp.Brit.* a short stick or club: *a policeman's truncheon.* **2** a staff of office or authority; baton: *a herald's truncheon.* —*v.* beat with a club. [ME < OF *tronchon,* ult. < *truncus.* See TRUNK.]

trun·dle (trun′dəl) *v.* **-dled, -dling;** *n.* —*v.* **1** roll or push along: *The workman trundled a wheelbarrow full of cement.* **2** roll or revolve.
—*n.* **1** the motion or sound of rolling. **2** a small wheel; caster. **3** trundle bed. **4** a low cart or wagon on small wheels. [ME, var. of *trindel* wheel, or of *trendle* << OE *trendel* ring, disk]

trundle bed a low bed on small wheels or casters that can be rolled under a higher bed when not in use; truckle bed.

trunk (trungk) *n.* **1** the main stem of a tree, as distinct from the branches and the roots. **2** the main or central part of something, especially the shaft of a column. **3** an enclosed compartment in an automobile for storing luggage, tools, etc. **4** a large, heavy box with a hinged lid, used for transporting or storing clothes and other personal property. **5** the body apart from the head, arms, and legs; torso. **6** the main body of a blood vessel, nerve, or similar structure as distinct from its branches. **7** the long, muscular, flexible snout of an elephant. **8** trunks, *pl.* very short pants worn by male athletes, swimmers, acrobats, etc. **9** a main channel or passage. **10** trunk line. [< L *truncus,* originally adj., mutilated]

trunk call *Brit.* a long-distance telephone call.

trunk hose short, full, baggy breeches reaching about halfway down the thigh, worn by men, especially in the 16th and 17th centuries.

trunk line 1 the main line of a railway, canal, etc. **2** a direct link

hat, āge, fär; let, ēqual, tèrm; it, īce
hot, ōpen, ôrder; oil, out; cup, put, rüle,
above, taken, pencəl, leman, circəs
ch, child; ng, long; sh, ship
th, thin; ᴛʜ, then; zh, measure

between two central telephone exchanges, for making connections between individual subscribers.

trun·nion (trun′yən) *n.* either of the two round projections of a cannon, one on each side, which support it on its carriage. [< F *trognon* trunk < L *truncus;* influenced by F *moignon* stump of an amputated limb]

A truss
supporting a roof

truss (trus) *v., n.* —*v.* **1** tie; fasten; bind (*often used with up*): *We trussed the burglar up and called the police.* **2** fasten the wings or legs of (a fowl) with skewers or twine in preparation for cooking. **3** support or strengthen with a truss or trusses. **4** *Archaic.* fasten or tighten (a garment).
—*n.* **1** a framework of beams or other braces for supporting a roof, bridge, etc. **2** a pad or other device worn as a support for a hernia. **3** a bundle or pack; especially in Britain, a bundle of hay having a specific mass. **4** on a ship or boat, an iron fitting by which a lower yard is fastened to the mast. [ME < OF *trusser,* ult. < L *torquere* twist]

trust (trust) *n., v.* —*n.* **1** a firm belief in the honesty, truthfulness, justice, or power of a person or thing; faith: *He put no trust in the strangers or their information.* **2** a person or thing trusted: *God is our trust.* **3** a confident expectation or hope: *Our trust is that she will soon be well.* **4** a group of individuals or companies controlling much of a certain kind of business: *a steel trust.* **5** a group of individuals or firms having a central committee that controls stock of the constituent companies, thus simplifying management and defeating competition. **6** something managed for the benefit of another; something committed to one's care. **7** the obligation or responsibility imposed on a person in whom confidence or authority is placed. **8** the condition of one in whom trust has been placed; being relied on: *A guardian is in a position of trust.* **9** keeping; care: *The will was left in my trust.* **10** *Law.* **a** a confidence reposed in a person by making him nominal owner of property, which he is to hold, use, or dispose of for the benefit of another. **b** an estate, etc. committed to a trustee or trustees. **c** the right of a person to enjoy the use or profits of property held in trust for him. **11** (adjl.) managing for an owner: *a trust company.* **12** (adjl.) of or having to do with a trust or trusts; held in trust: *a trust fund.* **13** confidence in the ability or intention of a person to pay at some future time for goods, etc.; business credit.
in trust, for the benefit of another: *The money was held in trust for her by her guardian.*
on trust, **a** on business credit; with payment later. **b** without evidence: *We took his assurances on trust.*
—*v.* **1** have faith; rely; be confident: *Trust in God.* **2** believe firmly in the honesty, truth, justice, or power of; have faith in: *He is a man to be trusted.* **3** rely on; depend on: *A forgetful man should not trust his memory.* **4** commit to the care of; leave without fear: *Can I trust the keys to him?* **5** confide or entrust something to the care of; invest: *Can I trust him with a large sum of money?* **6** hope; believe: *I trust you will soon feel better.* **7** give business credit to: *The butcher will trust us for the meat.* **8** allow to go somewhere or do something without misgiving or fear of consequences.
trust to, rely on; depend on: *Don't trust to luck.*
[ME < ON *traust*] —**trust′er,** *n.*

trust company a business concern formed primarily to act as a trustee but also often engaged in other financial activities normally performed by banks.

trus·tee (trus tē′) *n.* **1** a person responsible for the property or affairs of another person, of a company, or of an institution. **2** a person elected to a board or committee that is responsible for the schools in a district; school trustee. **3** a country made responsible for a trust territory.

trus·tee·ship (trus tē′ship) *n.* the position of trustee.

trust·ful (trust′fəl) *adj.* ready to confide; ready to have faith; believing. —**trust′ful·ly,** *adv.* —**trust′ful·ness,** *n.*

trust fund money, property, or other valuables held in trust.

trust·ing (trus′ting) *adj.* that trusts; trustful: *He has a trusting nature.* —**trust′ing·ly,** *adv.*

trust territory a territory placed under the administrative control of a particular country by the United Nations.

trust·wor·thy (trust′wèr′ᴛᴴē) *adj.* that can be depended on; reliable: *The class chose a trustworthy boy for treasurer.* —**trust′wor′thi·ly,** *adv.* —**trust′wor′thi·ness,** *n.*
☛ *Syn.* See note at **reliable.**

trust·y (trus′tē) *adj.* **trust·i·er, trust·i·est;** *n., pl.* **trust·ies.** —*adj.* that can be depended on; reliable: *a trusty servant.* —*n.* a prisoner who is given special privileges because of his good behavior. —**trust′i·ly,** *adv.* —**trust′i·ness,** *n.*

truth (trüth) *n., pl.* **truths** (trüᴛᴴz *or* trüths). **1** the quality or property of being in accord with fact or reality: *She doubted the truth of the story.* **2** something that is in accord with fact or reality: *to tell the whole truth. The truth is that I haven't seen him for over a year.* **3** a fixed or established principle, law, etc.; an accepted or proven doctrine or fact: *a basic scientific truth.* **4** true, exact, honest, sincere, or loyal quality or nature.
in truth, truly; really; in fact.
[OE *trīewth, trēowth < trīewe, trēowe* true]

truth·ful (trüth′fəl) *adj.* **1** telling the truth: *a truthful child.* **2** conforming to truth: *a truthful report.* —**truth′ful·ly,** *adv.* —**truth′ful·ness,** *n.*

truth serum *Informal.* any drug thought to make a person speak freely and openly when questioned.

try (trī) *v.* **tried, try·ing;** *n., pl.* **tries.** —*v.* **1** make an attempt or effort: *He tried to open the window, but it was stuck. You'll never know till you try. She's going to try for her lifesaving certificate next week.* **2** attempt to do or accomplish: *It seems easy until you try it.* **3** find out the quality or qualities of by experimenting or sampling: *Try your skill at trap-shooting. He tried the candy but didn't like it.* **4** find out the effectiveness or usefulness of (an action, process, or thing): *Try opening the window to get the smoke out. Did you try the hardware store to see if they had any?* **5** attempt to open (a door, window, etc.): *Try the doors to see if they are locked.* **6** *Law.* examine the evidence against in a court; determine the guilt or innocence of with respect to a particular accusation: *The woman was tried and found guilty.* **7** put to a severe test; strain: *His constant complaining tried her patience.* **8** subject to trials; afflict: *Job was greatly tried.* **9** *Archaic.* settle by test or investigation. **10** melt down or extract by melting (*often used with* **out**): *to try lard, to try out oil from blubber.*
try on, put on (clothing) to test the fit, looks, etc.: *to try on a new suit.*
try out, **a** test thoroughly by using: *She took the car onto the highway to try it out.* **b** take a test to show fitness for a particular role or place: *to try out for the hockey team, to try out for a part in a play. Are you going to try out?*
—*n.* **1** an attempt; endeavor; effort. **2** a trial; test; experiment. **3** *Rugger.* **a** the act of touching the ball to the ground behind the opponent's goal line. **b** the score (three points) so gained. [ME < OF *trier* cull; sift; origin uncertain]
☛ *Syn. v.* **1. Try, attempt, endeavor** = make an effort to or at. **Try** is the general word: *I tried to see him.* **Attempt** is used in more formal style or to suggest making a real effort, trying hard: *I attempted to obtain an interview.* **Endeavor,** fairly formal, suggests both great effort and great obstacles to be overcome: *The United Nations is endeavoring to establish peace.*
☛ *Usage.* **Try and** or **try to.** Although the formal idiom is **try to,** informal English has long used **try and.** Formal: *Let us try to get permission for the bazaar.* Informal: *Let's try and get permission for the bazaar.*

try·ing (trī′ing) *adj.* hard to endure; annoying: *It's been a trying day.*

try-on (trī′on′) *n. Informal.* the act or process of trying on an unfinished typewritten garment to check the fit, etc.; a fitting: *I have to go to the dressmaker's tomorrow for a try-on.*

try·out (trī′out′) *n.* a test made to determine fitness for a particular role or place: *The tryouts are tomorrow.*

tryp·sin (trip′sən) *n.* an enzyme in the digestive juice secreted by the pancreas. Trypsin changes proteins into peptones. [irregularly < Gk. *tripsis* rubbing < *tribein* rub]

try·sail (trī′sāl′ *or* trī′səl) *n.* a small fore-and-aft sail used in stormy weather on the foremast or mainmast.

try square an instrument for drawing right angles and testing the squareness of anything. See **square** for picture.

tryst (trist *or* trīst) *n.* **1** an agreement or appointment to meet at a certain time and place, especially an agreement by lovers for a secret meeting. **2** a meeting held by appointment. **3** a place of meeting. [ME < OF *triste,* in hunting, a place to which game used to be driven, probably < Scand.]

trysting place a place where a tryst is to be kept.

TS *Typing.* triple space.

tsar (zär) See **czar.**

tsar·e·vitch (zär′ə vich′) See **czarevitch.**

tsa·ri·na (zä rē′nə) See **czarina.**

tsar·ism (zär′iz əm) See **czarism.**

tsar·ist (zär′ist) See **czarist.**

TSE or **T.S.E.** Toronto Stock Exchange.

tset·se (tset′sē) *n.* tsetse fly. Also, **tzetze.**

tsetse fly any of several bloodsucking, two-winged flies (genus *Glossina*) of Africa that transmit various diseases, including sleeping sickness in human beings. [*tsetse* < Bantu]

T-shirt (tē′shèrt′) *n.* a light, knitted sport shirt or undershirt having no collar and, usually, short sleeves.

Tsim·shi·an (tsim′shē ən *or* chim′shē ən) *n., pl.* **-an** or **-ans. 1** a tribe of Indians who originally lived in the lower Skeena and Nass valleys in British Columbia. **2** a member of this tribe. **3** the language of this tribe.

tsp. teaspoon(s).

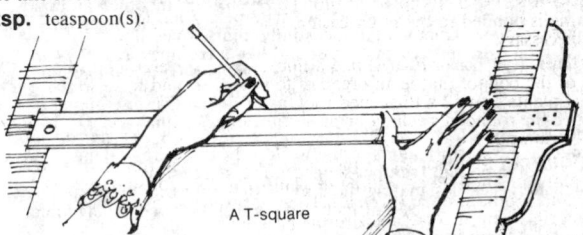

A T-square

T-square (tē′skwer′) a T-shaped ruler used for making parallel lines, etc. The shorter arm of a T-square slides up and down the edge of the drawing board, which serves as a guide.

T-strap (tē′strap′) *n.* **1** a T-shaped strap on a shoe, consisting of a strap along the instep joined to a strap around the ankle. **2** a shoe having such a strap.

tsu·na·mi (tsu nä′mē) *n.* a gigantic sea wave caused by an earthquake on the ocean floor, occurring especially in the Pacific Ocean and often causing great destruction in coastal regions. [< Japanese < *tsu* port + *nami* wave]

Tu. Tuesday.

T.U. Trade Union.

tu·an or **Tu·an** (tü′än) *n.* sir; lord; master; a title of respect originating in SE Asia. [< Malay]

Tua·reg (twä′reg) *n.* **1** a member of certain Moslem tribes of Berber or Libyan nomads of the Sahara. **2** the Hamitic language of these tribes.

tub (tub) *n., v.* **tubbed, tub·bing.** —*n.* **1** bathtub. **2** washtub. **3** *Informal.* bath: *He takes a cold tub every morning.* **4** a usually round, flat-bottomed, open container especially such a container made of wooden staves bound by hoops, used for holding butter, lard, etc. **5** as much as a tub can hold. **6** *Informal.* a clumsy, slow-moving boat or ship. **7** *Slang.* a fat person. —*v.* wash or bathe in a tub. [cf. MDu. or MLG *tubbe*]

A tuba

tu·ba (tyü′bə *or* tü′bə) *n.* **1** a large, brass musical wind instrument resembling a trumpet, having valves to vary the pitch. It has the lowest range of the brasses. **2** an organ stop that produces tuba-like tones. [< L *tuba* war trumpet]

tub·al (tyü′bəl *or* tü′bəl) *adj.* **1** of or having to do with a tube. **2** of, having to do with, or developing in a Fallopian tube: *a tubal ligation, a tubal pregnancy.*

tub·bing (tub′ing) *n.* a bath; washing.

tub·by (tub′ē) *adj.* **-bi·er, -bi·est. 1** like a tub in shape. **2** short

and fat or pudgy. **3** of a violin, etc., having a dull, wooden sound; not having proper resonance. —**tub′bi·ness,** *n.*

tub chair a usually upholstered armchair with a rounded back that extends forward on either side to form the arms.

tube (tyüb *or* tüb) *n., v.* **tubed, tub·ing.** —*n.* **1** a long, hollow cylinder, especially one used to hold or carry liquids or gases: *The mercury or alcohol of a thermometer is held in a glass tube. A plastic tube runs from the pump to the filter of our fish tank.* **2** a small cylinder of thin, flexible metal or plastic with a cap that screws onto the open end, used for holding paste substances, such as toothpaste or paint, ready for use. **3** a channel in an animal or plant body: *the bronchial tubes.* **4** *Botany.* the lower united portion of a gamopetalous corolla or a gamosepalous calyx. **5** a separate, inflatable cylinder of rubber that fits inside the outer casing of a tire; inner tube. **6** a pipe or tunnel through which something travels: *The subway runs under the city in a tube.* **7** *Informal.* subway. **8** electron tube. **9** the picture tube of a television set. **10** *Slang.* television: *What's on the tube tonight?*
—*v.* **1** furnish or fit with a tube or tubes; insert a tube in. **2** pass through or enclose in a tube. **3** make tubular. [< L *tubus*]
—**tube′less,** *adj.* —**tube′like,** *adj.*

tube·less tire (tyüb′lis *or* tüb′-) a type of tire in which an inner lining is bonded to the outer casing, making a separate inner tube unnecessary.

tu·ber (tyü′bər *or* tü′bər) *n.* **1** a thick, fleshy underground stem, as of the potato, that is an organ of food storage and from which new plants grow. **2** a thickened root, as of the dahlia, resembling a tuber. **3** a rounded swelling or projection in an animal body. [< L *tuber* lump]

tu·ber·cle (tyü′bər kəl *or* tü′bər kəl) *n.* **1** a small, rounded swelling or knob on an animal or plant. The roots of some plants, such as legumes, have tubercles. There is a tubercle near the end of each rib where it connects with the backbone. **2** a small, hard, abnormal lump in an organ or the skin, especially such a lump in the lungs that is characteristic of tuberculosis. [< L *tuberculum,* dim. of *tuber* lump]

tubercle bacillus the bacterium (*Mycobacterium tuberculosis*) that causes tuberculosis.

tu·ber·cu·lar (tyü bėr′kyə lər *or* tü bėr′kyə lər) *adj., n.* —*adj.* **1** tuberculous. **2** of, having to do with, or having tubercles. —*n.* a person having tuberculosis. —**tu·ber′cu·lar·ly,** *adv.*

tu·ber·cu·lin (tyü bėr′kyə lin *or* tü bėr′kyə lin) *n.* a sterile liquid prepared from a culture of the bacteria that cause tuberculosis, used in the diagnosis of the disease.

tu·ber·cu·lo·sis (tyü bėr′kyə lō′sis *or* tü bėr′kyə lō′sis) *n.* an infectious disease caused by the tubercle bacillus, affecting human beings and some other mammals, and characterized by the formation of tubercles in various tissues of the body. Tuberculosis in human beings usually affects the lungs. [< NL *tuberculosis* < L *tuberculum.* See TUBERCLE.]

tu·ber·cu·lous (tyü bėr′kyə ləs *or* tü bėr′kyə ləs) *adj.* **1** of, having to do with, or affected with tuberculosis: *a tuberculous patient.* **2** caused by the tubercle bacillus: *tuberculous ulcers in the lungs, a tuberculous infection.*

tube·rose (tyüb′rōz′ *or* tüb′-) *n.* a tropical plant (*Polianthes tuberosa*) of the agave family, having sword-shaped leaves and spikes of very fragrant, white, funnel-shaped flowers. The tuberose grows from a bulb. [< L *tuberosa,* fem. of *tuberosus* tuberous < *tuber* lump; interpreted as if from *tube* + *rose*]

tu·ber·os·i·ty (tyü′bər os′ə tē *or* tü′bər os′ə tē) *n., pl.* **-ties.**
1 the quality or condition of being tuberous. **2** a rounded knob or swelling, especially on a bone where muscles or ligaments are attached.

tu·ber·ous (tyü′bər əs *or* tü′bər əs) *adj.* **1** of, like, or having a tuber or tubers. **2** covered with rounded knobs or swellings. [< L *tuberosus* < *tuber* lump]

tub·ing (tyü′bing *or* tü′bing) *n.* **1** material in the form of a tube: *rubber tubing.* **2** a piece of tube. **3** a system of tubes.

tub thumper *Informal.* **1** a noisy preacher or speaker who thumps the table, etc.; a loud, emotional orator. **2** a press agent or spokesman.

tub thumping *Informal.* **1** the actions of a tub thumper. **2** ballyhoo; exaggerated publicity.

tu·bu·lar (tyü′byə lər *or* tü′byə lər) *adj.* **1** shaped like a tube; round and hollow: *The tuberose has tubular flowers.* **2** made of or provided with tube-shaped pieces: *tubular furniture.* **3** of or having to do with a tube or tubes. [< L *tubulus,* dim. of *tubus* tube, pipe]

tu·bu·late (tyü′byə lit *or* tü′byə lāt′; tyü′byə lāt *or* tü′byə lāt′) *adj., v.* **-lat·ed, -lat·ing.** —*adj.* tubular. —*v.* **1** form into a tube. **2** furnish with a tube. —**tu′bu·la′tion,** *n.*

tu·bule (tyü′byül *or* tü′byül) *n.* a very small tube, especially a narrow channel in an animal or plant. [< F < L *tubulus,* dim. of *tubus* pipe]

hat, āge, fär; let, ēqual, tėrm; it, īce
hot, ōpen, ôrder; oil, out; cup, put, rüle,
above, takən, pencəl, lemən, circəs
ch, child; ng, long; sh, ship
th, thin; ᴛʜ, then; zh, measure

tuck (tuk) *v., n.* —*v.* **1** put (something) into a narrow place or space where it is held tightly or concealed: *She tucked the newspaper under her arm. He tucked the letter away in an inside pocket.* **2** push the loose edge or end of (something) tightly into place: *Tuck your shirt in. He tucked a serviette under his chin.* **3** cover snugly by tucking in the bedclothes (*used with* in): *He always came up to tuck the children in.* **4** draw close together into a fold or folds; make shorter by gathering or folding together (*used with* up): *She tucked up her long skirt and waded into the lake.* **5** make a narrow, straight fold or folds in (a garment, etc.) for decoration or to shorten or control fullness: *a dress with a tucked bodice.* **6** fold (the legs) back or up when sitting or lying: *She sat with her legs tucked under her.* **7** eat heartily (*used with* away *or* in): *He tucked away a big meal.* **8** pull in or back (*used with* in): *to tuck in one's stomach.* **9** sew tucks.
—*n.* **1** a narrow, straight fold sewn into a garment, etc. for decoration or to shorten or control fullness. **2** *Diving, etc.* a position in which the knees are drawn up to the body. **3** *Brit. Slang.* food; eatables, especially sweets. **4** the part of the hull of a ship or boat under the stern where the planks or plates meet. [ME *tuke(n)* stretch < OE *tūcian* torment]

tuck·a·hoe (tuk′ə hō′) *n.* a large, edible fungus (*Poria cocos*) sometimes found on the roots of trees. [< Algonquian]

tuck·er¹ (tuk′ər) *n.* **1** a piece of lace, embroidered fabric, etc. worn by women in the 17th and 18th centuries as a yoke above a low-cut bodice. **2** a person or thing that makes tucks, especially an attachment or device on a sewing machine for making tucks. [< *tuck*]

tuck·er² (tuk′ər) *v. Informal.* tire; weary; exhaust (*usually used with* out): *We were all tuckered out after four hours of wandering around the zoo.* [cf. E dial. *tucked up* worn out, exhausted]

tuck shop *Esp.Brit.* a small shop, especially one near or connected with a school, etc., in which pastries, drinks, and candies are sold.

–tude *suffix forming nouns from adjective stems.* the state, quality, or condition of being, as in *aptitude, certitude.* [< F < L *-tudo, -tudinis*]

Tu·dor (tyü′dər *or* tü′dər) *adj., n.* —*adj.* **1** of or having to do with the royal family that ruled England from 1485 to 1603. **2** designating, having to do with, or characteristic of the time of the Tudors, especially of the style of architecture that was common then. Tudor architecture is characterized by shallow, pointed or slightly rounded arches, half-timbered construction, etc. —*n.* a member of the Tudor family. Elizabeth I was the last Tudor.

Tues. Tuesday.

Tues·day (tyüz′dē *or* tüz′dē, tyüz′dā′ *or* tüz′dā′) *n.* the third day of the week, following Monday. [OE *tīwesdæg* day of Tiw (god of war); translation of LL *Martis dies* day of Mars]

tu·fa (tyü′fə *or* tü′fə) *n.* **1** a soft porous form of limestone produced as a deposit from a spring or stream rich in lime. **2** tuff. [< Ital. *tufo* < L *tofus.* Doublet of TUFF.]

tuff (tuf) *n.* a soft, porous rock formed from volcanic ash or dust thrown out by an erupting volcano. Tuff can vary greatly in texture and composition. [< F *tuf* < Ital. *tufo* tufa < L *tofus.* Doublet of TUFA.]

tuft (tuft) *n., v.* —*n.* **1** a bunch of feathers, grass, threads, etc. growing from one place or held together at one end: *A goat has a tuft of hair on its chin.* **2** a bunch of short, fluffy, often decorative threads or lengths of yarn held together at one end, especially the ends of thread or yarn sewn through a comforter, mattress, cushion, etc. to keep the padding in place.
—*v.* **1** provide or decorate with a tuft or tufts. **2** secure the padding of (a comforter, etc.) by sewing through it at intervals. **3** grow in or form into tufts. [ME, ? < OF *touffe* < LL *tufa* helmet crest]

tuft·ed (tuf′tid) *adj.* **1** having or furnished with a tuft or tufts: *a tufted quilt.* **2** of a bird, having a tuft of feathers on the head; crested. **3** formed into a tuft or tufts.

tug (tug) *v.* **tugged, tug·ging;** *n.* —*v.* **1** pull with force or effort; pull hard: *I tugged the rope and it came loose. The child tugged at his mother's hand.* **2** move by pulling hard: *We tugged the boat up onto the sand.* **3** tow by a tugboat.
—*n.* **1** a hard pull. **2** a hard strain, struggle, effort, or contest. **3** tugboat. **4** a rope, chain, or strap used for pulling, especially the

harness trace. See **harness** for picture. [related to *tow*]
☛ *Syn. v.* **1.** See note at **pull.**

tug·boat (tug′bōt′) *n.* a small, powerful boat used to tow or push ships or boats.

tug–of–war (tug′əv wôr′) *n.* **1** a contest between two teams pulling at the ends of a rope, each trying to drag the other over a line marked between them. **2** any hard struggle for power.

tu·grik (tü′grēk) *n.* the basic unit of money in Mongolia, divided into 100 mongos. See table at **money.** [< Mongolian]

tu·i·tion (tyü ish′ən *or* tü ish′ən) *n.* **1** the price of or money paid for instruction: *Her yearly tuition is $1000.* **2** teaching; instruction: *The child made excellent progress under his capable tuition.* [< L *tuitio, -onis* protection < *tueri* watch over]

tu·i·tion·al (tyü ish′ən əl *or* tü ish′ən əl) *adj.* of or having to do with tuition.

tuk·tu (tuk′tü) *n. Cdn.* caribou. Also **tuktoo.** [< Inuktitut (Eskimo)]

tu·la·di (tü′lə dē′) *Cdn.* See **touladi.** [< Cdn.F *touladi* < Algonquian (Micmac)]

tu·la·re·mi·a (tü′lə rē′mē ə) *n.* an acute infectious bacterial disease of rabbits and other rodents, sometimes transmitted to human beings through insect bites or contact with diseased animals. [< NL *tularemia* < (*bacterium*) *tular*(*ense*), the organism that causes the disease (< *Tulare*, a county in California) + *-emia* < Gk. *haima* blood]

tu·lip (tyü′lip *or* tü′lip) *n.* **1** any of a genus (*Tulipa*) of plants belonging to the lily family, that grow from bulbs and have long, pointed leaves and large, cup-shaped, usually single flowers. There are many varieties of cultivated tulips. **2** the flower or bulb of a tulip. [< obs. Du. *tulipa* < F < Turkish *tülbend* < Persian *dulband* turban. Doublet of TURBAN.]

tulip tree a large North American hardwood tree (*Liriodendron tulipifera*) of the magnolia family having broad, lobed leaves and large, cup-shaped, greenish-yellow flowers that appear after the leaves. In Canada, this tree is native to extreme southern Ontario.

tu·lip·wood (tyü′lip wùd′ *or* tü′lip-) *n.* the wood of the tulip tree, used for cabinetwork.

tulle (tül) *n.* a fine, stiff, machine-made net, usually of silk or rayon, used especially for veils and ballet costumes. [< *Tulle*, a city in SW France]

tul·li·bee (tul′ə bē′) *n., pl.* **-bee** *or* **-bees.** *Cdn.* any of several ciscoes (genus *Coregonus*) found throughout most Canadian lakes from Quebec westward, particularly valued as a food fish. [< Cdn.F *touliibi* < Algonquian (Cree)]

tum·ble (tum′bəl) *v.* **-bled, -bling;** *n.* —*v.* **1** fall, especially helplessly, headlong, or end over end: *The child tumbled down the stairs.* **2** throw over or down; cause to fall: *The earthquake tumbled several buildings.* **3** roll or toss about. **4** move or go in a headlong or awkward way: *He tumbled out of bed to answer the phone. The excited children tumbled through the door.* **5** perform leaps, springs, somersaults, etc. **6** turn over and over; whirl: *to tumble clothes in a dryer.* **7** decline rapidly in amount, etc.: *The stock market tumbled.* **8** *Informal.* understand; catch on (*used with* **to**): *She tumbled to the trick right away.* **9** mix, cleanse, or polish in a tumbling box, or tumbler. —*n.* **1** a fall: *The tumble hurt him badly. He took a tumble on the ice.* **2** a state of confusion or disorder: *Her room was all in a tumble.* **3** a confused or disordered heap: *a tumble of clothes on the floor.* [ME, ult. < OE *tumbian* dance about]

tum·ble·bug (tum′bəl bug′) *n.* dung beetle (def. 1), especially any of numerous species that roll dung into balls in which they lay their eggs. The scarab (def. 1) is a tumblebug.

tum·ble·down (tum′bəl doun′) *adj.* ready to fall down; dilapidated.

tum·bler (tum′blər) *n.* **1** a person who performs leaps, springs, etc.; acrobat. **2** a glass for drinking out of, made without a handle or a foot or stem, and having a heavy, flat bottom. Tumblers originally had rounded or pointed bottoms so that they could not be set down until empty. **3** the amount a glass will hold: *to drink a tumbler of water.* **4** the part in a lock that must be moved from a certain position in order to release the bolt. **5** the part of a gunlock that forces the hammer forward when the trigger is pulled. **6** a kind of domestic pigeon that does backward somersaults while flying. **7** a toy figure with a rounded, weighted bottom that will rock when touched but will always right itself. **8** a revolving device that tumbles things for a particular purpose, such as a box or drum for polishing semiprecious stones or the drum in a clothes dryer. **9** a projecting part on a revolving or rocking shaft that moves another part. **10** a part in an automobile transmission that moves a gear into place.

tum·ble·weed (tum′bəl wēd′) *n.* any of various plants that after drying up in the fall break off from their roots and are blown about by the wind. Russian thistle is a tumbleweed.

tum·bling (tum′bling) *n.* the sport or practice of performing leaps, somersaults, and other gymnastic feats without the use of any apparatus.

tum·brel *or* **tum·bril** (tum′brəl) *n.* **1** a farmer's cart that can be tipped for emptying. **2** *Historical.* **a** an open cart used in the French Revolution to carry prisoners to the guillotine. **b** a two-wheeled covered cart for carrying ammunition and military tools. [probably < OF *tomberel* cart < *tomber* fall < Gmc.]

tu·me·fac·tion (tyü′mə fak′shən *or* tü′mə-) *n.* **1** the process of swelling or the condition of being swollen. **2** a swollen part.

tu·me·fy (tyü′mə fī′ *or* tü′mə fī′) *v.* **-fied, -fy·ing.** swell. [< L *tumefacere* < *tumere* swell + *facere* make]

tu·mes·cence (tyü mes′əns *or* tü mes′əns) *n.* the quality or state of being swollen.

tu·mes·cent (tyü mes′ənt *or* tü mes′ənt) *adj.* **1** becoming swollen; beginning to swell. **2** somewhat swollen. [< L *tumescens, -entis*, ult. < *tumere* swell]

tu·mid (tyü′mid *or* tü′mid) *adj.* **1** swollen. **2** of style, swollen with big words; bombastic. [< L *tumidus* < *tumere* swell] —**tu′mid·ly,** *adv.* —**tu′mid·ness,** *n.*

tum·my (tum′ē) *n., pl.* **-mies.** *Informal.* stomach.

tu·mor *or* **tu·mour** (tyü′mər *or* tü′mər) *n.* **1** an abnormal, separate mass of tissue in any part of the body, that develops from existing tissue, but has no physiological function. Tumors can be either benign (doing little or no harm) or malignant (cancerous). **2** any abnormal swelling. [< L *tumor* < *tumere* swell]

tu·mor·ous (tyü′mər əs *or* tü′mər əs) *adj.* **1** of or having to do with a tumor or tumors. **2** having a tumor or tumors.

tu·mour (tü′mər *or* tyü′mər) See **tumor.**

tump (tump) *n.* tumpline. [< Algonquian. Cf. METUMP.]

tump·line (tump′līn′) *n.* a kind of harness for carrying or pulling heavy loads, consisting of a long strap with a broad middle part that is placed around the forehead or chest, the two ends being attached to the pack or load. [< *tump + line*]

tu·mult (tyü′mult *or* tü′mult) *n.* **1** a violent disturbance or disorder; uproar: *We heard the tumult of the storm. The shout of "Fire!" caused a tumult in the theatre.* **2** a great disturbance of mind or feeling; confusion and excitement: *His mind was in a tumult.* [< L *tumultus*]

tu·mul·tu·ous (tyü mul′chü əs *or* tü mul′chü əs) *adj.* **1** characterized by tumult; very noisy or disorderly. **2** greatly disturbed. **3** rough; stormy: *Tumultuous waves beat upon the rocks.* —**tu·mul′tu·ous·ly,** *adv.* —**tu·mul′tu·ous·ness,** *n.*

tu·mu·lus (tyü′myə ləs *or* tü′myə ləs) *n., pl.* **-lus·es, -li** (-lī′ *or* -lē′). a mound of earth, especially over a grave. [< L]

tun (tun) *n.* **1** a large cask for holding liquids, especially wine, beer, or ale. **2** a unit formerly used for measuring the volume of liquids, equal to 252 gallons (about 954 L). [OE *tunne,* probably < Celtic]
☛ *Hom.* **ton, tonne.**

tu·na¹ (tü′nə *or* tyü′nə) *n.* **1** any of various large, spiny-finned food and game fishes (of genus *Thunnus* and other genera in family Scombridae) found in warm seas throughout the world, having a rounded, tapering body and a crescent-shaped tail. The largest and commercially most important tuna is the **bluefin tuna,** (*Thunnus thunnus*) which may weigh as much as 500 kilograms. **2** the flesh of a tuna, especially when canned for use as food. [< Am.Sp. *tuna,* ult. < L *thunnus.* See TUNNY.]

tu·na² (tü′nə) *n.* **1** any of various prickly pear cactuses, especially one (*Opuntia tuna*) of tropical America cultivated for its edible fruit. **2** the fruit of a tuna. [< Sp. < Haitian]

tun·a·ble *or* **tune·a·ble** (tyü′nə bəl *or* tü′nə bəl) *adj.* **1** capable of being tuned. **2** *Archaic.* harmonious; tuneful.

tuna fish **1** the flesh of a tuna, especially when canned for use as food. **2** (*adj.*) **tuna-fish,** made of tuna fish: *a tuna-fish casserole.*

tun·dra (tun′drə) *n.* a vast, level, treeless plain in the arctic regions. The subsoil of the tundra remains frozen all year round. [< Russian]

tune (tyün *or* tün) *n., v.* **tuned, tun·ing.** —*n.* **1** a succession of musical tones in a particular rhythm, forming a unit; melody: *He was humming a tune to himself as he worked.* **2** the proper pitch: *She can't sing in tune. The piano is out of tune.* **3** a mood or manner; attitude: *He was very cocky at first, but soon changed his tune.* **4** agreement; harmonious relation: *He's happier now that he's in tune with his surroundings again. She won't be elected because she's out of tune with the times.*

call the tune, have control; be in a position to dictate what will be done: *He talks big to the press, but it is his partner who calls the tune.*

sing a different tune, talk or behave differently: *She's singing a different tune since she lost her job.*

to the tune of, *Informal.* to the amount or sum of, especially when it is considered excessive: *He received a bill to the tune of $400 for car repairs.*

—*v.* **1** adjust to the proper pitch; put in tune: *to tune a piano or a violin.* **2** of an orchestra, adjust instruments to the proper pitch (*used with* up): *The orchestra was already tuning up when we arrived.* **3** adjust (a motor, etc.) for precise performance (*often used with* up). **4** adjust a radio or television set to receive a particular frequency of signals (*often used with* in): *He tuned his radio to the news from Moscow. Tune in tomorrow for another episode. We tuned in the new FM station.*

tune out, a adjust a radio or television set to cut out (interference or static). **b** *Slang.* turn one's mind away from; ignore: *Our boss tunes out complaints he doesn't want to hear.* [var. of *tone*]

tune·ful (tyün′fəl *or* tün′fəl) *adj.* musical; melodious: *That canary has a tuneful song.* —**tune′ful·ly,** *adv.* —**tune′ful·ness,** *n.*

tune·less (tyün′lis *or* tün′lis) *adj.* not tuneful; not having a pleasing or recognizable tune: *His absent-minded tuneless humming began to get on their nerves.*

tun·er (tyü′nər *or* tü′nər) *n.* **1** a person whose work is tuning musical instruments, especially pianos. **2** any person or thing that tunes.

tune–up (tyün′up′ *or* tün′-) *n.* adjustment of a motor, etc. to the proper running condition: *He took his car in for an engine tune-up.*

tung oil (tung) an oil obtained from the seeds of the tung tree, widely used as a drying oil in paints and varnishes, as a waterproofing agent, etc.

tung·sten (tung′stən) *n.* a hard, heavy, steel-grey metallic element with a very high melting point, used especially for the filaments of electric light bulbs and in making steel alloys; wolfram. Symbol: W; *at.no.* 74; *at.wt.* 183.85. [< Swedish *tungsten* < *tung* heavy + *sten* stone]

tung tree a tree (*Aleurites fordii*) of the spurge family native to China but now cultivated in other warm regions, having large, heart-shaped leaves and white flowers. The seeds of the tung tree yield oil.

tu·nic (tyü′nik *or* tü′nik) *n.* **1** a loose garment with or without sleeves, usually reaching to the knees, worn by the ancient Greeks and Romans. **2** a girls' or women's garment somewhat like a dress but shorter, worn over a skirt or long pants: *Sleeveless tunics, sometimes open at the sides, are often worn over blouses and skirts, etc.* **3** a hip-length overblouse. **4** a short, close-fitting coat or jacket worn as part of the uniform by soldiers, police officers, etc. **5** a covering or enclosing membrane of a plant or animal part. [< L *tunica,* ult. < Semitic]

tu·ni·cate (tyü′nə kit *or* tyü′nə kāt′, tü′nə kit *or* tü′nə kāt′) *n., adj.* —*n.* any of a subphylum (Tunicata, also called Urochordata) of marine chordate animals that includes the sea squirts, having in the adult stage a sacklike body with a tough, leathery outer covering (a tunic). —*adj.* **1** of, having to do with, or being a tunicate. **2** having or made up of concentric layers of tissue, as an onion bulb. [< L *tunicatus,* pp. of *tunicare* clothe with a tunic < *tunica.* See TUNIC.]

tuning fork a small, two-pronged steel instrument that sounds a fixed tone when struck, used to determine a standard pitch for singing or for tuning a musical instrument.

Tu·ni·sian (tù nē′zhən, tù nē′zē ən, *or* tù nē′shən) *n., adj.* —*n.* a native or inhabitant of Tunisia, a country in Africa, or its capital city, Tunis. —*adj.* of or having to do with Tunisia, Tunis, or the Tunisians.

tun·nel (tun′əl) *n., v.* **-nelled** *or* **-neled, -nel·ling** *or* **-nel·ing.** —*n.* **1** an artificial underground passage under a river, road, building, etc. or through a hill or mountain, for a railway, road, or walkway: *The railway passes through several tunnels on its way through the Rockies. There is a tunnel connecting the university residences with the food-services building.* **2** a nearly horizontal passageway in a mine (often used loosely for any drift, level, etc.). **3** any channel or conduit. **4** an animal's burrow.

—*v.* **1** make a tunnel: *The workmen are tunnelling under the river.* **2** make a tunnel through or under: *to tunnel a hill or river.* **3** make (one's way or a passage) by tunnelling: *She tunnelled a narrow passage through the snowdrift. They tunnelled their way under the prison wall.* [ME < OF *tonel* cask < *tonne* tun < Celtic] —**tun′nel·ler** *or* **tun′nel·er,** *n.*

tunnel vision 1 a very narrow field of vision; a field of vision that is restricted at the sides. **2** narrow-mindedness.

tun·ny (tun′ē) *n., pl.* **-nies** *or* **-ny.** tuna. [< F *thon* < Provençal < L *thunnus, thynnus* < Gk. *thynnos*]

tu·pek (tü′pək) *Cdn.* See **tupik.**

Tu·pi–Gua·ra·ni (tü pē′gwä′rä nē′) *n.* a linguistic stock of central South America—consisting principally of Tupi, the northern

hat, āge, fär; let, ēqual, tèrm; it, īce
hot, ōpen, ôrder; oil, out; cup, pút, rüle, əbove, takən, pencəl, lemən, circəs
ch, child; ng, long; sh, ship
th, thin; ᴛʜ, then; zh, measure

branch, and Guarani, the southern branch—occurring particularly along the lower Amazon.

tu·pik (tü′pək) *n. Cdn.* a compact, portable tent of skins, traditionally used by Inuit as a summer dwelling. Also, **tupek.** [< Inuktitut (Eskimo) *tupiq*]

tup·pence (tup′əns) See **twopence.**

tup·pen·ny (tup′ən ē) See **twopenny.**

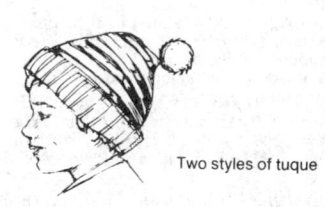

Two styles of tuque

tuque (tük *or* tyük) *n. Cdn.* **1** a knitted cap resembling a long stocking, usually knotted at the end: *Tuques are popular at the winter carnival.* **2** a tight-fitting, short knitted cap, often having a round tassel on top. [< Cdn.F var. of F *toque* cap]

Tu·ra·ni·an (tyü rā′nē ən *or* tü rā′nē ən) *adj. or n.* Ural-Altaic. [< Persian *Tūrān,* a district north of the Oxus]

A turban

tur·ban (tèr′bən) *n.* **1** a headdress for men worn especially by Moslems and Sikhs, consisting of a scarf wound around the head, sometimes over a cap. **2** any similar headdress, especially one worn by women, consisting of a scarf wound around the head or a close-fitting, brimless hat resembling this. [< Turkish < Arabic < Persian *dulband.* Doublet of TULIP.]

tur·baned (tèr′bənd) *adj.* wearing a turban.

tur·bid (tèr′bid) *adj.* **1** thick or cloudy with or as if with churned-up sediment; muddy: *a turbid river.* **2** confused or disordered: *a turbid and restless mind.* [< L *turbidus* < *turba* turmoil] —**tur′bid·ly,** *adv.* —**tur′bid·ness,** *n.*

tur·bid·i·ty (tèr bid′ə tē) *n.* the condition of being turbid.

tur·bi·nate (tèr′bə nit *or* tèr′bə nāt′) *adj., n.* —*adj.* **1** shaped like an upside-down cone. **2** shaped like a spiral or scroll. Many molluscs have turbinate shells. **3** having to do with or designating certain spongy, scroll-shaped bones in the nasal passages. —*n.* a turbinate shell or bone. [< L *turbinatus* < *turbo* whirling object or motion]

tur·bine (tèr′bīn *or* tèr′bən) *n.* a rotary engine or motor driven by a current of water, steam, or air that pushes against the blades of a wheel or system of wheels attached to a drive shaft, causing the wheel and drive shaft to turn. Turbines are used to turn generators that produce electric power. [< F < L *turbo, -binis* whirling object or motion]

turbo– *combining form.* consisting of or driven by a turbine, as in *turbojet.*

tur·bo·fan (tèr′bō fan′) *n.* **1** a turbojet engine in which a large fan driven by the turbine draws in additional air which is forced rearwards to increase the thrust of the jet. **2** the fan itself.

tur·bo·jet (tèr′bō jet′) *n.* **1** turbojet engine. **2** an aircraft powered by a turbojet engine or engines.

turbojet engine a jet engine using a turbine to drive an air compressor which supplies compressed air to the combustion chamber. A turbojet engine is started with an auxiliary power source that spins the turbine. Most military aircraft are powered by turbojet engines.

tur·bo·prop (tèr′bō prop′) n. 1 turboprop engine. 2 an aircraft powered by a turboprop engine or engines. [turbo- (< turbine) + propeller]

turboprop engine a jet engine using a propeller and a turbojet engine with two turbines. The turbojet engine is used mainly to turn the propeller, which supplies most of the power for the aircraft. The jet exhaust of a turboprop engine adds only a little to the power provided by the propeller.

tur·bot (tèr′bət) n., pl. **-bot** or **-bots.** 1 a large European flatfish (Scophthalmus maximus), valued as food. 2 any of various similar fishes. [ME < OF < OSwedish törnbut (< törn thorn, from the fish's prickles)]

tur·bu·lence (tèr′byə ləns) n. 1 the quality or state of being turbulent; disturbance or commotion: He was glad to retire from the turbulence of public life. 2 Meteorology. an unstable condition of the atmosphere, characterized by strong, irregular air currents.

tur·bu·lent (tèr′byə lənt) adj. 1 greatly disturbed or agitated; characterized by trouble or commotion: the turbulent sea, a turbulent state of mind. 2 causing disturbance; unruly; boisterous: a turbulent mob. [< L turbulentus < turba turmoil] —**tur′bu·lent·ly,** adv.

tu·reen (tù rēn′) n. a deep, covered dish for serving soup, etc. [< F terrine earthen vessel, ult. < L terra earth]

turf (tèrf) n., pl. **turfs** or (sometimes) **turves;** v. —n. 1 grass with its roots and the soil it is growing in, forming a thick layer like a mat. 2 a piece of turf; sod: We cut turfs from the back lawn to fill in bare spots in the front. 3 an artificial surface for a playing field, etc., made to resemble grass. 4 Usually, **the turf, a** a track for horse racing. **b** the sport or business of horse racing. 5 Informal. a particular territory or area: He could relax now that he was back on his own turf. 6 peat, especially a block of peat used for fuel. —v. 1 cover with turf. 2 Slang. dismiss or evict forcefully (usually used with out): The restaurant manager had turfed him out when he got rowdy. [OE]

turf·y (tèr′fē) adj. **turf·i·er, turf·i·est.** 1 covered with turf; grassy. 2 like turf. 3 full of or like peat. 4 of or having to do with horse racing. —**turf′i·ness,** n.

tur·ges·cence (tèr jes′əns) n. the process of swelling or the condition of being swollen.

tur·ges·cent (tèr jes′ənt) adj. becoming turgid; swelling. [< L turgescens, -entis, ppr. of turgescere begin to swell < turgere swell]

tur·gid (tèr′jid) adj. 1 swollen; bloated. 2 using big words and elaborate comparisons; bombastic; inflated; pompous. [< L turgidus < turgere swell] —**tur′gid·ly,** adv.

tur·gid·i·ty (tèr jid′ə tē) n. the quality or state of being turgid.

tur·gid·ness (tèr′jid nəs) n. turgidity.

Turk (tèrk) n. 1 a native or inhabitant of Turkey, a country in Asia Minor and SE Europe. 2 a native or inhabitant of the Ottoman Empire. 3 a member of any of the peoples traditionally speaking Turkic languages and inhabiting the region from the Adriatic Sea to eastern Siberia. [ME < Med.L Turcus < Persian]

Turk. Turkey; Turkish.

tur·key (tèr′kē) n., pl. **-keys.** 1 a large North American bird (Meleagris gallopavo) having a thickset body with metallic green, copper, and bronze plumage and a bare head and neck with wattles. Domestic turkeys are derived from a Mexican subspecies of this bird. 2 a similar bird (Agriocharis ocellata) of Central America and N South America which, together with the North American species, constitutes the gallinaceous family Meleagrididae. 3 the flesh of a domestic turkey, used for food: Turkey is associated especially with Christmas and Thanksgiving. 4 Cdn. esp.Prairie Provinces. sandhill crane. 5 Slang. a flop or failure, especially a play or motion picture that has failed. 6 Slang. an unattractive, stupid, or silly person: I don't want that turkey as a partner.
talk turkey, Informal. talk frankly and bluntly: They decided it was time to get together and talk turkey. [shortened from turkey-cock and turkey-hen, names orig. applied to the guinea fowl because it was first imported into England via Turkey, and later applied to the North American bird because it was at first confused with the guinea fowl]

turkey buzzard turkey vulture.

turkey·cock (tèr′kē kok′) n. 1 a male turkey. 2 a strutting, conceited person.

Turkey red 1 bright red. 2 a cotton cloth having this color.

turkey vulture a vulture (Cathartes aura) found in the western hemisphere as far north as southern Canada, having dark plumage and a red upper neck and head that are bare of feathers. The turkey vulture looks somewhat like a turkey.

Turk·ic (tèrk′ik) adj., n. —adj. 1 of, having to do with, or designating a subfamily of the Altaic family of languages, including Turkish, Turkoman, and Tartar. 2 of or having to do with the peoples speaking Turkic languages. —n. the Turkic languages.

Turk·ish (tèr′kish) n., adj. —n. the Turkic language of Turkey. —adj. of, having to do with, or characteristic of Turkey, its inhabitants, or their language.

Turkish bath 1 a kind of bath in which the bather stays in a hot, usually steam-filled room until he sweats freely and then is washed and massaged. 2 Often, **Turkish baths,** pl. a place used for such baths.

Turkish delight a fruit-flavored candy made of sugar and gelatin cut into cubes and dusted with powdered sugar.

Turkish Empire Ottoman Empire.

Turkish towel a thick towel made of cotton terry.

Turk·man (tèrk′mən) n., pl. **-men.** 1 a native or inhabitant of the Turkmen Soviet Socialist Republic in W Asia. 2 a native or inhabitant of Turkey; Turk.

Turk·men (tèrk′men for 1, -mən for 2) n. 1 a language of Turkestan. 2 pl. of **Turkman.**

Tur·ko·man (tèr′kə mən) n., pl. **-mans;** adj. —n. 1 a member of any of several Turkic peoples living mainly in the region around the Aral Sea in the Soviet Union. 2 the Turkic language of the Turkomans. —adj. of or having to do with the Turkomans or their language.

tur·mer·ic (tèr′mər ik) n. 1 a yellow powder prepared from the underground stem of an East Indian perennial herb (Curcuma longa), used as a seasoning, as a yellow dye, and in medicine. 2 the plant itself. 3 the underground stem of this plant. [earlier tarmaret < F < Med.L terra merita, literally, worthy earth < L terra earth + merere deserve]

tur·moil (tèr′moil) n. a commotion; disturbance; tumult. [origin uncertain]

turn (tèrn) v., n. —v. 1 move round as a wheel does; rotate: The merry-go-round turned. 2 cause to move round as a wheel does: I turned the crank three times. 3 move part way around; change from one side to the other: Turn over on your back. 4 cause to move around in order to open, close, raise, lower, or tighten: She turned the key in the lock. 5 perform by revolving, as a somersault. 6 take a new direction: The road turns to the north here. 7 give a new direction to: He turned his steps toward home. 8 change in direction or position; invert; reverse: to turn a page. 9 reverse the position of (the turf, soil, etc.) in ploughing or digging so as to bring the under parts to the surface: to turn a furrow. 10 alter or remake (a garment, etc.) by putting the inner side outward. 11 change so as to become: She turned pale. 12 transform or convert: The drop in temperature turned the rain to snow. They managed to turn defeat into victory. 13 change for or to a worse condition; sour; spoil: Warm weather turns milk. 14 give form to; make: He can turn pretty compliments. 15 change from one language into another; translate: Turn this sentence into Latin. 16 put out of order; unsettle: Too much praise turns his head. 17 depend: The success of the picnic turns on the weather. 18 cause to go, send, etc.: to turn a person from one's door. 19 drive back; stop: to turn a punch. 20 direct (one's thoughts or attention): He turned his thoughts toward home. 21 consider in different aspects; revolve (over) in the mind: to turn a problem in one's mind. 22 direct thought, eyes, etc.: He turned to his father for help. 23 put to use; apply: to turn money to good use. 24 move to the other side; go round; get beyond: to turn the corner. 25 shape on a lathe. 26 make or become sick; nauseate. 27 become dizzy. 28 give a curved or crooked form to; bend; twist. 29 pass or get beyond (a particular age, time, or amount): a man turning sixty. 30 cause (money or commodities) to circulate steadily. 31 of leaves, change color. 32 cause to recoil: His argument was turned against himself. 33 make antagonistic; prejudice: to turn friends against friends. 34 exchange for something else: to turn stock into cash. 35 adopt a different religion. 36 Obs. convert.
turn down, a fold down. **b** bend downward. **c** place with face downward. **d** Informal. refuse; reject: to turn down a plan. **e** lower by turning something.
turn in, a a turn and go in. **b** point (toes) inward. **c** Informal. go to bed. **d** hand in; deliver. **e** give back. **f** exchange: to turn an old bike in for a new one.
turn loose, free from restraint and allow to go where, or do as, one will: to turn a prisoner loose.
turn off, a shut off. **b** put out (a light). **c** turn aside. **d** do. **e** discharge. **f** Slang. make or become bored, uninterested, etc.
turn on, a start the flow of; put on. **b** attack; resist; oppose. **c** depend on. **d** have to do with. **e** Slang. take a narcotic; especially, smoke marijuana. **f** Slang. make or become stimulated and elated by, or as if by, the use of a psychedelic drug.

turn out, a put out; shut off. **b** let go out. **c** drive out. **d** come or go out: *We all turned out for hockey.* **e** go out on strike. **f** make; produce. **g** result. **h** become. **i** be found or known. **j** equip; fit out. **k** *Informal.* get out of bed.

turn over, a hand over; transfer: *He turned the job over to his assistant.* **b** think carefully about; consider in different ways: *She turned the idea over in her mind.* **c** buy and then sell (stock). **d** invest and get back (capital). **e** shift position, especially change from lying on one side to lying on the other. **f** convert to different use. **g** do business to the amount of (a specified sum).

turn to, a refer to. **b** go to for help. **c** get busy; set to work.

turn up, a fold up or over, especially so as to shorten; give upward turn to; bring upward to. **b** make (a lamp, etc.) burn stronger. **c** make (a radio, etc.) louder. **d** turn and go up. **e** be directed upwards. **f** appear.

—*n.* **1** a motion like that of a wheel: *At each turn, the screw goes in further.* **2** a single revolution, as of a wheel. **3** a change of direction: *a turn to the left.* **4** a place where there is a change in direction: *a turn in the road.* **5** the condition of being, or direction in which something is, twisted. **6** a change in affairs, conditions, or circumstances: *The sick man has taken a turn for the better.* **7** the time at which such a change takes place: *the turn of the year, the turn of a fever.* **8** a form; style: *a happy turn of expression, a serious turn of mind.* **9** a twist or bend: *Give that rope a few more turns around the tree.* **10** a time or chance to do something: *My turn comes after yours.* **11** a time or spell of action: *to have a turn at a thing.* **12** a deed; act: *One good turn deserves another.* **13** performance. **14** an inclination; bent: *He has a turn for mathematics.* **15** a walk, drive, or ride: *a turn in the park.* **16** a spell of dizziness or fainting. **17** *Informal.* a momentary shock caused by sudden alarm, fright, etc.: *to give someone a bad turn.* **18** form; mould; cast: *the turn of her arms.* **19** in music, an ornamental device of four tones, a principal tone, followed, usually, by one tone above and below it, and returning to the principal tone. The order in which the turn is performed is occasionally reversed.

at every turn, every time; without exception.

by turns, one after another.

in turn, in proper order.

out of turn, a not in proper order. **b** at an inappropriate time, stage, etc.: *He was tactless to speak out of turn.*

take turns, play, act, etc. one after another in proper order.

to a turn, to just the right degree.

turn about or **turn and turn about,** one after another in proper order.

[OE *turnian* < L *tornare* turn on a lathe < *tornus* lathe < Gk. *tornos.* Related to TOUR.]

☞ *Hom.* **tern.**

☞ *Syn. v.* **1. Turn, revolve, rotate** = move round in a circle. **Turn** is the general and common word, meaning "move in a circle" or in circle after circle, either on a pivot or axis or around a centre: *That wheel turns freely now.* **Revolve** means "turn round and round on a pivot" or, especially, in a circular path around something that serves as a centre: *The earth rotates (on its axis) once every 24 hours and revolves round the sun once each year.*

turn·a·bout (tèrn′ə bout′) *n.* **1** the act of turning so as to face the other way. **2** a changing to an opposite view, policy, etc.; about-face; reversal. **3** a merry-go-round.

turn·a·round (tèrn′ə round′) *n.* **1** an about-face or reversal. **2** a space for vehicles to turn around. **3** the time it takes a ship, airplane, etc. to unload, load, and undergo repairs and servicing before being ready to depart.

A turnbuckle, used for joining two lengths of wire

turn·buck·le (tèrn′buk′əl) *n.* a device for connecting and tightening metal rods, sections of wire, etc., consisting of a hollow metal link with an inside screw thread at either end or a swivel at one end and a screw thread at the other.

turn·coat (tèrn′kōt′) *n.* a person who changes his political party or principles; a person who goes over to the opposing side.

turn·down (tèrn′doun′) *adj., n.* —*adj.* that is or can be turned down; folded or doubled down: *a turndown collar.* —*n.* **1** a turning down; rejection. **2** a decline; downturn.

turn·er (tèr′nər) *n.* **1** a device or tool that is used for turning: *an egg turner.* **2** a person who forms or shapes things with a lathe.

turn indicator 1 a flashing light or other device on a motor vehicle for signalling turns. **2** a gyroscopic device that indicates any turning motion around the vertical axis of an airplane.

turning point a point in time at which a significant change takes place: *That experience was the turning point of his life.*

hat, āge, fär; let, ēqual, tèrm; it, īce
hot, ōpen, ôrder; oil, out; cup, pùt, rüle,
əbove, takən, pencəl, lemən, circəs

ch, child; ng, long; sh, ship
th, thin; ᴛʜ, then; zh, measure

tur·nip (tèr′nip) *n.* **1** a biennial plant (*Brassica rapa*) of the mustard family, having hairy leaves and a thick, round, whitish root. **2** the rutabaga, closely related to this plant. **3** the root of either of these plants, used as a vegetable. [probably ult. < ME *turn* (from its rounded shape) + *nepe* turnip < L *napus*]

turn·key (tèrn′kē′) *n., pl.* **-keys.** *Archaic.* a person in charge of the keys of a prison; the keeper of a prison.

turn·off (tèrn′of′) *n.* **1** the act of turning off. **2** a place where one can leave a highway, especially an exit ramp leading off an expressway: *It's two kilometres to the next turnoff.*

turn·out (tèrn′out′) *n.* **1** a gathering of people for a special purpose or event: *There was a good turnout at the dance.* **2** output. **3** the way in which a person or thing is equipped or dressed: *an elegant turnout.* **4** a carriage together with its horse or horses. **5** equipment; outfit. **6** *Esp.Brit.* a labor strike. **7** *Esp.U.S.* a wide place in a road for vehicles to pass. **8** *Esp.U.S.* a railway siding.

turn·o·ver (tèrn′ō′vər) *n.* **1** a small, filled pastry in the shape of a semicircle or triangle made by placing the filling on one half of a piece of rolled-out dough and folding the other half over it. **2** the rate at which people leave a job or company and have to be replaced: *The company has had a high turnover in the past year.* **3** the amount of business done in a given time: *There was a large turnover on the stock exchange this week.* **4** the paying out and getting back of the money involved in a business transaction: *The store reduced prices to make a quick turnover.* **5** *Football.* the act or an instance of losing possession of the ball to the opposing team through a fumble, pass interception, etc.: *Two touchdowns were scored as a result of turnovers.* **6** the act or an instance of turning over; upset or reversal. **7** (*adj.*) that can be or is designed to be turned over: *a turnover collar.*

turn·pike (tèrn′pīk′) *n.* **1** *Esp.U.S.* a road on which toll is or used to be charged, especially an expressway. **2** tollgate. [< *turn* + *pike* a sharp point; with reference to a spiked barrier across a road, turning on a vertical axis]

turn signal turn indicator (def. 1).

turn·spit (tèrn′spit′) *n.* a person or animal formerly employed to operate a device, such as a treadmill, for turning meat on a spit.

turn·stile (tèrn′stīl′) *n.* a barrier consisting of bars set into a revolving central post, allowing people to pass through only on foot, one at a time, and only in one direction.

turn·stone (tèrn′stōn′) *n.* any of a small genus (*Arenaria*) of migratory shore birds belonging to the same family as sandpipers, that use their flattened, slightly upturned bill to turn over stones in search of food.

turn·ta·ble (tèrn′tā′bəl) *n.* **1** on a record player, the revolving disk on which a record is placed to be played. **2** any similar disk or platform that revolves, such as a platform with track, used for turning a locomotive around.

tur·pen·tine (tèr′pən tīn) *n., v.* —*n.* **1** a thick, sticky fluid consisting of oil and resin, obtained from pines and various other coniferous trees. **2** a volatile oil distilled from this fluid, used especially as a solvent and thinner for paints, varnishes, etc. —*v.* apply turpentine to. [ME < OF < L *terebinthina* < Gk. *terebinthos* turpentine tree]

tur·pi·tude (tèr′pə tyüd′ *or* tèr′pə tüd′) *n.* a shameful wickedness; baseness. [< L *turpitudo* < *turpis* vile]

tur·quoise (tèr′kwoiz *or* tèr′koiz) *n., adj.* —*n.* **1** a sky-blue or greenish-blue precious stone or mineral, consisting of a phosphate of aluminum and copper, which is used as a gem. **2** a gem made from this stone. **3** light greenish-blue.
—*adj.* having the color turquoise. [< F *turquoise,* originally fem. adj., Turkish]

tur·ret (tèr′it) *n.* **1** a small tower, often on the corner of a building. **2** any of various low, rotating armored structures in which guns are mounted. **3** a cockpit in a military aircraft, usually enclosed by a strong, transparent plastic material and containing a machine gun or guns. **4** a kind of tower on wheels, formerly used in attacking walled castles, forts, or towns. [ME < OF *torete,* dim. of *tor* < L *turris* tower]

tur·ret·ed (tèr′ə tid) *adj.* **1** having a turret or turrets. **2** of a shell, having whorls forming a long spiral.

tur·tle¹ (tèr′təl) *n.* any of an order (Chelonia) of four-legged, toothless, generally slow-moving reptiles found throughout the

world, having the body encased in a protective bony shell with an outside layer of horny plates, or, in some species, tough skin. Most species of turtle can withdraw the head, legs, and tail into the shell for protection. Land turtles are often called tortoises.
turn turtle, turn bottom side up.
[< F *tortue* tortoise; influenced by E *turtle* turtledove]

tur·tle² (tėr′təl) *n. Archaic.* turtledove. [OE *turtle, turtla* < L *turtur*]

tur·tle·back (tėr′təl bak′) *n.* an arched projection erected over the deck of a steamer at the bow, and often at the stern also, to guard against damage from heavy seas.

tur·tle·dove (tėr′təl duv′) *n.* any of a genus (*Streptopelia*) of wild doves, especially a small, grey or brownish European wild dove (*S. turtur*) found in woods and around farms, noted for its sad-sounding cooing and the affection that it appears to have for its mate. [< *turtle²* + *dove¹*]

tur·tle·neck (tėr′təl nek′) *n.* 1 a high, snugly fitting, usually turned-over collar, especially on a sweater. See **collar** for picture. 2 a sweater having a turtleneck.

Tus·can (tus′kən) *n., adj.* —*n.* 1 a native or inhabitant of Tuscany, a district in central Italy. 2 the language of Tuscany, regarded as the classical form of Italian and forming the basis of modern standard Italian. —*adj.* 1 of or having to do with Tuscany or its people. 2 *Architecture.* of having to do with, or designating an order of architecture developed in ancient Rome, one of the five classical styles of architecture. The characteristic Tuscan column is seven diameters high, with an unfluted shaft and a capital and base having mouldings but no decoration. See **order** for picture.

Tus·ca·ro·ra (tus′kə rô′rə) *n., pl.* **-ra** or **-ras.** 1 a member of an Amerindian people of Iroquois stock who occupied what is now North Carolina at the time of their first contact with Europeans, but later migrated to New York and Ontario. The Tuscarora were the sixth nation to join the Iroquois Confederacy. 2 the Iroquoian language of the Tuscarora.

tush¹ (tush) *interj. or n.* an exclamation expressing impatience, contempt, etc.

tush² (tush) *n.* 1 a canine tooth of a horse. 2 tusk. [OE *tusc.* Related to TOOTH.]

tusk (tusk) *n., v.* —*n.* 1 a very long, large, pointed tooth, usually one of a pair projecting from the sides of the closed mouth in animals like the elephant, walrus, and wild boar. Animals with tusks use them for digging, as a weapon, etc. 2 any tooth or other object like a tusk. —*v.* gore, dig up, or tear with the tusks. [ME *tusk,* var. of OE *tux,* var. of *tusc* tush²]

tusk·er (tus′kər) *n.* an animal with well-developed tusks, such as a mature elephant, walrus, or wild boar.

tus·sah (tus′ə) *n.* 1 a coarse, strong silk from a wild or semi-domesticated silkworm (*Antheraea paphia*) of India and China. Undyed tussah is a brownish color. 2 the silkworm that produces this silk. The tussah feeds on oak or castor bean leaves and makes a larger cocoon than the domestic silkworm. Also called **tussore.** [< Hind. *tasar* shuttle]

tus·sle (tus′əl) *n., v.* **-sled, -sling.** —*n.* a scuffle or struggle: *There was a short tussle as everyone tried to get through the door first.* —*v.* struggle or wrestle: *The two sisters liked to tussle with one another.* [var. of *tousle*]

tus·sock (tus′ək) *n.* a tuft or clump of growing grass, etc. [origin uncertain]

tussock moth any of numerous dull-colored moths (family Lymantriidae) whose larvae have thick tufts of hair.

tus·sore (tus′ôr) *n.* tussah.

tut (tut) *interj., n., v.* **tut·ted, tut·ting.** —*interj. or n.* an exclamation of impatience, contempt, or rebuke. —*v.* exclaim in this way; utter a tut or tuts.

tu·te·lage (tyü′tə lij *or* tü′tə lij) *n.* 1 instruction: *They learned very quickly under his expert tutelage.* 2 guardianship; protection. 3 the condition of being in the care of a guardian. [< L *tutela* watching]

tu·te·lar (tyü′tə lər *or* tü′tə lər) *adj.* tutelary.

tu·te·lar·y (tyü′tə ler′ē *or* tü′tə ler′ē) *adj., n., pl.* **-lar·ies.** —*adj.* 1 protecting; guardian: *a tutelary saint.* 2 of or having to do with a guardian. —*n.* a tutelary saint, spirit, divinity, etc. [< L *tutelarius* < *tutela* protection < *tueri* watch over]

tu·tor (tyü′tər *or* tü′tər) *n., v.* —*n.* 1 a private teacher. 2 in certain colleges and universities, a teacher, especially an assistant teacher who gives extra instruction to students individually or in small groups. 3 in English universities, a college official appointed to advise students, direct their work, etc. —*v.* 1 teach; instruct, especially individually or privately. 2 act as

tutor. 3 *Informal.* be taught by a tutor. [ME < L *tutor* guardian < *tueri* watch over]

tu·to·ri·al (tyü tô′rē əl *or* tü tô′rē əl) *adj., n.* —*adj.* 1 of or having to do with a tutor: *tutorial authority.* 2 using tutors: *the tutorial system.* —*n.* in some colleges and universities, a class given by a tutor to an individual or a small group of students.

tu·tor·ship (tyü′tər ship′ *or* tü′tər-) *n.* the position, rank, or duties of a tutor.

tut·ti (tü′tē; *Italian,* tüt′tē) *adj., n., pl.* **-tis** (-tēz). *Music.* —*adj.* 1 all; all instruments or voices together. 2 to be performed by all instruments or voices. —*n.* a passage or section to be performed by all instruments or voices. [< Ital. *tutti,* pl. of *tutto* all]

tut·ti-frut·ti (tü′tē frü′tē) *n.* 1 a preserve of mixed fruits. 2 ice cream containing a variety of fruits or fruit flavoring. 3 (*adjl.*) flavored by mixed fruits. [< Ital. *tutti frutti* all fruits]

tu·tu (tü′tü; *French,* TY TY′) *n.* a ballet dancer's very short, frilly skirt. [< F *tutu,* alteration of *cucu,* child's reduplication of *cul* bottom < L *culus*]

tux (tuks) *n. Informal.* tuxedo.

tux·e·do (tuk sē′dō) *n., pl.* **-dos** or **-does.** 1 a man's semiformal jacket for evening wear, usually black with satin lapels and made without tails; dinner jacket. 2 a man's evening clothes including such a jacket. [< *Tuxedo* Park, New York, where it is supposed to have been first worn]

tu·yère (twē yer′ *or* twēr) *n.* a tube or pipe through which the blast of air enters a blast furnace, forge, etc. [< F *tuyère,* ult. < Gmc.]

TV or **tv** terminal velocity.

TV or **T.V.** (tē′vē′) *n., adj.* —*n.* 1 television. 2 a television set. —*adj.* of or having to do with television or television sets.

TV dinner a frozen, precooked, packaged dinner that is ready to serve after simply being heated in its aluminum container.

twad·dle (twod′əl) *n., v.* **-dled, -dling.** —*n.* silly, tiresome talk or writing; nonsense; drivel. —*v.* talk or write in a silly, tiresome way. [alteration of earlier *twattle,* ? < *tattle*] —**twad′dler,** *n.*

twain (twān) *n. or adj. Archaic or poetic.* two. [OE *twēgen*]

twang (twang) *n., v.* —*n.* 1 a sharp, ringing sound like that made by a bowstring or rubber band when plucked: *We could hear the twang of his bow as he shot the arrow.* 2 a sharp, nasal tone: *Some Nova Scotians speak with a twang.* —*v.* 1 make or cause to make a sharp, ringing sound: *The banjos twanged.* 2 play, pluck, shoot, etc. with a twang: *to twang a guitar. He twanged an arrow into the target.* 3 speak with a sharp, nasal tone. [imitative]

'twas (twoz *or* twuz; *unstressed,* twəz) it was.

tweak (twēk) *v., n.* —*v.* pull sharply and twist with the fingers: *She tweaked her little brother's ear and made him cry.* —*n.* a sharp pull and twist. [< var. of OE *twiccian* pluck]

tweed (twēd) *n.* 1 a woollen cloth with a rough surface, usually woven in a twill weave with yarns of two or more colors, used especially for suits and coats. 2 **tweeds,** *pl.* clothes made of tweed, especially a suit: *He was wearing tweeds.* 3 any of various similar fabrics. [said to be a misreading of *tweel,* var. of *twill*]

twee·dle (twē′dəl) *v.* **-dled, -dling.** play or produce shrill tones, such as those of a bagpipe or fiddle. [origin uncertain]

twee·dle·dum and twee·dle·dee (twē′dəl dum′ən twē′dəl dē′) 1 two persons or things that are practically identical. 2 **Tweedledum and Tweedledee,** identical twin brothers in Lewis Carroll's *Through the Looking Glass.* [imitative of the sounds of low-pitched and high-pitched instruments, probably from a rhyme by John Byrom (1692-1763), about a musical battle between Handel and Bononcini, giving them these names]

tweed·y (twē′dē) *adj.* 1 made of tweed; like tweed. 2 in the habit of wearing tweeds or other clothing suggestive of the outdoors.

'tween (twēn) *prep. Poetic.* between.

tweet (twēt) *n., interj., v.* —*n. or interj.* the sound made by a small or young bird or an imitation or representation of this sound. —*v.* utter a tweet or tweets. [imitative]

tweet·er (twēt′ər) *n.* a small high-fidelity loudspeaker used to reproduce sounds in the higher frequency range.

tweeze (twēz) *v.* pluck or remove with or as if with tweezers.

Tweezers

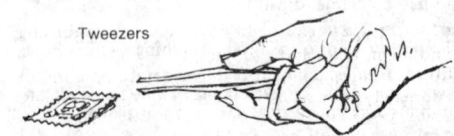

tweez·ers (twēz′ərz) *n.pl. or sing.* small pincers or tongs for

pulling out hairs or slivers, picking up small objects, etc. [< *tweeze* instrument case, ult. < F *étui* < OF *estuier* keep < VL *studiare* be zealous < L *studium* zeal]

twelfth (twelfth) *adj. or n.* **1** next after the 11th; last in a series of twelve; 12th. **2** one, or being one, of 12 equal parts.

Twelfth–day (twelfth'dā') *n.* January 6, the twelfth day after Christmas. On this day the feast of the Epiphany is celebrated. Formerly it marked the end of the Christmas season.

Twelfth–night (twelfth'nīt') *n.* the evening or eve of Twelfth-day, often celebrated as the end of Christmas festivities.

twelve (twelv) *n., adj.* —*n.* **1** two more than 10; 12. **2** the numeral 12: *The 12 is too small.* **3** the twelfth in a set or series. **4** a set or series of twelve persons or things. **5 the Twelve**, the twelve Apostles of Jesus. —*adj.* **1** being twelve. **2** being twelfth in a set or series (*used after the noun*): *Section Twelve.* [OE *twelf*]

twelve·fold (twelv'fōld') *adj., adv.* —*adj.* **1** twelve times as much or as many. **2** having twelve parts. —*adv.* twelve times as much or as many.

twelve·mo (twelv'mō) *n., pl.* -**mos**; *or adj.* duodecimo.

twelve·month (twelv'munth') *n.* a period of twelve months; a year.

Twelve Tables in ancient Rome, the first written code of laws, produced in 451 and 450 B.C.

twelve–tone (twelv'tōn') *adj.* **1** of or having to do with an atonal musical system developed by Arnold Schönberg, in which all the twelve tones of the chromatic scale are used in an arbitrarily chosen order but without the traditional tone centre or key. **2** using this musical system.

twen·ti·eth (twen'tē ith) *adj. or n.* **1** next after the 19th; last in a series of twenty; 20th. **2** one, or being one, of 20 equal parts.

twen·ty (twen'tē) *n., pl.* -**ties**; *adj.* —*n.* **1** two times ten; 20. **2** the numeral 20. **3** the twentieth in a set or series. **4** a 20-dollar bill. **5 twenties**, *pl.* twenty through twenty-nine, especially of a century or of a person's age: *He was in his twenties when his father died.* **6** a set or series of twenty persons or things. —*adj.* **1** being twenty. **2** being twentieth in a set or series (*used after the noun*): *Lesson Twenty.* [OE *twēntig*]

twen·ty·fold (twen'tē fōld') *adj., adv.* —*adj.* **1** twenty times as much or as many. **2** having 20 parts. —*adv.* twenty times as much or as many.

twenty–one (twen'tē wun') *n.* blackjack, a card game. [translation of F *vingt-et-un*]

twen·ty–twen·ty or **20/20** (twen'tē twen'tē) *adj.* of vision, normally acute: *I'm a bit short-sighted, but my sister has 20/20 vision.* [from a traditional test in which the standard for normal visual acuity is the ability to distinguish at a distance of 20 feet (about 6 m) a character ⅓ inch (about 8 mm) high]

'twere (twèr; *unstressed*, twər) *Archaic or poetic.* it were.

twice (twīs) *adv.* **1** two times: *twice a day. Twice two is four.* **2** doubly: *twice as much.* [ME *twies* < OE *twiga* twice]

twice–told (twīs'tōld') *adj.* told many times before; trite or very familiar: *twice-told tales.*

twid·dle (twid'əl) *v.* -**dled**, -**dling**; *n.* —*v.* **1** twirl: *to twiddle one's pencil.* **2** play with idly.

twiddle (one's) thumbs, a keep turning one's thumbs idly about each other. **b** do nothing; be idle. —*n.* a twirl. [origin uncertain]

twig[1] (twig) *n.* a slender shoot or branch of a tree or other woody plant. [OE *twigge*]

twig[2] (twig) *v.* **twigged**, **twig·ging**. *Informal.* **1** get the meaning; catch on (*often used with* to): *I didn't twig that he wanted a lift. They soon twigged to our plan.* **2** observe; notice. [originally thieves' slang, ult. < Irish *tuigim* I understand]

twi·light (twī'līt') *n.* **1** the faint light reflected from the sky before the sun rises and after it sets. **2** the period during which this light lasts, especially after sunset. **3** any faint light. **4** a period of gradual decline in fame, vigor, achievement, etc.: *the twilight of a golden age in history; twilight of one's life.* **5** any undefined or intermediate state or condition: *She lived in an uneasy twilight between sickness and health.* **6** (*adj.*) of, like, or produced by twilight: *the twilight hour, a twilight glow.* [ME *twilight* < *twi*- two, double + *light*[1]]

twilight sleep a semiconscious condition produced by the hypodermic injection of scopolamine and morphine. [translation of G *Dämmerschlaf*]

twilight zone an area or condition not clearly defined, as that between day and night, good and evil, etc.

twill (twil) *n., v.* —*n.* **1** a textile weave in which the crosswise threads pass alternately over one and then under two or more lengthwise threads, producing raised diagonal lines. See **weave** for picture. **2** fabric woven in this way. Denim is a twill. —*v.* weave (cloth) in the manner of a twill. [OE *twilic* < L *bilix* with a

hat, āge, fär; let, ēqual, tèrm; it, īce
hot, ōpen, ôrder; oil, out; cup, pút, rüle,
əbove, takən, pencəl, lemən, circəs

ch, child; ng, long; sh, ship
th, thin; ŧH, then; zh, measure

double thread < *bi*- two + *licium* thread, with substitution of *twi*- two for *bi*-]

'twill (twil) *Archaic or poetic.* it will.

twilled (twild) *adj.* woven in raised diagonal lines.

twin (twin) *n., v.* **twinned**, **twin·ning.** —*n.* **1** one of two children or animals born at the same time from the same mother. See also **fraternal** (def. 3) and **identical** (def. 3). **2** (*adj.*) being two or either one of two born at the same time from the same mother: *twin boys. That's his twin sister.* **3** one of two persons or things very much or exactly alike in structure, appearance, etc.: *This table is the twin of one we have at home.* **4** (*adj.*) being two persons or things very much or exactly alike; paired or matching: *twin houses, twin dresses.* **5** (*adj.*) having or consisting of two identical parts or units; double: *a twin-engined aircraft.* **6** (*adj.*) of bed linen, designed to fit a twin bed. **7** a composite crystal consisting of two crystals, usually equal and similar, united in reversed positions with respect to each other. **8 the Twins,** *Astronomy or astrology.* Gemini. —*v.* **1** give birth to twins. **2** join closely; pair. **3** match; duplicate. [OE *twinn*]

twin bed a single bed about one metre wide. Twin beds are often sold in matching pairs.

twine (twīn) *n., v.* **twined**, **twin·ing.** —*n.* **1** a strong thread or string made of two or more strands twisted together. **2** the act of twisting together, encircling or embracing. **3** something that is twisted together or interlaced. —*v.* **1** twist together: *She twined holly into wreaths.* **2** make or form by twisting: *to twine a wreath of flowers.* **3** wind or wrap around; cause to encircle or be encircled: *We are training the vine to twine around the post. He twined the string around his finger. They twined their arms around each other.* [OE *twīn*]

twin–en·gine (twin'en'jən) *adj.* twin-engined.

twin–en·gined (twin'en'jənd) *adj.* of an aircraft, powered by two engines.

twin–flow·er (twin'flou'ər) *n.* an evergreen trailing shrub (*Linnaea borealis*) of the honeysuckle family having pink or white, fragrant, bell-shaped flowers growing in pairs.

twinge (twinj) *n., v.* **twinged**, **twing·ing.** —*n.* **1** a sudden sharp, pinching pain that lasts only a moment: *a twinge of rheumatism.* **2** a sudden, brief mental pain; pang: *a twinge of remorse, a twinge of fear.* —*v.* feel or cause a twinge: *The theft occasionally twinged his conscience.* [OE *twengan* pinch]

twin·kle (twing'kəl) *v.* -**kled**, -**kling;** *n.* —*v.* **1** shine with quick little gleams: *The stars twinkled.* **2** of a person's eyes, light up or shine with amusement or fun: *Tony's eyes twinkled when he laughed.* **3** of the feet, move quickly: *The dancer's feet twinkled.* **4** wink or blink one's eyes. **5** cause to twinkle. —*n.* **1** a twinkling; sparkle; gleam. **2** a quick motion, especially of the feet in dancing. **3** a quick motion of the eyelid; a wink; blink. **4** the time required for a wink; twinkling: *He was gone in a twinkle.* [OE *twinclian*] —**twin'kler,** *n.*

twin·kling (twing'kling) *n.* **1** a little, quick gleam. **2** a very short period of time; instant.

twin–screw (twin'skrü') *adj., n.* —*adj.* of a steamship, having two screw propellers that revolve in opposite directions. —*n.* a steamship powered by such propellers.

twin·ship (twin'ship') *n.* **1** the fact or condition of being a twin or twins. **2** the relation existing between twins.

twin–size (twin'sīz') *adj.* **1** designating a twin bed. **2** designed for a twin bed: *a twin-size bedspread.* Compare **king-size, queen-size.**

twirl (twèrl) *v., n.* —*v.* **1** revolve rapidly; spin; whirl: *to twirl a top. The skaters twirled over the ice.* **2** turn or twist round and round idly with the fingers: *He twirled the ends of his mustache.* **3** *Baseball.* throw (a ball); pitch. —*n.* **1** the act of twirling; spin; whirl: *a twirl in a dance.* **2** a twist, curl, or flourish, as made in writing, etc. [cf. OE *thwirel* churn staff, and G *zwirlen* twirl] —**twirl'er,** *n.*

twist (twist) *v., n.* —*v.* **1** wind together; twine: *to twist flowers into a wreath.* **2** make by winding together: *to twist a wreath of flowers.* **3** wind (a cord, ribbon, wire, etc.) around something: *She twisted the wire around the post.* **4** give a spiral form to by turning one end while the other remains stationary or is turned in the

opposite direction: *to twist a rubber band. The belt is twisted at the back.* **5** move part way around: *He twisted around in his seat to see who had come in. She twisted the steering wheel sharply to the left.* **6** spin or twirl: *She twisted the ring on her finger.* **7** pull off or break by turning one end (*used with* **off**): *to twist off the stem of an apple.* **8** pull or force out of the natural shape or position: *I twisted my ankle when I fell. His face was twisted with pain. Your skirt is twisted.* **9** distort the meaning, purpose, or intent of: *Don't twist my words; I didn't mean that at all.* **10** have a winding shape; follow a winding course; have many curves or bends: *The path twists in and out among the rocks.* **11** give an abnormal bias or inclination to: *Years of bitterness had twisted his mind.* **12** dance the twist.
—*n.* **1** a wrench or sprain. **2** a twisting or being twisted: *There's a twist in the rope.* **3** something made by twisting, such as a roll or a loaf of bread made of twisted pieces of dough.
4 a strong, heavy kind of sewing thread usually made of silk or polyester: *buttonhole twist.* **5** a curve or bend: *a path full of twists and turns.* **6** an unexpected change or variation: *an old story with a new twist. The plot had several twists that kept us in suspense right to the end.* **7** a peculiar bias or inclination; quirk: *an action prompted by some mental twist.* **8** torsional strain or stress; torque. **9** *Sports.* **a** a lateral spin imparted to a ball in throwing or striking it. **b** a ball thus spun. **10** a dance in which the hips are vigorously turned back and forth while the dancer stands in one place. [OE *-twist,* as in *mæsttwist* mast rope, stay] —**twist′a·ble,** *adj.*

twist·er (twis′tər) *n.* **1** a tornado, whirlwind, etc. **2** any person or thing that twists or curves.

twist–tie (twist′tī′) *n.* a short length of thin wire between two narrow strips of paper or embedded in a narrow strip of soft plastic, used for closing plastic bags, tying up plants, etc.

twit (twit) *v.* **twit·ted, twit·ting;** *n.* —*v.* taunt lightly; make fun of; tease: *His friends twitted him about his schemes to make money.* —*n.* **1** the act of twitting. **2** *Informal.* an annoyingly silly or stupid person; fool; nitwit. [OE *ætwītan* < *æt* at + *wītan* blame]

twitch (twich) *v., n.* —*v.* **1** move with slight, quick jerks: *The child's mouth twitched as if she were about to cry.* **2** pull or move with a sudden tug; jerk: *He twitched the curtain aside.*
—*n.* **1** a quick, jerky movement of some part of the body. **2** a short, sudden pull or jerk. **3** a sharp pain; twinge. [related to OE *twiccian* pluck]

twitch grass couch grass.

twitch·y (twich′ē) *adj.* nervous or irritable.

twit·ter (twit′ər) *v., n.* —*v.* **1** make a series of light, trembling sounds; chirp: *Birds began to twitter just before sunrise.* **2** talk or laugh in a rapid, excited or nervous way; chatter or titter. **3** utter by twittering: *a sparrow twittering its morning song. She nervously twittered a greeting.* **4** tremble with excitement.
—*n.* **1** a series of light, trembling sounds; chirping: *the twitter of birds in the garden.* **2** an excited condition: *My nerves are in a twitter when I have to sing in public.* [imitative]

'twixt (twikst) *prep. Poetic or dialect.* betwixt; between.

two (tü) *n., pl.* **twos;** *adj.* —*n.* **1** one more than one; 2. **2** the numeral 2: *I can't see it very well, but I think it's a 2.* **3** the second in a set or series; especially, a playing card or side of a die having two spots: *the two of clubs.* **4** a two-dollar bill: *Do you have any twos?* **5** a set or series of two persons or things: *The audience came in in twos and threes.*
in two, in two parts or pieces: *She broke the cookie in two.*
put two and two together, form an obvious conclusion from the facts.
—*adj.* **1** being two. **2** being second in a set or series (*used mainly after the noun*): *Chapter Two tells about his childhood.* [OE *twā*]
☛ **Hom.** to, too.

two–bag·ger (tü′bag′ər) *n. Baseball.* a two-base hit.

two–base hit *Baseball.* a hit that allows the batter to reach second base.

two–bit (tü′bit′) *adj. Slang.* **1** worth or selling for twenty-five cents. **2** cheap, inferior, or insignificant; small-time: *a two-bit novel, a two-bit gangster.*

two bits *Slang.* twenty-five cents; a quarter.

two–by–four (tü′bī fôr′) *adj., n.* —*adj.* **1** especially of lumber, measuring two inches thick by four inches wide, untrimmed (about 5 by 10 cm): *They used two-by-four studs for the inside walls.* **2** *Informal.* small; narrow or limited: *a two-by-four apartment.* —*n.* a piece of lumber two inches thick by four inches wide. Two-by-fours are much used in building.

two cents' worth *Slang.* an individual point of view or opinion on a particular subject: *They said everyone would have a chance to put in his two cents' worth.*

two–di·men·sion·al (tü′di men′shən əl) *adj.* **1** having two

dimensions: *Drawing is a two-dimensional art form.* **2** of a character in a novel, play, etc., lacking depth or individuality.

two–edged (tü′ejd′) *adj.* **1** of a sword, etc., having two cutting edges; cutting both ways. **2** of a comment, etc., able to be taken in two ways; ambiguous: *a two-edged compliment.* **3** able to be used or to be effective in two ways: *a two-edged policy.*

two–faced (tü′fāst′) *adj.* **1** having two faces. **2** deceitful; hypocritical.

two–fac·ed·ly (tü′fā′səd lē′) *adv.* in a two-faced manner.

two–fac·ed·ness (tü′fā′səd nəs) *n.* the quality of being two-faced.

two–fist·ed (tü′fis′tid) *adj. Informal.* vigorous and aggressive: *a two-fisted bully.*

two·fold (tü′fōld′) *adj., adv.* —*adj.* **1** two times as much or as many; double. **2** made up of two parts or elements: *Her meaning was twofold; part joking and part serious.* —*adv.* two times as much or as many; doubly.

two–four (tü′fôr′) *adj.* of or designating a musical rhythm with two quarter notes to a bar.

two–hand·ed (tü′han′did) *adj.* **1** having two hands. **2** using both hands equally well. **3** involving the use of both hands; requiring both hands to wield or manage: *a two-handed sword.* **4** requiring two persons to operate: *a two-handed saw.* **5** engaged in by two persons: *a two-handed game.*

two–part time *Music.* a time or rhythm with two beats to the measure, or a multiple of two beats to the measure.

two–par·ty system (tü′pär′tē) a political system in which two political parties predominate over any others, one of the two generally having a majority in the legislature. This system originated in Great Britain in the 17th century, and has prevailed in Canada, the United States, and most countries of the English-speaking world.

two·pence (tup′əns) *n. Brit.* **1** the sum of two pence. **2** a former British silver coin worth two pence. Also, **tuppence.**

two·pen·ny (tup′ən ē) *adj. Brit.* **1** worth or costing two pence. **2** of little worth; cheap. Also, **tuppenny.**

two–piece (tü′pēs′) *adj., n.* —*adj.* of a dress, swimsuit, etc., consisting of separate, matching top and bottom parts. —*n.* a two-piece dress, swimsuit, etc.

two–ply (tü′plī′) *adj.* having two thicknesses, folds, layers, or strands.

two·some (tü′səm) *n.* **1** a group of two people. **2** a game played by two people. **3** the players in such a game.

two–step (tü′step′) *n.* **1** a dance in 2/4 time. **2** the music for such a dance.

two–time (tü′tīm′) *v.* **-timed, -tim·ing.** *Slang.* **1** be unfaithful to in love. **2** betray; double cross. —**two′-tim′er,** *n.*

two–tone (tü′tōn′) *adj.* having two colors or two shades of one color: *two-tone shoes. Her car is two-tone blue.*

'twould (twůd; *unstressed,* twəd) *Archaic or poetic.* it would.

two–way (tü′wā′) *adj.* **1** of a street, bridge, etc., allowing traffic to move in either direction. **2** of traffic, moving in both directions on the same street, etc. **3** designed for both sending and receiving messages: *a two-way radio.* **4** of or designating a valve, pipe, wire, etc. that connects with two outlets. **5** *Mathematics.* capable of variation in two ways or modes: *a two-way progression.*

two–wheel·er (tü′wēl′ər *or* -hwēl′ər) *n.* a vehicle having two wheels, especially a bicycle or motorcycle.

twp. township.

TX Texas.

-ty[1] *suffix.* tens, as in *sixty, seventy, eighty.* [OE *-tig*]

-ty[2] *noun-forming suffix.* the fact, quality, state, condition, etc. of being—, as in *safety, sovereignty, surety.* See also **-ity.** [ME < OF *-te, -tet* < L *-tas, -tatis*]

Ty. territory.

Ty·burn (tī′bərn) *n.* a former place of public execution in London.

ty·coon (tī kün′) *n. Informal.* a person who holds a very important position in business, industry, etc.; magnate. [< Japanese *taikun* < Chinese *tai* great + *kiun* lord]

ty·ee (tī′ē) *n., pl.* **ty·ee** (def. 2) or **ty·ees.** *Cdn.* **1** a spring salmon, especially one weighing more than about 13 kg. **2** *Esp.British Columbia.* **a** the chief of an Indian tribe or band. **b** any important person; boss. [< Chinook Jargon]

tyee salmon tyee (def. 1).

ty·ing (tī′ing) *v.* ppr. of **tie.**

tyke (tīk) *n.* **1** *Informal.* a small child. **2** a dog, especially an inferior or worthless one. **3** *Brit. dialect.* a low fellow; boor. [ME < ON *tík* bitch]

tym·pan (tim′pən) *n.* **1** a stretched membrane, or a sheet or plate of some thin material, in an apparatus. **2** *Archaic.* a drum. [< L < Gk. *tympanon.* Doublet of TYMPANUM, TIMBRE.]

tym·pa·ni (tim′pə nē′) *n.* See **timpani.**

tym·pan·ic (tim pan′ik) *adj.* **1** of, having to do with, or being the eardrum or the middle ear. **2** like a drum.

tympanic membrane eardrum.

tym·pa·nist (tim′pə nist) *n.* timpanist.

tym·pa·num (tim′pə nəm) *n., pl.* **-nums** or **-na** (-nə). **1** eardrum. **2** the middle ear. **3** a thin membrane covering the organ of hearing of an insect. **4** the diaphragm in a telephone. **5** *Architecture.* **a** the vertical recessed face of a pediment, enclosed by the cornices. **b** a slab or wall between an arch and the horizontal top of a door or window below. [< L *tympanum* drum < Gk. *tympanon.* Doublet of TIMBRE, TYMPAN.]

type (tīp) *n., v.* **typed, typ·ing.** —*n.* **1** a class or group having qualities or characteristics in common: *type O blood, a new type of engine. He doesn't like that type of work.* **2** a person or thing having the qualities or characteristics of a particular class or group; model, representative, or symbol: *She is a fine type of student.* **3** the general form, style, or character that distinguishes some class or group: *They weren't surprised when he got angry, because he was behaving true to type.* **4** *Informal.* an unusual or eccentric person: *He's a real type.* **5** *Printing.* **a** a block, usually of metal, having a raised letter, numeral, or sign in reverse on its upper surface, from which an inked impression can be made. **b** a collection of such pieces: *a box of type.* **c** a collection of letters, numerals, or signs that are reproduced photographically for printing. **d** a particular kind or size of letters, numerals, or signs: *The poem was set in italic type.* **6** printed or typewritten letters, numerals, or signs: *The page looks crowded with so much type on it.* **7** the figure, writing, or design on either side of a coin or medal. **8** *Biology.* **a** a species, genus, etc. whose characteristics are used as the basis for defining the next highest taxonomic group and for which the group is usually named. **b** the single specimen or series of specimens on which the description of a species for classification is based. —*v.* **1** classify according to type: *to type a blood sample. The new boy was immediately typed as a bully.* **2** typecast: *He's been typed as the boy next door ever since his first film.* **3** write with a typewriter. [< L < Gk. *typos* dent, impression]

☛ *Usage.* **Type of.** The idiom should not be shortened by omitting the **of,** as in *this type letter.* Standard usage requires *this type of letter.*

type·cast (tīp′kast′) *v.* **-cast, -cast·ing. 1** cast an actor in a role to fit his personality, appearance, etc. **2** cast an actor repeatedly in the same kind of role.

type·face (tīp′fās′) *n.* **1** the face, or printing surface, of type. **2** the design or style of type; face: *an ornate typeface.*

type·script (tīp′skript′) *n.* a typewritten manuscript.

type·set·ter (tīp′set′ər) *n.* a person, company, or machine that sets type for printing.

type·set·ting (tīp′set′ing) *n., adj.* —*n.* the act or process of setting type for printing. —*adj.* of, having to do with, or used for setting type: *typesetting machines, typesetting methods.*

type·write (tīp′rīt′) *v.* **-wrote, -writ·ten, -writ·ing.** write with a typewriter; type.

type·writ·er (tīp′rī′tər) *n.* **1** a machine for producing letters, numerals, and signs similar to those produced by printer's type, operated by means of a keyboard. When a key is struck, the corresponding type hits an inked ribbon, transferring the imprint of the letter, etc. onto paper behind the ribbon. **2** *Archaic.* typist.

type·writ·ing (tīp′rī′ting) *n.* **1** the act or skill of using a typewriter. **2** work done on a typewriter.

type·writ·ten (tīp′rit′ən) *adj., v.* —*adj.* written with a typewriter: *a typewritten letter.* —*v.* pp. of **typewrite.**

ty·phoid (tī′foid) *adj., n.* —*adj.* **1** of or having to do with typhoid fever. **2** like typhus. —*n.* typhoid fever. [< *typhus*]

typhoid fever a severe infectious disease caused by a bacterium (*Salmonella typhosa*) that enters the body in contaminated food or drink, most often from a polluted public water supply. Typhoid fever is characterized by fever, a rash of small red spots and, often, inflammation of the intestines.

ty·phoon (tī fün′) *n.* a violent tropical cyclone that forms over the Pacific Ocean. [< Chinese *tai fung* big wind; influenced by Gk. *typhōn* whirlwind]

ty·phus (tī′fəs) *n.* any of a group of very serious infectious diseases caused by any of several species of rickettsia which are carried especially by lice or fleas. Epidemic typhus, caused by *Rickettsia prowazekii,* is characterized by chills and fever, dark-red spots on the skin, and extreme weakness; it used to occur in epidemics in which many people died. [< NL < Gk. *typhos* stupor, originally, smoke]

typ·i·cal (tip′ə kəl) *adj.* **1** very much like others of the same type

hat, āge, fär; let, ēqual, tėrm; it, īce
hot, ōpen, ôrder; oil, out; cup, pùt, rüle,
ə above, takən, pencəl, lemən, circəs

ch, child; ng, long; sh, ship
th, thin; ᴛʜ, then; zh, measure

or kind; serving as an example; representative: *a typical Canadian. The typical Thanksgiving dinner has roast turkey as its main course.* **2** of, having to do with, or serving to distinguish a type; characteristic: *the hospitality typical of the pioneer. It was typical of him to sign it without reading it first.* **3** *Biology.* that is the type of the genus, family, etc. —**typ′i·cal·ly,** *adv.* —**typ′i·cal·ness,** *n.*

typ·i·fy (tip′ə fī′) *v.* **-fied, -fy·ing. 1** be a symbol of; signify or represent: *The dove typifies peace.* **2** have the common characteristics of; be an example of: *Alexander MacKenzie typifies the adventurous explorer.* **3** indicate beforehand. [< L *typus* type + E -*fy*] —**typ′i·fi·ca′tion,** *n.*

typ·ist (tīp′ist) *n.* a person who types, especially one whose work it is.

ty·po (tī′pō) *n. Informal.* a typographical error; a small mistake made in typing or in setting type.

ty·pog·ra·pher (tī pog′rə fər) *n.* printer.

ty·po·graph·ic (tī′pə graf′ik) *adj.* of or having to do with printing: *typographic errors.*

ty·po·graph·i·cal (tī′pə graf′ə kəl) *adj.* typographic. —**ty′po·graph′i·cal·ly,** *adv.*

ty·pog·ra·phy (tī pog′rə fē) *n.* **1** the art or process of printing with type; the work of setting and arranging type and of printing from it. **2** the arrangement, appearance, or style of printed matter. [< late Med.L < Gk. *typos* type + *-graphia* writing]

ty·po·log·i·cal (tī′pə loj′ə kəl) *adj.* of or having to do with typology.

ty·pol·o·gist (tī pol′ə jist) *n.* one who is skilled in typology.

ty·pol·o·gy (tī pol′ə jē) *n.* the classification and study of types, as of remains and specimens in archeology. [< Gk. *typos* type + E -*logy*]

Tyr (tēr) *n. Norse mythology.* the god of war, the son of Odin. [< ON]

ty·ran·nic (tə ran′ik *or* tī ran′ik) *adj.* tyrannical. [< L < Gk. *tyrannikos* < *tyrannos* tyrant]

ty·ran·ni·cal (tə ran′ə kəl *or* tī ran′ə kəl) *adj.* of or like a tyrant; arbitrary, cruel, or unjust: *a tyrannical king.* —**ty·ran′ni·cal·ly,** *adv.*

ty·ran·ni·cide (tə ran′ə sīd′ *or* tī ran′ə sīd′) *n.* **1** the act of killing a tyrant. **2** a person who kills a tyrant. [< L *tyrannicidium* the killing of a tyrant < *tyrannus* tyrant + *-cidium* act of killing (for def. 1); < L *tyrannicida* one who kills a tyrant < *tyrannus* + *-cida* killer (for def. 2)]

tyr·an·nize (tir′ə nīz′) *v.* **-nized, -niz·ing. 1** use power cruelly or unjustly (*used with* **over**): *Those who are strong should not tyrannize over those who are weaker.* **2** rule cruelly; oppress. **3** rule as a tyrant. —**tyr′an·niz·er,** *n.*

ty·ran·no·saur (ti ran′ə sôr′) *n.* tyrannosaurus.

ty·ran·no·sau·rus (ti ran′ə sô′rəs) *n.* a huge carnivorous dinosaur (*Tyrannosaurus rex*) of the late Cretaceous period in North America, noted for its ability to walk upright on its two hind legs. [< NL *Tyrannosaurus,* the genus name < Gk. *tyrannos* tyrant + *sauros* lizard]

tyr·an·nous (tir′ə nəs) *adj.* tyrannical; despotic. —**tyr′an·nous·ly,** *adv.*

tyr·an·ny (tir′ə nē) *n., pl.* **-nies. 1** cruel or unjust use of power. **2** severe or demanding conditions: *the tyranny of public opinion, living all one's life under the tyranny of the clock.* **3** a tyrannical act: *He had suffered many tyrannies.* **4** government by an absolute ruler. [< LL < Gk. *tyrannia* < *tyrannos.* See TYRANT.]

ty·rant (tī′rənt) *n.* **1** a person who uses his power cruelly or unjustly. **2** a cruel or unjust ruler. **3** a ruler with absolute power. Some tyrants in ancient Greece were kind and just rulers. [ME < OF < L < Gk. *tyrannos* (def. 3)]

tyre (tīr) *Brit.* See **tire².**

Tyr·i·an (tir′ē ən) *adj., n.* —*adj.* of or having to do with Tyre, a seaport in ancient Phoenicia. —*n.* a native of Tyre. [< L < Gk. *Tyrios*]

Tyrian purple **1** a crimson or purple dye highly prized by the ancient Greeks and Romans. It was obtained from certain molluscs. **2** a deep purplish red.

ty·ro (tī′rō) *n., pl.* **-ros.** a beginner in learning anything; novice; greenhorn. Also, **tiro.** [< L *tiro* recruit]

Ty·ro·le·an (tə rō′lē ən *or* tir′ə lē′ən) *n., adj.* —*n.* a native or inhabitant of Tyrol, a region in the Alps, partly in Austria and partly in Italy. —*adj.* of or having to do with Tyrol. Also, **Tirolean.**

Tyr·o·lese (tir′ə lēz′) *adj. or n.* Tyrolean. Also, **Tirolese.**

tzar (zär) *n.* czar.

tzar·e·vitch (zär′ə vich) *n.* czarevitch.

tza·ri·na (zä rē′nə) *n.* czarina.

tzet·ze (tset′sē) *n.* tsetse.

tzi·gane (tsē gän′) *n.* often, **Tzigane.** a Gypsy, especially a Hungarian one. [< F < Hungarian czigány. 19c.]

Uu

u or **U¹** (yü) *n., pl.* **u's** or **U's. 1** the twenty-first letter of the English alphabet. **2** any speech sound represented by this letter. **3** a person or thing identified as *u*, especially the twenty-first of a series. **4** something shaped like the letter U. **5** (*adj.*) of or being a U or u.

U² (yü) *adj. Esp.Brit. Informal.* belonging to or characteristic of the upper class. [< *upper class*]

u. 1 upper. **2** uncle.

U uranium.

U. University.

UAW United Automobile Workers (Union).

u·biq·ui·tous (yü bik′wə təs) *adj.* being or seeming to be everywhere at the same time; found or turning up everywhere: *He wanted a quiet place to read, but found it impossible to escape from his ubiquitous little sister.* [< *ubiquity*] —**u·biq′ui·tous·ly,** *adv.* —**u·biq′ui·tous·ness,** *n.*

u·biq·ui·ty (yü bik′wə tē) *n.* **1** the fact or condition of being or seeming to be everywhere at the same time. **2** the ability to be everywhere at once. [< NL *ubiquitas* < L *ubique* everywhere]

U–boat (yü′bōt′) *n.* a German submarine. [< G *U-boot,* short for *Unterseeboot* undersea boat]

U bolt a bolt shaped like the letter U, having both ends threaded to take securing nuts.

u.c. upper case; one or more capital letters.

U.C. 1 Upper Canada. **2** United Church.

ud·der (ud′ər) *n.* in a cow or female sheep or goat, etc., a large baglike organ containing two or more milk-producing glands, each gland provided with one teat. [OE *ūder*]

u·dom·e·ter (yü dom′ə tər) *n.* a rain gauge. [< L *udus* wet + E *-meter*]

U.E.L. United Empire Loyalist.

UFO (yü′ef ō′) *n., pl.* **UFOs** or **UFO's.** an unidentified flying object, especially a flying saucer or other object regarded as possibly being a spacecraft from another planet.

u·fol·o·gist (yü fol′ə jist) *n.* a person who studies UFOs, especially one who believes them to be from outer space.

u·fol·o·gy (yü fol′ə jē) *n.* the study of UFOs.

U·gan·dan (yü gan′dən) *n., adj.* —*n.* a native or inhabitant of Uganda, a country in E Africa. —*adj.* of or having to do with Uganda or its people.

ugh (ᴜн, u, ᴜн, *or* ug) *interj.* an exclamation expressing disgust or horror.

ug·li·fi·ca·tion (ug′lə fə kā′shən) *n.* the act or an instance of uglifying or the state of being uglified.

ug·li·fy (ug′lə fī′) *v.* **-fied, -fy·ing.** make ugly or more ugly: *uglifying the parkway with a lot of billboards.*

ug·ly (ug′lē) *adj.* **-li·er, -li·est. 1** very unpleasant to look at: *an ugly house, an ugly face.* **2** morally bad; objectionable; vile: *ugly rumors, an ugly deed.* **3** threatening; dangerous: *an ugly wound, ugly clouds.* **4** *Informal.* ill-natured or bad-tempered; quarrelsome: *an ugly dog. He gets ugly when he's drunk.* [ME < ON *uggligr* dreadful] —**ug′li·ness,** *n.*

☛ *Syn.* **1. Ugly, unsightly, homely** = not pleasing in appearance. **Ugly,** the opposite of **beautiful,** means "positively unpleasant or offensive in appearance": *There are five ugly lamps in that room.* **Unsightly** emphasizes being unpleasing to the sight, sometimes causing one to turn away to avoid seeing what is described: *Trains approach the city through an unsightly section.* **Homely** emphasizes lack of beauty or attractiveness, but does not suggest unpleasant or disagreeable qualities: *a homely child.*

ugly duckling a person or thing at first thought to be ugly, unpromising, etc. but that turns out to have unusual beauty, talent, value, etc. [with reference to the cygnet in a story by Hans Christian Andersen (1805-1875), that seems ugly in comparison with its duckling companions, but that grows up to be a swan]

U·gri·an (yü′grē ən *or* ü′grē ən) *n., adj.* —*n.* **1** a member of the branch of the Finno-Ugric peoples that includes the Magyars and certain groups from western Siberia. **2** the languages of these peoples. —*adj.* of or designating the Ugrians or their languages.

U·gric (yü′grik *or* ü′grik) *n.* the branch of the Finno-Ugric family of languages that includes Hungarian.

UHF or **U.H.F.** ultrahigh frequency.

uh–huh (ə hu′) *interj.* an expression of agreement or affirmation; yes.

uh·lan (ü′län *or* ü län′) *n. Historical.* **1** in certain European armies, a lancer and cavalry man of a type first known in Poland. **2** in the German army, a member of the heavy cavalry. [< G < Polish < Turkish *oghlān* boy]

uh–uh (uɴ′uɴ′) *interj.* an expression of disagreement, refusal, etc.; no.

UI or **U.I.** unemployment insurance.

UIC or **U.I.C.** Unemployment Insurance Commission.

U.K. United Kingdom.

u·kase (yü kās′ *or* yü′kās) *n.* **1** in Czarist Russia, an order or edict of the ruler or government. **2** any official proclamation or order. [< Russian *ukaz*]

Uke (yük) *n. or adj. Derogatory slang.* Ukrainian (def. 3).

Ukr. Ukraine; Ukrainian.

U·krain·i·an (yü krān′ē ən) *n., adj.* —*n.* **1** a native or inhabitant of the Ukraine, a constituent republic of the Soviet Union, situated in the SW part. **2** the Slavic language of the Ukrainians, closely related to Russian. **3** a person of Ukrainian descent: *There are many Ukrainians in Canada, especially in the West.* —*adj.* of or having to do with the Ukraine, its people, or their language.

Ukrainian Catholic 1 a member of an Eastern rite church within the Catholic Church, originating in E Europe and now active especially in the Ukraine, Canada, and the United States. **2** of or having to do with Ukrainian Catholics or their church.

u·ku·le·le (yü′kə lā′lē) *n.* a small guitar-shaped instrument having four strings. [< Hawaiian *ukulele,* literally jumping flea < *uku* flea + *lele* jump, leap]

ul·cer (ul′sər) *n.* **1** an open sore on the skin or a mucous membrane such as the lining of the stomach or the inside of the mouth. **2** a moral sore spot; corrupting influence. [< L *ulcus, ulceris*]

ul·cer·ate (ul′sər āt′) *v.* **-at·ed, -at·ing.** affect or be affected with an ulcer: *An ulcerated tooth may be very painful.* [< L *ulcerare* < *ulcus* ulcer]

ul·cer·a·tion (ul′sər ā′shən) *n.* **1** ulcerating or being ulcerated. **2** ulcer.

ul·cer·ous (ul′sər əs) *adj.* **1** having an ulcer or ulcers. **2** of or having to do with ulcers. —**ul′cer·ous·ly,** *adv.* —**ul′cer·ous·ness,** *n.*

ul·na (ul′nə) *n., pl.* **-nae** (-nē *or* -nī) or **-nas. 1** the bone of the forearm on the side opposite the thumb. See **arm¹** for picture. **2** a corresponding bone in the foreleg of an animal. [< NL < L *ulna* elbow]

ul·nar (ul′nər) *adj.* **1** of or having to do with the ulna. **2** in or supplying the part of the forearm near the ulna.

ul·ster (ul′stər) *n.* a long, loose, heavy overcoat, often belted at the waist. [< *Ulster,* a province of Ireland]

ult. 1 ultimo. **2** ultimate; ultimately.

☛ *Usage.* See note at **inst.**

ul·te·ri·or (ul tēr′ē ər) *adj.* **1** beyond what is seen or expressed; hidden, especially for a bad purpose: *an ulterior motive.* **2** more distant; on the farther side. **3** further; later. [< L *ulterior,* comparative of root of *ultra, ultro,* adv., beyond] —**ul·te′ri·or·ly,** *adv.*

ul·ti·ma (ul′tə mə) *n.* the last syllable of a word. [< L *ultima (syllaba)* last (syllable)]

ul·ti·mate (ul′tə mit) *adj., n.* —*adj.* **1** coming at the end; last possible; final: *He never stopped to consider the ultimate result of his actions.* **2** beyond which nothing further may be discovered by investigation or analysis; primary; basic: *the ultimate principle, the ultimate source.* **3** greatest possible. —*n.* an ultimate point, result, fact, etc. [< Med.L *ultimatus,* pp. of *ultimare* < Ital. *ultimare* bring to an end < L *ultimare* come to an

end < *ultimus* last]
☛ *Syn.* **1.** See note at **last**[1].

ul·ti·mate·ly (ul′tə mit lē) *adv.* finally; in the end.

ultimate strength *Physics.* the maximum stress or tension a substance can bear without tearing or breaking.

ultimate stress *Physics.* the stress or load needed to produce fracture or breakage.

ultima Thu·le (thü′lē) **1** the farthest north. **2** the farthest limit or point possible. **3** the uttermost degree attainable. [< L *ultima Thule* most remote Thule]

ul·ti·ma·tum (ul′tə mā′təm) *n., pl.* **-tums, -ta** (-tə). a final proposal, statement of conditions, or demand presented, especially one whose rejection may result in a breaking off of relations between negotiating parties or, sometimes, in international negotiations, a declaration of war. [< NL *ultimatum*, originally neut. of Med.L *ultimatus*. See ULTIMATE.]

ul·ti·mo (ul′tə mō′) *adv.* in or of last month. [< Med.L *ultimo* (*mense*) in the last (month)]

ul·tra (ul′trə) *adj., n.* —*adj.* beyond what is usual; very; excessive; extreme. —*n.* a person who holds extreme views or urges extreme measures. [< L *ultra* beyond]

ultra– *prefix.* **1** beyond a specified limit or range, as in *ultraviolet*. **2** very; extremely; unusually, as in *ultra-ambitious*, *ultrafashionable, ultramodest, ultraradical, ultrarefined.* [< LL *ultra-* < L *ultra*, adv. prep. beyond]

ul·tra·high frequency (ul′trə hī′) the range of radio frequencies between 300 and 3000 megahertz. Ultrahigh frequency is the range next above high frequency. *Abbrev.*: UHF or U.H.F.

ul·tra·ma·rine (ul′trə mə rēn′) *n., adj.* —*n.* **1** a deep blue. **2** a blue pigment made from powdered lapis lazuli. **3** a chemically similar pigment made from other substances. Artificial ultramarine is much cheaper than the natural pigment and also occurs in reddish and greenish hues.
—*adj.* **1** having the color ultramarine. **2** beyond or across the sea. [< Med.L *ultramarinus* < L *ultra* beyond + *mare* sea; used with reference to the source (Asia) of lapis lazuli]

ul·tra·mi·cro·scope (ul′trə mī′krə skōp′) *n.* a powerful instrument for making visible very tiny particles that are invisible to the common microscope. Light is thrown on the object from one side, over a dark background.

ul·tra·mi·cro·scop·ic (ul′trə mī′krə skop′ik) *adj.* **1** too small to be seen with an ordinary microscope. **2** having to do with an ultramicroscope.

ul·tra·mon·tagne (ul′trə mon′tān) *n., adj.* —*n. Historical.* a member of the extreme right wing of the Conservative Party in Quebec. —*adj.* of or having to do with this group. [< Cdn.F]

ul·tra·mon·tane (ul′trə mon′tān) *adj., n.* —*adj.* **1** beyond the mountains. **2** south of the Alps; Italian. **3** *Roman Catholic Church.* supporting a party or policy advocating extreme centralization of papal power, as opposed to a policy of decentralization.
—*n.* **1** a person living south of the Alps. **2** a supporter of ultramontane policies. [< Med.L *ultramontanus* < L *ultra* beyond + *mons, montis* mountain]

ul·tra·mon·tan·ism (ul′trə mon′tə niz′əm) *n.* a doctrine or policy favoring extreme centralization of papal power.

ul·tra·mon·ta·nist (ul′trə mon′tə nist) *n.* a supporter of ultramontanism.

ul·tra·mun·dane (ul′trə mun′dān) *adj.* **1** beyond the world; beyond the limits of the known universe. **2** beyond this present life. [< LL *ultramundanus* < L *ultra* beyond + *mundus* world]

ul·tra·son·ic (ul′trə son′ik) *adj.* of or designating sound waves having a pitch above the upper limit of human hearing, that is, a frequency above 20 000 Hz.

ul·tra·son·ics (ul′trə son′iks) *n.* (*used with a singular verb*) the branch of physics that deals with ultrasonic waves.

ul·tra·trop·i·cal (ul′trə trop′ə kəl) *adj.* **1** outside of the tropics. **2** warmer than the tropics; very hot.

ul·tra·vi·o·let (ul′trə vī′ə lit) *adj., n.* —*adj.* **1** of, having to do with, or designating the invisible rays, or waves, of the electromagnetic spectrum that are shorter than light rays but longer than X rays. **2** using such radiation. —*n.* the part of the electromagnetic spectrum with ultraviolet rays.

ultraviolet light ultraviolet rays.

ul·tra vi·res (ul′trə vī′rēz) *Latin.* going beyond the powers granted by authority or by law.

An ulu

u·lu (ü′lü) *n. Cdn.* a knife traditionally used by Inuit women, having a crescent-shaped blade and a handle of bone, ivory, wood, etc. Also, **ooloo.** [< Eskimo *ulu.* 19c.]

ul·u·lant (yül′yə lənt *or* ul′yə lənt) *adj.* howling or wailing.

ul·u·late (yül′yə lāt′ *or* ul′yə lāt′) *v.* **-lat·ed, -lat·ing. 1** of a dog, wolf, etc., howl. **2** lament loudly. [< L *ululare* howl]
—**ul′u·la′tion,** *n.*

U·lys·ses (yü lis′ēz) *n.* the Latin name for Odysseus, a Greek leader in the Trojan war and the hero of Homer's epic poem the *Odyssey.*

um·bel (um′bəl) *n.* a type of flower cluster in which stalks nearly equal in length spring from a common centre and form a flat or slightly curved surface, as in parsley. See **inflorescence** for picture. [< L *umbrella* parasol, dim. of *umbra* shade]

um·bel·lar (um′bəl ər) *adj.* umbellate.

um·bel·late (um′bəl it *or* um′bəl āt′) *adj. Botany.* **1** of or like an umbel. **2** having umbels; forming an umbel or umbels.

um·bel·lif·er·ous (um′bə lif′ər əs) *adj. Botany.* bearing an umbel or umbels. The parsley and carrot are umbelliferous.

um·ber (um′bər) *n., adj.* —*n.* **1** a heavy, brown earth, consisting mainly of ferric oxide and used in its natural state (**raw umber**) as a brown pigment, or after heating (**burnt umber**) as a reddish-brown pigment. **2** a brown or reddish brown. —*adj.* brown or reddish brown. [< Ital. (*terra*) *ombra* (earth of) shade, but (?) originally < *Umbria*, a district in central Italy]

um·bil·i·cal (um bil′ə kəl *or* um′bi li′kəl) *adj.* **1** of or having to do with the navel or umbilical cord. **2** formed, placed, or shaped like a navel or umbilical cord.

umbilical cord 1 in mammals, a cordlike structure through which a fetus in the womb receives food and discharges waste. The cord runs from the navel of the fetus to the placenta. **2** an electric cable, fuel line, or the like, connected to a rocket or spacecraft on its launching site and disconnected just before takeoff.

um·bil·i·cus (um bil′ə kəs *or* um′bə li′kəs) *n., pl.* **-ci** (-sī *or* -sē). **1** the navel; the depression in the middle of the abdomen, indicating the point where the umbilical cord was attached. **2** a navel-like formation, such as the hilum of a seed. [< L *umbilicus* navel]

um·bra (um′brə) *n., pl.* **-brae** (-brē *or* -brī). **1** a shadow of the earth or moon that completely hides the sun. See **eclipse** for picture. **2** the dark central part of a sunspot. **3** *Obsolete.* shade; shadow. [< L]

um·brage (um′brij) *n.* **1** a feeling that one has been slighted or insulted; resentment (*now used mainly in the phrases* **take umbrage** *and* **give umbrage**): *He took umbrage at the slightest criticism. She didn't say anything for fear of giving umbrage to her host.* **2** *Archaic or poetic.* **a** shade. **b** foliage that provides shade. [< F *ombrage*, ult. < L *umbra* shade]

um·bra·geous (um brā′jəs) *adj.* **1** likely to take offence. **2** giving shade. —**um·bra′geous·ly,** *adv.* —**um·bra′geous·ness,** *n.*

um·brel·la (um brel′ə) *n.* **1** a collapsible device used for protection against rain or sun, especially a small, light one meant to be carried in the hand and consisting of a circular, convex screen of cloth or plastic stretched over a framework of hinged ribs radiating from a central pole. **2** a screen of fighter aircraft or a barrage of gunfire to protect ground forces against enemy aircraft. **3** anything that protects or provides shelter. **4** a sphere of interest or control: *chartered banks under the umbrella of the Bank of Canada.* **5** an organization covering a broad range of activities, a wide sphere of interest, etc.: *The Community Chest is an umbrella for many local charities.* **6** (*adjl.*) serving as an umbrella. [< Ital. *ombrella*, ult. < L *umbra* shade]

Um·bri·an (um′brē ən) *n., adj.* —*n.* **1** a native or inhabitant of Umbria, a district in central Italy. **2** an Italic language of ancient S Italy. —*adj.* of or having to do with Umbria or its people.

An umiak

u·mi·ak (ü′mē ak) *n. Cdn.* a large, flat-bottomed boat made of

skins stretched over a wooden frame and propelled by paddles. Umiaks are used by Inuit for carrying freight and are usually worked by women. Also, **oomiak**. [< Eskimo *umiaq*. 18c.]

um·laut (ŭm′lout) *n., v.* —*n.* **1** in Germanic languages, a change in vowel sound because of the influence of a different vowel in the following syllable. **2** the sign (¨) used to indicate such a vowel, as in German *süss* sweet. **3** a vowel that is the result of such a change. —*v.* modify by umlaut. [< G *Umlaut* < *um* about + *Laut* sound]

um·pire (ŭm′pīr) *n., v.* **-pired, -pir·ing.** —*n.* **1** a person who rules on the plays in certain games: *The umpire called the ball a foul.* **2** a person chosen to settle a dispute. —*v.* **1** act as umpire. **2** act as umpire in. [earlier *a numpire* (taken as *an umpire*) < OF *nonper* not even, odd < *non* not (< L) + *per* equal < L *par*]

ump·teen (ŭmp′tēn′) *adj. Informal.* a great many: *I've heard umpteen different suggestions, but not one of them is practical.*

ump·teenth (ŭmp′tēnth′) *adj. Informal.* the last in an extremely long series: *I've just dialed his number for the umpteenth time, but there's still no answer.*

un-[1] *adjective-forming prefix.* not or the opposite of, as in *unequal, unjust, unobtrusive.* [OE]

☛ *Usage.* See note at **in-**[1].

un-[2] *verb-forming prefix.* do the opposite of or do what will reverse the act, as in *undress, unlock, untie.* [OE *un-, on-*]

UN or **U.N.** **1** United Nations. **2** Union Nationale.

un·a·bashed (un′ə basht′) *adj.* not embarrassed, ashamed, or awed. —**un′a·bash′ed·ly,** *adv.*

un·a·ble (un ā′bəl) *adj.* not able; lacking ability or power (*to*): *A newborn baby is unable to walk or talk.*

un·a·bridged (un′ə brijd′) *adj.* **1** not shortened; complete: *an unabridged book.* **2** of or designating any large dictionary more comprehensive than an ordinary desk dictionary, especially the largest one of a series.

un·ac·com·pa·nied (un′ə kum′pə nēd) *adj.* **1** not accompanied. **2** *Music.* without an accompaniment.

un·ac·count·a·ble (un′ə koun′tə bəl) *adj.* **1** that cannot be accounted for or explained; strange or puzzling: *He suddenly flew into one of his unaccountable rages.* **2** not obliged or bound to account for; not responsible: *The accused was judged insane and therefore unaccountable for his actions.* —**un′ac·count′a·bly,** *adv.*

un·ac·count·ed–for (un′ə koun′tid fôr′) *adj.* unexplained: *unaccounted-for atmospheric disturbances.*

un·ac·cus·tomed (un′ə kus′təmd) *adj.* **1** not used to; not accustomed. **2** not familiar; unusual; strange: *unaccustomed heat.*

un·ad·vised (un′əd vīzd′) *adj.* **1** not prudent or discreet; rash. **2** not advised; without advice.

un·ad·vis·ed·ly (un′əd vī′zid lē) *adv.* in an indiscreet manner; rashly.

un·af·fect·ed[1] (un′ə fek′tid) *adj.* not affected; not influenced: *unaffected by criticism.* [< *un-*[1] + *affected*[1]] —**un′af·fect′ed·ly,** *adv.* —**un′af·fect′ed·ness,** *n.*

un·af·fect·ed[2] (un′ə fek′tid) *adj.* simple and natural; sincere. [< *un-*[1] + *affected*[2]] —**un′af·fect′ed·ly,** *adv.* —**un′af·fect′ed·ness,** *n.*

un·al·ter·a·ble (un ol′tər ə bəl *or* un ôl′tər ə bəl) *adj.* that cannot be altered; not changeable. —**un·al·ter·a·bly,** *adv.*

un·a·neled (un′ə nēld′) *adj. Archaic.* without being anointed by a priest before death; not having received extreme unction. [< *un-* + *anele* give extreme unction to, ME *anelie*(n), ult. < OE *an-* on + *ele* oil < L *oleum*]

u·na·nim·i·ty (yü′nə nim′ə tē) *n.* the quality or state of being unanimous; complete accord or agreement.

hat, āge, fär; let, ēqual, tèrm; it, īce
hot, ōpen, ôrder; oil, out; cup, pût, rüle,
əbove, takən, pencəl, lemən, circəs

ch, child; ng, long; sh, ship
th, thin; ŦH, then; zh, measure

u·nan·i·mous (yü nan′ə məs) *adj.* **1** in complete accord or agreement; agreed: *The delegates were unanimous that the issue needed to be discussed further.* **2** formed by or showing complete accord; having the consent of everyone: *unanimous consent. The vote was unanimous.* [< L *unanimus* < *unus* one + *animus* mind] —**u·nan′i·mous·ly,** *adv.* —**u·nan′i·mous·ness,** *n.*

un·an·swer·a·ble (un an′sər ə bəl) *adj.* **1** that cannot be answered or has no answer: *unanswerable questions about life and death.* **2** that cannot be disproved: *an unanswerable argument.* —**un·an′swer·a·bly,** *adv.*

un·ap·proach·a·ble (un′ə prō′chə bəl) *adj.* **1** very hard to approach; aloof; distant. **2** unrivalled; without an equal. —**un′ap·proach′a·ble·ness,** *n.* —**un′ap·proach′a·bly,** *adv.*

un·apt (un apt′) *adj.* **1** not fit. **2** not likely. **3** not skilful. **4** not quick to learn. —**un·apt′ly,** *adv.* —**un·apt′ness,** *n.*

un·arm (un ärm′) *v. Archaic.* **1** take weapons or armor from; disarm. **2** lay down one's weapons. **3** take off armor.

un·armed (un ärmd′) *adj.* **1** without weapons or armor. **2** of plants and animals, without horns, teeth, prickles, spines, thorns, etc.

un·as·sum·ing (un′ə süm′ing *or* un′ə syüm′ing) *adj.* not putting on airs; modest. —**un′as·sum′ing·ly,** *adv.* —**un′as·sum′ing·ness,** *n.*

un·at·tached (un′ə tacht′) *adj.* **1** not attached. **2** not connected or associated with a particular body, group, organization, or the like; independent. **3** not married or engaged to be married.

un·at·tend·ed (un′ə ten′did) *adj.* **1** without attendants; alone. **2** not accompanied. **3** not taken care of; not attended to.

un·a·vail·ing (un′ə vā′ling) *adj.* not successful; useless. —**un′a·vail′ing·ly,** *adv.*

un·a·void·a·ble (un′ə void′ə bəl) *adj.* that cannot be avoided or prevented: *an unavoidable delay.* —**un′a·void′a·ble·ness,** *n.* —**un′a·void′a·bly,** *adv.*

un·a·ware (un′ə wer′) *adj.* not aware; ignorant: *They were unaware of her change in plans. He had gone out in the boat, unaware that there was a storm warning.* —*adv.* unawares.

un·a·wares (un′ə werz′) *adv.* **1** without being expected; by surprise: *The police caught the burglar unawares.* **2** without knowing or being aware: *We made the error unawares.*

un·backed (un bakt′) *adj.* **1** not backed, helped, or supported; unaided. **2** not bet on. **3** *Archaic.* not ridden.

un·bal·ance (un bal′əns) *n., v.* **-anced, -anc·ing.** —*n.* lack of balance; unbalanced condition; imbalance. —*v.* throw out of balance; disorder or derange.

un·bal·anced (un bal′ənst) *adj.* **1** not balanced. **2** mentally disordered; unstable or deranged.

un·bar (un bär′) *v.* **-barred, -bar·ring.** remove the bars from; unbolt.

un·bear·a·ble (un ber′ə bəl) *adj.* that cannot be endured:

un′a·bat′ed
un′ab·bre′vi·at′ed
un′a·bet′ted
un′ab·solved′
un′ab·sorbed′
un′ac·a·dem′ic
un′ac·cent′ed
un′ac·cen′tu·at′ed
un′ac·cept′a·ble
un′ac·cept′ed
un′ac·claimed′
un′ac·cli′ma·ted
un′ac·cli′ma·tized′
un′ac·com′mo·dat′ing
un′ac·com′plished
un′ac·cred′it·ed
un′ac·knowl′edged
un′ac·quaint′ed
un′ac·quit′ted
un·act′ed
un·ac′tion·a·ble
un·ac′tu·at′ed
un′a·dapt′a·ble
un′a·dapt′ed

un′ad·dressed′
un′ad·journed′
un′ad·just′a·ble
un′ad·just′ed
un′a·dorned′
un′a·dul′ter·at′ed
un′ad·van·ta′geous
un′ad·ver′tised
un′ad·vis′a·ble
un·af·fil′i·at·ed
un′a·fraid′
un′ag·gres′sive
un·aid′ed
un·aimed′
un·aired′
un′a·larmed′
un′a·ligned′
un′a·like′
un′al·layed′
un′al·lied′
un′al·low′a·ble
un′al·loyed′

un′al·pha·bet·ized′
un·al′tered
un′am·big′u·ous
un·am·bi′tious
un′a·mi′ca·ble
un′a·mused′
un′a·mus′ing
un′an·i·mat′ed
un′an·nounced′
un·an′swered
un·an′tic′i·pat′ed
un′a·pol′o·get′ic
un·ap′par·ent
un′ap·peal′ing
un′ap·peas′a·ble
un′ap·pe·tiz′ing
un′ap·pli·ca·ble
un′ap·plied′
un′ap·point′ed
un′ap·por′tioned
un′ap·pre′ci·at′ed

un′ap·pre′ci·a·tive
un′ap·pre·hen′sive
un′ap·proached′
un′ap·pro′pri·at′ed
un′ap·proved′
un·ar′gu·a·ble
un·ar′mored
un·ar·rest′ed
un·ar′tic′u·lat·ed
un·ar·tis′tic
un′as·cer′tain·a·ble
un′a·shamed′
un·asked′
un′as·pir′ing
un′as·sail′a·ble
un′as·sailed′
un·as·ser′tive
un′as·sessed′
un′as·sign·a·ble
un′as·signed′
un′as·sim′i·lat′ed
un′as·sist′ed
un′as·sort′ed

un′as·sumed′
un′a·toned′
un′at·tain′a·ble
un′at·tained′
un′at·tempt′ed
un′at·test′ed
un′at·trac′tive
un′aus·pi′cious
un·au·then′tic
un·au·then′ti·cat′ed
un·au′thor·ized′
un′a·vail′a·ble
un′a·venged′
un′a·vowed′
un′a·wak′ened
un·awed′
un·baked′
un·band′aged
un′bap·tized′
un·barbed′

unbearable suspense, unbearable pain. —**un·bear′a·ble·ness,** *n.*
—**un·bear′ab·ly,** *adv.*

un·beat·en (un bēt′ən) *adj.* 1 not defeated or surpassed. 2 not trodden; not travelled: *unbeaten paths.* 3 not beaten or pounded: *Add two unbeaten eggs.*

un·be·com·ing (un′bi kum′ing) *adj.* 1 not attractive; not suited to the wearer: *an unbecoming dress.* 2 not fitting or proper: *unbecoming behavior.* —**un′be·com′ing·ly,** *adv.*
—**un′be·com′ing·ness,** *n.*

un·be·known (un′bi nōn′) *adj. Informal.* not known.

un·be·knownst (un′bi nōnst′) *adj.* not known; unbeknown.

un·be·lief (un′bi lēf′) *n.* a lack of belief, especially in God or in a particular religion or doctrine.
► *Syn.* **Unbelief, disbelief** = lack of belief. **Unbelief** suggests only lack of belief in something offered or held as true, with no positive feelings one way or the other: *The Inquisition punished heretics for their unbelief.* **Disbelief** suggests a positive refusal to believe: *He expressed his disbelief in the value of universal military training.*

un·be·liev·a·ble (un′bi lē′və bəl) *adj.* beyond belief; too unlikely to believe; incredible: *an unbelievable story, a man of almost unbelievable strength.* —**un′be·liev′a·bly,** *adv.*

un·be·liev·er (un′bi lē′vər) *n.* 1 a person who does not believe. 2 a person who does not believe in a particular religion.

un·be·liev·ing (un′bi lē′ving) *adj.* not believing; doubting.
—**un′be·liev′ing·ly,** *adv.*

un·belt·ed (un′belt′əd) *adj.* without a belt: *He wore the coat unbelted.*

un·bend (un bend′) *v.* **-bent, -bend·ing.** 1 straighten. 2 release from strain. 3 relax: *The judge unbent and behaved like a boy.* 4 unfasten (a sail, rope, etc.).

un·bend·ing (un ben′ding) *adj., n.* —*adj.* 1 not bending or curving; rigid: *the unbending boughs of an old oak.* 2 not yielding; firm or inflexible: *an unbending attitude.* —*n.* a relaxing or freeing from constraint: *In a rare moment of unbending, he told us about his boyhood.* —**un·bend′ing·ly,** *adv.* —**un·bend′ing·ness,** *n.*

un·bent (un bent′) *v., adj.* —*v.* pt. and pp. of **unbend.** —*adj.* not bent or curved.

un·bi·assed or **un·bi·ased** (un bī′əst) *adj.* not biassed; impartial; fair: *an unbiassed account.*

un·bid·den (un bid′ən) *adj.* not bidden; not invited or not commanded.

un·bind (un bīnd′) *v.* **-bound, -bind·ing.** release from bonds or restraint; untie; unfasten; let loose. [OE *unbindan*]

un·bleached (un blēcht′) *adj.* not bleached; not made white by bleaching: *unbleached muslin.*

un·blem·ished (un blem′isht) *adj.* without blemishes; flawless: *smooth, unblemished skin, an unblemished reputation.*

un·blessed (un blest′) *adj.* 1 not blessed. 2 wicked, evil, or malignant: *a soul unblessed.* 3 unhappy; miserable; wretched. Also, **unblest.**

un·blush·ing (un blush′ing) *adj.* 1 not blushing. 2 shameless or unabashed: *unblushing impudence.* —**un·blush′ing·ly,** *adv.*

un·bod·ied (un bod′ēd) *adj.* 1 having no body; incorporeal. 2 disembodied.

un·bolt (un bōlt′) *v.* open or unlock a door, etc. by drawing back the bolt or bolts.

un·bolt·ed[1] (un bōl′tid) *adj.* not bolted or fastened: *an unbolted door.* [< *un-1* + *bolt*]

un·bolt·ed[2] (un bōl′tid) *adj.* not sifted: *unbolted flour.* [< *un-1* + *bolt2*]

un·bon·net·ed (un bon′ə tid) *adj.* wearing no bonnet or cap; bareheaded.

un·born (un bôrn′) *adj.* 1 within the mother's womb; not yet born: *an unborn child.* 2 not brought into being: *That joke should have stayed unborn.* 3 still to come; future: *unborn generations.*

un·bos·om (un buz′əm *or* un bü′zəm) *v.* 1 relieve (oneself) of (feelings, secrets, etc.) by revealing them. 2 reveal (thoughts, etc.). [< *un-2* + *bosom,* v.]

un·bound (un bound′) *adj.* 1 not fastened or bound together; loose: *unbound sheets of music.* 2 having no binding: *an unbound book.* 3 freed from bonds; released.

un·bound·ed (un boun′did) *adj.* not bounded; without bounds or limits; very great: *His unbounded good spirits cheered all of us up.*

un·bowed (un boud′) *adj.* 1 not bowed or bent. 2 not forced to yield or submit.

un·brace (un brās′) *v.* **-braced, -brac·ing.** 1 loosen, untie, or detach a brace, belt, article of clothing, etc. 2 loosen tension or relax. 3 weaken; make feeble.

un·braid (un brād′) *v.* separate the strands of.

un·break·a·ble (un brā′kə bəl) *adj.* not breakable; that cannot be easily broken: *an unbreakable toy.*

un·bri·dle (un brī′dəl) *v.* remove a bridle or restraint from: *to unbridle a horse.*

un·brid·led (un brī′dəld) *adj.* 1 not having a bridle on. 2 not controlled; not restrained.

un·bro·ken (un brō′kən) *adj.* 1 not broken; whole: *There was only one unbroken cup left in the whole set.* 2 not interrupted; continuous: *He had eight hours of unbroken sleep.* 3 not tamed: *an unbroken colt.* —**un·bro′ken·ness,** *n.*

un·buck·le (un buk′əl) *v.* **-led, -ling.** open the buckle or buckles of: *She unbuckled her belt and took it off.*

un·bur·den (un bėr′dən) *v.* 1 free from a burden. 2 relieve oneself or one's conscience or mind by confessing or revealing: *He decided to unburden himself of the problem. She unburdened her mind to her friend.*

un·busi·ness·like (un biz′nis līk′) *adj.* without system and method; not efficient.

un·but·ton (un but′ən) *v.* unfasten the button or buttons of.

un·but·toned (un but′ənd) *adj.* 1 not buttoned: *His coat was unbuttoned.* 2 unrestricted in expression or action; casual; informal: *He was in an unbuttoned mood, talking freely of his past.*

un·cage (un kāj′) *v.* **-caged, -cag·ing.** 1 release from a cage. 2 release.

un·called-for (un kold′fôr′ *or* un kôld′fôr′) *adj.* unnecessary and unjustified; impertinent or rude: *an uncalled-for remark.*

un·can·ny (un kan′ē) *adj.* 1 strange and mysterious; eerie: *The trees had uncanny shapes in the dim light.* 2 seeming to have or show powers beyond what is natural or normal: *an uncanny sense of timing, an uncanny knack for solving puzzles.* —**un·can′ni·ly,** *adv.* —**un·can′ni·ness,** *n.*
► *Syn.* See note at **weird.**

un·cap (un kap′) *v.* **-capped, -cap·ping.** 1 remove a cap or covering from: *to uncap a bottle.* 2 remove one's hat, especially in deference.

un·cer·e·mo·ni·ous (un′ser ə mō′nē əs) *adj.* 1 not ceremonious; informal. 2 not as courteous as would be expected; abrupt or rude: *an unceremonious dismissal.*
—**un′cer·e·mo′ni·ous·ly,** *adv.* —**un′cer·e·mo′ni·ous·ness,** *n.*

un·cer·tain (un sėr′tən) *adj.* 1 not known with certainty; not finally established; indefinite: *The election results are still uncertain. Her arrival time is uncertain.* 2 not sure; problematical: *an uncertain future.* 3 likely to change; unreliable: *a dog of uncertain temper. The weather remains uncertain.* 4 dubious or doubtful; hesitating: *an uncertain smile. He was uncertain about the reception he would get.* 5 not definite or defined; vague: *an uncertain shape in the mist.* 6 not constant; varying: *an uncertain flicker of light.* —**un·cer′tain·ly,** *adv.*
► *Syn.* 1. **Uncertain, insecure** = not sure in some way or about something. **Uncertain** emphasizes not knowing definitely or surely about something or not having complete confidence in a thing, a person, or oneself, and thus suggests the presence of doubt: *His plans for the summer are uncertain.* **Insecure** emphasizes not being protected from or guarded against danger or loss, and suggests the presence of fear or anxiety: *His position at the bank is insecure.*

un·cer·tain·ness (un sėr′tən nəs) *n.* the quality or state of being uncertain.

un·cer·tain·ty (un sėr′tən tē) *n., pl.* **-ties.** 1 the quality or state of being uncertain; doubt. 2 something uncertain: *Our trip is still an uncertainty.*

---

un·chain (un chān′) *v.* free from chains or as if from chains; set free.

un·change·a·ble (un chān′jə bəl) *adj.* that cannot be changed. —**un·change′a·ble·ness,** *n.* —**un·change′a·bly,** *adv.*

un·changed (un chānjd′) *adj.* not changed; the same.

un·chang·ing (un chān′jing) *adj.* not changing; constant: *listening to the unchanging roar of the sea.*

un·char·i·ta·ble (un char′ə tə bəl *or* un cher′ə tə bəl) *adj.* not generous; not charitable; severe; harsh. —**un·char′i·ta·ble·ness,** *n.* —**un·char′i·ta·bly,** *adv.*

un·chart·ed (un chär′tid) *adj.* not yet mapped; not recorded on a chart: *sailing uncharted seas.*

un·chaste (un chāst′) *adj.* not chaste; not virtuous. —**un·chaste′ly,** *adv.*

un·chas·ti·ty (un chas′tə tē) *n.* lack of chastity; unchaste character; lewdness.

un·checked (un chekt′) *adj.* not checked; not restrained.

un·chris·tian (un kris′chən) *adj.* **1** not Christian. **2** unworthy of Christians. **3** *Informal.* such as any civilized person would object to; barbarous; outrageous: *routed out of bed at a most unchristian hour.*

un·church (un chėrch′) *v.* **1** expel from a church; excommunicate. **2** deprive of status and rights as a church.

un·churched (un chėrcht′) *adj.* not belonging to or attending any church.

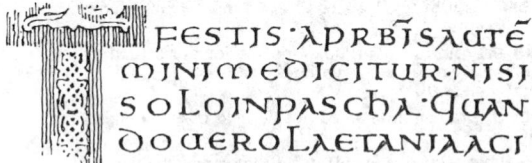

**FESTIS·APRBJSAUTĒ
MJNJMEDJCJTUR·NJSJ
SOLOJNPASChλ·QUAN
DOUEROLλETANJλλCI**

The first section of a page from the 6th-century Latin manuscript "Gregorius Magnus Papa, Liber sacramentorum," written in uncials

un·ci·al (un′shē əl *or* un′shəl) *n., adj.* —*n.* **1** a kind of letter or writing having heavy, rounded strokes, used especially in Greek and Latin manuscripts from the 4th to the 8th century. **2** manuscript written in uncial. —*adj.* having to do with or written in this style or such letters. [< L *uncialis,* in the sense "inch-high" < *uncia* inch]

un·ci·nate (un′sə nit *or* un′sə nāt′) *adj.* hooked; bent at the end like a hook. [< L *uncinatus,* ult. < *uncus* hook]

un·cir·cum·cised (un sėr′kəm sīzed′) *adj.* **1** not circumcised. **2** heathen.

un·civ·il (un siv′əl) *adj.* **1** not civil; rude; impolite. **2** not civilized. —**un·civ′il·ly,** *adv.*

un·civ·i·lized (un siv′ə līzd) *adj.* not civilized; barbarous or unenlightened.

un·clad (un klad′) *adj.* not dressed; not clothed; naked.

un·clasp (un klasp′) *v.* **1** unfasten. **2** release or be released from a clasp or grasp.

un·clas·si·fied (un klas′i fīd) *adj.* **1** not placed in a category or class. **2** not classified as secret or restricted: *Employees without security clearance have access only to unclassified information.*

un·cle (ung′kəl) *n.* **1** the brother of one's father or mother. **2** the husband of one's aunt. **3** *Informal.* a man considered as friend, adviser, etc. of a younger person or group.
say or **cry uncle,** *Informal.* give in; surrender: *She wouldn't let him up until he said uncle.*
[ME < AF < L *avunculus* one's mother's brother]

un·clean (un klēn′) *adj.* **1** not clean; dirty; filthy. **2** not pure morally; evil. **3** ceremonially unclean. [OE *unclǣne*]
—**un·clean′ness,** *n.*

un·clean·ly[1] (un klen′lē) *adj.* not cleanly; unclean. [< *un-*[1] + *cleanly*[1]] —**un·clean′li·ness,** *n.*

un·clean·ly[2] (un klēn′lē) *adv.* in an unclean manner. [< *unclean*]

un·clench (un klench′) *v.* open or become opened from a clenched state: *unclench one's fists.*

Uncle Sam (sam) *Informal.* the government or people of the United States. [< the initials *U.S.*]

Uncle Tom *Esp.U.S. Informal.* a black who behaves in a servile way toward whites in an attempt to win their approval. [for *Uncle Tom,* faithful Negro slave in *Uncle Tom's Cabin,* an antislavery novel by Harriet Beecher Stowe (1811-1896)]

un·cloak (un klōk′) *v.* **1** remove the coat from. **2** reveal; expose: *to uncloak an impostor.* **3** take off the cloak or outer garment.

un·clog (un klog′) *v.* free from an obstruction: *to unclog a drain.*

un·close (un klōz′) *v.* -closed, -clos·ing. open.

un·clothe (un klōŦH′) *v.* -clothed *or* -clad, -cloth·ing. **1** strip of clothes; undress. **2** lay bare; uncover.

un·co (ung′kō) *Scottish. adv., adj.* —*adv.* remarkably; very; extremely.
—*adj.* **1** unknown, strange, or unusual. **2** remarkable, extraordinary, or great. **3** uncanny. [ult. var. of *uncouth*]

un·coil (un koil′) *v.* unwind.

un·com·fort·a·ble (un kum′fər tə bəl) *adj.* **1** not comfortable: *I am uncomfortable in this chair.* **2** uneasy: *I feel uncomfortable at formal dinners.* **3** disagreeable; causing discomfort: *This is an uncomfortable chair.* —**un·com′fort·a·bly,** *adv.*
—**un·com′fort·a·ble·ness,** *n.*

un·com·mer·cial (un′kə mėr′shəl) *adv.* **1** not involving or concerned with commerce or business; non-commercial. **2** not following the principles or spirit of business; unbusinesslike.

un·com·mit·ted (un kə mit′id) *adj.* **1** not bound or pledged to a certain viewpoint, course, program, etc.: *an uncommitted candidate.* **2** not committed to prison or another institution.

un·com·mon (un kom′ən) *adj.* **1** not commonly encountered; rare; unusual: *The tulip tree is uncommon in most of Canada.* **2** remarkable: *uncommon strength, an uncommon grasp of the subject.* —**un·com′mon·ly,** *adv.* —**un·com′mon·ness,** *n.*

un·com·mu·ni·ca·tive (un′kə myü′nə kə tiv *or* un′kə myü′nə kā′tiv) *adj.* not giving out any information, opinions, etc.; silent and reserved; taciturn. —**un·com·mu′ni·ca′tive·ly,** *adv.*
—**un′com·mu′ni·ca′tive·ness,** *n.*

un·com·pro·mis·ing (un kom′prə mī′zing) *adj.* unyielding; firm; unwilling to compromise.
—**un·com′pro·mis′ing·ly,** *adv.*

un·con·cern (un′kən sėrn′) *n.* lack of care, interest, or anxiety; indifference: *The children looked with complete unconcern at their strange surroundings.*
► *Syn.* See note at **indifference.**

un·con·cerned (un′kən sėrnd′) *adj.* **1** free from care, interest, or anxiety; indifferent or nonchalant: *unconcerned about the results of the exam.* **2** not involved: *He was unconcerned with that aspect of the inquiry. They need an unconcerned person to settle the dispute.* —**un′con·cern′ed·ness,** *n.*

un·con·cern·ed·ly (un′kən sėr′nid lē) *adv.* in an unconcerned manner.

un·con·di·tion·al (un′kən dish′ən əl *or* un′kən dish′nəl) *adj.* without conditions; absolute: *unconditional surrender.*
—**un·con·di′tion·al·ly,** *adv.*

un·con·di·tioned (un′kən dish′ənd) *adj.* **1** without conditions; unconditional. **2** *Psychology.* not learned; not dependent on conditioning; natural or instinctive: *Withdrawing one's hand on contact with fire is an unconditioned reflex.*

un·con·form·i·ty (un′kən fôr′mə tē) *n., pl.* **-ties. 1** lack of conformity. **2** *Geology.* the surface of contact between rock strata of different ages, representing a period of erosion or non-deposition of rock, before the upper, younger bed was laid down.

un·con·nect·ed (un′kə nek′tid) *adj.* **1** separated; disconnected. **2** not connected; separate or unrelated: *What she had written was not a paragraph; it was just a series of unconnected sentences.*

un·con·quer·a·ble (un kong′kər ə bəl) *adj.* that cannot be conquered. **—un·con′quer·a·bly,** *adv.*

un·con·scion·a·ble (un kon′shən ə bəl) *adj.* **1** not influenced or guided by conscience; unscrupulous: *unconscionable business practices, an unconscionable liar.* **2** unreasonable; excessive: *to wait an unconscionable time for someone.* **—un·con′scion·a·bly,** *adv.*

un·con·scious (un kon′shəs) *adj., n.* **—adj. 1** not conscious; not able to feel or think: *to be knocked unconscious. He was unconscious for several days after the accident.* **2** not aware: *The general was unconscious of being followed by a spy.* **3** not meant; not intended: *unconscious neglect.* **—n. the unconscious,** the part of a person's mind of which the person is not normally aware, but which can affect behavior; a person's unconscious thoughts, desires, fears, etc. **—un·con′scious·ly,** *adv.* **—un·con′scious·ness,** *n.*

un·con·sti·tu·tion·al (un′kon stə tyü′shən əl *or* un′kon stə tü′shən əl) *adj.* contrary to the constitution; not constitutional. **—un′con·sti·tu′tion·al·ly,** *adv.*

un·con·sti·tu·tion·al·i·ty (un′kon stə tyü′shən al′ə tē *or* un′kon stə tü′shən al′ə tē) *n.* the fact, state, or condition of being contrary to the constitution.

un·con·trol·la·ble (un′kən trō′lə bəl) *adj.* not controllable; that cannot be controlled or held back: *I had to leave quickly because I felt an uncontrollable desire to laugh.* **—un′con·trol′la·bly,** *adv.*

un·con·ven·tion·al (un′kən vensh′nəl *or* un′kən ven′shən əl) *adj.* not bound by or conforming to convention, rule, or precedent; being out of the ordinary: *an unconventional way of dressing. She is an unconventional person.* **—un′con·ven′tion·al·ly′,** *adv.*

un·con·ven·tion·al·i·ty (un′kən ven′shən al′ə tē) *n.* the quality or state of being unconventional: *His unconventionality amused his friends.*

un·cork (un kôrk′) *v.* **1** pull the cork from. **2** let go or let out; release: *to uncork a vicious punch, to uncork one's pent-up feelings.*

un·count·ed (un koun′tid) *adj.* **1** not counted; not reckoned. **2** very many; innumerable.

un·cou·ple (un kup′əl) *v.* **-pled, -pling.** disconnect; unfasten.

un·cour·te·ous (un kėr′tē əs) *adj.* discourteous; impolite; rude. **—un·cour′te·ous·ly,** *adv.*

un·court·li·ness (un kôrt′lē nis) *n.* rudeness.

un·couth (un küth′) *adj.* **1** awkward or crude in appearance, conduct, etc.: *uncouth manners, an uncouth young man.* **2** *Archaic.* strange; outlandish: *They heard uncouth noises behind the locked door.* [OE *uncūth* < *un-*[1] + *cūth,* pp. of *cunnan* know] **—un·couth′ly,** *adv.* **—un·couth′ness,** *n.*

un·cov·er (un kuv′ər) *v.* **1** remove the cover from. **2** make known; reveal; expose. **3** remove the hat or cap of. **4** remove one's hat or cap in respect.

un·cov·ered (un kuv′ərd) *adj.* **1** having no cover or covering: *Don't leave the milk uncovered.* **2** not protected by insurance, etc. **3** not wearing a hat or cap.

un·cross (un kros′) *v.* change from a crossed position: *She uncrossed her legs and stretched them out.*

un·crown (un kroun′) *v.* take the crown from; depose.

un·crowned (un kround′) *adj.* **1** not crowned; not having yet assumed the crown. **2** having royal power without being king, queen, etc.

unc·tion (ungk′shən) *n.* **1** the act of anointing with oil, ointment, etc. for medical purposes or as a religious rite: *The priest gave the dying man extreme unction.* **2** the oil, ointment, etc. used for anointing. **3** something soothing or comforting: *the unction of flattery.* **4** a fervent or earnest quality in behavior or expression. **5** affected fervor or earnestness; unctuousness. [< L *unctio, -onis* < *unguere* anoint]

unc·tu·ous (ungk′chü əs) *adj.* **1** like an oil or ointment; oily or greasy. **2** of a person or a person's manner, very smooth, fervent, or earnest, especially in a false or affected way when trying to please or persuade: *The stranger's unctuous manner made us suspicious.* **3** of ground or soil, soft and clinging, but easily worked; rich in decayed organic matter. **4** of clay, very plastic. [ME < Med.L *unctuosus,* ult. < L *unguere* anoint] **—unc′tu·ous·ly,** *adv.* **—unc′tu·ous·ness,** *n.*

un·curl (un kėrl′) *v.* straighten out.

un·cut (un kut′) **1** not cut into or cut down: *The cake was on the table, still uncut.* **2** of a gem, not shaped: *uncut diamonds.* **3** of a book, having the folded edges of the leaves not cut open, or having untrimmed margins. **4** of a book, film, etc., not shortened; unabridged or unexpurgated: *They saw the uncut version of the film.*

un·daunt·ed (un don′tid *or* un dôn′tid) *adj.* not daunted; not discouraged or dismayed. **—un·daunt′ed·ly,** *adv.* **—un·daunt′ed·ness,** *n.*

un·de·ceive (un′di sēv′) *v.* **-ceived, -ceiv·ing.** free from error, illusion, or deception.

un·de·cid·ed (un′di sīd′id) *adj.* **1** not decided or settled. **2** not having one's mind made up. **—un′de·cid′ed·ly,** *adv.* **—un′de·cid′ed·ness,** *n.*

un·de·fined (un′di fīnd′) *adj.* **1** not defined or explained. **2** indefinite.

un·de·ni·a·ble (in′di nī′ə bəl) *adj.* **1** that cannot be denied; certain; indisputable: *the undeniable rudeness of his answer, undeniable excellence.* **2** unquestionably genuine or excellent: *Her references were undeniable.* **—un′de·ni′a·bly,** *adv.*

un·de·nom·i·na·tion·al (un′di nom′ə nā′shən əl *or* un′di nom′ə nāsh′nəl) *adj.* nondenominational.

un·der (un′dər) *prep., adv., adj.* **—prep. 1** in, at, or to a place or position directly below: *The marble rolled under the table. Write your name under mine.* **2** under and through to the other side of: *The road goes under that bridge.* **3** below the surface of: *under the ground, swimming under water.* **4** on the inside of; covered or hidden by: *She was wearing a heavy sweater under her parka. He has a soft heart under his gruff exterior.* **5** lower than the required or standard degree, amount, etc.: *under par. You cannot sign a contract if you are under age.* **6** less than: *It will cost under ten dollars.* **7** subject to the authority, control, influence, or guidance of: *He studied under a famous pianist. The soldiers acted under orders.* **8** during the time of: *England under King Charles I.* **9** in the position or state of being affected by: *under the new rules. He doesn't work well under pressure.* **10** within a particular group or category: *Books on gymnastics are classed under sports.* **11** represented by: *under a new name.* **—adv. 1** in or to a place or position below something: *We saw the swimmer go under.* **2** in or into a condition of subjection, failure, unconsciousness, etc.: *to knuckle under to a bully. His business went under.* **3** less than some quantity or limit: *ten dollars or under.* **—adj.** facing or projecting downward: *The under surface was rough.* [OE]

☛ *Syn. prep.* **1. Under, below, beneath** express a relation in which one thing is thought of as being lower than another in some way. **Under** suggests being directly lower: *A corporal is under a sergeant.* **Below** suggests being on a lower level, but not necessarily straight below nor without anyone or anything in between: *A corporal is below a major.* **Beneath** can be used in place of either

un′con·fused′	un′con·tra·dict′ed	un·court′ly	un·cur′tained	un′de·feat′a·ble
un′con·geal′a·ble	un′con·trived′	un′cre·at′ed	un·cus′tom·ar′y	un′de·feat′ed
un′con·gealed′	un′con·trolled′	un′cre·a′tive	un·dam′aged	un′de·fend′ed
un′con·gen′ial	un′con·tro·ver′sial	un·cred′it·ed	un·damped′	un′de·fen′si·ble
un′con·gest′ed	un′con·ver′sant	un·crit′i·cal	un·dat′ed	un′de·filed′
un·con′quered	un′con·vert′ed	un·crit′i·ciz′a·ble	un·daugh′ter·ly	un′de·fin′a·ble
un′con·sci·en′tious	un′con·vinced′	un·cropped′	un·daz′zled	un′de·fined′
un′con·se·crat′ed	un′con·vinc′ing	un·crowd′ed	un′de·bat′a·ble	un′de·formed′
un·con′sent′ing	un·cooked′	un·crys′tal·lized′	un·de·cayed′	un′de·layed′
un·con·sid′ered	un·cooled′	un·cul′ti·va·ble	un′de·ceiv′a·ble	un′de·liv′er·a·ble
un·con′soled′	un′co·op′er·a·tive	un·cul′ti·vat′ed	un′de·ceived′	un′de·liv′ered
un′con·strained′	un′co·or′di·nat′ed	un·cul′tured	un′de·ci′pher·a·ble	un′de·mand′ing
un·con′strict′ed	un·cor′dial	un·curbed′	un′de·ci′phered	un·dem′o·crat′ic
un·con′sumed′	un·corked′	un·cured′	un·decked′	un′de·mon′stra·ble
un′con·sum′mat·ed	un·cor·rect′ed	un·cur′i·ous	un′de·clared′	un′de·mon′stra·tive
un·con·tam′i·nat′ed	un′cor·rob′o·rat′ed	un·curled′	un′de·clin′a·ble	un·de′nied′
un·con′test′ed	un·cor·rupt′ed	un·cur′rent	un′de·clined′	un′de·pend′a·ble
un′con·tra·dict′a·ble	un·count′a·ble	un′cur·tailed′	un′dec′o·rat′ed	un′de·pre′ci·at′ed

under or **below**, but is usually more formal or literary: *He lies buried beneath an ancient oak tree. He is beneath notice.*

under– *prefix.* **1** in, on, or to a lower place or side; below or beneath, as in *underground, underline, underarm, underlip.* **2** on or for the inside; covered or concealed, as in *underwear.* **3** lower in rank; subordinate, as in *undersecretary.* **4** not enough; insufficiently, as *underfed, underripe.* **5** below normal, as in *undersized.*

un·der·a·chiev·er (un′dər ə chē′vər) *n.* a person, especially a student, who fails to work at the level of his ability.

un·der·age (un′dər āj′) *adj.* **1** of less than full age. **2** of less than the legal age for voting, marrying, drinking liquor in public bars, etc.

un·der·arm (un′dər ärm′) *adj., n., adv.* —*adj.* **1** on or under the inside of the arm where it joins the shoulder; on or under the armpit: *an underarm scar, the underarm seam in a shirt.* **2** armpit. **3** of, having to do with, or for the armpit: *underarm deodorant.* **4** underhand: *an underarm throw.*
—*n.* armpit.
—*adv.* underhand: *He threw the ball underarm.*

un·der·bel·ly (un′dər bel′ē) *n., pl.* **-lies. 1** the unprotected lower surface or part of the belly. **2** any unprotected or especially vulnerable part.

un·der·bid (un′dər bid′) *v.* **-bid, -bid·ding;** *n.* —*v.* **1** make a lower bid than, as in seeking a contract for work, at an auction, etc. **2** bid less than the full point value of: *to underbid a hand in bridge.*
—*n.* the act of underbidding. —**un′der·bid′der,** *n.*

un·der·bred (un′dər bred′) *adj.* **1** marked by lack of good breeding; ill-mannered or vulgar. **2** of a horse, dog, etc., not of pure breed.

un·der·brush (un′dər brush′) *n.* bushes and small trees growing under the large trees in a forest or wood; undergrowth.

un·der·car·riage (un′dər kar′ij *or* un′dər ker′ij) *n.* **1** the supporting framework of an automobile, carriage, etc. **2** the under part of an aircraft that receives the impact on landing and supports the aircraft on the ground or water; landing gear.

un·der·charge (*v.* un′dər chärj′; *n.* un′dər chärj′) *v.* **-charged, -charg·ing;** *n.* —*v.* **1** put an insufficient charge or load into. **2** charge less than the proper or fair price: *I think the clerk undercharged me. He undercharged me one dollar.* —*n.* **1** an insufficient charge or load. **2** a charge or price less than is proper or fair.

und·er·clothes (un′dər klōz′ *or* -klō̰ᴴz′) *n.pl.* underwear.

un·der·cloth·ing (un′dər klō̰ᴴ′ing) *n.* underwear.

un·der·coat (un′dər kōt′) *n., v.* —*n.* **1** a coat or layer of paint, etc. applied before the finishing coat. **2** the soft, thick fur of certain animals that is hidden by the longer, coarser hair of the outer coat.
—*v.* apply undercoating or an undercoat to: *to undercoat a car.*

un·der·coat·ing (un′dər kō′ting) *n.* a heavy, tarry coating sprayed on the underside of a motor vehicle to protect it against rust, etc.: *Every new car should have undercoating.*

un·der·cov·er (un′dər kuv′ər *or* un′dər kuv′ər) *adj.* working or done in secret: *The jeweller was an undercover man for the police.*

un·der·cur·rent (un′dər kèr′ənt) *n.* **1** a current flowing below the upper currents or the surface of a body of water, air, etc. **2** an underlying tendency that is often contrary to what is expressed or shown: *There was an undercurrent of sadness beneath his joking manner.*

un·der·cut (*v.* un′dər kut′; *n.* un′dər kut′) *v.* **-cut, -cut·ting;** *n.* —*v.* **1** cut under or beneath; cut away material from so as to leave a portion overhanging. **2** sell or work for less than a competitor. **3** cut a notch in (a tree) below the main cut to ensure falling in the desired direction or to prevent splitting. **4** *Golf, tennis, etc.* hit (a ball) with a downward slant to give it a backward spin.
—*n.* **1** the act or result of undercutting. **2** a notch cut in a tree below the main cut and on the side toward which the tree is to fall. An undercut prevents the tree from splitting when it falls. **3** *Esp.Brit.* the tenderloin or fillet of beef. **4** *Golf, tennis, etc.* the act or an instance of hitting a ball with a downward slant to give it a backward spin.

un·der·de·vel·oped (un′dər di vel′əpt) *adj.* **1** not developed in a normal way: *an underdeveloped limb.* **2** of a region, country, etc., poorly or inadequately developed in industry and commerce and having a relatively low standard of living.

un·der·dog (un′dər dog′) *n.* **1** a person or group that is expected to lose or is losing a struggle or contest. **2** a person or group that is a victim of persecution or injustice. **3** a dog having the worst of a fight.

un·der·done (un′dər dun′ *or* un′dər dun′) *adj.* not cooked enough; cooked very little.

un·der·em·ployed (un′dər em ploid′) *adj.* of a person in the work force, not adequately or fully employed.

un·der·es·ti·mate (*v.* un′dər es′tə māt′; *n.* un′dər es′tə mit *or* un′dər es′tə māt′) *v.* **-mat·ed, -mat·ing;** *n.* —*v.* estimate at too low a value, amount, rate, etc. —*n.* an estimate that is too low.

un·der·ex·pose (un′dər eks pōz′) *v.* **-posed, -pos·ing.** *Photography.* expose to light for too short a time.

un·der·ex·po·sure (un′dər eks pō′zhər) *n. Photography.* an exposure to the light for too short a time. Underexposure makes a photograph look dim.

un·der·feed (un′dər fēd′) *v.* **-fed, -feed·ing. 1** feed too little. **2** stoke with coal or other solid fuel from the bottom.

un·der·foot (un′dər fùt′) *adv.* **1** under one's foot or feet; down on or against the ground: *He walked straight through the flower bed, crushing several plants underfoot.* **2** at, before, or underneath one's feet: *enjoying the soft grass underfoot.* **3** in the way: *That dog is always underfoot.*

un·der·fur (un′dər fèr′) *n.* the soft, thick fur of certain mammals that is hidden by the longer, coarser hair of the outer coat.

un·der·gar·ment (un′dər gär′mənt) *n.* any garment worn under outer clothing, especially an article of underwear.

un·der·glaze (un′dər glāz′) *n.* a design, decoration, or color applied to a ceramic article before the glaze is put on.

un·der·go (un′dər gō′) *v.* **-went, -gone, -go·ing. 1** go through; be subjected to; experience: *The town has undergone many changes in the past few years.* **2** endure; suffer: *They underwent a great deal of hardship on the long trek.*
☛ *Syn.* See note at **experience.**

un·der·gone (un′dər gon′) *v.* pp. of **undergo.**

un·der·grad·u·ate (un′dər graj′ü it) *n., adj.* —*n.* a university student who has not yet received the first degree for a course of study; a student without a bachelor's degree. —*adj.* **1** for, having to do with, or designating undergraduates: *undergraduate activities.* **2** characteristic of undergraduates.

un·der·ground (*adv.* un′dər ground′; *adj., n.* un′dər ground′) *adv., adj., n.* —*adv.* **1** beneath the surface of the ground. **2** in or into concealment or secret operation: *The thieves went underground after the robbery.*
—*adj.* **1** being, working, or used beneath the surface of the ground: *underground telephone cables.* **2** done or operating secretly: *The revolution began as an underground movement in the cities.* **3** of, having to do with, or produced by a group or groups outside the establishment, especially avant-garde or radical groups: *an underground newspaper. Her first plays were produced by an underground theatre.*
—*n.* **1** *Esp.Brit.* an underground railway system in a city; subway. **2** place or space beneath the surface of the ground. **3** a secret organization of citizens or a grouping of such organizations, working to free a country from foreign domination or an autocratic regime. **4** any avant-garde or revolutionary movement in art, communications, or politics.

Underground Railroad *Historical.* a secret system set up by opponents of slavery in Canada and the United States before the Civil War to help slaves escape to freedom in the northern states and Canada.

un·der·growth (un′dər grōth′) *n.* **1** underbrush. **2** underfur.

un·der·hand (un′dər hand′) *adj., adv.* —*adj.* **1** not open or honest; secret and sly; underhanded. **2** with an upward movement of the hand from below shoulder level: *an underhand pitch.* —*adv.* **1** secretly and slyly underhandedly. **2** with an upward movement of the hand from below shoulder level: *to throw a ball underhand.*

un·der·hand·ed (un′dər han′did) *adj.* not open or honest; secret and sly: *an underhanded trick.* —**un′der·hand′ed·ly,** *adv.* —**un′der·hand′ed·ness,** *n.*

un·der·hung (un′dər hung′) *adj.* **1** of the lower jaw, projecting beyond the upper jaw: *A bulldog has an underhung jaw.* **2** having a projecting lower jaw. **3** resting on a track beneath, instead of being hung from above: *underhung sliding doors.* **4** underslung.

un·der·in·sured (un′dər in shürd′) *adj.* not carrying sufficient insurance.

un·der·lay (*v.* un′dər lā′; *n.* un′dər lā′) *v.* **-laid, -lay·ing;** *n.* —*v.* lay something under; raise, support, cushion, etc. with something laid underneath. —*n.* **1** something laid beneath to raise, support,

cushion, etc.: *The carpet has a foam rubber underlay.* **2** *Printing.* a piece or pieces of paper put under types, etc. to bring them to the proper height for printing. [OE *underlecgan*]

un·der·lie (un′dər lī′) *v.* **-lay, -lain, -ly·ing. 1** lie under; be beneath. **2** form the basis of; be a reason or cause for: *Strong resentment underlay his outburst.* [OE *underlicgan*]

un·der·line (un′dər līn′ *or* un′dər līn′) *v.* **-lined, -lin·ing;** *n.* —*v.* **1** draw a line or lines under. **2** emphasize; make emphatic or more emphatic: *His speech underlined the importance of co-operation.* **3** sew an underlining in (a garment).
—*n.* a line drawn underneath something: *The underline is too faint.*

un·der·ling (un′dər ling) *n.* a person of lower rank or position; inferior. [OE *underling* < *under* under + *-ling*]

un·der·lin·ing (un′dər lī′ning) *n.* a garment lining formed by attaching the individual sections separately to the corresponding garment sections, each garment section with its attached lining being treated as a unit when the garment is sewn together.

un·der·lip (un′dər lip′) *n.* the lower lip.

un·der·ly·ing (un′dər lī′ing) *adj., v.* —*adj.* **1** lying under or beneath. **2** fundamental; basic; essential. **3** not clearly evident or expressed; implicit: *His complementary remarks had an underlying tone of sarcasm.*
—*v.* ppr. of **underlie.**

un·der·manned (un′dər mand′) *adj.* having not enough crew, staff, etc.; understaffed: *The ship was undermanned, but still carried out its mission.*

un·der·mine (un′dər mīn′ *or* un′dər mīn′) *v.* **-mined, -min·ing. 1** wear away the base or foundations of: *The wave had undermined the cliff.* **2** injure or damage by secret or unfair means: *The editorial was obviously intended to undermine her influence in the community.* **3** weaken, wear out, or destroy gradually: *Several months of stress and insufficient sleep had undermined her health.* **4** make a passage or hole under; dig under: *to undermine a wall.*
—**un′der·min′er,** *n.*

un·der·most (un′dər mōst′) *adj. or adv.* lowest.

un·der·neath (un′dər nēth′) *prep., adv., adj., n.* —*prep.* **1** directly below; beneath; under: *a cellar underneath a house. Write the date underneath your name.* **2** on the inside of; covered or hidden by; under: *He wore a T-shirt underneath his shirt.*
—*adv.* **1** on the inside of or below something: *He crawled underneath. She was wearing her swimsuit underneath.* **2** on or at the lower part or surface: *The box is wet underneath.*
—*adj.* lower: *the underneath side.*
—*n.* the lower part or surface: *Let me see the underneath.* [OE *underneothan* < *under-* under + *neothan* below]

un·der·nour·ish (un′dər nėr′ish) *v.* provide with insufficient food for growth, health, etc.: *The children were badly undernourished.*

un·der·nour·ish·ment (un′dər nėr′ish mənt) *n.* not having enough food; lack of nourishment.

un·der·pants (un′dər pants′) *n.pl.* long or short pants worn as an undergarment.

un·der·pass (un′dər pas′) *n.* a way underneath, especially a road under railway tracks or under another road; subway.

un·der·pay (un′dər pā′) *v.* **-paid, -pay·ing.** pay too little.

un·der·pin (un′dər pin′) *v.* **-pinned, -pin·ning.** support or strengthen with props, stones, masonry, etc.

un·der·pin·ning (un′dər pin′ing) *n.* **1** the material or structure used to support a building or wall from below. **2** Often, **underpinnings,** *pl.* anything used as a foundation or support: *The new evidence provided a good underpinning for the detective's theory.*

un·der·play (un′dər plā′) *v.* **1** act (a role or scene) in a subdued or restrained manner. **2** play down.

un·der·priv·i·leged (un′dər priv′ə lijd) *adj.* **1** having fewer advantages than most people have, especially because of poor economic or social status. **2** (*noml.*) **the underprivileged,** *pl.* all persons who are underprivileged.

un·der·pro·duc·tion (un′dər prə duk′shən) *n.* production that is less than normal or less than there is a demand for.

un·der·rate (un′dər rāt′) *v.* **-rat·ed, -rat·ing.** rate or estimate too low; put too low a value on.

un·der·ripe (un′dər rīp′) *adj.* not completely ripe or not ripe enough: *The tomatoes were somewhat underripe, but edible.*

un·der·score (*v.* un′dər skôr′; *n.* un′dər skôr′) *v.* **-scored, -scor·ing;** *n.* —*v.* **1** underline. **2** emphasize. —*n.* an underscored line.

un·der·sea (*adj.* un′dər sē′; *adv.* un′dər sē′) *adj., adv.* —*adj.* being, carried on, or used beneath the surface of the sea: *an undersea cable, undersea explorations, undersea oil deposits.*
—*adv.* Often, **underseas,** beneath the surface of the seas: *exploring undersea.*

un·der·sec·re·tar·y (un′dər sek′rə ter′ē) *n., pl.* **-tar·ies.** an assistant secretary, especially of a government department.

un·der·sell (un′dər sel′) *v.* **-sold, -sell·ing. 1** sell things at a lower price than: *to undersell a competitor.* **2** sell (merchandise, etc.) at less than the actual value; sell at a loss. **3** promote or advertise (merchandise, etc.) in a restrained manner.

un·der·serv·ant (un′der sėr′vənt) *n.* a servant who does the simpler or lower tasks.

un·der·sexed (un′dər sekst′) *adj.* having a weaker sexual drive than is considered normal.

un·der·sher·iff (un′dər sher′if) *n.* a sheriff's deputy, especially one who acts when the sheriff is not able to act or when there is no sheriff.

un·der·shirt (un′dər shėrt′) *n.* a collarless, often sleeveless, knitted undergarment for the upper part of the body.

un·der·shoot (un′dər shüt′) *v.* **1** of an aircraft, come down short of (the runway or landing field). **2** shoot short of or below (a target, mark, etc.).

un·der·shorts (un′dər shôrts′) *n.pl.* short underpants worn by men and boys.

un·der·shot (un′dər shot′) *adj., v.* —*adj.* **1** of a water wheel, driven by water passing beneath. See **water wheel** for picture. **2** of the lower jaw, projecting beyond the upper; underhung. —*v.* pt. and pp. of **undershoot.**

un·der·side (un′dər sīd′) *n.* the surface lying underneath; the bottom side.

un·der·signed (un′dər sīnd′) *n., adj.* —*n.* **the undersigned,** the person or persons signing a letter or document: *The undersigned accepts the agreement. We, the undersigned, testify that we have read the document.* —*adj.* signed, or having signed at the end of a letter or document: *the undersigning witness.*

un·der·sized (un′dər sīzd′) *adj.* smaller than the usual, desired, or required size: *undersized trout.*

un·der·skirt (un′dər skėrt′) *n.* a skirt worn under another skirt: *a lace skirt with a satin underskirt.*

un·der·sleeve (un′dər slēv′) *n.* a sleeve worn under an outer sleeve, especially an ornamental inner sleeve extending below the other.

un·der·slung (un′dər slung′ *or* un′dər slung′) *adj.* **1** of a vehicle frame, suspended below the axles. **2** having an underslung frame. **3** of a jaw, undershot.

un·der·song (un′dər song′) *n.* a song that is sung as an accompaniment to another song.

un·der·staffed (un′dər staft′) *adj.* having too small a staff; having not enough personnel.

un·der·stand (un′dər stand′) *v.* **-stood, -stand·ing. 1** get the meaning of; comprehend: *Now I understand the message.* **2** get the meaning: *People listen to him but often do not understand.* **3** know how to deal with; know well; know: *A good teacher should understand children.* **4** comprehend as a fact; grasp clearly; realize: *You understand, don't you, that I will be away for three weeks?* **5** be informed; learn: *I understand that he is leaving town.* **6** take as a fact; believe: *It is understood that you will come.* **7** take as meaning; take as meant: *What are we to understand from his words?* **8** supply in the mind. In *He hit the tree harder than I,* the word *did* is understood after *I.*
understand each other, know each other's meaning and wishes; agree.
[OE *understandan*]
➤ *Syn.* **3.** See note at **know.**

un·der·stand·a·ble (un′dər stan′də bəl) *adj.* able to be understood. —**un′der·stand′a·bly,** *adv.*

un·der·stand·ing (un′dər stan′ding) *n., adj.* —*n.* **1** the mental process or state of one that understands; comprehension; knowledge: *a clear understanding of the problem.* **2** the ability to learn and know; intelligence: *The doctor was a man of understanding.* **3** knowledge of each other's meaning and wishes: *True friendship is based on understanding.* **4** agreement: *You and I must come to an understanding.*
—*adj.* intelligent and sympathetic: *an understanding reply.*
—**un′der·stand′ing·ly,** *adv.*

un·der·state (un′dər stāt′) *v.* **-stat·ed, -stat·ing. 1** state too weakly. **2** say less than the full truth about.

un·der·state·ment (un′dər stāt′mənt) *n.* **1** a statement that expresses a fact too weakly. **2** a statement that says less than could be said truly.

un·der·stood (un′dər stu̇d′) v. pt. and pp. of **understand.**

un·der·stud·y (un′dər stud′ē) n. **-stud·ies;** v. **-stud·ied, -stud·y·ing.** —n. a person who is ready to substitute in an emergency for an actor or any other regular performer. —v. **1** learn (a part) in order to replace the regular performer when necessary. **2** act as an understudy to.

un·der·sur·face (un′dər sėr′fis) n. underside.

un·der·take (un′dər tāk′) v. **-took, -tak·en, -tak·ing. 1** set about; try; attempt. **2** agree to do; take upon oneself. **3** promise; guarantee.

un·der·tak·er (un′dər tā′kər for 1; un′dər tā′kər for 2) n. **1** a person whose business is preparing the dead for burial and taking charge of funerals. **2** a person who undertakes something.

un·der·tak·ing (un′dər tā′king for 1 and 2; un′dər tā′king for 3) n. **1** something undertaken; task; enterprise. **2** a promise; guarantee. **3** the business of preparing the dead for burial and taking charge of funerals.

un·der·tone (un′dər tōn′) n. **1** a low or very quiet tone: to talk in undertones. **2** a subdued color; a color seen through other colors: There was an undertone of brown beneath all the gold and crimson of autumn. **3** a quality or feeling that is beneath the surface: an undertone of sadness in her gaiety.

un·der·took (un′dər tu̇k′) v. pt. of **undertake.**

un·der·tow (un′dər tō′) n. **1** any strong current below the surface, moving in a direction different from that of the surface current. **2** the backward flow from waves breaking on a beach.

un·der·val·u·a·tion (un′dər val′yü ā′shən) n. too low a valuation.

un·der·val·ue (un′dər val′yü) v. **-ued, -u·ing. 1** put too low a value on. **2** esteem too little; appreciate insufficiently.

un·der·vest (un′dər vest′) n. undershirt.

un·der·wa·ter (adj. un′dər wo′tər or -wô′tər; adv. un′dər wo′tər or -wô′tər) adj., adv. —adj. growing, done, or used below the surface of the water: underwater plants. A submarine is an underwater ship. —adv. below the surface of the water: She stayed underwater for two minutes.

under way in progress: Plans are under way for a new city hall.

un·der·wear (un′dər wer′) n. clothing worn under outer clothing and not meant to be visible when one is fully dressed.

un·der·weight (un′dər wāt′) adj., n. —adj. **1** of a person or animal, having a mass that is too small in proportion to height and build. **2** having less mass than is needed, desired, or specified: He claimed that the roast was underweight. —n. a mass that is less than needed, desired, or specified.

un·der·went (un′dər went′) v. pt. of **undergo.**

un·der·wood (un′dər wu̇d′) n. underbrush; undergrowth.

un·der·world (un′dər wėrld′) n. **1** the criminal part of society. **2** Greek and Roman mythology. the world of the dead; Hades. **3** the earth. **4** the opposite side of the earth.

un·der·write (un′dər rīt′ or un′dər rīt′) v. **-wrote, -writ·ten, -writ·ing. 1** insure (property) against loss. **2** sign (an insurance policy), thereby accepting the risk of insuring something against loss. **3** write under (other written matter); sign one's name to (a document, etc.). **4** agree to buy (all the stocks or bonds of a certain issue that are not bought by the public): The bankers underwrote the steel company's bonds. **5** agree to meet the expenses of; guarantee. [OE underwrītan, translation of L subscribere]

un·der·writ·er (un′dər rīt′ər) n. **1** a person who underwrites an insurance policy or carries on an insurance business; insurer. **2** an official of an insurance company who determines the risks to be accepted, the premiums to be paid, etc. **3** a person who underwrites (usually with others) issues of bonds, stocks, etc.

un·der·writ·ten (un′dər rit′ən or un′dər rit′ən) v. pp. of **underwrite.**

un·der·wrote (un′dər rōt′ or un′dər rōt′) v. pt. of **underwrite.**

un·de·sir·a·ble (un′di zīr′ə bəl) adj., n. —adj. objectionable; disagreeable. —n. a person that is not wanted.

un·de·vel·oped (un′di vel′əpt) adj. **1** not fully grown. **2** not put

hat, āge, fär; let, ēqual, tėrm; it, īce
hot, ōpen, ôrder; oil, out; cup, pu̇t, rüle,
above, takən, pencəl, lemən, circəs

ch, child; ng, long; sh, ship
th, thin; ₮H, then; zh, measure

to full use. **3** having resources not yet exploited; having little or no modern technology: undeveloped countries.

un·did (un did′) v. pt. of **undo.**

un·dine (un dēn′ or un′dēn) n. European folklore. a female water sprite who, by marrying a mortal and bearing a child, was supposed to be able to acquire a soul. [< NL Undina < L unda wave]

un·dis·ci·plined (un dis′ə plind) adj. not disciplined; without proper control; untrained.

un·dis·guised (un′dis gīzd′) adj. **1** not disguised. **2** unconcealed; open; plain; frank. —**un′dis·guis′ed·ly,** adv.

un·dis·put·ed (un′dis pyü′tid) adj. not disputed; not doubted. —**un·dis·put′ed·ly,** adv.

un·dis·turbed (un′dis tėrbd′) adj. not disturbed; not troubled; calm.

un·do (un dü′) v. **-did, -done, -do·ing. 1** unfasten, untie, unwrap, etc.: We quickly undid the package. I can't undo my shoelace. **2** do away with; cancel or reverse: We mended the roof, but a heavy storm undid our work. **3** bring to ruin; spoil; destroy. **4** Obsolete. explain or solve. [OE undōn] —**un·do′er,** n.

un·do·ing (un dü′ing) n. **1** a doing away with; spoiling; destroying. **2** a cause of destruction or ruin: Drink was his undoing.

un·done (un dun′) adj., v. —adj. **1** not done; not finished: to leave a job undone. **2** not fastened or done up: The top button was undone. **3** ruined. —v. pp. of **undo.**

un·doubt·ed (un dout′id) adj. not doubted; accepted as true.

un·doubt·ed·ly (un dout′id lē) adv. beyond doubt; certainly.

un·dress (v. un dres′; n. un′dres′ or un dres′; adj. un′dres′) v., n., adj. —v. **1** take the clothes off; strip. **2** to strip of ornament. **3** take dressing from (a wound). **4** take off one's clothes. —n. **1** loose, informal dress. **2** ordinary clothes. **3** lack of clothing; nakedness. —adj. of or having to do with informal or ordinary clothes.

un·due (un dyü′ or un dü′) adj. **1** not fitting; not right; improper. **2** too great; too much.

un·du·lant (un′jə lənt or un′dyə lənt) adj. waving; wavy.

undulant fever an infectious disease transmitted to man by bacteria in the milk of infected cattle, goats, etc. It brings on fever, spleen and bowel disorders, pain in the joints, etc.

un·du·late (un′jə lāt′ or un′dyə lāt′) v. **-lat·ed, -lat·ing;** adj. —v. **1** move in waves: undulating water. **2** have a wavy form or surface: undulating hair. **3** cause to move in waves. **4** give a wavy form or surface to. —adj. wavy. [< LL undula wavelet, L undulatus diversified as with waves < unda wave]

un·du·la·tion (un′jə lā′shən or un′dyə lā′shən) n. **1** a waving motion. **2** a wavy form. **3** one of a series of wavelike bends, curves, swellings, etc. **4** Physics. a wavelike motion in air or some other medium, as in the propagation of sound or light; vibration; wave.

un·du·la·to·ry (un′jə lə tô′rē or un′dyə lə tô′rē) adj. undulating; wavy.

un·du·ly (un dyü′lē or un dü′lē) adv. **1** excessively; too much: unduly harsh, unduly optimistic. **2** unjustly or improperly.

un·dy·ing (un dī′ing) adj. deathless; immortal; eternal. —**un·dy′ing·ly,** adv.

un·earned (un ėrnd′) adj. **1** not earned; not gained by labor or

un′de·scrib′a·ble	un′de·vi·at′ing	un′dis·charged′	un′dis·tin′guish·ing	un·drained′
un′de·served′	un′de·vout′	un′dis·closed′	un′dis·tort′ed	un′dra·mat′ic
un′de·serv′ing	un′di·ag·nosed′	un′dis·cour′aged	un′dis·tract′ed	un·drape′
un′des′ig·nat′ed	un′dif·fer·en′ti·at′ed	un′dis·cov′er·a·ble	un′dis·tressed′	un·draped′
un′de·sign′ing	un′di·gest′ed	un′dis·cov′ered	un′dis·trib′ut·ed	un·dreamed′
un′de·sired′	un′dig′ni·fied′	un′dis·crim′i·nat′ing	un′di·ver′si·fied′	un·dreamt′
un′de·spair′ing	un′di·lut′ed	un′dis·heart′ened	un′di·vid′ed	un·dressed′
un′de·stroyed′	un′di·min′ished	un′dis·mayed′	un′di·vulged′	un·dried′
un′de·tach′a·ble	un′di·min′ish·ing	un′dis·posed′	un·doc′u·ment·ed	un·drilled′
un′de·tached′	un·dimmed′	un′dis·so′ci·at′ed	un·do·mes′tic	un·drink′a·ble
un′de·tect′ed	un′dip·lo·mat′ic	un′dis·solved′	un·do·mes′ti·cat′ed	un·du′ti·ful
un′de·ter′mi·na·ble	un′di·rect′ed	un′dis·tilled′	un·dou′bled	un·dyed′
un′de·ter′mined	un′dis·cern′i·ble	un′dis·tin′guish·a·ble	un·doubt′a·ble	
un′de·terred′	un′dis·cern′ing	un′dis·tin′guished	un·doubt′ing	

service. 2 not deserved. 3 *Baseball.* scored because of a defensive error or errors.

unearned income income accruing from rents, investments, etc. and not from wages.

unearned increment increase in the value of property from natural causes, such as the growth of population, rather than from the labor, improvements, etc. put into it by the owner.

un·earth (un ėrth′) *v.* 1 dig up: *to unearth a buried city.* 2 find out; discover: *to unearth a plot.*

un·earth·ly (un ėrth′lē) *adj.* 1 not of this world; supernatural. 2 strange; weird; ghostly. 3 *Informal.* unnatural; extraordinary; preposterous. —**un·earth′li·ness,** *n.*

un·eas·y (un ēz′ē) *adj.* **-eas·i·er, -eas·i·est.** 1 restless; disturbed; anxious. 2 not comfortable. 3 not easy in manner; awkward. —**un·eas′i·ly,** *adv.* —**un·eas′i·ness,** *n.*

un·ed·u·cat·ed (un ej′ə kāt′id) *adj.* not educated; not taught or trained.
☞ *Syn.* See note at **ignorant.**

UNEF (yü′nef) United Nations Emergency Force.

un·em·ploy·a·ble (un′em ploi′ə bəl) *adj.* that cannot be employed.

un·em·ployed (un′em ploid′) *adj.* 1 not having a job; having no work: *an unemployed person.* 2 (*noml.*) **the unemployed,** people out of work. 3 not employed; not in use: *an unemployed skill.*

un·em·ploy·ment (un′em ploi′mənt) *n.* 1 a lack of employment; being out of work. 2 the number or percentage of persons unemployed at a particular time: *a period of high unemployment.* 3 unemployment insurance (def. 2).

unemployment insurance 1 a program providing regular payments of money for a fixed period to persons in the regular labor force who are temporarily unemployed due to layoffs, illness, maternity, etc. Unemployment insurance benefits in Canada are paid for through the contributions of employees, employers, and the federal government. 2 benefits paid through such a program: *He collected unemployment insurance for two months.*

un·e·qual (un ē′kwəl) *adj.* 1 not the same in amount, size, number, value, merit, rank, etc. 2 not balanced; not well matched. 3 not fair; one-sided: *an unequal contest.* 4 not enough; not adequate: *His strength was unequal to the task.* 5 not regular; not even; variable. —**un·e′qual·ly,** *adv.* —**un·e′qual·ness,** *n.*

un·e·qualled or **un·e·qualed** (un ē′kwəld) *adj.* not equalled; matchless.

un·e·quiv·o·cal (un′i kwiv′ə kəl) *adj.* 1 clear; plain. 2 of persons, not inclined to temporize, compromise, or equivocate; speaking frankly and bluntly. —**un′e·quiv′o·cal·ly,** *adv.* —**un′e·quiv′o·cal·ness,** *n.*

un·err·ing (un ėr′ing *or* un er′ing) *adj.* making no mistakes; exactly right. —**un·err′ing·ly,** *adv.* —**un·err′ing·ness,** *n.*

UNESCO (yü nes′kō) *n.* the United Nations Educational, Scientific, and Cultural Organization.

un·es·sen·tial (un′ə sen′shəl) *adj., n.* —*adj.* not essential; not of prime importance. —*n.* something not essential.

un·e·ven (un ē′vən) *adj.* 1 not level: *uneven ground.* 2 not equal; one-sided: *an uneven contest.* 3 of a number, leaving a remainder of 1 when divided by 2; odd. *Examples:* 9, 27, 781. 4 not uniform; irregular or variable: *It was an uneven performance, but on the whole very enjoyable.* [OE *unefen*] —**un·e′ven·ly,** *adv.* —**un·e′ven·ness,** *n.*

un·e·vent·ful (un′i vent′fəl) *adj.* without important or striking

occurrences. —**un′e·vent′ful·ly,** *adv.* —**un′e·vent′ful·ness,** *n.*

un·ex·am·pled (un′eg zam′pəld) *adj.* having no equal or like; without precedent or parallel; without anything like it: *This man's run of 100 metres in 9 seconds is unexampled.*

un·ex·cep·tion·a·ble (un′ek sep′shən ə bəl) *adj.* beyond criticism; wholly admirable. —**un′ex·cep′tion·a·bly,** *adv.*

un·ex·cep·tion·al (un′ek sep′shən əl) *adj.* 1 ordinary. 2 admitting of no exception. —**un′ex·cep′tion·al·ly,** *adv.*

un·ex·pect·ed (un′eks pek′tid) *adj.* not expected. —**un′ex·pect′ed·ly,** *adv.* —**un′ex·pect′ed·ness,** *n.*

un·fail·ing (un fā′ling) *adj.* 1 never failing; tireless; loyal. 2 never running short; endless. 3 sure; certain. —**un·fail′ing·ly,** *adv.*

un·fair (un fer′) *adj.* not fair; unjust. [OE *unfæger*] —**un·fair′ly,** *adv.* —**un·fair′ness,** *n.*

un·faith·ful (un fāth′fəl) *adj.* 1 not faithful; not true to duty or one's promises; faithless. 2 not accurate; not true to the original: *an unfaithful translation.* —**un·faith′ful·ly,** *adv.* —**un·faith′ful·ness,** *n.*

un·fa·mil·iar (un′fə mil′yər) *adj.* 1 not well-known; unusual; strange: *That face is unfamiliar to me.* 2 not acquainted: *He is unfamiliar with the Greek language.*

un·fa·mil·i·ar·i·ty (un′fə mil′yar′ə tē *or* -yer′ə tē, un′fə mil′ē ar′ə tē *or* -er′ə tē) *n.* lack of familiarity.

un·fas·ten (un fas′ən) *v.* undo; loose; open.

un·fath·om·a·ble (un faᴛʜ′əm ə bəl) *adj.* 1 so deep that the bottom cannot be reached. 2 too mysterious to be understood.

un·fath·omed (un faᴛʜ′əmd) *adj.* 1 not measured. 2 not understood.

un·fa·vor·a·ble or **un·fa·vour·a·ble** (un fā′vər ə bəl *or* un fāv′rə bəl) *adj.* 1 opposed or adverse: *Most of the reviews were unfavorable.* 2 not propitious or advantageous: *an unfavorable aspect.* —**un·fa′vor·a·ble·ness** or **un·fa′vour·a·ble·ness,** *n.* —**un·fa′vor·a·bly** or **un·fa′vour·a·bly,** *adv.*

un·feel·ing (un fē′ling) *adj.* 1 hard-hearted; cruel: *a cold, unfeeling person.* 2 not able to feel: *numb, unfeeling hands.* —**un·feel′ing·ly,** *adv.* —**un·feel′ing·ness,** *n.*

un·feigned (un fānd′) *adj.* sincere; real.

un·feign·ed·ly (un fān′id lē) *adv.* really; sincerely.

un·fet·ter (un fet′ər) *v.* remove fetters from; unchain.

un·fin·ished (un fin′isht) *adj.* 1 not finished; not complete. 2 without some special finish; not polished; rough; not painted: *unfinished furniture.*

un·fit (un fit′) *adj., v.* **-fit·ted, -fit·ting.** —*adj.* 1 not fit; not suitable. 2 not good enough; unqualified. 3 not adapted. —*v.* make unfit; spoil. —**un·fit′ness,** *n.*

un·fit·ted (un fit′id) *adj.* 1 inappropriate; not suitable. 2 not tailored or properly fitted: *an unfitted coat.*

un·fix (un fiks′) *v.* loosen; detach; unfasten.

un·flag·ging (un flag′ing) *adj.* not drooping or failing: *unflagging efforts.* —**un·flag′ging·ly,** *adv.*

un·flap·pa·ble (un flap′ə bəl) *adj. Informal.* having or showing self-control or coolness; imperturbable: *an unflappable teacher.*

un·fledged (un flejd′) *adj.* 1 of a bird, too young to fly; not having full-grown feathers. 2 undeveloped; immature.

un·flinch·ing (un flin′ching) *adj.* not drawing back from difficulty, danger, or pain; firm; resolute. —**un·flinch′ing·ly,** *adv.*

un·fold (un fōld′) *v.* 1 open the folds of; spread out: *to unfold a serviette.* 2 cause to be no longer bent, coiled, or interlaced; unbend and straighten out: *to unfold your arms.* 3 reveal; show; explain: *to unfold the plot of a story.* 4 open; develop: *Buds unfold into flowers.* [OE *unfealdan*]

---

un·eat′a·ble	un·end′ing	un·es·cap′a·ble	un·ex·pired′	un·fa·tigued′
un·eat′en	un·en·dorsed′	un·es·cort′ed	un·ex·plain′a·ble	un·fa′vored
un·e·clipsed′	un·en·dowed′	un·es·tab′lished	un·ex·plained′	un·fazed′
un·e·co·nom′ic	un·en·dur′a·ble	un·es′ti·mat′ed	un·ex·plic′it	un·fea′si·ble
un·e·co·nom′i·cal	un·en·dur′ing	un·eth′i·cal	un·ex·plod′ed	un·feath′ered
un·ed′i·ble	un·en·force′a·ble	un·e·vad′ed	un·ex·ploit′ed	un·fea′tured
un·ed′i·fy′ing	un·en·forced′	un·ex·ag′ger·at′ed	un·ex·plored′	un·fed′
un·ed′it·ed	un·en·gaged′	un·ex·am′ined	un·ex·posed′	un·fed′er·at′ed
un·ed′u·ca·ble	un·en·joy′a·ble	un·ex·ceed′ed	un·ex·pressed′	un·felt′
un·ef′faced′	un·en·larged′	un·ex·celled′	un·ex·pres′sive	un·fem′i·nine
un·e·lim′i·nat′ed	un·en·light′ened	un·ex·chang′a·ble	un·ex·pur·gat′ed	un·fenced′
un·e·man′ci·pat′ed	un·en·riched′	un·ex·cit′ed	un·ex·tend′ed	un·fer·ment′ed
un·em·bar′rassed	un·en·rolled′	un·ex·cit′ing	un·ex·tin′guished	un·fer′ti·lized′
un·em·bel′lished	un·en′tered	un·ex·cused′	un·fad′a·ble	un·fet′tered
un·e·mo′tion·al	un·en·ter·pris′ing	un·ex·cut′ed	un·fad′ed	un·filed′
un·em·phat′ic	un·en·ter·tain′ing	un·ex·er·cised′	un·fad′ing	un·fil′i·al
un·emp′tied	un·en·thu′si·as′tic	un·ex·haust′ed	un·fal′ter·ing	un·filled′
un·en·closed′	un·en′vi·a·ble	un·ex·pand′ed	un·fash′ion·a·ble	un·fil′tered
un·en·cour′aged	un·en′vied	un·ex·pend′ed	un·fas′tened	un·fired′
un·en·cum′bered	un·en′vi·ous	un·ex·pe′ri·enced	un·fath′om·a·ble	un·flat′ter·ing
un·en·dan′gered	un·e·quipped′	un·ex·pi·at′ed	un·fath′omed	un·fla′vored

un·forced (un fôrst′) *adj.* **1** not forced; not compelled; willing. **2** natural; spontaneous.

un·fore·seen (un′fôr sēn′) *adj.* not known beforehand; unexpected.

un·for·get·ta·ble (un′fər get′ə bəl) *adj.* that can never be forgotten. —**un′for·get′ta·bly,** *adv.*

un·formed (un fôrmd′) *adj.* **1** shapeless. **2** undeveloped. **3** *Biology.* unorganized.

un·for·tu·nate (un fôr′chə nit) *adj., n.* —*adj.* **1** not lucky; having bad luck. **2** not suitable; not fitting: *The child's outburst of temper was an unfortunate thing for the guest to see.* —*n.* an unfortunate person. —**un·for′tu·nate·ly,** *adv.* —**un·for′tu·nate·ness,** *n.*

un·found·ed (un foun′did) *adj.* without foundation; baseless: *an unfounded complaint.* —**un·found′ed·ly,** *adv.* —**un·found′ed·ness,** *n.*

un·fre·quent·ed (un′fri kwen′tid) *adj.* not frequented; seldom visited; rarely used.

un·friend·ed (un fren′did) *adj.* without friends.

un·friend·ly (un frend′lē) *adj.* **1** not friendly; hostile: *an unfriendly dog.* **2** not favorable: *unfriendly weather.* —**un·friend′li·ness,** *n.*
➤ *Syn.* **1.** See note at **hostile.**

un·frock (un frok′) *v.* deprive (a priest or minister) of his rank, position, and privileges.

un·fruit·ful (un früt′fəl) *adj.* not fruitful; barren; not productive.

un·furl (un fėrl′) *v.* spread out; shake out; unfold: *to unfurl a sail.*

un·gain·ly (un gān′lē) *adj.* awkward; clumsy. [ME *ungaynly* < *un-* not + *gaynly* agile] —**un·gain′li·ness,** *n.*
➤ *Syn.* See note at **awkward.**

un·gen·er·ous (un jen′ər əs) *adj.* not generous; mean. —**un·gen′er·ous·ly,** *adv.*

un·god·li·ness (un god′lē nis) *n.* lack of godliness; wickedness; sinfulness.

un·god·ly (un god′lē) *adj.* **1** irreligious. **2** wicked; sinful. **3** *Informal.* **a** very annoying; distressing; irritating: *an ungodly noise.* **b** outrageous; dreadful; shocking: *to pay an ungodly price.* **c** unbelievable: *to eat an ungodly amount.*

un·gov·ern·a·ble (un guv′ər nə bəl) *adj.* impossible to control; very hard to control or rule; unruly: *an ungovernable temper.* —**un·gov′ern·a·ble·ness,** *n.* —**un·gov′ern·a·bly,** *adv.*
➤ *Syn.* See note at **unruly.**

un·grace·ful (un grās′fəl) *adj.* not graceful; not elegant or beautiful; clumsy; awkward. —**un·grace′ful·ly,** *adv.* —**un·grace′ful·ness,** *n.*

un·gra·cious (un grā′shəs) *adj.* **1** not polite; rude. **2** unpleasant; disagreeable. —**un·gra′cious·ly,** *adv.* —**un·gra′cious·ness,** *n.*

un·grate·ful (un grāt′fəl) *adj.* **1** not grateful; not thankful. **2** displaying lack of gratitude: *an ungrateful silence.* **3** unpleasant; disagreeable. —**un·grate′ful·ly,** *adv.* —**un·grate′ful·ness,** *n.*

un·grudg·ing (un gruj′ing) *adj.* willing; hearty; liberal. —**un·grudg′ing·ly,** *adv.*

un·gual (ung′gwəl) *adj.* of, having to do with, bearing, or shaped like a nail, claw, or hoof. [< L *unguis* nail, claw, hoof]

un·guard·ed (un gär′did) *adj.* **1** not protected. **2** careless: *In an unguarded moment, she gave away the secret.* —**un·guard′ed·ly,** *adv.* —**un·guard′ed·ness,** *n.*

un·guent (ung′gwənt) *n.* an ointment for sores, burns, etc.; salve. [< L *unguentum* < *unguere* anoint]

un·gu·la (ung′gyə lə) *n., pl.* **-lae** (-lē′ *or* -lī′). **1** a hoof. **2** a nail; claw. **3** *Botany.* the claw-shaped base of a petal. **4** *Geometry.* a cylinder, cone, etc., the top part of which has been cut off by a plane oblique to the base. [< L *ungula,* dim. of *unguis* nail, claw, hoof]

un·gu·lar (ung′gyə lər) *adj.* of or like a hoof.

un·gu·late (ung′gyə lit *or* ung′gyə lāt′) *n., adj.* —*n.* **1** any of a

hat, āge, fär; let, ēqual, tėrm; it, īce
hot, ōpen, ôrder; oil, out; cup, pùt, rüle,
əbove, takən, pencəl, lemən, circəs

ch, child; ng, long; sh, ship
th, thin; ᴛʜ, then; zh, measure

large group of four-footed, plant-eating mammals having hoofed feet. Present-day ungulates comprise four orders: Perissodactyla (horses, rhinoceroses, etc.), Artiodactyla (deer, bovines, camels, etc.), Proboscidea (elephants), and Hydracoidea (hyraxes). This grouping is no longer used in formal classification. —*adj.* **1** having hoofs. **2** of or having to do with the ungulates. [< L *unglatus* < *ungula.* See UNGULA.]

un·hal·lowed (un hal′ōd) *adj.* **1** not made holy; not sacred. **2** wicked.

un·hand (un hand′) *v.* let go of; take the hands from.

un·hand·some (un han′səm) *adj.* **1** not good-looking; plain; ugly. **2** ungracious; discourteous; unseemly; mean. **3** not generous.

un·hand·y (un han′dē) *adj.* **1** not easy to handle or manage: *an unhandy tool.* **2** not skilful in using the hands: *an unhandy man.* —**un·hand′i·ly,** *adv.* —**un·hand′i·ness,** *n.*

un·hap·py (un hap′ē) *adj.* **-pi·er, -pi·est. 1** sad; sorrowful. **2** unlucky. **3** not suitable. —**un·hap′pi·ly,** *adv.* —**un·hap′pi·ness,** *n.*

un·har·ness (un här′nis) *v.* **1** remove the harness from; free from harness or gear: *unharness the horse.* **2** remove harness or gear. **3** *Archaic.* divest of armor.

un·health·ful (un helth′fəl) *adj.* bad for the health. —**un·health′ful·ly,** *adv.* —**un·health′ful·ness,** *n.*

un·health·i·ly (un hel′thə lē) *adv.* in a way that is not healthy.

un·health·i·ness (un hel′thē nis) *n.* **1** lack of health; sickness. **2** a condition harmful to health or causing disease.

un·health·y (un hel′thē) *adj.* **1** not possessing good health; not well: *an unhealthy child.* **2** characteristic of or resulting from poor health: *an unhealthy paleness.* **3** hurtful to health; unwholesome: *an unhealthy climate.* **4** morally harmful.

un·heard (un hėrd′) *adj.* **1** not perceived by the ear: *unheard melodies.* **2** not given a hearing: *to condemn a person unheard.* **3** *Archaic.* unheard-of.

un·heard-of (un hėrd′uv′ *or* -ov′) *adj.* **1** never heard of; unknown: *The electric light was unheard-of 200 years ago.* **2** not known before; unprecedented: *A price of $4 a dozen for eggs is unheard-of.*

un·hes·i·tat·ing (un hez′ə tāt′ing) *adj.* prompt; ready; immediate: *unhesitating acceptance.* —**un·hes′i·tat′ing·ly,** *adv.*

un·hinge (un hinj′) *v.* **-hinged, -hing·ing. 1** take (a door, etc.) off its hinges. **2** remove the hinges from. **3** separate from something; detach. **4** unsettle; disorganize; upset: *Trouble has unhinged this poor man's mind.*

un·his·tor·ic (un′his tôr′ik) *adj.* **1** not famous in history; unimportant. **2** unhistorical.

un·his·tor·i·cal (un′his tôr′ə kəl) *adj.* **1** not in accordance with the facts of history. **2** not recorded in history; legendary. **3** ignorant of the facts of history. —**un′his·tor′i·cal·ly,** *adv.* —**un′his·tor′i·cal·ness,** *n.*

un·hitch (un hich′) *v.* free from being hitched; unfasten.

un·ho·ly (un hō′lē) *adj.* **-li·er, -li·est. 1** not holy; wicked; sinful. **2** *Informal.* outrageous or dreadful: *They were raising an unholy row.* [OE *unhālig*] —**un·ho′li·ness,** *n.*

un·hook (un hùk′) *v.* **1** loosen from a hook. **2** undo by loosening a hook or hooks. **3** become loosed from hooks; become undone.

un·horse (un hôrs′) *v.* **-horsed, -hors·ing. 1** pull or knock from a horse's back; cause to fall from a horse: *The knight was unhorsed by the sharp thrust of his opponent's lance.* **2** dislodge; overthrow.

un′for·bear′ing	un·fought′	un·gift′ed	un·ham′pered	un·heat′ed
un′for·bid′den	un·found′	un·gird′	un·hand′i·capped′	un·heed′ed
un′force′a·ble	un·framed′	un·glam′or·ous	un·han′dled	un·heed′ful
un′fore·see′a·ble	un·free′	un·glazed′	un·hand′some	un·heed′ing
un′fore·seen′	un·fro′zen	un·gloved′	un·hanged′	un·helped′
un′fore·told′	un′ful·filled′	un·gov′erned	un·har′assed	un·help′ful
un′for·giv′a·ble	un·fun′ny	un·gram·mat′i·cal	un·hard′ened	un·her′ald·ed
un′for·giv′en	un·fur′nished	un·grat′i·fied	un·harmed′	un·he·ro′ic
un′for·giv′ing	un·fur′rowed	un·grat′i·fy′ing	un·harm′ful	un·hes′i·tant
un′for·got′ten	un·gal′lant	un·ground′ed	un·har·mo′ni·ous	un·hewn′
un′for·mu·lat′ed	un·gar′nished	un′guar·an·teed′	un·har′nessed	un·hin′dered
un′for·sak′en	un·gath′ered	un·guid′ed	un·har′rowed	un·hon′ored
un′forth·com′ing	un·gen·teel′	un·hack′neyed	un·har′vest·ed	un·hoped′for′
un′for·ti·fied′	un·gen′tle	un·hailed′	un·hatched′	un·housed′
	un·gen′tle·man·ly		un·healed′	

un·hu·man (un hyü′mən) *adj.* **1** not human; devoid of human qualities. **2** inhuman. **3** superhuman.

un·hurt (un hèrt′) *adj.* not hurt; not harmed.

uni– *combining form.* one: *unilateral.* [< L *unus* one]

U·ni·at (yü′nē at′), *n.*, *adj.* —*n.* a member of any Eastern Christian church that is in communion with the Roman Catholic Church and acknowledges the supremacy of the Pope but keeps its own liturgy and organization. —*adj.* of or having to do with such a church or its members. [< Russian *uniyat* < *uniya* union]

u·ni·cam·er·al (yü′nə kam′ər əl) *adj.* having only one house in a lawmaking body: *All Canadian provinces except Quebec have unicameral legislatures.* [< *uni-* + L *camera* chamber]

UNICEF (yün′i sef′) *n.* United Nations Children's Fund (originally, United Nations International Children's Emergency Fund).

u·ni·cel·lu·lar (yü′nə sel′yə lər) *adj.* of an organism, consisting of a single cell. *The amoeba is a unicellular animal.*

u·ni·corn (yü′nə kôrn′) *n.* **1** a legendary animal resembling a horse, and having a single long horn growing from the middle of its forehead. **2** a figure, picture, or representation of this animal, often used as a heraldic bearing. **3** in the Bible, a mistranslation of a Hebrew word referring to a two-horned animal, probably the aurochs (Deuteronomy 33:17). [< L *unicornis* < *unus* one + *cornu* horn]

u·ni·fi·ca·tion (yü′nə fə kā′shən) *n.* **1** a formation into one unit; union: *the unification of many states into one nation.* **2** a making or being made more alike: *The traffic laws of the different provinces need unification.* **3** the condition or state of being unified.

u·ni·form (yü′nə fôrm′) *adj.*, *n.*, *v.* —*adj.* **1** always the same; not changing: *The earth turns around at a uniform rate.* **2** all alike; not varying: *All the bricks are of a uniform size.* **3** not mixed or blended: *lawns of a uniform green.* **4** regular; even: *a uniform pace.* **5** in accordance or agreement with one another; conforming to one standard, rule, or pattern: *uniform answers.* —*n.* the distinctive clothes worn by the members of a group when on duty, by which they may be recognized as belonging to that group: *Soldiers, police officers, and nurses wear uniforms.* —*v.* clothe or furnish with a uniform. [< L *uniformis* < *unus* one + *forma* form] —**u′ni·form′ly,** *adv.* —**u′ni·form′ness,** *n.*
☛ *Syn.* 1, 3. See note at **even.**

u·ni·form·i·ty (yü′nə fôr′mə tē) *n.*, *pl.* **-ties.** a uniform condition or character; sameness throughout.

u·ni·fy (yü′nə fī′) *v.* **-fied, -fy·ing.** make or form into one; unite. [< LL *unificare* < L *unus* one + *facere* make] —**u′ni·fi′er,** *n.*

u·ni·lat·er·al (yü′nə lat′ər əl) *adj.* **1** of, on, or affecting one side only. **2** having all the parts arranged on one side of an axis; turned to one side; one-sided. **3** *Law.* of a contract, etc., affecting one party or person only; done by one side only; putting obligation on one party only: *unilateral disarmament.* **4** concerned with or considering only one side of a matter. **5** *Sociology.* related or descended on only one side of the family. —**u′ni·lat′er·al·ly,** *adv.*

u·ni·lat·er·al·ism (yü′nə lat′ə rə liz′əm *or* yü′nə lat′rə liz′əm) *n.* belief in or advocacy of a unilateral policy, especially in disarmament.

u·ni·lat·er·al·ist (yü′nə lat′ə rə list *or* yü′nə lat′rə list) *adj.*, *n.* —*adj.* of or having to do with unilateralism or unilateralists. —*n.* an advocate or follower of unilateralism.

u·ni·lin·gual (yü′nə ling′gwəl) *adj.* **1** having knowledge or use of only one language. **2** of or having one universal language.

u·ni·lin·gual·ism (yü′nə ling′gwə liz′əm) *n.* **1** the state, condition, or policy of being unilingual. **2** advocacy of or belief in one universal language.

un·im·peach·a·ble (un′im pēch′ə bəl) *adj.* free from fault; blameless. —**un′im·peach′a·bly,** *adv.*

un·in·spired (un′in spīrd′) *adj.* **1** not inspired. **2** dull; tiresome.

un·in·tel·li·gi·ble (un′in tel′ə jə bəl) *adj.* that cannot be understood. —**un′in·tel′li·gi·bly,** *adv.*

un·in·ter·est·ed (un in′tris tid *or* un in′tə res′tid) *adj.* not interested; showing no interest. —**un·in′ter·est·ed·ly,** *adv.*
☛ *Usage.* See note at **interested.**

un·in·ter·rupt·ed (un′in tə rup′tid) *adj.* without interruption; continuous. —**un′in·ter·rupt′ed·ly,** *adv.*

un·ion (yün′yən) *n.* **1** the act of uniting or the state of being united: *The United States was formed by the union of thirteen former British colonies.* **2** something formed by combining two or more members or parts: *The ten provinces of Canada form a union.* **3** a group of workers joined together to protect and promote their interests; labor union; trade union. **4** marriage. **5** any of various devices for connecting parts of machinery or apparatus, especially a piece to join pipes or tubes together. [ME < OF < LL *unio, -onis* < *unus* one]
☛ *Syn.* **1. Union, unity** = a forming or being one. **Union** emphasizes the joining together of two or more things, people, or groups to form a whole, or the state of being joined together as a unit: *A combat team is formed by the union of infantry and other forces.* **Unity** emphasizes and applies to the oneness of the whole that is formed: *The strength of any group is in its unity.*

un·ion·ism (yün′yən iz′əm) *n.* **1** the principle of union. **2** an attachment to a union. **3** the system, principles, or methods of labor unions.

un·ion·ist (yün′yən ist) *n.* **1** a person who promotes or advocates union. **2** a member of a labor union. **3 Unionist,** *Historical.* **a** a person who was in favor of union among the provinces of British North America, especially of Upper and Lower Canada. **b** a supporter of the federal government of the United States during the Civil War. **c** a person who opposed the political separation of Ireland from Great Britain. **d** a person who favors keeping Northern Ireland as part of the United Kingdom.

un·ion·i·za·tion (yün′yən ə zā′shən *or* -ī zā′shən) *n.* the act of unionizing or the state of being unionized.

un·ion·ize (yün′yən īz′) *v.* **-ized, -iz·ing. 1** form into a labor union. **2** organize under a labor union. **3** join in a labor union.

The Union Jack

Union Jack the red, white, and blue flag of the United Kingdom, formed by combining the crosses of St. George, St. Andrew, and St. Patrick, for England, Scotland, and Ireland respectively.

Union Na·tion·ale (nash′ē ən al′; *French*, Y nyôn′ nä syô näl′) a political party in Quebec, formed in the early 1930's.

union shop a business establishment that by agreement hires only employees who are, or will become, members of a labor union.

union station a station used jointly by two or more railways.

u·nique (yü nēk′) *adj.* **1** having no like or equal; being the only one of its kind. **2** *Informal.* rare; unusual. [< F < L *unicus*] —**u·nique′ly,** *adv.* —**u·nique′ness,** *n.*
☛ *Usage.* In formal English **unique** means 'being one of a kind,' and so it cannot be compared or qualified; something is either unique or not. In informal English **unique** is sometimes used with **more** or **most** and more often with a qualifier like **quite, rather,** or **really:** *Her clothes are rather unique.* This usage should be avoided in careful speech and writing.

u·ni·sex (yü′nə seks′) *adj.* of, having to do with, or designating clothing, hairstyles, etc. that are worn by members of both sexes.

u·ni·son (yü′nə sən *or* yü′nə zən) *n.* **1** doing together as one, at the same time, etc.: *The feet of marching soldiers move in unison. They spoke in unison.* **2** *Music.* **a** identity of pitch of two or more tones. **b** a performing together by voices, instruments, etc. of the

same′melody, etc., at the same pitch or an octave apart. **c** the interval between two tones of the same or different quality but identical pitch; prime[1]. [< Med.L *unisonus* sounding the same < LL *unisonus* in immediate sequence in the scale < L *unus* one + *sonus* sound]

u·nit (yü′nit) *n.* **1** a single thing or person. **2** any group of things or persons considered as one. **3** one of the individuals or groups of which a whole is composed: *The body consists of units called cells.* **4** a standard quantity or amount, used as a basis for measuring: *A metre is a unit of length; a minute is a unit of time.* **5** the smallest whole number; l. **6** regiment. **7** in schools, a section of a course, usually on one theme or topic. [probably < *unity*]

Unit. Unitarian.

U·ni·tar·i·an (yü′nə ter′ē ən) *n., adj.* —*n.* a member of a religious denomination based on the belief that God exists as one Being, not as the Father, the Son, and the Holy Spirit. Unitarians accept the moral teachings of Jesus and believe in reason, liberal social action, and tolerance of different religious views. —*adj.* of or having to do with Unitarians.

U·ni·tar·i·an·ism (yü′nə ter′ē ən iz′əm) *n.* the doctrines or beliefs of Unitarians.

u·ni·tar·y (yü′nə ter′ē) *adj.* **1** of or having to do with a unit or units. **2** having to do with unity. **3** like that of a unit; used as a unit.

u·nite (yü nīt′) *v.* **u·nit·ed, u·nit·ing.** **1** join together; make one; combine: *to unite bricks with mortar in a wall.* **2** bring together; amalgamate or consolidate into one body; join in action, interest, opinion, feeling, etc.: *Several firms were united to form one company.* **3** join by mutual pledging, covenant, or other formal bond; cause to become a union: *to unite a man and a woman in marriage.* **4** have or exhibit in union or combination: *a child uniting his father's temper and his mother's red hair.* **5** become one; join in action, etc. [< L *unitus,* pp. of *unire* < *unus* one] —**u·nit′er,** *n.*
☞ *Syn.* **1, 2.** See note at **join.**

u·nit·ed (yü nīt′id) *adj.* **1** joined together to make one. **2** joined together.

United Church of Canada a Christian church formed in 1924-1925 from a union of the Canadian Methodist and Congregationalist churches and two thirds of the congregations of the Canadian Presbyterian Church, whose doctrines combine the doctrines of the founding churches.

United Empire Loyalist any of the Loyalists in the American Revolution who emigrated to what are now Ontario and the Maritimes, or their descendants; especially, any of the people (or their descendants) who are officially recorded as having emigrated before the peace of 1783. Compare **Loyalist.**

United Nations **1** a world-wide organization devoted to establishing world peace and promoting economic and social welfare. The United Nations charter was put into effect on October 24, 1945. **2** the nations that belong to this organization: *Canada is one of the United Nations.* **3** the Allies (def. 2). *Abbrev.:* UN or U.N.

unit fraction a common fraction in which the numerator is l. *Examples:* $\frac{1}{8}, \frac{1}{100}.$

u·ni·ty (yü′nə tē) *n., pl.* **-ties.** **1** oneness; being united: *A circle has more unity than a row of dots. A nation has more unity than a group of tribes.* **2** a union of parts forming a complex whole. **3** harmony: *Brothers and sisters should live together in unity.* **4** the number one (l). **5** an arrangement and choice of material to give a single effect, main idea, etc.: *A pleasing picture has unity; so has a well-written composition.* **6 the unities,** *pl.* the rules of dramatic structure derived from Aristotle, according to which a play should have one main action occurring on one day in one place. [ME < L *unitas < unus* one]
☞ *Syn.* **1.** See note at **union.**

Univ. **1** University. **2** Universalist.

UNIVAC (yü′nə vak′) *n. Trademark.* an electronic computer having a binary numbering system. [< *Universal Automatic Computer*]

u·ni·va·lence (yü′nə vā′ləns *or* yü niv′ə ləns) *n.* the state of being univalent.

u·ni·va·lent (yü′nə vā′lənt *or* yü niv′ə lənt) *adj.* having a valence of one. [< *uni-* + L *valens, -entis,* ppr. of *valere* be worth]

u·ni·valve (yü′nə valv′) *n., adj.* —*n.* **1** a mollusc having a shell consisting of a single piece, called a valve. Gastropods are univalves. **2** the shell of such a mollusc. —*adj.* of, having to do with, or designating such molluscs.

u·ni·ver·sal (yü′nə vèr′səl) *adj., n.* —*adj.* **1** of, belonging to, concerning, or done by all: *Food, fire, and shelter are universal needs.* **2** of or having to do with the universe; existing everywhere:

hat, āge, fär; let, ēqual, tèrm; it, īce
hot, ōpen, ôrder; oil, out; cup, pùt, rüle,
əbove, takən, pencəl, lemən, circəs
ch, child; ng, long; sh, ship
th, thin; ᴛʜ, then; zh, measure

The law of gravity is universal. **3** covering a whole group of persons, things, cases, etc.; general. **4** adaptable to different sizes, angles, kinds of work, etc. **5** constituting, existing as, or regarded as a complete whole; complete; entire; whole: *the universal cosmos.* **6** accomplished in or comprising all, or very many, subjects; wide-ranging: *universal knowledge.* **7** allowing or providing for movement toward any direction: *a universal joint.*
—*n.* **1** a proposition that asserts or denies something of every member of a class. *Example:* All men are mortal. **2** something universal, especially a person or thing that is universally powerful, current, etc. [ME < L *universalis < universus.* See UNIVERSE.]
—**u·ni·ver′sal·ly,** *adv.*

U·ni·ver·sal·ism (yü′nə vèr′səl iz′əm) *n.* the doctrines or beliefs of Universalists.

U·ni·ver·sal·ist (yü′nə vèr′səl ist) *n., adj.* —*n.* a member of a Christian church holding the belief that all people will finally be saved. —*adj.* of or having to do with Universalists.

u·ni·ver·sal·i·ty (yü′nə vèr sal′ə tē) *n., pl.* **-ties.** the fact or condition of being universal.

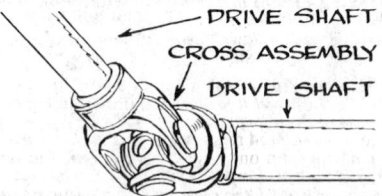

A universal joint on the drive shaft of an automobile

universal joint **1** a joint that moves in any direction. **2** a coupling for transmitting power from one shaft to another when they are not in line.

u·ni·verse (yü′nə vèrs′) *n.* **1** all things; everything that exists, including all space and matter. **2** the earth as inhabited by, and often including, mankind. **3** a field of thought, area of study, etc. considered as being complete and independent: *the universe of chemistry.* **4** universe of discourse. [< L *universum,* originally adj., whole, turned into one, neut. of *universus < unus* one + *vertere* turn]

universe of discourse *Logic and mathematics.* the set of things under discussion or consideration.

u·ni·ver·si·ty (yü′nə vèr′sə tē) *n., pl.* **-ties.** **1** an educational institution attended after secondary school for studies leading to a degree. Universities offer advanced courses in general subjects such as literature, history, and science, and also often have schools of law, medicine, business, etc. **2** a building or buildings used by a university. [ME < OF < Med.L *universitas* corporation < L *universitas* aggregate, whole < *universus.* See UNIVERSE.]

un·joint (un joint′) *v.* take apart the joints of.

un·just (un just′) *adj.* not just; not fair: *It is unjust to punish lawbreakers who are insane.* —**un·just′ly,** *adv.* —**un·just′ness,** *n.*

un·kempt (un kempt′) *adj.* **1** neglected; untidy. [< *un-*[1] + OE *cembed* combed, pp. of *cemban < camb* comb]

un·kind (un kīnd′) *adj.* harsh; cruel. —**un·kind′ness,** *n.*

un·kind·ly (un kīnd′lē) *adj., adv.* —*adj.* harsh; unfavorable. —*adv.* in an unkind way; harshly.

un·knit (un nit′) *v.* **-knit·ted** *or* **-knit, -knit·ting.** **1** untie or unfasten (a knot, etc.). **2** ravel out (something knitted). **3** smooth out (something wrinkled).

un·known (un nōn′) *adj., n.* —*adj.* not familiar or known; unidentified, unexplored, etc.: *an unknown country, an unknown number.* —*n.* **1** a person or thing that is unknown: *The diver descended into the unknown. The main actor in this movie is an unknown.* **2** *Mathematics.* a symbol, as in an equation, for a quantity whose value is to be found.

Unknown Soldier an unidentified soldier killed in battle, who is buried in a national monument and honored as the representative of all unidentified war dead of his country.

un·la·bored or **un·la·boured** (un lā′bərd) *adj.* 1 effortless; spontaneous; not stiff or stilted: *unlabored verses.* 2 not produced or cultivated by labor or effort: *unlabored fields.*

un·lace (un lās′) *v.* **-laced, -lac·ing.** undo the laces of.

un·lade (un lād′) *v.* **-lad·ed, -lad·en** or **-lad·ed, -lad·ing.** unload.

un·latch (un lach′) *v.* unfasten or open by lifting a latch.

un·law·ful (un lo′fəl *or* un lô′fəl) *adj.* 1 contrary to the law; against the law; forbidden; illegal. 2 *Archaic.* illegitimate. —**un·law′ful·ly,** *adv.* —**un·law′ful·ness,** *n.*

un·learn (un lern′) *v.* get rid of (ideas, habits, or tendencies); forget.

un·learn·ed (un ler′nid *for 1 and 4;* un lèrnd′ *for 2 and 3*) *adj.* 1 not educated; ignorant. 2 not learned; known without being learned: *A baby's ability to suck is unlearned.* 3 not showing education.

un·leash (un lēsh′) *v.* 1 release from a leash: *to unleash a dog.* 2 let loose: *to unleash one's anger.*

un·leav·ened (un lev′ənd) *adj.* not leavened. Unleavened bread is made without yeast.

un·less (ən les′ *or* un les′) *conj.* if it were not that; if not: *We'll go unless it rains.* [ME *on lesse* (*that*) *on* a less condition (than)]

un·let·tered (un let′ərd) *adj.* 1 not educated. 2 not able to read or write.

un·like (un līk′) *adj., prep.* —*adj.* 1 not like; different: *The two problems are quite unlike.* 2 different in size or number; unequal: *unlike weights.* 3 *Archaic or dialect.* unlikely. —*prep.* different from: *act unlike others.*

un·like·li·hood (un līk′lē hud′) *n.* improbability.

un·like·ly (un līk′lē) *adj.* 1 not likely; not probable: *He is unlikely to win the race.* 2 not likely to succeed: *an unlikely undertaking.* —**un·like′li·ness,** *n.*

un·like·ness (un līk′nis) *n.* the fact of being unlike; difference.

un·lim·ber (un lim′bər) *v.* 1 detach the limber or forepart of the carriage from an artillery piece. 2 prepare for action.

un·lim·it·ed (un lim′ə tid) *adj.* 1 without limits; boundless: *The boy seems to have unlimited energy.* 2 not restrained; not restricted: *a government of unlimited power.* —**un·lim′it·ed·ness,** *n.*

un·load (un lōd′) *v.* 1 remove (a load). 2 take the load from. 3 get rid of. 4 remove powder, shot, bullets, or shells from (a gun). 5 discharge a cargo: *The ship is unloading.* —**un·load′er,** *n.*

un·lock (un lok′) *v.* 1 open the lock of; open (anything firmly closed). 2 release; let loose. 3 disclose; reveal. 4 become unlocked.

un·looked–for (un lukt′fôr′) *adj.* unexpected; unforeseen.

un·loose (un lüs′) *v.* **-loosed, -loos·ing.** let loose; set free; release.

un·loos·en (un lü′sən) *v.* unloose; loosen.

un·love·ly (un luv′lē) *adj.* without beauty or charm; unpleasing in appearance; unpleasant; objectionable; disagreeable. —**un·love′li·ness,** *n.*

un·luck·y (un luk′ē) *adj.* 1 not lucky; unfortunate. 2 bringing or thought to bring bad luck: *The number 13 is unlucky.* —**un·luck′i·ly,** *adv.* —**un·luck′i·ness,** *n.*

un·make (un māk′) *v.* **-made, -mak·ing.** 1 undo; destroy; ruin. 2 deprive of rank or station; depose.

un·man (un man′) *v.* **-manned, -man·ning.** 1 deprive of the qualities of a man. 2 weaken or break down the spirit of. 3 deprive of virility or manhood; castrate. 4 deprive of men: *to unman a ship.*

un·man·ly (un man′lē) *adj.* not manly; weak; cowardly. —**un·man′li·ness,** *n.*

un·manned (un mand′) *adj.* not operated by or carrying a crew or other people: *an unmanned spacecraft.*

un·man·ner·ly (un man′ər lē) *adj., adv.* —*adj.* having bad manners; discourteous. —*adv.* with bad manners; rudely. —**un·man′ner·li·ness,** *n.*

un·mar·ried (un mar′ēd *or* un mer′ēd) *adj.* not married; single.

un·mask (un mask′) *v.* 1 remove a mask or disguise: *The guests unmasked at midnight.* 2 take off a mask or disguise from. 3 expose the true character of: *to unmask a hypocrite.* 4 reveal the presence of (guns, etc.) by firing: *to unmask a battery.*

un·match·a·ble (un mach′ə bəl) *adj.* that cannot be matched or equalled.

un·mean·ing (un mē′ning) *adj.* 1 without meaning. 2 without sense; without expression: *an unmeaning stare.* —**un·mean′ing·ly,** *adv.*

un·meas·ured (un mezh′ərd) *adj.* 1 not measured; unlimited; measureless. 2 unrestrained; intemperate.

un·meet (un mēt′) *adj.* not fit; not proper; unsuitable.

un·men·tion·a·ble (un men′shən ə bəl *or* un mensh′nə bəl) *adj., n.* —*adj.* that cannot be mentioned; not fit to be spoken about. —*n.* **unmentionables,** *pl.* things considered improper subjects of conversation; things not to be mentioned or discussed. —**un·men′tion·a·ble·ness,** *n.*

un·mer·ci·ful (un mèr′si fəl) *adj.* 1 having or showing no mercy; cruel. 2 excessive: *He kept us waiting an unmerciful length of time.* —**un·mer′ci·ful·ly,** *adv.* —**un·mer′ci·ful·ness,** *n.*

un·mind·ful (un mīnd′fəl) *adj.* regardless; heedless; careless: *He went ahead despite our warning and unmindful of the results.* —**un·mind′ful·ly,** *adv.*

un·mis·tak·a·ble (un′mis tāk′ə bəl) *adj.* that cannot be mistaken or misunderstood; clear; plain; evident. —**un′mis·tak′a·ble·ness,** *n.* —**un′mis·tak′a·bly,** *adv.*

un·mit·i·gat·ed (un mit′ə gāt′id) *adj.* 1 not softened or lessened: *unmitigated harshness.* 2 unqualified or absolute: *an unmitigated fraud.*

un·moor (un mür′) *v. Nautical.* 1 release the moorings of (a vessel). 2 weigh all the anchors of (a vessel) but one.

un·mor·al (un môr′əl) *adj.* neither moral nor immoral; not perceiving or involving right and wrong; amoral. —**un·mor′al·ly,** *adv.*

un·moved (un müvd′) *adj.* 1 not moved; firm. 2 not disturbed; indifferent.

un·muz·zle (un muz′əl) *v.* **-zled, -zling.** 1 take off a muzzle from (a dog, etc.). 2 free from restraint; allow to speak or write freely.

un·nat·u·ral (un nach′rəl *or* un nach′ə rəl) *adj.* 1 not in accordance with the usual course of nature. 2 at variance with natural feeling or normal decency, morality, etc.: *unnatural cruelty.* 3 artificial or affected: *an unnatural laugh.* —**un·nat′u·ral·ly,** *adv.* —**un·nat′u·ral·ness,** *n.*

un·nec·es·sar·y (un nes′ə ser′ē) *adj.* not necessary; needless. —**un·nec′es·sar′i·ly,** *adv.* —**un·nec′es·sar′i·ness,** *n.*

un·nerve (un nèrv′) *v.* **-nerved, -nerv·ing.** deprive of firmness or self-control.

un·num·bered (un num′bərd) *adj.* 1 not numbered; not counted: *The pages of the composition were left unnumbered.* 2 too many to count: *There are unnumbered fish in the ocean.*

UNO or **U.N.O.** United Nations Organization.

un·know′ing	un·lov′a·ble	un·matched′	un·min′gled	un·nav′i·ga·ble
un·la′belled	un·loved′	un·mat′ed	un·mirth′ful	un·nav′i·gat′ed
un·la′dy-like′	un·lov′ing	un·ma′tured′	un′mis·tak′en	un·need′ed
un·laid′	un·lu·bri·cat′ed	un·mixed′	un·mixed′	un·need′ful
un·la·ment′ed	un·mag′ni·fied′	un·meas′ur·a·ble	un·mod′i·fied′	un′ne·go′tia·ble
un·laun′dered	un·maid′en·ly	un·med′i·cal	un·mod′u·lat′ed	un′ne·go′ti·at′ed
un·leased′	un·mail′a·ble	un·med′i·cat′ed	un·mo′lest·ed	un·neigh′bor·ly
un·li′censed	un·mailed′	un·me′lo′di·ous	un·mo′ti·vat′ed	un·not′ed
un·life′like′	un·mal′le·a·ble	un·melt′ed	un·mould′ed	un·note′wor′thy
un·light′ed	un·man′age·a·ble	un·mem′or·a·ble	un·mount′ed	un·no′tice·a·ble
un·lik′a·ble	un′ma·nip′u·lat′ed	un·mem′o·rized′	un·mourned′	un·no′ticed
un·lined′	un·man′nered	un·mend′ed	un·mov′a·ble	un·nur′tured
un·link′	un′man·u·fac′tured	un·men′tioned	un·mov′ing	un·ob·jec′tion·a·ble
un·liq′ue·fied′	un·mapped′	un·mer′chant·a·ble	un·mown′	un·o·bliged′
un·liq′ui·dat′ed	un·marked′	un·mer′it·ed	un·mu′si·cal	un·o·blig′ing
un·lit′	un·mar′ket·a·ble	un′me·thod′i·cal	un·mys′ti·fied′	un·ob·scured′
un·lit′tered	un·marred′	un·met′ri·cal	un·nam′a·ble	un·ob·serv′a·ble
un·liv′a·ble	un·mar′riage·a·ble	un·mil′i·tar′y	un·named′	un·ob·serv′ant
un·lo′cat·ed	un·mas′tered	un·milled′	un·nat′u·ral·ized′	

un·ob·served (un′əb zėrvd′) *adj.* not observed; not noticed; disregarded.

un·ob·tru·sive (un′əb trü′siv) *adj.* not noticeable or intrusive; inconspicuous. —**un′ob·tru′sive·ly**, *adv.* —**un′ob·tru′sive·ness**, *n.*

un·oc·cu·pied (un ok′yə pīd′) *adj.* **1** not occupied; vacant: *an unoccupied parking space.* **2** not in action or use; idle: *an unoccupied mind.*

un·or·gan·ized (un ôr′gən īzd′) *adj.* **1** not formed into an organized or systematized whole. **2** not organized into labor unions. **3** not being a living organism. An enzyme is an unorganized ferment.

un·pack (un pak′) *v.* **1** take out (things packed in a box, trunk, etc.). **2** take things out of. **3** take out things packed.

un·paid (un pād′) *adj.* **1** not paid: *unpaid bills.* **2** without pay: *Candystripers are unpaid workers.*

un·pal·at·a·ble (un pal′ə tə bəl) *adj.* not agreeable to the taste; distasteful; unpleasant. —**un·pal′at·a·ble·ness**, *n.* —**un·pal′at·a·bly**, *adv.*

un·par·al·leled (un par′ə leld′ *or* un per′ə leld′) *adj.* having no parallel; unequalled; matchless.

un·par·lia·men·ta·ry (un′pär lə men′tə rē *or* un′pär lə men′trē) *adj.* not in acccordance with parliamentary practice.

un·peg (un peg′) *v.* **-pegged, -peg·ging. 1** remove the pegs from. **2** loosen or unfasten by removing pegs. **3** remove controls on the free rise and fall of (wages, prices, etc.).

un·peo·pled (un pē′pəld) *adj.* not inhabited; deprived of people.

un·pick (un pik′) *v.* remove or take out stitches from knitting, sewing, etc.

un·pile (un pīl′) *v.* **-piled, -pil·ing. 1** take or remove from a pile. **2** take a pile or heap apart.

un·pin (un pin′) *v.* **-pinned, -pin·ning.** take out a pin or pins from; unfasten.

un·pleas·ant (un plez′ənt) *adj.* not pleasant; disagreeable. —**un·pleas′ant·ly**, *adv.*

un·pleas·ant·ness (un plez′ənt nis) *n.* **1** the quality of being unpleasant. **2** something unpleasant. **3** a quarrel.

un·plug (un plug′) *v.* **-plugged, -plug·ging. 1** open or set free (something) by removing a plug or stopper. **2** disconnect (an electric light, appliance, etc.) by removing the plug from an outlet.

un·plumbed (un plumd′) *adj.* **1** not fathomed; not measured; of unknown depth. **2** not fully explored or understood: *an unplumbed area of physics.* **3** having no plumbing.

un·pop·u·lar (un pop′yə lər) *adj.* not generally liked: *an unpopular government policy. He was always unpopular with his colleagues.* —**un·pop′u·lar·ly**, *adv.*

un·pop·u·lar·i·ty (un′pop yə lar′ə tē *or* -ler′ə tē) *n.* lack of popularity; the fact of being unpopular.

un·prac·tised (un prak′tist) *adj.* **1** not skilled; not expert. **2** not put into practice; not used. Also, **unpracticed.**

un·prec·e·dent·ed (un pres′ə den′tid *or* un prē′sə den′tid) *adj.* having no precedent; never done before; never known before.

un·prej·u·diced (un prej′ə dist) *adj.* **1** without prejudice; impartial. **2** not impaired.

un·pre·pared (un′pri perd′) *adj.* **1** not made ready; not worked

hat, āge, fär; let, ēqual, tèrm; it, īce
hot, ōpen, ôrder; oil, out; cup, pùt, rüle,
əbove, takən, pencəl, lemən, circəs
ch, child; ng, long; sh, ship
th, thin; ŧH, then; zh, measure

out ahead: *an unprepared speech.* **2** not ready: *a person unprepared to answer.*

un·pre·tend·ing (un′pri tend′ing) *adj.* unassuming; modest. —**un′pre·tend′ing·ly**, *adv.*

un·pre·ten·tious (un′pri ten′shəs) *adj.* modest. —**un′pre·ten′tious·ly**, *adv.* —**un′pre·ten′tious·ness**, *n.*

un·prin·ci·pled (un prin′sə pəld) *adj.* lacking good moral principles; bad.
☛ *Syn.* See note at **unscrupulous.**

un·print·a·ble (un prin′tə bəl) *adj.* not fit to be printed.

un·pro·fes·sion·al (un′prə fesh′ən əl *or* un′prə fesh′nəl) *adj.* **1** contrary to professional etiquette; unbecoming in members of a profession. **2** not having to do with or connected with a profession. **3** not belonging to a profession. —**un′pro·fes′sion·al·ly**, *adv.*

un·prof·it·a·ble (un prof′ə tə bəl) *adj.* producing no gain or advantage. —**un·prof′it·a·ble·ness**, *n.* —**un·prof′it·a·bly**, *adv.*

un·pro·voked (un′prə vōkt′) *adj.* without provocation.

un·qual·i·fied (un kwol′ə fīd′) *adj.* **1** not qualified; not fitted. **2** not modified, limited, or restricted in any way: *unqualified praise.* **3** complete; absolute: *an unqualified failure.*

un·ques·tion·a·ble (un kwes′chən ə bəl) *adj.* **1** beyond dispute or doubt; certain: *an unquestionable advantage.* **2** impeccable in quality or nature; accepted without question; unexceptionable. —**un·ques′tion·a·ble·ness**, *n.* —**un·ques′tion·a·bly**, *adv.*

un·ques·tioned (un kwes′chənd) *adj.* not questioned; not disputed.

un·qui·et (un kwī′ət) *adj.* restless; disturbed; uneasy. —**un·qui′et·ly**, *adv.* —**un·qui′et·ness**, *n.*

un·quote (un kwōt′) *v.* **-quot·ed, -quot·ing.** mark the end of a quotation.

un·rav·el (un rav′əl) *v.* **-elled** *or* **-eled, -el·ling** *or* **-el·ing. 1** separate the threads of: *The kitten unravelled Grandma's knitting.* **2** come apart; ravel: *My knitted gloves are unravelling at the wrist.* **3** bring or come out of a tangled state; clear up: *to unravel a mystery.*

un·read (un red′) *adj.* **1** not read: *an unread book.* **2** not having read much: *an unread person.*

un·read·y (un red′ē) *adj.* **1** not ready; not prepared. **2** not prompt or quick. —**un·read′i·ly**, *adv.* —**un·read′i·ness**, *n.*

un·re·al (un rē′əl) *adj.* imaginary; not real; not substantial; fanciful. —**un·re′al·ly**, *adv.*

un·re·al·i·ty (un′rē al′ə tē) *n., pl.* **-ties. 1** lack of reality or substance; an imaginary or fanciful quality. **2** impractical or visionary character or tendency; impracticality. **3** something unreal: *Unrealities, such as elves and goblins, are fun to imagine.*

---

un′ob·serv′ing
un′ob·struct′ed
un′ob·tain′a·ble
un′ob·tained′
un′ob·trud′ing
un′ob·tru′sive
un′ob·tru′sive·ness
un·oc·ca′sioned
un′of·fend′ed
un′of·fend′ing
un′of·fen′sive
un·of′fered
un·of·fi′cial
un·of·fi′cious
un·oiled′
un·o′pened
un·op·posed′
un·op·pres′sive
un·or·dained′
un·or′dered
un·o·rig′i·nal
un·or′na·men·tal
un·or′na·ment·ed
un·or′tho·dox
un·os·ten·ta′tious
un·owned′
un·pac′i·fied′
un·paint′ed

un·paired′
un·pal′at·a·ble
un·par·don·a·ble
un·par′doned
un·par·ti′tioned
un·pas′teur·ized′
un·pa′tri·ot′ic
un·paved′
un·peace′a·ble
un·peace′ful
un·pen′sioned
un·pep′pered
un′per·ceived′
un′per·ceiv′ing
un′per·cep′tive
un·per·fect′ed
un·per·formed′
un·per·plexed′
un·per·suad′ed
un·per·sua′sive
un·per·turb′a·ble
un·per·turbed′
un·pe·rused′
un·phil·o·soph′ic
un·phil·o·soph′i·cal
un·pho·net′ic
un·pierced′
un·pit′ied
un·pit′y·ing

un·placed′
un·plagued′
un·planned′
un·plant′ed
un·play′a·ble
un·played′
un·pleased′
un·pleas′ing
un·pledged′
un·pli′ant
un·ploughed′
un·plowed′
un·plucked′
un·po·et′ic
un·po·et′i·cal
un·point′ed
un·poised′
un·po·lar·ized′
un·po·liced′
un·pol′ished
un·po·lit′i·cal
un·polled′
un·pol·lut′ed
un·pol′y·mer·ized′
un·pop′u·lat′ed
un·posed′
un·post′ed
un·prac′ti·ca·ble
un·prac′ti·cal

un·praised′
un·pre·dict′a·ble
un·pre·dict′ed
un·pre·med′i·tat′ed
un·pre·pos·sess′ing
un·pre·scribed′
un·pre·sent′a·ble
un·pre·served′
un·pressed′
un·pre·sump′tu·ous
un·pret′ty
un·pre·vail′ing
un·pre·vent′a·ble
un·print′ed
un·priv′i·leged
un·prized′
un·pro·cessed′
un·pro·claimed′
un·pro·cur′a·ble
un·pro·duc′tive
un·pro·faned′
un·pro·fessed′
un·pro·gres′sive
un·pro·hib′it·ed
un·pro·ject′ed
un·prom′is·ing
un·prompt′ed
un·pro·nounce′a·ble
un·pro·nounced′

un′pro·pi′tious
un′pro·por′tioned
un·pro·posed′
un·pros′per·ous
un·pro·tect′ed
un·pro·test′ed
un·pro·test′ing
un·proved′
un·prov′en
un·pro·vid′ed
un·pruned′
un·pub′li·cized′
un·pub′lished
un·punc′tu·al
un·pun′ished
un·pur′chas·a·ble
un·pu′ri·fied′
un·pur′posed
un·pur·su′ing
un·quail′ing
un·quelled′
un·quench′a·ble
un·quenched′
un·quot′a·ble
un·raised′
un·ran′somed
un·rat′ed
un·rat′i·fied′
un·read′a·ble

un·rea·son·a·ble (un rē′zən ə bəl or un rĕz′nə bəl) adj. 1 not reasonable; not sensible: an unreasonable fear of the dark. 2 not moderate; excessive: I think $90 is an unreasonable price for those shoes. —**un·rea′son·a·ble·ness**, n. —**un·rea′son·a·bly**,

un·rea·son·ing (un rē′zən ing or un rĕz′ning) adj. not reasoning; not using reason; reasonless. —**un·rea′son·ing·ly**, adv.

un·re·con·struct·ed (un′rē kən struk′tid) adj. not reconciled to change; adhering to old and outworn customs, standards, laws, etc.

un·reel (un rēl′) v. unwind from a reel.

un·re·gard·ed (un′ri gär′did) adj. disregarded; not heeded.

un·re·gen·er·a·cy (un′ri jen′ər ə sē) n. unregenerate condition; enmity toward God; wickedness.

un·re·gen·er·ate (un′ri jen′ər it) adj. 1 not born again spiritually; not turned to the love of God. 2 wicked; bad. —**un′re·gen′er·ate·ly**, adv. —**un′re·gen′er·ate·ness**, n.

un·re·lent·ing (un′ri len′ting) adj. 1 not yielding to feelings of kindness or compassion; merciless. 2 not slackening or relaxing in effort, determination, speed, etc. —**un′re·lent′ing·ly**, adv. —**un′re·lent′ing·ness**, n.
☛ Syn. 1. See note at **inflexible**.

un·re·li·a·bil·i·ty (un′ri lī′ə bil′ə tē) n. lack of reliability.

un·re·li·a·ble (un′ri lī′ə bəl) adj. not reliable; not to be depended on. —**un′re·li′a·bly**, adv.

un·re·li·gious (un′ri lij′əs) adj. 1 irreligious. 2 non-religious; not connected with religion.

un·re·mit·ting (un′ri mit′ing) adj. never stopping; not slackening; maintained steadily: unremitting vigilance. —**un′re·mit′ting·ly**, adv.

un·re·served (un′ri zėrvd′) adj. 1 frank; open: an unreserved manner. 2 not restricted or qualified; without reservation: unreserved praise. 3 not kept for a special person or purpose: unreserved seats.

un·re·serv·ed·ly (un′ri zėr′vid lē) adv. 1 frankly; openly. 2 without reservation or restriction.

un·rest (un rest′) n. 1 lack of ease and quiet; restlessness. 2 an agitation or disturbance amounting almost to rebellion.

un·re·strained (un′ri strānd′) adj. 1 not constrained; spontaneous or free: unrestrained joy. 2 immoderate or uncontrolled: unrestrained urban sprawl.

un·right·eous (un rī′chəs) adj. wicked; sinful; unjust. [OE unrihtwīs] —**un·right′eous·ly**, adv. —**un·right′eous·ness**, n.

un·ripe (un rīp′) adj. 1 not ripe; green. 2 of persons, plans, etc., not fully developed or grown; immature. —**un·ripe′ness**, n.

un·ri·valled or **un·ri·valed** (un rī′vəld) adj. having no rival; without an equal.

un·roll (un rōl′) v. 1 open or spread out (something rolled). 2 become opened or spread out. 3 reveal or become revealed, especially gradually: Our interest increased as the story unrolled.

UNRRA (un′rə) United Nations Relief and Rehabilitation Administration.

un·ruf·fled (un ruf′əld) adj. 1 not ruffled; smooth. 2 not disturbed; calm.

un·ruled (un rüld′) adj. 1 not kept under control; not governed. 2 not marked with lines: unruled paper.

un·ru·ly (un rü′lē) adj. hard to rule or control: an unruly crowd, an unruly horse. —**un·ru′li·ness**, n.
☛ Syn. Unruly, ungovernable = hard or impossible to control. Unruly = not inclined to obey or accept discipline or restraint, and suggests getting out of hand and becoming disorderly, contrary, or obstinately willful, resisting or defying attempts to bring under control: The angry mob become unruly. Ungovernable = incapable of being controlled or restrained, either because never subjected to rule or direction or because of escape from it: One of the circus lions became ungovernable.

un·sad·dle (un sad′əl) v. -dled, -dling. 1 take the saddle off (a horse). 2 cause to fall from a horse.

un·safe (un sāf′) adj. dangerous. —**un·safe′ly**, adv. —**un·safe′ness**, n.

un·said (un sed′) adj. not said or spoken.

un·sat·u·rat·ed (un sach′ə rā′tid) adj. 1 not saturated; not thoroughly wet. 2 of a solution, able to dissolve or absorb more of a substance. 3 of an organic compound, containing double or triple bonds between carbon atoms, thus able to undergo reactions in which other elements or radicals are taken on.

un·sa·vor·y or **un·sa·vour·y** (un sā′vər ē or un sāv′rē) adj. 1 tasteless. 2 unpleasant in taste or smell. 3 morally unpleasant; offensive: That man has an unsavory reputation. —**un·sa′vor·i·ly** or **un·sa′vour·i·ly**, adv. —**un·sa′vor·i·ness** or **un·sa′vour·i·ness**, n.

un·say (un sā′) v. -said, -say·ing. take back or cancel something said: What is said cannot be unsaid.

un·scathed (un skāᵺd′) adj. not harmed; uninjured.

un·schooled (un sküld′) adj. not schooled; not taught.

un·sci·en·tif·ic (un′sī ən tif′ik) adj. 1 not in accordance with the facts or principles of science: an unscientific notion. 2 not acting in accordance with such facts or principles: an unscientific farmer. —**un′sci·en·tif′i·cal·ly**, adv.

un·scram·ble (un skram′bəl) v. -bled, -bling. 1 reduce from confusion to order; bring out of a scrambled condition. 2 restore to the original condition, make no longer scrambled: unscramble a radio message. —**un·scram′bler**, n.

un·screw (un skrü′) v. 1 take out the screw or screws from. 2 loosen or take off by turning; untwist.

un·scru·pu·lous (un skrü′pyə ləs) adj. not careful about right or wrong; without principles or conscience: The unscrupulous gambler cheated. —**un·scru′pu·lous·ly**, adv. —**un·scru′pu·lous·ness**, n.
☛ Syn. Unscrupulous, unprincipled = having or showing no regard for what is morally right. Unscrupulous, describing a person's character, acts, or words, means not held back by any scruples of conscience, any doubts about the morality or justice of what one is doing or about to do, or by a sense of honor: He would stoop to any unscrupulous trick to avoid paying his bills. Unprincipled means being without, or showing an absence of, good moral principles: Only an unprincipled person would defend that man's conduct.

un·seal (un sēl′) v. 1 break or remove the seal of: unseal a letter. 2 open: The threat unsealed her lips.

un·search·a·ble (un sėr′chə bəl) adj. not to be searched into; that cannot be understood by searching; mysterious.

un·sea·son·a·ble (un sē′zən ə bəl or un sēz′nə bəl) adj. 1 not suitable to the season. 2 coming at the wrong time. —**un·sea′son·a·ble·ness**, n. —**un·sea′son·a·bly**, adv.

un·seat (un sēt′) v. 1 displace from a seat: The bronco unseated everyone who tried to ride it. 2 remove from office: Our previous M.P. was unseated in the last election.

un·seem·ly (un sēm′lē) adj., adv. not suitable; improper:

un′re·al·is′tic
un′re·al′ized
un·rea′soned
un·re·buked′
un·re·ceived′
un′re·cep′tive
un′re·cip′ro·cat·ed
un·reck′oned
un·re·claimed′
un·rec′og·niz′a·ble
un·rec′og·nized′
un·rec′om·mend′ed
un′rec·om·pensed′
un′rec·on·cil′a·ble
un·rec′on·ciled′
un·re·cord′ed
un·rec′ti·fied′
un·re·deemed′
un·re·fined′
un′re·flect′ing
un·re·formed′
un·re·freshed′
un·reg′i·ment·ed
un·reg′is·tered
un·reg′u·lat·ed

un′re·hearsed′
un·re·lat′ed
un·re·laxed′
un′re·lax′ing
un·re·li′a·ble
un′re·liev′a·ble
un·re·lieved′
un′re·mark′a·ble
un·rem′e·died
un′re·mem′bered
un′re·mit′ted
un′re·morse′ful
un·re·moved′
un·re·mu′ner·at·ed
un′re·mu′ner·a·tive
un·ren′dered
un·re·newed′
un′re·nowned′
un·rent′ed
un·re·paid′
un·re·paired′
un·re·pealed′
un·re·peat′a·ble
un·re·pent′ant
un′re·pent′ing

un·re·place′
un′re·port′ed
un′rep·re·sent′a·tive
un′rep·re·sent′ed
un′re·pressed′
un·re·prieved′
un·rep′ri·mand·ed
un′re·proached′
un·re·proved′
un·re·quest′ed
un·re·quit′ed
un·re·sent′ful
un·re·signed′
un·re·sist′ant
un·re·sist′ed
un′re·sist′ing
un·re·solved′
un′re·spect′ful
un′re·spon′sive
un·rest′ed
un′re·strict′ed
un′re·ten′tive
un′re·tract′ed
un′re·trieved′
un′re·turn′a·ble

un′re·turned′
un′re·vealed′
un′re·veal′ing
un′re·venged′
un·re·vised′
un·re·voked′
un·re·ward′ed
un·re·ward′ing
un·rhymed′
un·rhyth′mic
un·rhyth′mi·cal
un·rid′den
un·ri′fled
un·right′ful
un·rimed′
un·rip′ened
un·ro·man′tic
un·saint′ly
un·sal′a·ble
un·sal′a·ried
un·salt′ed
un·sanc′ti·fied′
un·sanc′tioned
un·san′i·tar′y
un·sat′ed

un·sa′ti·at·ed
un·sat·is·fac′to·ry
un·sat′is·fied′
un·sat′is·fy′ing
un·saved′
un·say′a·ble
un·scal′a·ble
un·scaled′
un·scanned′
un·scarred′
un·scent′ed
un·sched′uled
un·schol′ar·ly
un·scorched′
un·scoured′
un·scraped′
un·scratched′
un·screened′
un·scrip′tur·al
un·sculp′tured
un·sea′soned
un·sea·wor′thy
un·se·clud′ed
un·sec′ond·ed
un·se·cured′

unseemly laughter. —*adv.* improperly; unsuitably.
—**un·seem′li·ness,** *n.*

un·seen (un sēn′) *adj.* **1** not seen: *an unseen error.* **2** not visible: *an unseen spirit.*

un·self·ish (un sel′fish) *adj.* considerate of others; generous.
—**un·self′ish·ly,** *adv.* —**un·self′ish·ness,** *n.*

un·set·tle (un set′əl) *v.* **-tled, -tling.** make or become unstable; disturb; shake; weaken.

un·set·tled (un set′əld) *adj.* **1** disordered; not in proper condition or order. **2** not fixed or stable. **3** liable to change; uncertain: *The weather is unsettled.* **4** not adjusted or disposed of: *an unsettled estate, an unsettled bill.* **5** not determined or decided. **6** not inhabited.

un·sex (un seks′) *v.* deprive of sexual capacity or of the attributes of one's sex.

un·shack·le (un shak′əl) *v.* **-led, -ling.** remove shackles from; set free.

un·shak·en (un shā′kən) *adj.* not shaken; firm: *an unshaken belief in the faithfulness of a friend.*

un·sheathe (un shēтн′) *v.* **-sheathed, -sheath·ing.** draw (a sword, knife, etc.) from a sheath.

un·ship (un ship′) *v.* **-shipped, -ship·ping. 1** put off or take off from a ship: *to unship a cargo.* **2** remove from the proper place for use: *to unship an oar or tiller.*

un·shod (un shod′) *adj.* without shoes.

un·sight·ly (un sīt′lē) *adj.* ugly or unpleasant to look at.
—**un·sight′li·ness,** *n.*
☛ *Syn.* See note at **ugly.**

un·skil·ful or **un·skill·ful** (un skil′fəl) *adj.* awkward; clumsy.
—**un·skil′ful·ly** or **un·skill′ful·ly,** *adv.* —**un·skil′ful·ness** or **un·skill′ful·ness,** *n.*

un·skilled (un skild′) *adj.* **1** not skilled or trained: *Unskilled workers usually earn less than skilled workers.* **2** not requiring special skills or training: *unskilled labor.*

un·snap (un snap′) *v.* **-snapped, -snap·ping.** unfasten the snap or snaps of.

un·snarl (un snärl′) *v.* remove the snarls from; untangle.

un·so·cia·bil·i·ty (un′sō shə bil′ə tē) *n.* unsociable nature or behavior; lack of friendliness.

un·so·cia·ble (un sō′shə bəl) *adj.* not sociable; not associating easily with others: *unsociable behavior, an unsociable hermit.*
—**un·so′cia·ble·ness,** *n.* —**un·so′cia·bly,** *adv.*

un·sol·der (un sod′ər) *v.* **1** separate (something soldered). **2** break up; divide; dissolve.

un·so·phis·ti·cat·ed (un′sə fis′tə kāt′id) *adj.* not sophisticated; simple; natural.

un·sound (un sound′) *adj.* **1** not in good condition; not sound: *A diseased mind or body is unsound. Unsound walls are not firm. An unsound business is not reliable.* **2** not based on truth or fact: *an unsound doctrine, theory, etc.* **3** not restful; disturbed: *an unsound sleep.* —**un·sound′ly,** *adv.* —**un·sound′ness,** *n.*

un·spar·ing (un sper′ing) *adj.* **1** very generous; liberal. **2** not merciful; severe. —**un·spar′ing·ly,** *adv.* —**un·spar′ing·ness,** *n.*

un·speak·a·ble (un spē′kə bəl) *adj.* **1** that cannot be expressed in words: *unspeakable joy, an unspeakable loss.* **2** extremely bad;

hat, āge, fär; let, ēqual, tėrm; it, īce
hot, ōpen, ôrder; oil, out; cup, pût, rüle,
əbove, takən, pencəl, lemən, circəs
ch, child; ng, long; sh, ship
th, thin; тн, then; zh, measure

so bad that it can hardly be spoken of: *That was an unspeakable thing to do!* —**un·speak′a·bly,** *adv.*

un·spot·ted (un spot′id) *adj.* without spot or stain; pure.

un·sta·ble (un stā′bəl) *adj.* **1** not firmly fixed; easily moved, shaken, or overthrown. **2** not constant; variable. **3** *Chemistry.* easily decomposed; readily changing into other compounds.
—**un·sta′ble·ness,** *n.* —**un·sta′bly,** *adv.*

unstable element in chemistry, a radio-active element that eventually changes into a radio-active isotope.

un·stead·y (un sted′ē) *adj.* **1** not steady; shaky: *an unsteady voice, an unsteady flame.* **2** likely to change; not reliable: *unsteady winds.* **3** not regular in habits. —**un·stead′i·ly,** *adv.* —**un·stead′i·ness,** *n.*

un·step (un step′) *v.* **-stepped, -step·ping.** remove (a mast, etc.) from its step.

un·stop (un stop′) *v.* **-stopped, -stop·ping. 1** remove the stopper from (a bottle, etc.). **2** free from any obstruction; open.

un·strap (un strap′) *v.* **-strapped, -strap·ping.** loosen the strap of (a trunk, box, etc.).

un·string (un string′) *v.* **-strung, -string·ing. 1** take off or loosen the string or strings of. **2** take from a string. **3** weaken the nerves of; make nervous.

un·struc·tured (un struk′chərd) *adj.* having no formal or rigid structure or organization: *unstructured classes.*

un·strung (un strung′) *adj.* upset; emotionally disturbed. —*v.* pt. and pp. of **unstring.**

un·stud·ied (un stud′ēd) *adj.* not studied; not planned ahead; natural.

un·sub·stan·tial (un′səb stan′shəl) *adj.* not substantial; flimsy; slight; unreal. —**un·sub·stan′tial·ly,** *adv.*

un·suc·cess·ful (un′sək ses′fəl) *adj.* not successful; without success. —**un·suc·cess′ful·ly,** *adv.*

un·suit·a·bil·i·ty (un′sü tə bil′ə tē) *n.* being unsuitable.

un·suit·a·ble (un sü′tə bəl) *adj.* not suitable; unfit.
—**un·suit′a·bly,** *adv.*

un·suit·ed (un sü′tid) *adj.* not suited; unfit.

un·sung (un sung′) *adj.* **1** not sung. **2** not honored in song or poetry; unpraised.

un·sus·pect·ed (un′səs pek′tid) *adj.* **1** not under suspicion: *He had already committed several burglaries but was still unsuspected.* **2** not thought of, or known about: *an unsuspected danger.*

un·tan·gle (un tang′gəl) *v.* **-gled, -gling. 1** take the tangles out of; disentangle. **2** straighten out or clear up (anything confused or perplexing).

un·taught (un tôt′ *or* un tŏt′) *adj.* **1** not taught; not educated. **2** known without being taught; learned naturally.

un·think·a·ble (un thingk′ə bəl) *adj.* **1** that cannot be imagined or grasped by the mind; inconceivable: *the unthinkable vastness of the universe.* **2** that cannot be considered; out of the question: *It is unthinkable that she could be a thief.* —**un·think′a·bly,** *adv.*

un·think·ing (un thingk′ing) *adj.* **1** thoughtless; heedless; careless: *An unthinking comment can sometimes cause a lot of trouble.* **2** characterized by absence of thought: *blind, unthinking anger.* **3** not having the faculty of thought; unable to think. —**un·think′ing·ly,** *adv.*

un·thought–of (un thot′uv′ *or* un thôt′uv′, un thot′ov′ *or* un thôt′ov′) *adj.* not imagined or considered.

un·thread (un thred′) *v.* **1** take the thread out of. **2** unravel. **3** find one's way through.

un·ti·dy (un tī′dē) *adj.* not in order; not neat. —**un·ti′di·ly,** *adv.* —**un·ti′di·ness,** *n.*

un·tie (un tī′) *v.* **-tied, -ty·ing. 1** loosen; unfasten; undo: *to untie a knot.* **2** make free; release: *She untied her horse.* **3** make clear; explain; resolve. [OE *untīgan*]

un·til (ən til′ *or* un til′) *prep., conj.* —*prep.* **1** up to the time of: *It was cold from Christmas until April.* **2** before (*used only with a negative*): *She did not leave until morning.* —*conj.* **1** up to the time when: *He waited until the sun had set.* **2** before (*used only with a negative*): *He did not come until the meeting was half over.* **3** to the point or stage that: *He worked until he was too tired to do more.* [ME *untill* < ON *und* up to + *till* till[1]] ☛ *Usage.* See note at **till**[1].

un·time·ly (un tīm′lē) *adj., adv.* —*adj.* at a wrong time or season: *an untimely snowstorm.* —*adv.* too early; too soon: *an untimely death at age 32.* —**un·time′li·ness,** *n.*

un·tir·ing (un tīr′ing) *adj.* tireless; unwearying. —**un·tir′ing·ly,** *adv.*

un·ti·tled (un tī′təld) *adj.* **1** having no title. **2** not distinguished by a title; not of titled rank: *the gentry and other untitled classes.* **3** lacking lawful right; not entitled to rule.

un·to (un′tü; *before consonants often,* un′tə) *prep. Archaic or formal.* **1** to. **2** till; until: *The soldier was faithful unto death.* [ME *unto* < *un-* (see UNTIL) + *to*]

un·told (un tōld′) *adj.* **1** not told; not revealed. **2** too many to be counted; countless: *There are untold stars in the sky.* **3** not counted; immense: *untold wealth.*

un·touch·a·ble (un tuch′ə bəl) *adj., n.* —*adj.* **1** that cannot be touched; out of reach. **2** that must not be touched. —*n.* **1** *Historical.* in India, a person of the lowest caste whose touch supposedly defiled members of higher castes. **2** any person rejected by his social group; social outcast; pariah.

un·touched (un tucht′) *adj.* **1** not used, consumed, handled, etc.: *The cat left the milk untouched.* **2** not affected or moved: *The miser was untouched by the poor man's story.* **3** not dealt with: *The last topic was left untouched.*

un·tow·ard (un tôrd′ *or* un′tō wôrd′) *adj.* **1** unfavorable; unfortunate: *an untoward wind, an untoward accident.* **2** perverse; stubborn; willful. [< *un-*[1] + *toward*] —**un·to′ward·ly,** *adv.* —**un·to′ward·ness,** *n.*

un·tram·melled *or* **un·tram·meled** (un tram′əld) *adj.* not hindered; not restrained; free.

un·tried (un trīd′) *adj.* not tried; not tested.

un·true (un trü′) *adj.* **1** false; incorrect. **2** not faithful. **3** not true to a standard or rule. [OE *untrēowe*]

un·truss (un trus′) *v.* **1** unfasten; loose from a truss. **2** *Obsolete.* undress.

un·truth (un trüth′) *n.* **1** lack of truth; falsity. **2** a lie; falsehood. [OE *untrēowth*]

un·truth·ful (un trüth′fəl) *adj.* not truthful; contrary to the truth. —**un·truth′ful·ly,** *adv.* —**un·truth′ful·ness,** *n.*

un·tu·tored (un tyü′tərd *or* un tü′tərd) *adj.* untaught.

un·twine (un twīn′) *v.* **-twined, -twin·ing.** untwist.

un·twist (un twist′) *v.* **1** undo or loosen something twisted; unravel. **2** become untwisted.

un·used (un yüzd′) *adj.* **1** not in use; not being used: *an unused room.* **2** never having been used: *We'll keep the unused paper cups for our next picnic.*

unused to (un yüst′tü) not accustomed to: *The actor's hands were unused to manual labor.*

un·u·su·al (un yü′zhü əl) *adj.* not usual; beyond the ordinary; not common; rare. —**un·u′su·al·ly,** *adv.* —**un·u′su·al·ness,** *n.*

un·ut·ter·a·ble (un ut′ər ə bəl) *adj.* that cannot be expressed; unspeakable. —**un·ut′ter·a·bly,** *adv.*

un·var·nished (un vär′nisht) *adj.* **1** not varnished. **2** plain; unadorned: *the unvarnished truth.*

un·veil (un vāl′) *v.* **1** remove a veil from; disclose; reveal: *unveil a secret.* **2** take off one's veil; reveal oneself: *The princess unveiled.*

un·voiced (un voist′) *adj.* **1** not spoken; not expressed in words. **2** *Phonetics.* voiceless.

un·war·rant·a·ble (un wôr′ən tə bəl) *adj.* not justifiable; indefensible: *an unwarrantable invasion of privacy, unwarrantable rudeness.* —**un·war′rant·a·bly,** *adv.*

un·war·y (un wer′ē) *adj.* not cautious; not careful; unguarded. —**un·war′i·ly,** *adv.* —**un·war′i·ness,** *n.*

un·wea·ried (un wer′ēd) *adj.* **1** not weary; not tired. **2** never growing weary.

un·weave (un wēv′) *v.* **-wove, -wo·ven, -weav·ing.** take apart (something woven).

un·wel·come (un wel′kəm) *adj.* not welcome; not wanted.

un·well (un wel′) *adj.* ailing; ill; sick.

un·wept (un wept′) *adj.* **1** not wept for; not mourned. **2** not shed: *unwept tears.*

un·whole·some (un hōl′səm) *adj.* not wholesome; bad for the body or the mind; unhealthy. —**un·whole′some·ly,** *adv.* —**un·whole′some·ness,** *n.*

un·wield·y (un wēl′dē) *adj.* not easily handled or managed, because of size, shape, or weight; bulky and clumsy: *the unwieldy armor of knights.* —**un·wield′i·ness,** *n.*

un·will·ing (un wil′ing) *adj.* not willing; not consenting. —**un·will′ing·ly,** *adv.* —**un·will′ing·ness,** *n.*

un·wind (un wīnd′) *v.* **-wound, -wind·ing. 1** wind off; take from a spool, ball, etc. **2** become unwound. **3** disentangle. [OE *unwindan*]

un·wise (un wīz′) *adj.* not wise; not showing good judgment; foolish. [OE *unwīs*] —**un·wise′ly,** *adv.*

un·wit·ting (un wit′ing) *adj.* not knowing; unaware; unconscious; unintentional. —**un·wit′ting·ly,** *adv.*

un·won·ted (un wōn′tid *or* un wun′tid) *adj.* **1** not customary; not usual. **2** not accustomed; not used. —**un·wont′ed·ly,** *adv.* —**un·wont′ed·ness,** *n.*

un·world·ly (un wėrld′lē) *adj.* **1** not caring much for the things of this world, such as money, pleasure, and power. **2** naïve. **3** not of this world; spiritual. —**un·world′li·ness,** *n.*

un·wor·thi·ly (un wėr′тнē lē) *adv.* **1** in a way that is not worthy or honorable; shamefully. **2** not according to one's merits.

un·wor·thy (un wėr′тнē) *adj.* **1** not worthy; not deserving: *Such a silly story is unworthy of belief.* **2** not befitting or becoming; below

un·tem′pered	un·torn′	un·tuft′ed	un·vis′it·ed	un·wed′ded
un·tempt′ed	un·trace′a·ble	un·tun′a·ble	un·vit′ri·fied′	un·weed′ed
un·ten′a·ble	un·traced′	un·tuned′	un·wak′ened	un·weld′ed
un·ten′ant·ed	un·tracked′	un·tune′ful	un·walled′	un·wife′like′
un·tend′ed	un·tract′a·ble	un·turned′	un·want′ed	un·wife′ly
un·ter′ri·fied	un·trained′	un·typ′i·cal	un·war′like′	un·willed′
un·test′ed	un·trans·fer′a·ble	un·us′a·ble	un·warmed′	un·wink′ing
un·teth′ered	un·trans·formed′	un·u′ti·lized	un·warned′	un·wished′
un·thanked′	un·trans·lat′a·ble	un·ut′tered	un·war′rant·ed	un·with′ered
un·thank′ful	un·trans·lat′ed	un·vac′ci·nat′ed	un·washed′	un·wit′nessed
un·thatched′	un·trans·mit′ted	un·val′ued	un·wast′ed	un·wom′an·ly
un·thawed′	un·trav′elled	un·van′quished	un·watched′	un·won′
un·the·at′ri·cal	un·trav′ers·a·ble	un·var′ied	un·wa′tered	un·wood′ed
un·thought′	un·trav′ersed	un·va′ry·ing	un·wa′ver·ing	un·work′a·ble
un·thought′ful	un·treat′ed	un·ven′ti·lat′ed	un·weaned′	un·worked′
un·thrift′y	un·trimmed′	un·ver′i·fi·a·ble	un·wear′a·ble	un·work′man·like′
un·till′a·ble	un·trod′	un·ver′i·fied′	un·wea′ry	un·worn′
un·tilled′	un·trod′den	un·versed′	un·wea′ry·ing	un·wor′ried
un·tinged′	un·trou′bled	un·vexed′	un·weath′ered	un·wound′ed
un·tired′	un·trust′wor′thy	un·vi′a·ble	un·wed′	un·wrought′

the proper level or standard: *a gift not unworthy of a king.* **3** base; shameful: *unworthy conduct.* **4** lacking value or merit; worthless. —**un·wor′thi·ness,** *n.*

un·wound (un wound′) *v.* pt. and pp. of **unwind.**

un·wove (un wōv′) *v.* pt. of **unweave.**

un·wo·ven (un wō′vən) *v.* pp. of **unweave.**

un·wrap (un rap′) *v.* **-wrapped, -wrap·ping. 1** remove a wrapping from; open. **2** become opened.

un·wrin·kle (un ring′kəl) *v.* **-kled, -kling. 1** smooth the wrinkles from. **2** become smooth.

un·writ·ten (un rit′ən) *adj.* **1** not written. **2** understood or customary, but not actually expressed in writing. **3** not written on; blank.

unwritten law 1 common law. **2** a practice or rule established by general usage. **3** a principle or tradition that a person who commits a crime to avenge personal or family honor is entitled to lenient treatment.

un·yield·ing (un yēl′ding) *adj.* firm; not giving in: *an unyielding determination.*

un·yoke (un yōk′) *v.* **-yoked, -yok·ing. 1** free from a yoke; separate; disconnect. **2** remove a yoke.

up (up) *adv., prep., adj., n., v.* **upped, up·ping.** —*adv.* **1** from a lower to a higher place or condition; to, toward, or near the top: *The bird flew up.* **2** in a higher place or condition; on or at a higher level: *He stayed up in the mountains several days.* **3** from a smaller to a larger amount: *Prices have gone up.* **4** to or at any point, place, or condition that is considered higher: *He lives up north.* **5** above the horizon: *The sun is up.* **6** in or into an erect position: *Stand up.* **7** out of bed: *I usually get up at about seven o'clock.* **8** thoroughly; completely; entirely: *The paper burned up in a few minutes. My eraser is almost used up.* **9** at an end; over: *His time is up now.* **10** in or into being or action: *Don't stir up trouble.* **11** together: *Add these up.* **12** to or in an even position; not behind: *to catch up in a race, to keep up with the times.* **13** in or into view, notice, or consideration: *to bring up a new topic.* **14** in or into a state of tightness, etc.: *Shut him up in his cage.* **15** into safekeeping, storage, etc.; aside; by: *to store up supplies.* **16** *Baseball.* at bat. **17** of a score in tennis, etc., for each side: *The score is now 30 up.* **up against,** *Informal.* facing (something) as a thing to be dealt with. **up against it,** *Informal.* in difficulties. **up and down,** here and there; at various points; in many or different places throughout an area, etc.: *up and down the country.* **up for** in contention as a candidate or applicant for: *She is up for election to the committee.* **up to, a** occupied with; doing, scheming, planning, etc.: *She is up to some mischief.* **b** equal to; capable of doing: *Do you feel up to going out so soon after being sick?* **c** incumbent on, as a duty or task: *It's up to the judge to decide.* —*prep.* **1** along or through from the bottom to or toward the top of: *The cat ran up the tree. We walked up the hill. The smoke went up the chimney.* **2** along: *She walked up the street.* **3** toward the upper end or part of, especially toward the source of (a river): *They sailed up the St. Lawrence, from Quebec City to Montreal.* **4** at or in a higher part of: *There is soot up the chimney. They live further up the river.* —*adj.* **1** advanced; forward. **2** moving upward; directed upward: *an up trend.* **3** above the ground: *The wheat is up.* **4** out of bed: *The children were up at dawn.* **5** to or in an even position; not behind. **6** near; close. **7** with much knowledge or skill; well informed (*usually used with* **on**): *The engineer is up on the newest methods.* **8** *Baseball.* at bat. **9** ahead of an opponent by a certain number: *We are three games up.* **up and about,** active; occupied as usual, especially after an illness. **up and doing,** busy; active. —*n.* **1** an upward movement, course, or slope. **2** *Informal.* a period of good luck, prosperity, or happiness: *Her life is full of ups and downs.* **be on the up and up, a** *Informal.* increasing; rising; improving. **b** *Slang.* honest; legitimate. —*v.* **1** *Informal.* put, lift, or get up. **2** *Informal.* increase: *They upped the price of eggs.* [OE *upp(e)*]

up– *prefix.* up, as in *upcountry, upgrade, upkeep, uplift, upbringing.* [OE *up-*. Related to UP]

up-and-com·ing (up′ən kum′ing) *adj. Informal.* promising; enterprising; on the way to importance and success: *an up-and-coming actor.*

up-and-down (up′ ən doun′) *adj.* **1** characterized by alternate upward and downward motion; rising and falling; fluctuating: *up-and-down sales activity.* **2** vertical; perpendicular.

U·pan·i·shad (ü pan′ə shad′) *n.* any of a group of philosophical treatises in ancient Sanskrit, including those of the Vedanta. [< Skt.]

u·pas (yü′pəs) *n.* **1** a tall, SE Asian tree (*Antiaris toxicaria*) of the

hat, āge, fär; let, ēqual, tèrm; it, īce
hot, ōpen, ôrder; oil, out; cup, pùt, rüle,
above, takən, pencəl, lemən, circəs

ch, child; ng, long; sh, ship
th, thin; ᴛʜ, then; zh, measure

mulberry family having whitish bark and a poisonous, milky sap. **2** the sap of this tree, used as poison for arrows. [< Malay *upas* poison]

up·beat (up′bēt′) *n., adj.* —*n.* **1** *Music.* an unaccented beat; the beat at which the conductor's hand goes up. **2** revival; upswing. —*adj. Informal.* rising; hopeful; buoyant: *an upbeat market opening.*

up·borne (up bôrn′) *adj.* borne up; raised aloft; supported.

up·bound (up′bound′) *adj. or adv.* bound in an upward direction.

up·braid (up brād′) *v.* find fault with; blame; reprove: *The captain upbraided his men for falling asleep.* [OE *ūpbregdan* < *upp* up + *bregdan* weave, snatch, move suddenly] —**up·braid′er,** *n.* ☛ *Syn.* See note at **scold.**

up·braid·ing (up brād′ing) *n.* a severe reproof; scolding.

up·bring·ing (up′bring′ing) *n.* the care and training given to a child while growing up; especially, a particular way of training or educating a child: *a very casual upbringing, a Catholic upbringing.*

up·com·ing (up′kum′ing) *adj.* forthcoming; approaching.

up·coun·try (up′kun′trē) *n., adv., adj.* —*n.* the interior of a country. —*adv.* toward or in the interior of a country. —*adj.* remote from the coast or border; interior.

up·date (up dāt′) *v.* **-dat·ed, -dat·ing;** *n.* —*v.* bring up to date: *to update one's wardrobe. The files are updated once a month.* —*n.* the act or an instance of updating: *a monthly update.*

up·draft (up′draft′) *n.* an upward movement of gas, air, etc. Also, **updraught.**

up·draught (up′draft′) See **updraft.**

up·end (up end′) *v.* set on end; stand on end.

up·fold (up′fōld′) *n. Geology.* an upward fold; anticline.

up·grade (up′grād′) *n., adv., adj., v.* **-grad·ed, -grad·ing.** —*n.* an upward slope or incline. **on the upgrade,** rising; improving. —*adv. or adj.* uphill. —*v.* **1** improve the grade, quality, or rank of: *to upgrade livestock by selective breeding.* **2** promote to a higher position with a higher salary: *The company has set up a training program to upgrade its secretaries.*

up·growth (up′grōth′) *n.* **1** the process of growing up; development. **2** something that grows up.

up·heav·al (up hēv′əl) *n.* **1** the action or an instance of heaving or lifting up, especially of part of the earth's crust: *Geologists say that the Rocky Mountains were formed by an upheaval of the earth's crust.* **2** a sudden or violent agitation in affairs; social turmoil: *The sale of the family business caused a great upheaval.*

up·heave (up hēv′) *v.* **-heaved** or **-hove, -heav·ing. 1** heave up; lift up. **2** rise.

up·held (up held′) *v.* pt. and pp. of **uphold.**

up·hill (*adj.* up′hil′; *adv.* up′hil′) *adj.* **1** sloping or going up: *It is an uphill road all the way.* **2** difficult: *an uphill fight.* —*adv.* up the slope of a hill; upward: *We had to walk uphill for a kilometre.*

up·hold (up hōld′) *v.* **-held, -hold·ing. 1** give moral support to; confirm: *The principal upheld the teacher's decision.* **2** hold up; keep from falling; not let down: *We uphold the good name of our school.* **3** sustain; approve; confirm. —**up·hold′er,** *n.* ☛ *Syn.* **1.** See note at **support.**

up·hol·ster (up hōl′stər) *v.* provide (furniture) with cushions, springs, padding, etc. and a covering of cloth, leather, vinyl, etc. [back formation < *upholsterer*, ult. < obs. *uphold* keep in repair]

up·hol·ster·er (up hōl′stər ər) *n.* a person whose business is upholstering furniture.

up·hol·ster·y (up hōl′stər ē *or* up hōl′strē) *n., pl.* **-ster·ies. 1** padding, covering, springs, etc. of an upholstered piece of furniture. **2** the business or craft of upholstering.

up·hove (up hōv′) *v.* a pt. and a pp. of **upheave.**

UPI United Press International.

up·keep (up′kēp′) *n.* **1** maintaining or being maintained in good condition. **2** the cost of maintaining in good condition: *What's the upkeep on your car?*

up·land (up'lənd or up'land') n. 1 high land. 2 (adj.) of or found in high land: an upland meadow, upland flowers.

upland plover a North American sandpiper (Bartramia longicauda) found in open, grassy uplands, having streaked, buff-colored plumage, a long neck, and a small head with a straight, somewhat short bill.

up·lift (v. up lift'; n. up'lift') v., n. —v. 1 lift up; raise; elevate; especially, cause (a part of the earth's crust) to be raised. 2 improve mentally, socially, or morally: He had been greatly uplifted by his friends' cheerful optimism. —n. 1 the act, process, or result of lifting up. 2 mental, social, or moral improvement or a movement toward it: Good music gives her an uplift when she is discouraged. —**up·lift'er**, n.

up·most (up'mōst) adj. uppermost.

up·on (ə pon') prep. on. [ME upon < up + on]

up·per (up'ər) adj., n. —adj. 1 higher: the upper lip, the upper floor, the upper range of a singer's voice. 2 higher in rank, office, etc.; superior: the upper house of a parliament. 3 Upper, Geology and archaeology. of or designating a recent or late division or part of a specified period, epoch, system, or formation: Upper Cambrian. 4 farther upstream or inland: the upper St. Lawrence. 5 farther north. 6 of clothing, etc., covering the torso above the waist.
—n. 1 the part of a shoe or boot above the sole. 2 an upper berth or bunk: I had the upper, and my brother had the lower. 3 an upper tooth or denture: Her new uppers are much more comfortable than the old ones were. 4 Slang. any drug that acts as a stimulant.
on (one's) **uppers**, in financial difficulty; having very little or no money left: He was obviously on his uppers but refused to accept charity.

Upper Canada Cdn. 1 Esp.Maritimes. the province of Ontario. 2 until 1841, the official name of the region west of the Ottawa River and north of Lakes Ontario and Erie, now included in the province of Ontario. In 1841 Upper and Lower Canada were united in the Province of Canada. Upper Canada was so named because it lay farther up the St. Lawrence than Lower Canada. Abbrev.: U.C.

Upper Canadian Cdn. especially in the Maritimes, Ontarian.

upper case capital letters. Abbrev.: u.c.

up·per-case (up'ər kās') adj. capital; in capital letters.

Upper Chamber or **upper chamber** Upper House.

upper class the social class that has the greatest prestige or power in a society, usually due to wealth, birth, or education.

up·per-class (up'ər klas') adj. 1 having to do with, or suitable for the upper class of society: upper-class tastes. 2 in universities, schools, etc., of or having to do with the senior classes.

up·per-class·man (up'ər klas'mən) n., pl. **-men.** a senior student.

upper crust Informal. the upper classes.

up·per·cut (up'ər kut') n., v. **-cut, -cut·ting.** —n. Boxing. a short swinging blow directed upward and toward the chin. —v. strike with an uppercut.

upper hand a position of control; mastery or advantage: During the first two periods, the visiting team had the upper hand.

Upper House or **upper house** in a legislature having two branches, the branch that has the smaller number of members and is less representative. In some countries, the members of the Upper House are elected, as in the United States; in others they are appointed, as in Canada. The Senate is the Upper House of the Canadian Parliament.

Upper Lakes the most northerly of the Great Lakes; Lakes Superior and Huron and, sometimes, Lake Michigan.

up·per·most (up'ər mōst) adj., adv. —adj. 1 highest; topmost: the uppermost branches of a tree. 2 having the most force or influence; most prominent. —adv. 1 in or into the highest place: The watch lay with the back turned uppermost. 2 in or into the first or most prominent position.

up·pish (up'ish) adj. Informal. uppity. [< up, adv.]

up·pi·ty (up'ə tē) adj. Informal. inclined to put on airs; arrogant or conceited.

up·raise (up rāz') v. **-raised, -rais·ing.** raise or lift up.

up·rear (up rēr') v. lift up; raise.

up·right (adj., adv. up'rīt' or up rīt'; n. up'rīt') adj., adv., n.
—adj. 1 standing up straight; erect. 2 good; honest; righteous.
—adv. straight up; in a vertical position.
—n. 1 vertical or upright position. 2 something standing erect; a vertical part or piece: The boards for the fence were nailed across

the uprights. 3 upright piano. [OE upriht] —**up'right·ly**, adv. —**up'right·ness**, n.

☛ Syn. adj. 1. **Upright, erect** = straight up. **Upright** literally means "straight up," standing up straight on a base or in a base or in a position that is straight up and down, not slanting: After the earthquake not a lamp or chair was upright. **Erect**, describing the body, a thing, etc. means "held or set upright," not stooping or bent: At seventy she still walks erect.

upright piano a piano with a vertical frame and strings. Compare **grand piano**.

up·rise (v. up rīz'; n. up'rīz') v. **-rose, -ris·en, -ris·ing;** n. —v. 1 rise up. 2 slope upward. 3 increase in volume, amount, etc. —n. a rising up; upward rise.

up·ris·en (up riz'ən) v. pp. of uprise.

up·ris·ing (up'rī'zing or up rī'zing) n. 1 a revolt; rebellion: The revolution began with small uprisings in several towns. 2 Archaic. an upward slope; ascent.

up·riv·er (up'riv'ər) adj., adv. —adj. 1 belonging to or situated farther up, or toward the upper end of, a river. 2 leading or directed toward the source of a river. —adv. toward or in the direction of the source of a river.

up·roar (up'rôr') n. a noisy or violent disturbance; tumult; commotion: We heard an uproar in the hall and went to see what it was. There was a great uproar when the theft was discovered. [< Du. oproer insurrection, tumult; influenced by association with roar]

☛ Syn. See note at **noise**.

up·roar·i·ous (up rôr'ē əs or up rōr'ē əs) adj. 1 marked by uproar; noisy and confused: an uproarious disturbance. 2 loud and boisterous: uproarious laughter, in uproarious good spirits. 3 very funny: an uproarious comedy, an uproarious scene.
—**up·roar'i·ous·ly**, adv. —**up·roar'i·ous·ness**, n.

up·root (up rüt') v. 1 tear up by the roots: The storm uprooted two trees. 2 force away from: Famine uprooted many families from their homes in Ireland during the 1840's. —**up·root'er**, n.

up·rose (up rōz') v. pt. of uprise.

ups-a-dai·sy (up'sə dā'zē) interj. an expression of encouragement used especially to a small child when the child is being lifted or helped up after a fall.

up·set (v. up set'; n. up'set'; adj. up set' or up'set') v. **-set, -set·ting;** n., adj. —v. 1 tip over; overturn: to upset a boat. 2 disturb greatly; disorder: Rain upset our plans for a picnic. The shock upset her nerves. 3 overthrow; defeat: to upset a will, to upset an argument.
—n. 1 a tipping over; overturn. 2 a great disturbance; disorder. 3 an overthrowing; an unexpected defeat.
—adj. 1 tipped over; overturned. 2 greatly disturbed; disordered: an upset stomach.

upset price, the lowest price at which a thing offered for sale will be sold.

☛ Syn. v. 1. **Upset, overturn** = fall, or cause to fall, over or down. **Upset** suggests losing balance and tipping over from an upright or proper position as the result of a movement or action by some person or thing: He accidentally kicked the table and upset the vase of flowers. **Overturn** suggests turning upside down or, especially, over on one side from an upright position to one flat on the ground: He got up too quickly and overturned his chair.

up·shot (up'shot') n. the end result; outcome: The upshot of all the delays will probably be that we'll have to cancel the program.

up·side (up'sīd') n. the upper side.

upside down 1 having at the bottom what should be on top. 2 in complete disorder: The room was turned upside down. [alteration of ME up so down up as if down]

up·side-down cake (up'sīd doun') a cake baked with a layer of fruit on the bottom and served upside down with the fruit on top.

up·si·lon (yüp'sə lon') n. the 20th letter (Y, υ = English U, u, or Y, y) of the Greek alphabet.

up·stage (up'stāj') adv., adj., v. **-staged, -stag·ing.** —adv. toward or at the back of the stage of a theatre. —adj. 1 having to do with the back part of the stage. 2 toward or at the back of the stage. 3 haughty; snobbish: I didn't like his upstage manner.
—v. 1 force (another actor) to turn away from the audience by moving or staying upstage of him. 2 make oneself the centre of attention at the expense of another; steal the show from: She upstaged the hostess by welcoming everyone herself.

up·stairs (up'sterz') adv., adj., n. —adv. 1 up the stairs: I ran upstairs. 2 on or of an upper floor: She lives upstairs.
kick (someone) upstairs, get rid of a person by promoting him to a higher but ineffectual position.
—adj. on or of an upper floor: He is waiting in an upstairs hall.
—n. the upper storey or storeys (used with a singular verb): The upstairs of the house is very small.

up·stand·ing (up stan'ding) adj. 1 having integrity; honorable: a fine, upstanding young man. 2 standing up; erect.

up·start (up'stärt') n., adj. —n. 1 a person who has suddenly risen from a humble position to wealth, power, or importance. 2 an

unpleasant, conceited, and self-assertive person. —*adj.* **1** suddenly risen from a humble position to wealth, power, or importance. **2** conceited; self-assertive.

up·stream (up′strēm′) *adv. or adj.* in the direction opposite to the current of a stream: *It is hard to swim upstream. They stopped at an upstream camping site.*

up·stroke (up′strōk′) *n.* a stroke or movement in an upward direction: *the upstroke of a choir leader's baton.*

up·surge (*n.* up′sėrj′; *v.* up′sėrj′) *n., v.* **-surged, -surg·ing.** —*n.* sudden or rapid rise; a surge of growth, development, emotion, etc.: *an upsurge in prices, an upsurge of feeling.* —*v.* surge up; rise.

up·swept (up′swept′) *adj.* **1** curving or sloping upward. **2** of or having to do with a woman's hair style in which the hair is brushed upward and piled high on the head.

up·swing (up′swing′) *n., v.* **-swung, -swing·ing.** —*n.* **1** a swing or movement upward. **2** a marked improvement; strong advance. —*v.* undergo an upswing.

up·sy–dai·sy (up′sə dā′zē *or* up′sē dā′zē) *interj.* ups-a-daisy.

up·take (up′tāk′) *n.* **1** the act or process of taking or drawing up. **2** a flue or ventilating shaft.
quick (or **slow) on the uptake,** quick (or slow) to understand: *He's a very nice fellow, but a little slow on the uptake.*

up·thrust (up′thrust′) *n.* **1** an upward push. **2** a movement upward of part of the earth's crust.

up·tight (up′tīt′) *adj. Informal.* **1** angry and defensive: *Don't get uptight; she didn't mean anything by it.* **2** tense, worried, or anxious: *His mother gets uptight if he's late getting home.* **3** rigid and conformist in attitude; straitlaced: *an uptight approach to new ideas.* —**up′tight′ness,** *n.*

up-to-date (up′tə dāt′) *adj.* **1** extending to the present time; including the latest information: *an up-to-date record of sales, an up-to-date map of the city.* **2** keeping up with the times in style, ideas, or methods; modern: *an up-to-date dress shop. He's very up-to-date in his selling methods.*

up-to-the-min·ute (up′tə ㅜH ə min′it) *adj.* modern; up-to-date; latest.

up·town (*adv.* up′toun′; *adj.* up′toun′) *adv. or adj.* to or in a main part of a town or city that is higher, further north, or further from a lake, river, harbor, etc. than other parts: *to go uptown, an uptown store.*

up·turn (*v.* up tėrn′; *n.* up′tėrn′) *v., n.* —*v.* turn up or over. —*n.* **1** an upward turn. **2** improvement: *an upturn in business.*

up·turned (up tėrnd′) *adj.* **1** turned upside down; overturned: *He set the upturned chair on its feet.* **2** turned upward: *a mustache with upturned ends. She kissed the child's upturned face.*

UPU Universal Postal Union of the United Nations.

up·ward (up′wərd) *adv., adj.* —*adv.* **1** toward a higher place. **2** in the higher or highest position; uppermost: *to store baskets with the bottoms upward.* **3** toward a higher or greater rank, amount, age, etc.: *From public school upward, she studied French.* **4** above; more: *Children of five years and upward must pay carfare.* **5** to or toward the source: *to follow a river upward.*
upwards of or **upward of,** more than: *Repairs to the car will cost upwards of $800.*
—*adj.* directed or moving toward or situated in a higher place: *an upward glance.* [OE *upweard*]

up·ward·ly (up′wərd lē) *adv.* in an upward manner or direction; upward.

up·wards (up′wərdz) *adv.* upward.

Ur (ėr) *n.* an ancient city of Babylonia, on the Euphrates River.

U·ral–Al·ta·ic (yü′rəl al tā′ik) *adj., n.* —*adj.* **1** of the region embracing the Ural and Altaic Mountains. **2** of or having to do with a large family of languages spoken in northern Asia and eastern Europe, including the Finno-Ugric, Turkic, Mongolian, and some other languages. —*n.* the Ural-Altaic language family.

U·ra·ni·a (yü rā′nē ə) *n. Greek mythology.* the Muse of astronomy.

u·ran·i·nite (yü ran′ə nīt′) *n.* a blackish-green uranium mineral often found in crystal form. When found in veins, it is called **pitchblende.** *Formula:* UO_2

u·ra·ni·um (yü rā′nē əm) *n.* a heavy, white, radio-active metallic chemical element that occurs in pitchblende and certain other minerals. The uranium isotope, U^{235}, can sustain efficient chain reaction and is for this reason used in nuclear devices. *Symbol:* U; *at.no.* 92; *at.wt.* 238.03. [< NL *uranium* < *Uranus,* the planet]

U·ra·nus (yür′ə nəs *or* yü rā′nəs) *n.* **1** *Greek mythology.* the first god of the heavens, original ruler of the world and father of the Titans, the Cyclopes, and the Furies. He was overthrown by his son Cronus. **2** one of the larger planets. It is the seventh in order from the sun.

ur·ban (ėr′bən) *adj.* **1** of, having to do with, or in cities or towns:

hat, āge, fär; let, ēqual, tėrm; it, īce
hot, ōpen, ôrder; oil, out; cup, put, rüle,
ə above, tak ə n, pencil, lem ə n, circ ə s

ch, child; ng, long; sh, ship
th, thin; ㅜH, then; zh, measure

an urban district, urban planning, the urban population. **2** characteristic of cities or towns: *urban problems.* [< L *urbanus* < *urbs* city]

ur·bane (ėr bān′) *adj.* courteous and refined; smoothly polite; polished. [< L *urbanus,* originally, *urban.* See URBAN.] —**ur·bane′ly,** *adv.* —**ur·bane′ness,** *n.*

ur·ban·i·ty (ėr ban′ə tē) *n., pl.* **-ties. 1** the quality or state of being urbane. **2 urbanities,** *pl.* urbane acts; courteous, polite conduct.

ur·ban·i·za·tion (ėr′bə nə zā′shən *or* ėr′be nī zā′shən) *n.* the quality or state of being or becoming urbanized.

ur·ban·ize (ėr′bən īz′) *v.* **-ized, -iz·ing.** render urban: *to urbanize a district or its people.* —**ur′ban·i·za′tion,** *n.*

urban renewal a program, policy, or the process of rehabilitating or replacing rundown or substandard buildings in a city, especially in the downtown core.

urban sprawl the uncontrolled spreading of urban development, in the form of new subdivisions, shopping centres, etc., into rural areas.

ur·chin (ėr′chən) *n.* **1** a small child, especially a mischievous one. **2** sea urchin. **3** *Archaic.* hedgehog. **4** *Archaic.* a goblin or elf. [ME < OF *irechon* < L *ericius* an obstacle with spikes < *er* hedgehog]

Ur·du (ür′dü *or* ėr′dü) *n.* an Indic language closely related to Hindi. Urdu is an official language of Pakistan and is widely used in India.

–ure *noun-forming suffix.* **1** the act or fact of —ing, as in *failure.* **2** the state of being —ed, as in *pleasure.* **3** the result of —ing, as in *enclosure.* **4** the thing that —s, as in *legislature.* **5** the thing that is —ed, as in *disclosure.* **6** other special meanings, as in *procedure, sculpture, denture.* [< F *-ure* < L *-ura*]

u·re·a (yü rē′ə *or* yür′ē ə) *n.* a soluble crystalline compound present especially in the urine of mammals. Urea is manufactured synthetically for use in making fertilizers, adhesives, and plastics. *Formula:* $CO(NH_2)_2$ [< NL *urea,* ult. < Gk. *ouron* urine]

urea resin any of a group of thermosetting synthetic resins obtained chiefly from urea and formaldehyde, used for mouldings, adhesives, etc.

u·re·mi·a (yü rē′mē ə) *n. Medicine.* a condition resulting from the accumulation in the blood of waste products that should normally be eliminated in the urine. [< NL *uremia* < Gk. *ouron* urine + *haima* blood]

u·re·mic (yü rē′mik) *adj.* **1** of or having to do with uremia. **2** suffering from uremia.

u·re·ter (yü rē′tər *or* yür′ə tər) *n.* a duct that carries urine from a kidney to the bladder or the cloaca. See **kidney** for picture. [< NL < Gk. *ourētēr,* ult. < *ouron* urine]

u·re·thane (yü′rə thān′ *or* yü reth′ən) *n.* **1** a white crystalline compound and ethyl derivative used especially in the plastics industry to manufacture polyurethane and in medicine to treat certain forms of leukemia, etc. *Formula:* $C_3H_7NO_2$ **2** polyurethane.

u·re·thra (yü rē′thrə) *n., pl.* **-thrae** (-thrē *or* -thrī) **or -thras.** in most mammals, the duct by which urine is discharged from the bladder and also, in males, through which semen is discharged. [< LL < Gk. *ourēthra,* ult. < *ouron* urine]

u·re·thral (yü rē′thrəl) *adj.* of or having to do with the urethra.

urge (ėrj) *v.* **urged, urg·ing;** *n.* —*v.* **1** push, force, or drive: *The rider urged on his horse with whip and spurs.* **2** cause to hasten or gather speed; accelerate the pace of; speed up: *to urge a trotting horse into a gallop.* **3** try to persuade with arguments; ask earnestly: *They urged him to stay.* **4** plead or argue earnestly for; recommend strongly: *Motorists urged better roads.* **5** press upon the attention; refer to often and with emphasis: *to urge a claim, to urge an argument.*
—*n.* **1** a driving force, impulse, or desire. **2** the act of urging. [< L *urgere*]

ur·gen·cy (ėr′jən sē) *n., pl.* **-cies.** the quality or state of being urgent: *They said it was a matter of great urgency. His captors were moved by the urgency of his plea.*

ur·gent (ėr′jənt) *adj.* **1** demanding immediate action or attention; pressing; important: *He said the matter was urgent.* **2** insistent: *an urgent appeal for funds.* [< L *urgens, -entis,* ppr. of *urgere* urge] —**ur′gent·ly,** *adv.*

u·ric (yŭr′ik) *adj.* of, having to do with, or found in urine.

uric acid a white, odorless, tasteless, crystalline compound only slightly soluble in water, that is found in small quantities in the urine of mammals and in large quantities in the urine of birds and reptiles. *Formula:* $C_5H_4N_4O_3$

u·ri·nal (yŭr′ə nəl *or* yü rī′nəl) *n.* 1 an upright plumbing fixture into which to urinate, for use by men and boys. 2 a room or structure containing such fixtures. 3 a container for urine. [< LL *urinal*, ult. < L *urina*]

u·ri·nal·y·sis (yŭr′ə nal′ə sis) *n., pl.* **-ses** (-sēz′). a chemical analysis of a sample of urine. [alteration of British *uranalysis* < Gk. *ouron* urine + E *analysis*; influenced in spelling by *urine*]

u·ri·nar·y (yŭr′ə ner′ē) *adj., n., pl.* **-nar·ies.** —*adj.* 1 of, like, or having to do with urine. 2 of or having to do with the organs that secrete and discharge urine. —*n.* urinal.

u·ri·nate (yŭr′ə nāt′) *v.* **-nat·ed, -nat·ing.** discharge urine from the body. [< Med.L *urinare*]

u·ri·na·tion (yŭr′ə nā′shən) *n.* the act or process of urinating.

u·rine (yŭr′ən) *n.* waste material that is produced by the kidneys of vertebrates and that forms a clear, usually slightly acid fluid in mammals but is semisolid in birds and reptiles. [< L *urina*]

urn (ėrn) *n.* 1 a vase or similar vessel having a base or pedestal. Urns are often used for holding the ashes of the dead. 2 a large coffee pot or teapot with a tap. [< L *urna*]
☛ **Hom. earn.**

uro– *combining form.* urine; having to do with the urinary tract: *urology* = *the study of the urinary tract.*

u·ro·gen·i·tal (yŭr′ō jen′ə təl) *adj.* pertaining to or having to do with the urinary and genital organs. [< Gk. *ouron* urine + E *genital*]

u·ro·log·i·cal (yŭr′ə loj′ə kəl) *adj.* of or having to do with urology.

u·rol·o·gist (yü rol′ə jist) *n.* a specialist in urology.

u·rol·o·gy (yü rol′ə jē) *n.* the branch of medicine concerned with the study of the conditions, diseases, etc. of the urinary tract in the female or of the urogenital tract in the male. [< *uro-* + *-logy*]

Ur·sa Ma·jor (ėr′sə mā′jər) the most conspicuous northern constellation, situated near the north pole of the heavens and including the stars that form the Big Dipper; the Great Bear. [< L *ursa major* bigger bear]

Ur·sa Mi·nor (ėr′sə mī′nər) the northern constellation that includes the north pole of the heavens and the stars that form the Little Dipper; the Little Bear. [< L *ursa minor* smaller bear]

ur·sine (ėr′sīn *or* ėr′sən) *adj.* of, having to do with, or resembling a bear or the bear family; bearlike. [< L *ursinus* < *ursus* bear]

Ur·su·line (ėr′sə lin *or* ėr′syə lin, ėr′sə līn′ *or* ėr′syə līn′) *n., adj.* —*n.* a member of a Roman Catholic order of nuns founded in 1535 in Brescia, Italy, for the education of girls and for the care of the sick and needy. —*adj.* of or having to do with Saint Ursula, a British martyr of the fourth or fifth century, or the Ursulines.

ur·ti·car·i·a (ėr′tə ker′ē ə) *n.* hives. [< NL < L *urtica* nettle]

Uru. Uruguay.

U·ru·guay·an (yŭr′ə gwā′ən *or* yŭr′ə gwī′ən) *n., adj.* —*n.* a native or inhabitant of Uruguay, a country in SE South America. —*adj.* of or having to do with Uruguay or its people.

u·rus (yŭr′əs) *n.* aurochs (def. 1). [< L < Gmc.]

us (us; *unstressed,* əs) *pron.* the objective form of **we:** *Mother went with us.* [OE *ūs*]

U.S. United States (of America).

U.S.A. *or* **USA** United States of America.

us·a·bil·i·ty (yūz′ə bil′ə tē) *n.* the quality or state of being usable.

us·a·ble (yūz′ə bəl) *adj.* that can be used; fit for use. Also, **useable.** —**us′a·ble·ness,** *n.*

us·age (yüs′ij *or* yūz′ij) *n.* 1 a way or manner of using; treatment: *The car has had rough usage.* 2 a long-continued practice; customary use; habit; custom: *Travellers should learn many of the usages of the countries they visit.* 3 the customary way of using words: *In Shakespeare's time most unkindest was accepted usage.* [ME < OF *usage* < *us,* n., use < L *usus*]

us·ance (yūz′əns) *n.* 1 *Business.* the time allowed for payment of foreign bills of exchange. 2 the income of benefits of every kind derived from the ownership of wealth. [ME < OF *usance* < *user.* See USE.]

use (*v.* yüz; *n.* yüs) *v.* **used, us·ing;** *n.* —*v.* 1 put into action or

service; avail oneself of for a particular purpose: *We use our legs in walking. He used a knife to cut the meat. May I use your telephone?* 2 employ or practise actively; exercise, especially habitually or customarily: *to use one's knowledge, authority, or judgment, to use bad language.* 3 consume or expend by using: *We have used most of the money. The car uses too much gas.* 4 act toward; treat: *He used us well.* 5 act toward (a person or persons) in a particular way for one's own ends; exploit: *She uses people.*

used (yŭst *or* yüs) **to, a** accustomed to: *used to hardships.* **b** had as one's practice, custom, or state in the past: *He used to come by here every day. We used to sit and talk for hours.*

use up, a consume or expend entirely. **b** *Informal.* tire out; weary; exhaust.

—*n.* 1 the act of using: *the use of tools.* 2 the state of being used: *methods long out of use. Our telephone is in constant use.* 3 employment or usage resulting in or causing wear, damage, etc. 4 usefulness: *a thing of no practical use.* 5 the purpose that a thing is used for: *to find a new use for something.* 6 a way of using: *a poor use of materials.* 7 the fact or quality of serving the needs or ends (of a person or persons): *a park for the use of all the people.* 8 function; service; office: *the use of a catalyst in a chemical process.* 9 a need; occasion: *He had no further use for it.* 10 the power, right, or privilege of using: *to have the use of a boat for the summer.* 11 a custom; habit; usage: *It was his use to rise early.* 12 *Law.* **a** the act or fact of employing, occupying, possessing, or holding property so as to derive benefit from it. **b** the right of a beneficiary to the benefit or profits of land or tenements to which another has legal title in trust for the beneficiary. **c** a trust vesting title to real property in someone for the benefit of a beneficiary.

have no use for, a not need or want. **b** *Informal.* dislike.
make use of, use; employ: *Can you make use of these old curtains?*
put to use, make use of; utilize.
[ME < OF *us,* n., *user,* v., < L *usus,* pp. of *uti* to use] —**us′er,** *n.*
☛ *Syn. v.* 1. **Use, employ, utilize** = put into action or service. **Use,** the general and common word, emphasizes putting something or someone into service as a means or help in carrying out a purpose or getting what one wants: *He uses a typewriter for his homework.* **Employ,** more formal, often interchangeable with **use,** emphasizes putting to work for a special purpose or in a profitable way: *That architect frequently employs glass brick.* **Utilize** emphasizes making useful or turning to profitable use: *She utilizes every scrap of food.*
☛ *Pronun.* **Used to.** When **used,** either as past tense or participial adjective, is employed before the word **to** in sense 7 of the verb, it is pronounced (ŭst) or (üs), the (t) in the latter case being lost or assimilated before the same sound in the following word.

use·a·ble (yü′zə bəl) See **usable.**

used (yüzd) *adj.* not new; that has belonged to another or others: *a used car.*

use·ful (yüs′fəl) *adj.* of use; giving service; helpful. —**use′ful·ly,** *adv.* —**use′ful·ness,** *n.*

use·less (yüs′lis) *adj.* having no use or being of no use: *She is completely useless in the kitchen. That walkie-talkie is useless for any distance over a kilometre. It was useless to complain.* —**use′less·ly,** *adv.* —**use′less·ness,** *n.*

us·er (yü′zər) *n.* a person or thing that uses (*often used in compounds*): *users of a delivery service, a drug user.*

U-shaped (yü′shāpt′) *adj.* having the shape of the letter U: *a U-shaped kitchen counter.*

ush·er (ush′ər) *n., v.* —*n.* 1 a person who shows people to their seats in a church, theatre, etc. 2 a person who has charge of the door of a court, hall, or chamber. 3 *Brit.* an officer whose duty is to walk before a person of rank: *gentleman usher of the Black Rod.* —*v.* 1 act as usher to; conduct; escort: *The patrons were ushered to their seats.* 2 go or come before; introduce or inaugurate (*used with* **in**): *to usher in a new age. Winter was ushered in by a week of cold rains.* [ME < AF *usser,* OF *uissier* < VL *ustiarius* doorkeeper < *ustium,* var. of L *ostium* door]

ush·er·ette (ush′ər et′) *n.* a girl or woman acting as usher in a theatre.

U.S.S.R. *or* **USSR** Union of Soviet Socialist Republics.

u·su·al (yü′zhü əl) *adj.* 1 commonly done, used, occurring, etc.; ordinary or customary: *He didn't take his usual route home last night. It's the usual thing to tip a waiter in a restaurant.* 2 (*noml.*) **the usual,** something that is customarily done, used, etc.: *She sat down at our table and ordered the usual.*
as usual, in the usual manner.
[ME < LL *usualis* < L *usus* use, custom < *uti* to use] —**u′su·al·ly,** *adv.* —**u′su·al·ness,** *n.*
☛ *Syn.* 1. **Usual, customary** = often or commonly seen or found, especially in a certain place or at a given time. **Usual** emphasizes the familiar nature or quality of what is described, and applies to something that is in common use or that commonly or ordinarily happens or occurs: *This is the usual weather at this time of the year.* **Customary** describes something that is according to the usual practices or habits of a particular person or group: *He stayed up long past his customary bedtime.*

u·su·fruct (yü′zyə frukt *or* yü′syə frukt) *n. Law.* the right of using another's property without injuring or destroying it. [< L

usufructu, abl. of ususfructus, earlier usus (et) fructus use and enjoyment]

u·su·rer (yū′zhə rər) *n*. **1** a person who lends money at an extremely high or unlawful rate of interest. **2** *Archaic*. any money-lender. [ME < AF *usurer*, var. of OF *usurier* < LL *usurarius* moneylender < L *usurarius* at interest, for use < *usura* use < *uti* use]

u·su·ri·ous (yū zhùr′ē əs) *adj*. **1** taking extremely high or unlawful interest for the use of money; practising usury. **2** of, having to do with, or involving usury: *Fifty percent is a usurious rate of interest*.

u·surp (yū zėrp′ *or* yū sèrp′) *v*. seize and hold (power, position, authority, etc.) by force or without right: *The king's brother tried to usurp the throne*. [< L *usurpare*, ult. < *usu*, abl., through use + *rapere* seize] —**u·surp′er**, *n*.

u·sur·pa·tion (yū′zər pā′shən *or* yū′sər pā′shən) *n*. the act of usurping: *the usurpation of the throne by a pretender*.

u·su·ry (yū′zhə rē) *n*., *pl*. **-ries**. **1** the lending of money at an extremely high or unlawful rate of interest. **2** an extremely high or unlawful rate or amount of interest. **3** *Archaic*. the lending of money with an interest charge. [ME < Med.L *usuria*, alteration of L *usura*. See USURER.]

Ut. Utah.

UT Utah.

u·ten·sil (yū ten′səl) *n*. **1** a container or implement used for practical household purposes, especially in the kitchen. Pots, pans, kettles, and mops are utensils. **2** an instrument or tool used for some special purpose. Pens and pencils are writing utensils. [ME < Med.L *utensile* < L *utensilis* that may be used < *uti* use]

u·ter·ine (yū′tər in *or* yū′tər īn′) *adj*. **1** of or having to do with the uterus. **2** having the same mother, but a different father. Uterine brothers and stepbrothers born of the same mother. [ME < LL *uterinus* < L *uterus* uterus]

u·ter·us (yū′tər əs) *n*., *pl*. **-ter·i** (-tər ī′ *or* -tər ē′). in female mammals, a muscular organ lying within the pelvic cavity, that holds and nourishes the young till birth; womb. [< L]

u·til·i·dor (yū til′ə dôr′) *n*. *Cdn. North*. a large insulated tube mounted on short posts above ground and housing water, steam, and sewage pipes that supply services to buildings in a town or settlement built on permafrost.

u·til·i·tar·i·an (yū til′ə ter′ē ən) *adj*. **1** of, having to do with, or aimed at utility: *a utilitarian furniture design*. **2** of, having to do with, or designating utilitarianism: *utilitarian philosophy*. —*n*, a person who believes in utilitarianism.

u·til·i·tar·i·an·ism (yū til′ə ter′ē ən iz′əm) *n*. *Philosophy*. **1** the doctrine or belief that the greatest good of the greatest number should be the purpose of human conduct, especially as developed by Jeremy Bentham and John Stuart Mill. **2** the doctrine or belief that actions are good if they are useful. **3** a utilitarian quality or character.

u·til·i·ty (yū til′ə tē) *n*., *pl*. **-ties**. **1** the power to satisfy needs; usefulness: *The cottage was obviously designed more for utility than beauty*. **2** something that is useful. **3** (*adj*.) designed or serving strictly for usefulness rather than appearance or luxury: *utility furnishings*. **4** public utility. **5** the supplying of gas, water, electricity, etc. by a public utility: *They pay a lot more for utilities than we do*. **6** (*adj*.) designating, of, or having to do with the supplying of such services or the equipment used for this: *The car struck a utility pole*. **7** (*adj*.) designating the lowest and cheapest government grade of meat: *A utility grade turkey may be an A or B grade that has had the skin broken, or has a wing missing, etc*. **8** *Philosophy*. the greatest happiness of the greatest number. [ME < OF < L *utilitas*, ult. < *uti* use]

u·ti·li·za·tion (yū′tə lə zā′shən *or* -ī zā′shən) *n*. the act of utilizing or the state of being utilized.

u·ti·lize (yū′tə līz′) *v*. **-lized, -liz·ing**. make use of; put to some

hat, āge, fär; let, ēqual, tèrm; it, īce
hot, ōpen, ôrder; oil, out; cup, pút, rüle,
əbove, takən, pencəl, lemən, circəs

ch, child; ng, long; sh, ship
th, thin; ᴛʜ, then; zh, measure

practical use: *to utilize leftovers in cooking*. —**u′ti·liz′a·ble**, *adj*. —**u′ti·liz′er**, *n*.
☛ *Syn*. See note at **use**.

ut·most (ut′mōst) *adj*. **1** of the greatest or highest degree, amount, or quantity: *Sunshine is of the utmost importance to health*. **2** farthest or most distant; extreme: *the utmost ends of the earth*. —*n*. **1** the most that is possible; extreme limit: *He enjoyed himself to the utmost*. **2** all that one can do; the greatest or highest of one's powers or abilities: *She did her utmost to help him find a good job*. [OE *ūtemest* < *ūte* outside + *-mest* -most]

u·to·pi·a (yū tō′pē ə) *n*. **1** Utopia, an ideal commonwealth where perfect justice and social harmony exist, described in *Utopia*, by Sir Thomas More. **2** an ideal place or state with perfect laws. **3** a visionary, impractical system of political or social perfection. [< NL < Gk. *ou* not + *topos* place]

u·to·pi·an (yū tō′pē ən) *adj*., *n*. —*adj*. **1** Usually, **Utopian**, of, having to do with, or characteristic of Utopia. **2** of, having to do with, or like a utopia. **3** visionary; impractical. —*n*. **1** an ardent but impractical reformer; idealist. **2** Utopian, an inhabitant of Utopia.

u·to·pi·an·ism (yū tō′pē ən iz′əm) *n*. **1** the ideas, beliefs, and aims, of Utopians. **2** ideal schemes for the improvement of life, social conditions, etc.

u·tri·cle (yū′trə kəl) *n*. **1** *Botany*. **a** a small sac or baglike body, such as an air cell in seaweed. **b** a thin bladderlike seed vessel. **2** *Anatomy*. the larger of the two sacs of the internal ear. [< L *utriculus*, dim. of *uter* skin bag, skin bottle]

ut·ter[1] (ut′ər) *adj*. complete; total; absolute: *utter surprise, utter darkness, an utter failure*. [OE *ūtera* outer]

ut·ter[2] (ut′ər) *v*. **1** speak; make known; express: *the last words he uttered, to utter one's thoughts*. **2** give out as sound: *He uttered a cry of pain*. **3** *Law*. pass off (forged documents, counterfeit money, etc.) as genuine. [ME *uttren*, literally, put forth < OE *ūtor*, comparative of *ūt* out] —**ut′ter·a·ble**, *adj*. —**ut′ter·er**, *n*.

ut·ter·ance (ut′ər əns) *n*. **1** an uttering; expression in words or sounds: *The child gave utterance to his grief*. **2** the power or a way of speaking: *defective utterance*. **3** something uttered; a spoken word or words: *Some of his famous political utterances are included in the book*. **4** *Law*. the passing off of counterfeit money, forged cheques, etc.; uttering.

ut·ter·ly (ut′ər lē) *adv*. completely; totally; absolutely.

ut·ter·most (ut′ər mōst′) *adj*. *or n*. utmost.

u·vu·la (yū′vyə lə) *n*., *pl*. **-las** *or* **-lae** (-lē′ *or* -lī′). the small lobe of flesh hanging down from the soft palate in the back of the mouth. [< LL *uvula*, dim. of L *uva*, originally, grape]

u·vu·lar (yū′vyə lər) *adj*., *n*. —*adj*. **1** of or having to do with the uvula. **2** of a speech sound, produced or pronounced with vibration of the uvula. —*n*. a uvular speech sound.

ux. wife (for L *uxor*).

ux·o·ri·ous (uk sôr′ē əs *or* ug zôr′ē əs) *adj*. excessively or foolishly devoted to one's wife. [< L *uxorious* < *uxor* wife] —**ux·o′ri·ous·ly**, *adv*. —**ux·o′ri·ous·ness**, *n*.

Uz·bek (uz′bek) *n*., *adj*. —*n*. **1** a member of a Turkic people of Turkestan, a region in central Asia, especially of Uzbek, a republic of the U.S.S.R. **2** the Turkic language of the Uzbeks. —*adj*. of or having to do with Uzbek, its people, or their language.

Vv

v or **V** (vē) *n., pl.* **v's** or **V's. 1** the twenty-second letter of the English alphabet. **2** any speech sound represented by this letter. **3** a person or thing identified as *v,* especially the twenty-second in a series. **4** the Roman numeral for 5. **5** something shaped like the letter V. **6** (*adj.*) of or being a V or v.

v. 1 verb. **2** verse. **3** versus. **4** see (for L *vide*). **5** voice. **6** vice (used in titles). **7** volume. **8** von (used in names). **9** version. **10** violin. **11** velocity. **12** vocative. **13** very. **14** verso.

V 1 vanadium. **2** volt. **3** victory. **4** vector.

V. 1 Venerable. **2** Viscount. **3** Victoria. **4** Volunteer.

Va. Virginia (the state).

VA Virginia (the state).

V.A. Vicar Apostolic.

va·can·cy (vā′kən sē) *n., pl.* **-cies. 1** the state of being unoccupied or empty. **2** an unfilled post, office, or position: *The company has a vacancy for a sales representative.* **3** a space, room, apartment, etc. that is unoccupied and available: *There were no vacancies in the parking lot. The hotel had one vacancy.* **4** empty space; void: *He stared into the vacancy of the night.* **5** emptiness of mind; a lack of thought or intelligence. **6** *Archaic.* idleness or an interval of idleness.

va·cant (vā′kənt) *adj.* **1** empty; not occupied or filled: *a vacant house, a vacant chair, a vacant space.* **2** without thought or intelligence: *a vacant smile.* **3** having no expression: *a vacant face.* **4** free from work, business, etc.: *vacant time.* [ME < L *vacans, -antis,* ppr. of *vacare* be empty] **—va′cant·ly,** *adv.*

va·cate (və kāt′ *or* vā′kāt) *v.* **-cat·ed, -cat·ing. 1** go away from and leave empty or unoccupied; make vacant: *They will vacate the house next month.* **2** leave. **3** make void; annul; cancel. [< L *vacare* be empty]

va·ca·tion (və kā′shən *or* vā kā′shən) *n., v.* **—n. 1** a scheduled time of rest and freedom from work or activity, especially in schools and courts of law: *The school has a vacation at Christmas.* **2** a period of time spent away from work; holidays: *Is he taking a vacation this year? She spent her vacation at the cottage.* **3** the act or an instance of vacating.
—v. take or spend a vacation: *They are vacationing in the North.* [ME < L *vacatio, -onis* < *vacare* have time (off)] **—va·ca′tion·less,** *adj.*

va·ca·tion·er (və kā′shən ər *or* vā kā′shən ər) *n.* a person who is taking a vacation, especially away from home: *The resort town was crowded with vacationers.*

va·ca·tion·ist (və kā′shən ist *or* vā kā′shən ist) *n.* vacationer.

vac·ci·nate (vak′sə nāt′) *v.* **-nat·ed, -nat·ing. 1** inoculate with vaccine as a protection against smallpox or other diseases. **2** perform or practise vaccination.

vac·ci·na·tion (vak′sə nā′shən) *n.* **1** the act or process of vaccinating: *Vaccination has made smallpox a very rare disease.* **2** the sore or the scar left by vaccinating.

vac·cine (vak′sēn *or* vak sēn′) *n.* a preparation, often made of weakened viruses of a disease, used to inoculate a person in order to protect him from that disease: *Salk vaccine is used against polio.* [< L *vaccinus* pertaining to cows < *vacca* cow, used in the Mod.L phrase *virus vaccinus* virus of cowpox. This virus became the first vaccine when it was found to protect people against smallpox.]

vac·il·late (vas′ə lāt′) *v.* **-lat·ed, -lat·ing. 1** move first one way and then another; waver. **2** waver in mind or opinion: *A vacillating man finds it hard to make up his mind.* [< L *vacillare*]

vac·il·la·tion (vas′ə lā′shən) *n.* **1** the act or an instance of vacillating. **2** the inability to make up one's mind or take a stand.

va·cu·i·ty (va kyü′ə tē) *n., pl.* **-ties. 1** the quality or state of being empty or without thought or intelligence. **2** an empty space; vacuum. **3** something, such as an idea, that is foolish or stupid; inanity. **4** absence or lack (of something specified). [< L *vacuitas* < *vacuus* vacuous]

vac·u·ole (vak′yü ōl′) *n.* a tiny cavity in the cytoplasm of a living cell, containing fluid. [< F *vacuole* < L *vacuus* empty]

vac·u·ous (vak′yü əs) *adj.* **1** showing no thought or intelligence; foolish; stupid: *a vacuous statement.* **2** empty. [< L *vacuus*] **—vac′u·ous·ly,** *adv.*

vac·u·um (vak′yü əm) *n., pl.* **vac·u·ums** or (defs 1-3, 5) **vac·u·a** (vak′yü ə); *v.* **—n. 1** an empty space utterly devoid of matter, even air. **2** an enclosed space from which almost all air, gas, etc. has been removed. **3** a decrease of air pressure below normal atmospheric pressure. **4** (*adj.*) of, containing, using, or producing a vacuum: *vacuum brakes, a vacuum pump.* **5** an empty space; void: *His wife's death left a vacuum in his life.* **6** vacuum cleaner.
—v. clean with a vacuum cleaner: *to vacuum a rug. I was vacuuming when I heard the phone ring.* [< L *vacuum,* neut. adj., empty]

vacuum bottle a bottle or flask made with a vacuum between its inner and outer walls so that its contents will stay hot or cold for a long time.

vacuum cleaner an electrical appliance for cleaning carpets, curtains, floors, etc. by suction.

vacuum flask vacuum bottle.

vac·u·um–packed (vak′yü əm pakt′) *adj.* **1** of a container, having most of the air removed before being sealed in order to preserve the freshness, etc. of the contents: *Coffee, nuts, etc. are often sold in vacuum-packed tins.* **2** packed in airtight containers from which most of the air has been removed: *vacuum-packed tennis balls.*

vacuum pump 1 a pump or device by which a partial vacuum can be produced. **2** a pump in which a partial vacuum is utilized to raise water.

vacuum tube an electron tube from which almost all the air has been removed, leaving an almost perfect vacuum through which an electric current can pass freely.

va·de me·cum (vā′dē mē′kəm *or* vā′dē mā′kəm) **1** anything a person carries about with him because of its usefulness. **2** a book for ready reference; manual; handbook. [< L *vade mecum* go with me]

V.Adm. or **VAdm** vice-admiral.

vag·a·bond (vag′ə bond′) *n., adj.* **—n. 1** a wanderer, especially a tramp. **2** an idle, shiftless person; rascal.
—adj. 1 wandering: *Gypsies are traditionally a vagabond people.* **2** of, having to do with, or characteristic of a wanderer: *a vagabond life.* **3** shiftless and irresponsible. [ME < OF < L *vagabundus,* ult. < *vagus* rambling]

vag·a·bond·age (vag′ə bon′dij) *n.* the fact or state of being a vagabond; idle wandering.

va·gar·y (və ger′ē *or* vā′gə rē) *n., pl.* **-gar·ies. 1** an odd fancy; extravagant notion: *the vagaries of a dream.* **2** an odd action; caprice: *the vagaries of fashion.* [probably < L *vagari* wander < *vagus* roving]

va·gi·na (və jī′nə) *n., pl.* **-nas** or **-nae** (-nē *or* -nī). **1** in female mammals, the passage from the uterus to the vulva or external opening. **2** *Botany.* a sheathlike part in certain plants formed around the stem by the base of the leaf. [< L *vagina,* originally, sheath]

vag·i·nal (vaj′ə nəl *or* və jī′nəl) *adj.* **1** of or having to do with the vagina of a female mammal. **2** of or resembling a sheath.

vag·i·nate (vaj′ə nit *or* vaj′ə nāt′) *adj.* **1** having a vagina or sheath. **2** like a sheath.

vag·i·ni·tis (vaj′ə nīt′is) *n.* inflammation of the vagina.

va·gran·cy (vā′grən sē) *n., pl.* **-cies. 1** a wandering idly from place to place without proper means or ability to earn a living. **2** *Law.* the criminal offence of being a vagrant: *The tramp was charged with vagrancy.* **3** a wandering or digression of mind or thought.

va·grant (vā′grənt) *n., adj.* **—n. 1** a wanderer, especially a person who goes from place to place without a regular residence, often living by begging, etc. **2** *Law.* a beggar, prostitute, drunkard, etc. living without lawful or visible means of support. **—adj. 1** of, having to do with, or being a vagrant. **2** moving in no definite direction or course; wandering. [? alteration of AF *wacrant* (< Gmc.), influenced by F *vagant* straying (< L *vagari* wander)] **—va′grant·ly,** *adv.*

vague (vāg) *adj.* **va·guer, va·guest. 1** not clearly expressed or defined: *a vague statement, a vague notion, a vague longing.* **2** having no definite meaning or character: *"Nice" is a vague term.* **3** not thinking or expressing oneself clearly: *He was very vague*

about his plans. **4** having no definite outline: *a vague shape in the mist.* [< MF < L *vagus* wandering. Doublet of VAGUS.] —**vague′ly**, *adv.* —**vague′ness**, *n.*
☛ *Syn.* See note at **obscure.**

va·gus (vā′gəs) *n., pl.* **va·gi** (vā′jī *or* -jē). either of a pair of nerves extending from the brain to the heart, lungs, stomach, and other organs. [< L *vagus* wandering. Doublet of VAGUE.]

vail (vāl) *n. Archaic.* **1** lower; cause or allow to fall. **2** take off; doff. **3** yield; bow. [< OF *valer*, or < *avale* < OF *avaler*, both ult. < L *ad vallem* to the valley]

vain (vān) *adj.* **1** having too much pride in one's looks, ability, etc. **2** of no use; without effect or success; producing no good result: *a vain hope. He made several vain attempts to pull himself out of the icy water.* **3** of no value or importance; worthless; empty: *a vain boast.*
in vain, without effect or success: *My shout for help was in vain, for no one was near enough to hear me.*
[ME < OF < L *vanus*] —**vain′ly**, *adv.* —**vain′ness**, *n.*
☛ *Hom.* **vane, vein.**
☛ *Syn. adj.* **2. Vain, futile** = without effect or success. **Vain** describes thinking, action, effort, etc. that fails to accomplish what is hoped for and aimed at, or to produce any valuable result: *The principal made another vain appeal for better equipment in the high-school laboratories.* **Futile** adds and emphasizes the idea of being incapable of producing the desired, or any, result, and often suggests being useless or unwise to attempt: *Without modern antibiotics, early attempts to treat many diseases were futile.*

vain·glo·ri·ous (vān′glôr′ē əs) *adj.* excessively proud or boastful; extremely vain. —**vain′glo′ri·ous·ly**, *adv.*

vain·glo·ry (vān′glôr′ē) *n.* **1** an extreme pride in oneself; boastful vanity. **2** worthless pomp or show. [ME < OF < Med.L *vana gloria*]

vair (ver) *n.* **1** a grey-and-white squirrel fur used in the Middle Ages for lining and trimming the robes of nobles. **2** *Heraldry.* the representation of this fur by small shield-shaped or bell-shaped figures usually alternately silver and blue. [ME < OF < L *varius* variegated. Doublet of VARIOUS.]

val·ance (val′əns) *n.* **1** a short drapery or a decorative wooden or metal frame around the top of a window, used to hide curtain fixtures, etc. **2** a short curtain hanging around the edge of a bed, dressing table, etc. [probably from *Valence*, a town in SE France]

vale¹ (vāl) *n. Poetic.* valley. [ME < OF *val* < L *vallis*]

va·le² (vä′lē *or* vä′lā) *interj. or n. Latin.* good-bye; farewell.

val·e·dic·tion (val′ə dik′shən) *n.* the act or an instance of bidding farewell. [< L *valedict-*, pp. stem of *valedicere* bid farewell < *vale* be well! + *dicere* say]

val·e·dic·to·ri·an (val′ə dik tôr′ē ən) *n.* a student who gives the farewell address at the graduation of his class.

val·e·dic·to·ry (val′ə dik′tə rē *or* val′ə dik′trē) *n., pl.* **-ries**; *adj.*
—*n.* a farewell address, especially at the graduation exercises of a school or college. —*adj.* bidding farewell.

va·lence (vā′ləns) *n. Chemistry.* the quality of an atom or radical that determines the number of other atoms or radicals with which it can combine, indicated by the number of hydrogen atoms with which it can combine or which it can displace. Elements whose atoms lose electrons, such as hydrogen and the metals, have a positive valence. Elements whose atoms add electrons, such as oxygen and other non-metals, have a negative valence. Oxygen has a negative valence of two; hydrogen has a positive valence of one; one atom of oxygen combines with two of hydrogen to form a molecule of water. [< LL *valentia* strength < *valere* be strong]

Va·len·ci·a or **va·len·ci·a** (və len′shē ə *or* və len′shə) *n.* one of the most extensively cultivated varieties of sweet orange, having a thin skin and usually seedless pulp.

Va·len·ci·ennes (və len′sē enz′) *n.* a fine lace in which the pattern and background are made together of the same threads. [< *Valenciennes*, a city in N France, where this lace was first made]

va·len·cy (vā′lən sē) *n., pl.* **-cies.** valence.

val·en·tine (val′ən tīn′) *n.* **1** a greeting card or small gift sent or given on Saint Valentine's Day, February 14. **2** a sweetheart chosen on this day.

Valentine's Day (val′ən tīn′) Saint Valentine's Day, the day on which valentines are exchanged, February 14.

va·le·ri·an (və lēr′ē ən) *n.* **1** any of a genus (*Valeriana*) of perennial herbs, especially the common valerian (*V. officinalis*), a tall garden plant having clusters of small, very fragrant, white or reddish flowers and a strong-smelling root. **2** a drug made from the dried roots of the common valerian, formerly used in medicine. **3** (*adj.*) designating a family (Valerianaceae) of perennial or annual herbs or shrubs found mainly in the northern hemisphere. The valerian family includes the valerian and spikenard. [ME < OF

valeriane or Med.L *valeriana* < L *Valerius*, a Roman gens name]

val·et (val′it *or* val′ā) *n., v.* **-et·ed, -et·ing.** —*n.* **1** a male servant who takes care of a man's clothes, helps him dress, etc. **2** an employee of a hotel, etc. who cleans or presses clothes. —*v.* serve as a valet. [< F *valet*, var. of OF *vaslet*. See VARLET.]

val·e·tu·di·nar·i·an (val′ə tyü′də ner′ē ən *or* val′ə tü′-) *n., adj.*
—*n.* a weak or sickly person, especially one who thinks too much about being sick. —*adj.* of, having to do with, or characteristic of a valetudinarian. [< L *valetudinarius* sickly < *valetudo* (good or bad) health < *valere* be strong]

Val·hal·la (val hal′ə) *n. Norse mythology.* the hall where the souls of heroes slain in battle feast with the god Odin. [< NL < ON *valhöll* < *valr* those slain in battle + *höll* hall]

val·iant (val′yənt) *adj.* brave; courageous: *a valiant soldier, a valiant deed.* [ME < OF *vaillant*, ppr. of *valoir* be strong < L *valere*] —**val′iant·ly**, *adv.* —**val′iant·ness**, *n.*

val·id (val′id) *adj.* **1** supported by facts or authority; sound; true: *a valid argument.* **2** having legal force; legally binding: *A contract made by a person who is a minor is not valid.* **3** appropriate in a particular situation or for a particular goal or end; effective: *a valid approach to a problem, a valid excuse.* [< L *validus* strong < *valere* be strong] —**val′id·ly**, *adv.*
☛ *Syn.* **1. Valid, sound, cogent** = strong or convincing with respect to truth, rightness, or reasoning. **Valid**, describing reasons, objections, arguments, evidence, etc., emphasizes being based on truth or fact and supported by correct reasoning: *His objections to women doctors are not valid.* **Sound** emphasizes having a solid foundation of truth or right and being free from defects or errors in reasoning: *The author has sound views on opportunities today.* **Cogent**, a formal word, means "so valid or sound as to be convincing": *He gives cogent advice to young people.*

val·i·date (val′ə dāt′) *v.* **-dat·ed, -dat·ing.** **1** make or declare legally binding; give legal force to: *to validate election results.* **2** support by facts or authority; confirm: *The results of the experiments validated her hypothesis.*

va·lid·i·ty (və lid′ə tē) *n., pl.* **-ties.** the quality, fact, or condition of being valid: *He questioned the validity of the contract.*

va·lise (və lēs′) *n.* a travelling bag to hold clothes, etc. [< F < Ital. *valigia*]

Val·kyr·ie (val kēr′ē) *n. Norse mythology.* one of the handmaidens of Odin who ride through the air and hover over battlefields, choosing the heroes who are to die in battle and afterward leading them to Valhalla. [< ON *valkyrja* < *valr* those slain in battle + *kyrja* chooser]

val·la·tion (va lā′shən) *n.* a trench; rampart. [< LL *vallatio*, *-onis* < L *vallare* surround with a rampart < *vallum* rampart]

val·ley (val′ē) *n., pl.* **-leys. 1** low land between hills or mountains, usually having a stream or river flowing through it. **2** a wide region drained by a great river system: *the Ottawa valley.* **3** any hollow or structure like a valley. **4** *Architecture.* a trough formed where two slopes of a roof meet or where a roof meets a wall. [ME < OF *valee* < *val* vale < L *vallis*]

val·or or **val·our** (val′ər) *n.* bravery; courage. [ME < OF < LL *valor* < L *valere* be strong]

val·or·i·za·tion (val′ər ə zā′shən *or* val′ər ī zā′shən) *n.* the actual or attempted maintenance of certain prices for a commodity by a government. [< *valor*, in obs. sense of "value" < LL < L *valere* be worth]

val·or·ize (val′ər īz′) *v.* **-ized, -iz·ing. 1** assign a value to. **2** regulate the price of by valorization.

val·or·ous (val′ər əs) *adj.* valiant; brave; courageous.
—**val′or·ous·ly**, *adv.* —**val′or·ous·ness**, *n.*

valse (väls) *n. French.* waltz.

val·u·a·ble (val′yə bəl *or* val′yü ə bəl) *adj., n.* —*adj.* **1** having value; being worth something. **2** having great value. **3** that can have its value measured.
—*n.* Usually, **valuables,** *pl.* articles of value: *She keeps her jewellery and other valuables in a safe.* —**val′u·a·ble·ness**, *n.* —**val′u·a·bly**, *adv.*
☛ *Syn. adj.* **2. Valuable, precious** = worth much. **Valuable** describes something that is worth much money and would bring a high price if sold, or, often, something of great usefulness or benefit to the person (or group) that has it: *He has a valuable stamp collection.* **Precious** describes something that is very valuable because it is rare or scarce, or something of great worth which belongs to it by its very nature: *Many precious oriental art treasures are kept in the Royal Ontario Museum.*

val·u·a·tion (val′yü ā′shən) *n.* **1** value estimated or determined: *The jeweller's valuation of the necklace was $10 000.* **2** an estimating or determining of the value of something.

val·ue (val′yü) *n., v.* **-ued, -u·ing.** —*n.* **1** worth; excellence; usefulness; importance: *the value of education.* **2** the real worth; proper price: *He bought the house for less than its value.* **3** the power to buy: *The value of the dollar has varied greatly.* **4** an estimated worth: *He placed a value on his furniture.* **5** the meaning; effect; force: *the value of a symbol.* **6** a number or amount represented by a symbol: *The value of XIV is fourteen.* **7 values,** *pl.*

the established ideals of life. **8** *Music.* the relative length of a tone indicated by a note. **9** in speech, the special quality of sound. **10** in a painting, etc.: **a** the degree of lightness or darkness. **b** the relative importance or effect of an object, part, spot of color, etc.
—*v.* **1** rate at a certain value or price; estimate the value of. **2** think highly of; regard highly: *to value one's judgment.* [ME < OF *valu* < pp. of *valoir* be worth < L *valere*] —**val′u·er**, *n.*

☛ *Syn. v.* **2. Value, appreciate, esteem** = think highly of a person or thing. **Value** = think highly of people or things because we consider them extremely good, desirable, or important: *I value her friendship.* **Appreciate** = think highly of people or things because we can understand them enough to value or enjoy them: *His classmates appreciate her ready wit.* **Esteem** = value someone or something very highly, respect him, and at the same time feel an attachment to him: *One esteems a man like Churchill.*

val·ued (val′yüd) *adj.* **1** having its value estimated or determined. **2** regarded highly.

value judgment or **judgement** an assessment or judgment of the worth, excellence, desirability, etc. of an action, person, program, etc.

val·ue·less (val′yü lis) *adj.* without value; worthless.

val·vate (val′vāt) *adj.* **1** furnished with, or opening by, a valve or valves. **2** serving as or resembling a valve. **3** *Botany.* **a** meeting without overlapping, as the parts of certain buds do. **b** composed of, or characterized by, such parts. [< L *valvatus* having folding doors]

valve (valv) *n., v.* **valved, valv·ing.** —*n.* **1** a movable part that controls the flow of a liquid, gas, etc. through a pipe by opening and closing the passage. A tap is one kind of valve. **2** a flaplike membrane or structure in a hollow organ or part that works like a valve. The valves in the heart permit passage of blood in only one direction. **3** one of the two halves of the shell of an oyster, clam, etc. **4** *Botany.* **a** one of the sections formed when a seed vessel bursts open. **b** a section that opens like a lid when an anther opens. **5** *Esp.Brit.* a vacuum tube used in a radio. **6** *Music.* a device in certain wind instruments for changing the pitch of the tone by changing the direction and length of the column of air. Cornets, trumpets, and French horns have valves; they are pressed separately or in combination to produce tones between the 'open' tones.
—*v.* **1** furnish with a valve or valves. **2** control the flow of a liquid, gas, etc. by a valve. **3** discharge gas from a balloon by opening a valve. [< L *valva* one of a pair of folding doors] —**valve′less**, *adj.* —**valve′like′**, *adj.*

val·vu·lar (val′vyə lər) *adj.* **1** of or having to do with a valve, especially of the heart: *a valvular disorder.* **2** having the form of a valve. **3** furnished with or working by valves.

va·moose (va müs′) *v.* **-moosed, -moos·ing.** *Slang.* go away quickly. [< Sp. *vamos* let us go]

vamp¹ (vamp) *n., v.* —*n.* **1** the upper front part of a shoe or boot covering the instep and, sometimes, the toes. See **shoe** for picture. **2** a piece or patch added to an old thing to make it look new. **3** *Music.* an improvised musical accompaniment, introduction, etc. —*v.* **1** furnish or repair with a new vamp. **2** patch up; make (an old thing) look new (*usually used with* **up**). **3** invent, especially in order to deceive (*often used with* **up**): *He vamped up a big story about needing the money to help out a friend.* **4** *Music.* improvise an accompaniment, introduction, etc. [ME < AF *vampe*, OF *avanpie* forepart of the foot < *avant* before (< L *ab* from + *ante* before) + *pie* foot < L *pes*] —**vamp′er**, *n.*

vamp² (vamp) *Slang. n., v.* —*n.* a woman who seduces and exploits men; unscrupulous flirt. —*v.* act as a vamp; use wiles and charm on: *to vamp an unsuspecting man.* [< *vampire*]

vam·pire (vam′pīr) *n.* **1** an imaginary creature believed to be a corpse that comes back to life at night and sucks the blood of people while they sleep. **2** a person who ruthlessly takes advantage of others. **3** a woman who seduces and ruins men. **4** any of various tropical American bats (genera *Desmodus* and *Diphylla* of the family *Desmodontidae*) that live by sucking the blood of vertebrates and that can be dangerous to human beings and animals because they transmit diseases such as rabies. **5** any of various other species of bat that are believed to feed on blood but do not actually do so. [< F < Hungarian *vampir*; cf. Turkish *uber* witch]

van¹ (van) *n.* the front part of an army, fleet, or other advancing group; vanguard: *The magazine tries to be in the van of current fashion.* [< *vanguard*]

van² (van) *n.* **1** a large, enclosed motor truck or trailer used for moving furniture, etc. **2** a small, light motor truck with a completely enclosed body used as a camper, for delivering goods to customers, etc. **3** *Brit.* a railway car for luggage or freight. [< *caravan*]

va·na·di·um (və nā′dē əm) *n.* a rare, silvery grey, metallic chemical element used in making certain kinds of steel. *Symbol:* V; *at.no.* 23; *at.wt.* 50.942. [< NL < ON *Vanadis*, a name for Freya, the Norse goddess of love and beauty]

vanadium steel a steel alloy containing vanadium to make it tougher and harder.

hat, āge, fär; let, ēqual, tèrm; it, īce
hot, ōpen, ôrder; oil, out; cup, put, rüle,
əbove, takən, pencəl, lemən, circəs
ch, child; ng, long; sh, ship
th, thin; ᴛʜ, then; zh, measure

Van Al·len belt (van′al′ən) a broad zone or belt of high-intensity radiation above the earth's atmosphere, produced by a high concentration of charged particles trapped in the magnetic field of the earth.

van·dal (van′dəl) *n.* **1 Vandal, a** a member of a Germanic people originally living in the area south of the Baltic between the Vistula and the Oder, who ravaged Gaul, Spain, and North Africa and in A.D. 455 sacked Rome. Many books and works of art were destroyed by them. **b** (*adjl.*) of or having to do with the Vandals. **2** a person who willfully destroys or damages things, especially beautiful or valuable ones. **3** (*adjl.*) of or like a vandal; willfully or senselessly destructive. [< LL *Vandalus* < Gmc.]

van·dal·ism (van′dəl iz′əm) *n.* willful destruction or defacement of things, especially works of art or other valuable things or property.

van·dal·ize (van′də līz′) *v.* **-ized, -iz·ing.** destroy or damage willfully; subject to vandalism.

Van·dyke (van dīk′) *n.* **1** a short, pointed beard. **2** any of a series of V-shaped points forming a decorative edging on lace, cloth, etc. **3** a large collar, cape, etc. edged with such points. **4** (*adjl.*) in the style of dress characteristic of the portraits of the Flemish painter, Sir Anthony Van Dyck (1599-1641).

Vandyke brown 1 a medium to dark, earthy brown color. **2** a dark-brown organic pigment used by the painter Van Dyck; also, any of various other pigments made to imitate this.

vane (vān) *n.* **1** weather vane. **2** a blade, wing, or similar part attached to an axis, wheel, etc., so as to be turned by a current of air or liquid or to produce a current when turned. The vanes of a windmill are turned by the wind; the vanes of an electric fan produce air currents as they turn. **3** the flat, soft part of a feather. [OE *fana* banner]
☛ *Hom.* **vain, vein.**

van·guard (van′gärd′) *n.* **1** a body of soldiers marching ahead of the main part of an army to make sure the way is clear. **2** the foremost or leading position; van. **3** the leaders of a movement, especially persons who experiment or work with new ideas. [ME < MF *avantgarde* < OF < *avant* before (< L *ab* from + *ante* before) + *garde* guard < Gmc.]

va·nil·la (və nil′ə) *n.* **1** a food flavoring made from vanilla beans. **2** vanilla bean. **3** any of a genus (*Vanilla*) of tropical American orchids, especially *V. planifolia*, which is the chief source of the food flavoring. [< NL < Sp. *vainilla*, literally, little pod, ult. < L *vagina* sheath]

vanilla bean the long, beanlike fruit of a vanilla, especially *V. planifolia*, from which the flavoring vanilla is extracted.

van·ish (van′ish) *v.* **1** pass suddenly out of sight; disappear: *The sun vanished behind a cloud.* **2** cease to be: *Dinosaurs have vanished from the earth.* [ME < OF *esvaniss-*, a stem of *esvanir*, ult. < L *evanescere* < *ex-* out + *vanus* empty] —**van′ish·er**, *n.*
☛ *Syn.* **1.** See note at **disappear.**

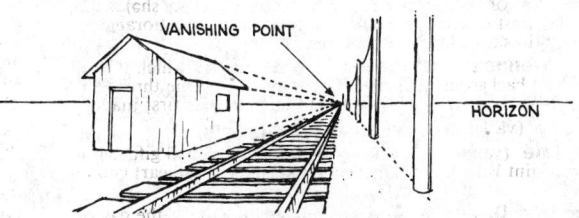

VANISHING POINT
HORIZON

vanishing point 1 the point toward which receding parallel lines seem to converge. **2** a point of disappearance.

van·i·ty (van′ə tē) *n., pl.* **-ties. 1** too much pride in one's looks, ability, etc. **2** a lack of real value; worthlessness: *the vanity of wealth.* **3** a useless or worthless thing. **4** worthless pleasure or display. **5** lack of effect or success. **6** vanity case. **7** dressing table. **8** a bathroom counter or cabinet with a built-in sink and storage space. [ME < OF < L *vanitas* < *vanus* empty]

vanity case a small travelling case used by women, containing a mirror and fitted for carrying cosmetics, etc.

Vanity Fair any place or scene, such as the world, a great city, or the world of fashion, regarded as given over to vain pleasure or empty show. [< *Vanity Fair*, a fair described in John Bunyan's *Pilgrim's Progress*, symbolizing the world of vain pleasure or empty show]

van·quish (vang′kwish) *v.* conquer; defeat; overcome. [ME < OF *vencus*, pp. of *veintre* or < OF *vainquiss-*, a stem of *vainquir*, both < L *vincere* conquer] —**van′quish·a·ble**, *adj.* —**van′quish·er**, *n.*

van·tage (van′tij) *n.* 1 a better position or condition; advantage. 2 the first point scored in a tennis game after deuce. [ult. < *advantage*]

vantage ground a position that gives one an advantage; a favorable position.

vantage point 1 a superior position from which a person can see to advantage. 2 a favorable condition that gives a person an advantage.

van·ward (van′wərd) *adj. or adv.* toward the front. [< *van*[1] + *-ward*]

vap·id (vap′id) *adj.* without much life or flavor; flat; dull. [< L *vapidus*] —**vap′id·ly**, *adv.* —**vap′id·ness**, *n.*

va·pid·i·ty (va pid′ə tē) *n.* insipidity; flatness of flavor.

va·por or **va·pour** (vā′pər) *n., v.* —*n.* 1 moisture in the air that can be seen; fog; mist. 2 steam from boiling water. 3 *Physics.* a gas formed by heating a substance that is usually a liquid or a solid. 4 **a** a substance, as alcohol, mercury, or benzoin, that has been changed into vapor for use medicinally, industrially, etc. **b** a mixture of a vaporized substance and air, as in an internal-combustion engine. **c** the emission or exhalation of such mixtures or of any substance in gaseous form. 5 something without substance; empty fancy. 6 **the vapors**, *Archaic.* low spirits.
—*v.* 1 pass off as vapor. 2 send out in vapor. 3 give out vapor. 4 boast; swagger; brag. [< L]

va·por·ish (vā′pər ish) *adj.* 1 like vapor. 2 abounding in vapor. 3 *Archaic.* in low spirits. 4 *Archaic.* having to do with or connected with low spirits: *vaporish fears.*

va·por·ize (vā′pər īz′) *v.* **-ized, -iz·ing.** change from a solid or liquid to a vapor: *To distil water, we first have to vaporize it.* —**va′por·iz′a·ble**, *adj.* —**va′por·i·za′tion**, *n.* —**va′por·iz′er**, *n.*

va·por·ous (vā′pər əs) *adj.* 1 full of vapor; misty. 2 like vapor. 3 soon passing; worthless.

vapor trail or **vapour trail** a white trail of water droplets or ice crystals that is sometimes seen in the wake of an aircraft flying at high altitudes. A vapor trail is caused by the condensation of moisture in the atmosphere or of exhaust gases from the aircraft.

va·por·y (vā′pər ē) *adj.* vaporous.

va·que·ro (vä ker′ō) *n., pl.* **-ros.** a cowboy or herdsman in Spanish America or the SW United States. [< Sp. *vaquero*, ult. < L *vacca* cow. Cf BUCKAROO.]

var. 1 variant; variation; variable. 2 variometer.

va·re·ny·ky (və ren′ə kē) *n.pl.* boiled dumplings filled with any of numerous fillings, such as cottage cheese, fruit, etc.

var·i·a·bil·i·ty (ver′ē ə bil′ə tē or var′ē ə bil′ə tē) *n.* 1 the fact or quality of being variable. 2 a tendency to vary.

var·i·a·ble (ver′ē ə bəl or var′ē ə bəl) *adj., n.* —*adj.* 1 apt to change; changeable; uncertain: *variable winds.* 2 likely to shift from one opinion or course of action to another; inconsistent: *a variable frame of mind.* 3 that can be varied: *This curtain rod is of variable length.* 4 *Biology.* deviating from the normal species, type, etc. 5 likely to increase or decrease in size, number, amount, degree, etc.; not remaining the same or uniform: *a constant or variable ratio.*
—*n.* 1 a thing, quality, or quantity that varies: *Temperature and rainfall are variables.* 2 a shifting wind. 3 **the variables**, the region between the northeast and the southeast trade winds.
—**var′i·a·ble·ness**, *n.* —**var′i·a·bly**, *adv.*

variable star any of several stars whose brightness varies in more or less regular periods.

var·i·ance (ver′ē əns or var′ē əns) *n.* 1 disagreement; dispute; difference of opinion: *She had had a slight variance with her brother over the matter.* 2 *Law.* a difference or discrepancy between two legal statements or documents, as between a writ and a complaint or evidence and an accusation, sufficient to make them ineffectual. 3 a varying or a tendency to vary; variation. 4 *Statistics.* the square of the standard deviation.
at variance, a differing; disagreeing; in disagreement: *His actions*

are at variance with his promises. **b** in a state of discord or dissension: *at variance with the neighbors.*

var·i·ant (ver′ē ənt or var′ē ənt) *adj., n.* —*adj.* 1 showing difference, disagreement, or variety: *variant readings of a poem, a variant pronunciation of a word.* 2 *Archaic.* variable; changing. —*n.* 1 something that is somewhat different from a standard or norm: *He showed us two variants of the original design.* 2 one of two or more slightly different things, especially forms, pronunciations, or spellings of one word: *The spellings color and colour are almost equally common variants.* [ME < OF < L *varians, -antis*, ppr. of *variare* change]

var·i·a·tion (ver′ē ā′shən or var′ē ā′shən) *n.* 1 a varying in condition, degree, etc.; change. 2 the act of changing in condition or degree. 3 the amount of change. 4 a varied or changed form. 5 *Music.* **a** a changing or ornamenting of a tune or theme. **b** one of a series of such modifications upon a theme. 6 *Biology.* **a** a deviation of an animal or plant from type. **b** an animal or plant showing such deviation or divergence. 7 *Astronomy.* the deviation of a heavenly body from its average orbit or motion.

var·i·col·ored or **var·i·col·oured** (ver′ē kul′ərd or var′ē kul′ərd) *adj.* having various colors.

var·i·cose (var′ə kōs or ver′ə kōs′) *adj.* 1 swollen or enlarged: *He has varicose veins in his legs.* 2 of, having to do with, or affected with, varicose veins. [< L *varicosus* < *varix, -icis* dilated vein]

var·i·cos·i·ty (var′ə kos′ə tē or ver′ə kos′ə tē) *n., pl.* **-ties.** 1 the state or condition of being varicose. 2 an abnormally dilated blood or lymph vessel.

var·ied (ver′ēd or var′ēd) *adj.* 1 of different kinds; having variety: *a varied assortment.* 2 changed; altered.

var·i·e·gate (ver′ē ə gāt′ or var′ē ə gāt′) *v.* **-gat·ed, -gat·ing.** 1 vary in appearance; mark, spot, or streak with different colors. 2 give variety to. [< L *variegare* < *varius* varied + *agere* drive, make]

var·i·e·gat·ed (ver′ē ə gā′tid or var′ē ə gā′tid) *adj.* 1 varied in appearance; marked with different colors: *variegated pansies.* 2 having variety.

var·i·e·ga·tion (ver′ē ə gā′shən or var′ē ə gā′shən) *n.* a variegating or being variegated; especially, variety of color.

va·ri·e·ty (və rī′ə tē) *n., pl.* **-ties.** 1 lack of sameness; difference; variation. 2 a number of different kinds: *The store has a great variety of toys.* 3 a kind; sort: *Which variety of cake do you prefer?* 4 *Biology.* a geographical grouping within an animal or plant species, based on inherited biological differences; subspecies. 5 variety show. [< L *varietas* < *varius* various]
☞ *Syn.* 2. **Variety, diversity** = a number of things of different kinds or qualities. **Variety** emphasizes absence of sameness in form or character, and may apply to a number of related things of different kinds or a number of different things of the same general kind: *A teacher has a wide variety of duties.* **Diversity** emphasizes unlikeness, complete difference, in nature, form, or qualities: *A person who has travelled widely has a diversity of interests.*

variety program or **programme** a variety show.

variety show an entertainment in a theatre or night club, on television, etc., made up of different kinds of acts such as songs, dances, and comic skits.

variety store a store selling a large variety of different things, especially small, inexpensive items such as sewing supplies, small toys, magazines, greeting cards, candy, and tobacco.

var·i·form (ver′ə fôrm′ or var′ə fôrm′) *adj.* varied in form; having various forms.

va·ri·o·la (və rī′ə lə) *n.* smallpox. [< Med.L *variola* < L *varius* various, spotted]

var·i·om·e·ter (ver′ē om′ə tər or var′ē om′ə tər) *n.* 1 an instrument for comparing the intensity of magnetic forces, especially the magnetic force of the earth at different points. 2 *Electricity.* an instrument for varying inductance, consisting of a fixed coil and a movable coil connected in series. [< L *varius* various + E *-meter*]

var·i·o·rum (ver′ē ô′rəm or var′ē ô′rəm) *n., adj.* —*n.* 1 an edition of a book that has the comments and notes of several editors, critics, etc. 2 an edition of a book containing variant versions of the text. —*adj.* of or like a variorum. [< L (*cum notis*) *variorum* (with notes) of various people]

var·i·ous (ver′ē əs or var′ē əs) *adj.* 1 differing from one another; different: *various opinions.* 2 several; many: *We have looked at various houses and have decided to buy this one.* 3 varied; many-sided: *lives made various by learning.* 4 varying; changeable. [< L *varius.* Doublet of VAIR.]

var·i·ous·ly (ver′ē əs lē or var′ē əs lē) *adv.* 1 in various ways or at various times: *She has been variously involved in editing, proofreading, and research.* 2 by various names or classifications: *He was known variously as Harry the Hooligan, Deadeye, and Jaws McGee.*

var·let (vär′lit) *n. Archaic.* a low fellow; rascal. [ME < OF *varlet*, var. of *vaslet*, originally, young man < Celtic]

var·mint (vär′mənt) *n. Informal or dialect.* **1** vermin. **2** an objectionable animal or person.

var·nish (vär′nish) *n., v.* —*n.* **1** a liquid that gives a smooth, glossy appearance to wood, metal, etc., made from resinous substances dissolved in oil or turpentine. **2** the smooth, hard surface made by this liquid when dry: *The varnish on the car has been scratched.* **3** a glossy appearance. **4** a false or deceiving appearance; pretence.
—*v.* **1** put varnish on. **2** give a false or deceiving appearance to. [ME < OF *vernis*, ult. ? < Gk. *Berenikē*, an ancient city in Libya] —**var′nish·er,** *n.*

var·si·ty (vär′sə tē) *n., pl.* **-ties. 1** *Informal.* university. **2** *Sports.* the principal team representing a school, college, or university.

varve (värv) *n.* one of a pair of stratified bands or layers of alternately light and dark sediment, deposited annually by melting glaciers and useful in determining the age of geological phenomena. [< Swedish *varv* layer]

varved (färvd) *adj.* arranged or deposited in varves.

var·y (ver′ē *or* var′ē) *v.* **var·ied, var·y·ing. 1** make or become different; change: *The driver can vary the speed of an automobile. The weather varies.* **2** *Music.* change or ornament (a basic tune or theme). **3** be different; differ: *The stars vary in brightness.* **4** give variety to: *to vary one's style of writing.* **5** alternate. **6** *Mathematics.* undergo or be subject to a change in value according to some law: *Pressure varies inversely as volume.* **7** *Biology.* exhibit or be subject to variation, as by natural or artificial selection. [ME < OF < L *variare* < *varius* various] —**var′y·ing·ly,** *adv.*
☛ **Hom. very** (ver′ē).

varying hare snowshoe hare.

vas (vas) *n., pl.* **va·sa** (vā′sə). *Anatomy.* a vessel or duct. [< L *vas* vessel]

vas·cu·lar (vas′kyə lər) *adj.* having to do with, made up of, or having vessels that carry blood, sap, etc.: *a vascular plant, vascular tissue.* [< NL *vascularis,* ult. < L *vas* vessel]

vascular bundle *Botany.* a unit of the system of specialized, tubelike cells by which food and water is carried through a plant.

vas·cu·lum (vas′kyə ləm) *n., pl.* **-lums** *or* **-la** (-lə). a covered, usually metal box used by botanists in the field for holding plant specimens. [< L *vasculum,* dim. of *vas* vase]

vas def·er·ens (def′ər ənz *or* -ə renz′) *pl.* **va·sa def·er·en·ti·a** (vā′sə def′ə ren′shē ə). especially in higher vertebrates, the duct that carries sperm from the testicles to the penis. [< NL < L *vas* vessel + *deferens,* ppr. of *deferre* to carry away. 16c.]

vase (vāz, väz, *or* voz) *n.* an open holder or container, usually taller than it is wide, used for ornament or for holding flowers. [< F < L *vas* vessel] —**vase′like′,** *adj.*

vas·ec·to·my (va sek′tə mē) *n., pl.* **-mies.** the surgical removal of part or all of the vas deferens, especially as a method of contraception. [< *vas* + *-ectomy*]

vas·e·line (vas′ə lēn′) *n.* **1** petroleum jelly. **2 Vaseline,** *Trademark,* a brand of petroleum jelly. [coined from G *Wasser* water + Gk. *elaion* oil]

vas·o·mo·tor (vas′ō mō′tər) *adj.* of or having to do with the nerves that regulate the size of the blood vessels. [< L *vas* vessel + E *motor,* adj.]

vas·sal (vas′əl) *n.* **1** in feudal times, a person who held land from a lord or superior, to whom in return he gave help in war or some other service. A great noble could be a vassal of the king and have many other men as his vassals. **2** (*adj.*) of or like a vassal. **3** a person in a subordinate position; a servant, slave, etc. [ME < OF < Med.L *vassallus* < LL *vassus* < Celtic]

vas·sal·age (vas′əl ij) *n.* **1** the state of being a vassal. **2** the homage or service due from a vassal to his lord or superior. **3** dependence; servitude. **4** the land held by a vassal.

vast (vast) *adj.* extremely great; immense: *a vast amount of money, a vast desert. Ontario and Alberta are vast provinces.* [< L *vastus*] —**vast′ly,** *adv.* —**vast′ness,** *n.*

vast·y (vas′tē) *adj. Poetic.* vast; immense.

vat (vat) *n., v.* **vat·ted, vat·ting.** —*n.* a large container for liquids; tank: *a vat of dye.* —*v.* place, store, or treat in a vat. [OE *fæt*]

Vat·i·can (vat′ə kən) *n.* **1** in Vatican City, the buildings of the Roman Catholic Church and the palace of the Pope. **2** the government, office, or authority of the Pope. [< L *Vaticanus* (*mons*) Vatican (hill), on which the palace of the Pope was built]

va·tic·i·nate (və tis′ə nāt′) *v.* **-nat·ed, -nat·ing.** prophesy. [< L *vaticinari* < *vates* seer] —**va·tic′i·na′tion,** *n.*

vau·de·ville (vo′də vil′ *or* vô′də vil′, vod′vil *or* vôd′vil) *n.* theatrical entertainment consisting of a variety of acts, such as singing, dancing, juggling, short plays, and animal acts. [< F

vaudeville < *Vau de Vire,* a valley in Normandy; first applied to the songs composed by Olivier Basselin, a poet of the 15th century, who lived in this valley]

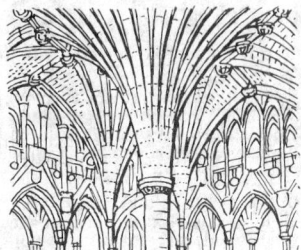

Vault¹: vaulted ceilings in the Houses of Parliament in Ottawa

vault¹ (volt *or* vôlt) *n., v.* —*n.* **1** an arched roof or ceiling; a series of arches. **2** an arched space or passage. **3** something like an arched roof. The **vault of heaven** means the sky. **4** an underground cellar or storehouse. **5** a place for storing valuable things and keeping them safe. Vaults are often made of steel. **6** a place for burial.
—*v.* **1** make in the form of a vault: *a vaulted roof.* **2** cover with a vault. [ME < OF *vaulte,* ult. < L *volvere* roll] —**vault′like′,** *adj.*

vault² (volt *or* vôlt) *v., n.* —*v.* jump or leap by resting on one or both hands or by using a pole: *He vaulted the fence. She vaulted from the saddle.* —*n.* the act of vaulting. [< OF *volter,* ult. < L *volvere* roll] —**vault′er,** *n.*

vault·ed (vol′tid *or* vôl′tid) *adj.* **1** in the form of a vault; arched. **2** built or covered with a vault.

vault·ing¹ (vol′ting *or* vôl′ting) *n.* **1** the art, practice, or operation of constructing vaults. **2** a vaulted structure. **3** vaults collectively.

vault·ing² (vol′ting *or* vôl′ting) *adj.* **1** reaching or leaping over. **2** too confident; overreaching: *vaulting ambition.* **3** for use in vaulting or gymnastics: *a vaulting-horse.*

vaunt (vont *or* vônt) *v. or n.* boast. [< F < LL *vanitare* < *vanus* vain] —**vaunt′ing·ly,** *adv.*

vb. verb; verbal.

V.C. 1 Victoria Cross. **2** vice-chairman. **3** vice-chancellor. **4** a person who has won a Victoria Cross. **5** vice-consul.

v.d. various dates.

V.D. *or* **VD** venereal disease.

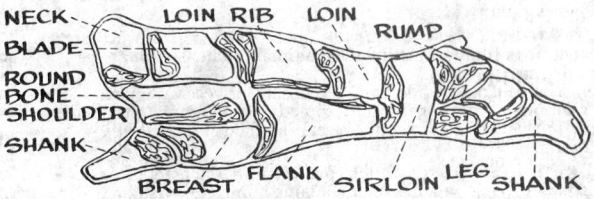

The main cuts of veal

veal (vēl) *n.* the flesh of a calf, used for food. [ME < OF *veel,* ult. < L *vitellus,* dim. of *vitulus* calf]

veal·er (vēl′ər) *n.* a calf that is less than 12 weeks old, raised for its tender meat.

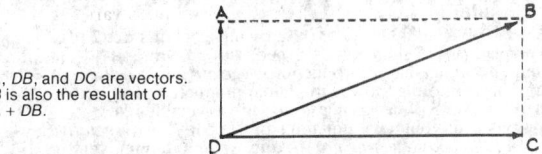

DA, DB, and *DC* are vectors. *DB* is also the resultant of *DA + DB.*

vec·tor (vek′tər) *n., v.* **1** *Mathematics.* **a** a quantity involving

direction as well as magnitude. **b** a line representing both the direction and the magnitude of some force, etc. **2** an agent, especially an insect, that transmits a disease-producing micro-organism from one host to another, either as a simple carrier or serving as a necessary host in the life cycle of the micro-organism. —*v.* guide (a pilot, aircraft, or missile) from one point to another within a given time by means of a vector: *He vectored the pilot back to the base.* [< L *vector* carrier < *vehere* carry]

Ve·da (vā′də *or* vē′də) *n.* any or all of the four collections of Hindu sacred writings. [< Skt. *veda* knowledge]

Ve·dan·ta (vi dän′tə *or* vi dan′tə) *n.* one of the leading schools of Hindu religious philosophy based on the Vedas, dealing with the relations of man and the universe with the Divine spirit. [< Skt. *veda* sacred knowledge + -*anta* end]

V–E Day the day of the Allied victory in Europe in World War II, May 8, 1945.

ve·dette (vi det′) *n.* **1** a mounted sentry stationed in advance of the outposts of an army. **2** a small naval vessel used for scouting. [< F < Ital. *vedetta*, ult. < L *videre* see]

Ve·dic (vā′dik *or* vē′dik) *adj., n.* —*adj.* having to do with or found in the Vedas. —*n.* the form of ancient Sanskrit in which the Vedas are written.

veer (vēr) *v., n.* —*v.* **1** change in direction; shift; turn: *The wind veered to the south. The talk veered to ghosts.* **2** change the direction of: *We veered our boat.* —*n.* a change in direction: *a veer to the left.* [< F *virer*]

veer·y (vēr′ē) *n., pl.* **veer·ies.** a common North American thrush (*Hylocichla fuscescens*) having a reddish-brown back and whitish under parts with very faint spotting on the breast. The veery winters in Central America and N South America. [probably imitative]

Ve·ga (vē′gə) *n. Astronomy.* a bluish-white star of the first magnitude, in the constellation Lyra. [< Med.L < Arabic (*al-nasr*) *al-wāqi'* the falling (vulture)]

veg·e·ta·ble (vej′tə bəl *or* vej′ə tə bəl) *n., adj.* —*n.* **1** a part of a plant, such as leaves, seeds, roots, stem, or fruit, used for food and usually eaten with the main part of the meal. Some common vegetables are potatoes, beans, peas, carrots, cabbage, tomatoes, sweet peppers, and spinach. **2** a usually non-woody plant grown for such parts. **3** *Rare.* any plant. **4** (*adj.*) of, having to do with, or like plants: *the vegetable kingdom, vegetable life.* **5** (*adj.*) consisting of or made from vegetables: *vegetable soup.* **6** a person apparently lacking in thought or feeling or one who has lost the use of his mind and, sometimes, limbs, etc. **7** (*adj.*) of or designating the life of such a person. [ME (*adj.*) < OF *vegetable*, or < LL *vegetabilis* vivifying, refreshing < *vegetus* vigorous]

vegetable marrow **1** any of several oblong varieties of summer squash having a smooth, whitish or green skin and white flesh. **2** the plant they grow on.

vegetable oil any fatty oil extracted from the seeds or fruit of plants, used in cooking.

veg·e·tal (vej′ə təl) *adj.* of, like, or having to do with plants or vegetables.

veg·e·tar·i·an (vej′ə ter′ē ən) *n., adj.* —*n.* **1** a person who eats no meat or fish and, sometimes, no animal products such as eggs, milk, or cheese. —*adj.* **1** of or having to do with vegetarians or vegetarianism. **2** containing no meat or fish and, sometimes, no animal products: *a vegetarian meal.* **3** serving only vegetarian foods: *a vegetarian restaurant.*

veg·e·tar·i·an·ism (vej′ə ter′ē ən iz′əm) *n.* the practice or principle of living on a diet that contains no meat or fish and, sometimes, no animal products.

veg·e·tate (vej′ə tāt′) *v.* -**tat·ed,** -**tat·ing.** **1** grow as plants do. **2** live with very little mental or physical activity; lead a dull, passive existence. [< L *vegetare* enliven < *vegetus* lively]

veg·e·ta·tion (vej′ə tā′shən) *n.* **1** plant life; growing plants: *There is not much vegetation in deserts.* **2** the process of vegetating. **3** a dull, passive existence. **4** any abnormal growth on a part of the body.

veg·e·ta·tive (vej′ə tā′tiv) *adj.* **1** growing as plants do. **2** of plants or plant life. **3** *Botany.* concerned with growth and development rather than reproduction: *vegetative root cells.* **4** causing or promoting growth in plants; productive; fertile: *vegetative mould.* **5** of or having to do with vegetable-like unconscious or involuntary functions of the body: *the vegetative processes of the body, such as growth and repair.* **6** having very little action, thought, or feeling. —**veg′e·ta′tive·ly,** *adv.* —**veg′e·ta′tive·ness,** *n.*

ve·he·mence (vē′ə məns) *n.* the quality or state of being vehement: *The vehemence of her retort surprised us.*

ve·he·ment (vē′ə mənt) *adj.* **1** having, showing, or caused by strong feeling; intense or passionate: *a vehement denial, vehement patriotism. He was vehement about not wanting to go.* **2** forceful; violent: *a vehement onslaught, a vehement wind.* [< L *vehemens, -entis* < *vehere* carry] —**ve′he·ment·ly,** *adv.*

ve·hi·cle (vē′ə kəl) *n.* **1** a carriage, cart, wagon, bicycle, automobile, sled, or any other conveyance used on land. **2** any form of conveyance or transportation: *a space vehicle.* **3** a means by which something is communicated, shown, done, etc.: *Language is the vehicle of thought.* **4** a painting medium, such as linseed oil, in which the pigment is suspended. [< L *vehiculum* < *vehere* carry]

ve·hic·u·lar (vē hik′yə lər) *adj.* of or having to do with vehicles.

veil (vāl) *n., v.* —*n.* **1** a length of cloth worn by women so as to fall over the head and shoulders and, sometimes, the face or part of the face. **2** a piece of very thin cloth or netting worn by women over the head or face as a protection or as an ornament. A veil is sometimes attached to a hat. **3** anything that covers or hides: *A veil of clouds hid the sun.* **4** **the veil,** the life of a nun in a religious order.
take the veil, become a nun.
—*v.* **1** cover with a veil: *In some places, Moslem women still veil their faces before going out in public.* **2** cover, screen, or hide: *Fog veiled the shore. His veiled threats had put them on their guard.* [ME < AF < L *velum* covering. Doublet of VELUM, VOILE.] —**veil′-like′,** *adj.*
☛ *Hom.* vale.

veil·ing (vā′ling) *n.* **1** a veil. **2** material for veils.

vein (vān) *n., v.* —*n.* **1** one of the membranous vessels or tubes that carry blood to the heart from all parts of the body. **2** a rib of an insect's wing. **3** one of the bundles of vascular tissue forming the principal framework of a leaf. **4** a distinct mass or bed of mineral or ore occurring in a crack in rock or between strata of rock: *a vein of copper.* **5** any streak or marking of a different shade or color in wood, marble, etc. **6** a strain or streak of some quality in character, conduct, writing, etc.: *There is a vein of fun in these poems. He has a vein of cruelty.*
—*v.* cover or mark with veins. [ME < OF < L *vena*] —**vein′less,** *adj.* —**vein′like′,** *adj.*
☛ *Hom.* vain, vane.

veined (vānd) *adj.* having veins or veinlike markings: *veined marble.*

vein·ing (vā′ning) *n.* an arrangement or pattern of veins.

vel. vellum.

ve·lar (vē′lər) *adj., n.* —*adj.* **1** of or having to do with a velum. **2** *Phonetics.* pronounced with the aid of the soft palate. *C* in *coo* has a velar sound. —*n. Phonetics.* a velar sound. [< L *velaris* < *velum* covering]

Vel·cro (vel′krō) *n. Trademark.* a type of fastener used for clothing, etc., consisting of two nylon strips or patches, one covered with tiny filaments formed into hooks and the other with loops. The fastener is closed by pressing the two surfaces together so that they lock, and opened by peeling them apart.

veld *or* **veldt** (velt *or* felt) *n.* in South Africa, open country having grass or bushes but few trees. [< Afrikaans *veld* < Du. *veld* field]

vel·lum (vel′əm) *n.* **1** the finest kind of parchment, originally made from calfskin, used especially for writing on or for binding books. **2** a manuscript written on vellum. **3** strong writing paper made to imitate vellum. **4** (*adj.*) of, resembling, or bound in vellum: *a vellum finish.* [ME < OF *velin* < *veel* calf. See VEAL.]

ve·loc·i·pede (və los′ə pēd′) *n.* **1** tricycle. **2** an early kind of bicycle or tricycle. **3** a railway handcar. [< F *vélocipède* < L *velox, -ocis* swift + *pes, pedis* foot]

ve·loc·i·ty (və los′ə tē) *n., pl.* -**ties.** **1** speed; swiftness; quickness of motion: *to fly with the velocity of a bird.* **2** the rate of motion in a particular direction: *The velocity of light is about 300 000 kilometres per second.* **3** the absolute or relative rate of operation or action. [< L *velocitas* < *velox, velocis* swift]

ve·lo·drome (vē′lə drōm′) *n.* a building having a track for bicycle racing and, usually, seats and other facilities for spectators.

ve·lour *or* **ve·lours** (və lür′) *n., pl.* **velours.** any of various fabrics with a nap or pile like velvet, used for upholstery, draperies, clothing, etc. [< F *velours* velvet, earlier *velous* < Provençal *velos*, ult. < L *villus* shaggy hair]

ve·lum (vē′ləm) *n., pl.* -**la** (-lə). a veil-like membrane or membranous part, especially the soft palate. [< L *velum* covering. Doublet of VEIL, VOILE.]

ve·lure (və lür′) *n.* **1** velvet or a fabric like it. **2** a soft pad used for smoothing silk hats. [var. of *velour.* See VELOURS.]

vel·vet (vel′vit) *n.* **1** cloth, usually of cotton, rayon, or nylon,

having a thick, short, cut pile that makes it smooth and soft to the touch. Velvet is made by weaving two layers of fabric together and then shearing the faces apart. **2** (*adj.*) made of or covered with velvet: *a velvet chesterfield.* **3** (*adj.*) like velvet; soft, smooth, rich, etc.: *the velvet paws of a kitten, a velvet voice.* **4** something like velvet or suggesting velvet, especially in softness or smoothness. **5** the soft, furry skin that covers and nourishes the growing antlers of a deer. **6** *Slang.* a clear profit or gain. **7** *Slang.* money won through gambling.

be on velvet, *Slang.* **a** have previous winnings available for gambling, speculating, etc. **b** be well supplied with money.
play on velvet, *Slang.* gamble or speculate with money won previously.
[ME < Med.L *velvetum,* ult. < L *villus* tuft of hair]

vel·vet·een (vel′və tēn′) *n.* **1** cotton or rayon cloth having a soft, cut pile similar to velvet, but which is woven singly instead of face to face like velvet. **2** (*adj.*) made of or covered with velveteen. [< *velvet*]

vel·vet·y (vel′və tē) *adj.* smooth and soft like velvet.

Ven. **1** Venerable. **2** Venice.

ve·na ca·va (vē′nə kā′və) *pl.* **venae cavae** (vē′nē kā′vē). either of the two large veins that in air-breathing vertebrates return blood to the right atrium of the heart. See **heart** for picture. [< L, literally, hollow vein]

ve·nal (vē′nəl) *adj.* **1** willing to sell one's services or influence basely; open to bribes; corrupt: *venal judges.* **2** influenced or obtained by bribery: *venal conduct.* [< L *venalis* < *venum* sale] —**ve′nal·ly,** *adv.*

ve·nal·i·ty (vē nal′ə tē) *n.* the quality of being venal.

ve·na·tion (vē nā′shən) *n.* **1** the arrangement of veins in a leaf or in an insect's wing. **2** such veins collectively. [< L *vena* vein]

vend (vend) *v.* sell, especially by peddling or hawking. [< L *vendere* < *venum dare* offer for sale]

vend·ee (ven dē′) *n.* a person to whom a thing is sold; buyer.

vend·er (ven′dər) *n.* vendor.

ven·det·ta (ven det′ə) *n.* a feud in which the relatives of a person who has been wronged or murdered try to take vengeance on the wrongdoer or killer or his relatives. [< Ital. < L *vindicta* revenge, ult. < *vindex, -icis* protector, avenger]

vend·i·bil·i·ty (ven′də bil′ə tē) *n.* salable quality; the quality of being marketable.

vend·i·ble (ven′də bəl) *adj., n.* —*adj.* salable. —*n.* a salable thing.

vending machine a coin-operated machine from which one may obtain coffee, candy, cigarettes, stamps, etc.

ven·dor or **ven·der** (ven′dər) *n.* **1** a person who sells, especially by peddling or hawking. **2** vending machine. [< AF *vendor* < *vendre* sell < L *vendere.* See VEND.]

ven·due (ven dyü′ or ven dü′) *n.* a public auction. [< Du. < OF *vendue* sale]

ve·neer (və nēr′) *n., v.* —*n.* **1** a thin layer of fine wood or other material covering a cheaper grade of wood, fibreboard, etc.: *a desk made of pine with a walnut veneer, a wall with a veneer of brick.* **2** surface appearance or show: *a veneer of honesty.* —*v.* **1** cover with a veneer. **2** conceal (something) under a superficial pleasantness or attractiveness. [earlier *fineer* < G *furnieren* < F *fournir* furnish] —**ve·neer′er,** *n.*

ven·er·a·bil·i·ty (ven′ər ə bil′ə tē) *n.* the fact or quality of being venerable.

ven·er·a·ble (ven′ər ə bəl) *adj.* **1** worthy of reverence; deserving respect because of age, character, or associations: *a venerable priest, venerable customs.* **2** designating an archdeacon of the Anglican Church (used as a title of respect). **3** *Roman Catholic Church.* designating a person recognized as having attained a degree of virtue but not yet recognized as beatified or canonized: *the Venerable Bede.* [ME < L *venerabilis* < *venerari* venerate] —**ven′er·a·bly,** *adv.*

ven·er·ate (ven′ər āt′) *v.* **-at·ed, -at·ing.** regard with deep respect; revere: *He venerates his father's memory.* [< L *venerari* < *Venus, Veneris,* originally, love]

ven·er·a·tion (ven′ər ā′shən) *n.* **1** deep respect; reverence. **2** the act of venerating or the state of being venerated.

ve·ne·re·al (və nēr′ē əl) *adj.* **1** of or having to do with sexual intercourse. **2** of a disease, transmitted by sexual intercourse. **3** of or having to do with diseases communicated by sexual intercourse. **4** infected with venereal disease. [< L *venereus* < *Venus, Veneris* Venus]

venereal disease a contagious disease that is transmitted only or mainly by sexual intercourse, such as gonorrhea or syphilis.

ven·er·y¹ (ven′ər ē) *n.* gratification of sexual desire. [< L *Venus, Veneris* Venus]

hat, āge, fär; let, ēqual, tėrm; it, īce
hot, ōpen, ôrder; oil, out; cup, pút, rüle,
əbove, takən, pencəl, lemən, circəs

ch, child; ng, long; sh, ship
th, thin; ᴛʜ, then; zh, measure

ven·er·y² (ven′ər ē) *n. Archaic.* hunting; the chase. [ME < OF *venerie,* ult. < L *venari* hunt]

Ve·ne·tian (və nē′shən) *n., adj.* —*n.* a native or inhabitant of Venice, a city on the NE coast of Italy. —*adj.* of or having to do with Venice or its people.

Venetian blind a window blind consisting of horizontal plastic, metal, or wooden slats that can be set at different angles to vary the amount of light that is let in.

Venetian glass a fine, very delicate kind of glassware. [< *Venice,* Italy, where it was first made]

Venez. Venezuela.

Ven·e·zue·lan (ven′ə zwē′lən or ven′ə zwä′lən) *n., adj.* —*n.* a native or inhabitant of Venezuela, a country in N South America. —*adj.* of or having to do with Venezuela or its people.

venge·ance (ven′jəns) *n.* **1** the inflicting of injury as a punishment for a wrong or injury; revenge: *to swear vengeance for a wrong, to take vengeance on an enemy.* **2** the desire to punish in this way: *There was vengeance in his heart.*
with a vengeance, a with great force or intensity: *By six o'clock it was raining with a vengeance. She started in on the job with a vengeance.* **b** to an unusual degree; extremely: *He was getting his own back with a vengeance. That escapade was adventure with a vengeance.*
[ME < OF *vengeance,* ult. < L *vindex* avenger]

venge·ful (venj′fəl) *adj.* **1** inflicting vengeance; serving as an instrument of vengeance. **2** seeking vengeance; inclined to avenge oneself; vindictive: *vengeful enemies.* **3** feeling or showing a strong desire for vengeance. —**venge′ful·ly,** *adv.* —**venge′ful·ness,** *n.*

ve·ni·al (vē′nē əl or vēn′yəl) *adj.* that can be forgiven; not very wrong; pardonable: *a venial sin, venial faults.* [ME < LL *venialis* < *venia* forgiveness]

venial sin *Theology.* a minor offence, or any offence that is not committed with full knowledge and consent and so can be forgiven. Compare **mortal sin.**

ve·ni·re (və nī′rē) *n. Law.* a writ authorizing the summoning of persons to serve on a jury. [< L *venire facias,* that you may cause (him) to come]

ven·i·son (ven′ə sən or ven′ə zən) *n.* the flesh of a deer, used for food; deer meat. [ME < OF < L *venatio* hunting < *venari* hunt]

venison bird *Cdn.* the Canada jay.

Ve·ni·te (vi nī′tē) *n.* the 95th Psalm (94th in the Vulgate). [< L *venite* come (2nd pers. pl. imperative), the first word in the Latin version]

ve·ni, vi·di, vi·ci (vē′nī vī′dī vī′sī or wā′nē wē′dē wē′kē) *Latin.* I came, I saw, I conquered (a report of victory made by Julius Caesar to the Roman Senate).

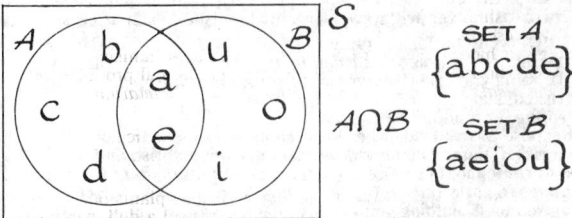

A Venn diagram showing the intersection of two sets having common elements. *S* is the set of all the letters of the alphabet, *A* is the set of the first five letters, and *B* is the set of vowels.

Venn diagram (ven) *Mathematics and logic.* a diagram using circles, rectangles, or ellipses to show the relationships between sets, propositions, etc. [< John Venn (1834-1923), an English logician]

ven·om (ven′əm) *n.* **1** the poison produced by some snakes, spiders, etc. and introduced into the body of prey or an enemy mainly by a bite or sting. **2** spite; malice: *There was venom in her voice.* [ME < OF *venin* < L *venenum* poison] —**ven′om·less,** *adj.*

ven·om·ous (ven′əm əs) *adj.* **1** poisonous: *Rattlesnakes are*

venomous. **2** spiteful; malicious. **—ven′om·ous·ly,** *adv.*
—ven′om·ous·ness, *n.*

ve·nous (vē′nəs) *adj.* **1** of, in, or having to do with veins: *venous blood.* **2** having veins: *the venous wings of insects.* [< L *venosus* < *vena* vein]

vent¹ (vent) *n., v.* **—n. 1** a hole; opening, especially one serving as an outlet. **2** an outlet; way out: *His great energy found vent in hard work.* **3** expression: *She gave vent to her grief in tears.* **4** the external opening of the intestine, especially in birds, fish, and reptiles. **5** the small opening in the barrel of certain old guns through which the powder was fired; touchhole. **6** in an automobile, etc., a small window that can be opened for indirect ventilation.
—v. 1 let out; express freely: *He vented his anger on the dog.*
2 make a vent in. [partly < MF *vent* wind < L *ventus*; partly < MF *évent* vent, blowhole, ult. < L *ex-* out + *ventus* wind]

vent² (vent) *n.* a slit or opening in a garment. [ME *vent*, var. of *fent(e)* < MF *fente* slit, ult. < L *findere* split]

vent·age (ven′tij) *n.* a vent; a small hole, especially for the escape or passage of air. The finger holes of a flute are ventages.

ven·ti·late (ven′tə lāt′) *v.* **-lat·ed, -lat·ing. 1** change the air in: *We ventilate a room by opening windows.* **2** purify by fresh air: *The lungs ventilate the blood.* **3** make known publicly; discuss openly: *to ventilate a grievance.* **4** furnish with a vent or opening for the escape of air, gas, etc. [< L *ventilare* fan < *ventus* wind]

ven·ti·la·tion (ven′tə lā′shən) *n.* **1** the act or process of ventilating. **2** a means of supplying fresh air: *That small window is the only ventilation in the warehouse.* **3** circulation of air: *The room has good ventilation.* **4** the circulation and exchange of gases in the lungs in the process of breathing.

ven·ti·la·tor (ven′tə lā′tər) *n.* any apparatus or means for changing or improving the air in an enclosed space.

ven·tral (ven′trəl) *adj.* **1** of or having to do with the belly; abdominal. **2** of, having to do with, or located on or near the part or surface opposite the back: *a ventral fin.* [< LL *ventralis* < L *venter* belly] **—ven′tral·ly,** *adv.*

ven·tri·cle (ven′trə kəl) *n.* **1** either of the two lower chambers of the heart that receive blood from the upper chambers and force it into the arteries. See **heart** for picture. **2** any of the series of four communicating cavities in the brain, which connect with the spinal cord and contain cerebrospinal fluid. See **brain** for picture. **3** any of various other small cavities in the body. [ME < L *ventriculus*, dim. of *venter* belly]

ven·tric·u·lar (ven trik′yə lər) *adj.* **1** of, having to do with, or being a ventricle. **2** having to do with the stomach. **3** swelling out; distended.

ven·tri·lo·qui·al (ven′trə lō′kwē əl) *adj.* having to do with ventriloquism.

ven·tril·o·quism (ven tril′ə kwiz′əm) *n.* the art or practice of speaking or uttering sounds without moving the lips so that the voice may seem to come from some source other than the speaker. [< L *ventriloquus* ventriloquist < *venter* belly + *loqui* speak]

ven·tril·o·quist (ven tril′ə kwist) *n.* a person who is skilled in ventriloquism, especially one who uses it to entertain an audience by appearing to carry on a conversation with a puppet manipulated by hand.

ven·tril·o·quy (ven tril′ə kwē) *n.* ventriloquism.

ven·ture (ven′chər) *n., v.* **-tured, -tur·ing. —n. 1** a risky or daring undertaking: *His courage was equal to any venture.* **2** a speculation to make money: *A lucky venture in oil stock made his fortune.* **3** the thing risked; stake.
at a venture, at random; by chance.
—v. 1 expose to risk or danger: *Men venture their lives in war.*
2 run a risk. **3** dare: *No one ventured to interrupt the speaker.*
4 dare to come, go, or proceed: *He ventured out on the thin ice and fell through.* **6** guess (at): *to venture at a reason.*
nothing ventured, nothing gained, advantage, profit, or other objectives are forfeited by overcautiousness or failure to risk danger.
[< *aventure*, an earlier form of *adventure*]
☛ *Syn. v.* **3.** See note at **dare.**

Ven·tur·er (ven′chə rər) *n.* a member, aged 14 to 17, of the Boy Scouts.

ven·ture·some (ven′chər səm) *adj.* **1** inclined to take risks; rash; daring: *a venturesome explorer.* **2** hazardous; risky: *A trip to the moon is a venturesome journey.* **—ven′ture·some·ly,** *adv.*
—ven′ture·some·ness, *n.*

ven·tu·ri (ven chür′ē *or* ven tür′ē) *n.* a short, narrow piece of tubing between wider sections in a pump or pipeline, used to measure or regulate the rate of flow of a liquid or gas. [< G.B. *Venturi* (1746-1822), an Italian physicist]

venturi tube venturi.

ven·tur·ous (ven′chər əs) *adj.* venturesome. **—ven′tur·ous·ly,** *adv.* **—ven′tur·ous·ness,** *n.*

ven·ue (ven′yü) *n.* **1** *Law.* **a** the place or neighborhood of a crime or cause of action. **b** the place where the jury is gathered and the case tried. A change of venue is allowed when strong local feeling may prevent a defendant from getting a fair trial. **2** the scene of a real or supposed action or event, in a novel or other literary work. [< OF *venue* coming, ult. < L *venire* come]

Ve·nus (vē′nəs) *n.* **1** *Roman mythology.* the goddess of love and beauty, corresponding to the Greek goddess Aphrodite. **2** any very beautiful woman. **3** the most brilliant planet, second in distance from the sun and coming closest to the earth.

Ve·nus's–fly·trap (vē′nəs iz flī′trap′) *n.* an insect-eating bog plant (*Dionaea muscipula*) of the sundew family native to the E United States, having hairy leaves with two lobes at the end that snap together to trap insects.

ver. **1** verse. **2** version.

ve·ra·cious (və rā′shəs) *adj.* **1** truthful. **2** true. [< L *verax, -acis* < *verus* true] **—ve·ra′cious·ly,** *adv.* **—ve·ra′cious·ness,** *n.*
☛ *Hom.* **voracious.**

ve·rac·i·ty (və ras′ə tē) *n., pl.* **-ties. 1** truthfulness. **2** correctness; accuracy: *to check the veracity of a statement.* **3** something that is true. [< Med.L *veracitas* < L *verax, -acis*. See VERACIOUS.]
☛ *Hom.* **voracity.**

ve·ran·da *or* **ve·ran·dah** (və ran′də) *n.* a large covered porch on one or more sides of a house. [< Hind. and other languages of India < Pg. *varanda* railing]

verb (vėrb) *n.* a word that expresses an act, happening, or state of being, and that in many languages has different forms for tense, voice, etc. The verb is the main part of the predicate of a sentence. *Examples: do, see, impose, introduce, think, be.* [< L *verbum*, originally, word]
☛ *Usage.* Verbs are classified on the basis of what follows them as a necessary part of the sentence structure. A verb followed by a noun or noun substitute as an object is called **transitive**: *She broke the mirror.* A verb not followed by an object is called **intransitive**: *She succeeded.* A verb followed by a noun or adjective as a complement referring to the subject is called a **linking verb**: *She became a lawyer. She seems better.* Many verbs in English can be either transitive or intransitive: *She broke the mirror. The mirror broke.*

ver·bal (vėr′bəl) *adj.* **1** in or of words: *A description is a verbal picture.* **2** expressed in spoken words; oral: *a verbal promise, a verbal message.* **3** word for word; literal: *a verbal translation from the French.* **4** *Grammar.* of, having to do with, or derived from a verb: *a verbal noun.*
—n. *Grammar.* a verb form that functions as a noun, adjective, or adverb. Participles, gerunds, and infinitives are verbals. [< LL *verbalis* < L *verbum* word, verb] **—ver′bal·ly,** *adv.*
☛ *Usage.* See note at **oral.**

ver·bal·ism (vėr′bəl iz′əm) *n.* **1** a verbal expression; word, phrase, etc. **2** too much attention to mere words. **3** a stock phrase or statement with little meaning.

ver·bal·ist (vėr′bəl ist) *n.* **1** a person who is skilled in the use or choice of words. **2** a person who pays too much attention to mere words.

ver·bal·ize (vėr′bəl īz′) *v.* **-ized, -iz·ing. 1** express in words. **2** use too many words; be wordy. **3** change (a noun, etc.) into a verb. **—ver′bal·i·za′tion,** *n.*

verbal noun gerund.
☛ *Usage.* See note at **gerund.**

ver·ba·tim (vėr bā′tim) *adv. or adj.* word for word; in exactly the same words: *His speech was printed verbatim in the newspaper.* [< Med.L *verbatim* < L *verbum* word]

ver·be·na (vər bē′nə) *n.* **1** any of a genus (*Verbena*) of chiefly New World plants having flowers of various colors growing in clusters or spikes. Some verbenas have long been cultivated as garden plants. **2** (*adj.*) designating a family (Verbenaceae) of mainly tropical herbs, shrubs, and trees. The verbena family includes the verbenas and also some trees important for timber, such as teak. [< L *verbena* leafy branch. Doublet of VERVAIN.]

ver·bi·age (vėr′bē ij) *n.* the use of too many words; abundance of useless words. [< F *verbiage*, ult. < L *verbum* word]

ver·bose (vėr bōs′) *adj.* containing or using too many words; wordy. [< L *verbosus* < *verbum* word] **—ver·bose′ly,** *adv.*
—ver·bose′ness, *n.*
☛ *Syn.* See note at **wordy.**

ver·bos·i·ty (vėr bos′ə tē) *n.* the use of too many words; wordiness.

ver·bo·ten (fer bō′tən) *adj. German.* forbidden, especially by authority.

ver·dan·cy (vėr′dən sē) *n.* the quality or state of being verdant; greenness.

ver·dant (vėr′dənt) *adj.* **1** green in color: *fields covered with*

verdant grass. **2** covered with growing green plants: *verdant fields.* [< *verdure*] —**ver′dant·ly,** *adv.*

ver·dict (vėr′dikt) *n.* **1** the decision of a jury: *The jury returned a verdict of not guilty.* **2** any decision or judgment: *the public's verdict, the verdict of history.* [ME < AF *verdit* < *ver* true (< L *verus*) + *dit,* pp. of *dire* speak < L *dicere*]

ver·di·gris (vėr′də grēs′ *or* vėr′də gris′) *n.* **1** a green or bluish coating that forms on brass, copper, or bronze when exposed to the air for long periods of time. **2** a green or bluish-green poisonous compound of copper and acetic acid, used as a pigment for paints. [ME < OF *vert de grece,* literally, green of Greece]

ver·dure (vėr′jər) *n.* **1** the fresh greenness of growing vegetation. **2** a flourishing growth of vegetation. **3** a condition of freshness and vigor. [ME < OF *verdure,* ult. < L *viridis* green]

ver·dur·ous (vėr′jər əs) *adj.* green and fresh.

verge¹ (vėrj) *n. or v.* **verged, verg·ing.** —*n.* **1** the point at which something begins or happens; brink: *His business is on the verge of ruin.* **2** a limiting belt, strip, or border of something. **3** a rod, staff, etc. carried as an emblem of authority. **4** *Architecture.* the shaft of a column.
—*v.* be on the verge; border: *Her silly talk verged on nonsense.* [ME < OF < L *virga* staff]

verge² (vėrj) *v.* **verged, verg·ing.** tend; incline: *She was plump, verging on fatness.* [< L *vergere*]

ver·ger (vėr′jər) *n.* **1** in some churches, an attendant who shows people to their seats, passes the collection plate, etc. **2** *Esp.Brit.* an officer or attendant who carries the staff or wand before a bishop, dean, etc. [< MF *verger* < *verge* verge¹ < L *virga* staff]

Ver·gil·i·an (vėr jil′ē ən) See **Virgilian.**

ver·i·est (ver′ē ist) *adj.* utmost: *the veriest nonsense.*

ver·i·fi·a·ble (ver′ə fī′ə bəl) *adj.* capable of being verified; that can be checked for truth or correctness.

ver·i·fi·ca·tion (ver′ə fə kā′shən) *n.* **1** verifying or being verified; proof by evidence or testimony; confirmation. **2** *Law.* an affidavit added to testimony or a statement by the pleading party declaring that his allegations are true.

ver·i·fy (ver′ə fī′) *v.* **-fied, -fy·ing. 1** prove (something) to be true; confirm: *The driver's report of the accident was verified by eyewitnesses.* **2** test the correctness of; check for accuracy: *Verify the spelling of a word by looking in a dictionary.* **3** *Law.* **a** testify or affirm to be true, formally or upon oath. **b** declare that one's allegations are true. [ME < OF < Med.L *verificare* < L *verus* true + *facere* make] —**ver′i·fi′er,** *n.*

ver·i·ly (ver′ə lē) *adv.* in truth; truly; really. [< *very* + *-ly*]

ver·i·sim·i·lar (ver′ə sim′ə lər) *adj.* appearing true or real; probable.

ver·i·si·mil·i·tude (ver′ə sə mil′ə tyüd′ *or* -tüd′) *n.* **1** appearance of truth or reality; probability: *A story must have verisimilitude to interest most people.* **2** something having merely the appearance of truth. [< L *verisimilitudo* < *verus* true + *similis* like]

ver·i·ta·ble (ver′ə tə bəl) *adj.* true; real; actual. [< OF *veritable* < *verité* < L *veritas.* See VERITY.] —**ver′i·ta·ble·ness,** *n.* —**ver′i·ta·bly,** *adv.*

ver·i·ty (ver′ə tē) *n., pl.* **-ties. 1** the quality or state of being true or real. **2** something that is true or real, especially a basic principle or belief: *the eternal verities.* [ME < OF < L *veritas* < *verus* true]

ver·juice (vėr′jüs′) *n.* **1** an acid liquor made from sour juice of crab apples, unripe grapes, etc. Verjuice was formerly used in cooking. **2** sourness, as of temper or expression. [ME < OF *verjus* < *vert* green (< L *viridis*) + *jus* juice < L]

ver·juiced (vėr′jüst′) *adj.* of or having to do with verjuice; sour.

ver·meil (vėr′māl *or* vėr′məl) *n. or adj.* **1** silver coated or plated with gold. **2** *Poetic.* vermilion. [ME < OF *vermeil* < L *vermiculus,* dim. of *vermis* worm]

ver·mi·cel·li (vėr′mə sel′ē *or* vėr′mə chel′ē; *Italian,* ver′mē chel′lē) *n.* a kind of pasta similar to spaghetti, but thinner. [< Ital. *vermicelli,* literally, little worms, ult. < L *vermis* worm]

ver·mi·cide (vėr′mə sīd′) *n.* any agent that kills worms; especially, a drug used to kill parasitic intestinal worms. [< L *vermis* worm + E *-cide²*]

ver·mic·u·lar (vėr mik′yə lər) *adj.* **1** of, having to do with, or characteristic of a worm or worms. **2** like a worm in nature, form, or method of movement. **3** like the wavy track of a worm. **4** marked with close wavy lines. **5** worm-eaten. [< Med.L *vermicularis,* ult. < L *vermis* worm]

ver·mic·u·lite (vėr mik′yə līt′) *n.* any of various silicate minerals in the form of small, lightweight granules or flakes that readily absorb water. Vermiculite is used as a medium for growing seedlings, for insulation, etc.

hat, āge, fär; let, ēqual, tėrm; it, īce
hot, ōpen, ôrder; oil, out; cup, pút, rüle,
əbove, takən, pencəl, lemən, circəs

ch, child; ng, long; sh, ship
th, thin; ŦH, then; zh, measure

ver·mi·form (vėr′mə fôrm′) *adj.* shaped like a worm. [< Med.L *vermiformis* < L *vermis* worm + *forma* form]

vermiform appendix a slender tube, closed at one end, growing out of the large intestine in the lower right-hand part of the abdomen. Appendicitis is inflammation of the vermiform appendix.

ver·mi·fuge (vėr′mə fyüj′) *n.* a medicine to expel worms from the intestines. [< F < L *vermis* worm + *fugare* cause to flee]

ver·mil·ion (vər mil′yən) *n., adj.* —*n.* **1** bright, somewhat orangy red. **2** a pigment having this color, especially one consisting of mercuric sulphide. —*adj.* having the color vermilion. [ME < OF *vermillon* < *vermeil.* See VERMEIL.]

ver·min (vėr′mən) *n. (usually functioning as plural)* **1** small animals that are troublesome, objectionable, or destructive, especially insects such as lice, fleas, and bedbugs, or rodents such as rats and mice. **2** *Esp.Brit.* animals or birds that destroy game, poultry, etc. **3** a vile, offensive, or dangerous person or persons. [ME < OF *vermin,* ult. < L *vermis* worm]

ver·min·ous (vėr′mən əs) *adj.* **1** infested with vermin. **2** caused by vermin. **3** like vermin; vile; worthless.

ver·mouth (vər müth′ *or* vėr′müth) *n.* a white wine flavored with herbs and used as a liqueur or in cocktails. Vermouth may be either dry or sweet, and ranges in color from pale yellow to reddish brown. [< F < G *Wermut(h)* wormwood, with which it was originally flavored]

ver·nac·u·lar (vər nak′yə lər) *n., adj.* —*n.* **1** a native language; language used by the people of a certain country or place. **2** everyday language; informal speech. **3** the language of a profession, trade, etc.: *the vernacular of the lawyers.* —*adj.* **1** used by the people of a certain country, place, etc.; native: *English is our vernacular tongue.* **2** of or in the native or everyday language, rather than a literary or learned language. [< L *vernaculus* domestic, native < *verna* home-born slave]

ver·nal (vėr′nəl) *adj.* **1** of, having to do with, or occurring in spring: *vernal green, vernal flowers, vernal months, the vernal equinox.* **2** like spring; fresh or new. **3** youthful: *Everyone admired the young girl's vernal freshness.* [< L *vernalis* < *ver* spring] —**ver′nal·ly,** *adv.*

vernal equinox the equinox that occurs about March 21.

ver·na·tion (vər nā′shən) *n. Botany.* the arrangement of leaves in a bud. [< NL *vernatio, -onis* < *vernare* bloom, renew itself]

ver·ni·er (vėr′nē ər *or* vėr′nēr) *n.* a small, movable scale for measuring a fractional part of one of the divisions of a fixed scale. [after Pierre Vernier (1580-1637), a French mathematician]

Ver·o·nal (ver′ə nəl, *or* ver′ə nol, *or* ver′ə nôl′) *n. Trademark.* barbital. [< G < *Verona,* a city in N Italy, where the inventor was when he proposed the name of the product]

ve·ron·i·ca (və ron′ə kə) *n.* **1** speedwell. **2** a cloth with an image of Christ's face, especially the cloth said to have been impressed with such an image after being used by St. Veronica to wipe the sweat from Christ's face on the way to Calvary. [< NL]

ver·sa·tile (vėr′sə tīl′ *or* vėr′sə təl) *adj.* **1** able to do many things well: *He is very versatile; he is an actor, a poet, a singer, and a language teacher.* **2** having many uses: *a versatile dress that is suitable for different occasions. A pocket knife is a versatile tool.* **3** *Zoology.* **a** capable of turning forward or backward: *the versatile toe of an owl.* **b** moving freely up and down and from side to side: *versatile antennae.* **4** *Botany.* attached at or near the middle so as to swing or turn freely: *a versatile anther.* **5** changeable; fickle; inconstant. [< L *versatilis* turning, ult. < *vertere* turn] —**ver′sa·tile·ly,** *adv.*

ver·sa·til·i·ty (vėr′sə til′ə tē) *n., pl.* **-ties.** the state or quality of being versatile.

verse (vėrs) *n.* **1** a form of literary expression using lines of words, the lines usually having a regularly repeated stress and often having rhyme; poetry. **2** a single line of verse. **3** stanza: *Sing the first verse of "O Canada."* **4** a type of verse; metre (def. 1): *blank verse, iambic verse.* **5** one of the short sections into which the chapters of the books of the Bible are traditionally divided. [late OE *vers* (replacing earlier *fers*) < L *versus,* originally, row, furrow < *vertere* turn around]

versed (vėrst) *adj.* experienced; practised; skilled: *A doctor should be well versed in medical theory.*

ver·si·cle (vėr′sə kəl) *n.* **1** a little verse. **2** one of a series of short

sentences said or sung by the minister or priest during services, to which the people make response. [< L *versiculus*, dim. of *versus.* See VERSE.]

ver·si·fi·ca·tion (vèr'sə fə kā'shən) *n.* **1** the making of verses. **2** the form or style of poetry; metrical structure. **3** a version in verse of a prose writing.

ver·si·fi·er (vèr'sə fī'ər) *n.* a person who makes verses.

ver·si·fy (vèr'sə fī') *v.* **-fied, -fy·ing. 1** write verses. **2** tell in verse. **3** turn (prose) into poetry. [< L *versificare* < *versus* verse + *facere* make]

ver·sion (vèr'zhən *or* vèr'shən) *n.* **1** a translation from one language to another; especially, a translation of the Bible: *the King James Version.* **2** a statement or description from a particular point of view: *Each of the three boys gave his own version of the quarrel.* **3** a special form or variant of something: *The tent trailer is a modern version of the travois.* [< L *versio, -onis,* originally, a turning < *vertere* turn]

vers li·bre (ver lē'brə) *French.* free verse; verse that follows no fixed metrical form.

ver·so (vèr'sō) *n., pl.* **-sos** (-səz). **1** *Printing.* **a** the back of a sheet of printed paper; the side that is to be read second. **b** the left-hand page of an open book. Compare **recto. 2** the reverse side of a medal or coin. [< L *verso folio* turned leaf < *versus,* pp. of *vertere* turn]

ver·sus (vèr'səs) *prep.* **1** against. **2** in contrast to: *the new versus the old, strength versus agility. Abbrev.*: v., vs. [< L *versus* turned toward, pp. of *vertere* turn]

ver·te·bra (vèr'tə brə) *n., pl.* **-brae** (-brā' *or* -brē') *or* **-bras.** one of the bones of the spinal column. See **spinal column** for picture. [< L < *vertere* turn]

ver·te·bral (vèr'tə brəl) *adj.* **1** of or having to do with a vertebra or the vertebrae. **2** composed of vertebrae.

ver·te·brate (vèr'tə brit *or* vèr'tə brāt') *n.* **1** any animal that has a segmented spinal column, or backbone. Fish, amphibians, reptiles, birds, and mammals are all vertebrates. **2** (*adj.*) of, having to do with, or designating the vertebrates. [< L *vertebratus* jointed < *vertebra.* See VERTEBRA.]

ver·te·bra·tion (vèr'tə brā'shən) *n.* division into segments like those of the spinal column; vertebrate formation.

ver·tex (vèr'teks) *n., pl.* **-tex·es** *or* **-ti·ces. 1** the highest point; top; summit. **2** *Mathematics.* **a** the point opposite to and farthest away from the base of a triangle, pyramid, etc. **b** the point of meeting of lines that form an angle. **c** a point where the axis of a hyperbola, parabola, or ellipse intersects it. **d** any point of a triangle or polygon. **3** *Astronomy.* a point in the heavens directly overhead. **4** *Anatomy.* the top of the head. [< L *vertex,* originally, whirl, n. < *vertere* turn]

ver·ti·cal (vèr'tə kəl) *adj., n.* —*adj.* **1** straight up and down; perpendicular to a level surface. A person standing up straight is in a vertical position. See **horizontal** for picture. **2** of or at the highest point; of the vertex. **3** directly overhead; at the zenith. **4** so organized as to include many or all stages in the production of some manufactured product: *a vertical union, vertical trusts.*
—*n.* a vertical line, plane, circle, position, part, etc. [< LL *verticalis* < *vertex* highest point. See VERTEX.] —**ver'ti·cal·ly,** *adv.*

ver·ti·ces (vèr'tə sēz') *n.* a pl. of **vertex.**

ver·ti·cil (vèr'tə sil) *n. Botany.* a whorl or circle of leaves, hairs, etc. growing around a stem or central point. [< L *verticillus,* dim. of *vertex.* See VERTEX.]

ver·tig·i·nous (vèr tij'ə nəs) *adj.* **1** whirling; rotary. **2** affected with vertigo; dizzy. **3** of the nature of or having to do with vertigo; likely to cause vertigo. **4** fickle; unstable. [< L *vertiginosus* suffering from dizziness < *vertigo.* See VERTIGO.]
—**ver·tig'i·nous·ly,** *adv.* —**ver·tig'i·nous·ness,** *n.*

ver·ti·go (vèr'tə gō') *n., pl.* **ver·ti·goes** *or* **ver·tig·i·nes** (vèr tij'ə nēz'). a sensation of dizziness or of giddiness. [< L *vertigo* < *vertere* turn]

ver·tu (ver tü' *or* vèr'tü) See **virtu.**

ver·vain (vèr'vān) *n.* verbena; especially, any of several wild North American herbs or a European species (*Verbena officinalis*) formerly used in medicine. [ME < OF < L *verbena* leafy bough. Doublet of VERBENA.]

verve (vèrv) *n.* enthusiasm; energy; vigor; spirit; liveliness. [< F]

ver·y (ver'ē) *adv. or adj.* **ver·i·er, ver·i·est.** —*adv.* **1** much; greatly; extremely: *The sun is very hot.* **2** absolutely; exactly: *in the very same place.*
—*adj.* **1** same; identical: *The very people who used to love her hate her now.* **2** mere; sheer: *The very thought of blood makes him sick. She wept from very joy.* **3** *Archaic.* real; true; genuine: *She seemed a very queen.* **4** actual: *He was caught in the very act of stealing.*

[ME < OF *verai,* ult. < L *verus* true]
☛ *Hom.* **vary.**

very high frequency the band of radio frequencies between 30 and 300 megahertz. Very high frequency is the range next above high frequency. *Abbrev.*: VHF, V.H.F.

Ver·y light (ver'ē) a colored light fired from a pistol as a signal or for temporary illumination. [< Edward W. *Very* (1847-1910), a U.S. naval officer who invented it]

very low frequency the band of radio frequencies between 3 and 30 kilohertz: Very low frequency is the range next above voice frequency. *Abbrev.*: VLF, V.L.F.

Very pistol a pistol for firing a Very light.

Very Reverend a title of respect for any of various ecclesiastical officials, such as a dean or canon or a rector of a college or seminary.

ves·i·cate (ves'ə kāt') *v.* **-cat·ed, -cat·ing.** cause blisters on; blister.

ves·i·cle (ves'ə kəl) *n.* **1** a small bladder, pouch, sac, or cyst in a plant or animal. **2** a small, abnormal, raised part in the outer layer of skin, containing a watery fluid; blister. **3** *Geology.* a small cavity in a rock or mineral. [< L *vesicula,* dim. of *vesica* bladder, blister]

ve·sic·u·lar (və sik'yə lər) *adj.* **1** of, having to do with, or having vesicles. **2** like a vesicle; having the form or structure of a vesicle.

ves·per (ves'pər) *n.* **1** *Archaic or poetic.* evening. **2** vespers *or* **Vespers,** *pl.* **a** a church service held in the late afternoon or in the evening. **b** the sixth of the canonical hours. **3** a bell calling people to vespers. **4** *Vesper,* the evening star. **5** (*adj.*) of or having to do with evening or vespers. [< Med.L < L *vespera* evening]

ves·per·tine (ves'pər tīn' *or* ves'pər tin) *adj.* **1** of or occurring in the evening: *vespertine.* **2** *Biology.* **a** of animals or birds, active in the evening. **b** of flowers, opening in the evening. **3** of stars, setting near the time of sunset. [< L *vespertinus* < *vesper* evening]

ves·pine (ves'pīn *or* ves'pən) *adj.* of or having to do with wasps or resembling a wasp. [< L *vespa* wasp]

ves·sel (ves'əl) *n.* **1** a ship or large boat. **2** an airship. **3** a hollow holder or container. Cups, bowls, pitchers, bottles, barrels, tubs, etc. are vessels. **4** a tube carrying blood or other fluid. Veins and arteries are blood vessels. **5** a person regarded as a container of some quality or as made for some purpose (used chiefly in or after Biblical expressions): *a vessel of purity.* [ME < OF < L *vascellum,* double dim. of *vas* vessel]

vest (vest) *n., adj.* —*n.* **1** a close-fitting, sleeveless, waistlength garment, usually buttoning up the front, worn by men or boys under a suit coat. **2** a similar garment worn by women. **3** an undershirt, especially for women and children. **4** *Archaic.* clothing; a garment. —*v.* **1** clothe; robe; dress in vestments: *The vested priest stood before the altar.* **2** furnish with powers, authority, rights, etc.: *Parliament is vested with power to declare war.* **3** put in the possession or control of a person or persons: *The management of the hospital is vested in a board of trustees.* [ME < OF *veste,* ult. < L *vestis* garment] —**vest'less,** *adj.*

ves·ta (ves'tə) *n.* a kind of short, usually wooden, friction match. [< Vesta]

Ves·ta (ves'tə) *n. Roman mythology.* the goddess of the hearth, corresponding to the Greek goddess Hestia. A sacred fire was always kept burning in the temple of Vesta.

ves·tal (ves'təl) *adj., n.* —*adj.* **1** of or having to do with the Roman goddess Vesta. **2** of or having to do with the vestal virgins. **3** chaste.
—*n.* **1** a chaste woman, especially a nun. **2** vestal virgin.

vestal virgin a virgin consecrated to the service of the Roman goddess Vesta. Six vestal virgins tended an undying fire in honor of Vesta at her temple in Rome.

vest·ed (ves'tid) *adj.* **1** *Law.* placed in the permanent possession or control of a person or persons; fixed; absolute: *vested rights.* **2** clothed or robed, especially in church garments: *a vested choir.*

vested interest 1 a legally established right to the possession of a real or personal property. **2** a self-interested concern for the preservation of a system, state of affairs, etc.: *Manufacturers have a vested interest in low freight rates.* **3** a person, group, or institution having such a concern.

vest·ee (ves tē') *n.* a fabric insert, with or without a collar, in the front of a dress, jacket, or blouse. [< vest + -ee, dim. suffix]

ves·tib·u·lar (ves tib'yə lər) *adj.* of or having to do with a vestibule.

ves·ti·bule (ves'tə byül') *n.* **1** a passage or hall between the outer door and the inside of a building. **2** the enclosed space at the end of a railway passenger car. **3** *Anatomy.* a cavity of the body that leads to another cavity. The vestibule of the ear is the central cavity of the internal ear. See **ear** for picture. [< L *vestibulum*]

ves·tige (ves'tij) *n.* **1** a slight remnant; trace: *Ghost stories are vestiges of a former widespread belief in ghosts.* **2** *Biology.* a part,

organ, etc. that is no longer fully developed or useful. **3** *Rare.* footprint. [< F < L *vestigium* footprint]
☛ *Syn.* **1.** See note at **trace.**

ves·tig·i·al (ves tij′ē əl) *adj.* **1** remaining as a vestige of something that has disappeared. **2** *Biology.* no longer fully developed or useful.

ALB   STOLE   CHASUBLE

Traditional Roman Catholic Mass vestments. The stole may be worn under or over the chasuble. The alb and stole are also sometimes worn without the chasuble.

vest·ment (vest′mənt) *n.* **1** an outer garment, especially for ceremonial or official wear. **2** any of the official garments worn by members of the clergy and assistants during church services. **3 vestments,** *pl.* clothing. [ME < OF *vestement*, ult. < L *vestis* garment]

vest–pock·et (vest′pok′it) *adj.* **1** able to fit into a vest pocket. **2** very small.

ves·try (ves′trē) *n., pl.* **-tries. 1** a room in a church, where vestments, etc. are kept; sacristy. **2** a room in a church or an attached building, used for Sunday school, prayer meetings, etc. **3** *Anglican Church.* **a** a committee that helps manage church business. **b** a meeting of parishioners on church business. [ME *vestry* < *vest* vest + -*(e)ry* -ery]

ves·try·man (ves′trē mən) *n., pl.* **-men.** a member of a committee that helps manage church business.

ves·ture (ves′chər) *n.* **1** clothing; garments. **2** a covering. [ME < OF *vesture*, ult. < L *vestis* garment]

Ve·su·vi·an (və sü′vē ən) *adj.* of, having to do with, or resembling Mount Vesuvius, an active volcano near Naples, Italy; volcanic.

vet¹ (vet) *n. or v.* **vet·ted, vet·ting.** *Informal.* —*n.* veterinarian. —*v.* **1** examine and care for as a veterinarian or, sometimes, as a doctor. **2** examine carefully; check: *to vet a report.* **3** be a veterinarian.

vet² (vet) *n. Informal.* veteran.

vet. 1 veteran. **2** veterinarian; veterinary.

vetch (vech) *n.* any of a genus (*Vicia*) of trailing or climbing plants of the pea family, including several species that are valuable fodder and soil-enriching plants. [< dial. OF < L *vicia*]

vet·er·an (vet′ər ən or vet′rən) *n., adj.* —*n.* **1** a person who has served in the armed forces, especially during wartime. **2** a person who has had much experience in war; an old soldier, sailor, or airman, etc. **3** (*adj.*) having had much experience in war: *Veteran troops fought side by side with new recruits.* **4** a person who has had much experience in some position, occupation, etc. **5** (*adj.*) grown old in service; having had much experience: *a veteran farmer.* [< L *veteranus* < *vetus, -teris* old]

vet·er·i·nar·i·an (vet′ər ə ner′ē ən or vet′rə ner′ē ən) *n.* a person trained to treat diseases and injuries of animals, especially one whose work it is.

vet·er·i·nar·y (vet′ər ə ner′ē or vet′rə ner′ē) *adj., n., pl.* **-nar·ies.** —*adj.* having to do with the medical or surgical treatment of animals. —*n.* veterinarian. [< L *veterinarius* < *veterinus* pertaining to beasts of burden and draft, probably < *vetus, veteris* old (i.e., good for nothing else)]

veterinary surgeon *Esp.Brit.* veterinarian.

ve·to (vē′tō) *n., pl.* **-toes;** *adj., v.* **-toed, -to·ing.** —*n.* **1** the right or power to forbid or reject: *The Senate has the power of veto over most bills passed in the House of Commons.* **2** the use of this right; a refusal of consent: *The Senate's veto kept the bill from becoming law.* **3** a statement of the reasons for disapproval of a bill passed by a legislature. —*adj.* having to do with a veto: *veto power.* —*v.* **1** reject by a veto. **2** refuse to consent to: *His parents vetoed his plan to buy a motorcycle.* [< L *veto* I forbid] —**ve′to·er,** *n.*

vex (veks) *v.* **1** anger by trifles; annoy; provoke. **2** disturb; trouble. [< L *vexare*]

vex·a·tion (veks ā′shən) *n.* **1** the quality or state of being vexed: *Her vexation at the delay was obvious.* **2** the act of vexing. **3** something that vexes.

vex·a·tious (veks ā′shəs) *adj.* vexing; annoying. —**vex·a′tious·ly,** *adv.* —**vex·a′tious·ness,** *n.*

vex·ed·ly (vek′sid lē) *adv.* with vexation; with a sense of annoyance or vexation.

vexed question a question causing difficulty and debate.

vex·il·lol·o·gist (vek′sə lol′ə jist) *n.* a person who studies flags.

vex·il·lol·o·gy (vek′sə lol′ə jē) *n.* the study of flags. [< L *vexillum* flag + -*logy.* 20c.]

VHF or **V.H.F.** very high frequency.

v.i. intransitive verb (for L *verbum intransitivum*).

V.I. 1 Vancouver Island. **2** Virgin Islands.

vi·a (vī′ə or vē′ə) *prep.* **1** by way of; by a route that passes through or along: *They travelled from Winnipeg to Saskatoon via Regina.* **2** by means or through the medium of: *We sent the package via airmail.* [< L *via,* abl. of *via* way]

vi·a·bil·i·ty (vī′ə bil′ə tē) *n.* the quality or state of being viable: *the viability of a plan.*

vi·a·ble (vī′ə bəl) *adj.* **1** able to stay alive. **2** able to keep operating or functioning: *a viable economy.* **3** of a fetus or newborn infant, sufficiently developed to maintain life outside the uterus. **4** *Botany.* capable of living and growing, as a spore or seed. [< F < *vie* life < L *vita*]

Vi·a Dol·o·ro·sa (vē′ə dol′ə rō′sə) *Latin.* **1** the road in Jerusalem travelled by Jesus from the judgment hall to Calvary. **2 via dolorosa,** a path of suffering or torment. [literally, sorrowful way]

vi·a·duct (vī′ə dukt′) *n.* a bridge, especially one consisting of a series of arches or short spans resting on high piers or towers, for carrying a road or railway over a valley, a part of a city, etc. [< L *via* road + *ductus* a leading; patterned on *aqueduct*]

vi·al (vī′əl) *n.* a small bottle, especially a glass bottle, for holding medicines, perfumes, etc. [var. of *phial*]
☛ *Hom.* **viol.**

vi·a me·di·a (vī′ə mē′dē ə) *Latin.* a middle way.

vi·and (vī′ənd or vē′ənd) *n.* Usually, **viands,** *pl.* articles of food, especially choice food. [ME < OF *viande* < LL *vivenda* things for living < L *vivenda,* pl., to be lived]

vi·at·i·cum (vī at′ə kəm or vē at′ə kəm) *n., pl.* **-ca** (-kə) or **-cums. 1** Holy Communion given to a person dying or in danger of death. **2** supplies or money for a journey. [< L *viaticum,* ult. < *via* road. Doublet of VOYAGE.]

vibes (vībz) *n.pl. Informal.* **1** vibraphone. **2** a distinctive emotional atmosphere; vibrations: *He left the party early because he said the vibes were bad.*

vi·brant (vī′brənt) *adj.* **1** vibrating. **2** throbbing with vitality, enthusiasm, etc.; full of life and vigor: *a vibrant personality.* **3** resounding or resonant: *a vibrant voice.* [< L *vibrans, -antis,* ppr. of *vibrare* vibrate] —**vi′brant·ly,** *adv.*

vi·bra·phone (vī′brə fōn′) *n.* a musical instrument similar to a xylophone but having motor-driven resonators and metal tubes that produce a vibrato.

vi·brate (vī′brāt) *v.* **-brat·ed, -brat·ing. 1** move or cause to move rapidly to and fro: *A piano string vibrates and makes a sound when a key is struck.* **2** swing or cause to swing to and fro; set in motion. **3** measure by moving to and fro: *A pendulum vibrates seconds.* **4** respond with feeling; thrill: *Their hearts vibrated to the appeal.* **5** resound: *The clanging vibrated in his ears.* [< L *vibrare* shake]

vi·bra·tile (vī′brə tīl′ or vī′brə til) *adj.* **1** capable of vibrating or of being vibrated. **2** having a vibratory motion. **3** having to do with vibration.

vi·bra·tion (vī brā′shən) *n.* **1** a rapid movement to and fro; quivering motion; vibrating: *The buses shake the house so much that we feel the vibration.* **2** a rapid or slow movement to and fro. **3** motion back and forth across a position of equilibrium. **4** an emotional stimulus or reaction. —**vi·bra′tion·less,** *adj.*

vi·bra·to (vī brä′tō) *n., pl.* **-tos.** *Music.* a vibrating or tremulous effect, produced by slight variations of pitch. [< Ital. < L *vibrare* to shake]

vi·bra·tor (vī′brā tər) *n.* **1** an electrical appliance or device that vibrates, used in massage. **2** a vibrating device in an electric bell or buzzer. **3** *Electricity.* **a** an apparatus for setting a given component

in vibration by means of continual impulses. **b** a device for causing oscillations.

vi·bra·to·ry (vī′brə tô′rē) *adj.* **1** vibrating or capable of vibration. **2** having to do with or causing vibration: *a vibratory force.* **3** consisting of vibration: *a vibratory movement.*

vi·bur·num (vī bėr′nəm) *n.* any of a genus (*Viburnum*) of shrubs and small trees of the honeysuckle family. The snowball is a viburnum. [< L]

vic·ar (vik′ər) *n.* **1** *Anglican Church.* a member of the clergy who carries out the duties of a parish but is not officially the rector. A rector may be responsible for several parishes, with a different vicar representing him in each one. **2** *Roman Catholic Church.* a deputy or representative of another official. The cardinal vicar of Rome is appointed to represent the pope. **3** any person who takes the place of another; a substitute or representative. [ME < OF < L *vicarius*, originally, adj., substitute < *vicis* (gen. of **vix* change)]

vic·ar·age (vik′ər ij) *n.* **1** the residence of a vicar. **2** the position or duties of a vicar.

vicar apostolic *Roman Catholic Church.* a missionary or titular bishop stationed either in a country where no episcopal see has yet been established, or in one where the succession of bishops has been interrupted.

vic·ar–gen·er·al (vik′ər jen′ər əl *or* -jen′rəl) *n., pl.* **vic·ars-gen·er·al. 1** *Roman Catholic Church.* a deputy of a bishop or an archbishop, assisting him in the government of the diocese. **2** *Anglican Church.* an ecclesiastical officer, usually a layman, who assists a bishop or an archbishop.

vi·car·i·ous (vī ker′ē əs *or* vi ker′ē əs) *adj.* **1** felt or realized by sharing in one's imagination the actual experience of another person: *She obtains a vicarious delight in foreign countries from reading travel books.* **2** done or suffered for others: *vicarious work, a vicarious sacrifice.* **3** taking the place of or doing the work of another: *As a ghost writer, he is a vicarious autobiographer.* **4** delegated: *vicarious authority.* **5** especially of menstrual bleeding, occurring in an unexpected or abnormal part of the body. [< L *vicarius.* See VICAR.] —**vi·car′i·ous·ly**, *adv.* —**vi·car′i·ous·ness**, *n.*

vic·ar·ship (vik′ər ship′) *n.* the office or position of a vicar.

vice[1] (vīs) *n.* **1** moral corruption; evil; wickedness. **2** an evil or immoral habit: *the vice of gluttony.* **3** a fault; a bad habit: *He said that his horse had no vices.* **4** prostitution. [ME < OF < L *vitium*]
☞ *Hom.* **vise.**

vice[2] (vīs) See **vise.**
☞ *Hom.* **vise.**

vi·ce[3] (vī′sē) *prep.* instead of; in the place of. [< L *vice* (abl. of **vix, vicis* turn, change]

vice– *prefix.* substitute; deputy; subordinate, as in *vice-president, vice-chairman, vice-chancellor.* [see VICE[3]]

vice–ad·mi·ral (vīs′ad′mə rəl) *n.* **1** *Canadian Forces.* in Maritime Command, the equivalent of a lieutenant-general. See chart at **rank**[1]. **2** a naval officer of similar rank in other countries. *Abbrev:* V.Adm. or VAdm

vice–chan·cel·lor (vīs′chan′sə lər) *n.* a person who substitutes for or acts as assistant to a chancellor.

vice–con·sul (vīs′kon′səl) *n.* a person next in rank below a consul.

vice·ge·ren·cy (vīs′jėr′ən sē) *n., pl.* **-cies.** the position of vicegerent.

vice·ge·rent (vīs′jėr′ənt) *n., adj.* —*n.* a person exercising the powers or authority of another; a deputy, especially of a ruler. —*adj.* acting as vicegerent. [< Med.L *vicegerens* < L *vice* instead (of) + *gerere* manage]

vi·cen·ni·al (vī sen′ē əl) *adj.* **1** of or for twenty years. **2** occurring once every twenty years. [< L *vicennium* twenty-year period < stem of *vicies* twenty times + *annus* year]

vice–pres·i·den·cy (vīs′prez′ə dən sē) *n.* the office or position of vice-president.

vice–pres·i·dent (vīs′prez′ə dənt) *n.* the officer next in rank to the president, who takes the president's place when necessary. *Abbrev:* V.P. or V.Pres.

vice–pres·i·den·tial (vīs′prez ə den′shəl) *adj.* of or having to do with the vice-president.

vice–re·gal (vīs rē′gəl) *adj.* of or having to do with a viceroy.

vice–re·gent (vīs′rē′jənt) *n.* a deputy of a regent.

vice·roy (vīs′roi) *n.* a person governing a province or colony as the representative of the sovereign. [< F *vice-roi* < *vice* vice[2] (< L) + *roi* king < L *rex*]

vice·roy·al·ty (vīs′roi′əl tē) *n.* the position or district of a viceroy.

vice ver·sa (vī′sə vėr′sə *or* vīs′ vėr′sə) the other way round; conversely: *John blamed Harry, and vice versa (Harry blamed John).* [< L]

Vich·y (vish′ē) *n.* Vichy water.

vi·chys·soise (vish′ē swäz′) *n.* a cream soup made chiefly of potatoes and leeks and sprinkled with chopped chives, usually served cold. [< F < *Vichy*, a city in France, where it originated]

Vichy water 1 a natural mineral water from springs at Vichy, France, containing sodium bicarbonate and other salts, used in the treatment of digestive disturbances, gout, etc. **2** a natural or artificial water of similar composition.

vic·i·nage (vis′ə nij) *n.* neighborhood; surrounding district; vicinity. [ME < OF < L *vicinus*. See VICINITY.]

vic·i·nal (vis′ə nəl) *adj.* **1** neighboring. **2** local. [< L *vicinalis* < *vicinus*. See VICINITY.]

vi·cin·i·ty (və sin′ə tē) *n., pl.* **-ties. 1** a region near or about a place; neighborhood; surrounding district: *He knew many people in Toronto and its vicinity.* **2** a nearness in place; closeness: *The vicinity of the school to the house was an advantage on rainy days.* [< L *vicinitas* < *vicinus* neighboring < *vicus* quarter, village]

vi·cious (vish′əs) *adj.* **1** depraved or wicked: *He had led a vicious life.* **2** dangerously aggressive or unruly: *a vicious dog, a vicious horse.* **3** fierce or violent: *a vicious brawl.* **4** spiteful; malicious: *a vicious rumor, a vicious retort.* **5** *Informal.* unpleasantly severe: *a vicious headache.* [ME < OF *vicieux* < L *vitiosus*] —**vi′cious·ly**, *adv.* —**vi′cious·ness**, *n.*

vicious circle 1 two or more undesirable things, each of which keeps causing the other. **2** in logic, false reasoning that uses one statement to prove a second statement when the first statement really depends upon the second for proof.

vi·cis·si·tude (və sis′ə tyüd′ *or* və sis′ə tüd′) *n.* **1** a change in circumstances, fortune, etc. that occurs by chance: *The viscissitudes of life may suddenly make a rich man poor or a poor man rich.* **2** constant change or variation; mutability. **3** a regular alternation or succession: *the vicissitude of day and night.* [< L *vicissitudo* < *vicis* (gen.) change. Cf. VICE[3].]

vi·comte (vē kôNt′) *n. French.* viscount.

vic·tim (vik′təm) *n.* **1** a person or animal injured, killed, sacrificed, or mistreated: *victims of war, a victim of heart disease, victims of an unjust economic system. She has been the victim of several harsh attacks in the press.* **2** a person tricked by another; dupe: *the victim of a swindler.* **3** a person or animal sacrificed as part of a religious rite. [< L *victima*]

vic·tim·i·za·tion (vik′təm ə zā′shən *or* -ī zā′shən) *n.* the act of victimizing or the state of being victimized.

vic·tim·ize (vik′təm īz′) *v.* **-ized, -iz·ing. 1** make a victim of; cause to suffer. **2** cheat; swindle. —**vic′tim·iz′er**, *n.*

vic·tor (vik′tər) *n.* **1** a winner; conqueror. **2** (*adjl.*) victorious. [< L *victor* < *vincere* conquer]

vic·to·ri·a (vik tô′rē ə) *n.* **1** a low, four-wheeled carriage with a folding top and a seat for two passengers: *A victoria is a type of phaeton.* **2** any of a genus (*Victoria*) of South American water lilies having huge rose-white flowers and very large leaves. [after Queen *Victoria* (1819-1901), Queen of Great Britain and Ireland from 1837 to 1901]

Victoria Cross a bronze medal in the shape of a Maltese cross, the highest award given in the Commonwealth to members of the armed forces for bravery in the presence of the enemy. See **medal** for picture.

Victoria Day in Canada, a national holiday falling on the Monday before or on the 24th of May, the birthday of Queen Victoria. Also called **Commonwealth Day** and, formerly, **Empire Day.**

Vic·to·ri·an (vik tô′rē ən) *adj., n.* —*adj.* **1** of or having to do with the reign of Victoria (1819-1901), Queen of Great Britain and Ireland from 1837 to 1901. **2** possessing characteristics attributed to Victorians, such as prudishness, smugness, bigotry, etc. **3** of or having to do with the city of Victoria, British Columbia. —*n.* **1** a person, especially an author, who lived during the reign of Queen Victoria. **2** a native or inhabitant of Victoria, British Columbia.

Victorian age the period during the reign of Queen Victoria, from 1837 to 1901.

Vic·to·ri·an·ism (vik tô′rē ən iz′əm) *n.* **1** the quality or state of being Victorian, especially in attitudes or tastes. **2** an idea, belief, etc. common during the Victorian age.

vic·to·ri·ous (vik tô′rē əs) *adj.* **1** having won a victory, conquering: *a victorious army.* **2** of or having to do with victory: *a victorious war.* —**vic·to′ri·ous·ly**, *adv.* —**vic·to′ri·ous·ness**, *n.*

vic·to·ry (vik′tə rē *or* vik′trē) *n., pl.* **-ries. 1** the total defeat of an enemy, antagonist, or opponent. **2** the achievement of success in a struggle against a difficulty or problem. [< L *victoria,* ult. < *vincere* conquer]

☛ *Syn.* **Victory, conquest, triumph** = success in a contest or struggle. **Victory** emphasizes winning a contest or fight of any kind, and suggests defeating the opponent or enemy: *We celebrated our victory.* **Conquest** adds and emphasizes bringing the defeated thing or country under complete or absolute control and reducing defeated people to subjects or slaves: *Some day we may complete the conquest of disease.* **Triumph** applies to a glorious victory or conquest: *The granting of the vote to women was a triumph for the suffragettes.*

vic·tro·la (vik trō′lə) *n.* **1 Victrola,** *Trademark.* a kind of phonograph. **2** *Archaic.* record player; phonograph.

vict·ual (vit′əl) *n., v.* **-ualled** *or* **-ualed, -ual·ling** *or* **-ual·ing.** —*n.* **victuals,** *pl.* food or provisions, especially when prepared for use. —*v.* **1** supply with food or provisions: *The captain victualled his ship for the voyage.* **2** take on a supply of food or provisions: *The ship will victual before sailing.* [ME < OF *vitaille* < LL *victualia,* pl., ult. < *vivere* live]

vict·ual·ler *or* **vict·ual·er** (vit′əl ər) *n.* **1** a person who supplies food or provisions to a ship, an army, etc. **2** *Esp.Brit.* the keeper of an inn, tavern, saloon, etc. **3** a ship that carries provisions for other ships or for troops.

vi·cu·ña (vi kün′yə *or* vi kyü′nə) *n.* **1** a wild animal (*Lama vicugna*) of South America closely related to the llama and alpaca, highly valued for its soft, fine wool. **2** the wool of a vicuna. **3** a cloth made from this wool, or from some substitute. [< Sp. < Quechua]

vid. vide.

vi·de (vī′dē *or* wē′dā) *v. Latin.* see.

vi·de in·fra (vī′dē *or* wē′dā in′frə) *Latin.* see below (in the same page, article, book, etc.).

vi·de·li·cet (və del′ə set′) *adv. Latin.* to wit; namely (*usually abbreviated to* **viz.**). [< *videre licet* it is permissible to see]

☛ *Usage.* See note at **viz.**

vid·e·o (vid′ē ō′) *adj., n.* —*adj.* of or used in the transmission or reception of television images. —*n.* **1** television. **2** the visual part, as opposed to the sound, of a film or television program. [< L *video* I see]

vid·e·o·phone (vid′ē ō fōn′) *n.* a telephone equipped to send and receive both audio and video signals so that the users can see as well as hear each other.

vid·e·o·tape (vid′ē ō tāp′) *n., v.* **-taped, -tap·ing.** —*n.* **1** a wide magnetic tape for recording the video and audio signals of a television production for later transmission. **2** a recording made on such a tape. —*v.* record on videotape.

vi·de su·pra (vī′dē *or* wē′dā sü′prə) *Latin.* see above (in the same page, article, book, etc.).

vi·dette (vi det′) See **vedette.**

vie (vī) *v.* **vied, vy·ing.** strive for superiority; contend in rivalry; compete. [< F *envier* challenge < L *invitare* invite]

Vi·en·nese (vē′ə nēz′) *n., pl.* **-nese;** *adj.* —*n.* a native or inhabitant of Vienna, the capital of Austria. —*adj.* of or having to do with Vienna or its people.

Vi·et·nam·ese (vē′ət nə mēz′ *or* vyet′nə mēz′) *n., adj.* —*n.* **1** a native or inhabitant of Vietnam, a country in SE Asia. **2** the official language of Vietnam. The relationship of Vietnamese to other languages has not yet been established. —*adj.* of or having to do with Vietnam, its people, or their language.

view (vyü) *n., v.* —*n.* **1** an act of seeing; sight: *It was our first view of the ocean.* **2** the power of seeing; the range of the eye: *A ship came into view.* **3** something seen; a scene: *The view from our house is beautiful.* **4** a picture of some scene: *Various views of the mountains hung on the walls.* **5** a mental picture; idea: *This book will give you a general view of the way the pioneers lived.* **6** a way of looking at or considering a matter; opinion: *A child's view of school is different from a teacher's.* **7** *Archaic.* aim or purpose. **8** a prospect; expectation: *with no view of success.*

in view, a in sight: *As the noise grew louder, the airplane came in view.* **b** under consideration: *Keep the teacher's advice in view as you try to improve your work.* **c** as a purpose or intention: *He works hard and has a definite aim in view.* **d** as a hope; as an expectation.

in view of, considering; because of.

on view, to be seen; open for people to see: *The exhibit is on view from 9 a.m. to 5 p.m.*

take a dim view of, look upon or regard with disapproval, doubt, pessimism, etc.

with a view to, a with the purpose or intention of: *He worked hard after school with a view to earning money for a new bicycle.* **b** with a hope of getting.

—*v.* **1** see; look at: *They viewed the scene with pleasure.* **2** consider; regard: *The plan was viewed favorably.* [ME < AF *vewe* < OF *veoir* see < L *videre*]

☛ *Syn. n.* **3. View, scene** = something seen. **View** emphasizes the idea of

hat, āge, fär; let, ēqual, tėrm; it, īce
hot, ōpen, ôrder; oil, out; cup, püt, rüle,
əbove, takən, pencəl, lemən, circəs

ch, child; ng, long; sh, ship
th, thin; ₮H, then; zh, measure

something actually seen through the eyes, and applies to what is presented to the sight, or within the range of vision, of someone looking from a certain point or position: *That new building spoils the view from our windows.* **Scene** emphasizes the idea of something that can be seen, and applies to a landscape or setting that is spread out before the eyes: *We have a fine view of the mountain scene.* **6.** See note at **opinion.**

view·er (vyü′ər) *n.* **1** a person who views: *a television viewer.* **2** a device for viewing, especially a small instrument for viewing photographic transparencies. **3** *Law.* a person appointed by a court to inspect and report on property.

view·find·er (vyü′fīn′dər) *n. Photography.* a camera device that shows the scene or area within view of the lens. Also, **view finder.**

view·less (vyü′lis) *adj.* **1** without views or opinions. **2** without a view: *a viewless room.*

view·point (vyü′point′) *n.* **1** the place from which one looks at something. **2** an attitude of mind; point of view: *A heavy rain that is good from the viewpoint of farmers may be bad from the viewpoint of tourists.*

vi·ges·i·mal (vī jes′ə məl) *adj.* **1** twentieth. **2** in or by twenties. [< L *vigesimus* twentieth]

vig·il (vij′əl) *n.* **1** a staying awake for some purpose; a watching; watch: *All night the mother kept vigil over the sick child.* **2** a night spent in prayer. **3** the day and night before a solemn church festival. **4** Often, **vigils,** *pl.* devotions, prayers, services, etc. on the night before a religious festival. [ME < OF < L *vigilia* < *vigil* watchful]

vig·i·lance (vij′ə ləns) *n.* the quality or state of being vigilant; watchfulness or alertness.

vigilance committee a self-appointed committee of citizens organized for protection or to maintain order and punish criminals in places or situations where official law enforcement appears inadequate.

vig·i·lant (vij′ə lənt) *adj.* watchful; alert: *a vigilant guard.* [< L *vigilans, -antis* watching < *vigil* watchful] —**vig′i·lant·ly,** *adv.*

☛ *Syn.* See note at **watchful.**

vig·i·lan·te (vij′ə lan′tē) *n.* a member of a vigilance committee. [< Sp. *vigilante* vigilant]

vi·gnette (vin yet′) *n., v.* **-gnet·ted, -gnet·ting.** —*n.* **1** a decorative design on a page of a book, especially on the title page. **2** a literary sketch; a short verbal description. **3** a short incident or scene, as in a movie or play. **4** an engraving, drawing, photograph, or the like, that shades off gradually at the edge. —*v.* **1** make a vignette of. **2** finish (a photograph or portrait) in the manner of a vignette. [< F *vignette,* dim. of *vigne* vine]

vig·or *or* **vig·our** (vig′ər) *n.* **1** active physical strength or force; flourishing physical condition. **2** mental energy or power. **3** strong or energetic action; intensity of action. **4** legal or binding force; validity: *a law in full vigor.* [ME < OF < L < *vigere* thrive]

vi·go·ro·so (vē′gō rō′sō) *adj., adv. Music.* —*adj.* vigorous; energetic. —*adv.* vigorously. [< Ital.]

vig·or·ous (vig′ər əs) *adj.* **1** full of vigor; strong and active: *The old man is still vigorous and lively.* **2** requiring or carried out with vigor; done energetically: *vigorous denial, vigorous exercises, a vigorous election campaign.* —**vig′or·ous·ly,** *adv.*

☛ *Syn.* **Vigorous, strenuous** = having or showing active strength or energy. **Vigorous,** describing a person or thing, emphasizes being full of healthy physical or mental energy or power and displaying active strength or force: *The old man is still vigorous and lively.* **Strenuous** emphasizes a constant driving force and indulgence in continuous energetic activity: *A diving champion leads a strenuous life.*

Vi·king *or* **vi·king** (vī′king) *n.* **1** one of the bands of Norsemen who raided the coasts of Europe during the eighth, ninth, and tenth centuries A.D. Some of them reached as far as North America. **2** any sea rover. **3** a Scandinavian. [< ON *vikingr;* cf. OE *wicing* < *wic* camp < L *vicus* village]

vil·a·yet (vil′ä yet′) *n.* in Turkey, a province or main governmental division. [< Turkish < Arabic *welāyet*]

vile (vīl) *adj.* **vil·er, vil·est. 1** despicable or evil: *a vile attempt to defraud an old man of his savings.* **2** physically repulsive: *the vile smell of rotting garbage.* **3** very bad or unpleasant: *vile language. The weather has turned really vile. She has a vile temper.* **4** degrading; mean and low: *He was reduced to the vile task of cleaning out the stables.* **5** *Archaic.* of little worth or account. [ME < OF < L *vilis* cheap] —**vile′ly,** *adv.* —**vile′ness,** *n.*

☛ *Syn.* **3.** See note at **base².**

vil·i·fi·ca·tion (vil′ə fə kā′shən) *n.* a vilifying or being vilified.

vil·i·fy (vil′ə fī′) *v.* **-fied, -fy·ing.** speak evil of; revile; slander. [ME < LL *vilificare* < L *vilis* vile + *facere* make] —**vil′i·fi′er,** *n.*

vil·la (vil′ə) *n.* a house in the country or suburbs, sometimes at the seashore. A villa is usually a large or elegant residence. [< Ital. < L]

vil·lage (vil′ij) *n.* **1** a group of houses, stores, schools, churches, etc. that together with the people living there form a community with fixed boundaries and some local powers of government. In Canada, a village is the smallest community that can have its own local government. **2** the people of a village: *The whole village was out to see the fire.* [ME < OF *village,* ult. < L *villa* country house]

vil·lag·er (vil′ij ər) *n.* a person who lives in a village.

vil·lain (vil′ən) *n.* **1** a scoundrel; wicked person. **2** a character in a play, novel, etc. whose evil motives or actions form an important element in the plot. **3** a person or thing blamed for a particular problem: *City health experts studying the epidemic decided the chief villain was overcrowding.* **4** villein. **5** *Informal.* rascal or rogue. **6** *Archaic.* a rude or clumsy person; boor. [ME < OF < Med.L *villanus* farmhand < L *villa* country house]
☛ *Hom.* villein.

vil·lain·ous (vil′ən əs) *adj.* **1** very wicked. **2** extremely bad; vile. —**vil′lain·ous·ly,** *adv.* —**vil′lain·ous·ness,** *n.*

vil·lain·y (vil′ən ē) *n., pl.* **-lain·ies. 1** great wickedness. **2** a very wicked act; crime.

vil·la·nelle (vil′ə nel′) *n.* a form of poem of 19 lines with two rhymes, written in five tercets with a final quatrain. [< F < Ital. *villanella* < *villa* villa]

vil·lein (vil′ən) *n.* in the Middle Ages, one of a class of half-free peasants. A villein was under the control of his lord, but in his relations with other men had the rights of a freeman. [var. of *villain*]
☛ *Hom.* villain.

vil·lein·age (vil′ən ij) *n.* **1** the fact or state of being a villein. **2** the conditions under which a villein held his land.

vil·li (vil′ī or vil′ē) *n.* pl. of **villus. 1** tiny hairlike parts growing out of the mucous membrane of the small intestine. The villi absorb certain substances. **2** soft, hairlike outgrowths on some plants, as on the stems of certain mosses. [< L *villi,* pl. of *villus* tuft of hair]

vil·lous (vil′əs) *adj.* having villi; covered with villi.

vil·lus (vil′əs) *n.* sing. of **villi.**

vim (vim) *n.* vitality and enthusiasm; energy: *full of vim after a good night's sleep.* [< L *vim,* accus. of *vis* force]

vin·ai·grette (vin′ə gret′) *n.* **1** an ornamental bottle or box for smelling salts, etc. **2** a salad dressing made of seasoned oil and vinegar, and, often, chopped chives or green onions, etc. Also called **vinaigrette sauce. 3** (*adj.*) served with vinaigrette: *artichokes vinaigrette.* [< F *vinaigrette* < *vinaigre.* See VINEGAR.]

vin·ci·ble (vin′sə bəl) *adj.* conquerable. [< L *vincibilis* < *vincere* conquer]

vin·cu·lum (ving′kyə ləm) *n., pl.* **-la** (-lə). **1** *Mathematics.* a line drawn over two or more terms in an expression to show that they are to be considered together. A vinculum is equivalent to parentheses. *Example:* $a + b \times c = (a + b) \times c.$ **2** *Anatomy.* a band or bandlike structure connecting parts. **3** *Rare.* a bond or tie. [< L *vinculum* bond < *vincire* bind]

vin·di·cate (vin′də kāt′) *v.* **-cat·ed, -cat·ing. 1** clear from suspicion, dishonor, hint, or charge of wrongdoing, etc.: *The verdict of "Not guilty" vindicated him.* **2** defend successfully against opposition: *He vindicated his claim to his uncle's fortune.* **3** confirm or justify: *Their faith in him has been vindicated.* [< L *vindicare* < *vindex, vindicis* defender] —**vin′di·ca′tor,** *n.*

vin·di·ca·tion (vin′də kā′shən) *n.* **1** the act or process of clearing from any charge of wrongdoing. **2** justification: *The successful invention was a vindication of his new idea.*

vin·dic·a·tive (vin dik′ə tiv or vin′də kā′tiv) *adj.* tending to vindicate; justifying.

vin·dic·tive (vin dik′tiv) *adj.* **1** feeling a strong tendency toward revenge; bearing a grudge: *He is so vindictive that he never forgives anybody.* **2** intended for revenge; involving revenge: *vindictive punishment.* **3** spiteful; malicious: *He has a vindictive nature. She writes a vindictive column in the local paper.* [< L *vindicta* revenge] —**vin·dic′tive·ly,** *adv.* —**vin·dic′tive·ness,** *n.*

vine (vīn) *n.* **1** any plant having a long, slender stem that does not stand up by itself, but creeps along the ground or climbs on a support by twining or by putting out tendrils: *Melons and pumpkins grow on vines. Ivy is a vine.* **2** grapevine: *the fruit of the vine.* [ME < OF < L *vinea* < *vinum* wine] —**vine′like′,** *adj.*

vin·e·gar (vin′ə gər) *n.* **1** a sour liquid produced by the fermentation of cider, wine, etc. and consisting largely of dilute, impure acetic acid. Vinegar is used in flavoring and preserving food. **2** speech or temper of a sour or acid character. [ME < MF *vinaigre* < *vin* wine (< L *vinum*) + *aigre* sour < L *acer*]

vin·e·gar·y (vin′ə gər ē or vin′ə grē) *adj.* of or like vinegar; sour.

vine·yard (vin′yərd) *n.* **1** a place planted with grapevines. **2** a field or sphere of activity, especially religious work. [< *vine* + *yard¹*]

vingt-et-un (vaN′tā œN′) *n.* twenty-one; blackjack (def. 5). [< F]

vi·nous (vī′nəs) *adj.* **1** of, like, or having to do with wine. **2** caused by drinking wine. [< L *vinosus* < *vinum* wine]

vin·tage (vin′tij) *n.* **1** the wine or grapes of one season from a particular vineyard: *The finest vintages cost much more than others.* **2** the year's harvest from which a particular wine was produced: *The vintage of this wine is 1978.* **3** the gathering of grapes for making wine. **4** the season of gathering grapes and making wine. **5** a particular period or year of origin: *songs of prewar vintage.* —*adj.* **1** of a good vintage; of superior quality: *a cellar full of vintage wines.* **2** being or representing the best example or model; classic: Sunshine Sketches of a Little Town *is vintage Stephen Leacock.* **3** of or belonging to an earlier time; old or old-fashioned: *shelves full of vintage comic books. She rattled around town in her vintage Ford.* [ME < AF *vintage,* alteration of OF *vendange* < L *vindemia* < *vinum* wine + *demere* take off; influenced by *vintner*]

vintage year 1 a year in which a vintage wine is produced: *The year 1972 was a vintage year.* **2** an outstandingly successful year: *a vintage year in the history of sports.*

vint·ner (vint′nər) *n.* a person who buys and sells wine; a dealer in wine. [earlier *vinter* < AF *vinetier,* ult. < L *vinum* wine]

vi·nyl (vī′nil or vī′il) *n.* **1** (*adj.*) of, designating, or containing a univalent group of atoms (CH_2CH-) derived from ethylene: *a vinyl polymer, vinyl acetate.* **2** a polymer of any of several organic compounds containing this group of atoms, used for the manufacture of floor and furniture coverings, toys, phonograph records, etc. **3** (*adj.*) made of such a polymer: *The car has a vinyl roof.*

vi·ol (vī′əl) *n.* one of a family of usually six-stringed musical instruments similar to the violin family, used mainly in the 16th and 17th centuries. Viols are played with a curved bow and have a softer, less rich and varied tone than the violin. [ME < OF *viole, vielle* < Med.L *vitula* fiddle < *Vituala* Goddess of Joy]
☛ *Hom.* vial.

vi·o·la¹ (vē ō′lə or vī ō′lə) *n.* a musical instrument of the violin family that is slightly larger and tuned a fifth lower than the violin. [< Ital.]

vi·o·la² (vī ō′lə or vī′ə lə) *n.* any of a genus (*Viola*) of plants that includes the violets and pansies; especially, any of numerous garden varieties that are hybrids, having yellow, purple, or white flowers somewhat smaller than pansies.

vi·o·la·ble (vī′ə lə bəl) *adj.* that can be violated. [< L *violabilis* < *violare.* See VIOLATE.]

vi·o·la da gam·ba (vē ō′lə dä gäm′bä) a bass member of the viol family, resembling a modern cello. It was the most important solo instrument of the family. Also called **bass viol.** [< Ital.; literally, violin for the leg]

vi·o·late (vī′ə lāt′) *v.* **-lat·ed, -lat·ing. 1** break (a law, rule, agreement, promise, etc.); act contrary to; fail to perform: *Speeding violates the traffic regulations.* **2** treat with disrespect or contempt: *The soldiers violated the church by using it as a stable.* **3** break in upon; disturb: *The sound of the explosion violated the usual calm of Sunday morning.* **4** trespass on; infringe on: *to violate the right of free speech.* **5** commit rape on. [ME < L *violare* < *vis* violence] —**vi′o·la′tor,** *n.*

vi·o·la·tion (vī′ə lā′shən) *n.* **1** violating or being violated; infringement of a law, rule, agreement, promise, etc. **2** an interruption or disturbance. **3** the treatment of a holy thing with disrespect or contempt. **4** rape.

vi·o·lence (vī′ə ləns) *n.* **1** rough force in action: *He slammed the door with violence.* **2** rough or harmful action or treatment. **3** harm; injury: *It would do violence to her principles to work on Sunday.* **4** the illegal or unjust use of physical force to injure or damage persons or property. **5** strength of feeling: *We were shocked by the violence of her hate.* **6** the improper treatment or use of a word; distortion of meaning or application. **7** rape. [ME < OF < L *violentia*]

vi·o·lent (vī′ə lənt) *adj.* **1** acting or done with strong, rough force: *a violent blow.* **2** caused by strong, rough force: *a violent death.* **3** showing or caused by very strong feeling, action, etc.: *violent language.* **4** severe; extreme; very great: *a violent pain.* **5** that tends to distort meaning. [ME < OF < L *violentus* < *vis* force] —**vi′o·lent·ly,** *adv.*

vi·o·let (vī′ə lit) *n.* **1** any of numerous plants (genus *Viola*) having small, solid-colored, usually yellow, white, or purple flowers. The purple violet (*V. papilionacea*) is the provincial flower of New Brunswick. **2** any plant of the genus *Viola*; viola. **3** the flower of a violet. **4** (*adj.*) designating a worldwide family (Violaceae) of herbs, shrubs, and small trees to which the violets belong. The violet family is made up of 800 species. **5** any of various unrelated plants having violet-like flowers: *dogtooth violet, African violet.* **6** a medium bluish-purple.
—*adj.* having the color violet. [ME < OF *violette*, ult. < L *viola*]

A violin

vi·o·lin (vī′ə lin′) *n.* **1** a musical instrument with four strings tuned at intervals of a fifth, played by drawing a bow across the strings: *The violin can produce tones of great variety and richness.* **2** (*adj.*) designating a family of stringed musical instruments of which the violin is the smallest. The other members of the violin family are the viola, cello, and double bass. [< Ital. *violino*, dim. of *viola* viol]

vi·o·lin·ist (vī′ə lin′ist) *n.* a person who plays the violin, especially a skilled player.

vi·ol·ist (vī′əl ist) *n.* a person who plays the viol, especially a skilled player.

vi·o·lon·cel·list (vī′ə lən chel′ist *or* vē′ə lən-) *n.* a cellist.

vi·o·lon·cel·lo (vī′ə lən chel′ō *or* vē′ə lən-) *n., pl.* **-los.** a cello. [< Ital. *violoncello*, ult. < *viola* viol]

vi·os·ter·ol (vī os′tər ol′ *or* vī os′tər ōl′) *n.* an oil containing a form of vitamin D, used as a medicine to prevent or cure rickets.

VIP *Informal.* very important person.

vi·per (vī′pər) *n.* **1** any of a family (Viperidae) of Old World poisonous snakes having hollow fangs in the upper jaw, through which poison is injected. The fangs are attached to movable bones and folded back when the mouth is closed. **2** pit viper. **3** any of various other snakes that are poisonous or thought to be poisonous. **4** an extremely spiteful or treacherous person. [< L *vipera* < *vivus* alive + *parere* bring forth]

vi·per·ine (vī′pər īn′) *n.* of, having to do with, or resembling a viper.

vi·per·ous (vī′pər əs) *adj.* like a viper; treacherous and malicious. —**vi′per·ous·ly,** *adv.* —**vi′per·ous·ness,** *n.*

vi·ra·go (və rä′gō *or* və rā′gō) *n., pl.* **-goes** *or* **-gos.** a violent, bad-tempered, or scolding woman. [< L *virago* < *vir* man]

vi·ral (vī′rəl) *adj.* of, having to do with, or caused by a virus: *viral pneumonia.*

vir·e·lay (vir′ə lā′) *n.* an old French form of short poem with two rhymes to a stanza. [ME < OF *virelai* < *vireli* a refrain]

vir·e·o (vir′ē ō′) *n., pl.* **-e·os.** any of a family (Vireonidae) of small, typically green-and-white, insect-eating, New World songbirds, resembling warblers, but less active and having a stouter bill that is hooked and notched at the tip. [< L *vireo* a small bird, possibly the greenfinch]

vi·res·cence (vī res′əns) *n.* greenness; a turning green.

vi·res·cent (vī res′ənt) *adj.* turning green; tending to a green color; greenish. [< L *virescens, -entis*, ppr. of *virescere* turn green]

Vir·gil·i·an (vèr jil′ē ən) *adj.* of, having to do with, or in the style of the Roman poet Virgil (70-19 B.C.).

vir·gin (vèr′jən) *n., adj.* —*n.* **1** a person, especially a woman, who has never had sexual intercourse. **2** an unmarried girl or young woman. **3** a member of any religious order of women who have vowed to remain virgins. **4** the Virgin, the Virgin Mary. **5** Virgin, a picture or statue of the Virgin Mary. **6** the Virgin, Astronomy or Astrology. Virgo.
—*adj.* **1** having to do with or suitable for a virgin: *virgin modesty.* **2** being a virgin. **3** pure or spotless: *virgin snow.* **4** not yet used or altered by human hands: *virgin forest.* **5** of wool, spun or woven only once or not yet spun at all. **6** initial; first: *a virgin effort.* [ME < OF < L *virgo, -inis*]

vir·gin·al¹ (vèr′jə nəl) *adj.* **1** of or suitable for a virgin; maidenly. **2** fresh; pure; unsullied; untouched. [ME < L *virginalis* < *virgo, -inis* maiden] —**vir′gin·al·ly,** *adv.*

vir·gin·al² (vèr′jə nəl) *n.* a musical instrument like a small

hat, āge, fär; let, ēqual, tèrm; it, īce
hot, ōpen, ôrder; oil, out; cup, pùt, rüle,
əbove, takən, pencəl, lemən, circəs

ch, child; ng, long; sh, ship
th, thin; ŦH, then; zh, measure

harpsichord, but set in a box without legs. It was much used, especially in England, in the 16th and 17th centuries. [apparently < *virginal¹*]

virgin birth or **Virgin Birth** the doctrine that Jesus had no human father, but was miraculously conceived by the Virgin Mary.

Virginia creeper a woody North American vine (*Parthenocissus quinquefolia*) of the grape family having compound leaves, bluish-black berries, and tendrils by means of which it climbs.

Virginia reel **1** a North American country-dance in which the partners form two lines facing each other and perform a number of dance steps. **2** the music for such a dance.

vir·gin·i·ty (vər jin′ə tē) *n.* the quality or state of being a virgin; maidenhood.

Virgin Mary the mother of Jesus Christ; Our Lady.

vir·gin's-bow·er (vèr′jənz bou′ər) *n.* any of several North American species of clematis having clusters of small white flowers, such as *Clematis virginiana.*

Vir·go (vèr′gō) *n.* **1** *Astronomy.* a constellation on the celestial equator thought of as having the form of a woman. **2** *Astrology.* **a** the sixth sign of the zodiac. The sun enters Virgo about August 22. See **zodiac** for picture. **b** a person born under this sign. [< L *virgo* maiden]

vir·gule (vèr′gyül) *n.* a slanting stroke (/) between two words, indicating that either word applies, as in *and/or.* [< L *virgula* little rod]

vir·i·des·cence (vir′ə des′əns) *n.* the condition of being viridescent.

vir·i·des·cent (vir′ə des′ənt) *adj.* greenish. [< LL *viridescens, -entis*, ppr. of *viridescere* turn green < L *viridis* green]

vir·ile (vir′īl *or* vir′əl) *adj.* **1** belonging to or characteristic of a man; masculine; manly. **2** having masculine vigor or forcefulness: *a virile writing style.* **3** of a male, capable of copulation; sexually potent. [< L *virilis* < *vir* man]

vi·ril·i·ty (və ril′ə tē) *n., pl.* **-ties.** the quality or state of being virile.

vi·ro·log·i·cal (vī′rə loj′ə kəl) *adj.* of or having to do with virology.

vi·rol·o·gist (vī rol′ə jist) *n.* a person who is trained in virology, especially one whose work it is.

vi·rol·o·gy (vī rol′ə jē) *n.* the study of viruses and virus diseases.

vir·tu (vèr tü′ *or* vèr′tü) *n.* **1** excellence or merit in an object of art because of its workmanship, rarity, antiquity, etc. **2** objects of art; choice curios. **3** a taste for objects of art; knowledge of objects of art. Also, **vertu.** [< Ital. *virtù* excellence < L *virtus* virtue. Doublet of VIRTUE.]

vir·tu·al (vèr′chü əl) *adj.* being something in effect, though not so in name or according to strict definition: *a virtual promise. The battle was won with so great a loss of soldiers that it was a virtual defeat. He is the virtual president, though his title is secretary.*

vir·tu·al·ly (vèr′chü ə lē) *adv.* almost entirely or for all practical purposes: *The house was virtually destroyed in the fire. The two houses are virtually identical.*

vir·tue (vèr′chü) *n.* **1** moral excellence; goodness. **2** a particular kind of goodness: *Justice and kindness are virtues.* **3** a good quality; merit or value: *There is virtue in making a detailed plan. He praised the virtues of his car.* **4** chastity, especially in a woman. **5** the power to produce effects: *There is little virtue in that medicine.*
by or **in virtue of,** relying on; because of; on account of: *By virtue of getting to the theatre early, they got the best seats. He was able to get a copy of the letter by virtue of his position in the company.*
make a virtue of necessity, do willingly what must be done anyway. [ME < L *virtus* manliness < *vir* man. Doublet of VIRTU.]
☛ **Syn. 1.** See note at **goodness.**

vir·tu·os·i·ty (vèr′chü os′ə tē) *n., pl.* **-ties.** **1** the character or skill of a virtuoso. **2** interest or taste in the fine arts.

vir·tu·o·so (vèr′chü ō′sō) *n., pl.* **-sos, -si** (-sē). **1** a person highly skilled in the methods of an art, especially in playing a musical instrument. **2** a person who has a cultivated appreciation of artistic excellence. **3** a student or collector of objects of art, curios, antiquities, etc. [< Ital. *virtuoso* learned]

vir·tu·ous (vèr′chü əs) *adj.* **1** good; moral; righteous. **2** chaste.
—**vir′tu·ous·ly,** *adv.* —**vir′tu·ous·ness,** *n.*

vir·u·lence (vir′yə ləns or vir′ə ləns) n. 1 the quality of being very poisonous or harmful; deadliness. 2 intense bitterness or spite; violent hostility.

vir·u·len·cy (vir′yə lən sē or vir′ə lən sē) n. virulence.

vir·u·lent (vir′yə lənt or vir′ə lənt) adj. 1 very poisonous or harmful; deadly: a virulent poison. 2 of disease, characterized by a rapid and severe malignant or infectious condition. 3 of a micro-organism, able to cause a disease by breaking down the protective mechanisms of the host. 4 intensely bitter or spiteful; violently hostile. [< L virulentus < virus poison] —**vir′u·lent·ly,** adv.

vi·rus (vī′rəs) n. 1 any of a large group of submicroscopic entities typically consisting of a core of RNA or DNA material surrounded by a coat of protein, that are capable of reproduction and growth only in living cells. Viruses are regarded either as the simplest micro-organisms or as very complex molecules. Many of them are agents of disease. 2 a disease caused by a virus. 3 a corrupting influence: the virus of prejudice. [< L virus poison]

vis (vis) n. Latin. force.

Vis. viscount.

vi·sa (vē′zə) n., v. -saed, -sa·ing. —n. an official document or endorsement on a passport allowing the person or persons identified in the passport to visit a particular country or region. Some countries will not allow a foreign traveller to enter without a visa. —v. give a visa to. [< F visa, ult. < L videre see]

vis·age (viz′ij) n. 1 the face, especially with reference to its form or expression: a grim visage, a visage of despair. 2 appearance; aspect: the sad visage of late autumn. [ME < OF visage < vis face < L visus a look < videre see]
☛ Syn. 1. See note at **face.**

vis-à-vis (vē′zə vē′) adv., adj., prep., n. —adv. or adj. face to face; opposite: We sat vis-à-vis. They found themselves in a vis-à-vis situation.
—prep. 1 face to face with; opposite: She sat vis-à-vis the guest of honor. The hotel is situated vis-à-vis the plaza. 2 in comparison with or in relation to: Vis-à-vis their competitors, they were doing very well.
—n. 1 a person or thing that is face to face with or opposite another. 2 a person who corresponds to one in another group, etc.; counterpart. [< F]

Visc. viscount.

vis·cer·a (vis′ər ə) n. pl. of **vis·cus** (vis′kəs). the internal organs of the body, especially those in the cavity of the trunk, such as the stomach, intestines, kidneys, and liver. [< L viscera, pl. of viscus]

vis·cer·al (vis′ər əl) adj. 1 of, having to do with, or affecting the viscera. 2 of or springing from instinct or emotion, rather than reason: a visceral reaction.

vis·cid (vis′id) adj. thick and sticky like heavy syrup or glue. [< LL viscidus < L viscum bird lime]

vis·cose (vis′kōs) n. 1 a viscous solution made from cellulose and used especially in making rayon. 2 rayon fibres, yarn, or fabric. 3 (adj.) of, having to do with, or made of viscose. [< L viscosus. See VISCOUS.]

vis·cos·i·ty (vis kos′ə tē) n., pl. -ties. 1 the quality or property of being viscous. 2 Physics. the property of a fluid that tends to prevent it from flowing; the frictional resistance of a fluid to the motion of its molecules.

vis·count (vī′kount) n. a nobleman ranking next below an earl or count and next above a baron. [ME < AF < OF visconte < vis-vice- + comte count²]

vis·count·cy (vī′kount sē) n. the title, rank, or dignity of a viscount.

vis·count·ess (vī′koun tis) n. 1 the wife or widow of a viscount. 2 a woman who holds in her own right a rank equivalent to that of a viscount.

vis·count·y (vī′koun tē) n. viscountcy.

vis·cous (vis′kəs) adj. 1 of a liquid, sticky; thick like syrup or glue; viscid. 2 Physics. having the property of viscosity. [ME < LL viscosus < viscum bird lime]

vise or **vice** (vīs) n., v. vised, vis·ing. —n. a tool having two jaws moved by a screw or lever, etc., used to hold an object firmly while work is being done on it. —v. hold, press, or squeeze with a vise, or as if with a vise. [ME < OF vis screw < VL vitium < L vitis vine]
☛ Hom. **vice.**

Vish·nu (vish′nü) n. Hinduism. one of the three great divinities of classical Hinduism, widely regarded as the highest god, and usually worshipped in one of his human forms, especially Krishna or Rama. [< Skt.]

vis·i·bil·i·ty (viz′ə bil′ə tē) n., pl. -ties. 1 the quality or state of being visible. 2 the condition of light, atmosphere, etc. with reference to the distance at which things can be clearly seen: Poor visibility was the main reason for the accident. 3 the distance at which things are clearly visible: Fog and rain decreased visibility to about 50 metres.

vis·i·ble (viz′ə bəl) adj. 1 that can be seen: The shore was barely visible through the fog. Bacteria are visible only with the aid of a microscope. 2 that can be observed; apparent; obvious: There was no visible improvement in the patient's condition. The tramp had no visible means of support. [ME < L visibilis < videre see]

vis·i·bly (viz′ə blē) adv. so as to be visible; plainly; evidently.

Vis·i·goth (viz′ə goth′) n. a member of the western division of the Goths. The Goths plundered Rome in A.D. 410, and formed a monarchy in France and N Spain about A.D. 418. [< LL Visigothi < Gmc.; taken as "the western Goths"]

vi·sion (vizh′ən) n., v. —n. 1 the power of seeing; sense of sight: He wears glasses because of poor vision. 2 the act or fact of seeing; sight. 3 the power of perceiving by the imagination or by clear thinking: a prophet of great vision. 4 something seen in the imagination, in a dream, in one's thoughts, etc.: The beggar had visions of great wealth. 5 a phantom. 6 a very beautiful person, scene, etc.
—v. imagine or envision. [ME < L visio, -onis < videre see]

vi·sion·ar·y (vizh′ən er′ē) adj., n., pl. -ar·ies. —adj. 1 having a tendency to indulge in fanciful and unpractical schemes or theories: a visionary thinker. 2 not practical; fanciful or utopian: a visionary scheme for a just society. 3 of, having to do with, or seen in a vision: The visionary scene faded and he awoke. 4 able or likely to see visions.
—n. 1 a person whose schemes or theories are fanciful and unpractical. 2 a person who sees visions.

vis·it (viz′it) v., n. —v. 1 make a call on or stay with for social reasons: I'm going to visit my aunt tomorrow. They're visiting friends in Europe this month. 2 go or come to see or stay at a place, especially for sightseeing, etc.: Last year we visited Newfoundland. 3 go or come to see officially in order to inspect or examine: The inspector visits the factory once a month. 4 make a call or stay as a guest: They are visiting in the country. 5 come upon; afflict: The poor old man was visited by many troubles. 6 send upon; inflict: He visited his anger upon them. 7 punish or avenge (a sin, etc.): to visit the sins of the fathers upon the children.
visit with, Informal. talk with.
—n. 1 a call or stay as a guest or for the purpose of inspection, etc.: They had to cut their visit short because he got sick. 2 Informal. a friendly talk or chat: We had a nice visit while we were waiting. [< L visitare, ult. < videre see]

vis·it·ant (viz′ə tənt) n., adj. —n. 1 a visitor, especially one thought to be supernatural. 2 Biology. a migrating bird in any of the places it stays temporarily. —adj. Archaic or poetic. paying a visit; visiting.

vis·it·a·tion (viz′ə tā′shən) n. 1 the act or an instance of visiting; especially, a visit for the purpose of making an inspection or examination: the visitation of a foreign ship. 2 a punishment or reward sent by God. 3 any severe affliction, blow, or trial.
4 **Visitation,** a the visit of the Virgin Mary to Elizabeth, her cousin (Luke 1:39-56). b a festival of the Roman Catholic Church, held July 2, in honor of this visit.

visiting card a calling card.

vis·i·tor (viz′ə tər) n. a person who visits or is visiting: I don't live here; I'm just a visitor. The zoo had more visitors than ever last summer.
☛ Syn. **Visitor, guest** = someone who comes to see or stay with another or in a place. **Visitor** is the general word, applying to anyone who comes to see a person or place or makes a call or stay, long or short, for any reason: Our visitors from the East arrived last night. **Guest** emphasizes the idea of being entertained, and applies especially to someone invited to come or stay: He usually entertains his guests at the club.

vi·sor (vī′zər) n., v. —n. 1 Historical. the movable front part of a helmet, covering the face. See **armor** for picture. 2 a projecting

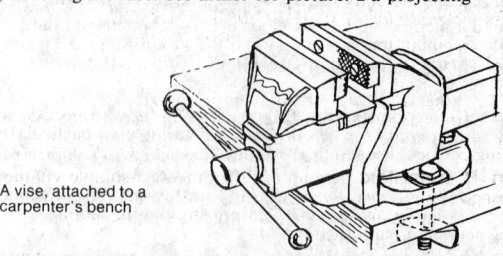

A vise, attached to a carpenter's bench

part, such as the peak of a cap, intended to protect the eyes from the sun or other strong light. See **cap** for picture. **3** a mask or disguise. **4** a small movable shade attached inside an automobile at the top of the windshield.
—*v.* cover or protect with a visor. Also, **vizor.** [ME < AF *viser* < *vis* face, ult. < L *videre* see]

vi·sored (vī′zərd) *adj.* furnished or equipped with a visor.

vis·ta (vis′tə) *n.* **1** a view seen through a narrow opening or passage: *The opening between two rows of trees afforded a vista of the lake.* **2** a mental view over a period of time or series of events in the past or future: *The book had opened up a new vista for her future.* [< Ital. *vista*, ult. < L *videre* see]

vis·u·al (vizh′ü əl) *adj., n.* —*adj.* **1** of, having to do with, or used in sight or vision: *Near-sightedness is a visual defect.* **2** that can be seen; visible: *the visual arts.* **3** done by sight only: *visual navigation.* **4** of the nature of a mental vision; produced or occurring as a picture in the mind: *to form a visual image of an author's description.*
—*n.* a visual device, such as a drawing, transparency, photograph, or film clip, used in a lecture, sales presentation, television newscast, etc. [< LL *visualis* < L *visus* sight < *videre* see]
—**vis′u·al·ly,** *adv.*

visual aid a device or means such as a chart, diagram, motion picture, etc. for aiding the learning process through the sense of sight.

vis·u·al·i·za·tion (vizh′ü əl ə zā′shən *or* -ī zā′shən) *n.* **1** the act or process of visualizing or the state of being visualized. **2** the thing visualized.

vis·u·al·ize (vizh′ü əl īz′) *v.* **-ized, -iz·ing. 1** form a mental picture of: *I can visualize his reaction when he hears the news.* **2** make visible; especially, make (an internal organ) visible by surgical means or X ray. **3** form mental pictures.

vi·ta (vē′tə) *n., pl.* **-tae** (-tī *or* -tē). an autobiographical sketch or summary; curriculum vitae. [< L *vita* life]

vi·tal (vī′təl) *adj., n.* —*adj.* **1** of, having to do with, or necessary to life: *vital forces. Eating is a vital function. The heart is one of the vital organs of the body.* **2** of the greatest importance; essential: *vital national interests. Perfect timing was vital to the success of their plan.* **3** causing death, failure, or ruin: *a vital wound, a vital blow to an industry.* **4** full of life and spirit; lively.
—*n.* **vitals,** *pl.* **a** the vital organs, such as the heart, brain, lungs, etc. **b** the essential parts or elements of anything. [ME < L *vitalis* < *vita* life] —**vi′tal·ly,** *adv.*

vi·tal·ism (vī′təl iz′əm) *n.* a doctrine that the behavior of a living organism is, at least in part, due to a vital force that cannot possibly be explained by physics and chemistry.

vi·tal·i·ty (vī tal′ə tē) *n., pl.* **-ties. 1** mental or physical vigor; liveliness: *She has great vitality.* **2** the power to endure or remain active: *the vitality of a tradition.* **3** vital force; the power to live; that which distinguishes the living from the non-living.

vi·tal·ize (vī′təl īz′) *v.* **-ized, -iz·ing. 1** put vitality into. **2** give life to. —**vi′tal·i·za′tion,** *n.* —**vi′tal·iz′er,** *n.*

vital signs physical signs of life, such as pulse, breathing, and temperature.

vital statistics 1 facts or data about births, deaths, marriages, etc. **2** *Informal.* a woman's bust, waist, and hip measurements. **3** *Informal.* any of various other kinds of numerical data, such as the achievements of an athlete, considered important.

vi·ta·min (vī′tə min) *n.* **1** any of certain complex organic substances required for the normal growth and nourishment of the body, found especially in milk, butter, raw fruits and vegetables, brewers' yeast, wheat, and cod-liver oil. Lack of vitamins in food causes such diseases as rickets and scurvy as well as general poor health. **2** (*adj.*) of, having to do with, or containing vitamins: *a vitamin deficiency, vitamin pills.* [< L *vita* life + E *amine* (< *ammonia*)]

vitamin A a fat-soluble vitamin occurring in two known forms, A_1 and A_2, and found especially in animal products such as milk, butter, cod-liver oil, egg yolk, liver, and leafy green vegetables. Vitamin A helps the body resist infection and prevents night blindness. *Formula for A₁:* $C_{20}H_{30}O$; *for A₂:* $C_{20}H_{28}O$.

vitamin B₁ thiamine.

vitamin B₂ riboflavin. Also, **vitamin G.**

vitamin B₆ pyridoxine.

vitamin B₁₂ a complex crystalline compound found especially in liver, that is necessary for blood formation and is used particularly in treating pernicious anemia. *Formula:* $C_{63}H_{90}N_{14}O_{14}PCo$

vitamin B complex a group of different water-soluble vitamins found especially in yeast, liver, eggs, and seed germs. They include thiamine, riboflavin, pyridoxine, vitamin B₁₂, biotin, choline, nicotinic acid, and pantothenic acid.

vitamin C a water-soluble compound found especially in citrus

fruits and also made synthetically; ascorbic acid. It is used especially for the prevention and treatment of scurvy. *Formula:* $C_6H_8O_6$

vitamin D any of several fat-soluble compounds that are necessary for normal growth of bones and teeth and found especially in fish-liver oils, egg yolk, and milk. The most abundant form of this vitamin is D₃, which is found in fish-liver oils and is also formed in the skin by the action of sunlight. *Formula (for D₃):* $C_{27}H_{43}OH$

vitamin E any of several fat-soluble vitamins found especially in leaves and seed germ oils. Lack of vitamin E is associated with sterility and degeneration of muscles in various animals. *Formula:* $C_{29}H_{50}O_2$

vitamin G vitamin B₂; riboflavin.

vitamin H biotin.

vi·ta·min·ize (vī′tə min īz′) *v.* **-ized, -iz·ing.** provide with vitamins.

vitamin K 1 either of two fat-soluble compounds necessary to the normal clotting of blood, found especially in leafy vegetables, alfalfa, etc. and formed in the intestines of mammals by the action of bacteria. *Formula for vitamin K₁:* $C_{31}H_{46}O_2$ *Formula for K₂:* $C_{41}H_{56}O_2$ **2** any of several synthetically produced compounds closely related to vitamins K₁ and K₂ and having a similar function.

vitamin L a vitamin found in beef liver (vitamin L₁) and yeast (vitamin L₂) that promotes normal lactation.

vitamin P a water-soluble vitamin obtained from citrus fruits and paprika and used to promote capillary resistance to hemorrhaging.

vi·tel·lin (vi tel′ən *or* vī tel′ən) *n.* a protein contained in the yolk of eggs. [< L *vitellus* egg yolk]

vi·ti·ate (vish′ē āt′) *v.* **-at·ed, -at·ing. 1** impair the quality of; spoil: *His illness vitiated his chances of success.* **2** destroy the legal force or authority of: *The contract was vitiated because one person signed under compulsion.* [< L *vitiare* < *vitium* fault]
—**vi′ti·a′tion,** *n.*

vit·i·cul·ture (vit′ə kul′chər *or* vī′tə kul′chər) *n.* the cultivation of grapes. [< L *vitis* vine + E *culture*]

vit·re·ous (vit′rē əs) *adj.* **1** of, having to do with, derived from, or consisting of glass. **2** like glass in texture, brittleness, etc.; glassy: *vitreous rocks.* **3** of or having to do with the vitreous humor. [< L *vitreus* < *vitrum* glass]

vitreous humor or **humour** the transparent, jelly-like substance that fills the interior of the eyeball behind the lens. See **eye** for picture.

vit·ri·fac·tion (vit′rə fak′shən) *n.* vitrification.

vit·ri·fi·ca·tion (vit′rə fə kā′shən) *n.* **1** the process of making or becoming glass or a glasslike substance. **2** something vitrified.

vit·ri·form (vit′rə fôrm′) *adj.* having the structure or appearance of glass. [< F < L *vitrum* glass + *facere* make]

vit·ri·fy (vit′rə fī′) *v.* change into glass or a glasslike substance by heat and fusion.

vit·ri·ol (vit′rē əl) *n.* **1** any of certain sulphates, as of copper (**blue vitriol**), iron (**green vitriol**), or zinc (**white vitriol**). **2** sulphuric acid. Vitriol burns deeply and leaves very bad scars. **3** very sharp speech or severe criticism. [ME < Med.L *vitriolum,* ult. < L *vitrum* glass]

vit·ri·ol·ic (vit′rē ol′ik) *adj.* **1** of or containing vitriol. **2** like vitriol. **3** bitterly severe; sharp: *vitriolic criticism.*

vi·tu·per·ate (vi tyü′pər āt′ *or* vī tü′pər āt′) *v.* **-at·ed, -at·ing.** find fault with in abusive words; revile. [< L *vituperare* < *vitium* fault + *parare* prepare]

vi·tu·per·a·tion (vi tyü′pər ā′shən *or* vī tü′pər ā′shən) *n.* bitter abuse in words; very severe scolding.

vi·tu·per·a·tive (vi tyü′pər ə tiv *or* vī tü′pər ə tiv) *adj.* abusive; reviling. —**vi·tu′per·a·tive·ly,** *adv.*

vi·va (vē′və) *interj., n.* —*interj.* an exclamation used as a salute or expression of approval. —*n.* a shout of applause or good will: *The crowd greeted him with a loud viva.* [< Ital.]

vi·va·ce (vē vä′chā) *adj., adv., n. Music.* —*adj.* quick; lively. —*adv.* in a lively manner.
—*n.* a lively movement or passage; composition to be played or sung in this manner. [< Ital. < L *vivax, -acis*]

vi·va·cious (vi vā′shəs *or* vī vā′shəs) *adj.* lively; sprightly;

animated: *a vivacious personality, a vivacious smile.* [< L *vivax, -acis*] —**vi·va′cious·ly,** *adv.* —**vi·va′cious·ness,** *n.*

vi·vac·i·ty (vi vas′ə tē *or* vī vas′ə tē) *n., pl.* **-ties.** liveliness; sprightliness; animation; gaiety. [< L *vivacitas < vivax, -acis* lively]

vi·var·i·um (vī ver′ē əm) *n., pl.* **-i·ums** *or* **-i·a** (-ē ə). an enclosed place for keeping animals in an environment as close as possible to their natural one. [< L]

vi·va vo·ce (vī′və vō′sē *or* vē′və vō′chā) **1** spoken; oral: *a viva voce examination.* **2** orally: *We voted viva voce instead of by ballot.* [< L *viva voce,* literally, by living voice]
☛ *Pronun.* The first pronunciation developed naturally from the term's use in Middle English; the second pronunciation shows the influence of modern Italian.

vive (vēv) *interj. French.* a word used in exclamation of praise or as a salute. *Vive la France!* means *Long live France!*

viv·id (viv′id) *adj.* **1** brilliant; strikingly bright: *Dandelions are a vivid yellow.* **2** full of life; lively: *a vivid description.* **3** clearly and strikingly perceived or felt: *a vivid impression, a vivid sensation.* **4** very strong and active: *a vivid imagination.* [< L *vividus < vivus* alive] —**viv′id·ly,** *adv.* —**viv′id·ness,** *n.*

viv·i·fy (viv′ə fī) *v.* **-fied, -fy·ing. 1** give life or vigor to. **2** enliven; make vivid. [< L *vivificare < vivus* alive + *facere* make] —**viv′i·fi·ca′tion,** *n.*

vi·vip·a·rous (vi vip′ə rəs *or* vī vip′ə rəs) *adj.* bringing forth living young, rather than eggs. Dogs, cats, cows, and human beings are viviparous. Compare **oviparous.** [< L *viviparus < vivus* alive + *parere* bring forth]

viv·i·sect (viv′ə sekt′ *or* viv′ə sekt′) *v.* **1** perform vivisection on: *to vivisect an animal.* **2** practise vivisection.

viv·i·sec·tion (viv′ə sek′shən) *n.* the act or practice of cutting into or experimenting on living animals for scientific study. [< L *vivus* alive + E *section*]

viv·i·sec·tion·ist (viv′ə sek′shən ist) *n.* **1** vivisector. **2** a person who favors or defends vivisection.

viv·i·sec·tor (viv′ə sek′tər) *n.* a person who practises vivisection.

vix·en (vik′sən) *n.* **1** a female fox. **2** a bad-tempered or quarrelsome woman. [OE **fyxen < fox* fox]

vix·en·ish (vik′sən ish) *adj.* ill-tempered; scolding.

Vi·yel·la (vī yel′ə) *n. Trademark.* a soft, lightweight, washable fabric, a blend of wool and cotton.

viz. to wit; namely (abbreviation of L *videlicet*): *Two members have been asked to attend the conference, viz., Ms. Sanchez and Mr. Faber.*
☛ *Usage.* **Viz.** is used mainly in rather formal documents or reference works. It is a written form that is not pronounced (viz), except humorously, but is usually spoken or read as "namely."

viz·ard (viz′ərd) *n.* a mask; visor (def. 3). [alteration of *visor*]

vi·zier (vi zēr′) *n.* in Moslem countries, especially in the former Turkish Empire, a high official or minister of state. [< Turkish < Arabic *wazīr,* originally, porter]

vi·zir (vi zēr′) See **vizier.**

vi·zor (vī′zər) See **visor.**

V–J Day the date of the Allied victory over Japan in World War II, either August 15, 1945 (when the fighting officially ended) or September 2, 1945 (the signing of the formal surrender).

VL *or* **V.L.** Vulgar Latin.

VLF *or* **V.L.F.** very low frequency.

V neck a garment neckline that is V-shaped at the front. —**V′-neck′** *or* **V′-necked′,** *adj.*

vo. verso.

VO voice-over.

vocab. vocabulary.

vo·ca·ble (vō′kə bəl) *n.* a word, especially as heard or seen without consideration of its meaning. [< L *vocabulum < vocare* call]

vo·cab·u·lar·y (və kab′yə lėr′ē *or* vō kab′yə ler′ē) *n., pl.* **-lar·ies. 1** the stock of words used by a person, class of people, profession, etc.: *Reading will increase your vocabulary.* **2** a collection or list of words, usually in alphabetical order, with their translations or meanings: *There is a vocabulary in the back of our French book.* **3** all the words of a language. **4** the characteristic expressions of a quality, feeling, etc.: *the vocabulary of prejudice.* [< Med.L *vocabularius < L vocabulum.* See VOCABLE.]

vo·cal (vō′kəl) *adj., n.* —*adj.* **1** of, by, for, with, or having to do

with the voice: *vocal organs, vocal power, a vocal message, vocal music.* **2** having a voice; giving forth sound: *We are vocal beings. The gorge was vocal with the roar of the cataract.* **3** aroused to speech; inclined to talk freely: *He became vocal with indignation.* **4** *Phonetics.* of a vowel.
—*n.* **1** a vocal sound. **2** *Music.* **a** a composition for the voice. **b** the part of a composition that is to be sung. [< L *vocalis < vox* voice. Doublet of VOWEL.] —**vo′cal·ly,** *adv.*

vocal bands vocal cords.

vocal cords either of two pairs of folds of membrane in the larynx. Voice is produced when the edges of the lower pairs of folds vibrate as air from the lungs passes between them. See **windpipe** for picture.

vo·cal·ic (vō kal′ik) *adj. Phonetics.* **1** of, having to do with, or consisting of a vowel or vowels: *a vocalic sound. I is a vocalic word.* **2** being or functioning as a vowel: *The word* pyre *has a vocalic* y.

vo·cal·ist (vō′kəl ist) *n.* singer.

vo·cal·ize (vō′kəl īz) *v.* **-ized, -iz·ing. 1** speak, sing, shout, etc. **2** make vocal; utter: *The dog vocalized its pain in a series of long howls.* **3** *Phonetics.* change into or pronounce as a vowel. —**vo′cal·i·za′tion,** *n.*

vo·ca·tion (vō kā′shən) *n.* **1** an occupation, business, profession, or trade: *He chose teaching as his vocation.* **2** an inclination or summons to a particular activity, especially to religious work: *Since childhood she felt a vocation for nursing.* [ME < L *vocatio, -onis,* literally, a calling < *vocare* call]
☛ *Usage.* **Vocation, avocation** are often confused. **Vocation** applies to a person's regular occupation, the way he earns his living. **Avocation** applies to a kind of work a person does in his spare time, a hobby: *Bookkeeping is her vocation, and photography is her avocation.*

vo·ca·tion·al (və kā′shən əl *or* vō kā′shən əl) *adj.* of or having to do with some occupation, trade, etc. Trades and skills such as carpentry, stenography, hairdressing, and printing are taught in vocational schools. —**vo·ca′tion·al·ly,** *adv.*

voc·a·tive (vok′ə tiv) *adj., n.* —*adj.* **1** *Grammar.* of, having to do with, or being the grammatical case, found in Latin and some other languages, that shows that a noun, pronoun, or adjective refers to a person or thing being addressed or invoked. **2** of, having to do with, or characterized by calling. —*n. Grammar.* **1** the vocative case. **2** a word or construction in the vocative case. [< L *vocativus < vocare* call] —**voc′a·tive·ly,** *adv.*

vo·cif·er·ant (və sif′ər ənt *or* vō sif′ər ənt) *adj., n.* —*adj.* vociferating. —*n.* a person who vociferates.

vo·cif·er·ate (və sif′ər āt′ *or* vō sif′ər āt′) *v.* **-at·ed, -at·ing.** cry out loudly or noisily; shout. [< L *vociferari < vox, vocis* voice + *ferre* bear]

vo·cif·er·a·tion (və sif′ər ā′shən *or* vō sif′ər ā′shən) *n.* a vociferating; noisy oratory or clamor.

vo·cif·er·ous (və sif′ər əs *or* vō sif′ər əs) *adj.* loud and noisy; shouting; clamoring: *a vociferous person, vociferous cheers.* [< L *vociferari.* See VOCIFERATE.] —**vo·cif′er·ous·ly,** *adv.* —**vo·cif′er·ous·ness,** *n.*

vod·ka (vod′kə) *n.* a colorless alcoholic liquor distilled from a mash of rye, wheat, etc. [< Russian *vodka,* dim. of *voda* water]

vogue (vōg) *n.* **1** something that is in fashion at a particular time; the popular style: *Hoopskirts were the vogue many years ago.* **2** general favor; popularity: *the colors that are in vogue this spring. This song had a great vogue at one time.* **3** a period of popularity: *a short vogue.* **4** (*adj.*) popular or fashionable: *vogue colors, a vogue word.* [< F *vogue* a rowing, course, success < *voguer* float < Ital. *vogare*]

voice (vois) *n., v.* **voiced, voic·ing.** —*n.* **1** the sound produced by the organs in the throat and uttered through the mouth and nose, especially the sounds human beings make in speaking, singing, shouting, etc.: *The voices of the children could be heard coming from the playground.* **2** such sound regarded as having a particular quality that distinguishes one person from another, expresses emotion, etc.: *to recognize someone's voice, a low voice, a gentle voice, an angry voice.* **3** such sounds: *His voice was gone because of a sore throat.* **4** anything thought of as being like speech or song: *the voice of the wind, the voice of one's conscience.* **5** *Music.* **a** a musical sound made by the vocal cords and resonated by several head and throat cavities; the tones made in singing. **b** ability as a singer: *He has a very good voice.* **c** singer: *The chorus consists of 70 voices.* **d** a part of a composition for one kind of singer or instrument. **6** expression: *They gave voice to their joy.* **7** an expressed opinion, choice, wish, etc.: *His voice was for compromise.* **8** a means or instrument of expression: *That newspaper claims to be the voice of the people.* **9** the right to express an opinion or choice: *We have no voice in the matter.* **10** *Grammar.* a form of a verb showing the relation of the subject of the verb to the action expressed by the verb. The active voice, as *sees* in *he sees,* shows that the subject is performing the action. The

passive voice, as *is seen* in *he is seen*, shows that the subject is receiving the action. **11** *Phonetics.* a sound uttered with vibration of the vocal cords, not with mere breath. **12** the proper use of the voice, as in acting or singing: *She is studying voice.*
in voice, in condition to sing or speak well.
lift up (one's) voice, a shout; yell. **b** protest; complain.
with one voice, unanimously.
—*v.* **1** express; utter: *They voiced their approval of the plan.* **2** *Phonetics.* utter with a sound made by vibration of the vocal cords, not with breath alone. The consonants *z, v,* and *d* are voiced; *s, f,* and *t* are not. **3** *Music.* **a** regulate the tone of (an organ, etc.). **b** write the parts of (a piece of music) for one kind of singer or instrument. [ME < OF *vois, voiz* < L *vox*]

voice box larynx.

voiced (voist) *adj.* **1** having a voice, especially of a particular kind (*usually used in compounds*): *deep-voiced.* **2** *Phonetics.* produced or uttered by means of vibration of the vocal cords. All vowel sounds are voiced; many consonants, such as *b, d,* and *g* are also voiced. Compare **voiceless.**

voice frequency the range of sound frequencies between 300 and 3000 hertz. Voice frequency is the second lowest range in the radio spectrum, above extremely low frequency.

voice·less (vois'lis) *adj.* **1** having no voice; mute. **2** *Phonetics.* produced or uttered without vibration of the vocal chords; not voiced. The consonants *p, t,* and *k* are voiceless. Compare **voiced.**

voice–o·ver (vois'ō'vər) *n.* **1** the voice of an unseen narrator or commentator in a motion picture or on television. **2** (*adj.*) made with an unseen narrator: *He does voice-over commercials for television.*

voice·print (vois'print') *n.* a graphic representation of an individual's voice. It is an electronic record of the duration, amplitude, and frequency of the sound or sounds uttered.

void (void) *adj., v., n.* —*adj.* **1** *Law.* without legal force or effect; not binding: *A contract made by a person under legal age is void.* **2** empty; vacant: *a void space.* **3** without effect; useless.
void of, devoid of; without; lacking.
—*v.* **1** *Law.* make invalid; nullify. **2** empty out. **3** *Archaic.* leave.
—*n.* an empty space: *The death of his dog left an aching void in Bob's heart.* [ME < OF *voide* < VL *vocitus,* ult. < var. of L *vacuus* empty] —**void′er,** *n.*

void·a·ble (void'ə bəl) *adj.* capable of being voided or given up: *The contract was voidable by either party after twelve months.*

voile (voil) *n.* a thin, sheer, somewhat crisp cloth in a plain weave, used for blouses, light dresses, curtains, etc. Voile is usually made of cotton or a cotton blend. [< F *voile,* originally, veil < L *vela,* pl. of *velum* covering. Doublet of VEIL, VELUM.]

voir dire *Law.* **1** a preliminary examination by a judge to determine the competency, interest, etc. of a trial witness or the voluntary nature of an accused person's confession to a police officer. **2** the oath administered to such a person. [< OF < *voire* truth + *dire* to speak. 17c.]

vol. 1 volume. **2** volunteer. **3** volcano.

vo·lant (vō'lənt) *adj.* **1** flying; able to fly. **2** *Heraldry.* represented as flying. **3** nimble; quick. [< L *volans, -antis,* ppr. of *volare* fly]

vol·a·tile (vol'ə tīl' *or* vol'ə təl) *adj.* **1** evaporating rapidly; changing into vapor easily at a relatively low temperature: *Gasoline is volatile.* **2** changing rapidly from one mood or interest to another; fickle; frivolous: *of a volatile disposition.* [< L *volatilis* flying < *volare* fly]

vol·a·tile·ness (vol'ə tīl'nəs) *n.* volatility.

vol·a·til·i·ty (vol'ə til'ə tē) *n.* the quality or state of being volatile.

vol·a·til·ize (vol'ə təl īz') *v.* **-ized, -iz·ing.** change into vapor; evaporate.

vol·can·ic (vol kan'ik) *adj.* **1** of, having to do with, or caused by a volcano: *a volcanic eruption.* **2** characterized by the presence of volcanoes. **3** made of materials from volcanoes: *volcanic rock.* **4** like a volcano in being likely to break forth violently: *a volcanic temper.*

volcanic glass a natural glass formed by the quick cooling of lava; obsidian.

vol·can·ism (vol'kən iz'əm) *n.* phenomena connected with volcanoes and volcanic activity.

vol·ca·no (vol kā'nō) *n., pl.* **-noes** *or* **-nos. 1** an opening in the earth's crust through which steam, ashes, and lava are expelled. **2** a hill or mountain around this opening, built up of the material that has been forced out. [< Ital. < L *Vulcanus* Vulcan]

vole (vōl) *n.* any of numerous rodents (family Cricetidae, especially in genus *Microtus*) resembling mice, but having a plumper body, a blunt nose, very short ears, and a short tail. The common field mouse is a vole. [< *volemouse* < *voll* field (< Scand.; cf. ON *vollr*) + *mouse*]

hat, āge, fär; let, ēqual, tèrm; it, īce
hot, ōpen, ôrder; oil, out; cup, put, rüle, əbove, takən, pencəl, lemən, circəs
ch, child; ng, long; sh, ship
th, thin; ŦH, then; zh, measure

vo·li·tion (vō lish'ən) *n.* **1** the act or an instance of using one's will to make a choice or decision: *He gave himself up to the police of his own volition.* **2** the power of making a choice or decision; will: *By a tremendous exercise of volition, she made one last effort.* [< Med.L *volitio, -onis* < L *volo* I wish]

vo·li·tion·al (vō lish'ən əl) *adj.* of or having to do with volition. —**vo·li′tion·al·ly,** *adv.*

vol·ley (vol'ē) *n., pl.* **-leys;** *v.* **-leyed, -ley·ing.** —*n.* **1** the discharge of a number of guns at once. **2** a shower of stones, bullets, arrows, etc. **3** a burst or outpouring of words, oaths, shouts, cheers, etc.: *A volley of questions met the prime minister as he stepped from the car.* **4** *Tennis, etc.* the hitting or return of the ball before it touches the ground.
—*v.* **1** discharge or be discharged in a volley: *Cannon volleyed on all sides.* **2** *Tennis, etc.* hit or return the ball before it touches the ground. [< F *volée* flight < *voler* fly < L *volare*]

vol·ley·ball (vol'ē bol' *or* -bôl') *n.* **1** a game played with a large ball and a high net. Two teams of players hit the ball with their hands back and forth across the net without letting it touch the ground. **2** the ball.

vol·plane (vol'plān') *v.* **-planed, -plan·ing;** *n. Archaic.* —*v.* glide toward the earth in an airplane without using motor power. —*n.* the act of gliding in this way. [< F *vol plané* gliding flight]

volt (vōlt) *n.* an SI unit for measuring the pressure, or push, of an electric current. One volt of pressure is needed to drive a current of one ampere through a conductor with a resistance of one ohm. *Symbol:* V [after Count Alessandro *Volta* (1745-1827), an Italian physicist]

volt·age (vōl'tij) *n.* the strength of electric pressure measured in volts. A current of high voltage is used in transmitting electric power over long distances.

vol·ta·ic (vol tā'ik) *adj.* of, having to do with, or producing direct electric current by chemical action; galvanic: *a voltaic cell.*

voltaic battery 1 a battery composed of voltaic cells. **2** voltaic cell.

voltaic cell an electrochemical cell.

vol·tam·e·ter (vol tam'ə tər) *n.* a device for measuring the quantity of electricity passing through a conductor by the amount of electrolysis it produces. [< *volta(ic)* + *meter²*]

volte face (volt'fäs'; *French,* vôlt fäs') *n.* an about-face; reversal in attitude. [< F < Ital. *voltafaccia* < *volta* a turning + *faccia* face < L *facies*]

volt·me·ter (vōlt'mē'tər) *n.* an instrument for measuring electromotive force.

vol·u·bil·i·ty (vol'yə bil'ə tē) *n.* **1** readiness to talk much; the habit of talking much. **2** a great flow of words.

vol·u·ble (vol'yə bəl) *adj.* characterized by a rapid or ready flow of words: *a voluble protest. He was voluble in his account of the accident.* [< L *volubilis,* originally, rolling < *volvere* roll] —**vol′u·bly,** *adv.*
☛ *Syn.* **2.** See note at **fluent.**

vol·ume (vol'yəm *or* vol'yüm) *n.* **1** a collection of printed or written sheets bound together to form a book; book: *We own a library of five hundred volumes.* **2** a book forming part of a set or series: *His memoirs were published in three volumes.* **3** a series of a periodical, usually all the issues published in one year. **4** space occupied, measured in cubic units: *The storeroom has a volume of 20 cubic metres.* **5** an amount or quantity, especially a large quantity: *Volumes of smoke poured from the chimneys of the factory.* **6** a degree of loudness and fullness of tone: *A pipe organ gives much more volume than a violin or flute.* **7** a roll of parchment, papyrus, etc. containing written matter (the ancient form of a book); scroll.
speak volumes, express much; be full of meaning: *His loving glance spoke volumes.*
[ME < OF < L *volumen* book roll, scroll < *volvere* roll]
☛ *Syn.* **4.** See note at **size¹.**

vol·u·met·ric (vol'yə met'rik) *adj.* of or having to do with measurement by volume.

vo·lu·mi·nous (və lü'mə nəs) *adj.* **1** of great size or volume; very bulky or full: *A voluminous cloak covered him from head to foot.* **2** forming or filling a large book or several books: *a voluminous report.* **3** writing or speaking much: *a voluminous*

author. [< LL *voluminosus* with many coils < L *volumen, -minis.* See VOLUME.] —**vo·lu′mi·nous·ly**, *adv.*

vol·un·tar·i·ly (vol′ən ter′ə lē) *adv.* of one's own free will; without force or compulsion.

vol·un·tar·y (vol′ən ter′ē) *adj., n., pl.* **-tar·ies.** —*adj.* **1** done, made, given, etc. of one's own free will; not forced or compelled: *Churches are supported by voluntary contributions.* **2** supported entirely by voluntary gifts: *She works for several voluntary organizations.* **3** acting of one's own free will or choice: *Voluntary workers built a road to the boys' camp.* **4** able to act of one's own free will: *a voluntary agent.* **5** *Law.* **a** done, given, or proceeding from the free or unconstrained will of a person: *a voluntary affidavit.* **b** acting or done without obligation or without receiving a valuable consideration: *a voluntary partition of land.* **c** deliberately intended; done on purpose: *voluntary manslaughter.* **6** *Physiology.* controlled by the will: *Talking is voluntary; breathing is only partly so.*
—*n.* **1** anything done, made, given, etc. of one's own free will. **2** *Music.* **a** a composition, often extemporized, that is used as a prelude. **b** an organ solo played before, during, or after a church service. **3** volunteer. [ME < L *voluntarius* < *voluntas* will < *volo* I wish]
☛ *Syn. adj.* **1. Voluntary, spontaneous** = done, made, given, etc. without being forced or compelled. **Voluntary** emphasizes the idea of something done of one's own free will or choice, not in obedience to the will of another: *The state is supported by taxes, the church by voluntary contributions.* **Spontaneous** emphasizes the idea of something neither compelled by another nor directed by one's own will, but done from natural impulse, without thought or intention: *The laughter at his jokes is never forced, but always spontaneous.*

vol·un·teer (vol′ən tēr′) *n., v.* —*n.* **1** a person who enters military service of his own free will. **2** a person who offers or performs a voluntary service, especially a public service. **3** (*adj.*) being, made up of, or done by volunteers: *a volunteer firefighter, a volunteer organization.* **4** a plant that grows from seed dropped by a previous crop or generation of plants, rather than from seed deliberately sown. **5** (*adj.*) designating such a plant or crop.
—*v.* **1** offer one's services as a volunteer: *As soon as war was declared, many men volunteered.* **2** offer of one's own free will: *He volunteered to do the job.* **3** tell or say voluntarily: *She volunteered the information.* [< F *volontaire*, originally adj. < L *voluntarius.* See VOLUNTARY.]

vo·lup·tu·ar·y (və lup′chü er′ē) *n., pl.* **-ar·ies.** a person who cares much for luxury and sensual pleasures. —*adj.* caring much for luxury and sensual pleasures. [< L *voluptuarius* < *voluptas* pleasure. See VOLUPTUOUS.]

vo·lup·tu·ous (və lup′chü əs) *adj.* **1** full of or giving pleasure to the senses: *voluptuous music, a voluptuous dance.* **2** occupied with or directed toward luxury and the pleasures of the senses. [ME < L *voluptuosus* < *voluptas* pleasure < *volup(e),* neut., agreeable] —**vo·lup′tu·ous·ly**, *adv.* —**vo·lup′tu·ous·ness,** *n.*

vo·lute (və lüt′) *n., adj.* —*n.* **1** a spiral or scroll-shaped thing or form. **2** *Architecture.* a spiral or scroll-like ornament, especially as an Ionic capital. See **order** for picture. **3** any of a family (Volutidae) of tropical marine gastropod molluscs typically having a short spiral shell. **4** the shell or one of the whorls of the shell of such a gastropod.
—*adj.* rolled up or spiral: *a volute spring.* [< F *volute* < Ital. < *voluta,* fem. pp. of *volvere* roll]

vom·it (vom′it) *v., n.* —*v.* **1** expel the contents of the stomach through the mouth; throw up what has been eaten. **2** throw up or out with force: *The chimneys vomited forth smoke.* **3** come out with force or violence.
—*n.* **1** the substance thrown up from the stomach in vomiting. **2** the act or an instance of vomiting. **3** *Archaic.* emetic. [ME < L *vomitus,* pp. of *vomere* spew forth]

voo·doo (vü′dü) *n., pl.* **-doos;** *adj., v.* **-dooed, -doo·ing.** —*n.* **1** a religion that originated in Africa and is still practised among some black peoples, especially in Haiti. Voodoo involves belief in the existence of spirits which act as guides or protectors of individuals or families and belief in the magical power of charms and spells. **2** a person who practises this religion.
—*adj.* of or having to do with voodoo.
—*v.* affect by voodoo sorcery, magic, or conjuration. [of Africa origin]

voo·doo·ism (vü′dü iz′əm) *n.* **1** the belief in or practice of voodoo. **2** voodoo rites or practices.

voo·doo·ist (vü′dü ist) *n.* a person who believes in or practises voodoo.

voo·doo·is·tic (vü′dü is′tik) *adj.* of or having to do with voodooism.

vo·ra·cious (vô rā′shəs *or* və rā′shəs) *adj.* **1** eating much; having an enormous appetite; ravenous: *voracious sharks.* **2** very eager;

unable to be satisfied: *She is a voracious reader.* [< L *vorax, -acis* greedy] —**vo·ra′cious·ly,** *adv.*
☛ *Hom.* **veracious** (va rā′shəs).

vo·ra·cious·ness (vô rā′shəs nəs *or* və rā′shəs nəs) *n.* the quality or state of being voracious; voracity.

vo·rac·i·ty (və ras′ə tē) *n.* the quality or state of being voracious.
☛ *Hom.* **veracity** (va ras′ətē).

vor·tex (vôr′teks) *n., pl.* **-tex·es** *or* **-ti·ces. 1** a whirling mass of water, air, etc. that sucks everything near it into its centre. A whirlpool is a kind of vortex. **2** a whirl of activity or other situation from which it is hard to escape: *The two nations were unwillingly drawn into the vortex of war.* [< L var. of *vertex.* See VERTEX.]

vor·ti·cal (vôr′tə kəl) *adj., n.* —*adj.* of or causing motion like that of a vortex; spinning; eddying. —*n.* a vortical motion.
—**vor′ti·cal·ly,** *adv.*

vor·ti·cel·la (vôr′tə sel′ə) *n., pl.* **-cel·lae** (-sel′ē *or* -sel′ī). any of a genus (*Vorticella*) of protozoans having a bell-shaped body with cilia at the oral end and a slender, contractile stalk at the other end, often found attached to a plant or other object under water. [< NL *vorticella,* dim. of L *vortex.* See VORTEX.]

vor·ti·ces (vôr′tə sēz′) *n.* a pl. of **vortex.**

vor·tig·i·nous (vôr tij′ə nəs) *adj.* moving in a vortex; vortical. [< L *vortigo, -inis,* var. of *vertigo* a whirling]

vot·a·ble (vōt′ə bəl) *adj.* capable of being submitted to a vote; that can be voted on.

vo·ta·ress (vō′tə ris) *n.* a female votary.

vo·ta·rist (vō′tə rist) *n.* votary.

vo·ta·ry (vō′tə rē) *n., pl.* **-ries. 1** a person devoted to something; devotee: *He was a votary of oriental music.* **2** a person, such as a monk or nun, bound by vows to a religious life. [< L *votum* vow]

vote (vōt) *n., v.* **vot·ed, vot·ing.** —*n.* **1** a formal expression of a person's opinion or decision in response to a specific question, a choice between candidates, etc.: *My vote is for peace. She won the election by twenty votes.* **2** the formal decision or expression of opinion by a group resulting from the majority of the individual choices of its members: *The vote may go against the government.* **3** the right to contribute to such a formal decision: *In our club, only those who have paid their fees have a vote.* **4** the written or printed slip, token, etc. used to indicate one's decision; ballot: *The votes were placed in a sealed box.* **5** what is expressed or decided by a majority of voters: *a vote of confidence, a vote of $200 000 for a new gymnasium.* **6** the total number of votes cast; votes collectively: *The vote was higher than in the last election.* **7** a particular group of voters or their votes: *the labor vote, the under-25 vote.* **8** the act or process of voting: *They decided to take a vote on the matter.*
—*v.* **1** give or cast a vote: *He voted for the Liberals. She has gone to vote.* **2** support by one's vote: *to vote Conservative.* **3** pass, determine, or grant by a vote: *The committee voted $30 000 for renovating the building.* **4** declare by general consent: *The trip was voted a success.* **5** *Informal.* suggest: *I vote that we go.*
vote down, defeat by voting against.
vote in, elect.
[ME < L *votum* vow. Doublet of vow.]

vote of confidence 1 in parliament, a majority vote of support for the government, especially in a crisis and when defeat of the government would have forced it to resign. **2** any show of support or approval.

vot·er (vō′tər) *n.* **1** a person who votes. **2** a person who has the right to vote.

voters' list at an election, a list giving the names, addresses, and occupations of all those entitled to vote in a given riding, ward, etc.

voting machine a mechanical device for registering and counting votes.

vo·tive (vō′tiv) *adj.* **1** done, given, etc. to fulfill a vow: *a votive offering.* **2** made up or expressive of a vow, desire, or wish: *a votive prayer.* [< L *votivus* < *votum* vow]

vouch (vouch) *v.* **1** be responsible; give a guarantee (*for*): *I can vouch for the truth of the story. The principal vouched for Bill's honesty.* **2** answer for; confirm; guarantee. **3** give evidence or assurance of a fact (*for*): *The success of the attack vouches for the general's ability.* **4** *Law.* call into court to give warranty of title. **5** sponsor or recommend (a person or thing); support; back. [ME < AF *voucher* < L *vocare* call]

vouch·er (vouch′ər) *n.* **1** a person or thing that vouches for something. **2** a written evidence of payment; receipt. Cancelled cheques returned from one's bank are vouchers.

vouch·safe (vouch sāf′) *v.* **-safed, -saf·ing.** be willing to grant or give; condescend to do or give: *The proud man vouchsafed no reply when we spoke to him.* [original meaning "guarantee," to *vouch* for as *safe*]

vous·soir (vü swär′) *n. Architecture.* any of the wedge-shaped

pieces forming an arch or vault. See **arch** for picture. [< F < VL *volsorium* < *volvere* roll]

vow (vou) *n., v.* —*n.* **1** a solemn promise: *a vow of secrecy.* **2** a promise made to God: *a nun's vows.*
take vows, become a member of a religious order.
—*v.* **1** make a vow. **2** make a vow to do, give, get, etc.: *to vow revenge.* **3** declare earnestly or emphatically: *She vowed she would never shop there again.* [ME < OF *vou* < L *votum* < *vovere* vow. Doublet of VOTE.]

vow·el (vou′əl) *n.* **1** a speech sound in which the vocal cords are vibrating and the breath is not blocked at any point in the mouth by the tongue, teeth, or lips. When you say *awe*, you are uttering a vowel. The vowel is the most prominent sound in a syllable. **2** a letter representing such a sound. The five vowels used in writing English are *a, e, i, o,* and *u*. **3** (*adj.*) of or having to do with a vowel. Voluntary *has four vowel sounds*; strength *has only one.* [ME < OF < L (*littera*) *vocalis* sounding (letter) < *vox* voice. Doublet of VOCAL.]

vox (voks) *n., pl.* **vo·ces** (vō′sēz). *Latin.* voice; sound; word; expression.

vox hu·ma·na (voks hyü mä′nə *or* hyü mā′nə) *n.* an organ reed stop, intended to be an imitation of the human voice. [< L *vox humana* the human voice]

vox po·pu·li (voks′ pop′yə lē′ *or* pop′yə lī′) *Latin.* the voice or opinion of the people.

voy·age (voi′ij) *n., v.* **-aged, -ag·ing.** —*n.* **1** a journey by water, especially a long journey: *a voyage to Japan.* **2** a journey through the air or through space: *an airplane voyage, the earth's voyage around the sun.* **3** a written account of a voyage, especially by sea. —*v.* make or take a voyage; travel by water or air: *Columbus voyaged on unknown seas.* [< F *voyage* < L *viaticum.* Doublet of VIATICUM.]
☛ *Syn. n.* **1.** See note at **trip.**

voy·ag·er (voi′ij ər) *n.* **1** a person who makes a voyage; traveller. **2** *Cdn.* voyageur.

vo·ya·geur (voi′ə zhèr′; *French,* vwä yä zhœr′) *n., pl.* **-geurs** (-zhèrz; *French,* -zhœr′). *Cdn.* **1** *Historical.* a canoeman or boatman, especially a French Canadian, in the service of the early fur-trading companies. **2** a person who travels the northern wilderness, especially by canoe. [< F *voyageur,* ult. < *voyage* voyage]

vo·yeur (vwä yèr′) *n.* a person who finds sexual gratification in observing the nude bodies or sexual acts of others. [< F *voyeur* < *voir* to see < L *videre*]

vo·yeur·ism (vwä yèr′iz əm) *n.* the habits and practices of a voyeur.

VP verb phrase.

V.P. *or* **V.Pres.** vice-president.

V.R. Queen Victoria (for L *Victoria Regina*).

V.Rev. Very Reverend.

vs. **1** versus. **2** verse.

v.s. vide supra.

V.S. Veterinary Surgeon.

V–shaped (vē′shāpt′) *adj.* shaped like the letter V.

v.t. transitive verb (for L *verbum transitivum*).

Vt. Vermont.

VT Vermont.

VTOL vertical takeoff and landing.

Vul. Vulgate.

hat, āge, fär; let, ēqual, tèrm; it, īce
hot, ōpen, ôrder; oil, out; cup, pùt, rüle,
əbove, takən, pencəl, lemən, circəs

ch, child; ng, long; sh, ship
th, thin; ℟H, then; zh, measure

Vul·can (vul′kən) *n. Roman mythology.* the god of fire and metalworking, corresponding to the Greek god Hephaestus.

vul·can·ite (vul′kən īt′) *n.* a hard black rubber made by treating crude rubber with sulphur and heating it to high temperatures; ebonite.

vul·can·ize (vul′kən īz′) *v.* **-ized, -iz·ing.** treat (crude rubber or a similar synthetic material) chemically, especially with sulphur and intense heat, to make it stronger and more elastic. [< *Vulcan*] —**vul′can·i·za′tion,** *n.* —**vul′can·iz′er,** *n.*

vulg. vulgar.

Vulg. Vulgate.

vul·gar (vul′gər) *adj.* **1** lacking good manners, taste, sensitivity, etc.; coarse; boorish: *vulgar language, vulgar ambition.* **2** in common use; ordinary. **3** of the common people: *Modern French, Italian, Portuguese, and Spanish developed from vulgar varieties of Latin.* **4** (*noml.*) **the vulgar,** *Archaic.* the common people. [ME < L *vulgaris* < *vulgus* common people] —**vul′gar·ly,** *adv.* —**vul′gar·ness,** *n.*
☛ *Syn. adj.* **1.** See note at **coarse.**

vul·gar·i·an (vul ger′ē ən) *n.* a vulgar person, especially a rich person who lacks good manners, taste, etc.

vul·gar·ism (vul′gər iz′əm) *n.* **1** a word, phrase, or expression that is regarded as substandard, coarse, or obscene. **2** vulgarity.

vul·gar·i·ty (vul gar′ə tē *or* vul ger′ə tē) *n., pl.* **-ties. 1** the quality or state of being vulgar. **2** an action, habit, etc. that is vulgar.

vul·gar·ize (vul′gər īz′) *n.* **-ized, -iz·ing. 1** make vulgar; make cheap or coarse. **2** make widely known; popularize. —**vul′gar·iz′er,** *n.*

Vulgar Latin the nonclassical, spoken form of ancient Latin, established as the main source of the Romance languages.

Vul·gate (vul′gāt) *n.* **1** the Latin translation of the Bible made by Saint Jerome in the fourth century A.D., used in subsequently revised form by the Roman Catholic Church as the authoritative text. **2 vulgate,** *Rare.* **a** the traditionally accepted text or reading of any author. **b** common speech; vernacular. [< L *vulgata* (*editio*) popular (edition)]

vul·ner·a·bil·i·ty (vul′nər ə bil′ə tē) *n.* the quality or state of being vulnerable; being open to attack or injury.

vul·ner·a·ble (vul′nər ə bəl) *adj.* **1** capable of being wounded or injured; open to attack: *The head is a vulnerable part of the body. The fort was vulnerable while the walls were being repaired.* **2** sensitive to or affected by certain influences (*used with* **to**): *Most people are vulnerable to ridicule.* **3** *Contract bridge.* in the position where penalties and premiums are increased. [< LL *vulnerabilis* wounding, ult. < *vulnus, -neris* wound] —**vul′ner·a·bly,** *adv.*

vul·ner·a·ble·ness (vul′nər ə bəl nəs) *n.* vulnerability.

vul·pine (vul′pīn *or* vul′pən) *adj.* of, having to do with, or like a fox. [< L *vulpinus* < *vulpes* fox]

vul·ture (vul′chər) *n.* **1** any of a family (Cathartidae) of large, carrion-eating, New World birds having a naked head and neck and relatively weak feet and claws, including the condors and the turkey vulture. **2** any of a subfamily (Aegypiinae) of similar, carrion-eating, Old World birds of the same family as hawks and eagles, also typically having a bare head. **3** a greedy, ruthless person who preys on others. [< L *vultur*]

vul·va (vul′və) *n., pl.* **-vae** (-vē *or* -vī) **or -vas.** the external parts of the genital organs of the female. [< L *vulva* womb]

vv 1 verses. **2** violins.

v.v. vice versa.

vy·ing (vī′ing) *v.* ppr. of **vie.**

Ww

w or **W** (dub′əl yü′) *n., pl.* **w's** or **W's. 1** the twenty-third letter of the English alphabet. **2** any speech sound represented by this letter. **3** a person or thing identified as *w*, especially the twenty-third in a series. **4** something shaped like the letter W. **5** (*adjl.*) of or being a W or w.

w. 1 week(s). **2** wide; width. **3** weight. **4** wife. **5** with.

W 1 watt. **2** west; western. **3** tungsten. **4** *W, Physics.* work; energy or force.

W. 1 Wednesday. **2** west; western. **3** Wales; Welsh.

WA Washington (state).

W.A. 1 Western Australia. **2** Women's Auxiliary.

WAAC or **W.A.A.C.** Women's Auxiliary Army Corps.

WAAF or **W.A.A.F.** Women's Auxiliary Air Force.

wab·ble¹ (wob′əl) See **wobble.**

wab·ble² (wob′əl) *n.* warble².

wab·bly (wob′lē) See **wobbly.**

wack·y (wak′ē) *adj. Slang.* unconventional in behavior; eccentric; crazy. Also, **whacky.**

wad (wod) *n., v.* **wad·ded, wad·ding.** —*n.* **1** a small, soft or loose mass of material, such as cotton batting or crumpled paper: *He plugged his ears with wads of cotton to keep out the noise. She stuck a wad of paper into the crack to keep the window from rattling.* **2** a small compact lump of something: *a wad of chewing gum.* **3** *Informal.* a roll of paper money: *He took a wad out of his pocket and counted off five tens.* **4** *Slang.* a large amount of money; wealth: *She made her wad in real estate.* **5** a round plug of felt, cardboard, etc. used in a gun or cartridge to hold powder and shot in place.
—*v.* **1** crush, press, or roll into a wad: *He wadded up the paper and threw it into the wastebasket.* **2** stuff with a wad: *to wad a gun.* **3** hold in place by a wad: *to wad a charge in a gun.* **4** pad or line with wadding. [origin uncertain]

wad·ding (wod′ing) *n.* **1** a soft material for padding, stuffing, packing, etc., especially carded cotton in sheets. **2** material for making wads for guns or cartridges. **3** a wad or wads.

wad·dle (wod′əl) *v.* **-dled, -dling;** *n.* —*v.* walk with short steps and an awkward, swaying motion, as a duck does. —*n.* an awkward, swaying gait. [< *wade*] —**wad′dler,** *n.*

wade (wād) *v.* **wad·ed, wad·ing;** *n.* —*v.* **1** walk through water, snow, sand, mud, or anything that hinders free motion. **2** walk about in shallow water for amusement: *We loved to go wading in the spring.* **3** cross or pass through by wading. **4** make one's way with difficulty (*used with* **through**): *to wade through an uninteresting book.* **5** *Informal.* attack or go to work on vigorously (*used with* **in** or **into**): *He waded right in and got the job done in half an hour.*
—*n.* the act of wading. [OE *wadan* proceed]

wad·er (wād′ər) *n.* **1** Usually, **waders,** *pl.* high waterproof boots and trousers used for wading, especially by fishermen, etc. **2** wading bird. **3** any person or thing that wades.

wa·di (wä′dē) *n., pl.* **-dis. 1** in parts of the Arabian peninsula, N Africa, etc., a valley or ravine through which a stream flows during the rainy season. **2** a stream or torrent running through such a ravine. **3** oasis. [< Arabic]

wading bird any long-legged bird that wades in water to look for food. Herons, cranes, sandpipers, and flamingos are wading birds.

wa·dy (wä′dē) *n., pl.* **-dies.** See **wadi.**

wa·fer (wā′fər) *n.* **1** a very thin, crisp biscuit or cookie: *an ice cream wafer.* **2** a very thin piece of candy: *a chocolate wafer.* **3** in some churches, a thin, round piece of unleavened bread used in the Communion service. **4** a small disk of paper or, formerly, dried paste, used as a seal on letters, documents, etc. [ME < AF *wafre* < Gmc.] —**wa′fer·like′,** *adj.*

wa·fer-thin (wā′fər thin′) *adj.* exceedingly thin: *wafer-thin cucumber slices.*

wa·fer·y (wā′fər ē) *adj.* like a wafer.

waf·fle¹ (wof′əl) *n.* a light, crisp, moulded cake made from a batter and baked in a waffle iron. [< Du. *wafel*]

waf·fle² (wof′əl) *v.* **-fled, -fling;** *n.* —*v.* **1** avoid making a decision or commitment by speaking ambiguously or evasively: *The ratepayers' association accused their MP of waffling on the airport issue.* **2** talk nonsense; prattle; talk on and on. —*n.* nonsense; foolish talk. [< Brit. dial. *waff* to yelp + *-le*]

waffle iron a device for cooking waffles, consisting of two hinged metal plates with a gridlike pattern of surface projections; the two plates close together and cook the waffles between them.

waft (waft *or* woft) *v., n.* —*v.* **1** carry over water or through air: *The waves wafted the boat to shore. The night wind wafted the sound of singing across the lake.* **2** transport or transfer very quickly or as if by magic: *be wafted by plane from Toronto to London.* **3** float: *A single feather wafted down to the ground.* **4** of a breeze, blow gently; stir.
—*n.* **1** the act of wafting. **2** a breath or puff of air, wind, etc. **3** something, such as a scent, wafted through the air. **4** a waving movement. [< earlier *wafter* convoy ship < Du. and LG *wachter* guard]

wag¹ (wag) *v.* **wagged, wag·ging;** *n.* —*v.* **1** move from side to side or up and down, especially rapidly and repeatedly: *He wagged his finger at me in disapproval. The dog's tail started wagging even before the car turned into the driveway.* **2** of a person's tongue, move in speaking, especially to chatter or gossip: *Tongues began to wag almost immediately after the police left.* **3** move (the tongue) in chatter or gossip: *They don't really know anything about it; they're just wagging their tongues.*
—*n.* the act of wagging. [ME; cf. OE *wagian*]

wag² (wag) *n.* a person who is fond of making jokes. [< *wag¹*]

wage (wāj) *n., v.* **waged, wag·ing.** —*n.* **1** Often, **wages,** *pl.* an amount paid for work, especially work on an hourly, daily, or piecework basis: *That company pays good wages.* **2** Usually, **wages,** something given in return (*used with a singular or plural verb*): *His illness taught him the wages of poor eating. "The wages of sin is death."* —*v.* carry on: *to wage war, to wage a campaign.* [ME < AF *wage,* var. of *gage.* See GAGE¹.] —**wage′less,** *adj.*
▸ *Syn.* See note at **salary.**

wage earner a person who works for wages or a salary.

wa·ger (wā′jər) *n., v.* —*n.* **1** an agreement between two persons that the one who is proved wrong about the outcome of an event will give a particular thing or sum of money to the person who is proved right; bet: *They made a wager on the result of the election.* **2** the thing or sum risked in a wager; stake: *What's your wager? He paid the wager promptly.* —*v.* make a wager; bet; gamble: *He wagered two dollars on the first race.* [ME < AF *wageure* < OF *wage* pledge. See WAGE.] —**wa′ger·er,** *n.*

wage·work·er (wāj′wėr′kər) *n.* wage earner.

wag·ger·y (wag′ər ē) *n., pl.* **-ger·ies. 1** joking or merriment. **2** a joke, especially a practical joke.

wag·gish (wag′ish) *adj.* **1** fond of making jokes. **2** done or made in fun; playful or funny: *a waggish look.* —**wag′gish·ly,** *adv.* —**wag′gish·ness,** *n.*

wag·gle (wag′əl) *v.* **-gled, -gling;** *n.* —*v.* move quickly and repeatedly from side to side; wag. —*n.* a wagging motion. [frequentative of *wag*]

wag·gon (wag′ən) *Esp.Brit.* See **wagon.**

wag·gon·er (wag′ən ər) *Esp.Brit.* See **wagoner.**

Wag·ne·ri·an (väg nēr′ē ən) *adj., n.* —*adj.* of or having to do with Richard Wagner (1813-1883), a German composer, especially of operas, his music, or his musical style. —*n.* an admirer of Richard Wagner's style or theory of music.

wag·on (wag′ən) *n.* **1** a four-wheeled vehicle, usually horse-drawn and especially one for carrying loads: *a milk wagon.* **2** a child's four-wheeled cart. **3** *Informal.* station wagon. **4** *Brit.* an open railway freight car.
hitch (one's) **wagon to a star,** have high hopes and ambitions; aim high.
off the wagon, *Slang.* drinking alcoholic liquors again after a period of abstaining from them.
on the wagon, *Slang.* no longer drinking alcoholic liquors. Also, **waggon.**
[< Du. *wagen.* Akin to WAIN.]

wag·on·er (wag′ən ər) *n.* a person who drives a wagon. Also, **waggoner.**

wag·on·ette (wag′ən et′) *n.* a four-wheeled, horse-drawn carriage with a seat in front running crosswise and two lengthwise seats facing each other.

wa·gon–lit (vä gôn lē′) *n. French.* in Europe, a railway sleeping car. [< F *wagon* railway coach + *lit* bed]

wag·on·load (wag′ən lōd′) *n.* the load that a wagon can carry.

wagon train 1 a group of wagons moving along in a line one after another, especially such a group carrying a company of settlers travelling together for protection. 2 *Esp.U.S.* a convoy of wagons carrying military supplies.

wag·tail (wag′tāl′) *n.* any of various small, chiefly Old World songbirds (family Motacillidae) having a very long tail that wags up and down as the birds walk or stand.

waif (wāf) *n.* 1 a person without home or friends, especially a homeless or neglected child. 2 anything without an owner; a stray thing, animal, etc. [ME < AF *waif*, probably < Scand.]

wail (wāl) *v., n.* 1 cry loud and long because of grief or pain. 2 make a mournful sound: *The wind wailed around the old house.* 3 lament; mourn. —*n.* 1 a long cry of grief or pain. 2 a sound like such a cry: *the wail of a hungry coyote.* [ME; ? < ON *væla* < *væ, vei*, interj., woe] —**wail′er**, *n.*
☛ Hom. **wale, whale.**

wain (wān) *n. Archaic or poetic.* wagon. [OE *wægn*]
☛ Hom. **wane.**

wain·scot (wān′skot′ *or* wān′skət) *n., v.* **-scot·ted** *or* **-scot·ed, -scot·ting** *or* **-scot·ing.** —*n.* 1 a facing of wood, usually in panels, on the walls of a room. 2 the lower part of the wall of a room when it is decorated differently from the upper part. —*v.* line with wood: *a room wainscotted in oak.* [ME < MLG *wagenschot* < *wagen* wagon + *schot* partition]

wain·scot·ting *or* **wain·scot·ing** (wān′skot′ing *or* wān′skət ing) *n.* 1 wainscot. 2 material used for wainscots.

wain·wright (wān′rīt′) *n.* a person who makes and repairs wagons.

waist (wāst) *n.* 1 the part of the human body between the ribs and the hips. 2 waistline. 3 a garment or part of a garment covering the body from the neck or shoulders to the waistline. 4 a narrow middle part: *the waist of a violin.* 5 the part of a ship amidships, as that between the forecastle and the quarterdeck of a sailing vessel, or between the forward and stern superstructure of an oil tanker. 6 the middle section of the fuselage of an aircraft, especially that of a bomber. [ME *wast*, probably < OE **wæst, weahst.* Related to WAX²]
☛ Hom. **waste.**

waist·band (wāst′band′) *n.* a band of cloth attached to the top of a skirt or trousers to fit around the waist: *a wide waistband. The waistband on these slacks is too loose.*

waist·cloth (wāst′kloth′) *n.* loincloth.

waist·coat (wāst′kōt′ *or* wes′kət) *n. Esp.Brit.* a man's vest. The modern waistcoat is basically the same garment as that worn by British and European men in the sixteenth century.

waist·line (wāst′līn′) *n.* 1 an imaginary line around the body at the smallest part of the waist. 2 the measurement around the body at this part: *Her waistline is 84 centimetres.* 3 the part of a garment that fits around the waist: *The dress has an elasticized waistline.* 4 the line where the bodice and skirt of a dress are joined together: *a loose-fitting dress without a waistline.*

wait (wāt) *v., n.* —*v.* 1 stay or be inactive until someone comes or something happens: *Let's wait in the shade. We waited for him for two hours.* 2 *Informal.* put off serving a meal: *Can you wait dinner for her?* 3 look forward expectantly: *waiting impatiently for the holidays.* 4 await; wait for: *wait one's chance. Wait your turn.* 5 be ready and available: *The car was waiting for us when we got there.* 6 be left undone; be put off: *That matter can wait till tomorrow.* 7 be a waiter or waitress (*usually used in the phrase* **wait at table**): *He waits at table in a hotel dining room.*
wait on, supply the wants of, as a clerk in a store, a waiter in a restaurant, etc.; serve: *A polite, elderly man waited on us.*
wait on *or* **upon, a** be a servant to: *He waits on the prince.* **b** pay a respectful visit to (a superior): *Tomorrow the prime minister will wait on the Queen.* **c** result from.
wait out, a do nothing until something has passed or is finished: *There was nothing to do but wait out the storm.* **b** *Baseball.* refrain from swinging at the pitches of (a pitcher), in the hope of getting a base on balls.
wait up, a delay going to bed until someone comes or something happens: *I'll probably be late, so don't wait up for me.* **b** *Informal.* stop and wait for someone to catch up: *Wait up! He's fallen behind again.*

—*n.* 1 the act or time of waiting: *I had a long wait at the doctor's office.* 2 *Theatre.* the time of an audience's waiting between acts, or of an actor's waiting between appearances on stage. 3 **waits,** *pl.* in England, a group of singers and musicians who go about the streets singing and playing at Christmas time.
lie in wait, stay hidden ready to surprise or attack: *Two assassins were lying in wait for the dictator.*
[ME < ONF *waitier*, originally, watch < Gmc.]
☛ Hom. **weight.**
☛ Usage. **Wait, await.** Wait chiefly means "stay inactive or in a place until something expected happens or comes," and only in a few phrases is followed directly by a grammatical object: *We can wait here until he comes.* **Await** almost always is followed by the grammatical object, and means "wait *for* someone or something," to look forward to or be ready for a coming or expected event or person: *We are eagerly awaiting your arrival.*

wait·er (wā′tər) *n.* 1 a man who waits on table in a hotel, restaurant, etc. 2 a person who waits. 3 a tray for carrying dishes.

wait·ing (wā′ting) *n., adj.* —*n.* the act of a person who waits. **in waiting,** in attendance on royalty: *in waiting to the king.* —*adj.* that waits.

waiting game a strategy whereby a person or group temporarily avoids action or a decision in the hope of being able to act or decide more effectively at a later date.

waiting list a list of people who have applied for something that may become available in the future: *There is already a long waiting list so you probably won't get on that flight.*

waiting maid a female servant or attendant.

waiting man a male servant or attendant.

waiting room a room at a railway station, doctor's office, etc. for people to wait in.

waiting woman a female servant or attendant.

wait-list (wāt′list′) *v.* enter on a list of persons waiting, especially for a seat on an airliner: *He is booked to fly tomorrow morning, but he is wait-listed for tonight's flight.*

wait·ress (wāt′ris) *n.* a woman who waits on table in a hotel, restaurant, etc.

waive (wāv) *v.* **waived, waiv·ing.** 1 refrain from claiming or pressing; give up or forgo: *The defendant's lawyer waived her right to cross-examine the witness.* 2 put off; postpone; delay. [ME < AF *weyver* abandon, probably < Scand. Related to WAIF]
☛ Hom. **wave.**

waiv·er (wā′vər) *n.* 1 *Law.* **a** a giving up of a right, claim, etc. **b** a written statement of this: *For $5000 the man signed a waiver of all claims against the railway.* 2 *Professional sports.* a condition in which the contract of a player is offered to other clubs in the league at a fixed price. If they decline, the contract may be taken up by a team from another league. [< AF *weyver*, infin. used as n. See WAIVE.]

wa·kan·da (wä kän′dä) *n.* among certain Plains Indians, a supernatural power found in living things and inanimate objects; Great Spirit. [< Siouan *wakanda* regard as sacred < *wakan* sacred spirit]

Wa·kash·an (wä kash′ən) *n., pl.* **-an** *or* **-ans.** a family of Amerindian languages of British Columbia and Washington, including Nootka, Kwakiutl, and Bella Bella.

wake¹ (wāk) *v.* **woke** *or* **waked, wo·ken** *or* **waked, wak·ing;** *n.* —*v.* 1 stop sleeping (*often used with* **up**): *to wake up early in the morning.* 2 rouse from sleep; cause to stop sleeping (*often used with* **up**): *The noise will wake the baby. Wake me up early.* 3 be or stay awake: *Waking or sleeping, he could not seem to get the accusation out of his mind.* 4 become alive or active (*often used with* **up**): *His conscience woke. The flowers wake in the spring.* 5 make alive or active; rouse to action, alertness, or liveliness (*often used with* **up**): *He needs some interest to wake him up.* 6 *Archaic or dialect.* **a** keep a watch or vigil, especially over a corpse. **b** keep watch over (a corpse) until burial.
wake (up) to, become conscious or aware of: *He finally woke up to the fact that his money was almost gone.*
—*n.* a watch held by the body of a dead person before burial, sometimes accompanied by festivities. [OE *wacian*]

wake² (wāk) *n.* 1 the track left behind a moving ship. 2 the track left by anything.
in the wake of, close behind; very soon after: *Floods came in the wake of the hurricane.*
[< MDu.]

wake·ful (wāk′fəl) *adj.* 1 not able to sleep: *still wakeful long after midnight.* 2 without sleep; sleepless: *They spent a wakeful night.* 3 watchful; alert. —**wake′ful·ly,** *adv.* —**wake′ful·ness,** *n.*

wak·en (wā′kən) *v.* wake. [OE *wæcnan*] —**wak′en·er,** *n.*

wake–rob·in (wāk′rob′ən) *n.* 1 trillium. 2 *Brit.* any of various plants of the arum family.

Wal·den·ses (wol den′sēz *or* wôl den′sēz) *n.pl.* a Christian sect formed by Peter Waldo in Lyons, France about 1170. They were

condemned by the popes and subjected to much persecution. Their present headquarters is in Italy.

Wal·den·si·an (wol den′sē ən *or* wôl-; wol den′shən *or* wôl-) *adj., n.* —*adj.* of or having to do with the Waldenses. —*n.* a member of the Waldenses.

wald·grave (wold′grāv′ *or* wôld′grāv′) *n.* in medieval Germany, an officer having jurisdiction over a royal forest. [< G *Waldgraf* < *Wald* woods < *Graf* count]

wale (wāl) *n., v.* **waled, wal·ing.** —*n.* **1** a streak or ridge made on the skin by a stick or whip; welt. **2** a long, narrow, raised surface, especially one of a series of parallel ribs or ridges in cloth such as corduroy. **3** Usually, **wales,** *pl.* a continuous line of thick, outside planking on the sides of a wooden ship.
—*v.* **1** mark with welts; raise welts on. **2** weave with ridges. [OE *walu*]
☛ *Hom.* **wail, whale.**

walk (wok *or* wôk) *v., n.* —*v.* **1** go on foot. **2** stroll for pleasure, exercise, etc.; take a walk or walks. **3** roam: *The ghost will walk tonight.* **4** go over, on, or through: *The captain walked the deck.* **5** make, put, drive, etc. by walking: *to walk off a headache.* **6** go slowly: *Walk, do not run.* **7** cause to walk: *The rider walked his horse.* **8** accompany or escort in walking; conduct on foot: *to walk a guest to the door.* **9** traverse on foot in order to measure, examine, etc.; pace off or over: *to walk the back line of a piece of property.* **10** of things, move or shake in a manner suggestive of walking. **11** *Baseball.* **a** go to first base after the pitcher has thrown four balls. **b** of a pitcher, give (a batter) a base on balls. **12** *Basketball.* take two or more steps while holding the ball. **13** conduct oneself in a particular manner; follow a particular course in life.
walk away from, progress much faster than.
walk off with, a take; get; win. **b** steal.
walk out, a *Informal.* go on strike. **b** leave suddenly. **c** *Informal.* go out with a person of the opposite sex; keep company; court.
walk out on, *Informal.* desert.
walk over, a defeat easily and by a wide margin. **b** *Informal.* treat contemptuously: *Don't let them walk over you.*
—*n.* **1** the act of walking, especially walking for pleasure or exercise: *a walk in the country.* **2** a distance to walk: *It is a long walk from here.* **3** a manner or way of walking; gait: *We knew the man was a sailor from his rolling walk.* **4** a route, sidewalk, or path for walking: *We always preferred the walk down by the river. I shovelled the snow off the walk.* **5** occupation or social position: *An electrician and a farmer are in different walks of life.* **6** *Baseball.* a batter's advance to first base on balls. **7** an enclosed place; tract: *a poultry walk.* [OE *wealcan* roll]
☛ *Syn. v.* **1. Walk, stride, plod** = go on foot at a pace slower than a run. **Walk** is the general word: *He walked downstairs.* **Stride** means "walk with long, regular steps," especially in haste, annoyance, or self-importance, or with healthy energy: *When we walk for exercise, we should stride briskly.* **Plod** means "walk heavily, slowly, and with effort": *The old horse plodded up the road.*

walk·a·way (wok′ə wā′ *or* wôk′-) *n. Informal.* an easy victory.

walk·er (wok′ər *or* wôk′ər) *n.* **1** a person who walks, especially one who walks in a particular way: *She's a fast walker.* **2** a framework on wheels designed to support a child learning to walk. **3** a framework designed to help a lame or crippled person walk.

walk·ie-talk·ie (wok′ē tok′ē *or* wôk′ē tôk′ē) *n., pl.* **-talk·ies.** a small, portable two-way radio set.

walk-in (wok′in′ *or* wôk′-) *adj., n.* —*adj.* large enough to be walked into: *a walk-in closet.* —*n.* a sure or easy victory.

walk·ing (wok′ing *or* wôk′ing) *n., adj.* —*n.* **1** the action of a person or thing that walks: *Walking is good exercise.* **2** the quality or condition of a road, etc. for walking: *The walking was treacherous after the ice-storm.*
—*adj.* **1** for use in walking: *Bring your walking shoes.* **2** including or consisting of the action of walking: *We went on a walking tour of the city centre.* **3** in human form; personified: *She's a walking encyclopedia.*

walking fern a North American fern (*Camptosorus rhizophyllus*) having long, tapering, evergreen fronds whose tips take root wherever they touch the ground, producing a new plant.

walking papers *Informal.* dismissal from a position, etc.

walking stick 1 a stick used for support in walking; cane. **2** stick insect, especially any of several North American species, such as *Diapheromera femorata.*

walk-on (wok′on′ *or* wôk′-) *n.* **1** a small part in a dramatic production in which an actor appears on stage but usually has no lines to speak. **2** an actor having such a part.

walk·out (wok′out′ *or* wôk′-) *n.* **1** a work stoppage; strike. **2** the departure of a group of people from a meeting, etc. as a protest.

walk·o·ver (wok′ō′vər *or* wôk′-) *n. Informal.* an easy victory.

walk-up (wok′up′ *or* wôk′-) *n.* **1** an apartment house or office building of more than two storeys having no elevator. **2** a room, apartment, or office above the ground floor in such a building.

hat, āge, fär; let, ēqual, tèrm; it, īce
hot, ōpen, ôrder; oil, out; cup, pút, rüle,
əbove, takən, pencəl, lemən, circəs

ch, child; ng, long; sh, ship
th, thin; ŦH, then; zh, measure

3 (*adjl.*) located above the ground floor in such a building: *a walk-up apartment.* **4** (*adjl.*) having several storeys and no elevator: *There is a walk-up annex.*

walk-way (wok′wā′ *or* wôk′-) *n.* **1** a pathway; passage; walk. **2** a framework or structure on which to walk.

walk·y-talk·y (wok′ē tok′ē *or* wôk′ē tôk′ē) *n., pl.* **-talk·ies.** See **walkie-talkie.**

wall (wol *or* wôl) *n., v.* —*n.* **1** the side of a building or room joining the floor or foundation and the ceiling or roof. **2** a solid structure of stone, brick, or other material built up to enclose, divide, support, or protect. **3** something like a wall in looks or use: *a wall of water four metres high.* **4** the side of any hollow thing: *the wall of a cylinder, the wall of the heart.*
come, be, etc. **up against a blank wall,** be completely unsuccessful, as when seeking information; be stymied: *She tried several angles, but always came up against a blank wall.*
drive or **push to the wall,** make desperate or helpless: *driven to the wall by debts.*
drive, send, etc. **up the wall,** *Informal.* make frantic with frustration or anger: *His constant whining drives me up the wall!*
go to the wall, a give way; be defeated. **b** fail in business.
with (one's) back to or **against the wall,** in an extreme or desperate situation.
—*v.* enclose, divide, protect, or fill with a wall, or as if with a wall: *The garden is walled. Workmen walled up the doorway.* [OE *weall* < L *vallum*] —**wall′-less,** *adj.* —**wall′-like′,** *adj.*

wal·la (wol′ə) See **wallah.**

wal·la·by (wol′ə bē) *n., pl.* **-bies** or (*esp.* collectively) **-by.** any of various small or medium-sized members of the kangaroo family, many of them no larger than a rabbit. [< native Australian *wolabā*]

wal·lah (wol′ə) *n.* **1** *Informal.* a chap; fellow. **2** *Anglo-Indian.* one who is connected with some special work or area: *a kitchen wallah.* Also, **walla.** [originally < Hindi *-vala,* adj. suffix, perhaps < Skt. *bala* boy]

wal·la·roo (wol′ə rü′) *n.* a large kangaroo (*Macropus robustus*) found in rocky regions of Australia, having thick, coarse, dark-grey or reddish-brown fur. [< native Australian *wolarū*]

wall·board (wol′bord′ *or* -bôrd′) *n.* any of various types of board, such as plasterboard, particleboard, or hardboard, used in place of plaster or wooden panelling to finish interior walls and ceilings.

walled (wold *or* wôld) *adj.* having walls: *a walled garden.*

wal·let (wol′it) *n.* **1** a small, flat, folding case, usually made of leather, having compartments for carrying paper money, credit cards, drivers licence, etc. and often coins. **2** *Archaic.* a bag for carrying food and small articles for personal use on a journey. [ME *walet;* origin uncertain]

wall-eye (wol′ī′ *or* wôl′-) *n.* **1** especially in a horse, an eye with an almost colorless iris. **2** an eye having an opaque, white cornea. **3** opacity of the cornea. **4** an eye that turns outward. **5** a condition of the eyes in which one or both eyes are turned outward because of an imbalance of the muscles. **6** a large, staring eye, as in some fish. **7** a common North American freshwater fish (*Stizostedion vitreum*) of the perch family that is one of the most important food and game fishes of Canada's inland waters, ranging in color from mainly olive brown to yellow, and occasionally greyish, speckled with gold or yellow, and having smoky, silvery eyes thought to resemble those of walleyed domestic animals. A bluish subspecies (the **blue walleye,** or **blue pike**) was formerly found in lakes Erie and Ontario. Also called **yellow walleye, pickerel, yellow pickerel, pikeperch, walleyed pike, doré,** and **dory.** [back-formation from *walleyed*]

wall-eyed (wol′īd′ *or* wôl′-) *adj.* having walleyes. [ME, by folk etymology < ON *vagl-eygr* < *vagl,* probably, speck in the eye + *auga* eye]

walleyed pike or **walleye pike** walleye (def. 7).

wall·flow·er (wol′flou′ər *or* wôl′-) *n.* **1** *Informal.* a person, especially a girl or woman, who remains on the sidelines at a dance, either from shyness or because of not being asked to dance. **2** any of numerous perennial plants (genera *Cheiranthus* and *Erysimum*) of the mustard family that often grow from chinks in walls. Several wallflowers having fragrant yellow, orange, or red flowers are widely cultivated.

wall hanging a large woven, knotted, appliquéd, etc. decoration hung on a wall.

Wal·loon (wo lün′) *n., adj.* —*n.* **1** a member of a people inhabiting chiefly the S parts of Belgium and adjacent regions in France. **2** their language, the French dialect of Belgium. —*adj.* of or having to do with the Walloons or their language. [< F *Wallon* < Med.L *Wallo* < Gmc.]

wal·lop (wol′əp) *v., n. Informal.* —*v.* **1** beat soundly; thrash. **2** hit very hard; strike with a vigorous blow. **3** defeat thoroughly, as in a game. —*n.* **1** a very hard blow. **2** the power to hit very hard blows: *He's got a real wallop!* [ME < ONF *waloper* gallop < Gmc.]

wal·lop·ing (wol′əp ing) *n., adj. Informal.* —*n.* **1** a sound beating or thrashing. **2** a thorough defeat. —*adj.* very big or impressive; whopping: *a walloping big baby.*

wal·low (wol′ō) *v., n.* —*v.* **1** roll about lazily or pleasurably, as animals in dust or mud: *The pigs wallowed in the cool mud.* **2** roll about clumsily or out of control: *The boat wallowed helplessly in the stormy sea.* **3** indulge oneself excessively in some pleasure, state of mind, way of living, etc.: *to wallow in luxury, to wallow in self-pity.* —*n.* **1** the act of wallowing. **2** a place where an animal wallows. [OE *wealwian* roll]

wall·pa·per (wol′pā′pər *or* wôl′-) *n., v.* —*n.* paper, usually having a printed or embossed design, used for covering the walls and, often, the ceiling of a room. —*v.* paste wallpaper on the walls of a room: *We decided to wallpaper the room instead of painting it. They spent all weekend wallpapering.*

Wall Street the money market or the financiers of the United States. [< *Wall Street*, a street in downtown New York City, the chief financial centre of the United States]

wal·nut (wol′nut′ *or* wôl′-, wol′nət *or* wôl′-) *n., adj.* —*n.* **1** any of a genus (*Juglans*) of hardwood trees found in many parts of the world, having compound leaves with from five to 23 toothed leaflets and fruit that is a large woody nut enclosed in a thick husk. Two species of walnut, the butternut and black walnut, are native to eastern Canada. **2** the roundish, edible nut of any of these trees. **3** the hard, dark wood of any of these trees, valued for making furniture, etc. **4** (*adj.*) designating a family (Juglandaceae) of trees, including the walnuts and hickories. **5** medium reddish brown. —*adj.* having the color walnut. [OE *wealhhnutu* < *wealh* foreign + *hnutu* nut]

Wal·pur·gis night (väl pür′gis) the night of April 30th, when witches were formerly supposed to hold revels with the devil.

wal·rus (wol′rəs *or* wôl′rəs) *n., pl.* **-rus** *or* **-rus·es.** a large sea mammal (*Odobenus rosmarus*) of the Arctic regions, resembling a seal but larger and having long tusks. Walruses have long been hunted, especially for their thick hide, their ivory tusks, and the oil obtained from their blubber. [< Du. *walrus, walros* < *wal(visch)* whale + *ros* horse]

waltz (wolts *or* wôlts) *n., v.* —*n.* **1** a smooth, even, gliding, ballroom dance in 3/4 time. **2** the music for such a dance. **3** any musical composition or part of a composition written in 3/4 time. —*v.* **1** dance a waltz. **2** move nimbly, quickly, or showily: *She waltzed through the room, cheerfully greeting all the guests.* **3** *Informal.* advance or proceed easily and successfully (*used with* **through**): *She waltzed through the exam in half the time it took me.* **4** *Informal.* approach boldly or abruptly; accost (*used with* **up**): *He just waltzed up to the foreman and said he was quitting.* **5** *Informal.* make a person go by or as if by taking him by the arm and leading him; march: *His mother waltzed him into the living room to apologize to his brother.* [< G *Walzer* < *walzen* roll] —**waltz′er,** *n.*

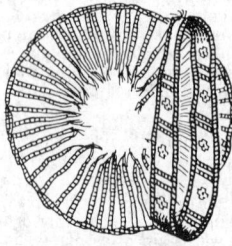

Wampum. The circular piece is the wampum record of the founding of the Iroquois League of Five Nations. It consists of an outer ring of shells with 50 separate strings representing the 50 chiefs of the League. The other piece is a standard Iroquoian wampum sash.

wam·pum (wom′pəm) *n.* **1** beads made from polished shells strung in belts and sashes, formerly used by eastern North American Indian peoples as money, as a reminder of a treaty, and as ornament. **2** *Slang.* money. [< Algonquian]

wan (won) *adj.* **wan·ner, wan·nest.** **1** pale and sickly; lacking natural color: *Her face looked wan after her long illness.* **2** looking worn or tired; faint or weak: *The sick boy gave the doctor a wan smile.* [OE *wann* dark] —**wan′ly,** *adv.* —**wan·ness,** *n.*

☛ *Syn.* **1.** See note at **pale.**

wand (wond) *n.* a slender stick or rod: *The magician waved his wand.* [ME < ON *vöndr*] —**wand′like′,** *adj.*

wan·der (won′dər) *v.* **1** move about without any special purpose: *I was too early for my appointment, so I wandered through the stores for awhile.* **2** go aimlessly over or through. **3** go from the right way; stray: *The dog wandered off and got lost.* **4** talk or think in a rambling or incoherent way; drift away in thought or be delirious: *The fever made his mind wander. As she talked, she kept wandering away from her subject and glancing at the door.* **5** of a river, path, etc., follow a winding, irregular course. [OE *wandrian*] —**wan′der·er,** *n.*

☛ *Syn.* **1. Wander, stray** = go from place to place more or less aimlessly or without a settled course. **Wander** emphasizes moving about from place to place without a definite course or destination: *We wandered through the stores, hoping to get ideas for Christmas presents.* **Stray** emphasizes going aimlessly beyond the usual or proper limits or away from the regular path or course, and often suggests getting lost: *Two of the children strayed from the picnic grounds.*

wandering Jew **1** any of several trailing or creeping plants (especially *Tradescantia Fluminensis* or *Zebrina pendula*) of the spiderwort family having showy leaves that are striped with white or cream on the upper side and are reddish purple beneath. Wandering Jews are commonly grown as house plants. **2 Wandering Jew,** in medieval legend, a Jew who insulted Christ on the way to the Crucifixion and was condemned to wander on earth till Christ's second coming.

wan·der·lust (won′dər lust′) *n.* a strong desire to wander: *His wanderlust led him all over the world.* [< G *Wanderlust* < *wandern* wander + *Lust* desire]

wane (wān) *v.* **waned, wan·ing;** *n.* —*v.* **1** of the moon, go through the regular decrease in the size of its visible portion: *The moon wanes after it has become full.* **2** become less brilliant or intense: *The light of day wanes in the evening.* **3** lose strength, power, or importance: *Her influence in the club has waned.* **4** of a period of time, draw to a close: *Summer wanes as autumn nears.* —*n.* the process of waning.

on the wane, growing less; waning: *His popularity was on the wane.* [OE *wanian*]

☛ *Hom.* **wain.**

wan·gan (wong′gən) *n.* wanigan.

wan·gle (wang′gəl) *v.* **-gled, -gling.** *Informal.* **1** manage to get by schemes, tricks, persuasion, etc. **2** make one's way through difficulties. **3** change (an account, report, etc.) dishonestly for one's advantage. [origin uncertain]

wan·i·gan (won′ə gən) *n. Cdn.* **1** a lumberman's chest or trunk. **2** a large sled equipped as living quarters and pulled by tracked vehicles as part of a train for carrying troops and supplies in the North. **3** a kind of boat used by lumbermen for carrying supplies, tools, etc. and as a houseboat. [< Algonquian *waniigan* trap, place for stray objects]

wan·nish (won′ish) *adj.* somewhat wan.

want (wont) *v., n.* —*v.* **1** wish for; desire: *He wants to become a singer. She wants a new car.* **2** be without what is desired or needed; lack: *a reply that wants courtesy. The building fund still wants several thousand dollars.* **3** need; require: *Plants want water. You want more exercise.* **4** suffer from a lack, especially of the necessities of life: *In spite of the new aid program, many people are still wanting. "Waste not, want not."* **5** wish to see, speak to, or use the help of a person: *Call me if you want me. You're wanted on the phone.* **6** seek or go after in order to question or arrest: *The police want him for questioning. She is wanted for theft.* **7** have or feel a shortage (*used with* **for**): *They are wealthy and want for nothing. She has never wanted for friends.* **8** *Informal.* ought (*to*): *You want to eat a balanced diet.* **9** *Informal.* wish to enter or leave (*used with* **in** *or* **out**): *The dog wants in. He was very enthusiastic at first, but now he wants out of the project.* **10** be short or lacking: *It wants an hour until train time.* —*n.* **1** something wanted; a desire or need: *The new park supplied a long-felt want. He is a man of few wants.* **2** the quality or state of lacking something desired or needed; shortage or lack: *The plant died for want of water.* **3** extreme poverty: *Many families were in want this past winter.* [ME < ON *vant* < *vanr* lacking]

☛ *Syn. v.* **2.** See note at **lack.** *n.* **3.** See note at **poverty.**

want ad *Informal.* a notice in a newspaper that an employee, job or position, apartment, car, etc. is wanted or that an apartment, car, etc. is for sale or rent.

want·ing (won′ting) *adj., prep.* —*adj.* **1** not coming up to a standard or need; not satisfactory: *The stranger was wanting in courtesy. "You have been weighed in the balance and found wanting."* **2** lacking; missing: *One volume of the set is wanting.*

—*prep.* **1** without: *an old chair wanting a back.* **2** minus; less: *a month, wanting three days.*

wan·ton (won′tən) *adj., n., v.* —*adj.* **1** without excuse or reason; senseless, reckless, or heartless: *a wanton attack, a wanton disregard of others' rights. His mistreatment of animals is wanton cruelty.* **2** sexually immoral; not chaste: *a wanton woman.* **3** *Poetic.* playful and unrestrained; frolicsome or frisky: *a wanton mood, a wanton child, a wanton breeze.* **4** *Archaic.* of vegetation, profuse in growth, luxuriant; rank.
—*n.* an immoral or unchaste person.
—*v. Poetic.* act in a wanton manner: *The wind wantoned with the leaves.* [ME *wantowen* < OE *wan-* deficient (related to WANE) + *togen* brought up, pp. of *tēon* bring] —**wan′ton·ly,** *adv.* —**wan′ton·ness,** *n.*

wap·i·ti (wop′i tē) *n., pl.* **-ti** or **-tis.** *Cdn.* the North American elk. See **elk** (def. 1). [< Algonquian]

war (wôr) *n., v.* **warred, war·ring.** —*n.* **1** open fighting carried on by armed forces between nations or parts of a nation. **2** any active struggle, strife, or conflict: *the war against disease, a gang war.* **3** the art or science of fighting against an opposing armed force; military science: *Soldiers are trained in war.* **4** (*adj.*) of, having to do with, or used in war: *war materials, war crimes.*
at war, taking part in a war.
go to war, a start a war. **b** go as a soldier.
—*v.* fight or contend; make war: *warring against poverty. Germany warred against France.* [ME *werre* < AF var. of OF *guerre* < Gmc.] —**war′less,** *adj.*
☛ *Hom.* **wore.**

War between the States the U.S. Civil War.

war·ble¹ (wôr′bəl) *v.* **-bled, -bling;** *n.* —*v.* **1** sing in a lilting, melodious way, with trills, quavers, etc.: *Birds warbled in the trees.* **2** make a sound like that of a bird warbling: *The brook warbled over its rocky bed.* **3** express by warbling: *to warble a greeting.*
—*n.* **1** the act of warbling. **2** a bird's song or a sound like it. [ME < ONF *werbler* < Gmc.]

war·ble² (wôr′bəl) *n.* **1** a small abscess under the hide, especially of cattle or horses, caused by a larva of the warble fly or botfly. **2** the larva of a warble fly. **3** a hard lump on a horse's back, caused by prolonged rubbing of a saddle. Also, **wabble.** [< Swedish *varbulde* < *var* pus + *bulde* swelling]

war·bled (wôr′bəld) *adj.* attacked or infected by warbles.

warble fly any of various two-winged flies (family Oestridae) whose larvae burrow under the hide of cattle, horses, and other mammals, causing warbles.

war·bler (wôr′blər) *n.* **1** any of a subfamily (Sylviinae, of the family Muscicapidae) of small, active, chiefly Old World songbirds typically having brown, dull olive-green, or greyish plumage, and including some species noted for their song. Some authorities classify warblers as a separate family (Sylviidae). **2** wood warbler. **3** any person or thing that warbles.

war bonnet a ceremonial headdress traditionally worn as a mark of honor among Amerindian peoples of the North American plains, consisting of a row or rows of feathers attached to a headband and trailing down the back.

war bride a woman who marries a soldier met during wartime, especially a foreign soldier.

war club a heavy club used as a weapon.

war crime any violation of the rules of warfare, especially atrocities against civilians, political prisoners, etc.

war criminal one who is convicted of committing a war crime.

war cry **1** a word or phrase shouted in fighting; battle cry. **2** a party cry in any contest.

ward (wôrd) *n.* **1** a division of a hospital, especially a section for a particular class or group of patients, consisting of one large room or a group of rooms: *a maternity ward, the children's ward.* **2** a division of a prison, such as a block of cells. **3** a district of a city, especially one represented by an alderman. **4** a person under the care of a guardian or of a court: *a ward of the Children's Aid Society.* **5** guard: *The soldiers kept ward over the castle.* **6** the state of being kept under guard or in custody. **7** *Fencing, etc.* a movement or position of defence. **8** a notch in a key. **9** the corresponding ridge in a lock. [OE *weard*, fem., a guarding]
—*v.* turn aside or keep away; avert (*usually used with* **off**): *He warded off the blow with his arm. She raised her collar to ward off the icy wind.* [OE *weardian* guard. Akin to GUARD.]

–ward *suffix.* in or to a particular direction or point in time, as *backward, seaward, upward.* See also **-wards.** [OE *-weard*]
☛ *Usage.* **-ward, -wards.** Of variants such as **downward—downwards** and **forward—forwards,** only the **-ward** form is used as adjective or noun: *a forward movement, looking to the westward.* Either variant may be used as adverb or preposition: *He fell forward* (or *forwards*). *He came toward me* (or *towards me*).

war dance a tribal dance performed before going to war or to celebrate a victory.

hat, āge, fär; let, ēqual, tėrm; it, īce
hot, ōpen, ôrder; oil, out; cup, pùt, rüle,
əbove, takən, pencəl, lemən, circəs

ch, child; ng, long; sh, ship
th, thin; ŦH, then; zh, measure

war·den (wôr′dən) *n.* **1** an official who enforces certain laws or rules: *a fire warden.* **2** a person in charge of the operation of a prison. **3** in certain colleges, churches, or other institutions, an official with administrative, academic, or supervisory duties. **4** *Cdn.* in provinces having county governments, the head of the county council, generally chosen by the members from among themselves. [ME < ONF *wardein,* var. of *g(u)arden,* ult. < Gmc. Doublet of GUARDIAN.]

ward·er (wôr′dər) *n.* **1** a guard or watchman. **2** jailer.

ward heeler *Esp.U.S. Informal.* a follower of a political boss, who goes around asking for votes, etc.

ward·robe (wôrd′rōb′) *n.* **1** a stock of clothes: *She is shopping for her spring wardrobe.* **2** a closet or piece of furniture for holding clothes. **3** a room in which clothes are kept. [ME < ONF *warderobe,* var. of OF *garderobe* < *garder* keep (< Gmc.) + *robe* gown (< Gmc.)]

ward·room (wôrd′rüm′ *or* -rùm′) *n.* on a warship, the living and eating quarters for all the commissioned officers except the commanding officer.

–wards *suffix.* in or to a particular direction or point in time, as *afterwards, backwards, towards.* See also **-ward.**
☛ *Usage.* **-wards.** Used originally and chiefly in adverbs. See note at **-ward.**

ward·ship (wôrd′ship) *n.* **1** guardianship or custody, especially over a minor or other ward. **2** the condition of being a ward, or under a legal or feudal guardian.

ware¹ (wer) *n.* **1** Usually, **wares,** *pl.* manufactured articles or goods for sale (as by merchants, peddlers, etc.); merchandise: *He peddled his wares from door to door.* **2** articles or goods of a particular kind or used for a particular purpose (*now used mainly in compounds*): *tinware, hardware, kitchenware. The silverware needs polishing.* **3** articles of fired clay; pottery: *blue-and-white ware from Delft. Biscuit ware is unglazed porcelain.* [OE *waru*]
☛ *Hom.* **wear, where.**

ware² (wer) *adj., v.* **wared, war·ing.** *Archaic or poetic.* —*adj.* aware. —*v.* look out (for); beware (of). [OE *wær*]
☛ *Hom.* **wear, where.**

ware·house (*n.* wer′hous′; *v.* wer′houz′ *or* -hous′) *n., v.* **-housed, -hous·ing.** —*n.* a building or large room where goods are stored. —*v.* store or keep in a warehouse.

ware·house·man (wer′hous′mən) *n.* **-men.** a person who owns or works in a warehouse.

war·fare (wôr′fer′) *n.* **1** war; fighting. **2** any struggle or contest. [ME *warfare* < *war* + *fare* a going, OE *faru* journey]

war game a training exercise that simulates war. It may be an exercise on a map or a computer, or it may be manoeuvres with actual troops, weapons, and equipment.

war·head (wôr′hed′) *n.* the forward part of a rocket, missile, torpedo, etc.: *The warhead contains the explosive charge.*

war horse **1** a horse used in war. **2** *Informal.* a person, especially a veteran soldier or a person in public life, who has survived many battles or struggles.

war·i·ly (wer′ə lē) *adv.* cautiously; carefully.

war·i·ness (wer′ē nis) *n.* caution; care.

war·like (wôr′līk′) *adj.* **1** fond of and ready for war: *a warlike nature, warlike peoples.* **2** threatening war; belligerent: *a warlike speech.* **3** of, for, or having to do with war: *warlike preparations.*
☛ *Syn.* **4.** See note at **military.**

war·lock (wôr′lok) *n.* a man who practises black magic; sorcerer. Compare **witch.** [OE *wærloga* traitor, oath-breaker < *wær* covenant + *-loga* one who denies]

war·lord (wôr′lôrd′) *n.* a military commander, especially one who has supreme civil authority in a particular region, often in defiance of a weak central government.

warm (wôrm) *adj., v.* —*adj.* **1** more hot than cold; having or giving forth some heat: *a warm fire. She sat in the warm sunshine.* **2** having a feeling of heat: *to be warm from running.* **3** that makes or keeps warm: *a warm coat.* **4** having or showing affection, enthusiasm, etc.: *a warm welcome, a warm friend, a warm heart.* **5** quick to show irritation or anger: *a warm temper.* **6** showing irritation or anger: *a warm dispute.* **7** of a trail, scent, etc., recent and strong. **8** *Informal.* in games, treasure hunts, etc., near what one is searching for. **9** of a color, suggesting warmth; mainly red or

yellow in tone. **10** uncomfortable; unpleasant: *to make things warm for a person.*
—v. 1 make or become warm: *to warm a room.* **2** make or become cheered, interested, friendly, or sympathetic: *The speaker warmed to his subject.*
warm up, a heat or cook again. **b** make or become more interested, friendly, etc. **c** practise or exercise for a few minutes before entering a game, contest, etc. **d** of an engine, etc., run or operate in order to reach a proper working temperature: *It takes the car a long time to warm up on cold mornings.* **e** run or operate (an engine, etc.) until it reaches a proper working temperature. [OE *wearm*] **—warm′er,** *n.* **—warm′ly,** *adv.* **—warm′ness,** *n.*

warm–blood·ed (wôrm′blud′id) *adj.* **1** having warm blood that stays about the same temperature regardless of the surrounding air or water. Warm-blooded animals have body temperatures between 36 and 44 degrees Celsius. **2** having or showing a passionate or ardent spirit.

warmed–o·ver (wôrmd′ō′vər) *adj.* **1** of food, warmed again; reheated: *warmed-over chili.* **2** of ideas, etc., not new or fresh or interesting; stale and trite.

warm front *Meteorology.* the front edge of a warm air mass advancing into and replacing a colder one.

warm–heart·ed (wôrm′här′tid) *adj.* having or showing a kind, sympathetic, or friendly nature: *a warm-hearted person, a warm-hearted response.*

warming pan a covered pan having a long handle and designed to hold hot coals, formerly used to warm beds.

warm·ish (wôrm′ish) *adj.* somewhat warm. **—warm′ish·ly,** *adv.* **—warm′ish·ness,** *n.*

war·mon·ger (wôr′mung′gər *or* -mong′gər) *n.* a person who is in favor of war or attempts to bring about war.

warmth (wôrmth) *n.* **1** the quality or state of being more hot than cold; being warm: *the warmth of an open fire.* **2** the quality or state of being lively, excited, fervent, etc.: *He spoke with warmth of the natural beauty of the countryside.* **3** a friendly, affectionate, or kind feeling or nature: *the warmth of family life.* **4** in painting, interior decorating, etc., a glowing effect produced by the use of reds and yellows.

warm–up (wôrm′up′) *n.* **1** the act or an instance of warming up: *a quick warm-up before the game.* **2** exercises or a routine used for warming up, as before a game, contest, etc.

warn (wôrn) *v.* **1** give notice to in advance about a possible or approaching unpleasantness or danger; put on guard: *The clouds warned us that a storm was coming. They had been warned against using the old bridge. She warned us to keep away from the dog.* **2** give notice of something that requires attention or action; inform: *His mother warned us that we would have to leave by 8 o'clock.* **3** give notice to stay away, go away, keep out, etc. (*used with* **off** *or* **away**): *There was a sign warning off trespassers.* **4** caution or admonish about certain actions, conduct, etc.: *They warned us not to smoke in the auditorium.* [OE *warnian*] **—warn′er,** *n.*
☛ *Syn.* **1. Warn, caution** = give someone notice of possible or coming danger, harm, risk, unpleasantness, consequences of an action or practice, etc. **Warn** emphasizes giving information or a hint that lets a person avoid or prepare for what is coming or likely to come: *Her mother warned her not to speak to strangers.* **Caution** emphasizes giving advice to be on one's guard against something (or someone) or suggesting steps that can be taken: *Drivers are cautioned against driving too long without a break.*

warn·ing (wôr′ning) *n., adj.* **—n.** something that warns; notice given in advance. **—adj.** that warns. **—warn′ing·ly,** *adv.*

War of 1812 a war between the United States and Great Britain, 1812-1815, fought on the Atlantic Ocean and in North America. This war confirmed Canada's independence of the United States.

War of Independence *U.S.* the Revolutionary War.

war of nerves a conflict or struggle characterized by the use of propaganda, bluffing, threats, etc. in order to break the morale of an opponent or enemy.

warp (wôrp) *v., n.* **—v. 1** bend or twist out of shape: *The heat from the radiator has warped the table. If you use green wood to build something, it is liable to warp.* **2** make or become perverted or distorted: *Prejudice warps our judgment. He has a warped sense of humor.* **3** move (a ship, etc.) by pulling on a rope fastened at one end to a fixed object. **4** arrange (threads or yarn) so as to form a warp.
—n. 1 a bend or twist in something that should be straight: *The board has a warp.* **2** a distortion of the mind, judgment, etc.; a bias or quirk. **3** a rope used for warping a ship or boat. **4** the threads stretched lengthwise in a loom, through which the crosswise threads are woven. See **weave** for picture. **5** the basis or foundation of something: *the warp of our society.* [OE *weorpan* throw]

warp·age (wôrp′ij) *n.* **1** a warping or being warped. **2** a charge for warping a ship into a harbor.

war paint 1 paint put on the face or body by certain peoples, such as formerly, some Amerindian peoples, before going to war. **2** *Informal.* make-up; cosmetics for the face. **3** *Informal.* ceremonial costume; full dress.

war·path (wôr′path′) *n.* the way or route taken by a fighting expedition of North American Indians.
on the warpath, a on a warlike expedition or at war. **b** looking for a fight; very angry.

war·plane (wôr′plān′) *n.* an aircraft used in war.

war·rant (wôr′ənt) *n., v.* **—n. 1** a written order giving legal authority for something, especially one authorizing a search, arrest etc.: *The police have a warrant for his arrest.* **2** something that gives a right; authorization or sanction: *Their vote of confidence was his warrant to continue his investigation.* **3** a good and sufficient reason for an action, belief, etc.; justification or grounds: *She had no warrant for her suspicions.* **4** a promise; guarantee. **5** a document certifying something, especially to a purchaser. **6** *Military. Historical.* the official certificate of appointment of a warrant officer.
—v. 1 justify: *It was a crisis that warranted immediate action.* **2** guarantee the quality, condition, etc. of: *to warrant the genuineness of goods purchased.* **3** *Informal.* declare positively or confidently: *I warrant I'll get there before you.* **4** authorize: *The law warrants his arrest.* [ME < ONF *warant* < Gmc.]

war·rant·a·ble (wôr′ən tə bəl) *adj.* capable of being warranted; justifiable. **—war′rant·a·ble·ness,** *n.* **—war′rant·a·bly,** *adv.*

war·ran·tee (wôr′ən tē′) *n.* a person to whom a warranty is made.

war·rant·er (wôr′ən tər) See **warrantor.**

warrant officer 1 *Canadian Forces.* a non-commissioned officer ranking next above a sergeant and below a master warrant officer. **2** a non-commissioned officer of similar rank in the armed forces of other countries. *Abbrev.:* W.O. or WO

war·ran·tor (wôr′ən tər *or* wôr′ən tôr′) *n.* a person who makes a warranty; guarantor.

war·ran·ty (wôr′ən tē) *n., pl.* **-ties. 1** a usually written promise or pledge that a product is what it is claimed to be and that the manufacturer will take the responsibility for repairing or replacing it if it proves to be defective. **2** authority or justification; warrant. [< OF *warantie* (var. of *guarantie*) < *warantir* warrant < *warant* a warrant < Gmc. Doublet of GUARANTY.]

war·ren (wôr′ən) *n.* **1** an area of ground having many interconnected burrows where rabbits live. **2** the rabbits living in a warren. **3** a crowded district or building. **4** *Esp.Brit.* an enclosed area where small game, such as rabbits or pheasants, are kept and bred. [ME < AF *warenne* < Celtic]

war·ri·or (wôr′ē ər) *n.* a fighting man; an experienced soldier. [ME < OF *werreieor* < *werreier* wage war < *werre* war. See WAR.] **—war′ri·or·like′,** *adj.*

War·saw Pact (wôr′so *or* wôr′sô) a collective defence alliance of Albania, Bulgaria, Czechoslovakia, the German Democratic Republic, Hungary, Poland, Romania, and the Soviet Union, signed in Warsaw on May 14, 1955.

war·ship (wôr′ship′) *n.* a ship used in war.

wart (wôrt) *n.* **1** a small, usually hard growth on the skin, caused by a virus. **2** anything resembling a wart, such as a hard lump on a plant. [OE *wearte*]

wart hog a wild pig (*Phacochoerus aethiopicus*) of Africa having two large tusks and two large wartlike growths on each side of its face.

war·time (wôr′tīm′) *n.* time of war.

wart·y (wôr′tē) *adj.* **wart·i·er, wart·i·est. 1** having warts or lumps that are like warts. **2** of or like a wart.

war whoop a war cry, especially of North American Indians.

war·y (wer′ē) *adj.* **war·i·er, war·i·est. 1** on one's guard against danger, deception, etc.; cautious and watchful: *a wary fox. Be wary of gossip. They were wary of the stranger.* **2** showing or done with caution: *He gave wary answers to all of the stranger's questions.* [< *ware²*]
☛ *Syn.* **2.** See note at **careful.**

was (wuz *or* woz; *unstressed,* wəz) *v.* the 1st and 3rd pers. sing., past indicative, of **be:** *I was late. Was he late, too?* [OE *wæs*]

wash¹ (wosh) *v., n.* **—v. 1** clean with water or other liquid: *to wash clothes, to wash one's face, to wash dishes.* **2** make clean: *washed from sin.* **3** remove (dirt, stains, paint, etc.) by or as if by the action of water: *to wash a spot out.* **4** wash oneself: *He washed before eating dinner.* **5** wash clothes: *She washes for a living.* **6** undergo washing without damage: *That cloth washes well.* **7** carry or be carried along or away by water or other liquid (*often used with* **away, out,** *etc.*): *The road was washed out during the storm.*

Wood is often washed ashore by the waves. **8** flow or beat with a lapping sound: *The waves washed upon the rocks.* **9** make wet: *The flowers are washed with dew.* **10** cover with a thin coating of color or of metal: *walls washed with blue, silver washed with gold.* **11** sift (earth, ore, etc.) by action of water to separate valuable material.

wash down, a wash from top to bottom or from end to end. **b** swallow liquid along with or after (solid food) to help in swallowing or digestion.

wash out, a wash the dirt from: *He washed out his socks.* **b** fail or cause to fail an examination. **c** lose color, body, or vigor. **d** *Informal.* cancel: *The whole program was washed out.*

wash up, a wash the hands and face, as before meals. **b** wash the dishes after meals: *We washed up right after supper.*
—*n.* **1** a washing or being washed. **2** a quantity of clothes washed or to be washed. **3** (*adj.*) that can be washed without damage: *a wash dress.* **4** the material carried along by moving water and then deposited as sediment: *A delta is formed by the wash of a river.* **5** the motion, rush, or sound of water: *We listened to the wash of the waves against the boat.* **6** a tract of land sometimes overflowed with water and sometimes left dry; a tract of shallow water; fen, marsh, or bog. **7** a liquid for a special use: *a hair wash, a mouth wash.* **8** waste liquid matter; liquid garbage. **9** washy or weak liquid food. **10** a thin coating of color or metal. **11** earth, etc. from which gold or the like can be washed. **12** the rough or broken water left behind a moving ship. [OE *wascan*]

wash² (wosh) *n. Cdn.* **1** any of the underwater exits from a beaver lodge. **2** a bear's den. [< Algonquian (Ojibway)]

Wash. Washington (state).

wash·a·ble (wosh'ə bəl) *adj.* **1** that can be washed without damage: *washable silk.* **2** that can be removed by washing: *washable paint or ink.*

wash–and–wear (wosh'ən wer') *adj.* of a fabric or garment, easily washed and dried and needing little or no ironing.

wash·ba·sin (wosh'bā'sən) *n.* a basin for holding water to wash one's face and hands, do laundry by hand, etc., especially a porcelain, metal, or plastic fixture in a bathroom, with attached water taps and a drain.

wash·board (wosh'bôrd') *n.* **1** a rectangular sheet of heavy glass, metal, etc. with a surface of rounded crosswise ridges, set in a wooden frame and used for rubbing the dirt out of clothes, etc. **2** a road having a surface with many crosswise ridges.

wash·bowl (wosh'bōl') *n.* a bowl for holding water to wash one's face and hands.

wash·cloth (wosh'kloth') *n.* **1** a small cloth for washing oneself; facecloth. **2** dishcloth.

wash·day (wosh'dā') *n.* a day when clothes and household linens are washed: *Monday is the traditional washday.*

washed–out (wosht'out') *adj.* **1** lacking color; pale or faded, as from much washing: *an old, washed-out shirt.* **2** *Informal.* lacking vigor or spirit; exhausted: *She was feeling washed-out after a day of meetings.*

washed–up (wosht'up') *adj. Informal.* **1** no longer able to function; failed; finished: *After three unsuccessful films, he is probably washed-up as a director.* **2** fatigued; washed-out.

wash·er (wosh'ər) *n.* **1** a person or thing that washes, especially an automatic washing machine. **2** a flat ring of metal, rubber, leather, etc. used to protect surfaces held by bolts or nuts, to seal joints, to reduce friction, etc.

wash·er·wom·an (wosh'ər wùm'ən) *n., pl.* **-wom·en.** a woman whose work is washing clothes and linens; laundress.

wash·ing (wosh'ing) *n.* **1** clothes or linens that have been washed or are to be washed; laundry; wash (def. 2). **2** Sometimes, **washings,** *pl.* material obtained in washing something: *washings of gold obtained from earth.* **3** the act of a person or thing that cleans with water.

washing machine a machine for washing clothes, etc.

washing soda a crystalline form of sodium carbonate, used dissolved in water for washing clothes, etc.

wash·out (wosh'out') *n.* **1** a washing away of earth, a road, etc. by rainfall, a flood, or other sudden rush of water. **2** the hole or break made by such action. **3** *Slang.* an utter failure: *The party was a complete washout. He turned out to be a washout as a salesman.*

wash·rag (wosh'rag') *n.* washcloth.

wash·room (wosh'rüm' *or* -rùm') *n.* **1** a room equipped with a toilet and sink, especially such a room in a public building: *Most restaurants and gas stations have washrooms for their customers.* **2** especially in industry, a room for washing fabrics or other materials being processed.

wash sale *Esp. U.S.* the illegal practice of buying and selling the same stocks in order to create a false impression of market activity.

wash·stand (wosh'stand') *n.* **1** a bowl with pipes and taps for

hat, āge, fär; let, ēqual, tėrm; it, īce
hot, ōpen, ôrder; oil, out; cup, pùt, rüle,
əbove, takən, pencəl, lemən, circəs

ch, child; ng, long; sh, ship
th, thin; ŦH, then; zh, measure

running water to wash one's hands and face. **2** a stand for holding a basin, pitcher, etc. for washing.

wash·tub (wosh'tub') *n.* a tub used to wash or soak laundry in.

wash·wom·an (wosh'wùm'ən) *n., pl.* **-wom·en.** washerwoman.

wash·y (wosh'ē) *adj.* **wash·i·er, wash·i·est. 1** too watery or thin: *washy tea.* **2** too weak; not having enough color, substance, or force; insipid: *washy colors, washy poetry.*

was·n't (wuz'ənt *or* woz'ənt) was not.

wasp (wosp) *n.* any of numerous winged insects (order Hymenoptera, especially family Vespidae) having biting mouthparts, a slender body with the abdomen attached to the thorax by a thin stalk, and, in the females and workers, a powerful sting. Some species of wasps live in colonies, but most do not. Wasps belong to the same order as bees, ants, and sawflies. [OE *wæsp*]

WASP or **Wasp** (wosp) *n. Often derogatory.* a person of N European, especially Anglo-Saxon, descent and Protestant background, thought of as belonging to the dominant, privileged class of society, especially in North America. [< *W*hite *A*nglo-*S*axon *P*rotestant]

wasp·ish (wos'pish) *adj.* **1** of or like a wasp. **2** irritable or snappish: *a waspish temper.* —**wasp'ish·ly,** *adv.* —**wasp'ish·ness,** *n.*

wasp waist a very slender waist.

wasp–waist·ed (wosp'wās'tid) *adj.* having a very slender waist.

was·sail (wos'əl, wäs'əl, *or* was äl') *n., v., interj.* —*n.* **1** a drinking party; revel with drinking of healths. **2** spiced ale or other liquor drunk at a wassail. **3** an old English toast meaning "Your health!"
—*v.* **1** take part in a wassail; revel. **2** drink to the health of.
—*interj.* "Your health!" [ME *wassayl* < ON *ves heill* be healthy! cf. OE *wes hāl*]

was·sail·er (wos'əl ər *or* was'əl ər) *n.* **1** reveller. **2** a drinker of toasts.

Was·ser·mann (wäs'ər mən) *n.* Wassermann test.

Wassermann test a test for syphilis, made on a sample of a person's blood or spinal fluid. [< August von *Wassermann* (1866-1925), a German physician who invented this test]

wast (wost) *v. Archaic or poetic.* 2nd pers. sing., past indicative of **be**: *Thou wast* means *you* (sing.) *were.*

wast·age (wās'tij) *n.* **1** loss by use, wear, decay, leakage, etc., especially preventable loss of something useful or valuable; waste. **2** the amount wasted.

waste (wāst) *v.* **wast·ed, wast·ing;** *n., adj.* —*v.* **1** make poor use of; spend uselessly; fail to get value from: *Don't waste time or money.* **2** wear down little by little; destroy or lose gradually: *The sick man was wasted by disease.* **3** damage greatly; destroy: *The soldiers wasted the enemy's fields.*
—*n.* **1** poor use; useless spending; failure to get the most out of something. **2** useless or worthless material; stuff to be thrown away: *Garbage or sewage is waste.* **3** bare or wild land; desert; wilderness. **4** a wearing down little by little; gradual destruction or loss. Both waste and repair are constantly going on in our bodies. **5** destruction or devastation caused by war, floods, fires, etc. **6** a vast, dreary, desolate, or empty expanse or tract, as of water or snow-covered land. **7** material left over or rejected during the manufacture of textiles, used to wipe off oil, dirt, etc.
go to waste, be wasted.
—*adj.* **1** thrown away as useless or worthless. **2** left over; not used. **3** not cultivated; that is a desert or wilderness; bare; wild. **4** in a state of desolation or ruin. **5** carrying off or holding refuse: *a waste drain.* **6** unused by or unusable to, and therefore excreted by, an animal or human body.
lay waste, damage greatly; destroy; ravage: *The invading army laid waste the countryside.*
[ME < ONF *waster,* var. of OF *guaster* < L *vastare* lay waste < *vastus* vast, waste; influenced in OF by cognate Gmc. word] ☞ *Hom.* waist.

waste·bas·ket (wāst'bas'kit) *n.* a basket or other open container for wastepaper, etc.

waste·ful (wāst'fəl) *adj.* using or spending too much. —**waste'ful·ly,** *adv.* —**waste'ful·ness,** *n.*

waste·land (wāst'land') *n.* **1** barren, uncultivated land: *desert*

wastelands. **2** a devastated, ruined region: *The advancing troops left a wasteland behind them.* **3** anything that has been improperly managed or is unproductive or barren: *Television has been described as a cultural wasteland.*

waste–lot (wāst′lot′) *n.* a vacant lot in a city, especially one neglected and left to run to weeds.

waste·pa·per (wāst′pā′pər) *n.* paper thrown away or to be thrown away as useless or worthless.

wastepaper basket wastebasket.

waste pipe a pipe for carrying off waste water, etc.

wast·er (wās′tər) *n.* a person or thing that wastes, especially a person who is a spendthrift.

wast·ing (wās′ting) *adj.* **1** gradually destructive to the body: *Tuberculosis is a wasting disease.* **2** laying waste; devastating.

wast·rel (wās′trəl) *n.* **1** waster. **2** a good-for-nothing.

wa·tap (wa täp′) *n. Cdn.* fibrous roots, especially of the spruce, once much used by North American Indians for sewing birchbark canoes, for weaving water-tight bowls and dishes, and for other purposes. Also, **watape, wattape.** [< Algonquian; cf. Ojibway *watapi*]

watch (woch) *v., n.* —*v.* **1** look attentively or carefully; observe closely: *The medical students watched while the doctor performed the operation.* **2** look at; observe; view: *to watch a play.* **3** look or wait with care and attention: *The boy watched for a chance to cross the busy street.* **4** keep guard: *He watched throughout the night.* **5** keep guard over; guard: *The dog watched the little boy.* **6** stay awake for some purpose: *The nurse watched with the patient.* **watch and ward,** guard. **watch out,** be careful; be on guard. **watch over,** guard or supervise; protect or preserve from danger, harm, error, etc. —*n.* **1** a careful looking; attitude of attention: *Be on the watch for cars when you cross the street.* **2** a protecting; a guarding: *A man keeps watch over the bank at night.* **3** *Historical.* a person or persons kept as a guard: *The man's cry aroused the town watch, who came running to his aid.* **4** a period of time for guarding: *a watch in the night.* **5** a staying awake for some purpose. **6** a spring-driven or electronic device for indicating time, small enough to be carried in a pocket or worn on the wrist. **7** *Nautical.* **a** the time of duty of one part of a ship's crew. A watch usually lasts four hours. **b** the part of a crew on duty at one time. [OE *wæccan*] —**watch′er,** *n.*

watch·band (woch′band′) *n.* a band or strap of leather, metal, etc. for holding a wristwatch on the wrist.

watch·case (woch′kās′) *n.* the outer covering for the works of a watch.

watch chain the chain attached to a watch and fastened to one's clothing or worn around one's neck.

watch·dog (woch′dog′) *n.* **1** a dog kept to guard property. **2** a watchful guardian.

watch fire a fire kept burning at night in camps, etc.

watch·ful (woch′fəl) *adj.* watching carefully; on the lookout; alert and vigilant: *a watchful guard. He is watchful of his health.* —**watch′ful·ly,** *adv.* —**watch′ful·ness,** *n.*

☞ *Syn.* **Watchful, vigilant, alert** = wide-awake and attentive or on the lookout for something good or harmful. **Watchful** is the general word, particularly suggesting paying close attention and observing carefully or keeping careful guard: *He is watchful of his health.* **Vigilant** suggests being constantly and keenly watchful for a definite reason or purpose, especially to see and avoid danger: *The new mayor is vigilant against attempts to take advantage of his lack of experience.* **Alert** emphasizes being wide-awake and ready to meet what comes: *The alert driver avoided an accident.*

watching brief **1** a brief directing a lawyer to observe proceedings on a client's behalf. **2** any position or task involving similar watchfulness.

watch·ma·ker (woch′mā′kər) *n.* a person who makes and repairs watches and clocks.

watch·mak·ing (woch′mā′king) *n.* the business of making and repairing watches.

watch·man (woch′mən) *n., pl.* **-men.** a person who keeps watch; guard: *A watchman guards the grounds at night.*

watch night New Year's Eve, observed in some churches with social gatherings and religious services which last until the arrival of the new year.

watch pocket a small pocket for holding a watch.

watch·tow·er (woch′tou′ər) *n.* a tower from which watch is kept for enemies, fires, ships, etc.

watch·word (woch′wėrd′) *n.* **1** a secret word that allows a person to pass a guard; password: *We gave the watchword, and the*

sentinel let us pass. **2** a motto; slogan: *"Forward" is our watchword.*

wa·ter (wo′tər *or* wô′tər) *n., v.* —*n.* **1** the liquid that falls as rain and makes up the seas, lakes, and rivers and that is also the main constituent of all living matter. Pure water is a transparent, colorless, odorless, tasteless compound of hydrogen and oxygen (H_2O) that can be converted into steam by heating it to $100°C$ and into ice by cooling it to $0°C$. **2** a body of water; a sea, river, lake, etc.: *He lived across the water from them.* **3** (*adj.*) found or living in or near water: *water rodents, water lilies, waterfowl.* **4** (*adj.*) in, on, or by means of water: *water sports, water power, water transport.* **5 waters,** *pl.* **a** a particular part of the ocean, a lake, etc.: *fishing in Canadian waters, the upper waters of the St. Lawrence, warm Pacific waters.* **b** mineral or spring water, as at a spa: *to take the waters.* **6** the water of a river, etc. with reference to the tide: *high or low water.* **7** the surface of a body of water: *to swim under the water.* **8** a liquid containing and resembling water: *rose water, soda water. When you cry, water runs from your eyes.* **9** the degree of clearness and brilliance of a precious stone. A diamond of the first water is a very clear and brilliant one. **10** the part of a crew on duty at one time. **11** *Business.* additional shares or securities issued without corresponding increase of capital or assets, so that the book value of the company's capital is inflated. **back water, a** make a boat go backward. **b** reverse one's course; withdraw from a position, claim, etc. **by water,** by means of a ship or boat: *He would rather travel by water than by air.* **hold water,** stand the test; be shown to be consistent, logical, effective, etc.: *That argument won't hold water.* **keep (one's) head above water,** keep out of trouble or difficulty, especially financial difficulty: *Business is so bad that he is finding it hard to keep his head above water.* **like water,** very freely or recklessly: *to spend money like water. Blood flowed like water.* **make** or **pass water,** urinate. **make water,** of a boat, ship, etc., take in water through leaks or over the side. **of the first water,** of the highest quality or most extreme degree: *a musical composition of the first water. He is a bungler of the first water.* **throw** or **pour cold water on,** actively discourage or belittle: *She didn't tell her friends her scheme because she knew they'd throw cold water on it.* **tread water,** keep afloat in the water, with the body upright and the head above the surface, by slowly moving the legs as if bicycling. —*v.* **1** sprinkle or wet with water: *to water the grass.* **2** provide with water to drink: *to water the horses.* **3** supply water to (a region, etc.): *British Columbia is well watered by rivers and brooks.* **4** fill with or discharge water: *Her mouth watered when she saw the cake. Strong sunlight can make your eyes water.* **5** weaken by adding water; adulterate with water: *It is against the law to sell watered milk.* **6** get or take in a supply of water: *A ship waters before sailing.* **7** of animals, drink water: *The cattle usually watered at the creek.* **8** make a wavy pattern on: *Watered silk is often called moiré.* **9** *Business.* increase (stock, etc.) by issue of additional shares or securities without a corresponding increase in capital or assets. **make (someone's) mouth water,** arouse one's appetite or desire: *a sports car to make your mouth water.* **water down, a** reduce in strength by diluting with water: *We watered down the punch because it was too strong.* **b** reduce the effectiveness or force of by altering; weaken: *The original bill had been watered down before being presented to Parliament.* [OE *wæter*] —**wa′ter·er,** *n.* —**wa′ter·less,** *adj.*

water bed a bed having a mattress that is a padded, water-filled plastic bag supported at the bottom and on all four sides by a wooden frame.

water beetle any of numerous beetles belonging to several different families, all having broad, fringed hind legs well adapted for swimming. Water beetles are found in freshwater streams and lakes.

water bird a bird that swims or wades in water.

water boatman any of various bugs (family Corixidae) that live in water and have paddle-like legs used in swimming.

water bomber an aircraft used for water bombing.

water bombing a means of fighting forest fires by dropping water on them from aircraft equipped with special tanks.

wa·ter-borne (wo′tər bôrn′ *or* wô′tər-) *adj.* **1** supported by water; floating. **2** conveyed by a boat or the like.

water bottle a bottle, bag, etc. for holding water.

wa·ter·buck (wo′tər buk′ *or* wô′tər-) *n.* any of several large African antelopes (genus *Kobus*) found near rivers and in marshy areas. [< Du. *waterbok*]

water buffalo the common buffalo (*Bubalus bubalis*) of S Asia

and the Philippines, having large, spreading horns. The water buffalo is used as a draft animal.

water bug 1 croton bug. 2 water boatman.

Water Carrier *Astronomy* or *Astrology*. Aquarius.

water chestnut 1 a Chinese sedge (*Eleocharis tuberosa*) having a button-shaped, edible tuber. 2 the tuber of this plant, used especially in Chinese cooking. 3 a floating, aquatic, Old World plant (*Trapa natans*) of the evening-primrose family having edible, nutlike fruit.

water clock an instrument for measuring time by the flow of water.

water closet 1 a room or compartment having a toilet with a bowl that can be flushed with water. 2 the toilet itself.

water color or **colour** 1 paint mixed with water instead of oil. 2 the art or skill of painting with water colors: *He is good at water color.* 3 a picture painted with water colors.

wa·ter·col·or or **wa·ter·col·our** (wo′tər kul′ər or wô′tər-) *adj.* made with water colors.

water cooler a device for cooling drinking water.

wa·ter·course (wo′tər kôrs′ or wô′tər-) *n.* 1 a stream of water; a river or brook. 2 a natural or artificial channel for water; a stream bed, canal, etc.

wa·ter·craft (wo′tər kraft′ or wô′tər-) *n., pl.* (def. 2) **-craft.** 1 skill in handling boats or in water sports. 2 a ship or boat.

wa·ter·cress (wo′tər kres′ or wôtər kres′) *n.* a perennial plant (*Nasturtium officinale*) of the mustard family that grows in running water and has crisp leaves often used in salads.

water cure the treatment of disease by the use of water; hydropathy.

water dog 1 a dog that swims well, especially one that retrieves game from water. 2 *Informal.* a man at home on or in the water, such as a sailor or a good swimmer.

wa·ter·fall (wo′tər fol′ or wô′tər fôl′) *n.* a stream or river falling over a cliff or down a very steep hill; cataract.

water flea any of numerous tiny aquatic crustaceans (order Cladocera) that swim with a skipping motion, by means of branched antennae.

wa·ter·fowl (wo′tər foul′ or wô′tər-) *n., pl.* (def. 1) **-fowl** or **-fowls.** 1 a water bird, especially one that swims. 2 **waterfowl,** *pl.* swimming game birds as a group, as opposed to shore birds, etc.

wa·ter·front (wo′tər frunt′ or wô′tər-) *n.* 1 the part of a city, town, etc. beside a river, lake, or harbor. 2 land at the water's edge. 3 (*adj.*) of, having to do with, or on the waterfront: *a waterfront hotel.*

water gap a gap in a mountain ridge through which a stream flows.

water gas a poisonous gas used for fuel or lighting, consisting of carbon monoxide and hydrogen with small amounts of methane, carbon dioxide, and nitrogen. It is produced by passing steam over very hot coal or coke.

water gate 1 a gate that controls the flow of water; floodgate. 2 a gate giving access to a river, etc., as from a building.

water glass 1 a glass to hold water; tumbler. 2 sodium or potassium silicate, a substance used especially to coat eggs in order to preserve them.

water hole a hole in the ground where water collects; small pond or pool.

water ice a confection or dessert consisting of a frozen mixture of water, sugar, and flavoring.

watering can a container with a handle and a spout for sprinkling or pouring water on plants, etc.

watering place 1 a place where water may be obtained, especially a pool, a part of a stream, etc. where animals go to drink. 2 *Informal.* a bar or tavern. 3 *Esp.Brit.* a resort with springs containing mineral water; spa. 4 *Esp.Brit.* a seaside resort.

watering pot watering can.

water jacket a casing with water or other liquid in it, surrounding something to keep it at a certain temperature; especially, in an internal-combustion engine, the part of the cylinder block that contains the coolant.

wa·ter·less (wo′tər ləs or wôtər ləs) *adj.* 1 not having water; dry. 2 not needing or using water: *waterless cooking.*

water level 1 the surface level of a body of water. 2 water table.

water lily any of a family (Nymphaeaceae) of water plants found in temperate and tropical parts of the world, having floating leaves and showy, fragrant flowers. The stems of a water lily grow from thick, creeping underground stems buried in the mud at the bottom of a pond, etc.

wa·ter·line (wo′tər līn′ or wô′tər līn′) *n.* 1 the line where the

hat, āge, fär; let, ēqual, tèrm; it, īce
hot, ōpen, ôrder; oil, out; cup, put, rüle,
ə above, takən, pencəl, lemən, circəs

ch, child; ng, long; sh, ship
th, thin; ŧH, then; zh, measure

surface of the water touches the side of a ship or boat. 2 any of several lines marked on a ship's hull to show the depth to which it sinks when unloaded, partly loaded, or fully loaded. 3 a line or mark showing how high water has risen or may rise; watermark (def. 1).

wa·ter·logged (wo′tər logd′ or wô′tər-) *adj.* 1 of a boat, etc., so full of water that it will barely float. 2 completely soaked with water.

Wa·ter·loo (wo′tər lü′ or wô′tər lü′) *n.* any decisive or crushing defeat: *She has met her Waterloo and will not run for election again. His first international tennis competition turned out to be his Waterloo.* [< *Waterloo,* a town in central Belgium, where Napoleon was finally defeated in 1815 by the allied armies under Wellington and Blücher]

water main a main pipe in a system of water pipes.

wa·ter·man (wo′tər mən or wô′tər-) *n., pl.* **-men.** 1 a boatman, especially one who rents out boats. 2 an oarsman.

wa·ter·mark (wo′tər märk′ or wô′tər-) *n., v.* —*n.* 1 a mark showing how high water has risen or may rise. 2 a faint mark produced on some paper by pressure of a projecting design during manufacture, indicating the maker, etc. The watermark may be seen by holding the paper up to the light. —*v.* put a watermark on: *Fine writing paper is often watermarked.*

wa·ter·mel·on (wo′tər mel′ən or wô′tər-) *n.* 1 a large, oblong or roundish edible fruit having sweet, juicy red, pink, or yellowish pulp with seeds scattered through it and a hard, thick green rind. 2 the trailing vine (*Citrullus vulgaris*) it grows on. The watermelon, which is native to Africa, is a member of the gourd family.

water meter a device that registers the quantity of water supplied to a house, etc. through a water supply system.

water milfoil any of a genus (*Myriophyllum*) of submerged or floating aquatic plants having whorls of finely divided leaves and tiny flowers. Some species are cultivated in ponds and aquariums.

water mill a mill whose machinery is run by water power.

water moccasin 1 a large, dark-colored, poisonous snake (*Agkistrodon piscivorus*), a kind of pit viper found in the swamps and rivers of the S United States. 2 any of various similar but harmless snakes, especially a water snake.

water nymph 1 a nymph or goddess associated with some body of water. 2 a nymph supposed to live in water.

water of crystallization water that is a constituent of certain crystalline substances and that usually is necessary to maintain a particular crystalline structure. When water of crystallization is removed by heating, the crystals usually break up into a powder.

water ouzel dipper (def. 2), a kind of bird.

water parsnip any of a genus (*Sium*) of marsh plants of the parsley family having primately compound leaves.

water pipe 1 a pipe for conveying water. 2 hookah.

water pistol a toy pistol designed to shoot a jet of water.

water polo a game played in a swimming pool by two teams of seven players who try to throw or push a round inflated ball into the opponents' goal.

water power 1 the power from flowing or falling water, used to drive machinery and make electricity. 2 a fall in a stream that can supply power.

wa·ter·proof (wo′tər prüf′ or wô′tər-) *adj., n., v.* —*adj.* that will not let water through; sealed, or treated or coated with something so as to keep water out: *a waterproof tarpaulin, a waterproof watch.* —*n.* 1 a waterproof material. 2 *Esp.Brit.* raincoat. —*v.* make waterproof.

water rat 1 a large vole (*Arvicola terrestris*) found along the banks of streams and lakes in Europe and Asia. 2 *Cdn.* muskrat. 3 any of various semi-aquatic rodents (subfamily Hydromyinae of family Muridae) of Australia, New Guinea, and the Philippines. 4 *Slang.* a waterfront petty thief or ruffian.

wa·ter·re·pel·lent (wo′tər ri pel′ənt or wôtər ri pel′ənt) *adj.* resistant to water; that repels water, but is not waterproof: *Most raincoats are water-repellent but those treated or coated with rubber or plastic are waterproof.*

wa·ter–re·sis·tant (woʹtər ri zisʹtənt or wôʹtər ri zisʹtənt) *adj.* water-repellant: *a water-resistant watch.*

wa·ter·shed (woʹtər shed' or wôʹtər-) *n.* **1** a high ridge of land that divides two areas drained by different river systems; a divide. On one side of a watershed, rivers and streams flow in one direction; on the other side, they flow in a different direction. **2** the region drained by one river system. [< *water* + *shed²*]

wa·ter·side (woʹtər sīd' or wôʹtər-) *n.* **1** land along the sea, a lake, a river, etc. **2** (*adj.*) of, at, or on the waterside: *a waterside park.*

water ski a broad ski, usually one of a pair, for skimming over the water while being towed by a boat.

wa·ter·ski (woʹtər skē' or wôʹtər-) *v.* **-skied, -ski·ing.** skim over the water on water skis. —**waʹter·skiʹer,** *n.*

wa·ter·ski·ing (woʹtər skē'ing or wôʹtər-) *n.* the practice or sport of skimming over the water on water skis.

water snake any of various snakes (family Colubridae) that live in or near water, especially any of numerous harmless snakes of genus *Natrix.*

wa·ter·soak (woʹtər sōk' or wôʹtər-) *v.* soak thoroughly with water.

water softener **1** a chemical added to hard water to soften it by dissolving and removing minerals. **2** a device using such a chemical and attached to a water supply.

water spaniel either of two breeds of spaniel, the Irish water spaniel or the American water spaniel, both having thick, curly, reddish-brown hair and often trained to retrieve game birds from water.

wa·ter·spout (woʹtər spout' or wôʹtər-) *n.* **1** a pipe that takes away or spouts water. **2** a rotating funnel-shaped or tube-shaped column of spray and water between a cloud and the surface of the ocean or a large lake, produced by the action of a whirlwind.

water sprite a sprite supposed to live in water.

water table the level below which the ground is saturated with water.

wa·ter·tight (woʹtər tīt' or wôʹtər-) *adj.* **1** so tight that no water can get in or out. Large ships are often divided into watertight compartments by watertight partitions. **2** leaving no opening for misunderstanding, criticism, etc.; perfect: *a watertight argument.*

water tower **1** an elevated tank or reservoir for storing water and maintaining a steady pressure in a water supply system. **2** any of several types of firefighting equipment designed to deliver water under pressure to a nozzle at a great height for fighting fires in the upper parts of tall buildings. The original water tower was a large, vertical, telescoping steel pipe with a nozzle at the top.

water vapor or **vapour** water in a gaseous state, especially when below the boiling point and fairly diffused, as in the atmosphere. Compare **steam.**

wa·ter·way (woʹtər wā' or wôʹtər-) *n.* **1** a river, canal, or other body of water that ships can go on. **2** a channel for water.

Water wheels. The overshot wheel (left) is turned by the force and weight of water falling on the blades. The undershot wheel (right) is turned by the force of the water pushing against the blades.

water wheel a wheel turned by running or falling water, used to supply power.

water wings a device consisting of two air-filled floats joined together, designed to give support to a swimmer or a person learning to swim. Water wings are worn under the arms, extending out behind the shoulders.

water witch a person who uses a divining rod to locate underground water sources.

wa·ter·works (woʹtər wėrks' or wôʹtər-) *n.pl. or sing.* **1** a system of pipes, reservoirs, water towers, pumps, etc. for supplying a city or town with water. **2** a building containing engines and

pumps for pumping water; pumping station. **3** *Slang.* a flow of tears, especially a sudden or violent flow.

wa·ter·worn (woʹtər wôrn' or wôʹtər-) *adj.* worn or smoothed by the action of water.

wa·ter·y (woʹtər ē or wôʹtər ē) *adj.* **1** too wet; soaked; sodden: *watery soil. The potatoes were overcooked and watery.* **2** of eyes, full of tears; tending to water: *The old man's eyes were watery.* **3** of a liquid, too thin; containing too much water: *watery soup, watery tea.* **4** like water in consistency or appearance: *A blister is filled with a watery fluid.* **5** weak or pale: *a watery blue, watery winter sunlight.* **6** indicating rain: *a watery sky.* **7** consisting of water: *a watery grave.*

watt (wot) *n.* an SI unit for measuring electric power, or energy available per second. One watt is equal to one joule of energy per second. *Symbol:* W [after James Watt (1736-1819), a Scottish engineer and inventor]
☛ **Hom. what.**

watt·age (wotʹij) *n.* electric power expressed in watts: *Our new heater has a higher wattage than our old one.*

wat·tap or **wat·tape** (wa täp') *Cdn.* See **watap.**

watt hour a unit of electric energy, equal to the power of one watt maintained for one hour. A watt hour is equal to 3.6 kilojoules. *Symbol:* W · h

wat·tle (wotʹəl) *n., v.* **-tled, -tling.** —*n.* **1** a construction of sticks interwoven with slender branches, twigs, or reeds to form a wall fence, etc.: *a hut built of wattle.* **2** Often, **wattles,** *pl.* poles used to support a roof of thatch. **3** (*adj.*) made or built of wattle. **4** the fleshy, wrinkled skin hanging down from the throat of certain birds. The wattle of a turkey is bright red. **5** the barbel of a fish. **6** *Australian.* any of various acacia trees whose long, pliant branches were used by early settlers for making wattle.
—*v.* **1** build or form of wattle: *to wattle a fence.* **2** twist or weave together into wattle: *to wattle twigs and branches.* [OE *watul*]

wat·tled (wotʹəld) *adj.* **1** having wattles. **2** formed by interwoven twigs; interlaced.

watt·me·ter (wotʹmē'tər) *n.* an instrument for measuring in watts the power developed in an electric circuit.

wave (wāv) *v.* **waved, wav·ing;** *n.* —*v.* **1** move back and forth or up and down from a fixed base, with a slow, sweeping or undulating motion, as in a current of air or water: *tall grasses waving. A flag waved in the breeze.* **2** make a signal or greeting with an up-and-down or back-and-forth movement of the hand or arm: *We waved until the train was out of sight.* **3** make a signal or greeting by such a movement of something held in the hand: *She waved her handkerchief.* **4** signal or direct by waving: *He waved us away. She waved goodbye.* **5** shake in the air; brandish: *He waved the stick at them.* **6** have a wavelike form or follow a curving line: *Her hair waves naturally.* **7** give a wavelike form or pattern to: *to wave hair.*
—*n.* **1** the action of waving, especially as a signal or greeting: *a wave of the hand.* **2** a moving ridge or swell of water, as on the sea: *The boat rose and fell on the waves.* **3** a group or one of a series of groups advancing in a surging or swelling movement, like ocean waves: *A wave of new settlers followed the completion of the railway.* **4** an emotion, activity, etc. passing from one person to the next in a group: *A wave of hysteria passed through the crowd.* **5** a swell or sudden temporary increase of emotion, influence, activity, etc.; upsurge or rush: *We're having a heat wave. A wave of fear swept over him.* **6** a curve or series of curves: *hair set in waves.* **7** permanent wave. **8** *Physics.* a periodic disturbance propagated through a medium or through space, in which energy is carried forward through local displacement of particles in a medium (as in a wave of water or sound) or through a change in temperature, strength of electromagnetic field, etc. (as in electromagnetic waves). **9** Often, **waves,** *pl. Poetic.* a body of water, especially the sea. [OE *wafian*] —**wave'like',** *adj.* —**wav'er,** *n.*
☛ **Hom. waive.**
☛ *Syn. n.* **1. Wave, breaker, ripple** = a moving ridge on the surface of water. **Wave** is the general word: *The raft rose and fell on the waves.* **Breaker** applies to a heavy wave of the ocean, that breaks into foam as it nears the shore or strikes rocks: *Our favorite sport is riding the breakers in.* **Ripple** applies to a tiny wave, such as one caused by the ruffling of a smooth surface by a breeze: *There is scarcely a ripple on the lake tonight.*

wave·length (wāvʹlength') *n.* **1** *Physics.* the distance between any point in a wave and the next point that is in the same phase, as from one peak to the next. Radio wavelengths are measured in metres. **2** *Informal.* a person's line of thought: *He and I were just never on the same wavelength.*

wave·less (wāvʹlis) *adj.* having no waves; still.

wave·let (wāvʹlit) *n.* a little wave.

wa·ver (wāʹvər) *v., n.* —*v.* **1** move unsteadily to and fro; flutter or totter. **2** vary in intensity; flicker: *a wavering light.* **3** hesitate between choices; be undecided in opinion, direction, etc.: *He wavered, not knowing which road to take.* **4** grow fainter, then louder, or change pitch up and down fairly quickly; quaver, tremble, or pulsate. **5** become unsteady; be about to give way;

falter: *The battle line wavered and then broke.*
—*n.* the act of wavering. [ult. < *wave*] —**wa′ver·er,** *n.*
—**wa′ver·ing·ly,** *adv.*
☛ *Hom.* waiver.
☛ *Syn. v.* 3. See note at hesitate.

wa·vey (wā′vē) *n. Cdn.* a wild goose, especially the snow goose.
[< *Cdn.*F < Cree]

wav·y (wā′vē) *adj.* **wav·i·er, wav·i·est. 1** having or marked by
undulations or curves: *wavy hair, a wavy line.* **2** moving or
proceeding in waves, or undulating curves. —**wav′i·ness,** *n.*

wa·wa (wä′wə *or* wä′wä) *n. Cdn.* wavey. [var. of WAVEY]

wax¹ (waks) *n., v., adj.* —*n.* **1** a yellowish, somewhat greasy,
pleasant-smelling substance secreted by bees for constructing their
honeycomb cells; beeswax. Wax is hard when cold, but can be
easily shaped when warm; it is used for candles, modelling, etc.
2 any of various substances resembling this. Paraffin, commonly
used for candles, etc., is often called wax. Sealing wax is a mixture
of resin and turpentine. Scale insects secrete a kind of wax. **3** (*adj.*)
made of wax: *a wax model for a sculpture.* **4** *Informal.* phonograph
record.
be wax in (someone's) **hands,** be totally under the influence of
someone.
—*v.* **1** rub or treat with wax or something like wax to polish, stiffen,
condition, etc.: *We wax that floor once a month.* **2** *Informal.* make a
phonograph recording of.
—*adj.* of wax. [OE *weax*] —**wax′like′,** *adj.*

wax² (waks) *v.* **1** of the moon, go through the regular increase in
the size of its visible portion. The moon waxes till it becomes full
and then it wanes. **2** grow bigger or greater; increase in size,
strength, prosperity, numbers, etc.: *During this period his wealth
waxed steadily.* **3** become: *to wax indignant. The party waxed
merry.* [OE *weaxan*]

wax bean 1 a variety of garden bean having yellow pods which
are used as a vegetable while still young and tender. **2** the immature
pod of this bean.

wax·en¹ (wak′sən) *adj.* **1** *Archaic.* made of or covered with wax.
2 like wax in being smooth, pale, and lustrous: *a waxen skin.*

wax·en² (wak′sən) *v. Archaic or poetic.* a pp. of wax².

wax myrtle or **wax–myr·tle** (waks′mèr′təl) *n.* **1** bayberry
(def. 1). **2** (*adj.*) designating a small family (Myricaceae) of aromatic
trees and shrubs found in many parts of the world. The wax-myrtle
family includes the bayberry and sweet gale.

wax paper or **waxed paper** paper coated with a waxy
substance such as paraffin, used mostly for wrapping food.

wax·wing (waks′wing′) *n.* any of a small genus (*Bombycilla,*
constituting the family Bombycillidae) of small, crested songbirds of
the northern hemisphere, having sleek, greyish or brownish
plumage, a narrow black stripe over the eye and, often, red,
waxlike tips on the secondary wing feathers. See also **bohemian
waxwing, cedar waxwing.**

wax·work (waks′wèrk′) *n.* **1** a figure or figures made of wax.
2 waxworks, *pl.* an exhibition of such figures, especially one
showing figures of famous or notorious people.

wax·y (wak′sē) *adj.* **wax·i·er, wax·i·est. 1** made of, containing, or
covered with wax: *Bayberries are waxy.* **2** like wax; smooth, glossy,
pale, etc.: *waxy skin.* —**wax′i·ness,** *n.*

way (wā) *n., adv.* —*n.* **1** a manner or style: *a queer way of talking.*
2 a method or means: *Doctors are using new ways of preventing
disease.* **3** a point or feature; respect; detail: *This plan is bad in
several ways.* **4** a direction: *Look this way.* **5** movement or progress
along a course: *The guide led the way.* **6** a distance: *The sun is a
long way off.* **7** a road; path; street; course: *a way through the
forest.* **8** a space for passing or going ahead. **9** Often, **ways,** *pl.* habit;
custom: *Don't mind his teasing; it's just his way.* **10** one's wish;
will: *A spoiled child wants his own way all the time.* **11** *Informal.* a
condition; state: *That sick man is in a bad way.* **12** a movement;
forward motion: *The ship slowly gathered way.* **13** the range of
experience or notice: *The best idea that ever came my way.* **14** a
course of life, action, or experience: *"The way of the ungodly shall
perish."* **15** *Informal.* district; area; region: *He lives out our way.*
16 ways, *pl.* the timbers on which a ship is built and launched.
by the way, a while coming or going. b in that connection;
incidentally.
by way of, a by the route of; through. b as; for: *By way of an
answer he just nodded.* c making a profession of or having a
reputation for (being or doing something): *He is by way of being a
clever cartoonist.*
come (one's) **way,** happen to one.
give way, a make way; retreat; yield. b break down or fall: *Several
people were hurt when the platform gave way.* c abandon oneself to
emotion: *give way to tears.*
go out of (one's) **way,** make a special effort.
have a way with one, be persuasive.
in a way, to some extent.

hat, āge, fär; let, ēqual, tèrm; it, īce
hot, ōpen, ôrder; oil, out; cup, pút, rüle,
above, takən, pencəl, lemən, circəs

ch, child; ng, long; sh, ship
th, thin; ғн, then; zh, measure

in the way, being an obstacle, hindrance, etc.
in the way of, a in a favorable position for doing or getting: *He put
me in the way of a good investment.* b in the matter or business of;
as regards: *We have a small stock in the way of hats.*
lose (one's) **way,** not to know any longer where one is.
make (one's) **way,** a go: *They made their way through the bushes
to the road.* b get ahead; succeed: *He's sure to make his way in the
world.*
make way, a give space for passing or going ahead; make room.
b move forward.
once in a way, occasionally.
out of the way, a so as not to be an obstacle, hindrance, etc.: *If we
take the chair out of the way, we can move the couch to that wall.*
b far from where most people live or go; awkward to reach.
c unusual; strange. d finished; taken care of: *I'd like to get this job
out of the way first.* e out of reach; not in danger. f improper or
wrong. g mislaid, hidden, or lost.
put out of the way, put to death; kill or murder.
see (one's) **way,** be willing or able.
take (one's) **way,** go.
under way, going on; in motion; in progress: *The program is under
way.*
—*adv. Informal.* at or to a great distance; far: *The cloud of smoke
stretched way out to the pier.* [OE *weg*]
☛ *Hom.* weigh, whey.
☛ *Syn. n.* **1, 2. Way, method, manner** = a mode or means of doing or
happening. **Way** is the common and general word, sometimes general in
meaning, sometimes suggesting a very personal or special manner or method:
The way in which she spoke hurt me. **Method** applies to an orderly way of
doing something, and suggests a definite arrangement of steps or a special
system: *Follow her method of cooking.* **Manner** applies to a characteristic or
individual method or particular way of acting or happening: *He rides in the
western manner.*
☛ *Usage.* **Way, ways. Way,** meaning distance (def. 6), is standard; **ways** is
non-standard: *a long way* (not *ways*) *off.*

way·bill (wā′bil′) *n.* a paper listing the goods in a shipment and
stating where the goods are to be shipped, by what route, and the
cost involved. The waybill is sent with the shipment.

way·far·er (wā′fer′ər) *n.* a traveller, especially one who travels
on foot.

way·far·ing (wā′fer′ing) *adj.* travelling, especially on foot.

way·laid (wā′lād′ *or* wā′lād′) *v.* pt. and pp. of waylay.

Wayland the Smith in Germanic and English legend, a
marvellously skilled smith who was normally invisible but became
visible under certain circumstances.

way·lay (wā′lā′ *or* wā′lā′) *v.* **-laid, -lay·ing. 1** lie in wait for and
attack; ambush: *Robin Hood waylaid and robbed rich travellers.*
2 stop (a person) on his way. [< *way* + *lay, v.,* after MLG or MDu.
wegelagen] —**way′lay′er,** *n.*

way–out (wā′out′) *adj. Slang.* far away from the ordinary; very
unconventional or experimental: *His clothes are way-out.*

–ways *suffix.* in a particular direction, position, or manner, as in
edgeways, sideways. [< *way*]

ways and means the resources, methods, etc. available to
accomplish a particular purpose: *The plan seemed attractive but the
committee still had to consider ways and means.*

way·side (wā′sīd′) *n., adj.* —*n.* the edge of a road or path.
—*adj.* along the edge of a road or path.

way station 1 a station between main stations on a railway, etc.
2 any stopping place along a route.

way train a railway train that stops at all or most of the stations
on its way.

way·ward (wā′wərd) *adj.* **1** tending to go against the advice,
wishes, or orders of others; wrong-headed; willful. **2** irregular;
unpredictable. [ME *weiward,* < *aweiward* turned away]
—**way′ward·ly,** *adv.* —**way′ward·ness,** *n.*

way·worn (wā′wôrn′) *adj.* wearied by travelling.

W.B. or **w.b.** way bill.

W.C. or **w.c.** *Brit. Informal.* water closet.

W.C. or **W/C** wing commander.

WCTU or **W.C.T.U.** Woman's Christian Temperance Union.

we (wē) *pron.pl., subj.* **we,** *obj.* **us,** *poss.* **ours. 1** the speaker or
writer plus the person or persons spoken or written to or about: *We*

are going to a movie; would you like to come? Bring your swimsuit so we can go to the pool. **2** the speaker or writer, thinking of himself as in a formal or official role. An author, a sovereign, a judge, or a newspaper editor sometimes uses *we* when others would say *I*. **3** people in general, including the speaker; one (def. 2); you (def. 2): *We need some starch in our diet.* [OE *we*]
☛ *Hom.* **wee.**

weak (wēk) *adj.* **1** lacking physical strength or health: *She is still weak from her illness. He realized he was too weak to move the rock.* **2** resulting from or showing lack of normal strength or health: *weak eyes. He spoke in a weak voice. She gave the door a weak push.* **3** that can too easily be broken, crushed, torn, overcome, etc.; inadequate, defective, etc.: *weak defences, a weak link in a chain, weak faith. The building collapsed because the foundation was weak.* **4** lacking authority, force, or power: *a weak government, a weak argument.* **5** lacking mental power: *a weak mind.* **6** lacking moral strength or firmness; not able to resist persuasion or temptation: *a weak character.* **7** containing less of the active ingredient or ingredients than is usual or desired: *a weak solution of boric acid. The tea is too weak.* **8** less strong or potent than is usual or normal: *a weak strain of a virus.* **9** lacking skill or aptitude: *The weaker students were given extra help in the subject.* **10** designating an aspect, field, etc. in which a person lacks skill or aptitude: *My weakest subject is history.* **11** lacking or poor in a particular thing: *The composition was weak in spelling, but otherwise quite good.* **12** *Business.* of prices on an exchange, etc.: **a** having a downward tendency; not firm. **b** characterized by a fluctuating or downward tendency: *a weak market.* **13** *Grammar.* **a** of verbs, inflected by the addition of consonants to the stem, not by an internal vowel change, as in the Germanic languages. English weak verbs form the past tense and past participle by adding *-ed, -d,* or *-t.* **b** of nouns and adjectives, having a majority of inflected endings with *-n,* as German *alten* and *Frauen* in *die alten Frauen.* **14** *Phonetics.* **a** of a syllable, not stressed. **b** of a stress, light; not strong. [ME < ON *veikr*]
☛ *Hom.* **week.**

weak·en (wē′kən) *v.* **1** make weak or weaker: *You can weaken tea by adding water. The new evidence weakened the case against him.* **2** become weak or weaker: *The patient was gradually weakening.* **3** take a less firm attitude; begin to give way: *He weakened when the child began to cry.* —**weak′en·er,** *n.*

weak·fish (wēk′fish′) *n., pl.* **-fish** or **-fish·es.** any of various spiny-finned marine fishes (family Sciaenidae) named for their weak mouths with easily torn flesh, especially a food and game fish (*Cynoscion regalis*) of the Atlantic coast of the United States. See also **sea trout.**

weak–kneed (wēk′nēd′) *adj.* lacking determination or resolution; giving in easily to opposition, intimidation, etc.

weak·ling (wēk′ling) *n.* a weak person or animal. [< *weak* + *-ling*]

weak·ly (wēk′lē) *adv., adj.* **-li·er, -li·est.** —*adv.* in a weak manner. —*adj.* weak; feeble; sickly. —**weak′li·ness,** *n.*

weak–mind·ed (wēk′mīn′did) *adj.* **1** having or showing little intelligence; feeble-minded. **2** lacking firmness of mind. —**weak′-mind′ed·ness,** *n.*

weak·ness (wēk′nis) *n.* **1** the condition of being weak; lack of power, force, or vigor. **2** a weak point; fault. **3** fondness: *She has a weakness for chocolate.*

weak stress *Phonetics.* the third in a series of three degrees of stress, the most prominent being primary, the next secondary. The last syllable of *opportunity* has a weak stress. Such stresses are not marked in this dictionary.

weal[1] (wēl) *n. Archaic.* well-being; prosperity; happiness: *Good citizens act for the public weal.* [OE *wela*]
☛ *Hom.* **we'll, wheal, wheel.**

weal[2] (wēl) *n.* a streak or ridge on the skin made by a stick or whip; welt. [var. of *wale*]
☛ *Hom.* **we'll wheal, wheel.**

weald (wēld) *n.* **1** *Archaic or poetic.* country or wilderness, either open or forested. **2 the Weald,** a district in SE England including parts of Kent, Surrey, and Sussex, formerly forested. [OE *weald* woods]

wealth (welth) *n.* **1** much money or property; riches. **2** *Economics.* all things that have money value or that add to the capacity for production. **3** a large quantity; abundance: *a wealth of hair, a wealth of words.* [< *well*[1] or *weal*[1]]

wealth·y (wel′thē) *adj.* **wealth·i·er, wealth·i·est.** having much money or property; rich. —**wealth′i·ly,** *adv.* —**wealth′i·ness,** *n.*
☛ *Syn.* See note at **rich.**

wean (wēn) *v.* **1** accustom (a child or young animal) to food other than its mother's milk. **2** accustom (a person) to do without something; cause to turn away: *The young delinquent was sent away to wean him from his bad companions.* [OE *wenian*]
☛ *Hom.* **ween.**

wean·ling (wēn′ling) *n., adj.* —*n.* a child or animal recently weaned. —*adj.* recently weaned.

weap·on (wep′ən) *n.* **1** any instrument or device designed or used to injure or kill, such as a sword, gun, bomb, club, or knife: *weapons of war. The murder weapon was a rock.* **2** an organ or part of an animal or plant used for fighting or protection, such as claws, horns, teeth, or stings. **3** a procedure or means used to get the better of an opponent: *Drugs are used as weapons against disease.* [OE *wæpen*] —**weap′on·less,** *adj.*

weap·on·ry (wep′ən rē) *n.* **1** weapons collectively. **2** the design and production of weapons.

wear (wer) *v.* **wore, worn, wear·ing;** *n.* —*v.* **1** have or carry on the body as clothing, adornment, etc.: *He always wears a suit to work. She was wearing pearls. He wore a sword.* **2** have habitually as part of one's person: *He wears a beard. I used to wear my hair long.* **3** carry on the body to assist or replace a natural part or organ: *He wears a hearing aid. She wore a brace on her leg.* **4** show as part of one's appearance: *wearing a grin. The old house wore an air of sadness.* **5** have as a quality or attribute; bear: *to wear one's honors modestly.* **6** of a ship, fly (a flag or colors). **7** change, make less, or damage by constant handling, using, rubbing, etc.: *These shoes are badly worn. Water had worn the stones smooth. The mountains were worn down by glacial action.* **8** suffer damage or deterioration from constant handling, using, rubbing, etc. (*often used with* **away** *or* **down**): *The cuffs of the shirt are starting to wear at the edges.* **9** produce gradually by rubbing, scraping, washing away, etc.: *I wore a hole in my shoe.* **10** tire; exhaust (*often used with* **out**): *The job was extremely wearing. A visit with him always wears me out.* **11** endure being used; last under use: *This coat has worn well. The shoes are beautiful but they won't wear.* **12** stand the test of experience, familiarity, criticism, etc.: *a friendship that did not wear.* **13** of time, pass or go gradually: *It grew hotter as the day wore on.* **14** pass time gradually (*used with* **away** *or* **out**): *to wear one's life away in regrets.* **15** hold the rank or office symbolized by (an ornament or article of dress): *"Uneasy lies the head that wears a crown." Who wears the pants in this family?* **16** of a ship, turn or be turned so that the bow is pointing away from the wind.
wear down, overcome by persistent effort: *He tried to wear his parents down by asking again and again why he couldn't go.*
wear off, become less: *As the freezing wore off, my tooth started to ache.*
wear out, a wear until no longer fit for use; make useless by long or hard wear: *She wore the shoes out in six months.* **b** become useless from long or hard wear: *I don't think this coat will ever wear out.*
wear thin, a become weak from being used too much: *My patience was wearing thin.* **b** become tiresome and unconvincing because of repetition: *That excuse of his is wearing thin.*
—*n.* **1** the act of wearing or the state of being worn: *clothing for summer wear.* **2** things worn or to be worn; clothing: *children's wear. Casual wear is sold on the second floor.* **3** damage or deterioration due to use: *The rug showed signs of wear.* **4** capacity for resisting deterioration and damage through use; lasting quality: *The shoes still have lots of wear in them.* [OE *werian*]
—**wear′a·ble,** *adj.* —**wear′er,** *n.*
☛ *Hom.* **ware, where.**

wear and tear damage or deterioration as a result of ordinary use over a period of time.

wea·ri·ness (wēr′ē nis) *n.* the quality or state of being weary.

wearing apparel clothes.

wea·ri·some (wēr′ē səm) *adj.* wearying; tiring; tiresome. —**wea′ri·some·ly,** *adv.* —**wea′ri·some·ness,** *n.*

wea·ry (wēr′ē) *adj.* **-ri·er, -ri·est;** *v.* **-ried, -ry·ing.** —*adj.* **1** tired: *weary feet. We were all weary after the long ride.* **2** causing tiredness; tiring: *a weary wait.* **3** having one's patience, liking, or tolerance exhausted (*used with* **of**): *She was weary of his stupid jokes.* **4** showing weariness: *a weary smile.*
—*v.* make or become weary. [OE *wērig*] —**wea′ri·ly,** *adv.*
☛ *Syn. adj.* **1.** See note at **tired.**

wea·sand (wē′zənd) *n. Archaic or dialect.* **1** windpipe. **2** throat. [OE *wǣsend*]

wea·sel (wē′zəl) *n., v.* **-selled** or **-seled, -sel·ling** or **-sel·ing.** —*n.* **1** any of several small, carnivorous mammals (genus *Mustela*) having a long, slender body, a long, flexible neck, short legs, and short, thick fur that is mainly reddish brown above and creamy below. Northern weasels turn white in winter. **2** (*adj.*) designating a family (Mustelidae) of carnivorous mammals that includes the weasels, minks, and otters. The weasel family is found throughout the world. **3** a sly and sneaky person.
—*v.* **1** use misleading or ambiguous words to avoid committing oneself or making a direct statement: *Stop weaselling and give me a straight answer.* **2** escape from or evade in a crafty way; get out of

a situation or obligation (*used with* **out**): *She had promised to help but weaselled out at the last minute.* [OE *weosule*]

weath·er (weᴛн′ər) *n., v.* —*n.* **1** the condition of the atmosphere at a particular time and place with respect to temperature, moisture, cloudiness, or windiness: *windy weather. The weather was beautiful for the entire trip.* **2** disagreeable conditions of the atmosphere, such as wind, rain, storm, or cold; bad weather: *a shelter for protection against the weather.* **3** (*adj.*) of or designating the side of a ship toward the wind; windward.

under the weather, *Informal.* **a** somewhat sick; ailing: *He's been feeling under the weather for several days.* **b** slightly drunk.

—*v.* **1** expose to the weather; subject to the action of sun, rain, frost, etc.: *Wood turns grey if weathered for a long time.* **2** become discolored or worn by air, rain, sun, frost, etc. **3** pass safely through (bad weather or a difficult time): *The ship weathered the storm.* **4** *Nautical.* sail to the windward of: *The ship weathered the cape.* **5** make (boards, tiles, etc.) overlap and slope downward so as to shed water. **6** resist the effects of the weather: *This paint weathers well.* [OE *weder*]

☛ *Hom.* **wether, whether.**

weather beam the side of a ship toward the wind.

weath·er–beat·en (weᴛн′ər bēt′ən) *adj.* worn or hardened by the wind, rain, and other forces of the weather.

weath·er·board (weᴛн′ər bôrd′) *n., v.* —*n.* **1** clapboard; siding. **2** the side of a ship toward the wind; weather beam. —*v.* cover with weatherboards.

weath·er–bound (weᴛн′ər bound′) *adj.* delayed by bad weather: *a weather-bound ship.*

weather breeder a fine clear day, popularly supposed to be a sign of a coming storm.

weath·er·cock (weᴛн′ər kok′) *n.* a weather vane, especially one in the shape of a rooster.

weather eye **1** the vision or watchful look of a person alert to signs of change in the weather. **2** a close watch for expected change of any kind: *The news media were keeping a weather eye on the labor situation.*

weath·er·glass (weᴛн′ər glas′) *n.* any of various instruments that measure atmospheric changes, especially a barometer.

weath·er·ing (weᴛн′ər ing) *n.* the destructive or discoloring action of air, water, frost, etc., especially on rocks.

weath·er·man (weᴛн′ər man′) *n., pl.* **-men.** *Informal.* **1** a person who forecasts the weather, especially a meteorologist. **2** a person who reports weather conditions and forecasts on radio or television.

weath·er·proof (weᴛн′ər prüf′) *adj., v.* —*adj.* protected against rain, snow, or wind; able to stand exposure to all kinds of weather. —*v.* make weatherproof.

weather strip a narrow strip to fill or cover the space between a door or window and the casing, so as to keep out rain, snow, and wind.

weath·er–strip (weᴛн′ər strip′) *v.* **-stripped, -strip·ping.** fit with weather strips.

weather stripping **1** a weather strip. **2** weather strips.

weather vane a device for showing the direction of the wind, consisting of a blade or a flat cutout figure mounted on a vertical axis in an exposed place, such as the peak of a roof or spire, so that it will turn with the wind.

weath·er–wise (weᴛн′ər wīz′) *adj.* skilful in forecasting the changes of the weather.

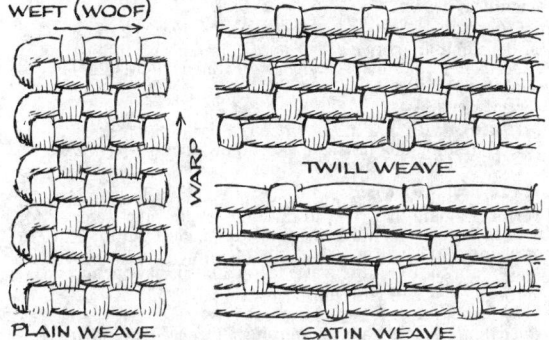

The three basic weaves for cloth

weave (wēv) *v.* **wove** or (rare) **weaved, wo·ven** or **wove, weav·ing;** *n.* —*v.* **1** form (threads or strips) into a texture or fabric; interlace.

---

hat, āge, fär; let, ēqual, tèrm; it, īce
hot, ōpen, ôrder; oil, out; cup, pùt, rüle,
əbove, takən, pencəl, lemən, circəs

ch, child; ng, long; sh, ship
th, thin; ᴛн, then; zh, measure

People weave thread into cloth, straw into hats, reeds into baskets. **2** make out of thread, etc.: *She is weaving a rug.* **3** work with a loom. **4** combine into a whole: *The author wove three plots together into one story.* **5** make by combining parts: *The author wove a story from three plots.* **6** make with care. **7** go or proceed by twisting and turning.

weave (one's) **way,** make one's way by twisting and turning.

—*n.* a method or pattern of weaving: *Homespun is a cloth of coarse weave.* [OE *wefan*]

☛ *Hom.* **we've.**

☛ *Usage.* **Woven, wove. Woven** is the regular past participle. **Wove** is now chiefly used in certain technical terms, such as *wire-wove* and *wove paper.*

weav·er (wē′vər) *n.* **1** a person who weaves, especially one whose work it is. **2** weaverbird.

weav·er·bird (wē′vər bèrd′) *n.* any of a family (Ploceidae) of Old World, seed-eating birds resembling finches, named for the elaborate woven nests made by many species.

web (web) *n., v.* **web·bed, web·bing.** —*n.* **1** a woven length of fabric, especially while on the loom or as it comes off the loom. **2** a cobweb or something similar produced by any of various insects. **3** any complicated network especially one that entangles like a cobweb: *a web of lies.* **4** the skin joining the toes of swimming birds and animals. **5** the vane of a feather. **6** a thin metal sheet or plate. **7** connective tissue. **8** a continuous sheet of paper as it is being manufactured or as it emerges from the paper machine. After the water is pressed out of the web, it enters the drying section. **9** an uncut roll of paper, especially newsprint, for use in rotary presses. **10** *Cdn.* snowshoe.

—*v.* **1** provide or cover with a web. **2** trap or entwine in a web. [OE *webb*] —**web′like′,** *adj.*

webbed (webd) *adj.* **1** formed like a web or with a web. **2** having the toes joined by a web. *Ducks have webbed feet.*

web·bing (web′ing) *n.* **1** cloth woven into strong strips, used in upholstery or for belts. **2** the plain foundation fabric left for protection at the edge of some rugs, etc. **3** skin joining the toes, as in a duck's feet.

web·foot (web′füt′) *n., pl.* **-feet. 1** a foot in which the toes are joined by a web. **2** a bird or animal having webfeet.

web–foot·ed (web′füt′id) *adj.* having the toes joined by a web.

web·toed (web′tōd′) *adj.* web-footed.

wed (wed) *v.* **wed·ded, wed·ded** or **wed, wed·ding. 1** marry. **2** unite. **3** be obstinately attached to (an opinion, one's own will, a habit, a faction, etc.). [OE *weddian*]

we'd (wēd; *unstressed,* wid) **1** we had. **2** we should; we would.

☛ *Hom.* **weed.**

Wed. Wednesday.

wed·ded (wed′id) *adj.* **1** married. **2** united. **3** devoted.

wed·ding (wed′ing) *n.* **1** the marriage ceremony. **2** an anniversary of the day of marriage, especially any of several specific anniversaries, such as the 25th (silver wedding) or the 50th (golden wedding). **3** a joining or uniting: *His writing shows a remarkable wedding of thought and language.* [OE *weddung*]

☛ *Syn.* **1.** See note at **marriage.**

Wedges being used to raise a support post

wedge (wej) *n., v.* **wedged, wedg·ing.** —*n.* **1** a piece of wood or metal with a tapering thin edge, used in splitting, separating, etc. **2** something shaped like a wedge: *He cut the big pie into ten wedges.* **3** something used like a wedge to make an opening or opportunity: *Her grand party was a wedge for her entry into society.* **4** *Golf.* a club used for high, short shots, lofting the ball out of traps, heavy grass, etc.

—*v.* **1** split or separate with a wedge. **2** fasten or tighten with a wedge. **3** thrust or pack in tightly; squeeze: *He wedged himself through the narrow window.* **4** force a way. [OE *wecg*]

Wedg·wood (wej′wùd) *n.* **1** a kind of fine, unglazed pottery having a raised, decorative design of white Greek and Roman models against a tinted ground. **2** a kind of fine china. **3** something made of either the pottery or the china. [after Josiah *Wedgwood* (1730-1795), an English potter, who originated it]

wed·lock (wed′lok) *n.* married life; marriage. [OE *wedlāc* pledge < *wedd* pledge + -*lāc*, noun suffix denoting activity]

Wednes·day (wenz′dē *or* wenz′dā) *n.* the fourth day of the week, following Tuesday. [OE *Wōdnes dæg* Woden's day; translation of LL *Mercurii dies* day of Mercury]

wee (wē) *adj.* **we·er, we·est.** very small; tiny. [from the phrase *a little wee* a little bit, OE *wǣg* weight]
☛ Hom. **we.**

weed¹ (wēd) *n., v.* —*n.* **1** a wild plant growing where it is not wanted, as in grainfields, gardens, lawns, pastures, etc., especially one that grows fast and is hard to get rid of. Russian thistle, milkweed, ragweed, and wild mustard are common weeds. **2** something useless, especially a horse unfit for racing or breeding. **3** *Informal.* a cigarette or cigar. **4** *Informal.* a marijuana cigarette. **5 the weed,** *Informal.* tobacco or marijuana.
—*v.* **1** take weeds out of: *to weed a garden.* **2** take out weeds: *I spent all morning weeding.* **3** remove or discard as not wanted (*usually used with* **out**): *The weak players were weeded out before the regular season began.* [OE *wēod*] —**weed′like′,** *adj.*
☛ Hom. **we'd.**

weed² (wēd) *n.* **1 weeds,** *pl.* mourning garments: *a widow's weeds.* **2** *Archaic.* garment. [OE *wǣd*]
☛ Hom. **we'd.**

weed·er (wē′dər) *n.* **1** a person who weeds. **2** a tool or machine for digging up weeds.

weed·y (wē′dē) *adj.* **weed·i·er, weed·i·est. 1** full of weeds: *a weedy garden.* **2** of or like a weed or weeds, especially in fast and vigorous growth. **3** thin and lanky: *a tall and weedy youth.* —**weed′i·ly,** *adv.* —**weed′i·ness,** *n.*

wee hours the hours after midnight; the early morning hours.

week (wēk) *n.* **1** seven days, one after another. **2** the time from Sunday through Saturday. **3** the working days of a seven-day period. A school week is five days.
Monday (or **Tuesday,** etc.) **week,** the Monday one week from this Monday (or Tuesday, etc.).
this day week, one week from today.
week in, week out, week after week. [OE *wice*]
☛ Hom. **weak.**

week·day (wēk′dā′) *n.* **1** any day except Sunday. **2** any day except Saturday or Sunday. **3** (*adj.*) of or on a weekday.

week·end (wēk′end′) *n., v.* —*n.* **1** Saturday and Sunday as a time for recreation, visiting, etc.; the time between the end of one week of work or school and the beginning of the next: *a weekend in the country, Thanksgiving weekend.* **2** (*adj.*) of or on a weekend.
—*v.* spend a weekend: *They are weekending at their cottage.*

week·ly (wēk′lē) *adj., adv., n., pl.* **-lies.** —*adj.* **1** of a week; for a week; lasting a week: *His weekly wage is $160.* **2** done or happening once a week: *a weekly letter home.*
—*adv.* once each week; every week.
—*n.* a newspaper or magazine published once a week.

ween (wēn) *v. Archaic.* think; suppose; believe; expect. [OE *wēnan*]
☛ Hom. **wean.**

weep (wēp) *v.* **wept, weep·ing;** *n.* —*v.* **1** shed tears; cry. **2** shed tears for; mourn. **3** spend in crying: *weep one's life away.* **4** let fall in drops; shed: *They wept bitter tears.* **5** give off moisture in drops; ooze or drip: *That basement wall sometimes weeps.* —*n.* a period or fit of weeping. [OE *wēpan*]

weep·er (wē′pər) *n.* **1** a person who weeps. **2** a person hired to weep at funerals; professional mourner.

weep·ing (wē′ping) *adj.* **1** that weeps. **2** having thin, drooping branches: *a weeping willow.*

weeping birch silver birch (def. 1).

weeping willow a large willow (*Salix babylonica*) native to E Asia, having long, feathery drooping branches. Weeping willows are often planted as ornamental trees.

wee·vil (wē′vəl) *n.* **1** any of a family (Curculionidae) of beetles having an elongated, usually downward-curving, snout, called a rostrum. Many weevils are serious agricultural pests, feeding on fruit, nuts, and grains, as well as on living plants. **2** any of various

other similar beetles, as of the family Bruchidae. [OE *wifel*]

wee·vil·ly or **wee·vil·y** (wē′vəl ē) *adj.* infested with weevils.

weft (weft) *n.* the threads running from side to side across a woven fabric; woof. See **weave** for picture. [OE *weft < wefan* weave]

weigh (wā) *v.* **1** determine the mass of by means of scales or a balance: *I weighed myself this morning.* **2** have as a measure of mass: *I weigh 45 kilograms.* **3** measure (a quantity of something) by mass (*usually used with* **out**): *The grocer weighed out two kilograms of potatoes.* **4** find how heavy a thing is at a certain altitude. **5** have as a measure by weight (def. 2): *Things weigh much less on the moon than on earth.* **6** balance in the mind; consider carefully: *He weighed his words before speaking.* **7** have importance or influence: *The amount of his salary does not weigh with Mr. Black at all, because he is very rich.* **8** bear down: *The mistake weighed heavily upon his mind.* **9** *Nautical.* **a** lift up (an anchor). **b** lift anchor.
weigh down, bend by weight; burden: *The boughs of the apple tree are weighed down with fruit. She is weighed down with many troubles.*
weigh in, find out one's weight before a contest.
weigh on, be a burden to.
[OE *wegan*] —**weigh′er,** *n.*
☛ Hom. **way, whey.**
☛ *Syn.* **4.** See note at **consider.**

weigh·mas·ter (wā′mas′tər) *n.* **1** an official in charge of public weighing scales. **2** a worker in charge of registering by weight the amount of a commodity produced, mined, etc.

weight (wāt) *n., v.* —*n.* **1** mass (def. 6): *The dog's weight is 20 kilograms.* **2** a piece of metal having a particular mass, used to weigh (def. 1) something on a balance: *a fifty-gram weight.* **3** how heavy a thing is; the quality of anything that makes it tend toward the centre of the earth: *Gas has hardly any weight at all. Your weight is a little less on a mountain than at sea level.* **4** a system of units for expressing mass: *avoirdupois weight, troy weight.* **5** a unit of such a system. **6** a quantity that has a certain mass: *a weight of gold dust.* **7** a heavy thing or mass: *A weight keeps the papers in place.* **8** a load or burden: *a weight of care.* Pillars support the weight of the roof. **9** influence or importance: *What he says carries a lot of weight around here.* **10** preponderant portion: *The weight of public opinion was against it.* **11** the relative heaviness of an article of clothing appropriate to the season's weather: *summer weight.* **12** *Statistics.* **a** a number assigned to an item in a statistical compilation, as in a cost-of-living index, to make its effect on the compilation reflect its importance. **b** the frequency of an item in a statistical compilation. **13** *Sports.* a metal ball thrown, pushed, or lifted in contests of strength.
by weight, measured by weighing.
pull (one's) weight, do one's part or share.
throw (one's) weight around or **about,** *Informal.* make too much use of one's rank or position; assert one's importance improperly or excessively.
—*v.* **1** load down; burden. **2** add weight to; put weight on: *The scales are weighted too heavily.* **3** attach importance or value to. **4** load (cloth or thread) with mineral to make it seem of better quality: *weighted silk.* **5** *Statistics.* give a weight to: *a weighted average.* **6** *Skiing.* direct all or most of the downward thrust onto: *to weight the left ski.* [OE *wiht < wegan* weigh]
☛ Hom. **wait.**

weight–arm (wāt′ärm′) *n.* in a lever, the distance from the weight to the fulcrum.

weight·less (wāt′lis) *adj.* **1** appearing to have no weight: *The snow was weightless on my shoulders.* **2** being free from the pull of gravity: *In outer space, all things are weightless.* —**weight·less·ly,** *adv.* —**weight·less·ness,** *n.*

weight·y (wā′tē) *adj.* **weight·i·er, weight·i·est. 1** heavy. **2** too heavy; burdensome: *weighty cares of state.* **3** important; influential: *a weighty speaker.* **4** convincing: *weighty arguments.* —**weight′i·ly,** *adv.* —**weight′i·ness,** *n.*
☛ *Syn.* **1.** See note at **heavy.**

Wei·ma·ra·ner (vī′mə rä′nər *or* wī′mə rä′nər) *n.* a breed of medium-sized hunting dog having a short, grey coat. [< *Weimar*, a city in Germany, where the breed was developed]

wei·ner (wē′nər) See **wiener.**

weir (wer) *n.* **1** a dam in a river to raise the level of the water or to divert its flow. **2** a fence of stakes or broken branches put in a stream or channel to catch fish. **3** an obstruction erected across a channel or stream to divert the water through a special opening in order to measure the rate of flow. [OE *wer*]
☛ Hom. **we're.**

weird (wērd) *adj.* **1** unearthly; mysterious: *They were awakened by a weird shriek.* **2** *Informal.* odd; fantastic; queer: *The shadows made weird figures on the wall.* **3** *Archaic or Scottish.* having to do with fate or destiny. [OE *wyrd* fate] —**weird′ly,** *adv.* —**weird′ness,** *n.*
☛ *Syn.* **1.** Weird, eerie, uncanny = mysteriously or frighteningly strange. **Weird**

describes something that seems not of this world or that is caused by something above or beyond nature: *All night weird cries came from the jungle.* **Eerie** suggests the frightening effect of something weird or ghostly or vaguely and evilly mysterious: *The light from the single candle made eerie shadows in the cave.* **Uncanny** suggests a strangeness that is disturbing because it seems unnatural: *I had an uncanny feeling that eyes were peering from the darkness.*

weird·o (wēr′dō′) *n. Slang.* a very odd or eccentric person; a person who is very strange or unconventional in appearance or behavior.

Weird Sisters 1 the Fates. 2 the witches in Shakespeare's *Macbeth.*

welch (welch *or* welsh) *v.* welsh.

wel·come (wel′kəm) *v.* **-comed, -com·ing;** *n., adj., interj.* —*v.* 1 greet in a friendly and kindly way: *to welcome a guest.* 2 receive gladly: *We welcome new ideas and suggestions.*
—*n.* a friendly and kindly reception. *You will always have a welcome here.*
wear out (one's) **welcome,** visit a person too often or too long.
—*adj.* 1 gladly received; pleasing: *a welcome visitor, a welcome letter, a welcome rest.* 2 gladly or freely permitted: *You are welcome to pick the flowers.* 3 as a reply to thanks, free to have or do something, to enjoy some favor, etc.: *You are quite welcome.*
—*interj.* an exclamation of friendly greeting: *Welcome!* [original meaning "agreeable guest," OE *wilcuma* < *wil-* (related to *will* pleasure) + *cuma* comer] —**wel′com·er,** *n.*

welcome mat 1 doormat. 2 *Informal.* any enthusiastic reception or welcome.

weld (weld) *v., n.* —*v.* 1 join together (metal, plastic, etc.) by hammering or pressing while hot and soft: *He welded the broken metal rod.* 2 unite closely: *Working together for a month welded them into a strong team.* 3 be welded or be capable of being welded: *Some metals weld better than others.*
—*n.* 1 a welded joint. 2 a welding. [< *well²,* v.] —**weld′er,** *n.*

wel·fare (wel′fer′) *n.* 1 health, happiness, and prosperity; a condition of being or doing well: *Uncle Charles asked about the welfare of everyone in our family.* 2 welfare work.
on welfare, receiving benefits from the government or from some organization to provide a basic standard of living: *There was no harvest and many families were on welfare.*
[ME *wel fare* < *wel* well < *fare* go]

welfare state a state whose government provides for the welfare of its citizens through old-age pensions, unemployment insurance, medical treatment, etc.

welfare work work done to improve the lives and living conditions of people who need help because of poverty, sickness, family problems, etc. Welfare work is carried on by governments, private organizations, and sometimes individuals.

welfare worker a person who does welfare work.

wel·kin (wel′kən) *n. Archaic.* the sky: *The welkin rang with the men's shouts.* [OE *wolcen* cloud]

well¹ (wel) *adv.* **bet·ter, best;** *adj., interj.* —*adv.* 1 in a satisfactory, favorable, or advantageous manner; all right: *The job was well done. Is everything going well at school?* 2 thoroughly; fully: *Shake well before using.* 3 to a considerable degree; much: *The fair brought in well over a hundred dollars.* 4 in detail; intimately: *He knows the subject well.* 5 easily or reasonably: *I couldn't very well refuse. You might well ask what he was doing there. They could well be here before dark.*
as well, a also; besides. **b** equally.
as well as, a in addition to; besides. **b** as much as.
—*adj.* 1 satisfactory; good; right: *It is well you came along.* 2 in good health: *I am very well.* 3 desirable; advisable: *It is always well to start a bit early.*
—*interj.* an expression used to show mild surprise, agreement, etc. or merely to fill in: *Well! Well! Here's Jack. Well, I'm not sure.* [OE *wel*]
☛ *Usage.* See note at **good.**

well² (wel) *n., v.* —*n.* 1 a hole dug or bored in the ground to get water, oil, gas, etc. 2 fountain or source: *Our class president is a well of ideas.* 3 something like a well in shape or use: *the well of a fountain pen.* 4 a shaft for light, or for stairs or an elevator, extending vertically through the floors of a building. 5 a compartment around the pumps on a ship. 6 a storage compartment for fish in the hold of a fishing boat, kept filled with water to keep the catch alive.
—*v.* spring; rise; gush: *Tears welled in her eyes.* [OE *wella,* n., *wiellan,* v.]

we'll (wēl; *unstressed,* wil) we shall; we will.
☛ *Hom.* **weal, wheal, wheel.**

well·a·day (wel′ə dā′) *interj. Archaic.* wellaway.

well-ad·just·ed (wel′ə jus′tid) *adj.* of persons, emotionally balanced and mature; able to cope with stress and change.

well-ad·vised (wel′əd vīzd′) *adj.* 1 proceeding with wisdom, care, or deliberation. 2 based on wise counsel or prudence.

hat, āge, fär; let, ēqual, tèrm; it, īce
hot, ōpen, ôrder; oil, out; cup, pút, rüle,
above, takən, pencəl, lemən, circəs

ch, child; ng, long; sh, ship
th, thin; ŦH, then; zh, measure

well-ap·point·ed (wel′ə poin′tid) *adj.* having good furnishings or equipment.

well-a·way (wel′ə wā′) *interj. Archaic.* alas!

well-bal·anced (wel′bal′ənst) *adj.* 1 rightly balanced, adjusted, or regulated. 2 sensible; sane.

well-be·haved (wel′bi hāvd′) *adj.* showing good manners or conduct.

well-be·ing (wel′bē′ing) *n.* health and happiness; welfare.

well-born (wel′bôrn′) *adj.* belonging to a good family.

well-bred (wel′bred′) *adj.* well brought up; having or showing good manners.

well-con·nect·ed (wel′kə nek′tid) *adj.* 1 of a well-known family; related to important or distinguished people. 2 put together well; carefully planned: *well-connected paragraphs.*

well-con·tent (wel′kən tent′) *adj.* highly pleased or satisfied.

well-de·fined (wel′di fīnd′) *adj.* clearly defined or indicated; distinct.

well-dis·posed (wel′dis pōzd′) *adj.* favorably or kindly disposed; having sympathetic or friendly feelings: *She was always well-disposed toward her nieces.*

well-do·ing (wel′dü′ing) *n.* the act of doing right; good conduct.

well-fa·vored or **well-fa·voured** (wel′fā′vərd) *adj.* of pleasing appearance; good-looking.

well-fed (wel′fed′) *adj.* showing the result of good feeding; fat; plump.

well-fixed (wel′fikst′) *adj. Informal.* well-to-do.

well-found (wel′found′) *adj.* supplied or equipped with what is needed.

well-found·ed (wel′foun′did) *adj.* rightly or justly founded: *a well-founded faith in discipline.*

well-groomed (wel′grümd′) *adj.* well cared for; neat and trim.

well-ground·ed (wel′groun′did) *adj.* 1 based on good reasons. 2 thoroughly instructed in the fundamental principles of a subject.

well-head (wel′hed′) *n.* 1 the source of a spring or stream. 2 source; fountainhead. 3 the top of a well or a structure built around it.

well-heeled (wel′hēld′) *adj. Slang.* prosperous; well-to-do.

well-in·formed (wel′in fôrmd′) *adj.* 1 having reliable or full information on a subject. 2 having information on a wide variety of subjects.

Wellington boot or **Wel·ling·ton** (wel′ing tən) *n.* 1 a very high leather boot that comes above the knee in front and is cut away behind. 2 a rubber boot coming nearly up to the knees. [worn by the first Duke of *Wellington* (1769-1852), a British general]

well-kept (wel′kept′) *adj.* well cared for; carefully tended.

well-knit (wel′nit′) *adj.* 1 firmly constructed or joined together; closely connected or linked. 2 of strong, supple build; well-built.

well-known (wel′nōn′) *adj.* fully or widely known.

well-man·nered (wel′man′ərd) *adj.* having or showing good manners; polite; courteous.

well-marked (wel′märkt′) *adj.* clearly marked or distinguished; distinct.

well-mean·ing (wel′mēn′ing) *adj.* 1 having good intentions. 2 proceeding from good intentions.

well-nigh (wel′nī′) *adv.* very nearly; almost.

well-off (wel′of′) *adj.* 1 in a good condition or position: *Your whole family is healthy, so you should consider yourself well-off.* 2 fairly rich; prosperous.

well-or·dered (wel′ôr′dərd) *adj.* ordered or arranged well; well-regulated.

well-placed (wel′plāst′) *adj.* 1 well aimed. 2 conveniently placed; accessible. 3 having a good official or social position.

well-pre·served (wel′pri zèrvd′) *adj.* showing few signs of age.

well-pro·por·tioned (wel′prə pôr′shənd) *adj.* having good or correct proportions; having a pleasing shape.

well-read (wel′red′) *adj.* having read much; knowing a great deal about books and literature.

Wells·i·an (wel′zē ən) *adj.* **1** of or having to do with H.G. (Herbert George) Wells (1866-1946), an English novelist and writer. **2** of or suggestive of his writings.

well–spo·ken (wel′spō′kən) *adj.* **1** speaking well, fittingly, or pleasingly; polite in speech. **2** spoken well.

well·spring (wel′spring) *n.* **1** fountainhead. **2** a source, especially of a supply that never fails.

well–suit·ed (wel′sü′tid) *adj.* suitable; convenient.

well sweep a device used to draw water from a well, consisting of a pole attached to a pivot and having a bucket at one end.

well–timed (wel′tīmd′) *adj.* timely.

well–to–do (wel′tə dü′) *adj.* having enough money to live well; prosperous.

well–turned (wel′tėrnd′) *adj.* **1** well shaped or rounded expertly. **2** gracefully or elegantly expressed: *a well-turned phrase.*

well–turned–out (wel′tėrnd′out′) *adj.* elegantly or fashionably dressed.

well–wish·er (wel′wish′ər) *n.* a person who wishes well to a person, cause, etc.

well–worn (wel′wôrn′) *adj.* **1** much worn by use. **2** used too much; trite; stale.

welsh (welsh) *v. Slang.* **1** cheat by failing to pay a bet. **2** evade the fulfilment of an obligation.
welsh on, fail to keep an agreement with. Also, **welch.**
[origin uncertain] —**welsh′er,** *n.*

Welsh (welsh *or* welch) *n., adj.* —*n.* **1 the Welsh,** *pl.* the people of Wales, a division of Great Britain. **2** the Celtic language of Wales. —*adj.* of or having to do with Wales,·its people, or their Celtic language. [OE *Welisc* < *wealh* stranger (a non-Saxon)]

Welsh·man (welsh′mən *or* welch′mən) *n., pl.* **-men. 1** a native or inhabitant of Wales. **2** a person of Welsh descent.

Welsh rabbit a mixture containing cheese, cooked and served on toast.

Welsh rarebit Welsh rabbit.

Welsh·wom·an (welsh′wum′ən) *n., pl.* **-wom·en. 1** a woman who is a native or inhabitant of Wales. **2** a woman of Welsh descent.

welt (welt) *n., v.* —*n.* **1** a strip of leather between the upper part and the sole of a shoe. **2** the narrow border, trimming, etc. on the edge of a garment or upholstery. **3** a seam similar to a flat fell seam, used in tailoring. **4** a streak or ridge made on the skin by a blow, especially from a stick or whip. **5** a heavy blow.
—*v.* **1** put a welt on. **2** *Informal.* beat severely. [ME *welte, walte*]

Welt·an·schau·ung (velt′än′shou′ùng) *n. German.* a mental scheme or conception of life, history, reality, etc.; one's way of looking at the world; literally, world view.

Welt·an·sicht (velt′än′zint) *n. German.* a special interpretation of reality; literally, world view.

wel·ter (wel′tər) *v., n.* —*v.* **1** roll or toss about; wallow. **2** lie soaked in some liquid; be drenched. —*n.* **1** a surging or confused mass: *The fighting children were a welter of arms and legs.*
2 confusion; commotion. [< MDu. and MLG *welteren*]

wel·ter·weight (wel′tər wāt′) *n.* a boxer weighing between 63.5 and 67 kilograms. [earlier *welter*, literally, beater (ult. < *welt*) + *weight*]

wen (wen) *n.* a harmless tumor of the skin. [OE *wenn*]

wench (wench) *n., v.* —*n.* **1** a girl or young woman. **2** *Archaic.* a female servant. —*v.* seek out and consort with wenches. [< *wenchel* child, OE *wencel*]

wend (wend) *v.* **wend·ed** *or* (archaic) **went, wend·ing. 1** direct (one's way): *We wended our way home.* **2** go. [OE *wendan*]

Wend (wend) *n.* a member of a Slavic people living in central Germany. [< G. *Wende*]

wen·di·go (wen′di gō′) *n., pl.* **-gos** for l; **-go** *or* **-gos** for 2. *Cdn.* **1** *Algonquian mythology.* an evil spirit of a cannibalistic nature. Also, **windigo. 2** a hybrid trout; splake. [< Algonquian (Ojibway) *weendigo* cannibal]

went (went) *v.* pt. of **go.** [originally pt. of *wend*]

wept (wept) *v.* pt. and pp. of **weep.**

were (wėr; *unstressed,* wər) *v.* **1** pl. and 2nd pers. sing., past indicative, of **be:** *The officers were obeyed by the soldiers.*
2 subjunctive of **be:** *If I were rich, I would travel.*
as it were, as if it were; so to speak.
[OE *wǣron*]
☞ *Hom.* **whir.**

☞ *Usage.* **Were.** For subjunctive uses, in expressing wishes not yet realized, conditions that are merely hypothetical, etc., **were** is used with all persons irrespective of number and tense: *I wish it were warmer. She looked as though she were ill.*

we're (wėr) we are.
☞ *Hom.* **weir.**

weren't (wėrnt *or* wernt) were not.

were·wolf (wėr′wúlf *or* wer′wúlf′) *n., pl.* **-wolves** (-wúlvz′). *Folklore.* a person, especially a man or boy, who has been changed into a wolf or who can change himself into a wolf, while retaining human intelligence. [OE *werwulf* < *wer* man + *wulf* wolf]

wert (wėrt *or* wert; *unstressed,* wərt) *v. Archaic.* 2nd pers. sing. past tense of **be.** *Thou wert* means *you* (sing.) *were.*

wer·wolf (wėr′wúlf *or* wer′wúlf′) See **werewolf.**

Wes·ley·an (wes′lē ən; *esp.Brit.* wez′lē ən) *n., adj.* —*n.* a member of the church founded by John Wesley (1703-1791), an English clergyman; Methodist. —*adj.* of or having to do with John Wesley or the Methodist Church.

west (west) *n., adv., adj.* —*n.* **1** the direction of the sunset; the point of the compass to the left as one faces north. **2** Also, **West,** the part of the world, or a given country or continent toward the west. **3 the West, a** *Cdn.* the western part of Canada or the United States. **b** the countries in Europe and America as distinguished from those in Asia, especially SW Asia. **c** the United States, the United Kingdom, and their allies as distinguished from Russia and her allies. **d** *Historical.* the Western Roman Empire.
out West, *Cdn.* **a** any point to the west of about Winnipeg. **b** in or towards any place west of about Winnipeg.
—*adv.* toward the west: *They travelled west for two days.*
—*adj.* **1** toward or farther toward the west. **2** from the west: *a west wind.* **3** situated or found in the west or the western part: *the west wing of a house.*
west of, farther west than: *Alberta is west of Saskatchewan.*
[OE]

west·bound (west′bound′) *adj.* going toward the west.

west·er (west′ər) *v., n.* —*v.* turn or move westward; shift to the west. —*n.* a wind or storm from the west.

west·er·ly (wes′tər lē) *adj., adv., n.* —*adj. or adv.* **1** toward the west: *walking in a westerly direction.* **2** from the west: *a westerly wind.* —*n.* a wind that blows from the west.

west·ern (wes′tərn) *adj., n.* —*adj.* **1** toward the west. **2** from the west. **3** of or in the western part of the world or a given country or continent: *Vancouver is a western port.* **4** of, in, or having to do with the West.
—*n. Informal.* **1** a story or motion picture dealing with life in the western part of North America, especially cowboy life in the United States in the late 19th century. **2** a western sandwich or western omelette.

Western Church the part of the Catholic Church that acknowledges the Pope as its spiritual leader and follows the Latin Rite; Roman Catholic Church.

Western civilization European and American civilization as contrasted with Oriental civilization.

Western Empire Western Roman Empire.

West·ern·er (wes′tər nər) *n.* a native or inhabitant of the West.

western hemlock 1 a tall hemlock (*Tsuga heterophylla*) found in the forest regions of British Columbia and the NW United States, an important timber-producing tree having flat needles and small, egg-shaped cones. **2** the moderately light, hard, and strong wood of this tree.

west·ern·i·za·tion (west′ər nə zā′shən *or* -nī zā′shən) *n.* the process of introducing or adopting western ideas, institutions, culture, etc.

west·ern·ize (west′ər nīz′) *v.* **-ized, -iz·ing.** introduce or adopt western ideas, customs, culture, etc. —**west′ern·i′zer,** *n.*

western juniper Rocky Mountain juniper.

western larch a very tall larch (*Larix occidentalis*) found mainly in the forests of southern British Columbia, often growing to heights of 30 to 50 metres, having oval cones and heavy, hard, strong wood. The western larch is one of the most important timber-producing trees in western Canada.

west·ern·most (wes′tərn mōst′) *adj.* farthest west.

western omelette *or* **omelet** an omelette made with eggs, chopped onions, and ham.

western red cedar a very large arborvitae (*Thuja plicata*) found along the Pacific coast and in interior British Columbia, a very long-lived tree often reaching a height of 45 to 60 metres and a diameter of 2.5 metres or more. The western red cedar was used by the Indians of the Pacific northwest for carving totem poles and building canoes and lodges.

Western Roman Empire the western part of the Roman Empire after the division in A.D. 395. The Western Roman Empire

came to an end in A.D. 476; the Eastern Empire continued as the Byzantine Empire until A.D. 1453.

Western saddle a saddle with a high pommel, originally to tie a rope to when lassoing cattle. See **saddle** for picture.

western sandwich a sandwich with a filling of scrambled eggs, minced ham, peppers, and onions.

western yew a yew (*Taxus brevifolia*) occurring as a small tree or shrub in the forests of British Columbia. The hard, strong wood of the western yew is valued for archery bows, canoe paddles, and carving.

West Germanic a subgroup of the Germanic languages comprising Afrikaans, Dutch, English, Flemish, Frisian, German, Yiddish, and the various dialects and earlier forms of these languages.

West Indian *n., adj.* —*n.* **1** a native or inhabitant of the West Indies, a large group of islands and island countries between Florida and South America. **2** a person whose recent ancestors came from the West Indies. —*adj.* of or having to do with the West Indies or the peoples of these islands.

West·min·ster (west′min′stər) *n. Brit. Informal.* Parliament, or the British government. [< *Westminster*, the part of London that contains the Houses of Parliament]

west–north·west (west′nôrth′west′) *n., adj., adv.* —*n.* a direction or compass point midway between west and southwest. —*adj. or adv.* in, toward, or from this direction.

West·pha·li·an (west fā′lē ən) *adj., n.* —*adj.* of or having to do with Westphalia, a region in NW West Germany. —*n.* a native or inhabitant of Westphalia.

west–south·west (west′south′west′) *n., adj., adv.* —*n.* a direction or compass point midway between west and northwest. —*adj. or adv.* in, toward, or from this direction.

west·ward (west′wərd) *adj., adv., n.* —*adj. or adv.* toward the west; west: *He walked westward* (adv.). *We live on the westward slope of the hill* (adj.). —*n.* a westward part, direction, or point.

west·ward·ly (west′wərd lē) *adj. or adv.* **1** toward the west. **2** of winds, from the west.

west·wards (west′wərdz) *adv.* westward.

wet (wet) *adj.* **wet·ter, wet·test;** *v.* **wet** or **wet·ted, wet·ting;** *n.* —*adj.* **1** covered or soaked with water or other liquid: *wet hands, a wet sponge.* **2** not yet dry: *Don't touch wet paint.* **3** rainy: *wet weather.* **4** watery; liquid: *Her eyes were wet with tears.* **5** *Informal.* having or favoring laws that permit making and selling of alcoholic drinks.
wet behind the ears, too young to know very much; green; inexperienced.
—*v.* **1** make or become wet. **2** pass urine; make wet by passing urine.
—*n.* **1** water or other liquid: *I dropped my scarf in the wet.* **2** wetness; rain. **3** *Informal.* a person who favors laws that permit the making and selling of alcoholic drinks. [ME *wett,* pp. of *wete(n),* OE *wǣtan*] —**wet′ly,** *adv.* —**wet′ness,** *n.*
☛ *Hom.* **whet.**
☛ *Syn. v.* **Wet, drench, soak** = make or become covered or spread through with liquid. **Wet** is the general word: *Wet the material well before applying soap.* **Drench** means "wet thoroughly" by pouring liquid: *Drench the ashes and ground before leaving a campfire.* **Soak** means "wet thoroughly" by putting and keeping, or lying, in or under liquid, especially until the liquid has spread through the fibres or substance of the thing: *Soak the stained spot in milk.*

wet blanket *Informal.* a person that has a discouraging or depressing effect.

wet cell an electrochemical cell having a liquid electrolyte.

weth·er (weᴛʜ′ər) *n.* a castrated male sheep. [OE]
☛ *Hom.* **weather, whether.**

wet·land (wet′land′) *n.* a marsh or swamp.

wet nurse a woman employed to suckle the infant of another.

wet–nurse (wet′nèrs′) *v.* **-nursed, -nurs·ing. 1** act as wet nurse to. **2** treat with special care; coddle; pamper.

wet strength a quality of some paper, enabling it to hold together and not tear or disintegrate even when wet.

wet suit a skin-tight suit of sponge rubber or a similar material that is not watertight but that will retain body heat, worn especially by skindivers in cold water.

wet·tish (wet′ish) *adj.* somewhat wet.

we've (wēv; *unstressed,* wiv) we have.
☛ *Hom.* **weave.**

w.f. or **wf** *Printing.* wrong font.

WFTU or **W.F.T.U.** World Federation of Trade Unions.

W.Ger. **1** West Germany. **2** West German.

W·h watt hour(s).

hat, āge, fär; let, ēqual, tèrm; it, īce
hot, ōpen, ôrder; oil, out; cup, pùt, rüle,
əbove, takən, pencəl, lemən, circəs
ch, child; ng, long; sh, ship
th, thin; ᴛʜ, then; zh, measure

whack (wak *or* hwak) *n., v.* —*n. Informal.* a sharp, resounding blow or the sound of such a blow.
have or **take a whack at,** *Slang.* make an attempt at; try: *I'd like to take a whack at flying a glider.*
out of whack, *Slang.* not in proper condition; out of order: *The timing of the engine is out of whack.*
—*v.* **1** *Informal.* strike with a sharp, resounding blow: *The batter whacked the ball out of the park.* **2** beat or win in a contest. **3** *Slang.* chop or take (*off*): *He whacked off a couple of branches with his axe.*
whack up, *Slang.* share; divide.
[? imitative]

whacked (wakt *or* hwakt) *adj. Esp.Brit. Slang.* exhausted; worn out.

whack·ing (wak′ing *or* hwak′ing) *adj. Slang.* large or tremendous: *a whacking success.*

whack·y (wak′ē *or* hwak′ē) *adj.* wacky.

whale¹ (wāl *or* hwāl) *n., pl.* **whales** or **whale;** *v.* **whaled, whal·ing.**
—*n.* any of an order (Cetacea) of aquatic mammals that are shaped like fish; especially, any of the larger members of this order (which are the largest known animals) as distinguished from the porpoises and dolphins. Whales breathe air and bear live young.
a whale of a, *Informal.* a big or impressive example or type of: *a whale of a car, a whale of a good time.*
—*v.* hunt and catch whales. [OE *hwæl*]
☛ *Hom.* **wail, wale** (wāl).

whale² (wāl *or* hwāl) *v.* **whaled, whal·ing.** *Informal.* **1** beat; whip severely. **2** hit hard. [apparently var. of *wale*]
☛ *Hom.* **wail, wale** (wāl).

whale·back (wāl′bak′ *or* hwāl′-) *n.* **1** especially on the Great Lakes, a freight steamer having a rounded upper deck shaped like a whale's back. **2** a humped hill, mound, etc. having the shape of a whale's back.

whale·boat (wāl′bōt′ *or* hwāl′-) *n.* a long, narrow rowboat, sharp at both ends, formerly much used in whaling.

whale·bone (wāl′bōn′ *or* hwāl′-) *n.* **1** baleen, the horny substance growing in the mouth of baleen whales. **2** a thin strip of this, especially as formerly used for stays in corsets, dresses, etc.

whal·er (wā′lər *or* hwā′lər) *n.* **1** a person who hunts whales. **2** a ship used for hunting and catching whales.

whal·ing (wā′ling *or* hwā′ling) *n.* **1** the hunting and killing of whales. **2** the industry concerned with the hunting, killing, and processing of whales.

wham (hwam) *n., interj., v.* **whammed, wham·ming.** *Informal.* —*n. or interj.* a loud bang; the sound of a hard impact. —*v.* hit with a bang; smash; beat. [imitative]

wham·my (wam′ē *or* hwam′ē) *n., pl.* **-mies.** *Slang.* a magical power or spell bringing bad luck; jinx: *The magician put the whammy on him.*

whang (wang *or* hwang) *n., v. Informal.* —*n.* a resounding blow or bang. —*v.* strike with a blow or bang. [imitative]

whap (wap *or* hwap) *v.* **whapped, whap·ping.** whop.

wharf (wôrf *or* hwôrf) *n., pl.* **wharves** or **wharfs.** a platform built on the shore or out from the shore, beside which ships can load and unload. [OE *hwearf*]

wharf·age (wôr′fij *or* hwôr′fij) *n.* **1** the use of a wharf for mooring a ship, storing and handling goods, etc. **2** the charge made for this. **3** wharves: *There are miles of wharfage in Montreal.*

wharf·in·ger (wôr′fin jər *or* hwôr′fin jər) *n.* a person who owns or has charge of a wharf. [for *wharfager* < *wharfage* with *n* added as in *passenger*]

wharves (wôrvz *or* hwôrvz) *n.* pl. of **wharf.**

what (wut *or* wot, hwut *or* hwot; *unstressed,* wət *or* hwət) *pron., adj., adv., interj., conj.* —*pron.* **1** as an interrogative pronoun a word used in asking questions about persons or things: *What is your name? What is the matter?* **2** as a relative pronoun: **a** that which: *I know what you mean.* **b** whatever; anything that: *Do what you please.*
and what not, and all kinds of other things.
give (one) **what for,** *Informal.* give one something to cry, suffer, or be miserable for; punish; castigate.
what for, why.

what have you, *Informal.* anything else like this; and so on.

what if, what would happen if.

what's what, *Informal.* the true state of affairs: *I'm still trying to find out what's what.*

what with, on account of or having regard to: *What with our long walk and all the excitement, we were exhausted.*

—*adj.* **1** as an interrogative adjective, a word used in asking questions about persons or things: *What time is it?* **2** as a relative adjective: **a** that...which; which: *Put back what money is left.* **b** whatever; any...that: *Take what supplies you will need.* **3** a word used to show surprise, doubt, anger, liking, etc. or to add emphasis: *What a pity!*

—*adv.* **1** how much; how: *What does it matter?* **2** a word used to show surprise, doubt, anger, liking, etc. or to add emphasis: *What a good time we had!*

—*interj.* a word used to show surprise, doubt, anger, liking, etc. or to add emphasis: *What? Are you late again?*

—*conj.*

but what, *Informal.* but that.

[OE *hwæt*]

☛ *Hom.* **watt** (wot).

what·ev·er (wɒt ev′ər *or* wot-, hwɒt ev′ər *or* hwot-) *pron., adj.* —*pron.* **1** anything that: *Do whatever you like.* **2** no matter what: *Whatever happens, he is safe.* **3** *Informal.* a word used for emphasis instead of *what: Whatever do you mean?* —*adj.* **1** any that: *Ask whatever girls you like to the party.* **2** no matter what: *Whatever excuse he makes will not be believed.* **3** at all: *Any person whatever can tell you.*

what·not (wut′not′ *or* wot′-, hwut′not′ *or* hwot′-) *n.* **1** a stand with several shelves for books, ornaments, etc. **2** a thing or person that may be variously named or described; nondescript.

what's (wuts *or* wots, hwuts *or* hwots) **1** what is: *What's the latest news?* **2** what has: *What's been going on here lately?*

what·so·ev·er (wut′sō ev′ər *or* wot′-, hwut′sō ev′ər *or* hwot′-, wɒt sō ev′ər *or* hwɒt-) *pron. or adj.* whatever.

wheal (wēl *or* hwēl) *n.* **1** a small burning or itching swelling on the skin. **2** a ridge on the skin made by a whip: welt. [cf. OE *hwelian* suppurate]

☛ *Hom.* **weal, we'll** (wēl), **wheel** (wēl *or* hwēl).

wheat (wēt *or* hwēt) *n.* any of a genus (*Triticum*) of cereal grasses bearing grain in dense spikes. There are thousands of varieties of wheat cultivated throughout the world. **2** the grain yielded by any of these plants, one of the world's most important sources of flour for bread, pasta, etc. [OE *hwǣte*]

wheat·ear (wēt′ēr′ *or* hwēt′-) *n.* any of a genus (*Oenanthe*) of small northern thrushes, especially *O. oenanthe*, having grey-and-black upper parts and light-brown underparts with a white rump.

wheat·en (wē′tən *or* hwē′tən) *adj.* made of wheat.

wheat germ the tiny, golden embryo of the wheat kernel, used as a cereal and as a vitamin supplement.

whee·dle (wē′dəl *or* hwē′dəl) *v.* **-dled, -dling. 1** persuade by flattery, smooth words, caresses, etc.; coax: *The children wheedled their mother into letting them go out.* **2** get by wheedling: *They finally wheedled the secret out of him.* [OE *wǣdlian* beg] —**whee′dler,** *n.* —**whee′dling·ly,** *adv.*

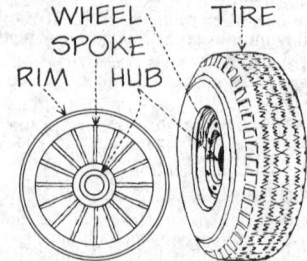

Wheels: a wagon wheel and a wheel for an automobile

wheel (wēl *or* hwēl) *n., v.* —*n.* **1** a round frame or disk that can turn on a pin or shaft in its centre. **2** any instrument, machine, apparatus, etc. shaped or moving like a wheel. A ship's wheel is used in steering. Clay is shaped into pots, etc. on a potter's wheel. **3** *Informal.* bicycle. **4** any force thought of as moving or propelling: *the wheels of government.* **5** a circling or circular motion or movement; rotation (not necessarily completed around); revolution. **6** a military or naval movement by which troops or ships in line change direction while maintaining a straight line. **7** *Informal.* big

wheel. **8 wheels,** *pl. Slang.* a motor vehicle, especially an automobile: *Do you have wheels?*

at the wheel, a at the steering wheel. **b** in control: *The variety night is bound to be a success with Peter at the wheel.*

wheels within wheels, complicated circumstances, motives, influences, etc.

—*v.* **1** *Informal.* ride a bicycle. **2** turn: *He wheeled around suddenly.* **3** move or perform in a curved or circular direction. **4** move on wheels: *The workman was wheeling a load of bricks on a wheelbarrow.* **5** travel along smoothly. **6** provide with wheels.

wheel and deal, *Slang.* do business or trade freely and rapidly, especially in an aggressive or somewhat unscrupulous way. [OE *hwēol*]

☛ *Hom.* **weal, we'll** (wēl), **wheal** (wēl *or* hwēl).

wheel·bar·row (wēl′bar′ō *or* wēl′ber′ō, hwēl′bar′ō *or* hwēl′ber′ō) *n.* a small vehicle for carrying loads, having one wheel at the front and two handles at the back.

wheel·base (wēl′bās *or* hwēl′-) *n.* in motor vehicles, the distance from the centre of the front axle to the centre of the rear axle, measured in millimetres.

wheel chair a chair mounted on wheels so that it can be pushed from behind or moved by the person sitting in it. Wheel chairs are used by invalids and people who are paralysed.

wheeled (wēld *or* hwēld) *adj.* having a wheel or wheels.

☛ *Hom.* **wield** (wēld).

wheel·er (wē′lər *or* hwēl′ər) *n.* **1** a person or thing that wheels. **2** a thing that has a wheel or wheels. **3** wheel horse.

wheel·er–deal·er (wē′lər dē′lər *or* hwē′lər-) *n. Slang.* a person who wheels and deals.

wheel horse 1 a horse nearest to the front wheels of the vehicle being pulled. **2** *Informal.* a person who works hard, long, and effectively.

wheel·house (wēl′hous′ *or* hwēl′-) *n.* a small, enclosed place on a ship to shelter the steering wheel and those that steer the ship; pilot house.

wheel·wright (wēl′rīt *or* hwēl′-) *n.* a man whose work is making or repairing wheels, carriages, and wagons.

wheeze (wēz *or* hwēz) *v.* **wheezed, wheez·ing;** *n.* —*v.* **1** breathe with difficulty and with a whistling sound. **2** make a sound like this: *The old engine wheezed, but it didn't stop.* **3** say with a wheeze. —*n.* **1** a whistling sound caused by difficult breathing. **2** *Slang.* a funny saying or story, especially one that has been told many times; an old or familiar joke. [? < ON *hvǣsa* hiss]

wheez·y (wē′zē *or* hwē′zē) *adj.* **wheez·i·er, wheez·i·est.** wheezing: *The old dog was fat and wheezy.* —**wheez′i·ly,** *adv.* —**wheez′i·ness,** *n.*

whelk¹ (welk *or* hwelk) *n.* any of a family (Buccinidae) of carnivorous marine gastropod molluscs typically having a thick, strong, spiral shell. [OE *weoloc*]

whelk² (welk *or* hwelk) *n.* pimple; pustule. [OE *hwylca*]

whelm (welm *or* hwelm) *v.* **1** overwhelm. **2** submerge. [related to OE *-hwelfan,* as in *āhwelfan* cover over; influenced by *helmian* cover]

whelp (welp *or* hwelp) *n., v.* —*n.* **1** a young animal, especially a puppy or wolf cub. **2** a good-for-nothing boy or young man. —*v.* give birth to a whelp or whelps. [OE *hwelp*]

when (wen *or* hwen; *unstressed,* wən *or* hwən) *adv., conj., pron., n.* —*adv.* at what time: *When does school close?* —*conj.* **1** at the time that: *Rise when your name is called.* **2** at any time that: *He is impatient when he is kept waiting.* **3** at which time; and then: *The dog growled till his master spoke, when he gave a joyful bark.* **4** although: *We have only three books when we need five.* **5** considering that; inasmuch as; since: *How can I help you when I don't know how to do the problems myself?* —*pron.* what time; which time: *Since when have they had a car?* —*n.* the time or occasion: *the when and where of an act.* [OE *hwænne*]

when·as (wen az′ *or* hwen-) *conj. Archaic.* when; while; whereas.

whence (wens *or* hwens) *adv., conj. Archaic.* —*adv.* from what place, source, or cause: *Whence do you come?* —*conj.* **1** from what place, source, or cause: *They wondered whence he had learned so much about their affairs.* **2** from which or from where: *Let him return to the country whence he came.* [ME *whennes* < OE *hwanone*]

whence·so·ev·er (wens′sō ev′ər *or* hwens′-) *conj.* from whatever place, source, or cause.

when·ev·er (wen ev′ər *or* hwen-) *conj. or adv.* at whatever time; when; at any time that.

when·so·ev·er (wen′sō ev′ər *or* hwen′-) *conj. or adv.* whenever; at whatever time.

where (wer *or* hwer) *adv., n., conj.* —*adv.* **1** in what place; at

what place: *Where is he?* **2** to what place: *Where are you going?* **3** from what place: *Where did you get that story?* **4** in which; at which: *the house where he was born.* **5** to which: *the place where he is going.* **6** in or at which place: *I don't know where he is.* **7** in what way; in what respect: *Where is the harm in trying?*
—*n.* **1** what place: *Where does he come from?* **2** the place or scene: *the when and the where of it.*
—*conj.* **1** to the place to which: *I will go where you go.* **2** in the place in which; at the place at which: *The book is where you left it.* **3** in any place in which; at any place at which: *Use the salve where the pain is felt.* **4** in or at which place: *They came to the town, where they stayed for the night.* **5** in the case, circumstances, respect, etc. in which: *Some people worry where it does no good.* [OE *hwær*]
☛ *Hom.* ware, wear (wer).

where·a·bout (wer′ə bout′ *or* hwer′-) *adv. or conj. or n.* whereabouts.

where·a·bouts (wer′ə bouts′ *or* hwer′-) *adv., conj., n.* —*adv. or conj.* where; near what place: *Whereabouts can I find a doctor? We did not know whereabouts we were.*
—*n.pl. or sing.* the place where a person or thing is: *Do you know the whereabouts of the cottage?*

where·as (wer az′ *or* hwer′-) *conj.* **1** on the contrary; but; while: *Some people like opera whereas others do not.* **2** considering that; since, often used at the beginning of a formal proclamation, resolution, etc.: *Whereas all men are human, so all men should show humanity.*

where·at (wer at′ *or* hwer-) *adv. or conj. Archaic.* at what; at which.

where·by (wer bī′ *or* hwer-) *adv. or conj.* by what; by which: *There is no other way whereby he can be saved.*

where·fore (wer′fôr *or* hwer′-) *adv., conj., n.* —*adv. Archaic.* **1** for what reason; why: *Wherefore do you weep?* **2** for which reason; therefore; so: *He has been found guilty, wherefore he must be banished.*
—*conj. Archaic or formal.* for what reason; why: *I think I know wherefore he is angry.*
—*n.* Usually, **wherefores**, *pl.* an explanation or reason: *I don't want to hear all the whys and wherefores.* [< where + fore, prep.]

where·from (wer from′ *or* wer frum′, hwer from′ *or* hwer frum′) *adv.* whence.

where·in (wer in′ *or* hwer-) *adv., conj. Archaic or formal.* —*adv.* in what place or respect: *Wherein had he erred?* —*conj.* in which place or respect: *the place wherein they lived.*

where·in·to (wer in′tü *or* hwer in′tü) *adv. or conj. Archaic.* into what; into which.

where·of (wer uv′ *or* -ov′, hwer′uv′ *or* -ov′) *adv. or conj. Archaic or formal.* of what, which, or whom.

where·on (wer on′ *or* hwer-) *adv. or conj. Archaic.* on which or what.

where·so·ev·er (wer′sō ev′ər *or* hwer′-) *conj. or adv. Archaic.* wherever.

where·to (wer tü′ *or* hwer-) *adv. or conj. Archaic or formal.* **1** to what; to which; where: *He went to that place whereto he had been sent.* **2** for what purpose; why: *Whereto do you lay up riches?*

where·un·to (wer un′tü *or* hwer-) *adv. or conj. Archaic.* whereto.

where·up·on (wer′ə pon′ *or* hwer′-) *adv. or conj.* **1** upon what; upon which. **2** at which; after which.

wher·ev·er (wer ev′ər *or* hwer-) *conj. or adv.* where; to whatever place; in whatever place: *Wherever are you going? Sit wherever you like.*

where·with (wer witH′ *or* -with′, hwer witH′ *or* -with′) *adv. or conj. Archaic.* with what; with which.

where·with·al (*n.* wer′witH ol′ *or* -ôl′, hwer′witH ol′ *or* -ôl′; *adv. and conj.* wer′witH ol′ *or* -ôl′, hwer′witH ol′ *or* -ôl′) *n., adv., conj.* —*n.* means, supplies, or money needed: *Does she have the wherewithal to pay for the trip?*
—*adv. or conj. Archaic.* with what; with which: *Wherewithal shall we be fed?*

wher·ry (wer′ē *or* hwer′ē) *n., pl.* **-ries. 1** a light, shallow rowboat for carrying passengers and goods on rivers. **2** a light rowboat for one person, used for racing. **3** *Esp.Brit.* a broad sailboat, used chiefly on rivers. [origin unknown]

whet (wet *or* hwet) *v.* **whet·ted, whet·ting;** *n.* —*v.* **1** sharpen by rubbing: *to whet a knife.* **2** stir up; awaken: *The smell of food whetted my appetite. An exciting story whets your interest.*
—*n.* **1** the act of whetting. **2** something that whets. **3** appetizer. [OE *hwettan*]
☛ *Hom.* wet (wet).

wheth·er (weTH′ər *or* hweTH′-) *conj., pron.* —*conj.* **1** *Whether* is a conjunction expressing a choice or an alternative: *It matters little*

hat, āge, fär; let, ēqual, tèrm; it, īce
hot, ōpen, ôrder; oil, out; cup, pút, rüle,
əbove, takən, pencəl, lemən, circəs

ch, child; ng, long; sh, ship
th, thin; TH, then; zh, measure

whether we go or stay. He does not know whether to work or play. **2** either: *Whether sick or well, she is always cheerful.* **3** if: *He asked whether he should finish the work.*

whether or no, in any case; no matter what happens.
—*pron. Archaic.* which of two: *"Whether is greater, the gift or the altar that sanctifieth the gift?"* [OE *hwether*]
☛ *Hom.* weather, wether (weTH′ər).
☛ *Usage.* See note at **if.**

whet·stone (wet′stōn′ *or* hwet′-) *n.* a stone for sharpening knives or tools.

whew (hwyü) *interj. or n.* an exclamation of surprise, relief, dismay, etc.: *Whew! it's cold!*

whey (wā *or* hwā) *n.* the watery part of milk that separates from the curd when milk sours and becomes coagulated or when cheese is made. [OE *hwæg*]
☛ *Hom.* way, weigh (wā).

which (wich *or* hwich) *pron., adj.* —*pron.* **1** as an interrogative pronoun, a word used in asking questions about one or more persons or things from a group: *Which seems the best plan?* **2** as a relative pronoun, a word used: **a** to connect a group of words with some other words in the sentence: *Take the book which is on the desk.* **b** in making statements about one or more persons or things from a group: *Tell me which you like best.* **3** a thing or fact that: *And, which was worse, he was late.*
which is which, which is one and which is the other: *They look so much alike, it's hard to tell which is which.*
—*adj.* **1** as an interrogative adjective, a word used in asking questions about one or more persons or things from a group: *Which boy won the prize? Which books are yours?* **2** a word used in connecting a group of words with some word in the sentence: *Be careful which way you turn.* **3** a word used in making statements about one or more persons or things from a group: *I don't know which dress to wear.* [OE *hwilc*]
☛ *Hom.* witch (wich).
☛ *Usage.* **Which.** As a relative pronoun **which** refers to things and to groups of people regarded impersonally: *They returned for his axe, which they had forgotten. The legislature, which passed the act this afternoon, deserves much credit.*
☛ *Usage.* See also the note at **that.**
☛ *Usage.* **Of which, whose.** See note at **who.**

which·ev·er (wich ev′ər *or* hwich-) *pron. or adj.* **1** any one that; any that: *Take whichever you want. Buy whichever hat you like.* **2** no matter which: *Whichever side wins, I shall be satisfied.*

which·so·ev·er (wich′sō ev′ər *or* hwich′-) *pron. or adj.* whichever.

whick·er (wik′ər *or* hwik′ər) *n. or v.* whinny. [imitative]

whiff (wif *or* hwif) *n., v.* —*n.* **1** a slight gust; puff; breath: *A whiff of fresh air cleared his head.* **2** a blow; puff. **3** a slight smell; puff of air having an odor. **4** a puff of tobacco smoke. **5** a slight outburst. **6** *Informal.* **a** in baseball, golf, etc., a swing at a ball without hitting it. **b** in baseball, a strikeout.
—*v.* **1** breathe in or out gently. **2** puff tobacco smoke from (a pipe, etc.); smoke. **3** *Informal. Baseball.* strike out or be struck out. [probably imitative; partly < ME *weffe* vapor, whiff]

whif·fet (wif′it *or* hwif′-) *n.* **1** *Informal.* an insignificant person or thing. **2** a small dog. [? < *whiff*]

whif·fle (wif′əl *or* hwif′-) *v.* **-fled, -fling. 1** blow in puffs or gusts. **2** veer; shift. **3** blow lightly; scatter. [< *whiff*]

whif·fler (wif′lər *or* hwif′-) *n.* one who whiffles, or shifts about in thought, opinion, intention, etc.

whif·fle·tree (wif′əl trē′ *or* hwif′-) *n.* whippletree.

Whig (wig *or* hwig) *n. Historical.* **1** a member or supporter of a British political party of the 18th and 19th centuries that favored sweeping social and political reforms. The Whig Party became the Liberal Party. **2** in the United States, a person living in any one of the Thirteen Colonies who supported the rebellion against Britain. **3** (*adj.*) composed of, having to do with, or characteristic of Whigs.

Whig·ger·y (wig′ər ē *or* hwig′-) *n.* the principles or practices of Whigs.

Whig·gish (wig′ish *or* hwig′-) *adj.* **1** of or having to do with Whigs. **2** like Whigs.

while (wīl *or* hwīl) *n., conj., v.* **whiled, whil·ing.** —*n.* **1** a time; space of time: *He kept us waiting a long while. The postman came*

a while ago. **2** *Archaic.* a particular time.
between whiles, at times; at intervals.
the while, during the time.
worth while, worth time, attention, or effort: *The visit to New York was certainly worth while.*
—*conj.* **1** during the time that; in the time that; in the same time that: *While I was speaking, he said nothing. Summer is pleasant while it lasts.* **2** in contrast with the fact that; although: *While I like the color of the hat, I don't like the style.*
—*v.* pass or spend in an easy, pleasant manner (*usually used with* **away**): *We whiled away the day playing at the beach.* [OE *hwīl*]
☛ Hom. **wile** (wīl).
☛ *Usage.* **While** is used principally as a subordinating conjunction introducing adverbial clauses of time: *They waited on the bank while he swam to the raft.* **While** is also used, rather weakly, in the sense of **although** or **but**: *While the doctor did all he could, he couldn't save her. Walnut is a hard wood, while pine is soft.* **While** is sometimes used for **and**, but not often: *The second number was an acrobatic exhibition, while the third was a trapeze artist.*

whiles (wīlz *or* hwīlz) *adv., conj. Archaic or dialect.* —*adv.* **1** sometimes. **2** in the meantime. —*conj.* while.

whi·lom (wī′ləm *or* hwī′-) *adj., adv. Archaic.* —*adj.* former: *a whilom friend.* —*adv.* formerly; once. [OE *hwīlum* at times, dat. pl. of *hwīl* while]

whilst (wīlst *or* hwīlst) *conj.* while.

whim (wim *or* hwim) *n.* **1** a sudden fancy or notion; freakish or capricious idea or desire: *Her whim for gardening won't last long.* **2** *Mining.* a kind of capstan used in hoisting. [probably < Scand.; cf. Icelandic *hvim* unsteady look]

whim·per (wim′pər *or* hwim′-) *v., n.* —*v.* **1** cry with soft, broken sounds: *The sick child whimpered.* **2** say with a whimper. **3** complain in a weak way; whine.
—*n.* a whimpering cry or sound. [probably imitative; cf. G *wimmern*] —**whim′per·er,** *n.* —**whim′per·ing·ly,** *adv.*

whim·sey (wim′zē *or* hwim′-) *n., pl.* **-seys.** See **whimsy.**

whim·si·cal (wim′zə kəl *or* hwim′-) *adj.* **1** having many odd notions or fancies; fanciful; odd. **2** full of whims. —**whim′si·cal·ly,** *adv.*

whim·si·cal·i·ty (wim′zə kal′ə tē *or* hwim′-) *n., pl.* **-ties.** **1** a whimsical character or quality. **2** a whimsical notion, speech, act, etc.

whim·sy (wim′zē *or* hwim′-) *n., pl.* **-sies.** **1** an odd or fanciful idea; whim: *It was just one of her whimsies; don't take it seriously.* **2** odd or fanciful humor; quaintness: *The story* Alice's Adventures in Wonderland *is full of whimsy.* **3** an object or creation showing whimsy. [< *whim*]

whin (win *or* hwin) *n.* furze. [cf. Icel. *hvingras* bent grass]
☛ Hom. **win** (win).

whine (wīn *or* hwīn) *v.* **whined, whin·ing;** *n.* —*v.* **1** make a soft, drawn-out, complaining cry or sound: *The dog whined to go out with us.* **2** complain in a peevish, childish way: *Some people are always whining about trifles.* **3** say with a whine.
—*n.* **1** a soft, drawn-out, complaining cry or sound. **2** a peevish, childish complaint. [OE *hwīnan*] —**whin′er,** *n.* —**whin′ing·ly,** *adv.*
☛ Hom. **wine** (wīn).

whin·ny (win′ē *or* hwin′ē) *n., pl.* **-nies;** *v.* **-nied, -ny·ing.** —*n.* the sound that a horse makes. —*v.* **1** of a horse, utter its characteristic call or cry. **2** express with such a sound. [related to WHINE]

whin·stone (win′stōn′ *or* hwin′-) *n.* basalt or some similar hard rock. [< *whin* whinstone (of uncertain origin) + *stone*]

whip (wip *or* hwip) *n., v.* **whipped, whip·ping.** —*n.* **1** a thing to strike or beat with, usually a stick with a cord at the end. **2** a whipping motion. **3** a dessert made by beating cream, eggs, etc. into a froth: *Prune whip is my favorite dessert.* **4 a** a member of a political party who controls and directs the other members in a lawmaking body, as by seeing that they attend meetings in which important votes are taken. **b** call made on members of a political party in a legislature to attend a given session or remain in attendance for it. **5** a person who manages the hounds of a hunting pack. **6** a driver; coachman. **7** a rope and pulley.
—*v.* **1** strike or beat with or as with a whip; lash: *He whipped the horse to make it go faster.* **2** move, put, or pull quickly and suddenly: *He whipped off his coat and whipped out his knife. The thief whipped behind a tree and escaped.* **3** bring, get, make, or produce by or as by whipping: *to whip the nonsense out of someone.* **4** incite; rouse; revive: *The speaker whipped his audience into a fervor.* **5** criticize or reprove with cutting severity. **6** *Informal.* defeat: *The mayor whipped his opponent in the election.* **7** summon (in, up) to attend, as the members of a political party in a legislative body, for united action. **8** beat (cream, eggs, etc.) to a froth. **9** sew with stitches passing over and over an edge. **10** wind (a rope, stick,

etc.) closely with thread or string; wind (cord, twine, or thread) around something. **11** cast a fish line with a motion like that of using a whip. **12** fish in: *whip a stream.*
whip up, a prepare or make quickly: *She whipped up some masks for us to wear on Halloween.* **b** stir up: *We are trying to whip up some interest in speed skating.*
[cf. MDu. and MLG *wippe* swing] —**whip′like′,** *adj.* —**whip′per,** *n.*

whip·cord (wip′kôrd *or* hwip′-) *n.* **1** a strong, twisted cord, sometimes used for the lashes of whips. **2** a strong worsted cloth with diagonal ridges on it.

whip hand **1** the hand that holds the whip while driving a horse-drawn vehicle. **2** a position of control; advantage: *A clever person often gets the whip hand over others.*

whip·lash (wip′lash′ *or* hwip′-) *n.* **1** a lash of a whip. **2** anything considered as similar to this: *the whiplash of fear.* **3** an injury to the neck caused by a sudden jolt that snaps the head backward and then forward. A person in a vehicle that is struck from behind by another vehicle can suffer whiplash.

whip·per–snap·per (wip′ər snap′ər *or* hwip′-) *n.* an insignificant person who thinks he is important.

whip·pet (wip′it *or* hwip′-) *n.* a breed of swift, lean racing and hunting dog that looks like a small greyhound. The whippet was developed from a cross between the greyhound and a terrier. [< *whip* in the sense of "move quickly"]

whip·ping (wip′ing *or* hwip′-) *n.* **1** a beating; flogging. **2** arrangement of cord, twine, or the like, wound about a thing: *We fastened the broken rod with a whipping of wire.*

whipping boy **1** *Historical.* a boy who was educated with a young prince and made to take punishment due to the prince. **2** any person who takes the blame for the wrongdoings of others; a scapegoat.

whipping post a post to which lawbreakers are tied to be whipped.

whip·ple·tree (wip′əl trē′ *or* hwip′-) *n.* the swinging bar of a carriage or wagon, to which the traces of a harness are fastened. [? < *whip*]

whip·poor·will (wip′ər wil′ *or* hwip′ər wil) *n.* a goatsucker (*Caprimulgus vociferus*) of central and E North America having soft, mottled brown-and-black plumage, a small bill, and an enormous mouth. Also, **whip-poor-will.** [imitative]

whip·saw (wip′sô′ *or* -sô′; hwip′sô′ *or* -sô′) *n., v.* —*n.* a long, narrow saw with its ends held in a frame. —*v.* **1** cut with a whipsaw. **2** *Informal.* get the better of (a person) no matter what he does.

whip·stitch (wip′stich′ *or* hwip′-) *v., n.* —*v.* sew with stitches passing over and over an edge. —*n.* a stitch made in whipstitching.

whip·stock (wip′stok′ *or* hwip′-) *n.* the handle of a whip.

whipt (wipt *or* hwipt) *v.* a pt. and pp. of **whip.**

whir *or* **whirr** (wêr *or* hwêr) *n., v.* **whirred, whir·ring.** —*n.* a buzzing noise as of something turning at high speed: *the whir of a small machine.* —*v.* operate or move with such a noise: *The motor whirred.* [cf. Danish *hvirre* whirl]

whirl (wêrl *or* hwêrl) *v., n.* —*v.* **1** turn or swing round and round; spin: *The leaves whirled in the wind.* **2** move round and round: *The dancers whirled about the room. He whirled the club.* **3** move or carry quickly: *We were whirled away in an airplane.* **4** become or be dizzy or giddy: *Her mind was whirling.*
—*n.* **1** a whirling movement. **2** something that whirls. **3** a dizzy or confused condition: *His thoughts were in a whirl.* **4** great activity; a rapid round of happenings, parties, etc.: *We had a rest after the whirl of Christmas holidays.* **5** an attempt or trial: *She had never been in a canoe before, but decided to give it a whirl.* [ME, probably < ON *hvirfla* < *hverfla* turn] —**whirl′er,** *n.*
☛ Hom. **whorl** (wêrl, hwêrl).

whirl·i·gig (wêr′lē gig′ *or* hwêr′lē-) *n.* **1** a toy that whirls. **2** a merry-go-round. **3** something that whirls round and round. [< *whirly-* (obs. var. of *whirl*) + *gig* something that whirls (of uncertain origin)]

whirligig beetle any of a family (Gyrinidae) of beetles usually seen in groups circling and spinning about on the surface of ponds or lakes.

whirl·pool (wêrl′pül′ *or* hwêrl′-) *n.* **1** water whirling round and round rapidly and violently. **2** anything like a whirlpool.

whirl·wind (wêrl′wind′ *or* hwêrl′-) *n.* **1** a current of air whirling violently round and round; whirling windstorm. **2** anything like a whirlwind. [< *whirl* + *wind*, after ON *hvirfilvindr*]

whirr (wêr *or* hwêr) *n. or v.* whir.

whish (wish *or* hwish) *n., v.* —*n.* a soft rushing sound; whizz; swish. —*v.* make a soft rushing sound. [imitative]

whisk (wisk *or* hwisk) *v., n.* —*v.* **1** remove, wipe, brush, etc. with a quick sweeping motion: *He whisked the crumbs from the table. She whisked the letter out of sight. The waitress whisked my plate*

away. **2** move or carry quickly or nimbly: *They whisked the children off to bed. The mouse whisked into its hole. The prime minister was whisked away in his limousine.* **3** beat or whip (eggs, etc.) to a froth. —*n.* **1** a quick sweeping or whipping movement: *with a whisk of the broom, a whisk of the horse's tail.* **2** whisk broom. **3** a small wire kitchen utensil for beating (eggs, cream, etc.) by hand. [ME *visk*, prob. < Scand.; cf. ON *visk* wisp]

whisk broom a small, short-handled broom for brushing away crumbs, dirt, etc.

whisk·er (wis′kər *or* hwis′kər) *n.* **1** Usually, **whiskers**, *pl.* the hair growing on a man's face, especially that on his cheeks and chin. **2** one of the hairs growing on a man's face. **3** any of the long, stiff sensory hairs growing near the mouth of a cat, rat, etc. [< *whisk*]

whisk·ered (wis′kərd *or* hwis′kərd) *adj.* having whiskers.

whisk·er·y (wis′kər ē *or* hwis′kər ē) *adj.* **1** whiskered. **2** resembling whiskers.

whis·key (wis′kē *or* hwis′kē) *n., pl.* **-keys.** See **whisky.**

whisk·y (wis′kē *or* hwis′kē) *n., pl.* **-kies.** a strong alcoholic drink made from grain. Also, **whiskey.** [short for *whiskybae* < Gaelic *uisge beatha*, literally, water of life]

whis·ky–jack (wis′kē jak′ *or* hwis′kē-) *n. Cdn.* Canada jay. Also, **whiskey-jack.** [< obs. *whisky-john*, alteration of Cree *wiskatjan*]

whisky sour a cocktail consisting of whisky, lemon juice, and sugar, usually served with an orange slice and a cherry.

whis·per (wis′pər *or* hwis′pər) *v., n.* —*v.* **1** speak very softly, with little or no vibration of the vocal cords: *We could hear them whispering behind us.* **2** tell secretly or privately: *It is whispered that his health is failing.* **3** make a soft, rustling sound: *The wind whispered in the pines.* **4** speak to very softly. —*n.* **1** the act or an instance of whispering: *She spoke in a whisper. They were speaking in whispers.* **2** something told secretly or privately. **3** a soft, rustling sound. **4** speech without vibration of the vocal cords. [OE *hwisprian*] —**whis′per·er,** *n.*

whist[1] (wist *or* hwist) *n.* a card game, resembling bridge, for two pairs of players. Auction and contract bridge developed from whist. [alteration of *whisk*, influenced by *whist*[2]]
☛ *Hom.* **wist** (wist).

whist[2] (wist *or* hwist) *interj., adj.* —*interj.* hush! silence! —*adj. Archaic.* hushed; silent.
☛ *Hom.* **wist** (wist).

whis·tle (wis′əl *or* hwis′əl) *v.* **-tled, -tling;** *n.* —*v.* **1** make a clear, shrill sound by forcing breath through one's teeth or pursed lips: *We heard him whistling as he walked along.* **2** make or utter a shrill sound resembling this: *The old steam engine whistled.* **3** produce or utter by whistling: *to whistle a tune.* **4** blow a whistle. **5** call, signal, or direct by a whistle: *The policeman whistled the automobile to stop.* **6** move with a shrill sound: *The wind whistled around the house.*
whistle for, *Informal.* go without; fail to get.
whistle in the dark, try to be courageous or hopeful in a fearful or trying situation.
—*n.* **1** the sound made by whistling. **2** a device for making shrill sounds by means of forced air or steam.
wet (one's) **whistle,** *Informal.* take a drink.
[OE *hwistlian*]

whis·tler (wis′lər *or* hwis′lər) *n.* **1** a person or thing that whistles. **2** any of various birds having a whistling call (such as the whistling swan) or making a whistling sound in flight (such as the goldeneye). **3** *Cdn.* hoary marmot.

whis·tle–stop (wis′əl stop′ *or* hwis′əl-) *n., v.* **-stopped, -stop·ping.** *Informal.* —*n.* **1** a small, little-known town along a railway line at which a train stops only when signalled. **2** a stop at such a town or station for a brief appearance or speech, as in a political campaign tour. **3** (*adj.*) of, having to do with, or characterized by whistle-stops: *a whistle-stop campaign.* —*v.* make a series of electioneering appearances or speeches at stations along a railway line.

whistling swan a North American swan (*Olor columbianus,* also classified as *Cygnus columbianus*) that nests in the Arctic, having white plumage and a black bill, named for its whistling call.

whit (wit *or* hwit) *n.* a very small bit: *The sick man is not a whit better.* [var. of OE *wiht* thing, wight]
☛ *Hom.* **wit** (wit).

white (wīt *or* hwīt) *n., adj.* **whit·er, whit·est.** —*n.* **1** the color of fresh snow or salt; the opposite of black. **2** the quality of being white; white coloration or appearance; whiteness. **3** a white coloring matter. **4** white clothing. **5** something white; a white or colorless part: *the white of an egg, the whites of the eyes.* **6** a member of a light-skinned race. **7** *Archery.* the central part of a butt (formerly painted white). **8** *Printing.* a blank space. **9** an ultraconservative; reactionary; royalist. **10** *Chess, checkers, or backgammon.* **a** the light-colored squares or other shapes on the board. **b** the white or

hat, āge, fär; let, ēqual, tèrm; it, īce
hot, ōpen, ôrder; oil, out; cup, pût, rüle,
abóve, takán, pencál, lemán, circás
ch, child; ng, long; sh, ship
th, thin; ₮H, then; zh, measure

light-colored pieces. **c** the player holding these pieces. —*adj.* **1** having the color of snow or salt; reflecting light without absorbing any of the rays composing it. **2** having a color that approaches it. **3** pale: *She turned white with fear.* **4** light-colored: *white wines, white meat.* **5** having a light-colored skin; of or having to do with the Caucasian race. **6** silvery or grey: *white hair.* **7** snowy: *a white winter.* **8** blank: *a white space.* **9** spotless; pure; innocent. **10** *Informal.* honorable; trustworthy; fair. **11** wearing white clothing. **12** ultraconservative; reactionary; royalist. **13** good; beneficent: *white magic.* **14** being at white heat.
bleed white, gradually use up or take away all of (someone's) money, strength, etc.
[OE *hwīt*] —**white′ness,** *n.*
☛ *Hom.* **wight** (wīt).

white ant termite.

white·bait (wīt′bāt′ *or* hwīt′-) *n., pl.* **-bait. 1** a young herring or sprat about 3 to 5 cm long. **2** any of various very small fish used for food.

white·bark pine (wīt′bärk′ *or* hwīt′-) **1** a small, often shrubby, mountain pine (*Pinus albicaulis*) of W North America having bluish-green needles, egg-shaped or almost round cones, and smooth, chalky-white bark on young stems. **2** the light, medium-soft wood of this tree.

white birch 1 a large North American birch (*Betula papyrifera*), common throughout most of Canada, noted especially for its papery white bark which can be readily peeled off in layers and which was traditionally used by North American Indian peoples of the eastern woodlands for making canoes, etc. **2** any of various other birches with white bark, such as the European silver birch. **3** the wood of a white birch.

white blood cell any of the white or colorless blood cells found in the blood and lymph of vertebrates; leucocyte. White blood cells help the body to fight infection.

white·cap (wīt′kap′ *or* hwīt′-) *n.* a wave with a foaming white crest.

white cedar 1 an arborvitae (*Thuja occidentalis*) of E North America, found in Canada from Nova Scotia to Manitoba. **2** the wood of this tree.

white clover a low-growing, creeping, Eurasian clover (*Trifolium repens*) having white flower heads, widely cultivated as a forage crop and also used in mixtures for lawn grass.

white coal *Cdn.* water used as a source of power.

white·coat (wīt′kōt′ *or* hwīt′-) *n.* **1** a young of a harp seal. It has a coat of white hair. **2** the skin of a whitecoat.

white·col·lar (wīt′kol′ər *or* hwīt′-) *adj.* of or having to do with clerical, professional, or business work or workers.

white corpuscle white blood cell.

whited sepulchre hypocrite.

white elephant 1 something rare or valuable that is expensive and troublesome to keep and take care of. **2** something very costly or elaborate that turns out to be useless or not worthwhile: *The new airport is just a white elephant.* **3** a possession that may have some intrinsic or potential value but is unwanted by its owner: *Several neighbors decided to have a garage sale to get rid of white elephants.* [with reference to a rare albino or pale-grey variety of Indian elephant held sacred in parts of S Asia]

white–faced (wīt′fāst′ *or* hwīt′-) *adj.* **1** wan; pallid; pale. **2** of an animal, having large white patches of hair on the head.

white feather a symbol of cowardice.
show the white feather, act like a coward.

white·fish (wīt′fish′ *or* hwīt′-) *n., pl.* **-fish** *or* **-fish·es.** any of a subfamily (Coregoninae, of the family Salmonidae) of silvery, large-scaled, freshwater fishes of northern regions that are important food fishes. Some authorities classify the whitefishes in a separate family (Coregonidae).

white flag a plain white flag used as a sign of truce or surrender.

white friar a Carmelite monk.

white garden lily Madonna lily.

white gold an alloy of gold, nickel or platinum, and some zinc and copper, that looks much like platinum and is used for jewellery.

White·hall (wīt′hol′ *or* -hôl′; hwīt′hol′ *or* -hôl′) *n.* **1** a former palace in London. **2** a street in London where many government

offices are located. **3** the British government or its policies.

white heat 1 extremely great heat at which things give off a dazzling, white light. **2** a state of extremely great activity, excitement, or feeling.

white heather *Cdn.* a small, evergreen shrub (*Cassiope tetragona*) of the heath family found in Arctic regions, having scalelike leaves and nodding bell-shaped flowers.

white hope *Slang.* a person of whom much is expected. [originally, a white challenger to a boxing title held by a black]

white–hot (wīt′hot′ *or* hwīt′-) *adj.* **1** white with heat; extremely hot. **2** very enthusiastic; excited; violent.

White House 1 the official residence of the President of the United States, in Washington, D.C. **2** *Informal.* the office, authority, opinion, etc. of the President of the United States.

white lead a heavy, white, poisonous compound of lead, used in making paint; basic carbonate of lead. *Formula:* 2PbCO₃Pb(OH)₂

white lie a lie about some small matter, especially one told to avoid being rude or hurting one's feelings.

white–liv·ered (wīt′liv′ərd *or* hwīt′-) *adj.* **1** *Archaic.* cowardly. **2** pale; unhealthy looking.

white man's burden the assumed task of the white race to govern and lead forward the peoples of allegedly less civilized countries, especially in Asia and Africa. [coined in *From Sea to Sea*, by Rudyard Kipling (1865-1936), an English author]

white matter tissue of the brain, spinal cord, etc. that consists chiefly of nerve fibres.

whit·en (wīt′ən *or* hwīt′ən) *v.* **1** make or become white: *to whiten sheets with bleach.* **2** make or become pale or paler: *He whitened when he heard the bad news.* —**whit′en·er,** *n.*

☛ *Syn.* **1. Whiten, bleach** = make white or nearly white. **Whiten,** the general word, often suggests applying a substance on the outside of something: *toothpaste that whitens one's teeth.* **Bleach** means to make white, lighter, or colorless by exposing to sunlight and air or by using chemicals: *Cotton can be bleached in the sun.*

white noise the sound produced by using the whole range of audible frequencies at once. Also, **white sound.** [by analogy with *white light,* which contains all the wave lengths of the visible spectrum]

white oak 1 a tall oak (*Quercus alba*) of E North America having shiny, bright-green, very deeply lobed leaves, light-grey or whitish bark, and a hard, durable wood. **2** any of various similar oaks. **3** the wood of a white oak, highly valued for lumber.

white·out (wīt′out′ *or* hwīt′-) *n. Cdn.* **1** an arctic weather condition in which the snow-covered ground, the cloudy sky, and the horizon become a continuous, shadowless mass of dazzling white. **2** a temporary blindness resulting from this condition. **3** a winter weather condition in which blowing snow completely fills the range of vision: *Many highway traffic accidents are caused by whiteouts.* [modelled on *blackout*]

white paper a government report concerning matters of lesser importance than those appearing in blue books.

white pepper a hot-tasting seasoning made by grinding the dried, husked berries of the black pepper vine.

white pine 1 any of various pines having soft, light wood, especially the eastern white pine (*Pinus strobus*) of the Great Lakes and St. Lawrence forest regions, and the western white pine (*P. monticola*) of southern British Columbia and the NW United States. **2** the wood of any of these trees, much used for building.

white plague tuberculosis.

white poplar 1 a large Eurasian poplar (*Populus alba*) having a dense covering of white, woolly hairs on the underside of the lobed leaves and on the twigs and buds. It is widely cultivated as an ornamental tree. **2** trembling aspen.

white potato the common potato.

White Russian 1 a Russian living in the western part of the Soviet Union, north of the Ukraine. **2** a Russian who recognizes the former czarist government of Russia as the legal government of that country.

white sauce a sauce made of milk, butter, flour, and, usually, seasonings cooked together.

white shark a large, ferocious shark (*Carcharodon carcharias*) widely distributed in temperate and tropical seas having a greyish back and white underside. The white shark is a maneater.

white slave 1 a woman forced to be a prostitute. **2** a white person held as a slave.

white slaver a person who keeps, controls, or deals in white slaves.

white slavery 1 the condition of white slaves. **2** traffic in white slaves.

white sound white noise.

white spruce a common spruce (*Picea glauca*) of the northern forest, also found throughout the rest of Canada, larger and taller than the black spruce, having long, slender cones, and bluish-green needles often covered with a whitish, powdery coating called a bloom.

white supremacist a believer in or supporter of white supremacy.

white supremacy the belief that the white race is superior to other races, especially the Negro race, and should therefore occupy the highest social, economic, and governmental positions.

white–tail (wīt′tāl′ *or* hwīt′-) *n.* white-tailed deer.

white–tailed deer (wīt′tāld′ *or* hwīt′-) a North American deer (*Odocoileus virginianus*) closely resembling the mule deer, but having a broad, relatively long tail with a wide, white fringe and underside, and antlers that arch forward.

white·thorn (wīt′thôrn′ *or* hwīt′-) *n.* hawthorn.

white·throat (wīt′thrōt′ *or* hwīt′-) *n.* **1** an Old World warbler (*Sylvia communis*) having mainly brownish plumage with a white throat. **2** white-throated sparrow.

white–throat·ed sparrow a common, grey-and-brown, North American sparrow (*Zonotrichia albicollis*) having broad stripes across the top of the head, from front to back, and a white throat patch.

white tie men's full evening dress with tails and white tie, as opposed to black tie.

white trash *U.S. Derogatory.* **1** poor whites considered collectively. **2** a poor white, or a person considered as one.

white·wash (wīt′wosh′ *or* hwīt′-) *n., v.* —*n.* **1** a liquid for whitening walls, woodwork, etc., usually made of lime and water. **2** a covering up of faults or mistakes. **3** anything that covers up faults or mistakes. **4** *Informal. Games.* a defeat without a score for the loser. —*v.* **1** whiten with whitewash. **2** cover up the faults or mistakes of. **3** *Informal.* defeat in a game without a score for the loser.

white water rapids.

white whale beluga (def. 1).

white·wood (wīt′wùd′ *or* hwīt′-) *n.* **1** a tree with light-colored wood, such as a tulip tree, linden, etc. **2** the wood of this tree.

whith·er (wiтн′ər *or* hwiтн′ər) *adv. or conj.* to what place; to which place; where. [OE *hwider*]

☛ *Hom.* wither (wiтнər).

whith·er·so·ev·er (wiтн′ər sō ev′ər *or* hwiтн′ər-) *adv. or conj.* wherever; to whatever place.

whit·ing¹ (wīt′ing *or* hwīt′-) *n., pl.* **-ing** *or* **-ings. 1** an important European marine food fish (*Merlangius merlangus,* also classified as *Gadus merlangus*) of the cod family. **2** any of various related or similar marine fishes. [ME < MDu. *wijting < wit* white; cf. OE *hwītling*]

whit·ing² (wīt′ing *or* hwīt′-) *n.* a powdered white chalk, used in making putty, whitewash, and silver polish. [< *white*]

whit·ish (wīt′ish *or* hwīt′-) *adj.* almost white.

whit·low (wit′lō *or* hwīt′-) *n.* a usually pus-filled inflammation of a finger or toe, especially near the nail; felon. [earlier *whitflaw,* probably < *white + flaw*]

Whit·mon·day (wit′mun′dē *or* -dā, hwit′mun′dē *or* -dā) *n.* the Monday after Whitsunday.

Whit·sun (wit′sən *or* hwit′-) *adj.* of or having to do with Whitsunday or Whitsuntide.

Whit·sun·day (wit′sun′dē *or* -dā, hwit′sun′dē *or* -dā) *n.* the seventh Sunday after Easter; Pentecost. [< *white + Sunday*]

Whit·sun·tide (wit′sən tīd′ *or* hwit′-) *n.* the week beginning with Whitsunday, especially the first three days.

whit·tle (wit′əl *or* hwit′əl) *v.* **-tled, -tling. 1** cut shavings or chips from (wood, etc.) with a knife. **2** shape or make by whittling: *to whittle a boat.*
whittle down or **away,** cut down little by little: *We tried to whittle down our expenses.*
[earlier *thwittle,* ult. < OE *thwītan* cut] —**whit′tler,** *n.*

whit·y (wī′tē *or* hwī′tē) *adj.* whitish.

whiz or **whizz** (wiz *or* hwiz) *v., pl.* **whiz·zes;** *v.* **whizzed, whiz·zing.** —*n.* **1** a humming or hissing sound. **2** *Slang.* a very clever person; an expert. —*v.* make a humming or hissing sound; move or rush with such a sound: *An arrow whizzed past his head.* [imitative]

who (hü; *unstressed relative,* ü) *pron.* **poss. whose,** *obj.* **whom. 1** as an interrogative pronoun, used in asking about the identity of a person or persons: *Who is she? Who told you?* **2** as a

relative pronoun: **a** used to connect a group of words with some previous word in the sentence: *The girl who spoke has left. We saw the men who were hired.* **b** used in making statements about the identity of a person or persons: *I don't know who will be there.* **who's who, a** which is one person and which is the other. **b** which people are important. [OE *hwā*]

☛ *Usage.* **Who** refers to people, to personified objects (such as a ship, a country), and occasionally to animals.

☛ *Usage.* See also the note at **that.**

☛ *Usage.* In informal English **who** is commonly used in both subject and object positions, though **whom** is obligatory immediately after a preposition: *Who did you speak to?* but *I saw the man to whom you spoke yesterday.*

☛ *Usage.* The use of **whose** as a relative referring to a non-personal antecedent (e.g. *generators whose combined capacity...*) is acceptable in both formal and informal situations when the construction **of which** would make the sentence seem clumsy.

WHO World Health Organization.

whoa (wō *or* hwō) *interj.* (used especially to horses) stop!

who'd (hüd) who would: *Who'd like to go along?*

who·dun·it (hü dun′it) *n. Slang.* a story or motion picture dealing with crime, especially murder, and its detection. [< *who* + *done* + *it*]

who·ev·er (hü ev′ər) *pron.* **1** who; any person that: *Whoever wants the book may have it.* **2** no matter who: *Whoever else goes hungry, he won't.*

whole (hōl) *adj., n.* —*adj.* **1** having all its parts or elements; complete: *He gave her a whole set of dishes.* **2** comprising the full quantity, amount, extent, number, etc.; entire: *a whole melon. He worked the whole day.* **3** not injured, broken, or defective: *to get out of a fight with a whole skin.* **4** in one piece; undivided: *to swallow a piece of meat whole.* **5** *Mathematics.* not fractional; integral: *a whole number.* **6** well; healthy. **7** having the same father and mother: *They are whole brothers.* **made out of whole cloth,** *Informal.* entirely false or imaginary. —*n.* **1** all of a thing; the total: *Four quarters make a whole.* **2** anything complete in itself; a system. **as a whole,** as one complete thing; altogether. **on the whole, a** considering everything. **b** for the most part. [dial. var. of ME *hole*, OE *hāl*] —**whole′ness,** *n.*
☛ *Hom.* hole.

whole–heart·ed (hōl′här′tid) *adj.* earnest; sincere; hearty; cordial. —**whole′-heart′ed·ly,** *adv.* —**whole′-heart′ed·ness,** *n.*

whole note *Music.* a note having the longest time value in standard notation, used as the basis for determining the time value of all other notes. It is equal to two half notes, four quarter notes, etc. See **note** for picture.

whole number a number denoting zero or one or more whole things or units; a number that does not contain a fraction; integer. *Examples:* 0, 1, 3, −47, 2052.

whole rest *Music.* a rest lasting as long as a whole note.

whole·sale (hōl′sāl′) *n., adj., adv., v.* **-saled, -sal·ing.** —*n.* the sale of goods in large quantities at a time, usually to retailers rather than to consumers directly: *He buys at wholesale and sells at retail.* —*adj.* **1** in large lots or quantities: *The wholesale price of this coat is $20; the retail price is $30.* **2** selling in large quantities: *a wholesale fruit business.* **3** broad and general; extensive and indiscriminate: *Avoid wholesale condemnation.* —*adv.* in large lots or quantities. —*v.* sell or be sold in large quantities: *They wholesale these jackets at $10 each. Such jackets usually wholesale for much less.*

whole·sal·er (hōl′sāl′ər) *n.* a merchant who sells goods wholesale.

whole·some (hōl′səm) *adj.* **1** good for the health; healthful: *wholesome food.* **2** healthy-looking; suggesting health: *a wholesome face.* **3** good for the mind or morals; beneficial: *wholesome books.* [ME *holsum* < *hol* whole + *-sum* -some] —**whole′some·ly,** *adv.* —**whole′some·ness,** *n.*
☛ *Syn.* 2. See note at **healthy.**

whole step *Music.* an interval consisting of two adjoining semitones and equal to one sixth of an octave, such as D to E, or E to F♯.

whole tone whole step.

whole–wheat (hōl′wēt′ *or* -hwēt′) *adj.* made of the entire wheat kernel.

who'll (hül) who will; who shall.

whol·ly (hō′lē) *adv.* to the whole amount or extent; completely; entirely; totally.
☛ *Hom.* holey, holy.

whom (hüm) *pron.* the objective form of **who.** [OE *hwām,* dat. of *hwā* who]
☛ *Usage.* See notes at **who** and **that.**

hat, āge, fär; let, ēqual, tėrm; it, īce
hot, ōpen, ôrder; oil, out; cup, pùt, rüle,
above, taken, pencəl, lemən, circəs
ch, child; ng, long; sh, ship
th, thin; ᴛʜ, then; zh, measure

whom·ev·er (hüm′ev′ər) *pron.* **1** whom; any person whom. **2** no matter who.

whom·so·ev·er (hüm′sō ev′ər) *pron.* any person whom.

whoop (hüp, wüp, *or* hwüp) *n., v.* —*n.* **1** a loud cry or shout: *When land was sighted, the sailor let out a whoop of joy.* **2** the cry of an owl, crane, etc.; hoot. **3** the loud, gasping noise a person with whooping cough makes after a fit of coughing. —*v.* **1** shout loudly. **2** call, urge, drive, etc. with shouts: *to whoop the dogs on.* **3** hoot. **4** make a whooping noise. **whoop it up,** *Slang.* make a noisy disturbance, as in celebrating. [imitative]
☛ *Hom.* hoop (hüp).

whoop-de-do (hüp′dē dü′, wüp′-, *or* hwüp′-) *n. Slang.* loud commotion or display; uproar.

whoop·ee (hü′pē *or* wùp′ē, hwü′pē *or* hwüp′ē) *interj., n.* —*interj.* an exclamation of hilarious, unrestrained joy or pleasure. —*n.* **1** a shout of whoopee. **2** loud excitement; hilarity. **make whoopee,** have a noisy, hilarious good time. [< *whoop*]

whoop·er (wü′pər, hwü′pər, *or* hü′pər) *n.* **1** whooping crane. **2** whooper swan. **3** a person or animal that whoops.

whooper swan a large, white, Old World swan (*Cygnus cygnus*) having a black bill with a yellow base, named for its whooping call.

whoop·ing cough (hü′ping) an infectious disease of children, characterized by fits of coughing ending with a loud, gasping sound.

Whooping cranes— about 135 cm long including the tail; height about 120 cm

whooping crane a very large white North American crane (*Grus americana*) having a long neck and legs, with black wing tips and a red patch on the face. The whooping crane, which is the tallest of Canadian birds, is almost extinct.

whop (wop *or* hwop) *v.* **whopped, whop·ping;** *n.* —*v.* **1** *Informal.* strike hard or beat. **2** defeat soundly. —*n.* a heavy blow or bump. Also, **whap.**

whop·per (wop′ər *or* hwop′ər) *n. Informal.* **1** something very large. **2** a big lie.

whop·ping (wop′ing *or* hwop′ing) *adj. Informal.* very large of its kind; huge.

whore (hôr) *n., v.* **whored, whor·ing.** —*n.* a promiscuous woman or one who is a prostitute. —*v.* **1** have intercourse with whores. **2** of a woman, be or act as a whore. [OE *hōre*]
☛ *Hom.* hoar.

whore·house (hôr′hous′) *n.* brothel.

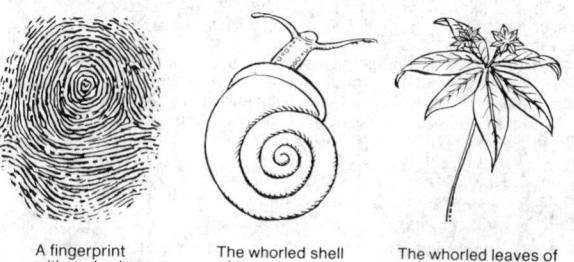

A fingerprint with a whorl | The whorled shell of a snail | The whorled leaves of the starflower, a North American wildflower

whorl (wėrl *or* hwėrl, wôrl *or* hwôrl) *n.* **1** a circle of leaves or flowers round a stem of a plant. **2** one of the turns of a spiral shell.

3 any coil or curl, especially of something that is whirling, or that suggests a whirling movement. **4** a type of fingerprint in which the ridges in the centre turn through at least one complete circle. [probably var. of *whirl*]
☛ Hom. **whirl** (wèrl, hwèrl).

whorled (wèrld *or* hwèrld, wôrld *or* hwôrld) *adj.* **1** having a whorl or whorls. **2** arranged in a whorl.
☛ Hom. **world** (wèrld).

whor·tle·ber·ry (wèr′təl ber′ē *or* hwèr′təl-) *n., pl.* **-ries. 1** a low-growing Eurasian shrub (*Vaccinium myrtillus*) closely related to the blueberry, having sweet, blackish, edible berries. **2** the berry of this shrub. Also called **bilberry.** [< *whortle* (ult. < OE *horte whortleberry*) + *berry*]

who's (hüz) who is.
☛ Hom. **whose.**

whose (hüz) *pron.* the possessive form of **who** and of **which;** of or relating to whom or which. [OE *hwæs*, gen. of *hwā* who; influenced in ME by nominative *who*]
☛ Hom. **who's.**
☛ Usage. **Whose** is always used when referring to people, but it can also be used for things, in order to make a long written or spoken sentence smoother. For instance, it is easier to read the second of the following sentences than the first: 1) *The plant has three new generators, the combined capacity of which is greater than that of the five we had before.* 2) *The plant has three new generators whose combined capacity is greater than that of the five we had before.*

whose·so·ev·er (hüz′sō ev′ər) *pron.* whose; of any person whatsoever: *I will accept whosesoever help is offered.*

who·so (hü′sō) *pron. Archaic.* whoever.

who·so·ev·er (hü′sō ev′ər) *pron.* whoever; anybody who.

why (wī *or* hwī) *adv., n., pl.* **whys; interj.** —*adv.* **1** for what cause, reason, or purpose: *Why did you do it? I don't know why I did it.* **2** for which; because of which: *That is the reason why he failed.* **3** the reason for which: *That is why he raised the question.* —*n.* the cause; reason: *I can't understand the whys and wherefores of her behavior.* —*interj.* an expression used to show surprise, doubt, etc. or just to fill in: *Why! The cage is empty. Why, yes, I will if you wish.* [OE *hwȳ*, instrumental case of *hwā* who and *hwæt* what]

WI Wisconsin.

WI *or* **W.I.** Women's Institute.

W.I. West Indies; West Indian.

wick[1] (wik) *n.* the part of an oil lamp or candle that is lighted, usually a loosely-twisted cord through which oil or melted wax is drawn up and burned. [OE *wēoce*]

wick[2] (wik) *v., n.* —*v. Curling.* curl a stone so that it glances off another already played. —*n.* a shot played in this way.

wick·ed (wik′id) *adj.* **1** bad; evil; sinful: *a wicked person, wicked deeds.* **2** mischievous; playfully sly: *a wicked smile.* **3** *Informal.* unpleasant; severe: *a wicked task, a wicked storm.* [< *wick* wicked, probably ult. < OE *wicca* wizard] —**wick′ed·ly,** *adv.*

wick·ed·ness (wik′id nis) *n.* **1** sin; the state of being wicked. **2** a wicked thing or act; something evil.

wick·er (wik′ər) *n.* **1** slender, easily bent branches or twigs that can be woven together. Wicker is used in making baskets and furniture. **2** (*adj.*) made of wicker. **3** (*adj.*) covered with wicker. **4** a slender, flexible branch or twig; withe. [ME < Scand.; cf. dial. Swedish *vikker* willow]

wick·er·work (wik′ər wèrk′) *n.* **1** twigs or branches woven together; wicker. **2** anything made of wicker. **3** the art or business of making things out of wicker.

wick·et (wik′it) *n.* **1** a small door or gate: *The big door has a wicket in it.* **2** a small window or opening, often protected by a screen or grating: *Buy your tickets at this wicket.* **3** a small gate or valve for emptying the chamber of a canal lock, or in the chute of a water wheel for regulating the passage of water. **4** *Croquet.* a wire arch stuck in the ground to knock the ball through. **5** *Cricket.* **a** either of the two sets of sticks that one side tries to hit with the ball. **b** the level space between these. **c** one batsman's turn. **d** the period during which two men bat together. [ME < AF *wiket*, ult. < Gmc., cf. MDu. *wicket*]

wick·et-keep·er (wik′it kēp′ər) *n. Cricket.* the player who stands behind the wicket.

wick·ing (wik′ing) *n.* material for lamp or candle wicks.

wick·i·up (wik′ē up′) *n.* a rude shelter, such as a lean-to; originally, a brush or mat-covered shelter among certain Algonquian Indians. [< Algonquian; cf. Fox *wikiyap* dwelling]

wid·der·shins (wid′ər shinz′) *adv. Scottish.* withershins.

wide (wīd) *adj.* **wid·er, wid·est;** *adv., n.* —*adj.* **1** filling much space

from side to side; not narrow; broad: *a wide street, the wide ocean.* **2** extending a certain distance from side to side, measured at right angles to length: *The door is 90 centimetres wide.* **3** full; ample; roomy: *wide shoes.* **4** of great range: *wide reading.* **5** far or fully open; distended: *stare with wide eyes.* **6** far from a named point, object, target, etc. **7** *Phonetics.* uttered with a relatively wide opening of the vocal organs.
—*adv.* **1** to a great or relatively great extent from side to side: *wide apart.* **2** over an extensive space or region: *They travel far and wide.* **3** to the full extent; fully: *Open your mouth wide.* **4** aside; astray.

wide of, far from: *His guess was wide of the truth. The shot was wide of the mark.*
—*n.* **1** a wide space or expanse. **2** *Cricket.* a ball bowled wide of the wicket, counting as a run for the batsman's side. [OE *wīd*]
—**wide′ness,** *n.*
☛ *Syn. adj.* **1, 2. Wide, broad** = far or large across. Although they are often used interchangeably, **wide** emphasizes the distance from one side to the other; **broad** emphasizes size or expanse of what is between the two sides, especially when it is larger than average: *A wide ocean separates Canada from Europe. Ships sail on the broad ocean.*

wide–a·wake (wīd′ə wāk′) *adj.* **1** with the eyes wide open; fully awake. **2** alert; keen; knowing.

wide–eyed (wīd′īd′) *adj.* **1** with the eyes wide open. **2** greatly surprised; astonished.

wide·ly (wīd′lē) *adv.* **1** to a great extent: *a widely distributed plant, a man is widely known, be widely read, widely opened eyes.* **2** very; extremely: *The boys gave two widely different accounts of the quarrel.*

wid·en (wīd′ən) *v.* make or become wide or wider: *He widened the path through the forest. The river widens as it flows.*
—**wid′en·er,** *n.*

wide–o·pen (wīd′ō′pən) *adj.* **1** opened as much as possible. **2** lax in the enforcement of laws, especially those having to do with the sale of liquor, with gambling, and with prostitution. **3** quite unsettled or undecided: *a wide-open question.*

wide·spread (wīd′spred′) *adj.* **1** spread widely or fully: *widespread wings.* **2** spread over a wide space: *a widespread flood.* **3** occurring in many places or among many persons far apart: *a widespread belief.*

widg·eon (wij′ən) *n., pl.* **-eon** *or* **-eons.** any of several freshwater ducks (genus *Anas*, also classified as *Mareca*), such as the North American baldpate; also, a Eurasian species (*A. penelope*), the male of which has mainly grey-and-white plumage with a reddish-brown head and breast. See also **baldpate.** [cf. MF *vigeon* wild duck]

wid·ow (wid′ō) *n., v.* —*n.* **1** a woman whose husband is dead and who has not married again. **2** *Card games.* a hand, or group of cards, not dealt to any player but capable of being used by a player who bids for it. **3** *Printing.* a word or group of words constituting less than a full line at the head of a column or page.
—*v.* make a widow or widower of: *She was widowed when she was only thirty years old.* [OE *widuwe*]

wid·ow·er (wid′ō ər) *n.* a man whose wife is dead and who has not married again. [ME, alteration of OE *widewa*]

wid·ow·hood (wid′ō hüd′) *n.* the condition or time of being a widow.

widow's mite a small amount of money given cheerfully by a poor person. [with reference to a poor widow's gift to the temple (Mark 12:42)]

widow's peak a V-shaped point formed by the hairline in the middle of the forehead. [from a belief that it was a sign of early widowhood]

width (width *or* witth) *n.* **1** how wide a thing is; distance across; breadth: *The width of the room is four metres.* **2** a piece of a certain width: *curtains taking two widths of cloth.* **3** extension or breadth in general; quality of wideness: *great width of mind, vision, etc.*

wield (wēld) *v.* hold and use; manage; control: *The soldier wielded his sword well. The people wield the power in a democracy.* [OE *wieldan*] —**wield′er,** *n.*

wie·ner (wē′nər) *n.* a reddish sausage usually made of beef and pork; frankfurter. [shortened form of *wienerwurst*]

wiener roast an outdoor social function at which wieners are roasted or boiled over an open fire. Also, **weiner roast.**

wie·ner·wurst (wē′nər wèrst′) *n.* wiener. [< G *Wienerwurst* Viennese sausage]

wife (wīf) *n., pl.* **wives. 1** a married woman, especially when considered with reference to her husband. **2** *Archaic.* a woman, as in *fishwife.*
take to wife, marry.
[OE *wīf*] —**wife′less,** *adj.*

wife·hood (wīf′hüd) *n.* the condition of being a wife.

wife·ly (wīf′lē) *adj.* **-li·er, -li·est.** of a wife; like a wife; suitable for a wife.

wig (wig) *n., v.* **wigged, wig·ging.** —*n.* an artificial covering of hair for the head: *The bald man wore a wig.* —*v.* **1** supply with, or cover with, a wig or wigs. **2** *Informal.* rebuke; scold. [< *periwig*]

wig·gle (wig′əl) *v.* **-gled, -gling;** *n.* —*v.* move with short, quick movements from side to side; wriggle: *The restless child wiggled in his chair.* —*n.* a wiggling movement. [cf. Du. *wiggelen*]

wig·gler (wig′lər) *n.* **1** a person or thing that wiggles. **2** the larva of a mosquito.

wig·gly (wig′lē) *adj.* **-gli·er, -gli·est. 1** wiggling: *a wiggly little caterpillar.* **2** wavy: *He drew a wiggly line under the heading.*

wight (wīt) *n. Archaic* or *dialect.* a human being; person. [OE *wiht*]
☛ *Hom.* **white.**

wig·wag (wig′wag′) *v.* **-wagged, -wag·ging;** *n.* —*v.* **1** move to and fro. **2** signal by movements of arms, flags, lights, etc. according to a code. —*n.* **1** signalling by movements of arms, flags, lights, etc. **2** the message signalled. [< *wig, v.* (related to WIGGLE) + *wag, v.*] —**wig′wag′ger,** *n.*

An Algonquian wigwam

wig·wam (wig′wom′) *n.* **1** a kind of dwelling traditionally used by Amerindian peoples from Manitoba to the Atlantic Provinces, consisting of an arched or cone-shaped framework of poles covered with hide, bark, mats made from rushes, etc. Compare **teepee.** **2** teepee. [< Algonquian (Ojibway)]

wild (wīld) *adj., n., adv.* —*adj.* **1** living or growing in the forests or fields; not tamed or cultivated: *The tiger is a wild animal. The daisy is a wild flower.* **2** with no people living in it: *wild land.* **3** not civilized; savage or primitive: *wild tribes.* **4** not checked; not restrained: *a wild rush for the ball.* **5** resisting control or restraint; unruly or insubordinate. **6** dissolute; dissipated; licentious: *to live a wild life.* **7** not in proper control or order: *wild hair.* **8** violently excited; frantic or distracted: *wild with rage.* **9** violent: *a wild storm.* **10** rash; crazy: *wild schemes.* **11** *Informal.* very eager. **12** unconventional, barbaric, or fanciful: *a wild tune or song.* **13** far from the mark. **14** *Card games.* of a card, able to be used to represent any number or suit.
run wild, live or grow without restraint.
wild and woolly, rough and uncivilized like the American West during frontier times; rough-and-tumble.
—*n.* **1** an uncultivated or desolate region or tract; waste; desert. **2 wilds,** *pl.* wild country.
—*adv.* in a wild manner or to a wild degree. [OE *wilde*] —**wild′ly,** *adv.* —**wild′ness,** *n.*

wild boar a wild pig (*Sus scrofa*) of Europe, N Africa, and Asia, from which most domestic breeds of pig have been derived.

wild carrot Queen Anne's lace.

wild·cat (wīld′kat′) *n., v.* **-cat·ted, -cat·ting.** —*n.* **1** any of various small or medium-sized wild members of the cat family, such as the lynx, bobcat, or ocelot. **2** a wild animal (*Felis sylvestris*) of Europe, resembling the domestic cat but somewhat larger and heavier and having a bushy tail. The wildcat is generally thought to be one of the ancestors of the domestic cat. **3** a person who has a wild temper or is a fierce fighter. **4** a well drilled for oil or gas in a region where none has been found before; a test well. **5** a risky or unsafe commercial enterprise. **6** a railway locomotive in operation without cars. **7** (*adj.*) of a strike, etc., begun or taking place illegally or without proper union approval. **8** (*adj.*) of, having to do with, or resulting from an unsound business enterprise.
—*v.* drill wells in regions not known to contain oil. —**wild′cat′ter,** *n.*

wild celery tape grass.

wild dog any of various wild members of the dog family, such as the dingo of Australia.

wil·de·beest (wil′də bēst′) *n.* the gnu, an African antelope. [< Afrikaans < Du. *wildebeest* wild beast]

wil·der (wil′dər) *v. Poetic* or *archaic.* **1** bewilder. **2** lose one's way; be perplexed. [apparently < *wilderness*] —**wil′der·ment,** *n.*

wil·der·ness (wil′dər nis) *n.* **1** a wild or desolate region with few or no people living in it. **2** a bewildering mass or collection: *a wilderness of streets.* [ME *wilderne* wild, OE *wildēorn,* ult. < *wilde*

hat, āge, fär; let, ēqual, tèrm; it, īce
hot, ōpen, ôrder; oil, out; cup, pùt, rüle,
əbove, takən, pencəl, lemən, circəs

ch, child; ng, long; sh, ship
th, thin; ŦH, then; zh, measure

wild + *dēor* animal]
☛ *Syn.* **1.** See note at **desert.**

wild–eyed (wīld′īd′) *adj.* **1** having wild eyes. **2** staring wildly or angrily.

wild·fire (wīld′fīr′) *n.* **1** a substance that burns fiercely and is hard to put out, formerly used in warfare. **2** will-o′-the-wisp; ignis fatuus. **3** any of various inflammatory, eruptive diseases, especially of sheep.
like wildfire, very rapidly: *The news spread like wildfire.*

wild·flow·er (wīld′flou′ər) *n.* **1** any flowering plant that grows in the woods, fields, etc.; an uncultivated plant. **2** a flower of such a plant. Also, **wild flower.**

wild·fowl (wīld′foul′) *n.* birds ordinarily hunted, such as wild ducks or geese, partridges, quail, and pheasants.

wild–goose chase (wīld′güs′) a useless search or pursuit.

wild·life (wīld′līf′) *n.* wild animals and birds as a group, especially those native to a particular area: *the northern wildlife.*

wild mustard one of the commonest Canadian weeds, an annual plant (*Sinapsis arvensis,* sometimes classified as *Brassica kaber*) growing up to one metre high, having somewhat hairy leaves and clusters of small, bright-yellow flowers. Wild mustard was introduced to North America from Europe and Asia.

wild oat 1 Usually, **wild oats, a** an Old World annual grass (*Avena fatua*) closely related to and resembling cultivated oats, that has been introduced to North America, where it has become a troublesome weed, especially in prairie grainfields. **b** any of several other wild grasses of the same genus. **2 wild oats,** youthful dissipation.
sow (one's) wild oats, indulge in youthful dissipation before settling down in life.

wild pansy a common European wildflower, a violet (*Viola tricolor*) having small, usually purple flowers. The pansy commonly found in gardens is derived mainly from the wild pansy.

wild rice *Cdn.* **1** a tall North American grass (*Zizania aquatica*) that grows in wet places, as along the edges of lakes. **2** its edible grain, which resembles rice.

wild rose *Cdn.* any uncultivated rose, especially the prickly rose. The wild rose is the floral emblem of Alberta.

wild West or **Wild West** the western United States during pioneer days.

wild·wood (wīld′wùd′) *n.* trees growing in their natural state; forest.

wile (wīl) *n., v.* **wiled, wil·ing.** —*n.* **1** a trick to deceive; a cunning way: *The serpent by his wiles persuaded Eve to eat the apple.* **2** subtle trickery; slyness; craftiness. —*v.* coax; lure; entice: *The sunshine wiled me from work.*
wile away, while away; pass easily or pleasantly.
[OE *wigle* magic]
☛ *Hom.* **while.**

wil·ful (wil′fəl) See **willful.** —**wil′ful·ness,** *n.*

wil·i·ness (wī′lē nis) *n.* the quality of being wily; craftiness; slyness.

will¹ (wil; *unstressed,* wəl) *v. pt.* **would,** *pres. sing.* or *pl.* **will.** an auxiliary verb used: **1** to express a promise: *"I will come at 4 o'clock" means that the speaker has made a definite appointment. The doctor will see you now.* **2** to refer to future happenings: *The train will be late. If they leave now, they will arrive in time for dinner.* **3** to introduce a polite request: *Will you please hand me that book?* **4** to express a capacity or power that something has: *This pail will hold eight litres.* **5** to refer to something done again and again: *She will read for hours at a time.* **6** as an imperative with the subject *you: Don't argue with me; you will do it at once!* [OE *willan*]
☛ *Usage.* **Will, shall.** Will is the usual auxiliary for forming the future tense: *I will be there. Tomorrow will come.* In formal English, however, some people still prefer to use **shall** when the subject is **I** or **we:** *We shall arrive before lunch.* For an emphatic future, the auxiliary (**will** or **shall**) is stressed in speech, but in writing **shall** is used with all subjects: *I shall not fail. You shall be home by midnight. This shall be done.*

will² (wil) *n., v.* **willed, will·ing.** —*n.* **1** the power of the mind to decide and do; deliberate control over thought and action: *A good leader must have a strong will.* **2** the act of choosing to do something, sometimes including also all deliberation that precedes

making the choice; volition. **3** purpose; determination: *the will to live.* **4** an order, command, or decree. **5** what is chosen to be done; (one's or its) pleasure. **6** wish; desire: *"Thy will be done."* **7** *Law.* **a** a legal statement of a person's wishes about what shall be done with his property after he is dead. **b** a document containing such a statement. **8** feeling toward another: *good will, ill will.*
at will, whenever one wishes.
do the will of, obey.
with a will, with energy and determination.
—*v.* **1** decide by using the power of the mind to decide and do; use the will: *She willed to keep awake.* **2** influence or try to influence by deliberate control over thought and action: *She willed the person in front of her to turn around.* **3** determine: *Fate has willed it otherwise.* **4** give by a will: *to will a house to someone.* **5** *Rare.* wish; desire. [OE]

willed (wild) *adj.* having a certain kind of will: *strong-willed.*

wil·let (wil′it) *n.* a large shore bird (*Catoptrophorus semipalmatus*) of the western hemisphere belonging to the same family as the sandpipers, having a long bill and grey, black, and white plumage. [< *pilly-will-willet*, imitative of its call]

will·ful or **wil·ful** (wil′fəl) *adj.* **1** wanting or taking one's own way; stubborn. **2** done on purpose; intended: *willful murder, willful waste.* [< *will²* + *full*] —**will′ful·ness** or **wil′ful·ness,** *n.*

will·ful·ly or **wil·ful·ly** (wil′fəl ē) *adv.* **1** by choice; voluntarily. **2** by design; intentionally. **3** selfishly; perversely; obstinately; stubbornly.

wil·lies (wil′ēz) *n. Informal.* a feeling of nervousness and uneasiness. [origin unknown]

will·ing (wil′ing) *adj.* **1** ready; consenting: *He is willing to wait.* **2** cheerfully ready: *willing obedience.* —**will′ing·ly,** *adv.* —**will′ing·ness,** *n.*

wil·li·waw (wil′ə wo′ or wil′ə wô′) *n.* **1** a sudden, violent gust of wind moving down to the sea from mountains along the coast. **2** any commotion or agitation. [origin unknown]

will-o'-the-wisp (wil′ə тнə wisp′) *n.* **1** a moving light appearing at night over marshy places, caused by the combustion of marsh gas. **2** something that deceives or misleads by luring on.

wil·low (wil′ō) *n.* **1** any of a genus (*Salix*) of trees and shrubs found mainly in the northern hemisphere, usually having long, narrow, pointed leaves arranged alternately on the twigs and flowers that appear in early spring before or at the same time as the leaves. Many willows have tough, slender branches that bend easily. **2** the wood of any of these trees or shrubs. **3** (*adj.*) made of willow. **4** (*adj.*) designating a family (Salicaceae) of trees and shrubs that consists of the willows and poplars. [ult. < OE *welig*]

willow herb any of several plants (genus *Epilobium*) of the evening-primrose family found in temperate and arctic regions, typically having narrow, willow-like leaves. See also **fireweed.**

willow ptarmigan a ptarmigan (*Lagopus lagopus*) found throughout the arctic regions of the world, having all-white winter plumage except for the black outer tail feathers, the male being distinguished in summer by its reddish-brown head, neck, and breast.

wil·low·y (wil′ō ē) *adj.* **1** like a willow; slender; supple; graceful. **2** having many willows.

will·pow·er (wil′pou′ər) *n.* power exercised by the will; self-control or determination: *He hasn't got enough willpower to keep to a diet.*

wil·ly-nil·ly (wil′ē nil′ē) *adv., adj.* —*adv.* **1** willingly or not; whether one wishes it or not: *He found himself involved willy-nilly in the promotion campaign.* —*adj.* that is or happens whether one wishes it or not: *a willy-nilly candidate.* [< *will I* (*he, ye*), *nill I* (*he, ye*); *nill* not will, OE *nyllan* < *ne* not + *willan* will]

wilt¹ (wilt) *v.* **1** become limp and drooping; wither. **2** lose strength, vigor, assurance, etc. **3** cause to wilt. [var. of *welt* wither, alteration of *welk*; cf. MDu. and MLG *welken*]

wilt² (wilt) *v. Archaic.* 2nd pers. sing. present tense of **will.** *Thou wilt* means *you* (sing.) *will.*

Wil·ton (wil′tən) *n.* a kind of velvety carpet. [< *Wilton*, a town in Wiltshire, England, famous for such carpets]

wil·y (wī′lē) *adj.* **wil·i·er, wil·i·est.** using subtle tricks to deceive; crafty; cunning; sly. —**wil′i·ly,** *adv.*

wim·ble (wim′bəl) *n.* a tool for boring. [ME < AF < MLG *wemel*]

wim·ple (wim′pəl) *n., v.* **-pled, -pling.** —*n.* a cloth draped closely about the face and covering the head and neck, worn by women in the Middle Ages and still forming part of the habit of some nuns. —*v.* **1** cover or muffle with a wimple. **2** ripple or cause to ripple. **3** *Archaic.* lie or lay in folds, as a veil. [OE *wimpel*]

win (win) *v.* **won, win·ning;** *n.* —*v.* **1** finish first in a race or competition: *to win a race. Her horse won by a length.* **2** gain (a prize, first place, etc.) in a race or competition: *Our display won first prize. They won the pennant.* **3** get victory or success: *You'll never win if the chairman is against the idea.* **4** gain (something) by effort, as if in a competition: *to win recognition for a new refining process.* **5** gain the favor or support of (often used with *over*): *The speaker soon won the audience. We won most of the undecided voters over to our side.* **6** gain the love, sympathy, etc. of; attract. **7** persuade to marry. **8** get to; reach, often by effort: *to win the summit of a mountain.*
win out, *Informal.* get victory or success; prevail: *Reason won out over stubbornness in the end.*
—*n. Informal.* the act or fact of winning; success; victory: *We had five wins and no defeats.* [OE *winnan*]
☛ *Hom.* **whin** (win).

wince (wins) *v.* **winced, winc·ing;** *n.* —*v.* draw back suddenly; flinch slightly: *The boy winced at the sight of the dentist's drill.* —*n.* the act of wincing. [ME < AF **wencir*, var. of OF *guencir* < Gmc.]

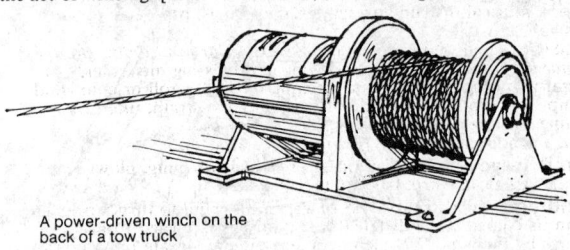

A power-driven winch on the back of a tow truck

winch (winch) *n., v.* —*n.* a machine for lifting or pulling, having a roller around which a rope or cable is wound. The crank of a winch is turned by hand or by an engine. —*v.* move by a winch. [OE *wince*]

Win·ches·ter (win′ches′tər or win′chis tər) *n.* a kind of breechloading repeating rifle, having a tubular magazine under the barrel and a bolt operated by a lever, invented and first made about 1866. Also, **Winchester rifle.** [< Oliver F. *Winchester* (1810-1880), an American manufacturer, who produced them]

wind¹ (*n.* wind *or, archaic or poetic,* wīnd; *v.* wind) *n., v.* **wind·ed, wind·ing.** —*n.* **1** air in motion. The wind may vary in force from a slight breeze to a strong gale. **2** a strong wind; gale. **3** a current of air filled with some smell: *The deer caught wind of the hunter and ran off.* **4** gas in the stomach or bowels. **5** *Music.* **a** a wind instrument. **b winds,** *pl.* the section of an orchestra or band composed of wind instruments. **6** power of breathing; breath: *A runner needs good wind.* **7** empty, useless talk. **8** vanity; conceit.
before the wind, in the direction toward which the wind is blowing.
between wind and water, a near the water line of a ship. **b** in a dangerous place.
down the wind, in the direction that the wind is blowing.
get wind of, a find out about; get a hint of: *Don't let him get wind of our plans.* **b** smell: *The deer soon got wind of the hunter.*
in the eye or **teeth of the wind,** directly against the wind.
in the wind, happening; about to happen; impending: *There's an election in the wind.*
into the wind, pointing toward the direction from which the wind is blowing.
off the wind, with the wind blowing from behind.
on the wind, as nearly as possible in the direction from which the wind is blowing.
sail close to the wind, a manage with close calculation or the utmost economy. **b** come very near to imprudence, dishonesty, indecency, etc.
take the wind out of (someone's) **sails,** take away one's advantage, argument, etc. suddenly or unexpectedly.
to the wind, to the point from which the wind blows.
up the wind, with the wind blowing from in front.
—*v.* **1** expose to wind or air. **2** follow by scent; smell. **3** put out of

A wimple, as worn in the early 14th century in England

breath; cause difficulty in breathing: *The fat man was winded by walking up the steep hill.* **4** let recover breath: *They stopped in order to wind their horses.* [OE]

☛ **Syn. n. 1. Wind, breeze** = air in motion. **Wind** is the general word: *The wind is from the north.* **Breeze,** except as a technical term (meteorology), means a light, gentle wind, especially one that is cool or refreshing: *We nearly always have a breeze at night.*

wind² (wīnd) *v.* **wound** or (rare) **wind·ed, wind·ing;** *n.* —*v.* **1** move this way and that; move in a crooked way; change direction; turn: *A brook winds through the woods. We wound our way through the narrow streets.* **2** proceed in a roundabout or indirect manner: *His speech wound slowly toward its conclusion.* **3** fold, wrap, or place about something: *The mother wound her arms about the child.* **4** cover with something put, wrapped, or folded around: *The man's arm is wound with bandages.* **5** roll into a ball or on a spool: *The old woman was winding yarn. Thread comes wound on spools.* **6** twist or turn around something: *The vine winds round a pole.* **7** be warped or twisted: *That board will wind.* **8** make (a machine) go by turning some part of it: *wind a clock.* **9** be wound: *This clock winds easily.* **10** haul or hoist by means of a winch, windlass, or the like. **11** of a musical instrument, tighten the strings, pegs, etc.; tune. **wind off,** unwind. **wind up, a** end; settle; conclude: *We expect to wind up the project tomorrow.* **b** *Baseball.* make swinging and twisting movements of the arm and body just before pitching the ball. **c** roll or coil; wind completely. **d** put into a state of tension, great strain, intensity of feeling, etc.; excite. —*n.* a bend; turn; twist. [OE *windan*] —**wind'er,** *n.*

wind³ (wīnd *or* wind) *v.* **wind·ed** or **wound, wind·ing.** blow: *The hunter winds his horn.* [special use of *wind¹*]

wind·age (win'dij) *n.* **1** the power of the wind to turn a missile from its course. **2** the distance that a missile is turned from its course by the wind. **3** a change in aim to compensate for windage. **4** atmospheric disturbance produced by the passage of a bullet, shell, or other missile. **5** the part of a ship's surface affected by the action of wind. **6** the slight difference between the diameter of a bullet, shell, etc. and of the bore of a gun of the same calibre.

wind·bag (wind'bag') *n. Slang.* a person who talks a great deal but does not say much that is significant.

wind–blown (wind'blōn') *adj.* **1** blown by the wind. **2** with the hair cut short and brushed forward.

wind–borne (wind'bôrn') *adj.* of pollen, seed, etc. carried by the wind.

wind·break (wind'brāk') *n. Cdn.* **1** a row or clump of trees or bushes planted to provide protection from the wind and, often, to prevent soil erosion. **2** any temporary shelter from the wind.

wind·break·er (wind'brā'kər) *n. Cdn.* a short outdoor jacket of wool, leather, nylon, etc. that closes to the neck and has close-fitting cuffs and waist.

wind–bro·ken (wind'brō'kən) *adj.* of horses, etc., having the breathing restricted or impaired; having the heaves.

wind–charg·er (wind'chär'jər) *n. Cdn.* **1** a windmill used to drive a generator. Wind-chargers were formerly much used on the Prairies to supply electricity for individual homes. **2** the generator of a wind-charger.

wind chill *Cdn.* the chilling effect of wind in combination with low temperature.

EXAMPLES OF WIND CHILL FACTOR

Wind Chill Factor	Description
700	Conditions considered comfortable when dressed for skiing.
1200	Conditions no longer pleasant for outdoor activities on overcast days.
1400	Conditions no longer pleasant for outdoor activities on sunny days.
1600	Freezing of exposed skin begins for most people, depending on the degree of activity and the amount of sunshine.
2300	Conditions for outdoor travel such as walking become dangerous. Exposed areas of the face freeze in less than 1 minute for the average person.
2700	Exposed flesh will freeze within half a minute for the average person.

Atmospheric Environment Service, Government of Canada

wind chill factor a measure of the combined chilling effect of wind and low temperature on living things or inanimate objects, expressed in watts per square meter.

wind·ed (win'did) *adj.* **1** out of breath. **2** having breath, or wind, of a specified kind or strength (*used only in compounds*): *short-winded.*

wind·fall (wind'fol' *or* -fôl') *n.* **1** fruit blown down by the wind:

hat, āge, fär; let, ēqual, tėrm; it, īce
hot, ōpen, ôrder; oil, out; cup, půt, rüle,
әbove, takәn, pencәl, lemәn, circәs
ch, child; ng, long; sh, ship
th, thin; ŦH, then; zh, measure

These apples are windfalls. **2** a tree blown down by the wind. **3** an unexpected piece of good luck.

wind·flow·er (wind'flou'ər) *n. Cdn.* in the West, any of several anemones, especially the prairie crocus.

win·di·go (win'di gō) *n., pl.* **-gos.** wendigo (def. 1).

wind·ing (wīn'ding) *n., adj.* —*n.* **1** the act of one that winds. **2** a bend; turn. **3** something that is wound or coiled. **4** *Electricity.* **a** a continuous coil of wire forming a conductor in a generator, motor, etc. **b** the manner in which the wire is coiled: *a series winding.* —*adj.* bending; turning. —**wind'ing·ly,** *adv.*

winding sheet a cloth in which a dead person is wrapped for burial.

wind instrument a musical instrument sounded by blowing air into it. Trumpets, flutes, clarinets, and oboes are wind instruments.

wind·jam·mer (wind'jam'ər) *n. Informal.* **1** in the merchant service, a sailing ship as opposed to a steamship. **2** a member of its crew.

wind·lass (wind'ləs) *n.* a machine for pulling or lifting things; winch. See **winch** for picture. [ME *windelass,* an alteration (influenced by ME *windel* wheel, winder) of ME *windass* < ON *vindáss* < *vinde* wind + *áss* beam, pole]

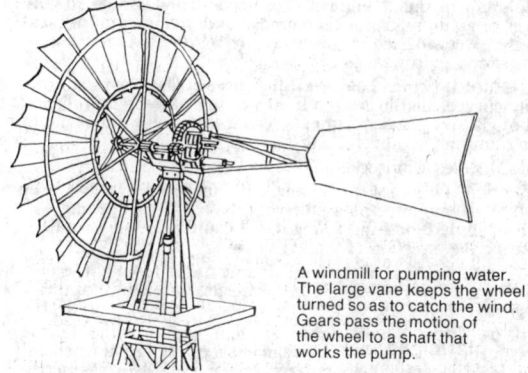

A windmill for pumping water. The large vane keeps the wheel turned so as to catch the wind. Gears pass the motion of the wheel to a shaft that works the pump.

wind·mill (wind'mil') *n.* **1** a mill or machine operated by the action of the wind upon a wheel of vanes or sails mounted on a tower. The motion thus produced is transmitted to a millstone, water pump, etc. **2** something that acts like or suggests a windmill, such as a pinwheel or helicopter.
tilt at or **fight windmills,** expend one's energy in futile attacks on what cannot be overcome or in a chase after imaginary foes (in allusion to the story of Don Quixote tilting at windmills under the illusion that they were giants).

win·dow (win'dō) *n., v.* —*n.* **1** an opening in the wall or roof of a building, boat, car, etc. to let in light or air. **2** such an opening with the frame, panes of glass, etc. that fill it. **3** the sashes and panes that fit such an opening: *to open the window.* **4** a windowpane: *to break a window.* **5 a** an opening like a window in shape or function, such as the transparent part of some envelopes through which the address is seen. **b** anything suggesting a window.
—*v.* furnish with windows. [ME < ON *vindauga* < *vindr* wind + *auga* eye] —**win'dow·less,** *adj.*

window box 1 a long, narrow box placed outside a window, or inside on a window sill, and used for growing plants and flowers. **2** a groove on the side of a window frame to hold the weights that counterbalance a vertically sliding sash.

window dresser a person who does window dressing.

window dressing 1 the art of attractively displaying merchandise in shop windows. **2** any display or statement made, often misleadingly, to create a favorable impression: *Much of the president's report was window dressing.*

win·dow·pane (win'dō pān') *n.* a piece of glass in a window.

window sash the frame for the glass in a window.

window seat a bench built into the wall of a room, under a window.

win·dow–shop (win′dō shop′) *v.* **-shopped, -shop·ping.** look at articles in store windows without going in to buy anything. —**win′dow-shop′per,** *n.*

window sill a piece of wood, stone, etc. across the bottom of a window.

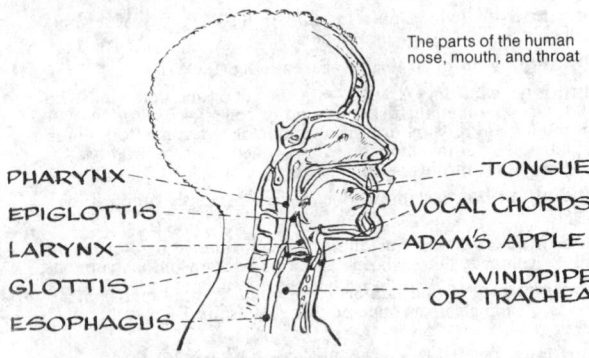

The parts of the human nose, mouth, and throat

PHARYNX — — TONGUE
EPIGLOTTIS — — VOCAL CHORDS
LARYNX — — ADAM'S APPLE
GLOTTIS — — WINDPIPE OR TRACHEA
ESOPHAGUS —

wind·pipe (wind′pīp′) *n.* the passage by which air is carried from the throat to the lungs; trachea. See **lung** for another picture.

wind·row (wind′rō′) *n., v.* —*n.* **1** a row of hay raked together to dry before being made into cocks or heaps. **2** any similar row, as of sheaves of grain, made for the purpose of drying; row of dry leaves, dust, etc. swept together by wind or the like. —*v.* arrange in a windrow or windrows. [< *wind¹* + *row¹*]

wind·shield (wind′shēld′) *n.* **1** the sheet of glass or plastic, usually curved, that forms the front window of a motor vehicle. **2** a sheet of glass or plastic forming a screen from the wind at the front of a motorcycle, motorboat, etc.

wind sleeve windsock.

wind·sock (wind′sok′) *n.* a long, cone-shaped canvas bag open at both ends, mounted on a pole with the narrower opening outward, so that the wind filling it will cause it to billow out, indicating the direction of the wind.

Wind·sor (win′zər) *n.* the family name of the royal house of Great Britain since 1917. [< *Windsor* Castle, a residence of the British sovereigns]

Windsor chair a kind of wooden chair, with or without arms, having a rounded spindle back, slanting legs, and a flat or slightly hollowed seat, especially popular in England and North America during the 18th century. [< *Windsor*, a town in Berkshire, England, where such chairs were first made]

Windsor tie a wide necktie of soft silk, tied in a loose bow.

wind·storm (wind′stôrm′) *n.* a storm with much wind but little or no rain.

wind·surf·ing (wind′sèr′fing) *n.* the sport of gliding over water on a board that is like a surfboard but is equipped with a sail. The operator controls the craft by leaning in a particular direction as he grasps one of the curved horizontal bars on either side of the sail. —**wind′surf′er,** *n.*

wind tunnel a tunnel-like chamber in which the effect of air pressures on aircraft, missiles, etc. can be calculated by means of artificially made winds.

wind–up (wīnd′up′) *n.* **1** a winding up; ending; close; conclusion. **2** *Baseball.* a series of movements made by a pitcher just before throwing the ball.

wind·ward (wind′wərd *or* win′dərd) *adv., adj., n.* —*adv.* **1** in the direction from which the wind is blowing. **2** toward the wind. —*adj.* **1** on the side toward the wind. **2** in the direction from which the wind is blowing. —*n.* the direction from which the wind is blowing: *They saw a ship to windward.*

wind·y (win′dē) *adj.* **wind·i·er, wind·i·est. 1** having much wind: *a windy street, windy weather.* **2** made of wind; empty: *windy talk.* **3** talking a great deal; voluble. **4** causing or having gas in the stomach or intestines. [OE *windig*] —**wind′i·ly,** *adv.* —**wind′i·ness,** *n.*

wine (wīn) *n., adj., v.* **wined, win·ing.** —*n.* **1** the juice of grapes that has been fermented and contains alcohol. **2** the fermented juice of other fruits of plants: *currant wine, dandelion wine.* **3** the color of red wine; a dark purplish-red. **4** something that exhilarates or intoxicates like wine.

new wine in old bottles, something new presented in an old form or style, or without a necessary change of form.
—*adj.* having the color wine.
—*v.* entertain with wine. [OE *wīn,* ult. < L *vinum*]
☞ *Hom.* **whine.**

wine·bib·ber (wīn′bib′ər) *n.* a person who drinks much wine. [(translation of G *Weinsäufer*) < *wine* + *bibber* < ME *bibbe(n)* drink, ? < L *bibere*]

wine cellar 1 a cellar where wine is stored. **2** the wine stored there.

wine gallon an old English gallon equal to 231 cubic inches (about 3.8 L), now the standard United States gallon.

wine·glass (wīn′glas′) *n.* a small drinking glass for wine.

wine·grow·er (wīn′grō′ər) *n.* a person who cultivates grapes and makes wine.

wine·grow·ing (wīn′grō′ing) *adj.* the business of a winegrower.

wine press 1 a machine for pressing the juice from grapes. **2** a vat in which grapes are trodden in the process of making wine.

win·er·y (wī′nər ē) *n., pl.* **-er·ies.** a place where wine is made.

Wine·sap *or* **wine·sap** (wīn′sap′) *n.* a variety of red winter apple.

wine·skin (wīn′skin′) *n.* a container made of the nearly complete skin of a goat, hog, etc. and used, especially in some Eastern countries, for holding wine.

wing (wing) *n., v.* —*n.* **1** the part of a bird, insect, or bat used in flying, or a corresponding part in a bird or insect that does not fly. **2** anything like a wing in shape or use, such as one of the major lifting and supporting surfaces of an airplane, the vanes of a windmill, and the feather of an arrow. **3** a part that sticks out from the main part or body, such as an extension at the side of a building, etc. **4** a part of an organization; faction. The radicals of a political group are called the left wing. **5** flying; winged flight. **6** *Sports.* a player whose position is on either side of the centre. **7** *Theatre.* **a** any of the pieces of side scenery on the stage. **b wings,** *pl.* the area at either side of the stage, out of sight of the audience. **8** either of the parts that project forward from the sides of the back of a wing chair. **9** an air-force unit made up of several squadrons. **10 wings,** *pl.* the insignia, or badge, of an aircraft pilot. **11** that part of a military force to the right or left of the main body. **12** *Facetious.* a foreleg or arm.
on the wing, a flying. **b** moving; active; busy. **c** going away.
take wing, fly away.
under (someone's) wing, under someone's protection or sponsorship.
—*v.* **1** fly or fly through: *The birds are winging south.* **2** supply with wings. **3** make able to fly; give speed to: *Terror winged his steps as the bear drew nearer.* **4** wound in the wing or arm: *The bullet winged the bird but did not kill it.* [ME < ON *væ̅ngr*] —**wing′less,** *adj.* —**wing′like′,** *adj.*

wing case either of the hardened front wings of certain insects.

wing chair a completely upholstered, high-backed armchair having wings on the sides of the back.

wing commander an air-force officer ranking next above a squadron leader and below a group captain. *Abbrev.:* W.C. or W/C

wing·ding (wing′ding′) *n. Slang.* **1** a lively, lavish party or celebration. **2** something remarkable or memorable of its kind: *a wingding of a fight.*

winged (wingd; *esp. poetic,* wing′id) *adj.* **1** having wings. **2** swift; rapid.

wing·spread (wing′spred′) *n.* the distance between the tips of the wings when they are spread out.

wink (wingk) *v., n.* —*v.* **1** close the eyes and open them again quickly. **2** close and open quickly. **3** close one eye and open it again as a hint or signal. **4** move by winking: *to wink back tears.* **5** twinkle: *The stars winked.* **6** give a signal or express a message by a winking of the eye, a flashlight, etc.
wink at, pretend not to see.
—*n.* **1** the act or an instance of winking. **2** a hint or signal given by winking. **3** a twinkle. **4** a very short time: *I didn't sleep a wink.* **5 winks,** *pl.* a short sleep; nap. [OE *wincian*]

wink·er (wingk′ər) *n.* **1** a person or thing that winks. **2** *Informal.* eyelash. **3** a blinder or blinker for a horse's eye.

win·kle (wing′kəl) *n.* periwinkle² (marine snail). [OE *-wincle* as in *pinewincle* periwinkle²]

win·ner (win′ər) *n.* a person or thing that wins.

win·ning (win′ing) *adj., n.* —*adj.* **1** that wins: *a winning team.* **2** charming; attractive: *a winning smile.* —*n.* **winnings,** *pl.* what is won; money won: *He pocketed his winnings.* —**win′ning·ly,** *adv.*

Win·ni·peg couch (win'ə peg') *Cdn.* a kind of couch having no arms or back and opening out into a double bed.

Winnipeg goldeye *Cdn.* goldeye.

win·now (win'ō) *v., n.* —*v.* **1** blow off the chaff from (grain); drive or blow away (chaff). **2** blow chaff from grain. **3** sort out; separate; sift: *to winnow truth from falsehood.* **4** *Archaic or poetic.* beat (the air) with or as if with wings. —*n.* **1** a contrivance for winnowing grain. **2** the act of winnowing or a motion resembling it. [OE *windwian* < *wind* wind[1]]

wi·no (wī'nō) *n.,* -**nos.** *Slang.* an alcoholic who is addicted to cheap wine.

win·some (win'səm) *adj.* charming; attractive; pleasing: *a winsome girl.* [OE *wynsum* < *wynn* joy] —**win'some·ly,** *adv.* —**win'some·ness,** *n.*

win·ter (win'tər) *n., v.* —*n.* **1** the coldest of the four seasons; the time of the year between fall and spring. **2** a year as denoted by this season: *a man of eighty winters.* **3** (*adj.*) of, having to do with, or characteristic of winter: *winter clothes, winter weather.* **4** (*adj.*) of the kind that may be kept for use during the winter: *winter apples.* **5** the last period of life. **6** a period of decline, dreariness, or adversity.
—*v.* **1** pass the winter. **2** keep, feed, or manage during winter: *We wintered our cattle in the warm valley.* [OE]

winter carnival a carnival that features winter sports and crafts.

win·ter·er (win'tər ər) *n. Cdn. Historical.* **1** a seasoned fur trader or voyageur who spent his winters in the fur country. **2** a wintering partner.

win·ter·green (win'tər grēn') *n.* **1** any of several evergreen shrubs (genus *Gaultheria*) of the heath family, especially a low-growing species (*G. procumbens*) of E North America having shiny, aromatic leaves and edible red berries. **2 oil of wintergreen,** an aromatic oil used for flavoring and in medicine, originally made from the leaves of the wintergreen, but now usually synthesized. **3** any of a genus (*Pyrola*) of perennial herbs of temperate and arctic regions having shiny, rounded leaves and fragrant, typically cup-shaped flowers. **4** any of various plants of related genera, such as the **one-flowered wintergreen** (*Moneses uniflora*). **5** (*adj.*) designating the family (Pyrolaceae) of low-growing perennial herbs that includes the wintergreens (genera *Pyrola, Moneses,* etc.) and pipsissewas.

winter ice sea ice that is more than about 20 centimetres thick and has formed and developed in one winter. It is therefore one year old or less.

wintering partner *Cdn. Historical.* **1** a stock-holding partner in the North West Company who represented the company the year round at trading posts in the fur country. **2** in the Hudson's Bay Company, a commissioned officer in charge of business at a trading post. He held no stock but received a share of the profits.

win·ter·ize (win'tər īz') *v.* -**ized,** -**iz·ing.** **1** make (an automobile, etc.) ready for operation or use during the winter. **2** prepare a building, such as a cottage, for use in winter. **3** safeguard an unoccupied building against damage in winter by draining taps, boarding windows, etc.

win·ter·kill (win'tər kil') *v., n.* —*v.* kill by or die from exposure to cold weather: *The rosebushes were winterkilled.* —*n.* death of plants and animals resulting from winter conditions.

winter solstice for the northern hemisphere, the time when the sun is farthest south from the equator, December 21 or 22.

winter squash 1 the large, edible fruit of a trailing vine (*Cucurbita maxima*) of the gourd family, greatly variable in size, shape, and color. The numerous varieties of winter squash are harvested in fall and can be stored many months. **2** a plant that produces such fruits.

win·ter·tide (win'tər tīd') *n. Archaic.* wintertime.

win·ter·time (win'tər tīm') *n.* the season of winter.

winter wheat wheat planted in the fall to ripen in the following spring or summer.

win·ter·y (win'tər ē *or* win'trē) *adj.* -**ter·i·er,** -**ter·i·est.** wintry.

win·tri·ness (win'trē nis) *n.* a wintry quality.

win·try (win'trē) *adj.* -**tri·er,** -**tri·est. 1** of or having to do with winter; like winter: *a wintry sky.* **2** devoid of fervor or affection; cold; chilling: *a wintry smile.* **3** destitute of warmth or brightness; dismal; dreary; cheerless: *a wintry gathering.*

win·y (wī'nē) *adj.* tasting, smelling, or looking like wine.

winze[1] (winz) *n. Scottish* an oath; curse. [< MDu. *wensch* wish]

winze[2] (winz) *n. Mining.* a small inclined shaft or passage connecting one level with another. [< earlier *winds,* perhaps < *wind*[2]]

wipe (wīp) *v.* **wiped, wip·ing;** *n.* —*v.* **1** rub with paper, cloth, etc. in order to clean or dry: *to wipe the table.* **2** take (away, off, or out) by rubbing: *Wipe away your tears. She wiped off the dust.*

hat, āge, fär; let, ēqual, tèrm; it, īce
hot, ōpen, ôrder; oil, out; cup, pút, rüle,
əbove, takən, pencəl, lemən, circəs
ch, child; ng, long; sh, ship
th, thin; ᴛʜ, then; zh, measure

3 remove: *The rain wiped away all the footprints.* **4** rub or draw (something) over a surface. **5** apply (a soft substance) by rubbing it on with a cloth, pad, etc.: *wipe wax on a table.* **6** form (a joint in lead pipe) by spreading solder with a leather pad.
wipe out, a destroy completely: *The pollution in the river has wiped out all the fish.* **b** cancel: *The generous man wiped out all the debts owed him.*
—*n.* the act of wiping: *He gave his face a hasty wipe.* [OE *wīpian*]

wip·er (wī'pər) *n.* **1** a person who wipes. **2** anything used for wiping.

wire (wīr) *n., v.* **wired, wir·ing.** —*n.* **1** metal drawn out into a thin, flexible rod or thread: *telephone wire.* **2** such metal as a material. **3** (*adj.*) made of or consisting of wire: *a wire fence.* **4** netting, etc. made of wire. **5** a piece of such metal: *He used a wire to connect the two batteries.* **6** something made of wire, such as a barbed-wire fence or a snare. **7** *Informal.* **a** telegraph: *He sent a message by wire.* **b** telegram. **8** a metal string of a guitar, piano, etc. **9** the finish line of a race course.
down to the wire, *Informal.* up to or at the very end or the very last moment.
get (in) under the wire, arrive or finish just before it is too late.
pull wires, *Informal.* pull strings.
—*v.* **1** furnish with wire or wiring: *to wire a house for electricity.* **2** fasten with wire: *He wired the two pieces together.* **3** fence (in) with wire. **4** stiffen with wire; place on a wire. **5** catch by a wire or wires. **6** *Informal.* telegraph: *to wire a birthday greeting.* [OE *wīr*]
—**wire'like',** *adj.* —**wir'er,** *n.*

wire cutter a tool for cutting wire.

wire·drawn (wīr'dron' *or* -drôn') *adj.* **1** drawn out into a wire. **2** protracted; prolonged; spun out. **3** treated with too much hairsplitting and refinement.

wire gauge a device, usually a disk with different-sized notches in it, for measuring the diameter of wire, the thickness of metal sheets, etc.

wire·haired (wīr'herd') *adj.* having coarse, stiff hair: *a wire-haired fox terrier.*

wire·less (wīr'lis) *adj., n., v.* —*adj.* **1** using no wires; transmitting by radio waves instead of by electric wires: *wireless telegraphy.* **2** *Esp.Brit.* radio.
—*n. Esp.Brit.* **1** a radio. **2** a message sent by radio.
—*v. Esp.Brit.* send or transmit by radio.

wire nail a small thin nail made from iron or steel wire, with a small head produced by compression of one end.

wire·pho·to (wīr'fō'tō) *n., v.* -**toed,** -**to·ing.** —*n.* **1** a method for transmitting photographs by reproducing a facsimile through electric signals. **2** a photograph transmitted in this fashion. —*v.* transmit by wirephoto.

wire puller *Informal.* a person who uses secret influence to accomplish his purposes.

wire pulling *Informal.* the use of secret influence to accomplish a purpose.

wire·tap (wīr'tap') *n., v.* -**tapped,** -**tap·ping.** —*n.* **1** wiretapping. **2** the information obtained by wiretapping. —*v.* **1** make a wiretap, legally or illegally. **2** record by wiretapping. Also, **wire tap.** [back formation < *wiretapping*]

wire·tap·per (wīr'tap'ər) *n.* a person who taps telephone wires secretly.

wire·tap·ping (wīr'tap'ing) *n.* the act or practice of making a secret connection with telephone or telegraph wires to find out the messages sent over them.

wire·worm (wīr'wèrm') *n.* the slender, hard-bodied larva of any of various click beetles. Wireworms feed on the roots of plants and do much damage to crops.

wir·ing (wīr'ing) *n.* a system of wires to carry an electric current.

wir·y (wīr'ē) *adj.* **wir·i·er, wir·i·est. 1** made of wire. **2** like wire. **3** lean, strong, and tough. —**wir'i·ly,** *adv.* —**wir'i·ness,** *n.*

wis (wis) *v. Archaic.* know (used only in *I wis,* parenthetically). [< *iwis* certainly (taken as *I wis*), OE *gewiss*]

Wis. or **Wisc.** Wisconsin.

wis·dom (wiz'dəm) *n.* **1** knowledge and good judgment based on experience; the quality of being wise. **2** wise conduct; wise words. **3** scholarly knowledge. [OE *wīsdōm* < *wīs* wise]

Wisdom of Solomon one of the books of the Apocrypha.

wisdom tooth the back tooth, or third molar, on either side of the upper and lower jaw, ordinarily appearing between the ages of 17 and 25.

wise¹ (wīz) *adj.* **wis·er, wis·est;** *v.* **wised, wis·ing.** —*adj.* **1** having knowledge and good judgment: *a wise counsellor.* **2** showing wisdom: *wise advice.* **3** having knowledge or information; informed: *We are none the wiser for his explanations.* **4** learned; erudite. **5** *Archaic.* having knowledge of occult or supernatural things. **get wise,** *Slang.* find out; understand; realize. **wise to,** *Slang.* aware of; informed about.
—*v.*
wise up, *Slang.* **a** inform or enlighten (a person). **b** become enlightened; gain awareness or understanding. [OE *wīs*] —**wise′ly,** *adv.* —**wise′ness,** *n.*
☛ *Syn.* **1.** **Wise, sage** = having or showing knowledge and good judgment in using and applying that knowledge. **Wise** emphasizes knowledge and understanding of people and of what is true and right in life and conduct, together with sound judgment in deciding and acting: *His wise father knows how to handle him.* **Sage** suggests deep wisdom based on wide knowledge and experience and profound thought and understanding: *The old professor gave us sage advice that we have never forgotten.*

wise² (wīz) *n.* way; manner: *John is in no wise a student; he prefers sports and machinery.* [OE *wīse.* Akin to GUISE.]

-wise *adverb-forming suffix.* **1** in — manner, as in *anywise* and *likewise.* **2** in a — ing manner, as in *slantwise.* **3** in the characteristic way of a —, as in *clockwise.* **4** in the — respect or case, as in *leastwise, otherwise.* **5** in the direction of —, as in *lengthwise.* **6** with regard to, as in *businesswise.* **7** special meanings, as in *sidewise.* [< *wise²*]
☛ *Usage.* **6.** In Old and Middle English -wise was freely added to nouns to form adverbs of manner. This usage has recently been revived and is popularly used to form words as needed: *He is doing well salarywise.* However, many people regard the usage as a fad appropriate only to informal speech and professional jargon. It should, therefore, be used with discretion, especially in writing.

wise·a·cre (wīz′ā′kər) *n.* a person who thinks that he knows everything. [< MDu. *wijssegger* soothsayer < G *Weissager*]

wise·crack (wīz′krak′) *n., v. Slang.* —*n.* a smart remark; a quick, witty reply. —*v.* make wisecracks. —**wise′crack′er,** *n.*

wi·sent (vē′zent) *n.* the European bison (*Bison bonasus*), somewhat smaller than the North American bison, or buffalo, and having a much smaller hump over the shoulder. The wisent is now nearly extinct as a wild animal, but survives in parks.

wish (wish) *v., n.* —*v.* **1** have a need or longing for; desire; want: *Do you wish to go home?* **2** have or express a desire or hope: *I wished for a new house. I wish that I had enough money to buy that model boat.* **3** have or express a desire or hope for: *We wish peace for all mankind.* **4** express a desire or hope with respect to the happiness, fortune, etc. of: *I wish you a Happy New Year.* **5** request or command (a thing or action, or a person to do something): *Do you wish me to send him in now?* **6** pass or impose (something undesirable or unwanted) on to; foist (*used with* **on**): *They wished the hardest job on him.*
—*n.* **1** the act or an instance of wishing: *What is your wish? He had no wish to be king.* **2** Usually, **wishes,** *pl.* the expressed desire for someone's happiness, fortune, etc.: *She sends you best wishes for a Happy New Year.* **3** the thing wished for: *They got their wishes.* [OE *wȳscan*] —**wish′er,** *n.*
☛ *Syn. v.* **1.** **Wish, desire** = want or long for something. **Wish** is the less emphatic word, sometimes suggesting only that one would like to have, do, or get a certain thing, sometimes suggesting a longing that can never be satisfied: *I wish I could travel round the world.* **Desire,** sometimes used as a formal substitute for **wish** or, especially, **want,** particularly suggests wishing strongly and usually a willingness or determination to work or struggle to get it: *He finally received the position he desired.*

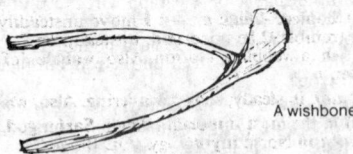

A wishbone

wish·bone (wish′bōn′) *n.* in poultry and other birds, the forked bone in the front of the breast.

wish·ful (wish′fəl) *adj.* having or expressing a wish; desiring; desirous. —**wish′ful·ly,** *adv.* —**wish′ful·ness,** *n.*

wishful thinking a believing something to be true that one wishes or wants to be true.

wish·y–wash·y (wish′ē wosh′ē) *adj.* **1** thin and weak; watery. **2** lacking in substantial qualities; feeble; inferior.

wisp (wisp) *n.* **1** a small bundle or bunch: *a wisp of hay.* **2** a small portion of anything; a little bit: *a wisp of smoke.* **3** a little thing: *a wisp of a girl.* [ME *wisp, wips;* cf. W. Frisian *wisp.* Akin to WIPE.]

wisp·y (wis′pē) *adj.* **wisp·i·er, wisp·i·est.** like a wisp; thin; slight.

wist (wist) *v. Archaic.* pt. and pp. of **wit.**
☛ *Hom.* **whist.**

wis·tar·i·a (wis ter′ē ə *or* wis tēr′ē ə) *n.* wisteria.

wis·te·ri·a (wis tēr′ē ə) *n.* any of a genus (*Wisteria*) of twining, mostly woody, vines of the pea family having compound leaves and large, drooping clusters of blue, purple, white, or rose flowers. Some wisterias are widely cultivated as ornamentals. [after Caspar Wistar (1761-1818), an American scientist]

wist·ful (wist′fəl) *adj.* **1** longing; yearning: *A child stood looking with wistful eyes at the toys in the window.* **2** pensive; melancholy. [< obs. *wist* attentive (< *wistly* intently, of uncertain origin) + -*ful*] —**wist′ful·ly,** *adv.* —**wist′ful·ness,** *n.*

wit¹ (wit) *n.* **1** the power to perceive quickly and express cleverly ideas that are unusual, striking, and amusing. **2** a person with such power. **3** the power of understanding; mind; sense: *People with quick wits learn easily. The child was out of his wits with fright. That poor man hasn't wit enough to earn a living.*
at (one's) wit's end, not knowing what to do or say.
have or keep (one's) wits about one, be alert: *You have to keep your wits about you to understand her lectures.*
live by (one's) wits, get one's living by clever or crafty devices rather than by any settled occupation.
[OE *witt*]
☛ *Hom.* **whit.**
☛ *Syn.* **1.** **Wit, humor** = power to see and express what is amusing or causes laughter. **Wit** = a mental sharpness and quickness in perceiving what is striking, unusual, inconsistent, out of keeping and in expressing it in cleverly surprising and amusing sayings: *Bernard Shaw was famous for his wit.* **Humor** = a power to see and show with warm sympathy and kindness the things in life and human nature that are funny or absurdly out of the ordinary: *Her sense of humor makes her popular.*

wit² (wit) *v. pres.* **1st pers. wot, 2nd pers. wost** (wost), **3rd pers. wot,** *pl.* **wit;** *pt. and pp.* **wist;** *ppr.* **wit·ting.** *Archaic.* know or learn.
to wit, that is to say; namely: *To my son I leave all I own—to wit, my house, what is in it, and the land on which it stands.* [OE *witan*]
☛ *Hom.* **whit.**

witch (wich) *n., v.* —*n.* **1** a person, especially a woman, who practises usually evil magic, often aided by the devil. Compare **warlock. 2** an ugly old woman. **3** *Informal.* a charming or fascinating girl or woman.
—*v.* **1** use the power of a witch on. **2** charm; fascinate; bewitch. [OE *wicce*]
☛ *Hom.* **which.**

witch·craft (wich′kraft′) *n.* **1** the practices and the cult of witches; the power or art of evoking supernatural forces or spirits to control or change the natural course of events, especially in order to work evil. **2** an influence or fascination suggesting such power or art.

witch doctor a professional practitioner of magic among certain nonliterate peoples, who uses his power especially in healing the sick.

witch·er·y (wich′ər ē *or* wich′rē) *n., pl.* **-er·ies. 1** witchcraft; magic. **2** charm; fascination.

witch hazel 1 any of a genus (*Hamamelis*) of shrubs and small trees native to E Asia and E North America having small clusters of yellow flowers, especially a North American species (*H. virginiana*) which is the source of a medicinal lotion. **2** the lotion prepared from the bark and leaves of the common North American witch hazel, used for cooling and soothing the skin.

witch hunt *Slang.* the persecuting or defaming of (a person) to gain an advantage, especially a political advantage. ✦

witch·ing (wich′ing) *adj.* bewitching; magical; enchanting. —**witch′ing·ly,** *adv.*

wit·e·na·ge·mot (wit′ə nə gə mōt′) *n.* the royal council of the Anglo-Saxons. [OE *witenagemōt* < *witena,* gen. pl. of *wita* councillor + *gemōt* meeting]

with (wiŧ *or* with) *prep.* **1** in the company of: *Come with me.* **2** among: *They will mix with the crowd.* **3** having, wearing, carrying, etc.: *a man with brains, a telegram with bad news.* **4** by means of; by using: *Cut meat with a knife.* **5** using; showing: *Work with care.* **6** as an addition to; added to: *Do you want sugar with your tea?* **7** including; and: *tea with sugar and lemon.* **8** in relation: *They are friendly with us.* **9** in regard to: *We are pleased with the house.* **10** in proportion to: *An army's power increases with its size.* **11** because of: *to shake with cold.* **12** in the keeping or service of: *Leave the*

dog with me. **13** in the region, sphere, experience, opinion, or view of: *It is day with us while it is night with the Chinese. High taxes are unpopular with many people.* **14** at the same time as: *With this event the field day ended.* **15** in the same direction as: *The boat floated along with the current.* **16** on the side of; for: *They are with us in our plan.* **17** from: *I hate to part with my favorite things.* **18** against: *We fought with that gang.* **19** receiving; having; being allowed: *I went with his permission.* **20** in spite of: *With all his size he was not a strong man.* **21** as a result of; because of; on account of: *green with age, eyes dim with tears.* **22** by adding, furnishing, filling, etc. a material to something: *a bottle filled with water.*
keep in with, *Informal.* keep acquaintance or friendship with.
with it, *Slang.* up to date; in the know; hep.
with that, when that occurred; whereupon: *The train reached the station, and, with that, our long trip ended.*
[OE *with* against]
☛ *Hom.* withe.
☛ *Syn.* 4. See note at **by.**

with– *prefix.* **1** against, as in *withstand.* **2** back; away, as in *withdraw, withhold.* **3** along with; alongside; toward, as in *withal, without, within.* [OE]

with·al (with ol′ *or* -ôl′, with ol′ *or* -ôl′) *adv., prep. Archaic.* —*adv.* with it all; as well; besides; also: *The lady is rich and fair and wise withal.* —*prep.* with. [< *with* + *all*]

with·draw (with dro′ *or* -drô′, with dro′ *or* -drô′) *v.* **-drew, -drawn, -draw·ing.** **1** draw back; draw away: *He quickly withdrew his hand from the hot stove.* **2** take back; remove: *Worn-out paper money is withdrawn from use by the government.* **3** go away: *She withdrew from the room.* **4** take back or retract a statement, motion, proposal, etc. [< *with-* away + *draw*]
☛ *Syn.* 3. See note at **depart.**

with·draw·al (with dro′əl *or* -drô′əl, with dro′əl *or* -drô′əl) *n.* **1** drawing back or taking back; taking away or going away: *The chairman noticed her withdrawal from the meeting.* **2** a mental condition during which a person ceases to communicate with others and draws back into himself.

with·drawn (with dron′ *or* -drôn′, with dron′ *or* -drôn′) *v., adj.* —*v.* pp. of **withdraw.** —*adj.* unsociable or unresponsive; introverted.

with·drew (with drü′ *or* with drü′) *v.* pt. of **withdraw.**

withe (with, with, *or* with) *n., v.* **withed, with·ing.** —*n.* **1** a willow twig. **2** any tough, easily bent twig suitable for binding things together. —*v.* bind with withes. [OE *withthe*]
☛ *Hom.* with.

with·er (with′ər) *v.* **1** lose or cause to lose freshness, vigor, etc.; dry up or fade: *a face withered with age. Flowers wither after they are cut.* **2** cause to feel ashamed or confused: *She blushed under her aunt's withering look.* [ME *wideren,* var. of *wederen* weather]
☛ *Hom.* whither.

with·ers (with′ərz) *n.pl.* the highest part of a horse's or other animal's back, behind the neck. See **horse** for picture. [OE *withre* resistance < *wither* against; from the fact that a horse opposes this part against the load he is pulling]

with·er·shins (with′ər shinz′) *adv. Scottish.* **1** in the opposite or contrary direction. **2** in a direction contrary to the apparent course of the sun, considered to be unlucky. Also, **widdershins.** [< earlier *widdershins* < MLG < MHG *widersinnes* < *wider* against, opposed + *-sind* way, direction + *-es* -s]

with·held (with held′) *v.* pt. and pp. of **withhold.**

with·hold (with hōld′) *v.* **-held, -hold·ing.** **1** refrain from giving or granting: *The play cannot be held if the principal withholds his consent.* **2** hold back; keep back: *The captain withheld his men from attack.* [< *with-* + *hold*]
☛ *Syn.* 2. See note at **keep.**

with·in (with in′ *or* with-) *prep., adv.* —*prep.* **1** inside the limits of; not beyond: *The task was within the man's powers. He guessed my weight within two kilograms.* **2** in or into the inner part of; inside of: *to see within the body by means of X rays.* **3** in the (inner) being, soul, or mind of.
—*adv.* **1** in or into the inner part; inside: *The house has been painted within and without. The curtains were white without and green within.* **2** in the inner being; in the being, soul, or mind; inwardly: *to keep one's grief within.* [OE *withinnan*]

with·out (with out′ *or* with-) *prep., adv., conj.* —*prep.* **1** with no; not having; free from; lacking: *A cat walks without noise. I drink tea without sugar.* **2** so as to omit, avoid, or neglect: *She walked past without looking at us.* **3** *Archaic.* outside of; beyond: *Soldiers are camped within and without the city walls.*
—*adv. Archaic or poetic.* on or at the outside; externally: *The house is clean within and without.*
do or **go without,** remain in want of something; manage in spite of not having a certain thing: *Either cook your own supper or go without.*
—*conj. Dialect.* unless. [OE *withūtan*]

---

hat, āge, fär; let, ēqual, tèrm; it, īce
hot, ōpen, ôrder; oil, out; cup, pút, rüle,
əbove, takən, pencəl, lemən, circəs
ch, child; ng, long; sh, ship
th, thin; ₮H, then; zh, measure

with·stand (with stand′ *or* with-) *v.* **-stood, -stand·ing.** stand against; hold out against; oppose, especially successfully: *The pioneers withstood many hardships. These shoes will withstand hard wear.* [OE *withstandan* < *with-* against + *standan* stand]
☛ *Syn.* See note at **oppose.**

with·stood (with stúd′ *or* with-) *v.* pt. and pp. of **withstand.**

with·y (with′ē *or* with′ē) *n., pl.* **with·ies.** **1** willow or osier; withe. **2** a band or halter made of withes. [OE *withig*]

wit·less (wit′lis) *adj.* lacking intelligence; stupid; foolish. —**wit′less·ly,** *adv.* —**wit′less·ness,** *n.*

wit·ness (wit′nis) *n., v.* —*n.* **1** a person who is present when something happens; one who has direct or first-hand knowledge of an event. **2** a person who gives evidence or testifies under oath before a judge, coroner, etc. **3** evidence; testimony. **4** a person who signs a document to show that another person's signature on it is genuine.
bear witness, be evidence; give evidence; testify: *A wife need not bear witness against her husband. The man's fingerprints bore witness to his guilt.*
—*v.* **1** see; perceive: *He witnessed the accident.* **2** testify to; give evidence of: *Her whole manner witnessed her surprise.* **3** give evidence; testify. **4** sign (a document) as a witness: *to witness a will.* [OE *witnes* knowledge < *wit* wit[1]]

witness box the place where a witness stands or sits to give evidence in a court of law.

witness stand *Esp.U.S.* witness box.

wit·ti·cism (wit′ə siz′əm) *n.* a witty remark. [< *witty;* on the model of *criticism*]

wit·ting·ly (wit′ing lē) *adv.* knowingly; intentionally.

wit·ty (wit′ē) *adj.* **-ti·er, -ti·est.** full of wit; clever and amusing: *a witty person, a witty remark.* [OE *wittig*] —**wit′ti·ly,** *adv.* —**wit′ti·ness,** *n.*

wive (wīv) *v.* **wived, wiv·ing.** *Archaic.* **1** marry a woman. **2** take as a wife. [OE *wīfian*]

wi·vern (wī′vərn) *n. Heraldry.* a two-legged, winged dragon with a barbed tail. [< *wiver* viper < dial. OF *wivre* < L *vipera*]

wives (wīvz) *n.* pl. of **wife.**

wiz·ard (wiz′ərd) *n., adj.* —*n.* **1** a man supposed to have magic power. **2** *Informal.* a very clever person; expert. —*adj.* magic. [ult. < *wise*[1]]

wiz·ard·ry (wiz′ərd rē) *n.* magic; magic skill.

wiz·ened (wiz′ənd) *adj.* dried up; withered; shrivelled: *a wizened apple, a wizened face.* [pp. of dial. *wizen,* OF *wisnian* shrivel]

wk. **1** week. **2** work.

wkly. weekly.

w.l. or **WL** **1** water line. **2** wavelength.

w.long. west longitude.

WMO World Meteorological Organization.

WNW or **W.N.W.** west-northwest.

wo (wō) *Archaic.* See **woe.**

W.O. **1** work order. **2** *Brit.* War Office.

W.O. or **WO** warrant officer.

woad (wōd) *n.* **1** a European herb (*Isatis tinctoria*) of the mustard family formerly cultivated for its leaves, from which a blue dye was made. **2** the dye itself. [OE *wād*]

wob·ble (wob′əl) *v.* **-bled, -bling;** *n.* —*v.* **1** move unsteadily from side to side; shake; tremble. **2** be uncertain, unsteady, or inconstant; waver. —*n.* a wobbling motion. Also, **wabble.** [cf. LG *wabbeln*] —**wob′bler,** *n.*

wob·bly (wob′lē) *adj.* unsteady; shaky; wavering. Also, **wabbly.**

Wo·den (wō′dən) *n.* the most important Anglo-Saxon god, corresponding to Odin in Norse mythology. [OE *Wōden*]

woe (wō) *n., interj.* —*n.* great grief, trouble, or distress: *Sickness and poverty are common woes.* —*interj. Archaic.* an exclamation of grief, trouble, or distress. [OE *wā,* interj.]

woe·be·gone (wō′bi gon′) *adj.* looking sad, sorrowful, or wretched.

woe·ful (wō′fəl) *adj.* **1** full of woe; sad; sorrowful; wretched: *a*

woeful expression. **2** pitiful: *a woeful sight.* **3** of wretched quality. —**woe′ful·ly,** *adv.* —**woe′ful·ness,** *n.*

wo·ful (wō′fəl) See **woeful.**

wok (wok) *n.* a wide, somewhat shallow metal cooking utensil used especially in Chinese cooking, having sides that curve in to a small, flat bottom.

woke (wōk) *v.* a pt. of **wake**[1].

wo·ken (wō′kən) *v.* a pp. of **wake**[1].

wold (wōld) *n.* high, rolling country, bare of woods. [OE *wald, weald* a wood]

wolf (wulf) *n., pl.* **wolves**; *v.* —*n.* **1** either of two wild members (genus *Canis*) of the dog family formerly widespread throughout the northern hemisphere but now greatly reduced in range and numbers, having a large, broad head, a deep, narrow chest, long legs, a long, bushy tail, and a coat that may be white, greyish, black, or reddish brown. The relatively small **red wolf** (*Canis rufus*) of south-central United States is considered by many authorities to be of the same species as the timber wolf (grey wolf). See also **timber wolf.** **2** any of several similar wild members of the dog family. **3** a cruel, savage, or greedy person. **4** *Slang.* a man who makes a habit of aggressively flirting with or trying to seduce women.
cry wolf, give a false alarm.
keep the wolf from the door, keep safe from hunger or poverty.
wolf in sheep's clothing, a person who pretends to be friendly or harmless, but intends to do harm.
—*v.* eat greedily (*often used with* **down**). [OE *wulf*] —**wolf′like′,** *adj.*

Wolf Cub a member, aged eight to ten, of the Boy Scouts.

wolf dog **1** any of various dogs used in hunting wolves. **2** a hybrid of a dog and a wolf. **3** in the North, an Eskimo dog or husky.

wolf eel wolf fish.

wolf·er (wul′fər) *n.* a wolf hunter.

wolf·fish or **wolf fish** (wulf′fish′) *n., pl.* **-fish** or **-fish·es.** any of a family (Anarhichadidae) of large fishes of the N Atlantic and Pacific oceans having long, pointed front teeth, especially a N Atlantic species (*Anarhichas lupus*) valued as a food fish. Wolffish belong to the same suborder as the blennies.

wolf·hound (wulf′hound′) *n.* any of several breeds of very large dog, such as the borzoi or the Irish wolfhound, formerly used in hunting wolves.

wolf·ish (wul′fish) *adj.* **1** of or having to do with wolves. **2** resembling a wolf: *a wolfish-looking dog.* **3** cruel, savage, or greedy: *He ate with wolfish impatience.* —**wolf′ish·ly,** *adv.* —**wolf′ish·ness,** *n.*

wol·fram (wul′frəm) *n.* **1** tungsten. **2** wolframite. [< G]

wolf·ram·ite (wul′frəm īt′) *n.* an ore consisting of compounds of tungsten with iron and manganese.

wolf's–bane or **wolfs·bane** (wulfs′bān′) *n.* aconite, especially a poisonous species (*Aconitum lycoctonum*) having dull-yellow flowers, found in the mountainous regions of Europe.

wolf spider any of a family (Lycosidae) of ground spiders ranging in size from a body length of about 6 mm to about 45 mm, that do not spin webs but leap on their prey. Some wolf spiders, such as the European tarantula, live in silk-lined burrows in the ground; others live in the open.

wolf willow or **wolf–wil·low** (wulf′wil′ō) *n. Cdn.* a North American shrub (*Elaeagnus commutata*) of the oleaster family found especially in the Prairies, having oblong, silvery leaves, small, fragrant flowers that are silver outside and yellow inside, and silvery fruit that is edible, but dry and mealy.

wol·ver·ine (wul′vər ēn′ *or* wul′vər ēn′) *n.* **1** a very powerful, heavily built, carnivorous mammal (*Gulo gulo*) of the weasel family found in the northern forests of North America and Eurasia, having a long, thick, coarse coat that is blackish brown with a light-brown stripe along each side of the body. **2** its fur. [earlier *wolvering < wolf*]

wolves (wulvz) *n.* pl. of **wolf.**

wom·an (wum′ən) *n., pl.* **wom·en** (wim′ən). **1** an adult female human being. A woman is a girl who has grown up. **2** women as a group; the average woman: *a magazine designed for the modern woman.* **3** (*adjl.*) female: *a woman cab driver. One of her women friends was asking about her.* **4** feminine nature or emotions; womanliness. **5** a female servant or attendant. **6** *Informal or dialect.* wife. **7** mistress; paramour. **8** a man considered as being womanish: *He's a fussy old woman.* [OE *wīfman < wīf* woman + *man* human

being] —**wom′an·less,** *adj.*
☞ *Usage.* See note at **lady.**

wom·an·hood (wum′ən hud′) *n.* **1** the condition or time of being a woman. **2** the character or qualities of a woman. **3** women as a group: *Marie Curie was an honor to womanhood.*

wom·an·ish (wum′ən ish) *adj.* **1** not suitable to a person, especially a man, of strong character: *womanish tears.* **2** effeminate: *He had a womanish way about him.* **3** characteristic of or suited for a woman or women; womanly. —**wom′an·ish·ly,** *adv.* —**wom′an·ish·ness,** *n.*

wom·an·ize (wum′ə nīz′) *v.* **-ized, -iz·ing. 1** of a man, indulge frequently in casual sexual relationships with women. **2** make effeminate. —**wom′an·iz′er,** *n.*

wom·an·kind (wum′ən kīnd′) *n.* women collectively.

wom·an·like (wum′ən līk′) *adj.* **1** like a woman; womanly. **2** suitable for a woman.

wom·an·ly (wum′ən lē) *adj.* **1** having or showing the best qualities of a woman: *a womanly nature. She is very womanly.* **2** proper or suitable for a woman: *Grandma says that hockey is not a womanly sport.* —**wom′an·li·ness,** *n.*

woman of the world a woman who has wide experience of different kinds of people and customs; a sophisticated and worldly-wise or practical woman.

woman suffrage **1** the political right of women to vote. **2** women's votes.

wom·an–suf·fra·gist (wum′ən suf′rə jist) *n.* a person who favors the right of women to vote.

womb (wüm) *n.* **1** uterus. **2** a place where something is conceived and developed. [OE *wamb*]

wom·bat (wom′bat) *n.* either of two burrowing Australian marsupials (*Vombatus ursinus* and *Lasiorhinus latifrons,* constituting the family Vombatidae, also called Phascolomidae) that resemble small bears. [< a native Australian language]

wom·en (wim′ən) *n.* pl. of **woman.**

wom·en·folk (wim′ən fōk′) *n.pl.* **1** women collectively. **2** a particular group of women, such as the female members of a family.

Women's Institute a society for women (originally, rural women) that promotes interest in agriculture and industry, home management, citizenship, and cultural activities. The first Women's Institute was formed in Stoney Creek, Ontario, in 1897. The movement spread to England in 1915. *Abbrev.:* WI or W.I.

women's rights social, political, and legal rights for women, equal to those of men.

won[1] (wun) *v.* pt. and pp. of **win.**
☞ *Hom.* **one.**

won[2] (wän) *n., pl.* **won. 1** the unit of money in South Korea. **2** the basic unit of money in North Korea, divided into 100 jun. See table at **money. 3** a coin or note worth one won. [< Korean]
☞ *Hom.* **one.**

won·der (wun′dər) *n., v.* —*n.* **1** a strange and surprising thing or event: *He saw the wonders of the city. It is a wonder he turned down the offer.* **2** the feeling caused by what is strange and surprising: *The baby looked with wonder at the Christmas tree.*
do wonders, do wonderful things; achieve or produce extraordinary results.
for a wonder, as a strange and surprising thing.
no wonder, a no marvel or prodigy: *The lecturer is no wonder.* **b** nothing surprising; not surprising: *No wonder he resigned.*
—*v.* **1** feel wonder: *We wonder at the splendor of the stars.* **2** feel some doubt or curiosity; wish to know or learn; speculate: *to wonder about his sudden departure.* **3** be surprised or astonished: *I shouldn't wonder if he wins the prize.* **4** be curious; be curious about; think about; wish to know: *I wonder what happened.* [OE *wundor*] —**won′der·er,** *n.* —**won′der·ing·ly,** *adv.*

won·der·ful (wun′dər fəl) *adj.* **1** causing wonder; marvellous; remarkable: *The explorer had wonderful adventures.* **2** *Informal.* excellent; splendid; fine: *We had a wonderful time at the party.* [OE *wunderfull*] —**won′der·ful·ly,** *adv.* —**won′der·ful·ness,** *n.*
☞ *Syn.* **Wonderful, marvellous** = causing wonder. **Wonderful** describes something so new and unfamiliar, out of the ordinary, beyond expectation, or imperfectly understood that it excites a feeling of surprise, admiration, puzzled interest, or, sometimes, astonishment: *The boys from Britain saw some wonderful sights on their first trip across Canada.* **Marvellous** describes something so extraordinary, surprising, or astonishing that it seems hardly believable: *The machine that can translate from a foreign language is a marvellous scientific invention.*

won·der·land (wun′dər land′) *n.* a land, realm, etc. full of wonders.

won·der·ment (wun′dər mənt) *n.* wonder; surprise.

won·drous (wun′drəs) *adj., adv.* —*adj.* wonderful. —*adv.* wonderfully. [alteration of *wonders* (gen. of *wonder*) wondrous, with the suffix *-ous* as in *marvellous*] —**won′drous·ly,** *adv.* —**won′drous·ness,** *n.*

won·ky (wong′kē) adj. Slang. likely to break down; in poor working order; shaky. [? alteration of dial. wankle, ult. < OE wancol shaky]

wont (wōnt) adj., n. —adj. accustomed: He was wont to read the paper at breakfast. —n. a custom or habit: He rose early, as was his wont. [originally pp., ult. < OE wunian be accustomed]
☞ Hom. won't.

won't (wōnt) will not.
☞ Hom. won't.

wont·ed (wōn′tid) adj. accustomed; customary; usual.

woo (wü) v. **1** seek to marry; court. **2** seek to win; try to get: Some people woo fame; some woo riches. **3** try to persuade; urge. [OE wōgian]

wood (wüd) n., v. —n. **1** the hard substance beneath the bark of trees and shrubs. **2** trees cut up for use: The carpenter brought wood to build a garage. **3** (adjl.) made of wood; wooden: a wood house. **4** something made of wood. **5** a cask; barrel; keg: wine drawn from the wood. **6** (adjl.) used for or on wood: We have a wood basket for the fireplace. **7** Printing. woodcuts collectively or a woodcut. **8** Music. **a** a wooden wind instrument; woodwind. **b** woods, pl. the woodwinds of a band or orchestra. **9** Often, woods, pl. a large number of growing trees; forest: looking for wildflowers in the woods. There is a large wood north of the village. **10** (adjl.) dwelling or growing in woods: wood moss.
out of the woods, out of danger or difficulty.
saw wood, Informal. **a** work steadily at one's task, without attention to anything else. **b** sleep heavily.
—v. **1** supply with wood; get wood for. **2** get supplies of wood. **3** plant with trees. [OE wudu]
☞ Hom. would.
☞ Usage. **Woods** is treated as singular and as plural. We speak of a woods but ordinarily use it with a plural verb: The woods are pretty in the fall. In proper names **woods** is frequently used with a singular verb. When used to qualify another noun, **woods** often refers particularly to forest areas as the site of logging operations: a woods camp, a woods superintendent.

wood alcohol methanol.

wood anemone any of several woodland anemones, especially Anemone quinquefolia of E North America and A. nemorosa of Europe.

wood·bine (wüd′bīn′) n. **1** honeysuckle, especially a common Eurasian species (Lonicera periclymenum) having fragrant yellow flowers. **2** Virginia creeper. [OE wudubind(e) < wudu wood + binde wreath]

wood block 1 a block of wood. **2** woodcut.

wood·carv·ing (wüd′kär′ving) n. **1** the art or craft of carving in wood. **2** an object or work of art made by carving in wood. —**wood′carv′er,** n.

wood·chuck (wüd′chuk′) n. groundhog. [< Algonquian (Ojibway) wejack; influenced by wood]

wood·cock (wüd′kok′) n., pl. **-cock** or **-cocks. 1** an Old World game bird (Scolopax rusticola) belonging to the sandpiper family, having reddish plumage, a long bill, and short legs. **2** a smaller shore bird (Philohela minor) of the same family, found in E North America. [OE wuducoc]

wood·craft (wüd′kraft′) n. **1** knowledge about how to get food and shelter in the woods; skill in hunting, trapping, finding one's way, etc. **2** skill in making things of wood.

wood·cut (wüd′kut′) n. **1** a block of wood with a pattern, design, or illustration cut into the surface, from which prints are made. **2** a print from such a block.

wood·cut·ter (wüd′kut′ər) n. a person who fells trees or chops wood.

wood·ed (wüd′id) adj. covered with trees: The park is well wooded.

wood·en (wüd′ən) adj. **1** made of wood. **2** stiff; awkward: The boy gave a wooden bow and left the stage. **3** dull; stupid. —**wood′en·ly,** adv. —**wood′en·ness,** n.

wood engraving 1 the art or process of making woodcuts. **2** woodcut.

wood·en–head·ed (wüd′ən hed′id) adj. Informal. dull; stupid.

wooden horse Trojan horse.

wood·en·ware (wüd′ən wer′) n. containers, utensils, etc. made of wood. Pails, tubs, and rolling pins are woodenware.

wood·land (wüd′lənd) n. **1** land covered with trees. **2** (adjl.) of, in, or having to do with woods.

wood·land·er (wüd′lən dər) n. a person who lives in the woods.

wood·lark (wüd′lärk′) n. a European lark (Lullula arborea), resembling the skylark, but somewhat smaller.

wood lice pl. of **wood louse.**

wood lily prairie lily.

hat, āge, fär; let, ēqual, tèrm; it, īce
hot, ōpen, ôrder; oil, out; cup, pút, rüle,
əbove, takən, pencəl, lemən, circəs
ch, child; ng, long; sh, ship
th, thin; ŦH, then; zh, measure

wood·lot (wüd′lot′) n. a piece of land on which trees are grown and cut; a bush lot.

wood louse 1 any of various small, terrestrial crustaceans (order Isopoda, especially genera Oniscus, Porcellio, etc.) found in dark, damp places, such as underneath stones, having a flattened, oval, segmented body covered with protective plates. Many species can roll into a ball if disturbed. **2** any of various small, wingless insects (order Corrodentia) that live under bark, in the woodwork of houses, etc.

wood·man (wüd′mən) n., pl. **-men. 1** woodcutter. **2** woodsman.

wood note a musical sound made by a bird or animal of the forest.

wood nymph 1 a nymph supposed to live in the woods. **2** a moth that destroys grapevines.

wood·peck·er (wüd′pek′ər) n. any of a family (Picidae) of climbing birds found almost worldwide, typically having showy, multicolored plumage, a long, straight, strong bill adapted for chiselling through the bark or wood of trees in search of insects, a long, extensile tongue with a horny spear at the tip for removing insects from deep cavities, and stiff tail feathers used in climbing.

wood pigeon a large Eurasian pigeon (Columba palumbus) having whitish patches on the neck and wings.

wood·pile (wüd′pīl′) n. a pile of wood, especially wood cut for fuel.

wood pulp wood made into pulp for making paper.

wood rat any of a genus (Neotoma) of rats of W North America having large ears, a furry tail, and thick grey fur. Wood rats are the only rats native to Canada.

wood·ruff (wüd′ruf′) n. any of several plants (genus Asperula) of the madder family, especially a Eurasian species (A. odorata), having small, fragrant flowers and narrow, pointed, fragrant leaves. [OE wudurōfe]

wood·shed (wüd′shed′) n. a shed for storing wood.

woods·man (wüdz′mən) n., pl. **-men.** a person who lives or works in the woods, especially one who is skilled in making his way in the woods and in hunting, fishing, trapping, etc.

wood sorrel any of a genus (Oxalis) of herbs found in temperate and tropical regions, having sour stem juice and compound leaves. The **white wood sorrel** (O. acetosella), which has leaves composed of three heart-shaped leaflets, is one of the plants considered to be the original shamrock.

woods·y (wüd′zē) adj. of or like the woods.

wood tar a dark-brown, sticky substance obtained from the distillation of wood and containing turpentine, resins, etc.

wood thrush a large thrush (Hylocichla mustelina) common in the thickets and woods of eastern North America.

wood turning the making of pieces of wood into various shapes by using a lathe.

wood warbler any of a New World family (Parulidae) of small, active, often brightly-colored songbirds similar to the Old World warblers but generally not having a musical song.

wood·wind (wüd′wind′) n. **1** woodwinds, pl. the wind instruments of an orchestra, including clarinets, oboes, etc. **2** any of this group of instruments. Woodwinds were formerly made of wood, but many are now made of metal. **3** (adjl.) of or having to do with woodwinds.

wood·work (wüd′wèrk′) n. things made of wood, especially the doors, stairs, mouldings, etc. inside a house.

wood·work·er (wüd′wèr′kər) n. a person who makes things of wood.

wood·work·ing (wüd′wèr′king) n. or adj. the act, process, or craft of making or shaping things of wood.

wood·worm (wüd′wèrm′) n. any of various insect larvae that bore in wood, especially the larva of a beetle (Anobium punctatum), that is destructive to furniture and buildings.

wood·y (wüd′ē) adj. **wood·i·er, wood·i·est. 1** having many trees; covered with trees: a woody hillside. **2** of a plant, having stems containing xylem, the tissue that is the main element of wood. Trees, shrubs, and some vines are woody plants. **3** consisting of wood: the woody parts of a shrub. **4** like wood: Turnips become woody when they are left in the ground too long. —**wood′i·ness,** n.

woo·er (wü′ər) *n.* one that woos; suitor.

woof (wüf) *n.* **1** the crosswise threads of a fabric; weft. **2** woven fabric or its texture. [ME *oof* < OE *ōwef* < *on* on + *wefan* weave]

wool (wül) *n.* **1** the soft, curly hair or fur of sheep and some other animals. **2** short, thick, curly hair. **3** something like wool: *Glass wool for insulation is made from fibres of glass.* **4** yarn, cloth, or garments made of wool. **5** (*adjl.*) made of wool.
pull the wool over (someone's) **eyes,** *Informal.* deceive someone. [OE *wull*]

wool·en (wül′ən) See **woollen.**

wool·gath·er·ing (wül′gaᴛʜ′ər ing *or* -gaᴛʜ′ring) *n., adj.* —*n.* absorption in thinking or daydreaming; absent-mindedness. —*adj.* inattentive; absent-minded; dreamy.

wool·grow·er (wül′grō′ər) *n.* a person who raises sheep for their wool.

wool·len *or* **wool·en** (wül′ən) *adj., n.* —*adj.* **1** made of wool: *a woollen suit.* **2** of or having to do with wool or cloth made of wool: *a woollen mill.* —*n.* Usually, **woollens** *or* **woolens,** *pl.* cloth or clothing made of wool.

wool·ly (wül′ē) *adj.* **-li·er, -li·est;** *n., pl.* **-lies.** —*adj.* **1** consisting of wool. **2** like wool. **3** covered with wool or something like it. **4** not definite; confused; muddled: *woolly thinking.* —*n. Informal.* an article of clothing made from wool. Also, **wooly.** —**wool′li·ness,** *n.*

wool·pack (wül′pak′) *n.* **1** a large cloth bag for packing wool. **2** *Historical.* a bundle or bale of wool weighing 240 pounds. **3** a round, fleecy cloud.

wool·sack (wül′sak′) *n.* **1** a bag of wool. **2** in the British House of Lords, the cushion on which the Lord Chancellor sits. **3** the office of Lord Chancellor.

wool·y (wül′ē) See **woolly.**

wooz·y (wü′zē) *adj. Slang.* **1** somewhat dizzy or weak: *to be just over an illness and still a little woozy.* **2** muddled; confused. **3** slightly drunk; tipsy.

Worces·ter·shire sauce (wüs′tər shər) *n.* a highly seasoned sauce made of soya sauce, vinegar, spices, etc. [< *Worcester,* a city in W England, where it was made originally]

word (wèrd) *n., v.* —*n.* **1** a sound or a group of sounds that has meaning and is an independent unit of speech. **2** the writing or printing that stands for a word. *Bat, bet, bit,* and *but* are words. **3** a short talk: *May I have a word with you?* **4** speech: *honest in word and deed.* **5** a brief expression or comment: *The teacher gave us a word of advice.* **6** a command; order: *We have to wait till she gives the word.* **7** a signal: *The word for tonight is "the King."* **8** a promise: *The boy kept his word.* **9** news: *No word has come from the battlefront.* **10** words, *pl.* **a** angry talk; a quarrel or dispute: *They had words about whose fault it was.* **b** the text of a song as distinguished from the music. **11 the Word, a** the Bible. **b** the message of the gospel. **c** the second person of the Trinity (John 1:1).
be as good as (one's) **word,** keep one's promise.
by word of mouth, by spoken words; orally.
eat (one's) **words,** take back what one has said; retract.
have the last word, in an argument, have the final, decisive say.
in a word, briefly.
in so many words, exactly; precisely.
man of his word, a man who keeps his promise.
mince words, avoid coming to the point, telling the truth, or taking a stand by using ambiguous or evasive words.
my word! an expression of surprise.
take (someone) **at his word,** take his words seriously and act accordingly.
take the words out of (someone's) **mouth,** say exactly what someone was just going to say.
the last word, a the last or latest thing or example in a class or field. **b** the final thing or example, beyond which no advance or improvement is possible.
upon my word, a I promise. **b** an expression of surprise.
word for word, in the exact words.
—*v.* put into words: *Word your ideas clearly.* [OE]

word·book (wèrd′bük′) *n.* a list of words, usually with explanations, etc.; dictionary; vocabulary.

word element combining form.

word·ing (wèr′ding) *n.* the way of saying a thing; the choice and use of words: *Careful wording helps you make clear to others what you really mean.*
☞ *Syn.* See note at **diction.**

word·less (wèrd′lis) *adj.* **1** without words; speechless. **2** not put into words; unexpressed. —**word·less·ly,** *adv.*

Word of God Bible.

word of honor *or* **honour** a solemn promise.

word order the arrangement of words in a sentence, phrase, etc.
☞ *Usage.* In English the usual word order for statements is subject + predicate, as in *John hit the ball. The ball hit John.* Some other patterns of word order (*Away ran John. Him the Almighty hurled..., Sweet are the uses of adversity.*) are chiefly rhetorical and poetic. In English, with its relatively few inflections, word order is the chief grammatical device for indicating the function of words and their relation to each other.

word processing a system for the input, editing, organization, storage, and retrieval of information, usually in the form of words, especially an automated system used to produce business correspondence.

word processor 1 a type of computer designed for use in word processing, including a keyboard, printer, storage, memory, and, usually, a display screen. **2** a person who operates a word processing system.

word·y (wèr′dē) *adj.* **word·i·er, word·i·est. 1** using too many words. **2** consisting of or expressed in words; verbal: *a wordy war.* —**word′i·ly,** *adv.* —**word′i·ness,** *n.*
☞ *Syn.* **Wordy, verbose** = using more words than are necessary. **Wordy** emphasizes the use of many words to say something that could be expressed more clearly and effectively in a few. Example: *There are many reasons that he has for going,* instead of *He has many reasons for going.* **Verbose,** a formal word used especially to describe public speakers, writers, speeches, and writings, adds the idea of using too many long, high-sounding words and long, roundabout sentences that do not express meaning clearly or interestingly: *The silvery, shimmering orb is a verbose way of saying the moon.*

wore (wôr) *v.* pt. of **wear.**
☞ *Hom.* **war.**

work (wèrk) *n., v.* **worked** *or* **wrought, work·ing.** —*n.* **1** the effort of doing or making something: *Moving the piano was hard work.* **2** something to do; occupation; employment: *He is out of work.* **3** something made or done, especially something creative; the result of effort: *The artist considers that picture to be his greatest work.* **4** a particular task, job, or undertaking: *to plan one's work for the day.* **5** material or a piece of material on which effort is expended: *The dressmaker took her work out on the porch.* **6 works,** *pl.* **a** a factory or other place for doing some kind of work: *His first job was in the boiler works.* **b** the moving parts of a machine or device: *the works of a watch.* **c** buildings, bridges, docks, etc. **d** actions; deeds: *good works.* **7** fortification. **8** *Physics.* **a** the transference of energy from one body or system to another. **b** that which is accomplished by a force when it acts through a distance. **9** the action, activity, or operation (of a person or thing), especially of a particular kind and with reference to result: *The medicine and suggestion have done their work.* **10** embroidery; needlework. **11** an engineering structure. **12 the works,** *Slang.* everything involved; the complete set, collection, or treatment: *He invested $50 000 and lost the works. The thugs caught the informer and gave him the works.*
at work, working.
in the works, *Informal.* in the planning stage; upcoming.
make short work of, do or get rid of quickly.
out of work, having no job; unemployed.
—*v.* **1** do work; labor: *Most people must work for a living.* **2** work for pay; be employed: *He works in a bank.* **3** carry on operations in (districts, etc.): *The salesman worked the Toronto area.* **4** put one's effort or labor into; perform a required or expected activity or on or in: *He worked his farm with success. The policeman was working his beat.* **5** act; operate, especially effectively: *This pump will not work. The plan worked.* **6** put into operation; use; manage: *to work a scheme.* **7** cause to do work: *He works his men long hours.* **8** treat or handle in making; knead; mix: *Dough is worked to mix it thoroughly.* **9** make, get, do, or bring about by effort: *He worked his way through college.* **10** move as if with effort: *His face worked as he tried to keep back the tears.* **11** bring about; cause; do: *The plan worked harm.* **12** go or do slowly or with effort: *The ship worked to windward. Work the cork loose.* **13** gradually become: *The window catch has worked loose.* **14** form; shape: *He worked a silver dollar into a bracelet.* **15** influence; persuade: *to work men to one's will.* **16** move; stir; excite: *Don't work yourself into a temper.* **17** solve: *Work all the problems on the page.* **18** *Informal.* use tricks on to get something: *to work a friend for a loan.* **19** ferment: *Yeast makes the brew work.*
work in, put in.
work off, get rid of.
work on or upon, try to persuade or influence.
work out, a plan; develop. **b** solve; find out. **c** use up. **d** give exercise to; practise. **e** accomplish. **f** result.
work to rule, of employees, work only as much as is demanded by terms of employment (without overtime, extraordinary effort, etc.), as a form or protest.
work up, a plan; develop. **b** excite; stir up. [OE *weorc,* n., *wyrcean,* v.]
☞ *Syn. n.* **1. Work, labor, toil** = effort or exertion turned to making or doing something. **Work** is the general word, applying to physical or mental effort or to the activity of a force or machine: *Keeping house is not easy work.* **Labor** applies to hard physical or mental work: *That student's understanding of his subjects shows the amount of labor he puts into his homework.* **Toil,** a word with some literary flavor, applies to long and wearying labor: *The farmer's toil was rewarded with good crops.*

work·a·ble (wėr'kə bəl) *adj.* that can be worked.

work·a·day (wėr'kə dā') *adj.* of or for working days; practical; commonplace; ordinary.

work·bag (wėrk'bag') *n.* a bag to hold the things that a person works with, especially a bag for sewing materials.

work·bench (wėrk'bench') *n.* a table at which a mechanic, carpenter, artisan, etc. works.

work·book (wėrk'būk') *n.* 1 a book containing outlines for the study of some subject, questions to be answered, etc.; a book in which a student does parts of his written work. 2 a book containing rules for doing certain work. 3 a book for notes of work planned or work done.

work·box (wėrk'boks') *n.* a box to hold the materials and tools that a person works with.

work·day (wėrk'dā') *n., adj.* —*n.* 1 a day for work; a day that is not a Sunday or a holiday. 2 the part of a day during which work is done. —*adj.* workaday.

work·er (wėr'kər) *n.* 1 a person or thing that works, especially a person who does a specified kind of work or works in a specified way: *a research worker, a volunteer worker. He's not a very good worker.* 2 a person who works hard: *She's really a worker.* 3 a manual laborer or one who works with industrial machines. 4 in a colony of bees, ants, wasps, or termites, one of a class of usually sterile individuals that care for the larvae, find food for the colony, etc.

work force 1 the total number of people employed by a particular company or working on a particular project, etc. 2 the total number of people potentially available for employment.

work·horse (wėrk'hôrs') *n.* 1 a horse used mostly for work, not for racing, hunting, or showing. 2 a person who is an exceptionally hard worker. 3 a machine that is especially powerful, productive, etc. Also, **work horse.**

work·house (wėrk'hous') *n. Esp.Brit. Historical.* a house where very poor people were lodged and were expected to perform some work in return.

work·ing (wėr'king) *n., adj.* —*n.* 1 the action, method, or performance of one that works. 2 Often, **workings.** operations; action: *the workings of one's mind. Do you understand the workings of this machine?* 3 Usually, **workings,** *pl.* the parts of a mine, quarry, tunnel, etc. where work is being done. —*adj.* 1 that works. 2 used in working. 3 used to operate with or by: *a working majority.* 4 **a** performing its function; that goes: *a working model of a train.* **b** that can be arranged or accomplished; workable: *a working agreement, a working arrangement.* 5 providing a basis for further work: *a working hypothesis.* 6 moving convulsively, as the features from emotion. 7 of liquor, etc., fermenting.

working capital 1 the amount of capital needed to operate a business. 2 the amount left when current liabilities are subtracted from current assets. 3 *Business.* the liquid, or immediately usable, capital of a business, as distinguished from frozen assets, such as property, machinery, etc.

working class a group thought of as including all those people who work for wages, especially manual and industrial workers.

working day workday.

work·ing–day (wėr'king dā') *adj.* workaday.

work·ing·man (wėr'king man') *n., pl.* **-men.** a man who works for wages, especially one who works with his hands or with machines.

working stiff *Slang.* workingman.

work·ing·wom·an (wėr'king wùm'ən) *n., pl.* **-wom·en.** a woman who works for wages, especially one who works with her hands or with machines.

work·load (wėrk'lōd') *n.* the amount of work assigned to a person, position, department, etc.

work·man (wėrk'mən) *n., pl.* **-men.** 1 workingman. 2 a person skilled in his trade or craft; craftsman.

work·man·like (wėrk'mən līk') *adj.* worthy of a good workman; skilful: *The job was done quickly and in a workmanlike manner.*

work·man·ship (wėrk'mən ship') *n.* 1 the art or skill of a workman; craftsmanship: *His workmanship is not always good.* 2 the quality of something that has been made: *jewellery of fine workmanship. The work done.*

workmen's compensation compensation for personal injuries suffered at work or diseases arising from work, that are not due to the employee's willful misconduct or gross negligence.

work of art 1 a product of any of the arts, especially a painting, statue, or literary or musical work. 2 anything done with great artistry or skill.

work·out (wėrk'out') *n. Informal.* 1 an exercise; practice. 2 a trial; test.

hat, āge, fär; let, ēqual, tėrm; it, īce
hot, ōpen, ôrder; oil, out; cup, pùt, rüle,
əbove, takən, pencəl, lemən, circəs

ch, child; ng, long; sh, ship
th, thin; ᴛн, then; zh, measure

work·peo·ple (wėrk'pē'pəl) *n.pl. Esp.Brit.* people who work, especially those who work with their hands or with machines.

work·place (wėrk'plās') *n.* 1 the specific location, as on an assembly line, at a desk, etc., where one does one's job: *Plant employees are not allowed to smoke at their workplace.* 2 the environment in which one works at one's job.

work·room (wėrk'rüm' *or* -rùm') *n.* a room set aside for working in: *We have a workroom in the basement.*

work·shop (wėrk'shop') *n.* 1 a room or building where work, especially manual work, is done. 2 a meeting of people for discussion, study, etc. of a particular subject: *The social-studies teachers had a workshop in September.*

work·ta·ble (wėrk'tā'bəl) *n.* a table to work at.

work·wom·an (wėrk'wùm'ən) *n., pl.* **-wom·en.** 1 a woman worker. 2 a woman who works with her hands or with machines.

world (wėrld) *n.* 1 the earth: *Ships can sail around the world.* 2 all of certain parts, people, or things of the earth: *the insect world, the ancient world, the Third World. The New World is North America and South America. The Old World is Europe, Asia, and Africa.* 3 a sphere of interest, activity, thought, etc.: *the world of music, the world of fashion.* 4 human affairs; the activities and circumstances of social, business, and public life: *a man of the world. The young graduate was ready to go out into the world.* 5 the things of this life and the people devoted to them: *Monks and nuns live apart from the world.* 6 the human race. 7 people in general; the public: *The whole world knows it.* 8 a star or planet, especially when considered as inhabited. 9 any time, condition, or place of life: *Heaven is in the world to come.* 10 all things; everything; the universe. 11 a great deal; very much; large amount: *The rest did her a world of good.*
all the world and his wife, everybody, male and female, especially everybody of any social pretensions.
bring into the world, give birth to.
come into the world, be born.
for all the world, a for any reason, no matter how great. **b** in every respect; exactly.
in the world, a anywhere. **b** at all; ever.
on top of the world, in high spirits: *I was on top of the world when I found out I had won.*
out of this world, *Informal.* **a** great; wonderful; distinctive: *Our plans for the decorations are out of this world.* **b** unearthly.
world without end, forever.
[OE *weorold*]
☛ *Hom.* whorled.
☛ *Syn.* 1. See note at **earth.**

World Bank the International Bank for Reconstruction and Development, an agency of the United Nations.

World Court a court made up of representatives of various nations, established as the Permanent Court of International Justice in 1920 under the covenant of the League of Nations to settle disputes between nations, and continued as the International Court of Justice under the United Nations.

world island *Geopolitics.* the land mass that constitutes Asia, Africa, and Europe.

world·li·ness (wėrld'lē nis) *n.* worldly ideas, ways, or conduct.

world·ling (wėrld'ling) *n.* a person who cares much for the interests and pleasures of this world. [< *world* + *-ling*]

world·ly (wėrld'lē) *adj.* **-li·er, -li·est.** 1 of this world; not of heaven: *worldly wealth.* 2 absorbed in or caring much for the interests and pleasures of this world. 3 worldly-wise.
☛ *Syn.* 1. See note at **earthly.**

world·ly–mind·ed (wėrld'lē mīn'did) *adj.* having or showing a worldly mind; caring much for the interests and pleasures of this world.

world·ly–wise (wėrld'lē wīz') *adj.* wise about the ways and affairs of this world.

World Series *Baseball.* the series of games played each fall between the winners of the two major league championships, to decide the professional championship of the United States.

World War I the war fought in Europe, Asia, Africa, and at sea, from July 28, 1914 to Nov. 11, 1918. The United Kingdom, France, Russia, Canada, the United States (1917-18), and their allies were on one side; Germany, Austria-Hungary, and their allies were on the other side.

World War II the war fought mainly in Europe, Asia, Africa, and at sea, from September 1, 1939 to August 14, 1945, beginning as a war between the United Kingdom, France, Poland, Canada, and their allies on one side and Germany and Italy on the other, ultimately involving most of the world's nations, notably the United States, Japan, and the Soviet Union.

world–wea·ry (wèrld′wēr′ē) *adj.* weary of this world; tired of living.

world·wide (wèrld′wīd′) *adj.* spread throughout the world.

worm (wèrm) *n., v.* —*n.* **1** any of numerous small, slender, elongated, often segmented invertebrates, usually soft-bodied and legless, such as the anclids (earthworms, etc.), flatworms (tapeworms, etc.), and nematodes (roundworms). **2** the wormlike larva of any of various insects. **3** something like a worm in shape or movement, such as the thread of a screw. **4** a short, continuously threaded shaft or screw, the thread of which gears with the teeth of a toothed wheel. **5** a force or agent that torments or slowly eats away from within. **6** a person who is the object of contempt or pity; wretch. **7 worms,** *pl.* a disease caused by parasitic worms in the body.
—*v.* **1** move like a worm; crawl or creep like a worm: *The soldier wormed his way toward the enemy's lines.* **2** make one's way insidiously (into): *He wormed himself into their confidence.* **3** wriggle (out of trouble, etc.). **4** work or get by persistent and secret means: *John tried to worm the secret out of me.* **5** look for or catch worms. **6** remove worms from. [OE *wyrm*] —**worm′er,** *n.* —**worm′like′,** *adj.*

worm–eat·en (wèrm′ēt′ən) *adj.* **1** eaten into by worms: *worm-eaten timbers.* **2** worn-out; worthless; out-of-date.

worm gear 1 worm wheel. **2** a worm wheel and an endless screw together. By a worm gear the rotary motion of one shaft can be transmitted to another shaft at right angles to it. See **gear** for picture.

worm·hole (wèrm′hōl′) *n.* a hole made by a worm.

worm wheel a wheel with teeth that mesh with the thread of a revolving screw called a worm.

worm·wood (wèrm′wùd) *n.* **1** any of various bitter herbs and shrubs (genus *Artemesia*) of the composite family, especially a European species (*A. absinthium*) that yields a bitter oil used in making absinthe. **2** something bitter or extremely unpleasant, such as a painful or mortifying experience. [OE *wermōd,* influenced by *worm, wood*]

worm·y (wèr′mē) *adj.* **worm·i·er, worm·i·est. 1** having worms; containing many worms. **2** damaged by worms. **3** contemptible; pitiable: *a wormy creature.* —**worm·i·ness,** *n.*

worn (wôrn) *v., adj.* —*v.* pp. of **wear.** —*adj.* **1** damaged by use: *worn rugs.* **2** tired; wearied: *a worn face.*

worn–out (wôrn′out′) *adj.* **1** used until no longer fit for use. **2** exhausted; fatigued.

wor·ri·ment (wèr′ē mənt) *n. Informal.* **1** worrying. **2** worry; anxiety.

wor·ri·some (wèr′ē səm) *adj.* **1** causing worry. **2** inclined to worry. —**wor′ri·some·ly,** *adv.*

wor·ry (wèr′ē) *v.* **-ried,-ry·ing;** *n., pl.* **-ries.** —*v.* **1** feel anxious or uneasy: *She will worry if we are late.* **2** cause to feel anxious or troubled: *The problem worried him.* **3** annoy; bother: *Don't worry me with so many questions.* **4** seize and shake with the teeth; bite at; snap at: *A dog will worry a rat.* **5** harass, as if by repeated biting, etc.; harry by rough treatment or repeated attacks.
worry along, manage somehow.
—*n.* **1** anxiety; uneasiness; trouble; care: *Worry kept her awake.* **2** a cause of trouble or care: *A mother of sick children has many worries.* [OE *wyrgan* strangle] —**wor′ri·er,** *n.*
☛ *Syn. v.* **2. Worry, annoy, harass** = disturb or distress a person with constant troubles, interference, etc. **Worry** emphasizes causing great uneasiness, care, or anxiety: *The change in his disposition and habits worries me.* **Annoy** particularly suggests constant interference, inconvenience, or irritation: *The new girl annoys her fellow workers by interrupting their work to ask foolish questions.* **Harass** emphasizes persistent or repeated demands or burdens: *He is harassed by business troubles and a nagging wife.*

worse (wèrs) *adj. comparative of* **bad;** *adv., n.* —*adj.* **1** more harmful, painful, regrettable, unpleasant, unfavorable, etc.: *It could be worse.* **2** more unattractive, unsuitable, faulty, incorrect, ill-advised, etc.: *His pen was poor and his writing even worse.* **3** more bad or evil: *He is dishonest enough, but his brother is much worse.* **4** of even lower quality or value; inferior: *The soil is worse in the valley.* **5** more ill: *The patient is worse today.* **6** less fortunate or well off.
—*adv.* in a worse manner or to a worse extent or degree: *It is raining worse than ever.*

—*n.* that which is worse: *He thought the loss of his property bad enough, but worse followed.* [OE *wyrsa*]

wor·sen (wèr′sən) *v.* make or become worse: *You will only worsen the situation if you talk about it. She was taken to hospital, but her condition worsened through the night.*

wor·ship (wèr′ship) *n., v.* **-shipped** or **-shiped, -ship·ping** or **-ship·ing.** —*n.* **1** great honor and respect paid to someone or something regarded as sacred: *the worship of God, idol worship.* **2** religious ceremonies or services in which one pays such respect: *Prayers and hymns are part of worship.* **3** great love and admiration: *hero worship.* **4 Worship,** a title used in addressing or referring to a mayor or, especially in Britain, to certain magistrates: *The letter was addressed to Her Worship the mayor. "Thank you, Your Worship," he said.*
—*v.* **1** pay great honor and respect to: *Moslems worship Allah.* **2** take part in a religious service. **3** consider extremely precious; hold very dear; adore: *A miser worships money.* [OE *weorthscipe < weorth* worth + *-scipe* -ship] —**wor′ship·per** or **wor′ship·er,** *n.*

wor·ship·ful (wèr′ship fəl) *adj.* **1** having or showing reverence: *worshipful silence.* **2** Often, **Worshipful,** *Esp.Brit.* a title of respect for mayors and certain other people of distinguished rank. **3** *Archaic.* worthy of respect and honor.

worst (wèrst) *adj. superlative of* **bad;** *adv., n., v.* —*adj.* **1** most harmful, painful, regrettable, unpleasant, unfavorable, etc.: *the worst diet imaginable, the worst sheep of the herd, the worst room in the hotel.* **2** most unattractive, unsuitable, faulty, incorrect, ill-advised, etc.: *That's the worst writing I've ever seen.* **3** most bad or evil: *It was the worst murder of the century.* **4** of the poorest quality or value: *This district has some of the worst soil in the province.*
—*adv.* in the worst manner or to the worst extent or degree: *He acts worst when he's tired.*
—*n.* that which is worst: *Yesterday was bad, but the worst is yet to come.*
at worst, under the least favorable circumstances.
give (someone) the worst of it, defeat one.
if (the) worst comes to (the) worst, if the very worst thing happens.
—*v.* beat; defeat: *The hero worsted his enemies.* [OE *wyrresta*]

wor·sted (wèr′stid or wùs′tid) *n.* **1** smooth, firm yarn or thread made from long wool fibres that have been combed. Worsted is used especially for firm, smooth-finished fabrics, carpets, and in knitting. **2** fabric made from worsted. **3** (*adj.*) made of worsted. [< *Worsted* (now Worstead), a town in E England, where it was made originally]

wort¹ (wèrt) *n.* the liquid made from malt that after fermentation becomes beer, ale, or other liquor. [OE *wyrt*]

wort² (wèrt) *n.* a plant, especially any of various herbaceous plants formerly used in medicine (*now used chiefly in compounds*): *liverwort, figwort.* [OE *wyrt*]

worth (wèrth) *adj., n.* —*adj.* **1** good or important enough for; deserving of: *Vancouver is a city worth visiting.* **2** equal in value to: *That stamp is worth at least twenty dollars.* **3** having property that amounts to: *That man is worth millions.*
for all (one) is worth, to the full extent of one's power or ability: *She ran for all she was worth.*
—*n.* **1** merit; usefulness; importance: *We should read books of real worth.* **2** value in money: *He needed money and had to sell his car for less than its worth.* **3** a quantity of something of specified value: *a dollar's worth of sugar.* **4** *Archaic.* property; wealth. [OE *weorth*]
☛ *Syn. n.* **1, 2.** See note at **merit.**

worth·less (wèrth′lis) *adj.* without worth; good-for-nothing; useless. —**worth′less·ly,** *adv.* —**worth′less·ness,** *n.*

worth·while (wèrth′wil′ or -hwil′) *adj.* worth time, attention, or effort; having real merit: *He ought to do some worthwhile reading.*

wor·thy (wèr′ᴛʜē) *adj.* **-thi·er, -thi·est;** *n., pl.* **-thies.** —*adj.* **1** having worth or merit: *She helps the worthy poor.* **2** deserving; meriting.
worthy of, **a** deserving. **b** having enough worth for.
—*n.* a person of great merit; an admirable person. —**wor′thi·ly,** *adv.* —**wor′thi·ness,** *n.*

wot (wot) *v. Archaic.* 1st and 3rd pers. sing. present tense, of **wit².** *I wot* means *I know.* [OE *wāt*]

would (wùd; *unstressed,* wəd) *v.* **1** an auxiliary verb used: **a** to introduce a request or command in a polite manner: *Would you please close the window?* **b** to soften a statement or express uncertainty: *I wouldn't like to ask him.* **c** to express an unlikely or an impossible condition: *If I asked him, he would say no. If I knew the way, I would tell you.* **d** to express repeated, or habitual, action in the past: *When we were small, we would spend hours playing in the sand.* **2** pt. of **will¹.** [OE *wolde*]
☛ *Hom.* **wood.**
☛ *Usage.* **Would** as the past tense of **will** is used most often in reported speech. Compare *He said, "I will come."* with *He said that he would come.* **Would**

rather is used to express a strong preference: *I would rather stay home than have to dance with him.*

would–be (wud′bē′) *adj.* **1** wishing or pretending to be. **2** intended to be.

would·n't (wud′ənt) would not.

wouldst (wudst) *v. Archaic or poetic.* 2nd pers. sing., past tense, of **will.** *Thou wouldst means you* (sing.) *would.*

wound¹ (wünd) *n., v.* —*n.* **1** a hurt or injury caused by cutting, stabbing, shooting, etc. **2** in a tree or plant, a similar injury due to external violence. **3** any hurt or injury to feelings, reputation, etc.: *The loss of his job was a wound to his pride.*
—*v.* **1** injure by cutting, stabbing, shooting, etc.; hurt. **2** injure in feelings, reputation, etc.: *His words wounded her.* [OE *wund*]

wound² (wound) *v.* pt. and pp. of **wind**².

wound³ (wound) *v.* a pt. and a pp. of **wind**³.

wove (wōv) *v.* pt. and a pp. of **weave.**

wo·ven (wō′vən) *v.* pp. of **weave.**

wow¹ (wou) *n.* **1** a wail. **2** a short explosive noise like a bark. **3** a variation in the sound pitch of a phonograph or tape recorder, caused by a slight irregularity in the speed of the driving mechanism. [imitative]

wow² (wou) *n., v., interj. Slang.* —*n.* **1** an exclamation of delight, admiration, etc. **2** a complete success; a hit: *The clown's act was a wow!*
—*v.* dazzle or impress: *My father really wowed everyone with his new suit.*
—*interj.* an exclamation of delight, admiration, etc.

wrack¹ (rak) *n., v.* —*n.* **1** wreckage. **2** ruin; destruction. **3** seaweed cast ashore.
—*v.* wreck; ruin. [< MDu. and MLG *wrak* wreck]
☛ Hom. **rack.**

wrack² (rak) *v.* **1** hurt very much; torture: *wracked by convulsions.* **2** stretch; strain. **3** torture on the rack. [var. of *rack*¹]
☛ Hom. **rack.**

wraith (rāth) *n.* **1** the ghost of a person seen before or soon after his death. **2** a ghost; spectre. [< Scottish, ? < ON *vörthr* guardian spirit]

wran·gle (rang′gəl) *v.* -gled,-gling; *n.* —*v.* **1** argue or dispute in a noisy or angry way; quarrel: *The children wrangled about who should sit in front.* **2** in the western parts of Canada and the United States, herd or tend (horses, etc.) on the range. —*n.* a noisy dispute or quarrel. [? < LG *wrangeln*]

wran·gler (rang′glər) *n.* **1** a person who wrangles. **2** in the western parts of Canada and the United States, a cowboy, especially one who looks after saddle horses.

wrap (rap) *v.* **wrapped** or **wrapt, wrap·ping;** *n.* —*v.* **1** cover by winding or folding something around: *She wrapped herself in a shawl.* **2** wind or fold as a covering: *Wrap a shawl around you.* **3** cover with paper and tie up or fasten: *to wrap a gift.* **4** cover; envelop; hide: *The mountain peak is wrapped in clouds. She sat wrapped in thought.*
wrapped up in, a devoted to; thinking mainly of: *She is wrapped up in her children.* **b** involved in; associated with.
wrap up, a put on warm outer clothes. **b** *Informal.* bring to a successful conclusion; clinch: *They wrapped up the game with three runs in the ninth.* **c** *Informal.* settle or finish: *to wrap up a meeting.*
—*n.* **1** a loose outer garment, especially one worn draped or wrapped about the shoulders, such as a shawl or cape. **2** wrapping paper: *gift wrap.*
under wraps, secret or concealed.
[ME *wrappen*]
☛ Hom. **rap.**

wrap·per (rap′ər) *n.* **1** a person or thing that wraps. **2** anything in which something is wrapped; covering; cover. **3** a woman's long, loose-fitting garment for wearing in the house. **4** the leaf or leaves rolled around smaller leaves or pieces to form the outside layer of tobacco in a cigar.

wrap·ping (rap′ing) *n.* Usually, **wrappings,** *pl.* the paper, or other material, in which something is wrapped.

wrapt (rapt) *v.* a pt. and a pp. of **wrap.**
☛ Hom. **rapt.**

wrasse (ras) *n.* any of a family (Labridae) of usually brightly-colored fishes of warm and temperate seas, having thick, fleshy lips, powerful teeth, and spiny fins. [< Cornish *wrach*]

wrath (rath *or* roth) *n.* very great anger; rage. [OE *wrǣththu*]
☛ Syn. See note at **anger.**

wrath·ful (rath′fəl *or* roth′-) *adj.* feeling or showing wrath; very angry. —**wrath′ful·ly,** *adv.* —**wrath′ful·ness,** *n.*

wrath·y (rath′ē *or* roth′ē) *adj.* **wrath·i·er, wrath·i·est.** wrathful.

wreak (rēk) *v.* **1** give expression to; work off (feelings, desires, etc.): *The bully wreaked his bad temper on his dog.* **2** inflict: *The*

hat, āge, fär; let, ēqual, tèrm; it, īce
hot, ōpen, ôrder; oil, out; cup, pût, rüle,
əbove, takən, pencəl, lemən, circəs
ch, child; ng, long; sh, ship
th, thin; ᴛʜ, then; zh, measure

hurricane wreaked havoc on the city. **3** *Archaic.* avenge. [OE *wrecan*]
☛ Hom. **reek.**

wreath (rēth) *n., pl.* **wreaths** (rēᴛʜz). **1** a ring of flowers or leaves twisted together. **2** something suggesting a wreath: *a wreath of smoke.* **3 Wreath,** Corona Australis (the Southern Crown), a southern constellation. [OE *wrǣth*]

wreathe (rēᴛʜ) *v.* **wreathed, wreath·ing. 1** make into a wreath; twist. **2** decorate or adorn with wreaths. **3** make a ring around; encircle: *Mist wreathed the hills.* **4** envelop: *wreathed in smiles.* **5** move in rings: *The smoke wreathed upward.* [partly < ME *wrethen,* pp. of *writhen* writhe, partly < *wreath*]

wreck (rek) *n., v.* —*n.* **1** the destruction of a ship, building, train, automobile, or aircraft: *The hurricane caused many wrecks.* **2** any destruction or serious injury: *Heavy rains caused the wreck of many crops.* **3** what is left of anything that has been destroyed or much injured: *The wreck of a ship was cast upon the shore.* **4** a person or animal that has lost physcial or mental health. **5** goods cast up by the sea, especially after a shipwreck.
—*v.* **1** cause the wreck of; destroy or ruin: *Their house was wrecked in the hurricane. The many years as a miner had wrecked his health.* **2** suffer wreck (used in the passive): *The ship was wrecked in a storm off the coast of Newfoundland.* **3** act as wrecker. [ME < AF < ON *wrek* < Gmc. *wrecan* to drive]
☛ Hom. **reck.**

wreck·age (rek′ij) *n.* **1** what is left by wreck or wrecks: *The shore was covered with the wreckage of ships.* **2** a wrecking or being wrecked: *the wreckage of one's hopes.*

wreck·er (rek′ər) *n.* **1** a person or machine that tears down buildings: *John operates the wrecker that is demolishing the vacant building.* **2** a person, car, train, or machine that removes wrecks. **3** a person or ship that recovers wrecked or disabled ships or their cargoes. **4** a person who causes shipwrecks by false lights on shore so as to plunder the wrecks.

wren (ren) *n.* any of a family (Troglodytidae) of small, energetic, insect-eating songbirds having mostly brownish plumage and a short, cocked tail. The North American **house wren** (*Troglodytes acdon*) is a common summer resident throughout much of Canada, often nesting near houses. The **winter wren** (*T. troglodytes*), the common wren of Britain, is a tiny wren found throughout the northern hemisphere. [OE *wrenna*]

Wren (ren) *n. Brit. Informal.* a member of the Women's Royal Naval Service. [< the initials, WRNS]

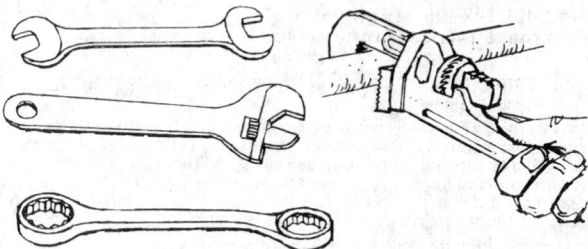

Wrenches. At left, from top to bottom, a double open-ended wrench, an adjustable wrench, and a double box wrench; at right, a pipe wrench in use

wrench (rench) *n., v.* —*n.* **1** a violent twist or twisting pull: *He broke the branch off the tree with a sudden wrench. He gave his ankle a wrench when he jumped off the bus.* **2** an injury caused by twisting. **3** grief; pain: *It was a wrench to leave our old home.* **4** a tool for holding, turning, or twisting something, such as a nut or bolt or a pipe. **5** distortion of the proper or original meaning, interpretation, etc.
—*v.* **1** twist or pull violently: *The policeman wrenched the gun out of the man's hand.* **2** injure by twisting: *He wrenched his back in falling from the horse.* **3** give pain or anguish to. **4** twist the meaning of. [OE *wrencan* twist]

wrest (rest) *v., n.* —*v.* **1** twist, pull, or tear away with force; wrench away: *He wrested the knife from his assailant.* **2** take by

force: *The usurper wrested the power from the king.* **3** twist or turn from the proper meaning, use, etc.
—*n.* **1** the act of wresting; a forcible twist, pull, or tear. **2** *Archaic.* a small, wrenchlike key used for turning the wrest pins on a harp or piano. [OE *wræstan*] —**wrest′er,** *n.*
☞ *Hom.* **rest.**

wres·tle (res′əl) *v.* **-tled, -tling;** *n.* —*v.* **1** fight or grapple with (an opponent) by holding, throwing, tripping, etc., but without striking with the fist. **2** engage or participate in such fighting or grappling. **3** struggle or contend (*with*): *wrestling with a problem, wrestling with inflation.* **4** move (something) laboriously, with or as if with wrestling movements: *He managed to wrestle the couch down the stairs.* —*n.* the act or an instance of wrestling; especially, a wrestling match. [ult. < *wrest*] —**wres′tler,** *n.*

wres·tling (res′ling) *n.* a sport or contest in which each of two opponents tries to throw or force the other to the ground. The rules for wrestling do not allow using the fists or certain holds on the body.

wrest pin one of the pins on a piano or harp around which one end of each string is coiled. The tension of the strings may be changed by turning the wrest pins.

wretch (rech) *n.* **1** a very unfortunate or unhappy person. **2** scoundrel. [OE *wrecca* exile]
☞ *Hom.* **retch.**

wretch·ed (rech′id) *adj.* **1** very unfortunate or unhappy. **2** very unsatisfactory; miserable: *a wretched hut.* **3** vicious; wicked; degenerate: *a wretched traitor.* —**wretch′ed·ly,** *adv.*
—**wretch′ed·ness,** *n.*
☞ *Syn.* **1. Wretched, miserable** = very unhappy or deeply disturbed. **Wretched** suggests a state of unhappinesss and extreme lowness of spirits marked by discouragement and hopelessness, caused by sorrow, sickness, worry, etc.: *He was wretched when he failed the examination again.* **Miserable** suggests a state of severe suffering or distress of mind, caused especially by conditions or circumstances such as poverty, humiliation, or misfortune: *After the loss of their savings and their home, they felt too miserable to see their old friends.*

wrick (rik) *v. or n.* sprain; wrench (def. 2, *n.* and *v.*). [ME *wricken* twist]
☞ *Hom.* **rick.**

wrig·gle (rig′əl) *v.* **-gled, -gling;** *n.* —*v.* **1** twist and turn: *Children wriggle when they are restless.* **2** move by twisting and turning: *A snake wriggled across the road.* **3** make one's way by tricks, excuses, etc.: *Some people can wriggle out of any difficulty.*
—*n.* the act of wriggling: *With one wriggle, he was under the bed.* [cf. Du. *wriggelen*]

wrig·gler (rig′lər) *n.* **1** a person who wriggles. **2** the larva of a mosquito.

wrig·gly (rig′lē) *adj.* twisting and turning.

wright (rīt) *n.* a person who makes or creates something (*usually used in compounds*): *wheelwright, shipwright, playwright.* [OE *wryhta,* var. of *wyrhta* < *weorc* work]
☞ *Hom.* **right, rite, write.**

wring (ring) *v.* **wrung, wring·ing;** *n.* —*v.* **1** twist and squeeze hard, especially so as to extract moisture (*often used with* **out**): *to wring clothes.* **2** force by twisting and squeezing: *The hikers wrung water from their soaking clothes.* **3** twist violently, especially out of place or relation; wrench: *to wring a chicken's neck.* **4** get by force, effort, or persuasion: *The old beggar could wring money from anyone by his sad story.* **5** clasp; press: *He wrung his old friend's hand.* **6** cause pain or pity in: *Their poverty wrung his heart.*
—*n.* the act of twisting and squeezing: *She gave her swimsuit a good wring.* [OE *wringan*]
☞ *Hom.* **ring.**

wring·er (ring′ər) *n.* a person or thing that wrings, especially a device or machine for squeezing water from clothes.
☞ *Hom.* **ringer.**

wrin·kle¹ (ring′kəl) *n., v.* **-kled, -kling.** —*n.* an irregular ridge or fold; crease: *An old man's face has wrinkles. When she unpacked the dress she found it was full of wrinkles.* —*v.* **1** make a wrinkle or wrinkles in: *He wrinkled his forehead.* **2** have or acquire wrinkles: *The label says the shirt won't wrinkle.* [cf. OE *gewrinclod,* pp., twisted, winding]

wrin·kle² (ring′kəl) *n. Informal.* a useful hint or idea; clever trick. [? special use of *wrinkle¹*]

wrin·kly (ring′klē) *adj.* **-kli·er, -kli·est.** wrinkled.

wrist (rist) *n.* **1** the part of the human arm between the palm of the hand and the forearm: *His wrists are thicker than mine.* See **arm** for picture. **2** a corresponding part of the forelimb of an animal. **3** the joint formed by the end of the larger bone of the forearm and the carpus, connecting the arm with the hand: *flexible wrists.* **4** one or more of the bones of this joint: *He broke his wrist when he fell.* **5** the part of a sleeve, glove, or mitten covering the wrist. [OE]

wrist·band (rist′band′) *n.* the band of a sleeve fitting around the wrist.

wrist·let (rist′lit) *n.* **1** a band worn around the wrist to keep it warm. **2** bracelet.

wrist pin a stud or pin projecting from the side of a crank, wheel, or the like, and forming a means of attachment to a connecting rod.

wrist shot *Sports.* a shot or stroke in which the power is provided by a flick of the wrist, rather than the arm.

wrist·watch (rist′wotch′) *n., pl.* **wrist·watches.** a small watch worn on a strap around the wrist.

writ¹ (rit) *n.* **1** something written; a piece of writing. The Bible is Holy Writ. **2** *Law.* a formal order directing a person to do or not to do something: *A writ from the judge ordered the man's release from jail.* [OE *writ* < *wrītan* write]

writ² (rit) *v. Archaic.* a pt. and a pp. of **write.**

write (rīt) *v.* **wrote, writ·ten, writ·ing.** **1** make letters or words with pen, pencil, chalk, etc.: *He learned to write.* **2** mark with letters or words: *to write a cheque.* **3** put down the letters, words, etc. of: *Write your name and address.* **4** give in writing; record: *She writes all that happens.* **5** make up (books, stories, articles, poems, letters, etc.); compose: *He writes for the magazines.* **6** be a writer: *Her ambition was to write.* **7** write a letter: *He writes to her every week.* **8** write a letter to: *I wrote him yesterday.* **9** show plainly: *Honesty is written on his face.*
write down, a put into writing: *Many early folk songs were never written down.* **b** put a lower value on.
write in, a insert (a fact, statement, etc.) in a piece of writing. **b** cast (a vote) for an unlisted candidate by writing his name on a ballot.
write off, a cancel as by entering in accounts as a loss: *My father agreed to write off my debt to him.* **b** U.S. note the deduction of for depreciation. **c** give up; treat as if nonexistent.
write out, a put into writing. **b** write in full: *She made quick notes during the interview and wrote out her report later.*
write up, a write a description or account of. **b** write in detail. **c** bring up to date in writing. **d** put a higher value on.
[OE *wrītan,* originally, scratch]
☞ *Hom.* **right, rite, wright.**

write–in (rīt′in′) *adj., n. U.S.* —*adj.* in an election, of or having to do with a person who is not officially listed as a candidate but who is voted for by his name being written in on a ballot. —*n.* a write-in candidate or vote.

write–off (rīt′ôf′) *n.* **1** something cancelled or recognized as a loss: *We treated the money we had lent him as a write-off.* **2** *Informal.* a total wreck, such as might be written off as a loss: *They weren't hurt badly in the accident, but their car was a write-off.*

writ·er (rīt′ər) *n.* a person who writes, especially one whose profession or business is writing, such as an author or journalist.

write–up (rīt′up′) *n. Informal.* a written description or account.

writhe (rīŦH) *v.* **writhed** or (*archaic or poetic*) **writh·en** (riŦHən), **writh·ing.** **1** twist and turn; squirm: *to writhe in pain.* **2** suffer intense embarrassment, shame, annoyance, etc.: *He writhed when he thought of the blunder he had made.* [OE *wrīthan*]

writ·ing (rī′ting) *n.* **1** written form: *Put your ideas in writing.* **2** handwriting. **3** something written; a letter, paper, document, etc. **4** a literary work; a book or other literary production: *the writings of Judge Haliburton.* **5** the profession or business of a person who writes. **6** (*adj.*) used in writing: *writing paper.*

writ·ten (rit′ən) *v.* a pp. of **write.**

WRNS or **W.R.N.S.** Women's Royal Naval Service.

wrong (rong) *adj., adv., n., v.* —*adj.* **1** not right; bad; unjust; unlawful: *It is wrong to tell lies.* **2** incorrect: *He gave the wrong answer.* **3** unsuitable; improper: *the wrong clothes for the occasion.* **4** in a bad state or condition; out of order; amiss: *Something is wrong with the car.* **5** not meant to be seen or shown: *the wrong side of the cloth.*
go wrong, a turn out badly. **b** stop being good and become bad.
—*adv.* in a wrong way, direction, etc.; so as to be wrong: *to guess wrong. You put the pieces together wrong.*
—*n.* **1** what is wrong; wrong thing or things: *Two wrongs do not make a right.* **2** an injustice; injury: *to do someone a wrong.*
in the wrong, at fault; guilty.
—*v.* **1** do wrong to; treat unjustly; injure: *He forgave those who had wronged him.* **2** discredit or dishonor unjustly by statement, opinion, etc.; impute evil to undeservedly. **3** cheat or defraud (a person of something). [OE *wrang* < ON **wrangr, rangr* crooked]
—**wrong′ly,** *adv.* —**wrong′ness,** *n.*

wrong·do·er (rong′dü′ər) *n.* a person who does wrong.

wrong·do·ing (rong′dü′ing) *n.* the doing of wrong; bad acts: *The thief was guilty of wrongdoing.*

wrong·ful (rong′fel) *adj.* **1** wrong; unjust. **2** unlawful.
—**wrong′ful·ly,** *adv.* —**wrong′ful·ness,** *n.*

wrong–head·ed (rong′hed′id) *adj.* **1** wrong in judgment or
opinion. **2** stubborn even when wrong. —**wrong′-head′ed·ly,** *adv.*
—**wrong′-head′ed·ness,** *n.*

wrote (rōt) *v.* pt. of **write.**
☞ *Hom.* **rote.**

wroth (roth) *adj. Archaic or poetic.* angry. [OE *wrāth*]

wrought (rot *or* rôt) *adj., v.* —*adj.* **1** shaped or formed with skill
and care; fashioned: *elegantly wrought vases.* **2** of metals, shaped
by hammering, etc.: *a plate of wrought silver.* —*v. Archaic.* a pt.
and a pp. of **work.**
☞ *Hom.* **rot** (rot).

wrought iron a tough, durable form of iron that is soft enough
to be easily forged and welded, but that will not break as easily as
cast iron. Wrought iron is often used for decorative furniture, gates,
or railings.

wrought–up (rot′up′ *or* rôt′-) *adj.* stirred up; excited.

wrung (rung) *v.* pt. and pp. of **wring.**
☞ *Hom.* **rung.**

wry (rī) *adj.* **wri·er, wri·est. 1** made by distorting the mouth or
other features to show disgust, bitterness, doubt, or irony: *a wry
face, a wry grin.* **2** marked by grim or bitter irony: *wry humor, wry
remarks.* **3** turned to one side in an abnormal way: *a wry nose.*
4 perversely wrong or inappropriate: *wry behavior.* [ult < OE
wrīgian turn] —**wry′ly,** *adv.*
☞ *Hom.* **rye.**

wry·neck (rī′nek′) *n.* **1** either of two Old World woodpeckers
(constituting the genus *Jynx* and the subfamily Jynginae) having
mottled greyish-brown plumage and differing from typical

hat, āge, fär; let, ēqual, tėrm; it, īce
hot, ōpen, ôrder; oil, out; cup, pút, rüle,
əbove, takən, pencəl, lemən, circəs

ch, child; ng, long; sh, ship
th, thin; ŦH, then; zh, measure

woodpeckers in having soft tail feathers, a small bill not adapted for
drumming on trees, and the habit of twisting their necks about when
disturbed. **2** a spasmodic or congenital contraction of the neck
muscles, causing the head to be pulled or twisted to the side.

WSW or **W.S.W.** west-southwest.

wt. weight.

wuth·er (wuŦH′ər) *v., n. Dialect.* —*v.* **1** a blow with a roar, as a
strong wind; bluster. **2** move or rush noisily; whiz. —*n.* a wuthering
sound. [< dial. *wuther* wither, *v.* < Scand.; cf. Norwegian *kvidra*
move quickly, related to *hvitha* wind squall]

WV West Virginia.

W.Va. West Virginia.

WY Wyoming.

Wy·an·dotte (wī′ən dot′) *n.* an American breed of
medium-sized, hardy chickens.

wye (wī) *n.* **1** the letter Y. **2** anything made or arranged in the
shape of the letter Y.

Wyo. Wyoming.

wy·vern (wī′vərn) *n.* See **wivern.**

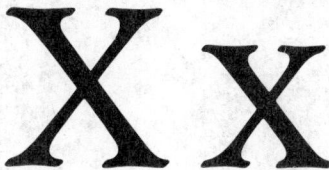

X x

x or **X** (eks) *n., pl.* **x's** or **X's. 1** the twenty-fourth letter of the English alphabet. **2** any speech sound represented by this letter. **3** a person or thing identified as *x,* especially the twenty-fourth of a series or the first of a pair or a series consisting of x, y, and sometimes z. **4** the Roman numeral for 10. **5** *Algebra.* **x,** an unknown quantity, as in $x + y = 5$. **6** *Geometry.* abscissa. **7 X,** an unidentified person or thing: *Mr. X.* **8** something shaped like the letter X. **9** (*adj.*) of or being an X or x. **10 x** is also used: **a** to indicate a certain place on a map, etc.: *X marks the spot.* **b** to symbolize a kiss. **c** to represent the signature of a person who cannot write.

x (eks) *v.* **x·ed** or **x'd, x·ing** or **x'ing. 1** mark with an x. **2** cancel or cross out with an x or a series of x's (*often used with* **out**): *to x out a mistake.*

X Christ; Christian.

Xan·thip·pe (zan tip′ē) *n.* a scolding woman; shrew. [< *Xanthippe,* the wife of Socrates, notorious as a scold]

xan·thous (zan′thəs) *adj.* **1** of or having to do with peoples having yellowish, reddish, or light-brown hair. **2** of or having to do with peoples having a yellowish skin, as the Mongolians. **3** yellow. [< Gk. *xanthos* yellow]

X chromosome one of the two chromosomes bearing the genes that determine sex in human beings and many animals. Each female body cell normally contains two X chromosomes and each egg cell contains one X chromosome. Compare **Y chromosome.**

Xe xenon.

xe·bec (zē′bek) *n.* a small, three-masted vessel of the Mediterranean. Also, **zebec.** [< F *xebec,* ult. < Arabic *shabbāk*]

xe·ni·a (zē′nē ə) *n. Botany.* the effects or changes in a seed resulting directly from cross-pollination. [< NL < Gk. *xenia* hospitality < Gk. *xenos* guest, stranger]

xeno– *combining form.* **1** stranger; foreigner: *xenophobia = fear of strangers.* **2** strange; foreign: *xenomorphic = of strange (different) form.* [< Gk. *xenos* guest, stranger]

xen·o·mor·phic (zen′ə môr′fik) *adj.* of rock, having a form distorted from the normal form as a result of pressure. [< *zeno–* + Gk. *morphē* shape + E *-ic*] **—xen′o·mor′phi·cal·ly,** *adv.*

xe·non (zē′non or zen′on) *n.* a rare, heavy, colorless, gaseous chemical element that is chemically inactive. It occurs in the air in minute quantities. *Symbol:* Xe; *at.no.* 54; *at.wt.* 131.30. [< Gk. *xenon,* neut. adj., strange]

xen·o·phobe (zen′ə fōb′) *n.* one who has a morbid fear or dislike of foreign persons or things. [< *xeno–* + *-phobe*]

xen·o·pho·bi·a (zen′ə fō′bē ə) *n.* a hatred or fear of foreigners or foreign things. [< NL < Gk. *xenos* stranger + *phobos* fear]

xero– *combining form.* dry; dryness: *xerophyte = a plant adapted to dry climate.* [< Gk. *xēros* dry]

xe·ro·graph·ic (zēr′ə graf′ik) *adj.* of or having to do with xerography.

xe·rog·ra·phy (zē rog′rə fē) *n.* a process for making copies of written or printed material, pictures, etc., by the action of magnetic attraction rather than ink and pressure. Tiny, negatively-charged particles are spread on positively-charged paper in an arrangement that exactly copies the printing, etc. on the original paper. [< *Xerography,* trademark]

xe·ro·phyte (zēr′ə fīt′) *n.* a plant that needs very little water and can grow in deserts or very dry ground. Cactuses, sagebrush, etc. are xerophytes. [< *xero–* + *-phyte*]

xe·ro·sis (zē rō′sis) *n.* abnormal dryness of the skin, eyes, or mucous membranes. [< *xero–* + *-osis*]

Xer·ox (zēr′oks) *n., v.* **—n. 1** *Trademark.* a copying process or machine using xerography. **2** Usually, **xerox,** a copy made on such a machine. **—v.** Usually, **xerox,** make copies on such a machine.

Xho·sa (kō′sä or kō′zä) *n., pl.* **-sa** or **-sas. 1** a member of a group of Bantu-speaking peoples of southern Africa. **2** the Bantu language of the Xhosa, closely related to Zulu and characterized by the use of clicks.

Xho·san (kō′sən or kō′zən) *adj.* of or having to do with Xhosa.

xi (sī, zī, or ksē) *n.* the 14th letter (Ξ, ξ = English X, x) of the Greek alphabet.

Xmas (kris′məs; *often, informally,* eks′məs) *n. Informal.* Christmas.

Xn. Christian.

X ray or **X–ray** (eks′rā′) *n.* **1** radiation of the same type as visible radiation (i.e. light) but having an extremely short wavelength. It can go through substances that ordinary light rays cannot penetrate, but will act in the same way as light does on a photographic film or plate to produce a picture. X rays are used to locate breaks in bones, a bullet lodged in the body, etc., and in treating certain diseases. **2** a picture obtained by means of X rays. **3** (*adj.*) **X-ray** or **x-ray,** made by or using X rays. [translation of G *X-Strahlen,* pl., < *X,* in sense of "unknown," + *Strahl* ray, beam]

X–ray or **x–ray** (eks′rā′) *v.* examine, photograph, or treat with X rays.

X's and O's tick-tack-toe.

Xtian. Christian.

Xty. Christianity.

xy·lem (zī′lem) *n.* the woody tissue in the vascular system of plants and trees that conducts water and mineral salts and supports the softer tissue. Compare **phloem.** [< G < Gk. *xylon* wood]

A xylophone

xy·lo·phone (zī′lə fōn′ or zil′ə fōn′) *n.* a musical percussion instrument consisting of two rows of wooden bars that are graduated in length to produce the tones of two octaves of the chromatic scale. It is played by striking the bars with wooden hammers. [< Gk. *xylon* wood + *phōnē* sound]

Yy

y or **Y** (wī) *n.* **y's** or **Y's.** **1** the twenty-fifth letter of the English alphabet. **2** any speech sound represented by this letter. **3** a person or thing identified as *y*, especially the twenty-fifth of a series or the second of a pair or a series consisting of x, y, and sometimes z. **4** *Algebra.* *y*, an unknown quantity, as in $2x + 3y = 7$. **5** *Geometry.* an ordinate. **6** something shaped like the letter Y. **7** (*adjl.*) of or being a Y or y.

–y¹ *suffix.* **1** full of, composed of, containing, having, or characterized by, as in *airy, cloudy, dewy, icy, juicy, watery.* **2** somewhat, as in *chilly, salty.* **3** inclined to, as in *chatty, fidgety.* **4** resembling; suggesting, as in *sloppy, sugary, willowy.* **5** in certain words, usually archaic or poetic, such as *stilly, vasty,* the -y was originally an intensifier. [OE *-ig*]

–y² *suffix.* used to indicate that someone or something is considered as small and attractive, thought of with affection, etc.: *doggy, dolly, mummy.* [ME]

–y³ *suffix.* **1** a state or quality, as in *jealousy, victory.* **2** an activity, as in *delivery, entreaty.* **3** a collective group of people or things: *soldiery, confectionery.* [< F *-ie* < L *-ia,* Gk. *-ia*]

y. **1** yard(s). **2** year(s).

Y **1** yttrium. **2** yen. **3** *Informal.* YMCA, YWCA, YMHA, or YWHA: *We spent the afternoon at the Y.*

yacht (yot) *n., v.* —*n.* **1** a light sailing vessel having graceful lines and designed for racing. **2** a similar vessel having sails, motor power, or both, luxuriously equipped, and used for private pleasure cruising. —*v.* sail, race, or cruise on a yacht. [< Early Mod. Du. *jaghte* (now *jacht*) < *jaghtschip* chasing ship]

yacht·ing (yot'ing) *n., adj.* —*n.* **1** the art of sailing a yacht. **2** the pastime of sailing on a yacht. —*adj.* **1** of yachting or yachts. **2** interested in yachting.

yachts·man (yots'mən) *n., pl.* **-men.** a person who owns or sails a yacht.

yachts·man·ship (yots'mən ship') *n.* skill or ability in handling a yacht.

yack (yak) *v. Slang.* See **yak².**

yah (yä) *interj.* a noise made to express derision, disgust, or impatience.

Ya·hoo (yä'hü *or* yä hü') *n.* **1** in Swift's *Gulliver's Travels,* a type of brute in human shape who works for a race of intelligent horses. **2** **yahoo,** any rough, coarse, or uncouth person.

Yah·veh or **Yah·ve** (yä'vä) See **Yahweh.**

Yah·weh or **Yah·we** (yä'wä) *n.* the name of God in the Hebrew Bible (the Old Testament). Also, **Yahveh, Yahve, Jahve, Jahveh.** [< Hebrew. See JEHOVAH.]

yak¹ (yak) *n.* a large, long-haired animal (*Bos grunniens*) of central Asia, related to the North American buffalo and to cattle. Yaks are often domesticated and used for food and as beasts of burden. [< Tibetan *gyag*]

yak² (yak) *v.* **yakked, yak·king;** *n. Slang.* —*v.* chatter; talk constantly. —*n.* persistent, idle chatter. [imitative]

yam (yam) *n.* **1** the edible, starchy tuber of any of several tropical and subtropical climbing vines (genus *Dioscorea,* of the family Dioscoreaceae), used as a staple food in tropical regions. **2** any of the vines that produce these tubers. **3** *U.S.* any of several varieties of sweet potato. [< Sp. *iñame,* ult. < Senegalese *nyami* eat]

yam·mer (yam'ər) *v., n.* —*v.* **1** whine or whimper in a complaining way. **2** utter (complaints, etc.) persistently. **3** howl, yell, or clamor: *dogs yammering for their food.* —*n.* a yammering sound or utterance.

yank (yangk) *v., n. Informal.* —*v.* pull with a sudden motion; jerk: *You almost yanked my arm off! She yanked the sweater out of the drawer.* —*n.* a sudden pull; jerk: *He gave the door a yank.* [origin uncertain]

Yank (yangk) *n. or adj. Slang.* Yankee.

Yan·kee (yang'kē) *n., adj.* —*n.* **1** a native of one of the six New England states of the northeastern part of the United States. **2** a native or inhabitant of any of the northern states of the United States. **3** a native or inhabitant of the United States; an American. —*adj.* of, having to do with, or characteristic of Yankees: *Yankee*

shrewdness. [probably ult. < Du. *Jan Kees* John Cheese (nickname), the *-s* being taken for pl. ending]

Yankee Doo·dle (dü'dəl) an American song, probably of English origin and taken over by the American soldiers in the Revolutionary War.

yap (yap) *n., v.* **yapped, yap·ping.** —*n.* **1** a snappish bark; yelp. **2** *Slang.* snappish, noisy, or foolish talk. **3** *Slang.* a peevish or noisy person. **4** *Slang.* the mouth. —*v.* **1** bark snappishly; yelp. **2** *Slang.* talk snappishly, noisily, or foolishly. **3** *Slang.* chatter or talk idly.

Ya·qui (yä'kē) *n., pl.* **-qui** *or* **-quis.** a member of an Amerindian people of S Arizona and NW Mexico.

yar·bor·ough (yär'bər ə) *n. Bridge, Whist.* a hand of 13 cards with no card higher than a nine. [after the second Earl of *Yarborough* (died 1897), who is said to have bet a thousand to one against the occurrence of such a hand. 19c.]

yard¹ (yärd) *n., v.* —*n.* **1** a piece of ground near or around a house, barn, school, etc. **2** a piece of enclosed ground for some special purpose or business: *a chicken yard.* **3** a space with tracks where railway cars are stored, shifted around, etc. **4** *Cdn.* a clearing where a group of moose or deer feed in winter. —*v.* **1** put into or enclose in a yard. **2** *Cdn.* of moose or deer, be in, settle, or come together in a yard (*often used with* up). [OE *geard*]

yard² (yärd) *n.* **1** a unit for measuring length, equal to 3 feet or 36 inches (about 91.4 cm). *Abbrev.*: y. *or* yd. **2** a long, slender beam, or spar, with tapered ends, fastened across a mast and used to support a sail. See **brig** for picture. **make yards, a** *Football.* advance the ball from the line of scrimmage. **b** *Informal.* advance; make headway: *He has already made yards in his new business.* [OE *gierd* rod]

yard·age¹ (yär'dij) *n.* **1** a length in yards. **2** a quantity of something, such as cloth, that is measured in yards: *a large yardage of silk.* **3** yard goods. **4** *Football.* the number of yards by which a team or player advances the ball from the line of scrimmage. **5** *Informal.* advance; gain; benefit.

yard·age² (yär'dij) *n.* **1** the use of a yard or enclosure, as in lading or unlading cattle, etc. at a railway station. **2** the charge made for such use.

yard·arm (yärd'ärm') *n.* either end of a yard supporting a sail on a square-rigged ship.

yard goods cloth, etc. sold by the yard.

yard·mas·ter (yärd'mas'tər) *n.* the manager of a railway yard.

yard of ale **1** the amount of ale or beer (between about 1 and 1.7 litres) contained in a very narrow, horn-shaped glass about one yard (90 cm) tall. **2** the glass itself.

yard sale an informal sale of personal possessions, furniture, etc., usually held in a private yard and patronized mostly by neighbors and passers-by. See also **garage sale.**

yard·stick (yärd'stik') *n.* **1** a stick one yard long, used for measuring. **2** any standard of judgment or comparison.

yar·mul·ke (yär'məl kə) *n.* a skullcap worn especially by Orthodox and Conservative Jewish men and boys for prayer and ceremonial occasions or, by strongly religious Jews, at all times. Also, **yarmulka.** [< Yiddish < Ukrainian and Polish *yarmulka* cap]

yarn (yärn) *n., v.* —*n.* **1** any spun thread, especially that prepared for weaving or knitting. **2** *Informal.* a tale; story: *Who told you that yarn?* **spin a yarn,** *Informal.* tell a story. —*v. Informal.* tell stories. [OE *gearn*]

yar·row (yar'ō *or* yer'ō) *n.* any of several plants (genus *Achillea*) of the composite family, especially the common yarrow (*A. millefolium*) having finely divided leaves and flat clusters of white or pink flowers. [OE *gearwe*]

yat·a·ghan (yat'ə gan') *n.* a sword used by Moslems, having no guard for the hand and no crosspiece, but usually a large pommel. [< Turkish]

yaw (yo *or* yô) *v., n.* —*v.* **1** turn from a straight course; go unsteadily. **2** of an aircraft, turn from a straight course by a motion about its vertical axis. —*n.* a movement from a straight course. [origin uncertain]

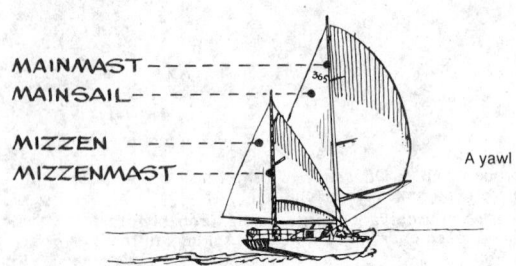

MAINMAST
MAINSAIL
MIZZEN
MIZZENMAST

A yawl

yawl (yol or yôl) n. **1** a boat similar to a ketch, having a large mast near the bow and a short mast near the stern. A yawl has its sails rigged fore-and-aft. **2** a ship's boat rowed by four or six oars. [< Du. *jol*]

yawn (yon or yôn) v., n. —v. **1** open the mouth widely and inhale deeply as an involuntary effect of sleepiness, boredom, etc. **2** utter while yawning. **3** be wide open, like a yawning mouth; gape: *A wide gorge yawned beneath our feet.* —n. the act or an instance of yawning. [OE *geonian*] —**yawn′er**, n.

yawp (yop or yôp) v., n. Dialect or informal. —v. utter a loud, harsh cry. —n. a loud, harsh cry. [imitative] —**yawp′er**, n.

yaws (yoz or yôz) n.pl. a contagious disease of the tropics, characterized by sores on the skin. [< Carib]

Yb ytterbium.

Y chromosome one of the two chromosomes bearing the genes that determine sex in human beings and many animals. Each male body cell normally contains one Y and one X chromosome and each sperm contains either a Y or an X chromosome. If an egg cell is fertilized by a sperm with an X chromosome, the resulting embryo will be a female; if the sperm is one with a Y chromosome, the embryo will be a male. Compare **X chromosome.**

y·cleped (i klept′ or i klēpt′) See **yclept.**

y·clept (i klept′) adj. Archaic. called; named; styled. [OE *gecleopod* named]

yd. yard(s).

Y.D.T. Yukon Daylight time.

ye¹ (yē; unstressed, yi) pron. Archaic, poetic, or dialect. you (plural); the ones spoken to: *"Come, all ye faithful."* [OE *gē*]

ye² (ᴛʜē; incorrectly, yē) definite article. an old way of writing the definite article "the."
☞ *Usage.* **Ye.** In Old and Middle English **the** was commonly written as þe. The early printers, who ordinarily did not have this consonant symbol (called "thorn") in their fonts, substituted *y* for it, but this was never intended to be read with the value of *y.*

yea (yā) adv., n. —adv. **1** aye; yes (used for affirmation or assent, as in voting). **2** Archaic. indeed; truly (used to introduce a clause). **3** Archaic. not only that, but also or more: *willing, yea eager.* —n. an affirmative vote or voter. [OE *gēa*]

yean (yēn) v. give birth to a lamb or kid. [OE *gēanian*; cf. *ēanian* yean, *gēan*, adj., pregnant]

yean·ling (yēn′ling) n. a lamb or kid; the young of a sheep or a goat.

year (yēr) n. **1** 12 months or 365 days; January 1 to December 31. A leap year has 366 days. **2** 12 months reckoned from any point. A **fiscal year** is a period of 12 months at the end of which the accounts of a government, business, etc. are balanced: *We moved here five years ago this week. They came with their six-year-old son.* **3** the part of a year spent in a certain activity: *The school year goes from September to June.* **4** the exact period of the earth's revolution around the sun. The **solar** or **astronomical year** is 365 days, 5 hours, 48 minutes, 46 seconds. **5** the time it takes for the apparent travelling of the sun from a given fixed star back to it again. The **sidereal year** is 20 minutes, 23 seconds longer than the solar year. **6** the time in which any planet completes its revolution around the sun. **7 years**, pl. **a** age: *a child of tender years.* **b** a very long time: *They hadn't seen each other for years.*
a year and a day, Law. a period constituting a term for certain purposes, in order to insure that a full year is completed.
year by year, with each succeeding year; as years go by.
year in, year out, always; continuously: *He has always worked hard, year in, year out.* [OE *gēar*]

year·book (yēr′bùk′) n. **1** a book or report published every year. **2** a school annual containing pictures and information about school activities.

year·ling (yēr′ling or yėr′ling) n. **1** an animal one year old: *The rancher decided to sell his yearlings.* **2** (adjl.) one year old: *a yearling colt.* [< year + -ling]

year·long (yēr′long′) adj. **1** lasting for a year. **2** lasting for years.

year·ly (yēr′lē) adj., adv. —adj. **1** once a year; in every year: *He takes a yearly trip to Toronto.* **2** lasting a year: *The earth makes a yearly revolution around the sun.* **3** for a year: *a yearly salary of $24 000.*
—adv. **1** once a year; annually: *A new volume comes out yearly.* **2** for a year: *He gets $24 000 yearly.*

yearn (yėrn) v. **1** feel a longing or desire; desire earnestly: *He yearns for home.* **2** feel pity; have tender feelings: *Her heart yearned for the homeless children.* [OE *giernan*]

yearn·ing (yėr′ning) n. an earnest or strong desire; longing.

year–round (yēr′round′) adj. or adv. throughout the year: *year-round residents.*

yeast (yēst) n. **1** a yellowish, frothy substance consisting mainly of cells of very small fungi (genus *Saccharomyces* and related genera), which grow especially on the surface of liquids containing sugar, producing fermentation. Yeast is used as a leavening agent for bread, in the making of beer and other alcoholic liquors, etc. **2** a yeast cell or fungus. **3** a product containing yeast, often in the form of a small pressed block or cake. **4** something that acts like yeast, in causing activity or ferment: *the yeast of rebellion.* **5** foam; froth. [OE *gist*]

yeast·y (yēs′tē) adj. **1** of, containing, or resembling yeast. **2** frothy or foamy: *yeasty waves.* **3** light or trifling; frivolous.

yegg (yeg) n. Slang. **1** a burglar who robs safes. **2** any burglar. [origin uncertain]

yell (yel) v., n. —v. **1** cry out with a strong, loud sound. **2** say with a yell. —n. **1** a strong, loud cry. **2** a special shout or cheer, especially one used by a school or college to encourage its sports team. [OE *giellan*]

yel·low (yel′ō) n., adj., v. —n. **1** the color of gold, butter, or ripe lemons. **2** a yellow pigment or dye. **3** something yellow, especially the yolk of an egg: *We used the whites of six eggs for cake and the yellows for custards.*
—adj. **1** having the color yellow. **2** having a yellowish-brown skin. **3** Informal. cowardly. **4** sensational: *a yellow journal.*
—v. **1** turn yellow: *Paper yellows with age.* **2** make yellow: *Buttercups yellowed the field.* [OE *geolu*] —**yel′low·ness**, n.

yel·low·bird (yel′ō bėrd′) n. any of various birds having yellow plumage, such as a North American goldfinch or the yellow warbler.

yellow cake Cdn. Slang. semirefined uranium ore.

yellow cypress or **cedar** a medium-large evergreen tree (*Chamaecyparis nootkatensis*) of the cypress family found along the Pacific coast of North America, usually about 25 metres tall, having small, sharply pointed, scale-like leaves and small, round, reddish-brown cones. The hard wood of the yellow cypress is much used for boat building.

yellow fever a dangerous, infectious disease of warm climates, caused by a virus transmitted by the bite of a mosquito and characterized by high fever, jaundice, vomiting, etc.

yel·low·ham·mer (yel′ō ham′ər) n. **1** a common Eurasian bunting (*Emberiza citrinella*) having mainly yellowish plumage. **2** the yellow-shafted flicker. See **flicker².** [earlier *yelambre* < OE *geolu* yellow + *amore*, a kind of bird; the *h* may have resulted from the influence of obs. *yellowham* of the same meaning < OE *geolu* yellow + *hama* covering, feathers]

yel·low·ish (yel′ō ish) adj. somewhat yellow.

yellow jack **1** yellow fever. **2** a yellow flag used as a signal of quarantine.

yellow jacket any of a genus (*Vespa*) of wasps having bright-yellow markings, that nest in colonies, usually in the ground.

Yel·low·knife (yel′ō nīf′) n., pl. -knife or -knives. **1** a group of North American Indians, closely allied to the Chipewyan, originally living in the region between the Great Bear Lake and the Great Slave Lake to the east. **2** a member of this group. **3** the Athapascan language of this people.

yel·low·legs (yel′ō legz′) n. either of two North American shore birds, the **greater yellowlegs** (*Tringa melanoleuca*) and the **lesser yellowlegs** (*T. flavipes*), belonging to the sandpiper family, having yellow legs, a brownish back streaked with white, and a white breast with brown markings.

yellow metal **1** gold. **2** a yellowish alloy containing copper and zinc.

yellow pages a telephone directory, or a part of one, that lists and advertises firms classified by the nature of their business. It is printed on yellow paper.

yellow peril the alleged danger from the growth and activities of Japan or China.

yellow pickerel walleye (def. 7).

yellow pine **1** any of several species of pine having relatively hard wood, especially the ponderosa pine. **2** the wood of any of these pines.

yellow walleye walleye (def. 7).

yellow warbler a New World warbler (*Dendroica petechia*) that is common throughout much of Canada, often found nesting in shrubbery around dwellings, having mainly yellowish-green plumage with bright-yellow patches on the tail.

yelp (yelp) *n., v. —n.* a quick, sharp bark or cry. —*v.* **1** make a quick, sharp bark or cry. **2** utter with a yelp. [OE *gielpan* boast]

Yem·e·ni (yem′ə nē) *n., adj. —n.* a native or inhabitant of the Yemen Arab Republic or the People's Democratic Republic of Yemen, neighboring countries in the S Arabian Peninsula. —*adj.* of or having to do with either of these countries or its inhabitants.

yen¹ (yen) *n., pl.* **yen. 1** the basic unit of money in Japan. See table at **money. 2** a coin worth one yen. [< Japanese]

yen² (yen) *n., v.* **yenned, yen·ning.** *Informal.* —*n.* a fanciful desire or longing: *a yen to see the world. You're free to do whatever you have a yen for.* —*v.* desire. [< Chinese (Pekinese) *yen* opium (lit. smoke)]

yeo·man (yō′mən) *n., pl.* **-men. 1** a naval petty officer, especially the chief signalman on a ship. **2** *Brit. Historical.* a member of a class of people who owned a small amount of land. **3** *Archaic.* a servant or attendant of a lord or king. **4** yeoman of the guard.
yeoman service or **yeoman's service,** extremely valuable service or assistance.
[ME *yoman*; origin uncertain]

yeo·man·ly (yō′mən lē) *adj., adv. —adj.* having to do with or suitable for a yeoman; sturdy; honest. —*adv.* like a yeoman; bravely.

yeoman of the guard in England, a member of a force once forming the sovereign's bodyguard, now having ceremonial duties and providing warders for the Tower of London.

yeo·man·ry (yō′mən rē) *n.* yeomen collectively.

yes (yes) *adv., n., pl.* **yes·es;** *v.* **yessed, yes·sing.** —*adv.* **1** a word used to indicate that one can or will, or that something is so; a word used to affirm, accept, or agree: *"Yes, five and two are seven," said Bob. Will you go? Yes.* **2** and what is more; in addition to that: *The soldier found that he could endure hardships, yes, even enjoy them.* —*n.* agreement; acceptance; consent: *You have my yes to that.* —*v.* say yes. [OE *gēse* < *gēa* yea + *sī* let it be]
☛ *Usage.* Yes and no, when used as adverbs, may modify a sentence (*Yes, you're right*) or may have the value of a co-ordinate clause (*No; but you should have told me*) or may stand as complete sentences (*Do you really intend to go with him? Yes.*).

Ye·shi·va (yə shē′və) *n., pl.* **Ye·shi·vas** or **Ye·shi·voth** (yə shē′vōt′). **1** a Jewish school for higher studies, often a seminary for the rabbinate. **2** a Jewish day school. [< Hebrew *yeshibah* sitting]

yes man *Slang.* a person who always agrees with his employer, superior officer, party, etc., especially one who does so obsequiously and in order to curry favor.

yes·ter·day (yes′tər dē *or* -dā′) *n., adv. —n.* **1** the day before today. **2** the recent past: *We are often amused by the fashions of yesterday.* —*adv.* **1** on the day before today. **2** recently. [OE *geostrandæg* < *geostran* yesterday + *dæg* day]

yes·ter·eve (yes′tər ēv′) *n. or adv. Archaic or poetic.* yesterday evening.

yes·ter·eve·ning (yes′tər ēv′ning) *n. or adv. Archaic or poetic.* yesterday evening.

yes·ter·morn (yes′tər môrn′) *n. or adv. Archaic or poetic.* yesterday morning.

yes·ter·night (yes′tər nīt′) *n. or adv. Archaic or poetic.* last night; the night before today.

yes·ter·year (yes′tər yēr′) *n. or adv. Poetic.* last year; the year before this.

yes·treen (yes′trēn′) *n. or adv. Scottish or poetic.* yesterday evening.

yet (yet) *adv., conj. —adv.* **1** up to the present time; thus far: *The work is not yet finished.* **2** now: *Don't go yet.* **3** then; at that time: *It was not yet dark.* **4** still; even: *speaking yet more loudly. Yet once more he urged them to reconsider.* **5** sometime: *The thief will be caught yet.* **6** but; nevertheless: *The story was strange, yet true.*
as yet, up to now.
—*conj.* but; nevertheless; however: *The work is good, yet it could be better.* [OE *gīet(a)*]

ye·ti (ye′tē) *n.* abominable snowman. [< Tibetan. 20c.]

yew (yü) *n.* **1** any of a genus (*Taxus*) of evergreen trees and shrubs of the northern hemisphere, having broad, flat needles that are dark green above and light green below and small, red, berrylike cones.

---

hat, āge, fär; let, ēqual, tėrm; it, īce
hot, ōpen, ôrder; oil, out; cup, pùt, rüle,
əbove, takən, pencəl, lemən, circəs
ch, child; ng, long; sh, ship
th, thin; ᴛʜ, then; zh, measure

2 the wood of the yew, especially the hard, fine-grained wood of the English yew (*T. baccata*), used in cabinetmaking and for archery bows. **3** (*adj.*) designating the family (Taxaceae) of evergreen trees and shrubs that includes the yews. [OE *īw*]

Ygg·dra·sil (ig′drə sil′) *n. Norse mythology.* the ash tree that binds together earth, heaven, and hell.

Yid·dish (yid′ish) *n., adj. —n.* a language that developed from a dialect of Middle High German, but nowadays containing many Hebrew and Slavic words, and written in Hebrew characters. Yiddish is spoken by Jews in eastern and central Europe and is much used in Jewish communities elsewhere. —*adj.* having to do with the Yiddish language. [< G *jüdisch* Jewish]

yield (yēld) *v., n. —v.* **1** produce; bear: *This land yields good crops. Mines yield ore.* **2** give; grant: *to yield one's consent.* **3** give up; submit; surrender: *The enemy yielded to our soldiers. I yielded to temptation and ate all the candy.* **4** give way: *The door yielded to his touch.* **5** give place: *We yield to nobody in love of freedom.* **6** *Archaic.* pay; reward.
—*n.* the amount yielded; product: *This year's yield from the silver mine was very large.* [OE *gieldan* pay]
☛ *Syn. v.* **3.** Yield, submit = give up to someone or something. **Yield** particularly suggests giving way before, or giving up to, a stronger force and, usually, ceasing to fight against it: *The obstinate man will not yield in an argument even when he is proved wrong.* **Submit** suggests giving up all resistance and giving in to the power, will, or authority of another: *Finally he submitted to the unjust treatment.* —*n.* See note at **crop.**

yield·ing (yēl′ding) *adj.* **1** not resisting; submissive: *a yielding nature.* **2** soft; giving way under weight or force: *We lay back in the yielding grass.*

yip (yip) *v.* **yipped, yip·ping;** *n. Informal.* —*v.* especially of dogs, bark or yelp briskly. —*n.* a sharp barking sound. [imitative]

-yl *combining form. Chemistry.* denoting a radical such as *ethyl* or *hydroxyl.* [< Gk. *hylē* wood, material]

YMCA or **Y.M.C.A.** Young Men's Christian Association.

YMHA or **Y.M.H.A.** Young Men's Hebrew Association.

Y·mir (ē′mir) *n. Norse mythology.* a giant from whose body the gods made the universe.

yo·del (yō′dəl) *v.* **-delled** or **-deled, -del·ling** or **-del·ing;** *n. —v.* sing or call with frequent, sudden changes from the ordinary voice pitch to a much higher pitch or to a falsetto in the manner of mountaineers of Switzerland and Tyrol. —*n.* the act or sound of yodelling. [< G *jodeln*] —**yo′del·ler** or **yo′de·ler,** *n.*

yo·dle (yō′dəl) *v.* **-dled, -dling;** *n.* See yodel. —**yo′dler,** *n.*

yo·ga or **Yo·ga** (yō′gə) *n.* a system to improve the condition of the body under the control of the mind and spirit through the practice of slow, rhythmic body movements, controlled breathing exercises, and complete relaxation of the body and the mind. Yoga originated in India about 6000 years ago as one of the six systems of Hindu philosophy. [< Hind. < Skt. *yoga* union]

yo·gi (yō′gē) *n., pl.* **-gis.** a person who practises or follows yoga.

yo·gurt (yō′gėrt) *n.* a semisolid food made from milk fermented by a bacterial culture and often sweetened and flavored with honey, fruit, etc. [< Turkish *yōghurt*]

yo-heave-ho (yō′hėv′hō′) *interj.* an exclamation used by sailors in pulling or lifting together.

yoicks (yoiks) *interj. Esp.Brit.* a cry used to urge on the hounds in fox hunting.

Yoke (def. 6):
a nightgown with a yoke

Yoke (def. 1):
a double yoke for oxen

yoke (yōk) *n., v.* **yoked, yok·ing.** —*n.* **1** a wooden frame which fits

around the neck of two work animals to fasten them together for pulling a plough or vehicle. **2** a pair fastened together by a yoke: *The plough was drawn by a yoke of oxen.* **3** any frame connecting two other parts: *The man carried two buckets on a yoke, one at each end.* **4** a separate upper section of a shirt, blouse, etc. that fits closely over the shoulder area. **5** a separate upper section of a skirt, fitting closely about the hips. **6** a modified crosshead used instead of a connecting rod between the piston and crankshaft in certain small engines. **7** a crossbar at the top of a rudder of a boat, and having two lines of ropes attached for steering. **8** a crossbar connecting the tongue of a wagon, carriage, etc. to the collars of two horses, mules, etc. **9** among the ancient Romans and others: **a** a contrivance similar to a yoke for oxen, etc. placed on the neck of a captive. **b** a symbol of this consisting of two upright spears with a third placed across them, under which captives were forced to walk. **10** something that binds together: *the yoke of marriage.* **11** something that holds people in slavery or submission: *Throw off your yoke and be free.* **12** rule; dominion: *Slaves are under their master's yoke.*
—*v.* **1** put a yoke on; fasten with a yoke. **2** harness or fasten a work animal or animals to: *The farmer yoked his plough.* **3** join; unite: *to be yoked in marriage.* [OE *geoc*]

yoke·fel·low (yōk′fel′ō) *n. Archaic.* a close companion, partner, or mate.

yo·kel (yō′kəl) *n. Derogatory.* a person who lives in or comes from a rural area, especially one who is unfamiliar with cities or with urban lifestyles, attitudes, etc. [origin uncertain]

yolk¹ (yōk) *n.* **1** the yellow and principal substance of an egg, as distinguished from the white. **2** the corresponding part in any animal ovum, which serves for the nutrition of the embryo. [OE *geolca* < *geolu* yellow]

yolk² (yōk) *n.* the fat or grease in sheep's wool. [? < earlier *yoak* < OE *ēowoca*, from Gmc. root of OE *ēowu* ewe; influenced by YOLK¹.]

Yom Kip·pur (yom kip′ər) the Day of Atonement, an annual Jewish day of fasting and atoning for sin, observed on the tenth day of Tishri, which is the first month of the Jewish civil year. [< Hebrew *yōm kippūr*]

yon (yon) *adj., adv., pron. Archaic or dialect* (*except in* **hither and yon**). —*adj. or adv.* yonder.
hither and yon See **hither**.
—*pron. Esp.Brit.* the one yonder: *Yon's the best man for the job.* [OE *geon*]

yond (yond) *adj. or adv. Archaic or dialect.* yonder. [OE *geond*]

yon·der (yon′dər) *adv., adj.* —*adv.* within sight, but not near; over there: *Look yonder.* —*adj.* **1** situated over there; being within sight, but not near: *He lives in yonder cottage.* **2** farther; more distant; other: *There is snow on the yonder side of the mountains.* [ME, extension of *yond*; cf. Gothic *jaindrē*]

yore (yôr) *n., adv.* —*n.*
of yore, of long ago; of time long past: *in days of yore.*
—*adv. Obsolete.* long ago; years ago. [OE *geāra*, gen. pl. of *gēar* year]

York (yôrk) *n.* **1** the royal house of England from 1461 to 1485. Its emblem was a white rose. **2** the name of Toronto from 1793 to 1834.

A York boat

York boat *Cdn. Historical.* a type of heavy freight vessel developed by the Hudson's Bay Company at York Factory on Hudson Bay and used especially on inland waterways.

York·ist (yôr′kist) *n., adj.* —*n.* an adherent or member of the English royal family of York, especially at the time of the Wars of the Roses (1455-1485). —*adj.* of or having to do with the English royal family of York.

York·shire pudding (yôrk′shər) a light, puffy, baked pudding made from a batter of flour, milk, and eggs, and traditionally served with roast beef. [< *Yorkshire*, a county in N England]

Yorkshire terrier a breed of small dog having long, silky, greyish-blue hair.

you (yü; *unstressed*, yə) *pron. sing. or pl., subj. or obj.* **you**, *poss.* **yours. 1** the person or persons spoken to: *Are you ready? I'll bring

you the book tomorrow.* **2** one; anybody: *You press this button to turn it on. You never can tell. His lectures put you to sleep.* [OE *ēow*, dat. and accus. of *gē* ye¹]
☛ *Usage.* The use of **you** and **your** to refer to people in general is common in speech: *The pay is good if you can stand the long hours.* In formal writing, however, most people prefer **one** or some other impersonal construction: *This work develops one's powers of concentration.* The important thing is to be consistent; avoid using **you** and **one** for the same purpose in the same piece of writing.

you'd (yüd; *unstressed*, yəd) **1** you had: *You'd better go quickly.* **2** you would: *You'd like this story.*

you'll (yül; *unstressed*, yəl) you will.

young (yung) *adj.* **young·er** (yung′gər), **young·est** (yung′gist); *n.* —*adj.* **1** in the early part of life or growth; not old: *A puppy is a young dog.* **2** having the looks or qualities of youth or a young person; youthful; lively: *She looks and acts young for her age.* **3** of youth; early: *one's young days.* **4** not so old as another: *Young Mr. Jones worked for his father.* **5** in an early stage; not far advanced: *The night was still young when we left the party.* **6** without much experience or practice: *He was too young in the business.*
—*n.* **1** young offspring: *An animal will fight to protect its young.* **2 the young,** *pl.* young people.
with young, pregnant.
[OE *geong*]
☛ *Syn. adj.* **3. Young, youthful, juvenile** = of or pertaining to persons between childhood and adulthood. **Young** emphasizes age, being in the early part of life: *too young to marry.* **Youthful** emphasizes having the qualities of a young person, especially freshness and vitality: *youthful vigor and enthusiasm.* **Juvenile** stresses immaturity, and describes things having to do with young people: *juvenile behavior, a juvenile novel.*

young blood 1 young people. **2** youthful vigor, energy, enthusiasm, etc.

young·ish (yung′ish) *adj.* rather young.

young·ling (yung′ling) *n., adj.* —*n.* **1** a young person, animal, or plant. **2** a novice; beginner. —*adj.* young; youthful. [OE *geongling*]

young·ster (yung′stər) *n.* **1** a child: *He is a lively youngster.* **2** a young person: *They have hired several youngsters for the summer.*

youn·ker (yung′kər) *n. Archaic.* a young fellow. [< MDu. *jonkher, jonchere* < *jonc* young + *here* lord, master]

your (yür; *unstressed*, yər) *adj.* **1** a possessive form of **you:** of, belonging to, or made or done by you or yourself: *Give me your hand. Is this your pen? We enjoyed your visit.* **2** of, having to do with, or belonging to one or oneself: *The government guarantees your basic freedoms.* **3** *Informal.* that you know or speak of: *your real lover of music, your modern girl.* **4 Your,** a word used as part of certain formal titles when using the title to address the person holding it: *Your Highness, Your Ladyship, Your Worship.* [OE *ēower*, gen. of *gē* ye¹]

you're (yür; *unstressed*, yər) you are.

yours (yürz) *pron. sing. and pl.* **1** a possessive form of **you:** that which belongs to you: *I think this scarf is yours. I don't like our set as well as yours.* **2** at your service: *yours sincerely. I am yours to command.*
of yours, belonging to or having to do with you: *Is he a friend of yours?*
yours truly, *Informal.* I, me, or myself: *Yours truly is going home.*

your·self (yür self′; *unstressed*, yər self′) *pron., pl.* **-selves. 1** a reflexive pronoun, the form used instead of **you** when referring back to the subject of the sentence: *You will hurt yourself if you aren't careful.* **2** a form of **you** used to make a statement stronger: *You yourself know the story is not true.* **3** your usual self: *Come see us when you feel better and are yourself again.*

your·selves (yür selvz′; *unstressed*, yər selvz′) *pron. pl. of* **yourself.**

yours truly 1 a phrase often used at the end of a letter, before the signature. **2** *Informal.* I; me.

youth (yüth) *n., pl.* **youths** (yüths *or* yü∓нz) *or* (collectively) **youth. 1** the fact or quality of being young: *He has the vigor of youth.* **2** the appearance, freshness, vigor, or some other quality characteristic of the young: *She keeps her youth well.* **3** the time between childhood and manhood or womanhood. **4** a young man. **5** young people collectively (*used with a singular or plural verb*). **6** the first or early stage of anything; the early period of growth or development: *during the youth of this country.* [OE *geoguth*]

youth·ful (yüth′fəl) *adj.* **1** young. **2** of youth; suitable for young people: *Everyone admired his youthful enthusiasm.* **3** having the looks or qualities of youth; fresh and lively: *The old man had a very happy and youthful spirit.* **4** early; new. —**youth′ful·ly,** *adv.* —**youth′ful·ness,** *n.*
☛ *Syn.* **2.** See note at **young.**

youth hostel a supervised, inexpensive lodging place for travelling young people, usually one of a system of such places.

you've (yüv; *unstressed*, yəv) you have: *You've gone too far.*

yowl (youl) *n., v.* —*n.* a long, distressful, or dismal cry; howl. —*v.* howl. [imitative]

yo-yo (yō′yō) *n., pl.* -**yos. 1** a small wheel-shaped toy made up of two disks, usually wooden, joined by a central peg to which is attached a long string. The string is held by one hand, and the toy is spun out and reeled in on the string. **2** *Slang.* a dull, stupid person, especially one who is gullible or easily manipulated. [< *Yoyo*, a trademark; origin uncertain]

yr. 1 year(s). **2** your; yours.

yrs. 1 years. **2** yours.

YST or **Y.S.T.** Yukon Standard Time.

YT Yukon Territory (*used esp. in computerized address systems*).

Y.T. Yukon Territory.

yt·ter·bi·a (i tẽr′bē ə) *n.* a heavy, white substance that forms colorless salts; ytterbium oxide. *Formula:* Yb_2O_3

yt·ter·bi·um (i tẽr′bē əm) *n.* a rare metallic chemical element belonging to the yttrium group. *Symbol:* Yb; *at.no.* 70; *at.wt.* 173.04. [< NL *yttrium*, ult. < *Ytterby*, a town in Sweden]

yt·tri·a (it′rē ə) *n.* a heavy, white powder; yttrium oxide. *Formula:* Y_2O_3

yt·tri·um (it′rē əm) *n.* a rare metallic chemical element. Compounds of yttrium are used for incandescent gas mantles. *Symbol:* Y; *at.no.* 39; *at.wt.* 88.905. [< NL *yttrium*, ult. < *Ytterby*, a town in Sweden]

yu·an (yü än′) *n., pl.* **yu·an. 1** the basic unit of money in the People's Republic of China, divided into 10 chiao and 100 fen. See table at **money.** **2** a coin or note worth one yuan. [< Chinese *yüan* round, a circle]

Yu·ca·tec (yü′kə tek′) *n.* **1** a member of an Amerindian people of the Yucatán peninsula in Mexico. **2** the Mayan language of the Yucatecs.

yuc·ca (yuk′ə) *n.* any of a tropical and subtropical American genus (*Yucca*) of plants of the lily family having long, stiff, sword-shaped leaves and a single erect cluster of large, white, lily-like flowers. [< NL < Sp. *yuca*]

hat, āge, fär; let, ēqual, tẽrm; it, īce
hot, ōpen, ôrder; oil, out; cup, pů̇t, rüle,
ə‌bove, tak‌ən, penc‌əl, lem‌ən, circ‌əs
ch, child; ng, long; sh, ship
th, thin; ŦH, then; zh, measure

Yu·go·slav (yü′gō slav′ *or* -släv′) *n., adj.* —*n.* a native or inhabitant of Yugoslavia, a country in SE Europe. —*adj.* of or having to do with Yugoslavia or its people. Also, **Jugoslav.**

Yu·go·sla·vi·an (yü′gō slav′ē ən *or* -slä′vē ən) *adj.* Yugoslav.

yuk (yuk) *n., v.* **yukked, yuk·king.** *Slang.* —*n.* a loud and hearty laugh. —*v.* laugh loudly and heartily.

Yu·kon·er (yü′kon ər) *n.* a native or long-term resident of the Yukon Territory.

Yule or **yule** (yül) *n.* **1** Christmas. **2** Yuletide. [OE *geōl*]

Yule log a large log burned at Christmas, originally one that burned as the base of a fire throughout the Christmas season.

Yule·tide or **yule·tide** (yül′tīd′) *n.* Christmas time; the Christmas season.

yum·my (yum′ē) *adj., n., pl.* -**mies.** *Slang.* —*adj.* delighting the senses, especially the taste; delicious. —*n.* something very tasty or delicious. [< *yum-yum*, an interjection expressing pleasure at something delicious]

yurt (yůrt) *n.* a portable, domed tent made of felt stretched over a framework of branches, used by the Mongolian nomads of Siberia. [< Russian *yurta* < Turkic]

YWCA or **Y.W.C.A.** Young Women's Christian Association.

YWHA or **Y.W.H.A.** Young Women's Hebrew Association.

y·wis (i wis′) *adv. Archaic.* certainly; indeed; iwis. [OE *gewis*, ult. < Gmc. **wid-* know]

Zz

z or **Z** (zed; *esp.U.S.*, zē) *n.*, *pl.* **z's** or **Z's**. **1** the twenty-sixth and last letter of the English alphabet. **2** any speech sound represented by this letter. **3** a person or thing identified as *z*, especially the twenty-sixth of a series or the last in a series consisting of x, y, and z. **4** *Algebra.* z, an unknown quantity. **5** something shaped like the letter Z. **6** (*adj.*) of or being a Z or z.

z. or **Z.** zone.

Z atomic number.

zai·bat·su (zī bät′sü) *n.pl.* or *sing.* the leading families of Japan, directing its industries. [< Japanese *zai* property + *batsu* family]

za·ire or **za·ïre** (zä ēr′) *n.*, *pl.* **zaire** or **zaïre**. **1** the basic unit of money in Zaire, divided into 100 makuta (*singular* likuta). See table at **money**. **2** a note worth one zaire.

Zam·bo·ni (zam bō′nē) *n. Trademark.* an apparatus for scraping off the surface of an ice rink and laying down a new surface in a single operation.

za·ny (zā′nē) *adj.* **-i·er, -i·est;** *n.*, *pl.* **-nies.** —*adj.* comically foolish or absurd. —*n.* **1** a zany person. **2** *Historical.* an assistant clown or buffoon in old comedies who tried to mimic the principal clown. [< F < dial. Ital. *zanni*, originally var. of *Giovanni* John]

zap (zap) *interj., n., v.* **zapped, zap·ping.** *Slang.* —*interj.* a word used to express or indicate a sudden, swift happening: *I was just standing there when—zap—something hit me on the head.* —*n.* the sound of a sudden slap, blow, blast, etc. —*v.* **1** hit with a hard blow. **2** kill. **3** beat; defeat. **4** move very fast; zip; zoom.

za·stru·gi (zə strü′gē) *n.pl.* sastrugi.

zeal (zēl) *n.* intense or fervent devotion to or enthusiasm for something or someone, as displayed in action. [ME < LL < Gk. *zēlos* < *zeein* to boil]

zeal·ot (zel′ət) *n.* a person who shows too much zeal; a fanatic. [< L *zelotes* < Gk. *zēlōtēs* < *zēlos* zeal]

zeal·ot·ry (zel′ət rē) *n.* too great zeal; fanaticism.

zeal·ous (zel′əs) *adj.* full of zeal; eager; earnest; enthusiastic: *The children made zealous efforts to clean up the house for the party.* [< Med.L *zelosus* < L *zelus* < Gk.] —**zeal′ous·ly**, *adv.* —**zeal′ous·ness**, *n.*

ze·bec (zē′bek) See **xebec**.

ze·bra (zē′brə or zeb′rə) *n.* any of several wild mammals (genus *Equus*) of Africa, closely related to and resembling the horse and donkey but marked with conspicuous black or brown stripes on a white or light tan background. [< Portuguese < Bantu]

ze·bu (zē′byü) *n.* any of numerous breeds of domestic cattle originally developed in India from an Asiatic wild ox (*Bos indicus*) closely related to the aurochs (the ancestor of European cattle), all breeds characterized by a hump over the shoulders, a long head, and loose folds of skin hanging from the throat and chest. Zebus are widely used in tropical Africa, Asia, and South America as draft animals and for milk and meat. [< F]

zech·in (zek′in) *n.* sequin, a former Italian gold coin.

zed (zed) *n.* the spoken form of the letter Z. [< F *zède* < LL < Gk. *zēta*]

zee (zē) *n. Esp.U.S.* zed.

Zeit·geist (tsīt′gīst′) *n. German.* a characteristic thought or feeling of a period of time; the spirit of the time. [< G *Zeit* time + *Geist* spirit]

zem·stvo (zemst′vō) *n.*, *pl.* **-stvos.** in Imperial Russia, a local assembly managing the affairs of a district. [< Russian *zemstvo* < *zemlya* country]

Zen (zen) *n.* **1** a mystical Japanese form of Buddhism that emphasizes contemplation and solitary study to achieve self-discipline and intuitive spiritual enlightenment. **2** (*adj.*) of, having to do with, or designating this religion. [< Japanese *zen* contemplation]

ze·na·na (ze nä′nə) *n.* in India and Persia, the part of the house set aside for the women. [< Hind. < Persian *zanāna* < *zan* woman]

Zen Buddhist a believer in or follower of Zen.

Zend (zend) *n.* the translation and explanation of the Zoroastrian Avesta.

Zend–A·ves·ta (zend′ə ves′tə) *n.* the sacred writings of the Zoroastrian religion.

ze·nith (zen′ith or zē′nith) *n.* **1** the point in the heavens directly overhead. See **nadir** for picture. **2** the highest or greatest point: *At the zenith of its power Rome ruled the whole of civilized Europe.* [ME < OF or Med.L *senit* < Arabic *samt* (*ar-rās*) the way (over the head)]

ze·o·lite (zē′ə līt′) *n.* any of various minerals consisting of hydrous silicates of aluminum, lime, and sodium, usually found in veins or cavities of basaltic rock. [< Swedish *zeolit* < Gk. *zēein* to boil + *-lite*, because it swells or boils under a blowpipe]

zeph·yr (zef′ər) *n.* **1** the west wind. **2** any soft, gentle wind; mild breeze. **3** a fine, soft yarn or worsted. [< L < Gk. *zephyros*]

Zeph·y·rus (zef′ər əs) *n. Greek mythology.* the personification of the west wind, thought of as the most gentle of gods.

Zep·pe·lin or **zep·pe·lin** (zep′ə lən or zep′lən) *n.* an early type of airship shaped like a cigar with pointed ends, having compartments for gas, engines, passengers, etc. [after Count Ferdinand von *Zeppelin* (1838-1917), a German airship builder]

ze·ro (zēr′ō) *n.*, *pl.* **-ros** or **-roes;** *adj., v.* **-roed, -ro·ing.** —*n.* **1** nought; the figure 0: *There are three zeros in 40 006.* **2** the point marked as 0 on the scale of a thermometer, etc. A Celsius thermometer reads up and down from zero. **3** the temperature that correpsonds to zero on the scale of a thermometer: *The forecast is zero. Water freezes at zero.* **4** the complete absence of quantity; nothing. **5** the lowest point: *The team's spirit sank to zero after its third defeat.* —*adj.* **1** of or at zero: *a zero score.* **2** not any; none at all: *a zero chance of survival, zero gravity.* **3** *Meteorology and aeronautics.* **a** designating a cloud ceiling limiting visibility to 15 metres or less. **b** designating a horizontal visibility of 50 metres or less. —*v.* adjust (an instrument or device) to zero point or line or to any given point from which readings will then be measured. **zero in,** adjust the sights of (a rifle) for a given range so a bullet will strike the centre of the target. **zero in on,** **a** get the range of by adjusting the sights of a firearm, etc. **b** direct with precision toward a target, etc. **c** locate as a target; find the range of. [< Ital. < Arabic *sifr* empty. Doublet of CIPHER.]

zero gravity a condition in which gravity does not operate; weightlessness.

zero hour **1** the time for beginning an attack, etc. **2** any point in time viewed as similar to this; crucial moment.

zero magnitude *Astronomy.* a degree of brilliance indicating a brightness 2½ times greater than that of first magnitude stars.

ze·ro–ze·ro (zēr′ō zēr′ō) *adj. Aeronautics and meteorology.* of or having to do with atmospheric conditions in which visibility is reduced to nothing in both vertical and horizontal directions.

zest (zest) *n., v.* —*n.* **1** keen enjoyment; relish: *The hungry man ate with zest.* **2** a pleasant or exciting quality, flavor, etc.: *Wit gives zest to conversation.* —*v.* give a zest to. [< F *zeste* orange or lemon peel]

zest·ful (zest′fəl) *adj.* characterized by zest. —**zest′ful·ly**, *adv.* —**zest′ful·ness**, *n.*

ze·ta (zā′tə or zē′tə) *n.* the sixth letter (Z, ζ = English Z, z) of the Greek alphabet.

Zeus (züs) *n. Greek mythology.* the god who is king of the gods and of mankind and husband of Hera. Zeus corresponds to the Roman god Jupiter.

zig·gu·rat (zig′ù rat′) *n.* an ancient Assyrian or Babylonian temple in the form of a pyramid of terraced towers. Also, **zikkurat.** [< Akkadian *ziqqurata* pinnacle, tower]

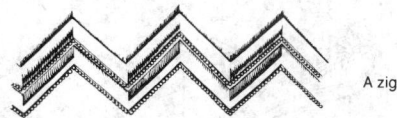

A zigzag design

zig·zag (zig′zag′) *adj., adv., v.* **-zagged, -zag·ging;** *n.* —*adj.* or

adv. with short, sharp turns, from one side to the other: *to go in a zigzag course. The path ran zigzag up the hill.*
—*v.* move in a zigzag way: *Lightning zigzagged across the sky.*
—*n.* 1 a zigzag line or course. 2 one of the short, sharp turns of a zigzag. [< F]

zik·ku·rat (zik′ů rat′) *n.* ziggurat.

zinc (zingk) *n., v.* **zincked** or **zinced** (zingkt), **zinck·ing** *or* **zinc·ing** (zingk′ing). —*n.* a bluish-white metallic chemical element, at ordinary temperatures very little affected by air and moisture. Zinc is used as a roofing material, in battery electrodes, in paint, in medicine, and for coating some metals. *Symbol:* Zn; *at.no.* 30; *at.wt* 65.37. —*v.* coat or cover with zinc. [< G *Zink*]

zinc ointment a salve containing zinc oxide, used especially in treating skin disorders.

zinc oxide an insoluble white powder used in making paint, rubber, glass, cosmetics, ointments, etc. *Formula:* ZnO

zing (zing) *n., v.* —*n.* 1 a sharp humming sound. 2 *Slang.* spirit; vitality; liveliness; zest. —*v.* make a sharp humming sound, especially in going fast: *A bullet zinged by her ear.* [imitative]

zin·ga·ro (tsēng′gä rō) *n., pl.* **-ri** (-rē). *Italian.* a gypsy.

zin·ni·a (zin′ē ə) *n.* any of a genus (*Zinnia*) of tropical and subtropical American plants of the composite family, cultivated in many varieties for their showy flower heads. [< NL; after Johann G. *Zinn* (1727-59), a German botanist]

Zi·on (zī′ən) *n.* 1 the hill in Jerusalem on which the royal palace and the temple were built. 2 Israel; the people of Israel. 3 heaven; the heavenly city. 4 the church of God. Also, **Sion.** [OE *Sion* < LL < Gk. *Seōn* < Hebrew *tsīyōn* hill]

Zi·on·ism (zī′ən iz′əm) *n.* a movement, begun in the late 19th century, to make modern Palestine (now Israel) a Jewish national state.

Zi·on·ist (zī′ən ist) *n.* an advocate of Zionism.

Zi·on·is·tic (zī′ə nis′tik) *adj.* of, having to do with, or resembling Zionism.

zip (zip) *n., v.* **zipped, zip·ping.** —*n.* 1 a sudden, brief, hissing sound, as of a flying bullet. 2 *Informal.* energy or vim. 3 *Esp.Brit.* zipper.
—*v.* 1 make a sudden, brief hissing sound. 2 *Informal.* proceed with energy. 3 fasten or close the zipper of: *He zipped up his jacket.* [imitative]

Zi·pan·gu (zi pang′gü) *n.* Marco Polo's name for Japan.

zip code 1 a system for addressing and sorting mail in the United States, in which a five-digit identifying number is assigned to each postal delivery area in the country. 2 an identifying number in this system. [< *Z*one *I*mprovement *P*lan]

zip·gun (zip′gun′) *n.* a home-made toy pistol or gun consisting of a piece of tubing, a wooden handle, and a rubber band or spring to fire the bullet.

zip·per (zip′ər) *n., v.* —*n.* a flexible fastening device for clothing, boots, cushion covers, etc., consisting of two parallel rows of plastic or metal coils or teeth on either side of an opening, which are locked together by means of a sliding tab to close the opening and unlocked by sliding the tab back again. —*v.* zip (def. 3). [< *Zipper*, a trademark]

zip·pered (zip′ərd) *adj.* equipped with a zipper: *a zippered jacket.*

zip·py (zip′ē) *adj.* **-pi·er, -pi·est.** *Informal.* full of energy; lively; gay.

zir·con (zėr′kon) *n.* 1 a crystalline mineral consisting of zirconium silicate, that occurs in various forms and colors. *Formula:* ZrSiO₄ 2 a gem made from this mineral. [probably < F < Arabic *zarqūn*]

zir·co·ni·um (zėr kō′nē əm) *n.* a rare metallic chemical element used in alloys for wires, filaments, etc. *Symbol:* Zr; *at.no.* 40; *at.wt.* 91.22 [< NL]

A zither

zith·er (zith′ər) *n.* a musical instrument having 30 to 40 strings

over a flat sounding board, played with a plectrum and the fingers. [< G *Zither* < L *cithara* < Gk. *kithara.* Doublet of CITHARA and GUITAR.]

zith·ern (zith′ərn) *n.* 1 cithern. 2 zither.

zit·tern (zit′ərn) *n.* zithern.

zlo·ty (zlô′tē) *n., pl.* **-tys** or **-ty.** 1 the basic unit of money in Poland, divided into 100 groszy. See table at **money.** 2 a coin worth one zloty. [< Polish]

Zn zinc.

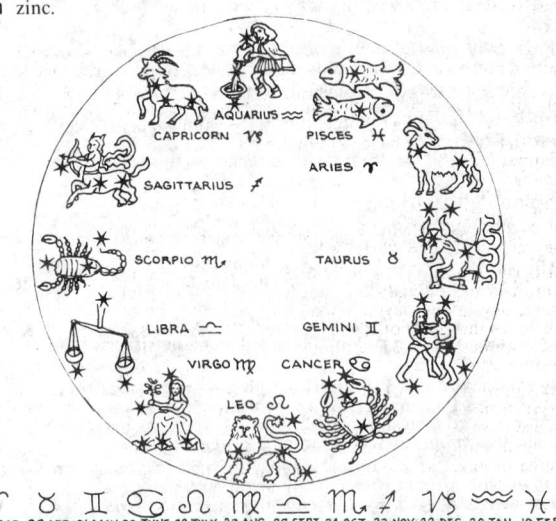

The constellations of the zodiac, with their astrological symbols and the traditional dates when the sun "enters" each sign

zo·di·ac (zō′dē ak′) *n.* 1 an imaginary belt of the heavens extending on both sides of the apparent yearly path of the sun. The zodiac is divided into 12 equal parts, called signs, named after 12 groups of stars. 2 a diagram representing the zodiac, used in astrology. [ME < OF < L < Gk. *zōdiakos* (*kyklos*), literally, (circle) of the animals, ult. < *zōion* animal]

zo·di·a·cal (zō dī′ə kəl) *adj.* 1 of or having to do with the zodiac. 2 situated in the zodiac.

Zoll·ver·ein (tsol′fer īn′ *or* tsôl′fer īn′) *n. German.* 1 a union of German states from 1819 to 1871 to promote uniform conditions of trade among themselves and between themselves and other nations. 2 any similar union of states or countries. [< G *Zollverein* toll union]

zom·bi (zom′bē) *n., pl.* **-bis.** zombie.

zom·bie (zom′bē) *n., pl.* **-bies.** 1 a corpse supposedly brought back to life by a supernatural power. 2 in certain West African voodoo cults, the python god. 3 the snake god of voodoo, derived from this. 4 a supernatural power or force by which the dead may be endowed with a capacity for mute trance-like action somewhat resembling life, alleged to be possessed by certain practitioners of West Indian voodoo. 5 *Cdn. Slang.* in World War II, a person conscripted for service in the army, primarily for home defence. 6 *Slang.* a very stupid, lethargic person. 7 a drink of several kinds of rum, fruit juice, sugar, and brandy. [< Haitian Creole *zôbi* < West African (Congo) *zumbi* good-luck fetish]

zon·al (zō′nəl) *adj.* 1 of a zone; having to do with zones. 2 divided into zones.

zone (zōn) *n., v.* **zoned, zon·ing.** —*n.* 1 an area, region, district, etc. set off as distinct from surrounding or neighboring areas, etc.: *a hospital zone, an industrial zone in a city. A combat zone is a region where fighting is going on.* 2 a region or area having a particular environment or climate and characterized by certain forms of plant and animal life. 3 *Mathematics.* a part of the surface of a sphere contained between two parallel planes. 4 *Poetic.* a belt; girdle. 5 an encircling or enclosing line, band, or ring, sometimes differing in color, texture, etc. from the surrounding medium.
—*v.* 1 set (an area or areas) apart for a special purpose, especially in a city or town: *This area is zoned for apartment buildings.* 2 divide into or mark with zones. 3 surround with or as if with a zone; encircle. [< L *zona* < Gk. *zōnē*, originally, girdle]

zoned (zōnd) *adj.* 1 marked with or having zones. 2 divided into zones.

zon·ing (zō′ning) *n.* building restrictions in an area of a city or town.

zoo (zü) *n.* a place where animals are kept and shown. [short for *zoological garden*]

zoo– *combining form.* living being; animal, as in *zoology.* [< Gk. *zōion* animal]

zo·o·ge·o·graph·ic (zō′ə jē ə graf′ik) *adj.* of or having to do with zoogeography.

zo·o·ge·og·ra·phy (zō′ə jē og′rə fē) *n.* the study of the distribution of animals over the surface of the earth.

zo·o·graph·ic (zō′ə graf′ik) *adj.* of or having to do with zoography.

zo·og·ra·phy (zō og′rə fē) *n.* the branch of zoology that describes animals and their habits; descriptive zoology.

zool. zoology; zoologist; zoological.

zo·o·lite (zō′ə līt′) *n.* a fossil animal. [< *zoo-* + *-lite*]

zo·o·log·i·cal (zō′ə loj′ə kəl *or* zü′ə loj′ə kəl) *adj.* 1 of animals and animal life. 2 having to do with zoology: *zoological science.* —**zo′o·log′i·cal·ly,** *adv.*

zoological garden zoo.

zo·ol·o·gist (zō ol′ə jist *or* zü ol′ə jist) *n.* a person trained in zoology, especially one whose work it is.

zo·ol·o·gy (zō ol′ə jē *or* zü ol′ə jē) *n.* 1 the science that deals with animals and animal life. Zoology deals with the form, structure, physiology, development, and classification of animals. It also includes the study of special groups such as birds, insects, snakes, mammals, etc. 2 a textbook or handbook dealing with this subject.

zoom (züm) *v., n.* —*v.* 1 of an aircraft, fly suddenly upward in a nearly vertical ascent at great speed: *The airplane zoomed.* 2 increase sharply or rapidly: *Prices zoomed.* 3 make a continuous, low-pitched humming or buzzing sound. 4 travel or move with a humming or buzzing sound. 5 move rapidly from one focus to another, as with a zoom lens. 6 move or travel rapidly. —*n.* 1 a sudden upward flight. 2 a humming or buzzing sound, especially of something moving.

zoom lens *Photography.* a type of lens that can be adjusted between telephoto close-ups and wide-angle shots without loss of focus.

zo·o·mor·phic (zō′ə môr′fik) *adj.* 1 depicting or using animal forms: *zoomorphic decoration.* 2 depicting a god or a superhuman being in animal shapes or motifs. [< E *zoo* + Gk. *morphē* form + E *-ic*]

zo·o·mor·phism (zō′ə môr′fiz əm) *n.* 1 *Art.* the depiction of animals or animal forms. 2 the representation of a god or other superhuman in the form or with the characteristics of an animal.

zo·on·o·sis (zō on′ə sis *or* zō′ə nō′sis) *n., pl.* **-ses** (-sēz). any infection or infestation that can be transmitted to man from lower vertebrates under natural conditions. [< NL < *zoo-* + Gk. *nosos* disease]

zo·o·phyte (zō′ə fīt′) *n.* any of various invertebrate animals that resemble plants in form, such as corals, sponges, or sea anemones. [< *zoo-* + *-phyte*]

zo·o·plast·ic (zō′ə plas′tik) *adj.* of or having to do with zooplasty.

zo·o·plast·y (zō′ə plas′tē) *n., pl.* **-ties.** plastic surgery in which living tissue from a lower animal is grafted on to a human body. [< *zoo-* + Gk. *plastikos,* ult. < *plassein* to form, shape]

zo·o·spore (zō′ə spôr′) *n. Botany.* a spore that has cilia, flagella, etc. and can move about. Some algae and fungi produce zoospores.

zo·o·tech·nic (zō′ə tek′nik) *adj.* of or having to do with zootechny.

zo·o·tech·ny (zō′ə tek′nē) *n.* the systematic breeding and care of animals in domestication. [< *zoo-* + Gk. *technē* art, science]

zoot suit (züt) *Slang.* a man's flashy suit with large shoulders, a long coat, and tight trouser cuffs.

Zo·ro·as·tri·an (zō′rō as′trē ən) *adj., n.* —*adj.* of or having to do with Zoroastrianism or Zoroaster. —*n.* a follower of Zoroaster or believer in Zoroastrianism.

Zo·ro·as·tri·an·ism (zō′rō as′trē ən iz′əm) *n.* a religion founded by the Persian prophet Zoroaster in the sixth century B.C. It is expounded in the Zend-Avesta and teaches that the supreme god Ormazd (or Ahura Mazda) is struggling continuously with

hat, āge, fär; let, ēqual, tėrm; it, īce
hot, ōpen, ôrder; oil, out; cup, put, rüle,
əbove, takən, pencəl, lemən, circəs
ch, child; ng, long; sh, ship
th, thin; ŦH, then; zh, measure

Ahriman, the spirit of evil, and needs the good deeds of mankind to help him ultimately to overcome evil.

Zou·ave (zü äv′ *or* zwäv′) *n.* 1 *Historical.* a member of a French infantry unit originally composed of Algerian recruits who were noted for their fighting ability, precision drilling, and colorful uniforms. 2 a member of any of various military units patterned after the French Zouaves, such as a body of volunteers called Papal Zouaves, originally organized at the call of the Pope for the protection of the Papal States in the 1860's. Zouaves were recruited in several cities of Quebec. [< F < *Zwāwa,* name of Algerian Berber tribe from which first Zouaves came]

zounds (zoundz) *interj. Archaic.* an oath expressing surprise or anger. [< *God's wounds!*]

Zr zirconium.

zuc·chi·ni (zü kē′nē) *n., pl.* **-ni** *or* **-nis.** 1 a small, oblong variety of summer squash having a smooth, dark green skin and white flesh with small seeds. 2 the plant it grows on. [< Ital. *zucchino,* dim. of *zuccho* gourd, squash]

Zu·lu (zü′lü) *n., pl.* **-lus** *or* **-lu;** *adj.* —*n.* 1 a member of a Bantu-speaking people of Natal in South Africa. 2 a Bantu language spoken by the Zulus. Zulu is an important literary language of southern Africa. —*adj.* of or having to do with the Zulus or their language.

Zu·ñi (zü′nyē *or* zü′nē) *n., pl.* **-ñi** *or* **-ñis.** 1 a member of an Amerindian people of W New Mexico. 2 the language of the Zuñi, of no known relationship to other languages. [< Am.Sp.]

zwie·back (swē′bak′, swē′bäk′, swī′bak′ *or* swī′bäk′; *German,* tsvē′bäk′) *n.* a kind of bread cut into slices and toasted dry in an oven. [< G *Zwieback* biscuit < *zwie-* two + *backen* bake]

Zwing·li·an (zwing′glē ən *or* tsving′lē ən) *adj., n.* —*adj.* of or having to do with Ulrich Zwingli (1484-1531), a Swiss Protestant reformer, or his doctrines. —*n.* a follower of Zwingli.

zygo– *combining form.* yoke; paired or yoked, as in *zygospore.* [< Gk. *zygon* yoke]

zy·go·spore (zī′gə spôr′ *or* zig′ə spôr′) *n. Botany.* a spore formed by the union of two similar gametes. [< Gk. *zygon* yoke + E *spore*]

zy·gote (zī′gōt *or* zig′ōt) *n.* any cell formed by the union of two gametes (i.e., reproductive cells). A fertilized egg is a zygote. [< Gk. *zygotos* yoked < *zygon* yoke]

zy·mase (zī′mās) *n.* an enzyme in yeast that changes sugar into alcohol and carbon dioxide. [< F < Gk. *zymē* leaven]

zyme (zīm) *n.* 1 any ferment, virus, etc. that causes an infectious or contagious disease. 2 any ferment or enzyme. [< Gk. *zymē* leaven]

zymo– *combining form.* fermentation, as in *zymology.*

zy·mol·o·gy (zī mol′ə jē) *n.* the science that deals with fermentation.

zy·mo·sis (zī mō′sis) *n.* 1 fermentation. 2 *Medicine.* a an internal process akin to fermentation, formerly supposed to cause an infectious disease. b any zymotic disease. [< NL *zymōsis* < Gk. *zymosis,* ult. < *zymē* leaven]

zy·mot·ic (zī mot′ik) *adj., n.* —*adj.* 1 having to do with, causing, or caused by fermentation. 2 having to do with or denoting any infectious disease caused by a fungus, originally thought to be caused by an internal process akin to fermentation. —*n.* a zymotic disease. [< Gk. *zymōtikos* causing fermentation] —**zy·mot′i·cal·ly,** *adv.*

zy·mur·gy (zī′mėr jē) *n.* the branch of chemistry dealing with the processes of fermentation, as in brewing, etc. [ult. < Gk. *zymē* leaven + *ergon* work]

Abbreviations

The following abbreviations and signs are used in this dictionary. Dates are approximate.

abbrev.	abbreviation	Mod.Gk.	Modern Greek (after 1500)
abl.	ablative	n.	noun
accus.	accusative	neut.	neuter
adj.	adjective	NL	New Latin (after 1500)
adv.	adverb	nom.	nominative
AF	Anglo-French	O	Old
Am.Ind.	American Indian	obj.	object, objective
Am.Sp.	American Spanish	obs.	obsolete
at.no.	atomic number	OE	Old English (before 1100)
at.wt.	atomic weight	OF	Old French (before 1400)
Austral.	Australian	OHG	Old High German (before 1100)
Brit.	British	OLG	Old Low German (before 1100)
c.	century	ON	Old Norse (before 1300)
Cdn.	Canadian	ONF	Old Northern French (before 1400)
Cdn.F.	Canadian French	OS	Old Saxon (800–1100)
cf.	compare	pers.	person
conj.	conjunction	Pg.	Portuguese
dat.	dative	pl.	plural
def.	definition	poss.	possessive
dial.	dialect, dialectal	pp.	past participle
dim.	diminutive	ppr.	present participle
Du.	Dutch	prep.	preposition
E	English	pres.	present
esp.	especially	pron.	pronoun
F	French	pronun.	pronunciation
fem.	feminine	pt.	past tense
fut.	future	Scand.	Scandinavian
G	German	sing.	singular
gen.	genitive	Skt.	Sanskrit
Gk.	Greek (from Homer to 200 A.D.)	Sp.	Spanish
Gmc.	Germanic	subj.	subject, subjective
HG	High German		*or*
Hind.	Hindi, Hindustani	subj.	subjunctive
Icel.	Icelandic	syn.	synonym
indic.	indicative	ult.	ultimately
infin.	infinitive	v.	verb
interj.	interjection	var.	variant
Ital.	Italian	VL	Vulgar Latin
L	Latin (200 B.C. to 300 A.D.)	voc.	vocative
lang.	language		
LG	Low German		
LGk.	Late Greek (200–700)		
LL	Late Latin (300–700)		
M	Middle		
masc.	masculine		
MDu.	Middle Dutch	<	taken from, derived from
ME	Middle English (1100–1500)	?	possibly
Med.	Medieval	*	unrecorded form
Med.Gk.	Medieval Greek (700–1500)		(assumed to have
Med.L	Medieval Latin (700–1500)		existed but not known
MF	Middle French (1400–1600)		to be recorded)
MHG	Middle High German (1100–1450)	=	equals, means
MLG	Middle Low German (1100–1450)	+	plus
Mod.	Modern	☞	fistnote (see p. xxix)